December 1, 1979

"Honoring Tomorrow's Leaders Today"

WHO'S WHO

AMONG AMERICAN

HIGH SCHOOL STUDENTS

1978-79

THIRTEENTH ANNUAL EDITION

VOLUME III

WHO'S WHO AMONG AMERICAN HIGH SCHOOL STUDENTS is a publication of Educational Communications, Inc. of Northbrook, Illinois and has no connection with "Who's Who In America" and its publisher, Marquis—Who's Who, Inc. Students featured in this volume attended school in the following states: Ohio, Indiana, Michigan and West Virginia.

Copyright 1979
Educational Communications, Inc.
3105 MacArthur Blvd.
Northbrook, Illinois 60062
Printed in U.S.A.
ISBN 0-915130-28-9
ISBN 0-915130-32-7 (8 Volume Set)
Library of Congress Catalog Card Number 68-43796

TABLE OF CONTENTS

Who's Who Review IV

Messages from Contributing Editors IX

Scholarship Award Winners XIX

Glossary of Abbreviations XXIV

Sample Biography XXV

Biographical Sketches 1

Students' Photographs P-1

WHO'S WHO REVIEW

When *WHO'S WHO AMONG AMERICAN HIGH SCHOOL STUDENTS* was first published in 1967, its *sole* purpose was to provide recognition for the positive achievements of outstanding junior and senior class secondary school students throughout the country. While this still remains as our primary goal, we have continuously strived to improve our program by adding new educational services which either directly or indirectly help WHO'S WHO students specifically and/or all high school students generally.

Within this review we wish to highlight some of these services to give readers a better idea of the scope and depth of the *total* WHO'S WHO activity program.

STUDENT SERVICES

SCHOLARSHIPS

In 1968, our second year of operation, a Scholarship Foundation was established to distribute funds to academically qualified students in need of financial assistance to continue their education. From a modest beginning of $4,000 in awards, the level of funding grew to $15,000 in 1974, $30,000 in 1976, $40,000 in 1978 and over $50,000 in 1979. Virtually all funds for this program are provided by the publishing company. Over $250,000 has been awarded to graduating high school students to date.

ANNUAL SURVEY OF HIGH ACHIEVERS

Since 1970 we have conducted an annual poll of student attitudes and opinions covering the major issues of the day. The purpose of this study is to provide a forum for students to make their opinions known to leaders in education and government who are in a position to respond. The results of the survey are distributed to the President of the United States, all U.S. Senators and Congressmen, Governors, key educators, research organizations and the press.

Survey stories have been reported in many journals, most newspapers and major broadcast media. (*U.S. News & World Report, Reader's Digest, Time, Parents Magazine, American Teacher, Today's Education, Face The Nation (CBS), State Legislatures, Denver Post, Atlanta Journal, Cleveland Press, Boston Globe, Chicago Tribune, Miami Herald, Tucson Daily Citizen, Detroit News, Los Angeles Times, New York Times* and *American Girl*, etc.).

THE COLLEGE REFERRAL SERVICE (CRS)

Through the CRS, WHO'S WHO sends announcements to colleges, universities and prospective employers informing them of the individual student's selection for listing and recognition. All WHO'S WHO students are sent a catalog of colleges and universities and an accompanying form and may initiate this service on a current or future basis. The major purpose of the CRS is to reinforce and substantiate the credentials of WHO'S WHO students seeking admission to college(s) or applying for employment. Several hundred institutions of higher education have informed us of the value and benefits of this service for *both* the students as well as the institutions. Over 50,000 referrals are made each year on behalf of WHO'S WHO students.

NEWSPAPER PUBLICITY FOR LISTED STUDENTS

Additional recognition for students is accomplished by providing local newspapers with data about students recognized in WHO'S WHO. Master listings of students who have authorized this service are sent to interested news media prior to publication. Many, many thousands of these articles have appeared in newspapers throughout the country.

A letter is sent each year to approximately 3,000 daily and weekly newspapers offering a listing of students from their communities. It is the responsibility of the newspapers to respond to this offer and notify us of their interest.

NEWSLETTER TO SCHOOL PAPER EDITOR—"WHO'S WHO REPORTS"

During the 1977-78 academic year we solicited all high school newspaper editors and advisors requesting news items from their individual schools. We received an overwhelming response of interesting items covering all areas of student and school activities, programs, features, curriculum innovations, sports, editorials, etc. Commencing with the 1978-79 academic year, these items have been published in newsletter format and distributed to all school newspaper editors to provide an idea exchange medium and a line of communications between schools.

FREE BOOK PROGRAM

WHO'S WHO sponsors the largest Free Book Program of any publisher in any field. Copies are offered to all participating high schools and youth organizations, all 7,500 public and private libraries and over 3,000 colleges and universities, junior colleges and accredited vocational/trade institutions. Between 10,000 and 15,000 complimentary copies with a retail value in excess of $200,000 are distributed each year through this program.

The major purpose of this extensive free distribution system is to provide meaningful, national recognition for listed students and to facilitate their ability to inspect their listing without necessitating purchase. Numerous participating high schools further comment that the book is well received in school libraries by all students and serves as an incentive in their overall pursuit of excellence.

GRANTS TO YOUTH ACTIVITY PROGRAMS

Since 1975 we have funded grants to youth organizations who require or desire financial support to continue or expand their programs and/or services on behalf of high school students. The amounts ranged from $100 to $10,000 and the scope from a local 4-H chapter to one of the largest national youth organizations in the country. The stipends fund scholarships in some instances or subsidize important educational publications or programs. We are only limited by imagination and our ability to identify worthwhile causes. Flexibility is one of our major assets. Following is a brief summary of grants issued or committed to date, totaling over $100,000:

Performing & Visual Arts Society (PAVAS),
$4,000, 2 Years
Funds chapter expansion mailings to high schools and resulted in numerous new chapters.

Contemporary-Family Life Curriculum,
$1,500, 1 Year
To curriculum author, Cliff Allen, Parkrose Senior High School, Parkrose, Oregon to fund formal request for grant from federal government. Result: Mr. Allen received $100,000 grant and has published textbook. Thousands of students now benefit from this exciting, contemporary subject matter.

Joint Council on Economic Education,
$10,000, 3 Years
The organization creates and distributes educational materials on economics for elementary, junior high, high schools and colleges, and is primarily concerned with educating students and teachers on economics.

Miss Teenage America Scholarship Program,
$18,000, 5 Years
For scholarship awards for each of the four semifinalists in this national competition. Contestants are selected on the basis of academic and leadership achievements, not beauty, poise or charm!

Distributive Education Clubs of America (DECA),
$10,000, 5 Years
We serve on the national Advisory Board of this major vocational/educational organization and sponsor the Finance & Credit Competency Based Award Program and the Registration Packet Brief Folios.

Office Education Association (OEA),
$12,000, 4 Years
We serve on the Advisory Board of this major vocational/educational organization also, and sponsor the OEA Awards Program and the Chapter Activities Manual, Secondary Level.

Foley, Minnesota 4-H Club,
$300, 1 Year
To sponsor a weekend retreat on career study for high school students.

Hamilton, Indiana Future Farmers
of America Chapter,
$100, 1 Year
This chapter received a 4½-acre site as a gift and was attempting to raise $2,000 from local businessmen to create a wildlife reserve for the pleasure and study of students and citizens. ECI employees made this contribution.

Animal Welfare Institute,
$1,000, 1 Year
For third edition of "Humane Biology Projects," a textbook for high school students presenting alternative laboratory experiments which do not involve stress or cruelty on or towards live animals.

Portland Christian Schools,
$1,000, 1 Year
For research to diagnose and assist children with specific language disability.

National Future Farmers of America Foundation,
$13,500, 4 Years
Sponsors a talent show at the National FFA Convention for the benefit of 20,000 attending students. This major vocational/educational organization serves over 500,000 high school students.

B'nai B'rith Career and Counseling Services,
$10,000, 3 Years
To revise "Starter File of Free Occupational Information," a B'nai B'rith publication for students seeking data on virtually all career fields. Publication will be available to all high school students and public libraries.

Modern Music Masters,
$4,000, 2 Years
For this national music honor society to produce literature for chapter expansion drive which we distribute to high school music departments.

Earthwatch,
$2,000, 2 Years
The organization conducts working scientific expeditions in many fields where qualified students work on a one-to-one basis with scientists and researchers. Our grants enable students to participate on a scholarship basis.

American Legion Boys Nation,
$3,500, 2 Years
For scholarships for the outstanding students elected President and Vice President of Boys Nation. The American Legion Boys State and Boys Nation's programs teach students valuable lessons about our democratic form of government.

American Legion Auxiliary Girls Nation,
$2,500, 1 Year
Provides $1,500 and $1,000 scholarships for the outstanding Girls Nation Citizen and Vice President respectively of this program which imparts valuable knowledge about functioning government.

Fellowship of Christian Athletes,
$5,300, 2 Years
Initial stipend of $2,800 sponsored a meeting of 600 athletic directors from all over the country who met in Louisville, Kentucky.

$2,500 has been designated for coaches' scholarships to attend FCA Coaches Conference during the summer of 1980. Conferences are held for coaches and their families, providing opportunities for spiritual, professional and family growth.

Mr. U.S.A. Teen Program,
$1,000, 1 Year
Scholarship for outstanding male student selected on the basis of leadership, citizenship, academic achievement and contributions to school, community and country.

Soroptimist International of the Americas, Inc.,
$1,000, 1 Year
Funds a scholarship of $1,000 to the finalist in their Youth Citizenship Awards program. Winner judged on service to school and community, leadership, dependability, integrity.

National Cheerleaders Association,
$1,800, 2 Years
Sponsoring scholarship awards for winners of state drill team contests.

Black United Fund,
$5,000, 1 Year
Funds scholarships for qualified black students selected by Black United Fund committee.

Law & Economic Center, University of Miami
School of Law,
$4,500, 1 Year
For a study of how to use mass media to communicate signficant issues on economics and public policy to the general public in an honest, provocative and understandable manner.

MAJOR POLICIES

Nominating Procedures

Each year all 21,000 public, private and parochial high schools are invited to nominate junior and senior class students who have achieved a "B" grade point average or better and demonstrated leadership in academics, athletics or extracurricular activities. The ultimate selections are left to the discretion of faculty members, but they may not select more than 15% of their eligible students. Most nominate less.

Recommendations are also received from churches of all denominations, scholarship agencies, civic and service groups and youth program sponsors at the national and local levels.

Editing Procedures

Recommendations and biographies are edited to assure compliance with our high standards. In the past three years alone, over 36,000 students who submitted biographies were deemed unqualified, necessitating the return of over $160,000 in orders. (Auditor's verification available upon request.)

The WHO'S WHO Board of Advisors met to define Standards and discuss general policies.

Verification of Data

To monitor the accuracy and integrity of data submitted by students, a nationally respected accounting firm is commissioned to conduct periodic, independent audits of published biographical data. Audits conducted in 1975 and 1978 reveal that up to 97.2% of the data published was substantially accurate. (Complete studies available upon request.)

Financial Policies

There are no financial requirements whatsoever contingent upon recognition in WHO'S WHO AMONG AMERICAN HIGH SCHOOL STUDENTS. The vast majority of students featured in all past editions have not purchased the book, but have received the recognition they have earned and deserve.

William C. Matney, Editor of WHO'S WHO AMONG BLACK AMERICANS, was introduced on the "Today Show" by book and theatre critic Gene Shalit. The publication has received numerous awards and honors.

WHO'S WHO supports Modern Music Masters, the largest High School Music Honor Society, through our grants program. Paul C. Krouse, WHO'S WHO Publisher, was honored at the last MMM Board of Directors meeting by their officers and directors.

OTHER PUBLICATIONS

Who's Who Among Black Americans

The second edition of WHO'S WHO AMONG BLACK AMERICANS was published by our organization in February of 1978. The book contains biographical sketches of 13,000 high-achieving black adults from all fields of endeavor.

This publication has been extremely well received by librarians, government agencies, educational institutions and major corporations. All four major library trade journals reviewed the publication and recommended it for their subscribers. The book was selected by the prestigious American Library Association as one of the "Outstanding Reference Books of the Year" for 1976, an honor comparable to an "Oscar" in the reference book field. It was also selected by *Black Scholar* as "A Notable Book" of 1976, one of only 19 publications to receive this distinction.

Most recently, WHO'S WHO AMONG BLACK AMERICANS was one of only 380 titles chosen by the Library of Congress to be exhibited at The White House Conference on Library & Information Services held in November, 1979.

The National Dean's List

The second annual edition of THE NATIONAL DEAN'S LIST was completed in September of 1979 and contains biographical sketches of 37,000 outstanding students from 1,200 colleges and universities. The 1979 edition is over 50% larger than last year's first edition. All students were selected by their respective deans because of their academic achievements. Each year, $5,000 in scholarship awards are distributed in $1,000 stipends to five distinguished students.

WHO'S WHO Executive Vice President, Jerald Lavin, receives sponsors award for FFA National Talent Show from Dan Reuwee, Former FFA Director of Information, and Bernie Staller, FFA Executive Director.

WHO'S WHO sponsors the annual Talent Show for the Future Farmers of America. WHO'S WHO VP Jerald Lavin joined the participants when they assembled in Kansas City.

WHO'S WHO sponsors four $1,000 scholarship awards for the four semifinalists of the Miss Teenage America Pageant. Awards are announced on the national telecast. WHO'S WHO Vice President Jerald Lavin is shown with Debbie Lewis, Miss Teenage Houston; Lori Heeren, Miss Teenage Sioux City; Laura Taylor, Miss Teenage Columbia; Kit Marchel, Miss Teenage Los Angeles.

WHO'S WHO sponsors the Chapter Activities Scrapbook event for the Office Education Association (OEA). From left, winning chapters are: Buckeye Hills Career Center, Caglipolis, Ohio; Aldine High School, Houston, Texas; Denton High School, Denton, Texas; David Crocket High School, Jonesboro, Tennessee; Dulles High School, Stafford, Texas; Algona High School, Algona, Iowa.

WHO'S WHO Executive Vice President, Jerald Lavin, with DECA Executive Director, Harry Applegate. WHO'S WHO supports DECA Competitive Events and serves on their National Advisory Board.

The Wooster family from Baltimore, Ohio were all featured in WHO'S WHO at different times. Shown above from left to right are Paul, featured 1977-78; Merrie Linn, featured 1973-74; Dee Ann, 1972-73; Debbie, 1970-71; and Iris, 1975-76.

WHO'S WHO sponsors a $1,500 scholarship award for the President and a $1,000 scholarship for the Vice President of the American Legion Boy's Nation program. Jerald Lavin and Paul Krouse presented Award Certificate to the 1978 President, Michael Lopez, J. K. Mullen H.S., Denver, Colorado at Boy's State Directors Conference in Indianapolis, Indiana.

PROFILE OF WHO'S WHO STUDENT
(Statistics from 1979 Edition)

Total number of Students 355,000

Academics
Total Juniors and Seniors enrolled
    during 1979 (%) 5%
Females (%) 61%
Males (%) 39%
Grade Point Average (%)
  "A" 67%
  "B" 32%
  "C" 1%
Local Honor Roll 252,684
National Honor Society 124,948
National Merit Ranking 16,071

Leadership Activities/Clubs
Student Council 82,202
Boys State/Girls State 30,471
Senior Class Officers 22,673
Junior Class Officers 34,876
Key Club 12,970

Major Vocational Organizations
4-H 37,394
Future Homemakers of America 30,937
Future Farmers of America 11,822
Distributive Education Clubs of America 7,091
Office Education Association 4,873

Varsity Athletics
Track....................................48,068
Basketball 46,912
Cheerleading/Pom Pon 36,130
Football 30,245
Baseball 25,265
Tennis 17,980
Fellowship of Christian Athletes 18,695

Music/Performing Arts
Orchestra/Band 104,037
Chorus 88,943
Drama..................................63,592

Miscellaneous
Church Activities 102,426
Yearbook 71,428
School Paper 63,027
Community Worker 39,913

MESSAGES FROM THE BOARD OF CONTRIBUTING EDITORS

JUDY HOUGHTON
*Executive Vice President
& General Manager
Miss Teenage America*

JUDY HOUGHTON

The MISS TEENAGE AMERICA Medallion bears five words—Integrity, Honor, Leadership, Knowledge and Achievement.

The young women who earn the right to wear the Medallions are truly representative of these qualities and accomplishments. By merit of the distinction of having been chosen to be recognized in this prestigious publication, it is obvious that you, too, possess these valuable traits.

I like to think of these as tools, of a sort, to build upon a successful future. Integrity and honor will win you the respect of others, as well as the inner satisfaction of self-respect. Achievement, knowledge and leadership offer you pride in accomplishment, an ability to help others and an opportunity to obtain that goal—and then the next goal—and then the next.

You will notice that I used the term, *earned,* instead of *won* in reference to the MISS TEENAGE AMERICA Medallions. You can't count on luck but you can count on sincere effort.

I have a favorite poem that perhaps says it best. The author is unknown.

Captains and Kings

Isn't it strange how Captains and Kings
And Clowns who caper in sawdust rings
And just plain folks like you and me
Are builders of our destiny.

To each is given a bag of tools,
A shapeless mass and a book of rules
And each must fashion, ere time has flown
A stumbling block...or a stepping stone.

The future is yours. I wish you many stepping stones.

MAJ. GEN.
DAVID B. EASSON
*Commandant
Air Force ROTC*

DAVID B. EASSON

A recent lecturer here at the Air Force's Air University was asked the question: Are today's young people worse than we were? This scholarly gentleman thought for a moment and answered, "Yes. The worse ones are worse, but that's only half the answer. The truth is that the ones who are better are so much better that if I had to choose for the future, I'd take today's kids."

His perception is much the same as mine. My business is molding young men and women into dedicated, responsible Air Force officers. That job is so much easier when we start with the best. And the young people coming into our program today are better than at any time in my memory. Their intelligence, maturity and sense of responsibility assure me that the future defense of our country will be in good hands.

Each year we receive upwards of 10,000 scholarship applications from high school seniors. Their academic achievements, involvement in school government, athletics, civic affairs and related activities, and their high moral values, speak well for America's future. Those of you selected for the high honor of being included in this edition of *Who's Who Among American High School Students* support that belief. It is noteworthy that our scholarship applicants, and you, represent all regions of the United States and all social strata, and include significant numbers of women and members of minority groups. You are truly a national resource.

The Air Force reflects this broad spectrum of our society. We are not a "mirror" image, nor do we try to be. Through the careful selection of people for admission to our profession, we attempt to project an image of what is right and good in America. We are often at the vanguard in such social issues as equal rights and opportunities for women and minorities. In this highly technological age, and with limited resources, we must actively seek out the best young men and women available without respect to race, religion, sex, or national origin. In this regard, we are competing with business and industry for your talent.

Whatever path to the future you choose for yourself, I encourage you to set lofty goals. There are sure to be obstacles along the way, but I have found that hard work and concerted effort are usually all that it takes to hurdle most obstacles. I prefer to think of these obstacles as "challenges." If there are no obstacles, your goals are not high enough.

Something I read recently, obviously written by someone with an analytical mind, may be worthy of your consideration: "You only have to be two per cent better than your peers to get 100 per cent ahead."

HARRY APPLEGATE
Executive Director
Distributive Education
Clubs of America

HARRY A. APPLEGATE

Aren't you lucky! Here we are on the threshold of the entire decade of the 1980's and everything at this point looks more promising than ever. During the next ten years all of us will witness events, discoveries and progress that probably was not yet thought of as the 1970's ended. And this immediate year ahead contains your open door to every bit of opportunity that you are willing to grasp!

We live in the greatest country in the world—the longest surviving Republic—the nation where your individual vote is requested and respected. We live as beneficiaries of a good foundation. And though it may be an accident that you were born in a nation where you were born free, and where it has been a privilege for you to enjoy that freedom, it is now your responsibility to see that you remain free. Free to choose, free to voice your opinion, free to live where you desire, free to choose your leaders, free to enjoy life.

You are to be congratulated on your accomplishments to date. Your selection to be recognized in this publication is ample testimony that you have made a running start. Now just settle in to a good, steady, progressive pace and start reaching and working for all you desire. You'll make it, I know. Because if you don't, someone else will, and there are too many persons counting on you for you to disappoint them. And may God be with you as you reach.

BERNIE L. STALLER
Executive Director
National FFA Foundation

BERNIE L. STALLER

Congratulations! Your efforts, your drive, your involvement and your dedication to a goal...have led to success...and to this recognition. For those characteristics you have been duly recorded in this, the 13th issue of *Who's Who Among American High School Students.*

It's a great start! It's a great foundation...a beginning! It is also a great waste...if you stop now. You have invested heavily in yourself and your future; so, too, have heavy investments been made by your parents, your teachers, your school and scores of others—will your investment and theirs...be profitable?

Will your chosen field advance in the years ahead because you were involved? Will your church, your school, and your community be better because you were there to lead and guide? Will your family enjoy the richness of love because of your devotion and dedication?

Only you know the answers. You have made a beginning, now continue to grow and expand, continue to learn and teach, and continue to respond and lead—the future is yours...and it's now!

MORTON TEMSKY
Chairman
Department of Law &
Business
Schenectady County
Community College

MORTON TEMSKY

Our world needs individuals who want to cope with and solve the many problems that build tension and fear.

You, the graduating seniors, shouldn't have to be faced with dilemmas such as solving: depression, inflation, disease, shortages, oppression, hunger. But you, just like every other generation, have to meet the challenge of the future.

Your skills, energy, and ingenuity have been nurtured in high school. You will sharpen them throughout college. But your true test will be to apply those attributes to bring solutions to those or other problems as listed, and more important, to bring freedom and peace in this our world.

DR. S. NORMAN FEINGOLD
National Director
B'nai B'rith Career &
Counseling Service

S. NORMAN FEINGOLD

It is again time for me to honor tomorrow's leaders today. You are the young adults who are listed in the prestigious *Who's Who Among American High School Students*. My response is written with a glow of professional satisfaction.

The future is now. The dedicated talents of young adults who are listed in this Directory bode well for a strong America both for the present and the future. Your superior achievements in school and community exhibit a quality of excellence and a deep concern for people at a time when too many people all over the world feel alienated and alone.

The changing, challenging world presents all kinds of exciting and volunteer opportunities. Look around you. Creative leadership is needed as never before. Youth leadership is the heart of a country's potential for further growth and development.

Each one of you described in this Directory is a part of a dynamic young leadership. Use it well. I am confident that you will do so in a style that reflects your goals and values.

As I peruse in depth applications for scholarships from candidates listed in this Directory, I find myself seeing hundreds and hundreds of dreams becoming fulfilled in ways that were never possible before.

The old saying comes to mind. Rank has its responsibilities as well as its privileges. Wear them well. I am confident that you will do so for you are our country's tomorrow. The baton is placed in your good hands.

CLIFF HUMPHREY
Director
Ecology Action
Educational Institute

CLIFF HUMPHREY

We know that energy performs work, and we know that our economy runs on stored energy. But would more energy solve the problems of our times? I don't think so.

I think we have an energy crisis all right, but not the kind of energy that comes in a barrel or is measured in BTU's. I'm concerned with creativity, vim and vigor, a real positive approach to life.

Here we sit in America, the world's most powerful nation—a nation that just exploded on the world scene in only 200 years. And we are sitting around waiting for something to happen. Are we waiting for the oil to run out or only until it reaches $5.00 a gallon before we do something?

We have built an economy that has taken energy for granted. Every indication is that energy will be more expensive in the future. Our wealth has come from mining resources and to a certain extent exploiting labor. But now our society is on record as being opposed to the exploitation of workers and our resources are being rapidly depleted. It is time to make some changes.

What are our options? Who knows? Does anyone know? Why not? Finding out these answers takes energy—lots of it! Do you have the energy to find out? The answers do not depend on what OPEC or the government is doing about "the energy crisis." The answers must come from all of you!

DR. WESLEY APKER
Executive Secretary
National Association
of State Boards
of Education

WESLEY APKER

William McFee in his *Tales of Hoffman* states that "the world is not interested in the storms you encountered, but did you bring in the ship?" There may be a tendency in these difficult times to complain too much, and concentrate too little on long-term solutions. There is also a tendency to seek easy remedies or to blame others. Your greatest human assets are your human spirit, your vision and capacity to stay focused on your goals. As you move into your university and adult years, do not lose those assets. Sharpen and expand them, for as McFee has said, the world cares little about the storms that toss you; it cares greatly, however, about bringing in the ship.

LESTER G. BENZ

LESTER G. BENZ
Executive Secretary
Emeritus
Quill & Scroll Society

Success! What is it? How does one achieve it? These are questions that every high school graduate faces today.

Those high achievers who apply for and receive college scholarships are usually asked to write a brief essay on their plans and hopes for the future. What do you want out of life? Most of these essays carry the thought, "I want to be successful." That is a lofty goal, but unless we have a plan for getting there, the objective may never be reached.

I recently heard one of our successful national leaders say, "The successful man is one who knows where he is going." In other words, success requires that we have a goal. To say, "I have a dream," is fine, but unless we translate that dream into reality and carry it through to achievement, we have not been successful.

How, then, do we achieve our goal? The answer is dedication. Dedication is singleness of purpose. It is the determination to achieve and to reach our goal in the face of discouragement. It is determination to overcome obstacles, of which there are always many in the path to success. Dedication often requires sacrifice. Many times we are tempted to take a detour from the path to success and in so doing we lose sight of where we are going. Remember that the successful man always knows where he is going and allows nothing to distract him from his goal.

Another theme that runs through a majority of the essays in scholarship applications is the ideal of service. "I want my life to benefit mankind and I want to contribute something that will make the world a better place in which to live." Such statements are common and reflect the high goals of today's high school graduate as he heads toward college in quest of success. Indeed, success and service are inseparable. The time honored motto of Rotary International is "He Profits Most Who Serves Best." This ideal of service has always been foremost in the lives of the world's most successful people.

So, in your pursuit of success, first establish your goal and then pursue it with dedication and determination, remembering that service is the most important goal you can set for yourself.

FRANCES HARLEY

FRANCES HARLEY
Executive Secretary
Modern Music Masters

If asked to sum up in three words the most important and integral ingredients for a happy and successful life, I would say "enthusiasm," "dedication," and "service."

All of you fine young men and women who have merited inclusion in this volume will surely press on to greater achievements throughout life, because you have already demonstrated that you are enthusiastic, dedicated and have been of service. You have been given special recognition by your teachers and administrators because you have been enthusiastic about all your activities and endeavors.

With enthusiasm you must address yourselves to the tasks which lie before you. It has been wisely said: "Years wrinkle the skin, but lack of enthusiasm wrinkles the soul." Always remember that enthusiasm can be the keynote to success!

Now we come to my second word—"dedication." If we are to lead a personally fulfilling life we must determine our priorities and must become wholly committed to them. First and foremost these priorities should best be idealistic in nature. When someone becomes dedicated to an ideal in any field of endeavor and strives to conduct himself in such a manner that at least one segment of the world will become better because he has lived and made a contribution toward this betterment, he will reap the richest rewards of the spirit. These cannot be interpreted in dollars and cents values.

You young high achievers have also demonstrated that you have become dedicated to a host of values not required by merely completing courses in your school curriculum. You have "gone the second mile" and have set a significant example to your fellow students.

Now we come to my third word—"service." Service to one's fellow-man, in whatever field his God-given talents lie, will bring untold personal rewards and insure a successful and happy life. Man is a spiritual being. It is not only "what is in one's head" that will bring about much needed reforms in today's world which is fraught with a multitude of seemingly unsolvable problems, but it is "what is in one's heart" that can make the ultimate difference. The challenges are great, but you have a great potential as tomorrow's leaders. You are vested with the responsibility of righting the wrongs which have been perpetrated by past generations. You have the opportunity to help bring into being a new dawn of peace, justice and equality for all, regardless of race, creed or color.

It is a mighty challenge, but you must meet it, if our great nation is to regain its former respected world leadership. And once again we come back to that word—"service." Whether one's career lies ahead in business, science, medicine, law, the arts, homemaking, or other fields, it will be by service to others in the family, school, church or temple, community and nation, that our influence for good will be felt.

So I congratulate all of you and know that with your enthusiasm, dedication and service, you will make a significant and lasting contribution to our country's great future.

VALERIE F. LEVITAN
Executive Director
Soroptimist International
of the Americas, Inc.

VALERIE F. LEVITAN

Congratulations! You've reached a major milestone and can be justly proud.

And now to college, where your courses can be more exploratory than ever before. Have fun! Select what you've been curious about—whether it's a special science class, a language like Chinese, a religion you've read about, a period of history or a course in sociology you've heard about. Enjoy museums! Take up a new sport. And most of all, travel—study abroad. Expand your horizons, for then you'll never be the same again!

And when you come home you'll see your family as people, not just relatives. You'll appreciate them for who they are, recognize their talents, and come to understand how their faith and trust in you has made you what you are and what you will be.

May all of you be amply rewarded! Your future ever bright and fulfilling!

ROBERT L. VAN ANDA
Paul Revere
Insurance Co.

ROBERT VAN ANDA

"Honoring Tomorrow's Leaders Today," a milestone in anyone's life. After all the handshaking, congratulations and the confetti stops falling around your shoulders you must face tomorrow. It is a new ball game, but nothing you cannot handle. You can handle it because you have already accepted the first challenge of life and you have prepared yourself well with a foundation that is made of mortar and steel and will stand the tests of tomorrow. But now you must continue to prepare as college is on the horizon and another challenge is about to present itself. You will undoubtedly handle this challenge the same as you did the last—one step at a time. You get to the top of the ladder one step at a time. The rungs are not made for resting, but are positioned to give you a boost to the next one. Do not stop, just "Keep On Keeping On."

As you continue to prepare for life you will find many obstacles that will present themselves. Some will seem almost insurmountable, but nothing you cannot handle. Mistakes will be made. Remember, erasers are put on the ends of pencils to correct errors and people that do not make mistakes once in a while are usually doing nothing. If I could give each of you one piece of advice, take God with you as a partner down the road of life. Let Him help you make the decisions and do not just turn to Him when your back is against the wall, but make Him a vital part of your everyday life. Let His goodness shine through you and He will give it unto you.

Certainly the world is rife with problems. If we look for the negatives we will most certainly find them, but try looking for the positive sides of life. Look for the good in your fellow man, in your community, your state and your country and then work towards trying to lift each just a little higher. Reach out and touch a life and you will feel better for it. Remember to give of yourself and then some.

SARA-ALYCE P. WRIGHT

SARA-ALYCE P. WRIGHT
Executive Director
National Board of the
Young Women's Christian
Association of the U.S.A.

Each year a new generation of high school graduates is advised, inspired and challenged to face a future filled with opportunities and responsibilities. We must hold to this practice in 1979 even as our thoughts ponder the meaning of the end of this decade and the beginning of a new one. The marking of time and history by decades has been used to define the dominant theme of a period, to measure its progress, and to identify directions for the next ten years.

During the seventies severe blows have been dealt to our nation's social, economic and political systems. More than ever it seems that the years immediately ahead will require a new determination to achieve the fundamental goals of a democratic society. Youth cannot be held in reserve for this task even though the older generation has always tried to "make things easier for youth than it was for them." Rather, those older must express confidence in and give support to young people.

Utilizing their natural faith and courage, young people must become immediately involved in working untiringly and creatively for solutions to the vast complexities of domestic and international issues and for the greater realization of the human potential.

ALFRED McELROY
Chairman
National Advisory Council
on the Education of
Disadvantaged Children

ALFRED Z. McELROY

It is difficult, sometimes, to contemplate statements to be made to the "cream of the American crop" of high school students; because each of you, in his own unique way, has made a mark on this nation through your dedicated educational endeavors.

Each of you has different dreams, hopes, and ambitions. However, no matter how various your aspirations, we all must agree on one thing—the mind can *successfully* handle only one set of thoughts at one time. Those thoughts associated with successful efforts usually result in rewarding benefits, while those associated with any and all aspects of failure result in failure.

As you have personally merited enrollment in this illustrious group, it is evident that you are motivated toward success, and possess the determination to pursue your future goals with great vigor. My personal recommendation, at this time, is that you not abandon the naive dreams that have brought you thus far. Turn back the pages of your high school career to page one—your ninth grade year. Remember the enthusiasm, excitement, and ambitions you had? Remember how hard you worked to achieve your goals? Even though you have now reached pages 200 and 300, and there are many more pages to come, it would be wise to remember that those pages only polish and improve the foundation you laid on page one.

However, do not let the polish and ambitions fade with future hazards that may be encountered. Never forget the hard and dedicated work it took to achieve the flow you now feel. For it is all these ingredients that will help you to build a stronger foundation in the years to come.

Each of the educational building blocks you handle with care and eagerness will play an intricate part in keeping your future efforts on a firm base, no matter how high you wish to project your life. I wish you continued good luck in all your lifelong pursuits, and many, many successes.

WALLY WIKOFF
Editor
Federal Intermediate
Credit Bank, 7th District

WALLY WIKOFF

Reading biographies of great leaders throughout history is not only fascinating reading, but excellent "homework" for becoming a leader oneself.

Inherent in the lives of all of those leaders is the fact that these people prepared for their roles by concentration, diligent effort and usually at a great sacrifice of some of those pleasures most of us prefer.

The great leaders are those who have, as a result of their dedication, performed a major service to humanity. In some cases that service is unique—such as the discovery of a cure for a frightful disease or perfecting a more efficient way to use nonrenewable fuel.

Too many, alas, give another service—lip service. There is an abundance of that. The choice of services in the future is yours. One is easy; the other is terribly difficult. All indications are that those listed in this book have already made the choice.

S. STOWELL SYMMES
Director of Curriculum
Joint Council on
Economic Education

S. STOWELL SYMMES

As citizens in an increasingly interdependent world, your greatest challenge will be to help fashion a better life for humankind; not only in your local communities, but also throughout the globe. It does not really matter whether you ultimately assume the mantle of "leader" or of "follower." After all, most persons play both roles to varying degrees during their lifetimes. What does matter, especially in an open society, is the realization that individuals significantly shape the world whenever they make decisions.

Much of your life will be spent weighing options and measuring the costs and benefits to yourself and to society, of the choices you make. How you choose to use time and money reflects your personal priorities and, when aggregated with the choices made by others, reflects the priorities of a community. Furthermore, how you respond to difficult issues dealing with environment, cities, energy, health care, poverty, taxation, and employment will determine the level of public dialogue and the quality of solution attempted. As an active participant in our growing complex economy you must face these challenges with wisdom and humble idealism. Decisions will not be easy.

You have the power to choose and thus to make a difference. Use that power generously, compassionately, and wisely. Our very existence as a civilized people depends upon the quality of your choices.

RANDY ST. CLAIR
Director
National Program Activities
Fellowship of
Christian Athletes

RANDY ST. CLAIR

The Spring day outside my window is crystal clear, with a deep blue sky, and brilliant sunshine. Earlier today, thunderstorms swept across the city, with low banks of grey clouds, and rain in sheets.

The change in the weather has prompted me to pen my thoughts to you, to offer my congratulations on your many accomplishments, and to wish you well as you continue your life's journey.

For me, the weather, and the seasons, are continuing reminders of the changes in my life, the opportunities that stand before me, and the richness of my memories. You stand today, filled with the experiences of high school, and challenged by the opportunities awaiting you, in the midst of your own personal growth and change.

An exciting time, to be sure. And I am grateful for the opportunity to share, at least momentarily, that time with you. Not long ago, I brought my thoughts together on the changes in the seasons and in our lives, and I would like to share them with you now. So, with my sincere wish for a happy, successful, and meaningful life, here is "The Passing of Seasons."

The cold October rain is beating
Quietly and steadily on my roof,
And the screen at the window
    Catches and streaks the shower,
    Caught in the reflection
    Of the light in the courtyard.

The reds and golds that decorate the Autumn
Fall to earth softly
As the sun drops toward the horizon,
Shaping long, lonely shadows
    in the western sky.

The day is darkening,
The grey sky is turning cold,
As Autumn passes into Winter.

Seeing myself in the season's change,
Looking back to Autumn's past,
I have known good and bad times,
    highs and lows.

Too often I have lost good moments,
        good memories,
Overcome by failure,
    defeat,
    sadness.

Now, in the beauty and promise of Fall,
I understand that nothing can change
Our moments after they're past.

I want to enjoy and learn
From my moments,
Not regret and hurt.

So, as the leaves fall outside,
And my breath turns foggy,
I am committed to not miss
Life
As Winter begins.

The weatherman said
The snow wouldn't miss this time.

He was right.

Driven by the wind,
Flakes became inches,
Piles and mounds,
    Fouling traffic,
        Driving walkers to cover.

Pubs became havens for respite from
    the storm,
Smoky, good-smelling rooms
of conversation, food,
        being together.

We shared community with one another,
Silent, but smiling greetings
For those who joined us,
    Their coats layered with ice,
        Hair in disarray.

As the evening approached,
The city grew quiet:
    Traffic signals blinked
        at empty intersections;
    Streetlights silhouetted
        the storm's last gasp;
    Sidewalks became highways
        for walkers,
            cross-country skiers,
        and even a bike rider.

Winter had kept us inside all day,
Driven together
By the snow and cold.

Now we celebrate the beauty of
Snowflakes and wind,
As we talk and walk and laugh,
Gathering at deli's and pizza parlors.

Funny, how we need a blizzard
to come together.

Winter
Is not a time to be alone,
You know.

But I am

Changes in my life
Have left me
By myself.

Homemade cookies,
Private jokes,
And quiet conversation
Are missed,
        to be sure.

But there is a 'newness' now,
A better understanding of me.

There is a freedom in my life,
And a willingness to reach out,
Beyond my 'aloneness.'

I want to participate in life;
I want to open up in my freedom;
I want to be honest with you,
            and me.

The Winter
Reminds me that this is
The season for straight lines
    and being honest.

God, I don't want to stay inside,
Driven behind the door
By snow and cold and hurt and failure.

I am anxious for Spring's
Warmth and sunshine,
    The passing from grey to green,
            cold to warm.

The hope of Spring—

Sweet smells and afternoon showers,
Open windows and birds singing,
Baseball and cookouts,
Bare feet and washing cars,
The sun on your face and in your bones—
    The reawakening to life.

Spring is the season of change,
            rebirth;
The world comes to life again,
Full of hope and promise.

God reminds us
In the beauty of blue skies
    and smiling faces that
Hey,
It's time to change.

The passing of seasons
Reminds us
That we're changing too.

Reds & golds to
        Snow & wind to
            Sunshine & warmth.

Loneliness to
    The importance of moments to
        Reaching out &
            Being honest.

We must never forget that Spring
    Always comes—

With hope
And freedom,

Through the changes
    in our lives,
And in the beauty
    of God's world.

DWIGHT LOKEN
Program Director
Office Education
Association

DWIGHT LOKEN

Congratulations on your outstanding high school achievements which have warranted your recognition in this year's edition of *Who's Who Among American High School Students*. It is my prayer in life that you will get to know your own real potential; that you will become the person you want to be! I offer the following suggestions as we approach the '80's...

"I will form good habits, and become their slave. I will be happier than I ever believed possible to be in this world of strife, sorrow, and pain. I will walk tall among men, and they will know me not, for today I am a new man, and a new life. I will greet each new day with love in my heart. And, when I am tempted to criticize, I will bite my tongue. And, when I move to praise, I will shout it from the housetop. I will persist until I see new success. I am nature's greatest miracle. I will live each day as if it were my last. I will master my emotions. Each day I will multiply my value a hundred fold. I will set my goals for today, for next week, and for next year, and the rest of my life. I WILL ACT NOW!"

PAUL DE FRANCIS
National Director
Performing and Visual
Arts Society

PAUL DE FRANCIS

Although the United States represents only 6% of the world's population, we consume 44% of the coal, 63% of the natural gas, and 33% of the petroleum that is consumed each year. On the other hand, over 80% of all newborns are raised in developing countries under conditions of hunger, malnutrition, disease, and inadequate housing. When over 80% of the world's newborn are raised in developing countries in conditions of hunger, malnutrition, disease, and inadequate housing, and when we use over one-sixth of the world's fuel, we had better take a good look at our values, our concern for mankind, and our own personal attitudes.

First, let us give thanks for what we have—food, shelter, transportation, education, and a security in knowing that our writings and thoughts won't land us in a concentration camp.

What can we do to help the developing countries? We can tighten our belts, eat moderately, drive moderately, heat and cool our homes and buildings moderately, and encourage our legislators to initiate advice and aid to those countries that request it. The world situation is "bigger than both of us," as the old saying goes. We are going to begin thinking in terms of the whole world, and not in terms of America only. If we don't think in terms of the entire world we will find ourselves in a very grave situation, one which will be catastrophic in dimension.

In summary: The problems of the world revolve around food, fuel, disease, housing, education, and government. Let us be thankful for the great gifts we possess, and let us do what we can to help the needy countries to help themselves.

BRIAN ROSBOROUGH
President
Earthwatch

BRIAN ROSBOROUGH

Think back. When you were being born, I stood where you are today, wondering what to study in school, where to point my life.

At the time, I worried that everything worth doing would be done, that there would be no new peaks to climb, no frontiers to explore, no problems left to solve—sound familiar?

But in your first seventeen years, a lot has happened.

Before you could walk, we put a man in space; as you learned to talk, we witnessed the assassination of a young president. Before you finished the sixth grade, America had lost its first war. As you started high school, another first, a U.S. president resigned.

Change creates opportunity. New problems beg solutions. New discoveries yield new frontiers.

In your seventeen years, biologists have discovered the origins of life, geologists have resolved the movement of continents, and astronomers have tracked the beginning of the universe to a point in time about 20 billion years ago. All that in 17 years!

We are told you are leaders, at least *Who's Who Among American High School Students* says so.

Well, I hope so, because we need fresh troops out here (after school) to help solve some fascinating problems. So hurry up. The world awaits your contribution.

CHRISTINE STEVENS
President
Animal Welfare Institute

CHRISTINE STEVENS

The campaign to save the whales has attracted support from stars of stage, screen, and television, urging us all to greater efforts to end the commercial killing of these mysterious giants.

John Denver, with his guitar, sang to the Commissioners of twenty-three nations gathered in London at the meeting of the International Whaling Commission, July 9-13, 1979. He told them how he had swum with whales, a mother and infant, and of the deep impression they had made on him, and he sang a song he had composed, "I Want to Live."

Before the meeting, Katharine Hepburn, Jack Lord, Gregory Peck and Jason Robards made recordings of messages to save the whales so that the Animal Welfare Institute could send them out to radio stations all over the country to play as public service announcements. All the stars generously donated their great talents and their precious time to help the cause.

Meantime, painstaking detective work has been carried out in different parts of the world about the pirate whalers who fly flags of convenience and hide their true identities in dummy companies in small countries. A Norwegian bank and a big Japanese fishing company have been written up in the press, with a photograph of the pirate whaler "Sierra" offloading meat to the Yamato Reefer shown in a documentary by Thames Television.

The pirates kill every whale they can find, regardless of how endangered the species is. They kill nursing mothers and infant whales, and they keep only the choicest cuts, throwing most of the dead whale overboard.

We must all work hard to stop the pirates and to end all commercial whaling while there is still time for the different species of whales to regenerate: the blue whale, biggest animal ever to live on earth; the humpback whale, whose beautiful songs can be heard for miles through the ocean—more than 100,000 recordings of the "Songs of the Humpback Whale" have been sold; the sperm whale, possessor of the biggest and most convoluted brain in the world; the sei whale, swiftest of all in swimming; the southern right whale, almost extinct but so playful it uses its huge flukes as a sail in the wind, sails in, then sounds and does it all over again; the gray whale, known to old-time whalers as a "devil fish" (an ignorant name, since whales are mammals that suckle their offspring) because the mothers were so determined in defending their young, holding a harpooned baby under one flipper and trying to bash the whaling boat with their flukes; the bowhead whales of the arctic almost wiped out by Yankee whalers, the object of an Alaskan Eskimo ritual; the Brydes' whale, long confused with the sei whale, the object of killing under so-called "scientific permits" by whalers who sold the meat and oil; the fin whale, central figure in Farley Mowat's well-known *A Whale for the Killing*; and last, the minke whale, so small that it was rejected by the huge factory ships as not worth the trouble to kill until the blue whales had become so scarce that they were said to be commercially extinct, and fin whales, the second largest, were heading in the same direction. Then the great antarctic whaling fleets with their spotter planes, helicopters and radar directed their war against the whales to the small minkes, curious, friendly creatures known for their "ship-seeking behavior" which makes them easy victims. More than 12,000 of them are scheduled to suffer long drawn out, painful deaths with "cold harpoons" incapable of killing quickly. This is the number allocated for the coming year to whaling nations belonging to the IWC. What the pirates will do besides, no one knows.

DANIEL K. INOUYE

It is with a sense of great personal pride and respect that I commend each of you for being selected for listing in the WHO'S WHO AMONG AMERICAN HIGH SCHOOL STUDENTS, 1978-79. This is an honor that your parents will never forget and one that will become more precious to you as you advance in your chosen careers.

Our world is becoming more and more complex and it is your generation that will have to aggressively address major national and international problems that mankind has never dreamed of before.

During the recent past, we have been blessed with an uncertain Peace, but our societal responsibilities have continued to grow. Approximately one out of every three children born will die before reaching the age of five, mostly from malnutrition-related causes. Our environment and especially our oceans are rapidly being overcome by toxic chemicals that were unknown to mankind just a few years ago; and there is every indication that our world's fossil fuel supply will be exhausted within our lifetime.

These are extraordinary challenges. However, I am confident that among you lay the solutions. Generations to come depend upon your success. Good luck!

THE HONORABLE
DANIEL K. INOUYE
Member of United States
Senate from Hawaii

DAVID LADD
Professor of Law
University of Miami
Law School

DAVID LADD

You are a superior person.

That is why your name appears in *Who's Who Among American High School Students*.

Someone—your teacher, your coach, your peer—has seen in you something better, something special, something worthy of respect, admiration and emulation. In mind, talent, character or achievement, in work, sports, or competition, you have distinguished yourself.

You are already a part of our elite. Be proud!

For nowadays, many people try to treat *elite* and *elitism* as dirty words. Undemocratic, they say.

Pure rubbish. After all, what does elite mean? "1. The choice or best of anything considered collectively. 2. ...persons of the highest class..." *Random House College Dictionary*, 1975, p. 429.

Now that you have been identified as one of the "best," and a person of the "highest class," what are your responsibilities? Primarily to develop your own unique talent and to insist that institutions allow extraordinary talent to be recognized and to be rewarded extraordinarily, wherever it appears. That is not only justice, but the way to achieve the best use of the talents of every person. Three cheers for inequality!

Of course, you say. Why make an obvious point? Because, obvious or not, a pernicious notion is abroad and growing: Everybody must be equal in status and wealth. Not equal in opportunity, but equal in fact. The notion is called equalitarianism (egalitarianism), and is rooted in one of the most unattractive human weaknesses—envy. Egalitarianism will inevitably produce equality in universal mediocrity.

So defend your gifts. Resist every pressure toward the ordinary.

Democracy does not mean an egalitarian leveling down to the lowest common denominator, but freedom in which you and every person may realize the best in him or her. Thus, every democracy can have an aristocracy in the sense of "any class or group considered to be superior."

You are already an aristocrat. Be proud!

DR. ROBERT MacVICAR
President
Oregon State University

ROBERT MacVICAR

I have had the privilege for several years of writing a brief message to a select group of young people who will shape the future of our nation for the next fifty years. Each of you whose names are in this book are blessed with unusual capacities and have greater potential than your fellows. Because of this fact, greater responsibilities will be yours during the careers which lie before you.

We in the developed nations of the world face unusually critical challenges in the decades ahead. We have come to depend upon machines to do an ever-increasing part of the tedious and physically demanding work—including computers to do many tasks which only human beings could do even a short 25 years ago. These machines, however, are costly to produce in terms of exhaustible resources and often demanding of energy in the form of fossil fuels or electrical power to operate. Both materials and energy are becoming increasingly scarce and changes in lifestyle may very well become necessary.

Whether we adjust to new and less material and energy consumptive patterns of living in a rational and orderly fashion or face some tremendous and worldwide "shoot out" over the dwindling supplies may well depend on you and your counterparts in the other countries of the world. Your demonstrated capacities for intellectual achievement and the many service-oriented projects to which you have so generously contributed your time are positive indicators that you will assume effectively the tasks of leadership which will be yours.

Regardless of how you prepare yourself for these awesome tasks—by formal education in college or university or by other means—you have much more to learn. I welcome you to the new challenges that graduation from secondary school will bring. I have confidence you will accept the challenges of the future in the same dynamic way you have met those of the present.

THE EDUCATIONAL COMMUNICATIONS SCHOLARSHIP FOUNDATION

During the 1978-79 academic year, approximately 20,000 students competed for scholarship awards sponsored by the Educational Communications Scholarship Foundation which is funded by the publishing company. Students competed by completing an application which requested data regarding achievement test scores, grade point average, extracurricular activities, work experience and general background information. Semifinalists were selected based on careful examination of all this information and were then requested to provide information regarding financial need. In addition, semifinalists were asked to write an essay from which the Scholarship Awards Committee attempted to evaluate the overall maturity of the students.

Fifty winners were selected and a total of $50,000 was awarded. Over $250,000 has been distributed through the ECI Scholarship Foundation to date.

1978-1979 SCHOLARSHIP WINNERS

Peter Mark Aupperle
Half Hollow Hills
High School East
Dix Hills, New York
Princeton University
Princeton, New Jersey

Jeanne Campanelli
Wellington C. Mepham
High School
Bellmore, New York
Georgetown University
Washington, D.C.

Judith Lynne Bell
Georgetown
Jr.-Sr. High School
Georgetown, Massachusetts
Dartmouth College
Hanover, New Hampshire

James H. Carson
Waynesboro Area Sr.
High School
Waynesboro, Pennsylvania
Dickinson College
Carlisle, Pennsylvania

Timothy Michael Berney
Lake Oswego High School
Lake Oswego, Oregon
Yale University
New Haven, Connecticut

Rosario S. Cassata
Patchogue-Medford
High School
Medford, New York
Drexel University
Philadelphia, Pennsylvania

Brian S. Bix
Robbinsdale Senior
High School
Robbinsdale, Minnesota
Washington University
St. Louis, Missouri

Elizabeth A. S. Clapp
Boulder High School
Boulder, Colorado
Bryn Mawr College
Bryn Mawr, Pennsylvania

Jacquelyn Marie Brewer
Henrico High School
Richmond, Virginia
Howard University
Washington, D.C.

Lawrence Rolande Clarke
Sharon Springs
Central School
Sharon Springs, New York
Princeton University
Princeton, New Jersey

1978-1979 Scholarship Winners (cont'd.)

Catherine R. Coolidge
Highland High School
Anderson, Indiana
Purdue University
West Lafayette, Indiana

David Michael Gauntt
Bedford High School
Bedford, Massachusetts
Massachusetts Institute
of Technology
Cambridge, Massachusetts

Michelle Coté
Windham High School
South Windham, Maine
University of Maine at Orono
Orono, Maine

Sandra Lynn Gossett
New Boston High School
New Boston, Texas
Texas A & M University
College Station, Texas

David Randolph Doss
Richard J. Reynolds
High School
Winston-Salem,
North Carolina
University of
North Carolina
Chapel Hill, North Carolina

Margaret Jacquelyn Green
St. Andrews Parish
High School
Charleston, South Carolina
Harvard University
Cambridge, Massachusetts

Edward C. DuMont
Piedmont High School
Piedmont, California
Yale University
New Haven, Connecticut

Monica Green
Montclair High School
Montclair, California
Loma Linda University
Riverside, California

Joseph F. Femia
T. R. Proctor High School
Utica, New York
Hamilton College
Clinton, New York

Keith E. Harp
Westside High School
Augusta, Georgia
Georgia Institute
of Technology
Atlanta, Georgia

René Brandon Fradd
Fort Pierce Central
High School
Fort Pierce, Florida
Columbia College,
Columbia University
New York, New York

Emma Hoo
George Washington
High School
San Francisco, California
Harvard University
(Radcliffe College)
Cambridge, Massachusetts

1978-1979 Scholarship Winners (cont'd.)

Ira M. Kaplan
South Shore High School
Brooklyn, New York
Princeton University
Princeton, New Jersey

Kenneth W. Merkitch
Plainedge High School
North Massapequa, New York
Northwestern University
Evanston, Illinois

Philip E. Keefer
Bellarmine College
Preparatory
San Jose, California
Washington University
St. Louis, Missouri

Kaelyn Morrill
Stevens High School
Rapid City, South Dakota
Brigham Young University
Provo, Utah

Sheila Maureen Kelleher
Magnificat High School
Rocky River, Ohio
Wellesley College
Wellesley, Massachusetts

Naomi Nishimura
Berkeley High School
Berkeley, California
Yale University
New Haven, Connecticut

Peter A. Kolodziej
University High School
Urbana, Illinois
Harvard University
Cambridge, Massachusetts

Judith Leah Passman
High School for
Engineering Professions
Houston, Texas
Massachusetts Institute
of Technology
Cambridge, Massachusetts

Anne Marie McAndrew
Klein High School
Spring, Texas
University of Dallas
Irving, Texas

Nicholas Poulos
Orange High School
Pepper Pike, Ohio
Johns Hopkins University
Baltimore, Maryland

Janet Marie McKissick
Floyd E. Kellam
High School
Virginia Beach, Virginia
University of Virginia
Charlottesville, Virginia

Alfred Puchala
Heath High School
Heath, Ohio
Yale University
New Haven, Connecticut

1978-1979 Scholarship Winners (cont'd.)

Elissa Meryl Sanders
Harriton High School
Rosemont, Pennsylvania
Boston University
Boston, Massachusetts

Harold Mitchell Tice
East Meadow High School
East Meadow, New York
Boston University
Boston, Massachusetts

Robert Savell
Northshore
Senior High School
Houston, Texas
Rice University
Houston, Texas

Sylvia Tillman
Ramapo Senior High School
Spring Valley, New York
University of Virginia
Charlottesville, Virginia

Brian Leland Slick
West Anchorage
Senior High School
Anchorage, Alaska
University of Oregon
Eugene, Oregon

Jenny Van Le
University High School
Los Angeles, California
Stanford University
Stanford, California

Patricia Anne Sowa
Aquinas High School
Southgate, Michigan
St. John's College
Annapolis, Maryland

Ann M. Wagner
Valley Central High School
Montgomery, New York
Adelphi University
Garden City, New York

Andrea Lee Spencer
Monmouth Regional
High School
Tinton Falls, New Jersey
Wesleyan University
Middletown, Connecticut

Kathleen M. Wagner
Marello Preparatory
Santa Cruz, California
University of California
Davis, California

Craig D. Steinley
Stevens High School
Rapid City, South Dakota
South Dakota School of
Mines and Technology
Rapid City, South Dakota

Jeffrey Richard Warren
State College Area
High School
State College, Pennsylvania
University of Virginia
Charlottesville, Virginia

1978-1979 Scholarship Winners (cont'd.)

Barry Weinberger
Oceanside High School
Oceanside, New York
Johns Hopkins University
Baltimore, Maryland

David Schroeder Wheeler
West Valley High School
Fairbanks, Alaska
Reed College
Portland, Oregon

Kristina Ellen Weisenstein
Webster Groves High School
Webster Groves, Missouri
Yale University
New Haven, Connecticut

Michael Charles Wiener
Asbury Park High School
Asbury Park, New Jersey
University of Rochester
Rochester, New York

AFS	American Field Service
Am Leg Awd	American Legion Award
Am Leg Boys St	American Legion Boys State
Am Leg Girls St	American Legion Girls State
Aud/Vis	Audio-Visual
Band	Band
Bausch & Lomb Awd	Bausch & Lomb Award
Beta Clb	Beta Club
Boy Scts	Boy Scouts
Boys Clb Am	Boys Clubs of America
Bsbl	Baseball
Bsktbl	Basketball
Btty Crckr Awd	Betty Crocker Award
C of C Awd	Chamber of Commerce Award
CAP	Civil Air Patrol
Chrh Wkr	Church Worker
Chrldng	Cheerleading
Chrs	Chorus
Cit Awd	Citizenship Award
Civ Clb	Civic Club
Cls Rep Frsh Cls	Class Representative—Freshman Class
Cls Rep Jr Cls	Class Representative—Junior Class
Cls Rep Soph Cls	Class Representative—Sophomore Class
Cls Rep Sr Cls	Class Representative—Senior Class
Cmnty Wkr	Community Worker
Cmp Fr Grls	Camp Fire Girls
Coach Actv	Coaching Activities
Crs Cntry	Cross Country
DAR Awd	Daughters of the American Revolution Award
Debate Tm	Debate Team
DECA	Distributive Education Clubs of America
Dnfth Awd	Danforth (I Dare You) Award
Drama Clb	Drama Club
Drl Tm	Drill Team
Drm Bgl	Drum & Bugle Corps
Drm Mjrt	Drum Majorette
Ed Sch Nwsp	Editor-in-Chief/Newspaper
Ed Yrbk	Editor-in-Chief/Yearbook
Elk Awd	Elks Award
Eng Clb	English Club
FBLA	Future Business Leaders of America
FCA	Fellowship of Christian Athletes
FDA	Future Doctors of America
FFA	Future Farmers of America
FHA	Future Homemakers of America
FNA	Future Nurses of America
4-H	4-H
4-H Awd	4-H Award
Fr Clb	French Club
FSA	Future Scientists of America
Ftbl	Football
FTA	Future Teachers of America
GAA	Girls Athletic Association
Ger Clb	German Club
Girl Scts	Girl Scouts
Glf	Golf
God Cntry Awd	God & Country Award
Gov Hon Prg Awd	Governor's Honor Program Award
Gym	Gymnastics
Hndbl	Handball
Hockey	Hockey
Hon Rl	Honor Roll
Hosp Ade	Hospital Aide (Candy Striper)
Hst Frsh Cls	Historian—Freshman Class
Hst Jr Cls	Historian—Junior Class
Hst Soph Cls	Historian—Sophomore Class
Hst Sr Cls	Historian—Senior Class
IM Sprt	Intramural Sports
JA	Junior Achievement
JA Awd	Junior Achievement Award
JC Awd	Jaycees Award
JETS Awd	Junior Engineering Technical Society Award
Jr NHS	Junior National Honor Society
Key Club	Key Club
Keyettes	Keyettes
Kiwan Awd	Kiwanis Award
Lat Clb	Latin Club
Lbry Ade	Library Aide
Lcrss	Lacrosse
Leo Clb	Leo Club
Lion Awd	Lions Club Award
Lit Mag	Literary Magazine
Mas Awd	Masonic Award
Mat Maids	Mat Maids
Mdrgl	Madrigal
Mgrs	Manager(s)
MMM	Modern Music Masters
Mod UN	Model UN
Mth Clb	Math Club
Natl Forn Lg	National Forensic League
Natl Merit Ltr	National Merit Letter
Natl Merit Schl	National Merit Scholarship
Natl Merit SF	National Merit Semi-Finalist
NCTE	National Council of Teachers of English Award
NHS	National Honor Society
OEA	Office Education Association
Off Ade	Office Aide
Opt Clb Awd	Optimist Club Award
Orch	Orchestra
PAVAS	Performing & Visual Arts Society
Pep Clb	Pep Club
Pol Wkr	Political Worker
Pom Pon	Pom Pon Squad
PPFtbl	Powder Puff Football
Pres Awd	President's Award
Pres Frsh Cls	President—Freshman Class
Pres Jr Cls	President—Junior Class
Pres Soph Cls	President—Sophomore Class
Pres Sr Cls	President—Senior Class
Quill & Scroll	Quill & Scroll

GLOSSARY OF ABBREVIATIONS

Red Cr Ade	Red Cross Aide	Stg Crw	Stage Crew
Rdo Clb	Radio Club	Stu Cncl	Student Council
Rotary Awd	Rotary International Award	Swmmng	Swimming
ROTC	Reserve Officers Training Corps		
Rptr Sch Nwsp	Reporter/School Newspaper	Ten	Tennis
Rptr Yrbk	Reporter/Yearbook	Tmr	Timer
Rus Clb	Russian Club	Trk	Track
		Trs Frsh Cls	Treasurer—Freshman Class
Sal	Salutatorian	Trs Jr Cls	Treasurer—Junior Class
SAR Awd	Sons of the American Revolution Award	Trs Soph Cls	Treasurer—Sophomore Class
		Trs Sr Cls	Treasurer—Senior Class
Sch Mus	School Musical	Twrlr	Twirler
Sch Nwsp	School Newspaper		
Sch Pl	School Play	USJC Awd	U.S. Jaycees Award
Sci Clb	Science Club	Val	Valedictorian
Scr Kpr	Score Keeper	VFW Awd	Veterans of Foreign Wars Award
Sct Actv	Scout Activities	VICA	Vocational Industrial Clubs of America
Sdlty	Sodality	Voice Dem Awd	Voice of Democracy Award
Sec Frsh Cls	Secretary—Freshman Class	VP Frsh Cls	Vice President—Freshman Class
Sec Jr Cls	Secretary—Junior Class	VP Jr Cls	Vice President—Junior Class
Sec Soph Cls	Secretary—Sophomore Class	VP Soph Cls	Vice President—Sophomore Class
Sec Sr Cls	Secretary—Senior Class	VP Sr Cls	Vice President—Senior Class
Socr	Soccer		
Soroptimist	Soroptimist	Wrstlng	Wrestling
Spn Clb	Spanish Club	Yrbk	Yearbook
Sprt Ed Nwsp	Sport Editor/School Newspaper	Y-Teens	Y-Teens
Sprt Ed Yrbk	Sport Editor/Yearbook	Yth Flsp	Youth Fellowship

EDITOR'S NOTE: The above abbreviations were compiled and utilized in order to conserve space and permit the listing of as much data per student as possible. Many biographies on the following pages contain abbreviations and symbols not listed here and for the most part were received from the student in that manner with no explanation given.

SAMPLE BIOGRAPHY

This sample is presented to familiarize the reader with the format of the biographical listings. Students are identified by name, school and location. Home addresses are not published in order to protect the privacy and integrity of all students.

KEY

1. Name
2. High School
3. Location
4. Class Year
5. Class Rank (when given)
6. Accomplishments
7. Future Plans

1 Wolk, Allan I.; **2** Beach H.S.; **3** Miami, FL; **4** Sr.; **5** 10-350; **6** Pres Stu Cncl; VP Sr Cls; Ftbl; 4-H; NHS; Cit Awd; Am Leg Awd; Sct Actv; **7** Harvard College; Biochemist

STUDENT BIOGRAPHIES

A

AARON, TYNOA; Emerson HS; Gary, IN; 5/149 Band; Drl Tm; Hon Rl; JA; NHS; ROTC; 4-H; Chrldng; Purdue Calumet Coll.

ABAD, KIMBERLY; Henry Ford Ii HS; Sterling Hts, MI; 9/438 Cmnty Wkr; Hon Rl; Hosp Ade; Orch; Stg Crw; Eastern Univ; Dietician.

ABASOLO, CARMELA; Morton Sr HS; Hammond, IN; Chrs; Hon Rl; Quill & Scroll; Rptr Sch Nwsp; Spn Clb; Ten; IM Sprt; Cit Awd; Spansih Essay Contst 79; Univ Of Illinois; Radio.

ABBAS, TOM; Canfield HS; Youngstown, OH; Boy Scts; Hon Rl; Sct Actv; Bsbl; Ftbl; IM Sprt; Youngstown State.

ABBERGER, SUE; Grace Baptist HS; S Bend, IN; Cls Rep Frsh Cls; Cl Rep Jr Cls; Chrs; Chrh Wkr; Hon Rl; Sch Pl; Yrbk; Chrldng;.

ABBOTT, APRIL; Marietta Sr HS; Marietta, OH; OEA; Bsktbl; Office Ed Assoc Ambassador Awd 79; St Bd Fo Ed Awd Of Distinction 79; Flag Corp Captain 79; Travel Agent.

ABBOTT, CHRIS; Pike Delta York Sr HS; Delta, OH; Cls Rep Frsh Cls; Hosp Ade; Off Ade; Pres Stu Cncl; Rptr Sch Nwsp; Pep Clb; Mgrs; Bowling Green SU; Mrktng Resrch.

ABBOTT, CINDY; Norton HS; Norton, OH; 35/300 Drl Tm; Drm Mjrt; Hon Rl; Stg Crw; Fr Clb; Trk; Mgrs; College; Chemistry.

ABBOTT, DENISE; Mooresville Consolidated HS; Mooresville, IN; 23/250 Band; Chrh Wkr; Girl Scts; Hon Rl; NHS; Pol Wkr; Sch Mus; Sch Pl; Drama Clb; Ger Clb; Purdue Univ; Comp Sci.

ABBOTT, GARY; Carson City Crystal HS; Muir, MI; 3/130 Am Leg Boys St; Hon Rl; NHS; Pres Stu Cncl; Yrbk; Sprt Ed Sch Nwsp; Lat Clb; Mth Clb; Letter Ftbl; Letter Trk; Michigan St Univ; Pre Vet.

ABBOTT, GEORGIA; Kenowa Hills HS; Grand Rapids, MI; Sec JA; NHS; Sch Mus; 4-H; Letter Trk; Pom Pon; Chmn PPFtbl; Cit Awd; 4-H Awd; Hope College; Psychoanalysis.

ABBOTT, JENNIFER; Loveland Hurst HS; Loveland, OH; Band; Girl Scts; Hon Rl; JA; NHS; Rptr Sch Nwsp; Drama Clb; Fr Clb; Key Clb; Univ; Engr.

ABBOTT, JOHN; Norton HS; Norton, OH; 35/287 Cls Rep Frsh Cls; Hon Rl; Jr NHS; Sci Clb; Ftbl; Univ Of Akron; Pre Med.

ABBOTT, MIKE; Salem HS; Salem, IN; Aud/Vis; Chrh Wkr; Cmnty Wkr; Hon Rl; Spn Clb; IM Sprt; College; Archi.

ABBOTT, SUZANNE; Cambridge HS; Cambridge, OH; 103/284 Chrs; Hon Rl; NHS; DECA; 4-H; 4-H Awd; Awd Of Distinct Outsdng Fem Stu 78; Dist Educ Progr 78; Ohio DECA Dist 12 Sec Treas 78; Bauder Fashion Coll; Fash Mdse.

ABBOTT, T LYNN; Bloomington HS South; Bloomington, IN; Cls Rep Frsh Cls; Cls Rep Soph Cls; Cl Rep Jr Cls; Girl Scts; Orch; Quill & Scroll; Stu Cncl; Yrbk; Sch Nwsp; Drama Clb; St Marys Univ; Poli Sci.

ABBOTT, WILLIAM; Eastwood HS; Pemberville, OH; 10/170 Band; Boy Scts; Hon Rl; Sct Actv; Univ Of Cincinnati; Archt.

ABBS, RONNY; Sturgis HS; Sturgis, MI; Capt Swmmng; Ferris State Coll; Machine Tool.

ABDALLA, MARY ANN; Stanton HS; Stratton, OH; Cls Rep Frsh Cls; Cls Rep Soph Cls; Cl Rep Jr Cls; Band; Chrs; Chrh Wkr; Cmnty Wkr; Hon Rl; NHS; Orch; Univ; Med Tech.

ABDELNOUR, JOSEPH; Lincoln West HS; Cleveland, OH; Debate Tm; Hon Rl; Sch Pl; Sci Clb; Cit Awd; Cleve State Univ; Law.

ABEL, JOSEPH R; Buckhannon Upshur HS; Buckhannon, WV; Pres Sr Cls; Band; Drm Mjrt; Hon Rl; 4-H; Letter Bsktbl; Trk; IM Sprt; 4-H Awd; YMCE Youth Leadership Camp; West Virginia Univ; Medicine.

ABEL, JULIA; Oregon Davis HS; Hamlet, IN; 16/58 Aud/Vis; Band; Chrs; Chrh Wkr; Cmnty Wkr; Drl Tm; Hon Rl; Yrbk; Rptr Sch Nwsp; Sch Nwsp; Perfct Attndnc 77 & 78; Ancilla Coll; Sci.

ABEL, VINCENT; Sandy Valley HS; Waynesburg, OH; Chrh Wkr; Cmnty Wkr; FCA; Yth Flsp; Ftbl; Wrstlng; Coach Actv; Akron Univ; Indstrl Mgmt.

ABELE, ADAM; Marietta Sr HS; Marietta, OH; 30/400 Hon Rl; VP NHS; Spn Clb; Ten; Univ.

ABELE, PATRICIA; Archbishop Alter HS; Kettering, OH; 21/289 Chrh Wkr; Drl Tm; Hon Rl; NHS; Stu Cncl; Fr Clb; Gym; GAA; IM Sprt; College; Chem Engr.

ABELE, SUE; Archbishop Alter HS; Kettering, OH; 25/350 Cls Rep Frsh Cls; Cls Rep Soph Cls; Pres Jr Cls; Cl Rep Jr Cls; Cls Rep Sr Cls; Chrs; Chrh Wkr; Cmnty Wkr; Drl Tm; Girl Scts; Miami Univ; Systems Analysis.

ABELE, SUSAN; Archbishop Alter HS; Kettering, OH; Cls Rep Frsh Cls; Cls Rep Soph Cls; Pres Jr Cls; Cl Rep Jr Cls; Cls Rep Sr Cls; Chrs; Chrh Wkr; Cmnty Wkr; Drl Tm; Girl Scts; Miami Univ; Systems Analysis.

ABELL, GARY; Benjamin Bosse HS; Evansville, IN; Band; Drm Mjrt; Hon Rl; Quill & Scroll; Rptr Yrbk; Yrbk; Rptr Sch Nwsp; Sch Nwsp; Cit Awd; Ball State Univ.

ABELL, JEFFREY A; Carroll HS; Dayton, OH; 4/271 Chrh Wkr; Hon Rl; Treas NHS; Treas Ger Clb; Pres Key Clb; JETS Awd; German Natl Hon Soc 1978; 3 Sprrs 3 Excllnt In Sci Comp; Mech Engr.

ABELS, DEBORAH; Coldwater HS; Coldwater, OH; Chrs; Hon Rl; Drama Clb; Spn Clb; Mgrs; Scr Kpr; Kiwan Awd; Reds Straight A Tickets; Univ.

ABELS, JEANETTE; Berea HS; Brookpk, OH; Chrs; Chrh Wkr; Hon Rl; Hosp Ade; Lbry Ade; NHS; Y-Teens; Trk; Honor For RSVP Work 79; Schlstc Awds For Lang 77; Schlstc Awd For Pt Avg 79; Ohio St Univ; Pre Vet.

ABELS, NANCY; St Henry HS; St Henry, OH; Band; Hon Rl; FHA; OEA; GAA; Bowling Green St Univ; Mktg.

ABER, DONALD M; Morgan HS; Malta, OH; Trs Jr Cls; Boy Scts; Hon Rl; Jr NHS; Sch Pl; Stg Crw; Yth Flsp; Yrbk; Drama Clb; Fr Clb;.

ABER, EVELYN; Bellbrook HS; Bellbrook, OH; 30/167 Sec Soph Cls; Band; Drl Tm; Girl Scts; Orch; Pep Clb; Spn Clb; Letter Bsktbl; GAA; IM Sprt; Miami Univ; Comp Analyst.

ABERNATHY, DARWYN; George Washington HS; E Chicago, IN; 64/263 Cls Rep Frsh Cls; Band; Bsbl; Ftbl; Wrstlng; Awrd For Moot Pins 2nd Plc In Sectnls Wrestling 77; Frosh Tourney 105 Lb Champ 77; B Tm Trnmnt Champ 78; Purdue Univ.

ABERNATHY, KURT; Covington HS; Covington, IN; Carpentry.

ABFALL, BETH; Lorain Cnty Voc Cntr; Avon, OH; Cls Rep Frsh Cls; Cls Rep Soph Cls; Cl Rep Jr Cls; Band; Cmnty Wkr; Girl Scts; Hon Rl; Stu Cncl; 4-H; OEA; Lorain Cnty Cmnty Coll; Sec.

ABNER, REGINA; Cass Technical HS; Detroit, MI; Chrh Wkr; Hon Rl; Wayne State Univ; Comp Prgmg.

ABNEY, BILL; Elston HS; Mich City, IN; 91/340 Cls Rep Frsh Cls; Cls Rep Soph Cls; Band; Boy Scts; Cmnty Wkr; FCA; Red Cr Ade; Sct Actv; Ftbl; Ind State Univ; Piolot Music.

ABNEY, BRUCE; Fountain Central Jr Sr HS; Hillsboro, IN; 27/135 Cls Rep Soph Cls; Cl Rep Jr Cls; Hon Rl; Stu Cncl; Yth Flsp; Rptr Sch Nwsp; Letter Ftbl; Letter Wrstlng; Purdue Univ; Indstrl Engr.

ABNEY, STEVEN P; Castle HS; Newburgh, IN; Hon Rl; NHS; Natl Merit SF; Indiana Univ; Linguistics.

ABRAHAM, DIANA; Vly Forge HS; Parma Hgts, OH; Chrs; Hon Rl; Bsbl; Trk; GAA; IM Sprt; USJC Awd; Coll; Child Care.

ABRAHAM, FRANK; Lincoln HS; Shinnston, WV; 1/198 Am Leg Boys St; Boy Scts; Chrh Wkr; Hon Rl; Hosp Ade; Pol Wkr; Sct Actv; Sci Clb; Spn Clb; Ftbl; Golden Horse Shoe WV Knowledge 76; Math Field Day Regional & Cnty 77; Math Field Day Cnty 78; Notre Dame Univ; Pre Med.

ABRAHAM, GREGORY; Liberty HS; Reynoldsville, WV; Band; Chrh Wkr; Hon Rl; Yth Flsp; Cit Awd;.

ABRAHAM, JUDITH; Cousino HS; Warren, MI; Hon Rl; Mth Clb; Spn Clb; Natl Merit Ltr; Wayne St Univ; Bio.

ABRAHAM, JULIE; Niles Mc Kinley HS; Niles, OH; 57/420 VP AFS; Hon Rl; Mdrgl; NHS; Off Ade; Treas Red Cr Ade; Sch Mus; Drama Clb; Key Clb; Pep Clb; Red Cross Serv Awd 78; Trumbull Memrl Hosp Schl Nrsng; RN.

ABRAHAM, LINDA; Southfield HS; Southfield, MI; Aud/Vis; Hon Rl; Stg Crw; Spn Clb; Univ; Pre Med.

ABRAHAMSEN, TERESA; Warren Central HS; Indpls, IN; Chrs; Girl Scts; Hon Rl; Pep Clb; Spn Clb; Gym; Trk; Chrldng; Pom Pon; 4-H Awd; Oral Roberts Univ; Phys Ther.

ABRAHAMSON, CLAYTON; Ludington HS; Ludington, MI; 39/247 Letter Ftbl; IM Sprt; Scr Kpr; Tmr; Elk Awd; Mi Comp Schlrshp 79; Michigan Tech Univ; Comp Prog.

ABRAM, JEWELL; Calvin Woodward HS; Toledo, OH; Band; Cmp Fr Grls; Pres Chrs; Chrh Wkr; VP JA; Sch Mus; Letter Ten; Trk; JA Awd; Voice Dem Awd; Jr Queen 78; Miss Teenag Oh Finlst 78; Bowling Green Univ; Music.

ABRAM, MARK A; Maumee Valley Cntry Day HS; Toledo, OH; 10/44 Cls Rep Sr Cls; Chrh Wkr; Hon Rl; JA; Rptr Sch Nwsp; Letter Bsbl; Letter Bsktbl; Letter Ftbl; Letter Trk; Natl Merit Ltr; 4 H Best Groomed Male Age Group; Brown Univ; Pre Med.

ABRAMS, CARLOS B; Clear Fork HS; Clear Creek, WV; Am Leg Boys St; Chrh Wkr; FBLA; Pep Clb; Sci Clb; Bsbl; Bsktbl; Ftbl; Am Leg Awd; Vocational Schl; Mine Foreman.

ABRAMS, DOUG; Manchester HS; Akron, OH; 20/215 Hon Rl; Letter Ftbl; Letter Trk; Univ Of Akron; Busns Admin.

ABRAMS, ERIC; Springboro HS; Lebanon, OH; Boy Scts; Chrh Wkr; Hon Rl; Univ.

ABRAMS, JANICE; Saginaw HS; Saginaw, MI; Cl Rep Jr Cls; Chrh Wkr; Hon Rl; Jr NHS; Off Ade; Red Cr Ade; Stu Cncl; Drama Clb; Bsktbl; Chrldng; Univ; Engr.

ABRAMS, LISA; Northeastern HS; Webster, IN; Hon Rl; 4-H; Lat Clb; Spn Clb; GAA; Twrlr; Indiana East Univ; Med Sec.

ABRAMSON, PENNY; East Canton HS; E Canton, OH; Chrs; Chrh Wkr; 4-H; Fr Clb; FHA; Pep Clb; VICA; Stark Tech; Acct.

ABRINKO, PAUL; Munster HS; Munster, IN; 5/440 Band; Chrh Wkr; Hon Rl; Orch; Sch Mus; De Paul Univ; Music.

ABROMAITIS, JEFFREY T; Chagrin Falls HS; Chagrin Fl, OH; 22/187 Band; Boy Scts; CAP; Hon Rl; NHS; Sct Actv; Mth Clb; IM Sprt; Schl Sponsored Schlrshp To Ohio Forestry Assoc Summer Camp 78; E Cntrl Region Delegt To 3rd World Scout For; Military Officer.

ABROMOWITZ, LESLIE; Meadowdale HS; Dayton, OH; 5/239 Hon Rl; NHS; Sch Pl; Letter Ten; Ohio St Univ; Medicine.

ABULS, MIKELIS; Cambridge HS; Cambridge, OH; Band; Hon Rl; NHS; Treas Key Clb; Letter Crs Cntry; Trk; Prudue Univ; Engr.

ABUNSSAR, MARY; Our Lady Of Mercy HS; Farmington Hls, MI; Cls Rep Frsh Cls; Chrh Wkr; Hosp Ade; NHS; Sch Pl; Ed Yrbk; Am Leg Awd; Cit Awd; College; Nurs.

ABUSAMRA, GARY; Mishawaka HS; Mishawaka, IN; 52/438 Hon Rl; JA; Swmmng; JA Awd; JETS Awd; Natl Merit Ltr; Purdue Univ; Elec Engr.

ACHESON, EDWARD; Moeller HS; Loveland, OH; 86/256 Boy Scts; Hon Rl; Off Ade; IM Sprt; SAR Awd; Bowling Green Univ; Bus Admin.

ACHESON, TERRY; Perry HS; Lima, OH; 10/69 Band; Chrs; Hon Rl; Yth Flsp; 4-H; Pep Clb; Spn Clb; 4-H Awd; Opt Clb Awd; Dietzel Schlrshp; U S Collegiate Wind Band European Tour; United Way Rep; Ohio Northern Univ; Music.

ACHKAR, ANTONIO A; Liberty HS; Youngstown, OH; Pres AFS; Am Leg Boys St; Chrs; Hon Rl; NHS; Stu Cncl; Fr Clb; Trumbull Cnty Wnr In Amer & Govt Test Of Amer Legion 77; 1st Pl In French Reading At YSU Foreign Lang 78; Univ.

ACHTERMANN, TERRESA; Little Miami HS; Morrow, OH; 8/201 Hon Rl; NHS; Scr Kpr; Univ Of Cincinnati; Hosp Pharm.

ACITELLI, ALFRED; Henry Ford HS; Detroit, MI; Hon Rl; Quill & Scroll; Sch Mus; Stg Crw; Ed Sch Nwsp; Rptr Sch Nwsp; Sch Nwsp; Natl Merit SF; Wayne St Univ; Acctg.

ACKELS, PHILIS; Ovid Elsie HS; Ovid, MI; 11/179 Hst Sr Cls; Hon Rl; NHS; Sch Pl; Rptr Sch Nwsp; PPFtbl; 4-H Awd; Central Michigan Univ; Acctg.

ACKER, JAN; Wapakoneta Sr HS; Wapakoneta, OH; 9/300 Band; Chrs; Chrh Wkr; Cmnty Wkr; Girl Scts; Hon Rl; Jr NHS; Red Cr Ade; Sch Mus; Yth Flsp; Univ; Music.

ACKERMAN, CARLA; Edison HS; Milan, OH; 2/164 Sal; Am Leg Aux Girls St; Band; Chrh Wkr; Drm Mjrt; Hon Rl; Jr NHS; NHS; Orch; Sch Mus; Bowling Green St Univ; Nursing.

ACKERMAN, DEAN; Reese HS; Vassar, MI; Am Leg Boys St; Hon Rl; FFA; Bsbl; Letter Bsktbl; Letter Ftbl; Letter Trk; Michigan St Univ; Acctg.

ACKERMAN, HEATHER; Emmerica Manual HS; Indianapolis, IN; 26/391 Am Leg Aux Girls St; Sec FCA; NHS; Quill & Scroll; Stu Cncl; Yrbk; VP Fr Clb; Bsktbl; Trk; GAA; Ind State; Public Relations.

ACKERMAN, KIMBERLY; Oxford HS; Oxford, MI; 8/214 Band; Chrs; Hon Rl; Jr NHS; NHS; Sch Mus; Sch Nwsp; Natl Merit Ltr; Eastern Michigan Univ; Music Ther.

ACKERMAN, MARY; Clarence M Kimball HS; Royal Oak, MI; Hon Rl; JA; Mod UN; NHS; Sch Mus; Sch Pl; Drama Clb; Ger Clb; Cit Awd; Natl Merit Ltr; Finlst Mi Math Test 79; Univ; Acctg.

ACKERMAN, RODERICK C; Brookside HS; Sheffield Lake, OH; Cls Rep Sr Cls; Band; NHS; PAVAS; Pol Wkr; FBLA; Sch Nwsp; Pres Drama Clb; Crs Cntry; Letter Wrstlng; General Motors Inst; Mktg.

ACKERMAN, SHARON; Sebring Mckinley HS; Sebring, OH; Band; Chrh Wkr; Hon Rl; Off Ade; Orch; Y-Teens; Rptr Sch Nwsp; FHA; Pep Clb; Chrldng; Akron Univ; Leg Sec.

ACKERSON, CATHY; South Range Raiders HS; Salem, OH; Chrh Wkr; Hon Rl; NHS; Drama Clb; Letter Bsktbl; Crs Cntry; Letter Trk; Coach Actv; PPFtbl; Scr Kpr; Letter Awd In Track; Schl Letter; Natl Hnr Soc; Hnr Mention For Bsktbl & Track All Stars; Ohio Coll; Nursing.

ACKLES, PEARO; Ovid Elsie HS; Ovid, MI; 3/179 VP Jr Cls; Hon Rl; NHS; Sch Nwsp; Fr Clb; Mth Clb; Crs Cntry; Ten; Natl Merit Schl; Michigan Tech Univ; Envir Engr.

ACKLEY, SHERYL LYNN; Adena HS; Frankfort, OH; Sec Frsh Cls; Sec Soph Cls; Sec Jr Cls; Chrs; Hon Rl; Off Ade; Sch Pl; Ed Sch Nwsp; Rptr Sch Nwsp; 4-H; Athens Univ; Jrnlsm.

AC MOODY, KEVIN; Coldwater HS; Coldwater, MI; DECA; IM Sprt; C of C Awd; Coldwtr Cmnty Schlrshp 79; 1st Pl DECA Regnl Comptn 79; 1st Pl DECA St Comptn 79; W Michigan Univ; Finance.

ACOFF, NORMA; Buchtel Univ HS; Akron, OH; 98/412 Ohi Univ; Fashion Merchandising.

ACOSTA, CLAUDIA; St Andrew HS; Inkster, MI; Hon Rl; NHS; Ed Yrbk; Rptr Sch Nwsp; FBLA; Pep Clb; Crs Cntry; IM Sprt; Scr Kpr; Univ; Cmnctns Std.

ACRA, BARBARA; Fenwick HS; Middletown, OH; 23/90 Band; Cmnty Wkr; Hon Rl; NHS; Orch; Sch Mus; Sch Pl; Fr Clb; Bsktbl; Dayton Univ.

ACRE, JAMES; Adelphian Academy; Otter Lk, MI; Chrh Wkr; Hon Rl; Pathfinder Club Master Guide Like Eagle Scout 79; Deacon Church 78; Merit Of Truth Awd 79; Univ Of Michigan.

ACRE, SCOTT; Adelphian Acad; Otter Lk, MI; Chrh Wkr; Univ Of Mich; Phys Ther.

ACREE, TROY; Herbert Hoover HS; Pinch, WV; Hon Rl; Quill & Scroll; Sprt Ed Sch Nwsp; Fr Clb; IM Sprt; Marshall Univ; Jrnlsm.

ACTON, AMY; Mitchell HS; Mitchell, IN; 36/151 Am Leg Aux Girls St; Band; Chrs; Chrh Wkr; Hon Rl; Jr NHS; FHA; Pep Clb; Bsktbl; GAA; Ind Univ; Telecomm.

ACTON, MARYANNA; Bloom Carroll HS; Lancaster, OH; Chrs; Cmnty Wkr; Drl Tm; Hon Rl; Red Cr Ade; 4-H; FFA; Pep Clb; Chrldng; GAA; Ohio St Agri Tech Inst; Equestrien.

ACTON, MIKE; Loogootee HS; Loogootee, IN; 18/160 Hon Rl; Letter Bsbl; Letter Bsktbl; Letter Ten; Ind State; Comp Sci.

ACUFF, RICHARD; Ross HS; Hamilton, OH; 7/140 Aud/Vis; Hon Rl; Lbry Ade; Yrbk; Sch Nwsp; Fr Clb; Sci Clb; Natl Merit Ltr; Coll; Comp Sci.

ACUNA, LOUIE; Walkerville HS; Walkerville, MI; 3/32 Pres Frsh Cls; Pres Soph Cls; VP Jr Cls; VP Sr Cls; Hon Rl; NHS; Capt Bsbl; Capt Bsktbl; Capt Trk; Pres Awd; West Shore Comm Coll; Electronics.

ADAM, GARY; Fitzgerald HS; Warren, MI; Band; Chrs; Hon Rl; NHS; Sch Mus; Ftbl; Wrstlng; Natl Merit Schl; Alma Coll.

ADAMCZYK, CONSTANCE; Holy Name Nazareth HS; Parma, OH; Chrh Wkr; Hon Rl; NHS; Drama Clb; Univ; Art Ther.

ADAMIEC, ROBERT; North Judson San Pierre HS; N Judson, IN; 12/125 Hon Rl; NHS; 4-H; FFA; Mth Clb; Sci Clb; Purdue Univ; Agri Engr.

ADAMIK, CHERYL; Meadowbrook HS; Byesville, OH; Trs Frsh Cls; Trs Soph Cls; Cl Rep Jr Cls; Hon Rl; Stu Cncl; Lat Clb; Mth Clb; Pep Clb; Letter Chrldng; PPFtbl; Univ; Pharm.

ADAMS, ALICE; Bremen HS; Bremen, IN; Cl Rep Jr Cls; Band; Cmp Fr Grls; Chrs; FCA; Hon Rl; Lbry Ade; Sch Pl; Stg Crw; Yth Flsp; Outstndng Scholastic Achvmnt Epsilon Pi Chapter 1976; Womans Relief Crps Essay Wnr 1976; Awd 1st Clrnt 1976; Ball St Univ; Marine Bio.

ADAMS, ALLISON; Fairbanks HS; Milford Center, OH; Am Leg Aux Girls St; Hon Rl; Hosp Ade; NHS; Off Ade; Stu Cncl; Ed Sch Nwsp; 4-H; FHA; Bsktbl; Clark Tech Coll; Legal Sec.

ADAMS, ALLISON; Lumen Christi HS; Jackson, MI; 32/247 Band; Hon Rl; JA; NHS; Sch Mus; Stg Crw; Ed Sch Nwsp; Drama Clb; Voice Dem Awd; Central Michigan Univ; Bus Admin.

ADAMS, AMY; Mc Comb HS; Custar, OH; Band; Chrs; Chrh Wkr; Hon Rl; Sch Pl; Yth Flsp; Rptr Yrbk; Trk; Mat Maids; Scr Kpr; Bowling Green St Univ; Poli Sci.

ADAMS, AMY; Perrysburg HS; Perrysburg, OH; 55/248 Band; Chrs; Girl Scts; Hon Rl; Yth Flsp; Spn Clb; Vocational Schl;cosmetology.

ADAMS, ANN; Otsego HS; Bowling Green, OH; 5/125 Hon Rl; NHS; Sprt Ed Yrbk; Drama Clb; Spn Clb; Letter Bsktbl; Socr; Letter Trk; PPFtbl; Scr Kpr; Ohio Univ; Medicine.

ADAMS, BELINDA; Immaculata HS; Detroit, MI; Chrh Wkr; Girl Scts; Hon Rl; Hosp Ade; Sct Actv; Yth Flsp; Yrbk; Cit Awd; Mich State Univ; Medicine.

ADAMS, BRIGITTE; Fraser HS; Fraser, MI; Letter Band; Letter Debate Tm; Hon Rl; Natl Forn Lg; NHS; Pol Wkr; Yth Flsp; Ger Clb; Socr; Voice Dem Awd; College.

ADAMS, CAROL; Plymouth HS; Plymouth, IN; 25/230 Am Leg Aux Girls St; Chrh Wkr; FCA; Hon Rl; FFA; Trk; PPFtbl; Ball St Univ; Cmnctns.

ADAMS, CHARLES; Waverly HS; Waverly, OH; Ftbl; Trk; Voc Schl; Comp Elec.

ADAMS, CHERI L; Glen Este HS; Batavia, OH; Hon Rl; NHS; 4-H; Pep Clb; Spn Clb; 4-H Awd; Spanish 3 Awd 79; Univ; Psych.

ADAMS, CINDY; Northrop HS; Ft Wayne, IN; 92/584 Hon Rl; Sch Mus; Spn Clb; International Bus Coll; Cosmetology.

ADAMS, DAN; Kenowa Hills HS; Grand Rapids, MI; Boy Scts; FCA; Sprt Ed Sch Nwsp; Rptr Sch Nwsp; Bsbl; Ftbl; Capt Hockey; Michigan St Univ; Bio Sci.

ADAMS, DANNY; Mt View HS; Davy, WV; Hon Rl; Univ; Bus.

ADAMS, DAVID; Edgewood HS; Ellettsville, IN; Aud/Vis; Cmnty Wkr; Off Ade; Key Clb; Letter Bsbl; Letter Bsktbl; Letter Ftbl; Purdue; Engr.

ADAMS, DEBBIE L; Guyan Valley HS; Branchland, WV; Chrs; Chrh Wkr; Hon Rl; Hosp Ade; Off Ade; PAVAS; Rptr Yrbk; Rptr Sch Nwsp; Mth Clb; Letter Trk; Marshall Univ; Law.

ADAMS, DEBRA; Wardensville HS; Wardensville, WV; 5/28 Band; Girl Scts; Sch Mus; Sch Pl; Sct Actv; 4-H; FBLA; FFA; Morris Harvey Coll; Nurse.

ADAMS, DIANA L; Patrick Henry HS; Grelton, OH; 3/126 VP Soph Cls; Sec Jr Cls; Treas Band; Pres Chrs; Hon Rl; VP NHS; Sch Mus; Treas Stu Cncl; Pres 4-H; Capt Bsktbl; Girls St Alternate; Univ.

ADAMS, DONALD; Mt Pleasant HS; Mt Pleasant, MI; Univ; Law.

ADAMS, DUANE; South Harrison HS; Jane Lew, WV; 11/83 Cls Rep Frsh Cls; Cls Rep Soph Cls; Pres Jr Cls; Boy Scts; Chrh Wkr; FCA; Hon Rl; Lbry Ade; NHS; Off Ade; WVU; Horticultural.

ADAMS, EDWARD A; Mariemont HS; Cincinnati, OH; 2/145 Capt Debate Tm; Natl Forn Lg; Pol Wkr; Sch Pl; Sec Stu Cncl; Rptr Sch Nwsp; Pres Key Clb; Natl Finalist Sons Of The Amer Rvltn Oratorial Contest 79; Reporter Cincinnati Enquirer Mag 79; Univ; Jrnlsm.

ADAMS, ELAINE; Carney Nadeau Public HS; Carney, MI; Sec Frsh Cls; Cls Rep Sr Cls; Band; Hon Rl; Sch Pl; Stu Cncl; Yrbk; Ed Sch Nwsp; Sch Nwsp; Drama Clb; Univ; Phys Ther.

ADAMS, ELIZABETH; Hamilton Township HS; R A F B, OH; 7/180 Hon Rl; NHS; Capt Bsktbl;

Vllybll 2 Yrs Lettered Yrs 76; Softball 1 Yr Lttrd 76; Champlain Coll; Dental Asstng.

ADAMS, EVE; Otsego HS; Bowling Green, OH; 5/125 Hon Rl; Pres Jr NHS; Pres NHS; Sch Pl; Sprt Ed Yrbk; Yrbk; Treas Drama Clb; Spn Clb; Letter Bsktbl; Letter Trk; Ohio Wesleyan Univ; Phys Therapy.

ADAMS, FRED; Hammond Baptist HS; Omaha, NE; Chrh Wkr; Sch Pl; Bsktbl; Letter Ftbl; Wrstlng; Homecoming King; Mr H B H S Male Stu; Hyles Anderson Coll; Special Ed.

ADAMS, JACQUELINE; Eau Claire HS; Eau Claire, MI; Band; Drl Tm; FCA; Girl Scts; Hon Rl; NHS; Chrldng; Mgrs; Mat Maids; Pom Pon; Ferris St Coll; Bus Cmmnctns.

ADAMS, JANE; Ben Davis HS; Indianapolis, IN; Chrs; Chrh Wkr; Hon Rl; Sch Mus; Sch Pl; Stg Crw; Drama Clb; Spn Clb; Trk; Univ; Music.

ADAMS, JANE; Central Montcalm HS; Stanton, MI; 2/123 VP Soph Cls; Pres Sr Cls; Hon Rl; Stu Cncl; Ed Sch Nwsp; Rptr Sch Nwsp; Spn Clb; Bsktbl; Trk; Mgrs; Alma Coll.

ADAMS, JEFF; Mt Pleasant HS; Mt Pleasant, MI; Boy Scts; Hon Rl; Sct Actv; Fr Clb; 4-H Awd; CMU.

ADAMS, JEFF; Akron Fairgrove HS; Fairgrove, MI; Band; Cmnty Wkr; Hon Rl; Jr NHS; Orch; Yth Flsp; Sprt Ed Yrbk; Yrbk; Bsbl; Hockey; Ferris State College; Law.

ADAMS, JEFFERY A; Lewis County HS; Weston, WV; Am Leg Boys St; FCA; Hon Rl; Stu Cncl; Key Clb; Pep Clb; VICA; Ftbl; Trk; IM Sprt; Voc Schl.

ADAMS, JILL; West Iron County HS; Princeton, MI; 38/128 Hon Rl; Off Ade; Yrbk; Fr Clb; Letter Gym; Gogebic Cmnty Coll; Cosmetologist.

ADAMS, JOHN; Padua Franciscan HS; Brunswick, OH; Cls Rep Soph Cls; Cmnty Wkr; FCA; Hon Rl; Bsktbl; Ftbl; Trk; IM Sprt; Scr Kpr; Tmr; 1 Yr Of Hnrs French 77; Univ; Elec.

ADAMS, JOHN; Princeton HS; Princeton, WV; 35/360 Am Leg Boys St; Hon Rl; Jr NHS; NHS; Sch Pl; Pres Drama Clb; Sci Clb; Cit Awd; Wv Univ; Chemistry.

ADAMS, JOHN Q; Arthur Hill HS; Vassar, MI; Boy Scts; Hon Rl; Yrbk; Sch Nwsp; Letter Wrstlng; Cit Awd; Boy Scout Eagle Awd; The Only Stu Rep To Regional Ed; Michigan Interscholastic Press Assn Awd Of Excellence; Brooks Inst; Photography.

ADAMS, JUDY; Franklin Sr HS; Franklin, OH; Chrs; Hon Rl; JA; Sch Mus; Sch Nwsp; FTA; Pep Clb;.

ADAMS, JUDY A; Springfield Local HS; New Middletown, OH; Cls Rep Soph Cls; Cl Rep Jr Cls; AFS; Band; Drl Tm; Hon Rl; Lbry Ade; Stu Cncl; Pep Clb; Spn Clb; YSU; Landscape Archt.

ADAMS, JULIA A; Fairborn Baker HS; Fairborn, OH; 70/335 Aud/Vis; Band; Boy Scts; Chrs; Capt Drl Tm; Hon Rl; Lbry Ade; Off Ade; Stg Crw; Drama Clb; Miami Univ; Opera.

ADAMS, JULIE A; John Glenn HS; New Concord, OH; 9/184 Chrs; Chrh Wkr; Girl Scts; Lbry Ade; Pres NHS; Sch Mus; Drama Clb; 4-H; Lat Clb; Miami Univ.

ADAMS, KAREN; Dominican HS; Mt Clemens, MI; Chrs; Capt Chrldng; Univ; Mdse Buying.

ADAMS, KAREN; Greenhills Sr HS; Cincinnati, OH; Orch; Sch Mus; Fr Clb; Trk; Chrldng; Duke Univ; Psych.

ADAMS, KENT; Bremen HS; Bremen, IN; 16/100 Am Leg Boys St; FCA; NHS; Fr Clb; Bsbl; Capt Bsktbl; Capt Ftbl; Trk; JC Awd; Kiwan Awd; College.

ADAMS, KERI L; Chesterton HS; Chesterton, IN; 19/453 Band; Chrs; Hon Rl; Mdrgl; Spn Clb; Letter Gym; Mat Maids; College; Law.

ADAMS, KIM; Upper Arlington HS; Columbus, OH; Val; Val; AFS; Chrh Wkr; NHS; Quill & Scroll; Ed Sch Nwsp; Pep Clb; Letter Mgrs; Stanford Univ; Business Law.

ADAMS, KIMBERLY; Chaminade Julienne HS; Dayton, OH; Band; Chrs; Chrh Wkr; Girl Scts; Orch; Sch Mus; Rdo Clb; Bsktbl; Capt Trk; JETS Awd; T Track Champ 100 Yds Dash St Runner Up 220 Yarddash 79; Radcliffe Univ; Archt.

ADAMS, L; Jefferson Area HS; Jefferson, OH; 2/176 AFS; Chrs; Girl Scts; Hon Rl; Lbry Ade; NHS; Sct Actv; Rptr Sch Nwsp; Fr Clb; Sci Clb; Coll; Spanish.

ADAMS, L RICHARD; A D Johnston HS; Bessemer, MI; Cls Rep Soph Cls; Hon Rl; Stu Cncl; Letter Bsbl; Letter Bsktbl; Letter Ftbl; Letter Trk; IM Sprt; Ferris St Univ; Auto Body Mech.

ADAMS, M; Catholic Ctrl HS; Mingo Jct, OH; Band; Hon Rl; Hosp Ade; Orch; Yrbk; FNA; Pep Clb; Univ; Nursing.

ADAMS, MARK A; Frankenmuth HS; Birch Run, MI; Boy Scts; Debate Tm; Hon Rl; JA; Sct Actv; IM Sprt; Michigan Tech Univ; Geological Engr.

ADAMS, MARVIN; Elgin HS; La Rue, OH; Band; Boy Scts; Drm Bgl; Hon Rl; 4-H; FFA; 4-H Awd; Elgin FFA Schlrshp Awd 76; All Star Drummer Otterbein Coll 76 & 77; Elgin Band Most Improved 79; Otterbein Coll; Music.

ADAMS, MARY; Cannelton HS; Tobinsport, IN; 1/30 Hst Sr Cls; Val; Chrh Wkr; NHS; 4-H; Chrldng; Purdue Univ; Pre Vet Med.

ADAMS, MARY; Man HS; Man, WV; 32/142 Band; Chrh Wkr; 4-H; Capt Bsktbl; Marshall Univ; Comp Progr.

ADAMS, MATTHEW D; Parkersburg HS; Vienna, WV; 5/740 Am Leg Boys St; Band; Cmnty Wkr; Hon Rl; Orch; Lat Clb; Pep Clb; Nugent Awd For Highest Schlstc Achvmnt In Schl System 76; 1st Chair French Hornist Solo In Wv All Star Orch; Univ Of Pennsylvania; Anthropology.

ADAMS, MICHAEL; Greenville Sr HS; Greenville, OH; 31/373 Hon Rl; Univ; Med.

ADAMS, MICHAEL; Portage Central HS; Galesburg, MI; 7/379 Band; Boy Scts; Debate Tm; Hon Rl; Treas Fr Clb; Natl Merit SF; Voice Dem Awd; Univ Of Michigan; Medieval Hist.

ADAMS, MICHAEL; Olentangy HS; Delaware, OH; 3/149 Aud/Vis; Hon Rl; Lbry Ade; NHS; Pres Fr Clb; Olentangy Acad Awd 77 78 & 79; Ohio St Univ; Data Proc.

ADAMS, MONICA; Erieview Catholic HS; Cleveland, OH; 7/100 Chrh Wkr; Hon Rl; Pol Wkr; Rptr Yrbk; Bsbl; Capt Bsktbl; Kiwan Awd; Univ; Spec Educ.

ADAMS, PAMELA; Madison Heights HS; Anderson, IN; 44/371 Cls Rep Frsh Cls; Cl Rep Jr Cls; Cls Rep Sr Cls; Band; Chrs; Chrh Wkr; FCA; Girl Scts; FDA; Spn Clb; Indiana Univ; Nursing.

ADAMS, PATRICIA; Baldwin HS; Idlewild, MI; 24/66 Sec Sr Cls; Cmp Fr Grls; Chrs; Chrh Wkr; Girl Scts; Hon Rl; Lbry Ade; Yrbk; Ed Sch Nwsp; Sch Nwsp; Muskegon Bus Coll; Data Proc.

ADAMS, RICH; Elyria HS; Elyria, OH; 2/565 Sal; Chrh Wkr; Hon Rl; Sch Pl; Sct Actv; Drama Clb; Glf; IM Sprt; Natl Merit SF; Ohio State Univ; Comp Engr.

ADAMS, ROBERT D; Grand Valley HS; Orwell, OH; 6/109 VP Frsh Cls; Hon Rl; NHS; Stu Cncl; Eng Clb; FHA; Letter Bsbl; Bsktbl; Letter Ftbl; Trk; Miami Univ Of Ohio; Bio Chemistry.

ADAMS, RUTH; Franklin HS; Franklin, OH; Band; Chrs; Drl Tm; Hon Rl; Sch Mus; Rptr Sch Nwsp; Fr Clb; Miami Univ Of Middletown; Eng.

ADAMS, SALLY; Eau Claire HS; Eau Claire, MI; Band; Chrh Wkr; Cmnty Wkr; FCA; Girl Scts; Hon Rl; Sch Mus; Sch Pl; 4-H; Pep Clb; Ferris St Univ; Court Reporter.

ADAMS, SCOTT; Dublin HS; Dublin, OH; 67/167 Aud/Vis; Hon Rl; Sct Actv; Eng Clb; Spn Clb; Ftbl; Ten; GAA; Toledo Univ; Elec Engr.

ADAMS, SHARON; Wirt County HS; Palestine, WV; Girl Scts; Off Ade; 4-H; FFA; Bsktbl; Trk; GAA; Mgrs; 4-H Awd; Forestry Camp; Delegate To St FFA Convention; Natl FFA Convention;.

ADAMS, SUSAN; Streetsboro HS; Streetsboro, OH; Girl Scts; Hon Rl; Jr NHS; NHS; Sch Pl; Ohio Tests Of Schlrshp Achievement; Honorable Mention In Algebra I; Ohio St Univ; Zoologist.

ADAMS, SUSAN; Saint Francis Desales HS; Columbus, OH; Hon Rl; Spn Clb; Franklin Univ; Bus.

ADAMS, SUSAN K; Independence HS; Coal City, WV; Band; Hon Rl; JA; Lit Mag; NHS; Yrbk; Rptr Sch Nwsp; 4-H; VP FHA; Pres Spn Clb; Chosen For Creative Writing Summer Prgrm At Berea C Ky; Berea Coll; Literature.

ADAMS, TAMARA; Laingsburg HS; Dewitt, MI; Band; Cmnty Wkr; Girl Scts; Hon Rl; Off Ade; Sct Actv; 4-H; FHA; Pep Clb; Lansing Com College; Horticulture.

ADAMS, TA MARLA J; Celina Sr HS; Celina, OH; Pres Chrs; Chrh Wkr; Hon Rl; Jr NHS; NHS; Sch Mus; Stg Crw; Sec Yth Flsp; Rptr Yrbk; FTA; Univ; Spec Educ.

ADAMS, TAMMY; Point Valley HS; Bainbridge, OH; Hon Rl; Hosp Ade; FHA;.

ADAMS, THERESA M; River Valley HS; Buchanan, MI; Cl Rep Jr Cls; Band; Hon Rl; Off Ade; Stu Cncl; 4-H; Spn Clb; Letter Trk; 4-H Awd; Pres Awd; College.

ADAMS, TINA; Cascade HS; Stilesville, IN; Hon Rl; FHA; Sci Clb; Trk; GAA; Mat Maids; Indiana St Univ; Geol.

ADAMS, TOM; Fremont HS; Fremont, IN; Hon Rl; Yth Flsp; Sch Nwsp; Fr Clb; OEA; Crs Cntry; Trk; Wrstlng; IM Sprt; Voc Schl.

ADAMS, TROY S; Brebeut Prep HS; Indianapolis, IN; Aud/Vis; Boy Scts; JA; Pol Wkr; Sct Actv; Commnd Natl Achievemnt Schlshp Prog 1978; Univ; Bus Mgmt.

ADAMS, WENDY; Jackson HS; Massillon, OH; 78/409 Trs Soph Cls; Off Ade; Stu Cncl; Y-Teens; Pep Clb; Spn Clb; Capt Chrldng; Keymate Of The Yr 79; Miss Jacksonite 79; Miss Oh Chrldr 78; Ohio St Univ; Archt.

ADAMS, WILLIAM; Logan Elm HS; Kingston, OH; Chrs; Cmnty Wkr; Hon Rl; Jr NHS; Sch Pl; Sprt Ed Sch Nwsp; Rptr Sch Nwsp; Ohi Univ; Pre Law.

ADAMSHICK, LIZ; St Francis De Sales HS; Columbus, OH; Chrh Wkr; Hon Rl; Lbry Ade; Stg Crw; Mgrs; Scr Kpr; Columbus Tech Inst; Acctg.

ADAMSON, AGNES; Marian HS; South Bend, IN; Cls Rep Sr Cls; Hon Rl; Sch Mus; Sch Pl; Stg Crw; Stu Cncl; Drama Clb; Pep Clb; Trk; IM Sprt; Indiana Univ; Bus Admin.

ADAMSON, KELLEY; Avon Jr Sr HS; Plainfield, IN; Hon Rl; 4-H; Pep Clb; Spn Clb; Capt Chrldng; 4-H Awd; Coll; Nurse.

ADAMSON, KIMBERLY; Emerson HS; Gary, IN; Am Leg Aux Girls St; Chrs; Hon Rl; NHS; OEA; Spn Clb; Trk; Chrldng; Purdue Univ; Phys Therapy.

ADAMSON, LORI; Northridge HS; Goshen, IN; 20/157 Band; Drl Tm; Pep Clb; Pom Pon; Ball State Univ; General Bsns.

ADAMSON, MELODY; Kenowa Hills HS; Grand Rapids, MI; Cmp Fr Grls; Girl Scts; Sct Actv; PPFtbl; Grand Rapids Jr Coll; Legal Sec.

ADAMSON, SUE; Rensselaer Central HS; Remington, IN; 14/154 Hon Rl; Hosp Ade; 4-H; Spn Clb; 4-H Awd; Mas Awd; St Elizabeths Schl; Nursing.

ADAMY, PAUL; Buckhannon Upshur HS; Buckhannon, WV; Boy Scts; Hon Rl; Sct Actv; 4-H; Bsktbl; Ftbl; Ten; IM Sprt; West Virginia Univ; Engr.

ADASTIK, BETHANNE; Forest Hills Northern HS; Ada, MI; Band; VP JA; Sch Pl; Ed Yrbk; Sch Nwsp; Cert Of Recognition In The St Of MI Schlrshp Comptn For Outstndg Academic Achvmnt 79; Aquinas Coll; Jrnlsm.

ADDAMS, JOHN S; Marysville HS; Marysville, OH; Band; Debate Tm; Natl Forn Lg; NHS; Orch; Letter Bsbl; IM Sprt; Univ; Law.

ADDERLEY, KRISTIN; Clawson HS; Clawson, MI; Band; Pres Drl Tm; Hon Rl; PPFtbl; Honorable Mention In Sci & Engr Fair Of Detroit; Cert From Marine Tech Soc U S Naval Inst; College; Veterinary Med.

ADDESSO, BETH; Bishop Gallagher HS; Detroit, MI; 7/332 Hon Rl; NHS; Letter Bsbl; Letter Bsktbl; College; Special Ed.

ADDIS, BRIAN; Zanesville HS; Zanesville, OH; FCA; Hon Rl; NHS; Pres Stu Cncl; Letter Bsbl; Letter Ftbl; Gym; Miami Univ; Archt.

ADDIS, LYNN; Harding HS; Marion, OH; Chrs; Chrh Wkr; FCA; Yth Flsp; Eng Clb; Spn Clb; Ftbl; IM Sprt; Scr Kpr; Tmr; Central Bible Coll; Aviation.

ADE, GEORGE; Valley Forge Sr HS; Parma Hgts, OH; 155/777 Chrs; Chrh Wkr; Cmnty Wkr; Hon Rl; Mdrgl; Yth Flsp; Fr Clb; Cit Awd; Case Western Reserve Univ; Chem Engr.

ADE, ROBERT; Northville HS; Northville, MI; Chrh Wkr; FCA; Natl Forn Lg; Ger Clb; Bsbl; Bsktbl; Am Leg Awd; Miami Of Ohi; Bus.

ADELMAN, FREDERIC; Garber HS; Essexville, MI; 6/175 Hon Rl; Ftbl; Ten; Scr Kpr; Cit Awd; DAR Awd; Univ; Jrnlsm.

ADELMAN, STEVEN; Essexville Garber HS; Essexville, MI; 35/180 Hon Rl; Bsktbl; Coach Actv; Cit Awd; College; Business.

ADELSBERGER, ANNETTE; London HS; West Jefferson, OH; Sec Frsh Cls; Cls Rep Frsh Cls; Sec Soph Cls; Cls Rep Soph Cls; Sec Jr Cls; Cl Rep Jr Cls; Sec Sr Cls; Cmnty Wkr; Hosp Ade; Off Ade; Outstandin 4 H St Leadership Camp; Tribe Of 1000; Co Chairperson Of Jr Fairboard; Ohio St Univ; Elem Ed.

ADELSTEIN, TERRI; Beachwood HS; Beachwood, OH; Cls Rep Sr Cls; Pres Debate Tm; Mod UN; Natl Forn Lg; Quill & Scroll; Stu Cncl; Ed Yrbk; Treas Fr Clb; Univ; Med.

ADEMA, ROGER; Coopersville HS; Coopersville, MI; 1/180 Am Leg Boys St; Chrh Wkr; Hon Rl; NHS; Letter Glf; Natl Merit SF; Univ Of Mic; Comp Sci.

ADEN, JANET; Warrensville Heights HS; Warrensville, OH; Cl Rep Jr Cls; Band; Cmp Fr Grls; Chrs; Chrh Wkr; JA; Orch; Sch Mus; Sch Pl; Stu Cncl; Internatl Quiz Tm For Cntrl Dist 79; Case Western Reserve Univ; Med.

ADKINS, ALANNA; Guvan Valley HS; Branchland, WV; VP Jr Cls; Band; Hon Rl; Stu Cncl; Yrbk; FBLA; Bsktbl; Trk; Chrldng; Honorarian; Marshall Univ; Cnslr.

ADKINS, ANNA; Huntington East HS; Huntington, WV; Chrh Wkr; Hon Rl; Jr NHS; Yth Flsp; Mth Clb; Spn Clb; Swmmng; Univ; Archt.

ADKINS, BARRY; South Point HS; South Point, OH; Boy Scts; Hon Rl; Letter Bsktbl; Virginia Tech Univ; Phys Educ.

ADKINS, BOB; Sidney HS; Sidney, OH; Hon Rl; NHS; Capt Ftbl; Capt Trk; Ashland Coll; Bus.

ADKINS, CATHY L; Hamlin HS; W Hamlin, WV; 16/61 Chrh Wkr; Hon Rl; Jr NHS; NHS; Yth Flsp; FBLA; Coll; Sec.

ADKINS, CONNIE; Highland HS; Marengo, OH; 18/124 Chrh Wkr; Girl Scts; NHS; Off Ade; Yth Flsp; College; Social Serv.

ADKINS, DAVID; Valley Local HS; Lucasville, OH; 10/110 Aud/Vis; Chrh Wkr; Hon Rl; Lbry Ade; NHS; 4-H; FTA; 4-H Awd; Shawnee St Coll; Chem.

ADKINS, JAMES R; Chesapeake HS; South Point, OH; 12/140 Hon Rl; Beta Clb; Wrstlng; Tech Schl; Weld Engr.

ADKINS, JEFF; Woodrow Wilson HS; Beckley, WV; 2/517 Sal; Treas NHS; Sci Clb; Letter Crs Cntry; Letter Ftbl; Letter Trk; Letter Wrstlng; Univ; Engr.

ADKINS, KATHLEEN J; Valley Local HS; Lucasville, OH; 1/110 Band; Capt Chrs; Drm Mjrt; Hon Rl; NHS; Sch Pl; Stu Cncl; Yth Flsp; Treas FTA; Pep Clb; Outstndg Member Awrd FTA 78; All Cnty Bands & Choirs Festvl 76 79; Shawnee St Cmnty Coll; Chem Engr.

ADKINS, MARCY; Beaver Local HS; E Liverpool, OH; 10/250 Am Leg Aux Girls St; Hon Rl; Jr NHS; NHS; Off Ade; VP Y-Teens; Eng Clb; 4-H; Sec Fr Clb; Mat Maids; Univ; Govt.

ADKINS, MARK; Vermilion HS; Vermilion, OH; 19/265 Hon Rl; Jr NHS; NHS; Quill & Scroll; Sch Pl; Stg Crw; Sprt Ed Yrbk; Fr Clb; OEA; Cit Awd; Trivia Contest Finalist; Bowling Green St Univ; Busns Admin.

ADKINS, METTA; Tecumseh HS; New Carlisle, OH; 37/344 Cls Rep Frsh Cls; AFS; Band; Chrs; Chrh Wkr; Cmnty Wkr; Hon Rl; Jr NHS; NHS; Sch Mus; Sinclair Comm Coll; Exec Sec.

ADKINS, PATSY; Guyan Valley HS; Ranger, WV; Band; Hon Rl; Hosp Ade; Jr NHS; Rptr Yrbk; Pep Clb; Bsbl; Bsktbl; Trk; United Airlines Oper Ctr; Stewardess.

ADKINS, RANDALL S; Holly HS; Davisburg, MI; 21/304 Band; Chrs; Hon Rl; Lit Mag; Orch; Sch Mus; 4-H; 4-H Awd; Central Michigan Univ; Music.

ADKINS, RANDY; Winfield HS; Pliny, WV; Boy Scts; Chrs; Cmnty Wkr; Hon Rl; Pol Wkr; Sct Actv; 4-H; Pep Clb; VICA; Ftbl; Wrestling 1st Cnty 1st Region & 3rd St 78; Track 1st Cnty Schl Record 75; Track Schl Record 76; Marshall Univ; HS Wrestling Coach.

ADKINS, ROBIN; West Washington HS; Hardinsburg, IN; Sec Chrh Wkr; Cmnty Wkr; Hon Rl; Sec Yth Flsp; Y-Teens; Sch Nwsp; VP 4-H; Trs Soph Cls; Sec Sci Clb; Spn Clb; Indiana Univ; Elem Educ.

ADKINS, RONDA; Nordonia HS; Macedonia, OH; 38/300 Band; Sch Mus; Sch Pl; Drama Clb; Univ; Music.

ADKINS, SHERRY; Saint Hedwig HS; Detroit, MI; Hon Rl; Mercy College; Social Sci.

ADKINS, SUSAN; Greenfield Central HS; Wilkinson, IN; 73/315 Chrs; VP Yth Flsp; Sec 4-H; Treas FFA; Ger Clb; Capt Bsktbl; Trk; GAA; 4-H Awd; FFA Section Star Farmer; Dist Sheep Proficiency; Ora Callahan Awd 4 H Citizenship; Purdue Univ; Animal Sci.

ADKINS, TIMOTHY; Washington HS; Massillon, OH; Boy Scts; DECA; Ger Clb; Kent St Univ; Advertising.

ADKINS, TINA; Gallia Acad; Gallipolis, OH; Chrs; Girl Scts; Yth Flsp; 4-H; Fr Clb; FTA; Key Clb; Sci Clb; Chrldng; SEOAL Hnrble Mention Sftbl; Marshall Univ; Nursing.

ADKINS, TINA; Huntington HS; Chillicothe, OH; Band; Hon Rl; Hosp Ade; Pep Clb; VICA; Pom Pon; Hocking Tech Coll; Nursing.

ADKINS, TODD; Huntington HS; Huntington, WV; 29/272 Cls Rep Soph Cls; Trs Jr Cls; Chrs; Chrh Wkr; Hon Rl; Mod UN; Sch Pl; Stu Cncl; Yth Flsp; Drama Clb; Stdnt Cncl Serv Awd 79; Music Awd Ldrshp Ability 79; Stdnt Body Chaplain 79; Marshall Univ.

ADKINS, VICKI; Paulding HS; Oakwood, OH; 11/198 Hon Rl; Univ; Educ.

ADLER, VICKI; Meadowdale HS; Dayton, OH; 11/239 Hon Rl; Lbry Ade; NHS; Off Ade; Rptr Sch Nwsp; Mgrs; Wright St Univ.

ADOLPHSEN, ARTHUR; Edgewood Sr HS; Ashtabula, OH; 59/247 Hon Rl; Sch Pl; Youngstown St Univ; Commercial Art.

ADORJAN, SHARON; Morton Sr HS; Hammond, IN; 80/419 Chrs; Hon Rl; Lbry Ade; Pol Wkr; College; Psych.

ADRIANOWYCZ, SONIA; James Ford Rhodes HS; Parma, OH; 1/310 Val; Hon Rl; NHS; Off Ade; Sch Pl; Sec Lat Clb; GAA; Scr Kpr; Cit Awd; Vllybl Letter 79; Oh Acad Regents Schlrshp 79; Math & Sci Dept Awds 79; Latin Awd; Girls Bsktbl; Worcester Polytech Inst; Engr.

ADRINE, ETHEL; Shaker Heights Sr HS; Shaker Hts, OH; Cl Rep Jr Cls; Chrs; Chrh Wkr; Hon Rl; Off Ade; Sch Mus; Sch Pl; Stu Cncl; Rptr Sch Nwsp; Sch Nwsp; Univ; Jrnlsm.

ADSIT, SUSAN; Douglas Mac Arthur HS; Sagianaw, MI; VP Frsh Cls; Cls Rep Soph Cls; Cl Rep Jr Cls; Hon Rl; Stu Cncl; VP Yth Flsp; Spn Clb; Bsktbl; PPFtbl; Operation Bently 2 Wk Gov Seminar Olivet Coll; 2nd Team All Cnfrnce Sftbl; Univ Of Michigan; Poli Sci.

ADY, KELLY; Perry HS; Massillon, OH; Cls Rep Frsh Cls; Yrbk; FHA; Stark Technical Coll.

ADZEMA, LISA; Mayfield Sr HS; Mayfield Hts, OH; Cls Rep Frsh Cls; Pres Jr Cls; Chrs; Hon Rl; NHS; Stu Cncl; Ed Yrbk; Drama Clb; Pep Clb; Scr Kpr; Univ; Educ.

ADZIA, GARY A; Morton Sr HS; Hammond, IN; 5/437 Pres Sr Cls; Am Leg Boys St; Hon Rl; NHS; Quill & Scroll; Sprt Ed Yrbk; Letter Bsktbl; Pres Awd; College.

AE BARD, SUN; Garrett HS; Garrett, IN; 9/117 Trs Soph Cls; Trs Jr Cls; Trs Sr Cls; Chrs; Hon Rl; Pres NHS; Pres Ger Clb; Univ Of Evansville; Phys Ther.

AEBI, JANET; West Branch HS; Alliance, OH; 6/256 Hon Rl; Hosp Ade; NHS; Sch Mus; Sch Pl; Yth Flsp; Pres FHA; FTA; Pep Clb; Natl Merit Ltr; Ohio St Univ; Med Tech.

AEDER, REBECCA; Waverly HS; Lansing, MI; 5/394 Band; Chrs; Chrh Wkr; Debate Tm; Girl Scts; Hon Rl; NHS; Ger Clb; Bausch & Lomb Awd; Natl Merit Ltr; Lansing Cmnty Coll Hon Schlrshp 79; Mi St Univ Awd For Acad Excllnc 79; Lansing Cmnty Coll; Foreign Lang.

AELING, JAMES; Minerva HS; Minerva, OH; 10/241 Boy Scts; Chrh Wkr; Cmnty Wkr; Hon Rl; Sct Actv; Pres 4-H; Pep Clb; Ftbl; Letter Wrstlng;.

AERTS, TODD; North Central Area HS; Powers, MI; Trs Soph Cls; Hon Rl; Mich Tech Univ; Engr.

AESCHLIMAN, KIM; Bluffton HS; Bluffton, IN; Sec Soph Cls; Sec Jr Cls; Am Leg Aux Girls St; Treas Chrh Wkr; Hon Rl; NHS; Y-Teens; Pep Clb; Spn Clb; Letter Bsktbl; Ball St Univ; Educ.

AFFHOLTER, JAMES E; Woodhaven HS; Woodhaven, MI; Band; Jr NHS; NHS; IM Sprt; Acceptd Lions Of Mich All St Band 1978; Univ Of Michigan; Solar Engr.

AFFHOLTER, PATRICK; Theodore Roosevelt HS; Wyandotte, MI; Am Leg Boys St; NHS; Pol Wkr; Letter Trk; College.

AGACINSKI, CYNTHIA; Catholic Central HS; Grand Rpds, MI; Sec Frsh Cls; Sec Soph Cls; Cls Rep Sr Cls; Hon Rl; Off Ade; Stu Cncl; Lat Clb; Aquinas; Phys Ther.

AGARDI, MIKE; South Amherst HS; S Amherst, OH; VP Frsh Cls; Cls Rep Frsh Cls; Cls Rep Soph Cls; VP Sr Cls; Hon Rl; Off Ade; Stu Cncl; Yrbk; Capt Bsktbl; Capt Ftbl;.

AGARWAL, NIKUNJ; George Washington HS; Charleston, WV; Cl Rep Jr Cls; Band; Jr NHS; Pres Mod UN; Orch; Pol Wkr; Pres Ed Sch Nwsp; Key Clb; Ohio St Univ; Poli Sci.

AGATEP, MARIA R C; St Florian HS; Detroit, MI; 3/75 Chrs; Hon Rl; Lbry Ade; Pres NHS; Sch Mus; Sch Pl; Stu Cncl; Ed Sch Nwsp; Rptr Sch Nwsp; Drama Clb; Wayne St Univ; RN.

AGATEP, MERILEEN; St Florian HS; Detroit, MI; 1/115 Trs Soph Cls; Pres Jr Cls; Chrs; Hon Rl; Sch Mus; Sch Pl; Stg Crw; Stu Cncl; Rptr Sch Nwsp; Sch Nwsp; Soc Of Dist Amer HS Stu; Cert Of Merit; Varsity Volleyball; Harvard Univ; Medicine.

AGEE, CARLA; Terre Haute North Vigo HS; Terre Haute, IN; 35/600 Hon Rl; JA; Y-Teens; GAA; Mgrs; JA Awd; Indiana State Univ; Bus.

AGEE, LISA; Central HS; Evansville, IN; 30/500 Cls Rep Frsh Cls; Cls Rep Soph Cls; Cl Rep Jr Cls; Cls Rep Sr Cls; Band; Hon Rl; NHS; Orch; Pol Wkr; Quill & Scroll; Ball St Univ; Bus Mgmt.

AGENS, JAMES; Lakeshore HS; St Joseph, MI; Hon Rl; Lit Mag; Off Ade; Quill & Scroll; Yth Flsp; Sch Nwsp; Drama Clb; Lake Mic College; Educ.

AGENS, KRISTINE; North HS; Willowick, OH; 10/706 Band; Hon Rl; NHS; Rptr Yrbk; Ger Clb; Univ; Bio.

AGIN, THOMAS; North College Hill HS; Cincinnati, OH; 12/162 Band; Pres Chrh Wkr; Hon Rl; NHS; Off Ade; Sch Mus; Spn Clb; Letter Bsktbl; Univ Of Cincinnati; Engr Sci.

AGLER, SUSAN; Holgate HS; Holgat4, OH; Hon Rl; Yth Flsp; Ed Sch Nwsp; 4-H; FHA; Mth Clb; Scr Kpr; College; Medical.

AGNE, BRIAN; Lakeview HS; Battle Creek, MI; Pres Sr Cls; Band; Cmnty Wkr; Hon Rl; NHS; Orch; Sch Mus; Stg Crw; Quiz Bowl Team Capt; DAR Good Citizen; Kiwanis Stu Of The Mth; Western Michigan Univ.

AGNEW, JOHN; Carroll HS; Xenia, OH; 19/320 Hon Rl; NHS; Letter Crs Cntry; Trk; IM Sprt; Vet.

AGOSTON, SHEILA; Lumen Cordium HS; Sagamore Hls, OH; Chrs; Drl Tm; Girl Scts; Hon Rl; Sch Mus; Sch Pl; Crs Cntry; GAA; College; Registered Nurse.

AGUILAR, JAVIER; Holy Redeemer HS; Detroit, MI; 1/130 Cls Rep Frsh Cls; Val; Chrh Wkr; Cmnty Wkr; Hon Rl; VP NHS; Treas Stu Cncl; Spn Clb; Letter Crs Cntry; Letter Trk; Wayne St Univ; Pharm.

AHEARN, DEBORAH; Meridian Sr HS; Sanford, MI; Hon Rl; Hosp Ade; JA; Pep Clb; Spn Clb; Letter Bsbl; JA Awd; Natl Merit SF; Voice Dem Awd; Univ.

AHL, KIMBERLY; South Spencer HS; Rockport, IN; 12/140 Chrs; Chrh Wkr; Hon Rl; NHS; Pol Wkr; Sch Mus; Drama Clb; Ger Clb; OEA; Bus Schl; Bus.

AHLBORN, BRIAN H; Penn HS; Mishawaka, IN; 8/475 Cls Rep Frsh Cls; FCA; Hon Rl; Mod UN; NHS; Mth Clb; Letter Ten; Univ; Actuarial Sci.

AHLE, CINDY; Old Fort HS; Tiffin, OH; Cls Rep Frsh Cls; Sec Soph Cls; Pres Jr Cls; VP Sr Cls; Band; Drm Mjrt; Hon Rl; Lbry Ade; NHS; Sch Pl; Ohio Northern Univ; Phys Ed.

AHLQUIST, ANNE; West Carrollton Sr HS; Dayton, OH; Am Leg Aux Girls St; Pres Chrs; Drl Tm; Hon Rl; Univ Of Dayton; Sec.

AHLRICHS, CHRISTINA A; Seton HS; Cincinnati, OH; 4/281 Hon Rl; Mod UN; NHS; Stu Cncl; Letter Bsktbl; Letter Swmmng; Letter Ten; Letter Trk; Univ Of Cincinnati; Mech Engr.

AHLRICHS, CHRISTINA; Seton HS; Cincinnati, OH; Cls Rep Frsh Cls; Hon Rl; Mod UN; NHS; Bsktbl; Swmmng; Ten; Capt Trk; GAA; General Motors Inst; Engr.

AHMAN, MARY L; Ottawa Glandorf HS; Ottawa, OH; Girl Scts; Hon Rl; NHS; Sch Mus; Ed Yrbk; Drama Clb; Fr Clb; Sec Sci Clb; GAA; Bowling Green St Univ; Educ.

AHMED, JERRY; Maple Hts HS; Maple Hgts, OH; Hon Rl; NHS; Letter Ftbl; Trk; Letter Wrstlng; College; Bus Admin.

AHO, KAREN; Negaunee HS; Negaunee, MI; Band; Debate Tm; Letter Bsktbl; Letter Trk; Michigan Tech Univ; Med Tech.

AHONEN, MARY; Wakefield HS; Wakefield, MI; Trs Jr Cls; Band; Chrs; Hon Rl; Stu Cncl; Pep Clb; Art.

AHR, NANCY; Seton HS; Cincinnati, OH; 6/266 Chrs; Hon Rl; Jr NHS; Treas NHS; Civ Clb; Fr Clb; Mth Clb; Treas Sci Clb; Oh Acad Schlrshp 79; Xavier Univ Pres Schlrshp 79; Xavier Univ; Mrktng.

AHRENS, LINDA; Ravenna HS; Ravenna, MI; 1/98 Hon Rl; NHS; Yrbk; Sch Nwsp; Western Mic Univ.

AHRENS, PHYLLIS; Mendon Cmnty HS; Mendon, MI; Band; Hon Rl; Hosp Ade; Red Cr Ade; Ftbl; Letter Swmmng; Letter Trk; PPFtbl; Glen Oaks Coll; Nursing.

AHRENS, SHARI; Plainwell HS; Plainwell, MI; 32/210 Chrs; Chrh Wkr; Hon Rl; Sch Mus; Yrbk; Sprt Ed Sch Nwsp; Sch Nwsp; Capt Bsktbl; Letter Trk; PPFtbl; Most Improved Alto Singer In Choir 75; Captn 4 Yr Letter Winner & MVP Vllybl 76 79; Kalamazoo Valley Coll; Sociology.

AHRMAN, ROXANNE; Peebles HS; Peebles, OH; Band; Drm Mjrt; Hon Rl; Hosp Ade; Lbry Ade; Stg Crw; Drama Clb; 4-H; Fr Clb; FTA; Univ; RN.

AIELLO, BECKY; Roosevelt Wilson HS; Clarksburg, WV; VP Frsh Cls; Trs Soph Cls; Cls Rep Sr Cls; Chrs; Hon Rl; Sch Mus; Sch Pl; Stu Cncl; Y-Teens; 4-H;.

AIELLO, GRACE; Benedictine HS; Detroit, MI; 6/180 Trs Frsh Cls; Chrs; Chrh Wkr; Hon Rl; Natl Forn Lg; NHS; Off Ade; Sch Pl; Wayne St Univ; Theatre.

AIKEN, DANIEL M; Bloomington HS North; Bloomington, IN; Band; Chrs; FCA; Sch Mus; DECA; Ger Clb; Trk; Tmr; 1st Plc IN DECA Advrtsng Srvcs Sllng 79; 3rd IN DECA Advrtsng Srvcs Oprtns 79; Indiana Univ; Bus.

AIKEN, DEBBIE; Nordonia Sr HS; Northfield, OH; VP Frsh Cls; Cmnty Wkr; Girl Scts; JA; Stu Cncl; Yth Flsp; Coach Actv; Voice Dem Awd; Univ; Bus.

AIKEN, KAREN; Champion; Warren, OH; Hon Rl; Stu Cncl; Spn Clb; Vocational; Dent Asst.

AIKENS, CRYSTAL; Hedgesville HS; Hedgesville, WV; Letter Band; Hon Rl; Lbry Ade; Drama Clb; 4-H; Pep Clb; Spn Clb; Capt Chrldng; Twrlr; 4-H Awd; Rcvd 1st & 2nd Premium Blue Ribbions 77; Held Offc Of Pres In 4 H 77; Univ; Law.

AIKENS, MARTHA; North Baltimore HS; N Baltimore, OH; 2/60 Sec Frsh Cls; Cls Rep Soph Cls; Sec Jr Cls; Sal; Band; Chrs; Girl Scts; Hon Rl; NHS; Off Ade; Univ Of Toledo; Respiratory Ther.

AIKMAN, KERRY; Greencastle HS; Greencastle, IN; 25/171 Cls Rep Soph Cls; Cl Rep Jr Cls; Hon Rl; Stu Cncl; Yth Flsp; Fr Clb; Pep Clb; Letter Trk; Chrldng; PPFtbl; College.

AIRGOOD, KAY; White Pigeon HS; White Pigeon, MI; 24/95 Hon Rl; NHS; Yrbk; Rptr Sch Nwsp; Sch Nwsp; Treas Fr Clb; FHA; Ferris State College; Bus Admin.

AIRHART, LISA; Girard HS; Girard, OH; 5/215 AFS; Girl Scts; NHS; Pres Y-Teens; Rptr Sch Nwsp; Ger Clb; Bsktbl; GAA; Youngstown State Univ; Accounting.

AIUTO, DINO; Warren HS; Sterling Hgts, MI; Letter Bsbl; Trk; Auto Mechanic.

AKARD, ALLYSON; Marion Adams HS; Sheridan, IN; 22/100 Girl Scts; Hon Rl; JA; Sct Actv; Yth Flsp; 4-H; FHA; Pep Clb; Crs Cntry; Swmmng; Ball State Univ; Teaching.

AKE, SHIRLEY; Whitehall HS; Whitehall, MI; 16/150 Band; Treas Chrs; Chrh Wkr; Girl Scts; Hon Rl; Treas NHS; Off Ade; Rptr Yrbk; Ten; PPFtbl; Muskegon Bus Coll; Med Asst.

AKENS, KONRAD; Zanesville HS; Zanesville, OH; Cls Rep Frsh Cls; Band; Hon Rl; Stu Cncl; College; Law.

AKENS, KONRAD R; Zanesville HS; Zanesville, OH; Cls Rep Frsh Cls; Band; Hon Rl; JA; Pol Wkr; Univ; Law.

AKER, LESLIE L; Bramwell HS; Bramwell, WV; 2/25 Band; Drm Mjrt; NHS; Stu Cncl; Yrbk; Letter Crs Cntry; Trk; Mgrs; Scr Kpr; Tmr; Bluefield St Coll; Elec Engr.

AKERS, JACQUELINE; Shortridge HS; Indianapolis, IN; Cls Rep Frsh Cls; Cls Rep Soph Cls; Cl Rep Jr Cls; Cls Rep Sr Cls; Hon Rl; NHS; Quill & Scroll; Sprt Ed Sch Nwsp; Rptr Sch Nwsp; Mat Maids; Ind Univ; Tele Communications.

AKERS, JOYCE; Woodhaven HS; Romulus, MI; 2/202 Sal; Chrh Wkr; Hon Rl; Jr NHS; NHS; Off Ade; Yrbk; 4-H; Ten; Michigan Tech Univ; Comp Engr.

AKERS, KAREN E; Coshocton HS; Coshocton, OH; 70/230 Band; Chrs; Drl Tm; Hon Rl; Lit Mag; Sch Pl; Sch Nwsp; Drama Clb; FTA; Spn Clb; Natl Council Of Teachers Of English Creative Writing Awd; Miami Univ; English.

AKERS, RADENE; Athens HS; Athens, WV; 7/63 Chrs; Hon Rl; Pres NHS; Sec Stu Cncl; Yrbk; Fr Clb; Pres FHA; Treas FTA; Treas Sci Clb; Concord College; Soc Work.

AKERS, RUSSELL; Chapmanville HS; Chapmanville, WV; Band; Chrs; Hon Rl; Marshall Univ; Law.

AKIN, JANA; Turpin HS; Cincinnati, OH; 16/357 Cls Rep Sr Cls; AFS; NHS; Yth Flsp; Letter Gym; Capt Chrldng; PPFtbl; Univ Of Georgia; Intl Bus.

AKIN, KEENAN; Hauser Jr Sr HS; Columbus, IN; 22/100 Aud/Vis; Chrh Wkr; Hon Rl; Lbry Ade; Mod UN; Purdue Univ; Aerospace Engr.

AKINS, MILLICENT; Mansfield Malabar HS; Mansfield, OH; 26/260 Drl Tm; Hon Rl; Jr NHS; Sch Pl; Drama Clb; Mth Clb; Kent St Univ; Elem Educ.

AKLEY, BELINDA; Vinson HS; Huntington, WV; 2/100 Band; Mod UN; NHS; Mth Clb; Treas Spn Clb; Marshall Univ; Chem.

AKMAN, LALE; North Farmington HS; Farm Hills, MI; Cls Rep Soph Cls; Cls Rep Sr Cls; Chrs; Hon Rl; Fr Clb; Gym; Univ; Psych.

AKRIDGE, APRIL; Inkster HS; Inkster, MI; 7/200 Chrh Wkr; Cmnty Wkr; Hon Rl; Lbry Ade; NHS; Orch; Stu Cncl; Yth Flsp; Rptr Yrbk; OEA; Phi Delta Kappa Sor Schlrshp; Miss Personality Of Phi Teen Group; Most Dependable Cheerleader; Univ Of Michigan; Acctg.

AKRIDGE, CINDY; Norwood HS; Norwood, OH; 13/348 Treas Band; Hon Rl; Treas Jr NHS; NHS; Orch; Sch Mus; Treas Key Clb; Coll.

ALAIMO, MARY; Centerline HS; Warren, MI; Band; Hon Rl; Jr NHS; NHS; Sch Pl; Stu Cncl; Sci Clb; Chrldng; Mic Univ; Medical.

ALAMAT, ELIZABETH; Pinckney HS; Brighton, MI; 18/257 Cl Rep Jr Cls; Sec Sr Cls; Band; Chrs; Sec Chrh Wkr; Hon Rl; NHS; Stu Cncl; Yth Flsp; FBLA; Spring Arbor Coll; Music Educ.

ALANIVA, HOWARD L; Crestwood HS; Dearborn Hts, MI; Hon Rl; IM Sprt; Am Leg Awd; Voice Dem Awd; Univ Of Michigan; Engr.

ALANO, CHRIS; Bloomfield HS; Bloomfield, IN; 10/100 Boy Scts; Hon Rl; Lbry Ade; Spn Clb; Purdue; Aerospace Engr.

ALASTANOS, JOHN; Washington Irving HS; Clarksburg, WV; 1/180 Chrh Wkr; Hon Rl; Pol Wkr; Lat Clb; Sci Clb; Trk; Wv Univ; Engr.

ALASTI, ISABELLA; Richmond Sr HS; Richmond, IN; Hon Rl; Ger Clb; Gov Hon Prg Awd; Natl Merit Schl; Rec Schlr Fr St Of Indiana; Particip In Natl German Contest; Purdue Univ; Pharm.

ALAVI, DAVID S; Steubenville HS; Steubenville, OH; Am Leg Boys St; Hon Rl; Orch; Ger Clb; Key Clb; Sci Clb; Letter Ten; College; Phys Sci.

ALBANESO, VIRGINIA; Wellsville HS; Wellsville, OH; Am Leg Aux Girls St; Band; Girl Scts; Sch Mus; Sch Pl; Y-Teens; Rptr Sch Nwsp; Drama Clb; FTA; Pep Clb; Anthropological Archlgst.

ALBANI, STEVE; Hubbard HS; Hubbard, OH; Hon Rl; Lbry Ade; Fr Clb; Key Clb; Ten; Opt Clb Awd; Ohio St Univ; Elec.

ALBAUGH, ANITA; Columbia City Joint HS; Columbia City, IN; Band; Chrh Wkr; Hosp Ade; Quill & Scroll; Sch Mus; Sch Pl; Stu Cncl; Sch Nwsp; Sec Civ Clb; VP 4-H; Univ; Radiology.

ALBEE, LORI A; Pocahontas Cnty HS; Dunmore, WV; Band; Quill & Scroll; Ed Yrbk; Rptr Sch Nwsp; Trk; Marshall Univ.

ALBER, MARGARET; Huntington North HS; Warren, IN; 23/604 Sec Frsh Cls; Cls Rep Soph Cls; Cl Rep Jr Cls; Cls Rep Sr Cls; Am Leg Aux Girls St; Band; Chrs; Sec Stu Cncl; Fr Clb; Brigham Young Univ; Comp.

ALBER, SUSAN; Big Rapids HS; Big Rapids, MI; Sec Jr Cls; VP Sr Cls; Hon Rl; NHS; Stu Cncl; Rptr Sch Nwsp; IM Sprt; Mgrs; Scr Kpr; College; Acctg.

ALBERRY, JUNE; Lakewood HS; Thornville, OH; 21/204 NHS; Capt Bsktbl; Letter Trk; Chrldng; Pres GAA; IM Sprt; College; Acct.

ALBERS, BARB; Berea HS; Brook Park, OH; 141/750 Band; Drl Tm; NHS; IM Sprt; Mat Maids; Ohi State Univ.

ALBERS, JOAN; Highland HS; Anderson, IN; 88/450 Band; Pres Boy Scts; Cmnty Wkr; Girl Scts; Hon Rl; Hosp Ade; Off Ade; Red Cr Ade; Sch Mus; Sct Actv; Whos Who Amony Amer HS Stu 77; Purdue Univ; Vet Med.

ALBERS, LYNNE; Strongsville Sr HS; Strongsville, OH; 4/435 Pres Jr Cls; Chrs; VP Jr NHS; NHS; Sct Actv; Treas Stu Cncl; Capt Bsktbl; Capt Chrldng; VP GAA; Capt PPFtbl; Miami Univ; Syst Analyst.

ALBERS, MARTHA; Ursuline Academy; Cincinnati, OH; 27/106 Sec Girl Scts; JA; Cit Awd; Biomed Engr.

ALBERS, MICHAEL; Versailles HS; Rossburg, OH; 26/130 Hon Rl; Letter Ftbl; Letter Trk; Letter Wrstlng; Univ; Lib Arts.

ALBERS, MICHELLE; Russia Local HS; Russia, OH; Pres Soph Cls; Pres Sr Cls; NHS; Stu Cncl; Rptr Yrbk; Pres 4-H; VP FHA; Spn Clb; Letter Chrldng; 4-H Awd;.

ALBERS, RITA; St Ursula Academy; Norwood, OH; 3/103 Cls Rep Frsh Cls; Pres Soph Cls; Cl Rep Jr Cls; Chrh Wkr; Hon Rl; NHS; Stu Cncl; College; Chemical Engineering.

ALBERT, JOHN; Columbian HS; Tiffin, OH; Hon Rl; Mth Clb; Spn Clb; Glf; Bus Schl; Comp Prog.

ALBERT, KATHLEEN; North Liberty HS; S Bend, IN; 6/101 Band; Chrs; Chrh Wkr; Hon Rl; NHS; Sprt Ed Sch Nwsp; 4-H; Ind Univ; Acctg.

ALBERT, PENNY; Martins Ferry HS; Martins Ferry, OH; Trs Soph Cls; Band; Chrh Wkr; Girl Scts; Hon Rl; Hosp Ade; Off Ade; Y-Teens; Sci Clb; Spn Clb; Ohio St Univ; Nursing.

ALBERT, SHAUNA; Hardin Northern School; Dola, OH; 12/59 Band; Chrs; Hon Rl; Stu Cncl; Rptr Sch Nwsp; 4-H; OEA; 4-H Awd; All Amer Hall Of Fame Band Hon 78; Red Ribbon In Solo Contest Drum 2 78; Letters & Pins For Band 78; Northwestern Bus Coll; Sec.

ALBERT, TED; Belding HS; Belding, MI; Am Leg Boys St; Band; Chrs; Chrh Wkr; Debate Tm; Hon Rl; NHS; Yth Flsp; FFA; Bsbl; Outstanding Jr Awd FFA; All Conf Catcher Of Yr; Natl FFA Conv Attendant; Michigan St Univ; Farm Mgmt.

ALBERTI, DEBBIE; Washington Catholic HS; Washington, IN; Chrs; Hon Rl; Sch Pl; Stg Crw; Yth Flsp; Drama Clb; Pep Clb; Chrldng; GAA; Vincennes Univ.

ALBERTINI, JANET; Bishop Donahue HS; Moundsville, WV; 2/54 Chrh Wkr; Girl Scts; Sec NHS; Stu Cncl; Yth Flsp; Ed Yrbk; Sec 4-H; GAA; Cit Awd; DAR Awd; West Liberty St Coll; Spec Educ.

ALBERTINI, MARCIA; Bishop Donahue HS; Moundsville, WV; 1/65 Hon Rl; NHS; Stu Cncl; Rptr Yrbk; Rptr Sch Nwsp; Pres 4-H; Spn Clb; GAA; Dnfth Awd; Lion Awd; Coll.

ALBERTS, MARIANNE; Imlay City HS; Attica, MI; 8/161 Hon Rl; Lbry Ade; Sec NHS; Rptr Yrbk; Imlay City Fed Of Tchrs Schlrshp 79; Times Herald Acad Achvmnt Awd 79; Yrbk Cert Of Awd 79; Hon Mentn Art; Ferris St Coll; Advertising.

ALBIN, MARIE; Meadowbrook HS; Cambridge, OH; Chrs; Chrh Wkr; Hon Rl; Yth Flsp; Sch Nwsp; 4-H; Pep Clb; Spn Clb; Univ; Nursing.

ALBRECHT, JONATHAN; Douglas Macarthur HS; Saginaw, MI; Boy Scts; Chrh Wkr; Yth Flsp; Lat Clb; Bsbl; Ftbl; IM Sprt; Pres Awd; Western Mic Univ; Bus Engr.

ALBRIGHT, BARBARA; Kelloggsville HS; Kentwood, MI; Cls Rep Frsh Cls; Letter Band; Cmnty Wkr; Hon Rl; Jr NHS; Cit Awd; Band Festv Medals 2nd Pl Solos; Nursing Cert For Nurses Aide; Kendall Schl Of Design Cert Of Course; Vocational Schl; Phys Therapy.

ALBRIGHT, JAMES; Jewett Scio HS; Jewett, OH; Am Leg Boys St; Hon Rl; NHS; Spn Clb; Letter Trk; Cit Awd; VFW Awd; Bowling Green State Univ; Elec.

ALBRIGHT, KAREN; David Anderson HS; Lisbon, OH; 22/95 FCA; Hon Rl; Yth Flsp; Sec Y-Teens; Fr Clb; Sec Sci Clb; Capt Bsktbl; College; Bus.

ALBRIGHT, KATRINA; Logan Sr HS; Logan, WV; VP Soph Cls; Sec Jr Cls; Jr NHS; NHS; Ed Yrbk; Pep Clb; Spn Clb; Gym; Chrldng; West Virginia Univ; Phys Ed.

ALBUS, DAVID; Madison HS; Madison, OH; Band; Boy Scts; Hon Rl; NHS; Sch Mus; Ger Clb; Pep Clb; Ftbl; Trk; College; Elec.

ALCORN, JANET; Broad Ripple HS; Indianapolis, IN; Band; Hon Rl; NHS; Off Ade; Univ; Comp Sci.

ALCORN, RAYMOND S; New Albany Sr HS; New Albany, IN; Boy Scts; Chrs; Hon Rl; JA; Sct Actv; 4-H; Pep Clb; Rdo Clb; IM Sprt; Mgrs; Eagle Scout 77; Order Of The Arrow 75; Univ; Med.

ALCOSER, NORA; Carson City Crystal Area HS; Carson City, MI; Sec Sr Cls; Am Leg Aux Girls St; FHA; Pep Clb; Trk; Chrldng; GAA; Am Leg Awd; Lion Awd; Voice Dem Awd; Alma Col; Nursing.

ALDA, ROTHER M; Columbian HS; Tiffin, OH; Hon Rl; Ten; Wrstlng; Univ Of Cincinnati; Aero Engr.

ALDERIGI, MARIA; Gallia Acad; Gallipolis, OH; Cls Rep Frsh Cls; Cls Rep Soph Cls; Band; Chrs; Girl Scts; Hosp Ade; Off Ade; Stu Cncl; Y-Teens; Sch Nwsp; Ohio Univ; Med.

ALDERING, GREGORY S; Bridgeport Comm HS; Saginaw, MI; 2/299 Am Leg Boys St; Band; Chrh Wkr; Hon Rl; NHS; Rptr Sch Nwsp; Sci Clb; Natl Merit SF; Univ; Astronomy.

ALDERMAN, KIM; Pocahontas Cnty HS; Millpoint, WV; 4-H; FBLA; FHA; Pep Clb; Socr; Trk; Bus Schl; Bus.

ALDERMAN, MARCIE; St Joseph Cntrl Catholic HS; Huntington, WV; Girl Scts; Hon Rl; Hosp Ade; Sct Actv; Rptr Yrbk; Keyettes; Pep Clb; VICA; Bsktbl; Hndbl; Marshall Univ; Soc Work.

ALDRICH, DANIEL; Waterloo Sr HS; Ottawa, OH; Boy Scts; Chrs; Chrh Wkr; Hon Rl; Sct Actv; Yth Flsp; Univ.

ALDRICH, DIANE M; Clare HS; Clare, MI; Chrs; Hon Rl; NHS; Mich Christian Coll; Eng.

ALDRICH, MARK; Midland HS; Midland, MI; Boy Scts; Hon Rl; Orch; Sct Actv; Ger Clb; Coll; Biomed Engr.

ALDRICH, SHARISE; Chesanina HS; Oakley, MI; Stu Cncl; Fr Clb; Chrldng; Art Clb; Cosmetology Voc Schl.

ALDRICH, STEPHANIE; Pellston HS; Carp Lake, MI; Hon Rl; Univ; History Tchr.

ALDRIDGE, KEMI J; Ripley HS; Kenna, WV; Trs Frsh Cls; Hst Jr Cls; Band; Treas Chrh Wkr; Drl Tm; Jr NHS; Sch Pl; Stg Crw; Rptr Yrbk; Beta Clb; Univ; Nursing.

ALERDING, PEGGY; Chatard HS; Indianapolis, IN; Pep Clb; Chrldng; PPFtbl; Indiana Univ; Phys Educ.

ALESSANDRINI, ANGELA; Cardinal Stritch HS; Oregon, OH; Cls Rep Frsh Cls; Sec Soph Cls; Cl Rep Jr Cls; Cls Rep Sr Cls; Band; Chrs; Hon Rl; Red Cr Ade; Sch Mus; Stu Cncl; Owens Tech Schl; Lab Tech.

ALESSI, RANDALL; Buckeye South HS; Yorkville, OH; 9/92 Hon Rl; NHS; Sch Pl; Ed Sch Nwsp; Drama Clb; Spn Clb; Bsktbl; Glf; College; Comp Sci.

ALESSI, VINCENT; Pontiac Central HS; Pontiac, MI; Cls Rep Soph Cls; Boy Scts; Chrh Wkr; Hon Rl; Stu Cncl; Letter Bsbl; Letter Crs Cntry; Capt Swmmng; Coach Actv; Tmr; Univ Of Michigan; Chem Engr.

ALEVIZOS, THOMAS; Rogers HS; Michigan City, IN; 5/480 Cls Rep Frsh Cls; Cl Rep Jr Cls; Pres Sr Cls; Chrh Wkr; Debate Tm; NHS; Quill & Scroll; Univ Of Mich;.

ALEXANDER, ANGELA; Father Joseph Wehrle Mem HS; Columbus, OH; 10/105 Sec Soph Cls; Sec Jr Cls; Girl Scts; Hon Rl; Sch Pl; Stu Cncl; Rptr Sch Nwsp; Drama Clb; Capt Mat Maids; Kiwan Awd; Dist Amer HS Stu Of Amer; Natl Awd Of Exc; Stu Of Month Awd; College; Nursing.

ALEXANDER, BILL; Portsmouth HS; Portsmouth, OH; 6/234 Hon Rl; Lat Clb; Ohi State Univ; Natural Resources.

ALEXANDER, CHRIS; Walnut Ridge HS; Columbus, OH; Cls Rep Frsh Cls; Cls Rep Soph Cls; VP Jr Cls; Pres Sr Cls; Hon Rl; Stu Cncl; Spn Clb; GAA; Mgrs; Ach Hnr Roll Yearly; College; Poli Sci.

ALEXANDER, COLLEEN; Wooster HS; Wooster, OH; 58/365 Sec Jr Cls; Am Leg Aux Girls St; Band; Chrh Wkr; Cmnty Wkr; Girl Scts; Hon Rl; Pol Wkr; Red Cr Ade; Sct Actv; Ohio St Univ; Educ.

ALEXANDER, CONNIE; Rockville HS; Rockville, IN; 4/82 Band; Chrh Wkr; Drl Tm; Drm Mjrt; Girl Scts; Hon Rl; NHS; Yth Flsp; Pep Clb; Twrlr; Univ Of Evansville; Rn.

ALEXANDER, CYNTHIA; Northfield Jr Sr HS; Wabash, IN; Chrh Wkr; Hon Rl; Hosp Ade; Lbry Ade; Yth Flsp; FHA; Univ; Health.

ALEXANDER, DONCELLA D; Independence Jr Sr HS; Columbus, OH; 19/216 Hon Rl; Jr NHS; Off Ade; Rptr Sch Nwsp; Sch Nwsp; Letter Trk; Natl Sci Foundtn Training Prog 1978; Natl Achiev Commd Stdnt 1978; Univ; Indust Engr.

ALEXANDER, FRED; Washington HS; Massillon, OH; Pres Frsh Cls; VP Sr Cls; Band; JA; VP DECA; Pres Jr Ach; Football Team Mascot; Cleve Broadcasting Inst; Announcer.

ALEXANDER, JAYNE E; Hagerstown Jr Sr HS; Hagerstown, IN; 5/172 Sec Band; Hon Rl; Treas NHS; Fr Clb; Sci Clb; Ball St Univ; Acctg.

ALEXANDER, JOANNE; Southfield HS; Southfield, MI; Debate Tm; Natl Forn Lg; NHS; Sch Mus; Sch Pl; Sct Actv; Rptr Sch Nwsp; Rdo Clb; Natl Merit Ltr; College; Communications.

ALEXANDER, JOSILYN; Roosevelt HS; Gary, IN; Sec Frsh Cls; Band; Hon Rl; JA; Jr NHS; Rptr Yrbk; Rptr Sch Nwsp; Fr Clb; College; Computer Science.

ALEXANDER, KATRINA; West Side Sr HS; Gary, IN; Cl Rep Jr Cls; Hon Rl; Orch; ROTC; Stu Cncl; VP Spn Clb; Natl Guards; Sec.

ALEXANDER, KENDALL; Lexington HS; Mansfield, OH; 23/271 Hon Rl; NHS; Mth Clb; Crs Cntry; Ftbl; Wrstlng; IM Sprt; Bowling Green St Univ; Math.

ALEXANDER, KERRY; Edon Northwest HS; Edon, OH; 3/68 VP Soph Cls; VP Jr Cls; VP Band; Hon Rl; Lbry Ade; Lit Mag; NHS; Sch Mus; Sch Pl; Rptr Yrbk; Univ Of Toledo; Pre Med.

ALEXANDER, KERRY; Edon HS; Edon, OH; 2/70 VP Soph Cls; VP Jr Cls; Sal; Band; Hon Rl; Lbry Ade; NHS; Orch; Sch Mus; Sch Pl; Ohio State; Medicine.

ALEXANDER, KLARA; Northmont HS; Brookville, OH; 130/517 Chrs; Girl Scts; Hon Rl; Sct Actv; Miami Valley Schl; Nursing.

ALEXANDER, LANA; Moorefield HS; Moorefield, WV; 8/91 VP Jr Cls; Am Leg Aux Girls St; Band; Chrh Wkr; Debate Tm; Hon Rl; Jr NHS; NHS; Off Ade; Sch Pl; West Virginia Univ; Medicine.

ALEXANDER, LAURIE A; John Hay HS; Cleveland, OH; 13/251 Cls Rep Sr Cls; Chrs; Chrh Wkr; Hon Rl; Hosp Ade; JA; Jr NHS; Lbry Ade; Off Ade; Red Cr Ade; Martha Haolden Jenning Schlshp Awd 77 & 78; Whos Who In Foreign Lang In Oh Schls 79; Ohio St Univ; Phys Ther.

ALEXANDER, LESLIE; Cloverdale HS; Cloverdale, IN; Chrs; Fr Clb; FTA;.

ALEXANDER, LISA; Hamilton Southeastern HS; Noblesville, IN; Girl Scts; Hon Rl; Sct Actv; Fr Clb; Cit Awd; Butler Univ; Med.

ALEXANDER, RENEE; Chelsea HS; Chelsea, MI; Girl Scts; Hon Rl; Pol Wkr; Natl Merit SF; Mic St Univ; Business.

ALEXANDER, RUTH; Berkeley Springs HS; Berkeley Spgs, WV; 24/133 Band; Chrh Wkr; Lbry Ade; Off Ade; Orch; Sch Mus; Sch Pl; Yth Flsp; Rptr Yrbk; Drama Clb; Whos Who Among Amer HS Stud 77; Womans Auxilary Nursing Schlrshp 79; Morgan Stud Aide Schlrshp 79; Shepherd Coll; Nursing.

ALEXANDER, SHARON; John Adams HS; Cleveland, OH; Cl Rep Jr Cls; Hon Rl; NHS; Bsbl; Bsktbl; Trk; Cit Awd; Vllybl Team Recevd A Lttr & Certifct 1977; Stenographers Lab Clb Treasrr 1978; Camera Clb Presdnt 1979; New Mexico Univ; Public Rel.

ALEXANDER, SUSAN; North Central HS; Indianapolis, IN; Girl Scts; Hon Rl; NHS; Off Ade; Cls Rep Frsh Cls; Sct Actv; Sec 4-H; Keyettes; Ball State; Acctg.

ALEXANDER, THEDA; North Posey Sr HS; New Harmony, IN; Chrs; Chrh Wkr; Hon Rl; NHS; Sch Mus; 4-H; FHA; 4-H Awd; Univ; Fshn Mdse.

ALEXANDER, VICKIE; Benjamin Logan HS; Bellefontaine, OH; Hon Rl; NHS; Sch Pl; Drama Clb; 4-H; Pres FHA; Pres OEA; Schlrshp Awd In Biology Home Ed II & Office Ed Assn; N W Business Coll; Med Ofc Asst.

ALEXANDER, WILLIAM P; Barberton HS; Barberton, OH; 109/442 Am Leg Boys St; Aud/Vis; Chrh Wkr; Hon Rl; Yth Flsp; IM Sprt; Hockins Tech Coll; Rec & Wildlife.

ALFARO, BERTHA; Delta HS; Delta, OH; FHA; Spn Clb; Toledo Univ; Child Card.

ALFERS, ELLEN; Stephen T Badin HS; Hamilton, OH; 6/435 Hon Rl; Hosp Ade; Sch Mus; Sch Pl; Stg Crw; Rptr Yrbk; Drama Clb; FHA; Letter Trk; IM Sprt; Univ; Nursing.

ALFLEN, ELIZABETH; Wayland Union HS; Wayland, MI; 5/205 VP Soph Cls; VP Jr Cls; Pres Sr Cls; Band; Chrs; Chrh Wkr; Debate Tm; Drl Tm; Girl Scts; Hon Rl; Awrd Academ Excel Mi St Univ 1979; Miss Teenage Amer Cand Final 1978; U S Army Certif Acheiv 1977; Michigan St Univ; Engr Arts.

ALFONSO, JACQUELINE; Copley HS; Akron, OH; 9/310 Chrs; Hon Rl; Hosp Ade; NHS; Off Ade; Spn Clb; Swmmng; IM Sprt; Tmr; Univ.

ALFONT, MICHELE L; Marion HS; Marion, IN; 20/710 Pres Frsh Cls; VP Jr Cls; Cls Rep Sr Cls; Am Leg Aux Girls St; Hon Rl; Sec NHS; PAVAS; Northwestern Univ; Theatre.

ALFORD, CHRIS; North Rop HS; Ft Wayne, IN; 80/587 Band; Bsbl; Ftbl; Ind Univ.

ALFORD, DENA; Switzerland Co Jr Sr HS; Vevay, IN; Trs Soph Cls; Band; Chrs; Drl Tm; MMM; Sch Mus; Treas Yth Flsp; Drama Clb; Pres 4-H; Sec Sci Clb; Courier Jrnl 4 H Awd 1977; Vincennes Univ; Acctg.

ALFORD, RICHELLE; Pike Central HS; Stendal, IN; NHS; FHA; Pep Clb; College; Social Work.

ALFORD, ROBIN; Stivers Patterson Co Op HS; Dayton, OH; 28/448 Cls Rep Frsh Cls; Cls Rep Soph Cls; Cl Rep Jr Cls; Hon Rl; Hosp Ade; Stu Cncl; Pres VICA; UICA Job Interview Contest Wnnr 1st & 2nd Pl 77 & 78; Univ Of Cincinnati; Nursing.

ALFREDSON, NANCY; Menominee HS; Menominee, MI; 54/273 Band; Hon Rl; Jr NHS; NHS; Bsktbl; Glf; Michigan Tech Univ; Med Tech.

ALFREY, STEVE; Little Miami HS; Morrow, OH; Boy Scts; Chrh Wkr; Hon Rl; Jr NHS; NHS; Stg Crw; Stu Cncl; Yth Flsp; Bsktbl; Crs Cntry; College; Engr.

ALFULTIS, CHARLES; North Ridgeville HS; N Ridgeville, OH; 30/340 Cls Rep Frsh Cls; Cls Rep Soph Cls; Cl Rep Jr Cls; Boy Scts; Chrs; Chrh Wkr; Hon Rl; NHS; Sct Actv; Yth Flsp; Pres Fields United Youth Fellowshp 78; Mbr Of Varsity R Lettermn Clb 77 78 & 79; Lorgin Cnty Cmnty Coll; Police Sci.

ALGER, HOLLY; Van Buren HS; Centerpoint, IN; Drl Tm; Girl Scts; Rptr Yrbk; Yrbk; Drama Clb; 4-H; FHA; Pep Clb; Sci Clb; Spn Clb; Coll; Archt Drafting.

ALGOE, ALISON; Mentor HS; Mentor On Lake, OH; Hon Rl; Math.

ALHADI, AZIZ; Brookfield HS; Masury, OH; 77/159 VP Soph Cls; Drl Tm; Sch Pl; Stg Crw; Pep Clb; IM Sprt; Voice Dem Awd; Coll; Interperter.

ALI, DUNCAN C; Reeths Puffer HS; Muskegon, MI; 17/330 Band; Hon Rl; NHS; Pep Clb; Spn Clb; Ten; Jr Varsity Letter For Tennis; College; Medicine.

ALICEA, ANNETTE; Washington HS; E Chicago, IN; Cl Rep Jr Cls; Chrs; Cmnty Wkr; Girl Scts; Hon Rl; NHS; FHA; Spn Clb; Perfect Attendance Certf 76 79; Univ; Bus Mgmt.

ALICEA, MILDRED; Westside HS; Gary, IN; Hon Rl; Lbry Ade; Lat Clb; VICA; Univ; Cosmetology.

ALICOX, LINDA; Elmhurst HS; Ft Wayne, IN; 192/420 Hst Sr Cls; Chrs; Girl Scts; Hon Rl; Red Cr Ade; DECA; Btty Crckr Awd; Cit Awd; Phys Educ Awd 73; Explrtry French Awd 74; Modeling.

ALIG, BARBARA; Coldwater HS; Coldwater, OH; 32/146 Hst Jr Cls; Hst Sr Cls; Band; Hon Rl; Hosp Ade; Off Ade; Ger Clb; Pep Clb; Trk; Chrldng; Voc Schl; Nursing.

ALIG, BOB; Archbishop Alter HS; Dayton, OH; 23/294 Chrs; Chrh Wkr; Cmnty Wkr; Hon Rl; NHS; Off Ade; PAVAS; Pol Wkr; Sch Mus; Sch Pl; College; Medicine.

ALKIRE, L; Nordonia HS; Northfield, OH; 79/444 Cls Rep Sr Cls; Sch Mus; Stg Crw; Stu Cncl; VICA; Letter Ftbl; Mgrs; Scr Kpr; Kent State Univ; Cmmrcl Art.

ALKIRE, LESA; Decatur Central HS; Indpls, IN; Cls Rep Frsh Cls; Cls Rep Soph Cls; Cls Rep Sr Cls; Band; Girl Scts; Hon Rl; Off Ade; Quill & Scroll; Sct Actv; Stu Cncl; Univ; Comp Tech.

ALKIRE, MARY; Bear Lake HS; Bear Lk, MI; 6/34 Cls Rep Frsh Cls; Chrh Wkr; Hon Rl; NHS; Trk; Vlybl Most Improved Player; Coll; Vet.

ALLAN, JANET; South Range HS; Canfield, OH; AFS; Band; Sch Mus; Univ; Nursing.

ALLAN, KAREN; Switzerland Cnty Jr Sr HS; Vevay, IN; 18/121 NHS; Ed Yrbk; Drama Clb; Pep Clb; Spn Clb; Bsktbl; Trk; Sterling Coll; Law.

ALLANSON, BARBARA; Regina HS; Univ Hts, OH; VP Frsh Cls; FCA; Girl Scts; Hon Rl; Stu Cncl; Bsbl; Bsktbl; Coach Actv; Pres GAA; IM Sprt; College; Health.

ALLARD, JENNIFER; Lebanon HS; Lebanon, OH; Cmp Fr Grls; Chrs; Hon Rl; Yth Flsp; Cit Awd; Ohi State Univ; Bus.

ALLARD, REBECCA; Charlevoix HS; Charlevoix, MI; 51/152 Trs Frsh Cls; Cl Rep Jr Cls; Am Leg Aux Girls St; Band; Stu Cncl; Ferris State College.

ALLBRIGHT, ANGELA; Rock Hill Sr HS; Pedro, OH; Girl Scts; Hon Rl; NHS; Sct Actv; Beta Clb; Mth Clb; Sci Clb; Ohio Univ HS Schlr 5 Free Coll Hours 79; Bus Schl.

ALLBRIGHT, JEFFERY; Bloomington HS; Bloomington, IN; 118/412 Band; Boy Scts; Boys Clb Am; Fr Clb; Bsktbl; Ftbl; Hndbl; Ind Univ; Sci.

ALLCORN, RODNEY; Sebring Mckinley HS; Sebring, OH; Treas Band; Letter Ftbl; IM Sprt; Tmr;.

ALLEGRA, CHRISTINE; St Joseph Acad; Cleveland, OH; NHS; Rptr Sch Nwsp; Mth Clb; College.

ALLEMAN, JAMES; Point Pleasant HS; Pt Pleasant, WV; Band; Boy Scts; Sch Mus; Sct Actv; Stu Cncl; Key Clb; Wrstlng; Marshall Univ; Music.

ALLEMEIER, JOHN; Greenfield Central HS; Greenfield, IN; Boy Scts; Hon Rl; Natl Forn Lg; Sct Actv; Yth Flsp; Boys Clb Am; Ger Clb; Mth Clb; Letter Wrstlng; Greenfield Bankng Co Schslhp Awd 78 & 79; Univ; Engr.

ALLEN, ANDRE; Warrensville Hts HS; Warrensville, OH; Cls Rep Frsh Cls; Boy Scts; Chrs; Bsbl; Ftbl; IM Sprt; Youngstown St Univ; Poli Sci.

ALLEN, BARRY; Upper Scioto Valley HS; Mc Guffey, OH; Cl Rep Jr Cls; Sec Band; Chrs; NHS; VP Stu Cncl; Yrbk; Beta Clb; Letter Bsbl; College.

ALLEN, BETH; R Nelson Snider HS; Ft Wayne, IN; 16/564 Chrs; Hon Rl; Fr Clb; Letter Glf; Natl Merit Ltr; Univ.

ALLEN, BONNIE; Jackson HS; Oak Hill, OH; Letter Band; Chrh Wkr; Girl Scts; Hon Rl; Off Ade; Sch Mus; Yrbk; Bsbl; Swmmng; Coach Actv; Hocking Tech; Nurse.

ALLEN, BOYD; Hubbard HS; Hubbard, OH; Chrh Wkr; Hon Rl; Sch Mus; Stg Crw; Yth Flsp; Key Clb; Capt Wrstlng; Thespians 1978; Univ Of Pittsburgh; Chem Engr.

ALLEN, BRIAN; Millington HS; Millington, MI; 6/150 Am Leg Boys St; Band; Hon Rl; NHS; Fr Clb; Ger Clb; Mich State Univ; Physics.

ALLEN, CAROL; Howell HS; Howell, MI; Chrs; Hon Rl; Mdrgl; NHS; Pom Pon; Opt Clb Awd; Mich State; Acctg.

ALLEN, CHERYL; Wilbur Wright HS; Dayton, OH; Chrs; Chrh Wkr; Drl Tm; Hosp Ade; Off Ade; Sch Nwsp; Outstanding Ach Awd In Business Law; College; Home Ec.

ALLEN, CONNIE; Winamac Community HS; Winamac, IN; Chrh Wkr; FHA; Sec FTA; Pep Clb; Spn Clb; Creative Writing.

ALLEN, CURT; Southmont HS; New Market, IN; Pres Frsh Cls; FCA; Hon Rl; Jr NHS; Stu Cncl; Pep Clb; Spn Clb; Bsktbl; College; Soc Std.

ALLEN, DEAN; Arsenal Technical HS; Indianapolis, IN; Boy Scts; Hon Rl; DECA; Wrstlng;.

ALLEN, DEBBIE; Beallsville HS; Clarington, OH; 12/80 Hst Frsh Cls; Pres Sr Cls; Pres Band; VP Chrs; Pres FCA; Hon Rl; Off Ade; Sch Mus; Sch Pl; Pres Drama Clb; All Cnty Band 4 Yrs; 1st Pl 4 H Cnty Fair Model; St Fair 4 H Model; Univ; Spec Educ.

ALLEN, DONALD D; Struthers HS; Struthers, OH; Chrs; Hon Rl; NHS; Sch Mus; Sch Pl; Stg Crw; Drama Clb; Ftbl; Trk; Ivy Schl; Commercial Art.

ALLEN, DONNA; Frank Cody HS; Detroit, MI; 12/450 Band; Drm Mjrt; Hon Rl; Sec NHS; OEA; PPFtbl; Cit Awd; Wayne St Mrt Schlshp Awd 1979; St Of Mi Cmpttv Schlshp Awd 1979; 1st Pl Mtrpltn Detroit Shrthnd Wnnr 1979; Wayne St Univ; Bus Admin.

ALLEN, FAWN; Warrensville Hts HS; Warrensville, OH; Cls Rep Frsh Cls; Hon Rl; Scr Kpr; Tmr; Cert Of Proficiency Century 21 Acctg; Cert Of Credit Busns Ed; Class Honors Merit Roll; Univ Of Cincinnati; Acctg.

ALLEN, GEORGE; Liberty HS; Girard, OH; 34/233 Letter Bsbl; Letter Bsktbl; Letter Ftbl; Univ; Engr.

ALLEN, GREG; Wadsworth Sr HS; Ashland, OH; 20/346 Hon Rl; Fr Clb; Lat Clb; Mth Clb; IM Sprt; Ohio St Univ; Vet.

ALLEN, GWENDOLYN; Corydon Cntrl HS; Corydon, IN; Sec Frsh Cls; Trs Frsh Cls; Sec Soph Cls; Trs Soph Cls; Sec Jr Cls; Trs Jr Cls; Hon Rl; NHS; Fr Clb; FBLA; Coll; Busns.

ALLEN, JAMES; Loy Norrix HS; Kalamazoo, MI; Chrh Wkr; Cmnty Wkr; Hon Rl; Yth Flsp; Swmmng; Exchange Stud To Spain With Internatl Youth For Understanding 78; YMCA Rifle Clb Pres V P & Treas; Univ; Hotel Mgmt.

ALLEN, JEFF; Bloomington HS North; Bloomington, IN; Aud/Vis; Band; Boy Scts; Chrh Wkr; Stg Crw; Purdue Univ; Comp Sci.

ALLEN, JOSEPH W; Turpin HS; Cincinnati, OH; JA; Ger Clb; IM Sprt; Natl Merit SF; Univ; Elec Engr.

ALLEN, KAREN; Horace Mann HS; Gary, IN; Sec Jr Cls; Pres Sr Cls; Chrh Wkr; Hon Rl; Jr NHS; NHS; Stu Cncl; Rptr Yrbk; Pep Clb; College; Math.

ALLEN, KAREN; Gallia Acad; Rio Grande, OH; Chrs; Chrh Wkr; Girl Scts; Hosp Ade; Off Ade; Sch Mus; Yth Flsp; FTA; Spn Clb; Trk; Rio Grande; Vet.

ALLEN, KIMBERLY; Bishop Noll Inst; Gary, IN; 109/321 Chrs; Chrh Wkr; Y-Teens; Civ Clb; College; Mgmt.

ALLEN, KIMBERLY; John Glenn HS; Bay City, MI; 9/328 Cls Rep Frsh Cls; Cls Rep Soph Cls; VP Jr Cls; Pres Sr Cls; Band; Chrh Wkr; Hon Rl; NHS; Stu Cncl; Capt Swmmng; Bay City Pro & Bus Womens Schlrshp 79; Delta Coll; Energy Research.

ALLEN, KYM; Robert S Rogers HS; Toledo, OH; Band; Hon Rl; Pres JA; Stu Cncl; Spn Clb; JA Awd; Columbus Coll Of Dsgn; Cmmrcl Art.

ALLEN, L; Windham HS; Windham, OH; Chrs; Hon Rl; NHS; Sch Pl; Drama Clb; Pres Spn Clb; Letter Trk; Univ Of Dayton; Elementary Ed.

ALLEN, LINDA; Worthington Jefferson HS; Worthington, IN; 12/40 Hon Rl; Lbry Ade;.

ALLEN, L TANYA; West Side Sr HS; Gary, IN; 66/650 Cls Rep Frsh Cls; Cls Rep Soph Cls; Cl Rep Jr Cls; Hon Rl; Lbry Ade; NHS; Stu Cncl; Trk; N Illinois Univ; Comp Sci.

ALLEN, MARLENE; Walnut Ridge HS; Columbus, OH; 82/424 Chrs; Sec Chrh Wkr; Cmnty Wkr; Girl Scts; Hon Rl; Hosp Ade; NHS; Red Cr Ade; Otterbein Coll; Nurse.

ALLEN, MARY; Penn HS; Osceola, IN; Band; Drl Tm; Hon Rl; Off Ade; Rptr Yrbk; Rptr Sch Nwsp; Pep Clb; Spn Clb; Mat Maids; 2 Gold Nisbova Medals Band 77 && 78; 1 Silver Nisbovia Medal Band 79; Indiana Univ; X Ray Tech.

ALLEN, MARY J; Hillsdale HS; Jeromesville, OH; 4/116 Band; Chrh Wkr; Hon Rl; Sec Lbry Ade; NHS; Sch Pl; Yth Flsp; FFA; Lat Clb; Am Leg Awd; Ohio State Univ; Computer Sci.

ALLEN, MAUREEN A; Bishop Watterson HS; Worthington, OH; 3/250 Cls Rep Soph Cls; Hon Rl; Hosp Ade; Jr NHS; NHS; Sch Mus; Rptr Sch Nwsp; Spn Clb; Mat Maids; Natl Merit Ltr; Univ Of Notre Dame; Bus.

ALLEN, MICHAEL; Terre Haute North Vigo HS; Terre Haute, IN; Hon Rl; Stu Cncl; Treas Key Clb; Letter Bsktbl; Coach Actv; IM Sprt; Mgrs; College.

ALLEN, MICHAEL; Oak Hill HS; Oak Hill, WV; Cls Rep Frsh Cls; Cls Rep Soph Cls; Hon Rl; Bsktbl; Letter Ftbl; Trk; Church League Bsktbll Awd 77; Univ; Engr.

ALLEN, MICHAEL J; Lawton Comm HS; Lawton, MI; 16/55 Am Leg Boys St; Boy Scts; Hon Rl; Sct Actv; Pres Stu Cncl; Sci Clb; Letter Bsbl; Letter Ftbl; Letter Wrstlng; All Conf Defense Ftbl; Most Valuable Lineman Ftbl; College; Busns Admin.

ALLEN, MICHELLE; Toronto HS; Toronto, OH; 2/140 Cls Rep Frsh Cls; Cls Rep Soph Cls; Cl Rep Jr Cls; Cls Rep Sr Cls; Am Leg Aux Girls St; Hon Rl; Pres Stu Cncl; Ed Sch Nwsp; Pep Clb; Spn Clb; Principals List; Schlrshp Tm; Hon Mention In Eng 2; Ohio St Univ; Health.

ALLEN, N; Norwayne HS; Creston, OH; Cmnty Wkr; Girl Scts; Hon Rl; Rptr Yrbk; 4-H; IM Sprt; Mgrs; Paeontology.

ALLEN, NANCY; Norwayne HS; Creston, OH; Cmnty Wkr; Girl Scts; Hon Rl; Sct Actv; Rptr Yrbk; 4-H; Mgrs; Voc Schl; Graphic Arts.

ALLEN, PATRICIA; East Technical HS; Cleveland, OH; 8/306 AFS; Drl Tm; Hon Rl; NHS; Rptr Yrbk; Rptr Sch Nwsp; Key Clb; OEA; Cit Awd; Kiwan Awd; Martha Holden Jennings Essay Schlrshp 78 & 79; Phi Delta Kappa Sorority Schlrshp 79; Miami Univ; Acctg.

ALLEN, RACHEL; Richmond HS; Richmond, MI; VP Sr Cls; Hon Rl; Stu Cncl; Rptr Yrbk; Natl Merit SF; St Johns Coll; Liberal Arts.

ALLEN, RANDY; Worthington Jefferson HS; Worthington, IN; 4/35 Hon Rl; NHS; Beta Clb; Am Leg Awd;.

ALLEN, REBECCA; Benton Harbor HS; Benton Harbor, MI; Hon Rl; Off Ade; Sct Actv; OEA; Chrs; JA; Jr NHS; College; Criminal Investigation.

ALLEN, RICHARD L; Bridgeport Sr HS; Bridgeport, WV; Band; Chrs; Chrh Wkr; Hon Rl; Jr NHS; NHS; Yth Flsp; Univ; Engr.

ALLEN, ROBERT J; Eastern Greene HS; Owensburg, IN; 27/70 Sec Frsh Cls; Pres Sr Cls; Boy Scts; NHS; Stu Cncl; Letter Bsbl; Letter Bsktbl; Letter Trk; Ind Central Univ; Bus Mgmt.

ALLEN, ROBERT M; Plainwell HS; Plainwell, MI; 42/220 Boy Scts; Hon Rl; Rptr Sch Nwsp; Glf; Coach Actv; IM Sprt; Scr Kpr; Mi Compttv Schslhp 79; Western Michigan Univ; Indust Engr.

ALLEN, ROYCE; Athens HS; Athens, MI; Chrh Wkr; Hon Rl; Jr NHS; NHS; Red Cr Ade; Spn Clb; Hillsdale Coll; Psych.

ALLEN, SERENA; Clare HS; Clare, MI; 10/131 Cls Rep Frsh Cls; Pres Soph Cls; Cl Rep Jr Cls; Pres Sr Cls; Band; Chrh Wkr; Debate Tm; Drm Mjrt; FCA; Girl Scts; Univ Of Michigan; Bus Admin.

ALLEN, SHARI; Johannesburg Lewiston HS; Lewiston, MI; 3/75 Sec Frsh Cls; Sec Jr Cls; Band; Girl Scts; Hon Rl; NHS; Off Ade; 4-H; FHA; Pep Clb; MVP Softball; MVP Basketball; Athlete Of The Year; All Amer Hall Of Fame Band; Lake Superior State Coll; Phys Ed.

ALLEN, SHARON L; Emerson HS; Gary, IN; Cl Rep Jr Cls; Band; Chrs; Chrh Wkr; Cmnty Wkr; Hon Rl; JA; Natl Forn Lg; Off Ade; Sch Mus; Schlstc Hon 77; Schlstc Or Achvmnt Hon 78; Hon & Forensics Awd 79; UCLA; Med.

ALLEN, TAMMY; Parkersburg South HS; Parkersburg, WV; Pres Soph Cls; Cls Rep Soph Cls; Cls Rep Sr Cls; Band; Drm Bgl; Orch; Stu Cncl; 4-H; Sci Clb; IM Sprt; W Virginia Inst Of Tech; Inter Desgn.

ALLEN, TODD; Jefferson HS; Dayton, OH; Band; Hon Rl; Boys Clb Am; Spn Clb; Ftbl; Trk; 2 Yr Awd In Ftbl & Track 79; Honor Roll Awd 79; Univ; Elec Engr.

ALLEN, TODD; Springboro HS; Lebanon, OH; 4-H; IM Sprt; 4-H Awd; College; Engr.

ALLEN, TONYA; Brookville HS; Metamora, IN; 1/196 Drl Tm; Girl Scts; Hon Rl; Rptr Sch Nwsp; 4-H; FHA; Pep Clb; GAA; College; Pharmacy.

ALLEN, TRACY; Oak Hill HS; Oak Hill, WV; 4/200 Chrs; Chrh Wkr; NHS; Yth Flsp; Chrldng; Vocational School; Beauty Culture.

ALLENICK, LISA; Glen Oak HS; Mayfield Hts, OH; Cls Rep Soph Cls; Pres Jr Cls; Cls Rep Sr Cls; Chrs; Cmnty Wkr; Sch Mus; Stg Crw; Stu Cncl; Pres Drama Clb; Chrldng; Coll Conservatory Of Music; Music.

ALLENSON, DONALD R; Parma HS; Broadview Hts, OH; 6/710 Hon Rl; NHS; Sci Clb; Natl Merit SF; Univ; Computer Sci.

ALLENSWORTH, GARY L; Jewett Scio HS; Uhrichsville, OH; 6/80 Sec Jr Cls; Boy Scts; Chrh Wkr; Hon Rl; Stu Cncl; Bsktbl; Ftbl; Kent St Univ; Bus.

ALLER, KATHY; Centerville HS; Centerville, OH; 70/680 NHS; Rptr Yrbk; Yrbk; Pep Clb; PPFtbl; Miami Univ; Applied Sci.

ALLERDING, SARAH; Harbor Springs HS; Hrbr Spgs, MI; Hon Rl; Stg Crw; Rptr Yrbk; Drama Clb; Letter Bsktbl; Trk; Chrldng; Michigan Tech Univ; Pro Archt.

ALLEVATO, GREG; Roosevelt Wilson HS; Clarksburg, WV; 6/132 Cls Rep Frsh Cls; Hon Rl; Sch Pl; Rptr Yrbk; Rptr Sch Nwsp; Drama Clb; VP Fr Clb; Leo Clb; Glf; Mgrs; College; Engr.

ALLEVATO, GREGORY; Roosevelt Wilson HS; Clarksburg, WV; 6/132 Cls Rep Frsh Cls; Am Leg Boys St; Hon Rl; NHS; Stu Cncl; Rptr Yrbk; Sprt Ed Sch Nwsp; VP Fr Clb; Glf; Dnfth Awd; College; Chem Engr.

ALLEX, MARK; Archbishop Alter HS; Kettering, OH; Band; Hon Rl; Sch Mus; Sch Pl; Drama Clb; Univ Of Dayton; Geol.

ALLEY, BRAD; Cannelton HS; Cannelton, IN; 5/35 Cmnty Wkr; Hon Rl; NHS; Stu Cncl; Pep Clb; Bsbl; Bsktbl; Crs Cntry; Trk;.

ALLEY, TROY; Iaeger HS; Big Sandy, WV; Hst Frsh Cls; Cls Rep Soph Cls; Hon Rl; JA; 4-H; Spn Clb; Ftbl; 4-H Awd; Natl Merit Ltr; Univ; Forest Ranger.

ALLGIRE, JULIE R; Stryker Local School; Stryker, OH; 15/50 VP Frsh Cls; Cls Rep Frsh Cls; Pres Soph Cls; Cls Rep Soph Cls; Cl Rep Jr Cls; Trs Sr Cls; Cls Rep Sr Cls; Band; Hon Rl; Pol Wkr; Bowling Green St Univ; Psych.

ALLGOOD, GWENDOLYN; Walnut Hills HS; Cincinnati, OH; Cl Rep Jr Cls; AFS; Girl Scts; Hon Rl; Pol Wkr; Letter Ten; Univ Of New Hampshire.

ALLINDER, MARGARET; Brookhaven HS; Columbus, OH; 54/402 Chrh Wkr; Hon Rl; Jr NHS; NHS; Pres Yth Flsp; Capital Univ; Psych.

ALLINGHAM, LAWRENCE L; Tecumseh HS; New Carlisle, OH; 5/400 Pres Soph Cls; Pres Jr Cls; Chrh Wkr; FCA; Hon Rl; Pres Jr NHS; Pres Stu Cncl; Fr Clb; Bsbl; Bsktbl; General Motors Inst; Mech Engr.

ALLISON, BRENDA S; Stryker HS; Stryker, OH; 15/57 Band; Chrs; Chrh Wkr; Girl Scts; Hon Rl; Lbry Ade; Sch Mus; Yth Flsp; FHA; Bsktbl; Univ.

ALLISON, C; Waverly HS; Waverly, OH; 30/178 Band; Hon Rl; Sch Pl; Fr Clb; FHA; Pep Clb; Trk; Mgrs; Scr Kpr; West Virginia Wesleyan Coll; Nursing.

ALLISON, ELIZABETH; Oak Glen HS; Chester, WV; Sec Jr Cls; Hon Rl; NHS; Sch Pl; Yth Flsp; Yrbk; 4-H; Fr Clb; Wv Univ; Lab Tech.

ALLISON, HENRY; Gallia Academy; Gallipolis, OH; Chrs; Fr Clb; Lat Clb; College; Bio Chem.

ALLISON, JANE; Baldwin HS; Baldwin, MI; Cls Rep Soph Cls; Sal; Pres Band; Hon Rl; Sec NHS; Pres Stu Cncl; Rptr Yrbk; Capt Bsktbl; Capt Trk; Alma Coll.

ALLISON, JEFFREY; Wm Mason HS; Mason, OH; 4/203 Am Leg Boys St; Chrs; Chrh Wkr; Cmnty Wkr; Hon Rl; Jr NHS; NHS; Yth Flsp; 4-H; Ohi State Univ; Vet.

ALLISON, JEFFREY; Eaton Rapids HS; Eaton Rapids, MI; 30/300 Pres Frsh Cls; Pres Soph Cls; Pres Jr Cls; Pres Sr Cls; Boy Scts; Chrh Wkr; Hon Rl; PAVAS; Sch Pl; Sct Actv; Alma Coll; Acctg.

ALLISON, LESLIE; Carroll HS; Dayton, OH; 22/285 Hon Rl; Mod UN; NHS; Stu Cncl; Spn Clb; Pres Jr Counc On World Affairs 79; OSU; Pre Med.

ALLISON, LISA; Univ Liggett; Grosse Pointe, MI; Hon Rl; Stg Crw; Yth Flsp; Sch Nwsp; Fr Clb; Chrldng; Mgrs; Univ Of Notre Dame.

ALLISON, MARLENE; Mt Vernon Acad; Mt Vernon, OH; Band; Hon Rl; Sch Mus; Andrews Univ; Nutrition.

ALLISON, MICHAEL; Mishawaka HS; Mishawaka, IN; 13/369 Hon Rl; Jr NHS; Lit Mag; NHS; Ed Yrbk; Rptr Yrbk; Rptr Sch Nwsp; Parsons Schl; Comm Dsgn.

ALLISON, MICHELLE; North Central HS; Indianapolis, IN; Cmp Fr Grls; Chrs; Hon Rl; Stu Cncl; Sprt Ed Yrbk; Fr Clb; Pep Clb; Letter Trk; IM Sprt; NCTE; Purdue Univ; Psych.

ALLISON, PEGGY S; Monrovia HS; Monrovia, IN; 4/109 Chrs; Chrh Wkr; Girl Scts; Hon Rl; NHS; Off Ade; Sch Mus; Yth Flsp; 4-H; Pep Clb; Indiana St Univ; Sec.

ALLISON, STEPHANIE A; Rogers HS; Toledo, OH; Cls Rep Sr Cls; Band; Chrh Wkr; Hon Rl; Treas JA; Lbry Ade; Orch; Red Cr Ade; Sci Clb; Spn Clb; GTCTM Cert Of Merit; Foreign Lang Day Superior Rating In Art Spanish; Participate In Whit Is Engr; Univ Of Toledo; Envir Health.

ALLMAN, DIANE; Washington Irving HS; Clarksburg, WV; 2/175 Sec Band; Hon Rl; Pres NHS; Yth Flsp; Lat Clb; Leo Clb; West Virginia Career Coll; Sec Sci.

ALLMAN, LESA; Buckhannon Upshur HS; Buckhannon, WV; Band; Hosp Ade; Sch Mus; Sch Pl; Y-Teens; FBLA; Pep Clb; Twrlr; West Virginia Univ.

ALLMAN, MICHAEL; Buckhannon Upshur HS; Buckhannon, WV; Chrs; Hon Rl; Fr Clb; Key Clb; Letter Ftbl; Swmmng; Letter Trk; IM Sprt; Mgrs; Pres Awd; Alderson Broaddus Univ; Coal Mn Mgmt.

ALLMAN, PENNY; West Washington HS; Campbellsbg, IN; VP Soph Cls; Pres Jr Cls; Pres Sr Cls; Cmnty Wkr; Hon Rl; Stu Cncl; Yrbk; Sch Nwsp; Pres Pep Clb; Bsktbl; Marion Univ; Jrnlsm.

ALLMANDINGER, LORNA L; Celina Sr HS; Celina, OH; Band; Chrs; Chrh Wkr; Girl Scts; Hon Rl; Lbry Ade; NHS; Sch Mus; FTA; Ger Clb;.

ALLMON, BARRY; Wintersville HS; Steubenville, OH; 30/300 Fr Clb; Trk; Univ; Chem Engr.

ALLMON, BILL; Grove City HS; Orient, OH; Band; Boy Scts; Hon Rl; NHS; Letter Bsbl; Bsktbl; Letter Ftbl; 1st Alt To Buckeye Boys State 1979; Amer Legion Basebl Team 1979; Whos Who Among Amer HS Stu 1978; Univ; Med.

ALLORI, MARY A; Heath HS; Heath, OH; Band; Chrs; Chrh Wkr; Hon Rl; NHS; Orch; Sec Yth Flsp; Sec Key Clb; Letter Bsktbl; Letter Trk; Ohio State Univ; Engr.

ALLOWAY, RUTH A; Fairview HS; Dayton, OH; 5/200 Cls Rep Frsh Cls; Cls Rep Soph Cls; Band; Hon Rl; Hosp Ade; JA; Jr NHS; NHS; Stg Crw; Stu Cncl; College; Math.

ALLS, TAMBERLYN; Coventry HS; Akron, OH; Girl Scts; Hon Rl; Lbry Ade; Quill & Scroll; Drama Clb; Spn Clb; Trk; Scr Kpr; Akron Univ; Criminal Justice.

ALLSHOUSE, JULIE; Prairie Heights HS; Angola, IN; 10/134 VP Jr Cls; Am Leg Aux Girls St; Band; Chrs; Stu Cncl; Yth Flsp; Sch Nwsp; College; Med.

ALLTOP, BRUCE; Jackson Milton HS; Lake Milton, OH; 8/105 Pres Frsh Cls; Cls Rep Soph Cls; VP Jr Cls; Pres Sr Cls; Trs Sr Cls; Am Leg Boys St; Hon Rl; NHS; Sch Mus; Sch Pl; Princeton Univ; Engr.

ALLWARDT, MATT; Tiffin Columbian HS; Tiffin, OH; Hon Rl; Letter Scr Kpr; Tmr; College; Computer Science.

ALLWINE, DAVID; Shelby Sr HS; Shelby, OH; 13/259 Band; Boy Scts; Chrh Wkr; Hon Rl; Sct Actv; FSA; Lat Clb; Rdo Clb; Sci Clb; Am Leg Awd; Runner Up Glenn F Cox Newsppr Achvmnt Awd 76; Ohio St Univ; Forestry.

ALLYN, DAVID; Flint S W HS; Flint, MI; Hon Rl; Michigan St Univ; Engr.

ALMASY, DOUGLAS; Mount Clemens HS; Mt Clemens, MI; Band; Chrh Wkr; Cmnty Wkr; Hon Rl; NHS; Orch; Yth Flsp; Bsktbl; Capt Trk; IM Sprt; General Motors Inst; Engineering.

ALMON, JOSEPH C; Decatur Central HS; Indnpls, IN; 19/380 Band; Hon Rl; Quill & Scroll; Rptr Yrbk; 4-H; Letter Glf; 4-H Awd; Purdue Univ; Chem Engr.

ALMOND, TED; Woodrow Wilson HS; Beckley, WV; 166/508 Hon Rl; VP Stu Cncl; Trk; Mgrs; Scr Kpr; West Virginia Tech Coll; Bio.

ALMY, LYNNE; Lakeview HS; Lakeview, MI; Band; Girl Scts; Hon Rl; NHS; Off Ade; Stu Cncl; Yrbk; Pres FHA; FTA; Pep Clb; Ferris State Coll; Acctg.

ALONZO, ENRIQUE; St Mary Prep HS; Canton, MI; 4/27 VP Frsh Cls; Chrs; Chrh Wkr; Crs Cntry; Gym; Swmmng; Trk; Univ Of Mic; Pre Med.

ALOUF, MAURICE; Fayetteville HS; Fayetteville, WV; 1/86 Val; Am Leg Boys St; NHS; Stu Cncl; Pres FBLA; 1st Pl In Acctg II At Wv St FBLA Conf 79; 2nd Pl Acctg 1 At Wv St FBLA Conf 78; Byrd Schlstc Recog Awd; W Virignia Inst Of Tech; Acctg.

ALPAY, SARA; Tiffin Columbian HS; Tiffin, OH; Cl Rep Jr Cls; Band; Chrs; Cmnty Wkr; Hon Rl; Hosp Ade; Stu Cncl; Rptr Yrbk; Rptr Sch Nwsp; Drama Clb; 1st Jr Jrnlsm Awrd 78; Univ; Jrnlsm.

ALQUIZA, DAVE; Osborn HS; Detroit, MI; Michigan Tech Univ; Fish Tech.

ALRED, JAMES H; Rogers HS; Michigan City, IN; 8/480 Band; Boy Scts; Chrh Wkr; Hon Rl; NHS; Sch Mus; Ger Clb; Ten; Purdue Univ; Elec Engr.

ALSMAN, JACKY; North Knox HS; Oaktown, IN; 72/145 Pres Frsh Cls; FCA; Fr Clb; Letter Bsktbl; Letter Ftbl; Letter Trk; Bsktbl Co MVP Rebound Awd All Cnfrnce All Sectnl; Most Recoveries & Steals Trophy Field Goal Trophy; College; Phys Ed.

ALSPACH, HOWARD; Hammond Tech Voc HS; Hammond, IN; Hon Rl;.

ALSPAUGH, CYNTHIA; Benjamin Logan HS; Zanesfield, OH; Hon Rl; Jr NHS; NHS; Sch Pl; Drama Clb; 4-H; OEA; Spn Clb; Chrldng; GAA; Schlrshp History 78; Merit History 79; Schlrshp Tm History 79; Patricia Stevens Coll; Int Design.

ALSPAUGH, PATTIE; Westerville South HS; Westerville, OH; Drl Tm; Quill & Scroll; Rptr Yrbk; Sch Nwsp; Drama Clb; Lieutenant Drill Team; Natl Winner Quill & Scroll; W Assoc; Ohio Univ; Journalism.

ALT, LINDA; Davison HS; Davison, MI; Band; Chrh Wkr; Girl Scts; Hon Rl; Orch; Stg Crw; Yth Flsp; Ger Clb; Letter Trk; Univ Of Mich; Physical Therapy.

ALTENA, S; Holland Christian HS; Holland, MI; Chrs; Sec Chrh Wkr; Debate Tm; Ger Clb; Gym; Coach Actv; Calvin; Cmmrcl Artist.

ALTENBURG, JOANN; Centerville HS; Spring Vly, OH; 80/680 Hon Rl; NHS; 4-H; Pep Clb; Letter Trk; IM Sprt; PPFtbl; Tmr; Miami Univ; Acctg.

ALTENBURGER, LARRY; Ottoville HS; Ottoville, OH; Trs Frsh Cls; Boy Scts; Chrs; Cmnty Wkr; Hon Rl; Boys Clb Am; Bsktbl; Letter Crs Cntry; Letter Trk; IM Sprt; Coll.

ALTENEDER, RACHEL; Perrysburg HS; Perrysburg, OH; 33/207 VP Soph Cls; VP Jr Cls; Pres Sr Cls; Hon Rl; NHS; Sch Mus; Sch Pl; Stg Crw; Stu Cncl; Drama Clb; Natl Thespians Soc; Univ; Pre Med.

ALTENHOF, MICHAEL; United Local HS; Kensington, OH; Pres Sr Cls; Hon Rl; Stg Crw; JC Awd; Delegate To Hugh Obrian Youth Leadrshp Seminar 78; Geneva Coll; Engr.

ALTHANS, GREGORY; Kenston HS; Chagrin Falls, OH; Cls Rep Frsh Cls; Cls Rep Soph Cls; Hon Rl; Rus Clb; Bsktbl; Letter Glf; Letter Ten; Russian Awd 77; Coll Of William & Mary; Law.

ALTHARDT, JOHN; Warren Central HS; Indianapolis, IN; Aud/Vis; Band; Chrh Wkr; Natl Forn Lg; Sch Pl; Yth Flsp; Sch Nwsp; Drama Clb; Ten; Opt Clb Awd; Indpls Nws Schlrshp To A 2 Wk Jrnlsm Sem 79; In St Sum Hon Progr For Rad TV 79; Sprtscstr Disk Jock; Ball St Univ; Mass Media.

ALTHAUS, CHERYL; Wadsworth Sr HS; Wadsworth, OH; 95/367 Band; FCA; Girl Scts; NHS; Pep Clb; Spn Clb; Letter Bsktbl; Capt Trk; Bluffton Coll; Elem Educ.

ALTHERR, ELAINE; Defiance Sr HS; Defiance, OH; Cmnty Wkr; Girl Scts; Hon Rl; JA; Jr NHS; NHS; Stg Crw; FTA; Pep Clb; Spn Clb; Bus Schl; Retail Mgr.

ALTHOFF, JANE M; Brownsburg HS; Brownsburg, IN; Hon Rl; 4-H; Spn Clb; Ind Univ; Nursing.

ALTHOUSE, STEPHEN; Southgate HS; Southgate, MI; Cls Rep Frsh Cls; Cls Rep Soph Cls; Cl Rep Jr Cls; Cls Rep Sr Cls; Am Leg Boys St; Stu Cncl; Rptr Sch Nwsp; Sch Nwsp; Letter Crs Cntry; Western Michigan Univ; Comp Sci.

ALTIERE, TAMMY; Windham HS; Windham, OH; Cls Rep Frsh Cls; Cls Rep Soph Cls; Cl Rep Jr Cls; Sec Sr Cls; Band; Chrs; Chrh Wkr; Pep Clb; Spn Clb; IM Sprt; Univ; Pre Med.

ALTIZER, TREVA; Centerburg HS; Centerburg, OH; Girl Scts; Hon Rl; Jr NHS; Lbry Ade; NHS; Off Ade; Yth Flsp; Yrbk; Drama Clb; Letter Bsktbl; Volleyball Letter 2; Trainer For All Sports; College; Phys Therapy.

ALTMAN, CYNTHIA S; New Buffalo HS; New Buffalo, MI; Hon Rl; Sch Mus; Stg Crw; Sch Nwsp; Spn Clb; Letter Trk; Anderson Coll.

ALTMAN, LINDA; Twin Lakes HS; Monticello, IN; 16/210 Chrs; Hon Rl; Lbry Ade; Natl Forn Lg; Sch Mus; 4-H; FHA; FTA; 4-H Awd; Indiana St Univ; Bus Mgmt.

ALTMAN, TINA; Plymouth HS; Plymouth, IN; 24/220 Band; Hon Rl; Lit Mag; Pres Eng Clb; Fr Clb; FTA; Mth Clb; Coll.

ALTON, ROBERT; John Marshall HS; Cleveland, OH; 96/602 Aud/Vis; Hon Rl; Pres JA; NHS; OEA; Cit Awd; JA Awd; Dale Carnegie Schlrshp; 4th Pl In OEA Contest Data Processing Computers;.

ALTSCHEFFEL, JANICE; Buena Vista HS; Saginaw, MI; Chrh Wkr; Hon Rl; Jr NHS; NHS; Yrbk; Ed Sch Nwsp; Sci Clb; Saginaw Bus Inst; Exec Sec.

ALTSCHULD, MATTHEW; James Ford Rhodes HS; Cleveland, OH; Hon Rl; Ger Clb; Letter Socr; Letter Trk; Wrstlng; IM Sprt; Cleveland St Univ.

ALTSTAETTER, JON; Mc Comb Local School; Mc Comb, OH; Boy Scts; Chrs; Off Ade; Sch Pl; Stu Cncl; Bsbl; Bsktbl; Letter Ftbl; Scr Kpr; Track Most Outstanding Runner Of Yr 79; Track Most Points Earned On Tm 79; Track Lettered 77 78 & 79; Univ; Archt.

ALTWIES, MARGIE; Carmel HS; Carmel, IN; 131/698 Hon Rl; Mat Maids; Univ; Med.

ALUISE, THOMAS; St Joseph Central Cath HS; Huntington, WV; Pres Frsh Cls; Cls Rep Soph Cls; Hon Rl; Lit Mag; Stu Cncl; Yrbk; Sprt Ed Sch Nwsp; Rptr Sch Nwsp; Eng Clb; Mth Clb; Univ; Jrnlsm.

ALVARADO, VICTOR; Harbor Springs HS; Cross Vlg, MI; Band; Boy Scts; Hon Rl; Sct Actv; Letter Bsbl; Letter Bsktbl; Letter Ftbl; Mathawd 79; Hon Stndt 79; Magna Cum Laude 79; Univ Of Michigan; Med Sci.

ALVARO, SHERRI L; Brooke HS; Weirton, WV; 79/404 Sec Frsh Cls; Chrs; Chrh Wkr; Cmnty Wkr; Hon Rl; JA; Sch Mus; Yth Flsp; Trk; IM Sprt; Bradford Schl; Sec.

ALVERSON, JILL; Colerain HS; Cincinnati, OH; 6/693 Chrs; Chrh Wkr; Cmnty Wkr; Hon Rl; Jr NHS; Mdrgl; NHS; Ger Clb; Miami Univ; Business Management.

ALVERSON, MICHAEL; Athens HS; Athens, MI; 8/82 Band; Hon Rl; Jr NHS; Sct Actv; Mgrs; Scr Kpr; Tmr; College.

ALVESTEFFER, ANGIE; Montague HS; Rothbury, MI; Chrs; Chrh Wkr; Hon Rl; Lbry Ade; NHS; Treas 4-H; Ger Clb; Letter Bsbl; Capt Crs Cntry; Letter Trk; Univ; Dent Work.

ALVESTEFFER, DIANA; Shelby Sr Shs; Shelby, MI; Hon Rl; Lbry Ade; NHS; Rptr Yrbk; Rptr Sch Nwsp; Fr Clb; Univ.

ALVEY, RICHARD; Sturgis HS; Sturgis, MI; Chrs; JA; Sch Mus; Ftbl; Trk; JA Awd; St Of Mi Schlshp For Coll 79; Rep Sturgis At Midwest Convntn 77; Central Michigan Univ; Religion.

ALVEY, RONALD; Springboro HS; Springboro, OH; Pres Frsh Cls; Hst Soph Cls; VP Jr Cls; Hon Rl; Off Ade; Letter Bsbl; Letter Ftbl; Coach Actv; IM Sprt; Am Leg Awd; Ohio State; Aviation.

ALVEY, TERRY; Mater Dei HS; Evansvl, IN; Cls Rep Soph Cls; Cl Rep Jr Cls; Aud/Vis; Boy Scts; Hon Rl; JA; Jr NHS; Sch Pl; Stg Crw; Stu Cncl; Co Chrmn Of Prom Comm 78; Indiana St Univ; Phys Ther.

ALWARD, MIKE; Monrovia HS; Monrovia, IN; 14/148 Hon Rl; Spn Clb; Letter Ftbl; Trk; Univ; Mech Engr.

AMABELI, TERESA; Sebring Mc Kinley HS; Sebring, OH; 6/91 Am Leg Aux Girls St; Band; Hon Rl; VP NHS; Quill & Scroll; Sch Nwsp; Lat Clb; Trk; GAA; Scr Kpr; Univ Of Akron; Bus Admin.

AMAMAN, TODD; Arthur Hill HS; Saginaw, MI; Cls Rep Sr Cls; Boy Scts; Chrh Wkr; Sch Pl; Stg Crw; Stu Cncl; Yth Flsp; Drama Clb; Ger Clb; Cit Awd; Concordia Univ; Theol.

AMAN, A; Lewis County HS; Camden, WV; Am Leg Aux Girls St; Band; Chrs; Chrh Wkr; Cmnty Wkr; Drm Mjrt; Hon Rl; Jr NHS; NHS; Wv Univ; Nursing.

AMAN, ANITA; Lewis County HS; Camden, WV; Band; Chrs; Hon Rl; Jr NHS; NHS; Sch Pl; Yth Flsp; Y-Teens; Rptr Sch Nwsp; Drama Clb; Mbr St Boniface Parish Cncl; Church Organist; West Virginia Univ; Nursing.

AMAN, MARY; West Catholic HS; Grand Rapids, MI; Chrs; Chrh Wkr; Hon Rl; Jr NHS; Mdrgl; NHS; Sch Mus; Sprt Ed Sch Nwsp; Rptr Sch Nwsp; Sch Nwsp; Central Mic; Nursing.

AMARAL, DONNA; Bedford Sr HS; Clinton, MS; Cmp Fr Grls; Girl Scts; Hon Rl; JA; Yrbk; FHA; Mth Clb; Spn Clb; Trk; Scr Kpr; S E Massachusetts Univ; Psych.

AMARI, FRANCESCA; Lakeview HS; Battle Creek, MI; Trs Frsh Cls; Cls Rep Frsh Cls; Trs Soph Cls; Cls Rep Soph Cls; Trs Jr Cls; Trs Sr Cls; Chrs; Hon Rl; JA; Natl Forn Lg; Whos Who In Outstndng HS Music Stu; Natl Schl Choral Awd; Homecoming Top Ten; Cntrl Michigan Univ; Broadcasting.

AMARO, DEBORA; Delton Kellogg HS; Delton, MI; Hon Rl; Spn Clb; Coll; Law.

AMASH, CAROLINE; Marietta Sr HS; Marietta, OH; AFS; Debate Tm; Hon Rl; NHS; Sch Mus; Sch Pl; Drama Clb; Marietta Coll; Modern Lang.

AMATO, LISA; St Thomas Aquinas HS; Canton, OH; Sec Soph Cls; Chrs; Lit Mag; Sch Mus; Yrbk; Pep Clb; Spn Clb; Trk; Letter Chrldng; GAA; Mbr Of Canton Ballet Co; Jr Hmcmng Attendant; 2 Art Awds; Univ Of Akron; Dance.

AMATO, NANCY; Lake Shore HS; St Clair Shores, MI; Cls Rep Soph Cls; Pres Jr Cls; VP Sr Cls; Band; Hon Rl; NHS; Stu Cncl; Pom Pon; PPFtbl; Macomb Comm Coll; Accounting.

AMBLE, ROBERT C; Davison Sr HS; Davison, MI; 1/430 Val; Am Leg Boys St; Aud/Vis; Band; Boy Scts; Debate Tm; Drl Tm; Hon Rl; Jr NHS; Lbry Ade; Massachusetts Inst Of Tech; Engr.

AMBURGEY, MICHAEL; Jackson Center HS; Wapakoneta, OH; Boy Scts; Sct Actv; Sprt Ed Sch Nwsp; Sch Nwsp; Lat Clb; Spn Clb; Bsktbl; Letter Trk; Am Leg Awd; Amer Lgn Amer Awd M8; Ohio Northern Univ; Law.

AMBURGEY, NITA; Parkway HS; Willshire, OH; 2/83 Hon Rl; Wright St Univ; Sec.

AMBURGEY, TERRI; Orchard View HS; Muskegon, MI; 34/200 Band; Hon Rl; Chrldng; PPFtbl; Muskegon Community College; Bus.

AMBURGY, LESA A; Little Miami HS; Morrow, OH; Chrh Wkr; Debate Tm; Girl Scts; Hon Rl; Jr NHS; Lbry Ade; Lit Mag; NHS; Off Ade; Pol Wkr; Eastern Kentucky Univ; Pre Law.

AMBUSKE, PAULETTE M; Bethel Local HS; New Carlisle, OH; Chrs; Hon Rl; Jr NHS; Treas NHS; Off Ade; Sch Mus; Sch Pl; Miami Valley Hosp Schl; RN.

AMELI, STEPHEN D; Brother Rice HS; Birmingham, MI; 25/251 Hon Rl; Jr NHS; NHS; Sch Nwsp; Letter Bsktbl; Coach Actv; IM Sprt; Natl Merit SF; College; Liberal Arts.

AMELL, LANE; Holly HS; Holly, MI; Hon Rl; Sprt Ed Sch Nwsp; Sch Nwsp; Letter Bsbl; Capt Bsktbl; Scr Kpr; Univ; Acctg.

AMELUXEN, TOM; Roscommon HS; Roscommon, MI; 8/142 Cl Rep Jr Cls; Band; Drm Mjrt; NHS; Orch; Sch Mus; Glf; Ferris St Coll; Mktg.

AMEND, JANET; Mcnicholas HS; Cincinnati, OH; 31/230 Hon Rl; Sch Pl; Chrldng; Coach Actv; GAA; IM Sprt; College; Lab Tech.

AMENDOLA, PETE; Central Catholic HS; Canton, OH; Hon Rl; Capt Crs Cntry; Letter Trk; IM Sprt; Walsh Coll; Pre Law.

AMENDOLARA, AIMEE; Ursuline HS; Youngstown, OH; 57/286 Pres Soph Cls; VP Sr Cls; VP Chrh Wkr; Hon Rl; Jr NHS; Treas NHS; Sch Pl; Stu Cncl; Glf; Scr Kpr; Bowling Green Univ; Scndry Tchr.

AMERMAN, DAVID; Clay City HS; Clay City, IN; 15/64 Trs Frsh Cls; Cls Rep Frsh Cls; Cls Rep Soph Cls; Trs Jr Cls; Band; Cmnty Wkr; Stu Cncl; VP Yth Flsp; VP FFA; Bsbl; Dist 7 Fruit & Veg Awd FFA 79; Indiana St Univ; Music.

AMES, DANNY; Leslie HS; Williamston, MI; Hon Rl; Letter Bsbl; Letter Bsktbl; Letter Glf; IM Sprt; Mgrs; Scr Kpr; Tmr; College; Math.

AMES, KAREN; Newaygo HS; Newaygo, MI; 2/100 Sal; Am Leg Aux Girls St; Band; Hon Rl; Mod UN; NHS; Sch Pl; Stu Cncl; DAR Awd; Natl Merit Schl; Michigan St Univ; Chem Engr.

AMES, STANLEY; Hudson Area HS; Hudson, MI; Am Leg Boys St; Boy Scts; Hon Rl; NHS; Rptr Yrbk; 4-H; Sci Clb; Spn Clb; Bsbl; Capt Ftbl; Attended Operation Bentley; St Qualifier At St Wrestling Tourney; College; Law.

AMES, VANESSA; Manchester HS; Manchester, MI; 2/109 Sec Sr Cls; Band; Chrs; Hon Rl; NHS; Sch Mus; Sch Pl; Stg Crw; Yth Flsp; Sec 4-H Awd; Michigan St Univ; Bus.

AMICK, KATHRYN; Covington HS; Covington, OH; Hon Rl; FHA; Upper Valley Voc Schl; Modeling.

AMICK, KATHY; Elwood Cmnty HS; Elwood, IN; JA; Drama Clb; 4-H; FBLA; Lat Clb; Leo Clb; Mdl 3 Yrs Straight A In Ltn 77; Pin 90 Wrld Per Mnt In Begn Shorthnd 79; Univ Of Arizona; Archaeology.

AMMAR, DOUGLAS; Charleston HS; Charleston, WV; VP Soph Cls; Pres Sr Cls; Am Leg Boys St; Band; Cmnty Wkr; Hon Rl; NHS; College; Law.

AMMAR, TREY; Bluefield HS; Bluefield, WV; 71/380 Cls Rep Soph Cls; Cl Rep Jr Cls; VP Sr Cls; Boy Scts; Cmnty Wkr; Hon Rl; Stu Cncl; Fr Clb; Key Clb; Ten; Bluefield State Coll; Bus Mgmt.

AMMERMAN, BRENNA; Chardon HS; Chardon, OH; 24/250 AFS; Chrs; Hon Rl; MMM; NHS; Off Ade; Sch Mus; Sch Pl; Drama Clb;.

AMMONS, BEVERLY J; St Johns Public HS; St Johns, MI; 3/350 Pres Frsh Cls; Cl Rep Jr Cls; Band; Chrs; FCA; Girl Scts; Hon Rl; Lbry Ade; Mdrgl; Sch Mus; Miss Michigan Natl Teen Pageant Finalist; Outstanding Youth Of Amer; College; Occupational Therapy.

AMMONS, TONYA; South HS; Akron, OH; 8/175 Cl Rep Jr Cls; Hon Rl; Stu Cncl; Key Clb; Pres Pep Clb; Gym; Ten; Kiwan Awd; Fayetteville Tech Inst; Sec Sci.

AMON, ELIZABETH; Canfield HS; Canfield, OH; Chrs; Hon Rl; Mdrgl; Off Ade; Sch Mus; Treas Y-Teens; Rptr Sch Nwsp; Fr Clb; Pep Clb; GAA; Univ.

AMON, JUDITH; Marion L Steele HS; Amherst, OH; 31/358 Band; Girl Scts; Hon Rl; NHS; Stg Crw; Drama Clb; 4-H; Ger Clb; College; Psych.

AMON, MICHAEL; Lakota HS; Middletown, OH; Hon Rl; NHS; Spn Clb; IM Sprt; Ohio State Univ; Elec Engineer.

AMONETT, TERESA; Yorktown HS; Muncie, IN; 14/206 Cls Rep Soph Cls; Cls Rep Sr Cls; FCA; Hon Rl; Hosp Ade; NHS; Treas Stu Cncl; Ball State Univ; Phys Ther.

AMOR, ANDREW; Grand Haven Sr HS; Grand Haven, MI; Band; Hon Rl; Orch; Sch Mus; Letter Swmmng; Grand Valley St Univ; Gnrl Archt.

AMORE, WENDY; Beavercreek HS; Xenia, OH; 68/800 Sec Frsh Cls; Cl Rep Jr Cls; Chrs; Chrh Wkr; Hon Rl; Lbry Ade; Sch Pl; Pres Yth Flsp; Sch Nwsp; Drama Clb; Wright St Univ; Elem Ed.

AMOS, DEBRA; The Andrews School; Painesville, OH; 2/71 Chrs; Chrh Wkr; Hon Rl; Pres NHS; Off Ade; GAA; Am Leg Awd; Gadsden St Jr Coll; Court Rprtr.

AMOS, PHYLLIS; Mannington HS; Mannington, WV; Cls Rep Frsh Cls; Cl Rep Jr Cls; Band; Chrh Wkr; Hon Rl; NHS; Sch Mus; Stu Cncl; Yth Flsp; Y-Teens; Wv Univ; Engr.

AMREIN, PATRICIA; Colerain Sr HS; Cincinnati, OH; 207/693 Chrs; Chrh Wkr; Cmnty Wkr; Off Ade; Sch Pl; Yth Flsp; 4-H; Pep Clb; GAA; Cit Awd; Cincinnati Tech Coll; Med Rcd Tech.

AMRHEIN, BARBARA; Brookville HS; Brookville, IN; 75/200 Cl Rep Jr Cls; Chrs; Stu Cncl; Yrbk; Cit Awd; Univ; Soc Work.

AMRHEIN, JULIE; Mona Shores HS; Muskegon, MI; Hon Rl; NHS; Yrbk; Fr Clb; Letter Swmmng; Trk; Univ.

AMRHEIN, MARY; Brookville HS; Brookville, IN; Chrs; Girl Scts; 4-H; Sec FHA; Pres Pep Clb; Letter Bsktbl; Letter Trk; Ind Vocational Tech; Comp Prog.

AMRHEIN, MARY C; Immaculate Conception Acad; Brookville, IN; 5/48 Pres Frsh Cls; Pres Sr Cls; Chrs; NHS; Orch; Quill & Scroll; Stu Cncl; Yrbk; DAR Awd; Xavier Univ; Medicine.

AMSBAUGH, DIANE; Marion Franklin HS; Columbus, OH; 106/312 Cls Rep Frsh Cls; Cl Rep Jr Cls; Cls Rep Sr Cls; Drl Tm; Stu Cncl; FHA; Mat Maids; Pom Pon; Ohio St Univ; Medicine.

AMSLER, DIAMANTINA; Marshall HS; Marshall, MI; 19/258 Hon Rl; Hosp Ade; JA; Jr NHS; NHS; Pol Wkr; JA Awd; Mi Comp Schlrshp 79; Amer Bus

Womens Schlrshp 79; Completed HS In Jan 79 & Attended Kellogg Cmnty Coll; Kellogg Cmnty Coll; Bus Admin.

AMSLER, ERIN; Rensselaer Ctrl HS; Rensselaer, IN; Chrh Wkr; Girl Scts; Hon Rl; NHS; Orch; Sch Mus; Sch Pl; Sct Actv; Stg Crw; Yth Flsp; St Elizabeth Schl; Nursing.

AMSTUTZ, TIM; Woodlan HS; New Haven, IN; Pres Frsh Cls; Pres Soph Cls; Trs Jr Cls; Trs Sr Cls; Band; Chrs; Drm Mjrt; Hon Rl; NHS; Sch Mus; College; Dancer.

AMSTUTZ, TODD; Jay Cnty HS; Portland, IN; Boy Scts; Sch Nwsp; Boys Clb Am; Mth Clb; Sci Clb; IM Sprt; Univ; Bus Admin.

AMUNDSON, PAUL; Greenfield Central HS; Greenfield, IN; 9/250 Am Leg Boys St; Chrs; Chrh Wkr; FCA; Hon Rl; Mdrgl; NHS; Sch Mus; Sch Pl; VP Stu Cncl; Univ Of South Dakota; Pre Med.

AMUSSEN, KIRSTEN; Clay HS; S Bend, IN; Cls Rep Soph Cls; Band; Drm Mjrt; Stg Crw; Rptr Sch Nwsp; Spn Clb; Swmmng; Purdue Univ; Fashion Designer.

AMY, ADEL; North Central HS; Indpls, IN; Cls Rep Frsh Cls; Cls Rep Soph Cls; Cl Rep Jr Cls; Hon Rl; Stu Cncl; Letter Chrldng; College; Education.

ANAMAN, TODD; Arthur Hill HS; Saginaw, MI; Cls Rep Sr Cls; Boy Scts; Chrh Wkr; Hon Rl; Sch Pl; Sct Actv; Stg Crw; Stu Cncl; Yth Flsp; Drama Clb; Concordia Coll; Theology.

ANCHOR, LISA; Hartford HS; Hartford, MI; Hon Rl; Bsbl; Bsktbl; Mgrs;.

ANDARSIO, CARLOS; Culver Military Acad; Springfield, OH; 31/204 Cls Rep Frsh Cls; Cl Rep Jr Cls; Cls Rep Sr Cls; Band; Chrh Wkr; Hon Rl; ROTC; Stu Cncl; Spn Clb; IM Sprt; College; Oral Surg.

ANDELSON, LESLIE; Rocky River HS; Rocky Rvr, OH; Aud/Vis; Chrh Wkr; Hon Rl; Lbry Ade; Natl Forn Lg; Sch Pl; Stg Crw; Drama Clb; Tmr; College.

ANDENORO, J; Linsly Military Inst; Sherrard, WV; Band; Hosp Ade; ROTC; Sch Mus; Rptr Sch Nwsp; Letter Socr; Letter Swmmng; Univ; Med.

ANDEREGG, ALFRED H; Buckhannon Upshur HS; Buckhannon, WV; Cls Rep Frsh Cls; Boy Scts; Cmnty Wkr; Hon Rl; NHS; Yth Flsp; 4-H; 4-H Awd; Univ.

ANDERER, KATHLEEN; White Cloud HS; White Cloud, MI; Sec Soph Cls; Chrh Wkr; Hon Rl; NHS; Sch Pl; VP Stu Cncl; Sch Nwsp; Uquinas College; History.

ANDERS, SHERYL; Madison Plains Local HS; Mt Sterling, OH; Cmp Fr Grls; Chrs; Hon Rl; 4-H; IM Sprt; 4-H Awd; Natl Merit Ltr; Bus Schl; Art.

ANDERSEN, LAURA; Yale HS; Emmett, MI; Hon Rl; Univ.

ANDERSEN, TERRI; Battle Creek Acad; Battle Creek, MI; 1/23 Sec Soph Cls; Trs Soph Cls; Trs Jr Cls; Val; NHS; Rptr Yrbk; Ed Sch Nwsp; Andrews Univ; Bus Admin.

ANDERSEN, THOMAS; Roy C Start HS; Toledo, OH; 3/400 Cls Rep Frsh Cls; Cls Rep Soph Cls; Cl Rep Jr Cls; Band; Hon Rl; JA; Jr NHS; NHS; Stu Cncl; Bsbl; Univ Of Toledo; Math.

ANDERSEN, TODD; Mooresville HS; Mooresville, IN; Hon Rl; Pol Wkr; Ger Clb; Ftbl; Univ; Civil Engr.

ANDERSLAND, MARK S; East Lansing HS; East Lansing, MI; 6/356 Debate Tm; NHS; Sch Nwsp; Socr; Coach Actv; JETS Awd; Natl Merit Ltr; Univ Of Michigan; Elec Engr.

ANDERSON, ANGIE; Pike Central HS; Winslow, IN; Hon Rl; NHS; Pep Clb; Chrldng; Cit Awd; Indiana Univ; Elem Educ.

ANDERSON, ANITA; Romeo Sr HS; Romeo, MI; Chrs; Hon Rl; Rptr Sch Nwsp; Sch Nwsp; Drama Clb; FTA; Okland Univ; Dietetics.

ANDERSON, ANTHONY; Mt Healthy HS; Cincinnati, OH; 22/572 Hon Rl; NHS; Spn Clb; Miami Univ; Vet Med.

ANDERSON, ARTHUR; Waldron Jr Sr HS; Waldron, IN; 12/63 Band; Chrs; Hon Rl; Rptr Yrbk; 4-H; FFA; Letter Bsbl; Letter Ten; 4-H Awd; Purdue Univ; Engr.

ANDERSON, BECKY; Shady Spring HS; Beckley, WV; Chrh Wkr; Hon Rl; 4-H; Lat Clb; Pep Clb; Capt Chrldng; Pom Pon; Bethany Lutheran Coll; Social Work.

ANDERSON, BRENDA; Thornapple Kellogg HS; Caledonia, MI; 6/151 Hon Rl; NHS; Sch Mus; Sch Pl; Ed Yrbk; Rptr Yrbk; PPFtbl; Univ Of Mic; Phys Ther.

ANDERSON, CAROL; Western HS; Auburn, MI; 14/465 Hon Rl; NHS; Red Cr Ade; Sch Pl; Drama Clb; Natl Merit Ltr; Northern Michigan Univ; Nursing.

ANDERSON, CATHERINE; George A Dondero HS; Royal Oak, MI; 42/400 Chrs; Chrh Wkr; Debate Tm; Hon Rl; NHS; Sch Mus; Sch Pl; Stg Crw; Drama Clb; Wayne State Univ; Nursing.

ANDERSON, CATHI; Traverse City HS; Traverse City, MI; Rptr Yrbk; Morthwestern Mic College.

ANDERSON, CHERYL; Dr Martin Luther King HS; Detroit, MI; Hst Jr Cls; FCA; Hon Rl; ROTC; Y-Teens; Ed Yrbk; DECA; FDA; Sci Clb; Bsbl; Michigan St Univ; Pre Law.

ANDERSON, CHERYL; Caseville Public School; Pigeon, MI; 1/13 Trs Frsh Cls; Cls Rep Soph Cls; Trs Jr Cls; Trs Sr Cls; Val; Am Leg Aux Girls St; Band; Hon Rl; NHS; Yth Flsp; Alma Coll; Music.

ANDERSON, CHRIS; Perry HS; Canton, OH; Chrs; Natl Forn Lg; Quill & Scroll; Sch Mus; Sch Pl; Rptr Sch Nwsp; Sch Nwsp; Drama Clb; Univ Of Cincinnati; Radio T V Prod.

ANDERSON, CHRISTINA; Gwinn HS; Ki Sawyer, MI; VICA; Glf; Voc Schl; Photog.

ANDERSON, CRYSTAL; Vrsvline HS; Campbell, OH; 82/345 Chrs; Drl Tm; Girl Scts; Hon Rl; Off Ade; Sct Actv; Stu Cncl; Fr Clb; Key Clb; Pep Clb; Ohio State; Programmer Analist.

ANDERSON, CYNTHIA; Arsenal Technical HS; Indianapolis, IN; Cl Rep Jr Cls; Am Leg Aux Girls St; Band; Pres Chrs; Chrh Wkr; Hon Rl; JA; Natl Forn Lg; Orch; Sch Pl; In St Officer Of OEA Dist 8 East VP 79; Jr Bsktbll Queen Queen Of Queens & Jr Prom Queen 79; Indiana Univ; Industrial Mgmt.

ANDERSON, CYNTHIA; West Washington HS; Fredericksburg, IN; 6/65 Chrs; Drl Tm; Hon Rl; NHS; Sch Pl; Drama Clb; 4-H; Spn Clb; 4-H Awd; Samford Univ; Pharmacist.

ANDERSON, DARCEY L; Frankfort Adena HS; Clarksburg, OH; Sec Frsh Cls; Chrs; Fr Clb; Bsktbl; Trk; Scr Kpr; 4-H Awd; Grove City Dental Asst Schl; Dent As.

ANDERSON, DAVE; Crestwood HS; Hiram, OH; 116/238 Pres Soph Cls; Cl Rep Jr Cls; Cls Rep Sr Cls; Stu Cncl; Fr Clb; Spartan School Of Aero; Pilot.

ANDERSON, DAVID; Bear Lake HS; Bear Lake, MI; Chrs; Hon Rl; Natl Forn Lg; Sch Pl; Letter Bsktbl; Letter Crs Cntry; Letter Trk; Scr Kpr; Tmr; 2 Yrs Var Track Capt & MVP 78; All Confrnc Track 2 Yrs All Confrnc Cross Cntry 78; 1 Yr Regnl Track; Ferris St Univ; Mgmt.

ANDERSON, DAVID; North Muskegon HS; North Muskegon, MI; 13/100 Chrs; Hon Rl; NHS; Orch; PAVAS; Sch Mus; Sch Pl; Stg Crw; Drama Clb; Mth Clb; Michigan Tech Univ; Elec Engr.

ANDERSON, DAWN; Oregon Davis HS; Grovertown, IN; Chrs; Drl Tm; Girl Scts; Hon Rl; Sch Pl; Drama Clb; 4-H; Ball State; Music.

ANDERSON, DEANNA; Oregon Davis HS; Walkerton, IN; 8/68 Hon Rl; NHS; Yrbk; 4-H; Pep Clb; Bsktbl; Trk; Chrldng; Pres GAA; Pom Pon; Franklin College; Bsns.

ANDERSON, DELLA; Muskegon HS; Muskegon, MI; Cls Rep Frsh Cls; Chrh Wkr; Hon Rl; JA; 4-H; Trk; 4-H Awd; College; Med Lab Tech.

ANDERSON, DONNA K; Charlestown HS; Charlestown, IN; 14/155 Band; Girl Scts; Hon Rl; JA; NHS; 4-H; FHA; Lat Clb; OEA; 4-H Awd; John Phillip Sousa Band Awd 79; Psi Iota Xi Sor Schlrshp 79; Indiana Hoosier Schlr 79; Indiana Univ S E; Vet Med.

ANDERSON, DORA; Churubusco Eagles HS; Churubusco, IN; Drl Tm; Hon Rl; Rptr Sch Nwsp; 4-H; FFA; FHA; Pep Clb; Trk; Pom Pon; 4-H Awd;.

ANDERSON, DOUG; Noblesville North HS; Noblesville, IN; VP Frsh Cls; Boy Scts; Chrs; Pol Wkr; Stg Crw; Stu Cncl; Yth Flsp; Fr Clb; Key Clb; Sci Clb; Purdue Univ; Law.

ANDERSON, DOUGLAS; North Montgomery HS; Darlington, IN; Band; Chrs; Hon Rl; Jr NHS; Sch Mus; Stg Crw; Rptr Sch Nwsp; 4-H; VP FHA; Pres Key Clb; Purdue Univ; Bus Mgmt.

ANDERSON, ELLIOTT; Marietta Sr HS; Marietta, OH; 4/465 Sal; VP NHS; Treas Yth Flsp; Treas Fr Clb; Key Clb; VP Rus Clb; Trk; Am Leg Awd; Natl Merit Ltr; Case Western Reserve Univ; Aero Engr.

ANDERSON, ELMER; Escanaba Area HS; Escanaba, MI; Boy Scts; Chrh Wkr; Sct Actv; IM Sprt; Northern Michigan Univ; Agri.

ANDERSON, ELVERA; Martin Luther King Sr HS; Detroit, MI; 5/200 Chrs; Chrh Wkr; Cmnty Wkr; Hon Rl; Lbry Ade; Off Ade; Rptr Yrbk; Fr Clb; Pom Pon; Cit Awd; Central St Univ; Psychology.

ANDERSON, ERIC C; St Francis De Sales; Toledo, OH; 10/200 Hon Rl; NHS; Rptr Sch Nwsp; Harvard Univ; Physics.

ANDERSON, GARY; Ypsilanti HS; Ypsilanti, MI; Cls Rep Sr Cls; Boy Scts; Chrs; Hon Rl; JA; Sch Mus; Sch Pl; Stg Crw; Stu Cncl; College; Actor.

ANDERSON, GLENN; West Side Sr HS; Gary, IN; Hon Rl; Spn Clb; Bsbl; Bsktbl; Cit Awd; Natl Merit Ltr; Purdue Univ; Educ.

ANDERSON, HOWARD; Troy HS; Troy, MI; Cls Rep Sr Cls; Debate Tm; Hon Rl; Natl Forn Lg; Pol Wkr; Sch Pl; Rptr Yrbk; Swmmng; Wayne St Univ; Pre Law.

ANDERSON, JAN; Okemos HS; Okemos, MI; 11/317 Sec Sr Cls; Chrs; Chrh Wkr; Hon Rl; NHS; Sch Mus; Yth Flsp; Hope College; Public Relations.

ANDERSON, JANE; Eisenhower HS; Saginaw, MI; 10/316 Debate Tm; Hon Rl; NHS; Off Ade; Bsktbl; Trk; Northern Michigan Univ; Acctg.

ANDERSON, JANET; Ansonia HS; Ansonia, OH; 13/70 Band; Chrs; Hon Rl; Stg Crw; Yth Flsp; Rptr Sch Nwsp; Drama Clb; OEA; GAA; College; Bus.

ANDERSON, JANET; Riverside HS; Painesville, OH; 23/300 Band; Hon Rl; Lbry Ade; Spn Clb; College; Bus Adm.

ANDERSON, JANINA; Covert HS; Covert, MI; Cls Rep Soph Cls; Cl Rep Jr Cls; Chrs; Hon Rl; Mod UN; NHS; Stu Cncl; FHA; Pep Clb; Bsktbl; College; Nursing.

ANDERSON, JANINE; Buchanan HS; Buchanan, MI; Cmp Fr Grls; Chrs; Chrh Wkr; Lbry Ade; Sch Pl; Yth Flsp; Alma Coll.

ANDERSON, JAY; Tippecanoe Valley HS; Mentone, IN; Aud/Vis; FCA; Hon Rl; Fr Clb; Spn Clb; IM Sprt; British Schl Of Mtr Racing; Rc Cr Dr.

ANDERSON, JEFF; Green HS; Uniontown, OH; Cls Rep Sr Cls; Chrh Wkr; Cmnty Wkr; FCA; Hon Rl; Sch Pl; Stg Crw; Pres Stu Cncl; Boys Clb Am; College; Law.

ANDERSON, JEFF; Hammond Baptist HS; Hobart, IN; Letter Bsktbl; Letter Crs Cntry; Letter Trk; Tennessee Temple Univ; Phys Ed.

ANDERSON, JEFF; Greenville Sr HS; Greenville, OH; Hon Rl; Bsbl; Univ.

ANDERSON, JEFFERY; North HS; Willoughby Hls, OH; 197/655 Hon Rl; Stg Crw; Drama Clb; Cleveland St Univ; Acctg.

ANDERSON, JEFFERY M; Baker HS; W Patterson Afb, OH; 10/335 Chrh Wkr; Hon Rl; NHS; Beta Clb; Mth Clb; Letter Glf; Letter Ten; IM Sprt; Gov Hon Prg Awd; Air Force Academy; Comp Sci.

ANDERSON, JEFFREY; Negaunee HS; Negaunee, MI; 17/150 Chrs; Hon Rl; Mi St 79; Ferris Coll; Dent Tech.

ANDERSON, JEFFREY; Frankfort HS; Frankfort, IN; Aud/Vis; Boy Scts; Drl Tm; ROTC; Sch Pl; Boys Clb Am; Fr Clb; Kemper Military School; Military Sci.

ANDERSON, JEFFREY; Whitmore Lake HS; Ann Arbor, MI; 10/98 Hst Jr Cls; Aud/Vis; Hon Rl; NHS; Letter Ftbl; Letter Trk; IM Sprt; General Motors Inst; Elec Engr.

ANDERSON, JOHN; Osborn HS; Detroit, MI; Aud/Vis; Debate Tm; Hon Rl; NHS; Sch Mus; Sch Nwsp; Drama Clb; Spn Clb; Candidate For Detroit Police Dept Outstanding Stu; Natl Merit Schlrshp; T V HS Representative; Michigan St Univ; Public Relations.

ANDERSON, JOHN; Lebanon HS; Lebanon, OH; Val; Debate Tm; Hon Rl; NHS; Spn Clb; IM Sprt; Natl Merit SF; Miami Univ; Systems Analysis.

ANDERSON, JOHN; Three Rivers HS; Three Rivers, MI; Band; Boy Scts; Chrs; Chrh Wkr; Hon Rl; Sct Actv; Stg Crw; Leo Clb; Rotary Awd; Western Michigan Univ; Comp Engr.

ANDERSON, JOHN; Alpena HS; Alpena, MI; Letter Ftbl; Wrstlng; Natl Merit Schl; Albion College; Law.

ANDERSON, JON; Columbus Acad; Bexley, OH; Cls Rep Sr Cls; Hon Rl; Yth Flsp; Rptr Sch Nwsp; Letter Bsbl; Letter Ftbl; IM Sprt; Natl Merit Schl; Harvard Univ.

ANDERSON, JOY; Pine River HS; Tustin, MI; Trs Soph Cls; Trs Jr Cls; Band; Chrh Wkr; Girl Scts; Hon Rl; Lbry Ade; NHS; Sch Mus; Yth Flsp; Bsns Schl; Sec.

ANDERSON, KAREN; Winchester Comm HS; Winchester, IN; Cmnty Wkr; Hon Rl; Jr NHS; NHS; Fr Clb; FHA; Chrldng; Ball St Univ; Math.

ANDERSON, KAREN; Stryker HS; Stryker, OH; 10/55 Pres Jr Cls; Band; Girl Scts; Hon Rl; 4-H; FHA; Gym; Chrldng; Mgrs; 4-H Awd; Univ; Law.

ANDERSON, KAREN; Bluffton HS; Bluffton, IN; Band; Hon Rl; Hosp Ade; Sch Mus; Y-Teens; Drama Clb; Ger Clb; IM Sprt; College.

ANDERSON, KARI; Onekama Consolidated HS; Kaleva, MI; Pres Jr Cls; Am Leg Aux Girls St; Band; Chrs; Hon Rl; Yrbk; FHA; College; Computers.

ANDERSON, KATHLEEN L; Clare HS; Clare, MI; Cls Rep Frsh Cls; Cls Rep Soph Cls; Cl Rep Jr Cls; Band; Debate Tm; FCA; Hon Rl; Sec NHS; Off Ade; Treas Stu Cncl; Univ; Med.

ANDERSON, KATHY; Medina HS; Medina, OH; NHS; Pep Clb; Letter Ftbl; Gym; Letter Ten; Letter Trk; GAA; PPFtbl; College.

ANDERSON, KEITH; Mid Peninsula HS; Rapid River, MI; 2/44 Pres Frsh Cls; Cls Rep Soph Cls; Cl Rep Jr Cls; Pres Sr Cls; Cls Rep Sr Cls; Sal; Am Leg Boys St; Band; Hon Rl; College; Engr.

ANDERSON, KELLY; Wayne Mem HS; Westland, MI; Chrs; Chrh Wkr; Girl Scts; Hon Rl; JA; Sch Mus; Sch Pl; Drama Clb; Ger Clb; Rdo Clb; Eastern Michigan Univ; Medicine.

ANDERSON, KELLY L; Liberty HS; Clarksburg, WV; 25/226 Chrs; Hon Rl; NHS; Sch Pl; Pres Y-Teens; Rptr Yrbk; Rptr Sch Nwsp; Drama Clb; Pres Pep Clb; Chrldng; West Virginia Univ; Bus Mgmt.

ANDERSON, KEVIN B; North Knox HS; Westphalia, IN; 12/150 FCA; Hon Rl; NHS; Treas Yth Flsp; FFA; Purdue Univ; Agri.

ANDERSON, KIMBERLY D; Liberty HS; Clarksburg, WV; 9/228 Trs Frsh Cls; Sec Sr Cls; Band; Chrs; Hon Rl; NHS; Stu Cncl; Y-Teens; Rptr Yrbk; DECA; Fairmont St Coll; Bus.

ANDERSON, LAURA; Niles HS; Niles, MI; 54/403 Chrs; VP Chrh Wkr; NHS; PAVAS; Pol Wkr; Sch Mus; Sch Pl; Sec Stu Cncl; Drama Clb; Rdo Clb; Top Ten Drama Stu Awd 77; Optimist Spch Contest Awds 1st Pl For City 75; Elks Outstndg Stu Awd 78; Northern Michigan Univ; Brdcstng.

ANDERSON, LE; Orchard View HS; Muskegon, MI; Sec Frsh Cls; Cls Rep Soph Cls; VP Jr Cls; VP Sr Cls; Band; Hon Rl; Off Ade; Red Cr Ade; Sch Pl; Stu Cncl; Grand Valley St Coll; Soc Sci.

ANDERSON, LISA; Upper Vly HS; Troy, OH; Trs Sr Cls; Chrs; Hon Rl; Hosp Ade; NHS; OEA; Sinclair Comm Coll; Bus Admin.

ANDERSON, LISA; National Trail HS; W Manchester, OH; 17/122 Sec Soph Cls; Am Leg Aux Girls St; Band; Chrh Wkr; Hon Rl; Lbry Ade; NHS; Off Ade; Ed Sch Nwsp; Ind Vocat Tech; Med Sec.

ANDERSON, LISA; John Adams HS; S Bend, IN; 79/395 Letter Swmmng; IM Sprt; Tmr; Univ; Elem Tchr.

ANDERSON, LISA R; Celina Sr HS; Celina, OH; Chrh Wkr; Hon Rl; NHS; Rptr Sch Nwsp; Sch Nwsp; GAA; IM Sprt; PPFtbl; Univ.

ANDERSON, LORI; Marysville HS; Marysville, OH; Chrh Wkr; Hon Rl; Spn Clb; Ohio St Agri Tech Schl; Equestrian.

ANDERSON, LORRAINE; Arthur Hill HS; Saginaw, MI; Hon Rl; NHS; Off Ade; Sch Pl; Pom Pon; Michigan St Univ; Sci.

ANDERSON, M; Catholic Ctrl HS; Stuebenvll, OH; 18/200 Girl Scts; Hon Rl; NHS; Spn Clb; Trk; Natl Merit SF; Univ; Chem.

ANDERSON, MARCIA; East Palestine HS; E Palestine, OH; Am Leg Aux Girls St; Band; Cmp Fr Grls; Chrh Wkr; Cmnty Wkr; Hon Rl; Trk; College; Nurse.

ANDERSON, MARIE; Fairless HS; Brewster, OH; Pres Band; Chrs; Girl Scts; Sch Mus; Sch Nwsp; Letter Trk; GAA; Kent St Univ; Hist.

ANDERSON, MARILYN; Mumford HS; Detroit, MI; Hon Rl; NHS; Fr Clb; Natl Honor Soc Awds; Wayne St Univ; Pharmacy.

ANDERSON, NEAL; Celina Sr HS; Celina, OH; Hon Rl; Univ; Graphic Arts.

ANDERSON, ONITTA; Emerson HS; Gary, IN; Chrh Wkr; Girl Scts; Hon Rl; ROTC; Y-Teens; Rptr Sch Nwsp; FHA; Pep Clb; Trk; Mgrs; College; Medical Technology.

ANDERSON, PAUL; Archbishop Alter HS; Miamisburg, OH; College; Journalism.

ANDERSON, PEGGY; Arch Bishop Alter HS; Kettering, OH; Treas Chrh Wkr; Cmnty Wkr; Hon Rl; Jr NHS; NHS; Y-Teens; Spn Clb; Letter Trk; Coach Actv; GAA; College; Communications.

ANDERSON, ROBBIN; Philo HS; Duncan Falls, OH; Fr Clb; GAA; Bowling Green Physical Educ.

ANDERSON, ROBERT; Waverly HS; Waverly, OH; Hon Rl; Lbry Ade; NHS; College; Physics.

ANDERSON, ROBERT; Toronto HS; Toronto, OH; Chrs; Hon Rl; Rptr Sch Nwsp; College.

ANDERSON, ROBERT W; Staunton HS; Brazil, IN; 1/48 Cls Rep Frsh Cls; Cls Rep Soph Cls; Cl Rep Jr Cls; Cls Rep Sr Cls; Val; NHS; Pres Stu Cncl; Key Clb; Letter Bsbl; Letter Trk; Univ; Sci.

ANDERSON, RONALD; Western HS; Kokomo, IN; 3/240 FCA; Hon Rl; NHS; Letter Bsktbl; Letter Ten; Univ; Engr.

ANDERSON, RUTH; St Ursula Academy; Toledo, OH; 3/113 Cls Rep Frsh Cls; Pres Sr Cls; Cmnty Wkr; Hon Rl; NHS; Stu Cncl; Swmmng; Coach Actv; Miami Univ; Zoology.

ANDERSON, SALLY; Schafer HS; Southgate, MI; 16/230 Pres Frsh Cls; Cls Rep Frsh Cls; Pres Soph Cls; Cls Rep Soph Cls; Pres Jr Cls; Cl Rep Jr Cls; Pres Sr Cls; Cls Rep Sr Cls; Band; Chrs; Western Michigan Univ; Music Ther.

ANDERSON, SCOTT; Mooresville HS; Mooresville, IN; Chrh Wkr; Cmnty Wkr; Hon Rl; Pol Wkr; Ger Clb; Ftbl; Letter Trk; Us Marine Corp.

ANDERSON, SCOTT; Penn HS; Granger, IN; 35/450 Hon Rl; NHS; Letter Bsbl; Letter Bsktbl; Bethel College.

ANDERSON, SCOTT; Field HS; Kent, OH; 9/270 Hon Rl; Gym; Coach Actv; Cit Awd; Univ; Math.

ANDERSON, SCOTT; La Porte HS; La Porte, IN; 95/500 Band; Chrs; Drm Bgl; Pres FCA; MMM; Sch Mus; Sch Pl; Ger Clb; Crs Cntry; Trk; College; Music.

ANDERSON, SHARON; Hoover HS; North Canton, OH; 69/422 Cls Rep Frsh Cls; Girl Scts; Hon Rl; JA; Off Ade; Stu Cncl; Pep Clb; Spn Clb; Swmmng; Trk; College.

ANDERSON, SHARON; Muncie Northside HS; Muncie, IN; 1/286 Am Leg Aux Girls St; Band; Girl Scts; Hon Rl; NHS; Ger Clb; Sci Clb; Letter Swmmng; Letter Ten; Natl Merit Schl; Carleton Coll.

ANDERSON, SHEILA; Spencer HS; Spencer, WV; Cls Rep Frsh Cls; Cls Rep Soph Cls; Cl Rep Jr Cls; Band; Girl Scts; Hon Rl; Lbry Ade; Sch Pl; Stg Crw; 4-H; Univ Of Charleston; Nursing.

ANDERSON, SHERRY; La Salle HS; South Bend, IN; 61/488 Cmp Fr Grls; Chrs; Chrh Wkr; Hon Rl; JA; NHS; Sch Mus; Sch Pl; Drama Clb; Spn Clb; Walkathon 20 Miles 77; Vlybl Tm Mbr 77; Tutored Math 76; Univ; Psych.

ANDERSON, SHIELL; Clyde Park HS; Livingston, MT; Pres Soph Cls; Cl Rep Jr Cls; Band; Debate Tm; Hon Rl; Jr NHS; Stu Cncl; Yrbk; 4-H; FFA; Univ Of Montana; Law.

ANDERSON, SONYA; River Valley HS; Marion, OH; VP JA; FHA; Bowling Green Univ; Marine Bio.

ANDERSON, SONYA; Waldo J Wood Memorial HS; Buckskin, IN; Hon Rl; Yth Flsp; Pep Clb; Pres Awd;.

ANDERSON, STEVE; Muskegon Sr HS; Muskegon, MI; Band; Hon Rl; Swmmng; Ten; Muskegon Cmnty Coll; Acctg.

ANDERSON, STEVE; Madison HS; Madison, OH; 11/295 Chrs; Hon Rl; Ger Clb; Crs Cntry; Trk; Univ; Sci.

ANDERSON, SUE; Cory Rawson HS; Bluffton, OH; 1/64 Cls Rep Soph Cls; Cl Rep Jr Cls; Val; Band; Chrs; Chrh Wkr; Hon Rl; NHS; Sch Mus; Sch Pl; Johnson Bible Coll; Nursing.

ANDERSON, SUE E; Laker HS; Pigeon, MI; Band; Sch Pl; Stu Cncl; Yth Flsp; 4-H; Bsktbl; Trk; IM Sprt; PPFtbl; Scr Kpr; 2nd Pl Art 1; 2nd Pl In Wmns Art Show; Numerous Horse Awds; College; Cosmetology.

ANDERSON, SUSAN; Chassell HS; Houghton, MI; Cl Rep Jr Cls; Girl Scts; Hosp Ade; Lbry Ade; Stu Cncl; 4-H; Letter Bsktbl; Trk; Chrldng; Northern Michigan Univ; Bookkeeping.

ANDERSON, SUSAN; Chassell HS; Chassell, MI; 1/23 Val; Hon Rl; Lbry Ade; Ed Yrbk; Mic Tech Univ; Med Tech.

ANDERSON, SUZANNE; Winchester Community HS; Winchester, IN; Band; NHS; FBLA; FHA; Spn Clb; College; Music.

ANDERSON, TERI; Mason HS; Mason, MI; Cls Rep Soph Cls; Band; Hon Rl; Orch; Stu Cncl; Trk; Letter Chrldng; Univ.

ANDERSON, TERRI; St Francis Central HS; Morgantown, WV; Chrs; Chrh Wkr; Hon Rl; Yrbk; Rptr Sch Nwsp; Pep Clb; Spn Clb; Letter Trk; West Virginia Univ; Pharm.

ANDERSON, TERRI; Wooster HS; Wooster, OH; 18/280 Chrh Wkr; NHS; Yrbk; Rptr Sch Nwsp; Wittenberg Univ; Elem Ed.

ANDERSON, THOMAS; Lake City Area HS; Lake City, MI; 3/69 VP Jr Cls; Trs Sr Cls; Am Leg Boys St; Band; Cmnty Wkr; Hon Rl; Jr NHS; NHS; 4-H; Letter Bsbl; Basic Ed Opportunity Grant 79; Mi Schlrshp Or Tuition Grant 79; Adrian Coll Grant 79; Adrian Coll; Pre Med.

ANDERSON, TIM; Pioneer HS; Ann Arbor, MI; 152/611 Cls Rep Frsh Cls; FCA; Hon Rl; Ftbl; Swmmng; Trk; Natl Merit Ltr; Univ; Pre Law.

ANDERSON, TIMOTHY; Ludington HS; Ludington, MI; Band; PAVAS; Sch Mus; Sch Pl; Stg Crw; Yth Flsp; Drama Clb; Fr Clb; Adrian College; Dramatic Arts.

ANDERSON, TIMOTHY W; Patterson Cooperative HS; Dayton, OH; Hon Rl; JA; 4-H; Bsbl; IM Sprt; Cit Awd; Natl Merit Ltr; Coll.

ANDERSON, TYANN; Wabash HS; Wabash, IN; 23/191 Chrs; Hon Rl; NHS; Pep Clb; Opt Clb Awd; Ball St Univ; Ofc Admin.

ANDERSON, WENDY; Fremont HS; Fremont, MI; 2/238 VP Soph Cls; Trs Sr Cls; Sal; Hon Rl; NHS; Stu Cncl; Letter Bsbl; Letter Bsktbl; Letter Trk; Natl Merit Ltr; Grand Vly St Coll.

ANDERSON, YOLANDA; Osborn HS; Detroit, MI; Trs Sr Cls; Drl Tm; Pres Girl Scts; Hon Rl; NHS; Off Ade; ROTC; Sct Actv; Mth Clb; Bsbl; Merit Schlrshp; Superior Jr Cadet Decoration Awd; Tennis M Lee Young Awd; Wayne St Univ; CPA.

ANDERSON, YVONNE S; Miami Trace HS; Washington C H, OH; Band; Chrs; Drl Tm; Drama Clb; FTA; College; Medicine.

ANDOCHICK, JAYNE; Madonna HS; Weirton, WV; 24/105 Chrh Wkr; Hon Rl; NHS; Letter Bsktbl; Letter Ten; Letter Trk; IM Sprt; Mat Maids; PPFtbl; Steubenville Coll.

ANDONIAN, C; Trinity HS; Garfield Hts, OH; Chrs; Letter Ftbl; Capt Hockey; Letter Wrstlng; PPFtbl; College; Architecture.

ANDRACKI, PATTY; Bishop Watterson HS; Columbus, OH; 99/250 Ohio St Univ; Cmnctns.

ANDRASIK, CANDY; Bellbrook HS; Bellbrook, OH; Cls Rep Frsh Cls; Cls Rep Soph Cls; Sec Jr Cls; Stu Cncl; Sec Lat Clb; Pep Clb; Crs Cntry; Letter Trk; Chrldng; GAA; College.

ANDRASSY, GREGG; Maple Heights HS; Maple Hgs, OH; Hon Rl; Natl Merit Ltr; Cleveland State; Wildlife Bio.

ANDRE, LINDA; Hudsonville HS; Hudsonville, MI; Sec Soph Cls; Cl Rep Jr Cls; Chrh Wkr; FCA; Hon Rl; Natl Forn Lg; Stu Cncl; Letter Ten; Chrldng; Univ Of Cosmetology.

ANDREA, DAVID; Hoover HS; N Canton, OH; Hon Rl; NHS; VP Sci Clb; Marquette Univ; Bus Admin.

ANDREADIS, PAUL; Anderson Sr HS; Cincinnati, OH; 12/417 Hon Rl; NHS; Fr Clb; Pres Lat Clb; Letter Wrstlng; Natl Merit Ltr; Univ; Bio Sci.

ANDREASSI, ANN; Cabrini HS; Allen Pk, MI; Drl Tm; Hon Rl; Univ Of Michigan; Early Chldhd Ed.

ANDREATTA, DALE A; Claymont HS; Uhrichsville, OH; 2/205 Band; Chrh Wkr; Hon Rl; Jr NHS; Fr Clb; Sci Clb; Crs Cntry; Letter Glf; Trk; Natl Merit SF; General Motors Inst; Mech Engr.

ANDREATTA, SUSAN; Claymont HS; Uhrichsville, OH; 27/200 Band; Capt Drl Tm; Hon Rl; NHS; Orch; Sch Mus; FTA; Pep Clb; Pom Pon; Muskingun Area Tech College; Radiol.

ANDREICHUK, VALERIE; Charlotte HS; Charlotte, MI; Chrh Wkr; Off Ade; Yth Flsp; Pep Clb; Trk; Chmn Chrldng; PPFtbl; Airline Training.

ANDREJCZUK, JOSEPH; Lawrence Public HS; Lawrence, MI; 1/56 Trs Soph Cls; Trs Jr Cls; Trs Sr Cls; Hon Rl; NHS; Sch Pl; Chmn Bsktbl; Mic State Univ; Mech Engr.

ANDREOLI, TOM; Cardinal Stritch HS; Walbridge, OH; Cls Rep Frsh Cls; Cls Rep Soph Cls; Cl Rep Jr Cls; Cls Rep Sr Cls; Chrs; Sch Pl; Stu Cncl; Ger Clb; Lat Clb; Bsbl; Univ; Comp Sci.

ANDRES, DEBORAH; Trinity HS; Seven Hills, OH; Cl Rep Jr Cls; VP Band; Cmnty Wkr; Sec Girl Scts; Hon Rl; Sch Mus; Stu Cncl; Pres 4-H; Fr Clb; Trk; Bowling Green St Univ.

ANDRESEN, NANCY; Concordia Lutheran HS; Ft Wayne, IN; 2/192 Hon Rl; NHS; Off Ade; FBLA; GAA; PPFtbl; Tri Kappa 1978; Acctg.

ANDRESKI, MONICA; Saint Clement HS; Detroit, MI; Chrs; Cmnty Wkr; Bsbl; Macomb; Photog.

ANDREW, TONYA; Switzerland Cnty Jr Sr HS; Vevay, IN; 23/121 Treas Band; Sec Chrs; Hon Rl; MMM; Off Ade; Sch Mus; Sch Pl; Pres Drama Clb; FHA; Pep Clb; Bus Schl; Bus.

ANDREWS, AMY; Berea HS; Berea, OH; Chrh Wkr; Girl Scts; Hon Rl; NHS; Orch; Sch Mus; Yth Flsp; Swmmng; Coll; Phys Therapy.

ANDREWS, AUDREY; John R Buchtel HS; Akron, OH; 50/471 Univ Of Akron; Chem Engr.

ANDREWS, BARBARA; Bellevue Sr HS; Bellevue, OH; 25/227 Am Leg Aux Girls St; Chrs; Chrh Wkr; Hon Rl; Sec NHS; Sch Mus; Sch Pl; Stg Crw; Yrbk; Rptr Sch Nwsp; Miami Univ; Mass Cmnctns.

ANDREWS, BILLY F; Floyd Central HS; Floyd Knobs, IN; Cls Rep Soph Cls; Trs Jr Cls; Cl Rep Jr Cls; Trs Sr Cls; Cls Rep Sr Cls; Chrs; Cmnty Wkr; Hon Rl; Mod UN; Sec NHS; Bus.

ANDREWS, BRIGID; St Joseph Academy; Cleveland, OH; Trs Soph Cls; Hon Rl; Stu Cncl; Rptr Yrbk; Univ; Eng.

ANDREWS, BRIGID; St Josephs Academy; Cleveland, OH; Trs Soph Cls; Hon Rl; Stu Cncl; Rptr Yrbk; Univ; Law.

ANDREWS, CAROLYN; Newbury HS; Newbury, OH; 2/80 Band; Chrh Wkr; Hon Rl; Jr NHS; NHS; Sch Pl; Drama Clb; 4-H; Sci Clb; Spn Clb; Harvard Univ; Med.

ANDREWS, DARRYL; John F Kennedy HS; Cleveland, OH; Band; Chrs; Chrh Wkr; Drm Bgl; Off Ade; Orch; Stg Crw; DECA; FBLA; OEA; UCLA; Law.

ANDREWS, DAVID; Washington HS; South Bend, IN; 3/323 Hon Rl; NHS; Ger Clb; Bausch & Lomb Awd; Elk Awd; Univ Of Notre Dame; Bio.

ANDREWS, DON; Stephen T Badin HS; Oxford, OH; 110/220 Cls Rep Frsh Cls; Cls Rep Soph Cls; Cls Rep Sr Cls; Chrh Wkr; Hon Rl; Sch Mus; Stu Cncl; Pres DECA; Drama Clb; Bsbl; DECA Student Of Year 1978; 1st Pl Dist Bus Ownership Mgmt 1979; Golden Trngl Honrbl Mentn Ftbl 1978; W Carolina Univ; Bus Mgmt.

ANDREWS, DOUG; Bexley HS; Bexley, OH; 1/185 Band; Hon Rl; NHS; Orch; Sch Pl; Stg Crw; Treas Lat Clb; JETS Awd; Univ; Math.

ANDREWS, GEOFFREY G; Oberlin HS; Oberlin, OH; 6/150 AFS; Am Leg Boys St; Boy Scts; Chrh Wkr; Cmnty Wkr; Debate Tm; Hon Rl; Sch Mus; Sch Pl; Sct Actv; Coll.

ANDREWS, JEFFREY; Wilbur Wright HS; Dayton, OH; Boy Scts; Hon Rl; Lbry Ade; Sct Actv; Boys Clb Am; Ftbl; Trk; IM Sprt; Scr Kpr; U S Naval Academy; Aero Engr.

ANDREWS, JEFFREY; Frankfort HS; Ridgeley, WV; Debate Tm; Hon Rl; NHS; Mth Clb; Letter Bsktbl; IM Sprt; West Virginia Univ.

ANDREWS, JOHN; Jackson HS; Massillon, OH; Debate Tm; Hon Rl; Mod UN; Natl Forn Lg; NHS; Letter Bsbl; Hnr Roll For U S Schl Band & Chorus Of Amer; European Tour; Outstanding Speaker Of House; Natl Forensic Dst; Ohio St Univ; Engr.

ANDREWS, KATHY; Celina Sr HS; Celina, OH; Chrs; Hon Rl; Lbry Ade; NHS; Off Ade; FHA; FTA; Ger Clb; GAA; IM Sprt; Univ.

ANDREWS, MATT; Girard HS; Girard, OH; Chrh Wkr; Cmnty Wkr; Off Ade; Rptr Yrbk; Sprt Ed Sch Nwsp; Bsktbl; Ftbl; Coach Actv; IM Sprt; John Carroll Univ; Bus.

ANDREWS, RICHARD; Sebring Mc Kinley HS; Sebring, OH; 22/90 Aud/Vis; Hon Rl; Letter Bsktbl; Don Wise Schlrshp Awd; A Average; Bowling Green St Univ; Info Systems.

ANDREWS, SCOTT; Huntington St Josephs HS; Huntington, WV; Cls Rep Frsh Cls; Hon Rl; Stu Cncl; Rptr Sch Nwsp; IM Sprt; Scr Kpr; Univ; Cmnctns.

ANDREWS, TAMMIE L; West Jefferson HS; W Jefferson, OH; Band; Chrs; Girl Scts; Hon Rl; Hosp Ade; 4-H; Bsktbl; Trk; Chrldng; GAA; Ohio St Univ; Law Enforcmnt.

ANDREWS, THOMAS; Franklin Comm HS; Franklin, IN; 4/260 Band; Chrs; Hon Rl; Pres JA; Jr NHS; Mdrgl; Pres NHS; Orch; Sch Mus; Sch Nwsp; Rector Schlrshp From De Pauw Univ; De Pauw Univ; Music.

ANDREWS, TIMOTHY; Hauser HS; Columbus, IN; 4/100 Trs Sr Cls; Chrh Wkr; Lbry Ade; Mod UN; Treas NHS; Quill & Scroll; Ed Yrbk; Pres FTA; Ball State Univ; Journalism.

ANDREWS, TOM; Lakeview HS; Cortland, OH; Pres Soph Cls; Pres Sr Cls; Am Leg Boys St; Chrh Wkr; Hon Rl; Lbry Ade; Ed Sch Nwsp; Rptr Sch Nwsp; Letter Ftbl; Letter Trk; College; Coast Gaurd.

ANDRISH, CATHERINE; Canfield HS; Canfield, OH; 9/258 Chrs; Girl Scts; Hon Rl; Mdrgl; NHS; Sch Mus; Stg Crw; Y-Teens; Fr Clb; Pep Clb; Univ; Nursing.

ANDRIZZI, MARK; Detroit Redford HS; Detroit, MI; Boy Scts; Hon Rl; Jr NHS; NHS; Crs Cntry; Swmmng; Ten; Trk; Natl Merit Ltr; Wayne St Univ; Sci.

ANDRULIS, EILEEN; Lake Michigan Cath HS; St Joseph, MI; Hon Rl; JA; 4-H; 4-H Awd; JA Awd;.

ANDRUS, DON; Hastings HS; Hastings, MI; Hon Rl; Pol Wkr; Rptr Yrbk; Fr Clb; Spn Clb; Natl Merit SF; Michigan St Univ; Linguistics.

ANDRUS, KIM; Lincoln West HS; Cleveland, OH; Cls Rep Frsh Cls; Val; Hon Rl; Jr NHS; NHS; Rptr Yrbk; Yrbk; Pep Clb; Sci Clb; Pres Awd; YWCA Bright Future Awd 79; Oh Acad Schslhp Prgor Cert 79; Excllnc In Eng 79; Cleveland St Univ; Bio.

ANDRUSIAK, MICHAEL; Caledonia HS; Caledonia, MI; Band; Chrh Wkr; Hon Rl; JA; Ftbl; Trk; Wrstlng; Coach Actv; JA Awd; Hope Coll; Bus Admin.

ANDUJAR, GLORIA; Bowling Green HS; Tulsa, OK; Girl Scts; FHA; VP Spn Clb; Univ Of Tulsa; Nursing.

ANELLI, ANDREA; Villa Angela Acad; Cleveland, OH; Cls Rep Sr Cls; Hon Rl; NHS; Sch Mus; Sch Pl; Stu Cncl; Drama Clb; Hiram Coll; Theatre.

ANGEL, TIMOTHY B; Portsmouth HS; Portsmouth, OH; Pres Frsh Cls; Cls Rep Frsh Cls; Cls Rep Soph Cls; Pres Jr Cls; Am Leg Boys St; Cmnty Wkr; Hon Rl; Hosp Ade; Jr NHS; Lbry Ade; Hugh O Brian Foundation Awd; Operation Yth; Eng & Bio Schlrshp Tms; Univ Of Cincinnati; Bio.

ANGELI, LARRY; Bishop Foley HS; Lake Orion, MI; Boy Scts; Hon Rl; Natl Forn Lg; Pol Wkr; Sch Pl; Stg Crw; Rdo Clb; Ftbl; Socr; Michigan St Univ; Bio.

ANGELL, RONALD; Detroit Cntry Day HS; Northville, MI; Chrs; 4-H; Capt Bsbl; Letter Ftbl; Letter Hockey; Letter Socr; Letter Ten; Ferris St Coll; Busns.

ANGELL, TAMMI; Hannan Trace HS; Crown City, OH; Sec Jr Cls; Band; Chrs; Hon Rl; Stu Cncl; Yrbk; Beta Clb; Pres 4-H; Rio Grande College; Nurs.

ANGELO, LINDA; Williamston HS; Williamston, MI; Sec AFS; Cmp Fr Grls; Sec Chrh Wkr; Cmnty Wkr; Hon Rl; Jr NHS; Lbry Ade; Lansing Comm Coll; Office Admin.

ANGELO, TERRI; Williamston HS; Williamston, MI; 1/152 VP AFS; Chrh Wkr; Hon Rl; Jr NHS; Lbry Ade; Dnfth Awd; Natl Merit Ltr; Lansing Comm College; Business.

ANGELO, TOM; Warren Western Reserve HS; Warren, OH; 72/465 Band; Chrh Wkr; Cmnty Wkr; Hon Rl; Orch; Sch Mus; Sch Pl; Stg Crw; Drama Clb; Jr & Sr Outstndng Boy Awd 78; Mbr Of N E Oh All Star Band 79; Schlshp From Dana Schl Of Music 79; Youngstown St Univ; Music Educ.

ANGELOTTI, STEVEN R; Midland HS; Midland, MI; Cls Rep Frsh Cls; Cls Rep Soph Cls; Cl Rep Jr Cls; Hon Rl; NHS; Pol Wkr; Stu Cncl; Yth Flsp; Ger Clb; Mth Clb; Univ.

ANGER, SHARON; Shawe Memorial HS; Madison, IN; 13/27 Trs Frsh Cls; FCA; Girl Scts; Hon Rl; Rptr Yrbk; Pep Clb; Univ Of Evansville; Spec Educ.

ANGLE, JANE; Buffalo HS; Huntington, WV; 8/141 Am Leg Aux Girls St; Band; Hon Rl; NHS; Sprt Ed Sch Nwsp; Rptr Sch Nwsp; FHA; Trk; Mgrs; Mat Maids; Busns Schl; Sec.

ANGLE, PATRICIA; Allegan HS; Allegan, MI; 25/191 Cls Rep Sr Cls; Band; Chrh Wkr; Girl Scts; Hon Rl; NHS; Lat Clb; Capt Bsktbl; Capt Trk; Coach Actv; Albion Coll; Wildlife Mgmt.

ANGLES, MIKE; Bluefield HS; Bluefield, WV; 38/312 Pres Soph Cls; Pres Jr Cls; Pres Sr Cls; Am Leg Boys St; Chrh Wkr; Cmnty Wkr; FCA; Hon Rl; NHS; Stu Cncl; Lee Coll; Missionary.

ANGLIM, PAUL; Gladstone Area HS; Gladstone, MI; 96/203 Am Leg Boys St; Boy Scts; Ftbl; Bay De Noc Cmnty Coll; Crmnl Justc.

ANGOTTI, JOHN D; Notre Dame HS; Clarksburg, WV; 1/54 VP Frsh Cls; VP Soph Cls; Pres Sr Cls; Val; Am Leg Boys St; Hon Rl; Pres NHS; Sch Pl; Treas Stu Cncl; Drama Clb; West Virginia Univ; C hemistry.

ANGOTTI, MARY E; Notre Dame HS; Clarksburg, WV; 2/54 Sec Frsh Cls; Cl Rep Jr Cls; Band; Chrs; Chrh Wkr; VP Natl Forn Lg; Sch Pl; Sec Stu Cncl; Drama Clb; Fr Clb; Participated In Hugh O Brain Youth Leadership Seminar 78; Participated In The Irl Allison Piano Aud 8yr 70; Wheeling Coll; Pre Med.

ANGOTTI, MARY J; Hinton HS; Hinton, WV; VP Frsh Cls; VP Soph Cls; Cl Rep Jr Cls; Girl Scts; Hon Rl; Jr NHS; Off Ade; Yrbk; Lat Clb; Chrldng; Spelling Awd 76; Yrbk Awd 79; West Virginia Univ; Bio Sci.

ANGSTEN, BETSY; Southfield HS; Southfield, MI; Jr NHS; NHS; Sch Mus; Sch Pl; Drama Clb; Spn Clb; Ten; Natl Merit Schl; Oakland Univ; Med Tech.

ANGWIN, KATHY; Luther L Wright HS; Ironwood, MI; Sec Soph Cls; Sec Jr Cls; Chrs; Hon Rl; Off Ade; Sch Mus; Rptr Yrbk; Yrbk; Rptr Sch Nwsp; Sch Nwsp; Univ; Sec.

ANKENBAUER, JERRY; St Xavier HS; Cincinati, OH; 28/270 Hon Rl; Yrbk; Pep Clb; Bsbl; Capt Bsktbl; Coach Actv; IM Sprt; Scr Kpr; Tmr; Natl Merit Ltr; College; Prelaw.

ANKENY, LAURA; Carroll HS; Dayton, OH; Stu Cncl; Ger Clb; Bsktbl; Univ.

ANKRAPP, SANDRA; St Clair HS; Richmond, MI; 2/209 Sal; Band; Chrh Wkr; Hon Rl; Treas NHS; Sch Pl; Stu Cncl; Ed Sch Nwsp; Letter Bsbl; Wayne St Univ; Liberal Arts.

ANKROM, ERNEST; Bloom Carroll HS; Carroll, OH; 23/170 Pres Frsh Cls; FCA; Hon Rl; NHS; Stu Cncl; Bsbl; Ftbl; Football Awds; College; Law Enforcement.

ANNE, DANA; Lake Shore HS; St Clair Shore, MI; VP Frsh Cls; Cls Rep Soph Cls; Cl Rep Jr Cls; Cls Rep Sr Cls; Hon Rl; Jr NHS; NHS; Stu Cncl; Ten; Mic State Univ; Bus.

ANNEKEN, MARY C; Seton HS; Cincinnati, OH; 26/283 Chrs; Hon Rl; Jr NHS; NHS; Off Ade; FBLA; Spn Clb; Coach Actv; Univ; Acctg.

ANNEN, DEBORAH; Vicksburg HS; Scotts, MI; 25/247 Pres Frsh Cls; Jr NHS; NHS; Sch Mus; Stu Cncl; Sprt Ed Yrbk; Rptr Yrbk; Sprt Ed Sch Nwsp; Rptr Sch Nwsp; Olivert College; Bio.

ANNES, ALAN; Decatur Central HS; Indianapolis, IN; Aud/Vis; Hon Rl; Pol Wkr; Sch Nwsp; 4-H; IM Sprt; 4-H Awd; IUPUI; Econ.

ANNO, JODI; Attica HS; Attica, IN; Trs Soph Cls; Trs Jr Cls; Hon Rl; Rptr Yrbk; Ed Sch Nwsp; Drama Clb; Pep Clb; Ind Bus College; Acctng.

ANSELMAN, ALAN; Marian HS; South Bend, IN; 46/165 Hon Rl; IM Sprt; Purdue Univ; Comp Sci.

ANSON, ELIZABETH; Walnut Hills HS; Cincinnati, OH; Chrh Wkr; Cmnty Wkr; Hon Rl; Hosp Ade; Lit Mag; Yth Flsp; Yrbk; Fr Clb; Trk; College; Art.

ANSPACH, SALLY; Buena Vista HS; Saginaw, MI; Band; Hon Rl; Lbry Ade; Trk; Central Michigan Univ; Sci.

ANSTETT, MELANIE; Cabrini HS; Allen Park, MI; 11/148 Hon Rl; Treas NHS; Quill & Scroll; Sch Mus; Stg Crw; Rptr Sch Nwsp; Drama Clb; Fr Clb; IM Sprt; Natl Merit SF; Northwestern Univ; Engr.

ANTASH, DEBRA; Milan HS; Milan, MI; 32/190 Hon Rl; Crs Cntry; Letter Swmmng; Letter Trk; Washtenaw Comm; Bus.

ANTAYA, KATHY; Our Lady Of Mercy HS; Detroit, MI; Chrh Wkr; Cmnty Wkr; Mod UN; Coll; Sci.

ANTCLIFF, SUSAN; South Newton Jr Sr HS; Goodland, IN; 12/112 Sec Soph Cls; Sec Jr Cls; Sec Sr Cls; Am Leg Aux Girls St; Band; Girl Scts; Hon Rl; Off Ade; Quill & Scroll; Yrbk; Univ; Bus.

ANTEAU, SANDRA K; St Mary Academy; Newport, MI; 5/130 Cmnty Wkr; Hon Rl; NHS; Fr Clb; Sci Clb; French Awd; Siena Heights Coll; Accounting.

ANTENUCI, LORI; Central Catholic HS; Canton, OH; 8/250 Cmnty Wkr; Hon Rl; Sch Mus; Sch Pl; Yth Flsp; Rptr Sch Nwsp; Drama Clb; OEA; Business Schl; Exec Sec.

ANTER, MARY JO; Port Huron HS; Mount Clemens, MI; 21/235 Pres Jr Cls; Hon Rl; NHS; Mth Clb; Capt Ten; Trk; Vllybl MVP 79; Girls Varsity Clb Pres 78; Hope Coll; Bus Admin.

ANTHONY, CATHERINE; Linden Mc Kinley HS; Columbus, OH; 27/259 Cls Rep Sr Cls; Chrh Wkr; Hon Rl; Lbry Ade; Stu Cncl; Rptr Yrbk; Spn Clb; Letter Bsktbl; Mgrs; Cert Of Recognition Ohio St Univ; MVP Softball 2 Letters; Linden Mc Kinley Stu Council Acad Awd; Bowling Green Univ; Public Relations.

ANTHONY, LAURIE; Madison Plains HS; London, OH; Trs Frsh Cls; Trs Soph Cls; Cl Rep Jr Cls; Am Leg Aux Girls St; Hon Rl; Hosp Ade; Jr NHS; NHS; Off Ade; Stu Cncl; Clark Tech Schl; Comp Prog.

ANTHONY, MARY A; Mount View HS; Gary, WV; Trs Soph Cls; VP Sr Cls; Chrh Wkr; Cmnty Wkr; Hon Rl; Jr NHS; Red Cr Ade; Yth Flsp; 4-H; FDA; Marshall Univ; Bio.

ANTHONY, PATRICK; Farmington HS; W Farmington, OH; Hon Rl; Stg Crw; Yrbk; Beta Clb; Bsbl; Bsktbl; Swmmng; Natl Merit Ltr; Ohio St Univ.

ANTHOS, ERIC; Theodore Roosevelt HS; Wyandotte, MI; Aud/Vis; Boy Scts; Hon Rl; NHS; Scr Kpr; Tmr; Univ Of Mic; Chem Engr.

ANTILL, BRADLEY; Norton HS; Clinton, OH; 9/250 Pres Jr Cls; Chrh Wkr; Hon Rl; Jr NHS; NHS; Letter Bsktbl; Letter Trk; Bio Hon 78; Univ; Forestry.

ANTILL, SANDI; Wintersville HS; Wintrsvl, OH; Cls Rep Frsh Cls; Band; Girl Scts; Hosp Ade; NHS; Stu Cncl; Fr Clb; FNA; GAA; Ohio Valley Schl Of Nursing; RN.

ANTINONE, CHARLES; Steubenville Cath Cntrl HS; Mingo Junction, OH; 51/204 Chrh Wkr; Cmnty Wkr; Hon Rl; Fr Clb; Letter Bsbl; Letter Glf; Trk; Coach Actv; IM Sprt; Univ; Engr.

ANTINONE, CHARLES; Catholic Central HS; Mingo Jct, OH; 51/204 Chrh Wkr; Cmnty Wkr; Hon Rl; Fr Clb; Letter Bsbl; Letter Glf; Trk; Coach Actv; IM Sprt; College; Engr.

ANTOLCZYK, CYNTHIA; Our Lady Of Mt Carmel HS; Wyandotte, MI; 2/63 Trs Soph Cls; Sal; Hon Rl; NHS; Pol Wkr; Ed Yrbk; Univ Of Detroit; Cmnctns.

ANTONELLI, LOUIS; Fairview HS; Fairview Pk, OH; 69/265 Am Leg Boys St; Aud/Vis; Hon Rl; JA; Stg Crw; Yrbk; Drama Clb; Univ; Law.

ANTONIW, MOTRIA; Holy Name Nazareth HS; Parma, OH; 9/289 Chrs; Hon Rl; Sct Actv; Case Western Reserve Univ; Chem Engr.

ANTOSZ, LINDA L; Archbishop Alter HS; Dayton, OH; Chrs; Cmnty Wkr; Hon Rl; Sch Pl; Stu Cncl; Yth Flsp; Chrldng; Tmr; Arizona St Univ; Spanish.

ANTRAM, THOMAS; Fitzgerald HS; Warren, MI; 21/308 Hon Rl; NHS; Sch Pl; Yth Flsp; Drama Clb; Crs Cntry; Trk; Mic Tech Univ; Elec Engr.

ANTUSH, VICKI; North Ridgeville HS; N Ridgeville, OH; Hon Rl; Hosp Ade; NHS; 4-H; Pep Clb; 4-H Awd; Lorian Cnty Cmnty Coll; Data Rroc.

ANUSZKIEWICZ JR, RICHARD; Lumen Christi HS; Jackson, MI; 51/242 Hon Rl; Jackson Comm College; Comp Engr.

ANWAY, JEROME; St Agatha HS; Detroit, MI; Hon Rl; Fr Clb; Letter Ftbl; GMI; Acctg.

ANZALONE, CHARLES A; Campbell Memorial HS; Campbell, OH; Capt Band; Chrh Wkr; Drm Bgl; Orch; Stu Cncl; Fr Clb; Mth Clb; Pep Clb; Sci Clb; Capt Ten; Coll.

ANZEVINO, HARRY; Boardman HS; Youngstown, OH; 69/567 Boy Scts; Hon Rl; NHS; Red Cr Ade; Sci Clb; Spn Clb; Youngstown St Univ; Busns.

ANZUILEWICZ, SHARON; Bluefield HS; Bluefld, WV; Cls Rep Frsh Cls; Cls Rep Soph Cls; Cl Rep Jr Cls; Hon Rl; Stu Cncl; Pep Clb; Spn Clb; GAA; Vpi; Business.

APARDIAN, GREGORY; St Francis De Sales HS; Toledo, OH; Aud/Vis; Band; Boy Scts; Hon Rl; Hosp Ade; Orch; Red Cr Ade; Sch Mus; Sct Actv; Toledo Univ; Elect Engr.

APEL, CHERI; Wheelersburg HS; Sciotoville, OH; Hon Rl; FHA; Pep Clb; Spn Clb; Outstndg Stu Awd 75; Shawnee St Coll; Resp Ther.

APICELLA, SUZANNE; Salem Sr HS; Salem, OH; Band; Hon Rl; Pep Clb; Spn Clb; Grove City Coll; Chem.

APISA, DEBRA; Mineral Ridge HS; Mineral Ridge, OH; 4/84 Band; Chrs; Hon Rl; Treas JA; NHS; Off Ade; Yth Flsp; Sch Nwsp; Beta Clb; Fr Clb; Youngstown St Univ; Nursing.

APITZ, WENDY; Akron East HS; Akron, OH; Hosp Ade; Stu Cncl; Yth Flsp; Rptr Sch Nwsp; Letter Gym; Letter Swmmng; Capt Chrldng; W Reserve Educ Fund Awd 79; Young Ctzns Awd 78; 12th Grd Cls Chaplain; Univ Of Akron; Med.

APO, JUDITH; Sts Peter & Paul Area HS; Saginaw, MI; Cmnty Wkr; Hon Rl; NHS; PAVAS; Rptr Sch Nwsp; Sch Nwsp; Pep Clb; Trk; GAA; PPFtbl; Univ; Health.

APPEDDU, TERESA A; Perrysburg HS; Perrysburg, OH; 2/251 Sal; Band; Girl Scts; Hon Rl; NHS; Orch;

Sct Actv; Fr Clb; Mth Clb; Sci Clb; Case Western Reserve Univ; Pre Med.

APPEL, BARBARA; East Clinton HS; Sabina, OH; 2/107 Sal; Am Leg Aux Girls St; Band; Drl Tm; NHS; Off Ade; Stg Crw; Yth Flsp; 4-H; Pres FHA; Pres Classroom For Young Americans; People To People HS Stu Ambassador Program; FHA St Homemakers Degree; Ohio Northern Univ; Engr.

APPEL, JENNIFER; Charleston Catholic HS; Scott Depot, WV; Am Leg Aux Girls St; Chrs; Debate Tm; Hon Rl; NHS; 4-H; Cit Awd; 4-H Awd; Phys Ther.

APPEL, SHARON; Lake Michigan Catholic HS; Benton Harbor, MI; 4/102 Pres Jr Cls; Cl Rep Jr Cls; Band; Chrs; Chrh Wkr; Debate Tm; Girl Scts; Hon Rl; NHS; Off Ade; University; Theatre.

APPELBAUM, TODD; Charles F Brush HS; Lyndhurst, OH; Am Leg Boys St; Aud/Vis; Boy Scts; Hon Rl; Stu Cncl; Key Clb; Socr; Ten; Trk; Coach Actv; Var Goalie Rated 8 In St 78; Capt Varl Goalie For S Euclid Landhurst Soccer Cleveland Champ 79; Ohio St Univ; Law.

APPELMANN, ROSANNE; New Richmond HS; New Richmond, OH; Sec Drl Tm; Hon Rl; Pres JA; NHS; Quill & Scroll; Rptr Sch Nwsp; Sch Nwsp; Fr Clb; Sci Clb; JA Awd; Univ.

APPLEBEE, SHERI; Ovid Elsie HS; Ovid, MI; Trs Jr Cls; VP Sr Cls; Girl Scts; Hon Rl; Jr NHS; Yth Flsp; Pep Clb; Letter Bsktbl; Coach Actv; Bus Sch; Bookeepper.

APPLEBY, MARIE; Springfield HS; Springfield, OH; Cls Rep Sr Cls; Band; Chrh Wkr; Drl Tm; Hon Rl; Orch; Pol Wkr; Stu Cncl; Civ Clb; Lat Clb; Univ; Econ.

APPLEBY, MATT; Ashland HS; Ashland, OH; Cl Rep Jr Cls; Hon Rl; VP JA; NHS; Stu Cncl; Sci Clb; JA Awd; College; Radio Broadcasting.

APPLEDORN, SCOTT; Holland HS; Holland, MI; 30/400 Hon Rl; NHS; Crs Cntry; Chmn Ten; IM Sprt; College; Bus.

APPLEGARTH, GEORGE; Buckeye South HS; Tiltonsville, OH; Band; Hon Rl; Sch Mus; Letter Ftbl; Glf; IM Sprt; Jefferson Cnty Tech Coll; Elec Engr.

APPLETON, C; Delphi Comm HS; Delphi, IN; Chrs; Chrh Wkr; Cmnty Wkr; Hon Rl; Sch Mus; Yth Flsp; 4-H; OEA; Spn Clb; 4-H Awd; Indiana Cntrl Univ; Nursing.

APPLETON, CYNTHIA; Shortridge HS; Indianapolis, IN; 51/379 VP Frsh Cls; Cls Rep Soph Cls; Chrs; Hon Rl; Off Ade; FSA; Letter Bsbl; Capt Trk; Mat Maids; JETS Awd; College.

APPOLONI, CATHY L; Three Rivers HS; Three Rivers, MI; Bsbl; Bsktbl; Mat Maids; 4-H Awd; College; Cosmotology.

APT, JAMES; John Adams HS; So Bend, IN; 30/420 Cl Rep Jr Cls; Cls Rep Sr Cls; Boy Scts; Hon Rl; NHS; Rptr Sch Nwsp; Sch Nwsp; Spn Clb; DAR Awd; College; Civil Engr.

AQUINO, THOMAS; Eastlake North HS; Eastlake, OH; CAP; Ftbl; Univ; Marine Bio.

ARACHIKAVITZ, KAREN; New Albany HS; New Albany, IN; Hon Rl; 4-H; 4-H Awd; College; Nursing.

ARAJ, NAHIL; Western HS; Detroit, MI; Sec Sr Cls; Hosp Ade; Lit Mag; Off Ade; OEA; Bsbl; Bsktbl; Ten; Gov Hon Prg Awd; Detroit College Of Bus.

ARBAUGH, CINDY; Fort Frye HS; Warner, OH; Trs Sr Cls; Hst Sr Cls; Drl Tm; Girl Scts; Hon Rl; Yth Flsp; 4-H; OEA; 4-H Awd; Otstndng OEA Prtcpnt 79; Rgnl 1st Plc Wnnr In OEA Job Intrvw 2 79; General Offc.

ARBAUGH, DARRELL; Valley Local HS; Lucasville, OH; 8/110 Hon Rl; Pep Clb; Capt Bsktbl; Trk; College; Envir Sci.

ARBAUGH, DEANNA; Valley Local HS; Lucasville, OH; Sec Sr Cls; Band; Chrs; Chrh Wkr; Cmnty Wkr; Girl Scts; NHS; Pol Wkr; Sch Pl; Yth Flsp; Kentucky Christian Coll; Missionary.

ARBOGAST, DAVID F; Whitmore Lake HS; Whitmore Lake, MI; Aud/Vis; Boy Scts; CAP; Hon Rl; Jr NHS; Lbry Ade; NHS; IM Sprt; Univ; Engr.

ARBOGAST, DIANA; Poca HS; Nitro, WV; 16/152 Band; Chrs; Girl Scts; Hon Rl; JA; Jr NHS; Rptr Sch Nwsp; Fr Clb; Putnam County Voc Tech Center; Sec.

ARBOGAST, LORI; Barboursville HS; Barboursville, WV; Sec FCA; Hon Rl; Jr NHS; Off Ade; FTA; Pep Clb; Spn Clb; Chrldng; Spanish II Award 7977; Spanish Honorary 1978; Marshall Univ; Lang.

ARBOGAST, NATALIE; Harman HS; Harman, WV; Sec Soph Cls; Band; Chrs; Chrh Wkr; Hon Rl; Sch Pl; FBLA; Pep Clb; Randolph Co Voc Tech Schl; Sec.

ARBUCKLE, JIM; Western HS; Russiaville, IN; Am Leg Boys St; Boy Scts; Chrs; Hon Rl; JA; Mdrgl; Natl Forn Lg; NHS; Sch Pl; Sct Actv; Univ; Engr.

ARBURN, GREG; Princeton Cmnty HS; Princeton, IN; 80/203 Chrh Wkr; FCA; Yth Flsp; 4-H; FFA; Letter Bsktbl; Letter Crs Cntry; Cit Awd; Dnfth Awd; 4-H Awd; Purdue Univ; Agri.

ARCE, WANDA; George Washington HS; E Chicago, IN; Chrs; Hon Rl; Hosp Ade; Sch Mus; Pep Clb; College; Law.

ARCERI, RONALD; Riverside HS; Dearborn Hts, MI; Cls Rep Sr Cls; Hon Rl; Stu Cncl; Coach Actv; IM Sprt; Univ Of Michigan; Engr.

ARCH, ANGIE; Bremen HS; Bremen, IN; FCA; Hon Rl; Sch Mus; Drama Clb; Pep Clb; Letter Ten; Chrldng; GAA; Ball St Univ; Elem Ed.

ARCHAMBAULT, JEFFREY; Farwell Area HS; Clare, MI; 1/112 Trs Soph Cls; NHS; Cntrl Mi Univ Bd Of Trustees Hon Schlrshp 78; Rotary Clb Schlrsp 79; Farwell Educ Assoc 79; Central Michigan Univ; Acctg.

ARCHAMBO, DUANE A; Cheboygan Area HS; Cheboygan, MI; Hon Rl; College; Construction.

ARCHBOLD, ROGER; Fenton Sr HS; Fenton, MI; Band; Boy Scts; Debate Tm; Hon Rl; Western Michigan Univ.

ARCHER, BRENT; Tyler County HS; Middlebourne, WV; Sec Soph Cls; Cl Rep Jr Cls; Hon Rl; Jr NHS; Stu Cncl; Ed Sch Nwsp; Sch Nwsp; Sci Clb; Bsktbl; IM Sprt; Marshall Univ; Journalism.

ARCHER, CYNTHIA; Crestwood HS; Mantua, OH; 30/238 Band; Hon Rl; NHS; Stg Crw; Beta Clb; Pres 4-H; Fr Clb; 4-H Awd; Youngstown St Univ; Music Educ.

ARCHER, JOHN; North Daviess HS; Odon, IN; 13/88 Am Leg Boys St; Chrs; Hon Rl; ROTC; Sch Mus; Beta Clb; Fr Clb; Cit Awd; Ind State Univ; Music Educ.

ARCHER, MARTHA; Regina HS; Highland Hts, OH; Cls Rep Soph Cls; Cl Rep Jr Cls; Hon Rl; Jr NHS; Sch Pl; Stu Cncl; Pep Clb; GAA; IM Sprt; College; Health.

ARCHER, SCOTT; Green HS; Uniontown, OH; 7/320 Cls Rep Soph Cls; VP Jr Cls; Cl Rep Jr Cls; VP Sr Cls; Cls Rep Sr Cls; Am Leg Boys St; FCA; Hon Rl; NHS; Stu Cncl; Stud Driver Of Yr 78; Pres Of Sunday Schl Class 78; Univ; Engr.

ARCHER JR, WILLIAM; Logan Elm HS; Circleville, OH; 3/200 Am Leg Boys St; Chrh Wkr; Hon Rl; NHS; Sch Pl; Yth Flsp; Letter Bsbl; Letter Bsktbl; IM Sprt; College; Law.

ARCHIE, CORINNE; Southeastern HS; Detroit, MI; Cl Rep Jr Cls; Chrs; Chrh Wkr; Hon Rl; VP NHS; Orch; Sch Mus; Stu Cncl; VP DECA; Cit Awd; Univ Of Michigan; Pre Dent.

ARCIELLO, GREGORY; Washington HS; Massillon, OH; Chrs; Hon Rl; VP Fr Clb; FHA; Letter Ftbl; Letter Wrstlng; Ohio St Univ; Bus.

ARDELIAN, DANIEL K; Southeast HS; Diamond, OH; Boy Scts; Hon Rl; Bsbl; Akron Univ; Bus Admin.

ARDERN, LIBBIE; West Geauga HS; Chesterland, OH; 4/352 Drl Tm; Hon Rl; Sec Jr NHS; NHS; Pres FNA; Pep Clb; Letter Bsbl; Univ Of Cincinnati; Nursing.

ARDVINI, ALAN; Northside HS; Muncie, IN; Purdue Univ; Chem Engr.

AREFORD, WENDY K; Univ HS; Morgantown, WV; 25/218 Hon Rl; Lbry Ade; Pol Wkr; Stg Crw; Drama Clb; FBLA; Sci Clb; West Virginia Univ; Law.

AREHART, DENISE M; Robert S Rogers HS; Toledo, OH; Cls Rep Soph Cls; Cl Rep Jr Cls; Cmp Fr Grls; Hon Rl; JA; Lbry Ade; Off Ade; Spn Clb; JA Awd; Bowling Green State Univ; Psych.

AREND, CAROL A; Archbold HS; Archbold, OH; Cmp Fr Grls; Chrs; Chrh Wkr; Hon Rl; Off Ade; Bsbl; Bsktbl; Trk; Mgrs; Scr Kpr; Univ Of Toledo; Jrnlsm.

AREND, JULIE A; Jackson County Western HS; Jackson, MI; Band; Chrs; Girl Scts; Hon Rl; Sch Mus; Sch Pl; Yth Flsp; 4-H; Gym; Scr Kpr; Coll; Elem Educ.

AREND, MICHAEL; Monroe HS; Monroe, MI; 78/542 Aud/Vis; Boy Scts; Hon Rl; Yrbk; Sch Nwsp; Spn Clb; Natl Merit Schl; Michigan St Univ; Engr.

ARENDS, J; Kalkaska HS; Kalkaska, MI; VP Soph Cls; Letter Bsktbl; Letter Ftbl; Letter Trk; College; Arch.

ARENDSEN, RODNEY; Zeeland HS; Holland, MI; Bsktbl; Ftbl; Ten; Rotary Awd; Mic Tech Univ; Mech Engr.

ARENDT, ANITA; Parma Sr HS; Parma, OH; 115/710 Band; Hon Rl; VP FFA; Coach Actv; Mgrs; State FFA Degree; 1st Pl FFA Proficiency Fruits & Veg; Leadership Awd; Ohio St Univ; Vocational Ag.

ARENS, MARIBETH; Ursuline HS; Girard, OH; 36/286 Fr Clb; Bsktbl; Youngstown St Univ; Forestry.

ARENS, MICHAEL J; Tinora HS; Defiance, OH; Am Leg Boys St; Band; Chrs; Hon Rl; 4-H; Letter Bsbl; Bsktbl; Crs Cntry; 4-H Awd; College.

ARENS, S; Holland Christian HS; Holland, MI; Am Leg Aux Girls St; Band; Chrh Wkr; Cmnty Wkr; 4-H; Ger Clb; Pep Clb; Calvin Coll; Med Tech.

AREVALO, DEBORAH; Mendon Jr Sr HS; Mendon, MI; Trs Soph Cls; Cls Rep Sr Cls; Chrh Wkr; Yth Flsp; Ed Yrbk; Rptr Yrbk; Yrbk; Rptr Sch Nwsp; 4-H; Letter Trk; Coll.

ARFT, DAVID; Armada Area HS; Romeo, MI; VP Frsh Cls; Cls Rep Soph Cls; Cl Rep Jr Cls; Cls Rep Sr Cls; Chrh Wkr; Hon Rl; NHS; Mich Tech Univ; Mech Engr.

ARGABRIGHT, PAM; Troy HS; Troy, OH; Hon Rl; OEA; IM Sprt; Mat Maids; Sinclair Comnty Bus Schl; Legal Sec.

ARGELINE, BARBARA; Howell HS; Howell, MI; 12/395 Sec Jr Cls; Chrs; Hon Rl; JA; NHS; Stu Cncl; Pep Clb; JA Awd; Michigan St Univ; Acctg.

ARGENT, JUDITH; Champion Twp HS; Champion Twp, OH; Girl Scts; Hon Rl; Off Ade; Univ Of Cincinnati; Animal Tech.

ARGYLE, JENNIFER; Kulkaska HS; Graham, TX; 1/135 Pres Jr Cls; Hon Rl; NHS; Sch Pl; Stu Cncl; Crs Cntry; Trk; Chrldng; GAA;.

ARIAS, JAMES; Washington HS; E Chicago, IN; 18/270 Am Leg Boys St; Band; Hon Rl; Orch; Sch Mus; Stu Cncl; Ten; Trk; IM Sprt; Am Leg Awd; Cit Awd; Univ; Engr.

ARIAS, NORMA; St Johns HS; St Johns, MI; Cls Rep Sr Cls; Hon Rl; Sch Mus; Stu Cncl;.

ARIGABRITE, SONYA; David Anderson HS; Lisbon, OH; Band; Treas Chrs; Hon Rl; Sch Mus; Treas Stu Cncl; Yth Flsp; Y-Teens; Rptr Yrbk; Fr Clb; Sec Sci Clb; Univ.

ARINI, JAMES; Sterling Heights HS; Warren, MI; Cls Rep Sr Cls; Hon Rl; Stu Cncl; Pep Clb; Letter Ftbl; IM Sprt; Wayne State Univ; Civil Engr.

ARIZMENDI, WANDA; Marshall HS; Marshall, MI; 51/246 Hon Rl; JA; Pol Wkr; Rptr Yrbk; Lat Clb; Spn Clb; IM Sprt; Davenport College Of Bus; Managmnt.

ARIZMENDY, L; Marshall HS; Marshall, MI; Cls Rep Frsh Cls; Cls Rep Soph Cls; Hon Rl; Spn Clb; Rotary Awd; College; Arch.

ARKENS, MARK; North Central Area HS; Powers, MI; 16/61 Aud/Vis; Sch Pl; Stg Crw; Ftbl; Trk; IM Sprt; Bay De Noc; Bus Admin.

ARKO, ANDREA; Tuslaw HS; Massillon, OH; Band; Hon Rl; NHS; Y-Teens; FTA; Pep Clb;.

ARLEDGE, WENDY; Berrien Springs HS; Berrien Spgs, MI; 35/160 Hon Rl; Sch Mus; Sch Pl; Stg Crw; Ed Yrbk; Rptr Sch Nwsp; Drama Clb; Spn Clb; Ten; Intl Thespian Soc 79; Univ; Cmnctns.

ARLING, LINDA; Minster HS; Minster, OH; 10/82 Am Leg Aux Girls St; Band; Chrh Wkr; Hon Rl; NHS; Sch Mus; FTA; Pep Clb; Spn Clb; Bowling Green Univ; Acctg.

ARLINGHAUS, BARB; St Joseph Acad; Cleveland, OH; 1/225 Val; Chrh Wkr; Cmnty Wkr; Hon Rl; Hosp Ade; NHS; Quill & Scroll; Red Cr Ade; Ed Sch Nwsp; Drama Clb; Purdue Univ; Engr.

ARMANINI, WANDA; Bryan HS; Bryan, OH; Hon Rl; Orch; Yrbk; Treas Fr Clb; GAA; Nw Tech College; Bus Mgmt.

ARMBRECHT, WILLIAM; Frankenmuth HS; Naperville, IL; 12/190 VP Jr Cls; Band; Sch Mus; 4-H; Concordia Coll; Comp Prog.

ARMBRUST, THOMAS; Richmond Sr HS; Richmond, IN; Cl Rep Jr Cls; Cls Rep Sr Cls; Band; FCA; Hon Rl; Stu Cncl; Sprt Ed Sch Nwsp; Capt Swmmng; Tmr; Indiana Univ; Busns.

ARMBRUSTER, DEBRA; Napoleon HS; Napoleon, OH; Am Leg Aux Girls St; Chrh Wkr; Hon Rl; Sec Yth Flsp; Treas 4-H; FHA; Lat Clb; 4-H Awd; Bowling Green State Univ; Home Ec.

ARMBRUSTER, HENRY T; St Edward HS; Cleveland, OH; 12/360 Sec Jr Cls; Chrh Wkr; Hon Rl; JA; Mod UN; NHS; Rptr Yrbk; Yrbk; Rptr Sch Nwsp; Sch Nwsp; College; Medicine.

ARMBRUSTER, LAURA; Bishop Dwenger HS; Ft Wayne, IN; Hon Rl; IUPU.

ARMBRUSTER, LOIS; South Dearborn HS; Aurora, IN; 4/300 Cl Rep Jr Cls; Hon Rl; Pres NHS; Stu Cncl; IM Sprt; Am Leg Awd; Purdue Univ; Math.

ARMBRUSTER, LORI; Napoleon HS; Napoleon, OH; Cls Rep Sr Cls; Am Leg Aux Girls St; Chrs; Chrh Wkr; Cmnty Wkr; Off Ade; Stg Crw; Stu Cncl; 4-H; Lat Clb; Bowling Green S Univ; Elem Ed.

ARMBRUSTER, MICHELLE; New Richmond HS; New Richmond, OH; 12/294 Chrs; Hon Rl; Sec JA; NHS; Sec Quill & Scroll; Yrbk; Sch Nwsp; Sec FHA; Pres FTA; Sec Socr; Univ Of Cincinnati; Elem Educ.

ARMBRUSTER, PHIL; Wynford HS; Bucyrus, OH; 4/125 VP Frsh Cls; Pres Soph Cls; Cls Rep Sr Cls; Am Leg Boys St; Band; Chrs; Hon Rl; Pres NHS; Stu Cncl; Key Clb; Univ; Acctg.

ARMENI, MARK; Boardman HS; Youngstown, OH; 34/594 Hon Rl; NHS; Treas Orch; Quill & Scroll; Sch Nwsp; Ger Clb; Sci Clb; Whos Who In Music 79; James A Garfield Schlrshp 79; Pres Merit Awd From Hiram Coll 79; Hiram Coll; Vet Med.

ARMENTROUT, CAROLYN; Jonathan Alder HS; Plain City, OH; Lbry Ade; Sch Pl; Y-Teens; Drama Clb; Pep Clb; Trk; Chrldng; College; Art.

ARMENTROUT, DAVID W; Chapmanville HS; Chapmanville, WV; 1/125 Am Leg Boys St; Jr NHS; NHS; Stu Cncl; Ed Yrbk; Sprt Ed Sch Nwsp; Beta Clb; Letter Bsbl; Letter Bsktbl; Letter Ftbl; Univ.

ARMER, CATHERINE; Bloomington South HS; Bloomington, IN; 24/314 Pres Sr Cls; Hon Rl; NHS; Pol Wkr; Quill & Scroll; Stg Crw; Stu Cncl; Ed Sch Nwsp; Rptr Sch Nwsp; Sch Nwsp; Georgetown Univ; Intl Jrnlsm.

ARMES, ROBBYN; Charlestown HS; Charlestown, IN; 37/196 Chrs; Hon Rl; Lbry Ade; Mdrgl; Sch Mus; Drama Clb; Spn Clb; S E Indiana Univ; Comp Sci.

ARMES, TEDDY; Clay Sr HS; South Bend, IN; Chrh Wkr; Hon Rl; Rptr Yrbk; Sch Nwsp; Lat Clb; Oregon Bible Coll; Eng.

ARMINIO, LISA M; Fairfield HS; Fairfield, OH; 141/600 Band; Chrs; Drm Mjrt; Hosp Ade; JA; Orch; Sch Mus; Sch Pl; OEA; Pep Clb; OOEA Regn 1 Job Interview 1 2nd Pl 78; 1st Pl Most Otstndng Drum Major 77; Univ; Clerk Steno.

ARMOCIDA, SUSAN; Ellet HS; Akron, OH; 12/363 Am Leg Aux Girls St; Chrs; Hon Rl; Jr NHS; NHS; Off Ade; VP Ger Clb; Letter Gym; Univ Of Akron; Law.

ARMS, BRENT; Franklin Heights HS; Grove City, OH; Pres Frsh Cls; Cls Rep Frsh Cls; Cls Rep Soph Cls; Cl Rep Jr Cls; Cls Rep Sr Cls; Band; Chrs; Chrh Wkr; Stu Cncl; Key Clb; Univ; Theol.

ARMS, DENISE; Lappeer West HS; Columbiaville, MI; 26/260 Band; NHS; Off Ade; Trk; Grand Rapids Baptist Coll; Phys Ther.

ARMSTRONG, ANGELA; Goshen HS; Goshen, IN; Cmp Fr Grls; Off Ade; Sch Mus; Sch Pl; Drama Clb; Spn Clb; Univ; Health.

ARMSTRONG, BONNIE; Shenandoah HS; New Castle, IN; 52/173 Cls Rep Sr Cls; Hon Rl; JA; Off Ade; Sch Pl; Sprt Ed Yrbk; Drama Clb; Pres FHA; Pep Clb; Bsktbl; Homecoming Queen Cand 79; Sr Sports Awd 79; Airline Schl; Stewardess.

ARMSTRONG, CAROL; Shelbyville Sr HS; Shelbyville, IN; Spn Clb; Voc Schl; Bus.

ARMSTRONG, CRAIG; Rochester HS; Rochester, IN; Hon Rl; Rptr Sch Nwsp; Ger Clb; Letter Bsbl; Univ; Cmnctns.

ARMSTRONG, CRAIG; Stow Lakeview HS; Stow, OH; Band; Debate Tm; Red Cr Ade; Stu Cncl; Rptr Yrbk; Lat Clb; Crs Cntry; Ftbl; Trk; IM Sprt; College; Premedicine.

ARMSTRONG, DARRYL; Orchard View HS; Muskegon, MI; 4/235 Trs Soph Cls; Trs Jr Cls; VP Sr Cls; Chrs; Hon Rl; Lbry Ade; NHS; Off Ade; Muskegon Community College; Theater.

ARMSTRONG, DAVID; New Harmony HS; Bowling Green, KY; 6/32 Boy Scts; Cmnty Wkr; Hon Rl; Sch Pl; Rptr Sch Nwsp; Lat Clb; Letter Bsktbl; Letter Crs Cntry; Capt Socr; Letter Trk; Western Ken Univ; Business Admin.

ARMSTRONG, DEB; Blackford HS; Hartford City, IN; 84/272 Band; Chrh Wkr; 4-H; OEA; Sci Clb; GAA; Mgrs; 4-H Awd; Ball St Univ; Bus Mgmt.

ARMSTRONG, DREW; Northrop HS; Ft Wayne, IN; Cls Rep Frsh Cls; Hon Rl; Letter Bsbl; Letter Hockey; Univ Of Nebraska; Spec Agent.

ARMSTRONG, FRANK; Holy Name Nazareth HS; Maple Hts, OH; Hon Rl; Jr NHS; NHS; Sch Pl; Fr Clb; Ftbl; IM Sprt; Cit Awd; Yuth Of Yr S E YMCA 77; YMCA Lifeguard 78; Red Cross Learshp Ctr Findlay Coll 78; Univ; Med.

ARMSTRONG, JEFFREY K; Turpin HS; Cincinnati, OH; 7/357 Cls Rep Frsh Cls; Pres NHS; Treas Stu Cncl; Letter Ftbl; Letter Trk; Letter Wrstlng; PPFtbl; Natl Merit SF; Jr Marshal At Graduation Ceremonies; Published Cartoonist THS 1st Solo Buzz Book; Univ.

ARMSTRONG, JOE; Eastern Greene HS; Springville, IN; 7/95 Band; Boy Scts; Hon Rl; NHS; Yth Flsp; VP 4-H; Pres FFA; Letter Bsktbl; Letter Trk; Participated In Natl FFA Soil Judging Contest 78; Recvd St Farmer Degree In FFA 79; Purdue Univ; Agri Econ.

ARMSTRONG, KYLE; East Kentwood HS; Kentwood, MI; Hon Rl; NHS; Fr Clb; PPFtbl; Awd Yth Talent Exhbt Shrt Stories 79; Awd Writng; Poetry Club Short Stories 79; Awd Schlstc Hnr Awd 79; Central Michigan Univ; Sci.

ARMSTRONG, MARK; Hilliard HS; Columbus, OH; Band; Hon Rl; Jr NHS; NHS; Pres Stg Crw; Mgrs; Univ; Comp Sci.

ARMSTRONG, MARK; Clear Fork HS; Belleville, OH; Cls Rep Frsh Cls; Cls Rep Soph Cls; Cl Rep Jr Cls; Yrbk; Sch Nwsp; Wrstlng; IM Sprt; Ohio Northern Univ; Business Admin.

ARMSTRONG, MARY G; Grand Blanc HS; Grand Blanc, MI; 5/690 Pres Frsh Cls; VP Soph Cls; Am Leg Aux Girls St; Cmnty Wkr; Hon Rl; NHS; Pol Wkr; Quill & Scroll; Stu Cncl; Sprt Ed Yrbk; Homecoming Qn; College; Medicine.

ARMSTRONG, MELISSA; Avondale HS; Pontiac, MI; AFS; Band; Pres NHS; Sch Mus; Sch Pl; Drama Clb; Capt Twrlr; Univ Of Michigan; Drama.

ARMSTRONG, NANCY; Alcona HS; Lincoln, MI; Boy Scts; Chrh Wkr; Girl Scts; Hon Rl; Sct Actv; Yth Flsp; 4-H; 4-H Awd; Muskegon Bus Coll; Acctg.

ARMSTRONG, NANCY J; Malabar HS; Mansfield, OH; Girl Scts; Off Ade; Stu Cncl; Rptr Yrbk; Mth Clb; GAA; Pres Awd; Coll; Nursing.

ARMSTRONG, PATRICIA; Maderia HS; Cincinnati, OH; 19/169 Band; Girl Scts; Hon Rl; Orch; Sch Mus; Yth Flsp; Spn Clb; Letter Swmmng; Univ; Bus.

ARMSTRONG, PATTI; Hesperia Sr HS; Hesperia, MI; 5/79 Band; Hon Rl; 4-H; 4-H Awd; Muskegon Comm Coll; Nursing.

ARMSTRONG, PAULA; Highland HS; Anderson, IN; 4/459 Cl Rep Jr Cls; Cls Rep Sr Cls; Band; Drl Tm; Hon Rl; NHS; Sch Mus; Stu Cncl; Fr Clb; Pep Clb; Jr Homecmng Princess 78; Prom Queen Attend 79; Jr Marshall 79; Univ; Comp Sci.

ARMSTRONG, RANDOLPH; Turpin HS; Cincinnati, OH; 8/362 Pres Jr Cls; Sch Pl; Stu Cncl; Letter Ftbl; Letter Trk; Letter Wrstlng; Univ; Med.

ARMSTRONG, REBECCA; Jefferson Area HS; Jefferson, OH; AFS; Sec Chrs; Lbry Ade; Sch Mus; Sch Pl; Stg Crw; Fr Clb; Spn Clb; Capt Bsktbl; GAA; J V Vllybll; J V Sftbll; Sr Class Prophecy; Kent St Univ; Elem Ed.

ARMSTRONG, RENEE; Cleveland Central Cath HS; Cleveland, OH; Sec Jr Cls; Cl Rep Jr Cls; Cls Rep Sr Cls; Chrs; Hon Rl; JA; NHS; Stu Cncl; Yrbk; Spn Clb; Ashland Coll; Elem Ed.

ARMSTRONG, RHEA; New Haven HS; New Haven, MI; Cls Rep Frsh Cls; Band; Chrh Wkr; Girl Scts; VP Stu Cncl; Yrbk; Rptr Sch Nwsp; Drama Clb; Pres OEA; Treas Chrldng; Busns Ofc Ed Club Stateswoman Awd; Ofc Ed Assn Ambassador Awd; Mi Competive Schlrshp Prog; Business Schl; Mgmt.

ARMSTRONG, ROBERT; Northview HS; Grand Rapids, MI; 50/289 Cls Rep Sr Cls; Band; Hon Rl; VP JA; Capt Socr; JA Awd; Michigan St Univ; Chem Engr.

ARMSTRONG, RODNEY; Portsmouth East HS; Sciotoville, OH; Aud/Vis; Boy Scts; Chrs; Lbry Ade; University; Math.

ARMSTRONG, ROSEMARY; Newcomerstown HS; Newcomerstown, OH; 23/105 Chrs; Hon Rl; Sch Pl; Stg Crw; 4-H; OEA; Bsbl; Kent State Univ; Nursing.

ARMSTRONG, SUE; Cadillac Sr HS; Cadillac, MI; 1/350 Band; Girl Scts; Hon Rl; NHS; Orch; Sch Mus; Yth Flsp; Michigan Tech Univ; Engr.

ARMSTRONG, THOMAS; Allegan HS; Allegan, MI; 11/200 Pres Sr Cls; Hon Rl; Pol Wkr; Sct Actv;

Stu Cncl; Rptr Yrbk; Spn Clb; Ten; Natl Merit Ltr; Kalamazoo Coll; Law.

ARMSTRONG, THOMAS G; Bishop Hartley HS; Reynoldsburg, OH; Boy Scts; Sch Mus; Sch Pl; Stg Crw; Drama Clb; Pep Clb; Chrldng; Mgrs; Ohio St Univ.

ARMSTRONG, TIMOTHY; Elkhart Central HS; Elkhart, IN; Band; Boy Scts; Chrs; Hon Rl; Sch Mus; Sct Actv; Stg Crw; Elk Awd; Indiana Univ; Bio Sci.

ARMSTRONG, YVETTE; Aquinas HS; Inkster, MI; Band; Orch; PAVAS; Sch Mus; Univ; Dent Hygnst.

ARNDT, ELIZABETH; East Lutheran HS; St Clair Shores, MI; Band; Chrs; Chrh Wkr; Hon Rl; NHS; Yth Flsp; Wayne St Univ; Law.

ARNDT, SHEL; Bethesda Christian HS; Indianapolis, IN; Trs Frsh Cls; Pres Jr Cls; Pres Sr Cls; Chrh Wkr; Off Ade; Yrbk; Ed Sch Nwsp; Bsktbl; Cedarville Coll.

ARNETT, AMY; Bexley HS; Bexley, OH; Pres Jr Cls; VP Sr Cls; Am Leg Aux Girls St; Hon Rl; NHS; Quill & Scroll; Stu Cncl; College; Med.

ARNETT, BETH; Ovid Elsie HS; Ovid, MI; Pres Jr Cls; Band; Hon Rl; Pep Clb; PPFtbl; Lansing Bus Inst; Exec Sec.

ARNETT, LARRY; Waverly HS; Waverly, OH; 17/175 Hon Rl; Rptr Sch Nwsp; 4-H; Bsktbl; Crs Cntry; Ftbl; Trk; Scr Kpr; Tmr; 4-H Awd; Ran In St Cross Cntry Meet Team Fnshd 14th 78; Qulfd In The 880 Yd Rn For The Dist Meet 78; Univ; Educ.

ARNETT, PEGGY; Sullivan HS; Merom, IN; 5/151 Chrs; VP FCA; Hon Rl; NHS; Sec Beta Clb; Spn Clb; Capt Gym; Ind State Univ; Comp Sci.

ARNEY, GORDON; Ridgewood HS; Fresno, OH; 13/150 Am Leg Boys St; Pres Band; Chrs; NHS; Pres Yth Flsp; VP 4-H; Pres Fr Clb; VP FTA; Dnfth Awd; 4-H Awd; Ohi State Univ; Floriculture.

ARNOLD, AARON; Waterford HS; Waterford, OH; 5/63 Pres Frsh Cls; Pres Soph Cls; Pres Jr Cls; Pres Sr Cls; Am Leg Boys St; Band; Chrh Wkr; Hon Rl; NHS; Sch Pl; Ohio Voc Tech Schl; Ag.

ARNOLD, CARRIE; St Ursula Acad; Toledo, OH; Cmp Fr Grls; Chrs; Chrh Wkr; Girl Scts; JA; Off Ade; Stg Crw; Spn Clb; Bsbl; Cit Awd; Dayton Univ; Exec Sec.

ARNOLD, CHRISTINE; North Posey HS; Poseyville, IN; 1/162 Hon Rl; NHS; 4-H; OEA; Pep Clb; Trk; GAA; 4-H Awd; College.

ARNOLD, CINDY; Belding HS; Belding, MI; Band; Cmnty Wkr; Girl Scts; Hon Rl; NHS; Sch Mus; Pres 4-H; VP FFA; Chrldng; 4-H Awd; Michigan St Univ; Vet.

ARNOLD, DALE; Strongsville HS; Strongsville, OH; 32/500 Chrh Wkr; Hon Rl; Jr NHS; NHS; Yth Flsp; Letter Wrstlng; Furman Univ; Bus.

ARNOLD, DAUN; Redford HS; Detroit, MI; Chrs; Hon Rl; NHS; PAVAS; Sch Mus; Chrldng; Cit Awd; Univ; Phys Ther.

ARNOLD, DEBBIE; Fort Frye HS; Beverly, OH; Cls Rep Soph Cls; Am Leg Aux Girls St; Band; Hon Rl; NHS; Sch Mus; Sch Pl; Treas Stu Cncl; Eng Clb; Pres Pep Clb; Univ; Jrnlsm.

ARNOLD, DIANA; Greenville Sr HS; Greenville, OH; 83/380 OEA; Coll; Sec.

ARNOLD, DON M; Mt Vernon HS; Fortville, IN; 1/161 Val; Am Leg Boys St; Band; Hon Rl; NHS; Sch Mus; Yth Flsp; Bsktbl; Ten; Trk; Gertrude Crouch Awd; Eugene C Pulliam Mem Schlrshp; Tri Kappa Serv Awd; Ball St Univ; Archt.

ARNOLD, DONNA; Crestwood HS; Ravenna, OH; Cls Rep Frsh Cls; Cls Rep Soph Cls; Cl Rep Jr Cls; Cls Rep Sr Cls; Chrs; Cmnty Wkr; Hon Rl; Stu Cncl; College; Pre Law.

ARNOLD, JEFFERSON; Harrison HS; W Lafayette, IN; Band; Boy Scts; Chrs; Debate Tm; Natl Forn Lg; Pol Wkr; Swmmng; Tmr; Purdue; Engineering.

ARNOLD, JULIE; Washington HS; Washington, IN; 4/204 Cls Rep Soph Cls; Cl Rep Jr Cls; Cls Rep Sr Cls; Am Leg Aux Girls St; Band; Drl Tm; Hon Rl; NHS; Pres Stu Cncl; Beta Clb; Indiana Univ; Med Tech.

ARNOLD, KIM; South Putnam HS; Cloverdale, IN; 17/100 Cls Rep Frsh Cls; Cl Rep Jr Cls; Cmnty Wkr; FCA; Hon Rl; 4-H; OEA; Pep Clb; Sci Clb; Spn Clb; Herron Schl Of Art Schlrshp 79; Univ Of Cincinnati; Archt.

ARNOLD, KIRSTEN; Whiteland HS; Franklin, IN; 4/208 Band; Cmp Fr Grls; Chrs; Chrh Wkr; Hon Rl; NHS; Sch Mus; Sch Pl; 4-H; 4-H Awd; Univ; Zoology.

ARNOLD, LARIN; Jackson HS; Jackson, MI; Cls Rep Soph Cls; Hon Rl; Lat Clb; Spn Clb; Ftbl; Trk; IM Sprt; PPFtbl; Scr Kpr; Tmr; Schlrshp From Albion Coll 79; Albion Coll; Mgmt.

ARNOLD, LORI; Mohawk HS; Tiffin, OH; Sec Soph Cls; Trs Jr Cls; Am Leg Aux Girls St; Band; Chrs; Hon Rl; NHS; Yth Flsp; Am Leg Awd; Cit Awd; Coll; Elem Ed.

ARNOLD, MATTHEW; Au Gres Sims HS; Augres, MI; Letter Bsktbl; Letter Trk; Univ; Tchr.

ARNOLD, MICQUE; Greenon HS; Enon, OH; Band; Girl Scts; Hon Rl; Sct Actv; FHA; FTA; Letter Ten; GAA; IM Sprt; Athens Ohio Univ; Home Ec.

ARNOLD, MONICA; Magnificat HS; Cleveland, OH; Chrs; Debate Tm; Pres Mod UN; Sch Mus; Sch Pl; Rptr Yrbk; Yrbk; Rptr Sch Nwsp; Drama Clb; Trk; College; Radiology.

ARNOLD, PAMELA; Field HS; Kent, OH; Cmnty Wkr; Girl Scts; Pol Wkr; Eng Clb; 4-H; Bsbl; Cit Awd; 4-H Awd; Outstndn Cnty Achvmntawd 78; Outstndng Cnty Horse Awd 78; Qtr Horse Ocngrss Sclshp 78; Akron Schl Of Prac Nursing; Nursing.

ARNOLD, REGINA; Danville HS; Danville, OH; Cls Rep Soph Cls; VP Jr Cls; Band; NHS; Stu Cncl; Yrbk; 4-H; Fr Clb; Letter Bsktbl; PPFtbl; Univ; Anatomy Tchr.

ARNOLD, RODERICK; Kettering HS; Detroit, MI; Boy Scts; Chrh Wkr; Cmnty Wkr; Hon Rl; JA; Jr NHS; NHS; Sch Mus; Sch Pl; Sct Actv; Straight A Awd; Computer Awd; Perfect Attendance Awd; 2nd In Spelling Bee; Marygrove Coll; Computer Sci.

ARNOLD, TERRY; Chadsey HS; Detroit, MI; Cls Rep Sr Cls; Pres Chrh Wkr; Girl Scts; Hon Rl; Off Ade; Sct Actv; Stu Cncl; Pep Clb; Cit Awd; Schlrshp Mercy Coll 79; Region Two Art Fair Awd 78; Mercy Coll; RN.

ARNOLD, TIMOTHY; Constantine HS; Constantine, MI; 6/105 Am Leg Boys St; Boy Scts; NHS; Sch Mus; Bsbl; Bsktbl; Ftbl; Hope Coll; Comp Sci.

ARNOLD, TRACY; Vinson HS; Huntington, WV; Chrs; Hon Rl; Hosp Ade; Off Ade; Sch Pl; Stu Cncl; Rptr Yrbk; Rptr Sch Nwsp; Eng Clb; Fr Clb; Marshall Univ; Social Work.

ARNOLD, VICKY; Upper Sandusky HS; La Rue, OH; Cls Rep Frsh Cls; Chrs; Girl Scts; Hon Rl; 4-H; 4-H Awd;.

ARNOLD, VIVIAN; Waterford HS; Waterford, OH; 4/67 Pres Frsh Cls; Pres Jr Cls; Am Leg Aux Girls St; Band; Hon Rl; Sec NHS; Sch Pl; Treas FHA; Sci Clb; Scr Kpr; Marietta Mem Hosp Schl; Radiology.

ARNOTO, RICHARD; Columbiana HS; Columbiana, OH; 6/100 VP Sr Cls; Am Leg Boys St; FCA; Hon Rl; Jr NHS; NHS; Yrbk; Spn Clb; Youngstown State Univ; Pre Med.

ARNOULD, THERESA; Lapeer West HS; Lapeer, MI; NHS; Red Cr Ade; Rptr Sch Nwsp; Fr Clb; Pep Clb; Spn Clb; Natl Merit Ltr; Univ Of Mich; Pre Med.

ARNOVITZ, JEFFREY; Warren Western Reserve; Warren, OH; 85/477 Chrh Wkr; JA; Rptr Sch Nwsp; Drama Clb; Ger Clb; JA Awd; Kent State Univ; Nurse.

ARNT, BARBARA; N Royalton HS; N Royalton, OH; Hon Rl; NHS; Sec Stu Cncl; Pep Clb; VICA; IM Sprt; Case Western Reserve Univ; Chemistry.

ARNT, KENNETH W; La Salle HS; South Bend, IN; 30/480 Hon Rl; Ind Univ; Biology.

ARONHALT, DAVID; Elk Garden HS; Elk Garden, WV; Chrs; Cmnty Wkr; Hon Rl; Sch Pl; Stu Cncl; Sprt Ed Sch Nwsp; Fr Clb; Letter Crs Cntry; Mgrs; Scr Kpr; Glenfield St Coll; Law Enforcement.

ARORA, NITA; Theodore Roosevelt HS; Kent, OH; Cls Rep Frsh Cls; VP AFS; Cmnty Wkr; Hon Rl; Hosp Ade; NHS; Off Ade; Red Cr Ade; Stu Cncl; 4-H; Kent St Univ; Med.

ARREGUIN, ANGELA; George Washington HS; E Chicago, IN; 12/269 Cls Rep Frsh Cls; Cls Rep Soph Cls; Cl Rep Jr Cls; Hon Rl; Jr NHS; NHS; Orch; Ind Univ; Airline Stewardess.

ARRENDONDO, FELICE M; Merrillville Sr HS; Merrillville, IN; Band; Girl Scts; Orch; Letter Swmmng; Kiwan Awd; Lion Awd; VFW Awd; Voice Dem Awd; Univ; Cmnctns.

ARRICK, CHRIS; Northfield HS; Wabash, IN; 3/120 FCA; JA; NHS; Stu Cncl; Spn Clb; Bsbl; Bsktbl; Ftbl; Pres Awd; College; Computer Sci.

ARRIGO, MARIE; St Joseph Acad; Cleveland, OH; Girl Scts; Hosp Ade; Orch; Sch Pl; Stg Crw; Ohio State Univ; Veterinary Med.

ARRINGTON, B; Newton HS; Newton, MS; Sec Soph Cls; Trs Soph Cls; Hon Rl; Hosp Ade; Off Ade; Stu Cncl; Letter Bsktbl; Meridian Jr College; Data Processing.

ARRINGTON, JANET; Jane Addams Voc HS; Cleveland, OH; Rptr Yrbk; Rptr Sch Nwsp; Drama Clb; VICA; Ten; Barbazoin Schl; Buyer.

ARRINGTON, RODERICK T; Oscoda Area HS; Oscoda, MI; 32/262 Boy Scts; Hon Rl; Ftbl; Wrstlng; Coach Actv; Scr Kpr; Tmr; Wolverine Boys St Amer Legion Rep 1978; Natl Achv Schol Prog 1978; Adrain Carleton Coll; Pre Med.

ARROWOOD, JACQUELI; Southwestern HS; Fenton, MI; VP Frsh Cls; Cls Rep Sr Cls; Band; Hon Rl; NHS; Off Ade; Red Cr Ade; Stu Cncl; Rptr Yrbk; Chrldng; Stud Council Leadrshp Awd 76; W Mi Acad Schlrshp 79; Acad Hon High Distinction 79; Western Michigan Univ; Chem.

ARROWSMITH, BRAD; Churubusco HS; Churubusco, IN; 37/125 Band; Hon Rl; Letter Ftbl; IM Sprt;.

ARSENAULT, JANET; Grosse Pointe South HS; Grss Pte Pk, MI; Chrs; Hon Rl; Hosp Ade; Sch Mus; Sch Pl; Drama Clb; Univ; Soc Work.

ARSIC, SINISA; Lincoln West HS; Cleveland, OH; Band; Chrs; Chrh Wkr; Hon Rl; NHS; Orch; Cit Awd; Martha Holden Jennings Awd 78; Honors Awd For Schl Serv 79; Cleveland Schlrshp Prog Awd 79; Cleveland St Univ; Comp Sci.

ARSULIC, ELLEN; Riverside HS; Painesville, OH; 13/300 VP Soph Cls; Am Leg Aux Girls St; Band; Hon Rl; Lbry Ade; Sec Stu Cncl; Fr Clb; Spn Clb; Coach Actv; Scr Kpr; Univ; Cmnctns.

ARTBAUER, MICHAEL; James Ford Rhodes HS; Cleveland, OH; 93/310 Cls Rep Frsh Cls; Cls Rep Soph Cls; Pres Stu Cncl; Yrbk; Capt Crs Cntry; Letter Trk; Kiwan Awd; Kent State Univ; Aerospace Tech.

ARTEAGA, KENNETH; Walled Lake HS; Union Lake, MI; 1/350 Cls Rep Sr Cls; Hon Rl; Jr NHS; Stu Cncl; Letter Bsbl; Letter Crs Cntry; Swmmng; Cit Awd; College; Pre Law.

ARTEBERRY, ALAN; South Spencer HS; Grandview, IN; Am Leg Boys St; Hon Rl; NHS; Yth Flsp; Bsktbl; Letter Ftbl; Swmmng; Mgrs; Scr Kpr; Western Kentucky Univ.

ARTEMIK, EDWARD; Niles Sr HS; Niles, MI; JA; Sch Pl; Drama Clb; Eng Clb; Fr Clb; Crs Cntry; Socr; Trk; Jrnlsm.

ARTER, JULIE; Crestline HS; Crestline, OH; 10/115 Sec Jr Cls; Am Leg Aux Girls St; Band; Hon Rl; Lbry Ade; VP NHS; Sch Mus; Ed Yrbk; Rptr Sch Nwsp; Sec 4-H; Ohio St Univ; Photog.

ARTERBERRIE, RHONDA Y; Central HS; Flint, MI; Band; Girl Scts; Hon Rl; Hosp Ade; Fr Clb; Univ; Comp Sci.

ARTERBURN, EVELYNN; George Washington HS; Indianapolis, IN; Am Leg Aux Girls St; Chrh Wkr; Girl Scts; Hon Rl; Off Ade; Sct Actv; Am Leg Awd; Voc Schl.

ARTH, DIANE; North Royalton HS; N Royalton, OH; Sec Soph Cls; Drl Tm; Girl Scts; Hon Rl; Hosp Ade; Off Ade; Treas Stu Cncl; Drama Clb; College.

ARTHUR, ALISON; Akron Garfield HS; Akron, OH; 34/396 Band; Chrs; Chrh Wkr; Debate Tm; Girl Scts; Hon Rl; Natl Forn Lg; NHS; Orch; Sch Pl; College; Phys Therapy.

ARTHUR, ANDREW; Jackson Co Western HS; Spring Arbor, MI; Ftbl; Michigan St Univ; Wildlife Mgmt.

ARTHUR, BRADFORD; Greenfield Ctrl HS; Greenfield, IN; Ger Clb; Letter Crs Cntry; Letter Trk; Purdue Univ; Engr.

ARTHUR, DEBRA; Calhoun HS; Creston, WV; Hon Rl; Drama Clb; Gym; College; Fashion Modeling.

ARTHUR, GREG; Paint Valley HS; Chillicothe, OH; Hon Rl; Rptr Yrbk; Univ Of Cincinnati; Pharm.

ARTHUR, GREGORY; Bath HS; Lima, OH; 8/190 Band; Boy Scts; Pres Chrs; Hon Rl; Pres NHS; Sch Mus; Sch Pl; Key Clb; Pep Clb; Spn Clb; Ohio St Univ; Acctg.

ARTHUR, KELLY; South Point HS; S Point, OH; Cls Rep Frsh Cls; VP Soph Cls; Trs Jr Cls; Trs Sr Cls; Chrh Wkr; Hon Rl; Capt Bsbl; Capt Bsktbl; Trk; Capt Chrldng;.

ARTHUR, SHELLEY; Milton HS; Ona, WV; 3/163 VP NHS; Quill & Scroll; Ed Sch Nwsp; 4-H; Pres Mth Clb; Sci Clb; Letter Chrldng; Marshall Univ; Journalism.

ARTIBEE, JANET; Carman HS; Flint, MI; Chrh Wkr; Girl Scts; Hon Rl; Sct Actv; Yth Flsp; Child Care Co Op Stud Of Yr Awd 78; Mi Christian Coll Acad Awd 79; MHEAA Grant Schlrshp 1200.

ARTMAN, J CURTIS; Jefferson Union HS; Toronto, OH; 16/150 Chrs; Hon Rl; Sch Mus; Beta Clb; Drama Clb; Letter Trk; Schl Record In 300 M Low Hurdles Set Jr & Sr Yr; Bowling Green St Univ.

ARTZNER, LORI; Euclid Sr HS; Euclid, OH; 110/725 Hon Rl; Sec OEA; JA Awd; Awd For Excllnc In Bus 76; CEA Regnl Contst 5th Pl In Shrthnd 78; Cert Of Achvmnt For Bus 76; Bus.

ARTZNER, THAIS; Sandy Valley HS; Waynesburg, OH; Hon Rl; NHS; OEA; Capt Gym; Monthly Schl Paper Honor Super Sr 1979; Sec.

ARULF, CURT; Princeton HS; Cincinnati, OH; 9/651 Band; Hon Rl; NHS; Sch Pl; Yrbk; Drama Clb; Natl Merit SF; Top Ten Student; Purdue Univ; Engr.

ARVIN, DOUG; Loogootee HS; Loogootee, IN; 29/144 Cls Rep Frsh Cls; Am Leg Boys St; Band; Chrh Wkr; Hon Rl; Stu Cncl; VP 4-H; IM Sprt; 4-H Awd; Purdue Univ; Engr.

ARVIN, STEVEN L; Loogootee Community HS; Loogootee, IN; Hon Rl; 4-H; Pep Clb; Capt Bsbl; Capt IM Sprt; College; Business Management.

ARY, DALE; Arcanum HS; Arcanum, OH; 36/99 Pres Frsh Cls; VP Soph Cls; Off Ade; Ed Sch Nwsp; Sprt Ed Sch Nwsp; Bsbl; Bsktbl; Capt Ftbl; IM Sprt; Cit Awd;.

ASCARELI, MIRIAM; West Lafayette HS; W Lafayette, IN; Sec Frsh Cls; Cls Rep Sr Cls; Debate Tm; Girl Scts; Hon Rl; Natl Forn Lg; NHS; Stu Cncl; Rptr Sch Nwsp; Ger Clb; Coll; Law.

ASCHENBRENNER, ELIZABETH; Pinckney HS; Pinckney, MI; 2/250 Sal; Band; Girl Scts; Hon Rl; Lit Mag; NHS; FBLA; Univ Of Michigan; Bus Admin.

ASH, ANNE; Big Bay De Noc HS; Fayette, MI; Band; Chrs; Hon Rl; Lbry Ade; 4-H; Bsbl; Letter Chrldng; 4-H Awd; Bay De Noc Coll; Real Estate.

ASH, DAVID; Greenhills HS; Cincinnati, OH; 1/255 Cl Rep Jr Cls; Cls Rep Sr Cls; Hon Rl; Pres JA; Mod UN; VP NHS; Quill & Scroll; Ed Sch Nwsp; Natl Merit SF; Northwestern Univ; Jrnlsm.

ASH, JENNIFER; Liberty HS; Clarksburg, WV; Chrs; Chrh Wkr; Hon Rl; Lbry Ade; Sch Pl; Fr Clb; FBLA; Bus Schl; Sec.

ASH, JUDITH; Liberty HS; Bristol, WV; Band; Hon Rl; Jr NHS; Orch; Stg Crw; 4-H; Sci Clb; Spn Clb; 4-H Awd; Farimont College; Science.

ASH, MARK; Warren G Harding HS; Warren, OH; Cls Rep Soph Cls; Cl Rep Jr Cls; Am Leg Boys St; Cmnty Wkr; Hon Rl; Jr NHS; NHS; Stu Cncl; Ftbl; Edinboro St Coll; Economics.

ASH, PETER; Interlochen Arts Academy; De Witt, IA; Band; Chrs; Hon Rl; Mdrgl; Orch; Sch Mus; Sch Pl; Guildhall Schl; Music.

ASH, STEVE; Dupont HS; Belle, WV; Am Leg Boys St; Hon Rl; Treas Jr NHS; Lat Clb; Pep Clb; Spn Clb; Bsktbl; IM Sprt; Scr Kpr; Virginia Tech Univ; Finance.

ASHANIN, MARINA; Shortridge HS; Indianapolis, IN; 2/287 Sec Frsh Cls; Girl Scts; NHS; Ed Yrbk; Fr Clb; Mth Clb; Butler Univ; Public Relations.

ASHBAUGH, JEFF; New Philadelphia HS; New Phila, OH; Band; Boy Scts; Chrs; Orch; Sct Actv; Yth Flsp; Ger Clb; Spn Clb; Trk; IM Sprt; Eagel Scout Awd 79; Culinary Inst Of Amer; Culinay Art.

ASHBROOK, BAMBI L; Revere Sr HS; Akron, OH; 40/290 Cls Rep Frsh Cls; Cls Rep Soph Cls; Cl Rep Jr Cls; VP AFS; Hon Rl; Lbry Ade; Off Ade; Sch Mus; Sch Pl; Stg Crw; Honor Thespian Awrd Drama Awrds 79; Best Female Thespian Of 79 Drama Awrds 79; N Cntrl Stdnt Evltng Team; Univ; Bus Admin.

ASHBY, KAREN; Warren Western Reserve HS; Warren, OH; 28/431 Hon Rl; Hosp Ade; JA; Jr NHS; NHS; Ed Sch Nwsp; Sch Nwsp; Ger Clb; Sec JA Awd; Voc Educ Home Ec Awd 77; Part In Proj Mars 78; Delegate To Regnl & Natl Jr Achvmnt Confrnc 78; Univ; Doctor.

ASHBY, REGINA; Washington Catholic HS; Washington, IN; Band; Chrs; Chrh Wkr; Cmnty Wkr; Hon Rl; Hosp Ade; 4-H; Ten; 4-H Awd; JC Awd; Musical Excllnc 77; Otstndng Performnc Band Awd 77; 1st Plc Poster Contest 73 76; Vincennes Univ; Nursing.

ASHBY, TERRY; Cameron HS; Cameron, WV; 11/69 Trs Soph Cls; Chrs; Mdrgl; NHS; Bell Schl Of Elec.

ASHCRAFT, LA RETA; Lincoln HS; Shinnston, WV; 160154 Cl Rep Jr Cls; Am Leg Aux Girls St; Band; Hon Rl; NHS; Sch Mus; Sec Drama Clb; VFW Awd; Fairmont St Coll; Cmnctns.

ASHCRAFT, LA RETA J; Lincoln HS; Shinnston, WV; 17/158 Am Leg Aux Girls St; Band; Hon Rl; NHS; Pol Wkr; Sch Mus; Sch Pl; Sec Drama Clb; Fairmont St Coll; Speech Commctns.

ASHCRAFT, MARGARET; New Haven HS; New Haven, MI; Band; Drm Mjrt; Girl Scts; Yrbk; Pep Clb; Spn Clb; Mic St Univ; Marine Bio.

ASHENFELTER, SHARLA; Gotebo HS; Gotebo, OK; Sec Jr Cls; Chrs; Chrh Wkr; Cmnty Wkr; Hon Rl; NHS; Sch Mus; Sch Pl; Yrbk; 4-H; S W Oklahoma State Univ.

ASHER, DONALD; Ypsilanti HS; Ypsilanti, MI; Hon Rl; Stg Crw; IM Sprt; College.

ASHER, EDWARD; St Ignatius HS; Bentleyville, OH; 98/312 Letter Hockey; Socr; IM Sprt; Univ; Aviation.

ASHLEY, ANGELA; Hudson Area HS; Hudson, MI; Trs Soph Cls; Trs Jr Cls; Trs Sr Cls; Am Leg Aux Girls St; Band; Hon Rl; Lbry Ade; NHS; Rptr Yrbk; Spn Clb; Jackson Cmnty Coll; Sec.

ASHLEY, BRUCE; St Albans HS; St Albans, WV; 8/409 VP Frsh Cls; Hon Rl; Jr NHS; NHS; Mth Clb; Spn Clb; Letter Bsbl; Coach Actv; Am Leg Awd; C of C Awd; Univ Of North Carolina; Math.

ASHLEY, DEBBIE; Franklin Cmnty HS; Franklin, IN; Hon Rl; Pres JA; Pep Clb; Bsktbl; Trk; Attend Awds 76 79; Var Vlybl; Univ; Vet.

ASHLEY, JAMES; Holly HS; Holly, MI; 1/285 Val; Boy Scts; NHS; Ftbl; Capt Trk; Central Michigan Univ.

ASHLEY, JOHN; Copley HS; Akron, OH; Am Leg Boys St; Band; Hon Rl; NHS; Crs Cntry; Trk; College.

ASHLEY, JULIA M; Meadowbrook HS; Pleasant City, OH; 5/179 Chrs; Chrh Wkr; Cmnty Wkr; Hon Rl; Lbry Ade; NHS; Off Ade; Sch Mus; Ed Sch Nwsp; 4-H; Univ Of Toledo; Physics.

ASHLEY, MICHAEL; Terre Haute South Vigo HS; Terre Haute, IN; Boy Scts; Hon Rl; Mod UN; Pol Wkr; Sct Actv; Pep Clb; Indiana Univ; Med Sci.

ASHLEY, RACHELLE; St Ursula Acad; Toledo, OH; Drl Tm; Orch; Sch Mus; Rptr Sch Nwsp; Drama Clb; Ger Clb; JA Awd; Bowling Green State College; Journal.

ASHLEY, SAUNDRA; Ripley Union Lewis HS; D, OH; Cl Rep Jr Cls; Chrs; Cmnty Wkr; Hon Rl; NHS; Stu Cncl; Rptr Yrbk; 4-H; Pep Clb; Spn Clb; College; Nursing.

ASHLOCK, IRVIN; John F Kennedy HS; Taylor, MI; Hon Rl; Rptr Sch Nwsp; Univ; Cinematography.

ASHMAN, CATHY; Franklin Central HS; Indianapolis, IN; Hosp Ade; College; Fashion Design.

ASHMAN, MICHAEL D; St Albans HS; St Albans, WV; 4/450 Am Leg Boys St; Hon Rl; Jr NHS; NHS; Fr Clb; Key Clb; Lat Clb; Wv Field Studies 79; HS History Bowl 79; Tm Part ACS Chem Test 79; Univ; Chem Engr.

ASHMAN, ROD; Jay County HS; Portland, IN; FCA; Hon Rl; Stu Cncl; Boys Clb Am; Letter Bsktbl; Letter Ftbl; Letter Trk; Univ; Coaching.

ASHMON, KATHY; Immaculate HS; Detroit, MI; Cls Rep Frsh Cls; Stu Cncl; College; Bus Admin.

ASHMORE, KATHRYN; Stockbridge HS; Stockbridge, MI; 1/126 Sec Frsh Cls; Pres Jr Cls; Pres Sr Cls; Val; Band; Chrh Wkr; Hon Rl; NHS; Off Ade; 4-H; Mi Comp Schlrshp 79; Adrian Coll; Bus Mgmt.

ASHWORTH, MELISSA; Hurricane HS; Hurricane, WV; Cls Rep Soph Cls; Trs Jr Cls; Band; Chrh Wkr; Hon Rl; Sdlty; Treas Stu Cncl; Y-Teens; 4-H; Bsktbl; West Virginia Univ; Psych.

ASKEW, ROSA; Roosevelt Sr HS; Gary, IN; Band; Chrh Wkr; Hon Rl; Lbry Ade; NHS; Pol Wkr; Cit Awd; Perf Attndnc Awd 77; Indiana Univ; Phys Ther.

ASKREN, GINA M; Lockland HS; Lockland, OH; Capt Chrldng; Clerical Offc Wrk.

ASKREN, TRACY; Attica HS; Attica, IN; 20/70 Hon Rl; Lit Mag; Spn Clb; Schslstc Hon Sweater 78; ISU; Pub Reltns.

ASMUS, FLORENCE; Ashtabula HS; Ashtabula, OH; AFS; Hon Rl; Lit Mag; NHS; Off Ade; Ger Clb; Mas Awd; Univ; Sci.

ASMUS, HEIDI; Otsego HS; Bowling Green, OH; Trs Frsh Cls; Pres Soph Cls; Trs Jr Cls; Cl Rep Jr Cls; Hosp Ade; Jr NHS; NHS; Stu Cncl; Capt Trk; Scr Kpr; Bowling Green St Univ; Acctg.

ASMUS, KARI; Eastwood HS; Pemberville, OH; 3/168 Am Leg Aux Girls St; Chrh Wkr; Hon Rl;

NHS; Rptr Sch Nwsp; Pres Fr Clb; Trk; Chrldng; Scr Kpr; College.

ASMUS, VICKI; Otsego HS; Bowling Green, OH; 1/150 Band; Chrh Wkr; Hon Rl; Jr NHS; NHS; Yth Flsp; 4-H; 4-H Awd; Bowling Green St Univ.

ASONS, IRISA; Hamilton Southeastern HS; Noblesville, IN; Sec Frsh Cls; Trs Frsh Cls; VP Soph Cls; Hst Sr Cls; Am Leg Aux Girls St; Hon Rl; NHS; Quill & Scroll; Rptr Sch Nwsp; Sch Nwsp; Natl Math Assn Awd; All Conf All Cntry Vlybl; Whos Who In Foreign Lang In Midwest; Indiana Univ.

ASPINWALL, SUSAN; A D Johnston HS; Bessemer, MI; 12/80 Cls Rep Frsh Cls; Cls Rep Soph Cls; Cl Rep Jr Cls; Cls Rep Sr Cls; Band; Chrs; Hon Rl; Gogebiz Community College; Exec Sec.

ASSENMACHER, KELLY; Northville HS; Northville, MI; Cls Rep Frsh Cls; Trs Jr Cls; Chrh Wkr; Cmnty Wkr; Hon Rl; Lbry Ade; NHS; Sch Mus; Yth Flsp; Ger Clb; Taylor Univ; Spec Ed.

ASSENMACHER, VICKI; St Mary Academy; Monroe, MI; Cmnty Wkr; Hon Rl; Hosp Ade; Letter Bsbl; Bsktbl; Coach Actv; GAA; Scr Kpr; Tmr; Univ; Dental Hygn.

ASSENMACHER, VICKI ANN; St Mary Academy; Monroe, MI; 9/130 Hon Rl; Hosp Ade; Letter Bsbl; Coach Actv; GAA; Mgrs; Tmr; Univ; Dental Hygiene.

ASTON, CHARLES; Warren G Harding HS; Warren, OH; 81/398 Boy Scts; Hon Rl; Ftbl; Oberlin Coll; Phys Ed.

ATANASOFF, MARCIA; Lansing Everett HS; Lansing, MI; NHS; Letter Ten; Cit Awd; Lansing Cmnty Coll; Flight Attendant.

ATCHESON, ATCHIE; Bexley HS; Bexley, OH; Red Cr Ade; Sct Actv; Bsktbl; Letter Socr; Coach Actv; Cit Awd; Univ; Bus.

ATCHISON, LISA; Central HS; Grand Rapids, MI; Band; Chrh Wkr; Girl Scts; Hon Rl; JA; Off Ade; Sch Mus; Yrbk; Gym; Letter Chrldng; Mic State Univ; Psych.

ATHANAS, MICHAEL; De Vilbiss HS; Toledo, OH; 21/320 Sec Jr Cls; Band; Chrs; Debate Tm; Hon Rl; NHS; Quill & Scroll; Sch Mus; Stg Crw; Yrbk; Univ Of Toledo; Psych.

ATHANAS, PETER; Thomas A Devilbiss HS; Toledo, OH; 1/310 Hon Rl; Jr NHS; NHS; Sch Nwsp; Socr; Natl Merit Ltr; Univ Of Toledo; Engr.

ATHEY, KRISTON J; Beavercreek HS; Xenia, OH; Chrh Wkr; Hon Rl; NHS; Yth Flsp; IM Sprt; Natl Merit SF; VFW Awd; Voice Dem Awd; College; Natural Science.

ATHEY, SHARON; Clay HS; S Bend, IN; 20/400 Chrs; Chrh Wkr; Treas Drl Tm; NHS; Stu Cncl; Rptr Yrbk; Fr Clb; FBLA; Letter Swmmng; Ten; Purdue Univ; Sci.

ATKINS, BRIAN J; Hayes HS; Cardiff, CA; Cmnty Wkr; Hon Rl; Pol Wkr; Stg Crw; Yrbk; Sch Nwsp; Drama Clb; Spn Clb; Letter Socr; Univ Of Ca lifornia.

ATKINS, CARLA; Garfield HS; Akron, OH; Chrh Wkr; Hon Rl; NHS; OEA; Swmmng; Chrldng; College; Legal Steno.

ATKINS, DANIEL; Mumford HS; Detroit, MI; Hon Rl; NHS; Letter Ftbl; Cit Awd; Voc Schl; Elec.

ATKINS, JACQUELYN K; Hobart HS; Hobart, IN; 12/395 AFS; Band; Hon Rl; Jr NHS; NHS; Quill & Scroll; Sch Mus; Sch Pl; Stg Crw; Rptr Sch Nwsp; Most Valu Staffer Schl Pap 1978; Most Imprvd Woowind Plyr 1977; De Pauw Honor Scholshp; De Pauw Univ; Radio.

ATKINS, JERMELL; Horace Mann HS; Gary, IN; Boy Scts; Chrs; Chrh Wkr; ROTC; Sch Mus; Sch Pl; Stg Crw; Boys Clb Am; Mgrs; Scr Kpr; Purdue Univ; Elec.

ATKINS, KEVIN J; Portage HS; Ogden Dunes, IN; 14/659 Am Leg Boys St; Band; Boy Scts; Hon Rl; Jr NHS; Lit Mag; NHS; Orch; Sch Mus; Sch Pl; Indiana Univ; Music Perfrm.

ATKINS, MARK; Sherman HS; Madison, WV; Band; Hon Rl; NHS; Ftbl; West Virginia Univ; Law.

ATKINS, MARY; Eastern HS; Beaver, OH; 20/64 Yth Flsp; Yrbk; Rptr Sch Nwsp; Ger Clb; Pep Clb; Spn Clb; Capt Bsktbl; Shawnee State Cmmnty College; Soc Te.

ATKINS, NATALIE; Poca HS; Nitro, WV; 10/153 Cls Rep Frsh Cls; Cls Rep Soph Cls; Cl Rep Jr Cls; Band; Chrs; Hon Rl; NHS; West Vir State College; Envir Engr.

ATKINS, PHYLLIS; Emerson HS; Gary, IN; Pres Jr Cls; Chrh Wkr; Hon Rl; College; Biology.

ATKINS, SARAH; Yale HS; Goodells, MI; CAP; Hon Rl; NHS; FHA; Spn Clb; IM Sprt; St Clair Cnty Cmnty Coll; Psych.

ATKINS, STEPHEN J; Maysville HS; So Zanesville, OH; VP Frsh Cls; Trs Soph Cls; FCA; Hon Rl; Stu Cncl; Key Clb; Pep Clb; Letter Bsbl; Letter Bsktbl; Letter Crs Cntry; Ohio St Univ; Elec.

ATKINS, TEIGHA; Princeton HS; Princeton, WV; Cl Rep Jr Cls; Hon Rl; Jr NHS; Stu Cncl; Pep Clb; Chrldng; East Tennessee St Univ; Psych.

ATKINSON, AMY; Dover HS; Dover, OH; Chrs; Pres FBLA; Trk; Kent State; Bus.

ATKINSON, J; Williamston HS; Williamston, MI; Swmmng; GMI; Engr Tech.

ATKINSON, JAMIE; Chelsea HS; Chelsea, MI; 39/210 Cls Rep Frsh Cls; Cls Rep Soph Cls; Cl Rep Jr Cls; Cls Rep Sr Cls; Band; Hon Rl; Off Ade; Quill & Scroll; Yrbk; Ed Sch Nwsp; Michigan St Univ; Jrnlsm.

ATKINSON, JOHN; Forest Hills Northern HS; Grand Rapids, MI; 25/150 FCA; Hon Rl; Bsbl; Ftbl; Hockey; Wrstlng; Albion Coll; Comp Sci.

ATKINSON, JUDY; Sissonville Sr HS; Charleston, WV; Girl Scts; Hon Rl; Jr NHS; Off Ade; Y-Teens; Rptr Yrbk; 4-H; Fr Clb; Pep Clb; Chrldng; College.

ATKINSON, KENNETH; Adlai Stevenson HS; Sterling Hgts, MI; Band; Chrh Wkr; Crs Cntry; Trk; Cert Of Recognitn St Schlrshp Prog Acad Achvmnt 79; Cert For Otstndng Schlstc Achvmnt From St Rep 79; Macomb Cnty Cmnty Coll; Lib Arts.

ATKINSON, LINDA; Ferndale HS; Oak Park, MI; 26/383 Band; Drm Mjrt; Natl Forn Lg; NHS; Orch; Quill & Scroll; Rptr Sch Nwsp; Sch Nwsp; Ger Clb; Voice Dem Awd; Oakland Univ; Eng.

ATKINSON, LISA; S Charleston HS; S Charleston, WV; Sec Frsh Cls; Trs Frsh Cls; Band; Girl Scts; Hon Rl; Rptr Sch Nwsp; FBLA; Spn Clb; Socr; College.

ATKINSON, REGINA; Griffith HS; Griffith, IN; Cls Rep Soph Cls; Cl Rep Jr Cls; Hon Rl; Jr NHS; Stu Cncl; Pep Clb; Coll; Soc Work.

ATKINSON, STEVE; Struthers HS; Struthers, OH; 75/278 Chrs; Hon Rl; Pres JA; PAVAS; Sch Pl; Rptr Yrbk; Drama Clb; Thespian Soc Pres; Cultural Arts PTA Reg Competition; Pittsburgh Art Inst; Art.

ATKINSON, TIM; Sault Area HS; Slt Ste Marie, MI; 3/325 Pres Frsh Cls; VP Jr Cls; Pres Band; Drm Mjrt; Hon Rl; NHS; Bsktbl; Ten; IM Sprt; College.

ATOR, C; R Nelson Snider HS; Ft Wayne, IN; 191/564 Band; Chrh Wkr; Hosp Ade; Yth Flsp; Fr Clb; Ten; Mgrs; College; Soc Work.

ATTARD, MARK; Bishop Borgess HS; Livonia, MI; Cls Rep Frsh Cls; Hon Rl; Jr NHS; NHS; Hockey; IM Sprt; Scr Kpr; Univ; Law.

ATWELL, MELISSA K; Monrovia Jr Sr HS; Monrovia, IN; 22/109 Cls Rep Sr Cls; Band; Chrh Wkr; Drl Tm; Hon Rl; Orch; Stu Cncl; 4-H; Pep Clb; Rdo Clb; Indiana St Univ; Busns.

ATWOOD, SHEILA; Emerson HS; Gary, IN; Sal; Band; Chrh Wkr; Cmnty Wkr; Hon Rl; Pres NHS; FHA; Spn Clb; Chrldng; Purdue Univ, Industrial Engr.

AUBE, HOWARD; Alpena HS; Alpena, MI; NHS; FFA; Ten; Wrstlng; Case Western Reserve Univ; Dent.

AUBE, NANCY; Alpena HS; Spruce, MI; Chrs; Chrh Wkr; Hon Rl; Ferris St Coll; Med Tech.

AUBRY, PATRICK S; St Francis De Sales HS; Toledo, OH; Hon Rl; JA; Sch Mus; Stg Crw; Rptr Sch Nwsp; Fr Clb; IM Sprt; Mgrs; Scr Kpr; JA Awd; Univ Of Toledo; Acctg.

AUCHARD, GREG; Malabar HS; Mansfield, OH; Band; Hon Rl; Stg Crw; Ftbl; Voc Schl; Airline Transport.

AUCREMANNE, JULIA; Notre Dame HS; Clarksburg, WV; 13/52 Cl Rep Jr Cls; NHS; Stg Crw; Sprt Ed Sch Nwsp; Drama Clb; 4-H; Fr Clb; Letter Bsbl; Letter Bsktbl; Letter Ftbl; Auburn Univ; Wildlife Mgmt.

AUDIA, KAREN; St Francis Central HS; Star City, WV; 29/68 Hon Rl; Stg Crw; Drama Clb; Pep Clb; Spn Clb; IM Sprt; Mgrs; Scr Kpr; Cit Awd; W Virginia Univ; Busns.

AUER, JAMES; St Ignatius HS; Bay Village, OH; 67/308 VP Frsh Cls; Cmnty Wkr; Hon Rl; Stu Cncl; Ftbl; IM Sprt; Notre Dame; Bus.

AUFDENAMO, CHERIE; Elmwood HS; Bloomdale, OH; Band; Chrh Wkr; Hon Rl; Yth Flsp; Pres 4-H; Pep Clb; Sci Clb; Mat Maids; College; Veterinary Asst.

AUFDENCAMP, CHERIE; Elmwood HS; Bloomdale, OH; Band; Sec Chrh Wkr; Hon Rl; Yth Flsp; Pres 4-H; Pep Clb; Sci Clb; Mat Maids; 4-H Awd; Ohio State; Vet Asst.

AUFDENKAMP, DIANE; Bowling Green Sr HS; Custar, OH; 24/322 Am Leg Aux Girls St; Chrh Wkr; Hon Rl; Jr NHS; NHS; Toledo Hospital Sch Of Nursing; RN.

AUGENSTEIN, TERESA; Marietta Sr HS; Marietta, OH; AFS; Chrh Wkr; Capt Drm Bgl; Girl Scts; NHS; Sch Pl; Sct Actv; Pres Yth Flsp; Drama Clb; Spn Clb; Univ; Bus.

AUGER, STEPHEN; Avondale HS; Auburn Heights, MI; Cl Rep Jr Cls; Rptr Yrbk; Rptr Sch Nwsp; Sch Nwsp; Boys Clb Am; Bsktbl; Capt Ftbl; Northern Mich; Architecture.

AUGSBURGER, JOAN; Cory Rawson HS; Bluffton, OH; VP Jr Cls; Band; Chrs; Sec Chrh Wkr; Drm Mjrt; Hon Rl; Sch Mus; Sch Pl; Pep Clb; Mat Maids; Hancock Cnty Strutting Champ 77; Tchr Of Baton Corp; Univ; Sec.

AUGSBURGER, JOHN; Bluffton HS; Beaverdam, OH; Hon Rl; Sch Nwsp; Letter Bsbl; Letter Ftbl; Ohio St Univ; Bus Admin.

AUGUSTA, JAMES; Gilmour Academy; South Euclid, OH; Sec Jr Cls; Awd For Outstndng Achvmnt In Spanish II 77; Awd For Outstndng Achvmnt Eng III 78; Bus Mgmt.

AUGUSTEIN, TAWNEE; Sebring Mc Kinley HS; Sebring, OH; 12/96 Band; Hon Rl; Off Ade; Rptr Yrbk; Yrbk; Treas FHA; Lat Clb; Bsktbl; Trk; Malone College; Busns Admin.

AUGUSTINE, ANNA; Geneva HS; Geneva, OH; 4/246 Cls Rep Frsh Cls; Cls Rep Soph Cls; Cl Rep Jr Cls; Band; NHS; Orch; Scr Kpr; Cleveland St Univ; Health.

AUGUSTINE, JEFF; Cory Rawson HS; Rawson, OH; 10/64 VP Frsh Cls; VP Sr Cls; Boy Scts; Chrs; NHS; Sch Pl; Stu Cncl; Yth Flsp; Yrbk; 4-H; Nashville Auto Diesel Coll; Ag Mech.

AUGUSTINE, JUDITH; Trenton HS; Trenton, MI; Band; Chrh Wkr; Hon Rl; Off Ade; Stg Crw; Ger Clb; Mat Maids; Univ; Med.

AUGUSTINE, SHERRY; South Range HS; North Lima, OH; 2/135 Sec AFS; Letter Band; Hon Rl; Sec NHS; Off Ade; Treas 4-H; Ger Clb; Trk; Univ; Nursing.

AUGUSTINIS, BRENDA; Cedar Lake Academy; Kalamazoo, MI; 3/80 Cls Rep Frsh Cls; VP Soph Cls; Cls Rep Sr Cls; Band; Chrs; Chrh Wkr; Hon Rl; Mdrgl; NHS; Rptr Sch Nwsp; Andrews Univ; Dentl Hygiene.

AUGUSTITUS, MARY; Utica HS; Utica, MI; 76/380 Hon Rl; Bsbl; Bsktbl;.

AUGUSTUS, CARLA; Sandusky HS; Sandusky, OH; 40/375 Cls Rep Frsh Cls; Cls Rep Soph Cls; Cl Rep Jr Cls; Band; Hst Frsh Cls; Drm Bgl; Girl Scts; Trs Frsh Cls; JA; Awd Miss Acad Awd 78; Natl Jr Achvrs Confrnc 79; Fred Waring Music Wrokshp Schslhp 79; Ohio St Univ.

AUKERMAN, BRUCE; North Vermillion HS; Newport, IN; FCA; Eng Clb; 4-H; Ftbl; Wrstlng; Coach Actv; Purdue Vet Schl; Vet.

AUKERMAN, ROBIN; Eaton HS; Eaton, OH; 13/175 Sec Soph Cls; Band; Hon Rl; Jr NHS; Off Ade; Orch; Yth Flsp; 4-H; Spn Clb; GAA; College; Med Tech.

AULL, JACKIE; Pike Central HS; Petersburg, IN; 45/192 Cls Rep Soph Cls; Cl Rep Jr Cls; Cls Rep Sr Cls; Hon Rl; NHS; Sch Pl; Yth Flsp; Rptr Sch Nwsp; Drama Clb; Pep Clb; Fashion Mdse.

AULT, AMBER; Marion Harding HS; Marion, OH; AFS; Band; Chrh Wkr; JA; Lit Mag; Orch; Sch Pl; Y-Teens; Rptr Sch Nwsp; Treas Drama Clb; Exchange Student To Lund Sweden ASSE; Jr Cnslr At Camp Mowana Lutheran Camp In Mansfield; College; Theatre.

AULT, BOBBI; Switz City Central HS; Lyons, IN; Cls Rep Frsh Cls; VP Soph Cls; Band; Drm Mjrt; Hon Rl; Orch; Stu Cncl; 4-H; Pep Clb; Letter Bsbl; Greene Cnty All St Tm Vlybl 77; Best Spikar 78; Indiana St Univ.

AULT, DON; Brooke HS; Wellsburg, WV; 65/403 Hon Rl; Quill & Scroll; Rptr Sch Nwsp; 4-H; Ger Clb; Letter Swmmng; IM Sprt; Univ; Sports Med.

AULT, WILLIAM; Rossford HS; Perrysburg, OH; 17/162 Pres Sr Cls; Cls Rep Sr Cls; Aud/Vis; Band; Hon Rl; NHS; Off Ade; Stu Cncl; Letter Bsktbl; Letter Crs Cntry; Winner Greatr Toledo Cncl Of Tchrs In Math; Superior Rating In St Band Cntst; Excel Rating In St Band; Bowling Green St Univ; CPA.

AUNE, KEVEN; Danville HS; Glenmont, OH; Carpenter.

AURAND, BRIAN; Jackson HS; Massillon, OH; 10/400 Hon Rl; NHS; Ger Clb; Natl Merit Ltr; College; Bus Admin.

AURAND, CYNTHIA; Saline HS; Saline, MI; VP Sr Cls; Chrs; Hon Rl; NHS; Off Ade; Yth Flsp; FHA; Sci Clb; Ten; Trk; Western Michigan Univ; Engr.

AUSENHEIMER, ANN; Bucyrus HS; Bucyrus, OH; Band; Chrh Wkr; Girl Scts; Hon Rl; NHS; Pres Yth Flsp; Rptr Sch Nwsp; Drama Clb; FTA; Pep Clb; Univ; Bus Admin.

AUST, LISA; Pike Central HS; Stendal, IN; Sec Soph Cls; Hon Rl; NHS; Off Ade; 4-H; FHA; Pep Clb; Sci Clb; Capt Chrldng; 4-H Awd; Evansville Univ; RN.

AUST, MARY; Ben Davis HS; Indianapolis, IN; FCA; Girl Scts; Off Ade; Quill & Scroll; Rptr Sch Nwsp; Beta Clb; Fr Clb; Glf; Swmmng; Trk; Arizona St Univ; Acctg.

AUSTERBERRY, MARY; Grosse Pointe South HS; Grosse Pte Pk, MI; 21/562 Hon Rl; NHS; Ger Clb; Swmmng; Letter Trk; PPFtbl; St Olaf Coll.

AUSTERMAN, ROBERT; William Mason HS; Mason, OH; Hon Rl; ROTC; Bsbl; Bsktbl; Socr; Ten; Trk; Bsktbl Letters & Participation Awd; Bsktbl Participation In Australia; Rugby & Soccer; Cincinnati Tech Coll; Hotel Mgmt.

AUSTIN, BETH; Brown Cnty HS; Nashville, IN; 6/209 Cls Rep Frsh Cls; Cls Rep Soph Cls; Band; Chrh Wkr; Hon Rl; JA; Lbry Ade; Stu Cncl; Yth Flsp; Beta Clb; Univ.

AUSTIN, BRADLEY; Cloverdale HS; Cloverdale, IN; Hon Rl; 4-H; 4-H Awd; Ivy Tech; Auto Body Repair.

AUSTIN, CRAIG; Southeast HS; Deerfield, OH; 3/196 Hon Rl; NHS; Sci Clb; Univ; Sci.

AUSTIN, DEANNA; Genoa Area HS; Genoa, OH; Sec Frsh Cls; Sec Soph Cls; Sec Jr Cls; Sec Sr Cls; Hon Rl; Off Ade; Yrbk; Gym; Chrldng; Owens Tech Coll; Aviation.

AUSTIN, DEDRIE; Whitehall HS; Twin Lake, MI; Hon Rl; Trk; Muskegon Bus College; Legal Sec.

AUSTIN, KAREN; Brown County HS; Nashville, IN; 5/149 Cmnty Wkr; Hon Rl; NHS; 4-H; Fr Clb; Pep Clb; 4-H Awd; Indiana Univ; Bus.

AUSTIN, KERRY; Warrensville Hts HS; Warrensville, OH; Aud/Vis; Hon Rl; Stg Crw; Letter Ftbl; Letter Trk; IM Sprt; Cit Awd; Univ Of Cincinnati; Chemical Eng.

AUSTIN, LAURIE; Central HS; Evansville, IN; 43/540 Cl Rep Jr Cls; Drl Tm; Hon Rl; Hosp Ade; Pres JA; Sec NHS; Pres Stu Cncl; Treas Civ Clb; Sec Lat Clb; Mgrs; Dist Lt Governr For Jr Civitan 78; Mbr Of Evansville Mayors Youth Councl 79; Univ; RN.

AUSTIN, MARY; Southgate HS; Southgate, MI; Val; Chrh Wkr; Hon Rl; NHS; Yth Flsp; Rptr Yrbk; Natl Merit SF; Michigan Tech Univ; Elec Engr.

AUSTIN, PATRICIA; Flushing HS; Flushing, MI; 14/523 Boy Scts; Cmnty Wkr; Girl Scts; Hon Rl; JA; NHS; Spn Clb; Bsktbl; Letter Trk; JA Awd; Lake Superior St Coll; Bio Sci.

AUSTIN, SANDRA; Carson City Crystal HS; Carson City, MI; 7/131 Cls Rep Frsh Cls; Chrh Wkr; Cmnty Wkr; Girl Scts; Hon Rl; NHS; Stu Cncl; 4-H; FHA; Mgrs; Ferris State College; Med.

AUSTIN, SCOTT; Corunna HS; Owosso, MI; Boy Scts; NHS; Letter Bsbl; Letter Bsktbl; Letter Ftbl; Coach Actv; Natl Merit Ltr; Michigan Tech Univ; Mech Engr.

AUSTIN, SUSAN; New Richmond HS; New Richmond, OH; Band; Orch; Fr Clb; Sci Clb; Bsktbl; Ohio St Univ; Vet.

AUSTIN, SUZANNE; Walled Lake Central HS; W Bloomfield, MI; Cl Rep Jr Cls; Chrs; Cmnty Wkr; Hon Rl; PAVAS; Sch Mus; Stu Cncl; Chrldng; Natl Merit Ltr; Oakland Univ; Lib Arts.

AUSTIN, TAWANA; Baldwin HS; Baldwin, MI; 10/67 Chrh Wkr; Hon Rl; Lbry Ade; NHS; Off Ade; Stu Cncl; Yrbk; Bsktbl; Capt Chrldng; Tmr; Western Michigan Univ; Data Proc.

AUTEN, LAURIE; Goodrich HS; Goodrich, MI; 22/140 Hon Rl; NHS; Off Ade; Yrbk; FFA; Bsktbl; Trk; Chrldng; IM Sprt; Mgrs; Central Michigan Univ; Social Work.

AUTRY, J ERIC; Southeast HS; Diamond, OH; Boy Scts; Hon Rl; Stu Cncl; Letter Bsbl; Letter Bsktbl; Coach Actv; Hot Stove Bsbl 70 79; West Virginia Univ; Bus Admin.

AUTUELINK, KURT; Calvin Christian HS; Grand Rapids, MI; Chrs; 4-H; Socr; IM Sprt; Univ; Math.

AUVENSHINE, JEFFREY; Mason Sr HS; Mason, MI; Cls Rep Frsh Cls; Chrs; Chrh Wkr; Hon Rl; Jr NHS; NHS; Sch Mus; 4-H; Letter Bsbl; IM Sprt; Bowlng League Pres 3 Yrs & Sprtsmnshp Awrd 76 79; St Finalst In All Amer Youth Bowling Tournmnt; Michigan St Univ; Dent.

AUVENSHINE, RHONDA; Holt HS; Lansing, MI; 85/360 Chrh Wkr; Off Ade; Fr Clb; Crldng; Univ; Soc Work.

AUVIL, ALTON; Sandy Valley HS; East Sparta, OH; 7/175 NHS; Rptr Yrbk; Letter Ftbl; Ten; Trk; Wrstlng; Ohio St Univ; Engr.

AUVIL, DAVID; Winfield HS; Scott Depot, WV; 16/133 Am Leg Boys St; Chrs; Hon Rl; VP Yth Flsp; Pep Clb; Letter Chrldng; Masonic Schlrshp; Soc Dstngshd Amer HS Stu; Mbr St AA Best Cheerleading Squad; Voted Most Talented Sr Cls; Marshall Univ; Business.

AUVINEH, STUART; North Central HS; Indianapolis, IN; 88/1065 Hon Rl; NHS; Sci Clb; Natl Merit Ltr; College.

AVASON, ANTHONY; East Detroit HS; East Detroit, MI; Hon Rl; Basic Grant; St Of Michigan Schlrshp; Detroit Coll Of Busns Schlrshp; Detroit Coll; CPA.

AVEDISIAN, PAUL; Southfield Christian HS; Southfield, MI; Cls Rep Frsh Cls; Band; Chrs; Hon Rl; Orch; Sch Pl; Stu Cncl; Cit Awd; DAR Awd; Univ Of Michigan; Earth Sci.

AVERESCH, MARLENE; Kalida HS; Kalida, OH; Am Leg Aux Girls St; Band; NHS; Sch Mus; Pres 4-H; FHA; 4-H Awd; Miami Univ; Psych.

AVERSA, NANCY; Richmond HS; Richmond, IN; 5/690 Cls Rep Frsh Cls; Cls Rep Soph Cls; Cl Rep Jr Cls; Cls Rep Sr Cls; Chrs; Chrh Wkr; Hon Rl; NHS; Stu Cncl; Y-Teens; Coll; Teaching.

AVERY, ALAN MATTHEW; Hagerstown Jr Sr HS; Greens Fork, IN; 7/172 Pres Frsh Cls; Boy Scts; VP NHS; Pres Sci Clb; Letter Ftbl; Letter Trk; Capt Wrstlng; Am Leg Awd; Cit Awd; Natl Merit SF; U S Coast Grd Acad; Ofcr Coast Grd.

AVERY, CARLA; Sault Area HS; Sault Ste Marie, MI; Hon Rl; 4-H; FFA; IM Sprt; 4-H Awd; Lake Superior St Coll; Comp Engr.

AVERY, GARY; Peck HS; Peck, MI; 11/50 Band; Boy Scts; Hon Rl; Bsbl; Bsktbl; Trk; IM Sprt; Scr Kpr; St Clair County Comm Coll; Elec.

AVERY, JEFFERY; Shortridge HS; Indianapolis, IN; 50/400 Voc Schl; Auto Design.

AVERY, JUDY; Mio Au Sable HS; Mio, MI; Trs Frsh Cls; Sec Soph Cls; Band; Chrs; Girl Scts; Hon Rl; NHS; Sch Mus; Sch Pl; Stg Crw; Outstndng Underclassmen Honor Awd Band; Chosen To Represent Soph Class In Homecoming; Univ; Spec Educ Tchr.

AVERY, LANCE N; Anderson HS; Anderson, IN; Am Leg Boys St; Band; Chrs; Drm Bgl; Drm Mjrt; Hon Rl; Orch; Sch Mus; Sch Pl; Stg Crw; Final Four For The Breedcove Ctznshp Awd Hoosier Boys St 79; Spanish Hnr Soc 77; Pres Of Drama Club 79; Air Force Academy; Comp Sci.

AVERY, LAURIE; Carroll HS; Bringhurst, IN; Girl Scts; Hon Rl; Sch Nwsp; 4-H; FHA; Spn Clb; Intl Bus Schl; Sec.

AVERY, MARSHA; Caro HS; Caro, MI; Girl Scts; Hon Rl; NHS; 4-H; Crs Cntry; Letter Trk; GAA; IM Sprt; 4-H Awd; Central Michigan Univ; Law.

AVERY, MERRILL; Baldwin Cmnty School; Baldwin, MI; Pres Jr Cls; Cmp Fr Grls; Girl Scts; Hon Rl; Off Ade; Stu Cncl; Ed Yrbk; 4-H; Letter Bsktbl; Univ.

AVERY, MERRILL; Baldwin Cmnty HS; Baldiwn, MI; Cls Rep Frsh Cls; Pres Jr Cls; VP Sr Cls; Girl Scts; Hon Rl; NHS; Stu Cncl; Ed Yrbk; Bsbl; Bsktbl; Ferris St Univ; CPA.

AVERY, ROBERT S; Parkside HS; Jackson, MI; Chrh Wkr; Orch; Ger Clb; IM Sprt; Western Michigan Univ; Acctg.

AVERY, STEVE; Marquette HS; Marquette, MI; Am Leg Boys St; Letter Ten; Mas Awd; College.

AVERY, TIMOTHY; Cedar Springs HS; Cedar Springs, MI; FCA; Bsktbl; Ftbl; Trk; Coach Actv; Rotary Awd; Cntrl Michigan Univ.

AVIS, MARCIA; Cedar Springs HS; Cedar Spgs, MI; Cl Rep Jr Cls; Pres Sr Cls; Cls Rep Sr Cls; Band; Chrh Wkr; Cmnty Wkr; Girl Scts; Hon Rl; Jr NHS; Off Ade; Central Michigan Univ; Chem.

AVIS, TODD; Valley Forge HS; Parma Hts, OH; 300/700 Cls Rep Soph Cls; Cl Rep Jr Cls; Chrh Wkr;

Cmnty Wkr; Red Cr Ade; Pres Stu Cncl; Y-Teens; Fr Clb; Muny Hockey League Best Defenseman Awd; Arizona State Univ; Bsns Admin.

AVONA, ELIZABETH; Bellbrook HS; Dayton, OH; Cls Rep Sr Cls; Band; Debate Tm; Hon Rl; NHS; Stu Cncl; Sprt Ed Yrbk; Rptr Yrbk; Yrbk; Rptr Sch Nwsp; Univ; Pre Med.

AVRADOPOULOS, VALARIE; Whetstone HS; Columbus, OH; Cmp Fr Grls; Chrs; Chrh Wkr; Girl Scts; Hon Rl; Jr NHS; NHS; Stu Cncl; Pres Yth Flsp; Sch Nwsp; Univ; Lang.

AWALD, JULIE; Oregon Davis HS; Walkerton, IN; 8/65 Pres Frsh Cls; Band; FCA; Hon Rl; 4-H; Letter Bsktbl; Letter Trk; Univ.

AWWILLER, DAWN; Fredericktown HS; Fredericktown, OH; 18/113 Am Leg Aux Girls St; Drl Tm; NHS; Treas Stu Cncl; Yrbk; Sec 4-H; VP Pep Clb; Ohi Dominican College; Bio Research.

AXE, TIM; St Francis De Sales HS; Toledo, OH; Hon Rl; Letter Wrstlng; IM Sprt; Natl Latin Hnr Soc 79; Univ; Physician.

AXELBERG, JOHN T; La Ville HS; Lakeville, IN; Pres Jr Cls; Val; Am Leg Boys St; Yth Flsp; Fr Clb; Sci Clb; IM Sprt; Am Leg Awd; Cit Awd; Natl Merit Schl; Sci Awd; Hoosier Scholar; Rector Scholar From De Pauw Univ; De Pauw Univ.

AXLEY, SALLY A; Ashland HS; Ashland, OH; VP Soph Cls; Cl Rep Jr Cls; VP Sr Cls; Am Leg Aux Girls St; Chrs; Cmnty Wkr; Hon Rl; Pol Wkr; Sch Mus; Stu Cncl; Ohio St Univ; Bio.

AXMAN, KATHLEEN S; Benzie Central HS; Beulah, MI; Band; Cmp Fr Grls; Girl Scts; Hon Rl; Lbry Ade; Sct Actv; 4-H; Chrldng; Pom Pon; Michigan St Univ; Journalism.

AXSOM, TIMOTHY; Edgewood HS; Bloomington, IN; 72/209.

AXTELL, JOHN; West Lafayette HS; W Lafayette, IN; Chrh Wkr; FCA; Hon Rl; Letter Ftbl; Glf; Mist Improvd Plyer Awd In Golf 78; Mentl Attitude Awd In Golf 79; Dan Cowger Awd In Glf 79; Purdue Univ; Engr.

AYDENT, LORI; Lake Catholic HS; Chardon, OH; 144/326 Band; Hon Rl; JA; Off Ade; Sch Mus; Sch Pl; Stg Crw; Yrbk; Mat Maids; PPFtbl; CPR Red Crss Cert 78; Thespian Soc 78; 2 Bnd Ribbons 78 & 79; Univ; Phys Ther.

AYERS, AVIS; Ripley HS; Ripley, WV; 17/259 Cls Rep Sr Cls; Chrs; Chrh Wkr; Cmnty Wkr; Hon Rl; Jr NHS; Natl Forn Lg; NHS; Off Ade; Quill & Scroll; Marshall Univ; Psych.

AYERS, CHRIS; Moorefield HS; Moorefield, WV; Am Leg Boys St; Hon Rl; Jr NHS; NHS; Sch Pl; Bsbl; Capt Bsktbl; Trk; Coach Actv; Cornell Univ Smmr Ssn 79; Univ; Math.

AYERS, CYNTHIA; Riverdale HS; Forest, OH; Chrs; PAVAS; Sch Mus; Sch Pl; Stg Crw; Drama Clb; 4-H; FHA; FTA; Scr Kpr;.

AYERS, REGINA; Holly Sr HS; Holly, MI; 20/293 Band; Hon Rl; NHS; Chrldng; Univ Of MI Regnts Almn Schlrshp Nominee 79; Whos Who In Musci 79; Univ Of Michigan; Pre Med.

AYERSMAN, KARLA J; University HS; Morgantown, WV; 22/146 Cl Rep Jr Cls; Hon Rl; Stu Cncl; Ger Clb; Letter Bsktbl; Trk; Chrldng; Coach Actv; GAA; IM Sprt; Univ; Phys Educ Tchr.

AYLSWORTH, KRISTINE; St Johns HS; St Johns, MI; 14/298 Chrs; Hon Rl; Jr NHS; Sch Pl; Stg Crw; Yth Flsp; Drama Clb; 4-H; Michigan St Univ; Nursing.

AYLSWORTH, LORI; Holy Rosary HS; Flint, MI; 3/57 Hon Rl; NHS; Rptr Yrbk; 4-H; 4-H Awd; Univ; Optmtst.

AYOOB, PERRY; Roosevelt Wilson HS; Clarksburg, WV; 9/122 Pres Frsh Cls; Am Leg Boys St; Band; Chrh Wkr; Hon Rl; NHS; Off Ade; Sch Pl; Pres Stu Cncl; Ed Yrbk; West Virginia Univ; Pharmacy.

AYOTTE, TOY; Douglas Mac Arthur HS; Saginaw, MI; 34/250 Hon Rl; NHS; Pep Clb; Delta Cmnty Coll; Dent Hygnst.

AYRES, CARRIE; Carroll HS; Bringhurst, IN; 1/139 Cl Rep Jr Cls; VP Sr Cls; Band; Hon Rl; NHS; Pres 4-H; Pres Spn Clb; Letter Swmmng;.

AYRES, DEBRA; Mississinewa HS; Marion, IN; Hon Rl; Jr NHS; Rptr Sch Nwsp; 4-H; Fr Clb; PPFtbl; 4-H Awd; Ball St Univ; Med Tech.

AYRES, STACY; Heritage Hills HS; Chrisney, IN; 1/211 FCA; Hon Rl; NHS; Stu Cncl; Pep Clb; Chrldng; Scr Kpr; Opt Clb Awd; Univ; Math.

AYSCUE, JUDY; Amelia HS; Cincinnati, OH; 57/280 Fr Clb; IM Sprt; Thomas More College; Nursing.

AZBELL, JANICE; William V Fisher Cath HS; Lancaster, OH; Sec Jr Cls; Hon Rl; Bsbl; Bsktbl; Letter Ten; Letter Chrldng; GAA; Ohio Univ.

AZBELL, PAULA; Westfall HS; Williamsport, OH; 1/141 Cls Rep Frsh Cls; Cls Rep Soph Cls; Cl Rep Jr Cls; VP Sr Cls; Am Leg Aux Girls St; Band; Girl Scts; Hon Rl; Jr NHS; NHS; Stdnts Active For Educ 77 78; Pickaway Cnty Fair Bd 78 79; Farm Bureau Camp Schlrshp 77; Univ Of Kentucky; Agronomy.

AZCONA, EDWARD S; Calumet HS; Gary, IN; 21/350 Hon Rl; JA; FSA; Sci Clb; Spn Clb; Univ; Vet.

AZER, AUDREY; St Peters HS; Mansfield, OH; Cmnty Wkr; Hon Rl; JA; NHS; Red Cr Ade; Sch Pl; Stg Crw; Stu Cncl; Rptr Yrbk; Civ Clb; Univ.

AZZANO, LAWRENCE; St Francis HS; Williamsburg, MI; 24/148 Band; Boy Scts; Debate Tm; Hon Rl; Sch Pl; Sct Actv; Stg Crw; IM Sprt; Scr Kpr; Tmr; Tech Schl; Mech Engr.

AZZOPARDI, JOHN; Fraser HS; Roseville, MI; 45/600 Hon Rl; NHS; Capt Ftbl; Adrian Coll; Acctg.

B

BAAB, CINDY; Garaway HS; Stonecreek, OH; Cls Rep Soph Cls; Trs Jr Cls; Trs Sr Cls; Am Leg Aux Girls St; Band; Chrs; Chrh Wkr; Cmnty Wkr; Hon Rl; Off Ade; Coll; X Ray Tech.

BAADE, BETH; Martinsville HS; Martinsville, IN; 81/490 Chrs; Hon Rl; Drama Clb; VP Lat Clb; Pep Clb; Gym; Tmr; Ind State Univ; Acctg.

BAAR, DAVID; Grand Rapids Christian HS; Holland, MI; Chrs; Chrh Wkr; Mdrgl; Sch Mus; Sch Pl; Yth Flsp; Hope Coll; Religion.

BAAR, SCOTT; West Ottawa HS; Holland, MI; Boy Scts; Sct Actv; Ftbl; Michigan Tech Univ; Engr.

BAAR, SHERYL; Hudsonville Public HS; Hudsonville, MI; 1/169 Sec Frsh Cls; Sec Soph Cls; Pres Jr Cls; Val; Chrs; Chrh Wkr; Mdrgl; Hope College; Music.

BABB, BRIAN; Springfield HS; Springfield, MI; Cl Rep Jr Cls; Stu Cncl; Bsktbl; Ftbl; Sports Writer.

BABB, LISA; Westfield Washington HS; Westfield, IN; Band; Hon Rl; NHS; Off Ade; Pep Clb; Spn Clb;.

BABCOCK, ANNE; Rocky River HS; Rocky River, OH; 3/310 VP Frsh Cls; VP Soph Cls; Am Leg Aux Girls St; Hon Rl; Hosp Ade; NHS; Sch Mus; Treas Stu Cncl; Mount Holycoke College.

BABCOCK, BRENDA; Anderson HS; Cincinnati, OH; 100/413 Chrs; Chrh Wkr; Yth Flsp; 4-H; Trk; Var Chrs; Tennessee Temple Univ; Bus.

BABCOCK, HOPE; John Glenn HS; Zanesville, OH; Hon Rl; NHS; 4-H; FHA; 4-H Awd;.

BABCOCK, JACQUELINE; Port Clinton HS; Pt Clinton, OH; Band; Chrh Wkr; GAA;.

BABCOCK, JANET K; John Glenn HS; New Concord, OH; 5/193 Chrh Wkr; Hon Rl; NHS; Off Ade; Stu Cncl; Pres 4-H; Spn Clb; Chrldng; 4-H Awd; Pres Awd; Bus Schl.

BABCOCK, JEFF; Port Clinton Sr HS; Port Clinton, OH; 12/269 Chrh Wkr; Hon Rl; NHS; Y-Teens; Fr Clb; Lat Clb; Crs Cntry; Wrstlng; Coach Actv; Hiram Coll; Zoology.

BABCOCK, PATRICK; Bishop Borgess HS; Dearborn Hts, MI; NHS; IM Sprt; Univ; Elec Engr.

BABCOCK, REGINA; Napoleon HS; Mc Clure, OH; Cls Rep Soph Cls; Cl Rep Jr Cls; Am Leg Aux Girls St; Chrs; Girl Scts; Hon Rl; Lbry Ade; Sch Mus; Sch Pl; Stg Crw; Bio St Schlrshp Team Honorable Mention; Ohio St Univ; Psych.

BABCOCK, SUSAN; Jackson County Western HS; Jackson, MI; Key Clb; Capt Crs Cntry; Letter Trk; Tmr; Western Michigan Univ; Bus Admin.

BABCOCK, TRESA; North Central HS; Pioneer, OH; Sec Chrs; Hon Rl; Hosp Ade; Lbry Ade; Sch Mus; Sch Pl; Rptr Yrbk; FTA; Pep Clb; Spn Clb; Toledo Univ; Eng Tchr.

BABER, DAWN; Northfield Jr Sr HS; Wabash, IN; Band; Drl Tm; FCA; Hon Rl; Quill & Scroll; Sch Pl; Stg Crw; Rptr Yrbk; Sch Nwsp; Drama Clb; Univ; Art.

BABICKA, GREGORY P; Andrean HS; Crown Point, IN; 105/253 Bsbl; Capt Hockey; IM Sprt; Univ.

BABILLA, TERRY; Andrean HS; Merrillville, IN; 50/275 Trs Frsh Cls; Hon Rl; Bsktbl; Letter Ftbl; Letter Glf; College; Law.

BABINEC, VENERINA; Ursuline HS; Lowellville, OH; Chrs; Hon Rl; Sch Mus; Yrbk; IM Sprt; Youngstown State Univ; Psych.

BABIUCH, TERESA A; Rogers HS; Toledo, OH; 15/450 Chrs; Hon Rl; Natl Forn Lg; Treas NHS; VP Y-Teens; FHA; Cit Awd; Univ Of Toledo; Nursing.

BAC, MICHELE; Morton HS; Hammond, IN; 39/399 Cls Rep Frsh Cls; Cls Rep Soph Cls; Sec Jr Cls; Stu Cncl; Yrbk; Mat Maids; Pom Pon; PPFtbl; Ind Univ; Business.

BACAK, ALICE; Port Clinton HS; La Carne, OH; Chrs; Hon Rl; College; Science.

BACCHI, JOE; Euclid HS; Euclid, OH; 180/704 Boy Scts; Hon Rl; Pol Wkr; Stg Crw; Bsbl; Letter Swmmng; IM Sprt; Tmr; Character Effort Citizenship Awd; Pres Phys Fitness Awd; Univ Of Toledo; Chem Engr.

BACEHOWSKI, KENNETH; West Catholic HS; Grand Rapids, MI; Band; Hon Rl; College; Psychology.

BACH, JAMES; Menominee HS; Wa Lace, MI; 1/260 Hon Rl; Jr NHS; NHS; Am Leg Awd; Natl Merit Ltr; Mich Tech Univ; Electrical Engr.

BACH, JULIA M; Immaculata HS; Detroit, MI; 3/96 Cmnty Wkr; Hon Rl; Lbry Ade; NHS; Off Ade; PAVAS; Pol Wkr; Sch Mus; Sch Pl; Ed Sch Nwsp; Michigan State Univ; Vet Med.

BACH, KAREN; Douglas Macarthur HS; Saginaw, MI; 29/300 Hon Rl; NHS; Lat Clb; Pep Clb; Ten; College; Bus Admin.

BACHANOV, ARLENE; Jared W Finney Sr HS; Detroit, MI; Chrh Wkr; Girl Scts; Treas NHS; Off Ade; Sct Actv; Rptr Sch Nwsp; Sch Nwsp; Glf; Assoc Ed Of On Target A City Stdnt Newsppr 77; Univ; Clinical Microbio.

BACHMAN, CARRIE; Annapolis HS; Dearborn Hgts, MI; 24/392 Cls Rep Frsh Cls; Cls Rep Soph Cls; Chrs; Cmnty Wkr; Girl Scts; Hon Rl; Sch Mus; Sch Pl; Sprt Ed Sch Nwsp; Rptr Sch Nwsp; Michigan St Univ; Journalism.

BACHMAN, G; Gaylord HS; Gaylord, MI; Cls Rep Frsh Cls; Cls Rep Soph Cls; Chrs; CAP; Debate Tm; Hon Rl; Pol Wkr; Sch Mus; Northern Mic Univ; Psych.

BACHMAN, GREGG; Bloom Carroll HS; Carroll, OH; Chrh Wkr; NHS; Yth Flsp; Treas FFA; Michigan St Univ; Horticulture.

BACHMAN, M; Rensselaer Central HS; Rensselaer, IN; Hon Rl; FFA; Iv Tech; Tool Die Mach.

BACHMAN, MARK; Rensselaer Ctrl HS; Rensselaer, IN; FFA; Top Soils Judge; 2nd Pl Natl Soil Tm; Ivy Tech Schl.

BACHMANN, KRIS; Floyd Central HS; New Albany, IN; 5/365 Band; Boy Scts; Hon Rl; Mod UN; Orch; Sch Mus; Sct Actv; Ger Clb; Purdue Univ; Engr.

BACHTEL, MARTHA; Canfield HS; Canfield, OH; 5/258 Chrs; Hon Rl; Jr NHS; NHS; Sch Mus; Sch Pl; Y-Teens; Drama Clb; Fr Clb; Chrldng; Univ; Public Rel.

BACIAK, SUSAN; James Ford Rhodes HS; Cleveland, OH; Cls Rep Soph Cls; Cl Rep Jr Cls; Capt Drl Tm; Hon Rl; NHS; Stu Cncl; Fr Clb; University; Soc Work.

BACK, KIM; William Henry Harrison HS; Cleves, OH; Hon Rl; Univ Of Cincinnati; Comp Prog.

BACK, STEVEN F; Highland HS; Wadsworth, OH; 54/240 Aud/Vis; Chrh Wkr; Cmnty Wkr; Hon Rl; Lbry Ade; 4-H; Pres Key Clb; IM Sprt; 4-H Awd; Univ Of Nevada; Mech Engr.

BACKER, ROBYN; Glen Este HS; Cincinnati, OH; Band; Cmp Fr Grls; Chrh Wkr; Drl Tm; Girl Scts; Hon Rl; Orch; Fr Clb; Trk; Pom Pon; Univ Of Cincinnati; Nursing.

BACKRATH, MARYBETH; Carroll HS; Dayton, OH; 23/285 VP Sr Cls; Drl Tm; Hon Rl; NHS; Stu Cncl; Boys Clb Am; Drama Clb; Pep Clb; Rus Clb; College.

BACKS, BRENDA; Marion HS; Marion, IN; Band; Chrs; Chrh Wkr; Drm Bgl; Hon Rl; Mod UN; NHS; Orch; Civ Clb; Pep Clb; Univ.

BACKUS, JACQUELINE; Berrien Springs HS; Berrien Spgs, MI; Hon Rl; NHS; 4-H; Ger Clb; Bsktbl; Trk; Coach Actv; 4-H Awd; Pres Awd; Mbr Of Vlybl & Bsktbl All Confernece Team; Mbr Of All Conference 880 Yd Relay Team; College; Industrial Design.

BACKUS, WENDALL; Salem HS; Salem, IN; Pres Frsh Cls; Pres Soph Cls; Pres Jr Cls; Pres Sr Cls; Lat Clb; Pep Clb; Mgrs;.

BACON, DEBBIE; Rockville HS; Rockville, IN; 12/93 Hon Rl; NHS; Yth Flsp; Yrbk; 4-H; Pep Clb; Letter Bsktbl; Trk; 4-H Awd; Vlybl Lettered 1 Yr 78; Bus Schl; Med Sec.

BACON, DOUGLAS; H H Dow HS; Midland, MI; Chrs; Hon Rl; Mod UN; Orch; Yth Flsp; Boys Clb Am; Letter Swmmng; Scr Kpr; Tmr; Trinity Univ; Elec Engr.

BACON, KAY; Northrop HS; Ft Wayne, IN; 39/500 Drl Tm; Hon Rl; JA; Rptr Sch Nwsp; OEA; JA Awd; Indiana Univ; Pre Law.

BACON, MOLLY; Chelsea HS; Gregory, MI; 19/225 Cls Rep Frsh Cls; Band; Chrs; Cmnty Wkr; Debate Tm; Girl Scts; Hon Rl; Hosp Ade; Lbry Ade; NHS; Univ; Comp Sci.

BACON, MOLLY A; Chelsea HS; Gregory, MI; Cls Rep Frsh Cls; Band; Chrs; Cmnty Wkr; Girl Scts; Hon Rl; Lbry Ade; NHS; Orch; Sch Mus; College; Comp Tech.

BACON, RONALD; Rockville HS; Rockville, IN; 8/85 Chrh Wkr; Hon Rl; NHS; Sci Clb; Glf; Trk; Letter Mgrs; Chess Club; Purdue Univ; Chem Engr.

BACON, SHARON; Science Hill HS; Johnson City, TN; Cls Rep Sr Cls; Band; Hon Rl; JA; Sch Nwsp; Beta Clb; Lat Clb; Pep Clb; JA Awd; E Texas St Univ; Comp Sci.

BADEN, BRENDA; Napoleon HS; Napoleon, OH; Band; Chrs; Chrh Wkr; Orch; Red Cr Ade; Sch Mus; Stg Crw; Lat Clb; Swmmng; Coll; Med Tech.

BADENHOP, SUSAN; Napoleon HS; Defiance, OH; 5/255 Hon Rl; NHS; Pres 4-H; Pres Fr Clb; Bsktbl; Trk; 4-H Awd; Defiance College; Bus Admin.

BADER, GEOFFREY; Haslett HS; Haslett, MI; Aud/Vis; Band; Debate Tm; Hon Rl; NHS; Orch; Natl Merit Ltr; College; Psych.

BADGER, F; Redford HS; Detroit, MI; Central Mic Univ; Drafting.

BADGETT, CAROL; Coldwater HS; Coldwater, OH; Band; Chrs; Yrbk; Ger Clb; Univ.

BADGLEY, MARY; Stephen T Badin HS; Hamilton, OH; Chrh Wkr; Cmnty Wkr; Hon Rl; Fr Clb; OEA; Tmr; Miami Univ; Bus.

BADGLEY, SAMUEL; Williamstown HS; Williamstown, WV; 6/110 Cls Rep Frsh Cls; Cls Rep Soph Cls; VP Jr Cls; Am Leg Boys St; Hon Rl; Stu Cncl; Bsktbl; Am Leg Awd; Lion Awd; Univ; Bus Admin.

BADILLO, FRANCISCO; Lorain Southview HS; Lorain, OH; Pres Sr Cls; Am Leg Boys St; Hon Rl; Ed Sch Nwsp; Sch Nwsp; Letter Trk; Bausch & Lomb Awd; Pres Awd; Univ; Jrnlsm.

BADOUR, JACQUELYN; Bullock Creek HS; Midland, MI; 5/150 Trs Sr Cls; Hon Rl; Hosp Ade; Jr NHS; NHS; Sch Pl; Stu Cncl; Pep Clb; GAA; Elk Awd; Bd Of Trustees Schlrshp For Delta Cmnty Coll; Delta Univ; Bus Admin.

BADRAN, CINDY; Ellet HS; Akron, OH; 33/364 Band; Sec Chrs; Hon Rl; Mdrgl; NHS; Sch Mus; Sch Pl; Akron Univ; Music.

BADRAN, CINDY; Ellet Sr HS; Akron, OH; 36/300 Band; Sec Chrs; Hon Rl; Mdrgl; NHS; Sch Mus; Sch Pl; Drama Clb; Akron Univ; Music Educ.

BADURINA, THERESE; Wehrle HS; Columbus, OH; 10/117 Sec Frsh Cls; Hon Rl; Rptr Yrbk; Sch Nwsp; Fr Clb; Lat Clb; GAA; Ohio St Univ; Pharmacy.

BADY, SHELTON; Buena Vista HS; Saginaw, MI; 7/187 VP Soph Cls; Cl Rep Jr Cls; VP Sr Cls; Chrs; Chrh Wkr; Hon Rl; NHS; Off Ade; Stu Cncl; Sci Clb; Outstndg Nws Carrier Awd; Wayne St Univ; Bus Admin.

BAECHLE, MARY; Aiken Sr HS; Cincinnati, OH; 5/576 Cls Rep Soph Cls; Chrh Wkr; Girl Scts; Hon Rl; Hosp Ade; NHS; Sct Actv; FTA; Pep Clb; Sec Spn Clb; Mt St Joseph Coll; R N.

BAEHL, CHERIE; North Posey HS; Poseyville, IN; Band; Chrh Wkr; Cmnty Wkr; FCA; Hosp Ade; Natl Forn Lg; Off Ade; Sch Mus; Sch Pl; Stg Crw; Ind State Univ; Interior Design.

BAEHL, LINDA; Mater Dei HS; Haubstadt, IN; 14/179 Chrs; Chrh Wkr; Cmnty Wkr; Hon Rl; NHS; Sch Mus; Pres 4-H; Pep Clb; Coach Actv; 4-H Awd; Deaconess Schl; Nursing.

BAEHR, BARBARA; Lake Ridge Academy; Lorain, OH; Cls Rep Frsh Cls; Chrs; Debate Tm; Hon Rl; Stg Crw; Yrbk; Sch Nwsp; Drama Clb; Fr Clb; Coll.

BAEHR, JOSEPH S; Logan Elm HS; Circleville, OH; 2/180 Sal; FCA; Hon Rl; NHS; Sch Pl; Stu Cncl; 4-H; Key Clb; Crs Cntry; Glf; College; Engr.

BAER, JACQUELINE; Regina HS; Lyndhurst, OH; Cls Rep Soph Cls; Sec Jr Cls; Hon Rl; Jr NHS; PAVAS; Sch Pl; Stu Cncl; GAA; Latin Excellence Awd; Envir Study Awd; Granted Fellowship At Case Wstrn Reserve Univ; College; Medicine.

BAER, KIMBERLY; Clarance M Kimball HS; Royal Oak, MI; Band; Chrh Wkr; JA; NHS; Sch Pl; U Of Mich; Med.

BAER, MARLENE; Springfield Local HS; Poland, OH; Cls Rep Frsh Cls; Trs Jr Cls; Band; Chrs; Chrh Wkr; Hon Rl; Lbry Ade; Yth Flsp; Pep Clb; Spn Clb; Malone Univ; Acctg.

BAER, MARY; Carroll HS; Dayton, OH; 123/285 Cls Rep Frsh Cls; Cls Rep Soph Cls; Cl Rep Jr Cls; Band; Drl Tm; Girl Scts; Stu Cncl; 4-H; Sec Spn Clb; Chrldng; Wendys All St Drill Team 79; Peace Corps Partnshp Progr Sec 78; Ski Club 78; Univ; Bus Admin.

BAER, RON; Edison HS; Norwalk, OH; Band; Boy Scts; Chrh Wkr; Hon Rl; Jr NHS; Sct Actv; Mth Clb; Sci Clb; Ohio Tests Fo Schlstc Achvmnt 1978; State Band Comp 1976; Terra Tech Coll; Math.

BAER, RONALD; Edison HS; Norwalk, OH; Band; Boy Scts; Chrh Wkr; Hon Rl; Sct Actv; Stg Crw; Mth Clb; Sci Clb; Univ; Elec Engr.

BAER, TIMOTHY; Lawrenceburg HS; Lawrenceburg, IN; Band; Boy Scts; Chrh Wkr; Hon Rl; JA; Lat Clb; Tri State Univ; Drafting.

BAERENWALD, PAUL; Cambridge HS; Cambridge, OH; 10/250 Cls Rep Frsh Cls; Cls Rep Soph Cls; Cl Rep Jr Cls; Hon Rl; NHS; Key Clb; Ftbl; Letter Ten; Letter Mgrs; College; Comp Sci.

BAER JR, RICHARD; Paint Valley HS; Bainbridge, OH; Letter Bsbl; Bsktbl; Letter Ftbl; Univ.

BAERMAN, CHRIS; Gull Lake HS; Galesburg, MI; 55/250 Cls Rep Frsh Cls; Hon Rl; Sci Clb; Letter Bsktbl; Crs Cntry; Letter Ftbl; Trk; Coach Actv; Natl Merit Ltr; Purdue Univ; E E.

BAERVELDT, LINDA; Scottsburg Sr HS; Scottsburg, IN; 9/200 Am Leg Aux Girls St; Band; Drl Tm; Girl Scts; Hon Rl; NHS; Sch Pl; Stg Crw; Drama Clb; Pres 4-H; Univ; Theatre.

BAFF, KAREN; Beachwood HS; Beachwood, OH; Girl Scts; Lit Mag; Sch Pl; Stg Crw; Spn Clb; Bsbl; Bsktbl; Trk; Scr Kpr; Univ.

BAFFER, DEBORAH; Riverside HS; Painesville, OH; 25/345 Hon Rl; Stu Cncl; Spn Clb; Bsktbl; Letter Swmmng; Letter Trk; College.

BAGAL, UJJVALA A; Centerville HS; Centerville, OH; Chrs; Hosp Ade; Stg Crw; Rptr Sch Nwsp; NCTE; Natl Merit SF; Entry Natl Anthlgy Of HS Ptry 1978; Hon Mntan In Oh Achvmnt Tst For Eng 1979; Univ; Pre Med.

BAGENT, SHARON LEE; Licking Valley HS; Newark, OH; 4/125 VP Sr Cls; Hon Rl; NHS; Stu Cncl; Yth Flsp; Y-Teens; Key Clb; Pep Clb; Mat Maids; Scr Kpr; Ohio St Univ; Pharmacy.

BAGGETT, JULIE; Garfield HS; Hamilton, OH; 4/300 Band; Chrs; Hon Rl; NHS; Sch Mus; Sch Pl; Spn Clb; Univ Of Cin.

BAGGETT, JULIE L; Garfield Sr HS; Hamilton, OH; 4/360 Band; Chrs; Hon Rl; Hosp Ade; Jr NHS; NHS; Sch Mus; Sch Pl; Spn Clb; Ten; Univ Of Cincinnati; Speech Therapy.

BAGINSKY, GRACE; Caro Community HS; Caro, MI; Aud/Vis; Chrs; Chrh Wkr; Cmnty Wkr; Hon Rl; Lbry Ade; NHS; Sch Mus; Sch Pl; Stg Crw; Mercy Coll Of Detroit; Liberal Arts.

BAGLEY, SHERLENE; Buchtel HS; Akron, OH; Trs Jr Cls; Pres Sr Cls; Chrh Wkr; Cmnty Wkr; Lbry Ade; Off Ade; VICA; GAA; Tmr; Patricia Stevens Car Coll; Fashion.

BAGWELL, HARRY; Coventry Sr HS; Akron, OH; Stark Tech Coll; Electronics.

BAHAS, KAREN; Cuyahoga Vly Christian Acad; Akron, OH; Chrs; Hon Rl; Hosp Ade; Sch Pl; Stg Crw; Drama Clb; Letter Trk; Univ; Med.

BAHENSKY, SUSAN; Lumen Cordium HS; Bedford, OH; Cls Rep Soph Cls; Hon Rl; Stg Crw; Stu Cncl; Bsbl; Bsktbl; Coach Actv; GAA; IM Sprt; Merit Awd Hnr Roll 79; Serv Awd Serv Other Than In Schl 79; Univ.

BAHLER, LISA J; Marlington HS; Louisville, OH; Chrs; Hon Rl; Off Ade; OEA; Scr Kpr;.

BAHNER, RICHARD S; Fairmont West HS; Kettering, OH; Boy Scts; Cmnty Wkr; FCA; Hon Rl; Sct Actv; Stu Cncl; Mth Clb; Sci Clb; Bsktbl; Crs Cntry; Univ; Med.

BAHORSKI, MARK; New Haven HS; Mt Clemens, MI; 5/100 Boy Scts; Hon Rl; NHS; Trk; IM Sprt; College.

BAHR, KATHRYN; Northrop HS; Ft Wayne, IN; Hon Rl; Rptr Yrbk; Sch Nwsp; Trk; Ind Univ; English.

BAHR, SUE; Onekama Consolidated HS; Manistee, MI; 1/70 Cls Rep Frsh Cls; Cls Rep Soph Cls; Sec Jr Cls; Trs Sr Cls; Val; Hon Rl; Lbry Ade; Ferris State College; A A S Acgt.

BAHRAMIS, GEORGE; Roosevelt HS; E Chicago, IN; 53/725 Cls Rep Frsh Cls; Cls Rep Soph Cls; Cl Rep Jr Cls; Stu Cncl; Sch Nwsp; Spn Clb; VICA; Ftbl; College; Industrial Arts.

BAIC, NICKOLA; Traverse City HS; Traverse City, MI; 17/800 Cls Rep Soph Cls; Trs Jr Cls; Cls Rep Sr Cls; Hon Rl; NHS; Stu Cncl; Pep Clb; Crs Cntry; Letter Trk; Natl Merit Ltr; Mich Tech Univ; Engr.

BAIFORE, LOUIS S; Reynoldsburg HS; Reynoldsburg, OH; 1/400 Pres Soph Cls; Hon Rl; Pres NHS; Ed Yrbk; 4-H; Socr; 4-H Awd; Univ.

BAIL, KELLY; Martinsburg HS; Martinsburg, WV; 12/214 Sec Soph Cls; Sec Jr Cls; Sec Sr Cls; Am Leg Aux Girls St; VP Band; Chrh Wkr; Hon Rl; NHS; Sch Mus; Sch Pl; Fairmont St Coll; Sci.

BAILEY, ANDREA; Cedarville HS; Yellow Spgs, OH; Hon Rl; VP Lbry Ade; NHS; Sch Pl; Rptr Sch Nwsp; Drama Clb; Treas Fr Clb; Pres Sci Clb; Acad C 77 78 & 79; Oh Schsltc Achvmnt Awd 77; NEDT Awd 78; Univ; Theatre Arts.

BAILEY, BEVERLEY; George Washington HS; Indianapolis, IN; Cls Rep Frsh Cls; Cl Rep Jr Cls; Chrh Wkr; Hon Rl; Yth Flsp; Bsktbl; GAA; Mgrs; Scr Kpr; Tmr; Univ; Eng.

BAILEY, BEVERLY; Withrow HS; Cincinnati, OH; Chrh Wkr; Hon Rl; Jr NHS; NHS; Yth Flsp; College.

BAILEY, BONNIE; Carmcl HS; Inidanapolis, IN, 48/721 Spanish Awd 2nd Yr 79; Indiana Univ; Bus.

BAILEY, BRET; Edwardsburg HS; Edwardsburg, MI; Univ Of Mic; Architect.

BAILEY, BRIAN D; Eastern HS; Pekin, IN; Band; Chrh Wkr; Hon Rl; NHS; 4-H; Letter Bsbl; Bsktbl; DAR Awd; Univ Of Evansville; Elec Engr.

BAILEY, CINDY; Loudonville HS; Loudonville, OH; 12/138 Hon Rl; Sch Pl; Yth Flsp; Rptr Sch Nwsp; Drama Clb; FHA; Scr Kpr; Univ; Bus Admin.

BAILEY, COLLETTA; West Side HS; Gary, IN; 26/650 Band; Chrs; Hon Rl; Jr NHS; NHS; Pol Wkr; Sch Mus; Y-Teens; Ind Univ Northwest; Acctg.

BAILEY, DANIEL; Watkins Memorial HS; Pataskala, OH; 2/202 Sal; Hon Rl; Lbry Ade; NHS; Wrstlng; Univ Of Cincinnati; Elec Engr.

BAILEY, DARREL; Greenville Sr HS; Greenville, OH; 41/398 Band; Hon Rl; NHS; Sch Mus; Ohio Northern Univ; Mech Engr.

BAILEY, DAVID; Princeton HS; Princeton, WV; 29/312 Hon Rl; Jr NHS; NHS; Pol Wkr; Quill & Scroll; Stg Crw; Rptr Sch Nwsp; 4-H; Key Clb; Sci Clb; Prfct Attndnce Of All 3 Yrs In HS 79; Copy Edtr Of Schl Nesppr Tiger Tribune 79; Bluefield Coll; Engr.

BAILEY, DEANNA; Lynchburg Clay HS; Lynchburg, OH; Band; Chrh Wkr; FCA; Hon Rl; Sch Pl; 4-H; Pep Clb; Bsktbl; Morehead State Univ; Phys Ed.

BAILEY, ELIZABETH; Watkins Memorial HS; Pataskala, OH; 19/202 Chrh Wkr; Cmnty Wkr; Hon Rl; Lit Mag; Yth Flsp; Sch Nwsp; Fr Clb; FHA; Swmmng; IM Sprt; Mt Carmel Schl; Nursing.

BAILEY, GALEN; Elmhurst HS; Ft Wayne, IN; 85/341 Pres Frsh Cls; Cls Rep Sr Cls; Band; Boy Scts; Hon Rl; JA; PAVAS; Quill & Scroll; Sch Mus; Rptr Yrbk; Indiana Univ.

BAILEY, GREGORY L; Montcalm HS; Rock, WV; Am Leg Boys St; Band; Chrs; Chrh Wkr; Cmnty Wkr; Hon Rl; Pol Wkr; Yth Flsp; Y-Teens; 4-H; West Virginia Univ; Engr.

BAILEY, HEATHER J; Bethel HS; Tipp City, OH; Trs Soph Cls; AFS; Cmp Fr Grls; Drl Tm; Hon Rl; Lit Mag; Rptr Yrbk; Rptr Sch Nwsp; FSA; Spn Clb; Wash Wkshp Semnr 79; Lamp Of Lrng Awd 79; Univ.

BAILEY, J; Lewis Cnty HS; Linn, WV; Chrs; Hon Rl; NHS; 4-H; Coll; Math.

BAILEY, JACOB; Northfork HS; Mc Dowell, WV; Hon Rl; Rptr Yrbk; 4-H; Fr Clb; FBLA; Key Clb; Bsktbl; Ftbl; Trk; Mgrs; 3 Letters For Athletic Acitivities 76 77 & 78; Perfect Attendance; Univ.

BAILEY, JAMES; West Side HS; Gary, IN; Cls Rep Frsh Cls; Cls Rep Soph Cls; Boy Scts; Chrs; Chrh Wkr; Hon Rl; PAVAS; Quill & Scroll; Stu Cncl; Yth Flsp; Indiana St Univ; Medicine.

BAILEY, JENNIFER; Iaeger HS; Panther, WV; VP Soph Cls; Pres Jr Cls; Hon Rl; NHS; Sec Stu Cncl; Sec Fr Clb; IM Sprt; Flag Corps 78; Sci Fair Ribbons 77 & 79; FMLA 78; West Virginia Univ; Pharm.

BAILEY, JOHN; Harper Creek HS; Battle Creek, MI; Chrh Wkr; Hon Rl; Key Clb; Letter Bsbl; Letter Bsktbl; Letter Ftbl; Brigham Young Univ; Bio.

BAILEY, JOHN; Adrian HS; Adrian, MI; Cls Rep Sr Cls; Hon Rl; Stu Cncl; Lat Clb; Bsbl; Bsktbl; Ftbl; IM Sprt; Rotary Awd; Michigan St Univ; Law.

BAILEY, JOHN; Mooresville HS; Mooresville, IN; Boy Scts; Chrh Wkr; Sct Actv; Yth Flsp; Ger Clb; God Cntry Awd; Kiwan Awd; Pres Awd; Voc Schl.

BAILEY, KARIN; Rochester Community HS; Rochester, IN; Hosp Ade; Sct Actv; FHA; Pep Clb; International Bus; Cpa.

BAILEY, KELLI; Green HS; N Canton, OH; Band; Chrs; Cmnty Wkr; Girl Scts; Yrbk; Univ; Phys Ther.

BAILEY, KENNETH; Gudwin Heisnts HS; Wyoming, MI; Band; Hon Rl; NHS; College; Comp Sci.

BAILEY, KEVIN; St Johns HS; Dewitt, MI; College; Carpenter.

BAILEY, KIM; Bellmont HS; Decatur, IN; Hosp Ade; DECA; California Coll; Imprt & Exprt Agent.

BAILEY, KIMBERLY S; Guyan Valley HS; Branchland, WV; Sch Pl; Rptr Yrbk; Rptr Sch Nwsp; Sci Clb; Mbr Gifted & Talented Progr 1977; Softbl Lincoln Cnty Yth Assoc 1978; Marshall Univ; Poli Sci.

BAILEY, LONNIE; Bloomfield HS; Bloomfield, IN; 12/85 Cl Rep Jr Cls; Band; Chrs; Hon Rl; NHS; Sch Mus; Sch Pl; Stu Cncl; Drama Clb; Spn Clb; Vincinnes; Bio.

BAILEY, LYNN; Morristown HS; Morristown, IN; 11/78 VP Frsh Cls; Pres Jr Cls; Am Leg Aux Girls St; Band; Chrs; Chrh Wkr; FCA; Girl Scts; Hon Rl; Stu Cncl; Indiana State Univ; Physical Ed.

BAILEY, MARCIA; Harrison Cmmty HS; Harrison, MI; Chrh Wkr; Hon Rl; Sch Pl; Stg Crw; Drama Clb; Trk; Central Michigan Univ; X Ray Tech.

BAILEY, MARK; Wirt Cnty HS; Elizabeth, WV; Cmnty Wkr; Hon Rl; NHS; Sch Pl; 4-H; FBLA; Letter Bsbl; Letter Ftbl; Coach Actv; 4-H Awd; West Virginia Univ; Elec Engr.

BAILEY, MARY; Cousino Sr HS; Warren, MI; Hon Rl; Pol Wkr; PPFtbl; Oakland Univ; Comp Prog.

BAILEY, MICHAEL; Marlette HS; Marlette, MI; 2/140 VP Sr Cls; Band; Hon Rl; VP NHS; Sch Nwsp; Pep Clb; Letter Crs Cntry; Alma College; Fine Arts.

BAILEY, OWEN; Mason Sr HS; Mason, MI; Cls Rep Frsh Cls; Hon Rl; Jr NHS; Ftbl; Pres Awd; Air Force; Airline Pilot.

BAILEY, PATRICK H; Poca HS; Poca, WV; Cls Rep Frsh Cls; Cls Rep Soph Cls; Pres Jr Cls; Am Leg Boys St; Aud/Vis; Band; Boy Scts; Chrh Wkr; Cmnty Wkr; Drm Mjrt; Outstanding 4 H Jr Leader Of Putnam Cnty 76 79; Army Awd At St Sci Fair 77; 1st Pl Drum Major 79; Univ Of Kentucky; Educ.

BAILEY, PHIL; Jay County HS; Portland, IN; 86/450 Cls Rep Frsh Cls; Cls Rep Soph Cls; Trs Jr Cls; Cl Rep Jr Cls; Cls Rep Sr Cls; Hon Rl; Jr NHS; NHS; VP Stu Cncl; Boys Clb Am; IVY Tech Schl; Carpentry.

BAILEY, REBECCA; Bergland Community School; Bergland, MI; VP Frsh Cls; Sec Soph Cls; Pres Jr Cls; Am Leg Aux Girls St; Band; Hon Rl; Sch Pl; Stu Cncl; 4-H; OEA; Univ; Bus Admin.

BAILEY, RHONDA; Allen East HS; Lima, OH; Cls Rep Soph Cls; Band; Chrs; Chrh Wkr; Hon Rl; Sch Pl; Sprt Ed Yrbk; Rptr Sch Nwsp; 4-H; FHA; College.

BAILEY, ROBERT; South Charleston HS; S Charleston, WV; Am Leg Boys St; Chrh Wkr; Hon Rl; NHS; Rdo Clb; Spn Clb; Natl Math Fld Day Wv Team 79; Spanish Natl Hon Soc 78; Cntrl Regnl Sci & Engr Fair 79; West Virginia Inst Of Tech; Elec Eng.

BAILEY, SANDY; Austintown Fitch HS; Youngstown, OH; 48/700 Cls Rep Frsh Cls; Cls Rep Soph Cls; Cmp Fr Grls; Hon Rl; Off Ade; Stu Cncl; Rptr Sch Nwsp; Sch Nwsp; Chrldng; PPFtbl; Certfct & Ribbon Chrledng 1977; Nom For Natl Honor Soc 1978; Letter Chrldng 1978; Kent St Univ; Speech Pathlgst.

BAILEY, SHARON S; Lewis County HS; Weston, WV; Band; Hon Rl; Stg Crw; Y-Teens; Pres 4-H; Trk; 4-H Awd; Mas Awd;.

BAILEY, STEVEN R; St Albans HS; St Albans, WV; Am Leg Boys St; Hon Rl; Jr NHS; NHS; Letter Bsbl; Letter Bsktbl; Letter Ftbl; Letter Trk; College; Comp Sci.

BAILEY, SUE; Southern Hills Joint HS; Sardinia, OH; 1/60 Val; Band; Girl Scts; Hon Rl; Sch Mus; Rptr Sch Nwsp; 4-H; Lat Clb; VICA; Bsbl; College; Elec Engr.

BAILEY, SUSAN; Upper Sandusky HS; Forest, OH; 67/225 Chrs; Hon Rl; Sch Pl; Drama Clb; Spn Clb; Letter Bsktbl; Gym; Trk; JC Awd; Sftbl 2 Lttr Vrsty 77 78 & 79; Vllybl Lttr Vrsty 78; Got An Awd For Making 1st Tm All NOL 78; Ohio St Univ; Phys Educ.

BAILEY, SUSAN; Poca HS; Poca, WV; 6/146 Cls Rep Frsh Cls; Cls Rep Soph Cls; Band; Girl Scts; Hon Rl; NHS; Off Ade; 4-H; Trk; Am Leg Awd; West Virginia St Univ; Nuclear Med.

BAILEY, TIMOTHY; John Glenn HS; Westland, MI; Hon Rl; Eastern Michigan Univ; Comp Sci.

BAILEY, TIMOTHY; Northeastern HS; Richmond, IN; Sec Soph Cls; Cls Rep Sr Cls; Pres Band; Hon Rl; NHS; Stu Cncl; Letter Bsktbl; Letter Ftbl; Ball St Univ; Architecture.

BAILEY, TOD A; Newton HS; Troy, OH; Cls Rep Sr Cls; Am Leg Boys St; VP Chrh Wkr; Hon Rl; Lbry Ade; Sct Actv; Stu Cncl; Bsbl; Bsktbl; Voc Schl; Mech.

BAILEY, TOM; Goshen HS; Goshen, IN; 1/246 Pres Soph Cls; Pres Jr Cls; Band; Boy Scts; Pres Chrs; Hon Rl; NHS; Stu Cncl; Yth Flsp; Sci Clb; Phil Eskew Award; Highest Schl Score Natl Math Test; Discus Throw Rec; Univ; Mech Engr.

BAILEY, TRINA; Clarkston Sr HS; Clarkston, MI; Band; Chrh Wkr; Hon Rl; Orch; Fr Clb; Michigan St Univ; Comp Sci.

BAILEY, VINCENT; Lutheran East HS; Cleveland, OH; FCA; MMM; Sch Mus; Sch Pl; Sct Actv; Stg Crw; Sch Nwsp; Drama Clb; FSA; Trk; UCLA; Comp Engr.

BAILHE, MARYANNE; Marian HS; Birmingham, MI; VP Frsh Cls; Cls Rep Soph Cls; Cl Rep Jr Cls; Hon Rl; Mod UN; Natl Forn Lg; NHS; College; Bus.

BAILOR, BRUCE; Fairfield Union HS; Pleasantville, OH; 3/158 Pres Soph Cls; Pres Jr Cls; Hon Rl; Pres Jr NHS; Stu Cncl; VP Yth Flsp; Treas FFA;.

BAIN, DONALD; Fairview HS; Fairview Pk, OH; Band; Boy Scts; Orch; Sch Pl; Sct Actv; Stg Crw; Ftbl; Trk; IM Sprt; Mgrs; Bowling Green Univ; Bus.

BAIN, JACKIE; Dunbar HS; Dunbar, WV; Trs Jr Cls; VP Sr Cls; Hon Rl; Jr NHS; NHS; VP FBLA; Pep Clb; Letter Crs Cntry; Letter Trk; Letter Chrldng; Wv State College; Bus.

BAIN, JANET; Farmington HS; Farmington, MI; Hon Rl; Pep Clb; Spn Clb; Ctrl Michigan Univ; Spanish.

BAIN, JENNIFER; Mohawk HS; Tiffin, OH; Band; Chrs; Chrh Wkr; Drm Bgl; Drm Mjrt; Girl Scts; Off Ade; Stg Crw; Y-Teens; Drama Clb; Tch Baton Lessons 79; Univ; Elem Tchr.

BAINBRIDGE, MARK; Monsignor J R Hackett HS; Kalamazoo, MI; Band; Boy Scts; Chrh Wkr; Off Ade; Sch Mus; Sch Pl; Sct Actv; Stg Crw; Yth Flsp; Pep Clb; College; Busns.

BAINES, LESLIE; Dearborn HS; Dearborn, MI; Girl Scts; Hon Rl; JA; Natl Forn Lg; NHS; Orch; IM Sprt; Univ Of Mich; Acctg.

BAIR, BRUCE A; New Philadelphia HS; New Phila, OH; Boy Scts; Chrh Wkr; Hon Rl; Univ Of New Mexico; Cmmrcl Pilot.

BAIR, ELIZABETH; Oakwood HS; Dayton, OH; Chrs; Hon Rl; NHS; Ed Sch Nwsp; Rptr Sch Nwsp; Bsktbl; Hockey; Ten; Chrldng; College; Home Ec.

BAIR, JANELL; Ben Davis HS; Indianapolis, IN; Pres Girl Scts; Mod UN; Stg Crw; Sch Nwsp; 4-H; Lat Clb; Coach Actv; PPFtbl; 4-H Awd; Perfect Serv Awd Indianapolis News; Grad For Toastmasters Intl; Purdue Univ; Bio.

BAIR, KIMBERLY; Teays Valley HS; Orient, OH; Chrh Wkr; Hon Rl; NHS; Rptr Yrbk; Lat Clb; Spn Clb; College; Animal Health.

BAIR, LISA; Napoleon HS; Napoleon, OH; Cls Rep Soph Cls; Cl Rep Jr Cls; Band; Hon Rl; Sch Mus; Lat Clb; Gym; BGSU; Occupational Therapist.

BAIRD, DANETTE; Lakeshore HS; St Joseph, MI; Chrh Wkr; College.

BAIRD, TAMI; Gallia Academy HS; Gallipolis, OH; 1/240 Am Leg Boys St; Chrs; Jr NHS; NHS; Off Ade; Stu Cncl; Rptr Sch Nwsp; FTA; Key Clb; Lat Clb; Ohio Univ; Scndry Educ.

BAISDEN, IVY; Wadsworth Sr HS; Wadsworth, OH; Chrh Wkr; Hosp Ade; Fr Clb; VICA; Hairdresser.

BAIZEL, JEAN; Villa Angela HS; Cleveland, OH; Chrs; Chrh Wkr; Debate Tm; Hon Rl; Sch Mus; Stg Crw; Yth Flsp; Drama Clb; Comp Progr.

BAJGROWICZ, E; Andrean HS; Gary, IN; Chrh Wkr; Wrstlng; IM Sprt; Univ; Electronics.

BAJKO, DONNA; Trinity HS; Seven Hills, OH; Cls Rep Frsh Cls; Cls Rep Soph Cls; Pres Sr Cls; Chrs; Hon Rl; Sch Mus; Stu Cncl; Fr Clb; Trk; Chrldng; Voted With Nicest Personality; Spirit & Friendliest 78; Schlrshp For 79 For Serv & 15000 Dollars 79; Univ.

BAJNOK, THOMAS; Newton Falls HS; Newton Falls, OH; Hon Rl; NHS; FSA; Sci Clb; Ftbl; Scr Kpr; Univ Of Cincinnati; Bio.

BAJOREK, CHRISTINE; Wadsworth Sr HS; Wadsworth, OH; 61/349 Am Leg Aux Girls St; Chrs; Girl Scts; NHS; 4-H; Fr Clb; Pep Clb; Letter Bsktbl; Glf; GAA; Univ Of Cincinnati; Law.

BAKALE, ROSEMARIE; Grand Haven HS; Grand Haven, MI; Sec Soph Cls; Cl Rep Jr Cls; Cls Rep Sr Cls; Chrh Wkr; Cmnty Wkr; Hon Rl; Jr NHS; NHS; Yrbk; DECA; Aquinas College.

BAKAN, ELIZABETH M; Archbishop Alter HS; Kettering, OH; 25/300 Drl Tm; Hon Rl; Jr NHS; Fr Clb; Keyettes; College; Comp Sci.

BAKAS, CATHERINE; Washington HS; E Chicago, IN; 2/286 Sal; Chrh Wkr; Hon Rl; NHS; Fr Clb; FTA; Key Clb; Bausch & Lomb Awd; DAR Awd; Elk Awd; Purdue Univ; Business Management.

BAKAS, CATHERINE; George Washington HS; East Chicago, IN; 2/278 Sal; Hon Rl; NHS; Fr Clb; FTA; Key Clb; Bausch & Lomb Awd; DAR Awd; Indiana Univ; Busns Admin.

BAKEMAN, CRAIG; White Pigeon HS; White Pigeon, MI; 5/94 Am Leg Boys St; Hon Rl; VP NHS; Quill & Scroll; Ed Yrbk; Bsbl; Bsktbl; Glf; Elk Awd; Rotary Awd; St Of Mi Compttv Schlshp; Michigan St Univ; Elec Engr.

BAKER, ALVIN; Claymont HS; Whrichsville, OH; 25/200 Cl Rep Jr Cls; Cls Rep Sr Cls; Ftbl; Wrstlng; Ohio Univ; Vet.

BAKER, BARBARA; Ovid Elsie HS; Ovid, MI; Chrs; Lbry Ade; Rptr Sch Nwsp; Am Leg Awd; Clinton Cnty Voc Schl; Cosmetology.

BAKER, BARRY; Reitz Memorial HS; Newburgh, IN; 3/217 Chrh Wkr; Cmnty Wkr; Hon Rl; NHS; Treas Sci Clb; Coach Actv; IM Sprt; C of C Awd; Rotary Awd; Purdue Univ; Mechanical Engineering.

BAKER, BONITA R; John Adams HS; Cleveland, OH; 1/509 Cls Rep Frsh Cls; Cl Rep Jr Cls; Val; Hon Rl; Jr NHS; Pres NHS; Off Ade; Stu Cncl; Pres OEA; Mas Awd; Cleveland St Univ; Banking.

BAKER, BRENDA; Reading HS; Reading, MI; 9/97 Band; Hon Rl; Off Ade; Stu Cncl; Sch Nwsp; FHA; Letter Gym; Jackson Cmnty Coll.

BAKER, BRENDA; Piqua Central HS; Piqua, OH; Off Ade; Bsktbl; Trk;.

BAKER, BRENDA; Southfield Christian HS; Orchard Lk, MI; 3/60 Sec Frsh Cls; Trs Frsh Cls; Cls Rep Soph Cls; VP Jr Cls; VP Chrs; Hon Rl; NHS; Stu Cncl; Letter Trk; Letter Chrldng; College; Medicine.

BAKER, BRIAN; Tyler County HS; Middlebourne, WV; 8/100 Band; Hon Rl; Beta Clb; Pres Mth Clb; Sci Clb; Bsbl; IM Sprt; West Virginia Univ; Medicine.

BAKER, BRIDGET; Divine Child HS; Dearborn, MI; Chrs; Sch Mus; Sch Pl; Stg Crw; Drama Clb; Fr Clb ; FTA; Pep Clb; Crs Cntry; Ten; Univ.

BAKER, BRUCE M; Jefferson Area HS; Jefferson, OH; 16/210 Cls Rep Frsh Cls; Cls Rep Soph Cls; Cl Rep Jr Cls; Am Leg Boys St; Band; Chrs; Hon Rl; Orch; Sch Mus; VP Stu Cncl; Ohio St Univ; Elec Engr.

BAKER, C; Tippecanoe Valley HS; Rochester, IN; Sec Soph Cls; Chrs; Hon Rl; Yth Flsp; 4-H; Pep Clb; Ten; Trk; IM Sprt; 4-H Awd; Vocational School.

BAKER, CARLA; Upper Sandusky HS; Upper Sandusky, OH; Band; Chrs; Chrh Wkr; Girl Scts; JA; Sch Pl; Sct Actv; Stg Crw; Yth Flsp; Y-Teens; Univ; Jrnlsm.

BAKER, CATHY A; Lawton HS; Lawton, MI; 2/55 VP Soph Cls; Pres Jr Cls; Pres Sr Cls; Band; Chrh Wkr; Cmnty Wkr; Hon Rl; NHS; Sch Mus; Stu Cncl; Univ; Comp Sci.

BAKER, CHARLOTTE; Coventry Sr HS; Akron, OH; 1/197 Val; Band; Chrh Wkr; Hon Rl; Fr Clb; Lat Clb; Natl Merit Ltr; Kent St Univ; Liberal Arts.

BAKER, CHERYL; New Albany HS; New Albany, OH; 4/85 Cls Rep Frsh Cls; Cls Rep Soph Cls; Cl Rep Jr Cls; Cls Rep Sr Cls; Chrh Wkr; Hon Rl; NHS; Stu Cncl; Yth Flsp; Yrbk; Accmp Pianist Study Conservatory Piano Instr Of Dr Douglas Starr; Franklin Univ; Banking.

BAKER, CHRIS; Hilliard HS; Galloway, OH; 32/350 Pres Jr Cls; FCA; Jr NHS; NHS; Sprt Ed Sch Nwsp; Rptr Sch Nwsp; Spn Clb; IM Sprt; College.

BAKER, CHRISTINE; New Miami HS; Overpeck, OH; 1/103 Trs Jr Cls; Trs Sr Cls; Val; Am Leg Aux Girls St; Treas NHS; Bsbl; Bsktbl; VFW Speech Contest Winner 2nd Pl; Received New Miami Ed Assn Schlrshp; Vlybl Capt MVP; Miami Univ; Math.

BAKER, CINDY; Twin Valley North HS; Lewisburg, OH; Chrs; Hon Rl; Yth Flsp; Yrbk; Rptr Sch Nwsp; Pep Clb; Univ Of Vermont; Acctg.

BAKER, COLLEEN; West Carrollton Sr HS; W Carrollton, OH; Sec Sr Cls; Trs Sr Cls; Band; Chrs; Chrh Wkr; Cmnty Wkr; Hon Rl; Jr NHS; NHS; Off Ade; Univ; Elem Educ.

BAKER, CYNTHIA; Paul Lawrence Dunbar HS; Dayton, OH; 9/209 Sal; Hon Rl; Sec NHS; Sec Off Ade; Rptr Sch Nwsp; Boys Clb Am; DECA; Pep Clb; Spn Clb; Letter Trk; Cert Of Honor Schlstc Ach; Outstanding Prospective Athlete; Ohio Univ; Telecommunications.

BAKER, CYNTHIA; Shenandoah HS; Shirley, IN; 22/139 Chrs; Chrh Wkr; Cmnty Wkr; Girl Scts; Hon Rl; Hosp Ade; Off Ade; Orch; Stg Crw; Y-Teens; Phys Instructer.

BAKER, DALE A; Edison HS; Berlin Hts, OH; Am Leg Boys St; Hon Rl; Lbry Ade; NHS; Sch Pl; Stg Crw; Drama Clb; Mth Clb; Univ.

BAKER, DANIEL; Newcomerstown HS; Newcomerstown, OH; Aud/Vis; Chrh Wkr; Cmnty Wkr; Off Ade; Sch Pl; Stg Crw; Letter Crs Cntry; Letter Trk; Kent St Univ; Bus.

BAKER, DANIEL T; Barberton HS; Barberton, OH; 170/520 Boy Scts; Cmnty Wkr; Hon Rl; Off Ade; Sct Actv; Yth Flsp; Capt Ftbl; Coach Actv; Youngstown State Univ; Engr.

BAKER, DEANNA; Port Clinton HS; Port Clinton, OH; 7/286 Am Leg Aux Girls St; Band; Hon Rl; NHS; Stu Cncl; Letter Trk; Mat Maids; Univ Of Kentucky; Pre Med.

BAKER, DEANNA; Port Clinton HS; , ; 7/286 Am Leg Aux Girls St; Band; Hon Rl; NHS; Stu Cncl; Lat Clb; Trk; Mat Maids; Univ Of Kentucky; Med.

BAKER, DEB; Indian Valley South HS; Port Washington, OH; Cl Rep Jr Cls; Sal; Am Leg Aux Girls St; Hon Rl; VP Yth Flsp; FHA; OEA; Pep Clb; Letter Trk; Kent St Univ; Acctg.

BAKER, DONNA; Granville HS; Granville, OH; Sec Frsh Cls; Trs Frsh Cls; Girl Scts; 4-H; OEA; Gym; Ambassadors Awrd In OEA 1978; Stateswomans Awrd In OEA 1978; 3rd Pl In Reg Constest For Typing 1978; Columbus Bus Univ; Bus.

BAKER, DORIS; Shaw HS; East Cleveland, OH; 13/487 Hon Rl; Off Ade; Orch; OEA; Cit Awd; Trophy For Straight A; 1st Pl Trophy For Stenographic; Cert For Achvmnt & Straight A; Vocational Schl; Med Sec.

BAKER, DOUG; Jonesville HS; Jonesville, MI; Hon Rl; Stg Crw; Rptr Sch Nwsp; Sch Nwsp; Trk; Scr Kpr; Tmr; Adrian Coll; Poli Sci.

BAKER, DOUGLAS; Lakeview HS; Battle Creek, MI; Hon Rl; St Of Mi Schlrshp 79; Oakland Univ Stud Life Schlrshp 79; Oakland Univ; Engr.

BAKER, DOUGLAS; Crooksville HS; Nw Lexington, OH; 1/100 Band; Chrh Wkr; Cmnty Wkr; Hon Rl; NHS; Sch Pl; Stg Crw; Treas Yth Flsp; Pres 4-H; Sci Clb; Univ; Chem Engr.

BAKER, ELIZABETH; Woodridge HS; Stow, OH; 2/100 Band; Cmnty Wkr; Girl Scts; VP JA; Jr NHS; NHS; Lat Clb; Letter Bsbl; Letter Crs Cntry; JA Awd; Finalist In Jr Achvmnt Achvr Of Yr Contest 79; 1 Rating At Ohio Music Educ Assoc Solo & Ensemble Contst 79; Univ; Engr.

BAKER, ELLEN; Reading HS; Hillsdale, MI; Pres Frsh Cls; Sec Soph Cls; Treas Band; Chrh Wkr; Hon Rl; Stu Cncl; Pres Yth Flsp; Sch Nwsp; Sec Fr Clb; PPFtbl; Univ; Elem Educ.

BAKER, FAYE; Central HS; Detroit, MI; Band; Chrs; Chrh Wkr; Lbry Ade; Sch Mus; Twrlr; Rochester Inst Of Tech; Grophic Arts.

BAKER, GAIL S; North Ridgeville Sr HS; N Ridgeville, OH; Cl Rep Jr Cls; Band; Drl Tm; Hon Rl; Jr NHS; NHS; Off Ade; Orch; Stg Crw; Stu Cncl; Univ; Botanical Sci.

BAKER, GARY; Clearcreek HS; Waynesville, OH; Cls Rep Soph Cls; Cl Rep Jr Cls; Chrs; Hon Rl; Stu Cncl; Agri.

BAKER, GLORIA; Graham HS; St Paris, OH; 15/187 Hon Rl; FFA; Pres FHA;.

BAKER, HOLLY; Wheeling Central Cath HS; Wheeling, WV; 2/135 Cl Rep Jr Cls; Cls Rep Sr Cls; Sal; Am Leg Aux Girls St; Chrh Wkr; Cmnty Wkr; Hon Rl; NHS; Stg Crw; Pres 4-H; Marshall Univ; Comp Sci.

BAKER, JACQUELYN; Kearsley HS; Davison, MI; 22/375 Girl Scts; Hon Rl; NHS; Off Ade; Red Cr Ade; Bsbl; Cit Awd; W Michigan Univ; Soc Work.

BAKER, JAMES D; Celina Sr HS; Celina, OH; 1/240 Boy Scts; Hon Rl; NHS; Fr Clb; Lat Clb; Letter Bsktbl; Ohio Northern Univ; Phrmcy.

BAKER, JOANN; Dublin HS; Dublin, OH; 22/157 Cls Rep Sr Cls; Chrs; Hon Rl; Sch Mus; Stu Cncl; Yth Flsp; Ed Sch Nwsp; Ohi State Univ; Bus Admin.

BAKER, JON; Claymont HS; Dennison, OH; 4/198 Chrh Wkr; Hon Rl; Jr NHS; NHS; Quill & Scroll; Yrbk; FTA; Lat Clb; Am Leg Awd; Natl Merit Ltr; Kent St Univ; Jrnlsm.

BAKER, JUDITH; Petoskey HS; Petoskey, MI; Chrs; Natl Forn Lg; NHS; Sch Mus; Pres Spn Clb; 60 Words Pin In Shrthnd 79; Cntrl Michigan Univ; Educ.

BAKER, JUDY; Southgate HS; Southgate, MI; 10/255 Cls Rep Soph Cls; Cl Rep Jr Cls; Cls Rep Sr Cls; Hon Rl; Jr NHS; NHS; Stu Cncl; Sch Nwsp; Pres OEA; Chrldng; Wayne St Univ; Acctg.

BAKER, JULIE; Big Walnut HS; Westerville, OH; 40/273 Band; Chrh Wkr; Lbry Ade; Y-Teens; Sci Clb; Letter Trk; Mgrs; College; Art.

BAKER, KATHY; Little Miami HS; Morrow, OH; Girl Scts; Hon Rl; JA; Jr NHS; Lit Mag; NHS; Off Ade; Stu Cncl; Pres Fr Clb; Pep Clb; Hon Given In Bio Gen Bus 76; Hon Given In Geom Acctg Hum Physiology 78; Hon Given In Socio 78; Univ; Bus.

BAKER, KELLY; Lake HS; Walbridge, OH; 12/155 Chrs; Chrh Wkr; Girl Scts; Hon Rl; NHS; Sch Mus; Stg Crw; Stu Cncl; Fr Clb; Pom Pon; Music Awd Solo In Com 78; Toledo Univ; Library Sci.

BAKER, KELLY; South Dearborn HS; Aurora, IN; Chrh Wkr; College; Law.

BAKER, KEVIN S; River Valley HS; Waldo, OH; Band; Mgrs; Tech Schl.

BAKER, KIM; Graham HS; Springfield, OH; 10/176 Chrs; Jr NHS; Off Ade; Stg Crw; Rptr Yrbk; Rptr Sch Nwsp; Ger Clb; Wright St Univ; Bio.

BAKER, KIMBERLY; Tippecanoe HS; Tipp City, OH; Chrs; Chrh Wkr; Cmnty Wkr; Hon Rl; Sch Pl; Stg Crw; Drama Clb; FHA; Sci Clb; Trk; Miami Univ; Physician.

BAKER, LAURIE; Turpin HS; Cincinnati, OH; 2/357 VP NHS; Off Ade; Fr Clb; Letter Bsktbl; PPFtbl; Hamilton Cnty All Star Vlybl 1978; Turpin Rep Rotary Club Semnr Cnty Govt; Vrsty Softbl Vlybl Captain 1976; Univ; Bus.

BAKER, LINDA; Mahoning Cnty Jt Voc Schl; Lake Milton, OH; Sec Jr Cls; Boy Scts; Chrh Wkr; Hon Rl; Off Ade; Sec Yth Flsp; Fr Clb; OEA; Spn Clb; Youngstown St Univ; Acctg.

BAKER, LORRY; Rogers HS; Michigan City, IN; Cls Rep Frsh Cls; Cls Rep Soph Cls; VP Jr Cls; Cls Rep Sr Cls; Aud/Vis; NHS; Pol Wkr; Stu Cncl; Yrbk; Drama Clb; Std Tchr Eng 79; Candeen Clb Pres 78; Eng Schlrshp Awd 79; Tri St Univ; Scndry Educ.

BAKER, MARK; Heath HS; Heath, OH; 21/155 FCA; Hon Rl; NHS; Spn Clb; Letter Bsbl; Letter Ftbl; Ohio St Univ; Engr.

BAKER, MARK; North Royalton HS; N Royalton, OH; Band; Boy Scts; Red Cr Ade; Sch Pl; 4-H; VICA; Letter Crs Cntry; IM Sprt; 4-H Awd; Ohio St Univ; Med Tech.

BAKER, MELISSA; St Joseph Central Cath HS; Fremont, OH; Cmp Fr Grls; Girl Scts; Hon Rl; 4-H; Vocational School; Social Work.

BAKER, MICHAEL; Attica HS; Attica, IN; 21/84 Trs Sr Cls; Aud/Vis; Yrbk; Sch Nwsp; FTA; Letter Bsbl; Letter Ten; College.

BAKER, MIKE; Worthington Jefferson HS; Worthington, IN; Aud/Vis; Band; Chrs; Chrh Wkr; Hon Rl; Sch Mus; Yth Flsp; Pep Clb; Bsktbl; Pep Band 1976; Univ; Engr.

BAKER, NANCY; Conotton Valley HS; Sherrodsville, OH; 7/59 Sec Frsh Cls; Hon Rl; NHS; Stu Cncl; Yrbk; Beta Clb; FHA; Pep Clb; Mgrs; Achvmtn Awd 79; Talntd Uth Semnr 79;.

BAKER, PAMELA L; Twin Valley North HS; Lewisburg, OH; Chrs; Hon Rl; Rptr Yrbk; Voice Dem Awd; Phys Ther.

BAKER, PATRICK; Cody HS; Detroit, MI; Cls Rep Frsh Cls; Boy Scts; Hon Rl; Off Ade; Ftbl; Cit Awd; Univ Of Mich; Elec Engr.

BAKER, PAUL; Jefferson Union HS; Richmond, OH; Hon Rl; 4-H; Letter Bsktbl; IM Sprt; Univ; Engr.

BAKER, RANDALL; Lincoln HS; Lumberport, WV; 1/158 Val; Hon Rl; NHS; Ed Yrbk; Fairmont St Coll; Math.

BAKER, RENEE; Bishop Noll Inst; E Chicago, IN; 33/337 Hon Rl; NHS; Pep Clb; Purdue Univ; Elem Ed.

BAKER, ROBERT; Gwinn HS; Little Lk, MI; Hon Rl; VICA; Ftbl; Mich Tech Univ; Civil Engr.

BAKER, ROBERT G; Wyoming Park HS; Wyoming, MI; Cls Rep Frsh Cls; Cls Rep Soph Cls; Cl Rep Jr Cls; FCA; Hon Rl; NHS; Sprt Ed Sch Nwsp; Sch Nwsp; Fr Clb; Bsbl; Univ.

BAKER, RODNEY; Washington Irving HS; Clarksburg, WV; Hon Rl; Yth Flsp; Fr Clb; Univ; Bus Admin.

BAKER, RONDA; Clyde HS; Clyde, OH; 10/120 Chrs; Hon Rl; JA; Lbry Ade; Sec Yth Flsp; Spn Clb; Crs Cntry; Trk; JA Awd; College; Psych.

BAKER, RONNIE; Peebles HS; Peebles, OH; Band; Boy Scts; Chrs; Chrh Wkr; Cmnty Wkr; Hon Rl; Lbry Ade; Sch Mus; Sch Pl; Sct Actv; Ohio St FFA Band; Adams Cnty Conservation Essay Wnnr; 2nd Pl Speech Contest FFA Chapter; Univ Of Cincinnati; Law.

BAKER, ROXANNE; Carrollton HS; Saginaw, MI; 22/127 Band; Pres Chrh Wkr; Debate Tm; Girl Scts; Sec MMM; Sec NHS; Orch; Sch Mus; Sch Pl; Pres Yth Flsp; Spring Arbor Coll; Fine Arts.

BAKER, SANDRA; Harrison HS; Evansville, IN; 22/500 Band; Chrs; Cmnty Wkr; Girl Scts; Hon Rl; Natl Forn Lg; Orch; Sch Mus; Stg Crw; Mth Clb; Clarinet All City & All St Band & Orchestra In Evansville Ing; Finalist In St Speech Meet; Purdue Univ; Pre Law.

BAKER, SCOTT; Boardman HS; Youngstown, OH; 4/600 Val; Boy Scts; Hon Rl; Pres NHS; Quill & Scroll; Sch Nwsp; 4-H; Pres Lat Clb; Mth Clb; Sci Clb; Univ Of Cincinnati; Chem Engr.

BAKER, SHARON; Dominican HS; Detroit, MI; Cls Rep Frsh Cls; Girl Scts; NHS; Univ Of Michigan; Med Tech.

BAKER, SHEILA; Calumet HS; Gary, IN; Off Ade; Yrbk; Pep Clb; Univ Of Alabama; Cmnctns.

BAKER, SHERRY; West Carrollton HS; W Carrollton, OH; Chrs; Chrh Wkr; Cmnty Wkr; Hon Rl; Off Ade; College; Nursing.

BAKER, SHERRY; Shakamak HS; Linton, IN; 17/98 Cls Rep Frsh Cls; Cls Rep Soph Cls; Cl Rep Jr Cls; Cls Rep Sr Cls; Chrs; Drl Tm; Quill & Scroll; Stu Cncl; Sprt Ed Yrbk; Yrbk; Indiana Univ; Bus.

BAKER, SHIRLEY; S Central HS; N Fairfield, OH; Am Leg Aux Girls St; Band; Sch Pl; Stu Cncl; Rptr Yrbk; Rptr Sch Nwsp; VP DECA; Drama Clb; 4-H; Scr Kpr; Voc Schl; Nuclear Engr.

BAKER, STEVE; Salem HS; Salem, IN; 39/160 Pres Band; Chrh Wkr; Debate Tm; NHS; Stg Crw; Drama Clb; Pres Lat Clb; Glf; Outstndng Bnd Mbr; Univ Of Evansville; Busns Admin.

BAKER, STEVEN; N Putnam Jr Sr HS; Greencastle, IN; FCA; Sci Clb; Spn Clb; Bsktbl; Ftbl; Trk; College; Laser Tech.

BAKER, STEVEN H; New London HS; New London, OH; 1/105 Am Leg Boys St; Hon Rl; VP NHS; Stu Cncl; Letter Glf; IM Sprt; Am Leg Awd; Natl Merit SF; Harvard Univ; Econ.

BAKER, SUSAN; Robert S Rogers HS; Toledo, OH; Pres Girl Scts; Sct Actv; Rptr Yrbk; Sch Nwsp; 4-H; Treas Ger Clb; Treas GAA; IM Sprt; Univ; Forestry.

BAKER, TERESA; Metro Dist Of Shakamak HS; Linton, IN; 19/89 Trs Jr Cls; Trs Sr Cls; Chrs; Drl Tm; Hon Rl; NHS; Quill & Scroll; Sprt Ed Yrbk; DECA; FHA; Indiana St Univ; Acctg.

BAKER, TERRI; Ansonia HS; Greenville, OH; 8/65 Trs Jr Cls; Chrs; Hon Rl; Off Ade; Stu Cncl; Yrbk; Ed Sch Nwsp; Drama Clb; FHA; OEA; Bus Schl.

BAKER, TERRY; Plymouth HS; Plymouth, OH; Am Leg Boys St; Band; Chrs; Chrh Wkr; Hon Rl; NHS; Sch Mus; Yth Flsp; College; Music.

BAKER, THEODORE; New Buffalo HS; Union Pier, MI; 2/97 Hon Rl; Stu Cncl; Spn Clb; Letter Trk; Mich State Univ; Math.

BAKER, TIMOTHY; Catholic Central HS; Livonia, MI; Hon Rl; Jr NHS; NHS; Pol Wkr; Sch Pl; Stg Crw; Rptr Sch Nwsp; Sch Nwsp; Drama Clb; Fr Clb; Univ Of Toronto; Psych.

BAKER, TONY; Chillicothe HS; Chillicothe, OH; AFS; Band; Boy Scts; Chrs; Hon Rl; Natl Forn Lg; Sch Mus; Sch Pl; Yth Flsp; Rptr Sch Nwsp; Columbus Coll; Art.

BAKER, TROY; Bremen HS; Bremen, IN; Cls Rep Sr Cls; Boy Scts; Chrh Wkr; Hon Rl; Stu Cncl; Yth Flsp; Fr Clb; Sci Clb; VICA; Bsktbl;.

BAKER, VINCENT; Kenmore HS; Akron, OH; Chrs; Hon Rl; Jr NHS; Mdrgl; NHS; Sch Mus; Coll; Electronics.

BAKER, WILLIAM; Morgantown HS; Morgantwn, WV; Pres Frsh Cls; Cl Rep Jr Cls; Hon Rl; Stu Cncl; Sprt Ed Yrbk; Mth Clb; Spn Clb; Letter Glf; IM Sprt; Spanish Hnr Soc HS & Natl Level; Math Hnr Soc; Univ; Dentistry.

BAKER, YON SUN; Northrop HS; Ft Wayne, IN; Chrs; Hon Rl; Lbry Ade; Off Ade; Schlrshp With Distinction 78; Achmvnt Awd 78;schlstc 76; Indiana Univ.

BAKI, MICHAEL A; Mansfield St Peters HS; Mansfield, OH; Am Leg Boys St; Chrh Wkr; Hon Rl; Stg Crw; Drama Clb; Bsbl; Bsktbl; Glf; Univ.

BAKI, MICHAEL A; St Peters HS; Mansfield, OH; Am Leg Boys St; Chrh Wkr; Cmnty Wkr; Hon Rl; Sch Mus; Sch Pl; Stg Crw; Drama Clb; Bsbl; Bsktbl; Univ.

BAKICH, DENISE; Weir Sr HS; Weirton, WV; 30/375 Cl Rep Jr Cls; Band; Pres Cmp Fr Grls; Drl Tm; Hon Rl; NHS; Y-Teens; Fr Clb; GAA; Mat Maids; Varsity Vlybl 2yr Letterwoman; John Philip Sousa Band Awd; Whohelo Medallion Awd; West Virginia Univ; Elem Ed.

BAKITA, TODD; St Johns Public HS; St Johns, MI; Am Leg Boys St; Hon Rl; NHS; VICA; Capt Bsktbl; Capt Ftbl; College; Engr.

BAKKE, MARK; Berkley HS; Berkley, MI; Boy Scts; NHS; Alma Coll.

BAKKER, MARGIE; Zeeland HS; Zeeland, MI; 5/150 Chrs; Chrh Wkr; Hon Rl; Jr NHS; Sch Mus; Ferris St Coll; X Ray Tech.

BAKOS, ANDREA; St Joseph Academy; Lakewood, OH; Cls Rep Frsh Cls; Chrh Wkr; Hon Rl; Lbry Ade; NHS; Mth Clb; Spn Clb; GAA; IM Sprt; Cleveland St Univ; Acctg.

BAKULA, LILLIAN; Villa Angela Academy; Richmond Hts, OH; Chrh Wkr; Cmnty Wkr; Hon Rl; Mod UN; Off Ade; Bsbl; Trk; Univ; Engr.

BAL, DONNA; Norway HS; Norway, MI; 2/89 Cl Rep Jr Cls; Sal; Hon Rl; NHS; Treas Stu Cncl; Ed Yrbk; Pres FBLA; Am Leg Awd; Michigan St Univ; Med Tech.

BALAGRIN, JAMES; Northwood HS; Northwood, OH; Trs Soph Cls; Trs Jr Cls; Band; Chrs; Hon Rl; JA; Stu Cncl; Sec Key Clb; Bsbl; JA Awd; # 1 Ratng In Dist Solo & Ensmbl 77; Univ.

BALAMUCKI, BRENDA; Chesaning Union HS; St Charles, MI; 1/242 Val; Band; Chrh Wkr; Hon Rl; Treas NHS; Sch Mus; Stg Crw; Drama Clb; Michigan Tech Univ; Engr.

BALASH, EVAN M; John Glenn HS; Bay City, MI; 23/384 Cls Rep Soph Cls; Band; Boy Scts; Chrs; Hon Rl; NHS; Sch Pl; Spn Clb; Letter Ftbl; Trk; Dodge Amvets Driver Excel Awd 78; St Of Mi Comptn Schlrshp 79; Cum Laude 79; Saginaw Valley St Univ; Bus.

BALASICK, KEVIN; L C Mohr HS; South Haven, MI; Ten; Lake Michigan Coll; Mortician.

BALASKO, GEORGE; Normandy HS; Parma, OH; 33/659 IM Sprt; Case Western Reserve Univ; Chem Engr.

BALASKY, GLENN; Hartland HS; Hartland, MI; 14/250 Band; Chrh Wkr; Drm Mjrt; Hon Rl; NHS; Sch Pl; Stg Crw; Drama Clb; Spn Clb; Trk; Univ Of Michigan.

BALATA, CHRISTINE; Lumen Cordium HS; Twinsburg, OH; Hon Rl; Fr Clb; IM Sprt; Inst Of Computer Mngmt; Comp Progr.

BALAZOWICH, DENISE; Green HS; Akron, OH; 131/315 Band; Chrh Wkr; Drm Mjrt; Hosp Ade; Orch; Yth Flsp; GAA; Twrlr; Cit Awd; Glenville St Coll; Admin Sci.

BALBER, MARY A; Lakeland HS; Union Lake, MI; Chrs; NHS; Sch Nwsp; PPFtbl; Univ; Cmnctns.

BALCERZAK, TAMMY; Ida HS; Petersburg, MI; Monroe Comunity Coll; Law.

BALCONI, NANCY; Sandusky HS; Sandusky, OH; OEA; Voc Schl; Acctg.

BALCONI, SUSAN; Ferndale HS; Pleasant Ridge, MI; Chrs; Hon Rl; Jr NHS; NHS; Rptr Yrbk; Letter Ten; GAA; PPFtbl; Mic State Univ; Sci.

BALDERSON, ELLEN; Morgan HS; Malta, OH; Girl Scts; Hon Rl; Jr NHS; Lbry Ade; 4-H; Spn Clb; GAA; IM Sprt; PPFtbl; 4-H Awd; Univ; Elem Tchr.

BALDIN, ANTOINETTE; Lake Central HS; Schererville, IN; 21/463 Chrs; Girl Scts; Hon Rl; NHS; Stg Crw; Drama Clb; Ger Clb; Purdue Univ; Chem Engr.

BALDINGER, RICK; Elgin Local Marion Cnty HS; Marion, OH; 15/155 Chrh Wkr; Hon Rl; NHS; 4-H; Lat Clb; Letter Bsktbl; Letter Crs Cntry; Letter Trk; Cit Awd; 4-H Awd; Citizenship Washington Focus 4 H Awd; Schlrshp Team; Top Hnrs In St In 4 H Woodworking; College; Sci.

BALDRIDGE, JEFFERY A; Princeton HS; Cincinnati, OH; Band; Orch; Sch Mus; Ohio St Univ; Admin Sci.

BALDWIN, BETH; Valley Forge HS; Parma, OH; Cls Rep Frsh Cls; Cls Rep Soph Cls; Cl Rep Jr Cls; Cls Rep Sr Cls; Chrs; Hon Rl; Stu Cncl; Yrbk; Pep Clb; Miami Univ; Art.

BALDWIN, CATHY; Bennett HS; Marion, IN; 1/25 Am Leg Aux Girls St; Girl Scts; Hon Rl; NHS; Quill & Scroll; Sct Actv; Rptr Sch Nwsp; Letter Bsktbl; Letter Ten; GAA; Marion Exchange Club Sportsman Awd Basketball; Soc Dstngshd Amer HS Stu; Varsity Club; College; Math.

BALDWIN, DARLENE; Finney HS; Detroit, MI; Drl Tm; Hon Rl; ROTC; Bsktbl; Letter Glf; Ferris State Univ; Prof Golfer.

BALDWIN, I; Valley Forge HS; Parma, OH; 85/777 Cls Rep Frsh Cls; Cls Rep Soph Cls; Sal; NHS; Off Ade; Stu Cncl; Yrbk; Spn Clb; Chrldng; Miami Univ; Spanish.

BALDWIN, JOHN; Highland HS; Anderson, IN; 93/450 Hon Rl; Stg Crw; Ten; Univ; Radio Brdcstng.

BALDWIN, LAUREL; Wadsworth Sr HS; Wadsworth, OH; Girl Scts; Hon Rl; Lbry Ade; Sch Pl; Stg Crw; Drama Clb; 4-H; Fr Clb; IM Sprt; 4-H Awd; Akron Univ; Ag.

BALDWIN, M; Flushing HS; Flushing, MI; Hon Rl; Letter Bsbl; Letter Bsktbl; Letter Ftbl; College.

BALDWIN, NORMAN; Fostoria HS; Fostoria, OH; 12/183 Boy Scts; Girl Scts; NHS; Yth Flsp; Spn Clb; Crs Cntry; Swmmng; Univ; Elec Engr.

BALDWIN, ROBIN; Jennings County HS; Butlerville, IN; Band; NHS; Stg Crw; 4-H; FTA; Cit Awd; 4-H Awd; Mas Awd; Natl Merit Ltr; Smith Coll; Elem Educ.

BALDWIN, SHERYL; Ionia HS; Ionia, MI; 22/272 Cls Rep Sr Cls; Hon Rl; NHS; Stu Cncl; Sci Clb; Grand Valley State College; Bio.

BALDWIN, TERRI; West Muskingum HS; Zanesville, OH; Cls Rep Frsh Cls; Cl Rep Jr Cls; Am Leg Aux Girls St; Chrs; Girl Scts; Hon Rl; NHS; Treas Stu Cncl; Y-Teens; Treas FHA; Vlybl Reserve Letter Varsity Letter; Sftbl Varsity Letter MVP Capt; College.

BALDWIN, THOMAS; Cadillac HS; Cadillac, MI; Hon Rl; Capt Bsbl; IM Sprt; Ltr From Major Lg Bsbl Team Reds 79; Jr Coll; Bsbl Player.

BALENSIEFER, KIM; Benton Central HS; Fowler, IN; 20/233 Am Leg Aux Girls St; Chrh Wkr; Hon Rl; NHS; Quill & Scroll; Sch Mus; Sch Pl; Stg Crw; Yrbk; Pres Drama Clb; Mike Schneidt Theatrical Awd; Martha Balensiefer Serv Awd; Keller Key Drama Awd; Ball State Univ.

BALENTINE, STEVEN; Traverse City Sr HS; Traverse City, MI; Hon Rl; NHS; Cit Awd; Natl Hnr Soc Schlrshp; Outstanding Sr In Math; Acad Ach; Michigan Tech Univ; Engr.

BALES, BRUCE; Randolph Southern HS; Winchester, IN; 4/79 Am Leg Boys St; Hon Rl; Sch Mus; Lat Clb; Rdo Clb; Spn Clb; Bsktbl; Crs Cntry; Ind Univ; Orthodonics.

BALES, CINDY; John Marshall HS; Indianapolis, IN; Band; Hon Rl; Quill & Scroll; Rptr Sch Nwsp; Eng Clb; Pres Ger Clb; Sci Clb; Pom Pon; PPFtbl; Indiana Univ; Medicine.

BALES, GARY L; Southeast HS; Atwater, OH; Band; Boy Scts; Treas MMM; Youngstown Univ; Music.

BALES, JEFF; Waynesfield Goshen HS; Waynesfield, OH; 2/60 Trs Frsh Cls; Band; Boy Scts; Chrs; Chrh Wkr; Cmnty Wkr; Hon Rl; JA; Lbry Ade; NHS; Florida South Univ; Marine Bio.

BALES, KIM; Blue River Valley Jr Sr HS; Mooreland, IN; 7/93 Am Leg Aux Girls St; Hon Rl; NHS; Off Ade; Pres Yth Flsp; Pres 4-H; FFA; VP Lat Clb; Ten; 4-H Awd; Jr Leaders Devotion Leader; Ball St Univ; Acctg.

BALES, KURT; Union HS; Lynn, IN; Pres Soph Cls; VP Sr Cls; Am Leg Boys St; Band; NHS; 4-H; Lat Clb; Letter Wrstlng; Purdue Univ; Veterinary Medicine.

BALES, TONY; Union HS; Mooreland, IN; 31/86 VP Frsh Cls; Aud/Vis; Chrh Wkr; Hon Rl; Lbry Ade; Yth Flsp; Rptr Yrbk; Rptr Sch Nwsp; 4-H; Spn Clb; Purdue Univ; Agri.

BALEY, CHRISTOPHER; Morrice Area Schl; Morrice, MI; VP Jr Cls; Am Leg Boys St; Hon Rl; NHS; Stu Cncl; Capt Bsbl; Bsktbl; Ftbl; Natl Merit Ltr; Pres Awd; Univ; Math.

BALFOUR, VALERIE; Stephen T Badin HS; Hamilton, OH; 18/200 Chrs; Chrh Wkr; Hon Rl; VP JA; NHS; Sch Mus; Drama Clb; Fr Clb; Opt Clb Awd; Optimist Club Awd 2 1st Pl In Oratorical Consts 78; Soph & Jr Yr Spec Hons For High Grds 78; Miami Univ; Psych.

BALGAVY, DENNIS; Breckenridge Jr Sr HS; Breckenridge, MI; 7/111 Band; Boy Scts; Chrs; Hon Rl; Mdrgl; NHS; Sch Mus; Sct Actv; Yth Flsp; Ftbl; Vocational Schl; Recording Engr.

BALKIN, LINDA; Loy Norrix HS; Kalamazoo, MI; Chrs; Hon Rl; Sch Mus; Letter Ten; Univ; Eng.

BALL, BRUCE; Lakeview HS; Lakeview, MI; 1/130 Trs Jr Cls; Trs Sr Cls; Val; Band; Hon Rl; VP NHS; Spn Clb; Letter Bsbl; Univ Of Michigan; Chem Engr.

BALL, CHARLES T; Richmond Sr HS; Richmond, IN; Debate Tm; Hon Rl; Jr NHS; Natl Forn Lg; NHS; Quill & Scroll; Sch Pl; Stu Cncl; Rptr Sch Nwsp; Univ; Law.

BALL, GREG; Scott HS; Ramage, WV; Hon Rl; Jr NHS; Stu Cncl; Marshall Univ; Dent.

BALL, HELEN; Whitemore Lake HS; Whitmore Lk, MI; Hon Rl; Jr NHS; NHS; Sch Mus; Sch Pl; Stg Crw; Yth Flsp; Rptr Yrbk; Drama Clb; Fr Clb; College; Cpa.

BALL, JANELL; Central HS; Switz City, IN; Sec Jr Cls; Chrs; Chrh Wkr; Hon Rl; Jr NHS; Lit Mag; Yrbk; 4-H; Pep Clb; GAA; College; Photography.

BALL, JEFF; Norwood HS; Norwood, OH; 102/348 Hon Rl; Sch Mus; DECA; Pep Clb; Crs Cntry; Wrstlng; 2nd Pl Team Mgmt; 1st Pl Busns Ownership; 3rd Pl St Comp Busns Ownership; Mbr Of Varsity N Club;.

BALL, JEFFREY; South Christian HS; Byron Center, MI; 1/186 Am Leg Boys St; Band; NHS; Glf; Ten; IM Sprt; Natl Merit Ltr; Natl Merit SF; U S Air Force Academy; Engr.

BALL, KAREN; Brookville HS; Brookville, IN; Hon Rl; Ger Clb; Univ; Psych.

BALL, KATHY; Columbia City Joint HS; Columbia City, IN; Cls Rep Frsh Cls; Cls Rep Soph Cls; Cl Rep Jr Cls; Sal; Chrs; Chrh Wkr; Cmnty Wkr; FCA; Hon Rl; Off Ade; Lutheran Schl Of Nursing; Nursing.

BALL, KATHY; Philip Barbour HS; Philippi, WV; Cmp Fr Grls; Chrs; Girl Scts; Hon Rl; NHS; Keyettes; Bus Schl; Sec.

BALL, KATHY; Sts Peter & Paul Area HS; Saginaw, MI; 6/117 Girl Scts; Hon Rl; Jr NHS; NHS; Off Ade; FTA; BEOG; Ach Awds In Art; Social Humanities Ach Awd; Delta Cmnty Coll; Data Processing.

BALL, LENA; Sherman HS; Ashford, WV; Cls Rep Frsh Cls; Cl Rep Jr Cls; NHS; Off Ade; Sch Pl; Stg Crw; Yrbk; 4-H; Ger Clb; Univ; Nursing.

BALL, MARCIE; Lake Orion HS; Oxford, MI; 7/460 Cls Rep Sr Cls; Band; Hon Rl; Jr NHS; VP NHS; 4-H; Trk; 4-H Awd; Natl Merit Ltr; University; Engr.

BALL, SANDRA; Forest Park HS; Crystal Falls, MI; Sec Frsh Cls; Sec Soph Cls; Sec Jr Cls; Cls Rep Sr Cls; Am Leg Aux Girls St; Band; Debate Tm; Drl Tm; Girl Scts; Hon Rl; Ferris St Coll; Archt Draftng.

BALL, TERESA; Scott HS; Ottawa, WV; Chrs; Hon Rl; Sch Pl; Pep Clb; Trk; Mgrs; Scr Kpr; Univ Of Charleston; Phys Ed.

BALL, THERESE; St Ursula Acad; Cincinnati, OH; Hon Rl; Stg Crw; Yrbk; Lat Clb; IM Sprt; Univ.

BALL, THOMAS; Onaway HS; Onaway, MI; 6/96 VP Sr Cls; Band; Chrh Wkr; Drm Bgl; Hon Rl; NHS; Sch Pl; Yth Flsp; Ftbl; IM Sprt; Ferris St Coll Schlrshp 79; Mi St Awd 79; Ferris St Coll; Pre Pharm.

BALL, TIM; Hurricane HS; Scott Depot, WV; 8/210 Sec Sr Cls; FCA; Hon Rl; JA; Letter Bsbl; Letter Bsktbl; Letter Ftbl; Coach Actv; IM Sprt; Lion Awd; Marshall Univ; Acctg.

BALL, TIMOTHY G; Hubbard HS; Hubbard, OH; Trs Jr Cls; Trs Sr Cls; Am Leg Boys St; Band; Boy

Scts; Chrh Wkr; Hon Rl; NHS; Orch; Sct Actv; Univ; Bio.

BALL, WHITNEY; Morgantown Sr HS; Morgantwn, WV; Chrh Wkr; Girl Scts; Hon Rl; Yth Flsp; Beta Clb; Fr Clb; Letter Trk; IM Sprt; Univ; Bus Admin.

BALLARD, BARRY; Huntington East HS; Huntington, WV; Pres Soph Cls; Hon Rl; Letter Bsbl; Letter Ftbl; Letter Trk; Coll.

BALLARD, KAREN; Roosevelt HS; Gary, IN; Band; Chrh Wkr; Cmnty Wkr; Hon Rl; Jr NHS; NHS; Bsktbl; IM Sprt; Cit Awd; Purdue Univ; Engr.

BALLARD, STEPHEN; Buchtel HS; Akron, OH; Chrh Wkr; Letter Glf; Mgrs; Cit Awd; Knights Of Columbus Schlrshp 75; Akron Univ; Law Enforcement.

BALLARD, TERESA; South Central Jr Sr HS; Elizabeth, IN; Band; Chrs; Lit Mag; NHS; 4-H; Spn Clb; Letter Bsktbl; 4-H Awd; Eastern Kentucky Univ.

BALLARD, THAMARA; Buena Vista HS; Saginaw, MI; Boy Scts; Chrs; Hon Rl; Red Cr Ade; 4-H; Ten; Trk; Pom Pon; JETS Awd; Pres Awd; Univ Of Mich; Med.

BALLAS, RHEA; Pickerington HS; Pickerington, OH; Boy Scts; Chrs; Chrh Wkr; Girl Scts; Hon Rl; Hosp Ade; NHS; VP Yth Flsp; Sch Nwsp; Sec FHA; Yng Adult Volunteer Akron Cty Hosp Awd 77; Ohio St Univ; Med.

BALLAS, TRACEY; Zanesville HS; Zanesville, OH; Cls Rep Frsh Cls; Chrs; Hon Rl; NHS; Off Ade; Sch Pl; Stu Cncl; Rptr Sch Nwsp; Sci Clb; Chrldng; Univ; Bus Admin.

BALLENGER, EDWARD; Bexley HS; Bexley, OH; Cls Rep Frsh Cls; Cl Rep Jr Cls; Band; Chrh Wkr; Hon Rl; Orch; Sch Mus; Sch Pl; Stu Cncl; Rptr Yrbk; Drum Major 78 80; Intl Thespian Soc For Troupe #2512 79; Univ; Cmmrcl Airline Pilot.

BALLERT, KELLY; High School; Toledo, OH; 51/910 Chrh Wkr; Girl Scts; Hon Rl; NHS; Quill & Scroll; Pres Yth Flsp; Sch Nwsp; Ger Clb; Pep Clb; PPFtbl; Ohio Univ; Journalism.

BALLESTER, SANDRA; Reeths Puffer HS; Muskegon, MI; 19/281 Chrs; Cmnty Wkr; Hon Rl; Hosp Ade; Jr NHS; NHS; Stu Cncl; Spn Clb; PPFtbl; Natl Merit Ltr; Basic Opprnty Grant 79; St Of Michigan Compt Schlrshp 79; Muskegon Cmnty Coll; Psych.

BALLEW, CRAIG; Struthers HS; Poland, OH; 5/277 Chrh Wkr; Cmnty Wkr; Hon Rl; NHS; Off Ade; Yth Flsp; Key Clb; Coach Actv; IM Sprt; Kiwan Awd; Youngstown Univ; Indust Engr.

BALLEW, DAVID; Bosse HS; Evansville, IN; Quill & Scroll; Yrbk; Sch Nwsp; College; Engr.

BALLEW, JONDA; Sissonville HS; Charleston, WV; Cls Rep Soph Cls; Girl Scts; Hon Rl; NHS; Stu Cncl; Yth Flsp; 4-H; Pep Clb; Trk; Chrldng; Math Awd; West Virginia Tech Coll; Archt.

BALLIEN, ELIZABETH A; Swan Valley HS; Saginaw, MI; 11/175 Band; Sec Chrh Wkr; Girl Scts; Hon Rl; NHS; Sch Pl; Sch Nwsp; English Awd; Tri State Music Festival; Vrsty Ski Team Conference Medal; Saginaw Valley State Coll; English.

BALLINGER, CHERYL; Licking Valley HS; Newark, OH; Hon Rl; Hosp Ade; Jr NHS; NHS; Y-Teens; Key Clb; Mat Maids; Camp Enterprise Participant; Diploma Of Merit In Spanish; Placed In High % In PSAT & ACT Test; Ohio State Univ; Bio Sci.

BALLINGER, MARY; Union County HS; Liberty, IN; 2/155 VP Soph Cls; VP Jr Cls; Am Leg Aux Girls St; Treas Band; Chrh Wkr; Cmnty Wkr; Drl Tm; Drm Mjrt; Hon Rl; NHS; Outstndng Acctg Stdnt 79; Bus Schl; Acctg.

BALLINGER, RANDY; National Trail HS; New Paris, OH; Pres Frsh Cls; Pres Soph Cls; Pres Jr Cls; Am Leg Boys St; Band; Chrh Wkr; Hon Rl; NHS; Off Ade; Letter Bsktbl; Dayton Flexible Sci Awd 79; Amer Leg Gov & Amer Test Dist Winner 78; Basktbl Desire Awd 79; Cincinnati Bible Coll.

BALLO, JUDITH; C S Mott HS; Warren, MI; 11/670 Chrs; Hon Rl; Jr NHS; NHS; Letter Chrldng; DAR Awd; Natl Merit Ltr; Michigan St Univ; Engr.

BALLOR, BARBARA; Pinconning Sr HS; Linwood, MI; Chrs; Cmnty Wkr; Hon Rl; Sch Mus; Sch Pl; Sct Actv; Drama Clb; PPFtbl; Central Michigan Univ; Soc Work.

BALLOU, AMY; Wayne HS; Dayton, OH; AFS; Chrh Wkr; Hosp Ade; Jr NHS; NHS; Yrbk; Sch Nwsp; Fr Clb; Opt Clb Awd; Summer Amer Abroad 79; 16th In St In Spanish Div 3 & 6th In Spanish Miami Univ In Ohio Test Of Achvmnt 79; Ohio St Univ; Foreign Lang.

BALLWEG, LISA; Marion Local HS; Chickasaw, OH; 4/88 Band; Hon Rl; NHS; 4-H; FTA; Pep Clb; Sci Clb; College; Engr.

BALMAS, DONNA; St Florian HS; Hamtramck, MI; 5/75 Trs Soph Cls; Pres Sr Cls; Chrs; Hon Rl; Natl Forn Lg; NHS; Ed Yrbk; Drama Clb; Sci Clb; Letter Bsbl; Univ Of Detroit; Busns Mgmt.

BALMER, C; Port Huron HS; Pt Huron, MI; Band; Cmp Fr Grls; Hon Rl; Lbry Ade; NHS; Stu Cncl; Yrbk; Letter Bsktbl; GAA; Univ Of Michigan; Med.

BALMER, KELLY; Whiteford HS; Sylvania, OH; Chrs; Hon Rl; Sch Mus; Spn Clb; Letter Bsktbl; Northwood Inst; Fshn Mdse.

BALMONS, JOHN; Garden City West Sr HS; Garden City, MI; Pres Ger Clb; Letter Ftbl; IM Sprt; Univ Of Michigan; Engr.

BALNKENSHIP, CHERYL; Utica HS; Utica, OH; 8/296 Chrs; Chrh Wkr; Drl Tm; Hon Rl; Jr NHS; NHS; Sch Mus; Sch Pl; Sch Nwsp; Drama Clb; Morehead State Univ; Communications.

BALOGH, D; Regina HS; Mayfield Hts, OH; Hon Rl; Rptr Sch Nwsp; Ten; Miami State Univ; Accounting.

BALOGH, DEANNA; Harry S Truman HS; Taylor, MI; 3/507 Chrh Wkr; Hon Rl; Sec NHS; Chrldng; Wayne State Univ; Occup Ther.

BALOGH, REBECCA W; La Ville Jr Sr HS; Plymouth, IN; 33/133 Band; Chrs; Mdrgl; Orch; Sch Mus; Stg Crw; Drama Clb; Fr Clb; Mth Clb; Sci Clb; Hazel Dell Neff Smelser Music Schlrshp; John Phillip Sousa Band Awd; Ball St Univ Music Honors Schlrshp; Ball St Univ; Music Ed.

BALSER, GARY; Bishop Dwenger HS; Ft Wayne, IN; Cl Rep Jr Cls; Chrs; Lbry Ade; Sch Mus; Sch Pl; Stg Crw; Stu Cncl; Drama Clb; Fr Clb; Letter Wrstlng; Purdue Univ; Engr.

BALSER, JEFFREY; William Henry Harrison HS; Evansville, IN; 1/459 Cl Rep Jr Cls; Cls Rep Sr Cls; Hon Rl; Treas NHS; Sch Mus; Sch Pl; Stu Cncl; Drama Clb; Mth Clb; Ten; Univ; Mad.

BALSMEYER, CINDY; Southridge HS; Huntngbrg, IN; Chrh Wkr; FCA; Hon Rl; Sch Mus; Yth Flsp; 4-H; Pep Clb; Letter Bsktbl; Letter Mgrs; PPFtbl; Univ; Bus.

BALSTER, CAROLYN; Coldwater HS; Coldwater, OH; 21/150 Band; Chrs; Chrh Wkr; Girl Scts; Hon Rl; Hosp Ade; NHS; Rptr Yrbk; 4-H; IM Sprt; Bowling Green St Univ; Pub Reltns.

BALSTER, DANIEL; Marion Local HS; Maria Stein, OH; Am Leg Boys St; Chrh Wkr; Hon Rl; NHS; FTA; Sci Clb; Crs Cntry; Trk;.

BALSTER, TINA; St Henry HS; St Henry, OH; Chrs; Hon Rl; NHS; Sch Mus; Drama Clb; OEA; Pep Clb; Spn Clb; GAA; Rank 4th In Reg OEA Talent Cntst 78; Ranked 3rd In Reg OEA Talent Cntst 79; Earned Exec Diplomat 77; Sec.

BALT, CHRISTINE; Andrean HS; Merrillville, IN; 96/251 Am Leg Aux Girls St; Hosp Ade; Sdlty; Stg Crw; Drama Clb; Ger Clb; Pep Clb; College; Nursing.

BALTHOUSE, WALTER; Kenowa Hills HS; Grand Rapids, MI; Band; Hon Rl; NHS; Univ.

BALTIMORE, SUSAN; Medina Sr HS; Fresno, CA; 2/341 Aud/Vis; Girl Scts; Hon Rl; Jr NHS; NHS; Red Cr Ade; 4-H; Lat Clb; Pep Clb; Letter Trk; Youth & Sci Convntn In Columbus Oh 78; Vllyb Mst Imprvd 78; Vlly Jr Var Capt 79; Univ Of California; Med.

BALTZELL, TAMI; Parkway HS; Rockford, OH; Cls Rep Frsh Cls; Band; Chrs; Chrh Wkr; Hon Rl; Stg Crw; Yth Flsp; 4-H; Lat Clb; Pep Clb; ITT; Elec.

BALZER, DAWN; Gladwin HS; Gladwin, MI; 2/180 Sec Jr NHS; Natl Forn Lg; NHS; Sch Pl; Stg Crw; VP Stu Cncl; Civ Clb; Drama Clb; Trk; Capt Chrldng; Univ.

BALZER, JOEL; North Canton Hoover HS; North Canton, OH; 70/490 Hon Rl; VP JA; Ger Clb; JA Awd; VFW Awd; Univ.

BALZER, RONDA; Reeths Puffer Sr HS; N Muskegon, MI; Trs Jr Cls; Hon Rl; Stu Cncl; Ed Yrbk; Rptr Yrbk; Fr Clb; Michigan St Univ; Elec Schl Tchr.

BALZHISER, JENI; Clermont Northeastern HS; Batavia, OH; Cls Rep Soph Cls; Band; Chrh Wkr; FCA; Girl Scts; Hon Rl; Pep Clb; Rdo Clb; Spn Clb; Chrldng; Captain Varsity Football Cheerleaders; Mem Of Jr Fair Board; In Charge Of Publicity At WCNE Radio; College; Sci.

BAMER, KELLI; Ironton HS; Ironton, OH; Rptr Yrbk; Ger Clb; Letter Trk; Mat Maids; Univ.

BAMHILL, TERESA; Ithaca HS; Ithaca, MI; Hon Rl; Ed Sch Nwsp; Rptr Sch Nwsp; Sch Nwsp; OEA; Pep Clb; Chrldng; Central Michigan College.

BAMMEL, BRIAN; Eisenhower HS; Utica, MI; 145/621 Chrh Wkr; FCA; Hon Rl; Yrbk; Sch Nwsp; VICA; Capt Bsktbl; Scr Kpr; Adrian Coll; Pre Med.

BAMMERLIN, DIANE; North Miami HS; Peru, IN; 1/120 Band; Hon Rl; NHS; Off Ade; Sch Pl; Yth Flsp; Drama Clb; Pep Clb; Spn Clb; Sch Rep For Dollrs For Schlrrs 78 & 79; Farrell See Bio Awd 78; Univ; Phys Ther.

BAMMERT, LINDA; Lake Linden Hubbell HS; Lake Linden, MI; Band; Hon Rl; Sch Pl; Michigan St Univ; Astronomy.

BANAL, DENISE; Buckeye N HS; Smithfield, OH; 17/106 Band; Drl Tm; Hon Rl; Jr NHS; NHS; Stu Cncl; Rptr Sch Nwsp; Sch Nwsp; Sci Clb; Spn Clb; Wheeling Park Schl; Radiology.

BANASZAK, SUSAN; George Rogers Clark HS; Whiting, IN; 17/218 Girl Scts; NHS; Bsktbl; Bus Schl.

BANASZEWSKI, SHERRI; High School; Holly, MI; 4/100 Band; Chrs; Girl Scts; Hon Rl; JA; Lbry Ade; Mdrgl; Drama Clb; Spn Clb; Oakland Cmnty Coll; Acctg.

BANCHICH, ROBERT S; Donald E Gauit Jr Sr HS; Hammond, IN; 50/250 Pres Frsh Cls; Cls Rep Soph Cls; Cl Rep Jr Cls; Am Leg Boys St; Hon Rl; MMM; Stu Cncl; Letter Socr; Letter Swmmng; Ten; Mst Outstndng Boy Stdnt Councl 77 79; Monterrey Univ; Pre Law.

BANCROFT, CHRISTINE; Cheboygan Area Public HS; Cheboygan, MI; Cls Rep Frsh Cls; Girl Scts; Hon Rl; Hosp Ade; Red Cr Ade; Sch Pl; Stg Crw; Fr Clb; VICA; Chrldng; Red Cross Lifesavng & Water Safety Adv 78; Voc Schl; RN.

BANCROFT, KAREN; Cheboygan Area HS; Cheboygan, MI; Trs Frsh Cls; Band; Chrh Wkr; Hon Rl; Hosp Ade; Sch Pl; Stu Cncl; Fr Clb; IM Sprt; Lawrence Inst Of Tech; Archt.

BANCROFT, KERI; Eastern HS; Lansing, MI; Cls Rep Soph Cls; Cl Rep Jr Cls; Chrh Wkr; Hon Rl; JA; Sch Pl; Stu Cncl; Yrbk; Fr Clb; Swmmng; Western Mic Univ.

BANDELOW, PATRICIA; The Andrews School; Eastlake, OH; 11/72 Chrs; Chrh Wkr; Hon Rl; Lit Mag; Mod UN; Pol Wkr; Red Cr Ade; Sch Mus; Sch Pl; Ed Sch Nwsp; Miami Univ; Systems Analysis.

BANDEMER, MELINDA; Lutheran E HS; E Detroit, MI; Chrh Wkr; Girl Scts; Hon Rl; Univ Michigan; Speech Pathology.

BANDFIELD, ROBERT T; Howell HS; Howell, MI; 160/395 Cls Rep Frsh Cls; Boy Scts; CAP; Hon Rl; Sct Actv; Ftbl; Hockey; Ten; Northwestern; Aviation.

BANDY, VINCENT; Lewis County HS; Weston, WV; Hon Rl; Jr NHS; NHS; Bsktbl; Letter Glf; Natl Merit Ltr; West Virginia Univ; Engr.

BANE, TINA; Oceana HS; Oceana, WV; VP Soph Cls; Band; Chrs; MMM; NHS; Stu Cncl; Beta Clb; Fr Clb; Pep Clb; Twrlr; West Virginia Univ; Med.

BANERJEE, DHRUVA; Miamisburg HS; Dayton, OH; 1/308 Debate Tm; Hon Rl; NHS; Y-Teens; Ger Clb; NCTE; Natl Merit SF; Nonors Seminars Of Metropolitian Dayton; Academic Ach By Ohio House Of Representatives; College; Aero Engr.

BANES, ROB; Frontier HS; Chalmers, IN; Trs Frsh Cls; Trs Soph Cls; Trs Jr Cls; Band; Cmnty Wkr; Hon Rl; Drama Clb; 4-H; Letter Bsbl; Letter Mgrs; Purdue; Marine Bio.

BANES, TRUDI J; North White HS; Monon, IN; 9/86 Band; Chrs; NHS; Sch Mus; Sch Pl; Stu Cncl; Ed Yrbk; Rptr Sch Nwsp; Pres Drama Clb; Ger Clb; Eng Awd 79; Univ Of Evansville; Cmnctns.

BANET, DEBORAH; Floyd Central HS; New Albany, IN; 5/368 Cls Rep Sr Cls; Chrh Wkr; Girl Scts; Hon Rl; NHS; Sct Actv; 4-H; Hst Frsh Cls; PPFtbl; Scr Kpr; Notre Dame; Business.

BANET, DUANE; Floyd Central HS; Floyd Knobs, IN; 40/382 Boy Scts; Hon Rl; Sprt Ed Sch Nwsp; Rptr Sch Nwsp; 4-H; 4-H Awd; In Schlr; Indiana Univ Southeast; Med.

BANEY, REBECCA S; Bay City Western HS; Kawkawlin, MI; 58/485 Band; Chrh Wkr; Cmnty Wkr; Girl Scts; Hon Rl; Hosp Ade; Pres Yth Flsp; 4-H; 4-H Awd; Kiwan Awd; Delta Coll; Psychology.

BANEZ, CARINA; Canton Central Catholic HS; Massillon, OH; Hon Rl; Drama Clb; College; Dietetics.

BANEZ, GERARD; Central Catholic HS; Massillon, OH; Cls Rep Soph Cls; VP Jr Cls; Am Leg Boys St; Hon Rl; Pres NHS; Sch Pl; VP Stu Cncl; Sch Nwsp; Spn Clb; Trk; Ralph Regulas Student Congress Council 79; Honors Prog 76; Univ; Med.

BANFIELD, CYNTHIA; Conneaut HS; Conneaut, OH; Cl Rep Jr Cls; VP Sr Cls; Am Leg Aux Girls St; Hon Rl; NHS; Opt Clb Awd; Inst Of Comp Mgmt; Comp Progr.

BANFIELD, DAWN; Roseville HS; St Clairshores, MI; 16/425 Cls Rep Frsh Cls; Band; Chrh Wkr; Hon Rl; Lbry Ade; Yth Flsp; OEA; Ten; Natl Merit Schl; Macomb Cnty Cmnty Coll; Legal Sec.

BANFILL, ROBERT; Kelloggsville HS; Kentwood, MI; Hon Rl; Jr NHS; Letter Ten; Cit Awd; College; Electronics.

BANFORD, TERRI; Clinton Massie HS; Wilmington, OH; VP Band; Chrs; Chrh Wkr; Cmnty Wkr; Hon Rl; Jr NHS; Sch Mus; Yth Flsp; 4-H; DAR Awd; Wright State; Airlines.

BANHART, JOHN E; Calumet HS; Gary, IN; 9/300 Chrh Wkr; Hon Rl; Jr NHS; NHS; Yth Flsp; 4-H; Wrstlng; Coach Actv; US Wrestling Federation Numerous Medals; AAU Jr Olympics Numerous Medals Grand Natl Qualifier; College; Education.

BANIEL, FRANK; Saginaw HS; Saginaw, MI; Letter Bsbl; Letter Ftbl; IM Sprt; 4-H Awd; Pres Awd; Western Michigan; Electrician.

BANK, LORI; Bridgeport Spaulding HS; Saginaw, MI; 7/332 Trs Jr Cls; Trs Sr Cls; Band; Chrs; Hon Rl; Hosp Ade; NHS; Ten; Univ Of Michigan; Med.

BANKER, JEFF; Sandusky HS; Sandusky, MI; 1/119 Val; Am Leg Boys St; NHS; Quill & Scroll; Pres Stu Cncl; Ed Sch Nwsp; Letter Bsbl; Letter Bsktbl; Letter Crs Cntry; Letter Trk; Univ Of Michigan; Engr.

BANKERT, MARK; Sandy Valley HS; Waynesburg, OH; Hon Rl; Rptr Sch Nwsp; Letter Glf; Ten; IM Sprt; College; Bus.

BANKO, ANDREA; Notre Dame HS; Clarksburg, WV; Band; Chrs; Drm Mjrt; Hon Rl; Rptr Yrbk; FNA; Mth Clb; Pep Clb; Bsktbl; Twrlr; Wv Univ; Civil Engr.

BANKS, ANGELO; Baldwin HS; Baldwin, MI; Trs Frsh Cls; Trs Jr Cls; Hon Rl; NHS; Off Ade; Bsbl; Capt Bsktbl; Dnfth Awd; Mic State Univ; Bus.

BANKS, BRAD; Cheboygan Area HS; Cheboygan, MI; VP Frsh Cls; Pres Sr Cls; Aud/Vis; Hon Rl; Sch Pl; Stu Cncl; Letter Ftbl; Letter Trk; Coach Actv; IM Sprt; Coll.

BANKS, CARL C; Atlanta HS; Atlanta, MI; Hon Rl; Sch Pl; Letter Bsbl; Letter Ftbl; Cit Awd; Michigan Tech Univ; Elec Engr.

BANKS, DANIEL K; Brownstown Central HS; Brownstown, IN; Band; Yrbk; Lat Clb; Sci Clb; Glf; IM Sprt; Purdue Univ.

BANKS, ELAUNDA; Calumet HS; Gary, IN; Chrh Wkr; Hon Rl; NHS; Cit Awd; Ind Voc; Data Pro.

BANKS, HARRIET; Columbia City Joint HS; Columbia City, IN; Hon Rl; JA; NHS; Off Ade; Spn Clb; College; Physical Therapy.

BANKS, JEFF; Carlisle HS; Carlisle, OH; Hon Rl; 4-H; Letter Bsbl; Bsktbl; Letter Ftbl; IM Sprt; Agri.

BANKS, JUANA; Father Joseph Wehrle Mem HS; Columbus, OH; Drl Tm; Girl Scts; Hon Rl; NHS; Spn Clb; Natl Merit Ltr; Univ; Poli Sci.

BANKS, KENNETH; Belmont HS; Dayton, OH; Cls Rep Frsh Cls; Cl Rep Jr Cls; Cls Rep Sr Cls; Boy Scts; Chrh Wkr; Hon Rl; NHS; Boys Clb Am; Wright St; Poli Sci.

BANKS, MARIAN; Franklin HS; Franklin, OH; Cls Rep Frsh Cls; VP Soph Cls; Chrs; Girl Scts; Lbry Ade; Off Ade; Sch Mus; Sch Pl; Sct Actv; Stg Crw; Miami Univ.

BANKS, SUSAN D; Cass Tech HS; Detroit, MI; Chrh Wkr; Girl Scts; Off Ade; Pol Wkr; Sct Actv; Stg Crw; FDA; Natl Merit SF; College; Medicine.

BANKS, TASCIA; Perry HS; Cridersville, OH; Sec Frsh Cls; Sec Soph Cls; Band; Chrs; Chrh Wkr; Girl Scts; Hon Rl; Rptr Yrbk; 4-H; Pep Clb; Univ Of Cincinnati; Bus Admin.

BANKSTON, EARNESTINE E; East HS; Columbus, OH; Drl Tm; Hon Rl; Lbry Ade; Off Ade; Sch Pl; Stu Cncl; Drama Clb; Mth Clb; Pep Clb; Chrldng; Ohio State Univ.

BANNHARD, DAVID; Carsonville Port Sanilac HS; Pt Sanilac, MI; 1/75 Hon Rl; NHS; Stu Cncl; Ed Yrbk; Sprt Ed Sch Nwsp; Letter Bsbl; Letter Bsktbl; Letter Ftbl; Letter Trk; Rookie Of Yr Bsktbl; Honorable Mention All League All Region Bsbl; College; Law.

BANNING, JIM; Calumet HS; Gary, IN; 4/260 Am Leg Boys St; Jr NHS; NHS; Letter Ftbl; Letter Trk; Am Leg Awd; Univ; Elec.

BANNINGA, GARTH; St Johns HS; St Johns, MI; Letter Bsktbl; Letter Ten; Univ.

BANNINGER, TERRI; Hammond Voc Tech HS; Hammond, IN; 1/207 Val; Am Leg Aux Girls St; Chrh Wkr; Hon Rl; NHS; DECA; Ball St Univ; Elem Ed.

BANNISTER, DESIREE; Redford HS; Detroit, MI; Cls Rep Frsh Cls; Cls Rep Soph Cls; Cl Rep Jr Cls; Cls Rep Sr Cls; Hosp Ade; Off Ade; Stu Cncl; Eng Clb; OEA; Detroit Coll Of Bus; Executive.

BANNISTER, JACKIE; Wadsworth HS; Wadsworth, OH; Cls Rep Frsh Cls; Cls Rep Soph Cls; Chrh Wkr; FCA; Stu Cncl; Yth Flsp; Pep Clb; Spn Clb; Swmmng; Trk; Bowling Green St Univ; Elem Educ.

BANNISTER, KARA; Marion HS; Marion, IN; 29/665 Band; Hon Rl; NHS; Pom Pon; Indiana Univ.

BANNISTER, LORNA; Crawfordsville HS; Crawfordsville, IN; 64/223 Aud/Vis; Chrs; Hon Rl; Sec JA; NHS; OEA; Pep Clb; Scr Kpr;.

BANNISTER, TOM; Jennings County HS; Scipio, IN; 6/351 Band; Hon Rl; NHS; Sch Pl; Ger Clb; Mth Clb; Natl Merit SF; Purdue Univ; Pharmacy.

BANNOW, SALLY JO; Mt Clemens HS; Mt Clemens, MI; Chrh Wkr; Hon Rl; NHS; Pres Orch; PAVAS; Sch Mus; Univ; Med.

BANREY, JOHN A; North Columbus HS; Columbus, OH; Chrs; JA; Sch Pl; Stu Cncl; Drama Clb; Pep Clb; VP VICA; Voc Schl; Heavy Diesel.

BANTA, PAUL F; North Central HS; Indianapolis, IN; 17/1200 Cls Rep Frsh Cls; Am Leg Boys St; Debate Tm; Hon Rl; Lit Mag; Mod UN; Natl Forn Lg; NHS; Stu Cncl; Mth Clb; Univ; Math.

BAPST, RICHARD; Hammond Tech Voc HS; Hammond, IN; 20/296 Hon Rl; Sch Mus; Sch Pl; Stg Crw; Drama Clb; Theaspiasn Troup #838; Purdue Univ; Bus Mgmt.

BAPTIST, THOMAS; L Anse Creuse HS; Mt Clemens, MI; 5/228 Hon Rl; NHS; Letter Ftbl; Capt Lcrss; Coach Actv; IM Sprt; Michigan St Univ; Mech Engr.

BARABAS, JOHN; Wadsworth HS; Wadsworth, OH; 85/351 Cls Rep Sr Cls; Am Leg Boys St; Band; Boy Scts; Chrh Wkr; Cmnty Wkr; NHS; Hocking Tech College; Forestry.

BARAN, BOHDANNA; Immaculate Conception HS; Detroit, MI; 5/33 Chrs; Hon Rl; Sec NHS; Sct Actv; Stu Cncl; Rptr Yrbk; Rptr Sch Nwsp; Fr Clb; Natl Merit SF; Wayne St Univ; Bus.

BARANCYK, STEVEN; Andrean HS; Merrillville, IN; 1/251 Cls Rep Soph Cls; Cl Rep Jr Cls; Am Leg Boys St; Hon Rl; Pres JA; NHS; Stu Cncl; Ed Yrbk; Rptr Yrbk; Drama Clb; College.

BARANIK, SUZANNE; Griffith Sr HS; Griffith, IN; Cls Rep Frsh Cls; Cl Rep Jr Cls; Hon Rl; Stu Cncl; Bsktbl; Gym; Swmmng; Letter Trk; Chrldng; GAA; Indiana Univ; Radiologic Tech.

BARANOUSKI, CYNTHIA J; Quincy HS; Quincy, MI; Band; Girl Scts; PAVAS; Sch Mus; Sch Pl; 4-H; Pep Clb; VICA; Trk; Opt Clb Awd; Natl VTCA Sec 78; John Edw Tomas Schlrshp 78; Pres Jr Fortnightly Musical Clb 78; Univ; Model.

BARANOWSKI, MIKE; Kalkaska HS; Maneclona, MI; Cls Rep Frsh Cls; Hon Rl; NHS; MI Farm Bureau Yng Peoples Ctznshp Seminar 79; Michigan Tech Univ; Chem Engr.

BARANSKI, KAREN; Fraser HS; Fraser, MI; Chrs; Pres Girl Scts; Hon Rl; NHS; Sch Mus; Sch Pl; Stg Crw; Yrbk; VP Drama Clb; Pres Fr Clb; Univ; Pre Med.

BARBER, ANDREA; Highland HS; Anderson, IN; Cl Rep Jr Cls; Band; Chrh Wkr; Cmnty Wkr; NHS; Stu Cncl; Treas Fr Clb; PPFtbl; Cit Awd; Lion Awd; Purdue Univ; Indus Engr.

BARBER, FRANCO; St Francis Desales HS; Columbus, OH; Chrs; Hon Rl; Jr NHS; Lbry Ade; Spn Clb; Socr; Mgrs; College; Engineering.

BARBER, KIM; Clarkston Sr HS; Drayton Pln, MI; Chrs; Chrh Wkr; Cmnty Wkr; FCA; Girl Scts; Hon Rl; Off Ade; Sct Actv; Yth Flsp; Pep Clb; Oral Roberts Univ; Music.

BARBER, KIMI; River Rouge HS; River Rouge, MI; VP Soph Cls; VP Jr Cls; Band; Chrh Wkr; Cmnty Wkr; Hon Rl; Stu Cncl; Michigan St Univ; Eng.

BARBER, MARY; Mt View HS; Welch, WV; 65/250 Cl Rep Jr Cls; Hon Rl; Lbry Ade; VP FBLA; Pres FHA; Univ Of Maryland; Law.

BARBER, MARYANN; Logan HS; Logan, WV; 1/294 Val; Am Leg Aux Girls St; Chrh Wkr; Cmnty Wkr; Hon Rl; Jr NHS; Treas NHS; Stu Cncl; Sec Fr Clb; Pep Clb; Marshall Univ; Comp Sci.

BARBER, MIKE; Madison Comprehensive HS; Mansfield, OH; Boy Scts; Chrs; Lbry Ade; Sch Pl; Sct Actv; Stg Crw; Rptr Sch Nwsp; DECA; 2nd Pl Dist & St Parlemntarn DECA 1978; 3rd Pl Dist Genrl Mdse DECA 1978; 2nd Pl Dist & St Gnrl Mdse 1979; Salesman.

BARBER, SUE; Taft Sr HS; Fairfield, OH; 10/475 Hon Rl; Jr NHS; NHS; Rptr Sch Nwsp; Ger Clb; Bsktbl; Ten; Univ Of Cincinnati.

BARBER, SUSAN; Sylvania Southview HS; Sylvania, OH; 25/370 Hon Rl; Sch Pl; Rptr Yrbk; Rptr Sch Nwsp; 4-H; Fr Clb; Pep Clb; PPFtbl; Scr Kpr; 4-H Awd; College; Medicine.

BARBER, TRACY; Perrysburg HS; Perrysburg, OH; 5/251 Hon Rl; Jr NHS; Treas NHS; Stg Crw; Fr Clb; Pep Clb; Sec Sci Clb; Socr; Trk; Mis State Univ; Engr.

BARBERA, MARGIE; Villa Angela Academy; Cleveland, OH; Girl Scts; Hon Rl; Stg Crw; Spn Clb; Kspelling Proficiency Cert 78; Geometry Schlrshp 78; Awd For Sci Display 72; Univ; Pre Engr.

BARBERY, KEVIN; Athens HS; Athens, WV; Band; Fr Clb; Key Clb; Bsktbl; Trk; Concord College; Bus.

BARBEY, JAMES; Lutheran HS E; Cleveland, OH; 4/46 Chrs; Chrh Wkr; Hon Rl;.

BARBOUR, ROGER; Stockbridge Community HS; Stockbridge, MI; Am Leg Boys St; Band; Chrh Wkr; Bsktbl; Ftbl; Trk; Albion College; Art.

BARBOUR, RUTH; Fairview HS; Berlin Hts, OH; 119/283 Treas Cmp Fr Grls; Hon Rl; Off Ade; Pol Wkr; Sch Mus; Sch Pl; Stg Crw; Pep Clb; Spn Clb; Capt IM Sprt; Bowling Green St Univ; Sci.

BARCHFELD, JOY; Marion L Steele HS; Amherst, OH; 99/360 Band; Stu Cncl; FTA; GAA; IM Sprt; Bnd Ltr 78; Univ; Spec Educ.

BARCIZ, K; Cardinal Stritch HS; Toledo, OH; Band; Hon Rl; Sch Mus; Pep Clb; Spn Clb; Ten; IM Sprt; College; Interior Decorator.

BARCLAY, CURT; Highland HS; Anderson, IN; Hon Rl; Sct Actv; Spn Clb; Hons 75; Purdue Univ; Acctg.

BARCUS, ANN M; Saint Clement HS; Warren, MI; VP Jr Cls; Hon Rl; Letter Bsbl; Coach Actv; GAA; IM Sprt; Univ; Math.

BARCUS, ELAINE; Berea HS; Berea, OH; 56/551 Cls Rep Soph Cls; Cl Rep Jr Cls; Hon Rl; NHS; Rptr Sch Nwsp; Pep Clb; Coach Actv; Tmr; Acad Achvmnt & Schlshp Awd; Acad Achvmnt In Math; Schlshp Dessert; Ohio Univ; Psych.

BARCUS, JEFFREY; Gallia Acad; Gallipolis, OH; NHS; 4-H; FFA; W Virginia Inst Of Tech; Comp Sci.

BARCUS, LESLIE; Dover HS; Dover, OH; VP Sr Cls; Band; Cmnty Wkr; Hon Rl; Sec Jr NHS; NHS; Stu Cncl; Yth Flsp; Pep Clb; Superior Ratng In Musc Compttns 79; Univ; Acctg.

BARCUS, LISA; Beavercreek HS; Dayton, OH; 152/702 AFS; Chrh Wkr; Cmnty Wkr; Hon Rl; Hosp Ade; NHS; Pep Clb; Ten; Us Merchant Marine Acad; Nautial Sci.

BARCZAK, STANISLAUS; Our Lady Of Mt Carmel HS; Wyandotte, MI; 4/65 Chrh Wkr; Hon Rl; NHS; Pep Clb; Letter Bsbl; Letter Bsktbl; Letter Ftbl; IM Sprt; College.

BARCZYKOWSKI, SANDRA; Washington HS; So Bend, IN; 32/337 Chrs; Drl Tm; Hon Rl; JA; Sch Mus; 4-H; Ger Clb; OEA; Pep Clb; 4-H Awd; Indiana Univ; Acctg.

BARDAR, JILL; Lorain Cath HS; Lorain, OH; 1/150 Trs Soph Cls; Cls Rep Soph Cls; VP Jr Cls; Cl Rep Jr Cls; Cls Rep Sr Cls; Hon Rl; Treas NHS; Stu Cncl; Pres 4-H; Pep Clb; NEDT Cert; Univ; Engr.

BARDEN, CHRIS; Grand Ledge HS; Lansing, MI; 1/450 Chrs; Cmnty Wkr; Girl Scts; Hon Rl; Mdrgl; NHS; Sch Mus; Sch Pl; Sct Actv; Spn Clb; Michigan St Univ; Psych.

BARDEN, DONNA; Penn HS; Mishawaka, IN; Hon Rl; Ind Voc Tech; Cmmrcl Art.

BARDONNER, PAMELA J; John Glenn HS; New Concord, OH; 2/193 AFS; Chrs; Hon Rl; NHS; Sch Pl; Drama Clb; Fr Clb; College; Writing.

BARDOSSY, ELIZABETH; St Augustine Acad; Cleveland, OH; 22/132 Mod UN; Pep Clb; Cle State Univ; Anthropology.

BARDOSSY, VICTORIA; Magnificat HS; Cleveland, OH; Pres JA; NHS; Yrbk; Sch Nwsp; Lat Clb; JA Awd; Natl Merit Ltr; Univ; Bus Admin.

BARE, MARIANNA; Mc Auley HS; Cincinnati, OH; Chrs; Chrh Wkr; Sch Mus; Stg Crw; Drama Clb; Edgecliff Coll; Art Ther.

BARESWILT, JUDY; Seton HS; Cincinnati, OH; 109/271 Chrs; Cmnty Wkr; Hon Rl; Sec JA; FBLA; JA Awd; Coll; Med Sec.

BARFELZ, DAWN; Bridgman HS; Bridgman, MI; Hon Rl; Sch Mus; Sch Pl; FHA; Bsbl; Chrldng; IM Sprt; Scr Kpr; Voc Schl; Interior Decorater.

BARGA, THERESA; Ansonia HS; Rossburg, OH; 14/70 Chrs; Hon Rl; Sch Mus; Sdlty; Sch Nwsp; FHA; OEA;.

BARGAHISER, HEIDI B; Madison Comprehensive HS; Mansfield, OH; Cls Rep Frsh Cls; Sec Soph Cls; VP Jr Cls; Stu Cncl; Spn Clb; Letter Bsktbl; Trk; GAA; IM Sprt; Univ.

BARGENQUAST, BRENT; Grand Ledge HS; Lansing, MI; Trk; Michigan St Univ; Engr.

BARGER, GORDON; Belding Area HS; Belding, MI; Band; Cmnty Wkr; Hon Rl; NHS; Mth Clb; Cit Awd; Voice Dem Awd; Central Michigan Univ; Psychology.

BARGER, JEFFREY; Rutherford B Hayes HS; Delaware, OH; AFS; Chrs; ROTC; Sch Mus; Sch Pl; Stg Crw; Drama Clb; Bsbl; Crs Cntry; Trk; Ohio St Univ.

BARGIEL, JOHN; St Hedwig HS; Detroit, MI; 5/70 Hon Rl; Off Ade; Fr Clb;.

BARGON, JENA; River Rouge HS; River Rouge, MI; 1/200 Sec Frsh Cls; Pres Soph Cls; Sec Soph Cls; Cl Rep Jr Cls; Chrh Wkr; Cmnty Wkr; Hon Rl; NHS; Stu Cncl; Drama Clb; Most Otstndng Jr Awrd Form Eastern Univ 78; Cert Of Otstndng Perfmnc In Acad Achvmnt From House Of Rep 75; Univ; Nursing.

BARGY, DANIEL W; Potterville HS; Potterville, MI; 1/68 Trs Frsh Cls; Trs Soph Cls; Val; Band; Hon Rl; Pres NHS; Off Ade; Orch; Letter Ten; Cit Awd; Mich State Univ; Acctg.

BARHOLOMAI, JAMES G; Jeffersonville HS; Jeffersonville, IN; 98/601 Cls Rep Sr Cls; Hon Rl; Pol Wkr; Yth Flsp; Yrbk; Sch Nwsp; Key Clb; Letter Gym; Letter Swmmng; Tmr; Indiana Univ; Pre Med.

BARHORST, GARRY; Anna Local HS; Anna, OH; 2/85 Sal; Am Leg Boys St; Band; Pres NHS; Stu Cncl; VP Drama Clb; Pres Sci Clb; Am Leg Awd; Univ Of Toledo; Math.

BARHORST, MARK; Sidney HS; Sidney, OH; Cls Rep Frsh Cls; Cls Rep Soph Cls; Band; Chrh Wkr; Orch; Sci Clb; Letter Bsbl; College; Vet.

BARHORST, MARY; Anna HS; Anna, OH; Val; Sal; Band; Cmnty Wkr; Hon Rl; NHS; Stu Cncl; FFA; FHA; Sci Clb; Miami Vly Schl; Nursing.

BARHORST, NANCY; Sidney HS; Sidney, OH; Trs Frsh Cls; Trs Soph Cls; Trs Jr Cls; Trs Sr Cls; Chrs; Chrh Wkr; VP NHS; Off Ade; Sch Mus; Drama Clb; Artist Cove Schl Of Techniques; Art.

BARHORST, TINA; Russia Local HS; Ft Loramie, OH; 4/44 Sec Frsh Cls; Trs Soph Cls; Band; Chrs; Hon Rl; NHS; Sch Pl; Drama Clb; Spn Clb; GAA; Dayton Univ; Forensic Med.

BARICKMAN, KATHRYN; Belpre HS; Little Hocking, OH; 5/150 Trs Frsh Cls; Trs Soph Cls; Trs Jr Cls; Chrs; Chrh Wkr; Hon Rl; NHS; Off Ade; Sch Pl; Yth Flsp; Columbus Tech Inst; Resp Ther.

BARIDO, RICHARD; Herber Hoover HS; Elkvw, WV; Hon Rl; Fr Clb; IM Sprt; Carnegie Mellon Univ; Archt.

BARINKA, SHAWN; Bridgman HS; Bridgman, MI; 17/92 Pres Sr Cls; Band; Hon Rl; NHS; Sch Pl; VP Stu Cncl; Sci Clb; Letter Bsbl; IM Sprt; Arizona St Univ.

BARKASI, LISA; Merrillville HS; Merrillville, IN; 182/604 Band; Chrh Wkr; Girl Scts; Hon Rl; Sch Mus; Stu Cncl; Pep Clb; IM Sprt; Pom Pon; PPFtbl; College; Journalism.

BARKEL, BARBARA S; W Michigan Christian HS; Muskegon, MI; NHS; Stg Crw; Rptr Yrbk; Pep Clb; MI Comptn Schlrshp 79; MI Comptn Schlrshp Awd For Outstndg Academic Achvmnt 79; Univ Of Michigan; Bio Med Engr.

BARKELEY, BILL; Catholic Central HS; Grand Rapids, MI; Cls Rep Soph Cls; Off Ade; Lat Clb; Crs Cntry; Trk; UCLA; Acctg.

BARKER, BARRY; Stonewall Jackson HS; Charleston, WV; Chrs; FCA; Hon Rl; Sch Mus; Lat Clb; Letter Ftbl; Letter Ten; Letter Trk; Letter Wrstlng; College; Math.

BARKER, BEULAH; Bluefield HS; Bluefield, WV; Chrh Wkr; Lbry Ade; Yth Flsp; Y-Teens; FHA; Pep Clb; Trk; College; Bus.

BARKER, BRADLEY; Mc Comb HS; Mc Comb, OH; 2/80 VP Soph Cls; VP Jr Cls; Trs Sr Cls; Chrs; Hon Rl; Jr NHS; NHS; Sch Pl; Yth Flsp; 4-H; Most Outstdg Jr Awd 79; Univ; Bio.

BARKER, CHERYL; Peck Cmnty Schools; Peck, MI; Girl Scts; Hon Rl; FHA; Pep Clb; Letter Bsbl; Letter Bsktbl; Letter Chrldng; Mgrs; Univ.

BARKER, DEBRA; Mason Sr HS; Mason, MI; Cls Rep Frsh Cls; Band; Hon Rl; Stu Cncl; Fr Clb; Pep Clb; Trk; IM Sprt; 4-H Awd; Pres Awd; College; Soc Fields.

BARKER, DEWAYNE; Du Pont Sr HS; Charleston, WV; Chrh Wkr; Hon Rl; Stg Crw; Ftbl; IM Sprt; West Virginia Univ; Chem Engr.

BARKER, DOUGLAS; Hart HS; Hart, MI; 4/144 Hon Rl; Rdo Clb; Sci Clb; Univ Of Michigan; Elec Engr.

BARKER, GEORGE; Menominee Area Public HS; Menominee, MI; 22/232 Cls Rep Sr Cls; Am Leg Boys St; NHS; VP Sci Clb; Trk; Michigan Tech Univ; Civil Engr.

BARKER, KATHERINE; Bay HS; Bay Vill, OH; Girl Scts; Off Ade; Yrbk; Spn Clb; Swmmng; IM Sprt; PPFtbl; Scr Kpr; Tmr; Univ Of Dayton; Psych.

BARKER, KIMBERLY; Vinton County Consldtd HS; Ray, OH; Am Leg Aux Girls St; Chrs; Chrh Wkr; Hon Rl; NHS; Off Ade; VP 4-H; Fr Clb; Pep Clb; Bsktbl; Ohio Univ; Bus.

BARKER, MARIANNA; Crestline HS; Crestline, OH; Am Leg Aux Girls St; Band; Chrs; Hon Rl; NHS; Orch; Sch Mus; Sch Pl; Stg Crw; Ger Clb; Spch & Drama Awd 79; Univ; Foreign Lang.

BARKER, MARK; La Crosse HS; Wanatah, IN; Am Leg Boys St; Ger Clb; Trk; Secondary Education.

BARKER, MARK; Northeastern HS; Williamsburg, IN; Hon Rl; Pol Wkr; Stu Cncl; 4-H; FFA; Crs Cntry; Trk; Wrstlng; 4-H Awd; Coll.

BARKER, MINDEE; Brooke HS; Weirton, WV; 103/415 Cmp Fr Grls; Chrh Wkr; Hon Rl; Drama Clb; Spn Clb; Hon Queen Bethel 4 Weirton Wv Intl Od Of Jobs Daughters 80; Pres Chstn Yth Fllwhsp 79; West Virginia Univ; Interior Design.

BARKER, PHILIP; St Matthew HS; Holt, MI; 1/6 Val; Chrs; Hon Rl; Sch Mus; Sch Pl; Yrbk; Letter Bsktbl; Letter Socr; Coach Actv; Spring Arbor Coll.

BARKER, RAY; Mississinewa HS; Marion, IN; Jr NHS; NHS; Key Clb; Letter Bsbl; Letter Bsktbl; Ftbl; Letter Ten; Univ; Med.

BARKER, ROBERTA; Kankakee Valley HS; De Motte, IN; Val; Am Leg Aux Girls St; Sec Band; Chrh Wkr; Hon Rl; Sec NHS; Off Ade; Mth Clb; Bsktbl; Trk; Indiana Univ; Lab Tech.

BARKER, SCOTT; North Putnam Jr Sr HS; Roachdale, IN; Boy Scts; Hon Rl; Jr NHS; NHS; Sct Actv; FFA; Sci Clb; Spn Clb; JETS Awd; Purdue Univ; Bio Chem.

BARKER, STEPHANIE; Amelia HS; Cincinnati, OH; Pres Band; Chrs; Chrh Wkr; Drl Tm; Drm Mjrt; Off Ade; Sch Mus; Stg Crw; Sec Yth Flsp; Band Awd Ltr 78; Tennessee Temple Univ; Educ.

BARKER, STEVE; Piketon HS; Piketon, OH; Pres Jr Cls; Hon Rl; 4-H; VICA; Voc Schl; Machine Trades.

BARKER, TIM; Martinsville HS; Martinsville, IN; Jr NHS; Bsbl; Letter Ten; IM Sprt; Scr Kpr; Bus Mgmt.

BARKER, TRACI; Bishop Donahue Memorial HS; Mc Mechen, WV; VP Frsh Cls; Band; Chrs; Girl Scts; Hon Rl; NHS; Pep Clb; Chrldng; West Liberty State College; Phys Ed.

BARKEY, ELISA; Copley Sr HS; Barberton, OH; Band; Girl Scts; Hosp Ade; Sct Actv; 4-H; Fr Clb; Spn Clb; Akron Univ; RN.

BARKHEIMER, SANDY; Perry HS; Navarre, OH; Chrh Wkr; Cmnty Wkr; Girl Scts; Hon Rl; Hosp Ade; NHS; Off Ade; Sct Actv; Spn Clb; VICA; 1st Class Girl Sct Awd 75; Girl Sct Wider Opport Buggies Bridges & Barndoors 78; Voc Schl; RN.

BARKLE, LISA; Kingsford HS; Kingsford, MI; 11/180 Hon Rl; NHS; Rptr Sch Nwsp; 4-H; FTA; Mgrs; PEO Sistrhd Schslhp 79; Michigan Tech Univ; Med Tech.

BARKLEY, ANN; Heritage HS; Ft Wayne, IN; 4/176 VP Frsh Cls; Trs Soph Cls; VP Jr Cls; VP Sr Cls; Band; Chrs; Chrh Wkr; Girl Scts; Hon Rl; Quill & Scroll; College; Nursing.

BARKS, BILLY; Ben Davis HS; Indianapolis, IN; Hon Rl; Boys Clb Am; Fr Clb; Bsktbl; Ten; Ind Univ.

BARLAGE, BRENDA K; Huntington HS; Chillicothe, OH; 5/93 Pres Sr Cls; Chrh Wkr; Cmnty Wkr; Hon Rl; NHS; Sch Pl; Yrbk; FTA; Ohio Univ; Xray Technologist.

BARLAGE, KATHY; Russia Local School; Houston, OH; 2/44 Pres Soph Cls; Band; Chrs; Hon Rl; NHS ; Drama Clb; Trk; Bus Schl; Acctg.

BARLAGE, KATHY; Russia Local HS; Houston, OH; 2/45 Pres Soph Cls; Band; Hon Rl; NHS; Off Ade; Drama Clb; Letter Trk; Business Schl; Acctg.

BARLAY, CYNTHIA; St Joseph Acad; Cleveland, OH; Hon Rl; Hosp Ade; NHS; Mth Clb; Spn Clb; Cnyahoga Community College; Rn.

BARLAY, KATHLEEN; St Joseph Academy; Cleveland, OH; Chrh Wkr; Cmnty Wkr; Hon Rl; Stg Crw; Sch Nwsp; Excellnc In Art 77; Cooper Schl Of Art; Artist.

BARLEKAMP, HAROLD C; Fostoria HS; Fostoria, OH; 1/200 Cls Rep Frsh Cls; Am Leg Boys St; Band; Chrs; Chrh Wkr; Hon Rl; Pres NHS; Sch Mus; Sch Pl; Yth Flsp; Whos Who In Foreign Lang 78; Partcpnt In Natl Sci Fdn Resrch Inst 78; Super Ratng Ohio Music Educ Assoc 76; Univ; Med.

BARLETT, DOUG; Streetsboro HS; Streetsboro, OH; 1/243 Pres Sr Cls; Am Leg Boys St; Band; Drm Mjrt; Hon Rl; NHS; Orch; Stg Crw; Sci Clb; Letter Trk; Univ; Aero Astro Engr.

BARLEY, JILL; Menominee HS; Menominee, MI; 50/285 Pres Frsh Cls; Cls Rep Soph Cls; Trs Jr Cls; AFS; Am Leg Aux Girls St; Chrh Wkr; Cmnty Wkr; Debate Tm; Hon Rl; Jr NHS; NHS; Real Estate Salesman.

BARLOW, BONNIE; South Newton Jr Sr HS; Goodland, IN; 6/100 Hon Rl; Sch Pl; Stu Cncl; FBLA; FHA; FTA; Letter Bsktbl; Letter Trk; Coach Actv; PPFtbl;.

BARLOW, DAVE; Reading HS; Reading, MI; Cl Rep Jr Cls; Cls Rep Sr Cls; Band; Chrs; Stu Cncl; Pep Clb; Crs Cntry; Cit Awd; Hillsdale College; Music.

BARLOW, REBECCA; Lutheran East HS; Detroit, MI; Hon Rl; Hosp Ade; Ed Sch Nwsp; Rptr Sch Nwsp; Sch Nwsp;.

BARLOW, ROBERTA; Wintersville HS; Wintersville, OH; 23/267 Band; Chrh Wkr; Hon Rl; Music Ensmbl & Band Awds 77; Music Solo & Ensmble & Band Awds 78; Univ; CPA.

BARLOW, VICKIE; Benedictine HS; Detroit, MI; Cls Rep Frsh Cls; Chrs; Hon Rl; Yth Flsp; Fr Clb; Pep Clb; Cit Awd; Miss French; Ath Vlybl Awd; Michigan St Univ.

BARMORE, BETH; Westfield Washington HS; Sheridan, IN; Band; Girl Scts; Hon Rl; Sch Mus; Sch Pl; Stg Crw; Drama Clb; 4-H; Fr Clb; Pep Clb; Indiana Univ; Speech Ther.

BARMORE, MATTHEW; Marion HS; Marion, IN; Band; Drm Mjrt; Hon Rl; Orch; Fr Clb; Psi Lota Xi Bnd Awd 79; Indiana Univ; Music Educ.

BARNARD, CAMEO; Clarkston Sr HS; Clarkston, MI; Chrs; Girl Scts; Hon Rl; Off Ade; Sch Mus; Sch Pl; Stg Crw; Drama Clb; Pontiac Bus Inst; Fshn Mdse.

BARNARD, DOUGLAS; Rossville HS; Rossville, IN; 3/50 Pres Jr Cls; Am Leg Boys St; Chrh Wkr; NHS; Pres Yth Flsp; Pres FFA; Letter Bsbl; Letter Crs Cntry; Letter Trk; Honor Roll 3 Yrs; Top Stu In Algebra II Class; Coll; Ag Engr.

BARNEKOW, DAVID; Buena Vista HS; Saginaw, MI; Boy Scts; Chrh Wkr; FCA; Hon Rl; NHS; Ed Sch Nwsp; Sci Clb; Ftbl; Awds Bio 78; Chem 78; Ctznshp Awd 78; Olivet Nazarene Coll; Bio Chem.

BARNELL, LA VONNE; Constantine HS; Constantine, MI; 5/100 Cls Rep Frsh Cls; Cls Rep Soph Cls; VP Sr Cls; Am Leg Aux Girls St; Band; Chrs; Hon Rl; Lit Mag; NHS; Off Ade; Ferris St Coll; Dent Asst.

BARNER, KAREN; Holly Sr HS; Holly, MI; 5/284 Chrs; Chrh Wkr; Girl Scts; Hon Rl; Mdrgl; NHS; Off Ade; Sch Mus; Sct Actv; Stg Crw; Michigan St Univ; Bus Admin.

BARNER, LEANNE; Everett HS; Lansing, MI; JA; NHS; Pol Wkr; Ed Yrbk; Rptr Sch Nwsp; FTA; Spn Clb; Cit Awd; Natl Merit Schl; 3 Stud Council Awds 75 76 & 77; Acad Achvmnt Awd 79; Lansing Cmnty Coll; Spec Educ Tchr.

BARNES, ALICE E; Delphos St Johns HS; Delphos, OH; 1/135 Pres Jr Cls; Am Leg Aux Girls St; Chrh Wkr; Cmnty Wkr; Girl Scts; Hon Rl; NHS; Sct Actv; Stu Cncl; Rptr Sch Nwsp; Schlrshp Tm Mbr 77 79; Excel & Superior Rtngs At Schl Dist Sci Fair 75 79; Rnks 8th In Adv Algebra 79; Ohio St Univ; Math.

BARNES, ANDY; Clermont Northeastern HS; Batavia, OH; Cls Rep Soph Cls; FCA; Hon Rl; Spn Clb; Letter Ftbl; College; Engr.

BARNES, BARBARA; Belpre HS; Belpre, OH; Girl Scts; Hon Rl; Off Ade; OEA; Ohio Offc Ed Assoc Chap Pres; Most Congenial Stu Awd; Exe Awd OEA; College; Accounting.

BARNES, BLAIR; Marysville HS; Marysville, OH; Cls Rep Soph Cls; Pres Jr Cls; Pres Sr Cls; Am Leg Boys St; Cmnty Wkr; Debate Tm; Natl Forn Lg; Red Cr Ade; Sch Mus; Stu Cncl; Ohi State Univ; Molecular Bio.

BARNES, CAROL A; William A Wirt HS; Gary, IN; 11/239 Chrh Wkr; Hon Rl; Jr NHS; NHS; Rptr Yrbk; IM Sprt; Natl Merit Ltr; Taylor Univ; Biology.

BARNES, CARRIE; Marysville HS; Marysville, MI; Band; Cmp Fr Grls; Debate Tm; Drl Tm; Drm Mjrt; Hon Rl; Hosp Ade; Stu Cncl; Sci Clb; GAA; College; Physical Therapy.

BARNES, DALE A; Franklin Cmnty HS; Franklin, IN; 6/260 Band; Boy Scts; Hon Rl; Lit Mag; NHS; Orch; Sch Mus; Lat Clb; Sci Clb; Natl Merit Ltr; Indiana St Univ; Music Educ.

BARNES, DOUGLAS; Madison Heights HS; Anderson, IN; 33/371 Band; Drm Bgl; NHS; Orch; Ball St Univ; Railroad Wrk.

BARNES, ERIC; Knightstown Community HS; Knightstown, IN; 14/145 VP Soph Cls; Trs Jr Cls; Am Leg Boys St; Band; FCA; Hon Rl; NHS; Spn Clb; Letter Bsbl; Letter Bsktbl; College; Pathology.

BARNES, ESTHER; Johnstown Monroe HS; Johnstown, OH; 5/140 Am Leg Aux Girls St; Band; Chrh Wkr; Hon Rl; Pres NHS; Sch Pl; Yth Flsp; Otterbein Coll; Elem Ed.

BARNES, EVELYN; Jane Addons Voc; Cleveland, OH; Cls Rep Frsh Cls; Cls Rep Soph Cls; Sec Jr Cls; Sec Sr Cls; Band; Cmp Fr Grls; Chrs; Chrh Wkr; Cmnty Wkr; Drl Tm; Community; Court Reporting.

BARNES, JANET; Manton Consolidated Schl; Manton, MI; 8/49 Hon Rl; NHS; Ferris St Coll; Data Proc.

BARNES, KAREN; Kelloggsville HS; Wyoming, MI; Cl Rep Jr Cls; Chrs; Hon Rl; Jr NHS; Off Ade; PAVAS; Stg Crw; Bsbl; Bsktbl; PPFtbl; Grand Rapids Jr Coll; Sec.

BARNES, KELLY S; Crestview Local HS; Leetonia, OH; Hon Rl; Pep Clb; Spn Clb; Bsktbl; Trk; Coach Actv; GAA; PPFtbl; Pres Awd; Univ.

BARNES, LAURIE; Paulding Exempted Vllg Schl; Paulding, OH; 16/172 Cls Rep Frsh Cls; Cl Rep Jr Cls; Chrs; Chrh Wkr; Hon Rl; PAVAS; Sch Mus; Sch Pl; Stg Crw; Stu Cncl; Univ Of Cincinnati; Graphic Design.

BARNES, LISA; Sycamore HS; Cincinnati, OH; Chrs; Drl Tm; Girl Scts; Hon Rl; NHS; Bsktbl; Coach Actv; IM Sprt; College Of Mt St Joseph; Physical Ed.

BARNES, MARGARET; National Trail HS; Eaton, OH; 3/125 Pres Frsh Cls; VP Soph Cls; VP Jr Cls; VP Sr Cls; Pres Band; Sec NHS; Pres Yth Flsp; Miami Univ; Acctg.

BARNES, MARY; Kenowa Hills HS; Grand Rapids, MI; Band; Drl Tm; 4-H; Pres Pep Clb; Gym; Mgrs; PPFtbl; 4-H Awd; Davenport Bus College; Acctg.

BARNES, MAURINE; Ashtabula HS; Ashtubula, OH; Band; Hon Rl; NHS; Rptr Yrbk; Sci Clb; Andrews Univ; Comp Sci.

BARNES, MICHAEL; West Lafayette HS; W Lafayette, IN; Band; Boy Scts; FCA; Hon Rl; Orch; Sch Mus; Sct Actv; Yth Flsp; Bsbl; Letter Ftbl; Purdue Univ; Bus Mgmt.

BARNES, MILTON; Hughes HS; Cincinnati, OH; Chrs; Sch Mus; Sch Pl; Stu Cncl; Boys Clb Am; Chrldng; IM Sprt; Cit Awd; Univ Cal; Foreign Languages.

BARNES, PAMELA; Redford HS; Detroit, MI; Cls Rep Frsh Cls; Michigan St Univ; Psych.

BARNES, SUE; Warren Western Reserve HS; Warren, OH; 55/467 Hon Rl; NHS; Y-Teens; Rptr Sch Nwsp; OEA; GAA; IM Sprt; Scr Kpr; Tmr; Govt.

BARNES, SUSAN; Morgan HS; Mc Connelsville, OH; Am Leg Aux Girls St; Hon Rl; Off Ade;.

BARNES, SUZANNE M; Marlington HS; Alliance, OH; 15/280 Hon Rl; JA; Rptr Sch Nwsp; Sch Nwsp; Akron Univ; Sec.

BARNES, TERESA; Rutherford B Hayes HS; Delaware, OH; Chrh Wkr; Hon Rl; Hosp Ade; Lit Mag; Sch Pl; Key Clb; Lat Clb; Volleyball Reserve 77 Co Capt 78; Univ; Psych.

BARNES, TERESA; Morton Sr HS; Hammond, IN; 32/419 Band; Chrh Wkr; Girl Scts; Hon Rl; Off Ade; Pol Wkr; Sct Actv; Stu Cncl; Bsktbl; Trk; Valparaiso Univ; Legal Secretary.

BARNES, THOMAS; Cascade HS; Clayton, IN; 10/150 Am Leg Boys St; Chrh Wkr; FCA; Hon Rl; NHS; Yth Flsp; Ed Sch Nwsp; Sprt Ed Sch Nwsp; Rptr Sch Nwsp; Bsbl; Social Studies Awd 79; Merit Awd 76; Liberty Baptist Coll; Ministry.

BARNES, TONI; Edwin Denby HS; Detroit, MI; Sec Jr Cls; Cl Rep Jr Cls; Chrs; Chrh Wkr; Hon Rl; Off Ade; Bsbl; Coach Actv; Schlshp For GPA 80; Awd Focus Hop For Attndng A Retreat 78; Univ; Med.

BARNES JR, WILLIAM; Huntington HS; Huntington, WV; Cls Rep Sr Cls; Chrh Wkr; Hon Rl; NHS; Stu Cncl; Yth Flsp; Fr Clb; Mth Clb; Letter Bsbl; Letter Bsktbl; Univ Of Tennessee; Engineering.

BARNET, ANNE; Archbishop Alter HS; Dayton, OH; Cls Rep Soph Cls; Cl Rep Jr Cls; Band; Hon Rl; NHS; Orch; Stu Cncl; Spn Clb; GAA; College; Bio Sci.

BARNETT, ANTHONY; Caldwell HS; Caldwell, OH; 37/104 Chrh Wkr; Cmnty Wkr; Sch Pl; Sct Actv; Rptr Sch Nwsp; Sch Nwsp; Spn Clb; Pittsburgh Art Inst; Cmmrcl Art.

BARNETT, DEBRA; Lamphere HS; Madison Hts, MI; Pres Frsh Cls; Hon Rl; NHS; Yrbk; Chrldng; Capt PPFtbl; Michigan St Univ; Acctg.

BARNETT, J MICHAEL; Elgin HS; Prospect, OH; 21/151 Cls Rep Soph Cls; Cl Rep Jr Cls; Cls Rep Sr Cls; Am Leg Boys St; Hon Rl; Jr NHS; Letter Bsktbl; Letter Trk; Scr Kpr; Univ.

BARNETT, JOHN; Fairbanks HS; Ostrander, OH; Yth Flsp; Letter Ftbl; Letter Ten; IM Sprt; Univ.

BARNETT, KEVIN; Jackson HS; Jackson, OH; Am Leg Boys St; Boy Scts; Hon Rl; NHS; Sct Actv; Stu Cncl; Yth Flsp; Sci Clb; Bsbl; Letter Bsktbl; Univ.

BARNETT, KEVIN; Franklin Comm HS; Franklin, IN; 19/280 Band; Chrh Wkr; Hon Rl; JA; Jr NHS; NHS; Orch; Sch Mus; 4-H; Sci Clb; Purdue Univ; Comp Sci.

BARNETT, LILLIE; Muskegon Heights HS; Muskegon Hts, MI; Chrh Wkr; Girl Scts; Hon Rl; Yrbk; 4-H; Cit Awd; 4-H Awd; Muskegon Bus College; Data Proc.

BARNETT, LUZVIMINDA; Trotwood Madison HS; Trotwood, OH; Hst Jr Cls; VP Sr Cls; Chrs; OEA; Trk; Letter Chrldng; Cit Awd; Vocational Schl; Legal Sec.

BARNETT, MARY; Princeton HS; Cincinnati, OH; 103/671 Boy Scts; Chrs; Drl Tm; Hon Rl; NHS; Sch Mus; Sch Pl; Stg Crw; Univ Of Cincinnati; Law Enforcement.

BARNETT, P; Rensselaer Central HS; Rensselaer, IN; 8/163 Cl Rep Jr Cls; Chrs; Hon Rl; NHS; Sch Mus; Stu Cncl; Pres 4-H; Veterinary Schl; Vet.

BARNETT, REGINA; Berkeley Springs HS; Berkeley Spg, WV; 12/133 VP Sr Cls; Girl Scts; Hon Rl; Hosp Ade; NHS; Off Ade; Red Cr Ade; Sch Mus; Stu Cncl; Wv Univ; Pre Phys Ther.

BARNETT, STEPHEN; North Muskegon HS; N Muskegon, MI; 24/108 Hon Rl; Glf; Univ.

BARNETT, VALERIE; Lorain Catholic HS; Lorain, OH; Treas Chrs; Cmnty Wkr; NHS; Drama Clb; Fr Clb; VP Pep Clb; Letter Ten; Commnded Stu Of Natl Achvmnt Schlrshp Progr 78; St Brd Of Ed Awd Of Distinctn 79; Cert For Stdy Of Frnch 78; Miami Univ; Acctg.

BARNETT, VETA; Marion HS; Marion, IN; Girl Scts; Off Ade; Y-Teens; Crs Cntry; Capt Trk; GAA; Mat Maids; Ball State Univ; Phys Ed.

BARNEY, SONIA; Mendon HS; Mendon, MI; Cl Rep Jr Cls; Band; FCA; Hon Rl; Hosp Ade; Red Cr Ade; 4-H; Trk; PPFtbl; 4-H Awd; Nazareth Univ; Nursing.

BARNEY, THOMAS; Grand Rapids Central HS; Grand Rapids, MI; Hon Rl; Jr NHS; Mod UN; NHS; Sch Pl; Lat Clb; Sci Clb; Mic Tech Univ; Pre Med.

BARNFIELD, ANDREA K; Carroll HS; Huntertown, IN; 6/221 Hon Rl; Natl Forn Lg; NHS; Sch Mus; Pres Fr Clb; Treas Sci Clb; Spn Clb; Bsktbl; Letter Crs Cntry; Letter Trk; Ft Wayne Chamber Of Cmrc Dist Stu Awd; Jr Engr Tech Soc Cert; Indiana Hoosier Schlrshp Awd; Purdue Univ; Biomed Engr.

BARNHARD, DORIS J; Fruitport HS; Fruitport, MI; Band; Chrs; Hon Rl; Jr NHS; NHS; Sch Mus; Pep Clb; Chrldng; Pom Pon; PPFtbl; St Of Mi Shclshp Awd 850 79; BEOG 79; Natl Dir Stdn Tloan 70079; Ferris St Coll; Pre Med.

BARNHART, CYNTHIA; Delaware Hayes HS; Delaware, OH; Cl Rep Jr Cls; Cls Rep Sr Cls; Hon Rl; Off Ade; Sch Pl; Stu Cncl; Sec Y-Teens; Rptr Sch Nwsp; Key Clb; Cert Pblc Sec.

BARNHART, FRANK; Rock Hill Sr HS; Pedro, OH; 5/175 Pres Jr Cls; Cls Rep Sr Cls; Band; Hon Rl; Jr NHS; NHS; Stu Cncl; Ed Sch Nwsp; Sch Nwsp; Beta Clb; Ohio Univ; Theater.

BARNHART, KARLA; Middletown HS; Middletown, OH; 4/519 Hon Rl; NHS; Pep Clb; GAA; Lion Awd; Magna Cum Laude Letter & Bar Earned; Herman H Lawrence Banquet; Cert Of Proficiency In Century 21 Acctg; Eastern Kentucky Univ; Elem Ed.

BARNHART, KENT T; Ewen Trout Creek HS; Ewen, MI; 3/50 VP Sr Cls; Cls Rep Sr Cls; Debate Tm; Hon Rl; Lbry Ade; Stg Crw; Stu Cncl; Letter Bsktbl; Letter Ftbl; Letter Trk; Michigan Tech Inst; Engr.

BARNHART, KIMBERLY; Lynchburg Clay HS; Hillsboro, OH; Cmp Fr Grls; Chrh Wkr; Cmnty Wkr; Sch Pl; Yth Flsp; Yrbk; Rptr Sch Nwsp; 4-H; Fr Clb; FFA; FFA Greenhand Degree 78; Girls Track 3 Yr Awd 79; Girls Bsktbl Letter 78; Southern St Univ; Indust Engr.

BARNHART, MELISSA; Tecumseh HS; New Carlisle, OH; 14/344 AFS; Chrs; Hon Rl; Jr NHS; NHS; Sch Mus; Sch Pl; Stg Crw; Pres Drama Clb; Fr Clb; Miami Jacobs Jr Coll; Fash Admin.

BARNHART, RANDY; Rutherford B Hayes HS; Delaware, OH; Boy Scts; Hon Rl; Pres JA; NHS; Sch Pl; Sct Actv; VP Spn Clb; Ftbl; JA Awd; Columbus Para Pro Inst; Comp Prog.

BARNHART, RHONDA; South Harrison HS; Mt Clare, WV; 9/86 Hon Rl; NHS; Stg Crw; Yth Flsp; Rptr Yrbk; Rptr Sch Nwsp; Letter Bsktbl; Trk; GAA; Scr Kpr; W Virginia Career Coll; Bookkeeping.

BARNHART, ROSE; Benjamin Logan HS; Rushsylvania, OH; Cls Rep Soph Cls; Chrh Wkr; Girl Scts; Hon Rl; Sch Pl; Stu Cncl; Yth Flsp; Drama Clb; FTA; Spn Clb; Univ; Scndry Educ Eng.

BARNHART, SHARI A; Edsel Ford HS; Dearborn, MI; AFS; Chrs; Cmnty Wkr; Hon Rl; NHS; PAVAS; Sch Mus; Ger Clb; Chrldng; Pom Pon; Eastern Michigan Univ; Elem Educ.

BARNHART, STEVE; Deerfield HS; Deerfield, MI; Cls Rep Frsh Cls; Trs Soph Cls; Trs Jr Cls; Trs Sr Cls; Band; Treas Stu Cncl; Letter Bsktbl; Letter Trk; Toledo Univ; Bus Admin.

BARNHART, THOMAS; Traverse City HS; Traverse City, MI; 20/683 Chrs; Mdrgl; NHS; Sch Pl; Univof Mic.

BARNHART, TONYA; Canal Winchester HS; Cnl Winchester, OH; Hon Rl; Off Ade; FHA; Spn Clb; Trk; Chrldng; PPFtbl; Paul C Hayes Tech Schl; Dental Asst.

BARNHILL, CINDY; Ben Davis HS; Indianapolis, IN; Chrh Wkr; Girl Scts; Hon Rl; Lbry Ade; Mod UN; Rptr Sch Nwsp; Spn Clb; Gym; Mgrs; IUPUI; Fshn Mdse.

BARNOVSKY, DAVID; Howland HS; Warren, OH; 45/472 Boy Scts; Chrh Wkr; Cmnty Wkr; Hon Rl; Sct Actv; Glf; IM Sprt; Univ; Chem Engr.

BARNTHOUSE, BRENDA; Lebanon HS; Mason, OH; Hst Sr Cls; Band; Chrh Wkr; Hon Rl; Lbry Ade; Yth Flsp; 4-H; FHA; OEA; Spn Clb; Deputy Clrk.

BARNWELL, JACQUELINE; Oakwood HS; Dayton, OH; AFS; Cmnty Wkr; FCA; Hon Rl; Jr NHS; NHS; Rptr Yrbk; Rptr Sch Nwsp; Pep Clb; Ten; 3rd Highst Avr Overal 77; Highst Spanish Avr 77 78 & 79; Bst Newsppr In Cincinnati HS 78; Univ; Foreign Serv.

BARON, ANNGEL; Ursuline HS; Campbell, OH; 121/342 FTA; Lat Clb; Youngstown State Univ; Medicine.

BARON, DANIELLE; Bay HS; Bay Vill, OH; Hon Rl; VP JA; Yth Flsp; Sprt Ed Yrbk; Swmmng; Ten; Trk; PPFtbl; JA Awd; Univ; Poli Sci.

BARON, DEBRA; Admiral King HS; Lorain, OH; 60/413 Trs Jr Cls; Band; Chrs; Hon Rl; NHS; OEA; Chrldng; AKAS Bwlng Lge 78; Mbr Co Op Off Educ 79; Whos Who Amer H S Stu 78; Lorain Cmnty Coll; Bus Admin.

BARON, EVA M; Robert S Rogers HS; Toledo, OH; 16/412 VP Jr Cls; VP Sr Cls; Hon Rl; NHS; Sch Mus; Sch Pl; Stg Crw; Drama Clb; Fr Clb; PPFtbl; Univ Of Toledo; Theatre.

BARONE, ANGELO; Southgate HS; Southgate, MI; Cl Rep Jr Cls; Cls Rep Sr Cls; Hon Rl; Sch Pl; Stu Cncl; Yrbk; Drama Clb; Ten; College; CPA.

BARONE, KATHRYN; Perkins HS; Sandusky, OH; 1/238 Pres Soph Cls; Pres Jr Cls; Pres Sr Cls; Val; Am Leg Aux Girls St; Sct Actv; Ed Sch Nwsp; Capt Trk; Am Leg Awd; Voice Dem Awd; Miami Univ; Cmmrcl Art.

BAROSK, NANCY; Parkside HS; Jackson, MI; Band; Hon Rl; Orch; Fr Clb; College.

BAROTH, JULIE; Harper Woods Scndry HS; Harper Woods, MI; Pres Frsh Cls; VP Soph Cls; Pres Jr Cls; Girl Scts; Hon Rl; Stu Cncl; Bsbl; Bsktbl; Letter Chrldng; IM Sprt; Michigan St Univ; Nursing.

BARR, ALAN; Manistique HS; Manistique, MI; 1/135 Pres Frsh Cls; Cls Rep Frsh Cls; Pres Soph Cls; Pres Sr Cls; Cls Rep Sr Cls; Val; Band; Boy Scts; Cmnty Wkr; Debate Tm; Univ Of Michigan; Pre Med.

BARR, CHERYL; J A Garfield Maplewood JVS; Garrettsville, OH; Drl Tm; JA; Lit Mag; Sch Mus; Sch Pl; Stu Cncl; Y-Teens; 4-H; OEA; Pep Clb; Maplewood JVS; Sec.

BARR, DEAN; Meadow Brook HS; Senecaville, OH; Band; Boy Scts; Chrh Wkr; Cmnty Wkr; Drm Bgl; Hon Rl; Yth Flsp; Key Clb; Bsbl; Wrstlng; Coll.

BARR, DOUG; Bridgeport Sr HS; Bridgeport, WV; Band; Boy Scts; Hon Rl; NHS; Sch Pl; Sct Actv; Stu Cncl; Ed Sch Nwsp; Sch Nwsp; Glf; West Virginia Univ; Marketing.

BARR, FREDERICK; Morgantown HS; Morgantwn, WV; Cl Rep Jr Cls; Boy Scts; Hon Rl; NHS; Sct Actv; Stu Cncl; Mth Clb; Spn Clb; College; Pre Med.

BARR, JEANETTE; Allen Park HS; Allen Pk, MI; Chrs; Hon Rl; Pep Clb; Univ Of Michigan; Pharm.

BARR, KRIS; Negaunee HS; Negaunee, MI; Chrs; Hon Rl; Pep Clb; Letter Gym; Letter Trk; IM Sprt; Univ; Bus.

BARR, MELODY; Candiz HS; Cadiz, OH; Cls Rep Frsh Cls; Sec Soph Cls; Sec Jr Cls; Chrs; Hon Rl; Sch Pl; Stu Cncl; Yth Flsp; Drama Clb; Lat Clb; Jr Attendant; Jr Prom Princess; Chose To Check At T R Charities All Star Game; Mount Union Coll; Psych.

BARR, MELODY; Cadiz HS; Cadiz, OH; Sec Frsh Cls; Sec Soph Cls; Sec Jr Cls; Chrs; Hon Rl; Hosp Ade; Sch Pl; Stu Cncl; Yth Flsp; Drama Clb; Mt Union Univ; Spec Ed.

BARR, MICHAEL; Malabar HS; Mansfield, OH; 1/275 Pres Frsh Cls; Pres Soph Cls; Am Leg Boys St; Band; Cmnty Wkr; Lit Mag; Orch; Key Clb; College; Bus Admin.

BARR, RHONDA; Buffalo HS; Kenova, WV; 2/150 Trs Soph Cls; Band; Hon Rl; Off Ade; Sch Pl; Yth Flsp; Yrbk; FHA; Mth Clb;.

BARR, RICHARD; R B Chamberlin HS; Twinsburg, OH; 2/170 Chrh Wkr; Hon Rl; NHS; Bsktbl; Glf; IM Sprt; Natl Merit Schl; Case Western Reserve Univ; Elec Engr.

BARR, SCOTT; Muskegon HS; Muskegon, MI; Band; Hon Rl; NHS; Orch; Sch Mus; Rptr Sch Nwsp; Drama Clb; Hockey; Michigan St Univ; Eng Educ.

BARR, STEPHEN; Clyde HS; Clyde, OH; 40/210 Aud/Vis; Hon Rl; Rptr Sch Nwsp; Bsbl; Bsktbl; Crs Cntry; Ftbl; Baldwin Wallace College; Bus.

BARR, STEVE; Clyde HS; Clyde, OH; 40/210 Aud/Vis; Hon Rl; Rptr Yrbk; Bsbl; Bsktbl; Ftbl; Coach Actv; Baldwin Wallace Coll.

BARRACO, N MARIA; Southgate HS; Southgate, MI; Band; Wayne St Univ.

BARRANGER, THERESA; Fairview HS; Fairview Pk, OH; 9/256 Hon Rl; NHS; Sci Clb; Cleveland St Univ; Engr.

BARRASS, CARLA; Niles Mc Kinley HS; Niles, OH; 42/329 Pres Band; Hon Rl; NHS; Sch Mus; Drama Clb; Key Clb; Cristom Awd For Most Outstanding Musician; Coca Cola Band Awd; Wash Elem PTA Schlrshp; Kent St Univ; Music.

BARREN, JOE; Revere HS; Richfield, OH; 12/282 NHS; VICA; 2nd Pl Nationwide Ivy Schl Fo Pro Art; 1st Pl Trophy & Medal VICA Skill Olympics Reg; Art Inst Coll; Visual Communications.

BARRERA, ANNETTE; Muskegon HS; Muskegon, MI; Hon Rl; Muskegon Community Coll; Law.

BARRERA, BRIAN; Douglas Mac Arthur HS; Saginaw, MI; Hon Rl; Sct Actv; Spn Clb; Univ; Comp Sci.

BARRETT, ALAN; Bexley HS; Bexley, OH; Hon Rl; Lat Clb; Crs Cntry; Socr; Trk; Univ.

BARRETT, B; Toronto HS; Toronto, OH; Band; Hon Rl; Off Ade; Sch Pl; Beta Clb; Pep Clb; Pom Pon; Coll.

BARRETT, BRADFORD; Cardinal Mooney HS; Canfield, OH; 3/288 Cls Rep Soph Cls; Cl Rep Jr Cls; Pres Sr Cls; Boy Scts; Chrh Wkr; Cmnty Wkr; Debate Tm; Hon Rl; Natl Forn Lg; NHS; Univ; Med.

BARRETT, CHARLES; Bishop Noll Inst; Calumet City, IL; 85/500 Cls Rep Frsh Cls; Hon Rl; Stu Cncl; Letter Bsktbl; Ftbl; Glf; Trk; Drake Univ; Mgmt.

BARRETT, DEBBIE; Flint Christian HS; Flint, MI; Trs Jr Cls; Chrs; Hon Rl; Sch Mus; Yth Flsp; Yrbk; Rptr Sch Nwsp; Pep Clb; IM Sprt; Scr Kpr; Univ Of Michigan; Law.

BARRETT, JEANNE; John Glenn HS; New Concord, OH; 20/193 Cl Rep Jr Cls; AFS; Chrs; Hon Rl; Lbry Ade; Yth Flsp; Lat Clb; Swmmng; College; Architect.

BARRETT, JERI; Triton HS; Tippecanoe, IN; 6/96 Cls Rep Frsh Cls; Cl Rep Jr Cls; Band; Chrs; FCA; Hon Rl; Sch Pl; Stu Cncl; Drama Clb; 4-H; Univ; CPA.

BARRETT, JULIANNE; Edgewood HS; Bloomingt on, IN; 4/180 Am Leg Aux Girls St; Chrs; Hon Rl; NHS; Sch Mus; Rptr Yrbk; Rptr Sch Nwsp; Gym; Trk; Lion Awd; Indiana Univ; Commnctns.

BARRETT, KEITH; Chaminade Julienne HS; Dayton, OH; Ohio St Univ; Agri Engr.

BARRETT, KENNETH C; Padua Franciscan HS; Seven Hills, OH; 40/258 Hon Rl; Music Aide; Soc Studies Club; Univ; Eng.

BARRETT, PAULA; Mc Comb HS; Mccomb, OH; 7/80 Hst Soph Cls; Aud/Vis; Chrs; Hon Rl; NHS; Rptr Yrbk; FHA; Bsktbl; Akron Univ; Acctg.

BARRETT, R; Brandon HS; Ortonville, MI; Cmnty Wkr; NHS; Trk; Wrstlng; Central Mic Univ; Med.

BARRETT, SHERI; Western Boone HS; Thorntown, IN; Hon Rl; Stu Cncl; Pep Clb; Ten; Chrldng; PPFtbl;.

BARRETT, TIM; Pike Central HS; Otwell, IN; VP Frsh Cls; FCA; Hon Rl; NHS; 4-H; Key Clb; Sci Clb; Letter Bsbl; Letter Bsktbl; Trk; Univ; Bus.

BARRETT, TODD; Gabriel Richard HS; Ann Arbor, MI; Pres Frsh Cls; Cls Rep Soph Cls; Chrh Wkr; Cmnty Wkr; Hon Rl; Sprt Ed Sch Nwsp; Capt Bsktbl; Capt Trk; All St Track 79; All Washtenaw Cnty Track 79; Youth Rep St Thomas Parish Cncl 78; Michigan St Univ; Speech.

BARRETTE, ANTHONY; Wakefield HS; Wakefield, MI; 6/60 Pres Soph Cls; Pres Jr Cls; Band; Drm Bgl; Hon Rl; Sch Pl; Stu Cncl; Drama Clb; Michigan St Univ.

BARRICK, APRIL; Notre Dame HS; Bridgeport, WV; 5/54 Band; Chrs; Chrh Wkr; Cmnty Wkr; Natl Forn Lg; Pol Wkr; Stg Crw; Drama Clb; FDA; Pres FTA; West Virginia Univ; Phys Therapy.

BARRICK, CHRISTOPHER; Yorktown HS; Muncie, IN; 10/205 Am Leg Boys St; Band; Drm Bgl; Hon Rl; MMM; NHS; Ger Clb; Sci Clb; College; Engr.

BARRICK, ELEANOR; Licking Valley HS; Nashport, OH; Band; Hon Rl; Stu Cncl; Pep Clb; Sci Clb; Chrldng; Univ; Sec.

BARRICKLOW, DEBRA; South Dearborn HS; Aurora, IN; 25/265 Band; Chrh Wkr; Hon Rl; Pres Yth Flsp; Yrbk; Pres 4-H; Pep Clb; 4-H Awd; Ball St Univ; Jrnlsm.

BARRICKLOW, LANA; Eastern HS; Sardina, OH; Chrh Wkr; Hosp Ade; Sch Pl; Pres 4-H; Fr Clb; Sec FFA; FTA; Pep Clb; Mgrs; 4-H Awd; FFA Ohio St Horse Proficiency Winner; Champ Saddle Seat Equitation; Chris Baltz Mem Trophy; Centre Coll; Busns Mgmt.

BARRIER, GERRLYN; Penn HS; Mishawaka, IN; Hon Rl; JA; Off Ade; Red Cr Ade; Rptr Yrbk; Yrbk; Sch Nwsp; Spn Clb; Mgrs; Mat Maids; Awd For Journalism; Ivy Tech Schl; Journalism.

BARRIGER, WILLIAM; All Saints Central HS; Bay City, MI; 6/167 Chrh Wkr; Cmnty Wkr; Hon Rl; Lbry Ade; NHS; Off Ade; Pol Wkr; Yrbk; Trk; Delta Coll; Pre Engr.

BARRINGER, OTIS T; Bay City Western HS; Auburn, MI; 32/484 Aud/Vis; Chrh Wkr; Hon Rl; Stg Crw; Coach Actv; Scr Kpr; Tmr; Delta Coll; Elec Tech.

BARRIOS, HEIDI; Maumee HS; Maumee, OH; 78/316 Chrh Wkr; Girl Scts; Lbry Ade; Orch; Sct Actv; Yth Flsp; Fr Clb; Trk; Mgrs; Scr Kpr; College; Rn.

BARRISH, DONNA; Eastlake North HS; Willowick, OH; Hon Rl; Off Ade; Rptr Sch Nwsp; Ger Clb; Spn Clb; Bsktbl; Associated Schls Inc; Airline.

BARRITT, LORI; St Johns Cnrl HS; Bridgeport, OH; Band; Cmp Fr Grls; Chrs; Cmnty Wkr; Girl Scts; Hon Rl; Sch Mus; Sct Actv; OEA; Pep Clb; Univ; Bus.

BARRON, BARBARA; Allen Park HS; Allen Park, MI; Girl Scts; Hon Rl; Fr Clb; GAA; College; Acctg.

BARRON, CHRIS; Monroe Catholic Central HS; Monroe, MI; 35/95 Sec Frsh Cls; Cls Rep Soph Cls; Cl Rep Jr Cls; Cls Rep Sr Cls; Hon Rl; Sec NHS; Stu Cncl; Rptr Yrbk; Letter Bsktbl; Monroe County Comm Coll.

BARRON, JEWEL A; Morton Sr HS; Hammond, IN; 14/451 Cls Rep Frsh Cls; Cl Rep Jr Cls; Am Leg Aux Girls St; Band; Chrs; Debate Tm; Hosp Ade; Jr NHS; Natl Forn Lg; NHS; Purdue Univ; Medicine.

BARRON, PANSY; Crothersville HS; Crothersville, IN; Trs Jr Cls; Trs Sr Cls; Drl Tm; Hon Rl; Off Ade; Yth Flsp; Pep Clb; Letter Pom Pon; Bus Schl; Bus.

BARRON, PEGGY; Kings HS; Loveland, OH; 1/175 Band; Hon Rl; NHS; Orch; Pres 4-H; Fr Clb; 4-H Awd; Kiwan Awd; Girls State; Med.

BARRON, VALERIE; Cass Technical HS; Detroit, MI; Cls Rep Soph Cls; Cl Rep Jr Cls; Band; Hon Rl; VP JA; Off Ade; Sct Actv; Spelman Univ; Ther.

BARROR, SHERRI L; Pike Delta York Sr HS; Delta, OH; 14/104 Chrh Wkr; Hon Rl; Jr NHS; NHS; Sch Pl; FHA; Mt Vernon Nazarene Coll; Co mp Sci.

BARROW, DEBBIE; Unioto HS; Chillicothe, OH; 5/120 Band; Girl Scts; Hon Rl; 4-H; FTA; Spn Clb; Bsktbl; Trk;.

BARROW, DIANA; Fremont HS; Fremont, IN; Chrh Wkr; Cmnty Wkr; Hon Rl; Stg Crw; Yth Flsp; Yrbk; FHA; FTA; Bsktbl; Chrldng; Business School; Sec.

BARROW, KIMBERLY; Corydon Central HS; Corydon, IN; 8/164 Chrs; Sec 4-H; FBLA; Pres FHA; Spn Clb; Bsktbl; Trk; GAA; Mgrs; Scr Kpr; Co Ed Rep For Schl 77; Indiana Central Univ; Nurse.

BARROW, SAMUEL; Dunbar HS; Dayton, OH; 10/199 Hon Rl; Hosp Ade; Sprt Ed Yrbk; Ed Sch Nwsp; Letter Bsktbl; Crs Cntry; Letter Ten; Letter Trk; Wright St Univ; Pre Med.

BARROW JR, HENRY; Central HS; Detroit, MI; Hon Rl; Wayne County Cmnty Coll; Engr.

BARRY, BRENDA; Hudson Area HS; Pittsford, MI; Am Leg Aux Girls St; Band; Chrs; Chrh Wkr; Hon Rl; NHS; Sch Pl; Jackson Community College; Acctg.

BARRY, CINDY; Hillsdale HS; Hillsdale, MI; Chrs; Hosp Ade; Lit Mag; Sch Mus; Sch Pl; Lat Clb; Basic Oppnty Grant 79; St Michigan Schlrshp 79; Albion Gift Asst 79; Albion Coll; Med.

BARRY, DAVID; Fremont HS; Fremont, IN; 5/75 NHS; Sch Mus; Spn Clb; Letter Bsbl; Letter Bsktbl; Letter Glf; Purdue Univ; Elec Engr.

BARRY, JAMES; Medina HS; Medina, OH; 37/360 Hon Rl; NHS; Capt Bsbl; IM Sprt; Ohio State Univ; Architecture.

BARRY, JAMES; Westwood HS; Ispeming, MI; 20/150 VP Frsh Cls; VP Soph Cls; Trs Jr Cls; Boy Scts; Hon Rl; NHS; Sct Actv; Ftbl; Ten; Coach Actv; Gogebic Cmnty Coll; Ski Area Mgmt.

BARRY, MATT; Napoleon HS; Napoleon, OH; Hon Rl; NHS; Sch Mus; Sch Pl; Stg Crw; Fr Clb; Letter Ftbl; Trk; Letter Wrstlng; Natl Merit Schl; Univ.

BARRY, MAUREEN; Our Lady Of The Elms HS; Akron, OH; Chrs; Hon Rl; Sch Pl; Stg Crw; Yrbk; Drama Clb; Cit Awd; Univ; Modern Lang.

BARRYMORE, VALERIE S; Bedford HS; Detroit, MI; Cmp Fr Grls; Chrs; Chrh Wkr; Capt FCA; Hon Rl; Natl Forn Lg; Sch Pl; Yth Flsp; Capt Chrldng; Cit Awd; 2nd Rnr Up In Michigan Christian Yth Conf 79; Univ; Cmnctns.

BARSAN, SHIRLEY; Avon Lake HS; Avon Lake, OH; 150/279 AFS; Band; Chrh Wkr; Girl Scts; Hosp Ade; Off Ade; Drama Clb; Lorain Comm Coll; Interntl Relations.

BARSOTTI, MARTITIA; Calumet HS; Calumet, MI; 1/175 Band; Chrs; Cmnty Wkr; Hon Rl; NHS; Orch; Sch Mus; Fr Clb; Letter Mgrs; Scr Kpr; Univ; Med.

BARTAWAY, RUTH; Central HS; Grand Rapids, MI; Chrh Wkr; Hon Rl; JA; Off Ade; ROTC; Yth Flsp; Spn Clb; JA Awd; House Of Rep For Schlstc Achvmnt 75; Principalsawd For Acad Exclinc 75; Cert Of Progress Voc Training 79; Bus Schl; Sec.

BARTELS, CYNTHIA F; Pioneer HS; Ann Arbor, MI; 61/644 Lit Mag; Natl Merit SF; Univ Of Michigan; Psych.

BARTELS, DAVID; Watterson HS; Columbus, OH; Aud/Vis; Boy Scts; Hon Rl; Jr NHS; NHS; Orch; Stg Crw; Rptr Sch Nwsp; Lat Clb; Ohi State Univ; Ceramic Engr.

BARTELS, MELISSA; Muncie Northside HS; Muncie, IN; 7/227 Hosp Ade; NHS; Stu Cncl; Ed Sch Nwsp; Mth Clb; Spn Clb; Indiana Univ; Nursing.

BARTELS, STEVE; Marquette HS; Michigan City, IN; FCA; College; Aviation.

BARTELS, WILLIAM; West Ottawa HS; Holland, MI; Cls Rep Frsh Cls; Cls Rep Soph Cls; Cl Rep Jr Cls; Cls Rep Sr Cls; JA; Rptr Yrbk; Sch Nwsp; Lake Superior St College; Conservati.

BARTELS, WILLIAM; Grosse Ile HS; Grosse Ile, MI; Band; Hon Rl; NHS; Letter Crs Cntry; Trk; Univ; Dent.

BARTELT, JACKIE; Southridge HS; Huntingburg, IN; Pres Jr Cls; Pres Sr Cls; Band; FCA; Hon Rl; Rptr Yrbk; Yrbk; Pep Clb; Spn Clb; Letter Bsktbl; Indiana State; Business.

BARTGES, JOSEPH; Charleston Catholic HS; Charleston, WV; 9/61 Am Leg Boys St; Band; Cmnty Wkr; Hon Rl; Key Clb; Sci Clb; Letter Wrstlng; IM Sprt; Mas Awd; Natl Merit Ltr; Marshall Univ; Spec Ed.

BARTHEL, CHRIS; Niles HS; Niles, MI; Hon Rl; Ger Clb; Notre Dame; Nuclear Engr.

BARTHEL, LINDA; Freeland HS; Freeland, MI; 17/115 Pres Sr Cls; Band; NHS; Stu Cncl; Sprt Ed Yrbk; Bsbl; Bsktbl; Trk; PPFtbl; Women In Engineering Schlrshp Michigan Tech Univ; Central Michigan Univ; Med Tech.

BARTHELD, ERIC; Turpin HS; Cincinnati, OH; Band; Boy Scts; Stg Crw; God Cntry Awd; Univ.

BARTHLOW, TAMARA; Alma HS; Alma, MI; 41/252 Cls Rep Soph Cls; Pol Wkr; Stu Cncl; Central Michigan Univ; Social Work.

BARTHOLOMEW, BARBARA; Highland Sr HS; Highland, IN; 35/494 Chrs; Hon Rl; NHS; Sch Mus; Stg Crw; Stu Cncl; Drama Clb; Hoosier Schlr 79; Accept To Purdue Univ With Distinct 79; Vet Sem Part; 2nd VP Of The Troop; NHC Tres; Purdue Univ; Med.

BARTHOLOMEW, BRAD; Clay HS; South Bend, IN; Band; Boy Scts; Cmp Fr Grls; Chrs; Chrh Wkr; Hon Rl; Sch Mus; Sch Pl; Norte Dame Univ; Engr.

BARTHOLOMEW, JOHN; Ravenna HS; Ravenna, OH; Hon Rl; Jr NHS; Ftbl; Trk; IM Sprt;.

BARTHOLOMEW, KAREN; Ursuline HS; Hubbard, OH; 88/322 Hon Rl; Fr Clb; Univ.

BARTHOLOMEW, LEDA; Big Bay De Noc HS; Garden, MI; Trs Frsh Cls; VP Soph Cls; Trs Jr Cls; Band; Chrs; Chrh Wkr; Hon Rl; NHS; 4-H; 4-H Awd; Univ.

BARTLEBAUGH, SCOTT; North HS; Eastlake, OH; 14/706 Hon Rl; NHS; Letter Socr; JETS Awd; Univ; Bio.

BARTLETT, BRYAN; Washington Irving HS; Clarksburg, WV; Band; Hon Rl; Swmmng; West Virginia Univ.

BARTLETT, CHARLES; Shaken Heights HS; Shaker Hts, OH; Red Cr Ade; Bsbl; All Ohio Baseball Team All St; Talent Awd Baseball Cuyahoga Comm Coll; Cert Of Apprecation Red Cross; Cuyahosa Comm Coll.

BARTLETT, CHERYL; Grafton HS; Grafton, WV; Cls Rep Soph Cls; Band; Chrs; Chrh Wkr; Hon Rl; NHS; Sch Mus; Fr Clb; Keyettes; Twrlr; Univ; Performing Arts.

BARTLETT, JACQUELYN; Hemlock HS; Hemlock, MI; 13/167 Cls Rep Soph Cls; Cl Rep Jr Cls; Chrh Wkr; Girl Scts; Hon Rl; Jr NHS; Lbry Ade; NHS; Stu Cncl; Treas Pom Pon; Lake Superior St Coll; Med Tech.

BARTLETT, LINDA; Whitehall HS; Whitehall, MI; Band; Chrs; Drm Mjrt; Hon Rl; NHS; Orch; Sch Mus; Ger Clb; Gym; Twrlr; Univ; Music.

BARTLETT, TWILA; Lincoln HS; Lumberport, WV; Cls Rep Frsh Cls; Band; Cmp Fr Grls; Drl Tm; Girl Scts; Hon Rl; Jr NHS; NHS; Off Ade; Sch Pl; Fairmont St Univ; Phys Educ.

BARTLETT, WILLIAM; South Harrison HS; W Milford, WV; Band; Boy Scts; Hon Rl; Sch Pl; Own Bus.

BARTLEY, BRENDA; Valley View HS; Frmrsvl, OH; Lbry Ade; Yth Flsp; FHA;.

BARTLEY, DAVID; Lake Orion HS; Lake Orion, MI; 48/435 Cls Rep Soph Cls; Am Leg Boys St; Band; Hon Rl; Jr NHS; Lit Mag; NHS; Sch Pl; Stg Crw; Rptr Sch Nwsp; Oakland Univ; Soc Std Tchr.

BARTLEY, GEORGE; Croswell Lexington HS; Croswell, MI; Am Leg Boys St; Sch Mus; Sch Pl; Sci Clb; Letter Ftbl; Trk; Wrstlng; Scr Kpr; Central Michigan Univ; Chem Engr.

BARTLEY, ROLAND; Clay Sr HS; Curtice, OH; 30/351 Am Leg Boys St; Band; FCA; Hon Rl; NHS; Stu Cncl; Sci Clb; Crs Cntry; Trk; IM Sprt; Univ Of Toledo; Chem Engr.

BARTLOW, MARK; Avon HS; Indianapolis, IN; 16/187 Band; Hon Rl; Sch Mus; Spn Clb; Letter Bsbl; IM Sprt; Indiana Univ; Premedicine.

BARTO, KRISTINE; Lockland HS; Lockland, OH; 15/60 Trs Jr Cls; Cl Rep Jr Cls; Drl Tm; Hon Rl; NHS; Stu Cncl; Pep Clb; Letter Bsktbl; Chrldng; IM Sprt; College; Acctg.

BARTOL, PATRICIA; Archbishop Alter HS; Dayton, OH; Band; Chrs; Chrh Wkr; Drm Mjrt; Pres Girl Scts; Hosp Ade; Mdrgl; College; Music.

BARTOLIN, LAURA J; Hubbard HS; Hubbard, OH; 16/350 Cmnty Wkr; Girl Scts; Hon Rl; Lbry Ade; Lit Mag; Off Ade; Quill & Scroll; Rptr Yrbk; Rptr Sch Nwsp; Sch Nwsp; Principals Banquet For High Achvrs 1978; Basic Studies Cert 1979; Awd Of Math Accomp 1977; Youngstown St Univ; Public Rel.

BARTON, BARBARA; Jefferson Area HS; Jefferson, OH; Pres Frsh Cls; Band; Chrs; Drm Mjrt; Lbry Ade; NHS; Sch Mus; 4-H; Fr Clb; Sci Clb; College; Nursing.

BARTON, BETH; Miami Trace HS; Jeffersonville, OH; AFS; Am Leg Aux Girls St; Band; Drm Bgl; Hon Rl; Sch Mus; Sch Pl; Rptr Sch Nwsp; Drama Clb; 4-H; Ohio St Univ; Agri.

BARTON, BETH; Lexington HS; Mansfield, OH; 28/269 Cls Rep Sr Cls; Hon Rl; NHS; Off Ade; Stu Cncl; Spn Clb; Letter Trk; Univ Of Rutgers; Bus Admin.

BARTON, BETH; Miami Trace HS; Jeffersonville, OH; AFS; Band; Drl Tm; Hon Rl; Sch Mus; Sch Pl; Rptr Sch Nwsp; Drama Clb; 4-H; FFA; Ohio St Univ; Agri.

BARTON, BETH M; Athens HS; Athens, MI; Trs Jr Cls; Band; Cmp Fr Grls; Hon Rl; Hosp Ade; Jr NHS; NHS; Off Ade; Pol Wkr; Quill & Scroll; Nazareth Coll; Nursing.

BARTON, CARRIE; David Anderson HS; Lisbon, OH; 6/120 Am Leg Aux Girls St; Band; Chrh Wkr; Hon Rl; Sch Mus; Yth Flsp; Y-Teens; Fr Clb; Sci Clb; VFW Awd; Ohio St Univ; Vet Sci.

BARTON, DAVID; Cardinal Stritch HS; Curtice, OH; 24/230 Am Leg Boys St; Pres Band; Hon Rl; NHS; Sch Mus; Fr Clb; Letter Wrstlng; College; Agri.

BARTON, DAVID; East Catholic HS; Detroit, MI; 3/74 Pres Soph Cls; Hon Rl; Sec Stu Cncl; Yrbk; Rptr Sch Nwsp; Sch Nwsp; Letter Crs Cntry; Letter Trk; Voice Dem Awd; Univ; Psych.

BARTON, KEITH; Clermont Northeastern HS; Batavia, OH; Boy Scts; Hon Rl; Stu Cncl; 4-H; Spn Clb; 4-H Awd; Otterbein College.

BARTON, KIMBERLY; Greenville Sr HS; Greenville, OH; 60/360 Cls Rep Soph Cls; Hon Rl; FHA; Letter Bsktbl; Letter Trk; IM Sprt; Bowling Green St Univ.

BARTON, MARY; Jefferson Area HS; Jefferson, OH; 11/180 Am Leg Aux Girls St; Band; Drm Mjrt; Pres NHS; Quill & Scroll; Sch Mus; Sch Pl; Treas Stu Cncl; Sch Nwsp; Natl Merit Ltr; Ohio Wesleyan Univ; English.

BARTON, PENNY; North Vermillion HS; Perrysville, IN; Am Leg Aux Girls St; Band; Chrs; Drl Tm; 4-H; FHA; OEA; Pep Clb; 4-H Awd; Lake Med Ctr Schl Of Nursing; Nurse.

BARTON, RACHEL L; Olney Friends HS; Barnesville, OH; Pres Sr Cls; Band; Chrs; Hon Rl; Stu Cncl; Ed Sch Nwsp; Letter Bsktbl; Letter Hockey; Pres GAA; Natl Merit SF; College; Liberal Arts.

BARTON, STEVEN C; Rocky River HS; Rocky River, OH; Am Leg Boys St; Hon Rl; Jr NHS; VP Stu Cncl; Letter Bsktbl; Letter Ftbl; Trk; GAA; IM Sprt; Am Leg Awd; College.

BARTONE, DANA; Traverse City Sr HS; Traverse City, MI; Hon Rl; NHS; Letter Bsbl; Capt Ftbl; Bos ton Univ; Aero Engr.

BARTOO, MICHAEL; Jackson HS; Massillon, OH; Band; Chrh Wkr; FCA; NHS; Ed Yrbk; Sprt Ed Yrbk; Key Clb; Spn Clb; Letter Bsbl; Letter Swmmng; Varsity Bsbl Batting Leadr 79; Camp Retupmoc For Comp Sci Rose Hulman Inst 79; Univ; Comp Sci.

BARTOS, JONATHAN; Hill Mc Cloy HS; Flushing, MI; Band; Boy Scts; Drm Bgl; Hon Rl; Ftbl; Swmmng; Letter Trk; Scr Kpr; Gen Cnty Ahtltc Hon Roll 79; Univ; Med.

BARTOSIEWICZ, CAROL; Dominican HS; Detroit, MI; Chrs; Cmnty Wkr; Girl Scts; Hon Rl; Mdrgl; NHS; Stg Crw; PPFtbl; Natl Merit SF; Univ.

BARTOSIK, CYNTHIA; Lumen Cordium HS; Walton Hills, OH; VP Frsh Cls; Drl Tm; Hon Rl; Hosp Ade; Stg Crw; Stu Cncl; Sprt Ed Yrbk; Drama Clb; GAA; IM Sprt; Merit Awrds For Having Over 3.0 Accum For 4 Sem & 6 Sem; Hiram Coll; Med Tech.

BARTOSZEK, JEFFREY; East Kentwood HS; Kentwood, MI; Band; Boy Scts; Hon Rl; NHS; Off Ade; Mth Clb; Bsbl; Ftbl; PPFtbl; Central Michigan Univ; Engr.

BARTRAM, DIANA S; Roncalli HS; Beech Grove, IN; 16/198 Chrs; Girl Scts; Off Ade; Stu Cncl; Spn Clb; Chrldng; IM Sprt; PPFtbl; Indiana Central Coll; Elem Ed.

BARTRAM, JULIE; Roncalli HS; Beech Grove, IN; 21/200 Chrs; Girl Scts; Hon Rl; Spn Clb; Chrldng; PPFtbl; Univ.

BARTRAM, KAREN; Tippecanoe Valley HS; Rochester, IN; Cls Rep Frsh Cls; Sec Soph Cls; Hon Rl; Sch Pl; Stu Cncl; Ger Clb; Chrldng; Mgrs; Scr Kpr; Bus Schl; Sec.

BARTRAND, TIMOTHY; Rogers HS; Wyoming, MI; 1/260 Val; Band; FCA; Hon Rl; Letter Crs Cntry; Letter Trk; Univ Of Notre Dame; History.

BARTROM, MELO; Marion HS; Marin, IN; Band; Girl Scts; Hon Rl; Jr NHS; Lbry Ade; NHS; Off Ade; OEA; Univ; Bus.

BARTZ, RICHARD; Alpena HS; Ossineke, MI; Band; Hon Rl; Orch; ACC; Law.

BARTZ, TERESA; Fraser HS; Fraser, MI; Band; Chrh Wkr; Hon Rl; Pol Wkr; Rptr Sch Nwsp; Voice Dem Awd; Macomb Cnty Cmnty Coll; Chiropractor.

BARWICK, GRANT W; Westerville North HS; Westerville, OH; Pres Soph Cls; Pres Jr Cls; Pres Sr Cls; AFS; Am Leg Boys St; NHS; Sch Mus; Sch Pl; Stg Crw; Drama Clb; Harold Carrick Memrl Awd 77; Ohio Dist Key Club Intl Oratorical Cntst 79; In The Know Team Mbr 78; Univ; Theater.

BASACCHI, WILLIAM; St Charles HS; St Charles, MI; Cmnty Wkr; Debate Tm; Hon Rl; Sch Pl; Stu Cncl; VICA; Bsktbl; Ftbl; College.

BASCO, RENE; Andrean HS; Hobart, IN; 13/251 Hon Rl; VP Y-Teens; Fr Clb; Bsktbl; DAR Awd; Valparaiso Univ; Bio.

BASEN, SHERRY; Edgewood HS; Kingsville, OH; 8/290 AFS; Girl Scts; Hon Rl; Yth Flsp; Yrbk; Sch Nwsp; Ger Clb; Sci Clb; GAA; Univ Of Akron; Accounting.

BASFORD, WAYNE R; Triway HS; Wooster, OH; Am Leg Boys St; Band; Jr NHS; Pres NHS; Stg Crw; Fr Clb; Mth Clb; Sci Clb; Letter Ten; Am Leg Awd; Akron Univ; Comp Sci.

BASHAM, KEN; East Liverpool HS; E Liverpool, OH; Cls Rep Soph Cls; Hon Rl; Key Clb; Spn Clb; IM Sprt; College; Elec Engr.

BASHAWATY, ALBERT; Franklin HS; Livonia, MI; Am Leg Boys St; Chrh Wkr; Hon Rl; Fr Clb; Am Leg Awd; Cit Awd; Mass Inst Of Tech; Physics.

BASHIAN, JACK; Solon HS; Solon, OH; 52/288 Aud/Vis; Chrh Wkr; Hon Rl; Yth Flsp; Ed Sch Nwsp; Sprt Ed Sch Nwsp; Sch Nwsp; Key Clb; Socr; IM Sprt; Ohio St Univ; Busns.

BASHOR, JANICE; Fairview HS; Sherwood, OH; 18/108 Band; Hon Rl; NHS; Off Ade; FHA; Mth Clb; Bsktbl; Mgrs; Tri St Univ; Engr.

BASIGER, CYNTHIA; Whitko HS; So Whitley, IN; Chrh Wkr; Hon Rl; Yth Flsp;.

BASIL, JOHN; Madonna HS; Weirton, WV; 17/100 Hon Rl; Sec Lit Mag; Treas NHS; VP Key Clb; Sci Clb; Letter Glf; IM Sprt; Univ Of Pittsburg; Dentistry.

BASIL, ROSANNE; Central Catholic HS; Wheeling, WV; 14/137 Chrh Wkr; Hon Rl; NHS; Rptr Yrbk; Rptr Sch Nwsp; Letter Bsktbl; Letter Trk; Mat Maids; Scr Kpr; Tmr; Future Medical Careers Treasurer; Soc Dstngshd Amer HS Stu; Volleyball; West Virginia Univ; Phys Therapy.

BASILE, CARLA; St Francis Central HS; Morgantown, WV; Hon Rl; Spn Clb; Bsktbl; Mgrs; Scr Kpr; Wv Univ; Psych.

BASISTA, JIM; John F Kennedy HS; Niles, OH; Hst Frsh Cls; Hst Soph Cls; Boy Scts; Chrh Wkr; Lit Mag; Sch Mus; Rptr Sch Nwsp; 4-H; Spn Clb; Letter Ftbl; Jrnlsm.

BASISTA, KAREN E; Struthers HS; Struthers, OH; 21/276 Pres Cmp Fr Grls; Sec Chrs; Hon Rl; Jr NHS; NHS; Off Ade; Y-Teens; Sch Nwsp; Pres FNA; Lat Clb; Natl Organ Guild; Youngstown State Univ; Nursing.

BASISTA, TAMMY D; Ursuline HS; Youngstown, OH; Sec Frsh Cls; Cls Rep Soph Cls; Hon Rl; Hosp Ade; Sch Pl; Ed Yrbk; Ed Sch Nwsp; Drama Clb; Chrldng; GAA; Yo Coll Of Bus; Sec.

BASNETT, KIM; Monongah HS; Fairmont, WV; Hon Rl; Y-Teens; Yrbk; Fr Clb; FHA; Pep Clb; Fairmont St Coll; Jrnlsm.

BASOM, SUSAN; Willow Run HS; Ypsilanti, MI; Pres Frsh Cls; Pres Soph Cls; Cl Rep Jr Cls; Band; Chrh Wkr; Stu Cncl; Sch Nwsp; IM Sprt; Cit Awd; EMU; Deaf Education.

BASORE, KEVIN; Niles Sr HS; Niles, MI; 10/388 Chrh Wkr; Hon Rl; Stu Cncl; Yth Flsp; Ftbl; Am Leg Awd; Opt Clb Awd; S W Michigan Coll; Comp Sci.

BASS, JOHN; Morton Sr HS; Hammond, IN; 31/419 Hon Rl; Quill & Scroll; Sprt Ed Sch Nwsp; Coach Actv; College; Math.

BASS, MARIE; South Side HS; Jackson, TN; Red Cr Ade; 4-H; FHA; Ut Martin Univ; Com Art.

BASS, MEETA; Catholic Ctrl HS; Steubenvll, OH; 3/203 Sec Frsh Cls; Sec Soph Cls; Band; Chrs; Girl Scts; Hon Rl; NHS; Sct Actv; Stu Cncl; Yth Flsp; St Dep Of Educ Cert Of Awd In Kent St Univ Dist; St Dept Of Educ Cert Of Awd In St Of Ohio; Spanish Awd; Univ; Law.

BASS, MONICA; Niles Sr HS; Niles, MI; Chrh Wkr; Cmnty Wkr; Hon Rl; Orch; Pep Clb; Bsbl; Trk; Chrldng; Southbend Youth Symphony 75& 76; Notre Dame Symphony Orch 78; Western Michigan Univ; Med Tech.

BASS, RIAN; Chesaning Union HS; Chesaning, MI; 40/300 Band; Hon Rl; NHS; Sch Mus; Sch Pl; Stg Crw; Yth Flsp; Drama Clb; Wrstlng; Grand Rapids Bapt Coll; Bible.

BASS, THOMAS; Southern HS; Syracuse, OH; Pres Chrh Wkr; Hon Rl; Yth Flsp; Fr Clb; FFA; Pep Clb; Bsbl; Letter Ftbl; Trk; Mgrs; Univ.

BASSETT, BECKY; Southwood Jr Sr HS; Wabash, IN; Am Leg Aux Girls St; Chrs; Chrh Wkr; FCA; Hon Rl; Lbry Ade; Natl Forn Lg; NHS; VP Yth Flsp; 4-H; Whos Who In Indiana & Kentucky HS Foreign Languages; College; Bsns.

BASSETT, CYNTHIA; East Noble School; Kendallville, IN; 33/259 Band; Hon Rl; JA; Yth Flsp; 4-H; Pep Clb; 4-H Awd; Hnrs Semnr In St Univ79; Univ; Brdcstng.

BASSETT, DAVID; New Haven HS; New Haven, IN; Band; Boy Scts; Hon Rl; Natl Forn Lg; Sch Mus; Sch Pl; Stg Crw; Rptr Yrbk; Rptr Sch Nwsp; Drama Clb; Indiana Univ; Theater.

BASSETT, GREGORY; Alexandria Monroe HS; Alexandria, IN; Band; Boy Scts; Sct Actv; Ger Clb; Univ; Comp Elec.

BASSETT, JEFF; Romulus HS; Romulus, MI; 10/300 Band; Hon Rl; NHS; Stu Cncl; God Cntry Awd; Kiwan Awd; Univ Of Michigan; Physics.

BASSETT, JENA L; Rogers HS; Toledo, OH; Cls Rep Soph Cls; Chrs; Chrh Wkr; Hon Rl; Sch Mus; Stu Cncl; FHA; Chrldng; Designer Schl; Cosmetology.

BASSETT, PAULA; Spencerville HS; Vendocia, OH; 15/100 Chrh Wkr; Hon Rl; Hosp Ade; IM Sprt; Univ.

BASSETT, TIMOTHY; Lake Orion Comm HS; Goodrich, MI; 70/456 Band; Chrs; Michigan St Univ; Sci.

BASSO, JOSEPH; Owosso HS; Owosso, MI; 32/406 Pres Sr Cls; Am Leg Boys St; Chrh Wkr; Hon Rl; NHS; Stu Cncl; Sprt Ed Sch Nwsp; Sch Nwsp; Lat Clb; Spn Clb; Rec Cert Mi Comp Schlrshp Prog 79; Michigan St Univ; Zoology.

BASTIN, BETTY S; Western HS; Detroit, MI; Pres Jr Cls; Chrs; Chrh Wkr; Hon Rl; NHS; Off Ade; Univ Of Michigan; Medicine.

BASTIN, KEVIN; Roosevelt Wilson HS; Mt Clare, WV; Pres Frsh Cls; Cls Rep Soph Cls; Cl Rep Jr Cls; Boy Scts; Chrh Wkr; Cmnty Wkr; Hon Rl; Off Ade; Stu Cncl; Yth Flsp; West Virginia Univ; Phys Ther.

BASYE, JUDITH A; Cuyahoga Vly Christian Acad; Akron, OH; Band; Chrs; Chrh Wkr; Hon Rl; Letter Bsktbl; Letter Hockey; College.

BASYE, RONETTA; Martinsville HS; Martinsville, IN; Rptr Yrbk;.

BASYE, SHELLY; Waverly HS; Waverly, OH; 22/157 Band; Girl Scts; Hon Rl; Off Ade; Stu Cncl; Pep Clb; Trk; Chrldng; Pom Pon; College; Med.

BATACLAN, GERALDINE; Benedictine HS; Detroit, MI; Hon Rl; JA; NHS; Yrbk; Modanna College; Nursing.

BATCHELDER, DEBBIE; Potterville HS; Grand Ledge, MI; 2/67 Hon Rl; Opt Clb Awd; Michigan St Univ.

BATCHELDOR, DOROTHY; Bullock Creek HS; Midland, MI; Band; Chrs; Drm Bgl; Girl Scts; Hon Rl; Yth Flsp; FSA; Central Mic Univ.

BATCHELLOR, TERRI; Indianapolis Baptist HS; Greenwood, IN; 6/41 Chrh Wkr; Hon Rl; Lbry Ade; Pol Wkr; Sch Pl; Stg Crw; Natl Merit Ltr; Nedt Certificated Highest In Schl Outstanding In Nation 75 76; Medals For Latin Typing 1 & 2 & Shorthand 76; Liberty Baptist Coll; Missionary.

BATCHELOR, GREGORY; Pontiac Central HS; Pontiac, MI; Aud/Vis; Band; Chrs; Chrh Wkr; Hon Rl; Mth Clb; Cit Awd; Lawrence Inst Of Tech Summer Sci Progr 79; Genrl Motors Inst; Engr.

BATCHELOR, KATE; Chagrin Falls HS; Chagrin Falls, OH; VP Soph Cls; Hon Rl; Stu Cncl; Yrbk; Sch Nwsp; Spn Clb; Bsktbl; Ten; PPFtbl; Univ.

BATCHIK, THOMAS; Ellet HS; Akron, OH; 5/363 Chrs; Hon Rl; Mdrgl; NHS; Quill & Scroll; Ed Sch Nwsp; Capt Crs Cntry; Letter Trk; Natl Merit SF;.

BATCHIK, TOM; Ellet HS; Akron, OH; Chrs; Hon Rl; Mdrgl; NHS; Quill & Scroll; Sch Mus; Ed Sch Nwsp; Spn Clb; Letter Crs Cntry; Letter Trk; Univ; Engr.

BATEMAN, ALAN; Lakota HS; W Chester, OH; Boy Scts; Hon Rl; Ger Clb; Rdo Clb; Letter Crs Cntry; Univ Of Cincinnati.

BATEMAN, CHRISTOPHER; West Jefferson HS; W Jefferson, OH; Am Leg Boys St; Chrs; Hon Rl; Quill & Scroll; VP Stu Cncl; Sprt Ed Sch Nwsp; Spn Clb; Letter Ftbl; Letter Wrstlng; Wittenburg Univ; Bus.

BATER, JEFF; Crestwood HS; Dearborn Hts, MI; Hon Rl; Lit Mag; Yth Flsp; Rptr Yrbk; Rptr Sch Nwsp; Mich State Univ; Bachelor Of Arts.

BATES, ALLISON; Waverly HS; Waverly, OH; 38/157 Band; Pep Clb; Bsbl; Chrldng; GAA; Mgrs; Pom Pon; Tmr; Ohi Univ; Fine Arts.

BATES, BARBARA A; Ben Davis HS; Indianapolis, IN; 339/864 Trs Soph Cls; Trs Jr Cls; Trs Sr Cls; FCA; Treas Stu Cncl; DECA; Gym; Letter Trk; Chrldng; PPFtbl; Nominated For Jr Sr Prom Court; Indiana Univ; Dental Hygiene.

BATES, BEVERLY; Southwestern HS; Detroit, MI; 22/225 Capt Drm Mjrt; Girl Scts; Hon Rl; VP NHS; Pol Wkr; DECA; FTA; Pep Clb; Am Leg Awd; Detroit NAACP Act 50 Silver Awd Essay; Michigan St Univ; Comp Sci.

BATES, DAN; Champion HS; Warren, OH; 3 Trs Jr Cls; Pres Sr Cls; Am Leg Boys St; Chrh Wkr; Letter Hon Rl; Sec Frsh Cls; Stu Cncl; Bsbl; Letter Ftbl; College.

BATES, DAVID; John F Kennedy HS; Taylor, MI; Boy Scts; Hon Rl; GMI; Drafting.

BATES, EDWIN C; Wadsworth Sr HS; Wadsworth, OH; 45/380 Am Leg Boys St; Hon Rl; NHS; Orch; Key Clb; Letter Wrstlng; Purdue Univ; Law.

BATES, ERIC; Jefferson HS; Shepherdstown, WV; 1/277 Val; Am Leg Boys St; Band; NHS; Ed Sch Nwsp; Pres Drama Clb; Spn Clb; Antioch Univ; Communications.

BATES, JEANNE; Valley HS; Jacksonburg, WV; Cls Rep Frsh Cls; Cls Rep Soph Cls; Cl Rep Jr Cls; Cls Rep Sr Cls; Band; Cmnty Wkr; Hon Rl; Sch Pl; Stu Cncl; Yrbk; West Virginia Career Coll; Sec.

BATES, JOE; Princeton Community HS; Princeton, IN; 61/222 Band; Boy Scts; Chrs; Chrh Wkr; Cmnty Wkr; FCA; Mdrgl; Sch Mus; Sch Pl; Stg Crw; Indiana St Univ; Bus Mgmt.

BATES, JUDIE; Cambridge HS; Cambridge, OH; Cls Rep Frsh Cls; Cls Rep Soph Cls; Cl Rep Jr Cls; Cls Rep Sr Cls; Hon Rl; Stu Cncl; Bsktbl; Letter Trk; GAA; Scr Kpr; West Liberty Univ; Dental Tech.

BATES, KERI; Elkhart Memorial HS; Elkhart, IN; Chrs; Hon Rl; Sch Mus; Sch Pl; Stu Cncl; Fr Clb; Pep Clb; Gym; Swmmng; Chrldng; College; Med Tech.

BATES, LAURA; Centerville HS; Centerville, OH; 140/680 Chrs; Chrh Wkr; Hon Rl; Mdrgl; Sch Mus; Sch Nwsp; Fr Clb; Lat Clb; OEA; Outstndng Stu Of The Year; Sinclair Coll; Exec Sec.

BATES, LINDA; South Sr HS; Columbus, OH; 22/342 Band; Chrh Wkr; Hon Rl; Jr NHS; NHS; OEA; IM Sprt; Kiwan Awd; Columbus Tech Inst; Sec.

BATES, MELANIE; Philo HS; Blue Rock, OH; 2/204 Sec Frsh Cls; Sec Soph Cls; Sec Jr Cls; Sec Sr Cls; Sal; Am Leg Aux Girls St; Band; Hon Rl; NHS; Rptr Yrbk; Ohio Univ; Cmnctns.

BATES, NAOMI; Corunna HS; Owosso, MI; Treas Chrh Wkr; Hon Rl; Lbry Ade; NHS; Ed Sch Nwsp; Rptr Sch Nwsp; Olivet Nazarene College; Radio.

BATES, RICHARD; Fowlerville HS; Fowlerville, MI; Pres Sr Cls; Am Leg Boys St; Chrh Wkr; Hon Rl; Lit Mag; NHS; 4-H; FFA; Letter Bsbl; Letter Bsktbl; College; Pre Med.

BATES, ROBERT; Algonac HS; Fair Haven, MI; Letter Ftbl; Univ Of Detroit; Dent.

BATES, SCOTT; Chalker HS; Southington, OH; VP Soph Cls; Am Leg Boys St; Hon Rl; Beta Clb; 4-H; Pep Clb; Spn Clb; Bsktbl; Letter Ftbl; Am Leg Awd; Ohio State Univ; Comp Tech.

BATES, SUE; Meadowbrook HS; , ; 7/179 Sec Jr Cls; Cl Rep Jr Cls; Hon Rl; Treas NHS; Sec Stu Cncl; Rptr Yrbk; Pep Clb; Sci Clb; Spn Clb; PPFtbl; College; Child Dvlpmnt.

BATES, TOM; Twin Vly North HS; Lewisburg, OH; Boy Scts; Hon Rl; Bsbl; Bsktbl; Ftbl;.

BATES, WAYNE L; Elizabeth A Johnson HS; Mt Morris, MI; Band; Chrh Wkr; Hon Rl; Stg Crw; Flint Univ; Aeronautical Engr.

BATH, ANNETTE; Washington HS; Washington, IN; Hon Rl; Off Ade; Sch Mus; Sch Pl; Stg Crw; Drama Clb; Fr Clb; Pep Clb; Wash Daviess Cntyart Lg Awd 79; Crafts Awd 79; 4 Yr French Cert Of Mert 79; Vincennes Univ; Bus Admin.

BATH, TERRY; Mt Notre Dame HS; Cincinnati, OH; 3/580 Cl Rep Jr Cls; Hon Rl; NHS; Stu Cncl; Pres Y-Teens; IM Sprt; Univ Of Dayton; Bus Admin.

BATISTA, CHERYL; Lorain Catholic HS; Lorain, OH; Cls Rep Soph Cls; Rptr Yrbk; Letter Bsktbl; Letter Trk; Univ; Bus Admin.

BATKIE, BARBARA J; Sandusky HS; Carsonville, MI; Cl Rep Jr Cls; Sal; Girl Scts; Hon Rl; Sec NHS; Off Ade; Sec Stu Cncl; Cit Awd; Oakland Univ; Bus Mgmt.

BATSON, JAMES; Kearsley HS; Burton, MI; Cls Rep Frsh Cls; Cls Rep Soph Cls; Cl Rep Jr Cls; Hon Rl; NHS; 3rd Pl In Regnl Compt Acctg 79; Part In HS Engr Inst At Mi St Univ 79; Univ; Engr.

BATSON, ROBERT; Niles Mc Kinley HS; Niles, OH; 9/425 VP Jr Cls; VP Sr Cls; AFS; Debate Tm; Natl Forn Lg; NHS; Sch Mus; VP Stu Cncl; VP Key Clb; Pres Awd; Univ Of Toledo Hnrs Schlrshp 79; Univ Of Toledo; Econ.

BATTAGLIA, AMY; Okemos HS; Okemos, MI; Pol Wkr; Treas Spn Clb; Trk; Mic State Univ; International Bus.

BATTERSHELL, KENNETH; Bishop Luers HS; Ft Wayne, IN; Chrh Wkr; Hon Rl; Sch Nwsp; Bsbl; Coach Actv;.

BATTISFORE, DONA; Charlotte HS; Potterville, MI; Chrs; Rptr Yrbk; Cit Awd; Cert Of Recgntn From St Of Mi 79; Whos Who Awd 79; Ctznshp 78; Spring Arbor Coll; Bus.

BATTJES, CAROLYN; Grandville HS; Grandville, MI; Hon Rl; Mercy Ctrl Schl; Nursing.

BATTLE, PHONDA D; Belleville HS; Ypsilanti, MI; 1/600 Cls Rep Sr Cls; Band; Hon Rl; NHS; Stu Cncl; Rptr Sch Nwsp; Sch Nwsp; Pep Clb; Spn Clb; Letter Chrldng; Univ Of Mich; Pre Med.

BATTLE, RAMONE; Muskegon Hts HS; Muskegon, MI; Cls Rep Soph Cls; Cl Rep Jr Cls; Trs Sr Cls; Chrh Wkr; Hon Rl; Stu Cncl; Sci Clb; 4-H Awd; JA Awd; Lion Awd; Western Univ; Bio.

BATTLE, SHELLEY; Clare HS; Clare, MI; Cls Rep Soph Cls; Cl Rep Jr Cls; Debate Tm; FCA; Girl Scts; Pres Stu Cncl; Rptr Yrbk; Fr Clb; Letter Trk; DAR Awd; Central Michigan Univ; CPA.

BATTLES, DONNA; Kenmore HS; Akron, OH; 26/305 Chrs; Hon Rl; Jr NHS; Mdrgl; NHS; Sch Mus; Pep Clb; Akron Univ.

BATTS, LORI; Jenison HS; Jenison, MI; 26/339 Sec Sr Cls; Band; Hon Rl; NHS; Red Cr Ade; Sch Pl; Stu Cncl; Yth Flsp; Natl Merit Schl; Western Mich Univ; Ther.

BAUCHER, JON; Celina Sr HS; Celina, OH; 10/225 Cls Rep Frsh Cls; Cls Rep Soph Cls; Cl Rep Jr Cls; Cls Rep Sr Cls; Cmnty Wkr; Hon Rl; Jr NHS; NHS; Pres Stu Cncl; FTA; Cincinnati Univ; Engr.

BAUCHER, MIKE; Coldwater HS; Coldwater, OH; Rptr Sch Nwsp; Bsbl; Bsktbl; IM Sprt; Wright State Dayton Ohio.

BAUCHLE, BONNIE; Southport HS; Indianapolis, IN; Cmp Fr Grls; Hon Rl; Yth Flsp; Key Clb; Ger Clb; Pep Clb; Gym; Chrldng; 4-H Awd; Coll; Fashion Dsgn.

BAUDO, JENNIFER; Green HS; Charlotte, NC; Cls Rep Frsh Cls; Chrs; Chrh Wkr; Hon Rl; Jr NHS; NHS; Stu Cncl; Central Piedmont College.

BAUER, ALBIN; Northwood HS; Northwood, OH; Am Leg Boys St; Band; Chrs; Hon Rl; Pres JA; NHS; Pres Stu Cncl; Key Clb; Letter Wrstlng; JA Awd; College; Medicine.

BAUER, BETH; Lincolnview HS; Van Wert, OH; 4/80 Treas Band; Cmp Fr Grls; Pres NHS; Yth Flsp; Pres Fr Clb; Letter Bsbl; Letter Trk; Univ.

BAUER, CHRIS; Groveport Madison HS; Groveport, OH; 31/377 Cls Rep Soph Cls; Cl Rep Jr Cls; Hon Rl; NHS; Stu Cncl; Yrbk; Chrldng; PPFtbl; Univ; Med.

BAUER, DANIEL; Unionvl Sebewaing Area HS; Sebewaing, MI; 18/113 Hon Rl; Bsbl; Bsktbl; Scr Kpr; Tmr; Ferris St Coll; Aviation.

BAUER, DEBORAH; Shelbyville HS; Shelbyville, IN; Chrs; Hon Rl; Hosp Ade; Sch Mus; Sch Pl; Drama Clb; Lat Clb; Pep Clb; Trk; Ball State Univ; Nursing.

BAUER, GREGORY; Western Reserve Acad; Kent, OH; Boy Scts; Chrh Wkr; Hon Rl; Off Ade; Red Cr Ade; Sct Actv; Ger Clb; Letter Bsbl; Socr; Letter Swmmng; Rice Univ; Pre Med.

BAUER, JEFFREY; Bryan HS; Bryan, OH; Pres Aud/Vis; Boy Scts; Chrh Wkr; Hon Rl; Pres JA; NHS; Pres 4-H; FFA; Pep Clb; Trk; Univ Of Cincinnati; Acctg.

BAUER, JOHN; Akron Garfield Sr HS; Akron, OH; 30/539 Trs Sr Cls; Band; Hon Rl; Natl Forn Lg; NHS; Stu Cncl; Fr Clb; Lat Clb; Letter Ftbl; Univ; Performing Art.

BAUER, JULIE; Reese HS; Reese, MI; 10/131 VP Frsh Cls; Pres Soph Cls; Pres Jr Cls; Pres Sr Cls; Hon Rl; Lbry Ade; MMM; NHS; Yth Flsp; Pep Clb; Western Michigan Univ; Acctg.

BAUER, KAREN; St Josephs HS; South Bend, IN; 18/265 Hon Rl; NHS; Quill & Scroll; Sch Pl; Stg Crw; Ed Yrbk; Drama Clb; 4-H; Pep Clb; Spn Clb; College; Journalism.

BAUER, KATHRYN; Kingswood HS; Lathrup Vlg, MI; Band; Chrs; Hon Rl; Lit Mag; Mdrgl; Sch Pl; Stg Crw; Yth Flsp; Rptr Sch Nwsp; Drama Clb; Univ; Eng.

BAUER, KOLLEEN; Medina Sr HS; Medina, OH; Cl Rep Jr Cls; Sec Sr Cls; Cls Rep Sr Cls; Chrs; Cmnty Wkr; Girl Scts; Hosp Ade; Red Cr Ade; Stu Cncl; Pep Clb; Ashland Coll; Sec Sci.

BAUER, LORI; Haslett HS; Haslett, MI; 20/179 Cmp Fr Grls; Chrs; Hon Rl; Lit Mag; NHS; Yth Flsp; Rptr Yrbk; Letter Bsktbl; Mi Comptn Schlrshp 79; Michigan St Univ; Hlth.

BAUER, MICHAEL; Purcell HS; Cincinnati, OH; Cls Rep Soph Cls; Cl Rep Jr Cls; Hon Rl; Stu Cncl; Ftbl; Capt Swmmng; Trk; Univ; Comp Sci.

BAUER, PAUL; Champion HS; Warren, OH; 190224 Aud/Vis; Chrh Wkr; Hon Rl; JA; Lbry Ade; NHS; Sch Pl; Stg Crw; Drama Clb; Fr Clb; 100 FTA Sclhsp; U S Air Force.

BAUER, RANDALL; Howland HS; Warren, OH; 20/436 Cls Rep Frsh Cls; Cls Rep Soph Cls; Cl Rep Jr Cls; Cls Rep Sr Cls; Cmnty Wkr; Hon Rl; Stu Cncl; Rptr Sch Nwsp; Drama Clb; Fr Clb; Univ; Chem Engr.

BAUER, RHONDA; Holgate HS; Holgate, OH; 5/60 Cl Rep Jr Cls; Trs Sr Cls; Chrs; Chrh Wkr; Hon Rl; Jr NHS; NHS; Sch Pl; Yth Flsp; Rptr Yrbk; Bowling Green St Univ.

BAUER, ROBERT; Parkside HS; Jackson, MI; Hon Rl; Crs Cntry; Trk; Wrstlng; Jackson Com College; Engineering.

BAUER, SALLY; Highlander Place HS; Aurora, IN; 65/265 Band; Pep Clb; Glf; Ten; IM Sprt; Univ; Natural Resources.

BAUER, SUZANNE; Inland Lakes HS; Indian River, MI; 2/90 Hon Rl; VP Stu Cncl; Rptr Yrbk; Sprt Ed Sch Nwsp; Letter Bsktbl; Letter Swmmng; Letter Trk; Voice Dem Awd; Univ; Sci.

BAUER, TAMMY; Williamsburg HS; Williamsburg, OH; Chrh Wkr; Hon Rl; Lbry Ade; NHS; Fr Clb; FHA; Univ.

BAUER, TRACY; Hicksville HS; Hicksville, OH; 11/99 Sec Jr Cls; Am Leg Aux Girls St; Band; Chrs; Chrh Wkr; Hon Rl; Hosp Ade; Lbry Ade; NHS; Univ Of Toledo; Med Tech.

BAUERBAND, JULIE; Attica HS; Attica, IN; 2/85 VP Soph Cls; Sal; VP Band; Chrs; VP NHS; Treas Stu Cncl; Yrbk; Pres Fr Clb; Trk; DAR Awd; Ball St Univ; Foreign Lang.

BAUERLE, HEIDI; Snider HS; Ft Wayne, IN; 99/525 Chrs; Chrh Wkr; Cmnty Wkr; Hon Rl; Sch Mus; Swing Chr; All City Chr; Nurse Aide Worker At Nursing Home; Indiana Univ; Occupt Ther.

BAUERMEISTER, CARYN; Northrop HS; Ft Wayne, IN; 33/587 Cls Rep Frsh Cls; FCA; Hon Rl; Rptr Sch Nwsp; Letter Bsktbl; Letter Gym; Capt Chrldng; IM Sprt; Cit Awd; Pres Awd; Bio Jrnlsm Typng & Attndnc Awds 76; Typng French Geom Awds 77; Purdue Univ; Bus Mgmt.

BAUERNFIEND, JUDY; Springs Vly HS; French Lick, IN; 14/88 Hon Rl; FHA; Spn Clb; Vincennes Univ; Radio Broadcasting.

BAUGHER, BOBBI JO; Triton HS; Bourbon, IN; 21/93 Sec Soph Cls; Band; Chrs; FCA; Hon Rl; Mdrgl; Off Ade; 4-H; FTA; Pep Clb; Vllybl Ltre 77; Typing Fastst Typer In Cls 78; Bus GPA 3.17 Acctg I 79; Homecoming Princss Soph Yr 78; Berea Univ; Phys Educ Tchr.

BAUGHER, KAREN; Bridgman HS; Bridgman, MI; Band; Chrs; Hon Rl; Lbry Ade; Off Ade; Sch Mus; Sch Pl; FHA; Pep Clb; Letter Bsktbl; Parsons Bus Schl.

BAUGHMAN, CAROL; Mogadore HS; Mogadore, OH; 2/96 Girl Scts; Hon Rl; Hosp Ade; Lbry Ade; NHS; Off Ade; FHA; Kent St Univ; Nursing.

BAUGHMAN, DAVID; Lucas HS; Perrysville, OH; Aud/Vis; Boy Scts; Hon Rl; NHS; Sch Pl; Y-Teens; 4-H; FFA; IM Sprt; 4-H Awd; State Farmer Awd Future Farmer Of America 1979; Work.

BAUGHMAN, J; Decatur Central HS; Indnpls, IN; Am Leg Aux Girls St; Chrs; Hon Rl; NHS; Sch Mus; Stg Crw; 4-H; Lat Clb; 4-H Awd; Natl Merit Ltr; Purdue Univ; Nursing.

BAUGHMAN, JULIE; Mathews HS; Cortland, OH; 26/150 Cls Rep Sr Cls; Band; Hon Rl; NHS; Stu Cncl; Y-Teens; Key Clb; VP Pep Clb; Spn Clb; 3rd Rnr Up As Queen Candidate In Fowler Fair 79; Northeastern Ohio Univ; Med.

BAUGHMANN, LORI; Our Lady Of Mercy HS; Redford, MI; NHS; Ger Clb; Am Leg Awd; Univ.

BAUKE, GREG; Purcell HS; Cincinnati, OH; Trs Sr Cls; Sal; Hon Rl; NHS; Pol Wkr; Stu Cncl; Lat Clb; Mth Clb; Capt Glf; Bausch & Lomb Awd; Xavier Univ; Pre Law.

BAUKE, GREGORY P; Purcell HS; Cincinnati, OH; 2/176 Trs Sr Cls; Hon Rl; NHS; Stu Cncl; FBLA; Lat Clb; Capt Glf; Xavier Univ; Acctg.

BAUKEMA, PAT; South Christian HS; Grand Rapids, MI; Band; Chrs; Drl Tm; Hon Rl; NHS; Calvin Coll; Registered Nurse.

BAUM, LORI; Tippecanoe Valley HS; Mentone, IN; 26/159 Hon Rl; NHS; Fr Clb; FTA; Pom Pon; Purdue Univ; Engr.

BAUM, TAMMY; Belding Area HS; Belding, MI; 12/144 Band; Hon Rl; NHS; Sch Mus; Univ Of Miami; Marine Bio.

BAUMAN, BETH; St Philip Catholic Cntrl HS; Battle Creek, MI; 6/70 Trs Soph Cls; Cls Rep Soph Cls; VP Jr Cls; Cl Rep Jr Cls; Sec Sr Cls; Hon Rl; Jr NHS; Stu Cncl; Lat Clb; VICA; Michigan St Univ; Travel Agent.

BAUMAN, BRIAN; La Salle HS; Cincinnati, OH; Hon Rl; JA; Ftbl; Trk; IM Sprt; UC.

BAUMAN, E SUE; East Knox HS; Howard, OH; VP Sr Cls; Cls Rep Sr Cls; Band; Chrs; Lit Mag; NHS; VP Quill & Scroll; Ohio Univ; Social Psyc.

BAUMAN, JAMES; Heritage Christian Schl; Indianapolis, IN; Debate Tm; Sch Pl; Stg Crw; Drama Clb; Spn Clb; Letter Bsktbl; Letter Socr; Grace Coll; Bus Admin.

BAUMAN, JANET; Lake Michigan Catholic HS; Benton Hrbr, MI; Hon Rl; Hosp Ade; Sch Mus; Sch Pl; Stg Crw; Drama Clb; Sci Clb; Voice Dem Awd; College; Nursing.

BAUMAN, JANET; Lake Michigan Cath HS; Benton Harbor, MI; Hon Rl; Sch Mus; Sch Pl; Drama Clb; Sci Clb; Univ Of Michigan; Nurse.

BAUMANN, DIANA; Stephen T Badin HS; Hamilton, OH; 20/220 Hon Rl; JA; NHS; Sch Mus; Sch Pl; Drama Clb; Treas Spn Clb; Natl Merit Ltr; College; Bio.

BAUMANN, JULIE; Oak Hills HS; Cincinnati, OH; Cl Rep Jr Cls; Cls Rep Sr Cls; Hon Rl; OEA; Printing.

BAUMANN, MELISSA J; Clear Fork HS; Bellville, OH; 3/165 Am Leg Aux Girls St; Chrh Wkr; Hosp Ade; NHS; Stu Cncl; Scr Kpr; DAR Awd; Mic Tech Univ; Chem Engr.

BAUMANN, ROBERT E; Cuyahoga Hts HS; Brklyn Hts, OH; Am Leg Boys St; Letter Crs Cntry; Trk; NEDT Highst In Schl 77 & 78; Achvmgnt Rating Of Exclng Dist Sci Day 79; Univ; Sci.

BAUMBERGER, MARY; Crestview HS; Mansfield, OH; Chrh Wkr; Hon Rl; Sct Actv; Yth Flsp; Yrbk; Drama Clb; Fr Clb; Mat Maids; Scr Kpr; Tmr; Univ; Nursing.

BAUMEISTER, MARK; River Valley School; Sawyer, MI; Chrh Wkr; Hon Rl; 4-H; Ger Clb; Bsktbl; Taylor Univ; Bus Admin.

BAUMER, BETH; Eastwood HS; Luckey, OH; Trs Jr Cls; Off Ade; Treas Yth Flsp; 4-H; Treas FHA; Sec Ger Clb; Pep Clb; Coll; Data Proc.

BAUMER, BEVERLY; Saint Ursula Acad; Cincinnati, OH; 7/85 Chrs; Chrh Wkr; Hon Rl; NHS; Rptr Yrbk; Spn Clb; Univ Of Cincinnati; Eng.

BAUMER, PATRICIA; Minster HS; Minster, OH; 19/80 Band; Girl Scts; Hon Rl; Rptr Sch Nwsp; Sch Nwsp; FTA; Pep Clb; Chrldng; College; Acctg.

BAUMERT, RITA J; Admiral King HS; Lorain, OH; 53/413 Hon Rl; NHS; OEA; Natl Merit Ltr; Lorain County Cmnty Coll; Bus Admin.

BAUMGARDNER, DAVE; Tri West HS; Jamestown, IN; Cls Rep Soph Cls; Stg Crw; Rptr Sch Nwsp; 4-H; Pep Clb; Letter Bsktbl; JETS Awd; Univ; Engr.

BAUMGARDNER, DAVE; Springboro HS; Springboro, OH; Hon Rl; Sch Pl; Yth Flsp; Yrbk; Glf; Wright State Univ.

BAUMGARDNER, KAREN M; Finneytown HS; Cincinnati, OH; 18/249 NHS; Ed Sch Nwsp; Drama Clb; Ten; Univ Of Cincinnati; Pre Med.

BAUMGARDNER, SARA; Delphos Jefferson Sr HS; Solon, OH; 12/112 Band; Chrs; Hon Rl; NHS; Sch Mus; Sec Yth Flsp; Spn Clb; Mgrs; Univ.

BAUMGART, JUDY; Lanesville HS; Lanesville, IN; 2/60 VP Frsh Cls; Trs Soph Cls; Cls Rep Soph Cls; Cl Rep Jr Cls; Cls Rep Sr Cls; Sal; Am Leg Aux Girls St; Band; Chrs; FCA; Indiana Univ; Elec Engr.

BAUMGARTNER, DAVE; Solon HS; Solon, OH; 70/300 Cl Rep Jr Cls; Hon Rl; Stu Cncl; Sec Key Clb; Bsktbl; Letter Ftbl; Letter Ten; PPFtbl; Albion Univ; Forestry.

BAUMGARTNER, DIANE; Clay Sr HS; Oregon, OH; 11/365 Hon Rl; NHS; Ed Yrbk; Yrbk; 4-H; Fr Clb; Letter Ten; 4-H Awd; Univ; Psych.

BAUMGARTNER, PAUL; East Kentwood HS; Kentwood, MI; Trs Jr Cls; Hon Rl; NHS; Letter Ftbl; Letter Wrstlng; Univ; Engr.

BAURLEY, JANET; South Ripley Jr Sr HS; Holton, IN; 9/104 Chrs; Hon Rl; NHS; 4-H; FNA; Pep Clb; Spn Clb; Letter Mgrs; 4-H Awd; Marian Univ; Biology.

BAVOLA, CAROL; Brookfield HS; Brookfield, OH; Cls Rep Frsh Cls; Pres Soph Cls; VP Sr Cls; Band; Off Ade; FNA; Pep Clb; Youngstown State; Nursing.

BAXTER, AMY; Griffith HS; Griffith, IN; 44/281 Cl Rep Jr Cls; Cls Rep Sr Cls; Chrs; Mdrgl; Quill & Scroll; Stu Cncl; Sch Nwsp; Comp Tech.

BAXTER, ANNE; Belleville HS; Belleville, MI; Chrh Wkr; Hon Rl; NHS; Stg Crw; Univ Of Mic; Nursing.

BAXTER, CRAIG; Minerva HS; Minerva, OH; 14/266 Hon Rl; NHS; Ftbl; Scr Kpr; Univ Of Toledo; Pre Med Sci.

BAXTER, JOHN R; Van Wert HS; Van Wert, OH; 21/230 Cl Rep Jr Cls; Cls Rep Sr Cls; Chrs; Hon Rl; Stu Cncl; Spn Clb; Crs Cntry; Trk; Univ; Engr.

BAXTER, KATHLEEN; Riverside HS; Painesville, OH; Sdlty; Yrbk; Rptr Sch Nwsp; Spn Clb;.

BAXTER, KENT; Pontiac Central HS; Pontiac, MI; Hon Rl; Cit Awd; Excel In Schlrshp 75; GMI; Archt.

BAXTER, MIKE; Snider HS; Ft Wayne, IN; Univ.

BAXTER, ROBERT; Brookville HS; Brookville, IN; Aud/Vis; Band; Hon Rl; Letter Bsbl; Univ.

BAXTER, SUSIN; Glen Lake Cmnty Schools; Glen Arbor, MI; 5/70 Sec Frsh Cls; Chrh Wkr; Hon Rl; Lbry Ade; Pres NHS; Off Ade; Sprt Ed Sch Nwsp; Fr Clb; Bsktbl; Ten; Bsktbl J V Mst Impvd 76; Hope Coll; Psych.

BAXTER, TAMI W; Hamilton S Eastern HS; Noblesville, IN; 2/135 Cls Rep Frsh Cls; Trs Sr Cls; Hon Rl; Stu Cncl; VP 4-H; Spn Clb; Chrldng; Mgrs; 4-H Awd; Top 5% Fresh Soph & Jr Yrs; Busns Schl; Acctg.

BAXTER, TIMOTHY; St Louis HS; Alma, MI; Pres NHS; Am Leg Awd; Rotary Awd; Michigan Tech Univ; Mech Engr.

BAY, LAURIE; East Noble HS; Kendallvile, IN; 40/271 Hon Rl; Intl Bus Coll; Acctg.

BAYBURN, DEBORAH L; Miami Trace HS; Jeffersonville, OH; 12/271 AFS; Band; Chrs; Chrh Wkr; Drl Tm; Drm Mjrt; Jr NHS; NHS; Stg Crw; Yth Flsp; Findlay Coll.

BAYER, JOHN; De Lasalle Collegiate HS; Gs Pt Pk, MI; Cls Rep Soph Cls; Hon Rl; Jr NHS; NHS; Sch Mus; Sch Pl; Stg Crw; IM Sprt; Mich State Univ; Engr.

BAYER, MARY; St Annes HS; Warren, MI; Sec Frsh Cls; Sec Soph Cls; Sec Jr Cls; VP Sr Cls; NHS; Ed Sch Nwsp; Drama Clb; Trk; Chrldng; Pom Pon; Coll.

BAYER, TED; Liberty Center HS; Liberty Ctr, OH; Hon Rl; 4-H; Fr Clb; FFA; 4-H Awd; Toledo; Engr.

BAYES, BRENDA; Taylor HS; Cleves, OH; Trs Frsh Cls; Cls Rep Frsh Cls; Sec Soph Cls; Cls Rep Soph Cls; Band; Drl Tm; Hon Rl; Hosp Ade; Off Ade; Stu Cncl; Mayfair Participtn 77; Buckeye St Yrbk Workshop Layout Awd 3rd 79 Design Awd Top 12 79; Cincinnati Acad; Cmmrcl Art.

BAYES, JANIE; Westfall HS; Orient, OH; Band; Chrs; Hosp Ade; 4-H; FNA; FTA; Spn Clb; Trk; Scr Kpr; 4-H Awd; Mt Carmel; Nursing.

BAYLERS, MICHAEL; Park Hills HS; Fairborn, OH; Hon Rl; Letter Socr; Coach Actv; IM Sprt;.

BAYLESS, PAULA; Poca HS; Bancroft, WV; 5/159 Band; Hon Rl; NHS; Pres Fr Clb; Natl Merit Schl; Ohio St Univ; Physics.

BAYLESS, PAUL N; Corunna HS; Corunna, MI; 31/222 Band; Rdo Clb;.

BAYLESS, R; Fairmont West HS; Kettering, OH; 14/500 Band; Hon Rl; Natl Forn Lg; Sch Mus; Sch Pl; Yth Flsp; Fr Clb; Rdo Clb; DAR Awd; Natl Merit Ltr; Foreign Service.

BAYLESS, ROSANN; Brooke HS; Wellsburg, WV; 11/403 Hon Rl; Lit Mag; NHS; Off Ade; Quill & Scroll; Spn Clb; W Liberty St Coll; Eng.

BAYLESS, VALERIE; Chillicothe HS; Chillicothe, OH; VP Jr Cls; Am Leg Aux Girls St; Chrs; Hon Rl; Natl Forn Lg; Orch; Sch Mus; Sch Pl; Stu Cncl; Letter Trk; Univ; Paramedics.

BAYLEY, CAROL; Kearsley HS; Flint, MI; 71/400 Band; Boy Scts; Hon Rl; Off Ade; Letter Bsktbl; Trk; Coach Actv; Mgrs; Univ Of Mic; Poli Sci.

BAYLEY, MARK; Sidney HS; Sidney, OH; Cls Rep Frsh Cls; Cls Rep Soph Cls; Hon Rl; 4-H; Letter Ftbl; IM Sprt; Ftbl Tm Cptn 79; Marine Corps; Vet Med.

BAYLIFF, JULIE; Waynesfield Goshen HS; Waynesfield, OH; Band; Chrs; Hon Rl; JA; Jr NHS; Sch Mus; Spn Clb; PPFtbl; College; Journalism.

BAYLISS, RICK; Harbor Springs HS; Hrbr Spgs, MI; Trs Frsh Cls; Trs Soph Cls; Trs Jr Cls; Trs Sr Cls; Hon Rl; Lbry Ade; Sch Pl; Bsbl; Bsktbl; Ftbl; Mesa San Diego State Univ; Bus Admin.

BAYLOR, CATHY; Kyger Creek HS; Gallipolis, OH; 2/67 Sal; Aud/Vis; Band; Hon Rl; Sec NHS; Sec Fr Clb; Treas Keyettes; Marshall Univ; Educ.

BAYNE, SHEILA; Strongsville Sr HS; Strongsville, OH; Ed Yrbk; Rptr Yrbk; Pres 4-H; FHA; GAA; PPFtbl; 4-H Awd; Coll; Food & Nutrition.

BAYS, JAMES M; Gallia Academy; Gallipolis, OH; Boy Scts; Hon Rl; Scholarship Team 78; Univ.

BAYS, JAMIE; Bloomfield HS; Bloomfield, IN; Am Leg Aux Girls St; Hon Rl; Fr Clb; Airline Hostess.

BAYS, LORIE; Midland Trail HS; Hico, WV; VP Frsh Cls; Cls Rep Soph Cls; Chrs; Girl Scts; Sch Mus; Yrbk; FBLA; VP FHA; Pep Clb; PPFtbl; Wv All St Chr 79; West Virginia Tech Univ; Music.

BAYS, SHERRY; Milton HS; Culleden, WV; Chrs; Chrh Wkr; Red Cr Ade; Pep Clb; College.

BAYS, TAMERA; Sherman HS; Peytona, WV; Band; Chrh Wkr; Cmnty Wkr; Girl Scts; Hon Rl; Lbry Ade; Sch Pl; Scr Kpr; Bus Schl; Bus Mgmt.

BAYSORE, JANE; Wm Mason HS; Mason, OH; 25/191 Hon Rl; Off Ade; Yth Flsp; 4-H; Pep Clb; Trk; Chrldng; IM Sprt; PPFtbl; R Walters Busns Schl; Exec Sec.

BAZIL, CARL W; Brother Rice HS; Birmingham, MI; 1/251 Val; Band; Debate Tm; Hon Rl; Mod UN; Natl Forn Lg; NHS; Sch Mus; Ed Yrbk; IM Sprt; Gold Awd For Excellence In Jr Year; Chariman Of Model Science; Michigan Competitive Schlrshp; College; Chemistry.

BAZINET, ARCHIE; Trenary HS; Trenary, MI; 5/11 Cls Rep Frsh Cls; VP Jr Cls; Pres Sr Cls; Am Leg Boys St; Sch Pl; Stg Crw; Crs Cntry; Cit Awd; Lion Awd; Michigan Tech Univ.

BAZINI, CHRISTINE; Tippecanoe Valley HS; Mentone, IN; 7/156 Band; Chrh Wkr; Hon Rl; NHS; Stg Crw; Yth Flsp; Sch Nwsp; Drama Clb; Spn Clb; Manchester Coll; Acctg.

BAZNER, DENISE; Divine Child HS; Dearborn, MI; Cmnty Wkr; Girl Scts; Hon Rl; NHS; Ger Clb; Sci Clb; Natl Merit SF; Wayne St Univ; Pharm.

BAZZARELLI, ROBERT; Collinwood HS; Cleveland, OH; 2/300 Cl Rep Jr Cls; Hon Rl; JA; Lbry Ade; NHS; Rptr Sch Nwsp; Sch Nwsp; JA Awd; Martha Holden Jennings Motivational Schlrshp 76; Jr Achvmnt Of Greater Cleveland VP Personnel 79; Case Western Reserve Univ; Comp Sci.

BAZZIE, REBA; Shady Spring HS; Daniels, WV; Cls Rep Soph Cls; Cl Rep Jr Cls; Pres Band; Cmnty Wkr; Drl Tm; Hon Rl; Pol Wkr; Stu Cncl; Yth Flsp; Drama Clb; Univ.

BAZZOLI, ELAINE; Tuscarawas Central Cath HS; Dover, OH; Hon Rl; NHS; Rptr Sch Nwsp; Pep Clb; Spn Clb; Scr Kpr; Univ.

BAZZOLI, SARA; Tuscarawas Central Cath HS; Dover, OH; 13/60 Hon Rl; NHS; Ed Yrbk; Sch Nwsp; Pep Clb; Letter Bsktbl; Letter Trk; Ohio St Univ; Elem Education.

BEACH, ALICE; Napoleon HS; Clarkdale, MI; Band; Boy Scts; Debate Tm; NHS; Orch; Sch Mus; 4-H; 4-H Awd; College; Engr.

BEACH, DAVID; Williamsburg HS; Batavia, OH; Fr Clb; Ftbl; Trk; Am Leg Awd; Univ; Sci.

BEACH, MARY; Alter HS; Centervl, OH; Chrs; Hosp Ade; Yrbk; Pep Clb; IM Sprt; Univ; Mech Drawing.

BEACH, ONEVA J; Switzerland County HS; Madison, IN; Rptr Yrbk; Rptr Sch Nwsp; Drama Clb; 4-H; Pep Clb; Ivy Tech; Acctg.

BEACH, SANDRA; Teays Valley HS; Ashville, OH; 1/200 Am Leg Aux Girls St; Chrs; Chrh Wkr; Hon Rl; NHS; Sch Mus; Pres Yth Flsp; Drama Clb; Lat Clb; Am Leg Awd; Ohio St Univ; Eng.

BEACH, SIMONE; Floyd Central HS; Floyd Knobs, IN; 16/360 Chrs; Hon Rl; NHS; Fr Clb; PPFtbl; Ltr For Hon Roll 77 ;swing Chr 78; Univ; Music.

BEACH, VENESSA; Bluffton HS; Bluffton, OH; Chrs; Hon Rl; Letter Bsktbl; Bluffton Coll.

BEACHY, JEFF; Northridge HS; Middlebury, IN; 1/143 Val; Hon Rl; Pres JA; NHS; Sch Mus; Ten; Mgrs; JC Awd; JETS Awd; Natl Merit Ltr; Purdue University; Electrical Engein.

BEACHY, LISA; West Jefferson HS; Galloway, OH; 6/108 Trs Frsh Cls; Trs Soph Cls; Trs Jr Cls; VP NHS; Ed Sch Nwsp; VP Fr Clb; Letter Trk; Scr Kpr; Miami Univ.

BEADIE, DOUG; Elmhurst HS; Ft Wayne, IN; 70/410 Cls Rep Frsh Cls; Cls Rep Soph Cls; Cls Rep Sr Cls; Quill & Scroll; Stu Cncl; Sch Nwsp; Crs Cntry; Ten; Univ; Ship Builder.

BEADLE, ANDREA; Traverse City Sr HS; Traverse City, MI; 24/800 Band; Chrh Wkr; Hon Rl; NHS; Orch; Sch Mus; Yth Flsp; Trk; Michigan St Univ; Soc Sci.

BEADLE, ANGELA; Washington HS; Massillon, OH; Cls Rep Frsh Cls; Cls Rep Soph Cls; Hon Rl; Stu Cncl; Rptr Sch Nwsp; DECA; FHA; Pep Clb; Bauder Voc Schl; Fshn Mdse.

BEADLE, BRIAN; Peck HS; Melvin, MI; Cls Rep Soph Cls; Pres Jr Cls; Stu Cncl; Pres 4-H; Letter Bsbl; Letter Ftbl; Voc Schl; Electrn.

BEADLE, CINDY; Southern Local HS; Salineville, OH; Pres Jr Cls; Hon Rl; Lbry Ade; Off Ade; Yrbk; FHA; FNA; Trk; Chrldng; Pom Pon; Work.

BEADLE, DIANNE; Fremont HS; Fremont, IN; 12/72 Trs Frsh Cls; Trs Soph Cls; VP Jr Cls; Band; Chrs; Girl Scts; Hon Rl; NHS; Sch Mus; Sch Pl; Finalst Dan Quayle Congrssnl Stu Progr 1978; 1st Pl St & Dist Saxaphone Quartet 1979; Indiana Central Univ; Phys Ther.

BEADLE, MIRTHA; Ottawa Hills HS; Grand Rapids, MI; Sec Chrh Wkr; Hon Rl; JA; Jr NHS; NHS; Off Ade; OEA; Spn Clb; Coed Corrspndnt Appeard In Coed Magzn 77; Andrews Univ; Engr.

BEAGAN, CELESTE; Northville HS; Northville, MI; Cls Rep Sr Cls; Chrs; Hon Rl; Off Ade; Stu Cncl; Adrian College; Acctg.

BEAGAN, CHERIE; Cody HS; Detroit, MI; College; Radiology.

BEAGAN, LYNETTE; Cherry Hill HS; Westland, MI; 1/250 Val; Cmp Fr Grls; Chrh Wkr; Cmnty Wkr; Hon Rl; NHS; Sch Pl; Stg Crw; Detroit Coll Of Bus; Legal Sec.

BEAGLE, ANN; North Decatur HS; Greensburg, IN; Cls Rep Soph Cls; VP Jr Cls; Drl Tm; Ten; Pom Pon;.

BEAL, DALE; Tri Village HS; New Madison, OH; Hon Rl; NHS; Fr Clb; Am Leg Awd; Univ Of Dayton; Enviro Engr.

BEAL, KAREN; Mother Of Mercy HS; Cincinnati, OH; Drl Tm; Girl Scts; Hon Rl; Sct Actv; Spn Clb; Gym; GAA; Scr Kpr; Twrlr; Kiwan Awd; Xavier Univ; Law.

BEAL, LINDA; Cedar Lake Academy; Charlevoix, MI; Band; Hon Rl; NHS; Andrews Univ.

BEAL, NADINE; Franklin Central HS; Indpls, IN; Chrs; Chrh Wkr; Cmnty Wkr; JA; NHS; Off Ade; Sch Mus; Pep Clb; Chrldng; Typist Of Yr 77; Typist Of Yr 78; Outstndng Hist Stndt Awd 78; Butler Univ; Music.

BEALE, BOBBI; Streetsboro HS; Streetsboro, OH; Cl Rep Jr Cls; Cls Rep Sr Cls; AFS; Chrs; Chrh Wkr; Cmnty Wkr; Girl Scts; Hon Rl; Lbry Ade; NHS; Eastern Mennonite College; Theatre.

BEALER, JAMES; Lake View HS; Cortland, OH; Aud/Vis; Hon Rl; Red Cr Ade; Yth Flsp; Ftbl; Trk; College; Engr.

BEALL, DONALD; Hedgesville HS; Hedgesville, WV; VP Band; Boy Scts; FCA; Hon Rl; MMM; Sch Mus; Letter Bsbl; James Rumsey; Electronic Tech.

BEALS, LISA; Northfield HS; Lagro, IN; 2/110 Sec Soph Cls; Cl Rep Jr Cls; Pres Sr Cls; Cls Rep Sr Cls; Am Leg Aux Girls St; Drl Tm; Hon Rl; VP NHS; Quill & Scroll; Stg Crw; Ball St Univ; Tchr.

BEALS, PATRICIA; River Valley HS; Marion, OH; Chrs; Quill & Scroll; Sch Mus; Yrbk; Ed Sch Nwsp; Bowling Green State Univ.

BEALS, SHAUNA; Hilltop HS; W Unity, OH; 4/64 Cls Rep Frsh Cls; Band; Chrs; Chrh Wkr; Hon Rl; NHS; Sch Mus; Sch Pl; Stg Crw; Stu Cncl; Best Spiker Awrd 1977; Academ Achiev Club 1975; 2nd Runner Up Egg N Fest Beauty Pag 1977; Montana St Univ; Sociology.

BEALS, THERESA; Tecumseh HS; New Carlisle, OH; Pres Soph Cls; Pres Jr Cls; AFS; Capt Drl Tm; Hon Rl; Jr NHS; Pres NHS; Off Ade; Sch Pl; Fr Clb; Miami Ctrl Cnfrnc Schlr Athlt Trck 1978; Bst Actrss 1979; Arrw Awd Mst Sprt 1979; Ohio St Univ; Optometry.

BEAM, DEBRA; Marysville HS; St Clair, MI; 75/175 Lbry Ade; OEA; Pep Clb;.

BEAMAN, REED S; East Lansing HS; East Lansing, MI; Band; Boy Scts; Hon Rl; NHS; Orch; Sch Mus; JA Awd; Natl Merit Schl; Univ; Bio Chem.

BEAMONT, TERESA; Stryker HS; Stryker, OH; Pres Sr Cls; Hon Rl; Yth Flsp; Rptr Yrbk; Rptr Sch Nwsp; Sec 4-H; FHA; OEA; Twrlr; 4-H Awd; OEA Executive Awd; Twirling Contest Awds; Cnty Honors For Beads 4 H Prjct;.

BEAN, JEFFERY A; Reeths Puffer HS; Muskegon, MI; 5/261 Band; Hon Rl; NHS; Spn Clb; Muskegon Comm Coll; Elec Engr.

BEAN, JIM; Connersville Sr HS; Connersville, IN; Hon Rl; NHS; 4-H; FFA; Sci Clb; IM Sprt; FFA Hoosier Farmer Degree 79; Otstndng Boy FFA Hon 79; Hoosier Schlr; Indiana Univ; Agri.

BEAN, T; Ortonville Brandon HS; Clarkston, MI; Pres Frsh Cls; Cls Rep Soph Cls; Cl Rep Jr Cls; Hon Rl; Bsbl; Ftbl; Trk; Wrstlng; Univ.

BEAN, WILLIAM; Mayville HS; Fostoria, MI; Cls Rep Frsh Cls; Cls Rep Soph Cls; Cl Rep Jr Cls; Pres Sr Cls; Cls Rep Sr Cls; Hon Rl; Lbry Ade; NHS; Delta College; Phys Ther.

BEANBLOSSOM, CYNTHIA; Decatur Central HS; Camby, IN; 5/396 A Pres Frsh Cls; NHS; VP Stu Cncl; Crs Cntry; Trk; Am Leg Awd; Dnfth Awd; Earlham College; Medicine.

BEANE, JOHN; Stonewall Jackson HS; Chrlstn, WV; 10/260 FCA; Hon Rl; JA; Jr NHS; Lbry Ade; NHS; Off Ade; Sch Pl; Rptr Yrbk; Drama Clb; West Virginia Univ; Med.

BEAN JR, RICHARD; Quincy HS; Quincy, MI; 1/125 Pres Frsh Cls; Pres Soph Cls; Pres Jr Cls; Am Leg Boys St; Aud/Vis; Boy Scts; Cmnty Wkr; Hon Rl; NHS; Pres Stu Cncl; Univ; Bus Admin.

BEAR, HELEN; Zionsville Cmnty HS; Zionsville, IN; 5/149 Cls Rep Sr Cls; Hon Rl; VP NHS; Pres Stu Cncl; Yrbk; Sec 4-H; Spn Clb; Am Leg Awd; JC Awd; Butler Univ; Bus Admin.

BEAR, JULIE; Huntington North HS; Roanoke, IN; Cls Rep Soph Cls; Trs Sr Cls; Am Leg Aux Girls St; Band; Chrs; Girl Scts; Hon Rl; College; Math.

BEARD, BEV; Clay HS; S Bend, IN; 108/496 Hon Rl; Hosp Ade; Off Ade; Fr Clb; Lat Clb; Pep Clb; Letter Trk; Univ Of Evansville; Phys Ther.

BEARD, LOIS; Elmhurst HS; Ft Wayne, IN; Band; Chrh Wkr; Hon Rl; Yth Flsp; Spn Clb; JA Awd; Lee College; Spanish.

BEARD, LORNA T; Lutheran East HS; Detroit, MI; 24/149 Chrh Wkr; Hon Rl; NHS; Yth Flsp; VP Lat Clb; Pep Clb; Letter Trk; Chrldng; PPFtbl; Scr Kpr; Jr Varsity Girls Basketball; Cert Of Ach In Career Exploration Prog; Handbell Choir; Michigan St Univ; Journalism.

BEARD, TERRI; Green HS; N Canton, OH; Chrs; Chrh Wkr; Hon Rl; NHS; Sch Pl; Stg Crw; Yth Flsp; Y-Teens; Drama Clb; Mgrs; Anderson Coll; Bus Admin.

BEARDMAN, JOAN; Ursuline HS; Youngstown, OH; Chrh Wkr; College; Nuclear Med.

BEARDMORE, CAROL; Clinton HS; Clinton, MI; 2/92 Sal; Band; Chrs; Girl Scts; Hon Rl; Jr NHS; Lbry Ade; Lit Mag; NHS; Off Ade; Michigan St Univ; Recreation.

BEARDSLEY, AMY; Fenton HS; Linden, MI; Cls Rep Frsh Cls; Cls Rep Soph Cls; Am Leg Aux Girls St; Cmp Fr Grls; Chrs; Chrh Wkr; Girl Scts; Hon Rl; Jr NHS; NHS; Michigan St Univ; Acctg.

BEARDSLEY, JOHN; Tecumseh HS; Tecumseh, MI; Cl Rep Jr Cls; Boy Scts; Hon Rl; NHS; Sct Actv; Stu Cncl; Yth Flsp; Y-Teens; Ed Yrbk; Sprt Ed Yrbk; US Air Force Acdmy; Hist.

BEARE, CONNIE; Austin HS; Scottsburg, IN; Pep Clb;.

BEARSS, GLENDA; Clawson HS; Clawson, MI; Chrs; Chrh Wkr; Hon Rl; NHS; Stu Cncl; Cit Awd; Principals Hon Roll 73; Schlstc Achvmnt 75 76 78 & 79; Excllnc In French 1 & 2 & 3 & 76 & 78;.

BEARY, JOHN D; Columbiana Village HS; Columbiana, OH; 2/110 Pres Frsh Cls; Pres Jr Cls; Am Leg Boys St; Chrh Wkr; Hon Rl; NHS; Off Ade; Stu Cncl; Rptr Sch Nwsp; Sch Nwsp; U S Military Acad; Engr.

BEASINGER, BARBARA; Henry Ford Ii HS; Sterling Hts, MI; Chrh Wkr; Cmnty Wkr; Girl Scts; Jr NHS; Natl Forn Lg; PAVAS; Sch Pl; Stg Crw; College; Speech Ther.

BEASLEY, BARBARA; Scecina Memorial HS; Indianapolis, IN; Hon Rl; Hosp Ade; NHS; Ten; GAA; Kiwan Awd; Ind State Univ; Med Tech.

BEASLEY, JUDY; Mitchell HS; Mitchell, IN; 4/148 Chrh Wkr; Cmnty Wkr; Hon Rl; Yth Flsp; Pres 4-H; Pres FHA; 4-H Awd; Rotary Stu Of Month; Schlstc M Awd;.

BEASLEY, KAY; Fountain Central HS; Veedersburg, IN; 4/150 Cl Rep Jr Cls; Band; Drl Tm; Girl Scts; Hon Rl; NHS; Stg Crw; Stu Cncl; Drama Clb; Pres 4-H; Indiana Univ; Tchr.

BEASLEY, LADONNA; Fountain Central HS; Veedersburg, IN; 4/150 Cl Rep Jr Cls; Sec Band; Drl Tm; Girl Scts; Hon Rl; NHS; Stg Crw; Stu Cncl; Drama Clb; Pres 4-H; Coll; Elem Tchr.

BEASLEY, MARK; Ben Davis HS; Indianapolis, IN; 4/835 Am Leg Boys St; Debate Tm; Natl Forn Lg; NHS; Fr Clb; 4-H Awd; Purdue Univ; Aero Engr.

BEASLEY, MARY; Southridge HS; Huntngbrg, IN; Band; Chrs; Chrh Wkr; Hon Rl; Sch Mus; Yrbk; FHA; Pep Clb; Spn Clb; ISUE; Business Management.

BEASLEY, RICHARD; Decatur Cntrl HS; Camby, IN; Cmnty Wkr; Hon Rl; Yth Flsp; 4-H; FTA; VICA; Wrstlng; IM Sprt; 4-H Awd; Mas Awd; Purdue Univ; Animal Sci.

BEASLEY, SANDRA; Ansonia HS; Rossburg, OH; 11/63 Chrs; Hon Rl; Off Ade; Rptr Yrbk; Rptr Sch Nwsp; 4-H; FHA; Edison State College; Acctg.

BEASTON, LAURA; Upper Sandusky HS; Upper Sandusky, OH; Band; Chrs; Chrh Wkr; Girl Scts; Hon Rl; Yth Flsp; 4-H; Mansfield Schl; Nursing.

BEAT, CHARLENE; Seneca East HS; Attica, OH; 19/90 Chrs; Chrh Wkr; Hon Rl; Sch Pl; Yrbk; Sch Nwsp; Drama Clb; 4-H; Cit Awd; 4-H Awd; Tiffin Univ; Acctg.

BEATON, KATHLEEN; O L Of Mt Carmel HS; Wyandotte, MI; 6/74 Hon Rl; Jr NHS; NHS; Sch Mus; Rptr Sch Nwsp; Pep Clb; Bsbl; Bsktbl; GAA; Univ; Medicine.

BEATTY, BRIAN; Canfield HS; Canfield, OH; Spn Clb; Univ; Nuclear Engr.

BEATTY, D; Triton HS; Bourbon, IN; 20/98 VP Jr Cls; Am Leg Boys St; Treas Chrs; NHS; Sch Mus; Letter Crs Cntry; Trk; Senator Richard Lugars Ldrshp Symposium; A M Proj At The Coast Guard Acad; Jr Sci & Humanities Symposium; Military Acad; Ocean Sci.

BEATTY, GREGORY T; Findlay HS; Findlay, OH; AFS; Am Leg Boys St; Boy Scts; NHS; Crs Cntry; Trk; Letter Wrstlng; Natl Merit Ltr; College.

BEATTY, JAMES; Williamstown HS; Williamstown, WV; 4/103 Boy Scts; Hon Rl; Treas NHS; Sch Pl; Treas Yth Flsp; Spn Clb; Letter Ftbl; Letter Glf; Letter Ten; God Cntry Awd; Sr Class Play; U S Naval Acad.

BEATTY, KAREN; Munising HS; Munising, MI; Pres Jr Cls; Band; Girl Scts; Sch Pl; FHA; Trk; Band Awd 78; Cosmetology.

BEATTY, KAREN; Beaver Local HS; E Liverpool, OH; Band; Cmp Fr Grls; Hon Rl; Jr NHS; Orch; Sch Mus; Eng Clb; Fr Clb; Mt Union Univ; Bus Admin.

BEATTY, MARC; Purcell HS; Cincinnati, OH; Band; Boy Scts; Chrh Wkr; Cmnty Wkr; Hon Rl; JA; Drama Clb; Harvard Univ; Bus Admin.

BEATTY, MARY; Briggs HS; Columbus, OH; 1/213 Val; Band; Girl Scts; Hon Rl; NHS; Off Ade; Orch; Sct Actv; Mth Clb; Spn Clb; Miami Univ.

BEATTY, TRINA A; Athens HS; Athens, MI; Trs Frsh Cls; Trs Soph Cls; Hon Rl; Jr NHS; Rptr Sch Nwsp; Pep Clb; Chrldng; Induction To The Natl Honor Soc; Soc Dstngshd Amer HS Stu; Exchange Stu To Brazil; Michigan St Univ; Psychology.

BEATY, PAM; Central Noble HS; Albion, IN; 3/120 Cls Rep Sr Cls; Am Leg Aux Girls St; Chrs; Capt Drl Tm; NHS; Sch Mus; Sch Pl; Stu Cncl; Drama Clb; Pres FTA; Algebra Honro Awrds 3 Awrds 77 79; Eng Acdmc Awrd 3 Awrds 77 79; Phys Sci Honor Awrd 79; Undiana Univ; Psych.

BEAUBIEN, JOYCE; East Detroit HS; E Detroit, MI; Chrh Wkr; Girl Scts; Hon Rl; Fr Clb; Tmr; College; Botany.

BEAUCHAMP, CATHY; Anderson HS; Anderson, IN; Girl Scts; Hon Rl; Hosp Ade; Lbry Ade; Ball State; Nursing.

BEAUCHAMP, JOHN; Knox Sr HS; Knox, IN; Pres Soph Cls; Cl Rep Jr Cls; Cls Rep Sr Cls; Hon Rl; Stg Crw; Ftbl; Letter Trk; Letter Wrstlng; Bus Schl; Archt.

BEAUCHAMP, LORI; Kelloggsville HS; Kentwood, MI; Band; Hon Rl; Trk; Coll; Nursing.

BEAUDIN, DIANE; Garber HS; Essexville, MI; Band; Hon Rl; Letter Trk; Cit Awd; Saginaw Vly St Coll; Bus Admin.

BEAUDOIN, MICHAEL; East Grand Rapids HS; Grand Rapids, MI; Cls Rep Frsh Cls; Cls Rep Soph Cls; Cl Rep Jr Cls; Cls Rep Sr Cls; Stu Cncl; Capt Ftbl; Capt Hockey; IM Sprt; Univ.

BEAUDRIE, JOHN; River Rouge HS; River Rouge, MI; Trs Frsh Cls; Cls Rep Soph Cls; Cl Rep Jr Cls; Cmnty Wkr; Hon Rl; Bsbl; Ftbl; IM Sprt; Cit Awd; Pres Awd; Outstndg Sportsmanshp 77; Principals Ctznshp Awd 79; Central Michigan Univ; Health.

BEAUFORE, MICHAEL J; Shrine HS; Royal Oak, MI; Pres Sr Cls; Cmnty Wkr; Hon Rl; Pol Wkr; Stg Crw; Stu Cncl; Yrbk; Soroptimist; IM Sprt; Cit Awd; Western Michigan Univ; Law.

BEAULIER, TERESA; Kingsford HS; Kingsford, MI; 33/190 Sec Sr Cls; Hon Rl; Yrbk; Pep Clb; PPFtbl; Michigan Tech Univ; Engr.

BEAUMAN, JEFF; Monroe HS; Monroe, MI; 132/603 Cls Rep Sr Cls; Aud/Vis; Hst Frsh Cls; Cmnty Wkr; JA; Sch Mus; Sch Pl; Stg Crw; Stu Cncl; Monroe Cnty Comm Coll; Comp Sci.

BEAUSAY, THOMAS; Perrysburg HS; Perrysburg, OH; FCA; Letter Ftbl; Letter Ten; Ohi State Univ; Chiropractic.

BEAVEN, THERESA; Reitz Mem HS; Evansville, IN; 22/226 Hon Rl; Hosp Ade; Stg Crw; 4-H; Fr Clb; Univ; Pediatrics.

BEAVER, ALICIA K; Grant HS; Kent Cty, MI; Band; Hon Rl; 4-H; FFA; Letter Ten; Cit Awd; 4-H Awd; College; Elementary Educ.

BEAVER, BILL; Springfield Local HS; Petersburg, OH; Boy Scts; Hon Rl; Sch Pl; Fr Clb; Mth Clb; Sci Clb; Spn Clb; Letter Ftbl; Trk; IM Sprt; Ohio State Univ;pre Med.

BEAVER, HELEN; Connersville Sr HS; Connersville, IN; 3/400 Cls Rep Soph Cls; Am Leg Aux Girls St; Hon Rl; Sct Actv; Yth Flsp; Ger Clb; Sci Clb; Letter Swmmng; Letter Trk; Chrldng; Univ; Med Tech.

BEAVER, LAURA; Rensselaer Central HS; Rensselaer, IN; Trs Sr Cls; Band; Chrs; Chrh Wkr; Hon Rl; Off Ade; Sch Mus; Rptr Yrbk; Spn Clb; Scr Kpr; Univ; Pre Schl Tchr.

BEAVER, MARK; Wheeling Ctrl Catholic HS; Wheeling, WV; Sch Pl; Stg Crw; Stu Cncl; Drama Clb; Ger Clb; Key Clb; Letter Ftbl; Trk; IM Sprt; Wheeling Coll; Bio.

BEAVER, PENNY; Hurricane HS; Hurricane, WV; Sec Frsh Cls; Cls Rep Soph Cls; Cl Rep Jr Cls; Chrh Wkr; Hon Rl; Stu Cncl; Yrbk; Bus Schl; Bus Mgmt.

BEAVER, PHILIP; R Nelson Snider HS; Ft Wayne, IN; Chrs; Sci Clb; Mech Engr.

BEAVERS, STACY; Piqua Central HS; Piqua, OH; 17/350 Sec Frsh Cls; VP Soph Cls; Hon Rl; Jr NHS; NHS; Stu Cncl; Sch Nwsp; 4-H; Lat Clb; Ohio Northern Univ; Pharmacy.

BEAVERS, VIRGINIA; Westland HS; Columbus, OH; Hon Rl; Lbry Ade; Off Ade; ROTC; FBLA; OEA; Pep Clb; IM Sprt; Columbus Busns Univ; Legal Sec.

BE BEE, INEZ M; Baldwin HS; Irons, MI; Drl Tm; Hon Rl; JA; Sch Pl; Sch Nwsp; Bsktbl; Trk; GAA; Cit Awd; Gov Hon Prg Awd;.

BEBKO, SARA; Yellow Springs HS; Yellow Sprg, OH; 6/80 Cl Rep Jr Cls; Band; NHS; Orch; Stu Cncl; Opt Clb Awd; Master Hon Carrier 77 78 & 79; French Spanich & History Awds 79; Rockford Coll; Lang.

BECERRA, FRANK; Elkins HS; Elkins, WV; Boy Scts; CAP; Yrbk; Key Clb; IM Sprt; Century III Leaders; Marshall Univ; Cinematography.

BECERRA, LISA C; E W Seaholm HS; Birmingham, MI; Cls Rep Sr Cls; Mod UN; Rptr Yrbk; Socr; IM Sprt; Schlrshp From Michigan St Univ 79 80; Michigan St Univ; Bus.

BECHER, WILLIAM; Cardinal Ritter HS; Brownsburg, IN; 2/180 Cls Rep Sr Cls; Hon Rl; NHS; Stu Cncl; Crs Cntry; Letter Trk; Purdue Univ; Law.

BECHINSKI, PAMELA; South Central HS; Hanna, IN; Pres Jr Cls; Chrs; Chrh Wkr; Hon Rl; NHS; Sch Mus; Sch Pl; Stg Crw; Yth Flsp; Drama Clb; Theatre.

BECHINSKI, RICHARD; La Crosse HS; La Crosse, IN; Am Leg Boys St; Hon Rl; NHS; Sch Pl; Drama Clb; Ger Clb; College; Med.

BECHSTEIN, SHARON; Otsego HS; Weston, OH; 11/125 Cls Rep Frsh Cls; Hon Rl; Jr NHS; Stu Cncl; Drama Clb; 4-H; Mat Maids; 4-H Awd; Owens Tech Schl; Acctg.

BECHT, DENISE; Floyd Central HS; Floyd Knobs, IN; Pres Frsh Cls; Cls Rep Frsh Cls; Pres Soph Cls; Cls Rep Soph Cls; Cl Rep Jr Cls; Hon Rl; Pep Clb; Pom Pon; PPFtbl;.

BECHT, KILEEN; Eau Claire HS; Sodus, MI; 14/100 Am Leg Aux Girls St; Chrh Wkr; Hon Rl; Letter Trk; Chrldng; Kalamazoo College; Poli Sci.

BECHTEL, GLORIA; Almont HS; Almont, MI; Band; Cmnty Wkr; Debate Tm; Hon Rl; Natl Forn Lg; Off Ade; Sprt Ed Yrbk; Rptr Yrbk; Ed Sch Nwsp; Iron Women Track 78; St Finalist Track Girls Discuss 77; Arthur Hunt Citznshp Awd 79; Olivet Coll; Criminal Justice.

BECHTEL, GREGORY; Walnut Hills HS; Cincinnati, OH; Band; Hon Rl; Stu Cncl; Ger Clb; University; Engr.

BECHTEL, KATHY; Wauseon HS; Wauseon, OH; Chrs; Hon Rl; Sch Mus; Sch Pl; Yth Flsp; Y-Teens; 4-H; Letter Gym; Letter Swmmng; Trk; College; Art.

BECHTEL, LAURIE B; Robert S Rogers HS; Toledo, OH; 22/409 FCA; Girl Scts; Jr NHS; NHS; Off Ade; Pol Wkr; Sch Mus; Stu Cncl; Rptr Yrbk; Sci Clb; Miami Univ; Educ.

BECHTEL, THOMAS; North Dariess HS; Elnora, IN; 22/84 Band; Chrh Wkr; FCA; Hon Rl; Sch Mus; Stu Cncl; Beta Clb; 4-H; Spn Clb; Capt Bsktbl; Vincennes Univ; Computer Tech.

BECHTLER, STU; Mansfield Christian School; Mansfield, OH; Hon Rl; Trk; Ohio St Univ; Livestock Prod.

BECHTOL, DEBRA; Harry S Truman HS; Taylor, MI; Band; Girl Scts; Hon Rl; Chrldng; College; Vet Med.

BECHTOLD, MARTIN; St Xavier HS; Ft Mitchell, KY; 125/264 Chrh Wkr; Cmnty Wkr; Hon Rl; Pol Wkr; Stu Cncl; Pep Clb; Wrstlng; Coach Actv; IM Sprt; Rotary Awd; Univ; Bus Admin.

BECHTOLD, VALERIE J; Union HS; Grand Rapids, MI; 75/400 Cls Rep Sr Cls; Band; Chrh Wkr; Cmnty Wkr; Hon Rl; Hosp Ade; JA; NHS; Orch; Quill & Scroll; Eastern Mich Univ; Occupational Ther.

BECK, BARRY; Forest Park HS; Cincinnati, OH; 64/356 Hon Rl; Ftbl; Trk; Wrstlng; Bowling Green St Univ; Bus.

BECK, BETH; Pettisville HS; Pettisville, OH; Band; Cmp Fr Grls; Chrs; Chrh Wkr; Hon Rl; Hosp Ade; Sch Pl; Yrbk; 4-H; Bowling Green St Univ.

BECK, CARTER; David Anderson HS; Lisbon, OH; 1/100 Am Leg Boys St; Band; Hon Rl; Jr NHS; NHS; Ed Yrbk; Am Leg Awd; Kiwan Awd; VFW Awd; Univ Of Cincinnati; Music.

BECK, CYNTHIA; Wauseon HS; Wauseon, OH; Sec Sr Cls; Band; Cmp Fr Grls; Chrh Wkr; Hon Rl; Sch Mus; Stg Crw; Yth Flsp; Y-Teens; Rptr Sch Nwsp; Univ; Educ.

BECK, DENIS; Highland HS; Fredericktown, OH; 8/124 Chrh Wkr; Sec NHS; 4-H; Sec Spn Clb; Cincinnati Bible Coll; Spec Educ.

BECK, DENISE; Ursuline HS; Lowellville, OH; 94/325 Hon Rl; JA; Fr Clb; Youngstown St Univ; Comp Tech.

BECK, DWAIN; Lapeer East HS; Metamora, MI; 67/258 Cmnty Wkr; Hon Rl; Lbry Ade; Rptr Yrbk; 4-H; Letter Glf; 4-H Awd; St Of Michigan Comp Schlrshp Prog; Grad With Hnrs; Ohio Inst Of Tech; Elec Tech.

BECK, ELIZABETH; Western Boone Jr Sr HS; Lebanon, IN; 50/150 FCA; Girl Scts; Hon Rl; 4-H; FHA; Pep Clb; Letter Bsktbl; Letter Trk; GAA; 4-H Awd; Kiwanis Athlete Of Wk Bsktbl & Vlybl; Purdue Univ; Pharmacy.

BECK, J; Flushing HS; Flushing, MI; 14/524 Band; Boy Scts; NHS; Orch; Sch Mus; Spn Clb; Glf; General Motors Inst; Engr.

BECK, KIMBERLY; Whiteford Agricultural HS; Ottawa Lk, MI; Am Leg Aux Girls St; Chrs; Hon Rl; NHS; Sch Mus; Stu Cncl; Rptr Yrbk; Rptr Sch Nwsp; Drama Clb; 4-H; College; Rn.

BECK, KRISTI; Brooke HS; Wellsburg, WV; 3/403 Chrs; Chrh Wkr; Hon Rl; NHS; Sch Mus; Pres Yth Flsp; Drama Clb; Fr Clb; Mat Maids; Milligan Coll; Human Relations.

BECK, MICHAEL; Southgate HS; Southgate, MI; Band; Hon Rl; Jr NHS; Treas NHS; Letter Glf; Univ Of Mic; Engr.

BECK, MICHELLE; Maplewood HS; Cortland, OH; 2/89 VP Frsh Cls; Cl Rep Jr Cls; Sal; Am Leg Aux Girls St; Chrs; Girl Scts; Hon Rl; Jr NHS; Ohi St Univ; Phys Ther.

BECK, MIKE; David Anderson HS; Lisbon, OH; Chrh Wkr; Hon Rl; Stu Cncl; Yth Flsp; Fr Clb; Key Clb; Letter Bsktbl; Letter Ftbl; Letter Trk; Univ; Bus Admin.

BECK, PAM; Wynford HS; Bucyrus, OH; 12/200 VP Frsh Cls; Cls Rep Soph Cls; Trs Sr Cls; Band; Chrs; Drm Mjrt; Hon Rl; Treas NHS; Off Ade; Sch Pl;.

BECK, PAM; Merrillville HS; Hobart, IN; 26/205 Lbry Ade; NHS; Pres Ger Clb; Natl Merit Ltr; Butler Univ; Pharmacy.

BECK, PHYLLIS; Hopkins Public HS; Dorr, MI; Band; Chrs; Hon Rl; Hosp Ade; Jr NHS; Letter Trk; Grand Rapids Jr Coll; Nurse.

BECK, RHONDA; Dunbar Sr HS; Dunbar, WV; Sal; Hon Rl; Mod UN; NHS; Off Ade; Stu Cncl; Ed Yrbk; Mth Clb; Spn Clb; Chrldng; Tuition Waver Schlrshp ACT Scores 79; BEOG Awd; Marshall Univ; Med Tech.

BECK, ROBERT; Frontier HS; Newport, OH; Boy Scts; Bsktbl;.

BECK, SALLY; St Johns HS; St Johns, MI; 25/339 Cl Rep Jr Cls; Band; Chrh Wkr; Hon Rl; Sch Mus; Sch Pl; Stg Crw; Stu Cncl; Yth Flsp; Drama Clb; Univ; Sci.

BECK, SHERRI; Jay County HS; Portland, IN; 80/475 Chrs; Chrh Wkr; Hon Rl; Jr NHS; NHS; Sec Yth Flsp; Y-Teens; Pep Clb; Univ; Elem Educ.

BECK, STEVE; Moeller HS; Edgewood, KY; 95/262 Cls Rep Soph Cls; Hon Rl; Off Ade; Boys Clb Am; Letter Bsbl; Ftbl; Trk; Coach Actv; IM Sprt; Scr Kpr; Zaferes Awd Ftbl 78; Defnsv Back Of Week For 2 Games 78; Western Kentucky Univ; Comp Sci.

BECK, STEVE; Anderson HS; Anderson, IN; Band; Chrs; Drm Bgl; JA; Ind Univ; Music.

BECK, WILLIAM; Connersville HS; Connersville, IN; 12/400 Cls Rep Frsh Cls; Cls Rep Soph Cls; Pres Sr Cls; Chrh Wkr; Hon Rl; Stu Cncl; Yrbk; Pres Drama Clb; 4-H; Sci Clb; College; Med.

BECKEL, BARBARA; Cardington Lincoln HS; Cardington, OH; 5/79 Am Leg Aux Girls St; Band; Chrh Wkr; Hon Rl; NHS; Sch Pl; Stg Crw; Marion Tech College; Bus Mgmt.

BECKEL, ROBERT D; Givinn HS; Apo New York, NY; Band; Boy Scts; Chrh Wkr; Hon Rl; Sct Actv; Stg Crw; Stu Cncl; Rptr Yrbk; Bsktbl; Ftbl; College.

BECKEL, SHARON; River Valley HS; Waldo, OH; 20/207 Band; Chrs; Chrh Wkr; Cmnty Wkr; FCA; NHS; Off Ade; Sch Mus; Stu Cncl; Yth Flsp; College; Social Work.

BECKELHEIMER, MARGARET; Charleston Catholic HS; Charleston, WV; Girl Scts; JA; Off Ade; Sch Pl; Sct Actv; Stg Crw; Drama Clb; Letter Bsktbl; IM Sprt; Glenville St Coll; Prim Educ.

BECKER, BERNARD; Castle HS; Elberfeld, IN; 5/340 Am Leg Boys St; Hon Rl; NHS; Stu Cncl; Key Clb; Sci Clb; Wrstlng; Univ Of Evansville; Engineering.

BECKER, BRENT; Crown Point HS; Crown Point, IN; Aud/Vis; 4-H; 4-H Awd; Ball St Univ; Archt.

BECKER, CATHY; Warren Local HS; Marietta, OH; Hon Rl; Hosp Ade; NHS; FHA; FNA; Pres OEA; GAA; Vocational Schl; Busns.

BECKER, CHRISTOPHER; Harrison HS; Evansville, IN; Cls Rep Sr Cls; Hon Rl; Sch Pl; Stu Cncl; Ftbl; Swmmng; IM Sprt; Cit Awd; Univ; Pre Med.

BECKER, DAVID; Coldwater HS; Coldwater, MI; 68/300 Band; Chrh Wkr; Cmnty Wkr; Hon Rl; Pres Yth Flsp; Ten; Eng Hnrs; Youth Group Pres; Spring Arbor Coll; Bio.

BECKER, DENNIS; Pike Central HS; Petersburg, IN; Band; Hon Rl; Jr NHS; NHS; Letter Swmmng; Bus Schl; Drafting.

BECKER, DOUG; Pike Central HS; Petersburg, IN; Band; Hon Rl; NHS; 4-H; Letter Swmmng; Navy.

BECKER, HENRY; Pickerington HS; Pickerington, OH; 13/196 Hon Rl; NHS; Ftbl; Letter Socr; Letter Wrstlng; IM Sprt; Univ; Elec Engr.

BECKER, JEFFREY; Gladwin HS; Gladwin, MI; Cls Rep Frsh Cls; Band; Hon Rl; Sct Actv; Stu Cncl; Letter Ftbl; Letter Trk; College; Farming.

BECKER, JUDITH; Badin HS; Hamilton, OH; 29/217 Cmnty Wkr; Hon Rl; JA; NHS; Y-Teens; Drama Clb; Spn Clb; Trk;.

BECKER, LAURA; Douglas Mac Arthur HS; Saginaw, MI; 60/310 Cl Rep Jr Cls; Pres Sr Cls; Chrs; Chrh Wkr; Hon Rl; JA; NHS; Stu Cncl; Yth Flsp; JA Awd; Univ; Nursing.

BECKER, LORI; West Union HS; W Union, OH; Girl Scts; Hon Rl; Hosp Ade; Sct Actv; Ed Yrbk; Drama Clb; Fr Clb; Alleghany College; Sociology.

BECKER, MARIA J; Mater Dei HS; Evansvl, IN; 20/180 Chrs; Hon Rl; Hosp Ade; Jr NHS; NHS; Sch Mus; Indiana St Univ; Psych.

BECKER, MARY E; St Alphonsus HS; Dearborn, MI; Chrs; Hon Rl; NHS; Sch Mus; Stu Cncl; Rptr Yrbk; Ed Sch Nwsp; Pep Clb; Chrldng; GAA; E Michigan Univ; Admin Mgmt.

BECKER, MICHAEL; Northwestern HS; W Salem, OH; VP Sr Cls; Band; Boy Scts; Chrs; Cmnty Wkr; Drm Bgl; Hon Rl; NHS; Sch Mus; Sch Pl; Coll.

BECKER, MIKE; Marian HS; S Bend, IN; 75/156 Boy Scts; Chrh Wkr; Sct Actv; IM Sprt; Hoosier Shclshp 78; Purdue Univ; Geo Sci.

BECKER, ROSE; Central Catholic HS; Wheeling, WV; Chrh Wkr; Hon Rl; Stg Crw; Drama Clb; FNA; Mgrs; English; History; Religion; Univ.

BECKER, SANDRA; Stow HS; Stow, OH; Treas AFS; Band; Drm Mjrt; Hon Rl; Stu Cncl; Fr Clb; Ger Clb; Capt Twrlr; Lion Awd; Univ; Linguistics.

BECKER, SUSAN; Pike Central HS; Petersburg, IN; 2/190 Sal; Band; Chrh Wkr; Drm Mjrt; Lit Mag; NHS; Pep Clb; IM Sprt; Natl Merit Ltr; Cntrl Sthrn In Mus Cntst 1st Pl Piano Solo 1976; Concordia Lutheran Coll; Soc Work.

BECKER, TERESA; Frontier HS; Marietta, OH; Chrh Wkr; Hon Rl; Sci Clb; Cit Awd; David Lipscomb College; Bio.

BECKER, THERESE; Eau Claire HS; Bangor, MI; 5/125 Chrh Wkr; Hon Rl; NHS; Sch Nwsp; 4-H; 4-H Awd; Natl Merit Ltr; Lake Michigan Coll; Math.

BECKER, WENDY; Kingswood School; Milford, MI; Cls Rep Frsh Cls; Cls Rep Soph Cls; Debate Tm; Hon Rl; Lit Mag; PAVAS; Yrbk; Chrldng; 7th Pl In Activity Achvmnt Awds 78; Qualified For Classes At Univ Of Salamanca Spain 79; Stanford Univ; Psych.

BECKERT, RICHARD; Cadiz HS; Cadiz, OH; 8/108 Aud/Vis; Band; Boy Scts; Chrh Wkr; Hon Rl; NHS; Sct Actv; Yth Flsp; Fr Clb; Rdo Clb; French I Awd 77; Trig Awd 79; Physics Awd 79; US Air Force Acad; Engr.

BECKETT, MICHAEL; Battle Creek Central HS; Battle Creek, MI; NHS; Pol Wkr; Letter Crs Cntry; Letter Trk; Natl Merit Ltr; B E Henry Memorial Schlrshp 79; US Navy.

BECKETT, MICHELLE; Ayersville HS; Defiance, OH; Sec Sr Cls; Chrs; Chrh Wkr; Hon Rl; Off Ade; Yth Flsp; Fr Clb; FHA; Pep Clb; Trk; Bus Schl; Stewardess.

BECKHAM, DENISE; Otsego HS; Bowling Green, OH; 13/133 Hon Rl; Jr NHS; Lbry Ade; NHS; Off Ade; Pol Wkr; Yrbk; Rptr Sch Nwsp; Sch Nwsp; Mth Clb; Univ; Acctg.

BECKHOLT, KENNETH; Mt Vernon Academy; Mt Vernon, OH; Cmnty Wkr; Hon Rl; Lbry Ade; Off Ade; Cit Awd; Kenyon Coll; Physics.

BECKINGER, BILL; Ida HS; Ida, MI; 25/160 Band; Hon Rl; ROTC; Capt Bsbl; Ftbl; Wrstlng; IM Sprt; Scr Kpr; Kiwan Awd; Military Coll; Offc.

BECKLEY, MARY BETH; Muskegon HS; Muskegon, MI; Cl Rep Jr Cls; Cls Rep Sr Cls; Chrh Wkr; Hon Rl; NHS; Off Ade; Pol Wkr; Stu Cncl; Yrbk; Musical Schlrshp To Interlochen Fine Arts Camp 78; Outstanding Work In English 77; Serv To The Orch 77; Muskegon Cmnty Coll.

BECKMAN, DAVID; Lutheran HS; Seven Hls, OH; Boy Scts; Hon Rl; Mod UN; Sct Actv; Ger Clb; Letter Bsktbl; Letter Ftbl; Trk; IM Sprt; Mich Tech; Biological Sci.

BECKMAN, HELEN; Delphos St Johns HS; Delphos, OH; Band; Hon Rl; NHS; Ed Sch Nwsp; Fr Clb; IM Sprt; Wright State.

BECKMAN, PAUL; Manistique HS; Lake Havasue, AZ; Boy Scts; Chrh Wkr; Cmnty Wkr; Pres Yth Flsp; VICA; Ftbl; Swmmng; Letter Ten; Wrstlng; Scr Kpr; Voc Schl; Welding.

BECKMAN, SHERRIE; Keyser HS; Keyser, WV; AFS; Band; Hon Rl; NHS; Stu Cncl; Yth Flsp; FBLA; Lat Clb; Chrldng; Pom Pon; Mineral Cnty Voc Tech; Acctg.

BECKMEYER, MADGE M; Seton HS; North Bend, OH; Hon Rl; Hosp Ade; Jr NHS; Mod UN; NHS; Orch; Red Cr Ade; Sch Mus; Pep Clb; Spn Clb; Univ; Law.

BECKNELL, RENEE; Norwood HS; Norwood, OH; 35/350 Cls Rep Frsh Cls; Hon Rl; Jr NHS; Stu Cncl; Yrbk; VP Key Clb; College; Bus.

BECKNER, STEPHEN; Pontiac Central HS; Pontiac, MI; Cl Rep Jr Cls; Glf; Swmmng; Tmr; Kalamazoo Coll; Pharm.

BECKS, BRIEN; Mumford HS; Detroit, MI; Hon Rl; NHS; Boys Clb Am; Trk; Cit Awd; Univ Of Detroit; Comp Engr.

BECKS, VANESSA; Jane Addams Vocational HS; Cleveland, OH; Cls Rep Frsh Cls; Cl Rep Jr Cls; Band; Cmp Fr Grls; Drl Tm; Girl Scts; Hon Rl; JA; Mgrs; Cit Awd; College; Data Proc.

BECKWITH, ANN; Highland HS; Medina, OH; 12/202 Band; Hon Rl; NHS; Lat Clb; Univ Of Akron; Chem.

BECKWITH, ANN; Gevan Valley HS; Saginaw, MI; Chrs; Hon Rl; JA; Pep Clb; Spn Clb; Trk; Scr Kpr; Saginaw Valley Univ; Spanish.

BECKWITH, ANN M; Swan Valley HS; Saginaw, MI; 29/188 Chrs; Hon Rl; JA; Spn Clb; Bsktbl; Trk; Manager Track; Saginaw Valley Coll; Languages.

BECKWITH, LEE G; South Charleston HS; S Charleston, WV; 1/297 Am Leg Boys St; Band; Boy Scts; Chrs; Hon Rl; Jr NHS; Lit Mag; MMM; NHS; Orch; Univ; Physician.

BECRAFT, MAX; Stivers Patterson Co Op HS; Dayton, OH; Chrh Wkr; VICA; 1st Plc In Charging Systems 77; Sec Automotive VICA 78; Diesel Mech.

BECTON, VENUS; Emerson HS; Gary, IN; 38/149 Sec Chrh Wkr; Hon Rl; JA; Sch Pl; FBLA; FHA; Univ Of Tennessee.

BEDDOW, BRUCE; Terre Haute North Vigo HS; Terre Haute, IN; Cls Rep Frsh Cls; Cls Rep Soph Cls; Cl Rep Jr Cls; Letter Glf; IM Sprt; Univ; Lib Arts.

BEDEL, KAREN; St Joseph Cntrl Catholic HS; Huntington, WV; Sec Jr Cls; Chrh Wkr; Drl Tm; Girl Scts; Lbry Ade; Rptr Yrbk; Rptr Sch Nwsp; Sch Nwsp; Pep Clb; Voice Dem Awd; Marshall Univ; Primary Educ.

BEDELL, HAROLD; Cheboygan Area HS; Cheboygan, MI; Hon Rl; Pres Fr Clb; Univ; Sci.

BEDELL, PAUL; Riverside HS; Dearborn Hts, MI; Am Leg Boys St; Band; Boy Scts; Cmnty Wkr; Hon Rl; Orch; Sct Actv; Ger Clb; Socr; Mi Comp Schlrshp Prog 80; Tchrs Aid Eng 79; Natl Merit Schlrshp Prog 80; Univ Of Michigan; Law.

BEDNAR, BERNADETTE; Lumen Cordium HS; Garfield Hts, OH; 10/100 Cls Rep Soph Cls; VP Jr Cls; Hon Rl; Stu Cncl; Rptr Sch Nwsp; Spn Clb; Coach Actv; IM Sprt; Univ; Cmnctns.

BEDNAR, JACQUELYN; Hubbard HS; Hubbard, OH; 15/333 Hon Rl; Yth Flsp; Fr Clb; Sci Clb; Youngstown St Univ; Med Tech.

BEDNARD, WALTER A; Charles S Mott HS; Warren, MI; Aud/Vis; Boy Scts; Hon Rl; JA; DECA; Ftbl; Mgrs; Cit Awd; JA Awd; MHEAA Grant Schlrshp 79; Mi Diff Grant 79; Brnz Merit Awd Dist Ed Pro Sls 78; Michigan Christian Coll; Bus.

BEDOSKY, JOSEPH; Padua Franciscan HS; N Royalton, OH; 26/300 Aud/Vis; Boy Scts; CAP; Ftbl; Trk; Wrstlng; Univ; Sci MD.

BEDSON, JAY A; Princeton HS; Springdale, OH; Band; Hon Rl; Quill & Scroll; Yth Flsp; Rptr Yrbk; Yrbk; Ed Sch Nwsp; Rptr Sch Nwsp; Rdo Clb; Cincinnati Post Awds 2nd Best City Wide General News Coverage; N Kentucky Univ; Mass Comm.

BEDWELL, BARBARA; Reeths Puffer HS; Muskegon, MI; Cl Rep Jr Cls; Lbry Ade; Spn Clb; Grand Valley State College; Psych.

BEE, AUDREY; Murray Wright HS; Detroit, MI; 31/450 Chrs; Chrh Wkr; Hon Rl; NHS; Off Ade; Sch Pl; Drama Clb; Cit Awd; Natl Merit Ltr; Univ Of Detroit; Med.

BEECH, DONALD; Clinton Central HS; Forest, IN; FCA; Lbry Ade; Sprt Ed Yrbk; Pep Clb; Bsbl; Letter Ftbl; Trk; Letter Wrstlng; Chrldng; Coach Actv; Univ; Phys Educ.

BEECHER, BRUCE D; Hauser Jr Sr HS; Columbus, IN; 23/105 Trs Frsh Cls; VP Sr Cls; Stu Cncl; Eng Clb; Trk; Ball St Univ.

BEECHER, DOREATHA; Emerson HS; Gary, IN; Cls Rep Frsh Cls; Cls Rep Soph Cls; Cl Rep Jr Cls; Band; Chrs; JA; Lbry Ade; Off Ade; Sch Mus; Purdue Univ; Engin Comp Sci.

BEECHLER, SUSAN; Alma HS; Alma, MI; Cls Rep Frsh Cls; Cls Rep Soph Cls; Cl Rep Jr Cls; Girl Scts; Hon Rl; Jr NHS; NHS; FFA; Spn Clb; Bsktbl; Trk; Western Mich Univ; Special Ed.

BEEGHLEY, JULIA; Dublin HS; Dublin, OH; 32/157 Band; Chrs; Hon Rl; NHS; Sch Mus; Sch Pl; Stg Crw; Yth Flsp; Lat Clb; Scr Kpr; Vlybl Varsity Letter; State Solo & Ensemble Contest; The John Philip Sousa Band Awd; Florida St Univ; Music.

BEEGLE, KEVIN; Walsh Jesuit HS; Univ Heights, OH; 9/170 Chrh Wkr; Hon Rl; Ftbl; IM Sprt; Univ Of Cincinnati; Finance.

BEEHLER, DAVID; Milan HS; Milan, MI; Boy Scts; CAP; Hon Rl; Sct Actv; Stu Cncl; Boys Clb Am; Bsktbl; Coach Actv; Mgrs; Scr Kpr; Lake Superior St Coll; Elec Tech.

BEEKER, CHERYL; Hauser HS; Hope, IN; 2/90 VP Jr Cls; VP Sr Cls; Am Leg Aux Girls St; Band; Hon Rl; NHS; Stu Cncl; Yth Flsp; 4-H; College; Bus Admin.

BEEKMAN, MIKE; Bay City All Saints HS; Bay City, MI; Hon Rl; Sch Nwsp; Letter Bsktbl; Letter Ftbl; Letter Trk; Univ; Med Sci.

BEELS, DENISE; Lakeview Sr HS; St Clair Shore, MI; 54/548 Aud/Vis; Girl Scts; Hon Rl; Hosp Ade; JA; NHS; Fr Clb; Mi Compttv Schlshp 78; Ferris Coll; Voc Educ.

BEEMER, DAVID A; Swartz Creek HS; Swartz Creek, MI; 9/453 Boy Scts; NHS; Drama Clb; Natl Merit SF; Naval Academy; Physics.

BEEMER, LORI; Clare HS; Clare, MI; Sec Frsh Cls; Band; Chrh Wkr; Girl Scts; Hon Rl; NHS; Quill & Scroll; Rptr Sch Nwsp; Pep Clb; Letter Bsbl; Graceland Coll; Bio.

BEEN, BETH A; Pickens HS; Pickens, WV; 2/13 VP Jr Cls; Trs Sr Cls; Am Leg Aux Girls St; Hon Rl; Pres NHS; Pres Stu Cncl; Ed Yrbk; Ed Sch Nwsp; Chrldng; DAR Awd; Univ; Med.

BEER, DAN; High School; Mansfield, OH; Band; NHS; Red Cr Ade; Sch Pl; Sch Nwsp; Pres 4-H; Ger Clb; Spn Clb; Univ.

BEERS, LU ANN; Peck Cmnty HS; Peck, MI; Cls Rep Soph Cls; Cl Rep Jr Cls; Hst Sr Cls; Hon Rl; NHS; Stu Cncl; DECA; 4-H; Chrldng; Bus Schl; Cashier.

BEERS, TRACIE; Waynesfield Goshen HS; Wapakoneta, OH; Sec Jr Cls; Chrs; Chrh Wkr; Hon Rl; Lbry Ade; Yth Flsp; Yrbk; Photog.

BEERWART, FRED; Oregon Davis HS; Hamlet, IN; Cls Rep Frsh Cls; Cls Rep Soph Cls; Am Leg Boys St; FCA; Hon Rl; NHS; Sch Pl; Rptr Sch Nwsp; Drama Clb; Treas Sci Clb; Rose Hullman Inst Of Tech.

BEESLEY, CATHERINE; Western Boone HS; Throntown, IN; 4/154 Cls Rep Soph Cls; Band; FCA; Hon Rl; NHS; Stu Cncl; Pep Clb; Chmn Bsktbl; Trk; GAA; College; Education.

BEESON, LYNETTE; Little Miami HS; Maineville, OH; Hon Rl; JA; Jr NHS; NHS; Red Cr Ade; Pep Clb; Ohio St Univ; Medicine.

BEETS, RAYMOND; Clinton Ctrl HS; Frankfort, IN; 7/105 Am Leg Boys St; Hon Rl; NHS; Mth Clb; Sci Clb; Am Leg Awd; Purdue Univ; Aerospace Engr.

BEGEOT, PAULA; Hubbard HS; Hubbard, OH; 5/330 Chrs; Drm Mjrt; Hon Rl; Sch Mus; Yth Flsp; Drama Clb; Fr Clb; FTA; Twrlr; Place In Internatl Dance Competition; Youngstown St Univ; Phys Ed.

BEGGS, DIANNE; Port Clinton Sr HS; Port Clinton, OH; Chrs; Girl Scts; Hon Rl; Ohio St Univ.

BEGIN, ALEXANDER; Detroit Country Day HS; Birmingham, MI; Chmn Aud/Vis; Lbry Ade; NHS; Chmn Drama Clb; Mth Clb; Scr Kpr; Tmr; Harvard; Economics.

BEGLEY, NANCY F; Arsenal Tech HS; Indianapolis, IN; Cls Rep Frsh Cls; Cls Rep Soph Cls; Cl Rep Jr Cls; Girl Scts; Hon Rl; Quill & Scroll; Sch Pl; Stu Cncl; Rptr Yrbk; Sch Nwsp; IUPUI; Eng.

BEGOVIC, MARY; Erieview Catholic HS; Cleveland, OH; 1/100 Hon Rl; Lit Mag; Pres Mod UN; Stg Crw; Stu Cncl; Yrbk; College; History.

BEHAN, MARY; Marian HS; Cincinnati, OH; Cls Rep Frsh Cls; Cls Rep Soph Cls; Am Leg Aux Girls St; VP NHS; Stu Cncl; Ten; Coach Actv; GAA; IM Sprt; Mgrs; Xavier Univ; Pre Law.

BEHLING, CYNTHIA; Lutheran North HS; Fraser, MI; 6/112 Chrs; Girl Scts; Hon Rl; NHS; Stu Cncl; Ed Yrbk; Pom Pon; DAR Awd; Natl Merit Ltr; Hillsdale Coll; Pre Med.

BEHM, MARCIE; Lakeland HS; Milford, MI; Hon Rl; NHS; Sch Mus; Stu Cncl; Pep Clb; Sci Clb; Letter Pom Pon; Michigan St Univ; Engr.

BEHM, MARY A; Grosse Pointe South HS; Grosse Pointe, MI; Cmnty Wkr; Hosp Ade; Off Ade; Stg Crw; OEA; Pep Clb; Bsbl; Swmmng; PPFtbl; Pres Awd; Aquinas Coll; Child Dev.

BEHNEN, LAURA; National Trail HS; New Paris, OH; Band; Vocational School; Animal Tech.

BEHNKE, ANNE JANE; Westerville South HS; Westerville, OH; Cl Rep Jr Cls; Girl Scts; Hon Rl; Sch Mus; Sch Pl; Stu Cncl; Pep Clb; Chrldng; Columbus Coll Of Art & Desgn; Art.

BEHNKE, DAWN; Pellston HS; Carp Lake, MI; Cls Rep Soph Cls; Pres Jr Cls; Band; Chrs; Chrh Wkr; Girl Scts; Hon Rl; NHS; Stu Cncl; Yth Flsp; Busns Schl; Sec.

BEHRENS, JACALYN; West Geauga HS; Novelty, OH; Chrs; Drl Tm; Hon Rl; Sch Mus; 4-H; Pep Clb; Trk; Pom Pon; PPFtbl; Rotary Awd; Purdue Univ; Interior Design.

BEHRINGER, DAVE; Defiance HS; Sherwood, OH; Boy Scts; Hon Rl; NHS; Sct Actv; Mth Clb; Bsktbl; Ftbl; Letter Trk; OSU; Orthedontist.

BEHRMANN, BARBARA; Hartland HS; Fenton, MI; Band; Hon Rl; Lit Mag; Sch Pl; Yth Flsp; Rptr Yrbk; Rptr Sch Nwsp; Drama Clb; Spn Clb; Letter Mgrs; Mich Stat Univ; Communications.

BEHRNDT, RONALD T; Springfield HS; Battle Crk, MI; 9/82 Band; Hon Rl; NHS; Ten; Mgrs; Kellogg Community; Acctg.

BEHROOZI, YASMIN; Shortridge HS; Indianapolis, IN; 47/444 Chrs; Girl Scts; Hon Rl; Orch; Quill & Scroll; Sch Mus; Sch Pl; Stg Crw; Rptr Yrbk; Rptr Sch Nwsp; Third Plc In The What Shortridge Means To Me Essay Contest; College; Theatre.

BEHYMER, BOB; Clermont Northeastern HS; Batavia, OH; Boy Scts; Hon Rl; Sci Clb; Spn Clb; IM Sprt; Univ; Forestry.

BEIGEL, JERRY; Sidney HS; Sidney, OH; Pres Sr Cls; Hon Rl; Pres NHS; Treas Stu Cncl; 4-H; Ger Clb; Key Clb; Letter Ftbl; Letter Wrstlng; Opt Clb Awd; Miami Univ.

BEIGEL, SHARON; Ursuline HS; Youngstown, OH; 50/317 Chrh Wkr; Girl Scts; Hon Rl; NHS; Sct Actv; Rptr Yrbk; FTA; Spn Clb; Univ; Optometry.

BEIGH, ROBERT; Arlington Local HS; Findlay, OH; Cls Rep Soph Cls; Pres Sr Cls; Hon Rl; NHS; Stu Cncl; Fr Clb; FFA; Letter Bsbl; Capt Ftbl; Capt Hockey; Ohio State Univ; Engr.

BEIMESCHE, JANE; St Ursula Acad; Cincinnati, OH; Hon Rl; VP Mod UN; NHS; Sch Pl; Drama Clb; Univ Of Cincinnati; Pre Med.

BEIN, CARY; Highland HS; Highland, IN; 70/494 Boy Scts; Hon Rl; Jr NHS; NHS; Ger Clb; Key Clb; Sci Clb; Bsktbl; Purdue Univ; Vet.

BEINDORF, ROBIN; Hudson Area HS; Hudson, MI; Chrs; Chrh Wkr; Girl Scts; Hon Rl; Hosp Ade; Lbry Ade; Sch Mus; Stg Crw; Rptr Yrbk; Yrbk; Univ; Bus Educ.

BEINING, BRIAN; Ottoville Local HS; Ft Jennings, OH; Chrh Wkr; Debate Tm; FCA; Hon Rl; Stg Crw; 4-H; FFA; Business Job Experience; Manager.

BEINING, LISA; Ottoville Local HS; Ottoville, OH; Band; Drm Mjrt; Hon Rl; Sch Mus; Sch Pl; Rptr Yrbk; Rptr Sch Nwsp; Pom Pon; Twrlr; 4-H Awd; Lima Tech Coll; Child Devlpmt.

BEISCHEL, JILL; Mc Auley HS; Cinti, OH; 3/252 Chrs; Hon Rl; Mod UN; Pres NHS; Natl Merit Ltr; Univ Of Cincinnati; Med Tech.

BEISCHEL, MICHELE; Mother Of Mercy HS; Cincinnati, OH; Cls Rep Frsh Cls; Cls Rep Soph Cls; Cl Rep Jr Cls; Chrs; Hon Rl; Sch Pl; Pep Clb; Soroptimist; Capt Bsktbl; Socr; Univ Of Cincinnati; Med.

BEISEL, ROBERT; Copley HS; Akron, OH; Cls Rep Sr Cls; Band; Chrs; Sch Mus; Yth Flsp; Rptr Yrbk; Key Clb; Spn Clb; Letter Ten; Mgrs; Ohio St Univ; Mech Engr.

BEITEL, BILL; Washington HS; Massillon, OH; 99/457 Hon Rl; Off Ade; Ger Clb; Bsbl; Capt Ftbl; Trk; Wrstlng; Univ; Hist.

BEITER, AMY; Pike HS; Indpls, IN; 5/303 Pres Soph Cls; Trs Jr Cls; Trs Sr Cls; Am Leg Aux Girls St; Band; Chrs; Hon Rl; Jr NHS; NHS; Stu Cncl; Purdue Univ; Vet.

BEITLER, LYN A; North Ridgeville Sr HS; N Ridgeville, OH; 5/375 Am Leg Aux Girls St; Band; Hon Rl; NHS; Off Ade; Ger Clb; Letter Swmmng; Letter Ten; Mgrs;.

BEITZ, GINA; Clio HS; Clio, MI; Band; Girl Scts; Hon Rl; Jr NHS; NHS; Stg Crw; PPFtbl; Mic State Univ; Business.

BEJARNO, KAY; Eastwood HS; Pemberville, OH; Sec Jr Cls; Band; Cmp Fr Grls; Chrs; Girl Scts; Hon Rl; Stu Cncl; 4-H; Pep Clb; Spn Clb; Bowling Green St Univ; Psych.

BELAK, MICHAEL; Padua Franciscan HS; Parma, OH; Band; Hon Rl; NHS; Orch; IM Sprt; All Oh St Fair Band Mbr 78; Ohio St Univ; Comp Sci.

BELANGER, JAY; Redford Union HS; Redford, MI; 4/600 Aud/Vis; Hon Rl; Lbry Ade; NHS; Natl Merit Schl; Mi Math Prize Awd Wnnr 77 79; Leg Awd 79; Univ Of Mi Regents Schlrshp 79; Univ Of Michigan; Math.

BELCHER, ARTHUR E; St Johns HS; Toledo, OH; Hon Rl; Lit Mag; Sch Pl; Sch Nwsp; Letter Wrstlng; IM Sprt; Natl Merit Ltr; Univ; Engr.

BELCHER, KATHY L; Eastmoor Sr HS; Columbus, OH; 10/293 Cls Rep Frsh Cls; Band; Chrh Wkr; Cmnty Wkr; Debate Tm; Hon Rl; NHS; Off Ade; Orch; 4-H; Recognition For Outstndng Schlstc Ach; Trophy MVP Bsktbl; Univ; Law.

BELCHER, PAM; Greenfield Central HS; Greenfield, IN; Band; Spn Clb; IUPUI.

BELCIK, TONI; Clay Sr HS; Oregon, OH; 6/385 Cl Rep Jr Cls; Am Leg Aux Girls St; Hon Rl; NHS; Pres Stu Cncl; Trk; Mat Maids; Pom Pon; Univ.

BELDON, ELIZABETH M; Huntington East HS; Huntington, WV; 62/315 Cls Rep Frsh Cls; Cls Rep Soph Cls; Cl Rep Jr Cls; Cls Rep Sr Cls; Cmp Fr Grls; Chrs; Hon Rl; Jr NHS; NHS; Off Ade; Marshall Univ.

BELFAST, DAMIAN; St Josephs Prep; Holton, MI; 2/8 Trs Jr Cls; VP Sr Cls; Chrs; Chrh Wkr; Cmnty Wkr; Hon Rl; NHS; Sch Pl; Stu Cncl; Aquinas College.

BELILE, KIMBERLY; Rogers HS; Wyoming, MI; 53/280 Hon Rl; NHS; Spn Clb; Bsktbl; Letter Ten; Aquinas Coll; Interior Dsgn.

BELILES, JOHN; Avon HS; Danville, IN; Cls Rep Soph Cls; Cl Rep Jr Cls; Chrs; Hon Rl; Mdrgl; Stu Cncl; Spn Clb; IM Sprt; College; Music.

BELILES, NANCY; Avon Jr Sr HS; Danville, IN; 89/198 Chrs; Pep Clb; Chrldng; IM Sprt; Vocational Schl; Nursing.

BELINSKI, CHARLES F; Stephen T Badin HS; Fairfield, OH; Am Leg Boys St; Letter Band; Chrs; Hon Rl; Lbry Ade; Sch Mus; VP Lat Clb; Pep Clb; Miami Univ.

BELISLE, JANE; Bloomington HS North; Bloomington, IN; Sec Frsh Cls; Sec Soph Cls; Cl Rep Jr Cls; Am Leg Aux Girls St; Chrs; Chrh Wkr; NHS; Stu Cncl; Bsktbl; Ten; Univ; Phys Educ.

BELKOWSKI, DEBORAH; Northville HS; Northville, MI; Band; Hon Rl; Marching Band 75 & 76; Flag Corps 77 & 78; Eastern Michigan Univ; Bus Admin.

BELL, ALICE; Marion Adams HS; Sheridan, IN; 20/92 Band; Chrs; Girl Scts; Jr NHS; 4-H; Earlham College; Psych.

BELL, ALLISON; South HS; Youngstwn, OH; 50/258 Cls Rep Soph Cls; Hon Rl; Hosp Ade; JA; Sch Mus; Stu Cncl; Y-Teens; Ed Sch Nwsp; Flo A & M; Business.

BELL, ANDRE; Ypsilanti HS; Ypsilanti, MI; Boy Scts; Chrs; Hon Rl; Boys Clb Am; Ftbl; Trk; Univ Of Tol; Math.

BELL, ANITA; Stivers Patterson Coop HS; Dayton, OH; 37/447 Band; Hon Rl; NHS; Orch; Stg Crw; All City HS Honors Band 76; Certf Of Recognition 76; Univ; Engr.

BELL, BARBARA; Riverdale HS; Arlington, OH; 1/96 Am Leg Aux Girls St; Band; Chrs; Chrh Wkr; Cmnty Wkr; Hon Rl; Jr NHS; NHS; Orch; Sch Mus; Bowling Green St Univ; Acctg.

BELL, BECKY; Canfield HS; Canfield, OH; Chrh Wkr; Hon Rl; JA; NHS; Sch Pl; Stg Crw; Yth Flsp; Fr Clb; Mth Clb; JA Awd; Univ; Intl Exec Sec.

BELL, BRIAN; Walled Lake Western HS; Walled Lk, MI; 6/463 Boy Scts; Hon Rl; Capt Hosp Ade; Orch; Sch Mus; Pep Clb; Letter Swmmng; Alma Coll; Pre Med.

BELL, CHARLES; Decatur Central HS; Indpls, IN; Aud/Vis; Boy Scts; Cmnty Wkr; Hon Rl; Sct Actv; Boys Clb Am; Pep Clb; Letter Ftbl; IM Sprt; PPFtbl; Indiana Central Univ; Law Enforcemnt.

BELL, CHARLES; West Preston HS; Newburg, WV; Boy Scts; Hon Rl; Sct Actv; FFA; Mth Clb; Sci Clb; VICA; Bsbl; Bsktbl; Preston Co Ed Center; Electrition.

BELL, DARRELL; Staunton HS; Brazil, IN; Hon Rl; Key Clb; Letter Trk; Awd For Outstndg Stu In Morning Bldg Trades Cl 78; Awd For Proficiency In Adv Math 78; Ivy Tech Voc Schl; Elec.

BELL, DARRYL; Colerain Vocational HS; Cincinnati, OH; Cl Rep Jr Cls; Chrs; Chrh Wkr; Hon Rl; JA; Off Ade; DECA; JA Awd; College; Busns.

BELL, DEBORAH L; Terre Haute N Vigo HS; Terre Haute, IN; 11/637 Band; Hon Rl; Treas JA; Off Ade; Orch; Y-Teens; 4-H; GAA; 4-H Awd; NEDT Awd; Toastmasters Awd; Track Official; Indiana St Univ.

BELL, DENISE; Loy Norrix HS; Kalamazoo, MI; Chrh Wkr; Cmnty Wkr; Girl Scts; Hon Rl; Lit Mag; Red Cr Ade; Yth Flsp; Rptr Sch Nwsp; 4-H; Fr Clb; Cottey Jr Coll; Soc.

BELL, DIANN; Dexter HS; Pinckney, MI; Girl Scts; Hon Rl; Univ; Sec.

BELL, DIATRICIA; Mt View HS; Anawalt, WV; Am Leg Aux Girls St; Band; Chrs; Chrh Wkr; Hon Rl; Jr NHS; NHS; Rptr Yrbk; Letter Trk; Univ; Soc Work.

BELL, DOUG; Muncie Southside HS; Muncie, IN; Chrs; Chrh Wkr; Hon Rl; Pol Wkr; Sch Mus; Sch Pl; Sprt Ed Sch Nwsp; Scr Kpr; Tmr; Ball St Univ; Poli Sci.

BELL, JACQUELINE; Ripley HS; Ripley, WV; 9/253 VP Frsh Cls; Cls Rep Soph Cls; Cl Rep Jr Cls; VP Sr Cls; Cls Rep Sr Cls; Band; Chrh Wkr; Cmnty Wkr; College; Fash Mdse.

BELL, JAMES; Brownsburg HS; Brownsburg, IN; Hon Rl; NHS; Bsktbl; Trk; Natl Merit Ltr; Opt Clb Awd; IUPUI; Grocery Merchandising.

BELL, JANE; Kenton HS; Kenton, OH; Chrs; Chrh Wkr; Cmnty Wkr; Girl Scts; Hon Rl; Mdrgl; Sch Mus; Yth Flsp; 4-H; Ger Clb; Voc Schl; Day Care.

BELL, JAYME; Van Buren HS; Brazil, IN; 20/90 Trs Frsh Cls; Trs Soph Cls; Trs Jr Cls; Trs Sr Cls; Band; Chrh Wkr; Girl Scts; Hon Rl; Off Ade; Stu Cncl; Ozark Bible Coll; Nursing.

BELL, JEFFREY; Niles HS; Niles, MI; Cls Rep Soph Cls; Cl Rep Jr Cls; Hon Rl; Stu Cncl; Ger Clb; Letter Wrstlng; Am Leg Awd; College; Chem Engr.

BELL, JEFFREY; Leslie HS; Leslie, MI; Cls Rep Frsh Cls; Off Ade; Bsbl; Ftbl; Wrstlng; Tmr; Univ.

BELL, JO; Cadillac Sr HS; Cadillac, MI; 5/325 VP Soph Cls; Pres Jr Cls; Cls Rep Sr Cls; Hon Rl; NHS; Stu Cncl; Letter Bsktbl; Ten; Coach Actv; GAA; Alma Coll; Bio Sci.

BELL, JOSEPH K; Doddridge County HS; Salem, WV; Chrh Wkr; Hon Rl; NHS; Mth Clb; Pep Clb; Trk; IM Sprt; Dnfth Awd; Univ; Chem Engr.

BELL, JUDY; Buckeye Valley HS; Ostrander, OH; 5/180 Cl Rep Jr Cls; Cls Rep Sr Cls; Band; Hon Rl; NHS; VP Stu Cncl; Mat Maids; Mt Carmel Schl Of Nursing; Nurse.

BELL, JULIE; John Glenn HS; Walkerton, IN; 16/100 Chrh Wkr; Hon Rl; NHS; Yth Flsp; Pep Clb; Letter Gym; Letter Chrldng; Scr Kpr; Indiana Univ; Comp Prog.

BELL, KAREN; Urbana HS; Urbana, OH; Cls Rep Soph Cls; Band; Chrs; Red Cr Ade; Sch Mus; Stu Cncl; Fr Clb; Rdo Clb; Berklee Coll Of Music; Music.

BELL, KATHRYN J; Eaton Rapids HS; Crystal, MI; 22/200 Aud/Vis; Mic Tech Univ; Engr.

BELL, KATHY; Marquette Sr HS; Marquette, MI; Band; Hon Rl; Letter Swmmng; Northern Michigan Univ; Med.

BELL, LISA; Pymatuning Valley HS; Andover, OH; Drl Tm; Off Ade; Sch Pl; Yth Flsp; 4-H; FHA; Spn Clb; Scr Kpr; 4-H Awd; Ken Delle Austintown Beaute Academe.

BELL, LORA J; Fostoria HS; Fostoria, OH; 69/190 Band; Chrs; Hon Rl; Lbry Ade; Natl Forn Lg; Sch Pl; Yrbk; Drama Clb; Fr Clb; Pep Clb; Vocational Schl; Modeling.

BELL, MARK; Buckeye South HS; Tiltonsville, OH; Boy Scts; Sct Actv; Drama Clb; Spn Clb; Syracuse Univ; Tele.

BELL, MICHAEL; Brown City HS; Brown City, MI; 4/86 Pres Chrs; Chrh Wkr; Hon Rl; NHS; Stu Cncl; Pres Yth Flsp; Yrbk; Pres 4-H; Letter Glf; 4-H Awd; General Motors Inst; Engr.

BELL, NINA; Morton Sr HS; Hammond, IN; 14/419 Cmp Fr Grls; Chrs; Chrh Wkr; Girl Scts; Hon Rl; Jr NHS; Pom Pon; Am Leg Awd; Piano Awards; Purdue Univ; Music.

BELL, PAMELA; Holt HS; Holt, MI; 1/271 Val; Chrs; Hon Rl; NHS; Sch Mus; Letter Chrldng; GAA; PPFtbl; John & Eliz Whiteley Commercial Awd & Bond; Lansing Comm Coll Busns Div Schlrshp; Top Ten Awd; Lansing Comm Coll; Busns.

BELL, RANDALL J; Fairfield Union HS; Lancaster, OH; 15/158 Trs Jr Cls; Hon Rl; Key Clb; Bsbl; Ftbl; Wrstlng; All Mid State League In Football 1978; Univ; Draftsmen.

BELL, RICKY; Benton Harbor HS; Benton Hrbr, MI; Cls Rep Soph Cls; Cl Rep Jr Cls; Chrs; Chrh Wkr; Cmnty Wkr; Hon Rl; PAVAS; FDA; Key Clb; Trk; Michigan St Univ; Bus Mgmt.

BELL, ROBERT; Traverse City Sr HS; Traverse City, MI; 40/700 Cls Rep Frsh Cls; Chrh Wkr; Hon Rl; NHS; Stu Cncl; Glf; Cit Awd; Law.

BELL, RODRICK; Kalkaska HS; Kalkaska, MI; Chrs; Hon Rl; NHS; Sch Pl; Bsktbl; Coach Actv; IM Sprt; Mgrs; Mich Tech; Tech Engr.

BELL, SAUNDRA SUE; Walter P Chrysler Memrl HS; New Castle, IN; 39/408 Chrh Wkr; Hon Rl; OEA; 6th Pl Acctg In Dist OEA Contest 79; 450.

BELL, SHANNA D; Mc Kinley HS; Sebring, OH; Chrs; Chrh Wkr; Hon Rl; NHS; Sch Mus; Sch Pl; Rptr Yrbk; Yrbk; Drama Clb; Bst Actrss In Minor Schl Pl Sight Unseen; Mt Union Univ; Bio.

BELL, STEFANIE; Mohawk HS; Sycamore, OH; Chrs; Girl Scts; Hon Rl; Y-Teens; 4-H; FHA; FTA; Pep Clb; Spn Clb; Swmmng;.

BELL, STEPHEN; Port Clinton HS; Pt Clinton, OH; 29/226 Boy Scts; Chrs; Chrh Wkr; Hon Rl; College.

BELL, SUSAN; Lakeland HS; Milford, MI; 26/450 Chrs; NHS; Stu Cncl; Rptr Yrbk; Pep Clb; Letter Ten; PPFtbl; Tmr; Central Michigan Univ; Poli Sci.

BELL, TARA; Wadsworth Sr HS; Wadsworth, OH; Chrs; Girl Scts; Hon Rl; Hosp Ade; Y-Teens; 4-H; Spn Clb; Letter Trk; Pres Awd; Univ; Nursing.

BELL, TEENA; Arlington HS; Indianapolis, IN; Cls Rep Frsh Cls; Cls Rep Soph Cls; Trs Jr Cls; Pres Sr Cls; Am Leg Aux Girls St; Hon Rl; JA; NHS; Sch Pl; Purdue Univ Top 5 Prog 78; In Bells Visitation Prog To Bell Labs 79; Purdue Univ; Engr.

BELL, TONYA; Fairfield Union HS; Thornville, OH; Cl Rep Jr Cls; Girl Scts; Stu Cncl; Pep Clb; Trk; Chrldng; Comp Prog.

BELL, TROY M; Bexley HS; Columbus, OH; Quill & Scroll; Stu Cncl; Ed Sch Nwsp; Socr; Letter Trk; Letter Wrstlng; Coach Actv; Kiwan Awd; Natl Merit Ltr; Natl Merit SF; Seminar Schlrshp Freedoms Foundation Valley Forge Columbus Branch; Quill & Scroll Awd; Press Clb News Awd; Dartmouth Univ; Chemistry.

BELL, VICKI; Fairview HS; Fairview, WV; Band; Chrs; Chrh Wkr; Drl Tm; Hon Rl; Hosp Ade; Lbry Ade; Sch Mus; Yth Flsp; Y-Teens; Fairmont St Univ.

BELL, WILLARD; Solon HS; Solon, OH; Chrh Wkr; FCA; Hon Rl; Pol Wkr; Fr Clb; Pep Clb; Letter Bsktbl; Glf; Letter Ten; Trk; Capt J V Basketbll Team 1977; Kenyon Coll; Bus Mgmt.

BELLA, JANICE; Shadyside HS; Shadyside, OH; 9/100 Am Leg Aux Girls St; Band; Chrs; Debate Tm; Drm Mjrt; Hon Rl; NHS; Y-Teens; Drama Clb; Spn Clb; W Liberty State Coll.

BELLA, WILLIAM; Shadyside HS; Shadyside, OH; 1/125 Am Leg Boys St; Band; Boy Scts; Chrh Wkr; Debate Tm; Hon Rl; Sch Mus; Sch Pl; Stu Cncl; Drama Clb; Coll; Engr.

BELLAMAH, LAURA; St Ursula Academy; Cincinnati, OH; 1/105 Hon Rl; NHS; Pep Clb; Pres Spn Clb; Ten; Coach Actv; GAA; IM Sprt; Scr Kpr; Natl Merit Ltr; Angeline Schlrshp 76; Partial Acad Schlrshp Ursuline Acad 76; Univ; Pre Med.

BELLAMY, GLENN; Lebanon HS; Lebanon, OH; 13/300 Band; Chrh Wkr; Drm Mjrt; Hon Rl; NHS; Sch Mus; Yth Flsp; Spn Clb; Univ Of Cincinnati; Med Tech.

BELLAMY, JAMES; Little Miami HS; Morrow, OH; JA; Jr NHS; NHS; Fr Clb; VICA; Bsbl; Wrstlng; IM Sprt; JA Awd; Warren Cnty Jt Voc Schl; Machinist.

BELLAMY, JOHN; Pike Central HS; Winslow, IN; 30201 Hon Rl; NHS; Sci Clb; Letter Bsbl; Letter Ten; Rose Hulman Inst Of Tech; Chem Engr.

BELLAND, JUDY; Galesburg Augusta HS; Kalamazoo, MI; 6/109 Band; Chrs; Cmnty Wkr; Hon Rl; 4-H; Scr Kpr; Univ; Music.

BELLAY, BARBARA; Warren G Harding HS; Warren, OH; 16 Am Leg Aux Girls St; Jr NHS; NHS; Gym; Chrldng; Case Western Reserve Univ; Engr.

BELLE, ANITA; Henry Ford HS; Detroit, MI; 3/500 Pres Frsh Cls; Pres Soph Cls; Pres Jr Cls; Sal; Chrh Wkr; Cmnty Wkr; Hon Rl; NHS; Sch Mus; Sch Pl; Michigan St Univ; Psych.

BELLE, KAREN; Henry Ford HS; Detroit, MI; Cls Rep Frsh Cls; Cls Rep Soph Cls; Cl Rep Jr Cls; Chrs; Hon Rl; Mdrgl; Sch Mus; Sch Pl; Pres Stu Cncl; Rdo Clb; College; Acting.

BELLEMAN, KEN; Purcell HS; Norwood, OH; 13/174 Pres Jr Cls; Hon Rl; Stu Cncl; Rptr Yrbk; Rptr Sch Nwsp; IM Sprt; Stdnt Cncl Pres 78; Prom Committee 78; Homecoming Committee 78; Xavier Univ; Hist.

BELLER, MELODY; William Henry Harrison HS; Harrison, OH; 11/218 Band; Hon Rl; JA; Jr NHS; Lbry Ade; NHS; Sch Mus; Sch Pl; Yrbk; College; Psych.

BELLETINI, EDWARD; St Agatha HS; Detroit, MI; Chrh Wkr; Hon Rl; Lbry Ade; PAVAS; Sch Pl; Yrbk; Drama Clb; Fr Clb; Letter Trk; Oakland Cmnty Coll; Cmmrcl Advtsng.

BELLEW, DONALD; Richmond HS; Richmond, IN; 83/550 Cls Rep Soph Cls; Cl Rep Jr Cls; Debate Tm; Hon Rl; Lbry Ade; Pol Wkr; Stu Cncl; Sch Nwsp; Letter Gym; Mgrs; College; Art.

BELLIN, SANDRA; Beachwood HS; Beachwood, OH; 1/157 Sec Frsh Cls; Sal; Am Leg Aux Girls St; Treas NHS; VP Quill & Scroll; Pres Stu Cncl; Chrldng; Bryn Mawr Coll.

BELLINGER, TIMOTHY; Sacred Heart Academy; Lake, MI; Chrs; Chrh Wkr; 4-H; Letter Bsktbl; Letter Ftbl; Letter Trk; 4-H Awd; Ftbl All Area Mt Pleasant & Saginaw 77; Ftbl All Area Mt Pleasant & Saginaw Hon Mention All St 78; Northwood Inst; Bus Admin.

BELLINI, JAMES; Glen Este HS; Batavia, OH; Chrh Wkr; Hon Rl; Eng Clb; Pep Clb; Spn Clb; Bsbl; Ftbl; Trk; Wrstlng; College; Bus.

BELLIS, GAYLE; Our Lady Of Mt Carmel HS; Southgate, MI; 10/65 Chrh Wkr; Hon Rl; NHS; Sch Mus; Sch Pl; Stg Crw; Pep Clb; Detroit Busns Inst; Acctg.

BELLIS, WENDI; Northrop HS; Fort Wayne, IN; 17/581 Band; Chrh Wkr; Drl Tm; Girl Scts; Hon Rl; NHS; Yth Flsp; C of C Awd; Cit Awd; Indiana Univ; Acctg.

BELLIVEAU, JOAN; St Annes Warren HS; Warren, MI; Trs Frsh Cls; Swmmng; Oakland Univ; Med Tech.

BELLMAN, TERESA; Seton HS; Cincinnati, OH; Chrs; Hon Rl; Sch Mus; Sch Pl; Cincinnati Tech Coll; Sec.

BELLNER, TAMARA; Pike Central HS; Stendal, IN; 6/192 Hst Jr Cls; Chrh Wkr; Cmnty Wkr; Hon Rl; NHS; Off Ade; 4-H; Pep Clb; Trk; Capt IM Sprt;.

BELLOR, ANNE; Pinconning Area HS; Linwood, MI; Cmnty Wkr; Hon Rl; NHS; 4-H; GAA; IM Sprt; Scr Kpr; Delta Coll; Sec.

BELLOT, TERRENCE; Andrean HS; Lake Station, IN; 104/225 Boy Scts; Hon Rl; Ftbl; Trk; Wrstlng; Univ.

BELLOTTE, JUSTINA; Notre Dame HS; Clarksburg, WV; Band; Chrs; FNA; Pep Clb; Twrlr; JA Awd; Jr Catholic Daughter Of Yr 76; Freshman Princess On Homecoming Ct 76; Modeling Schl; Modeling.

BELME, SUE; Wayne HS; Dayton, OH; 121/565 Cls Rep Frsh Cls; Cls Rep Soph Cls; Cl Rep Jr Cls; Chrh Wkr; Drl Tm; FCA; Ohio Univ; Liberal Arts.

BELMOSA, JOYLEVETTE; John F Kennedy HS; Cleveland, OH; Cl Rep Jr Cls; Cmnty Wkr; Girl Scts; Off Ade; Stu Cncl; Drama Clb; Merit Of Art Achvmnt 78; Brooks Coll; Interior Dsgnr.

BELOAT, GREG; North Posey HS; Poseyville, IN; Chrh Wkr; Hon Rl; Jr NHS; NHS; Rptr Sch Nwsp; Ger Clb; IM Sprt; Univ.

BELOBRADICH, MICHELLE; Ladywood HS; Plymouth, MI; Hon Rl; Quill & Scroll; Sch Mus; Yrbk; Drama Clb; Trk; Michigan State Univ; Psychology.

BELSHEE, FRANCES E; Greenbrier East HS; Whte Slphr Spg, WV; Band; Hon Rl; Pres Civ Clb; FTA; Concord Univ; Spec Educ.

BELSON, TAMARA; Mendon HS; Mendon, MI; 10/82 VP Frsh Cls; Am Leg Aux Girls St; Chrs; Chrh Wkr; FCA; Hon Rl; Lbry Ade; NHS; Stu Cncl; Yth Flsp; Athletic Schl Awd; Coll; Educ.

BELSTRA, AMY; Kankakee Valley HS; De Motte, IN; 17/190 Band; Chrh Wkr; Hon Rl; NHS; Sch Mus; Stg Crw; Rptr Yrbk; Drama Clb; College.

BELTMAN, THOMAS; Zeeland HS; Zeeland, MI; 17/193 Band; Hon Rl; NHS; Yth Flsp; Mgrs; Mich Tech Univ; Mech Engr.

BELTON, MICHAEL; Benedictine HS; Cleveland, OH; Hon Rl; Pres JA; Sch Mus; Drama Clb; Crs Cntry; Trk; IM Sprt; Pres JA Awd; Spanish Awd 77 78 & 79; Dale Carnegie Public Speaking Schlrshp 77; Drama Clb Awd; Univ; Zoology.

BELTZ, ANNE L; Marlington HS; Alliance, OH; 10/320 Am Leg Aux Girls St; Band; Drm Bgl; Girl Scts; Hon Rl; Lbry Ade; Off Ade; Orch; Sch Mus; Sch Pl; Univ; Communications.

BELTZ, DEBRA; Fraser HS; Fraser, MI; Hosp Ade; Spn Clb; College; Bio Sci.

BELTZ, LISA; Washington HS; Massillon, OH; 1/475 Val; Girl Scts; Hon Rl; Lbry Ade; NHS; Stg Crw; Drama Clb; Fr Clb; Pep Clb; Letter Trk; Oh Acad Schlrshp 4 Yr 79; Molone Acad Schlrshp 4 Yr 79; Malone Coll; Bio.

BELTZ, TIM; Harding HS; Marion, OH; NHS; Yth Flsp; Ashland Coll; Pre Vet.

BELUSAR, DAVID; Posen Consolidated HS; Posen, MI; Band; Fr Clb; FHA; Pep Clb; Letter Trk; Alpena Cmnty Coll; Sci.

BEMENDERFER, JOY; Indianapolis Baptist HS; Indianapolis, IN; 8/36 Chrs; Chrh Wkr; Hon Rl; Sch Pl; Rptr Sch Nwsp; Liberty Baptist Coll; Bus Educ.

BEMILLER, SUE; Ontario HS; Mansfield, OH; 47/165 Sec Jr Cls; Hst Sr Cls; AFS; Cmnty Wkr; Hon Rl; Stu Cncl; Rptr Yrbk; 4-H; Sch Clb; Ten; College; Elem Educ.

BEMIS, BRENDA; Winchester Comm HS; Winchester, IN; Chrh Wkr; Hosp Ade; Lbry Ade; Stg Crw; 4-H; FHA; FTA; Spn Clb; Anderson College; Elem Teacher.

BEMIS, DIANE; Versailles HS; Versailles, OH; 3/134 Hst Sr Cls; Am Leg Aux Girls St; Hon Rl; Fr Clb; FTA; Mth Clb; Spn Clb; Scr Kpr; Am Leg Awd; Voice Dem Awd; Ohio State Univ.

BENADUM, ELECTA; Zanesville HS; Zanesville, OH; 72/413 Hon Rl; Rptr Yrbk; Letter Ten; Letter Trk; Ohio St Univ; Bus Admin.

BENADUM, GREG; Fairfield Union HS; Lancaster, OH; 23/158 Band; Chrs; Hon Rl; Orch; Stg Crw; 4-H; Pep Clb; Music.

BENAK, KATHI; Elk Rapids HS; Williamsburg, MI; Band; Chrh Wkr; Debate Tm; Drm Mjrt; Hon Rl; NHS; Orch; Bob Jones Univ; Pre Med.

BENBOW, BRAD; Delta HS; Muncie, IN; 31/330 Cl Rep Jr Cls; Cls Rep Sr Cls; Aud/Vis; FCA; Hon Rl; Lbry Ade; Off Ade; Pol Wkr; Quill & Scroll; Stu Cncl; Wabash Univ; Corporate Law.

BENCETIC, KENNETH; Brookfield HS; Masury, OH; Cls Rep Frsh Cls; Cls Rep Soph Cls; Cl Rep Jr Cls; Aud/Vis; Debate Tm; Red Cr Ade; Stu Cncl; Bsbl; Bsktbl; Ftbl; Univ; Bus Mgmt.

BENCHEK, JAMES; Mayfield HS; Mayfield Hts, OH; Hon Rl; Letter Bsbl; College.

BENCIC, TIMOTHY; St Joseph HS; Euclid, OH; 17/295 Hon Rl; NHS; Letter Ftbl; Letter Trk; IM Sprt; Univ Of Toledo; Elec Engr.

BENDALL, CHERYL; High School; Jackson, MI; 8/250 Trs Soph Cls; Band; Chrh Wkr; Girl Scts; Hon Rl; NHS; Sch Mus; Mic State Univ; Horticulture.

BENDER, CATHERINE; Berea HS; Brook Park, OH; Cls Rep Frsh Cls; Cls Rep Soph Cls; Hon Rl; Mod UN; Stg Crw; Letter Swmmng; Case Western Reserve; Med.

BENDER, CHRISTOPHER; North Posey HS; Poseyville, IN; Hon Rl; JA; FFA; Bsbl; IM Sprt; Purdue Univ; Agri.

BENDER, DAVE; Berea HS; Brookpk, OH; 53/528 Chrh Wkr; Hon Rl; Mod UN; College; Law.

BENDER, DAWN; Bridgeport HS; Bridgeport, MI; Letter Trk; Pom Pon; Murphy M J Beauty Coll; Cosmotology.

BENDER, JENNIFER; Highland HS; Medina, OH; 14/210 Am Leg Aux Girls St; Band; NHS; Quill & Scroll; Rptr Yrbk; Sch Nwsp; Ger Clb; Key Clb; Pep Clb; Letter Bsktbl; Wittenberg Univ.

BENDER, JOHN; Berea HS; Brookpark, OH; 57/500 Hon Rl; Mod UN; Univ; Comp Sci.

BENDER, KATHRYN; Boonville HS; Boonville, IN; 32/222 Pres Soph Cls; Hon Rl; Jr NHS; Off Ade; Treas Stu Cncl; Rptr Sch Nwsp; Pep Clb; Chrldng; Indiana Univ; Optometry.

BENDER, LORI; Douglas Mac Arthur HS; Saginaw, MI; Pep Clb; Ten; Trk; Univ; Bus.

BENDER, RONALD; Goshen HS; Goshen, IN; 1/268 FCA; NHS; Sci Clb; Letter Bsbl; Letter Bsktbl; College; Math.

BENDING, KATRINA; Walter E Stebbins HS; Dayton, OH; Rptr Yrbk; Drama Clb; OEA; Pep Clb; Mgrs; Sinclair Comm College; Acctng.

BENDLIN, GREGORY J; Bay HS; Olmsted Falls, OH; 20/341 Am Leg Boys St; Boy Scts; Cmnty Wkr; Lit Mag; NHS; Red Cr Ade; Drama Clb; Spn Clb; JC Awd; Natl Merit Ltr; Univ; Intl Affairs.

BENE, RICHARD; William Mason HS; Mason, OH; 30/200 Boy Scts; Hon Rl; Sct Actv; Yth Flsp; Letter Bsbl; Coach Actv; IM Sprt; Am Leg Awd; Soph Homecoming Attendant; College; Engr.

BENEDETTI, VINCE; Bekley HS; Bexley, OH; Hon Rl; Rus Clb; Crs Cntry; Trk; IM Sprt; Tmr; Am Leg Awd; DAR Awd; VFW Awd; Voice Dem Awd; North Carolina State; Science.

BENEDETTO, BETTE; Parkside HS; Jackson, MI; 1/344 Val; Band; Hon Rl; Sec Stu Cncl; Letter Ten; Kalamazoo Coll.

BENEDICT, CAROLE; North Knox HS; Bicknell, IN; 20/174 Cls Rep Sr Cls; NHS; Stu Cncl; OEA; Pep Clb; Chrldng; Vincennes Univ; Med Sec.

BENEDICT, DAVID; Southfield Lathrup HS; Lathrup Vill, MI; Band; Hon Rl; Orch; Oakland Univ; Engr.

BENEDICT, DAWN; Winchester Comm HS; Winchester, IN; 4/155 Band; Hon Rl; NHS; FHA; Spn Clb; Ten; Letter Trk; Letter Mgrs; Indiana Schlrshp Honorary; Goodrich Schlrshp; Ball St Univ; Acctg.

BENEDICT, LAURIE; Battle Creek Acad; Battle Creek, MI; 5/23 Band; Chrs; Hon Rl; NHS; Stu Cncl; Yth Flsp; Beta Clb; Letter Bsktbl; Gym; Capt Socr; Andrews Univ; Nurse.

BENEFIELD, BELLANDRA; Beecher HS; Mt Morris, MI; 2/275 Cls Rep Soph Cls; Cl Rep Jr Cls; Sal; Cmnty Wkr; Girl Scts; Hon Rl; NHS; Stu Cncl; Trk; Chrldng; Michigan State Univ; Economics.

BENEFIELD, JOHN; Flint S W HS; Flint, MI; 21/450 Hon Rl; Off Ade; Quill & Scroll; Ed Sch Nwsp; Capt Crs Cntry; Capt Trk; Wrstlng; Coach Actv; Columbia Coll; Med.

BENEKER, SHARON; Brookville HS; Brookville, IN; 3/194 Chrs; Chrh Wkr; Hon Rl; NHS; Sec 4-H; FHA; Spn Clb; GAA; Univ; Early Childhood Ed.

BENFORD, MILLICENT; Woodward HS; Cincinnati, OH; Chrs; Hon Rl; MMM; Sch Pl; Rptr Sch Nwsp; Drama Clb; Bsbl; Wright State Univ; Drama.

BENGE, PATTY; Utica HS; Newark, OH; 12/200 Cl Rep Jr Cls; Hon Rl; Jr NHS; Lbry Ade; NHS; Rptr Yrbk; OEA; Pep Clb; Bsktbl; Trk; 3rd Pl In Acctg At Regional Contest; Reserve Vlybl Tm & Letter; Busns Schl; Data Processing.

BENGE, SUSAN; Utica HS; Newark, OH; 7/196 Sec Sr Cls; Hon Rl; NHS; Treas Civ Clb; Letter Bsktbl; Letter Trk; GAA; PPFtbl; Central Ohio Tech Coll; Acctg.

BENGELINK, JULIE; Calvin Christian HS; Grand Rapids, MI; Chrs; Cmnty Wkr; Hon Rl; Lbry Ade; Orch; Red Cr Ade; Sch Pl; Drama Clb; 4-H; Capt Pom Pon; Butterworth Schl; Nursing.

BENGRY, ALAN; Evart HS; Evart, MI; 8/104 Sec Jr Cls; Pres Sr Cls; Hon Rl; Natl Forn Lg; NHS; Sch Pl; Treas 4-H; Pres FFA; Trk; Mgrs; Ferris St Coll; Pharm.

BENHAM, BRADLEY; Orchard View HS; Muskegon, MI; Chrs; Chrh Wkr; Cmnty Wkr; Hon Rl; Glf; Letter Swmmng; MSU; Fisheries Science.

BENICK, BRIAN; Madison HS; Mansfield, OH; 14/500 Band; Ger Clb; Trk; Wrstlng; Kent State; Sci.

BENIFIELD, ROBIN; East HS; Youngstown, OH; 3/189 Pres Sr Cls; Girl Scts; Hon Rl; VP JA; NHS; Off Ade; Treas Stu Cncl; Y-Teens; Rptr Yrbk; Pep Clb; Rotary Clb Outstndg Jr Girl 1978; Oh Schlstc Achvmnt Awd 1975; Univ; Pre Law.

BENISH, DALE R; Millington HS; Millington, MI; 12/174 Cls Rep Frsh Cls; Trs Jr Cls; Cl Rep Jr Cls; Trs Sr Cls; Boy Scts; Cmnty Wkr; Hon Rl; Jr NHS; NHS; Sct Actv; I Am A Local Umpire 79; Ferris St Coll; Acctg.

BENJAMIN, KEITH; Riverdale HS; Mt Blanchard, OH; Chrs; Chrh Wkr; Hon Rl; Pres Yth Flsp; IM Sprt; Tech Schl; Archt.

BENJAMIN, LISA; Loogootee HS; Loogootee, IN; Band; Drl Tm; Hon Rl; Yrbk; 4-H; Pep Clb; Spn Clb; Trk; Chrldng; IM Sprt; Vllybl 78; Purdue Univ; Photog.

BENJAMIN, SCOTT; Carman HS; Flint, MI; Boy Scts; Hon Rl; NHS; Socr; Letter Ten; Natl Merit Ltr; Coll; Med.

BENJAMIN, SPRING; Reading HS; Reading, MI; Hon Rl; Bsktbl; Trk; College; Psych.

BENJAMIN, TED; Piqua Ctrl HS; Piqua, OH; 18/334 VP Frsh Cls; Pres Soph Cls; Pres Jr Cls; Am Leg Boys St; Band; Chrs; Chrh Wkr; Cmnty Wkr; Hon Rl; Jr NHS; Univ; Psych.

BENKERT, ROBIN; West Jefferson HS; W Jefferson, OH; 26/108 Cls Rep Frsh Cls; Cls Rep Soph Cls; Chrs; Chrh Wkr; Girl Scts; Hon Rl; Chrs; Chrh Wkr; Columbus Bus Univ; Med Sec.

BENKIEL, DANIEL; Morgantown HS; Morgantown, WV; 59/492 Cls Rep Frsh Cls; Cls Rep Soph Cls; Cl Rep Jr Cls; Cls Rep Sr Cls; Aud/Vis; Chrs; Hon Rl; Orch; Stu Cncl; Fr Clb; Wv Univ; Psych.

BENN, LAVITA; Jane Addams Vocational HS; Cleveland, OH; Cmp Fr Grls; Off Ade; Bsbl; Capt Bsktbl; Socr; Trk; IM Sprt; Cit Awd; Merit Roll Awd 78; Phys Fitness Awd 76; MVP Bstbl Tm 76; Univ; Legal Sec.

BENN, SUSAN; Morton Sr HS; Hammond, IN; Band; Chrh Wkr; Girl Scts; Hon Rl; Red Cr Ade; Sch Pl; Pep Clb; Sci Clb; Univ Of Calgary; Law.

BENNELL, KIMBERLY; Edison Sr HS; Lake Station, IN; Band; Drl Tm; Girl Scts; Hon Rl; Off Ade; Pres 4-H; Pep Clb; Sci Clb; Spn Clb; Gym; Coll.

BENNER, GARY; Cory Rawson HS; Findlay, OH; Sch Pl; FFA; VICA; Letter Wrstlng; Nashville Auto Diesel Coll; Mechanic.

BENNER, KELLY; South Newton Jr Sr HS; Goodland, IN; Am Leg Aux Girls St; Band; Sch Pl; FBLA; Lat Clb; PPFtbl; Attndnc Awd 76 & 77; IVY Tech Schl; Bank.

BENNER, LORI; Fulton HS; St Johns, MI; Band; Chrh Wkr; Hon Rl; Yth Flsp; Ed Sch Nwsp; Rptr Sch Nwsp; FHA; Mth Clb; Trk; Pom Pon; Univ.

BENNER, MIKE; Dekalb HS; Auburn, IN; 35/386 FCA; NHS; Y-Teens; Letter Bsktbl; Letter Ftbl; Letter Trk; Coach Actv; Purdue Univ; Aero Engr.

BENNET, SUE; Western Hills HS; Cincinnati, OH; 179/800 Cls Rep Soph Cls; Cl Rep Jr Cls; Cls Rep Sr Cls; Drl Tm; Hon Rl; Off Ade; Sch Mus; Stu Cncl; FHA; Miami Univ; Interior Dsgn.

BENNETT, ALBERT; Marlington HS; Alliance, OH; Boy Scts; Chrh Wkr; Univ; Balistics Exprt.

BENNETT, ALLEN; Laurel HS; Laurel, IN; Hon Rl; NHS; God Cntry Awd;.

BENNETT, ANDREW; Benzie Cnty Cntrl HS; Beulah, MI; Pres Frsh Cls; Pres Soph Cls; Am Leg Boys St; Band; Natl Forn Lg; Sch Mus; Pres Stu Cncl; Rptr Sch Nwsp; Drama Clb; Natl Merit Schl; 10 Pl St Forensics Tourn Informative Speaking; Professional Magician; Hmcmng King; Michigan St Univ; Broadcasting.

BENNETT, ANGELA; Cannelton HS; Cannelton, IN; 3/35 VP Frsh Cls; VP Soph Cls; VP Jr Cls; Band; Chrh Wkr; Drl Tm; Girl Scts; Hon Rl; Jr NHS; NHS; Varsity Volleyball Cptn; Univ.

BENNETT, ANGELA D; Jefferson Twp Local HS; Dayton, OH; Pres Jr Cls; Chrs; Chrh Wkr; Stu Cncl; FHA; OEA; Pep Clb; Trk; Pom Pon; C of C Awd; DEA Ambassador Awd Natl; DEA Stateswoman Awd St; Awd Of Distinction In Keypunch Operation;.

BENNETT, ARLA; Negaunee HS; Neagunee, MI; Cmp Fr Grls; 4-H; Pep Clb; Bsbl; 4-H Awd;.

BENNETT, B; Circleville HS; Cherry Grv, WV; Hon Rl; NHS; FBLA; Letter Bsktbl; Voice Dem Awd;.

BENNETT, BARBARA; Anderson HS; Cincinnati, OH; Cl Rep Jr Cls; Chrs; Hon Rl; Jr NHS; Stu Cncl; IM Sprt; PPFtbl; Cit Awd; JA Awd; Univ; Sci.

BENNETT, BRENDA; Warrensville Heights HS; Warrensvl Hts, OH; Cls Rep Frsh Cls; Cls Rep Soph Cls; Cl Rep Jr Cls; Cmp Fr Grls; Chrs; Drl Tm; Hosp Ade; JA; Stu Cncl; Bsbl; College; Nursing.

BENNETT, BRYAN; Clarkston HS; Clarkston, MI; Boy Scts; Hon Rl; Yth Flsp; Voc Of Mic; Engr.

BENNETT, CAROL; Niles Sr HS; Niles, MI; Band; Hon Rl; NHS; Chmn Stg Crw; Pres Yth Flsp; Yrbk; Drama Clb; Pep Clb; Twrlr; Top 10 Awd 77 & 79; Perfect Attndnc 77; Bethel Coll; Dent.

BENNETT, CATHERINE; Fairview HS; Fairview Park, OH; Sec Jr Cls; VP Chrs; Hon Rl; Hosp Ade; Pres NHS; Sch Mus; Drama Clb; Sci Clb; Chrldng; IM Sprt; Bowling Green St Univ; Nursing.

BENNETT, CATHY; Southview HS; Lorain, OH; 79/310 Chrh Wkr; Girl Scts; Hon Rl; Off Ade; Yth Flsp; OEA;.

BENNETT, CHRISTINE; Michigan Lutheran Seminary; Garden City, MI; Chrs; Hon Rl; Trk; IM Sprt; Dr Martin Luther Coll; Tchr.

BENNETT, DAG; Franklin Comm HS; Franklin, IN; 13/288 Cls Rep Frsh Cls; Cls Rep Soph Cls; Cl Rep Jr Cls; Pres Sr Cls; AFS; Band; Hon Rl; JA; Jr NHS; NHS; College; Medicine.

BENNETT, DANITA; Grove City HS; Grove City, OH; Cls Rep Frsh Cls; Cl Rep Jr Cls; Cls Rep Sr Cls; Hon Rl; Hosp Ade; Red Cr Ade; Stu Cncl; Yrbk; Pep Clb; Letter Bsktbl; E Kentucky Univ; Elem Ed.

BENNETT, DARRELL; Philip Barbour HS; Philippi, WV; Am Leg Boys St; Hon Rl; Key Clb; Sec VICA; Letter Ftbl; Letter Wrstlng; Scr Kpr; Am Leg Awd; VICA Camp 79; Voc Schl; Welding.

BENNETT, DONNA; South Harrison HS; Mc Whorter, WV; Cl Rep Jr Cls; Band; Hon Rl; NHS;.

BENNETT, EMILY; La Salle HS; South Bend, IN; 1/488 Cls Rep Soph Cls; Cl Rep Jr Cls; Cls Rep Sr Cls; Hon Rl; Pres NHS; Sch Mus; Stg Crw; Drama Clb; Swmmng; IM Sprt; Univ; Bus.

BENNETT, FRANK; Harper Creek HS; Battle Creek, MI; 24/250 Cls Rep Frsh Cls; Cls Rep Soph Cls; Hon Rl; NHS; Stu Cncl; Bsbl; Capt Ftbl; Wrstlng; Opt Clb Awd; Western Michigan Univ; Coaching.

BENNETT, GRAY; Eaton HS; Eaton, OH; Hon Rl; Yth Flsp; Civ Clb; Pres 4-H; Letter Ftbl; Letter Trk; Capt Wrstlng; Coach Actv; 4-H Awd; Delegate Rotary World Affairs Inst; Duke Univ; Law.

BENNETT, GREGG; Bishop Dwenger HS; Ft Wayne, IN; Hon Rl; Key Clb; Wrstlng; IM Sprt; Coll; Acctg.

BENNETT, JACKIE; Highland HS; Medina, OH; Band; Drl Tm; Hon Rl; Sch Pl; 4-H; Key Clb; Spn Clb; Mat Maids; 4-H Awd; Univ; Nursing.

BENNETT, JACQUELINE L; Federal Hocking HS; Stewart, OH; 25/130 Band; Girl Scts; Hon Rl; Sct Actv; 4-H; FBLA; 4-H Awd; Eng II Awd 77; Majorette; Hocking Tech Coll; Sec Sci.

BENNETT, JANEEN; Terre Haute North Vigo HS; Terre Haute, IN; 99/600 Cl Rep Jr Cls; Band; Hon Rl; JA; Lbry Ade; Stu Cncl; Y-Teens; GAA; PPFtbl; JA Awd; College; Busns.

BENNETT, JAY; Hubbard HS; Hubbard, OH; 17/350 Cls Rep Soph Cls; Band; Chrs; Hon Rl; Natl Forn Lg; NHS; Sch Mus; Sch Pl; Stg Crw; Drama Clb; Ohio Univ; Theatre.

BENNETT, JO; Buckhannon Upshur HS; Buckhannon, WV; Sec Soph Cls; Band; Chrh Wkr; Cmnty Wkr; Girl Scts; Hon Rl; Yth Flsp; Pep Clb; Mgrs; College; Acctg.

BENNETT, JOANNA; New Lexington Sr HS; New Lexington, OH; Chrs; Hon Rl; Sch Mus; Sch Pl; Stg Crw; Sch Nwsp; Drama Clb; Spn Clb; GAA; Mgrs;.

BENNETT, JOEY; Terre Haute North Vigo HS; Terre Haute, IN; Pres Sr Cls; Hon Rl; Off Ade; Quill & Scroll; Sprt Ed Sch Nwsp; Boys Clb Am; IM Sprt; Mgrs; Terre Haute Boys Clb Boy Of Yr; Indiana Boys Clb Boy Of Yr; Indiana St Univ; Journalism.

BENNETT, KAREN; Roseville HS; Roseville, MI; Chrs; Chrh Wkr; Hon Rl; Hosp Ade; Jr Mag; NHS; Yrbk; Rptr Sch Nwsp; Natl Merit SF; Voice Dem Awd; Macomb Cnty Comm Coll; Eng.

BENNETT, KIMBERLY; Rose D Warwick HS; Tekonsh, MI; 15/57 Chrs; Hon Rl; Sch Pl; Drama Clb; 4-H; Bsktbl; Trk; PPFtbl; Tmr; Vllybl Mst Valubl 79; Athlt Of Yr 79; Track Mst Valuable 79; Olivet Univ; Cmnctns.

BENNETT, LAURA; Union Scioto Loc Schls; Chillicothe, OH; 19/120 Cl Rep Jr Cls; Am Leg Aux Girls St; Chrs; Hon Rl; Off Ade; Quill & Scroll; Stu Cncl; Pep Clb; Spn Clb; Letter Bsktbl; 1st Fem Athlet Train 77; Lttrd Head Fem Train Bsktbll 2yrs Vllybll 3yrs 76; Lttrd Head Fem Mgr Bsktbll 76; Shawnee St Cmnty Coll; Radiology.

BENNETT, LAURI; Brighton HS; Brighton, MI; Band; Chrs; Chrh Wkr; Hon Rl; Yth Flsp; Fr Clb; College; Acctg.

BENNETT, LEAH; Circleville HS; Circleville, WV; 3/30 Sec Frsh Cls; Chrs; Chrh Wkr; Cmnty Wkr; Hon Rl; NHS; Stu Cncl; Yth Flsp; Rptr Yrbk; Rptr Sch Nwsp; West Virginia Univ.

BENNETT, LESLIE; West Branch Local HS; Salem, OH; 9/275 VP AFS; Band; Hon Rl; NHS; 4-H; FTA; College; Education.

BENNETT, LINDA; North Central HS; Pioneer, OH; Cls Rep Frsh Cls; Cls Rep Soph Cls; Cl Rep Jr Cls; Hon Rl; Off Ade; Stu Cncl; Rptr Sch Nwsp; FHA; FTA; Chrldng; Bus Schl; Sec.

BENNETT, MARK; Milan HS; Dillsboro, IN; 4/95 Band; Chrh Wkr; Hon Rl; NHS; Red Cr Ade; Stu Cncl; Treas Yth Flsp; Pres 4-H; FFA;.

BENNETT, MELISSA; South Harrison HS; Lost Creek, WV; Chrs; Hon Rl; NHS; Yrbk; Sch Nwsp; Pep Clb; Clarksburg Beauty Acadf Cosmotology.

BENNETT, MICHAEL; Zanesville Sr HS; Zanesville, OH; 47/383 FCA; NHS; Stu Cncl; Pres Sci Clb; Capt Bsbl; Capt Ftbl; Muskingum Univ; Law.

BENNETT, MIKE; Portsmouth East HS; Portsmouth, OH; 3/75 Am Leg Boys St; Hon Rl; Lbry Ade; NHS; Rptr Yrbk; Rptr Sch Nwsp; Pep Clb; VP Spn Clb; Bsktbl; Eng Schlrshp Team; Amer History Schlrshp Team; Shawnee St Univ; Acctg.

BENNETT, PATTI; Circleville HS; Circleville, WV; Sec Frsh Cls; Sec Soph Cls; Sec Jr Cls; Chrs; Hon Rl; VP FHA; Bsktbl; Chrldng; Mgrs; Voice Dem Awd; Univ; Sec.

BENNETT, PAULA; Chelsea HS; Gregory, MI; 26/152 Band; Hon Rl; NHS; Rptr Yrbk; Twrlr; Michigan State Univ; Soc Sci.

BENNETT, PENNY; Central Montcalm HS; Stanton, MI; Cls Rep Soph Cls; Cl Rep Jr Cls; Hon Rl; Pol Wkr; Stu Cncl; Collegef Sec.

BENNETT, RANDY; North Newton HS; Morocco, IN; VP Frsh Cls; Cls Rep Soph Cls; Hon Rl; NHS; Stu Cncl; 4-H; Mth Clb; Sci Clb; Spn Clb; Letter Bsktbl; Purdue Univ; Gen Aviation.

BENNETT, RENEA; Midland HS; Midland, MI; 218/486 Girl Scts; Hon Rl; Off Ade; Delta Coll.

BENNETT, RENEE; Jackson HS; Jackson, OH; Chrs; Girl Scts; Off Ade; Red Cr Ade; Stg Crw; Rptr Sch Nwsp; Sch Nwsp; 4-H; FHA; OEA; Montana St Univ; Soc Work.

BENNETT, RENEE; Gaylord HS; Gaylord, MI; Chrs; Girl Scts; Hon Rl; Natl Forn Lg; NHS; Off Ade; 4-H; PPFtbl; Univ; Math.

BENNETT, ROBERT; Servite HS; Detroit, MI; Rptr Yrbk; Fr Clb; IM Sprt; Mgrs; Natl Merit Ltr; Univ Of Detroit; Acctg.

BENNETT, ROBERTA; William Henry Harrison HS; W Laf, IN; 152/340 AFS; Chrs; Girl Scts; Orch; Sch Mus; Sch Pl; Sct Actv; Yth Flsp; Rptr Yrbk; College; Elem Educ.

BENNETT, ROBIN; Benton Central HS; Earl Park, IN; Band; Chrs; Girl Scts; Hon Rl; NHS; Drama Clb; 4-H; Spn Clb; Chrldng; College; Soc Work.

BENNETT, ROD; Zanesville Rosecrans HS; Zanesville, OH; 3/89 VP Jr Cls; Hon Rl; NHS; Stu Cncl; Sprt Ed Yrbk; Rptr Sch Nwsp; Pres Key Clb; Bsktbl; Letter Crs Cntry; Letter Trk; Ohio Univ; Comp Sci.

BENNETT, ROD; Warren Ctrl HS; Indianapolis, IN; 38/800 Band; Hon Rl; Jr NHS; NHS; Orch; Sch Mus; Univ; Music.

BENNETT, RONALD; Liberty HS; Clarksburg, WV; 8/250 Cls Rep Sr Cls; Am Leg Boys St; Band; Hon Rl; Jr NHS; NHS; Orch; Sch Mus; Sch Pl; Stg Crw; W Virginia Univ; Music Educ.

BENNETT, SHARI; Gallia Academy HS; Gallipolis, OH; Chrs; Yrbk; Sch Nwsp; FTA; Key Clb; Bowling Green St Univ; Intl Bus.

BENNETT, SHARON; Immaculata HS; Detroit, MI; Cls Rep Soph Cls; Cl Rep Jr Cls; Cls Rep Sr Cls; Hon Rl; NHS; Sprt Ed Sch Nwsp; Rptr Sch Nwsp; Bsbl; Bsktbl; Exc In Math Comp Cert; Art Exhibit Awd; All Cath Vlybl; Univ Of Michigan; Busns Admin.

BENNETT, SHARON; Tri Village HS; New Paris, OH; 1/63 Trs Soph Cls; Val; Band; Chrs; Chrh Wkr; Hon Rl; NHS; Off Ade; Sch Pl; DAR Awd; Olivet Nazarene Coll; Acctg.

BENNETT, SHARON; Covert HS; Coloma, MI; 2/34 Pres Frsh Cls; VP Soph Cls; Cl Rep Jr Cls; Band; Chrh Wkr; Girl Scts; Hon Rl; Jr NHS; Lbry Ade; Mod UN; Perfect Attndce 1975; Schl Hostess 1977; Univ; Bus.

BENNETT, SHIRLEY; Charles F Brush HS; S Euclid, OH; 37/620 Band; Chrs; Hosp Ade; NHS; Orch; Letter Swmmng; Tmr; Colllege Of Wooster; Biology.

BENNETT, STEVEN; Haslett HS; Haslett, MI; 21/154 Band; Drm Mjrt; Jr NHS; NHS; Crs Cntry; Wrstlng; Tmr; Michigan St Univ; Dairy Sci.

BENNETT, TERRY; Westfall HS; Orient, OH; Band; Hon Rl; NHS; Ohio State Uniff Architecture.

BENNETT, TIMOTHY; Winamac HS; Winamac, IN; Sec Soph Cls; VP Band; Chrh Wkr; Hon Rl; NHS; Orch; Yth Flsp; Purdue Univ; Civil Engr.

BENNETT, TRACEE; London City HS; London, OH; 13/133 Pres Frsh Cls; Trs Soph Cls; Sec Jr Cls; Hon Rl; NHS; Quill & Scroll; Stu Cncl; Rptr Yrbk; VP Fr Clb; Letter Trk; College.

BENNETT, TRACY; Caseville Public HS; Caseville, MI; 4/13 Cls Rep Frsh Cls; VP Soph Cls; Pres Jr Cls; Pres Sr Cls; Band; Chrs; Chrh Wkr; Northwood Inst; Bus Admin.

BENNETT, WILLIAM C; Ellet Sr HS; Akron, OH; 76/363 Sec Frsh Cls; Cls Rep Sr Cls; Chrs; Chrh Wkr; Cmnty Wkr; Debate Tm; Hon Rl; Natl Forn Lg; NHS; Sch Mus; Wooster Coll; Elem Ed.

BENNETT III, GEORGE; Cass Technical HS; Detroit, MI; College; Mechanical Engineer.

BENNIGAN, LORI; New Haven HS; New Haven, IN; Band; Drl Tm; Girl Scts; Hon Rl; Ger Clb; Pom Pon; Twrlr; Pres Awd; College; Ecol.

BENNING, CAROLYN; Newton HS; Pleasant Hl, OH; 5/52 Band; Chrs; Hon Rl; Treas NHS; Sch Mus; Stg Crw; Drama Clb; 4-H; Fr Clb; FTA; Miami Univ; Elem Ed.

BENNINGHOFEN, FREDRICK; Heath HS; Heath, OH; 14/165 Band; Hon Rl; Jr NHS; NHS; Sch Pl; Stg Crw; Drama Clb; Spn Clb; Cntrl Oh Tech Coll; Real Estate Tech.

BENNINGTON, MICHELLE; Bridgeport HS; Bridgeport, OH; Am Leg Aux Girls St; Band; VP Chrs; Girl Scts; Hon Rl; Sch Mus; Sch Pl; Drama Clb; Sci Clb; Chorus Awd 1st Soprano; Directors Band Awd; West Liberty State Coll; Music.

BENNINGTON, PATRICIA; Shadyside HS; Shadyside, OH; Chrh Wkr; Hon Rl; Off Ade; Florist.

BENNITT, LINDA; Switzerland Cnty HS; Vevay, IN; 11/116 Trs Jr Cls; VP Sr Cls; NHS; Off Ade; Sch Pl; Yrbk; Drama Clb; Pres FHA; Pep Clb; Chrldng; Vincennes Univ; Fshn Mdse.

BENNY, BETH; Wapakoneta HS; Wapakoneta, OH; Band; Yth Flsp; Spn Clb; Ten; Ohio Nothern Univ; Law.

BENOY, DEBORAH; Lemon Monroe HS; Monroe, OH; 3/300 Treas Am Leg Aux Girls St; Chrs; Hon Rl; NHS; Sch Mus; Sch Pl; Rptr Yrbk; Sch Nwsp; Drama Clb; Letter Ten; Won Essay Contst On Energy Stewardshp & A Paid Expense Trip To UN Wash DC Study Seminr 79; Univ; Jrnlsm.

BENSCH, DONNA; Lutheran East HS; Detroit, MI; 32/125 Cls Rep Sr Cls; Band; Hon Rl; NHS; Stg Crw; Stu Cncl; Yth Flsp; Ed Yrbk; Sprt Ed Sch Nwsp; Drama Clb; Central Mic; Legal Assistant.

BENSCH, DONNA; Lutheran HS East; Detroit, MI; Band; Girl Scts; Hon Rl; NHS; Sch Mus; Stg Crw; Stu Cncl; Yth Flsp; Ed Yrbk; Sch Nwsp; Central Michigan Univ.

BENSINGER, DOUGLAS; St Johns HS; St Johns, MI; Hon Rl; Rptr Yrbk; VICA; IM Sprt; Voc Schl; Archt.

BENSLEY, ROBERT; Mt Pleasant HS; Mt Pleasant, MI; Boy Scts; Hon Rl; Letter Ftbl; Letter Wrstlng; IM Sprt; C of C Awd; Cit Awd; Western Michigan St Univ; Math.

BENSON, BETH; Salem Sr HS; Salem, OH; 1/270 Cls Rep Frsh Cls; Cls Rep Soph Cls; Cls Rep Sr Cls; Band; Hon Rl; NHS; Sch Mus; Stu Cncl; Pres Y-Teens; Mth Clb; Brooks Writing Awd; Marie Burns Music Awd; Univ; Med.

BENSON, DENNIS; Southridge HS; Huntngbrg, IN; Boy Scts; Chrs; FCA; Hon Rl; 4-H; Letter Ftbl; Letter Ten; Letter Wrstlng; Chrldng; Coach Actv; Indiana St Univ; Bus Admin.

BENSON, LORI; Madeira HS; Cincinnati, OH; 41/148 Trs Jr Cls; Trs Sr Cls; Cmnty Wkr; Hon Rl; Lbry Ade; Off Ade; Stg Crw; Stu Cncl; Sch Nwsp; Drama Clb; College; Spec Ed.

BENSON, MARJORIE; Jonesville HS; Jonesville, MI; Band; Chrh Wkr; Cmnty Wkr; Hon Rl; NHS; Sch Nwsp; Pep Clb; Jackson Cmnty Coll; Bus.

BENSON, MARK; Highland HS; Highland, IN; Chrh Wkr; Hon Rl; Sch Mus; VICA; Bsktbl; College; Engr.

BENSON, NEAL; Philip Barbour HS; Philippi, WV; Band; Hon Rl; Stg Crw; 4-H; Sci Clb; 4-H Awd; Univ.

BENSON, S; Grand Rapids Ctrl HS; Grand Rapids, MI; 5/440 Hon Rl; NHS; Rptr Sch Nwsp; Lat Clb; Ten; IM Sprt; Am Leg Awd; DAR Awd; Natl Merit Ltr; Grand Rapids Jr Coll; Forestry.

BENSON, SCOTT; Grand Rapids Central HS; Grand Rapids, MI; 5/411 Hon Rl; Pres NHS; Rptr Sch Nwsp; Lat Clb; Ten; DAR Awd; Elk Awd; Grand Rapids Jr Coll; Forestry.

BENSON, TAMMY; North Central Area HS; Powers, MI; 3/63 Band; Hon Rl; NHS; Orch; Yrbk; 4-H; 4-H Awd; Lions Of Michigan All State Band; John Philip Sousa Awd; Cnty 4 H Key Clb Awd; N Michigan Univ; Music.

BENSON, TRACY A; Richmond Sr HS; Richmond, IN; Chrh Wkr; Hon Rl; NHS; Y-Teens; Pep Clb; Spn Clb; Univ; Pharm.

BENTGEN, CATHIE; La Salle HS; St Ignace, MI; 14/103 Pres Frsh Cls; Band; Chrh Wkr; Hon Rl; NHS; Sch Pl; Stg Crw; Stu Cncl; Drama Clb; Pep Clb; Mich State Univ; Business Admin.

BENTLEY, JODY; Southwood HS; La Fontaine, IN; 4/119 Band; Chrs; Chrh Wkr; FCA; Hon Rl; Sec Natl Forn Lg; Sch Mus; VP Yth Flsp; Rptr Yrbk; Rptr Sch Nwsp; Outstndng Home Ec Stu 1977; 4 H Awds In Goat & Photography 1975; Indiana Bus Coll; Acctg.

BENTLEY, PATRICIA; Olentangy HS; Powell, OH; 4/150 Hon Rl; Certificates Of Honor; Cert Of Merit In French; Columbus Busns Univ; Acctg.

BENTON, CHERYL; Edwardsburg HS; Edwardsburg, MI; Band; Chrs; Hon Rl; Sch Mus; Trk; Pom Pon; Southwestern Mic.

BENTON, JOYCE; Jefferson Union HS; Toronto, OH; Chrs; Chrh Wkr; Girl Scts; Hon Rl; Yth Flsp; PPFtbl; College; Spec Ed.

BENTON, KAREN; Toronto HS; Toronto, OH; 5/119 Cmp Fr Grls; Chrs; Chrh Wkr; Hon Rl; Fr Clb; Am Leg Awd; Cit Awd; Oh Bd Of Regnts Oh Acad Schlshp Progr 79; Awd Of Distinction 79; Ohio Vly Hosp Schl Of Nursing; Nurse.

BENTON, LISA; Galion Sr HS; Galion, OH; Cls Rep Soph Cls; Girl Scts; Hon Rl; Off Ade; Stu Cncl; Socr; Trk; Chrldng; Mat Maids; Univ.

BENTON, SHARON; Cass Tech HS; Detroit, MI; Chrh Wkr; JA; Off Ade; OEA; Pres Of Local Chptr For BOEC & OEA 78; 1st In Prlmntry Pro On Regnl Level 79; Wayne St Univ; Bus Admin.

BENTZ, PATRICIA A; Central Catholic HS; Wheeling, WV; 3/132 Chrh Wkr; Cmnty Wkr; Hon Rl; NHS; Sch Mus; Sch Pl; Rptr Yrbk; Rptr Sch Nwsp; Drama Clb; Natl Merit SF; Univ; Wildlife Bio.

BENYA, SUZANNE; Normandy Sr HS; Parma, OH; 24/649 Cl Rep Jr Cls; Band; Chrh Wkr; Girl Scts; Hon Rl; Lbry Ade; Sec NHS; Spn Clb; Cit Awd; Membr Of Ntnl Spnsh Hnr Scty; Univ; Med Dietetics.

BENZ, MARSHA L; Dexter HS; Dexter, MI; VP Soph Cls; Hon Rl; NHS; Sch Nwsp; Drama Clb; Letter Trk; Chrldng; Mgrs; Univ; Music.

BENZENBOWER, DOROTHEA; Highland HS; Anderson, IN; 10/400 Chrh Wkr; Hon Rl; Hosp Ade; NHS; Lat Clb; Ball State Univ; Nursing.

BERAHA, ELLIOT I; Deer Park HS; Cincinnati, OH; VP Sr Cls; Band; Hon Rl; NHS; Ten; The Oh Coun Of Tchr Of Math 79; Number 1 Chess Player On Tm 76 80; Attended Operation Yth 79; Univ; Chem Engr.

BERARDUCCI, MARY; Benedictine HS; Detroit, MI; Cls Rep Frsh Cls; Cls Rep Soph Cls; Cl Rep Jr Cls; Cls Rep Sr Cls; Hon Rl; Stu Cncl; Letter Bsbl; Twrlr; Mercy College; Medical Field.

BERBERICH, MONIKA; Lexington HS; Lexington, OH; 39/250 Band; Chrh Wkr; Cmnty Wkr; Lbry Ade; Pol Wkr; Red Cr Ade; Y-Teens; Ger Clb; Trk; Chrldng; German Awd At Wooster Coll; Univ; Public Relations.

BERBERICK, BRAD; Shelby HS; Shelby, OH; Band; Chrs; Chrh Wkr; Cmnty Wkr; Hon Rl; Orch; College; Music.

BERCIUNAS, HAROLD; Ben Davis HS; Indianapolis, IN; Band; Chrh Wkr; FCA; Hon Rl; Mod UN; Pres Fr Clb; Bsktbl; Ftbl; Wrstlng; IM Sprt; Hon Cert Indianapolis Star 73; Ministry.

BERDEN, PETER; Cheboygan Cath HS; Cheboygan, MI; 9/35 Pres Frsh Cls; Cls Rep Soph Cls; Hon Rl; Sch Mus; Sch Pl; Stg Crw; Stu Cncl; Ed Yrbk; Drama Clb; Kiwan Awd; Ferris St Univ; Acctg.

BERDOVICH, TERESA; Mannington HS; Mannington, WV; 32/100 Chrs; Chrh Wkr; Hon Rl; Lbry Ade; Off Ade; Sch Mus; Mat Maids; Glenville St Univ; Educ.

BERELSMAN, JOAN; Delphos St Johns HS; Spencerville, OH; 27/138 Chrs; Cmnty Wkr; Hon Rl; NHS; Sch Pl; 4-H; FHA; IM Sprt; Dnfth Awd; 4-H Awd; Ohio St Univ; Fshn Mdse.

BERELSMAN, RONALD; St Johns HS; Spencervll, OH; 49/153 Band; Cmnty Wkr; Drm Mjrt; Hon Rl; Orch; 4-H; FFA; Crs Cntry; IM Sprt; 4-H Awd; Ohio State; Engineering.

BERENS, ARDYTH; Unity Christian HS; Jenison, MI; Band; Hon Rl; Yth Flsp; Yrbk; Drama Clb; Spn Clb; Chrldng; IM Sprt; Davenport College; Accnt.

BERENS, DIANA; Tuslaw HS; Massillon, OH; Chrs; Girl Scts; Hon Rl; JA; Off Ade; Sch Mus; Sch Pl; Stg Crw; FHA; Univ; Amer Hist.

BERENS, TOM; Zeeland HS; Zeeland, MI; Boy Scts; Ger Clb; Grand Valley Univ; Bio Sci.

BERES, JOHN; Newbury HS; Newbury, OH; Trs Jr Cls; Treas Chrs; Jr NHS; Sch Mus; Sch Pl; Drama Clb; Ger Clb; College; English.

BERES, KEVIN; Marquette HS; Michigan City, IN; 6/73 Am Leg Boys St; Hon Rl; NHS; Letter Bsbl; Bsktbl; Crs Cntry; Scr Kpr; Tmr; Univ; Bus Admin.

BEREZO, JACKIE; Girard HS; Girard, OH; 2/200 Sec NHS; Yrbk; Fr Clb; OEA; Trk; Capt Chrldng; GAA; Youngstown St Univ; Med Asst.

BERG, DEBBIE; Copley HS; Copley, OH; Chrs; Chrh Wkr; Girl Scts; Hon Rl; Hosp Ade; NHS; Sch Mus; Yth Flsp; Rptr Yrbk; Fr Clb; Hiram Coll; Eng.

BERG, MICHAEL; Shaker Heights HS; Shaker Hts, OH; Band; Hon Rl; Stu Cncl; Rptr Yrbk; Letter Bsbl; Letter Ftbl; Letter Hockey; Univ.

BERGADINE, MARTHA; Hartland HS; Brighton, MI; 1/254 Hon Rl; Lit Mag; VP NHS; Sch Pl; Rptr Yrbk; DECA; Drama Clb; 4-H; Mgrs; Natl Merit Schl; Univ Of Michigan; Bus Admin.

BERGAN, PAMELA; Eau Claire HS; Eau Claire, MI; Sec Frsh Cls; Cl Rep Jr Cls; FCA; Hon Rl; Stu Cncl; Pep Clb; Letter Trk; College; Liberal Arts.

BERGEN, KAREN; Marietta Sr HS; Marietta, OH; 1/400 Sec Sr Cls; Trs Sr Cls; AFS; Am Leg Aux Girls St; Band; Hon Rl; NHS; Off Ade; Sch Mus; Yth Flsp; Univ; Math.

BERGEN, SUSAN; Marietta Sr HS; Marietta, OH; 50/456 VP Frsh Cls; Am Leg Aux Girls St; Chrh Wkr; Hon Rl; Lbry Ade; NHS; Off Ade; Sch Mus; Sch Pl; Stg Crw; Ohio Univ; Acctg.

BERGER, HOLLY; Leetonia HS; Leetonia, OH; Band; Cmp Fr Grls; Chrs; Hon Rl; Orch; Sch Mus; Sch Pl; 4-H; Pep Clb; Gym; College; Med Sec.

BERGER, JANET; Fayetteville HS; Fayetteville, OH; Sec Soph Cls; Pres Jr Cls; Chrs; Sch Mus; Sch Pl; Yrbk; Bsbl; Southern St Univ; Music.

BERGER, JOAN; Fr Joseph Wehrle Memrl HS; Columbus, OH; 7/120 VP Frsh Cls; Pres Soph Cls; Pres Jr Cls; Hon Rl; Jr NHS; Stu Cncl; Opt Clb Awd; Univ Of Cincinnati; Nursing.

BERGER, JODEE; Little Miami HS; Morrow, OH; 18/280 VP Sr Cls; Am Leg Aux Girls St; Chrs; Chrh Wkr; Hon Rl; JA; NHS; Off Ade; Sch Mus; Rptr Yrbk; Jr Achievement Shclrshp 79; Ohio Music Educ Assoc 78; Univ; Eng.

BERGER, JOSEPH; Mott HS; Warren, MI; FCA; Hon Rl; Sct Actv; Capt Bsktbl; Capt Ftbl; Trk; Cit Awd; Opt Clb Awd; Michigan St Univ.

BERGER, L; Versailles HS; Yorkshire, OH; 48/130 Boy Scts; Letter Ftbl; Letter Trk; Hocking Technical Coll; Forestry.

BERGER, MARTIN; Lakeview HS; Battle Creek, MI; Boy Scts; Hon Rl; Sch Mus; Sch Pl; Stg Crw; Rdo Clb; Letter Ftbl; Letter Trk; Letter Wrstlng; Oakland Univ; Engr.

BERGER, TAMMY; Jasper HS; Jasper, IN; 42/289 Am Leg Aux Girls St; Cmp Fr Grls; NHS; 4-H; Pep Clb; Letter Bsktbl; Letter Trk; Coach Actv; GAA; Mgrs; College; Bus.

BERGER, WANDA A; North HS; Youngstown, OH; 1/100 Trs Soph Cls; VP Jr Cls; Drl Tm; Girl Scts; Hon Rl; Hosp Ade; Off Ade; Stu Cncl; Yth Flsp; Y-Teens; Trumball Memorial Hosp; Nursing.

BERGERON, ARTHUR; Lakeview HS; Stow, OH; Wrstlng; College; Acctg.

BERGERON, BOB; Bishop Luers HS; Ft Wayne, IN; Letter Chrs; Letter Hon Rl; Letter Bsbl; Bsktbl; Letter Ftbl; IM Sprt; Coll; Elem Educ.

BERGERS, LESLIE; Kenowa Hills HS; Grand Rapids, MI; Sec Soph Cls; Chrs; Sch Mus; Rptr Sch Nwsp; Chrldng; Mat Maids; Pom Pon; PPFtbl; Olivet Nazarene Coll.

BERGERT, DANIEL L; David Anderson HS; Lisbon, OH; 5/120 Aud/Vis; Band; Chrh Wkr; Hon Rl; NHS; Sch Mus; Sch Pl; Rptr Sch Nwsp; Sci Clb; Scr Kpr; Boys St Alternate 79; Indstrl Bowling League; Ohio St Univ; Engr.

BERGHAUS, JOHN; Lutheran HS; Parma, OH; Band; Chrs; Orch; Sch Mus; Sch Pl; Ftbl; Wrstlng; College; Horticulture.

BERGHOFF, JEFF; Bishop Dwenger HS; Ft Wayne, IN; Band; Chrh Wkr; Cmnty Wkr; Orch; Sch Mus; Stg Crw; Lippin Awd Band HS Honor 78; Partcpt In Coll Orchestra 78; Univ; Music.

BERGLER, DENISE; Finney HS; Detroit, MI; 3/254 Chrh Wkr; Hon Rl; Hosp Ade; NHS; Off Ade; Spn Clb; Cit Awd; Wayne State Univ; Med Tech.

BERGMAN, CATHERINE; Cardinal Stritch HS; Genoa, OH; Cls Rep Frsh Cls; VP Soph Cls; Trs Jr Cls; Pres Sr Cls; VP Sr Cls; Hon Rl; NHS; Sch Mus; Stu Cncl; 4-H; Mount St Joseph.

BERGMAN, DOUG; Tipton HS; Atlanta, IN; 1/190 Hon Rl; NHS; Letter Bsbl; Letter Bsktbl; Indiana Univ; Acctg.

BERGNER, PAMELA; Walled Lake Central Sr HS; Union Lake, MI; Aud/Vis; Hon Rl; Lbry Ade; Sci Clb; Univ; Law Enfrcmnt.

BERGSTROM, KURT; Kingsford HS; Iron Mtn, MI; Cmnty Wkr; FCA; Hon Rl; Letter Ftbl; Letter Glf; College; Electronics.

BERINGER, MITZI; Northwest HS; Indianapolis, IN; 78/452 Hon Rl; Quill & Scroll; Stu Cncl; Yrbk; Chrldng; IM Sprt; Scr Kpr; Kiwan Awd; Indiana Univ; R N.

BERISH, JAMES; Valley Forge HS; Parma Hgts, OH; 204/750 Hon Rl; Sci Clb; Univ; Real Estate.

BERKEMEIER, STEVE; Lumen Christi HS; Jackson, MI; Boy Scts; Chrh Wkr; Cmnty Wkr; Hon Rl; Lbry Ade; Red Cr Ade; Yth Flsp; 4-H; IM Sprt; Univ Of Dayton.

BERKEMER, ANGELA; Fort Frye HS; Beverly, OH; 3/129 Am Leg Aux Girls St; Hon Rl; NHS; Quill & Scroll; Rptr Yrbk; Ed Sch Nwsp; Rptr Sch Nwsp; FHA; Treas FTA; Elizabeth Shaw Schlrshp; Outstanding English Awd; Hocking Tech Coll; Acctg.

BERKENKEMPER, MITCH; Webster County HS; Webster Sprgs, WV; 19/122 Hon Rl; Sch Pl; Yth Flsp; Pres 4-H; Bsktbl; Letter Wrstlng; 4-H Awd; Ribbons Won In Cntry Show 78; 4 H Conservation Awrd 79; 4 H Project Ribbons 70 78; Potomac St Coll; Med.

BERKEY, DAVID; St Marys Ctrl Catholic HS; Sandusky, OH; Boy Scts; Wrstlng; Vocational School.

BERLAGE, VICTOR J; Purcell HS; Cincinnati, OH; Cls Rep Soph Cls; VP Jr Cls; Boy Scts; Hon Rl; Mod UN; Stu Cncl; Mth Clb; IM Sprt; College.

BERLEKAMP, JOHN; Columbian HS; Tiffin, OH; Aud/Vis; Band; Rdo Clb; College; Electronics.

BERMAN, LEE; North HS; Columbus, OH; 23/335 Am Leg Boys St; Band; Hon Rl; Jr NHS; NHS; Orch; Pres Lat Clb; Trk; Capt Wrstlng; Am Leg Awd; Ohio St Univ; Engr.

BERMAN, ROBERT; Bishop Watterson HS; Columbus, OH; Band; Boy Scts; Hon Rl; NHS; Sch Mus; Sct Actv; Cert Of NEDT; MIT; Comp Design.

BERNABEI, ALVISE; Bishop Gallagher HS; Harper Wds, MI; 22/333 Cls Rep Frsh Cls; Cl Rep Jr Cls; Hon Rl; Letter Socr; Letter Ten; IM Sprt; Univ Of Michigan; Chem.

BERNADETTE, JONES; Bishop Noll Inst; Highland, IN; Chrs; Sch Mus; Stg Crw; Drama Clb; 4-H; Mat Maids; 4-H Awd; Ind Univ; Communications.

BERNARD, DEAN; Boardman HS; Youngstown, OH; Cmnty Wkr; Hon Rl; Am Leg Awd; Youngstown St Univ; Poli Sci.

BERNARD, EILEEN; Franklin HS; Livonia, MI; Chrs; Chrh Wkr; Hon Rl; Orch; Sch Mus; Yth Flsp; Ed Yrbk; Cit Awd; Univ; Comp Sci.

BERNARD, ELIZABETH; Liberty HS; Youngstown, OH; Pres Jr Cls; Drl Tm; Pol Wkr; Pres Stu Cncl; VP Lat Clb; Gym; Capt Chrldng; Am Leg Awd; Rotary Awd; Univ; Econ.

BERNARD, JEAN A; Andrean HS; Gary, IN; Chrh Wkr; JA; Fr Clb; Mth Clb; Letter Ftbl; Trk; Marian Coll; Chem.

BERNARD, LINDA; Bishop Watterson HS; Columbus, OH; Cmnty Wkr; Hon Rl; Rptr Yrbk; Sch Nwsp; Bsktbl; Coach Actv; IM Sprt; PPFtbl; Pres Awd; Ohio St Univ; Food Tech.

BERNARD, LISA; Fairview HS; Fairview Park, OH; 165/268 Girl Scts; Hon Rl; NHS; Rptr Yrbk; Rptr Sch Nwsp; Letter Swmmng; Scr Kpr; Univ; Law.

BERNARD, RICHARD J; Eastlake North HS; Eastlake, OH; Cls Rep Frsh Cls; Am Leg Boys St; Hon Rl; Off Ade; Sch Pl; Stu Cncl; Spn Clb; Letter Bsktbl; Letter Ftbl; Cit Awd; Univ; Bio.

BERNARDINELLI, JIM; Ursuline HS; Youngstown, OH; 32/292 Cmnty Wkr; Hon Rl; NHS; Sch Nwsp; Bsktbl; IM Sprt; Scr Kpr; Tmr; Youngstown St Univ; CPA.

BERNARDINI, MARY; Orchard View HS; Muskegon, MI; 1/225 Band; Hon Rl; NHS; Letter Trk; PPFtbl; Univ.

BERNATH, LAURA; Stryker HS; Stryker, OH; Sec Jr Cls; Am Leg Aux Girls St; Chrs; Hon Rl; Bsktbl; Bus Schl; Acctg.

BERNATH, SUSAN; Ovid Elsie HS; Ovid, MI; Hon Rl; FHA; PPFtbl; College; Tchr.

BERNDT, DEBRA; Merrillville HS; Hobart, IN; 65/604 Chrs; Hon Rl; Hosp Ade; Sprt Ed Sch Nwsp; Bsktbl; Letter Ten; Trk; Chrldng; Coach Actv; Capt PPFtbl; Miss Teen Indiana Pageant; Sftbl St Champs Pitcher; Valparaiso Univ; Educ.

BERNER, DEBRA; Switzerland Cnty Jr Sr HS; Cross Plains, IN; 1/118 Band; Hon Rl; MMM; NHS; 4-H; Pep Clb; Spn Clb; Letter Bsktbl; Letter Trk; Scr Kpr; Hanover Coll; Math.

BERNER, DOUGLAS; Bishop Foley HS; Madison Hts, MI; Boy Scts; Hon Rl; IM Sprt; Wayne State; Eng.

BERNER, PATRICIA; Niles HS; Niles, MI; 32/388 Hon Rl; NHS; Off Ade; Ten; Letter Trk; Letter Chrldng; Purdue Univ; Nursing.

BERNET, ANNE; Archbishop Alter HS; Dayton, OH; 7/290 Cls Rep Frsh Cls; Cls Rep Soph Cls; Cl Rep Jr Cls; Band; Hon Rl; NHS; Orch; Sch Mus; Stu Cncl; GAA; Univ; Bio.

BERNICKE, JEANNE; Napoleon HS; Napoleon, OH; 17/300 Band; Chrs; Drm Mjrt; Girl Scts; Hon Rl; Jr NHS; NHS; 4-H; Lat Clb; Gym; Bowling Green St Univ; Acctg.

BERNIER, LYNNE; St Alphonsus HS; Dearborn, MI; Cls Rep Frsh Cls; Sec Soph Cls; Sec Jr Cls; Sec Sr Cls; Chrs; Hon Rl; Stg Crw; Pep Clb; Letter Bsktbl; Chrldng; Univ.

BERNOCCO, THERESA; Divine Child HS; Dearborn, MI; Cmp Fr Grls; Chrs; Chrh Wkr; Girl Scts; JA; Lbry Ade; Sct Actv; Pep Clb; Spn Clb; Detroit Bus Schl; Sec.

BERNOSKY, DAVE; Watterson HS; Columbus, OH; Trs Jr Cls; Cl Rep Jr Cls; Stu Cncl; Sch Nwsp; Natl Merit Ltr; Schl Awd; Ohio St Univ; Geology.

BERNTHISEL, JEFFREY; Otsego HS; Bowling Grn, OH; Cls Rep Frsh Cls; Cls Rep Soph Cls; Cl Rep Jr Cls; Cls Rep Sr Cls; Am Leg Boys St; Boy Scts; Hon Rl; NHS; Sct Actv; Stu Cncl; Bowling Green St Univ; Bus Admin.

BEROLATTI, TINA; Lake Shore HS; St Clair Shores, MI; 1/588 Hon Rl; NHS; Off Ade; PAVAS; Sch Mus; Sch Pl; Stg Crw; Drama Clb; Chrldng; Wayne St Univ.

BEROS, SVETLANA; Euclid Sr HS; Euclid, OH; 47/747 Cls Rep Frsh Cls; Cls Rep Soph Cls; Cl Rep Jr Cls; Cls Rep Sr Cls; Chrs; Chrh Wkr; Cmnty Wkr; Hon Rl; NHS; Quill & Scroll; Coll; Law.

BEROSKE, KRISTIN; Evergreen HS; Delta, OH; Pres Sr Cls; Am Leg Aux Girls St; Sec Chrh Wkr; Hon Rl; NHS; Treas Leo Clb; Letter Trk; GAA; Pom Pon; Bowling Green St Univ.

BERQUIST, SUSAN; Jackson HS; Massillon, OH; 5/409 Band; Girl Scts; Hon Rl; NHS; Orch; Sch Mus; Sct Actv; Yth Flsp; Y-Teens; Treas Fr Clb; H C Sauder Awd For Most Outstndng Jr Bandsman; Januarys Teen Of The Month For The Massillon Independent; Bowling Green St Univ; Music.

BERRELEZ, DAVID; St Hedwig HS; Detroit, MI; Cls Rep Soph Cls; VP Jr Cls; Hon Rl; Stu Cncl; Pep Clb; Bsbl; Ftbl; Univ Of Michigan; Brdcstng.

BERRES, GLORIA; Delphos St Johns HS; Delphos, OH; Hon Rl; Ed Yrbk; 4-H; Treas FTA; IM Sprt; Scr Kpr; Tech College; Dental.

BERREY, SARA; North Canton Hoover HS; North Canton, OH; Am Leg Aux Girls St; Band; Boy Scts; Chrh Wkr; Hon Rl; Off Ade; Sct Actv; Yth Flsp; Rptr Sch Nwsp; Fr Clb; Univ; Phys Ther.

BERRODIN, NANCI; Pioneer HS; Ann Arbor, MI; Cl Rep Jr Cls; Cls Rep Sr Cls; Sec Band; Girl Scts; Hosp Ade; Treas Stu Cncl; Ger Clb; Letter Trk; Capt Chrldng; DAR Awd; Univ Of Colorado; Psych.

BERRY, ALLISON; Mc Kinley Sr HS; Canton, OH; Am Leg Aux Girls St; Hon Rl; NHS; Sprt Ed Yrbk; Spn Clb; Capt Swmmng; Chrldng; Am Leg Awd; Spanish Hnr Soc; Hmcmng Ct Bsktbl; Ohio St Univ.

BERRY, BONNIE K; Midland Trail HS; Danese, WV; Pres Jr Cls; Hon Rl; Sch Nwsp; Fr Clb; Pep Clb; Chrldng; PPFtbl; Scr Kpr; Soph Attnd To Homecoming Queen 77; West Virginia Univ; Psych.

BERRY, BRONWYN; Harper Creek HS; Battle Creek, MI; 44/240 Band; Drl Tm; Girl Scts; Hon Rl; NHS; 4-H; Spn Clb; Gym; Swmmng; Pom Pon; Daemen Coll; Med Rec Admin.

BERRY, CAROLYN; Highland HS; Wadsworth, OH; 38/202 Cls Rep Frsh Cls; Cls Rep Soph Cls; Chrs; Chrh Wkr; Cmnty Wkr; Chrh Wkr; NHS; Off Ade; Quill & Scroll; Stu Cncl; Univ Of Cincinnati; Nursing.

BERRY, CINDY; Berea HS; Berea, OH; Cls Rep Frsh Cls; Cl Rep Jr Cls; Chrs; Girl Scts; Hon Rl; Off Ade; Sct Actv; Stu Cncl; Drama Clb; Pep Clb; Most Valuable Swimmer Longbrooke Swim Team; Most Valuable Swimmer Country Club; Univ Of N Carolina; Psych.

BERRY, DANIEL; Trenton HS; Trenton, MI; Boy Scts; Hon Rl; NHS; Swmmng; IM Sprt; Univ Of Michigan; Aeronautical Engr.

BERRY, DAWN; Milan HS; Milan, MI; Cls Rep Frsh Cls; Cls Rep Soph Cls; Band; Hon Rl; Off Ade; Stu Cncl; 4-H; Swmmng; Trk; GAA; 2 Time St Finshr In Cls B St Swimmng 78; Steven Gustin Memrl Fund Band Schslhp 79; Dist & St Ban I Rtng 79; Univ; Phys Ther.

BERRY, DENA; Groveport Madison Sr HS; Columbus, OH; Cmp Fr Grls; Chrh Wkr; Hon Rl; Fr Clb; IM Sprt; Liberty Baptist Coll; Bio.

BERRY, DONNA; Washington HS; Washington, IN; Band; Chrh Wkr; Cmnty Wkr; Off Ade; Yth Flsp; Pep Clb; Vincennes Beauty College; Beautician.

BERRY, DWIGHT; Gladwin HS; Gladwin, MI; Cls Rep Frsh Cls; Cls Rep Soph Cls; Cl Rep Jr Cls; Chrh Wkr; Hon Rl; Stu Cncl; Rptr Yrbk; Rptr Sch Nwsp; Bsktbl; Ftbl; Rets Elec Schl; Comp.

BERRY, JAMES; Mc Kinley HS; Sebring, OH; 4/81 Pres Soph Cls; Am Leg Boys St; Hon Rl; Rptr Sch Nwsp; Pep Clb; Bsktbl; IM Sprt; Voice Dem Awd; Univ; Acctg.

BERRY, JOYCE; Cody HS; Detroit, MI; Aud/Vis; Hon Rl; Lbry Ade; Off Ade; Stg Crw; Stu Cncl; OEA; Stateswoman Awd 1979; Detroit Coll Of Bus; Leg Sec.

BERRY, LAURA; Hillsdale HS; Hillsdale, MI; 2/192 Sal; Band; Hon Rl; NHS; Orch; 4-H; FFA; 4-H Awd; Michigan St Univ; Agri.

BERRY, MARIANNE; East Canton HS; E Canton, OH; Am Leg Aux Girls St; Band; Chrs; Hon Rl; Jr NHS; Lbry Ade; NHS; 4-H; Fr Clb; FTA; Univ; Med Asst.

BERRY, MIKE; Norwalk HS; Norwalk, OH; Boy Scts; Chrh Wkr; FCA; Hon Rl; Sct Actv; Yth Flsp; 4-H; Bsbl; Bsktbl; Ftbl; College; Bus Acctg.

BERRY, PHILIP; Loy Norrix HS; Kalamazoo, MI; Cls Rep Frsh Cls; Trk; IM Sprt; Natl Merit Ltr; College.

BERRY, REBECCA A; Norwalk HS; Norwalk, OH; Chrs; Drl Tm; Hon Rl; Off Ade; Rptr Sch Nwsp; Sch Nwsp; Lat Clb; GAA; Mgrs; Univ.

BERRY, SUSAN; Marion Adams HS; Sheridan, IN; 17/99 Sec Frsh Cls; Sec Jr Cls; Hon Rl; Jr NHS; Pep Clb; Chrldng; Twrlr; Univ; Tchr.

BERRY, SUZETTE; East Kentwood HS; Kentwood, MI; Pres Soph Cls; Debate Tm; Hon Rl; NHS; Capt Ten; General Motore Institute; Mech Engr.

BERRY, TERRI LYNNE; Licking Valley HS; Newark, OH; 1/158 Cl Rep Jr Cls; Val; Capt Band; Chrs; Chrh Wkr; Hon Rl; VP NHS; Y-Teens; Ed Yrbk; Rptr Sch Nwsp; Camp Enterprize Rep 1978; Central Ohio Tech Coll; Admin Sec.

BERRY, VALGENIA; Princeton Community HS; Princeton, IN; 28/222 Band; Cmp Fr Grls; Chrs; Chrh Wkr; Sec FCA; Hosp Ade; NHS; Off Ade; Orch; Sch Mus; St Schlshp 79; Hoosier Schlr Awd 79; Indiana St Univ; Math.

BERRYHILL, PATRICIA; Onekama HS; Manistee, MI; Cls Rep Frsh Cls; Cls Rep Soph Cls; Pres Jr Cls; Band; Hon Rl; Sch Pl; Pres Stu Cncl; Drama Clb; FHA; Letter Bsktbl; Univ; Nursing.

BERRYMAN, BRADLEY; Standish Sterling Cntrl HS; Alger, MI; 25/150 Hon Rl; ROTC; Letter Ftbl; Letter Trk; Central Michigan Univ; Busns.

BERRYMAN, DEBBIE; Rosedale HS; Terre Haute, IN; Girl Scts; Drama Clb; Indiana Univ; Medicine.

BERSINGER, SUZANNE; Galion HS; Galion, OH; Chrs; Hon Rl; Hosp Ade; Yth Flsp; Letter Swmmng; Mt Vernon Nazarene Coll; Nursing.

BERT, TAMMY; Sebring Mc Kinley HS; Sebring, OH; 7/76 Am Leg Aux Girls St; Band; Chrs; Hon Rl; Sec NHS; Y-Teens; Rptr Yrbk; Trk; Chrldng; Rotary Awd; Awd For Quill & Scroll 78 79; Music Dir For Church 78 79; Graceland Coll; Sci.

BERTINI, WILLIAM J; John Glenn HS; New Concord, OH; 8/188 Hon Rl; NHS; Bsbl; Ftbl; College.

BERTKE, MARY; Marion Local HS; Maria Stein, OH; Hon Rl; Pep Clb; Sci Clb; Letter Bsktbl; IM Sprt; Bus Schl; Sec.

BERTLING, WILLIAM M; Clarkston HS; Clarkston, MI; Chrh Wkr; Cmnty Wkr; Hon Rl; Hosp Ade; Univ; Med.

BERTOLDI, PAUL; Kingsford HS; Kingsford, MI; Hon Rl; Jr NHS; NHS; Letter Bsktbl; Letter Ftbl; Univ; Bus Admin.

BERTOLDO, JEFF; Shawnee HS; Lima, OH; 5/246 Am Leg Boys St; Boy Scts; Chrs; NHS; Sct Actv; Fr Clb; Letter Swmmng; Brigham Young Univ; Zoology.

BERTOLINI, LAWRENCE E; Niles Mc Kinley HS; Niles, OH; Hon Rl; NHS; Red Cr Ade; Sci Clb; Univ.

BERTOLINO, SHARON; Buckeye W HS; Adena, OH; Pres Frsh Cls; Sec Jr Cls; Am Leg Aux Girls St; Band; Chrs; Hon Rl; Off Ade; Sch Nwsp; 4-H; FHA; Belmont Tech Coll; Comp Prog.

BERTOLONE, ANNE; Fairmont West HS; Kettering, OH; Cls Rep Sr Cls; Off Ade; Stu Cncl; Y-Teens; Chrldng; Univ; Bio.

BERTRAM, CHUCK; Mooresville HS; Mooresville, IN; 47/269 Hon Rl; Jr NHS; Sch Pl; DECA; Drama Clb; Ger Clb; Voc Schl; Elec.

BERTRAM, RANDAL; George Washington HS; Charleston, WV; Band; Chrs; Chrh Wkr; Hon Rl; Univ Of Kentucky; Elec Engr.

BERTSCH, KRISTINA; Lacrosse HS; Wanatah, IN; NHS; Yth Flsp; Ger Clb; Armed Forces.

BERTSCH, SUSAN; Central Cath HS; Canton, OH; Hon Rl; Rptr Yrbk; The Ohio St Univ; Indus Dsgn.

BERTSCHE, KAREN; Woodlan HS; Woodburn, IN; 4/150 Cl Rep Jr Cls; Sec Chrh Wkr; Hon Rl; PAVAS; Sch Mus; Drama Clb; FHA; Purdue Univ; Nuclear Engr.

BERTSCHY, LUANN; Mannington HS; Mannington, WV; Band; Hon Rl; NHS; Pres Yth Flsp; FHA; FTA; Trk; IM Sprt; College; Bio.

BERTZ, BRENDA J; Napoleon HS; Napoleon, OH; Cmnty Wkr; Hon Rl; Yth Flsp; Swmmng; Tmr; Univ; Comp Sci.

BERUS, LISA; Green HS; Akron, OH; Cls Rep Frsh Cls; Cls Rep Soph Cls; Sec Jr Cls; Cl Rep Jr Cls; Band; Chrs; Girl Scts; Hon Rl; Mdrgl; NHS; Univ.

BERWALD, KATHY; A D Johnston HS; Bessemer, MI; 3/85 Trs Frsh Cls; Sec Soph Cls; VP Jr Cls; VP Sr Cls; Hon Rl; Rptr Yrbk; Rptr Sch Nwsp; Letter Bsktbl; PPFtbl; VFW Awd; Ferris St Coll; Med Tech.

BERWELD, KIRT; Grand Ledge HS; Grnd Ldg, MI; Hon Rl; Lbry Ade; Rptr Yrbk; Spn Clb; Bsktbl; Letter Glf; Michigan St Univ; Chem Engr.

BERZONSKY, BARTHOLOMEW; Normandy HS; Seven Hills, OH; 10/649 Cl Rep Jr Cls; Hon Rl; Fr Clb; Univ; Music.

BESCH, JOHN; Marion Harding HS; Marion, OH; 1/475 Band; Orch; Sch Mus; Stu Cncl; Letter Bsbl; Natl Merit Ltr; College; Comp Sci.

BESEMER, DAVE; Algonac HS; Harsens Is, MI; Pres Soph Cls; Pres Jr Cls; Pres Sr Cls; Band; Hon Rl; NHS; Stu Cncl; Bsktbl; Glf; Ten; Univ; Law.

BESHARA, HELEN; Canfield HS; Canfield, OH; 38/258 Chrs; Girl Scts; Hon Rl; Lit Mag; Natl Forn Lg; Sch Mus; Sch Pl; Stg Crw; Y-Teens; Rptr Sch Nwsp; 1st Pl YSU Eng Fest Crestv Wrtng 79; Radcliffe Univ; Pre Med.

BESS, MIKE; Henry Ford Ii HS; Sterling Hts, MI; Chrh Wkr; Cmnty Wkr; Yth Flsp; Scr Kpr; Voc Schl; Automotive.

BESSOLO, MARY; Calumet HS; Ahmeek, MI; VP Frsh Cls; VP Soph Cls; Band; Cmp Fr Grls; Chrh Wkr; Hon Rl; NHS; Off Ade; Gogebic Comm College; Ct Reporting.

BEST, ALLAN; Portage Central HS; Portage, MI; Band; Chrh Wkr; Hon Rl; Socr; IM Sprt; Grand Rapids Baptist College; Aviati.

BEST, ANNETTE; Lapeer East HS; Lapeer, MI; Cls Rep Soph Cls; Cl Rep Jr Cls; Hon Rl; Off Ade; Stu Cncl; Pep Clb; Bsktbl; PPFtbl; Univ.

BEST, CARL; Edgewood HS; Ashtabula, OH; Yrbk; Sch Nwsp; Capt Crs Cntry; Capt Trk; Capt Wrstlng; Kent State Univ; Engr.

BEST, DIANA; Mackenzie HS; Detroit, MI; 7/350 Hon Rl; NHS; Detroit College Of Bus; Exec Sec.

BEST, KATHY L; Marietta Sr HS; Marietta, OH; 3/324 Chrs; Chrh Wkr; Hon Rl; NHS; Off Ade; Sch Pl; Drama Clb; VP OEA; Diplomat Awd In OEA 79; Gregg Typing Awd For Typing 50 WPM 79; Parkersburg Cmnty Coll; Bus.

BEST, LORI; Carroll HS; Bringhurst, IN; 47/101 Band; Hosp Ade; Off Ade; Stg Crw; 4-H; Pep Clb; PPFtbl; Scr Kpr; Tmr; Ivy Tech; Nurse.

BEST, MARIE; Marian HS; Birmingham, MI; Cls Rep Frsh Cls; Cls Rep Soph Cls; Cl Rep Jr Cls; Trs Sr Cls; Hon Rl; NHS; Letter Bsbl; Univ Of Michigan; Engr.

BEST, MATTHEW T; Steubenville Catholic HS; Jewett, OH; Chrs; Chrh Wkr; Hon Rl; NHS; 4-H; Sci Clb; Spn Clb; 4-H Awd; Ohio State Univ; Agricultural Engr.

BEST, RANDY; Upper Sandusky HS; Upper Sandusky, OH; Hon Rl; Business School; Managment.

BETEL, AARON; Southfield Lathrup HS; Southfield, MI; Debate Tm; Hon Rl; Lbry Ade; Treas Mod UN; Natl Merit SF; Univ; Pre Med.

BETEMPS, BEV; Withrow HS; Cincinnati, OH; Band; Girl Scts; Hon Rl; Jr NHS; NHS; Sch Mus; Yth Flsp; College.

BETHEL, KAREN J; Huntington HS; Chillicothe, OH; Chrh Wkr; Hon Rl; Lbry Ade; NHS; VP 4-H; OEA; Mgrs;.

BETHEL, KIMBERLY J; Huntington HS; Chillicothe, OH; 10/93 Am Leg Aux Girls St; Band; Pres Fr Clb; VP FTA; Pep Clb; Mgrs; HS Majorette 4 Yr 76; Seal Of Ohio Bnd 2 Yr 78; Won Ross Cnty Spelling Bee 11th In St Competition 76; Univ; Soc Serv.

BETHEL, STEVE; Hanover Horton HS; Horton, MI; 5/110 Cl Rep Jr Cls; Boy Scts; Hon Rl; Jr NHS; VP NHS; Sct Actv; Stu Cncl; Letter Ftbl; Letter Trk; Coach Actv; Jackson Cmnty Coll; Engr.

BETHKE, CARRIE; Pioneer HS; Ann Arbor, MI; Band; Chrh Wkr; Girl Scts; Yth Flsp; Ger Clb; Letter Gym; PPFtbl; Natl Merit Ltr; Univ; Bus Mgmt.

BETKER, MICHAELEEN; Theodore Roosevelt HS; Wyandotte, MI; 10/425 Band; Drm Bgl; Hon Rl; NHS; Orch; Sch Mus; E Michigan Univ; Acctg.

BETLER, ANNA; Buckhannon Upshur HS; Buckhannon, WV; Band; Hon Rl; NHS; Sch Mus; Stu Cncl; Pres Pep Clb; IM Sprt; Twrlr; Wv Univ; Interior Design.

BETLER, BRUCE; Pickens HS; Helvetia, WV; 1/11 Pres Frsh Cls; Cls Rep Soph Cls; VP Jr Cls; Hon Rl; NHS; Sch Pl; Drama Clb; 4-H; Bsktbl; IM Sprt; Notre Dame Univ; Theology.

BETLEY, RICK; Padua Franciscan HS; Parma, OH; Chrh Wkr; Hon Rl; JA; Mth Clb; Sci Clb; IM Sprt; JA Awd; Kent St Univ; Bus.

BETO, MICHELE; Notre Dame HS; Clarksburg, WV; Chrs; Chrh Wkr; Cmnty Wkr; Off Ade; Yrbk; Mth Clb; Pep Clb; Sci Clb; Twrlr; 1st Plc In Sci Fair Winner 76; West Virginia Univ.

BETONTE, AMY; Harbor HS; Ashtabula, OH; Cls Rep Soph Cls; Cl Rep Jr Cls; AFS; Debate Tm; Lit Mag; Off Ade; PAVAS; Sch Mus; Sch Pl; Stg Crw; Bus.

BETTE, KATHRYN; Bishop Gallagher HS; Detroit, MI; Hon Rl; Rptr Sch Nwsp; Sci Clb; Univ.

BETTEN, DIANE; Zeeland HS; Zeeland, MI; Chrh Wkr; Girl Scts; Hon Rl; Lbry Ade; Sch Pl; Stg Crw; Yth Flsp; 4-H; Letter Ten; IM Sprt; Bus Schl.

BETTER, WILLIAM E; Western Reserve Academy; Warren, OH; Cmnty Wkr; Yrbk; Sch Nwsp; Letter Bsbl; Letter Bsktbl; Letter Socr; Pres Phys Awd 74 75 76; Univ; Engr.

BETTERLY, TERESA; Dansville HS; Webberville, MI; Band; Hon Rl; Off Ade; Yth Flsp; 4-H; FHA; Letter Bsktbl; 4-H Awd; College; Nursing.

BETTERS, REBECCA; Gods Bible School; Fairbanks, AK; 4/40 Chrs; Chrh Wkr; Hon Rl; Sch Pl; Yrbk; Highest Grade Point Avg 76; Univ; Educ.

BETTGE, ELISABETH; Cloverdale HS; Cloverdale, IN; 2/105 Hon Rl; Hosp Ade; Orch; Sch Mus; Rptr Yrbk; Ed Sch Nwsp; Fr Clb; VP Sci Clb; Mat Maids; Ind Central Univ.

BETTINGER, KATE; Alter HS; Kettering, OH; Cls Rep Frsh Cls; Cls Rep Soph Cls; Cl Rep Jr Cls; Cls Rep Sr Cls; Chrh Wkr; FCA; Hon Rl; Stu Cncl; Yth Flsp; Gym; Miami Univ; Soc Psych.

BETTINGER, MARY; Benjamin Logan HS; Zanesfield, OH; 15/153 Am Leg Aux Girls St; Chrs; Girl Scts; Hon Rl; NHS; Sch Mus; Sch Pl; Sct Actv; 4-H; VP FHA; Ohio St Univ.

BETTINGER, WALT; Ada HS; Ada, OH; Hon Rl; NHS; Sch Pl; Sprt Ed Sch Nwsp; Spn Clb; Glf; Delta State Univ;.

BETTROSS, MARY LOUISE; Mahoning County Jnt Voc HS; Campbell, OH; Band; Girl Scts; OEA; Ohio Regnl Cmptn 1st 1979; Ohio St Compt 7th Acctg 1979; Univ; Acctg.

BETTS, BRENDA; Ovid Elsie HS; Elsie, MI; Am Leg Aux Girls St; Hon Rl; Pom Pon; Business School; Business.

BETTS, DAVID; Watkins Memorial HS; Pataskala, OH; 116/226 Band; Boy Scts; 4-H; FFA; De Kalb Ag Awd 1979; Outstndg Mbr Ffa 1979; 1st Pl Sheep Breedrs Awd 1979; Ohio St Univ; Animal Sci.

BETTS, JEANETTE; Holly HS; Holly, MI; 8/272 Hon Rl; Jr NHS; Lbry Ade; NHS; Red Cr Ade; Rptr Sch Nwsp; IM Sprt; PPFtbl; Photog.

BETTS, KATHRYN; Vinton Cnty HS; Mc Arthur, OH; Chrs; Chrh Wkr; Girl Scts; VP Stu Cncl; Yth Flsp; 4-H; Lat Clb; Spn Clb; Trk; PPFtbl;.

BETTS, MARLIN; Gods Bible HS; Beulah Hts, KY; Band; Chrs; Chrh Wkr; Hon Rl; DAR Awd; Gods Bible Schl.

BETTS, SUE; John Glenn HS; New Concord, OH; 5/193 Hon Rl; NHS; Sec Yth Flsp; Y-Teens; Sec 4-H; FFA; Voice Dem Awd; Ohio State Univ; Agriculture.

BETZ, ALAN; Ovid Elsie HS; Bannister, MI; Band; Boy Scts; Hon Rl;.

BETZ, MICHELLE; Argos Community HS; Plymouth, IN; Girl Scts; Hon Rl; FHA; Pep Clb; Business School; Sec.

BETZ, SHARON; Washington HS; Massillon, OH; Cls Rep Frsh Cls; Hon Rl; Off Ade; Sch Pl; Stg Crw; Yth Flsp; Rptr Sch Nwsp; Sch Nwsp; Drama Clb; Pep Clb; College; Journalism.

BETZ, THOMAS; North Canton Hoover HS; North Canton, OH; 42/425 Boy Scts; FCA; Hon Rl; Jr NHS; NHS; Sct Actv; Stu Cncl; Letter Ftbl; Capt Trk; Wrstlng; Cincinnati Univ; Nuclear Engr.

BEUCLER, PAM; Liberty Benton HS; Findlay, OH; Band; Hon Rl; NHS; Off Ade; Yth Flsp; Rptr Yrbk; Capt Chrldng; Stautzenburger Coll; Sec.

BEUKE, SANDI; Shortridge HS; Indianapolis, IN; Cls Rep Frsh Cls; Cls Rep Soph Cls; Cl Rep Jr Cls; Girl Scts; Hon Rl; Sch Pl; Ger Clb; Key Clb; Chrldng; Cit Awd; Butler Univ; Bus.

BEUTE, KAREN; Byron Center HS; Byron Center, MI; 8/140 Band; Hon Rl; Ger Clb; Grand Rapids Jr College; Rad Tech.

BEUTNER, THOMAS; Marquette HS; Michigan City, IN; Boy Scts; Hon Rl; Mth Clb; Sci Clb; Crs Cntry; Am Leg Awd; Cit Awd; DAR Awd; JETS Awd; Lion Awd; Univ.

BEUTTER, ELIZABETH; Penn HS; S Bend, IN; 103/486 Trs Sr Cls; Band; Cmp Fr Grls; Hon Rl; Stu Cncl; 4-H; Ger Clb; Swmmng; Trk; Pom Pon; Lions Club Yth Ambassador To Germany 79; Indiana Univ; Acctg.

BEUTTER, LORI; Mishawaka HS; Mishawaka, IN; 30/358 Cls Rep Frsh Cls; Cl Rep Jr Cls; Cls Rep Sr Cls; FCA; Hon Rl; NHS; Stu Cncl; Ball State Univ; Physical Ed.

BEVANS, BARBARA; Cadillac HS; Cadillac, MI; Band; Girl Scts; Hon Rl; Red Cr Ade; PPFtbl; College; Dog Trainer For Blind.

BEVER, KELLY; Covington HS; Covington, IN; 3/120 VP Band; Girl Scts; Hon Rl; Off Ade; Sch Pl; Pres Stu Cncl; Pres Yth Flsp; Drama Clb; Fr Clb; VP Pep Clb; Purdue Univ; Pre Med.

BEVER, KELLY L; Covington HS; Covington, IN; 3/120 VP Band; Hon Rl; Sch Mus; Sch Pl; Pres Stu Cncl; Yth Flsp; Drama Clb; Fr Clb; Pres Pep Clb; GAA; Coll; Medicine.

BEVERAGE, LAYTON H; Pocahontas Cnty HS; Marlinton, WV; 6/116 Pres Soph Cls; Pres Jr Cls; NHS; Yth Flsp; Drama Clb; 4-H; FFA; Bsktbl; Dnfth Awd; Voice Dem Awd; Univ; Law.

BEVERIDGE, KIMBERLY; Niles Mckinley HS; Niles, OH; 12/420 Chrs; Hon Rl; Mdrgl; NHS; Red Cr Ade; Sch Mus; Yrbk; Drama Clb; Chrldng; GAA; College.

BEVERLEY, JONI; Fayetteville HS; Fayetteville, WV; 32/88 VP Frsh Cls; VP Soph Cls; Cl Rep Jr Cls; Cls Rep Sr Cls; Sch Pl; Stg Crw; Stu Cncl; Drama Clb; VP Pep Clb; Spn Clb; W Virginia Tech Univ; Med Tech.

BEVERLY, CHERI; Olentangy HS; Galena, OH; Trs Jr Cls; Trs Sr Cls; Chrh Wkr; Drl Tm; Off Ade; Stg Crw; Drama Clb; Pep Clb; Spn Clb; Sunshine Girl 77 & 78; Bus Schl; Bus.

BEVILACQUA, LOU; St Francis De Sales HS; Columbus, OH; 16/182 Hon Rl; Wrstlng; Univ; Bus.

BEVINS, KIM; Arcanum Butler HS; Arcanum, OH; 16/111 VP Frsh Cls; Chrs; Hon Rl; NHS; Off Ade; Sch Mus; Pep Clb; Chrldng; Scr Kpr; Rotary Awd; Bsns Schl; Sec.

BEVIRT, BRUCE; Herbert Henry Dow HS; Midland, MI; Cls Rep Frsh Cls; Boy Scts; Chrs; Hon Rl; Sct Actv; Stu Cncl; Yth Flsp; Capt Ftbl; Coach Actv; PPFtbl; Soc Of Dist Amer HS Stu; Cert Of Recog Outstndng Acad Ach St Of Michigan Schlrshp Competition; N Michigan Univ; Med.

BEWLEY, LAURA; Morton Sr HS; Hammond, IN; Chrs; Chrh Wkr; Hon Rl; Mdrgl; Sch Mus; Yth Flsp; Pep Clb; College.

BEWLEY, MARC; Hammond Baptist HS; Crown Point, IN; 41/72 Pres Jr Cls; Pres Sr Cls; Chrs; Chrh Wkr; Sch Nwsp; Eng Clb; Ger Clb; Bsktbl; Letter Ftbl; Letter Socr; Ldrshp Awd; Music Awd; Hyles Anderson Coll; Theology.

BEWLEY, RONALD; Ben Davis HS; Indianapolis, IN; Band; Chrh Wkr; FCA; Hon Rl; Sch Mus; Sch Pl; 4-H; Fr Clb; Glf; Ivy Voc; Auto Body Repair.

BEX, JULIE; Bedford North Lawrence HS; Williams, IN; 46/483 Chrs; Chrh Wkr; Cmnty Wkr; Hon Rl; NHS; Stg Crw; Beta Clb; 4-H; Fr Clb; Pep Clb; Butler Univ; Pre Med.

BEYER, ANN; Villa Angela Acad; Wickliffe, OH; Boy Scts; Chrh Wkr; Girl Scts; Hon Rl; Hosp Ade; JA; NHS; Sch Mus; Drama Clb; Spn Clb; Spec Educ.

BEYER, LAURI; Colerain Senior HS; Cincinnati, OH; Hon Rl; Jr NHS; NHS; Capt Bsktbl; College; Physical Educ.

BEYER, MICHAEL G; Valley Forge Sr HS; Parma, OH; 6/704 Cls Rep Frsh Cls; Cls Rep Soph Cls; VP Jr Cls; Cl Rep Jr Cls; Cls Rep Sr Cls; Am Leg Boys St; Chrs; Hon Rl; Lit Mag; Mdrgl; Univ; Med.

BEYER, PAM; Waldron Jr Sr HS; Waldron, IN; 7/64 Cls Rep Sr Cls; Am Leg Aux Girls St; Hon Rl; Off Ade; Sch Pl; Stu Cncl; Rptr Yrbk; Pep Clb; Capt Chrldng; Ball State Univ; Sec.

BEYERLE, RICHARD A; Willoughby South HS; Willoughby, OH; 19/416 Hon Rl; NHS; Yrbk; Am Leg Awd; Case Western Reserve Univ; Engr.

BEYKE, GLENN; Jasper HS; Jasper, IN; 30/289 Am Leg Boys St; Hon Rl; 4-H; Letter Ftbl; Letter Trk; Indiana Univ; Bus.

BEYMON, LISA; Wintersville HS; Wintersville, OH; 40/267 Band; Hon Rl; Hosp Ade; Sch Pl; Stg Crw; Drama Clb; Spn Clb; Trk; GAA; PPFtbl; College; Med Tech.

BEYNON, LISA; Wintersville HS; Wintersville, OH; 40/282 Band; Hon Rl; Sch Pl; Stg Crw; Drama Clb; Pep Clb; Spn Clb; Trk; GAA; PPFtbl; College; Med Tech Pharm.

BEZAIRE, GERARD; Grosse Pte South HS; Grosse Pte Pk, MI; Mic State Univ; Acct.

BEZEK, DAVID; Milan HS; Maybee, MI; Chrh Wkr; Hon Rl; FFA; Chptr Farmer Awd FFA; FFA Spring Contest MSU; Michigan St Univ; Vet.

BEZEMEK, DAVID; Grandville HS; Grand Rapids, MI; Boy Scts; Hon Rl; Sch Nwsp; Swmmng; Davenport; Acct.

BEZENAH, ROBERT; Osborn HS; Detroit, MI; Hon Rl; Stg Crw; Yrbk; Boys Clb Am; Cit Awd; College; Mechanical Engr.

BEZZARRO, SUSAN; Ursuline HS; Youngstown, OH; 13/350 Chrs; Chrh Wkr; Hon Rl; NHS; Off Ade; Pep Clb; Tutor Awrd; Tutor; Italian Clb; Youngstown St Univ; Acctg.

BEZZARRO, TERESA; Ursuline HS; Youngstown, OH; Cl Rep Jr Cls; Cls Rep Sr Cls; Chrs; Chrh Wkr; Cmnty Wkr; Hosp Ade; Off Ade; Youngstown State Univ; Med.

BEZZO, DONALD; Our Lady Of Mt Carmel HS; Wyandotte, MI; 4/70 VP Frsh Cls; Cls Rep Soph Cls; Cl Rep Jr Cls; Pres Sr Cls; Hon Rl; Jr NHS; NHS; Sch Pl; Stu Cncl; Sprt Ed Yrbk; Boston Univ; Engr.

BHARDWAJ, ANU; Roosevelt HS; Kent, OH; Cls Rep Sr Cls; Cmnty Wkr; Hosp Ade; Orch; Stu Cncl; Sprt Ed Yrbk; Sci Clb; Soroptimist; Bsktbl; Hon Roll; Miss India In Banqt Held At E J Thoams Perfrmng Art Hall 78; Univ; Law.

BHARGAVA, VIVEK; Clay Sr HS; Oregon, OH; 2/366 Am Leg Boys St; Hon Rl; JA; Jr NHS; NHS; Stu Cncl; Yrbk; Sci Clb; Ten; JETS Awd; Quiz Bowl Team Toledo City Runner Up; Natl Sci Foundation Summer Research Prog; College; Medicine.

BHIRDO, TERESA; Bridgeport HS; Bridgeport, MI; 10/355 Band; Hon Rl; NHS; Off Ade; Ger Clb; Pres Pep Clb; Bsbl; Letter Trk; All Amer Hall Of Fame Band Hon 79; Acad Achvmnt Awd 76 79; Internatl Order Of Jobs Daughters Schlrshp 79; Univ; Lang Arts.

BHISITKUL, ROBERT; St Josephs HS; Niles, MI; Cls Rep Frsh Cls; Hon Rl; Stu Cncl; Letter Ten; Letter Trk; College; Med.

BIAGI, M CAROLINE; Reitz Mem HS; Evansville, IN; Hon Rl; PAVAS; Sci Clb; Univ.

BIAGLOW, MARY; Regina HS; Cleveland Hts, OH; Chrs; Hon Rl; Yrbk; Case Western Reserve Univ; Nursing.

BIALEK, JULIANA; West Lafayette HS; W Lafayette, IN; 25/179 Hon Rl; NHS; Rptr Yrbk; Keyettes; VP Pep Clb; Glf; Letter Ten; Univ.

BIALKOWSKI, CHERYL; R B Chamberlin HS; Twinsburg, OH; Trs Sr Cls; AFS; Girl Scts; Off Ade; Spn Clb; IM Sprt; Ohio St Univ; Biological Sciences.

BIALKOWSKI, MICHELLE; Normandy Sr HS; Seven Hills, OH; Chrs; Sch Mus; Fr Clb; Chrldng; IM Sprt; Economics.

BIANCO, BARRIE L; Wheeling Park HS; Wheeling, WV; Cmnty Wkr; Lbry Ade; Sch Pl; Stg Crw; Drama Clb; Carnegie Mellon Univ; Drama.

BIANCO, JOHN; St Edward HS; Lakewood, OH; 3/370 Chrh Wkr; Hon Rl; VP Jr NHS; Lit Mag; VP NHS; Off Ade; Pol Wkr; IM Sprt; Natl Merit SF; Eng I Math I Latin I Eng II Chem & U S Hist Awd; Univ.

BIAS, GARY; Milton HS; Milton, WV; 16/197 Am Leg Boys St; Band; Boy Scts; Hon Rl; Stu Cncl; Pres Yth Flsp; IM Sprt; Marching Field Commander 79; Eagle Scout 76; 2nd Yr Whos Who; Marshall Univ.

BIAS, PAULA; Milton HS; Milton, WV; 4/300 Hon Rl; NHS; Treas Yth Flsp; Mth Clb; Spn Clb; Letter Bsktbl; Letter Trk; Natl Merit Ltr; College; Biol.

BIAS, TINA; Milton HS; Milton, WV; Hon Rl; PAVAS; DECA; Cit Awd; Univ; Archt.

BIASI, ELLEN; James Ford Rhodes HS; Cleveland, OH; 22/309 Chrs; Drl Tm; NHS; Y-Teens; DECA; Ger Clb; Trk; Cuyahoga Cmnty Coll; Data Proc.

BIBB, CYNTHIA; Lutheran HS East; E Cleveland, OH; Chrs; Chrh Wkr; Drl Tm; Hosp Ade; JA; Off Ade; Sch Pl; Stg Crw; Stu Cncl; Yth Flsp; Kent St Univ; Cmnctn.

BIBB, PHILIP; Midland Trail HS; Ansted, WV; Hon Rl; 4-H; Pep Clb; VICA; Bsbl; Letter Ftbl; Letter Trk; Scr Kpr; Tmr; 4-H Awd; Fayette Plataeu Voc Schl; Machinist.

BIBLE, DANITA J; Carey HS; Carey, OH; Band; Drl Tm; Hon Rl; Lbry Ade; Y-Teens; FHA; Spn Clb; Tiffin Univ; Sec.

BIBLE, DIANE; Montpelier HS; Montpelier, OH; Band; Chrs; Off Ade; Treas 4-H; FTA; Letter Bsktbl; Letter Trk; Coach Actv; 4-H Awd; 1st Team Nw OAL & Dist 7 All Star Girls Basketball Team; 880 Medley Relay Team 3rd At State; Bowling Green St Univ; Elem Ed.

BIBLE, PAM; Kelloggsville HS; Wyoming, MI; Trs Sr Cls; Band; Hon Rl; Jr NHS; NHS; Sch Pl; Yrbk; Letter Chrldng; PPFtbl; Twrlr; Acad Letter 78; Perfect Attendnc 3 Yrs 78; Calvin Coll; Med.

BICAN, SUE; Erieview Catholic HS; Cleveland, OH; 3/100 Trs Frsh Cls; Pres Soph Cls; Cl Rep Jr Cls; Chrs; Hon Rl; Lit Mag; Mod UN; Sch Mus; Sch Pl; Stu Cncl; College; Conservation.

BICH THI NGOC, NGO; Central HS; Grand Rapids, MI; Cmp Fr Grls; Hon Rl; Lbry Ade; NHS; Off Ade; Sch Mus; Fr Clb; Mich State Univ; Chem Engr.

BICK, TRACY; Rochester HS; Rochester, IN; Trs Soph Cls; Sec Sr Cls; Chrs; Hon Rl; Mdrgl; Stu Cncl; Pep Clb; Ten; Trk; Chrldng; IUPU; Fshn Mdse.

BICKEL, CAROLYN S; Anderson HS; Anderson, IN; 21/428 Hon Rl; NHS; Treas Sct Actv; Ed Sch Nwsp; Rptr Sch Nwsp; Sch Nwsp; Treas Fr Clb; DAR Awd; Natl Merit SF; Indiana Univ; Medicine.

BICKEL, GARY; Corydon Central HS; Corydon, IN; Chrh Wkr; Cmnty Wkr; Hon Rl; Sch Pl; Stg Crw; Yth Flsp;.

BICKEL, JOSEPH; Bishop Luers HS; Ft Wayne, IN; Chrh Wkr; 4-H; Letter Ftbl; Capt Trk; Ftbl All City S Def Tackl 78; Bloomington Jr All St 1st Team Tckl 78; All St Hon Mntn Def Tckl 78; Univ.

BICKEL, KIMBERLY JO; East Clinton HS; New Vienna, OH; 39/100 Band; Chrh Wkr; Drl Tm; Hon Rl; Sch Mus; Yth Flsp; 4-H; FFA; FHA; Mth Clb; Outstndng Jr Dairymn Awd 75; 4 Yr Band Awd 78; 4 Yr Track Awd Hold Schl Recrd In Shot Put & Duscus 78; Ohio St Univ; Agri.

BICKEL, LESLIE; Upper Arlington HS; Columbus, OH; 89/610 Hon Rl; 4-H; Ger Clb; Univ Of Florida; Vet Med.

BICKEL, RANDY; Jay County HS; Portland, IN; Band; JA; Mdrgl; Mth Clb; JA Awd; Indiana St Univ.

BICKEL, SCOTT; Western HS; Kokomo, IN; Chrh Wkr; Hon Rl; Purdue Univ; Engr.

BICKERSTAFF, DEBBIE; Valley HS; Pine Grove, WV; Band; Hon Rl; NHS; Sch Pl; Stg Crw; Yrbk; FFA; Capt Trk; Chrldng; Coach Actv; Fairmont St Coll; Nursing.

BICKFORD, BARBARA; London HS; London, OH; 24/133 Hon Rl; Off Ade; Sch Pl; Rptr Yrbk; 4-H; Fr Clb; Letter Bsktbl; Crs Cntry; Trk; Mgrs; Univ; Fshn Dsgn.

BICKLE, KANDI; Rochester HS; Rochester, IN; Cls Rep Frsh Cls; VP Soph Cls; Cl Rep Jr Cls; Trs Sr Cls; FCA; Hon Rl; Sch Mus; Stu Cncl; Fr Clb; Pep Clb; Univ; Fshn Dsgn.

BICKNELL, ELLEN; Franklin HS; Franklin, OH; Band; Chrs; Chrh Wkr; Girl Scts; Hon Rl; JA; Sch Mus; Spn Clb; GAA; IM Sprt; Wright State; Med.

BICZAK, MARY A; Oakridge Sr HS; Muskegon, MI ; 5/150 Hon Rl; Jr NHS; NHS; Yth Flsp; Letter Bsbl; Letter Bsktbl; Letter Trk; IM Sprt; 4-H Awd; Phys Educ Awd Of Cls Of 80 77 79; MVP J V Vllybl 77; Outstndng Pitcher Sftbl 78; Univ.

BIDDINGER, CARMON; Washington HS; Washington, TN; 25/198 Chrs; Hon Rl; Lbry Ade; NHS; Sch Mus; Rptr Sch Nwsp; Sch Nwsp; Beta Clb; 4-H; Fr Clb; Vincennes Univ; Exec Sec.

BIDDINGER, KENT; Caro HS; Caro, MI; Boy Scts; Hon Rl; NHS; Yth Flsp; Ftbl; Swmmng; Trk; HSU; Med.

BIDDLE, DEBORAH; Ontario Sr HS; Crestline, OH; 52/176 Cls Rep Sr Cls; Band; Stu Cncl; Scr Kpr; Tmr; Ohio St Univ; Bus.

BIDDLE, DONNA; Bluffton HS; Bluffton, IN; Am Leg Aux Girls St; NHS; Off Ade; Y-Teens; Ger Clb; OEA; Pep Clb; Glf; Purdue Univ; Hotel Restaurant Mgmt.

BIDDLE, WILLIAM; Marlington HS; Limaville, OH; 29/300 Boy Scts; Hon Rl; Sec VICA; Bsbl; Ftbl; IM Sprt; Univ; Machine Trades.

BIDINGER, TANDY; Brandon HS; Ortonville, MI; Debate Tm; Hon Rl; Natl Forn Lg; NHS; Sch Mus; Sch Pl; Stu Cncl; Rptr Sch Nwsp; Sch Nwsp; Univ.

BIDLINGMEYER, KAREN; Seven Hills School; Cincinnati, OH; 3/50 Cmnty Wkr; Hon Rl; Sch Pl; Rptr Yrbk; Letter Bsbl; Letter Hockey; IM Sprt; Scr Kpr; Honorary Athletic Clb 78 80; 7 Up Clb Co Chairmn 79; Univ; Math.

BIEDEL, GINA; Waterford HS; Waterford, OH; 1/63 Cls Rep Frsh Cls; Band; Chrs; Chrh Wkr; Hon Rl; NHS; Sch Pl; Stu Cncl; Yth Flsp; Sci Clb; Univ; Comp Sci.

BIEDENBACH, J; Perry HS; Massillon, OH; Band; Orch; Univ; Oceanography.

BIEDENBENDER, MIKE; Elyria Catholic HS; Elyria, OH; Band; Hon Rl; Orch; Sch Mus; Ten; Natl Merit Ltr; Univ Of Cincinnati; Elec Engr.

BIEHL, JAY; Northfield HS; Urbana, IN; 4/110 Am Leg Boys St; Hon Rl; Pres NHS; Sch Pl; FFA; Capt Bsbl; Bsktbl; Lion Awd; Rotary Awd; Ball State Univ; Actuarial Sci.

BIEHL, JERRY; Tri Jr Sr HS; New Lisbon, IN; 11/80 Boy Scts; Hon Rl; Sct Actv; Spn Clb; Ftbl; IM Sprt; Scr Kpr; Purdue Univ; Carpentry.

BIEHL, REX; Northfield HS; Urbana, IN; Trs Frsh Cls; Trs Soph Cls; NHS; 4-H; FFA; Farm.

BIELAK, DAVID; Lake Catholic HS; Wickliffe, OH; Bsbl; Letter Bsktbl; College; Bus.

BIELEC, THOMAS; Flint Northern HS; Flint, MI; Band; Boy Scts; Hon Rl; NHS; Quill & Scroll; Stg Crw; Yrbk; Sch Nwsp; Trk; Eagle Scout Awd; Univ Of Michigan Regeants Alumin; Univ Of Michigan; History.

BIELICKI, JAMES; C S Mott HS; Warren, MI; Hon Rl; Jr NHS; NHS; Beta Clb; Letter Trk; College.

BIELSKI, DEBORAH J; Rossford HS; Rossford, OH; 10/146 Pres Band; Chrs; Chrh Wkr; Cmnty Wkr; Girl Scts; Hon Rl; Hosp Ade; NHS; Red Cr Ade; Sch Mus; Univ Of Toledo; Nursing.

BIELSKI, KAREN; Bishop Foley HS; Madison Hts, MI; Chrs; Chrh Wkr; Girl Scts; Hon Rl; Mdrgl; NHS; Rptr Yrbk; Bsbl; Capt Chrldng; GAA; Whos Who In Music; Most Outstanding Cheerleader; College; Busns Mgmt.

BIEN, SANDY; Big Walnut HS; Johnstown, OH; Cls Rep Frsh Cls; Cl Rep Jr Cls; Chrs; Yrbk; 4-H; Fr Clb; FHA; Ftbl; Busns Schl; Data Processing.

BIENVENUE, DAVID; Bexley HS; Columbus, OH; Trs Soph Cls; Hon Rl; Spn Clb; Wrstlng; Univ Of Ca; Engineering.

BIERCE, JEFF; Harding HS; Marion, OH; College; Dent.

BIERI, ROBERT; Lowell HS; Lowell, MI; Am Leg Boys St; Hon Rl; Stu Cncl; Sprt Ed Yrbk; Letter Bsktbl; Glf; Ten; Lion Awd; Rotary Awd; Hope Coll; Bus.

BIERMA, KENT; Kankakee Valley HS; De Motte, IN; Chrh Wkr; Hon Rl; NHS; Yth Flsp; Bsktbl; Capt Glf; Mr Defense Bsktbl 79; Calvin Coll; Engr.

BIERMA, SANDRA; Washington Township HS; Valparaiso, IN; 12/40 Sec Jr Cls; Chrs; Hon Rl; NHS; Sch Pl; 4-H; Bsktbl; Chrldng; 4-H Awd; College; Acctg.

BIERMANN, ANNE; Beaumont HS; Shaker Hts, OH; Chrs; Sch Mus; Sch Pl; Stg Crw; Drama Clb; Natl Merit Ltr; Natl Merit SF; Univ Of Toledo; Sociology.

BIERMANN, MARK; Gladwin HS; Gladwin, MI; Band; Chrh Wkr; Hon Rl; NHS; Sch Mus; Sch Pl; Stg Crw; Stu Cncl; Drama Clb; Lat Clb; Univ; Elec Engr.

BIERNACIK, CAROLYN; Andrean HS; Gary, IN; 72/279 Aud/Vis; Hosp Ade; Ill Benedictine; Medical Tech.

BIEROD, BRYAN; Floyd Central HS; Georgetown, IN; 3/359 Cls Rep Frsh Cls; Cls Rep Soph Cls; Cl Rep Jr Cls; Am Leg Boys St; Chrh Wkr; Hon Rl; NHS; Stu Cncl; Ger Clb; Opt Clb Awd; College; Comp Sci.

BIERSCHAUCH, R; Beal City HS; Mt Pleasant, MI; Band; Hon Rl; Lbry Ade; Letter Bsbl; Letter Bsktbl; Letter Ftbl; Scr Kpr; College; Comp Sci.

BIERWORTH, RICHARD; Lakeview HS; Cortland, OH; Am Leg Boys St; Band; Boy Scts; Hon Rl; JA; Sct Actv; Yth Flsp; Beta Clb; Lat Clb; JA Awd; College; Organic Chem.

BIERY, MICHELE; Hicksville HS; Hicksville, OH; Band; Chrs; Chrh Wkr; Girl Scts; Hon Rl; Sch Mus; Sch Pl; Yrbk; Rptr Sch Nwsp; Lat Clb; Ohio State Univ; Journalism.

BIESMAN, BRIAN; Carman HS; Flint, MI; Debate Tm; Hon Rl; NHS; Eng Clb; Trk; Univ Of Mic; Med.

BIESTEK, JOANNE; George Rogers Clark HS; Hammond, IN; 5/218 Treas NHS; Quill & Scroll; Yrbk; Ger Clb; Kiwan Awd; College; Eng.

BIESZKA, LINDA; W Catholic HS; Grand Rapids, MI; Cmnty Wkr; Hon Rl; Off Ade; Lat Clb; Pep Clb; Socr; Mic State Univ; Psych.

BIGALKE, LUANA; Esseville Garber HS; Essexville, MI; Sec Jr Cls; Sec Sr Cls; Chrs; Debate Tm; Natl Forn Lg; Sch Mus; Sch Pl; Stu Cncl; Cit Awd; College; Educ.

BIGAM, ROBYN; Westfall HS; Mt Sterling, OH; 16/128 Cls Rep Frsh Cls; Cls Rep Soph Cls; VP Jr Cls; VP Sr Cls; Am Leg Aux Girls St; Band; Hon Rl; Sch Pl; Stu Cncl; Yth Flsp; Grad Hnrs Stu 3.25 GPA Or Better 79; Capitol Univ; History.

BIGELOW, CHERYL; Highland HS; Anderson, IN; Band; IN Schl Of Music Assc Solo & Ensmble Contest Supr Rating 78 & 79; Outstndng Freshman Band Mbr Awd 77; Indiana Univ; Soc Wrk.

BIGELOW, GERTRUDE; Engadine Consolidated HS; Naubinway, MI; Trs Frsh Cls; Trs Soph Cls; Trs Jr Cls; Trs Sr Cls; Hon Rl; Lbry Ade; Sch Pl; Yrbk; Sch Nwsp; 4-H; N Central Mich College; Art.

BIGELOW, JEFFREY B; East Clinton HS; Sabina, OH; 3/113 Sec Frsh Cls; Pres Soph Cls; Am Leg Boys St; FCA; Hon Rl; NHS; Stg Crw; FTA; Mth Clb; Sci Clb; Coll.

BIGELOW, SANDRA; Pinconning Sr HS; Linwood, MI; 1/250 Trs Sr Cls; Girl Scts; Hon Rl; NHS; Yrbk; Chrldng; PPFtbl; Var Vllybl Ltr 77; Var Blly Ltr & Hon Mntn In Confrnc & 1st Pl In Confrnc 78; Michigan St Univ; Sci.

BIGGERS, KEVIN; Talcott HS; Talcott, WV; VP Frsh Cls; Pres Soph Cls; Pres Jr Cls; Chrh Wkr; Cmnty Wkr; Hon Rl; Stu Cncl; FBLA; Letter Bsktbl; Dnfth Awd; Univ; Comp Sci.

BIGGINS, SANDRA; Minerva HS; Minerva, OH; 17 Hon Rl; NHS; Sct Actv; FTA; Lat Clb; Pep Clb; GAA; Univ Of Akron; Speech.

BIGGS, HILDRED; Mississinewa HS; Gas City, IN; 21/230 Band; Chrs; Drm Bgl; Girl Scts; Hon Rl; Sc h Pl; Stg Crw; Yth Flsp; Sch Nwsp; Drama Clb; Indiana Univ; RN.

BIGGS, JOE; Brazil Sr HS; Brazil, IN; 3/191 Band; Chrh Wkr; Hon Rl; Rptr Yrbk; Ed Sch Nwsp; Rptr Sch Nwsp; Sci Clb; Spn Clb; Crs Cntry; Wrstlng; Purdue Univ; Vet Sci.

BIGGS, ROBERT L; Woodrow Wilson HS; Beckley, WV; 9/500 Cls Rep Soph Cls; Am Leg Boys St; Chrh Wkr; Cmnty Wkr; Hon Rl; NHS; Stg Crw; Key Clb; Lat Clb; Tmr; West Virginia Univ; Med.

BIGGS, TERESA; Maumee HS; Maumee, OH; 35/314 Girl Scts; Hon Rl; Hosp Ade; Lbry Ade; NHS; Y-Teens; 4-H; Bsktbl; Ten; Pres PPFtbl; Univ Of Toledo; Sci.

BIGHAM, STAN; Marquette Sr HS; Marquette, MI; Pres Frsh Cls; DECA; Cit Awd; Voice Dem Awd; N Michigan Univ; X Ray Tech.

BIGLER, CATHY; Augres Sims HS; Au Gres, MI; 5/48 VP Frsh Cls; Cl Rep Jr Cls; Cls Rep Sr Cls; Band; Chrh Wkr; Debate Tm; Hon Rl; Stu Cncl; 4-H; Chrldng; Central Mich Univ; Music.

BIGLER, GRANT; North Wood HS; Nappanee, IN; 41/191 Cls Rep Soph Cls; Chrh Wkr; Hon Rl; 4-H; Bsktbl; Ftbl; Wrstlng; IM Sprt; Mgrs; Purdue Univ; Mech Engr.

BIGLER, LINDA; Wadsworth HS; Wadsworth, OH; 83/365 Chrs; Chrh Wkr; Rptr Yrbk; Drama Clb; Pep Clb; Spn Clb; Scr Kpr; Mt Union College; Psych.

BIGLEY, JULIE; Schoolcraft HS; Schoolcraft, MI; Sec Frsh Cls; VP Soph Cls; Trs Jr Cls; Chrh Wkr; Hon Rl; NHS; Pres Stu Cncl; Rptr Yrbk; Chrldng; College; Bus Admin.

BIGNA, MICHAEL A; Taylor HS; Kokomo, IN; 1/300 Sal; Band; Boy Scts; Chrs; Hon Rl; NHS; Orch; Sch Pl; Ed Yrbk; Drama Clb; Rose Hulman Inst Of Tech; Physics.

BIHN, D; Cardinal Stritch HS; Oregon, OH; 38/230 Sec Jr Cls; Cls Rep Sr Cls; Boy Scts; Hon Rl; NHS; Sch Mus; Sch Pl; Sct Actv; Stu Cncl; Letter Crs Cntry; Univ; Engr.

BIHN, LYNN; Mother Of Mercy HS; Cheviot, OH; Chrs; Hon Rl; Fr Clb; Coach Actv; UC; Child Care.

BIHUN, CINDY; Port Clinton HS; Port Clinton, OH; 10/289 Cls Rep Frsh Cls; VP Jr Cls; AFS; Chrs; Hon Rl; Stu Cncl; Ger Clb; Mth Clb; Chrldng; College.

BIHUN, CYNTHIA; Port Clinton HS; Port Clinton, OH; 10/280 Cls Rep Frsh Cls; VP Jr Cls; Chrs; Chrh Wkr; Hon Rl; Stu Cncl; Ger Clb; Chrldng; Scr Kpr; College.

BIJAK, LAURA; Normandy HS; Parma, OH; 8/649 Chrs; Cmnty Wkr; Hon Rl; NHS; Rptr Yrbk; Yrbk; Fr Clb; Baldwin Wallace Coll; Acctg.

BIJAN, DONIA; Kingswood HS; Bloomfld Hls, MI; Cls Rep Frsh Cls; Sec Soph Cls; Girl Scts; Hon Rl; Chrldng; College; Journalism.

BILAS, MARY E; Woodrow Wilson HS; Youngstown, OH; 18/307 Lbry Ade; NHS; Youngstown St Univ; Comp Sci.

BILAS, ROGER B; North Olmsted Sr HS; North Olmsted, OH; 5/650 Am Leg Boys St; Hon Rl; Mod UN; NHS; Pres Key Clb; Capt Crs Cntry; Trk; Am Leg Awd; Natl Merit SF; Miami Univ; Law.

BILBREY, BRUCE; Wadsworth HS; Wadsworth, OH; Aud/Vis; Hon Rl; Sci Clb; VP VICA; Univ Of Akron; Elec Engr.

BILBY, LAURA; Douglas Mac Arthur HS; Saginaw, MI; 15/300 Chrh Wkr; Hon Rl; NHS; Sec Yth Flsp; Pres Spn Clb; Natl Merit Ltr; Graduated In Top 20 Of Class; Received Delta Coll Trustee Hnr Schlrshp; Delta Coll; Busns Admin.

BILBY, PAULA; Rochester HS; Rochester, IN; 41/166 Cmp Fr Grls; Chrh Wkr; Girl Scts; Hon Rl; Lbry Ade; Off Ade; 4-H; Ger Clb; 4-H Awd; Hon Roll Awd 76; German All A Awd 77 78 & 79; Math Sci & Home Ec Awd 74; Univ; Bus.

BILDZ, JUDY; Crown Point HS; Crown Point, IN; Hon Rl; Hosp Ade; Trk; Michigan Tech Univ; Chem Engr.

BILEK, GREG; Norton HS; Norton, OH; Aud/Vis; Boy Scts; Lbry Ade; Sct Actv; Akron Univ; Mech Engr.

BILGER, LAURA J; Bad Axe HS; Filion, MI; 24/130 Band; Chrs; Chrh Wkr; Drm Bgl; Hon Rl; Hosp Ade; Natl Forn Lg; NHS; Sch Mus; Yth Flsp; Grand Rapids Coll; Music Therapy.

BILITZKE, BARBARA; Caro Comm HS; Caro, MI; Trs Jr Cls; Cls Rep Sr Cls; FCA; Hon Rl; NHS; Sch Pl; Letter Bsbl; Letter Bsktbl; Letter Trk; Coach Actv; Central Michigan Univ; Sports.

BILKOVSKY, MARGIE; Brighton HS; Brighton, MI; Cls Rep Sr Cls; Band; Hon Rl; Quill & Scroll; Sch Mus; Ed Yrbk; Sci Clb; Letter Bsktbl; Trk; Natl Merit SF; Mich State; Med Tech.

BILL, JOSEPH; Broad Ripple HS; Indianapolis, IN; Cl Rep Jr Cls; Cls Rep Sr Cls; Chrs; FCA; Hon Rl; Mdrgl; PAVAS; Sch Mus; Sch Pl; Drama Clb; Indiana Univ; Theatre.

BILL, MARY J; Seton HS; Cincinnati, OH; 9/255 Hon Rl; Jr NHS; NHS; Fr Clb; FBLA; Mth Clb; Pep Clb; Bsktbl; College; Math.

BILLEG, STEPHEN; Upper Sandusky HS; Upper Sandusky, OH; Chrh Wkr; Hon Rl; NHS; Ftbl; Wrstlng; College; Comp Science.

BILLER, DEBORAH; Fairport Harding HS; Fairport Hbr, OH; VP Frsh Cls; Treas Band; Hon Rl; JA; Lbry Ade; Letter Bsktbl; Pres GAA; Lakeland Cmnty Coll; Comp Sci.

BILLERMAN, DONNA; Coldwater HS; Coldwater, OH; Band; Chrs; Girl Scts; Sct Actv; Bsktbl; Letter Trk; Mgrs; Tmr; Track Awd Field Events 79; Wright St Univ; Phys Educ.

BILLETER, BRIAN; Carrollton HS; Saginaw, MI; 32/152 Band; Boy Scts; Sch Mus; Sch Pl; Sct Actv; Stg Crw; Drama Clb; Bronze Hon Pin 52 Hon Pts 76; 2 Red Solo & Ensemble Medals 78; 1st & 2nd Yr Band Pins 77 & 78; Wildlife Conservation.

BILLIG, RON; Wickliffe Sr HS; Wickliffe, OH; 12/330 Hon Rl; NHS; Letter Trk; Case Western Reserve Univ; Chem Engr.

BILLINGS, GINA; Withrow HS; Cincinnati, OH; Chrh Wkr; Hon Rl; JA; Sch Mus; Stu Cncl; Yth Flsp; Pep Clb; VICA; Univ Of Cin; Wrd Prcsng.

BILLINGS, KELLY; Clay Sr HS; Oregon, OH; 54/323 Hon Rl; NHS; Off Ade; Sec Stu Cncl; Drama Clb; VP Pep Clb; Ten; Coach Actv; Univ Of Toledo; Bus Admin.

BILLINGSLEY, JEFF; Grand River Academy; E Liverpool, OH; Band; Boy Scts; Red Cr Ade; Sch Mus; Sct Actv; Stg Crw; Pep Clb; Bsktbl; Letter Socr; IM Sprt; Univ; Bus.

BILLMAN, ANITA; Buckeye Valley HS; Ostrander, OH; Sec Frsh Cls; Sec Soph Cls; Band; Hon Rl; Stg Crw; Ed Sch Nwsp; Drama Clb; 4-H; Fr Clb; FTA; Ohio St Univ; Agri Economics.

BILLS, DEBORAH; Lake Shore HS; St Cl Shores, MI; Chrs; Chrh Wkr; Hon Rl; NHS; Off Ade; Coach Actv; Northwood Inst; CPA.

BILLS, TERRENCE; Kalamazoo Loy Norrix HS; Kalamzoo, MI; Hon Rl; Swmmng; Coach Actv; Mgrs; Tmr; Cit Awd; College; Architecture.

BILLSBY, RICKY; Hebert Henry Dow HS; Midland, MI; Cls Rep Sr Cls; Am Leg Boys St; Hon Rl; Jr NHS; NHS; Stu Cncl; Letter Ftbl; Letter Trk; PPFtbl; Pres Awd; Alma Coll; Engr.

BILLY, MARK; Chaney HS; Youngstown, OH; 13/375 Chrh Wkr; Cmnty Wkr; Hon Rl; Jr NHS; NHS; Rptr Yrbk; Rptr Sch Nwsp; Youngstown State Univ; Dentistry.

BILO, JOHN; Ben Davis HS; Indianapolis, IN; Band; Boy Scts; Chrs; Chrh Wkr; NHS; Sch Mus; Sct Actv; Fr Clb; Indiana Univ; Tele Cmnctns.

BILO, SUSAN; Alexandria Monroe HS; Alexandira, IN; 3/163 Cl Rep Jr Cls; Cls Rep Sr Cls; Chrs; Girl Scts; Hon Rl; Jr NHS; NHS; Sch Mus; Sec Stu Cncl; Drama Clb; Purdue Univ; Clinical Psych.

BILODEAU, MARSHALL; Garber HS; Essexville, MI; 13/183 Band; Hon Rl; Letter Swmmng; Natl Merit Ltr; Natl Merit SF; Univ Center; Engr.

BILTZ, KATHY; Tipton HS; Tipton, IN; Chrs; Girl Scts; Hon Rl; Sct Actv; FBLA; OEA; Pep Clb; Bus Schl; Bus.

BINAU, ERIC; Bexley HS; Bexley, OH; Cls Rep Frsh Cls; Cls Rep Sr Cls; Band; Orch; Stu Cncl; Lat Clb; Letter Socr; Coach Actv; Stu Council Comm Chrmn; College; Biology.

BINDER, BARBARA A; Cathedral HS; Indianapolis, IN; 3/148 Hon Rl; Jr NHS; NHS; Sch Pl; Stu Cncl; Rptr Yrbk; Rptr Sch Nwsp; Fr Clb; IM Sprt; Scr Kpr; Advanc Plcemnt Eng Awd; Indianapolis Marion Cnty Creatv Writng Contst Hon Mention; Hoosier Scholr; Purdue Univ; Comp Sci.

BINDER, KIMBERLY; Sandusky HS; Snover, MI; 8/127 Chrh Wkr; Hon Rl; NHS; 4-H; FHA; Sec OEA; 4-H Awd; Baker Jr Coll; Clerk.

BINDER, SHERI; Wm V Fisher Catholic HS; Lancaster, OH; Chrh Wkr; Cmnty Wkr; Hon Rl; Hosp Ade; NHS; Stu Cncl; Yrbk; FNA; Ten; Chrldng; Mount Carmel Schl Nursng; Nurse.

BINEGAR, LINDA; Skyvue HS; Graysville, OH; Am Leg Aux Girls St; Pres Band; Hon Rl; VP NHS; Pres Stu Cncl; Ed Yrbk; Ed Sch Nwsp; Fr Clb; Purdue Univ; Med.

BING, ROBERT; Southeastern HS; Highland Pk, MI; Chrs; Chrh Wkr; Hon Rl; PAVAS; Pep Clb; Letter Bsbl; Letter Bsktbl; Letter Crs Cntry; Trk; Scr Kpr; Oakland Univ; Chem.

BINGAMAN, BRADFORD L; Fountain Central HS; Hillsboro, IN; 6/135 Cls Rep Sr Cls; Band; FCA; Hon Rl; NHS; Stu Cncl; Yth Flsp; Bsktbl; Crs Cntry; Ftbl; Coll; Engr.

BINGHAM, JAMES; Whetstone HS; Columbus, O H; 51/323 Aud/Vis; Hon Rl; NHS; PAVAS; Stg Crw; Drama Clb; IM Sprt; Ohi State Univ; Elec Engr.

BINGHAM, MARLOWE; So Newton HS; Brook, IN; 40 Cl Rep Jr Cls; Chrs; Girl Scts; Hosp Ade; Sch Pl; FBLA; FHA; Lat Clb; Pep Clb; Swmmng; Vincennes; Photography.

BINGHAM, ROGER; Clermont Northeastern HS; Batavia, OH; Chrh Wkr; Cmnty Wkr; NHS; Stg Crw; Spn Clb; IM Sprt; College.

BINGMAN, SARAH E; Eastmoor HS; Columbus, OH; 1/290 Val; Chrs; Hon Rl; Hosp Ade; Jr NHS; Lbry Ade; NHS; Orch; Sch Mus; Sch Pl; 17th In State Chemistry Examination; Craig A Paul Scholarship; College; Chem Engr.

BINION, WADE; Tri HS; Spiceland, IN; 14/80 Boy Scts; Hon Rl; NHS; Off Ade; 4-H; FFA; Spn Clb; Dnfth Awd; Purdue Univ; Vet.

BINIUS, CORRINA; West Branch HS; Alliance, OH; AFS; Chrh Wkr; Yth Flsp; Fr Clb; Pep Clb; Pom Pon; East Gate School; Wrk With Handicppd.

BINKLEY, BETH; Allen East HS; Harrod, OH; 1/115 Pres Sr Cls; Band; Hosp Ade; NHS; Yth Flsp; Yrbk; 4-H; FHA; Trk; Capt Chrldng; Miami Valley Schl Of Nursing; Nurse.

BINKLEY, JULIE; North Adams HS; Hillsdale, MI; 10/48 Treas Pep Clb; GAA; Ferris St Coll; Dent Asst.

BINKLEY, VALARIE; Allen East HS; Lima, OH; 5/105 Band; Girl Scts; Hon Rl; Hosp Ade; Lbry Ade; NHS; Sch Pl; Rptr Yrbk; Ed Sch Nwsp; 4-H; Ohio Northern Univ; Acctg.

BINKOWSKI, THERESA; Sacred Heart Academy; Mt Pleasant, MI; 2/55 Cl Rep Jr Cls; Cls Rep Sr Cls; Sal; Chrs; Chrh Wkr; JA; NHS; Stg Crw; Rptr Yrbk; Drama Clb; Ferris St Coll; Health.

BINNION, D; Charles F Brush HS; S Euclid, OH; Band; Chrs; Chrh Wkr; Girl Scts; Hon Rl; Chrldng; Univ; Phys Ther.

BINSBACHER, KATHY; Warren Central HS; Indianapolis, IN; Hon Rl; Fr Clb· Natl Merit Ltr; Natl Merit SF; Univ; Math.

BINZER, TONI; Immaculate Conception Acad; Cincinnati, OH; Chrs; Chrh Wkr; Hosp Ade; Orch; Sch Mus; Sch Pl; Spn Clb; Thomas Moore; Vet.

BIRCH, JOSEPH M; Whetstone Sr HS; Columbus, OH; VP Sr Cls; Am Leg Boys St; Chrs; Hon Rl; Spn Clb; Letter Bsktbl; IM Sprt; Univ; Law.

BIRCH, TONYA; Pellston HS; Pellston, MI; 1/72 Val; Band; Chrh Wkr; Hon Rl; NHS; Yth Flsp; 4-H; 4-H Awd; N Central Michigan Univ; Music.

BIRCHMEIER, STEVE; Chesaning Union HS; Chesaning, MI; Am Leg Boys St; Chrh Wkr; Hon Rl; NHS; Sci Clb; Bsbl; Bsktbl; Glf; Delta Coll; Drafting.

BIRD, KEITH; Matoaka HS; Matoaka, WV; Am Leg Boys St; Hon Rl; Pres NHS; Pres Stu Cncl; Pres Yth Flsp; Yrbk; Pres Key Clb; DAR Awd; Univ; Engr.

BIRD, PAMELA; Stonewall Jackson HS; Charleston, WV; Band; Drm Mjrt; Jr NHS; NHS; Off Ade; Yrbk; Fr Clb; Mth Clb; Sci Clb; College; Biochem.

BIRD, RANDY; South Haven HS; South Haven, MI; FCA; Hon Rl; Yth Flsp; 4-H; Letter Bsbl; Letter Bsktbl; Capt Glf; Tmr; 4-H Awd; Univ.

BIRD, THERESA; North HS; Eastlake, OH; Chrh Wkr; Hon Rl; Off Ade; Pep Clb; Sec Career.

BIRGY, STEVE; Kalkaska HS; Fifelake, MI; Fr Clb; Bsbl; Ftbl; Pres Awd; Central Michigan Univ; Forestry.

BIRHANZL, SUSAN M; Grove City HS; Grove City, OH; 57/525 Pres Soph Cls; Cls Rep Soph Cls; Cl Rep Jr Cls; Cls Rep Sr Cls; Cmp Fr Grls; Hon Rl; NHS; Stu Cncl; Yrbk; Fr Clb; Top 50 Stu 1979; Ohio St Univ; Fshn Mdse.

BIRKEL, KATHLEEN; Akron N HS; Akron, OH; 11/400 Chrh Wkr; Cmnty Wkr; Hon Rl; Jr NHS; Lbry Ade; NHS; Sch Mus; Sch Pl; Drama Clb; Pep Clb; Ohio St Univ; Sci.

BIRKENBERGER, LORI; Lake Catholic HS; Mentor, OH; Hon Rl; Hosp Ade; JA; Off Ade; Letter Swmmng; Tmr; Span I Awd 79; Univ; Bio.

BIRKHIMER, ELLEN; Midland HS; Midland, MI; Girl Scts; Hon Rl; NHS; Sct Actv; Yth Flsp; 4-H; Fr Clb; Letter Crs Cntry; Letter Trk; Natl Merit SF; Mi Math Prize Cmpttn Brnz Awd 1978; Dow Chem Co Life Is Fragile Art Cntst 3rd 1977; Univ; Cvl Engr.

BIRKHOFF, JOSEPHINE; Grandview Hts HS; Columbus, OH; 26/113 Sec Frsh Cls; Pres Soph Cls; Chrs; Rptr Yrbk; FHA; Sci Clb; Capt Hockey; GAA; IM Sprt; Mat Maids; Work Std Progr 78; Ohio St Univ; Bus.

BIRMAN, DIANE; Piqua Ctrl HS; Piqua, OH; 1/345 Cls Rep Frsh Cls; Sec Soph Cls; Cls Rep Soph Cls; Sec Jr Cls; Cl Rep Jr Cls; Am Leg Aux Girls St; Chrs; Chrh Wkr; Drl Tm; Hon Rl; Univ; Bus.

BIRMAN, KAREN; Gull Lake HS; Battle Creek, MI; Band; Chrh Wkr; FCA; Hon Rl; Sch Mus; Stg Crw; College; Recreation.

BIRR, BRYANT; West Branch HS; No Benton, OH; Boy Scts; Hon Rl; NHS; 4-H; IM Sprt; Am Leg Awd; 4-H Awd; Mount Union; Law.

BIRR, ELIZABETH; Western HS; Bay City, MI; 15/476 Chrh Wkr; Debate Tm; Hon Rl; NHS; Off Ade; Orch; Sch Mus; Sec Stu Cncl; Fr Clb; Lat Clb; Concordia Coll; Scndry Educ.

BIRTALAN, JUDY; East Canton HS; E Canton, OH; Sec Soph Cls; Chrs; Jr NHS; NHS; Off Ade; Yth Flsp; Rptr Yrbk; Fr Clb; Ohi State Univ; Dent Hygiene.

BIRTSAS, CHRISTINE; Robert S Rogers HS; Toledo, OH; Cl Rep Jr Cls; Band; Hon Rl; Lbry Ade; DECA; FBLA; Lat Clb; Spn Clb; IM Sprt; Ohio St Univ; Marketing.

BISCHER, MARY; Onaway HS; Onaway, MI; 16/96 Lbry Ade; Rptr Yrbk; Natl Merit Schl; Davenport Coll Fo Bus; Comp Progr.

BISCHOF, STEPHANIE; Wheeling Park HS; Wheeling, WV; Cls Rep Frsh Cls; Cls Rep Soph Cls; Sec Jr Cls; Cl Rep Jr Cls; Sec Sr Cls; Stu Cncl; Sch Nwsp; Trk; Chrldng; IM Sprt; West Virginia Univ; Med.

BISCHOFF, CATHY; Napoleon HS; Napoleon, OH; Chrs; Hon Rl; Trk; Scr Kpr; College.

BISCHOFF, JEFF; Napoleon HS; Napoleon, OH; Band; Boy Scts; Hon Rl; NHS; Orch; Sch Mus; Sch Pl; Sct Actv; Swmmng; Coll; Mech Engr.

BISCHOFF, TERESSA; Leslie HS; Leslie, MI; 4/119 Cls Rep Sr Cls; VP Band; Chrs; Chmn Drl Tm; Jr NHS; NHS; Sch Mus; Stu Cncl; Beta Clb; Chmn Chrldng; Mich State Univ; Dent Tech.

BISDORS, DIANE; Stephen T Badin HS; Hamilton, OH; 37/215 VP Band; Girl Scts; Pres JA; Sec NHS; Sch Mus; Stu Cncl; Fr Clb; Red Cr Ade; Univ Of Cincinnati; Bus Admin.

BISH, BRENDA; Edgewood HS; Ashtabula, OH; AFS; Band; Chrs; Chrh Wkr; Hon Rl; Sch Mus; Fr Clb; Sci Clb; Trk; Natl Merit Ltr; College; Sci.

BISHOP, BRENDA; Northrop HS; Ft Wayne, IN; 104/587 Hon Rl; VP JA; Off Ade; Orch; Sch Mus; Pres Yth Flsp; JA Awd; Home Ec & Perfect Attendance; Cert For English Algebra Health Orchestra; Perfect Attndnce & VP Of Prsnl; Indiana Purdue Univ; Elem Ed.

BISHOP, CARLA; High School; Barnesville, OH; Treas Band; Chrs; Chrh Wkr; FCA; Girl Scts; Hon Rl; Sch Mus; Sch Pl; Yth Flsp; Drama Clb; Belmont Tech Univ; Bus Mgmt.

BISHOP, CAROL J; Forest Park HS; Crystal Falls, MI; 2/91 Pres Soph Cls; Pres Jr Cls; Sal; Band; Hon Rl; Sch Pl; Stu Cncl; Yrbk; Drama Clb; Letter Trk; Michigan Tech Univ.

BISHOP, DANA; Bloom Local HS; South Webster, OH; Band; Chrs; Cmnty Wkr; Hon Rl; Stg Crw; OEA; Spn Clb; Capt Chrldng; IM Sprt; Pom Pon; Busns Schl; Sec.

BISHOP, DAVID; Fairfield Union HS; Bremen, OH; 6/158 Aud/Vis; Boy Scts; Chrs; Chrh Wkr; Hon Rl; Jr NHS; Lbry Ade; FFA; Univ Of Kentucky; Music.

BISHOP, DEBORAH; Daleville HS; Daleville, IN; Cls Rep Frsh Cls; Pres Soph Cls; Cl Rep Jr Cls; Band; Cmp Fr Grls; Chrs; Drl Tm; Girl Scts; Hon Rl; NHS; BSU Piano Contst Trophy 74 76; Mst Valbl Flag Corpn Mbr 79; Ltr Sweater Invllybl 79; Ball St Univ; Comp Tech.

BISHOP, DEREK; Warrensville Hts HS; Warrensville, OH; NHS; Red Cr Ade; Univ.

BISHOP, DONALD; Ursuline HS; Youngstown, OH; 51/300 Band; Boy Scts; Hon Rl; NHS; Red Cr Ade; Sch Mus; Sct Actv; Ger Clb; Trk; Wrstlng; Youngstown Univ; Med.

BISHOP, GERALD; Fairbanks HS; Milford Center, OH; 6/114 Band; Chrs; Chrh Wkr; Cmnty Wkr; Hon Rl; Lbry Ade; NHS; Sch Mus; Stu Cncl; Ed Yrbk; Concordia Univ.

BISHOP, GLENN; Kenton Sr HS; Kenton, OH; 7/200 Am Leg Boys St; Chrs; Hon Rl; Sch Mus; Drama Clb; Ger Clb; Letter Glf; Natl Merit Ltr; Univ; Chem Engr.

BISHOP, GREGORY; Owosso HS; Owosso, MI; Ohio Tech Univ; Elec.

BISHOP, IRMA; Onaway HS; Onaway, MI; 21/97 Chrh Wkr; Girl Scts; Lbry Ade; NHS; Off Ade; Sch Pl; 4-H; Bsktbl; Trk; GAA; Most Valuable Girls Trackster 77 & 79; Mbr Of HS Flag Corp 79; Eng & Bus Awd 79; Lake Superior St Univ; Bus Tchr.

BISHOP, JOSEPH; Hoover HS; N Canton, OH; Chrh Wkr; Hon Rl; Ftbl; Letter Trk; Univ; Forestry.

BISHOP, LARRY; Coshocton HS; Coshocton, OH; 24/231 Am Leg Boys St; Hon Rl; NHS; Spn Clb; Bsbl; Ftbl; Coach Actv; IM Sprt; Wooster College; Engineering.

BISHOP, LEE; Gilbert HS; Gilbert, WV; 12/72 Hon Rl; NHS; Off Ade; Rptr Sch Nwsp; 4-H; Sec FHA; 4-H Awd; S West Virginia Comm Coll; Exec Sec.

BISHOP, LORI; Martinsville HS; Martinsville, IN; 67/369 Girl Scts; Sct Actv; Stu Cncl; Ed Yrbk; Sprt Ed Yrbk; Rptr Yrbk; Yrbk; Rptr Sch Nwsp; Pres Fr Clb; Glf; Indiana Univ; Jrnlsm.

BISHOP, SHELLEY; Hamilton Hts HS; Arcadia, IN; Sec Frsh Cls; Hon Rl; Stg Crw; Stu Cncl; Drama Clb; 4-H; Fr Clb; Pep Clb; Sci Clb; Spn Clb; Purdue Univ; Vet.

BISHOP, TROY; Norwood HS; Norwood, OH; 10/350 Hon Rl; Jr NHS; NHS; Mth Clb; Letter Crs Cntry; Letter Trk; Univ; Elec Engr.

BISSA, MELINDA M; Grosse Pointe N HS; Grosse Pt Wds, MI; Hon Rl; DECA; 1st 2nd & 3rd Pl Awds In Deca Dist 9 Regionals; College; Finance.

BISSELL, DIANE; Midland HS; Midland, MI; Chrh Wkr; Hon Rl; Rptr Sch Nwsp; Sch Nwsp; Chrldng; Alma Coll; Acctg.

BISSELL, JANET; St Alphonsus HS; Detroit, MI; Univ; Psych.

BISSON, PEGGI; Stow HS; Stow, OH; AFS; Band; JA; Off Ade; Rptr Sch Nwsp; Drama Clb; Spn Clb; Military.

BIST, DALE; St Agatha HS; Detroit, MI; 10/95 Hon Rl; Univ Of Michigan; Engr.

BITEMAN, LAURA; Kenton Sr HS; Kenton, OH; Cls Rep Frsh Cls; Chrs; Chrh Wkr; Girl Scts; Hon Rl; Stg Crw; Yth Flsp; Yrbk; Ger Clb; Pep Clb; Miami Univ; Phys Ther.

BITTER, KRISTINE M; Seton HS; Cincinnati, OH; 4/256 Chrs; Hon Rl; JA; Sch Mus; Sch Pl; Stg Crw; Drama Clb; Pep Clb; Spn Clb; Capt Chrldng; Univ.

BITTIKOFER, RENEE; Willard HS; Plymouth, OH; Trs Frsh Cls; Trs Soph Cls; Trs Jr Cls; Band; Chrh Wkr; Girl Scts; Lbry Ade; Sct Actv; Yth Flsp; Rptr Yrbk; Bowling Green; Psychology.

BITTINGER, CYNTHIA M; Garfield HS; Hamilton, OH; 13/300 Sec Jr Cls; Drl Tm; Girl Scts; Hon Rl; Jr NHS; NHS; Off Ade; Stu Cncl; Yth Flsp; Y-Teens; Southern Ohio Bus Schl; Acctg.

BITTINGER, GAIL; Green HS; Uniontown, OH; Band; Chrs; Chrh Wkr; Sec 4-H; IM Sprt; College; Math.

BITTNER, JULIE; Reese HS; Reese, MI; 31/131 Chrh Wkr; Girl Scts; Hon Rl; Sec Sct Actv; VP Yth Flsp; Sec Pep Clb; Letter Trk; Concordiaa Coll; Educ.

BITTNER, THOMAS; Washington HS; Massillon, OH; Hon Rl; Yth Flsp; Boys Clb Am; Spn Clb; Bsktbl; Letter Glf; College; Aviation.

BITZ, LORI; Shakamak HS; Jasonville, IN; 7/86 Band; Chrs; Chrh Wkr; Hon Rl; NHS; Quill & Scroll; Yth Flsp; Yrbk; Drama Clb; Letter Trk; Indiana St Univ; Sec.

BITZINGER, LYNNE; Concordia Lutheran HS; Ft Wayne, IN; Chrh Wkr; ROTC; VP Soph Cls; Sch Nwsp; Purdue Univ; Med.

BIVENS, TWILA; Jefferson Twp HS; New Lebanon, OH; Chrs; Chrh Wkr; Debate Tm; Hon Rl; Hosp Ade; Lbry Ade; Fr Clb; Trk;.

BIXEL, ERIC A; Worthington HS; Worthington, OH; 13/563 Hon Rl; NHS; Rus Clb; Letter Crs Cntry; Trk; Natl Merit SF; Univ; Nuclear Engr.

BIXLER, BRIAN; Canfield HS; Canfield, OH; Cls Rep Frsh Cls; Cls Rep Soph Cls; VP Jr Cls; Cl Rep Jr Cls; Cls Rep Sr Cls; Am Leg Boys St; Chrs; Hon Rl; Jr NHS; Mdrgl; Honorable Mention In English 10 Div 2 In The Kent St Univ Dist In The Ohio Tests Of Scholastic Achvmnt; College; Liberal Arts.

BIXLER, LARRY; Centreville Public HS; Centreville, MI; 14/70 Boy Scts; Hon Rl; Lbry Ade; Rptr Yrbk; Rptr Sch Nwsp; Western Michigan Univ; Acctg.

BIXLER, RHONDA; Clyde Sr HS; Clyde, OH; 17/200 Band; Chrs; Hon Rl; Treas NHS; Sch Mus; Sch Pl; Stu Cncl; Ed Yrbk; Sec Drama Clb; Trk; Univ Of Alaska; Bus.

BIZIC, CHRISTINE M; Buckeye West HS; Adena, OH; Hon Rl; NHS; Off Ade; Drama Clb; FHA; OEA; Sci Clb; Letter Chrldng; GAA; Assistant Spanish Schlrshp Team; Varsity Volleyball Lettered; Business Schl; Accounting.

BIZON, SHEILA M; St Hedwig HS; Detroit, MI; Cl Rep Jr Cls; Yrbk; Voice Dem Awd; Cert For Optimist Clb Of W Detroit 77; 2nd Pl Voice Of Democ What Amer Means To Me 76; Bus Schl.

BIZYAK, EMILY; Berkshire HS; Burton, OH; Cmp Fr Grls; 4-H; Pep Clb; Trk; Scr Kpr; Bus School; Sec.

BIZZARRI, JO; Buckeye South HS; Rayland, OH; Cls Rep Soph Cls; Cl Rep Jr Cls; Hon Rl; Off Ade; Stu Cncl; Y-Teens; Yrbk; Drama Clb; Pep Clb; Spn Clb; Jeff Tech Bus Schl.

BJERRE, EMILY; Manchester HS; Akron, OH; Trs Jr Cls; NHS; Stu Cncl; Sec Yth Flsp; Rptr Yrbk; Akron Univ; Accounting.

BJORK, LISA; Inland Lakes HS; Indian Rvr, MI; 20/90 Aud/Vis; Girl Scts; Yth Flsp; 4-H; Letter Bsktbl; Trk; GAA; 4-H Awd; Coll; Dent Hygnst.

BJORNSON, ROBERT D; Grand Ledge HS; Lansing, MI; 30/500 Band; Hon Rl; NHS; Spn Clb; Natl Merit SF; College; Veterinarian.

BLACK, AMY; Randolph Southern HS; Lynn, IN; 1/79 Val; Band; Chrs; Chrh Wkr; Hon Rl; Sec NHS; Sch Pl; Stg Crw; Rptr Yrbk; Sec 4-H; Milligan Coll; Art.

BLACK, BILLIE; Buckhannon Upshur HS; Buckhannon, WV; 3/290 Chrs; Hon Rl; Sec Jr NHS; Sec NHS; Stu Cncl; VP Yth Flsp; Employment; Billing Clerk.

BLACK, CAROL; Southgate HS; Southgate, MI; 34/253 Hst Soph Cls; Cls Rep Soph Cls; Hst Jr Cls; Cl Rep Jr Cls; Cls Rep Sr Cls; Chrs; Hon Rl; Sch Mus; Sch Pl; Stg Crw; Schl Dramatics Awd 79; Alma Pres Schslhp 79; Mbr Of Outstndng Young Amer In Performng Arts 79; Alma Coll; Actress.

BLACK, CARRIE; Creston HS; Grand Rapids, MI; Pres Frsh Cls; Cls Rep Sr Cls; Cmp Fr Grls; Chrh Wkr; Cmnty Wkr; Jr NHS; NHS; Stu Cncl; OEA; Pep Clb; Davenport Bus Schl; Acctg.

BLACK, CATHERINE; Marian HS; S Bend, IN; Chrs; Hon Rl; JA; Sch Mus; Sch Pl; Trk; JA Awd; Ball State Univ; Nursing.

BLACK, DOUGLAS; Stonewall Jackson HS; Charleston, WV; Jr NHS; NHS; Treas Fr Clb; Mth Clb; Sci Clb; Letter Bsktbl; Letter Trk; College; Med.

BLACK, GENE E; Mississinewa HS; Marion, IN; Boy Scts; DECA; Spn Clb; Univ.

BLACK, JANE; Buckeye West HS; Adena, OH; 3/87 Band; Chrh Wkr; Hon Rl; NHS; Drama Clb; FTA; Pep Clb; Univ.

BLACK, JEANNE; Stryker HS; Stryker, OH; Trs Jr Cls; Chrs; Hon Rl; Stu Cncl; 4-H; Fr Clb; FHA; Spn Clb; Capt Bsktbl; Mat Maids; Univ; Art.

BLACK, JEFFREY; Milton HS; Barboursville, WV; 83/230 Hst Frsh Cls; VP Soph Cls; Trs Jr Cls; Cls Rep Sr Cls; Chrh Wkr; Hon Rl; Off Ade; Sch Mus; Sch Pl; Ed Sch Nwsp; Marshall Univ; Bookkeeping.

BLACK, JEFFREY; Brookside HS; Elyria, OH; Hon Rl; Letter Bsbl; Capt Bsktbl; Voc School; Comp Engr.

BLACK, JOSEPH; De Sales HS; Columbus, OH; Aud/Vis; Hon Rl; Jr NHS; Sch Pl; Fr Clb; Ftbl; Trk; IM Sprt; Ohio State; Ins Agent.

BLACK, KARL; Hopkins HS; Dorr, MI; 21/113 Chrs; Hon Rl; NHS; Off Ade; Sch Pl; Stu Cncl; Natl Merit SF; Grand Rapids Jr Coll; Elec Engr.

BLACK, LIBBY; Malabar HS; Mansfield, OH; 5/216 Cls Rep Soph Cls; Cl Rep Jr Cls; Cls Rep Sr Cls; Band; Hon Rl; VP NHS; Stu Cncl; Mth Clb; Cit Awd; Wooster Coll; Chem.

BLACK, LISA; Washington Irving HS; Clarksburg, WV; 26/139 Trs Frsh Cls; Pres Soph Cls; Pres Jr Cls; Chrs; NHS; Pres Stu Cncl; Sec Fr Clb; Pres Pep Clb; Letter Bsktbl; Capt Trk; W Va Wesleyan; Physcial Educ.

BLACK, LOIS; Hannan HS; Bottom, WV; Bsktbl; GAA; Glenville Coll.

BLACK, LORI; Bethesda Christian HS; Brownsburg, IN; Chrs; Chrh Wkr; Hon Rl; Sch Pl; Univ.

BLACK, MARGARET; La Salle HS; South Bend, IN; 15/488 Cls Rep Soph Cls; Cl Rep Jr Cls; Chrs; Hon Rl; NHS; Quill & Scroll; Sch Mus; Ed Sch Nwsp; Sch Nwsp; 4-H; Purdue Univ; Home Econ.

BLACK, MARY; John F Kennedy HS; Taylor, MI; Hon Rl; Jr NHS; Off Ade; Pol Wkr; Cit Awd; College.

BLACK, MARY L; Hannan HS; Fraziers Bottom, WV; Trs Frsh Cls; Sec Sr Cls; Val; Hon Rl; Lbry Ade; NHS; Off Ade; Stu Cncl; Yrbk; Pep Clb;.

BLACK, PAT; Muncie Southside HS; Muncie, IN; 17/327 Am Leg Boys St; Hon Rl; Jr NHS; NHS; Sch Pl; Sch Nwsp; Drama Clb; Lat Clb; Ball St Univ; Public Reltns.

BLACK, PATRICIA; Monroe HS; Monroe, MI; Sal; Hon Rl; NHS; Quill & Scroll; Ed Sch Nwsp; Letter Trk; PPFtbl; Natl Merit Ltr; Michigan St Univ; Engr.

BLACK, PAUL; Cooley HS; Detroit, MI; 7/400 Hst Jr Cls; Hst Sr Cls; Hon Rl; NHS; Off Ade; Swmmng; Mas Awd; Pres Awd; Univ Of Detroit; Engr.

BLACK, PENNY; Montcalm HS; Blulfield, WV; 8/57 Chrs; Hon Rl; Hosp Ade; Sch Mus; Rptr Yrbk; Pep Clb; Chrldng; Mgrs; Voice Dem Awd; Concord Coll.

BLACK, RENITA; Harman HS; Harman, WV; Band; Chrs; Cmnty Wkr; Hon Rl; FBLA; Pep Clb; Bsktbl; Chrldng; Scr Kpr; Twrlr; FBLA Treas 78; Tri Hi Y Treas 79; Coll; Comp Sci.

BLACK, SAMUEL; Sylvania Southview HS; Sylvania, OH; 12/296 Cls Rep Soph Cls; Trs Sr Cls; Hon Rl; JA; Natl Forn Lg; NHS; Sch Pl; Stu Cncl; Yth Flsp; Fr Clb; College; Computer Engr.

BLACK, SARA; Upper Arlington Sr HS; Columbus, OH; Cmp Fr Grls; Chrh Wkr; Girl Scts; Hon Rl; Hosp Ade; Lbry Ade; NHS; Fr Clb; School Art Awds 77; Part In Governors Art Show 76; Part In State Comp For French Level II 76; Univ; Psych.

BLACK, SCOT; Meadowbrook HS; Byesville, OH; Band; Chrh Wkr; Orch; Sch Pl; Yth Flsp; Yrbk; Letter Wrstlng; Bowling Green Univ; Elec Tech.

BLACK, SUSAN; Parkway HS; Willshire, OH; 6/82 Am Leg Aux Girls St; Sec Band; Chrs; Hosp Ade; Treas NHS; Lat Clb; Pep Clb; Bsbl; Trk; Univ; Nursing.

BLACK, SUSAN; Wayne Trace HS; Payne, OH; 13/122 Hon Rl; NHS; Rptr Yrbk; 4-H; OEA;.

BLACK, TROY; Princeton HS; Cincinnati, OH; 27/633 Hon Rl; Jr NHS; NHS; Hon By OSU Offc Of Minority Affairs 78; Spanish Hon Soc 77; Inducted Into Vikettes 79; Univ; Psych.

BLACK, YOLANDA M; Warrensville Hts HS; Warrensvlle Hts, OH; Cls Rep Frsh Cls; Cl Rep Jr Cls; Cls Rep Sr Cls; Drl Tm; Hon Rl; Jr NHS; Stu Cncl; Ed Sch Nwsp; DECA; Pep Clb; Fashion Apparel & Accessories Awd; Dyke Busns Schl; Retail & Fash Merch.

BLACKANN, HAROLD; Austintown Fitch HS; Youngstown, OH; Chrs; Chrh Wkr; Hon Rl; Pres Yth Flsp; VP Fr Clb; Youngstown Univ; Pre Law.

BLACKBURN, BRENT; Green HS; Akron, OH; Cls Rep Soph Cls; Cl Rep Jr Cls; Boy Scts; Chrs; Mdrgl; Sch Mus; Sch Pl; Stu Cncl; Yth Flsp; IM Sprt; Akron Univ; Criminology.

BLACKBURN, DALE; Oregon Davis HS; Francesville, IN; 2/68 Am Leg Boys St; Hon Rl; VP NHS; Sci Clb; Letter Bsbl; IM Sprt; Voice Dem Awd; Purdue Univ; Comp Sci.

BLACKBURN, DEANNA; Southern Local HS; Salineville, OH; Chrs; Girl Scts; Hon Rl; Jr NHS; NHS; Off Ade; Sct Actv; FHA; FNA; Coach Actv; Kent St Univ; Nursing.

BLACKBURN, DEBBIE; Zeeland HS; Zeeland, MI; Band; Girl Scts; Hon Rl; Natl Forn Lg; Lat Clb; Mth Clb; Sci Clb; Letter Ten; College; Math.

BLACKBURN, DEBORAH; Oceana HS; Oceana, WV; Hon Rl; FNA; JA Awd; Pineville Voc Tech Schl; LPN.

BLACKBURN, ELLEN; Parma HS; Parma, OH; 72/786 Cls Rep Frsh Cls; Cls Rep Soph Cls; Cl Rep Jr Cls; Band; Girl Scts; Hon Rl; Stu Cncl; College; Restaurant Mgnt.

BLACKBURN, GREG; Tippecanoe Valley HS; Mentone, IN; 12/168 Aud/Vis; Band; Hon Rl; NHS; Pep Clb; Pres Awd;.

BLACKENBERRY, ANGELA M; Marion Franklin HS; Columbus, OH; 36/312 Band; Hon Rl; NHS; Sct Actv; OEA; Pep Clb; 3rd Plc OEA Bulletin Board Competition; Tres Of IOE II; Columbus Tech Inst; Legal Sec.

BLACKER, NANCY; Centerville HS; Dayton, OH; 80/680 Cl Rep Jr Cls; Sec Sr Cls; Trs Sr Cls; Cls Rep Sr Cls; NHS; Quill & Scroll; Stu Cncl; Rptr Yrbk; Yrbk; Bsbl; Miami Univ; Mass Communications.

BLACKERT, LAURIE; Coventry HS; Akron, OH; Hosp Ade; Sch Pl; Pep Clb; Letter Bsbl; IM Sprt; Ohio St Univ; Psycho Ther.

BLACKFORD, ALLISON; Philo HS; Zanesville, OH; Band; Chrs; Sec Chrh Wkr; Hon Rl; JA; Sch Pl; Sec Yth Flsp; Sec 4-H; Ger Clb; Sci Clb; Ohio St Univ; Comp Sci.

BLACKFORD, JEFF; R Nelson Snider HS; Ft Wayne, IN; Hon Rl; Wrstlng; Ind Univ.

BLACKHURST, ERIC; Midland HS; Midland, MI; 22/490 Hon Rl; NHS; Quill & Scroll; Ed Sch Nwsp; Alma Coll; Pre Law.

BLACKMON, KEITH; Aero Mechanics Voc HS; Detroit, MI; Cls Rep Sr Cls; Aud/Vis; Boy Scts; Cmnty Wkr; Hon Rl; Cls Rep Frsh Cls; Pol Wkr; Sct Actv; Stu Cncl; Univ Of Michigan; Aero.

BLACKSTOCK, PATRICK; Ironton HS; Ironton, OH; 1/189 Val; Hon Rl; NHS; Spn Clb; Crs Cntry; Trk; Marshall Univ; H S Tchr.

BLACKWELL, BRIAN D; Bedford North Lawrence HS; Bedford, IN; 29/400 Cls Rep Frsh Cls; Pres Soph Cls; Pres Jr Cls; Pres Sr Cls; Band; Drm Bgl; Hon Rl; NHS; Orch; Pol Wkr; Univ Of Evansville; Engr.

BLACKWELL, CRYSTAL; Milton HS; Ona, WV; Cls Rep Soph Cls; Chrs; Girl Scts; Hon Rl; NHS; Stu Cncl; Pep Clb; Gym; Capt Chrldng; GAA; Huntington Bus Coll.

BLACKWELL, KATRINA; Brownstown Central HS; Brownstown, IN; 25/125 Band; Chrs; Girl Scts; Sch Mus; Yth Flsp; 4-H; FTA; Spn Clb; College; Education.

BLACKWELL, MICHAEL D; Brownstown Central HS; Brownstown, IN; Band; Boy Scts; Chrs; Hon Rl; Sch Mus; Sch Pl; Stg Crw; 4-H; Spn Clb; 4-H Awd; ITT; Recording Engr.

BLACKWELL, ROBERT; New Philadelphia HS; New Phila, OH; Aud/Vis; Boy Scts; Chrh Wkr; Hon Rl; Sct Actv; Bsbl; Trk; Wrstlng; Univ; Ministry.

BLACKWELL JR, JAN D; Muncie Central HS; Muncie, IN; 7/275 Am Leg Boys St; Band; Drm Mjrt; FCA; Hon Rl; Jr NHS; NHS; Sch Pl; Stg Crw; Yth Flsp; Purdue Univ; Math.

BLACKWOOD, JOHN; Cousino HS; Warren, MI; JA; Natl Forn Lg; Rdo Clb; Bsbl; Bsktbl; Glf; Hockey; IM Sprt; VFW Awd; Voice Dem Awd; College; Sociology.

BLADEN, ANN; Bloomfield HS; Bloomfield, IN; Cl Rep Jr Cls; Pres Chrh Wkr; FCA; Hon Rl; Sec NHS; Sch Mus; Sch Pl; Sec Stu Cncl; Drama Clb; Pep Clb; Purdue Univ; Genrl Psych.

BLADES, THERESA; Jared Finney HS; Detroit, MI; Cls Rep Frsh Cls; Band; Chrs; Chrh Wkr; Hon Rl; Lbry Ade; Off Ade; Stu Cncl; Yth Flsp; Cit Awd; Univ; Bus.

BLADUF, KATHY; Pt Clinton HS; Pt Clinton, OH; 69/233 Lbry Ade; Off Ade; Fr Clb; Pep Clb; GAA; Mgrs; Mat Maids; Tmr; Elk Awd; Tri Hi Y 77; Gym Aide 77 & 78; Terra Tech Bus Schl; Marketing.

BLADZIK, TIM; Manistee Catholic HS; Manistee, MI; Hon Rl; Letter Bsktbl; Letter Ftbl; Letter Trk; IM Sprt; Univ; Dential.

BLAGEFF, LILLIAN; Normandy HS; Parma, OH; 4/659 Cl Rep Jr Cls; Chrs; Cmnty Wkr; Lbry Ade; NHS; Sch Mus; Stu Cncl; Fr Clb; College; Law.

BLAIN, GREGORY; Point Pleasant HS; Apple Grove, WV; Band; Chrs; Chrh Wkr; NHS; Pep Clb; Trk; Coll; Music.

BLAIN, SUZETTE; St Clement HS; Detroit, MI; 8/150 Girl Scts; Hon Rl; Lbry Ade; Bsbl; GAA;

PPFtbl; Cit Awd; Hon Roll 77 78 & 79; Mercy Coll; RN.

BLAINE, J; Elizabeth A Johnson HS; Clio, MI; Cls Rep Frsh Cls; Cls Rep Soph Cls; VP Jr Cls; Boy Scts; Hon Rl; Jr NHS; Sct Actv; Stu Cncl; Letter Ftbl; Letter Trk; Central Michigan Univ.

BLAINE, PAULA A; Bloom HS; Wheelersburg, OH; Chrs; Chrh Wkr; Cmnty Wkr; Lbry Ade; Off Ade; OEA; College; Sec.

BLAIN JR, BRYCE D; High School; Medina, OH; 43/359 Boy Scts; Hon Rl; Jr NHS; NHS; Y-Teens; Key Clb; Spn Clb; Ftbl; Trk; Wrstlng; Miami Univ; Pre Law.

BLAIR, BARBARA; Medina HS; Medina, OH; 27/347 AFS; Chrh Wkr; Cmnty Wkr; Girl Scts; Hon Rl; NHS; Stg Crw; Drama Clb; Fr Clb; Pep Clb; Coll; Anthropology.

BLAIR, BENJAMIN; Logan Elm HS; Circleville, OH; Band; Chrs; Chrh Wkr; Cmnty Wkr; Hon Rl; NHS; Sch Pl; Yrbk; Circleville Swim Team Most Dedicated Swimmer; Schlrshp Team; Concert Band; Ohio St Univ; Engr.

BLAIR, CAROL; George Washington HS; Charleston, WV; Boy Scts; Chrh Wkr; Pres FCA; Sct Actv; Yth Flsp; DECA; Spn Clb; GAA; Univ Of E Kentucky; Agri.

BLAIR, F WARD; Lakota HS; W Chester, OH; 2/437 VP Soph Cls; Sal; Pres Band; Boy Scts; Chrs; Hon Rl; VP NHS; Sch Mus; Yth Flsp; Lat Clb; Wittenberg Presidential Scholar 79; Ohio Board Of Regents Acad Schlrshp 79; Womens Aux To Butler Conty Med; Wittenberg Univ; Bio.

BLAIR, JOANN; Carey HS; Carey, OH; Band; Chrs; Hon Rl; NHS; Yrbk; Lat Clb; Gym; Trk; IM Sprt; Beauty Schl; Beautician.

BLAIR, JOSEPH; Marsh Fork HS; Whitesville, WV; Cls Rep Soph Cls; Cl Rep Jr Cls; Debate Tm; Hon Rl; Jr NHS; Lbry Ade; Lit Mag; Mdrgl; NHS; PAVAS; West Virginia Univ; Engr.

BLAIR, KATHRYN; St Alphonsus HS; Detroit, MI; Cls Rep Sr Cls; Chrs; Hon Rl; Jr NHS; NHS; Sch Mus; Sch Pl; Stu Cncl; Pep Clb; Chrldng; Bus Schl.

BLAIR, KENDRA; Brookfield Sr HS; Brookfield, OH; Sec Soph Cls; Band; Drl Tm; Girl Scts; Hon Rl; Stu Cncl; Rptr Yrbk; Yrbk; Fr Clb; Pep Clb; Univ.

BLAIR, LARRY; Northfield HS; Lagro, IN; FCA; Hon Rl; Bsbl; Ftbl; Wrstlng; IM Sprt;.

BLAIR, LISA; West Lafayette HS; W Lafayette, IN; 13/188 Chrs; FCA; Girl Scts; Hon Rl; Jr NHS; Quill & Scroll; Treas Yth Flsp; Rptr Yrbk; Yrbk; Drama Clb; Univ; Med.

BLAIR, LORI A; Lebanon HS; Lebanon, OH; Cl Rep Jr Cls; Pres Sr Cls; Cls Rep Sr Cls; Chrs; Chrh Wkr; Girl Scts; Hon Rl; NHS; Sch Pl; Stu Cncl;.

BLAIR, MICHAEL; Springport HS; Barbeau, MI; Boy Scts; Chrs; Hon Rl; JA; Stg Crw; Yth Flsp; Boys Clb Am; Bsbl; Glf; JA Awd; Univ Of Mich; Comm Art.

BLAIR, PATTI; Gabriel Richard HS; River Rouge, MI; 11/185 Hon Rl; NHS; Bsktbl; Letter Trk; Capt Chrldng; Tmr; Michigan Tech Univ; Geological Engr.

BLAIR, PENNY; West Vigo HS; W Terre Haute, IN; Trs Jr Cls; Cmnty Wkr; Hon Rl; Mod UN; Sch Pl; Y-Teens; Rptr Sch Nwsp; Letter Swmmng; Letter Trk; Chrldng;.

BLAIR, REBECCA; Delta HS; Dunkirk, IN; Am Leg Aux Girls St; Hon Rl; FHA; OEA; Pep Clb; OEA Exec Awd 77 OEA Statesmn Awd 78; Ambassadr Awd 79; Treas Of OEA Sr Jr 78; Ball St Univ.

BLAIR, ROBERTA; Anderson HS; Anderson, IN; Chrh Wkr; Hon Rl; NHS; Yth Flsp; 4-H; Lat Clb; Coll; Math.

BLAIR, SHEILA; Wilbur Wright HS; Dayton, OH; Hon Rl; NHS; Off Ade; Stg Crw; Boys Clb Am; OEA; Ten; Scr Kpr; English 10 Awd; Typing I Awd; IOE Clerical I Awd; Wright St Univ; Pre Law.

BLAIS, MARY; Muskegon Catholic Centrl HS; Muskegon, MI; 7/178 Band; Hon Rl; Treas NHS; Fr Clb; Sci Clb; Aquinas College; Bio.

BLAISDELL, A; Flushing Sr HS; Flushing, MI; Band; Cmnty Wkr; Girl Scts; Hon Rl; NHS; Sch Pl; Stg Crw; Fr Clb; Socr; Michigan St Univ; Vet.

BLAIZE, NANCY J; Southfield Lathrup HS; Southfield, MI; Trs Jr Cls; Trs Sr Cls; Girl Scts; Hon Rl; NHS; Stg Crw; Stu Cncl; Pep Clb; Spn Clb; Trk; Michigan St Univ; Bio Med Engr.

BLAKE, APRIL; Lexington HS; Mansfield, OH; 4/270 Band; Hon Rl; Lbry Ade; NHS; Stg Crw; Drama Clb; 4-H; Fr Clb; Univ; Acctg.

BLAKE, GARY; Sandusky St Marys HS; Sandusky, OH; Rptr Yrbk; Letter Ftbl; Letter Wrstlng; IM Sprt; Ohio State Univ; Acct.

BLAKE, JEFF; New Albany HS; New Albany, IN; 38/565 Band; Chrh Wkr; Hon Rl; NHS; Orch; Yth Flsp; Yrbk; Ger Clb; Marion Coll; Pre Med.

BLAKE, PEGGY; Rosedale HS; Rosedale, IN; 2/55 Pres Frsh Cls; Pres Soph Cls; Pres Jr Cls; Hon Rl; Pres NHS; Quill & Scroll; Yrbk; Pep Clb; Chrldng; Pom Pon; Voted Miss Smart 78; St Marys Clg Math Contest; Indiana Voc Schl; Elec Tech.

BLAKE, PRISCILLA; Forest Park HS; Cincinnati, OH; Pep Clb; Letter Bsktbl; Letter Trk; College.

BLAKE, RICHARD; Lincoln Sr HS; Warren, MI; 1/327 Val; Band; Hon Rl; Pres Jr NHS; NHS; Orch; Red Cr Ade; Sch Mus; Natl Merit Ltr; Mi Delegate To Natl Yth Sci Camp In Wv 78; Hope Coll Pres Schlrshp 79; Hope Coll; Chem.

BLAKE, SANDRA K; Lewis County HS; Weston, WV; Hon Rl; Hosp Ade; Lbry Ade; Off Ade; 4-H; Pep Clb; Glennville St Coll.

BLAKE, SANDY; Groveport Madison HS; Columbus, OH; Band; Cmp Fr Grls; Hon Rl; Orch; Sch Mus; Sch Pl; Yth Flsp; PPFtbl; Southeastern Acad; Travel Agent.

BLAKE, SUSANNAH; Shortridge HS; Indianapolis, IN; 29/400 Cl Rep Jr Cls; Girl Scts; Hon Rl; Key Clb; Mth Clb; Trk; Chrldng; College.

BLAKE, TRENT; Milton HS; Ona, WV; Aud/Vis; Chrs; Hon Rl; Sch Mus; Sch Pl; Trk; Vocational Schl; Ind Elec.

BLAKEMAN, TERESA; Columbiana HS; Columbiana, OH; 8/100 Cmp Fr Grls; Chrs; Chrh Wkr; Hon Rl; JA; Treas Yth Flsp; 4-H; Sec Spn Clb; Girls Lg Hgh Avg In Bwlng Trophy Awd 79; Nomntd Into Thenatl Hnr Soc 78; Univ; Med.

BLAKER, TAWNYA; Carmel HS; Westfield, IN; 179/664 Cls Rep Sr Cls; Hon Rl; DECA; Sec 4-H; Trk; Purdue Univ; Animal Sci.

BLAKER, TAWYNA; Carmel HS; Westfield, IN; Cls Rep Sr Cls; Hon Rl; VP DECA; Sec 4-H; Trk; Purdue Univ; Animal Sci.

BLAKESLEE, DANIEL; John Marshall HS; Indianapolis, IN; 61/511 Boy Scts; Chrh Wkr; Hon Rl; JA; Sch Pl; Sct Actv; Stg Crw; Stu Cncl; Yth Flsp; Eng Clb; U S Navy; Nuclear.

BLAKLEY, JOHN; Watterson HS; Columbus, OH; Cls Rep Frsh Cls; Hon Rl; Sch Pl; College; Law.

BLALOCK, KIM; Highland Park Community HS; Highland Pk, MI; 6/273 Band; Chrh Wkr; Hon Rl; Univ Of Detroit; Dental Hygene.

BLANCHARD, KAREN; Chelsea HS; Chelsea, MI; Band; Girl Scts; Hon Rl; NHS; Yth Flsp; Rptr Yrbk;.

BLANCHARD, REENAE; Columbia City Joint HS; Columbia City, IN; JA; Off Ade; Pol Wkr; Stu Cncl; Spn Clb; Univ; Vet Sci.

BLANCHARD, TANYA; Cass Technical HS; Detroit, MI; Hon Rl; Orch; FTA; Univ; Spec Educ.

BLANCHORD, DEBBIE; Bay HS; Bay Vill, OH; 93/390 Chrs; Hon Rl; Lbry Ade; Sch Mus; Ten; Univ; Bus.

BLANCO, RICHARD; Chaney HS; Youngstown, OH; Band; Chrs; Hon Rl; Sch Mus; Sch Pl; Lat Clb; Spn Clb; Bsktbl; Ftbl; Coach Actv; Miami Dade Cmnty Coll.

BLAND, M; Flushing HS; Flushing, MI; NHS; Bsbl; Glf; Hockey; College.

BLAND, NATHAN E; Shortridge HS; Indianapolis, IN; Cls Rep Sr Cls; JA; ROTC; Sch Nwsp; Mth Clb; Letter Bsbl; Letter Wrstlng; GAA; College.

BLANDO, ALICIA; Andrean HS; Gary, IN; Hon Rl; Stg Crw; Mth Clb; IM Sprt; Am Leg Awd; Univ; Pre Med.

BLANEY, BARBARA; Bellmont HS; Decatur, IN; Girl Scts; Hon Rl; Hosp Ade; Yth Flsp; Drama Clb; Ger Clb; OEA; Trk; Intl Bus Coll; Sec.

BLANEY, DIANA; Teays Valley HS; Ashville, OH; 1/230 Chrs; Chrh Wkr; Girl Scts; NHS; Sch Mus; Drama Clb; Sci Clb; Spn Clb; Natl Merit Ltr; US Air Force Acad Summer Sci Seminar 79; State Sci Fair 79; Ohio St Univ; Engr Physics.

BLANEY, KATHLEEN; Newark Catholic HS; Newark, OH; Cl Rep Jr Cls; Chrs; Cmnty Wkr; Hon Rl; Fr Clb; Pep Clb; Letter Bsktbl; Trk; GAA; IM Sprt; Ohio Tst For Schlstc Acvmnt Fr 1 77; Frnch III 79; Voluntr Aide At A Nursng Hme; Part In Rlgn Serv Progr; Univ; Psych.

BLANEY, MARGARET; Bishop Noll Institute; Munster, IN; 100/400 Chrs; Chrh Wkr; Sch Mus; Stg Crw; Spn Clb; Purdue Univ; Business.

BLANEY, MICHELLE; John F Kennedy HS; Cleveland, OH; Cl Rep Jr Cls; JA; Stu Cncl; FTA; Chrldng; Tenn Intl Assoc Of Personnel In Emplymnt Security 79; Univ Of Cincinnati; Fshn Dsgn.

BLANEY, STEPHANIE; William A Wirt HS; Gary, IN; Hon Rl; Jr NHS; Sch Pl; Rptr Sch Nwsp; GAA;.

BLANFORD, MARY; Kalida HS; Ft Jennings, OH; Am Leg Aux Girls St; Hon Rl; NHS; Sch Mus; 4-H; IM Sprt; 4-H Awd; Univ; History.

BLANFORD, TAMARA; Benjamin Bosse HS; Evansville, IN; 9 Hon Rl; Pol Wkr; Stu Cncl; Treas FBLA; Pres OEA; Kiwan Awd; Opt Clb Awd; Employment; Co Oper.

BLANK, JOSEPH; Corydon Ctrl HS; Corydon, IN; 12/183 Cl Rep Jr Cls; Chrh Wkr; Hon Rl; NHS; Sch Nwsp; Pres Pep Clb; Letter Bsbl; Letter Bsktbl; Letter Crs Cntry; Purdue Univ; Psych.

BLANKE, TERRI; Northfield Jr Sr HS; Wabash, IN; 52/110 Band; Stg Crw; Yth Flsp; Rptr Yrbk; Rptr Sch Nwsp; Drama Clb; FHA; Pep Clb; Spn Clb; Pom Pon; Ball St Univ; Fash Merch.

BLANKEMEYER, ANGELA; Lincolnview HS; Van Wert, OH; 19/70 Am Leg Aux Girls St; Off Ade; 4-H; Sec Fr Clb; Bsktbl; Trk; GAA; IM Sprt; Scr Kpr; 4-H Awd; College; Elem Phys Ed.

BLANKEN, CELESTE; Tecumseh Sr HS; Medway, OH; Val; AFS; Hon Rl; Jr NHS; NHS; Off Ade; Stg Crw; Drama Clb; Fr Clb; Trk; Tecumseh Highsteppers Flag Corp; Honorable Mention In Sci Fair; Natl Merit Cert Of Commendation PSAT Test; Ohio Northern Univ; Bio.

BLANKENBERGER, CAROL; Mater Dei HS; Haubstadt, IN; 10/184 Hon Rl; 4-H; Bus Sch; Bus.

BLANKENBERGER, MARIA; North Posey HS; Cynthiana, IN; 14/175 Sec Sr Cls; Hon Rl; Natl Forn Lg; NHS; 4-H; FHA; IM Sprt; Purdue; Medical.

BLANKENSHIP, AARON; Nicholas County HS; Birch River, WV; 5/216 Cl Rep Jr Cls; Am Leg Boys St; Hon Rl; Lit Mag; NHS; Leo Clb; Letter Bsbl; Letter Wrstlng; Cit Awd; Marshal Univ; Chemistry.

BLANKENSHIP, BETH; Bucyrus HS; Bucyrus, OH; Sec Frsh Cls; Cls Rep Soph Cls; Cl Rep Jr Cls; Chrs; Chrh Wkr; Cmnty Wkr; Hon Rl; Off Ade; Sch Mus; Sch Pl; Ohio St Univ; Psych.

BLANKENSHIP, BOB; Lebanon Sr HS; Lebanon, IN; 46/256 Pres Frsh Cls; VP Jr Cls; Cls Rep Sr Cls; Aud/Vis; Boy Scts; Chrs; Hon Rl; Jr NHS; Mod UN; Natl Forn Lg; Rose Hulman Inst Of Tech; Elec Engr.

BLANKENSHIP, CARLA; Batavia HS; Batavia, OH; 1/75 Band; Hon Rl; NHS; Stu Cncl; Fr Clb; Pep Clb; Trk; Chrldng; PPFtbl; Sci Awrd Chem 78; Univ; Comp Sci.

BLANKENSHIP, GARY; Iaeger HS; Panther, WV; 12/123 Am Leg Boys St; Hon Rl; NHS; Letter Bsbl; Letter Bsktbl; Ftbl;.

BLANKENSHIP, JAMES R; Eastern HS; Greentown, IN; 7/125 Am Leg Boys St; Band; Chrh Wkr; FCA; Hon Rl; NHS; Pol Wkr; Lat Clb; Letter Swmmng; Natl Merit SF; Univ; Poli Sci.

BLANKENSHIP, KIMBERLY; Wayne HS; Wayne, WV; 10/154 VP Soph Cls; VP Jr Cls; VP Sr Cls; Chrs; Hon Rl; NHS; Sch Mus; Beta Clb; FBLA; DAR Awd; Marshall Univ; Legal Sec.

BLANKENSHIP, LAURA; Rock Hill Sr HS; Ironton, OH; Hon Rl; Pep Clb; Trk; GAA; Forester Aide.

BLANKENSHIP, MARVEL; Crestview HS; Mansfield, OH; Band; Chrs; Drm Mjrt; Off Ade; Rptr Yrbk; 4-H; 4-H Awd; U S Marines Corps; Air Trffc Cntrl.

BLANKENSHIP, PAMELA; Lima Perry HS; Lima, OH; Trs Jr Cls; VP Sr Cls; Chrs; Stu Cncl; Rptr Sch Nwsp; Trk; Bus Schl; Bus.

BLANKENSHIP, ROBIN; Oceana HS; Oceana, WV; 12/126 Pres Frsh Cls; Cls Rep Frsh Cls; NHS; Stu Cncl; Yrbk; Capt Bsktbl; Chrldng; Pres GAA; Marshall Univ; Educ.

BLANKENSHIP, SHERRY; Tippecanoe Valley HS; Warsaw, IN; 16/159 Sec Frsh Cls; Hon Rl; NHS; Sch Nwsp; FHA; OEA; TVHS Outstndng Rrc Rvw Rptrr 1977; 1st OEA Spch Sntst Reg 1978; Tms Unn WRSW Schlstc Awd Eng 1978; Manchester Univ; Eng.

BLANKENSHIP, TAMMY; Spanishburg HS; Kegley, WV; 4/42 Trs Soph Cls; Band; Chrs; Hon Rl; Yrbk; FBLA; FHA; Bluefield St Univ.

BLANKS, SHAWN; Inkster HS; Westland, MI; 20/225 Cl Rep Jr Cls; Cls Rep Sr Cls; Hon Rl; NHS; Stu Cncl; Ed Yrbk; Rptr Sch Nwsp; Outstndng Coop Awd 79; Black History Club Awd 79; 2nd Yr In Whos Who 78; Morehouse Coll; Bus Admin.

BLANTON, APRIL; Pike County Joint Voc HS; Piketon, OH; 1/19 Hon Rl; Rptr Sch Nwsp; 4-H; FHA; FTA; Spn Clb; VICA; Tech School; Electronics Technician.

BLANTON, KELLY; Switz City Central HS; Switz City, IN; Hon Rl; Lit Mag; NHS; Rptr Sch Nwsp; FHA; Vincennes Univ; Comp Tech Or Acctg.

BLANTON, SANDRA; Madison Comprehensive HS; Mansfield, OH; Chrs; JA; 4-H; FHA; Spn Clb; North Central Tech; Comp Program.

BLAQUIERE, JEANNE; Berkley HS; Berkley, MI; Chrs; Hon Rl; Jr NHS; Mdrgl; NHS; Univ; Pre Med.

BLASCAK, LISA; Austintown Fitch HS; Youngstown, OH; 49/679 VP Frsh Cls; VP Soph Cls; VP Jr Cls; VP Sr Cls; Treas Drl Tm; NHS; Y-Teens; Key Clb; Letter Gym; PPFtbl; Bowling Green St Univ; Elem Ed.

BLASCO, VIRGINIA; Lew Wallace HS; Gary, IN; 115/469 Band; Ed Sch Nwsp; Rptr Sch Nwsp; Sch Nwsp; Pres Spn Clb; Purdue; Journalism.

BLASKE, LUCIA; St Augustine Acad; Cleveland, OH; Chrs; Girl Scts; JA; Rptr Sch Nwsp; Drama Clb; Sci Clb; Control Data Inst; Comp Oper.

BLASKOWSKI, JOHN; Cheboygan Cath Ctrl HS; Cheboygan, MI; Cl Rep Jr Cls; Hon Rl; Sch Pl; Stg Crw; Letter Bsbl; Letter Bsktbl; Letter Ftbl; Voice Dem Awd; Univ.

BLATT, ALLISON L; Athens HS; Athens, WV; 4/74 Hon Rl; VP NHS; VP Stu Cncl; Sprt Ed Yrbk; Fr Clb; FTA; Pep Clb; Letter Bsbl; Capt Bsktbl; IM Sprt; Univ.

BLATT, DAN; Upper Arlington HS; Columbus, OH; 195/610 Cls Rep Frsh Cls; Hon Rl; Lit Mag; Quill & Scroll; Rptr Sch Nwsp; Sch Nwsp; Spn Clb; Ten; IM Sprt; Univ.

BLATT, JAMES; Magnolia HS; New Martinsvle, WV; Hon Rl; Bsktbl; Crs Cntry; Trk; Drafting.

BLATT, JOAN; Buffalo HS; Huntington, WV; Band; Drm Mjrt; Hon Rl; Yrbk; Rptr Sch Nwsp; Mat Maids; Marshall Cmnty Coll; Sec.

BLATTNER, KRISTI; Meadowbrook HS; Lore City, OH; 12/179 VP Jr Cls; Am Leg Aux Girls St; Hon Rl; Jr NHS; NHS; Sch Pl; Stu Cncl; Ed Yrbk; Key Clb; Pres Mth Clb;.

BLATZ, LAURIE; Wayne HS; Dayton, OH; Cmp Fr Grls; Chrh Wkr; Jr NHS; Stu Cncl; Pep Clb; IM Sprt; Mgrs; Natl Merit Ltr; Wright St Univ; Bus.

BLAUGH, DIAN; Washington HS; Massillon, OH; 71/482 Cls Rep Frsh Cls; Band; Hon Rl; NHS; Off Ade; Pres Y-Teens; Rptr Yrbk; Fr Clb; Pep Clb; Swmmng; Ohio St Univ.

BLAUSER, JEFF; St Marys HS; St Marys, WV; 8/122 Pres Soph Cls; VP Jr Cls; Pres Sr Cls; Am Leg Boys St; Aud/Vis; Band; Chrs; Chrh Wkr; Cmnty Wkr; Drm Mjrt; W Virginia Inst Of Tech; Elec Engr.

BLAUVELT, TAMRA; Madison Heights HS; Anderson, IN; Chrs; Girl Scts; NHS; Pres Drama Clb; FTA; Pep Clb; VP Spn Clb; Mgrs; Am Leg Awd; College; Secondary Ed.

BLAYLOCK, DAWN M; Lake Orion HS; Lake Orion, MI; 17/476 Hon Rl; Jr NHS; Natl Merit SF; Oakland Univ; Medicine.

BLAZEJEWSKI, GAIL; Our Lady Of Mercy HS; Livonia, MI; Cmnty Wkr; Hon Rl; Capt Bsktbl; Capt Hockey; GAA; NCTE; Mi Amateur Hockey Assoc St Champ 77; Diploma Of Merit In Spanish 77 78 & 79; Catholic Organ Bsktbll Tm 73; Univ.

BLAZEK, MICHELE; Jackson Milton HS; Lake Milton, OH; Am Leg Aux Girls St; Hon Rl; FHA; Chrldng; Am Leg Awd; Univ.

BLAZEK, MICHELE E; Jackson Milton HS; Lake Milton, OH; Hon Rl; Letter Chrldng; Am Leg Awd; 4-H Awd; Univ.

BLAZER, FRANCES; William V Fisher Cath HS; Canal Winchstr, OH; Hon Rl; Jr NHS; NHS; 4-H; Fr Clb; Valedictorian Of Graduating Freshman Class; Teachers Aide; College; Math.

BLAZER, WILLIAM E; Barboursville HS; Barboursville, WV; Am Leg Boys St; Boy Scts; Hon Rl; Jr NHS; Sch Pl; Sct Actv; Yrbk; Key Clb; Spn Clb; Bsktbl; Most Valuable Golfer 77; Chief Justice Of Supreme Ct Of Boys St 79; Cabinet Mbr Of E Cntrl Regnl Explorers; Military Acad; Engr.

BLEAK, TAMMY; Washington HS; So Bend, IN; 59/355 Chrh Wkr; Pres Orch; Sch Mus; Spn Clb; Bsktbl; Swmmng; Letter Mgrs; Scr Kpr; Tmr; Brigham Young Univ; Bus.

BLEECKER, JAMES; Adrian Sr HS; Clayton, MI; Chrh Wkr; Hon Rl; Sch Pl; Yth Flsp; 4-H; Sci Clb; 4-H Awd; Schlstc Awd For Achvmnt In Writing 78; Jr Holstein Freisian Awd 77; Michigan St Univ; Vet Sci.

BLEHA, JAMES; Elder HS; Cinn, OH; Hon Rl; Boys Clb Am; Bsbl; Bsktbl; Socr; Southern Ohio Coll; Machine Tooling.

BLEICHER, KAREN; Holy Rosary HS; Burton, MI; 6/57 Hon Rl; NHS; Sch Pl; Letter Crs Cntry; Letter Trk; Chrldng; Univ.

BLEILE, RICHARD C; Baraga HS; Baraga, MI; Hon Rl; Bsbl; Bsktbl; Letter Ftbl; Letter Trk; Ferris St College; Draftsman.

BLEITZ, BETH; Avondale Sr HS; Bloomfield Hls, MI; Aud/Vis; Cmnty Wkr; NHS; Quill & Scroll; Stu Cncl; Rptr Yrbk; Yrbk; Sch Nwsp; Boys Clb Am; Rdo Clb; Voted As 1 Of Top 3 Disc Jockeys At WAHS; VP Pres Promotional Dir Of WAHS; Intern At WABX FM; Mich St Univ; Telecommunications.

BLEND, BRUCE; Buckhannon Upshur HS; Buckhannon, WV; Pres Soph Cls; VP Sr Cls; Am Leg Boys St; Chrs; Hon Rl; Letter Bsktbl; Swmmng; 4-H Awd; Mas Awd; Pres Awd; College.

BLEND, BRUCE E; Buckhannon Upshur HS; Buckhannon, WV; Pres Soph Cls; VP Sr Cls; Am Leg Boys St; Chrs; Hon Rl; Stu Cncl; Letter Bsktbl; Swmmng; Mas Awd; Pres Awd; Univ.

BLESSING, GREGORY; Pleasant HS; Marion, OH; Hon Rl; Ohio Inst Of Tech; Elec Comm Tech.

BLESSING, MARK E; Concordia Lutheran HS; Ft Wayne, IN; Boy Scts; Chrh Wkr; Cmnty Wkr; Hon Rl; Pol Wkr; Ger Clb; IM Sprt; Scr Kpr; Indiana Univ; Actuary Sci.

BLESSINGER, KATHY; Southridge HS; Holland, IN; Am Leg Aux Girls St; Chrs; Hon Rl; Sch Mus; Stg Crw; Ger Clb; Letter Trk; PPFtbl;.

BLESSINGER, MICHELLE; Southridge HS; Holland, IN; Band; Girl Scts; Hon Rl; Sch Mus; Pres 4-H; FHA; Trk; 4-H Awd; Indiana Univ; Pediatric Nurse.

BLEVINS, CHRISTOPHER; Purcell HS; Cincinnati, OH; 12/280 Boy Scts; Chrh Wkr; Cmnty Wkr; Hon Rl; Yth Flsp; Boys Clb Am; Ftbl; Trk; Wrstlng; IM Sprt; Coll; Med.

BLEVINS, JAY D; R Nelson Snider HS; Ft Wayne, IN; 8/564 Hon Rl; Jr NHS; NHS; Off Ade; Bsbl; Wrstlng; IM Sprt; Cit Awd; Natl Merit Ltr; Ohio St Univ; Math.

BLEVINS, LANA; De Kalb HS; Auburn, IN; 21/305 Cls Rep Frsh Cls; Cls Rep Soph Cls; Pres Jr Cls; Chrh Wkr; Girl Scts; Hon Rl; NHS; Off Ade; Pol Wkr; Red Cr Ade; Auburns Bus & Prof Wmns Schlrshp 1979; Tri Kappa Honors Awd 1977; Voted Best Leader & Citizen By Sr Class; Internatl Bus Coll; Exec Sec.

BLEVINS, LORI; Brownstown Central HS; Brownstown, IN; 10/143 Am Leg Aux Girls St; Band; Chrs; Debate Tm; Hosp Ade; NHS; Sch Mus; Sch Pl; Yth Flsp; 4-H; De Pauw Univ; Nursing.

BLEVINS, MANDY; De Kalb HS; Auburn, IN; 34/281 JA; Off Ade; Pep Clb; Spn Clb; Bsktbl; Letter Gym; Chrldng; Pres IM Sprt; PPFtbl; JA Awd; Awrd Bat Girl 1977; Bus Schl; Math.

BLEVINS, RHONDA; Springfield North HS; Springfield, OH; Sec Jr Cls; Trs Jr Cls; Chrs; Drl Tm; Hon Rl; Orch; Stu Cncl; FBLA; Lat Clb; Mas Awd; Univ; Bus Admin.

BLEVINS, TRACY; Pike HS; Zionsville, IN; Band; Chrh Wkr; Girl Scts; Hon Rl; Off Ade; Pol Wkr; 4-H; Pep Clb; Trk; Pom Pon; Univ; Pharm.

BLEVINS, TWANA; Jonathan Alder HS; Plain City, OH; Trs Jr Cls; Off Ade; Sch Mus; Sch Pl; Y-Teens; Drama Clb; Pres 4-H; FHA; Pep Clb; Mgrs; Ohio St Univ; Phys Ther.

BLEVINS, VICKI; Shenandoah HS; Middletown, IN; 12/118 Band; Chrh Wkr; Girl Scts; Hon Rl; Yth Flsp; Sch Nwsp; Sec FTA; Ball St Univ; Photog.

BLEWITT, JENNIFER; Ursuline HS; Youngstown, OH; 27/260 Band; Chrh Wkr; Cmnty Wkr; Hon Rl; NHS; Sch Mus; Ohio Univ.

BLEWITT, SUSAN; Highland HS; Copley, OH; 36/202 Hon Rl; Lbry Ade; NHS; Off Ade; IM Sprt; Treas Mat Maids; Scr Kpr; Univ Of Akron; Poli Sci.

BLICKENSDERFER, DEANNE; West Branch HS; Homeworth, OH; AFS; Band; Chrs; Sec Chrh Wkr; Sch Mus; Sec 4-H; FHA; Pep Clb; Capt Pom Pon; College.

BLIKE, GEORGE; Central Hower HS; Akron, OH; 5/400 Boy Scts; Hon Rl; NHS; Orch; Red Cr Ade; Sct Actv; Rptr Yrbk; Letter Socr; Letter Swmmng; Univ; Med.

BLINN, LORE; Winamac Community HS; Star City, IN; 1/127 Am Leg Aux Girls St; Boy Scts; Chrh Wkr; Hon Rl; Jr NHS; NHS; Sch Mus; Sch Pl; Stu Cncl; Yth Flsp; Univ.

BLINN, LORIE; Southern Wells HS; Warren, IN; 25/95 Chrs; Ed Sch Nwsp; Rptr Sch Nwsp; 4-H; FHA; Pom Pon; Essay Contest 1st Pl St Of IN 1972;.

BLISCHAK, MATTHEW; Stanton HS; Stratton, OH; Boy Scts; Chrs; Hon Rl; NHS; Sch Mus; Bsktbl; Letter Crs Cntry; Letter Ftbl; Letter Trk; College; Engr.

BLISS, DANIEL; Owosso HS; Owosso, MI; 35/406 CAP; Hon Rl; NHS; Ten; IM Sprt; Mi Comptn Schlrshp 79; Emergecy Med Tech 79; Amelia Earhart Awd 79; Michigan Tech Univ; Chem Engr.

BLISS, ROBERT; Avon HS; Avon, OH; AFS; Hon Rl; 4-H; Bsktbl; Letter Ftbl; Letter Trk; IM Sprt; 4-H Awd; College; Engr.

BLISS, WALTE; High School; Upland, IN; 59/245 Lbry Ade; NHS; Yth Flsp; Letter Crs Cntry; Letter Swmmng; Letter Trk; Kiwan Awd; Taylor Univ.

BLISSICK, THOMAS; Michigan Center HS; Michigan Center, MI; Cls Rep Frsh Cls; Cls Rep Soph Cls; VP Sr Cls; Hon Rl; Stu Cncl; Bsktbl; Ftbl; IM Sprt; Soc Sci Acad Tm 79; Univ; Soc Work.

BLIVEN, MARGOT A; Connersville Sr HS; Connersville, IN; 1/400 Val; VP Band; Drm Mjrt; Hon Rl; VP JA; Pres NHS; Stu Cncl; Pres Ger Clb; VP Sci Clb; Natl Merit SF; Univ; Engr.

BLIZZARD, KYLE; Buckeye South HS; Rayland, OH; 4/125 VP Soph Cls; VP Jr Cls; Band; Hon Rl; NHS; Y-Teens; Rptr Sch Nwsp; Sec Drama Clb; Pep Clb; Spn Clb; Univ.

BLIZZARD, SHARON; Vinson HS; Huntington, WV; 27/120 Chrs; Hon Rl; Lbry Ade; NHS; FHA; Huntington Business College; Accnt.

BLOCH, PHILLP; Bexley HS; Columbus, OH; Chrh Wkr; Cmnty Wkr; Hon Rl; JA; Lbry Ade; Red Cr Ade; Sct Actv; Stg Crw; Rptr Sch Nwsp; Mth Clb; Superior Ratng Sci Fari 75; Aza Beau Sweetheart Awd 77; Ohio St Univ; Med.

BLOCK, CHERYL; Bishop Watterson HS; Worthington, OH; 8/249 Chrs; Hon Rl; Jr NHS; NHS; Rptr Yrbk; Rptr Sch Nwsp; Sch Nwsp; Mat Maids; Miami Univ.

BLOCK, DOUGLAS; Caro Community HS; Caro, MI; Chrh Wkr; Cmnty Wkr; FCA; Hon Rl; NHS; Yth Flsp; Rptr Sch Nwsp; Central Mic; Spec Ed.

BLOCK, JACK; Kalamazoo Central HS; Kalamazoo, MI; Am Leg Boys St; Hon Rl; Ftbl; Trk; Scr Kpr; Western Michigan Univ; Paper Engr.

BLOCK, L; Beal City HS; Weidman, MI; Sec Jr Cls; Chrs; Rptr Yrbk; Sch Nwsp; FHA; 4-H Awd; College; Soc Work.

BLOCK, RANDALL; Reitz Memorial HS; Evansville, IN; Band; Boy Scts; Hon Rl; PAVAS; Sch Mus; 4-H; Trk; Wrstlng; Cit Awd; 4-H Awd; ISUE; Elec Engr.

BLOCK, ROBERT; Ubly HS; Minden City, MI; 11/110 Hon Rl; NHS; Voc Schl; Audio Elec.

BLOCK, SANDRA; Hamtramck HS; Hamtramck, MI; 16/80 Cl Rep Jr Cls; Orch; Wayne St Univ; Med.

BLOCK, STEVEN; Columbus Acad; Worthington, OH; 5/45 Hon Rl; Lit Mag; Sch Pl; Rptr Sch Nwsp; Spn Clb; Letter Ftbl; Letter Wrstlng; Natl Merit SF; Cornell Univ.

BLOCKER, DENISE; Copley HS; Barberton, OH; Band; Girl Scts; Hon Rl; NHS; Sch Mus; Rptr Yrbk; Spn Clb; Trk; College.

BLODGETT, BRIAN; St Joseph Ctrl Catholic HS; Fremont, OH; 44/102 Cmnty Wkr; Y-Teens; Key Clb; IM Sprt; Ohio St Univ; Math.

BLODGETT, BRUCE; Charlotte HS; Charlotte, MI; 15/304 Hon Rl; NHS; Sct Actv; Stu Cncl; Y-Teens; Ten; Mic State Univ; Engr.

BLODGETT, GREG; Columbia Ctrl HS; Cement City, MI; 16/169 Band; Hon Rl; NHS; Bsbl; Bsktbl; Ftbl; JC Awd; Michigan Tech Univ; Mech Engr.

BLOGNA, BRENDA; Massillon Washington HS; Massillon, OH; 31/482 VP Soph Cls; VP Jr Cls; Cls Rep Sr Cls; Am Leg Aux Girls St; Hon Rl; Jr NHS; NHS; Quill & Scroll; Yrbk; Massillon Community Hosp; Nursing.

BLOGNA, JAMES; Washington HS; Massillon, OH; Cls Rep Frsh Cls; Boy Scts; Hon Rl; Boys Clb Am; Lat Clb; Letter Bsbl; Letter Ftbl; Letter Trk; Letter Wrstlng; Cit Awd; Florida Inst Of Tech; Marine Bio.

BLOIR, COLEEN; Edgerton HS; Edgerton, OH; 1/87 Chrh Wkr; Hon Rl; Jr NHS; NHS; Sch Mus; Sec Yth Flsp; Pep Clb; GAA; IM Sprt; Ft Wayne Bible Coll.

BLOME, ELIZABETH; Mother Of Mercy HS; Cincinnati, OH; 95/245 Cl Rep Jr Cls; Chrs; Drl Tm; Hon Rl; JA; Sct Actv; Stu Cncl; Fr Clb; Chrldng; IM Sprt; Univ; Dietic.

BLOMMEL, BRENDA; Carroll HS; Dayton, OH; Cmnty Wkr; Girl Scts; Hon Rl; NHS; Sch Pl; Stu Cncl; Trk; Univ; Wildlife Conservation.

BLOMMER, STEPHEN; Charlotte HS; Charlotte, MI; 56/306 Boy Scts; NHS; Sct Actv; Cit Awd; Ferris St Univ; Comp Tech.

BLOMQUIST, SUSAN; North Farmington HS; Farm Hills, MI; Chrs; Chrh Wkr; Cmnty Wkr; Hon Rl; Lbry Ade; NHS; Yth Flsp; Spn Clb; GAA; Taylor Univ.

BLOMSTROM, LYNN; Carrollton HS; Saginaw, MI; 31/150 Sec Sr Cls; Hosp Ade; Sec Pom Pon; Baker Jr Coll; Bus.

BLOODGOOD, LINDA; Greenfield Central HS; Greenfield, IN; 1/310 VP Soph Cls; Pres Chrs; Pres FCA; Treas NHS; Pol Wkr; Mth Clb; Pres Spn Clb; Purdue Univ.

BLOOM, MARK; Harbor HS; Ashtabula, OH; 49/199 AFS; Band; Boy Scts; FCA; Sch Mus; Sch Pl; Pres Drama Clb; Ger Clb; Crs Cntry; Ftbl; Univ; Theatre.

BLOOM, MARK; Shadyside HS; Shadyside, OH; Am Leg Boys St; Band; Hon Rl; Sch Pl; Stu Cncl; Pep Clb; Spn Clb; Crs Cntry; Swmmng; Letter Trk; Rpes Thespian Club 79; Pres Band; Bugler For Amer Lgn Chem Schlsp Team; Ohio St Univ; Med.

BLOOM, SALLIE; Malabar HS; Mansfield, OH; 16/278 Cls Rep Soph Cls; Cl Rep Jr Cls; Cls Rep Sr Cls; Band; Hon Rl; Jr NHS; NHS; Mth Clb; College; Elem Educ.

BLOSSER, JEFFREY; Fairfield Union HS; Lancaster, OH; 4/152 Hon Rl; 4-H; Key Clb; Letter Bsbl; Letter Glf; IM Sprt; Ohio St Univ; Archt.

BLOSSER, MELISSA; University HS; Morgantown, WV; Sec Frsh Cls; Trs Jr Cls; Girl Scts; Hon Rl; Quill & Scroll; Rptr Yrbk; Sch Nwsp; FHA; Scr Kpr; Univ Of Miami; Marine Bio.

BLOSSER, SHARON; Bridgman HS; Bridgman, MI; Band; Girl Scts; Hon Rl; Red Cr Ade; Sct Actv; FHA; Sci Clb; Gym; Letter Trk; GAA; College; Photography.

BLOSSER, TERRANCE; Morgantown HS; Morgantown, WV; Boy Scts; Chrh Wkr; Hon Rl; Sct Actv; Yth Flsp; Spn Clb; Ftbl; Trk; Coach Actv; IM Sprt; Forest Indust Of Wv Camp Schlrshp 79; Art Hon 78 79; West Virginia Univ; Forestry.

BLOSSER, TERRY; Spencer HS; Spencer, WV; Band; Chrh Wkr; Hon Rl; Jr NHS; Stg Crw; Mount Vernon Nazarene Coll; Acctg.

BLOUGH, DAN; Chelsea HS; Chelsea, MI; Am Leg Boys St; Debate Tm; Hon Rl; NHS; 4-H; God Cntry Awd;.

BLOUGH, MARY; Wadsworth Sr HS; Wadsworth, OH; 22/367 Am Leg Aux Girls St; Hon Rl; NHS; Rptr Yrbk; Fr Clb; Pep Clb; PPFtbl; Scr Kpr; Akron Univ; Bus Admin.

BLOUGH, PAMELA; Kelloggsville HS; Wyoming, MI; 6/141 Band; Cmp Fr Grls; Debate Tm; Hon Rl; NHS; Stg Crw; Yth Flsp; Letter Bsktbl; Trk; PPFtbl; Hugh O Brian Foundation Awd 77; Russell B Formisma Athlc Awd 79; Vllybll 3 Lttrs & 2 Yr Cpt 77 79; Michigan St Univ; Landscp Archt.

BLOUGH, ROBERT; Lynchburg Clay HS; Lynchburg, OH; 57/94 Band; Boy Scts; Chrs; Yth Flsp; Pep Clb; Mgrs; Most Improved Band 77; Newspaper Reporter For Bsktbl 78; Tech Coll; Food Serv.

BLOUGH, RONALD; Benzie Central HS; Honor, MI; NHS; Elec Engr.

BLOUGH, RUTHANN; Smithville HS; Smithville, OH; 1/97 Treas Band; Chrs; Hon Rl; NHS; Sch Pl; Stg Crw; Drama Clb; Pres 4-H; Wright St Univ; Nursing.

BLOUNT, JAMES; Union HS; Losantville, IN; 13/63 Band; Hon Rl; NHS; 4-H; Lat Clb; Spn Clb; Natl Merit SF; College; Computer Sci.

BLOUNT, MARIO; Notre Dame HS; Bridgeport, WV; 10/55 Cls Rep Frsh Cls; Boy Scts; FCA; Hon Rl; NHS; Yth Flsp; Key Clb; Mth Clb; Sci Clb; Letter Bsbl; Univ Of Virginia; Pre Law.

BLOUNT, PATRICIA; Franklin Heights HS; Grove City, OH; 9/254 Am Leg Aux Girls St; Band; Chrs; Drm Mjrt; FCA; Hon Rl; Sct Actv; OEA; Letter Bsktbl; Letter Trk; Clark Technical Coll; Court Reprtng.

BLOUNT, RICHARD; Walnut Hills HS; Cincinnati, OH; Hon Rl; NHS; Ger Clb; Mth Clb; Rdo Clb; Natl Merit Ltr; College; Mechanical & Electrical Eng.

BLOXSOM, JERRY; Gaylord HS; Gaylord, MI; Boy Scts; Hon Rl; Univ; Bus Admin.

BLOXSOM, JULIE A; Stevenson HS; Livonia, MI; 59/810 Chrs; Sch Mus; Sch Pl; Detroit News Schlstic Writing Awds Cert Of Merit; College; Music.

BLOYER, JILL; Boardman HS; Poland, OH; 120/600 Chrs; Chrh Wkr; Hon Rl; Mdrgl; PAVAS; Sch Mus; Stg Crw; Pres Ger Clb; Academic Excel Schlrshp YSU 79; Youngstown St Univ; Math.

BLUBAUGH, JUDI; St Francis De Sales HS; Columbus, OH; Drl Tm; Pep Clb; Gym; Chrldng; Ohio St Univ; Archt.

BLUBAUGH, LAURA M; Sullivan HS; Sullivan, IN; Trs Jr Cls; Am Leg Aux Girls St; Chrs; Drl Tm; Hon Rl; Off Ade; Sch Mus; Beta Clb; Lat Clb; Pep Clb; Indiana St Univ; Nursing.

BLUBAUGH, TERESA; North Canton Hoover HS; North Canton, OH; Chrh Wkr; Cmnty Wkr; Hosp Ade; Pep Clb; Spn Clb; Trk; College; Nursing.

BLUE, CYNTHIA; Miami Trace HS; Mt Sterling, OH; AFS; Am Leg Aux Girls St; Chrs; Off Ade; Sch Mus; 4-H; FBLA; 4-H Awd; Columbus Inst; Animal Health Tech.

BLUE, GORDON; Memorial HS; St Marys, OH; 18/222 Band; Chrs; NHS; Sch Mus; Sch Pl; Drama Clb; Fr Clb; Letter Ftbl; Letter Trk; U S Coast Guard Acad.

BLUE, JOHN G; Morgantown HS; Morgantown, WV; Boy Scts; Hon Rl; Rptr Yrbk; Sprt Ed Sch Nwsp; Mth Clb; Letter Bsbl; Bsktbl; Ftbl; Wrstlng; IM Sprt; Math Awd 77; West Virginia Univ; Dent.

BLUE, KIMBERLY; North Union HS; Richwood, OH; 24/121 Chrh Wkr; Girl Scts; Hon Rl; Lbry Ade; VP NHS; Pres 4-H; Pep Clb; Spn Clb; Bsbl; Letter Bsktbl; Vllybll 3 Var Letters; Schlrshp Tests In Spanish 2; Class Awds In Spanish 1 & 2 Art & Shorthand; Univ; Bus.

BLUE, STEVE; Edon Northwest HS; Edon, OH; 1/75 Pres Frsh Cls; Cl Rep Jr Cls; Band; Chrh Wkr; Hon Rl; Stu Cncl; Bsbl; Bsktbl; Letter Ftbl; IM Sprt; Placed The Upr 10 Per Cent Of Soc Of Profssnl Engr Math Contest 1977; Univ; Math.

BLUE, STEVE; Edon HS; Edon, OH; 1/70 Pres Frsh Cls; Pres Jr Cls; Am Leg Boys St; Band; Hon Rl; NHS; Yth Flsp; Spn Clb; Bsbl; Bsktbl; College; Math.

BLUEBAUGH, CHARLOTTE; Champion HS; Warren, OH; 13/217 Band; Cmnty Wkr; Hon Rl; NHS; Off Ade; Sch Pl; Treas 4-H; Pres FNA; 4-H Awd; Voice Dem Awd; Ohio Northern Univ; Bus Mgmt.

BLUHM, TRACY S; Muskegon Sr HS; Muskegon, MI; Boy Scts; Orch; Fr Clb; Letter Bsbl; Letter Glf; Muskegon Cmnty Coll; Pharm.

BLUM, CONNIE; Clawson Sr HS; Clawson, MI; Treas Chrs; Drl Tm; Girl Scts; Hon Rl; Stg Crw; Ten; Univ; Engr.

BLUM, JEANNE; Romeo Sr HS; Romeo, MI; 5/384 Band; Debate Tm; NHS; Sch Mus; Ed Yrbk; Yrbk; FBLA; De Pauw Univ; Music.

BLUM, KIM; Bellmont HS; Decatur, IN; Chrs; Drl Tm; Hon Rl; Hosp Ade; Yth Flsp; Drama Clb; Ger Clb; Sci Clb; Pom Pon; PPFtbl; Univ; Eng.

BLUM, TONY; St Charles Prep; Columbus, OH; Boy Scts; Hon Rl; Ftbl;.

BLUME, ROBERT; Moeller HS; Cincinnati, OH; Band; Chrs; Drl Tm; Drm Mjrt; Hon Rl; Orch; Sch Mus; Wright State Univ; Music.

BLUMENAU, SUSAN; Essexvle Hampton Garber HS; Essexville, MI; Cl Rep Jr Cls; Chrs; Sch Mus; Sch Pl; Stg Crw; Pep Clb; Letter Ten; Letter Chrldng; Pom Pon; Jr Town Meetng Leadr 79; Perfct Atttndnc Awd 79; Univ; Psych.

BLUMENKRANTZ, LYDIA; Covert 'S; Covert, MI; 2/38 Sec Frsh Cls; Sec Soph Cls; Sec Jr Cls; Sec Sr Cls; Sal; Band; Chrs; Chrh Wkr; Girl Scts; Hon Rl; Eastern Michigan Univ; Acctg.

BLUMENSCHEIN, ANTHONY; Marysville HS; Marysville, OH; Y-Teens; Letter Bsbl; Letter Bsktbl; Letter Ftbl; IM Sprt; Ftbl Otstndng Awd; 2nd Tm All Centra 78; Bsktbl; CBL League Assists Champ 78; Univ; Archt Engr.

BLUMENSCHEIN, GAYNELL L; Holly HS; Holly, MI; 10/283 Band; Chrs; Chrh Wkr; Girl Scts; Hon Rl; NHS; Sch Mus; Yth Flsp; 4-H; 4-H Awd; Band Mc Donald Awd; In Top 10 In Graduating Class; Whos Who In Music; Ferris St Coll; Pharmacy.

BLUMENTHALER, KATHY; Norton HS; Norton, OH; Hon Rl; Off Ade; Drama Clb; Fr Clb; College; Psychology.

BLUMER, BARBARA; Ursuline Acad; Cincinnati, OH; Cl Rep Jr Cls; Cls Rep Sr Cls; Stu Cncl; Pep Clb; Letter Swmmng; GAA; Miami Univ.

BLUMKA, MARY; Buchanan HS; Buchanan, MI; 3/126 Cmp Fr Grls; Chrs; Chrh Wkr; JA; NHS; Sch Mus; Sch Pl; Stg Crw; Sch Nwsp; College; Reg Occupational Therapist.

BLUNTSCHLY, THOMAS; Onsted HS; Onsted, MI; 25/120 Band; Hon Rl; Bsbl; Bsktbl; Ftbl; Bsbl Captain All LCAA 1st Tm All Cnty Hnrble Men; Eastern Michigan Univ; Comp Sci.

BLUST, BRIAN; Eisenhower HS; Rochester, MI; Aud/Vis; Band; Boy Scts; NHS; Pres 4-H; Pres VICA; Letter Ftbl; IM Sprt; 4-H Awd; Oakland Univ; Mech Engr.

BLYE, LESTER; Hughes HS; Cincinnati, OH; Aud/Vis; Band; Boy Scts; Hon Rl; Stg Crw; Ftbl; Ten; IM Sprt; Univ Of Cincinnati; Prepharmacy.

BOADWAY, RANDALL; Capac Jr Sr HS; Capac, MI; Band; Hon Rl; Orch; Sch Nwsp; Mgrs; Cit Awd; Cls Rep Frsh Cls;.

BOARD, DAVID; Lawrence Central HS; Indianapolis, IN; 97/400 Cls Rep Frsh Cls; Trs Soph Cls; Trs Jr Cls; Boy Scts; FCA; Hon Rl; NHS; Pres Key Clb; Letter Soroptimist; JETS Awd; Hoosier Schlr 79; Purdue Univ; Aero Engr.

BOARD, JENNY; Bloomington HS; Bloomington, IN; Swmmng; College.

BOARMAN, DENISE; La Ville Jr Sr HS; Lakeville, IN; 1/120 Cls Rep Frsh Cls; Cls Rep Soph Cls; Pres Jr Cls; Hst Jr Cls; Hst Sr Cls; Am Leg Aux Girls St; Aud/Vis; Hon Rl; NHS; 4-H; Purdue Univ; Engr.

BOATRIGHT, V; Hurricane HS; Hurricane, WV; Chrs; Chrh Wkr; Hon Rl; JA; Beta Clb; 4-H; Univ; Vet.

BOAZ, BRIAN; Anderson HS; Anderson, IN; 83/415 Hon Rl; Sch Pl; Lat Clb; Natl Merit Ltr; Indiana Univ; Neurosurgeon.

BOAZ, JOHN; Van Wert HS; Van Wert, OH; Ger Clb; Spn Clb; Ftbl; Letter Trk; IM Sprt; JA Awd; College; Elec Tech.

BOBB, RANDY; Brownstown Central HS; Crothersville, IN; 8/149 Chrs; NHS; Yth Flsp; 4-H; FFA; Sci Clb; Letter Ftbl; Most Improved Lineman BCHS Ftbll 78; Farming.

BOBBETT, CONNIE; Grass Lake HS; Grass Lake, MI; Girl Scts; Hon Rl; Lbry Ade; NHS; Rptr Yrbk; Ed Sch Nwsp; FHA; Eastern Mic Univ; Spec Ed.

BOBEK, LAURIE; Admiral King HS; Lorain, OH; Band; Chrs; Chrh Wkr; Cmnty Wkr; Girl Scts; Hon Rl; Sch Mus; Key Clb; Ten; College; X Ray Tech.

BOBERG, BRENDA; North Knox HS; Carlisle, IN; 7/160 Hon Rl; NHS; Yth Flsp; 4-H; FHA; FTA; Pep Clb; Vincennes Univ; Phys Ther.

BOBLENZ, LISA; River Valley HS; Marion, OH; 42/196 Band; Chrh Wkr; Girl Scts; Orch; Sch Mus; Stg Crw; Yth Flsp; Yrbk; Rptr Sch Nwsp; 4-H; College; Bio.

BOBLETT, ROBIN; Manton HS; Manton, MI; 7/50 Girl Scts; Hon Rl; Mod UN; NHS; Sct Actv; Rptr Yrbk; Natl Merit Schl; Merit Schlrshp Awd 79; Ferris St Coll; Bus Admin.

BOBLITT, LEEANN; Madison Heights HS; Anderson, IN; 8/376 Cls Rep Frsh Cls; Cls Rep Soph Cls; Cl Rep Jr Cls; Cls Rep Sr Cls; Band; NHS; Spn Clb; Am Leg Awd; DAR Awd; NCTE; Purdue; Pharmacy.

BOBO, LYNETTE; John F Kennedy Sr HS; Cleveland, OH; 7/300 Hon Rl; NHS; Off Ade; Rptr Yrbk; Natl Merit SF; Ferris St Coll; Court Rprtng.

BOBO, VALERIE F; Springfield HS; Holland, OH; Cls Rep Soph Cls; Am Leg Aux Girls St; Drm Bgl; Hon Rl; Lbry Ade; NHS; Sch Pl; FTA; Bsbl; Capt Bsktbl; Engr Schlrshp To Ohio St Univ 1979; Track Schlrshp To Ohio St Univ; Ohio St Univ; Aero Engr.

BOBON, BRENDA; Hudson Area HS; Hudson, MI; Chrs; Sch Pl; Rptr Yrbk; Yrbk; Drama Clb; FHA; Spn Clb; Mic State Univ; Social Work.

BOBOS, MARK; Bishop Noll Inst; Whiting, IN; 9/321 Cls Rep Frsh Cls; Hon Rl; Stu Cncl; Mth Clb; Purdue Univ; Physics.

BOBOVECZ, MARY B; Struthers HS; Struthers, OH; 51/275 Off Ade; Sch Pl; Stg Crw; Drama Clb; FNA; Pep Clb; Spn Clb; VFW Awd; Voice Dem Awd; Prospect Hall College; Mdse.

BOBOWSKI, BRAD; Morton Sr HS; Hammond, IN; 28/486 Cls Rep Soph Cls; Cl Rep Jr Cls; Cls Rep Sr Cls; NHS; Letter Bsbl; Letter Wrstlng; Evans Schlrshp 1978; Indiana Univ; Bus Admin.

BOBOWSKY, DIANE; George Rogers Clark HS; Hammond, IN; 32/218 Chrs; Spn Clb; IM Sprt; PPFtbl; Univ; Comp Sci.

BOBROSKI, MICHAEL; Riverside HS; Painesville, OH; 43/383 Hon Rl; NHS; 4-H; Letter Ftbl; Letter Swmmng; Letter Trk; IM Sprt;.

BOCCARDI, VINCENZO; Fairview HS; Fairview Pk, OH; Sch Mus; Sch Pl; Stg Crw; Drama Clb; Sci Clb; College; Lawyer.

BOCHENEK, GRACE; Bishop Gallagher HS; Detroit, MI; 64/322 Hon Rl; Capt Swmmng; Mgrs; Scr Kpr; Tmr; Cit Awd; Mic State Univ; Pre Dental.

BOCK, ANNE; Anderson HS; Anderson, IN; Sec Band; VP Chrh Wkr; Drm Bgl; FTA; Ball St Univ; Elem Educ.

BOCK, DAWN; Lowell HS; Lowell, MI; Chrs; Debate Tm; Hon Rl; NHS; Ger Clb; Letter Trk; Mic State Univ; Sci.

BOCK, JENNIFER; Upper Arlington HS; Columbus, OH; 43/610 Am Leg Aux Girls St; Chrs; Chrh Wkr; Cmnty Wkr; Hon Rl; NHS; Yth Flsp; Yrbk; Ger Clb; Chrldng; Univ.

BOCK, JENNY; Upper Arlington HS; Columbus, OH; Am Leg Aux Girls St; Band; Chrh Wkr; Cmnty Wkr; Hon Rl; Yth Flsp; Yrbk; Ger Clb; Pep Clb; Chrldng; College; Medicine.

BOCK, KRISTYN; Utica HS; Utica, MI; 12/300 Pres Soph Cls; Trs Jr Cls; Pres Sr Cls; Jr NHS; NHS; Sch Mus; Rptr Yrbk; Central Mich Univ; Accgt.

BOCK, MARY; North Putnam HS; Roachdale, IN; 2/156 Sec Frsh Cls; Band; FCA; Girl Scts; Hon Rl; NHS; Orch; Sch Mus; Sch Pl; Stu Cncl; Indiana St Univ.

BOCK, RICHARD; Lincoln HS; Shinnston, WV; Chrh Wkr; Hon Rl; Mod UN; Sprt Ed Sch Nwsp; Bsktbl; Ftbl; Trk; IM Sprt; Liberty Baptist Coll; Law.

BOCK, SUSAN; Stow HS; Munroe, OH; 75/515 Chrs; Hon Rl; Off Ade; Quill & Scroll; Sch Pl; Rptr Yrbk; Yrbk; Pep Clb; Capt Chrldng; Kent St Univ; Interior Dsgn.

BOCKBRADER, JANA; Elmwood HS; N Baltimore, OH; Chrh Wkr; Hon Rl; Yth Flsp; 4-H; FHA; Capt Bsktbl; Capt Trk; 4-H Awd; Ohio St Univ; Acctg.

BOCKBRADER, STEVEN; Wapakoneta HS; Cridersville, OH; 12/242 Natl Ed Dev Tests Top 10 Per Cent; College; Civil Engr.

BOCKELMAN, CONNIE; Upper Arlington HS; Columbus, OH; Chrh Wkr; Cmnty Wkr; Girl Scts; Hon Rl; NHS; Pres Quill & Scroll; Ed Sch Nwsp; Drama Clb; Fr Clb; Pep Clb; Univ Of Cincinnati; Jrnlsm.

BOCKELMAN, PEGGY; Mc Auley HS; Cinti, OH; Cmnty Wkr; Mod UN; Letter Gym; Letter Chrldng; Coach Actv; GAA; IM Sprt; Cls Rep Sr Cls; Cl Rep Jr Cls; Ohi Univ; Sports.

BOCKELMAN, SARAH; Napoleon HS; Napoleon, OH; 12/280 Am Leg Aux Girls St; Band; Hon Rl; Lit Mag; Natl Forn Lg; NHS; Sch Mus; Yth Flsp;.

BOCKHORN, TERRY; Fairmont West HS; Kettering, OH; 13/500 Cl Rep Jr Cls; AFS; Chrs; Hon Rl; Sch Mus; Stu Cncl; Pres Fr Clb; Mth Clb; Rdo Clb; Natl Merit Ltr; Morning Anncmnts; William & Mary Coll; Poli Sci.

BOCKOVER, WILLIAM; Anderson Highland HS; Anderson, IN; 82/407 Band; Boy Scts; Drm Bgl; Hon Rl; Lit Mag; Sch Mus; 4-H; Mercury Schlrshp From Ball St Univ; Outstndng Bag Pipe Player; Hoosier Merit Schlr; Ballstate Univ; Comp Prog.

BOCKRATH, VERNON; Continental HS; Cloverdale, OH; VP Soph Cls; Cl Rep Jr Cls; Cls Rep Sr Cls; Chrs; Hon Rl; NHS; Sch Mus; Stu Cncl; Spn Clb; Letter Ten; Ohi State Univ; Med.

BOCKSTAHLER, KURT; North Central HS; Indianapolis, IN; 257/114 Hon Rl; NHS; Off Ade; Drama Clb; Lat Clb; OEA; IUPUI; Comp Progr.

BOCOCK, SUSAN; Wheelersburg HS; Wheelersburg, OH; 6/162 Am Leg Aux Girls St; Aud/Vis; Band; Chrs; Girl Scts; Hon Rl; Lbry Ade; NHS; Sch Mus; Yth Flsp; Ohio State Univ; Home Ec.

BOCZAR, BOB; Maple Hts Sr HS; Maple Heights, OH; JA; Ger Clb; Cit Awd; JA Awd; John Carroll Univ; Chem.

BOCZAR, JOSEPH; Fitzgerald HS; Warren, MI; Boy Scts; Debate Tm; Hon Rl; Natl Forn Lg; NHS; Sct Actv; JETS Awd; Wayne State Univ; Mech Engr.

BODAGER, LISA; Rittman HS; Rittman, OH; 2/114 Pres Soph Cls; Sal; Sec Chrs; Hon Rl; NHS; Off Ade; Sch Pl; Ed Yrbk; Yrbk; Kenyon College.

BODAK, KIMBERLY; Admiral King HS; Lorain, OH; Boy Scts; Chrs; Chrh Wkr; Hon Rl; Hosp Ade; Lbry Ade; Ten; Lorain Cnty Cmnty Coll; Nursing.

BODARY, JOHN; Monroe Catholic Central HS; New Boston, MI; 5/85 Trs Jr Cls; Hon Rl; NHS; Sch Pl; Stg Crw; Rptr Yrbk; Yrbk; Trk; IM Sprt; Michigan St Univ; Engr.

BODDEN, CONNIE; Copley HS; Akron, OH; Chrh Wkr; Drl Tm; Hon Rl; NHS; Orch; Sch Mus; Yth Flsp; Yrbk; Letter Trk; Tmr; College.

BODDORF, CAROL J; Martins Ferry HS; Martins Ferry, OH; Band; Chrh Wkr; Girl Scts; Hon Rl; Off Ade; Sct Actv; Y-Teens; Yrbk; Sci Clb; Spn Clb; Univ; Math.

BODDORF, JUDY; Martins Ferry HS; Martins Ferry, OH; 32/215 Band; Chrh Wkr; Drm Mjrt; Girl Scts; Hon Rl; Hosp Ade; Sct Actv; Stu Cncl; Y-Teens; Sprt Ed Yrbk; West Liberty Univ; Lab Tech.

BODEN, LORRIE; Field HS; Suffield, OH; 30/239 Cmp Fr Grls; Hon Rl; Hosp Ade; Lbry Ade; Sdlty; Sch Nwsp; 4-H; Spn Clb; Cit Awd; 4-H Awd; Akron Univ; Sci.

BODENBACH, MICHELE; Clarence M Kimball HS; Royal Oak, MI; Chrs; Girl Scts; Hon Rl; Hosp Ade; NHS; Letter Bsktbl; Mercy College; Nursing.

BODENBENDER, BRENDA; Continental HS; Cloverdale, OH; Chrs; Hon Rl; Lbry Ade; Off Ade; Yrbk; Letter Bsktbl; Chrldng; IM Sprt; Voc Schl; Nursing.

BODENBENDER, LINDA; Continental Local HS; Cloverdale, OH; Chrs; Hon Rl; Lbry Ade; Off Ade; Sch Mus; Sch Pl; Sch Nwsp; Spn Clb; Bsktbl; Scr Kpr; Voc Schl; Interior Decorating.

BODENMILLER, DAN; Vandalia Butler HS; Vandalia, OH; 91/492 Pres Frsh Cls; Pres Soph Cls; Pres Jr Cls; VP Sr Cls; Am Leg Boys St; Hon Rl; Pol Wkr; Sch Pl; Stu Cncl; DECA; Gordon Jewelry Schlrshp Finalist; St Representative Ohio Assoc Of Stu Councils; Ohio DECA Male Stu Of Yr; Ohio St Univ; Busns Admin.

BODIE, MICHAEL J; St Francis De Sales HS; Toledo, OH; Boy Scts; Chrh Wkr; Hon Rl; Sct Actv; Lat Clb; IM Sprt; Best Jr Sailor At ILYA Put In Bay Wk; Holy Name Schlrshp; Excellent Rating For Sci Projects; Toledo Univ; Radiologist.

BODKINS, I RANDALL; Coalton HS; Norton, WV; Cls Rep Frsh Cls; Hon Rl; Stu Cncl; Yrbk; 4-H; Sci Clb; Letter Bsbl; Letter Bsktbl; IM Sprt; Garrett Cmnty Coll; Wildlife Mgmt.

BODLE, BRENDA; Heath HS; Heath, OH; 41/151 Band; Chrs; Hon Rl; Sch Mus; Sch Pl; Stg Crw; Drama Clb; 4-H; 4-H Awd; Central Ohio Tech Coll; Acctg.

BODLE, STEPHEN; West Lafayette HS; W Lfaayette, IN; FCA; Y-Teens; Rptr Yrbk; Letter Ftbl; IM Sprt; College; Finance.

BODMAN, MARIA; High School; Muskegon, MI; Band; Michigan St Univ; Poli Sci.

BODNAR, DEBORA; Green HS; Akron, OH; Trs Soph Cls; Cl Rep Jr Cls; Trs Sr Cls; Cls Rep Sr Cls; Hon Rl; NHS; Off Ade; College; Educ.

BODNAR, GAIL; Magnificat HS; Fairview Park, OH; Chrh Wkr; Cmnty Wkr; Hon Rl; NHS; Off Ade; Red Cr Ade; Stu Cncl; Pep Clb; IM Sprt; Ohio St Univ; Dent Hygnst.

BODNAR, MICHAEL; Garfield HS; Akron, OH; 1/460 Band; Hon Rl; Orch; Univ Of Akron.

BODNER, DAVID; Guernsey Catholic Cntrl HS; Cambridge, OH; 6/24 Hon Rl; Sch Pl; Stg Crw; Pep Clb; Letter Bsbl; Bsktbl; VFW Awd; Voice Dem Awd;.

BODNER, DAVID; Guernsey Catholic Ctrl HS; Cambridge, OH; 2/27 Chrs; Hon Rl; PAVAS; Pep Clb; Letter Bsktbl; Voice Dem Awd; Law Enforcement.

BODOR, CAROL; Hammond Technical Voc HS; Hammond, IN; 7/207 Hon Rl; NHS; Yrbk; Purdue Univ; Comp Progr.

BODY, CARMEN; Labrae HS; Warren, OH; 13/151 Am Leg Aux Girls St; Band; FTA; Spn Clb; Bsktbl; Trk; Kent State Univ; Speech Pathology.

BOEBEL, CHRISTOPHER; West Lafayette HS; West Lafayette, IN; 7/179 Debate Tm; Natl Forn Lg; NHS; Rptr Sch Nwsp; Fr Clb; Sci Clb; Letter Swmmng; NCTE; Natl Merit SF; Oberlin College.

BOECKMAN, KATHLEEN; Coldwater Exempted Vlg HS; Coldwater, OH; Chrs; Chrh Wkr; Hon Rl; Hosp Ade; Lbry Ade; Rptr Yrbk; Ed Sch Nwsp; Rptr Sch Nwsp; 4-H; FHA; Univ; Nursing.

BOEDECKER, DIANA; Linden Sr HS; Fenton, MI; Sec Band; Hon Rl; NHS; Off Ade; Sch Mus; Ed Yrbk; Coach Actv; Capt Pom Pon; LHS Style Show Awd 77; Mst Creative Sewing Stu 78; Placed Wreath On Tomb Of Unknown Soldier 79; Central Michigan Univ; Fshn Mdse.

BOEDECKER, REBECCA S; Carman HS; Flint, MI; Hon Rl; OEA; Letter Bsbl; Letter Bsktbl; GAA; College; Sec.

BOEGERT, RUTH; Parma Sr HS; Parma, OH; 78/782 Hon Rl; Quill & Scroll; Rptr Yrbk; Pep Clb; Univ; Art.

BOEGLI, STEVE; Edison HS; Milan, OH; Am Leg Boys St; Band; Boy Scts; Chrs; Chrh Wkr; Drama Clb; Glf; Univ; Music Educ.

BOEHLER, CATHERINE; Magnificat HS; Rocky River, OH; Chrs; Cmnty Wkr; Treas JA; NHS; Red Cr Ade; Sch Mus; Stu Cncl; Lang Awrd Spanish 3 78; Schlrshp To Magnificat HS 76; Upper 5% Of Stud Who Took Psat/nmsqt Test; Univ; Med.

BOEHM, BILL; Westerville South HS; Westerville, OH; 80/280 Band; FFA; Wrstlng; Ohi State Univ; Architecture.

BOEHM, FREDIE; Jasper HS; Jasper, IN; 40/289 Am Leg Boys St; Hon Rl;.

BOEHM, JOSEPH; St Ignatius HS; Rocky River, OH; 23/310 Cls Rep Frsh Cls; Cls Rep Soph Cls; Cl Rep Jr Cls; Stu Cncl; Yrbk; Letter Bsbl; Letter Bsktbl; Capt Ftbl; IM Sprt; Univ.

BOEHM, KAREN; Mcauley HS; Cincinnati, OH; Chrs; Chrh Wkr; Girl Scts; Hon Rl; JA; Stg Crw; Rptr Yrbk; Spn Clb; Xavier Univ; Bus Admin.

BOEHM, LORI; Bishop Ready HS; Grove City, OH; 95/146 Chrh Wkr; Drl Tm; Girl Scts; Off Ade; Pol Wkr; Sch Mus; Rptr Sch Nwsp; Coach Actv; Mat Maids; Univ; Elem Tchr.

BOEHM, MANFRED; St Joseph Sr HS; Saint Joseph, MI; 11/309 Hon Rl; Natl Merit Ltr; Michigan Tech Univ; Elec Engr.

BOEHM, MICHAEL; Chesterton HS; Porter, IN; 103/427 Aud/Vis; Band; Chrh Wkr; Hon Rl; Ger Clb; Pep Clb; Rdo Clb; Sci Clb; Univ Of Ari; Astrophysics.

BOEHM, S; Grand Ledge HS; Grnd Ldg, MI; Boy Scts; Hon Rl; Jr NHS; NHS; Crs Cntry; Trk; IM Sprt; Mich Tech; Mech Engr.

BOEHMAN, MICHAEL; Msgnr John R Hackett HS; Portage, MI; Pres Sr Cls; Natl Merit SF; Univ; Bus Admin.

BOEHN, JENNIE; Fairview HS; Sherwood, OH; 5/108 Band; Chrs; Chrh Wkr; Hon Rl; NHS; Sch Mus; Rptr Yrbk; Rptr Sch Nwsp; 4-H; Chrldng; Heldelberg Univ; Music.

BOEHNING, KIM; West Central HS; Francesville, IN; 16/100 Cls Rep Sr Cls; Band; Hon Rl; JA; NHS; Stu Cncl; 4-H; FTA; OEA; Pep Clb; Purdue Univ; Phys Educ.

BOEHNLEIN, PHILIP; Padua Franciscan HS; Parma, OH; Chrh Wkr; Cmnty Wkr; Hon Rl; JA; NHS; Yrbk; Sch Nwsp; Trk; IM Sprt; Dayton Univ; Advertising Photography.

BOEHNLEIN, ROBERT C; Mishawaka HS; Mishawaka, IN; 5/464 Chrs; Hon Rl; NHS; Sch Mus; Sch Pl; Crs Cntry; JETS Awd; Univ; Engr.

BOEKE, DEBRA; Minster HS; Minster, OH; 9/80 Band; Chrs; Drm Mjrt; Girl Scts; Hon Rl; Orch; Sch Mus; Sch Pl; Yrbk; Drama Clb; Bowling Green St Univ; Bus.

BOEKELOO, MARTIN; Sparta HS; Sparta, MI; Hon Rl; Yrbk; Fr Clb; Bsktbl; Ftbl; Michigan St Univ; Engr.

BOEKELOO, STUART; Portage Northern HS; Portage, MI; Hon Rl; Mod UN; NHS; Ger Clb; Capt Glf; Letter Ten; Albion Coll; Bio.

BOELCKE, MARK; Buchanan HS; Buchanan, MI; 12/160 Hon Rl; Spn Clb; Bsktbl; Letter Ftbl; College.

BOEMKER, TERRI; St Ursula Academy; Cincinnati, OH; 6/105 Hon Rl; Sch Pl; Natl Merit Ltr; Invitation To Apply For Telluride Assn Summer Programs; Half Tuition Schlrshp To St Ursula Acad; College; Education.

BOENSCH, MIKE; Reese HS; Saginaw, MI; Hon Rl; FFA;.

BOEPPLE, JILL; Edwardsburg HS; Edwardsburg, MI; Pres Frsh Cls; Chrs; JA; Sch Mus; Stu Cncl; Chrldng; Arizona State Univ; Art Educ.

BOEREMA, DOUGLAS; Landmark Christian HS; La Porte, IN; Band; Chrs; Chrh Wkr; Hon Rl; Fr Clb; Bsbl; Letter Bsktbl; Letter Ftbl; Socr; Coach Actv; Ping Pong 1st Pl; Tennis 2nd Trophy; Coll; Drafting.

BOERGER, CHRIS; Ansonia Local HS; Rossburg, OH; 6/67 Cls Rep Frsh Cls; Chrs; Hon Rl; NHS; Sch Pl; Stu Cncl; Ed Yrbk; Drama Clb; OEA; Pep Clb; Ohio St Univ; Dent.

BOERMA, JANE; St Joseph HS; St Joseph, MI; 3/300 Cls Rep Frsh Cls; Cls Rep Soph Cls; NHS; Stu Cncl; Sprt Ed Yrbk; Lat Clb; Sci Clb; Letter Swmmng; College.

BOERSEMA, DAWN; Hartland HS; Howell, MI; 25/237 Cmp Fr Grls; Chrs; Chrh Wkr; Hon Rl; Sch Pl; Stg Crw; Sec Yth Flsp; Yrbk; Drama Clb; Spn Clb; Spring Arbor Coll; Bio.

BOERSMA, CORNELIUS; Sidney HS; Sidney, OH; Am Leg Boys St; Debate Tm; Hon Rl; NHS; Ten; IM Sprt; College; Chem Engr.

BOES, MIRIAM; Arcadia Local School; Arcadia, OH; 3/64 Cls Rep Soph Cls; Sec Sr Cls; Band; NHS; 4-H; FHA; Bsktbl; Trk; IM Sprt; Mat Maids; Michael J Owens Tech Coll; Nursing.

BOES, ROBERTA; Calvert HS; Tiffin, OH; 13/100 Cls Rep Soph Cls; Cls Rep Sr Cls; Chrs; Hon Rl; VP NHS; Sch Mus; Sch Pl; Stu Cncl; Ed Yrbk; Cit Awd; Bawling Green Univ; Bus Admin.

BOESIGER, EDWARD A; Grosse Pointe North HS; Harper Woods, MI; 1/534 Cls Rep Frsh Cls; Hon Rl; NHS; Letter Bsbl; Bsktbl; Trk; Coach Actv; Natl Merit SF; Rensselaer Polytech Inst Math & Sci Awd 1978; Schl Winner Century III Leaders 1978; Ford Foundation Awd; Univ; Engr.

BOESKOOL, CINDY; Fremont HS; Fremont, MI; 87/238 Lbry Ade; Treas Yth Flsp; OEA; Muskegon Cmnty Coll; Elem Educ.

BOESKOOL, KIRK; Coopersville HS; Coopersville, MI; Am Leg Boys St; Aud/Vis; Chrh Wkr; Hon Rl; Mod UN; NHS; Sch Pl; Stu Cncl; Ferris State College; Engr.

BOETCHER, JACQULINE; Hobart Sr HS; Hobart, IN; Band; Chrh Wkr; Girl Scts; Hon Rl; Hosp Ade; Jr NHS; Lbry Ade; Sch Mus; Spn Clb; Bsktbl; Purdue Univ; Surg Nurse.

BOETTCHER, JOEL; Central HS; Evansville, IN; 6/505 Chrh Wkr; Hon Rl; NHS; Concordia Coll; History.

BOETTCHER, ROBERT; Reeths Puffer HS; N Muskegon, MI; 80/351 Boy Scts; Sch Mus; Sct Actv; Stg Crw; Letter Ftbl; Trk; Wrstlng; Tmr; College; Architect.

BOETTNER, JANET; Theodore Roosevelt HS; Wyandotte, MI; Band; Hon Rl; Jr NHS; NHS; Orch; Sch Mus; Michigan St Univ; Med Tech.

BOFENKAMP, BETH; Niles Mckinley HS; Niles, OH; 36/421 Hon Rl; NHS; Off Ade; Sprt Ed Sch Nwsp; Letter Bsktbl; Letter Ten; Trk; Coach Actv; GAA; PPFtbl; Bowling Green; Comp Sci.

BOFENKAMP, JILL; Niles Mc Kinley HS; Niles, OH; 116/400 Cls Rep Sr Cls; Band; Chrs; Stu Cncl; Rptr Yrbk; Letter Bsktbl; Letter Ten; Univ.

BOGAN, BILL; Edison HS; Milan, OH; Am Leg Boys St; Band; Boy Scts; NHS; Sch Mus; Sch Pl; Sct Actv; Stg Crw; Drama Clb; 4-H; Ohio St Univ; Indstrl Tech.

BOGAN, DAREN D; Clinton Massie HS; Wilmington, OH; 4/100 Band; Hon Rl; NHS; Sch Mus; Stu Cncl; Rptr Sch Nwsp; Letter Bsktbl; Letter Crs Cntry; Letter Trk; Scr Kpr; Ohio HS Athletic Assn Part In St Championships Track; Natl Youth Physi Fitness Prog Of Marine Corps; College.

BOGAN, TOM; Colnel Crawford HS; N Robinson, OH; FCA; Hon Rl; Sch Pl; Stu Cncl; Yth Flsp; Letter Bsbl; Bsktbl; Letter Ftbl; College.

BOGEN, THOMAS E; St Charles Prep; Columbus, OH; Boy Scts; Hon Rl; NHS; Ed Yrbk; Spn Clb; Ten; IM Sprt; Mgrs; Univ; Med.

BOGER, CAROL; Waldron HS; Waldron, IN; Off Ade; Rptr Yrbk; Rptr Sch Nwsp; Pep Clb; Blue River Voc Schl; Bus.

BOGER, SHIRLEY; Pettisville HS; Wauseon, OH; 4/51 Sal; Chrs; Hon Rl; Lbry Ade; NHS; Red Cr Ade; Sch Pl; Yrbk; FHA; FTA; Bowling Green State Univ; Home Ec.

BOGGESS, ANGELA; High School; Sandyville, WV; Chrh Wkr; Girl Scts; Sct Actv; Yth Flsp; Sci Clb; Sci.

BOGGESS, KELLY; Marsh Fork HS; Arnett, WV; Trs Frsh Cls; Cl Rep Jr Cls; Band; Chrs; Cmnty Wkr; Pep Clb; Spn Clb; Hndbl; IM Sprt; Raleigh Cnty Voc Sch; Data Proc.

BOGGESS, PATRICIA; Monongah HS; Fairmont, WV; Hon Rl; Y-Teens; Fr Clb; FHA; Clarksburg Beauty Acad; Beautician.

BOGGESS, WILLIAM; Groveport Madison HS; Groveport, OH; Hon Rl; Spn Clb; Bsbl; Ftbl; Coach Actv; Ohio State Univ; Communications.

BOGGS, CAROL; Berea HS; Berea, OH; Chrs; Girl Scts; Hon Rl; Off Ade; Yth Flsp; Fr Clb; Sci Clb; Letter Bsbl; Bsktbl; Coach Actv; Univ.

BOGGS, DEBORA A; Lewis County HS; Weston, WV; Letter Band; Chrh Wkr; Cmnty Wkr; Hon Rl; JA; Stg Crw; Yth Flsp; Y-Teens; Sch Nwsp; 4-H; Charting 4 H 78; W Virginia Univ; X Ray Tech.

BOGGS, PATSY; Pocahontas County HS; Hillsboro, WV; Chrs; Hon Rl; Yth Flsp; Gym; Scr Kpr; Tmr; Shorthand I Awd 79; Cmnty Coll; Legal Sec.

BOGGS, RHONDA; Columbia City Joint HS; Columbia City, IN; 9/291 Sec Soph Cls; Treas Chrs; Hon Rl; Natl Forn Lg; Sch Mus; Pres Stu Cncl; Sec Yth Flsp; Rptr Sch Nwsp; Sch Nwsp; VP 4-H; Purdue Univ; Comp Tech.

BOGGS, SUSAN; Richmond Sr HS; Richmond, IN; Cls Rep Frsh Cls; Hon Rl; Sch Pl; Stg Crw; Gym; PPFtbl; Ball St Univ; Psych.

BOGGS, TERRY; Perrysburg HS; Perrysburg, OH; Pres Frsh Cls; Cls Rep Soph Cls; VP AFS; Boy Scts; Chrh Wkr; Cmnty Wkr; FCA; Sch Mus; Sch Pl; Sct Actv; Univ; Internatl Bus.

BOGLIN, LORI; Withrow HS; Cincinnati, OH; 17/550 Cmp Fr Grls; Hon Rl; Off Ade; Pol Wkr; Stu Cncl; Cit Awd; Grad Top 10% Of Class 79; Tennessee St Univ; Bus Admin.

BOGNER, SONJA M; St Peters HS; Mansfield, OH; Drama Clb; Red Cross Club; CYO; Schl Variety Show; 2 Cert If Typing 77& 78; Univ; Legal Sec.

BOGNER, TAMRA; Malabar HS; Mansfield, OH; 10/211 Cls Rep Soph Cls; Sec Jr Cls; Cl Rep Jr Cls; Sec Sr Cls; Cls Rep Sr Cls; Chrs; Girl Scts; Purdue Univ; Pharm.

BOGOL, MELANIE M E; St Josephs HS; South Bend, IN; Cls Rep Soph Cls; Cl Rep Jr Cls; Cmp Fr Grls; Cmnty Wkr; Hon Rl; Hosp Ade; Lbry Ade; Off Ade; Sch Mus; Sch Pl; St Marys Coll; RN.

BOGUE, DEBBIE; Vanderbilt HS; Vanderbilt, MI; Cls Rep Frsh Cls; Cls Rep Soph Cls; VP Jr Cls; Chrs; Girl Scts; Stu Cncl; Ed Yrbk; Gym; Chrldng; Pom Pon; Ferris State Univ; Dental.

BOGUE, RANDY; Union HS; Modoc, IN; VP Frsh Cls; Cl Rep Jr Cls; Sec Sr Cls; VP Band; Boy Scts; Hon Rl; Pres NHS; Stu Cncl; 4-H; Letter Ten; U S Armed Serv; Comp Sci.

BOGUE, SCOTT; Taylor HS; Hemlock, IN; Aud/Vis; Chrh Wkr; Hon Rl; Lbry Ade; NHS; Purdue Univ; Agri.

BOGUSLAWSKI, WILLIAM; Grand Rapids Central HS; Grand Rapids, MI; Hon Rl; Crs Cntry; Ftbl; Capt Trk; Natl Merit Ltr; Natl Merit Schl; Varsity Letter Club Pres; Nominee For Gordon Scott Cup; Central Michigan Univ; Phys Therapy.

BOHACH, STEPHEN; Madonna HS; Weirton, WV; 48/100 Cls Rep Soph Cls; VP Jr Cls; Chrh Wkr; Hon Rl; Lit Mag; Stu Cncl; Yrbk; W Liberty State College; Bus Mgmt.

BOHACZ, BRIDGET; Bronson HS; Bronson, MI; 7/13 Sec Soph Cls; Cls Rep Soph Cls; Sec Jr Cls; Cl Rep Jr Cls; Sec Sr Cls; Cls Rep Sr Cls; Am Leg Aux Girls St; Hon Rl; NHS; Sch Mus; Michigan St Univ; Interior Dsgn.

BOHAN, LISA; Brownsburg HS; Brownsburg, IN; Cmp Fr Grls; Chrs; Chrh Wkr; Girl Scts; Hon Rl; JA; Mdrgl; Sch Mus; Sch Pl; Stg Crw; Harding Univ; Business.

BOHAYCHYK, CRYSTAL L; Marlington HS; Hartville, OH; 20/320 Am Leg Aux Girls St; Chrs; Girl Scts; Pres Lbry Ade; VP 4-H; Sec Spn Clb; Trk; 4-H Awd; God Cntry Awd; Language.

BOHLEN, DAN; Moeller HS; Cincinnati, OH; Hon Rl; Mdrgl; Quill & Scroll; Mth Clb; Rus Clb; Lcrss; PPFtbl; Opt Clb Awd;.

BOHLER, KARRIE; Greenville Sr HS; Greenville, OH; Hon Rl; Y-Teens; Spn Clb; Capt Chrldng; Univ; Health.

BOHLINGER, JILL E; Grosse Pointe North HS; G P Woods, MI; 26/534 FCA; Girl Scts; Hon Rl; Hosp Ade; NHS; Orch; Spn Clb; Capt Chrldng; Central Michigan Univ; Education.

BOHLMANN, JOHN; Eastmoor HS; Columbus, OH; Hon Rl; Fr Clb; Bsbl; Univ; Bio Sci.

BOHM, SCOTT; Reitz Memorial HS; Evansville, IN; 35/252 VP Frsh Cls; Cls Rep Soph Cls; Cl Rep Jr Cls; VP Sr Cls; Hon Rl; Natl Forn Lg; NHS; Stu Cncl; Rptr Sch Nwsp; Crs Cntry; College; Attorney.

BOHMAN, DEB; Coldwater HS; Coldwater, OH; Am Leg Aux Girls St; Band; Hon Rl; Ger Clb; Mgrs; Adv Pocmnt To Begin My Frsh Yr In Coll While Also Compltn My Sr Yr In HS; Univ Of Cincinnati; Pharm.

BOHMER, LORI; Rocky River HS; Rocky Rvr, OH; AFS; Band; Red Cr Ade; Stu Cncl; Pep Clb; Swmmng; Pom Pon; College.

BOHN, LAURIE; Sts Peter & Paul HS; Saginaw, MI; Hon Rl; Lbry Ade; NHS; FDA; Mich St Univ; Animal Tech.

BOHNENSTIEHL, TODD; Union HS; Grand Rapids, MI; 40/420 Cls Rep Soph Cls; VP Jr Cls; Debate Tm; Hon Rl; NHS; Sch Pl; Stu Cncl; Drama Clb; Ger Clb; Bsktbl; Univ Of Michigan; Pre Law.

BOHNERT, TONY; Jasper HS; Jaspe, IN; 1/270 Am Leg Boys St; VP JA; NHS; Pres 4-H; Pres Key Clb; Sci Clb; 4-H Awd; JA Awd; Purdue Univ; Vet.

BOHNEY, MARK; Bishop Noll Inst; Griffith, IN; 46/321 Band; Orch; Sch Mus; Mth Clb; Purdue Univ; Professional Pilot.

BOHNHOFF, CAROLE; Northfield HS; Wabash, IN; 6/114 Chrs; Hon Rl; NHS; Stg Crw; Yrbk; Drama Clb; Spn Clb; Indiana Univ.

BOHNKE, PAT; Concordia Lutheran HS; Monroeville, IN; 1/183 Treas Band; Sec Chrs; Hon Rl; NHS; Lat Clb; Sci Clb; GAA; PPFtbl; Franklin Coll; Bio.

BOHRER, RALPH; Wyoming Park HS; Wyoming, MI; 17/236 Pres Jr Cls; Cls Rep Sr Cls; NHS; Sch Mus; Sch Pl; Pres Stu Cncl; Letter Glf; Letter Trk; Dnfth Awd; DAR Awd; Hope Coll; Bus Admin.

BOILEK, SUE; Morton Sr HS; Hammond, IN; 2/436 Chrs; Drl Tm; Girl Scts; Hon Rl; Lbry Ade; NHS; Sch Mus; Sch Pl; Drama Clb; Fr Clb; Purdue Univ; Speech.

BOILON, LUANNA E; Lewis County HS; Weston, WV; Hon Rl; Hosp Ade; Lbry Ade; NHS; Pres Y-Teens; Rptr Sch Nwsp; Sch Nwsp; Mas Awd; West Virginia Career Coll; Sec.

BOISE, PERRY; Perry HS; Cridersville, OH; Band; Chrh Wkr; Cmnty Wkr; Yth Flsp; Sprt Ed Sch Nwsp; Spn Clb; Bsktbl; Ftbl; Trk; Bluffton College; Science.

BOK, PAULA; Fairview HS; Sherwood, OH; 12/106 Am Leg Aux Girls St; Band; Chrs; Hon Rl; NHS; Sch Mus; 4-H; FTA; Chrldng; Jr Homecmng Attend 78; Captn Of Var Cheerldrs 79; Pres Of CYO; Defiance Coll; Soc Wrk.

BOKAR, GREG; St Ignatius HS; Euclid, OH; 57/306 Cls Rep Frsh Cls; Cls Rep Soph Cls; Chrh Wkr; Cmnty Wkr; FCA; Hon Rl; Lat Clb; Bsbl; Letter Hockey; IM Sprt; College.

BOLALEK, DIANE; Bishop Noll Inst; Munster, IN; 15/321 Chrs; Girl Scts; Hon Rl; NHS; Stg Crw; Mth Clb; Crs Cntry; Purdue; Chem Engr.

BOLANDER, FREDERICK; Chagrin Falls HS; Richmond, VA; Boy Scts; Mth Clb; Crs Cntry; Univ Of Michigan; Elec Engr.

BOLANOWSKI, THOMAS; Bishop Noll Inst; Hammond, IN; 24/337 Boy Scts; Hon Rl; Mth Clb; Glf; Swmmng; Trk; IM Sprt; Indiana Univ; Bus.

BOLASH, PAMELA; Ursuline HS; Austintown, OH; 79/325 Cmp Fr Grls; Girl Scts; Hon Rl; Pres Fr Clb; Bsbl; Letter Chrldng; Youngstown St Univ.

BOLCHALK, NANCY; Hubbard HS; Hubbard, OH; Girl Scts; Hon Rl; Hosp Ade; Lit Mag; Off Ade; Quill & Scroll; Ed Sch Nwsp; Sch Nwsp; Fr Clb; FDA; Youngstown State Univ; Nursing.

BOLDEN, KIMBERLEY A; Midview HS; Elyria, OH; Cls Rep Frsh Cls; Cls Rep Soph Cls; Cl Rep Jr Cls; Aud/Vis; Girl Scts; Hon Rl; Stu Cncl; Rptr Yrbk; Yrbk; Rptr Sch Nwsp; Univ; Photog.

BOLDEN, MICHELLE; Brooke HS; Wellsburg, WV; Hon Rl; NHS; Ohio Valley Med Ctr Schl; Nurse.

BOLDING, JOYCE; John F Kennedy HS; Cleveland, OH; Sec Frsh Cls; Cls Rep Soph Cls; Cl Rep Jr Cls; Cls Rep Sr Cls; Cmnty Wkr; Hon Rl; Sch Nwsp; Spn Clb; Coach Actv; Cit Awd; Mert Roll 78; Hon Roll 76; Schslhp Ctznshp Roll 77; Harvard Univ; Law.

BOLDOSER, TODD; Logan Elm HS; Laurelville, OH; Chrh Wkr; Hon Rl; Pres FFA; Letter Bsktbl; Letter Trk; State Farmer Degree 1979; Univ; Agri.

BOLDRINI, LONELLE; Lakeview HS; Cortland, OH; Band; Hon Rl; Sch Pl; Y-Teens; Rptr Sch Nwsp; Beta Clb; Drama Clb; Lat Clb; Mt Union Univ; Law.

BOLEK, DEBORAH; Archbishop Alter HS; Bellbrook, OH; Hon Rl; Lbry Ade; GAA; Twrlr; Univ Of Dayton; Acctng.

BOLEN, DEBORAH J; Upper Scioto Valley HS; Mc Guffey, OH; Hst Frsh Cls; Trs Soph Cls; Pres Jr Cls;

VP Sr Cls; Cmp Fr Grls; Chrs; Chrh Wkr; Cmnty Wkr; Drl Tm; Girl Scts; Hardin Cnty Youth Arts Fest 79; Whos Who Elected 79; Otstndng Stud In Typing 79; Branch Univ; Singing.

BOLEN, JULIA; Independence HS; Crab Orchard, WV; Girl Scts; Hon Rl; JA; Sch Mus; Sch Pl; Beta Clb; 4-H; Fr Clb; FBLA; French & Biology Awds; Typing Certificate; Marshall Univ; Accounting.

BOLENBAUGH, GARY; R Nelson Snider HS; Ft Wayne, IN; 41/585 Cls Rep Frsh Cls; VP Soph Cls; Cls Rep Soph Cls; Pres Chrh Wkr; Treas JA; NHS; Stu Cncl; Crs Cntry; Ftbl; Letter Trk; Sr Of Yr 79; Comp Tech.

BOLENDER, PATRICIA; Eastern HS; Russellville, OH; Chrs; Chrh Wkr; Hon Rl; 4-H; FFA; FHA; Pep Clb; 4-H Awd; College; Interior Decorator.

BOLER, KAREN; Emerson Sr HS; Gary, IN; 29/155 Cls Rep Soph Cls; Pres Jr Cls; Pres Sr Cls; Chrs; Chrh Wkr; Cmnty Wkr; Drl Tm; Hon Rl; JA; Jr NHS;.

BOLES, K; La Ville Jr Sr HS; Lakeville, IN; 27/142 Chrs; Off Ade; FHA; Spn Clb; Am Leg Awd; Teachers Aid Cert; Indiana Univ; Comp Acctg.

BOLES, ROSALIND; Marian HS; Cincinnati, OH; Band; Spn Clb; Univ Of Cincinnati; Fshn Dsgn.

BOLES, RUTH; Marian HS; Cincinnati, OH; Treas Band; Spn Clb; College; Cmmrcl Art.

BOLES, SCOTT; Lapel HS; Lapel, IN; Cls Rep Frsh Cls; Cls Rep Soph Cls; Cl Rep Jr Cls; Cls Rep Sr Cls; Am Leg Boys St; Chrh Wkr; Stu Cncl; Sprt Ed Yrbk; Bsbl; Bsktbl; Univ; Engr.

BOLEY, LAURA J; Lancaster HS; Lancaster, OH; 15/567 Band; Hon Rl; Jr NHS; NHS; OEA; Spn Clb; Natl Merit SF; Michigan St Univ; Law.

BOLEY, ROBIN; Ionia HS; Ionia, MI; 29/272 Band; Hon Rl; NHS; Fr Clb; Sci Clb; Ten; Western Mic Univ; Bus Finance.

BOLEYN, GREGORY; Elmhurst HS; Ft Wayne, IN; Boy Scts; Hon Rl; Sct Actv; Ftbl; Trk; Wrstlng; ITT; Elec.

BOLGER, DONALD; Arthua Hill HS; Saginaw, MI; Hon Rl; NHS; Sci Clb; Mic Tech Univ; Engr.

BOLIN, CHERYL; Perry HS; Perry, MI; 40/150 Hon Rl; FHA; Spn Clb; Michigan St Univ; Pre Vet.

BOLINE, LORI; Dover HS; Columbiana, OH; 7/241 Chrs; Girl Scts; Hon Rl; Jr NHS; NHS; Off Ade; Red Cr Ade; Sch Mus; Sch Pl; Stg Crw; Whos Who In Frgn Lang In St Of Oh 78; Best Supporting Actress In Dist 78; Sic Awds 78; Univ; Elem Educ.

BOLING, BETH A; Pike HS; Indianapolis, IN; 3/313 Am Leg Aux Girls St; Band; Hon Rl; NHS; Orch; Pres Mth Clb; JETS Awd; Natl Merit Schl; Purdue Univ; Engr.

BOLINGER, CANDIS; Shakamak HS; Jasonville, IN; 20/74 Band; Chrh Wkr; Hon Rl; Sch Pl; Stg Crw; Treas Yth Flsp; VP Drama Clb; Rdo Clb; Cert Of Awd In Drama 76 & 77; Stage Mgr Awd 78; Chess Club 75; Trinity Bible Inst; Speech.

BOLINGER, LIZANN; Marion Harding HS; Marion, OH; Sal; Am Leg Aux Girls St; Chrh Wkr; FCA; Hon Rl; Lit Mag; NHS; Orch; Sch Mus; Pres Yth Flsp; Van Meter Schlshp Top Girls Stdn In Cls 79; Case Western Reserve Univ; Bio Chem.

BOLINGER, LORALEE; Coshocton HS; Coshocton, OH; 6/258 Chrh Wkr; Hon Rl; NHS; Orch; Stg Crw; Sec Fr Clb; Letter Bsktbl; Letter Ten; Letter Trk; Univ Of Akron.

BOLINGER, NANCY; Randolph Southern HS; Winchester, IN; 3/79 NHS; Pep Clb; Spn Clb; Natl Merit Ltr; Ball St Univ; Comp Sci.

BOLISH, ROBERT; John Glenn HS; Westland, MI; 225/765 Boy Scts; DECA; Crs Cntry; Ten; Eastern Michigan Univ; Acctg.

BOLLAERT, MICHELLE; Capac Jr Sr HS; Capac, MI; Band; Hon Rl; Sprt Ed Sch Nwsp; Rptr Sch Nwsp; Letter Bsktbl; Letter Trk; GAA; Area All Star Cagers Bsktbl 78; S Thomb Athltc Assoc Al Lg Selctn Bsktbl 78; SCCCC; Phys Educ.

BOLLAERT, RITA; Capac HS; Capac, MI; Band; Girl Scts; Hon Rl; Yrbk; 4-H; OEA; 4-H Awd; St Clair Cnty Cmnty Coll; Law Cmnctn.

BOLLENBACHER, BRUCE; Parkway HS; Rockford, OH; 36/97 VP Frsh Cls; Yth Flsp; Bsbl; Bsktbl; Coll; Appliances Repair.

BOLLENBACHER, JAMES; Laker HS; Bay Port, MI; Cls Rep Frsh Cls; Cl Rep Jr Cls; Am Leg Boys St; Band; Chrs; Hon Rl; Natl Forn Lg; NHS; Sch Mus; Sch Pl; Univ.

BOLLENBACHER, MARY; Champion HS; Warren, OH; 14/229 Chrh Wkr; Hon Rl; JA; Lbry Ade; NHS; Sch Pl; Rptr Yrbk; Pep Clb; Spn Clb; Outstndg Spch Stu 79; Kent St Univ; Acctg.

BOLLES, DANNA; Kirtland HS; Kirtland, OH; Cls Rep Soph Cls; Cl Rep Jr Cls; Am Leg Aux Girls St; Pep Clb; Spn Clb; Letter Hockey; PPFtbl; Scr Kpr; Homecoming Rep Jr 78; Outstndng Schlst Achvmnt Awd In Bus 79; Univ Of Miami; X Ray Tech.

BOLLHOEFER, DEBRA; Tippecanoe Valley HS; Rochester, IN; 14/160 Hon Rl; Lbry Ade; NHS; Treas FHA; Mgrs;.

BOLLIA, LORI; Mc Kinley Jr Sr HS; Sebring, OH; Cl Rep Jr Cls; Cls Rep Sr Cls; Chrs; Chrh Wkr; Girl Scts; Hon Rl; Stu Cncl; Y-Teens; Yrbk; 4-H; Youngstown St Univ; Police Sci.

BOLSER, SHERRY; Brookville HS; Brookville, IN; IM Sprt; 50% In Phys Ftnss J A 76; Pub Relations.

BOLSTER, RICHARD; Saint Ignatius HS; Euclid, OH; 8/309 Boy Scts; Hon Rl; Mod UN; IM Sprt; Natl Merit SF; College; Engr.

BOLT, RUTH; Calvin Christian HS; Wyoming, MI; Band; Hon Rl; Drama Clb; Bus Schl; Acctg.

BOLTON, BRENDA; Niles Sr HS; Niles, MI; 1/394 Val; Pres Chrs; Hon Rl; NHS; Sch Mus; Yrbk; Fr Clb; Letter Ten; Lion Awd; Rotary Awd; 4.0 Grd Pt Awd From Natl Hon Soc 79; Schlshp From S W Mi Coll 79; S W Michigan Univ; Cmmrcl Art.

BOLTON, DAWN; Cherry Hill HS; Westland, MI; Hon Rl; Henry Ford Comm College; Police Ofcr.

BOLTON, DEANNA R; Wheelersburg HS; Wheelersburg, OH; 43/162 Band; Chrs; Chrh Wkr; Girl Scts; Hon Rl; Lbry Ade; Yth Flsp; Lat Clb; Pep Clb; Sci Clb; Ohio Northern Univ; Elem Ed.

BOLTON, DON; Taylor Center HS; Taylor, MI; VICA; Ftbl; U Coll Mich; Tool & Die.

BOLTON, KATHLEEN; Archbishop Alter HS; Dayton, OH; Drl Tm; Hon Rl; Hosp Ade; NHS; Stu Cncl; Ger Clb; GAA; German Awd; First Honors; Sales Drive Rep Jr & Sr Yr For Class Money Making Proj; Parish Advisory Board; Miami Univ; Sci.

BOLTON, MARCIA; North Farmington HS; Farmington Hls, MI; 84/392 Oakland Univ; Comp Sci.

BOLTON, MARY; Walnut Hills HS; Cincinnati, OH; Band; Chrh Wkr; Cmnty Wkr; Hon Rl; Stu Cncl; Yrbk; Sch Nwsp; Natl Merit Ltr; Kenyon Coll; Psych.

BOLTON, TAMI; Ovid Elsie HS; Ovid, MI; Trs Frsh Cls; Cl Rep Jr Cls; Band; Girl Scts; Hon Rl; Sch Pl; Sch Nwsp; 4-H; PPFtbl; 4-H Awd; Perfect Attendance; JV Volleyball; United Teenager St Finalist; College.

BOLTZ, JAMES; St Joseph HS; St Joseph, MI; Rptr Sch Nwsp; Spn Clb; Mgrs; Univ; Jrnlsm.

BOLTZ, KEN; Martins Ferry HS; Bridgeport, OH; 1/217 Trs Frsh Cls; Chrh Wkr; Hon Rl; VP NHS; Treas Sci Clb; Ohio State Univ; Optometry.

BOLUS, SUSAN M; East Detroit HS; East Detroit, MI; Cls Rep Frsh Cls; Cls Rep Soph Cls; Pres Jr Cls; Cl Rep Jr Cls; NHS; Stu Cncl; Rptr Yrbk; Ten; Natl Merit SF; Girls Varsity Tennis Capt MVP & Letter; Stu Assembly Ldrshp Awd; Univ Of Michigan; Accounting.

BOMASTER, JILL; Franklin Central HS; Indpls, IN; Aud/Vis; Chrs; Chrh Wkr; Hon Rl; Sch Pl; Yth Flsp; Drama Clb; Pep Clb; Anderson; Music.

BOMETCH, JOHN; Marion Harding HS; Marion, OH; Chrs; Sch Mus; Sprt Ed Sch Nwsp; Letter Ten; IM Sprt; Capt Mgrs; Ohio St Univ; Jrnlsm.

BOMGAARS, DEBORAH; Lansing Christian HS; Grand Ledge, MI; Band; Chrs; Chrh Wkr; Hon Rl; Mdrgl; Orch; Sch Mus; Rptr Yrbk; Lat Clb; Mic State Univ; Rn.

BOMMARITO, LAURIE; St Stephen Area HS; Saginaw, MI; 7/84 Hon Rl; NHS; Red Cr Ade; Stu Cncl; Treas Pep Clb; Letter Swmmng; Letter Ten; Natl Merit Ltr; Univ Of Michigan; Nursing.

BOMMER, VICTORIA; Avon HS; Avon, OH; 18/146 Band; Hon Rl; Univ; Educ.

BONACE, JODI; Hubbard HS; Hubbard, OH; 18/330 Cls Rep Frsh Cls; Cl Rep Jr Cls; Hon Rl; Stu Cncl; Spn Clb; Chrldng;.

BONACE, JODY; Hubbard HS; Hubbard, OH; 18/330 Cls Rep Frsh Cls; Cl Rep Jr Cls; Cls Rep Sr Cls; Hon Rl; Stu Cncl; Pep Clb; Spn Clb; Chrldng; Cosmetology.

BONACKER, JOSEPH; Niles Mckinley HS; Niles, OH; Hon Rl; Pol Wkr; Ftbl; Trk; IM Sprt; College; Air Traffic Controller.

BONAFIELD, CYNTHIA; Morgantown HS; Morgantwn, WV; Band; Hon Rl; Keyettes; Mth Clb; Spn Clb; IM Sprt; Twrlr; Wv Univ; Dentistry.

BONANNI, LINDA; Belleville HS; Belleville, MI; 1/500 Val; Band; Hon Rl; NHS; Stu Cncl; Ed Yrbk; Rptr Sch Nwsp; Chrldng; Mgrs; Tmr; Univ Of Mi Regents Alumni Schlr 79; Yrbk Awd 79; Eastern Michigan Univ; Sci.

BONANSINGA, KATHRYN; Walnut Hills HS; Cincinnati, OH; Band; Chrh Wkr; Drl Tm; Hon Rl; Sch Mus; Sch Pl; Yrbk; Treas Fr Clb; Letter Trk; Chrldng; College; Bus Admin.

BONARDI, TIM; Harper Creek HS; Ceresco, MI; Cls Rep Soph Cls; Cl Rep Jr Cls; Cls Rep Sr Cls; Am Leg Boys St; Band; Boy Scts; Hon Rl; JA; NHS; Off Ade; St & Natl Hnrs In Horse 4 H 78 79; V P Natl Hnr Soc 79 80; Michigan St Univ; Comp Design.

BOND, ANDREA; East Grand Rapids HS; Grand Rpaids, MI; 10/250 NHS; Orch; Sch Mus; Lat Clb; Letter Bsktbl; Brown Univ.

BOND, BRENDA; Frontier HS; Newport, OH; 3/121 Am Leg Aux Girls St; Girl Scts; Hon Rl; NHS; Off Ade; Sch Pl; Stu Cncl; FHA; VP OEA; Bsktbl; Washington Tech Coll; Acctg.

BOND, C; Northeastern HS; Wllmsbrg, IN; 10/152 Band; Chrs; Chrh Wkr; Hon Rl; Hosp Ade; NHS; Spn Clb; Ball State; Nursing.

BOND, CYNTHIA; Shenandoah HS; Caldwell, OH; Sec Frsh Cls; Trs Soph Cls; Hon Rl; Off Ade; 4-H; Pep Clb; Spn Clb; Chrldng; Mat Maids; 4-H Awd; Miami Univ; Sci.

BOND, DEBORAH E; Robers HS; Toledo, OH; 16/412 Pres Frsh Cls; Jr NHS; NHS; Rptr Yrbk; Sprt Ed Sch Nwsp; Letter Bsktbl; Letter Ten; IM Sprt; PPFtbl; Ohio St Univ; Bus.

BOND, DEBRA; Walter E Stebbins HS; Dayton, OH; Defiance Coll; Soc Work.

BOND, GLENN; South Harrison HS; Mt Clare, WV; Cls Rep Frsh Cls; Cls Rep Soph Cls; Cl Rep Jr Cls; Cls Rep Sr Cls; Am Leg Boys St; Band; Chrs; Chrh Wkr; Hon Rl; NHS; Voc Schl.

BOND, JANINE; East Clinton HS; New Vienna, OH; 5/115 Cls Rep Frsh Cls; Cls Rep Soph Cls; Cl Rep Jr Cls; Chrh Wkr; Hon Rl; NHS; Stu Cncl; Yth Flsp; FTA; Mth Clb; Ohio St Univ.

BOND, KRISANN; Northrop HS; Ft Wayne, IN; Sec Band; Chrh Wkr; Girl Scts; Hon Rl; Hosp Ade; JA; Orch; Sch Mus; Yth Flsp; Yrbk; Purdue Univ; Animals.

BOND, LINDA; Newbury HS; Chagrin Falls, OH; 1/80 Trs Soph Cls; Pres Chrs; Pres Jr NHS; NHS; Pres Ger Clb; Sci Clb; VP Mat Maids; Bausch & Lomb Awd; College; Pre Med.

BOND, MARY K; North Knox HS; Oaktown, IN; VP Soph Cls; VP Jr Cls; FCA; Girl Scts; 4-H; Fr Clb; VP FHA; Pep Clb; Chrldng; 4-H Awd; Univ.

BOND, MICHAEL; Madeira HS; Madeira, OH; Chrs; Cmnty Wkr; Hon Rl; Sch Mus; Letter Bsbl; Letter Bsktbl; Coach Actv; PPFtbl; Northwestern Univ; Engr.

BONDS, RITA; East HS; Cleveland, OH; Cls Rep Frsh Cls; Cls Rep Soph Cls; Cl Rep Jr Cls; Band; Chrh Wkr; Cmnty Wkr; Drm Mjrt; Hon Rl; Jr NHS; Off Ade; Mntl Math 73; Case W Reserve Early Expsr To Engr 77; Rep Of 79 Tnng Inst On Alchl & Drugs 79; Univ Of Akron; Pre Nursing.

BON DURANT, LISA R; Greenview HS; Bowersville, OH; 1/200 VP Frsh Cls; Band; Chrs; Chrh Wkr; Hon Rl; Sch Mus; Sch Pl; Yth Flsp; Drama Clb; Fr Clb; Univ.

BONE, JOHN; Nitro HS; Charleston, WV; Chrs; Chrh Wkr; Hon Rl; Yth Flsp; Mth Clb; Letter Ftbl; IM Sprt; Kanawha Cmnty Sheriffs Youth Camp 75; All Cnty Chorus 75 79; Concert Choir 77 78 & 79; W Virginia Inst Of Tech; Chem Engr.

BONE, KAREN; Wood Memorial HS; Somerville, IN; Hon Rl; Lbry Ade; Univ Of Evansville; Language.

BONE, TOM; Woodrow Wilson HS; Beckley, WV; 38/510 Chrh Wkr; JA; NHS; Pol Wkr; Rptr Sch Nwsp; Key Clb; Sci Clb; JA Awd; Captain Quiz A Matic Bowl; Member Of History Bowl Team; West Virginia Univ; Poli Sci.

BONEK, MICHAEL; Washington HS; South Bend, IN; 23/354 Aud/Vis; Hon Rl; NHS; Bsbl; Ftbl; Letter Glf; Wrstlng; Cit Awd; College; Computer Science.

BONELLO, CAROL; Divine Child HS; Dearborn, MI; Hon Rl; Hosp Ade; Off Ade; Rptr Yrbk; Ger Clb; Gym; IM Sprt; Scr Kpr; Tmr; Voice Dem Awd; Univ; Sci.

BONEMA, JOHN; Spring Lake HS; Spring Lake, MI; 1/186 Val; Hon Rl; Mod UN; NHS; Sct Actv; Glf; IM Sprt; Elk Awd; Oakland Univ; Bio.

BONENBERGER, KATHY; Central Catholic HS; Wheeling, WV; 20/132 Hon Rl; Yrbk; Rptr Sch Nwsp; 4-H; Scr Kpr; Cit Awd; 4-H Awd; College.

BONEVICH, JAMES; Loy Norrix HS; Kalamazoo, MI; 12/300 Cls Rep Frsh Cls; Chrs; Hon Rl; Off Ade; Sch Mus; Sch Pl; Stg Crw; Letter Crs Cntry; Univ Of Michigan; Math.

BONEY, ANTHONY; North Baltimore HS; N Baltimore, OH; 6/56 VP Jr Cls; Pres Sr Cls; Am Leg Boys St; Band; Chrs; Chrh Wkr; Cmnty Wkr; Hon Rl; NHS; Off Ade; Univ Of Toledo; Pharm.

BONEY, RONALD; North Baltimore HS; N Baltimore, OH; 3/65 Hon Rl; Jr NHS; NHS; Capt Ftbl; Capt Trk; Capt Wrstlng; Ohio Northern Univ; Engr.

BONEY, STACIE; St Ursula Academy; Toledo, OH; Trs Frsh Cls; Cls Rep Soph Cls; Trs Sr Cls; Chrs; Hon Rl; Sch Mus; Stu Cncl; Letter Ten; Letter Trk; College; Engineer.

BONFIGLIO, RON; Greenville Sr HS; Greenville, OH; 7/380 Cls Rep Frsh Cls; Cls Rep Soph Cls; Trs Jr Cls; Cl Rep Jr Cls; Pres Sr Cls; Cls Rep Sr Cls; Am Leg Boys St; Hon Rl; Off Ade; Stu Cncl; Akron Univ; Med.

BONFIGLIO, TERRIE; Ashland HS; Ashland, OH; Chrs; Chrh Wkr; Off Ade; Sch Mus; Rptr Yrbk; Sch Nwsp; 4-H; Chrldng; IM Sprt; Am Leg Awd; Ohio State Univ; Vet.

BONHAM, ANDY; Wayne HS; Dayton, OH; Cls Rep Frsh Cls; Cls Rep Soph Cls; Chrh Wkr; FCA; Off Ade; Yth Flsp; Capt Socr; Grace College; Admin Bus.

BONHAM, BAMBI; Southside HS; Muncie, IN; Band; Hon Rl; JA; NHS; Off Ade; Stu Cncl; Sch Nwsp; Eng Clb; Univ; Jrnlsm.

BONHART, WILKES; St Johns HS; Toledo, OH; Socr; Boston Univ; Mech Engr.

BONIFAS, SAMUEL; Delphos Jefferson HS; Delphos, OH; Cl Rep Jr Cls; Aud/Vis; Chrs; Hon Rl; NHS; Sch Mus; Stu Cncl; Pres Spn Clb; Letter Bsbl; Letter Ftbl; College; Math.

BONIFAS, SHARON; Ottoville Local HS; Cloverdale, OH; Sec Soph Cls; Hon Rl; NHS; Sch Mus; Yrbk; 4-H; 4-H Awd; Univ; Comp Sci.

BONIFER, TOM; St Philip Catholic Cntrl HS; Battle Crk, MI; 2/48 Cls Rep Soph Cls; Cl Rep Jr Cls; Boy Scts; Hon Rl; NHS; Stu Cncl; Yrbk; Bsbl; Bsktbl; Glf; Univ.

BONINE, MARK; Ross Beatty HS; Vandalia, MI; 4/120 Cls Rep Frsh Cls; Hst Soph Cls; Pres Jr Cls; Band; Hon Rl; NHS; PAVAS; Univ Of Mic; Prelaw.

BONNE, MATTHEW; Penn HS; Mishawaka, IN; Hon Rl; 4-H; Ftbl; Wrstlng; 4-H Awd; Ball State Univ; Architecture.

BONNER, DRUCILLA; Jefferson Twp HS; Dayton, OH; Band; Hon Rl; Stu Cncl; Rptr Sch Nwsp; Spn Clb; College; Bus Admin.

BONNER, GAIL; East HS; Columbus, OH; Chrs; Cmnty Wkr; Hon Rl; Lbry Ade; NHS; Stu Cncl; Sprt Ed Sch Nwsp; 4-H; Pep Clb; Spn Clb; Central St Univ; Dr.

BONNER, PAM; Ellet HS; Akron, OH; Sec Sr Cls; Chrh Wkr; Drm Mjrt; Girl Scts; Hon Rl; JA; Lbry Ade; Off Ade; Pep Clb; VICA; Campus Life; Ohio St Univ; Horticulture.

BONNER, WILLIAM; Madonna HS; Burgettstown, PA; 7/100 Chrh Wkr; Hon Rl; NHS; Sch Nwsp; Sci Clb; Letter Trk; IM Sprt; Natl Merit Ltr; Rice Univ; Optometry.

BONNETT, RANDY; Cheboygan Area HS; Cheboygan, MI; Band; Hon Rl; Sch Pl; Bsktbl; Glf; IM Sprt; Ferris St Univ; Bus Mgmt.

BONNETTE, ROBIN; Streetsboro HS; Streetsboro, OH; VP Jr Cls; Drl Tm; Girl Scts; Off Ade; Stu Cncl; FHA; Pep Clb; Capt Chrldng; Scr Kpr; Tmr; Christmas Dance Qn; Cheerleading 4 Yrs; Busns Schl; Courtroom Clerk Typist.

BONO, JOHN; Lake Orion HS; Lake Orion, MI; Cls Rep Frsh Cls; Cls Rep Soph Cls; Cmnty Wkr; Awd Of Apprctn Dr Hogansons Tracvlng Disco Show & Rock N Roll Exrvgza 79; Univ.

BONSIGNORE, ANTHONY W; Buckeye South HS; Yorkville, OH; 3/110 Pres Soph Cls; Cls Rep Soph Cls; Cls Rep Sr Cls; Am Leg Boys St; NHS; Stu Cncl; Sprt Ed Sch Nwsp; Spn Clb; Bsktbl; Glf; Perfct Attndnc; Schlstc Team; Ohio St Univ; Pre Law.

BONTEMPO, SCOTT; North Ridgeville HS; N Ridgeville, OH; Band; Hon Rl; Orch; Stg Crw; Sch Nwsp; Drama Clb; Letter Glf; Capt Wrstlng; Coach Actv; Am Leg Awd; Stu Forum Stu Orgnztn For Commctns Between Stu & Bd Of Ed 1977; Varsity R Lettermans Club 1976; Univ.

BONTRAGER, GREGORY; Owosso HS; Owosso, MI; 67/406 Band; Chrs; Chrh Wkr; Cmnty Wkr; Hon Rl; NHS; Orch; VP Yth Flsp; Lat Clb; Bsbl; Mast Vlbl Plyr Var Bsbl 78; Bst Mrch Awd In #1 HS Mrch Band 78; Bst Sqd Awd Mrch Band 78; Spring Arbor Coll; Psych.

BONTRAGER, ROGER; Bethany Christian HS; Middlebury, IN; 43/68 VP Sr Cls; Chrs; Chrh Wkr; FCA; Hon Rl; Sch Mus; Sch Pl; VP Stu Cncl; Yth Flsp; Yrbk;.

BONTVAGER, GARY; Bethany Christian HS; Goshen, IN; 5/75 VP Jr Cls; Cl Rep Jr Cls; Chrh Wkr; Cmnty Wkr; Hon Rl; Stu Cncl; Yth Flsp; 4-H; Letter Bsbl; Letter Bsktbl; Varsity Ltr In Bsbl Bsktbl & Soccer; All Sectnl 1st Tm 1st Base Bsbl; Bsktbl Leading Scorer Varisty Team 78; Bus Schl; Acctg.

BONVISSUTO, JAMES; Holy Name HS; Maple Hts, OH; Cls Rep Frsh Cls; Cls Rep Soph Cls; Chrs; Hon Rl; Sprt Ed Yrbk; IM Sprt; Ohio Univ; Bus Admin.

BOODT, DOUGLAS; Ben Davis HS; Indianapolis, IN; FCA; NHS; Rdo Clb; Letter Gym; Indiana Univ; Cmnctns.

BOOG, JUDI; Ashley HS; Bannister, MI; 1/28 VP Sr Cls; Band; Hon Rl; NHS; Stu Cncl; FHA; FTA; Bsktbl; DAR Awd; Michigan St Univ; Home Ec.

BOOG, TAMMY; Ashley Comm HS; Bannister, MI; 2/28 Pres Frsh Cls; Cls Rep Soph Cls; Pres Jr Cls; Pres Sr Cls; Band; Hon Rl; NHS; Off Ade; Pol Wkr; Sch Pl; Lansing Comm Coll; Nursing.

BOOG, TAMMY; Ashley Cmnty HS; Bannister, MI; 2/28 Pres Frsh Cls; Pres Soph Cls; Pres Jr Cls; Pres Sr Cls; Band; Girl Scts; Hon Rl; NHS; Off Ade; Pol Wkr; Lansing Cmnty Coll; Nursing.

BOOHER, DON; Dayton Christian HS; Xenia, OH; Cls Rep Soph Cls; Cl Rep Jr Cls; Chrs; Hon Rl; Lbry Ade; Sch Mus; Stu Cncl; Yrbk; Drama Clb; Cit Aw d; Cedarville Coll; Bus.

BOOHER, SARAH; Laurel HS; Laurel, IN; Girl Scts; Hon Rl; NHS; Yrbk; Yrbk; Pres 4-H; 4-H Awd; Purdue Univ; Animal Sci.

BOOHER, SHAWNIE K; Dayton Christian HS; Xenia, OH; 6/95 Cls Rep Soph Cls; Cl Rep Jr Cls; Cls Rep Sr Cls; Chrs; NHS; Off Ade; Sch Mus; Stu Cncl; Cit Awd; Cedarville Coll.

BOOKER, CHERYL; Fayetteville HS; Fayetteville, WV; 27/86 Cls Rep Frsh Cls; Trs Jr Cls; Hon Rl; MMM; Stu Cncl; FBLA; FHA; Pep Clb; Spn Clb; Letter Bsktbl; West Virginia Inst Of Tech; Acctg.

BOOKER, LEIGH; Edwardsburg HS; Edwardsburg, MI; Hon Rl; Ed Sch Nwsp; Rptr Sch Nwsp; Sch Nwsp; 4-H; Fr Clb; Univ Of Notre Dame; Vet.

BOOKER, QULAR A; Princeton HS; Cincinnati, OH; 154/651 Hst Sr Cls; JA; NHS; DECA; Cincinnati Tech Coll; Acctg.

BOOKER, RUDOLPH E; Stivers Patterson Co Op HS; Dayton, OH; 96/428 Cls Rep Frsh Cls; Pres Soph Cls; Cls Rep Soph Cls; Cl Rep Jr Cls; Chrs; Chrh Wkr; Hon Rl; Boys Clb Am; DECA; Capt Ftbl; Free Entrps Compttn 3rd Pl 77; Free Entrps Hon Mntn 78; St Judo Champ 76; Harvard Univ; Personnel Mgmt.

BOOKER, STEPHANIE; Du Pont HS; Charleston, WV; Cl Rep Jr Cls; Sec Sr Cls; Chrs; Chrh Wkr; Cmnty Wkr; Hon Rl; JA; Jr NHS; Off Ade; Sch Mus; Thespian 77; Univ; Marketing.

BOOKER, TAMARA; W Washington HS; Hardinsburg, IN; Sec Frsh Cls; Band; Stu Cncl; DECA; Drama Clb; FHA; Pep Clb; VICA; Capt Chrldng; Mgrs;.

BOOKER, VALERIE; Frank Cody HS; Detroit, MI; Hon Rl; Lbry Ade; FDA; Pep Clb; Letter Glf; Letter Ten; GAA; Cit Awd; Cpt Of Vllybll Tml 79; Wayne St Mbrshp For H S Stdnts 79; Pres Of Med Careers Club 79; Oakland Univ; Vet Med.

BOOKMAN, DEBRA; Loudonville HS; Loudonville, OH; 9/133 Aud/Vis; Hon Rl; NHS; Sch Pl; Yth Flsp; Sch Nwsp; VP 4-H; 4-H Awd; N E Oh Sclstic Press Assoc 79; Pres Day Contest I Won 3rd In Spch Coverage; N Central Tech Coll; Comp Progr.

BOOKOUT, LAURA; Philip Barbour HS; Philippi, WV; Band; Hon Rl; NHS; Yth Flsp; 4-H; Fr Clb; Sci Clb; Trk; 4-H Awd; Anderson Broaddus Coll.

BOOMER, DORIE; Newberry HS; Newberry, MI; Cl Rep Jr Cls; Debate Tm; Hon Rl; Jr NHS; Natl Forn Lg; Sch Pl; Stu Cncl; Sch Nwsp; Bsbl; PPFtbl; Jackson Comm.

BOOMGAARD, MICHAEL; St Joseph Prep Seminary HS; Grand Haven, MI; Cls Rep Frsh Cls; Cls Rep Soph Cls; Trs Sr Cls; Chrh Wkr; Hon Rl; Jr

NHS; Sch Pl; Stu Cncl; Rptr Yrbk; Rptr Sch Nwsp; Aquinas Coll.

BOOMGAARD, MICHAEL D; St Joseph Prep Seminary; Grand Rapids, MI; Cls Rep Frsh Cls; Cls Rep Soph Cls; Cl Rep Jr Cls; Trs Sr Cls; Boy Scts; Chrh Wkr; Hon Rl; Jr NHS; Sch Pl; Stu Cncl; Aquinas Coll.

BOOMS, KAREN; Ubly HS; Minden City, MI; 17/110 Cls Rep Sr Cls; Hon Rl; NHS; Sch Pl; Stu Cncl; Ed Yrbk; Yrbk; 4-H; FHA; Pep Clb; Western Michigan Univ; Occptnl Ther.

BOON, BRIAN; Port Clinton Sr HS; Port Clinton, OH; 1/280 Band; Hon Rl; Ger Clb; Mth Clb; Bsktbl; Univ; Engr.

BOON, HEATHER; Lake Michigan Catholic HS; Benton Hrbr, MI; Chrs; JA; Rptr Yrbk; Yrbk; Fr Clb; Capt Chrldng; Michigan St Univ; Public Rel.

BOONE, CATHY; Lebanon Sr HS; Lebanon, IN; Am Leg Aux Girls St; Band; Chrs; Mdrgl; NHS; Sch Mus; 4-H; Tmr; 4-H Awd; Mas Awd; Purdue Univ; Elem Ed.

BOONE, ELIZABETH; Fremont HS; Fremont, IN; 8/49 Hon Rl; NHS; Pol Wkr; Sch Mus; Sch Pl; 4-H; Fr Clb; OEA; Ind Univ; Journalism.

BOONE, MARK; Hedgesville HS; Martinsburg, WV; Chrh Wkr; Cmnty Wkr; Hon Rl; ROTC; Sct Actv; Ger Clb; Ftbl; Trk; IM Sprt; Potomac State Univ; Elec Tech.

BOONE, MONICA; Warrensville Hts HS; Warrensvl Hts, OH; Cls Rep Frsh Cls; Drl Tm; Lbry Ade; Rptr Sch Nwsp; Ohio St Univ; Journalism.

BOONE, SHARI; Carman HS; Flint, MI; Cls Rep Frsh Cls; Cls Rep Soph Cls; Cl Rep Jr Cls; Cls Rep Sr Cls; Chrh Wkr; Cmnty Wkr; Hon Rl; NHS; Off Ade; Red Cr Ade; Fresh Talentawd For Jrnlsm Only One At Alma To Recv One 79; Pres Schlrshp Alma Coll 79; Mim Comptn Schlrshp; Alma Coll; Bus Admin.

BOONE, TERRY; Newton HS; Covington, OH; 2/47 VP Soph Cls; Pres Jr Cls; Cls Rep Sr Cls; Hon Rl; Lbry Ade; Lit Mag; NHS; Stu Cncl; Treas Yth Flsp; Treas FFA; Own Elec Bus.

BOONE, TRUDY; Elkhart Memorial HS; Elkhart, IN; Hon Rl; DECA; Chrldng; Bus Schl.

BOOP, ROBERT L; Triway HS; Orrville, OH; Hon Rl; Boys Clb Am; Bsktbl; Coach Actv; Wayne General; Business.

BOORN, MICHELLE; Bristol Local HS; Bristolville, OH; Cls Rep Soph Cls; Cl Rep Jr Cls; Hon Rl; Jr NHS; NHS; Stg Crw; Stu Cncl; Yth Flsp; College; Phys Ther.

BOOS, BRUCE; Edison HS; Norwalk, OH; Band; Hon Rl; NHS; VP Yth Flsp; Drama Clb; Pres 4-H; FFA; Treas Mth Clb; 4-H Awd; Opt Clb Awd; Ohio St Univ; Agri Ec.

BOOS, CATHY; Edison HS; Norwalk, OH; 4/164 Band; Chrs; Chrh Wkr; NHS; Sch Mus; Treas Stu Cncl; Pres Yth Flsp; Drama Clb; Sec 4-H; 4-H Awd; Oberlin Univ; Music.

BOOS, ELAINE; Winamac Community HS; Winamac, IN; Chrs; Hon Rl; Hosp Ade; Jr NHS; Pres NHS; Sch Mus; Stu Cncl; Drama Clb; 4-H; Pres Lat Clb; College; Acctg.

BOOS, SHARON; Huron HS; Sandusky, OH; 5 2/169 Hon Rl; NHS; Off Ade; Pres 4-H; Lat Clb; Letter Bsbl; Letter Mgrs; 4-H Awd; Ohio St Univ.

BOOSE, MICHELLE; West Geauga HS; Chesterland, OH; Aud/Vis; Chrs; Drl Tm; Girl Scts; Hon Rl; Lbry Ade; Sch Pl; Stg Crw; Rptr Sch Nwsp; College; Mass Communication.

BOOT, ELIZABETH; Forest Hills Northern HS; Grand Rapids, MI; Chrs; Sch Pl; Fr Clb; Grand Rapids Jr Coll; Med Tech.

BOOTH, ANGELA; Seeger Mem HS; Boswell, IN; Hon Rl; Sch Pl; Rptr Yrbk; Drama Clb; Spn Clb; Univ; Comm Art.

BOOTH, BECCIE; Indian Valley N HS; New Philadelph, OH; Trs Frsh Cls; Cl Rep Jr Cls; Cls Rep Sr Cls; Band; Chrs; Hon Rl; Jr NHS; NHS; Stu Cncl; Yrbk;.

BOOTH, BURTON; Coalton HS; Ellamore, WV; 12/32 Pres Frsh Cls; Band; Boy Scts; Hon Rl; Sch Pl; Stg Crw; Stu Cncl; Yth Flsp; Rptr Yrbk; 4-H;.

BOOTH, CHAS; St Vincent St Mary HS; Akron, OH; Hon Rl; NHS; Off Ade; Sch Mus; Mth Clb; Bsbl; Ftbl; Akron Univ; Acct.

BOOTH, JOHN; Johnstown Monroe HS; Johnstown, OH; Hon Rl; NHS; Crs Cntry; Trk; Bowling Green St Univ; Bus.

BOOTH, MARK W; Valley HS; Porters Falls, WV; Hon Rl; NHS; Letter Trk; Univ; Engr.

BOOTH, RICK; Washington County Voc HS; Wingett Run, OH; Pres 4-H; VICA; Bsbl; Bsktbl; Scr Kpr; Tmr; 4-H Awd; Westinghouse Elec Corp Awd; College; Archt.

BOOTHE, CARLEEN; Collinwood HS; Cleveland, OH; Cls Rep Soph Cls; Off Ade; Stu Cncl; Yrbk; Rptr Sch Nwsp; Ger Clb; Pep Clb; Twrlr; Cit Awd; Univ; Law.

BOOTHE, DONNA; Buckeye North HS; Smithfield, OH; Band; Chrs; Girl Scts; Hon Rl; NHS; Stu Cncl; Pep Clb; Spn Clb; Chrldng; Voc Schl.

BOOTHE, LORI; Ellet HS; Akron, OH; 2/363 Val; Chrs; Chrh Wkr; Cmnty Wkr; Hon Rl; Hosp Ade; Jr NHS; VP NHS; Orch; Stu Cncl; Natl Div In Piano Playing Auditions; PTA Schlrshp Awd; Univ Of Akron; Medicine.

BOOTON, ANITA; Fairland HS; Proctorvll, OH; 1/129 NHS; 4-H; Fr Clb; Mth Clb; Pep Clb; Letter Bsktbl; IM Sprt; 4-H Awd; Vllybl Ltr 2 Yr 77 & 78; Art Club Pres 78; Ohio St Univ; Dr Of Vet Med.

BOOTS, KAREN L; Southern Wells HS; Marion, IN; 14/100 VP Jr Cls; Am Leg Aux Girls St; Ed Yrbk; Yrbk; Drama Clb; PPFtbl;.

BOOTZ, ELON; Pinconning Area HS; Linwood, MI; 3/272 Sal; Cmnty Wkr; Hon Rl; Hosp Ade; Lbry Ade; NHS; Off Ade; Red Cr Ade; PPFtbl; Awd For Exc 79; St Of Michigan Comp Schlrshp Exam 79; Saginaw Valley St Coll; Vet Med.

BOOZER, FAITH; Dunbar HS; Charleston, WV; AFS; Pres Chrs; Chrh Wkr; Cmnty Wkr; Hon Rl; Lbry Ade; Off Ade; Pol Wkr; Sch Mus; Sch Pl; Soc Dist Amer HS Stu; Univ Of Tennessee; Fashion Design.

BOPRA, GENE; Carsonville Port Sanilac HS; Carsonville, MI; Cls Rep Sr Cls; Hon Rl; Sch Pl; Stg Crw; Stu Cncl; Yth Flsp; Fr Clb; FFA; Mic State Univ; Engr.

BORAWSKI, DEBORAH; Our Lady Of Mt Carmel HS; Wyandotte, MI; 2/72 Chrs; Hon Rl; Jr NHS; NHS; Sch Mus; Rptr Yrbk; Spn Clb; Letter Bsktbl; College; Reg Nurse.

BORBAS, TIMOTHY; Bramwell HS; Nemours, WV; 1/29 Pres Soph Cls; Hon Rl; NHS; VP Stu Cncl; Key Clb; Bsktbl; Crs Cntry; Trk; Univ.

BORCHERT, FRANK R; Cleveland Hts HS; Cleveland Hts, OH; 41/750 AFS; Am Leg Boys St; Band; Boy Scts; Chrh Wkr; Hon Rl; Orch; Sch Mus; Ed Sch Nwsp; Rptr Sch Nwsp; Swarthmore Coll; Poli Sci.

BORCK, BARB; Woodward HS; Toledo, OH; Hosp Ade; Red Cr Ade; FHA; Pep Clb; Sci Clb; Ten; Pres Of Health Club 78; Candy Striper Awd 78; Michael J Owens Tech Univ; Surgical.

BORCZON, M; Redford HS; Detroit, MI; Drm Mjrt; Hon Rl; Hosp Ade; Lbry Ade; NHS; Pol Wkr; Fr Clb; Am Leg Awd; Cit Awd; Univ; Engr.

BORDASH, DIANA; Toronto HS; Toronto, OH; Band; Drl Tm; Girl Scts; Hon Rl; Sch Mus; Fr Clb; Pep Clb; Trk; Pom Pon; Univ Of Akron; Resp Ther.

BORDEN, JULIE A; Shaw HS; Cleveland Hts, OH; Hst Jr Cls; Hon Rl; 4-H; OEA; Bsbl; Bsktbl; Gym; College; Stenographer.

BORDER, DIANA; Dover HS; Dundee, OH; Cls Rep Soph Cls; Cl Rep Jr Cls; Chrh Wkr; Hon Rl; Jr NHS; Lbry Ade; NHS; Stu Cncl; Yth Flsp; Y-Teens; Ohio St Univ; Fshn Mdse.

BORDERS, ANGELA; Immaculata HS; Detroit, MI; Hon Rl; Hosp Ade; JA; Pom Pon; JA Awd; Univ; Psych.

BORDNER, JODY; Hoover HS; North Canton, OH; Pres Sr Cls; Chrs; Hon Rl; NHS; Sch Mus; Stu Cncl; Cit Awd; College; Art.

BORDONARO, JOSEPH; Shaker Hts HS; Shaker Hts, OH; Boy Scts; Chrh Wkr; Hon Rl; Letter Ftbl; Coach Actv; IM Sprt; Univ Of Pennsylvania; Bus Admin.

BORDONARO, STEPHANIE; Beaumont School For Girls; Moreland Hls, OH; Aud/Vis; Debate Tm; Lit Mag; Pol Wkr; Rptr Sch Nwsp; Pep Clb; Spn Clb; Capt Socr; GAA; IM Sprt; Awd At Lk Erie Coll & Notre Dame Oh Frgn Lang Cntst 78; Awd At Schl Art Shows 77; Tampa Univ.

BOREK, MICHAEL; Lee HS; Wyoming, MI; 7/70 Pres Sr Cls; Chrs; Hon Rl; Pres NHS; Sch Mus; Sch Pl; Stu Cncl; Bsktbl; Letter Ftbl; Letter Trk; Western Mi Schlrshp 79; Michigan St Univ; Acctg.

BOREN, MICHAEL; Eastmoor HS; Columbus, OH; Capt Ftbl; Trk; Wrstlng; Univ; Bus.

BORER, GALE; New Riegel HS; New Riegel, OH; 1/51 Chrs; Girl Scts; NHS; Off Ade; Sch Mus; Rptr Yrbk; Bsbl; Am Leg Awd; Cit Awd; Tiffin Univ; Bus.

BORER, MARIANNE; Tiffin Calvert HS; Tiffin, OH; Chrh Wkr; Girl Scts; Stg Crw; Yth Flsp; Pep Clb; Mat Maids; Scr Kpr; Tmr; Terra Tech; Tchr.

BORES, BETSY; Monroeville HS; Monroeville, OH; VP Frsh Cls; Cls Rep Soph Cls; Cl Rep Jr Cls; Band; Hon Rl; NHS; Sch Pl; Stu Cncl; Pep Clb; Trk; Toledo Univ.

BORG, JOSEPHINE; Holy Redeemer HS; Detroit, MI; Cls Rep Frsh Cls; Cls Rep Soph Cls; Hon Rl; NHS; Rptr Sch Nwsp; Socr; Chrldng; UM; Advertising.

BORG, MARY; Marian HS; Southfield, MI; Cls Rep Soph Cls; Chrs; Hon Rl; Mod UN; NHS; Natl Merit Ltr; Oakland Univ; Nursing.

BORGEN, JAMES; Columbian HS; Tiffin, OH; Aud/Vis; Band; Boy Scts; Chrs; Hon Rl; Sct Actv; Drama Clb; Spn Clb; Trk; College.

BORGER, DEBRA; Amelia HS; Cincinnati, OH; 9/270 Hon Rl; Jr NHS; Lbry Ade; NHS; Off Ade; Stg Crw; Drama Clb; Treas Fr Clb; OEA; IM Sprt; Coll; Nursing.

BORGERT, SAM; Celina Sr HS; Celina, OH; Hon Rl; NHS; Lat Clb; Letter Bsktbl; Letter Ten; Univ.

BORGESON, DAVID; Grand Ledge HS; Grand Ledge, MI; NHS; Glf; IM Sprt; College.

BORGS, DACE; Columbia HS; Columbia Sta, OH; Chrs; Hon Rl; NHS; Fr Clb; Voice Dem Awd; 4th Pl In Ohio In Algebra II In Ohio Tests Of Scholastic Achvmnt; College; Research Sci.

BORIS, BARBARA; Villa Angela Academy; Euclid, OH; Sec Frsh Cls; Cls Rep Soph Cls; Cl Rep Jr Cls; Girl Scts; Stu Cncl; Pres Fr Clb; High Awds In Recitation Original Poetry Skits In French 76; Awd For Being Top Student In French 78; Univ; Spec Educ.

BORKOWSKI, JOHN; St Joseph HS; S Bend, IN; 1/263 Chrh Wkr; Hon Rl; NHS; Sch Pl; Letter Bsktbl; Cit Awd; DAR Awd; College.

BORN, DEAN; Benjamine Logan HS; Belle Cntr, OH; Pres Frsh Cls; Hon Rl; FFA; Letter Ftbl; Wrstlng; Voc Schl; Art.

BORN, DEBORAH; Perrysburg HS; Perrysburg, OH; 92/248 AFS; Chrs; Chrh Wkr; Cmnty Wkr; Girl Scts; Hon Rl; FTA; Ger Clb; Socr; DAR Awd; 1st Class Girl Scout 77; Mgr Of Dist Champ Vllybl Tm 78; Univ; Educ.

BORN, ERIC; Hagerstown Jr Sr HS; Hagerstown, IN; VP Jr Cls; Band; Boy Scts; Pres FCA; Hon Rl; Pres NHS; Sct Actv; Sprt Ed Yrbk; Sec Fr Clb; Capt Ftbl; Christian Athlete Of Yr 79; Tanker Of Yr 78; Most Valuable Swimmer 79; Univ; Pre Med.

BORN, RUTH A; Notre Dame HS; New Boston, OH; 2/60 Trs Soph Cls; Hon Rl; NHS; Stu Cncl; Mth Clb; Spn Clb; Bsbl; Bsktbl; Trk; Cit Awd; Shawnee St Cmnty Coll.

BORNAIS, CLAUDETTE; Walled Lake Western HS; Wixom, MI; Girl Scts; Hon Rl; Fr Clb; Coll.

BORNEMEIER, DEBRA; Henry Ford II HS; Sterling Hts, MI; 11/438 Band; Capt Drm Mjrt; Hon Rl; Hosp Ade; NHS; Stu Cncl; Yrbk; Capt Swmmng; Tmr; Northern Michigan Univ; Med.

BORNHORST, ELAINE; Minster HS; Ft Loramie, OH; Band; Chrs; Hon Rl; Off Ade; Sch Mus; Stg Crw; Scr Kpr; Lima Tech Univ; Elem Ed.

BORNMAN, CANDACE; Bethany Christian HS; Syracuse, IN; Chrs; Hon Rl; NHS; Orch; Yth Flsp; Sch Nwsp; Drama Clb; Crs Cntry; Trk; Chrldng; College; Cpa.

BORNTRAGER, ANNETTA; Northridge HS; Middlebury, IN; 1/150 Chrs; Chrh Wkr; Cmnty Wkr; Hon Rl; Hosp Ade; Lbry Ade; NHS; FHA; Cert Awd Getting All A's In German 1 78; Univ; Nursing.

BORODYCHUK, SHELLEY; Unionville Sebewaing AreaHS; Unionville, MI; 2/100 Band; Girl Scts; Hon Rl; Univ; Soc Work.

BOROFF, COY; Memorial HS; St Marys, OH; 12/250 Chrh Wkr; Hon Rl; FFA; OSU; Agri.

BOROSKI, LISA; Buckeye South HS; Rayland, OH; 2/130 Trs Soph Cls; Trs Jr Cls; Am Leg Aux Girls St; Band; Capt Drl Tm; Hon Rl; NHS; Y-Teens; Drama Clb; 4-H; Schlshp Team 77; Univ.

BOROWIAK, RICHARD M; Gaylord Community HS; Gaylord, MI; Hon Rl; NHS; Ftbl; College.

BOROWIAK, SANDY; St Marys Cathedral HS; Gaylord, MI; Yrbk; Sch Nwsp; Pep Clb; Letter Bsbl; Letter Bsktbl; Trk; Central Mich; Photog.

BOROWICZ, DEBORAH; Cheboygan Area HS; Cheboygan, MI; Hon Rl; NHS; Sch Pl; Rptr Yrbk; Univ; Comp Sci.

BOROWSKI, JOHN; St Stephens HS; Saginaw, MI; Cls Rep Frsh Cls; Cls Rep Soph Cls; Cl Rep Jr Cls; Cls Rep Sr Cls; Am Leg Boys St; Band; Boy Scts; Ed Sch Nwsp; Sprt Ed Sch Nwsp; Capt Hockey; N Mic Univ; Water Bio.

BORRADAILE, JOHN; Davison Cmnty HS; Davison, MI; .

BORRELLI, DENISE; Oregon Davis HS; Walkerton, IN; 2/58 Trs Frsh Cls; Trs Jr Cls; Cmnty Wkr; Sec FCA; Pol Wkr; Sch Pl; Rptr Yrbk; Sec 4-H; Pep Clb; Gym; College.

BORROR, GREGORY E; East Knox HS; Howard, OH; Chrh Wkr; Cmnty Wkr; Off Ade; Yth Flsp; 4-H; Pres 4-H; Pep Clb; Bsktbl; Letter Ftbl; 4-H Awd; Voc Schl; Diesel Mech.

BORS, LOUIS E; Holy Redeemer HS; Detroit, MI; Hon Rl; 4-H; IM Sprt; Scr Kpr; Mich State Univ.

BORST, JOHN M; Alba Public Schl; Alba, MI; 6/17 Sec Jr Cls; Hon Rl; Sprt Ed Yrbk; Sprt Ed Sch Nwsp; Bsktbl; Crs Cntry; Al Pena Cmnty Coll; Archt.

BORT, MARY; Chelsea HS; Gregory, MI; Chrs; Hon Rl; Mdrgl; Natl Forn Lg; Sch Mus; Letter Bsktbl; IM Sprt; Pres Awd; Univ; Theatre.

BORTHS, BOB; La Salle HS; Cincinnati, OH; 11/280 Sec Sr Cls; Hon Rl; NHS; Sch Mus; Rptr Sch Nwsp; Crs Cntry; Trk; Coach Actv; Ohio State Univ.

BORTON, ELIZABETH; West HS; Columbus, OH; VP Jr Cls; Chrs; Chrh Wkr; Cmnty Wkr; Drm Bgl; Hon Rl; Pres DECA; Pep Clb; DAR Awd; JA Awd; Distrib Edu DECA Stu Of Hte Yr 78; ESAA Adv Comm For Columbus Pub Schl; W HS Pres Cncl 77; Mt Carmel Schl Of Res Ther; Res Ther.

BORTON, GREGORY; Tecumseh HS; Tecumseh, MI; 82/250 Hon Rl; Letter Bsktbl; Letter Ftbl; Capt Trk; IM Sprt; Ftbl All League Defnsv Back & All Cnty Defnsv Back 78; Track St Qualifier In High Hurdles 78; Adrian Coll; Bus Admin.

BORTON, MARK; Arthur Hill HS; Saginaw, MI; 74/687 Yrbk; DAR Awd;.

BORTON, PETER; Minerva HS; Minerva, OH; Hon Rl; Stu Cncl; 4-H; College.

BORTZ, LISA; Chagrin Falls HS; Chagrin Falls, OH; AFS; Girl Scts; Hon Rl; NHS; Sch Nwsp; Ger Clb; Letter Bsktbl; Letter Ten; Univ; Bio Sci.

BORUCH, ALAN V; Hobart Sr HS; Hobart, IN; Hon Rl; Mth Clb; Sci Clb; Stanford Univ; Med.

BORUCKI, ANDREA; Portage HS; Portage, IN; Hon Rl; Jr NHS; Pep Clb; Gym; Chrldng; Ind Univ; Psych.

BORUCKI, DONNA; Bay City Central HS; Bay City, MI; 26/470 Hon Rl; NHS; Eng Clb; Pres Awd; College.

BORUFF, JANELL; Bloomfield HS; Bloomfield, IN; Trs Jr Cls; Band; Hon Rl; Stu Cncl; Drama Clb; Sci Clb; Chrldng; Scr Kpr; Hon Queen Of Jobs Daughters 78; Band Pres 78; Life Guard 78; Indiana St Univ; RN.

BORUTA, JOHN; Croswell Lexington HS; Lexington, MI; Cls Rep Frsh Cls; Band; Chrh Wkr; Orch; Sch Mus; Sch Pl; Stg Crw; Spn Clb; Bsktbl; Glf; Michigan St Univ; Comp Sci.

BORYCKI, BRENDA; Divine Child HS; Dearborn Hts, MI; Girl Scts; Hon Rl; Rptr Yrbk; Pom Pon; Univ.

BORYS, SUSAN; St Joseph Central Cath HS; Fremont, OH; Band; FTA; Univ; Spec Educ Tchr.

BORYSIAK, NANCY; Cabrini HS; Allen Pk, MI; Cmnty Wkr; Girl Scts; Hon Rl; NHS; Drama Clb; Spn Clb; Trk; Univ; Acctg.

BOS, LOREN; Holland Christian HS; Zeeland, MI; Pres Chrh Wkr; Letter Bsbl; Letter Socr; Letter Trk; IM Sprt; Calvin Coll.

BOSCH, BEVERLY; Hamilton Cmnty HS; Holland, MI; 11/130 Pres Soph Cls; Chrs; Hon Rl; Mdrgl; NHS; Sch Pl; Stg Crw; Stu Cncl; Rptr Yrbk; Ed Sch Nwsp; Michigan St Univ; Agri.

BOSCH, BRIAN; Holland Christian HS; Holland, MI; Cls Rep Frsh Cls; Cls Rep Soph Cls; Cl Rep Jr Cls; Cls Rep Sr Cls; Chrs; Chrh Wkr; Cmnty Wkr; Letter Bsbl; M S U; Horticulture.

BOSCH, KEVIN; Unity Christian HS; Hudsonville, MI; Pres Frsh Cls; Cls Rep Sr Cls; Hon Rl; Mod UN; Stu Cncl; Ger Clb; Trk; IM Sprt; Calvin College; Bus.

BOSCH, MARY; Wauseon HS; Wauseon, OH; Hon Rl; Y-Teens; Fr Clb; Gym; Univ; Sci.

BOSCH, ROBERT; Shelby HS; Shelby, MI; 23/122 Hon Rl; NHS; Glf; Mich State Univ; Veterinary Medicine.

BOSCO, FRED; Walnut Hills HS; Cincinnati, OH; Jr NHS; Lit Mag; Sch Pl; Spn Clb; Natl Merit SF; Williams College.

BOSE, PATTI; Buckeye West HS; Adena, OH; Chrh Wkr; Hon Rl; OEA; Belmont Tech Schl; Sales.

BOSECKER, CONNIE; South Spencer HS; Rockport, IN; Chrs; Chrh Wkr; Hon Rl; Rptr Sch Nwsp; 4-H; Ivy Tech.

BOSHART, TIM; Goshen HS; Goshen, IN; Band; Chrh Wkr; Hon Rl; Orch; Sch Mus; Yth Flsp; Outstndng Mrch Percssnst 77; Hon Sqd Mrch Band 78; Music Ltr & Jacket 78; Univ.

BOSKOVIC, CHRISTINE; Villa Angela Academy; Euclid, OH; Aud/Vis; Debate Tm; Hon Rl; Off Ade; Spn Clb; Second Honors; College; Nursing.

BOSLEY, PAMELA; Valley HS; Reader, WV; VP Frsh Cls; VP Soph Cls; Cl Rep Jr Cls; Band; Hon Rl; NHS; Sch Pl; Stu Cncl; Yrbk; Chrldng; All Trnmnt Cheerldr 78; Internatl Thespian Soc 79; Univ.

BOSLEY, SANDRA; Union HS; Mt Storm, WV; VP Frsh Cls; Cls Rep Soph Cls; Hst Sr Cls; Cls Rep Sr Cls; Hon Rl; NHS; Sch Pl; Beta Clb; Civ Clb; FHA; Potomac State College; Soc Work.

BOSLEY, SANDRA S; Union HS; Mt Storm, WV; Cls Rep Soph Cls; Hst Sr Cls; Cls Rep Sr Cls; Drl Tm; Hon Rl; Lbry Ade; Sch Pl; Stu Cncl; Pres Beta Clb; FHA; Potomac St Coll; Soc Work.

BOSMA, DEB; South Christian HS; Grand Rapids, MI; Hon Rl; Hosp Ade; Sch Pl; Stg Crw; Yth Flsp; College; Dental Asst.

BOSO, WILLIAM; Millersport HS; Millersport, OH; Cl Rep Jr Cls; Chrs; Chrh Wkr; Debate Tm; Hon Rl; Jr NHS; NHS; Tech Schl.

BOSS, C; West Ottawa HS; Holland, MI; 1/350 Pres Jr Cls; Am Leg Boys St; VP NHS; Letter Ten; Dnfth Awd; Brown Univ.

BOSS, JAMES; Cuyahoga Falls HS; Cuyahoga Falls, OH; Band; Chrs; Sch Mus; Univ; Comp Study.

BOSSERT, MELINDA; Acad Immaculate Conception; Batesville, IN; 33/68 Chrs; Chrh Wkr; Treas Girl Scts; Hon Rl; Sch Mus; Yrbk; Rptr Sch Nwsp; Spn Clb; Mgrs; Tuition Grant For ICA 77 80; Bus Schl; Bus.

BOSSERT, SUSAN; Union County HS; Liberty, IN; 4/123 VP Jr Cls; Cl Rep Jr Cls; Cls Rep Sr Cls; Drl Tm; FCA; Hon Rl; Lbry Ade; NHS; Pre Med.

BOSSIE, SHERRY; Dunbar HS; Dunbar, WV; Cls Rep Sr Cls; Hon Rl; Jr NHS; Mod UN; NHS; Off Ade; Stu Cncl; Rptr Sch Nwsp; Mth Clb; Sec Spn Clb; West Virginia Univ; Bus Mgmt.

BOST, PEGGY; Napoleon HS; Napoleon, OH; Chrs; Chrh Wkr; Hon Rl; Hosp Ade; Sch Mus; Yth Flsp; Drama Clb; Fr Clb; Gym; Swmmng; College; Nursing.

BOSTDORFF, JIM; Otsego HS; Bowling Green, OH; Am Leg Boys St; Chrh Wkr; Hon Rl; Yth Flsp; 4-H; FFA; Letter Bsktbl; Letter Crs Cntry; Letter Trk; 4-H Awd; 4 H Club Mbr; De Kalb Awd Winner Otsego FFA; State FFA Degree; College.

BOSTER, KRIS; Hurricane HS; Hurricane, WV; 5/235 Band; Chrh Wkr; Girl Scts; Hon Rl; VP JA; Treas NHS; Sch Mus; Y-Teens; VP 4-H; Pep Clb; All Cnty Vnd 77 78 & 79; All Area Bnd 77 78 & 79; Hon Ment In Cnty Wide Sci Fair 79; Typ Awd In 1st Yr 79; Univ; Engr.

BOSTER, TAMMY; Hurricane HS; Hurricane, WV; Hon Rl; Yth Flsp; Y-Teens; Pep Clb; Bsktbl; 4-H Awd; Business Schl.

BOSTIC, DARNISHA; Martin Luther King Jr HS; Detroit, MI; Cl Rep Jr Cls; Chrh Wkr; Cmnty Wkr; Hon Rl; Lbry Ade; Off Ade; Stu Cncl; Pres DECA; Pep Clb; Glf; Michigan St Univ; Busns Admin.

BOSTIC, TRACY LEE; Valley HS; Montgomery, VA; Chrh Wkr; Hon Rl; NHS; Stu Cncl; Swmmng; Chrldng; W Virginia Inst Of Tech; Busns Mgmt.

BOSTICK, CINDY; Crestview HS; Convoy, OH; Girl Scts; Hon Rl; Lbry Ade; Off Ade; FHA; Scr Kpr; Vantage Voc Schl; Fash Merch.

BOSTICK, JAMES; Shady Springs HS; Daniels, WV; Cl Rep Jr Cls; Band; Chrh Wkr; JA; Orch; Sch Mus; Pep Clb; Ten; Trk; Univ; Law.

BOSTICK, TIMOTHY R; Du Pont HS; Charleston, WV; 5/295 Am Leg Boys St; Chrs; Chrh Wkr; Hon Rl; Pres Stu Cncl; Yth Flsp; Lat Clb; Ten; IM Sprt;

ROTC Scholarship Awd; Massachusetts Inst Of Tech; Elec Eng.

BOSTON, BONNIE; Southern Local HS; Salineville, OH; 5/89 Pres Soph Cls; Pres Jr Cls; Band; Hon Rl; NHS; FNA; OEA; Letter Bsktbl; Chrldng; Mgrs; Univ; Acctg.

BOSTWICK, JUDY K; Kearsley HS; Burton, MI; 41/375 Chrs; Chrh Wkr; Girl Scts; Hon Rl; Hosp Ade; Red Cr Ade; Yth Flsp; Mgrs; Scr Kpr; Univ Of Michigan; Pre Med.

BOSTWICK, KRISTI; Fairview HS; Dayton, OH; Letter Drl Tm; Off Ade; Stg Crw; Art Inst Of Pittsburg; Art.

BOSTWICK, RAY; Sts Peter & Paul Area HS; Saginaw, MI; Chrs; Hon Rl; NHS; Trk; Saginaw Vly Coll; Music.

BOSWELL, LYNNE; Normandy Sr HS; Parma, OH; 11/649 Cls Rep Frsh Cls; Cls Rep Soph Cls; Chrs; Hon Rl; Lbry Ade; Pres NHS; Off Ade; Sch Mus; Sch Pl; VP Stu Cncl; Univ; Fine Arts.

BOTBYL, JEFFREY; North Muskegon HS; N Muskegon, MI; 26/108 Cls Rep Frsh Cls; Band; Chrs; Hon Rl; Jr NHS; NHS; Bsbl; IM Sprt; College; Engr.

BOTELLO, ROMAN; Olivet HS; Olivet, MI; 18/105 Band; Hon Rl; Lbry Ade; Sch Mus; Drama Clb; Key Clb; Pep Clb; Coach Actv; IM Sprt; PPFtbl; Kellog Cmnty Coll; Criminal Justice.

BOTSCHNER, ANDREW; North Canton Hoover HS; North Canton, OH; Am Leg Boys St; Band; Chrs; Hon Rl; Orch; Yth Flsp; Sci Clb; Glf; Ten; Am Leg Awd; Ohio Test Of Schlstc Achvmnt Amer Hist Hon Mention 79; Univ.

BOTSKO, KAREN; Brooklyn HS; Brooklyn, OH; 10/173 Band; Chrs; Cmnty Wkr; Hon Rl; Jr NHS; NHS; Off Ade; Orch; Sch Pl; Stg Crw; Outstanding Stu Busns; Amer Soc Of Wmn Accts; Co Capt Vlybl; Alpha & Beta Awds Isia; Nom Miss United Teen; College; CPA.

BOTSON, PAM; Magnificat HS; N Olmsted, OH; Girl Scts; Sch Pl; College; Math.

BOTT, LUCY; Chelsea HS; Grass Lake, MI; 9/210 Chrs; Hon Rl; Lbry Ade; NHS; 4-H; FFA; Trk; PPFtbl; 4-H Awd; Univ; Acctg.

BOTTEI, ROBERTA; Clay HS; South Bend, IN; 1/382 Val; Am Leg Aux Girls St; Chrh Wkr; Girl Scts; Pres NHS; Quill & Scroll; Stu Cncl; Univ Of Notre Dame; Political Sci.

BOTTI, SHARON; Holy Rosary; Flint, MI; 1/57 Hon Rl; Rptr Yrbk; Bsbl; Michigan St Univ; Accountant.

BOTTOMS, CHARLES W; St Ignatius HS; Cleveland, OH; Boy Scts; Cmnty Wkr; Hon Rl; JA; Lit Mag; Sct Actv; Yth Flsp; Y-Teens; Rdo Clb; Letter Trk; Won 4 Yr Schlrshp Writing Contest; Pres Youth Org; College; Engr.

BOTTORFF, ARTHUR; Washington HS; So Bend, IN; Rptr Yrbk; DECA; Fr Clb; Wrstlng; Mgrs; Distrib Educ St Tourn Finalist 79; Indiana Univ; Bus Admin.

BOTTS, KATHY; South HS; Columbus, OH; 33/300 Cmnty Wkr; Hon Rl; NHS; Off Ade; Sch Nwsp; OEA; Pep Clb; COE Stdnt Of Year 1979; V P COE; Sec.

BOTZMAN, JOHN; Lakeview HS; Stow, OH; Band; Boy Scts; Rptr Sch Nwsp; Letter Wrstlng; IM Sprt; Mgrs; Kent State Univ.

BOUCHARD, MICHELLE; Dover HS; Dover, OH; 114/243 Band; Chrs; Hosp Ade; Lbry Ade; Y-Teens; FBLA; Pep Clb; Bsbl; Trk; Scr Kpr; Ohi State Univ; Pub Relations.

BOUCHONNET, SANDRA; Scarlet Oaks HS; Cincinnati, OH; 26/635 Pres Jr Cls; VP Sr Cls; Trs Sr Cls; Hon Rl; Rptr Sch Nwsp; DECA; GAA; Academic Awd; 2nd Pl Poetry Contest; S Ohio Busns Coll; Retail Marketing.

BOUCKAERT, THEREASA; Garber HS; Essexville, MI; Band; Chrh Wkr; Cmnty Wkr; Girl Scts; Hon Rl; Sct Actv; 4-H; Cit Awd; 4-H Awd; Ferris Univ; Acctg.

BOUDREAU, MARC; Jenison HS; Jenison, MI; CAP; Hon Rl; JA; Stu Cncl; Rptr Yrbk; Rptr Sch Nwsp; Ger Clb; Mic Tech Univ; Orthodontistry.

BOUDRIE, TERRI; Jefferson HS; Monroe, MI; 7/179 Cmp Fr Grls; Chrs; Chrh Wkr; Cmnty Wkr; Hon Rl; Hosp Ade; JA; NHS; Red Cr Ade; Sch Pl; French Club 1978; Honor Roll 1976; Campfire Girls 1978; Monroe Cmnty Coll.

BOUGH, DONNA R; N Daviess Jr Sr HS; Odon, IN; 30/93 Cls Rep Frsh Cls; Cls Rep Soph Cls; Cl Rep Jr Cls; Am Leg Aux Girls St; Band; Chrs; Chrh Wkr; Drm Mjrt; FCA; Girl Scts; Indiana Univ; Phys Ther.

BOUGHEY, BECKY; Scott HS; Toledo, OH; Chrh Wkr; Hon Rl; Off Ade; Pol Wkr; Yth Flsp; OEA; Univ Of Toledo.

BOUGHNER, KATHY; Valley HS; Porters Fls, WV; Trs Jr Cls; Hon Rl; Letter Bsktbl; Letter Trk; Mgrs;.

BOUILLON, BETTY; New Riegel HS; New Riegel, OH; 2/48 Band; Hon Rl; NHS; 4-H; Pep Clb; Spn Clb;.

BOUILLON, JANET; New Riegel HS; New Riegel, OH; 10/48 Sec Soph Cls; Cls Rep Soph Cls; Sec Jr Cls; Band; Hon Rl; NHS; Stg Crw; Stu Cncl; 4-H; FTA; College.

BOUKAMP, MARK; North Muskegon HS; Twin Lake, MI; Hon Rl; NHS; Off Ade; Bsbl; Bsktbl; Ftbl; Trk; IM Sprt; Scr Kpr; Tmr; Muskegon Cmnty Coll; Bus Mgmt.

BOULDIN, DEBRA; Peterstown HS; Peterstown, WV; Hon Rl; NHS; Ed Yrbk; Rptr Sch Nwsp; Treas Fr Clb; Sec FHA; Sci Clb; Schlrshp Awd For Achieving 3.85 GPA 76 79; Bluefield St Coll; Nursing.

BOULLARD, GREGORY; Adlai Stevenson HS; Sterling Hghts, MI; 29/535 Cls Rep Frsh Cls; Cls Rep Soph Cls; Pres Jr Cls; Pres Sr Cls; Am Leg Boys St; Chrs; Chrh Wkr; Hon Rl; Toledo Univ; Pharmacy.

BOULTER, PANDORA; East Kentwood HS; Kentwood, MI; Hon Rl; Off Ade; Yth Flsp; IM Sprt; PPFtbl; Natl Merit Schl; W Michigan Univ; Bus Admin.

BOULTINGHOUSE, KATHY; South Spencer HS; Rockport, IN; 10/180 Cls Rep Soph Cls; Cl Rep Jr Cls; Cls Rep Sr Cls; Am Leg Aux Girls St; Band; Chrs; Drm Mjrt; Hon Rl; NHS; Sch Mus; Univ; Phys Ther.

BOULTON, DOUG; Potterville HS; Dimondale, MI; FCA; Hon Rl; NHS; Yth Flsp; Letter Bsktbl; Letter Ftbl; Scr Kpr; Tmr; Central Michigan Univ; Civil Engr.

BOULTON, JEFFREY; Fostoria HS; Fostoria, OH; Boy Scts; Hon Rl; NHS; 4-H; Fr Clb; Ten; Cincinnati Univ; Engr.

BOUMA, SUSAN; Calvin Chr HS; Wyoming, MI; Trs Jr Cls; Cl Rep Jr Cls; Hon Rl; Bsktbl; Trk;.

BOUNDS, JANE; Southridge HS; Huntngbrg, IN; Chrh Wkr; Cmnty Wkr; Girl Scts; Hosp Ade; Sec JA; FHA; Rdo Clb; JA Awd;.

BOUR, JOANN; Mohawk HS; Mc Cutchenville, OH; 2/126 Sal; Pres Band; Hon Rl; NHS; Rptr Yrbk; VP 4-H; Pres Spn Clb; Ohi State Univ; Pre Law.

BOUR, TOM; Mohawk Sr HS; Tiffin, OH; 1/120 Pres Soph Cls; Val; Band; Hon Rl; JA; Jr NHS; NHS; Stu Cncl; Ed Yrbk; Pres FTA; Toledo Univ; Pre Med.

BOURDEAU, BRIDGET; Lake Linden Hubbell HS; Lake Linden, MI; 4/53 Band; Hon Rl; Lbry Ade; Off Ade; Sch Pl; Ed Yrbk; Rptr Sch Nwsp; Bsktbl; Gym; Chrldng; Mich Tech; Forest Tech.

BOURDEAU, DOUGLAS; Troy HS; Troy, MI; Chrh Wkr; Off Ade; College; Vet.

BOURDEAU, JODI; Harbor HS; Ashtabula, OH; 13/177 AFS; Boy Scts; Fr Clb; OEA; Pep Clb; Lakeland Comm Coll; Data Processing.

BOURDON, RICHARD L; La Salle HS; South Bend, IN; 48/500 Band; Chrh Wkr; Drm Bgl; Hon Rl; Orch; Stu Cncl; Sprt Ed Sch Nwsp; Sci Clb; Letter Bsbl; Mgrs; 1st Plc USTA In St Champ Brass Solo 79; Univ; Music.

BOURGOIN, CAROL; Bishop Gallagher HS; St Clair Shores, MI; 14/328 Hon Rl; Ten; Univ Of Michigan; Engr.

BOURGUIGNON, MARY; Beaumont Girls HS; E Cleve, OH; Boy Scts; NHS; Sch Pl; Rptr Yrbk; Yrbk; Socr; Trk; Univ; Bio Chem.

BOURLAND, G; Whitmore Lake HS; Whitmore Lk, MI; 5/82 Hon Rl; Lbry Ade; NHS; Orch; Yth Flsp; Univ Of Mic; Orchestra Violinist.

BOURN, ROBERT; Braxton County HS; Rosedale, WV; 1/175 Cls Rep Soph Cls; Cl Rep Jr Cls; Val; Am Leg Boys St; Hon Rl; Jr NHS; NHS; 4-H; FFA; Am Leg Awd; FFA St Farmer Pin 78; Mbr Of 2nd Pl St FFA Landgudging Team 78; Mbr Of Cnty Area & St Math Team 77 M.; West Virginia Univ; Engr.

BOURNE, DAVID S; Marion L Steele HS; Amherst, OH; 7/342 Am Leg Boys St; Band; Hon Rl; NHS; Orch; Stg Crw; Drama Clb; Ger Clb; Sci Clb; Ten; Case Western Reserve Univ; Astronomy.

BOURNE, LISA; Jay County HS; Redkey, IN; 18/474 Hon Rl; JA; NHS; Sch Pl; Y-Teens; Sprt Ed Sch Nwsp; Fr Clb; Pep Clb; Gym; Chrldng; College; Psych.

BOUSCHOR, AMY; Traverse City Sr HS; Traverse City, MI; 7/700 Chrs; Girl Scts; Hon Rl; Mdrgl; NHS; Orch; Sch Mus; Yth Flsp; Drama Clb; Pep Clb; Yale Coll; Math.

BOUSSOM, MICHAEL; Lawton HS; Lawton, MI; 8/56 Band; Boy Scts; Hon Rl; 4-H; Voc Schl; Elec Engr.

BOUTCHER, BARB; Morton Sr HS; Hammond, IN; 12/465 Girl Scts; Hon Rl; NHS; Off Ade; Yrbk; Ger Clb; Univ Of So Carolina; Communications.

BOUTILIER, GAIL; Homer Community HS; Gladwin, MI; Chrh Wkr; Hon Rl; NHS; Gr Rapids Baptist Coll; Children.

BOUTYARD, TRINA; Martinsburg HS; Martinsburg, WV; Chrs; Girl Scts; Hon Rl; Hosp Ade; Red Cr Ade; 4-H; Pep Clb; Gym; Pom Pon; Berkeley Co Talent Show Dancing Catagory 1st Pl Overall 77; James Rumsey Voc Tech Schl; Lgl Sec.

BOUWKAMP, NANETTE; William Henry Harrison HS; W Laf, IN; Girl Scts; Hon Rl; Off Ade; Stg Crw; Stu Cncl; Yrbk; Sch Nwsp; Pep Clb; Spn Clb; Bsktbl; Ball State; English.

BOVA, JULIANA; Cardinal Mooney HS; Youngstown, OH; 18/288 Cmp Fr Grls; Debate Tm; Hon Rl; Natl Forn Lg; NHS; Stu Cncl; Drama Clb; Spn Clb; Highest Avg Speech Class 77; Qualified For St Speech 78; Tournament 78 & 79; Univ; Eng.

BOVEE, ANNETTE; Mc Comb Local HS; Mccomb, OH; 3/80 Am Leg Aux Girls St; Chrs; Hon Rl; Sch Mus; Stu Cncl; Sec Yth Flsp; Pres 4-H; Pres FHA; Sec Spn Clb; 4-H Awd; Bluffton College.

BOVENSCHEN, WAYNE; Armada Area HS; Armada, MI; Cls Rep Frsh Cls; Cl Rep Jr Cls; Band; Chrh Wkr; Hon Rl; NHS; Sch Mus; Stu Cncl; Yth Flsp; Letter Trk; Iron Man Awd Bskbl; 1st Chair League Band; Michigan St Univ; Data Processing.

BOWCOTT, MARY; Brooke HS; Wellsburg, WV; Am Leg Aux Girls St; Chrh Wkr; Cmnty Wkr; Fr Clb; Ohio Dominican Coll; Psych.

BOWDEN, CYNTHIA; Fairmont West HS; Kettering, OH; Chrs; Hon Rl; NHS; Sch Mus; Yth Flsp; Fr Clb; Mth Clb; Butler Univ; Bus.

BOWDEN, ROBIN; Warren HS; Warren, MI; Cmp Fr Grls; Girl Scts; Hon Rl; Adrian; Writer.

BOWE, MICHAEL; Dowagiac Union HS; Dowagiac, MI; Band; Chrh Wkr; Yth Flsp; Sprt Ed Sch Nwsp; IM Sprt; Mgrs; Scr Kpr; Mas Awd; St Of Mi Schshp 79; Adrian Grat 79; Adrian Coll; Phys Ther.

BOWE, STEVE; New Albany HS; New Albany, IN; 220/565 College; Mechanical Eng.

BOWELL, MELINDA; Beavercrook HS; Xenia, OH; 106/702 Cmnty Wkr; Hon Rl; Jr NHS; NHS; Off Ade; Pep Clb; Gym; Coach Actv; IM Sprt; Kettering Sch Med Art; Resp Tech.

BOWEN, CHRISTOPHER; Kirtland HS; Chesterland, OH; 5/125 Am Leg Boys St; Hon Rl; NHS; Yrbk; Sch Nwsp; Key Clb; Letter Bsktbl; Letter Ftbl; College; Photographer.

BOWEN, DENISE; South Point HS; Chesapeake, OH; 9/170 Chrh Wkr; NHS; Beta Clb; 4-H; FTA; Marshall Univ Tuition Waver; Lawrence Co Fair Qn Ct; Hilado Math Awd; Marshall Univ; Busns Admin.

BOWEN, DOUGLAS; Chelsea HS; Chelsea, MI; 130225 Hon Rl; JA; NHS; Glf; Univ; Engr.

BOWEN, JENNIFER; Clear Fork HS; Butler, OH; 19/169 Pres Band; Hon Rl; NHS; Quill & Scroll; Sch Nwsp; Coach Actv; Bowling Green Univ; Special Ed.

BOWEN, JUANITA; East Washington HS; Salem, IN; Cl Rep Jr Cls; Band; Chrh Wkr; Hon Rl; NHS; Sch Pl; Stu Cncl; Drama Clb; FHA; Pep Clb; Univ; Pediatrcn.

BOWEN, KEITH; Mississinewa HS; Gas City, IN; Band; Hon Rl; Fr Clb; Crs Cntry; Mgrs; Univ.

BOWEN, LESLIE; North Muskegan HS; N Muskegon, MI; Cl Rep Jr Cls; Band; Hon Rl; Orch; Sch Mus; Sch Pl; Stu Cncl; Univ Of Mich; Pharmacy.

BOWEN, ROGER; Jennings County HS; N Vernon, IN; 15/350 Band; Boy Scts; Hon Rl; Sch Pl; Yth Flsp; Rptr Sch Nwsp; 4-H; Ger Clb; Swmmng; VP 4-H Awd; Purdue Univ; Nuclear Engr.

BOWEN, STACY; Swan Valley HS; Saginaw, MI; 2/187 Trs Sr Cls; Chrh Wkr; Cmnty Wkr; JA; Lbry Ade; NHS; Pol Wkr; Sch Pl; Rptr Yrbk; Drama Clb; Michigan St Univ; Law.

BOWEN, STEPHANIE; Plmouth HS; Plymouth, IN; Cmp Fr Grls; Chrs; Hosp Ade; Lbry Ade; Drama Clb; Lat Clb; Mat Maids; Ind St Univ; Nrsg.

BOWEN, THOMAS R; Yorktown HS; Muncie, IN; Aud/Vis; Band; Hon Rl; Hosp Ade; Lbry Ade; Sch Mus; Fr Clb; Sci Clb; Cert CPR Instrctr Train Amer Hrt Asn 79; Ust Ml Jr Voluntr To Donat 1000 Hr In 1 Yr Ball Hosp 78; Wabash Univ; Med.

BOWEN, TODD; Jay County HS; Portland, IN; 37/450 AFS; Chrs; Chrh Wkr; Debate Tm; Hon Rl; Natl Forn Lg; NHS; Sch Pl; Stu Cncl; Fr Clb; College; Tchr.

BOWER, CHRIS; Patterson Co Op HS; Dayton, OH; Cls Rep Frsh Cls; Cls Rep Soph Cls; Cl Rep Jr Cls; Cmnty Wkr; Debate Tm; Lbry Ade; Yth Flsp; Ohi State; Mech.

BOWER, DANIEL; Groveport Madison HS; Columbus, OH; Boy Scts; Hon Rl; Sct Actv; Fr Clb; Letter Ten; Eagle Scout 76; World Conservation Awd 77; Selctd To Attend Gov Conservation Workshp 78; Ohio St Univ; Enviro Sci.

BOWER, RICHARD; Newbury HS; Chagrin Falls, OH; Rptr Yrbk; Rptr Sch Nwsp; Capt Bsktbl; IM Sprt; JC Awd;.

BOWER, STEVE; St Johns HS; St Johns, MI; 26/325 Chrs; Hon Rl; NHS; Swmmng; IM Sprt; Natl Merit Ltr; Lansing Community College; Engr.

BOWER, VICKI; Malvern HS; Malvern, OH; Trs Jr Cls; Chrs; Hon Rl; Off Ade; Sch Mus; 4-H; FHA; Pep Clb; Sci Clb; Chrldng; Bus Schl.

BOWER, VICKIE; Big Walnut HS; Galena, OH; Sec Frsh Cls; Sec Sr Cls; Band; Girl Scts; Hon Rl; NHS; 4-H; Fr Clb; Ohi St Univ.

BOWERMAN, JERI; Hillman Community Schools; Hillman, MI; Chrs; Girl Scts; Hon Rl; Lbry Ade; Sch Mus; Sch Pl; Sct Actv; Rptr Yrbk; Trk; Cit Awd; Univ.

BOWERMAN, KURT; Carson City Crystal Area HS; Carson City, MI; 6/127 Pres Frsh Cls; Am Leg Boys St; Band; Hon Rl; NHS; Off Ade; Stu Cncl; Bsbl; Letter Bsktbl; Letter Ftbl; Michigan Tech Univ; Elec Engr.

BOWERMAN, NANCY; Quincy HS; Quincy, MI; Chrs; Hon Rl; NHS; Off Ade; Ed Yrbk; Yrbk; Ed Sch Nwsp; 4-H; Mgrs; Scr Kpr;.

BOWERMAN, WILLIAM; William G Mather HS; Munising, MI; 2/104 Trs Frsh Cls; Sal; Band; Boy Scts; Hosp Ade; NHS; Sch Pl; Sct Actv; Rptr Sch Nwsp; Crs Cntry; Northern Michigan Univ; Pre Med.

BOWERS, BENEDICTE; Olivet HS; Olivet, MI; Trs Jr Cls; Hon Rl; NHS; Sch Mus; Stu Cncl; Yrbk; Spn Clb; Trk; Colorado St Univ; Interior Design.

BOWERS, BRENDA; Conotton Valley HS; Bowerston, OH; Band; Chrh Wkr; Girl Scts; Sch Mus; 4-H; FHA; Pep Clb; Sci Clb; Mgrs; 4-H Awd; Ohi State Univ; Bus Sci.

BOWERS, CAROL; Defiance Sr HS; Defiance, OH; Band; Hon Rl; Jr NHS; NHS; DECA; Fr Clb; FTA; Treas Sci Clb; Scr Kpr; Lutheran Hosp Schl Of X Ray; Radiolg.

BOWERS, CAROLYN; Whetstone Sr HS; Columbus, OH; Chrs; Hon Rl; Fr Clb; Tmr; Univ Of North Carolina; Psych.

BOWERS, DANIEL; Fountain Ctrl HS; Veedersburg, IN; 6/118 Cls Rep Frsh Cls; Cls Rep Soph Cls; Pres Jr Cls; Cl Rep Jr Cls; Pres Sr Cls; Cls Rep Sr Cls; Band; Boy Scts; FCA; Hon Rl; Purdue Univ; Elec Engr.

BOWERS, J; Norwayne HS; Creston, OH; Am Leg Boys St; Aud/Vis; Band; Chrs; FCA; Off Ade; Sch Mus; Sch Pl; Yth Flsp; IM Sprt; Bowling Green Univ; Cmnctns.

BOWERS, JAMES E; Coldwater HS; Coldwater, MI; DECA; Letter Ftbl; Western Michigan Univ.

BOWERS, J LYNNETTE; Whitko HS; Wabash, IN; Band; Hon Rl; Hosp Ade; Pom Pon; Univ; R N.

BOWERS, KAREN; University HS; Morgantown, WV; 10/146 Hon Rl; Jr NHS; Treas NHS; Yth Flsp; Rptr Yrbk; Rptr Sch Nwsp; FBLA; FHA; Special Journalism Awd; West Virginia Career Coll; Sec.

BOWERS, LINDA; Philip Barbour HS; Philippi, WV; Chrh Wkr; Hon Rl; Y-Teens; 4-H Awd; College; Med.

BOWERS, VICKI; Flemington HS; Shinnston, WV; 2/42 Hst Soph Cls; Band; Hon Rl; NHS; Sch Mus; Sprt Ed Yrbk; Sch Nwsp; Pres Fr Clb; FTA; Cit Awd; College; Acctg.

BOWERSOCK, CINDY; Wynford HS; Bucyrus, OH; Band; Chrs; Hon Rl; VP NHS; Sch Pl; Rptr Yrbk; S ec Drama Clb; 4-H; Pres Pep Clb; Sec Spn Clb; College; Nursing.

BOWERSOCK, DOUG; Perry HS; Cridersville, OH; Cls Rep Soph Cls; Chrs; Hon Rl; Bsktbl; Capt Glf; Trk; Mgrs; Outstanding Choir & Health Stu; Chamber Group; Lima Tech Coll; Mech Engr.

BOWERSOX, TODD; Wapakoneta Sr HS; Wapakoneta, OH; 2/320 Hon Rl; Jr NHS; NHS; Ftbl; NCTE; Hiram Coll; Bio.

BOWERSOX, JONATHAN W; Xenia HS; Xenia, OH; 3/450 Am Leg Boys St; Band; Chrs; Chrh Wkr; Hon Rl; NHS; Cedarville College; Pastor.

BOWKER, DEBBIE; Gull Lake HS; Richland, MI; 3/228 Chrs; Hon Rl; Jr NHS; NHS; Off Ade; Sch Mus; Drama Clb; 4-H; Ten; Chrldng; Univ; Music.

BOWLBY, MELINDA; Waldron Jr Sr HS; Shelbyville, IN; Band; Chrs; Chrh Wkr; Hon Rl; Lbry Ade; NHS; Yth Flsp; Fr Clb; Pep Clb;.

BOWLBY, MELINDA J; Waldron HS; Shelbyville, IN; Band; Chrs; Hon Rl; Lbry Ade; Yth Flsp; Fr Clb; Pep Clb; Coll.

BOWLES, DONNA; Carlisle HS; Franklin, OH; Cmp Fr Grls; Chrs; Chrh Wkr; Girl Scts; Hosp Ade; Lbry Ade; Yth Flsp; Pep Clb; Spn Clb; Branell Coll; Travel.

BOWLES, KIM; Belleville HS; Ypsilanti, MI; Hon Rl; JA; NHS; Eastern Mic Univ.

BOWLES, ROBIN; Corunna HS; Owosso, MI; 4/213 Band; Chrh Wkr; Hon Rl; NHS; Ed Yrbk; Sprt Ed Yrbk; Rptr Yrbk; Pres 4-H; Mi Bus Schls Lassoc Schlrshp 79; Future Sec Assoc 79; Baker Jr Coll; Exec Sec.

BOWLES, SCOTT; Western HS; Spring Arbor, MI; Cls Rep Soph Cls; Cl Rep Jr Cls; Debate Tm; VP Stu Cncl; Rptr Sch Nwsp; Spn Clb; Trk; GAA; Mgrs; Michigan Tech Univ; Physics.

BOWLES, STEVE; Chaminade Julienne HS; Dayton, OH; Chrs; Chrh Wkr; Hon Rl; Stg Crw; Drama Clb; Rdo Clb; Jrnlsm.

BOWLIN, CONNIE; Little Miami HS; Maineville, OH; Cls Rep Frsh Cls; Cls Rep Soph Cls; Sec Jr Cls; Hon Rl; Off Ade; Stu Cncl; Rptr Yrbk; Bus Schl.

BOWLING, GREG; Heath HS; Heath, OH; 1/150 Am Leg Boys St; Hon Rl; NHS; Letter Bsktbl; Letter Ftbl; Letter Trk; College; Engr.

BOWLING, KATHY R; Mt View HS; Tuscaloosa, AL; 55/257 Band; Drm Mjrt; Girl Scts; Hon Rl; Hosp Ade; NHS; Orch; VP Yth Flsp; Sch Nwsp; Ten; Univ Of Alabama; Phys Educ.

BOWLING, KEITH; Benjamin Bosse HS; Evansville, IN; Chrs; Chrh Wkr; Hon Rl; DECA; Cit Awd; Intrntl Bible College.

BOWLING, LORI; Austin HS; Austin, IN; 13/76 Chrh Wkr; Cmnty Wkr; Hon Rl; Jr NHS; Sch Pl; Pep Clb; Indiana St Univ; Jrnlsm.

BOWLING, RON; Richmond HS; Richmond, IN; Cls Rep Frsh Cls; Cl Rep Jr Cls; FCA; Hon Rl; Fr Clb; IM Sprt; College; English.

BOWLING, RON S; Richmond Sr HS; Richmond, IN; Cls Rep Frsh Cls; Cl Rep Jr Cls; FCA; Hon Rl; Yth Flsp; Fr Clb; Coll; Busns Admin.

BOWLING, TAMARA; Fairborn Park Hills HS; Fairborn, OH; 58/311 Girl Scts; Hon Rl; NHS; Stu Cncl; Scr Kpr; Tmr; Girls Volleyball Team 76 & 77; Varsity Footbl Statistion; Rec In Whos Who 77 Edition; Wright St Univ; Nursing.

BOWLING, TERESA; Belmont HS; Dayton, OH; Chrs; Cmnty Wkr; Off Ade; DECA; Spn Clb; Letter Bsktbl; Mgrs; Mas Awd; Miami Jacobs Jr Coll; Acctg.

BOWLING, TERESA; Taylor HS; Kokomo, IN; Aud/Vis; Chrs; Girl Scts; Lbry Ade; FHA; Pep Clb; Chrldng; IM Sprt; PPFtbl;.

BOWMAN, APRIL; Ross Sr HS; Hamilton, OH; 29/229 Cls Rep Frsh Cls; Cls Rep Soph Cls; Hon Rl; Spn Clb; GAA; Bowling Green Univ; Marine Bio.

BOWMAN, C DAVID; W Carrollton Sr HS; Dayton, OH; 5/450 Sec AFS; Hon Rl; Jr NHS; Lit Mag; NHS; Orch; Sch Mus; Sec Fr Clb; Dayton Philarmonic Youth Orchestra; S W Ohio Reg Orch; W Carrollton Soc Clb; Ohio Univ; Music.

BOWMAN, DAVID; Waterford Twp HS; Union Lake, MI; 10/400 Hon Rl; Rptr Yrbk; Natl Merit SF; Ancient History Awd; Gold Medal Ping Pong; Univ Of Michigan; Chem.

BOWMAN, DAVID; Houghton Lake HS; Roscommon, MI; Band; Hon Rl; NHS; Bsktbl; Ftbl; Letter Trk; Natl Merit SF; Univ.

BOWMAN, DONALD; Decatur Central HS; Indnpls, IN; Band; Boy Scts; Chrh Wkr; FCA; Sct Actv; Wrstlng; Perfect Attendance; Order Of Arrow Eagle Scout; College.

BOWMAN, GREG; Kings Mills HS; S Lebanon, OH; 4/175 Am Leg Boys St; Hon Rl; NHS; Spn Clb; Bsbl; Bsktbl; Ftbl; Trk; Coll; Elec Engr.

BOWMAN, JACKIE; Loudonville HS; Loudonville, OH; 35/133 Band; Hon Rl; Sch Mus; Sch Pl; Yrbk; Rptr Sch Nwsp; Drama Clb; 4-H; Spn Clb; Trk; North Central Tech Coll; Sec Sci.

BOWMAN, JANET; Blissfield HS; Palmyra, MI; 1/115 Chrh Wkr; Hon Rl; NHS; Rptr Yrbk; Pep Clb; Sec Spn Clb; Owens Tech; Optometric Assist.

BOWMAN, JEFFREY; Patterson Co Op HS; Dayton, OH; 7/458 Trs Jr Cls; Chrh Wkr; Hon Rl; NHS; Off Ade; Stu Cncl; OEA; Gym; 2 Time Winner Of Pres Phys Fitness Awrd 75; 2nd Plc In Dayton Middle Schls Track Meet 76; Univ.

BOWMAN, JEFFREY R; Southfield Christian HS; East Douglas, MA; Mi Compschlrshp Progr Cert For Academc Achvmnt 79; Univ; Mech Engr.

BOWMAN, JILL M; Rochester Adams HS; Rochester, MI; Chrh Wkr; Cmnty Wkr; Hosp Ade; Natl Forn Lg; Sch Mus; Sch Pl; Stg Crw; Stu Cncl; Drama Clb; Spn Clb; Univ; Psych.

BOWMAN, JOAN; Logan Elm HS; Laurelville, OH; Band; Drl Tm; Hon Rl; NHS; Stg Crw; Rptr Sch Nwsp; Sec 4-H; GAA; Scr Kpr; 4-H Awd; Univ; Math.

BOWMAN, JOHN; High School; Gallipolis, OH; Stg Crw; Sch Nwsp; 4-H; FFA; FHA; Letter Ftbl; Trk; Scr Kpr; Tmr; 4-H Awd; Voc Schl; Elec.

BOWMAN, KAREN S; Lincoln HS; Shinnston, WV; 35/150 Hon Rl; NHS; FHA; FTA; Pres Library Clb Mbr 78; Parkersburg Cmnty Coll; Rdlgc Tech.

BOWMAN, KATHY J; Switz City Central HS; Bloomfield, IN; 4/49 Hon Rl; Lit Mag; NHS; Rptr Yrbk; FHA; Letter Bsktbl; Pom Pon; Vincennes Univ; Acctg.

BOWMAN, KRISTI; Rock Hill HS; Ironton, OH; Hon Rl; Pep Clb; GAA; College; Photog.

BOWMAN, LEANNA; Edgewood HS; Gasport, IN; Chrh Wkr; Cmnty Wkr; FCA; Off Ade; Pol Wkr; 4-H; Ger Clb; 4-H Awd; Indiana Univ; Busns.

BOWMAN, LINDA; East HS; Columbus, OH; 36/270 Trs Jr Cls; Sec Sr Cls; Chrs; Chrh Wkr; Cmnty Wkr; Hon Rl; Lbry Ade; NHS; Off Ade; Sch Pl; Ohio Dominican Coll; Acctg.

BOWMAN, MARY PAT; Magnificat HS; N Olmstead, OH; Chrh Wkr; Cmnty Wkr; Chrldng; Coach Actv; Univ.

BOWMAN, MICHAEL; Griffith HS; Griffith, IN; 49/297 Quill & Scroll; Yrbk; Rptr Sch Nwsp; Sch Nwsp; College; Aviation Tech.

BOWMAN, MIKE; Mount Healthy HS; Cincinnati, OH; Cls Rep Sr Cls; Ger Clb; Bsbl; Letter Ftbl; Univ.

BOWMAN, REBECCA; Waverly HS; Waverly, OH; 25/172 Chrh Wkr; Hon Rl; Fr Clb; Pep Clb; Letter Trk; GAA; Capt Pom Pon; Scr Kpr; 4-H Awd; Univ; Nursing.

BOWMAN, ROY; Twin Valley South HS; W Alex, OH; Band; Bsktbl; Letter Crs Cntry; Ftbl; Letter Trk; Project Step; Tool & Die.

BOWMAN, SHERRY; Marsh Fork HS; Naoma, WV; Sec Jr Cls; Chrs; Hon Rl; Stu Cncl; Pep Clb; Concord Coll.

BOWMAN, STANLEY; Northfield HS; Lagro, IN; Band; Boy Scts; 4-H; FFA; Crs Cntry; Trk; IM Sprt; Natl Gold Key Finalist In Art 79; Track MIP Awd 79; Otstndng Jr Awd In Band 79; Coll; Indust Mgr.

BOWRON, JUDY; Scecina Memorial HS; Indianapolis, IN; 1/194 Trs Sr Cls; Hon Rl; NHS; Stu Cncl; Yrbk; Bsktbl; GAA; Univ; Comp Sci.

BOWSER, JACQUELINE; West Muskingum HS; Gratiot, OH; 1/168 VP Band; VP Chrs; Hon Rl; NHS; Fr Clb; Key Clb; Sci Clb; Socr; Natl Merit Ltr; Intl Thespian Soc 77; Coll; Acctg.

BOWSER, LISA R; Springfield HS; Holland, OH; VP Frsh Cls; Cls Rep Frsh Cls; Cls Rep Soph Cls; Cl Rep Jr Cls; Chrs; Hon Rl; Off Ade; Stu Cncl; 4-H; Spn Clb; Toledo Univ; Spanish Lang.

BOWSER, MARGIE; Hubbard HS; Masury, OH; Chrs; Chrh Wkr; Cmnty Wkr; Girl Scts; Hon Rl; Lit Mag; Quill & Scroll; Stg Crw; Yrbk; Rptr Sch Nwsp; Smmr Coll 1978; Girls State 2nd Rnnr Up 1978; Century III Schlrshp 1979; Univ; Elec Engr.

BOWSER, ROSEMARY; Fairborn Park Hills HS; Fairborn, OH; 1/325 Chrs; Capt Drl Tm; Hon Rl; Jr NHS; Lit Mag; NHS; Quill & Scroll; Rptr Yrbk; Wrstlng; Wright St Univ; Dent.

BOWSER, TERI; Montgomery Cnty Jt Voc HS; New Lebanon, OH; Chrs; Chrh Wkr; Drl Tm; Stu Cncl; OEA; Bsbl; Bsktbl; Trk; Ambassador Highest Awd Of DEA; Placed 3rd In Extemp Speaking At Reg Comp; Awd All Four Awd Of DEA Awd; Montgomery Cnty Joint Voc Schl; Sec.

BOWYER, LAURA; Hanover Central HS; Cedar Lake, IN; Chrs; Chrh Wkr; Girl Scts; Hon Rl; Jr NHS; Orch; Sch Pl; Stg Crw; Drama Clb; 4-H; Univ; Nursing.

BOX, ANN; Bay City Central HS; Bay City, MI; 6/512 Cls Rep Sr Cls; Band; Hon Rl; NHS; Orch; Stu Cncl; Eng Clb; PPFtbl; Bausch & Lomb Awd; Ferris St Coll; Pharm.

BOX, RITA; Eastern Greene Co HS; Springville, IN; Chrs; Chrh Wkr; Hon Rl; Pres FHA; Okland City Coll; Sec.

BOX, TERESA; Lexington HS; Lexington, OH; 2/32 Trs Frsh Cls; Band; Lbry Ade; NHS; Off Ade; Stu Cncl; Y-Teens; Bsktbl; Trk; Univ; Bus.

BOXHILL, JOHN H; Columbus East HS; Columbus, OH; 9/273 Cls Rep Frsh Cls; Cls Rep Soph Cls; Cl Rep Jr Cls; Cls Rep Sr Cls; Chrs; Drm Mjrt; Hon Rl; Jr NHS; NHS; Off Ade; Howard Univ; Dent.

BOXWELL, LAURIE; Marion Harding HS; Marion, OH; Capt Band; Capt Drm Bgl; Girl Scts; Hon Rl; Jr NHS; Spn Clb; Twrlr; Univ Of Michigan; Sci.

BOYCE, CHRISTINA; Grafton HS; Grafton, WV; Chrs; Hon Rl; Hosp Ade; NHS; Sch Mus; Sch Pl; VP Stu Cncl; Drama Clb; Letter Chrldng; PPFtbl; Vc Pres Of Niki Club 78; Jr Prom Prncss 79; Homcmngn Princss 76; Univ; TV Brdcstng.

BOYCE, JENNIFER; East Kentwood HS; Kentwood, MI; Sch Mus; Sch Pl; Drama Clb; Lat Clb; Central Michigan Univ; Psych.

BOYCE, JOHN; Cardinal Stritch HS; Toledo, OH; Chrh Wkr; Hon Rl; Stg Crw; Univ; Archt.

BOYD, ANITA; Cascade HS; Clayton, IN; 10/138 VP Soph Cls; VP Jr Cls; Am Leg Aux Girls St; Hon Rl; FBLA; Pep Clb; Spn Clb; Chrldng; Homecoming Candidate 76 79; Frosh Princess 76; Purdue Univ; Acctg.

BOYD, ANNETTE; Pickerington HS; Pickerington, OH; Chrh Wkr; Hon Rl; Yth Flsp; Y-Teens; VP Spn Clb; Univ; Comp Sci.

BOYD, BETH ANNE; Hedgesville HS; Hedgesville, WV; 43/250 Band; Girl Scts; Hon Rl; Hosp Ade; Off Ade; Orch; Stg Crw; Drama Clb; Fr Clb; Mth Clb; Shepherd Coll; Med Tech.

BOYD, CLEMENT W; Patterson Co Operative HS; Dayton, OH; 3/427 Cls Rep Frsh Cls; Trs Jr Cls; Cmnty Wkr; Hon Rl; NHS; Pol Wkr; Pres DECA; Ohi Univ; Communications.

BOYD, DEBORAH L; Buckeye West HS; Mt Pleasant, OH; 23/84 Sec Soph Cls; Chrs; Chrh Wkr; Cmnty Wkr; Girl Scts; Hon Rl; Off Ade; Sch Nwsp; OEA; Chrldng; Vocational Schl; Sec.

BOYD, DONNA; Deckerville Cmnty Schl; Snover, MI; Sec Frsh Cls; VP Soph Cls; Cl Rep Jr Cls; Sec Sr Cls; Hon Rl; NHS; Off Ade; Stu Cncl; OEA; Chrldng; Univ; RN.

BOYD, GORDON; Cedarville HS; Cedarville, OH; Bsbl; Coll; Bus Mang.

BOYD, JAMES L; Madison Comprehensive HS; Mansfield, OH; Ohio St Univ; Draftsman.

BOYD, JEFF; Marion Harding HS; Marion, OH; Bsktbl; Ftbl; Trk; IM Sprt; Univ; Comp Sci.

BOYD, JEFFREY S; Strongsville Sr HS; Strongsville, OH; Hon Rl; Bowling Green Univ; Bus.

BOYD, JENNIFER; Marysville HS; Marysville, OH; Hon Rl; Off Ade; Stg Crw; Lat Clb; Trk; Chrldng; GAA; IM Sprt; PPFtbl; Miami Univ.

BOYD, JENNY; Marysville HS; Marysville, OH; Cls Rep Frsh Cls; Hon Rl; Off Ade; Sch Mus; Lat Clb; Trk; Chrldng; GAA; IM Sprt; PPFtbl; Miami Univ; Computer Math.

BOYD, JERI; North Central HS; Indianapolis, IN; Off Ade; Pol Wkr; College; Law.

BOYD, LINDA; Shady Spring HS; White Oak, WV; Trs Soph Cls; Trs Jr Cls; Chrs; FCA; Sch Pl; Sct Actv; Pres Stu Cncl; Ed Sch Nwsp; Pep Clb; Letter Bsktbl; Musclr Dystrphy Assn Membr 1978; Volleyball 1976; Univ; Dent Hygienist.

BOYD, NANNETTE; Whitmer HS; Toledo, OH; 96/810 Cls Rep Frsh Cls; Trs Jr Cls; Trs Sr Cls; Jr NHS; NHS; Off Ade; Quill & Scroll; Stu Cncl; Yrbk; Spn Clb; Univ Of Toledo; Med Tech.

BOYD, NEAL; Riverdale HS; Forest, OH; Hon Rl; Yth Flsp; FTA; Glf; IM Sprt; College; Architect.

BOYD, PETER; Carman HS; Flint, MI; Band; Boy Scts; Hon Rl; Sct Actv; Natl Merit Ltr; Mic St Univ; Ba In History.

BOYD, QUINTON M; Carson City HS; Hubbardston, MI; Cls Rep Frsh Cls; VP Jr Cls; Debate Tm; Hon Rl; Stu Cncl; Rptr Yrbk; Letter Ftbl; Marine Bio.

BOYD, RAYMOND; North Harrison HS; Corydon, IN; 2/170 Sal; Am Leg Boys St; Band; Mod UN; NHS; Sch Mus; Stg Crw; JETS Awd; Natl Merit Ltr; Purdue Univ; Chem Engr.

BOYD, ROBIN; Mathews HS; Vienna, OH; 4/146 CAP; Hon Rl; NHS; Off Ade; Y-Teens; Yrbk; Sch Nwsp; FTA; Pep Clb; Spn Clb; Univ Of Akron.

BOYD, STEPHANIE; Immaculata HS; Detroit, MI; Cl Rep Jr Cls; Band; Chrs; Cmnty Wkr; Hon Rl; Hosp Ade; Pol Wkr; Yrbk; FDA; Lat Clb; Wayne St Univ; Dr.

BOYD, TAMMY; Central Catholic HS; Wheeling, WV; Hon Rl; Stu Cncl; Fr Clb; Wheeling Coll; Nursing.

BOYD, TERESA; Western HS; Waverly, OH; Am Leg Aux Girls St; Hon Rl; Sch Pl; 4-H; Fr Clb; Pep Clb; VICA; Bus Schl; Bus Mgmt.

BOYD, VANESSA; Portsmouth HS; Portsmouth, OH; 36/226 Hon Rl; Off Ade; FHA; Spn Clb; Univ Of Cincinnati; Bus Admin.

BOYD, WILLIAM; Shakamak HS; Jasonville, IN; 52/99 Chrh Wkr; Cmnty Wkr; Hon Rl; Yth Flsp; DECA; 4-H; FFA; Bsktbl; Hockey; Trk; DECA 2nd Petroleium Regnl 79; DECA 7th Petroleum St 79; DECA Petroleum Natl 79; Ivy Tech Voc Schl; Heavy Eqpt Opr.

BOYER, BRIAN; Springfield HS; Springfield, MI; Band; Hon Rl; Vocational School.

BOYER, CARRIE; Van Wert HS; Van Wert, OH; Chrs; Hon Rl; Sec JA; Lbry Ade; Yth Flsp; Y-Teens; Pep Clb; Spn Clb; Scr Kpr; Sec JA Awd; Wright St Univ; Elem Educ.

BOYER, DAVE; St Joseph Central Cath HS; Fremont, OH; Hon Rl; Ftbl;.

BOYER, JANICE; Champion HS; Warren, OH; 47/237 Chrh Wkr; Cmnty Wkr; Girl Scts; Hon Rl; Jr NHS; Off Ade; Sch Pl; Yth Flsp; Sch Nwsp; Fr Clb; Kent St Univ; Acctg.

BOYER, JANICE; Marion Adams HS; Sheridan, IN; 1/93 Val; Hon Rl; NHS; FHA; Letter Bsktbl; Purude Univ; Comp Sci.

BOYER, JEFF; Chelsea HS; Chelsea, MI; Aud/Vis; Band; Boy Scts; Chrh Wkr; Hon Rl; Sct Actv; Yth Flsp; Drama Clb; Letter Ftbl; Letter Trk; Jackson Comm Coll; Disc Jockey.

BOYER, JEFFREY; Mount View HS; Elbert, WV; Aud/Vis; Chrs; Bsbl; Mgrs; Concord Coll.

BOYER, LEANNE; Kenowa Hills HS; Grand Rapids, MI; 11/218 Cls Rep Sr Cls; Cmnty Wkr; Hon Rl; Hosp Ade; Lbry Ade; Pol Wkr; Stu Cncl; Pep Clb; Scr Kpr; Tmr; Butterworth Schl; Nursing.

BOYER, LISA; Hillsdale HS; Hayesville, OH; 11/120 Drm Mjrt; NHS; Sch Pl; Stg Crw; Stu Cncl; Sprt Ed Yrbk; Sec Drama Clb; VP 4-H; Pres FHA; Lat Clb; Musical Awd; Ohio State Univ; Law.

BOYER, MARY; Staunton HS; Sioux City, IA; 5/55 NHS; Key Clb; Letter Bsbl; Letter Bsktbl; Letter Crs Cntry; Purdue Univ.

BOYER, RACHEL; Bowling Green HS; Bowling Green, OH; Chrs; Chrh Wkr; Orch; Sch Mus; Stg Crw; 4-H; FFA; Sci Clb; Ten; 4-H Awd; Ohio State Univ; Horse Mgmt.

BOYER, RICK; Lakeview HS; Lamesa, CA; Band; Boy Scts; Drm Bgl; Orch; Sch Mus; Stg Crw; Letter Ftbl; Letter Trk; Cit Awd; College; Commercial.

BOYER, SCOTT; Newark Catholic HS; Newark, OH; Boy Scts; Hon Rl; Lat Clb; Bsktbl; Ftbl; Trk; College; Pre Dentistry.

BOYER, STEVEN; Castle HS; Newburgh, IN; 32/333 Aud/Vis; Band; Boy Scts; Chrh Wkr; Hon Rl; NHS; Yth Flsp; Key Clb; Sci Clb; Ftbl; Schlstc C 77 79; Purdue Univ; Elec Engr.

BOYER, STEVEN; West Muskingum HS; Zanesville, OH; Hon Rl; Trk; IM Sprt; Tmr; Ohio St Univ.

BOYER, SUE; Patrick Henry HS; Deshler, OH; Cls Rep Frsh Cls; Pres Jr Cls; Band; Chrs; Chrh Wkr; Girl Scts; Hon Rl; Sch Mus; Univ; Sociology.

BOYER, SUZANNE M; Aquinas HS; Taylor, MI; Hon Rl; Bsktbl; GAA; Western Michigan Coll; Psych.

BOYER, TAMMY; Monroe HS; Monroe, OH; 72/277 Sec Sr Cls; Drl Tm; Girl Scts; Hon Rl; NHS; Off Ade; Stu Cncl; Capt Chrldng; GAA; Middletown Hosp Tech; X Ray Tech.

BOYER, TARA; Federal Hocking HS; Athens, OH; Cls Rep Frsh Cls; Sec Jr Cls; Lbry Ade; Stu Cncl; Rptr Sch Nwsp; 4-H; Fr Clb; GAA; 4-H Awd; Ohio Univ.

BOYER, TERRY; Holy Rosary HS; Flint, MI; 3/41 Boy Scts; Hon Rl; NHS; Pol Wkr; Sch Pl; Sct Actv; Sch Nwsp; Letter Bsbl; Letter Bsktbl; Letter Crs Cntry; Univ Of Michigan; Dentistry.

BOYERS, TRACY; Vandercook Lake HS; Jackson, MI; Cl Rep Jr Cls; Band; Boy Scts; Chrh Wkr; FCA; Hon Rl; NHS; Stu Cncl; Yth Flsp; Bsktbl; General Motors Enst; Mechanic.

BOYES, KIM; Pinckney HS; Pinckney, MI; 3/256 Band; Chrh Wkr; Hon Rl; NHS; Sch Pl; Stg Crw; Natl Merit Ltr; Spring Arbor Coll; Bus Admin.

BOYLAN, RANDY; Stryker HS; Stryker, OH; 11/53 Hon Rl; Bsktbl; Crs Cntry; Letter Trk; Wrstlng; Northwest Tech Coll; Comp Progr.

BOYLAN, ROGER; Caro HS; Caro, MI; Chrh Wkr; NHS; Yth Flsp; Letter Bsbl; Letter Ftbl; Swmmng; Conservation.

BOYLE, BARBARA; New Richmond HS; New Richmond, OH; 9/194 NHS; Quill & Scroll; Pres Stu Cncl; Rptr Yrbk; Ed Sch Nwsp; Drama Clb; Pep Clb; Spn Clb; Harold G Rawlings Schlrshp; Jane Marsh Schlrshp For Stu Cncl; Discussion Ldr For 43rd Natl Stu Cncl Conf; Bowling Green St Univ; Broadcasting.

BOYLE, CATHERINE; Cathedral HS; Indianapolis, IN; Hon Rl; Stg Crw; Sch Nwsp; Marian College; Art.

BOYLE, KAREN; Lumen Christi HS; Jackson, MI; Band; Chrs; Hon Rl; NHS; Sch Mus; Stg Crw; Rptr Sch Nwsp; Drama Clb; Lat Clb; IM Sprt; Northern Mich Univ; Pre Med.

BOYLE, KENNETH R; Oregon Davis HS; Hamlet, IN; 2/58 Pres Frsh Cls; Sec Jr Cls; Chrh Wkr; Debate Tm; Hon Rl; NHS; Rptr Yrbk; Sprt Ed Sch Nwsp; IM Sprt; Mgrs; College; Optometry.

BOYLE, MAUREEN A; Ursuline Acad; Cincinnati, OH; Chrs; Cmnty Wkr; Natl Forn Lg; Pol Wkr; Sch Mus; Sch Pl; Stg Crw; Univ; Eng.

BOYLE, MICHAEL; Bishop Flaget HS; Chillicothe, OH; 12/40 Pres Soph Cls; Am Leg Boys St; Chrh Wkr; Hon Rl; Natl Forn Lg; Stu Cncl; Fr Clb; Letter Bsktbl; Letter Glf; Am Leg Awd; Bowling Green St Univ; Bus Admin.

BOYLE, PATRICIA; Marysville HS; St Clair, MI; 26/180 Cls Rep Frsh Cls; Cls Rep Soph Cls; Trs Jr Cls; Cls Rep Sr Cls; Hon Rl; Quill & Scroll; Sch Pl; Stg Crw; Stu Cncl; Rptr Sch Nwsp; St Clair Cnty Cmnty Coll; Jrnlsm.

BOYLE, STEVEN; Elmhurst HS; Ft Wayne, IN; 52/350 Hon Rl; Socr; Purdue; Science.

BOYLE, TONI; Beaver Local HS; E Liverpool, OH; 57/242 Sec Soph Cls; Am Leg Aux Girls St; Chrh Wkr; Hon Rl; Stu Cncl; Drama Clb; Eng Clb; Fr Clb; FHA; Pep Clb;.

BOYLES, GLENNA; Matoaka HS; Matoaka, WV; Pres Jr Cls; Am Leg Aux Girls St; Treas NHS; Stu Cncl; Yrbk; Sec Keyettes; Bluefield St Coll; Art.

BOYLES, JODY; Chillicothe HS; Chill, OH; 13/365 AFS; Cmnty Wkr; Debate Tm; Girl Scts; Hon Rl; Hosp Ade; Lbry Ade; Natl Forn Lg; NHS; Off Ade; Army; Med Tech.

BOYLL, ARLEEN; Marine City HS; Marine City, MI; Hon Rl; Hosp Ade; Sch Nwsp; Univ; Phys Ther.

BOYLL, KAREN; Terre Haute N Vigo HS; Terre Haute, IN; 50/593 Cls Rep Frsh Cls; Cls Rep Soph Cls; Cl Rep Jr Cls; Cls Rep Sr Cls; Aud/Vis; Band; Chrs; Drl Tm; FCA; Girl Scts; Indiana St Univ; Nursing.

BOYNE, ELLEN; Ursuline Acad; Cincinnati, OH; 19/106 Cmnty Wkr; Lit Mag; Rptr Yrbk; Purdue Univ; Advertising.

BOYS, DARLINDA; Anderson HS; Anderson, IN; 9/450 Hon Rl; NHS; Fr Clb; Lat Clb; Ball State Univ; Architecture.

BOYS, HOLLY; Shenandoah HS; Shirley, IN; Chrs; Chrh Wkr; Hon Rl; Lbry Ade; Off Ade; Yth Flsp; Ger Clb; IU Tech; Recptnst.

BOYS, SAMUEL; Plymouth HS; Plymouth, IN; 17/230 Pres Soph Cls; Am Leg Boys St; Band; Chrh Wkr; Hon Rl; MMM; Stu Cncl; Yth Flsp; Rptr Sch Nwsp; Mth Clb; Ball St Univ; Life Sci.

BOYTON, JOY; Stevenson HS; Livonia, MI; 45/740 Band; Girl Scts; Hon Rl; Off Ade; Pol Wkr; Sch Mus; Stg Crw; Cit Awd; Michigan St Univ; Materials Engr.

BOZELAK, JOHN J; Romulus Sr HS; Romulus, MI; 88/300 Boy Scts; Letter Bsbl; Letter Ftbl; Ferris St Coll; Envir Health.

BOZSONY, JOHN; Walsh Jesuit HS; Akron, OH; 5/179 Band; Hon Rl; Orch; Sch Mus; Sch Pl; Stg Crw; Yrbk; Rptr Sch Nwsp; Sch Nwsp; Akron Univ; Physics.

BOZUNG, CHRISTINE; St Patricks HS; Portland, MI; 1/46 VP Soph Cls; VP Jr Cls; Pres Sr Cls; Hon Rl; Jr NHS; NHS; Sch Pl; IM Sprt; Natl Merit SF; Michigan St Univ; Conservation.

BOZZELLI, JAMES M; Walsh Jesuit HS; Cuyahoga Falls, OH; 15/152 Cls Rep Frsh Cls; Pres Jr Cls; Hon Rl; Stu Cncl; Letter Ftbl; IM Sprt; Merit 1 Yr Schlrshp To Walsh Jesuit HS; Perfect Service Awd; Akron Beacon Journal; Fresh English Awd; College; Busns Admin.

BRABECK, PATRICK; Northeastern Wayne HS; Richmond, IN; Cls Rep Frsh Cls; Cls Rep Soph Cls; Cls Rep Sr Cls; Hon Rl; NHS; Stu Cncl; Treas Fr Clb; Treas FSA; Treas Sci Clb; Bsktbl; Indiana Univ; Mrktng.

BRACE, LORI; Northview HS; Grand Rapids, MI; Band; Chrh Wkr; Hon Rl; JA; NHS; Spn Clb; Glf; Trk; PPFtbl; Tmr; Mich State Univ.

BRACE, MICHAEL; Ashtabula Harbor HS; Ashtabula, OH; 30/200 Boy Scts; Off Ade; Sch Mus; Sch Pl; Stg Crw; Rptr Yrbk; Drama Clb; Univ; Elec.

BRACEY, JILL; Grosse Ile HS; Grosse Ile, MI; 3/238 VP Jr Cls; VP Sr Cls; Band; Chrh Wkr; Mdrgl; NHS; Sch Mus; Pres 4-H; Michigan State Univ; Psychology.

BRACEY, ROBERT; Grosse Ile HS; Grosse Ile, MI; Band; Chrs; Hon Rl; Sch Mus; Sch Pl; VP Drama Clb; Bsktbl; Trk; Michigan St Univ.

BRACKEN, CHUCK; Lasalle HS; Cincinnati, OH; 27/277 Cls Rep Soph Cls; Aud/Vis; Boy Scts; Chrh Wkr; Hon Rl; JA; NHS; FBLA; IM Sprt; JA Awd; Miami Coll; Busns Admin.

BRACKEN, SUSAN; Muskingum Area JVS; Zanesville, OH; Sec Jr Cls; Trs Sr Cls; Chrs; Girl Scts; Hon Rl; Lbry Ade; Off Ade; 4-H; OEA; 4-H Awd; Dipalmat; Execitive; 2nd Pl Typing Cont; Ohio Univ; Sec.

BRACKEN, WENDY; Cloverleaf Sr HS; Lodi, OH; 3/330 Am Leg Aux Girls St; Band; Hon Rl; Hosp Ade; NHS; Orch; FDA; Bsktbl; PPFtbl; DAR Awd; Coll; Pre Med.

BRACKENBURY, LENORA; Yale HS; Goodells, MI; 41/160 Cls Rep Frsh Cls; Chrs; Hon Rl; 4-H; Letter Bsktbl; Letter Trk; Chrldng; Michigan St Univ; Packaging.

BRACKETT, SUSAN; Berrien Springs HS; Berrien Spgs, MI; Band; Hon Rl; Sch Pl; Stg Crw; Spn Clb; Trk; Chrldng; Pres Awd; Dent Asst.

BRACKIN, PAMELA; Princeton Community HS; Hazleton, IN; 31/203 Trs Jr Cls; Chrs; Cmnty Wkr; Stu Cncl; Yth Flsp; 4-H; Mth Clb; Pep Clb; Bsktbl; Trk; Var Vllybl 76 78; Awd Mc Donalds Youth Salute Progr 79; Womns St Pitch Sftbl St Champ 77; Univ.

BRACKMAN, DAVID; Marion Local HS; Maria Stein, OH; Hon Rl; Off Ade; DECA; Mth Clb; Pep Clb; Sci Clb; Bsbl;.

BRACKMAN, LINDA; Marion Local HS; Maria Stein, OH; Hon Rl; Off Ade; Sec Stu Cncl; Rptr Yrbk; 4-H; FHA; Sec Pep Clb; Letter Trk; Capt Chrldng; IM Sprt; College; Bus Management.

BRACY, CARL; Lapeer East HS; Lapeer, MI; Chrh Wkr; Lbry Ade; Ed Yrbk; Sprt Ed Yrbk; Rptr Yrbk; Sch Nwsp; Letter Crs Cntry; Ftbl; Trk; Schlshp From Indepndnt Fundamntl Churches Of Amer 79; Moody Bible Inst.

BRADBURN, DOUGLAS; Bellmont HS; Decatur, IN; 15/400 Am Leg Boys St; Chrh Wkr; Hon Rl; NHS; Yth Flsp; Ger Clb; Letter Ftbl; Letter Trk; IM Sprt; Univ; Med.

BRADBURY, JUDITH A; Hurricane HS; Hurrican, WV; VP Frsh Cls; Cls Rep Frsh Cls; Band; Chrh Wkr; Cmnty Wkr; Drl Tm; Girl Scts; Hon Rl; Lbry Ade; NHS; Alderson Broaddus Coll; Religion.

BRADBURY, KATHY; Benton Harbor HS; Benton Hbr, MI; Band; Girl Scts; Hon Rl; Spn Clb; Bus Schl.

BRADDOCK, BECKY; Mt Vernon HS; Mt Vernon, OH; Trs Jr Cls; Trs Sr Cls; Chrh Wkr; Hon Rl; Jr NHS; NHS; Sch Pl; Yth Flsp; Ed Yrbk; 4-H; Univ Of Toledo; Chemistry.

BRADDOCK, LAURIE; Fredericktown HS; Fred, OH; Hon Rl; Yrbk; Pres 4-H; Letter Bsktbl; Letter Trk; 4-H Awd; College; Art.

BRADDOCK, MAE; Saginaw HS; Saginaw, MI; Chrs; Chrh Wkr; Cmnty Wkr; Girl Scts; JA; Jr NHS; Yth Flsp; Cit Awd; Univ; Pharm.

BRADEN, AMY; East Palestine HS; E Palestine, OH; 27/147 Cmp Fr Grls; Hon Rl; NHS; Off Ade; Sch Pl; Y-Teens; Drama Clb; Pres FHA; Pep Clb; Scr Kpr; Youngstown State Univ; Elem Educ.

BRADEN, TINA; Edgewood Sr HS; Kingsville, OH; Trs Jr Cls; Girl Scts; OEA; Univ; Crim Just.

BRADENBURG, TONYA; Union County HS; Brownsville, IN; 6/125 Trs Frsh Cls; Trs Soph Cls; Trs Jr Cls; Chrs; Chrs; Chrh Wkr; Drl Tm; Girl Scts; Hon Rl; College; Nursing.

BRADFIELD, BLAIR; Our Lady Of Mercy HS; Detroit, MI; Cmnty Wkr; Lbry Ade; Pol Wkr; Recognition Awd For Conducting & Org 1st Black Awareness Wk 79; Univ Of Michigan; Engr.

BRADFIELD, CARLA J; Terre Haute South Vigo HS; Terre Haute, IN; 92/668 Cls Rep Frsh Cls; Cl Rep Jr Cls; Chrh Wkr; Hon Rl; Hosp Ade; Off Ade; Pol Wkr; Yth Flsp; Y-Teens; Rdo Clb; Indiana St Univ; Educ.

BRADFIELD, CRAIG; Barnesville HS; Barnesville, OH; 9/130 Cls Rep Sr Cls; Debate Tm; Hon Rl; NHS; Stu Cncl; Key Clb; Bsktbl; Glf; Scr Kpr; Wake Forest Univ; Business.

BRADFIELD, JAMES; Elk Rapids HS; Elk Rapids, MI; VP Frsh Cls; Cls Rep Soph Cls; Pres Jr Cls; Debate Tm; Hon Rl; Bsbl; Bsktbl; Ftbl; College Baseball & Business.

BRADFIELD, J CRAIG; Barnesville HS; Barnesville, OH; 8/135 Cls Rep Sr Cls; Debate Tm; Hon Rl; NHS; Stu Cncl; Key Clb; Bsktbl; Letter Ftbl; Mgrs; Tmr; Wake Forest Univ; Bus.

BRADFIELD, LORI; Heritage HS; Monroeville, IN; Chrs; Cmnty Wkr; Girl Scts; Hon Rl; Y-Teens; 4-H; Pom Pon; Univ; Comp.

BRADFIELD, SUSAN; Indian Hill HS; Cincinnati, OH; Band; Drm Mjrt; Orch; Lat Clb; Mat Maids; Ribbon For Rating 2 In Piano Contest; Voted Most Outstanding Player In Concert Orchestra; College; Law.

BRADFORD, CELESTA; Frontier HS; Nw Mtmrs, OH; Band; Girl Scts; Hon Rl; NHS; Sch Pl; Rptr Yrbk; Yrbk; Chrldng; VP GAA; Muskingam Area Tech Coll; Med Lab.

BRADFORD, DONNA; Avon Jr & Sr HS; Danville, IN; Pres Frsh Cls; Cls Rep Frsh Cls; Band; Chrs; Chrh Wkr; Capt Drl Tm; Hon Rl; Stu Cncl; Drama Clb; Ger Clb; Indiana St Univ; Cmmrcl Advrtsng.

BRADFORD, REX; Wapokoneta Sr HS; Wapakoneta, OH; 23/242 Hon Rl; NHS; Pres 4-H; Treas FFA; 4-H Awd; FFA St Farmer Degree 2nd Dist Beef Awd 79; Trip To Ks City To Natl FFA Convntn 78; 4 H Jr Leader; Univ.

BRADFORD, ROBERT; Holland HS; Holland, MI; 6/300 Pres Jr Cls; VP Sr Cls; Trs Sr Cls; Am Leg Aux Girls St; Debate Tm; Hon Rl; JA; Mod UN; NHS; Pol Wkr; Univ; Soc Serv.

BRADFORD, SHANNON; Harry Hill HS; Lansing, MI; JA; Sch Mus; Sch Pl; Rptr Sch Nwsp; FTA; Chrldng; Mgrs; Twrlr; Lansing Community Coll; Elem Educ.

BRADFORD, TIMOTHY; Scott HS; Ramage, WV; Sch Pl; Stu Cncl; Trk; Marshal Univ; Poli Sci.

BRADFUTE, JENNIFER; Cedarville HS; Xenia, OH; 5/65 Cls Rep Sr Cls; Band; Hon Rl; NHS; Sch Pl; Stu Cncl; Rptr Yrbk; Yrbk; 4-H; Trk; Univ Of Toledo; Art.

BRADICK, LAURA; Parkway HS; Rockford, OH; 20/85 Band; Chrs; Sch Pl; Yth Flsp; 4-H; Keyettes; Lat Clb; Pep Clb; Sci Clb; Spn Clb; Anderson Coll.

BRADLEY, ANTHONY; Pontiac Central HS; Pontiac, MI; 122/476 Cls Rep Frsh Cls; Cls Rep Soph Cls; Cl Rep Jr Cls; Cls Rep Sr Cls; Hon Rl; Sch Mus; Stg Crw; 4-H; Ger Clb; Bsktbl; Lawrence Inst Of Tech; Elec Engr.

BRADLEY, BETH; Boardman HS; Canfield, OH; 241/591 Cmp Fr Grls; Chrh Wkr; Lbry Ade; Red Cr Ade; Yth Flsp; Y-Teens; Sec DECA; Fr Clb; FHA; GAA; Bradford Bus Schl; Fashion Mdse.

BRADLEY, CHARLES; Servite HS; Detroit, MI; Aud/Vis; Boy Scts; JA; Sch Pl; Stg Crw; RETS; Elec Engr.

BRADLEY, CHRISTINA R; Immaculata HS; Detroit, MI; Cls Rep Frsh Cls; Cls Rep Soph Cls; Cl Rep Jr Cls; Cls Rep Sr Cls; Sal; Aud/Vis; Chrs; Chrh Wkr; Cmnty Wkr; FCA; Volleyball Awd Varsity Letter Co Capt; Most Valuable Player Awd Bsktbl; Univ Of Texas; Computer Sci.

BRADLEY, DENNIS; Garfield HS; Akron, OH; Aud/Vis; Band; Chrs; Hon Rl; JA; Orch; Sch Pl; Drama Clb; Spn Clb; JA Awd; University; Music.

BRADLEY, ERIC; Wilbur Wright HS; Dayton, OH; 22/213 Boys Clb Am; Bsktbl; Mgrs; Bus Admin.

BRADLEY, KAREN; Lakeview HS; Stow, OH; Chrh Wkr; Hon Rl; Yth Flsp; VP 4-H; Fr Clb; Registerd Nurse.

BRADLEY, KIMM; River Valley HS; Marion, OH; Cmnty Wkr; JA; Lbry Ade; Sch Nwsp; Spn Clb; JA Awd; Bowling Green St Univ; Spec Ed.

BRADLEY, LORI; Peck HS; Melvin, MI; Cls Rep Frsh Cls; Trs Soph Cls; Chrs; Girl Scts; Hon Rl; NHS; Ed Yrbk; 4-H; Fr Clb; Bsktbl;.

BRADLEY, LORI; Peck Cmnty Schools; , ; 6/61 Trs Soph Cls; Chrs; Hon Rl; NHS; 4-H; Pep Clb; Bsktbl; Letter Trk; Chrldng; Coach Actv; Univ.

BRADLEY, LORIE; Hammond HS; Hammond, IN; Chrh Wkr; Hon Rl; Jr NHS; Purdue Univ; Reg Nurse.

BRADLEY, LUANNA; Goshen HS; Goshen, OH; 8/200 Trs Frsh Cls; Pres Jr Cls; Pres Sr Cls; Am Leg Aux Girls St; Chrs; Pres NHS; Rptr Yrbk; Sch Nwsp; Chrldng; Miami Univ.

BRADLEY, MARY; Warren Wshngtn Cnty Voc Schl; Marietta, OH; Sec Jr Cls; Band; Chrh Wkr; Girl Scts; Hon Rl; Yth Flsp; FNA; OEA; Pep Clb; Bsktbl; 1st In Regional KP Contest 1979; 10th In St KP Contest 1979; Top 20 Of Freshman Class 1977; Tech Coll; CPA.

BRADLEY, MELISSA; Mansfield Christian HS; Mansfield, OH; Cls Rep Frsh Cls; Cls Rep Soph Cls; Cl Rep Jr Cls; Cls Rep Sr Cls; Val; Hon Rl; Pres NHS; Pol Wkr; Drama Clb; Mth Clb; Miami Univ; Bus Law.

BRADLEY, MICHAEL; Garfield HS; Akron, OH; Hon Rl; Pres JA; Sch Pl; Treas Stu Cncl; VICA; JA Awd; Natl Jr Achvrs Confrnc 78; Jr Exec Awd 78; Co 3rd Plc In Dist For Co Of Yr JA 78; Univ; Machine Designer.

BRADLEY, MILTON; Jesup W Scott HS; Toledo, OH; 4/284 Hon Rl; Treas NHS; Stu Cncl; Bsktbl; Ohio State Univ; Archt.

BRADLEY, MOLLY; Sycamore HS; Cincinnati, OH; 12/445 Band; Hon Rl; Jr NHS; NHS; Letter Trk; Natl Merit Ltr; 1st Flute Mst Valuable Plyr Awd 77 & 78; Track Mst Valuable Relay Awd 79; Vlybl Varsity & Capt 77; Univ; Sci.

BRADLEY, NICOLE; Columbus E HS; Columbus, OH; Cls Rep Soph Cls; Sec Jr Cls; Cl Rep Jr Cls; Sec Sr Cls; Cls Rep Sr Cls; Hon Rl; JA; Jr NHS; NHS; Off Ade; Columbus Tech Inst; Sec Sci.

BRADLEY, PETER; Lee M Thurston HS; Redford, MI; Am Leg Boys St; Band; Hon Rl; NHS; Letter Bsbl; Letter Bsktbl; Letter Glf; Letter Trk; St Of Mi Compttv Schlshp Awd 79; Univ Of Michigan; Bus.

BRADLEY, REBECCA; Barr Reeve HS; Montgomery, IN; 2/49 Am Leg Aux Girls St; Band; Hon Rl; JA; Jr NHS; NHS; Off Ade; Stu Cncl; Yrbk; Beta Clb; Cert Of Awd In HS Placement Test Chem Bio & Exc In Advanced Bio; Purdue Univ; Vet.

BRADLEY, R LYNNE; Franklin Cmnty HS; Bargersville, IN; Chrs; Hon Rl; Jr NHS; Mdrgl; Sch Mus; Pep Clb; Purdue Univ; Vet Asst.

BRADLEY, SHERRY; Chaminade Julienne HS; Dayton, OH; 8/264 Band; Chrh Wkr; Hon Rl; Orch; Sch Mus; Letter Bsktbl; Trk; Directors Awd 79; Univ; Chem Engr.

BRADLEY, STEVE; Armada HS; Armada, MI; 4/128 VP Sr Cls; Boy Scts; Hon Rl; NHS; Stu Cncl; Pep Clb; Bsbl; Bsktbl; Glf; Coach Actv; Michigan St Univ; Acctg.

BRADLEY, SUSAN; Bedford HS; Bedford, OH; Cl Rep Jr Cls; Chrs; NHS; Off Ade; Sct Actv; Stg Crw; Drama Clb; Trk; College; Social Work.

BRADLEY, TAMMY; Madonna HS; Weirton, WV; 11/102 Hon Rl; Hosp Ade; Wheeling Coll; Nursing.

BRADLEY, THOMAS; John F Kennedy HS; Detroit, MI; Band; Boy Scts; Hon Rl; Wayne St Univ; Sound Engr.

BRADLEY, TOM; Orleans HS; Orleans, IN; 3/47 Am Leg Boys St; NHS; Letter Bsbl; Letter Bsktbl; Letter Glf; Kiwan Awd; Ind Univ; Acctg.

BRADLEY, TONI; Houghton Lake HS; Houghton Lk Hgt, MI; 6/140 Cmnty Wkr; Hon Rl; Hosp Ade; NHS; DAR Awd; Delta College; Physical Therapy.

BRADLEY, WALTER A; Tell City HS; Tell City, IN; 27/235 Band; Chrh Wkr; Cmnty Wkr; Hon Rl; Yth Flsp; Key Clb; IM Sprt; Scr Kpr; Tmr; Indiana Univ; Law.

BRADSHAW, DEBORAH; Cathedral HS; Indianapolis, IN; Drl Tm; Girl Scts; Hon Rl; Hosp Ade; Mod UN; NHS; Sch Pl; USAF Acad 79; U S Coast Guard Acad 79; Purdue Univ 79; USAF Acad; Comp Sci.

BRADSHAW, LISA; Van Buren HS; Carbon, IN; Cls Rep Frsh Cls; VP Jr Cls; Band; Hon Rl; NHS; Off Ade; Yth Flsp; 4-H; FTA; Pep Clb; College.

BRADSHAW, MORRIS; Hughes HS; Cincinnati, OH; Cls Rep Frsh Cls; Cls Rep Soph Cls; Boy Scts; Letter Ftbl; College; Computer Programer.

BRADSHAW, RITA; Clinton Central HS; Frankfort, IN; 5/105 Pres Frsh Cls; Pres Soph Cls; Pres Jr Cls; Pres Sr Cls; Am Leg Aux Girls St; Chrs; Chrh Wkr; FCA; Hon Rl; NHS; Vllybll Schlstc Awrd 78; Anderson Univ; Acctg.

BRADSHAW, ROB; Van Buren HS; Carbon, IN; 1/92 Sec Frsh Cls; Val; Chrh Wkr; Hon Rl; NHS; Pres Stu Cncl; Pres 4-H; Sec Key Clb; Letter Bsktbl; Letter Trk; De Pauw Univ; Math.

BRADTMILLER, KAREN; Concordia Lutheran HS; Ft Wayne, IN; Hon Rl; Letter Bsktbl; Trk; PPFtbl; Ball State Univ; Bus.

BRADY, ANGELA S; London HS; West Jefferson, OH; 21/133 Band; Chrh Wkr; Hon Rl; Off Ade; Orch; Yth Flsp; Pep Clb; Scr Kpr; Sec.

BRADY, BILL L; Pt Pleasant HS; Point Pleasant, WV; 1/250 Cl Rep Jr Cls; Am Leg Boys St; Band; Boy Scts; Chrs; NHS; Boy Scts; Stu Cncl; Pres Key Clb; Scr Kpr; College; Engr.

BRADY, BRIDGET; Pleasant HS; Marion, OH; 9/185 Cmnty Wkr; Hon Rl; Quill & Scroll; Rptr Sch Nwsp; Trk; IM Sprt; Scr Kpr; Rhode Island Schl Of Design; Archt.

BRADY, CHRISTOPHER; Charles S Mott HS; Warren, MI; Hon Rl; Jr NHS; Opt Clb Awd; College.

BRADY, DIANE; Philip Barbour HS; Philippi, WV; Hon Rl; NHS; Stu Cncl; Keyettes; Pep Clb; Bsktbl; Trk;.

BRADY, JILL; North Canton Hoover HS; North Canton, OH; Chrs; Hosp Ade; JA; Off Ade; Rptr Sch Nwsp; Pep Clb; JA Awd; Young Ctzns Awd YCA 78; Nursing Schl; RN.

BRADY, JOHN; Andrean HS; Hobart, IN; 24/251 Hon Rl; Univ.

BRADY, KEVIN; St Agatha HS; Redford, MI; Am Leg Boys St; Boy Scts; Hon Rl; NHS; Boys Clb Am; Spn Clb; Capt Bsktbl; Letter Trk; Univ Of Mic.

BRADY, KEVIN; Holland HS; Holland, MI; 13/300 Hon Rl; Mod UN; Rptr Sch Nwsp; Lat Clb; Natl Latin Exam Cum Laude Awd 79; Coll.

BRADY, LARRY; Frontier HS; New Matamoras, OH; Boy Scts; Debate Tm; Sch Pl; Stg Crw; Letter Ftbl; Ohio Univ; Elec Engr.

BRADY, LAURA; Wilmington HS; Cuba, OH; 7/297 Chrh Wkr; Cmnty Wkr; Hon Rl; NHS; Red Cr Ade; 4-H; Letter Bsbl; Letter Bsktbl; GAA; Pres Awd; Miami Univ; Athletic Trainer.

BRADY, MICKY; West Carrollton HS; W Carrollton, OH; 69/398 Hon Rl; Off Ade; Rptr Yrbk; Mgrs; PPFtbl; Univ Of Dayton; Bus Admin.

BRADY, NANCY; Chatard HS; Indianapolis, IN; 88/195 Chrh Wkr; Girl Scts; Hon Rl; Jr NHS; 4-H; Bsktbl; Trk; Phys Ther.

BRADY, ROSEANN; St Joseph Acad; Cleveland, OH; Trs Jr Cls; Cls Rep Sr Cls; Drl Tm; Hon Rl; Sch Pl; Stu Cncl; Drama Clb; FNA; Coach Actv; College; Pre Med.

BRADY, TOM; St Anne HS; Warren, MI; Trs Jr Cls; Pres Sr Cls; Boy Scts; Debate Tm; Sch Nwsp; Mic St Univ; Engr.

BRADY, V WAYNE; Carrollton HS; Saginaw, MI; Band; Boy Scts; Chrh Wkr; Hon Rl; JA; NHS; Stg Crw; Ftbl; Armed Forces.

BRAGG, BAMBA; Chesapeake HS; Chesapeake, OH; Band; Chrs; Photog.

BRAGG, FORREST; Midland Trail HS; Ansted, WV; Boy Scts; Cmnty Wkr; VICA; Mgrs; Welder.

BRAGG, SHERI; Heritage Christian HS; Lebanon, IN; Hon Rl; Sch Pl; VP Ger Clb; Trk; Cedarville Coll; Psychology.

BRAGG, STANLEY; Shady Spring HS; Shady Spring, WV; 1/155 Cls Rep Frsh Cls; Val; Am Leg Boys St; Band; Hon Rl; NHS; Orch; Stu Cncl; 4-H; Cit Awd; Outstanding Stu; All Area Band; All American Hall Of Fame; Concord Coll; Music.

BRAHAM, ROBIN; Beaver Local HS; E Liverpool, OH; 2/242 VP Sr Cls; Am Leg Aux Girls St; Chrs; Hon Rl; NHS; Off Ade; Sch Mus; Rptr Yrbk; Drama Clb; OEA;.

BRAHAM, ROBIN C; Beaver Local HS; E Liverpool, OH; 2/242 VP Sr Cls; Am Leg Aux Girls St; Band; Chrs; Cmnty Wkr; Drl Tm; Hon Rl; NHS; Off Ade; Sch Mus; Youngstown Coll Of Busns; Exec Sec.

BRAINARD, CAROL; Highland Sr HS; Highland, IN; 179/530 Girl Scts; Hon Rl; Sch Mus; Sct Actv; Stg Crw; Drama Clb; FHA; PPFtbl; Pres Awd; Univ Of Evansville; Nursing.

BRAINARD, RICHARD; Swan Valley HS; Saginaw, MI; Cls Rep Soph Cls; Stu Cncl; Letter Ftbl; Letter Ten; Coach Actv; Natl Merit SF; Western Michigan Univ; Flight Tech.

BRAINARD, TOM; Perry HS; Perry, OH; FCA; Hon Rl; 4-H; Key Clb; Letter Bsbl; Letter Ftbl; Wrstlng; Univ; Bus Admin.

BRAK, AARON; Bishop Donahue HS; Mc Mechen, WV; Chrs; Hon Rl; Spn Clb; Bsbl; Bsktbl; Crs Cntry; Trk; Wrstlng; College; Acct.

BRAKE, RANDY; Jefferson Union HS; Richmond, OH; Chrs; Cmnty Wkr; Hon Rl; Wrstlng; Coach A ctv; College.

BRAKE, TIMOTHY L; Mt Gilead HS; Cardington, OH; Am Leg Boys St; Hon Rl; 4-H; Letter Bsktbl; Letter Crs Cntry; Letter Trk; Am Leg Awd; 4-H Awd; Univ.

BRAKER, GLEN; Rensselaer Cntrl HS; Rensselaer, IN; 16/172 Chrs; Hon Rl; NHS; Sch Mus; Stg Crw; Yrbk; Rptr Sch Nwsp; 4-H; FFA; Individual In St Soil Judging Contest; Recipient Of Farm Builder Ag Engr Awd; Deb Campbell Mem Writing Awd; Purdue Univ; Landscape Archt.

BRAKORA, ANN; Big Rapids HS; Big Rapids, MI; 1/180 Val; Band; Hon Rl; NHS; Sch Mus; Sch Pl; Stg Crw; IM Sprt; Central Mic Univ; Music.

BRAKORA, SUZANNE; Hartland HS; Brighton, MI; Hon Rl; NHS; Fr Clb; Univ; Engr.

BRAKUS, MILAN M; Labrae HS; Warren, OH; 25/190 Am Leg Boys St; Aud/Vis; Chrh Wkr; Cmnty Wkr; Hon Rl; Spn Clb; IM Sprt; Am Leg Awd; College; Comp Engr.

BRAMAN, KENNETH; Norton HS; Doyltestown, OH; 9/370 Chrh Wkr; Hon Rl; Pres Jr NHS; Pres Yth Flsp; Pres Lat Clb; Sci Clb; Ftbl; Univ; Med.

BRAMAN, SHERRI; Rochester HS; Rochester, IN; 40/175 Chrs; FCA; Hon Rl; Pres 4-H; FFA; VP FHA; Pep Clb; 4-H Awd; 4 H Jr Leaders Vice Pres 1979; Purdue Univ; Home Ec.

BRAMBLE, S; L Benjamin Franklin HS; Livonia, MI; Chrs; Sch Pl; Stg Crw; Stu Cncl; Yrbk; Drama Clb; Sci Clb; Swmmng; Tmr; Natl Merit Ltr; Univ; Pre Law.

BRAMBLE, SHELLEY; Franklin HS; Livonia, MI; Chrs; Sch Pl; Stu Cncl; Yrbk; Sci Clb; Swmmng; Tmr; Natl Merit Ltr; Univ; Pre Law.

BRAMBLE, STEVEN; Winston Churchill HS; Livonia, MI; Cls Rep Soph Cls; Cls Rep Sr Cls; Am Leg Boys St; Chrs; Chrh Wkr; Yth Flsp; Sci Clb; Letter Swmmng; Tmr; Central Mic Univ; Bus Amdin.

BRAME, ANITA; Patterson Coop HS; Dayton, OH; 48/426 Cl Rep Jr Cls; Sec Sr Cls; Cls Rep Sr Cls; Chrs; Chrh Wkr; Hosp Ade; NHS; Sch Pl; VICA; Ohio State; Biology.

BRAMER, JOANNE; St Francis HS; Traverse City, MI; 11/130 Hon Rl; Mod UN; NHS; Bsktbl; Letter Trk; College; Medical Technology.

BRAMER, RANDALL; Harrison HS; W Lafayette, IN; Hon Rl; Yth Flsp; Rptr Sch Nwsp; 4-H; Crs Cntry; Trk; Opt Clb Awd; Purdue Univ; Agri.

BRAMMER, MINDY; Chesapeake HS; Chesapeake, OH; Hon Rl; NHS; Bsktbl; Trk; IM Sprt; Dnfth Awd; Univ.

BRAMMER, SAMANTHA; Switzerland County HS; Patriot, IN; 2/136 Am Leg Aux Girls St; Hon Rl; VP NHS; Pres 4-H; Crs Cntry; Spn Clb; Bsktbl; Trk; Dnfth Awd; Purdue Univ; Animal Science.

BRAMMER, SAMANTHA; Switzerland Cnty Jr Sr HS; Patriot, IN; 2/132 Am Leg Aux Girls St; Hon Rl; VP NHS; Pres 4-H; Pep Clb; Treas Spn Clb; Bsktbl; Letter Trk; Dnfth Awd; Coll; Animal Sci.

BRAMMER, SHARON; Pleasant HS; Marion, OH; Cls Rep Frsh Cls; Cl Rep Jr Cls; Hon Rl; Lbry Ade; Rptr Yrbk; Rptr Sch Nwsp; FHA; IM Sprt; Mat Maids; Scr Kpr; College; Broadcasting.

BRAMMER, TAMMY; Ironton HS; Ironton, OH; Cls Rep Frsh Cls; Cls Rep Soph Cls; Hon Rl; Stu Cncl; Ger Clb; Spn Clb; Letter Bsbl; Bsktbl; GAA; IM Sprt; Univ.

BRANCATO, LISA; Our Lady Of Mercy HS; Detroit, MI; Cls Rep Frsh Cls; Cls Rep Soph Cls; Cl Rep Jr Cls; Aud/Vis; Chrh Wkr; NHS; Off Ade; Sch Mus; Sch Pl; Stg Crw; Wayne St Univ; TV/RADIO Cmnctns.

BRANCH, CAROL; Napoleon HS; Jackson, MI; 10/159 VP Frsh Cls; NHS; Pres Stu Cncl; Ed Sch Nwsp; Capt Gym; Cntrl Michigan Univ; Jrnlsm.

BRANCH, KATIE; Shelby Sr HS; Shelby, OH; Band; Hon Rl; Orch; Fr Clb; Ohio St Univ; Photo Jrnlsm.

BRANCH, KENNETH; New Palestine HS; Cumberland, IN; 52/150 Chrh Wkr; Hon Rl; Treas Yth Flsp; Treas 4-H; Pres Key Clb; Spn Clb; Univ Of Eva; Comp Sci.

BRANCHEAU, CONNIE; Ida HS; Monroe, MI; Band; Stu Cncl; GAA; College; Chiro.

BRAND, BARBARA; Muncie Northside HS; Gaston, IN; Cls Rep Frsh Cls; Trs Soph Cls; Cls Rep Soph Cls; Cl Rep Jr Cls; Cls Rep Sr Cls; Girl Scts; Hon Rl; Stu Cncl; Ed Sch Nwsp; Rptr Sch Nwsp; Parsons Schl Of Design; Cmmrcl Art.

BRAND, CHRISTOPHER; St Francis De Sales HS; Toledo, OH; 19/223 Hon Rl; NHS; Letter Ftbl; Wrstlng; IM Sprt; Football All Academic 1978; FAA Pilots Exam; Univ; Aero Engr.

BRAND, GREG; Greenfield Central HS; Greenfield, IN; Cls Rep Frsh Cls; Hon Rl; Stu Cncl; Fr Clb; Swmmng; Ten; Trk; Pres Awd; College.

BRAND, ROBERT; Lawrence Central HS; Indianapolis, IN; Band; University; Engr.

BRANDEL, CAROLE; Southfield HS; Livonia, MI; Chrs; Chrh Wkr; Hon Rl; Detroit Bible College; Missions.

BRANDENBURG, JANET; Laurel HS; Laurel, IN; 5/29 Hon Rl; NHS; Yrbk; Spn Clb;.

BRANDENSTEIN, DIANNE; Cuyahoga Falls HS; Cuyahoga Fls, OH; Band; Chrs; Hon Rl; NHS; Trk; College; Veterinary Medicine.

BRANDEWIE, BART; Minster HS; Ft Loramie, OH; 30/80 Hst Soph Cls; Hst Jr Cls; Chrh Wkr; Yrbk; Rptr Sch Nwsp; FFA; Letter Bsbl; Letter Bsktbl; Letter Ftbl; Farming.

BRANDEWIE, TED J; Celina HS; Celina, OH; 5/245 Hon Rl; NHS; Stu Cncl; Lat Clb; Letter Bsktbl; Letter Glf; Letter Ten; IM Sprt; Natl Merit Ltr; Univ Of Dayton;electrical Engineer.

BRANDIMORE, J; Harry S Truman HS; Taylor, MI; Cls Rep Frsh Cls; Hon Rl; NHS; Stu Cncl; Natl Merit Ltr; Univ Of Michigan; Sci.

BRANDMAIR, BETH; John Glenn HS; Bay City, MI; Cls Rep Frsh Cls; Cls Rep Soph Cls; Hon Rl; Sch Mus; Yrbk; Sch Nwsp; Letter Bsbl; Letter Ten; Letter Trk; Chrldng; Delta Coll; Jrnlsm.

BRANDON, LISA; Wayne Mem HS; Westland, MI; 25/740 Hon Rl; NHS; Mth Clb; Pres OEA; Spn Clb; Central Michigan Univ.

BRANDT, BRAD; West Liberty Salem HS; West Liberty, OH; 2/80 Cls Rep Frsh Cls; Cls Rep Soph Cls; Cl Rep Jr Cls; Cls Rep Sr Cls; Sal; Hon Rl; NHS; Sch Pl; Stu Cncl; 4-H; College.

BRANDT, BRENDA; Admiral King HS; Lorain, OH; Cls Rep Sr Cls; Band; Hon Rl; Orch; Sch Mus; Stu Cncl; Bowling Green St Univ; Acctg.

BRANDT, DORINE; Arthur Hill HS; Saginaw, MI; Sec Frsh Cls; Band; Girl Scts; Hon Rl; 4-H; Letter Bsktbl; Letter Trk; Chrldng; Mgrs; 4-H Awd; Cert For Outstndng Abilities In Math; Vlybl Letter; Coll; Archt.

BRANDT, JIM; Dayton Christian HS; Kettering, OH; 25/140 Trs Frsh Cls; Pres Soph Cls; Cl Rep Jr Cls; Cls Rep Sr Cls; Chrh Wkr; Hon Rl; Stu Cncl; Letter Socr; Coach Actv; Voice Dem Awd; College; Armed Forces.

BRANDT, KIMBERLY; New Albany HS; New Albany, IN; Chrs; Hon Rl; Rptr Yrbk; Rptr Sch Nwsp; Ger Clb; PPFtbl; Univ; Jrnlsm.

BRANDT, LAURIE; Jeffers HS; Toivola, MI; Val; Am Leg Aux Girls St; Hon Rl; Pres NHS; Yrbk; Ed Sch Nwsp; Pres Ger Clb; IM Sprt; Kiwan Awd; Northern Michigan Univ; Avia Tech.

BRANDT, RALYNE; Willard HS; Willard, OH; Am Leg Aux Girls St; Band; Hon Rl; NHS; Yth Flsp; Rptr Yrbk; Trk; IM Sprt; Univ; Soc Work.

BRANHAM, DEBBIE; Blue Rvr Vly Jr Sr HS; New Castle, IN; 6/98 Hon Rl; NHS; Sch Mus; Sch Pl; OEA; Vocational Schl; Busns.

BRANHAM, RHONDA; Piketon HS; Waverly, OH; 1/96 Trs Jr Cls; Trs Sr Cls; Cls Rep Sr Cls; Val; Am Leg Aux Girls St; Chrh Wkr; Hon Rl; Treas NHS; Rptr Sch Nwsp; 4-H; Shawnee St Cmnty Coll; Microbio.

BRANHAM, SHARON; Carlisle HS; Franklin, OH; Band; FTA; College; Music.

BRANIFF, EMILEY; Brooke HS; Wellsburg, WV; 33/403 Chrs; Chrh Wkr; Hon Rl; Lbry Ade; Off Ade; Sch Mus; Yth Flsp; Sci Clb; Spn Clb; Letter Swmmng; Graceland Coll; Med Tech.

BRANIFF, GARY; Edwardsburg HS; Edwardsburg, MI; 8/148 Hon Rl; NHS; Bsktbl; Crs Cntry; Letter Trk; Natl Merit Ltr; Univ; Math.

BRANIFF, WILLIAM; Newaygo HS; Newaygo, MI; Natl Merit SF; Pres Awd; Mic Tech Univ; Engr.

BRANKAMP, ROB; William Henry Harrison HS; Harrison, OH; Aud/Vis; Hon Rl; Lat Clb; Trk; Metals I Awd Class Awd; Coll; Dentistry.

BRANKLE, NANCY; Warren Central HS; Indianapolis, IN; 100/873 Band; Chrh Wkr; Girl Scts; Hon Rl; NHS; Off Ade; Stg Crw; Fr Clb; OEA; IM Sprt; Indiana Univ; Para Legal.

BRANNEY, LINDA; Green HS; Uniontown, OH; Pres Frsh Cls; VP Soph Cls; Hon Rl; Y-Teens; Yrbk; Pep Clb; Trk; Chrldng; GAA; Voc Sch; Medical Assistant.

BRANNON, SUSAN M; Center Grove HS; Greenwood, IN; 3/6 Hon Rl; JA; Jr NHS; Lbry Ade; NHS; Sch Nwsp; Sec 4-H; Sci Clb; Spn Clb; PPFtbl; Indiana Univ; Zoology.

BRANNON, THOMAS J; Field HS; Mogadore, OH; Hon Rl; Letter Glf; Letter Ten; Chess Club 78; Cptn & MVP Tennis 79; Mst Imprvd Plyr Golf 78; Kent St Univ.

BRANSCUM, KIM; Lockland HS; Reading, OH; Cls Rep Frsh Cls; Trs Soph Cls; Cl Rep Jr Cls; Aud/Vis; Hon Rl; Off Ade; Sch Nwsp; Trk; Wrstlng; IM Sprt; Elec Schl; Elec.

BRANSON, DANIEL; River Valley HS; Harbert, MI; Pres Jr Cls; Cls Rep Sr Cls; Band; Boy Scts; Hon Rl; NHS; Orch; Red Cr Ade; Sct Actv; Stu Cncl; Univ; Math.

BRANT, ALICIA; Clinton Central HS; Frankfort, IN; Am Leg Aux Girls St; Chrs; Chrh Wkr; FCA; Girl Scts; Hon Rl; Lbry Ade; NHS; Andrews Univ; Nurse.

BRANT, SUSAN; Dundee HS; Maybee, MI; 5/107 Pres Soph Cls; Cls Rep Soph Cls; VP Jr Cls; Cl Rep Jr Cls; Pres Sr Cls; Cls Rep Sr Cls; NHS; Letter Trk; Letter Chrldng; Dnfth Awd; Michigan St Univ; Acctg.

BRANTLEY, DRAKE A; Central HS; Detroit, MI; Cl Rep Jr Cls; Cls Rep Sr Cls; Band; Hon Rl; NHS; Stu Cncl; Sci Clb; Glf; Natl Hon Soc 79; Genrl Elec Carboloy Schlrshp 79; Stud Of Yr 79; Univ Of Detroit; Elec Engr.

BRANZ, MARIE; Kingsford HS; Iron Mtn, MI; Band; Cmp Fr Grls; Debate Tm; Drl Tm; Girl Scts; Hon Rl; Sch Pl; Stg Crw; Rptr Yrbk; Yrbk; Precisionaires Drill Team 74 77; Ecology Poser Contst 72; Univ; Med Tech.

BRASCH, BIRCH; Sycamore HS; Blue Ash, OH; Chrs; Hon Rl; Sch Pl; Letter Pep Clb; Spn Clb; Letter Ftbl; Letter Trk; IM Sprt; Cit Awd; Awd Mr Track As Fresh 76; City Long Jump Record 75; Ran 9.90 As Soph In 100 Yd Dash Rcvd Spec Recogntn 78; W Virginia Univ; Lib Arts.

BRASHAW, CHERI; Bay City Central HS; Bay City, MI; 17/529 Hon Rl; Jr NHS; NHS; Sct Actv; Rptr Yrbk; Pres Fr Clb; Cit Awd; St Of Mi Dept Of Educ Schlrshp To Attend Ferris St 79; Acad Schlrshp To Western Mi Univ 79; Ferris St Coll; Pre Pharm.

BRASHEAR, ALLISON; Park Tudor HS; Indianapolis, IN; Hon Rl; Sch Pl; Stg Crw; Rptr Sch Nwsp; Sch Nwsp; VP Drama Clb; College; Busns Mgmt.

BRASIC, GREGORY; Sparta HS; Sparta, MI; 15/195 Aud/Vis; Boy Scts; Hon Rl; Sch Pl; Pres Sci Clb; Spn Clb; Michigan Comp St Schlrshp; Basic Ed Opportunity Grant; Michigan St Univ Grant; Michigan St Univ; Bio Chem.

BRASSELL, KERRY; Fraser HS; Fraser, MI; Debate Tm; Hon Rl; Lbry Ade; Sch Mus; Rptr Sch Nwsp; Fr Clb; College; Playwright.

BRASSELLE, TOM; Bridgeport HS; Bridgeport, WV; Am Leg Boys St; Hon Rl; Jr NHS; Sec Key Clb; Letter Bsktbl; Letter Glf; Univ.

BRASSEUR, JOHN; Penn HS; Mishawaka, IN; 1/499 Pres Sr Cls; Debate Tm; Hon Rl; Mod UN; NHS; Sch Pl; Spn Clb; Ten; Trk; Coach Actv; College; Engineering.

BRASSEUR, MICHELE; Inland Lakes School; Indian River, MI; 16/73 Sec Sr Cls; Band; Hon Rl; Stu Cncl; Trk; GAA; Northern Michigan Univ; Nursing.

BRASSEUR, SCOTT; Lewis Cnty HS; Weston, WV; Jr NHS; Stu Cncl; Wrstlng; Univ; Civil Engr.

BRASSIE, STEVEN; Scecina Memorial HS; Indianapolis, IN; 53/194 Band; Chrs; Hon Rl; Sch Mus; Fr Clb; College; Music.

BRASWELL, JAMES; East HS; Columbus, OH; 16/272 Boy Scts; Hon Rl; NHS; Ten; College; Tele Communication.

BRASWELL, JEFFREY J; Walsh Jesuit HS; Stow, OH; 20/170 Cl Rep Jr Cls; Cls Rep Sr Cls; Hon Rl; Sch Mus; Sch Pl; Stu Cncl; Yrbk; Sch Nwsp; Drama Clb; Pep Clb; Miami Univ; Communications.

BRATCHER, ALEXIS; Gladwin HS; Gladwin, MI; Girl Scts; Hon Rl; Lbry Ade; Off Ade; Sch Nwsp; Chrldng; Clerical Aide.

BRATCHER, DAVID; Gladwin HS; Gladwin, MI; Hon Rl; Natl Forn Lg; Sch Pl; Stg Crw; Crs Cntry; Coach Actv; Univ; Chem.

BRAUER, JENNIFER; Seton HS; Cincinnati, OH; Chrh Wkr; Hon Rl; JA; NHS; Mth Clb; Univ Of Cincinnati; Comp Tech.

BRAUN, COREY; Grand Haven Sr HS; Grand Haven, MI; 64/386 Am Leg Boys St; FCA; Hon Rl; Jr NHS; NHS; Yth Flsp; Letter Bsbl; Letter Bsktbl; Letter Ftbl; Trk; Albion Coll; Bus.

BRAUN, DANIEL; Warren Ctrl HS; Indianapolis, IN; 222/825 Boy Scts; Chrs; Hon Rl; JA; Yrbk; Sch Nwsp; VP 4-H; 4-H Awd; Indiana Univ; Bus.

BRAUN, ELIZABETH; Notre Dame Acad; Toledo, OH; Cls Rep Frsh Cls; Hon Rl; Orch; Yth Flsp; VP FBLA; Michael J Owens Tech Coll; Exec Sec.

BRAUN, JANET; Concordia Lutheran HS; Ft Wayne, IN; Cls Rep Frsh Cls; Cls Rep Soph Cls; Cl Rep Jr Cls; Treas Band; Hon Rl; Rptr Sch Nwsp; Trk; Univ; Med.

BRAUN, JOSEPH; Bishop Luers HS; Ft Wayne, IN; Hon Rl; Bsktbl; Socr; Letter Ten; PPFtbl; College; Pre Law.

BRAUN, MARY; Hale HS; Hale, MI; 1/65 Pres Soph Cls; VP Jr Cls; Cl Rep Jr Cls; VP Sr Cls; Cls Rep Sr Cls; Val; Am Leg Aux Girls St; Chrh Wkr; Cmnty Wkr; Hon Rl; Univ; Art.

BRAUN, MARY B; St Joseph Acad; Lakewood, OH; Girl Scts; Lit Mag; Fr Clb; FSA; Sci Clb; Univ; Geol.

BRAUN, SARA; Churubusco HS; Avilla, IN; Hon Rl; Rptr Yrbk; 4-H; FHA; Lat Clb; 4-H Awd; Indiana Univ; Busns.

BRAUSCH, JAMES; Clinton Massie HS; Clarksville, OH; Boy Scts; Hon Rl; NHS; Ftbl; Ten; Trk; Coll; Engr.

BRAUSE, KAREN; Buckeye Central HS; New Washington, OH; 3/99 Cls Rep Frsh Cls; Trs Jr Cls; Band; Chrs; Hon Rl; NHS; Stu Cncl; Pres Yth Flsp; 4-H; Pres FHA; Bowling Green Univ; Med Tech.

BRAWLEY, CHERYL; Richmond Sr HS; Richmond, IN; 100/520 Cmnty Wkr; Hon Rl; Hosp Ade; Quill & Scroll; Lat Clb; Indiana Univ East; Tchr Of Spec Educ.

BRAWLEY, JAMIE; Southeast HS; Newton Fls, OH; 18/196 Pres Frsh Cls; Hon Rl; Stu Cncl; 4-H; Bsktbl; Trk; IM Sprt; 4-H Awd; Sftbl All Star MVP Awd; Vlybl 2 Yr Letterman; Kent St Univ; Law.

BRAWNER, TIM; Southwestern HS; Hanover, IN; 7/100 Cls Rep Soph Cls; Trs Jr Cls; Cl Rep Jr Cls; Pres Sr Cls; Cls Rep Sr Cls; Am Leg Boys St; Hon Rl; NHS; Stu Cncl; 4-H; College.

BRAY, ANDREW P; Hawken HS; Pepper Pike, OH; 5/105 Hon Rl; Yrbk; Capt Wrstlng; Natl Merit SF; Univ; Engr.

BRAY, CHARLOTTE; Maconaquah HS; Grissom AFB, IN; 99/232 Hon Rl; Pep Clb; Chrldng;.

BRAY, JAMES; Roosevelt Wilson HS; Clarksbrg, WV; 10/132 Am Leg Boys St; Boy Scts; Pres NHS; Stu Cncl; Yth Flsp; Rptr Sch Nwsp; Pres 4-H; Leo Clb; Scr Kpr; Elk Awd; Univ.

BRAY, JAMES H; Roosevelt Wilson HS; Clarksburg, WV; 13/132 Cl Rep Jr Cls; Boy Scts; Hon Rl; Sch Pl; Stg Crw; Stu Cncl; Yth Flsp; Drama Clb; Pres 4-H; Leo Clb; College; Physics.

BRAY, JOHN; Shelbyville HS; Shelbyville, IN; 30/400 Band; Drm Bgl; Hon Rl; Pol Wkr; Spn Clb; Ind Univ; Political Sci.

BRAY, NANCY D; Tri West Hendricks HS; Pittsboro, IN; 3/125 Trs Jr Cls; Hon Rl; NHS; 4-H; Pep Clb; Spn Clb; DAR Awd; 4-H Awd; Univ; Pre Med.

BRAY, ROBIN; Monroe Gregg Jr Sr HS; Monrovia, IN; 6/110 Trs Soph Cls; Chrs; Hon Rl; Lbry Ade; NHS; Off Ade; Chrldng;.

BRAY, TRACEY; Norway Vulcan HS; Norway, MI; 25/87 Trs Frsh Cls; Trs Soph Cls; Trs Jr Cls; Trs Sr Cls; Hon Rl; Hosp Ade; DECA; Letter Trk; Letter Chrldng; N E Wisconsin Tech Inst.

BRAYNT, SHERRI; Tri West Hendricks HS; Brownsburg, IN; 58/121 Off Ade; Sch Pl; Drama Clb; 4-H; Pep Clb; Spn Clb; Mgrs; Pom Pon; PPFtbl; Am Leg Awd; Indiana Univ; Elem Ed.

BRAZ, ELIZABETH; Regina HS; N Randall, OH; Chrh Wkr; NHS; Off Ade; Sch Pl; Stg Crw; Drama Clb; John Carroll Univ; Engr.

BRAZELTON, DWAYNE; Francis Joseph Reitz HS; Evansville, IN; Hon Rl; JA; Jr NHS; NHS; Stu Cncl; Yth Flsp; 4-H; Treas FFA; Sci Clb; IM Sprt; Univ Of Evansville; Bio.

BRAZILE, VALERIE; Buchtel HS; Akron, OH; Chrh Wkr; Cmnty Wkr; Orch; Sch Mus; Trk; Univ.

BRAZO, JEFFREY L; Niles Sr HS; Niles, MI; 21/389 Hon Rl; JA; Stu Cncl; Yth Flsp; 4-H; VP FFA; Bsbl; Ftbl; Opt Clb Awd; Pres Awd; Runner Up Star Agri Bus Man Michigan FFA 79; State Winner Extemporaneous Public Speech 79; Orvill W Coolid; Southwestern Michigan Coll; Agri Bus.

BREAKFIELD, MICHAEL; Morrice HS; Bancroft, MI; Hon Rl; Lbry Ade; Sch Pl; Ftbl; Coach Actv; IM Sprt; Mgrs;.

BRECHBILL, LESLEE; Whitmer HS; Toledo, OH; Pres Chrs; Girl Scts; Hon Rl; NHS; Off Ade; Sch Mus; Sct Actv; Spn Clb; Univ Of Toledo; Med Tech.

BRECHT, MARCILLE; Shepherd HS; Shepherd, MI; Band; Hon Rl; NHS; Voice Dem Awd; Univ; Math.

BRECHTING, JOHN; West Catholic HS; Comstock Pk, MI; 240280 Hon Rl; Natl Merit Ltr; Mbr Of Natl Honor Soc 78 79 & 79 80; Michigan St Univ; Agri.

BRECKENRIDGE, STEPHEN K; Evansville Day HS; Evansville, IN; Cls Rep Frsh Cls; Cls Rep Soph Cls; Cl Rep Jr Cls; Hon Rl; VP Stu Cncl; Sprt Ed Yrbk; Letter Bsktbl; Letter Socr; Letter Ten; Natl Merit SF; Univ; Bus Admin.

BREDEHOEFT, JEFF; Leland Public HS; Lake Leelanau, MI; 3/34 Pres Frsh Cls; Pres Jr Cls; Cls Rep Sr Cls; Hon Rl; NHS; Stu Cncl; Letter Bsbl; Letter Bsktbl; Capt Socr; IM Sprt; Michigan St Univ; Military Sci.

BREDENFOERDER, DAVID; Mariemont HS; Terrace Pk, OH; 23/150 Cl Rep Jr Cls; Cls Rep Sr Cls; AFS; NHS; PAVAS; Sch Pl; Stu Cncl; Rptr Yrbk; Rptr Sch Nwsp; Drama Clb; Univ; Educ.

BREDEWEG, SARAH; L & M HS; Lyons, IN; Chrh Wkr; Hon Rl; Yth Flsp; Beta Clb; 4-H; FHA; Pep Clb; Pom Pon; 4-H Awd;.

BREEDING, DELILAH; Carlisle HS; Carlisle, OH; Aud/Vis; Off Ade; Yth Flsp; Spn Clb; Capt Ten; Trk; Wrstlng; Coach Actv; Miami Univ; Phys Ed.

BREEDLOVE, ANN; Northfield HS; Wabash, IN; 11/130 Pres Frsh Cls; Trs Soph Cls; Cl Rep Jr Cls; Hon Rl; Natl Forn Lg; NHS; Sch Pl; Stu Cncl; Pep Clb; Spn Clb; Uppr Wabash Career Voc Schl; Acctg.

BREEDLOVE, CANDY; Marion HS; Marion, IN; 32/710 Hon Rl; NHS; Quill & Scroll; Rptr Sch Nwsp; OEA; Spn Clb; Indiana Univ; Nursing.

BREEDLOVE, CORALEE; Southern Wells HS; Bluffton, IN; 21/90 Chrh Wkr; Hon Rl; Hosp Ade; NHS; Yth Flsp; 4-H; 4-H Awd; Hoosier Schlr 79; Coll; Acctg.

BREEDVELD, LAURIE; Jefferson Area HS; Ashtabula, OH; Band; 4-H; Fr Clb; 4-H Awd; College; Biology.

BREEN, DENNIS; Brooke HS; Follansbee, WV; 73/500 Hon Rl; Jefferson Tech Coll; Comp Sci.

BREEN, KATHLEEN; Green HS; Akron, OH; 1/325 Chrs; Chrh Wkr; Hosp Ade; NHS; Drama Clb; Pep Clb; Akron Univ; Elem Ed.

BREEN, KELLY D; Talawanda HS; Oxford, OH; 40/321 Band; Chrs; Girl Scts; Hon Rl; Jr NHS; NHS; Orch; 4-H; FHA; Pep Clb; Coop Office Educ; Miami Univ; Stewardess.

BREEN, MELINDA; Geneva Secondary HS; Geneva, OH; 13/243 Cls Rep Soph Cls; Cl Rep Jr Cls; AFS; Jr NHS; Lbry Ade; NHS; Fr Clb; Letter Chrldng; Univ.

BREEN, PAT; Jefferson HS; Newport, MI; 13/165 Band; Hon Rl; Jr NHS; Rptr Yrbk; Yrbk; Rptr Sch Nwsp; Sch Nwsp; Toledo Univ; Mgmt.

BREESE, DAVID L; Clay HS; Oregon, OH; FCA; Hon Rl; Bsbl; Wrstlng; Univ Of Toledo; Engr.

BREESE, THURLA; Mount Vernon Acad; Warren, OH; Chrh Wkr; Hon Rl; Rptr Sch Nwsp; Bsbl; Letter Wrstlng; Southern Missionery College.

BREGE, DAVID; Lutheran HS N; St Clair Shores, MI; 2/120 Cls Rep Frsh Cls; Cl Rep Jr Cls; Pres Sr Cls; Sal; Chrs; FCA; Hon Rl; NHS; Stu Cncl; Letter Bsbl; Univ; Pre Med.

BREGNI, CARLA; North Farmington HS; Farm Hills, MI; Cls Rep Soph Cls; Chrs; Cmnty Wkr; Debate Tm; Hon Rl; Off Ade; Sch Mus; Pep Clb; Chrldng; Western Univ; Psych.

BREHM, MICHAEL; Van Wert HS; Van Wert, OH; 7/230 VP Frsh Cls; Am Leg Boys St; Hon Rl; JA; NHS; Rptr Yrbk; Drama Clb; Lat Clb; Swmmng; JA Awd; Ohio St Univ; Pre Med.

BREHM, TONI; Arcanum Butler HS; Arcanum, OH; 9/99 Band; Chrh Wkr; Hon Rl; Stg Crw; Yrbk; 4-H; Miami Univ; Home Ec.

BREHMER, SHARI; Morton Sr HS; Hammond, IN; 42/436 Sec Frsh Cls; Hon Rl; Off Ade; Quill & Scroll; Stu Cncl; Yrbk; Pep Clb; Chrldng; GAA; PPFtbl; Indiana Univ; Comp Sci.

BREIVOGEL, TRACY; Reitz Memorial HS; Evansville, IN; Hon Rl; Pol Wkr; Pom Pon; Univ; Comp Sci.

BREJER, DONNA; St Joseph Academy; Cleveland, OH; Chrs; Chrh Wkr; Hon Rl; Red Cr Ade; Sch Pl; Stg Crw; Bsbl; Ten; Mgrs; Cleveland St Univ; Cmmrcl Art.

BREKRUS, SUSAN; La Salle HS; South Bend, IN; 21/488 Cl Rep Jr Cls; Hon Rl; Rptr Yrbk; Rptr Sch Nwsp; Spn Clb; Chrldng; IM Sprt; Indiana Univ; Optometry.

BRELSFORD, LETTRICIA; Piqua Central HS; Piqua, OH; Cls Rep Frsh Cls; Cl Rep Jr Cls; Cls Rep Sr Cls; Band; Sch Mus; Stg Crw; Stu Cncl; Yth Flsp; Drama Clb; 4-H; College; Soc Work.

BREMER, KAREN; Point Pleasant HS; Millersville, PA; 1/220 Val; Band; Girl Scts; Hosp Ade; NHS; Fr Clb; Lat Clb; DAR Awd; Natl Merit Ltr; Natl Merit SF; Millersville State Coll; Scndry Educ.

BREMNER, DAVID; Bellbrook HS; Bellbrook, OH; VP Frsh Cls; VP Soph Cls; Pres Jr Cls; Hon Rl; NHS; Stu Cncl; Lat Clb; Letter Bsbl; Letter Bsktbl; Glf; College.

BREMYER, JOHN; Calvert HS; Tiffin, OH; Cls Rep Frsh Cls; Jr NHS; NHS; Sch Mus; Stu Cncl; Letter Bsbl; Letter Ftbl; Cit Awd; Univ; Bio.

BRENDAHL, ANNETTE; Michigan Lutheran Seminary; St Charles, MI; Chrs; Hon Rl; Sch Pl; IM Sprt; PPFtbl; Merit Awd Young Writers Conf; Mich Lutheran Seminary Cert Of Honor & Activities Awd; Dr Martin Luther Coll; Education.

BRENNAN, BRIGID; Marian HS; Cincinnati, OH; Cls Rep Soph Cls; Chrh Wkr; Cmnty Wkr; Hosp Ade; Stu Cncl; FHA; GAA; College; Social Worker.

BRENNAN, COLLEEN; Gabriel Richard HS; Dearborn, MI; 19/154 Jr NHS; NHS; Mgrs; Scr Kpr; Tmr; Wayne State Univ; Pre Med.

BRENNAN, DEANNA; Breckenridge Jr Sr HS; Breckenridge, MI; Hon Rl; NHS; Sprt Ed Yrbk; Rptr Yrbk; Sprt Ed Sch Nwsp; FFA; Bsktbl; Letter Crs Cntry; Letter Trk; PPFtbl; Northern Michigan Univ; Phys Ed.

BRENNAN, JILL; Garber HS; Essexville, MI; Hon Rl; IM Sprt; Scr Kpr; Tmr; College; Bio.

BRENNAN, KELLY; R Nelson Snider HS; Ft Wayne, IN; 77/519 Drl Tm; Hon Rl; Hosp Ade; Pres Yth Flsp; Fr Clb; Trk; Pom Pon; Indiana Univ; Intl Bus Admin.

BRENNAN, KERRIN J; St Joseph HS; South Bend, IN; 20/263 Cmnty Wkr; Hon Rl; Orch; Sch Mus; Mth Clb; Sci Clb; Letter Wrstlng; JETS Awd; Natl Merit Schl; Univ Of Notre Dame; Physics.

BRENNAN, LISA; Ursuline HS; Youngstown, OH; 1/344 Cls Rep Frsh Cls; Cls Rep Soph Cls; Band; Hon Rl; Jr NHS; NHS; Orch; Sch Mus; Stu Cncl; Ed Yrbk; Univ; Engr.

BRENNAN, MARY; St Joseph Academy; N Olmsted, OH; Cmnty Wkr; JA; Sch Pl; Rptr Yrbk; Rptr Sch Nwsp; JA Awd; Cuyahoga Comm Coll; Journalism.

BRENNAN, MAUREEN; Madison HS; Madison, OH; 31/300 Pres AFS; Band; Hon Rl; NHS; VP Ger Clb; Pep Clb; Scr Kpr; Tmr; College; German.

BRENNAN, NANCY; Our Lady Of The Elms HS; Akron, OH; VP Frsh Cls; VP Soph Cls; Hon Rl; Sch Pl; Rptr Sch Nwsp; Sch Nwsp; Bsktbl; GAA; Top 10% In Ntl For NEDT 77; Univ; Eng.

BRENNAN, ROBERT; Zanesville HS; Zanesville, OH; FCA; Hon Rl; NHS; FFA; Spn Clb; Ftbl; NEDT 78; Oh Test Of Schlstc Achvmnt Hon Mntn 78; Univ; Math.

BRENNAN, SHARI; Jackson Milton HS; N Jackson, OH; 1/118 Cls Rep Sr Cls; Val; Hon Rl; Hosp Ade; Sec NHS; Sch Nwsp; Key Clb; Chrldng; Pres Awd; Kent St Univ; RN.

BRENNAN, SHARI L; Jackson Milton HS; North Jackson, OH; 1/118 Sec Jr Cls; Val; Hon Rl; Hosp Ade; Sec NHS; Yrbk; Sch Nwsp; 4-H; Key Clb; Chrldng; Kent St Univ; Nurse.

BRENNAN, SHEILA; St Joseph Acad; Fairview Pk, OH; Stg Crw; Rptr Yrbk; Rptr Sch Nwsp; Sch Nwsp; Spn Clb; IM Sprt; Univ; Bus Admin.

BRENNAN, STEPHANIE; Lehman HS; Sidney, OH; 9/87 Cls Rep Soph Cls; Cl Rep Jr Cls; Cls Rep Sr Cls; Band; Chrs; Hon Rl; Lbry Ade; Sch Pl; Treas Stu Cncl; Rptr Yrbk; Hon Stdnt; Acad Team; Schsp Team; Ohio St Univ; Psych.

BRENNAN, STEVEN; Yale HS; Emmett, MI; 10/178 Band; NHS; Sch Pl; Stu Cncl; Sci Clb; Crs Cntry; Ten; Trk; Mgrs; 4-H Awd; Michigan St Univ; Mech Engr.

BRENNAN, THOMAS; Chaminade Julienne HS; Dayton, OH; Chrh Wkr; Hon Rl; NHS; Stu Cncl; Natl Merit Ltr; Univ Of Dayton; Mech Engr.

BRENNEMAN, ANITA; Cory Rawson HS; Rawson, OH; 1/65 Val; Sec Chrs; Hon Rl; Lbry Ade; VP NHS; Sch Mus; Rptr Yrbk; Tmr; Dstngshd Stu Awd; Blanchard Vly Hosp Auxiliary Schlrshp; Acad Schlrshp From Lima Tech Coll; Lima Tech Coll; Radiologic Tech.

BRENNEMAN, LISA; Cabrini HS; Southgate, MI; Chrs; Hon Rl; Lbry Ade; Mdrgl; NHS; Sch Pl; Yth Flsp; Sch Nwsp; Drama Clb; Spn Clb; Alma College; Spanish.

BRENNEN, KIM; Howell HS; Brighton, MI; Girl Scts; Hon Rl; Lit Mag; Mod UN; Sec Stu Cncl; Ed Sch Nwsp; Sch Nwsp; PPFtbl; Columbia Univ; Jrnlsm.

BRENNER, ANA M B; Attica HS; Attica, IN; 9/78 Hon Rl; 4-H; Pep Clb; Spn Clb; Bsktbl; Ten; Trk; 4-H Awd; Univ; Art.

BRENNER, ANDREW; Perry HS; Owosso, MI; 8/160 Chrh Wkr; Hon Rl; NHS; Sch Pl; Yrbk; Sch Nwsp; Drama Clb; FHA; Bsktbl; College; Chem Engr.

BRENNER, ANNE; Boardman HS; Youngstown, OH; Cls Rep Sr Cls; Chrs; Chrh Wkr; Hon Rl; NHS; Sch Mus; Stu Cncl; Yth Flsp; Pres Sci Clb; Kenyon College; Chemistry.

BRENNER, EDWARD; Servite HS; Detroit, MI; Trs Jr Cls; Trs Sr Cls; Chrh Wkr; Hon Rl; Stu Cncl; Y-Teens; Bsbl; Bsktbl; Ftbl; IM Sprt; St Juliana Yhouth Sec; Bus Schl; CPA.

BRENNER, GEORGE; La Salle HS; Cincinnati, OH; 56/249 Band; Hon Rl; JA; Orch; Sch Mus; IM Sprt; College; Comp Prog.

BRENNER, JILL; Jackson Center HS; Jackson Cntr, OH; Trs Jr Cls; Hon Rl; NHS; 4-H; FHA; OEA; Trk; Am Leg Awd; 4-H Awd; Business School; Stenographer.

BRENNER, RICHARD; Mater Dei HS; Evansvl, IN; 62/150 Boy Scts; Chrh Wkr; Hon Rl; Univ.

BRENNER, ROBIN; Uppervalley Joint Voc HS; Jackson Center, OH; Cls Rep Sr Cls; Am Leg Aux Girls St; Chrh Wkr; Hon Rl; Lit Mag; Sec NHS; Stg Crw; Stu Cncl; 4-H; Pres FHA; Northwestern Bus College; Med Tech.

BRENNER, TIMOTHY; Perry Public HS; Owosso, MI; 2/117 Sal; Hon Rl; NHS; Letter Bsktbl; Letter Ftbl; IM Sprt; Mgrs; Scr Kpr; Univ; Acctg.

BRENTLINGER, REED; Heath HS; Heath, OH; 28/151 Hon Rl; Bsbl; Trk; Ferris St; Marketing.

BRESLIN, KELLY; Tecumseh HS; New Carlisle, OH; FCA; Hon Rl; Jr NHS; NHS; FBLA; Pres Pep Clb; Letter Chrldng; Am Leg Awd; Volleyball; College; Bsns Admin.

BRESNAHAN, MAUREEN; Grosse Ile HS; Grosse Ile, MI; Band; Drl Tm; Girl Scts; Hon Rl; Trk; Chrldng; GAA; Pres Awd; 2 Schlrshps To Blue Lakes Fine Arts Camps; Alma Coll Schlrshp; Alma Coll; Busns Admin.

BRESSER, KIMBERLY J; Dondero HS; Bloomfield Hls, MI; Cls Rep Frsh Cls; Hon Rl; Lit Mag; Mod UN; Rptr Yrbk; Rptr Sch Nwsp; Bsktbl; Letter Swmmng; Trk; Chrldng; Michigan St Univ; Psych.

BRESSETTE, JULIE; Marquette Sr HS; Marquette, MI; 21/430 Am Leg Aux Girls St; Fr Clb; Am Leg Awd; Mbr Safe YMCA Of Mi Youth Council; Stud Rep Marquette Indian Parent Comm; Kaufman Schlrshp; Michigan St Univ; Attorney.

BRESSLER, BRETT; Walnut Ridge HS; Columbus, OH; Hst Frsh Cls; Cls Rep Soph Cls; Cl Rep Jr Cls; Ftbl; Wrstlng; Pres Awd; 3rd Pl City Wrstlng Tournmnt 78; Univ; Pre Med.

BRESSLER, MIKE; Lexington HS; Mansfield, OH; 9/280 Hon Rl; NHS; Sct Actv; Ger Clb; Mth Clb; C of C Awd; Univ; Poli Sci.

BRESTER, MICHAEL; Indian Creek HS; Morgantown, IN; 11/148 Hon Rl;.

BRETES, M; Lumen Christi HS; Jackson, MI; Chrh Wkr; Hon Rl; Hosp Ade; NHS; College; Nursing.

BRETT, ERIC; Chagrin Falls HS; Chagrin Fl, OH; Sch Pl; Sct Actv; Stg Crw; Ger Clb; College; Physics.

BRETT, KIMBERLY; John Glenn HS; Westland, MI; 50/720 Cls Rep Frsh Cls; Hon Rl; Hosp Ade; Jr NHS; Lbry Ade; NHS; Sch Pl; Rptr Sch Nwsp; OEA; Spn Clb; Cntrl Mi Bd Of Trusts Hon Schlshp 79; St Of Mi Sclcshp 79; Cntrl Michigan Univ; Indust Engr.

BRETTELL, DENISE; Buckeye North HS; Mingo Jct, OH; 1/109 Sec Frsh Cls; Sec Soph Cls; Sec Jr Cls; Hst Sr Cls; Am Leg Aux Girls St; Band; Chrh Wkr; Cmnty Wkr; Girl Scts; Hon Rl; Miami Of Ohio Univ; Child Psych.

BRETTHAUER, KURT; Clay HS; South Bend, IN; Hon Rl; Bsktbl; Purdue Univ; Chemistry.

BRETZ, CARIE; Utica HS; Newark, OH; 35/198 Hon Rl; Letter Bsktbl; Letter Trk; PPFtbl; Ohio St Univ; Surgical Nurse.

BRETZ, CHRISTOPHER; Patrick Henry HS; Mc Clure, OH; 6/100 Hon Rl; Treas 4-H; FFA; 4-H Awd; Bio Scholarship Team; Chem Scholarship Team; Defiance Math Test; Ohio St Univ; History.

BRETZ, KATHLENE; Little Miami HS; Morow, OH; Girl Scts; Hon Rl; JA; Lit Mag; NHS; Yrbk; VP Fr Clb; Bsktbl; Socr; Trk; Top Stu In Human Phys; Univ.

BRETZ, RUTH; North HS; Willowick, OH; Band; Chrh Wkr; Cmnty Wkr; Hon Rl; Ger Clb; Marching Band Letter; Cleveland St Univ; Speech Pathology.

BREUER, D; Beal City HS; Mt Pleasant, MI; VP Jr Cls; Band; Chrs; Hon Rl; 4-H; Spn Clb; Chrldng; Lion Awd; VFW Awd; Voice Dem Awd; College; Music.

BREUTZMAN, LINDA; Coloma HS; Coloma, MI; Chrs; Chrh Wkr; Hon Rl; Orch; Yth Flsp; Bsktbl; IM Sprt; PPFtbl; Immanuel Luthern College; Teacher.

BREUTZMAN, MARY; Coloma HS; Coloma, MI; 5/227 Hon Rl; NHS; Sch Pl; Drama Clb; Pep Clb; Chrldng; PPFtbl; DAR Awd; Eastern Mi Univ; Phy Ed.

BREUTZMAN, ROSE; Coloma HS; Coloma, MI; Chrh Wkr; Hon Rl;.

BREVING, JUDY; Batavia HS; Batavia, OH; Cls Rep Soph Cls; Hon Rl; Sch Pl; Stu Cncl; Drama Clb; FHA; Spn Clb; Trk; Chrldng; GAA; Univ Of Cincinnati.

BREWCZAK, NANCY; Mt Clemens HS; Mt Clemens, MI; 3/300 Sec Band; Hon Rl; Lit Mag; Ed Sch Nwsp; Sprt Ed Sch Nwsp; Rptr Sch Nwsp; VP Key Clb; Mic State Univ; Journ.

BREWER, ANITA; Springs Valley HS; French Lick, IN; 35/71 Chrs; Sch Pl; Rptr Sch Nwsp; Pres FHA; Pres OEA; Trk; Sullian Jr Coll; Admin Acctg.

BREWER, BRENT; London HS; London, OH; 7/140 Cls Rep Frsh Cls; Am Leg Boys St; Boy Scts; Cmnty Wkr; Hon Rl; Stg Crw; Stu Cncl; Boys Clb Am; 4-H; Fr Clb; Eagle Scout; Scout Of Yr Awd; Order Of Arrow Scout Awd; College; Mech Engr.

BREWER, BRIAN; Barboursville HS; Barboursville, WV; Am Leg Boys St; Chrs; Chrh Wkr; FCA; Hon Rl; Jr NHS; VP NHS; Pres Key Clb; Mth Clb; Capt Crs Cntry; Univ; Soc Work.

BREWER, CATHERINE; Clyde Sr HS; Clyde, OH; Hon Rl; Tutor English; Nurses Aide; Humane Award; Terra Tech Coll; Acctg.

BREWER, CHRIS; Linton Stockton HS; Linton, IN; Band; Girl Scts; Hon Rl; NHS; Pol Wkr; Sch Mus; Sch Pl; Yth Flsp; 4-H; Pep Clb; Vllybl Letter 78; Sftbl Letter 78; Indiana Univ; Med.

BREWER, CINDY; Wilmington HS; Wilmington, OH; 34/312 Chrs; Hon Rl; Stg Crw; Drama Clb; 4-H; Fr Clb; VP Pep Clb; Chrldng; 4-H Awd; Mas Awd; Phi Delta Sigma 77; Jr Leadrshp 77 78 & 79; 4 H Camp Cnslr 77 78 & 79; Univ Of Cincinnati; Bus.

BREWER, DARRIN; Jennings County HS; No Vernon, IN; 12/351 NHS; Pep Clb; Letter Bsbl; Ftbl; Wrstlng; Purdue Univ; Mechanical Engineering.

BREWER, DEBORAH; Salem HS; Salem, IN; Val; Am Leg Aux Girls St; Band; NHS; Sch Mus; Sch Pl; Yth Flsp; Pres Drama Clb; Lat Clb; Purdue Univ; Vet.

BREWER, ELVIS; Hammond Technical Voc HS; Hammond, IN; Aud/Vis; Chrh Wkr; Civ Clb; Rdo Clb; VICA; VALPO; Elec Tech.

BREWER, JAMES; Bishop Noll Institute; Gary, IN; Capt Debate Tm; Natl Forn Lg; VP NHS; Quill & Scroll; Sch Mus; Sch Nwsp; Mth Clb; Spn Clb; Natl Hist Day Finstl 79; Nalt Jr Achvrs Conf Elec Comm Validtn Co Chrmn 79; Univ; Poli Sci.

BREWER, MICHAEL R; Wood Memorial HS; Oakland City, IN; Hon Rl; Pol Wkr; Evansville Univ Voc Schl; Welding.

BREWER, RICK; Euclid Sr HS; Euclid, OH; Hocking Tech Schl; Wildlife Mgmt.

BREWER, SANDRA; Canton South HS; Canton, OH; Cls Rep Frsh Cls; Natl Forn Lg; Pol Wkr; Drama Clb; Treas 4-H; Lat Clb; Rdo Clb; Scr Kpr; Akron Univ; Enviro Engr.

BREWER, SANDRA L; Beechcroft Sr HS; Columbus, OH; 13/215 Am Leg Aux Girls St; Letter Chrs; Hon Rl; NHS; Yrbk; VP Fr Clb; Bsbl; Wrstlng; Chrldng; PPFtbl; PTA Scholastic Achievemnt Awds; OSAT Tests For French I & II; COSI Kiwanis Leadership Conf; Ohio St Univ; Med Tech.

BREWER, STEVEN; Salem HS; Salem, IN; 4/150 Cls Rep Soph Cls; Am Leg Boys St; Chrs; Pres NHS; Stu Cncl; Treas Yth Flsp; Lat Clb; Sci Clb; Cummins Engine Sclshp Fdn; Richard Lugars Sympsm On Natl Affairs; Debt Club Vc Pres; Indiana Univ S E.

BREWER, TERESA; Greenville Sr HS; Greenville, OH; 10/380 Cls Rep Frsh Cls; Cls Rep Soph Cls; Cl Rep Jr Cls; Girl Scts; Hon Rl; Jr NHS; NHS; Quill & Scroll; Stu Cncl; Yth Flsp; State Repr 4 H Hunt Div 1976; Univ; Communication Arts.

BREWER, TERRY; Clinton Massie HS; Waynesville, OH; Chrh Wkr; Sch Pl; 3rd Pl Tri St Regnl Bible Quiz 79; Shclshp Hon Awd 75; 6th Pl Amer Hist Test Of Shclst Achvmtn 79; Navy; Amer Hist.

BREWER, WILLIAM; North Farmington HS; Farmingtn Hls, MI; 25/390 Boy Scts; Cmnty Wkr; Hon Rl; NHS; Sprt Ed Yrbk; Fr Clb; Letter Swmmng; Coach Actv; IM Sprt; Tmr; Phi Beta Kappa Cert Of Commendation 79; French Awd 79; Forensics Awd 2nd In Extemporaneous Speaking 76; Yale Univ; Law.

BREWSTER, ANITA K; Western HS; Piketon, OH; 1/42 VP Jr Cls; Sec Sr Cls; Band; Chrs; Chrh Wkr; Hon Rl; NHS; Sch Pl; Ed Yrbk; 4-H; Ohio Univ; Education.

BREWSTER, JEFF; Streetsboro HS; Streetsboro, OH; Boy Scts; Chrh Wkr; Cmnty Wkr; Sct Actv; Yth Flsp; Letter Crs Cntry; Letter Ten; Ohio State Univ; Business.

BREWSTER, LISA K; Burch HS; Delbarton, WV; Sec Frsh Cls; VP Soph Cls; Sec Jr Cls; Chrs; Hon Rl; Beta Clb; FTA; Pep Clb; Bsbl; Gym; Marshall Univ; Nursing.

BREWSTER, STEVE; Cheboygan Catholic HS; Cheboygan, MI; Trs Jr Cls; Boy Scts; Hon Rl; Sch Mus; Stg Crw; Letter Bsktbl; Capt Ftbl; Letter Trk; Mech.

BREWSTER, VENEETA; Hughes HS; Cincinnati, OH; 3/428 Sec Jr Cls; VP Sr Cls; Hon Rl; NHS; Stu Cncl; Pep Clb; Chrldng; Pom Pon; C of C Awd; DAR Awd; Young Mens Mercantile Library; Cincinnati Congressional Schlrshp Prog; Attending Rensselear Poly Inst; Coll; Elec Engr.

BREWTON, CHARLES A; Princeton HS; Cincinnati, OH; Cls Rep Frsh Cls; Cls Rep Soph Cls; Band; JA; Orch; PAVAS; Sch Mus; Stu Cncl; Lat Clb; OMEA Solo Contest; OMEA Dist XIV Symphonic Band; Cincinnati Yth Symphony Orchestra; Oberlin Coll; Music.

BREYER, DAVID; Cedar Lake Academy; Cedar Lake, MI; Pres Soph Cls; Chrh Wkr; Hon Rl; NHS; Yrbk; Sprt Ed Sch Nwsp; Bsktbl; IM Sprt; Andrews Univ; Medicine.

BREYFOGLE, KATHLEEN; Loy Norrix HS; Kalamazoo, MI; Girl Scts; Hon Rl; Yth Flsp; Rptr Yrbk; Fr Clb; Letter Swmmng; Letter Trk; Tmr; Hope Univ; Comp Sci.

BREZA, KELLY; Pinconning Area HS; Pinconning, MI; Band; Girl Scts; Hon Rl; Off Ade; Pep Clb; VICA; Bsbl; PPFtbl; Delta Univ.

BREZNAK, RONALD J; Ellet HS; Akron, OH; 58/366 Chrh Wkr; Jr NHS; NHS; Yth Flsp; Kent St Univ; Law Enforcement.

BREZNY, RASTISLAV; Middletown HS; Middletown, OH; 26/517 Band; Boy Scts; Hon Rl; NHS; Yrbk; Sch Nwsp; Ger Clb; Mth Clb; Trs Sr Cls; Ohio State Univ; Chemical Engr.

BRIA, LISA A; Valley HS; Charlton Hts, WV; Cls Rep Soph Cls; Chrh Wkr; Cmnty Wkr; Sprt Ed Yrbk; Rptr Yrbk; DECA; Swmmng; Ten; Letter Chrldng; West Virginia Inst Of Tech; Med Rec.

BRIANS, JENNIFER; Walnut Hills HS; Cincinnati, OH; Chrs; Girl Scts; Hon Rl; FSA; Northern Ken Univ.

BRICE, CAPRICE; Covert HS; Covert, MI; Chrs; Mod UN; Sch Nwsp; DECA; FHA; Pep Clb; Chrldng; Davenport College; Marketing.

BRICHACEK, MICHELLE; Holy Name HS; Garfield Hts, OH; Girl Scts; Spn Clb; Letter Bsbl; Letter Bsktbl; IM Sprt; Scr Kpr; Univ.

BRICKER, BARBARA; Big Walnut HS; Sunbury, OH; 37/243 Chrh Wkr; Girl Scts; JA; Lbry Ade; Rptr Sch Nwsp; 4-H; Fr Clb; FHA; JA Awd; Jr Degree 77; Chapt Degree 78; St Degree 789; Columbus Tech Inst; Acctg.

BRICKER, CEDRIC; Jay County HS; Portland, IN; Hon Rl; NHS; 4-H; Letter Trk; 4-H Awd; College; Drafting.

BRICKER, CONNIE; Yale HS; Yale, MI; 2/160 Hst Sr Cls; Band; Hon Rl; NHS; Sch Mus; Sch Pl; Yth Flsp; Rptr Sch Nwsp; St Clair Cnty Cmnty Coll; Bus Admin.

BRICKER, DON; Yale HS; Yale, MI; 6/180 Aud/Vis; Band; Hon Rl; NHS; Yth Flsp; Sci Clb; Letter Crs Cntry; Letter Trk; Univ; Mech Engr.

BRICKER, PAMELA; Carlisle HS; Carlisle, OH; Band; Chrs; Chrh Wkr; Hon Rl; NHS; Stu Cncl; FTA; Treas Spn Clb; Letter Scr Kpr; College; Ed.

BRICKER, SARA; Boyne City HS; East Jordan, MI; 10/111 Band; Hon Rl; Sch Mus; Capt Bsktbl; Letter Trk; Vllybl Letter 3 Yrs All Confrnc & MVP 78 79; Band John Philip Sousa Awd 79; Top Girl Athlete 79; Michigan St Univ; Music.

BRICKER, SUSAN; Columbiana HS; Columbiana, OH; Cmp Fr Grls; Chrs; Chrh Wkr; Drl Tm; Hon Rl; Yth Flsp; Fr Clb; Sec Pep Clb; Chrldng; Youngstown State Univ.

BRICKLEY, KEVIN; Warren HS; Sterlings Hts, MI; Aud/Vis; Debate Tm; Hon Rl; Lbry Ade; Natl Forn Lg; Sch Mus; Sch Pl; Sct Actv; Stg Crw; Drama Clb; San Diego Univ; Criminal Law.

BRICKMAN, JUDY; Mccomb Local HS; Mccomb, OH; 1/80 Pres Frsh Cls; Hon Rl; NHS; Off Ade; Stu Cncl; Pep Clb; Trk; Scr Kpr; Bluffton College.

BRICKNER, BRIAN; Tiffin Columbian HS; Tiffin, OH; Cls Rep Frsh Cls; Boy Scts; Hon Rl; Jr NHS; Sch Pl; Sct Actv; Stg Crw; Stu Cncl; Yth Flsp; Y-Teens; Univ Of Cct; Pharmacy.

BRICKNER, JULIE; Seton HS; Cincinnati, OH; 8/284 Hon Rl; Jr NHS; NHS; Orch; Sch Mus; Sch Pl; Sec Mth Clb; Pep Clb; Spn Clb; Letter Bsktbl; Univ; Vet.

BRICKNER, KATHRYN; Calvert HS; Tiffin, OH; Chrs; Hon Rl; Hosp Ade; Sch Mus; Stu Cncl; Pep Clb; Swmmng; Mat Maids; Cit Awd; Univ; Child Psych.

BRICKNER, KEITH; Calvert HS; Tiffin, OH; Chrs; Chrh Wkr; Sch Pl; Letter Ftbl; Letter Wrstlng; Univ; Bus.

BRICKNER, LOUIS; Tiffin Calvert HS; Tiffin, OH; Boy Scts; Chrs; Chrh Wkr; FCA; Sch Mus; Ftbl; IM Sprt; Cit Awd; Univ.

BRIDENBAUGH, DONALD; Eastwood HS; Luckey, OH; Hon Rl; Pol Wkr; Fr Clb; Key Clb; Letter Glf; Trk; IM Sprt; Norwich Univ; Military Std.

BRIDENSTINE, JANICE; Ridgedale HS; Morral, OH; 23/108 Cls Rep Frsh Cls; Chrs; Cmnty Wkr; Hon Rl; Lit Mag; Quill & Scroll; Sch Mus; Sch Pl; Yrbk; Rptr Sch Nwsp; Univ; Cmnctns.

BRIDGE, DANIEL; Rockville HS; Rockville, IN; 24/98 Am Leg Boys St; FCA; Hon Rl; NHS; Letter Ftbl; Letter Wrstlng; Univ; Civil Engr.

BRIDGE, LISA; Frontier HS; Monticello, IN; Band; Hon Rl; Off Ade; Yth Flsp; Drama Clb; 4-H; Pep Clb; Mbrshp In Sunshine Soc; Univ; Cmnctns.

BRIDGE, MAUREEN; Wylie E Groves HS; Birmingham, MI; AFS; Band; Chrs; Cmnty Wkr; Girl Scts; Hon Rl; PAVAS; Sch Mus; Sch Pl; Northern Mic Univ; Natural Sci.

BRIDGELAND, E; Mason HS; Mason, MI; Band; Hon Rl; NHS; Orch; Rptr Yrbk; Rptr Sch Nwsp; 4-H; Fr Clb; 4-H Awd; Mich State Univ; Animal Science.

BRIDGES, BRUCE; Milton Union HS; Laura, OH; 43/218 Cmnty Wkr; Lat Clb; Univ Of Dayton; Bio.

BRIDGES, DARRYL K; Charles F Kettering HS; Detroit, MI; Drl Tm; Hon Rl; Off Ade; ROTC; Cit Awd; Central St Univ; Accounting.

BRIDGES, GINA; Lake HS; Walbridge, OH; Sec Frsh Cls; Trs Soph Cls; Band; Chrs; Drm Mjrt; FCA; Girl Scts; Hon Rl; Sch Mus; Bowling Green Univ; Journalism.

BRIDGES, MELISA; Ecorse HS; Ecorse, MI; Cls Rep Soph Cls; Cl Rep Jr Cls; Band; Cmnty Wkr; Girl Scts; Jr NHS; Stu Cncl; FHA; Spn Clb; Trk; College.

BRIEDE, BEV; Seton HS; Cincinnati, OH; Hon Rl; NHS; Spn Clb; Deaconess Hosp Schl; Nursing.

BRIER, DANIEL E; Cardinal Ritter HS; Indianapolis, IN; 7/158 Boy Scts; Hon Rl; Sct Actv; Rptr Yrbk; Crs Cntry; Trk; Univ; Bio.

BRIER, MARK; Caldwell HS; Caldwell, OH; 1/104 Hon Rl; Spn Clb; Ohio St Univ; Aerospace Engr.

BRIGANDI, JOSEPH; Garfield HS; Akron, OH; Pres Sr Cls; Cmnty Wkr; NHS; Stu Cncl; Sch Nwsp; Spn Clb; Letter Trk; Am Leg Awd; Young Citizens Awd 78; Western Reserve Educ Fnd Awd 79; Stu Cncl Most Valuab Male 79; Univ; Music.

BRIGGS, COLLEEN; Reeths Puffer HS; Muskegon, MI; Band; Chrh Wkr; Cmnty Wkr; Rptr Sch Nwsp; Spn Clb; Coll; English.

BRIGGS, CYNTHIA J; Highland HS; Wadsworth, OH; Cls Rep Frsh Cls; Band; Chrs; Hon Rl; Off Ade; Sch Mus; Stu Cncl; Key Clb; Lat Clb; Letter Crs Cntry; Univ; Dsgn In Art.

BRIGGS, FREDRICK; North Adams HS; Hillsdale, MI; 48/60 Cl Rep Jr Cls; Band; Hon Rl; Sch Pl; Rptr Sch Nwsp; Drama Clb; Pep Clb; Ftbl; IM Sprt; Aircraft Mech.

BRIGGS, GERALD; North HS; Youngstown, OH; 6/80 Hon Rl; Jr NHS; NHS; Sch Pl; Bsktbl; Cit Awd; Rotary Awd;.

BRIGGS, JAMES; Cuyahoga Falls HS; Cuyahoga Falls, OH; Chrs; Hon Rl; Pres JA; Pres NHS; Sch Mus; Ftbl; Trk; Rotary Awd; College.

BRIGGS, JULIE; Cameron Dragons HS; Cameron, WV; Band; Chrs; Hon Rl; Yth Flsp; Y-Teens; FHA; Bsbl; Bsktbl; GAA; PPFtbl;.

BRIGGS, KARI; Adena HS; Frankfort, OH; 10/85 VP Sr Cls; Band; Hon Rl; NHS; Stu Cncl; Rptr Yrbk; Rptr Sch Nwsp; Ohio Univ; Sec.

BRIGGS, RHONDA; Cambridge HS; Cambridge, OH; Cls Rep Frsh Cls; Cls Rep Soph Cls; Cl Rep Jr Cls; Cls Rep Sr Cls; Chrh Wkr; Hon Rl; Jr NHS; NHS; Stu Cncl; Yth Flsp; Knoxville Coll; Business.

BRIGGS, RITA; Vassar HS; Tuscola, MI; Chrh Wkr; Quill & Scroll; Yth Flsp; Yrbk; Rptr Sch Nwsp; FHA; Spn Clb; College; Data Processing.

BRIGGS, ROGER; Waterford Mott HS; Pontiac, MI; Cert Of Recgntn Of St Of Mi Compttv Schslshp 79; Lawrence Inst Of Tech; Bus Admin.

BRIGGS, THOMAS; North Miami HS; Macy, IN; Cls Rep Frsh Cls; Cls Rep Soph Cls; Cl Rep Jr Cls; Cls Rep Sr Cls; Am Leg Boys St; Band; Chrs; Chrh Wkr; Hon Rl; Mdrgl; Lincoln Tech; Auto Mech.

BRIGHAM, CHERYL A; North Central HS; Indianapolis, IN; 39/1194 Hon Rl; Hosp Ade; Mod UN; NHS; Rptr Sch Nwsp; Natl Merit SF; Univ Of Michigan.

BRIGHAM, GREGORY; Madeira HS; Madeira, OH; Sch Mus; Sch Pl; Sct Actv; Drama Clb; Spn Clb; Letter Crs Cntry; College.

BRIGHT, CARL P; Benzie Central HS; Empire, MI; 20/130 Hon Rl; NHS; Pep Clb; Letter Bsbl; Letter Ftbl; Bsbl Region U Class C All Star Tm Awd 77 & 78; Bsbl All St Class 1st Tm 77; Bsbl All St Class C 2nd Tm 78; Central Michigan Univ; Bus.

BRIGHT, CAROLYN; Immaculata HS; Detroit, MI; 1/96 Cls Rep Soph Cls; Cl Rep Jr Cls; Hon Rl; JA; Mod UN; NHS; Pol Wkr; Stg Crw; Stu Cncl; Ed Sch Nwsp; E Mi Univ Mst Outstndng Jr Awd 79; 1200 Schlsp Awd To E Mi Univ 79; Univ; Archt.

BRIGHT, CARRIE; Fisher Catholic HS; Lancaster, OH; Sec Frsh Cls; Cls Rep Soph Cls; Chrh Wkr; Cmnty Wkr; Hon Rl; Jr NHS; NHS; Ten; Univ Of San Diego; Bus Admin.

BRIGHT, LAURA; Black River HS; West Salem, OH; Band; Chrh Wkr; Drm Mjrt; Hon Rl; Sch Pl; Yth Flsp; Yrbk; Fr Clb; Pep Clb; Sci Clb; Bus Schl; Med Sec.

BRIGHT, MELISSA; South Charleston HS; S Charleston, WV; Band; Chrs; Chrh Wkr; Girl Scts; Hon Rl; Sec Jr NHS; NHS; Sch Mus; Sch Pl; Treas Stu Cncl; Spanish Natl Hon Soc Sec & Treas 78 79 & 80; Math Awd 3rd Pl Math Field Day 77; Spanish Awd Otstndng Stud; Univ; Acctg.

BRIGHT, PENNY; Arcanum Butler HS; Arcanum, OH; 8/99 Hon Rl; Lbry Ade; NHS; Sch Pl; Yrbk; FHA; Trk; IM Sprt; Mgrs; Scr Kpr; Schlrshp Consistnt High Pt Grd Avrg 75; Silver Libertys Of Lang 77; Univ.

BRIGHT, PHILIP; Mansfield Christian HS; Mansfield, OH; VP Jr Cls; Chrh Wkr; Orch; Letter Wrstlng; Grace College; Music.

BRIGHT, TERRI; Westerville South HS; Columbus, OH; Chrs; Debate Tm; Drl Tm; Drm Mjrt; Hon Rl; Lbry Ade; Off Ade; College; Bus.

BRIGLE, KERRY; Edon HS; Edon, OH; 7/68 Trs Sr Cls; Am Leg Boys St; Aud/Vis; Hon Rl; NHS; Stu Cncl; Mth Clb; Spn Clb; Letter Bsbl; Capt Crs Cntry; OHSAA St Cross Country Meet; Ohio St Hwy Patrol Academy Jr Cadet; 3 Yr Chess Club Champion; Univ; Psych.

BRIGNER, KIM; Chippewa Hills HS; Barryton, MI; Cls Rep Sr Cls; Band; Hon Rl; Trk; Chrldng; CMU; Med.

BRILL, DAVID; Fenwick HS; Middletown, OH; Boy Scts; Chrh Wkr; Hon Rl; Crs Cntry; Trk; Wrstlng; IM Sprt; Pres Awd; Univ Of Dayton; Elec Engr.

BRILL, JANIE; Keyser HS; Keyser, WV; 6/245 AFS; Band; Chrs; Hon Rl; NHS; Orch; Sch Pl; Stg Crw; Yrbk; Rptr Sch Nwsp; West Virginia Univ; Drama.

BRILL, MICHELLE; Griffith HS; Griffith, IN; 46/353 Cls Rep Soph Cls; Cl Rep Jr Cls; Chrs; Chrh Wkr; Cmnty Wkr; Hon Rl; Jr NHS; Off Ade; Pol Wkr; Sch Mus; Schl Letter For Choir; Final To Ms Teen Indiana Pageant; Purdue Calumet Univ; Psych.

BRILL, TIM; Goshen HS; Goshen, IN; 36/297 Cls Rep Frsh Cls; Band; Hon Rl; Orch; Stu Cncl; Rptr Yrbk; Rptr Sch Nwsp; Pep Clb; Ftbl; Trk; Univ; Med.

BRIM, JANE; Kenton Sr HS; Kenton, OH; 33/190 Chrs; Cmnty Wkr; Hon Rl; Sch Mus; IM Sprt; Cit Awd; Univ; Acctg.

BRIMMER, DOUGLAS; Robert S Rogers HS; Toledo, OH; Band; Boy Scts; Jr NHS; NHS; Orch; Sch Mus; Sct Actv; Fr Clb; Letter Bsbl; Letter Ftbl; College; Engr.

BRIMMER, PAUL; Mt Vernon Acad; Sanborn, NY; Chrs; Chrh Wkr; God Cntry Awd; Southern Missionary.

BRIMMER, PAUL; Mt Vernon Academy; Sanborn, NY; Chrs; Chrh Wkr; Boys Clb Am; Southern Missionary Coll.

BRINCEFIELD, MARY; Lincolnview HS; Middle Pt, OH; Chrs; Lbry Ade; NHS; Red Cr Ade; FHA; Sci Clb; College.

BRINCEFIELD, THOMAS L; Lincolnview HS; Elgin, OH; Chrs; Hon Rl; Sch Mus; Sct Actv; Yth Flsp; Fr Clb; Sci Clb; Huntington Coll; Youth For Chrst Dir.

BRINCKS, MICHAEL; Bridgman HS; Bridgman, MI; Am Leg Boys St; Band; Boy Scts; Chrs; Chrh Wkr; Hon Rl; Sch Mus; Sch Pl; Sct Actv; Stg Crw;.

BRINDIAR, JOHN; Mahoning Cnty Jnt Voc HS; Lowellville, OH; Boy Scts; Sch Pl; Drama Clb; 4-H; Fr Clb; OEA; 4-H Awd; Sixth Pl Reg Acctg Reltd I 1978; Youngstown St Univ; CPA.

BRINDLEY, KELLI; Ashtabula Harbor HS; Ashtabula, OH; 4/169 Trs Frsh Cls; Trs Soph Cls; Trs Jr Cls; AFS; JA; NHS; Letter GAA; IM Sprt; JA Awd; Univ Of Akron; Civil Engr.

BRINEGAR, MARK; Edgewood HS; Ellettsville, IN; Debate Tm; Off Ade; Sch Mus; Sch Pl; Stg Crw; Yth Flsp; Drama Clb; Ger Clb; Natl Merit Ltr; Collegea; Law.

BRINER, NANCY; Coldwater HS; Coldwater, OH; 1/150 Pres Chrs; Chrh Wkr; Hon Rl; NHS; VP Stu Cncl; Ed Yrbk; Spn Clb; IM Sprt; JC Awd; Wright St Univ; Acctng.

BRINGEDAHL, DEWEY; Muskegon Sr HS; Muskegon, MI; Band; Hon Rl; Jr NHS; Ger Clb; Ferris St Coll; Pharmacy.

BRINK, ELAINE; Bishop Ready HS; Columbus, OH; Cls Rep Frsh Cls; VP Soph Cls; Cl Rep Jr Cls; Cmp Fr Grls; Chrh Wkr; FCA; Hon Rl; Off Ade; Quill & Scroll; Univ; Modeling.

BRINK, JEANNE; Holland HS; Holland, MI; 29/296 Cmp Fr Grls; Chrh Wkr; Hon Rl; NHS; Orch; Yth Flsp; Spn Clb; Hope Coll; Psych.

BRINK, MELISSA; U S A HS; Akron, MI; Band; Hon Rl; Lat Clb; Capt Chrldng; College; Humanities.

BRINKER, ANITA; Bishop Dwenger HS; Ft Wayne, IN; Chrs; Hon Rl; NHS; Rptr Yrbk; Pres 4-H; Fr Clb; 4-H Awd; Univ; Botany.

BRINKER, DEBORAH L; Carmel HS; Carmel, IN; 9/698 Hon Rl; NHS; Lat Clb; Trackettes 77 79; Racketteers 77; Butler Univ; Acctg.

BRINKER, JAY; Greenville Sr HS; Greenville, OH; 2/380 Hon Rl; NHS; Rptr Yrbk; Key Clb; Spn Clb; Letter Crs Cntry; Letter Trk; Univ Of Cincinnati; Engr.

BRINKER, SUE; Leetonia HS; Leetonia, OH; 28/87 Band; JA; Sch Mus; Rptr Yrbk; Kent State Univ; Music.

BRINKER, WARREN; Durand HS; Durand, MI; 57/215 Debate Tm; Hon Rl; Yrbk; Univ Of Mic; Bus Admin.

BRINKERHOFF, SCOTT; Wooster HS; Wooster, OH; 33/365 Jr NHS; 4-H; Spn Clb; Letter Ftbl; Trk; IM Sprt; 4-H Awd; All Conf Footbll Best Lineman 1979; Amer Schlrshp Awd 1979; Keystone Brdcstng 1979; Alll Star Bsktball; Univ; Engr.

BRINKMAN, CARI; Caro HS; Caro, MI; Cmp Fr Grls; Girl Scts; Hosp Ade; Lbry Ade; Sch Pl; Stg Crw; Sch Nwsp; 4-H; FHA; Bsbl; Delta Bus Schl; Legal Sec.

BRINKMAN, DAVID; Centerville HS; Centerville, OH; Chrh Wkr; Cmnty Wkr; Natl Forn Lg; Sch Mus; Sch Pl; Stg Crw; VP Yth Flsp; Drama Clb; Ger Clb; Key Clb; Sprv & Admin Mgmt Class Clb 77 79; Miami Univ Of Ohio; Acctg.

BRINKMAN, FREDRICK J; Whiteland Community HS; Whiteland, IN; 31/215 FCA; Jr NHS; Sch Mus; Ten; Mas Awd; College; Pre Med.

BRINKMAN, LYNN; Bedford Sr HS; Temperance, MI; Band; Pol Wkr; Lat Clb; Edsel Richardson Schlrshp; Michigan St Univ; Vet.

BRINKMAN, TERESA; Our Lady Of Mercy HS; Farm Hls, MI; Chrh Wkr; Hon Rl; Sch Pl; Rptr Yrbk; Univ; Interior Dsgn.

BRINKMANN, DALE; Moeller HS; West Chester, OH; Hon Rl; Bsktbl; IM Sprt; College; Acctg Or Comp Progr.

BRINKMOELLER, LISA; Immaculate Conception Acad; Batesville, IN; 1/68 Trs Sr Cls; Am Leg Aux Girls St; Chrs; Chrh Wkr; Hon Rl; Hosp Ade; JA; NHS; Red Cr Ade; Sch Mus; Tuition Grant Of 75 Renewbl Each Yr; Hugh O Brian Outstndng Soph 78; I U Hon Spanish Std Progr 79; Univ; Pre Med.

BRIOLAT, SHERRY; Ubly HS; Ubly, MI; Cls Rep Frsh Cls; Band; Girl Scts; Hon Rl; Hosp Ade; Lbry Ade; Off Ade; Sch Pl; Stg Crw; 4-H; Saginaw St Clare Univ; Nursing.

BRISCOE, ANNA; Salem HS; Salem, IN; Lit Mag; Sprt Ed Sch Nwsp; Rptr Sch Nwsp; Lat Clb; Pep Clb; Ten; Ind Univ; Nursing.

BRISCOE, VALORIEN; East HS; Columbus, OH; Sec Jr Cls; Drl Tm; Hon Rl; Jr NHS; NHS; OEA; Pep Clb; Franklin College; Bus Admin.

BRISKE, JEFF; Orchard View HS; Moskegon, MI; 4/215 Chrh Wkr; Hon Rl; NHS; Letter Bsktbl; Univ; Elec Engr.

BRISKE, KIRBY J; Manistee HS; Manistee, MI; 5/200 Cls Rep Frsh Cls; Cls Rep Sr Cls; Am Leg Boys St; Debate Tm; Hon Rl; Lit Mag; Natl Forn Lg; NHS; Sch Mus; Sch Pl; 1st Place Stu Division Manistee World Of Arts & Crafts; One Man Art Exhibit West Shore Comm Coll; Univ Of Michigan; Archt.

BRISKEY, BARBARA; Waldron HS; Waldron, MI; 6/39 Sec Frsh Cls; Sec Jr Cls; Hon Rl; Ed Yrbk; Trk;.

BRISKEY, JO; Pettisville HS; Wauseon, OH; 1/51 VP Soph Cls; Chrs; Hon Rl; NHS; Sch Pl; Stu Cncl; Yrbk; College; Acctg.

BRISLINGER, CHRISTY; Fisher Catholic HS; Logan, OH; Girl Scts; Hon Rl; NHS; Off Ade; 4-H; Ohio St Univ; Dental Hygiene.

BRISTOL, WILLIAM; Moeller HS; Cincinnati, OH; Hon Rl; Lit Mag; Socr; Trk; IM Sprt; Best Genrl Bus Stdnt In Schl 77 78; Miami Univ; Acctg.

BRISTOW, DENIS; Piqua Central HS; Piqua, OH; Orch; Lat Clb; Spn Clb; Univ; Law.

BRISTOW, MICHAEL E; Bloomington HS North; Bloomington, IN; Band; Boy Scts; Chrs; Chrh Wkr; Lbry Ade; Orch; Sct Actv; Sch Nwsp; Natl Merit SF; Order Of Arrow Boy Scts Of Amer 1976; Photos In The Whole Press 1978; Indiana Univ; Comp Progr.

BRISTOW, SHARON; Port Clinton HS; Pt Clinton, OH; Hon Rl; Off Ade; Mat Maids; Bowling Green State Univ.

BRITIGAN, ROBERT D; Gull Lake HS; Richland, MI; VP Frsh Cls; Cls Rep Frsh Cls; Cls Rep Soph Cls; Cl Rep Jr Cls; Cls Rep Sr Cls; Hon Rl; Off Ade; Stu Cncl; Sch Nwsp; Fr Clb; Sprtsmnshp Awd; Jr Tennis Champ; Sailing Awd; Univ.

BRITT, DONATA; Finney HS; Detroit, MI; Voc Schl; Data Proc.

BRITT, MARLA; Jackson HS; Jackson, OH; 12/228 Hon Rl; NHS; FHA; Ohio Univ; Spec Educ Tchr.

BRITT, NANCY; Whittemore Prescott HS; Turner, MI; 5/120 VP Frsh Cls; Band; Chrh Wkr; Hon Rl; NHS; Stu Cncl; 4-H; Bsktbl; Twrlr;.

BRITT, SUSAN; Thomas W Harvey HS; Painesville, OH; Hon Rl; NHS; Swmmng; Ladeland Community College.

BRITT, THOMAS; Fairmont West HS; Kettering, OH; Chrh Wkr; Cmnty Wkr; Hon Rl; JA; Fr Clb; Pep Clb; Rdo Clb; Socr; Trk; IM Sprt; Univ Of D; Comp Sci.

BRITTAIN, GLENN; Durand Area HS; Lennon, MI; 16/208 Cls Rep Sr Cls; Chrs; Chrh Wkr; Hon Rl; Lbry Ade; NHS; Natl Merit Ltr; Univ Of Michigan; Elec Engr.

BRITTAIN, RANDY; Northmont HS; Dayton, OH; Chrh Wkr; IM Sprt; 2nd Appearance In Whos Who; Liberty Coll; Acctg.

BRITTON, ANNETTE; Atlanta Community HS; Atlanta, MI; 7/49 Band; Chrh Wkr; Hon Rl; NHS; Off Ade; Sch Pl; Stu Cncl; Yrbk; 4-H; FHA; Schlstc Achvmtn Awd 75 79; Acctg Awd 79; Evangel Coll; Elem Educ.

BRITTON, JERILYN; Rockville HS; Rockville, IN; Cmp Fr Grls; Girl Scts; Hon Rl; Y-Teens; FHA; Pep Clb; Spn Clb; Gym; Beauty Schl.

BRITTON, SABRINA; Carroll HS; Flora, IN; 7/105 NHS; Stu Cncl; Fr Clb; 100.

BRITVEC, KEL; Battle Creek Central HS; Battle Creek, MI; Cls Rep Frsh Cls; Cls Rep Soph Cls; Cl Rep Jr Cls; Cls Rep Sr Cls; Hon Rl; Pol Wkr; Stu Cncl; Central Mic Univ; Psyco.

BRNILOVICH, ROBERT; Nordonia HS; Macedonia, OH; 53/610 Pres Jr Cls; Chrh Wkr; Ftbl; Trk; Wrstlng; Coach Actv; Scr Kpr; Coll; Bus.

BROADBENT, MARY; East Liverpool HS; E Liverpool, OH; Cls Rep Soph Cls; Cl Rep Jr Cls; Cls Rep Sr Cls; Am Leg Aux Girls St; Band; Cmp Fr Grls; Chrs; Chrh Wkr; Sch Mus; Sch Pl; Ohio St Univ; Bus Ed.

BROADNAX, VAUGHN M; Xenia HS; Xenia, OH; Cls Rep Frsh Cls; Am Leg Boys St; Boy Scts; Chrh Wkr; Hon Rl; Orch; Sct Actv; Letter Ftbl; Letter Trk; Us Naval Acad; Structural Design.

BROADSTREET, KATHY J; Martinsville HS; Martinsville, IN; 111/425 Cls Rep Frsh Cls; Cls Rep Soph Cls; Cl Rep Jr Cls; Off Ade; Stg Crw; Stu Cncl; Chrldng; Indiana Busns Coll; Sec.

BROADSTREET, SHELLY; South Putnam HS; Fillmore, IN; Band; Chrs; Cmnty Wkr; FCA; Sch Mus; Sch Pl; Stg Crw; Yth Flsp; Drama Clb; 4-H; Cosmetology.

BROADUS, HELEN; Walnut Hills HS; Cincinnati, OH; Chrs; Hon Rl; Ger Clb; Capt Chrldng; Univ Of Cincinnati; Med Tech.

BROADWATER, MARK A; Parkersburg HS; Vienna, WV; Am Leg Boys St; Band; Boy Scts; Chrh Wkr; Yth Flsp; Boys Clb Am; Glf; IM Sprt; Mas Awd; Univ.

BROADWAY, NOLA; Western HS; Spring Arbor, MI; Chrs; Debate Tm; Natl Forn Lg; Off Ade; Red Cr Ade; Stu Cncl; Fr Clb; Natl Forensic League Acceptance 77; Jackson Cmnty Coll; LPN.

BROBST, JANET; Windham HS; Windham, OH; 2/77 Sec Sr Cls; Sal; Chrs; Hon Rl; NHS; Fr Clb; Spn Clb; Lion Awd; Columbus Tech Inst; Animal Hlth Tech.

BROCIOUS, LISA; Hubbard HS; Hubbard, OH; Band; Hon Rl; FTA; Youngstown State Univ; Acctg.

BROCK, BYRON; Marysville HS; Marysville, MI; Am Leg Boys St; Drama Clb; Ten; Univ; Engr.

BROCK, DENISE C; Lebanon HS; Lebanon, OH; 28/295 Band; Chrs; Girl Scts; Hon Rl; Jr NHS; Sch Mus; Sch Pl; Drama Clb; FTA; Spn Clb; Won Musical Ach Awd; In Movie Harper Vly PTA As Extra; Lebanon Singers & Dancing Group; Music Schlrshp; Univ Of Cincinnati; Music.

BROCK, DONNA; West Carrollton Sr HS; Dayton, OH; 42/392 VP Chrs; Chrh Wkr; Hon Rl; Jr NHS; NHS; Pol Wkr; Stu Cncl; VP Yth Flsp; VP Fr Clb; Sec OEA; Outstndng Cooperative Office Ed Stu; Outstndng Shorthand Stu; Recipient Of Natl Ambassador Awd In OEA; Sinclair Comm Coll; Busns.

BROCK, J; Hamilton Southeastern HS; Indianapolis, IN; Boy Scts; Chrh Wkr; Hon Rl; JA; Lbry Ade; Sct Actv; Stg Crw; Rdo Clb; Sci Clb; Univ; Bus.

BROCK, PAMELA; Norwood HS; Norwood, OH; Hon Rl; JA; Rptr Sch Nwsp; Fr Clb; Voc Schl; Mass Cmnctns.

BROCK, PATRICK; Princeton HS; Cincinnati, OH; Boy Scts; Hon Rl; Scalet Oaks Voc Schl; Auto Body Mngr.

BROCK, REGINA; Norwood HS; Norwood, OH; Chrs; Girl Scts; Hon Rl; Sch Mus; Pep Clb; Letter Bsbl; Letter Bsktbl; GAA; Univ; Artist.

BROCK, STEVE; Knightstown Community HS; Spiceland, IN; 7/130 Trs Soph Cls; Pres Jr Cls; Am Leg Boys St; NHS; Stu Cncl; Sprt Ed Sch Nwsp; Letter Crs Cntry; Letter Trk; Am Leg Awd; Ball St Univ; Archt.

BROCK, WILLIAM; Cooley HS; Detroit, MI; Cls Rep Frsh Cls; Aud/Vis; Hon Rl; NHS; Stg Crw; FBLA; FTA; Pep Clb; Rdo Clb; Detroit College Of Bus; Acctg.

BROCKER, TERRI; Heritage Christian HS; Indianapolis, IN; Sec Frsh Cls; Sec Soph Cls; Sec Jr Cls; Sec Sr Cls; Sec Band; Hon Rl; Quill & Scroll; Sch Pl; Ed Sch Nwsp; Ger Clb; College; Special Ed.

BROCKERT, CAROL; Wapakoneta Sr HS; Wapakoneta, OH; Chrs; Chrh Wkr; Hon Rl; Sch Mus; Sch Pl; Stg Crw; DECA; Drama Clb; Spn Clb; Univ; Criminal Law.

BROCKETT, LISA; Bryan HS; Bryan, OH; 3/199 Hon Rl; NHS; Letter Trk; GAA; IM Sprt; Ohi State; Financing.

BROCKETTE, RENEE; Northview HS; Grand Rapids, MI; Band; Cmp Fr Grls; Hon Rl; JA; Pol Wkr; Yth Flsp; Key Clb; Letter Glf; Letter Swmmng; Pom Pon; Ferris St Coll; Marketing.

BROCKHOFF, NANCY; Northridge HS; Goshen, IN; Hon Rl; 4-H; Ten; Dnfth Awd; 4-H Awd; JA Awd; Purdue Univ.

BROCKMAN, STEPHEN R; Floyd Central HS; New Albany, IN; 1/343 Val; VP Band; Chrh Wkr; Hon Rl; Jr NHS; NHS; Orch; Letter Ten; Letter Trk; JETS Awd; Floyd Ctnrl HS Athltc Schlstc Awd 1979; Purdue Pres Honor Awd 1979; Edmund K Scott Memrl Fund Schlrshp; Purdue Univ; Civil Engr.

BROCKMAN, TRACY; Lanesville HS; Georgetown, IN; Chrs; FCA; Hon Rl; NHS; Sch Mus; Stu Cncl; Yth Flsp; Rptr Yrbk; 4-H; Pep Clb;.

BROCKMAN, VICKI; Battle Creek Cntrl HS; Battle Crk, MI; 11/466 Band; Hon Rl; NHS; Orch; Sch Mus; Stg Crw; Rptr Sch Nwsp; Drama Clb; Kellogg Comm Coll Bd Of Trustees Awd For Acad Exc; Cert Of Recog St Of Mich Comp Schlrshp Prog; Coll; Pharm.

BROCKMEYER, BETH; Mother Of Mercy HS; Cincinnati, OH; 6/237 Cmnty Wkr; Hon Rl; Lbry Ade; Mod UN; NHS; Thomas More Coll; Psych.

BROCKMEYER, BOBBI; Hilliard HS; Amlin, OH; AFS; Band; Girl Scts; Jr NHS; Lbry Ade; Stg Crw; Stu Cncl; Spn Clb; Swmmng; Jones Count Jr Coll; Coaching.

BROCKMYRE, MICHAEL; St Johns Public HS; St Johns, MI; FCA; Hon Rl; NHS; 4-H; Letter Crs Cntry; Letter Gym; Letter Trk; Coach Actv; IM Sprt; Natl Merit Ltr; Mich State Univ; Pre Med.

BROCKSCHMID, BRETT; Northview HS; Grand Rapids, MI; Ed Sch Nwsp; Mas Awd; Michigan St Univ; Busns Admin.

BROCKSCHMIDT, DIANA; Anderson HS; Cincinnati, OH; 9/377 Cl Rep Jr Cls; Chrs; Girl Scts; Hon Rl; Yth Flsp; Letter Swmmng; Letter Ten; Chrldng; Tmr; SAR Awd; Miami Univ; Educ.

BROCKWAY, ROXANN; Kalkaska HS; Kalkaska, MI; 7/113 Cls Rep Soph Cls; Cl Rep Jr Cls; Band; Lbry Ade; NHS; Sch Pl; Stu Cncl; Rptr Yrbk; Rptr Sch Nwsp; Fr Clb; Michigan Tech Univ; Bus Admin.

BROCKWAY, RUSSELL; Riverside HS; Painesville, OH; Cls Rep Frsh Cls; Pres Soph Cls; Cls Rep Soph Cls; Cl Rep Jr Cls; Boy Scts; Sct Actv; Stu Cncl; Spn Clb; Letter Bsbl; Letter Ftbl; Coll; Busns.

BRODACKI, CAROLYN; Armada HS; Richmond, MI; 6/109 Sec Soph Cls; VP Jr Cls; Pres Band; Hon Rl; Sec NHS; Sch Mus; Sec Stu Cncl; Pep Clb; Letter Trk; Mercy Coll Of Detroit; R N.

BRODE, KEVIN; Fairless HS; Brewster, OH; Cls Rep Frsh Cls; Cls Rep Soph Cls; Cl Rep Jr Cls; Am Leg Boys St; Sch Mus; Sch Pl; Stu Cncl; Drama Clb; Pep Clb; Letter Glf; Univ; Engr.

BRODERICK, LISA; Cathedral HS; Indianapolis, IN; 12/150 Cls Rep Frsh Cls; Chrs; Girl Scts; Hon Rl; Eng Clb; Lat Clb; Chrldng; GAA; IM Sprt; PPFtbl; Honorary Schlrshp To Purdue Univ; Homecoming Qn; Univ Of Dayton; Dentistry.

BRODERICK, MARY E; Marian HS; Berkley, MI; Cls Rep Frsh Cls; Cl Rep Jr Cls; VP Sr Cls; Cls Rep Sr Cls; Aud/Vis; Debate Tm; Hon Rl; Mod UN; Off Ade; Sch Mus; Loyola Univ; Business.

BRODZINSKI, KELLY; La Ville Jr Sr HS; Lakeville, IN; Cls Rep Frsh Cls; Cls Rep Soph Cls; Cl Rep Jr Cls; Cls Rep Sr Cls; Am Leg Aux Girls St; Sec Aud/Vis; Band; Girl Scts; Stu Cncl; 4h Outstndg Jr Ldr Townshp 78; Hnr Bnd & All Conf Band 79; Univ; Forestry.

BRODZINSKI, RHONDA; Buckeye North HS; Smithfield, OH; 23/106 Aud/Vis; Band; FCA; Hon Rl; Lbry Ade; NHS; Sprt Ed Sch Nwsp; Jefferson Tech College; Leg Sec.

BROECKER, MONICA; Lake Fenton HS; Fenton, MI; Band; Chrh Wkr; Hon Rl; NHS; Sch Mus; Cit Awd; Univ Of Michigan; Sec.

BROERING, ELAINE; Marion Local HS; Maria Stein, OH; Sec Soph Cls; VP Jr Cls; Band; Hon Rl; NHS; Off Ade; Sdlty; 4-H; FHA; Pep Clb; College; Nurse.

BROGDON, BONITA; Mount View HS; Thorpe, WV; VP Jr Cls; Band; Chrh Wkr; Hon Rl; 4-H; FHA; Pep Clb; Bus School; Bus Admin.

BROIDA, CAROLINE; North Farmington HS; Farm Hills, MI; Hon Rl; Univ; Med Sci.

BROIDA, CLARK; Copley HS; Akron, OH; Chrs; JA; Rptr Yrbk; Spn Clb; Trk; JA Awd; Univ; Urban Geography.

BROKAMP, MICHAEL G; Jennings Local HS; Ft Jennings, OH; 1/45 Pres Jr Cls; Am Leg Boys St; Band; Chrs; Hon Rl; Orch; Sch Mus; Sch Pl; Stu Cncl; Rptr Sch Nwsp; Univ Of Dayton; Comp Sci.

BROKOB, WILLIAM H; Swan Valley HS; Saginaw, MI; Boy Scts; NHS; Sct Actv; Swmmng; Trk; Natl Merit SF; Michigan State Univ; Sci.

BROMAN, CARL E; Bluffton HS; Bluffton, IN; Am Leg Boys St; Ger Clb; Ftbl; Wrstlng; Univ; Engr.

BROMLEY, ELIZABETH; West Muskingum HS; Brownsville, OH; Chrs; Hon Rl; NHS; Spn Clb; Univ.

BROMLEY, PAMELA J; Pentwater Public HS; Wakefield, MI; Chrh Wkr; Lbry Ade;.

BRONALD, MOLLY; Shelby HS; Shelby, MI; Pres Frsh Cls; Pres Jr Cls; Hon Rl; Jr NHS; NHS; Sch Pl; Stu Cncl; Rptr Sch Nwsp; Drama Clb; Letter Ten; 1/2 Tuition Concssn For Courses At St Bonaventure Univ Smr 79; Univ; Psych.

BRONDOS, JANET; Wintersville HS; Bloomingdale, OH; 4/267 Am Leg Aux Girls St; Band; Chrh Wkr; Girl Scts; Hon Rl; NHS; Pres 4-H; Akron Univ; Pre Med Phys.

BRONISH, LOUISE; Lakewood HS; Lakewood, OH; 40/750 Cls Rep Frsh Cls; Cls Rep Soph Cls; Cls Rep Sr Cls; Hon Rl; JA; NHS; OEA; Rus Clb; JA Awd; Kiwan Awd; The Carnegians Jr Achvmnt Chaptr 79; Louis & Marion Seltzer Awd In Voc Training 79; Jr Achvmnt Schlrshp 79; Cleveland St Univ; Bus.

BRONNER, DARRYL; Cass Technical HS; Detroit, MI; 401/901 Band; Boy Scts; Drl Tm; Mod UN; Off Ade; Sch Mus; Sct Actv; Boys Clb Am; OEA; Data Proc Kypnch At BOEC Reg Comp 1979; Extmprns Verbl Cmmnctns At BOEC Reg 1979; Cond For Ofce Of P 1978; Michigan St Univ; Comp Sci.

BRONSON, DREW; Cheboygan Area HS; Cheboygan, MI; 51/197 Cmnty Wkr; Hon Rl; Fr Clb; Spn Clb; Mich Tech Univ; Comp Sci.

BRONSON, MICHELLE; Marian HS; Cincinnati, OH; Band; FCA; Yrbk; Xavier Univ; Eng.

BRONSON, PAMELA; Memphis HS; Memphis, MI; Band; Girl Scts; Hon Rl; Sch Nwsp; Michigan St Univ; Vet Sci.

BRONSON, SHERRY M; John Adams HS; Cleveland, OH; Girl Scts; Hon Rl; Jr NHS; NHS; Off Ade; FNA; FTA; Univ Of Akron; Nursing.

BROOKE, BARBARA; Cowan HS; Muncie, IN; 8/80 Cls Rep Frsh Cls; Pres Sr Cls; Am Leg Aux Girls St; Band; Debate Tm; Drl Tm; Girl Scts; Hon Rl; Jr NHS; NHS; St Mary Of The Woods; Med Tech.

BROOKER, MATT; Fort Frye HS; Marietta, OH; Hon Rl; NHS; 4-H; Capt Bsktbl; Washington Tech Coll; Mech Engr.

BROOKER, ROBERT F; Anthony Wayne HS; Whitehouse, OH; 4/285 Hst Frsh Cls; Cls Rep Frsh Cls; Cls Rep Soph Cls; Cl Rep Jr Cls; Cls Rep Sr Cls; Band; Hon Rl; NHS; Sci Clb; Letter Bsbl; Toledo; Engineering.

BROOKEY, THOMAS; Park Hills HS; Fairborn, OH; Cls Rep Frsh Cls; Cls Rep Soph Cls; Cl Rep Jr Cls; Chrs; Hon Rl; NHS; Off Ade; VP Stu Cncl; Spn Clb; Mgrs; College; Business.

BROOKHART, ADINA L; Celina Sr HS; Celina, OH; 22/240 NHS; Yth Flsp; FHA; IM Sprt; Wright St Univ; Acctg.

BROOKHART, ANGELA R; Celina Sr HS; Celina, OH; 1/240 Band; Girl Scts; Hon Rl; NHS; Rptr Yrbk; FBLA; Lat Clb; Pep Clb; Capt Chrldng; GAA; Ohio St Univ.

BROOKHART, JULIE; Columbiana HS; Columbiana, OH; 16/101 Sec Sr Cls; Pres Chrs; Hon Rl; Mdrgl; NHS; Rptr Yrbk; Pres Pep Clb; Chrldng; Northern Cmnty Hosp; Radiogcl Tech.

BROOKINS, ANDY; Fredericktown HS; Fredericktown, OH; Hon Rl; VICA; Ohio St Univ; Archt.

BROOKMAN, CHERYL; Lima HS; Lima, OH; Am Leg Aux Girls St; Band; Drm Bgl; Hon Rl; Civ Clb; DECA; Technical Coll; Nurse.

BROOKOVER, DONALD; Wirt County HS; Elizabeth, WV; Cmnty Wkr; Hon Rl; NHS; VP 4-H; Bsktbl; Trk; Coach Actv; 4-H Awd; West Virginia Univ; Acctg.

BROOKOVER, JOE; Windham HS; Garrettsville, OH; 16/110 Band; Chrs; Sch Pl; Drama Clb; Spn Clb; College; Drafting.

BROOKS, ALBERT; Buena Vista HS; Saginaw, MI; Hon Rl; Rptr Sch Nwsp; Sch Nwsp; Bsktbl; Capt Ftbl; IM Sprt; Delta Coll; Archt Design.

BROOKS, AMY; Colerain HS; Cincinnati, OH; Band; Hon Rl; Lbry Ade; Yth Flsp; Sch Nwsp; Fr Clb; Bsktbl; Trk; Natl Merit Ltr;.

BROOKS, BEVERLY; East HS; Akron, OH; 7/320 Sec Sr Cls; Chrs; Drl Tm; Hon Rl; NHS; Off Ade; Sch Mus; Sci Clb; Letter Gym; Letter Swmmng; Univ Of Akron; Busns Admin.

BROOKS, BRUCE; Youngstown South HS; Youngstown, OH; Debate Tm; JA; Off Ade; Sch Pl; Stu Cncl; Drama Clb; Univ; Elec Engr.

BROOKS, CAROL; Divine Child HS; Dearborn Ht, MI; Chrs; Hon Rl; Hosp Ade; Pep Clb; Spn Clb; Letter Trk; GAA; E Michigan Univ; Spec Ed.

BROOKS, CHARLES; Brexton County HS; Sutton, WV; Am Leg Boys St; Band; Boy Scts; Cmnty Wkr; Drm Bgl; Hon Rl; Jr NHS; NHS; Sch Mus; Sch Pl; Univ; Chem Engr.

BROOKS, DARLENE; Jane Addams Vocational HS; Cleveland, OH; Trs Jr Cls; Hon Rl; JA; Jr NHS; Off Ade; Red Cr Ade; Sch Pl; Stu Cncl; Control Data Inst; Comp Prog.

BROOKS, DIANNA; Springboro HS; Springboro, OH; Cmp Fr Grls; Chrs; Chrh Wkr; Hon Rl; Jr NHS; NHS; Yth Flsp; Pep Clb; Chrldng; IM Sprt; Kent Christian Coll; Christ Educ.

BROOKS, EDWIN; North Muskegon HS; North Muskegon, MI; Chrh Wkr; Cmnty Wkr; Sch Mus; Sch Pl; Stg Crw; Rptr Sch Nwsp; Drama Clb; Western Mic Univ; Art Curriculum.

BROOKS, GARY; Northrop HS; Ft Wayne, IN; Crs Cntry; Letter Trk; Yth Incentive Schlrshp From Mc Culloch Ctr 79; Most Improved Track Man Of 79; Indiana Univ; Bus.

BROOKS, GEORGE; Roosevelt HS; Gary, IN; Band; Boy Scts; Chrh Wkr; Hon Rl; JA; Pres FSA; Spn Clb; Math Awd 78; Summr Hon Semnr In St Univ 79; Mite Progr Purdue Univ 79; Indiana St Univ; Comp Sci.

BROOKS, GINA; Alexandria Monroe HS; Alexandria, IN; Spn Clb; 4-H Awd; Ball St Univ; Elem Educ.

BROOKS, GREGORY; Berkeley Springs HS; Berkeley Sp, WV; Cls Rep Frsh Cls; Am Leg Boys St; Boy Scts; Hon Rl; Lbry Ade; Sch Pl; Sct Actv; Stg Crw; Stu Cncl; Sci Clb; College; Pre Med.

BROOKS, GREGORY; Forest Hills Central HS; Ada, MI; Chrh Wkr; Hon Rl; Yth Flsp; Wrstlng; Western Mic Univ; Com Engr.

BROOKS, JACQUELYN R; Crispus A Hucks HS; Indpls, IN; Chrh Wkr; Hon Rl; JA; NHS; Off Ade; Yth Flsp; Lat Clb; St Fnlst In Miss United Teenagr Pageant 79; 2nd Yr Algebra Awd 79; Awd For Mainttng An 8.000 Grd Pt Avg 79; IUPUI; Acctg.

BROOKS, JAMES; Frankfort HS; Ridgeley, WV; Hst Jr Cls; AFS; Hon Rl; NHS; Yrbk; Mth Clb; Trk; Rt Art Awd Glenvl St Coll Art Exhbt 79; 1st Pl 79 Minrl Co & St Soc Studies Fair 79; Frankfrt Hgh Art Hnrs; Fairmont St Coll; Art.

BROOKS, JANET; Pineville HS; Pineville, WV; Band; Cmnty Wkr; Hon Rl; Lbry Ade; Pep Clb; Band Awds 77 78 & 79; Univ; Elem Tchr.

BROOKS, JEFF; Lewis County HS; Weston, WV; Cls Rep Frsh Cls; Cls Rep Soph Cls; Cl Rep Jr Cls;

VP Sr Cls; Chrs; FCA; Pres Key Clb; Capt Ftbl; Letter Trk; Kiwan Awd; Ftbl Schlrshp To Fairmont Coll 79; Mbr Of St Track Tm 78; Fairmont St Coll; Bus Admin.

BROOKS, JENNIFER; Imlay City HS; Imlay City, MI; Band; Girl Scts; Hon Rl; Treas NHS; Yth Flsp; Bsktbl; Crs Cntry; Trk; PPFtbl; 4-H Awd; Michigan St Univ; Earth Sci.

BROOKS, JO L; Ironton HS; Ironton, OH; 38/180 Band; Lbry Ade; Mod UN; NHS; Orch; Quill & Scroll; Rptr Yrbk; Univ Of Cincinnati; Pharmacy.

BROOKS, JONATHAN; Avon HS; Danville, IN; Chrs; Chrh Wkr; Hon Rl; Pol Wkr; Pres Yth Flsp; Sprt Ed Sch Nwsp; Rptr Sch Nwsp; Ger Clb; Sci Clb; Ball St Univ; Jrnlsm.

BROOKS, JOSEPH W; Baldwin HS; Baldwin, MI; 8/68 Band; Chrh Wkr; Cmnty Wkr; Hon Rl; NHS; Sch Pl; Yth Flsp; Sprt Ed Yrbk; Yrbk; Sch Nwsp; Univ; Engr.

BROOKS, K; Northeastern HS; Fountain Cy, IN; 6/148 Trs Frsh Cls; Sec Soph Cls; Sec Jr Cls; Sec Sr Cls; NHS; Sec Stu Cncl; Fr Clb; Letter Gym; Letter Trk; College; Educ.

BROOKS, KAREN; Bullock Creek HS; Midland, MI; 1/152 Trs Jr Cls; VP Sr Cls; Val; Band; Hon Rl; Pres NHS; Yth Flsp; Rptr Yrbk; Rptr Sch Nwsp; 4-H; Michigan Tech Univ; Chem Engr.

BROOKS, KATHY; Olentangy HS; Westerville, OH; Cl Rep Jr Cls; Hon Rl; Lbry Ade; NHS; Stu Cncl; Pep Clb; Spn Clb; Letter Trk; Bowling Green State Univ; Acctg.

BROOKS, KENNETH; Owosso HS; Owosso, MI; Hon Rl; JA; Sch Nwsp; JA Awd; Air Force; Elec.

BROOKS, KIM; North Posey HS; Wadesville, IN; Chrh Wkr; Hon Rl; Fr Clb; Pep Clb; VICA; GAA; Pres Awd; Ambassador Coll.

BROOKS, LAURA; Scottsburg Sr HS; Scottsburg, IN; Cls Rep Sr Cls; Off Ade; Stu Cncl; Rptr Sch Nwsp; 4-H; Fr Clb; Pep Clb; Gym; Chrldng; GAA; Univ Of Kentucky; Comp Oper.

BROOKS, LAURA; Midview HS; Columbia St, OH; 42/260 Band; Girl Scts; Hon Rl; Sct Actv; Stg Crw; 4-H; Spn Clb; Trk; Letter Chrldng; 4-H Awd; Univ Of Toledo; Physics.

BROOKS, MARY; Cathedral HS; Indianapolis, IN; 7/148 AFS; Drl Tm; Hon Rl; NHS; Ed Yrbk; Rptr Yrbk; Rptr Sch Nwsp; Carleton College; Chem.

BROOKS, MICHAEL; Cari Brablec HS; Roseville, MI; Letter Bsbl; Letter Bsktbl; Macomb County Cmnty Coll; Engr.

BROOKS, MICHAEL J; Eisenhower HS; Saginaw, MI; Boy Scts; NHS; Letter Trk; Natl Merit SF; Michigan Tech; Chem Engr.

BROOKS, MICHAEL K; Point Pleasant HS; Letart, WV; Band; Sch Mus; FFA; Pep Clb; VICA; Bsbl; Mgrs; 4-H Awd; Voc Schl; Mech.

BROOKS, PENNY R; Independence HS; Pemberton, WV; Sec Frsh Cls; Cls Rep Soph Cls; Pres Jr Cls; Hon Rl; VP JA; Sec Stu Cncl; Yrbk; Beta Clb; 4-H; FBLA; Sci Fair Awd 1975; Prncpl Awd 1976; Univ; Bus.

BROOKS, RAY; Hobart HS; Hobart, IN; 44/395 Hon Rl; Jr NHS; NHS; Stu Cncl; Letter Bsbl; Letter Ftbl; College; Law.

BROOKS, RENEE; Huntington North HS; Huntington, IN; Cls Rep Soph Cls; Chrs; Chrh Wkr; Hosp Ade; Off Ade; Pres Yth Flsp; Pres 4-H; Pep Clb; 4-H Awd; Lutheran Hosp Schl; Nursing.

BROOKS, RHONDA; Jewett Scio HS; Scio, OH; Band; Girl Scts; Hon Rl; 4-H; FHA; Pep Clb; Gym; Chrldng; 4-H Awd; Columbus Bus Schl.

BROOKS, ROBIN; Midland HS; Midland, MI; Cmp Fr Grls; Chrs; Hon Rl; Lbry Ade; Stu Cncl; Chrldng; College; Commercial Art.

BROOKS, SALLY; Bellefontaine HS; Bellefontaine, OH; 5/210 Am Leg Aux Girls St; Chrs; Chrh Wkr; FCA; Hon Rl; NHS; Sch Mus; Sch Pl; Drama Clb; Chrldng; Ohio Northern Univ; Pharm.

BROOKS, SUSAN; Clyde Sr HS; Green Spg, OH; Am Leg Aux Girls St; Hon Rl; Schlrshp 77; Bus Schl; Offc Sec.

BROOKS, SUZANNE; Hazel Park HS; Ferndale, MI; Chrs; Chrh Wkr; Girl Scts; Sch Mus; Sct Actv; Rptr Sch Nwsp; Drama Clb; Wayne St Univ; Soc Work.

BROOKS, SUZIE; Philip Barbour HS; Belington, WV; Cmp Fr Grls; Chrs; Hon Rl; Sch Pl; Stg Crw; 4-H; Chrldng; Coach Actv; IM Sprt; 4-H Awd; Univ; Art.

BROOKS, TIMOTHY S; Walnut Hills HS; Cincinnati, OH; AFS; Boy Scts; Capt Ftbl; Capt Wrstlng; Natl Merit Commended Stu 1978; Univ; Bus Admin.

BROOME, CHERYL; Washington Cnty Voc Schl; Warner, OH; Band; Chrs; Chrh Wkr; Girl Scts; Hon Rl; Sch Mus; Sch Pl; Sct Actv; 4-H; OEA; Stark Tech Coll; Data Proc.

BROOME, CHERYL L; Washington Co Voc HS; Warner, OH; Band; Chrs; Chrh Wkr; Girl Scts; Hon Rl; Sch Mus; Sch Pl; VP Yth Flsp; 4-H; OEA; Ohio Academic Schlrshp; Best All Around Stu; Data Processing 1st Pl; Stark Tech Coll; Computer Prog.

BROPHEY, JOSEPH; East Liverpool HS; E Liverpool, OH; Key Clb; Lat Clb; Kent St Univ; Law Enforcement.

BROPHEY, MARSHA; East Liverpool HS; E Liverpool, OH; 18/351 Am Leg Aux Girls St; Hon Rl; NHS; Stg Crw; Ed Yrbk; Rptr Yrbk; Drama Clb; Keyettes; Pep Clb; Spn Clb; Indpndnt Std Progr 79; Ohio Tests Of Schlstc Achvmnt Spanish I Bio I & Algbr II; Univ.

BROPHY, SHAWNE; Bishop Ready HS; Columbus, OH; Cls Rep Frsh Cls; Cmp Fr Grls; Hon Rl; Pep Clb; Spn Clb; Coach Actv; Spanish 2nd Yr Awd For Excellnc 77; Spanish 3rd Yr Awd For Excellnc 78; Texas A & M Univ; Elem Spec Educ.

BROSCH, KATHY; North Ridgeville HS; N Ridgeville, OH; Band; Girl Scts; Hon Rl; NHS; Stg Crw; Drama Clb; Ohio St Univ; Engr.

BROSCHART, DONNA; Mc Nicholas HS; Cincinnati, OH; 30/250 Am Leg Aux Girls St; Hon Rl; Lit Mag; NHS; Quill & Scroll; Ed Sch Nwsp; Xavier Univ; Communications.

BROSEY, MARY; Ursuline Academy; Cincinnati, OH; 11/110 Pres Frsh Cls; Cls Rep Sr Cls; Hon Rl; VP NHS; Pol Wkr; Stu Cncl; Fr Clb; Capt Socr; Spec Art Awd For Pottery; Co Chairmn Of Shillitos Tn Bd; Univ; Bus.

BROSH, RICHARD; Wheeling Central Cath HS; Wheeling, WV; Cls Rep Frsh Cls; Cls Rep Soph Cls; Cl Rep Jr Cls; Chrh Wkr; Cmnty Wkr; Hon Rl; Stu Cncl; Key Clb; Trk; Scr Kpr; West Virginia Univ; Engr.

BROSIUS, DIANE; Beaver Local HS; E Liverpool, OH; Trs Frsh Cls; VP Soph Cls; Chrs; Chrh Wkr; Hon Rl; NHS; Sch Mus; Rptr Sch Nwsp; Drama Clb; Eng Clb; Jr Nike Of Yr Awrd 78 79; Best Supporting Actress 78 79; Girls St Rep 79; Univ; Nursing.

BROSKI, JOSEPH; Holy Name Nazareth HS; Maple Hts, OH; 11/320 Hon Rl; Jr NHS; NHS; IM Sprt; Scr Kpr; Cit Awd; Univ; Comp Sci.

BROSKO, KATHRYN; Springfield Local HS; New Midd, OH; 39/158 Cmp Fr Grls; Hon Rl; Off Ade; Yth Flsp; Civ Clb; Pep Clb; Spn Clb; Bsktbl; Honors Diploma; Youngstown St Univ; Elec Engr.

BROSMER, PATRICIA; Jasper HS; Jasper, IN; Hon Rl; JA; Off Ade; Pep Clb; PPFtbl; JA Awd; College; Nursing.

BROSNAHAN, MARY; Dearborn HS; Dearborn, MI; Chrs; Hon Rl; Hosp Ade; Gym; Mercy College; Med.

BROSNAN, JOHN; St Francis De Sales HS; Columbus, OH; Boy Scts; Cmnty Wkr; Hon Rl; Sct Actv; Letter Crs Cntry; Letter Trk; Pres Awd; Scouting Cathlc Relgs Medl 76; Eagle Scout Awd 78; Math Assoc Of Amer Awd 79; Ohio St Univ; Comp Sci.

BROSNAN, KEVIN; Heritage Christian HS; Indianapolis, IN; Am Leg Boys St; Hon Rl; Sch Pl; Pres Stu Cncl; Crs Cntry; Letter Trk; Univ; Bible.

BROSS, BETSY; Wyle E Groves HS; Franklin, MI; Chrs; Hon Rl; Lbry Ade; Yth Flsp; Mich State; Speech Pathologist.

BROSS, CATHY; Seton HS; Cincinnati, OH; 19/255 Cls Rep Frsh Cls; Cls Rep Soph Cls; Girl Scts; Hon Rl; Jr NHS; NHS; Sct Actv; Stu Cncl; FBLA; Lat Clb; Xavier Univ; CPA.

BROSS, JANICE; Bridgman HS; Bridgman, MI; Chrs; Hon Rl; Lbry Ade; Sch Mus; Sch Pl; Letter Trk; Beauty College; Cosmotologist.

BROSS, KAREN; Chelsea HS; Chelsea, MI; Band; Chrs; Chrh Wkr; Hon Rl; Off Ade; Orch; Rptr Sch Nwsp; 4-H; Ger Clb; 4-H Awd; E Michigan Univ; Busns.

BROSSMAN, ROBERT; Linsly Military Inst; Wheeling, WV; Cls Rep Frsh Cls; Cls Rep Soph Cls; Cl Rep Jr Cls; Cls Rep Sr Cls; Band; Drm Bgl; Orch; ROTC; Sch Mus; Stg Crw; W Vir Univ; Aerodynamic Engr.

BROST, MARY; Three Rivers HS; Three Rivers, MI; 12/286 Chrs; Chrh Wkr; Hon Rl; NHS; Yth Flsp; Rptr Sch Nwsp; Ger Clb; Pep Clb; Western Mich Univ.

BROSTOWSKI, MARK; Saint Alphonsus HS; Dearborn Hts, MI; Pres Frsh Cls; Pres Soph Cls; Cl Rep Jr Cls; Band; Chrs; Hon Rl; NHS; Sch Mus; Stu Cncl; College.

BROTHERS, TERESA; Southern Local HS; Salineville, OH; Sec Jr Cls; Girl Scts; Hon Rl; NHS; FHA; OEA; Bus Schl; Comp Progr.

BROTHERS, THERESA; Centreville HS; Sturgis, MI; Band; Hon Rl; Sch Mus; FTA; Spn Clb; Awd For Band 75 78; Awd For Phys Educ 78; Glen Oaks Cmnty Coll; Tchr.

BROTT, CHERI; Geneva Secondary Schl; Geneva, OH; 1/240 Band; Pres NHS; Sch Mus; Rptr Yrbk; Drama Clb; Pres Fr Clb; DAR Awd; Natl Merit Schl; Case Western Reserve Univ; Engr.

BROTT, KENNETH; Green HS; Uniontown, OH; Debate Tm; Hon Rl; Mdrgl; NHS; Sch Mus; Sch Pl; Drama Clb; Letter Crs Cntry; Letter Ten; IM Sprt; Univ; Poli Sci.

BROTT, VICKI; Mona Shores HS; Muskegon, MI; Band; Chrh Wkr; Hon Rl; Bsktbl; Muskegon Community College; Med.

BROUGH, JULIE; Pt Clinton HS; Port Clinton, OH; Am Leg Aux Girls St; Hon Rl; NHS; 4-H; Letter Bsktbl; GAA; Dnfth Awd; 4-H Awd; Acctg.

BROUGH, JULIE; Port Clinton HS; Port Clinton, OH; 4/270 Am Leg Aux Girls St; Hon Rl; NHS; 4-H; Bsktbl; GAA; Dnfth Awd; 4-H Awd; Tiffin Univ; Acctg.

BROUGHTON, RONALD V; Monroe Catholic HS; Monroe, MI; 7/95 Trs Jr Cls; JA; NHS; Rptr Sch Nwsp; Bsktbl; Swmmng; Trk; IM Sprt; Civil Air Ptrl Squadrn Commndr; Vice Pres Ski Clb; Graduated With Hghst Hon From Cath H S; Univ; Engr.

BROUILLET, CAROLE; Elisabeth A Johnson Mrl HS; Mt Morris, MI; Letter Bsbl; Letter Bsktbl; IM Sprt; MSU; Sec Studies.

BROUILLETTE, HELEN; Crown Point HS; Crown Point, IN; 11/490 Chrs; Hon Rl; Mdrgl; MMM; NHS; Sch Mus; Sch Pl; Sec FHA; Lat Clb; Indiana St Univ; Music.

BROUILLETTE, SHERRY; Benton Central Jr Sr HS; Fowler, IN; Am Leg Aux Girls St; FCA; Jr NHS; NHS; Off Ade; OEA; Trk; GAA; IM Sprt; PPFtbl; Voc Schl; Busns.

BROULLIRE, THOMAS; Manistique HS; Manistique, MI; Cls Rep Frsh Cls; Cls Rep Soph Cls; Cl Rep Jr Cls; Treas Stu Cncl; Y-Teens; Letter Swmmng; Letter Trk; Coach Actv; Letter Mgrs; Scr Kpr; Northern Michigan Univ; Mortuary Sci.

BROUSSEAU, JAMES; Imlay City Cmnty HS; Imlay City, MI; Chrs; Natl Forn Lg; Red Cr Ade; Sch Mus; Stu Cncl; Yth Flsp; Sprt Ed Yrbk; Rptr Yrbk; FFA; Treas Sci Clb; Outstndng Chorale Mbr; Morris Speech Improvement Forensics; Eastern Michigan Dept Schlrshp; Eastern Michigan Univ; Music.

BROUWER, JACKIE; Bishop Dwenger HS; Ft Wayne, IN; Girl Scts; Hon Rl; Hosp Ade; Sec JA; College.

BROVONT, JEFF; Rochester HS; Rochester, IN; Am Leg Boys St; Band; FCA; Hon Rl; Ftbl; Letter Swmmng; Letter Trk; Engr.

BROW, RICHARD; Crooksville HS; Crooksville, OH; 19/83 VP Frsh Cls; Hon Rl; Lbry Ade; Stu Cncl; Eng Clb; Pep Clb; Spn Clb; College; Rad Broad.

BROW, WENDY; Northport Public HS; Northport, MI; 6/26 Trs Frsh Cls; Pres Soph Cls; Band; Girl Scts; Jr NHS; NHS; Stu Cncl; 4-H; Pep Clb; Bsktbl; College; Tchr.

BROWDER, ANN; Parkside HS; Jackson, MI; Band; Chrs; Girl Scts; Sct Actv; Yth Flsp; Pep Clb; Gym; Swmmng; Coach Actv; Penn State Univ.

BROWER, C; Nordonia HS; Macedonia, OH; 106/442 FCA; Bsbl; Bsktbl; Letter Ftbl; College; Comp Sci.

BROWER, DAVID; Rossville HS; Rossville, IN; Hon Rl; 4-H; Key Clb; Letter Bsbl; Letter Bsktbl; Voc Schl; Archt Engr.

BROWER, LAURIE; Tri Jr Sr HS; Cambridge, IN; 9/95 Band; Chrh Wkr; Hon Rl; NHS; Sch Pl; Stg Crw; 4-H; Trk; Hnr Roll 1 Full Yr 78; Ohio St Univ; Florist.

BROWER, MARLENE; Cedar Lake Academy; Holland, MI; Sec Soph Cls; Band; Chrh Wkr; Hon Rl; NHS; Off Ade; Stu Cncl; Ed Yrbk; IM Sprt; Cit Awd; Andrews Univ; Nursing.

BROWER, WILLIAM C; Tri Jr Sr HS; Cambridge, IN; 27/92 Band; Chrh Wkr; Hon Rl; Sch Pl; Stg Crw; Drama Clb; Ten; Trk; Wrstlng; SAR Awd; Ohio St Univ; Horticulture.

BROWN, ANGELA; Cass Tech HS; Detroit, MI; Chrs; Chrh Wkr; Cmnty Wkr; Hon Rl; Yth Flsp; Sci Clb; GAA; Cit Awd; Natl Merit Schl; Wayne St Univ; Soc Work.

BROWN, ANGELA; Worthington Jefferson HS; Worthington, IN; 4/40 Am Leg Aux Girls St; Chrs; Chrh Wkr; FCA; Hon Rl; NHS; Stu Cncl; Beta Clb; Sec Ger Clb; Dnfth Awd; Indiana St Univ; Nursing.

BROWN, ANN; Paint Valley HS; Bainbridge, OH; 7/90 VP Soph Cls; VP Jr Cls; Chrh Wkr; Hon Rl; Yth Flsp; Rptr Yrbk; 4-H; Pres FHA; Lat Clb; Sec Sci Clb; Soc Dstngshd Amer HS Stu; Hospital Aide Awrd; College; Medicine.

BROWN, ANTHONY; Warren Western Reserve HS; Warren, OH; Cl Rep Jr Cls; JA; Ftbl; Trk; Capt Wrstlng; Capt IM Sprt; Univ; Jrnlsm.

BROWN, BARRY; Southern Wells HS; Montpelier, IN; 4/96 Pres Soph Cls; Am Leg Boys St; Aud/Vis; Hon Rl; Jr NHS; NHS; Stu Cncl; 4-H; Letter Bsbl; Letter Bsktbl; Univ; Elec Engr.

BROWN, BECKY; Hampshire HS; Augusta, WV; 18/213 Band; Chrs; Chrh Wkr; Drl Tm; Hon Rl; Hosp Ade; NHS; Sch Pl; Yth Flsp; Rptr Yrbk; Fairmont St Univ; Nursing.

BROWN, BRIAN; Alpena HS; Ossineke, MI; Chrh Wkr; Hon Rl; Bsbl; Ftbl; Alpena Comm Coll; Forestry.

BROWN, BRUCE; Ayersville HS; Defiance, OH; 12/88 Hon Rl; Stu Cncl; 4-H; Spn Clb; Letter Bsktbl; Letter Crs Cntry; Letter Trk; Coach Actv; Coll; Elem Educ.

BROWN, CAMILLE; Williamstown HS; Williamstown, WV; Trs Sr Cls; AFS; Pep Clb; Letter Mgrs; Potomac St Univ; Elem Educ.

BROWN, CARLA; Marian HS; Detroit, MI; Chrh Wkr; Girl Scts; Hon Rl; JA; Sch Pl; Yth Flsp; Trk; Chrldng; Twrlr; Cit Awd; College; Busns Admin.

BROWN, CARLA; Southern Local HS; Lisbon, OH; 19/82 Cmp Fr Grls; Chrs; Chrh Wkr; Hon Rl; Off Ade; FNA; Trk; Chrldng; Photography Schl; Photog.

BROWN, CARLIE; Kent Roosevelt HS; Kent, OH; Band; Chrs; Drl Tm; Hon Rl; Pep Clb; Swmmng; Pom Pon; Honorable Mention In Ohio Tests Of Scholastic Ach; 1st Yr Spanish Div I; Schlrshp Awds 3.5 Avg; Miami Univ Of Ohio; Law.

BROWN, CAROL; Defiance HS; Defiance, OH; Chrs; Hon Rl; Jr NHS; Sch Mus; Sch Pl; Stg Crw; Rptr Sch Nwsp; Pres 4-H; Spn Clb; 4-H Awd; College; Surgeon.

BROWN, CATHERINE M; Alma HS; Alma, MI; 13/250 Cls Rep Soph Cls; Trs Sr Cls; Band; NHS; Letter Trk; Chrldng; Natl Merit SF; Univ Of Michigan; Jrnlsm.

BROWN, CATHERINE R; Wadsworth Sr HS; Rittman, OH; 5/350 Cls Rep Frsh Cls; Chrs; Girl Scts; Hon Rl; NHS; Stu Cncl; Rptr Yrbk; 4-H; Fr Clb; Pep Clb; Ohio State Univ; Vet.

BROWN, CEDRIC M; Belmont HS; Dayton, OH; Chrh Wkr; Hon Rl; Sct Actv; DECA; Spn Clb; VICA; 3rd Pl Awd Schl Woodshop Display Craftmanship; Wright State Univ; Mgmt.

BROWN, CHANDRA; Romulus Sr HS; Romulus, MI; 62/308 Hon Rl; NHS; Stu Cncl; 4-H; Capt Bsktbl; Trk; Chrldng; Cit Awd; 4-H Awd; Kiwan Awd; Awd Th Athletic Dr Awd 79; Schlrshp Wayne Cnty Cmnty Coll For Summer Schl 79; Tuskegee Inst Univ; Youth Ldrshp.

BROWN, CHARLES; Du Pont Sr HS; Belle, WV; Chrh Wkr; Hon Rl; Jr NHS; Sct Actv; Stu Cncl; Fr Clb; Letter Bsktbl; Letter Trk; IM Sprt; Kanawha Cnty Sheriffs Camp 76; West Virginia Inst Of Tech; Engr.

BROWN, CHARLES; Holland HS; Holland, MI; Pres Frsh Cls; Cls Rep Soph Cls; Cl Rep Jr Cls; Cls Rep Sr Cls; Boy Scts; Stu Cncl; Yrbk; Ger Clb; Glf; Most Valuable Officer 77; Univ; Archt.

BROWN, CHARLES A; Shortridge HS; Indianapolis, IN; Cls Rep Frsh Cls; Cls Rep Soph Cls; Cl Rep Jr Cls; Hon Rl; JA; Key Clb; Mth Clb; Bsbl; Trk; JA Awd; Univ; Engr.

BROWN, CHRIS; Chillicothe HS; Chillicothe, OH; Cls Rep Frsh Cls; Am Leg Boys St; Chrs; Chrh Wkr; Cmnty Wkr; Hon Rl; NHS; Sch Pl; Bsbl; Am Leg Awd; Liberty Baptist Coll; Youth Ministry.

BROWN, CINDA; Lawrence Central HS; Indianapolis, IN; Cmnty Wkr; Girl Scts; Hon Rl; Jr NHS; NHS; Off Ade; Pol Wkr; Sct Actv; Yth Flsp; Beta Clb; College; Tchr.

BROWN, CINDY; Cambridge HS; Cambridge, OH; 10/270 Cl Rep Jr Cls; Trs Sr Cls; Band; Chrs; Hon Rl; JA; NHS; Sec Stu Cncl; Letter Trk; Purdue Univ; Sci.

BROWN, CINDY; Norwood HS; Norwood, OH; Band; Hon Rl; Off Ade; Orch; Sch Mus; Sct Actv; Lat Clb; Tmr; Berklee Schl Of Music; Composer.

BROWN, CINDY; Boardman HS; Youngstown, OH; 53/585 Chrs; Chrh Wkr; Hon Rl; Y-Teens; Fr Clb; Youngstown State; Radiology.

BROWN, CINDY; Brookville HS; Brookville, IN; 4/196 Cl Rep Jr Cls; Cmnty Wkr; Hon Rl; Pol Wkr; Stu Cncl; Rptr Yrbk; Yrbk; GAA; College; Rn.

BROWN, CONNIE; Medina Sr HS; Barberton, OH; 9/341 AFS; Am Leg Aux Girls St; Girl Scts; Hon Rl; NHS; 4-H; Capt Crs Cntry; Letter Trk; Univ Of Cincinnati; Aero Engr.

BROWN, CYNTHIA; Churubusco HS; Churubusco, IN; Chrh Wkr; Hon Rl; Treas FTA; VP OEA; Acad Schlshp 79; Michigan Christian Coll; Bus Admin.

BROWN, CYNTHIA; Cass Tech HS; Detroit, MI; Chrh Wkr; Cmnty Wkr; Hon Rl; ROTC; Y-Teens; FTA; Cit Awd;.

BROWN, CYNTHIA; Whitehall Yearling HS; Whitehall, OH; Cl Rep Jr Cls; Drl Tm; Girl Scts; Hon Rl; Treas NHS; Red Cr Ade; Fr Clb; Scr Kpr; Coll; Elem Ed.

BROWN, CYNTHIA MARI; Colerain HS; Cincinnati, OH; Chrh Wkr; Hon Rl; Jr NHS; NHS; Off Ade; Drama Clb; Fr Clb; Natl Merit SF; William And Mary; Eng Lit.

BROWN, DANIEL; Fairless HS; Navarre, OH; 18/235 Pres Sr Cls; Aud/Vis; Hon Rl; Jr NHS; NHS; Stu Cncl; Chmn Drama Clb; Mgrs; Akron Univ; Elec Tech.

BROWN, DANIEL; Holgate HS; Holgate, OH; Cl Rep Jr Cls; Chrh Wkr; Cmnty Wkr; Hon Rl; Stu Cncl; Yth Flsp; Mth Clb; VICA; Bsbl; Letter Bsktbl; Univ; Engr.

BROWN, DARLING; Elk Garden HS; Elk Garden, WV; Band; Chrs; Hon Rl; Sch Pl; Sch Nwsp; Letter Bsktbl; Scr Kpr; Voice Dem Awd; Univ; Nursing.

BROWN, DAVID; Grove City HS; Orient, OH; 1/480 Pres Soph Cls; Cls Rep Soph Cls; Pres Jr Cls; Cl Rep Jr Cls; Pres Sr Cls; Cls Rep Sr Cls; Band; Hon Rl; Jr NHS; VP Stu Cncl; Rotary Intl Camp Entprs 1979; Univ; Bus Mgmt.

BROWN, DAVID; Westfield Washington HS; Westfield, IN; Chrh Wkr; Ftbl; Trk; Wrstlng; IM Sprt; Bus Schl; Rest Mgmt.

BROWN, DAVID; Quincy HS; Quincy, MI; 10/179 Boy Scts; Chrh Wkr; Hon Rl; NHS; Letter Bsktbl; Scr Kpr; Tmr; 4-H Awd; Univ; Bus Admin.

BROWN, DAVID; Little Miami HS; Maineville, OH; Cl Rep Jr Cls; Chrs; Hon Rl; NHS; Letter Bsbl; Letter Bsktbl; Letter Ftbl; College.

BROWN, DEBORAH; Dublin HS; Dublin, OH; 48/153 Am Leg Aux Girls St; Band; Cmp Fr Grls; Chrh Wkr; Hon Rl; Orch; Stg Crw; Yth Flsp; Ed Yrbk; Yrbk; Univ Of Cincinnati; Archt.

BROWN, DEBRA; Austin HS; Austin, IN; 10/100 Chrh Wkr; Hon Rl; Ed Sch Nwsp; Sch Nwsp; FTA;.

BROWN, DEBRA P; Our Lady Of Angels HS; Cincinnati, OH; Chrs; Chrh Wkr; Girl Scts; Hon Rl; Lbry Ade; Sch Pl; Sct Actv; Sdlty; Beta Clb; Spn Clb; 1st Pl Awd For Black Hstry Essay Contest 78; 2nd Pl Awd For 79 Sci Fair; Ldrshp Wrkshp Recognition 79; Univ Of Cincinnati; Pharm.

BROWN, DECELIA; East Knox HS; Howard, OH; Band; Hon Rl; Sch Pl; Sch Nwsp; DECA; Drama Clb; Pep Clb; Spn Clb; Capt Bsktbl; Ftbl; College; Phys Ed.

BROWN, DEIDRE; Colonel Crawford HS; Bucyrus, OH; Band; Chrh Wkr; Hon Rl; NHS; Pres 4-H; 4-H Awd; Univ; Med.

BROWN, DENISE; John F Kennedy HS; Taylor, MI; Cls Rep Frsh Cls; Hon Rl; Off Ade; Yrbk; Coll.

BROWN, DENISE; Defiance HS; Defiance, OH; Hon Rl; Jr NHS; Off Ade; Orch; Stg Crw; Stu Cncl; Rptr Sch Nwsp; 4-H; Spn Clb; Mgrs; Coll; Comm Art.

BROWN, DEREK T; Stivers Patterson HS; Dayton, OH; 210/428 Cmp Fr Grls; Chrs; Chrh Wkr; Hon Rl; Sch Pl; Yrbk; Ftbl; JETS Awd; Univ Of Cincinnati; Engr.

BROWN, DIANE; Flemington HS; Flemington, WV; 6/47 Band; Chrs; NHS; Yth Flsp; Rptr Yrbk; Pres 4-H; Fr Clb; VP FHA; Dnfth Awd; 4-H Awd; Warren Wilson Coll; Journalism.

BROWN, DIANE; Lynchburg Clay HS; Lynchburg, OH; Band; FCA; Girl Scts; Hon Rl; Sch Pl; Stu Cncl; Pep Clb; Bsktbl; Letter Trk; Gym; College; Nurse.

BROWN, DONNA; West Catholic HS; Conklin, MI; Chrh Wkr; Hon Rl; NHS; Yrbk; 4-H; Fr Clb; PPFtbl; Voc School; Med.

BROWN, DONNA K; Fort Frye HS; Lowell, OH; 9/123 Am Leg Aux Girls St; Band; Chrh Wkr; Hon Rl; NHS; Sch Mus; Sch Pl; Yth Flsp; 4-H; Spn Clb; Englsih Honorary Soc; Art Honorary; Marching Band Awd; College; Journalism.

BROWN, DOUGLAS; Gladwin HS; Gladwin, MI; Chrs; Chrh Wkr; Hon Rl; NHS; Rptr Sch Nwsp; Bsktbl; Crs Cntry; Trk; Univ.

BROWN, DWIGHT; Champion HS; Warren, OH; Band; Chrs; Chrh Wkr; Hon Rl; Yth Flsp; Bsktbl; IM Sprt; Olivet Nazerene Coll; Bus.

BROWN, EDDIE L; Garaway HS; Sugarcreek, OH; Pres Frsh Cls; Cls Rep Soph Cls; VP Jr Cls; Am Leg Boys St; Boy Scts; Hon Rl; NHS; Sch Pl; Stu Cncl; Yrbk; Eagle Scout 1978; St F F A Degree 1978; Ohio St Univ; Educ.

BROWN, ELAINE; Stivers Patterson Co Op HS; Dayton, OH; 120/428 Cls Rep Frsh Cls; Chrs; Chrh Wkr; Cmnty Wkr; Hon Rl; Hosp Ade; Stu Cncl; Yth Flsp; Boys Clb Am; VICA; Amer Natl Red Cross Cert Of First Aid & CPR 79; Univ; Med.

BROWN, ELAINE; Clarksville HS; Clarksville, IN; 3/175 Sec Soph Cls; Hon Rl; VP JA; NHS; Quill & Scroll; Stu Cncl; Rptr Yrbk; Rptr Sch Nwsp; Civ Clb; Drama Clb; Indiana Univ S E.

BROWN, ELIZABETH A; Jonesville HS; Jonesville , MI; 1/95 Cls Rep Sr Cls; Val; Hon Rl; NHS; Pol Wkr; Stu Cncl; Pres 4-H; Letter Trk; 4-H Awd; Harvard Univ; Juvenile Law.

BROWN, ELIZABETH; Upper Arlington HS; Columbus, OH; FCA; Lbry Ade; Off Ade; Yth Flsp; FHA; Pep Clb; Spn Clb; VICA; Coach Actv; Mgrs; Ohio St Univ; Bus.

BROWN, ELIZABETH; Southfield HS; Southfeld, MI; Band; Chrs; Sch Mus; Sch Pl; Drama Clb; Trk; Chrldng; Tmr; Univ; Pre Med.

BROWN, ERICA L; South HS; Columbus, OH; Cls Rep Frsh Cls; Pres Jr Cls; VP Jr Cls; Hon Rl; Jr NHS; Sch Pl; Drama Clb; OEA; Bsbl; Bsktbl; Univ; Bus Admin.

BROWN, ERIN; Kelloggsville HS; Kentwood, MI; Chrs; Drm Bgl; Girl Scts; PAVAS; Sch Mus; Sch Pl; Civ Clb; Spn Clb; Hndbl; Mgrs; Barbizon School; Cosmotology.

BROWN, GAIL R; Lakola HS; W Chester, OH; 40/446 Band; Hon Rl; NHS; Red Cr Ade; Spn Clb; GAA; IM Sprt; Mgrs; Excel In Spnsh 76 79; Straight A 76 79; Perfect Attend Awd 76; Univ Of Kentucky; Bus Admin.

BROWN, GEORGE A; Troy HS; Sherman Oaks, CA; 65/315 Pres Frsh Cls; Cls Rep Frsh Cls; Pres Soph Cls; Cls Rep Soph Cls; Pres Jr Cls; Cl Rep Jr Cls; Hon Rl; NHS; Stu Cncl; VICA; Univ Of S California; Bio.

BROWN, GLEN; Jefferson Area HS; Jefferson, OH; Am Leg Boys St; Chrs; Bsktbl; Crs Cntry; Coach Actv; Univ; Finance.

BROWN, GLENN; Brighton HS; Brighton, MI; Chrh Wkr; FCA; Hon Rl; Lawrence Inst Tech Univ; Bus Admin.

BROWN, GREG; Taft HS; Hamilton, OH; Band; Boy Scts; Chrh Wkr; Hon Rl; Jr NHS; Lit Mag; Sct Actv; Yth Flsp; Wrstlng; Miami Univ; Banking.

BROWN, HEATHER H; Andrews HS; Westfield, NY; Hon Rl; Y-Teens; Culinary Inst Of Amer; Foods.

BROWN, HEATHER H; Andrews School; Westfield, NY; Hon Rl; Y-Teens; 100 Schlshp For Foods Major From Foods Tchrs 79; 3rd Pl Andrews Schl Fall House Show 79; Culinary Inst Of Amer; Food Prep.

BROWN, HUGH; Memorial HS; St Marys, OH; 36/223 Band; Boy Scts; Chrs; Chrh Wkr; Hon Rl; Stg Crw; Yth Flsp; 4-H; Lat Clb; Ten; Univ; Vet Sci.

BROWN, HUGH H; Memorial HS; St Marys, OH; 36/223 Chrs; Hon Rl; Jr NHS; NHS; Sch Mus; Stg Crw; Yth Flsp; Rptr Yrbk; Rptr Sch Nwsp; 4-H; Univ; Vet.

BROWN, INGE; Bluefield HS; Bluefield, WV; 68/365 Girl Scts; Hon Rl; Off Ade; Spn Clb; Bsktbl; GAA; Mgrs; Scr Kpr; Cit Awd; Natl Merit Ltr; Bible Cert Awd 77; Bluefield St Coll; Crim Law.

BROWN, JACKIE; Tuslaw HS; N Lawrence, OH; 12/168 Chrh Wkr; Hon Rl; OEA; R G Drage Educ Ctr; Acctg.

BROWN, JAMES; Glen Este HS; Mt Carmel, OH; Am Leg Boys St; Boy Scts; Hon Rl; NHS; SAR Awd; Miami Univ; Pre Med.

BROWN, JANET; Rockville HS; Rockville, IN; 21/93 Aud/Vis; Band; Hon Rl; Pres Lbry Ade; Rptr Sch Nwsp; Fr Clb; Pep Clb; Mgrs; Scr Kpr; Tmr; Gran Ambassdr Of Good Will Intl Ord Of Rainbow Girls 76; St Sec In Stdnt Media Assoc 79; Vincennes Univ; French Tchr.

BROWN, JANICE; Hamilton Southeastern HS; Noblesville, IN; Chrs; Hon Rl; NHS; 4-H; Treas OEA; Ten; 4-H Awd; Perfect Attndnc; Jr Schlrshp; Ball St Univ; Acctg.

BROWN, JANIE C; Emerson HS; Gary, IN; Band; Hon Rl; Stu Cncl; Drama Clb; Letter Trk; Capt Chrldng; Indiana Univ N W.

BROWN, JAY; Bedford N Lawrence HS; Bedford, IN; 39/420 Band; Boy Scts; Hon Rl; NHS; Sct Actv; Ger Clb; Sci Clb; Univ Of Evansville; Engr.

BROWN, JEFF; Eastman Sr HS; Columbus, OH; Aud/Vis; Hon Rl; Crs Cntry; Capt Swmmng; Trk; Univ; Computers.

BROWN, JEFFREY; Williamston HS; Williamston, MI; 10/160 Band; Drm Mjrt; PAVAS; Sch Mus; Sch Pl; Rptr Yrbk; Yrbk; Rptr Sch Nwsp; Sch Nwsp; Drama Clb; MSU; Motion Picture Arts.

BROWN, JENNIFER; Oceana HS; Oceana, WV; Girl Scts; Hon Rl; PAVAS; Rptr Yrbk; Spn Clb; IM Sprt; Concord Coll; Elem Ed.

BROWN, JENNIFER; Sandusky HS; Monroeville, OH; 95/404 Lbry Ade; DECA; BGSU.

BROWN, JENNIFER; Oceana HS; Oceana, WV; Cmp Fr Grls; Chrh Wkr; Cmnty Wkr; FCA; Girl Scts; PAVAS; Pol Wkr; Sch Pl; Yth Flsp; Concord College; Bus Mgmt.

BROWN, JENNIFER L; Seton HS; Cincinnati, OH; 21/272 Cl Rep Jr Cls; Hon Rl; NHS; College; Pharmacy.

BROWN, JILL; Morgan HS; Mc Connelsville, OH; Band; Drm Bgl; Hon Rl; Jr NHS; NHS; Sch Mus; Pep Clb; Spn Clb; Letter Gym; Chrldng; Cincinnati Univ; Dent Hygnst.

BROWN, JIM; Jackson HS; Wellston, OH; 144/228 Chrs; Chrh Wkr; Sch Mus; Sch Pl; Yth Flsp; 4-H; 4-H Awd; Ohio St Univ; Animal Sci.

BROWN, JOHN C; River Valley HS; Sawyer, MI; 1/150 Cl Rep Jr Cls; Pres Sr Cls; NHS; Stu Cncl; VP Ger Clb; Natl Merit Ltr; Univ; Comp Systems.

BROWN, JOY; Fairfield Union HS; Lancaster, OH; 56/150 Band; Hon Rl; Rptr Yrbk; Rptr Sch Nwsp; Ohio Univ Lancaster; Med Sec.

BROWN, JULIANNE; Stephen T Badin HS; Hamilton, OH; 5/217 Cls Rep Frsh Cls; Cl Rep Jr Cls; VP Sr Cls; Hon Rl; NHS; Ed Yrbk; Fr Clb; Scr Kpr; Lion Awd; Rotary Awd; Univ Of Tenn; Sci.

BROWN, JULIE; Carey HS; Carey, OH; Band; Chrs; Hon Rl; NHS; Orch; Sch Mus; Yth Flsp; Drama Clb; Lat Clb; DAR Awd; Wittenberg Univ; Medicine.

BROWN, JULIE; Jay County HS; Dunkirk, IN; 15/500 Band; Hon Rl; Jr NHS; Lit Mag; NHS; Y-Teens; Mth Clb; Sci Clb; Letter Ten; College.

BROWN, JULIE; John Marshall HS; Indianapolis, IN; Hon Rl; JA; Quill & Scroll; Rptr Yrbk; Yrbk; Spn Clb; College; Journalism.

BROWN, JULIE A; Waynesfield Goshen HS; Lakeview, OH; 4/60 Chrs; Chrh Wkr; Hon Rl; NHS; Yth Flsp; Rptr Yrbk; Spn Clb; Univ; Psych.

BROWN, KAREN; Edison HS; Milan, OH; 11/185 VP Frsh Cls; Sec Sr Cls; Chrs; Hon Rl; NHS; Sch Pl; Stg Crw; Drama Clb; Mth Clb; Mgrs; Univ; Pre Med.

BROWN, KAREN; Marietta Sr HS; Marietta, OH; AFS; Chrs; Chrh Wkr; Spn Clb; College; Education.

BROWN, KATHIE; Brighton HS; Brighton, MI; Hon Rl; Baker Jr Coll; Acctg.

BROWN, KATHLEEN; Dominican HS; Detroit, MI; Trs Soph Cls; Trs Sr Cls; Chrs; Mdrgl; Sch Mus; Swmmng; Chrldng; Pom Pon; PPFtbl; Mic State Univ; Rn.

BROWN, KATHRYN; Princeton HS; Cincinnati, OH; Chrh Wkr; Hon Rl; Off Ade; DECA; OEA; E Kentucky Univ; Exec Sec.

BROWN, KAYE; Harper Creek HS; Battle Creek, MI; Cls Rep Frsh Cls; Trs Sr Cls; Chrs; Drl Tm; Hon Rl; NHS; Sch Mus; Drama Clb; Glf; Capt Pom Pon; Broward Cmnty Coll; Tchr.

BROWN, KELLY; Franklin HS; Franklin, OH; Hon Rl; GAA; IM Sprt; College; Engineering.

BROWN, KENDRA; Rock Hill HS; Kitts Hill, OH; Band; Chrh Wkr; Cmnty Wkr; Hon Rl; Yth Flsp;.

BROWN, KIM; Pendleton Heights HS; Anderson, IN; Sec Frsh Cls; Trs Soph Cls; Cl Rep Jr Cls; Band; Drl Tm; Off Ade; Quill & Scroll; Rptr Yrbk; Rptr Sch Nwsp; Sch Nwsp; Ball St Univ; Jrnlsm.

BROWN, KIMBERLY; Maumee HS; Toledo, OH; 24/335 Am Leg Aux Girls St; Band; Hon Rl; Lbry Ade; NHS; Quill & Scroll; Sch Pl; Ed Yrbk; Rptr Sch Nwsp; Pres DECA; Frat Order Of Egls N Smith Mem Schlrshp 79; Oh Brd Of Regents Academic Achvmnt Progr 3rd Pl Cert 79; Columbus Coll Of Art; Fshn Dsgn.

BROWN, KIMBERLY; Grafton HS; Graftan, WV; Chrh Wkr; Hon Rl; Yth Flsp; Fr Clb; Fairmont St Coll; Med Lab Tech.

BROWN, KIMBERLY; Maumee HS; Toledo, OH; 24/335 Am Leg Aux Girls St; Band; Hon Rl; Lbry Ade; NHS; Quill & Scroll; Sch Pl; Ed Yrbk; Rptr Sch Nwsp; DECA; Columbus Coll Art & Design; Fshn Dsg.

BROWN, KIMBERLY; Shadyside HS; Shadyside, OH; Band; Chrs; Hon Rl; Sch Mus; Sch Pl; Yth Flsp; Y-Teens; Drama Clb; Spn Clb; GAA; College; Nursing.

BROWN, KIMBERLY; Madison HS; Madison, OH; Cls Rep Frsh Cls; Cls Rep Soph Cls; Cl Rep Jr Cls; Hon Rl; Stu Cncl; Y-Teens; Bsktbl; Trk; Tmr; College; Med.

BROWN, KIRSTEN C; Norwalk HS; Norwalk, OH; VP Frsh Cls; Hon Rl; Sch Pl; Stu Cncl; Rptr Sch Nwsp; Drama Clb; Fr Clb; Pep Clb; Chrldng; GAA; Thunderstorms Of Thought Hon Mention Poetry Awd 1978; Pep Club Awd 1976; Univ; Jrnlsm.

BROWN, KURT; Morgantown HS; Morgantwon, WV; Cls Rep Frsh Cls; Cls Rep Soph Cls; Cl Rep Jr Cls; VP Sr Cls; Hon Rl; Bsbl; Letter Ftbl; Wrstlng; Wv Univ; Dentistry.

BROWN, KURT; Orchard View HS; Muskegon, MI; 6/213 Sec Sr Cls; Trs Sr Cls; Boy Scts; Hon Rl; JA; NHS; Trk; Western Mich Univ; Bus Admin.

BROWN, L; Delphos Jefferson Sr HS; Delphos, OH; Band; Chrs; Hon Rl; Sch Mus; Rptr Yrbk; Spn Clb; Lima Tech Schl; Nursing.

BROWN, LAURA; Marshall HS; Marshall, MI; Chrs; Chrh Wkr; Debate Tm; Hon Rl; Mdrgl; Natl Forn Lg; NHS; Sch Mus; Sch Pl; Stg Crw; Awd For Otstndng Work In Drama 79; Awd For Otstndng Work In Eng 79; Awd For Particptn In St SSA Hon Choir; Univ; Musical Theatre.

BROWN, LAURA; Madison Hts HS; Anderson, IN; Am Leg Aux Girls St; FCA; Hon Rl; Pres NHS; Letter Ten; Am Leg Awd; Univ.

BROWN, LESLIE; Shaker Heights HS; Shaker Hts, OH; Cls Rep Frsh Cls; VP Soph Cls; VP Jr Cls; Pres Sr Cls; Drl Tm; Hon Rl; Red Cr Ade; Stu Cncl; Sch Nwsp; GAA; Spelman Coll; Biomedical Engr.

BROWN, LESLIE; Clinton Massie HS; Harveysburg, OH; 10/115 Cls Rep Frsh Cls; Sec Band; Drl Tm; Drm Mjrt; NHS; Sch Mus; Stu Cncl; 4-H; Bsbl; PPFtbl; College; Communications.

BROWN, LESLIE J; Buckeye North HS; Smithfield, OH; 25/119 Band; Chrh Wkr; FCA; Hon Rl; NHS; Sch Pl; Stu Cncl; Sci Clb; Ftbl; Wrstlng;.

BROWN, LINDA; Reynoldsburg HS; Reynoldsburg, OH; Chrh Wkr; Hon Rl; JA; Lbry Ade; Pol Wkr; Ed Yrbk; Rptr Yrbk; Rptr Sch Nwsp; Natl Merit Ltr; Ohio Tests Of Schlstc Achievement Eng 9 Honorable Mention In Dst 77; NEDT Top 10%; Spice Club Lang Std; Univ; Pre Law.

BROWN, LINDA; Battle Creek Central HS; Battle Creek, MI; Trs Soph Cls; Band; JA; Police Cmnty Rltns Yth Awd 79; Mi Brd Of Ed Schlrshp 79; Western Michigan Univ; Archt.

BROWN, LINDA; Bosse HS; Evansville, IN; 11/329 Cls Rep Soph Cls; Trs Jr Cls; Cl Rep Jr Cls; Cls Rep Sr Cls; Hon Rl; NHS; Quill & Scroll; Sec Stu Cncl; Sch Nwsp; Pep Clb; Univ.

BROWN, LISA; Portage Township HS; Houghton, MI; Band; Girl Scts; Hon Rl; Natl Forn Lg; Ed Sch Nwsp; Letter Trk; Pres Awd; Alma Coll; Languages.

BROWN, LISA K; Cardinal Ritter HS; Indianapolis, IN; 10/147 Cls Rep Frsh Cls; Pres Soph Cls; Cl Rep Jr Cls; Chrs; Drl Tm; Girl Scts; Hon Rl; Mdrgl; MMM; NHS; Honor Awrd In Eng 1 & 2; Honor Awrd In Speech 1 & 2; Cntrl Ind Music Cont Vocal 76 79; Univ; Dent Hygiene.

BROWN, LISE; Bloomington HS; Bloomington, IN; 1/393 Val; Chrs; Girl Scts; Hon Rl; NHS; Sch Mus; Letter Swmmng; College; Research Sci.

BROWN, LORELLE R; William A Wirt HS; Gary, IN; 21/220 VP Frsh Cls; Sec Soph Cls; Trs Soph Cls; VP Jr Cls; Trs Sr Cls; Band; Chrs; Chrh Wkr; Girl Scts; Hon Rl; Indiana Univ; Tele Communications.

BROWN, LORI S; Edison Sr HS; Merriville, IN; Hon Rl; VP OEA; Coach Actv; Chrldng; Voc Ed Awd At The Gary Area Career Cntr 79; Typing II 3rd Pl Awd At The Gary Area Career Cntr 79; Mc Cormick Voc Schl; Steno.

BROWN, LOU; Mt Gilead HS; Mt Gilead, OH; 10/105 Chrh Wkr; Hon Rl; Lbry Ade; VP Spn Clb; Letter Gym; Capital Univ; Library Sci.

BROWN, LYNN; Northwood HS; Nappanee, IN; C mp Fr Grls; Chrs; Hon Rl; Off Ade; Pep Clb; Letter Gym; Trk; Chrldng; GAA; IM Sprt; College; Nurse.

BROWN, MARCY; William A Wirt HS; Gary, IN; Hon Rl; GAA; Bus Schl; Comp Progr.

BROWN, MARIA; John Hay HS; Cleveland, OH; Cls Rep Soph Cls; Chrs; Jr NHS; Sch Pl; Stu Cncl; Drama Clb; Trk; Coll; Law.

BROWN, MARIFRAN; Interlochen Arts Academy; Traverse City, MI; Cls Rep Frsh Cls; Chrh Wkr; Cmnty Wkr; Hon Rl; Orch; Pol Wkr; Sch Mus; Stu Cncl; Yth Flsp; Cit Awd; Univ Of Michigan; Sci.

BROWN, MARK; Big Walnut HS; Sunbury, OH; Chrh Wkr; FCA; Yth Flsp; Fr Clb; Leo Clb; Bsktbl; Trk; Scr Kpr; Tmr; Univ.

BROWN, MARK; Seaholm HS; Birmingham, MI; Cls Rep Frsh Cls; VP Soph Cls; Pres Jr Cls; Band; Boy Scts; Debate Tm; Natl Forn Lg; Sch Pl; Stg Crw; Stu Cncl; Michigan St Univ; Bus Admin.

BROWN, MARK; N Canton Hoover HS; North Canton, OH; Cmnty Wkr; Hon Rl; Orch; Sct Actv; Letter Swmmng; Tmr; College; Creative Writing.

BROWN, MARK R; Milford HS; Highland, MI; Aud/Vis; Chrs; Chrh Wkr; Mod UN; PAVAS; Sch Mus; Sch Pl; Stg Crw; Drama Clb; Wrstlng; Ball State Univ; Drama.

BROWN, MARTIN E; North Central HS; Indianapolis, IN; 25/1065 Boy Scts; Hon Rl; NHS; Pol Wkr; Natl Merit Ltr; Amer Chem Soc Test Hon Mntn; Cross Cntry Team Mst Imprvd Runner; Indiana Univ; Chem.

BROWN, MELANIE D; Lewis County HS; Weston, WV; Hon Rl; Jr NHS; NHS; Ed Yrbk; Yrbk; Sch Nwsp; 4-H; Cert Of Merit For Jrnlsm 79; Trip To Europe 78; Fairmont St Coll.

BROWN, MICHELE D; Cass Tech HS; Detroit, MI; Cmnty Wkr; Hon Rl; Letter Ten; Letter Trk; Chrldng; College; Medicine.

BROWN, MORRIS; Eisenhower HS; Saginaw, MI; Cl Rep Jr Cls; Hon Rl; Stu Cncl; Yth Flsp; Capt Ftbl; IM Sprt; Western Michigan Univ; Aviation Engr.

BROWN, NEIL; Bellbrook HS; Bellbrook, OH; Chrh Wkr; Fr Clb; Lat Clb; Collegez; Teacher Of Handicapped.

BROWN, PAMELA; Tipton HS; Tipton, IN; 58/188 Hon Rl; Sch Pl; Pres Yth Flsp; 4-H; Pep Clb; Ball St Univ; Archt.

BROWN, PAMELA; Magnolia HS; New Martinsvle, WV; Aud/Vis; Band; Chrh Wkr; Girl Scts; Hon Rl; Yth Flsp; FTA; Pep Clb; W Liberty State; Elem Educ.

BROWN, PAMELA; Shaker Hts HS; Shaker Hts, OH; Cls Rep Soph Cls; Treas Chrs; Lbry Ade; Stg Crw; Stu Cncl; Drama Clb; Bsktbl; Hockey; Trk; GAA; Michigan St Univ; Hotel/rest Mgmt.

BROWN, PAUL; Elkhart Memorial HS; Elkhart, IN; Bsbl; Ftbl; Coach Actv; IM Sprt; Univ; Phys Ther.

BROWN, PAUL; Hilliard HS; Hilliard, OH; Band; FCA; Hon Rl; Stu Cncl; Yth Flsp; Swmmng; Univ.

BROWN, PAYNE; Northrop HS; Ft Wayne, IN; 132/600 Cls Rep Frsh Cls; Am Leg Boys St; Cmnty Wkr; Pol Wkr; Sct Actv; Bsktbl; Letter Glf; Am Leg Awd; Boys St Attorney Genrl St Senate & Councilman 79; Hon Awd Soc Studies 77; Univ; Attorney.

BROWN, PENNY; Atherton HS; Burton, MI; Hon Rl; Jr NHS; Rptr Sch Nwsp; Letter Bsktbl; Letter Trk;.

BROWN, PERRY; Fredericktown HS; Fred, OH; Band; Trs Frsh Cls; Sch Mus; Sch Pl; Yth Flsp; Spn Clb; IM Sprt; Univ; Comp Sci.

BROWN, PHILLIP; Monroe Gregg HS; Mooresville, IN; Aud/Vis; Band; Boy Scts; Cmnty Wkr; Hon Rl; Orch; Pol Wkr; Sch Pl; Sct Actv; Stg Crw; Military Serv.

BROWN, REGINA; Pershing HS; Detroit, MI; Chrs; Drl Tm; Girl Scts; Hon Rl; Jr NHS; Off Ade; ROTC; Y-Teens; FHA; Sci Clb; Univ Of Detroit; Busns.

BROWN, REGINALD; North Marion HS; Monongah, WV; Cls Rep Frsh Cls; Trs Soph Cls; Band; Chrs; Hon Rl; Stu Cncl; Yrbk; Fr Clb; Trk; Fairmont State; Bus Admin.

BROWN, RICHARD; Madison Plains HS; Mt Sterling, OH; Cmnty Wkr; Hon Rl; Stu Cncl; Bsbl; Bsktbl; Honor Was Selected As HS All Amer For Basketball; Best Offensive On Reserve Best Off Varsity; College.

BROWN, ROBERT; Stow HS; Munroe Falls, OH; Band; Boy Scts; Chrs; Hon Rl; JA; Sch Pl; Stg Crw; IM Sprt; JA Awd; Kent St Univ; Art.

BROWN, ROBIN; Wayne HS; Dayton, OH; Cl Rep Jr Cls; Cls Rep Sr Cls; VP Drl Tm; Hon Rl; Boys Clb Am; Pep Clb; Chrldng; Scr Kpr; Superior & Excllnt Rating In Christian Music Tchg Clb Piano Cntst 78; Wright St Univ; Psych.

BROWN, ROCHELLE; East HS; Columbus, OH; Stu Cncl; Fr Clb; Coll; Psych.

BROWN, ROGER; Gladwin HS; Gladwin, MI; Hon Rl; Ftbl; IM Sprt; Central Mic Univ; Physics.

BROWN, ROGER; Liberty Benton HS; Findlay, OH; Am Leg Boys St; Chrs; Hon Rl; Jr NHS; Sch Mus; Pres Yth Flsp; Pres FFA; Letter Bsbl; Letter Bsktbl; Opt Clb Awd;.

BROWN, ROGER E; Liberty Benton HS; Findlay, OH; Am Leg Boys St; Chrs; Hon Rl; Jr NHS; Sch Mus; Pres Yth Flsp; Pres FFA; Letter Bsbl; Letter Bsktbl; Opt Clb Awd; Coll; Construction.

BROWN, ROWENA; Eastern HS; Waverly, OH; 17/66 Chrs; Hon Rl; Sch Mus; Sch Pl; Yth Flsp; Rptr Yrbk; Drama Clb; FTA; Pep Clb; Pom Pon; College; Education.

BROWN, SALLY; Perry HS; Massillon, OH; Chrh Wkr; Girl Scts; Hon Rl; Jr NHS; NHS; Off Ade; Sct Actv; Rptr Yrbk; Swmmng; Ohio St Univ; Public Rltns.

BROWN, SANDRA; Buckhannon Upshur HS; Rock Cave, WV; Band; Girl Scts; Hon Rl; Lbry Ade; Yrbk; Sch Nwsp; Fr Clb; Spn Clb; Letter Bsktbl; Mgrs; Clarksburg Acad; Cosmetology.

BROWN, SANDRA; Tippecanoe Vly HS; Warsaw, IN; Hon Rl; Yth Flsp; 4-H; 4-H Awd;.

BROWN, SARAH; Elmhurst HS; Ft Wayne, IN; 40/342 Chrh Wkr; Hon Rl; Mat Maids; Purdue Univ; Educ.

BROWN, SARAH S; Central Hower HS; Akron, OH; 13/413 Am Leg Aux Girls St; Hon Rl; NHS; Red Cr Ade; Stu Cncl; Ed Yrbk; Ed Sch Nwsp; FHA; Lat Clb; Pep Clb; Akron Univ; Med.

BROWN, SHARI; Anderson HS; Cincinnati, OH; Chrs; Chrh Wkr; Hon Rl; Orch; Sct Actv; Yth Flsp; Spn Clb; Ten; Univ Of Cincinnati; Engr.

BROWN, SHARON; Grafton HS; Grafton, WV; Hon Rl; NHS; Fairmont St Coll; Med Rec Tech.

BROWN, SHARON; Maumee HS; Maumee, OH; 29/316 Band; Chrh Wkr; FCA; Hon Rl; Yth Flsp; Y-Teens; Spn Clb; PPFtbl; Owens Tech College; Dental Hygiene.

BROWN, SHARON; Nordonia HS; Northfld Ctr, OH; 8/434 Cls Rep Frsh Cls; Cls Rep Soph Cls; Chrs; Drl Tm; Girl Scts; Hon Rl; NHS; Yth Flsp; Drama Clb; Univ Of Akron; Dietician.

BROWN, SHARON; Switzerland County Jr Sr HS; Florence, IN; 14/120 Am Leg Aux Girls St; Band; Chrs; Hon Rl; Lbry Ade; MMM; NHS; Sch Mus; Sch Pl; Drama Clb;.

BROWN, SHARON; Switzerland Coutny Jr Sr HS; Florence, IN; 17/122 Am Leg Aux Girls St; Band; Chrs; Hon Rl; Lbry Ade; MMM; NHS; Drama Clb; 4-H; FHA;.

BROWN, SHARON A; Independence Jr Sr HS; Columbus, OH; Hon Rl; NHS; Sec FHA; OEA; JA Awd; Franklin Univ; Acctg.

BROWN, SHEILA; Central HS; Evansville, IN; 92/482 Chrh Wkr; Stu Cncl; 4-H; Mth Clb; Rdo Clb; 4-H Awd; ISUE; Comp Sci.

BROWN, SHELLEY A; Buena Vista HS; Saginaw, MI; 22/158 Chrs; Hon Rl; JA; Off Ade; 4-H; Mic St Univ; Legal Secretary.

BROWN, STANLEY; Madison Hts HS; Anderson, IN; Cls Rep Frsh Cls; Hon Rl; Quill & Scroll; Yrbk; Sch Nwsp; Ten; Mgrs; International Bus Coll; Acctg.

BROWN, STANLEY; Merrill Community HS; Merrill, MI; Band; Boy Scts; Chrh Wkr; Hon Rl; Sct Actv; Treas FFA; Letter Ftbl; Saginaw Valley State College; Mec En.

BROWN, STEFAN; Yellow Springs HS; Yellow Sprg, OH; Band; Boy Scts; Chrh Wkr; Orch; Letter Bsktbl; Letter Socr; Mst Imprvd Plyr In Soccer Awd 78; Mst Imprvd Plyr In Bsktbl Awd 79; Univ; Banking.

BROWN, STEVEN; Holt HS; Holt, MI; Band; Boy Scts; Chrh Wkr; NHS; Yth Flsp; Pres Spn Clb; Letter Trk; God Cntry Awd; Lansing Community Coll; Data Proc.

BROWN, SUSAN; Crestview HS; Ohio City, OH; Cls Rep Soph Cls; Cl Rep Jr Cls; Aud/Vis; Chrs; Cmnty Wkr; Hon Rl; Lbry Ade; NHS; Sch Mus; Sch Pl; Parliamentary Proc Team; Ballpark Qn; FHA Northwest Dist Qn; College; Photography.

BROWN, TAMARA; Mater Dei HS; Evansvl, IN; Chrs; Chrh Wkr; Girl Scts; Hon Rl; Pol Wkr; Sch Pl; Sct Actv; GAA; IM Sprt; PPFtbl; Univ.

BROWN, TAMARA; Meadowbrook HS; Byesville, OH; Cls Rep Frsh Cls; Cls Rep Soph Cls; Cl Rep Jr Cls; Hon Rl; Stu Cncl; Rptr Yrbk; Mth Clb; Pep Clb; VICA; Scr Kpr; College; Pre Law.

BROWN, TAMMY; Hillsdale HS; Ashland, OH; 2/100 Band; Hon Rl; NHS; Lat Clb; Pep Clb; GAA; Univ; Vet.

BROWN, TAMMY; Indianapolis Baptist HS; Indianapolis, IN; 1/36 Val; Band; Chrh Wkr; Hon Rl; Pol Wkr; Yrbk; Pep Clb; Mgrs; Scr Kpr; Medals Spanish II Typing Geometry 77; Medals Algebra II US History Band 78; Bob Jones Univ; Math Tchr.

BROWN, TANIA; Columbus East HS; Columbus, OH; Band; Debate Tm; Hon Rl; Jr NHS; NHS; Orch; Pep Clb; Letter Bsktbl; Univ; Pharm.

BROWN, TANYA; Murray Wright HS; Detroit, MI; Lbry Ade; Off Ade; OEA; Univ Of Detroit; Cpa.

BROWN, TERESA; Avon HS; Indpls, IN; Girl Scts; Univ; Elem Teacher.

BROWN, TERESA L; North Central HS; Pioneer, OH; 25/72 Trs Frsh Cls; Trs Soph Cls; Trs Jr Cls; Trs Sr Cls; Band; Pres Chrs; Hon Rl; Sch Pl; Pep Clb; Bsktbl; Bowling Green State Univ; Phy Ther.

BROWN, TESSY; North Adams HS; Seaman, OH; 2/93 VP Jr Cls; Am Leg Aux Girls St; Band; Chrs; Cmnty Wkr; Hon Rl; Hosp Ade; Southern State Comm College.

BROWN, THEODORE; Ursuline HS; Youngstown, OH; 141/345 Cls Rep Soph Cls; Cl Rep Jr Cls; Chrh Wkr; Cmnty Wkr; Stu Cncl; Pres Lat Clb; Bsktbl; Shcl Rep For Daybreak 79; Rep On Schl History Tm 78; Pres Of Latin Clb 77; Cincinnati St Univ; Bus Admin.

BROWN, THOMAS; Troy HS; Southfield, MI; Pres Frsh Cls; Cls Rep Frsh Cls; Cls Rep Soph Cls; Cl Rep Jr Cls; Hon Rl; NHS; Stu Cncl; Spn Clb; Ftbl; PPFtbl; USC; Law.

BROWN, TIM; Sts Peter & Paul HS; Pittsburgh, PA; 6/11 Pres Soph Cls; Boy Scts; Stu Cncl; Yrbk; Ger Clb; Letter Bsktbl; Letter Socr; IM Sprt; Scr Kpr; Fr Hector Bellinatos Mem Schlrshp; Most Improved Player Awd Soccer; Fr Henry Paleari Mem Schlrshp; Vocational Schl; Construction.

BROWN, TINA; Champion HS; Warren, OH; 21/214 Band; NHS; Off Ade; Sch Pl; Y-Teens; VP FTA; Pres OEA; Scr Kpr; Best Typist Intensive Ofc Ed; Summer Sftbl St Champs; Busns Schl; Stenographer.

BROWN, TINA; Daleville HS; Yorktown, IN; 30/70 Chrs; Girl Scts; Yth Flsp; Fr Clb; FHA; Pep Clb; Swmmng; Opt Clb Awd; St Petersburg Jr Coll; Photog.

BROWN, TODD; Olentangy HS; Westerville, OH; 25/149 Band; Chrh Wkr; Hon Rl; Sch Mus; Yth Flsp; 4-H; Spn Clb; Oral Roberts Univ; Pre Med.

BROWN, TONYA; Pittsford HS; Osseo, MI; Sec Frsh Cls; Band; Off Ade; 4-H; Pep Clb; Letter Trk; Letter Chrldng; 4-H Awd; Reserve Champ Halter Horse At Fair; Grand Champ Halter Horse At Fair For 4 H; Jackson Bus Schl; Sec.

BROWN, TRACEY; Springs Valley HS; French Lick, IN; 43/88 Band; Girl Scts; Hon Rl; Off Ade; FHA; Pep Clb; Ivy Tech; Paramedic.

BROWN, TRACY; Greenville Sr HS; Greenville, OH; Hon Rl; Yth Flsp; Rptr Yrbk; Drama Clb; 4-H Awd; College; Communications.

BROWN, VIRGILENE; Clermont Northeastern HS; Batavia, OH; Chrh Wkr; Drl Tm; Hon Rl; NHS; Sch Pl; Drama Clb; Fr Clb; Ohio Univ; Rec Ther.

BROWN, VIVIAN; Tuslaw HS; N Lawrence, OH; 15/177 Pres Soph Cls; Hon Rl; NHS; Stu Cncl; VICA; Bsktbl; Trk; GAA; Vocational School; Cosmetology.

BROWN, WILLIAM; Midland Trail HS; Lansing, WV; Boy Scts; Chrh Wkr; Hon Rl; Yth Flsp; Pep Clb; VICA; Bsktbl; Ftbl; Trk; JA Awd; West Virginia Tech Univ; Indust Arts.

BROWN, WILLIAM; Jefferson Area HS; Jefferson, OH; 2/188 AFS; Band; Pres Chrs; VP NHS; Sch Mus; Sch Pl; Fr Clb; FTA; Pep Clb; Am Leg Awd; Cedarville Coll; Busns Admin.

BROWN, WILLICE; Kettering HS; Detroit, MI; Hon Rl; Wayne State Univ; Accounting.

BROWN, WINFRED; North HS; Youngstown, OH; Sec Sr Cls; Am Leg Boys St; Chrh Wkr; Hon Rl; Off Ade; Sch Pl; Boys Clb Am; Sci Clb; Am Leg Awd; Cit Awd; Med Schl; Bio.

BROWNE, JULIE; Flushing Sr HS; Flushing, MI; Band; Yth Flsp; Fr Clb; PPFtbl; Univ Of Michigan; Sociology.

BROWNE, MARGARET P; Fr Joseph Wehrle Memrl HS; Columbus, OH; 20/110 Chrh Wkr; Hon Rl; Sch Mus; Sch Pl; Stg Crw; Rptr Sch Nwsp; Sch Nwsp; Drama Clb; Natl Merit SF; Ohio Univ; Botany.

BROWNELL, AMY; Athens HS; Troy, MI; 87/450 Cls Rep Frsh Cls; Cl Rep Jr Cls; Cls Rep Sr Cls; Chrh Wkr; Debate Tm; Hon Rl; Natl Forn Lg; NHS; Stu Cncl; Rptr Sch Nwsp; Mic State Univ; Communication Arts.

BROWNELL, DAVID M; Mentor HS; Mentor, OH; 12/700 Band; Hon Rl; Ed Yrbk; Sch Nwsp; Pres Sci Clb; Natl Merit SF; College; Engr.

BROWNING, BILL; Aiken HS; Cincinnati, OH; 15/560 Cl Rep Jr Cls; Cls Rep Sr Cls; Band; Drm Bgl; Hon Rl; Orch; Sch Mus; Sch Pl; Stu Cncl; Yth Flsp; Cadet Of The Year Queen City Cadets Drum & Bugle Corps; Stu Of Month In Music; Aiken Frn Lang Honor Society; Berklee Coll Of Music; Jazz.

BROWNING, CHERYL; Flat Rock Sr HS; Flat Rock, MI; Band; Chrh Wkr; Drl Tm; Girl Scts; Hon Rl; NHS; Sch Mus; Stg Crw; Sci Clb; EMU History Day Awd 2nd Pl In Jr Class; College; Science.

BROWNING, GREGORY; Paul Laurenc Dunbar HS; Dayton, OH; 8/200 Hon Rl; NHS; Univ; Mech Engr.

BROWNING, JAMES; Carlisle HS; Carlisle, OH; Pres Sr Cls; Band; Chrs; Chrh Wkr; NHS; Sch Pl; Stu Cncl; Yrbk; Sch Nwsp; Letter Bsktbl; Univ; Art.

BROWNING, JENNIFER; North Central HS; Indianapolis, IN; Cl Rep Jr Cls; Cmnty Wkr; Girl Scts; Sch Pl; Stu Cncl; Civ Clb; Pep Clb; Trk; Chrldng; PPFtbl; Indiana Univ; Psych.

BROWNING, JOANN; Ross HS; Hamilton, OH; Hon Rl; Jr NHS; Photography.

BROWNING, KENNETH; Crooksville HS; Crooksville, OH; Hst Soph Cls; Hst Jr Cls; Am Leg Boys St; Debate Tm; NHS; Sch Pl; Sci Clb; VICA; Bsbl; Bsktbl; Univ; Comp Sci.

BROWNING, LISA; Lynchburg Clay HS; Lynchburg, OH; Band; Girl Scts; Sch Mus; Sch Pl; Stg Crw; 4-H; Fr Clb; FHA; Pep Clb; Swmmng; Schlrshp Team; Mc Alpins Teen Board; Univ; Law.

BROWNING, LISA K; Nitro HS; Nitro, WV; Hon Rl; Chrldng; Mgrs; Mat Maids; Scr Kpr; Pres Awd; West Virginia St Univ.

BROWNING, ROBERT; L Anse HS; Lanse, MI; Band; Hon Rl; Hosp Ade; Sch Nwsp; N Cntrl Michigan Univ; Resp Therapy.

BROWNING, TRISH; Seton HS; Cincinnati, OH; Girl Scts; Hon Rl; Jr NHS; NHS; Pol Wkr; Fr Clb; Mth Clb; Letter Ten; Coach Actv; GAA; Univ; Comp Sci.

BROWNING JR, JOSEPH; South Charleston HS; S Charleston, WV; Cls Rep Frsh Cls; Cl Rep Jr Cls; Jr NHS; NHS; Ed Sch Nwsp; Spn Clb; Opt Clb Awd; Marshall Univ; Brdcst.

BROWN JR, MICHAEL; Warren Sr HS; Troy, MI; Boy Scts; Chrs; NHS; Letter Bsktbl; Letter Ftbl; Letter Trk; IM Sprt; Tmr; Opt Clb Awd; Most Outsdng Athlete 76; Most Outsdng 9th Grade Stu 76; Michigan Univ; Engr.

BROWNLEE, JOSEPH; Washington HS; Massillon, OH; 4/463 Band; Hon Rl; NHS; Orch; Natl Merit Ltr; Univ Of Akron; Music.

BROWNLEE, WENDI; Hartland HS; Fenton, MI; Chrh Wkr; Hon Rl; Off Ade; Yth Flsp; Spn Clb; Letter Trk; Mgrs; Scr Kpr; Tmr; Am Leg Awd; Central Univ.

BROWNSWORD, SUE; Perry HS; Canton, OH; Band; Chrh Wkr; Girl Scts; Hon Rl; Hosp Ade; NHS; Univ; Music.

BROYLES, TAMARA; Watkins Mem HS; Pataskala, OH; 16/226 Band; Girl Scts; Hon Rl; Sch Mus; Treas Yth Flsp; Rptr Sch Nwsp; 4-H; IM Sprt; Ohio Univ; Acctg.

BROZENICK, NORMAN J; St Joseph Prep; Vienna, WV; 3/19 Chrs; Jr NHS; NHS; Ed Sch Nwsp; Letter Crs Cntry; Letter Ten; Natl Spanish Honor Soc; Southeastern Ohio Lang Fair; 1st Pl In Folksinging; Amer Reg Theater; Hghst Schlast; College.

BRUAL, BARB; Ursuline Academy; Celina, OH; 28/105 Chrh Wkr; Trs Frsh Cls; Chrh Wkr; Cmnty Wkr; Hosp Ade; Off Ade; Mat Maids; Scr Kpr; Tmr; Serv Awd 79; Ackwnldgmnt Of Lit Serv 79; Exclnnc In Piano From Oh Music Tchr Assoc 76; Mt St Joseph Coll; Nursing.

BRUBAKER, GAYLE; Rossford HS; Rossford, OH; 5/150 Band; Chrs; Chrh Wkr; Hon Rl; Lbry Ade; NHS; Red Cr Ade; Sch Mus; Sch Nwsp; Drama Clb; Oberlin Coll; Education.

BRUBAKER, JOHN M; Farmington HS; Farmington, MI; Band; Chrh Wkr; Cmnty Wkr; Hon Rl; Orch; Sch Mus; JC Awd; Awd For Creatvty Inart; Hon Mntn In Sci Fair; Univ; Pre Med.

BRUBAKER, PAUL; Austintown Fitch HS; Youngstown, OH; Pres Soph Cls; Pres Jr Cls; Pres Sr Cls; Am Leg Boys St; Cmnty Wkr; Hon Rl; Natl Forn Lg; Beloit College; Pre Law.

BRUBAKER, ROGER; Whitko HS; N Manchester, IN; FFA; IM Sprt; Lincoln Tech Inst; Mechanic.

BRUCE, BECKY; Wood Memorial HS; Oakland City, IN; Pep Clb; Photog.

BRUCE, CHARLENE; Hubbard HS; Hubbard, OH; 2/330 Band; Chrh Wkr; Hon Rl; VP Spn Clb; Youngstown St Univ; Sci.

BRUCE, CHARLES; Tippecanoe HS; Tipp City, OH; Aud/Vis; Chrh Wkr; Lbry Ade; 4-H; Ftbl; IM Sprt; 4-H Awd; Wright St Univ; Engr.

BRUCE, DAVID; Carman HS; Flint, MI; 1/355 NHS; Sch Mus; Natl Merit SF; Univ Of Michigan; Med.

BRUCE, DAVID W; Harrison HS; Harrison, MI; 44/158 Boy Scts; Hon Rl; Sch Pl; Stg Crw; Central Mic Univ; Acctg.

BRUCE, DENICA; Hamilton Township HS; Columbus, OH; 3/187 Cls Rep Soph Cls; Cl Rep Jr Cls; Am Leg Aux Girls St; Girl Scts; VP NHS; Stu Cncl; Pres Spn Clb; Capt PPFtbl; Sftbl Var Ltr 77; Vllybl Var Ltr 78; Indiana St Univ; Phys Educ.

BRUCE, GEORGE A; Hubbard HS; Hubbard, OH; 34/360 Cls Rep Frsh Cls; AFS; Band; Chrs; Hon Rl; Lit Mag; Sch Mus; Sch Pl; Sct Actv; Treas Stu Cncl; Kent St Univ; Pre Med.

BRUCE, JOAN; Hastings HS; Hastings, MI; 25/323 Chrs; Cmnty Wkr; Hon Rl; Beta Clb; Fr Clb; Sci Clb; PPFtbl; Univ; Med.

BRUCE, KELLY; Coleman HS; Coleman, MI; 8/96 Cls Rep Sr Cls; Girl Scts; Hon Rl; NHS; Stu Cncl; Bsktbl; Trk; Michigan St Univ; Vet.

BRUCE, ROBERT; Huntington HS; Huntington, WV; 23/252 Band; Chrh Wkr; Hon Rl; Jr NHS; NHS; Stg Crw; Lat Clb; Mth Clb; Marshall Univ; Comp Sci.

BRUCE, TERESA; Du Pont HS; Charleston, WV; Cl Rep Jr Cls; Band; Chrh Wkr; Cmnty Wkr; Hon Rl; Mod UN; Stu Cncl; Rptr Yrbk; FBLA; Lat Clb; W V Jr Clscl Lg Pres 79; Marjorette 78 80; West Virginia St Univ.

BRUCHNAK, AL; Wayne Memorial HS; Wayne, MI; Cls Rep Frsh Cls; Band; Hon Rl; Jr NHS; NHS; Pol Wkr; Stu Cncl; Mth Clb; Bsbl; Mic Tech Univ; Metelluirgical.

BRUCK, LISA; St Mary Academy; Anderson, MI; 11/130 Cmnty Wkr; Hon Rl; Sch Nwsp; 4-H; 4-H Awd; Michael Owens Tech Coll; Dent Hygnst.

BRUCKELMEYER, ELIZABETH; Benjamin Logan HS; N Chicago, IL; 2/13 Chrs; Hon Rl; FHA; OEA; Ohio Hi Poin Jus; Data Acctg.

BRUCKEN, NANCY; Shaker Heights HS; Shaker Hts, OH; 34/575 Chrh Wkr; Girl Scts; Lbry Ade; Yth Flsp; Bsktbl; GAA; IM Sprt; Marietta Coll; Math.

BRUCKER, KATHRYN; Notre Dame Acad; Toledo, OH; Chrs; Drl Tm; Sch Pl; Stu Cncl; Pep Clb; College; Social Work.

BRUCKNER, KRISTY; Walnut Ridge Sr HS; R, OH; 83/300 Chrs; Hon Rl; NHS; Off Ade; Sch Mus; Rptr Yrbk; Fr Clb; Pep Clb; PPFtbl; Scr Kpr; Bowling Green St Univ; Optometry.

BRUDERICK, RICHARD; Harbor Beach Cmnty HS; Minden City, MI; 26/141 Chrh Wkr; Hon Rl; Natl Forn Lg; NHS; Sch Mus; Stu Cncl; Yth Flsp; Yrbk; Rptr Sch Nwsp; Sch Nwsp; Calvin Coll; Elec Tech.

BRUECK, CORINNE; Lake Shore HS; Baroda, MI; Hon Rl; JA; Treas 4-H; FHA; OEA; Kiwan Awd; Mi Bus Schools Schlrshp 79; Davenport Coll; Acctg.

BRUEGGEMAN, JILL; Concordia Lutheran HS; Ft Wayne, IN; 12/187 VP Sr Cls; Chrh Wkr; Hon Rl; Stu Cncl; Ed Yrbk; Ger Clb; Pep Clb; College; English.

BRUEMMER, CHRISTINE; Ravenna HS; Ravenna, OH; Hon Rl; Lbry Ade; Off Ade; Stg Crw; Drama Clb; Spn Clb; GAA; ATI; Botany.

BRUENING, DANIEL; Moeller HS; Deer Pk, OH; 9/253 Cl Rep Jr Cls; Cls Rep Sr Cls; Hon Rl; NHS; Stu Cncl; Rptr Sch Nwsp; IM Sprt; Scr Kpr; 1st Hnr Evry Qtr 2nd Hghst Fr 1 76; 1st Hnr Evry Qtr Hst Avg Soph Bio & Hghst Av Fr 2 77; Hghst Avg In Frt; Univ; Jrnlsm.

BRUESSOW, MICHELLE M; Bridgeport HS; Bridgeport, MI; Cl Rep Jr Cls; Cls Rep Sr Cls; Band; Chrs; Drl Tm; Hon Rl; Off Ade; Stu Cncl; Ger Clb; Pep Clb; Univ.

BRUEY, SHARON; Perry HS; Massillon, OH; 82/570 Hon Rl; NHS; Yth Flsp; Yrbk; Sch Nwsp; Treas FHA; Pep Clb; Spn Clb; Tech College.

BRUGGEMEIER, LISA; N Royalton HS; N Royalton, OH; Chrs; Hon Rl; Mdrgl; Sch Mus; Sch Pl; Stg Crw; Drama Clb; Kent St Univ; Bus Mgmt.

BRUHN, DEBORAH; Concord HS; Spring Arbor, MI; Band; Girl Scts; Hon Rl; FHA; USMC; Electronics.

BRUHN, TIM; Whiteland Comm HS; Greenwood, IN; 17/219 Hon Rl; Indiana Univ; Busns.

BRULEY, MARY; Lake Michigan Catholic HS; St Joseph, MI; JA; JA Awd; College; Math.

BRUMAGE, CHERYL; Licking Valley HS; St Louisville, OH; 13/165 Band; Chrh Wkr; Drl Tm; Girl Scts; Hon Rl; NHS; Sprt Ed Yrbk; Rptr Sch Nwsp; Pep Clb; Sci Clb; Central Ohio Tech; Engr.

BRUMBAUGH, CHARLA; North Baltimore HS; N Baltimore, OH; 3/67 Cls Rep Frsh Cls; Pres Jr Cls; Band; Cmp Fr Grls; Chrs; Hon Rl; NHS; Off Ade; Sch Mus; Stu Cncl; Univ Of Toledo.

BRUMBAUGH, LISA; Richmond Sr HS; Richmond, IN; 83/580 Chrs; Debate Tm; Hon Rl; Jr NHS; VP Y-Teens; Rptr Sch Nwsp; Spn Clb; Indiana Univ; Acctg.

BRUMBAUGH, LISA K; Richmond Sr HS; Richmond, IN; 80/580 Chrs; Debate Tm; Hon Rl; Jr NHS; VP Y-Teens; Rptr Sch Nwsp; Spn Clb; Indiana Univ; Acctg.

BRUMBAUGH, ROBERT; Whitko HS; So Whitley, IN; Boy Scts; Yth Flsp; 4-H; Letter Glf; Univ; Math.

BRUMBAUGH, ROBIN; Bradford HS; Bradford, OH; Trs Jr Cls; Band; Drl Tm; Hon Rl; Off Ade; FHA; OEA; Pom Pon; Lion Awd;.

BRUMBERG, ANNETTE; Lemon Monroe HS; Monroe, OH; 6/252 Am Leg Aux Girls St; Band; Chrs; Chrh Wkr; Cmnty Wkr; Girl Scts; Hon Rl; NHS; Sch Mus; Sch Pl; Univ Of Cincinnati; Nursing.

BRUMELS, KAREN; Comstock Park HS; Comstock Park, MI; Sec Soph Cls; Sec Jr Cls; Am Leg Aux Girls St; Band; Chrs; Chrh Wkr; Cmnty Wkr; Hon Rl; Lbry Ade; Natl Forn Lg; Grand Rapids Baptist Coll; Bus Admin.

BRUMFIEL, TRACY; Laurel HS; Laurel, IN; 5/31 Boy Scts; Hon Rl; NHS; Ger Clb; Bsbl; Scr Kpr; Tmr; Indiana Univ; Acctg.

BRUMFIELD, CYNTHIA D; Barboursville HS; Le Sage, WV; 47/349 Trs Sr Cls; Band; Sec Chrh Wkr; Pres FCA; Hon Rl; Sch Pl; Stu Cncl; Rptr Yrbk; Drama Clb; Pres Fr Clb; Miss Teenage Amer Semi Finalist; Marshall Univ; Psych.

BRUMFIELD, JOYCE; Fairland HS; Proctorville, OH; 16/153 Cl Rep Jr Cls; Cls Rep Sr Cls; Chrh Wkr; Hon Rl; NHS; Off Ade; Stu Cncl; Yth Flsp; Ed Yrbk; Rptr Yrbk; Correspondent To Huntington Advertiser; Jr Attendent; Ohio Univ HS Scholar Cert; Shawnee St Univ; Health.

BRUMFIELD, LAURA; Springboro HS; Waynesville, OH; Band; Hon Rl; Jr NHS; Letter Orch; Stg Crw; Rptr Yrbk; 4-H; Spn Clb; IM Sprt; PPFtbl; College; Medicine.

BRUMLEY, CONNIE; Union HS; Losantville, IN; Band; Yrbk; FHA; Gym; Chrldng; DAR Awd; Bus Schl; Legal Sec.

BRUMMEL, BETH; Kenowa Hills HS; Grand Rapids, MI; Chrh Wkr; Hon Rl; PPFtbl; Davenport Coll; Acctg.

BRUMMETT, ROBIN; Martinsville HS; Martinsville, IN; Band; Cmnty Wkr; Lbry Ade; Orch; Pres 4-H; Pep Clb; Dnfth Awd; 4-H Awd; School Delegate 79; Indiana Univ; Spch.

BRUNDZA, JOSEPH; Bloomington N HS; Bloomington, IN; 29/400 VP Sr Cls; Boy Scts; Chrh Wkr; Hon Rl; Sct Actv; Yrbk; Spn Clb; IM Sprt; Opt Clb Awd; Eagle Scout; Recpiient Of The Ad Altare Dei Emblem; Recipient Of The Pope Piux XII Emblem; Coll; Law.

BRUNE, JOHN; Brighton HS; Brighton, MI; Boy Scts; Hon Rl; Sct Actv; Crs Cntry; Wrstlng; IM Sprt; PPFtbl; Mi St Univ HS Engr Isnt 77; Personal Photog Inclusion In Meteor Photo Co Image Lib; Michigan Tech Univ; Elec Engr.

BRUNE, LAURIE; Zanesville HS; Zanesville, OH; Pres Frsh Cls; Sec Jr Cls; Sec Sr Cls; Chrs; Drl Tm; Hon Rl; NHS; Stu Cncl; Ohio State Univ; Cosmetology.

BRUNE, LIANNE; Zanesville HS; Zanesville, OH; Chrs; Capt Drl Tm; Hon Rl; Jr NHS; NHS; Off Ade; Spn Clb; Ohi State Univ; Interior Decorating.

BRUNEEL, LAURIE; Harper Woods Secondary Schl; Harper Woods, MI; Sec Frsh Cls; Sec Soph Cls; VP Jr Cls; Cmnty Wkr; Hon Rl; Stu Cncl; Univ; Nutrition.

BRUNEEL, PATRICIA; Reese HS; Reese, MI; 13/130 Girl Scts; Hon Rl; Lbry Ade; NHS; Off Ade; Yth Flsp; Pep Clb; Capt Chrldng; Cit Awd; Kellogg Comm College; Dent Hygienist.

BRUNELL, DAVID; Annapolis HS; Dearborn Hts, MI; 55/378 Cls Rep Soph Cls; VP Jr Cls; Cl Rep Jr Cls; VP Sr Cls; Cls Rep Sr Cls; Chrs; Hon Rl; Eastern Mic Univ; Public Relations.

BRUNETTI, DONNA; Notre Dame HS; Clarksburg, WV; Rptr Yrbk; FTA; Pep Clb; Ten; IM Sprt; Fairmont St Coll; Elem Ed.

BRUNETTI, JOHN; Bridgeport Sr HS; Bridgeport, WV; Band; Boy Scts; Sch Mus; Sch Pl; Sct Actv; Stu Cncl; DECA; 4-H; Pres Key Clb; Wrstlng; Marshall Univ.

BRUNFIELD, THOMAS; Huntington HS; Huntington, WV; 1/400 Am Leg Boys St; Hon Rl; Jr NHS; NHS; Key Clb; Mth Clb; Bsbl; Ftbl; Wrstlng; Stu Body VP 79; Univ; Med.

BRUNI, THERESA M; Harry E Wood HS; Indianapolis, IN; Cls Rep Frsh Cls; Cmnty Wkr; Debate Tm; Hon Rl; JA; Jr NHS; NHS; Sch Mus; Sch Pl; Drama Clb; Italian Club 76; Grant For 961 Dollars 79; Indiana Univ; Psych.

BRUNK, KAREN; Valley View HS; Germantown, OH; Chrh Wkr; Hon Rl; NHS; Sec Yth Flsp; Sec 4-H; Spn Clb; Mgrs; 4-H Awd; College.

BRUNK, SHARON; Valley View HS; Germantown, OH; Chrh Wkr; Hon Rl; NHS; Yth Flsp; 4-H; Spn Clb; 4-H Awd; Univ.

BRUNKE, LINDA; Benjamin Logan HS; Bellefontaine, OH; Drl Tm; Hon Rl; Rptr Yrbk; FBLA; Gym; GAA; Beauty College.

BRUNN, BOB; Jackson Memorial HS; Canton, OH; Cls Rep Soph Cls; Band; Hon Rl; NHS; Orch; Sch Mus; Stu Cncl; Yth Flsp; Drama Clb; VP Ger Clb; Superior Ratings At Solo & Ensemble Contest; College.

BRUNN, STEVE; James A Garfield HS; Ravenna, OH; Band; Chrh Wkr; Hon Rl; NHS; Sch Mus; Yth Flsp; Yrbk; Sci Clb; Spn Clb; Letter Bsktbl; Hiram College; Bio.

BRUNN, STEVEN; James A Garfield HS; Ravenna, OH; Hon Rl; NHS; Red Cr Ade; Yth Flsp; Rptr Yrbk; Sci Clb; Spn Clb; Bsktbl; College; Science.

BRUNNER, JEFFERY; Lowell HS; Cedar Lk, IN; 39/230 Pres Yth Flsp; 4-H; Sec FFA; Letter Swmmng; 4-H Awd; Kiwan Awd; Purdue Univ; Engr.

BRUNNER, MICHELE; Pike Delta York HS; Delta, OH; Chrs; Girl Scts; Hon Rl; Off Ade; Sch Mus; Sch Pl; Stu Cncl; Rptr Sch Nwsp; Glf; Socr; Adrian Univ; Bus.

BRUNNER, SUSAN; Central Catholic HS; N Canton, OH; Band; Girl Scts; Hosp Ade; JA; Sct Actv; Spn Clb; Pres Awd; Barbizon Fshn Schl; Fshn Mrchnd.

BRUNO, CHRISTINA; Grandville HS; Wyoming, MI; Cmp Fr Grls; Chrs; Girl Scts; JA; Yrbk; Pep Clb; Spn Clb; PPFtbl; Cit Awd; Jr Coll; Med.

BRUNO, LORI; Cadiz HS; Hopedale, OH; Cl Rep Jr Cls; Chrs; Hon Rl; NHS; Sch Pl; Stu Cncl; Ed Sch Nwsp; Drama Clb; Spn Clb; Capt Chrldng; Ohio St Univ; Hist.

BRUNO, RITA; Madonna HS; Burgettstown, PA; 20/103 VP Jr Cls; Cl Rep Jr Cls; Chrs; Hon Rl; Jr NHS; NHS; Sch Pl; Rptr Sch Nwsp; Pep Clb; Sci Clb; Duquesne Univ; Pharmacy.

BRUNO, SCOTT; Wapakoneta Sr HS; Wapakoneta, OH; 3/340 Hon Rl; NHS; Sch Nwsp; Spn Clb; Bsktbl; Natl Merit SF; Xavier Univ; Comp Sci.

BRUNOW, AMY; Concordia Lutheran HS; Ft Wayne, IN; 4/181 Hon Rl; Yrbk; Letter Bsktbl; Letter Trk; Mgrs; Univ; Med.

BRUNS, BETSY; Mother Of Mercy HS; Cincinnati, OH; Chrh Wkr; Girl Scts; Hon Rl; Off Ade; Stg Crw; Graphic Design.

BRUNS, DIANE; St Henry HS; St Henry, OH; Sec Frsh Cls; Pres Sr Cls; Band; Chrh Wkr; Hon Rl; Jr NHS; Pres NHS; Yrbk; Pres OEA;.

BRUNS, GREGG; St Xavier HS; Cincinnati, OH; 49/259 Boy Scts; Chrh Wkr; Cmnty Wkr; Hon Rl; Sch Mus; Sch Pl; Stg Crw; Ftbl; College; Pre Med.

BRUNS, JOANNE C; Alter HS; Kettering, OH; 5/350 Hon Rl; Pres NHS; Spn Clb; Capt Chrldng; GAA; IM Sprt; Natl Merit SF; Univ Of Dayton; Engr.

BRUNS, KAREN; Seton HS; Cincinnati, OH; Chrh Wkr; Hon Rl; Orch; Rptr Yrbk; Spn Clb; Ohio Visual Art Inst; Photog.

BRUNS, LINDA; Napoleon HS; Napoleon, OH; Band; Chrh Wkr; Hon Rl; Orch; 4-H; Lat Clb; 4-H Awd; Bus Schl; Sec.

BRUNS, MICHAEL A; Wapakoneta Sr HS; Wapakoneta, OH; 7/308 Cls Rep Sr Cls; Boy Scts; NHS; Sct Actv; Stu Cncl; Spn Clb; Letter Wrstlng; IM Sprt; Univ.

BRUNS, RODNEY; Brookfield HS; Brookfield, OH; VP Jr Cls; Boy Scts; Chrh Wkr; NHS; Fr Clb; Bsktbl; Letter Trk; Univ; Agronomy.

BRUNS, RONALD; Chaminade Julienne HS; Dayton, OH; 88/275 Boy Scts; Chrh Wkr; JA; Sct Actv; Letter Socr; Univ Of Cincinnati; Bio Chem.

BRUNS, TIM; Marion Local HS; Celina, OH; Chrh Wkr; Cmnty Wkr; Debate Tm; Sch Pl; Sdlty; Eng Clb; 4-H; FFA; IM Sprt; 4-H Awd; Agricultural.

BRUNS, TIM; Hagerstown Jr Sr HS; Hagerstown, IN; 32/184 Hon Rl; NHS; Sch Mus; Sch Pl; Rptr Sch Nwsp; Rdo Clb; Sci Clb; Purdue Univ; Elec Engr.

BRUSH, CHRIS; Celina Sr HS; Celina, OH; Chrh Wkr; Hon Rl; NHS; Lat Clb; Univ; Writing.

BRUSNAHAN, LINDA; Rensselaer Central HS; Rensselaer, IN; 38/154 Sch Nwsp; Drama Clb; Letter Swmmng; Tmr; Evansville Univ; Cmnctns.

BRUSS, GEORGE; Jackson Milton HS; N Jackson, OH; 3/106 Am Leg Boys St; Hon Rl; Ger Clb; Key Clb; Letter Bsktbl; Letter Glf; Mgrs; Scr Kpr; Tmr; Am Leg Awd; Youngstown St Univ; Bus Admin.

BRUSS, GEORGE; Jackson Milton HS; North Jackson, OH; 3/106 Am Leg Boys St; Hon Rl; Ger Clb; Key Clb; Letter Glf; Am Leg Awd; Youngstown State Univ; Bus Admin.

BRUSS, RACHEL; Union City Comm HS; Union City, IN; Band; Chrs; Drm Mjrt; Hon Rl; Hosp Ade; Sch Mus; Yth Flsp; FSA; Pep Clb; Gym; Cecilian Club Award Outstndng In Field Of Music; John Phillip Sousa Band Awrd; Lutheran Hosp Schl; Nursing.

BRUSSEAU, KIMBERLEY; Inter City Christian HS; Allen Park, MI; 9/43 Girl Scts; NHS; Off Ade; Yth Flsp; Scr Kpr; Henry Ford Comm Coll; Acctg.

BRUSSEL, SHERYL; St Johns Public HS; St Johns, MI; Cls Rep Frsh Cls; FCA; Hon Rl; Stu Cncl; Drama Clb; Ten; Chrldng; IM Sprt; Mic State Univ.

BRUSSO, JAMES; Calumet HS; Laurium, MI; 6/142 Am Leg Boys St; Hon Rl; NHS; Sch Pl; Crs Cntry; Letter Hockey; IM Sprt; Pres Awd; Michigan Tech Univ; Metal Engr.

BRUST, CHRIS; Eastern HS; Beaver, OH; Am Leg Boys St; Band; Boy Scts; Hon Rl; Pres NHS; Yrbk; Pres 4-H; Scr Kpr; 4-H Awd; Pres Of Pike Cnty Jr Fair Bd 78; Ohio St Univ; Vet Med.

BRUST, MARY BETH; Archbishop Alter HS; Centervl, OH; Hosp Ade; Capt Bsktbl; GAA; Scr Kpr; Baldwin Wallace Univ; Phys Ther.

BRUST, MARY BETH; Archbishop Alter HS; Centerville, OH; 150/290 Cmnty Wkr; Bsktbl; GAA; College; Phys Ed.

BRUTSCHE, PAULA; Greenville Sr HS; Greenville, OH; Chrs; Hon Rl; NHS; Pres Yth Flsp; Drama Clb; Sci Clb; Treas Spn Clb; College.

BRYAK, PAUL; Hammond HS; Hammond, IN; Aud/Vis; Hon Rl; Ind Univ; Computer Sci.

BRYAN, BECKY; Northrop HS; Ft Wayne, IN; 67/534 Cls Rep Frsh Cls; Cls Rep Soph Cls; Band; Hon Rl; Orch; Sch Mus; Capt Bsktbl; Cit Awd; Ill Univ; Law.

BRYAN, DENISE; West Branch HS; Salem, OH; AFS; Band; Yth Flsp; 4-H; Lat Clb; Pep Clb; Trk;.

BRYAN, DOUGLAS; Zanesville HS; Zanesvile, OH; Chrh Wkr; Debate Tm; FCA; Hon Rl; NHS; Glf; Kent Christian Coll; Bible.

BRYAN, LA MAR; Colon HS; Colon, MI; Band; Hon Rl; VP NHS; Treas Stu Cncl; Rptr Sch Nwsp; 4-H; FFA; Trk; Mgrs; DAR Awd; Michigan St Univ; Jrnlsm.

BRYAN, MAUREEN; Munster HS; Munster, IN; 4/431 Hon Rl; Natl Forn Lg; NHS; Sch Pl; Sch Nwsp; Drama Clb; Bausch & Lomb Awd; Natl Merit Schl; Pres Awd; Purdue Univ; Metallurgical Engr.

BRYAN, RUTH; Reynoldsburg HS; Reynoldsburg, OH; Hon Rl; Hosp Ade; Yrbk; Sch Nwsp; Columbus Tech Inst; Med Tech.

BRYAN, SUE; Merrill Community HS; St Charles, MI; Chrs; Vocational Schl; Cosmetology.

BRYANT, BARBARA; Edinburgh Community HS; Franklin, IN; 2/59 FCA; Hon Rl; VP NHS; Sch Pl; VP Stu Cncl; Drama Clb; Fr Clb; Pep Clb; Letter Bsktbl; Am Leg Awd; Purdue Univ; Comp Sci.

BRYANT, CARLA; Blue River Valley HS; New Castle, IN; Cls Rep Frsh Cls; Cls Rep Soph Cls; Cl Rep Jr Cls; VP Sr Cls; Hon Rl; Natl Forn Lg; NHS; Sch Pl; Stu Cncl; Yrbk; Manchester College; Speech Comm.

BRYANT, CHARALENA; West Union HS; W Union, OH; Chrh Wkr; Hon Rl; NHS; Rptr Yrbk; Rptr Sch Nwsp; OEA; 1st In OEA Extemporaneous Speech 78; 2nd In OEA St Comp Extemporaneous Speech 78;f 18th In Natl Comp 78; Morhead Univ; X Ray Tech.

BRYANT, CINDY; Kings HS; Morrow, OH; Cls Rep Soph Cls; Sec Jr Cls; Sec Sr Cls; Drl Tm; Hon Rl; Off Ade; Sch Mus; Stu Cncl; Pep Clb; Chrldng; Busns Schl.

BRYANT, CINDY; Bridgeport Sr HS; Bridgeport, WV; Band; Chrs; Girl Scts; Hon Rl; Hosp Ade; Jr NHS; NHS; Yth Flsp; Trk; Univ; Med.

BRYANT, DOUGLAS; Carroll Sr HS; Cutler, IN; Am Leg Boys St; Boy Scts; Hon Rl; Spn Clb; Mgrs; Gov Hon Prg Awd; Natl Merit SF; Natl Merit Schl; Honorary Schlrshp From Indiana Univ; GMI Schlrshp; General Motors Inst; Engr.

BRYANT, ELIZABETH; Trinity HS; Cleveland, OH; Cls Rep Soph Cls; Chrs; Drl Tm; Rptr Sch Nwsp; Fr Clb; Trk; Pom Pon; Univ; Bus Admin.

BRYANT, EVON; East HS; Youngstown, OH; Cmp Fr Grls; Chrs; Hon Rl; NHS; Red Cr Ade; Y-Teens; Pep Clb; Spn Clb; Letter Bsktbl; Letter Trk; Cert Of Merit Scholastic Achievement 1977 78; Cert Of Serv Of The Mayor 1972 73;cert Of Recognition 1973; Youngstown St Univ; Nursing.

BRYANT, FELICIA; Southeastern HS; Detroit, MI; Chrs; Chrh Wkr; Hon Rl; JA; NHS; Cit Awd; JA Awd; Opt Clb Awd; Perfct Attndnc Awd Chem 79; Bio Awd Keypunch Awd & Typing Awd 78; Univ; Engr.

BRYANT, GLENDA; Milan HS; Milan, IN; 11/80 Band; Chrs; Chrh Wkr; Hon Rl; Lbry Ade; NHS; Yth Flsp; Drama Clb; Bsktbl; Bus Schl; Comp Progr.

BRYANT, JAMES; Dunbar HS; Dunbar, WV; Hon Rl; Mod UN; Stu Cncl; Spn Clb; College; Lawyer.

BRYANT, JANET; Eastern HS; Waverly, OH; Chrs; Hon Rl; Yrbk; Pep Clb; Shawnee St Univ; Nursing.

BRYANT, KAREN; Elkins HS; Elkins, WV; 3/220 Cls Rep Soph Cls; NHS; Y-Teens; VP Tri Hi Y 79; Stu Cncl Rep 77; Intl Stu Exchng Progr 79; Span Hon Soc; Univ; Pre Law.

BRYANT, KAREN; Chapmanville HS; Chapmanville, WV; Chrs; Hon Rl; Jr NHS; Sch Pl; Rptr Sch Nwsp; Beta Clb; Pep Clb; Spn Clb; Bsktbl; IM Sprt; Southern W Virginia Coll; Med.

BRYANT, L; Cardinal Mooney HS; Youngstown, OH; Band; Cmnty Wkr; Drl Tm; Orch; Ohio State Univ; Veterinarian Med.

BRYANT, LORI; Struthers HS; Struthers, OH; 8/270 Cmp Fr Grls; Hon Rl; Jr NHS; NHS; Yth Flsp; FNA; Lat Clb; Pep Clb; IM Sprt; Opt Clb Awd; Youngstown St Univ; Med Tech.

BRYANT, RHONDA; Marion HS; Marion, IN; Lbry Ade; Quill & Scroll; Ed Yrbk; Rptr Yrbk; Univ; Spec Educ.

BRYANT, SANDRA; West Jefferson HS; W Jefferson, OH; 7/96 Pres Frsh Cls; Pres Soph Cls; Pres Jr Cls; Cls Rep Sr Cls; Hon Rl; NHS; Quill & Scroll; Sch Pl; Ohi State Univ; Journalism.

BRYANT, SHEILA; Springfield HS; Battle Crk, MI; Chrh Wkr; Hon Rl; NHS; Off Ade; Perfct Attndnc 77; Wrights Beauty Acad; Beautician.

BRYANT, SHELLEY; Eastern HS; Salem, IN; 9/94 Pres Sr Cls; Chrh Wkr; Hon Rl; NHS; FHA; Pep Clb; Spn Clb; Mgrs; Indiana St Univ.

BRYANT, SUSAN; Zanesville HS; Zanesville, OH; Chrs; Girl Scts; Hon Rl; NHS; Orch; Red Cr Ade; Sch Pl; Stu Cncl; Yth Flsp; Sci Clb; Univ; Bus Admin.

BRYANT, SUZANNA; Central Catholic HS; Canton, OH; Sec Soph Cls; Sec Jr Cls; Sec Sr Cls; Cmnty Wkr; Off Ade; Pol Wkr; Yrbk; Fr Clb; Pep Clb; Ten; Southern Methodist Univ.

BRYANT, VALERIE; Covert HS; Covert, MI; 1/38 Pres Frsh Cls; Cls Rep Soph Cls; Pres Jr Cls; Val; Band; Hon Rl; Mod UN; NHS; Orch; Stu Cncl; Mem Of Ron Nelson 1978 All Star Band; Attended Interlochen Michigan All St Music Camp; Univ Of Michigan; Medicine.

BRYANT III, JAMES; West Side HS; Gary, IN; Boy Scts; Chrh Wkr; Drl Tm; Hon Rl; ROTC; Boys Clb Am; Ftbl; Trk; College; Engineering.

BRYCE, CRAIG; Brown City HS; Brown City, MI; Pres Soph Cls; Band; NHS; Yth Flsp; Letter Bsbl; Letter Glf; Voice Dem Awd; Univ; Bus Admin.

BRYCE, MARGARET; Waterford Kettering HS; Drayton Plains, MI; 49/395 Cls Rep Frsh Cls; Sec Sr Cls; Cls Rep Sr Cls; Hon Rl; Jr NHS; NHS; Stu Cncl; Ten; Chrldng; Mich State Univ.

BRYCK, ANNETTE; Plainwell HS; Plainwell, MI; Sec Soph Cls; VP Jr Cls; VP Sr Cls; Girl Scts; Hon Rl; NHS; Rptr Yrbk; Yrbk; Sec Fr Clb; Letter Bsktbl; Univ; Sci.

BRYENTON, ELISABETH; Fairview HS; Fairview Pk, OH; Cmnty Wkr; Girl Scts; Hon Rl; Jr NHS; Lit Mag; NHS; Ger Clb; Sci Clb; Capt Ten; US Army Grand Prize Winner 79; Genrl Motors 1st Plc Awd 79; US Rep To Japan Stud Sci Fair 79; Princeton Univ; Botany.

BRYNER, VAUGHN; John Adams HS; So Bend, IN; 13/400 Chrs; Chrh Wkr; Lit Mag; NHS; Orch; Sch Mus; VP Yth Flsp; College; Music.

BRYSON, BARRY; Buffalo HS; Huntington, WV; Am Leg Boys St; Chrh Wkr; Pol Wkr; Sch Pl; Sprt Ed Sch Nwsp; Rptr Sch Nwsp; Sch Nwsp; Drama Clb; Fr Clb; Socr; Ohio Valley Coll; Theology.

BRYSON, BARRY E; Buffalo HS; Huntington, WV; Am Leg Boys St; Band; Chrh Wkr; Cmnty Wkr; Hon Rl; Mod UN; PAVAS; Pol Wkr; Sch Pl; Sprt Ed Sch Nwsp; Univ; Religion.

BRZEZICKI, MIKE; Deer Park HS; Cincinnati, OH; 1/210 VP Soph Cls; Pres Jr Cls; Boy Scts; Hon Rl; NHS; Stu Cncl; Sprt Ed Sch Nwsp; Letter Bsktbl; Letter Crs Cntry; Capt Ten; 1st Plc In OCTM Local Math Contest 79; Activity Awd 76 79; Its Acad Tm Local Quiz Comp 78 79 & 80; Harvard Univ; Dr.

BRZEZINSKI, TERESE; Bay City All Sts Central HS; Bay City, MI; 8/170 Cl Rep Jr Cls; Cmnty Wkr; Hon Rl; NHS; Pol Wkr; Red Cr Ade; Rptr Yrbk; Trk; Pom Pon; Saginaw Vly Triskelion Merit Schlrshp 79; Bay City Pro & Bus Wmns Club Schlrshp 79; MI Comptn Schlrshp 79; Saginaw Valley St Univ; Acctg.

BRZOZOWY, ROBIN; Theodore Roosevelt HS; Wyandotte, MI; 36/413 Hon Rl; Jr NHS; NHS; Ed Yrbk; Letter Twrlr; Natl Merit SF; Univ Of Mic; Hospital Admin.

BRZUZIEWSKI, G; Cuyahoga Heights HS; Brklyn Hts, OH; 2/75 Hon Rl; Bsktbl; Ftbl; Trk; Tmr; College; Physics.

BUANNO, ANDREA; Euclid Sr HS; Euclid, OH; 106/703 Hon Rl; Lit Mag; NHS; Quill & Scroll; Rptr Sch Nwsp; Notre Dame Coll; Journalism.

BUBALO, ANN; Kankakee Valley HS; Wheatfield, IN; 7/190 Hon Rl; NHS; 4-H; Sci Clb; Spn Clb; 4-H Awd; Purdue Univ; Nursing.

BUBALO, JOE; Kankakee Vly HS; Wheatfield, IN; 18/183 Am Leg Boys St; Hon Rl; Lbry Ade; NHS; Sch Nwsp; 4-H; Mth Clb; Sci Clb; 4-H Awd; Univ.

BUBLITZ, SHELLEY; Reese HS; Reese, MI; 17/131 Cls Rep Frsh Cls; Cls Rep Soph Cls; Cl Rep Jr Cls; Cls Rep Sr Cls; Hon Rl; Off Ade; Stu Cncl; Pres Ger Clb; Pep Clb; PPFtbl; Northwood Inst; Acctg.

BUBLITZ, STEPHEN; Bridgeport HS; Bridgeport, MI; Band; Boy Scts; Chrh Wkr; Cmnty Wkr; Hon Rl; Sch Pl; Sct Actv; Stg Crw; Yth Flsp; Letter Crs Cntry; Ctrl Michigan St Univ; Bus Admin.

BUCATA, DIANE; Aquinas HS; Dearborn Hts, MI; Band; Chrs; Hosp Ade; Sch Mus; Sch Pl; Stg Crw; Stu Cncl; VP Drama Clb; College; Nursing.

BUCCANERO, TRACEY; Ontanagon Area HS; Ontonagon, MI; Cls Rep Sr Cls; Val; Band; Hon Rl; NHS; Off Ade; Sch Pl; Stu Cncl; Drama Clb; Bsktbl; Michigan Tech Univ; Nursing.

BUCCARELLI, DINO; Mount View HS; Welch, WV; Cmnty Wkr; Hon Rl; Jr NHS; Natl Merit Ltr; West Virginia Univ.

BUCCELLATO, PATRICIA; Adlai Stevenson HS; Sterling Hts, MI; 120/612 Chrh Wkr; Cmnty Wkr; Girl Scts; Hon Rl; Off Ade; Pol Wkr; Sct Actv; Stg Crw; Sch Nwsp; Leo Clb; Voc Schl; Bus Admin.

BUCCI, DOMINIC; Grand River Academy; Pittsburgh, PA; Hon Rl; Rptr Sch Nwsp; Bsktbl; Socr; Ten; Math Assoc Of Amer Awd 79; Univ; Comp Analysis.

BUCCI, ENRICO; Rocky River HS; Rocky Rvr, OH; Cls Rep Frsh Cls; Hon Rl; Capt Socr; Cit Awd; Coll; Acctg.

BUCCI, ROSEMARY; Elwood Cmnty HS; Elwood, IN; 4/186 Cl Rep Jr Cls; Cls Rep Sr Cls; Pres NHS; Sch Pl; Stu Cncl; Yth Flsp; Drama Clb; Sec FBLA; Mth Clb; Pep Clb; Butler Univ; Acctg.

BUCEY, STEVE; Buckeye North HS; Mingo Junction, OH; 24/120 Sci Clb; Letter Wrstlng; Univ; Physics.

BUCEY, STEVEN W; Buckeye North HS; Mingo Jct, OH; 24/120 Band; Boy Scts; Hon Rl; Mth Clb; Sci Clb; Letter Wrstlng; Univ; Physics.

BUCHANAN, GLENDA; Leetonia HS; Salem, OH; 5/86 Hon Rl; Lbry Ade; Sch Pl; Am Leg Awd; Natl Merit Ltr; Excllnc In Home Ec 76; Spanish III Honor Stdnt 78; 13th In Dist For Eng II Schlrshp Test 78; Malone Coll; Med.

BUCHANAN, JANET; Wirt County HS; Elizabeth, WV; 20/96 Trs Jr Cls; Band; Chrs; Chrh Wkr; Cmnty Wkr; Hon Rl; NHS; Off Ade; Yth Flsp; 4-H; Parkersburg Community College; Denta.

BUCHANAN, KARIN; West Lafayette HS; W Lafayette, IN; 86/179 Chrs; Hon Rl; Sch Mus; Drama Clb; Ger Clb; Pep Clb; Pom Pon; Purdue Univ; Mgmt.

BUCHANAN, LARRY; Cascade HS; Coatesville, IN; Band; Chrs; Chrh Wkr; FCA; Sch Pl; 4-H; Letter Gym; Swmmng; Outstndg Yth Awd & Essay Contest 76; Solo Contst Piano 1st At Area Contst 1st At St 78; Bob Jones Univ; Piano.

BUCHANAN, ROBINA; Jane Addams Vocational HS; Cleveland, OH; Hon Rl; Hosp Ade; NHS; Stg Crw; Cit Awd; Western Rescue Univ; Rn.

BUCHANAN, VICKI; Big Creek HS; Berwind, WV; 16/107 Chrs; Hon Rl; Lbry Ade; FHA; Southwest Virginia Cmnty Coll; Psych.

BUCHER, BOB; Lima Sr HS; Lima, OH; Off Ade; Yth Flsp; Lima Branch Of Ohio St; Acctg.

BUCHER, DENISE; Valley HS; Reader, WV; Pres Frsh Cls; Band; Chrs; Chrh Wkr; Drm Mjrt; Girl Scts; Hon Rl; NHS; Sch Pl; Treas Stu Cncl; West Liberty St Coll; Educ.

BUCHER, LEANNE; La Crosse HS; La Crosse, IN; Trs Frsh Cls; Pres Jr Cls; Pres Sr Cls; Band; Hon Rl; Lbry Ade; NHS; 4-H; Ger Clb; Pep Clb; Univ; Soc Work.

BUCHER, RICHARD; Walnut Hills HS; Cincinnati, OH; Cl Rep Jr Cls; Band; Y-Teens; Rptr Yrbk; Rptr Sch Nwsp; Capt Socr; Dartmouth Coll; Journalism.

BUCHHOLZ, LYNDA; Central Montcalm HS; Stanton, MI; Band; Chrs; Girl Scts; Hon Rl; Lbry Ade; MMM; Sct Actv; Rptr Sch Nwsp; 4-H; Mgrs; Cntrl Michigan Univ.

BUCHHOP, JEFF; Hillsdale HS; Hillsdale, MI; 28/182 Boy Scts; Chrs; Jr NHS; NHS; Sct Actv; Key Clb; Michigan St Univ; Pre Vet.

BUCHHOP, TRACEY; Four County Jnt Voc Schl; Liberty Center, OH; 1/533 Trs Frsh Cls; Cls Rep Soph Cls; VP Jr Cls; Val; Band; Chrh Wkr; Hon Rl; NHS; Off Ade; Red Cr Ade; Sec.

BUCHMAN, GERALD; Calvert HS; Tiffin, OH; Cls Rep Frsh Cls; Cls Rep Soph Cls; Cl Rep Jr Cls; Cls Rep Sr Cls; Hon Rl; NHS; Stu Cncl; Rptr Sch Nwsp; Wrstlng; Mgrs; Outstanding Soph Awd; Kiwanis Eldon Wert Awd; Ohio St Univ; Vet.

BUCHNER, KITTY; Mendon HS; Mendon, MI; Chrh Wkr; Hon Rl; 4-H; PPFtbl; Glen Oaks; Sec.

BUCHNER, PAUL; St Ignatius HS; Parma, OH; 90/309 Hon Rl; Mod UN; Pres Sct Actv; Lat Clb; Trk; IM Sprt; Georgetown Univ; Poli Sci.

BUCHSIEB, CHRISTINE; Centerville HS; Dayton, OH; 112/587 Cls Rep Frsh Cls; Cls Rep Soph Cls; Cl Rep Jr Cls; Band; NHS; Sch Mus; Stu Cncl; Capt Chrldng; Miami Univ; Finance.

BUCINSKI, ELAINE; Pine River Jr Sr HS; Le Roy, MI; Band; Chrs; Hon Rl; Sch Mus; FHA; Gym; Swmmng; Trk; IM Sprt; Twrlr; Ferris St Univ; Nursing.

BUCK, CHERYL A; Grand Valley HS; Windsor, OH; 23/114 Trs Sr Cls; Hon Rl; Drama Clb; 4-H; FHA; OEA; 4-H Awd; Busns Schl; Computer Operator.

BUCK, DEBBIE; Celina Sr HS; Celina, OH; Hon Rl; Wright St Univ; Bus.

BUCK, ELIZABETH; Federal Hocking HS; Gu ysville, OH; Girl Scts; Red Cr Ade; Ohi Univ; Psych.

BUCK, KEITH; Suttons Bay HS; Suttons Bay, MI; 3/63 Cls Rep Frsh Cls; Cls Rep Soph Cls; Cl Rep Jr Cls; Cls Rep Sr Cls; Hon Rl; Stu Cncl; Bsbl; Bsktbl; Ftbl; Letter Ftbl; N W Michigan Coll; Maritime Acad.

BUCK, SUSAN; Ross HS; Hamilton, OH; 5/240 Chrs; Girl Scts; Hon Rl; NHS; Stg Crw; Rptr Yrbk; Rptr Sch Nwsp; Drama Clb; Spn Clb; Natl Merit Ltr; College; English.

BUCKBEE, JEANNE; Hampshire HS; Romney, WV; 4/205 Cl Rep Jr Cls; Chrs; Hon Rl; Stu Cncl; Pom Pon; College.

BUCKEL, STEVE; Scecina Mem HS; Indianapolis, IN; 38/196 Chrh Wkr; Hon Rl; JA; Ten; JA Awd; Indiana Univ; Bus.

BUCKENMEYER, PHILIP; Algonac HS; Algonac, MI; 50/250 Hon Rl; NHS; Rus Clb; Spn Clb; Natl Merit Ltr; Michigan St Univ.

BUCKINGHAM, DARLENE; Willard HS; Willard, OH; Am Leg Aux Girls St; Band; Hon Rl; NHS; Rptr Yrbk; VP 4-H; FHA; Crs Cntry; Trk; Am Leg Awd; Coll; Nursing.

BUCKINGHAM, FRANCES; South Bend Washington HS; South Bend, IN; 88/385 Girl Scts; Hon Rl; Stu Cncl; Indiana Univ; Exec Sec.

BUCKINGHAM, SUSAN; Portage Northern HS; Portage, MI; Hon Rl; VP DECA; Fr Clb; Pep Clb; Chrldng; Michigan St Univ; Bus.

BUCKLE, SHEILA; Belleville HS; Belleville, MI; Hon Rl; Letter Crs Cntry; Letter Gym; Letter Swmmng; Letter Trk; Chrldng; Eastern Univ; Occupational Therapy.

BUCKLES, DIANA; Tell City HS; Tell City, IN; 34/229 Cls Rep Frsh Cls; Am Leg Aux Girls St; Lit Mag; Stu Cncl; Drama Clb; Fr Clb; Pep Clb; Mat Maids; Indiana Univ; Bus.

BUCKLES, PATTY; Coventry HS; Akron, OH; 12/200 Hon Rl; Quill & Scroll; Rptr Yrbk; Rptr Sch Nwsp; GAA; Univ Of Akron; Math.

BUCKLESS, MELISSA; Brighton HS; South Lyon, MI; 50/300 Cl Rep Jr Cls; Am Leg Aux Girls St; Band; Pres Chrs; Hon Rl; Mdrgl; Sch Mus; Stu Cncl; Drama Clb; Letter Trk; Mich State Univ; Vocal Music.

BUCKLEY, CINDY; Franklin HS; Farnklin, OH; Chrs; Hon Rl; Off Ade; Sch Mus; Treas Yth Flsp; Fr Clb; Sec FTA; Anderson Coll; Art.

BUCKLEY, MARVIN E; Arsenal Tech HS; Indianapolis, IN; Pres Frsh Cls; Pres Soph Cls; Pres Jr Cls; Pres Sr Cls; Band; Hon Rl; PAVAS; Sch Mus; Mth Clb; Rdo Clb; ITT Tech Inst; Elec Engr.

BUCKLEY, RHONDA; Carl Brablec HS; Roseville, MI; Band; Hon Rl; Jr NHS; Sch Mus; Treas Stu Cncl; Trk; Capt Chrldng; Coach Actv; Central Michigan Univ; Music.

BUCKLEY, TERRI; Garfield HS; Akron, OH; Cl Rep Jr Cls; Sec Sr Cls; Cls Rep Sr Cls; Band; Hon Rl; NHS; OEA; Letter Trk;.

BUCKMAN, JOHN; Patterson Co Op HS; Dayton, OH; Band; Hon Rl; Stu Cncl; Coll; Elec Tech.

BUCKMAN, JULIA; Marquette Sr HS; Marquette, MI; 89/427 Band; Spn Clb; Mi Compt Schlshp 79; Michigan St Univ; Bus Law.

BUCKMASTER, DENNIS R; De Kalb HS; Ashley, IN; 4/285 Am Leg Boys St; Band; NHS; Yth Flsp; Pres 4-H; Sec FFA; Pres Sci Clb; 4-H Awd; Tri Kappa HS Honor Banquet; Purdue Univ; Ag Engr.

BUCKMASTER, JOE; Napoleon HS; Napoleon, OH; Band; Boy Scts; Chrh Wkr; Cmnty Wkr; Hon Rl; Sch Mus; Sch Pl; Stg Crw; Letter Wrstlng; IM Sprt; University.

BUCKNELL, THERESE; Southfield HS; Southfield, MI; Hon Rl; Off Ade; Scr Kpr; Northern Mic Univ; Nursing.

BUCKNER, A; Brookhaven HS; Columbus, OH; Band; Chrs; Debate Tm; Lit Mag; Orch; Stg Crw; Ed Sch Nwsp; Drama Clb; Fr Clb; Rdo Clb; Univ; Literature.

BUCKNER, CYNTHIA; John F Kennedy HS; Cleveland, OH; 180403 Cls Rep Sr Cls; Aud/Vis; Chrh Wkr; Hon Rl; NHS; Stg Crw; Stu Cncl; OEA; Rdo Clb; Cit Awd; J F K Chapt Of Cleveland Tchr Union Shclshp 79; J F K Radio Clyub Excllnc In Progr Awd 79; Baldwin Wallace Coll; Acctg.

BUCKNER, STACY; Brownsburg HS; Brownsbrg, IN; 35/314 Cls Rep Frsh Cls; Cls Rep Soph Cls; Cl Rep Jr Cls; Hon Rl; NHS; Letter Trk; Mat Maids; Univ; Bus.

BUCSI, CONNIE; Owosso HS; Owosso, MI; Band; Hon Rl; Off Ade; 4-H; Lat Clb; Gym; Twrlr; Cit Awd; 4-H Awd; Univ; Modeling.

BUCSI, JIM; Corunna HS; Owosso, MI; Hon Rl; FFA; Mech.

BUCY, RANDALL; Warren Western Reserve HS; Warren, OH; Chrh Wkr; Pol Wkr; Kent State; Criminal Justice.

BUCZEK, ANTON; West Catholic HS; Grand Rapids, MI; Hon Rl; Mic Tech; Civil Eng.

BUCZKIEWICZ, JAN E; Copley HS; Fairlawn, OH; Trs Sr Cls; Hon Rl; NHS; Rptr Yrbk; Letter Bsktbl; Letter Trk; Coach Actv; GAA; Univ; Med.

BUCZKOWSKI, LISA; Washington HS; South Bend, IN; 32/355 Hon Rl; JA; 4-H; Fr Clb; 4-H Awd; Indiana Univ; Acctg.

BUDA, DENYSE L; Davison HS; Davison, MI; Band; Chrs; Debate Tm; Girl Scts; Hon Rl; Off Ade; Sch Pl; Drama Clb; 4-H; College; Journalism Or Data Proc.

BUDA, DINIPE; Davison Sr HS; Davison, MI; Band; Chrs; Debate Tm; Girl Scts; Hon Rl; Off Ade; Sch Pl; 4-H; Ger Clb; Pep Clb; Jrnlsm.

BUDAJI, THERESE; Normandy Sr HS; Parma, OH; 2/649 Chrs; Cmnty Wkr; Hon Rl; Lbry Ade; NHS; Sch Pl; Fr Clb; Coll; Math.

BUDAK, MARY; Marquette HS; Michigan City, IN; Chrs; Hon Rl; NHS; Pol Wkr; Sch Mus; Stg Crw; Yrbk; Sch Nwsp; Ger Clb; Sci Clb; Valparaiso Univ; Nursing.

BUDAY, DOUGLAS; Charlevoix HS; Charlevoix, MI; Cl Rep Jr Cls; Cls Rep Sr Cls; Am Leg Boys St; Band; Boy Scts; Fr Clb; Bsktbl; Ftbl; Trk; IM Sprt; Michigan St Univ; Comp Progr.

BUDD, JIMMY R; Brandon HS; Goodrich, MI; Cls Rep Frsh Cls; Pres Soph Cls; Pres Jr Cls; Pres Sr Cls; Hon Rl; Stu Cncl; Sch Nwsp; Ftbl; Pres Awd; Hist Civil War Awd 77; Univ Of Michigan; Law.

BUDD, PHILIPPA; Notre Dame Academy; Toledo, OH; Hon Rl; NHS; Sch Pl; Fr Clb; Univ; Nursing.

BUDDE, FRANK; Saint Xavier HS; Cincinnati, OH; 41/264 Cmnty Wkr; Hon Rl; NHS; Spn Clb; Letter Glf; IM Sprt; Univ Of Notre Dame; Business Admin.

BUDDE, GERALD; Moeller HS; Cincinnati, OH; 12/256 Hon Rl; Bsktbl; Chrldng; Univ Of Dayton; Acctg.

BUDDE, JULIA; Salem Sr HS; Salem, OH; Boy Scts; Sci Clb; Spn Clb; Univ; Med Sci.

BUDDELMEYER, RICHARD; Holgate Local HS; New Bavaria, OH; 22/58 Hon Rl; Bsbl; Bsktbl; Ftbl; Mgrs; Northwestern Tech; Nursing.

BUDDELMEYER, WANETA; Northridge HS; Johnstown, OH; 6/116 Am Leg Aux Girls St; Band; Chrs; Chrh Wkr; Hon Rl; NHS; Sch Mus; Stg Crw; Stu Cncl; Sch Nwsp; John Galbruth Schslhp To Oh Univ 79; Century III Leardshp Finlst 79; Oh Bd Of Regnst Schlshp 79; Ohio Univ; Brdcstng.

BUDICH, CHRISTOPHER; Chaminade Julienne HS; Dayton, OH; Cmnty Wkr; Hon Rl; Socr; College; Med Tech.

BUDIN, PAMELA; Malabar HS; Mansfield, OH; 6/261 Cls Rep Frsh Cls; Cls Rep Soph Cls; Cl Rep Jr Cls; Cls Rep Sr Cls; Band; Hon Rl; NHS; Orch; VP Stu Cncl; Hon Rl; Mayor For A Day; Univ; Pre Law.

BUDLONG, CYNTHIA; Bay HS; Bay Vill, OH; Cls Rep Soph Cls; Cl Rep Jr Cls; Cls Rep Sr Cls; Chrs; Off Ade; Stu Cncl; Pep Clb; Capt Chrldng; IM Sprt; PPFtbl; Southern Seminary; Sec Sci.

BUDNIK, THOMAS; Littlefield Public HS; Brutus, MI; 2/45 Pres Frsh Cls; VP Soph Cls; VP Jr Cls; Hon Rl; NHS; VP Stu Cncl; Letter Bsbl; Letter Crs Cntry; Letter Trk; Harvard Univ; Law.

BUDNY, THOMAS; Parma Sr HS; Parma, OH; Cls Rep Frsh Cls; Cl Rep Jr Cls; Cls Rep Sr Cls; Sch Pl; Stu Cncl; Drama Clb; Ftbl; Univ.

BUDNY, TRACY; Bloomfield HS; Bloomfield, IN; 16/85 Boy Scts; Chrh Wkr; Hon Rl; Treas NHS; Yrbk; Sci Clb; Spn Clb; Summer Schlrshp Rose Hulman Comp Sci Camp; Univ; Comp Sci.

BUDZINSKI, CINDY; Cleveland Central Cath HS; Cleveland, OH; 8/183 Cls Rep Frsh Cls; Pres Jr Cls; Hon Rl; NHS; Sch Mus; Sch Pl; Rptr Sch Nwsp; Drama Clb; Spn Clb; Capt Chrldng; Spanish Poetry Declamation 1st Pl; Whos Who In Foreign Lang Stu; Cleveland St Univ; Law.

BUDZINSKI, CYNTHIA; Cleveland Cntrl Catholic HS; Cleveland, OH; 8/180 Cls Rep Frsh Cls; Pres Jr Cls; Cls Rep Sr Cls; Hon Rl; NHS; Sch Mus; Rptr Sch Nwsp; John Carroll Univ; Psych.

BUECHE, JOSEPH; Rogers HS; Wyoming, MI; 19/255 VP Band; Boy Scts; Hon Rl; NHS; IM Sprt; 4-H Awd; Michigan Tech Univ; Indus Engr.

BUECHLER, LESA; Jasper HS; Jasper, IN; Chrh Wkr; Cmnty Wkr; Lbry Ade; PAVAS; Rptr Sch Nwsp; Pep Clb; Voc Schl.

BUECHLER, MIKE; Forest Park HS; Ferdinand, IN; Hon Rl; Ger Clb; Bsktbl; Crs Cntry; Trk; IM Sprt; Voc Schl; Diesel Mech.

BUECHNER, PENELOPE; Groveport Madison HS; Groveport, OH; Hon Rl; FHA; Pep Clb; Spn Clb; Chrldng; JETS Awd; Univ.

BUEHL, JOY; Hastings HS; Hastings, MI; Cmp Fr Grls; Chrs; Hon Rl; Lbry Ade; Beta Clb; Fr Clb; PPFtbl; Jr Coll.

BUEHLER, SUE; Clay HS; Oregon, OH; Band; FCA; Hon Rl; Bsktbl; Trk; Coll; Acctg.

BUEHRER, JENNY; Archbold Area HS; Stryker, OH; Cl Rep Jr Cls; Band; Chrs; Hon Rl; Sch Mus; Stu Cncl; Yth Flsp; Pep Clb; Capt Chrldng; Coll; Elem Ed.

BUEHRER, REGGIE; Stryker Public HS; Stryker, OH; Am Leg Boys St; Chrs; Hon Rl; Letter Wrstlng; Am Leg Awd; Toledo Univ; Busns.

BUELL, BRAIN; Franklin HS; Franklin, OH; Hon Rl;.

BUETTNER, BART; East Kentwood HS; Kentwood, MI; Mgrs; Natl Merit Ltr; Ferris St Coll; Bus Admin.

BUETTNER, JOSEPH; Delphos Saint Johns HS; Delphos, OH; 68/137 Band; Hon Rl; Orch; Sch Mus; Sch Pl; Fr Clb;.

BUETTNER, JULIE; Delphos St Johns HS; Delphos, OH; Band; Hon Rl; Hosp Ade; 4-H; FTA; Trk; Chrldng; Twrlr; 4-H Awd; College; Nursing.

BUETTNER, KEVIN; Ottoville Local HS; Ft Jennings, OH; Cls Rep Soph Cls; Chrs; Chrh Wkr; Hon Rl; Stu Cncl; Yth Flsp; 4-H; Fr Clb; Bsktbl; Trk; Factory Work.

BUETTNER, LORRAINE; Groveport Madison Sr HS; Canal Winchstr, OH; Pres Frsh Cls; Pres Soph Cls; Pres Jr Cls; Am Leg Aux Girls St; Drl Tm; Hon Rl; NHS; Stu Cncl; Rptr Sch Nwsp; 4-H; Ohio St Univ; Home Ec.

BUEY, JOSEPH W; Bridgeport HS; Bridgeport, WV; Am Leg Boys St; Hon Rl; Jr NHS; Yrbk; Key Clb; West Liberty Univ.

BUFFALOE, CHRIS; Decatur Central HS; Indpls, IN; 2/450 Hon Rl; Mod UN; NHS; Lat Clb; Trk; IM Sprt; Indiana Univ; Law.

BUFFER, THOMAS; Upper Arlington HS; Columbus, OH; 99/660 Band; Hon Rl; NHS; Sch Pl; Sct Actv; Drama Clb; Pres Ger Clb; Natl Merit Schl; Ohio State Univ.

BUFFINGTON, STEVE; Anderson HS; Anderson, IN; Cls Rep Soph Cls; Cl Rep Jr Cls; Cls Rep Sr Cls; Boy Scts; Hon Rl; Sct Actv; Stu Cncl; Yth Flsp; Rptr Sch Nwsp; Sch Nwsp; Univ; Engr.

BUFFO, RICHARD; Hoover HS; North Canton, OH; Cls Rep Soph Cls; Cl Rep Jr Cls; Hst Sr Cls; Cls Rep Sr Cls; Chrs; Hon Rl; Sch Mus; College.

BUFLER, MARCIA; Stephen T Badin HS; Hamilton, OH; Sec Frsh Cls; VP Soph Cls; Cl Rep Jr Cls; Hon Rl; Stu Cncl; FHA; Gym; Chrldng; College.

BUGAI, ALAN; Traverse City Sr HS; Traverse City, MI; Aud/Vis; Hon Rl; Lbry Ade; Lit Mag; Rptr Sch Nwsp; Sch Nwsp; Cit Awd; Key Awds Acad Ach; St Of Michigan Competitive Schlrshp; N W Michigan Coll; Public Health.

BUGEDA, MARY; Kirtland HS; Kirtland, OH; 10/125 VP Jr Cls; Capt AFS; Drl Tm; Hon Rl; NHS; Sch Mus; Stu Cncl; Sch Nwsp; College.

BUGGELE, SHARON; Edison HS; Milan, OH; 9/125 VP Soph Cls; Band; Hon Rl; NHS; Sch Pl; St g Crw; Drama Clb; Mth Clb; Sci Clb; Tmr; College.

BUGGS, GEMI R; South HS; Youngstown, OH; 5/293 Sec Frsh Cls; Cl Rep Jr Cls; Cls Rep Sr Cls; Hon Rl; Jr NHS; NHS; Off Ade; Stu Cncl; Letter Trk; Chrldng; Arizona State Univ; Engr.

BUGH, DAVID; Bedford N Lawrence HS; Bedford, IN; Boy Scts; Red Cr Ade; Sct Actv; Yrbk; Boys Clb Am; Drama Clb; Spn Clb; Ftbl; Trk; Cit Awd; Schl Schlrshp Awd; Purdue Univ; Science.

BUGHER, RICHARD; New Haven HS; Ft Wane, IN; 8/274 Fr Clb; Letter Wrstlng; Univ.

BUHAGIAR, ROSEMARIE; St Andrew HS; Detroit, MI; Sec Frsh Cls; Sec Soph Cls; Sec Jr Cls; Sec Sr Cls; Chrh Wkr; Hon Rl; NHS; Madonna College; Reg Nurse.

BUHNGIAR, ROSEMARIE; St Andrew HS; Detroit, MI; Sec Frsh Cls; Sec Soph Cls; Sec Jr Cls; Sec Sr Cls; Chrh Wkr; Hon Rl; NHS; Sch Pl; Stg Crw; Stu Cncl; Univ; Nursing.

BUI, DUNG Q; Ben Davis HS; Indianapolis, IN; Fr Clb; Swmmng;.

BUICE, CHERYL; Adlai E Stevenson HS; Sterling Hgts, MI; Chrh Wkr; Ger Clb; Natl Merit SF; Wayne State Univ; Liberal Arts.

BUICK, DAVID; Kearsley HS; Flint, MI; Cls Rep Frsh Cls; Pres Soph Cls; Pres Jr Cls; Boy Scts; Chrh Wkr; Hon Rl; NHS; Pol Wkr; Sch Pl; Sct Actv; Mi Press Assoc Otstndng Carrier Of Yr 77; Natl Carrier Of Yr 77; Participant Lions Internatl Youth Camp 79; Univ; Med.

BUICKEL, LARRY L; Central HS; Evansville, IN; 7/500 Boy Scts; Cmnty Wkr; Hon Rl; NHS; Sch Pl; Sct Actv; Stu Cncl; Drama Clb; Lat Clb; Bsbl; Univ Of Evansville; Comp Sci.

BUIE, SYLVIA A; Immaculata HS; Detroit, MI; 4/93 Debate Tm; Hon Rl; Hosp Ade; VP JA; NHS; Red Cr Ade; Mgrs; Natl Achv Schol Prog For Negro Stu 1978; Semi Finalist Mich Competitive Schol Prog 1978; Univ Of Akron; Med.

BUIKEMA, SANDRA; Mendon HS; Mendon, MI; Band; Hon Rl; Lbry Ade; NHS; Sch Mus; Yth Flsp; Fr Clb; Letter Trk; Mat Maids; PPFtbl; Parsons Bus Schl; Sec.

BUIST, SHERYL; South Christian HS; Byron Center, MI; 6/173 Pres Frsh Cls; Band; Chrh Wkr; Drl Tm; Hon Rl; Sch Pl; 4-H; Pep Clb; Chrldng; Calvin Coll; Social Work.

BUIT, STEPHEN; Mona Shores HS; Muskegon, MI; NHS; Crs Cntry; Trk; IM Sprt; Hope Coll; Engr.

BUJOLD, MARY; Marian HS; Troy, MI; Band; Girl Scts; Hon Rl; Mod UN; Rptr Sch Nwsp; Spn Clb; Swmmng; Trk; IM Sprt; Scr Kpr; St Marys Of Notre Dame; Business.

BUKER, VICKY; William Henry Harrison HS; W Lafayette, IN; 3/302 VP Jr Cls; Band; Hon Rl; Sec NHS; Sch Mus; Stu Cncl; Fr Clb; Keyettes; Pres Mth Clb; Letter Trk; College; Arch.

BUKOVCIK, RONALD; Ovid Elsie HS; Henderson, MI; 18/170 Hon Rl; NHS; 4-H; Letter Bsbl; Letter Ftbl; Coach Actv; IM Sprt; 4-H Awd; Mi Schslhp Progr 79; Cntrl Michigan Univ.

BUKOVEC, SUE; Euclid Sr HS; Euclid, OH; 30/720 Hon Rl; Swmmng; Mgrs; Cit Awd; Univ; Drftsmn.

BUKOWICZ, JOHN; Bishop Gallagher HS; Roseville, MI; 40/348 Hon Rl; Sch Pl; IM Sprt; Natl Merit Ltr; Natl Merit Schl; Wayne St Univ; Busns Admin.

BUKRIM, SHARON A; University HS; Mount Morris, PA; 7/175 Band; Chrs; Hon Rl; Jr NHS; NHS; Rptr Yrbk; Rptr Sch Nwsp; Pep Clb; IM Sprt; Scr Kpr; West Virginia Univ; Acctg.

BULACH, JAMES; Eaton HS; Eaton, OH; 9/170 Band; Hon Rl; Lbry Ade; NHS; FFA; Lat Clb; Perfct Attndnc 78; Phy Ftns Awd Pres 76; Tech Schl; Farming.

BULETKO, ANDY; Canfield HS; Canfield, OH; Hon Rl; Key Clb; Lat Clb; Spn Clb; Letter Bsbl; Letter Ftbl; All Mahoning Vly Conf Tm 78; All NEO Tm 78; Youngstown St Univ; Bus.

BULGER, JIM; Bellaire HS; Jacobsburg, OH; 79/237 Sec Sr Cls; Cls Rep Sr Cls; Hon Rl; Stu Cncl; Beta Clb; Fr Clb; Letter Ftbl; IM Sprt; Earlham Coll; Chem Engr.

BULICK, TINA; Milan HS; Sunman, IN; 8/95 Chrs; Chrh Wkr; Hon Rl; NHS; Off Ade; Rptr Yrbk; FTA; Art School.

BULINGTON, PATTY; La Crosse HS; La Crosse, IN; 5/40 Sec Sr Cls; Trs Sr Cls; NHS; Rptr Yrbk; FHA; Pres Ger Clb; Pep Clb; Bsktbl; Trk; Pom Pon; Photog.

BULKA, MARY; Notre Dame HS; Clarksburg, WV; Chrs; Pep Clb; Bsktbl; Trk; Alderson Broaodus Univ; Phys Ther.

BULKOWSKI, ELIZABETH; Fostoria HS; Fostoria, OH; Chrs; Hon Rl; Hosp Ade; Sec NHS; Sch Mus; Ed Yrbk; Coach Actv; Bowling Green State Univ; Med.

BULKOWSKI, M L; Nordonia HS; Northfield, OH; Cls Rep Sr Cls; Chrh Wkr; Cmnty Wkr; Stu Cncl; Yth Flsp; Pep Clb; IM Sprt; Mgrs; Mat Maids; College; Bus.

BULLA, DWAYNE; Highland Sr HS; Highland, IN; 46/511 Chrs; Hon Rl; NHS; Sch Mus; Sch Pl; Pres Key Clb; IM Sprt; Mgrs; Perfect Attendance Awd; Recognition Awd From Muscular Dystrophy Assc; Most Valuable Player; Michigan Coll; Law.

BULLARD, GENEVA; Lincoln HS; Cambridge, IN; Chrs; Girl Scts; Hon Rl; Y-Teens; 4-H; OEA;.

BULLINGER, RUTH; Ottoville HS; Cloverdale, OH; Chrh Wkr; Hon Rl; Lbry Ade; FHA; Mgrs; Busns Schl; Busns.

BULLION, CHRIS; Valley HS; Lucasville, OH; 45/107 Band; Chrs; Hon Rl; Sch Pl; 4-H; FHA; FTA; Morehead State Univ; Music.

BUMB, CAROLYN; Seneca East HS; Bellevue, OH; Sec Frsh Cls; Cls Rep Soph Cls; VP Jr Cls; Chrs; Hon Rl; Jr NHS; NHS; Sch Pl; Stu Cncl; Drama Clb; Voc Schl; English.

BUMBUL, KARL; Woodhaven HS; Trenton, MI; 7/202 Cmnty Wkr; Jr NHS; NHS; 4-H; Crs Cntry; Swmmng; Trk; Ferris State College; Electronics.

BUMBUL, KEVIN; Woodhaven HS; Trenton, MI; Jr NHS; NHS; 4-H; Letter Bsktbl; Letter Trk; IM Sprt; 4-H Awd; Wahue Cnty Cmnty Coll; Auto Mech.

BUMGARDNER, ERIC; Wahama HS; New Haven, WV; 7/95 Am Leg Boys St; Hon Rl; NHS; 4-H; Ftbl; Trk; W Vir Inst Of Tech; Civil Engr.

BUMGARDNER, JEFFREY; Wahama HS; Mason, WV; Am Leg Boys St; Band; Boy Scts; Chrh Wkr; Hon Rl; Sch Mus; Treas Yth Flsp; Key Clb; Rdo Clb; West Virginia Tech Univ; Comp Sci.

BUMGARNER, LISA; Spencer HS; Spencer, WV; Band; Cmnty Wkr; Hon Rl; Pep Clb; Chrldng; Univ; Archt.

BUMKE, LISA; Marion HS; Marion, IN; Chrs; Chrh Wkr; Girl Scts; Hon Rl; Jr NHS; NHS; Sch Mus; Sec Yth Flsp; Yrbk; Natl Merit Ltr; Purdue Univ; Interior Dsgn.

BUMPUS, PAM; Madison Comprehensive HS; Mansfield, OH; Cl Rep Jr Cls; Band; FHA; OEA; Tech School; Bus.

BUNCH, STANLEY; Medina HS; Medina, OH; 61/365 Chrs; Chrh Wkr; NHS; Red Cr Ade; Sch Mus; Sch Pl; Drama Clb; Letter Gym; Coach Actv; Mgrs; Buckeye Coll; Data Proc.

BUNDY, CHERYL; Northrop HS; Ft Wayne, IN; 13/645 Band; Hon Rl; Off Ade; Orch; Sci Clb; Trk; Cit Awd; Earlham; Bio.

BUNDY, PAULA; Weir HS; Weirton, WV; 4/355 Band; Chrh Wkr; Pres Hosp Ade; Jr NHS; NHS; Orch; Sch Mus; Yth Flsp; Rptr Yrbk; Sch Nwsp; Washington & Jefferson Coll; Pre Med.

BUNDY, ROGER; Salem HS; Salem, IN; Hon Rl; NHS; Stu Cncl; Sci Clb; Letter Bsktbl; Letter Crs Cntry; Letter Trk; Indiana State; Bus.

BUNDY, SHERRELL; New Palestine HS; Greenfield, IN; 1/189 VP Band; Sec NHS; Sch Mus; Stg Crw; Stu Cncl; Drama Clb; Fr Clb; DAR Awd; Purdue Univ; French.

BUNDY, SUSAN; Columbia City Joint HS; Columbia City, IN; Cls Rep Frsh Cls; Cls Rep Soph Cls; Cl Rep Jr Cls; Cls Rep Sr Cls; Chrs; FCA; NHS; Quill & Scroll; Stu Cncl; Ed Yrbk; Nursing Schl; Nurse.

BUNEMANN, L; Trenton HS; Trenton, MI; 1/500 Band; Chrs; Chrh Wkr; Cmnty Wkr; Drm Bgl; Hon Rl; NHS; Off Ade; Sch Mus; Sch Pl; Solon Ensemble Six Time Awd Winner; Beloit Coll; Pre Med.

BUNEVICH, WILLIAM; Holy Name Nazareth HS; Parma, OH; Aud/Vis; Boy Scts; Stg Crw; Letter Bsbl; Letter Ftbl; Wrstlng; Coach Actv; IM Sprt; Cit Awd; Akron Univ; Pharmacy.

BUNGE, DAVID; Van Buren HS; Findlay, OH; VP Soph Cls; Band; Chrs; FCA; Rptr Yrbk; Rptr Sch Nwsp; Letter Bsbl; Letter Bsktbl; College.

BUNGE, DENISE; Van Buren HS; Findlay, OH; Trs Frsh Cls; AFS; Band; Cmp Fr Grls; Chrs; Hon Rl; Sch Mus; Rptr Yrbk; Drama Clb; Scr Kpr; College; Foreign Language.

BUNGE, ROBIN; Brown County HS; Nashville, IN; Band; Sec FCA; NHS; Sch Mus; Sch Pl; Stu Cncl; Rptr Yrbk; VP Pep Clb; Trk; Pom Pon; Univ; Music.

BUNKER, BELINDA; Sault Area HS; Sault Ste Marie, MI; 25/300 Hon Rl; NHS; Quill & Scroll; Rptr Yrbk; Trk; IM Sprt; Natl Merit Schl; Ferris State College; Data Proc.

BUNN, TIMOHTY; Wilbur Wright HS; Dayton, OH; Am Leg Boys St; Drm Mjrt; Mdrgl; Off Ade; Red Cr Ade; Sprt Ed Yrbk; Sprt Ed Sch Nwsp; FFA; FHA; FTA; Sinclair Cmnty Coll.

BUNNING, TAMARA J; La Porte HS; Laporte, IN; 10/480 Am Leg Aux Girls St; Band; Chrs; Chrh Wkr; Drm Mjrt; Girl Scts; Hon Rl; Lbry Ade; MMM; Natl Forn Lg; Indiana Univ; Dental Hygiene.

BUNOFSKY, LORENE; Struthers HS; Struthers, OH; Hon Rl; Drama Clb; FNA; Pep Clb; Spn Clb; Univ; Nursing.

BUNSEY, LAURA; Nordonia HS; Northfield, OH; Chrh Wkr; Cmnty Wkr; NHS; Ed Yrbk; Rptr Yrbk; PPFtbl; Akron Univ.

BUNT, KATHLEEN; Sandusky HS; Sandusky, OH; Cls Rep Frsh Cls; VP Soph Cls; Cls Rep Soph Cls; Cl Rep Jr Cls; Cls Rep Sr Cls; Chrs; Lbry Ade; Off Ade; Stu Cncl; Rptr Yrbk; Bus Schl.

BUNTING, THERESA; Belding HS; Belding, MI; 1/147 Val; Band; Chrh Wkr; Hon Rl; Lbry Ade; NHS; Orch; PAVAS; Sch Pl; Drama Clb; Michigan St Univ.

BUNTON, EDWIN; Lake Michigan Cath HS; Benton Hrbr, MI; Cl Rep Jr Cls; 4-H; Bsktbl; Ftbl; Michigan St Univ; Jrnlsm.

BUNYOFF, KATHI; Austintown Fitch HS; Youngstown, OH; 20/600 Hon Rl; NHS; Ed Sch Nwsp; Montery Inst; Interpreter.

BURA, ROBERT; Padua Franciscan HS; Parma, OH; 21/268 Chrh Wkr; Cmnty Wkr; Hon Rl; NHS; Boys Clb Am; Mth Clb; IM Sprt; Pres Of St Columbkille CYO 78; Org 2 Musclr Dystrophy Dance Marathons 78; Cleveland St Univ; Systems Analyst.

BURACK, KIMBERLY; Tecumseh HS; Tecumseh, MI; 58/234 Band; Drl Tm; Hon Rl; Lit Mag; NHS; Sch Pl; Sec Stu Cncl; Sec Yth Flsp; Sch Nwsp; Sec Fr Clb; St Of Michigan Competitive Schlrshp Awd; Michigan St Univ; Psych.

BURAND, BETH; Perrysburg HS; Perrysburg, OH; Chrh Wkr; Hon Rl; NHS; Treas Stu Cncl; Ger Clb; Natl Merit Ltr; Bowling Green St Univ; Nursing.

BURBANK, MICHAEL; Elk Rapids HS; Rapid City, MI; 7/105 Pres Frsh Cls; Hon Rl; Letter Ftbl; Letter Wrstlng; Natl Merit Schl; Great Lakes Maritime Acad; Engr.

BURCH, BETSY J; Turpin HS; Cincinnati, OH; 1 5/357 Cls Rep Frsh Cls; VP Soph Cls; Pres Chrs; Girl Scts; NHS; Pres Orch; Sch Mus; Pres Stu Cncl; Yth Flsp; Letter Socr; Miami Univ; Business.

BURCH, BONNIE; Struthers HS; Struthers, OH; 79/252 Chrs; Sch Mus; Sch Pl; Stg Crw; Yth Flsp; Drama Clb; 4-H; FTA; 4-H Awd; Mas Awd; Youngstown St Univ; Stewardess.

BURCH, EDWARD A; Eastmoor Sr HS; Columbus, OH; 28/292 Boy Scts; Chrs; Chrh Wkr; Cmnty Wkr; Hon Rl; Orch; Pol Wkr; Sch Mus; Sch Pl; Sct Actv; Northwestern Univ; Broadcasting.

BURCH, LORI; Muskegon HS; Muskegon, MI; Chrh Wkr; Girl Scts; Hon Rl; Hosp Ade; Bsbl; Swmmng; IM Sprt; College; Interior Designer.

BURCH, MARIANNE; Charleston Catholic HS; S Charleston, WV; Chrs; Chrh Wkr; Cmnty Wkr; Girl Scts; Hon Rl; Hosp Ade; Off Ade; Sct Actv; Keyettes; Spn Clb; Univ; Marine Bio.

BURCH, THELMA; Reitz Memorial HS; Evansville, IN; Hon Rl; Pom Pon; College.

BURCH, TONI F; Pontiac Northern HS; Pontiac, MI; Chrh Wkr; Hon Rl; Jr NHS; NHS; Yth Flsp; Fr Clb; FTA; Cit Awd; Natl Merit Ltr; Spellman Coll; Biochem.

BURCH, TRACY; New Albany HS; New Albany, IN; Pres Frsh Cls; Cls Rep Soph Cls; Debate Tm; Hon Rl; Stu Cncl; Yrbk; Ger Clb; Letter Bsktbl; IM Sprt; Pres Awd; Ohio St Univ; Brdcstng.

BURCHAM, KAREN; Chesapeake HS; Chesapeake, OH; Lbry Ade; Sch Pl; Rptr Yrbk; Drama Clb; Univ; Hotel Mgmt.

BURCHAM, LISA; South Ripley Jr Sr HS; Versailles, IN; 1/112 Cls Rep Soph Cls; Sec Jr Cls; Cl Rep Jr Cls; Chrs; Girl Scts; Hon Rl; Stu Cncl; Yth Flsp; Sec 4-H; Pep Clb; Perfect Attendance; Judson Coll.

BURCHARD, KAREN; Central HS; Grand Rapids, MI; Debate Tm; Drl Tm; Hon Rl; NHS; ROTC; Sch Mus; Fr Clb; Spn Clb; DAR Awd; Opt Clb Awd; Foreign Languages.

BURCHETT, JIMMY; North Vermillion HS; Cayuga, IN; FCA; Bsbl; Bsktbl; Glf;.

BURD, CHERYL; Midland HS; Midland, MI; Hon Rl; W Mich Univ; Pre Architecture.

BURD, TERRI; Lawrence Cnty Joint Voc Schl; Proctorville, OH; 26/318 Sec Jr Cls; Band; Chrh Wkr; Hon Rl; Jr NHS; NHS; Yth Flsp; Rptr Sch Nwsp; Sec 4-H; OEA; Top 10% Of Jr Cls Recvd 5 Free Hrs From Oh Univ 1979; Marshall Univ; Sec.

BURDEN, DONALD; Botkins HS; Botkins, OH; 10/48 Am Leg Boys St; Chrs; Chrh Wkr; Hon Rl; Fr Clb; FTA; Sci Clb; College; Acctg.

BURDETT, CAROL; Beechcroft HS; Columbus, OH; DECA; Pep Clb; Trk;.

BURDETT, VICKY; Stonewall Jackson HS; Charleston, WV; Cls Rep Frsh Cls; Chrh Wkr; Girl Scts;

Hon Rl; Pol Wkr; Sct Actv; Stu Cncl; Yth Flsp; Ed Yrbk; Sprt Ed Yrbk; Morris Harvey Univ; Bus Educ.

BURDETTE, MELODY; Barnesville HS; Piedmont, OH; Hon Rl; Off Ade; Sch Mus; Treas Yth Flsp; Rptr Sch Nwsp; Drama Clb; Fr Clb; FTA; Gov Hon Prg Awd; Ohi State Univ; Physical Therapy.

BURDETTE, MONTY; Mississinewa HS; Gas City, IN; 12/225 FCA; Hon Rl; Jr NHS; NHS; Spn Clb; Bsktbl; Crs Cntry; Glf; College.

BURDETTE, RICHARD A; Spencer HS; Spencer, WV; 3/158 Am Leg Boys St; FCA; Hon Rl; Jr NHS; Lbry Ade; Treas NHS; Sch Pl; Sprt Ed Yrbk; Bsktbl; Trk; Univ Of Charleston; Comp Sci.

BURDETTE, TAMIE; Perry HS; Canton, OH; Band; Chrs; Chrh Wkr; Girl Scts; Hon Rl; VP JA; Stg Crw; FHA; Treas OEA; Univ; Acctg.

BURDI, CAROLYN; Cousino Sr HS; Warren, MI; Cls Rep Frsh Cls; Cls Rep Soph Cls; Chrs; Chrh Wkr; Girl Scts; Hon Rl; Jr NHS; Mdrgl; NHS; Sch Mus; Univ Of Detroit; Acctg.

BURDICK, COLLEEN; Imlay City HS; Imlay City, MI; Band; Chrs; Girl Scts; Hon Rl; Sch Mus; Sct Actv; Stg Crw; Fr Clb; Ten; IM Sprt; Cntrl Michigan Univ; Bio.

BURDICK, DAKIN; Warsaw Cmnty HS; Warsaw, IN; Cls Rep Soph Cls; Boy Scts; Hon Rl; Sch Nwsp; Fr Clb; Spn Clb; Princeton Univ; Comp Prog.

BURDICK, MARIE; Allen Park HS; Allen Park, MI; 39/360 Band; Drm Bgl; Girl Scts; Jr NHS; Yth Flsp; Fr Clb; Michigan St Univ; Med Tech.

BURDICK, MARK; Parkside HS; Jackson, MI; 19/360 Pres Chrh Wkr; Cmnty Wkr; Hon Rl; Letter Ftbl; Wrstlng;.

BURDINE, BOBBY; Cascade HS; Clayton, IN; 15/150 Hon Rl; Letter Bsktbl; Letter Trk; Indiana St Univ; Car Painter.

BURDINE, VICKIE; Western Boone Jr Sr HS; Jamestown, IN; Band; Chrs; Chrh Wkr; Drl Tm; FCA; Girl Scts; Off Ade; Sch Mus; Sprt Ed Sch Nwsp; Rptr Sch Nwsp; Vocational Schl; Cosmetology.

BURDO, JULIE; Maumee HS; Maumee, OH; 15/316 Band; Orch; College.

BURDORF, ELIZABETH; Northside HS; Muncie, IN; 63/250 Sec Sr Cls; NHS; Off Ade; Spn Clb; Indiana Univ; Bus.

BURDSALL, JOHN; Elwood Cmnty HS; Elwood, IN; 19/189 Hon Rl; Lbry Ade; Mod UN; NHS; Pres Stu Cncl; Y-Teens; Mth Clb; Sci Clb; Spn Clb; Ftbl; Rose Hulman Inst; Mech Engr.

BURDSALL, PAUL; Clermont Northeastern HS; Batavia, OH; 124/256 Band; Chrh Wkr; FCA; Yth Flsp; Sch Nwsp; 4-H; FFA; Wrstlng; IM Sprt; 4-H Awd; Animal Sci.

BUREAN, MELISSA; Jackson Center HS; Jackson Cntr, OH; 4/37 Sec Frsh Cls; Cls Rep Frsh Cls; Pres Jr Cls; Cl Rep Jr Cls; Cls Rep Sr Cls; Am Leg Aux Girls St; Band; Chrs; Hon Rl; VP NHS; Coll; Med.

BUREK, D; Belleville HS; Belleville, MI; 2/500 Hon Rl; NHS; Sch Mus; Bsktbl; Michigan St Univ; Med Tech.

BURFORD, CHERYL; Stryker HS; Stryker, OH; 1/59 Sec Band; Drl Tm; Hon Rl; Rptr Yrbk; Rptr Sch Nwsp; FHA; Letter Trk; Am Leg Awd; Ohio St Univ; Preoptometry.

BURFORD, SANDFORD; Dunbar HS; Charleston, WV; Boy Scts; Hon Rl; Jr NHS; NHS; Mth Clb; Spn Clb; VICA; Elk Elec School; Service Man.

BURG, MARY; Pinckney HS; Pinckney, MI; 8/250 Girl Scts; Hon Rl; NHS; Yth Flsp; Yrbk; 4-H; Natl Merit Ltr; Mic State Univ; Law.

BURGAN, JOHNNY; River Valley HS; Caledonia, OH; Chrh Wkr; FCA; Sct Actv; Spn Clb; Bsktbl; Letter Crs Cntry; Letter Trk; Capt IM Sprt; College; Elec Engr.

BURGE, ANNETTE; Everett HS; Lansing, MI; 34/443 Cmnty Wkr; Lbry Ade; NHS; Stu Cncl; Rptr Sch Nwsp; Sch Nwsp; FTA; Pep Clb; Cit Awd; Mi Competitive Schlrshp 79; Ctrl Mi Univ Hon Schlrshp 79; Central Michigan Univ; Spec Educ.

BURGE, GERALDINE; Griffith Sr HS; Griffith, IN; 14/300 Pres Soph Cls; Cl Rep Jr Cls; Hon Rl; Jr NHS; NHS; Off Ade; Pep Clb; Letter Gym; Letter Swmmng; Chrldng; Univ; Pre Med.

BURGEI, CAROLYN; Ottoville Local HS; Cloverdale, OH; Cls Rep Frsh Cls; Cmp Fr Grls; Chrs; Girl Scts; Hon Rl; Sch Mus; Sch Pl; Stu Cncl; Rptr Yrbk; Eng Clb; Coll.

BURGEI, PATRICIA; Delphos St Johns HS; Elido, OH; 40/140 Cls Rep Frsh Cls; Trs Sr Cls; Band; Hon Rl; Sch Mus; 4-H; FTA; IM Sprt; Northwestern Busns Coll; Legal Sec.

BURGER, ANDY; Greenbrier East HS; Whte Slphr Spg, WV; 56/375 Boy Scts; Chrh Wkr; FCA; Hon Rl; Jr NHS; Off Ade; Sprt Ed Yrbk; Yrbk; Rptr Sch Nwsp; Sch Nwsp; Marshall Univ; Bus Admin.

BURGER, MARK C; Monroe Catholic Central HS; Maybee, MI; 9/95 Band; Boy Scts; Hon Rl; NHS; Sct Actv; Natl Merit Ltr; Adrian Coll; Acctg.

BURGER, THERESE; Newark Catholic HS; Newark, OH; Chrs; Hon Rl; Lbry Ade; Sch Mus; Sch Pl; Stg Crw; Stu Cncl; VP Drama Clb; Fr Clb; GAA; Ohio St Univ; Theater.

BURGESS, ANITA; Peebles HS; Peebles, OH; Hon Rl; Lbry Ade; Lit Mag;.

BURGESS, BRENDA; Oakridge HS; Muskegon, MI; 3/165 Trs Frsh Cls; Trs Soph Cls; Trs Jr Cls; Jr NHS; NHS; Stu Cncl; Pep Clb; Univ; Bus.

BURGESS, CINDY; Shady Spring HS; Daniels, WV; Band; Hon Rl; Hosp Ade; Drama Clb; Pep Clb; Chrldng; Marshall Univ; Psych.

BURGESS, CONNIE L; Perry HS; Lima, OH; Cls Rep Frsh Cls; Chrs; Hon Rl; Lbry Ade; Off Ade; Stu Cncl; 4-H; Bsktbl; Trk; Scr Kpr; Bus Schl.

BURGESS, DIANNE; Newberry HS; Newberry, MI; 15/110 Cmp Fr Grls; Hon Rl; NHS; Off Ade; Sch Pl; Stg Crw; GAA; IM Sprt; PPFtbl; St Of Mi Schkshp 79; Michigan Tech Univ; Engr.

BURGESS, EDWARD; Our Lady Of Mt Carmel HS; Taylor, MI; Capt Ftbl; Coach Actv; IM Sprt; Defensive Plyr Of The Yr Ftbl 79; Northwood Inst; Bus Admin.

BURGESS, GARY L; Withrow HS; Cincinnati, OH; Rptr Sch Nwsp; College.

BURGESS, JOHN; Vestaburg HS; Blanchard, MI; Cls Rep Soph Cls; Cl Rep Jr Cls; Pres Sr Cls; Boy Scts; Debate Tm; Hon Rl; NHS; Off Ade; Pol Wkr; Stu Cncl; Univ Of Michigan; Law.

BURGESS, KATHY; West Branch HS; Beloit, OH; 11/231 Chrs; Debate Tm; Girl Scts; Hon Rl; Jr NHS; Natl Forn Lg; Sch Mus; Letter Bsktbl; Letter Trk; Letter Wrstlng; Univ; Educ.

BURGESS, L; Corunna HS; Corunna, MI; Band; Drm Mjrt; JA; Pol Wkr; Sch Pl; JA Awd; Voc Schl; Printing.

BURGESS, LAURA; Lamphere HS; Madison Hts, MI; Hon Rl; NHS; Fr Clb; Pom Pon; PPFtbl; Oakland Cmnty Coll; Acctg.

BURGESS, MARILYN; Brown City HS; Brown City, MI; 3/87 VP Frsh Cls; Pres Soph Cls; Pres Jr Cls; Band; Chrs; Chrh Wkr; Cmnty Wkr; Drm Mjrt; Girl Scts; Hon Rl; CMU Truestees Schlrshp 1980; Principals Awd 1979; St Of Mich Competitive Schlrshp; Central Michigan Univ.

BURGESS, MARY; Marquette HS; Michigan City, IN; 22/81 Cls Rep Frsh Cls; Cls Rep Soph Cls; Hon Rl; Sch Mus; Stu Cncl; Rptr Yrbk; Drama Clb; Fr Clb; Letter Swmmng; Letter Ten; Purdue Univ; Bio.

BURGESS, PAM; Bridgeport HS; Bridgeport, WV; Chrh Wkr; Girl Scts; Hon Rl; Hosp Ade; Lbry Ade; Yth Flsp; Y-Teens; Womens Club Awd; College; Medicine.

BURGESS, RANDALL; Loy Norrix HS; Kalamazoo, MI; Band; Chrh Wkr; Hon Rl; Yth Flsp; Bsktbl; Univ.

BURGESS, SANDY; Mount Hope HS; Mt Hope, WV; Cls Rep Frsh Cls; Trs Soph Cls; VP Jr Cls; Hon Rl; Off Ade; Sch Pl; Stu Cncl; FBLA; Chrldng; Natl Merit Ltr; Marshall Univ; Law.

BURGESS, T ROBIN; Carlisle Sr HS; Carlisle, OH; Chrs; Cmnty Wkr; Girl Scts; 4-H; FTA; OEA; Spn Clb; Trk; Tmr; 4-H Awd; Carlisle Educ Regoc Assoc 77; Recvd A Ltr In Concert Chr 78; Bus Schl; Sec.

BURGETT, PAMELA; Creston HS; Grand Rapids, MI; 1/417 FCA; Hon Rl; NHS; Letter Gym; Swmmng; Letter Trk; Capt Chrldng; Kiwan Awd; Mic State Univ; Engr.

BURGHY, JORDANA; Unionville Sebewaing HS; Pearce, AZ; Hon Rl; Chrldng; Coll; Bookkeeping.

BURGMEIER, JOHN; Chaminade Julienne HS; Dayton, OH; Hon Rl; JA; Socr; Hocking Tech; Wildlife & Recreation.

BURGOS, EVA; Logansport HS; Logansport, IN; Sec FCA; Hosp Ade; Off Ade; Sch Pl; Stg Crw; Yrbk; Ge r Clb; Mth Clb; Ten; GAA; Cass County Girls Tennis Campionship 78; Hoosier Honorary Schlrshp 78; Mbr Of Mu Alpha Theta Natl HS Club; Indiana Univ; Psych.

BURGOYNE, JEFF; Covington HS; Covington, IN; 11/120 Band; Debate Tm; Hon Rl; Sch Pl; Fr Clb; Chrldng; Cit Awd; DAR Awd; Wabash Coll; Law.

BURGUARD, RENATA; Summerfield HS; Petersburg, MI; 5/83 VP Jr Cls; Pres Sr Cls; Pres Band; Cmp Fr Grls; Chrs; Hon Rl; NHS; Pres Stu Cncl; Yrbk; Sci Clb; Leon Wells Schlrshp; St Of Michigan Competitive Schlrshp; Thomas Staples Schlrshp; Cntrl Michigan Univ; Law Enforcement.

BURIAN, RONEE; New Buffalo Consolidated HS; New Buffalo, MI; Pres Frsh Cls; Cls Rep Soph Cls; Band; Hon Rl; Rptr Sch Nwsp; Mgrs; Tmr;.

BURIANEK, KEVIN J; Brighton HS; Brighton, MI; Band; Boy Scts; Hon Rl; Sch Mus; Sch Pl; Stg Crw; Crs Cntry; Trk; Kiwan Awd; Northwestern Michigan Univ; ATP Lic.

BURICH, MARY; Memorial HS; Campbell, OH; 5/210 Cmnty Wkr; Hon Rl; NHS; Off Ade; Pol Wkr; Fr Clb; Mth Clb; Ten; Trk; Youngstown St Univ; Journalism.

BURICH, RAY; Streetsboro HS; Streetsboro, OH; Hon Rl; Rptr Sch Nwsp; Rdo Clb; Univ.

BURIE, CINDY; Menominee HS; Menominee, MI; 10/256 Hon Rl; NHS; Twrlr; N Michigan Univ; Data Proc.

BURIG, JENNIFER; Wheeling Park HS; Wheeling, WV; 17/500 Cl Rep Jr Cls; Chrs; Hon Rl; Hosp Ade; Natl Forn Lg; NHS; Stu Cncl; Drama Clb; Mat Maids; Univ; Health.

BURIN, SUZANNE M; Clawson HS; Clawson, MI; Cls Rep Frsh Cls; Cls Rep Soph Cls; Cl Rep Jr Cls; Chrs; Hon Rl; GAA; PPFtbl; Natl Merit Ltr; College; Biochemistry.

BURK, BARBARA; Jefferson HS; Lafayette, IN; Chrs; Girl Scts; Hon Rl; Jr NHS; Sch Pl; Stu Cncl; Sch Nwsp; Coach Actv; Mat Maids; Scr Kpr; Vin; Architectoral Designer.

BURK, DANIEL; Fremont HS; Fremont, MI; 4/238 Cls Rep Soph Cls; VP Jr Cls; VP Sr Cls; Am Leg Boys St; Hon Rl; NHS; Letter Bsktbl; Letter Ftbl; Natl Merit Ltr; Kalamazoo Coll.

BURK, DEBI; Switzerland Co HS; Vevay, IN; Cls Rep Frsh Cls; Cls Rep Soph Cls; Cl Rep Jr Cls; Cls Rep Sr Cls; Chrs; Girl Scts; Hon Rl; Off Ade; Pep Clb; Bsktbl;.

BURK, ROBERT W; Parkersburg HS; Parkersburg, WV; 1/700 Cls Rep Sr Cls; Am Leg Boys St; Hon Rl; Stu Cncl; Yth Flsp; Fr Clb; Pres Pep Clb; Bsbl; Gym; IM Sprt; Outstanding Freshman 76; Univ; Engr.

BURKE, BRENDA; Northeast Dubois HS; Dubois, IN; 18/79 Hon Rl; Beta Clb; Ger Clb; Pep Clb; Bsktbl; Ten; IM Sprt; PPFtbl; Marian College.

BURKE, BRIAN P; Fairmont W HS; Kettering, OH; Boy Scts; Cmnty Wkr; Hon Rl; Pol Wkr; Sch Pl; Sct Actv; Stu Cncl; Drama Clb; 4-H; Key Clb; 1st Honors Awds; Univ Of Notre Dame; Dentistry.

BURKE, CHRISTINE; Adlai Stevenson HS; Sterling Hgts, MI; Band; Girl Scts; Hon Rl; Sch Pl; Sct Actv; Drama Clb; Ger Clb; OEA; Oakland Univ; Comp Info Sci.

BURKE, DEBBIE; Corydon Central HS; Corydon, IN; Letter Bsktbl; Letter Ten; Letter Trk; Letter GAA; Vlybl Ldrshp Awd; Univ Of Louisville; Phys Ed.

BURKE, DENNIS; Orleans HS; Orleans, IN; 1/72 Am Leg Boys St; Hon Rl; NHS; Yth Flsp; Letter Bsktbl; Letter Crs Cntry; Letter Trk; Coach Actv; Pres Awd; Schlshp Awd 76 & 77; Univ.

BURKE, DOREEN; Bishop Ready HS; Columbus, OH; 40/144 Hon Rl; Off Ade; Letter Gym; Letter Ten; Capt Trk; Coach Actv; Ohio St Univ.

BURKE, MARGARET; Dominican HS; Detroit, MI; Band; Chrs; Mdrgl; NHS; Sch Mus; Sch Pl; Treas Drama Clb; College.

BURKE, MARY E; Our Lady Of Mercy HS; Brighton, MI; Chrh Wkr; NHS; Sch Pl; Fr Clb; Sci Clb; Trk; Pom Pon; Univ Of Michigan; Optometry.

BURKE, THERESE; Rocky River HS; Rocky Rvr, OH; Chrs; Jr NHS; Stu Cncl; Pep Clb; Swmmng; IM Sprt; Tmr; Univ; Oceanography.

BURKE, THOMAS; Holly Sr HS; Davisburg, MI; Aud/Vis; Hon Rl; NHS; Spn Clb; Crs Cntry; Letter Ten; Univ Of Michigan; Law.

BURKE, TOM; Mendon HS; Mendon, MI; FCA; Hon Rl; NHS; 4-H; Ftbl; Trk; Tmr; 4-H Awd; Grand Rapids Schl; Bible.

BURKE, WILLIAM; Bexley HS; Bexley, OH; Trs Frsh Cls; Cls Rep Frsh Cls; Pres Soph Cls; Cl Rep Jr Cls; Pres Sr Cls; Cls Rep Sr Cls; Am Leg Boys St; Pres Band; Hon Rl; Jr NHS;.

BURKE, WILLIAM J; Bexley HS; Bexley, OH; Trs Frsh Cls; Pres Soph Cls; Pres Sr Cls; Am Leg Boys St; Band; Hon Rl; NHS; Sch Pl; College; Chemistry.

BURKET, MARK; Tuscarawas Valley HS; Dover, OH; 10/150 Am Leg Boys St; Chrs; Chrh Wkr; Hon Rl; Jr NHS; NHS; Sch Pl; Stg Crw; Ohi St Univ; Chem Engr.

BURKETT, BILLIE; Princeton HS; Princeton, WV; 12/370 Cl Rep Jr Cls; Hon Rl; Jr NHS; NHS; Off Ade; VP Stu Cncl; VP Fr Clb; Pep Clb; Pom Pon; Cit Awd; Schlrshp Awd; Cert Of Part; Univ; Archt Engr.

BURKETT, DENISE; Bellevue HS; Bellevue, MI; 2/100 Pres Soph Cls; Val; Band; Hosp Ade; Sch Mus; Sch Pl; Stg Crw; Pres Drama Clb; Treas Spn Clb; Central Michigan Univ; Medicine.

BURKETT, HERBERT; Breckenridge Jr Sr HS; Breckenridge, MI; 52/109 Band; Chrs; Chrh Wkr; Hon Rl; Orch; Drama Clb; 4-H; FFA; Key Clb; VICA; Saginaw Vly St Coll; Agri.

BURKETT, MIKE J; Brookville HS; Brookville, OH; 3/150 Hst Frsh Cls; Hst Soph Cls; Hon Rl; NHS; Treas Sci Clb; 18th Bio Tests 1978; 10% Jets Neas Test 1979; General Motors Inst; Mech Engr.

BURKETT, WILLIAM; Washington HS; Massillon, OH; 7/500 Am Leg Boys St; Pres Jr NHS; Stu Cncl; Pres Yth Flsp; Pres Lat Clb; Letter Socr; Trk; Georgia Tech Univ; Aerospace Engr.

BURKEY, KERRY; Monroe Cath Central HS; Monroe, MI; Hon Rl; Orch; Sch Mus; John Phillip Sousa Bnd Awd; St Of Michigan Tuition Grant Sienna Hgts Coll; BEOG Monroe Cnty Comm Coll; Monroe Cnty Comm Coll; Bus.

BURKHAMER, JEFFREY; Williamstown HS; Williamstown, WV; 9/116 VP Frsh Cls; Am Leg Boys St; Hon Rl; Bsbl; Bsktbl; Ftbl; IM Sprt; Tmr; College.

BURKHAMMER, JILL; Lewis County HS; Weston, WV; Am Leg Aux Girls St; Band; FCA; Hon Rl; Pres Jr NHS; Treas NHS; Stg Crw; Stu Cncl; Sprt Ed Sch Nwsp; Sch Nwsp; Peom Published In Natl Musicians Mag 77; 59th Pl Out Of 6000 Entrants In Essay Contest 78; Bsktbl Tm 76; Fairmont St Univ; Vet Sci.

BURKHAMMER, LOU; Federal Hocking HS; Coolville, OH; Band; Hon Rl; Yth Flsp; Treas 4-H; Mth Clb; Pep Clb; Spn Clb; Letter Trk; Capt Chrldng; 4-H Awd; Ohio St Univ; Med.

BURKHARD, IVAN; Harbor Beach Cmnty HS; Harbor Beach, MI; 11/124 Cls Rep Sr Cls; Band; Chrh Wkr; Hon Rl; NHS; Orch; Sec Yth Flsp; Rptr Sch Nwsp; Treas 4-H; Pep Clb; Delta Coll; Residential Constr.

BURKHARDT, D; Nordonia HS; Macedonia, OH; Cleveland Univ; Archaeology.

BURKHARDT, D; Fairmont West HS; Kettering, OH; 90/471 Hon Rl; Fr Clb; Letter Socr; IM Sprt; College.

BURKHARDT, ROBIN; Caro HS; Caro, MI; 1/160 Val; Band; Chrh Wkr; Hon Rl; NHS; Rotary Awd; MSU; Physics.

BURKHART, ANITA; Zanesville HS; Zanesville, OH; Cls Rep Frsh Cls; Band; Cmp Fr Grls; Chrs; Chrh Wkr; Cmnty Wkr; Girl Scts; Hon Rl; Hosp Ade; Orch; Coll; Spec Educ.

BURKHART, ELAINE; Holgate Local HS; New Bavaria, OH; Band; Girl Scts; Hon Rl; Lbry Ade; NHS; Bsktbl; Voice Dem Awd; Nursing School; Rn.

BURKHART, JULIA A; Tri West Hendricks HS; North Salem, IN; 5/140 Cls Rep Frsh Cls; Trs Soph Cls; Cls Rep Soph Cls; Cl Rep Jr Cls; Band; Drl Tm; Drm Mjrt; Hon Rl; NHS; Stu Cncl; Univ.

BURKHART, JULIE; Lexington HS; Mansfield, OH; 47/263 Cl Rep Jr Cls; Lbry Ade; Off Ade; Stg Crw; Stu Cncl; VP Y-Teens; Rptr Yrbk; FTA; Key Clb; Spn Clb; Lexington Local Safety Town Teacher; Kiwanis Essay Awd; Slippery Rock Coll; Elem Ed.

BURKHART, PEGGY; Beaumont Girls HS; Univ Hts, OH; 5/120 Hon Rl; Lit Mag; NHS; Fr Clb; Univ; Sci.

BURKHART, TANIA; Martinsburg Sr HS; Martinsburg, WV; Hon Rl; Sch Mus; Sch Pl; Rptr Yrbk; Yrbk; Rptr Sch Nwsp; 4-H; Pep Clb; Sci Clb; Chrldng; Shepherd Coll; Park Admin.

BURKHOLDER, DAVID; Cory Rawson HS; Bluffton, OH; Cls Rep Frsh Cls; Cls Rep Soph Cls; VP Jr Cls; Pres Sr Cls; Am Leg Boys St; Chrs; Hon Rl; NHS; Stu Cncl; Ohi Northern College; Engr.

BURKHOLDER, KAREN; Stryker HS; Stryker, OH; 3/59 Trs Frsh Cls; Cl Rep Jr Cls; Cls Rep Sr Cls; Capt Drl Tm; FCA; Hon Rl; Lbry Ade; NHS; College; Exec Sec.

BURKHOLDER, KAREN; Stryker Local HS; Stryker, OH; Trs Frsh Cls; Cl Rep Jr Cls; Drl Tm; Sec Stu Cncl; Yth Flsp; 4-H; FHA; Gym; Chrldng; Univ.

BURKHOLDER, KEITH; High School; Bluffton, OH; 9/93 Bsktbl; Letter Glf; Letter Wrstlng; Voc Schl.

BURKHOLDER, ROBERT; Tri Village HS; Greenville, OH; 3/96 VP Frsh Cls; Cls Rep Soph Cls; Band; Chrs; Hon Rl; NHS; Sch Mus; Sch Pl; Stu Cncl; 4-H; Chem Awd 2nd In Cnty Test; Algbr II Awd; Bst Frsh In Band Awd; Univ; Chem Engr.

BURKHOLDER, SARAH; Elston Sr HS; Mich Cit, IN; 110/316 Chrh Wkr; Off Ade; Fr Clb; Ten; Varsity Tennis 79; Stu Aide 79; French Club 77 79; Boston Coll; Pre Law.

BURKING, BROOK C; Pike HS; Indianapolis, IN; Band; Hon Rl; Jr NHS; Lit Mag; Treas NHS; Pol Wkr; Yth Flsp; Natl Merit SF; Natl Achvmnt 78; Outstndng Yng Amer; Purdue Univ; Elec Engr.

BURKITT, YVETTE; Williamston HS; Williamston, MI; Sec Soph Cls; Band; Cmp Fr Grls; Hon Rl; Jr NHS; Letter Ten; College.

BURKLOW, THOMAS; Central HS; Evansville, IN; 20/528 Band; Boy Scts; Hon Rl; Hosp Ade; JA; NHS; Sct Actv; Sec Stu Cncl; Mth Clb; Sci Clb; Cornell Univ; Biophysics.

BURKS, LEONARD; Mount View HS; Welch, WV; Am Leg Boys St; Chrh Wkr; Hon Rl; Jr NHS; Mod UN; NHS; Treas Stu Cncl; Am Leg Awd; Golden Horseshoe 1976; Math Field Day 1977; Univ.

BURKS, LEONARD W; Mountview HS; Welch, WV; Am Leg Boys St; Chrh Wkr; Hon Rl; Jr NHS; Mod UN; NHS; Treas Stu Cncl; Boy Scts; College.

BURKS, LISA; Lakeland HS; Milford, MI; Cls Rep Frsh Cls; Cls Rep Soph Cls; Cl Rep Jr Cls; Cls Rep Sr Cls; Cmnty Wkr; Stu Cncl; Yrbk; Ed Sch Nwsp; Sprt Ed Sch Nwsp; Rptr Sch Nwsp; Michigan St Univ; Journalism.

BURKS, LORI; Avon HS; Indpls, IN; 27/158 Cls Rep Frsh Cls; Pres Soph Cls; Cls Rep Soph Cls; Cl Rep Jr Cls; Drl Tm; Hon Rl; NHS; Stu Cncl; Bsktbl; Pom Pon; College.

BURKS, PAMELA; Whiteland Cmnty HS; New Whiteland, IN; 28/232 Cl Rep Jr Cls; FCA; Hon Rl; NHS; Off Ade; Stu Cncl; Pep Clb; Trk; Mgrs; Mat Maids; Stu Cncl Pres 80; Sunshine Soc 79; Vincennes Univ; Soc Work.

BURKY, ALVIN; Pickens HS; Pickens, WV; 3/13 Cmnty Wkr; Hon Rl; NHS; Rptr Yrbk; Rptr Sch Nwsp; Pres 4-H; Capt Bsktbl; Cit Awd; DAR Awd; 4-H Awd; Davis & Elkins Coll.

BURLEIGH, ROGER; Otsego HS; Otsego, MI; Cls Rep Sr Cls; Band; Chrs; Mdrgl; Mod UN; NHS; Sch Mus; Sch Pl; Sprt Ed Yrbk; Letter Swmmng; Olivet Coll; Communications.

BURLEW, CAROL; Anderson HS; Cincinnati, OH; 33/342 Sec Frsh Cls; Band; Chrh Wkr; Hon Rl; NHS; Orch; Fr Clb; Pep Clb; Kiwan Awd; Ohio Northern Univ; Chem.

BURLEY, BETH; Green HS; Akron, OH; 21/325 Am Leg Aux Girls St; Boy Scts; Chrs; Debate Tm; Hon Rl; Hosp Ade; NHS; Sch Mus; College; Phys Asst.

BURLEY, P; Elizabeth A Johnson Mem HS; Clio, MI; Chrh Wkr; Hon Rl; Yth Flsp; 4-H; 4-H Awd; Univ.

BURMAN, PETER; Charles F Brush HS; S Euclid, OH; Univ; Elec Engr.

BURNELL, CARY; Whitehall Sr HS; N Muskegon, MI; 18/150 Letter Band; Yrbk; Bsktbl; Mgrs; Hnrbl Mention In Watecolors 78 HS Art Show 78; Univ; Sports Admin.

BURNER, CURT; Bridgeport Sr HS; Bridgeport, WV; VP Jr Cls; Am Leg Boys St; Hon Rl; Jr NHS; NHS; Stu Cncl; Key Clb; Spn Clb; Letter Ftbl; Letter Glf; U S Military Acad; Medicine.

BURNER, DAVID; Patrick Henry HS; Deshler, OH; Band; Hon Rl; Orch; Letter Trk; Owens Tech College.

BURNER, JAMIE; Philip Barbour HS; Philippi, WV; Hon Rl; Stu Cncl; Yrbk; Pep Clb; Mat Maids; Fairmont St Coll; Phys Educ.

BURNETT, ANDREW S; Avon Jr Sr HS; Indianapolis, IN; Band; Hon Rl; JA; Ger Clb; Sci Clb; Letter Glf; Mbr Of 1st Symphnc Band At Avon Sr HS 76; Butler Univ; Pharm.

BURNETT, CLARE; Magnificat HS; Cleveland, OH; Chrs; Hon Rl; NHS; Red Cr Ade; Sch Pl; Rptr Sch Nwsp; Drama Clb; Crs Cntry; Ten; Natl Merit Ltr; College; Technical Engineering.

BURNETT, CLINTON; The Leelanau HS; Flint, MI; 3/26 VP Sr Cls; Boy Scts; Hon Rl; Sct Actv; Stu Cncl; Rptr Yrbk; Socr; Ten; Wrstlng; Coach Actv; Alma College.

BURNETT, GREGORY; Parkside HS; Jackson, MI; Band; Hon Rl; Ten; 1st Div Lating On Snare Drum Mi St Bnd &3 Orch St Fest 77; 1st Div Ratng On Xylophone Same Fest 77; Michigan St Univ; Bus.

BURNETT, JAMES W; North Central HS; Indianapolis, IN; 108/999 Hon Rl; Mod UN; NHS; Pol Wkr; Yrbk; Sci Clb; JETS Awd; In Bell Tele Awd From Reg Sci Fair 1976; Mbr Of The ACM; Mbr Of The IEEE; Butler Univ; Physics.

BURNETT, JILL; Heritage HS; Monroeville, IN; Hon Rl; Bsktbl; College; Phys Educ.

BURNETT, JILL; Eastern HS; Pekin, IN; Pres Sr Cls; VP NHS; 4-H; Spn Clb; Natl Merit Ltr; Purdue Univ; Biology.

BURNETT, KELLY; Marian HS; South Bend, IN; Cl Rep Jr Cls; Cls Rep Sr Cls; Chrs; Chrh Wkr; Cmnty Wkr; Hon Rl; Mdrgl; Sch Mus; Sch Pl; Stg Crw; Purdue Univ; Bus.

BURNETT, MELISSA; Ursuline Acad; Cincinnati, OH; Cmnty Wkr; Girl Scts; Chrldng; Coach Actv; Business School; Business Mgmt.

BURNETT, NICOL; Heath HS; Heath, OH; Cls Rep Frsh Cls; Cls Rep Soph Cls; Cl Rep Jr Cls; Cls Rep Sr Cls; Hon Rl; NHS; Stu Cncl; Sprt Ed Yrbk; Spn Clb; Ohio Northern Univ; Foreign Lang.

BURNETT, PAT; Harrison Community Schools; Harrison, MI; Hon Rl; Lbry Ade; 4-H; Pep Clb; PPFtbl; 4-H Awd; Mid Michigan Cmnty Coll; Hist Tchr.

BURNETT, ROBIN; Gallia Academy HS; Gallipolis, OH; Pres Jr Cls; Chrs; Hosp Ade; Sch Mus; Stu Cncl; Yrbk; Sch Nwsp; FNA; Chrldng; Scr Kpr; Ohio St Univ; Nursing.

BURNETTE, JENNIFER; Whiteland Comm HS; New Whiteland, IN; 6/220 FCA; Hon Rl; Yth Flsp; FBLA; Pep Clb; Letter Bsktbl; PPFtbl; College; Bio Sci.

BURNETTE, TERRI; Spanishburg HS; Kegley, WV; 4/33 Chrs; Hon Rl; Pres FBLA; FHA; Sec Pep Clb; Pres Awd; College; Acctg.

BURNEY, JOEL; John Adams HS; Cleveland, OH; Boy Scts; Stu Cncl; Sci Clb; Spanish Awd 79; Case Western Reserve; Bus Mgmt.

BURNEY, KEVIN; Highland Park Community HS; Highland Pk, MI; Boy Scts; Cmnty Wkr; Hon Rl; JA; NHS; Stu Cncl; Stg Crw; Boys Clb Am; UCLA; Law.

BURNHAM, ROXANNE; Laingsburg HS; Laingsburg, MI; Band; Hon Rl; NHS; Sch Pl; 4-H; FHA; Pep Clb; 4-H Awd; Mic State Univ; Medical Secretary.

BURNIS, MARK; Manistique HS; Manistique, MI; Aud/Vis; Band; Boy Scts; Red Cr Ade; Sct Actv; Pep Clb; Capt Ftbl; Trk; Univ; Engr.

BURNS, BARBARA; Elwood Community HS; Elwood, IN; 15/350 Hon Rl; Jr NHS; Lbry Ade; NHS; Stu Cncl; Rptr Yrbk; Pep Clb; Spn Clb; Letter Gym; Chrldng; Indiana Univ; Phys Ther.

BURNS, CONNIE; Fairbanks HS; Ostrander, OH; 11/102 Hon Rl; Hosp Ade; Lbry Ade; Sch Nwsp; Drama Clb; Spn Clb; PPFtbl; Voice Dem Awd; Columbus Coll Art & Dsgn; Int Desgn.

BURNS, CYNTHIA; Cass Tech HS; Detroit, MI; Chrh Wkr; Hon Rl; Cit Awd; Univ Of Michigan; Pre Med.

BURNS, DANIEL; Avon HS; Plainfield, IN; 20/200 Cls Rep Frsh Cls; Cl Rep Jr Cls; Pres Sr Cls; Am Leg Boys St; VP FCA; Hon Rl; Jr NHS; NHS; Off Ade; Stu Cncl; Coll; Med.

BURNS, DONALD; Watkins Memorial HS; Pataskala, OH; Aud/Vis; Band; Chrh Wkr; Hon Rl; Spn Clb; IM Sprt; Amer Schl Of Brdcstng; Disc Jockey.

BURNS, ELLEN; La Porte HS; Laporte, IN; 28/543 Chrs; Hon Rl; NHS; Fr Clb; Swmmng; Trk; GAA; Univ Of Iowa; Sci.

BURNS, G; Mathews HS; Vienna, OH; Hon Rl; Jr NHS; NHS; Y-Teens; FTA; Pres Key Clb; Pep Clb; Spn Clb; Sec Chrldng; Scr Kpr; Cllege.

BURNS, GREG; Sebring Mckinley HS; Sebring, OH; Bsbl; IM Sprt; Kent State Univ; Comp Progr.

BURNS, JAMES; Thornapple Kellogg HS; Middleville, MI; Hon Rl; NHS; Western Mic Univ; Bus.

BURNS, JOHN; Zanesville HS; Zanesville, OH; Cls Rep Frsh Cls; FCA; Hon Rl; NHS; Stu Cncl; Glf; Ten; College; Optometry.

BURNS, JOHN A; Central HS; Evansville, IN; 33/600 Cls Rep Soph Cls; Hon Rl; JA; NHS; Pres VICA; Ftbl; Socr; Cit Awd; Kiwan Awd; Univ Of Evansville; Comp Engr.

BURNS, KEITH; Liberty HS; Girard, OH; Band; Boy Scts; Letter Wrstlng; Hon Mntn In Kent St Dist For 1st Yr Bio 78; 3rd Sict Wrstlng & Howland Invi Tourn 78; Natl Hon Soc; Univ; Air Force.

BURNS, LAURA; W Bloomfield HS; W Bloomfield, MI; Cl Rep Jr Cls; Trs Sr Cls; Chrs; Girl Scts; Hon Rl; Jr NHS; NHS; Sch Pl; Stu Cncl; Pep Clb; Michigan St Univ; Bio.

BURNS, LISA; Shaker Heights HS; Shaker Hts, OH; 250/600 Hon Rl; Hosp Ade; Lbry Ade; Off Ade; Sch Pl; Stg Crw; Spn Clb; IM Sprt; Howard Univ; Chem.

BURNS, MARY A; Coleman HS; Coleman, MI; 15/94 Band; Chrh Wkr; Girl Scts; Hon Rl; NHS; Sch Pl; Drama Clb; C Michigan Univ; Psych.

BURNS, MIKE; St Josephs HS; S Bend, IN; 129/260 Band; Chrh Wkr; Hon Rl; Stg Crw; Fr Clb; Gov Hon Prg Awd; A Hoosier Schlrshp; Dept Awd; Excel In Art For Drawing & Graphics; Indiana Univ; Art.

BURNS, M SHAWN; Our Lady Of Mercy HS; Detroit, MI; Cls Rep Frsh Cls; Cls Rep Soph Cls; Cls Rep Sr Cls; Girl Scts; Mod UN; Sch Mus; Sch Pl; Stg Crw; Drama Clb; FSA; Univ; Bus Mgmt.

BURNS, NANCY; Lancaster HS; Winnetka, IL; 31/567 Am Leg Aux Girls St; Chrs; NHS; Sch Mus; Drama Clb; Fr Clb; Ten; GAA; AFS; Hon Rl; Lat Clb; Univ Of Rochester; English.

BURNS, PATRICIA; Catholic Central HS; Wyoming, MI; Chrh Wkr; Hon Rl; NHS; Quill & Scroll; Rptr Sch Nwsp; Lat Clb; Natl Merit SF; Michigan St Univ; Dr Of Vet Med.

BURNS, PAULA; Salem HS; Salem, IN; 27/176 Band; Drl Tm; Drm Bgl; Hon Rl; JA; Off Ade; Stu Cncl; Rptr Yrbk; Drama Clb; Lat Clb; Indiana Univ; Med.

BURNS, RITA; Grove City HS; Grove City, OH; Chrs; Chrh Wkr; Orch; Sch Mus; Sch Pl; OEA; Bsktbl; College; Court Reporter.

BURNS, ROBERT; Newark Catholic HS; Newark, OH; Cmp Fr Grls; Cmnty Wkr; Hon Rl; Letter Ftbl; IM Sprt; Ohio St Univ; Elec Engr.

BURNS, SALLY; Fairbanks HS; Milford Center, OH; 3/96 Sec Jr Cls; Chrs; Hon Rl; NHS; Sch Mus; Stg Crw; Rptr Yrbk; Drama Clb; 4-H; Spn Clb; Univ.

BURNS, SHERRIE; Gaylord HS; Gaylord, MI; Cls Rep Frsh Cls; Cls Rep Soph Cls; Cmnty Wkr; Debate Tm; Hon Rl; Natl Forn Lg; NHS; Pol Wkr; Red Cr Ade; Stu Cncl; Michigan St Univ; Law.

BURNS, STEVE; Staunton HS; Brazil, IN; 4/50 Cl Rep Jr Cls; Cls Rep Sr Cls; Band; Chrh Wkr; Hon Rl; NHS; VP Stu Cncl; Key Clb; Mgrs; Scr Kpr; Indiana St Univ; Math Tchr.

BURNS, STEVEN; Plymouth HS; Plymouth, IN; 49/250 Band; Boy Scts; Hon Rl; Stg Crw; Sch Nwsp; 4-H; Spn Clb; Letter Glf; 4-H Awd; Ohio Univ; Photojournalism.

BURNS, SUSAN; Ferndale HS; Pleasant Ridge, MI; 11/250 Band; NHS; Stg Crw; Rptr Yrbk; Drama Clb; Fr Clb; Mic State Univ; Zoology.

BURNS, TAMMY; Wilbur Wright HS; Dayton, OH; Trs Soph Cls; Cl Rep Jr Cls; Band; Cmnty Wkr; Hosp Ade; Lbry Ade; Sec Fr Clb; Sec Ger Clb; Trk; Germn 2 78; Stndt Of Mont 79; Elem Educ.

BURNS, TAMMY; Austin HS; Austin, IN; 9/100 Band; Chrs; Hosp Ade; Sch Mus; FTA; Pep Clb; Spn Clb; Mgrs; Coll; System Analysis.

BURNS, TERESA; Chillicothe HS; Chillicothe, OH; Chrs; Hon Rl; NHS; College; Med Asst.

BURNS, WILLIAM; Loy Norrix HS; Kalamazoo, MI; Aud/Vis; Boy Scts; Chrh Wkr; Hon Rl; Yth Flsp; FDA; Ten; Wrstlng; Michigan St Univ; Vet Med.

BURNSIDE, BETH; Bridgeport Sr HS; Bridgeport, WV; Hon Rl; Jr NHS; NHS; Y-Teens; Pep Clb; Letter Trk; Fairmont St Coll.

BURNSIDE, CHRIS; Barboursville HS; Barboursville, VA; Boy Scts; Chrs; Fr Clb; Letter Socr; Letter Ten; Univ; Eng.

BURNSIDE, DAPHNE; West Side HS; Gary, IN; 29/650 Hon Rl; Jr NHS; Lbry Ade; Yrbk; Indiana St Univ; Spanish.

BURNSIDE, JULIE; William Mason HS; Mason, OH; 20/180 AFS; Chrs; Hon Rl; NHS; Sci Clb; IM Sprt; RN.

BURNSIDE, PAUL; Delaware Hayes HS; Delaware, OH; AFS; Pres Chrs; Chrh Wkr; Sch Mus; Sch Pl; Ohio Wesleyan Univ; Musicology.

BURNSIDE, PHIL; Mohawk HS; Sycamore, OH; Sch Pl; Stg Crw; Yth Flsp; Drama Clb; FTA; IM Sprt; Cit Awd; Work.

BURNSIDE, SANDRA K; Lewis County HS; Weston, WV; Band; Hon Rl; Yth Flsp; Y-Teens; 4-H; Pep Clb; PPFtbl; 4-H Awd; West Virginia Univ; Medicine.

BURNSWORTH, KATHY; Southern Wells; Bluffton, IN; 7/100 Aud/Vis; Girl Scts; Hon Rl; Lbry Ade; NHS; Sch Mus; 4-H; Pep Clb; Internatl Bus Coll; Acctg.

BURR, DIANE; Marlington HS; Alliance, OH; 78/289 Hon Rl; Lbry Ade; Sch Mus; Sch Pl; Yth Flsp; Ed Sch Nwsp; Drama Clb; Fr Clb; Rdo Clb; VICA; Univ; Jrnlsm.

BURR, RONDA; Anchor Bay HS; New Haven, MI; Hon Rl; Eastern Univ; Data Proc.

BURRELL, ANN; Walnut Hills HS; Cincinnati, OH; Band; Hon Rl; Lit Mag; Pol Wkr; Sch Pl; Stu Cncl; Rptr Sch Nwsp; Socr; NCTE; Univ; Eng.

BURRELL, CINDY; Muskingum Area Joint Voc Sch; Zanesville, OH; 3/13 Sec Jr Cls; Sec Sr Cls; Cmp Fr Grls; Chrs; Girl Scts; Hon Rl; NHS; Y-Teens; DECA; 4-H; Bus Schl; Restaurant Mgr.

BURRELL, DIANA; Hubbard HS; Hubbard, OH; Band; Cmp Fr Grls; Chrs; Hon Rl; Sch Mus; FTA; College.

BURRELL, PAMELA D; William A Wirt HS; Gary, IN; 6/230 Sec Frsh Cls; Am Leg Aux Girls St; Hon Rl; Pres NHS; Sch Pl; Sec Stu Cncl; Yrbk; Pres Pep Clb; Chrldng; GAA; Indiana Univ; Medicine.

BURRELL, RICHARD; Walkerville Cmnty School; Walkerville, MI; Pres Frsh Cls; Trs Soph Cls; Pres Jr Cls; Pres Sr Cls; Boy Scts; Sch Pl; Sct Actv; Yrbk; Rptr Sch Nwsp; 4-H; Ferris St Coll; Pre Engr.

BURRESS, STEVEN; Start HS; Toledo, OH; College.

BURRESS, YVONNE; Scottsburg Sr HS; Scottsburg, IN; 3/203 Chrh Wkr; Treas FCA; Hon Rl; NHS; 4-H; Treas Fr Clb; Sci Clb; Univ; Nursing.

BURRIER, GAIL; New Philadelphia HS; Pt Washngtn, OH; 23/289 Jr NHS; Pres 4-H; 4-H Awd; Cert Of Honor Alg 78; Spanish Awd 77; Kent St Univ; Acctg.

BURRIS, BRENDA; Chandon HS; Chesterland, OH; AFS; Cmnty Wkr; Hon Rl; Hosp Ade; NHS; Fr Clb; FBLA; Bsktbl; Crs Cntry; Chrldng; Ohi Univ; Educ.

BURRIS, BRIAN D; Toronto HS; Toronto, OH; 31/179 Aud/Vis; Boy Scts; Chrh Wkr; Sch Mus; Sch Pl; Sct Actv; Stg Crw; Spn Clb; Bsktbl; Ten; Kent St Univ; Bus Admin.

BURRIS, LISA; Elgin HS; Larue, OH; 9/138 Band; Chrs; Hon Rl; NHS; Rptr Sch Nwsp; Lat Clb; Ohio Valley Coll; Bio Sci.

BURRIS, SUSAN; Eastmoor Sr HS; Columbus, OH; 30/290 Cls Rep Frsh Cls; Chrs; Drl Tm; Hon Rl; DECA; Swmmng; Mgrs; Pom Pon; PPFtbl; Ohio St Univ; Educ.

BURRISS, DAVID M; Waverly HS; Waverly, OH; Hon Rl; Yth Flsp; 4-H; Letter Bsbl; Letter Crs Cntry; Coach Actv; IM Sprt; Univ; Educ.

BURROUGHS, CONNIE J; Fairlawn HS; Sidney, OH; 1/48 VP Soph Cls; Chrs; Hon Rl; Hosp Ade; Sch Mus; Yth Flsp; Rptr Yrbk; 4-H; FHA; Ten; Wright St Univ; Educ.

BURROUGHS, DAVE; Barberton HS; Barberton, OH; Cls Rep Frsh Cls; Chrh Wkr; Cmnty Wkr; Stu Cncl; Letter Ftbl; Letter Trk; IM Sprt; Univ; Bnkg.

BURROUGHS, KIMBERLY; St Martin De Porres HS; Detroit, MI; Cls Rep Frsh Cls; Cls Rep Soph Cls; Cl Rep Jr Cls; Cls Rep Sr Cls; Chrs; Chrh Wkr; Drl Tm; Girl Scts; Hosp Ade; Sch Pl; Sienia Hts Coll; Law Enfrcmnt.

BURROUGHS, SHERRY; Hinton HS; Jumping Branch, WV; Band; Drm Mjrt; Hon Rl; Off Ade; Sch Mus; Rptr Sch Nwsp; 4-H; West Virginia Univ; Med Tech.

BURROWAY, JAMES; Portsmouth HS; Portsmouth, OH; Aud/Vis; Band; Boy Scts; Chrh Wkr; Cmnty Wkr; Hon Rl; NHS; Spn Clb; DAR Awd; Woodsman Of World Amer Hist Awd; Teen Inst On Alcohol & Other Drugs; Portsmouth Orzaba Mexico Sister Cities; Univ Of Cincinnati; Elec Engr.

BURROWNS, DEBRA; Roosevelt Wilson HS; Nutter Fort, WV; 19/122 Am Leg Aux Girls St; Band; Chrh Wkr; Cmnty Wkr; Girl Scts; Hon Rl; Hosp Ade; NHS; Off Ade; Sch Pl; Alderson Broaddus Coll; Nursing.

BURROWS, DEBRA; Roosevelt Wilson HS; Nutter Fort, WV; Am Leg Aux Girls St; Band; Chrh Wkr; Girl Scts; Hon Rl; Hosp Ade; NHS; Off Ade; Sch Pl; VP Yth Flsp; Alderson Broaddus Coll; Nursing.

BURROWS, HOWARD; Dexter HS; Pinckney, MI; Band; Hon Rl; NHS; Orch; Ger Clb; Kalamazoo College; Sci.

BURRUS, GINA M; Jefferson HS; Newport, MI; 11/218 Cls Rep Frsh Cls; Cls Rep Soph Cls; Hon Rl; Sch Mus; Sch Pl; Stu Cncl; Drama Clb; Fr Clb; Pep Clb; Chrldng; Monroe Cmnty Coll; Psych.

BURRUS, JAMES; Jefferson HS; Newport, MI; 15/186 Cls Rep Frsh Cls; Cls Rep Soph Cls; Cl Rep Jr Cls; Cls Rep Sr Cls; Hon Rl; NHS; Rptr Yrbk; Rptr Sch Nwsp; Sch Nwsp; Ftbl; Michigan St Univ; Law.

BURSA, J; Tiffin Calvert HS; Tiffin, OH; 4/98 Band; Pres Girl Scts; JA; NHS; Orch; Sct Actv; Pep Clb; Ohi Northern Univ; Pharmacy.

BURSA, JILL; Calvert HS; Tiffin, OH; 4/99 Band; Drm Mjrt; Pres Girl Scts; Hon Rl; JA; NHS; Orch; Pep Clb; IM Sprt; Cit Awd; Ohio Northern Univ; Pharm.

BURSKEY, JUDITH; Walled Lake Central HS; Union Lake, MI; 7/364 Chrs; Chrh Wkr; Cmnty Wkr; Hon Rl; NHS; PAVAS; Sch Mus; Yth Flsp; Wayne St Univ; Soc Work.

BURSLEM, JEFFREY G; Jackson HS; Massillon, OH; Am Leg Boys St; Debate Tm; Hon Rl; JA; Natl Forn Lg; NHS; Off Ade; Pol Wkr; Spn Clb; College; Comp Science.

BURSON, JANA; Meigs HS; Shade, OH; 1/212 Band; Chrh Wkr; Hon Rl; Pres NHS; Spn Clb; DAR Awd; Natl Merit Ltr; Ohio Univ; Med Tech.

BURSON, JOHN; Vinton County HS; Mc Arthur, OH; 5/150 Band; Chrs; Chrh Wkr; Hon Rl; Jr NHS; NHS; Pol Wkr; Treas Pol Wkr; Lat Clb; Letter Ten; Bowling Green State Univ; Music.

BURT, ANN; Lake Orion Comm HS; Lake Orion, MI; Am Leg Aux Girls St; Hon Rl; Lit Mag; Off Ade; Stu Cncl; Ed Yrbk; Yrbk; Grand Rep To St Of Fl Internatl Order Of Rainbow For Girls; St Grand Ofcr Of Internatl Ordr Of Rnbw For Grl; College; Medicine.

BURT, BRIAN; Elmhurst HS; Ft Wayne, IN; 1/413 Pres Frsh Cls; Pres Soph Cls; Pres Jr Cls; VP Sr Cls; Am Leg Boys St; Hon Rl; Stu Cncl; Rptr Yrbk; Rptr Sch Nwsp; Fr Clb; Univ; Comp Sci.

BURT, JANET; Belding HS; Belding, MI; 3/140 Band; Hon Rl; NHS; Ten; Chrldng; Central Mic Univ; Fashion Design.

BURT, JANET; Calumet HS; Gary, IN; 5/300 Hon Rl; Jr NHS; NHS; Sch Nwsp; Fr Clb; Pep Clb; Pom Pon; PPFtbl; Indiana Univ.

BURT, JEFFREY S; A D Johnston HS; Bessemer, MI; 7/82 Chrh Wkr; Hon Rl; Pol Wkr; ROTC; Letter Bsbl; Letter Bsktbl; Letter Ftbl; St Of Mi Comp Schlrshp Winner; Mi Math Prize Comp Finalist; Top Ten; Michigan Tech Univ; Comp Sci.

BURT, JENNIFER; Parma Sr HS; Parma, OH; 63/782 Debate Tm; Hon Rl; Natl Forn Lg; NHS; Quill & Scroll; Ed Sch Nwsp; Rptr Sch Nwsp; Sch Nwsp; Ten; Scr Kpr; Slap Shot Shouters Hockey Booster Group; Univ Of Nebraska; Journalism.

BURT, KIMBERLY; W Muskingum HS; Newark, OH; VP Frsh Cls; Band; Chrh Wkr; Girl Scts; Hon Rl; Jr NHS; Lbry Ade; Sch Pl; Stu Cncl; Y-Teens; Coll; Acctg.

BURTCH, MICHELLE; Chesaning Union HS; Burt, MI; Cls Rep Frsh Cls; Cl Rep Jr Cls; Aud/Vis; Hon Rl; Stu Cncl; Bus Schl; Sec.

BURTON, ANDREW J; Luther L Wright HS; Ironwood, MI; 1/170 Am Leg Boys St; Band; Boy Scts; Hon Rl; NHS; Sct Actv; Letter Crs Cntry; Letter Wrstlng; Natl Merit SF; Michigan St Univ.

BURTON, DONNIE; Lockland HS; Cincinnati, OH; 8/60 Hon Rl; NHS; Fr Clb; Bsbl; Ftbl; Scr Kpr; Vocational Schl; Broadcasting.

BURTON, DORTHEA A; Mumford Sr HS; Detroit, MI; Chrs; Chrh Wkr; Girl Scts; Hon Rl; JA; NHS; Off Ade; Y-Teens; FTA; OEA; Ferris St Coll; Bus Admin.

BURTON, DOUGLAS; Madison Comp HS; Mansfield, OH; 12/450 Hon Rl; Jr NHS; NHS; VP Spn Clb; Bsbl; Glf; Coach Actv; IM Sprt; Univ.

BURTON, DRENNA; Hundred HS; Wileyville, WV; 6/47 Cls Rep Frsh Cls; Cls Rep Soph Cls; Band; Chrs; Hon Rl; Lbry Ade; VP NHS; Wv Univ; Music.

BURTON, FLOYD R; Springs Valley HS; French Lick, IN; 1/72 Band; Chrh Wkr; Hon Rl; Fr Clb; Rose Hulman Inst Of Tech; Med.

BURTON, FRANK; Wirt County HS; Elizabeth, WV; Letter Bsbl; Letter Ftbl; Letter Wrstlng; PPFtbl; Welding.

BURTON, GREGORY K; Mumford Sr HS; Detroit, MI; 12/550 Band; Hon Rl; Treas NHS; Stu Cncl; Spn Clb; Crs Cntry; Ftbl; Trk; Cit Awd; Opt Clb Awd; Music Award; MESA Prgm Lawrence Hall Of Sci; Police Youth Athletic Band; Univ; Med.

BURTON, GWENDOLYN D; South HS; Cleveland, OH; Cmp Fr Grls; Chrh Wkr; Cmnty Wkr; Drl Tm; Hon Rl; JA; Jr NHS; NHS; Off Ade; PAVAS; Natl Merit Commended Stu; Math STI At Phillips Acad; Captain Of Vrsty Fencing Team; Miami Univ; Systems Engr.

BURTON, JACKIE; Henryville HS; Jeffersonville, IN; 2/249 Hon Rl; Jr NHS; NHS; Spn Clb; Whos Who In Frgn Lang 78; Univ; Elem Ed Tchr.

BURTON, JENNY; North Putnam HS; Greencastle, IN; Chrs; Hon Rl; Mdrgl; 4-H; OEA; 4-H Awd; Ind State Univ; Sec Sci.

BURTON, JOYCE A; Center Grove HS; Greenwood, IN; 5/300 Chrh Wkr; Hon Rl; Fr Clb; FTA; Natl Merit SF; Bio Jr; Cert De Merite French Soph & Jr; Univ; Elem Educ.

BURTON, KELLY; Salem HS; Salem, IN; JA; Drama Clb; 4-H; Sec Spn Clb; Letter Crs Cntry; Letter Trk; College; Archt.

BURTON, KILA; Flemington HS; Flemington, WV; Trs Soph Cls; Sec Jr Cls; Band; Hon Rl; NHS; Off Ade; FBLA; Bus Schl; Sec.

BURTON, LATANYA; John Adams HS; Cleveland, OH; 11/408 Cls Rep Sr Cls; Chrs; Hon Rl; FTA; Pep Clb; Cit Awd; Outstndng Stdnt In Physics 79; Eng Bkkpng & Typing Awd 79; Dyke Coll; Acctg.

BURTON, LUCINDA; Wirt County HS; Elizabeth, WV; Band; Chrh Wkr; Hon Rl; NHS; Off Ade; Yth Flsp; 4-H; FBLA; Pep Clb; Trk; Parkersburg Community College; Sec.

BURTON, MARILYN; Elmwood HS; Wayne, OH; 3/120 Sec Sr Cls; Pres Band; Hon Rl; Treas NHS; Sec Yth Flsp; Sec 4-H; FTA; Bsktbl; College.

BURTON, MICHAEL; Springs Valley HS; French Lick, IN; Cl Rep Jr Cls; Am Leg Boys St; Band; Hon Rl; Lbry Ade; Stu Cncl; Bsktbl; Ftbl; Trk; Purdue Univ; Engr.

BURTON, PEGGY; David Anderson HS; Lisbon, OH; 30/95 FCA; Girl Scts; Hon Rl; Lbry Ade; Sch Mus; Yth Flsp; Y-Teens; Rptr Sch Nwsp; Fr Clb; FSA; Slippery Rock Univ; Acctg.

BURTON, RALPH; Padva Franciscan HS; Middleburg Hts, OH; Letter Bsktbl; College; Phys Educ.

BURTON, RICHARD; Attica HS; Attica, IN; 27/75 Boy Scts; Chrs; Ftbl; IM Sprt; Purdue; Mech Engr.

BURTON, RICKY; Lockland HS; Lockland, OH; Rptr Yrbk; Bsktbl; Glf; Ten; Wrstlng; Cincinnati Tech Coll; Elec.

BURTON, ROBIN; Washington HS; Washington, IN; 11/216 VP Frsh Cls; Cls Rep Frsh Cls; VP Soph Cls; Cls Rep Soph Cls; Cl Rep Jr Cls; Hon Rl; Stu Cncl; Fr Clb; Pep Clb; Indiana St Univ; Medicine.

BURTT, CHRISTINE; Pymatuning Valley HS; Williamsfield, OH; Pres Jr Cls; Cl Rep Jr Cls; Cls Rep Sr Cls; Sal; Band; Chrs; Hon Rl; NHS; Stu Cncl; 4-H; Ashtabula Cnty Joint Voc Schl.

BURTT, KIM; Northridge HS; Goshen, IN; Drl Tm; Hon Rl; 4-H; Pep Clb; Spn Clb; Capt Pom Pon; Ball St Univ; Busns Admin.

BURWELL, LOUIS; Ironton HS; Ironton, OH; 16/189 Band; NHS; Letter Ten; Ohio St Univ; Comp Sci.

BURWELL, RODNEY; East Akron HS; Akron, OH; VP Frsh Cls; Cls Rep Soph Cls; Hst Jr Cls; Chrs; Chrh Wkr; Sch Mus; Sprt Ed Sch Nwsp; Sci Clb; Capt Socr; Capt Wrstlng; Iowa Univ; Phys Educ.

BURWINKEL, JAMES; St Francis Sem; Cincinnati, OH; 1/12 Pres Frsh Cls; Val; Chrs; Hon Rl; Sch Pl; Ed Sch Nwsp; Letter Socr; IM Sprt; Natl Merit Ltr; Xavier Univ; Honors Ab Program.

BURY, DIANA; Benton Harbor HS; Benton Hbr, MI ; Cls Rep Soph Cls; Cl Rep Jr Cls; Band; Chrh Wkr; Girl Scts; Hon Rl; NHS; Sch Mus; Stu Cncl; Rptr Yrbk; Univ.

BURZINSKI, BARB; Rogers HS; Toledo, OH; Pres Jr Cls; Band; Cmp Fr Grls; Jr NHS; NHS; Stu Cncl; Sci Clb; Socr; Letter Ten; PPFtbl; College; Science.

BURZINSKI, JOSEPH E; Robert S Rogers HS; Toledo, OH; 11/512 VP Band; NHS; Orch; Sch Mus; Sci Clb; Univ Of Louisville; Music.

BURZYNSKI, SHELLEY; Lumen Christi HS; Jackson, MI; Cls Rep Frsh Cls; VP Soph Cls; Pres Jr Cls; Am Leg Aux Girls St; Pol Wkr; Red Cr Ade; Stu Cncl; Ed Yrbk; Pep Clb; IM Sprt; Jackson Community College;advertisin.

BUSACK, FREDERICK L; St Joseph Central Cath HS; Fremont, OH; 12/100 Pres Jr Cls; Band; Hon Rl; NHS; Orch; Stu Cncl; Pep Clb; Most Outstndng Musician 1977; Selected For All OH Band 1979; Selected For Amer Yth Symphony Tour Of Europe; Univ; Geology.

BUSANA, BONNIE; Jefferson Union HS; Steubenvill, OH; Band; Chrs; Hon Rl; Y-Teens; OEA; Pep Clb; GAA; Pres Awd; Busns Schl; Legal Sec.

BUSARD, LYMAN W; Laville Jr Sr HS; Plymouth, IN; 10/135 Boy Scts; Chrh Wkr; NHS; Mth Clb; VP Spn Clb; Bsbl; Bsktbl; Ftbl; College; Chemical Engineer.

BUSAROW, KERRY; Springfield North HS; Springfield, OH; Band; Chrs; Hon Rl; Orch; Sch Mus; Letter Trk; IM Sprt; Natl Merit SF; Wittenberg Univ; Chem.

BUSBY, JOANNA; Oak Hill HS; Oak Hill, WV; Chrh Wkr; Hon Rl; NHS; Yth Flsp; Fr Clb; Sci Clb; Univ; Psych.

BUSBY, JOSANNA; Lapel HS; Anderson, IN; Hon Rl; Off Ade; Rptr Yrbk; Lat Clb; Pep Clb; Sci Clb; Ball State Univ; Acctg.

BUSCH, AMANDA; Elkins HS; Elkins, WV; 15/241 Cl Rep Jr Cls; Am Leg Aux Girls St; Band; NHS; Stu Cncl; Letter Bsktbl; Letter Ten; Chrldng; Pres GAA; Scr Kpr; College; Communications.

BUSCH, JEFF; Western Reserve Acad; Parma, OH; Band; Boy Scts; Orch; Sch Mus; Stg Crw; Rptr Sch Nwsp; Capt Crs Cntry; Letter Trk; College; Law.

BUSCHE, MARSHA; Eastside Jr Sr HS; Hicksville, OH; 1/92 Val; Hon Rl; NHS; Off Ade; Stu Cncl; Rptr Yrbk; Fr Clb; Pep Clb; Sci Clb; Mgrs; Top Acctg Stu Amer Outstndng Names Faces; Highest GPA In Class; Honorary Hoosier Schlr Century III Ldrs; Purdue Univ; Labor Law.

BUSCHELMANN, KIMBERLY; Reading Community HS; Reading, OH; 4/218 Am Leg Aux Girls St; Girl Scts; Hon Rl; Jr NHS; NHS; Rptr Sch Nwsp; Ger Clb; Coach Actv; Scr Kpr; JETS Awd; Mt St Joseph Univ; Resp Ther.

BUSCHKOETTER, SHARLA; Jasper HS; Jasper, IN; Hon Rl; JA; Drama Clb; 4-H; Pep Clb; JA Awd; College; Comp Sci.

BUSCHMANN, JILL; Marian HS; Bloomfield Hl, MI; Chrs; Mdrgl; Mod UN; Natl Forn Lg; College; Graphic Design.

BUSCHOR, DAN; Archbishop Alter HS; Dayton, OH; 6/298 Aud/Vis; Chrs; Hon Rl; NHS; Sch Pl; Pres Stg Crw; Yrbk; Letter Bsbl; IM Sprt; U S Air Force Acad; Aviation.

BUSENBARK, KELLI; Whitko HS; S Whitley, IN; FCA; Pol Wkr; Rptr Sch Nwsp; Fr Clb; Letter Bsktbl; Letter Trk; Coach Actv; GAA; Indiana Ctrl Univ; Phys Ed.

BUSH, BETH; Mogadore HS; Mogadore, OH; 36/97 VP Chrs; Chrh Wkr; JA; Mdrgl; PAVAS; Sch Mus; Drama Clb; Sec FHA; Sci Clb; Voice Dem Awd; Eckerd Coll; Art.

BUSH, BEVERLY A; Mona Shores HS; Muskegon, MI; Cls Rep Frsh Cls; Chrs; Chrh Wkr; Hon Rl; Lbry Ade; NHS; Sch Pl; Stu Cncl; Sci Clb; Crs Cntry; Sci Dept Awds Bio 77 & Chem 78; Eng Dept Awd Runner Up 79; Pres Schlr Grand Valley St Univ 79; Grand Valley St Univ; Med Tech.

BUSH, BRENDA; Charlestown HS; Charlestwon, IN; Cl Rep Jr Cls; Chrs; JA; Off Ade; FHA; JC Awd; Mas Awd;.

BUSH, CYNTHIA; Norwood HS; Norwood, OH; Band; Chrs; Hon Rl; JA; Sch Mus; Yrbk; Pep Clb; Coll; Music Educ.

BUSH, DEANNA; Morgantown HS; Westover, WV; Hon Rl; Jr NHS; Rptr Yrbk; Fr Clb; DAR Awd; West Virginia Univ; Medicine.

BUSH, DEBBIE; Seymour HS; Seymour, IN; 11/358 Hon Rl; Pol Wkr; Yth Flsp; 4-H; Ger Clb; Pep Clb; Letter Bsktbl; Letter Trk; Coach Actv; GAA; All St Sftbl Team 76 78; Whos Who In For Lang Germn 78; Who Whos Among Amer HS Stdtn 78; Bus Awd 79; Indiana Cntrl Univ; Acctg.

BUSH, ERIC; East Canton HS; E Canton, OH; Band; Hon Rl; Yth Flsp; Spn Clb; Bsktbl; Capt Crs Cntry; Gym; Trk; Capt IM Sprt; College; A F Rotc, 1 Yr In A F.

BUSH, GLENNA; Hammond Technical Voc HS; Hammond, IN; 103/219 PAVAS; Sch Pl; Stg Crw; Sch Nwsp; Pep Clb; Business School.

BUSH, HOPE; Perry HS; Laingsburg, MI; Hon Rl; NHS; FHA; Spn Clb; Mich State Univ; Dentistry.

BUSH, JEFFREY; Springboro HS; Springboro, OH; Band; Boy Scts; Chrs; Chrh Wkr; Hon Rl; PAVAS; Sct Actv; Stg Crw; Yth Flsp; FTA; Coll; Busns.

BUSH, JOSEPH; Padua Franciscan HS; Cleveland, OH; 60/225 Cls Rep Frsh Cls; Cl Rep Jr Cls; Hon Rl; NHS; Stu Cncl; Bsbl; Ftbl; IM Sprt; Natl Merit Ltr; College; Acctg.

BUSH, JULIE; John Marshall HS; Indianapolis, IN; 8/463 Hon Rl; NHS; Off Ade; Quill & Scroll; Ed Sch Nwsp; Sprt Ed Sch Nwsp; Rptr Sch Nwsp; Letter Bsktbl; Trk; PPFtbl; Ball State Univ; Journalism.

BUSH, KAREN; Washington HS; Massillon, OH; Cls Rep Soph Cls; Cl Rep Jr Cls; AFS; Chrs; Hon Rl; Sch Mus; Sch Pl; Stg Crw; College; Public Relations.

BUSH, LISA; Williamstown HS; Williamstown, WV; Cls Rep Frsh Cls; Cl Rep Jr Cls; AFS; Band; Stu Cncl; Fr Clb; Pep Clb; Letter Trk; Letter Chrldng; College; Health.

BUSH, LYNNE; Zanesville HS; Zanesville, OH; Hon Rl; Lbry Ade; NHS; Off Ade; Lat Clb; College.

BUSH, NANCY; Rocky River HS; Rocky Rvr, OH; Hon Rl; Jr NHS; Ten; Univ.

BUSH, PAMELA; Central Hower HS; Akron, OH; 17/340 Chrh Wkr; VP JA; Lit Mag; NHS; Rptr Sch Nwsp; Pep Clb; Akron Univ; Education.

BUSH, PAMELA; South Range HS; Canfield, OH; 10/131 Hon Rl; NHS; Off Ade; Yrbk; Drama Clb; VP Ger Clb; Univ; Nursing.

BUSH, PATRICIA; Concord HS; Concord, MI; 3/70 Trs Soph Cls; Pres Jr Cls; Chrh Wkr; Hon Rl; Natl Forn Lg; Orch; Sch Mus; VP Stu Cncl; Yth Flsp; Opt Clb Awd; Univ; Lib Arts.

BUSH, RICHARD; Seeger Mem HS; Wlmsprt, IN; Chrs; Cmnty Wkr; Hon Rl; Lbry Ade; Pol Wkr; 4-H; Ten; Chrldng; Cheerleading Trophy For Winning Sectional; Published Essay; Indiana St Univ; Acctg.

BUSH, ROBERT; Douglas Macarthur HS; Saginaw, MI; 20/400 Hon Rl; Jr NHS; NHS; Sci Clb; Letter Bsbl; Letter Ftbl; Pres Awd; Mich State; Sci.

BUSH, RONNI; Olivet HS; Olivet, MI; Band; Hon Rl; Off Ade; PPFtbl; Kellogg Cmnty Coll; Bus Ed.

BUSH, RUSSELL; Southwestern HS; Flat Rock, IN; 10/53 Band; Chrh Wkr; Yrbk; Rptr Sch Nwsp; Mth Clb; Pep Clb; Spn Clb; Gov Hon Prg Awd; Eli Lilly Hon Prog 79; Ball St Univ.

BUSH, SCOTT; Edgewood HS; Middletown, OH; Hon Rl; NHS; Sch Pl; Ger Clb; Coral Gables; Marine Bio.

BUSH, SHARON; Buchtel University HS; Akron, O H; 144/452 Hon Rl; Upward Bound Hon Soc Kent St Univ 79; Univ; Finance.

BUSH, VIVIAN; Franklin Central HS; Indianapolis, IN; Cmp Fr Grls; Chrs; Chrh Wkr; Off Ade; Yth Flsp; FNA; Lat Clb; Pep Clb; Spn Clb; Chrldng; Sftbl Sportsmanship Awd 79; Jobs Daughters Hon Queen 79; Clark Coll; Med Asst.

BUSH, WESLEY; Morgantown HS; Winnetka, IL; 1/400 Hon Rl; Treas NHS; Stu Cncl; Pres Mth Clb; Am Leg Awd; DAR Awd; Kiwan Awd; Natl Merit Schl; Rensselaer Math & Sci Awd 78; Wv Delegate To Natl Youth Sci Camp 79; MIT; Elec Engr.

BUSHART, CHUCK; Milan HS; Maybee, MI; 8/192 Pres Frsh Cls; Pres NHS; FFA; Ftbl; Eastern Mich Univ; Computer Science.

BUSHAW, MICHELE; John Glenn HS; Westland, MI; Band; Chrs; Chrh Wkr; Girl Scts; Hon Rl; Jr NHS; Lbry Ade; Orch; Western Mic Univ; Sci.

BUSHEY, DOUGLAS; Edwardsburg HS; Edwardsburg, MI; Hon Rl; Letter Bsbl; Letter Glf; Univ; Chem Engr.

BUSHEY, MARY; Mancelona HS; Bellaire, MI; Cls Rep Frsh Cls; Band; Hon Rl; Jr NHS; VP Stu Cncl; Rptr Sch Nwsp; 4-H; Letter Trk; Ferris St Coll; Pharm.

BUSHMAN, BRENDA; Eastwood HS; Pemberville, OH; Cls Rep Soph Cls; Cl Rep Jr Cls; Band; Hon Rl; Off Ade; Stu Cncl; 4-H; Chrldng; Bowling Green St Univ; Busns.

BUSHMAN, KAREN S; Madison Comprehensive HS; Mansfield, OH; Chrs; Sec Chrh Wkr; Rptr Sch Nwsp; Sch Nwsp; Treas FHA; Spn Clb; N Ctrl Tech Coll; Comp Progr.

BUSHNELL, BETSY; Riverside HS; Painesville, OH; Band; Chrh Wkr; Hon Rl; College.

BUSHNELL, BROOKS; North Bloomington HS; Bloomington, IN; 5/488 FCA; NHS; Sch Pl; Boys Clb Am; Ger Clb; Natl Merit SF; Indiana Univ; Bus Admin.

BUSHNELL, J ANTHONY; Central HS; Evansville, IN; Cls Rep Soph Cls; Cl Rep Jr Cls; Aud/Vis; Ten; Chmn Chrldng; 4-H Awd; God Cntry Awd; College; Mgmt.

BUSHONG, DENISE; Marysville HS; Marysville, OH; Cls Rep Frsh Cls; Pres Soph Cls; Chrs; Chrh Wkr; Natl Forn Lg; Sch Mus; Stu Cncl; Chrldng; GAA; PPFtbl; Bowling Green State Univ; Bus Admin.

BUSHOUSE, SUSAN; Portage Central HS; Portage, MI; 9/370 Band; Debate Tm; Hon Rl; Lbry Ade; Natl Forn Lg; Orch; Sch Mus; Sch Pl; Stg Crw; Rptr Yrbk; Oakland Univ; Anthropology.

BUSHUE, ROSE M; Covington HS; Covington, IN; Cl Rep Jr Cls; Chrs; Chrh Wkr; Hon Rl; Stu Cncl; 4-H; Pep Clb; Letter Bsktbl; Trk; Mgrs; Ball State Univ; Phys Educ.

BUSHYAGER, KAREN; Boardman HS; Poland, OH; Chrs; Hon Rl; Stg Crw; Youngstown Univ; Art.

BUSICK, KARMEN; Bellmont HS; Decatur, IN; 43/244 Cl Rep Jr Cls; Cls Rep Sr Cls; Chrs; Drl Tm; Hon Rl; Sch Mus; Stu Cncl; Yth Flsp; 4-H; OEA; 4 H Awd Many Trips; 4 H Round Up Jr Ldr Confrnc 78; Univ; Bus Educ.

BUSKARD, JOLANE; Grandville Public HS; Grand Rapids, MI; Chrh Wkr; Cmnty Wkr; 4-H; Bsbl; Mat Maids; PPFtbl; 4-H Awd; Univ; Pre Law.

BUSKEY, JOHN; Centerville HS; Centerville, IN; Aud/Vis; FCA; PAVAS; Sch Pl; Drama Clb; Letter Ten; Letter Trk; Singing In Univ Of S CA Choir 76; Nettle Creek Players Inc 79; Drama.

BUSKIRK, ANGELA; Bangor HS; Bangor, MI; 40/98 Chrh Wkr; Hon Rl; Lbry Ade; Off Ade; Key Clb; Pep Clb; Spn Clb; Davenport College Of Bus; Comp Progr.

BUSKIRK, CARLA; Diamond Oaks Career Dvlpmnt; Harrison, OH; VP Jr Cls; Pres Sr Cls; Am Leg Aux Girls St; Girl Scts; Hon Rl; Stu Cncl; DECA; Sec 4-H; Pep Clb; Trk; Dist DECA Vc Chrprsn; Bus Schl; Retail Mgmt.

BUSKIRK, HOWARD; Hastings HS; Hastings, MI; Cls Rep Frsh Cls; Trs Soph Cls; Sec Jr Cls; Trs Jr Cls; NHS; Pol Wkr; Sch Pl; Drama Clb; Fr Clb; Univ Of Mic; Journalism.

BUSKO, JOY; Warren Western Reserve HS; Warren, OH; 62/470 Girl Scts; Hon Rl; NHS; Red Cr Ade; Capt Bsbl; Bsktbl; IM Sprt; Kent St Univ; Comp Tech.

BUSLER, SUSAN; Carrollton HS; Carrollton, OH; 40/255 Aud/Vis; Chrs; Chrh Wkr; Hon Rl; Sch Mus; Sch Pl; Stg Crw; Drama Clb; 4-H; Fr Clb; Natl 4 H Club Congress Delegate In Sheep 1978; Kent St Univ; Rec Ther.

BUSMAN, LORI; Vestaburg HS; Vestaburg, MI; 5/76 Hon Rl; NHS; Off Ade; Stu Cncl; Yth Flsp; Spn Clb; Letter Chrldng; PPFtbl; Ctrl Michigan Univ; Acctg.

BUSONIK, SHARON; Campbell Memorial HS; Campbell, OH; Cls Rep Frsh Cls; Cls Rep Soph Cls; Cl Rep Jr Cls; Cls Rep Sr Cls; Hon Rl; NHS; Off Ade; Key Clb; Mth Clb; Pep Clb; College; Comp Sci.

BUSSA, MARGARET; Elk Rapids HS; Rapid City, MI; Band; Hon Rl; Sch Pl; Ed Yrbk; Rptr Yrbk; 4-H; 4-H Awd; Univ; Photog.

BUSSE, ALVIN E; Chaminade Julienne HS; Dayton, OH; Pres Sr Cls; Chrh Wkr; Hon Rl; JA; NHS; Stu Cncl; Bsktbl; Tmr; JA Awd; Univ; Cmnctns.

BUSSE, BOB; Milton Union HS; Ludlow Fl, OH; 19/216 Am Leg Boys St; Band; Chrh Wkr; Hon Rl; NHS; Pol Wkr; Sch Pl; Stu Cncl; FTA; Ten; Outsdng Bndsmn 78; Oh Univ Amer Hstry Test Finalist 78; Univ Of Dayton; Law.

BUSSE, MARY A; St Anne HS; Warren, MI; Cls Rep Frsh Cls; Cls Rep Soph Cls; Cl Rep Jr Cls; Girl Scts; Hon Rl; JA; Jr NHS; NHS; Pol Wkr; Sct Actv; Univ; Astronomy.

BUSSELL, LINDA; Lockland HS; Cincinnati, OH; 3/65 VP Soph Cls; Hon Rl; Chmn NHS; Sec Stu Cncl; Rptr Yrbk; Trk; Chmn Chrldng;.

BUSSELLE, RICK; Otsego HS; Grand Rapids, OH; 95/125 Pres Frsh Cls; VP Jr Cls; Boy Scts; Spn Clb; Ftbl; Trk; Capt Wrstlng; Univ.

BUSSEN, DEREK; Hazel Park HS; Hazel Park, MI; Hon Rl; NHS; Sch Mus; Sch Pl; Drama Clb; Crs Cntry; Michigan St Univ; Theatre.

BUSSENGER, TERRY; Frankenmuth HS; Frankenmuth, MI; Am Leg Boys St; Band; Capt Bsbl; Capt Bsktbl; Capt Ftbl; Northwood Inst; Bus Admin.

BUSSER, JOHN; Padua Fransiscan HS; Cleveland, OH; Hon Rl; NHS; Ftbl;.

BUSSEY, ALAN R; Arlington HS; Indianapolis, IN; 6/399 Cl Rep Jr Cls; Boy Scts; Hon Rl; JA; NHS; Spn Clb; Pres VICA; Capt Trk; Natl Merit SF; Genl Mtrs Inst; Elec Engr.

BUSSEY, DEANNA; Portsmouth East HS; Wheelersburg, OH; Val; Am Leg Aux Girls St; Chrs; Chrh Wkr; Girl Scts; Hon Rl; Lbry Ade; NHS; Off Ade; Sch Mus; Shawnee St Coll; Acctg.

BUSSING, TONY; St Xavier HS; Cincinnati, OH; 85/265 Socr; Univ Of Cincinnati; Aeronautical Eng.

BUSSMAN, DEBBIE; Grove City HS; Grove City, OH; 1/509 VP Soph Cls; VP Jr Cls; Val; Cmp Fr Grls; Hon Rl; NHS; Sec Stu Cncl; Ed Yrbk; Sec Fr Clb; Kiwan Awd; Rotary Intl Camp Enterprs 1978; Most Ambitious Sr 1979; Ohio Univ; Comp Sci.

BUSSON, JULIE; St Vincent St Mary HS; Akron, OH; 23/271 Chrh Wkr; Cmnty Wkr; Hon Rl; Lbry Ade; NHS; Sch Pl; Mth Clb; Ten; Miami Univ; Comm.

BUSWELL, ALAN; South Newton HS; Kentland, IN; 3/110 Am Leg Boys St; Chrh Wkr; Hon Rl; NHS; Yth Flsp; 4-H; Treas Ger Clb; Sci Clb; Letter Bsktbl; Crs Cntry; Coll.

BUSWELL, BEN D; John R Buchtel Univ HS; Akron, OH; Chrh Wkr; Cmnty Wkr; Sch Nwsp; Treas VICA; IM Sprt; Univ Of Akron; Mech Engr.

BUTCHER, BECKY; Ellet Sr HS; Akron, OH; 13/363 Chrs; Hon Rl; Jr NHS; Mdrgl; NHS; Quill & Scroll; Sch Mus; Sch Pl; Rptr Yrbk; Ed Sch Nwsp; Akron Univ; Foreign Lang.

BUTCHER, CARLA; Reed City HS; Reed City, MI; Band; Hon Rl; FHA; Trk; Mgrs; Central Michigan Univ; Comp Sci.

BUTCHER, JEAN; Bentley HS; Livonia, MI; Band; Hon Rl; Trk; Scr Kpr; Cert Of Recogntn For Acad Achvmnt In St Of Mi Schlrshp Comp 79; Central Michigan Univ; Bus Admin.

BUTCHER, KAREN A; Bellmont HS; Decatur, IN; 3/274 Hon Rl; NHS; Treas Yth Flsp; Sci Clb; Spn Clb; Trk; Letter Mgrs; JETS Awd; Purdue Univ; Med.

BUTCHER, KIMBERLY; John F Kennedy HS; Taylor, MI; Chrh Wkr; Hon Rl; Off Ade; College; Nursing.

BUTCHER, LETHA; Lewis County HS; Weston, WV; Am Leg Aux Girls St; Band; Chrs; Chrh Wkr; Hon Rl; Lbry Ade; NHS; Sch Pl; Stg Crw; Yth Flsp; All Area Band White 78; All Area Band Blue 77; Univ Of West Virginia; Music Ed.

BUTCHER, MARCIA R; Owosso HS; Owosso, MI; Cl Rep Jr Cls; Am Leg Aux Girls St; Chrs; Hon Rl; Hosp Ade; Treas NHS; Stu Cncl; Y-Teens; 4-H; Lat Clb; Alma College.

BUTCHER, R; Loogootee HS; Loogootee, IN; 20/150 Cl Rep Jr Cls; Cls Rep Sr Cls; Chrh Wkr; Cmnty Wkr; Hon Rl; Lbry Ade; Pol Wkr; Sch Pl; Stg Crw; Stu Cncl; Rose Hulman Univ; Engr.

BUTCHKO, DOREEN; St Ladislaus HS; Detroit, MI; 7/112 Chrs; Hon Rl; Sch Nwsp; Pep Clb; College; Busns.

BUTERA, SALLEE; Perry HS; Massillon, OH; Cls Rep Frsh Cls; Chrs; FCA; Hon Rl; Natl Forn Lg; NHS; Quill & Scroll; Sch Mus; Sch Pl; Stu Cncl; Univ; Optometrist.

BUTERA, SALLY; Perry HS; Massillon, OH; 1/563 Am Leg Aux Girls St; Cmp Fr Grls; Chrs; FCA; Natl Forn Lg; NHS; Sch Mus; Ed Sch Nwsp; FDA; Chrldng; Ind; Optometry.

BUTKE, BETH; Southridge HS; Huntingburg, IN; 2/200 Chrs; Pres Chrh Wkr; Hon Rl; Hosp Ade; Sch Mus; Pres FHA; Pep Clb; Indiana Univ; Phys Ther.

BUTKIEWICZ, MARY ELLEN; Admiral King HS; Lorain, OH; Chrh Wkr; Hon Rl; JA; Rptr Yrbk; Yrbk; Bsktbl; Mgrs; Scr Kpr; Essay Awd From Polish League Of American Veterans 76; Univ; Elec Engr.

BUTLER, ANDRE; Paul Laurence Dunbar HS; Dayton, OH; Band; Boy Scts; Drm Bgl; Hon Rl; NHS; Orch; Beta Clb; IM Sprt; ITT Tech; Repairman.

BUTLER, AUDREY; Larel Oaks Career Dev Cmps; Hillsboro, OH; Cls Rep Sr Cls; Chrs; Hon Rl; Off Ade; 4-H; OEA; Pep Clb; GAA; 4-H Awd; Voctl Trning Area Cert 1979; LDS Bus Coll; Med Sec.

BUTLER, CHRIS; Licking Valley HS; Newark, OH; 1/154 4-H; Key Clb; Letter Ftbl; Letter Trk; Letter Wrstlng;.

BUTLER, CHRISTILA; Carman HS; Flint, MI; Cmnty Wkr; Hon Rl; Hosp Ade; Sch Pl; Gym; PPFtbl; College; Med Tech.

BUTLER, CINDY; Shadyside HS; Shadyside, OH; Chrh Wkr; Girl Scts; Hon Rl; JA; Off Ade; Sct Actv; Yth Flsp; Wv Northern Comm College; Art.

BUTLER, D; Martinsburg HS; Inwood, WV; Chrh Wkr; Cmnty Wkr; Hon Rl; NHS; Off Ade; Sch Pl; Stg Crw; Yth Flsp; Drama Clb; 4-H; WVU; Engr.

BUTLER, DARLENE; Addison HS; Manitou Beach, MI; 14/111 Chrs; Chrh Wkr; MMM; Girl Scts; Hon Rl; Sch Mus; 4-H; Ger Clb; Chrldng; Ten Temple Univ.

BUTLER, DENISE; Columbia City HS; Columbia City, IN; 6/273 Sec Frsh Cls; Sec Soph Cls; Sec Jr Cls; Sec Sr Cls; Am Leg Aux Girls St; NHS; FHA; Spn Clb; Letter Trk; 4-H Awd; Purdue Univ; Elem Educ.

BUTLER, DENISE; Caldwell HS; Caldwell, OH; Band; Chrs; Chrh Wkr; Hon Rl; Yth Flsp; Pep Clb; Letter Bsktbl; Letter Trk; Coach Actv; Natl Merit Ltr; College; Psychology.

BUTLER, DIANA; Brooke HS; Beech Bottom, WV; 60/466 Chrs; Hon Rl; NHS; Drama Clb; Fr Clb; W Liberty State College; Office Admn.

BUTLER, DONALD; Pike Central HS; Winslow, IN; Sct Actv; Yrbk; Drama Clb; Letter Bsbl; Wrstlng; Hon Mntn Drafting Fair 79; Univ; Mech Engr.

BUTLER, E; Mason HS; Mason, MI; Band; Chrh Wkr; Hon Rl; Sch Mus; Sch Nwsp; 4-H; Letter Chrldng; IM Sprt; Ill State Univ; Communications.

BUTLER, FRANKY; Warsaw Community HS; Warsaw, IN; 1/360 Cls Rep Frsh Cls; Val; Hon Rl; Natl Forn Lg; Sch Pl; Drama Clb; FDA; Ball State Univ; Pre Med.

BUTLER, GEORGE; Romulus Sr HS; Romulus, MI; 15/303 Cls Rep Sr Cls; Band; Hon Rl; Rptr Yrbk; Spn Clb; Capt Wrstlng; IM Sprt; Gov Hon Prg Awd; Kiwan Awd; Natl Merit Schl; Tri State Univ; Mech Engr.

BUTLER, JANET; Cntrl Montcalm HS; Stanton, MI; 10/120 Cls Rep Frsh Cls; Pres Jr Cls; Band; Cmnty Wkr; Girl Scts; Hon Rl; Off Ade; Sch Mus; Sch Pl; Sct Actv; Cntrl Michigan Univ; Child Dev.

BUTLER, JEANNINE A; St Marys Of Redford Sr HS; Detroit, MI; Pres Sr Cls; Cmnty Wkr; Hon Rl; JA; Stu Cncl; Fr Clb; Pep Clb; Natl Merit Ltr; Natl HS Inst Stu Northwestern Univ; Perfect Attendence; Interpreting Literature; College; Journalism.

BUTLER, JEFF; Triway HS; Wooster, OH; Drama Clb; Letter Ftbl; Letter Wrstlng; IM Sprt; Recvd Dist Qualification In Wrestlng; Ohio Univ; Poli Sci.

BUTLER, JIM C; Richmond HS; Richmond, IN; Band; Chrs; Chrh Wkr; Hon Rl; Mdrgl; Red Cr Ade; Sch Mus; Yth Flsp; Rptr Sch Nwsp; Sch Nwsp; Oral Roberts Univ; Bus.

BUTLER, JOSEPH; Rossville HS; Rossville, IN; Band; Hon Rl; Sch Mus; Pep Clb; Sci Clb; Bsbl; Crs Cntry; IM Sprt; Scr Kpr; Univ.

BUTLER, JULIE; Marian HS; Cincinnati, OH; Cls Rep Frsh Cls; Cl Rep Jr Cls; Band; Chrs; Girl Scts; Hosp Ade; Lit Mag; Off Ade; PAVAS; Pol Wkr; Cnslr Schlrshp 79; Univ Schlrshp 79; Ohio Univ; Pre Dent.

BUTLER, KELLY; Holt HS; Holt, MI; 11/313 Band; Chrs; Debate Tm; Hon Rl; Natl Forn Lg; NHS; PAVAS; Mic St Univ; Pre Law.

BUTLER, KENNETH; St Francis De Sales HS; Toledo, OH; 24/200 Chrh Wkr; Hon Rl; Letter Ftbl; IM Sprt; Ucollegium Honarum; Univ; Pre Med.

BUTLER, KEVIN; St Francis Desales HS; Columbus, OH; 12/186 Hon Rl; Letter Crs Cntry; Trk; Letter Mgrs; College; Comp Sci.

BUTLER, KIMBERLY; Coventry Sr HS; Akron, OH; 8/204 Cl Rep Jr Cls; Cls Rep Sr Cls; Hon Rl; Quill & Scroll; Stu Cncl; Fr Clb; Capt Chrldng; Akron Univ; Bus Admin.

BUTLER, LISA; Dekalb HS; Auburn, IN; Pres Soph Cls; Cls Rep Soph Cls; VP Jr Cls; Am Leg Aux Girls St; Chrs; Hosp Ade; NHS; Off Ade; Sch Mus; Sch Pl; IUPU; Elem Educ.

BUTLER, LORI; Eau Claire HS; Eau Claire, MI; 1/100 Hon Rl; Treas NHS; 4-H; Pep Clb; Bsktbl; Ten; Natl Merit Ltr; Western Michigan Univ; Data Proc.

BUTLER, MICHELLE; Cass Technical HS; Detroit, MI; Chrh Wkr; Hon Rl; Lbry Ade; NHS; Off Ade; Pres Stu Cncl; Sec Pep Clb; Natl Merit SF; Homecoming Court; Univ Of Michigan; Medicine.

BUTLER, PATRICK; Padua Franciscan HS; Brecksville, OH; Hon Rl; Pres JA; Yth Flsp; 4-H; Spn Clb; JA Awd; JETS Awd; American Univ.

BUTLER, ROBERT; Iaeger HS; Iaeger, WV; Band; Hon Rl; Pep Clb; Wrstlng; Univ.

BUTLER, SANDY; Licking Valley HS; Newark, OH; 4/150 Band; Chrh Wkr; Hon Rl; Lbry Ade; Off Ade; Y-Teens; Rptr Sch Nwsp; 4-H; OEA; College; Busns Mgmt.

BUTLER, SHARON; North Sr HS; Columbus, OH; Chrh Wkr; Hon Rl; NHS; OEA; Dnfth Awd; Voc Schl; Exec Sec.

BUTLER, SHELLY; Milan HS; Moores Hill, IN; VP Jr Cls; Band; Chrs; Hon Rl; NHS; Sch Mus; Sch Pl; Drama Clb; Pep Clb; Spn Clb; Ind Univ; Bus.

BUTLER, SHERI; Fowlerville HS; Fowlerville, MI; 13/147 Am Leg Boys St; Am Leg Aux Girls St; Hon Rl; NHS; Stu Cncl; 4-H; FFA; Letter Bsktbl; Trk; 4-H Awd; Spring Arbor Coll; Phys Educ.

BUTLER, TENIA L; Godwin Heights HS; Wyoming, MI; 9/181 Band; Cmp Fr Grls; Chrs; Hon Rl; NHS; Sch Mus; Yrbk; Ger Clb; Letter Trk; IM Sprt;.

BUTLER, UNRENEE; Mumford HS; Detroit, MI; Hon Rl; NHS; Off Ade; Stu Cncl; Yrbk; Sec FHA; Mth Clb; Natl Merit Ltr; Bagley Elem Schl Honor Society; Hampton Jr High Honor Society; Mumford HS Natl Honor Society; Wayne State Univ; Busns Admin.

BUTLER, VALERIE; Gabriel Richard HS; Wyandotte, MI; 60/160 Hon Rl; Ed Sch Nwsp; Sprt Ed Sch Nwsp; Rptr Sch Nwsp; Sch Nwsp; Fr Clb; Pep Clb; Mi Competitive Schlrshp 79; Wayne St Univ; Psych.

BUTLERBAUGH, ARTEENA; Southeastern HS; Londonderry, OH; Chrs; Hon Rl; Stu Cncl; 4-H; Lat Clb; OEA; Mgrs; College; Teacher.

BUTNER, TOM; St Edward HS; Cleveland, OH; Pres Soph Cls; Cls Rep Soph Cls; Cl Rep Jr Cls; JA; Jr NHS; Ftbl; Wrstlng; West Virginia Univ; Sci.

BUTTERS, FRED; Homer Cmnty HS; Homer, MI; 19/81 Boy Scts; Hon Rl; NHS; Sct Actv; FFA; Ftbl; Natl Merit SF; Slvr Palm Eagle Scout 78; Teetonkah #206 Ord Of Arrow 78; Michigan Dept Educ Schlrshp 79; Lawrence Inst Of Tech; Archt.

BUTTRESS, MARYBETH; Bishop Ready HS; Columbus, OH; 1/135 VP Jr Cls; Val; Chrh Wkr; Hon Rl; NHS; Sch Pl; Yrbk; Ohio State Univ; Occupational Ther.

BUTTS, ANDREA; Holy Rosary HS; Burton, MI; Trs Frsh Cls; Cls Rep Frsh Cls; Trs Soph Cls; Cls Rep Soph Cls; Cl Rep Jr Cls; Hon Rl; Sch Nwsp; FBLA; Trk; Chrldng; Ctrl Michigan St Univ; Bus.

BUTTS, ANDY; Loudonville HS; Loudonville, OH; Aud/Vis; Hon Rl; NHS; Sch Pl; Stg Crw; Rptr Sch Nwsp; Lat Clb; Letter Bsbl; Ohio St Univ; Aero Engr.

BUTTS, AVIS; Western HS; Detroit, MI; 6/200 Sec Sr Cls; Chrh Wkr; Hon Rl; NHS; Stu Cncl; Mth Clb; General Mtrs Inst; Indus Admin.

BUTTS, BARBARA J; Chippewa Hills HS; Remus, MI; 4-H; Fr Clb; Spn Clb; Scr Kpr; 4-H Awd; Michigan St Univ; Vet.

BUTTS, CHARLES L; Lima Sr HS; Lima, OH; Pres Frsh Cls; Cls Rep Soph Cls; Cl Rep Jr Cls; Am Leg Boys St; Pres Band; Chrs; Hon Rl; Orch; Stu Cncl; Ten; Lima Area Yth Symphony Orch 78; Miami Univ; Pre Dent.

BUTTS, DENISE; Ripley HS; Gay, WV; 13/257 Chrh Wkr; Hon Rl; Lbry Ade; NHS; Off Ade; Stg Crw; FBLA; Mth Clb; Natl Merit Ltr; West Virginia Univ; Acctg.

BUTTS, LINDA; Graham HS; Rosewood, OH; 27/165 Chrs; Chrh Wkr; Hon Rl; Jr NHS; NHS; Off Ade; Sch Mus; Sch Pl; Stg Crw; Yth Flsp; Clark Tech Coll; Human Serv.

BUTTS, ROBERT J; Western Brown Sr HS; Georgetown, OH; 16/190 Treas Am Leg Boys St; Hon Rl; Pres NHS; Yth Flsp; VP 4-H; Spn Clb; 4-H Awd; Highest Achvmnt In Drafting 77; Attended Workshop On Paper Tech At Miami Univ 79; Univ; Elec.

BUTTS, VICKI; Piqua Central HS; Piqua, OH; Chrs; Chrh Wkr; CAP; Girl Scts; Hon Rl; Pol Wkr; Sct Actv; FBLA; OEA; Hyles Anderson Bapt Coll; Elem Ed.

BUTZ, DAVID E; Gilmour Academy; Gates Mls, OH; 15/70 Band; Boy Scts; Hon Rl; Sch Mus; Spn Clb; Socr; Coach Actv; IM Sprt; Spanish Achvmnt Awrd 77; Art Achvmnt Awrd 77; Band Achvmnt Awrd 77; Bethany Univ; Bus Mgmt.

BUTZ, STEPHANIE; Avon HS; Indianapolis, IN; 42/187 Sec Soph Cls; Cls Rep Soph Cls; Sec Jr Cls; Cl Rep Jr Cls; Cls Rep Sr Cls; Band; NHS; VP Stu Cncl; Letter Bsktbl; Ten; Indiana St Univ; Busns.

BUTZER, JUDY; Smithville HS; Marhallvl, OH; Aud/Vis; Hon Rl; Lbry Ade; Stg Crw; Rptr Yrbk; Yrbk; Rptr Sch Nwsp; Kent St Univ.

BUTZU, CAROLINE; Lutheran East HS; Detroit, MI; Chrs; Chrh Wkr; Hon Rl; Yth Flsp; Rptr Sch Nwsp; Univ Of Detroit; Eng.

BUXTON, ALAN; Celina HS; Celina, OH; Vocational School; Equip Oper.

BUXTON, JAMES; John Glenn HS; Westland, MI; 10/705 Hon Rl; NHS; Sci Clb; Natl Merit Ltr; Oakland Univ; Mgmt.

BUXTON, KARA; Leslie HS; Onondaga, MI; Band; Hon Rl; 4-H; Ten; 4-H Awd; Meredith Manor Voc Schl; Equitation.

BUXTON, RICHARD; Kimball HS; Royal Oak, MI; Band; VP Chrs; Chrh Wkr; Hon Rl; Mdrgl; NHS; Sch Mus; Sch Pl; Yth Flsp; Drama Clb; College;.

BUYACK, BRIDGET; Goodrich HS; Goodrich, MI; Chrs; Chrh Wkr; Hon Rl; Lbry Ade; NHS; Yth Flsp; 4-H; Fr Clb; Am Leg Awd; 4-H Awd; Univ Of Mic; Comp Progr.

BUYS, LORI; Jenison HS; Jenison, MI; Hon Rl; Pom Pon; Chic Univ; Cosmetology.

BUYSSE, THOMAS; De Lasalle Collegiate HS; St Clair Shore, MI; 15/120 Boy Scts; Hon Rl; NHS; Sprt Ed Sch Nwsp; Fr Clb; Swmmng; Letter Trk; IM Sprt; Univ Of Detroit; Math.

BUZALSKI, GREGORY; West Catholic HS; Grand Rapids, MI; Band; Ten; IM Sprt; College; Architectural Landscaping.

BUZEK, DONNA M; Cloverleaf Sr HS; Spencer, OH; Hon Rl; Jr NHS; Off Ade; 4-H; Ohio St Univ; Equestrian.

BUZGA, JEANNE; Ursuline HS; Youngstown, OH; 26/285 Band; Chrs; Hon Rl; Hosp Ade; Orch; Red Cr Ade; Yrbk; Drama Clb; Lat Clb; Scr Kpr; Ohio Univ; Communications.

BUZZELL, DIANNA; Beaverton HS; Beaverton, MI; 4/163 Chrh Wkr; Cmnty Wkr; Hon Rl; Lbry Ade; NHS; Yth Flsp; Spn Clb; Central Michigan Univ; Elem Ed.

BUZZO, MICHAEL; North Dickinson County HS; Iron Mtn, MI; Pres Soph Cls; Aud/Vis; Band; Boy Scts; Hon Rl; Lbry Ade; Sct Actv; IM Sprt; Mgrs; Cit Awd; College; Engr.

BYARD, SANDRA; Pellston Public HS; Levering, MI; 1/53 Trs Frsh Cls; Pres Soph Cls; VP Jr Cls; Chrh Wkr; Hon Rl; NHS; Yth Flsp; FTA; Trk; Rep Queens Ct 77; John Wesley Coll.

BYAS, STANLEY; Linden Mc Kinley HS; Columbus, OH; 27/387 Cls Rep Frsh Cls; Cls Rep Soph Cls; Cl Rep Jr Cls; Cls Rep Sr Cls; Band; Boy Scts; Drm Bgl; Hon Rl; Jr NHS; NHS;.

BYE, FRANCES; Corydon Central HS; Corydon, IN; 8/198 Chrh Wkr; Hon Rl; Lbry Ade; NHS; Yth Flsp; Fr Clb; Mth Clb; Trk; Mgrs; Univ.

BYERLEY, BETH; Memorial HS; St Marys, OH; Pres Jr Cls; Val; Band; Hon Rl; Jr NHS; NHS; Off Ade; Sch Mus; Stu Cncl; Y-Teens; Ohio St Univ; Lang.

BYERLY, CHERYL; Madison Plains HS; London, OH; Band; Chrs; Hon Rl; Mod UN; Stg Crw; Rptr Yrbk; 4-H; Spn Clb; Scr Kpr; 4-H Awd; Stud Recogntn Day At Miami Univ 78; Univ; History.

BYERLY, TERESA L; Bloom Carroll HS; Carroll, OH; 5/156 Hon Rl; Sec NHS; Off Ade; 4-H; OEA; Capt Crs Cntry; 4-H Awd; Ohio State Univ; Economics.

BYERS, CHERON; Marion L Steele HS; Amherst, OH; Cls Rep Soph Cls; Hon Rl; JA; Lbry Ade; Ed Sch Nwsp; Drama Clb; IM Sprt; Mas Awd; A Grand Appntmnt Grand Lectures To Dist 78; Grand Cross Of Color 79; Lorain Cmnty Coll; Bus.

BYERS, DAVID; Bishop Flaget HS; Chillicothe, OH; 7/38 Hon Rl; NHS; Sch Pl; VP Stu Cncl; Capt Bsktbl; Trk; Coach Actv; Scr Kpr; Tmr; Walsh Coll; Spec Educ.

BYERS, DONNA; Toronto HS; Toronto, OH; Band; Sec FCA; Girl Scts; Hon Rl; Sch Pl; Drama Clb; Fr Clb; Pep Clb; Bsktbl; Trk; Schlrshp Team 76; Jefferson Tech Coll; Med Asst.

BYERS, GARY; Elmwood HS; Wayne, OH; Lbry Ade; Pol Wkr; Yth Flsp; IM Sprt;.

BYERS, HOLLY; Terre Haute S Vigo HS; Terre Haute, IN; 92/630 Cls Rep Frsh Cls; Pres Jr Cls; Pres Sr Cls; Sec Sr Cls; Girl Scts; Hon Rl; NHS; Stu Cncl; Drama Clb; PPFtbl; Indiana St Univ; Elem Educ.

BYERS, JAY; Ann Arbor Huron HS; Ypsilanti, MI; Cls Rep Frsh Cls; Am Leg Boys St; Pres Debate Tm; Hon Rl; Jr NHS; Lbry Ade; Pres Sci Clb; Letter Ten; Natl Merit Ltr; Beloit Coll; Govt.

BYERS, JEFFREY; Austintown Fitch HS; Youngstown, OH; Band; Boy Scts; Hon Rl; Sct Actv; Spn Clb; J H Ludt Awd Outstndng Persnl Achvmnt Scouts 79; Hist Day 1s T Dist 2nd S 79; Youngstown St Univ; Comp Sci.

BYERS, JON; Loudonville HS; Loudonville, OH; Am Leg Boys St; Hon Rl; Jr NHS; NHS; Pol Wkr; Rptr Sch Nwsp; 4-H; FFA; Cit Awd; 4-H Awd; Ohio St Univ; Agri.

BYERS, KAREN; Weir HS; Weirton, WV; 44/344 Band; Hon Rl; NHS; Sec Y-Teens; Lat Clb; Mat Maids; W Virginia Univ; Pharm.

BYERS, MICHELE; Steubenville Cath Ctrl HS; Mingo Junction, OH; 36/217 Hon Rl; Stg Crw; Yrbk; Pep Clb; Letter Bsktbl; Letter Trk; IM Sprt; Bradford/pitt Pa; Accounting.

BYERS, PAUL; Madison Hts HS; Anderson, IN; 14/391 Am Leg Boys St; Band; Boy Scts; Chrh Wkr; Cmnty Wkr; Hon Rl; NHS; Off Ade; Sct Actv; Yth Flsp; Indiana Univ; Dentistry.

BYERS, WHITNEY; Theodore Roosevelt HS; Kent, OH; Chrs; Bsbl; Letter Trk; Univ; Airline Pilot.

BYLER, WILLIAM; Fredericktown HS; Fredericktown, OH; 38/113 Cl Rep Jr Cls; Cls Rep Sr Cls; Am Leg Boys St; Pres Band; NHS; Stu Cncl; Spn Clb; Ohio Univ; Music Ed.

BYNDON, ELAINE; Our Lady Of Angels HS; Cincinnati, OH; Trs Frsh Cls; Sec Soph Cls; VP Jr Cls; Hon Rl; Off Ade; Stu Cncl; Rptr Sch Nwsp; Honorary City Solictor In Yth In City Govt Prog 78; Univ; Cmnctns.

BYNUM, PATRICK; Bangor HS; Grand Jct, MI; Band; Boy Scts; Chrs; Hon Rl; Sch Mus; Letter Crs Cntry; Letter Trk; Letter Mgrs; Univ; Music.

BYRD, BECKY; Princeton HS; Cincinnati, OH; 85/650 Cl Rep Jr Cls; Pres Sr Cls; Chrs; Chrh Wkr; Hon Rl; NHS; Red Cr Ade; Stg Crw; Ed Sch Nwsp; Rptr Sch Nwsp; Won 1st Pl Regional & St Competitive Events; Southern Ohio Coll.

BYRD, CHERYL M; Oak Park HS; Oak Park, MI; 140/386 Chrs; Chrh Wkr; Cmnty Wkr; Hon Rl; Off Ade; DECA; Pres OEA; Detroit Coll Of Bus Schlshp 2yrs 1979; Schl Serv Awd 1979; Detroit Coll Of Bus; Offc Clerk.

BYRD, CINDY; South Putnam HS; Greencastle, IN; Trs Jr Cls; Band; Hon Rl; Yrbk; 4-H; VP FHA; VP OEA; Chrldng; Bus Schl; Leg Sec.

BYRD, DAPHNE; Union City Comm HS; Union City, IN; 1/102 Cls Rep Frsh Cls; Cls Rep Soph Cls; Cl Rep Jr Cls; Band; Treas Chrs; Hon Rl; NHS; Sch Mus; Sec Stu Cncl; Eng Clb; Univ; Nursing.

BYRD, DARLA D; East Sr HS; Akron, OH; Chrs; Chrh Wkr; Girl Scts; Off Ade; Quill & Scroll; Rptr Yrbk; Rptr Sch Nwsp; Fr Clb; Pep Clb; Urban Journalism & Minority Broadcasting Wrkshp Schlrshp; Outstndng Underclassman In The Caravan Nwspr; Oral Roberts Univ; News Commentator.

BYRD, DEBA; Clermont Northeastern HS; Batavia, OH; Cls Rep Sr Cls; FCA; Girl Scts; Hon Rl; NHS; Sch Pl; Eng Clb; 4-H; Spn Clb; Scr Kpr; Wilmington Coll; Agri Comm.

BYRD, JEFFREY; Emerson HS; Gary, IN; 1/150 Pres Frsh Cls; Pres Soph Cls; Val; Am Leg Boys St; Hon Rl; Jr NHS; NHS; Boys Clb Am; Bsbl; Am Leg Awd; Univ; Engr.

BYRD, LIZA; Harper Creek HS; Battle Creek, MI; Cmp Fr Grls; Chrh Wkr; Girl Scts; Hon Rl; JA; Off Ade; Yth Flsp; Pep Clb; PPFtbl; College; Chem.

BYRD, MICHELLE E; Cass Technical HS; Detroit, MI; 29/960 Band; Chrh Wkr; Girl Scts; Hon Rl; NHS; Orch; Spn Clb; Spelman Coll; Chem.

BYRD, STEPHEN L; Lake HS; North Canton, OH; 6/220 Am Leg Boys St; Boy Scts; NHS; Sch Pl; Pres Yth Flsp; Mth Clb; Letter Ftbl; Wrstlng; DAR Awd; Natl Merit SF; Capt Of Lk Hgh Academc Challng Tm 1978; Univ; Pre Med.

BYRD, TYRONE; Jesup W Scott HS; Toledo, OH; Cls Rep Frsh Cls; Cl Rep Jr Cls; Sprt Ed Yrbk; Ftbl; Trk; Univ; Comp Tech.

BYRER, LISA; Northrop HS; Ft Wayne, IN; Chrs; Hon Rl; JA; Sch Mus; JA Awd; Univ.

BYRGE, DONALD K; Jay County HS; Dunkirk, IN; Cls Rep Frsh Cls; Cls Rep Soph Cls; Aud/Vis; Hon Rl; Sch Mus; Sch Pl; Stg Crw; Pep Clb; Bsbl; Ftbl; Coll; Radiology.

BYRNE, JOAN; Regina HS; E Cleveland, OH; Pres Frsh Cls; Cls Rep Soph Cls; Hon Rl; NHS; Yrbk; Rptr Sch Nwsp; Drama Clb; Chrldng; Coach Actv; Univ; Jrnlsm.

BYRNE, JOHN; Jenison HS; Jenison, MI; 33/365 Chrh Wkr; Hon Rl; NHS; Capt DAR Awd; Letter Ftbl; PPFtbl; Alma Coll.

BYRNE, JOHN; Baraga HS; Baraga, MI; NHS; Sch Pl; Trk; College; Engineering.

BYRNE, JOHN; St Philip Catholic Ctrl HS; Battle Creek, MI; 34/67 Letter Crs Cntry; Trk; Michigan Tech Univ; Geology.

BYRNES, KEVIN H; Aquinas HS; Taylor, MI; Yth Flsp; Rptr Sch Nwsp; Crs Cntry; Ten; Coach Actv; IM Sprt; Univ Of Detroit; Communications.

BYRSKI, DEBORAH; Hamady Sr HS; Flushing, MI; Chrh Wkr; Girl Scts; Hon Rl; NHS; Bsktbl; Letter Ten; Northern Michigan Univ; Psych.

BYRUM, BETH; Greenville Sr HS; Greenville, OH; VP Soph Cls; Cls Rep Soph Cls; VP Jr Cls; VP Sr Cls; Chrs; Girl Scts; Off Ade; Stu Cncl; Yth Flsp; 4-H; Bus Schl.

BYSTRY, ROBERT; Bronson HS; Bronson, MI; 19/150 Pres Sr Cls; Sal; Boy Scts; Cmnty Wkr; Hon Rl; Bsktbl; Ftbl; Hndbl; Socr; Capt Trk; Michigan St Univ; Comp Sci.

C

CABACUNGAN, GENEVIE R; Taft Sr HS; Hamilton, OH; Treas AFS; Chrs; Drl Tm; Girl Scts; Hon Rl; Jr NHS; NHS; Ed Yrbk; Drama Clb; Ger Clb; Miami Univ; Accounting.

CABACUNGAN, GUILLERMO R; Taft Sr HS; Hamilton, OH; 7/350 Pres Frsh Cls; Debate Tm; Hon Rl; Jr NHS; Natl Forn Lg; NHS; Orch; Sch Mus; Stu Cncl; Ed Sch Nwsp; City Dir Youth Civic Day; 1st Pl Clb Level 2nd Pl Zone Level Optimist Oratorical; 1st Pl St Finals; Coll; Law.

CABELL, DAVID; St Xavier HS; Cincinnati, OH; 16/264 Boy Scts; Hon Rl; Univ Of Cincinnati; Pre Med.

CABI, ABIDIN; Howland HS; Warren, OH; 135/430 Cls Rep Frsh Cls; Cls Rep Soph Cls; Cl Rep Jr Cls; Band; Hon Rl; Quill & Scroll; Ed Yrbk; Yrbk; Ten; IM Sprt; Ohio St Univ; Pre Law.

CABLE, CHERYL; R B Chamberlin HS; Twinsburg, OH; 1/200 Sec Jr Cls; Sec Sr Cls; Sec FCA; Hon Rl; NHS; Cit Awd; College; Math.

CABLE, DEENA; Toronto HS; Toronto, OH; 53/119 Sec Frsh Cls; Sec Soph Cls; Pres Jr Cls; Band; Sch Mus; DECA; Spn Clb; GAA; IM Sprt; Gregg Shorthand & Typing Awds; Filing Awd; Wilma Boyd Career Schl; Sec.

CABLE, PHILIP; Gilmour Academy; Canton, OH; Trs Soph Cls; Trs Sr Cls; Hon Rl; Sch Mus; Sch Pl; Sct Actv; Stu Cncl; Rptr Sch Nwsp; Drama Clb; IM Sprt; Headmasters List; Participated In Intl Stu Ldrshp Inst; Scuba Diving Clb;.

CABOT, JOHN; West Geauga HS; Chesterland, OH; 105/352 Boy Scts; Cmnty Wkr; FCA; Hon Rl; Sprt Ed Yrbk; Letter Bsbl; Letter Ftbl; Hndbl; Socr; Trk; Jr Achvmnt For Honor Roll 75; Baseball 2 Ltrs & A ll Conf & MVP 76 79; Ftbl 2 Ltrs & All Conf & All County; Ohio Univ.

CABRERA, JUAN; Harrison HS; Evansville, IN; 20/450 Boy Scts; Sct Actv; Rptr Sch Nwsp; Fr Clb; Ftbl; Capt Socr; Trk; Schlshp H Schl Awd For Acad 78 & 79; Indiana Univ; Pre Med.

CACCAVARI, PETER; Anderson HS; Cincinnati, OH; 3/377 Chrh Wkr; Hon Rl; NHS; Lat Clb; Dnfth Awd; Natl Merit Ltr; College; Acctg.

CACKOWSKI, DAVID; Chanel HS; Macedonia, OH; Chrh Wkr; IM Sprt; Cuyahoga Cmnty Coll.

CADDELL, MILDRED; Valley View HS; Farmersville, OH; Am Leg Aux Girls St; Band; Chrs; Chrh Wkr; Girl Scts; Hon Rl; Lbry Ade; Pol Wkr; Yth Flsp; Rptr Sch Nwsp; Ohio St Univ; Pre Law.

CADEAU, GABE; Bergland HS; Begland, MI; Boy Scts; Chrs; Hon Rl; Lbry Ade; Stg Crw; VICA; Gym; Cit Awd; College; Electonics.

CADGER, DEBRA; Clawson HS; Clawson, MI; Band; Girl Scts; Swmmng; College; Engr.

CADICK, JOHN; South Spencer HS; Grandview, IN; Pres Jr Cls; Am Leg Boys St; Hon Rl; Off Ade; Bsbl; Bsktbl; Ftbl; Mgrs; Univ; Poli Sci.

CADIENTE, EILEEN; Indiana Academy; Indpls, IN; Sec Frsh Cls; Trs Soph Cls; Band; Chrs; Stu Cncl; Rptr Sch Nwsp; Andrews Univ; Dent Hygnst.

CADLE, CARLA J; Independence HS; Princewick, WV; 15/149 Cls Rep Frsh Cls; Sec Sr Cls; Chrh Wkr; Hon Rl; Lbry Ade; Sec NHS; Treas Beta Clb; 4-H; Pres FBLA; Pep Clb; Raleigh Co Vo Tech; Data Processing.

CADLE, ROBERT; Hurricane HS; Hurricane, WV; 14/227 Chrh Wkr; FCA; Hon Rl; Off Ade; 4-H; Mth Clb; Bsktbl; Ten; Marshall Univ; Bus Law.

CADORETTE, CAROL; Bedford Sr HS; Bedford Hts, OH; 44/564 Hon Rl; Hosp Ade; JA; Jr NHS; NHS; Fr Clb; Bsktbl; GAA; Cuyahoga Cmnty Coll; Chem.

CADWALLADER, BRUCE; Blanchester HS; Blanchester, OH; 12/160 Pres Soph Cls; Pres Jr Cls; Pres Sr Cls; Am Leg Boys St; Band; Boy Scts; FCA; Hon Rl; NHS; Sch Mus; Ohio Univ; Communications.

CADWALLADER, CYNTHIA L; Harper Creek HS; Battle Creek, MI; 30/244 Hon Rl; NHS; Off Ade; Rptr Sch Nwsp; Fr Clb; Spn Clb; PPFtbl; Kellogg Cmnty Coll; Bus Mgmt.

CADWALLADER, JONDA; Lynchburg Clay HS; Lynchburg, OH; Band; Hon Rl; Stg Crw; 4-H; Pep Clb; Trk; Chrldng; 4-H Awd; R Walters Tech Coll; Dent Hygnst.

CADWELL, LYNNE; Benton Harbor HS; Benton Hbr, MI; 18/400 Band; Lbry Ade; Sch Mus; Sch Pl; Stu Cncl; Rptr Yrbk; Yrbk; Ten; Trk; Univ Of California; Busns Admin.

CADWELL, MACHELLE; Southwestern HS; Detroit, MI; 20/180 Cls Rep Frsh Cls; Cmnty Wkr; Hon Rl; Jr NHS; NHS; Pep Clb; Central Min Univ; Drama.

CADY, BARBARA; Chatard HS; Indianapolis, IN; 13/195 Sec Sr Cls; Hon Rl; NHS; Rptr Sch Nwsp; Crs Cntry; Letter Trk; IM Sprt; Capt Mat Maids; Univ.

CADY, CHRISTINE; Gladwin Comm HS; Gladwin, MI; 10/147 C Michigan Univ; Busns Admin.

CADY, JEFFREY; Romulus Sr HS; Romulus, MI; Band; Boy Scts; Meteorology.

CADY, MELINDA; Holy Rosary HS; Flint, MI; Hon Rl; Yrbk; Fr Clb; OEA; Letter Bsktbl; Letter Trk; Univ; Office Admin.

CADY, VERNON; Bear Lake HS; Bear Lake, MI; 8/35 NHS; Bsbl; Letter Bsktbl; Northwestern Mich Coll; Acctg.

CAESAR, RONALD; Carson City Crystal Area HS; Fowler, MI; Letter Crs Cntry; Letter Trk; Vocational Schl; Elec Engr.

CAFARO, BETH A; St John HS; Ashtabula, OH; 30/121 Sec Jr Cls; VP Sr Cls; Girl Scts; NHS; FHA; Gym; PPFtbl; Walsh Coll; Education.

CAFFREY, DEBORAH; Moorefield HS; Purgitsville, WV; Cls Rep Frsh Cls; Band; Chrh Wkr; Girl Scts; Hon Rl; NHS; Red Cr Ade; Yth Flsp; 4-H; Pep Clb; Univ; Comp Sci.

CAGLE, MONICA; Jackson Center HS; Jackson Cntr, OH; Am Leg Aux Girls St; Chrs; Girl Scts; Hon Rl; Quill & Scroll; Sch Pl; Stu Cncl; Yrbk; Sch Nwsp; FHA; Ohio State Univ; English.

CAGLE, STUART; New Palestine HS; New Palestine, IN; FCA; Hon Rl; NHS; Fr Clb; Glf; IM Sprt; Purdue Univ; Turf Mgmt.

CAHALAN, ELIZABETH; Groose Ile HS; Grosse Ile, MI; Treas Band; VP NHS; Sch Mus; Fr Clb; Dnfth Awd; Univ Of Michigan.

CAHILL, BARBARA; La Salle HS; St Ignace, MI; Band; Girl Scts; Hon Rl; NHS; Sch Pl; Spn Clb; Bsktbl; Letter Trk; Chrldng; Pres Awd; Western Univ; Phys Ed.

CAHILL, RENATE; Northville HS; Northville, MI; Hon Rl; Ger Clb; Schoolcraft Comm Coll; Busns.

CAHOON, CARLA; Carsonville Port Sanilac HS; Carsonville, MI; Band; Chrs; Cmnty Wkr; Hon Rl; Lbry Ade; Off Ade; Sch Mus; Pep Clb; Letter Bsktbl; Twrlr; College; Dent Asst.

CAIN, ANGELA; London HS; London, OH; 6/160 Am Leg Aux Girls St; Chrh Wkr; Hon Rl; NHS; Sch Mus; Sch Pl; Rptr Sch Nwsp; Drama Clb; Fr Clb; Trk; Wright St Univ; Vocal Music.

CAIN, CANDY; Tipton HS; Tipton, IN; 8/120 Band; Girl Scts; NHS; 4-H; Lat Clb; 4-H Awd; ISU; Nursing.

CAIN, DI ANNE A; Our Lady Of Mercy HS; Milford, MI; Cls Rep Frsh Cls; Cls Rep Soph Cls; Cl Rep Jr Cls; Band; Hon Rl; NHS; Stu Cncl; IM Sprt; Organizer Of Radio Marathon 77; Office Mgr Of Bus Class & Candy Store; Notre Dame Univ; Mgr.

CAIN, JOHN; Airport Comm HS; Monroe, MI; Band; Chrh Wkr; Cmnty Wkr; Hon Rl; Sch Mus; Yth Flsp; Sci Clb; Monroe County Comm College; Elec.

CAIN, KATHY; Fremont HS; Angola, IN; Chrs; Girl Scts; Hon Rl; Y-Teens; Sch Nwsp; Sec OEA; Pep Clb; Trk;.

CAIN, LINDA; Logan Elm HS; Circleville, OH; Band; Hon Rl; NHS; Red Cr Ade; Sch Pl; College.

CAIN, MELODY; Berkeley Springs HS; Berkley Spg, WV; 9/133 Cls Rep Frsh Cls; Cls Rep Soph Cls; Cl Rep Jr Cls; Trs Sr Cls; Cls Rep Sr Cls; Hon Rl; Jr NHS; Treas NHS; Off Ade; Stu Cncl; Shephred College; Bus Admin.

CAIN, MICHELE; Brooke HS; Follansbee, WV; 115/450 Hon Rl; Hosp Ade; JA; FNA; Lat Clb; IM Sprt; West Liberty St Coll; Nursing.

CAIN, PEGGY; Brooke HS; Follansbee, WV; Chrh Wkr; Hon Rl; JA; Lat Clb; Mat Maids; JA Awd; Amer Famous Names & Faces 78; Smithsonian Intership 79; Whos Who 77; West Virginia Univ; Vet.

CAIN, ROBERT A; Beaver Local HS; East Liverpool, OH; 11/221 Band; Chrs; Hon Rl; NHS; Sch Mus; Stg Crw; Drama Clb; Eng Clb; Lat Clb; Sci Clb; Univ Of Pittsburg; Pre Med.

CAIN, ROSA; Philip Barbour HS; Philippi, WV; Hon Rl; Stu Cncl; 4-H; Keyettes; Pep Clb; Bsktbl; Trk; West Virginia Univ; Nursing.

CAIN, TIM; Tri Cnty Middle Sr HS; Remington, IN; Hon Rl; Pep Clb; Letter Bsbl; IM Sprt; Scr Kpr; Tmr; Univ; Phys Ed.

CAIN, WAYNE; Maplewood HS; Cortland, OH; Hon Rl; Jr NHS; 4-H; 4-H Awd; College;.

CAINE, DONNA; Central HS; Detroit, MI; Band; Spn Clb; College; Special Ed.

CAINE, MARYBETH; Father Joseph Memorial HS; Columbus, OH; 10/107 Drl Tm; Hon Rl; Rptr Sch Nwsp; Univ; Math.

CAIRNDUFF, JUDY; Fenton HS; Fenton, MI; Pres Soph Cls; Pres Jr Cls; VP Sr Cls; Am Leg Aux Girls St; Chrh Wkr; Girl Scts; Hon Rl; Lbry Ade; Univ Of Mic; Physical Therapy.

CAIRO, TANIA R; Thomas A De Vilbiss HS; Toledo, OH; 30/320 Sec Band; Chrh Wkr; Hon Rl; NHS; Orch; Pres Yth Flsp; Young Womens Recognition Awd For Church; OMEA Solo & Ensemble Awd; College; Music.

CAITO, MICHAEL; Medina Sr HS; Medina, OH; 22/370 Sec Sr Cls; Hon Rl; NHS; Key Clb; Letter Ten; Kiwan Awd; Case Western Reserve Univ; Pre Dent.

CAJKA, MICHELLE; St Joseph Academy; Fairview Park, OH; Cmnty Wkr; Debate Tm; Hon Rl; NHS; Pol Wkr; Sch Mus; Sch Pl; Stg Crw; Yrbk; Sch Nwsp; Univ.

CALABRESE, ELISA; Lorain Catholic HS; Lorain, OH; Am Leg Aux Girls St; Chrh Wkr; Hon Rl; NHS; Off Ade; Orch; Pol Wkr; Pep Clb; Lorain Cnty Comm College.

CALABRESE, ROBERTA; Staunton HS; Brazil, IN; Sec Jr Cls; Chrs; Capt Drl Tm; Hon Rl; Ger Clb; Pep Clb; Indiana St Univ; Aviation Tech.

CALABRIA, JUDY; Catholic Central HS; Steubenvll, OH; 1/203 Hon Rl; Sec NHS; FHA; Spn Clb; Bsktbl; Letter Ten; IM Sprt; College.

CALABRO, DEBORAH J; Port Huron Northern HS; Port Huron, MI; Cls Rep Sr Cls; Chrh Wkr; Girl Scts; Hon Rl; NHS; Sct Actv; Stu Cncl; Yth Flsp; GAA; St Of Mich Comp Schlrshp Tuition Grant Awd; St Of Mich Comp Schlrshp Cert Of Recog; St Clair Cnty Comm Coll; Busns Admin.

CALAMITA, LISA; Mayfield HS; Mayfield Hts, OH; Chrs; Drl Tm; Hon Rl; Mod UN; Rptr Sch Nwsp; Pom Pon; Principals List Awd; College; Psych.

CALDEMEYER, CAROLYN; Pike Central HS; Winslow, IN; Chrs; Chrh Wkr; Hon Rl; NHS; Sch Mus; 4-H; 4-H Awd; Mas Awd; Indiana Univ.

CALDEMYER, MARK; Southridge HS; Holland, IN; 1/180 Band; Drm Bgl; FCA; Hon Rl; Pres Yth Flsp; Spn Clb; Bsktbl; Glf; Ten; Cert Of Hnr Pres By Huntingburg Study Clb; Indiana Univ; Med.

CALDER, KATHLEEN; Kimball HS; Royal Oak, MI; Band; Chrh Wkr; NHS; Univ; Math.

CALDERONE, MARIA; East Detroit HS; E Detroit, MI; Girl Scts; Hon Rl; Sct Actv; Wayne St Univ; Spec Ed.

CALDREN, CONNI; Green HS; Uniontown, OH; Chrs; Hon Rl; PAVAS; Sch Mus; Sch Pl; Yth Flsp; Drama Clb; Fr Clb; Dancer.

CALDWELL, CAREY; Anderson HS; Anderson, IN; VP Frsh Cls; Band; Boy Scts; JA; Sch Mus; Stg Crw; Stu Cncl; Yth Flsp; Ger Clb; Socr; Anderson Coll.

CALDWELL, CARLA; Jackson HS; Massillon, OH; Chrs; Debate Tm; Girl Scts; Hon Rl; NHS; Sch Mus; Y-Teens; Ger Clb; Jazz Dancing Lessons & Tennis Lessons; Eng Horseback Riding Lessons; Univ Of Akron; Engr.

CALDWELL, CAROLYN; Cambridge HS; Cambridge, OH; Cls Rep Frsh Cls; Cls Rep Soph Cls; Cl Rep Jr Cls; Chrh Wkr; Hon Rl; Jr NHS; Pres Stu Cncl; Yrbk; Ed Sch Nwsp; Pres 4-H; Ohi State Univ.

CALDWELL, CHARMA R; John Marshall HS; Brookly, OH; Cls Rep Sr Cls; Chrh Wkr; Cmnty Wkr; Rptr Yrbk; Letter Bsbl; Letter Bsktbl; GAA; Cit Awd; Selected For The 2nd Yr In A Row To Whos Who 79; Central St Univ; Data Proc.

CALDWELL, CHERYL; Cambridge HS; Cambridge, OH; 1/270 Cls Rep Frsh Cls; Sec Soph Cls; Pres Jr Cls; Val; Am Leg Aux Girls St; Chrh Wkr; Cmnty Wkr; Ohi State Univ; Vet Med.

CALDWELL, CURTIS; Bellefontaine Sr HS; Bellefontaine, OH; 35/241 Boy Scts; Chrs; Hon Rl; Sct Actv; Stu Cncl; Yth Flsp; Civ Clb; Sci Clb; Spn Clb; Mgrs; Miami Univ; Archt.

CALDWELL, DAVID; Buffalo HS; Wayne, WV; Hon Rl; Pres FFA; Spn Clb; Coll.

CALDWELL, GREGORY; St Marys Of Redford HS; Detroit, MI; 16/153 Cls Rep Frsh Cls; Chrs; Chrh Wkr; Cmnty Wkr; Hon Rl; Quill & Scroll; Sch Pl; Univ Of Detroit; Educ.

CALDWELL, JENNIFER; St Ursula Academy; Toledo, OH; Chrh Wkr; Cmnty Wkr; Sch Pl; Stg Crw; Drama Clb; Fr Clb; FDA; Lat Clb; Pep Clb; Chrldng; Med.

CALDWELL, JOE; Hackett HS; Kalamazoo, MI; Am Leg Boys St; Boy Scts; Chrs; Sch Mus; Sch Pl; Sct Actv; Sprt Ed Yrbk; Rptr Yrbk; Rptr Sch Nwsp; Western Michigan Univ; Law.

CALDWELL, KRISTY; Princeton HS; Princeton, WV; 62/367 Cls Rep Frsh Cls; Stu Cncl; Pep Clb; Spn Clb; Pom Pon; Coll.

CALDWELL, MARK; Dunbar HS; Dunbar, WV; Cls Rep Frsh Cls; Band; Chrs; Hon Rl; 4-H; Fr Clb; Pep Clb; IM Sprt; Voice Dem Awd; Univ Of Miami; Aviation.

CALDWELL, MICHAEL B; Covington HS; Covington, OH; Aud/Vis; Hon Rl; Sch Pl; Stg Crw; Yrbk; Rptr Sch Nwsp; DECA; Key Clb; Kiwan Awd; Radio T V Sound Tech.

CALDWELL, REBECCA; Elgin HS; Marion, OH; 1/151 Chrs; Chrh Wkr; Hon Rl; Mod UN; Yth Flsp; Lat Clb; Mt Vernon Nazarene Coll; Nursing.

CALDWELL, REGINA; Northfork HS; Elkhorn, WV; 7/140 Trs Frsh Cls; Sec Soph Cls; Sec Jr Cls; Stu Cncl; Hon Rl; Sch Pl; Drama Clb; Fr Clb; FHA; Sci Clb; Bluefield St Coll; Nurse.

CALDWELL, STEPHEN J; Lasalle HS; Jesper, IN; 111/468 Chrh Wkr; Hon Rl; Yth Flsp; Rptr Yrbk; Rptr Sch Nwsp; Sch Nwsp; Fr Clb; Lat Clb; Crs Cntry; Trk; Univ.

CALDWELL, TEISHA K; Bloom Local HS; Wheelersburg, OH; Band; Chrs; Sch Pl; Drama Clb; FHA; Twrlr; Sextette 1 Rating 78; Scioto County Music Fest 77 78 & 79; Grange 78; Univ Of Dayton; Cmmrcl Art.

CALDWELL, TOI L; Warrensville Hts HS; Warrensville Ht, OH; Cls Rep Frsh Cls; Trs Jr Cls; Trs Sr Cls; Chrs; Red Cr Ade; Stu Cncl; Rptr Yrbk; Drama Clb; Pep Clb; Ten; Univ; Bus Mgmt.

CALDWELL, TOMMY; Provine HS; Jackson, MS; Hon Rl; Jackson State Univ; Pilot.

CALDWELL, VIRGIL; Constantine HS; Constantine, MI; Hon Rl; Rptr Yrbk; Yrbk; Rptr Sch Nwsp; Sch Nwsp; Sci Clb; Natl Merit Ltr; Adrian College; Bio.

CALEF, TAMMY; Roosevelt Wilson HS; Stonewood, WV; Chrs; Hon Rl; Sch Pl; Stu Cncl; Y-Teens; Rptr Sch Nwsp; Pres Drama Clb; FHA; Bsktbl; Ten; Fairmont St Univ; Phys Ed.

CALEY, JANIE B; Schoolcraft HS; Vicksburg, MI; Band; Chrs; Girl Scts; Hon Rl; NHS; Sch Mus; 4-H; Capt Tw.rlr; Kalamazoo Vly Comm Coll; Nursing.

CALEY, JOHANNAH; Lapeer East HS; Metamora, MI; Cl Rep Jr Cls; Band; Chrs; Hon Rl; NHS; Sch Mus; Sch Pl; Drama Clb;.

CALHOON, SARAH S; Hilliard HS; Hilliard, OH; 17/353 Am Leg Aux Girls St; Band; Cmnty Wkr; Hon Rl; Jr NHS; NHS; Stu Cncl; Ed Sch Nwsp; Sprt Ed Sch Nwsp; 4-H; Mbr Of Oh St Univ Pres Club; Outstndg Sr Awd Hilliard HS 79; Natl Marching Band Contest Whitewater Wi 79; Ohio St Univ; Home Ec.

CALHOUN, DARYL; Washington HS; Massillon, OH; Hon Rl; Ftbl; College.

CALHOUN, DOUGLAS; Onsted HS; Onsted, MI; 3/123 Am Leg Boys St; Band; Hon Rl; NHS; Red Cr Ade; Stu Cncl; Rptr Sch Nwsp; Letter Ftbl; Letter Trk; Grand Valley St Coll; Acctg.

CALHOUN, ELIZABETH; Whetstone HS; Columbus, OH; 39/320 Am Leg Aux Girls St; Band; Chrs; Cmnty Wkr; Hon Rl; Hosp Ade; NHS; Off Ade; Orch; Sch Mus; Grinnell Coll; Soc Sci.

CALHOUN, FRANCES; Belleville HS; Belleville, MI; Cmp Fr Grls; Chrs; Hon Rl; Lbry Ade; DECA;.

CALHOUN, LYNN; Greenville Sr HS; Greenville, MI; 6/230 VP Frsh Cls; Pres Jr Cls; Am Leg Boys St; VP Stu Cncl; Fr Clb; Mth Clb; Spn Clb; Letter Bsbl; Letter Ftbl; IM Sprt; MI St Alumni Distnghsd Schlrshp Participant 79; Stu Coun Ldrshp Awd 79; Michigan St Univ; Acctg.

CALHOUN, MISTII A; Mt Healthy HS; Cincinnati, OH; 296/507 VP Frsh Cls; Cmnty Wkr; Off Ade; Stu Cncl; Rptr Sch Nwsp; Pep Clb; Trk; Exec Sec.

CALHOUN, NATHANIEL; Buena Vista HS; Saginaw, MI; Pres Frsh Cls; VP Soph Cls; Sec Jr Cls; Pres Sr Cls; Chrs; Chrh Wkr; Cmnty Wkr; Hon Rl; MMM; Pol Wkr; Most Outstanding Male; Michigan St Univ; Law.

CALHOUN, TIMOTHY; Vinson HS; Huntginton, WV; Ftbl; Trk;.

CALISI, PERRY; Grosse Pointe North HS; Grosse Pt Wds, MI; Pres Jr Cls; Cls Rep Sr Cls; VP Chrs; Hon Rl; PAVAS; Sch Pl; Stu Cncl; Drama Clb; Ftbl; Michigan St Univ; Bus Law.

CALISSLE, FRED; Bishop Donahue HS; Wheeling, WV; Boy Scts; Chrs; Hon Rl; NHS; Sch Pl; Stu Cncl; 4-H; Key Clb; Letter Ftbl; Mgrs; Bus.

CALKINS, FAYE; Andrews HS; Mentor, OH; Trs Soph Cls; Cl Rep Jr Cls; Chrh Wkr; Girl Scts; Hon Rl; Mod UN; NHS; Sct Actv; Stu Cncl; Yth Flsp; Coll; Math.

CALKINS, L; Parkside HS; Jackson, MI; Debate Tm; Hon Rl; Natl Forn Lg; Pol Wkr; Lat Clb; Mat Maids; Univ; Pre Law.

CALKINS, LINDA; Eastern HS; Bloomfield, IN; Pres Frsh Cls; Drl Tm; Hon Rl; NHS; FHA; Pep Clb; GAA; Pom Pon; Bus Schl; Legl Sec.

CALKINS, LINDA; Athens HS; Troy, MI; Cls Rep Soph Cls; Cl Rep Jr Cls; Cls Rep Sr Cls; Band; Girl Scts; Hon Rl; Sch Pl; Stu Cncl; Yth Flsp; Swmmng; Letter Chrldng; Northwood Inst; Fshn Mdse.

CALKINS, NANETTE; South Harrison HS; Lost Creek, WV; 12/86 Chrs; Hon Rl; Hosp Ade; Jr NHS; Treas NHS; Pres 4-H; FTA; Bsktbl; Trk; 4-H Awd; W Virginia Univ; Bio.

CALLAGHAN, DOUGLAS; Hartland HS; Fenton, MI; Band; Hon Rl; Lit Mag; Yrbk; Sch Nwsp; Fr Clb; Ftbl; Ten; Wrstlng; Cit Awd; Michigan St Univ; Med.

CALLAHAN, ALTA; Lockland HS; Cincinnati, OH; 9/71 Band; Girl Scts; Hon Rl; NHS; Socr; Chrldng; Univ Of Cincinnati; Psych.

CALLAHAN, ARLENE; St Alphonsus HS; Detroit, MI; 24/180 Hon Rl; Lbry Ade; Sch Mus; Sch Pl; Trk; Univ; Drama.

CALLAHAN, BRIAN S; Morristown HS; Shelbyville, IN; 1/77 Cls Rep Soph Cls; Cl Rep Jr Cls; Val; Band; Chrh Wkr; Hon Rl; Jr NHS; NHS; Stu Cncl; Yth Flsp; Whos Who Foreign Lang In Indiana 1977; General Motors Inst; Mech Engr.

CALLAHAN, D; Massillon Perry HS; Canton, OH; 13/470 Am Leg Aux Girls St; Hon Rl; NHS; Off Ade; Letter Bsktbl; Letter Trk; Ohio Northern Univ; Pharmacy.

CALLAHAN, DEBORAH; Westfall HS; Orient, OH; 5/140 Cmp Fr Grls; Hon Rl; NHS; Off Ade; Sch Mus; Sch Pl; Rptr Yrbk; Rptr Sch Nwsp; FTA; Mat Maids; Shorthand I & II Awds 78 & 79; Govt Awd 79; Eng Awds 78 & 79; Legal Sec.

CALLAHAN, JAMES; West Lafayette HS; W Lafayette, IN; 5/185 Am Leg Boys St; FCA; NHS; Letter Bsbl; Letter Ftbl; IM Sprt; Natl Merit Ltr; Participate In U S Military Acad Invitational Acad Workshop; Participate In U S Naval Acad Engr/sci Seminar; U S Military Academy.

CALLAHAN, LISA; Green HS; N Canton, OH; Chrs; Chrh Wkr; Drm Bgl; Hon Rl; Sch Mus; Yth Flsp; IM Sprt; Malone Coll; Math.

CALLAHAN, LYNN; Rossford HS; Perrysburg, OH; 9/147 Girl Scts; Hon Rl; VP JA; Lbry Ade; NHS; VP Yth Flsp; Drama Clb; Fr Clb; Spn Clb; Crs Cntry; Ohio State Univ.

CALLAHAN, MARY; Ontario HS; Mansfield, OH; 76/178 Girl Scts; Hon Rl; Y-Teens; Fr Clb; Swmmng; Trk; Scr Kpr; Tmr; Univ; Bus Mgmt.

CALLAHAN, TRACY; Meadowbrook HS; Senecaville, OH; Hon Rl; Jr NHS; Yth Flsp; Yrbk; 4-H; Mth Clb; Pep Clb; Sci Clb; PPFtbl; Ohi State Univ.

CALLAWAY, JOHN; Chagrin Falls HS; Chagrin Fl, OH; Drama Clb; Letter Crs Cntry; Trk; Univ; Forestry.

CALLENDER, JUDY; Port Huron Northern HS; North Street, MI; 23/400 Hon Rl; NHS; Natl Merit Schl; Kurt Edie Memrl Shclshp 79; The Times Herald Cert Of Awm 75 79; St Clair Cnty Cmnty Coll; Nursing.

CALLIHAN, TAMMY; Girard HS; Girard, OH; Band; Fr Clb; Ger Clb; Sci Clb; Univ.

CALLON, SUSAN; Sault Area HS; Sault Ste Marie, MI; Band; Lake Superior St Coll; Sec.

CALLOW, AMY; Bellmont HS; Decatur, IN; 37/244 Hon Rl; NHS; Spn Clb; Swmmng; Univ; Spanish.

CALOMENI, REGINA; Cousino HS; Warren, MI; Hon Rl; Letter Mgrs; Letter Tmr; Michigan State Univ; Criminal Just.

CALOVINI, THERESA; Union Local HS; Holloway, OH; 8/144 Cls Rep Frsh Cls; Cls Rep Soph Cls; Cl Rep Jr Cls; Cls Rep Sr Cls; Debate Tm; Treas NHS; VP Stu Cncl; Yrbk; Fr Clb; Pres FHA; Univ Of Akron; Pre Law.

CALRELAGE, MICHAEL D; Fremont HS; Angola, IN; Hon Rl; Univ; Engr.

CALVELAGE, KRISTINA; Ft Jennings HS; Fort Jennings, OH; Trs Soph Cls; Trs Sr Cls; Band; Chrs; Girl Scts; Hon Rl; Sch Mus; Sch Pl; 4-H; Fr Clb; Bowling Green St Univ; Spec Ed.

CALVELAGE, LARRY; Delphos St Johns HS; Delphos, OH; Cls Rep Frsh Cls; Cls Rep Soph Cls; Cl Rep Jr Cls; Cls Rep Sr Cls; Aud/Vis; Hon Rl; Sch Pl; Ohio Univ; Comp Sci.

CALVELAGE, MIKE; Fremont HS; Angola, IN; 6/76 Hon Rl; Letter Wrstlng; Purdue Univ; Mech Engr.

CALVERT, BRAIN; New Albany HS; New Albany, OH; Pres Frsh Cls; Cl Rep Jr Cls; Band; Chrh Wkr; FCA; Stu Cncl; Crs Cntry; Trk; College.

CALVERT, DEBRA; Decatur Central HS; Indianapolis, IN; 63/385 Chrs; Cmnty Wkr; Debate Tm; Hon Rl; JA; Mdrgl; Off Ade; Quill & Scroll; Sch Mus; Sch Pl; Most Imprvd Spch Tm Mbr 78; Spch Tm Sec Champ Dramatic Duo 78; Indiana Central Univ; Jrnlsm.

CALVERT, FRANCINE; Worthington Jefferson HS; Worthington, IN; 4/40 Sec Frsh Cls; Hst Jr Cls; Band; Chrh Wkr; Hon Rl; NHS; Off Ade; Yth Flsp; College.

CALVERT, LISA; Lumen Christi HS; Jackson, MI; Hon Rl; Hosp Ade; Lbry Ade; NHS; Rptr Sch Nwsp; Pep Clb; Spn Clb; IM Sprt; MSU; Med.

CALVERT, SANDRA; Wapakoneta HS; Cridersville, OH; Cmnty Wkr; Hon Rl; Off Ade; Lat Clb; Bsktbl; Ten; Trk; Coach Actv; College; English Teacher.

CALVIN, CHRISTINE D; Highland HS; Highland, IN; 15/520 Sec Frsh Cls; Band; Hon Rl; NHS; Sch Mus; Pres 4-H; FHA; Ger Clb; Letter Swmmng; 4-H Awd; Indiana Univ Honors Prgrm In Foreign Languages; College.

CALVIN, CINDY; Mahoning Cnty Joint Voc Schl; Salem, OH; Cl Rep Jr Cls; Hon Rl; Jr NHS; Lbry Ade; Stu Cncl; Sch Nwsp; OEA; Pep Clb; Letter Bsktbl; Pom Pon; Mahoning Cnty Voc Schl; Word Proc Sp.

CALVIN, TAMARA; John Adams HS; So Bend, IN; 77/400 Band; Hon Rl; Orch; Sch Mus; Lat Clb; Trk; PPFtbl; Indiana Univ; Med.

CALVO, LIAN; Bexley HS; Bexley, OH; FCA; Stu Cncl; Rptr Sch Nwsp; Pep Clb; Spn Clb; GAA; IM Sprt; Wright St Univ; Psych.

CAMACHO, ELIZABETH; Admiral King HS; Lorain, OH; Hon Rl; Hosp Ade; JA; Akron Univ; Nursing.

CAMARATA, TONI; Tuslaw HS; Massillon, OH; Band; Hon Rl; Stu Cncl; VP Y-Teens; Yrbk; FNA; VP Pep Clb; Scr Kpr; Aultman Hosp Nursing Schl; Lpn.

CAMBRE, ERIC; Sycamore HS; Cincinnati, OH; Chrs; Hon Rl; Stg Crw; Univ.

CAMBURN, TROY; Lansing Everett HS; East Lansing, MI; Hon Rl; NHS; Letter Ten; Coach Actv; Mic State Univ; Pre Med.

CAMECHIS, RON; Fairfield Union HS; Thornville, OH; Pres Frsh Cls; Cl Rep Jr Cls; Aud/Vis; Chrh Wkr; Hon Rl; Jr NHS; Lbry Ade; Sch Pl; Stu Cncl; FFA; Hocking Tech; Forestry.

CAMELLA, JANICE; St Marys Central Cath HS; Sandusky, OH; Band; Hon Rl; 4-H; Ger Clb; Sci Clb; Bsktbl; Letter Ten; GAA; IM Sprt; 4-H Awd; Bowling Green State Univ; Spec Ed.

CAMERATA, LYNN; Cuyahoga Falls Sr HS; Cuyahoga Fls, OH; Pres Frsh Cls; Cls Rep Frsh Cls; Cls Rep Soph Cls; Cl Rep Jr Cls; Sec Sr Cls; Chrs; Hon Rl; JA; NHS; Sch Pl; Akron Univ; Elec Engr.

CAMERON, ANDREW; Southfield HS; Southfield, MI; Cls Rep Soph Cls; Boy Scts; Hon Rl; Jr NHS; Quill & Scroll; Sct Actv; Y-Teens; Rptr Yrbk; Rptr Sch Nwsp; Spn Clb; Mich State Univ; Social Sci.

CAMERON, BRUCE; Brebeuf Prep; Indpls, IN; Boy Scts; Chrh Wkr; Hon Rl; Lbry Ade; Mdrgl; Yrbk; Sch Nwsp; Rdo Clb; Earlham Univ; Pre Med.

CAMERON, DANA; George Washington HS; Indianapolis, IN; 11/412 Am Leg Aux Girls St; Band; Hon Rl; JA; NHS; Sch Pl; Spn Clb; Letter Trk; Chrldng; Am Leg Awd; Freedoms Fdn Vly Forge Awd 79; Univ; Pediatrician.

CAMERON, JEFF; Gallia Academy; Gallipolis, OH; 1/250 Boy Scts; Chrh Wkr; Cmnty Wkr; NHS; Sch Pl; Sct Actv; Rptr Sch Nwsp; Drama Clb; Lat Clb; Letter Bsktbl; Coll; Med.

CAMERON, JEFFREY; Gladwin HS; Gladwin, MI; Cls Rep Sr Cls; Cmnty Wkr; Hon Rl; Letter Bsbl; Natl Merit Ltr; St Of Mighigan Comp Schlrshp 79; Ferris St Coll; Bus Admin.

CAMERON, MARK; Barberton HS; Barberton, OH; 8/470 VP Frsh Cls; Cls Rep Soph Cls; Cl Rep Jr Cls; Hon Rl; JA; Jr NHS; NHS; Stu Cncl; Ger Clb; Capt Swmmng; Univ; Archt.

CAMERON, WILLIAM; Sandy Vly HS; Magnolia, OH; Hon Rl; Univ; Acctg.

CAMMET, DEBI; Belleville HS; Ypsilanti, MI; 56/500 Cls Rep Frsh Cls; Hon Rl; Lbry Ade; NHS; Yrbk; Ger Clb; Crs Cntry; Chrldng; Eastern Mich; Pharmacy.

CAMP, DENISE E; West Muskingum HS; Zanesville, OH; Chrs; Hon Rl; Stg Crw; 4-H; Spn Clb; Trk; 3.5 Schlshp Awd 76 & 78; Univ; Sci.

CAMP, JAMES; St Joseph Cntrl Cath HS; Fremont, OH; Band; Hon Rl; Ftbl; Coll; Engr.

CAMP, JOYCE; Monroeville HS; Monroeville, OH; Band; Hon Rl; NHS; Sch Pl; 4-H; Spn Clb; Chrldng; Scr Kpr; Twrlr; 4-H Awd; College; Athletic Trainer.

CAMP, KATHRYN L; Waverly HS; Waverly, OH; Chrh Wkr; Off Ade; FHA; FTA; Spn Clb; Sftbl Sportsmanship Trophy Circleville Bible Coll 77; Zone Champ Bible Quiz Trophy 78 & 79; Columbus Tech Univ; Nurse.

CAMP, LINDA A; East Canton HS; E Canton, OH; Sec Frsh Cls; Cls Rep Soph Cls; Sec Jr Cls; Cls Rep Sr Cls; Am Leg Aux Girls St; Band; Cmp Fr Grls; Chrs; Chrh Wkr; Hon Rl; Coll; Phys Therapy.

CAMP, LYNNE; Lakewood HS; Buckeye Lake, OH; Band; Chrs; Chrh Wkr; Cmnty Wkr; Girl Scts; Hon Rl; Jr NHS; NHS; Sct Actv; Yth Flsp; French Natl Hnr Soc 78; Explr Pst Pres 79; Cert For Tutrng Stds 77; Ohio St Univ; Dent Hygn.

CAMP, SYLVESTER; Hannan HS; Ashton, WV; Sec Soph Cls; Hon Rl; Lbry Ade; NHS; Ed Yrbk; Drama Clb; Sec FFA; Cit Awd; DAR Awd; Marshall Univ; Acctg.

CAMP, TRACY; Pike Central HS; Velpen, IN; Hst Jr Cls; Sec Sr Cls; Stg Crw; Pep Clb; Swmmng; 4-H Awd; Univ; Beautician.

CAMPAGNA, MARIA; Rockville HS; Rockville, IN; Hon Rl; Sch Pl; Stg Crw; PPFtbl; Bus Schl.

CAMPANA, GREG; Stow HS; Munroe Falls, OH; 25/550 Cl Rep Jr Cls; Band; Boy Scts; Hon Rl; Pres NHS; Orch; Sch Pl; Sct Actv; Stg Crw; Stu Cncl; Univ; Archt.

CAMPAU, ROXANNE; Zeeland HS; Zeeland, MI; 5/200 Band; Pres Chrh Wkr; Hon Rl; NHS; Letter Trk; Chrldng; Michigan St Univ; Art.

CAMPBELL, ANNETTE; Wahama HS; New Haven, WV; Sec Frsh Cls; Trs Frsh Cls; Pres Soph Cls; Cl Rep Jr Cls; Chrs; Chrh Wkr; Hon Rl; Sec Stu Cncl; Pres Yth Flsp; FHA; Univ; Child Devlpmt.

CAMPBELL, BEN; Gallia Academy HS; Gallipolis, OH; Cls Rep Frsh Cls; Boy Scts; Chrs; Chrh Wkr; Pol Wkr; Sch Mus; Rptr Sch Nwsp; Pep Clb; Coach Actv; Cit Awd; Univ; Law.

CAMPBELL, BEVERLY; Put In Bay Schl; Put In Bay, OH; 3/6 VP Frsh Cls; Am Leg Aux Girls St; Chrs; Girl Scts; Hon Rl; Red Cr Ade; Sch Mus; Sch Pl; Stg Crw; Stu Cncl; Univ; Theatre Arts.

CAMPBELL, BRENDA K; Midland Trail HS; Sharon, PA; Sch Pl; Stg Crw; VP Drama Clb; Keyettes; Pennsylvania St Univ.

CAMPBELL, CARLA; Niles Mc Kinley HS; Niles, OH; 70/420 AFS; Band; Red Cr Ade; Sch Mus; Sch

Pl; Stg Crw; Drama Clb; Ger Clb; Trk; PPFtbl; Youngstown St Univ; Acctg.

CAMPBELL, CARLOS; Hannan Trace HS; Crown, OH; Cls Rep Frsh Cls; Cls Rep Soph Cls; Cmnty Wkr; Hon Rl; NHS; Stu Cncl; Beta Clb; 4-H; Pep Clb; Bsktbl; Latin I Awd; Marshall Univ.

CAMPBELL, CAROL; Withrow HS; Cincinnati, OH; Band; Chrh Wkr; Hon Rl; Lbry Ade; Univ Of Cinn; Nurse.

CAMPBELL, CARYN; Sacred Heart Academy; Mt Pleasant, MI; 18/54 Cl Rep Jr Cls; Cls Rep Sr Cls; Chrs; Chrh Wkr; Cmnty Wkr; Girl Scts; Hon Rl; Lbry Ade; Lit Mag; Stu Cncl; Cntrl Michigan Univ; Jrnlsm.

CAMPBELL, CLAYTON; Manchester HS; Akron, OH; Boy Scts; Chrh Wkr; Lbry Ade; Yth Flsp; Crs Cntry; College; Accntg.

CAMPBELL, DALE; Carlisle HS; Carlisle, OH; Boy Scts; Hon Rl; Letter Bsktbl; Letter Trk; Coach Actv; Scr Kpr; Bowling Green St Univ; Sci.

CAMPBELL, DANNY; Pine River HS; Cadillac, MI; Cls Rep Frsh Cls; Letter Ftbl; Wrstlng; Wexford Mesuakee VS; Elec.

CAMPBELL, DARLENE; Clinton Central HS; Frankfort, IN; Chrs; Sch Mus; Sch Pl; Stg Crw; Drama Clb; Pep Clb; Letter Mgrs; Cit Awd; Indiana Univ; Archt Design.

CAMPBELL, DAVID; Cedarville HS; Cedarvl, OH; Pres Frsh Cls; Trs Jr Cls; VP Sr Cls; Hon Rl; NHS; 4-H; FFA; 4-H Awd; Univ; Animal Sci.

CAMPBELL, DAVID H; Linsly Military Inst; Toronto, OH; Band; Boy Scts; Debate Tm; Hon Rl; ROTC; Sct Actv; Stu Cncl; Beta Clb; Fr Clb; Rdo Clb; Acad Ach Awd; Hnr Awd For First & Second Hnr; Coll; Law.

CAMPBELL, DIANE; Penn Township HS; Mishawaka, IN; Chrh Wkr; Sch Pl; Yrbk; Ger Clb; IM Sprt; Univ.

CAMPBELL, DON; Eaton HS; Eaton, OH; 25/180 Band; Chrs; Chrh Wkr; PAVAS; Sch Mus; Sch Pl; Stg Crw; Drama Clb; Spn Clb; Univ Of Cin; Theatre.

CAMPBELL, DONALD; Grant HS; Grant, MI; Hon Rl; Mth Clb; Sci Clb; Letter Bsktbl; Ten; Cit Awd; Univ Of Michigan; Med.

CAMPBELL, DONNA J; Jeffersonville HS; Jeffersonville, IN; 55/601 FCA; Hon Rl; Capt Gym; Chrldng; IM Sprt; PPFtbl; Indiana Univ; Elem Ed.

CAMPBELL, ED; Marlington HS; Homeworth, OH; 17/303 Am Leg Boys St; Hon Rl; NHS; Yth Flsp; Pres 4-H; Pres FFA; IM Sprt; Ohio St Univ; Agri Ed.

CAMPBELL, ELIZABETH; Barnesville HS; Barnesville, OH; Am Leg Aux Girls St; Chrs; Chrh Wkr; Hon Rl; Lbry Ade; Sch Pl; Rptr Sch Nwsp; Sch Nwsp; Fr Clb; FTA; Statistician For Bsktbl; Ohio St Univ; Busns Admin.

CAMPBELL, ERIC; Bristol Local HS; Bristolville, OH; Hon Rl; 4-H; Ohio St Univ; Vet.

CAMPBELL, GARY; Pine River Jr Sr HS; Cadillac, MI; Letter Ftbl; Letter Wrstlng; Univ; Forestry.

CAMPBELL, GUWYNE; Trimble Local HS; Glouster, OH; Hon Rl; NHS; Fr Clb; Bsktbl; Glf; IM Sprt; Univ.

CAMPBELL, J; Kalkaska HS; Kalkaska, MI; Band; Chrh Wkr; DECA; College; Bus.

CAMPBELL, J; Sault Area HS; Slt Ste Marie, MI; 2/315 Hon Rl; Hosp Ade; NHS; Red Cr Ade; Sch Pl; Yth Flsp; Pep Clb; Lake Superior State Coll.

CAMPBELL, JACKIE; Marion Harding HS; Marion, OH; Band; Chrs; Chrh Wkr; Cmnty Wkr; Girl Scts; Hon Rl; Off Ade; Orch; Sct Actv; Stg Crw; Mt Vernon Nazarene Coll; Psych.

CAMPBELL, JAMES H; George Washington Sr HS; Charleston, WV; 18/350 Band; Hon Rl; Jr NHS; Sch Mus; Yth Flsp; Bausch & Lomb Awd; SAR Awd; Hon Grad 79; Kanawha Cnty All Cnty Band 76 79; Disngshd Musicn Cert Of U S Marine Youth Fdn 79; Washington & Lee Univ; Pre Dent.

CAMPBELL, JAN; Barr Reeve HS; Montgomery, IN; Cls Rep Soph Cls; VP Band; Drm Mjrt; Hon Rl; Sch Pl; VP Stu Cncl; Yrbk; Beta Clb; Pep Clb; Chrldng; Vocational Schl; Sec.

CAMPBELL, JEANETTE; Barr Reeve HS; Montgomery, IN; 14/66 Sec Jr Cls; Sec Sr Cls; Band; Chrh Wkr; Drm Mjrt; Hon Rl; Off Ade; Sch Pl; Rptr Yrbk; Beta Clb; Univ Of Evansville; Dent Hyg.

CAMPBELL, JENNIFER; Peterstown HS; Peterstown, WV; Trs Frsh Cls; Hon Rl; NHS; Sch Pl; Drama Clb; Fr Clb; FTA; Pep Clb; Concord Coll; Psych.

CAMPBELL, JOAN; Charlotte HS; Charlotte, MI; 1/310 Sec Frsh Cls; Val; Band; Pres NHS; Sch Mus; Stg Crw; Treas Spn Clb; Letter Glf; PPFtbl; Natl Merit Ltr; Michigan St Univ; Poli Sci.

CAMPBELL, JUDY; Heath HS; Heath, OH; 1/170 Band; Chrs; Debate Tm; Girl Scts; Hon Rl; Natl Forn Lg; NHS; Yrbk; Spn Clb; Ohio Univ; Tchr.

CAMPBELL, KATHLEEN M; Villa Angela Academy; Cleveland, OH; 12/192 Cmnty Wkr; Hon Rl; Pol Wkr; Rptr Yrbk; Natl Merit SF; Voice Dem Awd; Science Award 76; Ohio Test Of Schol Acheiv English 77; Univ; Engr.

CAMPBELL, KIM; Northrop Sr HS; Ft Wayne, IN; 95/587 Band; Chrs; Drl Tm; Girl Scts; Univ; Stewardess.

CAMPBELL, KRISTEN; Fenton Sr HS; Fenton, MI; 24/267 Band; Hon Rl; NHS; Trk; PPFtbl; Cntrl Mi Univ Bd Of Trustees Hon Schslhp 79; ACP Acad Recngnt 79; Recgntn For Part In Mi Law Day 79; Cntrl Michigan Univ; Law.

CAMPBELL, LAUREL; Midview HS; Grafton, OH; VP Jr Cls; Chrs; Hon Rl; Jr NHS; Lit Mag; NHS; Off Ade; Stu Cncl; Rptr Yrbk; Rptr Sch Nwsp; Univ; Cmnctns.

CAMPBELL, LEE A; Ursuline Academy; Golf Manor, OH; Chrh Wkr; Cmnty Wkr; Hon Rl; Hosp Ade; NHS; Pol Wkr; Bsbl; Chrldng; Coach Actv; Sci Fair Awd; Yth Aid To Retarded; Spelling Awd; Comm Serv St Rita Schl For Deaf; Univ Of Cincinnati; Spec Ed.

CAMPBELL, LESLIE; Wheeling Park HS; Wheeling, WV; Band; Drl Tm; Hon Rl; Lit Mag; NHS; Quill & Scroll; Yrbk; Fr Clb; Pep Clb; Mat Maids; West Liberty St Coll; Advrtsng.

CAMPBELL, LISA; Beaumont Schl For Girls; Cleveland, OH; Chrh Wkr; Cmnty Wkr; Hon Rl; NHS; Off Ade; Fr Clb; FNA; FTA; Cit Awd; Alt Winner In Alpha Kapa Alpha Sor Essay Contest 79; Univ.

CAMPBELL, LORI; Henryville HS; Underwood, IN; Hon Rl; Ivy Tech Schl.

CAMPBELL, LYNDA; Riverview Cmnty HS; Riverview, MI; 17/253 Band; Drm Mjrt; Hon Rl; NHS; Twrlr; Henry Ford Cmnty Coll; Comp Sci.

CAMPBELL, MARCIA; Bexley HS; Columbus, OH; 12/178 VP Frsh Cls; VP Soph Cls; Chrs; Jr NHS; Quill & Scroll; Stu Cncl; Ed Sch Nwsp; Letter Swmmng; Letter Chrldng; Am Leg Awd; Freedoms Found At Vly Forge Yth Seminar; Kiwanis Internation Yth Ldrshp Conf; Buckeye Girls St; Coll; Med.

CAMPBELL, MARIANNA; Upper Scioto Valley HS; Alger, OH; 3/75 Chrs; Hon Rl; Jr NHS; NHS; Stg Crw; Yrbk; Beta Clb; Pres Fr Clb; GAA; JA Awd; Accomponist Awd 76; Outsdng French Stu Awd 76; Top Grd Pnt Aver 77; Ohio St Univ; Elem Educ.

CAMPBELL, MARK; Barberton Sr HS; Barberton, OH; 118/490 Boy Scts; Sct Actv; Beta Clb; Ger Clb; Ftbl; Ohio St Univ; Welding.

CAMPBELL, MONIQUE; Jefferson Area HS; Rock Creek, OH; AFS; Aud/Vis; Chrs; Chrh Wkr; Cmnty Wkr; Drl Tm; Girl Scts; Hon Rl; JA; Jr NHS; Tech Schl; Data Proc.

CAMPBELL, NADINE; Carson City Crystal Area Sch; Crystal, MI; Girl Scts; Hon Rl; NHS; Yth Flsp; 4-H; FHA; Spn Clb; Univ; Elem Educ.

CAMPBELL, NANCY; John Glenn HS; Cambridge, OH; Sec Frsh Cls; Sec Soph Cls; Sec Jr Cls; Band; Chrs; Hon Rl; Letter Bsbl; Bsktbl; Muskingum Area Tech College; Account.

CAMPBELL, PAM; Borden HS; Borden, IN; Hon Rl; Fr Clb; IV Tech Coll; Photog.

CAMPBELL, PATRICIA; Holy Redeemer HS; Detroit, MI; Cls Rep Frsh Cls; Cls Rep Soph Cls; Sec Jr Cls; Chrs; Hon Rl; NHS; Chrldng; Univ Of Mich; Doctor.

CAMPBELL, PATSY; Lemon Monroe HS; Middletown, OH; 7/287 Band; Chrs; Chrh Wkr; Girl Scts; Hon Rl; JA; NHS; Sch Mus; Sec Yth Flsp; God Cntry Awd; Natl Frat Of Stndt Musicn 74 78; Natl Fedtn Of Music Clubs 74 78; Miami Univ; Elem Educ.

CAMPBELL, RANDALL; Reading HS; Reading, OH; Chrh Wkr; Y-Teens; 4-H; FFA; Key Clb; Pep Clb; Sci Clb; Ftbl; College.

CAMPBELL, REBECCA; Crooksville HS; Crooksville, OH; 6/112 Am Leg Aux Girls St; Band; Girl Scts; Hon Rl; NHS; Sch Pl; Yth Flsp; Rptr Sch Nwsp; 4-H; FHA; Schlrshp Tm 76 77; Jefferson Tech Schl; Acctg.

CAMPBELL, RHONDA; William Mason HS; Mason, OH; 8/178 AFS; Am Leg Aux Girls St; VP Band; Chrh Wkr; Hon Rl; VP NHS; Orch; Yth Flsp; Sec Sci Clb; NCTE; Miami Univ; Science.

CAMPBELL, RICHARD M; Dayton Christian HS; Miamisburg, OH; 11/130 Cls Rep Frsh Cls; Cls Rep Soph Cls; Cl Rep Jr Cls; Hon Rl; VP Stu Cncl; Letter Bsktbl; Capt Socr; Oral Roberts Univ; Phys Ther.

CAMPBELL, ROSEMARY; Springboro HS; Springboro, OH; Band; Girl Scts; Hon Rl; Rptr Yrbk; Sch Nwsp; 4-H; 4-H Awd; Art Club Serv Awd Tri Cty Show Winner; O M E A Super & Exc Rtng; All Oh St Fair Bnd; Warren Cnty Fair;.

CAMPBELL, ROXANNA; Fredericktown HS; Fred, OH; 2/130 Am Leg Aux Girls St; Band; Hon Rl; Off Ade; Quill & Scroll; Yth Flsp; Rptr Yrbk; Yrbk; Rptr Sch Nwsp; 4-H; Slctd To Attnd Women In Engr Workshp Mich Tech U 79; 2 Yr Membr Ohio Tests Of Schlstc Achvmnt Schlrshp Team; Univ; Math.

CAMPBELL, RUSSELL K; Rockville HS; Rockville, IN; 15/100 FCA; NHS; Lat Clb; Sci Clb; Letter Bsktbl; Letter Crs Cntry; Letter Glf; College; Med Doctor.

CAMPBELL, S; Redford HS; Detroit, MI; College; Law.

CAMPBELL, SCOTT; River Valley HS; Caledonia, OH; 5/200 Band; NHS; Orch; Sch Mus; Yth Flsp; 4-H; Fr Clb; Sci Clb; Ohio St Univ; Sci.

CAMPBELL, SCOTT; Berrien Springs Public HS; Berrien Spgs, MI; 35/111 Band; FCA; Hon Rl; Sct Actv; Rptr Sch Nwsp; Mth Clb; Sci Clb; Letter Trk; Capt IM Sprt; Lake Michigan Coll; Music.

CAMPBELL, STEVE; Wynford HS; Marion, OH; 8/140 Hon Rl; Pres NHS; Stu Cncl; Key Clb; Bsktbl; Letter Ftbl; Letter Trk; Capt Wrstlng; Ohio Northern Univ; Elec Engr.

CAMPBELL, STEVE; Malabar HS; Mansfield, OH; 33/288 Hon Rl; Stu Cncl; Key Clb; Mth Clb; Mgrs; Mu Alpha Theta Math Awd 79; Ohio St Univ; Forestry.

CAMPBELL, SUSAN; Oakridge HS; Muskegon, MI ; Chrh Wkr; Hon Rl; Bsktbl; Musk Community College; Regist Nurse.

CAMPBELL, SUSAN; Farmington Sr HS; Farmington, MI; Cls Rep Frsh Cls; Sec Sr Cls; Girl Scts; Hon Rl; NHS; Fr Clb; Pep Clb; Letter Ten; Letter Trk; GAA; Central Michigan Univ; Educ.

CAMPBELL, SUSIE; Bishop Ready HS; Columbus, OH; Chrh Wkr; Cmnty Wkr; Pol Wkr; Rptr Sch Nwsp; Univ; Jrnlsm.

CAMPBELL, TAMARA; Eastside Jr/sr HS; Butler, IN; Cls Rep Frsh Cls; Cls Rep Soph Cls; Drl Tm; Hon Rl; Off Ade; Sch Pl; Rptr Yrbk; Spn Clb; Pom Pon; Mas Awd; Intl Busns Coll; Busns.

CAMPBELL, TAMMY; Bellefontaine HS; Bellefontaine, OH; Chrs; Chrh Wkr; Off Ade; Sch Mus; Yth Flsp; Y-Teens; 4-H; FTA; Mth Clb; 4-H Awd;.

CAMPBELL, TERESA; Hicksville HS; Hicksville, OH; 20/110 Band; Chrh Wkr; Girl Scts; Hon Rl; Stg Crw; 4-H; Pep Clb; Spn Clb; 4-H Awd; College; Earth Sci.

CAMPBELL, THOMAS; Greenbrier East HS; Lewisburg, WV; 1/315 Val; FCA; Hon Rl; NHS; Stu Cncl; Yrbk; Sci Clb; Letter Ten; IM Sprt; Mgrs; West Virginia Univ; Engr.

CAMPBELL, VALERIE; Champion HS; Warren, OH; 4/230 Trs Frsh Cls; Cls Rep Frsh Cls; Trs Soph Cls; Cls Rep Soph Cls; Cl Rep Jr Cls; Cls Rep Sr Cls; Am Leg Aux Girls St; Band; Chrh Wkr; Cmnty Wkr; Ohio State Univ; Phys Ther.

CAMPBELL, WILLIAM; Wirt County HS; Palistine, WV; Chrh Wkr; Cmnty Wkr; Lbry Ade; 4-H; FFA; Ftbl; Mgrs; Voc Schl; Diesel Mech.

CAMPBELL, WILLIAM; Bloomington South HS; Bloomington, IN; FCA; Jr NHS; Bsktbl; Ftbl; Univ; Pre Med.

CAMPEAU, STEVEN; Cheboygan Area HS; Cheboygan, MI; Pres Frsh Cls; Cls Rep Frsh Cls; Band; Hon Rl; Orch; Sch Pl; Stu Cncl; Fr Clb; Ftbl; Hockey;.

CAMPENSA, ROSS; Euclid Sr HS; Euclid, OH; 6/650 Band; Chrs; Cmnty Wkr; Hon Rl; Sch Mus; Sch Pl; Drama Clb; Bsktbl; Ftbl; Hockey; Distinguished Schlr Awd 76 79; Goalie On All Star Tm 76; Goalie For Cleveland Sts Hockey Tm 78; Case Western Reserve Univ; Med.

CAMPERMAN, RICHARD; Donald E Gavit HS; Hammond, IN; 32/218 Chrh Wkr; Hon Rl; JA; Spn Clb; JA Awd; Gabit A Hnr Roll Awd 79; Indiana St Univ; Math.

CAMPLESE, KATHLEEN; Edgewood HS; Kingsville, OH; AFS; Band; Chrs; Girl Scts; Pres 4-H; Lat Clb; Sci Clb; Swmmng; Cit Awd; College; Acctg.

CAMPO, MARK; Admiral King HS; Lorain, OH; Lbry Ade; Sprt Ed Yrbk; Bsbl; Ftbl; Wrstlng; College; Bus.

CAMPOLA, JACKIE; East Lake North HS; Willowick, OH; 42/699 Hon Rl; Letter Trk; Univ; Fashion Mdse.

CAMPOLITO, RALPH; Canfield HS; Canfield, OH; Hon Rl; Fr Clb; Spn Clb; Ohio St Univ; Bus Admin.

CAMPOLO, AMY; Southeastern HS; Springfield, OH; 9/68 Hon Rl; Rptr Yrbk; Fr Clb; Univ; Vet.

CAMPREDON, PAULA; Walnut Ridge HS; Reynoldsburg, OH; Chrs; Chrh Wkr; NHS; Quill & Scroll; Yrbk; Fr Clb; Pep Clb; Sweet Briar Coll; Languages.

CAMPTON, D; Washington Catholic HS; Washington, IN; 16/70 Bus Schl.

CAMSTRA, MICHAEL; Miami Trace HS; Jamestown, OH; 37/249 Boy Scts; Sch Pl; Rptr Sch Nwsp; 4-H; FFA; Letter Ftbl; Letter Trk; Letter Wrstlng; Kiwan Awd; Ohio St Univ; Pre Law.

CAMUSO, BARBARA; Cardinal Mooney HS; Youngstown, OH; 11/302 Chrh Wkr; Hon Rl; Jr NHS; NHS; Off Ade; Quill & Scroll; Ed Sch Nwsp; Lat Clb; Mth Clb; Am Leg Awd; Youngstown State Univ; Educ.

CANADA, BARBARA; Reading Community HS; Cincinnati, OH; Chrs; Chrh Wkr; Girl Scts; Hon Rl; Hosp Ade; Lbry Ade; Sch Mus; Sct Actv; Rptr Yrbk; Spn Clb; Univ; Nursing.

CANADAY, BONNIE; Wood Memorial HS; Oakland City, IN; Aud/Vis; Chrs; Chrh Wkr; Cmnty Wkr; Hon Rl; Lbry Ade; Sch Mus; Stg Crw; Y-Teens; Nazarene World Youth Delegate 78; Mbmr Of Nazarene Teen Care Corp 79; Mid Amer Nazarene Coll; Chrstn Educ.

CANADAY, CONNIE; Wood Memorial HS; Oakland City, IN; Chrs; Chrh Wkr; Cmnty Wkr; Lbry Ade; Orch; Sch Mus; Sch Pl; Stg Crw; Yth Flsp; Cit Awd; Chsn As Mbr Of The Teen Care Corps Wrkd In Virgin Islands 79; Chsn As A Delegt To Intl Inst Estes Pk Co 78; Mid America Nazarene Coll; Phys Ther.

CANADAY, LORI; Hammond Baptist HS; Schererville, IN; Chrs; Chrh Wkr; Hon Rl; Lbry Ade; Sch Mus; Sch Pl; Yth Flsp; Spn Clb; Capt Chrldng; IM Sprt; Univ; Elem Educ.

CANADY, IRVIN; Ben Davis HS; Indianapolis, IN; Cl Rep Jr Cls; Hon Rl; Mod UN; Stg Crw; Cit Awd; Purdue; Mech Engr.

CANADY JR, ALBERT; Shakamak HS; Midland, IN; 25/86 Hon Rl; Quill & Scroll; Sch Nwsp; Conservation Officer.

CANAN, CRYSTAL; Bradford HS; Bradford, OH; 4/65 Hon Rl; NHS; Stu Cncl; Yrbk; Pres FHA; Letter Bsktbl; Letter Trk; PPFtbl; Lion Awd; Univ; Bus Admin.

CANARD, GINGER; Litchfield HS; Litchfield, MI; 1/52 Val; Chrh Wkr; Debate Tm; Hon Rl; Off Ade; Sch Mus; Sch Pl; Rptr Yrbk; Fr Clb; Trk; Michigan St Univ; Sci.

CANARD, SHEILA; Western HS; Russiaville, IN; 29/200 Band; Girl Scts; JA; Univ; Pre Vet.

CANARY, EDWARD; Loogootee Cmnty HS; Loogootee, IN; 5/150 Chrh Wkr; Hon Rl; Letter Bsbl; Letter Bsktbl; Rose Hulman Univ; Engr.

CANDELA, JON; Harbor HS; Ashtabula, OH; 11/195 AFS; NHS; Sch Mus; Sch Pl; Stu Cncl; Drama Clb; Spn Clb; College; Cmmrcl Communications.

CANFIELD, BRIGETTE; Cadillac Sr HS; Cadillac, MI; Band; Hon Rl; Northern Michigan Univ; Med Tech.

CANFIELD, MIRANDA; Crawford Au Sable HS; Grayling, MI; 24/166 Band; Chrs; Girl Scts; Hon Rl; NHS; Sch Mus; Yth Flsp; 4-H; 4-H Awd; Michigan St Univ; Vet.

CANFIELD JR, JOHN; Charleston Catholic HS; Charleston, WV; Cls Rep Frsh Cls; Boy Scts; Hon Rl; JA; NHS; Pol Wkr; Sct Actv; College; Polit Sci.

CANGANELLI, ENZA; C F Brush HS; Lyndhurst, OH; Hosp Ade; Pres JA; Lbry Ade; Univ.

CANIZARO, NANCY; Ursuline HS; Youngstown, OH; Cls Rep Soph Cls; Cl Rep Jr Cls; VP Sr Cls; Lbry Ade; Off Ade; Stu Cncl; Univ; Bus.

CANN, HILARIAN; Notre Dame HS; Clarksburg, WV; 26/62 Am Leg Boys St; Chrs; Chrh Wkr; Hon Rl; Jr NHS; NHS; Yth Flsp; Drama Clb; Key Clb; Bsbl; Kings Coll; CPA.

CANN, LARRY; Notre Dame HS; Clarksburg, WV; Chrs; Chrh Wkr; Hon Rl; Sch Pl; Fr Clb; Key Clb; Mth Clb; Sci Clb; Bsbl; Ftbl; W Virginia Univ; Law.

CANNADAY, GWENDOLYN; Mount View HS; Anawalt, WV; Cl Rep Jr Cls; Band; Chrs; Chrh Wkr; Cmnty Wkr; Hon Rl; Sprt Ed Sch Nwsp; 4-H; FBLA; Pep Clb; Benjamin Franklin Bus Admin; Acctg.

CANNATTI, CARLA; Ursuline HS; Youngstwon, OH; 11/283 Cl Rep Jr Cls; Hon Rl; Red Cr Ade; Stu Cncl; Letter Trk; Youngstown State Univ.

CANNELL, CHRISTINE; Sebring Mc Kinley HS; Sebring, OH; Off Ade; Quill & Scroll; Ed Yrbk; Sprt Ed Yrbk; Rptr Yrbk; Yrbk; Fr Clb; Letter Bsktbl; GAA; Scr Kpr; Aultman Univ; Nursing.

CANNON, CAROL; Taylor HS; Kokomo, IN; 7/189 Am Leg Aux Girls St; Chrs; Sec Girl Scts; Hon Rl; NHS; Sct Actv; 4-H; Fr Clb; PPFtbl; Rcvd 1st Cl Awd In Girl Scouts 77; Indiana Univ; Elem Ed.

CANNON, KAYETTA; Hinton HS; Hinton, WV; Cls Rep Frsh Cls; Cls Rep Soph Cls; Band; Cmnty Wkr; Hon Rl; Sch Pl; FBLA; Schlrshp Schl Of Choice County Jr Miss 79; Savings Bond County Jr Miss 79; Univ; Comp Sci.

CANNON, KEVIN; Clio Area HS; Clio, MI; Hon Rl; Jr NHS; NHS; Yth Flsp; Letter Bsbl; Letter Bsktbl; Capt Ftbl; NCTE; Univ.

CANNON, MIKE; Solon HS; Solon, OH; Boy Scts; Chrh Wkr; Cmnty Wkr; Hon Rl; Pol Wkr; Key Clb; Spn Clb; Ftbl; IM Sprt; Univ; Law Enforcement.

CANNON, RUSSELL; Patterson Cooperative HS; Dayton, OH; Cls Rep Soph Cls; Boy Scts; Hon Rl; JA; Stu Cncl; VICA; IM Sprt; College; Printing.

CANRIGHT, JANE; Chesterton HS; Chesterton, IN; 2/420 Band; Chrs; Mdrgl; NHS; Sch Mus; Scr Kpr; Univ; Math.

CANSECO, JORGE; Culver Military Academy; Laredo, TX; 107/191 Cls Rep Frsh Cls; Boy Scts; Hon Rl; Pol Wkr; ROTC; Stu Cncl; Socr; IM Sprt; Grad From Culver Summer Naval Schl 78; Co Won The E In Sum Nav Schl Culver Ind Sum 78; Univ; Bus.

CANSWELL, JAMES K; Jesup W Scott HS; Toledo, OH; Bsktbl; Ftbl; Law.

CANTANON, GREGORY S; Independence HS; Coal City, WV; Pres Soph Cls; Am Leg Boys St; Hon Rl; NHS; Stu Cncl; Pres Beta Clb; Bsbl; Ftbl; Capt Wrstlng; Ohio Inst Of Tech; Elec Tech.

CANTARELLI, AILEEN; Jackson HS; Massillon, OH; Chrs; Girl Scts; Hon Rl; NHS; Y-Teens; Spn Clb; Swmmng; College; Math.

CANTER, LINDA; Washington HS; Massillon, OH; 23/483 Cl Rep Jr Cls; Cls Rep Sr Cls; Chrs; Hon Rl; NHS; Off Ade; Quill & Scroll; Sch Mus; Sch Pl; Y-Teens; Coll Of Wooster; Elem Educ.

CANTER, MARY; Miller HS; Shawnee, OH; Chrs; Hon Rl; Yrbk; Sch Nwsp; Drama Clb; 4-H; FBLA; Ohio State; Computer Science.

CANTER, PAT; Troy HS; Troy, OH; Trs Jr Cls; VP Sr Cls; Hon Rl; Pres OEA; Mat Maids; Scr Kpr; Ohio Univ; Poli Sci.

CANTER, ROBIN G; Oak Hill HS; Oak Hill, OH; Sec Frsh Cls; Trs Soph Cls; Trs Jr Cls; Band; Chrs; Hon Rl; Hosp Ade; Sch Mus; Sch Pl; Beta Clb; Rio Grande Coll; Elem Ed.

CANTERBURY, JEFF; Green HS; Uniontown, OH; Band; Chrs; Chrh Wkr; Debate Tm; Mdrgl; Sch Pl; Drama Clb; Emory Univ; Optometrist.

CANTLEY, CONNIE; Sherman HS; Orgas, WV; Cls Rep Frsh Cls; Chrh Wkr; Cmnty Wkr; Hon Rl; Jr NHS; NHS; Off Ade; Sch Pl; Yth Flsp; Sch Nwsp; Voc Schl; Exec Sec.

CANTON, MARK; Campbell Memorial HS; Campbell, OH; 4/208 Boy Scts; Hon Rl; NHS; Mth Clb; Sci Clb; Spn Clb; Letter Ftbl; College; Chem Engr.

CANTON, RAYMOND; Canfield HS; Youngstown, OH; Band; Hon Rl; Spn Clb; College; Air Force Rotc.

CANTOR, D; Linsly Inst; Wheeling, WV; Band; Drm Bgl; ROTC; Sch Mus; Sch Nwsp; Fr Clb; Mgrs; Scr Kpr; Tmr; College; Math.

CANTRELL, BOBBY; Iaeger HS; Jolo, WV; Am Leg Boys St; Aud/Vis; Hon Rl; Jr NHS; Lbry Ade; Natl Forn Lg; Sch Pl; Stu Cncl; Drama Clb; Rdo Clb; Bluefield St Coll; Mining Engr.

CANTRELL, STEVE; Sharples HS; Sharples, WV; Cls Rep Frsh Cls; Cls Rep Soph Cls; VP Jr Cls; Am Leg Boys St; Hon Rl; Jr NHS; NHS; Off Ade; Stu Cncl; Ed Sch Nwsp; West Virginia Tech Univ; Radio Prog.

CANTRELL, WILLIAM K; Grand Ledge HS; Grand Ledge, MI; 48/453 Boy Scts; Chrh Wkr; Hon Rl; NHS; Pol Wkr; Lat Clb; Letter Bsbl; Ftbl; Socr;

Hillsdale Merit Schlrshp Awd 79 83; Merit Schlrshp Mi 79 83; Hillsdale Coll; Physics.

CAPARON, DAVID; H H Dow HS; Midland, MI; Aud/Vis; Band; Boy Scts; Orch; Sch Mus; Sch Pl; Sct Actv; Stg Crw; Delta Mic State; Bio.

CAPEN, MARY ANN; Ursuline HS; Canfield, OH; 20/352 Cmnty Wkr; Hon Rl; Jr NHS; NHS; 4-H; Ger Clb; 4-H Awd; Good News Prog Working With Retarded 78; Tutor For Algebra Awrd From Schl 78; Univ.

CAPERS, DEBBIE; Buckeye West HS; Cadiz, OH; 30/84 Trs Jr Cls; Trs Sr Cls; Chrh Wkr; Hon Rl; Off Ade; FHA; OEA;.

CAPES, ANDREW E; St Joseph HS; St Joseph, MI; Crs Cntry; Trk; College.

CAPES, LISA; Jennings County HS; No Vernon, IN; 14/351 Band; Chrh Wkr; NHS; Sch Pl; 4-H; Ger Clb; Pep Clb; Trk; 4-H Awd;.

CAPKA, KEN; St Edward HS; Fairview Pk, OH; 10/375 Hon Rl; JA; Lit Mag; Yrbk; Scr Kpr; JA Awd; College.

CAPLIS, THERESE M; Chesterton HS; Valpariaso, IN; Band; Hon Rl; JA; Jr NHS; NHS; Off Ade; Yth Flsp; Ger Clb; Pep Clb; Spn Clb; Purdue Univ; Vet Med.

CAPOGRECO, JENNINE; Girard HS; Girard, OH; 13/209 Jr NHS; Treas NHS; Stu Cncl; Treas Y-Teens; Yrbk; Rptr Sch Nwsp; Treas OEA; Capt Chrldng; GAA; Bus Schl; Sec.

CAPONE, JOSEPH; Valley View HS; Germantown, OH; Chrs; Hon Rl; Stu Cncl; Ftbl; Trk; IM Sprt; College; Med.

CAPORUSCIO, CONCETTA; Trinity HS; Bedford, OH; 6/126 Chrs; Hon Rl; Spn Clb; Hiram College; Foreign Languages.

CAPOUCH, PATRICIA; Kankakee Vly HS; Rensselaer, IN; 48/250 Hon Rl; NHS; Stu Cncl; Letter Bsktbl; GAA; Scr Kpr; Vlybl Letter Earned; Track Letter Earned; Lettermans Clb; Purdue Univ; Eng.

CAPOZIELLO, JOHN; St Francis De Sales HS; Columbus, OH; CAP; Red Cr Ade; Sci Clb; Spn Clb; 1st NASA Awd On Expermntl Jet Eng 79; Army Awd On Exprmntl Jet Engn 79; Superr Ratng Oh Acad Of Sci 79; Ohio St Univ; Meterology.

CAPPA, TINA M; Fairfield Sr HS; Fairfield, OH; 137/556 Girl Scts; Off Ade; Pol Wkr; Quill & Scroll; Rptr Yrbk; Spn Clb; Bsktbl; Trk; Capt Chrldng; GAA; Vllybll Grtr Miami Confrnc Team Champs 1975; World Affairs Delegate 1976; Miami Hamilton Campus Univ.

CAPPARELLI, SHERRY; Rochester HS; Rochester, MI; VP Band; NHS; Yth Flsp; Letter Trk; Univ Of Michigan; Med.

CAPPAS, CONSTANCE; Grosse Pointe North HS; Grosse Pt Shrs, MI; Girl Scts; Hon Rl; Hosp Ade; Letter Mgrs; PPFtbl; Letter Tmr; 5 Yr Awd In Dancing Cls 77; Univ; Archt.

CAPPEL, CATHERINE A; Seton HS; Cincinnati, OH; 7/282 Chrs; Girl Scts; Hon Rl; Jr NHS; NHS; Pol Wkr; Sch Mus; Fr Clb; Pep Clb; Cit Awd; Univ; Psych.

CAPPELLETTI, DANA; Martins Ferry HS; Martins Ferry, OH; 10/214 VP Soph Cls; Band; Hon Rl; NHS; Yrbk; Fr Clb; Sci Clb; Wheeling Coll; Respiratory Ther.

CAPPELLETTI, KATHRYN; Shaker Hts HS; Shaker Hts, OH; Cls Rep Soph Cls; Cl Rep Jr Cls; Chrs; Hon Rl; Stu Cncl; Fr Clb; Swmmng; Univ; Spec Ed.

CAPPOCCIAMI, TONI; Grove City HS; Grove City, OH; 33/452 Sec Soph Cls; Cls Rep Soph Cls; Trs Jr Cls; Cl Rep Jr Cls; Sec Sr Cls; Cls Rep Sr Cls; Hon Rl; NHS; Stu Cncl; Rptr Yrbk; Summer Schlr Ohio Univ 79; Ohio Univ; Cmnctns.

CAPPS, BECKY; Hammond Technical Voc HS; Hammond, IN; Hst Jr Cls; Am Leg Aux Girls St; Chrh Wkr; Girl Scts; Hon Rl; NHS; Sec Stu Cncl; Ger Clb; VICA; Purdue Cal Campus.

CAPRANICA, ANDREA; Champion HS; Warren, OH; 47/226 Band; Chrs; NHS; Sch Mus; Spn Clb; Youngstown St Univ; Med Lab.

CAPRARO, FERNANDA; Woodhaven HS; Woodhaven, MI; 9/206 Pres Jr Cls; Chrh Wkr; Hon Rl; Jr NHS; Pres NHS; Off Ade; Stu Cncl; Treas Spn Clb; Natl Merit Ltr; Eastern Michigan Univ; Fshn Mdse.

CAPREZ, RAPHAEL; Akron North HS; Akron, OH; 5/400 Hon Rl; Jr NHS; Pres NHS; Orch; Spn Clb; Glf; Ten; IM Sprt; Cit Awd; Natl Merit Schl; Chrysler Awd 79; Acad Schrlshp 79; Awd Of Distinction 79; Univ Of Akron; Law.

CAPUANO, BETTINA; Mc Kinley Sr HS; Carton, OH; 7/553 Chrs; Chrh Wkr; Sec Girl Scts; Hon Rl; Jr NHS; NHS; Sch Mus; Stg Crw; Spn Clb; Natl Merit Ltr; Oh Tst Of Schlstc Achievmt Span Ii Hon Mntn 1977; Sociedad Honraria Hiapanica 1978; Univ; Elem Educ.

CAPUTO, FELICIA; Bridgeport Sr HS; Bridgeport, WV; Sec Frsh Cls; Band; Drm Mjrt; Hon Rl; Jr NHS; NHS; Stu Cncl; Y-Teens; Pep Clb; Cert From The Natl Ed Deve Test; West Virginia Univ; Acctg.

CAPWILL, DIANA M; Solon HS; Solon, OH; Boy Scts; Girl Scts; Hon Rl; JA; Lbry Ade; NHS; Off Ade; Rptr Yrbk; Pep Clb; Bsbl; Ursuline Coll; Elem Ed.

CAPWILL, DIANE M; Solon HS; Solon, OH; Boy Scts; Girl Scts; JA; Lbry Ade; NHS; Off Ade; Rptr Yrbk; Pep Clb; Letter Bsbl; Letter Chrldng; Ursuline Coll; Lib Arts.

CARABALLO, ARTURO; Washington HS; E Chigco, IN; 21/270 Am Leg Boys St; Chrh Wkr; Cmnty Wkr; NHS; Am Leg Awd; A & B Hon Roll 77; Univ; Bus Mgmt.

CARABALLO, DANIEL; Theodore Roosevelt HS; E Chicago, IN; 8/199 Pres JA; Natl Forn Lg; NHS; Latino Schlr Awd From Indiana Univ 79; Univ; Engr.

CARABIN JR, THOMAS; St Paul HS; Norwalk, OH; 2 Cls Rep Soph Cls; Sal; Boy Scts; Hon Rl; Fr Clb; Bsktbl; Natl Merit Schl; Firelands Of Bwlg Green; Bus Admin.

CARABOOLAD, CYNTHIA; St Augustine Academy; Cleveland, OH; Cls Rep Frsh Cls; Trs Soph Cls; Cl Rep Jr Cls; Hon Rl; NHS; Stu Cncl; Pep Clb; Sci Clb; Chrldng; IM Sprt; Ohio Northern Univ; Pharm.

CARADONNA, SULLY; Bishop Watterson HS; Hilliard, OH; Hon Rl; Jr NHS; Lat Clb; Ftbl; College; Med.

CARAMELLA, ALAN; Maple Hts HS; Maple Heights, OH; Pres Chrs; Chrh Wkr; Jr NHS; NHS; Sch Mus; Sch Pl; Stg Crw; Sec Drama Clb; Capt Ten; Brigham Young Univ; Pre Law.

CARAMELLA, MICHAEL; White Pine HS; White Pine, MI; Cls Rep Frsh Cls; Cls Rep Soph Cls; Cl Rep Jr Cls; Cls Rep Sr Cls; Am Leg Boys St; Band; Chrh Wkr; Cmnty Wkr; Hon Rl; Jr NHS; Michigan Tech Univ; Acctg.

CARANO, KARLA; Campbell Memorial HS; Campbell, OH; Debate Tm; Hon Rl; NHS; VP Fr Clb; Key Clb; Mth Clb; Sci Clb; Univ; Pre Med.

CARANO, LU ANN; Campbell Memorial HS; Campbell, OH; Pres Soph Cls; Trs Sr Cls; Drm Mjrt; Hosp Ade; Natl Forn Lg; NHS; Off Ade; Red Cr Ade; Sch Pl; Stu Cncl; Univ Of Cincinnati; Poli Sci.

CARANO, THOMAS; South Lyon HS; South Lyon, MI; Cl Rep Jr Cls; Cls Rep Sr Cls; Hon Rl; Fr Clb; Letter Bsktbl; Letter Crs Cntry; Letter Glf; Natl Merit Ltr; Natl Merit SF; Pres Awd; Alma College.

CARAWAY, CHRISTINE; Everett HS; Lansing, MI; Pres Jr Cls; IM Sprt; Voyageurs Clb; Cert Of Awd For Academc Achvmnt 78; Var Vllybl 75 79; Co Captn & Mst Dedicated Awd For Vlybl; Michigan St Univ; Bio Sci.

CARBARY, ROXIANNE; Whitmore Lake HS; Whitmore Lk, MI; 17/85 Chrs; Hon Rl; Jr NHS; Natl Forn Lg; NHS; PAVAS; Sch Mus; Sch Pl; Yrbk; Drama Clb; Central Michigan Univ; Bus Mgmt.

CARBENO, DAVID; Eisenhower HS; Saginaw, MI; Band; Boy Scts; Cmnty Wkr; Hon Rl; Sct Actv; Stg Crw; Letter Ten; Northwood Inst; Hotel Mgmt.

CARBONE, CAROL; Magnificat HS; North Olmsted, OH; NHS; Stg Crw; Yrbk; Letter Crs Cntry; Rotary Awd; Univ; Archt Engr.

CARD, KATHY; Kearsley Community HS; Flint, MI; 27/378 Band; Boy Scts; Chrh Wkr; Hon Rl; Natl Forn Lg; NHS; Sch Pl; Mic State; Pre Vet.

CARD, SUZANNE; Merrill HS; Midland, MI; 2/120 Sal; Hon Rl; NHS; Off Ade; Delta College; Bus Mgmy.

CARDAMAN, SCOTT; Maple Hts Sr HS; Maple Hgts, OH; Cls Rep Sr Cls; Bsktbl; Letter Ftbl; Trk; Letter Wrstlng; Coll; Law.

CARDER, ALICIA A; Covington HS; Covington, OH; 23/80 VP Soph Cls; Hon Rl; Lbry Ade; Fr Clb; Letter Bsktbl; Coach Actv; PPFtbl; Varsity Girls Sftbl Ltr 9 10 11 2nd Tm All Lg 79; Varsity Girls Bsktbl Hnrbl Mention All Lg 10 & 11th; Univ; Asst Vet.

CARDER, JACKQUELYN; Liberty HS; Salem, WV; Am Leg Aux Girls St; Chrh Wkr; Hon Rl; Jr NHS; Sch Mus; Stg Crw; Yth Flsp; Drama Clb; Fr Clb; Univ; Paralegal.

CARDER, MARTY; Monongah HS; Four States, WV; 10/52 VP Sr Cls; Am Leg Boys St; Treas NHS; Stu Cncl; Fr Clb; Capt Bsktbl; Capt Ftbl; Trk; Am Leg Awd; Elk Awd; Fairmont St Coll.

CARDER, MICHELE; Marysville HS; Marysville, OH; Band; Chrs; Drl Tm; Sch Mus; Sch Pl; 4-H; Lat Clb; Sci Clb; Scr Kpr; Univ; Hist.

CARDER, RHONDA; Flemington HS; Grafton, WV; 4/48 Pres Soph Cls; Trs Sr Cls; Band; Chrh Wkr; Hon Rl; Pres NHS; Pep Clb; Pres VICA; Bsktbl; Chrldng; Alderson Broddus Coll; Med Asst.

CARDOSI, SHARON M; St Ursula Acad; Cincinnati, OH; Hon Rl; NHS; College; Nurse.

CARDUCCI, LAURA; Mount Vernon Academy; Ashtabula, OH; Band; Chrs; Girl Scts; Hon Rl; Orch; Sch Pl; Letter Trk; GAA; IM Sprt; Tmr; Band Awd 78; Swimming 10 Miles 76; Andrews Univ; Conservtn.

CARDWELL, ANITA; Ironton HS; Ironton, OH; Band; Chrh Wkr; Cmnty Wkr; Sch Mus; 4-H; 4-H Awd; Ohio State; Social Work.

CARDWELL, JULIE; Ben Davis HS; Indianapolis, IN; 112/853 FCA; Quill & Scroll; Stu Cncl; Sch Nwsp; Lat Clb; Pep Clb; Letter Glf; Trk; Mat Maids; PPFtbl; Indiana Univ; Cmnctns.

CARDWELL, SCOTT; Crestview HS; Mansfield, OH; Sec Band; Hon Rl; Pres Yth Flsp; VP Spn Clb; Letter Bsbl; Letter Bsktbl; Bowling Green State Univ; Phys Ther.

CARDWELL, STAN; Hedgesville HS; Hedgesville, WV; 10/250 Hon Rl; Sci Clb; Trk; Marshal Univ; Biological.

CARDY, CHERYL; Whitehall Sr HS; Whitehall, MI; Hon Rl; NHS; Ed Yrbk; Sch Nwsp; Univ.

CAREK, JERRY; Brookside HS; Sheffield Lake, OH; Mth Clb; Sci Clb; Bsktbl; Ftbl; Wrstlng; Toledo College; Med.

CARELS, JACQUELINE A; Warren HS; Sterling Hgts, MI; 1/403 Chrs; Debate Tm; Hon Rl; Natl Forn Lg; NHS; Pol Wkr; Sch Mus; Sch Pl; Drama Clb; Opt Clb Awd; Wayne St Univ; Math.

CARENDER, NEIL H; Eastern Hancock Jr Sr HS; Charlottesville, IN; 2/108 VP Sr Cls; Hon Rl; Pres NHS; Rptr Yrbk; Letter Ten; Natl Merit SF; Univ; Elec Engr.

CARESS, PATRICIA M; Park Tudor HS; Indianapolis, IN; Pres Frsh Cls; Cls Rep Soph Cls; Chrs; Chrh Wkr; Girl Scts; Hon Rl; Sch Mus; Sch Pl; Stg Crw; Civ Clb; Cum Laude Comm 1975; Univ; Bus Admin.

CAREY, ANNE; Holland HS; Holland, MI; VP Frsh Cls; Cls Rep Frsh Cls; Cls Rep Soph Cls; Cls Rep Sr Cls; Pres Band; Drm Mjrt; Hon Rl; NHS; Off Ade; Treas Stu Cncl; Hope Coll; Psych.

CAREY, ANNE; Farmington HS; Farmington, MI; Hon Rl; Pep Clb; Spn Clb; Loyola Univ; Lang.

CAREY, ARTHUR M; Chalker HS; Southington, OH; 3/85 Band; Chrs; Beta Clb; Bsbl; Musician.

CAREY, DANIEL; Walnut Hills HS; Cincinnati, OH; Hon Rl; Lit Mag; Sch Nwsp; Crs Cntry; Trk; Tmr; Univ; Zoology.

CAREY, DAVID L; Solon HS; Solon, OH; 23/288 Cmnty Wkr; Hon Rl; Pol Wkr; Key Clb; Bsbl; Bsktbl; Miami Univ; Bus Admin.

CAREY, ELIZABETH; John F Kennedy HS; Taylor, MI; 10/414 Band; Chrh Wkr; Hon Rl; NHS; Cit Awd; Wayne St Univ; Lib Arts.

CAREY, GLORIA; Marine City Ward Cottrel HS; Marine City, MI; 12/200 Hon Rl; Hosp Ade; NHS; Sch Pl; Rptr Yrbk; Rptr Sch Nwsp; Ten; Trk; Chrldng; Pom Pon; Michigan St Univ; Mktg.

CAREY, JENNIFER; North HS; Springfield, OH; Band; Chrs; Cmnty Wkr; Hon Rl; Orch; Sch Mus; Sch Pl; Rptr Sch Nwsp; Eng Clb; Univ.

CAREY, JON; Dexter HS; Dexter, MI; Am Leg Boys St; Band; Hon Rl; Lit Mag; Stg Crw; Drama Clb; Ger Clb; Letter Crs Cntry; Natl Merit Ltr; Michigan St Univ.

CAREY, KRISTI; Orchard View HS; Muskegon, MI; Cl Rep Jr Cls; Band; Hon Rl; Red Cr Ade; Stu Cncl; Rptr Yrbk; Rptr Sch Nwsp; Sch Nwsp; Pom Pon; Tmr; Muskegon Bus Coll; Acctg.

CAREY, LISA; Springfield HS; Springfield, MI; Chrs; Chrh Wkr; Cmnty Wkr; Hon Rl; Hosp Ade; Sch Mus; Sch Pl; Stg Crw; Drama Clb; Schslp Cert 78 & 79; Western Michigan Univ; Cmnctns.

CAREY, LYNN; Turpin HS; Cincinnati, OH; Sec Jr Cls; Chrh Wkr; Orch; Sch Mus; Yth Flsp; Letter Gym; Chrldng; Univ.

CAREY, RHONDA; Wilmington HS; Wilmington, OH; Stu Cncl; Fr Clb; Pep Clb; Bsbl; Chrldng; IM Sprt; Mat Maids; Coll; Teaching.

CAREY, ROBIN; Sidney HS; Sidney, OH; Chrs; Sch Mus; VP Stu Cncl; Yrbk; Treas Drama Clb; Pres 4-H; Ger Clb; Socr; Coach Actv; 4-H Awd; Miami Univ; Photo Journalism.

CARINELLI, JEANNEINE; Bluefield HS; Bluefld, WV; 17/350 Pres Frsh Cls; Cls Rep Soph Cls; Cl Rep Jr Cls; Cls Rep Sr Cls; Hon Rl; NHS; Fr Clb; Chrldng; Cit Awd; Bluefield State; Nursing.

CARINO, TERESA; Marian HS; Troy, MI; Cls Rep Sr Cls; Chrh Wkr; Girl Scts; Hon Rl; Mod UN; IM Sprt; Scr Kpr; Univ; Law Enforcement.

CARK, BRENDA; Clinton HS; Tipton, MI; Band; Cmp Fr Grls; Chrs; Chrh Wkr; Girl Scts; Hon Rl; Sct Actv; Sprt Ed Sch Nwsp; Rptr Sch Nwsp; Pep Clb; Bowling Green St Univ; CPA.

CARL, JANET; Brooke HS; Colliers, WV; 46/408 Hon Rl; Jr NHS; NHS; Pol Wkr; Spn Clb; College; Nursing.

CARL, KATHLEEN; Sylvania Northview HS; Toledo, OH; Pres AFS; Chrs; Hon Rl; Natl Forn Lg; Miami Univ; Bus.

CARL, PATRICIA S; Edgewood HS; Bloomington, IN; 10/223 Band; Hon Rl; Sch Mus; Sch Pl; Drama Clb; Ger Clb; Indiana Univ; Music.

CARLE, PATTY; Westfall HS; Circleville, OH; 1/120 Trs Sr Cls; Am Leg Aux Girls St; Band; Chrh Wkr; Hon Rl; NHS; Orch; VP FNA; FTA; Sci Clb; Univ; Acctg.

CARLETON, ALLISON; Delaware Hayes HS; Delaware, OH; AFS; Treas Band; Hon Rl; Y-Teens; Letter Gym; Natl Merit SF; Selectd To Rep Class In Eng Div OTSA 79; Bronze Medl For Acad Achvmnt 78; Silver Medl For Acad Achvmnt 79; Ohio St Univ.

CARLETON, LISA; Talawanda HS; Oxford, OH; 6/321 AFS; Am Leg Aux Girls St; Band; Chrh Wkr; Hon Rl; Jr NHS; NHS; Drama Clb; Capt Hockey; Letter Trk; Miami Univ; Envir Sci.

CARLIN, DIANE; Newark Cath HS; Newark, OH; Hon Rl; NHS; PAVAS; 4-H; Pep Clb; Gym; Chrldng; GAA; IM Sprt; Univ Of San Diego; Vet.

CARLIN, KAREN; Corunna HS; Corunna, MI; 60/300 Cls Rep Soph Cls; Cl Rep Jr Cls; Cls Rep Sr Cls; Chrs; Chrh Wkr; Cmnty Wkr; Drm Mjrt; Girl Scts; JA; Off Ade; Univ; Data Processing.

CARLINI, THOMAS; Jackson HS; Canton, OH; 63/409 Boy Scts; FCA; Yth Flsp; Key Clb; Crs Cntry; Trk; Massillon Indepndnts Teenager Of Month 79; Natl Hon Soc Schlshp 79; Y Teen Man Of Month 79; Univ Of Arizona; Civil Engr.

CARLISLE, ALAN; Greenhills HS; Cincinnati, OH; 90/254 Chrh Wkr; Capt Glf; Coll; Comp Sci.

CARLISLE, JAMES; Washington HS; Massillon, OH; Boy Scts; Chrh Wkr; Hon Rl; Sct Actv; Fr Clb; Sci Clb; Spn Clb; Letter Swmmng; Trk; Coach Actv; Amer River Coll; Forestry.

CARLISLE, JOYCE; Mt View HS; Vivian, WV; Pres Frsh Cls; Sec Jr Cls; Band; Chrh Wkr; Drl Tm; Hon Rl; Hosp Ade; Jr NHS; Stu Cncl; Yth Flsp; 2nd Pl In FBLA Conf At Concord Coll 79; Youngstown Univ; Exec Sec.

CARLISLE, LORI C; Grandview Heights HS; Columbus, OH; Aud/Vis; Chrs; Chrh Wkr; Drl Tm; Sch Mus; Stu Cncl; Yth Flsp; Yrbk; Pep Clb; Hockey; Otterbein Private Methodist Coll.

CARLISLE, MARCY; Jonesville HS; Jonesville, MI; Cmp Fr Grls; Cmnty Wkr; Off Ade; Mgrs; Bus Schl; Fshn Mdse.

CARLISLE, TIM; Indian Valley North HS; New Philadelph, OH; Cls Rep Frsh Cls; Pres Jr Cls; Band; Hon Rl; NHS; Stg Crw; Stu Cncl; Yrbk; Sch Nwsp; FTA; Univ.

CARLISLE, TIMOTHY; Indian Vly North HS; New Phila, OH; Cls Rep Frsh Cls; Pres Jr Cls; Band; Hon Rl; Stu Cncl; Yrbk; Sch Nwsp; FTA; Spn Clb; Ten; Univ.

CARLISLE, WILMA; Northridge HS; Dayton, OH; 10/225 Cls Rep Sr Cls; Am Leg Aux Girls St; Lit Mag; NHS; Stu Cncl; Yth Flsp; Sprt Ed Yrbk; Pres Key Clb; Letter Hockey; Letter Trk; Whos Who 78 79; Wright St Univ; Bus.

CARLOCK, MICHAEL; Hartford HS; Hartford, MI; Ftbl; Wrstlng;.

CARLOW, DEBORAH; Switzerland Cnty Jr Sr HS; Vevay, IN; 6/130 Hon Rl; NHS; 4-H; Fr Clb; Pep Clb; Letter Bsktbl; 4-H Awd; Univ.

CARLSON, BETH; St Joseph HS; Galesburg, MI; Cl Rep Jr Cls; Band; Cmnty Wkr; Hon Rl; Orch; Sch Mus; Rptr Yrbk; Drama Clb; Trk; Michigan Tech Univ; Med.

CARLSON, CATHY; South Newton Jr Sr HS; Brook, IN; 23/125 Band; Cmnty Wkr; Girl Scts; Hon Rl; Hosp Ade; Sch Mus; Sch Pl; Pres 4-H; VP FBLA; FHA; Univ; Bus.

CARLSON, CHRISTOPHER; Clermont Northeastern HS; Batavia, OH; Cls Rep Soph Cls; Band; Boy Scts; Chrh Wkr; FCA; Stu Cncl; Yth Flsp; 4-H; Bsktbl; Ten; Univ; Music.

CARLSON, COLLEEN; R Nelson Snider HS; Ft Wayne, IN; 32/560 Chrh Wkr; Hon Rl; Sch Mus; Sch Pl; Fr Clb; Univ; Med Tech.

CARLSON, ERIC; Big Rapids HS; Big Rapids, MI; 1/190 Trs Frsh Cls; Cls Rep Frsh Cls; Cls Rep Soph Cls; Cl Rep Jr Cls; Band; Debate Tm; Hon Rl; Jr NHS; Natl Forn Lg; NHS; Univ; Elec Engr.

CARLSON, J; Ontario HS; Mansfield, OH; 8/180 Cls Rep Frsh Cls; Cls Rep Soph Cls; AFS; Band; Chrh Wkr; Jr NHS; Sec Stu Cncl; Ed Yrbk; Bsktbl; GAA; College; Bus.

CARLSON, JAN; Ontario HS; Mnsfld, OH; 8/180 Cls Rep Frsh Cls; Cls Rep Soph Cls; AFS; Band; Chrh Wkr; Hon Rl; Jr NHS; NHS; Stu Cncl; Ed Yrbk; Univ; Bus.

CARLSON, JANA; Lowell HS; Ada, MI; 6/217 Band; Cmp Fr Grls; Chrh Wkr; Hon Rl; JA; Spn Clb; Trk; Butterworth Schl Of Nursing; Nurse.

CARLSON, JEAN M; Valparaiso HS; Valparaiso, IN; 1/475 Am Leg Aux Girls St; Chrs; Chrh Wkr; FCA; Hon Rl; NHS; Stu Cncl; Eng Clb; Spn Clb; Letter Swmmng; Univ; Chem.

CARLSON, LAURA; Yellow Springs HS; Yellow Sprg, OH; 9/75 Sec Frsh Cls; Sec Soph Cls; Sec Jr Cls; Band; Chrs; NHS; Sch Mus; Letter Socr; College.

CARLSON, LINDA; Troy HS; Sandy, UT; Band; Hon Rl; NHS; Swmmng; Trk; College; Communications.

CARLSON, MARK; Princeton Community HS; Princeton, IN; Band; Chrh Wkr; Drl Tm; Hon Rl; Mth Clb; Sci Clb; Letter Bsbl; Coach Actv; Am Leg Awd; Univ; Sci.

CARLSON, NANCY; Hammond Tech Voc HS; Hammond, IN; 1/220 Hon Rl; NHS; Pres PAVAS; Sch Mus; Sch Pl; Stg Crw; Yrbk; Letter Bsktbl; Capt Trk; Am Leg Awd; Indiana Univ; Performing Arts.

CARLSON, PETE; Pine River HS; Tustin, MI; VP Sr Cls; Hon Rl; NHS; Ferris St Coll; Medicine.

CARLSON, RAINE; Merrillville HS; Merrillville, IN; 148/603 Chrh Wkr; Girl Scts; Hon Rl; Sct Actv; VP FTA; Ger Clb; GAA; PPFtbl; 1st Class Girl Scout 77; Indiana St Univ; Bus Admin.

CARLSON, RAYMOND; Decatur HS; Dowagiac, MI; VP Frsh Cls; VP Soph Cls; Hon Rl; NHS; Wrstlng; Coll; Bio.

CARLSON, RAYMOND; Canfield HS; Canfield, OH; Boy Scts; Cmnty Wkr; Hon Rl; Sprt Ed Yrbk; Rptr Sch Nwsp; Spn Clb; Bsbl; Bsktbl; IM Sprt; Ohio Northern Univ; Pharm.

CARLSON, ROGER; Maplewood HS; Cortland, OH; 11/89 Chrh Wkr; Hon Rl; VP NHS; Pres Yth Flsp; Beta Clb; Crs Cntry; Trk; Tmr; Natl Merit SF; Youngstown St Univ; Mass Cmnctns.

CARLSON, SCOTT; Flushing Sr HS; Flushing, MI; Boy Scts; Chrh Wkr; Hon Rl; NHS; Stu Cncl; Letter Bsbl; Letter Bsktbl; Letter Ftbl; Coach Actv; Cit Awd; Pres Of Natl Hon Soc 79; Mi Youth Leadrshp Smnr As Outstndng Soph For Hugh O Brian Leadrshp Progr 78; Coll; Pre Med.

CARLSON, SHARON; Cadillac Sr HS; Cadillac, MI; Chrs; Chrh Wkr; Hon Rl; Letter Natl Forn Lg; Sch Mus; 4-H; PPFtbl; Central Michigan Univ.

CARLSON, SUSANMARIE; Belleville HS; Belleville, MI; Band; Drm Mjrt; Hon Rl; Lbry Ade; Yth Flsp; Mgrs; Twrlr; 1st Pl In Schl Wide Art Show 79; Western Michigan Univ; Art Educ.

CARLSON, TRACY; Calumet HS; Mohawk, MI; 3/159 Hon Rl; NHS; ROTC; Stu Cncl; Rptr Sch Nwsp; Varsity & Jr Varsity Rifle Team Ctpn 78 79; Recpt Schl Suptnd Ldrshp 79; Slctd Gattalion Cmdr JROTC 79; Michigan Tech Univ; Engr.

CARLSON, VICKI; Grand Ledge HS; Lansing, MI; 1/475 Band; Chrh Wkr; Cmnty Wkr; Debate Tm; Hon Rl; NHS; Stg Crw; Spn Clb; Lansing Comm Coll; Psych.

CARLSTROM, SANDY L; Hartland HS; Hartland, MI; Hon Rl; Pom Pon; College.

CARMAN, BRAD; Fort Frye HS; Beverly, OH; Band; Hon Rl; NHS; Orch; Sch Mus; Yth Flsp; Eng Clb; Bsktbl; Univ; Physician.

CARMAN, CHARLES D; Stow HS; Stow, OH; Chrh Wkr; Hon Rl; NHS; Sch Pl; Stg Crw; Mth Clb; Bsktbl; IM Sprt; Acad Challenge Team Mbr 78; Superior Achvmnt Recgntn In St Math Exam 79; David Lipscomb Coll; Math.

CARMEAN, JOHN; Malabar HS; Mansfield, OH; VP Soph Cls; Hon Rl; Letter Trk; IM Sprt; Univ; Bus.

CARMEN, CATHY; Whiteland Community HS; Franklin, IN; 11/219 AFS; Chrs; Cmnty Wkr; Drl Tm; FCA; Hon Rl; Sch Pl; Stu Cncl; Yth Flsp; 4-H; Univ; Soc Sci.

CARMER, CINDY; Plymouth Salem HS; Plymouth, MI; Chrh Wkr; Hon Rl; Off Ade; Grand Rapids Schl Of Bible; Music.

CARMICHAEL, AMY; East Liverpool HS; E Liverpool, OH; 1/366 Val; Chrh Wkr; Girl Scts; Hon Rl; NHS; Stg Crw; Sch Nwsp; Spn Clb; Letter Bsktbl; Chosen For Independent Study Progr 78; Univ; Pre Med.

CARMICHAEL, ANITA; Hartford HS; Watervliet, MI; Trs Jr Cls; Band; Hon Rl; Mod UN; NHS; Off Ade; Sch Pl; Sch Nwsp; Chrldng; Pom Pon; College; Journalism.

CARMICHAEL, FELECIA; Linden Mc Kinley HS; Columbus, OH; 11/268 Cls Rep Frsh Cls; Cl Rep Jr Cls; Cls Rep Sr Cls; Hon Rl; JA; Stu Cncl; Bsktbl; Ten; Capital Univ; Law.

CARMICHAEL, MARK; Shaker Heights HS; Shaker Hts, OH; 74/556 Chrs; Hon Rl; Jr NHS; NHS; Letter Crs Cntry; Letter Ftbl; Letter Trk; IM Sprt; Natl Merit SF; San Diego St Univ; Bus Admin.

CARMONY, KEVIN; St Francis De Sales HS; Perrysburg, OH; 16/223 Cls Rep Frsh Cls; Cls Rep Soph Cls; Cl Rep Jr Cls; Hon Rl; NHS; Stu Cncl; Rptr Sch Nwsp; Capt Swmmng; Coach Actv; IM Sprt; John Carroll Univ; Pre Med.

CARNAGUA, D JEFFREY; Franklin Central HS; Indianapolis, IN; 8/247 Treas NHS; Quill & Scroll; Sch Pl; Stu Cncl; Sch Nwsp; Pep Clb; Letter Crs Cntry; Trk; Natl Merit SF; Indiana Central; Acctg.

CARNAHAN, DENNIS; Ayersville HS; Defiance, OH; Boy Scts; Chrs; Hon Rl; Boys Clb Am; Wrstlng; Northwest Tech Schl; Drafting.

CARNAHAN, SANDRA; Howell HS; Howell, MI; 17/435 Hon Rl; NHS; 4-H;.

CARNEGIE, JYME; Bloomington HS N; Bloomington, IN; Chrh Wkr; Girl Scts; Hon Rl; Jr NHS; NHS; Off Ade; Yrbk; Mat Maids; PPFtbl; Hoosier Schlr 79; Photo Ed Awd 79; Indiana Univ; Dent Hygn.

CARNEGIS, KEN; Dayton Christian HS; Dayton, OH; Hon Rl; Letter Ten; Letter Trk; Voice Dem Awd; Univ Of Cincinnati; Mech Engr.

CARNES, BRUCE; Tippecanoe Valley HS; Rochester, IN; 15/180 Band; Hon Rl; NHS; 4-H; Swmmng; 4-H Awd; Purdue Univ; Aviation.

CARNES, CATHE; Southern Wells Jr Sr HS; Poneto, IN; 11/96 Chrs; Hon Rl; NHS; Sec 4-H; Dnfth Awd; 4-H Awd; Butler Univ; Fashion Mdse.

CARNES, KELLY; Southern Wells HS; Poneto, IN; Hon Rl; NHS; Pep Clb; Pom Pon; PPFtbl; Ball St Univ; Bus Instrctr.

CARNES, KEVIN; Richmond HS; Richmond, IN; 165/602 Cls Rep Frsh Cls; Cl Rep Jr Cls; Cls Rep Sr Cls; Hon Rl; Jr NHS; Lit Mag; Quill & Scroll; Stu Cncl; Y-Teens; Rptr Sch Nwsp; Miami Univ; Systems Analysis.

CARNES, L; Galesburg Augusta HS; Galesburg, MI; 1/109 Sec Frsh Cls; Band; Hon Rl; Stu Cncl; Sch Nwsp; 4-H; Key Clb; Chrldng; Cit Awd; Dnfth Awd; Univ; Art.

CARNES, LORIE; Malvern HS; Malvern, OH; VP Frsh Cls; Cl Rep Jr Cls; Hon Rl; Off Ade; Stu Cncl; Yrbk; Pep Clb; Trk; Chrldng; Cit Awd; Bowling Green Univ; Health.

CARNES, SHIRLEY E; Heath HS; Heath, OH; 8/160 Band; Hon Rl; NHS; Sch Pl; Pres Yth Flsp; Drama Clb; Attending Cumberland Coll In Summer On Schlrshp 79; Univ.

CARNEY, DENISE; Oakridge HS; Muskegon, MI; 1/118 Val; Band; Hosp Ade; NHS; Dnfth Awd; Western Mic Univ; Dent.

CARNEY, GARY; Cardinal HS; Middlefield, OH; 2/104 AFS; Chrs; Hon Rl; Pres NHS; Sch Mus; Sch Pl; Yrbk; Rptr Sch Nwsp; Letter Crs Cntry; Mgrs; Danforth I Dare You Awd 79; Kiwanis Outstanding Freshman Awd 77; Schlstc Tm 77 78 & 79; Univ Of Connecticut; Psych.

CARNEY, JOSEPH B; Park Tudor HS; Indianapolis, IN; VP Frsh Cls; VP Soph Cls; Pres Jr Cls; Band; Hon Rl; Orch; Sch Mus; Sct Actv; Yth Flsp; Key Clb; Track Coach Awd; College; Math.

CARNEY, LANCE; Dunbar HS; Dunbar, WV; 5/168 Boy Scts; Hon Rl; Jr NHS; NHS; Off Ade; Stu Cncl; Rptr Yrbk; Mth Clb; Pep Clb; Spn Clb; Camp Horseshoe Ldrshp Camp 78; Tuiton Schlrshp Marshall Univ 79; Top Ten Stu 79; Marshall Univ; Pharm.

CARNEY, PAIGE; Winfield HS; Scott Depot, WV; Cls Rep Frsh Cls; Hon Rl; Jr NHS; Fr Clb; FHA; Pep Clb; Glf; Ten; Chrldng; College; Education.

CARNINE, GLENN; Southwestern Shelby Co HS; Flat Rock, IN; 12/64 Boy Scts; Chrs; Chrh Wkr; FCA; Sct Actv; Yth Flsp; FSA; Key Clb; Pep Clb; Sci Clb; Univ Of Evansville; Engr.

CARNLEY, CINDY E; Grant HS; Grant, MI; Girl Scts; Hon Rl; FBLA; Pep Clb; Dietician.

CARO, DINORAH; Calvin Christian HS; Grandville, MI; Band; Hosp Ade; Lbry Ade; Red Cr Ade; Stg Crw; Ed Sch Nwsp; Rptr Sch Nwsp; Sch Nwsp; Drama Clb; Letter Pom Pon; Calvin Coll; Home Ec.

CARO, JOSEPH; Huntington HS; Huntington, WV; Cl Rep Jr Cls; Am Leg Boys St; Hon Rl; Jr NHS; NHS; Pol Wkr; Red Cr Ade; Pres Stu Cncl; VP Lat Clb; Mth Clb; Comp In Wv St Track Tournmt 79; Univ; Bus Admin.

CAROLAN, KIRK; Owendale Gagetown HS; Gagetown, MI; VP Frsh Cls; VP Sr Cls; Hon Rl; Sch Pl; Bsbl; Ftbl; Trk; Coach Actv; Univ; Phys Educ.

CAROLEN, CAROLYN; Highland Park Comm HS; Highland Pk, MI; Cmp Fr Grls; Chrs; Chrh Wkr; Cmnty Wkr; JA; Lbry Ade; PAVAS; Sch Mus; Sch Pl; Pep Clb; Michigan St Univ; Busns Comm.

CAROW, JANELLE T; Marquette HS; Michigan City, IN; 19/75 Chrs; Hon Rl; NHS; Sch Mus; Stg Crw; Stu Cncl; Rptr Sch Nwsp; Drama Clb; Ger Clb; Sci Clb; Indiana Univ.

CARPENTER, BRIAN; Amanda Clearcreek HS; Lancaster, OH; Boy Scts; Chrh Wkr; Hon Rl; Stg Crw; Stu Cncl; College.

CARPENTER, BRIAN; Columbia HS; Columbia Sta, OH; Hon Rl; Bsktbl; Ftbl; Lorian Cnty Joint Voc Schl; Elec.

CARPENTER, BUDDY; Windham HS; Windham, OH; Am Leg Boys St; Chrs; Chrh Wkr; Hon Rl; Sch Pl; Stu Cncl; Ed Yrbk; Spn Clb; Bsktbl; Trk; Mount Vernon Nazarene Coll; Coach.

CARPENTER, CARMEN; Plymouth Canton HS; Canton, MI; Chrs; Girl Scts; Hon Rl; JA; Off Ade; Sch Pl; Drama Clb; 4-H; FDA; Coll; Nursing.

CARPENTER, CAROLINE; Upper Arlington HS; Columbus, OH; 108/617 Cmnty Wkr; Hon Rl; Hosp Ade; FDA; Ger Clb; Ten; GAA; JA Awd; Pres Awd; Air Force Academy.

CARPENTER, CARRIE; Cass City HS; Deford, MI; Cls Rep Frsh Cls; Cls Rep Soph Cls; Band; Debate Tm; Girl Scts; Hon Rl; Jr NHS; Natl Forn Lg; NHS; Off Ade; Michigan St Univ; Comp Mktg.

CARPENTER, CRAIG; Hillsdale HS; Hillsdale, MI; Cls Rep Frsh Cls; Boy Scts; Chrh Wkr; Pres Yth Flsp; 4-H; 4-H Awd; Mic State Univ; Vet.

CARPENTER, DEBRA; Carlisle Sr HS; Franklin, OH; Drl Tm; Off Ade; Spn Clb; Letter Bsbl; Trk; Univ.

CARPENTER, DEIDRE; Brookhaven HS; Columbus, OH; 72/429 Cmp Fr Grls; Chrs; Drl Tm; Hon Rl; Ed Yrbk; Rptr Yrbk; DECA; Fr Clb; Scr Kpr; Ohio St Univ; Psych.

CARPENTER, DIANE; John Glenn HS; Bay City, MI; Hon Rl; Sch Mus; Rptr Yrbk; Gym; Chrldng; PPFtbl; Michigan St Univ; Bus.

CARPENTER, DONNA; Wayne Memorial HS; Westland, MI; Cls Rep Soph Cls; Cl Rep Jr Cls; Cls Rep Sr Cls; Chrs; Cmnty Wkr; Debate Tm; Girl Scts; Hon Rl; NHS; Off Ade; Outstndng Service Awd From Intl Order Of Rainbow For Girls; Univ Of Michigan; Psych.

CARPENTER, DONNA; Fairland HS; Proctorvll, OH; VP Frsh Cls; Cls Rep Frsh Cls; VP Soph Cls; Cls Rep Soph Cls; Cl Rep Jr Cls; Cls Rep Sr Cls; Band; Girl Scts; Hon Rl; Stu Cncl; College.

CARPENTER, ELIZABETH; St Marys HS; St Marys, WV; Am Leg Aux Girls St; Band; NHS; Red Cr Ade; Sch Pl; Rptr Yrbk; Rptr Sch Nwsp; Drama Clb; PPFtbl; Glenville St Coll; Elem Ed.

CARPENTER, JULIE; Chillicothe HS; Chillicothe, OH; 24/380 AFS; Hon Rl; Jr NHS; NHS; Off Ade; VP Spn Clb; Natl Merit Ltr; Ohio Board Of Regents Schlshp Awd 79; Ohio Univ Anonymous Schlrhp 79; Ohio Univ; Comp Tech.

CARPENTER, K; Port Clinton HS; Pt Clinton, OH; Cls Rep Frsh Cls; Cls Rep Soph Cls; Cl Rep Jr Cls; Band; Hon Rl; Stu Cncl; Ger Clb; Trk; Univ; Foreign Languages.

CARPENTER, KATHY; Dondero HS; Royal Oak, MI; 62/400 Hon Rl; Chrldng; Mgrs; Mat Maids; PPFtbl; Scr Kpr; Coll; Busns Mgmt.

CARPENTER, KIMBERLY; Bloomfield School District; Newberry, IN; 13/83 Sec Sr Cls; Band; FCA; Hon Rl; Yrbk; Drama Clb; Pep Clb; Spn Clb; Mgrs; Indiana St Univ.

CARPENTER, LESLIE; Washington Irving HS; Clarksburg, WV; 23/139 Am Leg Boys St; Chrs; Hon Rl; Mdrgl; NHS; Sch Mus; Sch Pl; Lat Clb; Pres Leo Clb; SAR Awd; Fairmont State Coll; Acctg.

CARPENTER, LYNDA; Pittsford HS; Pittsford, MI; 8/58 Chrh Wkr; Hon Rl; NHS; Stu Cncl; FHA; Spn Clb; Houghton Coll; Elem Educ.

CARPENTER, LYNN; Yellow Springs HS; Yellow Springs, OH; 2/78 VP Frsh Cls; VP Soph Cls; Sec Jr Cls; Sec Sr Cls; Sal; Jr NHS; NHS; Sch Pl; Letter Spn Clb; Letter Socr; Wright St Univ.

CARPENTER, MARY; Barnesville HS; Barnesville, OH; 10/102 Girl Scts; Hon Rl; Hosp Ade; Sec 4-H; Fr Clb; FHA; GAA; IM Sprt; Scr Kpr; 4-H Awd; Otterbien Univ; Forest Ranger.

CARPENTER, NANCY; Paw Paw HS; Paw Paw, MI; Hon Rl; NHS; Off Ade; Letter Trk; Natl Merit Schl; Western Michigan Univ.

CARPENTER, NINA; Hagerstown Jr Sr HS; Hagerstown, IN; Cmnty Wkr; FCA; Girl Scts; Hon Rl; Y-Teens; Rptr Yrbk; OEA; Pep Clb; Ten; Chrldng; 3rd Pl Job Manual Unemployed At Indiana St Ofc Ed Assn Cont; Ball State Univ; Data Processing.

CARPENTER, REGENIA; Cedar Lake Academy; South Haven, MI; 10/100 VP Frsh Cls; Cls Rep Frsh Cls; Sec Soph Cls; Cls Rep Soph Cls; Cl Rep Jr Cls; Chrh Wkr; Hon Rl; NHS; Off Ade; Stu Cncl; Columbia Union Coll; Med.

CARPENTER, RENEE; Groveport Madison HS; Winchester, OH; Pres Frsh Cls; Pres Soph Cls; Chrs; Hon Rl; Sch Pl; Stu Cncl; Drama Clb; College; Phystry.

CARPENTER, RONALD; Webster County HS; Webstersprg, WV; Boy Scts; Chrs; Rptr Sch Nwsp; Wv Univ; Mining Engr.

CARPENTER, S; Comstock Park Secondary HS; Comstock Pk, MI; Hon Rl; Sch Mus; Sch Pl; Sprt Ed Yrbk; Letter Ftbl; Letter Trk; Letter Wrstlng; Coll; Archt.

CARPENTER, SHARON; Cadiz HS; Cadiz, OH; Chrs; Hosp Ade; Lbry Ade; Mgrs; College; Nursing.

CARPENTER, SHENAN L; Kenton Sr HS; Kenton, OH; Hon Rl; Sch Mus; Sch Pl; Stg Crw; Rptr Yrbk; Rptr Sch Nwsp; Pres Drama Clb; Bluffton Coll; Elem Ed.

CARPENTER, STEPHANIE; Broad Ripple HS; Indianapolis, IN; Chrs; Cmnty Wkr; Hon Rl; NHS; Orch; PAVAS; Sch Mus; Sch Pl; College; Forestry.

CARPENTER, TERI; Jenison HS; Jenison, MI; 1/342 Cls Rep Frsh Cls; Cls Rep Soph Cls; VP Jr Cls; Band; Hon Rl; NHS; Sch Pl; Stu Cncl; Pep Clb; Letter Chrldng; College; Broadcasting.

CARPENTER, TERRI; Athens HS; Athens, MI; 17/87 Hon Rl; Lbry Ade; NHS; Off Ade; Yth Flsp;.

CARPENTER, TIM; Collinwood HS; Cleveland, OH; 27/224 Hon Rl; Jr NHS; NHS; Glf; IM Sprt; Cit Awd; College; Bus.

CARPENTER, VAL; Atherton HS; Burton, MI; Band; Girl Scts; Hon Rl; Sch Pl; Sct Actv; Sci Clb; Mat Maids; Univ Of Michigan; Phys Ther.

CARPENTER, VICKI; Willard HS; Willad, OH; Chrh Wkr; Jr NHS; Orch; Sch Mus; Yth Flsp; Capt Crs Cntry; Letter Trk; Capt Chrldng; IM Sprt; Tech College.

CARPENTER, WESLEY; Independence HS; Coal City, WV; 3/157 Cls Rep Frsh Cls; Cls Rep Soph Cls; Cl Rep Jr Cls; Hon Rl; Treas NHS; Pres Stu Cncl; Beta Clb; FHA; Pres VICA; Dnfth Awd; Chemistry Awd; 4 H; Masonic; Concord Coll; Acctg.

CARPER, JEFFRY D; Madison Heights HS; Anderson, IN; Cls Rep Frsh Cls; Bowling; Mgr Of T League Team; Ball St Univ; Busns.

CARPER, KIMBERLEY; Jefferson HS; Charlestown, WV; Band; Hon Rl; Lbry Ade; Bsbl; Bsktbl; Coach Actv; GAA; IM Sprt; College; Phsyical Educ.

CARPICO, JOSEPH; Jefferson Union HS; Bloomingdale, OH; 1/156 Pres Jr Cls; Val; Am Leg Boys St; Boy Scts; Chrs; Hon Rl; Sch Mus; Sct Actv; VP Stu Cncl; Rptr Sch Nwsp; U S Air Force Acad; Engr.

CARPICO, LAWRENCE; Jefferson Union HS; Bloomingdale, OH; Am Leg Boys St; Am Leg Aux Girls St; Chrs; Hon Rl; Sch Mus; Stu Cncl; Yrbk; Beta Clb; Drama Clb; 4-H; Ohi State Univ; Med.

CARPIO, DENNIS; Garrett HS; Garrett, IN; Bsktbl; Indiana Univ; Pre Med.

CARR, BOBBIN; Sistersville HS; Sistersville, WV; 30/60 Rptr Yrbk; Drama Clb; FBLA; Pep Clb; Chrldng; GAA; IM Sprt; Fairmont St Coll; Bus Educ.

CARR, CATHY D; Southport HS; Indianapolis, IN; 2/410 Am Leg Aux Girls St; Capt Band; Cmp Fr Grls; Hon Rl; NHS; Orch; Sch Mus; Stu Cncl; Sec Fr Clb; FTA; Srptmst Youth Ctznshp Awd 1st Pl Cnty 1979; Southport Dept Awd For Sci 1979; P H Robbins Music Awd 1979; Indiana Univ; Pre Med.

CARR, CHRISTINA; Marquette HS; Michigan City, IN; Trs Frsh Cls; VP Soph Cls; Cl Rep Jr Cls; Chrh Wkr; Cmnty Wkr; Off Ade; Sch Mus; Sch Pl; Stu Cncl; Pep Clb; Univ Of Evansville; Earley Child Ed.

CARR, DARRYLE; East HS; Cleveland, OH; Boy Scts; Chrs; Hon Rl; Jr NHS; NHS; Sct Actv; Univ; Art.

CARR, DAVINE; Les Cheneaux Comm HS; Cedarville, MI; Cls Rep Frsh Cls; Cls Rep Soph Cls; Band; Chrs; Hon Rl; NHS; Stu Cncl; Yth Flsp; Yrbk; 4-H; College; Special Ed.

CARR, DOROTHY; Scottsburg HS; Scottsburg, IN; 9/255 Girl Scts; Hon Rl; Hosp Ade; NHS; Sch Pl; Sch Nwsp; Drama Clb; Fr Clb; Opt Clb Awd; Voc Schl; Med.

CARR, JAMES; Switzerland Co Jr Sr HS; Vevay, IN; Band; MMM; Stg Crw; Sci Clb; Trk; Mgrs; Kiwan Awd; Most Outstanding Fresh Band Mem; Most Outstanding Jr Band Mem; College; Law Enforcement.

CARR, KELLIE; Marquette HS; Marquette, MI; Chrs; Sch Mus; Natl Merit Schl; N Mic Univ; Acctg.

CARR, LINDA; Bishop Dwenger HS; Ft Wayne, IN; Cl Rep Jr Cls; Chrs; Cmnty Wkr; Hon Rl; NHS; Sch Mus; Sct Actv; Stu Cncl; Indiana Univ.

CARR, LUANNE; Taylor HS; Cleves, OH; 14/150 Band; FCA; Hon Rl; Stg Crw; Rptr Yrbk; Rptr Sch Nwsp; Drama Clb; Pep Clb; Univ Of Cincinnati; Scndry Educ.

CARR, MERRY; William G Mather HS; Munising, MI; 51/96 Chrh Wkr; Cmnty Wkr; Hon Rl; Yth Flsp; Sch Nwsp; 4-H; Bsbl; Bsktbl; Cit Awd; 4-H Awd; Suomi Coll; Bus.

CARR, MICHAEL; Deer Park HS; Cincinnati, OH; Band; Boy Scts; Chrh Wkr; Hon Rl; Lbry Ade; NHS; Stg Crw; Rptr Sch Nwsp; Ten; Brigham Young Univ.

CARR, MICHELE S; Beecher HS; Mt Morris, MI; 10/250 Cls Rep Soph Cls; Hon Rl; NHS; Spn Clb; Chrldng; PPFtbl; Honor Roll All Year 1976; Outstanding Attendance 1976; Mbr Ntl Honor Soc 1977; UCLA; Pre Law.

CARR, MIKE; Perrysburg HS; Perrysburg, OH; Ftbl; College; Bus Admin.

CARR, PATRICK; River Valley HS; Marion, OH; 19/243 VP Soph Cls; Am Leg Boys St; FCA; Hon Rl; NHS; Orch; Sch Mus; College; Physical Therapy.

CARR, RHONDA; Immaculata HS; Detroit, MI; Cls Rep Soph Cls; Trs Jr Cls; Cl Rep Jr Cls; Cmnty Wkr; Girl Scts; Hon Rl; NHS; PAVAS; Sch Pl; Sct Actv; Univ; Engr.

CARR, ROSETTA; John Adams HS; Cleveland, OH; 2/470 Cl Rep Jr Cls; Sec Sr Cls; Sal; Hon Rl; Jr NHS; NHS; Off Ade; VP Stu Cncl; OEA; Rotary Awd; Ohio State Univ; Rn.

CARR, STEVEN L; Garfield Sr HS; Hamilton, OH; 45/330 Boy Scts; Pres Chrs; Hon Rl; Jr NHS; Mod UN; NHS; Off Ade; Sct Actv; Rptr Yrbk; Rptr Sch Nwsp; Ohio Univ; Sci Ed.

CARR, TAMMY; Moorefield HS; Moorefield, WV; 24/88 Trs Sr Cls; Sec Band; Hon Rl; Lbry Ade; Sec NHS; Off Ade; Sch Pl; Stu Cncl; Rptr Sch Nwsp; Pres FHA; Potomac St Coll; Acctg.

CARR, THERESA; Stanton HS; Empire, OH; 8/67 Hon Rl; Sec NHS; Ed Sch Nwsp; Pep Clb; Capt Chrldng; GAA; IM Sprt;.

CARR, VERNON; Bluefield HS; Bluefield, WV; Chrs; Chrh Wkr; Rptr Sch Nwsp; Key Clb; Treas Spn Clb; Trk; Most Otstndng Christian Character 77; Univ; Tech Engr.

CARRASCO, JAMES; Norwalk HS; Norwalk, OH; Hon Rl; Stu Cncl; Letter Ftbl; Trk; College; Elec.

CARRASCO, RICHARD; Norwalk Sr HS; Norwalk, OH; 34/200 Band; Hon Rl; NHS; Orch; Bsktbl; Ftbl; Trk; St Bd Of Educ Awd Of Distnctn 79; MVP Track 77; All N Oh Lg Track Sprinter 77; Ohio St Univ; Phys Ther.

CARRAUTHERS, MICHAEL B; Cass Technical HS; Detroit, MI; Band; Orch; Sch Mus; Pep Clb; Trk; St Champ Trckmn 78; MSBOA Solo & Ens Fest Awrd 78; MSBOA Band & Orch Fest Awrd 78; Michigan St Univ; Music.

CARREATHERS, EVA; Aquinas HS; Inkster, MI; Chrs; Hon Rl; Yth Flsp; Letter Trk; Cit Awd; Polish Amer Congress Of Mi 76; Polish Lang Comp 2nd Plc 78; Chosen As Bd Mbr For 17 Mag 79; Arizona St Univ; Child Psych.

CARRELL, DAVID; Barberton HS; Barberton, OH; 10/480 Band; Hon Rl; Jr NHS; NHS; Ger Clb; Key Clb; Ftbl; Trk; Wrstlng; IM Sprt; Akron Univ; Elec Engr.

CARRELL, REBECCA L; Flushing Sr HS; Flushing, MI; Chrh Wkr; Cmnty Wkr; NHS; Stg Crw; Fr Clb; Univ Of Michigan; Sci.

CARRICK, AMY; Daleville HS; Moore, OK; Chrs; JA; Sch Mus; Fr Clb; JA Awd; Ball State.

CARRICO, DEBRA; Newcomerstown HS; Newcomerstown, OH; Cl Rep Jr Cls; Chrs; Chrh Wkr; Hon Rl; Hst Frsh Cls; Stu Cncl; OEA; Secretarial Job.

CARRIER, JOSEPH; East Detroit HS; E Detroit, MI; 93/633 Cls Rep Frsh Cls; Cls Rep Sr Cls; Hon Rl; Jr NHS; NHS; Stu Cncl; Bsbl; Bsktbl; Coach Actv; Am Leg Awd; Coll; Busns Admin.

CARRIER, LAWRENCE; Grandville HS; Grandville, MI; Cls Rep Soph Cls; Cl Rep Jr Cls; Band; Hon Rl; NHS; Bsktbl; Trk; Univ; Bus.

CARRIER, LISA; South Amherst HS; Elyria, OH; 1/60 Chrh Wkr; Hon Rl; Lbry Ade; NHS; Sec Fr Clb; Sci Clb; Voice Dem Awd; Rep The Oh Jr Acad Of Sci 80; Outsdng Bio Stu Awd 78; Part In Sci Fairs Loc Sup Rtng Dist 78; Univ; Bio.

CARROLL, ANITA; New Albany HS; New Albany, OH; Natl Forn Lg; Ger Clb; Pep Clb; Bsktbl; Cit Awd; College; Work With Handicapped.

CARROLL, BECKY; Conotton Valley HS; Sherrodsville, OH; 1/55 VP Frsh Cls; Cl Rep Jr Cls; Band; Chrs; Drm Mjrt; Mdrgl; Sch Mus; Stu Cncl; Treas Beta Clb; Capt Bsktbl; Arion Awrd In Band 79; Hon Mention Amer Legions St Test 79; Wittenberg; Pre Law.

CARROLL, CARLA; Little Miami HS; Morrow, OH; Band; Hon Rl; Lbry Ade; NHS; Sct Actv; Rptr Yrbk; Letter Ten; College; Bus.

CARROLL, CHARLES E; Mumford HS; Detroit, MI; Hon Rl; NHS; Rptr Yrbk; Spn Clb; Ftbl; Trk; Natl Merit Ltr; Univ Of Michigan; Architect Engr.

CARROLL, CHRIS; Midpark HS; Brook Park, OH; Band; Hon Rl; Hosp Ade; JA; Fr Clb; Letter Trk; Cuyahoga Community College.

CARROLL, CYNDY; Mc Nicholas HS; Cincinnati, OH; 30/230 VP Soph Cls; VP Jr Cls; Trs Sr Cls; NHS; Sprt Ed Yrbk; Bsbl; Bsktbl; Trk; Scr Kpr; IM Sprt; Coll.

CARROLL, DAVE; Clear Fork HS; Butler, OH; 24/160 VP Frsh Cls; Pres Jr Cls; Chrs; Hon Rl; NHS; Sch Mus; Stu Cncl; Spn Clb; Ftbl; Muskingum College; Educ.

CARROLL, DEBORAH; Bloom Carroll HS; Carroll, OH; Drl Tm; Hon Rl; NHS; Orch; Ed Yrbk; Fr Clb; Flag Corps Squad Leader; Schlrshp Teams; Bsns Schl; Graphics Communications.

CARROLL, JEANETTE; Maple Vly HS; Nashville, MI; Cmp Fr Grls; Girl Scts; Hon Rl; Lit Mag; Off Ade; Sch Pl; Stu Cncl; Sch Nwsp; 4-H; Spn Clb; Lansing Cmnty Coll; Sec.

CARROLL, JOSEPH; John Adams HS; S Bend, IN; 64/395 Hon Rl; Univ; Sci.

CARROLL, KAREN; Huntington North HS; Warren, IN; 32/572 Aud/Vis; Band; Chrh Wkr; Cmnty Wkr; FCA; Hon Rl; IM Sprt; International Bus Coll; Sec.

CARROLL, KIM; Montezuma HS; Montezuma, IN; 6/35 Cls Rep Frsh Cls; VP Soph Cls; Sec Sr Cls; Chrs; Hon Rl; Pep Clb; Letter Bsktbl; Letter Ten; IM Sprt; Mgrs; Tech Ivy Tech; Math.

CARROLL, KIMILEN; Logan HS; Logan, WV; VP Sr Cls; Chrh Wkr; Hon Rl; Hosp Ade; Off Ade; FBLA; Keyettes; Pep Clb; Gym; Chrldng; Concord Coll; Art.

CARROLL, MARK; Midview HS; Columbia St, OH; 60/268 Band; Pres Chrh Wkr; Stg Crw; Pres Yth Flsp; Pep Clb; Mgrs; Mbr Of All Oh St Fair Band 78; Lorain Cnty Cmnty Coll.

CARROLL, MARY; St Joseph Ctrl Cath HS; Huntington, WV; 6/53 Pres Soph Cls; Am Leg Aux Girls St; Chrh Wkr; Hon Rl; Keyettes; Pep Clb; Letter Ten; Letter Chrldng; Univ; Comm Art.

CARROLL, MATTHEW; Bishop Gallagher HS; Detroit, MI; 4/322 Boy Scts; Hon Rl; NHS; Sct Actv; Stu Cncl; Bsktbl; Ftbl; Natl Merit Schl; Univ Of Detroit; Engr.

CARROLL, MAUREEN; St Francis De Sales HS; Columbus, OH; Hon Rl; Yrbk; Fr Clb; Mat Maids; Ohio St Univ; Retail Mdse.

CARROLL, PATRICK J; St Francis De Sales HS; Toledo, OH; 2/191 Sec Frsh Cls; Cls Rep Soph Cls; Debate Tm; Natl Forn Lg; NHS; Rptr Sch Nwsp; Letter Trk; Univ; Banking.

CARROLL, PATSY; Morley Stanwood HS; Morley, MI; 18/104 Hon Rl; Lbry Ade; NHS; Off Ade; Stg Crw; Great Lakes Bible Coll; Eng.

CARROLL, SANDRA; Withrow HS; Silverton, OH; Pres Jr Cls; Girl Scts; Hon Rl; VICA; Cit Awd; Voca Schl; Cosmetology.

CARROLL, SARAH; George Washington HS; Charleston, WV; Cmnty Wkr; Hon Rl; Jr NHS; NHS; Yrbk; Fr Clb; PPFtbl; Natl Merit SF; Duke Univ; Comp Sci.

CARROLL, SHAWN; Cloverdale HS; Cloverdale, IN; 1/90 Pres Frsh Cls; Cls Rep Sr Cls; Val; Am Leg Aux Girls St; Band; Capt Drl Tm; Pres FCA; Capt Girl Scts; Hon Rl; Lbry Ade; Purdue Univ; Vet.

CARROLL, STEPHANIE; Warren Central HS; Indpls, IN; 151/862 Am Leg Aux Girls St; Cmp Fr Grls; NHS; Yth Flsp; 4-H; Pep Clb; Spn Clb; De Pauw Univ; Pre Law.

CARROLL, SUSAN; West Branch HS; Beloit, OH; 6/265 Girl Scts; Hon Rl; Natl Forn Lg; NHS; Stg Crw; Pres 4-H; FTA; 4-H Awd; Rotary Awd; Voice Dem Awd; Youngstown Univ; Sci.

CARROLL, SUSAN; New Buffalo HS; New Buffalo, MI; Cls Rep Soph Cls; Sec Jr Cls; Girl Scts; Hon Rl; Rptr Yrbk; Trk; Capt Chrldng; Coll.

CARROW, STEVEN; Braxton County HS; Gassaway, WV; 1/185 Am Leg Boys St; Band; Boy Scts; Chrh Wkr; Hon Rl; Jr NHS; NHS; Sct Actv; 4-H; Mth Clb; Natl 4 H Confrnc 79; Natl Math Assoc Hon Roll 79; Atlantic Region Math League Meet 79; Univ; Math.

CARRUTHERS, RANDY; Clinton Massie HS; Wilmington, OH; 19/100 Boy Scts; Chrs; Hon Rl; 4-H; Letter Bsbl; Bsktbl; Ftbl; Ten; Trk; Eastern Kentucky Univ; Comp Tech.

CARRUTHERS, SCOTT; Berea HS; Berea, OH; Boy Scts; Chrs; Off Ade; Sch Mus; Sch Pl; Pep Clb; Crs Cntry; Trk; IM Sprt; Tmr; Univ; Bus Mgmt.

CARSON, BETSY; Ben Davis Sr HS; Indianapolis, IN; 32/826 Cls Rep Frsh Cls; Cls Rep Soph Cls; Band; Debate Tm; Hon Rl; Stu Cncl; Treas Fr Clb; Pep Clb; Chrldng; Am Leg Awd; Indiana St Univ; Elem Educ.

CARSON, CARMELA; Collinwood HS; Cleveland, OH; 1/235 Chrs; Capt Drl Tm; Hon Rl; NHS; Pep Clb; Letter Trk; Anthros Motivationl Awd 79; M H Jennings Awd 77; Georgia Inst Of Tech; Bio Med.

CARSON, DAVID; Little Miami HS; Loveland, OH; 30/300 Boy Scts; Hon Rl; Stg Crw; Ftbl; IM Sprt; Natl Merit Ltr; Fla Tech; Comp.

CARSON, DENISE; Edgewood Sr HS; Ashtabula, OH; Pres Frsh Cls; Chrs; Stu Cncl; Lat Clb; Sci Clb; Scr Kpr; Cit Awd; Bus.

CARSON, DIANE; Stanton HS; Irondale, OH; Band; Chrs; Chrh Wkr; Off Ade; Sch Mus; Yrbk; Fr Clb; Pep Clb; Bsktbl; Trk; Voc School.

CARSON, LYNN; Port Huron HS; Port Huron, MI; Cls Rep Frsh Cls; Cls Rep Soph Cls; Cl Rep Jr Cls; Cls Rep Sr Cls; Band; Cmp Fr Grls; Girl Scts; Off Ade; Letter Bsbl; Letter GAA; St Clair Cnty Cmnty Coll; Legal Sec.

CARSON, MARGARET; St Johns HS; St Johns, MI; Hon Rl; Sch Pl; Yth Flsp; Drama Clb; Chrldng; Central Michigan Univ; Spanish.

CARSON, PATTI; Garfield Hts Sr HS; Garfield Hts, OH; 11/354 Chrh Wkr; Hon Rl; Jr NHS; NHS; Off Ade; Yth Flsp; Pep Clb; VICA; Bus Schl; Legl Sec.

CARSON, PATTI; Garfield Heights Sr HS; Garfield Hts, OH; 15/346 Chrs; Chrh Wkr; Hon Rl; Jr NHS; NHS; Off Ade; Yth Flsp; Boys Clb Am; OEA; GAA; Cleveland St Univ; Law Enforcement.

CARSON, TONYA R; East HS; Columbus, OH; Aud/Vis; Band; Chrs; Chrh Wkr; Drama Clb; VICA; Trk; Natl Merit Ltr; Ohio St Univ; Law.

CARSTENS, LINDA; Lakeview HS; Battle Creek, MI; Chrs; Hosp Ade; JA; PPFtbl; Univ; Bus.

CARTAR, KATRINA; Southwestern HS; Detroit, MI; 10/210 Cls Rep Frsh Cls; Cls Rep Soph Cls; Cl Rep Jr Cls; Cls Rep Sr Cls; Band; Chrs; Hon Rl; Lbry Ade; Off Ade; Stu Cncl; Wayne St Univ; Bus Admin.

CARTER, ALLISON; Benedictine HS; Detroit, MI; Cl Rep Jr Cls; Chrh Wkr; Hon Rl; NHS; Stu Cncl; Yrbk; Fr Clb; FSA; New York Univ; Pre Law.

CARTER, ANTRIECE; Kettering HS; Detroit, MI; Cl Rep Jr Cls; Hon Rl; NHS; Glf; Cit Awd; College; Child Psychologist.

CARTER, BARB; North Miami HS; Peru, IN; 6/118 VP Chrs; Hon Rl; MMM; Sec NHS; Yth Flsp; Sec Drama Clb; Sec OEA; Pres Spn Clb; GAA;.

CARTER, CONNIE; Leslie HS; Onondaga, MI; Hon Rl; 4-H; FFA; Bsktbl; Letter Trk; PPFtbl; 4-H Awd; Mic State Univ; Vet Sci.

CARTER, CYNTORIA E; Princeton HS; Cincinnati, OH; Sec Sr Cls; Chrs; Hon Rl; JA; NHS; Sch Mus; Sch Pl; Stg Crw; Stu Cncl; Rptr Yrbk; Ball St Univ; Radio TV.

CARTER, DALE A; Jefferson Union HS; Steubenville, OH; Band; Chrh Wkr; Cmnty Wkr; Girl Scts; Hon Rl; NHS; Orch; Sch Mus; Yrbk; Beta Clb; Kent Christian Coll; Teaching.

CARTER, DEBRA; Kettering Sr HS; Detroit, MI; Hon Rl; Jr NHS; NHS; Cit Awd; Univ; Phys Ther.

CARTER, DOUGLAS; Tippecanoe HS; Tipp City, OH; Cls Rep Frsh Cls; Band; Chrs; Drm Mjrt; Hon Rl; Mod UN; NHS; Sch Pl; Stg Crw; Pres Drama Clb; Whos Who Among Amer HS Stud 77; Best Drum Major At Chaminade Julienne Band Fest 78; Internatl Thespn 3 Yrs; Ohio Wesleyan Univ; Econ.

CARTER, EMILY A; Dayton Christian HS; Dayton, OH; 11/95 Chrh Wkr; Hon Rl; Hosp Ade; NHS; Off Ade; Spn Clb; Cit Awd; Pres Awd; Wright St Univ; Nursing.

CARTER, GILBERT; Elwood Cmnty HS; Elwood, IN; Leo Clb; Spn Clb; Univ; Food Mktg.

CARTER, IRENE; Colerain HS; Cincinnati, OH; Cls Rep Soph Cls; Chrs; Stg Crw; Stu Cncl; Drama Clb; Natl Merit Ltr; Univ; Bus.

CARTER, JACQUELINE; Ferndale HS; Ferndale, MI; 28/410 Chrs; Chrh Wkr; Hon Rl; Jr NHS; NHS; Orch; Sch Mus; Letter Bsktbl; Letter Trk; GAA; Michigan St Univ; Comp Sci.

CARTER, JANET; Lockland HS; Lockland, OH; 7/70 Cl Rep Jr Cls; Hon Rl; Stu Cncl; Fr Clb; Univ Of Cincinnati; Zoology.

CARTER, JANETTA; Fountain Central HS; Kingman, IN; Chrs; Chrh Wkr; Hon Rl; JA; Off Ade; Sch Mus; Yth Flsp; 4-H; Lat Clb; JA Awd; Bus Schl; Acctg.

CARTER, JILL; Reynoldsburg HS; Reynoldsburg, OH; 10/420 Hon Rl; NHS; Yth Flsp; Capt Bsktbl; Opt Clb Awd; Var Vllybl 7;. Tennis Statistcn 78; Univ; RN.

CARTER, JIMMY; John J Pershing HS; Detroit, MI; Drl Tm; Hon Rl; NHS; ROTC; Rptr Sch Nwsp; Cit Awd; Amherst; Computor Engineer.

CARTER, JOYCE; Parkside HS; Jackson, MI; Chrh Wkr; Girl Scts; Orch; Yth Flsp; 4-H; 4-H Awd; Jackson Community Coll; Nursing.

CARTER, JULIA; Athens HS; Troy, MI; 1/500 Hon Rl; Hosp Ade; NHS; Red Cr Ade; 4-H; Fr Clb; Socr; 4-H Awd; Pres Awd; Univ Of Michigan; Med.

CARTER, KAREN; Marlette HS; Marlette, MI; Cls Rep Soph Cls; Band; Boy Scts; Hon Rl; NHS; Stu Cncl; Rptr Yrbk; Yrbk; OEA; Spn Clb; Volleyball 3yrs Varisity Letter; OEA Diplomat Stateswomen & Various Other Awd; Ferris St Coll; Acctg.

CARTER, KENDA; Field HS; Mogadore, OH; 16/300 Girl Scts; Hon Rl; JA; NHS; Pres Stu Cncl; Sch Nwsp; GAA; Scr Kpr; Kty State Univ; Phys Ther.

CARTER, KIM; Bloom Local HS; Franklin Fce, OH; 9/84 Sec Jr Cls; Chrs; Chrh Wkr; Hon Rl; Stu Cncl; FHA; Letter Trk; Chrldng; Pres Awd;.

CARTER, LINDA; Bellaire HS; Bellaire, OH; 54/243 Chrs; Drl Tm; Hon Rl; Sch Mus; Sch Pl; Stg Crw; Drama Clb; Fr Clb; Trk; Duquesne Univ; Music.

CARTER, LORETTA; Oceana HS; Oceana, WV; 1/119 Val; Chrh Wkr; Hon Rl; NHS; Quill & Scroll; Ed Yrbk; Treas Spn Clb; Marshall Univ; Comp Sci.

CARTER, MELINDA; Bellbrook HS; Xenia, OH; Chrh Wkr; Hon Rl; Yth Flsp; Anderson Coll; Art.

CARTER, MIKE; Bishop Foley HS; Fraser, MI; Band ; Hon Rl; NHS; Lat Clb; Natl Merit Ltr; Wayne St Univ; Bio Sci.

CARTER, MIMI; Wellsville HS; Wellsville, OH; Girl Scts; Hon Rl; Sct Actv; Y-Teens; Rptr Sch Nwsp; FTA; Trk; Univ; Pediatrician.

CARTER, PAMELA; William G Mather HS; Munising, MI; 4/105 Pres Sr Cls; Band; Hon Rl; NHS; Sch Pl; Stg Crw; Rptr Yrbk; Capt Bsktbl; Trk; College; Dentistry.

CARTER, PHILIP; Brighton HS; Brighton, MI; Hon Rl; Letter Wrstlng; Univ Of Michigan; Engr.

CARTER, PRECIOUS A; Morrison R Waite HS; Toledo, OH; Pres Chrs; Pres JA; 4-H; FHA; Bsbl; Pom Pon; 4-H Awd; JA Awd; Central State Univ; Computer Prog.

CARTER, ROBBI; Clare HS; Clare, MI; 8/136 Chrh Wkr; NHS; Yth Flsp; 4-H; Fr Clb; 4-H Awd; Mi Comptn Schlrshp Recpnt 78; Trustee Hnrs Schlrshp Mid MI Cmnty Coll 79; Mbr Of New Life Singing Grp 77; Mid Michigan Cmnty Coll; Bus Admin.

CARTER, ROBERT D; Stantion HS; Irondale, OH; 1/70 Aud/Vis; Hon Rl; Lbry Ade; NHS; 4-H; Bsktbl; Crs Cntry; Trk; Mgrs; 4-H Awd; Univ Of Cincinnati; Mech Engr.

CARTER, ROBYN; Elmwood HS; Cygnet, OH; 2/105 Band; Chrs; Chrh Wkr; Cmnty Wkr; Girl Scts; Hon Rl; Treas MMM; Sec NHS; Orch; Sch Mus; Oh Acad Schlrshp 79; Whos Who In Music 78; Otstndng Jr 77; U S Collegiate Wind Band 79; Wood City Fest Band; Ohio St Univ; Animal Sci.

CARTER, SHERRIE; Sparta HS; Sparta, MI; Chrh Wkr; Hon Rl; Spn Clb; Grand Rapids Baptist College.

CARTER, TERESA; Coloma HS; Coloma, MI; 3/200 Hon Rl; NHS; Lat Clb; Pom Pon; Natl Merit Ltr; Western Mi Univ; Bus Admin.

CARTER, WALTER; Milton HS; Milton, WV; Band; Stu Cncl; Letter In Band; W Virginia Univ; Law.

CARTRIGHT, KELLY; New Washington HS; Otisco, IN; 2/48 Sal; Hon Rl; NHS; Stu Cncl; Rptr Yrbk; Rptr Sch Nwsp; Pep Clb; Ind Univ Se; Elem Ed.

CARTWRIGHT, ANGELA; Miami Trace HS; Washington Ch, OH; AFS; Am Leg Aux Girls St; Chrs; Hon Rl; NHS; Sch Mus; Sch Pl; Drama Clb; Pres 4-H; FHA; Ohio St Sci Fair Spr Rtg 77 & 79; St Encounter Degree FHA 79; Hon Mtn Schlstc Achvmnt Tst 77; Coll; Pre Law.

CARTWRIGHT, JANICE; East Canton HS; E Canton, OH; 1/110 Val; Treas Chrs; Hon Rl; Jr NHS; NHS; Off Ade; Sch Pl; Drama Clb; Pres Fr Clb; Sec Pep Clb; I Dare You Awd 79; Booster Club Ath Acad Achvmnt Awd 79; Teenager Of The Mnth Of Dec 78; Stark Tech Univ; Comp Progr.

CARTWRIGHT, KEN; Ernest W Seaholm HS; Birmingham, MI; Boy Scts; Chrh Wkr; Cmnty Wkr; Mod UN; Sct Actv; Socr; Trk; Natl Merit Ltr; Univ.

CARTWRIGHT, MARY J; Henry Ford Ii HS; Stelring Hts, MI; 5/423 Hon Rl; Jr NHS; NHS; Off Ade; PAVAS; Mich St; Aero Eng.

CARTWRIGHT, SHARON; Scottsburg HS; Scottsburg, IN; 9/232 Hon Rl; NHS; Fr Clb; Mgrs; Acad Awd; Voc Awd; Bus Schl; Sec.

CARTWRIGHT, TERESA; Unionville Sebewaing Area; Unionville, MI; 4/120 Cls Rep Soph Cls; Band; Chrh Wkr; Hon Rl; Ed Yrbk; Rptr Yrbk; 4-H; FHA; Bsbl; Chrldng; Delta Coll; Acctg.

CARTWRIGHT, THOMAS; Woodrow Wilson HS; Youngstown, OH; Boy Scts; Chrh Wkr; Ftbl;.

CARTY, DYANN; South Vermillion HS; Clinton, IN; 10/180 Trs Jr Cls; Trs Sr Cls; Hon Rl; Jr NHS; NHS; Stg Crw; Rptr Sch Nwsp; 4-H; Treas Fr Clb; Pep Clb; Indiana St Univ; Art.

CARUANA, LISA; Saint Francis Cabrini HS; Allen Pk, MI; Chrh Wkr; Drl Tm; Hon Rl; Pom Pon; College; Nurse.

CARULLI, PATRICIA; Kennedy HS; Taylor, MI; 24/375 Chrh Wkr; Hon Rl; Lbry Ade; NHS; Off Ade; Rptr Yrbk; Rptr Sch Nwsp; Treas Ger Clb; PPFtbl; Cit Awd; Univ Of Detroit; Dental Hygiene.

CARUSO, ANTHONY; St Xavier HS; Cincinnati, OH; 26/263 Cmnty Wkr; Hon Rl; NHS; Rptr Yrbk; Bsbl; Bsktbl; IM Sprt; DAR Awd; College; Law.

CARUSO, ROBERT J; Sidney HS; Sidney, OH; Cls Rep Soph Cls; Boy Scts; Chrs; Debate Tm; Sct Actv; Stu Cncl; Sch Nwsp; College; Comp Sci.

CARUSO, STEVE; West Branch HS; Alliance, OH; Band; Boy Scts; Hon Rl; NHS; Orch; Sch Mus; Stg Crw; Glf; Mgrs; Scr Kpr; College.

CARUSO, THOMAS; Notre Dame HS; Clarksburs, WV; Cls Rep Frsh Cls; VP Soph Cls; Boy Scts; Chrs; Chrh Wkr; Hon Rl; Stu Cncl; Key Clb; Letter Ftbl; Letter Ten; West Virginia Univ; Busns Admin.

CARVER, CAROLINE; South Vigo HS; Terre Haute, IN; Chrs; Hon Rl; Sch Mus; Fr Clb; Show Chr Swing Chr 78; Indiana Hoosior Schlrshp 79; St Mary Of The Woods Univ; French.

CARVER, LORA; Valley Local HS; Lucasville, OH; 1/110 Trs Soph Cls; Band; Hon Rl; NHS; Stu Cncl; Ed Yrbk; FBLA; FHA; FTA; VP 4-H Awd; Soc Disting Amer HS Stu 1978; Jr Fair Bd Asst 1978; Univ.

CARVER, RICHARD N; Buckeye Sr HS; Medina, OH; 14/173 Hon Rl; Yrbk; Akron Univ; Chem Engr.

CARVER, RICK; Oxford HS West Campus; Oxford, MI; 18/260 Band; Pres Chrs; Chrh Wkr; Hon Rl; Jr NHS; NHS; Sch Mus; Sch Pl; Drama Clb; Rotary Awd; Western Michigan Univ; Theater.

CARY, JACQUELYN; Milford HS; Milford, MI; Cls Rep Soph Cls; Chrh Wkr; Cmnty Wkr; Off Ade; Fr Clb; Gym; Trk; IM Sprt; PPFtbl; 4-H Awd; Eastern Michigan Univ; Spec Educ.

CASANOVA, BRUCE; Norway HS; Norway, MI; Boy Scts; Chrh Wkr; Hon Rl; Sprt Ed Yrbk; Ed Sch Nwsp; 4-H; Key Clb; Letter Bsktbl; Letter Ftbl; Letter Glf; Lake Superior State College; Busines.

CASBAR, DEBORAH; Amelia HS; Amelia, OH; 12/280 Hon Rl; NHS; Stu Cncl; Spn Clb; Am Leg Awd; Exccln Cin Spansih III & Amer Govt 78; Univ Of Cincinnati; Pre Bus Admin.

CASE, BRIAN; Lakeview HS; Cortland, OH; 1/180 Am Leg Boys St; Band; Hon Rl; NHS; Stg Crw; Yth Flsp; Beta Clb; Lat Clb; Mth Clb; Univ; Physics.

CASE, CAROLINE A; Swan Valley HS; Saginaw, MI; 2/182 Cmnty Wkr; JA; Jr NHS; Lbry Ade; NHS; Sch Nwsp; Spn Clb; Natl Merit SF; Voice Dem Awd; Michigan St Univ; Bus Admin.

CASE, CONNIE; Nicholas County HS; Summersville, WV; 1/214 Pres Soph Cls; Pres Jr Cls; Val; Band; Drm Mjrt; NHS; Sec Stu Cncl; Pres VICA; Letter Trk; IM Sprt; West Virginia Univ; Nursing.

CASE, JAMES; Arthur Hill HS; Zilwaukee, MI; Boy Scts; PAVAS; Sch Pl; Merit Achvmnt Awd 76; Univ; Fire Fighting.

CASE, JAY; Union City Comm HS; Union City, IN; 3/112 Pres Frsh Cls; Pres Soph Cls; Pres Jr Cls; Hon Rl; NHS; Sch Mus; Sprt Ed Yrbk; Eng Clb; Letter Bsbl; Letter Bsktbl; Taylor Univ; Computer Prog.

CASE, MARK; West Ottawa HS; Holland, MI; 35/352 Hon Rl; JA; NHS; Off Ade; Rptr Sch Nwsp; DECA; FFA; Spn Clb; Elk Awd; Ctrl Michigan St Univ.

CASEBEER, ANN; Tekonsha HS; Tekonsha, MI; Sec Frsh Cls; Chrs; Chrh Wkr; Hon Rl; Treas Stu Cncl; Yth Flsp; Bsktbl; College; Bus.

CASEY, DEBORAH; Medina Sr HS; Medina, OH; Chrs; Girl Scts; Off Ade; Sch Mus; Sct Actv; Pep Clb; Letter Gym; Letter Trk; Letter Chrldng; GAA; College.

CASEY, DIXIE; Edwardsburg HS; Edwardsburg, MI; Lbry Ade; Yth Flsp; Ed Sch Nwsp; Bsktbl; IM Sprt; S W Michigan Univ; Nursing.

CASEY, JEFF; Lima Sr HS; Wapakoneta, OH; Aud/Vis; Chrs; Chrh Wkr; Hon Rl; Lbry Ade; PAVAS; Sch Mus; Yth Flsp; High Hon In Vocal Music 77; Univ; Psych.

CASEY, JEFFERY B; North Baltimore HS; N Baltimore, OH; Am Leg Boys St; Boy Scts; Chrh Wkr; Hon Rl; Sch Mus; Sch Pl; Sct Actv; Stg Crw; 4-H; Ftbl; N Baltimore Tech Schl; Mech Engr.

CASEY, KATHLEEN; Hackett HS; Kalamazoo, MI; Cls Rep Frsh Cls; Hon Rl; NHS; Letter Swmmng; Ten; College; English.

CASEY, LINDA; Catholic Central HS; Grand Rpds, MI; 12/211 Chrh Wkr; Cmnty Wkr; Girl Scts; Hon Rl; Hosp Ade; Red Cr Ade; Pres Ger Clb; Siena Hts Coll; Acctg.

CASEY, LORRAINE K; Bay HS; Bay Vill, OH; AFS; Drl Tm; Girl Scts; Hosp Ade; JA; Lbry Ade; Off Ade; Sct Actv; Sch Nwsp; DECA; Cleveland St Univ.

CASEY, MICHAEL; Catholic Central HS; Grand Rapids, MI; 55/233 Cls Rep Frsh Cls; Boy Scts; Chrh Wkr; Debate Tm; Hon Rl; JA; Stg Crw; Lat Clb; Mic Tech; Elec Engr.

CASH, JEFFREY; Jeffersonville HS; Jeffersonville, IN; 50/633 FCA; Hon Rl; Jr NHS; Letter Bsbl; Bsktbl; JC Awd; Indiana Univ; Acctg.

CASH, KENNETH; Columbia City Joint HS; Columbia City, IN; Cls Rep Frsh Cls; Cls Rep Soph Cls; Cl Rep Jr Cls; FCA; JA; Spn Clb; IM Sprt; Opt Clb Awd; Univ; Bus.

CASH, LAURA; Terre Haute North Vigo HS; Rosedale, IN; Band; Chrs; Cmnty Wkr; Hon Rl; JA; Mod UN; Quill & Scroll; Ind Univ; Pediatrician.

CASH, PATRICK D; Purcell HS; Cincinnati, OH; 9/175 Cls Rep Soph Cls; Cl Rep Jr Cls; Band; Chrh Wkr; Hon Rl; Jr NHS; NHS; Stu Cncl; Rdo Clb; Letter Bsktbl; Univ Of Cincinnati; Engr Sci.

CASH, PHILIP C; Cloverdale HS; Cloverdale, IN; 21/86 Band; Chrh Wkr; Hon Rl; Sch Mus; Sch Nwsp; Fr Clb; Univ.

CASHBAUGH, SANDRA; Muskegon HS; Muskegon, MI; Band; Chrh Wkr; Girl Scts; Hon Rl; NHS; Sct Actv; Fr Clb; Ferris State Univ; Pharmacy.

CASHNER, ELIZABETH; East Canton HS; E Canton, OH; Band; Chrs; JA; Mod UN; PAVAS; Rptr Sch Nwsp; Sch Nwsp; Drama Clb; 4-H; FHA; Cert Of Recgntn For Serv To HS Newpaper 78; Cert Of Recgntn For Being In Art Show 78; Oh PTA Cltrl Art 78; Jane Skinner Modeling Acad; Actress.

CASIANO, ADA; Washington HS; E Chicago, IN; 73/275 Chrs; Off Ade; Orch; Stu Cncl; FHA; FTA; Spn Clb; Bsbl; Bsktbl; Cit Awd; College; Airline Stewardess.

CASIELLO, NANCY L; Hagerstown Jr Sr HS; Williamsburg, IN; 2/172 Hon Rl; Mod UN; Pres NHS; VP 4-H; Fr Clb; Pres FHA; Sci Clb; 4-H Awd; Ball St Univ; Nurse.

CASILLAS, TERRI; Libbey HS; Toledo, OH; Hon Rl; JA; Jr NHS; Red Cr Ade; Treas FFA; Sci Clb; Most Otstndng Jr In Animal Care 78; Toledo Med Educ Cntr; Vet Asst.

CASIMER, GREGORY; John Adams HS; So Bend, IN; 5/395 Pres Frsh Cls; Pres Soph Cls; Pres Jr Cls; Chrh Wkr; NHS; PAVAS; Stu Cncl; Yrbk; College; Engineering.

CASITY, JANET L; Springfield Local HS; New Springfield, OH; 14/148 Band; Hon Rl; NHS; 4-H; Treas FTA; Pep Clb; Spn Clb; 4-H Awd; Univ Of Akron; RN.

CASKEY, JAMES; Madison Plains HS; London, OH; 20/143 Hon Rl; Stg Crw; Spn Clb; Chess Clb; Ohio Natl Guards; Art Clb; Lake Choctau Twirlers; Quick Recall; College; Art.

CASLAVKA, SHARON; Catholic Central HS; Grand Rpds, MI; Cls Rep Soph Cls; Cls Rep Sr Cls; Chrs; Hon Rl; Jr NHS; NHS; Stu Cncl; Fr Clb; Pep Clb; Trk; Michigan St Univ; Busns Mgmt.

CASNER, KATHY; Zanesville HS; Zanesville, OH; Aud/Vis; Chrs; Chrh Wkr; Drl Tm; Hon Rl; NHS; Off Ade; Sch Pl; Stg Crw; Yth Flsp; 4 Dollr Awd Frsh; Athltc Trainer Soph & Jr; Univ; Law.

CASON, CYNTHIA; Valley View HS; Farmersville, OH; Sec Frsh Cls; Sec Soph Cls; Chrs; Cmnty Wkr; Drl Tm; Hon Rl; Lbry Ade; Bus.

CASON, JEFFREY; La Salle HS; South Bend, IN; 7/480 Hon Rl; Jr NHS; Orch; Quill & Scroll; Yrbk; Sch Nwsp; Sci Clb; Natl Merit Ltr; Univ; Pre Med.

CASPER, REBECCA; Clay HS; South Bend, IN; 82/430 Hon Rl; Rptr Sch Nwsp; Pep Clb; Pom Pon; Coll; Spec Ed.

CASPERS, JANET; Bay City Ctrl HS; Bay City, MI; 11/512 Cls Rep Soph Cls; Hon Rl; Pres NHS; Stu Cncl; PPFtbl; Distin Amer HS Awd; Cum Laude Grad; Michigan Competitive Schlrshp Awd; Michigan Tech Univ; Engr.

CASSADY, PAUL; Galion HS; Galion, OH; Boy Scts; Chrh Wkr; Cmnty Wkr; Debate Tm; Hon Rl; Sct Actv; Cit Awd; Awd For Taking Eng Test For Galion HS At Hiedelburg Coll 77; Ohio St Univ; Math.

CASSADY, PERRY; Floyd Central HS; New Albany, IN; Hon Rl; 4-H; Spn Clb; Purdue Univ; Med.

CASSAR, ANN; Our Lady Of Mercy HS; Farmington Hls, MI; College; Bus.

CASSAR, CARMELINE; Holy Redeemer HS; Detroit, MI; Cls Rep Frsh Cls; Hon Rl; Trk; Cit Awd; Stud Govt & Stud Serv 77; Activities Awd & Schlrshp Cert 78; Serv Awd & Serv Pin 79; Univ; Bus.

CASSEL, KEITH; Roosevelt HS; Gary, IN; Hon Rl; Natl Forn Lg; Forensics Part 79; Otstndng Achvmnt In Math 79; Univ; Psych.

CASSEL, MARTHA; Oakwood HS; Dayton, OH; 2/170 Trs Jr Cls; AFS; Cmnty Wkr; Hon Rl; Ger Clb; Socr; Letter Wrstlng; College; Bio Med.

CASSEL, TED; Greenville HS; Greenville, OH; Boy Scts; Sct Actv; Yth Flsp; Fr Clb; Lat Clb; Spn Clb; Univ Of Cin; Bus Admin.

CASSELL, CHRIS; Cathedral HS; Indianapolis, IN; Am Leg Boys St; Hon Rl; NHS; Rptr Sch Nwsp;

Capt Bsbl; Bsktbl; Capt Ftbl; Miami Of Ohio Univ; Bus.

CASSELL, KATHI; Frankfort Sr HS; Frankfort, IN; 46/247 Cls Rep Frsh Cls; Cls Rep Soph Cls; Cl Rep Jr Cls; Chrs; Sch Pl; Stu Cncl; Yth Flsp; OEA; Pep Clb; Chrldng; Ball St Univ; Acctg.

CASSIDY, EDWARD; Columbia HS; Columbia Sta, OH; Aud/Vis; Boy Scts; Hon Rl; Sch Mus; Sch Pl; Drama Clb; Fr Clb; Univ; Chem.

CASSIDY, GLENN; Archbishop Alter HS; Kettering, OH; 155/310 Boy Scts; Key Clb; Letter Bsbl; Wrstlng; Univ; Bus.

CASSIDY, KEVIN; Eminence HS; Stilesville, IN; 2/42 Hon Rl; NHS; Sprt Ed Yrbk; Boys Clb Am; Fr Clb; Bsbl; Bsktbl; Crs Cntry; Trk; Cit Awd; Purdue Univ; Vet.

CASSIDY, LYNN; Churubusco HS; Churubusco, IN; 33/110 VP Jr Cls; Band; Chrs; Hon Rl; PAVAS; Sch Mus; Sch Pl; College; Music.

CASSIDY, MICHAEL; Oakridge HS; Muskegon, MI; Band; Hon Rl; Jr NHS; Natl Forn Lg; NHS; Pep Clb; Letter Bsktbl; Crs Cntry; Trk; Coll; Music.

CASTANIER, KARI; John Glenn HS; Bay, MI; Band; Girl Scts; Hon Rl; Sch Mus; Chrldng; Univ; Acctg.

CASTEEL, CARLA; Buckeye West HS; Adena, OH; Band; Drm Mjrt; Hon Rl; NHS; Rptr Yrbk; Drama Clb; Sec FTA; Pres OEA; Letter Bsktbl; GAA; Outstndng Preficncy Awd Acctg I 1979; Attended 3oea Regnl Contst For Acctg I 1979; Bradford Bus Schl; Acctg.

CASTEEL, ELLEN D; Hagerstown Jr Sr HS; Hagerstown, IN; 4/142 Hon Rl; Spn Clb; Bsbl; Bsktbl; PPFtbl; Natl Soc Of Distngsh HS Students 1978; Sportsmanship Award 1976; Univ Of Arizona; Comp Prog.

CASTEEL, JACQUELINE; Woodridge HS; Cuyahoga Fls, OH; Trs Soph Cls; VP Jr Cls; Band; Jr NHS; Stu Cncl; Lat Clb; Pep Clb; Scr Kpr; Univ; Psych.

CASTELLS, JAIME; Lakota HS; Cincinnati, OH; Aud/Vis; Hon Rl; Rptr Yrbk; Pres Sci Clb; Spn Clb; Natl Merit Ltr; Univ Of Cincinnati; Nuclear Engr.

CASTER, BETH; Solon HS; Solon, OH; 7/288 Chrs; FCA; Hon Rl; Mdrgl; MMM; Sec NHS; Stu Cncl; Letter Crs Cntry; Letter Swmmng; Letter Trk; Miami Univ; Music.

CASTER, MELVIN; South Decatur HS; Greensburg, IN; 5/110 Band; NHS; Drama Clb; Fr Clb; Crs Cntry; Letter Trk; Letter Wrstlng; Ind Univ; Astronomy.

CASTERLINE, SILVIA; Berea HS; Brook Pk, OH; VP Jr Cls; Aud/Vis; Chrs; Hon Rl; Jr NHS; Lbry Ade; Stu Cncl; Rptr Yrbk; Rptr Sch Nwsp; Ger Clb;.

CASTILLO, BILL; Ridgedale HS; Marion, OH; 7/96 Pres Frsh Cls; Cls Rep Frsh Cls; Cls Rep Soph Cls; Cl Rep Jr Cls; Am Leg Boys St; Aud/Vis; Chrh Wkr; FCA; Hon Rl; Jr NHS; West Point; Engr.

CASTILLO, ELIZABETH; Port Clinton HS; Pt Clinton, OH; 22/235 Cl Rep Jr Cls; Cls Rep Sr Cls; Chrs; Hon Rl; Jr NHS; NHS; Sch Pl; Treas Stu Cncl; Sec 4-H; Bowling Green St Univ; Elem Ed.

CASTILLO, LEE; Ottawa Glandorf HS; Ottawa, OH; VP Jr Cls; Cl Rep Jr Cls; Cmnty Wkr; Hon Rl; Ftbl; Trk; IM Sprt; College.

CASTILLO, THELMA; St Alphonsus HS; Detroit, MI; Cmnty Wkr; Hon Rl; Yth Flsp; Coach Actv; Univ; Law.

CASTILOW, KATHRYN; Bishop Donahue HS; Glendale, WV; Cl Rep Jr Cls; Cls Rep Sr Cls; Chrh Wkr; Hon Rl; Pep Clb; Spn Clb; GAA; College; Industrial Hygenist.

CASTLE, BRAD; North Newton HS; Demotte, IN; 31/196 Hon Rl; Apprentice; Plumbing.

CASTLE, CHERYL; Bridgeport Spaulding HS; Birch Run, MI; Band; Hon Rl; Hosp Ade; NHS; Sch Pl; Rptr Yrbk; Pep Clb; Trk; Chrldng; Treas Pom Pon; College; Psych.

CASTLE, DAVID; Southeastern HS; Londonderry, OH; Cls Rep Frsh Cls; Cls Rep Soph Cls; Cl Rep Jr Cls; Hon Rl; Jr NHS; NHS; Yrbk; 4-H; Fr Clb; Lat Clb; Univ; Agri.

CASTLE, DAVID; Heath HS; Heath, OH; NHS; Spn Clb; Letter Crs Cntry; Letter Trk; Lion Awd; Ohio St Univ; Comp Sci.

CASTLE, LON; West Geauga HS; Novelty, OH; 8/352 Cls Rep Sr Cls; Pres Debate Tm; Hon Rl; Natl Forn Lg; NHS; Sch Pl; Stu Cncl; Rptr Sch Nwsp; Sch Nwsp; IM Sprt; Oh Test Of Schlstc Achvmnt Bio 77; Oh Councl Of Tchr Of Math 78 & 79; Bucknell Univ; Pre Med.

CASTNER, BECKY; Greenhills HS; Cincinnati, OH; 67/245 Chrs; Chrh Wkr; PAVAS; Letter Trk; Letter Chrldng; Miami Univ; Education.

CASTNER, KENNETH; Stow HS; Stow, OH; 40/500 Debate Tm; Natl Forn Lg; Sch Pl; Stu Cncl; Drama Clb; Mth Clb; Ten; Natl Merit Ltr; Case Western Reserve Univ; Comp Engr.

CASTO, ALICE; David Anderson HS; Lisbon, OH; 21/98 Pres Cmp Fr Grls; Chrs; Hon Rl; NHS; Off Ade; Y-Teens; Rptr Sch Nwsp; Sci Clb; Mgrs; Art Club 2nd Pl Awd In Area Comptn 79; Youngstown St Univ; Dietetic Tech.

CASTO, CATHY; Hurricane HS; Hurricane, WV; Band; Chrs; Chrh Wkr; Girl Scts; Hon Rl; JA; Orch; Yth Flsp; Rptr Sch Nwsp; 4-H; All Area Band; V P Bible Club; Univ; Music.

CASTO, CHERYL; Marietta Sr HS; Marietta, OH; 83/405 Band; Hon Rl; Off Ade; Bowling Green Univ; Med Tech.

CASTO, CYNTHIA; Green HS; Unontown, OH; Chrs; Rptr Yrbk; DECA; Fr Clb; Portage Lakes Voc Schl.

CASTO, JOAN; Marion Harding HS; Marion, OH; 2/500 Cls Rep Frsh Cls; AFS; Am Leg Aux Girls St; Band; Hon Rl; Lbry Ade; Off Ade; Orch; Sch Mus; Sch Pl; Brass Chr Symphonette Woodwind Ensemble Pep Bnd ; Slctd Field Commndr For Marchng Bnd Stu Dir 79; Akron Univ; Sci.

CASTO, JOHNDA B; West Jefferson HS; W Jefferson, OH; 50/110 VP Frsh Cls; VP Soph Cls; Band; Chrs; Drl Tm; Girl Scts; Hosp Ade; Off Ade; Sch Pl; Stg Crw; Tech Schl; Med Asst.

CASTO, KERRY; Ripley HS; Ripley, WV; Cls Rep Frsh Cls; Cls Rep Soph Cls; Cl Rep Jr Cls; Cls Rep Sr Cls; Chrs; Hon Rl; Jr NHS; Quill & Scroll; Sch Pl; Stg Crw; Marshall Univ; Brdcstng.

CASTO, LAURIE; Barberton HS; Barberton, OH; 192/499 Cl Rep Jr Cls; Hon Rl; Off Ade; Stu Cncl; FTA; OEA; Spn Clb; Treasurer Of COE Class; Sr Prom Queen; Business Schl.

CASTONGIA, ROGER; North Newton HS; Morocco, IN; 18/140 Band; Boy Scts; Hon Rl; NHS; Stg Crw; Ed Yrbk; Rptr Yrbk; Boys Clb Am; Spn Clb; Glf; Hoosier Schlr Awd 79; Amer Lg Aux Sclshp 79; Ball St Univ; Archt.

CASTOR, CHERYL; West Jefferson HS; W Jefferson, OH; Cls Rep Frsh Cls; Am Leg Aux Girls St; Band; Chrs; Girl Scts; Hon Rl; NHS; Sch Mus; Sch Pl; Pep Clb; Wittenberg Univ.

CASTOR, ROGER; Elwood Community HS; Elwood, IN; 11/187 Band; Boy Scts; Hon Rl; Jr NHS; NHS; Sch Mus; Sch Pl; Stg Crw; Drama Clb; Mth Clb; Basic Educ Opprt Grant; Ball St Univ; Music.

CASTRICONE, SUZANNE; St Francis Desales HS; Columbus, OH; Cls Rep Soph Cls; Cl Rep Jr Cls; Cls Rep Sr Cls; Drm Mjrt; Quill & Scroll; Sch Pl; Stg Crw; Stu Cncl; Sprt Ed Sch Nwsp; Rptr Sch Nwsp; Ohi State Univ; Communications.

CASTRODALE, JEANMARIE; Ursuline HS; Campbell, OH; 55/319 Girl Scts; Hon Rl; Sct Actv; IM Sprt; Itialian Club; Youngstown St Univ.

CASTRONOVO, DAVID P; Chesterton HS; Valparaiso, IN; Band; Drm Bgl; Hon Rl; Orch; Sch Mus; Stg Crw; Sci Clb; Designated Finalist For NROTC Schlrshp 79; Structural Engr.

CASWELL, BOB; Seaholm HS; Troy, MI; Cls Rep Frsh Cls; Cls Rep Soph Cls; Cl Rep Jr Cls; Aud/Vis; Boy Scts; Chrh Wkr; Lbry Ade; Off Ade; Sch Pl; Stu Cncl; NSF Mech Engr Fuel Economy; Wayan St Univ; Univ Of Michigan; Engr.

CASWELL, CHRISTINE; Walled Lake Central HS; Union Lake, MI; Cls Rep Frsh Cls; Cls Rep Soph Cls; Hon Rl; PAVAS; Stu Cncl; Crs Cntry; Trk; GAA; IM Sprt; Oakland Comm College; Med.

CASWELL, CYNTHIA; Green HS; No Canton, OH; Chrs; Chrh Wkr; Sch Mus; Treas Y-Teens; Pep Clb; Pom Pon; Mt Vernon Nazarene Coll; Music.

CASWELL, MARGARET; Struthers HS; Struthers, OH; Lbry Ade; DECA; Spn Clb;.

CATA, CEFERINO; Archbishop Alter HS; Centerville, OH; 27/280 Hon Rl; NHS; Pres Sct Actv; Key Clb; Spn Clb; IM Sprt; College; Med.

CATANZARITE, LAURIE; Sandusky HS; Marlette, MI; 1/150 Trs Jr Cls; Cl Rep Jr Cls; Debate Tm; Girl Scts; Hon Rl; NHS; Sch Mus; Stu Cncl; Fr Clb; Letter Trk; Univ; Med.

CATANZARO, JOENETT; Seton HS; Cincinnati, OH; Drl Tm; Girl Scts; Hon Rl; Sct Actv; Stg Crw; 4-H; Spn Clb; GAA; Scr Kpr; 4-H Awd; Univ Of Cincinnati; Nursing.

CATANZARO, LUCIE; Archbishop Alter HS; Miamisburg, OH; Cls Rep Frsh Cls; Cmp Fr Grls; Chrh Wkr; Chmn Stu Cncl; Drama Clb; Fr Clb; Letter Bsktbl; Letter Ten; IM Sprt; Scr Kpr; Medicine.

CATE, ANDREW E; Lawrence North HS; Indianapolis, IN; 16/356 Band; Hon Rl; NHS; Sch Mus; Mth Clb; JETS Awd; Hon Schlshp Rose Hulman Inst Of Tech 1979; Crtfct Of Mrt 10th Pl 1979; Durdue Univ Crtfct Rcgntn Acad 1979; Rose Hulman Inst Of Tech; Engr.

CATELLA, VICTOR; Aquinas HS; Woodhaven, MI; Cls Rep Sr Cls; Hon Rl; NHS; Stu Cncl; Sprt Ed Yrbk; Letter Bsbl; Coach Actv; Scr Kpr; Tmr; Univ; Acctg.

CATES, ANNETTE; Covington HS; Kingman, IN; 3/120 Band; FCA; Hon Rl; Yth Flsp; 4-H; Fr Clb; Pep Clb; Bsktbl; GAA; 4-H Awd; Purdue Univ; Comp Sci.

CATES, DALE; Covington HS; Kingman, IN; 3/121 Band; FCA; Hon Rl; Yth Flsp; Pres 4-H; Pep Clb; Letter Bsktbl; GAA; 4-H Awd; Whos Who In Music 78; Purdue Univ; Comp Sci.

CATES, MARK; Madison Comp HS; Mansfield, OH; Band; Boy Scts; Fr Clb; Key Clb; Letter Ftbl; Letter Wrstlng; Ohio Univ; Optometry.

CATEY, LAURIE; Muskegon HS; Muskegon, MI; Band; Hon Rl; Pres NHS; Orch; Yth Flsp; Fr Clb; Pep Clb; Am Leg Awd; Mich Tech Univ; Bio.

CATHCART, JOE; Scecina Memorial HS; Indianapolis, IN; 47/190 Cl Rep Jr Cls; FCA; Hon Rl; Letter Bsktbl; Capt Ftbl; History.

CATHELL, JEFF; Bridgeport HS; Bridgeport, WV; Cls Rep Frsh Cls; Hon Rl; Jr NHS; NHS; Yrbk; Letter Bsktbl; Letter Ftbl; Letter Trk; College; Engr.

CATHER, CHRISTINE; Bremen HS; Bremen, IN; Pres Sr Cls; FCA; Lit Mag; Off Ade; Sch Mus; Sch Pl; Stu Cncl; Yth Flsp; Rptr Yrbk; Rptr Sch Nwsp; IUSB; Mdse.

CATHER, MARY LOU; Medina County Voc Schl; Wellington, OH; 6/79 Trs Frsh Cls; Trs Jr Cls; Chrs; Hon Rl; Off Ade; Sch Nwsp; Beta Clb; Pres 4-H; OEA; Pep Clb; 1st OOEA Regnl Test Typing 1978; 1st OOEA State Test Tyuping 1978; 15th OEA Natl Test Typing 1978; Bus Schl; Leg Sec.

CATO, ANGIE; Pike Central Middle HS; Velper, IN; Hon Rl; Lbry Ade; Stg Crw; Drama Clb; 4-H; Univ.

CATO, TERRENCE; Adelphian Academy; W Bloomfield, MI; Pres Band; Chrh Wkr; Cmnty Wkr; Hon Rl; Sch Mus; Sch Pl; Stg Crw; Ed Yrbk; Yrbk; Sch Nwsp; John Philip Sousa Band Awd 77; Courtesy Ct; MIT; Archt.

CATOLINE, MARYBETH; Ursuline HS; Youngstown, OH; 15/319 Chrs; Hon Rl; Jr NHS; Lit Mag; NHS; Stg Crw; Drama Clb; Eng Clb; Ger Clb; Key Clb; Math Team 77; Americas Outstndg Names & Faces 79; Univ Of Rochester; Genetics.

CATRON, KEVIN; Coldwater HS; Coldwater, OH; Air Force.

CATT, MARTHA; Charles F Brush HS; S Euclid, OH; 23/595 AFS; Chrs; Cmnty Wkr; NHS; Sch Mus; Sch Pl; Stu Cncl; Rptr Sch Nwsp; Pres Drama Clb; Pep Clb; Northwestern Univ; Eng.

CATTELL, DEBBIE; Loy Norrix HS; Kalamazoo, MI; Band; Girl Scts; Hon Rl; Red Cr Ade; Sct Actv; Cit Awd; Western Mich Univ; Occupational Ther.

CATTLEDGE, ANDREA; Hammond HS; Hammond, IN; VP Soph Cls; Sec Jr Cls; Chrs; Girl Scts; JA; Sch Mus; Stu Cncl; Drama Clb; Letter Bsktbl; Citzn Apprenticeship Progr 79; Sftbl Lg 79; Univ; Poli Sci.

CATTRELL, JODY; Southern Local HS; Wellsville, OH; Sec Sr Cls; Band; Hon Rl; NHS; Orch; Sch Pl; Treas FHA; FNA; Chrldng; Mgrs; Kent State; Business.

CAUBLE, DENISE; Orleans HS; Orleans, IN; 14/70 Am Leg Boys St; Chrs; Drl Tm; Hon Rl; NHS; Sch Pl; Stu Cncl; Yth Flsp; Yrbk; 4-H; Natl Choral 79; Vlybl Ltd 3 Yrs 76 78; ASCS Conservation 75; ISU; Eng Tchr.

CAUDEL, DEBRA; Grosse Ile HS; Grosse Ile, MI; Pres Frsh Cls; Cls Rep Soph Cls; Sec Jr Cls; Sec Sr Cls; Band; Chrs; Chrh Wkr; Girl Scts; Hon Rl; Mdrgl; Homcmng Queen 78; Albion Coll; Econ.

CAUDILL, ANTHONY; Whitko HS; Pierceton, IN; Cls Rep Soph Cls; Hon Rl; Sch Mus; Stu Cncl; Yth Flsp; Rptr Sch Nwsp; Drama Clb; Ger Clb; Sci Clb; Letter Glf;.

CAUDILL, JACK; Moeller HS; Cincinnati, OH; 19/262 Chrh Wkr; Hon Rl; NHS; Rptr Sch Nwsp; Sch Nwsp; IM Sprt; Ohio Univ; Broadcasting.

CAUDILL, JULIA; Sandy Valley HS; Sandyville, OH; Pres Soph Cls; Chrs; Jr NHS; Pres Lbry Ade; Natl Forn Lg; Stu Cncl; Rptr Sch Nwsp; Spn Clb; Gym; Chrldng; Stark Tech Coll; Comp Progr.

CAUDILL, JULIE A; Dundee Community HS; Maybee, MI; 10/107 Chrs; Chrh Wkr; Hon Rl; Treas NHS; Off Ade; Ed Yrbk; Rptr Sch Nwsp; FTA; Yrbk Key 79; Grand Valley St Coll Schlrshp 79; ACT Schlrshp Finalist 78; Grand Valley St Coll; Nursing.

CAUDILL, LAURIE A; Dansville Agricultural HS; Dansville, MI; Chrs; Girl Scts; Hon Rl; Lbry Ade; NHS; Off Ade; Sec FHA; Pep Clb; Busns Schl; Busns.

CAUDILL, LA VERTA; Peru HS; Peru, IN; 22/260 Hon Rl; Lbry Ade; NHS; Fr Clb; Ger Clb; GAA; Wghos Who Forgn Lang 78 & 79; Ball St Univ.

CAUDILL, ROBIN; Belding HS; Belding, MI; Band; Chrh Wkr; Hon Rl; NHS; Orch; Drama Clb; Arizona St Univ; Law.

CAUDILL, SHERRI; Ironton HS; Ironton, OH; Band; JA; Lat Clb; GAA; IM Sprt; Nursing.

CAUDILL, STEVE; Federal Hocking HS; Coolville, OH; Am Leg Boys St; Sec Band; Boy Scts; Chrs; NHS; Sct Actv; Pres Yth Flsp; Yrbk; Ohio State; Studio Recording.

CAUDLE, DEBBIE; Montgomery Cnty Jnt Voc HS; Clayton, OH; Hst Jr Cls; VP Sr Cls; Hon Rl; OEA; Sinclair Univ; Acctg.

CAULK, DAVID; Ben Davis HS; Indianapolis, IN; Cls Rep Soph Cls; Pres Jr Cls; Cl Rep Jr Cls; Chrs; Cmnty Wkr; FCA; Hon Rl; Stu Cncl; Y-Teens; DECA; DECA V P Dist 8 1979; DECA Pres Dist 8 1980; Outstndg Stdnt DECA 1979; Univ; Mngr Bus.

CAUPP, CAROLYN; Smith Green Cmnty HS; Churubusco, IN; Hon Rl; Bsktbl; Trk; IM Sprt; Mgrs; Univ; Math.

CAUSBY, BARB; Conotton Valley HS; Sherrodsville, OH; 3/59 Trs Soph Cls; Trs Jr Cls; Trs Sr Cls; Hon Rl; Rptr Yrbk; Rptr Sch Nwsp; Beta Clb; Treas FHA; 4-H Awd;.

CAUSEY, DIANE; Madison HS; Madison, OH; 21/295 Band; Hon Rl; Yth Flsp; Scr Kpr; Kent St Univ; Hrng Imprd Tchr.

CAUSEY, DOROTHY; Horace Mann HS; Gary, IN; Hon Rl; JA; NHS; Cit Awd; I V Tech; Bus.

CAVADEAS, SUSANNE; Escanaba Area Public HS; Cornell, MI; 27/450 Hon Rl; JA; Lbry Ade; NHS; Pol Wkr; JA Awd; Natl Merit Schl; Delgt To Operation Bentley Olivet Coll 78; Anna C Norton Memrl Schslhp 79; Mayor Of Stdnt Govt Day 78; Michigan St Univ; Bus Admin.

CAVALLI, CATHY C; Eastlake North HS; Willowick, OH; Band; Cmp Fr Grls; Chrs; Hon Rl; Hosp Ade; Jr NHS; Lbry Ade; NHS; Off Ade; School Guard Lieutenant; Clinic Aid; Pioneer Girl Of The Yr Awd; College; Nursing.

CAVANAUGH, BONNIE; Beaverton HS; Beaverton, MI; 2/144 Sec Frsh Cls; Cls Rep Soph Cls; Cl Rep Jr Cls; Hon Rl; NHS; Stu Cncl; Rptr Sch Nwsp; Pep Clb; Spn Clb; Letter Bsbl; Univ; Med.

CAVANAUGH, CASEY; Catholic Central HS; Detroit, MI; 17/217 Trs Frsh Cls; Cls Rep Frsh Cls; Sec Soph Cls; Trs Soph Cls; Sec Jr Cls; Trs Jr Cls; Cls Rep Sr Cls; Mic State Univ; Pro Frisbee.

CAVANAUGH, DARREN; Stow Lakeview HS; Stow, OH; Hon Rl; NHS; Letter Ten; Trk; JETS Awd; Natl Merit Ltr; Oh Counsl Of Tchr Of Math Awd 79; Oh Test Of Schltc Achvmtn Awd 78; Oh Cert Of Superior Acvhmtn Math 79; Univ; Engr.

CAVANAUGH, DON; Beaverton HS; Beaverton, MI; Boy Scts; Chrs; Hon Rl; NHS; Sch Pl; Stu Cncl; Rptr Yrbk; Rptr Sch Nwsp; Boys Clb Am; Letter Crs Cntry; Northern Michigan Univ; Consrvtn.

CAVANAUGH, JACKIE; R Nelson Snider HS; Ft Wayne, IN; Aud/Vis; Band; Chrs; Drl Tm; Girl Scts; Hon Rl; Pol Wkr; Rptr Yrbk; Fr Clb; Pom Pon; Ball St Univ; Nursing.

CAVE, KIM; Madison Plains HS; London, OH; Chrs; Chrh Wkr; Girl Scts; Hon Rl; Mod UN; Stg Crw; Yth Flsp; Sch Nwsp; VP 4-H; Pres FHA; Coll; Soc Work.

CAVELL, JUDITH; Beachwood HS; Beachwood, OH; Debate Tm; Natl Forn Lg; NHS; Orch; Stu Cncl; Yrbk; Rptr Sch Nwsp; Fr Clb; Natl Merit SF; Ohio Test Of Schlrshp Ach In Engl II; Coll.

CAVEN, BOB; Hubbard HS; Hubbard, OH; 10/350 Chrh Wkr; Hon Rl; NHS; Lat Clb; Letter Crs Cntry; Letter Trk; Natl Sci Foundation Chemistry Program; American Chemical Soc HS Chemistry Awd; College; Engr.

CAVENDER, KIMBERLEE; Sherman HS; Seth, WV; Cls Rep Frsh Cls; Cls Rep Soph Cls; Cl Rep Jr Cls; Hon Rl; Stu Cncl; Rptr Sch Nwsp; 4-H; Pep Clb; Capt Chrldng; Pom Pon; Boone County Voc Schl; Tchrs Aid.

CAVENDER, MICHAEL; Bethel Local HS; Tipp City, OH; 8/99 Cls Rep Frsh Cls; Cls Rep Soph Cls; Pres Band; Hon Rl; Jr NHS; Lbry Ade; NHS; Orch; Sch Mus; Sch Pl; Purdue Univ; Chem.

CAVENDER, ROBERT; South Charleston HS; S Charleston, WV; Hon Rl; Jr NHS; NHS; Rptr Sch Nwsp; Sci Clb; Natl Merit Ltr; Duke Univ; Pre Med.

CAVERLY, SHEILA; Marysville HS; Marysville, MI; 90/173 Band; Chrh Wkr; Cmnty Wkr; Drm Bgl; Hosp Ade; Sch Mus; Drama Clb; Abilene Christian Univ; Psych.

CAWLEY, GALEN; Bridgeman HS; Buchanan, MI; 1/92 Pres Frsh Cls; Cls Rep Soph Cls; Pres Jr Cls; Am Leg Boys St; Boy Scts; Chrs; Chrh Wkr; Hon Rl; NHS; Sch Pl; Univ Of Michigan; Econ.

CAY, KATHLEEN; Meridian HS; Sanford, MI; 4/125 Hon Rl; NHS; Ed Sch Nwsp; Pep Clb; Chrldng; College; Med.

CAYABYAB, LOUISE; Solon HS; Solon, OH; Cls Rep Frsh Cls; Chrs; NHS; Off Ade; Stu Cncl; Ger Clb; Pep Clb; Trk; Chrldng; Mgrs; Southern Methodist Univ; Pre Med.

CAYLOR, JAMES; Bluffton HS; Bluffton, IN; 30/133 Sch Nwsp; Ger Clb; Natl Merit Ltr; College; Journalism.

CAYLOR, PATRICIA; East Palestine HS; E Palestine, OH; Cls Rep Frsh Cls; Cls Rep Soph Cls; Cl Rep Jr Cls; Cls Rep Sr Cls; Stu Cncl; Pres Fr Clb; Bsbl; Letter Chrldng; Spring Sports Attendant; Winter Sports Attendant; Coll; Phys Therapy.

CAYTON, BOBBY; Lewis County HS; Weston, WV; VP Frsh Cls; Chrh Wkr; Treas FCA; Hon Rl; Stu Cncl; Yth Flsp; Pres 4-H; Key Clb; Pep Clb; Letter Bsbl; I Dare You For Qualities Of Leadership 4 H; West Virginia Tech; Mining Engr.

CAYTON, TERESA; Pontiac Central HS; Pontiac, MI; Band; Cmp Fr Grls; Chrh Wkr; FCA; Girl Scts; Hon Rl; Lbry Ade; Sch Mus; Sch Pl; Sct Actv; Band Letter & Awd 79; Drama Awd 79; Tennessee St Univ; Cmnctns.

CEBAK, KATHY; Struthers HS; Struthers, OH; Band; Cmnty Wkr; Drm Mjrt; Hon Rl; Orch; Y-Teens; Lat Clb; Twrlr; Youngstown St Univ; X Ray Tech.

CECELONES, CATHERINE S; Catholic Central HS; Steubenville, OH; 38/205 Treas Band; Hon Rl; NHS; PAVAS; Drama Clb; Lat Clb; College; Acctg.

CECELONES, MARIANN; Catholic Central HS; Steubenville, OH; 21/228 Band; Hon Rl; NHS; Orch; Yth Flsp; Rptr Yrbk; Drama Clb; FTA; VP Lat Clb; Kent State Univ; English & Law.

CECH, MICHAEL; Saginaw HS; Saginaw, MI; Am Leg Boys St; Aud/Vis; Band; Drm Bgl; Hon Rl; Hockey; Am Leg Awd; Drum & Bugle Corp Drmmr Of Yr 78; Amer Lgn Boys St Sprtsman Of Yr 79; Frosh Perf Attndnc; Univ; Sci.

CECIL, BETH; Howland HS; Warren, OH; 50/450 Hon Rl; NHS; Sprt Ed Yrbk; Yrbk; Fr Clb; Pep Clb; Ten; IM Sprt; Scr Kpr; Tmr; Miami Univ; Secondary Educ.

CECIL, CARLA; Vinton County Consolid HS; Allensville, OH; 13/160 Cls Rep Frsh Cls; VP Soph Cls; VP Jr Cls; VP Sr Cls; Lbry Ade; NHS; Yrbk; 4-H; Rio Grande College; Phys Educ.

CECIL, ERICK; Cameron HS; Cameron, WV; Band; Chrs; Chrh Wkr; Hon Rl; Mdrgl; Quill & Scroll; Sch Mus; Spn Clb; Gym; W Liberty State; Art Tchr.

CECIL, LISA; Newton Local HS; Pleasant Hl, OH; Sec Frsh Cls; Sec Sr Cls; Band; Treas NHS; Rptr Sch Nwsp; Letter Bsktbl; Chrldng; Pres GAA; College; Nurse.

CECIL, TERESA; Matoaka HS; Matoaka, WV; FHA; Pep Clb; Spn Clb; Bluefield St Coll; RN.

CECKOWSKI, DIANE; Bishop Dwenger HS; Ft Wayne, IN; 2/457 Chrs; Girl Scts; Rptr Yrbk; Sch Nwsp; Key Clb; Univ; Dent Hygnst.

CEDRON, RHONDA; Mona Shores HS; Muskegon, MI; Cls Rep Frsh Cls; Cmnty Wkr; NHS; Pep Clb; Gym; Univ; Radio TV Cmnctns.

CELAREK, CARYN; Hamilton Southeastern HS; Noblesville, IN; Chrs; Girl Scts; Hon Rl; NHS; Pep Clb; House Of James Voc Schl; Cosmetolgst.

CELAREK, JOSEPH; Bishop Luers HS; Ft Wayne, IN; 18/190 Boy Scts; Chrh Wkr; Cmnty Wkr; Hon Rl; Treas Key Clb; Capt Glf; Dnfth Awd; Kiwan Awd; Tri Kappa Schlrshp For 18 Of Jr Class 78; Free Awd For Ldrshp & Ctznshp; Low Qualifier In The Yth Golf; Univ; CPA.

CELESTE, JOSE; Gilmour Acad; Mayfield Hts, OH; 2/80 Cl Rep Jr Cls; Cmnty Wkr; Hon Rl; NHS; Stu

Cncl; Rptr Sch Nwsp; Bsbl; Letter Bsktbl; Letter Ftbl; College; Pre Medicine.

CENCELEWSKI, CARYLE; Washington HS; South Bend, IN; 9/355 Hon Rl; NHS; Sci Clb; Am Leg Awd; Chicago Mtr Club 76; Pres 8th Grd Holy Family Schl 75; Univ; Forestry.

CENTEA, MARK; Wadsworth Sr HS; Wadsworth, OH; Hon Rl; Letter Wrstlng; Univ; Research.

CENTERS, DIANNE; Lincoln HS; Cambridge, IN; 20/138 Band; Drl Tm; Hon Rl; Y-Teens; OEA; Spn Clb; Mas Awd; Bus Schl.

CENTLIVRE, CYNTHIA; Bishop Dwenger HS; Ft Wayne, IN; Am Leg Aux Girls St; Chrh Wkr; Girl Scts; Hosp Ade; Lbry Ade; Stg Crw; Ed Yrbk; 4-H; Ger Clb; IM Sprt; Z Club Sec 79; Univ; Banking.

CENZER, ROBERT; Milford HS; Milford, MI; 13/366 Cls Rep Frsh Cls; Cls Rep Soph Cls; Cl Rep Jr Cls; VP Sr Cls; Am Leg Boys St; Band; Chrh Wkr; Debate Tm; Hon Rl; Mod UN; Univ Of Mic; Comp Engr.

CERAR, MARY; Galion HS; Galion, OH; 47/275 Chrs; Chrh Wkr; Cmnty Wkr; Girl Scts; Hon Rl; Hosp Ade; Sec JA; Lbry Ade; Red Cr Ade; Sch Mus; Galion Elks Clb 200 Mst Valbl Stdnt Schlshp 1979; Galion Board Of Educ Scholarshp For 250 Per Yr 3 Yrs 1979; Ohio St Univ; Spec Educ.

CERBIN, HEIDI; Euclid Sr HS; Euclid, OH; 73/714 Sec Band; Sec Girl Scts; NHS; Sch Mus; Sct Actv; Tmr; Cleveland St Univ; Elem Ed.

CERCONE, BARBARA; Tuscarawas Ctrl Catholic HS; New Phila, OH; Girl Scts; Pep Clb; Spn Clb; College; Lab Tech.

CERCONE, JACQUELINE; Brooke HS; Follansbee, WV; Cls Rep Frsh Cls; Cls Rep Soph Cls; Sal; Quill & Scroll; Rptr Yrbk; Lat Clb; Letter Chrldng; Wv Univ.

CERGOL, ANN; Nordonia HS; Northfield, OH; 2/430 VP Sr Cls; Sal; Hon Rl; Hosp Ade; Jr NHS; NHS; Pep Clb; Capt Chrldng; IM Sprt; Cit Awd; Ohio Wesleyan Univ; Math.

CERNI, CRISTINA; Howland HS; Warren, OH; 9/481 Pres Frsh Cls; Chrs; Hon Rl; Red Cr Ade; Sprt Ed Yrbk; Pep Clb; Ten; Trk; PPFtbl; Pres Awd; Youngstown State Univ; Med.

CERNY, DENISE; St Johns HS; St Johns, MI; 13/298 Cls Rep Soph Cls; Band; Chrh Wkr; Girl Scts; Hon Rl; NHS; Orch; Sct Actv; Sec Stu Cncl; Yth Flsp; Michigan St Univ; Horticulture.

CERRONE, FRANK; Linsly Institute HS; Wheeling, WV; Hst Frsh Cls; Hst Soph Cls; Hst Jr Cls; Hon Rl; Pol Wkr; ROTC; Y-Teens; Lat Clb; IM Sprt; Mgrs; Univ; Engr.

CERVANTES, PHILLIP; St Francis De Sales HS; Oregon, OH; Hon Rl; Bsktbl; Ftbl; IM Sprt; Coll; Educ Admin.

CERVO, NANCY; Cardinal Ritter HS; Indianapilis, IN; 38/148 Cls Rep Soph Cls; Cl Rep Jr Cls; Cls Rep Sr Cls; Hon Rl; Stu Cncl; Spn Clb; Mat Maids; Pom Pon; PPFtbl; Tmr; IUPUI; Nursing.

CESARIO, JAYME; Buckeye South HS; Dillonvale, OH; Pres Frsh Cls; Am Leg Aux Girls St; Hon Rl; Sch Pl; Y-Teens; Rptr Yrbk; Drama Clb; Pep Clb; Spn Clb; Ohio St Univ; Law.

CESTKOWSKI, GENEVIEVE; Watersmeet Township HS; Land O Lakes, WI; VP Jr Cls; Band; Chrs; Girl Scts; Lbry Ade; Natl Forn Lg; Rptr Yrbk; Rptr Sch Nwsp; Bsktbl; Chrldng; Bus Mgmt.

CHACALOS, MICHELE; Bridgeport HS; Bridgeport, OH; Hon Rl; FHA; Spn Clb; Coll; Travel Agent.

CHACON, JUANA M; Hammond HS; Hammond, IN; 32/343 Cls Rep Soph Cls; Band; Chrh Wkr; Hon Rl; Jr NHS; NHS; Orch; Fr Clb; Indiana Univ; Lab Tech.

CHADBOURNE, DENISE; Anderson HS; Anderson, IN; 19/415 Cls Rep Frsh Cls; Trs Sr Cls; Am Leg Aux Girls St; Hon Rl; NHS; Stu Cncl; Yth Flsp; Ten; Pres Awd; Purdue Univ; Marketing.

CHADD, DORIS; Calumet HS; Gary, IN; 9/297 Hon Rl; Sec NHS; VP Quill & Scroll; Sch Pl; Rptr Yrbk; Yrbk; OEA; Treas Pep Clb; Sci Clb; Mas Awd; Bus Schl; Court Steno.

CHADDA, JYOTI; Trenton HS; Trenton, MI; Sch Mus; Sch Pl; Mth Clb; Swmmng; Univ Of Michigan; Med.

CHADRICK, KENT; Fairborn Park Hills HS; Fairborn, OH; 58/307 Band; Chrs; Chrh Wkr; Drm Mjrt; Hon Rl; NHS; Yth Flsp; Letter Gym; Letter Trk; Pres Awd; Ohio St Univ; Archt.

CHADWICK, ALAN; Beaver Local HS; Negley, OH; Trs Soph Cls; Am Leg Boys St; Hon Rl; Ftbl; IM Sprt; Tmr; Embry Riddle Univ; Aerospace.

CHADWICK, DAVID; Mt Vernon Sr HS; Butler, OH; Hon Rl; NHS; Quill & Scroll; Ed Yrbk; Sch Nwsp; 4-H; Spn Clb; Elk Awd; Kiwan Awd; Bowling Green St Univ; Bus Mgmt.

CHAFFEE, MARYANN; Ovid Elsie HS; Ovid, MI; 25/170 Hon Rl; NHS; Sch Pl; Rptr Sch Nwsp; Pres Pep Clb; Central Michigan Univ; Psych.

CHAFFEE, TOM; Taylor HS; Kokomo, IN; Aud/Vis; Cmnty Wkr; Hon Rl; Lbry Ade; Letter Bsbl; Letter Ftbl; IM Sprt; Indiana Univ; Bus.

CHAFFIN, ALICE F; Kermit HS; Kermit, WV; 5/40 Pres Frsh Cls; Sec Jr Cls; Band; Chrh Wkr; Hon Rl; Beta Clb; FBLA; FHA; Spn Clb; Twrlr; College; Elem Ed.

CHAFFIN, BARRY; Ithaca HS; Ithaca, MI; Hon Rl; Letter Ftbl; Letter Ten; Letter Wrstlng; Rotary Awd; Selected To Atttened Rotary Leadership Camp; College; Engr.

CHAFFIN, JOANNA; Edgewood HS; Bloomington, IN; Band; Chrh Wkr; Drl Tm; FCA; Girl Scts; Hon Rl; Treas Ger Clb; Indiana Univ.

CHAFFIN, L; Brookhaven HS; Columbus, OH; Band; Girl Scts; Hon Rl; JA; Jr NHS; Lbry Ade; Lit Mag; Letter Bsbl; Ohi State; Med.

CHAFFIN, SHERE; Central HS; Grand Rapids, MI; Hon Rl; NHS; Stu Cncl; Rptr Sch Nwsp; Bsktbl; IM Sprt; Univ Of Mich; Phys Educ.

CHAFFINS, PAULA; Rock Hill Sr HS; Kitts Hill, OH; 7/142 Band; Chrh Wkr; Hon Rl; Civ Clb; 4-H; Chrldng; 4-H Awd;.

CHAKY, JOANETTE; Holy Name Nazareth HS; Parma, OH; Cls Rep Soph Cls; Chrs; Hon Rl; Mdrgl; NHS; Bsbl; Mgrs; Cit Awd;.

CHALICH, LOIS T; Hartland HS; Howell, MI; Band; Hon Rl; Lbry Ade; Lit Mag; NHS; Yrbk; Letter Bsktbl; Mgrs; Michigan St Univ; Archt.

CHALKER, DONNA; Green HS; Akron, OH; 8/316 Chrs; Chrh Wkr; Hon Rl; Lbry Ade; Yrbk; Univ; Stewardess.

CHALKER, ROBERT H; Girard HS; Girard, OH; Treas AFS; Am Leg Boys St; Band; Boy Scts; Hon Rl; NHS; Sct Actv; Yrbk; VP Ger Clb; Key Clb; Univ; Engr.

CHALKO, JENNIFER; Andrean HS; Gary, IN; Hon Rl; NHS; Stu Cncl; Lat Clb; Pres Mth Clb; Opt Clb Awd; Butler Univ; Actuarial Sci.

CHALOUPKA, FRANK J; Walsh Jesuit HS; Northfield, OH; 14/180 Cmnty Wkr; Hon Rl; Rptr Sch Nwsp; Sch Nwsp; Schlrshp To HS; College; Medicine.

CHALTRY, GERRY; Mather HS; Munising, MI; Band; Boy Scts; Hon Rl; Sct Actv; Bsktbl; Crs Cntry; IM Sprt; Univ; Engr.

CHALUPA, ANNE; Parma HS; Parma, OH; 13/710 Cls Rep Sr Cls; Hon Rl; Mth Clb; Swmmng; Chrs; Chrh Wkr; Cmnty Wkr; Rptr Yrbk; Miami Univ.

CHALUT, MIKE; Holy Rosary HS; Flint, MI; Hon Rl; Bsbl; Ftbl; Trk; College.

CHAMBERLAIN, AMY; Franklin HS; Franklin, OH; 2/300 Treas Band; Girl Scts; Hon Rl; Off Ade; Stu Cncl; Rptr Yrbk; Sec 4-H; Mth Clb; Sci Clb; Spn Clb; Ohio St Univ; Vet.

CHAMBERLAIN, CATHERINE; Houghton HS; Houghton, MI; 32/114 Sec Band; Chrs; Natl Forn Lg; Sch Mus; Bsktbl; Glf; Capt Swmmng; Trk; PPFtbl;.

CHAMBERLAIN, CRAIG D; Celina Sr HS; Celina, OH; 14/241 Pres Band; Chrs; Hon Rl; NHS; Sch Mus; Sch Pl; Yth Flsp; Sec Drama Clb; Ohio St Univ; Law.

CHAMBERLAIN, DAVE; St Josephs Ctrl Cath HS; Fremont, OH; 20/102 Cls Rep Frsh Cls; Am Leg Boys St; Hon Rl; Stu Cncl; Key Clb; Letter Ftbl; Wrstlng; Univ.

CHAMBERLAIN, JUDY; Belleville HS; Belleville, MI; 173/479 Band; Chrh Wkr; Hon Rl; Hosp Ade; Lbry Ade; Yth Flsp; BEOG 79; Marion Univ; Nursing.

CHAMBERLAIN, KATHLEEN; Little Miami HS; Morrow, OH; Band; Girl Scts; Hon Rl; JA; NHS; Off Ade; Ger Clb; Pep Clb; Letter Bsktbl; GAA; Univ.

CHAMBERLAIN, LYNDA; Lamphere HS; Madison-heights, MI; 79/331 Hon Rl; Off Ade; Sch Pl; Letter Ten; PPFtbl; Natl Merit SF; Acknowldgmnt Schlrshp 78; Michigan St Univ; Pre Med.

CHAMBERLAIN, SANDRA; Walter P Chrysler Mem HS; New Castle, IN; AFS; Band; FCA; Sch Mus; Stg Crw; Ed Sch Nwsp; Drama Clb; Pep Clb; Brigham Young Univ.

CHAMBERLAIN, WANDA L; Independence HS; Midway, WV; 6/150 Sec Frsh Cls; Sec Soph Cls; Sec Jr Cls; Drl Tm; Hon Rl; NHS; Sec Stu Cncl; Yrbk; Mat Maids; Pom Pon; West Virginia Univ.

CHAMBERLIN, GAYLA; Northwestern HS; Wooster, OH; Aud/Vis; Band; Chrs; Hon Rl; Sch Mus; Drama Clb; Sec 4-H; Fr Clb; FTA; Pep Clb; College; Foreign Languages.

CHAMBERS, ANGELA; Cascade HS; Clayton, IN; Sec Soph Cls; Sec Jr Cls; Band; Pep Clb; Letter Gym; Letter Trk; Chrldng; Indiana St Univ; Gym Coach.

CHAMBERS, ARNESE; Beaumont School For Girls; Clevelnd, OH; Chrs; Chrh Wkr; Hon Rl; Lit Mag; Pol Wkr; Rptr Sch Nwsp; Lat Clb; Ten; IM Sprt; Natl Merit Ltr; Interracial Schlrshp Awd 76 80; Georgetown Univ; Poli Sci.

CHAMBERS, BECKY; Herbert Hoover HS; Elkview, WV; Band; Hon Rl; Jr NHS; Off Ade; Yth Flsp; Drama Clb; FHA; Sec Pep Clb; Chrldng; GAA; Sec.

CHAMBERS, BELINDA; Seeger Memorial HS; West Lebanon, IN; 4/126 Capt Drl Tm; FCA; Hon Rl; Hosp Ade; Treas NHS; Red Cr Ade; Yth Flsp; Pep Clb; Letter Trk; Capt Pom Pon; Indiana Univ.

CHAMBERS, CECILIA; Theodore Roosevelt HS; Kent, OH; 100/355 AFS; Band; Chrh Wkr; Cmnty Wkr; Girl Scts; Hon Rl; NHS; Drama Clb; Univ Of Cincinnati; Social Work.

CHAMBERS, DAVID; Western Reserve Acad; New Castle, PA; 38/89 Cls Rep Frsh Cls; Hon Rl; Sch Mus; Sch Pl; Mth Clb; Sci Clb; Letter Lcrss; IM Sprt; Univ; History.

CHAMBERS, ELLEN; Gallia Academy HS; Gallipolis, OH; Am Leg Aux Girls St; Band; Sch Mus; Yth Flsp; Rptr Yrbk; Rptr Sch Nwsp; 4-H; FTA; Lat Clb; Sci Clb; Mid American Nazarene Coll; Elem Edu.

CHAMBERS, KEITH; Kyger Creek HS; Gallipolis, OH; Boy Scts; Chrs; Chrh Wkr; Hon Rl; Yth Flsp; Lat Clb; USN; Nuclear Power.

CHAMBERS, LINDA; Marsh Fork HS; Dry Creek, WV; Chrs; Hon Rl; Hosp Ade; NHS; Off Ade; Yrbk; Pep Clb; Letter Bsktbl; Trk; Chrldng; Beckley Coll; Nursing.

CHAMBERS, MARY A; Bedford N Lawrence HS; Bedford, IN; 26/398 Am Leg Aux Girls St; Chrs; Pres Debate Tm; Hon Rl; Mdrgl; Natl Forn Lg; NHS; Yrbk; VP Beta Clb; Ger Clb; Univ Of Evansville; Communications.

CHAMBERS, RICKY; Bellefontaine Sr HS; Bellefontaine, OH; 66/241 Band; Boy Scts; Sct Actv; Yth Flsp; 4-H; Ger Clb; Sci Clb; IM Sprt; 4-H Awd; Univ; Elec Engr.

CHAMBERS, TERESA; Kyger Creek HS; Gallipolis, OH; Chrh Wkr; Girl Scts; Hosp Ade; Yth Flsp; 4-H; Spn Clb; Ten; 4-H Awd; Univ; Deaf Tchr.

CHAMBERS, TIMOTHY; Hemlock HS; Hemlock, MI; 90/200 Glf; Hockey; Ten; IM Sprt; Northwood Inst; Automotive Marketnig.

CHAMBERS, WILLA; Whiteoak HS; Hillsboro, OH; Sec Soph Cls; Drl Tm; Hon Rl; Lbry Ade; Off Ade; Sec 4-H; Pres Fr Clb; Bsktbl; Trk; Coll; Phys Ed.

CHAMNESS, WILLIAM S; Holland HS; Holland, MI; 1/309 Cls Rep Soph Cls; Cl Rep Jr Cls; Cls Rep Sr Cls; Boy Scts; Chrh Wkr; Hon Rl; Pres NHS; Orch; Treas Yth Flsp; Ger Clb; Harvard Prize Book Awd 1978; Jr Rotarian 1978; Univ.

CHAMPAGNE, FRANCES; North Huron HS; Kinde, MI; 5/54 Trs Frsh Cls; VP Sr Cls; Hon Rl; NHS; Stu Cncl; FBLA; Pres OEA; Capt Bsktbl; Trk; Oakland Univ; Econ.

CHAMPAGNE, KAREN; John F Kennedy HS; Taylor, MI; Hon Rl; Jr NHS; NHS; Sch Pl; Drama Clb; College.

CHAMPAGNE, KATHY; Elkton Pigeon Bay Port HS; Kinde, MI; 24/135 Rptr Sch Nwsp; Sch Nwsp; FHA; Pep Clb; Chrldng; IM Sprt; PPFtbl; Mic State Univ.

CHAMPER, LESA; Madison Plains HS; London, OH; Drl Tm; Hon Rl; PAVAS; Sch Pl; Sch Nwsp; Pres 4-H; Trk; Cit Awd; 4-H Awd; JA Awd; Mbro Of Madison Cnty Jr Fair Bd 79; Hon At Schl Hon Banquet 79; Hon At Schl Band Banquet For Flag Corps 79; Defiance Coll; Art.

CHAMPION, BRENDA; Elwood Community HS; Elwood, IN; 60/282 Sprt Ed Yrbk; 4-H; Spn Clb; Ball St Univ.

CHAMPION, STEVEN; Galesburg Augusta HS; Galesburg, MI; 37/110 Pres Jr Cls; Band; Orch; Sch Mus; Stu Cncl; 4-H; Glf; 4-H Awd; Natl Rifle Assoc Pro Marksman Awd 74; Smll Engn Awd 4 H 73; 1 Rating Solo Ensmbl Compt 79; Western Michigan Univ; Music.

CHAMPNEY, LARRY; Concord HS; Horton, MI; Am Leg Boys St; Aud/Vis; Chrh Wkr; Hon Rl; NHS; Sch Mus; Stu Cncl; Yth Flsp; Yrbk; Sch Nwsp; Annual Michigan Industrial Educ Soc; Coll; Aviation.

CHAMPOUX, HEIDI; Huron HS; Ann Arbor, MI; Chrs; Sch Mus; Natl Merit SF; Wheaton Coll.

CHAN, SUSAN; Dublin HS; Dublin, OH; 53/153 Chrs; Hon Rl; JA; Lbry Ade; Lit Mag; Off Ade; Rptr Yrbk; Yrbk; College; Acctg.

CHAN, TAN S; South Bend Washington HS; South Bend, IN; 5/355 Hon Rl; NHS; Yrbk; Univ; Bus Mgmt.

CHANCE, JANIS; Richmond Sr HS; Richmond, IN; Cls Rep Soph Cls; Band; FCA; Hon Rl; Pol Wkr; Stu Cncl; Y-Teens; 4-H; Key Clb; Spn Clb; #1 Indv 4 H Livestock Judge In Area Comptn 78; 4 H Beef Showmanshp; 4 H Sheep Showmanshp; Univ; Phys Ed.

CHANCE, MICHAEL; Indian Valley South HS; Gnadenhutten, OH; Chrh Wkr; Hon Rl; JA; Jr NHS; NHS; Sch Pl; Treas Stu Cncl; Rptr Yrbk; Yrbk; Am Leg Awd; Ohio State; Medicine.

CHANDLER, BONNIE; Salem Sr HS; Salem, OH; 75/250 Pres Jr Cls; Cl Rep Jr Cls; Pres Sr Cls; Cls Rep Sr Cls; Am Leg Aux Girls St; Chrh Wkr; Cmnty Wkr; Drl Tm; FCA; Girl Scts; Kent St Univ; Home Ec.

CHANDLER, COLLEEN; Bedford Sr HS; Toledo, OH; Cls Rep Soph Cls; Cl Rep Jr Cls; Sec Sr Cls; Band; Hon Rl; Hosp Ade; Rptr Sch Nwsp; Mat Maids; Honorable Mention Detroit Free Press Journalism Cont; Michigan St Univ; Social Work.

CHANDLER, CONSTANCE; Pontiac Northern HS; Pontiac, MI; Band; Cmp Fr Grls; Chrs; Chrh Wkr; Cmnty Wkr; Drm Mjrt; Girl Scts; Hon Rl; Off Ade; Stu Cncl; Univ; Pre Med.

CHANDLER, DEBORAH; North Putnam HS; Coatesville, IN; 25/150 Cmp Fr Grls; Chrs; Chrh Wkr; FCA; Hon Rl; NHS; Sch Mus; Sch Pl; Stg Crw; Stu Cncl; Schlrshp To Math Sci Inst For HS Stu At Indiana Univ; Symposium For Tomorrows Leaders Sponsored By Senator; Indiana Univ.

CHANDLER, LARRY; Princeton Cmnty HS; Princeton, IN; 4/205 Am Leg Boys St; FCA; Jr NHS; NHS; Bsbl; Letter Bsktbl; Letter Ftbl; Letter Glf; Univ.

CHANDLER, LISA; Herbert Hoover HS; Clendenin, WV; 15/285 Cls Rep Frsh Cls; Hon Rl; Jr NHS; Yth Flsp; 4-H; FTA; Pep Clb; Trk; Chrldng; GAA; Univ; Med.

CHANDLER, LISA J; Bridgeport Sr HS; Bridgeport, WV; Am Leg Aux Girls St; Boy Scts; Chrs; Chrh Wkr; Hon Rl; Off Ade; Sch Pl; Yth Flsp; Y-Teens; Drama Clb; West Virginia Univ; Pre Dent.

CHANDLER, MICHELLE; Brookhaven HS; Columbus, OH; 7/436 Band; Chrs; Chrh Wkr; Drm Mjrt; Hon Rl; Jr NHS; NHS; Sch Pl; Rptr Sch Nwsp; Drama Clb; Oh Merit Schlrshp 79; PTA Schlrshp 79; Benner Schlrshp Nazarene Coll 79; Mt Vernon Nazarene Coll; Med Admin.

CHANDLER, MIKE; Decatur Jr Sr HS; Lawton, MI; 6/74 Boy Scts; Hon Rl; Letter Bsktbl; Ftbl; IM Sprt; Top 10 Of Class 78; Capt Of JV Ftbl Tm 77; Voc Schl; Heating & Air Cond Tech.

CHANDLER, RETHA; Zanesville HS; Zanesville, OH; Chrs; Hon Rl; NHS; Sch Pl; Spn Clb; Mgrs; Univ; Dent.

CHANDLER, ROBYN; Hurricane HS; Hurricane, WV; Chrh Wkr; Girl Scts; Hon Rl; Yth Flsp; Y-Teens; Pep Clb; Marshal Univ; Paralegal.

CHANDLER, WILLIAM E; Tri West Hendricks HS; Pittsboro, IN; 10/112 Band; Chrs; Chrh Wkr; CAP; Debate Tm; Hon Rl; NHS; Orch; Sch Mus; Sch Pl; Delgt To Sympsm Fo Rtommorow Leadr 78; In Schl Music Assn Solo Ensmlb Conts 1st Div; Indiana St Univ; Pro Musician.

CHANEY, DIANA; Norwood Sr HS; Norwood, OH; Chrs; JA; Jr NHS; Off Ade; Sch Mus; Rptr Yrbk; Yrbk; Mth Clb; Spn Clb; Schlstc Art Awrd Finalist; Univ Of Cincinnati; Bus Mgmt.

CHANEY, ELIZABETH; Miami Trace HS; Washington Ch, OH; 40/234 Band; Chrs; Chrh Wkr; Drm Mjrt; Hon Rl; Sch Mus; Sch Pl; Drama Clb; FTA; Ohi State Univ; English Educ.

CHANEY, KELLY; Newton HS; Pleasant Hl, OH; 13/47 Band; Hon Rl; Rptr Yrbk; Yrbk; Ed Sch Nwsp; Pres 4-H; Mgrs; Wright St Univ; History.

CHANEY, KIMBERLY S; Huntington HS; Chillicothe, OH; Band; Chrh Wkr; Hon Rl; Hosp Ade; Lbry Ade; NHS; Orch; Sct Actv; Yth Flsp; Yrbk; Ohio St Univ; Med Tech.

CHANEY, LARRY L; Paint Valley HS; Chillicothe, OH; 1/80 Chrh Wkr; FCA; Hon Rl; Lbry Ade; NHS; Yth Flsp; Lat Clb; Am Leg Awd; Amer Legion Awd In Most Subjects; Natl Honor Soc 1977; Trophies Bible Quiz 1975; Ohio Univ.

CHANEY, PEGGY; Bishop Dwenger HS; Ft Wayne, IN; Trs Frsh Cls; Stu Cncl; Mgrs; Tmr; College; Law.

CHANEY, ROBIN; Hurricane HS; Hurricane, WV; Band; Drl Tm; Girl Scts; Hon Rl; JA; Y-Teens; 4-H; Mth Clb; Pep Clb; 4-H Awd; Univ; Pre Vet.

CHANEY, WILLIAM T; Schl Creative & Perf Arts; Cincinnati, OH; Cl Rep Jr Cls; Cls Rep Sr Cls; Band; Chrs; Chrh Wkr; Sch Mus; Yth Flsp; Letter Bsbl; Letter Bsktbl; Cit Awd; Morehouse Coll; Music.

CHANLEY, BONITA; Lauesville HS; Lanesville, IN; Chrs; FCA; Hon Rl; NHS; Sch Mus; Rptr Yrbk; FHA; Trk; Chrldng; Indiana Univ; Speech.

CHANNELL, RICHARD; Springfield Local HS; New Springfield, OH; 11/140 AFS; Hon Rl; Sch Nwsp; Fr Clb; Bsktbl; Ftbl; Trk; IM Sprt; Coll; Law.

CHANT, CARL; Morrice HS; Owosso, MI; Boy Scts; Hon Rl; Lbry Ade; Yth Flsp; Sprt Ed Yrbk; Rptr Yrbk; 4-H; 4-H Awd; Mas Awd;.

CHAO, YUN SENG; Princeton HS; Springdale, OH; 5/633 Hon Rl; Lbry Ade; NHS; Orch; Yrbk; Mth Clb; Natl Merit Ltr; College; Aerospace Engr.

CHAPARIAN, MICHAEL; Edsel B Ford HS; Dearborn, MI; AFS; Debate Tm; Hon Rl; 4-H; Ger Clb; Bsbl; IM Sprt; Gold Sci Awd 6 Sem Of Only A In Dept 79; Michigan Tech Univ; Chem Engr.

CHAPDELAINE, STEPHEN; Lapeer East HS; Lapeer, MI; Band; Chrs; Hon Rl; Natl Forn Lg; NHS; Sch Mus; Sch Pl; Stg Crw; Drama Clb; Fr Clb; Natl Thespian Soc 79; Univ Of Michigan; Music.

CHAPELOW, JODY; Sebring Mc Kinley HS; Sebring, OH; 21/93 Band; Drm Mjrt; Quill & Scroll; Rptr Yrbk; Rptr Sch Nwsp; Ger Clb; Lat Clb; Kent State Univ; Bus.

CHAPIN, SCOTT; Schoolcraft HS; Schoolcraft, MI; Pres Frsh Cls; Band; Boy Scts; Hon Rl; Sct Actv; 4-H; Letter Trk; Western Michigan Univ; Bio.

CHAPIN, TIMOTHY; Walled Lake Central HS; Union Lake, MI; Boy Scts; Hon Rl; Rptr Yrbk; Rptr Sch Nwsp; Trk; IM Sprt; Cit Awd; Natl Assoc Mbr Of Natl Wildlife Fed 79; Michigan St Univ; Writer.

CHAPIN, TONI L; Springfield HS; Toledo, OH; Chrs; Chrh Wkr; FCA; Hon Rl; Rptr Yrbk; Fr Clb; Pep Clb; Trk; Chrldng; PPFtbl; Cheerleading Awds; Soloist St Competitions; Intl Fine Arts Coll; Interior Dec.

CHAPLIN, GARY; Akron Garfield HS; Akron, OH; Pres Frsh Cls; Band; Hon Rl; Jr NHS; NHS; Stg Crw; VICA; IM Sprt; Am Leg Awd; Heritage Baptist Univ; Missionary.

CHAPMAN, ANNETTE; St Bernard Elmwood Pl HS; Hamilton, OH; Sec Sr Cls; Band; Drl Tm; Hon Rl; Lbry Ade; Off Ade; Sch Pl; Stu Cncl; Rptr Sch Nwsp; Bus Schl.

CHAPMAN, BARBARA; Western Reserve Acad; Hudson, OH; 4/84 Hon Rl; Stg Crw; Yrbk; Hockey; College; Biology.

CHAPMAN, BERT; Marion HS; Marion, IN; Chrh Wkr; Hon Rl; NHS; Orch; Sch Mus; Yth Flsp; Ger Clb; Newspaper Hon Carrier 78; Demolay Recognitn Awd 79; Deacon Westminster Presbytrn Church In Marion 78 80; Taylor Univ; Poli Sci.

CHAPMAN, BRIAN; Midland Trail HS; Victor, WV; 2/113 Sal; Hon Rl; NHS; Rptr Yrbk; Bsktbl; Letter Ftbl; Letter Trk; Coach Actv; IM Sprt; Wv Inst Of Tech; Engr.

CHAPMAN, CAROL; Greenfield Central HS; Greenfield, IN; 1/315 Am Leg Aux Girls St; VP FCA; Hon Rl; NHS; Rptr Yrbk; Pres 4-H; FFA; Mth Clb; Spn Clb; Letter Trk; Univ.

CHAPMAN, CAROLINE; Our Lady Of Mercy HS; Detroit, MI; Cmnty Wkr; Yth Flsp; Bsbl; Bsktbl; Coach Actv; Univ; Law Enforcmnt.

CHAPMAN, CRAIG; William V Fisher HS; Logan, OH; Pres Frsh Cls; Pres Soph Cls; Am Leg Boys St; Boy Scts; Hon Rl; Off Ade; Pol Wkr; Sct Actv; Stu Cncl; Yth Flsp; Sec Of Poli Sci Club 77; Univ; Pre Law.

CHAPMAN, DAVID; Washington HS; Washington, IN; 32/203 Am Leg Boys St; Pres Chrh Wkr; Debate Tm; Hon Rl; NHS; Pol Wkr; Red Cr Ade; Sch Pl; Stg Crw; Beta Clb; Purdue Univ; Horticulture.

CHAPMAN, DAVID; Washington HS; Washington, IN; Am Leg Boys St; Chrh Wkr; Hon Rl; NHS; Pol Wkr; Red Cr Ade; Sch Pl; Stg Crw; Yth Flsp; Beta Clb; Purdue Univ; Horticulture.

CHAPMAN, DIANA; Covington HS; Covington, IN; 7/104 Sec Sr Cls; Trs Sr Cls; Chrh Wkr; Hon Rl; NHS; Sec Stu Cncl; FHA; Sec FTA; GAA; DAR Awd; Ball St Univ; Nursing.

CHAPMAN, JENNIFER L; Richwood HS; Richwood, WV; Cls Rep Soph Cls; Cl Rep Jr Cls; Hon Rl; Stu Cncl; Sec Rptr Sch Nwsp; VP Pep Clb; Glf; Capt Chrldng; Sec Rotary Awd; Amer Outstndng Names & Faces; West Virginia Univ; Psych.

CHAPMAN, JOSEPH; Chapmanville HS; Chapmanville, WV; Cls Rep Frsh Cls; Cls Rep Soph Cls; Cl Rep Jr Cls; Boy Scts; Chrh Wkr; Cmnty Wkr; Sct Actv; Yth Flsp; Beta Clb; Key Clb; Alderson College.

CHAPMAN, J RODRICK; Lewis Cnty HS; Roanoke, WV; Aud/Vis; Band; Hon Rl; Sch Mus; Sch Pl; Stg Crw; Stu Cncl; Sch Nwsp; Mgrs; Tmr; Prod Engr For Adult Basic Ed TV Productions; West Virginia Coll; Electronics.

CHAPMAN, KIMBERLY; Lawton HS; Lawton, MI; Cmnty Wkr; Hon Rl; Hosp Ade; Lbry Ade; Off Ade; Stg Crw; Rptr Sch Nwsp; Trk; Michigan St Univ; Med.

CHAPMAN, LINDA; Chapmanville HS; Chapmanville, WV; Cmp Fr Grls; Girl Scts; Hon Rl; Beta Clb; VP FBLA; FHA; Keyettes; Pep Clb; Chrldng; Cit Awd; Business; Comercial.

CHAPMAN, MARK; Milton HS; Milton, WV; Hon Rl; Ftbl; Voc Schl; Draftsman.

CHAPMAN, MARY; Northern HS; Detroit, MI; Debate Tm; Hon Rl; Jr NHS; Natl Forn Lg; NHS; Pol Wkr; Quill & Scroll; Ed Sch Nwsp; DAR Awd; Wayne State Univ; Mass Comm.

CHAPMAN, MICHELLE; Columbian HS; Tiffin, OH; Cls Rep Frsh Cls; Band; Chrs; Hon Rl; Sch Pl; Stu Cncl; Drama Clb; 4-H; Fr Clb; 4-H Awd; Univ; Dent Hygn.

CHAPMAN, PAMELA; J F Kennedy Sr HS; Cleveland, OH; Hon Rl; Letter Bsktbl; Coach Actv; IM Sprt; Cit Awd; Coll Of Wooster; Child Psych.

CHAPMAN, RICHARD; Port Clinton HS; Pt Clinton, OH; Hon Rl; Natl Forn Lg; Ger Clb; Cert Of Awd For Chem St Dept Of Ed; Delegate To Oh Jr Sci Humanities Symposium; Chess Club Pres 2 Yrs; Ohio St Univ; Chemistry.

CHAPMAN, ROBIN; Norwalk HS; Norwalk, OH; Cls Rep Frsh Cls; Cls Rep Soph Cls; Cl Rep Jr Cls; Band; Hon Rl; Jr NHS; NHS; Off Ade; Stu Cncl; Yth Flsp; College; Nurse.

CHAPMAN, SANDRA C; North Ridgeville HS; N Ridgeville, OH; Cls Rep Sr Cls; ROTC; Chrs; Stu Cncl; Girl Scts; Hon Rl; Mdrgl; Sch Mus; Stu Cncl; Sch Nwsp; Baldwin Wallace Univ; Crmnl Law.

CHAPMAN, STEVE; Willoughby S HS; Eastlake, OH; Cls Rep Soph Cls; Cl Rep Jr Cls; Cls Rep Sr Cls; Am Leg Boys St; Hon Rl; NHS; Stu Cncl; Capt Ftbl; Capt Wrstlng; Dnfth Awd; Coll; Engr.

CHAPMAN, SUSAN; Coshocton HS; Coshocton, OH; 12/230 Hon Rl; NHS; Sch Pl; Stu Cncl; Rptr Sch Nwsp; Fr Clb; Sec Lat Clb; PPFtbl; Ohio St Univ; Educ.

CHAPMAN, T; Triton HS; Bourbon, IN; Chrs; FCA; Hon Rl; Mdrgl; Off Ade; Sch Mus; Stu Cncl; FNA; Pep Clb; Sci Clb; Voc Schl; Wholesale Mdse.

CHAPMAN, TAMI; Ridgedale HS; Marion, OH; Cls Rep Soph Cls; Pres Sr Cls; Band; Chrs; Chrh Wkr; Cmnty Wkr; Drl Tm; Hon Rl; College; Speech.

CHAPMAN, VICKI; Beechcroft Jr Sr HS; Columbus, OH; Girl Scts; Hon Rl; Lbry Ade; Sch Mus; OEA; Capital Univ; Crt Rptr.

CHAPOTON, WILLIAM; Bishop Gallagher HS; Mt Clemens, MI; 43/333 Hon Rl; Off Ade; Sch Pl; Wayne State Univ; Acctg.

CHAPPANO, PERRY; St Joseph Prep Seminary; Vienna, WV; 4/19 Cls Rep Frsh Cls; Cls Rep Soph Cls; Pres Sr Cls; NHS; Sch Pl; Stu Cncl; VP Key Clb; Letter Bsbl; Capt IM Sprt; Cit Awd; Georgetown Univ; Foreign Serv.

CHAPPELEAR, LORA; Fairbanks HS; Milford Center, OH; 1/90 VP Soph Cls; Am Leg Aux Girls St; Hon Rl; NHS; Sch Pl; FHA; Trk; GAA; College.

CHAPPELL, JACKIE; Tri West Hendricks HS; Pit tsboro, IN; Trs Jr Cls; Trs Sr Cls; Band; Drl Tm; Girl Scts; Hon Rl; NHS; Fr Clb; Pep Clb; Trk; St Josephs Coll; Bio.

CHAPPELL, JACQUELINE A; Tri West Hendricks HS; Pittsboro, IN; 2/120 Trs Jr Cls; Trs Sr Cls; Band; Girl Scts; Hon Rl; NHS; Fr Clb; Pep Clb; Swmmng; Trk; Univ.

CHAPPELL, JOHN; Liberty HS; Bristol, WV; Cls Rep Frsh Cls; Cls Rep Soph Cls; Boy Scts; Chrs; Chrh Wkr; FCA; Hon Rl; ROTC; Stu Cncl; Yth Flsp;.

CHAPPELL, KITTY; Pike Central HS; Petersburg, IN; Hst Frsh Cls; FCA; Hon Rl; NHS; Stu Cncl; 4-H; Sci Clb; Letter Swmmng; Mgrs; 4-H Awd; Indiana Univ; Nuclear Med.

CHAPPELL, LORI; Griffith HS; Griffith, IN; Sec Soph Cls; Cls Rep Soph Cls; Cl Rep Jr Cls; Cls Rep Sr Cls; Hon Rl; NHS; Pom Pon; PPFtbl; Purdue Univ; Nursing.

CHAPPLE, REBECCA; Kenston HS; Chagrin Fls, OH; Pres Jr Cls; Chrs; Hon Rl; Sch Pl; Drama Clb; Rus Clb; Chrldng; PPFtbl; Pres Intensive Ofc Ed Sec Clb; Outstndng Stu Awd IOE Class; Will Be Pres Of Sr Class; Coll; Intl Busns.

CHAPPO, RICHARD; John F Kennedy HS; Taylor, MI; Sprt Ed Sch Nwsp; Letter Ftbl; Letter Wrstlng; Eastern Michigan Univ; Radio.

CHARBONEAU, MICHAEL; Luke M Powers HS; Grand Blanc, MI; Debate Tm; Jr NHS; Natl Forn Lg; NHS; Sch Pl; Sch Nwsp; Ftbl; IM Sprt; Natl Merit SF; Opt Clb Awd; Mich State Univ; Pre Med.

CHARBONNEAU, ROBERT; Tri Township HS; Rapid Rvr, MI; Hon Rl; Letter Trk; Voc Schl.

CHARCANDY, SHERRI; Scott HS; Madison, WV; Band; Girl Scts; Hon Rl; Jr NHS; Stu Cncl; Yth Flsp; Pep Clb; Twrlr; Center Coll; Acctg.

CHARGO, JANICE; Ithaca HS; Ithaca, MI; Cls Rep Frsh Cls; Cls Rep Soph Cls; Am Leg Aux Girls St; Band; Debate Tm; Drm Mjrt; Hon Rl; Natl Forn Lg; NHS; Sch Mus; Olivet College; Music.

CHARGO, RENEE; Durand Area HS; Lennon, MI; 9/220 Hon Rl; NHS; Sprt Ed Yrbk; Rptr Yrbk; Yrbk; Rptr Sch Nwsp; Sch Nwsp; Baker Jr Coll Of Bus; Exec Sec.

CHARI, VEENA; Grosse Pointe North HS; Grosse Pt Wds, MI; Hon Rl; Jr NHS; NHS; Sch Pl; Drama Clb; Fr Clb; Spn Clb; Wayne State Univ; Physician.

CHARLES, CHRISTOPHER; Princeton HS; Princeton, WV; 2/350 Am Leg Boys St; Band; Chrs; Chrh Wkr; Hon Rl; Jr NHS; Mdrgl; NHS; Quill & Scroll; Sch Nwsp; Wv All St Chrs 78; Whos Who In Music 78; 1st Pl St WVU HS Jrnlsm Comp 78; Shcl Rep Wv H O Brien Leadr 77; West Virginia Univ; Med.

CHARLES, JAMES; Gwinn HS; Cornell, MI; Aud/Vis; Bay De Noc; Mech.

CHARLES, TAMMY; Chesapeake HS; Chesapeake, OH; 6/128 Hon Rl; NHS; Tennessee Temple Coll; Bio.

CHARME, MICHAEL; Meadowdale HS; Dayton, OH; Hon Rl; Jr NHS; NHS; Ftbl; Letter Glf; B Nai Brith Yth Org St At Arms Sec & Treas; Dayton Jewish Ctr Traveling Bsktbll Team Capt; Univ Of Florida; Acctg.

CHARNAS, JOHN; Warren Western Reserve HS; Warren, OH; 19/500 Am Leg Boys St; Boy Scts; Hon Rl; NHS; Sct Actv; Swmmng; Univ; Chem.

CHARR, JEFFREY S; View HS; Anawalt, WV; 20/240 Cls Rep Frsh Cls; Cls Rep Soph Cls; Cl Rep Jr Cls; Boy Scts; Hon Rl; NHS; Quill & Scroll; Red Cr Ade; Stu Cncl; Yrbk; Outstndg Male Soph 1978; Wrestlng Champ Mc Dowell Cnty 1979; Dist Sec Key Club 1979; West Virginia Univ; Med.

CHARTER, DAVID; Northport HS; Northport, MI; 10/28 Trs Jr Cls; Trs Sr Cls; Band; Boy Scts; Yrbk; Rptr Sch Nwsp; Bsbl; Bsktbl; Socr; Mgrs; E Michigan Univ; Bus Admin.

CHARTIER, LORI; Port Huron N HS; Port Huron, MI; Cls Rep Frsh Cls; Cls Rep Sr Cls; Chrh Wkr; Hon Rl; NHS; Stu Cncl; St Clair Co Comm Coll; Forestry.

CHARVILLE, DAVE; Edison HS; Milan, OH; Band; Sch Mus; FFA; Univ; Bus.

CHASE, CAROL; Alexander HS; Albany, OH; Cls Rep Sr Cls; Girl Scts; Hon Rl; NHS; Stg Crw; Stu Cncl; 4-H; FHA; Pep Clb; Trk; Hocking Tech Coll; Med Records.

CHASE, CAROL ANN; Alexander HS; Albany, OH; Girl Scts; Hon Rl; Jr NHS; NHS; Stg Crw; Stu Cncl; 4-H; FHA; Pep Clb; Trk; Hocking Tech Coll; Bus.

CHASE, CYNTHIA; Norwalk HS; Norwalk, OH; 9/185 VP Sr Cls; Band; Chrh Wkr; Hon Rl; Yth Flsp; Sprt Ed Sch Nwsp; Letter Trk; GAA; Scr Kpr; College; Comp Sci.

CHASE, DENNIS; Highland HS; Fredericktown, OH; 14/127 Pres Frsh Cls; Pres Soph Cls; Am Leg Boys St; FCA; NHS; Stu Cncl; 4-H; FFA; Capt Ftbl; Agri.

CHASE, LAWRENCE R; Switzerland Cnty Jr Sr HS; Vevay, IN; Am Leg Boys St; NHS; Rptr Sch Nwsp; Bsktbl; Trk; Coll.

CHASE, LEE; Westland HS; Columbus, OH; Cls Rep Frsh Cls; Aud/Vis; Chrs; Chrh Wkr; Cmnty Wkr; Pol Wkr; Sch Mus; Sch Pl; Yth Flsp; Ftbl; Black Belt In Karate 79; Ohio St Univ; Pub Relations.

CHASE, LINDA; Alexander HS; Albany, OH; 8/132 Trs Sr Cls; Hon Rl; NHS; Stg Crw; 4-H; FHA; Pep Clb; Trk; Chrldng; GAA; Hocking Tech Coll; Sec Sci.

CHASE, MICHAEL; Merrillville HS; Merrillville, IN; Hon Rl; NHS; Univ; Bus.

CHASE, PENNY; Amanda Clearcreek HS; Lancaster, OH; Am Leg Aux Girls St; Cmp Fr Grls; Hon Rl; NHS; Rptr Sch Nwsp; Lat Clb; Pres Sci Clb; IM Sprt; Cit Awd; Regnl Schlr Prog 78; Newark Schlrshp Test #11 76; Otstndng Stud Awd 73 74 & 75; Univ.

CHASE, STEPHEN P; Ansonia Local HS; Galveston, TX; 1/70 Val; Am Leg Boys St; Pres NHS; Stu Cncl; Spn Clb; Pres VICA; Trk; Am Leg Awd; Bausch & Lomb Awd; DAR Awd; Rice Univ; Sci.

CHASTAIN, DEBBIE; Salem HS; Salem, IN; 7/147 Pres JA; NHS; 4-H; OEA; Letter Crs Cntry; Letter Trk; Cit Awd; Ind Univ.

CHASTAIN, KAREN; Canton South HS; Canton, OH; Cls Rep Frsh Cls; Cl Rep Jr Cls; Hon Rl; NHS; Off Ade; Sch Nwsp; Mth Clb; Pep Clb; Sci Clb; Stark Tech; Acctg.

CHASTAIN, REBEKAH; Southwestern HS; Flat Rock, IN; 17/60 Band; Chrs; Lbry Ade; Bsktbl; Univ; Nursing.

CHASTAIN, ROGER; Orleans HS; Orleans, IN; 1/70 Hon Rl; Trk; IM Sprt; College; Elec.

CHASTEEN, DEANNA; Lebanon HS; Lebanon, OH; Chrs; Hon Rl; Lbry Ade; Fr Clb; FTA; Univ; French.

CHATFIELD, DAVID; Normandy HS; Parma, OH; 13/649 Boy Scts; Chrs; Cmnty Wkr; Hon Rl; Pol Wkr; Swmmng; Natl Merit Ltr; Cleveland St Univ; Law.

CHATFIELD, PETER W; Cardinal HS; Huntsburg, OH; 2/115 Sec Jr Cls; Trs Jr Cls; Sal; Pres AFS; Am Leg Boys St; Chrs; Chrh Wkr; Hon Rl; Pres NHS; Sch Mus; Wesleyan Univ.

CHATMAN, ERNEST; Martin Luther King HS; Detroit, MI; Band; Debate Tm; Drl Tm; FCA; JA; Lit Mag; Off Ade; ROTC; Sch Pl; Sprt Ed Yrbk; College.

CHATO, CAROL; Meadowdale HS; Dayton, OH; 19/275 Cls Rep Frsh Cls; Cls Rep Soph Cls; Cl Rep Jr Cls; Cls Rep Sr Cls; Hon Rl; NHS; Off Ade; Stg Crw; Drama Clb; Univ Of Dayton; English.

CHATOS, TINA; Perry Baptist HS; Laingsburg, MI; Band; Chrh Wkr; Hon Rl; Stu Cncl; Yth Flsp; FHA; Bsktbl; Grand Rapids Bptst Cllge; Spec Ed.

CHATREAU, CHERIE; Bedford Sr HS; Lambertville, MI; Cls Rep Frsh Cls; Cls Rep Soph Cls; Cl Rep Jr Cls; VP Sr Cls; Chrs; Drl Tm; Sch Mus; Stu Cncl; Yrbk; Bsktbl; Northern Michigan Univ; Psych.

CHATTERSON, PATRICIA; Rochester Sr HS; Rochester, MI; 68/360 Chrs; Hosp Ade; Mdrgl; NHS; Sch Mus; Stg Crw; Treas Pep Clb; Mgrs; Tmr; Kiwan Awd; Michigan St Univ; Nursing.

CHATTERTON, DALE; Buffalo HS; Huntington, WV; Band; Chrs; Chrh Wkr; Hon Rl; Mod UN; Sch Pl; Rptr Yrbk; Mth Clb; Capt Socr; West Virginia Tech Univ; Elec Tech.

CHATTIN, LORI; South Knox HS; Vincennes, IN; 9/125 Cls Rep Frsh Cls; Pres Soph Cls; Cls Rep Soph Cls; Cl Rep Jr Cls; Band; Hon Rl; NHS; Sec Stu Cncl; 4-H; Fr Clb; Purdue Univ; Vet Med.

CHAURIN, LISA; Edison HS; Norwalk, OH; 8/164 Trs Soph Cls; Band; Chrs; Hon Rl; Jr NHS; NHS; Sch Mus; Sch Pl; Stg Crw; Drama Clb; Ohio Univ; Speech.

CHAVEZ, SHELLY; De Kalb HS; Auburn, IN; 69/295 Girl Scts; Stu Cncl; Yrbk; Pep Clb; Chrldng; PPFtbl; Vocational Schl; Dental Hygiene.

CHEADLE, KIM; Montpelier HS; Montpelier, OH; 13/105 VP Soph Cls; Band; Drl Tm; Hon Rl; Sch Mus; 4-H; Letter Bsktbl; Letter Trk; College; Computer Sciences.

CHEATHAM, LINDA; Stephen T Badin HS; Hamilton, OH; Chrh Wkr; Cmnty Wkr; Hon Rl; Rptr Sch Nwsp; Pep Clb; Gym; Capt Chrldng; IM Sprt; Scr Kpr; Tmr; Miami Univ; Soc.

CHEATHAM, SHERYL; Daleville HS; Daleville, IN; Cl Rep Jr Cls; Hon Rl; NHS; Stu Cncl; Fr Clb; Letter Gym; Trk; Letter Chrldng; Mat Maids; Purdue Univ; Fashion Merch.

CHEATUM, TY; Broad Ripple HS; Indianapolis, IN; Cls Rep Sr Cls; Chrs; Hon Rl; Mdrgl; NHS; Off Ade; Sch Mus; Sch Pl; Spn Clb; Letter Bsbl; Hoosier Schlr 79; Purdue Mert Schsp 79; Purdue Univ; Elec Engr.

CHECK, JEANNE; Our Lady Of Mercy HS; Redford, MI; Cmnty Wkr; Girl Scts; JA; Pep Clb; Gym; Swmmng; Coach Actv; Univ Of Michigan; Psych.

CHECK, RAYMOND B; Univ Of Detroit HS; Detroit, MI; 12/150 Cls Rep Frsh Cls; Cl Rep Jr Cls; Cmnty Wkr; Debate Tm; Hon Rl; Mod UN; NHS; Sch Pl; Rptr Yrbk; Natl Merit SF; Univ.

CHECKLEY, MARK; Blissfield HS; Howell, MI; 23/111 Pres Soph Cls; Pres Jr Cls; Pres Sr Cls; Cmnty Wkr; Hon Rl; NHS; Fr Clb; Key Clb; Letter Bsbl; Letter Ftbl; St MHEAA Schlrshp; BEOG NOSL; Western Michigan Univ; Busns.

CHEEK, KEITH E; Bloom Carroll HS; Lancaster, OH; Pres Soph Cls; Cls Rep Soph Cls; Pres Sr Cls; Am Leg Boys St; Boy Scts; Hon Rl; Jr NHS; Lbry Ade; Stu Cncl; Capt Bsktbl; All Dist 1st Team Ftbl; All Mid State League Bsktbl; Hall Of Fame Ftbl; College.

CHEEK, KIMBERLEE; Alma HS; Alma, MI; Chrh Wkr; Letter Bsktbl; Johnson Bible Coll; History.

CHEEK, LORI A; St Stephen T Badin HS; Hamilton, OH; 9/211 Chrh Wkr; Drl Tm; Girl Scts; Hon Rl; Sch Mus; Sch Pl; Bsbl; Bsktbl; Trk; Rotary Awd;.

CHEEK, TAMI; De Kalb HS; Waterloo, IN; 69/281 4-H; Ger Clb; Pep Clb; Letter Gym; Letter Trk; Chrldng; IM Sprt; Twrlr; 4-H Awd; De Paw Univ; Sociology.

CHEESEMAN, JEAN; Brookhaven Sr HS; Columbus, OH; Cls Rep Frsh Cls; Cl Rep Jr Cls; VP Sr Cls; Cls Rep Sr Cls; Chrh Wkr; Hon Rl; Lit Mag; Off Ade; Stu Cncl; Yth Flsp; Knight Chanodor Awd 77; Ohio St Univ; Phys Educ.

CHEESMAN, STEVEN; Moeller HS; Cincinnati, OH; 97/300 Trs Jr Cls; Cls Rep Sr Cls; Hon Rl; Stu Cncl; Rptr Sch Nwsp; Bsktbl; Letter Ftbl; Letter Glf; Letter Ten; IM Sprt; Univ Of Dayton; Acctg.

CHEKOURAS, KEVE; Admiral King HS; Lorain, OH; JA; Orch; Sch Mus; Univ; Law.

CHEN, AL; Liberty HS; Youngstown, OH; Chrs; YSU; Dentistry.

CHENAULT, JAMES C; St Francis De Salles HS; Temperance, MI; Band; Chrs; Rptr Sch Nwsp; Drama Clb; Letter Mgrs; Mich Solo & Ensemble Festival; Superior Rating Tuba Solo; Tuba Schlrshp To Interlochen; All State Band; College; Physics.

CHENEVEY, J ALAN; Orrville HS; Orrville, OH; Pres Frsh Cls; FCA; Hon Rl; Bsbl; Bsktbl; IM Sprt; Coll; Indus Arts.

CHENEY, DENISE; Mason HS; Mason, MI; Chrs; Chrh Wkr; Cmnty Wkr; Hon Rl; Jr NHS; Sch Mus; Stu Cncl; Yth Flsp; Ed Yrbk; Albion Coll; Bus, Public Relations.

CHENEY, PAUL; Ithaca HS; Ithaca, MI; Band; Hon Rl; Sch Mus; Stg Crw; Yth Flsp; 4-H; Ftbl; 4-H Awd; Mic Tech Univ; Comp Sci.

CHENEY, SANDRA C; Upper Sandusky HS; Upper Sandusky, OH; 2/212 Drl Tm; Hon Rl; Hosp Ade; NHS; Stu Cncl; Drama Clb; 4-H; VP FNA; 4-H Awd; Bluffton; Pre Med.

CHENEY, SUSAN M; Sidney HS; Sidney, OH; 7/250 Girl Scts; Hon Rl; NHS; Off Ade; Stg Crw; Stu Cncl; Natl Merit Ltr; Natl Merit SF; Vanderbilt Univ; Civil Engr.

CHENGELIS, EVELYN; Boardman HS; Boardman, OH; 77/558 Hon Rl; NHS; Fr Clb; Sci Clb; College; Nursing.

CHEPOLIS, BILL; Park Hills HS; Fairborn, OH; Hon Rl; Jr NHS; Letter Crs Cntry; Ftbl; Socr; Letter Trk; Ore State Univ; Comp Sci.

CHERRY, LORI; Mc Comb HS; Mc Comb, OH; 4/81 Hst Jr Cls; Am Leg Aux Girls St; Chrs; Hon Rl; NHS; Sch Pl; Rptr Sch Nwsp; Pres 4-H; Pres FHA; College; Vet.

CHERRY, SCOTT; Edison Jr Sr HS; Lake Station, IN; Boy Scts; Spn Clb; Letter Bsbl; Letter Bsktbl; Crs Cntry; Letter Ftbl; Coach Actv; Univ; Engr.

CHERRY, SHELLI; Smithville HS; Marshallvil, OH; Cls Rep Soph Cls; Band; Chrs; Drm Mjrt; Girl Scts; Fr Clb; Trk; GAA; Twrlr; Muskingum College; Bus.

CHERRY, STEVEN; Northwestern HS; Burbank, OH; Chrs; Cmnty Wkr; 4-H; Bsbl;.

CHERRYHOLMES, SHARA; Waynesville HS; Waynesville, OH; Trs Soph Cls; Sec Band; Girl Scts; Hon Rl; NHS; Stu Cncl; Ed Yrbk; College; Acctng.

CHERUP, MARCIA; Westland HS; Columbus, OH; Band; Chrh Wkr; Drl Tm; Hon Rl; Drama Clb; Pep Clb; Crs Cntry; Trk; IM Sprt; Tmr; College; Nursing.

CHESNEY, JACQUELINE; Theodore Roosevelt HS; Wyandotte, MI; Hon Rl; NHS; Stu Cncl; Mercy Coll; Nursing.

CHESNEY, KELLY; Howell HS; Howell, MI; Hon Rl; Y-Teens; Ger Clb; Letter IM Sprt; Cit Awd; Univ.

CHESS, JIMMY R; Bath HS; Lima, OH; 2/200 Boy Scts; Chrs; Hon Rl; NHS; Sch Mus; Stu Cncl; Ed Yrbk; 4-H; Fr Clb; Letter Ftbl; College; Engr.

CHESSER, CHARLES; Alexander HS; Athens, OH; Pres Frsh Cls; Pres Soph Cls; Boy Scts; Chrh Wkr; Hon Rl; NHS; Fr Clb; Lat Clb; Spn Clb; Letter Bsbl; Ohio Univ; Acctg.

CHESSER, SUSAN L; Galien HS; Galien, MI; Chrh Wkr; Hon Rl; NHS; Sch Pl; Rptr Yrbk; Rptr Sch Nwsp; Letter Bsktbl; Scr Kpr; Tmr; Manchester Coll; Elem Tchr.

CHESTNUT, CONNIE; Cloverdale HS; Cloverdale, IN; 3/88 VP Soph Cls; Band; Hon Rl; NHS; Sch Pl; Treas Stu Cncl; Sprt Ed Yrbk; Pep Clb; GAA; Scr Kpr; Univ.

CHESTNUT, JEFFREY; North Daviess HS; Odon, IN; 45/100 Chrh Wkr; FFA; Spn Clb; IM Sprt; College; Math.

CHEVRETTE, MIKE; Negaunee HS; Negaunee, MI; Chrs; Cmnty Wkr; Hon Rl; Mdrgl; Stg Crw; VICA; Bsktbl; Ftbl; Trk; Wrstlng; Voc Schl; Carpntr.

CHEW, CONNIE; Tri HS; New Castle, IN; Sec Soph Cls; Trs Jr Cls; Trs Sr Cls; Lbry Ade; Off Ade; FHA; VP OEA; Chrldng; GAA; Mat Maids; Indiana Univ East; Sec/recpt.

CHEW, DENNIS; North Vermillion HS; Cayuga, IN; Am Leg Boys St; Letter Bsbl;.

CHEW, RICHARD; New Buffalo HS; Union Pier, MI; Sec Frsh Cls; Cls Rep Frsh Cls; VP Soph Cls; Cls Rep Soph Cls; Cl Rep Jr Cls; Cls Rep Sr Cls; Aud/Vis; Band; Boy Scts; Chrs; Pepperdine Univ; Drama.

CHEZEM, MARY; William Henry Harrison HS; W Laf, IN; Girl Scts; Hon Rl; Sch Mus; Sct Actv; Stg Crw; Rptr Yrbk; Rptr Sch Nwsp; Ger Clb; Pep Clb; Trk; Purdue Univ; Intr Decor.

CHIACCHIERO, JOHN; Harbor HS; Ashtabula, OH; 25/200 Cls Rep Frsh Cls; VP Soph Cls; VP Jr Cls; Sec Aud/Vis; FCA; Yrbk; Pres Spn Clb; Bsbl; Letter Bsktbl; Letter Ftbl; Univ; Pre Med.

CHIAN CHAO, IN; Ravenna HS; Solon, OH; Chrs; Hon Rl; NHS; Fr Clb; Univ; Med.

CHIAPELLA, KAREN; Warren Woods HS; Warren, MI; Cls Rep Frsh Cls; Cls Rep Soph Cls; Cl Rep Jr Cls; Cls Rep Sr Cls; Chrs; NHS; Sch Mus; Sch Pl; Stu Cncl; Capt Chrldng; Oakland Univ; Theatre.

CHICK, GREG; Fairborn Park Hills HS; Xenia, OH; Cls Rep Frsh Cls; Aud/Vis; Hon Rl; Stg Crw; Sch Nwsp; Capt Bsktbl; Letter Socr; Pres Awd; Yale Univ; Law.

CHICK, MARTIN; Thomas N Harvey HS; Painesville, OH; Band; Rptr Sch Nwsp; Letter Crs Cntry; Letter Trk; College; Bus Mngmnt.

CHIDESTER, DEBORAH; Beaver Local HS; Lisbon, OH; 27/221 Band; Chrs; Chrh Wkr; Hon Rl; NHS; Sch Mus; Stg Crw; Yrbk; Drama Clb; Eng Clb; Univ; Med Tech.

CHIDSEY, DARRYL; Buckeye Sr HS; Valley City, OH; 20/180 Hon Rl; NHS; FTA; Lat Clb; Bsbl; Bsktbl; Ftbl; IM Sprt; Scr Kpr; Tmr; Pres Of Lttrmns Clb 78; Bst Dfnsv Back On Ftbll Tm 78; 1st Tm Medina Cnty Gazette Ftbll Tm 78; Bowling Green St Univ; Bus Admin.

CHILCOTE, GARY; Upper Arlington HS; Columbus, OH; 230/610 Boy Scts; Drama Clb; Fr Clb; IM Sprt; Scr Kpr; Ohio State Univ; Engineering.

CHILCOTE, LARRY; Upper Arlington HS; Columbus, OH; 223/610 Boy Scts; Ohi State Univ.

CHILD, DEBRA; St Clair HS; St Clair, MI; 12/200 Cls Rep Sr Cls; Band; Hon Rl; Sec NHS; Letter Bsktbl; Capt Trk; IM Sprt; Mgrs; St Clair Cnty Cmnty Coll; Offc Educ.

CHILDERS, BRENDA; Springfield North HS; Springfield, OH; Cl Rep Jr Cls; Sec Sr Cls; Trs Sr Cls; Chrs; Cmnty Wkr; Girl Scts; Hon Rl; Orch; Pol Wkr; Sct Actv; Outstanding Stu Awd In Biology; Miami Univ; Business Admin.

CHILDERS, C; Brandon HS; Ortonville, MI; Chrh Wkr; FCA; Hon Rl; Letter Ftbl; Letter Ten; College; Sci.

CHILDERS, GLENN; Lawrenceburg HS; Lawrenceburg, IN; Cls Rep Frsh Cls; Pres Band; Drm Mjrt;

Hon Rl; NHS; Sch Mus; Stu Cncl; Key Clb; Pres Sci Clb; VP Spn Clb; Indiana Univ; Comp Sci.

CHILDERS, JEFF; Peru HS; Peru, IN; VP Sr Cls; Aud/Vis; Stg Crw; Stu Cncl; Rptr Sch Nwsp; Ger Clb; Pep Clb; Ftbl; IM Sprt; Ind Univ; Bus.

CHILDERS, JENNIFER; Arsenal Tech HS; Indianapolis, IN; Hon Rl; Off Ade; Lat Clb; Mth Clb; 1st Geometry & Math 79; Mu Alpha Theta Math Clb Sec 79; Bus Schl; Math.

CHILDERS, P; Regina HS; Cleveland, OH; Chrs; Drl Tm; JA; Sch Pl; Beta Clb; Drama Clb; JA Awd; De Paul Univ; Acctg.

CHILDRESS, DONALD; Mississinewa HS; Marion, IN; Chrh Wkr; Hon Rl; NHS; Sch Mus; Sch Pl; Stg Crw; Drama Clb; Pres Fr Clb; Voice Dem Awd; Univ Of Nc; Law.

CHILDS, CINDY; Kingston Cmnty HS; Kingston, MI; Chrh Wkr; Hon Rl; NHS; Ten; Detroit Bible Coll.

CHILDS, DENISE; Saginaw HS; Saginaw, MI; 2/350 Hon Rl; JA; Jr NHS; NHS; Fr Clb; JA Awd; College; Engineering.

CHILDS, KELLIE; Central HS; Detroit, MI; Drl Tm; Hon Rl; Jr NHS; Lbry Ade; Stu Cncl; Pep Clb; Cit Awd; Michigan St Univ; Nursing.

CHILDS, PATRICIA; Dunbar HS; Dayton, OH; Wright State Univ; Theatre.

CHILDS, R; Northern HS; Detroit, MI; Chrh Wkr; Cmnty Wkr; Hon Rl; Pol Wkr; Drama Clb; Sci Clb; Hnr Awd For Outstndng Ach In Art; Wayne St Univ; Med.

CHILDS, RICK; Adams Central HS; Decatur, IN; Hon Rl; PAVAS; Sch Pl; Sprt Ed Sch Nwsp; Drama Clb; Mth Clb; Spn Clb; Bsbl; Letter Ftbl; Glf; Purdue Univ; Sci.

CHILLEMI, CHRISTOPHER; Rocky River HS; Rocky River, OH; Hon Rl; Ftbl; Wrstlng; IM Sprt; Voc Schl; Auto Mech.

CHILTON, DEBRA; Eastlake North HS; Eastlake, OH; Cls Rep Frsh Cls; Cls Rep Soph Cls; Cl Rep Jr Cls; Am Leg Aux Girls St; Band; Chrh Wkr; Cmnty Wkr; Drm Mjrt; Hon Rl; College.

CHILTON, ROBIN; Indianapolis Baptist HS; Indianapolis, IN; Am Leg Aux Girls St; Chrs; Chrh Wkr; Girl Scts; Hon Rl; Lbry Ade; Mdrgl; Pol Wkr; Rptr Yrbk; Rptr Sch Nwsp;.

CHIN, HEATHER J; Immaculata HS; Detroit, MI; 5/93 Pres Sr Cls; VP Sr Cls; Hon Rl; NHS; Stu Cncl; Spn Clb; Central Michigan Univ; Comp Sci.

CHIN, HILARY C; Immaculata HS; Detroit, MI; 6/93 VP Jr Cls; Hon Rl; VP NHS; Sec Stu Cncl; Spn Clb; Cntrl Michigan Univ; Psychology.

CHIN, SHERMAN; Whitehall Yearling HS; Whitehall, OH; Am Leg Boys St; Hon Rl; Stu Cncl; Letter Bsbl; Bsktbl; Am Leg Awd; College; Business.

CHIODO, CATHIE; Berea HS; Berea, OH; Cls Rep Frsh Cls; Trs Soph Cls; Chrs; Chrh Wkr; Cmnty Wkr; Hon Rl; Hosp Ade; JA; NHS; Off Ade; Coll; Med.

CHIODO, VALERIE; Madonna HS; Follansbee, WV; 1/105 Val; Am Leg Aux Girls St; NHS; Sec Stu Cncl; Rptr Yrbk; Yrbk; Letter Ten; Alderson Broaddus College; Rn.

CHIOLDI, MARIO; St Edward HS; Middleburg Hts, OH; Trs Frsh Cls; Cls Rep Soph Cls; Debate Tm; Hon Rl; Lit Mag; Mod UN; Natl Forn Lg; NHS; Rptr Sch Nwsp; Key Clb; English III Awd; Ohio Univ Summer Scholars Program; College.

CHIPPS, CHERYL; Hoover HS; North Canton, OH; 96/430 Cls Rep Frsh Cls; Chrs; Cmnty Wkr; Girl Scts; Hon Rl; Hosp Ade; Off Ade; Sct Actv; Idabelle Firestone Schl Of Nursing.

CHIPPS, JAMES P; Roosevelt Wilson HS; Clarksburg, WV; 5/122 VP Frsh Cls; Pres Jr Cls; Am Leg Boys St; Band; Hon Rl; NHS; Orch; Sch Pl; VP Stu Cncl; Yth Flsp; Elks Mst Vlbl Stdnt 79; Kiwanas Boy Of Month 79; West Virginia Univ; Engr.

CHIRALOS, TONY; Copley HS; Akron, OH; Crs Cntry; Letter Trk; Univ.

CHISHOLM, DARCY; Arthur Hill HS; Saginaw, MI; Band; Chrh Wkr; Hon Rl; Hosp Ade; Sec JA; Off Ade; Pres Yth Flsp; Rptr Yrbk; Rptr Sch Nwsp; JA Awd; Delegate To Natl Jr Achvmnt Confrnc 79; Michigan St Univ; Nursing.

CHISHOLM, SUSAN M; Sycamore HS; Cincinnati, OH; 8/400 Boy Scts; Girl Scts; Hon Rl; NHS; Red Cr Ade; Swmmng; Natl Merit SF; Univ; Archt.

CHITTOCK, CHRISTOPHER; Kenston HS; Chargin Fl, OH; 82/217 VP Sr Cls; Boy Scts; Chrh Wkr; Cmnty Wkr; FCA; Quill & Scroll; Stu Cncl; Ed Sch Nwsp; Ftbl; Trk; College; Law.

CHITWOOD, KIMBERLY; Culver Girls Academy; Louisville, KY; 26/193 Cls Rep Soph Cls; Cl Rep Jr Cls; Cls Rep Sr Cls; Girl Scts; Hon Rl; Lbry Ade; Lit Mag; Stu Cncl; Rptr Sch Nwsp; Pep Clb; Univ; Law.

CHIZMADIA, GERALD L; Lakeville Memorial HS; Columbiaville, MI; 18/189 VP Sr Cls; Chrh Wkr; Hon Rl; NHS; Stg Crw; Natl Merit Schl; Opt Clb Awd; Rotary Awd; Repair & Maintain Farm Equip 73 79; 3.5 Comm Mbr Of Lakeville HS 78; Michigan Tech Univ; Mech Engr.

CHLEBEK, MICHELE; La Salle HS; South Bend, IN; 11/500 Hon Rl; Lit Mag; NHS; Quill & Scroll; Rptr Sch Nwsp; Sch Nwsp; Letter Bsbl; NCTE; Ind Univ; Advertising.

CHMELOVSKI, LINDA; Madonna HS; Follansbee, WV; 6/100 Hon Rl; Lit Mag; NHS; W Liberty St Coll; Acctg.

CHMIELEWSKI, JANET; Dominican HS; Hamtramck, MI; Chrh Wkr; Hon Rl; Hosp Ade; NHS; IM Sprt; Natl Merit Schl; Mic Tech Univ; Med Tech.

CHMIELEWSKI, PAUL; Gabriel Richard HS; Ann Arbor, MI; 10/75 Cls Rep Frsh Cls; Cls Rep Soph Cls; Cl Rep Jr Cls; Am Leg Boys St; Boy Scts; Hon Rl; NHS; VP Stu Cncl; Am Leg Awd; Natl Merit SF; Univ Of Notre Dame; Optometry.

CHMIELIEWSKI, SHERRI; Manistee Catholic Ctrl HS; Manistee, MI; Girl Scts; Hon Rl; Red Cr Ade; Rptr Sch Nwsp; 4-H; Letter Bsktbl; Trk; Coach Actv; 4-H Awd; Aquinas College; Accountant.

CHO, JUDY; Centennial HS; Columbus, OH; 1/213 Band; Hon Rl; Hosp Ade; Jr NHS; NHS; Orch; Treas Stu Cncl; Spn Clb; IM Sprt; Natl Merit SF; Univ; Pre Med.

CHO, PEGGY; East Kentwood HS; Kentwood, MI; Hon Rl; Lit Mag; Sch Mus; Yth Flsp; Eng Clb; Letter Ten; 1st Plc In Schls Poetry Writing Contest 79; Univ Of Michigan; Engr.

CHOAT, RONI L; Mt Vernon HS; Gambier, OH; Cl Rep Jr Cls; Drl Tm; Lbry Ade; NHS; 4-H; FHA; FTA; Spn Clb; Gym; College; Elem Ed.

CHOBAN, GARY; Buckannon Upshur HS; Buckhannon, WV; Band; Hon Rl; Pol Wkr; Crs Cntry; Trk; IM Sprt; West Virginia Univ.

CHOCOLA, JOSEPH C; Williamston HS; Okemos, MI; 20/180 Boy Scts; Hon Rl; Jr NHS; Sct Actv; Rptr Yrbk; 4-H; Bsbl; Bsktbl; Capt Glf; Capt Ten; Hillsdale Coll; Bus.

CHOI, CHUL; Greenville Sr HS; Greenville, MI; Am Leg Boys St; Chrh Wkr; Cmnty Wkr; Hon Rl; JA; Orch; Stu Cncl; Fr Clb; IM Sprt; Supereme Ct Justice 79; Mst Outstndng Orch 77; Blue Lake Fine Arts Camp Schlsp 77 & 78; Univ; Med.

CHOI, JIM; Madena HS; Cincinnati, OH; Hon Rl; NHS; Pol Wkr; Fr Clb; Bsktbl; Ftbl; Cit Awd; JA Awd; Washington Univ; Chem Engr.

CHOINSKI, MARLENE; Saint Alphonsus HS; Dearborn, MI; 10/173 Cl Rep Jr Cls; Chrs; Hon Rl; NHS; Pep Clb; Chrldng; GAA; College.

CHOISON, JERRI J; Bishop Noll Inst; Gary, IN; Fresh Class Rep To Stu Coun; Piano Comptn For 3 Yrs Where 2 Rcvd 2 Superior Rtngs Gld Mdl & Slvr Mdl; Univ; Archt.

CHOITZ, CAROLYN; Gladwin HS; Gladwin, MI; 55/149 Lbry Ade; Rptr Yrbk; Central Michigan Univ; Bio.

CHOLEK, P; Seven Hills HS; Cincinnati, OH; Hon Rl; Sci Clb; Bsbl; C of C Awd; Natl Merit SF; College; Math.

CHOLER, DEBBIE; Walled Lake Central HS; Union Lake, MI; Cls Rep Soph Cls; Cl Rep Jr Cls; Hon Rl; NHS; Orch; Sch Mus; Ger Clb; Ten; 3rd Prize In The Artrain Poster Contest; Awds From Paintings Entered In Contests; Art Club; Kendall Schl Of Design; Art.

CHONTOS, TODD E; Martins Ferry HS; Martins Ferry, OH; Pres Frsh Cls; Cls Rep Soph Cls; Chrs; Sch Mus; Stu Cncl; Bsktbl; Amer Indstr & Resources Corp Award 1975; Ohio State Univ; Pharmacy.

CHORDAS, FRED; Hubbard HS; Hubbard, OH; 14/330 Hon Rl; Fr Clb; Bsktbl; College; Optometry.

CHOREY, CHRIS; Meadowbrook HS; Lore City, OH; Band; Sec Key Clb; Lat Clb; Mth Clb; Rus Clb; Sci Clb; College.

CHOU, WINSTON; Morgantown HS; Morgantwn, WV; Cls Rep Soph Cls; Cl Rep Jr Cls; Boy Scts; Hon Rl; NHS; Sct Actv; Stu Cncl; Rptr Yrbk; Mth Clb; Spn Clb; Univ; Archt.

CHRISMAN, SUSAN; De Kalb HS; Auburn, IN; 2/283 Cls Rep Frsh Cls; VP Jr Cls; VP Sr Cls; Am Leg Aux Girls St; Band; Boy Scts; Drl Tm; JA; VP NHS; Sch Mus; Invited To Tri Kappa Honor Banquet; Received 1st Rating At Vocal Contest; College; Financing.

CHRIST, RICH; Leslie HS; Leslie, MI; Pres Sr Cls; Am Leg Boys St; Band; Boy Scts; Chrh Wkr; Hon Rl; Stu Cncl; Yth Flsp; Letter Glf; Letter Wrstlng; College.

CHRISTEN, MARLA; Rogers HS; Toledo, OH; Chrs; Chrh Wkr; Yth Flsp; Fr Clb; Sci Clb; GAA; College; Pharmacy.

CHRISTENSEN, CHRISTINE; Whiteford Ag HS; Ottawa Lk, MI; Hon Rl; NHS; Off Ade; Pep Clb; Mgrs; Univ; Bus.

CHRISTENSEN, JO ANN; East Kentwood HS; Kentwood, MI; Pres Frsh Cls; Cmnty Wkr; Off Ade; Rptr Yrbk; Eng Clb; Pep Clb; Letter Chrldng; GAA; PPFtbl; Natl Merit SF; Mi Comp Schlrshp Recogntn 79; Whos Who 77; Aquinas Coll; Psych.

CHRISTENSEN, KAREN; Lake City Area HS; Lake City, MI; Sec Frsh Cls; Hst Jr Cls; Hst Sr Cls; Band; Chrs; Hon Rl; Jr NHS; NHS; Sch Mus; Sch Pl; Univ; Dent Hygnst.

CHRISTENSEN, RICHARD; Hartland HS; Hartland, MI; Boy Scts; Hon Rl; Stu Cncl; Fr Clb; FTA; Letter Bsktbl; Letter Crs Cntry; Letter Trk; Varsity Club; Most Valuable For Cross Country; Most Improved For B B; Colorado Air Force Academy; Aviation.

CHRISTENSEN, ROBERT; Westfall HS; Orient, OH; 17/160 Am Leg Boys St; Band; Chrs; Hon Rl; NHS; Orch; Ed Yrbk; Yrbk; Sch Nwsp; 4-H; Photography; Band Serv; Vocational Schl; Photography.

CHRISTENSEN, SHEILA; Edwardsburg Public HS; Niles, MI; Chrs; Hon Rl; Stu Cncl; Letter Crs Cntry; Capt Trk; Kendall; Interior Design.

CHRISTENSEN, SUSAN; Edwardsburg HS; Edwardsburg, MI; Band; Chrh Wkr; Orch; Sch Mus; Yth Flsp; Rptr Sch Nwsp; Univ; Med Asst.

CHRISTIAN, KENT C; Cascade HS; Clayton, IN; 3/137 Pres Sr Cls; Am Leg Boys St; Band; Hon Rl; NHS; Stu Cncl; 4-H; Bsbl; Bsktbl; Ftbl; Indiana St Univ.

CHRISTIAN, LARRY; Newton HS; Troy, OH; 7/44 Cls Rep Frsh Cls; FCA; Hon Rl; NHS; Stu Cncl; Rptr Sch Nwsp; Bsbl; Bsktbl; Crs Cntry; Socr; Edison St Coll.

CHRISTIAN, SCHONDRA; South HS; Youngstown, OH; 18/316 Sec Frsh Cls; Chrh Wkr; Hon Rl; Off Ade; Stu Cncl; Y-Teens; Rptr Yrbk; Letter Trk; Letter Chrldng; Bronz Award 77; Univ; Med.

CHRISTIAN, SUSAN B; Sandusky HS; Sandusky, OH; Pres Soph Cls; Pres Jr Cls; Pres Sr Cls; AFS; Am Leg Aux Girls St; Band; Chrs; NHS; College; Med.

CHRISTIAN, TERRI; Chesapeake HS; Chesapeake, OH; 21/140 Sec Frsh Cls; Sec Soph Cls; Sec Jr Cls; Aud/Vis; Hon Rl; Lbry Ade; Off Ade; Stu Cncl; Pep Clb; Huntington Coll; Bus Educ.

CHRISTIAN, TERRI; Field HS; Suffield, OH; 44/256 Band; Cmp Fr Grls; Chrs; Hon Rl; NHS; Off Ade; 4-H; Bsktbl; GAA; Bowling Green Univ.

CHRISTIAN, THOMAS; North Dickinson HS; Sagola, MI; 11/47 Band; NHS; Sch Pl; Sprt Ed Sch Nwsp; Letter Ftbl; Gust K Newberg Schlrshp 79; Alpha Beta Awd; Natl Hon Soc; Michigan Tech Univ; Civil Engr.

CHRISTIANER, MICHAEL; New Haven HS; Ft Wayne, IN; Cl Rep Jr Cls; Band; FCA; JA; Stu Cncl; Trk;.

CHRISTIANSEN, LISA; Williamston HS; Williamston, MI; Hon Rl; Jr NHS; Sch Pl; 4-H; Capt Bsktbl; Swmmng; Ten; Chrldng; GAA; IM Sprt; Mich State Univ; Fashion Mrchndsg.

CHRISTIANSEN, SCOTT; Plymouth HS; Plymouth, IN; 12/215 Band; Chrh Wkr; Hon Rl; Sch Mus; Stg Crw; Yth Flsp; Fr Clb; Mth Clb; Letter Ftbl; IM Sprt; Purdue Univ; Science.

CHRISTIANSEN, TODD; St Marys Central Cath HS; Sandusky, OH; Cls Rep Soph Cls; JA; Lbry Ade; Sch Nwsp; JA Awd; Kiwan Awd; Coll; Elec Tech.

CHRISTIDES, SCOTT; High School; Hunt Woods, MI; Hon Rl; NHS; Univ Of Michigan; Arts.

CHRISTIE, JANET; Northfield Jr Sr HS; Urbana, IN; Band; Chrh Wkr; Hon Rl; Yth Flsp; Rptr Sch Nwsp; 4-H; Pep Clb; Spn Clb; Mgrs; 4-H Awd; Univ; Elem Ed.

CHRISTIE, MICHAEL L; Shaker Hts HS; Shaker Hts, OH; Cls Rep Soph Cls; Cl Rep Jr Cls; Cls Rep Sr Cls; Chrh Wkr; Debate Tm; Hon Rl; Rptr Sch Nwsp; Letter Crs Cntry; Trk; Letter Wrstlng; Haverford Coll; Law.

CHRISTIE, SAMUEL H; North Harrison HS; Depauw, IN; 6/170 Band; Chrs; Hon Rl; Jr NHS; Mod UN; NHS; Stg Crw; Yth Flsp; Yrbk; Sch Nwsp; Rose Hulman Inst Of Tech; Elec Engr.

CHRISTIN, AMY; Anderson Sr HS; Cincinnati, OH; 1/377 Pres Jr Cls; Pres Sr Cls; Sec AFS; Am Leg Aux Girls St; Hon Rl; Jr NHS; NHS; Ed Sch Nwsp; Rptr Sch Nwsp; Am Leg Awd; Brown Univ Awd Outstndng Eng Expression; Natl Merit Testing For Eng; Straight A; Univ Of Denver; Eng Lit.

CHRISTL, BEVERLY; Berrien Springs HS; Berrien Spgs, MI; 1/140 VP Band; Hon Rl; VP NHS; VP Ger Clb; VP Mth Clb; VP Sci Clb; Michigan St Univ; Acctg.

CHRISTLE, ROXANN; Wabash HS; Wabash, IN; VP Jr Cls; Pres Sr Cls; Am Leg Aux Girls St; Chrs; Hon Rl; Sch Mus; Stu Cncl; Trk; PPFtbl; Purdue Univ; Education.

CHRISTMAN, ERICH; Revere HS; Bath, OH; Chrh Wkr; Hon Rl; Yth Flsp; 4-H; Letter Crs Cntry; Letter Wrstlng; IM Sprt; Pres Awd; Univ; Acctg.

CHRISTMAN, JEFF; Patrick Henry HS; Deshler, OH; 18/120 Hon Rl; Bsktbl; Ftbl; Trk; College.

CHRISTMAN, LINDA; Philo HS; Zanesville, OH; Band; Chrs; Hon Rl; Stu Cncl; Fr Clb; FTA; Sci Clb; Twrlr; Bowling Green Univ; Psych.

CHRISTMAS, CHRISTINA; Mason Cnty Cntrl HS; Scottville, MI; 5/130 Trs Frsh Cls; Cls Rep Soph Cls; Pres Jr Cls; Pres Sr Cls; Band; Chrh Wkr; Hon Rl; Pres NHS; Off Ade; Stu Cncl; David Chase Mem Awd Ctznshp In Music; Harbison Walker Schlrshp; Go To Farm Bureau Yng Pepoles Ctznshp Semnr; Grand Rapids Bapt Coll; Busns Admin.

CHRISTMON, KEVIN; Pontiac Central HS; Pontiac, MI; Band; Boy Scts; Chrs; Chrh Wkr; Hon Rl; Sch Mus; Sch Pl; Stu Cncl; Drama Clb; Pep Clb; Michigan St Univ; Vet.

CHRISTNER, LINDA; Crestline HS; Crestline, OH; 11/114 Chrs; Hon Rl; Sec JA; Jr NHS; Off Ade; Orch; Sch Mus; Trk; Kiwan Awd; Oh St Univ Bk Awrd 79; Perfect Attendnc Awrd 79; Ohio St Univ; Sci.

CHRISTOF, MARY; George Rogers Clark HS; Whiting, IN; 3/218 Band; Chrs; Chrh Wkr; JA; Jr NHS; Orch; Sch Mus; Sch Pl; Stg Crw; Rptr Sch Nwsp; Univ.

CHRISTOFIELD, JOANNA; Indian Hill HS; Cincinnati, OH; Chrh Wkr; Cmnty Wkr; Girl Scts; Hon Rl; Hosp Ade; Eng Clb; Fr Clb; Pep Clb; Trk; IM Sprt; College.

CHRISTOFORIDIS, JOHN; St Johns HS; Toledo, OH; Cls Rep Frsh Cls; Cls Rep Soph Cls; Boy Scts; Chrh Wkr; Hon Rl; Stu Cncl; Fr Clb; Socr; Ten; Trk; Univ.

CHRISTOPH, LORNA; La Crosse HS; Wanatah, IN; Chrs; Hon Rl; Yth Flsp; Fr Clb; Jr Coll; Health.

CHRISTOPHER, ALAN; Morgantown HS; Morgantwn, WV; Cls Rep Soph Cls; Cl Rep Jr Cls; Hon Rl; Stu Cncl; IM Sprt; West Va Univ; Engr.

CHRISTOPHER, CARLIN; Merrillville HS; Merrillville, IN; 72/600 Aud/Vis; Boy Scts; Hon Rl; Purdue Univ; Engr.

CHRISTOPHER, DALE; Galion HS; Galion, OH; Band; Hon Rl; Mth Clb; Letter Glf; College; Comp Science.

CHRISTOPHER, SCOTT; Tri County HS; Wolcott, IN; Aud/Vis; FCA; Hon Rl; Sct Actv; Stg Crw; 4-H; FFA; Letter Ftbl; Voc Schl; Agric Bus.

CHRISTOPHERSON, DEBORAH; Three Rivers HS; Three Rivers, MI; Band; Chrh Wkr; Hon Rl; NHS; Treas Yth Flsp; Rptr Yrbk; Rptr Sch Nwsp; Ger Clb; Scr Kpr; Grand Rapids Baptist Coll.

CHRISTY, GAYLE; Otsego HS; Liberty Center, OH; Band; Girl Scts; Hon Rl; Jr NHS; NHS; 4-H; 4-H Awd;.

CHRISTY, SHERYL; Troy HS; Troy, MI; Chrs; Hon Rl; NHS; Sch Pl; Rptr Sch Nwsp; Sch Nwsp; Pres Drama Clb; Kalamazoo Coll; Theatre Arts.

CHRISWELL, KAREN; Ravenna HS; Ravenna, OH; Chrs; Chrh Wkr; Hon Rl; Sch Mus; Sch Pl; Pres OEA; Gym; IM Sprt; Most Businesslike Person Award 79; Jr High Choir Mbr 77; Honor Award For Pt Average In OEA 79; Kent St Bus Coll; Office Mgmt.

CHRITIANSON, CAROL; William Mason HS; Mason, OH; Trs Soph Cls; Sec Jr Cls; Pres Sr Cls; Sec Band; Chrs; Chrh Wkr; Drm Bgl; Girl Scts; Hon Rl; Off Ade; Univ; Forestry.

CHRNKO, JOLYNNE; Brookfield Sr HS; Masury, OH; Band; Hon Rl; NHS; Off Ade; Stu Cncl; Yrbk; Beta Clb; Fr Clb; FDA; FTA; Youngstown St Univ; Dent Hygiene.

CHRONINGER, BONNIE; Edon HS; Montpelier, OH; 7/78 Band; Hon Rl; Rptr Sch Nwsp; 4-H; Spn Clb; 4-H Awd; Voice Dem Awd; College; Equestrian Field.

CHRONISTER, AMY; Wellsville HS; E Liverpool, OH; 23/156 Sec Sr Cls; NHS; Ed Yrbk; FTA; Am Leg Awd; Ohi State Univ; Vet Med.

CHUBA, DANIEL; Dexter HS; Dexter, MI; Hon Rl; Bsktbl; Capt Crs Cntry; Capt Trk; Eastern Michigan Univ; BBA.

CHUBB, MARK; Carroll HS; Xenia, OH; 66/285 Boy Scts; Chrs; Chrh Wkr; Sct Actv; Ger Clb; VP Key Clb; Rdo Clb; Cert Of Recognition Cath Comm; Ad Altare Dei Cath Del Emblem; 2nd Pl Oratory Awd Ohio Dist Key Club; Univ Of Dayton; Philosophy.

CHUBE, RENEE; Andrean HS; Gary, IN; 116/259 Hon Rl; Sdlty; Stu Cncl; VP Fr Clb; Chrldng; Pom Pon; 4-H Awd; Opt Clb Awd; College; Lawyer.

CHUBNER, ROBERT; Fairborn Baker HS; W Patterson, OH; 14/300 FCA; Hon Rl; NHS; Beta Clb; Fr Clb; Mth Clb; Capt Bsktbl; IM Sprt; Natl Merit Schl; Ga Tech; Elec Engr.

CHUDAKOFF, ROBERT; Charles F Brush HS; Lyndhurst, OH; Band; Debate Tm; Hon Rl; Natl Forn Lg; IM Sprt; Attended 79 St Debate Tourn In Dayton 79; Have Attained The Degree Of Distinct In Natl Forensics Leag 79; Univ Of Michigan; Law.

CHUDZINSKI, HELEN; St Joe Central Catholic HS; Fremont, OH; Cmp Fr Grls; Girl Scts; Hon Rl; JA; Y-Teens; Rptr Yrbk; Yrbk; Sch Nwsp; 4-H; Pep Clb; Vanguard Vocational; Bus.

CHUEY, NICHOLAS; Clawson HS; Clawson, MI; 23/300 Hon Rl; NHS; Pol Wkr; Am Leg Awd; Ferris St Univ; Mech Engr.

CHUMLEY, CHRIS; Covington HS; Covington, IN; Boy Scts; Chrh Wkr; Yrbk; Peace Corps.

CHUMLEY, GINA; Trenton HS; Trenton, MI; Letter Band; Hon Rl; NHS; Rptr Sch Nwsp; Letter Bsktbl; Letter Trk; Lawrence Tech; Architect.

CHUMLEY, JONATHAN; Broad Ripple HS; Indianapolis, IN; Cmnty Wkr; Hon Rl; JA; NHS; Pol Wkr; Sprt Ed Yrbk; Boys Clb Am; Cit Awd; JA Awd; Marion Cnty Journalism & Math Day Prizes; College; Meteorology.

CHUMNEY, DOUG; Tri Village HS; New Paris, OH; 4/71 Cls Rep Soph Cls; Hon Rl; Stu Cncl; Glf; Wright St Univ; Bus.

CHUNYO, DOUGLAS; Padua Franciscan HS; Parma, OH; Hon Rl; Ftbl; IM Sprt; Natl Merit Ltr; Ohio St Univ; Vet.

CHUPARKOFF, STEPHEN; Mc Donald HS; Mc Donald, OH; 1/96 Am Leg Boys St; Aud/Vis; Hon Rl; JA; Sch Pl; Rptr Yrbk; College; Law.

CHURCH, AMANDA; Meadow Bridge HS; Meadowbrdg, WV; Cls Rep Frsh Cls; Cls Rep Soph Cls; Cl Rep Jr Cls; Cls Rep Sr Cls; Chrs; Hon Rl; NHS; Fr Clb; Keyettes; Pep Clb; Concord Coll; Medicine.

CHURCH, CHERYL; Eastern Local HS; Jackson, OH; 6/66 Hon Rl; Paul D Camp Community Coll; Sec.

CHURCH, J C; Marion Harding HS; Marion, OH; Cls Rep Frsh Cls; Cmnty Wkr; Sprt Ed Yrbk; Rptr Yrbk; Yrbk; Sch Nwsp; Capt Crs Cntry; Trk; IM Sprt; Tmr; Cross Cntry MVR Captall Time Schl Cls Recrd Of 12;48 2 1/2 Mils & 1st Team All Buckeye Confrnc 78; Uni; Bus Admin.

CHURCH, JOHN; Ithaca HS; Alma, MI; 4/125 Cls Rep Frsh Cls; Cls Rep Soph Cls; Cl Rep Jr Cls; VP Sr Cls; Am Leg Boys St; Band; Boy Scts; Chrs; Debate Tm; Hon Rl; Ctrl Michigan Univ; Econ.

CHURCH, KARON; Marian HS; Cincinnati, OH; Chrh Wkr; Cmnty Wkr; JA; Lbry Ade; Pol Wkr; Yrbk; Spn Clb; Trk; Fisk Univ; Bus Mgmt.

CHURCH, PATRICIA; Green HS; Uniontown, OH; 27/321 Band; Chrh Wkr; Girl Scts; Hon Rl; Yth Flsp; Rptr Yrbk; College; Early Child Educ.

CHURCHES, LINDA; Grand Blanc HS; Grand Blanc, MI; 1/625 Cls Rep Frsh Cls; VP Soph Cls; Cls Rep Soph Cls; Cl Rep Jr Cls; Cls Rep Sr Cls; Val; Stu Cncl; Letter Pom Pon; PPFtbl; Am Leg Awd; Migh State Univ.

CHURCHFIELD, JEFFORY; Arthur Hill HS; Saginaw, MI; Hon Rl; Sci Clb; Ftbl; Swmmng; Coach Actv; Valparaiso Univ; Elec Engr.

CHURCHILL, CHRISTY; Lorain Catholic HS; Lorain, OH; Pres Frsh Cls; Cls Rep Soph Cls; Girl Scts; Hon Rl; Sct Actv; Rptr Sch Nwsp; Crs Cntry; Trk; PPFtbl; Scr Kpr; Univ; Pre Med.

CHURCHILL, LAURA; Beaumont Girls HS; Univ Hts, OH; Cls Rep Frsh Cls; Cmnty Wkr; Hon Rl; Lit Mag; Stu Cncl; Rptr Yrbk; Gym; Trk; Coach Actv; Univ.

CHURILLA, DENNIS W; Morton Sr HS; Hammond, IN; 20/465 Boy Scts; NHS; Sct Actv; Pres Sci Clb; Bsktbl; Letter Ftbl; Glf; Coach Actv; IM Sprt; Natl Merit Ltr; Rose Hulman Univ; Computer Sci.

CHURILLA, SCOTT; Wheeling Park HS; Wheeling, WV; AFS; Natl Forn Lg; Sch Pl; Stg Crw; Stu Cncl; Drama Clb; Fr Clb; Glf; Pres Of Thespain Trp Mbr 1942 79; Univ; Pre Law.

CHURNESS, EMORY; Robert S Rogers HS; Toledo, OH; Chrs; Hon Rl; Cert Of Mert Toledo Councl Of Math Tchr Contst 27th Out Of 255 78; Spanish Diploma Of Mert Third Yr 78; Univ Of Toledo; Pharm.

CHWALIK, THERESA; James Ford Rhodes HS; Cleveland, OH; Cl Rep Jr Cls; NHS; Off Ade; OEA; Bus Schl; Bus Educ.

CHYCHLYK, STEVEN; Western Reserve Academy; Parma Hts, OH; 30/86 Chrh Wkr; Stu Cncl; Bsbl; Letter Ftbl; Letter Wrstlng; Univ.

CHYLINSKI, PATRICIA; Bishop Gallagher HS; Detroit, MI; 80/330 Cls Rep Soph Cls; Cl Rep Jr Cls; Cls Rep Sr Cls; Hon Rl; Sch Pl; Stu Cncl; Chrldng; PPFtbl; Coll.

CIABATTONI, CAROL; Maplewood HS; Cortland, OH; 9/89 Hon Rl; Off Ade; Sch Pl; Beta Clb; Drama Clb; 4-H; FTA; Elizabeth Stewart Hon Schlrshp 79; Thiel Univ; Med Tech.

CIALKOWSKI, MARIANNE; St Frances Cabrini HS; Allen Pk, MI; Drl Tm; Girl Scts; Hon Rl; Spn Clb; Pres Awd; Univ.

CIAMACCO, BRIDGET; Brookhaven HS; Columbus, OH; Band; Hon Rl; NHS; Orch; Sch Pl; Stu Cncl; Drama Clb; Pres Spn Clb; Knight Chancellor Awd 77; Ohio St Univ; Med.

CIAMMAICHELLA, MIKE; Highland HS; Hinckley, OH; 11/210 NHS; Key Clb; Letter Bsbl; Letter Ftbl; Letter Wrstlng; Case Western Reserve Univ; Engr.

CIARNIELLO, ANITA; Springfield Local HS; Poland, OH; Sec Soph Cls; Pres Jr Cls; Cl Rep Jr Cls; Chrh Wkr; Hon Rl; Hosp Ade; Stu Cncl; Yth Flsp; 4-H; Pom Pon; College; Medicine.

CIBULL, MARSHA; Bosse HS; Evansville, IN; Cls Rep Frsh Cls; Cls Rep Soph Cls; Cmnty Wkr; Off Ade; Pol Wkr; Stu Cncl; Yrbk; Sch Nwsp; Pep Clb; Ind Univ.

CICHON, DE LANE; Buckeye W HS; Adena, OH; 2/92 NHS; Drama Clb; FHA; Pep Clb; Sci Clb; Chrldng; Ohio Valley Schl Of Nursing; Rn.

CICHY, EDWARD A; Rossford HS; Perrysburg, OH; 13/150 Cls Rep Frsh Cls; Am Leg Boys St; Chrs; Hon Rl; Pres Stu Cncl; Toledo; Educ.

CICIRELLA, LEONETTE; Lumen Cordium HS; Maple Hts, OH; 1/107 Hon Rl; Sch Pl; Yrbk; Sprt Ed Sch Nwsp; Spn Clb; College; Journalism.

CICIRELLI, LONNIE; Wickliffe Sr HS; Wickliffe, OH; 14/325 Am Leg Aux Girls St; Hon Rl; Sec NHS; Off Ade; Sch Mus; Sch Pl; VP Stu Cncl; Drama Clb; Mat Maids; Pres Awd; John Carroll Univ; Pre Vet.

CIELENSKY, AMY; Ravenna HS; Ravenna, OH; 8/360 Cls Rep Frsh Cls; Cls Rep Soph Cls; Cl Rep Jr Cls; Cls Rep Sr Cls; Band; Hon Rl; NHS; Sch Mus; Stu Cncl; Yth Flsp; Honorable Mention Kent St Univ Dist In Ohio Test Of Scholastic Achvmnt; College; Computer Sci.

CIESLIK, JOSEPH; Alpena HS; Alpena, MI; 28/714 Chrh Wkr; Debate Tm; Hon Rl; NHS; Rptr Yrbk; Natl Merit SF; Alpena Comm College; Bio.

CIESLINSKI, DARREN; All Saints Central HS; Bay City, MI; Cl Rep Jr Cls; Cls Rep Sr Cls; Hon Rl; Lit Mag; Sch Pl; Stg Crw; Ed Sch Nwsp; Sprt Ed Sch Nwsp; Boys Clb Am; Letter Ftbl; SUSC.

CIFUENTES, GILDA; John F Kennedy HS; Taylor, MI; Cls Rep Soph Cls; Band; Off Ade; Yrbk; Bsktbl; Gym; Letter Chrldng; GAA; Pom Pon; PPFtbl;.

CIGOLLE, HENRY D; Girard HS; Girard, OH; Boy Scts; Yth Flsp; Key Clb; Letter Bsktbl; Letter Ftbl; Trk; Mahoning Vly Athltc Conf 1978; All Trumbull Cnty 1st Tm 1978; Univ.

CIHLA, EDWARD; Midview HS; Elyria, OH; Band; Hon Rl; JA; Spn Clb; Ten; College; Busns.

CILENSEK, LISA; Lake Cath HS; Wickliffe, OH; Stu Cncl; Scr Kpr; Am Leg Awd; Coll; Med.

CIMINELLO, JEFFREY R; Newark HS; Newark, OH; Boy Scts; Chrs; Hon Rl; PAVAS; Sch Mus; Sch Pl; Stg Crw; Yth Flsp; Drama Clb; Letter Wrstlng;.

CIMINI, TINA; Union Local HS; Belmont, OH; Treas Band; Hon Rl; Hosp Ade; NHS; Orch; Stu Cncl; Rptr Yrbk; Rptr Sch Nwsp; Sch Nwsp; Fr Clb; Pres Classrm For Young Amer 79; Ohio Valley Genrl Hosptl; RN.

CIMPERMAN, ANTHONY J; Lake Catholic HS; Mentor, OH; 12/300 Pres Frsh Cls; Cls Rep Sr Cls; Boy Scts; Chrs; Chrh Wkr; Hon Rl; NHS; Sch Mus; Stu Cncl; Yrbk; John Carroll Univ; Engr.

CINGEL, CYNTHIA; Holy Name HS; Cleveland, OH; Cls Rep Frsh Cls; Cls Rep Soph Cls; Cl Rep Jr Cls; Cls Rep Sr Cls; Chrs; Drl Tm; Hon Rl; Hosp Ade; Jr NHS; Lbry Ade; Typing Awd 76; 1st P 2nd Hon 75 79; Cmnty Serv Awd 200 Hrs Volntr 78; Bowling Green St Univ; Nursing.

CINGLE, ANDREA; Normandy HS; Parma, OH; 39/649 Aud/Vis; Band; Drm Bgl; Girl Scts; Hon Rl; Hosp Ade; Off Ade; Sch Pl; Stg Crw; Drama Clb; Kent St Univ; Med.

CINQUINA, GLORIA; Mcauley HS; Cincinnati, OH; 5/262 Aud/Vis; Chrh Wkr; Cmnty Wkr; Girl Scts; Hon Rl; Sct Actv; Spn Clb; Univ Of Cinncinnati; Animal Tech.

CIOCCA, ANN; Mogadore HS; Mogadore, OH; Chrs; Girl Scts; Lbry Ade; Mdrgl; Red Cr Ade; Sch Mus; Sch Pl; Sct Actv; Stg Crw; Stu Cncl; St Thomas Hosp Schl; Nursing.

CIOFANI, TERRI; Bellaire HS; Bellaire, OH; Cls Rep Frsh Cls; Cls Rep Soph Cls; Cl Rep Jr Cls; Band; Chrs; Chrh Wkr; Hon Rl; Stu Cncl; Y-Teens; Spn Clb; Cheerleading Letters; Frosh Track Attendant; Vocational Schl; Cosmetology.

CIOLEK, GLENN; Paul K Cousino HS; Warren, MI; Debate Tm; Lit Mag; NHS; Natl Merit Ltr; Wayne State Univ; Astronomy.

CIPITI, BARBARA; Maple Hts Sr HS; Maple Hgts, OH; Letter Band; Hon Rl; Letter Bsktbl; Letter Trk; IM Sprt; Pres Awd; Ashland Coll; Photog.

CIPOLETTI, LINDA; Brooke HS; Wellsburg, WV; 44/404 NHS; VP Pol Wkr; Sch Mus; Treas Stu Cncl; Y-Teens; Yrbk; IM Sprt; WVU; Rn.

CIPOLLA, LEONETTE; St Alphonsus HS; Dearborn, MI; 8/177 Chrh Wkr; Hon Rl; Hosp Ade; Henry Ford Comm College; Rn.

CIRA, CHARLES; High School; Morgantown, WV; Chrh Wkr; Fr Clb; Letter Bsbl; Bsktbl; Ftbl; West Virginia Univ; Engr.

CIRA, SANDY; Madison Comp HS; Mansfield, OH; Cl Rep Jr Cls; Cls Rep Sr Cls; Band; Chrh Wkr; Hon Rl; NHS; Y-Teens; Fr Clb; IM Sprt; Twrlr; Ohio St Univ; Comp Prog.

CIRNER, KATHLEEN; Lumen Cordium HS; Bedford, OH; Drl Tm; Hon Rl; Fr Clb; Coach Actv;.

CIRONI, LOUIS; Alliance HS; Alliance, OH; 27/321 Aud/Vis; Debate Tm; Hon Rl; Lbry Ade; NHS; FBLA; Key Clb; Sci Clb; Ftbl; IM Sprt; Mt Union Univ; Bus.

CIROTA, REGINA; Euclid Sr HS; Euclid, OH; 142/703 Hon Rl; OEA; Night Schl; Busns.

CISARIK, KIMBERLY; Andrean HS; Hobart, IN; 72/251 Hon Rl; Mod UN; Fr Clb; Pep Clb; GAA; PPFtbl; Butler Univ; Pre Law.

CISKAL, CAROLYN; Admiral King HS; Lorain, OH; Band; Chrh Wkr; Hon Rl; NHS; Pep Clb; Univ Of Toledo; Sci.

CISKAL, JUDITH; Admiral King HS; Lorain, OH; Chrh Wkr; Hon Rl; Orch; Y-Teens; Univ; Horticulture.

CITRON, GREGG; Southfield HS; Southfield, MI; Hon Rl; Lbry Ade;. IM Sprt; Michigan St Univ; Dentist.

CIUK, SHARON; Divine Child HS; Dearborn, MI; Band; Chrs; Chrh Wkr; Pep Clb; VP Spn Clb; Trk; Pom Pon; Voice Dem Awd; Univ Of Michigan; Dental Hyg.

CIVIELLO, MICHAEL; Tuscarawas Ctrl Catholic HS; New Phila, OH; 3/75 Pres Soph Cls; Cls Rep Soph Cls; Pres Jr Cls; Am Leg Boys St; Boy Scts; Jr NHS; NHS; Pres Stu Cncl; Letter Bsbl; Letter Wrstlng; Case Western Reserve; Elec Engr.

CLAAR, JILL; Tri HS; New Lisbon, IN; 18/82 Hon Rl; 4-H; Bsktbl; Indiana St Univ; Zoology.

CLAAR, JULIE; Sndsky Stmarys Ctrl Cath HS; Sandusky, OH; 10/135 Cls Rep Frsh Cls; Cls Rep Soph Cls; Hon Rl; NHS; Spn Clb; Letter Trk; Capt Chrldng; GAA; Tenative Bgsu; Phys Ther.

CLAAR, RANDY E; Paint Valley HS; Chillicothe, OH; 2/90 Chrh Wkr; Hon Rl; Yth Flsp; Lat Clb; Sci Clb; Letter Bsbl; Letter Bsktbl; Scr Kpr; Am Leg Awd; Air Force Acad; Geography.

CLAAR, SANDRA L; Paint Valley HS; Chillicothe, OH; 1/90 Pres Soph Cls; Pres Jr Cls; Chrh Wkr; Drl Tm; Hon Rl; Hosp Ade; Yth Flsp; Rptr Frbk; FHA; Lat Clb; Volleyball Letter 1978; 9th Pl Dist Ohio Test Of Schlstc Achievmnt 1978; Ohio State Univ; Med.

CLADY, SHARON; Bucyrus HS; Bucyrus, OH; Hon Rl; NHS; Stg Crw; Univ; Art.

CLAERHOUT, DON; U S A HS; Unionville, MI; Chrh Wkr; Stu Cncl; FFA; Bsktbl;.

CLAEYS, MARY; Lake Michigan Cath HS; Benton Hrbr, MI; Hon Rl; NHS; Sci Clb; Letter Bsktbl; IM Sprt; Scr Kpr; Univ; Med Tech.

CLAEYS, MARY; Lake Michigan Catholic HS; Benton Harbor, MI; 5/95 Hon Rl; Fr Clb; Letter Bsktbl; IM Sprt; Mgrs; Scr Kpr; College.

CLAGETT, STEVEN B; Fairmont HS; Fairmont, WV; 2/255 Am Leg Boys St; Chrs; Hon Rl; Stu Cncl; Mth Clb; Spn Clb; Letter Ftbl; Wv Univ; Engr.

CLAGGETT, STEVE; Buckeye Vly HS; Delaware, OH; Hon Rl; 4-H; Letter Ten; Letter Trk;.

CLAJUS, KRISTIN; Walnut Hills HS; Cincinnati, OH; Chrs; Hon Rl; Lit Mag; Sch Mus; Yrbk; Capt Chrldng; Hanover Coll; Jrnlsm.

CLAMPITT, CORT; New Palestine HS; New Palestine, IN; Chrs; Chrh Wkr; JA; Letter Bsbl; Ten; Letter Wrstlng; IM Sprt; Cit Awd; JA Awd; Most Musical Talent 78; Most Hustle Bsbl 74; Univ; Acctg.

CLANCY, DEIRDRE T; Shrine HS; Royal Oak, MI; 12/176 Cmnty Wkr; Pres Girl Scts; Hon Rl; NHS; Pol Wkr; Rptr Sch Nwsp; Sch Nwsp; Coach Actv; Natl Merit SF; College; Medicine.

CLANCY, MAUREEN; Bishop Luers HS; Ft Wayne, IN; Cls Rep Soph Cls; Cl Rep Jr Cls; Cls Rep Sr Cls; Chrs; Hon Rl; Sch Mus; Chrldng; IM Sprt; PPFtbl; JA Awd; Purdue Univ; Vet Med.

CLANCY, PAUL M; Aquinas HS; Lincoln Park, MI; Boy Scts; Hon Rl; Sch Nwsp; Letter Bsbl; Letter Bsktbl; Crs Cntry; Letter Ftbl; Trk; Cit Awd; Notre Dame Univ; Marine Bio.

CLAPP, RUSSELL; Grand Haven Sr HS; Grand Haven, MI; Cls Rep Soph Cls; Cl Rep Jr Cls; Hon Rl; Jr NHS; NHS; Stu Cncl; Ger Clb; Letter Mgrs; Natl Merit Ltr; Univ; Comp Engr.

CLAPP, TAMARA L; Montezuma HS; Montezuma, IN; Cls Rep Frsh Cls; Sec Soph Cls; Cl Rep Jr Cls; Pres Stu Cncl; Yth Flsp; Pres 4-H; Pep Clb; Letter Bsktbl; Letter Ten; Letter Trk; Indiana St Univ.

CLARK, ALTON; Patterson Co Op HS; Dayton, OH; Band; Boy Scts; Chrh Wkr; Sch Mus; Boys Clb Am; VICA; Bsbl; Voc Schl.

CLARK, ANGELA; Jonathan Alder HS; Plain City, OH; 4/99 Band; Hon Rl; NHS; Yrbk; Bausch & Lomb Awd; Natl Merit Ltr; Ohio St Univ; Mech Engr.

CLARK, ANGELA D; Chesapeake HS; Proctorville, OH; 25/140 Chrs; Chrh Wkr; Hon Rl; Sch Mus; Sch Pl; Yth Flsp; Beta Clb; 4-H; Cit Awd; 4-H Awd; Ohio Univ; Jrnlsm.

CLARK, ANN; Johnstown Monroe HS; Johnstown, OH; 5/139 Band; Hon Rl; NHS; Stu Cncl; Pres Yth Flsp; Y-Teens; 4-H; Pres FHA; Spn Clb; Ohio St Univ; Home Ec Educ.

CLARK, BELINDA; Park Hills HS; Fairborn, OH; Chrh Wkr; Girl Scts; Hon Rl; NHS; Yth Flsp; Univ Of Ken; Acctg.

CLARK, BETH E; Belleville HS; Wayne, MI; 28/519 Cl Rep Jr Cls; Hon Rl; Jr NHS; Lbry Ade; NHS; Stu Cncl; Rptr Sch Nwsp; Sch Nwsp; Rdo Clb; Mgrs; 2nd Plc Writing Cont; Cert Of Merit In French Language; Univ Of Michigan; Journalism.

CLARK, BONITA; Northwestern Community HS; Flint, MI; Hon Rl; JA; Stu Cncl; Y-Teens; Scr Kpr; Tmr; Mic State Univ; Pre Med.

CLARK, BRENDA; Morgan HS; Malta, OH; Hon Rl; Lbry Ade; NHS; Yth Flsp; Rptr Sch Nwsp; 4-H; Spn Clb; IM Sprt; 4-H Awd; Muskingum Tech Schl; Radiology.

CLARK, BRIAN; Saginaw HS; Saginaw, MI; Chrh Wkr; Hon Rl; Sch Pl; Bsktbl; Central Michigan Univ; Bus Admin.

CLARK, BRIGITTE; Bishop Donahue HS; Moundsville, WV; Cls Rep Sr Cls; Band; Chrh Wkr; Cmnty Wkr; Girl Scts; Hon Rl; Pol Wkr; Stu Cncl; Rptr Yrbk; Rptr Sch Nwsp; Univ.

CLARK, BRYAN; Licking Heights HS; Johnstown, OH; Am Leg Boys St; Band; Chrs; 4-H; Ger Clb; Mth Clb; Sci Clb; Trk; Wrstlng; Ohio State Univ; Med.

CLARK, CANDY L; Martinsburg HS; Martinsburg, WV; Cls Rep Soph Cls; Cl Rep Jr Cls; Band; Hon Rl; 4-H; VP Keyettes; Pep Clb; Chrldng; Univ; Bus Admin.

CLARK, CARLA; Milton HS; Milton, WV; Band; Rptr Sch Nwsp; Pep Clb; College; Law.

CLARK, CAROLYN; Marion HS; Marion, IN; Chrh Wkr; Hon Rl; FNA; Indiana Univ; Nursing.

CLARK, CATHERINE; Flushing Sr HS; Flint, MI; Cls Rep Frsh Cls; Trs Soph Cls; Pres Jr Cls; Cmnty Wkr; Girl Scts; Hon Rl; Hosp Ade; NHS; Off Ade; Red Cr Ade; Lansing Cmnty Coll; Med.

CLARK, CATHERINE; Terre Haute North Vigo HS; Terre Haute, IN; Cls Rep Soph Cls; Band; Girl Scts; Hon Rl; Orch; Sch Mus; Y-Teens; 4-H; Fr Clb; Swmmng; Univ; Spec Ed.

CLARK, CHARLENE; Bristol HS; Bristolville, OH; Band; Hon Rl; Sch Mus; Yrbk; Pep Clb; Trk; Chrldng; Trade Sch For Csmtlgy; Btcn.

CLARK, CHERYL; Hamlin HS; Hamlin, WV; 5/62 Hst Sr Cls; Band; Chrh Wkr; Cmnty Wkr; Drm Mjrt; Hon Rl; Jr NHS; St Marys Schl Of Nursing; Rn.

CLARK, CHRISTINE M; Alcona Community HS; Harrisville, MI; 5/124 Hon Rl; Jr NHS; Off Ade; Yrbk; Pep Clb; Spn Clb; N Michigan Univ; Nursing.

CLARK, CRAIG; Milton HS; Milton, WV; Cls Rep Frsh Cls; Cls Rep Soph Cls; Cl Rep Jr Cls; Am Leg Boys St; Boy Scts; NHS; Mth Clb; Spn Clb; Letter Ten; Stdnt Council Exec Cabinet 79; Mod Bio Awd 77; Earth Sci Awd 77; Univ; Chem.

CLARK, DAVID; Carmel HS; Carmel, IN; Pres Frsh Cls; Cls Rep Soph Cls; Pres Jr Cls; Chrs; FCA; Stu Cncl; Letter Bsktbl; IM Sprt; Selectd To Attend LAB At Wabash Coll 79; Univ; Engr.

CLARK, DAVID; Greenville HS; Greenville, OH; VP NHS; Crs Cntry; Trk; Natl Merit SF; Kent St Univ; Physics.

CLARK, DAVID; Wilmington HS; Wilmington, OH; Cls Rep Frsh Cls; Cls Rep Soph Cls; Pres Jr Cls; Band; Chrs; Cmnty Wkr; FCA; Sch Mus; Stg Crw; Ohio St Univ.

CLARK, DEIRDRA; Immaculata HS; Detroit, MI; Hon Rl; JA; Stg Crw; Fr Clb; Univ Of Michigan; Psych.

CLARK, DEIRDRE; Davison Sr HS; Davison, MI; Chrh Wkr; Cmnty Wkr; Girl Scts; Hon Rl; Bsktbl; IM Sprt; Mgrs; PPFtbl; Univ Of Michigan; Archt.

CLARK, DENISE; Cathedral HS; Indianapolis, IN; 25/148 Cls Rep Soph Cls; Cl Rep Jr Cls; Cls Rep Sr Cls; Hon Rl; NHS; Off Ade; Sch Mus; Sch Pl; Stg Crw; VP Stu Cncl; Cathedral HS Brd Of Turstees Awd 79; Sr Class Spirit Awd 79; Acctg Awd 797; Marquette Univ; Acctg.

CLARK, DONNA; Adrian Sr HS; Adrian, MI; Hon Rl; Rptr Yrbk; Pep Clb; Trk;.

CLARK, ERIC W; Edwardsburg HS; Edwardsburg, MI; Band; Hon Rl; Bsktbl; Ftbl; Trk; Univ; Tchr.

CLARK, GINA; Stanton HS; Irondale, OH; 20/66 Hon Rl; Lbry Ade; Off Ade; Sch Mus; Sch Pl; Stg Crw; Rptr Yrbk; Sprt Ed Sch Nwsp; Rptr Sch Nwsp; Bsktbl; Acctg Club 77 78 & 79; Jefferson Tech Coll; Med Asst.

CLARK, GREGORY; Bishop Chatard HS; Indianapolis, IN; Sct Actv; 4-H; Spn Clb; Letter Bsktbl; Letter Trk; Scr Kpr; Tmr; Cit Awd; JC Awd; Univ; Bus.

CLARK, JACKIE; Cambridge HS; Cambridge, OH; Cls Rep Frsh Cls; Cls Rep Soph Cls; Stu Cncl; Pep Clb; Gym; Chrldng; Univ.

CLARK, JACQUELINE; Horace Mann HS; Gary, IN; Chrh Wkr; ROTC; Yth Flsp; Yrbk; Pep Clb; Mat Maids; Cit Awd; Ivy Tech Coll; Acctg.

CLARK, JAMES; Ontonagon Area HS; Ontonagon, MI; Aud/Vis; Chrh Wkr; Hon Rl; Pol Wkr; Sch Pl; Stg Crw; Drama Clb; Trk; IM Sprt; Univ Of Michigan; Med.

CLARK, JAMES; Rockford Sr HS; Rockford, MI; 6/365 Am Leg Boys St; Band; Hon Rl; NHS; Orch; Sci Clb; Natl Merit Ltr; Michigan Tech Univ; Chem Engr.

CLARK, JAMES R; Madison Heights HS; Anderson, IN; Am Leg Boys St; Band; Pres Stu Cncl; Fr Clb; Ftbl; Coach Actv; Dnfth Awd; Rotary Awd; In HS Speech Confrnc & Stud Legisltv Assembly 76; Corp Law.

CLARK, JAMIE L; Norwood Sr HS; Norwood, OH; Band; Pres Chrs; Sec Chrh Wkr; Girl Scts; Hon Rl; Off Ade; Sch Mus; Sct Actv; Stu Cncl; Yrbk; Univ; Spec Ed.

CLARK, JANET; Doddridge County HS; Salem, WV; Band; Chrh Wkr; Cmnty Wkr; Hon Rl; Stu Cncl; Yth Flsp; FBLA; FHA; Pep Clb; Typing Awd 78; 4 H Charting Pin 77; Univ; Nurse.

CLARK, JEFF; Grand Ledge HS; Grand Ledge, MI; 8/418 Band; Hon Rl; NHS; Red Cr Ade; Sch Mus; Spn Clb; Mi Comp Schlrshp 79; Michigan St Univ; Acctg.

CLARK, JEFF; Bishop Ready HS; Columbus, OH; Cls Rep Frsh Cls; Cls Rep Soph Cls; Chrh Wkr; Cmnty Wkr; Hon Rl; Letter Bsbl; Letter Bsktbl; Scr Kpr; JA Awd; Ohio State Univ; Math.

CLARK, JEFFREY; Belleville HS; Belleville, MI; 127/490 Band; Boy Scts; Drm Bgl; Hon Rl; NHS; Sch Mus; Sct Actv; Rdo Clb; Crs Cntry; Trk; Outstndng Sr Bandsman At Marching Bnd Camp 79; St Of Michigan Comp Schlrshp Prog Certf Of Recognition 79; Michigan St Univ; Vet Med.

CLARK, JOE; Pontiac Central HS; Pontiac, MI; FCA; Hon Rl; Off Ade; Boys Clb Am; Fr Clb; Key Clb; Bsbl; Bsktbl; Ftbl; Cit Awd; Univ Of Detroit; Dentistry.

CLARK, JOHN; Cardington Lincoln HS; Cardington, OH; 4/79 FCA; NHS; Yth Flsp; Fr Clb; N Central Tech Coll; Comp Prog.

CLARK, JOHN; Bellmont HS; Decatur, IN; 21/231 Am Leg Boys St; Band; Hon Rl; Mdrgl; NHS; Sch Mus; Lat Clb; Sci Clb; Indiana Central Univ; Music Educ.

CLARK, JOHN; Scecina HS; Indianapolis, IN; 54/190 Chrh Wkr; Hon Rl; Rptr Yrbk; Coll; Acctg.

CLARK, JONI; Wahama HS; Letart, WV; 1/96 Sec Jr Cls; Sec Sr Cls; Val; Am Leg Aux Girls St; Band; Sec NHS; Stu Cncl; Pres 4-H; Sec FHA; Pep Clb; Marshall Univ; Elem Ed.

CLARK, JOYCE; John Glenn HS; Norwich, OH; 12/193 Trs Soph Cls; Trs Jr Cls; Chrs; Chrh Wkr; Hon Rl; NHS; 4-H; Spn Clb; Bsktbl; Pres Awd; Ohio Vly; Teaching Handicapped.

CLARK, JULIE; Bloomington HS South; Bloomington, IN; 13/395 Chrh Wkr; Hon Rl; Jr NHS; Yth Flsp; Treas OEA; 3rd Pl Shrthnd OEA Reg Cmpttn 1979; Vc Prsdnt Ftr Sec Assoc; Indiana Univ; Med.

CLARK, K; Ursuline Acad; Cincinnati, OH; 25/106 Chrs; Cmnty Wkr; IM Sprt; College; Arts.

CLARK, KAHTLEEN; Van Buren HS; Brazil, IN; Chrh Wkr; Drl Tm; Hosp Ade; Pep Clb; Sci Clb; Trk; GAA; Scr Kpr; Vincennes Univ; Physical Therapy.

CLARK, KAREN; Tri West HS; North Salem, IN; 20/111 Band; Chrs; Hon Rl; NHS; Fr Clb; Pep Clb; Spn Clb; Swmmng; Trk; Mgrs;.

CLARK, KAREN; Chesapeake HS; Chesapeake, OH; Band; Cmp Fr Grls; Chrs; Chrh Wkr; Yth Flsp; 4-H; Univ; Paramedic.

CLARK, KAREN; Edinburgh Cmnty HS; Edinburg, IN; 6/61 Am Leg Aux Girls St; Chrs; FCA; Girl Scts; Hon Rl; Hosp Ade; Jr NHS; NHS; Quill & Scroll; Sch Pl; Purdue Univ; Nursing.

CLARK, KAREN; Richmond HS; Richmond, IN; 52/532 Chrh Wkr; Hon Rl; Pres NHS; Quill & Scroll; Yrbk; Sec 4-H; Spn Clb; Ind State Univ; Nursing.

CLARK, KATHLEEN; Bishop Dwenger HS; Ft Wayne, IN; Chrs; Cmnty Wkr; Girl Scts; Hon Rl; NHS; Rptr Yrbk; Keyettes; Univ; Phys Ther.

CLARK, KATHLEEN; Columbus Schl For Girls; Columbus, OH; VP Sr Cls; Am Leg Aux Girls St; Chrs; Hon Rl; Lbry Ade; Pol Wkr; Sch Mus; Stu Cncl; Rptr Sch Nwsp; Rus Clb; Univ Of Notre Dame; Math.

CLARK, KATHLEEN M; Servite HS; Detroit, MI; Girl Scts; Hon Rl; JA; Lbry Ade; Sec NHS; Fr Clb; JA Awd; Natl Merit SF; Adrian Coll; Bio Chem.

CLARK, KENT; Port Huron Northern HS; Pt Huron, MI; Cls Rep Frsh Cls; Cls Rep Soph Cls; Cl Rep Jr Cls; Am Leg Boys St; Cmnty Wkr; Stu Cncl; Bsktbl; Ftbl; Trk; Albion.

CLARK, KERRY; Daleville HS; Daleville, IN; 24/70 Anderson Area Voc Sch.

CLARK, KIMBERLY; Shawnee HS; Lima, OH; 9/343 Treas Chrs; Hon Rl; Sec NHS; Stu Cncl; Y-Teens; Yrbk; Fr Clb; Gym; Capt Chrldng; GAA; Graceland Coll; Comp Sci.

CLARK, KIM K; Ovid Elsie HS; Elsie, MI; 1/170 Pres Soph Cls; Trs Jr Cls; Band; Hon Rl; VP NHS; Yth Flsp; Treas Pep Clb; PPFtbl; 4-H Awd; Natl Merit SF; Central Mic Univ; Computer Science.

CLARK, LINDA; Mc Bain Rural Agri School; Mc Bain, MI; Chrs; Cmnty Wkr; Girl Scts; Hon Rl; Pres 4-H; Bsktbl; Trk; Mat Maids; 4-H Awd; MVP; Best Sprinter On Tm; Varsity Ltr In Track Fresh Yr; 1st At The Conf Mt In 100 Yd Dsh & 3rd In Hgh Jmp; Michigan St Univ; Animal Tech.

CLARK, LINDA; Lawrenceburg HS; Lawrenceburg, IN; 34/139 Aud/Vis; Band; Hon Rl; JA; Jr NHS; 4-H; Key Clb; Pep Clb; Vincennes Univ; Comp Progr.

CLARK, LINDA; River Rouge HS; River Rouge, MI; Cls Rep Frsh Cls; Cls Rep Soph Cls; Band; Hon Rl; NHS; Orch; Stu Cncl; Bsktbl; Ten; Scr Kpr; Univ Of Boston; Engr.

CLARK, LINDA; Cameron HS; Cameron, WV; Band; Chrs; Hon Rl; Sch Pl; FFA; FHA; Pep Clb; West Liberty St Univ; Spch.

CLARK, LISA; Greenville Sr HS; Greenville, OH; 10/378 Cls Rep Frsh Cls; Trs Soph Cls; Cls Rep Soph Cls; Cl Rep Jr Cls; Chrs; Hon Rl; Stu Cncl; Yth Flsp; Rptr Sch Nwsp; Drama Clb; Bowling Green St Univ; Corporate Law.

CLARK, LORA R; Hurricane HS; Hurricane, WV; Hon Rl; 4-H; Mth Clb; Letter Trk; IM Sprt; 4-H Awd; Berea Coll; Vet Med.

CLARK, LOUDWELLA; Emerson HS; Gary, IN; Chrh Wkr; Hon Rl; Jr NHS; Sch Pl; Yrbk; Drama Clb; FBLA; College.

CLARK, MAGGIE; Gallia Academy HS; Gallipolis, OH; 17/227 Band; 9th Plc In Spanish 2 Of Oh Tests Of Schlstc Achvmnt 78; Univ; Med Tech.

CLARK, MARY; Clare HS; Midland, MI; FCA; Hon Rl; NHS; Rptr Yrbk; Rptr Sch Nwsp; Fr Clb; Letter Bsbl; Letter Bsktbl; Swmmng; Michigan St Univ; Vet.

CLARK, MARY; St Peter & Paul Area HS; Saginaw, MI; Band; Chrs; Chrh Wkr; Girl Scts; Hon Rl; JA; NHS; Sch Mus; Drama Clb; Spn Clb; Louisiana St Univ; Med Tech.

CLARK, MARY C; West Geauga HS; Chesterland, OH; Drl Tm; Hon Rl; Pep Clb; Ten; IM Sprt; College ; Bus Mgmt.

CLARK, MECHELLE; Westfall HS; Orient, OH; Cls Rep Frsh Cls; Cls Rep Soph Cls; Drm Mjrt; Hosp Ade; Jr NHS; NHS; FNA; Pres FTA; Scr Kpr; 4-H Awd; College; Nursing.

CLARK, MICHAEL; Northrop HS; Ft Wayne, IN; 121/589 Chrs; Sch Mus; Sch Pl; Ten; Lion Awd; Opt Clb Awd; Oral Roberts Univ; Drama.

CLARK, MICHAEL; Maysville Sr HS; Zanesville, OH; Chrs; Sch Mus; Yth Flsp; Yrbk; 4-H; Bsktbl; Ftbl; Trk; Wrstlng; 4-H Awd; Ohio St Univ; Elec Engr.

CLARK, MICHAEL; High School; Toledo, OH; Boy Scts; Sct Actv; FDA; Mth Clb; Sci Clb; Spn Clb; Ftbl; Wrstlng; Toledo Univ; Pre Med.

CLARK, MISSEY; La Porte HS; Laporte, IN; Cmp Fr Grls; Hon Rl; Off Ade; Sch Mus; Stu Cncl; 4-H; Fr Clb; Pep Clb; VICA; Pom Pon; Girl Res Forml Winter Dance Queen 79; Indiana Univ; Dent Hygnst.

CLARK, NANCY; Zeeland HS; Zeeland, MI; Band; Debate Tm; Off Ade; Ger Clb; Gym; Chrldng; Mat Maids; PPFtbl; Scr Kpr; Voc Schl.

CLARK, NANCY; Reed City HS; Reed City, MI; Hon Rl; Spn Clb; GAA; Patricia Stevens Coll; Fashion.

CLARK, PATRICK; Concord HS; Concord, MI; Band; Chrh Wkr; Hon Rl; NHS; Sch Pl; Yth Flsp; Trk; Wrstlng; Ferris St Univ; Acctg.

CLARK, PAUL; Gibsonburg HS; Gibsonburg, OH; 4-H; FFA; Letter Bsktbl; 4-H Awd; Terra Tech Voc Schl; Welding.

CLARK, PHILIP; Lehman HS; Sidney, OH; 10/98 Band; Chrh Wkr; Hon Rl; Fr Clb; Bsbl; Ftbl; Ohi State Univ; Chem Engr.

CLARK, REGINA; Monongah HS; Shinnston, WV; 11/49 Band; Chrh Wkr; Girl Scts; Hon Rl; Yth Flsp; Y-Teens; Fr Clb; FHA; Pep Clb; Voc Schl.

CLARK, RICHARD; Princeton Community HS; Princeton, IN; Cls Rep Sr Cls; Stu Cncl; Boys Clb Am; DECA; Mth Clb; Pep Clb; Ten; Coach Actv; Mgrs; Scr Kpr; Wabash Univ; Pre Law.

CLARK, RICK; Fort Frye HS; Beverly, OH; Cls Rep Frsh Cls; Cls Rep Soph Cls; VP Jr Cls; Chrh Wkr; Hon Rl; NHS; Stu Cncl; Letter Bsktbl; Letter Ftbl; Am Leg Awd; Marietta Coll; Pre Med.

CLARK, SHERYL; Western Boone HS; Lebanon, IN; 17/146 Sec Jr Cls; Band; Hon Rl; NHS; VP 4-H; Fr Clb; Pep Clb; Letter Trk; GAA; 4-H Awd; Whos Who Among Amer HS Foreign Language Stu; Most Outstndng Girl 4 H Clb; College; Education.

CLARK, STEPHEN; Wadsworth HS; Wadsworth, OH; 9/365 Band; Boy Scts; Chrh Wkr; NHS; Sct Actv; Yth Flsp; Lat Clb; Natl Merit SF; Univ Of Toledo; Mechanical Engineer.

CLARK, STEVEN; Jackson HS; North Canton, OH; 1/409 Cls Rep Frsh Cls; Val; Am Leg Boys St; Chrh Wkr; FCA; Hon Rl; JA; David Lipsomb College; Psych.

CLARK, STUART; Defiance Sr HS; Defiance, OH; Cls Rep Frsh Cls; Cls Rep Soph Cls; Band; Hon Rl; JA; Sch Mus; Sch Pl; Stu Cncl; Mth Clb; Sci Clb; Univ; Aviation.

CLARK, SUSAN; Berkshire HS; Burton, OH; Cls Rep Soph Cls; Cmnty Wkr; Hon Rl; Off Ade; Stu Cncl; Pep Clb; Bsbl; Socr; Chrldng; Scr Kpr; Ind Univ; Bus.

CLARK, SUZANNE; Ben Davis HS; Indianapolis, IN; 99/834 Debate Tm; Hon Rl; Mod UN; Fr Clb; Gym; Swmmng; Trk; Mgrs; Texas Christian Univ; Tchr Of Blind.

CLARK, SUZETTE; Edwardsburg HS; Edwardsburg, MI; Chrh Wkr; Cmnty Wkr; Girl Scts; Hon Rl; Off Ade; Fr Clb; Pep Clb; Sci Clb; Letter Chrldng; Mst Vlbl Chrldr 79; Michigan St Univ.

CLARK, TAMARA S; Hannan HS; Fraziers Bottom, WV; Pres Jr Cls; Band; Chrh Wkr; Hon Rl; NHS; Yth Flsp; Rptr Yrbk; FHA; Pep Clb; Chrldng; Marshall Univ; Forestry.

CLARK, TODD R; Oak Hills HS; Cincinnati, OH; 22/875 Band; Hon Rl; NHS; Ger Clb; Swmmng; IM Sprt; Cit Awd; Natl Merit SF; Case Western Reserve Univ; Engr.

CLARK, TOKI M; Eastmoor Sr HS; Columbus, OH; 24/290 Pres Frsh Cls; Cls Rep Soph Cls; Trs Jr Cls; Sec Sr Cls; Am Leg Aux Girls St; Chrh Wkr; Girl Scts; Off Ade; Sch Pl; Sct Actv; Miami Univ; Communications.

CLARK, WALTER B; Howell HS; Howell, MI; Band; Hon Rl; Sch Mus; Stg Crw; Ed Sch Nwsp; Rptr Sch Nwsp; Sch Nwsp; 4-H; Spn Clb; Ftbl; Jrnlsm 1978; Michigan St Univ; Hotel Mgmt.

CLARK, WILLIAM; Walter E Stebbins HS; Dayton, OH; Soc For Acad Excllnc 78; Univ; Elec Engr.

CLARK, WILLIAM A; Alpena HS; Alpena, MI; Hon Rl; Natl Merit SF; Alpena Comm College; Archtctr.

CLARKE, ANN; Holly Sr HS; Holly, MI; 10/298 Treas Band; Chrs; Hon Rl; NHS; Sch Mus; 4-H; PPFtbl; Michigan St Univ; Music Educ.

CLARKE, CHRISTIE; Eaton Rapids HS; Eaton Rapids, MI; 17/280 Band; Chrs; Hon Rl; Orch; Sch Mus; College; Music Educ.

CLARKE, CORY; Mississinewa HS; Gas City, IN; 76/200 Drl Tm; Hon Rl; Rptr Sch Nwsp; Sch Nwsp; Fr Clb; FHA; FNA; Pep Clb; Pom Pon; PPFtbl; Indiana Univ; Nursing.

CLARKE, DONNA; Amelia HS; Amelia, OH; 4/280 Band; Chrh Wkr; Drl Tm; Hon Rl; NHS; Sch Mus; Yth Flsp; Bob Jones Univ; Music.

CLARKE, DORA; Dowagiac Union HS; Dowagiac, MI; 1/217 Pres Soph Cls; Val; Hosp Ade; NHS; Sch Nwsp; Sec Sci Clb; Bsbl; GAA; DAR Awd; Elk Awd; Andrews Univ; Psych.

CLARKE, KAREN; Oregon Davis HS; Walkerton, IN; VP Jr Cls; Band; Hon Rl; Drama Clb; DAR Awd; Purdue Univ; Psych.

CLARKE, RICHARD; Bremen HS; Bremen, IN; 44/103 Hon Rl; Pol Wkr; Pep Clb; Crs Cntry; IM Sprt; Scr Kpr; 3rd Plc In Intramural Bsktbll Playoff 79; 4th Plc In Intramural Bsktbll Playoff 78; Butler Univ; Math.

CLARKE, RUTH; Shaker Sr HS; Cleveland, OH; Chrs; Chrh Wkr; Coll; Nursing.

CLARKE, SHARI; Alter HS; Dayton, OH; 105/350 Chrs; Natl Merit Ltr;.

CLARK III, ROBERT; Gardway HS; Sugarcreek, OH; Aud/Vis; Hon Rl; NHS; Treas Stu Cncl; Spn Clb; Letter Trk; IM Sprt; Tmr;.

CLARK JR, ROBERT; Butler HS; Vandalia, OH; 1/388 Cls Rep Frsh Cls; Cl Rep Jr Cls; Val; Hon Rl; Pres NHS; Pol Wkr; Yth Flsp; Spn Clb; Letter Bsktbl; Capt Ten; Miami Univ; Bus Mgmt.

CLARKSON, DAVID; Croswell Lexington HS; Croswell, MI; Aud/Vis; Band; Chrh Wkr; Hon Rl; Orch; Stg Crw; Yth Flsp; Ed Sch Nwsp; St Clair Cnty Cmnty Coll; Fireman.

CLARKSON, LORI; Durand Area HS; Swartz Crk, MI; Chrs; Girl Scts; Hon Rl; Lbry Ade; NHS; Yth Flsp; 4-H; Univ Of Mich; Library Sci.

CLARKSON, MARY M; Ripley Union Lewis HS; Georgetown, OH; Chrh Wkr; Off Ade; Sch Pl; Stg Crw; Y-Teens; 4-H; Bsktbl; Trk; IM Sprt; 4-H Awd; Xavier Univ.

CLARY, JOHN; East Grand Rapids HS; Grand Rapids, MI; Cls Rep Frsh Cls; Cls Rep Soph Cls; VP Sr Cls; Chrs; Cmnty Wkr; Hon Rl; JA; Pol Wkr; Sch Mus; Sch Pl; Wesleyan Univ; Orthodontist.

CLASH, TAMMY; Kingsford HS; Kingsford, MI; Band; Chrs; Cmnty Wkr; Hon Rl; Off Ade; Orch; Y-Teens; IM Sprt; George Williams Coll; Behavioral Sci.

CLASS, REBECCA; Dover HS; Dover, OH; 28/243 Band; Hon Rl; Hosp Ade; Jr NHS; Yth Flsp; FTA; Pep Clb; Spn Clb; Aultman Schl; RN.

CLATON, LORI; Tri County HS; Remington, IN; Drl Tm; Hon Rl; Off Ade; Yrbk; Pep Clb; Chrldng; Pom Pon; Moody Bible Inst.

CLATTERBUCK, ELIZABETH M; Green Township HS; N Canton, OH; Aud/Vis; Band; Chrs; Chrh Wkr; Drm Mjrt; Hon Rl; JA; Mdrgl; NHS; Orch; Miami Univ; Secondary Ed.

CLATTERBUCK, LIZ; Green HS; North Canton, OH; Band; Chrs; Hon Rl; Mdrgl; NHS; Orch; FTA; College; Educa.

CLATWORTHY, SANDRA; Huntington East HS; Huntington, WV; Cl Rep Jr Cls; Chrs; Girl Scts; Off Ade; Sch Mus; Keyettes; Trk; College.

CLAUDY, LORI; Whiteland HS; Whiteland, IN; 21/250 Rptr Yrbk; 4-H; Fr Clb; FBLA; FTA; Letter Bsktbl; 4-H Awd; Ball State Univ; Pre Law.

CLAUS, JERRI L; Buena Vista HS; Saginaw, MI; 13/157 Hon Rl; Sch Nwsp; Sci Clb; Air Force.

CLAUSEN, GREG; Little Miami HS; Morrow, OH; 1/210 Aud/Vis; Pres Band; Hon Rl; Sch Mus; Ger Clb; Socr; Letter Ten; Natl Merit Ltr; Univ Of Cincinnati; Elec Engr.

CLAUSING, JAMES A; Miamisburg Sr HS; Miamisburg, OH; 1/300 Am Leg Boys St; Band; Chrh Wkr; Hon Rl; NHS; Orch; Sch Mus; Yth Flsp; Scr Kpr; Univ.

CLAUSING, KIM; Portsmouth HS; Portsmouth, OH; 64/226 VP Frsh Cls; VP Soph Cls; Cmnty Wkr; Girl Scts; Hon Rl; Lbry Ade; Off Ade; Sct Actv; Civ Clb; Univ Of Cincinnati; Nursing.

CLAUSING, W; Bishop Watterson HS; Worthington, OH; 24/283 Chrh Wkr; NHS; Trk; College; Architecture.

CLAUSON, LINDA; Rochester Cmnty HS; Rochester, IN; 47/165 Am Leg Aux Girls St; FCA; Hon Rl; Hosp Ade; Off Ade; Yth Flsp; Pres 4-H; FHA; VP Ger Clb; Key Clb; Indiana Central Univ; R N.

CLAUSS, ANN; Washington Catholic HS; Washington, IN; 5/58 Trs Jr Cls; Band; Chrs; Chrh Wkr; FCA; Hon Rl; NHS; Sch Mus; Sch Pl; Ind State Univ; Bus.

CLAWSON, LISA; Attica HS; Attica, IN; 1/80 Trs Frsh Cls; Cls Rep Soph Cls; Pres Jr Cls; Pres Sr Cls; Val; Band; NHS; Stu Cncl; Letter Bsktbl; Letter Trk; AES Schrdshp 1973; Studnt Cncl Most Vlbl Mbr 1977; AES Art & Sci 1973; Purdue Univ; Mgmt Bus.

CLAWSON, MARY A; Attica HS; Attica, IN; Sec Frsh Cls; Band; Chrh Wkr; Hon Rl; NHS; Sch Pl; Yth Flsp; Drama Clb; Hst Frsh Cls; Pep Clb; College.

CLAY, BRENT; Chesapeake HS; Chesapeake, OH; 27/140 Aud/Vis; Chrs; Hon Rl; Glf; Marshall Univ; Radio Broadcasting.

CLAY, CAROLE; Grosse Pointe N HS; Grosse Pte Wds, MI; 15/536 Band; Chrh Wkr; Cmnty Wkr; FCA; Girl Scts; Hon Rl; Lit Mag; NHS; Sct Actv; Rptr Yrbk; Michigan St Univ; Engr.

CLAY, CHARLES; North HS; Columbus, OH; 5/325 Hon Rl; Lit Mag; NHS; Yrbk; Ed Sch Nwsp; Rptr Sch Nwsp; Spn Clb; Ohio St Univ; Elec Engr.

CLAY, CHARLES E; Pennfield HS; Battle Creek, MI; 34/172 Cls Rep Frsh Cls; Band; JA; Drama Clb; Letter Bsktbl; Letter Ftbl; Letter Trk; Coach Actv; JA Awd; Natl Merit Ltr; Bus Admin.

CLAY, GREGORY C; Barboursville HS; Barboursville, WV; Cls Rep Frsh Cls; Am Leg Boys St; Hon Rl; Jr NHS; Stu Cncl; Sch Nwsp; 4-H; Key Clb; Spn Clb; Wrstlng; West Virginia Tech Univ; Engr.

CLAY, JACKI LYNN; Martinsville HS; Martinsville, ID; 74/425 Hon Rl; Stu Cncl; DECA; Gym; Chrldng; Pres Awd; Indiana Univ; Law.

CLAY, JEFFERY; Pineville HS; Saulsville, WV; 1/97 Pres Frsh Cls; Pres Soph Cls; Chrh Wkr; Jr NHS; NHS; Stu Cncl; 4-H; Letter Ten; Dnfth Awd; 4-H Awd; Math Field Days St 75 79; Chess Club St Tournmnt 78; Wv Golden Horse Shoe Awd 76; Voc Schl; Elec.

CLAY, KIMBERLY; Paul Harding HS; Fort Wayne, IN; Band; Pom Pon; College; Wildlife Mgmt.

CLAY, MELISSA; Van Wert HS; Van Wert, OH; Lbry Ade; Capt Bsktbl; Capt Trk; IM Sprt; Coll; Educ.

CLAY, PATRICIA E; Mid America Christian HS; Barboursville, WV; 3/35 Band; Chrs; Chrh Wkr; Cmnty Wkr; Girl Scts; Hon Rl; Hosp Ade; Lbry Ade; Yrbk; Fr Clb; Spanish Honor Awd; Pensacola Christian Coll; Medicine.

CLAY, PENNI; Beechcroft Jr Sr HS; Columbus, OH; 16/209 Cmp Fr Grls; Chrs; Treas Chrh Wkr; Girl Scts; Hon Rl; Jr NHS; NHS; Off Ade; Sch Pl; VP DECA; Univ Of Cincinnati; Interior Design.

CLAY, SONYA; Carlisle HS; Carlisle, OH; Pres Soph Cls; Pres Jr Cls; Am Leg Aux Girls St; Chrs; Chrh Wkr; Drl Tm; Girl Scts; Ken Univ; Med.

CLAYA, MICHAEL; Austintown Fitch HS; Youngstown, OH; Chrh Wkr; Debate Tm; JA; Natl Forn Lg; Rptr Sch Nwsp; Ger Clb; JA Awd; College.

CLAYMAN, COLLEEN; Ashtabula Harbor HS; Ashtabula, OH; 4/197 AFS; Band; JA; NHS; Stu Cncl; FTA; Sec Ger Clb; Pep Clb; Treas Spn Clb; Chrldng; Fac Math Awd 3 Yrs; Fac Eng III Awd 78; Oh Test Of Schlstc Achvmnt Awd Geom 77; Univ; Math.

CLAYPOOL, LAURA; Northrop HS; Ft Wayne, IN; 1/589 Val; Hon Rl; Sprt Ed Sch Nwsp; Trk; PPFtbl; Purdue Univ; Engr.

CLAYTON, CONNYE; Southeastern HS; Detroit, MI; 7/191 Chrh Wkr; Cmnty Wkr; Hon Rl; NHS; Off Ade; OEA; Cit Awd; Admin Mgmt Soc Schlrshp; S E Outstndng Busns Stu; Univ Of Detroit; Mktg.

CLAYTON, DONNA; Monrovia HS; Monrovia, IN; 1/140 Chrh Wkr; Hon Rl; NHS; Spn Clb; GAA; Mgrs; Indiana Univ; Medicine.

CLAYTON, JANET; Fairmont Sr HS; Fairmont, WV; 6/233 Am Leg Aux Girls St; Hon Rl; NHS; Spn Clb; Bsktbl; Trk; Mas Awd; Marshall Univ; Bio.

CLAYTON, LAURIE; Monroeville HS; Monroeville, OH; 25/88 Band; Girl Scts; Hon Rl; Sct Actv; Bsktbl; GAA; PPFtbl; Coll; Educ.

CLAYTON, MICHAEL; Sidney City HS; Sidney, OH; Hon Rl; Ger Clb; Bsbl; Bsktbl; Socr; Univ.

CLAYTOR, SARAH; Tri Jr Sr HS; Dunreith, IN; Chrs; Hon Rl; NHS; VP FHA; Trk; GAA; Elk Awd; Ball St Univ; Nursing.

CLEAR, BRADLEY; John Adams HS; South Bend, IN; Band; Chrh Wkr; Hon Rl; JA; Yth Flsp; Univ; Bus Mgmt.

CLEARY, CHRISTOPHER; New Richmond HS; New Richmond, OH; 15/195 Pres Band; Hon Rl; Treas NHS; Orch; Sch Mus; FSA; Rose Hulman Inst Of Tech; Math.

CLEARY, KATIE; Holy Name Nazareth HS; Cleveland, OH; 28/330 Band; Hon Rl; Hosp Ade; Orch; Pol Wkr; Lat Clb; College; Psych.

CLEARY, R MICHAEL; Washington Sr HS; Washington C H, OH; AFS; Am Leg Boys St; Aud/Vis; Band; Boy Scts; Chrs; Chrh Wkr; Drl Tm; Hon Rl; Lbry Ade; Miami Univ.

CLEAVENGER, BRIGETTA; Philip Barbour HS; Philippi, WV; Band; Hon Rl; Jr NHS; NHS; Sch Mus; Stg Crw; Drama Clb; Alderson Broddaus College; Educ.

CLEAVER, WANDA; Centerville Sr HS; Centerville, IN; 3/160 FCA; NHS; Off Ade; Pol Wkr; Y-Teens; Ball St Univ; Acctg.

CLEGG, MARK; Ida HS; Petersbrg, MI; 2/165 Am Leg Boys St; Boy Scts; VP NHS; Sct Actv; Ftbl; Wrstlng; IM Sprt; Whos Who In For Lang Amon Mid W HS 78; Eagle Scout 78; Univ Of Toledo.

CLEGHORN, ELLEN; Maumee HS; Maumee, OH; 24/316 Girl Scts; Hon Rl; Y-Teens; Spn Clb; IM Sprt; PPFtbl; Bowling Green St Univ; Bus.

CLEMANS, LORI; Madison Plains HS; London, OH; Band; Chrs; Hon Rl; Lbry Ade; Mod UN; NHS; Sch Pl; 4-H; Fr Clb; 4-H Awd; Quick Recall Team 78; Hon Mntn Eng St Test 76; Oh Half Arabn Horse Assoc Queen 78 & 79; Ohio St Univ; Horse Trainer.

CLEMENCE, CATHY; Athens HS; Athens, MI; VP Sr Cls; Hon Rl; Jr NHS; NHS; Off Ade; Quill & Scroll; Stu Cncl; Yrbk; Bsktbl; Trk; Michigan St Univ; Animal Tech.

CLEMENS, ARLO; Ogeman Heights HS; West Branch, MI; 46/188 Boy Scts; NHS; Sct Actv; Stu Cncl; 4-H; FFA; Key Clb; Dnfth Awd; 4-H Awd; Davenport Busns Schl; Busns.

CLEMENS, DOUG; Stryker HS; Stryker, OH; Pres Frsh Cls; Band; Boy Scts; Chrs; Hon Rl; 4-H; FFA; Wrstlng; Univ; Engr.

CLEMENS, MARGERY; Normandy HS; Seven Hills, OH; Aud/Vis; Chrs; Cmnty Wkr; Hon Rl; Sch Mus; Sch Pl; Drama Clb; 4-H; Fr Clb; Kent St Univ; Math.

CLEMENS, MARTY; Arthur Hill HS; Saginaw, MI; Bsbl; Glf; Scr Kpr; Michigan St Univ; Math.

CLEMENS, TEENA; High School; Burr Oak, MI; 11/31 Sec Frsh Cls; Chrs; Hon Rl; Off Ade; Sch Mus; Sch Pl; Rptr Sch Nwsp; Chrldng; Mgrs; PPFtbl; Beauty Schl; Beautician.

CLEMENT, JIM; Hammond Baptist HS; Merrillville, IN; Boy Scts; Bsbl; Bsktbl; Ftbl; Bob Jones Univ; History.

CLEMENT, KEVIN; Delphos St Johns HS; Delphos, OH; 40/150 Cls Rep Frsh Cls; Cls Rep Soph Cls; VP Sr Cls; Chrh Wkr; Cmnty Wkr; PAVAS; Sch Mus; Sch Pl; Stu Cncl; 4-H; Miami Univ; Zoology.

CLEMENT, MICHAEL D; Sand Creek HS; Adrian, MI; 1/73 Val; Aud/Vis; Cmnty Wkr; Debate Tm; Hon Rl; Lbry Ade; NHS; Stg Crw; Yrbk; Ed Sch Nwsp; Jrnlsm 1 & 2 Acctg 1 & 2 Awds; Eng Amer History Awds; Mi Comp Schlrshp; Jrnlsm 3 Awd; Century 2 Ldrs Comp; Adrian Coll; Speech.

CLEMENTE, DIANE; Niles Mckinley HS; Niles, OH; Hon Rl; Pres OEA; Pep Clb; Chrldng; College; Comp Tech.

CLEMENTS, DANIEL; W E Groves HS; Birmingham, MI; Boy Scts; Letter Swmmng; Mic St Univ.

CLEMENTS, LARRIANN; Bosse HS; Evansville, IN; Pres Soph Cls; Sec Sr Cls; Am Leg Aux Girls St; Chrs; Hon Rl; NHS; Spn Clb; NCTE;.

CLEMENTS, MARK; Alpena Sr HS; Alpena, MI; 13/744 Band; Boy Scts; Chrh Wkr; CAP; Sct Actv; Yrbk; Lat Clb; Elk Awd; Natl Merit Ltr; Michigan St Univ.

CLEMENTS, MARTIN; Catholic Central HS; Bloomingdale, OH; 12/204 Chrh Wkr; Hon Rl; NHS; 4-H; VICA; Akron Univ; Engr.

CLEMENTS, MICHELLE; Haworth HS; Kokomo, IN; 60/422 Cmnty Wkr; Hon Rl; NHS; Sch Mus; 4-H; Key Clb; 4-H Awd;.

CLEMENTS, REGINA; Blissfield HS; Blissfield, MI; 16/122 Band; Hon Rl; NHS; FBLA; GAA; Toledo Univ; Elem Educ.

CLEMENTS, RENE S; North Montgomery HS; Crawfordsville, IN; Cls Rep Soph Cls; Cl Rep Jr Cls; Cmp Fr Grls; Chrs; Drl Tm; Hon Rl; Sch Mus; Sch Pl; Stg Crw; Yth Flsp; Coll; Jrnlsm.

CLEMENTS, THERESA; Riverdale HS; Mt Blanchard, OH; 13/99 Aud/Vis; Chrs; Hon Rl; NHS; Off Ade; Rptr Sch Nwsp; OEA; Scr Kpr; Hon Medallion 79; Bowling Green St Univ; Acctg.

CLEMMONS, CINDY; Paint Valley HS; Bainbridge, OH; 45/85 Lbry Ade; 4-H; Fr Clb; GAA; Mgrs; Selctd As Mbr Into Youth Conservation Corps 78; Hocking Tech Coll; Forestry.

CLEMMONS, MICHELE; Franklin HS; Westland, MI; 3/600 Girl Scts; Hon Rl; Stu Cncl; Rptr Yrbk; Letter Socr; College.

CLEMONS, BARRY; North Miami HS; Macy, IN; 8/122 Hon Rl; FFA;.

CLEMONS, BRENT; North Miami HS; Macy, IN; 13/122 Hon Rl; FFA;.

CLEMONS, DEAN; Danbury HS; Marblehead, OH; 15/65 Boy Scts; Hon Rl; NHS; Off Ade; Sch Pl; Stg Crw; Sci Clb; Spn Clb; Capt Bsktbl; Ftbl; Findlay Coll.

CLEMONS, PAUL; Mahoning Cnty Joint Voc Schl; Lake Milton, OH; Hon Rl; DECA; FFA; Retail Mdse.

CLENDENIN, JEFFREY; Nitro HS; Charleston, WV; Mth Clb; IM Sprt; Marshall Univ; Acctg.

CLENDENING, DANNY; Ionia HS; Ionia, MI; 21/271 Am Leg Boys St; Hon Rl; Jr NHS; NHS; 4-H; 4-H Awd; Lake Superior State College; Elec.

CLERC, JANETTE; Midland HS; Midland, MI; 27/486 Girl Scts; Hon Rl; Yrbk; Fr Clb; Mic Tech Univ; Engr.

CLEVELAND, KELLY; Columbian HS; Tiffin, OH; Band; Chrs; Lbry Ade; Stu Cncl; Drama Clb; Spn Clb; Gym; Bowling Green St Univ; Bus.

CLEVENGER, CYNTHIA; Jefferson Union HS; Steubenville, OH; Band; Chrs; Hon Rl; Y-Teens; Beta Clb; OEA; Pep Clb; Pres Awd; Perfect Attendance 78 79; Capt Flag Corps 78 79; Jefferson Tech Coll; Med Asst.

CLEVENGER, DEBRA K; North Ridgeville Sr HS; N Ridgeville, OH; 13/350 Hon Rl; NHS; Off Ade; OEA; Spn Clb; Ten; Sec.

CLEVENGER, DENNIS A; Jonathan Alder HS; Plain City, OH; Am Leg Boys St; Band; Hon Rl; NHS; Sch Mus; Sch Pl; Stg Crw; Drama Clb; Mth Clb; Ohi State Univ; Pharmacy.

CLEVENGER, EDWARD; Union County HS; Liberty, IN; 17/130 Am Leg Boys St; Hon Rl; Sch Mus; Yth Flsp; Glf; IM Sprt; Mgrs; College; Banking.

CLEVENGER, KEVI M; Lima Sr HS; Lima, OH; Chrs; Sec Chrh Wkr; Hon Rl; Hosp Ade; Off Ade; Yth Flsp; Yrbk; Rptr Sch Nwsp; DECA; 5th Pl In DECA Job Interview Contest 79; Voc Educ.

CLEVENGER, LORI A; Muncie Northside HS; Muncie, IN; Chrs; FCA; MMM; Sch Mus; Sch Pl; Pep Clb; Chrldng; Tmr; Ball St Univ; Music Tchr.

CLEVENGER, MARGARET S; Jonathan Alder HS; Plain City, OH; 3/106 Chrs; Hon Rl; Sec NHS; Y-Teens; Yrbk; Rptr Sch Nwsp; Drama Clb; Fr Clb; Spn Clb; Chrldng;.

CLEVENGER, MIKE; Portsmouth East HS; Sciotoville, OH; Chrs; Sch Mus; Yrbk; Spn Clb; Letter Bsbl; Letter Ftbl; Shawnee St Coll; Bus Admin.

CLEVENGER, STUART; Elgin HS; Prospect, OH; 25/180 Chrh Wkr; Hon Rl; Yth Flsp; College; Elec Engr.

CLICK, DARLENE; Labrae HS; Southington, OH; 11/130 Cls Rep Soph Cls; Cl Rep Jr Cls; Hon Rl; Stu Cncl; Spn Clb; Kent State; Law.

CLICK, DEBORAH; Northwestern HS; Kokomo, IN; 14/173 Band; Chrh Wkr; Hon Rl; NHS; Yth Flsp; 4-H; Ger Clb; Pep Clb; Chrldng; C of C Awd; Indiana Univ; Pre Med.

CLIFFORD, MARIA; Liberty HS; Youngstown, OH; Hon Rl; Lit Mag; Stg Crw; Drama Clb; Fr Clb; Pep Clb; Youngstown State Univ; Art.

CLIFFORD, MARSHA; Davison Sr HS; Davison, MI; Girl Scts; Hon Rl; Off Ade; Baker Jr Coll; Sec.

CLIFFORD, ROBERT; Heath HS; Heath, OH; Band; Pres Yth Flsp; Letter Crs Cntry; Letter Trk; Univ; Educ.

CLIME, MARY; Marcellus HS; Marcellus, MI; 23/70 VP Frsh Cls; Pres Soph Cls; Band; Chrs; Drl Tm; Treas Girl Scts; Hon Rl; Sch Pl; Sct Actv; Sch Nwsp; Honor Awd 76; Stu Service Awd 76; Mi Competitive Schlrshp 78; Southwestern Michigan Coll; Law.

CLIMER. KATHY; Southeastern HS; Londonderry, OH; FTA; Spn Clb; Bsktbl; Trk; Univ; Psych.

CLIMES, ROBIN; North Canton Hoover HS; Greentown, OH; Chrs; Chrh Wkr; Hon Rl; Lbry Ade; Pol Wkr; Ger Clb; Univ Of Akron; Nursing.

CLIMIE, DONNA M; South Lyon HS; So Lyon, MI; Cmp Fr Grls; Chrs; Girl Scts; Hon Rl; PAVAS; Sch Mus; Sch Pl; Sct Actv; Stg Crw; Drama Clb; Eastern Univ; Drama.

CLINDANIEL, JIM; Centerburg HS; Centerburg, OH; 9/63 Cls Rep Sr Cls; Hon Rl; Pres 4-H; Spn Clb; Letter Bsbl; Letter Swmmng; Letter Wrstlng; PPFtbl; Ohio Northern Univ; Pharm.

CLINE, ALICIA; Olentangy HS; Westerville, OH; Band; Chrs; Hon Rl; Mdrgl; NHS; 4-H; Fr Clb; Pep Clb; Trk; Chrldng; Bowling Green Univ; Bus Engr.

CLINE, BARBARA; Stow HS; Cuyahoga Falls, OH; Cmp Fr Grls; Chrs; Hon Rl; Off Ade; Sch Pl; Stu Cncl; Rptr Yrbk; Yrbk; Drama Clb; Lat Clb; Akron Univ; Nursing.

CLINE, BONITA; Independence HS; Sophia, WV; Cls Rep Soph Cls; Cl Rep Jr Cls; Hon Rl; JA; Treas Stu Cncl; Beta Clb; 4-H; FBLA; Pep Clb; Letter Trk; Science Fair; College.

CLINE, BRIAN; Marion Adams HS; Sheridan, IN; 42/98 Chrh Wkr; VP Yth Flsp; VP 4-H; Letter Bsbl; Letter Bsktbl; Coach Actv; IM Sprt; Mgrs; Scr Kpr; Tmr; College; Accounting.

CLINE, CELESTE; Bellbrook HS; Bellbrook, OH; 6/162 Band; Chrh Wkr; Hon Rl; Off Ade; Letter Bsktbl; GAA; IM Sprt; Scr Kpr; Tmr; Mt Vernon Nazarene Coll; Acctg.

CLINE, CINDY; Shepherd HS; Shepherd, MI; Cls Rep Frsh Cls; Trs Soph Cls; VP Jr Cls; Sec Sr Cls; Chrh Wkr; Girl Scts; Hon Rl; Off Ade; Stu Cncl; FHA; Central Michigan Univ; Stenographer.

CLINE, DAWN M; Athens HS; Athens, MI; Band; Hon Rl; NHS; Pol Wkr; Quill & Scroll; Ed Yrbk; Yrbk; Trk; College.

CLINE, JENNIFER; Oceana HS; Lynco, WV; Band; Chrs; Chrh Wkr; Hon Rl; MMM; NHS; Beta Clb; College; Med.

CLINE, JOSEPH I; Mentor HS; Mentor, OH; Hon Rl; Jr NHS; NHS; Key Clb; Natl Merit SF; Univ Of Vir; Physical Science.

CLINE, KEVIN; Bishop Ready HS; Columbus, OH; Am Leg Boys St; Hon Rl; Jr NHS; NHS; Spn Clb; Bsktbl; Ten; Bowling Green Univ; Mechanical Engr.

CLINE, LORA; Unioto HS; Chillicothe, OH; Band; Chrs; Hon Rl; Hosp Ade; Jr NHS; Pres NHS; Quill & Scroll; Sch Mus; Stg Crw; Rptr Yrbk; Capital Univ; Music.

CLINE, MICHELLE; Greencastle HS; Greencastle, IN; Cmnty Wkr; Hon Rl; Red Cr Ade; FHA; FTA; Pep Clb; Spn Clb; Swmmng; Chrldng; Mgrs; Ind State Univ; Physical Educ.

CLINE, PATRICIA; Mt View HS; Welch, WV; Chrs; Chrh Wkr; Cmnty Wkr; Hon Rl; Off Ade; Sch Pl; Rptr Sch Nwsp; Sch Nwsp; FBLA; FNA; Univ.

CLINE, PHILIP A; Huntington East HS; Huntington, WV; Am Leg Boys St; Chrs; Hon Rl; Natl Forn Lg; Pol Wkr; Yrbk; Rptr Sch Nwsp; Fr Clb; Key Clb; Mth Clb; Attended & Giftd HS Stu 77 80; St Forensics Tournmnt 5th Pl Oratorical Contest; Univ.

CLINE, RHONDA; Wayne HS; Wayne, WV; Chrs; Hon Rl; NHS; Sch Mus; Yrbk; Beta Clb; Marshall Univ.

CLINE, ROBIN; Grandview Hts HS; Columbus, OH; 19/119 Chrs; Hon Rl; IM Sprt; Cit Awd; Schlshp Awd 79; Fred Wring Music Worksp Schslhp 78; Bus.

CLINE, SUSAN; Jennings Cnty HS; N Vernon, IN; 1/350 Cls Rep Frsh Cls; Cls Rep Soph Cls; Val; NHS; Pres Stu Cncl; Yrbk; FTA; Spn Clb; Dnfth Awd; Gov Hon Prg Awd; Indiana Central Univ; Elem Ed.

CLINE, TAMARA L; Barnesville HS; Barnesvile, OH; 7/101 Cl Rep Jr Cls; Am Leg Aux Girls St; Hosp Ade; NHS; Sch Mus; Stu Cncl; VP 4-H; VP Fr Clb; VP FHA; FTA; Muskingum Univ; Scndry Educ.

CLINGAN, LINDA C; Hedgesville HS; Martinsburg, WV; Hon Rl; Sch Mus; Stu Cncl; 4-H; Pep Clb; Sci Clb; Capt Chrldng; DAR Awd; Best Cheerleaders Awd; All Bi State Team Softball; Treas Of Varsity Club; Bauder Fash Coll; Fash Design.

CLINGENPEEL, JULIE; Lincoln HS; Cambridge, IN; Chrh Wkr; Drl Tm; Hon Rl; NHS; Spn Clb; College; Bilingual Busns.

CLINGER, RUTH; Ridgedale HS; Marion, OH; Sal; Am Leg Aux Girls St; Chrh Wkr; Hon Rl; NHS; Pol Wkr; IM Sprt; Scr Kpr; Ohio St Univ.

CLINGERMAN, CHARLOTTE; Allen Park HS; Allen Park, MI; Band; Chrs; Girl Scts; Hon Rl; Sct Actv; 4-H; Sci Clb; 4-H Awd; Plague Of Recognition For Proficiency In Amer History; Ribbon For Scoring Highest Number Of Pts In Archery; College; Acctg.

CLINK, C; Hillman Comm HS; Hillman, MI; 14/59 Pres Frsh Cls; Cl Rep Jr Cls; Cls Rep Sr Cls; Band; Hon Rl; Sch Pl; Stu Cncl; Rptr Sch Nwsp; Sch Nwsp; Letter VICA; Alma Coll; Pre Med.

CLINK, D; Comstock Park HS; Comstock Pk, MI; 2/160 Sal; Band; Hon Rl; NHS; Pep Clb; Coach Actv; GAA; Pres Pom Pon; PPFtbl; Aquinas College.

CLINKENBEARD, CINDI; Snider HS; Ft Wayne, IN; 1/550 Debate Tm; Hon Rl; Orch; Stg Crw; Spn Clb; Bsktbl; Trk; Letter Chrldng; PPFtbl; Tri Kappa Scholastic Awd; Academic Plaque Top 3 Stu Awd; Snider Scholastic Awds; College; Communications.

CLINTON, SUSAN; Plymouth Centennial Educ Pk; Plymouth, MI; 42/540 Girl Scts; Hon Rl; NHS; Yth Flsp; Swmmng; Michigan St Univ; Med Tech.

CLIPPINGER, DEB; Sheridan HS; Glenford, OH; Cls Rep Frsh Cls; Chrs; Chrh Wkr; FCA; Hon Rl; Jr NHS; Lbry Ade; NHS; Off Ade; PAVAS; Central Ohio Tech; Radiographic Tech.

CLIPPINGER, MICHAEL; Utica HS; Utica, OH; 40/210 Sec Sr Cls; Am Leg Boys St; Chrs; Sch Mus; Sch Pl; Pres Stu Cncl; Pres Drama Clb; Letter Bsbl; Cit Awd; Ctrl Ohio Tech Coll; Drafting.

CLITES, LORI; North Newton HS; Morrocco, IN; 1/141 Val; Band; Hon Rl; NHS; Sch Pl; 4-H; Natl Merit Ltr; St Josephs College; Mathematics.

CLOAT, KATHY; Switzerland Co Jr Sr HS; Vevay, IN; 20/120 Girl Scts; Hon Rl; Pep Clb; Spn Clb;.

CLODFELTER, RITA; North Putnam Jr Sr HS; Roachdale, IN; 1/107 Cls Rep Frsh Cls; Cls Rep Soph Cls; Cl Rep Jr Cls; Val; FCA; Sch Mus; Girl Scts; Pres Stu Cncl; Drama Clb; 4-H; Purdue Univ; Acctg.

CLONCS, JEFFREY; Willard HS; Willard, OH; 65/181 Bsbl; Bsktbl; Ftbl; Wrstlng; IM Sprt; Indiana Univ; Bus Admin.

CLORE, KRISTA; Davison HS; Davison, MI; Cls Rep Soph Cls; Band; Chrs; Chrh Wkr; Girl Scts; Hon Rl; Orch; Sch Mus; Stg Crw; Stu Cncl; Fredrick Chopin Piano Awd 79; Schlrshp To Blue Lke Fine Arts Cmp 75; MI Dist & Five St Reg Teens Inv Wnnr; Bob Jones Univ; Music Educ.

CLOSE, TAMMY; Loudonville HS; Loudonville, OH; Hon Rl; Off Ade; Rptr Yrbk; Treas Spn Clb; Cit Awd; Homecoming Queen 78; Reserve Bsktbl 77 78; Best Drawing In Schls Art Contest 78; Voc Schl; Beautician.

CLOSSMAN, L; Tri Valley HS; Nashport, OH; 29/223 Chrh Wkr; Hon Rl; Yth Flsp; 4-H; Lat Clb; Crs Cntry; Ftbl; IM Sprt; Ohio St Univ.

CLOSSON, NENA; Roosevelt Wilson HS; Clarksburg, WV; Band; Chrs; Chrh Wkr; Hon Rl; Pol Wkr; Sch Mus; Sch Pl; Y-Teens; 4-H; Fr Clb; Jrnlsm Awd; Sportsmanship Awd; Class Favorite; Fairmont St Univ; Phys Educ.

CLOTZ, MICHAEL; Admiral King HS; Lorain, OH; Band; Chrs; Orch; Sch Pl; Yrbk; Drama Clb; Ten; Univ Of Toledo; Pharmacy.

CLOUD, SHIRLEY; Decatur Central HS; Indnpls, IN; 56/364 Band; Letter Bsktbl; Letter Ten; Indiana St Univ; Lab Tech.

CLOUGH, DEBORAH; Fordson HS; Dearborn, MI; 15/600 Band; Hon Rl; NHS; Sprt Ed Yrbk; Mth Clb; Letter Bsktbl; GAA; IM Sprt; Vlybl Ltr 78; Sftbl Ltr 78; Wayne St Univ Merit Schlrshp 79; Wayne St Univ; Bus Mgmt.

CLOUGH, JUDY; Flushing Sr HS; Flushing, MI; Lbry Ade; Sch Nwsp; Art Hnr Soc 78; Coll; Photog.

CLOUSE, ANTHONY; A Leon Clouse HS; Losantville, IN; Cls Rep Frsh Cls; Cls Rep Soph Cls; Cl Rep Jr Cls; Letter Bsktbl; Letter Crs Cntry; Letter Trk; Lettermans Club; Ball St Univ; Archt.

CLOUSE, JACKIE; Sheridan HS; Somerset, OH; 2/180 VP Frsh Cls; FCA; Hon Rl; NHS; Treas Stu Cncl; 4-H; FHA; FTA; Capt Bsktbl; Scr Kpr; Miami Univ.

CLOUSE, JANE; New Riegel HS; New Riegel, OH; 7/48 Cls Rep Frsh Cls; Pres Soph Cls; Trs Jr Cls; Hon Rl; Jr NHS; NHS; Stu Cncl; FTA; Mgrs; 4-H Awd; College.

CLOUSE, JULIA; Brookhaven HS; Columbus, OH; Chrs; Chrh Wkr; Hon Rl; NHS; Spn Clb; IM Sprt; Scr Kpr; Tmr; Univ; Nursing.

CLOUSE, KAREN; Eastmoor HS; Columbus, OH; 3/290 Chrs; Jr NHS; NHS; Yrbk; Rptr Sch Nwsp; FTA; Pep Clb; College; Poli Sci.

CLOUSE, KEVIN; Monrovia HS; Martinsville, IN; Chrs; Chrh Wkr; Hon Rl; Yth Flsp; Spn Clb; Coll; Elec Engr.

CLOUSE, SARALYNN; North Central HS; Farmersbg, IN; 4/100 VP Chrs; Chrh Wkr; Hon Rl; Jr NHS; NHS; Treas Yth Flsp; Lat Clb; Indiana St Univ; Music Educ.

CLOUSE, YVONNE; New Riegel HS; New Riegel, OH; Band; NHS; VP 4-H; Spn Clb; Letter Bsktbl; Cit Awd; Pres Awd; BGSU; Chem.

CLOUSER, CONNIE; South Amherst HS; So Amherst, OH; Band; Chrs; Drm Mjrt; Hon Rl; NHS; Off Ade; Sch Mus; Pep Clb; Trk; PPFtbl;.

CLOUTHIER, DAWN; Lake Linden Hubbell HS; Lake Linden, MI; 6/60 Trs Jr Cls; Cmp Fr Grls; Chrh Wkr; Hon Rl; 4-H; Pep Clb; Bsktbl; Letter Trk; Scr Kpr; Tmr; NEDT Awd 77; Univ; Chem.

CLOUTIER, CHARLES; Lake Linden Hubbell HS; Lake Linden, MI; 3/60 Am Leg Boys St; Band; Hon Rl; Letter Bsktbl; Letter Ftbl; Trk; Natl Merit Ltr; Univ; Elec Engr.

CLOUTIER, RITA; St Marys Of Redford HS; Detroit, MI; Chrh Wkr; Hon Rl;.

CLOVESKO, ANITA; Rocky River HS; Rocky Rvr, OH; AFS; Chrs; Chrh Wkr; Girl Scts; Hon Rl; Jr NHS; Sch Mus; Spn Clb; Letter Bsktbl; Letter Trk; College; Teach.

CLUCK, T; Harrison HS; Evansville, IN; Chrs; Chrh Wkr; Hosp Ade; JA; FBLA; Pep Clb; Pom Pon; Cit Awd; Coll; Interior Decorating.

CLUGSTON, HANS; Big Rapids HS; Big Rapids, MI; Hon Rl; NHS; Yrbk; Rptr Sch Nwsp; Case Western Reserve Univ; Physics.

CLUNK, DAVID; Whitmer Sr HS; Toledo, OH; 67/810 Chrh Wkr; Cmnty Wkr; Hon Rl; Stu Cncl; VICA; Coach Actv; PPFtbl; Outstanding Serv Awd At Whitmer; Toledo Univ; Elec Engr.

CLUP, MARK; Columbiana HS; Columbiana, OH; 7/100 Glf; Kent State; Business.

CLUTTER, ANGIE; Boonville HS; Boonville, IN; 21/210 Sec Soph Cls; Sec Jr Cls; Am Leg Aux Girls St; Band; Chrh Wkr; Hon Rl; Off Ade; Stu Cncl; Yth Flsp; Pep Clb; College.

CLUTTER, KAREN; Crestline HS; Crestline, OH; Cls Rep Soph Cls; Cls Rep Sr Cls; Cmp Fr Grls; Chrs; Chrh Wkr; Cmnty Wkr; Girl Scts; Hon Rl; College; Elem Ed.

CLUTTER, KEVIN; Toronto HS; Toronto, OH; Hon Rl; Ftbl; Trk; Am Leg Awd; U S Army; Chem Engr.

CLUTTER, PENNY; Webster County HS; Parcoal, WV; Cls Rep Frsh Cls; Hon Rl; NHS; Sch Pl; Stg Crw; Stu Cncl; Ed Sch Nwsp; Pep Clb; Chrldng; IM Sprt; West Virginia Univ; Pre Law.

CLUTTER, TODD; Marshall HS; Marshall, MI; Hon Rl; JA; Bsbl; Letter Ftbl; Letter Trk; Rotary Awd; Univ; Med.

CLUXTON, ALLAN; Peebles HS; Peebles, OH; 20/110 Pres Frsh Cls; VP Soph Cls; Trs Jr Cls; Hst Sr Cls; Band; Chrh Wkr; Hon Rl; FFA; Bsktbl; Farming.

CLYDE, GEORGIA; New Albany HS; New Albany, OH; 11/100 Trs Frsh Cls; Trs Soph Cls; Am Leg Aux Girls St; Girl Scts; Hon Rl; Orch; Bsbl; Capt Bsktbl; IM Sprt; PPFtbl; Coll; Health.

CLYMER, NANCY; Cheboygan Catholic HS; Cheboygan, MI; 1/32 Cls Rep Frsh Cls; Cls Rep Soph Cls; Val; Hon Rl; Rptr Yrbk; Rptr Sch Nwsp; Letter Trk; Mgrs; Central Mich Univ; Acctg.

COADY, PATRICK; St Charles Prep; Columbus, OH; Aud/Vis; Chrh Wkr; Cmnty Wkr; Sch Pl; Stg Crw; Ger Clb; Lat Clb; Ftbl; Ohio St Univ; Bus.

COAKLEY, JAMES; Gilmour Academy; Cleveland Hts, OH; VP Frsh Cls; Hon Rl; NHS; Pol Wkr; Sch Pl; Stu Cncl; Rptr Sch Nwsp; Fr Clb; FDA; Crs Cntry; French Awd; Merit Achvmnt Awd Whos Who; Georgetown Univ; Med.

COALMER, NANCY; Beaver Local HS; E Liverpool, OH; Am Leg Aux Girls St; Hon Rl; Jr NHS; Off Ade; Y-Teens; Eng Clb; Fr Clb; Pep Clb; Sci Clb; Crs Cntry; Alderson Broaddus Univ; Phys Asst.

COAN, MARK; Centerville HS; Centerville, OH; 152/687 Hon Rl; Bsktbl; Ftbl; Trk; IM Sprt; PPFtbl; Kiwan Awd; Vir Military Inst.

COAN, PAMELA; Fairhaven Christian Academy; Chesterton, IN; Band; Chrs; Chrh Wkr; Hon Rl; Yth Flsp; Yrbk; Chrldng; College; English.

COASTER, SANDRA; Reed City HS; Reed City, MI; 21/165 Trs Soph Cls; Sec Jr Cls; Sec Sr Cls; Band; Hon Rl; Hosp Ade; NHS; Sch Pl; Stu Cncl; Chrldng; Ferris St Coll; Nursing.

COATES, BONNIE; Chillicothe HS; Chillicothe, OH; 20/380 AFS; Aud/Vis; Girl Scts; Hon Rl; NHS; Orch; Y-Teens; Bsbl; Bsktbl; St Francis Coll; Med Tech.

COATES, DOUGLAS; Tuscarawas Valley HS; E Sparta, OH; 19/142 Band; Chrs; Chrh Wkr; Debate Tm; Hon Rl; Natl Forn Lg; NHS; Sch Mus; Sch Pl; Stu Cncl; John Philip Sousa Awd 79; Natl Schl Choral Awd 79; Best Male Actor 79; Kent State Univ; Music Educ.

COATES, JEAN; Shadyside HS; Shadyside, OH; Band; Hon Rl; Y-Teens; Spn Clb; Ohio Vlly Hosp Schl Of Nurs; Nurse.

COATES, MARK; Shadyside HS; Shadyside, OH; 25/103 Hon Rl; NHS; Sch Mus; Spn Clb; Letter Ftbl; Trk; Ohio St Univ.

COATES, TAVA; Waynesfield Goshen HS; Wapakoneta, OH; VP Jr Cls; Band; Chrs; Chrh Wkr; Hon Rl; Jr NHS; NHS; Sch Mus; FHA; Pep Clb; Banking.

COATS, STEPHANIE; Bloomfield HS; Bloomfield, IN; 9/75 Pres Sr Cls; Hon Rl; NHS; Lat Clb; Sci Clb; Univ.

COATSOLONIA, DINA; Kouts HS; Kouts, IN; 2/52 Cls Rep Frsh Cls; Cls Rep Soph Cls; Cl Rep Jr Cls; Cls Rep Sr Cls; Aud/Vis; Band; Hon Rl; NHS; Off Ade; Sch Pl; Purdue Univ.

COBB, ABONIS; John F Kennedy HS; Cleveland, OH; Trk; Mgrs; Cit Awd; Cleveland St Univ; Doctor.

COBB, BARRY; Harbor HS; Ashtabula, OH; 8/167 NHS; Stu Cncl; Fr Clb; Pres Mth Clb; Letter Glf; Faculty Awd French; Ohio Awd Of Distinction; Ohio Bd Of Regents Awd; Ohio St Univ; Engr.

COBB, JANELLE; Aquinas HS; Westland, MI; Cl Rep Jr Cls; Band; Chrh Wkr; Cmnty Wkr; Hon Rl; Stu Cncl; Yth Flsp; Congressmens Medal Of Merit Awd; William Ford 15th Dist Michigan; Coll; Med.

COBB, JEFFREY B; University HS; Aurora, OH; Sch Pl; Stg Crw; Yrbk; Sch Nwsp; Sci Clb; Natl Merit SF; Cornell Univ; Elec Engr.

COBB, KATHERINE; Thomas A De Vilbiss HS; Toledo, OH; Hon Rl; NHS; Quill & Scroll; Sct Actv; Stu Cncl; Sprt Ed Yrbk; VP Rus Clb; PPFtbl; Pres Pay A El Sa Soc Serv Club 1979; Student Rep Century III Ldrshp Prog 1979; Univ Of Texas; Law.

COBB, KATHRYN; Everett HS; Lansing, MI; Orch; Ger Clb; Pep Clb; Lansing Cmnty Coll; Elem Educ.

COBB, LAURA; Northrop HS; Ft Wayne, IN; 32/587 Chrs; Chrh Wkr; Hon Rl; JA; Mdrgl; Music Letter 79; Univ; Eng.

COBB, MICHELE S; Flushing HS; Flushing, MI; Hon Rl; JA; Fr Clb; Sci Clb; Bsbl; Socr; Swmmng; Trk; Coach Actv; IM Sprt; Voc Schl.

COBB, PATTY; Herbert Hoover HS; Clendenin, WV; VP Frsh Cls; Band; Chrs; Hon Rl; Jr NHS; Stu Cncl; Drama Clb; 4-H; Pep Clb; Mgrs; All Cnty Band 76 79; All Area Band 78; All Cnty Chorus 77 78 & 79; WVMTA Dist 3 Piano 78; Marshall Univ; Music.

COBB, TAMMY; West Side Sr HS; Gary, IN; Cls Rep Frsh Cls; Cls Rep Soph Cls; Cl Rep Jr Cls; Band; Chrh Wkr; Hon Rl; JA; Stu Cncl; Pep Clb; Pom Pon; Summer Coll Courses 79; Numerous Jr Achievement Awds 77 78; Numerous Music Awds & Sftbll Trophies 75 79; Purdue Univ; Med Tech.

COBBLE, BRIAN; West Ottawa HS; Holland, MI; Aud/Vis; Band; Hon Rl; Lbry Ade; Stg Crw; College; Astrophysics.

COBBLE, DEAN; Hobart Senior HS; Hobart, IN; 16/395 Am Leg Boys St; Pres FCA; Hon Rl; Jr NHS; NHS; Stu Cncl; Yth Flsp; Ger Clb; Letter Bsktbl; Letter Ftbl; De Pauw Univ; Pre Law.

COBERLY, REBECCA; Gilmer Cnty HS; Glenville, WV; 1/98 Sec Sr Cls; Val; Chrh Wkr; Hon Rl; Natl Forn Lg; Pres NHS; Off Ade; Stu Cncl; Ed Yrbk; Ed Sch Nwsp; Glenville St Coll.

COBERLY, THOMAS; Summerfield HS; Petersburg, MI; Band; Boy Scts; Hon Rl; Michigan Univ; Vet.

COBLENTZ, KRISTI; Greenville Sr HS; Greenville, OH; 3/380 Cls Rep Soph Cls; Chrh Wkr; Hon Rl; Pres 4-H; Sci Clb; Sec Spn Clb; Soc Of Dist Amer HS Stu; Coll.

COBOURN, SHANE; Salem Sr HS; Salem, OH; Boy Scts; Sct Actv; God Cntry Awd; Swiss Alpine Guide Schl; Mtn Guide.

COBURN, DEBORAH; Mannington HS; Farmington, WV; Cmnty Wkr; Girl Scts; Hon Rl; Sch Pl; Yrbk; Fr Clb; Bsktbl; Trk; Fairmont State; Astronomy.

COBURN, LINDA; Rock Hill Sr HS; Kitts Hill, OH; Cls Rep Soph Cls; Band; Hon Rl; Yrbk; Sch Nwsp; 4-H; Sci Clb; Bsktbl; Trk; GAA;.

COBURN, TERRI; Lincoln HS; Shinnston, WV; Hon Rl; Rptr Yrbk; FBLA; Sci Clb;.

COBURN, TIMOTHY J; Fremont HS; Fremont, IN; Sec Jr Cls; Chrs; Hon Rl; NHS; Sch Mus; Rptr Sch Nwsp; Pres FTA; Pres OEA; Spn Clb; Univ; Psych.

COBY, CHARLES; Moorefield HS; Moorefield, WV; Cmnty Wkr; Hon Rl; Stg Crw; 4-H; FFA; Bsktbl; Glf; 4-H Awd; Potomac St Coll; Forestry.

COCANOUR, MICHELLE; Springs Valley HS; French Lick, IN; 1/72 Hst Frsh Cls; Trs Jr Cls; VP Sr Cls; Band; Chrh Wkr; Drm Mjrt; Hon Rl; NHS; Fr Clb; Lat Clb; Indiana Univ; Ther.

COCH, CAROL; Theodore Roosevelt HS; Wyandotte, MI; Band; Cmp Fr Grls; Hon Rl; Hosp Ade; Jr NHS; NHS; Sch Mus; Sch Pl; Drama Clb; Fr Clb; Wayne St Univ; Nurse.

COCHENOUR, DAVE; N Canton Hoover HS; North Canton, OH; 59/421 Boy Scts; Cmnty Wkr; FCA; Hon Rl; Pol Wkr; Spn Clb; Bsbl; Letter Ftbl; Coll; History.

COCHERL, DONNA; Marion Harding HS; Marion, OH; Cls Rep Soph Cls; Cl Rep Jr Cls; Band; Girl Scts; Hon Rl; Lbry Ade; Off Ade; Sct Actv; Stu Cncl; 4-H; 1st Girl To Recieve Varsity Ltr At Harding High 78; Bowling Green Univ; Bus Admin.

COCHRAN, ALLEN; Cambridge HS; Cambridge, OH; Cmnty Wkr; Hon Rl; VP NHS; Red Cr Ade; Key Clb; Letter Ten; Ohio St Univ.

COCHRAN, BARB; Snider HS; Holland, MI; 10/580 Band; Chrh Wkr; Cmnty Wkr; Hon Rl; JA; Rptr Sch Nwsp; Fr Clb; Chrldng; Univ Of Michigan; Bus & Mgmt.

COCHRAN, BARBARA; R Nelson Snider HS; Holland, MI; 8/500 Chrh Wkr; Hon Rl; Orch; Rptr Sch Nwsp; Fr Clb; Pep Clb; Chrldng; Univ Of Mic; Bus Admin.

COCHRAN, CAROL; Winchester Community HS; Winchester, IN; Hon Rl; Fr Clb; FBLA; FHA; Ball St Univ; Tch Elem Schl.

COCHRAN, DARBY; Greenville Sr HS; Greenville, OH; Hon Rl; OEA; Sci Clb; Ftbl; Edison St Cmnty Coll; Acctg.

COCHRAN, IRENA F; Shady Spring HS; Beckley, WV; Cls Rep Frsh Cls; Cls Rep Soph Cls; Chrs; FCA; Hon Rl; Off Ade; Sch Mus; Stu Cncl; Yth Flsp; 4-H; Raleigh Co Vo Tech Ctr; Data Proc.

COCHRAN, JOSEPH R; Frontier HS; New Matamoras, OH; Aud/Vis; Band; Chrh Wkr; Washington Co Tech Schl; Comp Prog.

COCHRAN, KELLY; Saint Peters HS; Mansfield, OH; Girl Scts; Hon Rl; JA; Red Cr Ade; Rptr Sch Nwsp; Key Clb; GAA; IM Sprt; College; Math.

COCHRAN, LAURA; Barberton HS; Barberton, OH; Sec Sr Cls; Band; Chrs; Hon Rl; Jr NHS; Off Ade; Stu Cncl; Yth Flsp; Y-Teens; Rptr Sch Nwsp; Bauder Fashion Coll; Fshn Mdse.

COCHRAN, LYNN; Mason Sr HS; Mason, MI; Chrs; Hon Rl; Pres Hosp Ade; Mdrgl; Sch Mus; Rptr Yrbk; Pres 4-H; Pep Clb; Sec Spn Clb; 4-H Awd; Michigan St Univ; Bi Lingual Lawyer.

COCHRAN, MICHAEL; Sherman HS; Bloomingrose, WV; Band; Boy Scts; Chrh Wkr; Hon Rl; NHS; Sct Actv; Yth Flsp; VICA; Wva Tech; Drafting.

COCHRAN, PAUL; Peru Sr HS; Peru, IN; 19/289 Hon Rl; JA; Natl Forn Lg; NHS; Fr Clb; Purdue Univ; Sci.

COCHRAN, PHYLLIS; Crestline HS; Crestline, OH; 5/120 Hon Rl; Jr NHS; NHS; Sch Nwsp; 4-H; 4-H Awd; Ohio St Univ; Zoology.

COCHRAN, SUE; Frontier HS; N Matamoras, OH; 25/122 Mountain St Univ; Data Processing.

COCHRAN, TONY; Gorham Fayette HS; Fayette, OH; Cmnty Wkr; Hon Rl; Stu Cncl; Rptr Yrbk; Fr Clb; Scr Kpr; Univ Of Toledo; Comp Sciences.

COCHRANE, MARK; Brookside HS; Sheffield Lake, OH; Band; Boy Scts; Cmnty Wkr; Hon Rl; NHS; PAVAS; Sch Mus; Sch Pl; Wrstlng; Cit Awd; Kent State Univ; Bus Admin.

COCKERHAM, KATHY; Pike Ctrl Middle HS; Petersburg, IN; Hst Soph Cls; Chrs; Chrh Wkr; Hon Rl; Lbry Ade; NHS; Sch Mus; Sch Pl; Stu Cncl; Ed Yrbk; Oakland City Coll; Legal Sec.

COCKERHAM, RUTH; Springfield HS; Akron, OH; 37/381 Chrs; Chrh Wkr; Hon Rl; Jr NHS; MMM; NHS; Sch Mus; Yth Flsp; Fr Clb; Pep Clb; Akron Univ; Home Econ.

COCKFIELD, NANCY; Redford Union HS; Redford, MI; Hon Rl; Red Cr Ade; Wayne St Univ; Phys Ther.

COCKING, LLOYD; Trenton HS; Trenton, MI; 5/539 Hon Rl; NHS; Crs Cntry; Wrstlng; Mi St Univ Acad Excell Awd 79; Michigan St Univ; Air Force ROTC.

COCKLIN, ALESIA; Mohawk HS; Sycamore, OH; Band; Chrh Wkr; Cmnty Wkr; Lbry Ade; Orch; Stg Crw; Yth Flsp; Drama Clb; FHA; FTA; Miss Teenage U S Finlst For Ohio 79; BGSU; Intr Dsgn.

COCKRELL, ANGELA; Robert A Taft HS; Cincinnati, OH; 6/150 Pres Frsh Cls; Cls Rep Soph Cls; Pres Jr Cls; VP Sr Cls; Drl Tm; Hon Rl; Rptr Yrbk; Treas OEA; Cit Awd; College; Court Stenographer.

COCUZZA, JOAN; Niles HS; Niles, MI; 1/350 Band; Hon Rl; Sch Pl; Stg Crw; Yrbk; Pep Clb; Spn Clb; Bsktbl; College.

CODDINGTON, POLLY; Middletown HS; Middletown, OH; 9/519 Am Leg Aux Girls St; Band; Chrs; Chrh Wkr; Cmnty Wkr; Drm Bgl; Hon Rl; Jr NHS; Lbry Ade; Lit Mag; De Pauw Univ; Theatre.

CODDINGTON, SANDRA; Stow Sr HS; Stow, OH; 65/523 Cls Rep Frsh Cls; AFS; Girl Scts; Hon Rl; Sct Actv; Lat Clb; Pep Clb; GAA; PPFtbl; Natl Merit Ltr; Kent St Univ.

CODER, PAMELA; North Union HS; Marysville, OH; 3/155 Sec Frsh Cls; Cl Rep Jr Cls; Cls Rep Sr Cls; Cmnty Wkr; Drl Tm; Hon Rl; Off Ade; Sch Pl; Stu Cncl; Sec 4-H; 1st In Art For 3 Yrs 78; Art Clb 78; Ohio St Univ.

CODY, ANNE K; Lake Central HS; Crown Point, IN; 5/550 Cls Rep Frsh Cls; Trs Soph Cls; Am Leg Aux Girls St; Capt Drl Tm; Jr NHS; NHS; Sch Mus; Drama Clb; OEA; DAR Awd; Indiana Univ.

CODY, JUDITH; Ionia HS; Lansing, MI; 12/272 Chrs; Hon Rl; NHS; Yth Flsp; 4-H; Spn Clb; Letter Bsbl; 4-H Awd; Lansing Cmnty Coll; Acctg.

CODY, ROBIN; Central HS; Columbus, OH; Cls Rep Frsh Cls; Hon Rl; Letter Bsktbl; Univ; Dentistry.

COE, ROBERT; West Catholic HS; Grand Rapids, MI; Hon Rl; Letter Ftbl; Univ; Bus.

COE, ROBIN; Jonesville Community HS; Jonesville, MI; Cl Rep Jr Cls; Chrs; Hon Rl; NHS; Stu Cncl; Chrldng; College; Bus.

COE, SHARON; Lakeview HS; Cortland, OH; Cls Rep Frsh Cls; VP Jr Cls; Cls Rep Sr Cls; Band; Hon Rl; NHS; Stu Cncl; Yth Flsp; Y-Teens; Beta Clb; College.

COE, STEPHEN; Wapakoneta Sr HS; Pottstown, PA; Lbry Ade; Fr Clb; Crs Cntry; Trk; Wrstlng; NEDT Top %; Coll.

COE, STEVE; Miami Trace HS; Washington C H, OH; Hon Rl; Stu Cncl; Yth Flsp; FFA; Capt Bsktbl; Coach Actv; Am Leg Awd; Cit Awd; 4-H Awd; Rotary Awd; Ohio State; Agri.

COE, STEVEN; Eastlake North HS; Willowick, OH; 33/670 Hon Rl; Univ Of Akron; Chem Engr.

COEBURN, PATRICIA; Reading HS; Reading, MI; Bsktbl; IBM Opr.

COFER, ANTHONY; Paoli HS; West Baden, IN; 40/118 Band; Boy Scts; Chrs; Hon Rl; Sch Nwsp; Spn Clb; Bsbl; JETS Awd; Purdue Univ; Aero Engr.

COFFER, KAREN L; Indianapolis Baptist HS; Indianapolis, IN; Trs Jr Cls; Band; Chrs; Chrh Wkr; Hon Rl; NHS; Sch Pl; FHA; Spn Clb; Scr Kpr; Awd For Most Spiritual & Best Academic Yr; Liberty Baptist Coll; Data Processng.

COFFEY, CAROL; Jeffers HS; South Range, MI; 2/52 VP Sr Cls; Sal; Band; Chrs; Drl Tm; Girl Scts; Hon Rl; Hosp Ade; NHS; Off Ade; N Michigan Univ; Health.

COFFEY, DENISE; St Clement HS; Warren, MI; Chrh Wkr; Cmnty Wkr; Hon Rl; Orch; Quill & Scroll; Sprt Ed Yrbk; Rptr Sch Nwsp; College; Music.

COFFEY, JACQUELINE; Mount Vernon HS; Indianapolis, IN; Hon Rl; Rptr Yrbk; OEA; Trk; IM Sprt; Ambassador Awd 78; Stateswmn Awd 78; 4th Pl Receptionist Contest Regional 78; Ball St Univ; Spec Educ.

COFFEY, KELLY; Morgan HS; Mc Connelsville, OH; 12/253 Am Leg Aux Girls St; Band; Chrs; Chrh Wkr; Girl Scts; Hon Rl; Jr NHS; Lbry Ade; NHS; Sch Mus; Ohio Univ; Elem Educ.

COFFEY, LAVONNA S; Lockland HS; Lockland, OH; Drl Tm; Hon Rl; JA; Stg Crw; Rptr Yrbk; Sch Nwsp; Drama Clb; Bsbl; Bsktbl; IM Sprt; Soc Work.

COFFEY, SONDRA; Sidney HS; Sidney, OH; Chrs; Chrh Wkr; Cmnty Wkr; Hon Rl; Orch; PAVAS; FHA; Ohio State Univ; Medicine.

COFFEY, TERESA; Warren Ctrl HS; Indpls, IN; Hon Rl; NHS; Stg Crw; Drama Clb; Spn Clb; Ball St Univ; Corporate Finance.

COFFINDAFFER, DONNA; Winfield HS; Scott Depot, WV; Pres Chrs; Chrh Wkr; Hon Rl; Jr NHS; NHS; VP Yth Flsp; 4-H; 4-H Awd; West Virginia Univ; Comp Sci.

COFFINDAFFER, TERRY; Scott HS; Madison, WV; Hon Rl; Jr NHS; Letter Bsbl; Letter Ftbl; Univ; Engr.

COFFMAN, C; Centerville HS; Richmond, IN; 7/150 Chrh Wkr; Cmnty Wkr; Drl Tm; Girl Scts; Hon Rl; Jr NHS; NHS; Sch Mus; Sch Pl; Pres Yth Flsp; Ball St Univ; Speech Path.

COFFMAN, CATHY; Doddridge Cnty HS; New Milton, WV; VP Frsh Cls; Cls Rep Soph Cls; Cl Rep Jr Cls; Cls Rep Sr Cls; Band; Yrbk; Fr Clb; FHA; FTA; Pep Clb; Fairmont St Coll; Mental Health.

COFFMAN, JAY; Brown Cnty HS; Nineveh, IN; Hon Rl; 4-H; 4-H Awd; Voc Schl; Indus Drafting.

COFFMAN, JENNIE; Our Lady Of The Elms HS; Barberton, OH; 5/35 Chrs; Hon Rl; Hosp Ade; Sch Pl; Rptr Sch Nwsp; Univ; Pre Med.

COFFMAN, LISA; Ben Davis HS; Indianapolis, IN; Chrs; Chrh Wkr; Cmnty Wkr; JA; Mod UN; Off Ade; Fr Clb; Pep Clb; Univ.

COFFMAN, MARITA; Winchester Comm HS; Winchester, IN; Band; Drl Tm; Hon Rl; NHS; Yth Flsp; Fr Clb; Am Leg Awd; Ind State; Bus Admin.

COFFMAN, ROGER; Big Walnut HS; Westerville, OH; 5/233 Am Leg Boys St; Band; Hon Rl; Treas Jr NHS; NHS; Sch Mus; Fr Clb; Bsktbl; Letter Ftbl; Letter Wrstlng; Ohio St Univ; Engr.

COFFMAN, TERESA; Central Catholic HS; Lafayette, IN; Cls Rep Soph Cls; Chrs; Cmnty Wkr; Jr NHS; Sch Mus; Pep Clb; Letter Swmmng; 4-H Awd; Flight Attendent.

COFIELD, JULIE; South Ripley HS; Versailles, IN; 17/112 Am Leg Aux Girls St; Band; Drm Mjrt; Hon Rl; Quill & Scroll; Rptr Yrbk; Rptr Sch Nwsp; Pep Clb; Spn Clb; Mgrs; College; Elementary Ed.

COGAR, CHERYL; Rocky River Sr HS; Rocky Rvr, OH; Hosp Ade; NHS; Orch; Mgrs; PPFtbl; Univ.

COGAR, SAMUAL; Perry HS; Perry, OH; Ohio Northern; Pharmacy.

COGASDALE, MYRLE; Gull Lake HS; Richland, MI; 7/240 Band; Girl Scts; Hon Rl; Sch Mus; Stg Crw; Fr Clb; Letter Ten; Trk; Univ; Theatre.

COGLEY, NANETTE; Riverdale HS; Arlington, OH; 1/105 Band; Hon Rl; NHS; Sch Mus; Stu Cncl; Sch Nwsp; FTA; Univ; Radio/tv.

COGLEY, TERRI; Ravenna HS; Ravenna, OH; 22/327 AFS; Cmnty Wkr; Hon Rl; Hosp Ade; NHS; Yth Flsp; Rptr Yrbk; 4-H; Fr Clb; Kent State Univ; Medicine.

COGSWELL, CAROLYN; Trenton HS; Trenton, MI; Chrs; Girl Scts; Hon Rl; Natl Forn Lg; Sch Mus; Sch Pl; Stg Crw; Drama Clb; Pep Clb; Univ Of Michigan; Marine Bio.

COGSWELL, TERESA; Owen Valley HS; Spencer, IN; 24/198 Girl Scts; Hon Rl; Rptr Yrbk; Pep Clb; Ind Univ; Acctg.

COHAN, KURT; Negaunee HS; Negaunee, MI; Hon Rl; Bsbl; Ftbl; Ten; IM Sprt; N Michigan Univ.

COHEE, DONALD; Hale HS; S Branch, MI; Lbry Ade; Off Ade; Letter Bsbl; Letter Ftbl; IM Sprt; Mgrs;.

COHEN, ANDREW; Wheeling Park HS; Wheeling, WV; 35/598 AFS; Chrh Wkr; Cmnty Wkr; Fr Clb; Letter Ten; IM Sprt; Univ.

COHEN, CATHY J; Thomas A De Vilbiss HS; Toledo, OH; 1/260 Pres Jr Cls; Pres Sr Cls; Debate Tm; Hon Rl; NHS; Letter Bsktbl; PPFtbl; Natl Merit Ltr; Opt Clb Awd; Yth Recogn Optimist Club 1978; Univ; Poli Sci.

COHEN, LINDA S; Eastmoor HS; Columbus, OH; Hon Rl; Hosp Ade; Jr NHS; Lbry Ade; Mgrs; Ohio St Univ; Dental Hygnst.

COHEN, SHELLY; Deer Park HS; Cincinnati, OH; Am Leg Aux Girls St; Band; Chrs; Hon Rl; Sch Mus; Sct Actv; Stg Crw; Drama Clb; Am Leg Awd; 4th Dist Pres In Ohio; Pres Of Jr Girls At Unit 111 Woodlawn Oh; Univ Of California; Exec Sec.

COHEN, SHERRIE; Eastmoor HS; Columbus, OH; Cls Rep Frsh Cls; Sec Sr Cls; Chrs; Drl Tm; Hon Rl; Hosp Ade; Lbry Ade; Off Ade; PAVAS; College.

COHEN, TRACY; Rayen HS; Youngstown, OH; VP Sr Cls; Cls Rep Sr Cls; Band; Chrs; Hon Rl; Sch Mus; Rptr Yrbk; Rptr Sch Nwsp; Youngstown State Univ; Music Educ.

COHN, JUDY; John Adams HS; South Bend, IN; Hon Rl; NHS; Sch Nwsp; Natl Merit SF; Indiana Univ; Sociology.

COHN, MORTON; Summerfield HS; Petersburg, MI; Cls Rep Soph Cls; Cl Rep Jr Cls; Cls Rep Sr Cls; Chrh Wkr; Hon Rl; Sch Pl; Stu Cncl; Rptr Yrbk; Sci Clb; Trk; Detroit News Schlstc Awd For Achvmnt In Writng 7;8 Rabbi Leon I Fever Awd For Lit Exprssn 77; Univ Of Michigan; Hist.

COILE, KIM; Pleasant HS; Marion, OH; 16/160 Chrh Wkr; Hon Rl; NHS; Quill & Scroll; Stg Crw; Stu Cncl; Sec Yth Flsp; Ed Sch Nwsp; Drama Clb; FHA; Univ; Jrnlsm.

COLA, CATHLEEN; Berea HS; Berea, OH; 213/608 Drl Tm; Sch Mus; Bsktbl; Letter Gym; Letter Swmmng; Trk; Tmr; Swimming Spirit Awd 78; Bowling Green Univ; Fshn Mdse.

COLA, KATHLEEN; Struthers HS; Struthers, OH; 78/272 Cmp Fr Grls; Chrs; Chrh Wkr; Cmnty Wkr; Hon Rl; Hosp Ade; Off Ade; Red Cr Ade; Yth Flsp; Drama Clb; Youngstown St Univ; Elem Ed.

COLABUNO, CHRISANN; Riverside HS; Painesville, OH; Cl Rep Jr Cls; Hon Rl; Lit Mag; Stu Cncl; Rptr Yrbk; Yrbk; Rptr Sch Nwsp; Sch Nwsp; Spn Clb; Univ; Jrnlsm.

COLALUCA, LINDA; Woodrow Wilson HS; Youngstown, OH; 71/343 Band; Cmp Fr Grls; Chrs; Girl Scts; Hon Rl; Sct Actv; OEA; Twrlr; Bus School; Sec.

COLANER, VICKI; Huron HS; Ann Arbor, MI; Girl Scts; Hon Rl; Lbry Ade; Orch; Stg Crw; Rptr Yrbk; Sch Nwsp; 4-H; 4-H Awd; Natl Merit SF; Outstanding Awd In Busns; Univ Of Michigan; Cosmetology.

COLANGELO, SCOTT; Heath HS; Heath, OH; Cls Rep Frsh Cls; FCA; Hon Rl; Ftbl; Glf; Letter Trk; Ohio St Univ; Civil Engr.

COLARELLI, PATRICIA; Creston HS; Grand Rapids, MI; Cls Rep Frsh Cls; Hon Rl; Jr NHS; NHS; Letter Gym; Letter Swmmng; Chrldng; GAA; IM Sprt; Mich State Univ; Vet.

COLARUSSO, RONAELE J; Shoals HS; Shoals, IN; 15/65 Hst Frsh Cls; Hst Soph Cls; Hst Jr Cls; Hst Sr Cls; Drl Tm; Beta Clb; Fr Clb; Letter Bsktbl; Capt Chrldng; Pom Pon; Bus Schl; Legal Sec.

COLBERT, ANGELA; Southeast HS; N Benton, OH; Cls Rep Frsh Cls; Cls Rep Soph Cls; Cl Rep Jr Cls; Cls Rep Sr Cls; Aud/Vis; Band; Drm Mjrt; FCA; Girl Scts; Orch; Univ; Agric Tchr.

COLBERT, PAMELA S; Roosevelt Wilson HS; Nutter Fort, WV; 10/132 Hon Rl; Lbry Ade; Y-Teens; Pep Clb;.

COLBERT, ROBIN; John Marshall HS; Indianapolis, IN; 41/611 Hon Rl; IUPUI; Xray Tech.

COLBERT, TERRI; Pickerington HS; Cnl Wichters, OH; Girl Scts; Hon Rl; NHS; FHA; Spn Clb; College; Med.

COLBURN, JOHN; Alma HS; Elwell, MI; FFA; Ftbl; College.

COLBURN, RANDE; Cedar Lake Acad; Muskegon, MI; IM Sprt; Cit Awd; Muskegon Cmnty Coll; Construction.

COLBURN, SHERRY; Caledonia Sr HS; Caledonia, MI; VP Jr Cls; VP Sr Cls; Band; Chrs; Hon Rl; Off Ade; Sch Mus; Sch Pl; Drama Clb; Letter Trk; Univ; Cosmetology.

COLBY, CRAIG; Houston HS; Houston, OH; 3/62 Hon Rl; NHS; VP FFA; Bsktbl; Crs Cntry; Trk; 4-H Awd; Amer Lgn Leadrshp Awd 79; Farm.

COLBY, JENNIFER; Rossville HS; Rossville, IN; 4/78 Sec Band; Chrs; Natl Forn Lg; NHS; Pres Stu Cncl; Trk; DAR Awd; Ball St Univ; Personnel Mgmt.

COLBY, ROB; Northmont HS; Dayton, OH; Cl Rep Jr Cls; Hon Rl; JA; Stu Cncl; Sch Nwsp; Pep Clb; Letter Ten; Coach Actv; Mgrs; Tmr; Miami St Univ; Psych.

COLCHAGOFF, WICK R; Rogers HS; Toledo, OH; Jr NHS; NHS; Orch; Stu Cncl; Pres Sci Clb; Letter Ftbl; Letter Trk; Letter Wrstlng; Outstanding Jr Rogers; All St Band; Pres Varsity Clb; College; Phys Ed.

COLDREN, TRACY; Hayes HS; Delaware, OH; Cls Rep Frsh Cls; AFS; Cmnty Wkr; FCA; Sch Pl; Stu Cncl; Drama Clb; FTA; Pres Sci Clb; Capt Chrldng; Univ Of Colo; Psychology.

COLE, ALICIA; Admiral King HS; Lorain, OH; Cls Rep Frsh Cls; Cls Rep Soph Cls; Cl Rep Jr Cls; Cls Rep Sr Cls; Girl Scts; Hon Rl; Off Ade; Pres Stu Cncl; FHA; Bsktbl; Stud Council Most Active Jr Rep 78; Nominatd To Run For Miss Oh US Teenager 79; Oh St Sec For NAACP 77; Coll; Law.

COLE, ANTOINETTE; Horace Mann HS; Gary, IN; Sec Frsh Cls; Sec Soph Cls; Hon Rl; Jr NHS; Lbry Ade; NHS; Stu Cncl; Mth Clb; Tmr; College; Pharmaceutical.

COLE, BARRY; Bullock Creek HS; Midland, MI; 11/160 Hon Rl; NHS; Bsktbl; Ftbl; Trk; Michigan Tech Univ; Elec Engr.

COLE, BRIAN; Nordonia HS; Macedonia, OH; Ftbl; IM Sprt; College; Psycology.

COLE, CATHERINE; Calvin Christian HS; Wyoming, MI; 1/160 Val; Chrs; Chrh Wkr; Debate Tm; Hon Rl; NHS; Ger Clb; IM Sprt; Natl Merit Ltr; Calvin Coll; Math.

COLE, CHERYL; West Lafayette Sr HS; W Lafayette, IN; Cls Rep Frsh Cls; Chrh Wkr; Hon Rl; NHS; Y-Teens; Fr Clb; Pep Clb; Trk; Chrldng; DAR Awd; Univ; Sci.

COLE, CHRIS; Grant HS; Bailey, MI; Hon Rl; Lbry Ade; Off Ade; Yth Flsp; Sci Clb; Bus Schl.

COLE, DARRYL L; Paul Laurence Dunbar HS; Dayton, OH; 30/205 Cls Rep Frsh Cls; Cls Rep Soph Cls; Cl Rep Jr Cls; Cls Rep Sr Cls; Aud/Vis; Boy Scts; Chrh Wkr; Cmnty Wkr; Debate Tm; FCA; Kent St Univ; Bus Mgt.

COLE, DAVID; Mohawk HS; Sycamore, OH; Am Leg Boys St; Hon Rl; NHS; Crs Cntry; Trk; IM Sprt; Scr Kpr; Cit Awd; Natl Merit Ltr; Tiffin Univ; Acctg.

COLE, GEORGENE; Regina HS; Cleveland, OH; Hon Rl; JA; Sch Nwsp; Ohio St Univ; Comp Prog.

COLE, GREGORY; Whitmer HS; Toledo, OH; Hon Rl; Bsbl; Ftbl; IM Sprt; Univ; Astronomy.

COLE, H; Central Hower HS; Akron, OH; Band; Boy Scts; Chrs; Drm Bgl; Fr Clb; Crs Cntry; Ftbl; Trk; Wrstlng; Univ; Chem.

COLE, JAMES; Lapel HS; Lapel, IN; Chrs; Chrh Wkr; Cmnty Wkr; Hon Rl; Yth Flsp; Bsbl; Bsktbl; Ftbl; Scr Kpr; College; Engineer.

COLE, JANE; Kimball HS; Royal Oak, MI; Cmnty Wkr; Girl Scts; Hon Rl; Y-Teens; Letter Bsbl; Gym; Coach Actv; IM Sprt; Northwood Institute; Fashion Mdse.

COLE, JAY; Decatur Central HS; Indianapolis, IN; 25/310 Am Leg Boys St; Hon Rl; Civ Clb; Lat Clb; IM Sprt; Purdue Univ; Wildlife Bio.

COLE, JENNIFER; Copley Sr HS; Akron, OH; 2/316 Am Leg Aux Girls St; Chrs; Hon Rl; NHS; Sch Mus; Sprt Ed Yrbk; Pep Clb; Spn Clb; Letter Swmmng; Tmr; General Motors Inst; Indust Admin.

COLE, JOHN D; Martinsburg HS; Martinsburg, WV; 1/220 Cls Rep Frsh Cls; Am Leg Boys St; Hon Rl; NHS; Stu Cncl; Sprt Ed Yrbk; Pres Key Clb; Bsktbl; Letter Ftbl; Letter Glf; College.

COLE, JUDY; Wheelersburg HS; Wheelersburg, OH; 22/135 Band; Chrs; Chrh Wkr; Hon Rl; Stg Crw; FHA; Spn Clb; Twrlr; Barbizon Modeling Schl; Model.

COLE, JULIE; Avondale Sr HS; Auburn Hts, MI; Band; Off Ade; Quill & Scroll; Sch Mus; Yth Flsp; Rptr Sch Nwsp; Sch Nwsp; Cit Awd; Central Michigan Univ; Journalism.

COLE, KATHRYN; Muskegon Cath Central HS; Muskegon, MI; Girl Scts; Hon Rl; Hosp Ade; Sprt Ed Yrbk; Drama Clb; Spn Clb;.

COLE, KENNETH; Taylor HS; Kokomo, IN; 21/250 Band; NHS; Drama Clb; Fr Clb; Pep Clb; IM Sprt; Natl Merit Ltr; Indiana Univ; Micro Bio.

COLE, LEE; Malabar Sr HS; Mansfield, OH; 21/286 VP Soph Cls; VP Jr Cls; Band; Cmnty Wkr; Hon Rl; NHS; Orch; Sch Pl; Stu Cncl; Mth Clb; Univ; Psych.

COLE, LISA; Fulton HS; Middleton, MI; Cmnty Wkr; Hon Rl; Lbry Ade; Civ Clb; Mth Clb;.

COLE, LUCINDA; Byron HS; Byron, MI; 7/79 Cls Rep Frsh Cls; Cls Rep Soph Cls; Band; Chrs; Chrh Wkr; Drm Mjrt; Girl Scts; Hon Rl; Hosp Ade; Baker Jr College; Acctng.

COLE, MARK; Elyria Catholic HS; Elyria, OH; Hon Rl; NHS; Stg Crw; Ed Yrbk; Sch Nwsp; Drama Clb; Spn Clb; NCTE; College; Chem.

COLE, MARYLEE; Houghton Lake HS; St Helen, MI; Cmnty Wkr; Hon Rl; Hosp Ade; NHS; 4-H; Fr Clb; Spn Clb; 4-H Awd; Kirtland Cmnty Coll; Nursing.

COLE, NANCY; Concord HS; Concord, MI; Chrs; MSU; Horticulture.

COLE, PATTY; Clermont Northeastern HS; Marathon, OH; Band; Chrh Wkr; FCA; Girl Scts; Hon Rl; Sch Pl; Yth Flsp; 4-H; FFA; Rdo Clb; Cincinnati Tech Coll; Med Asst.

COLE, PHYLLIS; Riverdale HS; Mt Blanchard, OH; Sec Soph Cls; VP Jr Cls; VP Sr Cls; Band; Cmp Fr Grls; Chrs; Chrh Wkr; Debate Tm; Hon Rl; Jr NHS; Univ; Literature.

COLE, RANDY; L & M HS; Lyons, IN; Hon Rl; Beta Clb; FFA; Bsbl; Bsktbl; Capt Crs Cntry; Trk; MVP Cross Cntry 77; Conservation.

COLE, RANDY; William Henry Harrison HS; W Lafayette, IN; 16/281 Pres Soph Cls; Pres Jr Cls; Pres Sr Cls; Band; Hon Rl; Natl Forn Lg; NHS; Off Ade; Sch Pl; Sct Actv; Wabash Coll; Law.

COLE, RANDY; Eaton HS; Eaton, OH; 25/175 Pres Frsh Cls; VP Frsh Cls; Am Leg Boys St; Hon Rl; Y-Teens; Bsbl; Bsktbl; Ftbl; Trk; IM Sprt; College; Business Admin.

COLE, RENEE; Penn HS; Mishawaka, IN; 16/465 Sec Frsh Cls; Chrs; Hon Rl; Sch Mus; Yth Flsp; Spn Clb; Bus Schl; Steno.

COLE, ROBIN; Immaculata HS; Detroit, MI; Chrs; Cmnty Wkr; Girl Scts; Sch Mus; Sct Actv; FNA; Univ; RN.

COLE, SANDI; Traverse City Sr HS; Traverse City, MI; 114/800 Chrs; Cmnty Wkr; Hon Rl; Mdrgl; Sch Mus; Sch Pl; Stg Crw; Civ Clb; Natl Merit SF; Central Michigan Univ; Music.

COLE, SHELIA; Mooresville HS; Mooresville, IN; Chrh Wkr; Hon Rl; Jr NHS; Yth Flsp; FHA; Pep Clb; Mgrs; PPFtbl; Univ; Med.

COLE, SUE; Tecumseh HS; Tecumseh, MI; 28/241 Chrh Wkr; Hon Rl; NHS; Fr Clb; Malone Univ; Drafting.

COLE, VICKI L; Bridgeport Sr HS; Bridgeport, WV; Hon Rl; Hosp Ade; FNA; Storer Schlr 79; United Hosp Axlry Candystripper Schlr 79; Alderson Broaddus Coll; Nursing.

COLE, WALTER; Gwinn HS; Sawyer Afb, MI; Hon Rl; NHS; Rptr Sch Nwsp; Indust Arts Merit Awd; Univ; Photog.

COLEBROOK, PATRICIA; Northwood HS; Northwood, OH; Chrs; Hon Rl; JA; Off Ade; Rptr Yrbk; Bsbl; Bsktbl; GAA; Mgrs; Mat Maids; College; Science.

COLEFF, CHARITY; Vermilion HS; Vermilion, OH; OEA; Bank Cnslr.

COLE JR, JAMES; West Side HS; Gary, IN; 1/650 Val; Chrh Wkr; Jr NHS; NHS; Pol Wkr; Lat Clb; Rdo Clb; Cit Awd; Ill Inst Of Tech; Mech.

COLELLA, RICHARD; Marion L Steele HS; Lorain, OH; 7/358 NHS; Stu Cncl; Fr Clb; Letter Ftbl; Letter Trk; IM Sprt; Natl Merit Ltr; Univ; Pre Law.

COLEMAN, ADAM; Triway Local HS; Shreve, OH; 7/167 Band; Chrh Wkr; Hon Rl; NHS; Stg Crw; Natl Merit Schl; Rose Hulmon Inst Of Tech; Physics.

COLEMAN, CELEST; St Marys Of Redford HS; Detroit, MI; 16/157 Chrh Wkr; Girl Scts; Hon Rl; NHS; Stu Cncl; Trk; Hampton Institute; Bio.

COLEMAN, CHARLENE; New Riegel HS; New Riegel, OH; 1/48 Trs Soph Cls; Band; Chrs; Hon Rl; NHS; Sch Pl; Stg Crw; 4-H; FHA; Pep Clb; Bowling Green St Univ; Library Sci.

COLEMAN, CHARLENE M; New Riegel HS; New Riegel, OH; 1/48 Band; Chrs; Hon Rl; NHS; Sch Mus; Stg Crw; Treas 4-H; FHA; Pep Clb; Spn Clb; College; Acctg.

COLEMAN, CHARLES; East Liverpool HS; E Liverpool, OH; 14/341 Am Leg Boys St; Band; Chrs; Chrh Wkr; Drm Mjrt; NHS; Yth Flsp; Lat Clb; Twrlr; Asbury Coll; Christian Ed.

COLEMAN, DEBBRA; Western Reserve HS; Wakeman, OH; Band; Girl Scts; Hon Rl; Hosp Ade; Lbry Ade; NHS; 4-H; Spn Clb; 4-H Awd; Cert Of Awd For Schlstc Acvhmtn & Eng Team 76; Cert Of Awd For Schlshp Team Albbr 77; M B Johnson Schl Of Nursing; RN.

COLEMAN, DEBORAH J; Elyria Catholic HS; Elyria, OH; Band; Hon Rl; Pol Wkr; Sch Mus; Y-Teens; Drama Clb; Pep Clb; Spn Clb; Ten; Univ; Pediatrician.

COLEMAN, GREGORY; Martin Luther King HS; Detroit, MI; Band; Hon Rl; NHS; Voc Schl; Music.

COLEMAN, JACK D; North Ridgeville HS; N Ridgeville, OH; Cls Rep Frsh Cls; Cls Rep Soph Cls; Cl Rep Jr Cls; Cls Rep Sr Cls; Chrh Wkr; Cmnty Wkr; Hon Rl; Ed Yrbk; Sprt Ed Yrbk; Rptr Yrbk; Football Co Capt 1978; 1st Pl In Drawing Banner 1978; Cmmrcl Art.

COLEMAN, JACQUELINE; Cass Technical HS; Detroit, MI; Cmnty Wkr; Hon Rl; Lbry Ade; Fr Clb; Sci Clb; Michigan St Univ; Chem Engr.

COLEMAN, JAMES; East HS; Columbus, OH; Cmnty Wkr; Debate Tm; Natl Forn Lg; Letter Ftbl; Trk; Flo A & M Univ; Pharmacy.

COLEMAN, JEANETTE; Shakamak HS; Jasonville, IN; 45/86 Chrs; DECA; 4-H; Bsktbl; Indiana Voc Tech Schl; Sec.

COLEMAN, J TODD; L & M HS; Lyons, IN; 9/33 Cls Rep Frsh Cls; Pres Soph Cls; Pres Jr Cls; Pres Sr Cls; Stu Cncl; 4-H; FFA; Letter Bsbl; Letter Bsktbl; Letter Crs Cntry; Future Farmers Of Amer Outstanding Greenhand; Purdue Univ; Ag Ed.

COLEMAN, KIM; Richmond Sr HS; Richmond, IN; Hon Rl; Orch; 4-H; 4-H Awd; Univ; Nursing.

COLEMAN, LINDA; Tri County HS; Wolcott, IN; 4/73 Cl Rep Jr Cls; Am Leg Aux Girls St; Band; Chrs; Drl Tm; NHS; Sch Mus; College; Music.

COLEMAN, NEAL E; Munice Northside HS; Muncie, IN; Am Leg Boys St; Band; Boy Scts; Chrh Wkr; Debate Tm; Pres JA; VP Natl Forn Lg; NHS; Letter Wrstlng; JA Awd; Purdue Univ; Chem Engr.

COLEMAN, PAMELA K; Washington HS; Washington, IN; 12/194 Band; Hon Rl; Jr NHS; NHS; Off Ade; Beta Clb; Fr Clb; Pep Clb; Vincennes Univ; Comp Prog.

COLEMAN, SHAWNA L; John Glenn HS; New Concord, OH; 82/172 Aud/Vis; Chrs; Chrh Wkr; Drl Tm; Hon Rl; Lbry Ade; Off Ade; Sch Mus; Sch Pl; Y-Teens; All Ohio St Fair Yth Choir; European St Fair Yth Choir;.

COLEMAN, SHEILA; Willow Run HS; Ypsilanti, MI; VP Frsh Cls; Trs Jr Cls; Hon Rl; NHS; Letter Crs Cntry; Letter Trk; Letter Mat Maids; Mic St; Acctg.

COLEMAN, STAN; De Kalb HS; Waterloo, IN; 7/314 Pres Frsh Cls; VP Jr Cls; Pres Sr Cls; Chrh Wkr; NHS; Letter Wrstlng; DAR Awd; Kiwan Awd; Ball St Univ; Jrnlsm.

COLEMAN, TERRY; Ludington HS; Ludington, MI; Chrh Wkr; FCA; Hon Rl; NHS; Rptr Yrbk; Yrbk; Capt Bsbl; Capt Wrstlng; Elk Awd; Mich Christian; Journalism.

COLEMAN, THELMA; East HS; Columbus, OH; Hon Rl; Bsktbl; Trk; Texas A & M Univ; Communctns.

COLEMAN, TRACEY E; Bloomington N HS; Bloomington, IN; 109/432 Cmnty Wkr; Hon Rl; Rptr Sch Nwsp; Sch Nwsp; Pep Clb; Chrldng; PPFtbl; Tmr; College; Advertising.

COLES, GREGORY E; Hawken HS; Cleveland Hts, OH; Chrs; Chrh Wkr; Cmnty Wkr; Debate Tm; Yth Flsp; Trk; Wrstlng; Mgrs; Rutgers Univ; Accounting.

COLESCOTT, GAYLE; Crestwood HS; Mantua, OH; Cl Rep Jr Cls; Cls Rep Sr Cls; Hon Rl; Hosp Ade; Off Ade; Stu Cncl; Beta Clb; 4-H; Fr Clb; Pep Clb; Med Careers Progr Awd 78; Most Imprvd Plyer Girls Bsktbl 76; Bake Off Semi Fnlst 78; St Thomas Hosp Schl Of Nursing; RN.

COLETTA, SHARON; Princeton HS; Cincinnati, OH; Boy Scts; Hon Rl; NHS; Quill & Scroll; Yrbk; Gym; Pres Awd; Bowling Green Univ; Acct.

COLGROVE, JUDITH; Dominican HS; Detroit, MI; Pres Frsh Cls; Girl Scts; Yrbk; Rptr Sch Nwsp; Sch Nwsp; Trk; Chrldng; Mgrs; Ctr For Creatv Studies; Photo Jrnlsm.

COLGROVE, LISA; Winamac Cmnty HS; Winamac, IN; Trs Frsh Cls; Aud/Vis; Band; Girl Scts; Hon Rl; Hosp Ade; Lat Clb; Pep Clb; Indiana Univ; Pre Med.

COLIP, JANET; Buchanan HS; Buchanan, MI; Chrs; Chrh Wkr; Hon Rl; JA; Off Ade; PAVAS; Sch Mus; Rptr Sch Nwsp; Spn Clb; 4-H; Univ; Bus.

COLLARD, MICHAEL L; Field HS; Magadore, OH; Sec Boy Scts; Hon Rl; NHS; Sct Actv; Fr Clb; Univ; Elec Engr.

COLLER, WILLIAM; Hubbard HS; Hubbard, OH; 70/320 Sprt Ed Sch Nwsp; Letter Glf; College; Computer Sci.

COLLERAN, MARY K; Cherry Hill HS; Inkster, MI; 17/200 Hon Rl; Jr NHS; Rptr Yrbk; Rptr Sch Nwsp; Pep Clb; Capt Chrldng; Michigan St Univ; Med Tech.

COLLESEL, CHRIS; Amelia HS; Amelia, OH; 4/280 Chrh Wkr; Hon Rl; Treas NHS; Spn Clb; Am Leg Awd; Univ Of Cincinnati; Chem Engr.

COLLEY, JANE; Maumee HS; Maumee, OH; 14/316 Cmnty Wkr; Girl Scts; Hon Rl; Off Ade; Y-Teens; Yrbk; Fr Clb; GAA; IM Sprt; PPFtbl; Univ Of Toledo; Pharm.

COLLEY, TINA; Marion Harding HS; Marion, OH; Chrs; Hon Rl; Off Ade; Sch Mus; FHA; Scr Kpr; Medicine.

COLLIER, ANTOINETTE; Seymour HS; Seymour, IN; 42/354 Band; Chrs; Chrh Wkr; Debate Tm; Hon Rl; Hosp Ade; Orch; Sch Mus; FBLA; FTA; Indiana St Univ; Music.

COLLIER, BETSY; Lexington HS; Lexington, OH; 28/280 Sec Frsh Cls; Sec Soph Cls; Sec Jr Cls; Sec Sr Cls; Band; Drl Tm; Hon Rl; Lbry Ade; Orch; Stu Cncl; Bowling Green Univ; Interior Design.

COLLIER, CAROLYN; Collinwood HS; Cleveland, OH; Trs Frsh Cls; Cls Rep Frsh Cls; Cls Rep Soph Cls; Cl Rep Jr Cls; Chrs; Hon Rl; Lbry Ade; Off Ade; Stu Cncl; Univ; Comp Sci.

COLLIER, KENNETH; Chagrin Falls HS; Chagrin Falls, OH; Boy Scts; Hon Rl; VICA; College; Math.

COLLIER, KIM; Patrick Henry HS; Deshler, OH; 2/121 Cl Rep Jr Cls; VP Sr Cls; Chrh Wkr; Hon Rl; Pres NHS; Off Ade; Stu Cncl; Yth Flsp; Letter Bsktbl; Letter Trk; Univ; Life Sci Educ.

COLLIER, LISA; Waldron HS; Shelbyville, IN; Cls Rep Frsh Cls; Cl Rep Jr Cls; Band; Drl Tm; Hon Rl; Off Ade; Stu Cncl; Yrbk; 4-H; Lat Clb; Univ; Elem Ed.

COLLIER, MARK A; Valparaiso HS; Valparaiso, IN; 26/453 Cls Rep Frsh Cls; Chrh Wkr; Hon Rl; Jr NHS; Lbry Ade; NHS; Stu Cncl; Yth Flsp; Natl Merit Ltr; Natl Merit SF; Purdue Univ; Comp.

COLLIER, MARY R; Mifflin Sr HS; Columbus, OH; Cl Rep Jr Cls; Hon Rl; Off Ade; Stu Cncl; Pep Clb; Gym; Capt Chrldng; Vrsty Chrldr Awd 77; Gym Awd 77; Univ; Real Est.

COLLIER, MELISSA; Williamsburg HS; Williamsburg, OH; 2/90 Sal; Am Leg Aux Girls St; Chrs; Chrh Wkr; Drl Tm; Girl Scts; NHS; Off Ade; Sch Mus; Spn Clb; Univ Of Cincinnati; Bus Admin.

COLLIER, TERESA; Waldron HS; Shelbyville, IN; 11/64 Cls Rep Sr Cls; Band; Hon Rl; NHS; Sch Pl; Rptr Yrbk; Drama Clb; 4-H; Fr Clb; Pep Clb; Indiana Univ; Acctg.

COLLINGS, CHRISTOPHER; Upper Arlington HS; Columbus, OH; JA; Stg Crw; Yrbk; Ger Clb; Univ; Comp Tech.

COLLINGS, KATHY; Eastern HS; Bloomfield, IN; 5/84 Trs Jr Cls; VP Band; Chrh Wkr; NHS; Rptr Yrbk; 4-H; Am Leg Awd; Bus Schl; Sec.

COLLINGS, SARAH; Scottsburg HS; Scottsburg, IN; Band; Chrh Wkr; Girl Scts; Sch Pl; Drama Clb; Fr Clb; Gym; DAR Awd; Univ; Bio Physics.

COLLINS, ANTONIO; Woodrow Wilson HS; Beckley, WV; 12/500 Am Leg Boys St; Chrh Wkr; Hon Rl; NHS; Univ; Archt.

COLLINS, BETH; Bexley HS; Bexley, OH; 77/184 Cl Rep Jr Cls; Cls Rep Sr Cls; Chrs; Drl Tm; Hon Rl; PAVAS; Pol Wkr; Sch Mus; Stu Cncl; Drama Clb; Miami Univ; Pre Law.

COLLINS, BRIAN; Graham HS; St Paris, OH; 20/165 Hon Rl; Crs Cntry; Trk; Wrstlng; Ohio State Univ; Chem Engr.

COLLINS, CAROL; Laurel HS; Metamora, IN; 10/29 Chrh Wkr; Hon Rl; NHS; Sec 4-H; OEA; Pres Spn Clb; Indiana St Univ; Bus Educ.

COLLINS, CATHY L; Wm H Harrison HS; Evansville, IN; 11/373 Chrs; Chrh Wkr; Hon Rl; NHS; Pol Wkr; Sch Mus; Sch Pl; Stg Crw; Stu Cncl; Yth Flsp; North Central Evaluation Stu Member For Social Studies; Sr Prom Chairman Jr Prom Committee; David Lipscomb Coll; Fash Merch.

COLLINS, CHARLES; Windham HS; Windham, OH; Hon Rl; NHS; Spn Clb; Bsktbl; Letter Glf; Coach Actv; Scr Kpr; Univ.

COLLINS, CHARLES; Alpena HS; Alpena, MI; 5/759 Chrh Wkr; Hon Rl; NHS; Letter Bsktbl; Letter Trk; Mich Tech Univ; Chem Engr.

COLLINS, CHARLES W; Brookhaven HS; Columbus, OH; 19/434 Band; Chrs; Chrh Wkr; Hon Rl; NHS; Orch; Rus Clb; Rotary Awd; Mt Vernon Nazarene Coll; Bio.

COLLINS, CHRISTOPHER; Morgantown HS; Morgantown, WV; Chrh Wkr; Hon Rl; NHS; VP Fr Clb; Mth Clb; Letter Crs Cntry; Glf; Letter Wrstlng; Voice Dem Awd; West Virginia Univ; Mech Engr.

COLLINS, CHRISTY; Union Local HS; Bethesda, OH; 8/153 Band; Hon Rl; NHS; Yth Flsp; Yrbk; Rptr Sch Nwsp; Pres 4-H; VP FHA; FTA; Sci Clb; Pres Classroom For Young Amer; Ohio Univ; Education.

COLLINS, COLIN; St Xavier HS; Cincinnati, OH; 73/264 Chrs; Chrh Wkr; Cmnty Wkr; Hon Rl; Sch Mus; FSA; Mth Clb; Bsktbl; IM Sprt; JETS Awd; College; Electrical Engin.

COLLINS, CORRINE; Big Bay De Noc HS; Fayette, MI; 1/50 VP Frsh Cls; Pres Soph Cls; VP Jr Cls; Pres Sr Cls; Val; Chrh Wkr; Hon Rl; Sec NHS; Ed Yrbk; 4-H; Michigan Tech Univ; Math.

COLLINS, CURTIS J; St Martin De Porres HS; Detroit, MI; 18/72 Boy Scts; Hon Rl; Sct Actv; Pep Clb; Univ Of Detroit; Mech Engr.

COLLINS, DAWN; Hobart HS; Hobart, IN; Sec Soph Cls; Hon Rl; Jr NHS; Stu Cncl; 4-H; FTA; Pep Clb; Spn Clb; Mat Maids; Outsdng 9th Grd Stu 1976; Whos Who In Spanish 1977; Perfect Attend Awds 1976; Univ Of Indiana; Bus.

COLLINS, DENISE; Liberty HS; Bristol, WV; 6/228 VP Sr Cls; Band; Hon Rl; Jr NHS; Sec NHS; Sch Mus; Stu Cncl; Sec Yth Flsp; Treas Spn Clb; Scr Kpr; Fairmont St Coll; Social Work.

COLLINS, J; Versailles HS; Versailles, OH; VP Frsh Cls; Pres Sr Cls; Band; Chrs; Chrh Wkr; Sch Mus; Sch Pl; Stg Crw; Drama Clb; Spn Clb; Univ Of Cincinnati; Registered Nurse.

COLLINS, J; Gallia Acad; Crown City, OH; 60/227 Band; Hon Rl; 4-H; FFA; Lat Clb; Sci Clb; Bsbl; Ftbl; Trk; Wrstlng; OSU; Vet.

COLLINS, JACQUELINE; Rutherford B Hayes HS; Delaware, OH; AFS; Band; Chrs; Drm Mjrt; Hon Rl; NHS; Sch Mus; Stg Crw; Y-Teens; Drama Clb; Whos Who In Music 79; Schl Of Hartford Ballet; Ballet.

COLLINS, JAN; Gallia Academy; Crown City, OH; VP 4-H; Pres FFA; Lat Clb; Ftbl; Trk; Dnfth Awd; 4-H Awd; Ohio St Univ; Vet.

COLLINS, JUDITH; Harrison Community HS; Harrison, MI; 9/133 Trs Jr Cls; Cmnty Wkr; Hon Rl; NHS; Treas Stu Cncl; Yth Flsp; Yrbk; VP Pep Clb; Sci Clb; Mgrs; Univ Of Michigan; Archt.

COLLINS, KATHLEEN; Notre Dame Academy; Toledo, OH; Band; Hon Rl; Hosp Ade; Jr NHS; NHS; Sch Nwsp; Spn Clb; Hnr Ribbon No Absenteeism 77; Right To Life 78; Univ Of Dayton; Photog.

COLLINS, KATHRYN S; Buffalo HS; Prichard, WV; 8/103 Cl Rep Jr Cls; Cls Rep Sr Cls; Am Leg Aux Girls St; Band; Drm Mjrt; Hon Rl; NHS; Red Cr Ade; Sch Pl; Rptr Sch Nwsp; W Virginia Jr Miss Schlrshp; Whos Who In Music; Physiology Awd; St Marys Schl; Nursing.

COLLINS, KELLY; Grove City HS; Grove City, OH; 56/509 Sch Pl; Stg Crw; Drama Clb; Fr Clb; Ger Clb; Pep Clb; Letter Gym; Natl Merit SF; Ohio St Univ; Geology.

COLLINS, KEVIN; Upper Sandusky Sr HS; Upper Sandusky, OH; Hon Rl; NHS; Pres 4-H; FFA; Spn Clb; Letter Bsbl; Letter Bsktbl; 7th Pl In St FFA Poultry & Egg Judging 78; 1st Pl In St FFA Poultry & Egg Judging 79; Ohio St Univ; Law.

COLLINS, KIMBERLY; Western Reserve Acad; Canton, OH; Chrs; Hon Rl; Off Ade; Sch Mus; Yrbk; Bsktbl; Crs Cntry; College; Art.

COLLINS, LARRY G; Bellefontaine HS; Bellefontaine, OH; 14/241 Chrh Wkr; Sci Clb; IM Sprt; College; Comp Sci.

COLLINS, LAURIE; Fredericktown HS; Fredericktown, OH; 7/118 Am Leg Aux Girls St; Chrh Wkr; NHS; Off Ade; Rptr Sch Nwsp; 4-H; FHA; Mas Awd; Miami Univ; Acctg.

COLLINS, MARY JO; Clear Fork; Beckley, WV; 3/26 Sal; Hon Rl; NHS; Off Ade; Yrbk; Natl Merit SF; Rotary Awd; Morris Harvey Univ; Med Tech.

COLLINS, MAUREEN; Sardusky Saint Marys Central; Sandusky, OH; Cls Rep Soph Cls; Hon Rl; NHS; Sci Clb; Spn Clb; GAA; College; Business.

COLLINS, MICHAEL; Pontiac Central HS; Pontiac, MI; Chrh Wkr; Hon Rl; Sch Nwsp; Voc Schl; Auto Mech.

COLLINS, MICHAEL; St Joseph HS; St Joseph, MI; FCA; Rptr Sch Nwsp; Sch Nwsp; Letter Ftbl; Letter Ten; Univ.

COLLINS, MIKANN; Buchtel Univ HS; Akron, OH; 1/452 Chrh Wkr; Hon Rl; NHS; Off Ade; Orch; Sch Mus; Sch Pl; Stg Crw; Letter Socr; Ten; Univ.

COLLINS, NANCY; Big Walnut HS; Galena, OH; 48/214 Cls Rep Sr Cls; AFS; Band; Pep Clb; Bsbl; Bsktbl; Ftbl; Gym; Wrstlng; PPFtbl; College; Landscape Archt.

COLLINS, PETER; Pennsboro HS; Pennsboro, WV; VP Frsh Cls; Pres Jr Cls; Am Leg Boys St; Boy Scts; Hon Rl; Natl Forn Lg; NHS; Off Ade; Sch Pl; Stu Cncl;.

COLLINS, ROBBIN; Chesterton HS; Chesterton, IN; 106/464 Girl Scts; Hon Rl; Sct Actv; Valparaiso Univ; Nursing.

COLLINS, ROBERT; Northrop HS; Ft Wayne, IN; Chrh Wkr; JA; Yth Flsp; Bsktbl; Ten; Trk; Cit Awd; JA Awd; Germn Achvmtn Awd; Purdue Univ; Aero Engr.

COLLINS, ROBERT; Beaverton HS; Beaverton, MI; 3/140 Band; Boy Scts; Hon Rl; NHS; Sch Pl; Sprt Ed Yrbk; 4-H; Spn Clb; 4-H Awd; Natl Merit Ltr; Michigan St Univ; Chem.

COLLINS, ROBIN; Kenton Sr HS; Kenton, OH; 42/211 Band; Chrs; Chrh Wkr; Hon Rl; Quill & Scroll; Sch Mus; Sch Pl; Yrbk; Drama Clb; 4-H; Schlrshp Awd 77 & 78; Youth Fitness Achvmnt Awd 77; Oh Music Educ Assoc Awds 79; Univ; Lib Sci.

COLLINS, ROSANNA; Saginaw HS; Saginaw, MI; Cl Rep Jr Cls; Chrs; Chrh Wkr; Hon Rl; OEA; Bsktbl; Mgrs; Elk Awd; JA Awd; Saginaw Valley St Coll; Nursing.

COLLINS, ROXANE; Wellston HS; Wellston, OH; 17/105 Cls Rep Sr Cls; Band; Girl Scts; Hon Rl; NHS; Gym; Capt Chrldng; Twrlr; Mas Awd; Rotary Awd; Rio Grande Coll; Med Lab Tech.

COLLINS, SHEILA R; Upper Sandusky Sr HS; Upper Sandusky, OH; Hon Rl; Hosp Ade; Sch Pl; Stu Cncl; Drama Clb; FBLA; Pres FNA; Spn Clb; Natl Merit Ltr; Captain Of Flag Line; Actors Actor Awd For Jr Class Play; Two Superior Ribbons For Flag Competion; College; Law.

COLLINS, TAMARA; Medina Sr HS; Medina, OH; 51/341 AFS; Hon Rl; NHS; Stg Crw; Drama Clb; Pep Clb; Scr Kpr; Univ Of Akron; Bus Admin.

COLLINS, TAMI; Washington HS; Washington, IN; 5/219 Band; Chrh Wkr; Drm Mjrt; Hon Rl; Sch Mus; Yth Flsp; Beta Clb; Fr Clb; Pom Pon; Purdue St Univ; Pharmacy.

COLLINS, TIM; Bishop Ready HS; Columbus, OH; Pres Soph Cls; Hon Rl; NHS; Letter Ten; Comp Prog.

COLLINS, TOL; Pickerington HS; Pickerington, OH; Hon Rl; Crs Cntry; Trk; Ohio St Univ; Navy.

COLLINS, TRACY; Saginaw HS; Saginaw, MI; Cls Rep Sr Cls; Band; Cmp Fr Grls; Girl Scts; Lbry Ade; Sch Pl; Drama Clb; Sci Clb; Bsktbl; Gym;.

COLLINS, WILLIAM; Hartland HS; Howell, MI; 2/250 Am Leg Boys St; Hon Rl; NHS; Sch Pl; Drama Clb; Spn Clb; Natl Merit Ltr; Univ Of Michigan; Comp Sci.

COLLINS II, EDWARD L; Midpark HS; Middleburg Hgts, OH; 54/644 Am Leg Boys St; Band; Boy Scts; Hon Rl; NHS; Key Clb; Letter Swmmng; Chrh Wkr; College; Electrical Engr.

COLLINSWORTH, TAMMY; Chelsea HS; Chelsea, MI; 20/214 VP Sr Cls; Girl Scts; Hon Rl; NHS; Capt Bsktbl; Coach Actv; IM Sprt; PPFtbl; Scr Kpr; Tmr; Central Michigan Univ.

COLLISON, CHARLOTTE; Arthur Hill HS; Saginaw, MI; Hon Rl; Rptr Yrbk; Rptr Sch Nwsp; Sci Clb; JC Awd; Outstanding Soph 78; Outstanding Jr 79; Vllybll Tm 74 & 79; Univ.

COLLISON, LORI; Big Bay De Noc HS; Manistique, MI; Chrs; Cmnty Wkr; Hon Rl; Lbry Ade; 4-H; Scr Kpr; Univ.

COLLIVER, ANN; Heath HS; Heath, OH; Cmnty Wkr; Hon Rl; Lbry Ade; Sch Pl; Drama Clb; Rdo Clb; Spn Clb; Columbus Bus Univ; Fshn Mdse.

COLLIVER, MICHELE; Grandview Hts HS; Columbus, OH; Band; Girl Scts; Off Ade; Quill & Scroll; Rptr Yrbk; Ed Sch Nwsp; Drama Clb; Spn Clb; Mat Maids; Scr Kpr; Schlrshp Club; Thespian Drama; State Band Contest; Ohio St Univ; Communications.

COLLOREDO, LINDA; Minerva HS; Minerva, OH; 3/241 Sec Soph Cls; Cls Rep Soph Cls; Band; Chrh Wkr; Hon Rl; NHS; Off Ade; Stu Cncl; Yth Flsp; Pep Clb; College; Computer Prgrm.

COLMAN, CORY; Warsaw Community HS; Merrillville, IN; 105/360 Chrh Wkr; Hon Rl; JA; Ed Sch Nwsp; DECA; JA Awd; Grace College; Bus.

COLMAN, REBECCA J; Martins Ferry HS; Martins Ferry, OH; 11/215 Girl Scts; Hon Rl; NHS; Sch Pl; Stu Cncl; Y-Teens; Sprt Ed Yrbk; Drama Clb; 4-H; Pep Clb; Goucher Coll; Public Rel.

COLMERY, ROBIN; Aurora HS; Aurora, OH; 25/163 Cls Rep Sr Cls; NHS; Stu Cncl; Mth Clb; Pep Clb; Capt Chrldng; Miami Univ; Communications.

COLON, BRENDA; Wauseon HS; Wauseon, OH; Cl Rep Jr Cls; Chrs; Stu Cncl; Treas Y-Teens; FTA; Trk; Chrldng; College.

COLONEL, GWENDOLENE; New Richmond HS; New Richmond, OH; Chrs; Chrh Wkr; Hon Rl; JA; Jr NHS; NHS; Sch Mus; 4-H; Fr Clb; FTA; Univ.

COLSON, MARCELLA; Brecksville HS; Broadview Hts, OH; Trs Jr Cls; Cl Rep Jr Cls; Cls Rep Sr Cls; Hon Rl; NHS; Off Ade; Sch Mus; Stu Cncl; Pres Fr Clb; Ger Clb; Miami Univ; Med Tech.

COLSTON, KAREN; John Hay HS; Cleveland, OH; Val; Hon Rl; Jr NHS; Lbry Ade; NHS; Yrbk; Schlrshp Ohio Bd Of Receiving 79; Univ Of Cincinnati; Phys Ther.

COLTER, J; Taylor HS; Kokomo, IN; Hon Rl; College; Business.

COLTER, TINA; Mt Notre Dame HS; Loveland, OH; 16/143 Band; Chrh Wkr; Drl Tm; Girl Scts; Hon Rl; NHS; Sch Mus; Ed Sch Nwsp; Drama Clb; Miami Univ; Acctg.

COLTHAR, KAREN; Lynchburg Clay HS; Lynchburg, OH; Sec Sr Cls; Chrs; Drl Tm; Hon Rl; NHS; 4-H; FHA; OEA; 4-H Awd;.

COLTHARP, JAMES; Talawanda HS; Oxford, OH; 1/290 Val; Am Leg Boys St; NHS; Pol Wkr; Stu Cncl; Letter Ten; Dnfth Awd; DAR Awd; Rochester Univ; Pblc Policy Analysis.

COLTON, ROSE; Parma HS; Parma, OH; Cmnty Wkr; Hon Rl; Pol Wkr; College; Bus.

COLUCCI, ELLA; Ashtabula HS; Ashtabula, OH; 16/225 Cls Rep Frsh Cls; Sec Soph Cls; Cl Rep Jr Cls; Am Leg Aux Girls St; Hon Rl; Jr NHS; Stu Cncl; 4-H; FTA; Ger Clb; Findlay Coll; Equestrian Studies.

COLVILLE, BRENDA; Arcanum Butler HS; Arcanum, OH; 1/99 Band; Chrs; Chrh Wkr; Hon Rl; NHS; Sch Mus; Sch Pl; Stu Cncl; Voc Schl.

COLVIN, DAVID; Loogootee HS; Loogootee, IN; Hon Rl; Drama Clb; 4-H; Fr Clb; Ten; IM Sprt; 4-H Awd; Ind State Univ; Bus.

COLVIN, EDWARD; Medina Sr HS; Medina, OH; 43/341 Boy Scts; Hon Rl; NHS; Treas Key Clb; Capt Crs Cntry; Letter Trk; Amer HS Athlete Cross Cntry 78; Univ; Pre Med.

COLVIN, JEFFERY; Springboro HS; Springboro, OH; Boy Scts; FCA; Hon Rl; Sct Actv; Letter Ftbl; Letter Trk; Letter Wrstlng; IM Sprt; College.

COLVIN, JOHN; Washington Catholic HS; Montgomery, IN; Univ; Engr.

COLVIN, LAURA; Marion HS; Marion, IN; Hon Rl; Sch Pl; Yrbk; Drama Clb; College.

COLWELL, DANNY; Defiance HS; Defiance, OH; Am Leg Boys St; Hon Rl; NHS; Eng Clb; 4-H; Fr Clb; Sci Clb; Dnfth Awd; Natl Merit Ltr; Pres Awd; Univ Of Vir; Botany Or Law.

COLWELL, ELIZABETH; Jefferson Union HS; Richmond, OH; 3 Cls Rep Frsh Cls; Cls Rep Soph Cls; Cl Rep Jr Cls; Chrs; Hon Rl; Stu Cncl; Beta Clb; Letter Glf; Univ Of Akron; Accounting.

COLWELL, MARY; Meigs HS; Vinton, OH; Chrh Wkr; Cmnty Wkr; Hon Rl; Stu Cncl; Rptr Sch Nwsp; 4-H; OEA; Pep Clb; Mgrs; Scr Kpr; Hocking Tech Coll; Sec Sci.

COLYER, TRACEY; Lapeer East HS; Attica, MI; Cls Rep Sr Cls; NHS; Fr Clb; Mich State Univ; Biochem.

COMAN, PAM; Fairview HS; Fairview Park, OH; 33/239 Chrs; Chrh Wkr; Girl Scts; Hon Rl; JA; Rptr Yrbk; Sci Clb; Univ; Med.

COMBEN, MARGARET; Pellston HS; Indian River, MI; Chrh Wkr; Girl Scts; Hon Rl; Hosp Ade; NHS; Mich State Univ; Bio.

COMBES, LAURA; Beaumont Girls HS; Shaker Hts, OH; Chrs; Drl Tm; Sch Mus; Sch Pl; Drama Clb; Lat Clb; College; Communications.

COMBS, ANDREA; Marysville HS; Marysville, OH; Hosp Ade; College; Nurse.

COMBS, BRIAN L; East Clinton HS; Sabina, OH; Cls Rep Frsh Cls; Band; Hon Rl; NHS; Sch Pl; Pep Clb; Sci Clb; Spn Clb; Southern St Univ.

COMBS, JEANNE; Preble Shawnee HS; Gratis, OH; Cls Rep Frsh Cls; Cls Rep Soph Cls; Trs Jr Cls; Cls Rep Sr Cls; Band; Chrs; Hon Rl; Sch Mus; Stu Cncl; Yth Flsp; Miami Univ; Data Processing.

COMBS, JOHNNIE; Whiteland Cmnty HS; Greenwood, IN; Trs Sr Cls; Chrh Wkr; FTA; Pep Clb; IM Sprt; Franklin Coll; Hstry.

COMBS, MATTHEW; Cuyahoga Falls HS; Cuyahoga Falls, OH; JA; Ger Clb; New York Univ; Film Director.

COMBS, PAUL; W Jefferson HS; W Jefferson, OH; Hon Rl; Jr NHS; Letter Bsbl; Letter Bsktbl; Letter Crs Cntry; Letter Ftbl; Bowling Green Univ.

COMBS, SUZETTE; Springboro HS; Springboro, OH; Chrs; Chrh Wkr; Drl Tm; Hon Rl; NHS; Sch Pl; Yrbk; Rptr Sch Nwsp; God Cntry Awd; JC Awd; Kty Christian Coll; Eng.

COMBS, TAMMI; Bedford North Lawrence HS; Avoca, IN; 28/380 Band; Chrs; Chrh Wkr; Cmnty Wkr; Hon Rl; Mdrgl; NHS; Pol Wkr; Beta Clb; Fr Clb; Olivet Nazarene Coll; Music.

COMBS, TERRY; Lakeville Memorial HS; Columbiaville, MI; Chrh Wkr; Cmnty Wkr; Debate Tm; Hon Rl; Natl Forn Lg; Pol Wkr; Sct Actv; Letter Bsbl; Art Awd; Cntrl Michigan Univ; Mid Schl Tchr.

COMBS, TOD; Paint Valley HS; Chillicothe, OH; 30/88 Am Leg Boys St; Boy Scts; 4-H; Bsktbl; Ftbl; Trk; Mgrs; Univ; Archt.

COMBS, TOD A; Paint Valley HS; Chillicothe, OH; 30/88 Am Leg Boys St; Boy Scts; Sct Actv; 4-H; Bsktbl; Ftbl; Trk; Letter Mgrs; Univ; Archt.

COMBS, VICKI; Norwood Sr HS; Norwood, OH; Cls Rep Frsh Cls; Hon Rl; JA; Jr NHS; Lit Mag; Stg Crw; Rptr Sch Nwsp; Lat Clb; Spn Clb; Ohio Visual Arts Univ; Cmnrcl Art.

COMELLA, DAWN; Valley Forge HS; Parma, OH; 122/777 Girl Scts; Hon Rl; Jr NHS; Yth Flsp; College.

COMENSOLI, MICHAEL; Negaunee HS; Negaunee, MI; Chrs; Chrh Wkr; Debate Tm; Hon Rl; Ten; IM Sprt; Scr Kpr; North Mic Univ.

COMER, ALEXIS; West Side HS; Gary, IN; Hon Rl; Quill & Scroll; Sch Nwsp; Ball St Univ; Jrnlsm.

COMER, ARNITA; West Side HS; Gary, IN; Hon Rl; Y-Teens; Pep Clb; Tmr; College; Mec Tech.

COMER, JANICE; Marian HS; Birmingham, MI; Cls Rep Soph Cls; Cmnty Wkr; FCA; Hon Rl; Pol Wkr; GAA; IM Sprt; Univ; Radiology.

COMERZAN, BENJAMIN; Our Lady Of Mount Carmel HS; Ecorse, MI; Hon Rl; NHS; Ed Yrbk; Yrbk; Treas Sci Clb; Spn Clb; Art.

COMISSO, LAURIE; Allen Park HS; Allen Pk, MI; Chrs; Girl Scts; Hon Rl; Jr NHS; Bsbl; GAA; PPFtbl; Univ; Vet Tech.

COMITO, CARLA M; Our Lady Of Mercy HS; Redford, MI; 2/306 Cls Rep Soph Cls; Sal; Chrs; JA; Jr NHS; Lbry Ade; Mod UN; NHS; Orch; Sch Mus; Wayne St Univ; Acctg.

COMMAGER, TOM; Benjamin Logan HS; Zanesfield, OH; Band; Boy Scts; Hon Rl; Bsbl; Bsktbl; Swmmng; Voc Schl; Comp Design.

COMMENT, PAM; De Kalb HS; Ashley, IN; Chrh Wkr; Hon Rl; NHS; Sec Yth Flsp; Pep Clb; Sec Sci Clb; College; Acctg.

COMMISSO, CARMELA; Lake Shore HS; St Clair Shore, MI; Cmp Fr Grls; Chrs; Debate Tm; Hon Rl; Jr NHS; Yrbk; Sch Nwsp; Crs Cntry; Scr Kpr; Tmr; Michigan St Univ.

COMO, MELANIE; St Josephs HS; Granger, IN; Cls Rep Frsh Cls; Pres Soph Cls; Cl Rep Jr Cls; Debate Tm; Hon Rl; Stu Cncl; Chrldng; IM Sprt; PPFtbl; Opt Clb Awd; Notre Dame; Psych.

COMODECA, JAMES A; Normandy HS; Parma, OH; 59/649 VP Frsh Cls; Pres Soph Cls; Pres Jr Cls; Am Leg Boys St; Boy Scts; Chrs; Chrh Wkr; Cmnty Wkr; Hon Rl; Pol Wkr; Univ; Envrmntl Engr.

COMP, PAULA; Fenton HS; Fenton, MI; Chrh Wkr; Girl Scts; Hon Rl; Letter Trk; Tmr; College; Bus.

COMPAGNONE, GIUSEPPINA; St Alphonsus HS; Dearborn, MI; 25/180 Hon Rl; Sch Mus; Sch Pl; Detroit Coll Of Busns; Sec.

COMPETTI, JUDY; Wm V Fisher Catholic HS; Lancaster, OH; Cl Rep Jr Cls; Chrs; Hon Rl; NHS; Sec Fr Clb; FTA; 4-H Awd; Ohio Univ Lancaster; Acctg.

COMPTON, BOBBIE; Deer Park HS; Cincinnati, OH; Pres Frsh Cls; Chrs; Chrh Wkr; Girl Scts; Hon Rl; Sch Mus; Sch Pl; Pres Stu Cncl; Sec Drama Clb; Univ Of Cincinnati; Music.

COMPTON, DIANA; Taylor HS; Cincinnati, OH; Cl Rep Jr Cls; Am Leg Aux Girls St; Band; FCA; Hon Rl; Pres Jr NHS; VP NHS; College; Engr.

COMPTON, KAREN; St Francis De Sales HS; Columbus, OH; Sch Nwsp; PPFtbl; Tmr; Busns Schl; Acctg.

COMPTON, KATHLEEN; Park Tudor HS; Indianapolis, IN; Cls Rep Frsh Cls; Cls Rep Soph Cls; Hon Rl; Stg Crw; Rptr Yrbk; Fr Clb; Sci Clb; Hockey; Ten; IM Sprt; Univ; Med.

COMPTON, MARGARET M; Forest Hills Central HS; Ada, MI; Band; Drm Bgl; Sch Mus; Sch Pl; Stg Crw; Drama Clb; PPFtbl; Pres Awd; Western Mic Univ; Music.

COMPTON, ROBIN KAY; Waldron HS; Waldron, IN; 10/72 Band; Hon Rl; Off Ade; Rptr Yrbk; 4-H; Lat Clb; Pep Clb; Univ.

COMRIE, DOREEN; Wyoming Park HS; Wyoming, MI; 10/227 Band; NHS; Sct Actv; Ger Clb; Natl Merit Schl; Eng Awd 79; Michigan St Univ; Pre Vet Med.

CONANT, LISA; Fremont Public HS; Fremont, MI; 54/234 Chrh Wkr; Cmnty Wkr; Hon Rl; Lbry Ade; Red Cr Ade; Yth Flsp; 4-H; Pep Clb; Mgrs; PPFtbl; Nazareth Coll; Nursing.

CONANT, TAMMIE; Jenison HS; Jenison, MI; Cl Rep Jr Cls; Cls Rep Sr Cls; Val; Cmnty Wkr; Hon Rl; NHS; Sch Pl; Stu Cncl; Yth Flsp; Rptr Sch Nwsp; Grand Valley St Univ.

CONARTON, LORI; Holt HS; Dimondale, MI; 15/345 Trs Jr Cls; Cmnty Wkr; Hon Rl; NHS; Ed Yrbk; Rptr Sch Nwsp; Sch Nwsp; Letter Ten; Coach Actv; IM Sprt; Ferris State; Journalism.

CONATSER, RONNIE; Wilbur Wright HS; Dayton, OH; 8/211 Chrh Wkr; Hon Rl; NHS; Sct Actv; Rets Tech Center Inc; Elec.

CONAWAY, DOUGLAS; Ironton HS; Ironton, OH; 1/183 Val; Mod UN; NHS; Sch Mus; Ed Sch Nwsp; JC Awd; Kiwan Awd; Natl Merit Schl; Miami Univ; Chem Engr.

CONAWAY, TOM; Crooksville HS; Crooksville, OH; Boy Scts; Hon Rl; Sch Pl; Sct Actv; Stg Crw; Yth Flsp; Sch Nwsp; Fr Clb; FSA; Sci Clb; Bus Schl.

CONCHA, JOHN; Beavercreek HS; Fairborn, OH; 125/702 Pres AFS; Band; NHS; IM Sprt; Ohio St Univ; Engr.

CONDER, STEVEN; Goshen HS; Goshen, IN; VP Jr Cls; Band; Chrh Wkr; Hon Rl; NHS; Stu Cncl; Sci Clb; Swmmng; Amer HS Ath All Amer 77; Univ; Archt.

CONDES, DEBBIE; Kankakee Vly HS; De Motte, IN; 22/198 Chrs; Hon Rl; Sch Mus; Stg Crw; Rptr Yrbk; Drama Clb; Ger Clb; Sci Clb; PPFtbl; Outstndng In German; Univ; Nursing.

CONDIC, ERIC; Kalamazoo Central HS; Kalamazoo, MI; Boy Scts; Chrs; Debate Tm; Hon Rl; Natl Forn Lg; Yrbk; Fr Clb; Western Mich Univ; Geol.

CONDIT, JENIFER; St Ursula Acad; Cincinnati, OH; Cls Rep Soph Cls; VP Jr Cls; Cls Rep Sr Cls; Cmnty Wkr; Stu Cncl; Pep Clb; Spn Clb; GAA; Cit Awd; College; Pub Relations.

CONDON, CELESTE; St Marys Cntrl Cath HS; Sandusky, OH; Cl Rep Jr Cls; Cls Rep Sr Cls; Rptr Yrbk; Pep Clb; Spn Clb; Chrldng; GAA; IM Sprt; College; Fash Merch.

CONDON, JAN M; Clay Sr HS; Oregon, OH; Pres Frsh Cls; Cls Rep Soph Cls; FCA; Hon Rl; NHS; Off Ade; Sec Stu Cncl; Ed Yrbk; FTA; Cit Awd; Univ Of Toledo; Nursing.

CONDON, JEFFREY; White Pine HS; Ontonagon, MI; 9/41 Pres Frsh Cls; Cls Rep Soph Cls; Trs Jr Cls; Band; Hon Rl; Yrbk; Sch Nwsp; Ftbl; Trk; Michigan St Univ; Med Asst.

CONDON, TIMOTHY; Moelled HS; Cincinnati, OH; 60/262 Aud/Vis; Cmnty Wkr; Hon Rl; Off Ade; Yrbk; Coach Actv; IM Sprt; DAR Awd; Miami Univ; Advertising Graphics.

CONDRA, JOHN; Athens HS; Troy, MI; Am Leg Boys St; Boy Scts; Hon Rl; Sct Actv; Oakland Univ; Forestry.

CONDRON, CATHY; Bishop Foley HS; Troy, MI; Girl Scts; Hon Rl; Sct Actv; Bsbl; Bsktbl; GAA; PPFtbl; Western Michigan Univ; Occptnl Ther.

CONE, HOLLY; Mason Sr HS; Mason, MI; Sal; Band; Hon Rl; Hosp Ade; Jr NHS; NHS; Sch Mus; Denison Univ; Pre Med.

CONGER, MEG; Ursuline Academy; Cincinnati, OH; 26/104 Cmnty Wkr; Hon Rl; Bsktbl; Tmr; Pres Awd; Miami Univ; Bus.

CONGLETON, JILL; Washington Cnty Voc School; Belpre, OH; Pres Jr Cls; Band; Chrs; Girl Scts; Hon Rl; JA; Sct Actv; 4-H; OEA; 4-H Awd;.

CONIGLIARO, JOYCE; Crestwood HS; Hiram, OH; Sec Frsh Cls; Cls Rep Frsh Cls; Pres Soph Cls; Cls Rep Soph Cls; Pres Jr Cls; Cl Rep Jr Cls; Cls Rep Sr Cls; Chrs; Girl Scts; Hon Rl; Betty Crocker Conserv Of Energy Awd 78; Kent St Univ; Child Psych.

CONIGLIO, LISA; Three Rivers HS; Three Rivers, MI; 23/234 Hon Rl; NHS; Sec 4-H; Pep Clb; Spn Clb; Trk; PPFtbl; Central Michigan Univ.

CONIGLIO, SHIRLEY; Canfield HS; Canfield, OH; 56/273 Chrh Wkr; Hon Rl; Ed Yrbk; Rptr Yrbk; Rptr Sch Nwsp; Key Clb; Youngstown St Univ; Pre Law.

CONINE, JILL; Athens HS; Athens, MI; 19/87 Hon Rl; Hosp Ade; NHS; Red Cr Ade; Sch Pl; FNA; Pep Clb; VICA; S Central Schl Of Prctcl Nrsg; Nurse.

CONING, JERRY; Madison Comprehensive HS; Mansfield, OH; Boy Scts; Cmnty Wkr; Hon Rl; Spn Clb; Letter Ftbl; Letter Trk; Letter Wrstlng; Coach Actv; Ashland Col; Comp Progr.

CONKLE, KAREN; Garrett HS; Garrett, IN; 12/130 Cls Rep Soph Cls; Sec Jr Cls; Chrs; Hon Rl; VP NHS; Stu Cncl; Y-Teens; 4-H; Ger Clb; Pep Clb; Univ; Phys Ther.

CONKLIN, JEFF; Yorktown HS; Muncie, IN; Stu Cncl; Capt Bsktbl; Capt Ftbl; Capt Glf; Cit Awd; Indiana Univ;.

CONKLIN, JEFFREY; St Francis Desales HS; Toledo, OH; Hon Rl; IM Sprt; Ohi State; Bus Admin.

CONKLIN, JOSEPH; Vicksburg HS; Vicksburg, MI; JA; Fr Clb; Ftbl; Univ; Math.

CONKLIN, LEANNE; Geneva HS; Geneva, OH; 29/250 Cls Rep Frsh Cls; Cls Rep Soph Cls; Cl Rep Jr Cls; Cls Rep Sr Cls; Girl Scts; JA; Sct Actv; FBLA; JA Awd; Univ; CPA.

CONKLIN, LISA; Northland HS; Columbus, OH; 52/393 Girl Scts; Hon Rl; NHS; Ger Clb; Lat Clb; Ohio St Univ; Law.

CONKLING, WINIFRED; Bloomington HS South; Bloomington, IN; Trs Sr Cls; NHS; Quill & Scroll; Ed Yrbk; Pom Pon; Kiwan Awd; Northwestern Univ; Jrnlsm.

CONLAN, MICHAEL; Hubbard HS; Hubbard, OH; Cmnty Wkr; Hon Rl; Sprt Ed Yrbk; Rptr Yrbk; Yrbk; Sch Nwsp; Mth Clb; Youngstown St Univ; Math.

CONLEY, BARBARA; Lockland HS; Cincinnati, OH; 6/63 Chrs; Chrh Wkr; Cmnty Wkr; Drl Tm; NHS; Sch Mus; Stg Crw; Fr Clb; Spn Clb; GAA; Milligan Coll; Bus.

CONLEY, CAROL; Eastern HS; Lucasville, OH; Band; Chrs; Chrh Wkr; Nursing.

CONLEY, CHERYL; Ubly Cmnty HS; Bad Axe, MI; Chrs; Girl Scts; Hon Rl; Lbry Ade; Sch Pl; Stg Crw; FHA; Trk; PPFtbl; Univ.

CONLEY, DAVID; Patterson Co Operative HS; Dayton, OH; Univ; Elec.

CONLEY, GREG; Carey HS; Carey, OH; Chrh Wkr; Hon Rl; NHS; Drama Clb; Bsktbl; Crs Cntry; Trk; IM Sprt; Mgrs; Terra Tech; Electro Mechanical Eng.

CONLEY, JEAN; Imlay City Community HS; Lum, MI; Cl Rep Jr Cls; Hon Rl; Lbry Ade; NHS; Stu Cncl; Letter Chrldng;.

CONLEY, LORI; Jackson HS; Jackson, OH; Trs Soph Cls; Hst Jr Cls; Chrs; Hon Rl; Off Ade; Rptr Sch Nwsp; Sch Nwsp; FHA; OEA; Trk; Jr And Chptr Degree In FHA; Jr Fair Board; Business School; Med Sec.

CONLEY, LYN; Lake Central HS; Dyer, IN; 37/518 Cmp Fr Grls; Chrs; Girl Scts; Hon Rl; NHS; Quill & Scroll; Ed Sch Nwsp; Rptr Sch Nwsp; Bsktbl; IM Sprt; Rookie Yr Paper 1979; Best Scout Booster 1979; Univ; Mass Cmnctns.

CONLEY, MARK; Warsaw Community HS; Silver Lake, IN; Am Leg Boys St; Band; Boy Scts; Hon Rl; Sct Actv; 4-H; FFA; Letter Bsbl; FFA St Band 77 78; FFA Natl Band 77 78 & 79; Schl Band Awds 77 78 & 79; Purdue Voc Schl; Agri.

CONLEY, PATRICIA A; Portsmouth East HS; Portsmouth, OH; Band; Drm Mjrt; Hon Rl; Lbry Ade; NHS; Off Ade; Sch Mus; Capt College; Pre Law.

CONLEY, REBECCA; Amelia HS; Cincinnati, OH; Cls Rep Soph Cls; Girl Scts; Stu Cncl; Chrldng; GAA; Xavier Univ; Radiology Tech.

CONLEY, SANDY; Tecumseh HS; New Carlisle, OH; FCA; Hon Rl; Jr NHS; Letter Ten; Chrldng; Bus Schl; Bus.

CONLEY, SHERYL; Hesperia Comm HS; Muskegon, MI; 6/79 Pres Jr Cls; Band; Girl Scts; Hon Rl; Sch Pl; Sct Actv; Stg Crw; Drama Clb; Pep Clb; Letter Chrldng;.

CONLEY, SUSAN; Cardinal HS; Middlefield, OH; 14/128 AFS; Chrs; Hon Rl; Stg Crw; Yrbk; Trk; GAA; Ohi State Univ; Architecture.

CONLEY, TERESA; Birmingham Seaholm HS; Troy, MI; 338/620 Chrs; Chrh Wkr; Off Ade; Sec Yth Flsp; Albion Coll Gift 79; Albion Coll; Spec Educ.

CONLEY, TOBIN P; Traverse City St Francis HS; Traverse City, MI; Pres Frsh Cls; Pres Sr Cls; Band; Cmnty Wkr; Hon Rl; Mod UN; NHS; Sch Pl; Stu Cncl; Rptr Sch Nwsp; Rotary Intl Yth Exchg Student 78; Univ; Soc Sci.

CONLEY, YALE; Parkersburg HS; Vienna, WV; Cmnty Wkr; FCA; Hon Rl; Pep Clb; Letter Ftbl; IM Sprt; Marshall Univ; Pre Dent.

CONLIN, DANIEL; Taft Sr HS; Hamilton, OH; Hon Rl; Jr NHS; Ger Clb; Bsktbl; IM Sprt; Univ; Engr.

CONLON, BARB; Cedar Lake Academy; Grand Rapids, MI; 3/82 Band; Chrs; Chrh Wkr; Hon Rl; NHS; Orch; Crs Cntry; Trk; IM Sprt; Scholastic Hnrs Awd; Honorable Mention Museum Talent Exhibit; Award Plaque Earning Letter In Track; Andrews Univ; Nursing.

CONLON, CINDIE; St Francis HS; Traverse City, MI; Band; Hon Rl; NHS; Ed Yrbk; Pep Clb; Northwestern Mic College; Journalism.

CONLON, CYNTHIA; Marian HS; Cincinnati, OH; Sec Frsh Cls; Sec Soph Cls; Fr Clb; FBLA; Univ Of Cincinnati; Bus Mgmt.

CONN, LESLIE; Ferndale HS; Milford, MI; Hon Rl; Sch Pl; Stg Crw; DECA; Bsktbl; Trk; Univ.

CONN, MARK; Holt HS; Holt, MI; Cls Rep Frsh Cls; Cls Rep Soph Cls; Cls Rep Sr Cls; Hon Rl; Lbry Ade; Stu Cncl; Glf; Ten; Coach Actv; IM Sprt; Lansing Cmnty Coll; Flight Tech.

CONNAIR, BRIAN; Archbishop Alter HS; Kettering, OH; Chrs; Mdrgl; NHS; Yrbk; Drama Clb; College; Archt.

CONNAWAY, JO; Carroll HS; Camden, IN; 5/100 Am Leg Aux Girls St; Chrs; Girl Scts; Hon Rl; NHS; Sch Mus; Sch Pl; Stu Cncl; Drama Clb; Fr Clb; Hanover Coll.

CONNELL, DEBBIE; Chelsea HS; Gregory, MI; Sec Jr Cls; Pres Sr Cls; Girl Scts; Hon Rl; Yth Flsp; Rptr Sch Nwsp; FFA; GAA; IM Sprt; Scr Kpr; Daytona Cmnty Coll; Criminal Justice.

CONNELL, JEFFEREY; Everett HS; Lansing, MI; Cls Rep Frsh Cls; Boy Scts; Hon Rl; JA; Yth Flsp; Wrstlng; College; Math.

CONNELL, KATHLEEN; Nordonia HS; Northfield, OH; 28/448 Band; Hon Rl; NHS; Sch Mus; Sch Pl; Stg Crw; Pep Clb; PPFtbl; Scr Kpr; Outstndng Musicn Awd 78; Asst Choreogrphr For Schl Ply 78; Choreg For Jr Cls Play 79; Kent St Univ; Dance.

CONNELL, LYNNE; Buckeye North HS; Brilliant, OH; Am Leg Aux Girls St; Band; Chrh Wkr; Cmnty Wkr; Girl Scts; Hon Rl; Off Ade; Sch Pl; Sct Actv; Yth Flsp; Schl Of Cosmetology; Cosmetology.

CONNELL, REBECCA; Mooresville HS; Mooresville, IN; 22/255 AFS; NHS; Sch Mus; Drama Clb; Ger Clb; Sci Clb; Ten; Purdue Univ; Speech Pathology.

CONNELL, THOMAS R; Buckeye North HS; Brilliant, OH; 2/106 Am Leg Boys St; Band; Boy Scts; Chrh Wkr; Hon Rl; NHS; Sct Actv; Rptr Yrbk; Spn Clb; Glf; 1st Prize Science Fair; Eagle Scout; Univ; Chem Engr.

CONNELLY, CONNIE; Badin HS; Hamilton, OH; 84/211 Gym; Swmmng; Ten; Chrldng; Tmr; Univ Of Dayton; Phys Ed.

CONNELLY, DEBBIE; Rocky River HS; Rocky River, OH; Cl Rep Jr Cls; Girl Scts; Off Ade; Stu Cncl; Swmmng; Chrldng; Bowling Green Univ.

CONNELLY, JAMES; Walled Lake Central HS; Union Lake, MI; Hon Rl; Cit Awd; Univ Of Michigan; Archt.

CONNELLY, LINDA; Green HS; Akron, OH; 1/325 Drl Tm; Girl Scts; Hon Rl; NHS; Pep Clb; Sec GAA; Pom Pon; Univ; Comp Prog.

CONNELLY, RUTH; Niles Mckinley HS; Niles, OH; Pres Soph Cls; AFS; Hon Rl; Jr NHS; NHS; Red Cr Ade; Stg Crw; Stu Cncl; Drama Clb; PPFtbl; College; Botanist.

CONNER, BUDDY; Benjamin Bosse HS; Evansville, IN; Pres Frsh Cls; VP Soph Cls; Cl Rep Jr Cls; Cls Rep Sr Cls; Hon Rl; Red Cr Ade; Sct Actv; Stu Cncl; Letter Bsbl; Capt Ftbl; Univ; Archt.

CONNER, JOHN; Heritage Christian HS; Indianapolis, IN; Pres Frsh Cls; Cls Rep Frsh Cls; Pres Jr Cls; Cl Rep Jr Cls; Chrs; Chrh Wkr; Pol Wkr; Sch Mus; Stg Crw; Stu Cncl; College; Busns Admin.

CONNER, RHONDA; Bath Sr HS; Lima, OH; Chrs; Girl Scts; Hon Rl; NHS; Sch Pl; 4-H; Letter Bsktbl; PPFtbl; Varsity Softball 3 Letters; College; Science.

CONNER, SHEILA; Indian Creek HS; Morgantown, IN; 19/164 Am Leg Aux Girls St; Band; Hon Rl; NHS; Rptr Yrbk; 4-H; Pep Clb; Rdo Clb; Ten; GAA; Business Mgmt.

CONNER, TERESA; Collinwood HS; Cleveland, OH; Cls Rep Frsh Cls; Cls Rep Soph Cls; Cl Rep Jr Cls; Sal; Chrs; Drl Tm; Hon Rl; Yth Flsp; Sch Nwsp; Drama Clb; Baldwin Wallace Coll; Poli Sci.

CONNER, THOMAS; Wheeling Park HS; Wheeling, WV; Band; Boy Scts; Chrs; Hon Rl; Mod UN; Orch; Pol Wkr; Sct Actv; Pres Key Clb; Treas Mth Clb; West Liberty St Coll; Poli Sci.

CONNER, TIMOTHY; Bluffton HS; Bluffton, IN; 23/132 Cls Rep Frsh Cls; Cls Rep Soph Cls; Cl Rep Jr Cls; Band; Hon Rl; Pol Wkr; Sch Mus; Stu Cncl; Yth Flsp; Pres Ger Clb; College; History.

CONNER, TIMOTHY; Stonewall Jackson HS; Charleston, WV; Sec Am Leg Boys St; Aud/Vis; Jr NHS; Sct Actv; Drama Clb; Lat Clb; Mth Clb; Sci Clb; Letter Crs Cntry; Letter Trk; Math Fld Day Awd 79; West Virginia Univ; Pre Med.

CONNER, TRACY L; Barboursville HS; Huntington, WV; Cls Rep Frsh Cls; Cls Rep Soph Cls; Band; FCA; Girl Scts; Off Ade; Y-Teens; 4-H; OEA; Pep Clb; 4th Talent Show Gymnastics; West Virginia Univ; Spanish.

CONNERS, KEVIN; Hayes HS; Delaware, OH; Pres Frsh Cls; Pres Soph Cls; Chrh Wkr; Cmnty Wkr; JA; Pol Wkr; Stu Cncl; Sch Nwsp; FBLA; Key Clb; College; Busns.

CONNOLLY, JOHN R; Purcell HS; Cincinnati, OH; Cls Rep Soph Cls; Cl Rep Jr Cls; Pres Sr Cls; Hon Rl; Stu Cncl; Letter Bsbl; Letter Ftbl; IM Sprt; Univ; Civil Engr.

CONNOLLY, JOLINE; Defiance Sr HS; Defiance, OH; 25/295 Cmnty Wkr; Hon Rl; Jr NHS; Off Ade; Sch Pl; Stu Cncl; Pep Clb; Spn Clb; Letter Gym; Chrldng; Homemaking; Ohio Univ; Business.

CONNOLLY, LISA; Ashtabula Harbor HS; Ashtabula, OH; 50/198 AFS; Chrs; Rptr Yrbk; Rptr Sch Nwsp; Spn Clb; Univ; Jrnlsm.

CONNOLLY, MARY; St Alphonsus HS; Dearborn, MI; Sec Jr Cls; Chrs; Hon Rl; NHS; Sch Mus; Stu Cncl; Pep Clb; Chrldng; GAA;.

CONNOLLY II, T; Hoover HS; North Canton, OH; Hon Rl; NHS; Fr Clb; Sci Clb; College; Science.

CONNOR, DAVID; Pontiac Northern HS; Pontiac, MI; Hon Rl; Letter Ftbl; Letter Wrstlng; HS Record

In Wrestling Fastest Pin In 0.07 Seconds; Reg Hnrs Michigan Industria Ed Awd; College; Engr.

CONNOR, KEITH; Shaker Heights Sr HS; Shaker Hts, OH; Cls Rep Frsh Cls; Boy Scts; Chrh Wkr; Hon Rl; Off Ade; Sch Mus; Sch Pl; Sct Actv; Stg Crw; Drama Clb; Univ; Bio.

CONNOR, KIMBERLY; St Ursula Academy; Toledo, OH; Cls Rep Soph Cls; Chrs; Chrh Wkr; JA; Stu Cncl; Yth Flsp; Fr Clb; Ten; JA Awd; 3 Blue Ribbons & Red Ribbon From OMTA Music 76; Univ; Poli Sci.

CONNOR, TIM; Wilmington HS; Wilmington, OH; 25/280 Band; Chrs; Sch Mus; Sch Pl; Stg Crw; Ed Sch Nwsp; Sprt Ed Sch Nwsp; Rptr Sch Nwsp; Sch Nwsp; Drama Clb; College; Sci.

CONNORS, JEFFREY; St Clair HS; Marine City, MI; Hon Rl; NHS; Sch Pl; Stg Crw; Wrstlng; Rotary Awd; Oakland Univ; Engr.

CONNORS, KEVIN; R Nelson Snider HS; Notre Dame, IN; 19/550 Band; Treas JA; Lat Clb; Sci Clb; C of C Awd; JA Awd; Univ Of Notre Dame; Engr.

CONOMEA, JAMIE; Brooklyn HS; Brooklyn, OH; Band; Boy Scts; Chrs; Orch; Sct Actv; Stu Cncl; Boys Clb Am; Key Clb; Spn Clb; Bsktbl; Conf Champs Ftbl & Wrestling; College; Archt.

CONOVER, LINDA; Glen Este HS; Cincinnati, OH; Hon Rl; Hosp Ade; Off Ade; Sch Mus; Pep Clb; Spn Clb; Univ Of Cincinnati; Xray Tech.

CONOVER, MELISSA; Southwestern HS; Flat Rock, IN; 3/60 Hon Rl; NHS; Ed Sch Nwsp; Drama Clb; Pep Clb; Bsktbl; IUPUI; Mech Engr.

CONRAD, CARLIN; Springs Valley HS; French Lick, IN; Hon Rl; Stg Crw; 4-H; Fr Clb; Pep Clb; Letter Crs Cntry; Letter Trk; IM Sprt; Mgrs; Scr Kpr; Indiana Univ; Busns Admin.

CONRAD, CHRIS; Penn HS; Osceola, IN; 134/487 Chrh Wkr; FCA; Yth Flsp; Spn Clb; Bethel Coll; Phys Educ.

CONRAD, DENISE; Magnificat HS; N Olmstead, OH; Girl Scts; NHS; Bsktbl; Glf; IM Sprt; College; Stewardess.

CONRAD, DENNIS; Spencer HS; Reedy, WV; 10/162 Boy Scts; Cmnty Wkr; Hon Rl; Pol Wkr; Sch Pl; Sct Actv; Rptr Sch Nwsp; Wheeling Coll; Law.

CONRAD, GARY; Federal Hocking HS; Coolville, OH; Cls Rep Frsh Cls; Cls Rep Soph Cls; Cl Rep Jr Cls; Hon Rl; Yrbk; 4-H; Pep Clb; Bsktbl; IM Sprt; Scr Kpr; Ohio Univ.

CONRAD, JAMES; Whiteland Community HS; Franklin, IN; 19/220 VP Jr Cls; AFS; FCA; Jr NHS; 4-H; FFA; FTA; Letter Bsktbl; Letter Ftbl; Letter Trk; Univ; Engr.

CONRAD, JOEL; De Kalb HS; Ashley, IN; 39/287 Band; Chrs; Chrh Wkr; Jr NHS; NHS; Yth Flsp; VP 4-H; Pres FFA; Bsbl; Ftbl; Purdue Univ; Ag.

CONRAD, KEELY; Springs Valley HS; French Lick, IN; 13/81 Trs Frsh Cls; Trs Soph Cls; Cl Rep Jr Cls; Trs Sr Cls; Band; Capt Drm Bgl; Girl Scts; Hon Rl; Treas Stu Cncl; Fr Clb; Purdue Univ; Pharm.

CONRAD, KELLY; Fostoria HS; Fostoria, OH; Hon Rl; Hosp Ade; NHS; VP FHA; Letter Bsktbl; Letter Ten; Fostoria Athltc Boosters Hon Awd For Tennis 7.; Tech Coll; Comp Progr.

CONRAD, KEVIN; South Dearborn HS; Aurora, IN; 31/265 Am Leg Boys St; Hon Rl; NHS; Pep Clb; Letter Bsbl; Letter Ten; Univ; Math.

CONRAD, KRISTI; North Union HS; Magnetic Spg, OH; Pres Frsh Cls; Band; Hon Rl; Stu Cncl; Spn Clb; Capt Bsktbl; Trk; Coach Actv; IM Sprt; PPFtbl; Vllybll Capt 1st Tm League 78; Bowling Green St Univ.

CONRAD, KRISTINE; Napoleon HS; Napoleon, OH; Cls Rep Sr Cls; Band; Hon Rl; NHS; Sch Mus; Stu Cncl; Lat Clb; Capt Swmmng; Tmr; Natl Merit Ltr; College.

CONRAD, LISA R; Meadowbrook; Byesville, OH; Cls Rep Frsh Cls; Cls Rep Soph Cls; Hon Rl; Sch Pl; Stu Cncl; Y-Teens; Fr Clb; Chrldng; Ohio State Univ.

CONRAD, LOUIS; Lapeer East Sr HS; Lapeer, MI; Am Leg Boys St; NHS; Ftbl; Trk; Univ.

CONRAD, LYNN V; Liberty HS; Bristol, WV; Cls Rep Soph Cls; Cl Rep Jr Cls; Chrh Wkr; Hon Rl; Jr NHS; Sch Mus; Stu Cncl; Yth Flsp; Rptr Yrbk; Drama Clb; Univ; Optometry.

CONRAD, NANCY; Lake Michigan Catholic HS; Benton Hrbr, MI; Girl Scts; Hon Rl; Sci Clb; Spn Clb; Cit Awd; Bus Schl; Bus Admin.

CONRAD, RALPH; Sandy Valley HS; E Sparata, OH; 6/160 Band; Boy Scts; Chrs; Cmnty Wkr; Drm Bgl; Hon Rl; JA; Natl Forn Lg; NHS; Orch; St Qualifier In Forensics; Pres Of Natl Forensic League 79; Pres Of Chess Clb 78 79 & 80; Cornell Univ; Law.

CONRAD, ROBERT; Madison Comprehensive HS; Mansfield, OH; Val; Am Leg Boys St; Lbry Ade; Pres NHS; Stu Cncl; Ger Clb; Natl Merit SF; Univ Of Cin; Electrical Engr.

CONRAD, RON; Garrett HS; Garrett, IN; Boy Scts; Chrh Wkr; FCA; Hon Rl; Sct Actv; Yth Flsp; Pres Spn Clb; Ftbl; Trk; Wrstlng; College; Math.

CONRAD, RONALD; Garrett HS; Garrett, IN; Boy Scts; Chrh Wkr; Cmnty Wkr; FCA; Hon Rl; Yth Flsp; Pres Spn Clb; Bsbl; Letter Ftbl; Letter Trk; Univ.

CONRAD, SUE; Ellet HS; Akron, OH; 5/365 Chrs; Hon Rl; Jr NHS; Sec NHS; Off Ade; Ger Clb; Spn Clb; Kent St Univ.

CONRAD, TONY; Greenville Sr HS; Greenville, OH; Hon Rl; Sci Clb; Perfect Attendance Awrd; College; Math.

CONRADT, MARY J; Stephen T Badin HS; Hamilton, OH; 2/200 Hon Rl; VP 4-H; Spn Clb; Gym; Chrldng; 4-H Awd; 4 H Horse Reserve Grand Champ 1975; Univ; Bus.

CONRATH, CHRISTOPHER; Marietta HS; Marietta, OH; 22/407 Band; Boy Scts; Hon Rl; Jr NHS; NHS; Orch; Sct Actv; Yth Flsp; College; Med.

CONROY, BRIGID; Catholic Central HS; Spring Lake, MI; Chrh Wkr; Hon Rl; NHS; Yrbk; Spn Clb; Letter Swmmng; PPFtbl; Tmr; Univ.

CONROY, CRAIG; River Valley HS; Marion, OH; 11/210 Cl Rep Jr Cls; Cls Rep Sr Cls; Am Leg Boys St; FCA; JA; Jr NHS; NHS; Stu Cncl; Yth Flsp; Yrbk; Defiance Coll; Busns Admin.

CONROY, KAREN; Catholic Central HS; Steubenville, OH; Drl Tm; Hon Rl; NHS; Yrbk; Spn Clb; Doctor Of Mtrs Stu Citation 77; Florida Inst Of Tech; Env Tech.

CONROY, KATHY; Utica HS; Utica, MI; Band; Drl Tm; Hon Rl; NHS; Off Ade; Orch; Twrlr; Oakland Univ; Mech Engr.

CONROY, MICHAEL; Avon HS; Plainfield, IN; FCA; Letter Ftbl; Letter Trk; Scr Kpr; Tmr; Elk Awd; JC Awd; USJC Awd; Indiana Univ; Mrktng.

CONROY, RANDALL; Kimball HS; Royal Oak, MI; 189/604 Hon Rl; Letter Bsbl; IM Sprt; Central Mic; Env Engr.

CONROY, THOMAS; Aquinas HS; Allen Pk, MI; Boy Scts; Chrh Wkr; Hon Rl; Jr NHS; Sct Actv; Stg Crw; Yrbk; Swmmng; Univ; Chem Engr.

CONSER, JAN; R Nelson Snider HS; Ft Wayne, IN; 29/564 Band; Chrs; Hon Rl; Lbry Ade; Orch; Sch Mus; Univ; Music.

CONSIGLIO, DONNA; Bishop Gallagher HS; Detroit, MI; 85/356 Girl Scts; Hon Rl; Off Ade; Sch Pl; Ed Yrbk; Spn Clb; PPFtbl; Natl Merit Ltr; Michigan St Univ; Bio Sci.

CONSTAND, ELAINE; Chippewa Valley HS; Mt Clemens, MI; Sec Frsh Cls; Hst Jr Cls; Chrs; Chrh Wkr; Hon Rl; Mdrgl; Mod UN; NHS; Sch Mus; Stu Cncl; Univ Of Michigan; Busns Admin.

CONTINI, GEORGE; Dover HS; Dover, OH; Cls Rep Sr Cls; Am Leg Boys St; Aud/Vis; Pres Band; Chrs; Cmnty Wkr; Hon Rl; Natl Forn Lg; VP NHS; Off Ade; Baldwin Wallace Coll; Theatre.

CONTINO, MICHAEL S; Circleville HS; Circleville, OH; VP Sr Cls; Am Leg Boys St; Hon Rl; NHS; Stu Cncl; Rptr Yrbk; Lat Clb; Letter Ftbl; Letter Trk; Wrstlng; Eng Mert Soc 78; Latin Hon Soc 78; Univ.

CONTOS, CARYN; Central Catholic HS; Toledo, OH; Cls Rep Frsh Cls; Cmnty Wkr; Hon Rl; NHS; Quill & Scroll; Rptr Sch Nwsp; Sch Nwsp; Fr Clb; Pep Clb; Mat Maids; Univ Of Toledo; Tchr.

CONTRA, BENJAMIN; Malabar HS; Mansfield, OH; 70/250 Boy Scts; Chrh Wkr; Key Clb; Mth Clb; Bsktbl; College; Bus.

CONTRERA, LAURA; Valley Forge HS; Parma, OH; 23/777 Chrs; Girl Scts; Hon Rl; NHS; Lat Clb; Bsbl; Bsktbl; College; Marine Biologist.

CONTRERAS, KAREN; Holy Redeemer HS; Detroit, MI; Hon Rl; Spn Clb; Letter Bsbl; Letter Bsktbl; Letter Chrldng; College; Exec Sec.

CONTRERAZ, RAIMUNDO; Paulding HS; Paulding, OH; Chrh Wkr; Cmnty Wkr; Hon Rl; Lbry Ade; NHS; Off Ade; Yrbk; OEA; DAR Awd; Defiance Crescent News Carrier Of Yr 1978; Ohio Reg 6 OEA Reg Contest 2nd Pl Acct I 1979; Northurst Tech Coll; Acctg.

CONTROGUERRA, S; Steubenville Cath Ctrl HS; Steubenvll, OH; 40/204 Cls Rep Frsh Cls; Cls Rep Soph Cls; Cl Rep Jr Cls; Hon Rl; NHS; Sch Mus; Sch Pl; Stu Cncl; Yrbk; Drama Clb; Univ; Nursing.

CONVERY, YVES; Yale HS; Yale, MI; Hon Rl; Sci Clb; Crs Cntry; Trk; College; Elec Tech.

CONWAY, CATHERINE; Marian HS; Birmingham, MI; Girl Scts; Hon Rl; NHS; Stg Crw; Drama Clb; Chrldng; IM Sprt; Univ; Bus.

CONWAY, CHRIS; Ridgedale HS; Marion, OH; Hon Rl; Bsbl; Bsktbl; Ftbl; IM Sprt; Business School.

CONWAY, JOANNE; Bloomfield HS; Bloomfield, IN; Cls Rep Sr Cls; Boy Scts; FCA; Hon Rl; NHS; Orch; Yrbk; Drama Clb; Pep Clb; Sci Clb; Schlrshp To Purdue Academic Ldrshp Seminar 78; Schlrshp To ISU Summer Honors Seminar 79; Univ; Elem Educ.

CONWAY, KATHLEEN; Clarkston HS; Drayton Plns, MI; 28/360 Hon Rl; NHS; Bsbl; Bsktbl; Gym; Trk; Chrldng; Coll; Physical Therapy.

CONWAY, KEVIN; Lumen Christi HS; Jackson, MI; Cls Rep Frsh Cls; Stu Cncl; Letter Bsbl; Letter Bsktbl; Crs Cntry; Letter Ftbl; Coach Actv; Albion College; Acctg.

CONWAY, LAURA; Ernest W Seaholm HS; Birmingham, MI; 6/650 Chrs; Chrh Wkr; Hon Rl; Jr NHS; Lbry Ade; NHS; Stg Crw; Bausch & Lomb Awd; Natl Merit SF; College; Engr.

CONWAY, RUCHELLE; Struthers HS; Struthers, OH; Hon Rl; JA; Lbry Ade; Y-Teens; Drama Clb; FNA; FTA; Lat Clb; JA Awd; Univ; Law.

CONWELL, CARL; Southern Wells HS; Warren, IN; Hon Rl; NHS; Sch Pl; Stg Crw; Drama Clb; Univ; Math.

CONYERS, SINGLETON; St Ursula Academy; Cincinnati, OH; Chrs; Sch Pl; Stg Crw; Fr Clb; IM Sprt; Univ Of Cincinnati; Pre Med.

CONYNGHAM, PAM; Magnificat HS; North Olmsted, OH; NHS; Quill & Scroll; Sch Mus; Stg Crw; Rptr Yrbk; Ed Sch Nwsp; Drama Clb; IM Sprt; Medl For French III Excellnc 79; Intl Thespian Soc 79; 1st Pl French III Poetry Compostn 79; Univ; Cmnctns.

COOCH, THOMAS; Pittsford Area HS; No Adams, MI; Chrh Wkr; Hon Rl; NHS; Fr Clb; FFA; Ftbl; Trk; Cit Awd; 4-H Awd; Voc Schl.

COOGAN, LYNNE; Magnificat HS; Westlake, OH; Cls Rep Soph Cls; NHS; Red Cr Ade; Sch Pl; Drama Clb; Mth Clb; Gym; GAA; College; Nurse.

COOK, ALEXANDER; Wayne Memorial HS; Westland, MI; Wayne St Univ; Lib Arts.

COOK, BELINDA; Southridge HS; Huntingburg, IN; Cls Rep Frsh Cls; Cls Rep Soph Cls; Band; Drl Tm; FCA; Hon Rl; Stu Cncl; Rptr Yrbk; Spn Clb; Letter Swmmng; All Amer Shout It Out Cheerleader At Sr Bowl; Marched In Cotton Bowl Parade; Purdue Univ.

COOK, BETTY J; Brown City HS; Melvin, MI; Trs Sr Cls; Band; Chrs; Hon Rl; NHS; Stu Cncl; Yth Flsp; VP FHA; VP FTA; Letter Pom Pon; Ferris St Coll; Receptionist.

COOK, BILL; Lima Sr HS; Lima, OH; Hon Rl; Pres DECA; Ger Clb; Pep Clb;.

COOK, BRENDA; St Johns Public HS; De Witt, MI; Band; Chrh Wkr; Lbry Ade; Off Ade; Orch; Yth Flsp; Fr Clb; Spurgeon; Christian Educ.

COOK, CARI; Lake HS; Walbridge, OH; 3/150 Chrs; Girl Scts; Hon Rl; NHS; Sch Mus; Stu Cncl; Sch Nwsp; Letter Bsbl; Letter Bsktbl; Top Jr Girl In Eng 78; Top Chem Stdnt 78; Hon In Geom P Spanish II 77; Univ.

COOK, CARLENE; Midland HS; Midland, MI; Cls Rep Frsh Cls; Hon Rl; DECA; Ger Clb; 4-H Awd; Western Mic Univ; Bus.

COOK, CATHLEEN; Tecumseh HS; Tecumseh, MI; Cmp Fr Grls; Chrs; Chrh Wkr; Girl Scts; Hon Rl; Lit Mag; Sch Pl; Stg Crw; Yth Flsp; Hope College; Hist.

COOK, CHARLENE; Belleville HS; Belleville, MI; 7/499 Am Leg Aux Girls St; Band; Hon Rl; Hosp Ade; NHS; Sch Mus; Tmr; Kiwan Awd; Lion Awd; Natl Merit SF; Eastern Mich Univ; Elem Education.

COOK, CHRISTOPHER; St Joseph Catholic HS; Fremont, OH; Hon Rl; Sch Pl; 4-H; IM Sprt; 4-H Awd; College; Biological Science.

COOK, DAVID; Mullens HS; Mullens, WV; 6/87 Cls Rep Frsh Cls; Cls Rep Soph Cls; Cl Rep Jr Cls; Hon Rl; Jr NHS; NHS; Stu Cncl; Beta Clb; Bsktbl; Letter Ftbl; Hon Guard 79; St Track Meet 79; Vc Pres Of Conservtn Club; West Virginia Inst Of Tech; Chem Eng.

COOK, DAVID; Little Miami HS; Blanchester, OH; Cls Rep Soph Cls; Cl Rep Jr Cls; Band; Boy Scts; Drm Mjrt; Hon Rl; Orch; ROTC; Sct Actv; 4-H;.

COOK, DEBORAH; Lumen Cordium HS; Cleveland, OH; Chrs; Drl Tm; Hon Rl; JA; Sch Nwsp; JA Awd; Univ Of Ala; Communications.

COOK, DEBRA; Western Reserve HS; Berlin Center, OH; Cl Rep Jr Cls; Cls Rep Sr Cls; Band; Chrs; Hon Rl; NHS; Stu Cncl; Pres 4-H; Treas OEA; 4-H Awd;.

COOK, DONNA; East HS; Cleveland, OH; 6/250 VP Sr Cls; Hon Rl; NHS; Quill & Scroll; Rptr Yrbk; Ed Sch Nwsp; Swmmng; Trk; Chrldng; IM Sprt; Univ Of Cincinnati.

COOK, ED; North Vigo HS; Terre Haute, IN; 1/614 Val; Band; Hon Rl; Letter Crs Cntry; Trk; Natl Merit SF; Rose Hulman Inst Of Tech; Engr.

COOK, ELIZABETH; Marietta HS; Marietta, OH; AFS; Hon Rl; Off Ade; Sch Pl; Rptr Sch Nwsp; Ger Clb; Spn Clb; Mat Maids; Scr Kpr; College; Bio Sci.

COOK, ELLEN T; Broad Ripple HS; Indianapolis, IN; 56/355 Chrh Wkr; Hon Rl; Univ; Vet.

COOK, ERIC; Allen Park HS; Allen Park, MI; Band; Hon Rl; Sct Actv; Ftbl; Glf; Trk; Wrstlng; Michigan St Univ; Chem Engr.

COOK, FLEMING; Cass Technical HS; Detroit, MI; Chrs; Chrh Wkr; Hon Rl; Yth Flsp; IM Sprt; Scr Kpr; St Of Mi Schlrshp Awd 79; Eastern Michigan Univ; Bus Admin.

COOK, JAMES; Northrop HS; Ft Wayne, IN; 177/35 Chrs; Sch Mus; Sch Pl; Letter Ten; Flo State; Bus.

COOK, JANET; South Newton Jr Sr HS; Brook, IN; 8/118 Chrh Wkr; Girl Scts; Hon Rl; Red Cr Ade; Sct Actv; Yth Flsp; Lat Clb; Swmmng; Natl Merit Ltr; Ball St Univ; Comp Sci.

COOK, JEFF; Centerville Sr HS; Centerville, IN; 27/156 Cl Rep Jr Cls; Band; Boy Scts; Debate Tm; FCA; Hon Rl; Sch Mus; Stu Cncl; Yth Flsp; Yrbk; Univ; Computer Sci.

COOK, JO ANNE; Parchment HS; Kalamazoo, MI; 15/164 Boy Scts; Girl Scts; Hon Rl; JA; NHS; 4-H; JA Awd; Adrian Coll; Bus.

COOK, JOSEPH; Ubly Community HS; Ruth, MI; Cls Rep Frsh Cls; Band; Hon Rl; Natl Forn Lg; NHS; Sch Pl; IM Sprt; Central Michigan Univ; Pre Law.

COOK, JUDITH; Rossford HS; Toledo, OH; 6/150 Sec Frsh Cls; Trs Sr Cls; Band; Hon Rl; Sec NHS; Orch; Sch Pl; Stu Cncl; Yrbk; Drama Clb; Univ Of Michigan.

COOK, JULIE; Barberton HS; Barberton, OH; Hon Rl; Ger Clb; Graceland Coll; Foreign Lang.

COOK, KELLY; Waldron Area HS; Waldron, MI; 8/39 Cls Rep Sr Cls; Pres Band; Chrh Wkr; Hon Rl; NHS; Sch Pl; Stu Cncl; VP FHA; VP Spn Clb; Mgrs; Huntington Coll; English Ed.

COOK, KELLY; Crooksville HS; Crooksville, OH; Band; Drl Tm; 4-H; Pep Clb; Spn Clb; Chrldng; College.

COOK, KEVIN; Terre Haute South HS; Terre Haute, IN; Hon Rl; Spn Clb; Letter Bsbl; Evansville; Broadcasting.

COOK, LEANNE; Penn HS; Granger, IN; 4/486 Hon Rl; NHS; Off Ade; Spn Clb; PPFtbl; Scr Kpr; Purdue Univ; Chem Engr.

COOK, LEISA; Vandalia Butler Sr HS; Vandalia, OH; Chrs; Hon Rl; NHS; PAVAS; Sch Pl; Rptr Sch Nwsp; Lat Clb; Pep Clb; IM Sprt; Hnr For Citizenship 78; Kent St Univ Hnrs Schl 79; Pres Of Latin Club 78 79; Wittenberg Univ; Dent.

COOK, MARIA; West HS; Garden City, MI; Hon Rl; Ger Clb; Letter Trk; Albion College; Archaeology.

COOK, MARIA; Chippewa HS; Doylestown, OH; Cls Rep Frsh Cls; Pres Soph Cls; Pres Jr Cls; Cl Rep Jr Cls; Cls Rep Sr Cls; Girl Scts; Hon Rl; Pres NHS; Sch Pl; Drama Clb; Akron Univ; Bio.

COOK, MARK; Columbian HS; Tiffin, OH; VP Frsh Cls; Band; Boy Scts; Drm Bgl; Hon Rl; JA; Sct Actv; Stu Cncl; Trk; Wrstlng; Ohio St Univ; Music.

COOK, MARK A; Walter E Stebbins HS; Dayton, OH; 45/434 Aud/Vis; Band; Hon Rl; MMM; Sch Mus; Rptr Sch Nwsp; Ftbl; Trk; NCTE; Ohio State Univ.

COOK, MATTHEW A; Madison Comp HS; Mansfield, OH; Band; Chrs; Chrh Wkr; Mdrgl; Orch; Pep Clb; Spn Clb; Ohio State Univ; Audio Engr.

COOK, MAUREEN; Pewamo Westphalia HS; Lyons, MI; 5/117 Cls Rep Soph Cls; Cls Rep Sr Cls; Hon Rl; NHS; Stg Crw; Ed Sch Nwsp; 4-H; Letter Bsbl; Letter Bsktbl; Western Michigan Univ; Bus Admin.

COOK, PAM; Spencer HS; Spencer, WV; 37/138 Chrh Wkr; Cmnty Wkr; Girl Scts; Hon Rl; Lbry Ade; Rptr Sch Nwsp; 4-H; Trk; IM Sprt; 4-H Awd;.

COOK, PATRICIA O; Cass Tech HS; Detroit, MI; Cmnty Wkr; Hosp Ade; Red Cr Ade; Yrbk; Sec Civ Clb; Natl Merit Ltr; Recognition In Michigan Comp Schlshp Prog 1978; Michigan St Univ; Pediatrician.

COOK, RANDY; Norwood HS; Norwood, OH; Boy Scts; Chrh Wkr; Hon Rl; Sct Actv; Yth Flsp; Boys Clb Am; Bsbl; Ftbl; Wrstlng; Univ Of Cincinnati; Acctg.

COOK, RAYMOND; Napoleon HS; Jackson, MI; Yrbk; Letter Trk; Univ; Archt.

COOK, REBECCA L; Solon HS; Solon, OH; Hon Rl; Hosp Ade; NHS; Fr Clb; Pep Clb; Capt Ten; Trk; PPFtbl; Natl Merit Ltr; Univ; Bio Sci.

COOK, RICK; De Kalb HS; Ashley, IN; 51/287 Cl Rep Jr Cls; Chrs; Chrh Wkr; Natl Forn Lg; NHS; Pol Wkr; Sch Mus; Sch Pl; Stg Crw; VP Stu Cncl; Ball St Univ; Theatre.

COOK, ROBERT G; Floyd Central HS; Georgetown, IN; 1/342 Cl Rep Jr Cls; Trs Sr Cls; Cls Rep Sr Cls; Val; Am Leg Boys St; Band; Chrs; Chrh Wkr; Cmnty Wkr; Pres Debate Tm; Purdue Univ; Engr.

COOK, ROBYN; Ridgedale HS; Marion, OH; 10/75 Pres Soph Cls; FCA; Hon Rl; Sch Nwsp; Leo Clb; Bsbl; Bsktbl; Trk; DAR Awd; Ohio Northern Univ; Bus Mgmt.

COOK, RODNEY A; Ravenna HS; Ravenna, OH; AFS; Aud/Vis; Band; Boy Scts; Chrs; Chrh Wkr; Cmnty Wkr; Hon Rl; Red Cr Ade; Sch Mus; Mbr Of Boys Od Of Arrow 76; Eagle 79; Ohio St Univ; Engr.

COOK, S; Beal City Public HS; Mt Pleasant, MI; 4/70 Chrh Wkr; Hon Rl; Off Ade; Rptr Sch Nwsp; Sci Clb; Mgrs; Central Michigan Univ; Bio.

COOK, STACIA; Southmont HS; Crawfordsville, IN; Chrs; Hon Rl; Stg Crw; Rptr Sch Nwsp; Drama Clb; 4-H; FHA; Ger Clb; Bus Schl; Acctg.

COOK, SUSAN; Ludington HS; Ludington, MI; 5/250 Cls Rep Sr Cls; Sec Band; Chrh Wkr; Hon Rl; Pres NHS; Stu Cncl; Yth Flsp; John Brown Univ; Elem Educ.

COOK, SUSAN; Aiken Sr HS; Cincinnati, OH; 2/400 Sec Band; Hon Rl; Jr NHS; Spn Clb; Miami Univ; Math.

COOK, TAMARA; John Glenn HS; Westland, MI; Debate Tm; Jr NHS; Telluride Assoc Summer Progr At Cornell Univ 79; Univ; Eng.

COOK, THOMAS; Athens HS; Princeton, WV; Cls Rep Frsh Cls; Pres Soph Cls; VP Jr Cls; Hon Rl; NHS; Stu Cncl; FTA; Letter Bsktbl; Trk; Univ.

COOK, TIM; Pike Central HS; Winslow, IN; Hon Rl; NHS; VP Yth Flsp; Letter Bsbl; Bsktbl; Letter Ftbl; Trk; Wrstlng; Natl Hnr Soc 1978; Varsity Reserve Mst Vlbl 1976; Football Var Mst Prmsng 1977; Univ; Comp Tech.

COOK, VINCE; Garfield HS; Akron, OH; 74/443 Hon Rl; Off Ade; Fr Clb; College; Forestry.

COOK, YVONNE; North Adams HS; North Adams, MI; Sec Soph Cls; Sec Jr Cls; Hosp Ade; Sch Pl; Drama Clb; FDA; FTA; Chrldng; GAA; Central Mic Univ; Child Psych.

COOKE, ALANE; Andrean HS; Gary, IN; Sec Jr Cls; VP Sr Cls; Hon Rl; JA; Stu Cncl; Pep Clb; IM Sprt; Pom Pon; Purdue Univ; Acctg.

COOKE, DAVID W P; Maumee HS; Maumee, OH; Hon Rl; Lit Mag; Crs Cntry; Socr; Wrstlng; IM Sprt; Bates Coll; Law.

COOKE, JUDITH; Brecksville Sr HS; Broadview Hts, OH; 7/369 Hon Rl; NHS; Quill & Scroll; Ed Yrbk; Pres Beta Clb; Ger Clb; Cit Awd; Univ Of Akron; Fine Arts.

COOKE, PHILLIP; Pineville HS; Pineville, WV; 14/97 Cl Rep Jr Cls; Cls Rep Sr Cls; Boy Scts; Hon Rl; Jr NHS; NHS; Stu Cncl; Spt Ed Sch Nwsp; 4-H; Pep Clb; Bsktbll All Trnmnt All Cnty 78; Bsktbll All St Hon Mention 79; Concord Coll; Acctg.

COOKSEY, NEIL C; Boardman HS; Youngstown, OH; 103/592 Cls Rep Frsh Cls; VP Soph Cls; Cls Rep Soph Cls; Pres Jr Cls; Pres Sr Cls; FCA; Yth Flsp; Lat Clb; Letter Ftbl; Natl Merit SF; Univ.

COOKSEY, TIA J; Hubbard HS; Hubbard, OH; 21/350 Band; Cmp Fr Grls; Hon Rl; Yrbk; Fr Clb; Coach Actv; Scr Kpr; Kent Tms Algebra; Ohio St Univ; Health.

COOLEY, ANNE M; Mason Sr HS; Mason, MI; Chrs; Chrh Wkr; Girl Scts; Hon Rl; Jr NHS; Sch Mus; Stu Cncl; Rptr Yrbk; VP 4-H; Sci Clb; Voc; Floriculture.

COOLEY, CHRIS; Hastings HS; Hastings, MI; Cls Rep Frsh Cls; Cls Rep Soph Cls; Cl Rep Jr Cls; Chrs; Hon Rl; Sch Mus; Stu Cncl; Fr Clb; Key Clb; Pep Clb; Ferris St Univ; Pharm.

COOLEY, GARY; North Union HS; Richwood, OH; Chrs; Hon Rl; FFA; Pres Awd;.

COOLEY, JENNIFER; Tri Valley HS; Frazeysburg, OH; 4/215 Am Leg Aux Girls St; Hon Rl; Lbry Ade; NHS; Yrbk; FHA; Sec Spn Clb; Ohio Univ; Nursing.

COOLEY, KAREN; Lamphere HS; Madison Hts, MI; 35/330 Chrs; Chrh Wkr; Girl Scts; Hon Rl; NHS; Off Ade; Chrldng; PPFtbl; Miami Univ Of Ohio; Marketing.

COOLEY, LYNN; Oregon Davis HS; Hamlet, IN; Cl Rep Jr Cls; Hon Rl; NHS; Sch Pl; Stg Crw; Stu Cncl; Drama Clb; 4-H; Pep Clb; Bio.

COOLEY, SUE; Borden HS; Borden, IN; 9/73 Hon Rl; FFA; FHA;.

COOLEY, SUSAN; Mason Sr HS; Mason, MI; Chrs; Chrh Wkr; Hon Rl; Mdrgl; Sch Mus; Sch Pl; 4-H; Univ.

COOLEY, YOLANDA; Mumford HS; Detroit, MI; Boy Scts; Chrh Wkr; NHS; FTA; OEA; Rus Clb; Sci Clb; Cit Awd; Mary Grove Coll; Acctg.

COOLIDGE, CATHERINE R; Highland HS; Anderson, IN; 1/400 Band; NHS; Sch Pl; Yth Flsp; Drama Clb; Pres Lat Clb; DAR Awd; Natl Merit SF; Purdue Univ; Chem Engr.

COOMBS, LORI; South Dearborn HS; Aurora, IN; 3/580 Chrs; Chrh Wkr; Girl Scts; Sct Actv; Drama Clb; Pep Clb; Ten; IM Sprt; PPFtbl; College; Elem Teaching.

COOMES, JAY; Central HS; Evansville, IN; Cls Rep Sr Cls; Boy Scts; Cmnty Wkr; Natl Forn Lg; NHS; NCTE; Voice Dem Awd; Oral Roberts Univ; Med.

COON, BARBARA; Jackson County Western HS; Jackson, MI; 5/172 Cls Rep Sr Cls; Hon Rl; NHS; Stu Cncl; Spn Clb; Bsktbl; Glf; DAR Awd; Hope Coll; Chem.

COON, CHRISTINA L; Westland HS; Columbus, OH; 31/496 VP Jr Cls; Trs Sr Cls; Cmp Fr Grls; Hon Rl; Stu Cncl; OEA; GAA; Mat Maids; Scr Kpr; Most Likely To Succeed; Most Outstanding Jr Steno Stdnt 1977; 6th Pl Regional OEA Shorthand Contest 1978; Bowling Green Univ; Law.

COON, DANIEL; Fowlerville HS; Fowlerville, MI; 8/170 Band; Hon Rl; Jr NHS; NHS; Sch Pl; Stg Crw; Letter Ftbl; Trk; Capt Wrstlng; PPFtbl; Alma College; Tchr.

COON, DEBBIE; Owosso HS; Owosso, MI; 1/406 Hon Rl; JA; NHS; Yth Flsp; Lat Clb; DAR Awd; JA Awd; Natl Merit SF; Voice Dem Awd; Central Mich Univ; Marketing.

COON, JEFFREY; Taylor HS; Kokomo, IN; Chrs; Hon Rl; NHS; Spn Clb; Lion Awd; Ind Univ; Music Ed.

COON, KATHY; Allen East HS; Lima, OH; 1/107 VP Jr Cls; Chrs; Chrh Wkr; Hon Rl; NHS; Sch Pl; Fr Clb; College; Nursing.

COON, KENNETH; Glen Este HS; Batavia, OH; Hon Rl; Stg Crw; Univ; Art.

COON, PAMELA; Fowlerville HS; Fowlerville, MI; Trs Sr Cls; VP Band; Drm Mjrt; Hon Rl; Jr NHS; Stu Cncl; Rptr Sch Nwsp; 4-H; Trk; Chrldng; Univ; Nursing.

COON, ROBIN; Hart HS; Hart, MI; 8/143 Trs Frsh Cls; Pres Jr Cls; Am Leg Aux Girls St; Chrh Wkr; Hon Rl; Hosp Ade; Natl Forn Lg; VP NHS; Sch Pl; Ed Sch Nwsp; Univ Of Miami; Drama.

COON, WILLIAM; Loudonville HS; Loudonville, OH; Hon Rl; ROTC; Sch Pl; Rptr Sch Nwsp; Lat Clb; Bsbl; Bsktbl; College; Oceanography.

COONE, SANDRA; Benton Harbor HS; Coloma, MI; Band; Hon Rl; JA; NHS; Univ; Vet.

COONEY, HUGH; Kalamazoo Central HS; Kalamazoo, MI; Pres Sr Cls; Cmnty Wkr; Sprt Ed Yrbk; Letter Ftbl; Letter Trk; Kalamazoo Coll; Physics.

COONEY, KENDA; West Carrollton Sr HS; W Carrollton, OH; 22/330 Chrh Wkr; Drl Tm; Hon Rl; JA; Jr NHS; NHS; Sch Pl; Drama Clb; Mat Maids; JA Awd; Sinclair Cmnty Coll; Exec Sec.

COONEY, MICHAEL; Kalamazoo Central HS; Kalamazoo, MI; Letter Glf; Letter Hockey; Natl Merit SF; Kalamazoo Coll; Physics.

COONEY, PEGGY; St Peters HS; Mansfield, OH; Chrh Wkr; Hosp Ade; Hosp Ade; VP NHS; Sch Pl; Stu Cncl; Yrbk; Letter Bsbl; Coach Actv; IM Sprt; College; Pre Med.

COONS, ELIZABETH I; Versailles HS; Bradford, OH; Hon Rl; NHS; Stu Cncl; Fr Clb; Crs Cntry; Trk; Univ; Med.

COOPER, ANITA; Spencer HS; Spencer, WV; Cls Rep Frsh Cls; Cl Rep Jr Cls; Chrh Wkr; Hon Rl; Lbry Ade; Sch Pl; Stu Cncl; Sprt Ed Sch Nwsp; Drama Clb; IM Sprt; Marshall Univ; Journalism.

COOPER, AUSTIN; Lutheran HS East; Cleveland Hts, OH; VP Jr Cls; Chrh Wkr; Cmnty Wkr; Orch; Sch Mus; Stg Crw; Stu Cncl; Yth Flsp; Sprt Ed Sch Nwsp; Wrote Article For HS Newspaper & Was Published In Plain Dealer 78; Recvd A Music Camp Schlrshp To U Of Ks; Morehouse Coll; Pre Law.

COOPER, BETH; Rockville HS; Rockville, IN; 12/94 Chrs; Chrh Wkr; Cmnty Wkr; FCA; Hon Rl; Off Ade; Yth Flsp; Pep Clb; Spn Clb; Chrldng; College; Elem Educ.

COOPER, BILL; Chillicothe HS; Chillicothe, OH; Aud/Vis; Chrh Wkr; Hon Rl; NHS; Sct Actv; Pres Yth Flsp; Lat Clb; Trk; Wrstlng; Scr Kpr; Awd Of Partcptn In Vacation Bible Schl 74; Ohio St Univ; Pre Med.

COOPER, BRADLEY; Broad Ripple HS; Indianapolis, IN; Pres Frsh Cls; Cls Rep Soph Cls; Cl Rep Jr Cls; Chrs; Hon Rl; NHS; Sch Mus; Drama Clb; Letter Ten; IM Sprt; Ind Univ.

COOPER, CAROLYN; Lynchburg Clay HS; Lynchburg, OH; Hon Rl; NHS; Voice Dem Awd; Bus Schl; Sec.

COOPER, CONNIE; St Johns HS; St Johns, MI; Chrh Wkr; Hosp Ade; Off Ade; Yth Flsp; Fr Clb; 4-H Awd; Olivet Nazarene; Nurse.

COOPER, DEBORAH; Washington HS; Albuquerque, NM; Cls Rep Frsh Cls; Cls Rep Soph Cls; Hst Jr Cls; Am Leg Aux Girls St; Debate Tm; Girl Scts; Hon Rl; Chrldng; Univ Of Albuquerque; Pol Science.

COOPER, ELECCA; Harman HS; Harman, WV; Pres Jr Cls; Band; Chrs; Chrh Wkr; Hon Rl; Pres Yth Flsp; Pres FBLA; Bsbl; Bsktbl; Band Awd Best Drummer; Sunday Schl Teaching Awd; Perfect Attendance Awds; Vocational Schl.

COOPER, ELIZABETH; Southeast HS; Atwater, OH; 24/175 Band; Chrs; Treas MMM; Stu Cncl; Rptr Sch Nwsp; Pres Pep Clb; American Legion Americanism Test Awd; Outstndng Ser Awd Rainbow Girls; College; Communications.

COOPER, ELIZABETH; South Haven HS; S Haven, MI; Band; Cmnty Wkr; Girl Scts; Hon Rl; NHS; Stg Crw; Yth Flsp; Pep Clb; Natl Merit Ltr; College; Chem.

COOPER, ELIZABETH; Valley Forge HS; Parma Heights, OH; 21/704 Chrs; Girl Scts; Hon Rl; Jr NHS; Lbry Ade; Treas NHS; Off Ade; Yth Flsp; Pep Clb; Spn Clb; Grove City Coll; Busns Admin.

COOPER, GAIL; Mendon HS; Three Rivers, MI; Chrh Wkr; Cmnty Wkr; FCA; Hon Rl; Yth Flsp; Chrldng; Parsons Bus Schl; Sec.

COOPER, JACQUELYN; Southwestern HS; Detroit, MI; Cmp Fr Grls; Chrs; Chrh Wkr; Hon Rl; JA; Off Ade; Stu Cncl; Sch Nwsp; Sci Clb; Cit Awd; College; Occupational Therapy.

COOPER, JEFFREY L; Wauseon HS; Ostrander, OH; Band; Chrs; Chrh Wkr; Debate Tm; Hon Rl; Lbry Ade; Yth Flsp; Fr Clb; Sci Clb; Letter Swmmng; I Was Alternate To The Inter Natl Sci & Engr Fair 79; Navy Sci Awd 79; Univ; Comp Sci.

COOPER, KATHY; Jackson HS; Jackson, OH; 22/250 Sec Frsh Cls; Hst Jr Cls; Band; Hon Rl; Lbry Ade; Off Ade; VP Stu Cncl; Lat Clb; OEA; Pep Clb; Bus Schl; Exec Sec.

COOPER, KEITH; New Albany HS; New Albany, OH; Cls Rep Sr Cls; Band; Boy Scts; Hon Rl; Stu Cncl; Letter Crs Cntry; Ftbl; Trk; Wrstlng; Ohi State.

COOPER, KELLY; Reynoldsburg HS; Reynoldsburg, OH; Cmnty Wkr; Girl Scts; Hon Rl; Sct Actv; Bsktbl; IM Sprt; PPFtbl; Scr Kpr; God Cntry Awd; Var Sftbl Var Letter 78; 1st Yr Reserve Vllybl Reserve Letter 78; Knights Of Colubus Freethrow Contest Won; Ohio St Univ; Educ Tchr.

COOPER, KEVIN; Elkins HS; Elkins, WV; Cls Rep Frsh Cls; Hon Rl; JA; Stu Cncl; Bsbl; Bsktbl; IM Sprt; JA Awd; Pres Awd; West Virginia Inst Of Tech; Draft.

COOPER, KEVIN; New Albany HS; New Albany, OH; 9/95 Trs Soph Cls; VP Jr Cls; Cls Rep Sr Cls; Am Leg Boys St; Hon Rl; NHS; Yrbk; Sci Clb; Ftbl; Swmmng; Ohio State Univ; Comp Sci.

COOPER, KIEL D; Port Huron Northern HS; Warren, MI; Cl Rep Jr Cls; Band; Boy Scts; Chrh Wkr; Pol Wkr; Sct Actv; Stu Cncl; Yth Flsp; Opt Clb Awd; Coll; Broadcasting.

COOPER, KRISTEN; Morgantown HS; Morgantwn, WV; Cls Rep Soph Cls; Cl Rep Jr Cls; Hon Rl; Spn Clb; W Va; Agriculture.

COOPER, LORI; Cass Technical HS; Detroit, MI; Cmp Fr Grls; Chrh Wkr; Civ Clb; JETS Awd; Lawrence Inst Of Tech; Mech Engr.

COOPER, MARGARET; Edison Sr HS; Lk Station, IN; 11/17 Sec Frsh Cls; Sec Soph Cls; Sec Jr Cls; VP Sr Cls; Am Leg Aux Girls St; Aud/Vis; Hon Rl; NHS; Stu Cncl; VP Pep Clb; Univ; Pre Law.

COOPER, MARY J; Madison HS; Madison, OH; Cls Rep Sr Cls; Chrs; Hon Rl; Off Ade; Stu Cncl; Pep Clb; Bsbl; Bsktbl; Natl Merit Ltr; NEC Lpitcher Hnrbl Mention 79; Lakeland Cmnty Coll; Interior Dsgn.

COOPER, MELISSA; Cadillac HS; Cadillac, MI; 42/302 Sec Chrs; Hon Rl; NHS; Off Ade; Sch Mus; Chrldng; Scr Kpr; Ferris State College; Pre Sci.

COOPER, PATRICIA; Ursuline Academy; Cincinnati, OH; 4/106 Chrs; Rptr Sch Nwsp; Natl Merit Ltr; Univ.

COOPER, RENELL; Murray Wright HS; Detroit, MI; Hst Sr Cls; Hon Rl; NHS; Stu Cncl; Pres Pep Clb; Cit Awd; Wayne State Univ; Liberal Arts.

COOPER, RICKY; Tippecanoe Valley HS; Rochester, IN; Hon Rl; Bsbl; IM Sprt; Pres Awd; Most Stolen Bases On Bsbl Tm 79; Rookie Of Yr Bsbl Tm 78; All Confrnc Hon Mention 79; Grace Coll; History.

COOPER, RICKY; Atherton HS; Burton, MI; 22/150 Hon Rl; Ten; College; Comp Progr.

COOPER, ROBIN; Cardington Lincoln HS; Cardington, OH; Pres Soph Cls; Pres Jr Cls; Hon Rl; Stu Cncl; Rptr Sch Nwsp; 4-H; FFA; Letter Ftbl; 4-H Awd; Cert From Wmns Auxiliary Of Amer Institute Of Mining Metallurgical & Petroleum Engrs; College; Agri Journalism.

COOPER, SHARON; Maysville HS; S Zanesville, OH; Chrh Wkr; FCA; Hon Rl; NHS; Yth Flsp; 4-H; FTA; Letter Trk; 4-H Awd; Wooster Ag Tech; Horticulture.

COOPER, SUSAN; Maysville HS; Zanesville, OH; Band; FCA; Hon Rl; 4-H; FTA; Bsktbl; Trk; 4-H Awd; Univ.

COOPER, TARI; Taft Sr HS; Hamilton, OH; 2/400 Cls Rep Soph Cls; Cl Rep Jr Cls; Band; Chrs; Drl Tm; Hon Rl; Jr NHS; NHS; Sch Mus; Stu Cncl; Valedictorian Of Wilson Jr HS 77; Hon Mention In Oh Schlstc Achvmnt Test Eng 9 77; Miami Univ; Math.

COOPER, TERRI; Eminence HS; Paragon, IN; Hon Rl; FHA; Pep Clb; Chrldng; Am Leg Awd; College; Lpn.

COOPER, TERRY; Monrovia HS; Mooresville, IN; VP Sr Cls; Band; FCA; Sch Pl; Stu Cncl; 4-H; Spn Clb; Letter Bsktbl; Letter Crs Cntry; Capt Trk; Louis Armstrong Jazz Awd 79; Trophy Bst Free Throw Pct Jr Var Bsktbl 7;8 Trophy Cross Cntry Mst Imprvd 77; Music.

COOPER, TRACY; Tippecanoe HS; Tipp City, OH; Sec Jr Cls; Band; Drm Bgl; Hon Rl; Hosp Ade; NHS; Off Ade; Rptr Yrbk; 4-H; Twrlr; Have Been Fresh & Jr Homecoming Attendant; Twirling Trophys & Medals; College; Med Tech.

COOPER, TRIS T; Eastern HS; Winchester, OH; Pres Frsh Cls; Hon Rl; Sch Pl; Pres Stu Cncl; 4-H; Fr Clb; Sec FFA; FTA; Bsbl; Bsktbl; Fern Baird Schlrshp Wilmington Coll78; Schlrshp Team 11th Eng; Wilmington Coll; Agri.

COOPER, WILLIAM L; West Muskingum HS; Zanesville, OH; Chrs; Chrh Wkr; Hon Rl; Sch Mus; 4-H; FFA; Mgrs; 4-H Awd; Ohio St Univ; Ag.

COOPER, WILLIAM M; New Albany HS; Westerville, OH; 19/100 Cls Rep Sr Cls; Hon Rl; Stu Cncl; Sci Clb; Ohio St Univ; Forest Bio.

COOPER, WYNN; Crestview HS; Columbiana, OH; Hon Rl; Glf; College.

COOPER, YVONNE COOPE; Woodrow Wilson HS; Beckley, WV; Hon Rl; Stu Cncl; Yrbk; Lat Clb; Pep Clb; Chrldng; Univ; Pre Dental.

COORS, MARY; Mc Auley HS; Cinti, OH; 17/252 Cmp Fr Grls; Hon Rl; JA; Sch Pl; Stg Crw; Pep Clb; Spn Clb; Bsbl; Coach Actv; GAA; Univ Of Cincinnati; Med Sec.

COOTS, CAROL; Midland Trail HS; Lookout, WV; Hon Rl; Mgrs; Univ; Nursing.

COPAS, CHRISTINA; Wehrle HS; Columbus, OH; Band; Chrh Wkr; FCA; Hon Rl; Jr NHS; Red Cr Ade; Rptr Yrbk; Chrldng; Letter GAA; Mgrs; Ohio St Univ; Med Tech.

COPAS, JERRY; New Abany HS; New Albany, IN;

COPAT, MARCELO; Mooresville HS; Mooresville, IN; Boy Scts; Hon Rl; Sct Actv; Drama Clb; Sci Clb; Spn Clb; Trk; Wrstlng; IUPUI.

COPE, BARRY; Heritage Christian HS; Indianapolis, IN; Am Leg Boys St; Hon Rl; Quill & Scroll; Sch Pl; Stg Crw; Ed Sch Nwsp; Mgrs; College; Journalism.

COPE, DIANE; Preble Shawnee HS; Camden, OH; Chrh Wkr; Cmnty Wkr; Debate Tm; Girl Scts; Hon Rl; Sch Pl; Yth Flsp; Drama Clb; Fr Clb; Pres FHA; Rep Youth Leadership 1979; Creative Writing Club 1978; 1st Pl FHA Hero St Ralley Speech 1979; Dayton Univ; Poli Law.

COPE, LISANN; Toronto HS; Toronto, OH; 18/119 Cmnty Wkr; Hon Rl; Stg Crw; Rio Grande College; Med Lab.

COPELAND, BARBARA; Lakeland HS; Milford, MI; Am Leg Aux Girls St; Hosp Ade; NHS; Stu Cncl; Rptr Yrbk; Sch Nwsp; Sec Ger Clb; Pep Clb; Univ; Pre Med.

COPELAND, DEBRA; Wapakoneta HS; Wapakoneta, OH; Cl Rep Jr Cls; Band; Chrh Wkr; Cmnty Wkr; Girl Scts; Hon Rl; Off Ade; Red Cr Ade; 4-H; Lat Clb; Ohio Northern Univ; Sci.

COPELAND, JOYCE; Avon HS; Plainfield, IN; 1/186 Val; Band; Hon Rl; NHS; Sprt Ed Sch Nwsp; Fr Clb; Letter Bsktbl; Letter Ten; Ball State; Bus.

COPELAND, MICHAEL J; Perry HS; Canton, OH; Sprt Ed Yrbk; Rptr Yrbk; Key Clb; Letter Swmmng; Ashland Coll; Food Serv.

COPELAND, ROBERTA; Henry Ford HS; Detroit, MI; 99/432 Chrh Wkr; CAP; Girl Scts; Hon Rl; JA; Pres Yth Flsp; Glf; Swmmng; Univ; Forestry.

COPELAND, VINCE; Avon HS; Plainfield, IN; 23/158 Hon Rl; 4-H; Spn Clb; Ftbl; Trk; Letter Wrstlng; College; Engineering.

COPELYN, TANZETTA; Kearsley HS; Flint, MI; Cls Rep Frsh Cls; Band; Cmp Fr Grls; Girl Scts; Hon Rl; Jr NHS; NHS; Univ Of Mic; Psych.

COPHER, ELIZABETH; Pike HS; Indianapolis, IN; 36/303 Band; Drm Mjrt; FCA; Girl Scts; Hon Rl; Jr NHS; Pol Wkr; Quill & Scroll; Sct Actv; Yth Flsp; Ind Univ; Journalism.

COPLEN, MICHAEL; Tippecanoe Valley HS; Akron, IN; Hon Rl; NHS; Spn Clb; Bsbl; Letter Bsktbl; Ten;.

COPLEY, GREGORY; Williamson HS; Chattaroy, WV; Hon Rl; NHS; Stu Cncl; Sch Nwsp; 4-H; JA Awd; S W Vir Community College; Bus.

COPLIN, MARK L; Olivet HS; Charlotte, MI; Band; Chrh Wkr; FCA; Hon Rl; Sch Mus; Sch Pl; Sct Actv; Drama Clb; 4-H; Letter Bsktbl; LCC; Law Enforcement.

COPNEY, P; Finney HS; Detroit, MI; Girl Scts; Hon Rl; Off Ade; Yrbk; Wayne St Univ; Phys Ed.

COPNEY, PRISCILLA; Finney HS; Detroit, MI; Girl Scts; Hon Rl; Hosp Ade; JA; Off Ade; Sch Mus; Wayne State Univ; Phy Ed.

COPPERNOLL, RICHARD; Peru Sr HS; Peru, IN; 4/278 Am Leg Boys St; Boy Scts; Cmnty Wkr; Hon Rl; NHS; Fr Clb; Coach Actv; Elk Awd; Kiwan Awd; Whos Who In Foreign Lang 77 79; Purdue Univ; Bio Sci.

COPPOCK, TAMMY; Pickaway Ross Joint Voc Schl; Waverly, OH; Cls Rep Frsh Cls; Cls Rep Soph Cls; Chrh Wkr; Hon Rl; Stu Cncl; 4-H; OEA; Pep Clb; Bsktbl; Letter Trk; Soph Attnd Miss Huntington Ct 1977; Cheerleader 3 Yrs; High Jump Sectionl & Dist Winner 1978; Vlybl Letter;.

CORACE, GILDA; Lutheran HS E; Mt Clemens, MI; Chrs; Chrh Wkr; Hon Rl; Sch Pl; Ed Yrbk; Rptr Yrbk; Drama Clb; Natl Merit Ltr; NEDT Hnr Crt 78; Univ Of Michigan; Sci.

CORAK, FRANK; Divine Child HS; Dearborn, MI; Sec Band; Hon Rl; Orch; Sch Pl; Stg Crw; Crs Cntry; Ftbl; College.

CORAZZI, SUSAN; R Nelson Snider HS; Ft Wayne, IN; Hon Rl; Cert Of Awd For Soc Std 78; Indiana Univ; Bus.

CORBAN, RUTH; Tuslaw HS; Massillon, OH; 15/183 Trs Frsh Cls; Pres Chrs; Hon Rl; NHS; Sch Mus; Y-Teens; Rptr Yrbk; FTA; Pep Clb; Chrldng;.

CORBETT, BRIDGET; Warsaw Community HS; Warsaw, IN; Band; Hon Rl; Hosp Ade; Sch Pl; DAR Awd; Univ; Vet Med.

CORBETT, CAROL; Northwestern HS; Wooster, OH; Chrs; Girl Scts; Hon Rl; Sch Mus; Sch Pl; Stg Crw; Drama Clb; 4-H; FFA; FTA; Ohio St Univ; Animal Sci.

CORBETT, J; Mathews HS; Fowler, OH; Cmp Fr Grls; Hon Rl; Y-Teens; 4-H; FTA; Key Clb; Pep Clb; Spn Clb; Letter Chrldng; College.

CORBETT, RONALD D; Sidney HS; Sidney, OH; Hon Rl; Key Clb; College; Biology.

CORBIN, BRAD; Flat Rock HS; Flat Rock, MI; 3/113 Hon Rl; NHS; C of C Awd; Tri State Univ; Chem Engr.

CORBIN, JAMI L; Bloomfield HS; Bloomfield, IN; Chrh Wkr; Girl Scts; Hon Rl; NHS; Stg Crw; Pep Clb; Rotary Awd; Ind Univ; Advertising.

CORBIN, PATTY; Newark HS; Newark, OH; Cls Rep Frsh Cls; Cl Rep Jr Cls; Cls Rep Sr Cls; Chrs; Drl Tm; Drm Bgl; Girl Scts; Hon Rl; JA; Stu Cncl; College; Nursing.

CORBIN, STUART; Anderson HS; Anderson, IN; 212/499 Boy Scts; Off Ade; Sct Actv; Fr Clb; Purdue Univ; Mech Engr.

CORBIN JR, JOHN; Hampshire HS; Springfield, WV; AFS; Chrh Wkr; Cmnty Wkr; Hon Rl; Letter Bsbl; Letter Ftbl; James Rumsey Voc Schl; Indus Elec.

CORBITT, DIANE; Shepherd HS; Mt Pleasant, MI; Girl Scts; Hon Rl; Hosp Ade; Lbry Ade; Mt Pleasant Voc Schl; Nursing.

CORCOGLIONITI, MICHELE; Roosevelt Wilson HS; Stonewood, WV; Chrs; Hon Rl; Lbry Ade; Y-Teens; Leo Clb; Fairmont State Coll; Acctg.

CORCORAN, BOB; Niles Mc Kinley HS; Niles, OH; 20/440 Hon Rl; Rptr Yrbk; Rptr Sch Nwsp; Lat Clb; West Point Univ; Math.

CORCORAN, MARY L; Fraser HS; Fraser, MI; Hon Rl; Coll; Bus Admin.

CORCORAN, ROBERT; Niles Mc Kinley HS; Nills, OH; 23/440 Hon Rl; Sch Mus; Sch Pl; Rptr Yrbk; Rptr Sch Nwsp; Lat Clb; Univ; Engr.

CORD, REBECCA; Waldron HS; Shelbyville, IN; 6/65 Trs Sr Cls; Band; Chrs; Hon Rl; NHS; Off Ade; Sch Pl; Yrbk; Drama Clb; 4-H; Indiana Univ; Tele Cmnctns.

CORDELL, PAT; Richmond HS; Richmond, IN; Hon Rl; Glf; Ind Univ; Acctg.

CORDEN, PATRICIA; Traverse City Sr HS; Traverse City, MI; Cl Rep Jr Cls; Sec Sr Cls; Cls Rep Sr Cls; Chrh Wkr; Stu Cncl; Rptr Sch Nwsp; Pep Clb; Cit Awd; Legal Sec.

CORDER, DOLLY; Clay Battelle HS; Blacksville, WV; Band; Girl Scts; Hon Rl; Hosp Ade; FFA; FNA; VICA; Comp 450 Hrs Of Nursing At Monongalla Cnty Voc Tech Cntr 78; West Virginia Univ; RN.

CORDES, DEBORAH; Deer Park HS; Cincinnati, OH; Chrs; Girl Scts; Off Ade; Sch Mus; Rptr Yrbk; Pep Clb; Gym; Trk; Capt Chrldng; Mat Maids; College; Phys Educ.

CORDIAK, JAMES; St Edward HS; Brook Park, OH; 30/360 Cls Rep Soph Cls; Pres Jr Cls; Pres Sr Cls; Hon Rl; Jr NHS; Stu Cncl; Capt Ftbl; Capt Trk; Coach Actv; Computer Sci Sales.

CORDIAL, MARILYN; Olentanay HS; Powell, OH; Cls Rep Frsh Cls; Cls Rep Soph Cls; Aud/Vis; Band; Chrs; Chrh Wkr; FCA; Girl Scts; Hon Rl; Lbry Ade; Rollins Coll; Interior Design.

CORDLE, CATHY; St Charles Cmnty HS; St Charles, MI; 15/120 Cls Rep Soph Cls; Chrh Wkr; NHS; Stu Cncl; Yth Flsp; Pep Clb; Voice Dem Awd; St Of Mi Schlrshp Awd 79; Delta Brd Of Trustee Schlrshp Awd 79; Hnr Cert & Slvr Cord At Sr Hnr Convctn 79; Delta Coll; Fshn Dsgnr.

CORDLE, VICKI; Monroe HS; La Salle, MI; 40/556 Cls Rep Frsh Cls; Cls Rep Soph Cls; Cls Rep Sr Cls; Chrs; Hon Rl; NHS; Stg Crw; Sec Yth Flsp; Anderson Coll; Bus Admin.

CORDOVA, DANIEL; Baker HS; Dayton, OH; Boy Scts; Hon Rl; Sch Pl; Sct Actv; Stg Crw; Treas Stu Cncl; Drama Clb; VP Sci Clb; Crs Cntry; Trk; Intl Thespian Soc 78; Univ; Bio.

CORDRAY, DIANE; Garrett HS; Avilla, IN; 2/150 Cls Rep Frsh Cls; Cls Rep Soph Cls; Cl Rep Jr Cls; Sal; Band; Chrs; Chrh Wkr; Treas Debate Tm; Girl Scts; Hon Rl; Ft Wayne Univ; Jrnlsm.

CORDRAY, JAMES; Grove City HS; Grove City, OH; 1/509 Hon Rl; NHS; Pres Fr Clb; Sci Clb; Letter Crs Cntry; Letter Trk; Am Leg Awd; Kiwan Awd; Natl Merit SF; Ohio St Univ; Engr.

CORDRAY, JUSTY; Muskingum Area Joint Voc HS; Somerset, OH; Hst Jr Cls; Chrs; Chrh Wkr; Girl Scts; Hon Rl; Jr NHS; Lbry Ade; Off Ade; Sch Pl; Pres OEA; Muskingum Tech Bus Schl; Clrcl.

CORDREY, TONI; Mt Vernon Sr HS; Mt Vernon, OH; Drl Tm; Girl Scts; Hon Rl; Hosp Ade; JA; Jr NHS; Pres 4-H; FHA; OEA; 4-H Awd;.

CORDS, LAURA; Frank Cody HS; Detroit, MI; Sec Soph Cls; Sec Jr Cls; Band; Hon Rl; NHS; Swmmng; GAA; PPFtbl; Scr Kpr; Schlr Athlete Medal 79; Michigan St Univ; Comp Sci.

CORE, CARLA; Shadyside HS; Shadyside, OH; 1/120 Cls Rep Frsh Cls; Cls Rep Soph Cls; Am Leg Aux Girls St; Hon Rl; NHS; Sch Pl; Stu Cncl; Y-Teens; 4-H; Spn Clb; Ohio Northern Univ; Pharmacy.

CORE, CAROL; Shadyside HS; Shadyside, OH; Band; Chrs; Chrh Wkr; Debate Tm; Hon Rl; NHS; Sch Pl; Y-Teens; Drama Clb; IM Sprt; Ohio Univ; Sociology.

CORE, DAWN; Clay Battelle HS; Wadestown, WV; 13/90 Band; Chrh Wkr; Cmnty Wkr; Hon Rl; Sch Mus; Sch Pl; Stu Cncl; Sec Yth Flsp; Drama Clb; 4-H; West Virginia Univ; Law.

CORELLA, MARC; Wintersville HS; Steubnvl, OH; Cl Rep Jr Cls; Stu Cncl; Spn Clb; Ftbl; Ten; IM Sprt; Ashland Coll; Chem.

COREY, KAREN; Whittemore Prescott HS; Prescott, MI; 24/107 Trs Jr Cls; Trs Sr Cls; Chrh Wkr; Hon Rl; Sch Pl; Sch Nwsp; Cit Awd; Central Michigan Univ.

CORFMAN, RHONDA; Liberty Benton HS; Findlay, OH; Cls Rep Soph Cls; Chrh Wkr; Hon Rl; NHS; Off Ade; Stu Cncl; Yth Flsp; 4-H; 4-H Awd;.

CORK, SANDY; Speedway HS; Speedway, IN; 22/200 Sec Frsh Cls; FCA; Hon Rl; Mdrgl; NHS; Yth Flsp; Sec Pep Clb; Trk; Chrldng; IM Sprt; College; Education.

CORKLE, ROXANN; Morenci Area HS; Morenci, MI; 18/80 Sec Jr Cls; Am Leg Aux Girls St; Band; Chrs; Hosp Ade; Sch Mus; 4-H; Pep Clb; 4-H Awd; College; Data Proc.

CORKREAN, BARBARA; High School; Huntington, WV; Girl Scts; Hon Rl; Keyettes; Bsktbl; Cit Awd; College; Nurse.

CORLETT, PAULA; Negaunee HS; Palmer, MI; Band; Cmnty Wkr; Girl Scts; Hon Rl; PPFtbl; Michigan Tech Univ; Comp Tech.

CORLETZI, ED; Cardinal Mooney HS; Youngstown, OH; Band; Hon Rl; Lat Clb; IM Sprt; Ohio St Univ; Bus.

CORLEW, BRADLEY; Edgewood HS; Ashtabula, OH; 45/256 Boy Scts; Hon Rl; JA; Yrbk; Fr Clb; Letter Bsktbl; Ftbl; Socr; Ten; Ohio St Univ; Bio Chem.

CORLEY, CHARLES A; Philip Barbour HS; Philippi, WV; Am Leg Boys St; Hon Rl; NHS; Letter Bsbl; Letter Ftbl; Voc Sch; Elec.

CORLEY, STEVEN B; Coalton HS; Coalton, WV; 1/35 Sec Jr Cls; Chrh Wkr; Cmnty Wkr; Hon Rl; Lbry Ade; Sch Pl; Drama Clb; 4-H; Sci Clb; Univ; Tchr.

CORLEY, WALTER; Elkins HS; Elkins, WV; Ftbl Awd; 1st Yr Auto Body 2 Yr Course; Lab Asst Awd; College; Auto Mech.

CORLSON, ROBERT; Walled Lake Central HS; Union Lake, MI; Aud/Vis; Boy Scts; Hon Rl; PAVAS; Sch Mus; Stg Crw; GMI; Engr.

CORMANY, JILL; Marysville HS; Marysville, OH; 20/240 Cls Rep Frsh Cls; Cl Rep Jr Cls; Band; Chrs; Chrh Wkr; Drm Mjrt; Hosp Ade; Jr NHS; Sch Mus; Stu Cncl; Univ; Med Lab Tech.

CORMANY, SUSAN; Columbia City Joint HS; Columbia City, IN; 10/300 Am Leg Aux Girls St; Chrh Wkr; Cmnty Wkr; Hon Rl; Jr NHS; NHS; Yth Flsp; Yrbk; 4-H; FHA; Univ; Tchr.

CORNACHIONE, JILL; Chippewa HS; Doylestown, OH; Cls Rep Soph Cls; Sec Jr Cls; Hon Rl; NHS; Sch Pl; Stu Cncl; Pres 4-H; Pep Clb; Letter Bsktbl; Letter Trk; Shorthand & Typing Awd From Cnty Bus Contest; Natl Hon Soc Serv Awd; Achvmnt Awd Otstndng Accomplshmnt Math; Akron Univ; Math.

CORNELIS, CAROL; St Joseph HS; South Bend, IN; 21/229 Hon Rl; NHS; Sch Pl; Stg Crw; Bsbl; Bsktbl; IM Sprt; Ball St Univ; Pharmacy.

CORNELISON, LOREE; Morton Sr HS; Hammond, IN; 12/419 Chrs; Hon Rl; Pep Clb; PPFtbl; 1st Pl State Comp; Univ.

CORNELISON, SUE; South Knox HS; Wheatland, IN; 18/106 Chrh Wkr; Drl Tm; Girl Scts; Hon Rl; NHS; 4-H; FHA; FNA; Pep Clb; 4-H Awd; Indiana Univ; Phys Ther.

CORNELIUS, DEBORAH; Wilmington HS; Wilmington, OH; 1/284 Band; Chrh Wkr; Hon Rl; NHS; Yth Flsp; GAA; IM Sprt; Cedarville College; Math.

CORNELIUS, JEFFREY; Brookville HS; Brookville, IN; 4/200 Am Leg Boys St; Hon Rl; NHS; Sci Clb; Bsbl; Bsktbl; Ten; Ball St Univ; Busns Admin.

CORNELIUS, SHELLY; Kewanna HS; Kewanna, IN; Cls Rep Frsh Cls; Trs Soph Cls; Sec Jr Cls; Cmp Fr Grls; Chrh Wkr; Girl Scts; Lbry Ade; Stu Cncl; Yrbk; 4-H; Beauty School; Beautician.

CORNELL, ALLISON; Washington HS; Massillon, OH; Chrs; Chrh Wkr; Cmnty Wkr; Red Cr Ade; Sch Mus; Sch Pl; Stg Crw; Yth Flsp; Y-Teens; Rptr Yrbk; Mont State Univ; Journalism.

CORNELL, CAROL; Tippecanoe HS; Tipp City, OH; Hon Rl; NHS; FHA; Sinclair Community Coll.

CORNELL, JAMES; New Richmond HS; New Richmond, OH; Chrs; Chrh Wkr; Hon Rl; NHS; Quill & Scroll; Glf; IM Sprt; Univ Of Cincinnati; Archt.

CORNELL, JUDY; Williamstown HS; Williamstown, WV; 20/115 Band; Chrs; Chrh Wkr; Girl Scts; Hon Rl; Pep Clb; Valley Bty Schl; Csmtlgst.

CORNELL, KEITH; Kenton HS; Kenton, OH; Spn Clb; Letter Bsbl; Letter Ftbl; Wrstlng; Univ.

CORNELL, LISA; Charleston Catholic HS; S Charleston, WV; Chrs; Chrh Wkr; Cmnty Wkr; Pres JA; Off Ade; Stu Cncl; Rptr Yrbk; Ed Sch Nwsp; Fr Clb; Pep Clb; Univ Of Kentucky; Bio.

CORNELL, MARK D; Wyoming HS; Cincinnati, OH; 80/200 Sch Mus; Sch Pl; Stg Crw; Drama Clb; Sci Clb; IM Sprt; Natl Merit SF; College; Marine Science.

CORNER, BEVERLY; Walnut Ridge HS; Columbus, OH; 3/500 Chrs; Chrh Wkr; Cmnty Wkr; Drl Tm; FCA; Yth Flsp; Fr Clb; Bsbl; Coll; Law.

CORNER, BRENDA; La Salle HS; South Bend, IN; 125/488 Debate Tm; Drama Clb;.

CORNER, STEPHEN; Cass Tech HS; Detroit, MI; Aud/Vis; Hon Rl; Stg Crw; Swmmng; IM Sprt; Michigan St Univ; Mech Engr.

CORNETT, CHERYL; Northfield Jr Sr HS; Wabash, IN; Girl Scts; Hon Rl; JA; Lbry Ade; Off Ade; Stg Crw; Rptr Sch Nwsp; 4-H; FHA; OEA; Upper Wabash Career Ctr.

CORNETT, DONALD R; Marlington HS; Minerva, OH; 35/289 Hon Rl; Stg Crw; FFA; VICA; Vocational Schl; Nuclear Research.

CORNETT, JULIE; Maysville HS; S Zanesville, OH; 6/215 Hon Rl; NHS; Stu Cncl; Ed Yrbk; Rptr Yrbk; Sch Nwsp; College.

CORNETT, MARISSA; Eaton HS; Eaton, OH; 1/178 Sec Jr Cls; Chrs; Hon Rl; Jr NHS; Sch Pl; Stu Cncl; Drama Clb; Pep Clb; Pres Spn Clb; GAA; Miami Univ; Physician.

CORNETT, PEGGY; Eminence HS; Cloverdale, IN; 20/42 Fr Clb; Univ; Nursing.

CORNISH, DALE A; Hoover HS; North Canton, OH; 129/422 VP Boy Scts; Sct Actv; Sci Clb; Spn Clb; Bsktbl; Letter Ten; College; Mech Engr.

CORNS, TAUWANTA; Hamilton Twp HS; Columbus, OH; 33/260 Chrh Wkr; Cmnty Wkr; Hon Rl; Yth Flsp; Yrbk; Fr Clb; FTA; Shawnee St Univ; Med Lab Tech.

CORNWELL, CHRISTINE; Mason HS; Mason, MI; Band; Drm Mjrt; Girl Scts; NHS; Orch; Sch Mus; Ten; Hon Rl; Alma Coll; Art.

CORNWELL, JULIA; North Central HS; Indianapolis, IN; 203/999 Chrs; Girl Scts; Hon Rl; Lbry Ade; NHS; Sch Mus; Sct Actv; Stu Cncl; Yth Flsp; OEA; Schlshp To Oakland City Coll 79; Offc Educ Assoc Diplomt St Womans & Ambssdr Awd 79; Indiana Univ; Bus.

CORNWELL, KAREN; Upper Arlington HS; Columbus, OH; Cls Rep Frsh Cls; Band; Chrs; Hon Rl; Quill & Scroll; Stu Cncl; Rptr Sch Nwsp; Miss Teenage Columbus 79; Co Capt Vllybll Team 77; Ohio St Univ; Jrnlsm.

CORNWELL, KAY; Buckhannon Upshur HS; Buckhannon, WV; VP Frsh Cls; Pres Jr Cls; Sec Yth Flsp; IM Sprt; Univ; Med.

CORNWELL, LAURA; N Muskegon HS; N Muskegon, MI; 16/108 Band; Chrs; Chrh Wkr; Girl Scts; Hon Rl; NHS; Orch; Sct Actv; Yth Flsp; Yrbk; Coll; Marine Bio.

CORNWELL, MICHELLE; Norwood HS; Norwood, OH; Cls Rep Frsh Cls; Cls Rep Soph Cls; Cl Rep Jr Cls; Chrs; Drl Tm; Hon Rl; Off Ade; DECA; Fr Clb; Mth Clb; Univ Of Cincinnati.

CORON, ROBERT; Meadowdale HS; Dayton, OH; Letter Ten; College.

CORP, DEBBIE; Crooksville HS; Corning, OH; 12/90 Sec Soph Cls; Sec Jr Cls; Chrh Wkr; Drl Tm; Hon Rl; NHS; Sch Pl; Yth Flsp; Ed Yrbk; Yrbk; Voc Schl; Interior Dec.

CORPUS, J THOMAS; Rocky River HS; Rocky River, OH; Cls Rep Frsh Cls; Cmnty Wkr; Hon Rl; Letter Ftbl; Letter Trk; Wrstlng; IM Sprt; Univ; Podiatry.

CORRELL, JEFFREY; Central Catholic HS; Canton, OH; Am Leg Boys St; Debate Tm; Treas Natl Forn Lg; Treas FBLA; Ohio FBLA Public Speaking 1st Pl; Stu Congress Cncl Co Rep; Natl Forensic League Degree Of Distinction; Boston Univ; Poli Sci.

CORRIE, TERRI; North Newton HS; De Motte, IN; 2/140 Pres Frsh Cls; Pres Soph Cls; Pres Jr Cls; Cl Rep Jr Cls; Cls Rep Sr Cls; Sal; Am Leg Aux Girls St; Purdue Univ; Nursing.

CORRIGAN, DAVID; Bark River Harris HS; Wilson, MI; 12/51 Cls Rep Soph Cls; Pres Jr Cls; Boy Scts; Hon Rl; NHS; Stu Cncl; Letter Bsktbl; Baydenoc Community College; Tech.

CORRIGAN, JEFFREY; Carlisle Sr HS; Carlisle, OH; Letter Band; Cmnty Wkr; Hon Rl; Orch; Civ Clb; Pep Clb; Ftbl; Trk; Mgrs; 3 Yrs Carlisle Educ Recogntn Assoc 76; Jazz Band 76; Bike Racin 75; Univ; Engr.

CORRIGAN, JOSEPH; Padua Franciscan HS; Lakewood, OH; Hon Rl; IM Sprt; Univ.

CORRY, MIRIAM; Taylor HS; Cleves, OH; Chrs; Hon Rl; Off Ade; Stg Crw; Key Clb; Coll.

CORSALE, JOHN; Girard HS; Girard, OH; 1/200 AFS; Cmnty Wkr; Debate Tm; Stu Cncl; Ed Sch Nwsp; Rptr Sch Nwsp; Pres Fr Clb; Pres Key Clb; Sci Clb; Ftbl; Univ; Jrnlsm.

CORSON, MAUREEN; Thornapple Kellogg HS; Middleville, MI; 2/156 Pres Sr Cls; Val; Sch Pl; Stu Cncl; Eng Clb; FSA; Mth Clb; Sci Clb; Swmmng; Bausch & Lomb Awd; Mich State Univ; Pre Vet Med.

CORTOPASSI, JOHNNA; La Salle HS; San Clemente, CA; 21/104 Hon Rl; Rptr Sch Nwsp; Bsktbl; Letter Chrldng; Natl Merit SF; Adrian Coll.

CORWELL, BECKY; Frankfort HS; Ridgeley, WV; Cl Rep Jr Cls; Cls Rep Sr Cls; Hon Rl; Stu Cncl; FHA; Pep Clb; Chrldng; Mat Maids; Univ.

CORWIN, DALE K; Carlisle HS; Franklin, OH; Band; Chrs; Chrh Wkr; Drm Bgl; FCA; Hon Rl; 4-H; Letter Ten; IM Sprt; 4-H Awd; Miami Univ; Educ.

CORWIN, MALINDA; New Richmond HS; New Richmond, OH; 3/196 Hst Sr Cls; Cls Rep Sr Cls; Hon Rl; Jr NHS; NHS; Pol Wkr; Stu Cncl; Rptr Yrbk; Wright St Univ.

CORY, DAWN; Colonel Crawford HS; Bucyrus, OH; Band; Chrh Wkr; Cmnty Wkr; Girl Scts; Hon Rl; Orch; Yrbk; Pep Clb; Trk; College.

CORY, JILL; Colonel Crawford HS; Bucyrus, OH; Band; Chrh Wkr; Cmnty Wkr; Hon Rl; NHS; Off Ade; Sch Pl; Gym; Trk; Univ; Drama.

CORY, TAWNY; Bloomington HS N; Bloomington, IN; 131/420 Bsktbl; Chrldng; PPFtbl; Indiana Univ; Nursing.

CORYA, TERRY; Yorktown HS; Yorktown, IN; 45/180 OEA; Spn Clb; Ivy Tech; Acctg.

CORZATT, ROB; Miami Trace HS; Leesburg, OH; 10/242 VP Sr Cls; AFS; Hon Rl; NHS; Ed Sch Nwsp; Rptr Sch Nwsp; Pres 4-H; FFA; Trk; 4-H Awd; FFA Public Speaking Awd; 4 H & FFA Horse Judging Awds; FFA Leadership Awd; Ohio State Univ; Natural Resources.

COSCARELLY, CATHERINE; Trenton HS; Trenton, MI; 43/560 Pres Frsh Cls; Cls Rep Soph Cls; Cl Rep Jr Cls; Chrh Wkr; Hon Rl; Natl Forn Lg; Quill & Scroll; Sch Mus; Sch Pl; Stg Crw; Eastern Michigan Univ; Theatre.

COSENTINO, LENNY; Chagrin Falls HS; Chagrin Falls, OH; Letter Ftbl; Letter Wrstlng; Coach Actv; IM Sprt; College; Bus.

COSGRAVE, HEIDI; Maysville HS; S Zanesville, OH; Chrs; Hon Rl; Hosp Ade; Stu Cncl; Rptr Yrbk; Pep Clb; Spn Clb; Trk; GAA; Coll; Doctor.

COSGRIFF, SUSAN; St Hedwig HS; Detroit, MI; Chrs; Chrh Wkr; Hon Rl; NHS; Yrbk; Fr Clb; Univ Of Detroit; Music.

COSGROVE, BRONWYN D; H H Dow HS; Midland, MI; Hon Rl; Rptr Sch Nwsp; Sch Nwsp; Letter Glf; Letter Ten; NCTE; Central Mic Univ; Journalism.

COSMA, CATHERINE; St Joseph Academy; Cleveland, OH; 80/220 Chrs; Hon Rl; NHS; Quill & Scroll; Sch Mus; Ed Sch Nwsp; Cuyahoga Cmnty Coll; Ct Reportr.

COSME, ELAINE; Blissfield HS; Blissfield, MI; 29/104 Cmnty Wkr; Hon Rl; IM Sprt; Mich State Univ; Sociology.

COSMO, DIANE; Martins Ferry HS; Martins Ferry, OH; Band; Hon Rl; Treas Stu Cncl; Yth Flsp; Y-Teens; Fr Clb; Sci Clb; Ten; GAA; Cit Awd; College.

COSS, NATALIE M; River HS; Hannibal, OH; 10/162 Cls Rep Frsh Cls; Cls Rep Soph Cls; Band; Pres Chrs; Chrh Wkr; FCA; Hon Rl; Hosp Ade; Sch Mus; FTA; Univ; Sec.

COSS, PAMELA J; Lordstown HS; Warren, OH; 16/58 Sec Jr Cls; Hon Rl; NHS; Sch Pl; Stu Cncl; OEA; Pep Clb; Capt Chrldng; College; Social Work.

COSTA, CATHERINE; Athens HS; Athens, WV; 6/78 Chrs; Hon Rl; Jr NHS; Sec NHS; Stu Cncl; Sprt Ed Yrbk; Fr Clb; FHA; Keyettes; Pep Clb; Concord Coll; Bio.

COSTA, MARIA; Lorain Catholic HS; Lorain, OH; Chrs; Chrh Wkr; Hon Rl; Hosp Ade; Ed Yrbk; Rptr Yrbk; Rptr Sch Nwsp; VP Fr Clb; VP Spn Clb; Bsktbl; Univ; Jrnlsm.

COSTA, STEPHEN; Ursuline HS; Youngstown, OH; 27/317 Am Leg Boys St; Band; Chrs; Chrh Wkr; Debate Tm; Hon Rl; Sct Actv; Sch Nwsp; Key Clb; Histry Day 1st Pl Grp Perfrmnces Lcl Regnl & St 76; Youngstown St Univ; Soc.

COSTANZA, JENNIFER; Andrean HS; Portage, IN; Aud/Vis; Jr NHS; NHS; Yrbk; Rptr Sch Nwsp; Pep Clb; Kalamazoo Coll.

COSTANZA, LOUANN; Eau Claire HS; Sodus, MI; 7/150 VP Soph Cls; Band; FCA; Hon Rl; NHS; Orch; Stu Cncl; Rptr Sch Nwsp; 4-H; Pep Clb; S W Michigan Univ; Data Processing.

COSTANZO, JAMES; Crestview HS; New Waterford, OH; Am Leg Boys St; Hon Rl; Spn Clb; Letter Bsktbl; Letter Ftbl; Letter Trk; College.

COSTAR, DAVID W; Okemos HS; Okemos, MI; 29/326 Band; Lit Mag; Orch; Natl Merit SF; Univ; Physics.

COSTELAC, DAVE; Lincoln HS; Shinnston, WV; Hon Rl; NHS; Sci Clb; Spn Clb; Letter Ftbl; Letter Trk; Letter Wrstlng; College; Med.

COSTELLO, JOHN; Moeller HS; Cincinnati, OH; 13/249 Cls Rep Frsh Cls; Cls Rep Soph Cls; Cl Rep Jr Cls; Sal; Hon Rl; Natl Forn Lg; NHS; Stu Cncl; Ed Sch Nwsp; Sprt Ed Sch Nwsp; Univ Of Cincinnati; Actuarial Sci.

COSTELLO, JOHN M; Moeller HS; Cincinnati, OH; 15/251 Cls Rep Frsh Cls; Cls Rep Soph Cls; Cl Rep Jr Cls; Cls Rep Sr Cls; Hon Rl; Pres NHS; Pol Wkr; Stu Cncl; Ed Sch Nwsp; Sprt Ed Sch Nwsp; Univ Of Cincinnati; Actuarial Sci.

COSTELLO, KATHLEEN; Walnut Ridge HS; Columbus, OH; 22/429 Chrs; Hon Rl; Hosp Ade; Jr NHS; NHS; Orch; Sch Mus; Sch Pl; VP Drama Clb; Treas Fr Clb; Ohio St Univ; Elem Educ.

COSTELLO, KYLE; Washington Irving HS; Clarksburg, WV; Hon Rl; Fr Clb; Leo Clb; Letter Ftbl; Pres Of Explorers Post Dent Clb 79; West Virginia Univ; Engr.

COSTELLO, NANCY; Sandy Valley HS; Magnolia, OH; Hon Rl; Spn Clb; Trk; Univ Of Akron; Accgt.

COSTELLO, ROBERT W; St Joseph HS; Cleveland, OH; 17/243 Sec Frsh Cls; Boy Scts; Debate Tm; Hon Rl; Natl Forn Lg; NHS; Spn Clb; Opt Clb Awd; Booster Club; Univ; Comp Sci.

COSTICK, MIKE; Hubbard HS; Hubbard, OH; Band; Chrh Wkr; Hon Rl; Vocational Schl; Elec.

COSTIGAN, TAMMY; Amelia HS; Amelia, OH; Band; Chrs; Sch Mus; Sch Pl; Spn Clb; Twrlr; Univ; Nursing.

COSTIN, BELINDA M; Notre Dame Academy; Perrysburg, OH; Hon Rl; Orch; Stu Cncl; Yth In Govt YMCA; First Hnr Fresh & Soph; Second Hnr Jr Yr; Coll; Med.

COSTIN, KENNETH; Eminence HS; Stilesville, IN; 10/47 VP Soph Cls; Pres Sr Cls; NHS; Sprt Ed Yrbk; FFA; Bsbl; Capt Bsktbl; Capt Crs Cntry; Trk; Gov Hon Prg Awd; Purdue Univ; Acctg.

COSTOLO, LAURA; Grafton HS; Grafton, WV; Sec Frsh Cls; Cls Rep Soph Cls; Band; Drl Tm; Hon Rl; Stu Cncl; Rptr Yrbk; Rptr Sch Nwsp; IM Sprt; Fairmont State College; Psych.

COSTON, REBECCA; Carson City Crystal HS; Fenwick, MI; Trs Jr Cls; Chrh Wkr; Yth Flsp; FHA; Pep Clb; Bsktbl; IM Sprt; College; Teacher.

COSTON, ROBERT; Buckhannon Upshur HS; Buckhannon, WV; Band; Boy Scts; Chrh Wkr; Hon Rl; Sch Mus; Stg Crw; Yth Flsp; Drama Clb; 4-H; IM Sprt; Del To Un Meth Annual Conf 79; Univ; History.

COSTYN, CAROL; St Alphonsus HS; Detroit, MI; Drm Mjrt; Hon Rl; Trk; Twrlr; Univ; Bus.

COTA, MARJORIE; South Vigo HS; Terre Haute, IN; Cls Rep Frsh Cls; Cls Rep Soph Cls; Cl Rep Jr Cls; Aud/Vis; Chrs; Debate Tm; Hon Rl; Ind State; Marine Bio.

COTCHER, DEBORAH; Fenton Sr HS; Fenton, MI; 33/275 Band; Chrh Wkr; Cmnty Wkr; Hon Rl; Jr NHS; NHS; Yth Flsp; IM Sprt; PPFtbl; Tmr; Michigan St Univ; Engr.

COTE, DIANE; Upper Arlington HS; Columbus, OH; 16/610 Band; Cmp Fr Grls; Hon Rl; NHS; Yth Flsp; Fr Clb; GAA; Mgrs; Tmr; Natl Merit Ltr; French Natl Hon Soc 78; Univ; Pre Med.

COTE, MONIQUE; Port Huron Central HS; Port Huron, MI; Lbry Ade; DECA; Fr Clb; St Clair Comm Coll; Education.

COTE, PHILIP; Benzie Central HS; Beulah, MI; Cls Rep Frsh Cls; Cls Rep Soph Cls; Cl Rep Jr Cls; Band; Hon Rl; NHS; Stu Cncl; Letter Wrstlng; College; Med Tech.

COTTA, ALEX; Mc Nicholas HS; Cincinnati, OH; 25/230 Boy Scts; Hon Rl; Jr NHS; NHS; Sct Actv; Rptr Yrbk; Ftbl; IM Sprt; Univ; Dent.

COTTER, GINGER; Ontario HS; Mansfield, OH; 12/180 Band; Hon Rl; Tech College.

COTTER, KAREN; Sacred Heart Acad; Mt Pleasant, MI; Pres Jr Cls; Stu Cncl; Lat Clb; Bsbl; Bsktbl; Letter Trk; Pres Awd; Nazareth College; Nurse.

COTTER, KENNETH; Penn HS; Mishawaka, IN; 38/499 Am Leg Boys St; Debate Tm; FCA; Hon Rl; Mod UN; NHS; Letter Bsbl; Letter Ftbl; Coach Actv; College; Poli Sci.

COTTER, LORIE; Howell Sr HS; Howell, MI; Band; Girl Scts; Hon Rl; Pol Wkr; Sct Actv; Univ Of Michigan.

COTTER, TRACY P; St Alphonsus; Dearborn, MI; 7/789 Cls Rep Frsh Cls; Cls Rep Soph Cls; VP Jr Cls; Cls Rep Sr Cls; Val; NHS; Sch Mus; Stu Cncl; Lcrss; IM Sprt; Harvard Univ; Dent.

COTTER JR, JOHN; Pewamo Westphalia HS; Pewamo, MI; 1/118 Cls Rep Frsh Cls; Cls Rep Soph Cls; Cl Rep Jr Cls; Val; Band; Hon Rl; NHS; Sch Pl; Glf; Trk; Aquinas Coll; Acctg.

COTTERMAN, K; Sidney HS; Sidney, OH; Hon Rl; Hosp Ade; VP 4-H; Spn Clb; IM Sprt; Ohio St Univ; Pre Vet.

COTTERMAN, KAREN; Piqua Central HS; Piqua, OH; 25 Cmnty Wkr; Drm Mjrt; NHS; Sch Pl; Stu Cncl; Ed Yrbk; Rptr Yrbk; VP Drama Clb; Pres Spn Clb; Letter Bsktbl; Miami Univ; Bus Admin.

COTTON, BETH; Bishop Donahue HS; Glen Dale, WV; Cls Rep Frsh Cls; Girl Scts; Hon Rl; Stu Cncl; Pep Clb; Spn Clb; Chrldng; West Liberty St Coll.

COTTON, DIANNA; United Local HS; Kensington, OH; 26/128 Chrh Wkr; Hon Rl; Hosp Ade; Stg Crw; Rptr Yrbk; 4-H; FHA; Ger Clb; Trk; Rotary Awd; Past Worthy Advsr Of Intl Order Of Rainbow 77; Membr Of Record Brkng CPR Marathon 79; Ohio St Univ; Pharm.

COTTON, DONNA L; Marlington HS; Alliance, OH; Trs Frsh Cls; Trs Soph Cls; Trs Jr Cls; Trs Sr Cls; Band; Drm Mjrt; VP OEA; Trk; Stark Tech Schl; Comp Prog.

COTTON, JED; Big Rapids HS; Big Rapids, MI; Band; Hon Rl; NHS; Letter Bsbl; Letter Ftbl; IM Sprt; Cit Awd; Data Proc.

COTTON, LLOYD; Muskegon Sr HS; Muskegon, MI; Band; Chrs; Chrh Wkr; Drm Mjrt; Hon Rl; Mdrgl; NHS; Yth Flsp; Rptr Sch Nwsp; Letter Ten; Michigan St Univ.

COTTON, MICHAEL; East HS; Columbus, OH; 6/272 VP Frsh Cls; Cls Rep Soph Cls; Cl Rep Jr Cls; Cls Rep Sr Cls; Boy Scts; Hon Rl; Jr NHS; NHS; Off Ade; Sch Pl; Ohio St Univ; Medicine.

COTTON, PAMELA; Ashtabula Harbor HS; Ashtabula, OH; 32/199 AFS; Yth Flsp; 4-H; Fr Clb; Pep Clb; Letter Bsktbl; Coach Actv; GAA; IM Sprt; Scr Kpr; Business School.

COTTON, PAUL A; Marlington HS; Alliance, OH; 84/289 Letter Wrstlng; IM Sprt; College; Bsns Admin.

COTTON, SARA M; Harper Creek HS; East Leroy, MI; 18/240 Cls Rep Frsh Cls; Cls Rep Soph Cls; Cl Rep Jr Cls; Cls Rep Sr Cls; Hon Rl; NHS; Pol Wkr; Pep Clb; Spn Clb; Ten; Central Michigan Univ.

COTTONGIM, ED; Plainfield Jr Sr HS; Plainfield, IN; Band; Orch; Spn Clb; Wrstlng; Mental Attitude

Awd Bsbl; Outstanding Ldrshp Awd Band; Ball St Univ; Engr.

COTTRELL, KAZUO O; Fenwick HS; Middletown, OH; Chrh Wkr; Hon Rl; NHS; Rptr Yrbk; Ed Sch Nwsp; College; Med.

COTTRELL, MARGARET; Dominican HS; Detroit, MI; Trs Frsh Cls; Cls Rep Soph Cls; Girl Scts; Sct Actv; Stu Cncl; Letter Swmmng; Letter Trk; Awrd Most Imprvd Swimmer 77; Acctg.

COTTRILL, CAROL A; Huntington HS; Chillicothe, OH; 3/20 Band; Cmnty Wkr; Hon Rl; Sch Nwsp; 4-H; Fr Clb; OEA; Trk; Chrldng; Pom Pon; Exec Awrd 79; 4 H Awrds; Bus Schl; Steno.

COTTRILL, KATHRYN; Stonewall Jackson HS; Charleston, WV; Cls Rep Frsh Cls; Band; Cmnty Wkr; Drm Mjrt; Hon Rl; Lbry Ade; Stu Cncl; Y-Teens; Sch Nwsp; Pep Clb; Coll; Tchr.

COTTRILL, MARK; Stow HS; Monroe Fls, OH; Aud/Vis; Sch Pl; Stg Crw; Rptr Sch Nwsp; Ftbl; Coach Actv; Lion Awd; Case Western Reserve.

COTTRILL, REONA; Washington Irving HS; Clarksburg, WV; Hon Rl; Fairmont Coll; Acctg.

COTTRILL, SHEILA; Gilmer County HS; Shock, WV; Chrh Wkr; Hon Rl; Hosp Ade; Yth Flsp; 4-H; FHA; Pep Clb; VICA; Fairmont State Coll; Nursing.

COTTS, CHERYL; Zeeland HS; Hudsonville, MI; 10/213 Hon Rl; NHS; 4-H; IM Sprt; 4-H Awd; Bus Schl; Comp Prog.

COUCH, MARK; Huntington North HS; Huntington, IN; 5/603 Band; Letter Wrstlng; IM Sprt; JETS Awd; NEDT 77; Univ; Chem Engr.

COUCH, NANCY; Rosedale HS; Rosedale, IN; Hon Rl; NHS; Quill & Scroll; Yrbk; Sch Nwsp; FTA; Pep Clb; Chrldng; Capt Pom Pon; Tchrs Aid; Homecoming Queen Attendent; Chrmn Of Prom Comm; IV Tech; Comp Progr.

COUCH, PAMELA; Fitzgerald HS; Warren, MI; Pres Frsh Cls; VP Sr Cls; Band; Hon Rl; Stu Cncl; Twrlr; Opt Clb Awd; Band Pres 79; Macomb County Cmnty Coll; Bus.

COUCH, SALLY; Eastern HS; Smithville, IN; Chrs; Chrh Wkr; Hon Rl; NHS; Sch Mus; Yth Flsp; 4-H; FHA; Pep Clb; Trk;.

COUDEN, JOSEPH; St Charles Prep; Blacklick, OH; Letter Wrstlng; College; Dentist.

COUGHENOUR, JOHN; W Ottawa HS; Holland, MI; Band; Chrs; Chrh Wkr; Mdrgl; Orch; PAVAS; Sch Mus; Sch Pl; VP Stu Cncl; Drama Clb; Hope Coll.

COUGHLIN, CAROLYN; Ursuline HS; Youngstown, OH; 42/319 Debate Tm; Hon Rl; NHS; Off Ade; Rptr Sch Nwsp; Lat Clb; Trk; Scr Kpr; Irish Way Schlrshp Summer Prog In Ireland 79; Oh Schlstc Achvmnt Awd Eng; Univ; Law.

COUGHLIN, JEFFREY; Lorain Catholic HS; Avon Lake, OH; Aud/Vis; Chrs; Chrh Wkr; Cmnty Wkr; Hon Rl; Rptr Sch Nwsp; Sch Nwsp; Ftbl; Trk; Coach Actv; Univ; Bus Mgmt.

COUGHLIN, PATRICIA; Bexley HS; Columbus, OH; Chrs; Sprt Ed Yrbk; Rptr Yrbk; Sch Nwsp; Spn Clb; Letter Gym; Letter Hockey; Trk; Letter Chrldng; Univ; Educ.

COUGLIN, STEVE; Kingsford HS; Kingsford, MI; Cls Rep Frsh Cls; Hon Rl; Stu Cncl; IM Sprt; Scr Kpr; Univ; Acctg.

COUGRAS, CATHERINE; Campbell Memorial HS; Campbell, OH; Cls Rep Frsh Cls; Pres Soph Cls; Cl Rep Jr Cls; VP Sr Cls; Chrh Wkr; Cmnty Wkr; NHS; Off Ade; Stu Cncl; Rptr Yrbk; Youngstown St Univ; Elem Ed.

COULTAS, KEITH; Perry Central HS; Tell City, IN; Band; Drm Mjrt; Sch Pl; Stg Crw; Drama Clb; 4-H; Fr Clb; Pep Clb; Twrlr; 4-H Awd; College; Music.

COULTER, BRENDA; South Central HS; Elizabeth, IN; VP Jr Cls; Hon Rl; 4-H; Mth Clb; VP Spn Clb; IM Sprt; 4-H Awd; Ind Univ; Acctg.

COULTER, KEVIN; Lapeer East Sr HS; Lapeer, MI; Am Leg Boys St; Hon Rl; NHS; Stu Cncl; Letter Ft bl; Natl Merit Ltr; Univ Of Michigan; Astronomy.

COULTER, PAUL; New Albany HS; New Albany, IN; 87/565 Cl Rep Jr Cls; Aud/Vis; Band; Boy Scts; Hon Rl; Ger Clb; Mgrs; Ind Univ; Math.

COULTER, RHONDA; Lake Orion HS; Lake Orion, MI; 43/435 Band; Chrh Wkr; Girl Scts; Hon Rl; Jr NHS; NHS; Off Ade; Sct Actv; Yth Flsp; Oakland Univ; Engr.

COULTER, SHAWN; Whitehall Yearling HS; Columbus, OH; FCA; Pol Wkr; Letter Ftbl; Letter Trk; Letter Wrstlng; VFW Awd; Rcvd Schlstc Awd For 3.6 Grd Avg For Sr Yr; Lstd In Whos Who Amng Amer HS Stu 77 79; Cptn Of Ftbl Tm; U S Naval Academy; Officer.

COUNTISS, JOHN; Upper Arlington HS; Columbus, OH; 1/622 Am Leg Boys St; Hon Rl; NHS; Ger Clb; Kiwan Awd; Natl Merit Schl; Valedictorian 79; Deans Schlshp Washington Univ 79; Washington Univ; Med.

COUNTRYMAN, KIMBERLY; Middletown HS; Middletown, OH; 10/528 Chrs; Chrh Wkr; Hon Rl; Lit Mag; NHS; Orch; Sch Mus; Ashland College; Economics.

COUNTRYMAN, SUSAN; Paint Valley HS; Lyndon, OH; Tech Schl; Interior Dsgn.

COURNEENE, CINDY; Escanaba Area Public HS; Escanaba, MI; 76/451 Band; Chrs; Chrh Wkr; Girl Scts; Hon Rl; Jr NHS; NHS; Orch; Sch Mus; Sct Actv; Carroll Coll; Elem Ed.

COURNOYER, HELENE; Lumen Cordium HS; Maple Hts, OH; Cmp Fr Grls; Hon Rl; Bsktbl; Gym; Coach Actv; GAA; Univ; Sci.

COURSER, KATHRYN; Chippewa Hills HS; Mt Pleasant, MI; Hon Rl; NHS; Ferris State College; Pharmacist.

COURSON, KIMBERLY; Wyoming Park HS; Wyoming, MI; 12/227 Chrh Wkr; Cmnty Wkr; Lbry Ade; NHS; Fr Clb; Spn Clb; Calvin College; Lang.

COURT, DENISE; Harper Creek HS; Battle Creek, MI; 5/244 Sec Frsh Cls; Sec Soph Cls; Sec Jr Cls; Hon Rl; Hosp Ade; NHS; Sec Fr Clb; Letter Glf; Letter Ten; Chrldng; College; Nursing.

COURTAD, DIANNE; Traverse City HS; Traverse City, MI; Girl Scts; JA; 4-H; Pep Clb; JA Awd; Northwestern Mich Coll; Data Proc.

COURTAD, GREGG; North HS; Columbus, OH; 22/325 Am Leg Boys St; Lit Mag; VP NHS; Sch Mus; Sch Pl; Pres Stu Cncl; Rptr Sch Nwsp; Drama Clb; Lat Clb; Spn Clb; Kenyon Coll; Journalism.

COURTER, AMY; Bullock Creek HS; Midland, MI; Cmnty Wkr; Hon Rl; Pres JA; NHS; Pol Wkr; Stg Crw; 4-H; Spn Clb; GAA; Capt IM Sprt; Univ; Soc Work.

COURTER, CONNIE; Lawrenceburg HS; Lawrenceburg, IN; 6/165 Girl Scts; Hon Rl; NHS; Off Ade; Ed Sch Nwsp; Pep Clb; Chrldng; GAA; Indiana Univ.

COURTER, THOMAS; Bullock Creek HS; Midland, MI; 12/160 Chrh Wkr; Cmnty Wkr; Capt Debate Tm; Hon Rl; Pres JA; Natl Forn Lg; Chmn NHS; Pol Wkr; Sch Pl; VP FSA; Selected To Natl Achievers Assoc 77; Selected As Midland Areas Soph Of Yr 77; Central Michigan Univ; Bus Admin.

COURTNEY, CAROL; Alexandria Monroe HS; Alexandria, IN; 7/200 Trs Jr Cls; Trs Sr Cls; Chrs; Drl Tm; Hon Rl; Yrbk; 4-H; Pep Clb; Spn Clb; Twrlr; Soph Tri Kappa Awd Of Excellence 78; Purdue Univ; Med Tech.

COURTNEY, CAROLYN; Boardman HS; Youngstwn, OH; 100/658 Chrs; Cmnty Wkr; Debate Tm; Girl Scts; Hon Rl; Hosp Ade; Natl Forn Lg; Red Cr Ade; Sch Mus; Sch Pl; Youngstown St Univ; Tele Cmnctns.

COURTNEY, JAMES; Lewis County HS; Jane Lew, WV; Am Leg Boys St; Chrs; Chrh Wkr; Hon Rl; NHS; Key Clb; Bsbl; Bsktbl; Ftbl; Lion Awd; West Virginia Univ; Dent.

COURTNEY, KELLY; Sturgis HS; Sturgis, MI; Jr NHS; NHS; Stg Crw; Bsktbl; PPFtbl; Univ Of Michigan.

COURTNEY, KIM; Staunton HS; Brazil, IN; 1/50 Trs Jr Cls; Band; Chrh Wkr; Drl Tm; Hon Rl; NHS; 4-H; Ger Clb; Pep Clb; 4-H Awd; Purdue 4h Roundup Awrd 1978; Indiana St Univ; Sci.

COURTNEY, LESLI; Bishop Fenwick HS; Mason, OH; Drl Tm; Hon Rl; NHS; Sch Mus; 4-H; Letter Pom Pon; 4-H Awd; Natl Merit Ltr; Southern Ohi College; Sec Sci.

COURTNEY, MARYLYNNE; Belleville HS; Belleville, MI; Band; Chrh Wkr; Hon Rl; Hosp Ade; Sch Pl; Stg Crw; Yth Flsp; Mgrs; Univ Of Mich; Phys Ther.

COURTNEY, MICHELE J; North Daviess HS; Elnora, IN; 44/93 Cls Rep Soph Cls; Cl Rep Jr Cls; FCA; Girl Scts; Hon Rl; Off Ade; Stu Cncl; Yrbk; Pep Clb; Chrldng; Vincennes Univ; Horticulture.

COURTS, CRAIG; Thornapple Kellogg HS; Caledonia, MI; 4/152 Boy Scts; Chrh Wkr; Hon Rl; Jr NHS; NHS; Bsktbl; Ten; W Mich Univ; Acctg.

COURY, THERESA; Magnificat HS; Brookpark, OH; Chrh Wkr; Cmnty Wkr; Hon Rl; Hosp Ade; NHS; Stg Crw; Yth Flsp; Pep Clb; Trk; College; Math.

COURY, TINA; Zanesville HS; Zanesville, OH; Sec Frsh Cls; Trs Frsh Cls; Trs Jr Cls; Trs Sr Cls; Chrs; Hon Rl; NHS; Off Ade; Stu Cncl; Lat Clb; Ohi State Univ; Fash Merch.

COUSINEAU, C; Redford HS; Detroit, MI; Boy Scts; Hon Rl; Art Coll; Graphic Illustration.

COUSINO, COLLEEN S; Notre Dame Acad; Erie, MI; 2/134 Cls Rep Frsh Cls; Cls Rep Soph Cls; NHS; Stu Cncl; Fr Clb; Natl Merit SF; Designer Of Erie Twnshp Logo; Cert Outstdng Ach In The St Of Mich Schlrshp Cntst; Notre Dame Coll; Chemistry.

COUSINO, DIANE M; Robert S Rogers HS; Toledo, OH; 3/412 Chrs; Hon Rl; Hosp Ade; NHS; Pres Lat Clb; Sci Clb; NCTE; Natl Merit Ltr; Bowling Green St Univ.

COUSINO, JEANETTE; Saint Marys Cntrl Cath HS; Sandusky, OH; 40/128 Cl Rep Jr Cls; Band; Chrs; Chrh Wkr; VP JA; Pres Stu Cncl; Letter Bsktbl; Letter Ten; GAA; JA Awd; Schl Panthers Mascot; Ohio State Univ; Fashion Merch.

COUSINS, BRENDA; George Washington HS; East Chicago, IN; 13/283 Cls Rep Frsh Cls; Cls Rep Soph Cls; Cl Rep Jr Cls; Cls Rep Sr Cls; Hon Rl; JA; NHS; Stu Cncl; FHA; Pep Clb; Top Ten Stu Block Jr HS 1974; Purdue Univ; Comp Sci.

COUSSENS, JULIE; Marian HS; Granger, IN; 11/145 Hon Rl; NHS; Yrbk; Pep Clb; Swmmng; Trk; IM Sprt; Univ; Bus Admin.

COVATCH, MICHAEL; Bishop Foley HS; Sterling Hts, MI; Boy Scts; Chrh Wkr; Cmnty Wkr; Hon Rl; Sacred Heart Seminary; Priest.

COVAULT, VICKI; Sidney HS; Sidney, OH; Sec Sr Cls; Girl Scts; Hon Rl; Off Ade; Orch; OEA; Pep C lb; Mas Awd; Best Typing II 1977; Most Edicated Worker 1978; Grad High Honors Top 12 1978; Edison St Univ; Acctg.

COVENTRY, RHONDA; Lapeer West Sr HS; Columbiaville, MI; 11/265 Band; NHS; Fr Clb; Trk; Cedarville Coll; Math.

COVENTRY, SHARON; Lapeer West HS; Columbiaville, MI; Band; NHS; Spn Clb; Letter Trk; #1 Typ In Typing II Class 79; Bus Schl; Bus Sec.

COVER, AIMEE; Chelsea HS; Chelsea, MI; 13/210 Band; Chrh Wkr; FCA; Hon Rl; Jr NHS; NHS; Beta Clb; 4-H; FHA; Natl Merit SF; E Michigan Univ; Occuptnl Ther.

COVERT, CHRISTINE; Clarence M Kimball HS; Royal Oak, MI; Girl Scts; Hon Rl; NHS; Sct Actv; Treas Yth Flsp; Y-Teens; Spn Clb; Trk; Voice Dem Awd; Univ.

COVERT, MARIE; St Agatha HS; Detroit, MI; Hon Rl; NHS; Rptr Yrbk; Fr Clb; Mth Clb; Sci Clb; Wayne St Univ; Chem Engr.

COVERT, YVONNE; West Sr HS; Garden City, MI; Cls Rep Soph Cls; Cl Rep Jr Cls; Cls Rep Sr Cls; Chrs; Hon Rl; Jr NHS; Off Ade; Stu Cncl; Sch Nwsp; Pom Pon; College; Liberal Arts.

COVEYOU, JONATHON; Petoskey HS; Petoskey, MI; Lat Clb; Natl Merit Schl; Mic Tech Univ; Sci Engr.

COVIAK, THERESA; Gaylord St Marys HS; Gaylord, MI; Hon Rl; JA; ROTC; Stg Crw; Rptr Yrbk; Rptr Sch Nwsp; Drama Clb; 4-H; Lat Clb; Pep Clb; College; Psychologist.

COVILLE, KAREN; Climax Scotts HS; Climax, MI; 10/64 Hon Rl; Natl Forn Lg; NHS; Stg Crw; FHA; College; Sec.

COVINGTON, DAWN; River Rouge HS; River Rouge, MI; 5/150 Cls Rep Frsh Cls; Cls Rep Soph Cls; Cl Rep Jr Cls; Cls Rep Sr Cls; Band; Chrs; Chrh Wkr; Cmnty Wkr; Girl Scts; Hon Rl; Dist Pores Of Chrstn Youth Fllshp 79; Smmr Sci Inst 79; Wayne St Univ; Math.

COVINGTON, ZENARA; Ecorse HS; Ecorse, MI; Cls Rep Soph Cls; Pres Jr Cls; Pres Sr Cls; Band; Chrh Wkr; Hosp Ade; Jr NHS; NHS; Rptr Yrbk; Pres Awd; Univ Of Michigan; Medicine.

COVY, DALE; Bishop Borgess HS; Livonia, MI; Boy Scts; Chrh Wkr; Hon Rl; Jr NHS; Yth Flsp; Sci Clb; Letter Ftbl; Trk; IM Sprt; Natl Merit Ltr; Phi Betta Kapa 79; St Of Mi Comptv Schshp Recgntn 79; W Mi Acad Schslp; Michigan St Univ; Vet Med.

COWAN, VICKIE; Union HS; Losantville, IN; Girl Scts; Hon Rl; Red Cr Ade; Yrbk; FHA; Pep Clb; Sci Clb; Spn Clb; Letter Bsktbl; Mgrs; Morton Memorial; Dental Technology.

COWARD, RHODA; Quincy HS; Quincy, MI; Band; Chrh Wkr; NHS; 4-H; Fr Clb; IM Sprt; French Awd; Perfect Attendance; Grand Rapids Bapt Coll; Bus Admin.

COWDERY, JANE; St Peters HS; Mansfield, OH; Am Leg Aux Girls St; Band; NHS; Sprt Ed Yrbk; Rptr Yrbk; VP Spn Clb; Bsktbl; Capt Swmmng; College; Science.

COWDERY, JOAN; St Peters HS; Mansfield, OH; Band; Hon Rl; Sprt Ed Yrbk; Yrbk; Drama Clb; Sci Clb; Spn Clb; Letter Bsbl; Letter Bsktbl; Capt Swmmng; Univ; Marine Bio.

COWDREY, CHRISTINE; Batavia HS; Batavia, OH; Am Leg Aux Girls St; NHS; Off Ade; Stu Cncl; Rptr Yrbk; Ed Sch Nwsp; Drama Clb; Pres Fr Clb; PPFtbl; Cit Awd; Univ; Bus.

COWELL JR, RONALD; Mackinac Island Public HS; Mackinaw Island, MI; 2/7 Hon Rl; Yrbk; Ed Sch Nwsp; 4-H; IM Sprt; Fersirs; Air Cond Plumbing Heating.

COWELS, CAMILLE; Otsego HS; Otsego, MI; Girl Scts; Lat Clb; Spn Clb; Bsktbl; Mem Of Amer Jr Polled Hereford Assn; Mbr S W Mi Polled Hereford Assn; Princess For 2yrs Of Above Assn; College; Nursing.

COWEN, VIRGINIA; Bishop Luers HS; Ft Wayne, IN; Chrs; Girl Scts; Hon Rl; Sch Mus; Sch Pl; Stg Crw; Rptr Sch Nwsp; Chrldng; GAA; IM Sprt; Tri St Hon Chr 78; Nisbova 4 1st Pl 2 2nd Pl Awd 77 79; Univ.

COWGER, RENEE; Coventry HS; Akron, OH; Cls Rep Frsh Cls; Cls Rep Soph Cls; VP Jr Cls; Band; Chrs; Stu Cncl; Rptr Yrbk; Rptr Sch Nwsp; Gym; Chrldng; Univ; Psych.

COWGILL, SCOTT; Lakeshore HS; Stevensville, MI; 51/291 Chrh Wkr; Hon Rl; Natl Forn Lg; Sch Mus; Sch Pl; Stg Crw; Ger Clb; Crs Cntry; Glf; Southwestern Mich Coll; Comp Progr.

COWGILL, TERESA; Bishop Ready HS; Columbus, OH; Cmnty Wkr; VP JA; Pol Wkr; Sch Pl; Rptr Yrbk; Gym; Trk; Scr Kpr; Tmr; JA Awd; Univ.

COWLES, CARRIE; Belding HS; Belding, MI; Aud/Vis; Band; Hon Rl; Lbry Ade; NHS; Drama Clb; Pep Clb; College; Vet.

COWLES, JACK D; Battle Creek Central HS; Battle Creek, MI; 2/550 Sal; Chrs; Hon Rl; NHS; Sch Mus; Sch Pl; Ftbl; Univ Of Mic; Law.

COWLEY, KEVEN; Deckerville Community Schls; Deckervll, MI; Hon Rl; Off Ade; Mgrs; Univ; Aero Engr.

COWLIN, WILLIAM J; Cranbrook HS; Crystal Lake, IL; Orch; Sch Mus; Rptr Sch Nwsp; Sch Nwsp; Crs Cntry; Letter Trk; Natl Merit SF; Bus Admin.

COX, A; Brookhaven HS; Columbus, OH; VP Band; Hon Rl; NHS; Sch Pl; VP Fr Clb; Tmr; Ohio State Univ.

COX, BILLIE; Benjamin Bosse HS; Evansville, IN; Chrs; Chrh Wkr; Hon Rl; Jr NHS; NHS; Lat Clb; Pep Clb; NCTE; Natl Merit SF; Campbellsville College; Psych.

COX, BOB; Sidney HS; Sidney, OH; 21/250 Hon Rl; Key Clb; Letter Crs Cntry; Trk; Miami Univ; Finance.

COX, C; R Nelson Snider HS; Ft Wayne, IN; 52/564 Drl Tm; Hon Rl; Stu Cncl; Letter Trk; Pom Pon;.

COX, CAMILLA; N Montgomery HS; Darlington, IM; Band; Chrh Wkr; Hon Rl; Hosp Ade; Off Ade; Sch Mus; Stg Crw; Drama Clb; 4-H; OEA; Ivy Tech Voc Schl; Bus.

COX, DANIEL; Stephen T Badin HS; Hamilton, OH; Chrh Wkr; Hon Rl; Letter Ftbl; Letter Trk; Letter IM Sprt; Univ Of Dayton; Psych.

COX, DARRELL; Warsaw Comm HS; Warsaw, IN; 13/450 Hon Rl; Letter Crs Cntry; Letter Trk; Natl Merit Ltr; Times Union WRSW Radio Schlstc Awd For Math; Indiana Univ; Med.

COX, DAVID; Columbia City Joint HS; Columbia City, IN; 21/273 Am Leg Boys St; Hon Rl; Treas NHS; Stu Cncl; Pres FTA; Key Clb; Spn Clb; College; Computer Science.

COX, DEBORAH; Watkins Memorial HS; Pataskala, OH; Band; Spn Clb; Trk; Ohio State Univ; Med.

COX, DENEICE L; Edwardsburg HS; Edwardsburg, MI; Chrs; Hon Rl; Lbry Ade; Rptr Yrbk; Yrbk; Fr Clb; S W Michigan Univ; Health.

COX, GARY; Ridgewood HS; W Lafayette, OH; 50/150 Cls Rep Soph Cls; Cl Rep Jr Cls; Am Leg Boys St; Boy Scts; Hon Rl; Rptr Sch Nwsp; Letter Bsktbl; College Of Steubenville; Bus Admin.

COX, GREG; Yorktown HS; Muncie, IN; 21/172 Hon Rl; Fr Clb; Bsktbl; Mgrs; Ball St Univ; Acctg.

COX, GREGORY; North Adams HS; Hillsdale, MI; Trs Frsh Cls; Trs Soph Cls; Boy Scts; Hon Rl; Off Ade; Sprt Ed Yrbk; Letter Bsbl; Letter Bsktbl; Letter Ftbl; Letter Trk; Ferris State; Marketing.

COX, JANE; Hannan Trace HS; Crown City, OH; Cls Rep Soph Cls; Band; Chrs; Hon Rl; 4-H; Pep Clb;.

COX, JOYCE; Rivet HS; Vincennes, IN; Rptr Sch Nwsp; FHA; Pep Clb; Chrldng; IM Sprt; Vincennes Univ; Education.

COX, KAREN; Winchester Community HS; Winchester, IN; Band; Chrh Wkr; Hon Rl; Jr NHS; Lbry Ade; NHS; Orch; Sch Mus; Stu Cncl; Yth Flsp; College; Rn.

COX, KATHY; North Putnam HS; Greencastle, IN; 28/155 NHS; 4-H; FHA; Lat Clb; Pep Clb; GAA; Ivy Tech Voc Schl; Acctg.

COX, KIMBERLEE; Evergreen Local HS; Berkey, OH; Cls Rep Frsh Cls; Cls Rep Soph Cls; Cl Rep Jr Cls; Cmp Fr Grls; Chrh Wkr; Cmnty Wkr; Girl Scts;.

COX, LAURIE; Madison Hts HS; Anderson, IN; Hon Rl; Treas Lat Clb; Pep Clb; Ball Hosp; Sci.

COX, LISA; Brighton HS; Birghton, MI; Chrs; Girl Scts; Hon Rl; Pol Wkr; Fashion Designer.

COX, LORAINE; St Marys HS; St Marys, WV; Off Ade; 4-H; FHA; 4-H Awd; Parkersburg Cmnty Coll.

COX, MARK A; Charlestown HS; Charlestown, IN; 1/176 Hon Rl; VP NHS; Pres Stu Cncl; Yrbk; FTA; VP Lat Clb; IM Sprt; Am Leg Awd; In St Univ Physics Semnr 79; Stdnt Leadrhp Inst In Univ 79; Jrnlsm Inst In Univ 79; Univ; Chem.

COX, MELISSA D; Mississinawa Valley HS; Union City, OH; Sec Band; Hon Rl; NHS; Stu Cncl; Sec Yth Flsp; Drama Clb; Pres 4-H; FHA; OEA; Pep Clb; Vocational Schl; Modeling.

COX, MICHELLE; Richmond HS; Richmond, IN; Chrs; Hon Rl; Lbry Ade; NHS; Pol Wkr; Y-Teens; 4-H; Trk; IM Sprt; Purdue Univ; Bio Chem.

COX, MONICA; Mc Auley HS; Cincinnati, OH; Cmp Fr Grls; Girl Scts; JA; Pep Clb; IM Sprt; JA Awd; Xavier Univ; Acctg.

COX, PATRICIA; Northern HS; Detroit, MI; 36/236 Hon Rl; Off Ade; Hockey; Swmmng; GAA; Scr Kpr; Univ Of Detroit; Med Tech.

COX, PHILLIP; North Posey HS; Poseyville, IN; Cls Rep Frsh Cls; Cls Rep Soph Cls; VP Sr Cls; Boy Scts; Hon Rl; Sct Actv; Stu Cncl; Pep Clb; Crs Cntry; Capt Trk; Univ; Bus.

COX, RICHARD; Tri HS; New Castle, IN; Aud/Vis; Band; Drm Mjrt; Lbry Ade; VICA; Barber Or Hairstylist.

COX, ROBBIN J; West Branch Sr HS; Beloit, OH; Band; Chrh Wkr; Debate Tm; Hon Rl; NHS; VP FFA; Tech Schl; Landscape Desgn.

COX, ROBIN; Muskegon Sr HS; Muskegon, MI; Hon Rl; NHS; Wrstlng; Coach Actv; Letter In Wrestling Also Baguba Awd Most Valuable Player; Grand Vly St Coll Hnr Schlrshp; Michigan St Comp; Grand Vly St Coll; Acctg.

COX, SALLY; Portsmouth HS; Portsmouth, OH; 21/226 Sec Frsh Cls; Band; Drl Tm; Hon Rl; Hosp Ade; NHS; Lat Clb; PPFtbl; Shawnee St Cmnty Coll; Dent Hygn.

COX, SANDY; Lebanon HS; Lebanon, OH; Chrs; Chrh Wkr; Drl Tm; Treas Girl Scts; Hon Rl; Lbry Ade; NHS; FTA; Spn Clb; IM Sprt; Miami Univ; Scndry Educ Math.

COX, STEPHANIE; Washington HS; Massillon, OH; Sec Jr Cls; Sec Sr Cls; Am Leg Aux Girls St; Chrs; Hon Rl; Jr NHS; NHS; Off Ade; Red Cr Ade; College.

COX, SUSAN; High School; Huntington, WV; Aud/Vis; Band; Chrs; Chrh Wkr; Girl Scts; Hon Rl; Off Ade; Sch Mus; Yth Flsp; Mth Clb; Marshall Univ; Bus.

COX, TAMMY; Midland Trail HS; Ramsey, WV; Chrs; Off Ade; Pep Clb; Univ; Bus Mgmt.

COX, THERESA; Lockland HS; Lockland, OH; Girl Scts; Hon Rl; Stu Cncl; Yrbk; Fr Clb; Pep Clb; Spn Clb; Trk; Chrldng; GAA; Exec Sec.

COX, THOMAS; R B Hayes HS; Delaware, OH; Cls Rep Sr Cls; AFS; Band; Chrh Wkr; Hon Rl; Jr NHS; Stu Cncl; Key Clb; Capt Ftbl; Wrstlng; Miami Univ Of Ohio.

COX, VELVET; Pickaway Ross HS; Chillicothe, OH; Trs Jr Cls; Chrs; Chrh Wkr; Debate Tm; Girl Scts; Hon Rl; Hosp Ade; Lbry Ade; NHS; Yth Flsp; Ohio Univ; CPA.

COX, VELVET; Pickaway Ross Joint Voc HS; Chillicothe, OH; Trs Jr Cls; Chrs; Chrh Wkr; Debate Tm; Hon Rl; Hosp Ade; Lbry Ade; Bus Schl; Cpa.

COX, WILLIAM F; Richmond Sr HS; Richmond, IN; Boy Scts; Chrh Wkr; Hon Rl; JA; Lbry Ade; NHS; JA Awd; Chess Club Tm Capt; Top Bd 78; 8

Sem Perf Attndc 75; 23 Consecutive Mos Carrier Hon Roll; Paladium Hem 77; Univ; Med.

COY, JENNIFER; Waynesfield Goshen HS; New Hampshire, OH; Band; Drl Tm; Hon Rl; 4-H; FHA; Spn Clb; Gym; Trk; Chrldng; PPFtbl; Univ; Spec Ed.

COY, KELLY; Hamilton Southeastern HS; Noblesville, IN; 43/135 Chrs; Hon Rl; Sch Mus; Sch Pl; Stg Crw; Drama Clb; Ball State; Pre Med.

COY, NICKY; Stryker Local School; Stryker, OH; Band; Hon Rl; Sch Pl; Stg Crw; Pres Stu Cncl; Yrbk; Pres 4-H; VP FHA; Letter Trk; 4-H Awd; Spec Schl; Interior Design.

COY, SUSAN; Jay Cnty HS; Portland, IN; 28/474 Cmnty Wkr; Hon Rl; Jr NHS; NHS; Y-Teens; 4-H; Spn Clb; Letter Trk; 4-H Awd; Univ; Home Ec.

COYLE, CATHY; Elmhurst HS; Ft Wayne, IN; 38/400 AFS; Hon Rl; Rptr Yrbk; PPFtbl; Univ; Engr.

COYLE, RUTH; Belmont HS; Dayton, OH; Girl Scts; Hon Rl; Lbry Ade; Off Ade; Sct Actv; Pres Spn Clb; Socr; Ohi State Univ; Forestry.

COYNE, DAVID; Euclid Sr HS; Euclid, OH; 10/700 Hon Rl; Pol Wkr; Civ Clb; Key Clb; Capt Crs Cntry; Letter Swmmng; Trk; Wrstlng; Natl Merit Ltr; Cleveland St Univ; Civil Engr.

COYNE, EDWARD J; Linsly Inst; Wheeling, WV; Pres Frsh Cls; FCA; Hon Rl; ROTC; Sch Mus; Stu Cncl; Ger Clb; Bsbl; Bsktbl; Ftbl;.

COYNE, ERIN; Wheeling Central HS; Wheeling, WV; Hon Rl; Chrldng; Mat Maids; West Virginia Univ; Bus Mgmt.

COYNE, JOSEPH H; University Of Detroit HS; Detroit, MI; Boy Scts; Chrh Wkr; Hon Rl; Sch Pl; St g Crw; Spn Clb; Ftbl; Opt Clb Awd;.

COYNE, KELLY S; Newark Sr HS; Newark, OH; Hon Rl; Jr NHS; NHS; Univ; Math.

COYNE, KIMBERLY; Eastlake North HS; Timberlake, OH; 55/708 Am Leg Aux Girls St; Hon Rl; Stu Cncl; Pep Clb; Spn Clb; Trk; Univ; Acctg.

COZ, LAURA; Windham HS; Garrettsville, OH; Band; Chrs; Chrh Wkr; Hon Rl; NHS; Sch Pl; Stg Crw; Spn Clb; Scr Kpr; Univ; Zoology.

COZAD, MICHAEL; Wheeling Park HS; Wheeling, WV; 119/599 Lbry Ade; Trk; Wv Univ; Med.

CRABB, JEFF; Hanover Central HS; Cedar Lake, IN; 46/137 Chrh Wkr; Hon Rl; Sch Nwsp; Indiana Univ; Law.

CRABBE, LAURA; Amanda Clearcreek HS; Stoutsville, OH; VP Sr Cls; Band; Chrh Wkr; Hon Rl; Yth Flsp; Rptr Yrbk; 4-H; Sci Clb; Bsbl; Chrldng; Ohio St Univ; Obstitrition.

CRABBS, CHRIS; Shelby Sr HS; Shelby, OH; Boy Scts; Chrs; Hon Rl; Fr Clb; Wrstlng; Ohio St Univ; Mech Engr.

CRABILL, JOHN G; La Salle HS; South Bend, IN; 5/417 Cls Rep Soph Cls; VP Jr Cls; Cls Rep Sr Cls; Band; Boy Scts; Pres Debate Tm; NHS; Yrbk; Ten; Univ; Mission Work.

CRABLE, RHONDA P; St Francis De Sales HS; Columbus, OH; Drl Tm; Spn Clb; Gym; Ten; PPFtbl; Miss Outstndg Awd Drill Tm Camp 1978; Univ; Mdse.

CRABTREE, DAVID; Kyger Creek HS; Addison, OH; VP Soph Cls; Band; Hon Rl; Mod UN; NHS; Stu Cncl; Fr Clb; Key Clb; Bsbl; Letter Ten; Sandy Niniger Awd; College; Medicine.

CRABTREE, DOUG; Stow HS; Stow, OH; Chrh Wkr; Debate Tm; Hon Rl; Natl Forn Lg; NHS; Socr; Natl Hnr Soc 10th Grd Fairfield Oh; Attended Austrian Public Schls German Speaking; Evangel Coll; Bible.

CRABTREE, JUDITH; Hartford HS; Hartford, MI; 3/97 Sec Soph Cls; Sec Jr Cls; Sec Band; Hon Rl; Pres NHS; Rptr Yrbk; Yrbk; VP Pep Clb; Spn Clb; Pom Pon; Western Mi Univ Acad Schlrshp 79; St Of Mi Competitive Schlrshp 79; Western Michigan Univ.

CRABTREE, KATHLEEN S; South Point HS; South Point, OH; Cl Rep Jr Cls; Cmp Fr Grls; Hon Rl; OEA; Pep Clb; Univ Of Cincinnati; Bus.

CRABTREE, KATHRYN; Fairview HS; Fairvw Pk, OH; 4/285 Cls Rep Sr Cls; AFS; Aud/Vis; Cmnty Wkr; Drl Tm; Hon Rl; NHS; Pol Wkr; Rptr Sch Nwsp; Pres Rdo Clb; Northwestern Univ; Broadcasting.

CRABTREE, LU ELLA; Dawson Bryant HS; Coal Grove, OH; 26/122 Sec Sr Cls; Cls Rep Sr Cls; Debate Tm; Hon Rl; NHS; Off Ade; Yth Flsp; FHA; Pep Clb; GAA;.

CRABTREE, NORMA; Northwest HS; Lucasville, OH; 5/148 Hon Rl; Jr NHS; Lbry Ade; Quill & Scroll; Sch Pl; Rptr Yrbk; FTA; Univ Of Cin; Chemcial Engr.

CRABTREE, PATRICIA; Eastern HS; Beaver, OH; Band; Chrs; Hon Rl; Treas MMM; Yrbk; Sch Nwsp; FHA; Columbus Tech Inst; Sec.

CRABTREE, SANDY; Walter P Chrysler Memrl HS; New Castle, IN; 12/400 Hon Rl; Jr NHS; NHS; VP OEA; Hon Jckt Winner 3.8 Avrg For 6 Sems 78; Hon Cert Recgnt 77 & 78; Regnl St & Natl Offc Educ Assoc 79; Voc Schl; Bus Admin.

CRABTREE, SOPHIA Y; Tri Valley HS; Frazeysburg, OH; Chrs; Chrh Wkr; Hon Rl; Yth Flsp;.

CRABTREE, TONDA; Benjamin Logan HS; Zanesfield, OH; 23/157 Chrs; Chrh Wkr; Hon Rl; FTA; OEA;.

CRABTREE, TRACY D; Alexandria Monroe HS; Alexandria, IN; Cls Rep Soph Cls; Cl Rep Jr Cls; Pres Sr Cls; Chrs; Hon Rl; Sch Nwsp; Bsbl; Bsktbl; Ftbl; Hockey; Arizona St Univ; Tchr.

CRABTREE JR, GLENN; Hampshire HS; Romney, WV; 57/250 AFS; Band; Hon Rl; Pol Wkr; Sch Pl; Stu Cncl; Drama Clb; West Virginia Univ; Acctg.

CRACKEL, DANIEL; Owosso HS; Owosso, MI; 16/406 Hon Rl; NHS; Lat Clb; Letter Bsbl; Crs Cntry; Michigan St Univ; Elec Engr.

CRADY, SANDRA; Gwinn HS; K I Sawyer Afb, MI; Pres Jr Cls; VP Jr Cls; Sec Jr Cls; Hon Rl; Hosp Ade; NHS; Stu Cncl; Univ Of Mic Ann Arbor; Pre Med.

CRAFT, CHERYL; Portsmouth E HS; Portsmouth, OH; 14/81 Hon Rl; Lbry Ade; NHS; Lat Clb; Spn Clb; Cit Awd; Hnr Awrd 3 Yrs Stu Librarian 79; Citizenship Awrd 74; Honor Roll Cert 76 79; Mercy Hosp; Med Tech.

CRAFT, CHERYL; Chaminade Julienne HS; Dayton, OH; Chrs; Hon Rl; Off Ade; Miami Jacobs; Fashion Mdse.

CRAFT, DEB; Wapakoneta Sr HS; Wapakoneta, OH; 54/335 Am Leg Aux Girls St; Chrs; Girl Scts; Hon Rl; Red Cr Ade; Sch Mus; Sct Actv; Yth Flsp; Drama Clb; OEA; Ohio Univ; Travel Agent.

CRAFT, LES; Mansfield Christian HS; Crestline, OH; VP Frsh Cls; Cl Rep Jr Cls; Stu Cncl; Voc Schl; Carpentry.

CRAFT, LLOYD E; Fairmont Sr HS; Fairmont, WV; Trs Jr Cls; Am Leg Boys St; Band; Chrs; Hon Rl; Jr NHS; Mdrgl; NHS; Sch Mus; Sch Pl; West Virginia Univ; Pharm.

CRAFT, SUSAN; Westland HS; Grove City, OH; DECA; Ohio State Univ.

CRAFT, SUSAN; Hamilton Taft HS; Hamilton, OH; Trs Frsh Cls; Cls Rep Frsh Cls; Cls Rep Soph Cls; Cl Rep Jr Cls; Band; Chrs; Drl Tm; Hon Rl; Off Ade; Sch Pl; Univ Of Cincinnati; Retailing.

CRAFT, WESLEY; Mansfield Christian HS; Crestline, OH; Pres Frsh Cls; Cl Rep Jr Cls; Stu Cncl; Bsktbl; Factory Work.

CRAGO, DONALD; Madonna HS; Weirton, WV; Boy Scts; Chrh Wkr; Hon Rl; Lit Mag; Sct Actv; Yrbk; West Virginia Univ; Engr.

CRAIG, CINDY; Peck Community HS; , ; Sec Frsh Cls; Cls Rep Soph Cls; Cl Rep Jr Cls; Cls Rep Sr Cls; Chrh Wkr; Cmnty Wkr; NHS; Sch Pl; Yth Flsp; Drama Clb; St Clair Comm Coll; Special Ed.

CRAIG, CYNTHIA; Groveport Madison Fresh Schl; Columbus, OH; Rptr Sch Nwsp; Scr Kpr; Ohio St Univ; Phys Ther.

CRAIG, CYNTHIA; Bellbrook HS; Bellbrook, OH; Band; Girl Scts; Sch Mus; Yrbk; Rptr Sch Nwsp; Sch Nwsp; Lat Clb; Pep Clb; Ten; GAA; Ohio State; Clothing Buyer.

CRAIG, DIANE; Akron Fairgrove HS; Fairgrove, MI; Trs Jr Cls; Band; Chrh Wkr; Sec Girl Scts; Hon Rl; NHS; Treas Stu Cncl; Yth Flsp; FHA; Letter Bsbl; Acad Awrd History 79; FHA St Convention 1st Plc In Market Place 79; Jobs Daughters Grand Bethel Rep 79; Univ; Med.

CRAIG, JULIA; North Lawrence HS; Bedford, IN; 6/417 Girl Scts; Hon Rl; NHS; 4-H; Mth Clb; Spn Clb;.

CRAIG, JULIA; Bedford N Lawrence HS; Bedford, IN; 7/380 Girl Scts; Hon Rl; NHS; 4-H; Spn Clb; Am Leg Awd; Univ; Comp Sci.

CRAIG, KIMBERLY; Norton HS; Norton, OH; Hon Rl; Hosp Ade; FHA; FNA; Mth Clb; Gym; Chrldng; GAA; Twrlr; Cit Awd; St Louis Univ; Nursing.

CRAIG, LESLIE; Chaminade Julienne HS; Dayton, OH; Chrs; Chrh Wkr; Cmnty Wkr; Red Cr Ade; Yth Flsp; Spn Clb; Alpha Beta Kappa Schlrshp Awrd 75; Amer Natl Red Cross Recog Awrd 77; Ohio St Univ; Occptnl Ther.

CRAIG, LISA A; Marion Franklin Sr HS; Columbus, OH; Cl Rep Jr Cls; Chrs; Cmnty Wkr; Hon Rl; Sch Pl; Stu Cncl; Fr Clb; OEA; Excepted At Northwest Career Center Vocational Schl Financial Clerk Prog; Univ Of California; Theatre.

CRAIG, MARY; Saints Peter & Paul Area HS; Sgnw, MI; Sec Jr Cls; Sec Frsh Cls; Mdrgl; Sch Mus; Stu Cncl; Rptr Yrbk; Coach Actv; GAA; PPFtbl; College; Med.

CRAIG, MARY; New Buffalo Sr HS; New Buffalo, MI; 5/95 VP Sr Cls; Band; Off Ade; Spn Clb; Letter Bsktbl; Cit Awd; Univ; Aviation.

CRAIG, MOLLIE S; Ridgemont HS; Ridgeway, OH; 6/70 Hst Soph Cls; VP Jr Cls; Band; Drl Tm; Drm Mjrt; Hon Rl; NHS; Yrbk; College; Art.

CRAIG, NANCY; Elston HS; Michigan City, IN; 15/301 Pres Soph Cls; Band; NHS; Sch Mus; Sch Pl; Stg Crw; Stu Cncl; Drama Clb; Lion Awd; College; Bio Chem.

CRAIG, PAMELA; Milan HS; Milan, MI; Trs Jr Cls; Trs Sr Cls; Drm Mjrt; Girl Scts; Hon Rl; Swmmng; Trk; Chrldng; GAA; Twrlr; Washtenaw Comm Coll; Dental Asst.

CRAIG, PETER; Shortridge HS; Indianapolis, IN; Band; Hon Rl; Mth Clb; Rus Clb; Am Leg Awd; Univ; Comp Tech.

CRAIG, REBECCA; Fountain Central HS; Veedersburg, IN; 26/118 Trs Sr Cls; Hon Rl; NHS; Off Ade; Sch Mus; Drama Clb; Pep Clb; Vincennes Univ; Recreation Lesier.

CRAIG, SUSAN; Clarksville HS; Clarksville, IN; 12/147 Hon Rl; Quill & Scroll; Yrbk; Rptr Sch Nwsp; Sec DECA; OEA; Spn Clb; Indiana St Univ; Acctg.

CRAIGIE, GLEN M; Walled Lake Western HS; Walled Lk, MI; Boy Scts; Hon Rl; UM; Aero Engr.

CRAIGO, CANDICE; Normandy HS; Parma, OH; 44/649 Chrs; Chrh Wkr; Hon Rl; Pep Clb; Spn Clb; Chrldng; Univ; Health Serv.

CRAIN, RUTH; Benjamin Logan HS; West Mansfield, OH; 13/153 Hon Rl; Jr NHS; NHS; Sch Pl; FTA; OEA; Pres Spn Clb; L Lockwood & B Logan Ed Assoc Schlrshp 79; Hnrbl Mntn In St Schlstc Test Eng 12 79; Basic Ed Opp Grnt 79; Morehead St Univ; Bus Educ.

CRALL, MARTHA; Bullock Creek HS; Midland, MI; 2/160 Cl Rep Jr Cls; Pres Sr Cls; Sal; Hon Rl; NHS; Ed Sch Nwsp; Sprt Ed Sch Nwsp; Pep Clb; DAR Awd; Natl Merit SF; HS Co Op Dow Chemical Co; Sports Correspondent & Columnist Midland Daily News; Univ Of Michigan; Journalism.

CRAMER, DARLENE; Fulton HS; Middleton, MI; Band; Chrs; Chrh Wkr; Yth Flsp; 4-H; FHA; Pep Clb; Trk; 4-H Awd; Univ; Spec Educ Tchr.

CRAMER, DAVID; Lincolnview HS; Van Wert, OH; Cl Rep Jr Cls; Chrs; Chrh Wkr; Stu Cncl; Yth Flsp; 4-H; FFA; Trk; Wrstlng; 4-H Awd; Wilmington Univ; Phys Ed.

CRAMER, DEBORAH; Goodrich HS; Grand Blanc, MI; VP Frsh Cls; Hon Rl; Sch Pl; Stg Crw; Ed Yrbk; Rptr Yrbk; Rptr Sch Nwsp; Pres Fr Clb; Letter Bsktbl; Letter Trk; Ctrl Mich Univ; Phys Educ.

CRAMER, DOUGLAS; Garrett HS; Garrett, IN; Hst Frsh Cls; Hon Rl; VP Yth Flsp; Rptr Sch Nwsp; VP Ger Clb; Sci Fair 1st Pl 74; Tri Kappa Hon Roll 75 & 76; Indiana Univ; Comp Sci.

CRAMER, JANICE; Buckeye HS; Litchfield, OH; 2/181 Sal; Chrs; Chrh Wkr; NHS; 4-H; FHA; Spn Clb; Natl Merit Schl; Voice Dem Awd; Oberlin Coll; Bio.

CRAMER, JEFF; Mona Shores HS; Muskegon, MI; Band; Mich State; Elec Engr.

CRAMER, KENNETH; Magnolia HS; New Martinsvle, WV; 5/200 Am Leg Boys St; Band; Chrh Wkr; Debate Tm; Hon Rl; NHS; Treas Mth Clb; College; Electrical Engr.

CRAMER, MICHELLE; Loudonville HS; Perrysville, OH; 11/133 Band; Hon Rl; Lbry Ade; NHS; Sch Mus; Stg Crw; Sch Nwsp; GAA; The Ohi State Univ; Phys Ther.

CRAMER, PHILLIP; Culver Military Acad; Culver, IN; Band; FCA; Hon Rl; ROTC; Yth Flsp; Bsktbl; Ftbl; IM Sprt; Cit Awd; College.

CRAMPTON, CATHY; St Stephen Area HS; Saginaw, MI; 20/84 Sec Frsh Cls; Sec Soph Cls; Sec Jr Cls; Hon Rl; NHS; Sch Pl; Stg Crw; Beta Clb; Drama Clb; Pep Clb; Ctrl Michigan Univ; Bus Admin.

CRANDELL, MARCIE; Swartz Creek HS; Gaines, MI; Band; Hon Rl; 4-H; Trk; Scr Kpr; Tmr; 4-H Awd; Michigan St Univ; Animal Tech.

CRANE, CINDY; Ross Beatty HS; Cassopolis, MI; Chrh Wkr; Hon Rl; NHS; Rptr Sch Nwsp; 4-H; FFA; Bsktbl; Trk; FFA Greenhand Farmer 76; FFA Chap Farm 77; FFA Outdoor Recreation Awd 78; Kansas Cty Mtrpltn Jr Coll; PE Tchr.

CRANE, ELLEN; Perry HS; Perry, MI; 15/150 Band; Hon Rl; NHS; Yth Flsp; FHA; Univ; Law.

CRANE, JEFF; Attica Jr Sr HS; Attica, IN; 2/76 Trs Frsh Cls; Cl Rep Jr Cls; Cmnty Wkr; Hon Rl; NHS; Pol Wkr; Bsbl; Letter Ftbl; IM Sprt; Wabash College; Law.

CRANE, JILL; Edwardsburg HS; Edwardsbg, MI; 38/151 Chrh Wkr; Sch Mus; Sct Actv; Stg Crw; Yth Flsp; Rptr Yrbk; Drama Clb; Fr Clb; Mic State Univ ; Pre Med.

CRANE, LORI; Westfield Washington HS; Carmel, IN; Hon Rl; Pep Clb; Spn Clb; PPFtbl; College; Bus.

CRANE, MARIE; Edwardsburg HS; Edwardsburg, MI; Debate Tm; Fr Clb; Bsktbl; Tmr; College; Special Education.

CRANE, MICHAEL; Cass Tech HS; Detroit, MI; Hon Rl; NHS; OEA; Natl Merit SF; 1st Pl Date Process BOEC Region Compt 1979; Michigan St Univ; Comp Sci.

CRANE, SCOTT J; North Central HS; Indianapolis, IN; 58/1194 Cls Rep Frsh Cls; Cls Rep Soph Cls; Hon Rl; JA; Red Cr Ade; Stu Cncl; Ger Clb; Sci Clb; IM Sprt; JA Awd; Northwestern Univ; Med.

CRANFORD, CHERYL; Amanda Clearcreek HS; Amanda, OH; Cmp Fr Grls; Hon Rl; Yrbk; FSA; Sci Clb; GAA; IM Sprt; Ohio St Univ; Phys Ther.

CRANKSHAW, MARC; Lapeer East HS; Lapeer, MI; Hon Rl; Lbry Ade; NHS; Letter Ftbl; Trk; Tmr; MVP & Co Capt Of Frosh Bsktbl Tm 76; Univ Of Michigan; Space Sci.

CRANOR, NANCY; Ben Davis HS; Indianapolis, IN; 3 Sec.

CRANSTON, WILLIAM; Wheeling Park HS; Wheeling, WV; 7/599 Cls Rep Frsh Cls; Cls Rep Soph Cls; Cl Rep Jr Cls; Band; Boy Scts; Chrs; Chrh Wkr; Hon Rl; Stu Cncl; Mth Clb; Univ; Bus Admin.

CRARY, CAREN; William Henry Harrison HS; Lafayette, IN; Band; Mth Clb; Gym; Purdue Univ; Elem Ed.

CRASE, SHEENA; Galion Sr HS; Galion, OH; 16/272 Band; Hon Rl; Hosp Ade; Yth Flsp; OEA; GAA; Mat Maids; Bus Schl.

CRAVEN, MARKHAM; Mt Gilead HS; Mt Gilead, OH; Band; Boy Scts; Hon Rl; Sch Pl; Sct Actv; Stg Crw; Drama Clb; Pres Fr Clb; Metorious Thespian Serv; Eagle Scout; Wright St Univ; Engr Physics.

CRAVEN, PENNY; Fraser HS; Mt Clemens, MI; Girl Scts; Hon Rl; JA; Jr NHS; Stu Cncl; Gym; Chrldng; Tampa Univ; Psych.

CRAVEN, TERRI; Woodrow Wilson HS; Beckley, WV; Hon Rl; Off Ade; Pep Clb; Letter Ten; Chrldng; W Virginia Univ; Dent Hygiene.

CRAVENS, MARGIE; Crothersville Community HS; Crothersville, IN; Sec Sr Cls; Drl Tm; Hon Rl; NHS; Yth Flsp; Yrbk; 4-H; Oral Roberts Univ.

CRAVER, KIMBERLY; Nordonia Hills HS; Northfield, OH; Arizona St Univ; Bus.

CRAVER, STEPHANIE; Union HS; Grandrapids, MI; 10/400 Pres Soph Cls; Cls Rep Soph Cls; Cl Rep Jr Cls; Cls Rep Sr Cls; Hon Rl; Mod UN; NHS; Sch Pl; Pres Stu Cncl; Yth Flsp; Western Michigan Univ; Speech Path.

CRAWFIS, SANDI; Bellefontaine Sr HS; Bellefontaine, OH; 7/245 Sec Frsh Cls; Am Leg Aux Girls St; Chrs; Cmnty Wkr; Hon Rl; Jr NHS; NHS; Off Ade; Sch Mus; Sch Pl; Coll; Med.

CRAWFORD, BECKY; West Union HS; West Union, OH; Am Leg Aux Girls St; Hon Rl; NHS; Stu Cncl; Yth Flsp; Yrbk; Sec Eng Clb; Pres FHA; Pep Clb; Mgrs; Schlrshp Team 3 Yrs; College; Education.

CRAWFORD, BIANCA M; Bishop Noll Institute; Gary, IN; 179/321 Cls Rep Frsh Cls; Band; Chrh Wkr; Cmnty Wkr; Hon Rl; Pol Wkr; Stu Cncl; Y-Teens; Serv Club 79; Xinos SH Sclstc Club Of Phi Delta Kappa 78; Univ Of Michigan; Pediatric Nursing.

CRAWFORD, BRENDA; East HS; , ; 3/276 Hon Rl; Jr NHS; NHS; Off Ade; Stu Cncl; OEA; Spn Clb; 4-H Awd; JA Awd; Columbus Tech Inst; Comp Sci.

CRAWFORD, CATHERINE; Southfield HS; Southfield, MI; Chrs; Chrh Wkr; Cmnty Wkr; Hon Rl; Lbry Ade; NHS; Off Ade; ROTC; Sch Mus; Sch Pl; Univ Of Mich; Psych.

CRAWFORD, CYNTHIA; Columbia Central HS; Brooklyn, MI; 10/170 Cls Rep Frsh Cls; Cls Rep Soph Cls; Am Leg Aux Girls St; Chrs; Hon Rl; NHS; Stg Crw; 4-H; Gym; Chrldng; Univ Of Toledo; Elem Ed.

CRAWFORD, DAN; Felicity Franklin HS; Bethel, OH; Cls Rep Frsh Cls; Aud/Vis; Sch Pl; Stu Cncl; Pres FFA; Bsktbl; Crs Cntry; Capt Trk; Mgrs; Clermont County All Star Track Tm 78 79; Univ; Cmnctns.

CRAWFORD, DOUG; Lima Sr HS; Lima, OH; Chrh Wkr; Hon Rl; Sct Actv; Yth Flsp; DECA; 2nd Advtsng Comp 1979; Top Ten Ad Comp St 1979; 1st Flag Dsgn 1977; Univ Of Dayton; Cmrcl Dsgn.

CRAWFORD, DWENDOLYN; Inkster HS; Inkster, MI; Cmnty Wkr; Hon Rl; JA; Sch Pl; Ten; JA Awd; Natl Merit Ltr; Nursing Schl; RN.

CRAWFORD, JANI; Avon Jr Sr HS; Danville, IN; Chrs; Chrh Wkr; Drl Tm; Hon Rl; Lbry Ade; NHS; Yth Flsp; Fr Clb; Pom Pon;.

CRAWFORD, JEFF; Waverly HS; Lansing, MI; 74/369 Aud/Vis; FCA; Jr NHS; Letter Ftbl; Letter Trk; IM Sprt; PPFtbl; Varsity Club Mbr 77 79; Mi Comptn Schlrshp 79; Michigan St Univ; Fisheries.

CRAWFORD, JIM; St Ignatius HS; Lakewood, OH; Debate Tm; Hon Rl; Hosp Ade; JA; VP Mod UN; Pol Wkr; Stu Cncl; Pep Clb; JA Awd; John Carroll Univ; Law.

CRAWFORD, JOANNE; Hillman Cmnty HS; Hillman, MI; 4/60 Chrs; Hon Rl; NHS; Sch Pl; Stu Cncl; Rptr Sch Nwsp;.

CRAWFORD, JODI; Montabella HS; Edmore, MI; Pres Jr Cls; Band; Chrh Wkr; Drl Tm; Hon Rl; Chrldng; PPFtbl; Central Michigan Univ.

CRAWFORD, JOHN; Amelia HS; Cincinnati, OH; Cls Rep Soph Cls; Boy Scts; Hon Rl; Ftbl; Hockey; Wrstlng; IM Sprt; Univ; Bus.

CRAWFORD, JOY; School Craft HS; Schoolcraft, MI; Band; Chrs; Drm Mjrt; Hon Rl; Sch Pl; Capt Bsktbl; Trk; Twrlr; Univ; Phys Ed.

CRAWFORD, KATHI; Champion HS; Warren, OH; 53/214 Trs Jr Cls; Off Ade; Stu Cncl; Sch Nwsp; Pres 4-H; Sec OEA; 4-H Awd; Kent St Univ; Office Admin.

CRAWFORD, KAY; Northmor HS; Mt Gilead, OH; 3/120 Chrh Wkr; FCA; Girl Scts; Hon Rl; NHS; Stu Cncl; Yth Flsp; Ed Sch Nwsp; Sec 4-H; VP FHA; Bluffton Coll; Elem Ed.

CRAWFORD, KEVIN; Highland HS; Anderson, IN; Band; Pres Chrh Wkr; Lbry Ade; Lat Clb; Div Rating In Indianan Cntrl S Schl Music Assn Solo; Art Ach Awd; Spec Mention Ach Awd; Coll; Music.

CRAWFORD, KIMRICK; Warrensville Hts HS; Warrensvl Hts, OH; Rptr Sch Nwsp; Crs Cntry; Trk; Natl Merit Ltr;.

CRAWFORD, LAURIE; W Branch HS; Beloit, OH; 13/240 Sec Sr Cls; Am Leg Aux Girls St; Chrs; Chrh Wkr; Girl Scts; Hon Rl; NHS; Sct Actv; Yth Flsp; Grove City Coll; Educ.

CRAWFORD, MARIBETH; Hoover HS; North Canton, OH; Band; Hon Rl; Sch Mus; 4-H; Sci Clb; Spn Clb; 4-H Awd; College; Music Perform.

CRAWFORD, MELANIE; S Harrison HS; Jane Lew, WV; Cls Rep Frsh Cls; Cls Rep Soph Cls; Chrh Wkr; Girl Scts; Hon Rl; Sch Pl; Stu Cncl; Yth Flsp; FHA; FTA; Pep Clb; Fairmont St Univ; Sec.

CRAWFORD, MICHAEL; Hazel Park HS; Ferndale, MI; 1/306 Chrh Wkr; Hon Rl; Mic State; Chem Engr.

CRAWFORD, MITCHELL; Barnesville HS; Barnesville, OH; Cls Rep Frsh Cls; VP Soph Cls; Cl Rep Jr Cls; Boy Scts; Hon Rl; VP Stu Cncl; Fr Clb; FTA; Key Clb; Bsktbl; Ohio Univ; Ind Art Tchr.

CRAWFORD, MOLLY; Tuslaw HS; Navarre, OH; 32/183 Am Leg Aux Girls St; Chrs; Girl Scts; Hon Rl; Hosp Ade; Sch Mus; Sch Pl; Y-Teens; Pep Clb; GAA; Stark Tech Coll; Civil Construction.

CRAWFORD, ROGER; Lynchburg Clay HS; Sardinia, OH; 7/106 Cl Rep Jr Cls; Chrh Wkr; Hon Rl; Pres Jr NHS; Sch Pl; Stu Cncl;.

CRAWFORD, SALLY; Madison HS; Madison, OH; 20/295 Sec Chrh Wkr; Hon Rl; Lbry Ade; Treas Keyettes; Spn Clb; Bob Jones Univ; Acctg.

CRAWFORD, SUSAN; Wayne Trace HS; Grover Hill, OH; Hon Rl; JA; FHA; OEA; Wright St Univ; Sec.

CRAWFORD, TANGI; Norwood HS; Cincinnati, OH; Hon Rl; NHS; Sch Mus; Stg Crw; Fr Clb; Rdo Clb; Letter Ten; Univ Of Cin; Med Tech.

CRAWLEY, BRIAN; Turpin HS; Cincinnati, OH; 9/371 Boy Scts; Sch Pl; Drama Clb; Ftbl; Trk; Univ; Math.

CRAWLEY, ERIN; Turpin HS; Cincinnati, OH; 26/357 Boy Scts; NHS; Sch Pl; Sct Actv; Pres Drama Clb; Natl Merit Ltr; Univ; German.

CRAWMER, CHRISTYE; Bexley HS; Columbus, OH; Sec Soph Cls; Boy Scts; Cmp Fr Grls; Chrs; Orch; Pres Yth Flsp; Tmr; Univ.

CRAYCRAFT, JEFF; Franklin HS; Franklin, OH; Mgrs; Univ.

CREA, DONNA J; Hubbard HS; Hubbard, OH; 36/356 VP Frsh Cls; AFS; Band; Chrs; Girl Scts; Hon Rl; Quill & Scroll; Sch Mus; Stg Crw; Pres Y-Teens; St Elizabeth Schl Of Nursing; Nurse.

CREAGAN, KAREN; Decatur Jr Sr HS; Decatur, MI; Chrh Wkr; Hon Rl; NHS; Off Ade; Stu Cncl; Letter Bsktbl; Mgrs; Scr Kpr; Camp Miniwanka 79; Volleyball Letter 79; Softball Letter 77; Notre Dame Univ; Med.

CREAGAN, ROBERT; Decatur HS; Decatur, MI; 4/80 Pres Jr Cls; Trs Sr Cls; Am Leg Boys St; Chrh Wkr; NHS; Sch Pl; Pres Stu Cncl; Ed Yrbk; Letter Trk; St Meinrad College; Philosophy.

CREAGER, DENISE; Napolean HS; Napoleon, OH; Band; Chrs; Chrh Wkr; Hon Rl; Orch; Lat Clb; Letter Swmmng; Univ.

CREASAP, LAURA B; River Valley HS; Marion, OH; 18/185 Chrh Wkr; Hon Rl; NHS; Off Ade; Stg Crw; Yth Flsp; FBLA; PPFtbl; Scr Kpr; Tmr; Bookkeeping Awd; Scie Fair; College; Data Acctg.

CREASEY, ERROL; Wood Memorial HS; Oakland City, IN; 5/97 Cls Rep Soph Cls; Pres Jr Cls; Am Leg Boys St; Chrh Wkr; Ftbl; Glf; Wrstlng; Am Leg Awd; Voice Dem Awd; Univ; Navy Engr.

CRECELIUS, SARA; Central HS; Newberry, IN; 3/27 Trs Frsh Cls; Sec Soph Cls; Band; Chrs; Chrh Wkr; Hon Rl; 4-H; Pep Clb; Spn Clb; Bsktbl; Vincennes Univ; Accounting.

CRECHIOLO, LORAINE; Aquinas HS; Dearborn Hts, MI; Cls Rep Soph Cls; Cl Rep Jr Cls; Girl Scts; Hon Rl; NHS; Sch Mus; Stg Crw; Bsbl; Capt Chrldng; IM Sprt; Art & Design Coll; Art.

CREDEN, STEPHEN; Niles Sr HS; Niles, MI; Boy Scts; Chrh Wkr; JA; Sct Actv; Hockey; Opt Clb Awd; Coll; Elec Engr.

CREDIT JR, NORMAN; Buffalo HS; Huntington, WV; Boy Scts; Hon Rl; FFA; FHA; Mth Clb; Letter Ftbl; Cit Awd; Air Force.

CREECH, KIMBERLY; Walker Thomas Memorial HS; Indianapolis, IN; Hon Rl; Cit Awd; JC Awd; Bus Schl; Sec.

CREECH, SUZANNE; Bay HS; Bay Vill, OH; Cls Rep Soph Cls; Cl Rep Jr Cls; Yth Flsp; Pep Clb; PPFtbl; Tmr; Univ; Family Relations.

CREECH, TRACY; Western Brown Sr HS; Willmsbrg, OH; Cls Rep Frsh Cls; Cls Rep Soph Cls; Cl Rep Jr Cls; Chrh Wkr; Hon Rl; Off Ade; Sch Pl; Stu Cncl; Yth Flsp; Rptr Sch Nwsp; Southern St Coll; Med Asst.

CREED, LAWRENCE; Hubbard HS; Hubbard, OH; Band; Boy Scts; Hon Rl; Sct Actv; Fr Clb; Boy Scout Sr Patrol Ldr 78; Perfect Attndnc 77; Youngstown St Univ; Civil Engr.

CREED, NATALIE; Logan Elm HS; Circleville, OH; Girl Scts; Hon Rl; NHS; Sct Actv; Coach Actv; Mgrs; Acctg.

CREED, PAT; Lasalle HS; South Bend, IN; 60/488 Pres Frsh Cls; VP Soph Cls; VP Jr Cls; NHS; Letter Swmmng; Trk; IM Sprt; Pom Pon; Scr Kpr; Tmr; Purdu; Engr.

CREED, STEPHANIE; Shaker Hts HS; Shaker Hts, OH; Cls Rep Soph Cls; Cl Rep Jr Cls; AFS; Hon Rl; Lit Mag; Sch Pl; Stg Crw; College; Law.

CREEL, SCOTT R; Walsh Jesuit HS; Akron, OH; 3/175 Band; Hon Rl; Sch Nwsp; Crs Cntry; Trk; College; Vet.

CREEMERS, PAULINE; Chippewa Hills HS; Remus, MI; Hon Rl; FHA; Spn Clb; Crs Cntry; Gym; Trk; Aquinas College; Rn.

CREGO, KELLY; Urbana HS; Urbana, OH; Cmp Fr Grls; Chrs; Cmnty Wkr; Hon Rl; Hosp Ade; Lbry Ade; Lit Mag; Natl Forn Lg; Off Ade; Red Cr Ade; Ohio St Univ; Nursing Practtnr.

CREIGHTON, MARTYNA; Perry HS; Painesville, OH; Band; Chrs; Girl Scts; Lbry Ade; Sch Mus; Pep Clb; Spn Clb; Lakeland; Social Sciences.

CRELIN, JAMES W; Boardman HS; Boardman, OH; 60/556 Boy Scts; Chrh Wkr; FCA; Hon Rl; NHS; Yth Flsp; Letter Bsbl; IM Sprt; Scr Kpr; Univ; CPA.

CREMA, LAURA; Mt Notre Dame HS; Cincinnati, OH; 19/180 Pres Soph Cls; Am Leg Aux Girls St; Hon Rl; Yrbk; Spn Clb; Miami Univ; Pre Law.

CREMEANS, ROBERT B; Huntington East HS; Huntington, WV; Am Leg Boys St; Boy Scts; PAVAS; Pol Wkr; Sct Actv; Stu Cncl; Key Clb; Univ; Art.

CREMEANS, SHANDA R; Crown Point HS; Crown Point, IN; 45/584 Band; Drl Tm; Hon Rl; Lit Mag; NHS; 4-H; Lat Clb; Pep Clb; Letter Trk; Pom Pon; Indiana Univ; Bus.

CREMER, LISA; St Francis Cntrl HS; Morgantown, WV; Chrs; Hon Rl; NHS; Stu Cncl; Ed Sch Nwsp; Rptr Sch Nwsp; Drama Clb; Fr Clb; Mth Clb; Pep Clb; West Virginia Univ; Busns Mgmt.

CREMER, MICHELE; St Francis Central HS; Morgantown, WV; 2/56 Cls Rep Soph Cls; Cl Rep Jr Cls; Cls Rep Sr Cls; Am Leg Aux Girls St; Pres NHS; VP Stu Cncl; Ed Yrbk; Letter Bsktbl; Letter Trk; Cit Awd; West Virginia Univ; Pre Nursing.

CREMIN, ANN; Ann Arbor Pioneer HS; Ann Arbor, MI; Band; Hon Rl; Ger Clb; Letter Swmmng; IM Sprt; Natl Merit Ltr; Univ; Bus.

CREPEAU, DANIEL; Detour Area HS; Goetzville, MI; Debate Tm; NHS; 4-H; Letter Bsbl; Letter Ftbl; 4-H Awd; Michigan Tech Univ; Engr.

CREPS, DAVID; Perrysburg HS; Perrysburg, OH; Hon Rl; Sch Mus; Ten; Coll; Bus.

CRESPO, SYLVIA M; East HS; Youngstown, OH; Chrs; Debate Tm; Hon Rl; NHS; Off Ade; Stu Cncl; OEA; Rdo Clb; Youngstown Univ; Law.

CRESSMAN, GREGORY; W E Groves HS; Southfield, MI; 100/575 Band; Boy Scts; Chrs; Hon Rl; Sch Mus; Wrstlng; St Louis Univ; Engr.

CRESSMAN, JOHN; Chagrin Falls HS; Chagrin Fl, OH; Band; Hon Rl; Ger Clb; Pres VICA; Letter Socr; Univ; Mech Engr.

CRESWELL, SUSAN; East Grand Rapids HS; E Grand Rpd, MI; Trs Frsh Cls; Trs Soph Cls; Trs Jr Cls; Yrbk; Trk; Pom Pon; PPFtbl; Michigan St Univ.

CREVELING, JANE; Shortridge HS; Indianapolis, IN; Cl Rep Jr Cls; Cls Rep Sr Cls; Chrs; Quill & Scroll; Yth Flsp; Yrbk; Sch Nwsp; Fr Clb; Key Clb; Mth Clb; Univ; Spec Ed.

CREVISTON, LAURA; North Putnam HS; Bainbridge, IN; 6/155 Am Leg Aux Girls St; FCA; Hon Rl; Hosp Ade; NHS; Sch Mus; FHA; Pep Clb; Spn Clb; Graceland College; Forestry.

CREW, CHRISTOPHER; Wauseon HS; Wauseon, OH; Chrs; Orch; Sch Mus; Yth Flsp; Fr Clb; Pep Clb; Glf; College; Bus.

CREW, SHARON; Wilbur Wright HS; Dayton, OH; 30/217 Chrs; Chrh Wkr; Cmnty Wkr; Stu Cncl; Yth Flsp; Fr Clb; OEA; Cit Awd; Cntrl St Coll Academic Schlrshp; Delta Sigma Theta Schlrshp; Central St Univ; Acctg.

CREWS, AMY; Southern Local HS; Wellsville, OH; 4/82 Sec Frsh Cls; Cmp Fr Grls; Hon Rl; NHS; FNA; OEA; Bsktbl; Chrldng; Scr Kpr; College; Acctg.

CREWS, BRENDA; Kettering Sr HS; Detroit, MI; Chrh Wkr; Cmnty Wkr; Drl Tm; Hon Rl; Hosp Ade; Hosp Ade; Lbry Ade; Off Ade; ROTC; FHA; Mercy Coll; Nursing.

CREWS, DAVID; Wellsville HS; Wellsville, OH; Hon Rl; NHS; Rptr Yrbk;.

CREWS, ISAAC; Washington HS; Massillon, OH; Cls Rep Frsh Cls; Am Leg Boys St; Chrs; Chrh Wkr; Off Ade; Stu Cncl; Rptr Sch Nwsp; Boys Clb Am; Am Leg Awd; Cit Awd; College; Architecture.

CRIBBINS, SUSAN; Yale HS; Goodells, MI; Chrs; Hon Rl; JA; Stu Cncl; Yrbk; 4-H; Pep Clb; Letter Bsbl; Letter Bsktbl; Letter Trk; St Clair Comm Coll.

CRIBBS, MITCH; Mona Shores HS; Muskegon, MI; Boy Scts; Hon Rl; Letter Wrstlng; Mgrs; Michigan St Univ; Aerospace Engr.

CRIBLEZ, RUTH; Bluffton HS; Bluffton, OH; Am Leg Aux Girls St; Chrs; Hon Rl; Treas Yth Flsp; Pres 4-H; 4-H Awd; College; Computer Science.

CRICKENBERGER, KATHERINE; Pocahontas County HS; Hillsboro, WV; 11/130 Band; Chrh Wkr; Cmnty Wkr; NHS; Orch; Quill & Scroll; Sch Pl; Concord College; Soc Std.

CRICKENBERGER, SARA; Pocahontas County HS; Hillsboro, WV; 6/130 NHS; Stg Crw; Stu Cncl; VP Yth Flsp; Ed Yrbk; Drama Clb; VP 4-H; Pep Clb; Natl Merit Ltr; 3rd Dist Soil Conserv Spch Contest 79; 2nd Know Your United Natns Contst 78; Univ; Med.

CRIDER, REX A; Shawnee Sr HS; Lima, OH; 37/247 Am Leg Boys St; Hon Rl; Rptr Yrbk; Pres Spn Clb; Cit Awd; Univ; Law.

CRIDER, VICKI; Upper Arlington HS; Columbus, OH; 77/610 AFS; Debate Tm; Hon Rl; Treas JA; Pres Natl Forn Lg; Fr Clb; Mgrs; Scr Kpr; Upper Arlington Educ Assoc Schlrshp Awd 79; French Natl Hnr Soc 78; Univ.

CRIDGE, MICHAEL; Madison Heights HS; Anderson, IN; 58/371 Hon Rl; Spn Clb; Letter Glf; Univ.

CRIGGER, BARBARA; Edison HS; Berlin Hts, OH; Lbry Ade; Univ.

CRIHFIELD, DIANNIA; Walton Jr Sr HS; Harmony, WV; 6/34 VP Sr Cls; Cls Rep Sr Cls; Band; Drm Mjrt; Hon Rl; Jr NHS; NHS; Sch Pl; Stu Cncl; Yth Flsp; Glenville St Coll; Busns.

CRIMINSKI, SCOTT; Linsly Institute; Wheeling, WV; 1/70 Chrh Wkr; Hon Rl; NHS; ROTC; Sch Mus; Letter Bsbl; Letter Ftbl; Letter Wrstlng; Univ; Chem.

CRINER, BARBARA; South Harrison HS; Clarksburg, WV; Band; Chrs; Stg Crw; Yrbk; Rptr Sch Nwsp; Trk; GAA;.

CRINER, BRIAN; Roscommon HS; Roscommon, MI; 20/118 Band; Chrs; Chrh Wkr; Orch; Yth Flsp; IM Sprt; Natl Merit Schl; Univ; Music.

CRINER, CHRISTINE M; Liberty HS; Clarksburg, WV; Cls Rep Soph Cls; Cl Rep Jr Cls; Band; Hon Rl; Jr NHS; Natl Forn Lg; Sch Mus; Sch Pl; Stu Cncl; Y-Teens; Univ; Drama.

CRING, SUSAN; Big Walnut HS; Sunbury, OH; 7/250 Am Leg Aux Girls St; Band; Chrh Wkr; NHS; Yth Flsp; Yrbk; 4-H; Fr Clb; Bsktbl; Ohio St Univ; Nursing.

CRINO, BONNIE; Memorial HS; Campbell, OH; Cls Rep Frsh Cls; Rptr Yrbk; FHA; Key Clb; Mth Clb; Pep Clb; Michigan State College; Arts.

CRIPE, DONALD D; Mt Healthy HS; Cincinnati, OH; 13/672 Hon Rl; Jr NHS; Univ Of Cincinnati; Med.

CRIPE, JACQUIE; Greensburg Comm HS; Greensburg, IN; 21/211 Cls Rep Soph Cls; VP Jr Cls; Pres Sr Cls; Chrs; Chrh Wkr; Hon Rl; Jr NHS; Mdrgl; NHS; Off Ade;.

CRIPE, MELODIE; Goshen HS; Goshen, IN; 20/268 Band; Pres FCA; Hon Rl; Lbry Ade; NHS; Orch; Stu Cncl; VP Yth Flsp; VP 4-H; Letter Bsktbl; Coll; Phys Therapy.

CRIPLIVER, TOM; Thomas A Edison HS; Lake Station, IN; 32/173 Cls Rep Frsh Cls; VP Soph Cls; Am Leg Boys St; Band; Chrs; Hon Rl; Off Ade; Sch Mus; Sch Pl; Stg Crw; Student Council V P 1977; Student Council Pres 1978; Univ; Tchr.

CRIPPS, DONNA; Twin Valley South HS; W Alex, OH; Cmnty Wkr; Drl Tm; Hon Rl; Sch Pl; Stu Cncl; Sch Nwsp; DECA; FBLA; Rdo Clb; Mgrs; Montgomery Cnty JVS; Fshn Mdse.

CRISLER, TIMOTHY; New Haven HS; New Haven, IN; Band; Off Ade; Stu Cncl; Bsbl; Trk; Wrstlng; Outstndng Soph Of Stndt Councl 77; Bandsman Awd 77; Univ.

CRISLIP, MELINDA L; Ashtabula HS; Ashtabula, OH; 19/269 AFS; Band; Chrs; Chrh Wkr; Hon Rl; VP JA; NHS; Sch Mus; Drama Clb; VP Key Clb; Univ; Creative Writing.

CRISLIP, MICHELLE; Wellsville HS; Wellsville, OH; Band; Cmnty Wkr; Girl Scts; Sct Actv; Y-Teens; Rptr Sch Nwsp; FTA; Pep Clb; Ohio St Univ; Interior Decorating.

CRISON, GREG; Yale HS; Goodells, MI; Hon Rl; JA Awd; Univ.

CRISP, DANIEL; London HS; London, OH; Cls Rep Frsh Cls; Boy Scts; Chrh Wkr; Hon Rl; NHS; PAVAS; Sch Pl; Stg Crw; Stu Cncl; Pres Yth Flsp; U S Naval Acad; Ocean Engr.

CRISS, REBECCA; North Ridgeville Sr HS; N Ridgeville, OH; 10/333 Band; Hon Rl; NHS; Off Ade; Orch; Yth Flsp; Bowling Green St Univ; Mrktng.

CRISS, WAYNE P; Lincoln HS; Lumberport, WV; 9/158 Hon Rl; NHS; Yrbk; Fairmont St Coll.

CRIST, DONNA; Midland Trail HS; Ansted, WV; Band; Chrh Wkr; Drl Tm; Hon Rl; Stu Cncl; Yth Flsp; Fr Clb; Pep Clb; Scr Kpr; Wv Inst Of Tech; Music.

CRIST, FREDRICK; Woodsfield HS; Woodsfield, OH; Band; Boy Scts; Sch Pl; Rptr Yrbk; Yrbk; Drama Clb; 4-H; Fr Clb; 4-H Awd; God Cntry Awd; Elec.

CRIST, JEANETTA; Midland Trail HS; Hico, WV; Cls Rep Frsh Cls; Sec Soph Cls; Hon Rl; NHS; Stu Cncl; Yrbk; Fr Clb; Pep Clb; Chrldng; Univ; Elem Ed.

CRIST, JOANNA; Winfield HS; Pliny, WV; Chrh Wkr; Hon Rl; VICA; Voc Sch; Printing.

CRIST, LISA; Calvert HS; Tiffin, OH; Hon Rl; JA; Scr Kpr;.

CRIST, NATALIE; Edon HS; Edon, OH; 20/75 Chrs; Chrh Wkr; Cmnty Wkr; Hon Rl; Off Ade; Stg Crw; Yth Flsp; Rptr Yrbk; Yrbk; Sch Nwsp; Voc Schl; Photog.

CRIST, PATRICIA; Sheridan HS; Glenford, OH; Am Leg Aux Girls St; Chrs; Chrh Wkr; Cmnty Wkr; FCA; Hosp Ade; Lbry Ade; 4-H; FHA; Ohio State Univ.

CRIST, RHONDA; Tecumseh HS; New Carlisle, OH; VP Jr Cls; VP Sr Cls; AFS; VP Band; Treas Chrs; FCA; Hon Rl; Jr NHS; NHS; Orch; Word Of Life Bible Inst.

CRITCHLEY, SHERRI; Meadow Bridge HS; Danese, WV; 5/60 Trs Sr Cls; Band; Chrs; NHS; Yrbk; Rptr Sch Nwsp; Fr Clb; Treas FTA; Dnfth Awd; Concord College; Spec Ed.

CRITES, DENNIS; Bloomfield HS; Bloomfield, IN; FCA; Hon Rl; Sci Clb; Spn Clb; Letter Bsbl; Letter Bsktbl; Letter Trk; College.

CRITES, NENA; Federal Hocking HS; Coolville, OH; Drl Tm; Hon Rl; Rptr Sch Nwsp; FBLA; Pep Clb; Trk; GAA; Scr Kpr; 4-H Awd; Hocking Tech Coll; Bus.

CRITES, STEVEN; Washington HS; Massillon, OH; 6/492 Cls Rep Soph Cls; Cl Rep Jr Cls; Sal; AFS; Hon Rl; Sec NHS; Stu Cncl; Spn Clb; Univ Of Akron; Acctg.

CRITES II, DONALD; Moorefield HS; Old Fields, WV; 1/88 Val; Jr NHS; NHS; Yrbk; Rptr Sch Nwsp; Mas Awd; SAR Awd; VFW Awd; Wv Univ; Aerospace Engr.

CRITTENDEN, DAVID A; Jackson Parkside HS; Jackson, MI; 1/325 Cls Rep Frsh Cls; Cls Rep Soph Cls; Cl Rep Jr Cls; Band; Cmnty Wkr; Debate Tm; Hon Rl; Univ Of Mic; Archt.

CRNARICH, MARIANN; Mahoning County JVS HS; Poland, OH; Trs Jr Cls; VP Sr Cls; Chrs; Lbry Ade; Off Ade; Sch Pl; Y-Teens; OEA; IM Sprt; Scr Kpr; Gnrl Clercl I 1st Rgnl 2nd Natl 1978; Art Exhibit 1st & Ind Pl Hon Mentn 1975; Bus Schl; Admin Sec.

CROCE, SUZANNE; Westerville North HS; Westerville, OH; 69/477 VP Frsh Cls; Chrs; Capt Drl Tm; Hon Rl; Lit Mag; NHS; VP Stu Cncl; Yth Flsp; Drama Clb; Coco Cola All Amer Drill Team; Miami Univ; Mass Communctn.

CROCKER, MARTIN; Franklin Comm HS; Franklin, IN; 11/266 AFS; Boy Scts; Girl Scts; NHS; Sct Actv; Rptr Sch Nwsp; Boys Clb Am; 4-H; Lat Clb; Sci Clb; Rose Hulman Inst Tech; Bio Med Engr.

CROCKER, MARTIN C; Franklin Cmnty HS; Franklin, IN; 7/264 Cls Rep Frsh Cls; AFS; Boy Scts; Chrh Wkr; Cmnty Wkr; Hon Rl; Sec NHS; Pol Wkr; Sct Actv; Stu Cncl; Rose Hulman Inst Of Tech; Bio Med.

CROCKER, NORMAN; Cuyahoga Vlly Chrstn Academy; Akron, OH; 1/55 VP Jr Cls; Pol Wkr; Pres Stu Cncl; Ed Sch Nwsp; Sprt Ed Sch Nwsp; Rptr Sch Nwsp; Ger Clb; Capt Socr; Capt Trk; Natl Merit SF; Houghton Coll; Med.

CROCKETT, CARMEN; Boardman HS; Youngstown, OH; 175/600 Chrh Wkr; Hon Rl; Sch Pl; Drama Clb; Fr Clb; Letter Trk; Univ Of Sthern Cal; Intntl Relations.

CROCKETT, JO ANNE; Elmhurst HS; Ft Wayne, IN; Aud/Vis; Chrh Wkr; Hon Rl; Off Ade; Stu Cncl; OEA; Intl Bus Coll; Bus.

CROCKETT, SANDRA; Bedford HS; Bedford, OH; Band; Chrs; Hosp Ade; JA; Off Ade; Sch Mus; Spn Clb; Tmr; College; Med Lab.

CROFT, KIMBERLY; Perry Local HS; Cridersville, OH; VP Jr Cls; Chrs; Girl Scts; Hon Rl; Off Ade; Stu Cncl; VP 4-H; Pres Spn Clb; Bsktbl; Trk; Ohio St Univ; Elem Ed.

CROFT, RANDALL; Griffith HS; Griffith, IN; Chrh Wkr; Cmnty Wkr; Hon Rl; Bsktbl; Trk; IM Sprt; Voc Schl; Carpentry.

CROFT, RENEE; Tuslaw HS; N Lawrence, OH; 1/167 Pres Frsh Cls; Pres Soph Cls; Pres Jr Cls; Hon Rl; Treas Lbry Ade; NHS; Stu Cncl; Y-Teens; Rptr Yrbk; Yrbk; Ohio State Univ; Physical Therapy.

CROMER, DARYL; Lockland HS; Cincinnati, OH; 10/72 Cls Rep Frsh Cls; VP Soph Cls; Cls Rep Soph Cls; Aud/Vis; Chrh Wkr; Hon Rl; Jr NHS; Stu Cncl; Fr Clb; Mth Clb; Univ Of Cincinnati; Lab Tech.

CROMPTON, THOMAS; West Jefferson HS; W Jefferson, OH; 19/92 Hon Rl; Sch Pl; Stg Crw; FFA; Columbus Tech Inst; Mgmt.

CROMWELL, CINDY; Haslett HS; Haslett, MI; 32/160 Cmp Fr Grls; Chrs; Girl Scts; Hon Rl; Jr NHS; Off Ade; Stu Cncl; Spn Clb; Chrldng; Cit Awd; Univ; Physiology.

CROMWELL, TODD; Hicksville HS; Hicksville, OH; 21/109 Lit Mag; Sch Pl; Yrbk; Sch Nwsp; Tech School; Real Estate.

CRONE, LAURIE; Van Wert HS; Van Wert, OH; 10/214 Band; Chrs; Chrh Wkr; Hon Rl; NHS; Yth Flsp; Ger Clb; Spn Clb; Whos Who In Foreign Lang In Oh 79; Univ; Elem Educ.

CRONIGER, COLLEEN; Regina HS; Euclid, OH; Cmnty Wkr; Girl Scts; Hon Rl; NHS; Stg Crw; Yth Flsp; Sch Nwsp; Drama Clb; French Awd 77 78 & 79; Ecology Creek Projct 77; Newspaper Awd 78; Univ; Sci.

CRONIN, BRENDA; Stanton HS; Hammondsville, OH; Hon Rl; NHS; Sec Fr Clb; Capt Bsktbl; Letter Trk; GAA; IM Sprt; Twrlr; Mount Union Coll; Math.

CRONIN, CHRISTINE C; Our Lady Of Mercy HS; Livonia, MI; 3/334 Cls Rep Soph Cls; Cl Rep Jr Cls; Cmnty Wkr; Girl Scts; Lbry Ade; Mod UN; Natl Forn Lg; NHS; Pol Wkr; Red Cr Ade; College; Engr.

CRONIN, SHERI; Oak Glen HS; N Cumberland, WV; Band; Chrs; Cmnty Wkr; Girl Scts; Hon Rl; Hosp Ade; NHS; Sch Nwsp; 4-H; Fr Clb; Ohio Vly Schl; Nursing.

CRONLEY, MARK; St Francais De Sales HS; Columbus, OH; Boy Scts; Fr Clb; Ten; Wrstlng; Ohio St Univ; Bus Admin.

CROOK, NANCY E; Central HS; Evansville, IN; 1/528 Trs Frsh Cls; Trs Jr Cls; Trs Sr Cls; Band; Hon Rl; NHS; 4-H; Glf; Letter Ten; PPFtbl; Purdue Univ; Agri.

CROOKS, JOHN; Montabella HS; Stanton, MI; Chrh Wkr; Hon Rl; NHS; Bsbl; Bsktbl; Grand Rapids Baptist College; Farmng.

CROOKS, LISA; RB Chamberlin HS; Twinsburg, OH; Chrs; Chrh Wkr; Cmnty Wkr; FCA; Hon Rl; Off Ade; Stu Cncl; Yth Flsp; Pep Clb; GAA; 5th & 7th Annual Schlstc Awrd 77; Schlrshp Awrd 77; Anderson Coll; Eng.

CROOKS, MARQUIDA L; Akron South HS; Akron, OH; 15/154 Girl Scts; Hon Rl; Lbry Ade; Off Ade; Sec FHA; Ger Clb; Gym; Chrldng; Akron Univ; Acctg.

CROOKS, MERRIAM; Olivet Comm HS; Olivet, MI; Band; Chrs; Chrh Wkr; Girl Scts; Hon Rl; Lbry Ade; Sch Mus; Sch Pl; Yth Flsp; Rptr Yrbk; Hope Coll; Biology.

CROOKS, MONIQUE; Central Hower HS; Akron, OH; Chrh Wkr; Hon Rl; Off Ade; Stu Cncl; Pep Clb; Gym; Trk; Coll Of Wooster; Psych.

CROOKS, SHELLY; Benzie County Central HS; Benzonia, MI; Cls Rep Frsh Cls; Cls Rep Soph Cls; Cl Rep Jr Cls; Band; Girl Scts; Hon Rl; NHS; Stu Cncl; Yth Flsp; Yrbk; Farm Bureau Ctznshp Seminar 79; Ferris St Coll; Bus Admin.

CROOKSTON, FRED; Gull Lake HS; Kalamazoo, MI; 13/228 Cls Rep Sr Cls; Hon Rl; NHS; Sprt Ed Yrbk; Letter Bsbl; Letter Bsktbl; Most Imprvd Varsity Baseball 1979; Pres Studt Senate 1979; Stdnt Serv Awd 1978; Roofer.

CROSBY, ARDIS; Brighton HS; Brighton, MI; Hon Rl; Univ; Art.

CROSBY, JERILYN; Fairview HS; Dayton, OH; 16/160 Cl Rep Jr Cls; Sec Sr Cls; Cls Rep Sr Cls; Girl Scts; Hon Rl; Sch Mus; FHA; Trk; JA Awd; DBA Awd Dayton Bar Assn; Wright St Univ; Medicine.

CROSBY, K SUE; Bellaire HS; Bellaire, OH; 91/215 Girl Scts; Hon Rl; Spn Clb; Bus.

CROSBY, NICOLLETTEE; Charlestown HS; Louisville, KY; 20/191 Chrs; Drl Tm; Girl Scts; Hon Rl; Jr NHS; NHS; Fr Clb; Ten; Trk; Varsity Letterman Jacket 78 79; Univ Of Louisville.

CROSBY, PAUL; Yellow Springs HS; Yellow Springs, OH; Band; Sch Mus; Letter Crs Cntry; Letter Trk; Opt Clb Awd; Ohio State Univ; Med.

CROSLEY, TAMMY; Blanchester HS; Midland, OH; VP Jr Cls; Band; Chrs; Chrh Wkr; Yth Flsp; 4-H; Bsktbl; Trk; GAA; 4-H Awd; Coll; Tchr.

CROSS, CLAUDIA; Shadyside HS; Shadyside, OH; Band; Cmnty Wkr; Y-Teens; Drama Clb; GAA; Nation Wide Beauty Academy; Tchr.

CROSS, ELLEN; Detour Area HS; Detour Vlg, MI; Cmp Fr Grls; Chrs; Hon Rl; NHS; Stu Cncl; Capt Trk; Mgrs; Lake Superior State; Cmmrcl.

CROSS, JACQUELINE; Galion HS; Galion, OH; Girl Scts; Hon Rl; NHS; Yth Flsp; Y-Teens; Scr Kpr; DAR Awd; Ohio Northern Univ; Pharmacy.

CROSS, JAMES; Buckeye South HS; Yorkville, OH; Cls Rep Soph Cls; Hon Rl; Stu Cncl; Letter Wrstlng; Ohio State Univ; Elec.

CROSS, JESSICA; Eastern HS; Springville, IN; 14/90 VP Jr Cls; Band; Chrs; NHS; Sct Actv; Rptr Yrbk; Pres FFA; Trk; Chrldng; Purdue Univ; Agri.

CROSS, JUDITH; Brooke HS; Follansbee, WV; 80/466 Band; Chrh Wkr; Hon Rl; NHS; Off Ade; W Virginia Northern Cmnty Coll; Sec.

CROSS, JULIA; Dowagiac Union HS; Dowagiac, MI; Hon Rl; 4-H; IM Sprt; 4-H Awd; Lion Awd; SMC; Acctg.

CROSS, KIMBERLY; Bullock Creek Midland HS; Midland, MI; Hon Rl; Natl Forn Lg; NHS; Pep Clb; Capt Pom Pon; Univ Of Kan; Med.

CROSS, LINDA; Washington HS; South Bend, IN; 40/355 Hon Rl; Pep Clb; Spn Clb; College; Acting.

CROSS, LISA; Stow Sr HS; Stow, OH; Band; Chrh Wkr; Hon Rl; Sch Pl; Stu Cncl; Rptr Sch Nwsp; 4-H; College; Fine Arts.

CROSS, NANCY; Alexander HS; Athens, OH; Chrs; Cmnty Wkr; Hon Rl; Hosp Ade; Lbry Ade; Off Ade; Sch Pl; Yth Flsp; 4-H; FHA; Holzer Medical Coll; Nursing.

CROSS, PATRICIA A; Walter P Chrysler Memm HS; New Castle, IN; 22/414 Chrs; Chrh Wkr; Capt Drl Tm; Hon Rl; NHS; Pres Yth Flsp; Treas OEA; Bible; Business.

CROSS, RHONDA; Shaker Heights HS; Shaker Hts, OH; Chrs; Sec Chrh Wkr; Girl Scts; Hon Rl; Hosp Ade; Sch Mus; Stu Cncl; Rptr Sch Nwsp; Bsbl; GAA; Schlrshp Key 77; Wnr Of Essay Cntst; 1st Pl In Lake Erie League Solo & Ensemble Cntst; Univ Of Dayton; Chem Engr.

CROSS, RHONDA; Edgewood HS; Bloomington, IN; Chrs; Hon Rl; 4-H; Pep Clb; 4-H Awd; Itt Tech; Keypunch Operator.

CROSS, STEVE; St Marys Ctrl Cath HS; Sandusky, OH; Hon Rl; Ger Clb; Letter Bsbl; Letter Glf; Univ; Phys Sci.

CROSS, TAMI; Laurel Oaks Career Dev Cmpus; Greenfield, OH; Sec Jr Cls; Drl Tm; Jr NHS; FTA; OEA; Tmr; College; Busns.

CROSS, TIMOTHY P; Catholic Central HS; Bloomfield Hls, MI; 33/217 Sec Soph Cls; Trs Jr Cls; Cls Rep Sr Cls; Hon Rl; NHS; PAVAS; Pol Wkr; Stu Cncl; Rptr Sch Nwsp; Sci Clb; College.

CROSSER, ROBERT J; Port Clinton HS; Pt Clinton, OH; VP Soph Cls; Pres Jr Cls; Cl Rep Jr Cls; Am Leg Boys St; Chrs; Hon Rl; Stu Cncl; DECA; Univ; Bio Chem.

CROSSFIELD, ROSEMIE; Culver Girls Academy; Oyster Bay, NY; Cls Rep Frsh Cls; Band; Chrs; Chrh Wkr; Drl Tm; Girl Scts; Lbry Ade; ROTC; Sct Actv; Stu Cncl; Wake Forest Univ; Med.

CROSSLAND, KENNETH; Shortridge HS; Indianapolis, IN; Cls Rep Frsh Cls; Cls Rep Soph Cls; Cl Rep Jr Cls; Band; Boy Scts; Cmnty Wkr; FCA; JA; Orch; Stu Cncl; Coll; Auto Mech.

CROTS, MARLENE; Whiteford HS; Ottawa Lake, MI; 1/94 Val; Band; Hon Rl; Hosp Ade; NHS; Sec Yth Flsp; 4-H; Spn Clb; Natl Merit Ltr; Bio Awd 77; Chem Awd 78; Math Awd 79; Univ Of Toledo; Nursing.

CROUCH, BOB; Western HS; Parma, MI; Fr Clb; Bsbl; Ftbl; IM Sprt; Coll.

CROUCH, CAROLINE; Brown County HS Coop; Columbus, IN; Band; Hon Rl; Sch Mus; FHA; Sci Clb; Spn Clb; Hist.

CROUCH, JOHN; Merrillville Sr HS; Merrillville, IN; Band; Hon Rl; Trk; Univ; Indus Arts.

CROUCH, LEIGH; Whiteland Comm HS; Franklin, IN; 62/213 Cls Rep Soph Cls; Cl Rep Jr Cls; Band; Drl Tm; Drm Mjrt; Sch Mus; Stu Cncl; Pep Clb; Mat Maids; Pom Pon; College; Busns.

CROUCH, MARY; John Marshall HS; Indianapolis, IN; 11/466 Chrs; Hon Rl; NHS; Quill & Scroll; Sch Mus; Sch Pl; Ed Yrbk; Key Clb; DAR Awd; Z Club Pres; Indiana Univ; Journalism.

CROUCH, PAULA J; Shady Spring HS; Blue Jay, WV; Sec Frsh Cls; Band; Chrh Wkr; FCA; Girl Scts; Hon Rl; Stu Cncl; Yth Flsp; 4-H; Pep Clb; Bus Schl; Legal Sec.

CROUCH, RENEE; Tecumseh HS; Springfield, OH; 2/345 Sal; AFS; Girl Scts; Hon Rl; Jr NHS; NHS; Sct Actv; 4-H; Spn Clb; Scr Kpr; Wright St Univ; Medicine.

CROUCH, TERESA; Bedford N Lawrence HS; Bedford, IN; 23/403 Am Leg Aux Girls St; Hon Rl; NHS; Pol Wkr; Beta Clb; Keyettes; Pep Clb; Bsktbl; Capt Trk; PPFtbl; Purdue Univ; Industrial Engr.

CROUCHER, CONNIE; Lemon Monroe HS; Middletown, OH; Chrs; Chrh Wkr; Cmnty Wkr; Girl Scts; Hon Rl; Sch Mus; Sch Pl; Stg Crw; Miami Univ; Music.

CROUSE, BRENDA; Hamilton Southeastern HS; Noblesville, IN; 13/140 Band; Chrh Wkr; Girl Scts; Hon Rl; JA; NHS; Sct Actv; Yth Flsp; OEA; Pep Clb; Bus Schl; Bus Admin.

CROUSE, NANCY; Kimball HS; Royal Oak, MI; 107/604 Debate Tm; Girl Scts; Hon Rl; NHS; OEA; PPFtbl; Oakland Cmnty Coll; Bus.

CROUSE, RAYMOND R; Paw Paw HS; Paw Paw, MI; 7/200 Cmnty Wkr; Hon Rl; NHS; Crs Cntry; Michigan St Univ; Chem Engr.

CROUSE, STEVE; Carson City Crystal HS; Carson City, MI; Cls Rep Frsh Cls; Cls Rep Soph Cls; Band; Chrh Wkr; Cmnty Wkr; Hon Rl; NHS; Yth Flsp; Letter Bsbl; Bsktbl; Bible Coll; Lords Work.

CROUSE, TERRY; Hampshire HS; Romney, WV; 1/213 Band; Boy Scts; Hon Rl; Sch Pl; Drama Clb; FFA; Bausch & Lomb Awd; Voice Dem Awd; WVU; Agri Info.

CROW, CAROL; Bentley HS; Burton, MI; Hon Rl; Lbry Ade; NHS; Ed Yrbk; Yrbk; Univ Of Michigan; Med.

CROW, CHESTER H; Western Boone Jr Sr HS; Lebanon, IN; 1/163 VP Frsh Cls; VP Soph Cls; Pres Jr Cls; Pres Sr Cls; Val; Letter Swmmng; Am Leg Awd; DAR Awd; 4-H Awd; Kiwan Awd; Rose Hulman Tech Inst; Mech Engr.

CROW, GLENN; L C Mohr HS; South Haven, MI; College.

CROW, KATHY; Fairview HS; Ney, OH; Hon Rl; 4-H; Letter Bsktbl; Letter IM Sprt; Am Leg Awd; 4-H Awd; Tech College; Clerical.

CROW, LAURA; Upper Sandusky HS; Upper Sandusky, OH; Chrh Wkr; Drl Tm; FCA; Hon Rl; NHS; VP Stu Cncl; VP Yth Flsp; Pres 4-H; Bsktbl; Trk; Nursing School; Rn.

CROW, LISA; Herbert Henry Dow HS; Midland, MI; 6/405 Hon Rl; Sec JA; NHS; Spn Clb; Letter Gym; Letter Trk; Cert Of Recognition St Of Mich Comp Schlrshp Prog; Gymanstics Awd; Skill Day Awds; Shorthand Transcription; Cntrl Michigan Univ; Eng.

CROW, LYNETTA; Cory Rawson HS; Rawson, OH; Aud/Vis; Band; Lbry Ade; Stg Crw; 4-H; FHA; Pep Clb; 4-H Awd; Voc Schl; Child Care.

CROW, REBECCA L; Southern HS; Racine, OH; 33/109 Trs Soph Cls; VP Jr Cls; Trs Sr Cls; Band; Chrs; Hosp Ade; MMM; Sch Pl; Rptr Yrbk; Ed Sch Nwsp; Ohio Univ.

CROWDER, DORRINE; John Adams HS; Cleveland, OH; 3/480 Cls Rep Sr Cls; Chrs; Hon Rl; Treas NHS; Sch Mus; Stu Cncl; Pep Clb; Pres GAA; Pom Pon; Cit Awd; Perfct Attndnc 6 Yrs 79; Finlst In Cleveland Schlshp Progr 79; Hon At Rotary Lunchn 79; Ohio St Univ; Psych.

CROWDER, JOY; Springs Valley HS; French Lick, IN; 18/97 Trs Frsh Cls; Hon Rl; Stu Cncl; Rptr Yrbk; Fr Clb; Pres Pep Clb; Purdue Univ.

CROWDUS, DANA; North Central HS; Indianapolis, IN; Girl Scts; Hon Rl; JA; Mod UN; Off Ade; Sct Actv; Fr Clb; Inidana St Univ Summer Hnrs Prog; Coll; Law.

CROWE, ALVIN J; Northeastern HS; Williamsburg, IN; Hon Rl; Yrbk; Sch Nwsp; Fr Clb; VP Of Spec Olypcs 78; Cadet Tchr Spnsh I 78; Univ; Cargo Pilot.

CROWE, CHRISTINE L; Eastlake North HS; Eastlake, OH; 13/690 Hon Rl; Jr NHS; NHS; Sch Nwsp; Bsktbl; Trk; GAA; Columbus Coll Of Art Design; Art.

CROWE, CONNIE; Salem HS; Vallonia, IN; 4/180 Cls Rep Frsh Cls; VP Soph Cls; VP Jr Cls; VP Sr Cls; Am Leg Aux Girls St; Chrh Wkr; Hon Rl; NHS; Stu Cncl; FHA; Indiana Univ; Bus Mktg.

CROWE, DAVID; Rock Hill Sr HS; Kitts Hill, OH; 1/190 Chrh Wkr; Hon Rl; Jr NHS; NHS; Yth Flsp; Beta Clb; Mth Clb; Sci Clb; Algbr I Health Awd & Sci Awd 76; World Hist Spanish II Eng II Bio P Geom Awds 77; Chem Amer Hist Awd 78; Univ; Dent.

CROWE, DUANE L; Perry HS; Cridersville, OH; Hon Rl; Letter Bsktbl; Letter Ftbl; Letter Trk;.

CROWE, LAURA; Heritage Christian School; Indianapolis, IN; JA; Rptr Yrbk; Yrbk; Mgrs; Mike & Type Awd 79; Ball St Univ; Acctg.

CROWE, LYNN; Bedford HS; Bedford, OH; Band; Cmp Fr Grls; Band; Hon Rl; Jr NHS; NHS; Quill & Scroll; Rptr Sch Nwsp; Spn Clb; Bowling Green Univ; Acctg.

CROWE, RANDALL; Brownsburg HS; Brownsbg, IN; Boy Scts; Spn Clb; Ten; IM Sprt; Ball St Univ; Archt.

CROWE, RICHARD; Bosse HS; Evansville, IN; 42/370 Hon Rl; VP JA; Pol Wkr; OEA; Spn Clb; Cit Awd; JA Awd; Anna Bosse Schlrshp; Indiana St Schlrshp; U E Admin With Distinction; Univ Of Evansville; Comp Prog.

CROWE, SHIRL; Brighton HS; Brighton, MI; Chrh Wkr; Hon Rl; Yth Flsp; Rptr Sch Nwsp; 4-H; Fr Clb; Ten; Mic St Univ; Denistry.

CROWE, THERESA; Hardin Northern HS; Dunkirk, OH; 3/65 Pres Frsh Cls; Band; Chrh Wkr; Hon Rl; JA; Stu Cncl; Yth Flsp; 4-H; Fr Clb; Pep Clb; Univ; Med.

CROWE, TINA; Whiteoak HS; Sardinia, OH; Cmp Fr Grls; Chrh Wkr; Cmnty Wkr; Hon Rl; Off Ade; Sch Pl; Yrbk; Eng Clb; 4-H; FHA; Southern St Coll; Exec Sec.

CROWE, TONY; Hardin Northern HS; Dunkirk, OH; 39/69 Band; Chrs; Cmnty Wkr; Pol Wkr; Stg Crw; Yth Flsp; Yrbk; FFA; Pres Key Clb; Bsbl; Hocking Tech; Paramedic.

CROWELL, KATHY; Forest Park HS; Cincinnati, OH; 7/387 Chrs; Drl Tm; Hon Rl; JA; NHS; Off Ade; Sch Mus; Sch Pl; Drama Clb; Spn Clb; Ohio St Univ; Sci.

CROWELL, SHEILA K; Hedgesville HS; Martinsburg, WV; Chrh Wkr; Hon Rl; Sch Pl; Stu Cncl; Drama Clb; Pep Clb; Chrldng; Shepherd Coll; Sec.

CROWL, HAROLD S; Lewis County HS; Weston, WV; Cls Rep Soph Cls; Am Leg Boys St; Hon Rl; Jr NHS; Pres NHS; Stu Cncl; Yrbk; Elect Pres Natl Hon Soc 79; Know Your St Govt Day; West Virginia Univ; Med.

CROWL, JAMIE; East Palestine HS; E Palestine, OH; Cmp Fr Grls; Chrs; Off Ade; Sch Mus; Sch Pl; Sct Actv; Stg Crw; Univ; Med.

CROWLEY, BARBARA; Carrollton HS; Saginaw, MI; 10/125 Girl Scts; NHS; Sch Mus; Sch Pl; Stg Crw; Drama Clb; Fr Clb; Mic State Univ; Hotel Mgnt.

CROWLEY, COLLEEN; Clio HS; Clio, MI; VP Jr Cls; VP Sr Cls; Band; Chrh Wkr; Hon Rl; Sch Mus; Sch Pl; Stu Cncl; 4-H; PPFtbl; Univ Of Michigan; Law.

CROWLEY, DAVID; Waterford Mott HS; Pontiac, MI; Hon Rl; Jr NHS; NHS; Stg Crw; Coach Actv; Natl Merit Ltr; Natl Merit SF; Mich State Univ; Profession Engr.

CROWLEY, MARGARET; Regina HS; Euclid, OH; Cls Rep Soph Cls; Pres Jr Cls; Hon Rl; Hosp Ade; NHS; Treas Stu Cncl; Rptr Yrbk; Carlow College; Nursing.

CROWLEY, MARY; Notre Dame HS; Clarksburg, WV; 4/60 Hon Rl; NHS; Y-Teens; Rptr Yrbk; FBLA; Chrldng; College.

CROWLEY, MICHAEL J; Urbana HS; Urbana, OH; Sec Frsh Cls; Pres Soph Cls; Pres Jr Cls; Cls Rep Sr Cls; Am Leg Boys St; Band; Chrs; Hon Rl; Lbry Ade; Lit Mag; College; Science.

CROWLEY, RICHARD B; Notre Dame HS; Clarksburg, WV; 4/54 Am Leg Boys St; VP Band; Hon Rl; NHS; Stg Crw; Rptr Yrbk; IM Sprt; Marshall Univ; Music.

CROXFORD, DAVID; Gibsonburg HS; Helena, OH; 16/101 Band; Boy Scts; Chrs; Sch Mus; Sch Pl; Rptr Yrbk; Rptr Sch Nwsp; 3rd & 7th In Dist French I & II BGSU Schlrshp Tests; Honorable Mention St French I; Kent St Univ; Law.

CROY, PAUL; Greensburg Cmnty HS; Greensburg, IN; Band; Chrs; Drm Bgl; Hon Rl; Mdrgl; Sch Mus; Sch Pl; Fr Clb; Pep Clb; Sci Clb; West Point; Military Acad Band.

CROYDON, ROBERT; St Francis De Sales HS; Toledo, OH; 18/203 Band; Chrh Wkr; Hon Rl; NHS; Fr Clb; College; Oceanography.

CROYLE, STEVEN; Parkersburg Catholic HS; Davisville, WV; 2/48 Chrh Wkr; Hosp Ade; NHS; Rptr Sch Nwsp; Pres IM Sprt; Univ Of Fla; Architecture.

CROYSDALE, JOYCE; Chaney HS; Youngstown, OH; Hon Rl; NHS; Off Ade; Y-Teens; Sch Nwsp; Pep Clb; Letter Bsktbl; Letter Ten; Letter Trk; PPFtbl; College; Law.

CRUFF, LONNY; Hopkins HS; Dorr, MI; 8/112 Band; Chrh Wkr; Hon Rl; Jr NHS; NHS; Sch Pl; Yth Flsp; FFA; Pep Clb; Mgrs; St Winner Pub Speaking Mi Assn FFA 79; St Winner Demonst Mi Assn FFA 78; Class Speaker At Grad Drmny 79; Michigan St Univ; Dairy Sci.

CRULL, MICHAEL; Highland HS; Anderson, IN; 32/439 Hon Rl; NHS; Bsktbl; Scr Kpr; Tmr; Pres Awd; Coll; Mech Engr.

CRULO, KELLY; Bedford N Lawrence HS; Avoca, IN; Chrh Wkr; Hon Rl; Beta Clb; Fr Clb; Pep Clb;.

CRUM, BARRY M; Clyde Sr HS; Clyde, OH; Am Leg Boys St; Chrs; Hon Rl; Letter Ftbl; Letter Trk; Bowling Green Ohio St Univ; Tchr.

CRUM, D; Albion Sr HS; Albion, MI; Hon Rl; Letter Bsbl; Letter Bsktbl; Letter Ftbl; Letter Glf; Letter Ten; Kiwan Awd;.

CRUM, EDWARD; Chippewa Hills HS; Remus, MI; 16/250 Cls Rep Frsh Cls; Trs Jr Cls; Band; Hon Rl; Spn Clb; Bsbl; Ftbl; Wrstlng; Air Force Acad; Law.

CRUM, LAWERENCE; Central HS; Detroit, MI; Cls Rep Frsh Cls; Cls Rep Soph Cls; Cl Rep Jr Cls; Cls Rep Sr Cls; Band; Yth Flsp; Bsbl; Bsktbl; Ftbl; Gym; Univ Of Detroit.

CRUM, MIA; Coopersville Public HS; Coopersville, MI; Chrs; Hon Rl; Jr NHS; NHS; Sch Mus; Stu Cncl; FHA; FNA; Ger Clb; Lat Clb; Voc Schl.

CRUM, SCOTT; Cardington Lincoln HS; Cardington, OH; Chrh Wkr; FFA; Bsbl; IM Sprt; Coll.

CRUM, TIM; Kermit HS; Kermit, WV; 1/37 Band; Hon Rl; Lbry Ade; Yrbk; Rptr Sch Nwsp; Beta Clb; 4-H; Spn Clb; Bsktbl; Marshall Univ; Pharmacy.

CRUM, VIRGINIA; Magnolia HS; Matewan, WV; Cls Rep Frsh Cls; Cls Rep Soph Cls; Cl Rep Jr Cls; Cls Rep Sr Cls; Band; Chrs; Chrh Wkr; Hon Rl; 4-H; S West Virginia Comm Coll; Gen Busns.

CRUMBACK, TRACY; Caledonia HS; Caledonia, MI; 6/179 Pres Frsh Cls; Cls Rep Soph Cls; Boy Scts; Debate Tm; Hon Rl; NHS; Stu Cncl; Yth Flsp; Letter Bsbl; Bsktbl; Central Michigan Univ; Acctg.

CRUMET, DIANNE; Niles HS; Niles, MI; Cls Rep Frsh Cls; Band; Hon Rl; 4-H; Letter Bsktbl; Cit Awd; 4-H Awd; Coll; Acctg.

CRUMLEY, CHARMONETTE; Columbus E HS; Columbus, OH; Chrs; Drl Tm; Off Ade; Fr Clb; Cit Awd; Univ; Chem Engr.

CRUMLEY, PAUL; Wheeling Park HS; Triadelphia, WV; 19/623 Pres Band; Chrs; Mdrgl; Sct Actv; Mth Clb; Natl Merit SF; Univ; Elec Engr.

CRUMP, ANDREA; Horace Mann HS; Gary, IN; Cl Rep Jr Cls; Hon Rl; JA; Jr NHS; NHS; Stg Crw; Cit Awd; Oakwood Coll; Nursing.

CRUMP, CHRIS; Malabar HS; Mansfield, OH; 16/278 Cls Rep Soph Cls; Cl Rep Jr Cls; Cls Rep Sr Cls; Boy Scts; VP NHS; Pres Key Clb; Mth Clb; Bsbl; Letter Crs Cntry; Letter Wrstlng; West Point Acad.

CRUMPTON, JENNIFER; Utica HS; Utica, MI; Hon Rl; Off Ade; Ger Clb; IM Sprt; Oakland College; English Tchr.

CRUMRINE, DONNA; Holgate HS; New Bavaria, OH; Band; Chrs; Girl Scts; Hon Rl; Stu Cncl; 4-H; Mth Clb; Sci Clb; Chrldng; Voice Dem Awd; Owens Tech Coll.

CRUMRINE, MARY BETH; St Ursula Acad; Cincinnati, OH; Cmp Fr Grls; Chrs; Hon Rl; JA; NHS; Drama Clb; Fr Clb; Swmmng; Univ; Bus Admin.

CRUSE, PHYLLIS; Taylor HS; Cincinnati, OH; VP Sr Cls; Drl Tm; Hon Rl; Hosp Ade; Off Ade; Pep Clb; Trk; College.

CRUSE, SANDRA G; Ravenswood HS; Ravenswood, WV; Cls Rep Soph Cls; VP Jr Cls; Cls Rep Sr Cls; Band; Hon Rl; JA; NHS; Stu Cncl; Chrldng; GAA; West Virginia Univ.

CRUSER, DIRK; Jennings County HS; Westport, IN; 4/365 Hon Rl; NHS; Ger Clb; Indiana St Univ; Math.

CRUZ, MARCEA; Flushing HS; Flushing, MI; Chrs; Girl Scts; Fr Clb; Ten; Trk; PPFtbl; Michigan St Univ; Interior Design.

CRUZ, RUTH A; Lewis Cnty HS; Weston, WV; 9/263 Am Leg Aux Girls St; Chrs; Hon Rl; Treas Jr NHS; Sec NHS; Pep Clb; IM Sprt; PPFtbl; W Virginia Univ; Med Tech.

CRYDERMAN, ANN; Les Cheneaux Community HS; Cedarville, MI; Chrs; Hon Rl; St Marys Inst Inc; Cosmetologist.

CSAKY, KATALIN; Copley Sr HS; Barebrton, OH; Chrh Wkr; Hon Rl; NHS; Off Ade; 4-H; Spn Clb; 4-H Awd; Univ Of Akron; Bus.

CSAPO, MICHAEL; Lakeville HS; Otisville, MI; 4/189 Hon Rl; NHS; Sch Pl; Ed Sch Nwsp; Crs Cntry; Trk; Wrstlng; Coach Actv; Natl Merit Schl; Univ Of Mic; Philosophy.

CSENAR, THOMAS; South Bend Lasalle HS; South Bend, IN; Cls Rep Soph Cls; Cl Rep Jr Cls; Hon Rl; NHS; Pep Clb; Letter Bsbl; Letter Ftbl; Coach Actv; IM Sprt; Univ; Math.

CSIZI, EDWARD; Morrison R Waite HS; Toledo, OH; 39/269 Cl Rep Jr Cls; Cls Rep Sr Cls; Pres Chrs; Hon Rl; NHS; Off Ade; Pol Wkr; Sch Mus; Stu Cncl; Yrbk; Class Of 79 Serv Awd; Ohio DECA Dist Awd Bsns Mgmt Test 3rd Pl; Kent State Univ; Child Psych.

CSIZIK, FRANK; Benedictine HS; Cleveland, OH; 24/102 Boy Scts; Chrh Wkr; Sct Actv; Ger Clb; John Carol Coll.

CUBBERLEY, ALAN J; Chagrin Falls HS; Chagrin Falls, OH; Lat Clb; Sci Clb; Crs Cntry; IM Sprt; Mgrs; Miami Univ; Marine Bio.

CUBIA, PERRY E; Pontiac Central HS; Pontiac, MI; Band; Boy Scts; Hon Rl; Hosp Ade; Yth Flsp; Boys Clb Am; Mth Clb; Sci Clb; Bsktbl; Trk; Sel By Schl To Represent Stu Govt; Accepted At Lawrence Inst Of Tech For Summer Sci Inst; Univ Of Michigan; Medicine.

CUBICEC, DOINA; Forest Park HS; Cincinnati, OH; 31/339 Band; Girl Scts; Hon Rl; Lbry Ade; Sch Mus; Sch Pl; Drama Clb; Coll; Med.

CUCCIARRE, MICHAEL; Fairview HS; Fairview Pk, OH; 47/268 Band; Orch; Letter Crs Cntry; Letter Trk; Miami Univ; Mechanical Engineering.

CUCCO, LILLIAN; Firelands HS; Amherst, OH; 56/156 Chrs; Hon Rl; Mdrgl; Sch Mus; 4-H Awd; Heidelberg Coll; Voice.

CUCKLER, MICHAEL; Federal Hocking HS; Athens, OH; Cls Rep Frsh Cls; Cls Rep Soph Cls; Cl Rep Jr Cls; Am Leg Boys St; Hon Rl; Pres 4-H; Bsktbl; Ftbl; 4-H Awd; Bsktbll Defnsv Plyr Of The Yr 79; 4 H Judging Awrds 77 & 78; Univ.

CUCKOVICH, LINDA; Western Reserve HS; Warren, OH; Hon Rl; Rptr Sch Nwsp; College.

CUDDY, WILLIAM; Fayetteville HS; Fayetteville, WV; 8/86 Chrh Wkr; NHS; Yth Flsp; Cit Awd; Wv Inst Of Tech.

CUDKOWICZ, ALEXANDER; Fairmont West HS; Kettering, OH; 5/525 Band; Chrs; Hon Rl; NHS; Orch; Sch Mus; Sch Pl; Fr Clb; Mth Clb; Kalamazoo College; Veterinary Med.

CUKELJ, CAROLINE; St Joseph Academy; Cleveland, OH; Cls Rep Sr Cls; Hon Rl; Yrbk; Rptr Sch Nwsp; Fr Clb; Ger Clb; GAA; Univ; Nursing.

CULBERT, ANNETTE; Coldwater HS; Coldwater, MI; Band; Cmp Fr Grls; Chrs; Hon Rl; NHS; Fr Clb; Trk; IM Sprt; Lake Superior State Coll; Nurse.

CULBERTSON, LEE; Greenville HS; Greenville, OH; 1/385 Hon Rl; NHS; Yth Flsp; Rptr Yrbk; Bsktbl; Letter Glf; Northwestern Univ; Engr.

CULBERTSON, M; Hartford HS; Hartford, MI; Am Leg Aux Girls St; Hon Rl; NHS; Sch Pl; Pep Clb; Crs Cntry; Mich State; Pharmacist.

CULEY, ANDREW; Manistique Ctrl HS; Manistique, MI; Hon Rl; Bsktbl; Ftbl; Trk; Hnr Roll;.

CULLEN, ANTONIO H; Baldwin HS; Baldwin, MI; Chrh Wkr; Hon Rl; Rptr Sch Nwsp; Boys Clb Am; Bsbl; Bsktbl; Ftbl; Mgrs; College; Electronics.

CULLEN, MOLLY; Clyde HS; Clyde, OH; 6/185 Cls Rep Frsh Cls; Cls Rep Soph Cls; Band; Chrs; Hon Rl; NHS; Sch Mus; VP Stu Cncl; Rptr Sch Nwsp; 4-H; College; Bus.

CULLEN, SEAN; Clyde Sr HS; Clyde, OH; Cl Rep Jr Cls; Am Leg Boys St; Chrs; Hon Rl; NHS; Sch Mus; Sch Pl; Rptr Yrbk; Drama Clb; VP Spn Clb; Bowling Green St Univ; Music.

CULLEN, TERRY; Point Pleasant HS; Letart, WV; VP Sr Cls; Hon Rl; 4-H; FFA; IM Sprt; 4-H Awd; Potomac St Coll; Ag Tech.

CULLEN, TERRY L; Point Pleasant HS; Letart, WV; VP Sr Cls; Chrh Wkr; 4-H; FFA; 4-H Awd; Potomac St Univ; Agri.

CULLER, ROBERTA; Fairview HS; Edgerton, OH; Chrs; Chrh Wkr; Hon Rl; NHS; Off Ade; Sch Mus;

Yth Flsp; Sch Nwsp; 4-H; Letter Bsktbl; Univ; Comp Progr.

CULLEY, CATHLEEN; Magnificat HS; Bay Village, OH; Cls Rep Frsh Cls; Cmnty Wkr; Girl Scts; NHS; Orch; Red Cr Ade; Sch Mus; Sct Actv; Y-Teens; Drama Clb; Niagara Univ; Nursing.

CULLISON, KENDALL; Eastern HS; Bloomfield, IN; Sec Sr Cls; Band; Chrh Wkr; Hon Rl; Jr NHS; Lbry Ade; NHS; Ind Univ; Welder.

CULLOM, CATHY; Beavercreek HS; Dayton, OH; 18/702 Chrs; Chrh Wkr; Hon Rl; NHS; Yth Flsp; Pep Clb; Socr; Swmmng; Scr Kpr; Tmr; Ohio St Univ; Med Dietetics.

CULLY, THOMAS; Rogers HS; Toledo, OH; Hon Rl; DECA; Fr Clb; Glf; Cit Awd; Ohi State Univ; Acctg.

CULMAN, SHIRLEY; Mother Of Mercy HS; Ci ncinnati, OH; 51/243 Hon Rl; FHA; Pep Clb; GAA; Kiwan Awd; Univ Of Cincinnati; Mktg.

CULP, CYNTHIA; Chalker HS; Southington, OH; 6/80 Cls Rep Frsh Cls; Sec Jr Cls; Trs Jr Cls; Am Leg Aux Girls St; Hon Rl; Hosp Ade; Sec NHS; Off Ade; Stu Cncl; Y-Teens; Southington Vol Firemns Fest Queen 78; Bio Club Vc Pres 78; Ohio Univ; Devlpmt Psych.

CULP, DEBORAH; Jesup W Scott HS; Toledo, OH; 4/270 Cls Rep Soph Cls; Cl Rep Jr Cls; Trs Sr Cls; Chrh Wkr; Hon Rl; Sec NHS; Stu Cncl; Ed Yrbk; Treas Fr Clb; Pep Clb; Univ Of Michigan.

CULP, KENDELL; Rennsselaer Central HS; Rensselaer, IN; 15/172 Hon Rl; NHS; Pol Wkr; Quill & Scroll; Ed Sch Nwsp; Sprt Ed Sch Nwsp; VP 4-H; FFA; Outstanding Soph; District Star Farmer; Purdue Univ; Agriculture.

CULP, KENDELL; Rensselaer Central HS; Rensselaer, IN; 15/163 Hon Rl; NHS; Pol Wkr; Quill & Scroll; Ed Sch Nwsp; Sprt Ed Sch Nwsp; VP 4-H; FFA; Scr Kpr; 4-H Awd; Purdue Univ; Agri.

CULP, SCOTT; Triad HS; North Lewisburg, OH; 1/48 Trs Soph Cls; VP Jr Cls; Hon Rl; 4-H; FFA; Letter Crs Cntry; Letter Trk; Mgrs; Scr Kpr; Twrlr; Ohio Weslyan Univ; Physcst.

CULP, SHIRELLE; Southeastern HS; Detroit, MI; Hon Rl; Off Ade; Cit Awd; Coll; Nursing.

CULP, TODD; Triad HS; North Lewisburg, OH; 12/75 Cls Rep Frsh Cls; Sec Soph Cls; Hon Rl; Sch Pl; Stu Cncl; 4-H; FFA; Bsktbl; Crs Cntry; Trk; Otterbein Coll; Biology.

CULPEPPER, CONNIE; Elmhurst HS; Ft Wayne, IN; 59/440 Cls Rep Frsh Cls; Chrh Wkr; Cmnty Wkr; Drl Tm; Hon Rl; JA; Sch Pl; Stu Cncl; Pres DECA; Capt Bsktbl; Indiana Univ; Pediatrcn.

CULROSS, JAMES; Taylor HS; Kokomo, IN; Mod UN; NHS; Sch Pl; Sct Actv; Stu Cncl; Pres Drama Clb; Pres Sci Clb; IM Sprt; Purdue Univ; Chem Engr.

CULTER, RONALD; Marysville HS; Smith Creek, MI; Bsbl; Letter Ftbl; Letter Trk; Awrd Weight Lifting & Agility Hnr Soc 77; Univ; State Trooper.

CULVER, DEBRA; Southwestern HS; Franklin, IN; Band; Girl Scts; Sch Mus; Sch Pl; Sct Actv; Stg Crw; Bsktbl; Trk; GAA; Franklin College.

CULVER, MARY; Manton Consolidated Schools; Manton, MI; Cls Rep Frsh Cls; Cl Rep Jr Cls; Band; Hon Rl; Lit Mag; NHS; Stg Crw; Sch Nwsp; 4-H; Trk; Art Awd 79; Best Stu 74; Schlrshp Awd 75; Univ.

CULY, BRIAN; Hagerstown Jr Sr HS; Hagerstown, IN; 6/135 Pres Soph Cls; FCA; Hon Rl; NHS; NHS; Stu Cncl; Fr Clb; Sci Clb; Letter Crs Cntry; Letter Swmmng; Purdue Univ; Pilot.

CULY, JUDY; Union HS; Losantville, IN; 1/80 Am Leg Aux Girls St; Sec Band; Chrs; Girl Scts; Hon Rl; NHS; Off Ade; Sch Pl; Drama Clb; 4-H; Univ.

CULY, STEVE; Union HS; Losantville, IN; 5/65 Am Leg Boys St; Treas Band; Boy Scts; Hon Rl; NHS; Sch Pl; Rptr Yrbk; Drama Clb; 4-H; Sci Clb; Washington Univ; Astronomy.

CUMBOW, JUDITH; Lutheran HS; Detroit, MI; 2/149 Chrh Wkr; Girl Scts; Hon Rl; Lbry Ade; VP NHS; Sch Pl; Drama Clb; Ger Clb; Pres Pep Clb; DAR Awd; College; Mech Engr.

CUMMING, BARBARA; Ferndale HS; Pleasant Ridge, MI; 27/400 Hon Rl; NHS; Sch Mus; Ed Yrbk; Drama Clb; Rotary Awd; Kalamazoo Coll; Bio.

CUMMING, NANCY; Ferndale HS; Pleasant Ridge, MI; 24/400 Hon Rl; NHS; Sch Mus; Sch Pl; Ed Yrbk; Drama Clb; Rotary Awd; Kalamazoo College; Eng.

CUMMINGS, ANITA; Muskegon Hts HS; Muskegon Ht, MI; 1/270 Pres Frsh Cls; Chrh Wkr; Drm Mjrt; Girl Scts; Pres NHS; Sch Pl; Stu Cncl; Mas Awd; Opt Clb Awd; Miss Fashionette Teen Queen; 1st Runner Up Miss Debutante; Michigan St Univ; Chem Engr.

CUMMINGS, BRIAN; Hillman HS; Hillman, MI; Pres Frsh Cls; Cl Rep Jr Cls; Band; Cmnty Wkr; Pol Wkr; Stg Crw; Stu Cncl; Sprt Ed Sch Nwsp; Rptr Sch Nwsp; Civ Clb; Stu Of The Year In Soc Sci & Economics; Golden Helmet Awd & All St Kicker Ftbl; Homecoming King; Northern Mich Univ; Dentistry.

CUMMINGS, C; Eastern HS; Lansing, MI; Band; Girl Scts; Hon Rl; Trk; Lansing Community Coll; Vet.

CUMMINGS, CHRISTINE; Dwight D Eisenhower HS; Saginaw, MI; 2/327 Cls Rep Soph Cls; VP Jr Cls; Cls Rep Sr Cls; Sal; Natl Forn Lg; Rptr Yrbk; VP Pep Clb; Capt Chrldng; Awd For Academic Excel From I St Univ 79; Saginaw Ed Emp Credit Union Schlrshp 79; Michigan St Univ; Financial Admin.

CUMMINGS, DEBRA; Benton Harbor HS; Benton Harbor, MI; 36/417 Band; Chrh Wkr; Cmnty Wkr; Hon Rl; Off Ade; DECA; Central Michigan Univ; Busns Admin.

CUMMINGS, GARY; Keyser HS; Keyser, WV; 28/248 Boy Scts; Hon Rl; NHS; Mth Clb; Potomac State College; Eng.

CUMMINGS, JOE; Barr Reeve HS; Cannelburg, IN; 6/49 Trs Soph Cls; VP Sr Cls; Am Leg Boys St; Band; Hon Rl; Beta Clb; 4-H; Fr Clb; FFA; Pep Clb; Univ.

CUMMINGS, JOHN; Bowling Green Sr HS; Bowling Green, OH; 17/325 Hon Rl; NHS; Spn Clb; Letter Crs Cntry; Letter Trk; IM Sprt; Kiwan Awd; Bowling Green St Univ; Pre Med.

CUMMINGS, JOHN; Lumen Christi HS; Jackson, MI; Band; Sch Mus; Sch Pl; Stg Crw; Sch Nwsp; Drama Clb; Bsbl; Coach Actv; Univ; Bus Admin.

CUMMINGS, KELLY; Put In Bay HS; Put In Bay, OH; 1/13 Val; Chrs; Hon Rl; Sch Pl; Yrbk; 4-H; Am Leg Awd; St Mary Of The Woods Coll; Psych.

CUMMINGS, MARK; Sherman HS; Ashford, WV; Ger Clb; VICA; College; Math.

CUMMINGS, MARY; Wheeling Park HS; Triadelphia, WV; Cls Rep Frsh Cls; Chrs; Natl Forn Lg; Sch Mus; Sch Pl; Stg Crw; Stu Cncl; Drama Clb; Fr Clb; Bsktbl; Coll; Theatre.

CUMMINGS, PAMELA; Wayne Memorial HS; Westland, MI; Chrs; Chrh Wkr; Girl Scts; Orch; Sct Actv; Ger Clb; Hndbl; Ten; IM Sprt; Btty Crckr Awd; Coll; Nurse.

CUMMINGS, STEPHEN; Jackson Parkside HS; Jackson, MI; 12/270 Cls Rep Frsh Cls; Cls Rep Soph Cls; Cl Rep Jr Cls; Band; Hon Rl; Orch; Letter Ten; Michigan St Univ; Bus Admin.

CUMMINGS, STEVE; Wapakoneta HS; Wapakoneta, OH; 20/308 Band; Boy Scts; Hon Rl; NHS; Sct Actv; Stg Crw; Yth Flsp; Mth Clb; Letter Crs Cntry; Letter Trk;.

CUMMINS, DENISE; Manchester HS; Clinton, OH ; 27/21 Band; Chrs; Drl Tm; NHS; Sch Mus; Sch Pl; Treas Stu Cncl; Rptr Yrbk; Fr Clb; Sec Pep Clb; Akron Univ; Nursing.

CUMMINS, HUGH; Indian Hill HS; Cincinnati, OH; Chrh Wkr; Rptr Yrbk; Ger Clb; Lat Clb; IM Sprt; College; Bus Ec.

CUMMINS, KATHY; Malabar HS; Mansfield, OH; 21/265 Sec Chrh Wkr; Cmnty Wkr; Girl Scts; Hon Rl; NHS; Stu Cncl; Ed Yrbk; Rptr Yrbk; Mth Clb; Ten; Miami Univ.

CUMMINS, MICHAEL D; Northeastern Wayne HS; Fountain City, IN; Hon Rl; Pres NHS; Letter Ftbl; Letter Trk; IM Sprt; Univ.

CUMMINS, PEGGY; Southington Chalker HS; Southington, OH; 21/80 Hon Rl; Hosp Ade; NHS; Stu Cncl; Y-Teens; Yrbk; Beta Clb; 4-H; FNA; Lat Clb; College; Bilingual Sec.

CUMMINS, RUSSELL; Hicksville HS; Hicksville, OH; Cls Rep Soph Cls; Chrs; Stu Cncl; Lat Clb; Letter Bsbl; Letter Ftbl; College; Phys Ther.

CUMMISKEY, JAYNE; Bishop Watterson HS; Worthington, OH; Chrs; Chrh Wkr; Girl Scts; Hon Rl; NHS; Off Ade; Rptr Sch Nwsp; Spn Clb; OSU; Math.

CUMPSTON, GAIL; Cameron HS; Cameron, WV; 20/103 VP Frsh Cls; Band; Hon Rl; Off Ade; Y-Teens; Rptr Sch Nwsp; GAA; PPFtbl; Univ; Acctg.

CUNNINGHAM, AMY; John Marshall HS; Indianapolis, IN; 37/611 Band; Cmp Fr Grls; Chrh Wkr; Hon Rl; Yth Flsp; Block Ltr M For 6 Sem Of Bnd 79; Mbr Of JMHS Bnad Won Super Ratng 78; Univ; Chem Engr.

CUNNINGHAM, BARB; Salem Sr HS; Salem, OH; AFS; FHA; Pep Clb; Univ; Nursing.

CUNNINGHAM, BRENT; Orrville HS; Orrville, OH; FCA; Hon Rl; NHS; Stu Cncl; Boys Clb Am; Fr Clb; FTA; Ten; IM Sprt; Special Awds Ftbl FCA Stu Tutor Honor Roll & Special History Awd; College; Math.

CUNNINGHAM, CHRISTINE; Valley HS; Reader, WV; 3/78 VP Jr Cls; Hst Sr Cls; Chrs; Chrh Wkr; Hon Rl; NHS; Quill & Scroll; Sch Pl; Stu Cncl; Yth Flsp; Fairmont St Coll; Comp Prog.

CUNNINGHAM, CRAIG; Clear Fork HS; Bellville, OH; 8/180 Pres Frsh Cls; Cl Rep Jr Cls; Boy Scts; Hon Rl; NHS; Stu Cncl; Letter Bsktbl; College.

CUNNINGHAM, CRAIG; Scarlet Oaks HS; Reading, OH; 66/217 VP Jr Cls; Trs Sr Cls; Hon Rl; Stu Cncl; DECA; DECA Food Mrktng Awrds Dstrct 2nd Plc & St 9th Plc 77; Awrd Of Dstnctn OH Brd Of Educ; Bus Schl; Mgmt.

CUNNINGHAM, DANITA; Roosevelt Wilson HS; Clarksburg, WV; Band; Girl Scts; Hon Rl; NHS; Orch; Sch Pl; Y-Teens; FBLA; Leo Clb; Mgrs;.

CUNNINGHAM, DAPHNEY; Warrensville Heights HS; Warrensville Ht, OH; Cl Rep Jr Cls; Chrs; Chrh Wkr; Cmnty Wkr; Hon Rl; Sch Mus; Sch Pl; Kent State Univ; Telecommunications.

CUNNINGHAM, DEBORAH; Delphi Community HS; Delphi, IN; Chrs; Lbry Ade; Sch Mus; Sch Pl; Stg Crw; Drama Clb; Pep Clb; Spn Clb; Bus Schl; Sec.

CUNNINGHAM, DIANA; Lincoln HS; Lumberport, WV; Hon Rl; Y-Teens; Coll; Jrnlsm.

CUNNINGHAM, FAYE; Stivers Patterson Co Op HS; Dayton, OH; Cls Rep Soph Cls; Cl Rep Jr Cls; Boy Scts; Stu Cncl; 4-H; OEA; Pep Clb; UCLA; Bus Admin.

CUNNINGHAM, FLORENCE; Hubbard HS; Hubbard, OH; 10/320 Cls Rep Sr Cls; Am Leg Aux Girls St; Band; Chrh Wkr; Hon Rl; Lit Mag; NHS; Quill & Scroll; Stu Cncl; VP Yth Flsp; Kent St Univ.

CUNNINGHAM, JEAN; Wilmington HS; Wilmington, OH; 20/200 Band; Chrh Wkr; Cmnty Wkr; Lit Mag; NHS; Sch Mus; Stg Crw; Yth Flsp; College.

CUNNINGHAM, JILL; Minerva HS; Minerva, OH; Cls Rep Frsh Cls; Am Leg Aux Girls St; Band; Girl Scts; Hon Rl; Stu Cncl; 4-H; Pep Clb; Spn Clb; Chrldng; Miami Univ; Acctg.

CUNNINGHAM, JOAN; Dexter HS; Dexter, MI; 17/168 Trs Frsh Cls; Trs Soph Cls; Trs Jr Cls; Hon Rl; Jr NHS; NHS; Trk; Chrldng; Eastern Michigan Univ; Math.

CUNNINGHAM, KERRY; Stow HS; Stow, OH; Hon Rl; Sprt Ed Sch Nwsp; Letter Bsbl; Letter Bsktbl; Ftbl; Pres Awd;.

CUNNINGHAM, KIM; Kearsley HS; Davison, MI; Band; Girl Scts; Hon Rl; Rptr Sch Nwsp; Univ Of Michigan.

CUNNINGHAM, KIMBERLY M; Southeastern HS; Chillicothe, OH; Band; Drl Tm; Hon Rl; Jr NHS; NHS; Ed Yrbk; FTA; Lat Clb; Pep Clb; Am Leg Awd;.

CUNNINGHAM, M; Holy Name HS; Middleburg Ht, OH; 86/330 Cls Rep Frsh Cls; Chrh Wkr; Hon Rl; Off Ade; Stu Cncl; Fr Clb; Pep Clb; IM Sprt; Scr Kpr; Cit Awd; Toledo Univ; Pharm.

CUNNINGHAM, MARCIA; Calumet HS; Gary, IN; Cls Rep Frsh Cls; Band; Pres Chrs; Off Ade; Pres Sch Mus; Sch Pl; Y-Teens; Drama Clb; Fr Clb; FNA; Creative Hair Styling; Cosmtlgy.

CUNNINGHAM, MARK; West Lafayette HS; W Lafayette, IN; FCA; Ftbl; IM Sprt; Purdue Univ.

CUNNINGHAM, MARY; Lumen Christi HS; Jackson, MI; 100/242 Pol Wkr; ROTC; Lat Clb; Swmmng; Trk; IM Sprt; PPFtbl; Central Michigan Univ; Bus Admin.

CUNNINGHAM, MICHELLE; Edward Lee Mc Clain HS; Greenfield, OH; 3/143 Chrh Wkr; NHS; Pres Yth Flsp; Fr Clb; Spn Clb; Natl Merit SF; Whos Who In Amer HS Aws For Religious Art 78; World Affairs Inst Cincinnati Oh By Rotary Club 79; Ohio Univ; Acctg.

CUNNINGHAM, NANCY; Covington HS; Covington, IN; FHA;.

CUNNINGHAM, ROBERT; Wheelensburg HS; Wheelersubrg, OH; Fr Clb; IM Sprt; Scr Kpr; Tmr; Mental Health Assn 76 79; Coll.

CUNNINGHAM, RUTH; John Glenn HS; Westland, MI; Cls Rep Frsh Cls; Cl Rep Jr Cls; Cmp Fr Grls; Hon Rl; NHS; Red Cr Ade; Stu Cncl; Gym; Letter Trk; Cit Awd; Ferris State; Pharmacy.

CUNNINGHAM, SALLY; Covington HS; Covington, IN; 4/120 Am Leg Aux Girls St; Band; Chrh Wkr; Cmnty Wkr; Drl Tm; Sec FCA; Girl Scts; Hon Rl; Sch Pl; Sct Actv; Univ; Comp Progr.

CUNNINGHAM, SALLY S; Covington Comm HS; Covington, IN; 4/120 Am Leg Aux Girls St; Band; Sec Chrh Wkr; Drl Tm; Treas FCA; Sch Mus; Sch Pl; Sct Actv; Rptr Sch Nwsp; VP Eng Clb; Honor Jacket 5 Chevrons Trojan Honor Pin; College; Law.

CUNNINGHAM, SARAH; Medina HS; Seville, OH; Band; Chrs; Chrh Wkr; Cmnty Wkr; Girl Scts; Off Ade; Sch Mus; Sct Actv; Stg Crw; Rptr Yrbk; College; Soc Work.

CUNNINGHAM, SHARI; Southmont Jr Sr HS; Waveland, IN; 2/196 Band; Cmp Fr Grls; Sec Chrh Wkr; Girl Scts; Hon Rl; Hosp Ade; Jr NHS; NHS; Stg Crw; Stu Cncl; Butler Univ; Pre Med.

CUNNINGHAM, SHEILA; Garfield HS; Akron, OH; 1/403 Trs Frsh Cls; Sec Sr Cls; Chrh Wkr; Hon Rl; Jr NHS; NHS; Stu Cncl; Drama Clb; OEA; Am Leg Awd; Med Stenographer.

CUNNINGHAM, TAMARA; Kearsley Community HS; Davison, MI; Band; Girl Scts; Hosp Ade; Nott Community College; Registernurs.

CUNNINGHAM, TERESA; Madison Heights HS; Anderson, IN; 62/390 Cls Rep Frsh Cls; Cls Rep Soph Cls; Cl Rep Jr Cls; Cls Rep Sr Cls; Aud/Vis; FCA; Hon Rl; Spn Clb; Swmmng; Tmr; Marian College Of Ind; Bus.

CUNNINGHAM, TERESA; East Liverpool HS; E Liverpool, OH; 22/342 Trs Frsh Cls; Cls Rep Soph Cls; Sec Jr Cls; VP Sr Cls; Band; Drl Tm; NHS; Sch Mus; Sch Pl; Ohi Univ; Psych.

CUNNINGHAM, TERESA K; Waldo J Wood Memorial HS; Oakland City, IN; VP Soph Cls; Band; Chrs; Chrh Wkr; Hon Rl; Lbry Ade; Orch; Sch Nwsp; 4-H; FHA; Vincennes Univ; Phys Therapy.

CUNNYNGHAM, KATHRYN L; Whetstone HS; Columbus, OH; 1/330 AFS; Cmp Fr Grls; Chrs; Hon Rl; Lbry Ade; NHS; Sch Pl; Rptr Sch Nwsp; Pres Fr Clb; Natl Merit SF; College.

CUPP, MEGAN; Buckhannon Upshur HS; Buckhannon, WV; Chrs; Chrh Wkr; Cmnty Wkr; Sch Mus; Stu Cncl; 4-H; Wv Wesleyan Coll; History.

CUPP, NATALIE; New Richmond HS; Amelia, OH; 8/196 Chrh Wkr; Hon Rl; Hosp Ade; NHS; Quill & Scroll; Fr Clb; FHA; FTA; Univ.

CURKENDALL, TERRI; Philip Barbour HS; Philippi, WV; Chrs; Hon Rl; Sec NHS; Sch Pl; Stu Cncl; Sec Drama Clb; Pres 4-H; Pep Clb; Sec Spn Clb; Chrldng; West Virginia Univ; Gnrl Forestry.

CURL, CONNIE; Fairfield HS; Hamilton, OH; 42/596 Hon Rl; VP JA; NHS; DECA; VP Lat Clb; Letter Swmmng; Natl Merit Ltr; Outstndng Achvmnt In Latin 78; Univ; Pre Med.

CURL, PATRICIA; Switzerland Cnty HS; Madison, IN; 10/143 Sec Jr Cls; Band; Drm Mjrt; Girl Scts; Hon Rl; 4-H; Pep Clb; 4-H Awd;.

CURLEY, CAROLYN G; Highland HS; Wadsworth, OH; Cls Rep Sr Cls; Chrs; Off Ade; Stu Cncl; Lat Clb; Akron Univ; Bus.

CURLIN, PAUL; Switzerland Cnty HS; Vevay, IN; Hon Rl; NHS; Sch Mus; Sch Pl; Drama Clb; Best Actor Jr Class Play 1978; Outstnd Perfmc Jr; Top Ten 7th Grade And 8th Grade; Rose Hulman Inst Of Tech; Comp Sci.

CURLISS, LAURA; Blanchester HS; Blanchester, OH; 3/164 Cl Rep Jr Cls; Cls Rep Sr Cls; Band; Chrs; Girl Scts; Hon Rl; NHS; Red Cr Ade; Sch Mus; Sch Pl; Univ; Law.

CURNOW, THOMAS; Harbor Springs HS; Harbor Springs, MI; Am Leg Boys St; Hon Rl; Letter Ftbl; Lake Superior St Coll; Elec.

CURRAN, CATHY; Columbiana Cnty Jnt Voc Schl; Rogers, OH; Trs Jr Cls; Hon Rl; Sch Pl; Stg Crw; Y-Teens; Pres 4-H; Treas OEA; Pep Clb; Trk; 4-H Awd; Meredith Manor; Horse Bus.

CURRAN, JOHN; Marian HS; Mishawaka, IN; Hon Rl; NHS; Bsktbl; Letter Ftbl; Voice Dem Awd; Univ Of Notre Dame.

CURRAN, JOHN; Pontiac Central HS; Pontiac, MI; Letter Swmmng; Univ; Acctg.

CURRAN, MICHAEL; Orchard View HS; Muskegon, MI; 17/223 Sec Frsh Cls; Band; Hon Rl; NHS; Rptr Sch Nwsp; Glf; Capt Swmmng; Letter Ten; VFW Awd; Voice Dem Awd; Mi Competive Schlrshp Prog 79; Whos Who Among Amr HS Stu 77; Ferris St Univ; Pharm.

CURRAN, RANDY; South Ripley Jr Sr HS; Versailles, IN; 11/120 Aud/Vis; Chrh Wkr; Hon Rl; Lbry Ade; VICA; Ivy Tech Inst; Electrician.

CURREN, CAMILLA; North Ridgeville HS; N Ridgeville, OH; Band; VP Girl Scts; Hon Rl; Lit Mag; Sec Yth Flsp; Yrbk; Pres 4-H; Sec Ger Clb; Honorable Mention; Ohio Tests Of Scholastc Ach; Reprtr Photographer For Newspaper; Article Expert; Softball; College; Bio Chem.

CURREN, GARRY; Harding HS; Marion, OH; Band; Boy Scts; Chrs; NHS; Sch Mus; Sch Pl; Fr Clb; Bsbl; Capt Ftbl; Gym; Vanderbilt Univ; Elec Engr.

CURRENCE, BECKY; Washington HS; Massillon, OH; Cl Rep Jr Cls; Cls Rep Sr Cls; Chrs; Hon Rl; Jr NHS; Sch Mus; Yth Flsp; Fr Clb; Letter Swmmng; Ohio St Univ; Comp Engr.

CURREY, BETH; Brookhaven HS; Columbus, OH; 248/434 Chrs; Hon Rl;.

CURRIE, CHRISTOPHER; University Of Detroit HS; Farmington, MI; Debate Tm; Hon Rl; Mod UN; NHS; Sch Mus; Natl Merit Ltr; Mi Comp Schslhp 79; Univ Of Detroit Trustees Grant 79; Univ Of Detroit; Archt.

CURRIE, DEBBIE; J F Rhodes HS; Cleveland, OH; Band; Jr NHS; Orch; Sch Mus; Stu Cncl; Ger Clb; OEA; Ten; College; Comp Sci.

CURRIE, MAXINE; Kettering Sr HS; Detroit, MI; Band; Chrs; Chrh Wkr; Drl Tm; Girl Scts; Hon Rl; Jr NHS; NHS; Off Ade; Sct Actv; Senior Intensfd Prog 1978; 3rd Runr Up Homecoming Crt 1978; Michigan St Univ; RN.

CURRIE, STEPHEN; William A Wirt HS; Gary, IN; 129/230 Cls Rep Sr Cls; Pres Chrh Wkr; Cmnty Wkr; Pres Stu Cncl; Yth Flsp; Civ Clb; Crs Cntry; Trk; University; Busns Mgmt.

CURRIER, JEFF; Caro Comm HS; Caro, MI; Am Leg Boys St; Boy Scts; Hon Rl; NHS; Sch Pl; Fr Clb; Trk; Am Leg Awd; Mich State Univ; Natural Sciences.

CURRY, ANITA; Cardinal HS; Middlefield, OH; 4/103 AFS; Cmp Fr Grls; Chrs; Chrh Wkr; Cmnty Wkr; Girl Scts; Hon Rl; Jr NHS; NHS; Off Ade; Schlrshp Tm French 2 78 & Algebra 2 79; Algebra 2 Awd 79; Bowling Green Univ; Sociology.

CURRY, DAVID; Buckhannon Upshur HS; Buckhannon, WV; Chrs; Hon Rl; Yth Flsp; 4-H; 4-H Awd;.

CURRY, DAVID A; West Lafayette HS; W Lafayette, IN; 95/185 Boy Scts; Ger Clb; 2nd Prize German Test For HS Stu; Purdue Univ; Horticulture.

CURRY, DEBRA; Westfall HS; Orient, OH; Band; Chrs; Hon Rl; Sch Mus; FHA; Letter Chrldng; Banner Auxilary For Band Letter; Busns Schl; Corp Sec.

CURRY, DENISE; Broad Ripple HS; Indianapolis, IN; Am Leg Aux Girls St; Cmp Fr Grls; Chrs; Girl Scts; Hon Rl; NHS; ROTC; Rptr Sch Nwsp; Ger Clb; Am Leg Awd; Univ Of Evansville; Journalism.

CURRY, EDWARD; Georgetown HS; Georgetown, OH; 8/64 VP Sr Cls; Am Leg Boys St; Chrs; Hon Rl; VP NHS; Sch Mus; Rptr Yrbk; 4-H; Fr Clb; Cit Awd; Univ Of New Orleans; Elem Educ.

CURRY, KEVIN; Chesapeake HS; Chesapeake, OH; Cl Rep Jr Cls; Boy Scts; Band; Hon Rl; Off Ade; Stu Cncl; Yrbk; Beta Clb; Marshall Univ; Comp Sci.

CURRY, REX; Waterford HS; Waterford, OH; 6/69 Sec Frsh Cls; Trs Sr Cls; Hon Rl; Sch Pl; Sci Clb; Spn Clb; Bsbl; Crs Cntry; Ohio Univ; Bus Admin.

CURRY, SABRINA; Chadsey HS; Detroit, MI; Cmp Fr Grls; Chrs; Chrh Wkr; Cmnty Wkr; Drl Tm; Girl Scts; Hon Rl; Red Cr Ade; Sch Mus; Sct Actv; Univ.

CURRY, SANDY; Hamlin HS; Hamlin, WV; Band; Hon Rl; Jr NHS; NHS; Sch Pl; Yth Flsp; 4-H; Ger Clb; Pep Clb; Letter Bsktbl;.

CURRY, VERNA; East HS; Youngstown, OH; 1/190 Cls Rep Frsh Cls; Cls Rep Soph Cls; Pres Jr Cls; Cls Rep Sr Cls; Val; Pres Chrh Wkr; Cmnty Wkr; Hon Rl; JA; Jr NHS; Principles Awd 1978; Spainish Awd 1978; Natl Hnr Soc 1977; Youngstown St Univ; Med.

CURRY, YOLONDA L; East HS; Columbus, OH; Hon Rl; JA; NHS; Lat Clb; Pep Clb; Trk; Coach Actv; Mgrs; Scr Kpr; Tmr; Howard Univ; Law.

CURTIN, KEVIN; Lake Linden Hubbell HS; Lake Linden, MI; Boy Scts; Chrh Wkr; Hon Rl; Sct Actv; Sch Nwsp; Ftbl; Hockey; Coach Actv; Scr Kpr; Tmr; Mich Tech Univ; Engr.

CURTIS, ALICE; Noblesville HS; Noblesville, IN; Band; Rptr Yrbk; Pres OEA; Twrlr; 4-H Awd; Indian Busns Coll; Busns.

CURTIS, BETSY; Pinckney HS; Pinckney, MI; Cls Rep Frsh Cls; Cls Rep Soph Cls; Cl Rep Jr Cls; Band; Pres Chrs; Hon Rl; Mdrgl; Natl Forn Lg; NHS; Stu Cncl; Mic State Univ; Music Educ.

CURTIS, CHRIS; Madison Comprehensive HS; Mansfield, OH; Hon Rl; Ger Clb; Trk; Wrstlng; College; Math.

CURTIS, CRAIG; Wilmington HS; Wilmington, OH; 350284 VP Frsh Cls; Cl Rep Jr Cls; Band; 4-H; FFA; Pep Clb; Cit Awd; 4-H Awd; FFA Leadshp Awd 78; Jr Leadrshp 4 H Awd 78; 4 H Showmnshp Awd 74 & 78; Ohio St Univ; Acctg.

CURTIS, JAMES D; East Clinton HS; New Vienna, OH; 25/125 Boy Scts; Chrh Wkr; FCA; Hon Rl; NHS; Yth Flsp; 4-H; Treas Sci Clb; Letter Bsbl; Letter Ftbl; Tech Coll; Comp Tech.

CURTIS, JERRY; St Johns HS; De Witt, MI; Boy Scts; Sct Actv; Letter Ten; IM Sprt; Univ; Public Relations.

CURTIS, KIM; Bedford HS; Bedford, OH; Cl Rep Jr Cls; Band; Univ; Med Research.

CURTIS, MARK; Concord HS; Jackson, MI; Am Leg Boys St; Boy Scts; Hon Rl; Sct Actv; Rptr Sch Nwsp; Sch Nwsp; Letter Wrstlng; ROTC; Pilot.

CURTIS, MARY; Laingsburg HS; Laingsburg, MI; Band; Girl Scts; Hon Rl; 4-H; FHA; Ger Clb; Pep Clb; Letter Chrldng; GAA; PPFtbl; Univ; Vet Asst.

CURTIS, MARY; Harper Creek HS; Battle Creek, MI; 7/240 Chrs; Chrh Wkr; Girl Scts; Hon Rl; NHS; Off Ade; Sch Mus; Pres Yth Flsp; Rptr Yrbk; Drama Clb; Univ; Bus Mgmt.

CURTIS, RENATE; Big Rapids HS; Big Rapids, MI; Band; Debate Tm; Drl Tm; Natl Forn Lg; NHS; Sch Mus; Sch Pl; Stg Crw; Drama Clb; Fr Clb; Michigan St Univ; Civil Engr.

CURTIS, TAMMY; North Vigo HS; Rosedale, IN; 90/583 VP Sr Cls; Band; Hon Rl; JA; Off Ade; Y-Teens; Rptr Sch Nwsp; Ivy Tech; Lpn.

CURTON, CARMAN; Mattawan HS; Schoolcraft, MI; 16/136 Chrs; Yth Flsp; Ed Yrbk; Yrbk; College; Psych.

CUSHMAN, KATHY J; West Liberty Salem HS; West Liberty, OH; 10/80 Cmp Fr Grls; Chrh Wkr; Cmnty Wkr; Hon Rl; Jr NHS; Lbry Ade; NHS; Off Ade; Sch Mus; Sch Pl;.

CUSHMAN, PAMELA; Otsego HS; Otsego, MI; 10/222 VP Soph Cls; Cls Rep Soph Cls; Cl Rep Jr Cls; Pres Sr Cls; Cls Rep Sr Cls; Band; Chrs; Girl Scts; Hon Rl; Mod UN; Hope Coll; Elem Ed.

CUSICK, COLLEEN; Fairview HS; Fairvw Pk, OH; Band; Chrs; Hon Rl; Lit Mag; Orch; Sch Mus; Stg Crw; Yth Flsp; Drama Clb; Tmr; Bowling Green St Univ; Music Educ.

CUSICK, DOUG; Linsly Institute; Follansbee, WV; Hon Rl; JA; ROTC; Key Clb; Lat Clb; Spn Clb; UCLA; Med.

CUSICK, E; Roy C Start HS; Toledo, OH; Chrs; JA; Sch Mus; Sch Pl; Spn Clb; Univ.

CUSICK, JEFFERY L; Marion HS; Marion, IN; Am Leg Boys St; Band; Chrh Wkr; Hon Rl; NHS; Sct Actv; Yth Flsp; Sci Clb; Bsbl; Bsktbl; Purdue Univ; Chem Engr.

CUSICK, MIKE; Warsaw Comm HS; Warsaw, IN; Pres Sr Cls; Cls Rep Sr Cls; Boy Scts; Cmnty Wkr; Girl Scts; Pol Wkr; Sch Pl; Letter Stu Cncl; Sch Nwsp; Pres DECA; St Josephs Busns School; Busnsmgmt.

CUSTER, DANA; Bellmont HS; Decatur, IN; 31/244 Cl Rep Jr Cls; Cls Rep Sr Cls; Drl Tm; Trs Frsh Cls; NHS; Stu Cncl; Spn Clb; Ind Univ Of Purdue.

CUSTER, JAMES; United Local HS; Hanoverton, OH; 43/120 Hon Rl; Lbry Ade; Pres 4-H; FFA; 4-H Awd; Mbr Of United FFA Chptr 4th In St; 1sat Pl FFA Pub Spkng At Local & Dist Gld Mdl At St; Brdcstng.

CUSTER, KATHLEEN; Andrean HS; Valparaiso, IN; 45/254 Cls Rep Frsh Cls; Hon Rl; Jr NHS; NHS; Chrldng; Opt Clb Awd; Purdue Univ; Psych.

CUSTIS, MARTHA; Lebanon HS; Lebanon, OH; Debate Tm; Hon Rl; JA; 4-H; FBLA; FHA; Sci Clb; Letter Hockey; 4-H Awd; Miami Univ Middletown; Bus.

CUSTODIO, BAMBI; De Kalb HS; Auburn, IN; 2/309 AFS; JA; NHS; Stu Cncl; Fr Clb; Pep Clb; JA Awd; 12th Annl Hon Bnqt 12th Grd; Hon Awd 12th Grd; Univ.

CUTHBERTSON, JAMES; Arthur Hill HS; Saginaw, MI; 5/600 Hon Rl; Natl Merit Ltr; College; Bio.

CUTHRELL, RANDY; Clawson HS; Clawson, MI; Chrh Wkr; Hon Rl; Spn Clb; Letter Mgrs; Univ; Lang Intrptr.

CUTI, JONATHON; Spring Lake HS; Spring Lake, MI; 31/185 Am Leg Boys St; Boy Scts; Chrh Wkr; FCA; Hon Rl; Sch Mus; Stg Crw; Bsktbl; Hope College; Bus.

CUTICCHIA, ANNE; Upper Arlington HS; Columbus, OH; 1/620 AFS; Am Leg Aux Girls St; Cmnty Wkr; Hon Rl; NHS; Quill & Scroll; Sch Nwsp; Fr Clb; Spn Clb; Ten; College; Business.

CUTLER, ANNE; Central HS; Evansville, IN; Cls Rep Frsh Cls; Cls Rep Soph Cls; Cl Rep Jr Cls; Cls Rep Sr Cls; Hon Rl; Stu Cncl; Rptr Yrbk; Beta Clb; Gym; Trk; Natl Fed Music Club Awd Solo ISUE 78 & 79; Natl Fed Music Club Awd Duet ISUE 79; Indiana Univ; Drafting.

CUTLER, BECKY; Piketon HS; Waverly, OH; 9/115 Chrs; Hon Rl; Sch Mus; Sprt Ed Sch Nwsp; Rptr Sch Nwsp; 4-H; FHA; FTA; OEA; Pep Clb; Univ.

CUTLER, JOHN; Gods Bible Schl HS; Cincinnati, OH; 2/40 VP Frsh Cls; Chrs; Hon Rl; Sch Pl; Yth Flsp; Drama Clb; Spn Clb; Bsktbl; Gym; IM Sprt; Univ; Offc Mach.

CUTLER, LAURA; Timken Sr HS; Canton, OH; Band; Chrs; Drm Bgl; Girl Scts; Hon Rl; Sec JA; Lbry Ade; NHS; Sch Mus; Sch Pl; College; Bio Sci.

CUTLIP, CRIS; Miami Trace HS; Bloomingburg, OH; 45/242 AFS; Sec Band; Drl Tm; Hon Rl; Stu Cncl; Y-Teens; Drama Clb; Pres 4-H; FTA; Twrlr;.

CUTLIP, LUANN; Hillsdale HS; Jeromesville, OH; Pres Soph Cls; Band; Hon Rl; NHS; Sch Pl; Drama Clb; Lat Clb; Chrldng; GAA; Ashland Coll; Med Tech.

CUTRIGHT, JEAN M; Buckhannon Upshur HS; Tallmansville, WV; Stg Crw; Sec.

CUTSHALL, DEIRDRE; Southwestern HS; Lexington, IN; Cls Rep Frsh Cls; Cls Rep Soph Cls; Cl Rep Jr Cls; Cls Rep Sr Cls; Chrh Wkr; Hon Rl; Lbry Ade; 4-H; FHA; GAA; Univ; Bus Law.

CUTT, ANDREA; Lutheran West HS; Rocky River, OH; 10/99 Chrh Wkr; Hon Rl; NHS; Off Ade; Orch; Red Cr Ade; Sch Mus; Rptr Yrbk; GAA; Ohio State Univ; Architecture.

CUTTER, KIM; Richmond Sr HS; Richmond, IN; 6/550 Cls Rep Frsh Cls; Trs Jr Cls; Sec Band; Hon Rl; Hosp Ade; Mod UN; NHS; Stu Cncl; Yth Flsp; Y-Teens; Indiana Univ; Elem Ed.

CUTTER, REBECCA L; Warren Sr HS; Warren, MI; 32/400 Band; Hon Rl; NHS; Michigan St Univ; Zoology.

CUTTERIDGE, RONDA; Central HS; Evansville, IN; 47/520 Cls Rep Frsh Cls; Hon Rl; NHS; Stu Cncl; Ed Sch Nwsp; Rptr Sch Nwsp; VP DECA; Pres OEA; Kiwan Awd; Rotary Awd; Benjamine & Anna Bosse Schlrshp 79; OEA Dist St & Natl Awd 79; Univ Of Evansville; Bus Educ.

CUTTS, MARY; North HS; Youngstown, OH; 7/112 Cls Rep Sr Cls; Chrs; Chrh Wkr; Hon Rl; Jr NHS; NHS; Off Ade; Stu Cncl; Y-Teens; Fr Clb; Howard Univ; Law.

CUYLER, KELLIE; Issac C Elston HS; Michigan City, IN; 58/308 Band; Hon Rl; Off Ade; Mth Clb; Spn Clb; Southern Ill Univ; Dental Hygiene.

CVENGROS, GARY; A D Johnston; Bessemer, MI; Chrs; Hon Rl; Lbry Ade; Red Cr Ade; Sch Nwsp; Letter Ftbl; Western Mich; Aviator.

CVENGROS, JOSPEH; Center Line HS; Warren, MI; Hon Rl; Bsbl; Bsktbl; Ftbl; Trk; General Motors Inst; Draftsman.

CYBULSKI, J; Lumen Christi HS; Grass Lk, MI; Cmnty Wkr; Hon Rl; 4-H; Lat Clb; Wrstlng; 4-H Awd; Mich State Univ; Drafting.

CYGAN, CHRISTOPHER; Warren Woods HS; Warren, MI; Letter Band; Hon Rl; Orch; Sch Mus; Pep Clb; St Of Mi Compt Schslhp E Mi Univ Regnl HS Scslhp 79; John Phillip Sousa Band Awd 79; Eastern Michigan Univ; Music.

CYGAN, DAVID M; Warren Woods HS; Warren, MI; Hon Rl; NHS; OEA; U S Merchant & Marine Acad 79; Mi Comp Schlrshp 79; Regnl HS Schlrshp To E Mi Univ 79; Eastern Michigan Univ; Math.

CYHANICK, M; Martinsburg HS; Martinsburg, WV; 27/220 Cl Rep Jr Cls; Girl Scts; Hon Rl; Sct Actv; Stu Cncl; Letter Trk; Univ.

CYMANSKI, CHRISTINE; Elyria Catholic HS; N Ridgeville, OH; Chrs; Chrh Wkr; Hon Rl; Treas 4-H; Spn Clb; 4-H Awd; Cleveland St Univ.

CYPHER, TERESA; St Vincent St Mary HS; Cuyahoga Falls, OH; Chrs; Hon Rl; JA; Jr NHS; NHS; Off Ade; Sch Pl; Bsbl; Bsktbl; JA Awd; Akron Univ; Jrnlsm.

CYPHERT, JOANNA; St Francis HS; Morgantown, WV; Letter Bsktbl; Letter Trk; Scr Kpr; Univ.

CYR, YVONNE; Fairmont East HS; Kettering, OH; AFS; Am Leg Aux Girls St; FCA; Girl Scts; Hon Rl; NHS; Sprt Ed Yrbk; Miami University.

CYRUS, ANGELA; Dunbar HS; Dunbar, WV; Cls Rep Frsh Cls; Boy Scts; Cmp Fr Grls; Chrs; Chrh Wkr; Hon Rl; Lbry Ade; Stu Cncl; Yth Flsp; Y-Teens; French Hon Soc 79; Typing I Awd 79; West Virginia St Coll; Comp Sci.

CYRUS, PAMELA; Milton HS; Milton, WV; 1/250 Trs Soph Cls; Cls Rep Soph Cls; Band; Chrs; Hon Rl; VP Jr NHS; NHS; Stu Cncl; Fr Clb; Mth Clb; St & Cnty Wnr Soc Studies Fair 78; Student Body V P 79; Math Field Day Tm 78; Univ; Med.

CYRUS, SHERRY D; Buffalo HS; Prichard, WV; Band; Chrh Wkr; Drm Mjrt; Hon Rl; Sch Mus; FBLA; FHA; Marshall Univ.

CYRUS, TIMOTHY; New Richmond HS; Bethel, OH; Chrh Wkr; JA; Sci Clb; JA Awd; Univ; History.

CYRUS, TRESSA; Milton HS; Milton, WV; Cls Rep Soph Cls; Am Leg Aux Girls St; Band; Chrs; Pres Chrh Wkr; Girl Scts; Hon Rl; Jr NHS; NHS; Sch Mus; West Virginia Baptist St Yth Committee Conv 78 80; Eng Awd 75 & 77; Geo Awd 78; Univ; Psych.

CZACHOR, ANN M; St Alphonsus HS; Detroit, MI; 11/181 Girl Scts; Hon Rl; Fr Clb; Univ; Engr.

CZACHOR, MARY L; St Alphonsus HS; Detroit, MI; 14/181 Girl Scts; Hon Rl; Fr Clb; Univ; Engr.

CZAIJKA, ANN; Marian HS; Birmingham, MI; Hon Rl; Chrldng; Michigan Univ; Law.

CZAJKA, CINDY; St Andrew HS; Detroit, MI; Trs Frsh Cls; Chrs; FCA; Hon Rl; Jr NHS; NHS; Sch Mus; Sch Pl; Chrldng; IM Sprt; Michigan St Univ; Spec Educ.

CZAPKO, LAURA K; North Newton HS; Lk Village, IN; Band; Chrs; Sch Pl; Sch Nwsp; Key Clb; FBLA; Pep Clb; Spn Clb; Trk; 4-H Awd; College; Theatre Arts.

CZAPLICKI, DAWNA; Vly Forge HS; Parma, OH; 177/650 Hon Rl; Hosp Ade; Sch Pl; Drama Clb; Spn Clb; VICA; Sec Mat Maids; Cit Awd; Natl Merit Ltr; Ohio St Univ; Respiratory Therapy.

CZAPLICKI, VICKY; St Alphonsus HS; Detroit, MI; Band; Chrs; Drm Mjrt; Hon Rl; Hosp Ade; Sch Mus; Pep Clb; Twrlr; Mercy Coll; Med Asst.

CZARNAPYS, MARY; West Catholic HS; Grand Rapids, MI; Hon Rl; VP NHS; Sch Pl; Pres Lat Clb; Aquinas College; Law.

CZARNECKI, DANIEL; Comstock Park HS; Comstock Pk, MI; Boy Scts; Natl Forn Lg; NHS; Rptr Yrbk; Letter Ftbl; Trk; Wrstlng; Mgrs; Cit Awd; Mich Tech Univ; Civil Eng.

CZARNIK, CAROLYN; Franklin HS; Westland, MI; Girl Scts; Hon Rl; Sct Actv; Letter Bsbl; GAA; Cit Awd; Coll.

CZARNIK, MARY; St Florian HS; Detroit, MI; 8/75 NHS; Spn Clb; College; Engr.

CZARNOMSKI, CAROL; East Detroit HS; East Detroit, MI; Band; FCA; Hon Rl; NHS; Ed Yrbk; Yrbk; PPFtbl; Macomb Cnty Cmnty Coll; Mrktng.

CZARNOTA, JAN; Paul K Cousino Sr HS; Warren, MI; Cls Rep Frsh Cls; Cls Rep Soph Cls; Cl Rep Jr Cls; Hon Rl; Jr NHS; NHS; PAVAS; Stu Cncl; Mth Clb; Pep Clb; Wayne St Univ Merit Schlrshp 79; Western Univ Schlrs Prog 79; Warren Cultural Arts Theatre Schlrshp 79; Wayne St Univ; Bus.

CZARNOWSKI, V; Brandon HS; Ortonville, MI; Band; Chrs; Chrh Wkr; Cmnty Wkr; Hon Rl; Orch; Sch Mus; Rptr Sch Nwsp; Trk; Natl Merit Ltr; Univ Of Michigan; Archt.

CZARNOWSKI, VINCENT; Brandon HS; Ortonville, MI; Band; Chrs; Chrh Wkr; Hon Rl; Sch Mus; Rptr Sch Nwsp; Trk; Natl Merit Ltr; UM; Archt.

CZEBATUL, CYNTHIA; Fraser HS; Fraser, MI; Cls Rep Frsh Cls; Cls Rep Soph Cls; Hon Rl; NHS; Stu Cncl; Sch Nwsp; 4-H; Bsktbl; Ten; Mic Tech Univ; Med Tech.

CZECH, ALINA; Valley Forge HS; Parma, OH; 5/704 Cl Rep Jr Cls; Cls Rep Sr Cls; Hon Rl; Jr NHS; NHS; Sch Pl; Stu Cncl; Sch Nwsp; Fr Clb; Pep Clb; Northwestern Univ; Intl Bus Admin.

CZERKAWSKI, GREGORY A; Reitz Memorial HS; Newburgh, IN; 50/215 Band; Chrs; Hon Rl; Sch Mus; Sch Pl; Indiana Univ; Music.

CZERNIAWSKI, LINDA; St Florian HS; Hamtramck, MI; 4/114 Hon Rl;.

CZESTKOWSKI, ANN; Bishop Borgess HS; Detroit, MI; Hon Rl; Am Leg Awd; Univ Of Michigan; Law.

CZICH, THERESA; Central Catholic HS; Dennison, OH; Band; Chrs; Hon Rl; Hosp Ade; NHS; Treas Pep Clb; Ohio St Univ; Phys Ther.

CZOKNIJ, ZENON; Immaculate Conception HS; Hamtramck, MI; 6/33 Cl Rep Jr Cls; Chrs; Chrh Wkr; Hon Rl; NHS; Stu Cncl; Sprt Ed Sch Nwsp; Wayne State Univ; Med.

CZUCHRAN, DENNY; Buckeye South HS; Rayland, OH; Ftbl; Carpenter.

CZYMBOR, MARY; Hemlock HS; Saginaw, MI; 10/166 Sec Soph Cls; Cls Rep Sr Cls; Band; Hon Rl; NHS; Sch Pl; Stu Cncl; Saginaw Valley State; Acctg.

CZYZYK, WILLIAM; Catholic Ctrl HS; Grand Rapids, MI; Band; Hon Rl; Trk; Aquinas Coll; Music.

D

DAAVETTILA, NEIL; South Lyon HS; Northville, MI; 7/269 Hon Rl; NHS; IM Sprt; Mic Technological Univ; Engr.

DABERTIN, D; George Rogers Clark HS; Whiting, IN; Cls Rep Frsh Cls; Cls Rep Soph Cls; Cl Rep Jr Cls; Am Leg Boys St; Cmnty Wkr; NHS; Quill & Scroll; Stg Crw; Stu Cncl;.

D ACHILLE, JANET; Capac HS; Emmett, MI; Band; Hon Rl; Pres NHS; Sch Nwsp; VP 4-H; VP FFA; Bsktbl; Chrldng; GAA; 4-H Awd; MSU; Med Lab Tech.

DACK, JEFF; Springport HS; Springport, MI; Pres Jr Cls; CAP; NHS; Letter Bsktbl; Letter Glf; Scr Kpr; Tmr; College; Rotc Military.

DADABBO, MARK; Holy Redeemer HS; Detroit, MI; 1/176 Cls Rep Frsh Cls; Cls Rep Soph Cls; Cl Rep Jr Cls; Hon Rl; NHS; Stu Cncl; Bsbl; Bsktbl; Crs Cntry; Eastern Michigan Univ; Educ.

DADAIAN, MICHELLE; Fairview HS; Fairview Pk, OH; Cls Rep Frsh Cls; Cls Rep Soph Cls; Cl Rep Jr Cls; Cls Rep Sr Cls; Sal; Band; Chrh Wkr; Hon Rl; JA; Off Ade; Schlrs Recognition 78 79; Univ; Poli Sci.

D ADAMS, JOY; Amanda Clearcreek HS; Stoutsville, OH; Sec Soph Cls; VP Jr Cls; Band; NHS; Off Ade; Stu Cncl; Yrbk; 4-H; Sci Clb; Bsbl;.

DADOSKY, MARGARET; Mc Nicholas HS; Cincinnati, OH; 4/250 Cls Rep Frsh Cls; Hon Rl; NHS; Stu Cncl; 4-H; Univ; Med.

DAENZER, SHELBY; Kearsley HS; Flint, MI; Trs Frsh Cls; Cls Rep Frsh Cls; Cls Rep Soph Cls; Hon Rl; NHS; Stu Cncl; Yrbk; Letter Bsktbl; Coach Actv; Mgrs; Univ; Med.

DAFLUCAS, MONICA A; St Francis De Sales HS; Columbus, OH; 21/185 Chrh Wkr; Hon Rl; Sch Mus; Sch Pl; Rptr Yrbk; GAA; Capt Mat Maids; Scr Kpr; Tmr; Miami Univ; Home Economics.

DAGGY, CAROL; Richmond HS; Richmond, IN; Hon Rl; NHS; Orch; Sch Mus; Stu Cncl; Natl Merit Ltr; Eartham College; French.

DAGHLIAN, JACKIE; Warsaw Community HS; Winona Lake, IN; 25/370 Band; Chrh Wkr; Hon Rl; Sch Mus; Grace Coll.

D AGOSTINO, JEFFERY; St Francis Central HS; Morgantown, WV; Am Leg Boys St; Hon Rl; NHS; Fr Clb; Letter Bsbl; Elk Awd; Marietta Univ; Cmmrcl Archt.

DAGOSTINO, LISA; Canfield HS; Canfield, OH; 5/250 Chrs; Chrh Wkr; Girl Scts; Hon Rl; Lit Mag; NHS; Stg Crw; Y-Teens; Fr Clb; Key Clb; Art Contst Winner 79; Outstndng Manes & Faces Awd 79; Ohio St Univ; Sci.

DAGUE, TAMMY; Johnstown Monroe Sr HS; Johnstown, OH; Trs Jr Cls; Band; Chrs; Drm Mjrt; Hon Rl; Sch Pl; FTA; Mas Awd; Res Of Futr Tchr Of Amer 78; Drill Team 79;grand Offcr For Rainbow In Oh 78; Otterbein Coll; Drama.

DAGUE, TERRY; Floyd Central HS; New Albany, IN; 70/359 Chrs; Hon Rl; Sch Pl; Pom Pon; Univ.

DAHER, PATRICIA; Marquette HS; Michigan City, IN; 20/64 Cls Rep Sr Cls; Hon Rl; Jr NHS; NHS; Red Cr Ade; Stu Cncl; Fr Clb; Swmmng; Scr Kpr; Indiana Univ; Pre Dentistry.

DAHL, KEVIN; Coopersville HS; Coopersville, MI; Boy Scts; Hon Rl; Capt Ten; Bus Schl; Mgmt.

DAHLKAMP, SUE; Munster HS; Munster, IN; AFS; Girl Scts; Stg Crw; Stu Cncl; OEA; Scr Kpr; Tmr; Marion Awd; Ambassador Awd; First Class Awd; Calumet Coll; Acctg.

DAHLKE, PEGGY; Stevenson HS; Livonia, MI; Centrl Mic Univ; Accnt.

DAHM, MAUREEN; Bishop Dwenger HS; Ft Wayne, IN; Aud/Vis; Chrs; Chrh Wkr; Cmnty Wkr; Pol Wkr; Civ Clb; Pom Pon; Srgnt Of Arms City Wide Sorority 1977; VP City Wide Sorority 1978; Nominated Member Natl Cheerleader Staff; Xavier Univ; Psych.

DAHMS, CAROL; Munster HS; Hammond, IN; Chrs; Chrh Wkr; Cmnty Wkr; Hon Rl; Hosp Ade; Jr NHS; NHS; Off Ade; Red Cr Ade; Yth Flsp; Purdue Univ; Sci.

DAIBER, MARK; Medina Sr HS; Medina, OH; 19/350 Hon Rl; NHS; Ger Clb; Letter Ftbl; Trk; Letter Wrstlng; IM Sprt; Univ Of Michigan; Geology.

DAIGNAULT, LAURIE; Arthur Hill HS; Saginaw, MI; Cls Rep Soph Cls; Cl Rep Jr Cls; Hon Rl; NHS; Off Ade; PAVAS; Sch Pl; Stg Crw; Drama Clb; Pep Clb; Saginaw Valley St Coll.

DAILER, CINDY; Bishop Donahue HS; Benwood, WV; 21/54 Cls Rep Soph Cls; Cmp Fr Grls; Chrs; Chrh Wkr; Cmnty Wkr; Girl Scts; Hon Rl; Lbry Ade; Off Ade; Pol Wkr; West Virginia Cmnty Coll; Med.

DAILEY, DIANA; Linton Stockton Jr Sr HS; Linton, IN; 4/99 Hon Rl; NHS; Y-Teens; Rptr Yrbk; Treas FBLA; Spn Clb; Bus.

DAILEY, JAMES; Columbiana HS; Columbiana, OH; 10/105 Cls Rep Soph Cls; Am Leg Boys St; Hon Rl; NHS; Off Ade; Spn Clb; Bsbl; Ftbl; Wrstlng; Coach Actv; 8 Yr Awd Varsity Ltrs 78; Booster Club Awd Schlrshp 78; 3.5 Above Awd 78; Youngstown St Univ; Math Educ.

DAILEY, KAREN; Our Lady Of Mercy HS; Farm Hls, MI; Chrs; Cmnty Wkr; Girl Scts; Hosp Ade; NHS; Stg Crw; Sec Ger Clb; Tmr; Univ; Nurse.

DAILEY, LISA; Cardington Lincoln HS; Cardington, OH; 14/79 Pres Jr Cls; Rptr Yrbk; Fr Clb;.

DAILEY, N; Mississinewa HS; Jonesboro, IN; 17/205 Hst Frsh Cls; Hst Jr Cls; Hon Rl; NHS; FHA; OEA; Pep Clb; Gym; Chrldng; Mat Maids; Prospect Hall Coll; Travel.

DAILEY, W H; Culver Military Acad; Shreveport, LA; 3/191 Cmnty Wkr; Drl Tm; Hon Rl; Jr NHS; ROTC; Ger Clb; Socr; Ten; Wrstlng; IM Sprt; Walter G Roberts Awd 77; Col G T Gunston Med 77 & 78; Univ Of Virginia; Law.

DAILY, CHRISTOPHER; Whiteland Community HS; Franklin, IN; 40/200 Am Leg Boys St; Pres FCA; NHS; Key Clb; Ftbl; IM Sprt; Ball State Univ; Acctg.

DAILY, DON; Wintersville HS; Wintersville, OH; 11/282 Am Leg Boys St; Hon Rl; NHS; Fr Clb; Bsbl; Bsktbl; Ftbl; Coach Actv; IM Sprt; Am Leg Awd; College; Engr.

DAILY, DONALD; Wintersville HS; Wintersville, OH; 11/282 Am Leg Boys St; Hon Rl; NHS; Fr Clb; Bsbl; Bsktbl; Ftbl; Coach Actv; IM Sprt; Am Leg Awd; Coll; Engr.

DAILY, KIMBERLY; Eaton Rapids HS; Eaton Rapids, MI; 20/245 Chrs; Hon Rl; NHS; Off Ade; Yth Flsp; Yrbk; Trk; PPFtbl; Hon Schlrshp Fr Ctrl Mi Univ 78; St Of Mi Cmptve Schlrshp Awd 79; Two Hon Ment In Crtve Wrtng Yth Tal Exhbt; Joan Jewett Career Schl; Travel Agnt.

DAILY, MARCIA; Loogootee HS; Loogootee, IN; Band; Chrh Wkr; Hon Rl; Off Ade; Rptr Yrbk; Fr Clb; Pep Clb; Chrldng; IM Sprt; Scr Kpr; Univ.

DAIN, DEBORAH; Columbiana HS; New Springfield, OH; 22/101 Chrs; Chrh Wkr; Drl Tm; Hon Rl; Mdrgl; NHS; Off Ade; Yrbk; Pep Clb; Spn Clb; Aultman Hosp; Nursing.

DAKIN, MAUREEN; Plainfield HS; Plainfield, IN; 11/283 Cls Rep Frsh Cls; Cls Rep Soph Cls; Chrs; Cmnty Wkr; Hon Rl; Mdrgl; NHS; Sch Mus; Stg Crw; Stu Cncl; Concerto Contest Played Piano Indlps Symphony Orchestra; Jr Miss Talent Awd; All St Choir Member; College; Music.

DAKIN, SUSAN J; Middletown HS; Middletown, OH; Chrs; Hon Rl; Fr Clb; Pep Clb; Mat Maids; Ohio Univ; Speech.

DAKOSKE, CATHERINE; Canton Central Catholic HS; N Canton, OH; Cl Rep Jr Cls; Hon Rl; Stu Cncl; Rptr Yrbk; Ten; Univ Of Michigan; Dent Hygnst.

DAKOSKE, JOSEPH; Traverse City Sr HS; Traverse City, MI; Boy Scts; Debate Tm; Letter Ten; Kiwan Awd; Northwestern Michigan Coll.

DALE, LARRY; Northfork HS; Mc Dowell, WV; Band; Hon Rl; Sprt Ed Yrbk; Mgrs; W Va Univ; Aerospace Tech.

DALE, MICHELE; Hartland HS; Fenton, MI; 7/254 Band; Hon Rl; Hosp Ade; Lit Mag; NHS; Sch Pl; Rptr Yrbk; DECA; Drama Clb; Mgrs; Univ Of Michigan; Dent Hygn.

DALE, N; Eastbrook HS; Van Buren, IN; Chrs; Cmnty Wkr; 4-H; Purdue Univ; Forestry.

DALEN, DUWAYNE; Farwell HS; Lake, MI; Hon Rl; NHS; Ger Clb; Letter Trk; Central Michigan Univ; Elec.

DALES, ELDON; Lebanon HS; Lebanon, OH; 4/200 Band; Pres Chrh Wkr; Hon Rl; NHS; ROTC; Sch Mus; Sch Pl; Stg Crw; Sci Clb; Wilmington Coll Otstndng Sci Achvmnt Awd 79; AFJROTC 1st Lieutenant 79; AFJROTC Ace Acad Achvmnt 79; Univ Of Cincinnati; Chem Engr.

DALEY, CAROL; Lapeer East HS; Lapeer, MI; Cl Rep Jr Cls; Cls Rep Sr Cls; Chrs; Chrh Wkr; Debate Tm; Girl Scts; Hon Rl; Treas NHS; Oakland Univ; Soc Studies.

DALEY, LISA; Lexington Sr HS; Lexington, OH; Band; Chrs; Cmnty Wkr; Hon Rl; Lbry Ade; Orch; Stu Cncl; Sec Y-Teens; Rptr Yrbk; FTA; Mbr All Richladn Cnty Chr 79; Ltr Orch Band & Chr 79; Univ; Cmnctns.

DALLER, JOSEPH; Belding HS; Belding, MI; Chrs; Chrh Wkr; Cmnty Wkr; Hon Rl; NHS; Y-Teens; Sch Nwsp; Letter Bsbl; Letter Ftbl; Letter Wrstlng; Captn Of Varsty Bsbl Tm 79; 2nd Tm All Confrnc Var Ftbl 79; Most Valuable Lineman Ftbl 79; Ferris St Univ; Archt.

DALLEY, JEFFREY; Taylor Center HS; Taylor, MI; Debate Tm; Hon Rl; Natl Forn Lg; NHS; Sch Mus; Fr Clb; IM Sprt; Wayne State Univ; Premed.

DALTON, DAPHNE; Marion HS; Marion, IN; 1/750 Chrs; Chrh Wkr; Hon Rl; NHS; Rptr Yrbk; Ed Sch Nwsp; Ger Clb; Sci Clb; Letter Swmmng; Letter Ten; Ambssdrs 79; Forming Tr Club For Girls M Club 79; Pres 'S Sor 79; Univ; Chem.

DALTON, DIANE; Knightstown Community HS; New Castle, IN; Chrs; Chrh Wkr; Drl Tm; Hon Rl; Sch Mus; Stg Crw; Yth Flsp; VP Drama Clb; FTA; Univ; Music.

DALTON, DOUG; Sidney HS; Sidney, OH; Band; Chrs; Chrh Wkr; Hon Rl; NHS; Off Ade; Stg Crw; Yth Flsp; Key Clb; Bsktbl; Univ Of Cincinnati; Elec Engr.

DALTON, FREDDIE; Rock Hill Sr HS; Ironton, OH; 45/161 Boy Scts; Capt Bsktbl; Letter Ftbl; Letter Trk;.

DALTON, JOHN; Madison Heights HS; Anderson, IN; 25/371 Hon Rl; NHS; Pol Wkr; Ger Clb; Letter Glf; Ball St Univ; Acctg.

DALTON, LARRY L; Henryville HS; Henryville, IN; 1/70 Pres Sr Cls; Val; Pres Band; Hon Rl; Pres NHS; Sch Pl; Letter Crs Cntry; Letter Trk; Am Leg Awd; Dnfth Awd; Purdue Univ; Civil Engr.

DALTON, MARY; Merrillville HS; Merrillville, IN; Band; Chrh Wkr; Hon Rl; NHS; Drama Clb; Spn Clb; Natl Merit Schl; Indiana Univ; Spanish.

DALTON, R; Kalkaska HS; Rapid City, MI; 1/120 Pres Frsh Cls; Chrh Wkr; NHS; Sch Pl; Letter Bsbl; Natl Merit Ltr;.

DALTON, TERRY; Monrovia HS; Mooresville, IN; Sec Soph Cls; Band; Hon Rl; Spn Clb; Tmr; Jazz Band Concert Bvand Marchng Band 76 80; Spnsh Club Off 79; Univ; Radio.

DALTON, WENDELL; West Muskingum HS; Zanesville, OH; Cls Rep Frsh Cls; Cls Rep Soph Cls; Hon Rl; Stu Cncl; Fr Clb; FFA; Bsbl; Bsktbl; Ftbl; Pres Awd; College.

D ALTORIO, ALFONSO; Struthers HS; Struthers, OH; 63/276 Boy Scts; DECA; Rdo Clb; Bsbl; Youngstown St Univ; Communications.

DALTORIO, VIRGINIA; Struthers HS; Struthers, OH; 39/280 Hon Rl; Lbry Ade; Y-Teens; Rptr Yrbk; Drama Clb; FNA; Lat Clb; Pep Clb; Rdo Clb; Sci Clb; Youngstown St Univ; Dental Hygnst.

DALVERNY, CARLY; Winamac Community HS; Winamac, IN; Girl Scts; Hon Rl; Sct Actv; Y-Teens; Pep Clb; Spn Clb; GAA; Pom Pon; Scr Kpr; Drill Team Superstars; Nominated For Semal A Queen; College; Medicine.

DALVERNY, CARLY; Winamac Cmnty HS; Winamac, IN; Girl Scts; Hon Rl; Sct Actv; Fr Clb; Pep Clb; Spn Clb; Mgrs; Mat Maids; Pom Pon; De Pauw Univ; Pre Med.

DALY, ANN; Muncie Northside HS; Muncie, IN; 30/250 Cl Rep Jr Cls; Cls Rep Sr Cls; Cmnty Wkr; Jr NHS; NHS; Orch; Pres Stu Cncl; Rptr Sch Nwsp; Ger Clb; Sci Clb; Pratt Inst; Art.

DALY, CHRISTINE; Pontiac Central HS; Pontiac, MI; Hon Rl; Sch Mus; Drama Clb; Fr Clb; Coach Actv; College; Drama.

DALY, TIMOTHY; Muncie Northside HS; Muncie, IN; Cl Rep Jr Cls; Cls Rep Sr Cls; Hon Rl; Ger Clb; Lat Clb; Mth Clb; Pep Clb; Sci Clb; Ind Univ; Optometry.

DALZOTTO, LINDA; New Buffalo HS; New Buffalo, MI; 2/69 Sal; Hon Rl; Jr NHS; NHS; Stu Cncl; Ed Yrbk; Sprt Ed Yrbk; Trk; Chrldng; Natl Merit SF; Cntrl Michigan Univ; Jrnlsm.

DAME, ROBERT A; Kalamazoo Central HS; Kalamazoo, MI; 9/425 Band; Chrh Wkr; Hon Rl; NHS; Hope Coll; Comp Programming.

DAMIANI, MICHAEL; St Alphonsus HS; Dearborn, MI; Chrh Wkr; Debate Tm; Hon Rl; Stg Crw; Yrbk; Drama Clb; Mgrs; Univ Of Mic; Engineering.

DAMIANI, PAUL; Grandview HS; Columbus, OH; AFS; Band; Boy Scts; Chrs; FCA; Sct Actv; Stg Crw; Rptr Sch Nwsp; Pep Clb; Rdo Clb; Music Hnr Awd Vocal 79; Ord Of The Arrow Scts 77; Univ; Cmmrcl Pilot.

DAMIANI, RUDY; Grandview Hts HS; Columbus, OH; 15/135 Hon Rl; Ftbl; Letter Wrstlng; IM Sprt; Schlrshp Awd Soph & Jr Yrs 78; Univ.

D AMICO, BEVERLY; Mayfield HS; Highland Hts, OH; AFS; Chrs; Drl Tm; Hon Rl; Hosp Ade; Red Cr Ade; Rptr Sch Nwsp; Sch Nwsp; Drama Clb; Bsbl; Clevelnd Press Awd 3d Pl 1978; Spec Achvmnt In Jrnlsm 1978; Five Super Ribbons From Super Star Drll Tm Camp; Univ.

D AMICO, LORRI; Trinity HS; Warrensville, OH; 47/150 Chrs; Chrh Wkr; Capt Drl Tm; Hon Rl; Univ; Eng.

DAMMINGA, JEAN; Benjamin Franklin HS; Westland, MI; Am Leg Aux Girls St; Band; Chrs; Hon Rl; Orch; Stu Cncl; Univ; Elem Vocal Music.

DAMON, JUANITA; Brethren Christian HS; South Bend, IN; 2/29 Band; Chrs; Hon Rl; Sch Pl; Treas Stu Cncl; Yth Flsp; Letter Chrldng; Grace Coll; Music.

D AMOUR, JAMES C; Sparta HS; Sparta, MI; Am Leg Boys St; Hon Rl; NHS; Pol Wkr; Stu Cncl; VP Fr Clb; VP Sci Clb;.

DAMRON, CHONCHITA D; Almont HS; Almont, MI; Treas Chrs; Girl Scts; Hon Rl; Hosp Ade; NHS; Sch Mus; Sct Actv; Drama Clb; Bsbl; Chrldng; Western Michigan Univ; Art Educ.

DAMRON, GERALDINE; Kermit HS; Kermit, WV; 5/36 Hst Jr Cls; Band; Hon Rl; Beta Clb; FHA; Pep Clb; Spn Clb; Concord Univ; Busns.

DAMRON, KIMBERLY; Marion HS; Marion, IN; Band; Drl Tm; Girl Scts; Hon Rl; Hosp Ade; NHS; Stu Cncl; Yrbk; Pom Pon; Twrlr; Ball St Univ; Dent Hygnst.

DAMSCHRODER, KATHRYN; Gibsonburg HS; Gibsonburg, OH; 1/110 Trs Jr Cls; Val; Am Leg Aux Girls St; Band; Chrs; Chrh Wkr; Cmnty Wkr; Girl Scts; Hon Rl; Hosp Ade; Ohio Bd Of Regents Outstndng Acad Ach; Bowling Green St Univ Most Outstndng HS Jr Awd; USAF Acad; Aeronautical Engr.

DANAHER, DEBBIE; Fairview HS; Fariview Pkar, OH; Band; Drl Tm; Girl Scts; Hon Rl; Yth Flsp; GAA; IM Sprt; Tmr; Cit Awd; Bowling Green Univ; Eng.

DANALS, STUART; Loudonville HS; Perrysville, OH; 21/131 Sec Frsh Cls; Boy Scts; Hon Rl; Jr NHS; Spn Clb; Bsktbl; Ftbl; Trk; N Central Tech College; Mech Engr.

DANCHO, MARCIE; Centerville Sr HS; Richmond, IN; 9/150 Chrh Wkr; FCA; Hon Rl; NHS; Y-Teens; Pres Fr Clb; Letter Bsktbl; IM Sprt; Manchester Univ; Bio.

DANCIE, RENEE; Jane Addams Vocational HS; Cleveland, OH; Girl Scts; Hon Rl; JA; Y-Teens; Akron Univ; Pre Med.

DANDAR, ANNA; Edison HS; Berlin Hts, OH; Cls Rep Frsh Cls; Cls Rep Soph Cls; Sec Jr Cls; Cl Rep Jr Cls; Cls Rep Sr Cls; AFS; Am Leg Aux Girls St; Band; Chrs; Chrh Wkr; Univ; Nursing.

DANDAR, MARY; Cardinal Stritch HS; Toledo, OH; 1/212 Boy Scts; Hon Rl; NHS; Fr Clb; CYO Softball; Chess Club & Team; Public Relations Comm; Univ; Acctg.

DANDRIDGE, BEVERLY; Covert HS; Covert, MI; 4/38 VP Frsh Cls; VP Soph Cls; Cl Rep Jr Cls; Pres Sr Cls; Band; Chrh Wkr; Drm Mjrt; Girl Scts; Hon Rl; Mod UN; Eastern Michigan Univ; Busns.

DANDROW, MARY; Hopkins HS; Hopkins, MI; Cls Rep Soph Cls; Pres Jr Cls; Hon Rl; Stu Cncl; Pres FFA; Scr Kpr; Mich State; Agri.

DANEMAYER, CHRIS; Lasalle HS; Cincinnati, OH; Hon Rl; NHS; Yrbk; Wrstlng; College; Comercial Art.

DANESTEN, MANDANA; Andrews School; Cleveland, OH; Sec Frsh Cls; Chrs; Hon Rl; Yrbk; Sch Nwsp; Gym; Hndbl; Socr; Swmmng; 500 Schslhpt From Andrews Schl For Acad Achvmnt 79; Univ; Med.

DANEVICH, KIM; Lorain Catholic HS; Lorain, OH; Chrs; Drm Bgl; Hon Rl; Gym; Trk; Pom Pon; Natl Merit Ltr; Akron Univ; Accounting.

DANG, DZUNG; St Mary Of Redford HS; Detroit, MI; 8/152 Hon Rl; NHS; Rptr Yrbk; Mth Clb; Sci Clb; Socr; Letter Trk; IM Sprt; MSU; Comp Sci.

DANG, T; West Ottawa HS; Holland, MI; Orch; Spn Clb; Univ; Educ.

DANGELO, DONNA; Wintersville HS; Steubenville, OH; 17/289 Hon Rl; Sch Pl; Stg Crw; Yrbk; Drama Clb; Spn Clb; Spn Clb; Trk; GAA; Wittenburg Univ; Bio.

DANGELO, NICHOLAS; Morton Sr HS; Hammond, IN; Am Leg Boys St; Hon Rl; Sprt Ed Sch Nwsp; Ftbl; Glf; Coach Actv; IM Sprt; Cit Awd; Bage In Genrl Assbly 79; Univ; Pre Law.

DANGELO, THOMAS; Southern Local HS; Summitvll, OH; Cl Rep Jr Cls; Cls Rep Sr Cls; Am Leg Boys St; Hon Rl; Jr NHS; NHS; Stu Cncl; Lat Clb; Bsktbl; Ftbl; College; Computer.

DANGELO, VINCENT; Mt Hope HS; Glen Jean, WV; 33/90 Chrs; Chrh Wkr; Sch Pl; Sprt Ed Yrbk; Ftbl; Glf; Trk; IM Sprt; Wv Univ; Bus.

DANGLER, CHRIS; Crestview HS; Convoy, OH; Cls Rep Frsh Cls; Cls Rep Soph Cls; Cl Rep Jr Cls; Chrh Wkr; Cmnty Wkr; Hon Rl; Lbry Ade; Sch Mus; 4-H; FHA; Busns Schl; Sec.

DANGLER, PATRICIA; Springfield HS; Battle Crk, MI; Hon Rl; NHS; Stg Crw; Drama Clb; 4-H; 4-H Awd; Beloit Coll; Archeology.

DANGLER, PENNY; Continental Local HS; Continental, OH; Hon Rl; Lbry Ade; FHA; College; Interior Design.

DANGLER, TRACIE; Napoleon HS; Napoleon, OH; Cls Rep Frsh Cls; Cls Rep Soph Cls; Cl Rep Jr Cls; Am Leg Aux Girls St; Chrs; Chrh Wkr; Cmnty Wkr; Hon Rl; Red Cr Ade; Sch Mus; Bowling Green St Univ; Tchr.

DANIEL, BARBARA; Cory Rawson HS; Rawson, OH; Band; Chrh Wkr; Hon Rl; NHS; Sch Pl; Yth Flsp; Yrbk; Pep Clb; Trk; Chrldng; Nationwide Beauty Schl.

DANIEL, BRENDA; Mannington HS; Mannington, WV; 1/103 Cls Rep Frsh Cls; Cls Rep Soph Cls; Cl Rep Jr Cls; Am Leg Aux Girls St; Chrh Wkr; Hon Rl; Mod UN; MMM; NHS; Quill & Scroll; Fairmont St Coll; Art.

DANIEL, BRENDA S; Northfield Jr Sr HS; Wabash, IN; 8/109 Chrs; Chrh Wkr; Hon Rl; Natl Forn Lg; Sec NHS; Sch Mus; FNA; Pep Clb; Spn Clb; Parkview Methodist Schl; Nursing.

DANIEL, CLATTE; Jane Addams Vocational HS; Cleveland, OH; Cls Rep Sr Cls; JA; Stu Cncl; JA Awd; Cleveland St Univ; Med Lab Tech.

DANIEL, CYNTHIA; Tippecanoe Valley HS; Akron, IN; 10/158 Hon Rl; Lbry Ade; NHS; FSA; Pep Clb; Spn Clb; Letter Swmmng; Trk; Coach Actv; IM Sprt; Outstndng Sr Math Awd; Purdue Univ; Engr.

DANIEL, ELIZABETH D; Liberty HS; Lester, WV; Cls Rep Soph Cls; Cmnty Wkr; Hon Rl; Stu Cncl; FHA; Pep Clb; Trk; IM Sprt; Pom Pon; Scr Kpr; College; Med Tech.

DANIEL, FRANKIE; Perry Central Comm HS; Rome, IN; Hst Frsh Cls; Girl Scts; Hon Rl; Lbry Ade; NHS; 4-H; Fr Clb; FHA; Bsktbl; Trk; College; Nursing.

DANIEL, KEITH; Russia Local HS; Russia, OH; 6/44 Am Leg Boys St; Boy Scts; Hon Rl; NHS; Sch Pl; Stg Crw; Stu Cncl; Drama Clb; Spn Clb; Letter Bsbl; GMI; Elec Engr.

DANIEL, KELLEY; Fairfield Union HS; Thornville, OH; 23/147 Band; Chrs; Drm Mjrt; Jr NHS; NHS; Sch Pl; Rptr Yrbk; FTA; OEA; Spn Clb; Outstndng Fresh Marching Band Mem;.

DANIEL, MARC; Columbia City Joint HS; Columbia City, IN; 70/275 Quill & Scroll; Yrbk; FTA; Pres Key Clb; Spn Clb; Ftbl; Univ.

DANIEL, MARIANNE; Farmington HS; Farmington, MI; Band; Chrs; Chrh Wkr; NHS; Orch; Yth Flsp; Fr Clb; Swmmng; Ten; Cit Awd; Cnsv Of Music.

DANIEL, MARK; Mannington HS; Mannington, WV; Hon Rl; Stu Cncl; FHA; Bsktbl; Letter Ftbl; Trk; IM Sprt; Voc Schl; Indust Elec.

DANIEL, PEARL; Carrollton HS; Minerva, OH; Aud/Vis; Girl Scts; Hon Rl; Pres 4-H; FHA; Treas Spn Clb; Bsktbl; Trk; Dnfth Awd; 4-H Awd; Marines; Acctg.

DANIEL, RACHEL; Avon Jr Sr HS; Danville, IN; 9/181 Band; Chrh Wkr; Girl Scts; Hon Rl; Sec NHS; Pol Wkr; VP Yth Flsp; Rptr Sch Nwsp; 4-H; Pres Fr Clb; 1st Yr French Outstnsng Stdtn 78; 2 1st In In St Music Contst 78; 1st Altrtn Girls St 79; Olivet Nazarene Coll.

DANIELL, JULIA A; Tyler County HS; Middlebourne, WV; 3/90 VP Jr Cls; Band; Hon Rl; Jr NHS; Stu Cncl; Yrbk; Rptr Sch Nwsp; FTA; Sci Clb; Univ; Art.

DANIELS, DAVID; Fayetteville HS; Fayetteville, WV; Cls Rep Frsh Cls; Cls Rep Soph Cls; Am Leg Boys St; Chrs; Hon Rl; Sch Mus; Sch Pl; Stg Crw; Pres Stu Cncl; Rptr Yrbk; West Virginia Univ; Vet.

DANIELS, JAMES; Maysville HS; Zanesville, OH; Boy Scts; Hon Rl; Sct Actv; 4-H; Wrstlng; Coach Actv; Scr Kpr; Tmr; Coll; Automotive Engr.

DANIELS, KIM; Springport HS; Albion, MI; Band; Cmnty Wkr; Hon Rl; NHS; Rptr Sch Nwsp; 4-H; Trk; 4-H Awd; Univ; Med.

DANIELS, RINDA; East HS; Akron, OH; VP Frsh Cls; Band; Drm Mjrt; Hon Rl; Sch Mus; FHA; Pep Clb; Spn Clb; Twrlr; Univ; Lawyer.

DANIELS, SHELIA; Independence HS; Glen White, WV; NHS; 4-H; FBLA; Univ; Bus Mgmt.

DANIELS, SONIA; Washington HS; Massillion, OH; Am Leg Aux Girls St; Chrs; Hon Rl; Jr NHS; VP NHS; Off Ade; Sch Mus; Ger Clb; Univ.

DANIELS, STEVE; Bellevue HS; Nashville, TN; Band; Hon Rl; Fr Clb; Letter Ten; IM Sprt; Univ; Comp Prog.

DANIELS, URSULA; Pershing HS; Detroit, MI; 10/280 Hon Rl; Pres NHS; VP Y-Teens; Treas FNA; Letter Ten; Michigan St Univ; Phys Ther.

DANIELS, URSULA; John J Pershing HS; Detroit, MI; Hon Rl; Pres NHS; VP Y-Teens; Yrbk; Treas FDA; OEA; Ten; Mic State Univ.

DANIELSON, MICHELLE; Houghton HS; Houghton, MI; 1/125 Band; Chrs; Hon Rl; Sch Mus; Sch Pl; Rptr Yrbk; Letter Bsktbl; Letter Trk; Coach Actv; Mgrs; N Michigan Univ; Scndy Educ.

DANISON, JODI; Philo HS; Roseville, OH; Cls Rep Frsh Cls; Pres Soph Cls; Cls Rep Soph Cls; Cls Rep Sr Cls; Band; Chrh Wkr; Hon Rl; Lit Mag; Off Ade; Stu Cncl; Univ; Dent Hygnst.

DANISON, MARY; Tecumseh HS; New Carlisle, OH; 13/364 Cl Rep Jr Cls; Trs Sr Cls; Band; Hon Rl; Jr NHS; NHS; Off Ade; Sch Mus; Sec Drama Clb; Trk; Band Board Rep; Honors Awd For Conducting; Honor Grad; Miami Univ; Math.

DANKE, DANIEL; Cadillac HS; Cadillac, MI; 9/300 Hon Rl; Glf; Natl Merit Ltr; Michigan Tech Univ; Civil Engr.

DANKO, ROBERT; Danbury HS; Marblehead, OH; Boy Scts; Sct Actv; Stg Crw; Sci Clb; Bsktbl; Letter Ftbl; Letter Trk; Scr Kpr; Tmr; Terra Tech; Law Enforcement.

DANKO, ROSANNE; Bedford Sr HS; Bedford, OH; Chrs; JA; NHS; Off Ade; Quill & Scroll; Sch Pl; Stg Crw; Rptr Yrbk; Ed Sch Nwsp; Drama Clb; Univ; Drama.

DANKOWSKI, MARGARET; Ontario HS; Galion, OH; VP Jr Cls; Band; Stu Cncl; Yrbk; Spn Clb; Letter Bsktbl; Letter Trk; DAR Awd; 4-H Awd; East Tenn Univ; Communications.

DANNEFFEL, TINA; Hartford HS; Watervliet, MI; Band; Chrs; Sec Chrh Wkr; Cmnty Wkr; FCA; Hon Rl; Mod UN; Sch Pl; Rptr Yrbk; Rptr Sch Nwsp; Blue Lk Fine Art Camp Shclhsp 77 79; Hartford Jazz Band Awd 78 & 79; Whos Who In Music 77; River Forest Univ; Music.

DANOWSKI, LISA; Northview HS; Grand Rapids, MI; Chrs; Cmnty Wkr; Hon Rl; JA; Off Ade; Pep Clb; PPFtbl; Davenport Bus Coll; Comp Progr.

D ANSELMI, LAURIE D; Liberty HS; Clarksburg, WV; 60/228 Cls Rep Frsh Cls; Band; Hon Rl; Y-Teens; Sch Nwsp; Drama Clb; 4-H; FNA; Pep Clb; Bsktbl; Parkersburg Cmnty Coll; Radiolgy.

DANTER, JEFF; Bexley HS; Bexley, OH; VP Band; Mth Clb; Capt Crs Cntry; Trk; College.

DANTIMO, JULIE; Nordonia HS; Northfield, OH; Band; Drl Tm; Girl Scts; Sch Mus; Sch Pl; Drama Clb; Ten; IM Sprt; Pom Pon; Scr Kpr; Cuyahoga Commnty College; Phys Asst.

D ANTONI, MARK; Chesapeake HS; Chesapeake, OH; 3/156 Hon Rl; NHS; Beta Clb; Letter Bsktbl; Univ; Bus Mgmt.

DANTUONO, MARK; Bettsville HS; Tiffin, OH; 1/20 Pres Jr Cls; Am Leg Boys St; Band; Hon Rl; NHS; Am Leg Awd; Cit Awd; Univ.

DANZEBRINK, NORBERT; Crawfordsville HS; Crawfordsville, IN; Band; Boy Scts; FCA; Hon Rl; Boys Clb Am; Key Clb; Bsbl; Glf; Letter Ten; Mgrs; Marquette Univ; Pre Law.

DAPORE, MARK; Versailles HS; Versailles, OH; 10/138 Band; Chrs; Chrh Wkr; FCA; Hon Rl; FFA; Bsbl; Letter Crs Cntry; Letter Trk; Univ; Engr.

DAPRILE, JEANETTE; Ursuline HS; Youngstown, OH; Cl Rep Jr Cls; Stu Cncl; Spn Clb; Youngstown St Univ; Offc Mgmt.

DARA, DAVID; De La Salle Collegiate HS; Detroit, MI; 2/129 Sal; Hon Rl; NHS; Spn Clb; Letter Ten; Natl Merit SF; Michigan Tech Univ; Elec Engr.

DARATONY, JAMES; Plymouth Salem HS; Plymouth, MI; FCA; Hon Rl; NHS; Off Ade; Ftbl; Rotary Awd; Hillsdale College; Comp Sci.

DARBRO, JILL; Switzerland County Jr Sr HS; Vevay, IN; Cls Rep Frsh Cls; Cls Rep Soph Cls; Cl Rep Jr Cls; Cls Rep Sr Cls; Chrs; FHA; Pep Clb; Sec Awd In Mixed Choir 79; Sullivan Jr Coll Of Bus; Bus Admin.

DARBY, CHRISTIE L P; River Rouge HS; River Rouge, MI; JA; Stu Cncl; Pep Clb; Spn Clb; Bsbl; Hockey; Chrldng; College; Nrsgn.

DARBY, PAM; Shady Spring; Beaver, WV; Band; Drm Mjrt; FCA; Girl Scts; Hon Rl; Sch Pl; Drama Clb; Pep Clb; Letter Mat Maids; Letter Twrlr; Marshall Univ; Tchr.

DARBY, RAY; Midland HS; Freeland, MI; Cls Rep Frsh Cls; Hon Rl; Letter Trk; Letter Wrstlng; Mic Tech Univ; Chem Engr.

DARBYSHIRE, JONN; Clayton Northmont HS; Englewood, OH; Chrs; Hon Rl; Sch Mus; Letter Ftbl; Letter Wrstlng; Univ; Bus.

DARDINGER, ANN; West HS; Columbus, OH; 3/330 Am Leg Aux Girls St; Chrs; Cmnty Wkr; Hon Rl; Hosp Ade; Jr NHS; NHS; Off Ade; FTA; Spn Clb; Univ Of Dayton; Dietetics.

DARE, DAVID; Padua Franciscan HS; Parma Hts, OH; Chrh Wkr; Cmnty Wkr; Stu Cncl; Sprt Ed Sch Nwsp; Letter Bsbl; IM Sprt; Scr Kpr; Creighton Univ; Jrnlsm.

DARIN, CHRISTINE; Nordonia HS; Northfield, OH; Cls Rep Frsh Cls; Sec Jr Cls; Sec Sr Cls; Band; Chrs; Chrh Wkr; Cmnty Wkr; Girl Scts; Lbry Ade; Off Ade; Univ; Dietitian.

DARK, JANE; Fountain Central HS; Veedersburg, IN; 29/135 Trs Jr Cls; Band; Chrh Wkr; Drl Tm; Hon Rl; Sch Mus; Yrbk; Rptr Sch Nwsp; 4-H; FHA; Ball St Univ; Jrnlsm.

DARLING, DARLING F; Elk Garden HS; Elk Garden, WV; Band; Chrs; Hon Rl; Sch Pl; Sch Nwsp; Letter Bsktbl; Scr Kpr; Voice Dem Awd; Univ; Nursing.

DARLING, DORIS J; Linden Mc Kinley HS; Columbus, OH; 19/250 Trs Frsh Cls; Drl Tm; Hon Rl; Stu Cncl; Bsbl; Bsktbl; Trk; Chrldng; Clerk Typist.

DARLING, KEVIN; Dublin HS; Dublin, OH; 15/156 Band; Chrs; Hon Rl; NHS; Sch Mus; Stg Crw; Ed Yrbk; Rptr Yrbk; Rptr Sch Nwsp; Lat Clb; Yearbook Service Awd; Miami Univ; Medicine.

DARLING, ROSE; Central HS; Grand Rapids, MI; Band; Girl Scts; Hon Rl; JA; NHS; Yrbk; OEA; Pep Clb; Outstg Achvmnt Sociology 78; PTA Schlrshp 79; Grnd Rpds Jr Coll Schlrshp 79; Grand Rapids Jr Coll; Bus.

DARLING, SCOT; Salem HS; Salem, OH; VP Sr Cls; Key Clb; Letter Ten;.

DARLSON, DANIEL; Griffith HS; Griffith, IN; Hon Rl; Jr NHS; Off Ade; Letter Bsbl; Letter Ftbl; IM Sprt; Purdue; Bus Mgmt.

DARNELL, BEVERLY; Philip Barbour; Belington, WV; Cls Rep Soph Cls; Band; Hon Rl; Stu Cncl; 4-H; Keyettes; Am Leg Awd; 4-H Awd; Lab Technician.

DARNELL, DOUGLAS; Norton HS; Norton, OH; Band; Boy Scts; Hon Rl; Orch; Sch Mus; Sch Pl;.

DARR, LINDA; Dublin HS; Dublin, OH; 19/157 Band; Chrs; Hon Rl; NHS; Orch; Sch Mus; Yth Flsp; Drama Clb; 4-H; Ohio Univ.

DARR, LORAINE; Fremont St Josephs Cntrl HS; Fremont, OH; 2/95 Am Leg Aux Girls St; Hon Rl; Pres NHS; Dnfth Awd; Coll; Nursing.

DARR, LORAINE L; St Joseph Cntrl Catholic HS; Fremont, OH; 1/85 Hon Rl; NHS; 4-H; IM Sprt; Univ; Nursing.

DARRAGH, TERRI; Mcauley HS; Cincinnati, OH; Chrh Wkr; Hon Rl; Sch Pl; Stg Crw; Drama Clb; Chrldng; College.

DARRAH, LINDA; Canton South HS; Canton, OH; Band; Hon Rl; Lit Mag; NHS; Off Ade; Y-Teens; Pep Clb; College; Bus.

DARRAH, MATTHEW; Kent Roosevelt HS; Kent, OH; Chrs; Sprt Ed Sch Nwsp; Bsbl; Kent St Univ; Bus.

DARRAH, SHERRI; Tyler County HS; Middlebourne, WV; 18/105 Band; Girl Scts; Hon Rl; Yth Flsp; Treas Sci Clb; Treas Spn Clb; Ctznshp Awrd 74; Vllybll Partcptn Awrd 77; Salem Coll; Vet Med.

DARRAH, SHERRI; Tyler Cnty HS; Middlebourne, WV; 18/105 Band; Girl Scts; Hon Rl; Yth Flsp; Treas Sci Clb; Treas Spn Clb; Cit Awd; Salem Coll; Vet.

DARRALL, MICHELE; Fairview Park HS; Fairview Pk, OH; 12/268 Girl Scts; Hon Rl; Hosp Ade; Pres JA; NHS; Yrbk; Sci Clb; JA Awd; Excellent & Superior Ratings In Local Dst & St Sci Fair S 79; 75 Dlr Awd For Excellence In North E Ohio Sci; Univ; Chem.

D ARRIGO, ANTONINO; Monroe HS; Monroe, MI; 115/520 Stu Cncl; Monroe Cmnty Coll; Electronics.

DARROW, JUDY; Jackson HS; Jackson, MI; Cl Rep Jr Cls; Cls Rep Sr Cls; Hon Rl; Fr Clb; IM Sprt; PPFtbl; Mic State Univ; Animal Husbandry.

DARTER, ALICE; Muncie Northside HS; Muncie, IN; FCA; Hon Rl; Jr NHS; NHS; Spn Clb; Letter Swmmng; Chrldng; Ball State Univ; Phys Ther.

DAS, SHEELA; North Muskegon HS; N Muskegon, MI; 21/109 Cls Rep Soph Cls; Band; Hon Rl; NHS; Sch Mus; Stu Cncl; Yrbk; Rptr Sch Nwsp; Fr Clb; Capt Chrldng; Univ; Bio Sci.

DASCENZO, JANINE; Cardinal Mooney HS; Youngstown, OH; 57/288 Debate Tm; Hon Rl; Stu Cncl; Ten; Coach Actv; College; Poli Sci.

DASCENZO, STACEY E; Dominican HS; Warren, MI; Hosp Ade; JA; NHS; Wayne State Univ; Pharmacy.

DASELER, TIM; Brown Cnty HS; Nineveh, IN; 1/208 Hon Rl; Sch Pl; Sct Actv; 4-H; VP Fr Clb; Pres Sci Clb; Bsbl; 4-H Awd; Univ; Engr.

DASEN, SUE; Corunna HS; Corunna, MI; Band; Hon Rl; 4-H; Swmmng; GAA; Scr Kpr; 4-H Awd; Michigan St Univ.

DASHER, ALAN; Moorefield HS; Moorefield, WV; Jr NHS; NHS; 4-H; FFA; Glf; College.

DASHER, MICHAEL; Elkins HS; Elkins, WV; Hon Rl; Key Clb; Spn Clb; IM Sprt; Univ; Engr.

DASSAY, SUSAN L; Gladwin HS; Gladwin, MI; Hon Rl; Spn Clb; Chrldng; PPFtbl; Pres Awd; Mid Michigan Coll; Exec Sec.

DATINI, MICHELLE; Aquinas HS; Lincoln Pk, MI; Hon Rl; Univ.

DATO, JACQUELINE; Ladywood HS; Canton, MI; Hon Rl; Quill & Scroll; Stg Crw; Rptr Yrbk; Drama Clb; Wayne St Univ.

DATORNEY, ROBERT; Western Reserve HS; Warren, OH; 23/430 Hon Rl; NHS; College.

DATTE, STEVEN; Bay City Western HS; Auburn, MI; 21/450 Hon Rl; NHS; Letter Ftbl; Letter Trk; Oakland Univ; Comp Sci.

DATTILO, LISA; Shawe Memorial HS; Madison, IN; 8/32 Sec Frsh Cls; Trs Frsh Cls; Girl Scts; Hon Rl; Jr NHS; NHS; Sch Nwsp; 4-H; Pep Clb; Letter Trk; J V Vllybll MVP 78; Varsity Vllybll Letter 78; Hanover Coll; Sec.

DATZ, JERRY; Archbishop Alter HS; Kettering, OH; 68/332 Pres Sr Cls; Chrs; Chrh Wkr; Hon Rl; Jr NHS; Stu Cncl; Crs Cntry; Coach Actv; IM Sprt; Mgrs; Miami Univ.

DATZ, TERRI; Hilliard HS; Amlin, OH; 5/332 AFS; Chrs; Chrh Wkr; Hon Rl; NHS; VP Yth Flsp; 4-H; Letter Bsktbl; GAA; Natl Merit Ltr; Varsity Sftbl 2 Letters All League Hnr Mention; Varsity Vlybl 1 Letter; Coll.

DAUGHERTY, BETH; Medina Sr HS; Medina, OH; 52/450 Pres AFS; Band; NHS; Univ; Intl Bus.

DAUGHERTY, CARALEE; South Lake HS; St Clair Shore, MI; Cl Rep Jr Cls; Hon Rl; Hosp Ade; Pol Wkr; Red Cr Ade; Ed Yrbk; Ten; Tmr; Mi Compttv Schshp 79; Detroit News Writng Awd 79; Cls Spkr At Grad 79; Albion Univ; Govt.

DAUGHERTY, CHRISTINE; Lake Orion Comm HS; Lake Orion, MI; 12/400 Cls Rep Soph Cls; Jr NHS; NHS; Rdo Clb; Bsbl; Capt Bsktbl; Coach Actv; Mgrs; Univ Of Michigan; Comp Sci.

DAUGHERTY, JAMES; Lapel HS; Lapel, IN; Aud/Vis; Band; Boy Scts; Sch Mus; Sct Actv; Stg Crw; Sci Clb; Wrstlng; Univ.

DAUGHERTY, JULIA A; Highland HS; Anderson, IN; 4/407 Girl Scts; NHS; Sch Pl; Drama Clb; Spn Clb; 4-H Awd; Natl Merit SF; Ball State Univ.

DAUGHERTY, MICHAEL; Lutheran HS; Warren, MI; 48/130 Aud/Vis; Band; Boy Scts; Chrs; Hon Rl; Sch Pl; Sct Actv; Trk; Wrstlng; Mich Tech Univ; Elec Engr.

DAUGHERTY, PATRICIA; St Ursula Academy; Villa Hls, KY; 39/85 Chrs; Chrh Wkr; Mdrgl; Mod UN; Sch Mus; Sch Pl; Northern Kentucky Univ; Spec Educ.

DAUGHERTY, PAULA; North Union HS; Richwood, OH; Band; Chrs; Hon Rl; Sch Mus; 4-H; Lat Clb; Gym; 4-H Awd; College; Interior Design.

DAUGHERTY, REGINA; Belmont HS; Dayton, OH; Cls Rep Frsh Cls; Cl Rep Jr Cls; Chrs; Chrh Wkr; Cmnty Wkr; Lbry Ade; Drama Clb; Trk; IM Sprt; Cit Awd; Wright St Univ; Poli Sci.

DAUGHERTY, RHONDA; Cascade HS; Clayton, IN; Trs Soph Cls; Trs Jr Cls; Trs Sr Cls; Chrs; Chrh Wkr; FCA; Girl Scts; Hon Rl; Stu Cncl; Rptr Yrbk; Homcmng Princss 75 & 77; Tlnt Awd In Plainfield Jr Miss Pgnt 79; Univ; Music.

DAUGHERTY, RICK; Chippewa HS; Doylestown, OH; Joint Voc Wayne Cnty Schl; Carpentry.

DAUGHERTY, TIMOTHY; Ontario HS; Mansfield, OH; 17/197 Band; Drm Bgl; Hon Rl; Sch Mus; Sch Pl; Sct Actv; Stg Crw; College; Comp.

DAUGHERTY, WILLIAM; Mona Shores HS; Muskegon, MI; 4/400 Hon Rl; Jr NHS; NHS; Bsbl; Bsktbl; Ftbl; Coach Actv; IM Sprt; Cit Awd; Central Michigan Univ; Busns.

DAULT, KAREN; Chelsea HS; Grass Lk, MI; Drl Tm; Hon Rl; Natl Forn Lg; Stg Crw; College; Spec Educ.

DAULT, MARY; William A Wirt HS; Gary, IN; Ed Yrbk; Sprt Ed Yrbk; Rptr Yrbk; Yrbk; Pep Clb; Sci Clb; Spn Clb; Indiana Univ; Respitory Ther.

DAUM, KRISTA; Marion Harding HS; Marion, OH; Band; Hon Rl; 4-H; Spn Clb; Typing Contest Bus Univ Col 79; Bus Schl; Bus.

DAUNHAUER, JUDITH; Notre Dame Acad; Toledo, OH; Trs Frsh Cls; Chrs; Chrh Wkr; Hon Rl; Mod UN; NHS; Stu Cncl; Spn Clb; College; Architecture.

D AURORA, ROBERT M; St Joseph Prep Seminary; Follansbee, WV; Pres Frsh Cls; Pres Soph Cls; Pres Jr Cls; Aud/Vis; Chrs; Chrh Wkr; Jr NHS; NHS; Stu Cncl; Lat Clb; DE Corra Awd 76;.

DAUSCH, CHRISTOPHER; Triton Ctrl HS; Fairland, IN; 9/170 Boy Scts; FCA; NHS; Rptr Sch Nwsp; Fr Clb; Bsktbl; Crs Cntry; Trk; Pres Awd; Univ; Engr.

DAVEE, LYNN; Mooresville HS; Mooresville, IN; 45/265 Band; Chrh Wkr; Hon Rl; Hosp Ade; Mdrgl; NHS; Sch Mus; Stg Crw; Fr Clb; Ind State Univ; Bus Mgmt.

DAVENPORT, DENISE; Lima HS; Lima, OH; Cl Rep Jr Cls; Cls Rep Sr Cls; Band; Chrs; Capt Drl Tm; Lbry Ade; Sch Mus; Stu Cncl; Pep Clb; Gym; College.

DAVENPORT, KAREN; Blanchester HS; Plsnt Pln, OH; Cls Rep Frsh Cls; Hon Rl; GAA; JA; Off Ade; Sch Pl; Yth Flsp; Drama Clb; Fr Clb; Scr Kpr; Raymond Walters College; Dental Hygi.

DAVENPORT, KAREN L; Maumee HS; Maumee, OH; 36/360 Chrh Wkr; Hon Rl; Yrbk; VP Spn Clb; Univ Of Toledo; RN.

DAVENPORT, MARSHA; Adelphian Academy; Lapeer, MI; Hon Rl; Rptr Sch Nwsp; IM Sprt; Andrews Univ; History.

DAVENPORT, PATRICIA; Deer Park HS; Cincinnati, OH; Band; Drl Tm; Hon Rl; NHS; Sch Mus; Y-Teens; Drama Clb; Letter Bsbl; Chrldng; GAA; College; Computer Annalyst.

DAVENPORT, SUSAN; Marion Local HS; Osgood, OH; Am Leg Aux Girls St; Hon Rl; NHS; 4-H; FHA; OEA; Sci Clb; 4-H Awd; Bus Schl; Sec.

DAVET, BOB; R B Chamberlin HS; Twinsburg, OH; 62/172 Band; Boy Scts; Chrh Wkr; Sch Pl; Sct Actv; Stg Crw; Yth Flsp; Bsbl; Bsktbl; IM Sprt; John Philip Sousa Band Awd; Busns Schl; Comp Prog.

DAVEY, KIM; Hartland HS; Brighton, MI; 35/250 Cl Rep Jr Cls; Hon Rl; Off Ade; Fr Clb; Bsbl; Ten; Chrldng; Mgrs; JC Awd; Michigan St Univ; Cmntns.

DAVEY, TIM; Clay HS; Oregon, OH; 100/354 Cls Rep Frsh Cls; Cls Rep Soph Cls; Chrh Wkr; FCA; Hon Rl; Yth Flsp; Mth Clb; Spn Clb; Bsktbl; Trk; Anderson Coll; Bus Admin.

DAVID, DALE; Elmwood HS; Wayne, OH; 8/114 Pres Jr Cls; Pres Sr Cls; Am Leg Boys St; MMM; VP NHS; Sch Mus; Stu Cncl; Yth Flsp; Pres Drama Clb; Sec FFA; Bowling Greeen St U; Fine Arts.

DAVID, MARK; Columbia City Joint HS; Columbia City, IN; Boy Scts; FCA; Yth Flsp; 4-H; Spn Clb; Ftbl; Swmmng; Wrstlng; Indiana Univ; Business.

DAVID, MICHELLE; Miami Valley School; Centerville, OH; Chrh Wkr; Cmnty Wkr; Lbry Ade; Off Ade; Sch Mus; Sch Pl; Yth Flsp; Rptr Sch Nwsp; Chrldng; Scr Kpr; Univ; Psych.

DAVID, RODGERS; Knox Sr HS; Knox, IN; 28/158 Letter Bsktbl; Letter Ftbl; Coll; Bus.

DAVID, SHARON; Petoskey HS; Boyne Falls, MI; Girl Scts; Hon Rl; Hosp Ade; Red Cr Ade; Yth Flsp; 4-H; FFA; FHA; FNA; Pep Clb; Grand Rapids Of Bible & Music.

DAVIDGE, KATHLEEN; Lee M Thurston HS; S Redford Twp, MI; 442/484 Band; Girl Scts; Jr NHS; Lbry Ade; NHS; Sct Actv; Yth Flsp; Madonna Coll; Nursing.

DAVIDO, SCOTT; Valley Forge HS; Parma, OH; 3/704 Lit Mag; NHS; Lat Clb; Case Western Reserve Univ; Econ.

DAVIDOVIC, MILA; James Ford Rhodes HS; Cleveland, OH; 4/309 Chrh Wkr; Hon Rl; NHS; Sec Stu Cncl; Treas Lat Clb; Cit Awd; Case Western Univ; Pre Med.

DAVIDS, DARRELL; Berkeley Springs HS; Berkeley Spgs, WV; 56/139 Cls Rep Frsh Cls; Cls Rep Sr Cls; Aud/Vis; Band; Boy Scts; Chrs; Hon Rl; Sch Mus; Sct Actv; Hagerstown Jr College; Mech Engr.

DAVIDS, ROBERT M; John Marshall HS; Indpls, IN; 120/600 Off Ade; Stu Cncl; Key Clb; Bsbl; Bsktbl; IM Sprt; Kiwan Awd; College.

DAVIDSON, BARBARA; Old Trail HS; Sagamore Hl, OH; Cls Rep Sr Cls; Chrh Wkr; Girl Scts; Hon Rl; Stu Cncl; Spn Clb; Letter Hockey; Mgrs; Univ.

DAVIDSON, DARRYL; Andrean HS; Gary, IN; Chrh Wkr; Hon Rl; Jr NHS; Sct Actv; Yth Flsp; Lat Clb; Mth Clb; Sci Clb; Spn Clb; Bsktbl; College; Med.

DAVIDSON, HARRYL; Andrean HS; Gary, IN; Chrh Wkr; Cmnty Wkr; Hon Rl; Jr NHS; Sct Actv; Yth Flsp; Lat Clb; Mth Clb; Bsktbl; Trk; College; Pre Med.

DAVIDSON, JACQUELINE; L & M HS; Bloomfield, IN; 8/24 Pres Frsh Cls; VP Soph Cls; Sec Jr Cls; Drl Tm; Hon Rl; Yrbk; Beta Clb; FHA; Pep Clb; GAA; Indiana St Univ.

DAVIDSON, JACQUELINE; Canton South HS; Canton, OH; 1/260 Cls Rep Soph Cls; Band; Hon Rl; NHS; Fr Clb; Mth Clb; Rdo Clb; Sci Clb; Ten; Rotary Awd;.

DAVIDSON, JAMES; Milton HS; Culloden, WV; Cls Rep Soph Cls; Am Leg Boys St; Band; Pres Chrs; Chrh Wkr; Cmnty Wkr; Hon Rl; Off Ade; Sch Mus; Sch Pl; Amer Lgn Bosy St Auditor 78; Mrch Chr Field Marshall 77 79; Amer Lg Boys St Jr Cnslr 79; Marshall Univ; Bus Mgmt.

DAVIDSON, KIM; Cadiz HS; Hopedale, OH; Hosp Ade; FHA; Bsktbl; College; Psych.

DAVIDSON, KIM; Bellevue HS; Bellevue, MI; 9/102 Chrs; Hon Rl; Sec NHS; Off Ade; Sch Mus; Sch Pl; Stu Cncl; Rptr Yrbk; Chrldng; PPFtbl; Kellogg Community Coll; Fire Sci.

DAVIDSON, LORI; Logansport HS; Logansport, IN; 1/349 Val; Am Leg Aux Girls St; Band; Chrs; Natl Forn Lg; Capt Drama Clb; Capt Sci Clb; Trk; DAR Awd; Kiwan Awd; Hanover College; Medical Field.

DAVIDSON, MICHAEL; South Newton Jr Sr HS; Goodland, IN; 28/126 Pres Frsh Cls; Cls Rep Soph Cls; Cl Rep Jr Cls; Quill & Scroll; Sch Pl; Yrbk; Pres Lat Clb; Letter Ftbl; Letter Glf; Letter Wrstlng; Purdue Univ.

DAVIDSON, NANETTE; Guyan Valley HS; Branchland, WV; VP Soph Cls; Band; Hon Rl; Sch Pl; Drama Clb; Letter Trk; Capt Chrldng; Mgrs; 4-H Awd; Marshall Univ; Phys Educ.

DAVIDSON, PEGGIE A; Southeast HS; Ravenna, OH; Chrs; Chrh Wkr; Cmnty Wkr; Girl Scts; Sct Actv; Yth Flsp; 4-H; Pep Clb; Cit Awd; 4-H Awd; Papergirl Of The Month 76; Kent St Univ; RN.

DAVIDSON, PETER S; Greenwood Comm HS; Greenwood, IN; Hon Rl; NHS; Pol Wkr; Bsktbl; Letter Ftbl; Letter Trk; IM Sprt; Letter Mgrs; JETS Awd; AFROTC Schlrshp; Pres Honor Awd; Basketball Statistician Letter; Purdue Univ; Computer Sci.

DAVIDSON, SANDRA; Michigan Lutheran Sem; St Louis, MI; Chrs; Hon Rl; Rptr Yrbk; Pep Clb; PPFtbl;.

DAVIDSON, STEVE; Meadowdale HS; Dayton, OH; 3/230 Cl Rep Jr Cls; Hon Rl; NHS; Capt Wrstlng; Ohio State Univ; Engr.

DAVIDSON, TERRI; Licking Cnty Joint Voc Schl; Granville, OH; 18/186 VP Jr Cls; Pres Sr Cls; Hon Rl; NHS; OEA; Letter Bsktbl; PPFtbl;.

DAVIDSON, TERRY; Lynchburg Clay HS; Hillsboro, OH; Chrh Wkr; Debate Tm; Hon Rl; Sch Pl; Pres 4-H; VP FFA; Bsktbl; 4-H Awd; Bankers Awd Dairy Production Crop Production Schlrhsp Awd In FFA; Intermediate Showmanship At Co Fair; Univ.

DAVIDSON, TIMOTHY; South Charleston HS; Spring Hill, WV; VP Sr Cls; Chrs; Hon Rl; Jr NHS; MMM; NHS; Sch Mus; Stu Cncl; College.

DAVIES, CATHY; Washington HS; Massillon, OH; 72/460 Sec Soph Cls; Sec Jr Cls; Sec Sr Cls; AFS; Chrs; Girl Scts; Hon Rl; NHS; Quill & Scroll; Drama Clb; Runner Up For Miss Massillonian 79; Ca ndidate For Homecoming Queen 79; Miss Congeniality 79; Ohio St Univ; Acctg.

DAVIES, LUCIA; Terre Haute South Vigo HS; Terre Haute, IN; 114/630 Cls Rep Frsh Cls; Chrs; Hon Rl; Mod UN; Sch Mus; Y-Teens; Rptr Sch Nwsp; 4-H; Ind State Univ; Dent Hygiene.

DAVIES, MELANIE; Canfield HS; Canfield, OH; Girl Scts; Hon Rl; Pep Clb; Spn Clb; IM Sprt; Pres Awd; College; Law.

DAVIES, TERESA; North Putnam Jr Sr HS; Bainbridge, IN; 5/103 Band; Hon Rl; Lbry Ade; Natl Forn Lg; NHS; Orch; Sch Mus; Sch Pl; Treas Drama Clb; Lat Clb;.

DAVIRRO, MICHAEL; Madison HS; Madison, OH; Pres Soph Cls; Pres Jr Cls; Chrs; Red Cr Ade; Sch Pl; Key Clb; Univ; Hist.

DAVIS, ADAM B; University Liggett HS; Grosse Pointe, MI; Lit Mag; Sch Mus; Sch Pl; VP Stu Cncl; Ed Sch Nwsp; Sch Nwsp; Letter Ftbl; Natl Merit SF; Univ Of Michigan; Bus Admin.

DAVIS, ALLISON; University HS; Morgantown, WV; 1/166 Hon Rl; Jr NHS; Lbry Ade; NHS; Ger Clb; Bsktbl; Scr Kpr; Attended The World Conference Convention; Publications Board; West Virginia Univ; Chem.

DAVIS, ANGELA; East Tech HS; Cleveland, OH; 57/312 Cls Rep Soph Cls; Cl Rep Jr Cls; Hon Rl; Stu Cncl; Rptr Yrbk; FHA; Spn Clb; Cit Awd; Bowling Green St Univ; Dietitics.

DAVIS, ANGELA; Danville Community HS; Danville, IN; Chrs; Chrh Wkr; FCA; Hon Rl; NHS; Sch Mus; 4-H; Spn Clb; Bus.

DAVIS, ANGELA; Charles E Chadsey HS; Detroit, MI; Chrs; Girl Scts; Hon Rl; JA; Jr NHS; NHS; Stu Cncl; Mth Clb; Pep Clb; JA Awd; Univ Of Detroit; Dental Hygiene.

DAVIS, ANTOINETTE; George Washington HS; East Chicago, IN; 29/250 NHS; Purdue Univ; Music.

DAVIS, APRIL; Washington HS; Washington, IN; 9/216 Band; Hon Rl; Pres JA; Beta Clb; Pres 4-H; Treas Lat Clb; Pom Pon; JA Awd; IU; Science.

DAVIS, BARBARA; Jewett Scio HS; Cadiz, OH; Sec Jr Cls; Band; Chrh Wkr; Girl Scts; Hon Rl; Sch Mus; Sch Pl; Yth Flsp; Rptr Yrbk; 4-H; Grand Lecturer Dist 18 Order Of Rainbow Girls; Bowling Green St Univ; Bio.

DAVIS, BARBARA; Hampshire HS; Augusta, WV; 34/200 AFS; Band; Chrh Wkr; Hon Rl; Off Ade; Stg Crw; Yth Flsp; College; Soc Work.

DAVIS, BELINDA; Rock Hill HS; Ironton, OH; 59/187 Cmp Fr Grls; Girl Scts; Hon Rl; Stu Cncl; Bsktbl; Chrldng; Scr Kpr; Mas Awd; Coll; Airline Hostess.

DAVIS, BETH; Charleston HS; Charleston, WV; 3/270 Sec Sr Cls; Cls Rep Sr Cls; Hon Rl; Jr NHS; Lit Mag; NHS; Stu Cncl; Civ Clb; Lat Clb; Mas Awd; Marshall Univ; Speech Pathology.

DAVIS, BETH; Franklin Hgts HS; Columbus, OH; 11/196 Am Leg Aux Girls St; Hon Rl; NHS; Off Ade; Sch Pl; Drama Clb; OEA; Spn Clb; Capt Gym; Capt Chrldng; Mt Carmel Schl Of Nursing; RN.

DAVIS, BETH; Franklin Hts HS; Columbus, OH; 14/193 Hon Rl; NHS; Off Ade; OEA; Spn Clb; Capt Gym; Capt Chrldng; Capital Univ; Paralegal.

DAVIS, BETH; Martins Ferry HS; Martins Ferry, OH; 55/218 Sec Soph Cls; Sec Jr Cls; Band; Stu Cncl; Y-Teens; Sec Fr Clb; Ohio State; Physicatherapist.

DAVIS, BETSY; Pymatuning Valley HS; Andover, OH; AFS; Band; Chrs; Chrh Wkr; Cmnty Wkr; Girl Scts; Lbry Ade; Sct Actv; Yth Flsp; Drama Clb; Coll; Psych.

DAVIS, BEVERLY C; Williamson HS; Williamson, WV; 14/165 Sec Frsh Cls; Cl Rep Jr Cls; Chrs; Girl Scts; Hon Rl; NHS; Off Ade; Stu Cncl; Yth Flsp; Drama Clb; College; Phys Ed.

DAVIS, BONNY M; Williamstown HS; Williamstown, WV; AFS; Chrs; Chrh Wkr; Cmnty Wkr; Sch Pl; Yth Flsp; Sec Drama Clb; Coach Actv; IM Sprt; Univ; Educ.

DAVIS, BRENDA; River Valley HS; Three Oaks, MI; Cmnty Wkr; Hon Rl; Lbry Ade; Spn Clb; Bsktbl; Scr Kpr; Univ Of Haw; Phys Educ.

DAVIS, BRENDA D; Stivers Patterson Coop HS; Dayton, OH; Cls Rep Frsh Cls; Chrs; Chrh Wkr; Hon Rl; JA; Sch Mus; Stg Crw; Boys Clb Am; VICA; Natl Merit Ltr; Wright St Univ; Nursing.

DAVIS, BRYAN; Madison HS; Madison, OH; 37/310 Boy Scts; Hon Rl; Sct Actv; 4-H; Spn Clb; Ohio St Univ; Vet.

DAVIS, CARLA; Franklin HS; Franklin, OH; Band; Chrh Wkr; Cmnty Wkr; Hon Rl; NHS; Off Ade; Sch Mus; Stg Crw; Yth Flsp; Coll; Univ; Med.

DAVIS, CARLA; Warrensville Heights HS; Warrensville, OH; 3/220 Cls Rep Frsh Cls; Cl Rep Jr Cls; VP Sr Cls; Aud/Vis; Band; Chrs; Girl Scts; Hon Rl; NHS; Off Ade; Florida Inst Of Tech; Enviro Engr.

DAVIS, CAROL; N Central Area HS; Powers, MI; 6/63 Trs Frsh Cls; VP Soph Cls; Sec Jr Cls; Sec Sr Cls; Band; Cmnty Wkr; Hon Rl; Red Cr Ade; Sch Pl; Yrbk; Earle Schlrshp; Basic Equal Opportunity Grant; Lake Superior St Coll; Tech Acctg.

DAVIS, CAROL; Marian HS; South Bend, IN; 16/152 Sec Soph Cls; Hon Rl; NHS; Stu Cncl; Pep Clb; Spn Clb; Trk; Chrldng; IM Sprt; College; Medicine.

DAVIS, CAROLYN; Southeastern HS; Detroit, MI; Hon Rl; Orch; Sch Mus; Sch Pl; Stu Cncl; Drama Clb; Typing Awd 77; Outstndng Contrvtn In Drama Awd 78; Humn Reltns Awd 79; Alabama A & M Univ; Bus Admin.

DAVIS, CAROLYN; Elwood Community HS; Elwood, IN; 47/312 Band; Girl Scts; Jr NHS; VP Spn Clb; Ball State; Educator.

DAVIS, CATHERINE; Guernsey Noble Voc School; Caldwell, OH; Hon Rl; Lat Clb; Bsktbl; Univ; Law.

DAVIS, CATHERINE; Highland Park Comm HS; Highland Park, MI; Hon Rl; NHS; Rptr Yrbk; Rptr Sch Nwsp; OEA; Cit Awd; Univ Of Mich; Business.

DAVIS, CHALRES; Whitehall Yearling HS; Whitehall, OH; Band; Chrh Wkr; Sch Pl; Drama Clb; Crs Cntry; Socr; Swmmng; Johnson Bible Coll.

DAVIS, CHARLES; Morgantown HS; Morgantown, WV; Cls Rep Soph Cls; Pres Jr Cls; Cl Rep Jr Cls; Am Leg Boys St; Band; Boy Scts; Chrh Wkr; College; Law.

DAVIS, CHARLES M; Morgantown HS; Morgantown, WV; 2/474 Cls Rep Soph Cls; Pres Jr Cls; Sec Jr Cls; Am Leg Boys St; Band; Hon Rl; NHS; Bsktbl; Letter Ten; DAR Awd; College; Poli Sci.

DAVIS, CHERYL; St Clair HS; St Clair, MI; 17/220 Pres Jr Cls; Cl Rep Jr Cls; Pres Sr Cls; Cls Rep Sr Cls; Chrs; Chrh Wkr; Cmnty Wkr; Girl Scts; Hon Rl; NHS; MI All State Honors Choir 1975; Yth For Understanding Exchange St To Japan 1978; Schlr Ath Awd 1977; St Clair Cmnty Coll; Nursing.

DAVIS, CHRISTINE; Warren Western Reserve HS; Warren, OH; 22/465 Band; Hosp Ade; Lbry Ade; Lit Mag; NHS; Off Ade; Y-Teens; Univ Of Akron; R N.

DAVIS, CHRISTOPHER; Shaw HS; Cleveland, OH; Band; Chrs; Chrh Wkr; Cmnty Wkr; Off Ade; Pol Wkr; Red Cr Ade; Y-Teens; Ftbl; Trk; N E YMCA Youth Of The Yr 79; Senator Rep City Of Cleveland Oh Youth & Govt Prog 79; Univ; Poli Sci.

DAVIS, CHRISTOPHER; St Francis De Sales HS; Toledo, OH; 18/203 Pres Frsh Cls; Pres Soph Cls; Chrh Wkr; Hon Rl; NHS; Sct Actv; Stu Cncl; Rptr Sch Nwsp; Ftbl; Trk; Wrstlng; Notre Dame Univ; Med.

DAVIS, CINDY; Jackson HS; Jackson, OH; Am Leg Aux Girls St; Band; Girl Scts; Yth Flsp; Rptr Yrbk;

4-H; Lat Clb; Pep Clb; Sci Clb; PPFtbl; Ohio St Univ; Elem Educ Tchr.

DAVIS, CLARENCE; Clear Fork HS; Artie, WV; Cls Rep Soph Cls; Cl Rep Jr Cls; Band; Hon Rl; JA; Mth Clb; Letter Bsktbl; Letter Glf; Letter Trk; Earth Science Award; Beckley Voc School.

DAVIS, CONNIE; Lenore HS; Naugatuck, WV; 7/70 Chrs; Hon Rl; Quill & Scroll; Yrbk; Rptr Sch Nwsp;.

DAVIS, CYNTHIA; Anderson HS; Cincinnati, OH; 35/355 Cls Rep Frsh Cls; Am Leg Aux Girls St; VP Chrs; Hon Rl; NHS; Sec Stu Cncl; Letter Gym; Miami Unif; Systems Analysis.

DAVIS, DANA; Concordia Lutheran HS; Ft Wayne, IN; Chrs; Sch Mus; FBLA; GAA; Mgrs; PPFtbl; Ball St Univ; Criminal Justice.

DAVIS, DANIEL A; Mitchell HS; Mitchell, IN; Voc Schl; Elec.

DAVIS, DANNA; Oak Hill HS; Oak Hill, WV; 26/194 VP Sr Cls; Am Leg Aux Girls St; Chrs; Chrh Wkr; Cmnty Wkr; Hon Rl; Stu Cncl; Yth Flsp; Pep Clb; Concord Coll Undergrad Schlrshp 79; Pres Oak Hill Jrs 79; Treas Tri Hi Y 79; Spec Music Awd 79; Concord Coll; Poli Sci.

DAVIS, DAVID; Princeton Community HS; Princeton, IN; Boy Scts; Chrh Wkr; Yrbk; Boys Clb Am; 4-H; Ftbl; 4-H Awd; Natl Merit Ltr; Wabash Valley Coll; Radio Brdcstng.

DAVIS, DE ANN; Liberty HS; Salem, WV; 14/228 Chrh Wkr; Jr NHS; NHS; Stu Cncl; Mth Clb; Pep Clb; Chrldng; IM Sprt; Scr Kpr; Tmr; Partcpt Math Day; Homecoming Princess; E Tennessee St Univ.

DAVIS, DEBORA; North Ctrl HS; Hymera, IN; Band; Chrh Wkr; Hosp Ade; Lbry Ade; Yth Flsp; Drama Clb; FBLA; FSA; Pep Clb; Sci Clb; Vincennes Univ; Nursing.

DAVIS, DEBORAH; Dayton Christian HS; Dayton, OH; 10/96 Chrh Wkr; Hon Rl; Cit Awd; Liberty Baptist Coll; Acctg.

DAVIS, DEBRA J; Shenandoah HS; Fargo, ND; 7/102 Cls Rep Soph Cls; Pres Jr Cls; Chrs; Hon Rl; Lbry Ade; Stu Cncl; Sch Nwsp; 4-H; Mth Clb; Pep Clb; Univ.

DAVIS, DIANA; Brandywine HS; Niles, MI; Hon Rl; Sch Mus; Sch Pl; Drama Clb; PPFtbl; Mich State; Drama.

DAVIS, DONNA; Hopewell Loudon HS; Fostoria, OH; 12/90 Hon Rl; Letter Trk; Clemson Univ; Sociology.

DAVIS, DORIAN; South HS; Cleveland, OH; 167/410 Aud/Vis; Band; Boy Scts; Chrs; Chrh Wkr; Cmnty Wkr; Lbry Ade; Orch; Pol Wkr; Sch Pl; Ohio St Univ; Law.

DAVIS, DOUGLAS; Ironton HS; Ironton, OH; 46/184 Chrh Wkr; Hon Rl; Spn Clb; Letter Bsbl; Ohio U Frex Achvmnt Schlrshp 79; Ohio Univ.

DAVIS, DREMA; Webster County HS; Webster Spgs, WV; 17/127 Band; Chrh Wkr; Hon Rl; NHS; 4-H; Sci Clb; Bsktbl; 4-H Awd; J Philips Sousa Band Awd 79; Sci Fair Awd 78; Island Creek Band Camp Awd 78; West Virginia Univ; Nursing.

DAVIS, ELIZABETH; Mineral Ridge HS; Mineral Ridge, OH; Sec Jr Cls; Chrs; Hon Rl; 4-H; PPFtbl; Youngstown St Univ; Nursing.

DAVIS, ERNEST; Columbus North HS; Columbus, OH; 40/325 Band; Chrs; FCA; Hon Rl; NHS; Ger Clb; OEA; Ftbl; Trk; Letter Wrstlng; Franklin Univ; CPA.

DAVIS, GABRIELLE; Rossford HS; Rossford, OH; VP Soph Cls; Pres Jr Cls; Pres Sr Cls; Stu Cncl; Yrbk; Letter Bsktbl; Coach Actv; Univ.

DAVIS, GAIL; Maplewood Area Joint Voc Sch; Kent, OH; Band; Hon Rl; 4-H; OEA; Cit Awd; 4-H Awd; Outstndng Stdnt Awd 1978; Receptionst Contst 2nd Pl OOEA Regn 9 1978; Cierfct Of Hon & 2nd Yr Hon Pin 1977; Univ; CPA.

DAVIS, GAIL; Tuslaw HS; Massillon, OH; 7/178 VP Frsh Cls; Cls Rep Soph Cls; Chrs; Girl Scts; Hon Rl; Jr NHS; Sch Mus; Stu Cncl; Y-Teens; 4-H; Akron Univ; Exec Sec.

DAVIS, GEOFFREY; Mt Healthy HS; Cincinnati, OH; 53/575 Hon Rl; Stu Cncl; Civ Clb; Letter Ftbl; Letter Trk; Univ; Personnel Admin.

DAVIS, GEORGE; Beechcroft HS; Columbus, OH; 24/213 Hon Rl; Treas NHS; VP OEA; Letter Bsktbl; Trk; Coach Actv; IM Sprt; Natl Merit Ltr; Natl Achvmnt 1977; Class Speaker 1979; OEA Amb 1978; 1st Pl St Data Proc 1979; Cornell Univ.

DAVIS, GEORGE; Beechcroft HS; Columbuus, OH; 29/196 Hon Rl; Treas NHS; OEA; Letter Bsktbl; Trk; Natl Merit Ltr; Cornell Univ; Engr.

DAVIS, GERRY; Goshen HS; Goshen, IN; 1/280 Chrs; Hon Rl; Mdrgl; NHS; Letter Ftbl; Letter Trk; Depauw Univ; Pre Law.

DAVIS, HARVEY; Pontiac Central HS; Pontiac, MI; Cls Rep Sr Cls; Boy Scts; Chrh Wkr; Debate Tm; FCA; Hon Rl; JA; Natl Forn Lg; Yth Flsp; Boys Clb Am; Pres Chrch Yth Usher Brd; VP Crystal Lk Yth Dept; Chem Asst; Saginaw Vly St Univ; Elec Engr.

DAVIS, J; Lorain Catholic HS; Lorain, OH; Chrh Wkr; Hon Rl; Lorain County Comm College; Math.

DAVIS, JAMES; Gibsonburg HS; Gibsonburg, OH; 12/104 Hst Sr Cls; Chrh Wkr; Hon Rl; Fr Clb; Sec FFA; Sci Clb; Ftbl; Tmr; FFA Awds Star Granhand Pub Spkng & Attndnc 77; FFA Awds Pub Spkng Palmntry Prod Attnndnc 78; Ohio St Univ; Agri Bus.

DAVIS, JAMES B; Buffalo HS; Huntington, WV; Band; Hon Rl; 4-H; Wrstlng; 4-H Awd; Marshall Univ.

DAVIS, JAMES E; Garfield Sr HS; Hamilton, OH; Hon Rl; Jr NHS; NHS; Spn Clb; College; Math.

DAVIS, JAMES W; Athens HS; Princeton, WV; Hon Rl; Trk; Concord College; Engr.

DAVIS, JEANNE; Lorain Catholic HS; Lorain, OH; Chrh Wkr; Cmnty Wkr; Hon Rl; Loran Comm College; Math.

DAVIS, JEANNETTE S; Clay City HS; Center Point, IN; 1/59 Val; Hon Rl; NHS; Off Ade; Yrbk; 4-H; Pres OEA; Pep Clb; Letter Trk; GAA; Indiana St Univ; Elem Educ.

DAVIS, JEFFREY; Elyria Catholic HS; Elyria, OH; Band; Chrs; Chrh Wkr; Cmnty Wkr; Hon Rl; Sch Mus; Sch Pl; Univ Of Ohi; Zoology.

DAVIS, JENNIE; Pittsford HS; Osseo, MI; Band; Girl Scts; Lbry Ade; FHA; Trk; Siena Height Col; Sec.

DAVIS, JENNIE M; Jane Addams HS; Cleveland, OH; Off Ade; Stu Cncl; Rptr Yrbk; Rptr Sch Nwsp; Swmmng; Trk; Chrldng; IM Sprt; Cit Awd; JA Awd; Univ; Child Psych.

DAVIS, JENNIFER; Groveport Madison HS; Groveport, OH; Am Leg Aux Girls St; Chrs; Chrh Wkr; CAP; Girl Scts; NHS; Drama Clb; Spn Clb; Mat Maids; Univ Of S Ala; Bus.

DAVIS, JENNIFER; Penn HS; Mishawaka, IN; 90/454 Band; Boy Scts; Hon Rl; Sch Pl; Sct Actv; Fr Clb; Ball State Univ; Soc Work.

DAVIS, JESSICA; Morgantown HS; Morgantwn, WV; Band; Chrs; Hon Rl; Sch Mus; Sch Pl; Stg Crw; Drama Clb; 4-H; Keyettes; Pep Clb; Coll; Nursing.

DAVIS, JILL; Harbor HS; Ashtabula, OH; AFS; Band; Chrs; Chrh Wkr; Yth Flsp; Rptr Yrbk; Rptr Sch Nwsp; Spn Clb; College; Jounalism.

DAVIS, JILL S; Western Reserve Acad; Hudson, OH; 6/89 Cls Rep Frsh Cls; Band; Chrs; Chrh Wkr; Hon Rl; Sch Mus; Stg Crw; Stu Cncl; Yth Flsp; Ten; Coll; Music.

DAVIS, JOANN; Buckeye South HS; Tiltonsville, OH; 3/120 Girl Scts; Jr NHS; NHS; Spn Clb; Belmont Joint Voc Schl; Nursing.

DAVIS, JOHN; Hubbard HS; Hubbard, OH; Pres Sr Cls; Hon Rl; Stu Cncl; Letter Glf; Letter Wrstlng; Univ.

DAVIS, JOHN R; Newton Falls HS; Newton Falls, OH; Am Leg Boys St; Band; Chrh Wkr; Hon Rl; NHS; Pol Wkr; Sch Pl; Stg Crw; Yth Flsp; Rptr Sch Nwsp; Arthur J Prescott Schlrshp 79; 1st Plc Tm Winner Oh Tests Of Schlstc Achvmnt 79; Miami Univ; Soc Studies.

DAVIS, JONI; Girard HS; Girard, OH; 3/224 Cls Rep Sr Cls; AFS; Am Leg Aux Girls St; Chrs; Debate Tm; Capt Drl Tm; Girl Scts; Mdrgl; Pres NHS; Sch Mus; Ohio State Univ; Journalism.

DAVIS, JUDY ANNE; Evergreen HS; Swanton, OH; Band; Chrh Wkr; Cmnty Wkr; Drl Tm; Girl Scts; Hon Rl; Lit Mag; FTA; Spn Clb; Mgrs; Band Librarian 78 80; All Cnty Band Fulton Cnty 1st Chair 79; Partcptd In 2 Hist Day Contsts 78 & 79; Univ; Med.

DAVIS, JULIA L; Wayland Union HS; Shelbyville, MI; Cls Rep Frsh Cls; Cls Rep Soph Cls; Band; Girl Scts; Hon Rl; NHS; Sch Mus; Sch Pl; Treas Stu Cncl; Rptr Sch Nwsp; Michigan St Univ; Acctg.

DAVIS, KANARDO; Jesup W Scott HS; Toledo, OH; Hon Rl; Rptr Yrbk; Boys Clb Am; Ftbl; Cit Awd; Ohio St Univ; Archt.

DAVIS, KAREN; Ripley HS; Kentuck, WV; Band; Chrs; Cmnty Wkr; Girl Scts; Hon Rl; Hosp Ade; Jr NHS; Lbry Ade; Off Ade; Drama Clb; Schlrshp From Med Careers Club At Schl 79; St Finalist In Miss Teen USA Pageant 79; George Mason Univ; Music Ed.

DAVIS, KAREN; Ashtabula HS; Ashtabula, OH; 16/208 Chrs; Chrh Wkr; Hon Rl; Jr NHS; Lit Mag; Off Ade; Sch Mus; Yth Flsp; Rptr Yrbk; Natl Merit Schl; Anderson Coll; Music.

DAVIS, KAREN; Turpin HS; Cincinnati, OH; 8/342 Chrh Wkr; Girl Scts; Hon Rl; Sct Actv; FHA; Ger Clb; Swmmng; College; Math.

DAVIS, KAREN; Ashtabula Cnty Joint Voc HS; Jefferson, OH; 7/200 Chrs; Treas JA; Pres NHS; Sch Pl; OEA; Pep Clb; Spn Clb; 1st Pl Reg II OEOA Speech 1978; Honor Mentn Ohio Tests Schol Achiev; Kent St Dist Spanish I & II 1976; Univ; Bus Admin.

DAVIS, KAREN; Greenville HS; Greenville, MI; Chrh Wkr; Hon Rl; Hosp Ade; Yth Flsp; Rptr Yrbk; Sec Pep Clb; ACT Finlst 79; Grand Rapids Schl For Nusing; RN.

DAVIS, KAREN; Walnut Ridge HS; Columbus, OH; Rptr Yrbk; Sch Nwsp; Pep Clb; Spn Clb; College; Advertising.

DAVIS, KATHERINE D; Reitz Memorial HS; Evansville, IN; Chrs; Girl Scts; Hon Rl; Hosp Ade; Sch Mus; Sch Pl; Fr Clb; Pom Pon; Tigerette Dance Group Monogram 78; Western Kentucky Univ; Interior Dsgn.

DAVIS, KATRINA; Medora HS; Medora, IN; 5/21 Sec Frsh Cls; Trs Soph Cls; Band; Hon Rl; Sch Pl; Yth Flsp; Yrbk; Beta Clb; Sci Clb; Spn Clb; Sullivan Business Schl; Accounting.

DAVIS, KATY; Mother Of Mercy HS; Cincinnati, OH; Cmp Fr Grls; Hon Rl; Hosp Ade; NHS; Fr Clb; Good Samaritan Schl; Nursing.

DAVIS, KEITH; Hamilton Southeastern HS; Noblesville, IN; 8/136 Trs Jr Cls; Am Leg Boys St; Band; Boy Scts; Drm Mjrt; Hon Rl; VP MMM; NHS; Sch Mus; Treas Stu Cncl; Univ.

DAVIS, KEVIN; Woodsfield HS; Woodsfield, OH; 18/71 VP Frsh Cls; Cls Rep Soph Cls; Cl Rep Jr Cls; Cls Rep Sr Cls; Hon Rl; Bsbl; Capt Bsktbl; Capt Ftbl; Waynesburg Coll; Bus.

DAVIS, KEVIN; Madison Comprehensive HS; Mansfield, OH; 13/370 Aud/Vis; NHS; Ger Clb; Letter Glf; Ohio Northern Univ; Elec Engr.

DAVIS, KEVIN; Lima Sr HS; Lima, OH; 146/536 Cls Rep Frsh Cls; Cls Rep Soph Cls; Cl Rep Jr Cls; Cls Rep Sr Cls; Band; PAVAS; Sch Pl; Stg Crw; Stu Cncl; Drama Clb; Ohio St Univ; Actor.

DAVIS, KEVIN; Madison Comprehensive HS; Mansfield, OH; 15/464 Aud/Vis; NHS; Ger Clb; Letter Glf; Mgrs; Univ.

DAVIS, KIM; Spanishburg HS; Kegley, WV; Trs Frsh Cls; Band; Chrs; Cmnty Wkr; Hon Rl; Stu Cncl; Rptr Yrbk; FHA; Sci Clb; Bsbl; Concord Coll; Elem Ed.

DAVIS, KIMBERLY; Laingsburg HS; Laingsburg, MI; Pres Frsh Cls; Cmnty Wkr; Hon Rl; Off Ade; Lansing Comm Coll; Industrial Mgmt.

DAVIS, KIMBERLY; Clinton Central Jr Sr JS; Forest, IN; 13/124 Band; Capt Chrs; Pres FCA; Sch Mus; Sec 4-H; Sec OEA; Pep Clb; Bsbl; Pom Pon; Office Work.

DAVIS, KYLE S; Center Grove HS; Greenwood, IN; Chrs; Hon Rl; NHS; Sch Nwsp; Ger Clb; Bsktbl; Capt Ftbl; Trk; Wrstlng; Indiana Univ; Busns Admin.

DAVIS, LAMONT; Southeastern HS; Detroit, MI; 12/265 Band; Chrs; Chrh Wkr; Hon Rl; Orch; PAVAS; Sch Mus; Sch Pl; Stg Crw; Rptr Yrbk; Western Michigan Univ; Bio Med.

DAVIS, LARRY; Eau Claire HS; Riverside, MI; Boy Scts; Hon Rl; Ftbl; Letter Wrstlng; Denver Automotive; Auto Body.

DAVIS, LAURA; North Judson San Pierre HS; North Judson, IN; 18/126 Cls Rep Frsh Cls; Cls Rep Soph Cls; Cl Rep Jr Cls; Pres Sr Cls; Band; Hon Rl; Stu Cncl; Bsktbl; Trk; Mgrs; Ind State Univ; Phys Educ.

DAVIS, LAURIE A; Benjamin Logan HS; Bellefontaine, OH; Band; Chrh Wkr; NHS; 4-H; Fr Clb; FTA; Letter Gym; Chrldng; Mgrs; Pres Awd; Schlrshp Tm For French 2 78; Schlrshp Tm For Chem 1 79; Ohio St Univ; Nursing.

DAVIS, LAWRENCE C; Bellbrook Sr HS; Bellbrook, OH; 24/160 Cls Rep Frsh Cls; Cls Rep Soph Cls; Cl Rep Jr Cls; Sct Actv; Stu Cncl; Crs Cntry; Trk; Univ Of New Mexico; Architecture.

DAVIS, LEE; Lincoln HS; Shinnston, WV; 11/152 Cls Rep Frsh Cls; Cls Rep Soph Cls; Band; Chrh Wkr; Hon Rl; Jr NHS; NHS; Orch; Stu Cncl; Y-Teens; West Virginia Univ; Econ.

DAVIS, LEESA; River Vly HS; Waldo, OH; 10/203 Band; NHS; Orch; Pres 4-H; Capt PPFtbl; 4-H Awd; Univ.

DAVIS, LEESA; River Valley HS; Waldo, OH; 10/193 Band; NHS; Orch; VP 4-H; PPFtbl; 4-H Awd; College.

DAVIS, LILI; Winamac Cmnty HS; Winamac, IN; Chrh Wkr; Off Ade; Univ.

DAVIS, LINDA; East HS; Akron, OH; Hon Rl; JA; Pep Clb; College; Acctg.

DAVIS, LINDA K; Indian Valley North HS; New Philadelphi, OH; Sec Jr Cls; Pres Sr Cls; Sal; Chrs; Hon Rl; NHS; Sch Pl; Muskingum College; Journalism.

DAVIS, LINDA K; Indian Valley North HS; New Phila, OH; 1/74 Cls Rep Soph Cls; Sec Jr Cls; Pres Sr Cls; Chrs; Hon Rl; NHS; Stu Cncl; Yrbk; Sch Nwsp; Pres FTA; College; Journalism.

DAVIS, LISA; Philo HS; Chandlersville, OH; 20/208 Band; Chrs; Chrh Wkr; Hon Rl; Jr NHS; Lit Mag; NHS; Off Ade; Sch Nwsp; 4-H;.

DAVIS, LISA; Kenston HS; Chagrin Fls, OH; Chrh Wkr; Drm Mjrt; Girl Scts; Hon Rl; Sct Actv; Yth Flsp; Twrlr; College; Acctg.

DAVIS, LORELEA; Grosse Pointe South HS; Grosse Pte Pk, MI; Hon Rl; Hosp Ade; JA; JA Awd; Natl Merit Schl; Michigan St Univ; Pre Med.

DAVIS, M; Grand Ledge HS; Grand Ledge, MI; 1/500 Cls Rep Soph Cls; Band; NHS; Michigan St Univ; Elec Engr.

DAVIS, MARK; Liberty HS; Wilsonburg, WV; 40/270 Band; Hon Rl; Mth Clb; Trk; Farimont State Univ; Elec.

DAVIS, MARTHA; South Christian HS; Caledonia, MI; Cls Rep Soph Cls; Chrs; Chrh Wkr; FCA; Lbry Ade; Off Ade; Stg Crw; Yth Flsp; 4-H; Ger Clb; Univ; Banking.

DAVIS, MARTHA; Arthur Hill HS; Saginaw, MI; Off Ade; Ed Yrbk; Rptr Sch Nwsp; Saginaw Vly Univ; Agri.

DAVIS, MARY; Bishop Watterson HS; Worthington, OH; 56/260 Chrh Wkr; Girl Scts; Hon Rl; Hosp Ade; Sch Mus; Sch Pl; Stg Crw; Rptr Sch Nwsp; 4-H; Lat Clb; Kent St Distinguished Schlr Nominee 79; Univ; Spec Educ.

DAVIS, MARY A; St Agatha HS; Redford, MI; 6/98 Sec Jr Cls; Hon Rl; Lbry Ade; NHS; Stu Cncl; Bsbl; Bsktbl; PPFtbl; Scr Kpr; College; Accounting.

DAVIS, MICHAEL; Eastbrook HS; Marion, IN; Band; Hon Rl; Orch; Fr Clb; Letter Ftbl; Letter Trk; Letter Wrstlng; Coach Actv; Ball St Univ; Phys Ther.

DAVIS, MICHELE; John Adams HS; Cleveland, OH; Cls Rep Frsh Cls; Hon Rl; Jr NHS; NHS; Off Ade; Stu Cncl; Ten; Ohio State Univ; Psych.

DAVIS, MICHELLE; Greenfield Central HS; Pendleton, IN; Band; Girl Scts; Y-Teens; Sec 4-H; Spn Clb; Pom Pon; PPFtbl; 4-H Awd; Superior Ratng In In Schl Music Assoc Contst Fest 78 & 79; Cherry Blossm Fest In Wash Dc 79; Ball St Univ; Zoology.

DAVIS, MIKE; Greenhills HS; Cincinnati, OH; 6/254 Trs Jr Cls; Pres Sr Cls; Chrs; FCA; Hon Rl; Lbry Ade; Mod UN; NHS; Off Ade; Quill & Scroll; Miami Univ; Bus Admin.

DAVIS, MITCHELL; Merrillville HS; Merrillville, IN; 85/604 Chrs; Hon Rl; Yrbk; Letter Ftbl; UCLA; Law.

DAVIS, NANCY; Piqua Central HS; Piqua, OH; 21/350 Band; Chrs; Girl Scts; Hon Rl; Jr NHS; Lbry Ade; NHS; Orch; Sch Mus; Sch Pl; Univ; Hotel Mgmt.

DAVIS, NEIL; Northwestern HS; West Salem, OH; Hon Rl; Glf; IM Sprt; Ohio St Univ; Civil Engr.

DAVIS, NICOLE; Walnut Hills HS; Cincinnati, OH; 1/450 Cmnty Wkr; Hon Rl; Lit Mag; NHS; Fr Clb; College; Pre Med.

DAVIS, PAMELA; Brookside HS; Sheffield Lake, OH; Band; Chrh Wkr; Girl Scts; JA; NHS; Sch Mus; Sch Pl; Drama Clb; Fr Clb; FTA; Olivet Nazarene College; Nursig.

DAVIS, PAMELA; Moorefield HS; Moorefield, WV; 22/96 Cls Rep Sr Cls; Hon Rl; NHS; Stu Cncl; FFA; FHA; Pep Clb; Trk; Chrldng; Outstanding Sr Track 78; Project Idea 78; Shepherd Coll; Cmmrcl Art.

DAVIS, PAMELA; Bloomington HS North; Bloomington, IN; 10/484 Lbry Ade; Fr Clb; Pres OEA; Indiana Univ; Bus Admin.

DAVIS, PAULA; Fremont Ross HS; Fremont, OH; Girl Scts; Hon Rl; Off Ade; Yrbk; Sch Nwsp; OEA; Trk; Terra Tech Bus Schl; Mdse.

DAVIS, PEGGY; Central HS; Bay City, MI; Band; Sch Mus; Stu Cncl; Rptr Sch Nwsp; Sch Nwsp; Bsktbl; PPFtbl; Western Michigan Univ.

DAVIS, PENNY; Newcomerstown HS; Guernsey, OH; Band; Chrh Wkr; Hon Rl; NHS; 4-H; FTA; Capt Bsktbl; Trk; PPFtbl; 4-H Awd; All Amer Hall Of Fame Band Hon 78; Quernsey Co Jr Fair Bd 77 78 & 79; Hon Mention Bsktbl 78; Larson Schl; Radiology Tech.

DAVIS, PRISCILLA; Onekama HS; Onekama, MI; Cl Rep Jr Cls; Hon Rl; NHS; Yth Flsp; Yrbk; Drama Clb; FHA; Typing Awd 76; Math Awd 76 79; Acctg Awd 78; Univ; Acctg.

DAVIS, RAE JEAN; Fredericktown HS; Fredericktown, OH; 10/125 Cls Rep Frsh Cls; Am Leg Aux Girls St; Band; Treas Chrs; Girl Scts; Hon Rl; VP NHS; Sch Mus; Stu Cncl; Yrbk; Busns Schl; Sec.

DAVIS, RAYMOND P; Northwestern HS; Detroit, MI; Boy Scts; Cmnty Wkr; Drl Tm; Hon Rl; Lbry Ade; NHS; Off Ade; FBLA; FTA; Mth Clb; Univ Of Detroit; Acctg.

DAVIS, REBECCA; Hinton HS; Hinton, WV; Chrh Wkr; Girl Scts; Hon Rl; Jr NHS; NHS; Stu Cncl; Rptr Yrbk; Rptr Sch Nwsp; Fr Clb; FHA; Univ; Commrcl Artist.

DAVIS, RENEE; Brookhaven HS; Columbus, OH; 32 Sec Sr Cls; Hon Rl; Jr NHS; NHS; Stu Cncl; Rptr Yrbk; Ed Sch Nwsp; Ohi College; Foreign Language.

DAVIS, RHONDA; Sidney HS; Sidney, OH; Chrh Wkr; Debate Tm; Girl Scts; Hon Rl; NHS; Off Ade; Sct Actv; Stg Crw; Yth Flsp; FHA; Univ; Bio.

DAVIS, ROBERT; Mineral Ridge HS; Mineral Ridge, OH; 18/80 VP Frsh Cls; Lbry Ade; Stg Crw; Bsbl; Bsktbl; Ftbl; Gym; Ohio St Univ; Pharm.

DAVIS, RODGER; Pontiac Central HS; Pontiac, MI; 124/477 Chrh Wkr; Hon Rl; Sch Pl; Sci Clb; Letter Ftbl; Letter Trk; Letter Coach Actv; Mgrs; PPFtbl; Cit Awd; Dallas Inst Of Mortuary; Mortician.

DAVIS, ROGENA; Glen Este HS; Cincinnati, OH; 30/250 Chrh Wkr; Hon Rl; NHS; Off Ade; Yrbk; Honor Awds; Staff Achvmnt Awd Yrbk Journalism; Achvmnt Awd In Busns; Univ Of Cincinnati; Retail Mgmt.

DAVIS, RONDA; Warren Local HS; Belpre, OH; Ch rs; Chrh Wkr; Off Ade; Pres Yth Flsp; Sec FHA; Ohio Univ; Comp Sci.

DAVIS, RUBY; Buena Vista HS; Saginaw, MI; 35/157 Chrs; Chrh Wkr; Hon Rl; Bsktbl; Trk; Coach Actv; GAA; IM Sprt; Pom Pon; PPFtbl; White Pine Conf Track Team Honors; All Conf & Hon Mention Bsktbl; Jessie Johnson Mem Schlrshp Fund; Tennessee St Univ; Busns.

DAVIS, RUTH; Clermont Northeastern HS; Batavia, OH; 10/200 Band; FCA; Hon Rl; NHS; Spn Clb; Scr Kpr; Eastern Ky Univ; Occupational Ther.

DAVIS, SANDRA; West Sr HS; Garden City, MI; 5/415 Sec Soph Cls; Pres Jr Cls; Cls Rep Sr Cls; Chrh Wkr; Hon Rl; NHS; Off Ade; Stu Cncl; Bsbl; Letter Bsktbl; Phi Beta Capa Awd 79; Homecoming Ct 79; Mi St Awd Of Acad Excllnc 79; Acad Athlete 79; Bus Awd 79; Michigan St Univ; Comp Sci.

DAVIS, SANDRA; Shaw HS; Cleveland Hts, OH; Pres Frsh Cls; Hon Rl; Jr NHS; Red Cr Ade; Sprt Ed Sch Nwsp; OEA; Gym; Trk; Chrldng; Cit Awd; Tennessee St Univ.

DAVIS, SHAWN; Brown Cnty HS; Nashville, IN; 7/205 Chrh Wkr; Hon Rl; NHS; Sch Mus; Sch Pl; Stg Crw; Drama Clb; Sci Clb; Letter Ten; Univ; Ministry.

DAVIS, SHELLEY; Williamston HS; Williamston, MI; Hosp Ade; Jr NHS; Lansing Cmnty Coll; RN.

DAVIS, SHELLEY; Franklin Heights HS; Columbus, OH; 10/300 VP Jr Cls; VP Sr Cls; Girl Scts; Hon Rl; Lbry Ade; NHS; Sch Pl; Stg Crw; Stu Cncl; Drama Clb; Univ; Public Rel.

DAVIS, STACIE; Park Hills HS; Fairborn, OH; 17/334 Chrs; Chrh Wkr; Hon Rl; Stu Cncl; Waitress Of Month For May From Employer; Sinclair Cmnty Coll; RN.

DAVIS, STEPHAN C; Liberty HS; Clarksburg, WV; 48/228 Pres Soph Cls; Cmnty Wkr; Jr NHS; Stu Cncl; DECA; Mth Clb; Bsktbl; Capt Crs Cntry; Trk; Lion Awd; Clemson Univ; Bus Mgmt.

DAVIS, STEPHANIE; Warsaw Community HS; Leesburg, IN; 84/405 Trs Jr Cls; Cmnty Wkr; Hon Rl; Stu Cncl; Mat Maids; College; Law.

DAVIS, STEPHANIE J; University HS; Morgantown, WV; 9/146 Pres Frsh Cls; Pres Soph Cls; VP Sr Cls; Band; Chrh Wkr; Hon Rl; Pres Jr NHS; Pres NHS; Pol Wkr; Sch Mus; West Virginia Univ.

DAVIS, STEVE; Madeira HS; Madeira, OH; 60/175 AFS; Band; Boy Scts; Hon Rl; Stg Crw; Rptr Yrbk;

Rptr Sch Nwsp; Drama Clb; Lat Clb; Univ; Chem Engr.

DAVIS, STEVE; Riverside HS; De Graff, OH; 1/85 Val; Band; Chrh Wkr; Hon Rl; NHS; Yth Flsp; Pres FFA; Bsbl; Bsktbl; Natl Merit Schl; Baptist Bible Coll.

DAVIS, SUE; Notre Dame Academy; Toledo, OH; Cls Rep Soph Cls; Trs Jr Cls; Hon Rl; Treas JA; Stg Crw; Stu Cncl; Spn Clb; GAA; IM Sprt; CYO St Finlst In Bsktbl 7,; Univ; Soc Work.

DAVIS, SUSAN; Colerain HS; Cincinnati, OH; VP Soph Cls; VP Jr Cls; Chrh Wkr; Drl Tm; Hon Rl; NHS; Stu Cncl; College; Math.

DAVIS, SUSAN; Richmond Sr HS; Richmond, IN; Cls Rep Soph Cls; Cl Rep Jr Cls; Band; Chrs; Hon Rl; Hosp Ade; NHS; Orch; Sch Pl; Stu Cncl; Univ; Bus.

DAVIS, SUSAN; Morgan HS; Mc Connelsville, OH; Cls Rep Frsh Cls; Trs Soph Cls; Trs Jr Cls; Cls Rep Sr Cls; Am Leg Aux Girls St; Hon Rl; NHS; Off Ade; Sch Pl; Stu Cncl; Ohio St Univ; Fshn Mdse.

DAVIS, SUSAN; Northwest HS; Mc Dermott, OH; 8/143 VP Soph Cls; Sec Sr Cls; Am Leg Aux Girls St; Girl Scts; Hon Rl; NHS; Sch Pl; Stu Cncl; Sec FTA; Letter Trk; Miami Univ; Acctg.

DAVIS, SUZANNE; East Canton HS; E Canton, OH; VP Frsh Cls; Am Leg Aux Girls St; VP Chrs; Girl Scts; Ed Yrbk; FTA; Sci Clb; Letter Trk; IM Sprt; Univ; Spec Educ.

DAVIS, TAMMY; Poca HS; Poca, WV; 32/125 Chrh Wkr; Cmnty Wkr; Girl Scts; Hon Rl; JA; Yth Flsp; FBLA; Chrldng; Univ; Bus.

DAVIS, TAUNA; Hamlin HS; Hamlin, WV; 12/60 Hst Frsh Cls; Band; Drm Mjrt; Hon Rl; Jr NHS; NHS; Ed Yrbk; Pep Clb; Twrlr; Mas Awd; Marshall Univ; Med Lab Tech.

DAVIS, TERESA; Otsego HS; Otsego, MI; 1/150 Boy Scts; Hon Rl; NHS; Sch Mus; Stg Crw; Cls Rep Frsh Cls; Spn Clb; College; Engr.

DAVIS, TERRI; Cascade HS; Amo, IN; 4/137 Am Leg Aux Girls St; Letter Chrs; FCA; Hon Rl; NHS; Bsktbl; Crs Cntry; Letter Trk; College; Spec Educ.

DAVIS, THOMAS; Lakeview HS; Battle Creek, MI; Boy Scts; FCA; Sct Actv; Lat Clb; Letter Ftbl; IM Sprt; God Cntry Awd; Ferris State College; Optometry.

DAVIS, TIMOTHY; South Haven HS; South Haven, MI; 17/230 Band; FCA; Hon Rl; Pres NHS; Stu Cncl; Letter Swmmng; Hope College; Chem.

DAVIS, TIMOTHY L; Rensselaer Ctrl HS; Rensselaer, IN; 21/154 Band; Hon Rl; Letter Bsktbl; Letter Ftbl; Letter Trk; Dnfth Awd; Univ; Engr.

DAVIS, TROY; Greenville HS; Troy, MI; Cl Rep Jr Cls; Boy Scts; Cmnty Wkr; Hon Rl; Stu Cncl; Rptr Yrbk; Yrbk; Rptr Sch Nwsp; Sch Nwsp; Spn Clb; Greenville Bd Of Educ Schlrshp 79; Michigan St Univ; Pre Law.

DAVIS, VERNIECE; George Washington HS; Indianapolis, IN; Chrh Wkr; Cmnty Wkr; Hon Rl; JA; Off Ade; Red Cr Ade; ROTC; Pep Clb; JA Awd; JETS Awd; 2nd Pl Math Rally Minor Engr Adv Ach Awd Progr IUPUI 78; Outsdng Tailor Stu Hon Awd 79; Most Outgoing Awd; Purdue Univ; Elec Engr.

DAVIS, VICKI; Newcomerstown HS; Newcomerstown, OH; 9/102 Trs Sr Cls; Band; Hon Rl; NHS; Stg Crw; Yth Flsp; PPFtbl; Dollars For Scholars Schlrshp; Aultman Hosp Schl; Radiology.

DAVIS, VON R; Bellefontaine HS; Belle Fontaine, OH; 91/243 Cls Rep Frsh Cls; Cls Rep Soph Cls; Am Leg Boys St; Band; Chrh Wkr; Cmnty Wkr; Debate Tm; Hon Rl; Orch; Pol Wkr; Howard Univ; Law.

DAVIS, WALTER; Central HS; Evansville, IN; 83/528 Cls Rep Frsh Cls; Cls Rep Sr Cls; FCA; Hon Rl; JA; Stu Cncl; Bsktbl; Cit Awd; Murray St Univ; Archt Drawing.

DAVIS, WENDY; Harbor HS; Ashtabula, OH; Chrs; Chrh Wkr; Girl Scts; Lit Mag; Off Ade; Quill & Scroll; Sch Pl; Rptr Yrbk; Spn Clb; Chrldng; General Knowledge Contest Olympics 3rd Plc; APMIA Camp Awd; Rex Coll; Law.

DAVIS, WILLIAM K; Lebanon HS; Lebanon, OH; 13/300 Cls Rep Frsh Cls; Am Leg Boys St; Hon Rl; Lbry Ade; NHS; Stu Cncl; Swmmng; DAR Awd; Rotary Awd; Univ; Law.

DAVIS JR, EUGENE; Columbia HS; Columbia Sta, OH; Stg Crw; Letter Bsbl; Bsktbl; Ftbl; Lorain Cnty Joint Voc Schl.

DAVISON, JANE; Littlefield Public HS; Oden, MI; Cls Rep Frsh Cls; Trs Soph Cls; Trs Jr Cls; Hon Rl; Off Ade; Ed Yrbk; Rptr Sch Nwsp; 4-H; Pep Clb; Bsktbl; Executive Sec.

DAVISON, JILL A; Catholic Central HS; Steubenvll, OH; 6/204 Chrs; Hon Rl; NHS; Drama Clb; Fr Clb; FNA; Pep Clb; IM Sprt; College; Nurse.

DAVISON, JOHN; Lake Catholic HS; Mentor, OH; Boy Scts; Miami Univ; Architecture.

DAVISON, LORI; Indian Hill HS; Cincinnati, OH; 29/270 Chrs; Hon Rl; Mod UN; Sch Mus; Yth Flsp; Ed Sch Nwsp; Sprt Ed Sch Nwsp; Rptr Sch Nwsp; Pres Spn Clb; Letter Swmmng; Univ.

DAVISON, MARK; Clinton Central HS; Frankfort, IN; 16/101 Band; Chrs; Chrh Wkr; Drm Mjrt; FCA; Sch Mus; Stg Crw; Purdue; Engr.

DAVISSON, BARRY; Lincoln HS; Shinnston, WV; Cl Rep Jr Cls; VP Sr Cls; Am Leg Boys St; Hon Rl; Jr NHS; NHS; Stu Cncl; Bsktbl; Letter Ftbl; Letter Trk; Fairmont St Univ; Elect Engr.

DAVISSON, CARMA; Lewis Cnty HS; Weston, WV; Chrs; Chrh Wkr; FCA; Hon Rl; Stu Cncl; Pep Clb; Rdo Clb; Trk; PPFtbl;.

DAVISSON, DAN; Greensburg Comm HS; Greensburg, IN; 71/209 Band; Chrs; Chrh Wkr; Hon Rl; Mdrgl; Yth Flsp; Y-Teens; Sprt Ed Sch Nwsp; Letter Glf; Kiwan Awd; Walter E Lowe Jrnlsm Wrkshp Awd Ball St Univ 1978; Univ Of Evansville; Commnctn.

DAVISSON, MAXIUM; Elmwood HS; Wayne, OH; Chrs; Chrh Wkr; Sch Mus; Sch Pl; Stg Crw; Yth Flsp; Bsbl; IM Sprt; Coll.

DAVISSON, MELISSA; Greensburg Community HS; Greensburg, IN; 16/200 Band; Chrs; Chrh Wkr; Hon Rl; Mdrgl; Sch Mus; Yth Flsp; Y-Teens; Drama Clb; Letter Glf; Ball State Univ; Art Educ.

DAVISSON, TERRENCE M; Elmwood HS; Fostoria, OH; Cls Rep Frsh Cls; Band; Chrs; Chrh Wkr; MMM; Sch Mus; Stu Cncl; Rptr Sch Nwsp; Ftbl; Wrstlng; Univ Of Toledo; Elec Engr.

DAWES, BOB; Bishop Ready HS; Galloway, OH; 30/140 Cls Rep Frsh Cls; Cls Rep Soph Cls; Cl Rep Jr Cls; Pres Sr Cls; Am Leg Boys St; Hon Rl; NHS; Stu Cncl; Letter Bsbl; Bsktbl; Univ; Bus Admin.

DAWES, CHRIS; Bishop Flaget HS; Chillicothe, OH; Band; FCA; Hon Rl; Sch Mus; Stg Crw; Rptr Yrbk; Rptr Sch Nwsp; Bsbl; Bsktbl; Crs Cntry; Univ; Bus.

DAWES, JOHN; Springboro HS; Springboro, OH; Band; Chrh Wkr; Hon Rl; Ftbl; IM Sprt; College; Music.

DAWIDOWICZ, PETER; St Florian HS; Hamtramck, MI; Pres Frsh Cls; Pres Soph Cls; VP Soph Cls; Cl Rep Jr Cls; Pres Sr Cls; Hon Rl; PAVAS; Sch Mus; Stu Cncl; Sprt Ed Sch Nwsp; Eastern Michigan Univ; Dentist.

DAWKINS, GREGORY J; Cass Tech HS; Detroit, MI; Boy Scts; Chrs; Chrh Wkr; FCA; Hon Rl; Yth Flsp; Rptr Sch Nwsp; Univ Of Notre Dame; Theology.

DAWSON, ANGELA; Magnificat HS; Bayvillage, OH; Chrs; Chrh Wkr; Girl Scts; Sch Mus; Sch Pl; Sct Actv; Stg Crw; Rptr Sch Nwsp; Drama Clb; Key Clb; Psych.

DAWSON, CAROL; Dayton Christian HS; Brookville, OH; Cls Rep Sr Cls; Chrs; Hon Rl; Lbry Ade; Stu Cncl; Yth Flsp; Spn Clb; Cit Awd; Coll; Computer Sci.

DAWSON, CASSANDRA; East HS; Cleveland, OH; Cl Rep Jr Cls; Cls Rep Sr Cls; Stu Cncl; Dyke College; Accounting.

DAWSON, CHARLES J; Hampshire HS; Romney, WV; AFS; Band; Hon Rl; Bsktbl; IM Sprt;.

DAWSON, DARLA; Lakeview HS; Cortland, OH; Am Leg Aux Girls St; Off Ade; Stu Cncl; FDA; Ger Clb; Spn Clb; Bsbl; Trk; GAA; College; Med.

DAWSON, DENISE C; Garfield HS; Hamilton, OH; 11/376 Hon Rl; Hosp Ade; Jr NHS; Mod UN; NHS; Ed Yrbk; Spn Clb; Belmont Coll; Busns Admin.

DAWSON, DOUG; Ashtabula County Jt Voc Schl; Dorset, OH; 3/300 Pres Jr Cls; Sec Sr Cls; Hon Rl; NHS; Stu Cncl; Lat Clb; OEA; Awd Of Honor Schlrshp Recog; Lakeland Comm Coll; Data Processing.

DAWSON, GEORGE; Buckhannon Upshur HS; French Creek, WV; 6/290 Pres Soph Cls; VP Jr Cls; Am Leg Boys St; Hon Rl; Pres NHS; Sch Mus; Key Clb; Ftbl; IM Sprt; Fairmont St Coll; Pharm.

DAWSON, JEFFREY; Colonel Crawford HS; Galion, OH; Hon Rl; NHS; Letter Bsbl; Letter Bsktbl; Letter Ftbl; Univ.

DAWSON, JOHN; Charles M Russell HS; Great Falls, MT; 2/581 Sal; Hon Rl; Jr NHS; NHS; Orch; Yth Flsp; Montana State Univ; Mech Engr.

DAWSON, JON; Short Ridge HS; Indianapolis, IN; Band; Chrh Wkr; Voc Schl; Decorating.

DAWSON, LATISHA; Benedictine HS; Detroit, MI; Hon Rl; JA; Sch Pl; Letter Trk; Michigan St Univ; Liberal Arts.

DAWSON, LORA; Buckhannon Upshur HS; Buckhannon, WV; Chrldng; Coll.

DAWSON, PAMELA; Gladstone Area HS; Gladstone, MI; 24/202 VP Soph Cls; VP Jr Cls; VP Sr Cls; Cls Rep Sr Cls; Band; Chrh Wkr; Hon Rl; Hosp Ade; NHS; Western Mic Univ; Occup Ther.

DAWSON, PENNY; Adena Local HS; Washington Ch, OH; 12/80 Trs Jr Cls; Trs Sr Cls; Band; Chrs; Hon Rl; Jr NHS; NHS; Sch Pl; Yth Flsp; Y-Teens; Voc Schl; Vet.

DAWSON, TONI; Cody HS; Detroit, MI; VP Jr Cls; Hon Rl; Off Ade; FNA; Pep Clb; Chrldng; GAA; College; Reg Nurse.

DAY, APRIL; Princeton HS; Princeton, WV; Chrh Wkr; Drl Tm; NHS; Yrbk; Pep Clb; Spn Clb; Bluefield St Coll; Nursing.

DAY, CLARK; West Ottawa HS; Holland, MI; 42/342 Hon Rl; NHS; Sch Mus; Sch Pl; Stg Crw; Yth Flsp; Pres Drama Clb; Spn Clb; Grand Vly St Univ; Criminal Justice.

DAY, DAVID; Marion Harding HS; Marion, OH; 2/450 Band; Chrs; Chrh Wkr; Mdrgl; Orch; Sch Mus; Spn Clb; Capt Swmmng; Univ; Educ.

DAY, DEBBIE; Salem HS; Salem, IN; 12/175 Chrh Wkr; Hon Rl; NHS; Sec 4-H; Lat Clb; Pep Clb; Spn Clb; Letter Crs Cntry; Letter Trk; Chrldng; Abilene Christian Univ; Elem Educ.

DAY, DIANE L; Heath HS; Heath, OH; Sec Frsh Cls; Sec Soph Cls; Sec Jr Cls; Sec Sr Cls; Cls Rep Sr Cls; Hon Rl; Jr NHS; Lbry Ade; NHS; Letter Bsktbl; Univ.

DAY, DIANNE; St Peters HS; Mansfield, OH; Chrh Wkr; Cmnty Wkr; Hon Rl; NHS; Sch Pl; Stg Crw; Rptr Yrbk; Drama Clb; Biology.

DAY, ELIZABETH; Pike HS; Indianapolis, IN; 51/303 Hon Rl; Jr NHS; Y-Teens; Rptr Sch Nwsp; College; Journalism.

DAY, JAMES; Mason HS; Mason, MI; Cl Rep Jr Cls; Band; Boy Scts; Chrh Wkr; Hon Rl; Jr NHS; NHS; Sci Clb; Univ Of Mic; Mech Engr.

DAY, JULIE; Shelby Sr HS; Shelby, OH; Band; Hon Rl; JA; Off Ade; Sch Mus; JA Awd; Tech Schl; Steno.

DAY, MARK S; Park Tudor HS; Indianapolis, IN; Chrs; Hon Rl; Mdrgl; Sch Mus; Sch Pl; Sch Nwsp; Sec Fr Clb; Mgrs; Natl Merit SF; Rose Hulman Inst Of Tech; Comp Sci.

DAY, MIKE; La Salle HS; Cincinnati, OH; 21/280 Rptr Yrbk; Bsktbl; Univ Of Cincinnati.

DAY, MONICA; Eastern HS; Salem, IN; Band; NHS; 4-H; Pep Clb; Spn Clb; Scr Kpr; 4-H Awd; Ind State Univ; History.

DAY, ROBERT; Mason Sr HS; Mason, MI; Band; Boy Scts; Hon Rl; Jr NHS; 4-H; Sci Clb; Letter Swmmng; Tmr; College; Sci.

DAY, SUSAN; East Washington HS; Salem, IN; Hon Rl; NHS; FHA; Sci Clb; Univ; Bus.

DAYER, TANYA; St Ursula Acad; Toledo, OH; Cls Rep Frsh Cls; Hon Rl; Lbry Ade; Rptr Sch Nwsp; VP Lat Clb; Univ; Acctg.

DAYTON, JANET; Thomas W Harvey HS; Painesville, OH; 6/170 Chrh Wkr; Hon Rl; NHS; Stg Crw; Fr Clb; Scr Kpr; Lakeland Cmnty Coll; Children.

DAYTON, LOU A; Morgantown HS; Morgantown, WV; Band; Chrs; Fr Clb; Pep Clb; W V Weslyan; Pre Med.

DAZLEY, MICHAEL; Genoa Area HS; Genoa, OH; 50/176 Band; Sch Mus; Key Clb; Letter Bsktbl; Letter Ftbl; Letter Trk; IM Sprt; Findlay Coll; Educ.

D BENEDETTO, MICHAEL; Catholic Central HS; Wintersvll, OH; Band; Hon Rl; Jr NHS; Sch Mus; College; Elec Engr.

DEACON, ELIZABETH; Redford Union HS; Redford, MI; 50/550 Hst Soph Cls; Cls Rep Sr Cls; Band; Cmp Fr Grls; Hon Rl; Red Cr Ade; Stu Cncl; Pep Clb; GAA; Mich State Univ; Nurse.

DEAHL, STEVE; Heritage HS; Ft Wayne, IN; 2/175 Am Leg Boys St; Band; VP Chrs; Drm Mjrt; Hon Rl; Sch Mus; Sch Pl; Yth Flsp; Letter Crs Cntry; Trk; Univ; Comp Sci.

DEAK, CAROL; Jimtown HS; Elkhart, IN; 6/96 VP Soph Cls; Cls Rep Soph Cls; Sec Jr Cls; Cl Rep Jr Cls; Hon Rl; NHS; Rptr Yrbk; Sch Nwsp; Drama Clb; FHA; College; Education.

DEAKINS, MATTHEW; Chassell HS; Chassell, MI; Pres Soph Cls; Boy Scts; Hon Rl; Lbry Ade; Sch Pl; 4-H; College.

DEAL, BARRON; Collinwood HS; Cleveland, OH; Aud/Vis; Band; Boy Scts; Drl Tm; Sct Actv; Letter Bsbl; Letter Socr; IM Sprt; Mas Awd; Cleveland St Univ; Engr.

DEAL, FRANCHESKA; Benjamin Bosse HS; Evansville, IN; Hon Rl; Pol Wkr; Sch Mus; Sch Pl; Stu Cncl; Rptr Yrbk; Rptr Sch Nwsp; Sch Nwsp; Pep Clb; Gym; Univ; X Ray Tech.

DEAL, KIMBERLY D; Guyan Valley HS; Banger, WV; Cl Rep Jr Cls; Chrs; Hon Rl; Sch Mus; Stu Cncl; Rptr Sch Nwsp; Marshall Univ; Nursing.

DEAL, NANCY; Hubbard HS; Hubbard, OH; Cmp Fr Grls; Drm Mjrt; Hon Rl; Hosp Ade; Off Ade; Yth Flsp; PPFtbl; Univ; Bus Admin.

DEAL, PAM; Douglas Mac Arthur HS; Saginaw, MI; Chrs; Girl Scts; Hon Rl; Rptr Sch Nwsp; Ten; Chrldng; PPFtbl; Coll; Phys Ther.

DEAL, TAMARA; Meridian HS; Sanford, MI; Sec Soph Cls; Hosp Ade; VP JA; NHS; Sch Mus; Stu Cncl; 4-H; Pep Clb; Natl Merit SF; Voice Dem Awd; College; Nurse.

DEAN, ANDREA; Henry Ford HS; Detroit, MI; Chrs; Hon Rl; Sch Mus; Oakland Univ; Psych.

DEAN, BERNIE; Breckenridge HS; Merrill, MI; 22/109 Chrh Wkr; Debate Tm; Hon Rl; FFA; Letter Bsbl; Capt Bsktbl; Scr Kpr; Central Michigan Univ.

DEAN, BETTYE; Northrop HS; Ft Wayne, IN; Cls Rep Frsh Cls; Pres Soph Cls; Pres Jr Cls; Pres Sr Cls; Chrs; Stu Cncl; Letter Trk; PPFtbl; Cit Awd; College.

DEAN, EDWARD; Michigan Center HS; Michigan Cente, MI; Letter Trk; Cert Of Recognition From Mich; Schlrshp From Mich St; Cert Of Ach In Basic Solid St Prog;.

DEAN, GAIL; Washington HS; Massillon, OH; 8/483 AFS; Am Leg Aux Girls St; Band; Chrs; Chrh Wkr; Hon Rl; Jr NHS; Ohi Wesleyan Univ; Hist.

DEAN, GERALD; Armada HS; Armada, MI; Hon Rl; NHS; Stg Crw; Letter Bsktbl; Univ.

DEAN, JACK; River Valley HS; Cardington, OH; 32/207 Ohio State; Acctg.

DEAN, JEFFREY; Malvern HS; Malvern, OH; 2/71 Cl Rep Jr Cls; Sal; Am Leg Boys St; Band; NHS; Yrbk; Sci Clb; Bowling Green State Univ; Computer.

DEAN, JOSEPH; Niles Mc Kinley HS; Niles, OH; Cls Rep Frsh Cls; Cls Rep Soph Cls; Pres Jr Cls; Pres Sr Cls; Am Leg Boys St; Capt Debate Tm; Pres Natl Forn Lg; NHS; Pres Stu Cncl; Key Clb; Teenager Of Mnth 79; Stud Council Schl Serv Schlrshp 79; Pres Of Teenager Of Mnth Bd 78; Youngstown St Univ; Educ.

DEAN, KAREN; River Valley HS; Cardington, OH; Pres Jr Cls; Am Leg Aux Girls St; Girl Scts; Hon Rl; VP NHS; Stu Cncl; Treas Spn Clb; PPFtbl; Ohi State Univ.

DEAN, KATHY; Rock Hill HS; Pedro, OH; Hon Rl; Business School; Secretary.

DEAN, KELLY; North Union HS; W Mansfield, OH; Band; Treas Chrh Wkr; Hon Rl; Lbry Ade; NHS; Orch; Pres 4-H; Letter Trk; PPFtbl; 4-H Awd; College; Engr.

DEAN, KIMBERLY; Franklin HS; Livonia, MI; Sec Soph Cls; Chrs; Chrh Wkr; Cmnty Wkr; FCA; Hon Rl; Stu Cncl; Cit Awd; Sec Of Stdnt Counclawd 78; Pres Of Girls Chrs Hon 78; Univ; RN.

DEAN, LISA; Poca HS; Poca, WV; Sec Frsh Cls; Band; Girl Scts; 4-H; Letter Trk; Chrldng; GAA; Mgrs; Scr Kpr; College; Physc Educ.

DEAN, MARTY; Our Lady Of Providence HS; New Albany, IN; 27/168 Chrs; Chrh Wkr; Hon Rl; Lbry Ade; Off Ade; Pol Wkr; Univ Of Louisville; Pre Law.

DEAN, MICHAEL; Vandalia Butler HS; Vandalia, OH; Cls Rep Soph Cls; Cl Rep Jr Cls; Band; Hon Rl; Mod UN; NHS; Sch Mus; Spn Clb; College; Computer Engineering.

DEAN, MICHAEL; Schafer HS; Southgate, MI; 1/250 Trs Frsh Cls; Cls Rep Soph Cls; Trs Jr Cls; Trs Sr Cls; Val; Band; NHS; Stanford Univ; Comp Sci.

DEAN, ROBERT; North Royalton HS; N Royalton, OH; 47/287 Cls Rep Sr Cls; Boy Scts; IM Sprt; Am Leg Awd; Mas Awd; Cleveland State Univ; Acctg.

DEAN, SAM; Norton HS; Norton, OH; 26/287 Boy Scts; Chrh Wkr; FCA; Hon Rl; Jr NHS; Sct Actv; Yth Flsp; Wooster College.

DEAN, SAMUEL J; Pine River HS; Luther, MI; Hon Rl; Sct Actv; Letter Ftbl; Letter Trk; Ferris St Coll; Bus Mgmt.

DEAN, SUSAN; Bluefield HS; Bluefield, WV; 16/284 Cl Rep Jr Cls; Hon Rl; NHS; Stu Cncl; Spn Clb; Letter Bsktbl; Letter Glf; Mgrs; Univ; Acctg.

DEAN, SUZY; Western Brown Sr HS; Mt Orab, OH; Sec Frsh Cls; VP Jr Cls; VP Sr Cls; Sch Pl; Stu Cncl; Rptr Yrbk; Drama Clb; Fr Clb; Chrldng;.

DEAN, TONYA; Buckhannon Upshur HS; Buckhannon, WV; Chrs; Girl Scts; Hon Rl; NHS; Stu Cncl; College; Bus.

DEARDORF, MARGARET; Carroll HS; Dayton, OH; Hon Rl; NHS; Rptr Sch Nwsp; Spn Clb; Letter Trk; Univ Of Dayton; Brdcstng.

DEARDORF, STEPHANIE; De Kalb HS; Auburn, IN; 3/287 Cls Rep Soph Cls; Cl Rep Jr Cls; Cls Rep Sr Cls; FCA; Pres NHS; Off Ade; Stu Cncl; Yrbk; VP Ger Clb; Pres Pep Clb; Ball St Univ; Landscape Archt.

DEARDORFF, JENNIFER; George Washington HS; Charleston, WV; Hosp Ade; Sch Mus; Sch Pl; Yrbk; Keyettes; West Virginia Univ; Vet Med.

DEARDOURFF, DOUG; Greenville Sr HS; Greenville, OH; Hon Rl; Ohio St Univ.

DEARDUFF, DEE; North Newton HS; Morrocco, IN; 10/148 VP Jr Cls; Am Leg Aux Girls St; Band; Chrh Wkr; Cmnty Wkr; Girl Scts; Hon Rl; NHS; Red Cr Ade; Yth Flsp; Purdue Univ; Psych.

DEARDURFF, MARK; Carroll HS; Fairborn, OH; 7/290 Hon Rl; NHS; Sct Actv; Ger Clb; Letter Trk; Texas A & M Univ; Elec Engr.

DEARING, HUGH; Pontiac Central HS; Pontiac, MI; Cmnty Wkr; Hon Rl; Lbry Ade; Off Ade; Pol Wkr; Fr Clb; Ftbl; Letter Ten; Coach Actv; Mich State Univ.

DEARING, THEODORE; Battle Creek Central HS; Battle Creek, MI; VP Frsh Cls; NHS; Sch Mus; Stg Crw; Stu Cncl; Letter Ftbl; Letter Ten; College; Music.

DEARTH, CRAIG; Wayne HS; Dayton, OH; 125/620 Boy Scts; JA; ROTC; Boys Clb Am; Wright State Univ; Communications.

DEARTH, SUSAN; Allen East HS; Lafayette, OH; Sec Jr Cls; Band; Sec Chrh Wkr; Cmnty Wkr; Sch Mus; Treas Yth Flsp; Rptr Sch Nwsp; VP FHA; Tmr; Twrlr; North Western Bus Coll; Sec.

DEARY, SANDRA; Western HS; Detroit, MI; 5/200 Drl Tm; Hon Rl; NHS; Off Ade; ROTC; Stu Cncl; Yrbk; Rptr Sch Nwsp; Sch Nwsp; Natl Sojourness Awd ROTC 78; Natl Hon Soc Schlrshp 1st Pl 78; Natl Hon Soc Schlrshp 2nd Plc 79; Michigan St Univ; Psych.

DEASON, DIANE; Huron HS; New Boston, MI; 23/163 Cls Rep Frsh Cls; Cls Rep Soph Cls; Cl Rep Jr Cls; Cls Rep Sr Cls; Hon Rl; Hosp Ade; NHS; Stu Cncl; PPFtbl; Scr Kpr; Mi Comptn Schlrshp 79; Adrian Coll; Acctg.

DEATER, BILL; Hesperia HS; Hesperia, MI; Cls Rep Frsh Cls; Pres Soph Cls; Band; Hon Rl; Lbry Ade; Stu Cncl; Mth Clb; Letter Glf; U S Air Force; Elect.

DEATHERAGE, LESLIE; Barberton HS; Barberton, OH; 5/478 Chrh Wkr; Cmnty Wkr; Hon Rl; Lbry Ade; NHS; Yth Flsp; Ger Clb; Univ.

DEATHERAGE, LINDA; Norton HS; Norton, OH; Chrh Wkr; Hon Rl; Lit Mag; Fr Clb; Pep Clb; Scr Kpr; Akron Univ; Accntg.

DEATON, GARY; Lemon Monroe HS; Middletown, OH; 40/273 VP Sr Cls; Am Leg Boys St; VP Chrs; Chrh Wkr; Hon Rl; Sch Mus; Sch Pl; Miari Univ; Bus.

DEATON, JENNIFER; Lemon Monroe HS; Middletown, OH; 4/259 Cl Rep Jr Cls; Band; Treas Chrs; Drl Tm; Hon Rl; NHS; Sch Mus; Sec Stu Cncl; Miami Univ; Bus.

DEATON, ROGER; Austin HS; Austin, IN; Letter Bsbl; Coach Actv; Indiana Univ S E; Engr.

DEATON, RUSSELL; Cadiz HS; New Athens, OH; 3/143 Cls Rep Frsh Cls; Boy Scts; Chrs; Hon Rl; Jr NHS; NHS; Sch Pl; Stu Cncl; Spn Clb; Glf; College; Math.

DEATON, TODD; Switzerland Co Jr Sr HS; Vevay, IN; 1/120 Pres Soph Cls; Am Leg Boys St; Hon Rl; NHS; Sprt Ed Sch Nwsp; Letter Bsktbl; Crs Cntry; Letter Trk; College; Comp Sci.

DEAVER, STEPHANIE; Federal Hocking HS; Coolville, OH; 12/120 VP Band; Hon Rl; Sch Pl; Rptr Sch Nwsp; 4-H; Pep Clb; Spn Clb; Trk; Chrldng; College; Bus.

DEBAR, BRIAN; Grand Ledge HS; Lansing, MI; Band; Chrs; Chrh Wkr; JA; Mdrgl; Sch Mus; Sch Pl; Stg Crw; College; Avionics.

DE BARGE, MARY; Munster HS; Munster, IN; 94/402 Chrs; Girl Scts; Sct Actv; Dance Ballet Toe Tap Jazz & Acrobatic; Awd Dance Schlrshp; Tchrs Dance Asst; Coll; Resp Ther.

DE BAUN, ANDREA; Olivet HS; Bellevue, MI; Band; Drl Tm; Drm Mjrt; Hon Rl; Sprt Ed Sch Nwsp; Rptr Sch Nwsp; Drama Clb; Bsktbl; Trk; Tmr; Full Schlrshp Vlybl Camp; All Conf Vlybl & Track; Kellogg Comm Coll; Sec.

DE BEE, REX A; Oak Glen HS; Chester, WV; Band; Jr NHS; NHS; Yrbk; Sprt Ed Sch Nwsp; Sch Nwsp; Reading Awd 105 Books In 27 Weeks 76; Earth Sci Awd 76; Typing Awd 76; Pennsylvania Tech Schl; Elec.

DEBELAK, MAUREEN; North HS; Willowick, OH; Chrs; Drm Mjrt; Hon Rl; Jr NHS; Off Ade; Stu Cncl; Rptr Sch Nwsp; Pep Clb; Letter Chrldng; Mgrs; Voc Schl; Crt Reprtng.

DEBELISO, MARK; Redford Saint Marys HS; Detroit, MI; 7/156 VP Jr Cls; Chrh Wkr; FCA; Hon Rl; NHS; Letter Bsbl; Letter Ftbl; Univ Of Detroit; Engr Mech.

DE BERRY, JEFF; Bishop Borgess HS; Detroit, MI; FCA; Pep Clb; Letter Bsbl; Letter Bsktbl; Capt Ftbl; Adrian Coll.

DEBIEN, MARILYN; Franklin HS; Westland, MI; Chrs; Hon Rl; Sch Mus; Chrldng; College; Bus Admin.

DEBLER, DIANE; Charlotte HS; Charlotte, MI; Cmp Fr Grls; Chrh Wkr; Hon Rl; Lbry Ade; Off Ade; Pep Clb; Cit Awd; Lansing Bus Inst; Sec.

DE BLOSSIO, JIMMY; Lincoln HS; Shinnston, WV; Hst Sr Cls; Am Leg Boys St; Hon Rl; NHS; Stu Cncl; Sprt Ed Sch Nwsp; Pep Clb; Bsbl; Bsktbl; Ftbl; Fairmont St Univ; Mining Tech.

DEBO, DONA; Madison Comprehensive HS; Mansfield, OH; Sec Frsh Cls; Am Leg Aux Girls St; Band; Lbry Ade; NHS; Sch Pl; Fr Clb; Natl Merit Ltr; Mansfield Exchng Club Outsdng Soph 78; Univ; Educ.

DE BOER, JOHN; Bridgman HS; Bridgman, MI; Boy Scts; Chrh Wkr; Hon Rl; NHS; Sct Actv; Yth Flsp; Letter Bsbl; IM Sprt; Am Leg Awd; God Cntry Awd; Univ Of Mich; Arch.

DE BOER, JOSEPH R; Kenowa Hills HS; Comstock Pk, MI; Chrh Wkr; Hon Rl; NHS; Pres 4-H; Crs Cntry; Letter Trk; Univ.

DE BOER, MARY; Ottawa Hills HS; Grand Rapids, MI; Hon Rl; NHS; Orch; Sch Mus; Trk; Grand Rapid Jr College; Business.

DE BOER, NANCY; Kenowa Hills HS; Grand Rapids, MI; Band; Girl Scts; Hosp Ade; NHS; Pep Clb; Sci Clb; Letter Ten; Trk; Pres Awd; Kalamazoo College; Bio Research.

DE BOLT, DANIELLE; Bellmont HS; Decatur, IN; Hon Rl; JA; Yrbk; Drama Clb; Spn Clb; Univ; Bus Mgmt.

DE BOR, MICHAEL; Reeths Puffer HS; Muskegon, MI; 28/272 Band; Boy Scts; Hon Rl; NHS; Letter Ten; Muskegon Comm College; Comp Srvc.

DEBORAH, THAYER; Midland HS; Midland, MI; Chrh Wkr; Cmnty Wkr; Hon Rl; Sec Sct Actv; Drama Clb; Glf; Ten; IM Sprt; PPFtbl; Cit Awd; Delta College; Botanist.

DE BORD, JULIE; Medina HS; Medina, OH; VP Band; Cmp Fr Grls; Chrs; Chrh Wkr; FCA; Girl Scts; Yth Flsp; Pep Clb; Ten; Bowling Green; Flight Attendant.

DE BOUVER, ROB; Van Buren Local HS; Findlay, OH; Band; Chrs; Hon Rl; Sch Mus; Sch Pl; Stg Crw; Lat Clb; Pep Clb; IM Sprt; College; Music.

DE BOW, ANDRIA; George Washington HS; Indianapolis, IN; Sec Jr Cls; Cls Rep Sr Cls; Chrh Wkr; Debate Tm; Hon Rl; JA; Off Ade; Stu Cncl; IUPUI; Bus.

DE BOY, KEVIN; Rossville HS; Rossville, IN; Chrh Wkr; Hon Rl; Yth Flsp; Rptr Sch Nwsp; 4-H; Fr Clb; FFA; Letter Bsktbl; Glf; Letter Trk; Bus Schl; Ag.

DE BOY, LISA; William Henry Harrison HS; W Lafayette, IN; Cls Rep Soph Cls; Cl Rep Jr Cls; Sal; Band; Hon Rl; NHS; Off Ade; Stu Cncl; VP 4-H; Pres Keyettes; Purdue Univ; Humanities.

DE BROSSE, JEFFREY; Whetstone HS; Columbus, OH; Boy Scts; Hon Rl; NHS; Sct Actv; Ger Clb; Awd Eagle Scout 79; Univ; Banking.

DE BROSSE, JEROME; Coldwater HS; Coldwater, OH; Pres Soph Cls; Am Leg Boys St; Boy Scts; Chrs; Chrh Wkr; Hon Rl; NHS; Ger Clb; Sci Clb; Am Leg Awd; Ohio St Univ; Zoology.

DE BROSSE, MARK E; Lehman HS; Piqua, OH; Hon Rl; Chmn Crs Cntry; College; Engr.

DE BRUIN, ANDREA; Ottawa Hills HS; Grand Rapids, MI; VP Frsh Cls; Cls Rep Frsh Cls; Trs Jr Cls; Cl Rep Jr Cls; Trs Sr Cls; Cls Rep Sr Cls; Cmp Fr Grls; Chrh Wkr; Hon Rl; College; Acctg.

DE BUSK, GERALD; Oak Hill HS; Oak Hill, WV; 2/196 Cl Rep Jr Cls; Cls Rep Sr Cls; Sal; Am Leg Boys St; Chrh Wkr; Hon Rl; NHS; Yth Flsp; IM Sprt; Dnfth Awd; George Hand Gladys H Cunningham Schlrshp 79; 1st Pl Cnty Math Field Day 79; Hon Mention Sci & Engr Fair 79; Virginia Polytech Inst; Acctg.

DE CAIR, SHERI; Napoleon HS; Napoleon, OH; Chrs; Chrh Wkr; Hon Rl; Stg Crw; Y-Teens; Drama Clb; Lat Clb; Swmmng; Univ; Elem Ed.

DECAIRE II, DENNIS; Quincy HS; Quincy, MI; Band; Chrh Wkr; Drm Mjrt; Hon Rl; Yth Flsp; FHA; FFA; Mgrs; Voc Schl; Auto Body Repair.

DE CAMP, SAM; Valley School; Flint, MI; Sch Pl; Stg Crw; Spn Clb; Socr; IM Sprt; Univ; Econ.

DE CARLO, SUSAN; Northrop HS; Ft Wayne, IN; Cls Rep Frsh Cls; Chrs; Hon Rl; Off Ade; Stu Cncl; Gym; Chrldng; Cit Awd; Natl Merit Ltr; Pres Awd;.

DE CATO, DEBORAH A; Cardinal Mooney HS; Boardman, OH; Chrh Wkr; Cmnty Wkr; Off Ade; Spn Clb; Trk; GAA; Volunteer Service Of Assumption Nursing Home 77 79; Univ; Marine Bio.

DE CECCO, ANITA; Scecina Memorial HS; Indianapolis, IN; 12/189 Hon Rl; Rptr Sch Nwsp; College; Spanish.

DE CELLES, CINDY; Chesterton HS; Chesterton, IN; 100/749 Band; Hon Rl; NHS; Off Ade; Yth Flsp; VP OEA; Am Leg Awd; Exec Dipmt Stswm Ambsr Torch 78 79; 2nd Pl Recds Mgmt Dist 78; 4th Pl Recd Mgmt St 78; Purdue Univ; Natl Park Serv.

DE CESARO, MARY; Upper Arlington HS; Middletown, OH; Hon Rl; Pep Clb; GAA; Mgrs; Miami Univ; Med.

DE CESSNA, PAUL; Perrysburg HS; Perrysburg, OH; 36/251 Pres Stu Cncl; Crs Cntry; Ftbl; Trk; Selected To Attnd Scientific Sem 79; Reciev 1st Team All Leag Hon In 300 Meters Low Hurdles 79; U S Air Force Academy; Psych.

DECHANT, HILLARY; Glen Oak School; Beachwood, OH; Chrh Wkr; PAVAS; Sch Mus; Sch Pl; Drama Clb; Natl Merit Ltr;.

DE CHENE, MICHELLE; Romulus Sr HS; Romulus, MI; Sec Frsh Cls; Cls Rep Frsh Cls; Cls Rep Soph Cls; Cl Rep Jr Cls; Pres Sr Cls; Am Leg Aux Girls St; Chrs; Chrh Wkr; Cmnty Wkr; Girl Scts; Busns Ofc Ed Class; Ski Club; Rep For HS Citizens Advisory Comm; Univ Of Michigan; Law.

DECHMEROWSKI, PHIL; Field HS; Mogadore, OH; Chrs; Hon Rl; Letter Bsbl; Pittsburg Univ; Math.

DE CHRISTOFARO, CARMEN; Niles Mc Kinley HS; Niles, OH; 31/400 Hon Rl; Stu Cncl; Letter Ftbl; IM Sprt; Mayor Or Youth Day 79; Jr Attendant At Jr Sr Prom 79; Church League Bsktbl; Youngstown St Univ.

DE CHRISTOFARO, JULIE; Berea HS; Berea, OH; AFS; Chrs; Debate Tm; Hon Rl; Natl Forn Lg; NHS; Fr Clb; Sci Clb; Gym; Letter Swmmng; Foreign Language Awd; Natl Awd For Fossil Showcase; Asst In Charge Of Uniform Roles; Marietta Coll; Petroleum Engr.

DE CHRISTOFARO, LOU; Niles Mc Kinley HS; Niles, OH; Hon Rl; Natl Forn Lg; NHS; Sch Mus; Stu Cncl; Drama Clb; Ten; Chrldng; Speech Team St Finals 17th In St Original Oratory; College; Comp Sci.

DECK, DEBORAH; Merrillville HS; Merrillville, IN; 16/601 Hon Rl; NHS; Spn Clb; Bsktbl; Purdue Univ; Acctg Cpa.

DECK, DOUGALS; Merrillville HS; Merrillville, IN; 65/605 Hon Rl; Letter Bsbl; Letter Bsktbl; Ark Univ; Bus Mngt.

DECK, LISA; North Liberty HS; S Bend, IN; Chrs; Chrh Wkr; Hon Rl; Yrbk; Fr Clb; Southeastern Acad; Travel Agent.

DECKARD, DEBBIE; Randolph Southern Jr Sr HS; Winchester, IN; 12/70 Band; Chrh Wkr; Cmnty Wkr; Hon Rl; Hosp Ade; NHS; Sch Pl; Sec Stu Cncl; Pres Yth Flsp; Sprt Ed Yrbk; Highest Serving % On Vllybl Tm 78; 2 Reserve Champ Horse In 4 H Clb 77; Univ; Med.

DECKARD, JAY; Brownstown Ctrl HS; Brownstown, IN; 27/145 Band; Hon Rl; Lat Clb; Sci Clb; Glf; Indiana Univ; Bus.

DECKARD, PAMELA S; Danville Community HS; Danville, IN; NHS; Yrbk; Pep Clb; Spn Clb; Mat Maids; 2 Spanish Awd For 1st & 2nd Yr Hon 77 & 78; Schlstc Art Awds Gold Key Finlst 77 & 78; Winona Schl Of Photog; Photog.

DECKARD, SHELLEY; Whiteland Cmnty HS; New Whiteland, IN; 16/200 VP Jr Cls; Hon Rl; NHS; Quill & Scroll; Ed Yrbk; Rptr Yrbk; FTA; Key Clb; Pep Clb; Pom Pon; Indiana Voc Tech Coll; Surgical Tech.

DECKER, ALLYN; Gladwin HS; Gladwin, MI; Chrh Wkr; Cmnty Wkr; Hon Rl; Natl Forn Lg; NHS; Sch Mus; Sch Pl; VP Stu Cncl; Yth Flsp; Rptr Yrbk; Mooddy Bible Inst.

DECKER, CHRIS; Mona Shores HS; Muskegon, MI; Hon Rl; FBLA; FHA; Pep Clb; Chrldng; Mat Maids; Scr Kpr; Tmr; Muskegon Bus; Comp Progr.

DECKER, CINDY; Kenton HS; Kenton, OH; Chrs; Cmnty Wkr; Hon Rl; Lbry Ade; PAVAS; Quill & Scroll; Ed Yrbk; Rptr Sch Nwsp; Drama Clb; FTA; Marion College; Audio.

DECKER, DONALD; Indian Valley North HS; Tuscarawas, OH; VP Frsh Cls; VP Soph Cls; Cl Rep Jr Cls; Band; Boy Scts; Chrs; Chrh Wkr; Hon Rl; NHS; Sch Mus; College; Computer Programmer.

DECKER, DOUGLAS; Lutheran East HS; Detroit, MI; Band; Boy Scts; Hon Rl; Lbry Ade; NHS; Stu Cncl; Bsktbl; Letter Ftbl; Wayne St Univ; Law.

DECKER, FREDERICK; Columbian HS; Tiffin, OH; Spn Clb; Letter Ftbl; Trk; Wrstlng; IM Sprt; Bus Schl; Salesman.

DECKER, KAREN; Warsaw Community HS; Claypool, IN; 81/360 Chrs; Hon Rl; JA; 4-H; Key Clb; 4-H Awd; JA Awd; Chr Awd 78; Perfct Attndnc For 4 Yrs 79; Ball St Univ; Elem Educ.

DECKER, KIMBER; Chippewa Hills HS; Remus, MI; 20/224 VP Soph Cls; Pres Jr Cls; VP Chrs; Chrh Wkr; Mdrgl; Orch; Sch Mus; Stu Cncl; Treas Yth Flsp; Pres FFA; U S Naval Acad; Aero Engr.

DECKER, LORETTA; Southwestern HS; Franklin, IN; 6/66 Trs Frsh Cls; Sec Jr Cls; Trs Sr Cls; Band; NHS; Ed Yrbk; Drama Clb; Capt Pom Pon; DAR Awd; Indiana St Univ; Psych.

DECKER, MICHELLE; Our Lady Of Mercy HS; Orchard Lake, MI; Hon Rl; Tmr; 2nd Pl In AAA Postr Contst 77; 1st Pl In AAA Poster Contst Out Of Shcl 77; 7th Pl In SAE Feul Econ 78; Univ.

DECKER, PAMLA; Ashley HS; Ashley, MI; Pres Frsh Cls; Pres Soph Cls; Pres Jr Cls; VP Sr Cls; Hon Rl; Trs Frsh Cls; Treas Stu Cncl; FTA; College.

DECKER, SCOTT; Traverse City HS; Traverse City, MI; 30/680 Hon Rl; Lit Mag; NHS; Stg Crw; Crs Cntry; Trk; Mic State Univ; Wildlife Mngmnt.

DECKER, THOMAS; Lakewood HS; Lake Odessa, MI; Band; Chrs; FCA; Hon Rl; Orch; Sch Mus; Sch Pl; Letter Ftbl; Letter Trk; Natl Merit Ltr; Central Mich Univ; Comp Sci.

DECKER, WILLIAM; Bridgeport Sr HS; Bridgeport, WV; 27/170 Band; Boy Scts; Hon Rl; Sct Actv; Stu Cncl; Wrstlng; Eagle Scout Awd; U S Air Force Acad; Civil Engr.

DECKERT, CARLA; Amelia HS; Cincinnati, OH; 50/280 Pres Band; Girl Scts; Hon Rl; NHS; Orch; Sch Mus; Fr Clb; Pep Clb; Letter Bsbl; GAA; Univ Of Cincinnati; Acctg.

DECKERT, MICHAEL B; Bedford N Lawrence HS; Newburgh, IN; 48/420 Cls Rep Sr Cls; Band; Boy Scts; Chrs; Chrh Wkr; Hon Rl; Mdrgl; NHS; Orch; Sch Mus; Ball St Univ; Broadcast Advrtsng.

DE COCQ, DAWN; South Bend G Washington HS; S Bend, IN; 13/355 Chrs; NHS; Sch Mus; Sch Pl; Drama Clb; 4-H; Capt Pom Pon; Tmr; DAR Awd; 4-H Awd; Univ; Art Educ.

DE COE, MARY BETH; Vassar HS; Vassar, MI; 1/180 Cls Rep Frsh Cls; Cl Rep Jr Cls; Band; Hon Rl; NHS; Stg Crw; Stu Cncl; 4-H; Spn Clb; Trk; Michigan Tech Univ; Engr.

DE COOK, BRIAN; Gull Lake HS; Richland, MI; 26/210 Cls Rep Soph Cls; Chrh Wkr; Hon Rl; NHS; Sprt Ed Yrbk; Letter Bsbl; Letter Bsktbl; Ftbl; College; Indian River Comm College.

DE COOMAN, LAURA; Fenton HS; Fenton, MI; 64/264 Band; Hon Rl; NHS; Off Ade; Mgrs; Tmr; Recognition For Outstanding Acad Ach In St Of Mi Schlrshp Comp; Sr Hnrs; Schlrhsp For High Act Score; C S Mott Comm Coll; Dental Hygiene.

DE COSTE JR, ROBERT; Lakeview HS; St Clair Shores, MI; Boy Scts; Cmnty Wkr; Red Cr Ade; Sct Actv; Letter Ftbl; Hndbl; Letter Swmmng; IM Sprt; Scr Kpr; Tmr; Macomb Comm College; Liberal Arts.

DECOT, KEVIN DALE; Bloom Carroll HS; Carroll, OH; 4/170 Boy Scts; Hon Rl; NHS; Sct Actv; Rptr Yrbk; Yrbk; Letter Glf; DAR Awd; Wagnalls Memorial Scholarship.

DE CRANE, JOAN; Regina HS; Lyndhurst, OH; Pres Soph Cls; Cl Rep Jr Cls; Hon Rl; Jr NHS; Pres Stu Cncl; Ten; GAA; IM Sprt; Univ; Sci.

DE CRANE, TRICIA; Tuscarawas Ctrl Catholic HS; New Phila, OH; Chrs; Chrh Wkr; Cmnty Wkr; Hon Rl; Off Ade; Rptr Yrbk; Ed Sch Nwsp; Rptr Sch Nwsp; Pep Clb; Bsktbl; Jrnlsm.

DEDENBACH, COLLEEN L; Cheboygan HS; Cheboygan, MI; 6/197 Band; Hon Rl; Orch; Sch Pl; Fr Clb; Eastern Michigan Univ.

DE DOMENIC, MICHELE; Ashtabula Harbor HS; Ashtabula, OH; 13/180 Sec Frsh Cls; Sec Soph Cls; Band; NHS; Off Ade; Stu Cncl; Treas Fr Clb; Treas FTA; GAA; Typing Awd 77; Bowling Green Univ; Bus Mgmt.

DEEDRICK, LORA; Zanesville HS; Zanesville, OH; Chrh Wkr; Cmnty Wkr; Hon Rl; Lbry Ade; NHS; Yth Flsp; Sci Clb; West Liberty St Coll; Dent Hygiene.

DEEGAN, AMY; Watterson HS; Columbus, OH; Chrs; Girl Scts; Hon Rl; Jr NHS; Fr Clb; Chrldng; Scr Kpr; Univ.

DEEGAN, KEVIN; Linsly Military Institute; Wheeling, WV; Hon Rl; ROTC; Letter Bsbl; Letter Ftbl; College; Bus.

DEEKS, MELISSA J; Cuyahoga Falls HS; Cuyahoga Falls, OH; 148/754 Band; Chrs; NHS; Yth Flsp; Ger Clb; NCTE; Cuyahoga Fls HS Eng Achvmnt Awrd 79; Kent St Univ; Jrnlsm.

DEEL, DAVID; Hazel Park HS; Hazel Park, MI; 94/306 Band; Hon Rl; Orch; PAVAS; Sch Mus; Sch Pl; Pep Clb; Cit Awd; LIT; Archt.

DEEM, JEFFERY; Williamstown HS; Williamstown, WV; 33/115 4-H; Bsktbl; Trk; 4-H Awd; Lion Awd; Coll.

DEEM, JOAN; Lincoln HS; Fairmont, WV; Hon Rl; NHS; Treas Spn Clb; Stu Active In Educ Club; Math Field Day; W Virginia Univ; Math.

DEEMS, DAVID; Crestline HS; Galion, OH; 3/122 Am Leg Boys St; Hon Rl; NHS; Sch Mus; Sch Pl; Yth Flsp; Rptr Yrbk; 4-H; Trk; 4-H Awd; Boston Univ; Bio Med Engr.

DEEN, STEVEN C; Corydon Central HS; Corydon, IN; 13/162 Band; Yth Flsp; Fr Clb; Pep Clb; IM Sprt; Indiana Univ; Arts & Sci.

DEER, LISA; New Palestine HS; New Palestine, IN; 15/125 Am Leg Aux Girls St; Cmp Fr Grls; Drl Tm; Hon Rl; NHS; Sch Pl; Rptr Yrbk; Ten; Pom Pon; Purdue Univ; Pilot.

DEER, WILLIAM K; Lawrence Central HS; Indianapolis, IN; 13/388 Hon Rl; Pol Wkr; Sch Pl; Stg Crw; Drama Clb; Natl Merit SF; College; Law.

DEES, KONDA; Richmond Sr HS; Richmond, IN; 33/690 Hon Rl; NHS; Spn Clb; Univ; Spanish.

DEES, MICHAEL; St Josephs Central Cath HS; Port Clinton, OH; Band; Chrs; Rptr Yrbk; Letter Glf; Coach Actv; Cincinnati Univ; Music Educ.

DEES, MITCH; Northwest Sr HS; Fairfield, OH; Cl Rep Jr Cls; Band; Chrh Wkr; Hon Rl; Jr NHS; NHS; Pres Stu Cncl; Lat Clb; SAR Awd; Natl Latin Exam Magna Cum Laude; Ohio Music Ed Assn Solo & Ensemble; 2nd Pl Chem Div Schl Sci Fair; College; Pre Law.

DEETER, CHRIS; Greenville Sr HS; Greenville, OH; 16/380 Hon Rl; NHS; Yth Flsp; Key Clb; Letter Bsktbl; Letter Ftbl; College; Busns Admin.

DEETER, DEBBIE; Northfield HS; Wabash, IN; Sec Jr Cls; Chrh Wkr; NHS; Quill & Scroll; Rptr Yrbk; Sch Nwsp; Drama Clb; FHA; Pep Clb; Purdue Univ; Med Asst.

DEETER, KRIS; Greenville Sr HS; Greenville, OH; 8/360 Chrs; Chrh Wkr; Girl Scts; Hon Rl; NHS; Orch; Drama Clb; Lat Clb; Sci Clb; 4-H Awd; Defiance Coll; Special Ed.

DEETER, TAMARA; Northfield HS; Wabash, IN; Cls Rep Frsh Cls; Cls Rep Soph Cls; Cl Rep Jr Cls; Cls Rep Sr Cls; Am Leg Aux Girls St; FCA; Hon Rl; VP NHS; Quill & Scroll; VP Stu Cncl; Univ; Math.

DE FABIO, JAMI; Kirtland HS; Kirtland, OH; Cls Rep Frsh Cls; Cls Rep Soph Cls; Chrs; Hon Rl; Lakeland Cmnty Coll; Stenography.

DEFALLO, JEANNE; Catholic Central HS; Steubenville, OH; 68/210 Cls Rep Sr Cls; Hon Rl; Hosp Ade; Red Cr Ade; Rptr Sch Nwsp; FHA; Pep Clb; Bsbl; Bsktbl; Trk; Business Schl; Secretarial.

DEFEVER, LEANNE; Davison Sr HS; Davison, MI; 6/400 Chrs; NHS; Pres Ger Clb; Letter Trk; Mat Maids; PPFtbl; Oakland Univ.

DEFEVER, NANCY; Corunna HS; Corunna, MI; Trs Sr Cls; Stu Cncl; Rptr Yrbk; Pres 4-H; Sec FFA; Bsktbl; 4-H Awd; Mic State.

DEFFENBAUGH, CARL R; Leetonia HS; Leetonia, OH; Am Leg Boys St; Boy Scts; FCA; Hon Rl; Yth Flsp; VICA; Ftbl; C of C Awd;.

DEFIBAUGH, DEBRA D; Benjamin Logan HS; Belle Fontaine, OH; 41/156.

DE FINA, DAVID; Bishop Noll Institute; Calumet City, IL; 11/337 Chrh Wkr; Hon Rl; Sch Pl; Ed Sch Nwsp; Bsbl; Swmmng; IM Sprt; Kiwan Awd; Bradley Univ; Engineering.

DEFLEY, LAURA; Immaculate Conception Acad; Pt Sulphur, LA; Pres Soph Cls; Band; Chrs; Chrh Wkr; Girl Scts; Hon Rl; Yth Flsp; Yrbk; College; Psych Soc Work.

DEFOURNY, LISA; Bishop Watterson HS; Columbus, OH; 55/250 Chrs; Cmnty Wkr; Hon Rl; Sch Nwsp; Tmr; Ohi St Univ;.

DE FOUW, DOUGLAS; West Geauga HS; Chester Isl, OH; Cls Rep Soph Cls; Chrs; Chrh Wkr; Hon Rl; Mdrgl; Sch Mus; Sch Pl; Stg Crw; Stu Cncl; Yth Flsp; Univ; Mgmt.

DE FRANCES, CAROL; Cardinal Mooney HS; Youngstown, OH; 22/296 Cls Rep Soph Cls; Cl Rep Jr Cls; Chrh Wkr; Hon Rl; JA; Jr NHS; Natl Forn Lg; NHS; Stu Cncl; Spn Clb; College; Economics.

DE FRANCIS, ANN; Archbishop Alter HS; Centerville, OH; 1/345 Val; NHS; Sec Civ Clb; VP Spn Clb; Socr; Coach Actv; Univ; Chem.

DE FUR, DEBRA; New Harmony HS; New Harmony, IN; Am Leg Aux Girls St; Hon Rl; Stu Cncl; Ed Yrbk; Rptr Sch Nwsp; 4-H; OEA; Pep Clb; IM Sprt; Pom Pon; Lockyear Coll; Comp Prog.

DE GARMO, TRACY; Milford HS; Milford, MI; Band; Drl Tm; Hon Rl; NHS; Sec Stu Cncl; Rptr Yrbk; Yrbk; Rptr Sch Nwsp; Sch Nwsp; Spn Clb; Acad High Hon 4 Yrs; General Motors Inst; Mech Engr.

DE GENARO, STEPHEN; Hubbard HS; Hubbard, OH; Hon Rl; Lit Mag; Quill & Scroll; Ed Yrbk; Rptr Sch Nwsp; Lat Clb; Youngstown St Univ; Soc Std.

DEGITZ, JULIA; Anderson HS; Anderson, IN; 32/429 Hon Rl; NHS; Stu Cncl; Fr Clb; C of C Awd; Indiana Univ; Nursing.

DE GRAAF, PAM; Kenowa Hills HS; Grand Rpds, MI; Band; Chrh Wkr; Girl Scts; Hon Rl; Off Ade; Orch; Sch Mus; Sch Pl; Stg Crw; Yth Flsp; Lake Superior St Coll; Archt.

DE GRAAF, PAM; Kenowa Hills HS; Grand Rapids, MI; Band; Orch; Sch Mus; Sch Pl; Stg Crw; Rptr Yrbk; Ed Sch Nwsp; PPFtbl; Natl Merit Schl; Lake Superior State Univ; Architecut.

DE GRAFF, RHONDA; Pickerington HS; Pickerington, OH; 42/198 Cl Rep Jr Cls; Stu Cncl; Spn Clb; Univ; Bio.

DE GRANDCHAMP, PAUL; Mt Pleasant Sr HS; Mount Pleasant, MI; Pres Frsh Cls; Pres Soph Cls; Boy Scts; Chrs; Chrh Wkr; Hon Rl; Mdrgl; Sch Mus; Sch Pl; Yth Flsp; St Of Michigan Competitive Schlrshp; CMU HS Music Camp Vocalist Of Yr; Valedictorian; Central Michigan Univ; Liberal Arts.

DE GRANDE, LYNN; Marlette Comm HS; Brown City, MI; 2/131 Sal; Hon Rl; NHS; Sch Pl; Stu Cncl; Sec 4-H; Pres OEA; Letter Ten; 4-H Awd; Delta Kappa Gamma Awd For Outstndg Citizen; OEA Diplomat & Stateswoman Awds; College; Advertising.

DE GREGORIO, DENISE; Southgate HS; Southgate, MI; 4 Hon Rl; Off Ade; Stu Cncl; Letter Mgrs; Mat Maids; Scr Kpr; Tmr; College; Fshn Dsgn.

DEGRENDEL, AMY; Rochester HS; Rochester, MI; 61/370 Drl Tm; Hon Rl; Hosp Ade; Jr NHS; Univ Of Hawaii.

DE GROAT, JACQUELINE S; Ernest W Seaholm HS; Birmingham, MI; 117/660 Cls Rep Soph Cls; Cl Rep Jr Cls; Cls Rep Sr Cls; Band; Chrh Wkr; Cmnty Wkr; Hon Rl; Jr NHS; Yth Flsp; Natl Merit SF; Univ Of Mic; Pre Med.

DE GROFF, PETE; Hilltop HS; W Unity, OH; Cls Rep Frsh Cls; VP Jr Cls; Band; Chrh Wkr; Hon Rl; Orch; Sch Mus; Ftbl; Univ.

DE GROOT, JAMES; Olivet HS; Olivet, MI; Band; Boy Scts; Chrs; Chrh Wkr; Debate Tm; FCA; Hon Rl; NHS; Sch Pl; Sct Actv; All League Tight End In

Ftbl; Awd In 4 H In Raising Hogs & Woodworking; Coll.

DE GUISE, MARY; Merrill HS; Merrill, MI; VP Soph Cls; Pres Jr Cls; Band; Drm Bgl; Girl Scts; Hon Rl; Letter Bsbl; Letter Bsktbl; GAA; PPFtbl; College; Music.

DE GUZMAN, MARIA N; Highland Park Cmnty HS; Highland Park, MI; Cls Rep Sr Cls; Hon Rl; NHS; Off Ade; Quill & Scroll; Capt Ten; Dist Educ Awd 77; Office Aide Awd 79; Northwood Inst; Fshn Mdse.

DE HAAN, DAWN; Grand Rapids Christian HS; Grand Rapids, MI; Chrs; Red Cr Ade; Yrbk; PPFtbl; Ferris St College; Radiology Tech.

DE HAAN, JOLENE E; Cedar Springs HS; Grand Rapids, MI; Chrh Wkr; Hon Rl; Lbry Ade; NHS; Rptr Yrbk; FHA; Pep Clb; Schslshp From Mi Dept Of Educ 79; Kent Skills Ctr For 2 Yrs & Took Eng & Drafting Progr 77 79; Grand Rapids Jr Coll; Engr.

DE HAAN, LYNETTE; Reese HS; Reese, MI; Am Leg Aux Girls St; Girl Scts; Hon Rl; Hosp Ade; NHS; Sct Actv; 4-H; Treas Ger Clb; Letter Trk; Ferris; Pharm.

DE HART, DONALD E; Indian Creek HS; Franklin, IN; 5/148 VP Jr Cls; VP Sr Cls; Am Leg Boys St; Pres FCA; Jr NHS; Treas NHS; VP Stu Cncl; Rptr Sch Nwsp; Letter Crs Cntry; Letter Trk; Purdue Univ; Aeronautical Engr.

DE HART, PATRICK; Oak Hill HS; Oak Hill, WV; Pres Sr Cls; NHS; Stu Cncl; Capt Bsbl; W Va Inst Of Tech; Lawyer.

DE HATE, DOREEN; Pinconning Area HS; Pinconning, MI; Treas Boy Scts; Hon Rl; Univ; Nursing.

DE HAVEN, JANET; James A Garfield HS; Garrettsville, OH; 1/140 VP Soph Cls; Band; Hon Rl; NHS; Orch; Fr Clb; Univ; Engr.

DEHMLOW, BRIAN; Concordia Lutheran HS; Ft Wayne, IN; 1/180 Band; Hon Rl; Ger Clb; Pres Sci Clb; Univ; Physics.

DEHN, JEFF; South Haven HS; South Haven, MI; Cl Rep Jr Cls; Chrs; FCA; Hon Rl; Orch; Sch Mus; Stu Cncl; Rptr Yrbk; Letter Bsbl; Bsktbl; Univ.

DEHNE, MICHAEL; New Buffalo Area HS; New Buffalo, MI; Band; Bsktbl; Letter Ftbl; Letter Trk; Scr Kpr; CEI; Comp Tech.

DEHNE, SUSAN; Seton HS; Cincinnati, OH; Girl Scts; Hon Rl; Orch; Sch Mus; Sct Actv; Univ; Art.

DE HOFF, BETTY; Boardman HS; Canfield, OH; 65/598 Hon Rl; Natl Forn Lg; NHS; Stg Crw; Stu Cncl; Yth Flsp; Y-Teens; Pres Fr Clb; Marion Coll; Nursing.

DEIBEL, JILL; Ridgewood HS; Fresno, OH; 2/150 Sal; Band; Chrs; Chrh Wkr; Hon Rl; Off Ade; Univ Of Ohi; Law.

DEIBEL, LAVONNE; Smithville HS; Wooster, OH; 5/100 Cls Rep Frsh Cls; Sec Jr Cls; Sec Sr Cls; Band; Chrs; Hon Rl; NHS; Mount Union College; Acct.

DEICHLER, KAREN; Brookfield HS; Brookfield, OH; Chrs; Girl Scts; Hon Rl; NHS; Off Ade; Sch Mus; Sch Pl; Stg Crw; Stu Cncl; Rptr Yrbk; SPAN 79; Univ; Med.

DEISING, RANDY; Manistee Catholic Cent HS; Manistee, MI; Hon Rl; NHS; Letter Bsktbl; Letter Ftbl; Ferris State College; Accnt.

DEITERING, VICTORIA; Lehman HS; Piqua, OH; Cls Rep Soph Cls; Trs Jr Cls; Chrs; Chrh Wkr; Girl Scts; Hosp Ade; Sch Mus; Sch Pl; Sct Actv; Sdlty; Science.

DEITERS, JULIE; Anna HS; Anna, OH; 4/69 Am Leg Aux Girls St; Hon Rl; NHS; Sch Pl; Spn Clb; Bsktbl; GAA; IM Sprt; Am Leg Awd; Schlrshp Team Algebra II Top Cnty Team; Volleyball Varsity Letter; Pep Clb Sec; Wright St Univ; Acctg.

DEITZEN, VINCENT; Hillsdale HS; Osseo, MI; FCA; Jr NHS; NHS; Letter Ftbl; Lloyd Morningstar Mmrl Schlrshp 79; Cert Of Recogntn St Of Mi Schlrshp Comp 79; Sr Athletic Awrd 79; Farmer.

DEJANOVICH, MICHAEL J; Bishop Noll Inst; Chicago, IL; 37/340 Boy Scts; Hon Rl; NHS; Mth Clb; Trk; Univ Of Chicago; Poli Sci.

DE JARNATT, DAWN; Sturgis Sr HS; Sturgis, MI; JA; Lbry Ade; Glen Oaks Comm Coll; Library Sci.

DE JARNETT, RONALD; Princeton Cmnty HS; Princeton, IN; 14/205 Trs Frsh Cls; Hon Rl; Rptr Yrbk; Rptr Sch Nwsp; Mth Clb; Sci Clb; Univ; Mech Engr.

DE JESUS, CHUCHU; Plymouth HS; Plymouth, IN; Trs Frsh Cls; AFS; Band; Hon Rl; Jr NHS; NHS; Off Ade; Sch Mus; Stu Cncl; Eng Clb; Stdnt Leadership Inst Schlrshp 1976; Indiana Univ; Bus Admin.

DE JONG, JONATHAN; Berkley HS; Berkley, MI; 63/580 Aud/Vis; Pres Band; Chrs; Chrh Wkr; Hon Rl; Orch; Sch Mus; Yth Flsp; Pres Pep Clb; Swmmng; Marine Bio.

DE JONGE, THOMAS; Shelbyville Sr HS; Shelbyville, IN; VP Soph Cls; VP Jr Cls; Pres Sr Cls; Cmnty Wkr; Hon Rl; Jr NHS; Stu Cncl; Rptr Sch Nwsp; Lat Clb; Bsktbl; College; Busns Admin.

DE JONGH, JOHN C; East Catholic HS; Detroit, MI; Aud/Vis; Hon Rl; NHS; Stu Cncl; Wayne St Univ; Pharm.

DE JULIAN, MICHELE; Trenton HS; Trenton, MI; Girl Scts; Hon Rl; Stu Cncl; Pep Clb; Spn Clb; Chrldng; Figure Skating Wyandotte Figure Skating Club Slvr Medlst 77; Hillsdale Coll; Psych.

DE JUTE, DAVID; St Johns HS; Toledo, OH; 1/241 Cls Rep Frsh Cls; Cls Rep Soph Cls; Pres Jr Cls; Pres Sr Cls; VP Band; Hon Rl; Sch Pl; Stu Cncl; Rptr Yrbk; Rptr Sch Nwsp; Outstnndg Jr In N W Oh 79; Hertz Mert Schshlp 76; Berchmans Awd 79; Univ; Art.

DE KEMPER, DONNA; Princeton Cmnty HS; Princeton, IN; Cls Rep Frsh Cls; Cls Rep Soph Cls; Cl Rep Jr Cls; Band; DECA; 4-H; FSA; Pep Clb; Sci Clb; 4-H Awd; Indiana St Univ; Med.

DE KIEP, LORI; Grand Haven HS; Grand Haven, MI; 1/385 Val; Band; Hon Rl; Hosp Ade; Jr NHS; NHS; Orch; Sch Mus; Ferris State College; Med Tech.

DEKLE, ROSS; Henry Ford HS; Detroit, MI; VP Frsh Cls; VP Soph Cls; VP Jr Cls; Band; Chrh Wkr; Hon Rl; Lbry Ade; Lawrencwe Institute Of Tech; Arch.

DE KLERK, HILDA; Lapeer East Sr HS; Lapeer, MI; 10/258 Chrs; Hon Rl; NHS; VP Yth Flsp; Bsktbl; Mgrs; JC Awd; Cert Of Recogntn St Of Mi Comp Schlrshp Prog 79; Univ Of Mi Regnts Alumni Schlrshp 79; William Jennings Bryan Coll; Psych.

DE KLERK, JAYNE; Lapeer East Sr HS; Lapeer, MI; Trs Frsh Cls; Cls Rep Soph Cls; Chrh Wkr; Hon Rl; NHS; Stu Cncl; Letter Trk; Mgrs; Bryan Coll; Elem Ed.

DE KOCK, SHARON; Kankakee Valley HS; Fair Oaks, IN; 19/190 Chrs; Chrh Wkr; Hon Rl; NHS; Off Ade; Sch Mus; Sch Pl; Stu Cncl; Yth Flsp; Rptr Yrbk; Office Educ Assn Contest Reg Adv Typing 1st Pl 79; Schl Awd In Adv Typing 79; Calvin Coll; Bus Admin.

DE KRAKER, CANDACE; South Christian HS; Moline, MI; Band; Chrh Wkr; Cmnty Wkr; Debate Tm; Hon Rl; Natl Forn Lg; Sch Pl; Yth Flsp; Rptr Yrbk; 4-H; College.

DE LAAT, DOUGLAS; Ashtabula Harbor HS; Ashtabula, OH; 62/210 AFS; Chrh Wkr; FCA; Pep Clb; Spn Clb; Bsktbl; Glf; IM Sprt;.

DE LAAT, JACKIE; West Geauga HS; Chesterland, OH; Cls Rep Frsh Cls; Aud/Vis; Chrs; Girl Scts; Hon Rl; Off Ade; Stu Cncl; Sprt Ed Yrbk; Pep Clb; Letter Bsktbl; Univ; Phys Ther.

DELAHANTY, LAWRENCE; Vicksburg Community HS; Vicksburg, MI; 13/233 Boy Scts; Chrh Wkr; Fr Clb; Trk; Michigan Tech Univ; Engr.

DELAINE, VALERIE; Western Hills HS; Cincinnati, OH; Cls Rep Frsh Cls; Cls Rep Soph Cls; Cl Rep Jr Cls; Chrh Wkr; FCA; JA; Yth Flsp; Fr Clb; Harvard Univ; Law.

DE LAND, CONSTANCE; Millington HS; Millington, MI; 20/167 Sec Frsh Cls; Band; Drm Mjrt; Hon Rl; NHS; Twrlr; Univ; Math.

DE LANEY, JULIE; Carroll HS; Dayton, OH; Cls Rep Frsh Cls; Cls Rep Soph Cls; Cl Rep Jr Cls; Drl Tm; Sch Pl; Boys Clb Am; Drama Clb; Fr Clb; GAA; Pom Pon; Voc Schl; Modeling.

DE LANEY, KENNETH; Ovid Elsie HS; Owosso, MI; Band; Boy Scts; Drm Bgl; Hon Rl; Sch Pl; Rdo Clb; College; Broadcasting.

DE LANEY, MICHAEL; Bishop Foley HS; Troy, MI; Hon Rl; NHS; College; Banking Finance.

DE LANG, JAMES; Robert S Tower Sr HS; Warren, MI; 1/400 Hst Jr Cls; Val; Band; NHS; Letter Bsbl; Letter Ftbl; Letter Trk; Michigan St Univ; Civil Engr.

DELAPLAINE, CHRIS; Bedford North Lawrence HS; Bedford, IN; 160/400 Pol Wkr; Beta Clb; Key Clb; Letter Ftbl; Letter Trk; Coach Actv; Full Athletic Schlrshp To Indiana St Univ 79; Indiana St Univ.

DELAPLANE, KEITH S; Logansport HS; Logansport, IN; 31/340 Aud/Vis; Chrs; Chrh Wkr; Hon Rl; Natl Forn Lg; Sch Mus; Sch Pl; Yrbk; Drama Clb; Fr Clb; Butler Univ; English.

DE LA ROSA, DULCINA; Cass Tech HS; Detroit, MI; Band; Hon Rl; ROTC; VP Y-Teens; Univ; Child Psych.

DELAUDER, SHERRI L; Morgantown HS; Morgantwn, WV; Cls Rep Frsh Cls; Cls Rep Soph Cls; Cl Rep Jr Cls; Band; Drm Mjrt; Jr NHS; Stu Cncl; VP Pep Clb; Fresh Schlrshp Awd; All County Chorus Awd; College; Nursing.

DE LAVERN, DONNA; Bridgeport HS; Saginaw, MI; 24/335 Hon Rl; JA; Ger Clb; Cum Laude; German Awd; Merit Roll Awd; Saginaw Vly St Coll; Animal Tech.

DE LAY, MICHELE; Brandywine HS; Niles, MI; 3/136 Trs Soph Cls; VP Jr Cls; Pres Sr Cls; AFS; NHS; Sch Mus; Sch Pl; Stg Crw; Yrbk; Drama Clb; Central Michigan Univ; Elem Ed.

DEL BELLO, CAROLYN; Boardman Sr HS; Youngstown, OH; 9/600 Girl Scts; Hon Rl; Jr NHS; Orch; Sch Mus; Sct Actv; Fr Clb; Am Leg Awd; Univ; Soc Work.

DELBERT, STEPHANIE; Philo HS; Roseville, OH; 45/208 Chrs; Cmnty Wkr; Hon Rl; NHS; Orch; Sch Mus; Sch Pl; Yth Flsp; Spn Clb; Chrldng; Ohio Univ; Psychology.

DEL CAMP, DINAH D; Newton HS; Plesant Hill, OH; 3/50 Am Leg Aux Girls St; Band; Chrs; Drm Mjrt; FCA; Hon Rl; Lbry Ade; NHS; Sch Pl; Stg Crw; Ohio St Univ; Phys Ther.

DE LEON, TAMMY; Jonathan Alder HS; Plain City, OH; Chrs; Y-Teens; FHA; Chrldng; GAA; Sec.

DE LEONARDIS, DOREEN; Catholic Central HS; Steubenville, OH; 27/204 Hon Rl; Yth Flsp; Treas Pep Clb; Spn Clb; Tmr; Shorthnd Awd 78; Bus Schl; Sec.

DE LEONE, SUE; Roosevelt HS; Kent, OH; Cls Rep Soph Cls; Trs Jr Cls; Cl Rep Jr Cls; Trs Sr Cls; Red Cr Ade; Stu Cncl; Rptr Yrbk; 4-H; Pep Clb; Chrldng; Vllybl Letter 78; Schlrshp Awd 77 78; Univ.

DELEWSKY, MARIE; Adlai E Stevenson HS; Livonia, MI; 45/815 Cls Rep Frsh Cls; Cls Rep Soph Cls; Cl Rep Jr Cls; Cls Rep Sr Cls; Band; Chrs; Chrh Wkr; Cmnty Wkr; Drm Mjrt; Girl Scts; Wayne St Univ; Pre Med.

DEL GADO, BRENDA; Woodrow Wilson HS; Youngstown, OH; Hst Frsh Cls; Y-Teens; VICA; Tech Schl; Dental Lab.

DEL GADO, DAVID M; Bloom Carroll HS; Canal Winchestr, OH; Boy Scts; Hon Rl; NHS; Sct Actv; Rptr Yrbk; FFA; Bsbl; Letter Crs Cntry; Mgrs; Air Force Academy; Math.

DELGARBINO, MARK; Warren G Harding HS; Warren, OH; 38/385 Am Leg Boys St; Treas FCA; Hon Rl; NHS; Letter Bsbl; Letter Ftbl; Univ; Archt.

DEL GRECO, PATRICIA; Napoleon HS; Napoleon, OH; Chrs; PAVAS; Sch Mus; Sch Pl; Stg Crw; VP Drama Clb; Ohio St Univ; Cosmotology.

DE LISLE, CATHY; Lincoln HS; Vincennes, IN; FCA; Fr Clb; FHA; FTA; Sci Clb; Chrldng; Vincennes Univ; Phys Therapy.

DELKER, KRAIG; Chesapeake HS; Chesapeake, OH; Cl Rep Jr Cls; Hon Rl; Stu Cncl; Pep Clb; Letter Bsktbl; IM Sprt; College.

DELL, MICHAEL; Goodrich HS; Lapeer, MI; VP Sr Cls; Band; Vocational School.

DELLAPOSTA, BRUCE; Carlisle HS; Franklin, OH; Sct Actv; Boys Clb Am; Letter Bsbl; Letter Ftbl; Letter Wrstlng; College; Forestry.

DELLINGER, ELIZABETH; Chagrin Falls HS; Chagrin Falls, OH; Pres AFS; Pres Debate Tm; Sec Girl Scts; Hon Rl; Hosp Ade; Lit Mag; Natl Forn Lg; NHS; Rptr Sch Nwsp; SAR Awd; College; Economics Law.

DELLINGER, JOHN; Hedgesville HS; Falling Wtrs, WV; Cls Rep Frsh Cls; Pres Soph Cls; Cl Rep Jr Cls; Boy Scts; Hon Rl; Jr NHS; NHS; Stu Cncl; Yth Flsp; Mth Clb; W Virginia Univ; Wildlife Mgmt.

DE LONEY, TODD; Roosevelt HS; Gary, IN; VP Frsh Cls; Cls Rep Soph Cls; Cl Rep Jr Cls; Pres Chrs; Chrh Wkr; Hon Rl; Stu Cncl; Sec Fr Clb; FTA; Flo A&m; Law.

DE LONG, CINDY; Wylie E Groves HS; Birmingham, MI; Chrs; Chrh Wkr; Girl Scts; Hon Rl; Yth Flsp; IM Sprt; Michigan St Univ; Intl Relations.

DE LONG, DONNA; Bishop Hartley HS; Columbus, OH; Hon Rl; Swmmng; Chrldng; Mat Maids; Job As Sec.

DE LONG, ELIZABETH; Mt Pleasant HS; Mt Pleasamt, MI; Band; Girl Scts; Hon Rl; Yrbk; Pep Clb; Bsbl; GAA; IM Sprt; PPFtbl; Scr Kpr; Ferris St Univ; Draftsman.

DE LONG, JEFF; Bishop Flaget HS; Chillicothe, OH; Boy Scts; Chrh Wkr; Hon Rl; Jr NHS; Lbry Ade; NHS; Sct Actv; Stg Crw; Fr Clb; Ohio Univ; Acctg.

DE LONG, JOHN R; Tiffin Calvert HS; Tiffin, OH; 25/101 Band; Boy Scts; Hon Rl; JA; Sch Mus; Rptr Sch Nwsp; Pep Clb; Letter Wrstlng; Am Leg Awd; JA Awd; Univ; Scndry Educ.

DE LONG, KAREN; Whiteland HS; Indianapolis, IN; 27/208 Hon Rl; Sec 4-H; FTA; Univ.

DE LONG, PATRICIA; Armada HS; Armada, MI; 6/96 Cls Rep Frsh Cls; Trs Soph Cls; Cl Rep Jr Cls; Cls Rep Sr Cls; Band; Hon Rl; Lbry Ade; Off Ade; Sch Mus; Stu Cncl; Central Michigan Univ; Acctg.

DE LONG, SUSAN; New Richmond HS; Bethel, OH; 16/194 Sec Soph Cls; VP Sr Cls; Hon Rl; NHS; Quill & Scroll; Rptr Sch Nwsp; Fr Clb; Pep Clb; Capt Chrldng; GAA; Univ Of Cincinnati; Brdcstng.

DE LORIA, JOAN; Petoskey HS; Petoskey, MI; Chrh Wkr; Debate Tm; Girl Scts; Hon Rl; Natl Forn Lg; NHS; Sch Mus; Sch Pl; Aguinas College; Drama.

DE LORME, FELICIA; Whitko HS; Pierceton, IN; 14/151 Cl Rep Jr Cls; Cls Rep Sr Cls; Chrs; FCA; Hon Rl; NHS; Sch Mus; Sch Pl; Stu Cncl; Rptr Yrbk; Distngd Amer HS Stu 1977; Purdue Univ.

DE LORME, TAMMY; Crestview HS; Wren, OH; Chrs; Chrh Wkr; Sch Mus; Stg Crw; Stu Cncl; Rptr Sch Nwsp; Treas FHA; Pep Clb; Trk; Univ; Lab Tech.

DELOST, ELIZABETH; Magnificat HS; Fairview Pk, OH; Chrs; Girl Scts; Sch Mus; Sct Actv; Fr Clb; Chrldng; Pres Awd; Coll; Comm Art.

DELPH, ILENE; Marietta Sr HS; Marietta, OH; 17/450 NHS; Yth Flsp; FTA; Spn Clb; Letter Bsktbl; Ohio St Univ; Elem Ed.

DELPHIA, BRIAN; Whetstone HS; Columbs, OH; Aud/Vis; Band; Boy Scts; Hon Rl; Sch Mus; Sct Actv; Stu Cncl; Rptr Yrbk; 4-H; Lat Clb; Ohio St Univ; Biochem.

DEL POZO, ROBERT; Linsly HS; Wheeling, WV; Sec Soph Cls; Hon Rl; Mod UN; ROTC; Drama Clb; FDA; Sci Clb; Spn Clb; Swmmng; College; Medicine.

DEL PRINCE, MICHAEL; Ashtabula Harbor HS; Ashtabula, OH; 20/200 Chrh Wkr; FCA; Lat Clb; Spn Clb; Letter Bsbl; Letter Glf; IM Sprt; Ashtabula Area HS Stdnt Of Mnth 79; Univ; Acctg.

DEL SIGNORE, THOMAS; Struthers HS; Struthers, OH; Lit Mag; Sch Nwsp; VP DECA; Lat Clb; IM Sprt; Univ; Photo Proc.

DEL TORO, DAVID; Morton Sr HS; Hammond, IN; 2/436 Cls Rep Frsh Cls; Cls Rep Soph Cls; Cl Rep Jr Cls; Cls Rep Sr Cls; Sal; Am Leg Boys St; Hon Rl; JA; Natl Forn Lg; NHS; Rose Hulman Inst Of Tech; Mech Engr.

DEL TORO, LISA; Morton Sr HS; Hammond, IN; 38/419 Cls Rep Soph Cls; Debate Tm; Hon Rl; Rptr Sch Nwsp; Pep Clb; PPFtbl; Twrlr; Univ; Flight Attendant.

DE LUCA, DAVID; Ravenna HS; Ravenna, OH; Cls Rep Soph Cls; Chrh Wkr; Hon Rl; NHS; Ed Yrbk; Ftbl; Trk; College.

DE LUCA, TIM; Padua Franciscan HS; Brook Pk, OH; Treas Chrs; Chrh Wkr; Treas JA; Univ; Elec Engr.

DE LUCIO, TAMARA; Richmond HS; Richmond, IN; Drl Tm; Girl Scts; Hosp Ade; Y-Teens; Yrbk; 4-H; Spn Clb; Univ; Sec Educ.

DEL VAL, SAN JUANITA; Grant HS; Bailey, MI; Hon Rl; Lbry Ade; FNA; Spn Clb; Letter Trk; PPFtbl; Cit Awd; Univ; Med.

DEL VALLE, ELENA; Marian HS; Blmfld Hls, MI; Cls Rep Frsh Cls; Cmnty Wkr; Hon Rl; Stu Cncl; Natl Schlrstic Art Awd Gold Key Pencil Drwng 78; Univ; Chem.

DEL VALLE, JEAN; Trenton HS; Trenton, MI; 22/539 Band; Girl Scts; NHS; Ger Clb; Pep Clb; Letter Bsktbl; Capt Trk; Mich State Univ.

DELVENTHAL, REX; Napoleon HS; Napoleon, OH; 6/275 Hon Rl; NHS; Sch Mus; Sch Pl; Lat Clb; Capt Swmmng; Bausch & Lomb Awd; Univ Of Cin; Aero Engr.

DELVENTHAL, SCOTT; Bryan HS; Hornell, NY; Hon Rl; Pep Clb; Letter Bsbl; Letter Bsktbl; Ftbl; Letter Socr; College; Engr.

DE MAIOLO, DENISE; Niles Mc Kinley HS; Niles, OH; 29/420 AFS; Chrs; Hon Rl; Hosp Ade; Jr NHS; Mdrgl; Natl Forn Lg; NHS; Stg Crw; Drama Clb; Ohio St Univ; Phys Ther.

DEMAK, RONALD; Berkley HS; Oak Park, MI; Band; Cmnty Wkr; IM Sprt; HS Hon Sci Prgr 78; Delgt T Onatl Jr Sci &humnts Symposm 79; Semi Finlst St Of Mi Comp Schlshp; Michigan St Uni; Bio Chem.

DEMAN, KENNETH; Grosse Pointe North HS; Grosse Pt Shrs, MI; 1/500 Chrs; Chrh Wkr; Hon Rl; NHS; Ger Clb; IM Sprt; Natl Merit Ltr; Univ; Med.

DE MARAY, CAROL; Peck HS; Melvin, MI; Chrs; Chrh Wkr; Hon Rl; NHS; Yth Flsp; 4-H; Pep Clb; Bsktbl; 4-H Awd; College.

DE MARCO, ANDREW; Canfield HS; Youngstown, OH; Cls Rep Sr Cls; Aud/Vis; Hon Rl; Hosp Ade; Jr NHS; Lbry Ade; NHS; Stu Cncl; Spn Clb; College; Med.

DE MARCO, DIANE; North Farmington HS; Farm Hills, MI; Cls Rep Frsh Cls; Cls Rep Soph Cls; Cl Rep Jr Cls; Cmp Fr Grls; Chrs; Hon Rl; Mdrgl; Natl Forn Lg; Calvin College; German.

DE MARCO, KATHY; Euclid Sr HS; Euclid, OH; 89/746 Cl Rep Jr Cls; Chrs; Hon Rl; NHS; Quill & Scroll; Treas Stu Cncl; Yrbk; OEA; Character Effort & Citizenship Awd; Cert Of Recognition Busns & Typing; Cert Of Merit French; College; Medical Sec.

DE MARCO, SAM; Lincoln HS; Shinnston, WV; 20/200 Pres Frsh Cls; Am Leg Boys St; Hon Rl; NHS; Stu Cncl; Sprt Ed Yrbk; Letter Bsbl; Letter Bsktbl; Letter Ftbl; Letter Trk; Univ; Math.

DE MARCO, SAMMY J; Lincoln HS; Shinnston, WV; 20/200 Pres Frsh Cls; Am Leg Boys St; Hon Rl; Jr NHS; NHS; Sprt Ed Yrbk; Pep Clb; Sec Spn Clb; Letter Bsbl; Letter Bsktbl; College; Math Tchr.

DEMAREE, CAROL; Noblesville HS; Noblesville, IN; 25/256 Trs Frsh Cls; Chrs; Hon Rl; Pol Wkr; Pres 4-H; Lat Clb; Treas OEA; 4-H Awd; Kiwan Awd; Lion Awd; Butler Univ; Cmnctns.

DE MARY, BETTY; Monongah HS; Monongah, WV; Cls Rep Frsh Cls; Cls Rep Soph Cls; Cl Rep Jr Cls; Hon Rl; Stu Cncl; Y-Teens; Yrbk; 4-H; Fr Clb; FHA; Fairmont St Coll; Med Records Tech.

DE MARY, KIMBERLY; Monongah HS; Fairmont, WV; 8/51 Hon Rl; NHS; Off Ade; Fr Clb; Mth Clb; Elk Awd; 4-H Awd; Voice Dem Awd; Fairmont State Coll; Foreign Lang.

DE MATAS, LISA G; Immaculata HS; Detroit, MI; 8/93 Trs Jr Cls; Hon Rl; NHS; Outstanding Schlrshp In Art; Diploma Merit In Spanish; Cert Service To The School; Wayne State Univ.

DE MATAS, RANDY; Benedictine HS; Detroit, MI; Hon Rl; Vocational Schl; Technology.

DE MATTIA, DEBORAH; North Farmington HS; Farm Hills, MI; Cls Rep Frsh Cls; Hon Rl; Jr NHS; Lbry Ade; NHS; Stu Cncl; Letter Swmmng; Mgrs; JA Awd; Michigan St Univ; Bio Sci.

DEMBCZYNSKI, PATRICIA; Eau Claire HS; Sodus, MI; 1/107 Sec Jr Cls; Band; Hon Rl; Pres NHS; Rptr Yrbk; Rptr Sch Nwsp; Ten; Var Ltr & Pin For Acad Achvmnt 78 & 79; Genrl Bus Awd 79; U S Hist Awd 79; Western Michigan Univ; Cnslr.

DEMBSKI, JULIE J; Lehman HS; Piqua, OH; VP Jr Cls; Pres Sr Cls; Hon Rl; Off Ade; Sch Mus; Sch Pl; Stu Cncl; Drama Clb; OEA; Pep Clb;.

DEMBY, BARBARA; Midview HS; Grafton, OH; 1/270 Am Leg Aux Girls St; Chrh Wkr; Hon Rl; Hosp Ade; Jr NHS; Lbry Ade; Mod UN; NHS; Off Ade; Sch Pl; Boston Univ; Physician.

DEMECHKO, EDWARD A; Woodrow Wilson HS; Youngstwn, OH; 16/345 Boy Scts; Chrh Wkr; NHS; Letter Bsbl; Letter Bsktbl; Letter Ftbl; Trk; Univ; Math.

DE MENT, CHRIS; Adena HS; Frankfort, OH; Am Leg Boys St; Band; Hon Rl; NHS; NHS; Stu Cncl; Pres 4-H; Pres FFA; Pep Clb;.

DE MENT, JOHN T; Nordonia HS; Macedonia, OH; 1/450 Boy Scts; Cmp Fr Grls; Hon Rl; NHS; Sct Actv; Sci Clb; Capt Ten; GAA; IM Sprt; Scr Kpr; Case Western Reserve Univ; Research.

DEMERS, GUY; Upper Arlington HS; Upper Arlington, OH; Cmnty Wkr; Sch Pl; Drama Clb; Fr Clb; Crs Cntry; Trk; IM Sprt; Ohio St Univ; Dentistry.

DE METER, DEBORA A; Highland HS; Highland, IN; 126/494 Hon Rl; Lbry Ade; NHS; Ger Clb; Key Clb; Sci Clb; Ind State Univ; R N.

DE MICCO, ANNA; Roosevelt Wilson HS; Mt Clare, WV; Cl Rep Jr Cls; Band; Treas Boy Scts; Hon Rl; Stu Cncl; VP Y-Teens; Fr Clb; Leo Clb; IM Sprt; Twrlr; W Virginia Univ; Fash Merch.

DEMIDOVICH, JILL; Van Wert HS; Van Wert, OH; 18/215 Band; Drm Mjrt; Hon Rl; Lbry Ade; NHS; Y-Teens; Fr Clb; Pep Clb; Sci Clb; IM Sprt; Miami Univ; Psych.

DEMING, KRIS; Caseville Public HS; Caseville, MI; Cls Rep Frsh Cls; VP Soph Cls; Band; Boy Scts; Hon Rl; Jr NHS; NHS; Sch Pl; Stu Cncl; Drama Clb; Univ Of Michigan; Med.

DE MIO, CARMEN; Holy Name Nazareth Acad; Cleveland, OH; Chrs; Hon Rl; Hosp Ade; Pol Wkr; Pres Y-Teens; Spn Clb; Bsbl; Cleveland State Univ; Tchr.

DEMIRJIAN, LISA; Kenston HS; Aurora, OH; Chrh Wkr; Drl Tm; Hon Rl; Univ; Tchr.

DEMIS, ELISA; Washington HS; Massillon, OH; Band; Chrs; VP Chrh Wkr; Girl Scts; Hon Rl; NHS; VP Lat Clb; Pep Clb; IM Sprt; Univ; Law.

DEMKO, DAVID; North Farmington HS; Farmington Hls, MI; 46/390 Band; Chrs; Hon Rl; NHS; Orch; Sch Mus; Rptr Yrbk; Yrbk; Natl Merit SF;.

DEMKO, RONALD; Cardinal Stritch HS; Oregon, OH; 27/225 FCA; Hon Rl; NHS; Sch Mus; Sch Pl; Stg Crw; Letter Bsktbl; Letter Ftbl; Letter Trk; Coach Actv; Univ Of Toledo; Med Tech.

DEMLER, MARY; John Adams HS; South Bend, IN; 28/385 Pres Chrs; Hon Rl; NHS; Sch Mus; Yth Flsp; Drama Clb; Natl Merit Ltr; Memorial Hospital Schl; Nursing.

DE MORE, GERALDETTA; Glen Oak HS; Cleveland, OH; Aud/Vis; Chrh Wkr; Hon Rl; Jr NHS; Off Ade; Yth Flsp; Yrbk; Scr Kpr; Mst Otstndng Math Stud 76; N E Oh Sci Fair 77; Univ; Comp Sci.

DE MOSS, ROSE M; Shelbyville Sr HS; Shelbyville, IN; 35/299 Am Leg Aux Girls St; Chrh Wkr; Cmnty Wkr; Hon Rl; Hosp Ade; Off Ade; Red Cr Ade; Pep Clb; Spn Clb; IM Sprt; Sec Of Spanish Club 77; Sec Of Sunshine Soc 79; Florida St Univ; Acctg.

DE MOTT, DOUG; Northwest HS; Jackson, MI; Hon Rl; NHS; St Of Mich Competitive Merit Schlrshp 79; Presidential Schlrshp Jackson Cmnty Coll 79; Jackson Cmnty Coll; Bus Admin.

DE MOTT, GERALD; Davison HS; Davison, MI; Cls Rep Soph Cls; Boy Scts; Sch Pl; Sct Actv; Stu Cncl; Fr Clb; Bsbl; Glf; God Cntry Awd; Univ Of Michigan; Engr.

DEMPSEY, BRIAN T; Harper Creek HS; Battle Creek, MI; 11/253 Boy Scts; Hon Rl; NHS; Yrbk; Letter Ftbl; Letter Ten; Letter Wrstlng; Opt Clb Awd; Univ Of Michigan; Engr Naval Archt.

DEMPSEY, DENISE; Athens HS; Athens, MI; 4/87 Hon Rl; NHS; Quill & Scroll; Sct Actv; Yth Flsp; Rptr Yrbk; Sec.

DEMPSEY, KELLY; William Henry Harrison HS; Evansville, IN; 24/461 Cls Rep Frsh Cls; VP Soph Cls; Cls Rep Soph Cls; Cl Rep Jr Cls; Cls Rep Sr Cls; Hon Rl; NHS; Sec Stu Cncl; Pep Clb; Capt Chrldng; Coll; Law.

DEMSHAR, DENISE; North Royalton HS; N Royalton, OH; Girl Scts; Hon Rl; Sch Pl; Stg Crw; Stu Cncl; Treas Drama Clb; College; Sociology.

DE MUNDO, MELINDA L; Notre Dame HS; Clarksburg, WV; 8/52 Chrh Wkr; NHS; Stg Crw; Sch Nwsp; Lat Clb; Bsbl; Academic Schrlshp 77; Davis & Elkins Coll.

DENBA, SALLY; Our Lady Of Mercy HS; W Bloomfield, MI; Girl Scts; Hon Rl; Jr NHS; NHS; Cit Awd;.

DENBOW, JAMIE; Morgan HS; Mc Connelsville, OH; Pres Frsh Cls; Cls Rep Soph Cls; Am Leg Aux Girls St; Band; Hon Rl; NHS; Mth Clb; Pep Clb; IM Sprt; PPFtbl; Future Sec Of America 1978; Muskingum Area Tech Coll; Sec Work.

DENDINGER, LINDA; River Valley HS; Marion, OH; Chrh Wkr; JA; Yth Flsp; DECA; 4-H; FFA; Ohio St Univ; Acctg.

DENDLER, JEFFREY; Central Baptist HS; Sharonville, OH; Cls Rep Soph Cls; Cl Rep Jr Cls; Chrs; Stu Cncl; Bsktbl; Socr; IM Sprt; Univ Of Cincinnati; Communications.

DE NEFF, THERESE; Gabriel Richard HS; Ann Arbor, MI; NHS; Fr Clb; Letter Bsbl; Letter Bsktbl; St Marys College; Bio.

DENEKAMP, JOHANNES G; Henry Ford Ii HS; Sterling Hts, MI; 16/418 CAP; Debate Tm; Hon Rl; Natl Forn Lg; NHS; Sch Pl; Stg Crw; Wayne St Univ; Med.

DENEKAS, LORI; St Joseph HS; Saint Joseph, MI; Cls Rep Sr Cls; Band; FCA; Hon Rl; NHS; Orch; Sch Mus; Stu Cncl; Yth Flsp; Hope Coll; Psych.

DENEWETH, EDWARD; Servite HS; Detroit, MI; Hon Rl; Jr NHS; Sch Pl; Spn Clb; Letter Ftbl; Letter Trk; IM Sprt; Univ; Bus.

DENEWETH, MICHAEL; Servite HS; Detroit, MI; 10/97 Hon Rl; Jr NHS; NHS; Capt Ftbl; IM Sprt; Tmr; Univ.

DEN HARTOG, DANIEL J; Hastings HS; Hastings, MI; Am Leg Boys St; Boy Scts; Chrh Wkr; NHS; Trk; NCTE; Natl Merit Ltr; Natl Merit SF; Natl Merit Schl; Hope Coll; Mech Engr.

DE NIKE, ELIZABETH; Troy HS; Troy, MI; 9/293 Band; Hon Rl; NHS; Rptr Sch Nwsp; Wayne St Univ; Vet Med.

DENISI, LAURA; Niles Sr HS; Niles, MI; Girl Scts; Hon Rl; JA; Off Ade; Stg Crw; Yth Flsp; Yrbk; Drama Clb; Cert Of Merit In French 77; Hnr Stu Awd 77; Univ; Soc Sci.

DENKHAUS, ROBERT; Firestone HS; Akron, OH; 70/380 Cmnty Wkr; JA; Univ; Forestry.

DENLINGER, KENT; Milton Union HS; W Milton, OH; 1/220 VP Sr Cls; Am Leg Boys St; Chrh Wkr; Hon Rl; NHS; FTA; Bsbl; Bsktbl; Crs Cntry; Cit Awd; Grace Coll.

DENMARK, MICHAEL; Garfield HS; Hamilton, OH; Band; Chrs; Hon Rl; Sch Mus; Stu Cncl; Boys Clb Am; Cls Rep Frsh Cls; Cls Rep Soph Cls; Cl Rep Jr Cls; Sal; Miami Univ; Bio & Bus.

DENNEHY, JOAN; Our Lady Of The Sea HS; Grse Pt Pk, MI; Cls Rep Frsh Cls; Pres Soph Cls; Cl Rep Jr Cls; VP Sr Cls; Chrh Wkr; Cmnty Wkr; Hon Rl; Ten; GAA; IM Sprt; Aquinas Coll; Educ.

DENNEY, CAROLYN; Elmhurst HS; Ft Wayne, IN; 71/346 Aud/Vis; Band; Chrh Wkr; Orch; Yth Flsp; Ind Univ; Music.

DENNEY, DAVID; Watkins Memorial HS; Pataskala, OH; Band; Debate Tm; Hon Rl; Spn Clb; Natl Merit Ltr; Sax Quartet Superior Rtng 77 78 & 79; Ohio St Univ; Physics.

DENNEY, DIANE; Huntington North HS; Huntington, IN; Off Ade; Pol Wkr; Yth Flsp; Fr Clb; FNA; Nursing.

DENNEY, SUZAN; Athens HS; Athens, MI; Band; Hon Rl; Jr NHS; NHS; Red Cr Ade; Stu Cncl; Pep Clb; Bsktbl; PPFtbl; Univ; Nursing.

DENNING, BERNITA; Mt Vernon Sr HS; Mt Vernon, IN; 4-H; FFA; Ger Clb; Busns Schl; Drafting.

DENNING, JACKIE; Southport HS; Indianapolis, IN; 60/485 Cmnty Wkr; FCA; Hon Rl; Off Ade; Stu Cncl; FBLA; FTA; Pep Clb; Chrldng; GAA; Nominee Strawberry Fest Queen & Valentines Queen; Sec/tres Foreign Stu Club; Indiana Univ; X Ray Tech.

DENNIS, ANTHONY; Green HS; Uniontown, OH; Cls Rep Frsh Cls; Cls Rep Soph Cls; Aud/Vis; Chrs; Hon Rl; Lbry Ade; Eng Clb; Lat Clb; Mth Clb; Oh Test Of Schsltc Achvmtn Hon Mntn; Ohio St Univ; Vet Med.

DENNIS, BRENT; Clearview HS; Lorain, OH; NHS; Bsktbl; Letter Ftbl; Letter Trk; Univ; Dent.

DENNIS, CONNIE; Loudonville HS; Loudonville, OH; 2/135 Hon Rl; NHS; Sch Pl; Ed Yrbk; Sch Nwsp; Drama Clb; 4-H; Pres FHA; Cit Awd; Bsktbl Statistician; Zion Luther League News Reporter; Ashland Coll; Acctg.

DENNIS, CYNTHIA K; Miami Trace HS; New Holland, OH; AFS; Band; Cmp Fr Grls; Chrs; Drl Tm; Sch Pl; Stg Crw; Yth Flsp; Drama Clb; Pres 4-H; Moorhead Univ.

DENNIS, DEBORAH; Maumee HS; Maumee, OH; 52/316 Hon Rl; Off Ade; Gym; Trk; IM Sprt; PPFtbl; Univ; Med.

DENNIS, IDA; Maysville HS; Zanesville, OH; Hon Rl; Hosp Ade; Pep Clb;.

DENNIS, KAREN; Laingsburg HS; Laingsburg, MI; Band; Girl Scts; Hon Rl; Lbry Ade; NHS; Off Ade; Sct Actv; 4-H; Ger Clb; Capt Trk; Baker Jr Coll; Fshn Mdse.

DENNIS, KELLY; Whiteland Comm HS; Franklin, IN; VP Frsh Cls; Cls Rep Soph Cls; Cl Rep Jr Cls; Band; FCA; Stu Cncl; Letter Bsktbl; Capt Trk; PPFtbl; Franklin Coll; Eng.

DENNIS, LINDA J; Anderson HS; Anderson, IN; 2/402 Cls Rep Frsh Cls; Cls Rep Soph Cls; Hon Rl; Jr NHS; Pol Wkr; Y-Teens; Mth Clb; Pep Clb; Spn Clb; Ftbl; Indiana Univ; Medicine.

DENNIS, ROBERT R; Claymont HS; Uhrichsville, OH; Trs Jr Cls; Am Leg Boys St; Hon Rl; Stu Cncl; Yrbk; Ftbl; Wrstlng; Univ.

DENNIS, SCOTT; Elk Rapids HS; Elk Rapids, MI; Trs Frsh Cls; Trs Soph Cls; Trs Jr Cls; Debate Tm; Hon Rl; Natl Forn Lg; Sch Mus; Sch Pl; Drama Clb; Ftbl; I Was Accepted At And Attended Operation Bentley 79; Qualified For The St Of Mim Competitive Schlrshp 80; Univ; Sci.

DENNIS, SCOTT; Ann Arbor Pioneer HS; Ann Arbor, MI; 6/606 Chrs; Hon Rl; Lit Mag; Mdrgl; Sch Mus; NCTE; Natl Merit SF; Natl Merit Schl; Univ Of Chicago.

DENNIS, SCOTT; Buchanan HS; Niles, MI; Hon Rl; Off Ade; VICA; Vocation School; Serv Manager.

DENNIS, SUSAN; Marlette Comm HS; Marlette, MI; Band; Cmp Fr Grls; Chrh Wkr; Cmnty Wkr; Hon Rl; NHS; Pol Wkr; Red Cr Ade; Stu Cncl; Yth Flsp; 1st Plc Information Comm II Mi St BOEC Conf; Pearl Baxter Schlrshp Awd Marlette HS; Natl Lifesaving Awd; Northwood Inst Univ; Exec Sec.

DENNIS, TAMMY; Shenandoah HS; Caldwell, OH; 4/90 Pres Soph Cls; Pres Sr Cls; Pres Band; Chrs; Hon Rl; NHS; Sch Mus; Sch Pl; Muskingum Area Tech ; Data Proc.

DENNISON, DAWNA K; Liberty HS; Clarksburg, WV; Cls Rep Frsh Cls; Cls Rep Soph Cls; Cl Rep Jr Cls; Band; Cmp Fr Grls; Chrs; Girl Scts; Hon Rl; Jr NHS; Red Cr Ade; WVU; Interior Decorator.

DENNISON, DENISE; Ovid Elsie HS; Owosso, MI; 7/170 Band; Drl Tm; Hon Rl; NHS; Sch Mus; 4-H; Pep Clb; Pom Pon; PPFtbl; Mic State Univ; Med Tech.

DENNISON, KIMBERLY; Lewis Cnty HS; Camden, WV; Hst Soph Cls; Cls Rep Soph Cls; Hst Jr Cls; Cl Rep Jr Cls; Hst Sr Cls; Cls Rep Sr Cls; Boy Scts; Chrh Wkr; Cmnty Wkr; Hon Rl; Natl Schlstc Writing Awd; Natl Yth Ideals Awd; Stu Meritorious Awd; Chatham Coll; Poli Sci.

DENNISON, RHONDA; South Central HS; Laconia, IN; Cls Rep Soph Cls; Cl Rep Jr Cls; Cls Rep Sr Cls; Hon Rl; Stu Cncl; Yth Flsp; 4-H; FHA; Mth Clb; Bsktbl;.

DENNISON JR, RANDAL; Central HS; Evansville, IN; 25/490 Chrh Wkr; Hosp Ade; NHS; Stu Cncl; Pres Yth Flsp; Pres Ger Clb; Natl Merit SF; Univ Of Evansville; Law.

DENNISTON, DAVID; Greenville Sr HS; Greenville, OH; 6/360 Hon Rl; NHS; Sch Mus; Yth Flsp; Drama Clb; 4-H; Sci Clb; Pres Spn Clb; 4-H Awd; Spanish Awd; Carried Flag For Graduation; Ohio St Univ; Natural Resources.

DENNISTON, PAULA; Center Line HS; Center Line, MI; Cl Rep Jr Cls; Cls Rep Sr Cls; Band; Hon Rl; NHS; Stu Cncl; Rptr Sch Nwsp; Fr Clb; Scr Kpr; Univ; Sociology.

DENNISTON, ROBERTA; Arcanum Butler HS; Arcanum, OH; 42/99 Chrs; Chrh Wkr; Cmnty Wkr; Hosp Ade; Lbry Ade; FHA; FHA Jr & Chapter Degree; Busns Schl; Bookkeeping.

DENNY, ALLEN; Catholic Central HS; Grand Rapids, MI; Band; Hon Rl; Pres JA; Pep Clb; Trk; IM Sprt; JA Awd; Most Valubl Delegate NAJAC Grand Rapids Area 77; Mi Comp Schlrshp 79; Michigan St Univ; Acctg.

DENNY, BRIAN; Georgetown HS; Georgetown, OH; 4/91 Am Leg Boys St; Boy Scts; Hon Rl; NHS; Sct Actv; Rptr Yrbk; Fr Clb; Treas Sci Clb; Bsktbl; Trk; Univ; Chem Engr.

DENNY, CYNTHIA; Cooley HS; Detroit, MI; Cls Rep Sr Cls; Chrs; Chrh Wkr; Hon Rl; NHS; Off Ade; Stu Cncl; Cit Awd; St Of Mi Schlrshp 78; Genrl Elec Carbolouy Schlrshp 79; Univ Of Detroit; Engr.

DENNY, DOUG; Napoleon HS; Napoleon, OH; Hon Rl; Stg Crw; Ftbl; Trk; IM Sprt; College.

DENSFORD, BRIAN; Crothersville HS; Austin, IN; Band; Chrh Wkr; Hon Rl; Yth Flsp; Rptr Yrbk; 4-H; FFA; Pep Clb; Trk; 4-H Awd; Star Chapt Farmer FFA 78; Plcmnt In Agri Prod FFA 78; Univ; Conservation.

DENSFORD, MONTY; Crothersville Cmnty HS; Austin, IN; VP Frsh Cls; Pres Soph Cls; Band; Hon Rl; Sct Actv; Yth Flsp; Rptr Yrbk; Pres 4-H; FFA; Bsktbl; Voc Schl; Mech.

DENSMORE, DEANNA; Morenci Area HS; Morenci, MI; 6/66 Am Leg Aux Girls St; Chrs; Hon Rl; NHS; 4-H; Key Clb; Spn Clb; Jackson Comm Coll; Law.

DENSON, DONNA; East Canton HS; E Canton, OH; 1/104 Val; Chrs; Hon Rl; Jr NHS; Lbry Ade; NHS; Stg Crw; Rptr Sch Nwsp; Drama Clb; Sci Clb; Voc Schl; Nursing.

DENSON, JOHN; Highland Park Cmnty HS; Highland Park, MI; 10/350 Hon Rl; Orch; Sch Nwsp; Massachusetts Inst Tech; Elec Engr.

DENSON, LAVERNE; George Washington HS; E Chicago, IN; 34/270 Pres Soph Cls; Chrh Wkr; Hon Rl; Orch; Sch Mus; Stu Cncl; Yth Flsp; Boys Clb Am; Ind State Univ; Med Lab Tech.

DENSTEDT, WILLIAM F; Hale HS; Hale, MI; 3/67 Trs Soph Cls; Trs Jr Cls; Am Leg Boys St; Band; Hon Rl; Lbry Ade; NHS; Sch Pl; Drama Clb; Pres Class Of 80 Sr Trip Club For Grd 12 Elec Grd 11; Ski Club Throughout HS; Michigan St Univ; Ind Engr.

DENT, JOHN N; H H Dow HS; Midland, MI; 51/480 Band; Boy Scts; Chrh Wkr; Hon Rl; Orch; Sch Mus; Lat Clb; Capt Swmmng; Natl Merit SF; Univ Of Michigan.

DENT, LAURA J; Robert S Rogers HS; Toledo, OH; Hon Rl; NHS; Mth Clb; Pres Sci Clb; Spn Clb; Crs Cntry; Trk; GAA; IM Sprt; PPFtbl; Cert Of Merit; Spanish Honorary & Cert Of Merit; Case Western Reserve Univ; Bio.

DENT, MIRIAM; Eastlake North HS; Willowick, OH; 12/706 Trs Soph Cls; Trs Jr Cls; Trs Sr Cls; Am Leg Aux Girls St; Hon Rl; Jr NHS; NHS; Sch Pl; Sch Nwsp; Drama Clb; College; Law.

DENTINO, D ARCY; Kenston HS; Chagrin Fl, OH; 24/220 Cls Rep Frsh Cls; Cls Rep Soph Cls; Trs Jr Cls; Cls Rep Sr Cls; Chrs; Hon Rl; FHA; Gym; Chrldng; Mat Maids; Jr Homecmng Attndnt 78; Jr Prom Attdndnt 79; Homecmng & Chrstmns Dance Comm 78; Univ; Theater Arts.

DENTON, HELEN; Greenwood Cmnty HS; Greenwood, IN; 67/275 Cls Rep Sr Cls; Band; Cmnty Wkr; Hon Rl; FBLA; Pep Clb; Cit Awd; Univ; Bus.

DENTON, JOHN L; Northmer HS; Galion, OH; Cls Rep Soph Cls; Am Leg Boys St; Band; Chrs; Hon Rl; NHS; Orch; Sch Mus; Stu Cncl; Spn Clb; Optometry.

DENTON, TERESA; Grant HS; Howard Cty, MI; Cls Rep Frsh Cls; Band; Chrh Wkr; Cmnty Wkr; Hon Rl; Hosp Ade; Lbry Ade; Orch; Sch Pl; VP Stu Cncl; Univ; Nursing.

DENTON, WENDELL; Southwestern HS; Franklin, IN; 43/72 Pres Sr Cls; Aud/Vis; Sch Mus; Sch Pl; Stg Crw; Yrbk; Sch Nwsp; Drama Clb; Pres FDA; FFA; Ivy Tech Schl; Elec.

DEOBALD, BRIAN; Western Reserve Acad; Aurora, OH; 27/86 Cl Rep Jr Cls; Hon Rl; Sch Mus; Sch Pl; Stu Cncl; Rptr Sch Nwsp; Letter Swmmng; IM Sprt; College; Policitcal Scic.

DE PAEPE, DENISE; Penn HS; Mishawaka, IN; 92/500 Hon Rl; Mod UN; NHS; Sch Pl; Spn Clb; PPFtbl; Peer Cnsrl Grp Called The Trust Co 2 Yrs; Ball St Univ; Spec Educ.

DE PALMA, RALPH L; University HS; Cleve Hts, OH; 1/87 Val; Boy Scts; Pres Chrs; Hon Rl; Sch Mus; Key Clb; Letter Crs Cntry; Harvard Univ.

DE PAS, DOREEN; Carney Nadeau Public HS; Wilson, MI; 3/22 Hst Jr Cls; Band; Hon Rl; Sch Pl; Stu Cncl; Ed Sch Nwsp; Rptr Sch Nwsp; Sch Nwsp; Drama Clb; Voc Sch; Commerical Arts.

DE PASCALE, GINNY; Cardinal Mooney HS; Youngstown, OH; 87/296 Hon Rl; College; Nursing.

DE PAUL, VINCENT; Stow Lakeview HS; Stow, OH; Rptr Sch Nwsp; Ftbl; Kent State; Law.

DE PEW, DARIN; Lemon Monroe HS; Monroe, OH; 42/278 Chrh Wkr; Hon Rl; NHS; Yth Flsp; Ger Clb; Glf; Mt Vernon Nazarene Coll; Soc Sci.

DE PEW, STERLING; Northrop HS; Ft Wayne, IN; Band; Hon Rl; Orch; Sch Mus; Crs Cntry; Music.

DE PIETRO, JERI; Louisville HS; Louisville, OH; Band; Chrs; Chrh Wkr; Cmnty Wkr; Lbry Ade; Sch Mus; College; Art.

DE PINET, BARBARA; Tiffin Calvert HS; Tiffin, OH; Band; Girl Scts; Hon Rl; Orch; Sch Mus; 4-H; Ger Clb; Mat Maids; Tmr; 4-H Awd; Univ; Early Childhood Ed.

DE PINET, CINDY; Seneca East HS; Bloomvile, OH; VP Frsh Cls; VP Soph Cls; Cl Rep Jr Cls; Am Leg Aux Girls St; Band; Sec Chrs; Hon Rl; Sch Pl; Stu Cncl; Drama Clb; Vocational Schl; Busns Sec.

DE PLANTY, LUANNE; Rockville Jr Sr HS; Rockville, IN; 9/85 Am Leg Aux Girls St; Band; Chrs; FCA; Hon Rl; NHS; Indiana St Univ; Elem Ed.

DE PUGH, TRACY A; Huntington HS; Waverly, OH; 17/98 Am Leg Boys St; Hon Rl; Bsbl; Bsktbl; Ftbl; Trk; Appointed Tp Rep Schl For Boys St Best Foul Shooting Percentage Trophy 79; Univ.

DEPUTY, SUSAN; Wood Memorial HS; Oakland City, IN; 25/125 Band; Drl Tm; FCA; Girl Scts; Hon Rl; Sct Actv; Sch Nwsp; Vincennes Univ; Med Sec.

DERALAS, DEAN; Barberton HS; Barberton, OH; Cls Rep Frsh Cls; Cl Rep Jr Cls; Chrh Wkr; Hon Rl; Stu Cncl; Yth Flsp; Yrbk; Beta Clb; Key Clb; Lat Clb; Akron Univ; Bus.

DE RAMO, TAMMY; Bristol HS; Bristolville, OH; Trs Frsh Cls; Chrs; Sch Pl; Stu Cncl; Rptr Yrbk; Bsktbl; Voc Schl; Sci.

DE RAUD, MICHELE; Plymouth Salem HS; Canton, MI; 13/535 Hon Rl; NHS; Sch Pl; Stu Cncl; Coach Actv; Capt Pom Pon; Natl Merit Ltr; Hillsdale Coll Pres Schlrshp 79; Individual Achvmnt Trophy At Pom Pon Camp 79; Principals Academic Awd 79; Hillsdale Coll; Poli Econ.

DERBIN, JANICE; Clay HS; South Bend, IN; Trs Sr Cls; Chrs; Chrh Wkr; Hon Rl; NHS; Quill & Scroll; Chmn Stu Cncl; Pres Yth Flsp; Sch Nwsp; Fr Clb; Bethel Coll.

DERDA, JULIE; La Salle HS; South Bend, IN; 49/448 Cmp Fr Grls; Chrs; Chrh Wkr; Girl Scts; Hon Rl; Hosp Ade; Sch Mus; Sdlty; Eng Clb; 4-H; Winner Creative Writing Contest La Salle 79; Notre Dame Univ; Eng.

DERECKI, BARBARA; Hartland HS; Brighton, MI; 1/250 VP Soph Cls; Cls Rep Soph Cls; VP Jr Cls; Hon Rl; Lit Mag; NHS; Rptr Yrbk; College.

DEREICH, MARK; Struthers HS; Struthers, OH; 16/276 Debate Tm; Lat Clb; Univ.

DEREMER, DIANA; Canton South HS; Canton, OH; Hon Rl; Off Ade; Sch Pl; Drama Clb; Rdo Clb; Mgrs; Scr Kpr; Tmr; Univ Of Akron; Bus.

DERICKO, DEBORAH; Grandview Heights HS; Columbus, OH; 3/132 Pres Frsh Cls; Drl Tm; Girl Scts; Hon Rl; Jr NHS; Yrbk; Fr Clb; Lat Clb; Hockey; Trk; Ohio Tests Of Schlstc Achvmnt; Franklin Univ; Acctg.

DE RICO, HELEN L; Buckhannon Upshur HS; Buckhannon, WV; Chrh Wkr; Hon Rl; Lbry Ade; Off Ade; Stu Cncl; FBLA; Sec.

DERISI, TOM; Crown Point HS; Crown Point, IN; Cls Rep Frsh Cls; Cls Rep Soph Cls; Hon Rl; Jr NHS; Sch Nwsp; Ftbl; Indiana Univ; Chem.

DERKS, DOUGLAS; Sparta HS; Conklin, MI; Trs Frsh Cls; Band; Hon Rl; Treas Rptr Yrbk; Letter Glf; Letter Ten; Western Michigan Univ; Marketing.

DE RONGHE, BETH; Dominican HS; Detroit, MI; Cls Rep Frsh Cls; Cl Rep Jr Cls; Sch Mus; Sch Pl; Stg Crw; Stu Cncl; Univ; Med.

DE RONNE, DIANE; Our Lady Star Of The Sea HS; Grosse Pt Park, MI; Girl Scts; Hon Rl; Sch Mus; Sch Pl; Yrbk; GAA; IM Sprt; Univ Of Detroit; Dent Hygenist.

DE RONNE, DIANE; Our Lady Star Of The Sea HS; Grse Pt Pk, MI; Girl Scts; Hon Rl; Sch Mus; Sch Pl; Sct Actv; Yrbk; GAA; IM Sprt; Univ Of Detroit.

DE ROSA, SUZY; Buckeye Valley HS; Ashley, OH; 14/289 Hosp Ade; Sch Mus; Stg Crw; Ed Sch Nwsp; 4-H; Key Clb; Pep Clb; Capt Gym; Trk; Ohio St Univ; Phys Ther.

DERR, JANINE; Holland HS; Holland, MI; 11/365 Cls Rep Frsh Cls; Chrs; Chrh Wkr; Cmnty Wkr; Hon Rl; Hosp Ade; NHS; Off Ade; Sch Pl; Drama Clb; Bronson Methodist Schl; RN.

DERR, JEFFREY W; Huntington North HS; Huntington, IN; 16/600 Am Leg Boys St; Boy Scts; Chrs; Chrh Wkr; Hon Rl; Stg Crw; Ger Clb; Boy Of Month 76; Optimist Clb; NEDT Awrd 77; Chosen Arch Acolyte 79; Univ; Comp Sci.

DERR, VICKIE; Tuslaw HS; No Lawrnece, OH; Band; Drm Mjrt; Girl Scts; Hon Rl; Orch; Sch Mus; Stg Crw; Y-Teens; FTA; Spn Clb; Stark Tech Coll; Real Estate.

DERRICKSON, MIKE; Tri Jr Sr HS; New Lisbon, IN; 28/84 Cls Rep Frsh Cls; Boy Scts; Letter Bsbl; Letter Bsktbl; Letter Crs Cntry; Scr Kpr; Tmr; Bsbl All Conf Most Stolen Bases 78; Bsktbl Awd 78; Univ; Mech Engr.

DERROW, JEANIE; Put In Bay HS; Put In Bay, OH; 6/13 Cl Rep Jr Cls; Pres Sr Cls; Chrs; Cmnty Wkr; Hon Rl; NHS; Sch Pl; Rptr Yrbk; Drama Clb; St Mary Of The Woods Univ; Theatre.

DERSCH, DAVID M; Heritage Hall Christian HS; Muncie, IN; 1/7 Pres Frsh Cls; VP Jr Cls; Sch Pl; Ed Yrbk; Capt Bsktbl; Capt Socr; C of C Awd; Natl Merit Ltr; Opt Clb Awd; SAR Awd; College;.

DERSE, JAYNE; Groves HS; Birmingham, MI; Cls Rep Frsh Cls; Pres Soph Cls; AFS; Chrh Wkr; Girl Scts; Hon Rl; Mod UN; Orch; Sch Pl; Stu Cncl; Bloomfield Twnshp Cmnty Serv 77; Univ; Bus Admin.

DERSHEM, E S; Van Wert HS; Van Wert, OH; 40/206 Band; Chrs; Jr NHS; Sch Pl; Fr Clb; IM Sprt; God Cntry Awd; JA Awd; Univ Of Cincinnati; Engr Sci.

DERUSHA, SUSAN; Engadine Consolidated HS; Naubinway, MI; 2/38 VP Frsh Cls; VP Soph Cls; VP

Jr Cls; Cls Rep Sr Cls; Sal; Hon Rl; Stu Cncl; Trk; Chrldng; Cit Awd; Ferris State Coll; Bus.

DERWACTER, KENDRA; Maysville HS; Zanesville, OH; 29/201 Band; Chrs; Drl Tm; Girl Scts; Hon Rl; NHS; Off Ade; Yth Flsp; Sec FTA; Letter Trk; Organ Merit 75; Hon Merit Talent Contest For Organ 75; Tech Schl; Dent Hygiene.

DERY, JEANNETTE; Ladywood HS; Livonia, MI; 1/74 Val; Chrs; Hon Rl; JA; Lbry Ade; Lit Mag; NHS; Pres Orch; Red Cr Ade; Sch Mus; Wayne St Univ; Comp Sci.

DERY, JULIE; Bishop Foley HS; Washington, MI; Band; Girl Scts; Hon Rl; Off Ade; Sch Mus; Sch Pl; Fr Clb; Pom Pon; Oakland Univ; Jeweler.

DERYCK, CHRIS; Buchtel HS; Akron, OH; Cls Rep Soph Cls; Band; Hon Rl; Stg Crw; Lat Clb; Capt Crs Cntry; Letter Swmmng; Letter Trk; Columbia Univ; Envir Sci.

DE RYCKERE, ANDREW J; South Bend Washington HS; South Bend, IN; 18/450 Am Leg Boys St; Hon Rl; NHS; Yrbk; Lang Clb; Youth For Undrstndng Foreign Exchng Stndt Sweden; Univ; Acctg.

DERYCK JR, RICHARD C; Garfield HS; Akron, OH; 35/400 Cmnty Wkr; NHS; Lat Clb; Letter Ftbl; College.

DE SALVO, CAROL; Windham HS; Windham, OH; Cls Rep Frsh Cls; Cls Rep Soph Cls; Cl Rep Jr Cls; Chrh Wkr; Hon Rl; Sch Pl; Rptr Yrbk; Yrbk; Drama Clb; Hiram College; Comp.

DESANA, RAYMOND; Trenton HS; Wyandotte, MI; 98/535 Hon Rl; NHS; Stu Cncl; Bsbl; Ftbl; Hockey; IM Sprt; Natl Merit SF; Albion Coll; Bus Admin.

DESANTIAGO, STEVE; Griffith HS; Griffith, IN; 20/230 Cmnty Wkr; Hon Rl; NHS; Wrstlng; Am Leg Awd; Lion Awd; Natl Merit Schl; Ind Ball State; Architect.

DE SANTIS, ANNE; Bishop Gallagher HS; Harper Woods, MI; 11/332 Cls Rep Frsh Cls; Cls Rep Soph Cls; Cl Rep Jr Cls; VP Sr Cls; Girl Scts; Hon Rl; NHS; Sch Pl; Stu Cncl; Letter Mgrs; Central Michigan Univ; Commrcl Desgn.

DE SANTIS, KATHLEEN; Fraser HS; Fraser, MI; 11/620 Hon Rl; Jr NHS; NHS; Pres Stu Cncl; Rptr Sch Nwsp; Pres Spn Clb; IM Sprt; PPFtbl; Cit Awd; Dnfth Awd; Wayne St Univ; Pre Med.

DE SANTIS, LAWRENCE; Chanel HS; Maple Hts, OH; 16/109 Hon Rl; Lbry Ade; Off Ade; Gym; Cleveland State Univ; Chem Engr.

DESCH, JENNIFER; Brown County HS; Nashville, IN; 3/208 Band; Quill & Scroll; Sch Pl; Rptr Yrbk; 4-H; Letter Trk; Chrldng; College; Phys Therapy.

DESCH, JOSEPH M; Archbishop Alter HS; Dayton, OH; Cls Rep Frsh Cls; Cl Rep Jr Cls; Boy Scts; PAVAS; Sch Mus; Pres Sct Actv; Stu Cncl; VP Key Clb; Pep Clb; Rdo Clb; Ohio St Univ; Bus Advertising.

DESCH, MAGGIE; Coldwater HS; Coldwater, OH; 1/150 Band; Chrs; Hon Rl; NHS; Sch Mus; Drama Clb; Ger Clb; Letter Bsktbl; Letter Crs Cntry; Letter Trk; Univ.

DE SELLEM, MARLENE; Southern Local HS; Salineville, OH; Band; Yth Flsp; 4-H; FNA; Lat Clb; Pep Clb; Trk; GAA; Coll; Vet.

DESERO, TINA; Richmond HS; Richmond, MI; 11/161 Chrs; Hon Rl; NHS; Sch Mus; Sch Pl; St Clair Cmnty Coll; Elem Educ.

DESHANO, BRIAN; Bullock Creek HS; Freeland, MI; Band; Hon Rl; 4-H; 4-H Awd; Univ.

DESHON, GORDON; Valley View HS; Frmrsvl, OH; FCA; Yth Flsp; FFA; Wrstlng; IM Sprt; Or U.

DE SIMPELARE, TOM; Unionville Sebewaing HS; Unionville, MI; Band; Hon Rl; NHS; Sch Nwsp; 4-H; FFA; Bsbl; Bsktbl; 4-H Awd; Delta Coll; Elect.

DESKINS, DEBBIE; Big Creek HS; Coalwood, WV; 2/148 Sec Frsh Cls; VP Soph Cls; Pres Jr Cls; Am Leg Aux Girls St; Aud/Vis; Band; Chrh Wkr; Hon Rl; Hosp Ade; NHS; Marshall Univ; Acctg.

DESKINS, SANDRA J; Shady Spring HS; Daniels, WV; 10/164 Cls Rep Soph Cls; Band; Chrh Wkr; FCA; Hon Rl; JA; NHS; Stu Cncl; Yth Flsp; Rptr Yrbk; Bluefield Coll; Phys Therapy.

DE SMET, KATHRYN; Servite HS; East Detroit, MI; VP Soph Cls; Hon Rl; Jr NHS; NHS; Stu Cncl; Rptr Sch Nwsp; Pep Clb; Letter Trk; Letter Chrldng; Detroit Bus College; Acctng.

DESNOYER, C; Lumen Christi HS; Jackson, MI; Hon Rl; Y-Teens;.

DESOFF, BETTY; Cody HS; Detroit, MI; Band; Hon Rl; PPFtbl; Univ Of Mic; Computer Program.

DESOTELL, MARK; Menominee HS; Menominee, MI; 3/260 Am Leg Boys St; Cmnty Wkr; Hon Rl; Stu Cncl; Boys Clb Am; Civ Clb; Mth Clb; Mic State; Engr.

DE STEFANO, KAREN; Edgewood HS; Ellettsville, IN; 15/230 Band; Cmnty Wkr; Drl Tm; Hon Rl; Off Ade; Sch Mus; Stg Crw; Stu Cncl; Rptr Yrbk; Drama Clb; Ind Univ; Bus.

DESTRAMPE, LORI; Gladstone Area HS; Gladstone, MI; 8/300 Sec Soph Cls; Cls Rep Soph Cls; Band; Girl Scts; Hon Rl; Quill & Scroll; Sch Pl; Stg Crw; Stu Cncl; Rptr Sch Nwsp; Univ; Jrnlsm.

DESTRO, KIMBERLY; Brunswick HS; Brunswick, OH; 9/465 Treas Band; Chrh Wkr; Debate Tm; Hon Rl; NHS; Sch Mus; Drama Clb; Akron Univ; Computer Science.

DE TEMPLE, BONNY; Bishop Donahue HS; Mc Mechen, WV; Chrh Wkr; Cmnty Wkr; Hon Rl; NHS; Sch Mus; Sch Pl; Capt Chrldng; GAA; Business School; Secretarial.

DETKE, JOHN; St Anne HS; Warren, MI; Cls Rep Soph Cls; Cmnty Wkr; Hon Rl; Pol Wkr; Stu Cncl; Univ Of Mic; Engr.

DETMER, PATRICIA; Dominican HS; Detroit, MI; Cls Rep Frsh Cls; Cmp Fr Grls; Girl Scts; Hon Rl; NHS; Off Ade; College; Grade Schl Teacher.

DE TORAKIS, KALLIOPE; Ellet Sr HS; Akron, OH; 14/363 Chrh Wkr; Hon Rl; Jr NHS; NHS; Off Ade; Orch; Fr Clb; Akron Univ; Spec Educ.

DETRICK, TAMMY; Dublin HS; Dublin, OH; 5/160 Sec Frsh Cls; Cls Rep Frsh Cls; Trs Soph Cls; VP Jr Cls; Pres Sr Cls; Am Leg Aux Girls St; Band; Chrs; Hosp Ade; NHS; Miami Univ; Pre Med.

DETROW, PAUL; Crestview Local HS; Leetonia, OH; 2/84 Cls Rep Soph Cls; Pres Jr Cls; Sal; Pres Chrs; Chrh Wkr; Hon Rl; NHS; Sch Mus; Stu Cncl; 4-H; Malone Coll; Bus Admin.

DETTERER, SUE; Patrick Henry HS; Napoleon, OH; Chrh Wkr; Hon Rl; Bsktbl; Trk; GAA; IM Sprt; Vollyball Award 1978; Sports Hall Of Fame 1977; Univ; Nursing.

DETTMER, LORETTA; Struthers HS; Struthers, OH; Band; Hon Rl; Lbry Ade; Y-Teens; Fr Clb; FTA; Geneva Univ; Psych.

DETWEILER, JULIE; Wayne HS; Ft Wayne, IN; 22/301 Am Leg Aux Girls St; Chrh Wkr; Hon Rl; JA; NHS; Off Ade; Orch; Pol Wkr; OEA; Shorthnd Awd 150 Wrds Per Min 1979; Prepared Verbl Cmnctns Top 1/ In St 1979; Outstndng Bus Educ Stdnt 79; Baptist Bible Coll; Bus.

DETWILER, JEFFREY S; Walled Lake Central HS; Walled Lake, MI; Cls Rep Sr Cls; Cmnty Wkr; Hon Rl; Jr NHS; NHS; Off Ade; Stu Cncl; Letter Bsbl; Bsktbl; Capt Ftbl; Princeton Univ; Engr.

DETWILER, LYNN; Grant HS; Bailey, MI; Hon Rl; Stg Crw; Spn Clb; Coll; Marine Bio.

DETWILER, SCOTT; Marcellus Community HS; Decator, MI; Hon Rl; Lit Mag; NHS; Letter Bsbl; Letter Bsktbl; Letter Ftbl; Letter Trk; Amos Alonzo Stagg Schlr Athlete Schlrshp 79; 1st Tm All S W Athletic Confernc Split End Ftbl 78; Univ Of Chicago; Law.

DETWILER, SHARON; Tippicanoe Valley HS; Warsaw, IN; 62/160 Band; Chrs; Hon Rl; Sch Mus; Sch Pl; Drama Clb; 4-H; Pep Clb; Spn Clb; 4-H Awd; One Of 15 Finalists In St Fair Fshn Review 78; Previouse Hnr Of Whos Who Last Year 78; Intl Bus Coll; Sec.

DEUBER, CATHY; Barberton HS; Barberton, OH; 3/460 AFS; Chrh Wkr; Jr NHS; NHS; Sct Actv; Ger Clb; Rotary Awd; Voice Dem Awd; Univ; Sci.

DEUEL, LYNNE; Onsted Community HS; Onsted, MI; 2/120 Sec Jr Cls; Hon Rl; NHS; Letter Trk; Chrldng; Western Michigan Univ; Acctg.

DEUERING, GREG; Memorial HS; Evansville, IN; Hon Rl; VICA; Indiana Voc Tech Schl; Comp Tech.

DEUITCH, MATT; Greenfield Central HS; Greenfield, IN; 1/325 Pres Frsh Cls; Am Leg Boys St; VP Chrs; NHS; Sch Pl; Treas Drama Clb; Ger Clb; Pres Mth Clb; College; Mathematics.

DEULEY, ROBERT; Calhoun HS; Mt Zion, WV; VP Frsh Cls; Sec Jr Cls; Hon Rl; 4-H; Mth Clb; Sci Clb; Bsbl; Bsktbl; Ftbl; Trk; 2nd Plc In Area Sci Fair 77; West Virginia St Univ; Comp Prog.

DEUR, DWIGHT; Fremont HS; Fremont, MI; 36/238 Band; Hon Rl; Northwestern Mic College; Data Proc.

DE VANE, LAURA; George Washinton HS; Charleston, WV; JA; Keyettes; West Virginia Univ; Comp Sci.

DE VANEY, DARRYL; Lapeer East HS; Lapeer, MI; Am Leg Boys St; Band; Hon Rl; Natl Forn Lg; NHS; PAVAS; Sch Pl; Stg Crw; 4-H; Am Leg Awd; Le Tourneau Coll; Elec Engr.

DE VAUL, SUSAN; Mannington HS; Mannington, WV; Am Leg Aux Girls St; Chrh Wkr; Hon Rl; NHS; Fr Clb; IM Sprt; Mat Maids; Univ; Med Tech.

DE VAULT, LINDA; Father Joseph Wehrle Mem HS; Columbus, OH; 4/115 Cmp Fr Grls; Chrs; Girl Scts; Hon Rl; NHS; Stu Cncl; Capt Chrldng; Mat Maids;.

DE VAULT, LIZ; Lowell HS; Lowell, IN; 56/235 Hon Rl; Fr Clb; OEA; PPFtbl; Bus Schl; Exec Sec.

DE VAULT, MARK; Fairless HS; Beach City, OH; Boy Scts; Sct Actv; Stu Cncl; Rptr Sch Nwsp; Trk; IM Sprt; Mgrs; Scr Kpr; R G Drage Voc Schl; Distributive Ed.

DEVENPORT, EARL; La Brae HS; Newton Falls, OH; 30/200 Band; Boy Scts; Chrh Wkr; Hon Rl; Sct Actv; 4-H; Fr Clb; Pep Clb; Spn Clb; Bsbl; Youngstown St Univ; Comp Mech.

DEVERS, JULIA; Piqua Ctrl HS; Piqua, OH; Band; Chrs; Chrh Wkr; Hon Rl; Jr NHS; NHS; Orch; Sch Mus; Sch Pl; Sec Drama Clb; Univ; Med.

DEVETSKI, DANIEL L; John Adams HS; So Bend, IN; Cls Rep Frsh Cls; Chrh Wkr; Cmnty Wkr; Hon Rl; NHS; Letter Ten; Natl Merit SF; Univ; Med.

DE VILLE, DAVE; Leetonia HS; Leetonia, OH; Boy Scts; Hon Rl; 4-H; Bsbl; Bsktbl; Ftbl; Trk; Coach Actv; College; Drafting.

DE VINE, KEVIN; Charlestown HS; Chrlstn, IN; 50/159 Hon Rl; Crs Cntry; IM Sprt; Ind Univ Southeast; Bus.

DE VITA, PATRICIA; Dwight D Eisenhower HS; Utica, MI; 139/602 Trs Jr Cls; Pres Sr Cls; Band; Cmnty Wkr; Hon Rl; PAVAS; Stu Cncl; FBLA; Elk Awd; Natl Merit Schl; Creative Studies Ctr; Advertising.

DE VITO, DIRK; Shelby Sr HS; Shelby, OH; Cls Rep Frsh Cls; Cls Rep Soph Cls; Cl Rep Jr Cls; Sal; Am Leg Boys St; Hon Rl; Stu Cncl; Letter Bsbl; Letter Ftbl; Letter Wrstlng; Univ; Math.

DEVLIN, JOHN; Warren Western Reserve HS; Warren, OH; 49/477 Cmnty Wkr; Hon Rl; Jr NHS; NHS; Red Cr Ade; Ed Sch Nwsp; Fr Clb; Ohio Univ; Journalism.

DEVLIN, MEGAN A; Andover HS; Birmingham, MI; 1/420 VP Soph Cls; Val; Cmnty Wkr; Debate Tm; Lit Mag; NHS; Stu Cncl; Ed Sch Nwsp; Rptr Sch Nwsp; Sch Nwsp; College; Secondary Ed.

DEVNEY, EDWARD; Lake Catholic HS; Painesville, OH; Chrh Wkr; Hon Rl; Stu Cncl; Ger Clb; Letter Ftbl; IM Sprt; John Carroll Univ; Marketing.

DE VOL, ROBERT; Centerville HS; Centerville, OH; 83/687 Cls Rep Sr Cls; Boy Scts; Hon Rl; Jr NHS; NHS; Letter Ftbl; IM Sprt; College; Bio.

DE VOR, MARGARET; Lapeer East Sr HS; Lapeer, MI; Hon Rl; 4-H; 4-H Awd; Ferris St Coll; Dent Asst.

DE VOR, THERESE; Lapeer East HS; Lapeer, MI; Chrs; Hon Rl; Mdrgl; NHS; Sch Mus; 4-H; Spn Clb; 4-H Awd; Central Michigan Univ; Hist.

DE VORE, LINDA; Frankfort HS; Frankfort, IN; Drl Tm; ROTC;.

DE VOS, PAMELA; Calvin Christian HS; Grand Rapids, MI; Hon Rl; Davenport Coll; Acctg.

DE VOWE, DAVID; Bergland HS; Bergland, MI; Aud/Vis; Band; Michigan Tech Univ.

DE VRIES, BONITA; Whitehall HS; Whitehall, MI; NHS; Ger Clb; Natl Merit SF; Calvin; Eng.

DE VRIES, CRAIG; Calvin Christian HS; Byron Center, MI; Band; Hon Rl; Sch Pl; Stg Crw; Drama Clb; IM Sprt; Calvin Coll.

DE VRIES, DOUG; West Ottawa HS; Holland, MI; Lee Coll; Ministry.

DE VRIES, ERIC; Holland Christian HS; Zeeland, MI; Chrs; Chrh Wkr; Hon Rl; Orch; Sch Pl; Yth Flsp; Bsktbl; Socr; Trk; IM Sprt; Davenport College; Acctg.

DE VRIES, J; East Kentwood HS; Kentwood, MI; Hon Rl; Jr NHS; NHS; Mic Tech; Industrial Engr.

DE VRIES, JACK; Hanover Central HS; Cedar Lake, IN; 3/137 Hon Rl; Jr NHS; NHS; Letter Bsktbl; Letter Trk; DAR Awd; College; Oceanographical Engr.

DE VRIES, LEXIE; Fairmont West HS; Kettering, OH; 1/490 Band; FCA; Hon Rl; Fr Clb; Mth Clb; Letter Bsktbl; Letter Hockey; Pres Awd; Hghst Grd Pt For Schlr Ath Awd 79; Rcvd Cert For Superior Performance Onthe NEDT 77; Indiana Univ; Acctg.

DE VRIES, LORI; Reed City HS; Paris, MI; Cls Rep Frsh Cls; Band; Girl Scts; Hon Rl; Stu Cncl; Rptr Sch Nwsp; 4-H; GAA; 4-H Awd;.

DE VRIES, MARY S; Holland HS; Holland, MI; Chrh Wkr; Hon Rl; Orch; 4-H; Letter Swmmng; Tmr; Hope Univ; Vet Asst.

DEVUONO, LINDA; Sycamore HS; Montgomery, OH; Hon Rl; Rptr Yrbk; Key Clb; Gym; College; Law.

DEWA, ANDREW; Warren Woods HS; Warren, MI; 1/335 Band; Debate Tm; Hon Rl; NHS; College; Physics.

DE WALD, DEBBIE; Homestead HS; Ft Wayne, IN; 12/250 Sec Jr Cls; Hon Rl; NHS; Sch Pl; Stu Cncl; Yth Flsp; Rptr Yrbk; Yrbk; Chrldng; PPFtbl; Ohio St Univ; Acctg.

DE WALD, ROGER; Au Gres Sims HS; Au Gres, MI; Band; Boy Scts; Hon Rl; 4-H; Letter Bsbl; Letter Bsktbl; Letter Ftbl; 4-H Awd; College; Horticultural.

DE WALT, JEANNINE; Hillsdale HS; Hillsdale, MI; Jr NHS; NHS; Sch Nwsp; Fr Clb; Pep Clb; Chrldng; Allegheny College.

DEWAR _II, WESLEY D; Hauser HS; Hope, IN; 2/103 Chrh Wkr; Hon Rl; Lbry Ade; Mod UN; NHS; Quill & Scroll; Rptr Yrbk; Ind Univ; Public Admin.

DEWATERS, RONALD; Hartland HS; Brighton, MI; Band; Chrh Wkr; Hon Rl; NHS; Orch; Cit Awd; Univ Of Mich; Comp Science.

DE WEERD, JUDY; West Ottawa HS; Holland, MI; 9/316 Band; Chrh Wkr; Hon Rl; Hosp Ade; NHS; Orch; Sch Mus; Stu Cncl; Yth Flsp; Hope Coll; Chem.

DE WEESE, BARRY; South Spencer HS; Rockport, IN; 2/147 Cl Rep Jr Cls; Trs Sr Cls; Cls Rep Sr Cls; Sal; Chrs; Hon Rl; Jr NHS; Pres NHS; Sch Mus; Sch Pl; Western Kentucky Univ.

DE WEESE, MARGY; Fairlawn HS; Sidney, OH; Sec Jr Cls; Band; Chrs; Drl Tm; Hon Rl; Lbry Ade; NHS; Sch Mus; Yth Flsp; Rptr Yrbk; Ohio St Univ; Phys Therapy.

DEWESE, DAVID; Kenton HS; Kenton, OH; Am Leg Boys St; Chrs; Chrh Wkr; Hon Rl; NHS; Sch Pl; Stu Cncl; Yth Flsp; Rptr Sch Nwsp; Cincinnati Bible College; Ministry.

DEWEY, DALE; East Grand Rapids HS; E Grand Rapids, MI; Cls Rep Frsh Cls; Hon Rl; Sch Mus; Sch Pl; Rptr Yrbk; Lat Clb; Letter Glf; Coach Actv; Scr Kpr; Univ.

DEWEY, ELIZABETH; Maumee Valley Cntry Day Schl; Lambertville, MI; Hon Rl; Stg Crw; Sch Nwsp; Drama Clb; Art.

DEWEY, LINDA; Eau Claire HS; Eau Claire, MI; 10/100 Band; Chrh Wkr; Hon Rl; Pres Yth Flsp; Pres 4-H; Adrian Coll; Cpa.

DEWEY, R; Mancelona HS; Bellaire, MI; Band; Sch Nwsp; Pep Clb; Northwestern Mic College; Radio.

DEWHURST, KIM; Gods Bible Schl HS; Rutland, OH; Boy Scts; Chrs; Chrh Wkr; Hon Rl; Sct Actv; 4-H; Mth Clb; Pep Clb; Ftbl; Dnfth Awd; Gods Bible Schl; Missionary.

DE WILDE, JUDI C; Grandview Hts HS; Columbus, OH; Cmp Fr Grls; Chrs; Chrh Wkr; Drl Tm; FCA; Lbry Ade; Yth Flsp; Yrbk; Letter Hockey; GAA; Fred Waring Music Schlrshp 1977; Dist Solo Contest Ssuperior Rating 1978; 4 Yrs Choir; Western Kentucky Univ; Elem Educ.

DE WILDE, MATTHEW; Capac HS; Capac, MI; Band; Hon Rl; FFA; VICA; Letter Trk; Gemini Schl Of Fine Arts; Paint.

DE WIND, JOHN; Reeths Puffer Sr HS; Muskegon, MI; 7/325 Cls Rep Soph Cls; Cl Rep Jr Cls; Band; Hon Rl; NHS; Stu Cncl; Tage Band Jazz Band; Univ; Comp Sci.

DE WINDT, ANN; Grand Rapids Baptist HS; Grandville, MI; Hon Rl; Lbry Ade; Pep Clb; PPFtbl; Grand Rapids Jr Coll; Med.

DE WITT, DAWN; Zeeland HS; Zeeland, MI; Chrh Wkr; Debate Tm; Drm Mjrt; Girl Scts; Hon Rl; Natl Forn Lg; Chrldng; PPFtbl; Twrlr; Univ; Soc Work.

DE WITT, JANET; Princeton HS; Princeton, WV; 70/372 Cls Rep Frsh Cls; Cls Rep Soph Cls; Band; Sec Chrh Wkr; Off Ade; Stu Cncl; Mat Maids; W Vir Tech; Dental Hygenist.

DE WITT, KELLY; Taylor Center HS; Taylor, MI; Band; Girl Scts; Hon Rl; Letter Bsbl; Letter Bsktbl; IM Sprt; Mgrs; PPFtbl; Michigan St Univ; Med Tech.

DE WITT, MICHAEL; Roscommon HS; Roscommon, MI; Cls Rep Soph Cls; Band; Boy Scts; Hon Rl; Orch; Sch Mus; Glf; Michigan St Univ; Engr.

DE WITT, MICHAEL S; Rowlesburg HS; Rowlesburg, WV; Cl Rep Jr Cls; Am Leg Boys St; Boy Scts; Hon Rl; NHS; Sch Pl; Yrbk; Bsbl; Bsktbl; Best Citznshp Awd 77 78 & 79; Typing Awd 78; Nominatd All Amer Athlete 77; Univ; Med.

DE WITT, STEVEN; Wyoming Park HS; Wyoming, MI; NHS; Ger Clb; Ftbl; Davenport Bus Schl; Bus Mgmt.

DEWITZ, NANCY; Oak Harbor HS; Oak Harbor, OH; 1/193 Trs Jr Cls; Band; Chrs; Hon Rl; Pres 4-H; Mat Maids; Scr Kpr; 4-H Awd; Jr Hmcmng Attendant; Suburban Lakes League Wrestng Qn; Future Farmers Of Amer FFA Attendant; College; Math.

DE WOLF, DAVID; Pinckney Community HS; Hamburg, MI; Chrh Wkr; Hon Rl; NHS; Letter Crs Cntry; Letter Trk; IM Sprt; Mic Tech Univ; Elec Engr.

DE WOLFF, DEA; Kalamazoo Christian HS; Kalamazoo, MI; 8/130 Chrh Wkr; Hon Rl; NHS; Yth Flsp; Pep Clb; Natl Merit Ltr; Top 10% Of Class 77 78 & 79; St Of Mi Competitive Schlrshp 79; Hope Coll; Psych.

DEWS, DAVID; Benedictine HS; Cleveland, OH; 5/103 Cls Rep Frsh Cls; Hon Rl; NHS; Fr Clb; Bsktbl; Crs Cntry; Trk; IM Sprt;.

DEWS, DAVID M; Benedictine HS; Cleveland, OH; 6/104 Hon Rl; NHS; Fr Clb; Bsktbl; Crs Cntry; Trk;.

DEXTER, DAVID; Muskegon Sr HS; Muskegon, MI; NHS; Stu Cncl; Yth Flsp; Letter Ten; Elected Stu Council Pres For Schl Yr; Selected To Part In Natl Leadership Training Ctr Prog; College; Law Enforcement.

DEXTER, GREGG; Williamston HS; Williamston, MI; Hon Rl; 4-H; Bsbl; Ftbl; Michigan St Univ; Mtlrgcl Engr.

DEY, JEFFREY; Lake HS; Millbury, OH; 9/156 Band; Hon Rl; JA; NHS; Quill & Scroll; Rptr Sch Nwsp; Fr Clb; Letter Ten; NCTE; Bowling Green St Univ; Comp Sci.

DEY, LORI; Oscoda Area HS; Saginaw, MI; 11/240 Band; Girl Scts; Hon Rl; NHS; Fr Clb; IM Sprt; Mich State Univ; Med Technologist.

DEYE, MARY; St Ursula Academy; Cincinnati, OH; NHS; Rptr Yrbk; Capt Glf; Chrldng; 1st Hon Pin 78; Univ.

DEYHLE, RICHARD; Mc Nicholas HS; Cincinnati, OH; 27/239 Hon Rl; NHS; IM Sprt; Univ; Comp Sci.

DEYLING, J; Nordonia HS; Northfield, OH; 4/420 Chrh Wkr; Hon Rl; NHS; Bsktbl; IM Sprt; Letter Mgrs; PPFtbl; College; Bus Mgmt.

DE YOUNG, BOBBIE; Harper Creek HS; Battle Creek, MI; Hon Rl; Ten; Chrldng; Hope Coll; Bus.

DE YOUNG, JEFFREY J; Lakeland HS; Milford, MI; 33/420 Band; Mod UN; NHS; Letter Bsbl; Letter Bsktbl; Letter Ftbl; Letter Trk; Scr Kpr; Tmr; Oakland Cmnty Coll; Liberal Arts.

DE YOUNG, MARY; Comstock Park HS; Comstock Pk, MI; 1/160 Val; Hon Rl; Lbry Ade; Natl Forn Lg; NHS; Yrbk; Pep Clb; Mgrs; Davenport Coll; Acctg.

DE YOUNG, MATTHEW; Holt HS; Holt, MI; 57/360 Michigan St Univ; Chem Engr.

DE ZARN, CHARLES; La Salle HS; Cincinnati, OH; Cl Rep Jr Cls; Cls Rep Sr Cls; Aud/Vis; Band; Hon Rl; Orch; Sch Mus; Stu Cncl; IM Sprt; Cit Awd; Vice Pres Of Lasalles Band; Univ Of Cincinnati; Business.

DHONDT, ARTHUR; St Johns HS; St Johns, MI; Sch Pl; Sct Actv; 4-H; Ten; College; Agri Bus.

DIAB, AMALIE; Kirtland HS; Kirtland, OH; AFS; Band; Girl Scts; Fr Clb; Twrlr; Mas Awd; College; Political Science.

DIAL, DEBBIE; Zionsville Cmnty HS; Zionsville, IN; 13/149 Chrs; Hon Rl; MMM; Sch Mus; Fr Clb; Indiana Univ; Music Ther.

DIANA, CATHY; Mathews HS; Vienna, OH; Pres Jr Cls; Chrs; Chrh Wkr; Hon Rl; Hosp Ade; Off Ade; Red Cr Ade; Sch Pl; Stu Cncl; Y-Teens; Youngstown St Univ; Nursing.

DIANA, GINA; Washington HS; Massillon, OH; Trs Jr Cls; Chrs; Hon Rl; Jr NHS; Sch Mus; Yrbk; Spn Clb; Chrldng; Stark Technical College; Engr Tech.

DI ANGELIS, TAMMY; Weir HS; Weirton, WV; Band; Cmp Fr Grls; Chrh Wkr; Cmnty Wkr; Drl Tm; Hon Rl; Hosp Ade; Off Ade; Yth Flsp; Y-Teens;

May Court Queen Queen Victoria XXXVIII 79; Homecoming Court 79; St Joseph Yng Adult 79; Wilma Boyd Career Schl; Airlines.

DIAN MOORE, LISA; Van Buren HS; Brazil, IN; Band; FCA; Hon Rl; Off Ade; Pres Stu Cncl; 4-H; Fr Clb; FTA; Treas Sci Clb; Chrldng; College; Educ.

DI ANTONIO, LISA; Madonna HS; Weirton, WV; 17/99 Boy Scts; Hon Rl; JA; NHS; Sch Mus; Pep Clb; Univ; Nursing.

DI ASIO, JEFFREY; Edgewood HS; Ashtabula, OH; 100/350 Band; Rptr Yrbk; Rptr Sch Nwsp; Spn Clb; Ftbl; Trk; Wrstlng; IM Sprt; College; Business.

DIAZ, BRETT; Edgewood Sr HS; Ashtabula, OH; Cls Rep Frsh Cls; Cls Rep Soph Cls; Cl Rep Jr Cls; Cls Rep Sr Cls; AFS; Cmnty Wkr; Debate Tm; Off Ade; Stg Crw; Stu Cncl; Univ; Psych.

DIAZ, JOSE; Calumet HS; Gary, IN; Hon Rl; FSA; Pep Clb; Sci Clb; Ftbl; Letter Trk; Purdue Univ; Indust Sales Engr.

DIAZ, MARIO; Rogers HS; Wyoming, MI; 75/268 Boys Clb Am; FSA; Mth Clb; Sci Clb; Spn Clb; Gym; Trk; Univ Of Miami; Comp Sci.

DIAZ, VERONICA; Aiken HS; Cincinnati, OH; 57/576 Trs Soph Cls; Cls Rep Soph Cls; VP Jr Cls; Cl Rep Jr Cls; Hon Rl; Jr NHS; Off Ade; Stu Cncl; Rptr Yrbk; FTA; Univ Of Cincinnati; Spanish.

DIBA, LINDA; Struthers HS; Struthers, OH; Hon Rl; Jr NHS; NHS; Drama Clb; Treas OEA; Pep Clb; Youngstown State Univ; Accounting.

DIBBLE, KEITH; Servite HS; Detroit, MI; Letter Ftbl; IM Sprt; Ferris St Univ; Plumbing.

DIBLE, CHRISTINE; London HS; London, OH; Cls Rep Soph Cls; Cl Rep Jr Cls; Band; Hon Rl; NHS; Off Ade; Sch Pl; Stg Crw; Stu Cncl; Sch Nwsp; Univ Of Cincinnati; Med Illstrn.

DI CESARE, FRANCIS; Steubenville Cath Ctrl HS; Wintersville, OH; 21/204 Band; Hon Rl; NHS; Key Clb; Trk; College; Poli Sci.

DICESARE, THOMAS; Fostoria St Wendelin HS; Fostoria, OH; 13/79 Hon Rl; Letter Bsbl; Letter Bsktbl; Letter Ftbl; Bowling Green St Univ; Sec Ed.

DI CHIRO, CHRISTINE; North Ridgeville HS; N Ridgeville, OH; Cmnty Wkr; Drl Tm; Hon Rl; NHS; Off Ade; Spn Clb; Letter Swmmng; Letter Ten; Pom Pon; Tmr; Edgecliff Coll; Home Ec.

DICK, DAVID; Franklin Hts HS; Columbus, OH; Chrh Wkr; Yth Flsp; Glf; Ten; Wrstlng; Coll; Busns Admin.

DICK, DIANA; Milton HS; Milton, WV; Band; DECA; FHA; Pep Clb; Marshall Univ; Bus Mgmt.

DICK, DIANA; Lincoln HS; Cambridge, IN; 15/130 VP Sr Cls; Drl Tm; Hon Rl; Stu Cncl; 4-H; OEA; Spn Clb; Letter Pom Pon; IVY; Office Management.

DICK, JANE; Hedgesville HS; Hedgesville, WV; Hon Rl; FHA; Voc Schl; Cosmetology.

DICK, KEVIN; Franklin HS; Livonia, MI; 24/600 Univ Of Mich; Elec Engr.

DICK, KIMBERLY; Adlai Stevenson HS; Sterling Hts, MI; Girl Scts; Hon Rl; NHS; Natl Merit Ltr; Oakland Univ; Comp Progr.

DICK, STEVE; Lincoln HS; Cambrid E, IN; 2/132 Hon Rl; NHS; 4-H; FFA; Spn Clb; Univ.

DICKE, LINDA; New Knoxville Local HS; New Bremen, OH; Band; Chrh Wkr; Cmnty Wkr; Hon Rl; Orch; Sch Pl; Yth Flsp; 4-H; Ohio State Schl Of Cosmetics; Cosmet.

DICKENDESHER, MARY B; New Albany HS; New Albany, OH; Cls Rep Sr Cls; Drl Tm; Hon Rl; NHS; Off Ade; Scr Kpr; Columbus Tech Inst; Sec.

DICKENS, T; Marsh Fork HS; Naoma, WV; 4/25 Sec Frsh Cls; Band; Chrs; Hon Rl; Sch Nwsp; Pep Clb; Letter Chrldng; Concord Coll; Nursing.

DICKERSON, BARBARA; Kenton Sr HS; Kenton, OH; Band; Chrh Wkr; Drl Tm; Hon Rl; Yth Flsp; Spn Clb; Cit Awd; Flag Corp Captn; Univ.

DICKERSON, DAVID; Midland Trail HS; Rainelle, WV; Hon Rl; NHS;.

DICKERSON, DEBRA; Western Boone Jr Sr HS; Jamestown, IN; 15/167 Band; Chrh Wkr; Drl Tm; Hon Rl; NHS; Red Cr Ade; Sch Mus; 4-H; Pep Clb; DAR Awd;.

DICKERSON, MARY E; Bluefield HS; Bluefield, WV; Hon Rl; Y-Teens; Spn Clb; NCTE; Knoxville Univ.

DICKERSON, NATALIE; Taylor HS; Cincinnati, OH; Band; Chrs; Hon Rl; Hosp Ade; Sch Mus; Sch Pl; Stu Cncl; Drama Clb; Pep Clb; Chrldng; Cincinnati Tech Univ; Real Estate.

DICKERSON, R; Withrow HS; Cincinnati, OH; Hon Rl; Stg Crw; Rptr Yrbk; Yrbk; Rptr Sch Nwsp; Sch Nwsp; Pep Clb; Wrstlng; Bricklayer.

DICKERSON, TERESA M; Clare HS; Clare, MI; Trs Frsh Cls; Cls Rep Frsh Cls; Trs Soph Cls; Cls Rep Soph Cls; Sec Jr Cls; Cl Rep Jr Cls; Sec Sr Cls; Cls Rep Sr Cls; Band; FCA; Aquinas Coll; Journalism.

DICKES, BRUCE; Napoleon HS; Napoleon, OH; Band; Hon Rl; Orch; 4-H; Toledo Univ; Elec Engr.

DICKEY, CHARLENE; Peterstown HS; Peterstown, WV; NHS; Sch Pl; Rptr Yrbk; Rptr Sch Nwsp; Drama Clb; Fr Clb; Pep Clb; Univ; Bus Admin.

DICKEY, CYNTHIA; Fairview HS; Sherwood, OH; Sec Soph Cls; Cl Rep Jr Cls; Chrs; Hon Rl; NHS; Sch Mus; Stu Cncl; Yth Flsp; Spn Clb; Natl Merit Schl; St Francis College; Elem Educ.

DICKEY, D; La Porte HS; Laporte, IN; Chrs; Chrh Wkr; MMM; Orch; PAVAS; Sch Mus; Fr Clb; College; Instrumental Music.

DICKEY, DEIDRE; La Porte HS; La Porte, IN; Cmp Fr Grls; Chrs; Girl Scts; MMM; Orch; PAVAS; Sch Mus; Yth Flsp; Fr Clb; Pep Clb; Oberlin Coll; Music.

DICKEY, MICHAEL G; Anderson HS; Anderson, IN; 70/460 Band; Boy Scts; Drm Bgl; Hon Rl; NHS; Orch; Sch Mus; Sct Actv; Spn Clb; Indiana Univ; Acctg.

DICKINSON, DARRYL; Western HS; Jackson, MI; Boy Scts; Ftbl; Trk; Mich State; Communications.

DICKINSON, JOSEPH; Wadsworth Sr HS; Wadsworth, OH; Chrh Wkr; Drm Mjrt; FCA; Hon Rl; Stu Cncl; Yth Flsp; Spn Clb; Bsbl; Bsktbl; Coach Actv; All City Bslb Team Al L Star Team 74 76; Pioneer Confrnc 1st Team Mst Valbl Hitter 79; Univ; Bsbl.

DICKINSON, JULIE; Kearsley HS; Davison, MI; Band; Girl Scts; Hon Rl; Letter Bsbl; Letter Hndbl; Letter Ten; Grand Valley State Coll; Med.

DICKINSON, KENDRA; Western HS; Spring Arbor, MI; Band; Chrs; Chrh Wkr; Cmnty Wkr; Girl Scts; Hon Rl; Mdrgl; NHS; Orch; Sch Mus; Spring Arbor Coll; Fine Arts.

DICKINSON, TAMARA; Piqua Central HS; Piqua, OH; Sec Sr Cls; Trs Sr Cls; Band; Chrs; Chrh Wkr; Off Ade; Sch Mus; Sch Pl; Stg Crw; Stu Cncl; Univ; Art.

DICKINSON, TODD; Fairview HS; Mark Center, OH; Sec Frsh Cls; Trs Frsh Cls; Hon Rl; Stg Crw; Mth Clb; Bsbl; Scr Kpr; College; Agri.

DICKISON, PHILIP D; Union HS; Mooreland, IN; Sec Frsh Cls; Pres Jr Cls; Band; Chrs; Hon Rl; NHS; Sch Pl; Drama Clb; Lat Clb; Coll; Medicine.

DICKOW, DIANE; Our Lady Of Mercy HS; Southfield, MI; Natl Forn Lg; Stg Crw; Drama Clb; Pep Clb; Spn Clb; Lawrence Inst Of Tech; Engr.

DICKS, RALPH E; Monrovia HS; Mooresville, IN; 7/109 Band; Boy Scts; Hon Rl; NHS; Rptr Yrbk; Bsbl; Bsktbl; Purdue Univ; Elect Engr.

DICKSON, ANDREW C; Port Huron Northern HS; Port Huron, MI; 28/408 Aud/Vis; Band; Hon Rl; NHS; Sch Nwsp; Univ; Astro Engr.

DICKSON, CHARLA; Fairfield Union HS; Lancaster, OH; 9/158 Chrs; Chrh Wkr; Hon Rl; Jr NHS; Pep Clb; Spn Clb; Univ; Fash Mdse.

DICKSON, DEANNE M; Whittemore Prescott HS; Prescott, MI; 4/120 Band; Hon Rl; NHS; Rptr Yrbk; Rptr Sch Nwsp; Perfect Attend 76 78; Peace Corps Serv Awd Chairman 77; Kirtland Cmnty Coll; Sociology.

DICKSON, EVERETT J; Union HS; Jasonville, IN; 13/48 Band; Chrs; Stg Crw; 4-H; Pep Clb; 4-H Awd; In St Sclhsp 79; Hoosier Schlr Awd 79; Bnd & Chrs Awd 79; Vincennes Univ; Geol.

DICKSON, JANICE; Marietta HS; Marietta, OH; 85/430 VP Jr Cls; VP Sr Cls; Band; Chrs; Girl Scts; Hon Rl; Sch Pl; Stg Crw;.

DICKSON, LORI; Pleasant HS; Marion, OH; 22/150 Cl Rep Jr Cls; Girl Scts; Hon Rl; Hosp Ade; NHS; Quill & Scroll; Yrbk; Rptr Sch Nwsp; Drama Clb; Fr Clb; College; Bus.

DICKSON, MARY; Sandusky HS; Sandusky, MI; Band; Chrs; Chrh Wkr; Girl Scts; Hon Rl; Sch Pl; Sct Actv; Stg Crw; Rptr Sch Nwsp; 4-H; Univ.

DICKSON, THOMAS; Beavercreek HS; Morrow, GA; 36/702 Chrh Wkr; Debate Tm; Natl Forn Lg; NHS; Yth Flsp; Pep Clb; Bsbl; Ten; Univ Of Geo; Poli Sci.

DI DIO, MARY B; Fraser HS; Roseville, MI; Hon Rl; Jr NHS; NHS; Yth Flsp; Fr Clb; Ten; College; Bus.

DIDION, PAULETTE; St Marys Ctrl Catholic HS; Sandusky, OH; Chrh Wkr; Cmnty Wkr; Hon Rl; Jr NHS; NHS; 4-H; Ger Clb; Sci Clb; GAA; 4-H Awd; Michigan Univ; Med.

DI DOMENICO, KEVIN; Wintersville HS; Wintersville, OH; 101/267 Cls Rep Frsh Cls; Stu Cncl; Rptr Yrbk; Spn Clb; Letter Bsbl; Letter Ftbl; Babe Ruth Bsbl Ath Of The Yr 75; Ohio St Univ; Soc Sci.

DIDOMIZIO, TINA; Hazel Park HS; Detroit, MI; 9/306 Chrs; Hon Rl; NHS; Sch Mus; Sch Pl; Drama Clb; Trk; Am Leg Awd; Elk Awd; Voice Dem Awd; Adrian Coll; Med Tech.

DIDUR, MARISA; Grosse Pointe North HS; Grosse Pte Farm, MI; Hon Rl; Hosp Ade; NHS; Rptr Sch Nwsp; DECA; Communications.

DIEDERICK, JUNE; Midview HS; Elyria, OH; 68/247 JA; ROTC; 4-H; JA Awd; Lorain Cnty Cmnty Coll; Elec Engr.

DIEFENBACH, LENARD; Lee M Thurston HS; Redford, MI; Boy Scts; Chrh Wkr; JA; Lawrence Inst Tech; Elec Engr.

DIEFENTHALER, LORI; Morrison R Waite HS; Toledo, OH; 1/300 Val; Am Leg Aux Girls St; Hon Rl; VP NHS; Stu Cncl; Pres Fr Clb; Bausch & Lomb Awd; Cit Awd; Kiwan Awd; Ohio Academic Schlrshp 79; Natl Hon Society Schlrshp 79; Waite HS Alumni Schlrshp 79; Ohio St Univ.

DIEFFENBAUGHER, LORI; Jackson HS; North Canton, OH; Band; FCA; Girl Scts; Hon Rl; NHS; Off Ade; Orch; Y-Teens; Pep Clb; Spn Clb; Stark Tech Schl; Data Comp Progr.

DIEGEL, GAIL; Grosse Pointe North HS; Harper Wds, MI; FCA; Hon Rl; Ger Clb; PPFtbl; Scr Kpr; College; Med.

DIEGEL, VICKI; Belleville HS; Belleville, MI; 11/480 Chrs; Chrh Wkr; Hon Rl; Mdrgl; NHS; PAVAS; Sch Mus; Sch Pl; Natl Merit Ltr; Natl Merit Schl; Michigan Competive Scholarship; Whos Who In Music; Brigham Young Univ; Music Perf.

DIEHL, CAROL; Aiken Sr HS; Cincinnati, OH; Band; Cmp Fr Grls; Chrs; Chrh Wkr; Cmnty Wkr; Hon Rl; Jr NHS; Lbry Ade; NHS; Stu Cncl; Volunteer Wrk For Handicapped; Nelson Schwab Awd; Day Bequest Card; Marshall Univ; Special Ed.

DIEHL, CHRISTOPHER; Woodsfield HS; Columbus, OH; 8/69 Band; Boy Scts; Chrs; Hon Rl; NHS; Sch Pl; Sct Actv; Eng Clb; Fr Clb; Capt Glf; Miami Univ; Archt.

DIEHL, DEBRA; Unionville Sebewaing HS; Unionville, MI; Band; Girl Scts; Hon Rl; Bsbl; Bsktbl; Trk; Chrldng; Lake Superior St Coll; Bio Sci.

DIEHL, HELEN; Notre Dame Acad; Toledo, OH; Girl Scts; JA; Ger Clb; College; Med.

DIEHL, JOHN W; Union HS; Alderson, WV; 1/95 Am Leg Boys St; Band; Chrh Wkr; Hon Rl; Jr NHS; Sch Pl; Beta Clb; FFA; Liberty Baptist Coll; Ministry.

DIEHL, MICHAEL; Milton HS; Ona, WV; Boy Scts; FFA; Bsbl; Glf; Cabell Cnty Career Ctr; Electrician.

DIEHLMAN, SHARI; Reeths Puffer HS; Muskegon, MI; 42/346 Band; Chrh Wkr; Cmnty Wkr; Hon Rl; Rptr Sch Nwsp; Chrldng; Scr Kpr; Michigan St Univ.

DIEHR, JOHNNY; Notre Dame HS; St Clair Shore, MI; 7/198 Hon Rl; Rptr Sch Nwsp; Swmmng; IM Sprt; Kalamazoo College; Medicine.

DIEKEMA, KATHERINE; Fremont Sr HS; Fremont, MI; 96/225 Chrh Wkr; Hon Rl; Hosp Ade; Orch; Red Cr Ade; Yth Flsp; 4-H; Ger Clb; PPFtbl; Nazareth Coll; Nursing.

DIEKER, LARRY; St Charles Prep HS; Upper Arlington, OH; Boy Scts; Chrh Wkr; FCA; Hon Rl; NHS; Fr Clb; Glf; Univ; Jrnlsm.

DIEKMANN, DIANA; Field HS; Mogadore, OH; 5/240 Girl Scts; Hon Rl; NHS; Sec 4-H; Fr Clb; Pep Clb; Trk; Univ Of Akron; Comp Prog.

DIEKMANN, FRANK; Moeller HS; Loveland, OH; Boy Scts; Lit Mag; Sct Actv; Stu Cncl; Sch Nwsp; Pep Clb; Univ Of Cincinnati; Journ.

DIEM, CRAIG; Patrick Henry HS; Deshler, OH; 7/120 Boy Scts; Chrh Wkr; Hon Rl; Sct Actv; Bsbl; Bsktbl; Ftbl; Univ Of Toledo; Engr.

DIEMER, JENNY I; Defiance Sr HS; Defiance, OH; 44/295 Hon Rl; Hosp Ade; Jr NHS; Off Ade; Yrbk; Spn Clb; Cinncinatti Univ; Med.

DIEMER, TAMARA; Ottawa Glandorf HS; Glandorf, OH; 34/179 Hon Rl; Sch Mus; Yrbk; Sch Nwsp; Drama Clb; Lima Tech Schl; Radiologic Tech.

DIENER, DAWN; Kearsley HS; Flint, MI; 10/320 Cls Rep Frsh Cls; Cl Rep Jr Cls; Band; Hon Rl; Natl Forn Lg; NHS; Stu Cncl; Yth Flsp; Rptr Yrbk; Pres Fr Clb; State Champion Volleyball Team Mbr; College; Special Ed.

DIENER, JONATHAN; Bedford HS; Temperance, MI; 1/482 Pres Band; Hon Rl; NHS; Sch Mus; Sch Pl; Stg Crw; Drama Clb; IM Sprt; Univ Of Toledo Merit Schlrshp 79; John Philip Sousa Awd; Directors Awd; Univ Of Toledo; Elec Engr.

DIERINGER, MARK; Lima HS; Lima, OH; 11/550 Band; Chrs; Debate Tm; Drm Bgl; Hon Rl; Orch; Sch Mus; Ohio State Univ; Engineering.

DIERINGER, SANDY; Defiance HS; Defiance, OH; Band; Cmnty Wkr; Hon Rl; JA; NHS; Sch Mus; Mth Clb; Spn Clb; JA Awd; Ohio State Univ; Pharmacy.

DIERNA, JOHN S; Elyria Cath HS; Elyria, OH; 24/200 Pres Jr Cls; Am Leg Boys St; Hon Rl; Jr NHS; Quill & Scroll; Pres Stu Cncl; Ed Sch Nwsp; Sprt Ed Sch Nwsp; Letter Trk; Dnfth Awd; Acad Letter Schlstc Ach; Univ; Med.

DIETERICH, MICHELE; Old Trail HS; Cuyahoga Fl, OH; 1/14 VP Soph Cls; Cl Rep Jr Cls; Cmnty Wkr; Hon Rl; Yrbk; Rptr Sch Nwsp; Spn Clb; Hockey; College; Public Relations.

DIETERICH, ROY; Hedgesville HS; Falling Waters, WV; 6/225 Cl Rep Jr Cls; Am Leg Boys St; Chrh Wkr; Hon Rl; NHS; Pres Stu Cncl; Yth Flsp; Mth Clb; Bsbl; Letter Ftbl; Univ; Engr.

DIETRICH, CORRINE; Highland HS; Hinckley, OH; 47/202 Band; Chrs; Chrh Wkr; Hon Rl; Sec Yth Flsp; Ger Clb; Pensacola Christian Coll; Nursing.

DIETRICH, JEAN; Sparta HS; Conklin, MI; Chrh Wkr; Hon Rl; Jr NHS; NHS; Off Ade; Stu Cncl; 4-H; Pep Clb; Spn Clb; Grandvallet College; Nursing.

DIETSCH, DELICE; Valley HS; Smithfield, WV; Jr NHS; NHS; Sch Pl; Stu Cncl; Rptr Yrbk; Ed Sch Nwsp; College; Journalism.

DIETZ, BRIAN; Walnut Hills HS; Cincinnati, OH; Hon Rl; Pol Wkr; Sch Mus; Stu Cncl; Sch Nwsp; Mth Clb; Spn Clb; Natl Merit SF; College; Econ.

DIETZ, DALE; Warren Central HS; Indianapolis, IN; NHS; VP Key Clb; IUPIU; Chem Engr.

DIETZ, HOPE L; Ft Frye HS; Beverly, OH; Cls Rep Soph Cls; Cl Rep Jr Cls; Drl Tm; Stg Crw; Stu Cncl; Pep Clb; Chrldng; GAA; 4-H Awd; 3 1/2 Wk Tour In Spain With Spansih Csl 79; Univ; Soc Worker.

DIETZ, MARK; Kalkaska Public HS; Kalkaska, MI; Chrh Wkr; Cmnty Wkr; FCA; Univ; Sci.

DIETZ, MARLA; Cardinal Mooney HS; Poland, OH; Band; Chrh Wkr; Cmnty Wkr; Hon Rl; Off Ade; Lat Clb; Gym; Swmmng; Chrldng; Scr Kpr; Youngstown State Univ.

DIETZ, MICHAEL; Ayersville HS; Defiance, OH; 10/90 Am Leg Boys St; VP Band; Boy Scts; Chrs; Hon Rl; NHS; Sch Mus; Fr Clb; Swmmng; Ten; Univ; Mech Engr.

DIETZ, NORMA; Wapakoneta Sr HS; Wapakoneta, OH; 1/308 Band; Hon Rl; NHS; Treas Quill & Scroll; Rptr Yrbk; 4-H; Lat Clb; Mth Clb; Exc Rating In St Sci Fair Superior Dist; Summa Cum Laude In Natl Latin Exam; 13th Plc In Ohio Cncl Of Math; Univ; Med.

DIETZEN, CHARLES; Northwestern HS; Kokomo, IN; 1/171 Am Leg Boys St; Boy Scts; Chrh Wkr; Cmnty Wkr; Hon Rl; JA; NHS; Pol Wkr; Sch Pl; Sct Actv; Purdue Univ; Engr.

DIEZ, DAVID C; Malabar HS; Mansfield, OH; Band; Boy Scts; Chrs; Hon Rl; NHS; Orch; Red Cr Ade; Sch Mus; Sch Pl; Stg Crw; Univ; Music.

DIFAZIO, DAVID; Fordson HS; Dearborn, MI; 59/550 Boy Scts; Hon Rl; Sct Actv; Ftbl; Wayne State Univ; Pharmacy.

DI FRANCO, MARK; Padua Franciscan HS; Seven Hills, OH; Boy Scts; Chrs; JA; Ed Yrbk; Letter Trk; Coach Actv; Mgrs; JA Awd; Roman Catholic Awd Boy Scts 76; Pope Pius XII Roman Cathlc Awd Boy Scts 78; Coll; Env Bio.

DIGBY, BOB; Otsego HS; Grand Rapids, OH; Am Leg Boys St; Band; Boy Scts; Hon Rl; Sct Actv; Yth Flsp; 4-H; FFA; 4-H Awd; God Cntry Awd; Pres Beaver Creek Boosters 4 H; VP Of Otsego Chapt FFA; High Indiv At Dist FFA Soil Judging Cont; Bowling Green St Univ; Comp Sci.

DIGBY, JEFFREY; Tiffin Columbian HS; Tiffin, OH; Hon Rl; Glf; Voc Schl; Comp Progr.

DI GENOVA, JOHN; Wabash HS; Wabash, IN; Chrh Wkr; Hon Rl; Ger Clb; Ftbl; Wrstlng; IM Sprt; Ivy Tech Kokomo; Tech Mech.

DI GERONIMO, MARY; Clinton Massie HS; Wilmington, OH; Cls Rep Frsh Cls; Cls Rep Soph Cls; Cl Rep Jr Cls; Hon Rl; Lbry Ade; Off Ade; Ambassador Clb; Art.

DIGGINS, SHA REA; Horace Mann HS; Gary, IN; Cls Rep Frsh Cls; Cls Rep Soph Cls; Cl Rep Jr Cls; Chrs; Hon Rl; Hosp Ade; JA; Mdrgl; NHS; Sch Pl; Natl Jr Honor Soc; Natl Jr Honor Soc; Univ; Med.

DIGGS, CHUCK; Howell HS; Howell, MI; 84/395 Cls Rep Frsh Cls; Chrs; Hon Rl; Sch Pl; Stu Cncl; 4-H; Sci Clb; Bsbl; Crs Cntry; Trk; Michigan State Univ.

DI GIACOMO, FRANK; Boardman HS; Youngstown, OH; 31/596 Hon Rl; Natl Forn Lg; NHS; Quill & Scroll; Sch Mus; Stu Cncl; Ed Sch Nwsp; 1st Pl Spanish Drama Foreign Lang Day Westminster Coll; Coll; Psych.

DI GIACOMO, MICHAEL; Bay HS; Bay Vill, OH; Cls Rep Frsh Cls; Boy Scts; FCA; Hon Rl; Sch Nwsp; Fr Clb; Rdo Clb; Capt Hockey; Coach Actv; IM Sprt; New Hampshire Bus Schl; Bus.

DI GIOIA, DAVID M; Marquette HS; Beverly Shores, IN; 4/66 Hon Rl; NHS; Ger Clb; Sci Clb; Socr; Natl Merit SF; Univ; Physics.

DI GIOIA, DIANE; Marquette HS; Beverly Shores, IN; Chrs; Hon Rl; Sch Mus; Sch Nwsp; Drama Clb; Lion Awd; College; English.

DI GIROLAMO, JAMES; Madonna HS; Weirton, WV; 24/98 Hon Rl; Jr NHS; NHS; Key Clb; Sci Clb; Univ; Law.

DIGMAN, ROBERT; Wellsville HS; Wellsville, OH; Boy Scts; Chrs; Sch Pl; FTA; Key Clb; Ftbl; Trk; IM Sprt; Am Leg Awd; Cit Awd; Univ; Bookkeeping.

DI GREGORIO, MARIANNA C; East Detroit HS; East Detroit, MI; Chrs; Girl Scts; Sch Pl; Stg Crw; Rptr Yrbk; Rptr Sch Nwsp; Pres Drama Clb; Most Promising Actress; Best Actress; Best Supporting Actress; Univ Of Detroit; Journalism.

DIJAK, TIMOTHY; St Stephen Area HS; Saginaw, MI; Hon Rl; Sprt Ed Yrbk; Rptr Yrbk; Rptr Sch Nwsp; Letter Glf; Saginaw Vly St Coll; Bus.

DI LABIO, LISA; Grosse Pointe N HS; Grosse Pt Fms, MI; Chrh Wkr; Cmnty Wkr; Hon Rl; Hosp Ade; NHS; Spn Clb; History Cert Of Honor; Spanish Diploma Of Merit; College; Medicine.

DILE, CYNTHIA; Princeton HS; Cincinnati, OH; 167/671 Chrh Wkr; Western Kentucky Univ; Bus Admin.

DILGER, JAMES; St Edward HS; Cleveland, OH; Hon Rl; Lit Mag; NHS; Sch Pl; Drama Clb; Key Clb; IM Sprt; Oh Poetry Day Contst 1st Awd 78; 9th Annl Defiance Coll Poetry Day Hon Mntn 79; Univ; Jrnlsm.

DI LISIO, GERALDINE M; Woodrow Wilson HS; Youngstown, OH; Chrs; Cmnty Wkr; Pres Hosp Ade; JA; Lbry Ade; Off Ade; Pres Red Cr Ade; 4-H; FNA; VICA; The Apri Ca Basic Mdlng & Fnshng Course Awd 77; Sci Fair 76; Choffin Career Center Voc Schl; LPN.

DILL, LEE ANN K; Holt HS; Holt, MI; 2/343 Chrh Wkr; Hon Rl; NHS; Sch Pl; Yth Flsp; Civ Clb; Mgrs; Cit Awd; Schlstc Awd; Acctg Awd; Four Yr Camping Awd; Brigham Yng Univ; Acctg.

DILL, SUSAN; Vandalia Butler HS; Dayton, OH; AFS; Chrs; Hon Rl; NHS; Sch Mus; Sch Pl; Drama Clb; Fr Clb; Miami Univ.

DILL, TRACI; Mott HS; Pontiac, MI; 63/400 Sec Frsh Cls; Chrs; Debate Tm; Girl Scts; Hon Rl; Lit Mag; Sch Mus; Stu Cncl; Rptr Yrbk; Kalamazoo Coll; Intl Law.

DILLARD, DIANA; Coloma HS; Coloma, MI; Cls Rep Frsh Cls; Cls Rep Soph Cls; Chrs; Chrh Wkr; Girl Scts; Hon Rl; Stg Crw; Stu Cncl; Rptr Yrbk; Yrbk; Bus.

DILLARD, HAROLD R; Springs Valley HS; West Baden, IN; 18/81 Band; Boy Scts; Hon Rl; Orch; ROTC; Sch Pl; 4-H; Fr Clb; 4-H Awd; SAR Awd; Eagle Scout 1978; Order Of Arrow 1975; 4 Yr ROTC Award 1978; Indiana Univ; Psych.

DILLARD, PATRICIA; North HS; Columbus, OH; 1/325 Val; Band; Hon Rl; Lit Mag; NHS; Orch; Stu Cncl; Sec Fr Clb; Natl Merit Schl; Univ Of Pennsylvania; Computer Engr.

DILLBACK, CYNTHIA; North HS; Evansville, IN; 60/358 Pres Soph Cls; Band; Girl Scts; Quill & Scroll; Sch Mus; Stu Cncl; Ed Yrbk; 4-H; Pep Clb; Mgrs; Ball St Univ; Spec Ed.

DILLE, MARK; Brownsburg HS; Brownsburg, IN; 36/300 Boy Scts; Chrs; Hon Rl; Indiana St Univ; Chem.

DILLER, KAREN; Cuyahoga Falls HS; Cuyahoga Fls, OH; Cl Rep Jr Cls; Hon Rl; Jr NHS; NHS; Off Ade; Stu Cncl; Pres Spn Clb; Ten; Pres Akron Univ; Engr.

DILLER, MITZI; Clare HS; Farwell, MI; Cls Rep Frsh Cls; Sec Soph Cls; Pres Jr Cls; Band; Debate Tm; Girl Scts; NHS; Off Ade; Stu Cncl; Rptr Sch Nwsp; Aquina Univ; Med.

DILLERY, DARRYL; Albion Sr HS; Albion, MI; 10/220 Cls Rep Frsh Cls; Hon Rl; NHS; Sch Pl; Stu Cncl; Swmmng; Albion Coll; Econ.

DILLEY, BRENDA; Okemos HS; East Lansing, MI; 1/291 Val; NHS; Letter Ten; Hope Coll; Biology.

DILLEY, DONNA; Pocahontas County HS; Marlinton, WV; 28/120 Band; Chrs; Drl Tm; Girl Scts; Hon Rl; Hosp Ade; Lbry Ade; Sch Pl; Stg Crw; Drama Clb; YMCA Leadership Cert; Miss West Virginia Teen Contestant; West Virginia Weslyan Coll; Nursing.

DILLEY, GARY; Riley HS; Clrksbrg, WV; Boy Scts; Hon Rl; Ftbl; Trk; Wrstlng; Notre Dame Univ; Law.

DILLEY, JACQUELINE; Rock Hill Sr HS; Ironton, OH; Girl Scts; Hon Rl; Jr NHS; NHS; Stu Cncl; Rptr Yrbk; Beta Clb; Sci Clb; Chrldng;.

DILLEY, JACQUELINE; Rockhill HS; Ironton, OH; Hon Rl; Hosp Ade; Jr NHS; NHS; Stu Cncl; Yrbk; Beta Clb; Mth Clb; Capt Chrldng; Business School.

DILLEY, PAMELA; Pocahontas County HS; Marlinton, WV; 26/134 Sch Pl; Drama Clb; 4-H; VP FHA; FTA; Pep Clb; Bsktbl; Trk; Fairmont St Coll; Bus.

DILLEY, SUSAN; Ironton HS; Ironton, OH; Chrh Wkr; Hon Rl; Ger Clb; Bob Jones Univ; Nursing.

DILLHOFF, DARLENE; Carroll HS; Xenia, OH; Band; Cmnty Wkr; Girl Scts; Mgrs; Scr Kpr; Var Lttr In Band 76; Var Lttr In Sftbl As Stattcn & Mgr 78; Wright St Univ; Acctg.

DILLICK, LOIS A; Buchtel HS; Akron, OH; 6/452 Hon Rl; Lbry Ade; NHS; Bsktbl; College; Medicine.

DILLING, KENT; Northfield HS; N Manchester, IN; Pres Frsh Cls; Pres Soph Cls; Pres Jr Cls; Cls Rep Sr Cls; Chrs; Hon Rl; Sch Mus; Sch Pl; Pres Stu Cncl; Drama Clb; Purdue Univ; Agri.

DILLION, ELWOOD; London HS; London, OH; 16/130 Am Leg Boys St; Hon Rl; NHS; Fr Clb; Letter Hndbl; Letter Trk; Kiwan Awd; Ohio Univ; Med.

DILLION, KARMEN; London HS; London, OH; 14/150 Hon Rl; NHS; Quill & Scroll; Sch Pl; Sch Nwsp; Drama Clb; Letter Trk; Wittenberg Univ; Fine Arts.

DILLION, RUSTY; London HS; London, OH; 16/130 Am Leg Boys St; Hon Rl; NHS; Off Ade; Fr Clb; Letter Ftbl; Letter Trk; Kiwan Awd; Ohio Univ; Med.

DILLMAN, MARY S; Rutherford B Hayes HS; Delaware, OH; Cls Rep Soph Cls; Sec Jr Cls; Cls Rep Sr Cls; Pres AFS; Chrs; Pres Orch; Sch Mus; Stu Cncl; Yth Flsp; Y-Teens; Ohio St Univ; Music Ed.

DILLMAN, MIKE; Purcell HS; Cincinnati, OH; 161/180 Hon Rl; Coach Actv; IM Sprt; Natl Merit Ltr; Univ Of Cin; Bus Admin.

DILLMAN, MITCHELL F; Lawrence Central HS; Indianapolis, IN; 4/379 Chrs; Hon Rl; NHS; Yth Flsp; Key Clb; Sci Clb; Letter Ten; JETS Awd; Kiwan Awd; Top Percent In Natl Ed Deve Test; Top Percent In Amer Chem Soc Schlrshp Test; Leadershp & Sportsmanshp Awd; Purdue Univ; Chem Engr.

DILLON, CELESTE; Minerva HS; Paris, OH; 21/216 Am Leg Aux Girls St; Band; Hon Rl; Natl Forn Lg; Off Ade; Orch; Sch Pl; Drama Clb; Pres Fr Clb; FTA; Miami Univ; Foreign Languages.

DILLON, CHARLES; James A Garfield HS; Garrettsvle, OH; Pres Frsh Cls; VP Sr Cls; Hon Rl; Pres NHS; Stu Cncl; Fr Clb; Sci Clb; Letter Ftbl; Letter Wrstlng; College; Computer Science.

DILLON, DAVID; Chesterton HS; Chesterton, IN; 163/406 Boy Scts; Lbry Ade; Rdo Clb; Sec Spn Clb; IM Sprt; ISU; Math.

DILLON, DONNA; Bluefield HS; Bluefield, WV; Hon Rl; Y-Teens; Rptr Sch Nwsp; FHA; Univ.

DILLON, G C; Marysville HS; Raymond, OH; Girl Scts; Hon Rl; Hosp Ade; 4-H; FHA; Otterbein Coll; Elem Educ.

DILLON, JOE; Sandy Valley HS; East Sparta, OH; 60/170 Hon Rl; Ftbl; Malone Univ; History Tchr.

DILLON, JULIA; St Peters HS; Mansfield, OH; Cls Rep Frsh Cls; Sec Soph Cls; Cl Rep Jr Cls; JA; Yrbk; Drama Clb; IM Sprt; Mgrs; Mat Maids; College; Nursing.

DILLON, KAREN E; Huntington E HS; Huntington, WV; 1/340 Trs Jr Cls; Trs Sr Cls; Band; Drm Mjrt; NHS; VP FHA; Sec Keyettes; Mth Clb; DAR Awd; Elk Awd; Marshall Univ.

DILLON, MARY E; Bedford Sr HS; Temperance, MI; Chrs; Stu Cncl; Rptr Sch Nwsp; Mgrs; St Marys Coll; Nursing.

DILLON, MICHELE; Jackson HS; North Canton, OH; 25/400 Cls Rep Frsh Cls; Chrh Wkr; FCA; Hosp Ade; NHS; Pol Wkr; Sch Pl; Yth Flsp; Spn Clb; Letter Swmmng; Miami Univ; Law.

DILLON, SAMUEL; Woodsfield HS; Woodsfield, OH; Bsbl; Mgrs; Stdnt Councl Talent Show Winner 77; Engr Schl; Civil Engr.

DILLON, TIMOTHY; Bishop Dwenger HS; Ft Wayne, IN; Cls Rep Frsh Cls; Cls Rep Soph Cls; Chrh Wkr; Hon Rl; NHS; Off Ade; Sch Pl; Pres Fr Clb; College; Law.

DILLON, TONY; Princeton Cmnty HS; Princeton, IN; 1/203 Am Leg Boys St; Band; Chrh Wkr; NHS; Orch; Sch Mus; Yth Flsp; Mth Clb; Pres Spn Clb; Lion Awd; Mbr Of 1976 Marching Tigers Class B St Champ 76; Mbmr Of IN Pres Inauguration Band 77; Purdue Univ; Pre Vet.

DILLON, VICTORIA; Powers Catholic Central HS; Flint, MI; 8/272 Sec NHS; Fr Clb; Mott Cmnty Coll; Dent Asst.

DILMAN, DEBORAH; Mayville HS; Mayville, MI; 9/82 NHS; PPFtbl; Natl Merit Ltr; Western Mic Univ; Bus Admin.

DI LORETO, DANIEL; Massillon Washington HS; Massillon, OH; Hon Rl; Off Ade; OEA; Spn Clb; Letter Bsbl; Bsktbl; Letter Ftbl; Letter Trk; IM Sprt; College; Pre Med.

DILSAVER, SHEILA; Otsego HS; Weston, OH; 14/130 Cls Rep Soph Cls; Cl Rep Jr Cls; Hon Rl; Jr NHS; NHS; Stu Cncl; Yth Flsp; Yrbk; Drama Clb; Chrldng; Bowling Green St Univ; Computer Sci.

DILTS, WILLIAM; Philo HS; Ironsport, OH; Band; Drm Bgl; Hon Rl; NHS; Orch; Sch Mus; Sci Clb; Spn Clb; Letter Trk; All Ohio St Fair Band; College; Music.

DILTZ, LORA; Bradford HS; Covington, OH; Sec Soph Cls; Band; Drl Tm; Girl Scts; Hon Rl; Hosp Ade; NHS; Off Ade; Stu Cncl; College; Nursing.

DILWORTH, CYNTHIA; East Palestine HS; E Palestine, OH; Cmp Fr Grls; Chrs; Treas FHA; Trk; Scr Kpr; Youngstown St Univ; Interior Dsgn.

DI MARCO, JOHN; Bellefontaine Sr HS; Bellefontaine, OH; 10/250 Am Leg Boys St; Sec Band; Debate Tm; Hon Rl; NHS; Sch Pl; Drama Clb; Ger Clb; Sci Clb; Natl Merit Ltr; Coll; Engr.

DIMARIO, GREG; Padua Franciscan HS; Parma, OH; Hon Rl; Wrstlng; IM Sprt; Scr Kpr; Miami Univ; Business.

DIMAS, SYLVIA; Hartford HS; Hartford, MI; Band; Hon Rl; Lat Clb; Spn Clb; Letter Bsbl; Trk; PPFtbl; Univ; Bus Admin.

DI MASCIO, PAULA A; Akron Garfield HS; Akron, OH; 29/450 Pres Band; Chrh Wkr; Girl Scts; Lit Mag; NHS; Orch; Stg Crw; Fr Clb; Lat Clb; Akron Univ; Health.

DI MASSA, SALVATORE F; North Royalton HS; N Royalton, OH; Boy Scts; Letter Bsktbl; Ftbl; Coach Actv; IM Sprt; Univ; Bus.

DIMATTIO, CYNTHIA; Newbury HS; Novelty, OH; Band; Chrs; Girl Scts; Yth Flsp; Rptr Sch Nwsp; Bsktbl; Trk; Chrldng; Mat Maids; John Caroll Univ; Journalist.

DIMBATH, KAREN; Centerville HS; Centerville, OH; 132/687 Band; NHS; Sct Actv; Christ Hosp Schl Nrsng; Nursing.

DIMEFF, BOB; Akron Ellet HS; Akron, OH; 1/363 Am Leg Boys St; Hon Rl; Jr NHS; NHS; Red Cr Ade; Spn Clb; Letter Ftbl; Ten; IM Sprt; Univ Of Akron; Med.

DIMIT, JEFFREY; Fort Wayne N Side HS; Ft Wayne, IN; 6/456 Aud/Vis; Letter Crs Cntry; Wrstlng; Univ Of Illinois; Civil Engr.

DIMITROFF, SASHE; The Valley HS; Flint, MI; Hon Rl; Lbry Ade; Orch; Sch Pl; Sct Actv; Fr Clb; Crs Cntry; Socr; IM Sprt; Cit Awd; Univ Of Michigan; Medicine.

DIMOND, STEVE; Delton Kellogg HS; Delton, MI; 7/160 Hon Rl; Davenport Coll; Mach Mrktng.

DIMOND, TERRI; Bethel HS; Tipp City, OH; Sec Soph Cls; VP Jr Cls; Cmp Fr Grls; Chrs; Drl Tm; Hon Rl; Sch Mus; Sch Pl; Stg Crw; Stu Cncl; College; Interior Decorator.

DIMOVICH, PETER; Frank Cody HS; Detroit, MI; Hon Rl; NHS; Letter Crs Cntry; College; Chem.

DIMOVICH, VELKO; Frank Cody HS; Detroit, MI; NHS; Off Ade; Univ Of Michigan; Engr.

DIN, NAVEED A; Linsly Military Institute; Bethlehem Whlng, WV; 5/65 Cls Rep Soph Cls; Cl Rep Jr Cls; Band; Chrs; Cmnty Wkr; Debate Tm; Drl Tm; Drm Bgl; Hon Rl; Pres Lbry Ade; Sgt Major 78; Bst Non Commissnd Offcr Awd From U S Army 78; Sr Perfctt Attndnc 79; Pre Med.

DINAN, KEVIN; Zanesville Bishop HS; Zanesville, OH; VP Sr Cls; Hon Rl; Jr NHS; NHS; Rptr Yrbk; Yrbk; Rptr Sch Nwsp; Sch Nwsp; Key Clb; Bsbl; Ohio Univ; Engr.

DI NARDO, ELLEN; Cabrini HS; Allen Pk, MI; Chrh Wkr; Cmnty Wkr; Hon Rl; Jr NHS; NHS; Sch Mus; Sch Pl; Stg Crw; Sec Drama Clb; French Awd 78; Morality & Media Contst 79; Mercy Univ; Nursing.

DI NARDO, JOHN; Cabrini HS; Allen Park, MI; 3/145 Hon Rl; Jr NHS; NHS; Sch Mus; Sch Pl; VP Drama Clb; Am Leg Awd; Kiwan Awd; Natl Merit Ltr; Univ Of Mich; Law.

DINEEN, MARK; Boardman HS; Boardman, OH; 98/612 Hon Rl; NHS; Spn Clb; Crs Cntry; Trk;.

DINES, MARY K; Montmorency Atlanta Comm HS; Atlanta, MI; Pres Jr Cls; Hon Rl; Sch Pl; Stg Crw; Yrbk; 4-H; FHA; Pep Clb; Bsbl; Letter Trk; College; Stewertist.

DINGEMAN, MARK; St Agatha HS; Detroit, MI; 3/135 Boy Scts; Hon Rl; NHS; Sch Pl; Sct Actv; Spn Clb; Letter Trk; Scr Kpr; Voice Dem Awd; Wayne State Univ; Busns Admin.

DINGER, DEB; Clear Fork HS; Butler, OH; 20/170 Chrs; Girl Scts; Hon Rl; Lbry Ade; Lit Mag; Sch Mus; Sch Nwsp; 4-H; Pep Clb; Spn Clb; Bowling Green Univ; Jrnlsm.

DINGWELL, MICHELLE; Vale HS; Goodells, MI; Girl Scts; Hosp Ade; Lbry Ade; Sch Nwsp; 4-H; Bsbl; Bsktbl; Ftbl; Hndbl; Socr; St Clair Comm Coll; Comm Art.

DINKA, JOHN; Grosse Pointe South HS; Grosse Pointe, MI; 1/548 Cmnty Wkr; Debate Tm; Hon Rl; NHS; Pres Ger Clb; Trk; Cit Awd; Univ Of Detroit Insignis Schlrshp 79; Congressmn Medl Of Merit 79; Mi Legislative Merit Awd 79; Univ Of Detroit; Med.

DIONNE, MIDGE; Airport HS; Monroe, MI; Cmp Fr Grls; Chrs; Debate Tm; Sch Mus; Drama Clb; Fr Clb; Pep Clb; Pom Pon;.

DI ORIO, K; Kettering Fairmont West HS; Kettering, OH; Sec Soph Cls; Sec Jr Cls; Cls Rep Sr Cls; Hon Rl; Stu Cncl; Yth Flsp; Fr Clb; Twrlr; College; Special Educ.

DIORKA, SANDRA; Essexville Garber HS; Essexville, MI; 7/179 Band; Chrh Wkr; Girl Scts; Hon Rl; Sct Actv; Yth Flsp; 4-H; God Cntry Awd; Art Carvd Name Game Drawng Winner 1000 78; Girls Scout 1st Scl 77; Western Michigan Univ; Med Tech.

DI PANGRAZIO, SHARON; Holyname Nazareth HS; Parma, OH; Cmnty Wkr; Hosp Ade; Lit Mag; Lat Clb; Ten; Ohi State Univ; Dent.

DI PERSI, RENEE; Liberty HS; Youngstown, OH; Cl Rep Jr Cls; AFS; Chrs; Chrs; Girl Scts; Hon Rl; Natl Forn Lg; Sch Mus; Stg Crw; Drama Clb; Children Civic Theater Of Youngstown Stge Mgr Of Yr 79; Cls A Solo Compt Of Oh 2 Rating 79; Univ; Music.

DIPERT, RICHARD; Oregon Davis HS; Walkerton, IN; Band; Boy Scts; Chrh Wkr; Sct Actv; God Cntry Awd; Eagle Scout; Pep Band; Indiana St Univ; Psych.

DI PIETRANTONIO, ANTOINETTE; St Ursula Academy; Cincinnati, OH; VP Frsh Cls; Chrh Wkr; Girl Scts; NHS; Stu Cncl; Yth Flsp; Spn Clb; Chrldng; Coach Actv; GAA; Most Outstndng Stu; Sci Fair Awds; College; Archt.

DI PIETRO, JOSEPH; Cardinal Mooney HS; Youngstown, OH; 72/288 Cls Rep Sr Cls; Hon Rl; Stu Cncl; Ftbl; IM Sprt; College; Optometry.

DIPPEL, MICHAEL; Muskegon Catholic Ctrl HS; Muskegon, MI; Trs Frsh Cls; Cls Rep Soph Cls; Pres Jr Cls; Cls Rep Sr Cls; Hon Rl; Sch Pl; Stu Cncl; Drama Clb; Letter Bsbl; Letter Ftbl; Muskegon Comm College.

DI RENZO, TERESA; Boardman HS; Youngstown, OH; Cls Rep Frsh Cls; Cls Rep Soph Cls; Cl Rep Jr Cls; Cls Rep Sr Cls; Hon Rl; Jr NHS; Stu Cncl; Y-Teens; Pep Clb; Chrldng; Mount Union Univ; Med Tech.

DIRIG, SCOTT; Elmhurst HS; Ft Wayne, IN; Elmhurst High Acad Achvmnt Awd 77 & 78; Air Force Acad; Comp Engr.

DIRKS, LINDA; Rocky River HS; Rocky River, OH; 11/312 Hon Rl; Lit Mag; NHS; Tmr; Cleveland State Univ; Engineering.

DIRKSEN, CARLA; Marion Local HS; Maria Stein, OH; 20/88 Hon Rl; NHS; Stu Cncl; 4-H; FHA; FTA; Sci Clb; Letter Trk; 4-H Awd; College; Computer Sci.

DIRKSEN, TERESA; Marion Local HS; Maria Stein, OH; Am Leg Aux Girls St; Band; Hon Rl; NHS; FHA; Pep Clb; Sci Clb; IM Sprt; Scr Kpr; 2nd Pl Bio II & World Hist; 2nd Pl Chem; 3rd Pl Eng III; Participated In Project Sci Scholar Prog; Univ Of Dayton; Med Tech.

DIRLAM, DANA; Delta HS; Muncie, IN; 5/330 Chrh Wkr; FCA; Girl Scts; Hon Rl; JA; NHS; Stu Cncl; Yth Flsp; FHA; Sci Clb; High Sales JA 78; Treas Of The Hr JA 79; Univ; CPA.

DIRLAM, JOHN E; Delta HS; Muncie, IN; 8/300 Hon Rl; NHS; Yth Flsp; Fr Clb; Spn Clb; Wrstlng; Purdue Univ; Mech Engr.

DI SALVO, LISA; Carroll HS; Dayton, OH; Drl Tm; Natl Merit Ltr; Ohio St Univ; Bus.

DISHAW, SHARON; Forest Park HS; Crystal Falls, MI; 18/85 Sec Frsh Cls; Sec Soph Cls; Band; Hon Rl; Stu Cncl; 4-H; Trk; Capt Chrldng; IM Sprt; 4-H Awd; Ferris St Univ; Food Serv.

DISHER, SUSAN; Triton Jr Sr HS; Bourbon, IN; 6/79 Band; Hon Rl; Pres NHS; 4-H; FBLA; FTA; Pep Clb; GAA; Cit Awd; DAR Awd; Bnd Pin; Bnd Medals 77; Typing Cert 78; Bnd Cert; Hstry Cert; Acctg II Cert 79; Ivy Tech Univ; Bus.

DISHMAN, LOUETTA; Union HS; Mooreland, IN; 14/60 Hon Rl; Lat Clb; Ivy Tech Voc Schl; Comp Progr.

DISHON, CARLA; Greenon HS; Springfield, OH; 52/405 Chrh Wkr; Girl Scts; Hon Rl; JA; Sch Mus; Sch Pl; Stg Crw; Rptr Sch Nwsp; Sch Nwsp; Drama Clb; Univ; Eng.

DISMORE, TERRI; Henryville HS; Henryville, IN; Girl Scts; Hon Rl; Off Ade; Red Cr Ade; Sch Pl; Sct Actv; DECA; 4-H; FHA; Ind Univ Se; Tchr.

DISSELKOEN, LORI; Zeeland HS; Zeeland, MI; 3/200 Am Leg Aux Girls St; Band; Chrh Wkr; Hon Rl; Mod UN; MMM; NHS; Treas Yth Flsp; Mth Clb; Letter Ten; Univ Of Mich; Comp Sci.

DISSINGER, JULIE; Heath HS; Heath, OH; Am Leg Aux Girls St; Band; Sec Chrs; FCA; Hosp Ade; Mdrgl; Sch Mus; VP FNA; Trk; Univ; Nursing.

DISTEL, BRETT; Mohawk HS; Tiffin, OH; Cls Rep Frsh Cls; Cls Rep Soph Cls; Boy Scts; Chrs; Hon Rl; NHS; Sct Actv; Stu Cncl; FTA; Ger Clb; Bowling Green Univ; Transportation.

DISTEL, GREG; Calvert HS; Tiffin, OH; Letter Ftbl; Wrstlng; Coach Actv; Toledo Univ; Bus.

DITMER, ROY E; Eaton HS; Eaton, OH; Chrs; Sch Mus; Sch Pl; Stg Crw; Bsktbl; Ftbl; Trk; Univ; Indus Ed.

DITS, DAVID; Marian HS; South Bend, IN; 4/150 Cmnty Wkr; Hon Rl; NHS; Spn Clb; Socr; Univ Of Notre Dame; Engr.

DITTENBER, SUSAN; Au Gres Sims HS; Au Gres, MI; Pres Frsh Cls; Pres Soph Cls; Cl Rep Jr Cls; Band; Girl Scts; Hon Rl; Natl Forn Lg; VP NHS; Stu Cncl; Yrbk; Coll.

DITTMANN, KAREN; Seton HS; Cincinnati, OH; 15/280 Chrs; Girl Scts; Hon Rl; Sec Jr NHS; NHS; Treas Orch; Sch Mus; Sct Actv; Fr Clb; Univ Of Cincinnati; Music.

DITTMANN, KAREN M; Seton HS; Cincinnati, OH; 13/254 Chrs; Girl Scts; Hon Rl; Jr NHS; NHS; Orch; Red Cr Ade; Sch Mus; Sct Actv; Sch Nwsp; Univ Of Cincinnati; Music.

DITTMER, JEFF; Capitol City Christian HS; Lansing, MI; VP Sr Cls; Chrs; Hon Rl; NHS; Letter Bsbl; Letter Bsktbl; Letter Crs Cntry; Letter Socr; Letter Trk; Letter Wrstlng; Grand Rapids Baptist Coll; Bus.

DITTMER, TERRI M; Firelands HS; Berlin Heights, OH; Band; Drm Mjrt; Girl Scts; Hon Rl; Off Ade; Sct Actv; Y-Teens; 4-H; 4-H Awd; Pep Band Cncert Band Marching Band; 4h Pres; Comp Progr.

DITTNER, MARK; Northwest HS; Canal Fulton, OH; Hon Rl; NHS; Lat Clb; Bsbl; Ftbl;.

DITTO, KATHY; Delphos St Johns HS; Delphos, OH; Pres Frsh Cls; Val; Band; Hon Rl; Jr NHS; NHS; Orch; Sch Pl; Rptr Sch Nwsp; FTA; Univ Of Toledo; Pharm.

DITZ, PATRICIA; Springfield North HS; Springfield, OH; Cls Rep Soph Cls; Cl Rep Jr Cls; Chrh Wkr; Girl Scts; Hon Rl; NHS; Stu Cncl; Rptr Sch Nwsp; College; Juvenile Delinguents.

DIVER, BONITA; Deerfield HS; Deerfield, MI; Trs Frsh Cls; Am Leg Aux Girls St; Band; Chrh Wkr; Hon Rl; NHS; Yth Flsp; 4-H; 4-H Awd; Voc Schl; Dent Asst.

DIVITO, RAFFAELA; St Augustine Academy; Cleveland, OH; Chrh Wkr; Girl Scts; Hon Rl; Natl Jr Tennis League Parks Tourney Doubles Runner Up 76; Bsktbl Our Lady Of Mt Carmel Most Imprvd Playr 76;.

DIWYK, IRENE; Andrean HS; Gary, IN; 21/251 Sec Jr Cls; Pres Sr Cls; Am Leg Aux Girls St; Hon Rl; Ger Clb; Mth Clb; Coll; Comp Sci.

DIX, CARLA; Cory Rawson HS; Findlay, OH; 12/65 Trs Frsh Cls; Aud/Vis; Band; Chrh Wkr; Hon Rl; NHS; Off Ade; College; Office Med Asst.

DIX, KEVIN; Paulding HS; Paulding, OH; Hon Rl; Spn Clb; Univ Of Ala; Wildlife Mgmt.

DIXIT, SUDHAKAR; Park Hills HS; Fairborn, OH; 36/366 Am Leg Boys St; Hon Rl; NHS; Mth Clb; Swmmng; Am Leg Awd; JA Awd; Wright St Univ; Med.

DIXON, BRYAN K; St Charles Prep; Westerville, OH; Sec Sr Cls; Hon Rl; NHS; Letter Bsbl; Letter Ftbl; IM Sprt; Dnfth Awd; Notre Dame; Law.

DIXON, CHARLOTTE L; Saginaw HS; Saginaw, MI; Sec Frsh Cls; Cls Rep Soph Cls; Cl Rep Jr Cls; Band; Chrh Wkr; Hon Rl; Drama Clb; Outstng Sut 76; 8th Annual Black Hnr Convocation Awd 78; Sec Sunday Schl Dept Lion Baptst Chrch 79; Univ Of Michigan; Law.

DIXON, CINDY; Elk Garden HS; Elk Garden, WV; 1/38 Sec Soph Cls; Trs Soph Cls; Sec Jr Cls; Am Leg Aux Girls St; Band; Chrh Wkr; Hon Rl; Sch Mus; Sch Pl; Yth Flsp; Potomac St Univ; Soc Work.

DIXON, DANIEL; Waverly HS; Waverly, OH; 6/175 Band; Boy Scts; Hon Rl; NHS; Letter Crs Cntry; Letter Trk; Am Leg Awd; Oh Univ HS Schlr 79; Univ.

DIXON, DAVID; Piketon HS; Piketon, OH; 7/115 Chrh Wkr; Hon Rl; Jr NHS; NHS; Sch Nwsp; Pep Clb; Bsbl; Bsktbl; Letter Trk; IM Sprt; Univ; Acctg.

DIXON, DIANNE; Harper Creek HS; Battle Creek, MI; 3/240 Band; Hon Rl; NHS; Orch; Bsktbl; Swmmng; Capt Chrldng; Univ; Writer.

DIXON, HEBREW L; Stivers Patterson HS; Dayton, OH; Cls Rep Frsh Cls; VP Jr Cls; Band; Chrs; Drm Mjrt; Hon Rl; JA; Sch Pl; Boys Clb Am; VICA; Optimist Internatl Oratorical Contest; Pl In Annual Midwest Ceramic Show; Pl In M D Bowlerama; Cincinnati Univ; Archt.

DIXON, JOHN; Scecina HS; Indianapolis, IN; Hon Rl; Rptr Sch Nwsp; Letter Ftbl; Letter Wrstlng; Lincoln Tech Inst.

DIXON, KATHY; Ridgedale HS; Marion, OH; 1/96 Sec Soph Cls; Drl Tm; Hon Rl; NHS; Rptr Yrbk; Pres FHA; Leo Clb; College; Pre Med.

DIXON, KIM; Little Miami HS; Morrow, OH; Cl Rep Jr Cls; Girl Scts; Hon Rl; Jr NHS; Lit Mag; NHS; Off Ade; Rptr Yrbk; Fr Clb; Bsbl; Top 10% PSAT 79; Otstndng Acctg Stud Cert 78; Univ; Bus Admin.

DIXON, LINDA; Ross Sr HS; Hamitlon, OH; 41/226 Band; Chrs; Drm Mjrt; Girl Scts; Hon Rl; NHS; Rptr Yrbk; 4-H; Sec Fr Clb; Letter Trk; Univ.

DIXON, PAUL; Lincolnview Local HS; Van Wert, OH; 12/78 Am Leg Boys St; Hon Rl; NHS; Pol Wkr; Treas DECA; Bsktbl; Wright St Univ; Finance.

DIXON, SARA; Lincolnview HS; Van Wert, OH; 4/80 Hon Rl; Jr NHS; Sec NHS; Pol Wkr; 4-H; Fr Clb; FFA; GAA; College; Argi.

DIXON, SUZANNA; Groveport Madison HS; Columbus, OH; 72/377 Band; Chrs; Girl Scts; Sch Nwsp; 4-H; Fr Clb; Trk; Chrldng; College; Journ.

DIZE, KATHY; New Haven HS; Ft Wayne, IN; 32/344 Cls Rep Frsh Cls; Cls Rep Soph Cls; Cl Rep Jr Cls; Band; Chrs; Chrh Wkr; Drl Tm; Hon Rl; Sct Actv; Stu Cncl; Indiana Univ; Med.

DLOUHY, KIMBALL; Elkhart Bapt Christian HS; Union, MI; Cls Rep Frsh Cls; Pres Soph Cls; Val; Band; Chrs; Chrh Wkr; Hon Rl; Sch Pl; Sct Actv; Stu Cncl; Grand Rapids Bapt Coll; Educ.

DLUGOPOLSKI, PAUL; Clintondale HS; Mt Clemens, MI; 15/270 Cl Rep Jr Cls; Cls Rep Sr Cls; Hon Rl; NHS; Stu Cncl; Key Clb; Letter Ftbl; Wayne St Univ; Civil Engr.

DLUGOS, JENNIFER; St Francis HS; Star City, WV; Capt Drl Tm; VP Hon Rl; Sch Mus; Rptr Yrbk; Rptr Sch Nwsp; Drama Clb; Fr Clb; Pep Clb; Letter Trk; West Virginia Univ.

DOAK, ANGIE; Tyler County HS; Middlebourne, WV; 17/100 Trs Soph Cls; Cl Rep Jr Cls; Band; Hon Rl; NHS; Off Ade; Pol Wkr; Stu Cncl; Yrbk; Ed Sch Nwsp; Ohio Valley Coll; Sec Sci.

DOAKS, MARCUS; Washington HS; So Bend, IN; Boy Scts; Chrh Wkr; Hon Rl; Sct Actv; Letter Bsbl; Letter Ftbl; Univ; Bus.

DOANE, KERRY C; Lakewood HS; Lake Odessa, MI; 12/180 Cls Rep Sr Cls; Band; Hon Rl; Jr NHS; NHS; Treas Stu Cncl; Rptr Yrbk; Pep Clb; Trk; Capt Chrldng; Michigan State Univ; Bsns Admin.

DOBBEN, BRIAN; Mansfield Christian HS; Ashland, OH; Band; Treas NHS; Natl Merit Ltr; Le Tourneau College; Mech Eng.

DOBBINS, MICHELE; Braxton County Sr HS; Frametown, WV; Cls Rep Frsh Cls; Hst Soph Cls; Hst Jr Cls; Hst Sr Cls; FCA; Hon Rl; Stu Cncl; Yrbk; Pep Clb; Trk; Alderson Broaddus Coll; Med.

DOBBS, JILL; Lincoln HS; Vincennes, IN; Hon Rl; Off Ade; Rptr Sch Nwsp; IM Sprt; Vincennes Univ; Commrcl Art.

DOBBS, RANDY; John Marshall HS; Indianapolis, IN; 40/612 Hon Rl; IM Sprt; Ind Univ; Bus.

DOBECK, TIMOTHY G; Valley Forge Sr HS; Parma, OH; 101/703 Pres Soph Cls; Pres Jr Cls; Pres Sr Cls; NHS; Pol Wkr; Stu Cncl; Y-Teens; Yrbk; Rptr Sch Nwsp; Letter Bsbl; Cleveland St Univ; Poli Sci.

DOBER, LISA; Port Clinton HS; Pt Clinton, OH; Hon Rl; Off Ade; Yrbk; Pep Clb; Spn Clb; Mgrs; Ohio State Univ.

DOBLER, STEVE; Peru HS; Peru, IN; 13/260 Cls Rep Frsh Cls; Pres Soph Cls; Hon Rl; NHS; Stu Cncl; Pep Clb; Ftbl; Wrstlng; Purdue Univ; Elec Engr.

DOBSON, BETH; Wellsville HS; Wellsville, OH; 6/145 Cls Rep Frsh Cls; Cls Rep Soph Cls; Pres Jr Cls; Am Leg Aux Girls St; Pres Band; Hon Rl; NHS; Sch Mus; Sch Pl; Stg Crw; Intl Paper Co Essay Contest Runnr Up 79; Univ; Phys Ther.

DOBSON, CATHY; Vassar HS; Vassar, MI; 26/214 Band; Drl Tm; Girl Scts; Hon Rl; JA; Sct Actv; Stg Crw; Yth Flsp; Fr Clb; Spn Clb; French Outstdg 79; Natl Majorette Camp 76; Top 20% Class 79; Univ Of Florida; Emergcy Med.

DOCKERY, RAMONA; North HS; Evansville, IN; 53/360 Off Ade; PPFtbl; Hnry St Schlrshp 79; Whos Who In Amer HS Stu 77; Indiana St Univ; Spanish.

DODAK, BETHANY; Chesaning Union HS; Burt, MI; Band; Cmp Fr Grls; Drl Tm; Hon Rl; Hosp Ade; Pol Wkr; Yrbk; Swmmng; College; Retail Fash Merch.

DODD, CHERYL; Jesup W Scott HS; Toledo, OH; Pres Frsh Cls; Pres Soph Cls; Pres Jr Cls; Chrs; Hon Rl; Off Ade; Quill & Scroll; Sch Mus; Stu Cncl; Pep Clb; Univ; Marketing.

DODD, KAREN; Firelands HS; Amherst, OH; 7/170 Pres Jr Cls; Band; Hon Rl; NHS; 4-H; Chrldng; 4-H Awd; College; Math.

DODD, LEE A; Roosevelt Wilson HS; Clarksburg, WV; Band; Debate Tm; Hon Rl; Lbry Ade; Red Cr Ade; Sch Pl; Y-Teens; FTA; Lat Clb; Pep Clb; Salem Coll; Law.

DODD, ROBIN; Anderson HS; Anderson, IN; Chrs; Hon Rl; Pep Clb; Anderson Coll; Nurse.

DODD, TONIA; Whetstone HS; Columbus, OH; 76/365 Band; Cmp Fr Grls; Chrs; Chrh Wkr; Hon Rl; Hosp Ade; JA; MMM; NHS; Orch; Miss Congeniality; Who He Lo Medallion Comp Fire Girls Eagle Scout; Ohio St Univ; Music.

DODDERER, TODD; Johnstown Monroe HS; Johnstown, OH; 34/145 Pres Soph Cls; Pres Jr Cls; Pres Sr Cls; Cmnty Wkr; Debate Tm; 4-H; FFA; Pep Clb; Letter Bsktbl; Letter Glf; College.

DODDERER, TODD; Johnstown Monroe HS; , ; 34/139 Pres Soph Cls; Pres Jr Cls; Pres Sr Cls; Cmnty Wkr; Sch Pl; Yth Flsp; 4-H; FFA; Letter Bsktbl; Letter Ftbl; Wilmington Coll.

DODDS, FAYE; North Branch HS; North Branch, MI; 28/170 Band; Chrs; Chrh Wkr; Drl Tm; Hon Rl; 4-H; Spring Arbor Coll; Bio.

DODDS, G ALFRED; Culver Military Acad; Brunswick, OH; 4/191 Drl Tm; Lbry Ade; NHS; ROTC; Glf; IM Sprt; Natl Merit Ltr; Univ; Med.

DODGE, JENNIFER; North Canton Hoover HS; North Canton, OH; 14/425 Am Leg Aux Girls St; Band; Chrh Wkr; Cmnty Wkr; Hon Rl; NHS; Yth Flsp; Pep Clb; Spn Clb; Pres Awd; College; Bus.

DODGE, MARTIN; Jackson HS; Jackson, MI; Hon Rl; Quill & Scroll; Sprt Ed Sch Nwsp; Ger Clb; Letter Ftbl; W Michigan Univ; Computer Sci.

DODMAN, PAMELA; Turpin HS; Cincinnati, OH; 10/357 NHS; Capt Bsktbl; Letter Ten; Capt PPFtbl; Miami Univ; Psychology.

DOENGES, PHILIP; Concordia Lutheran HS; Ft Wayne, IN; 50/200 Chrs; Chrh Wkr; Drl Tm; Capt ROTC; FBLA; Lat Clb; Sci Clb; Univ; Comp Tech.

DOERFLEIN, JOSEPH; Brookville HS; Metamora, IN; 58/200 Aud/Vis; Hon Rl; 4-H; Coll; Chem.

DOERFLER, KEVIN; Mc Comb HS; Mccomb, OH; Cl Rep Jr Cls; Am Leg Boys St; Chrs; Chrh Wkr; Hon Rl; Sch Pl; Rptr Yrbk; Rptr Sch Nwsp; Sch Nwsp; 4-H; Valparaiso Coll; Journalism.

DOERFLER, MICHAEL; Northwestern HS; Wooster, OH; Hst Soph Cls; Band; Chrs; Chrh Wkr; Hon Rl; NHS; Sch Pl; Stu Cncl; Drama Clb; Pres Fr Clb; Univ; Dsgn Engr.

DOERING, LISA; Jimtown HS; Elkhart, IN; Band; Chrs; Chrh Wkr; Hon Rl; Sch Pl; Yth Flsp; DECA; Bsktbl; Pom Pon; PPFtbl; Univ.

DOGAN, JOHN; Coldwater HS; Coldwater, MI; Letter Ftbl; Letter Ten; Letter Trk; Albion Coll; Bus Admin.

DOGGETT, DE ANNA; Bellbrook HS; Bellbrook, OH; Pres Frsh Cls; Trs Jr Cls; NHS; Sch Pl; Pres Yth Flsp; Treas Fr Clb; FFA; Lat Clb; Chrldng; Twrlr; Oral Roberts Univ.

DOGGETT, RANDALL; Madison Plains Local HS; London, OH; NHS; Mgrs; Natl Merit Ltr; Univ; Chem.

DOHERTY, COLLEEN; Amelia HS; Amelia, OH; Girl Scts; Hon Rl; Off Ade; Fr Clb; Good Samaritan School Of Nurse Nurse.

DOHERTY, LOUISE; Mt Notre Dame HS; Cincinnati, OH; 11/173 Cls Rep Soph Cls; Cl Rep Jr Cls; Cmnty Wkr; Hon Rl; Jr NHS; NHS; Sch Pl; Stu Cncl; Rptr Sch Nwsp; Spn Clb; Univ Of Cincinnati; Busns Mgmt.

DOHM, KATHY; Traverse City HS; Traverse City, MI; 8/700 NHS; Pep Clb; Trk; Natl Merit Ltr; Nw Mich Coll; Med.

DOHNER, DEBORAH; South Newton HS; Kentland, IN; Chrh Wkr; Drl Tm; Girl Scts; Sch Pl; Yth Flsp; Ed Yrbk; Lat Clb; Pep Clb; College;.

DOING, PAULA; Berkshire HS; Burton, OH; 3/128 AFS; Band; Hon Rl; Jr NHS; MMM; NHS; 4-H; 4-H Awd; Natl Merit SF; Mt Vernon Nazarene Coll; Natural Res.

DOKES, JENNIFER; Buckeye North HS; Smithfield, OH; 4/110 Sec Frsh Cls; Trs Soph Cls; VP Sr Cls; Chrh Wkr; Hon Rl; Treas NHS; Stu Cncl; Rptr Sch Nwsp; Pep Clb; Bsktbl; Soc Of Distinguished H S Students; Coll Of Steubenville; Communications.

DOL, GEORGE; La Salle HS; S Bend, IN; Hon Rl; Y-Teens; Pep Clb; Indiana Univ; Math.

DOLAN, DIANE; Memphis HS; Memphis, MI; 5/95 Sec Frsh Cls; Trs Soph Cls; Trs Jr Cls; Trs Sr Cls; Hon Rl; Rptr Sch Nwsp; Letter Bsktbl; Letter Trk; PPFtbl; Univ; Bus Mgmt.

DOLAN, JAMES; Pocahontas County HS; Arbovale, WV; 8/130 Hon Rl; NHS; Letter Bsktbl; IM Sprt; Fairmont St Coll; Bus.

DOLAN, P; Greenbrier East HS; Ronceverte, WV; FCA; Girl Scts; Hon Rl; Yth Flsp; Bsktbl; Trk; College; Physical Education.

DOLAN, VALERIE; East Canton HS; East Canton, OH; 2/115 Band; Chrs; Hon Rl; Jr NHS; NHS; Pres FTA; Pep Clb; Sci Clb; Pres Spn Clb; Bsktbl; Univ; Math.

DOLATOWSKI, TOM; Parma Sr HS; Parma, OH; 69/710 NHS; Sch Pl; Pres FFA; Ohio St Univ; Horticulture.

DOLD, MARYELLEN; Servite HS; Detroit, MI; 3/96 Pres Frsh Cls; Pres Soph Cls; Pres Jr Cls; Hon Rl; Jr NHS; NHS; Red Cr Ade; Letter Bsbl; Letter Bsktbl; Letter Trk; Walsh Inst; Bus.

DOLE, JOHN; Grandville HS; Walker, MI; 10/360 Hon Rl; Jr NHS; Stg Crw; Rptr Yrbk; 4-H; 4-H Awd; Natl Merit Ltr; Michigan St Univ; Bio.

DOLES, TERESA; Vinton Co Consolidated HS; Londonderry, OH; 18/155 Chrh Wkr; Spn Clb; Voc Schl; Keypunch Operator.

DOLEZAN, STEPHEN; Hartford HS; Hartford, MI; Band; Hon Rl; Stg Crw; Bsbl; Bsktbl; Cert Of Mert In Basic Design Field Std 77; Genrl Bus & World Geog Merts 76; Sr & Stage Band Awds 76 79; ITT; Elec.

DOLIN, APRIL; Northwest HS; Canal Fulton, OH; Am Leg Aux Girls St; Band; Chrh Wkr; Hon Rl; Hosp Ade; Jr NHS; Sec Natl Forn Lg; NHS; Off Ade; Sch Mus; Coll; Nursing.

DOLL, LARRY J; North Knox HS; Bicknell, IN; Chrh Wkr; NHS; Red Cr Ade; 4-H; US Air Force Acad; Aero Engr.

DOLL, LYNN; Bath HS; Dewitt, MI; 19/101 Hon Rl; Off Ade; Vllybl Awd A Bee 78; Lansing Cmnty Coll; Acctg.

DOLL, MARY BETH; Mother Of Mercy HS; Cincinnati, OH; Cls Rep Soph Cls; Girl Scts; Hon Rl; Fr Clb; GAA; IM Sprt; Cit Awd; Stud Of Wk 77; Marian Awd Girl Scouts 76; Univ Of Cincinnati; Math.

DOLL, MYRNA; Pennsboro HS; Pennsboro, WV; 3/50 Cls Rep Soph Cls; Band; Chrh Wkr; Cmnty Wkr; Drm Mjrt; Natl Forn Lg; NHS; Sch Pl; Stu Cncl; College; Radio Tech.

DOLL, RENEE; Rivet HS; Vincennes, IN; 4/47 Cls Rep Frsh Cls; Am Leg Aux Girls St; Chrs; Hon Rl; Sch Mus; Sch Pl; Stu Cncl; Fr Clb; Bsktbl; Crs Cntry; Notre Dame Univ; Medicine.

DOLL, SABRINA; Rivet HS; Vincennes, IN; Cls Rep Frsh Cls; Cl Rep Jr Cls; Chrs; Hon Rl; Sch Mus; Sch Pl; Stu Cncl; Drama Clb; Pep Clb; Bsktbl; College; Medicine.

DOLLER, CHERYL; Forest Park HS; Cincinnati, OH; 1/360 Hon Rl; NHS; Spn Clb; Univ; Elem Educ.

DOLLHOPF, KENNETH; Wayne Memorial HS; Westland, MI; 9/750 Band; Drm Mjrt; Hon Rl; NHS; Orch; Sch Mus; Mth Clb; IM Sprt; Michigan Tech Univ; Engr.

DOLORESCO, JENNIFER; Northwest HS; Cincinnati, OH; 1/438 Sec Frsh Cls; Cls Rep Frsh Cls; Cls Rep Sr Cls; Val; NHS; Ed Yrbk; Beta Clb; Bausch & Lomb Awd; JETS Awd; Kiwan Awd; Purdue Univ; Chem Engr.

DOLPH, DEBORAH K; Chesterton HS; Chesterton, IN; 18/409 Hon Rl; NHS; Sch Pl; Stg Crw; Ftbl; Trk; Wrstlng; Mgrs; Mat Maids; Scr Kpr; Colorado St Univ; Sci.

DOLSEN, RONALD; Au Gres Sims HS; Au Gres, MI; Chrh Wkr; Hon Rl; Natl Forn Lg; Sch Pl; Stg Crw; Ger Clb; Cit Awd; U S Navy; Nuclear.

DOLSKY, CHARLES; Stephenson HS; Stephenson, MI; Cls Rep Frsh Cls; Trs Soph Cls; Pres Jr Cls; Hon Rl; NHS; Stu Cncl; Letter Bsktbl; Mic State Univ; Math.

DOLSON, JIM; Lumen Christi HS; Jackson, MI; 22/231 Band; Boy Scts; Hon Rl; NHS; Sct Actv; Yth Flsp; Michigan Tech Univ; Comp Engr.

DOMAKO, KEN; Beaverton HS; Beaverton, MI; Cl Rep Jr Cls; Band; Chrh Wkr; Hon Rl; NHS; Orch; Stu Cncl; Pep Clb; Univ Of Michigan; Aerodynamic Engr.

DOMBI, KAREN; Cardinal Stritch HS; Toledo, OH; Cls Rep Soph Cls; VP Jr Cls; Trs Sr Cls; Chrh Wkr; Hon Rl; NHS; Sch Mus; Stu Cncl; Pep Clb; Spn Clb; Coll; Sci.

DOMBKOWSKI, JULIE; Clay HS; Oregon, OH; 16/325 Band; Girl Scts; Hon Rl; JA; NHS; Stg Crw; Drama Clb; 4-H; 4-H Awd; Natl Merit Ltr; Northwestern; Journalism.

DOMBRAUSKY, NANCY; Muskegon Sr HS; Muskegon, MI; Chrs; NHS; Sec Orch; Sch Pl; Stu Cncl; Yth Flsp; Rptr Sch Nwsp; Sci Clb; Am Leg Awd; Cit Awd; Michigan Tech Univ; Mech Engr.

DOMBROSKI, KAREN; Edgewood HS; Conneaut, OH; 30/275 AFS; Aud/Vis; Chrs; Spn Clb; Chrldng; Cit Awd; College.

DOMBROSKY, PATRICIA; Brooke HS; Wellsburg, WV; 1/461 Cls Rep Sr Cls; Val; Chrh Wkr; Hon Rl; Lit Mag; NHS; VP Quill & Scroll; Red Cr Ade; Sch Mus; Ed Sch Nwsp; Natl Sci Found Stu Sci Training Progr 78; Outstndg Chem Stu 78; Outstndg Jrnlst 79; Bucknell Univ; Chem.

DOMBROWSKI, ANN; Msgr Hackett HS; Kalamazoo, MI; 30/140 Band; Chrs; Capt Drl Tm; Hon Rl; NHS; Sch Mus; Sch Pl; Drama Clb; Letter Glf; Parsons Bsns Schl; Legal Sec.

DOMBROWSKI, CHRISTOPHER; Tri Cnty HS; Remington, IN; 7/83 Chrh Wkr; Cmnty Wkr; Hon Rl; NHS; Sch Mus; Sch Pl; Drama Clb; Spn Clb; Purdue Univ; Chem Engr.

DOME, WILLIAM; Bangor John Glenn HS; Bay City, MI; Pres Frsh Cls; Cls Rep Soph Cls; Cl Rep Jr Cls; Cls Rep Sr Cls; Band; NHS; Stu Cncl; Yth Flsp; Letter Ftbl; Letter Ten; Alma Coll; Poli Sci.

DOMENICO, MICHAEL; Tuscarawas Ctrl Catholic HS; New Phila, OH; Letter Bsbl; Capt Ftbl; Coach Actv; Marietta Univ; History.

DOMER, MITCHELL; Marlington HS; Hartville, OH; 50/300 Chrs; Chrh Wkr; Yth Flsp; Spn Clb; IM Sprt; Baptist Bible Schl; Youth.

DOMER, MITCHELL P; Marlington HS; Hartville, OH; 55/300 Chrs; Chrh Wkr; Yth Flsp; Spn Clb; IM Sprt; Liberty Baptist Coll; Missions.

DOMER, SHIRLEY; Triway HS; Shreve, OH; 1/162 Val; Band; Chrs; Hon Rl; Jr NHS; Lbry Ade; Treas NHS; Sch Mus; Sch Pl; Ed Yrbk; Youngstown St Univ; Comp Sci.

DOMER, SHIRLEY J; Triwày HS; Shreve, OH; 1/162 Val; Band; Chrs; Hon Rl; Jr NHS; Lbry Ade; Treas NHS; Youngstown State Univ; Comp Sci.

DOMIENIK, STEVEN; Grosse Pointe North HS; Harper Woods, MI; Chrs; Cmnty Wkr; PAVAS; Sch Mus; Sch Pl; Stg Crw; Drama Clb; Fr Clb; Letter Wrstlng; IM Sprt; Central Mich Univ; Broadcasting.

DOMINGUEZ, IRMA; Horace Mann HS; Gary, IN; Sec Jr Cls; Drl Tm; Jr NHS; ROTC; Stu Cncl; Yrbk; VP Spn Clb; Letter Kiwan Awd; Candt In Hugh O Brien Ldrshp Fndtn 77; Univ Of Texas; Psych.

DOMINICK, CARLOS; Collinwood HS; Cleveland, OH; 35/300 Cls Rep Frsh Cls; Cls Rep Soph Cls; Hon Rl; Stu Cncl; IM Sprt; Cit Awd; Ltr In Bowling 78; Pin In Bowling 79; Case Western Reserve Univ; Engr.

DOMM, SUSAN; Garden City East HS; Garden City, MI; 80/400 Chrs; Bsktbl; Crs Cntry; Capt Trk; Univ Of Michigan; Med.

DOMMER, WALTER; Liberty Benton HS; Findlay, OH; Boy Scts; Hon Rl; NHS; Letter Bsbl; Letter Bsktbl; College; Petro Eng.

DOMOKUR, DEBBIE; Springfield Local HS; N Springfield, OH; Trs Sr Cls; Cls Rep Sr Cls; VP AFS; Band; Hon Rl; NHS; Stu Cncl; Fr Clb; Bob Jones Univ; Educ.

DONAHUE, BRIAN P; Franklin Heights HS; Columbus, OH; Am Leg Boys St; NHS; Bsktbl; Letter Ftbl; Trk; College;.

DONAHUE, FAUNA; North Gallia HS; Vinton, OH; 1/65 Cl Rep Jr Cls; Am Leg Aux Girls St; Band; Debate Tm; Hon Rl; Lbry Ade; NHS; Orch; Sch Pl; Stu Cncl; Rio Grand Univ; Educ.

DONAHUE, JONI; Gladwin HS; Gladwin, MI; Chrh Wkr; Girl Scts; Hon Rl; Red Cr Ade; Sch Pl; Sct Actv; Stg Crw; Yth Flsp; Trk; PPFtbl; Bob Jones Univ; Business Admin.

DONAHUE, KEITH C; Benedictine HS; Highland Hts, OH; 7/95 Cls Rep Frsh Cls; Cls Rep Soph Cls; Cls Rep Sr Cls; Aud/Vis; Cmnty Wkr; Hon Rl; Jr NHS; Lbry Ade; NHS; Sch Mus; Bucknell Univ; Elec Engr.

DONAHUE, TIMOTHY R M; Strongsville HS; Strongsville, OH; Band; Boy Scts; Drm Bgl; Sch Pl; Sct Actv; Stg Crw; Fr Clb; Sci Clb; Ohi State Univ; Conservationist.

DONALDSON, LAURA; Father Wehrle Memorial HS; Columbus, OH; Hon Rl; Hosp Ade; Letter Bsbl; Wrstlng; Ohio St Univ; Medicine.

DONATHAN, DANIEL; Kalkaska HS; Fife Lk, MI; Band; Hon Rl; Univ; Law Enforcement.

DONATHAN, SUZAN; Western Brown Sr HS; Mt Orab, OH; 5/200 Cls Rep Soph Cls; Hon Rl; NHS; Treas Spn Clb; Letter Chrldng; Univ; Legal Sec.

DONER, JEFF J; Lincolnview HS; Van Wert, OH; Am Leg Boys St; Treas Band; NHS; VP Yth Flsp; VP 4-H; VP FFA; Pres Sci Clb; Letter Trk; Cit Awd; 4-H Awd; College; Pre Med.

DONES, DONALD F; South Central HS; Elizabeth, IN; 1/68 Pres Frsh Cls; Cls Rep Soph Cls; Cl Rep Jr Cls; Hon Rl; NHS; Pres Stu Cncl; Pres Fr Clb; Letter Bsbl; Letter Bsktbl; Letter Crs Cntry; Univ.

DONEY, KAREN; Edison HS; Milan, OH; 3/164 Sec Soph Cls; Val; Sal; Hon Rl; Drama Clb; FHA; Mth Clb; Pep Clb; Soroptimist; Univ; Chem.

DONLEY, CYNTHIA; Whitehall HS; Whitehall, MI; 8/150 Treas Band; Chrs; Pres Girl Scts; Hon Rl; Sec NHS; Sch Mus; Pres Ger Clb; Stephens College; Communications.

DONLEY, DONNA; Martins Ferry HS; Bridgeport, OH; 50/214 Hon Rl; Bsktbl; Letter Trk; GAA; 2 Yr Ltr In Vlybl 77 79; All Time OVAC Record In Shot Put 79; West Liberty St Univ; Acctg.

DONLEY, KEVIN; St Alphonsus HS; Dearborn, MI; 4/171 Cls Rep Frsh Cls; Trs Soph Cls; Cl Rep Jr Cls; Boy Scts; Hon Rl; NHS; Stu Cncl; Letter Crs Cntry; Letter Swmmng; Letter Trk; Univ.

DONLEY, KOLLEEN; Buckeye West HS; Adena, OH; Chrs; Hon Rl; Off Ade; Yrbk; Drama Clb; FHA; OEA; Mgrs; Bradford Bus Schl; Sec.

DONLEY, RICHARD; Greenon HS; Springfield, OH; Band; Hon Rl; Fr Clb; FTA; Lat Clb; Univ.

DONLIN, COLLEEN; Madison HS; Madison, OH; 10/290 Band; Cmp Fr Grls; Chrs; Chrh Wkr; Cmnty Wkr; Girl Scts; Hon Rl; Lit Mag; NHS; Orch; Century III Leadrshp Awd 78; Oh Bd Of Regents Schlrshp Awd 79; Ohio St Univ; Speech Path.

DONN, COLETTE; Gladwin HS; Gladwin, MI; 34/178 Hon Rl; 4-H; Bsktbl; Letter Trk; Chrldng; PPFtbl; 4-H Awd; Lansing Bus Inst; Exec Sec.

DONNELLAN, MARGARET; Yale Public HS; Emmett, MI; 1/183 Am Leg Aux Girls St; Chrh Wkr; CAP; Debate Tm; Hon Rl; NHS; 4-H; Spn Clb; IM Sprt; St Claire Cnty Cmnty Coll; Engr.

DONNELLON, DAN; Moeller HS; Cincinnati, OH; Cls Rep Frsh Cls; Pres Natl Forn Lg; NHS; Pol Wkr; Stu Cncl; Rptr Sch Nwsp; Pep Clb; Trk; Its Acad Team Captain; Stu Mayor Montgomery Ohio; Ohio St Univ; Attorney.

DONNELLON, MARY; Marian HS; Cincinnati, OH; Cls Rep Frsh Cls; Cl Rep Jr Cls; Chrh Wkr; Fr Clb; FHA; Pep Clb; Socr; Ohi State Univ; Journalism.

DONNELLON, SHEILA; Marian HS; Cincinnai, OH; Cl Rep Jr Cls; FHA; Ten; GAA; Xavier Univ; Pol Sci.

DONNELLY, CHRIS; Whiteford School; Ottawa Lk, MI; Cls Rep Frsh Cls; Cls Rep Soph Cls; Cl Rep Jr Cls; Boy Scts; Off Ade; Sct Actv; Ftbl; Trk; Wrstlng; Capt Mgrs; Michigan Univ; Mech.

DONNELLY, DANIEL; R Nelson Snider HS; Ft Wayne, IN; Hon Rl; Fr Clb; Natl Merit Ltr; IVPU.

DONNELLY, TED; St Ignatius HS; S Euclid, OH; Cls Rep Frsh Cls; Cls Rep Soph Cls; Wrstlng; IM Sprt; Univ.

DONNENWIRTH, ELLEN; Indian Hill HS; Cincinnati, OH; Band; Hon Rl; Hosp Ade; Lbry Ade; Off Ade; Coll; Music.

DONOHER, GARY T; Archbishop Alter HS; Dayton, OH; 55/332 Cls Rep Frsh Cls; Cls Rep Soph Cls; Cl Rep Jr Cls; Chrs; Hon Rl; NHS; Pol Wkr; Sch Mus; Sch Pl; Stu Cncl; Univ Of Dayton; Theatre.

DONOHOE, ELLEN; Athens HS; Athens, OH; Am Leg Aux Girls St; Hon Rl; Jr NHS; NHS; 4-H; FBLA; FHA; Pep Clb; Chrldng; Am Leg Awd; Marietta Coll; Bus Admin.

DONOHOE, LISA; Tuscarawas Cntrl Cath HS; Uhrichsville, OH; Cl Rep Jr Cls; Hon Rl; NHS; Sch Pl; Rptr Yrbk; Rptr Sch Nwsp; Drama Clb; Pep Clb; Bsktbl; Chrldng; Univ.

DONOHUE, TRINA; West Branch HS; Homeworth, OH; Trs Jr Cls; Cl Rep Jr Cls; Chrs; Hon Rl; NHS; Stu Cncl; Ed Sch Nwsp; Pres FTA; Sec Lat Clb; Kent St Univ; Bus Admin.

DONOVAN, ANGELA; Holy Name Nazareth HS; Parma, OH; 14/325 Sec Soph Cls; Sec Jr Cls; Hon Rl; Sch Mus; Sch Pl; Stu Cncl; Cit Awd; Natl Merit SF; Univ Of Notre Dame; Poli Sci.

DONOVAN, JOHN; Rensselaer Central HS; Rensselaer, IN; 30/163 Band; Chrs; Hon Rl; Orch; Sch Mus; Pep Clb; Letter Ftbl; Letter Swmmng; Purdue; Engr.

DONOVAN, JOHN; Berea HS; Berea, OH; Hon Rl; NHS; Orch; Sct Actv; Mth Clb; College; Engr.

DONOVAN, MICHAEL; Brighton Area HS; Brighton, MI; 14/420 Am Leg Boys St; Cmnty Wkr; Hon Rl; NHS; Capt Bsktbl; Capt Ftbl; Eastern Michigan Univ; Envrnmntl Bio.

DONOVAN, NEYSA; Mcauley HS; Cincinnati, OH; Chrs; Swmmng; JA Awd; Cincinnati Tech Coll; Med Asst.

DONOVAN, THERESA; Bishop Ready HS; Columbus, OH; 15/130 Chrh Wkr; Cmnty Wkr; Drl Tm; Hon Rl; NHS; Pol Wkr; Yrbk; Ohio Northern Univ; Pharmacy.

DONTA, DENISE; Fairland HS; Proctorvll, OH; 8/152 Hst Soph Cls; Hon Rl; NHS; Fr Clb; Mth Clb; Pep Clb; Clemson Univ; Nursing.

DOOGE, MARY; Creston HS; Grand Rpds, MI; Cls Rep Soph Cls; Chrs; FCA; Hon Rl; Hosp Ade; Jr NHS; Sch Mus; Yth Flsp; Letter Swmmng; Tmr; Grand Rapids Jr Coll; Pharm.

DOOLAN, JEAN; Lakeshore HS; St Joseph, MI; 20/292 Chrs; Chrh Wkr; Cmnty Wkr; Girl Scts; Hon Rl; Pres JA; NHS; Quill & Scroll; Sch Mus; Sch Pl; Jr Achmnt Schlrshp 79; Marian Guild Schlrshp 79; Ctrl Michigan Univ Schlrshp 79; Central Michigan Univ; Jrnlsm.

DOOLEY, KAREN; Cannelton HS; Cannelton, IN; 1/35 Band; Girl Scts; Hon Rl; Jr NHS; NHS; Rptr Yrbk; Pep Clb; Letter Bsktbl; Letter Trk; Chrldng; Univ; Math.

DOOLITTLE, MELANIE; Rose Warwick HS; Tekonsha, MI; Cls Rep Soph Cls; Band; Chrs; Girl Scts; Hon Rl; Stu Cncl; Kellogg Community College; Phys Ther.

DOOLITTLE, WILLIAM; Glendview Hts HS; Columbus, OH; Hon Rl; Jr NHS; Ftbl; Kiwan Awd; Univ Of Michigan; Chem.

DOOTENGN, PATTY; Western Reserve HS; Norwalk, OH; 7/119 Pres Frsh Cls; Cls Rep Soph Cls; Cl Rep Jr Cls; Pres Sr Cls; Cmp Fr Grls; Hon Rl; Jr NHS; NHS; Sch Pl; Rptr Sch Nwsp; Ohio St Univ; Mrktng.

DOPERALSKI, NORA; Elston HS; Michigan City, IN; 41/326 Am Leg Aux Girls St; Girl Scts; Hon Rl; Sec NHS; Stu Cncl; Sprt Ed Yrbk; Fr Clb; GAA; Mat Maids; Univ Of Dayton; Pre Law.

DOPF, RONALD W; Fairmont West HS; Kettering, OH; 1/505 Val; Band; Hon Rl; Treas JA; NHS; Sch Pl; Rptr Sch Nwsp; Treas Ger Clb; Miami Univ; Bus.

DOPP, SUSAN; Geneva HS; Geneva, OH; 46/242 AFS; Chrs; Chrh Wkr; Off Ade; Stg Crw; Univ Of Dayton; Med Tech.

DORAN, CAROL; New Riegel HS; Carey, OH; 2/51 Trs Frsh Cls; Am Leg Aux Girls St; Band; Chrs; Chrh Wkr; Cmnty Wkr; Hon Rl; Jr NHS; NHS; Sch Mus; Bowling Green St Univ; Nursing.

DORAN, JULIA; East Palestine HS; E Palestine, OH; VP Soph Cls; Band; Cmp Fr Grls; Hon Rl; NHS; Pep Clb; Letter Bsktbl; College; Bio.

DORAN, KATHY; Parma Sr HS; Parma, OH; Girl Scts; Hon Rl; Lbry Ade; OEA; Bus Schl; Sec.

DORANDO, RUTH; Farmington HS; Farmington Hls, MI; Hosp Ade; Y-Teens; Pres 4-H; Tmr; 4-H Awd; Michigan St Univ; Vet Sci.

DORANTICH, JON; Newton Falls HS; Newton Falls, OH; Boy Scts; Chrs; Hon Rl; Ger Clb; Sci Clb; Bsktbl; Ftbl; Trk; IM Sprt; Univ; Math.

DORBUSCH, GERALD; Oakwood HS; Dayton, OH; 63/162 Hon Rl; Mgrs; College; Med.

DORCEY, PAUL; Frankenmuth HS; Frankenmuth, MI; 5/180 Am Leg Boys St; Band; Hon Rl; NHS; Ftbl; Coach Actv; IM Sprt; Tmr; Natl Merit Ltr; Univ; Engr.

DORCEY, WILLIAM J; Swan Valley HS; Saginaw, MI; 12/188 Band; JA; NHS; Yth Flsp; Bsbl; JA Awd; Voice Dem Awd; Final Navy NROTC 4 Yr Schlrshp 1979; Univ Of Michigan; Chem.

DORE, MARISA; Franklin HS; Livonia, MI; Chrs; Hon Rl; Capt Ten; Coach Actv; Mgrs; Cit Awd; Western Mic; Fine Arts.

DOREMUS, KARLA; Otsego HS; Bowling Green, OH; 1/140 Cls Rep Frsh Cls; Cls Rep Soph Cls; Chrs; Hon Rl; Pres Jr NHS; NHS; Sch Pl; Stu Cncl; Drama Clb; Spn Clb; Univ.

DORFMAN, CELIA; Maumee Valley Cntry Day HS; Lambertville, MI; Chrs; Hon Rl; Hosp Ade; Yrbk; Rptr Sch Nwsp; Sch Nwsp; Fr Clb; College; Liberal Arts.

DORGER, ROBERT; St Xavier HS; Cincinnati, OH; 175/275 Cls Rep Frsh Cls; Cls Rep Soph Cls; Cl Rep Jr Cls; Cls Rep Sr Cls; Letter Ftbl; Letter Socr; Letter Ten; IM Sprt; Ind Univ.

DORIA, DAWN; St Vincent St Mary HS; Akron, OH; Cmnty Wkr; JA; Sch Pl; Rptr Yrbk; Rptr Yrbk; Yrbk; Drama Clb; Pep Clb; JA Awd; Akron Univ; Preschl Tchr.

DORIA, DIANE; Chadsey HS; Detroit, MI; Hon Rl; Trs Frsh Cls; Sch Pl; Stu Cncl; Rptr Sch Nwsp; Sch Nwsp; Drama Clb; Lat Clb; Michigan St Univ; Vet.

DORICH, ANNETTE; Madonna HS; Weirton, WV; 18/98 Sec Soph Cls; Chrh Wkr; Cmnty Wkr; Hon Rl; NHS; Pep Clb; Mat Maids; Bus Awd 79; Ineract Club 78; West Virginia Univ; Ind Engr.

DORINGO, BARBARA; Ellet HS; Akron, OH; 25/363 Cls Rep Sr Cls; Chrh Wkr; Girl Scts; Hon Rl; Jr NHS; NHS; Off Ade; Red Cr Ade; Sch Mus; Stu Cncl; Akron Univ; Med Tech.

DORITY, P; Withrow Sr HS; Cincinnati, OH; Band; Boy Scts; Hon Rl; Hosp Ade; JA; Stu Cncl; Morehouse Univ; Acctg.

DORMAN, ELLEN; Au Gres Sims HS; Au Gres, MI; Trs Soph Cls; Chrh Wkr; Hon Rl; Lbry Ade; Off Ade; 4-H; Bsktbl; Trk; Mgrs; Scr Kpr; Ctrl Michigan Univ; Soc Work.

DORN, JILL; Miami Trace HS; Washington Ch, OH; 12/300 Cls Rep Frsh Cls; AFS; Am Leg Aux Girls St; Chrh Wkr; Hon Rl; NHS; Off Ade; Stu Cncl; 4-H; Chrldng; Univ Of Ken; Business.

DORN, LORI; Archbishop Alter HS; Dayton, OH; 30/331 Chrs; Cmnty Wkr; Hon Rl; Hosp Ade; NHS; Stu Cncl; Bsbl; Bsktbl; Coach Actv; GAA; Univ Of Dayton; Educ.

DORN, PHIL; Madison Plains HS; South Solon, OH; 1/145 VP Jr Cls; Aud/Vis; Hon Rl; NHS; Stu Cncl; Yrbk; Sch Nwsp; 4-H; FFA; Spn Clb; FFA Scholarship Awd; FFA Crop & Livestock Awds; Ohio St Univ; Animal Sci.

DORN, TAMARA; Gladwin HS; Gladwin, MI; Chrs; Hon Rl; Sch Mus; Rptr Yrbk; Rptr Sch Nwsp; Sch Nwsp; Bsbl; IM Sprt; Saginaw Bus Institute; Secretary.

DORNBOS, SHERYL; South Christian HS; Grand Rapids, MI; Hon Rl; Jr NHS; Yrbk; Letter Bsbl; Letter Bsktbl; Coach Actv; Michigan St Univ; Vet.

DORNBUSCH, RAYMOND; Midland HS; Midland, MI; Hon Rl; JA; Yth Flsp; Univ Of Mic; Elec Engr.

DORNER, D; Galesburg Augusta HS; Galesburg, MI; Hon Rl; Sci Clb; Spn Clb; Michigan St Univ; Vet.

DORNER, EVA; Beaumont HS; Cleve Hts, OH; Pres Frsh Cls; Cmp Fr Grls; Girl Scts; Sch Pl; Socr; Trk; Natl Merit Ltr; College; Art.

DORNOFF, ANTHONY; St Alphonsus HS; Dearborn Hts, MI; Boy Scts; Hon Rl; Off Ade; Eastern Michigan Univ; Spec Ed.

DOROHOFF, LORI; Hicksville HS; Hicksville, OH; 3/90 Band; Hon Rl; Hosp Ade; NHS; Sch Pl; Yth Flsp; Lat Clb; Univ; Phys Ther.

DORONY, LORAINE; Ithaca HS; Alma, MI; Band; Debate Tm; Girl Scts; Hon Rl; Hosp Ade; 4-H; FHA; 4-H Awd; Nazareth Coll; RN.

DORONY, LORIE; Ithaca HS; Alma, MI; Band; Debate Tm; Girl Scts; Hon Rl; Hosp Ade; 4-H; FHA; 4-H Awd; Nazareth Coll; Nurse.

DOROTINSKY, WILLIAM; John F Kennedy HS; Taylor, MI; 1/450 Cls Rep Frsh Cls; Cls Rep Soph Cls; Cl Rep Jr Cls; Cls Rep Sr Cls; Am Leg Boys St; Cmnty Wkr; Hon Rl; Jr NHS; NHS; Off Ade; Cert Of Merit Fr Univ Of Ia 78; Cert Of Merit Fr Mi Legislature 78; Pres Of Natl Honor Soc 79; Univ Of Michigan; Physician.

DOROW, KATHERINE; Whitehall HS; Whitehall, MI; Trs Frsh Cls; Band; Chrs; Hon Rl; NHS; Sch Mus; Stu Cncl; Ger Clb; Lat Clb; GAA; College.

DORRIER, SARA; Edwardsburg HS; Cassapolis, MI; Sec Soph Cls; Band; Hon Rl; NHS; Orch; Sch Mus; Sch Pl; Stg Crw; Pep Clb; Acad Awd For Excellnc 79; Univ; Med.

DORRIS, LORRIE; Shadyside HS; Shadyside, OH; Band; Chrs; Chrh Wkr; Drm Mjrt; Girl Scts; Hon Rl; Sch Mus; Sch Pl; Sct Actv; Sdlty; West Liberty St Coll; Comp Sci.

DORRIS, TERESA; Holly HS; Holly, MI; 1/325 Band; Hon Rl; NHS; Yth Flsp; 4-H; 4-H Awd; Natl Merit SF; General Motors Inst; Acctg.

DORSEY, DANIEL; Walnut Ridge HS; Columbus, OH; 36/450 Cls Rep Frsh Cls; Cls Rep Soph Cls; Chrs; Cmnty Wkr; Hon Rl; NHS; Sch Mus; Stu Cncl; Ger Clb; Letter Ftbl; Miami Univ; Bus.

DORSEY, LINDA; Tippecanoe Valley HS; Warsaw, IN; 12/159 Band; Girl Scts; Hon Rl; NHS; Pres Yth Flsp; FTA; OEA; Spn Clb; Letter Bsktbl; Letter Trk; Ivy Tech Univ; Busns.

DORSEY, MARY; Crothersville Community HS; Crothersville, IN; 3/60 Am Leg Aux Girls St; Drl Tm; Hon Rl; NHS; Pres Stu Cncl; Pres 4-H; FHA; College; Engr.

DORSEY, TOM; Riverside HS; Quincy, OH; 6/85 Am Leg Boys St; Band; Hon Rl; NHS; Sch Pl; Stg Crw; Rptr Yrbk; IM Sprt; Public Relations.

DORSKI, RONALD L; Port Clinton HS; Port Clinton, OH; 3/285 Bcy Scts; Hon Rl; NHS; Red Cr Ade; Sct Actv; 4-H; FFA; Mth Clb; Letter Crs Cntry; Letter Swmmng; Univ.

DORSTEN, JONILLA M; Archbishop Alter HS; Kettering, OH; 10/353 Hon Rl; NHS; Sch Mus; Sch Pl; Chmn Stu Cncl; Spn Clb; Swmmng; IM Sprt; PPFtbl; Natl Merit SF; Univ Of Virginia; Archt.

DORSTEN, PEG; St Henry HS; Celina, OH; 30/122 Chrh Wkr; Cmnty Wkr; Drm Mjrt; Hon Rl; NHS; Sch Pl; Drama Clb; 4-H; OEA; Spn Clb; Albssr Awd In Offc Educ Assoc 79; 6th In Shrthnd I Comp In OEA 78; Wright St Univ; Bus Admin.

DORTCH, ROBIN; London HS; W Jefferson, OH; 40/133 Pres Band; Hon Rl; Yrbk; Rptr Sch Nwsp; Sch Nwsp; Pep Clb; Bsktbl; Letter Trk; GAA; Ohio St Univ; Photo Jrnlsm.

DORTON, VANESSA A; Independence Jr Sr HS; Columbus, OH; Cls Rep Frsh Cls; Cls Rep Soph Cls; Chrh Wkr; Drl Tm; FCA; VP Stu Cncl; Civ Clb; Fr Clb; Gym; Ten; Natl Honor Soc; Ashland Coll; Acctg.

DORZEL, SUSAN M; Seton HS; Cincinnati, OH; Band; Chrs; Chrh Wkr; Hon Rl; Jr NHS; Mdrgl; NHS; Orch; Sch Mus; Pep Clb; Univ; Marketing.

DOSA, JOHN J; Marlington HS; Alliance, OH; 5/312 Am Leg Boys St; Band; Chrs; Drm Bgl; Hon Rl; Orch; Sch Mus; Sch Pl; Stg Crw; Yth Flsp; Spanish Awd; Biology Awd; College; Aero Engr.

DOSCH, JOHN; West Muskingum HS; Zanesville, OH; 4-H; Pres FFA; Key Clb; VICA; 4-H Awd; Hocking Tech Coll; Forestry.

DOSECK, KEVIN; Memorial HS; St Marys, OH; Chrs; Chrh Wkr; CAP; Sch Mus; Pres Yth Flsp; Navy.

DOSH, KRISTINE; Athens HS; Athens, MI; 2/87 Chrh Wkr; Hon Rl; Hosp Ade; NHS; Off Ade; Red Cr Ade; Yth Flsp; Yrbk; Pep Clb; Kellogg Comm Coll.

DOSMANN, CATHY; Brethren Christian HS; South Bend, IN; 2/17 Sal; Band; Chrs; Chrh Wkr; Girl Scts; Hon Rl; NHS; Orch; Yth Flsp; Drama Clb; Awana Awds; College; Secondary Ed.

DOSMANN, ROSEMARIE; Penn HS; Granger, IN; 38/496 Cmp Fr Grls; Hon Rl; NHS; Rptr Yrbk; Ed Sch Nwsp; 4-H; Spn Clb; IM Sprt; PPFtbl; Indiana Univ; Acctg.

DOSS, CATHY; Baptist Academy; Indianapolis, IN; Val; Band; Chrs; Chrh Wkr; Hon Rl; Mdrgl; Sch Mus; Sch Pl; 4-H; Whos Who In Music; Highest Academic Average Of Schl; 3rd Place ACE Natl Comp Piano Solo; College; Music.

DOSS, CHERYL; Fairland HS; Proctorvll, OH; 10/132 Am Leg Aux Girls St; Hon Rl; Jr NHS; Sec NHS; Stu Cncl; Mth Clb; Pep Clb; Capt Chrldng; Jr Pom Pon; Hr Scshlp At Oh Univ 78; Scslhp Comm For Mu Alph Theta 78; Prom Comm 78; Nalt Eng Mert Test 77; Marshall Univ; Med Tech.

DOSSETTE, LISA; Wayne Memorial HS; Westland, MI; Hon Rl; Univ Of Michigan; Dentistry.

DOSTER, DAWN; Wayne Trace HS; Paulding, OH; Trs Jr Cls; Band; Chrh Wkr; Hon Rl; Hosp Ade; FHA; Mth Clb; VICA; Twrlr; Coll; Asst Phys Therapy.

DOSTER, WENDY; South HS; Akron, OH; Chrs; Chrh Wkr; Key Clb; Kiwan Awd; Akron Univ; Elem Ed.

DOSWALD, CAROLINE S; Kent Roosevelt HS; Kent, OH; AFS; Hon Rl; VP 4-H; Fr Clb; Pep Clb; Letter Swmmng; Letter Trk; Tmr; 4-H Awd; Natl Merit SF; Ohio State Univ; Vet Med.

DOTSON, BERNARD; Emerson HS; Gary, IN; 5/145 VP Sr Cls; Hon Rl; JA; NHS; FBLA; Spn Clb; Cit Awd; College; Engr.

DOTSON, BETH A; Lawrenceburg HS; Lawrenceburg, IN; 6/146 Chrh Wkr; Girl Scts; Hon Rl; Lbry Ade; NHS; Sch Mus; Rptr Yrbk; Pres 4-H; Pep Clb; Sec Spn Clb; Ball St Univ; Journalism.

DOTSON, BRAD; Marysville HS; Broadway, OH; 23/230 Rptr Sch Nwsp; VP FFA; Bsbl; IM Sprt; Univ.

DOTSON, CRISTAL; Franklin Heights HS; Columbus, OH; 36/290 Band; Chrs; Girl Scts; Orch; Sct Actv; Yth Flsp; Pep Clb; Mat Maids; Scr Kpr; Tmr; Head Majorette 78; Christian Teens 77; Univ; Law.

DOTSON, DAVID M; Wynford HS; Nevada, OH; 10/134 Cls Rep Soph Cls; Cl Rep Jr Cls; Cls Rep Sr Cls; Am Leg Boys St; Chrs; NHS; Rptr Yrbk; Rptr Sch Nwsp; Letter Bsktbl; Letter VICA; Univ Of Toledo.

DOTSON, JOHN; Paint Valley HS; Bainbridge, OH; 27/67 FFA; Letter Ftbl; College.

DOTSON, KELLY; South Charleston HS; S Charleston, WV; 1/240 Am Leg Aux Girls St; Band; Drm Mjrt; Hon Rl; Jr NHS; NHS; Stu Cncl; Yth Flsp; Spn Clb; Rensselaer Awd; College.

DOTSON, KIM; Wayne Memorial HS; Wayne, MI; 1/660 Debate Tm; Hon Rl; NHS; Mth Clb; Spn Clb; Recvd Gold Medal For A Avg Through HS 79; Regents Schlr Awd 79; Sue Ross Memrl Schlrshp In Foreign Lang 79; Eastern Michigan Univ; Spanish.

DOTSON, LISA; Clay Sr HS; Oregon, OH; Band; Drl Tm; Girl Scts; Hon Rl; Hosp Ade; Rptr Yrbk; Fr Clb; Trk; Toledo Univ; Nursing.

DOTSON, MARK; Wayne HS; Dayton, OH; 62/600 Cl Rep Jr Cls; Cls Rep Sr Cls; Aud/Vis; Hon Rl; Jr NHS; NHS; Quill & Scroll; Yth Flsp; FBLA; Letter Bsbl; Ohio Univ; Bus Admin.

DOTSON, MELISSA; Groveport Madison Sr HS; Groveport, OH; Chrs; Drl Tm; Hon Rl; Sch Mus; Sch Pl; Yrbk; VP FHA; Mat Maids; PPFtbl; FHA Queen Jr Chap & St Degrres; Hon Chrs Part In Oh Wesleyan 78; Bus.

DOTSON, TAMIE; Milton HS; Culloden, WV; Hon Rl; Sch Mus; Sprt Ed Sch Nwsp; Pep Clb; Bsktbl; Hndbl; Trk; Chrldng; GAA; IM Sprt; Marshall; Bus Mngmt.

DOTTAVIO, LINDA; Washington HS; Massillon, OH; Girl Scts; Hon Rl; Rptr Sch Nwsp; DECA; Drama Clb; Bus Schl; Fashion Mdse.

DOTY, DAVID; Edon HS; Edon, OH; 4/78 Band; Hon Rl; Bsbl; Bsktbl; DAR Awd; Oral Roberts Univ; Math.

DOTY, DONNA; Lincoln HS; Pershing, IN; 7/150 Chrh Wkr; Hon Rl; Lbry Ade; NHS; Sec Spn Clb; C of C Awd; Univ; Elem Educ.

DOUBLER, DONNA; Brecksville HS; Brecksville, OH; 300/367 Band; Hon Rl; Sch Mus; Sch Pl; Drama Clb; ICM; Systems Anaylist.

DOUD, THOMAS; St Philip Catholic HS; Battle Creek, MI; Hon Rl; NHS; Fr Clb; Hockey; Central Mic Univ; Chem.

DOUDS, KELLY; Revere HS; Bath, OH; 70/285 Cl Rep Jr Cls; Band; Debate Tm; Hon Rl; JA; Natl Forn Lg; Sch Pl; Ed Sch Nwsp; Rptr Sch Nwsp; Sch Nwsp; Michigan St Univ; Bus.

DOUGHERTY, DEBRA; Newark Sr HS; Newark, OH; Chrh Wkr; Jr NHS; NHS; Yth Flsp; Ger Clb; Ten; GAA; Mgrs; Scr Kpr; Grove City Coll; Med.

DOUGHERTY, JEFFREY; Lemon Monroe HS; Middletown, OH; Chrs; Hon Rl; VICA; Trk; Univ; Arc ht.

DOUGHERTY, STEPHEN; Lakota HS; W Chester, OH; Band; Hon Rl; Jr NHS; Orch; Sch Mus; Rptr Yrbk; Fr Clb; Key Clb; Trk; College; Law.

DOUGHMAN, J SHANE; Gallia Academy HS; Gallipolis, OH; VP Frsh Cls; Sec Soph Cls; Sec Jr Cls; Annapolis Univ; Aero Engr.

DOUGLAS, BETH E; Fairview HS; Fairview Pk, OH; 3/300 Trs Sr Cls; Band; Hon Rl; NHS; Sch Nwsp; VP Fr Clb; Sci Clb; Letter Bsktbl; Letter Swmmng; Natl Merit SF; Girls Volleyball 78; Pres Of Luther League 79; Outstndg French Stu; Ohio St Univ; Bio Med Engr.

DOUGLAS, DEANA; Edison HS; Lake Station, IN; Girl Scts; Off Ade; Sch Pl; Stg Crw; Spn Clb; Cumberland College; Eng.

DOUGLAS, JAMES; Huntington E HS; Huntington, WV; 13/313 Chrh Wkr; NHS; Pres DECA; Marshall Univ; Distributive Ed.

DOUGLAS, JIM; Vandalia Butler HS; Dayton, OH; 27/400 Boy Scts; Chrs; Hon Rl; Natl Forn Lg; NHS; PAVAS; Sch Mus; Sch Pl; Stg Crw; Ed Yrbk; Ohio St Univ.

DOUGLAS, JOY; Brown Cnty HS; Nineveh, IN; Cmp Fr Grls; DECA; Univ; Conservation.

DOUGLAS, KELLY; Clio Area HS; Clio, MI; Off Ade; OEA; Univ Of Michigan.

DOUGLAS, MARIANNE; Lumen Cordium HS; Twinsburg, OH; 4/91 Cls Rep Soph Cls; Cl Rep Jr Cls; Trs Sr Cls; Chrs; Drl Tm; Girl Scts; Hon Rl; Jr NHS; NHS; Off Ade; Akron Univ; Engr.

DOUGLAS, MARK; Nitro HS; Poca, WV; Cls Rep Frsh Cls; Cls Rep Soph Cls; Cl Rep Jr Cls; Band; Chrh Wkr; Hon Rl; NHS; Stu Cncl; 4-H; Sci Clb; Marshall Univ; Med.

DOUGLAS, RUTH; Springboro HS; Springboro, OH; Sec Frsh Cls; Cls Rep Soph Cls; Trs Jr Cls; Trs Sr Cls; Band; Hon Rl; Stu Cncl; Yth Flsp; 4-H; Pep Clb; Miami Univ; Nursing.

DOUGLAS, TERESA; Cambridge HS; Cambridge, OH; 34/270 Am Leg Aux Girls St; Cmnty Wkr; Hon Rl; JA; Lbry Ade; NHS; Off Ade; 4-H; Trk; 4-H Awd; Muskingum Area Tech Coll; Vet Asst.

DOUGLAS, VALERIE; Libbey HS; Toledo, OH; Pres Frsh Cls; Pres Soph Cls; Band; Chrh Wkr; Hon Rl; NHS; Pres Stu Cncl; Yrbk; DECA; 4-H; Best Stu Of The DECA & Amer Hstry Class 78; JA 1 Yr VP Of Personal; 2nd Yr Tres; 3rd Yr Pres; Univ; Bus.

DOUGLASS, WILLIAM D; Bedford HS; Lambertville, MI; FCA; Letter Ftbl; Letter Wrstlng; Weight Lifting Mi St HS Champ 198 Lbs 78; Univ; Phys Ther.

DOUNTZ, STACI; Westfall HS; Mt Sterling, OH; Band; Drm Bgl; Sch Pl; Rptr Sch Nwsp; Sch Nwsp; 4-H; FHA; Sci Clb; GAA; IM Sprt; Hocking Tech Voc Schl; Emergency Med.

DOUP, JEFF A; Fredericktown HS; Fred, OH; 16/138 Cls Rep Frsh Cls; Band; Hon Rl; Stu Cncl; Yth Flsp; FFA; Pep Clb; Bsktbl; Ohio St Univ; Sci.

DOUTHIT, DOROTHY; Interlochen Arts Academy; Concord, MI; Band; Hon Rl; NHS; Orch; Sch Mus; Sch Pl; Stg Crw; Drama Clb; Trk; Tuesday Musicale Scholarships 1977; Baldwin Wallace Cons Of Music; Music.

DOUTHITT, PHIL; Frankfort HS; Fort Ashby, WV; Pres Jr Cls; Hon Rl; Lbry Ade; NHS; Sch Mus; Sch Pl; Ed Yrbk; 4-H; Fr Clb; FTA; French Awd 1976; Hist Awd 1976; Geomtry 1977; Potomac St Coll; Bus.

DOVE, CRYSTL L; Mathias HS; Mathias, WV; 1/20 Val; Am Leg Aux Girls St; Pres NHS; Sec Stu Cncl; Bsktbl; Capt Chrldng; DAR Awd; Voice Dem Awd; W Virginia Univ; Med Tech.

DOVE, L; Circleville HS; Riverton, WV; 7/30 VP Sr Cls; Hon Rl; Lbry Ade; VICA; Lion Awd; Shepherd Coll; Reg Nurse.

DOVE, LORRI; Hedgesville HS; Hedgesville, WV; Cl Rep Jr Cls; Band; Chrh Wkr; Cmnty Wkr; Hon Rl; Sec NHS; Sec Stu Cncl; Pres FTA; Univ; Chem.

DOVENBARGER, EDDIE; Ridgewood HS; Coshocton, OH; 14/150 VP Sr Cls; Hon Rl; NHS; Off Ade; Sch Pl; Yrbk; Pres FTA; Trk; Chrldng; JC Awd; Kent St Univ; Bus Ed.

DOVICHI, LORI; Marian HS; Blmfld Hls, MI; Mod UN; Sch Mus; Sch Pl; Stg Crw; Sch Nwsp; Fr Clb; Letter Swmmng; GAA; IM Sprt; Tmr; Univ; Jrnlsm.

DOWD, LARRY; Muskegon Cath Ctrl HS; Muskegon, MI; 20/200 Hon Rl; Sch Pl; Stg Crw; Bsbl; Ftbl; Coach Actv; IM Sprt; Natl Merit Schl; Muskegon Cmnty Coll; Mech Engr.

DOWDELL, JENNIFER; Yellow Springs HS; Yellow Sprg, OH; 11/76 Cls Rep Frsh Cls; Cls Rep Soph Cls; Mod UN; Orch; Sch Mus; Stu Cncl; Bsbl; Socr; Hstry Awd 77 79; Purdue Minority Engr Smmr Progr 79; Appointmnt To Gov Brown Yth Adv Comm Eng Awd 79; Purdue Univ; Metal Engr.

DOWDEN, ELIZABETH; Bishop Hartley HS; Columbus, OH; 32/177 Chrs; Chrh Wkr; Girl Scts; Hon Rl; NHS; Sch Mus; Sch Pl; Sct Actv; Stg Crw; Rptr Yrbk; Miami Univ; Elem Ed.

DOWELL, DAVID; Brown County HS; Nashville, IN; Hon Rl; Spn Clb; Ten; Tmr; College.

DOWELL, GREGORY; Clermont N E HS; Goshen, OH; Cls Rep Frsh Cls; Cls Rep Soph Cls; Band; Cmnty Wkr; FCA; Mod UN; Fr Clb; Ftbl; IM Sprt; Grant & Loan Hanover Coll; Hanover Coll; Busns Admin.

DOWELL, TERESA; Kankakee Valley Jr Sr HS; Wheatfield, IN; Girl Scts; Lbry Ade; Sct Actv; Rptr Sch Nwsp; Treas 4-H; Sci Clb; GAA; Purdue Univ; Law.

DOWIATT, JAN; Mansfield St Peters HS; Mansfield, OH; VP Soph Cls; VP Sr Cls; Chrh Wkr; Cmnty Wkr; Girl Scts; Hon Rl; NHS; Treas Off Ade; Pres Orch; Red Cr Ade; Univ.

DOWKER, CLARK; Johannesburg Lewiston HS; Johannesburg, MI; 4/57 Aud/Vis; Band; Hon Rl; Lbry Ade; NHS; Yrbk; Rptr Sch Nwsp; Kirtland Comm College; Engineering.

DOWLER, BOB; Groveport Madison HS; Groveport, OH; Cls Rep Frsh Cls; Chrs; Yth Flsp; FFA; Ftbl; Conf Luther Leag Offc 1978; Local Leag Pres 1979; Ohio St Univ; Agri Bus.

DOWLER, LYNN; Groveport Madison HS; Groveport, OH; 30/391 Treas Band; Sec Chrh Wkr; Hon Rl; NHS; Sch Mus; Yth Flsp; Pep Clb; All Ohio St Fair Band; Whos Who Among Foreign Lang Stu; Ohio Scholastic Ach Test French I & II; Ohio Univ.

DOWLER, SANDRA; Heritage Jr Sr HS; New Haven, IN; 39/179 Trs Jr Cls; Trs Sr Cls; Band; Chrs; Hon Rl; Yth Flsp; Sprt Ed Sch Nwsp; Pep Clb; Spn Clb; Bsktbl; Ball St Univ; Public Rel.

DOWLING, CYNTHIA D; West Technical HS; Cleveland, OH; Pres Sr Cls; Hon Rl; Jr NHS; NHS; Sch Pl; Stu Cncl; Yrbk; Trk; IM Sprt; Cit Awd; Outstanding Academic Achievement Plaque 1976; 2nd Pl Regional Contest Wnr 1978; 7th Pl Regional Contst; OSU; CPA.

DOWLING, DENNIS; Adrian Sr HS; Adrian, MI; 113/390 Boy Scts; Chrh Wkr; Cmnty Wkr; Pol Wkr; Lat Clb; Ftbl; Trk; IM Sprt; St Of Mi Comp Schlrshp Prog 78; Central Michigan Univ; Psych.

DOWLING, JACKIE; Seeger Memorial HS; Williamsport, IN; 7/128 Cls Rep Sr Cls; Chrh Wkr; Hon Rl; Lit Mag; NHS; Sch Mus; Stg Crw; Stu Cncl; Yth Flsp; Ed Sch Nwsp; Lakeview Schl Of Nursing.

DOWMONT, DINEEN; United HS; Salem, OH; Band; Drm Bgl; Hon Rl; Off Ade; Stu Cncl; Yrbk; Sch Nwsp; 4-H; Pep Clb; God Cntry Awd; Vocational Schl; Stewardess.

DOWNARD, BECKY; Piketon HS; Lucasville, OH; 1/115 Chrs; Hon Rl; MMM; Sch Mus; Stu Cncl; Yrbk; 4-H; FTA; Spn Clb; Chrldng; Univ; Guidance Cnslr.

DOWNARD, PAULA; Southern Local HS; Irondale, OH; Chrs; Chrh Wkr; Hon Rl; Yth Flsp; 4-H; FNA; Lat Clb; 4-H Awd;.

DOWNEN, DIANA; North Posey Sr HS; Wadesville, IN; Fr Clb; Pep Clb; GAA; Indiana St Univ.

DOWNER, ROSALIND F; Ecorse HS; Ecorse, MI; 8/160 Cls Rep Frsh Cls; Cls Rep Soph Cls; VP Jr Cls; Cls Rep Sr Cls; Band; Chrh Wkr; Hon Rl; NHS; Off Ade; Stu Cncl; Adrian Coll; Acctg.

DOWNEY, BOB; Fenwick HS; Franklin, OH; VP Sr Cls; NHS; Stu Cncl; Sprt Ed Yrbk; Rptr Yrbk; Glf; IM Sprt; Natl Merit Ltr; Coll; Engr.

DOWNEY, CAROL; Berea HS; Berea, OH; 8/563 AFS; Hon Rl; Hosp Ade; NHS; Red Cr Ade; Sch Mus; Ed Yrbk; Drama Clb; Capt Swmmng; 4-H Awd; Miami Univ; Archt.

DOWNEY, DEBRA J; Berea HS; Berea, OH; 123/550 Cls Rep Frsh Cls; Band; Chrh Wkr; Hon Rl; Natl Forn Lg; Sch Mus; Stg Crw; Stu Cncl; Yth Flsp; 4-H; Pres Of Heritate Congregational Church 78; Rep To Natl Assoc 76 79; Pilgrim Fellowship; Univ; Educ.

DOWNEY, MARK J; City HS; Grand Rapids, MI; Boy Scts; Cmnty Wkr; Jr NHS; Lit Mag; Sct Actv; Yrbk; Mas Awd; Outstanding Acad Awd; Registered As Mbr Soc Dstngshd Amer HS Stu; Life Scout In Scouts; Ma Inst Of Tech; Aerospace Engr.

DOWNEY, MONICA; Marian HS; Birmingham, MI; Cmnty Wkr; Hon Rl; Mod UN; NHS; Off Ade; Stg Crw; Fr Clb; Letter Trk; IM Sprt; Purdue; Aeronautical Engin.

DOWNEY, W; William Henry Harrison HS; W Lafayette, IN; Hosp Ade; Yth Flsp; Rdo Clb; Socr; Purdue Univ; Computer Programming.

DOWNIE, ALAN A; Lake Ridge Acad; Lorain, OH; 1/21 Cls Rep Frsh Cls; Cls Rep Soph Cls; Trs Jr Cls; Cl Rep Jr Cls; Boy Scts; Hon Rl; NHS; Sct Actv; Letter Lcrss; Letter Socr; Univ; Med.

DOWNING, DONALD; Marion Harding HS; Marion, OH; Stu Cncl; IM Sprt; Univ; Pre Med.

DOWNING, ELIZABETH; Malabar HS; Mansfield, OH; 2/278 Cls Rep Frsh Cls; Cls Rep Soph Cls; Cl Rep Jr Cls; Hon Rl; NHS; PAVAS; Pol Wkr; Mas Inst Of Tech; Aerospace.

DOWNING, LINDA; High School; Beaverton, MI; VP Frsh Cls; Cls Rep Frsh Cls; Cls Rep Soph Cls; Cl Rep Jr Cls; Trs Sr Cls; Cls Rep Sr Cls; Hon Rl; NHS; Off Ade; Stu Cncl; Central Michigan Univ; Sec.

DOWNING, SHARON; Warren Western Reserve HS; Warren, OH; Hon Rl; PAVAS; Sch Mus; Sch Pl; Stg Crw; Drama Clb; Ger Clb; Ken State; Psychiatry.

DOWNING, TAMI; Margaretta HS; Vickery, OH; Sec Jr Cls; Band; Yth Flsp; Sec 4-H; Pep Clb; Chrldng; 4-H Awd; Yth In Government; Alternate To Girls State; Tech Schl; Fash Dsgn.

DOWNS, ALAN; Anderson HS; Cincinnati, OH; Chrs; Bsbl; Glf; Cit Awd; Schlrshp YBA Jr King Of TV Bowling 79; Natl Holiday Tournmnt 78; High Series In St Bowling 10th Nation; Univ Of Cincinnati; Pro Bowler.

DOWNS, AMY; Colonel Crawford HS; Bucyrus, OH; Trs Sr Cls; Am Leg Aux Girls St; Band; Chrs; Chrh Wkr; FCA; Hon Rl; Bsktbl; Olivet Nazarene Coll; Nurse.

DOWNS, DALE; Edgewood HS; Gosport, IN; 42/200 Band; Chrh Wkr; Cmnty Wkr; Hon Rl; 4-H; Spn Clb; Mgrs; Cit Awd; Ind Univ; Pre Med.

DOWNS, KARA; Clinton Prairie Jr Sr HS; Frankfort, IN; 6/94 Am Leg Aux Girls St; Chrs; Chrh Wkr; Girl Scts; Hon Rl; NHS; Sch Mus; FHA; FTA; Pep Clb; Ball St Univ; Nursing.

DOWSE, DLORAH; Farmington Sr HS; Farmington, MI; Chrs; Girl Scts; Hon Rl; Rptr Yrbk; Pep Clb; Hockey; Letter Socr; GAA; Cit Awd; Univ; Bookkeeping.

DOWSETT, KATHY; Our Lady Of The Lakes HS; Draytonplains, MI; Cmnty Wkr; Girl Scts; Hon Rl; NHS; Sct Actv; Fr Clb; Mth Clb; Sci Clb; Univ Of Dayton.

DOYEN, DEAN; Gwinn HS; Gwinn, MI; Hon Rl; Red Cr Ade; Sch Nwsp; Bsktbl; Ftbl; Coach Actv; IM Sprt; Scr Kpr; Tmr; Central Mic Univ; Journalism.

DOYLE, CAROLYN; Scecina Memorial HS; Indianapolis, IN; 13/194 Cmnty Wkr; Hon Rl; Rptr Sch Nwsp; Whos Who In Midwestern Lang Stud 79; PSAT Scores Top 5% 79; Indiana Univ; Jrnlsm.

DOYLE, CINDY; Medina Sr HS; Medina, OH; Girl Scts; Hon Rl; Off Ade; 4-H; Pep Clb; Letter Bsbl; Letter Ten; Letter Chrldng; GAA; ICM Comp Schl; Comp Analysist.

DOYLE, DARLENE; Warren Woods HS; Warren, MI; 24/364 Band; Chrh Wkr; Hon Rl; NHS; Sch Mus; Sch Pl; Eastern Michigan Univ; Med Tech.

DOYLE, DAVID; Loogootee HS; Loogootee, IN; Band; Boy Scts; Chrh Wkr; Hon Rl; Sct Actv; Fr Clb; Pep Clb; IM Sprt; Bus Math Awrd 78; Purdue Univ; Bldg Trade Mgmt.

DOYLE, DIANE; Huntington Local HS; Chillicothe, OH; 11/90 Am Leg Aux Girls St; Band; Hon Rl; NHS; Fr Clb; FTA; Pep Clb; Mgrs; Univ; Nurse.

DOYLE, EDWARD; Ainsworth HS; Swartz Creek, MI; Band; Boy Scts; Hon Rl; Rptr Sch Nwsp; Crs Cntry; Ten; Trk; Wrstlng; Michigan Tech Univ; Forestry.

DOYLE, KARI; Hartland HS; Brighton, MI; Trs Soph Cls; Trs Sr Cls; Hon Rl; Lbry Ade; Lit Mag; NHS; Yrbk; Capt Chrldng; College; Acctg.

DOYLE, KELLY; Schafer HS; Southgate, MI; 11/263 Band; Hon Rl; NHS; Stg Crw; Drama Clb; Pep Clb; Letter Bsktbl; Letter Trk; IM Sprt; Michigan Tech Univ; Med Tech.

DOYLE, KYLE; Loogootee HS; Loogootee, IN; 18/147 Am Leg Aux Girls St; Band; Cmp Fr Grls; Chrh Wkr; Girl Scts; Hon Rl; Yrbk; 4-H; OEA; Pep Clb; Univ.

DOYLE, PATRICE; Bishop Luers HS; Ft Wayne, IN; Chrs; Girl Scts; Hon Rl; Y-Teens; Drama Clb; Pep Clb; Spn Clb; Gym; Swmmng; Univ.

DOYLE, RICHARD; Ross Beatty HS; Cassopolis, MI; Boy Scts; Chrs; Sct Actv; 4-H; FFA; 4-H Awd; Southwestern Univ; Mechinac.

DOYLE, SARAH M; R Nelson Snider HS; Ft Wayne, IN; 7/564 Chrs; Hon Rl; Fr Clb; Principals List 78; Swing Choir 79; Univ Of Evansville; Acctg.

DOYLE, SHARON A; Grand Ledge HS; Grnd Ldg, MI; Hon Rl; NHS; Lat Clb; Latin Club Sec 76 & 77; Hugh O Brian Leadrshp Awd Nominee 77; Nalt Latin Exam 79; Univ; Engr.

DOYLE, TERESA; Scecina Mem HS; Indianapolis, IN; 3/194 Hon Rl; Treas NHS; Off Ade; Sch Mus; Yrbk; Fr Clb; GAA; Mgrs; Ach In Hnrs Algebra; Cert For French III; Schlrshp Pin Completion Hnrs Prog; College; Law.

DOYLE, TONY; Brown County HS; Nineveh, IN; Cls Rep Frsh Cls; Cls Rep Soph Cls; Chrs; Fr Clb; Glf; 4-H Awd; Ind State; Pga Golf Pro.

DOYLE, WILLIAM; Huntington HS; Chillicothe, OH; Cl Rep Jr Cls; Cls Rep Sr Cls; Am Leg Boys St; Band; Hon Rl; Sch Pl; Stu Cncl; Fr Clb; Pep Clb; Letter Bsbl; Voc Schl; Mechanics.

DOYLY, RENEE; Grand Haven Sr HS; Grand Haven, MI; 1/397 Am Leg Aux Girls St; Band; Hon Rl; Treas NHS; Orch; Sch Mus; Letter Bsktbl; Letter Trk; Ferris St Univ; Acctg.

DOZIER, JEAN A; Celina Sr HS; St Marys, OH; 12/241 AFS; Band; Debate Tm; Hon Rl; Natl Forn Lg; NHS; Orch; Sch Mus; Sch Pl; Yth Flsp; Univ; Med.

DOZIER, SHARI; Withrow HS; Cincinnati, OH; 29/563 Cls Rep Sr Cls; Chrs; Hon Rl; NHS; Pol Wkr; Sch Pl; Stu Cncl; Wilberforce; Psych.

DRABEK, SCOTT; Padua Franciscan HS; Parma, OH; Band; Hon Rl; Orch; Sch Mus; Sch Pl; Stu Cncl; Ftbl; Ten; Chrldng; Univ; Chem Engr.

DRABICK, R STEVEN; Canton South HS; Canton, OH; Trs Sr Cls; Chrs; Chrh Wkr; Hon Rl; NHS; Y-Teens; Mth Clb; Sci Clb; Spn Clb; Bsbl; Hon Mntn Dist Oh Schlshp Test Bio 78; Akron Univ.

DRABICKI, KATHLEEN; St Alphonsus HS; Detroit, MI; 32/171 Band; Girl Scts; Hon Rl; Lbry Ade; Sct Actv; Bsbl; Letter Trk; IM Sprt; Scr Kpr; Tmr; Henry Ford; Medicine.

DRABISON, LINDA; Austintown Fitch HS; Youngstown, OH; 50/700 Drl Tm; Girl Scts; NHS; Off Ade; Stu Cncl; Spn Clb; Youngstown St Univ; Poli Sci.

DRAEGER, SUE; Clay Sr HS; Oregon, OH; Band; Drm Bgl; Drm Mjrt; Hon Rl; Off Ade; Pep Clb; Mat Maids; Twrlr; St Fancy Strut Champ; St Military Strut Champ; 1st Runner Up Miss Majorette Ohio; Owens Tech Coll; Med.

DRAG, PATTI; Gull Lake HS; Richland, MI; Hon Rl; Jr NHS; NHS; Off Ade; Spn Clb; Letter Bsbl; Letter Bsktbl; Aviation.

DRAGGOO, REX; Prairie Hts HS; Orland, IN; Chrs; Bsktbl;.

DRAGOMIR, LINDA; West Branch HS; Alliance, OH; Sec Sr Cls; Am Leg Aux Girls St; VP Band; Chrh Wkr; Hon Rl; NHS; VP Yth Flsp; Treas FHA; Univ.

DRAGON, ELIAS; Harbor HS; Ashtabula, OH; 30/204 Cls Rep Soph Cls; Aud/Vis; FCA; Stu Cncl; Rptr Yrbk; Fr Clb; Mth Clb; Bsbl; Ftbl; IM Sprt; Pennsylvania St Univ; Chem Engr.

DRAGUN, ANDREW; Osborn HS; Detroit, MI; Cl Rep Jr Cls; Boy Scts; Chrs; Hon Rl; Stu Cncl; Ten; Coll; Mech Engr.

DRAHER, AMY; Marlette HS; Marlette, MI; 6/132 Trs Frsh Cls; Cls Rep Frsh Cls; Trs Soph Cls; Hon Rl; NHS; Stu Cncl; Rptr Sch Nwsp; OEA; Pep Clb; Trk; Sec.

DRAIME, TIMOTHY; Canton South HS; Canton, OH; Cls Rep Soph Cls; Cl Rep Jr Cls; Band; Boy Scts; Chrh Wkr; FCA; Hon Rl; Lbry Ade; Sct Actv; Bsbl; Stark Tech Inst; Auto Body Mech.

DRAIN, SELWYN; Elida HS; Lima, OH; 60/275 Cls Rep Soph Cls; Cl Rep Jr Cls; Cls Rep Sr Cls; Am Leg Boys St; Chrh Wkr; Hon Rl; NHS; Rptr Sch Nwsp; Sch Nwsp; Ftbl; Ball State Univ; Comp Sci.

DRAK, GERALD J; Fruitport HS; Nunica, MI; 23/281 Band; Hon Rl; NHS; Bsktbl; Outstndng Sr Ml Athlt 79; St Of Mi Schslp 79; Muskegon Cmnty Coll Bd Of Trustee Schlshp 7.; Muskegon Cmnty Coll; Chem.

DRAKE, ALECIA; Benedictine HS; Detroit, MI; Cls Rep Frsh Cls; Cls Rep Soph Cls; Trs Jr Cls; Chrs; Chrh Wkr; Hon Rl; JA; NHS; Sch Mus; Sch Pl; Wayne St Univ; Comp Sci.

DRAKE, ANN; Turpin HS; Cincinnati, OH; 17/371 Cls Rep Frsh Cls; Cls Rep Soph Cls; Cl Rep Jr Cls; Girl Scts; Stu Cncl; Bsktbl; Letter Socr; Letter Trk; PPFtbl; College; Liberal Arts.

DRAKE, CONNIE; Seeger HS; Williamsport, IN; 23/141 Cls Rep Soph Cls; Cl Rep Jr Cls; Band; Cmp Fr Grls; Chrs; Drl Tm; Hon Rl; Stu Cncl; 4-H; FHA; Hon Roll Hon Schlrshps 77 78 & 79; Indiana St Univ; CPA.

DRAKE, DAVID; Rogers HS; Michigan City, IN; 34/480 Am Leg Boys St; Aud/Vis; Chrs; Hon Rl; NHS; Rptr Yrbk; Mth Clb; Sci Clb; Bsktbl; Glf; Butler Univ; Dent.

DRAKE, DAVID; Whitmer Sr HS; Toledo, OH; Boy Scts; Hon Rl; Off Ade; Lat Clb; Ohio St Univ; Vet Med.

DRAKE, DONNA; Reese HS; Richville, MI; Band; Debate Tm; Girl Scts; Hon Rl; NHS; 4-H; Ger Clb; Letter Trk; 4-H Awd; Univ; Med Lab.

DRAKE, GLENDA; North Vigo HS; Terre Haute, IN; Band; Girl Scts; Hon Rl; Sec JA; Lbry Ade; Sch Mus; Y-Teens; Pres DECA; 4-H; Pep Clb; Indiana St Univ; Mktg.

DRAKE, J; Warren Ctrl HS; Indpls, IN; JA; Jr NHS; Lat Clb; Ten; IM Sprt; JA Awd; Bus Schl; Bus.

DRAKE, JAMES; Oregon Davis HS; Hamlet, IN; Boy Scts; Hon Rl; Lbry Ade; Sch Pl; Sct Actv; Rptr Sch Nwsp; Drama Clb; FHA; Sci Clb; Ball St Univ; Indust Artist.

DRAKE, JEFFREY; Upper Arlington HS; Columbus, OH; 78/610 Debate Tm; FCA; Hon Rl; Natl Forn Lg; Fr Clb; Bsbl; Ftbl; Lcrss; Wrstlng; Capt Of Var Wrstlng; Univ; Law.

DRAKE, JIM; Southern Local HS; Kensington, OH; 2/100 Chrh Wkr; Hon Rl; NHS; Yth Flsp; Treas 4-H; Lat Clb; Bsktbl; IM Sprt; 4-H Awd; Ohio St Univ; Engr.

DRAKE, JUDY; Port Huron Northern HS; Port Huron, MI; 156/408 Cl Rep Jr Cls; Cls Rep Sr Cls; Drl Tm; Hon Rl; Letter Stu Cncl; Rptr Yrbk; Letter Pom Pon; Kiwan Awd; St Clair County Com Coll; Law Enfr.

DRAKE, JULIANNE; Kingsford HS; Iron Mtn, MI; Trs Soph Cls; Band; Cmnty Wkr; Hon Rl; Stu Cncl; Y-Teens; Ed Yrbk; Pep Clb; Letter Gym; Letter Trk; College.

DRAKE, KAREN; University HS; Morgantown, WV; Hon Rl; Lbry Ade; Ger Clb; Pep Clb; Chrldng; Univ; Data Proc.

DRAKE, LISA A; Springfield Local HS; Holland, OH; Trs Sr Cls; Band; Chrs; Chrh Wkr; Cmnty Wkr; Hon Rl; JA; Lbry Ade; NHS; Off Ade; Future Medical Careers Assoc; Bowling Green State Univ; Speech.

DRAKE, NANCY; Springboro HS; Springboro, OH; Chrh Wkr; Hon Rl; Off Ade; Sch Pl; Stu Cncl; Rptr Yrbk; Sprt Ed Sch Nwsp; Swmmng; College; Textiles.

DRAKE, PAMELA; Rogers Sr HS; Michigan City, IN; 3/535 Cl Rep Jr Cls; Am Leg Aux Girls St; Chrh Wkr; Hon Rl; NHS; Spn Clb; Letter Ten; Rotary Awd; Vllybl 2 Ltr 77 &78; Univ.

DRAKE, PATRICIA; Parma HS; Brooklyn, OH; 120/740 Chrh Wkr; Cmnty Wkr; Girl Scts; Hon Rl; Hosp Ade; NHS; Yth Flsp; Swmmng; Hiram College; Nursing.

DRAKE, RANDALL; Zanesville HS; Zanesville, OH; Cls Rep Frsh Cls; Hon Rl; NHS; Sch Pl; Stg Crw; 4-H; 4-H Awd; College; History.

DRAKE, ROBERT; Charleston Catholic HS; Charleston, WV; Debate Tm; Hon Rl; Lbry Ade; NHS; Rptr Yrbk; Yrbk; Rptr Sch Nwsp; Sch Nwsp; Ger Clb; Cit Awd; Marshall Univ; Jrnlsm.

DRAKE, STEPHEN; Fairfield HS; Hamilton, OH; 62/640 Chrs; Hon Rl; Sch Mus; Sch Pl; Stg Crw; Pres Drama Clb; Ger Clb; Intl Thespian Soc Trp 390 Pres 79; Choraliers Swing Chr 78; 11 Plays Part In 3 Yrs 76 79; Univ; Law.

DRAKE, THOMAS J; Yorktown HS; Yorktown, IN; 72/180 Sec Jr Cls; Letter Bsktbl; Coach Actv; Courtesey & Ldrshp Awd 79; All Delaware Cnty Tourney Bsktbl Tm 79; All Muncie Sec Tourney Bsktbl Tm 79; Math.

DRAKOS, LINDA; Weir Sr HS; Weirton, WV; 109/343 Cls Rep Sr Cls; Hon Rl; Stu Cncl; GAA; IM Sprt; W Liberty St Coill Art Mert Awd 79; Ohio Vly Hosp Schl Of Nursing; Nurse.

DRANSFIELD, SHERRY; Franklin HS; Livonia, MI; Cls Rep Frsh Cls; Chrs; Hon Rl; Off Ade; Stu Cncl; Sch Nwsp; Trk; Chrldng; Cit Awd; Central Mich Univ; Educ.

DRAPER, JEFFREY; Northfield HS; Roann, IN; 1/108 VP Sr Cls; Val; Am Leg Boys St; Boy Scts; Hon Rl; NHS; Yrbk; Crs Cntry; Glf; Coach Actv; Whos Who In Indiana HS Foreign; Jr Assistant Scout Master; MVP Golf Team Golf Medalist; Butler Univ; Bsns Admin.

DRAPER, LISA; Bellaire HS; Bellaire, MI; 2/47 Sal; Band; Girl Scts; Hon Rl; Letter Bsktbl; Letter Trk; Western St Coll; Mktg.

DRAPER, MELISSA; Pickerington HS; Pickerington, OH; Cmp Fr Grls; Chrs; Chrh Wkr; Hon Rl; NHS; Red Cr Ade; Spn Clb; Tmr; Miami Univ.

DRAPER, TREVA; Whitehall Yearling HS; Whitehall, OH; Aud/Vis; Chrs; Chrh Wkr; Drm Bgl; FCA; Sch Mus; Sch Pl; Stg Crw; Stu Cncl; Drama Clb; Valley Forge Freedom Awd 78; Muskinghum Univ; Soc Psych.

DRAWL, DAVID; Maplewood HS; Cortland, OH; Am Leg Boys St; Hon Rl; NHS; Pres Beta Clb; Letter Bsbl; Bsktbl; Univ.

DRAY, CATHY; Arcadia HS; Findlay, OH; 1/65 Trs Frsh Cls; Cl Rep Jr Cls; Band; Chrs; Hon Rl; Jr NHS; Orch; Sch Mus; Stu Cncl; Yrbk; University; Math.

DRAYTON, KATHERINE; Fenton Sr HS; Fenton, MI; Girl Scts; Hon Rl; Hosp Ade; NHS; Red Cr Ade; Sct Actv; Trk; Mgrs; Tmr; Honor Guard 79; Univ; Med.

DRAZGA, MICHAEL; Hamilton J Robichaud HS; Dearborn Hts, MI; 12/167 Band; Chrh Wkr; Hon Rl; Lbry Ade; Ed Yrbk; Rptr Yrbk; Rptr Sch Nwsp; Boys Clb Am; Capt Crs Cntry; Trk; Michigan St Univ; Telecmmnctns.

DRDA, REGINA; Lorain Catholic HS; Avon, OH; Cls Rep Frsh Cls; Cl Rep Jr Cls; Band; Chrh Wkr; Hon Rl; NHS; Univ.

DREDGE, MISTY; Vandercook Lake HS; Jackson, MI; Band; Hon Rl; NHS; Sch Pl; Capt Gym; JACC; Acctg.

DREES, KEVIN; Marion Local HS; Yorkshire, OH; Hon Rl; NHS; Pep Clb; Letter Bsbl; Letter Ftbl; IM Sprt;.

DREES, SHARON; Versailles HS; Bradford, OH; Cls Rep Frsh Cls; Cls Rep Soph Cls; Cl Rep Jr Cls; Cls Rep Sr Cls; Band; Chrs; Sch Mus; Sch Pl; Stu Cncl; 4-H Awd; Miami Univ; English.

DREFFS, CYNTHIA; Whitmore Lake HS; Whitmore Lk, MI; 13/96 VP Frsh Cls; Sec Soph Cls; Pres Jr Cls; Girl Scts; Hon Rl; Jr NHS; NHS; Sch Pl; College; Attorney.

DREGER, MICHELLE; Ravenna HS; Ravenna, OH; Band; Chrs; Hon Rl; Hosp Ade; NHS; Sch Mus; Stu Cncl; Trk; Cit Awd; Lion Awd; Ohio St Univ; Vet.

DREHER, SHERRI; W Vigo HS; W Terre Haute, IN; 7/187 Hon Rl; NHS; Red Cr Ade; Sch Pl; Y-Teens; Rptr Sch Nwsp; FTA; Indiana St Univ; Busns Mgmt.

DREILING, MARGARET; Canfield HS; Canfield, OH; 41/270 Cmnty Wkr; Girl Scts; Hon Rl; Hosp Ade; Jr NHS; Lit Mag; Y-Teens; Ed Yrbk; Ed Sch Nwsp; Rptr Sch Nwsp; Kent St Univ; Spec Ed.

DREMANN, AMY; High School; Fredricktown, OH; 13/113 Am Leg Aux Girls St; Chrh Wkr; Drl Tm; Hon Rl; NHS; Off Ade; Sch Mus; 4-H; FHA; Spn Clb; Bowling Green St Univ; Arts & Sci.

DRENNAN _III, JOHN F; Sts Peter & Paul Area HS; Saginaw, MI; 47/116 Band; Hon Rl; Sprt Ed Sch Nwsp; Rptr Sch Nwsp; Sch Nwsp; Bsbl; Bsktbl; Opt Clb Awd; Serv Awd In Jr Class; Virginia Military Inst; Journalism.

DRENTEN, ROBERT; Zeeland HS; Zeeland, MI; 17/200 Hon Rl; Iowa St Univ; Meteorology.

DRENTH, PAMELA; Holland Christian HS; Holland, MI; Chrs; Chrh Wkr; Cmnty Wkr; Hosp Ade; Yth Flsp; Ger Clb; IM Sprt; Univ; Spec Educ.

DRESBACH, NORMAN; Teays Valley HS; Circleville, OH; 13/189 Hon Rl; NHS; 4-H; Treas FFA; Letter Bsktbl; V Pres Jr County Fair Board; St Farmer Degree FFA; Farm Bureau Youth Council; Agricultural Tech Inst; Ag Mech.

DRESBACH II, JOE N; Southeastern Ross HS; Chillicothe, OH; Chrs; Chrh Wkr; Hon Rl; 4-H; FFA; Bsktbl; Trk; 4-H Awd; Univ; Agri.

DRESHER, JONI; Centerville HS; Dayton, OH; Band; Girl Scts; OEA; Scr Kpr; Bowling Green Univ; Sec.

DRESS, LAURIE; Put In Bay HS; Put In Bay, OH; 2/6 Pres Frsh Cls; Chrs; Girl Scts; Hon Rl; Sch Pl; Stg Crw; Stu Cncl; Rptr Yrbk; Ed Sch Nwsp; Drama Clb; Terra Tech Univ; Real Estate.

DREW, GREGG A; Piqua Central HS; Piqua, OH; 60/215 Chrh Wkr; Cmnty Wkr; Hon Rl; Red Cr Ade; Pres Key Clb; VP Sci Clb; Letter Socr; Letter Ten; Wittenberg Univ; Chem.

DREW, KATIE; Cathedral HS; Indianapolis, IN; 9/161 Sec Frsh Cls; Chrh Wkr; Girl Scts; Hon Rl; NHS; Sch Mus; Stg Crw; Stu Cncl; Yrbk; Drama Clb; Hoosier Schlrshp 78; Acctg Awd 77; Univ Of Dayton; Bus.

DREW, NANCY E; Chelsea HS; Chelsea, MI; Hon Rl; Lbry Ade; NHS; Yrbk; Univ; Acctg.

DREW, RHONDA; Tecumseh HS; Elberfeld, IN; Cls Rep Frsh Cls; Drama Clb; FBLA; Pep Clb; Trk; Chrldng; PPFtbl; 4-H Awd; Bus.

DREWNO, GREGORY; Taylor Center HS; Taylor, MI; Aud/Vis; Band; Hon Rl; JA; Yrbk; Rptr Sch Nwsp; Swmmng; Mic State; Chiropractor.

DREWS, MICHELLE; Wayne Memorial HS; Wayne, MI; Cmp Fr Grls; Chrs; Chrh Wkr; Girl Scts; Hon Rl; NHS; Off Ade; PAVAS; Sch Mus; Cit Awd; Eastern Michigan Univ; Geographer.

DRICKHAMER, JENNIFER; Our Lady Of The Elms HS; Akron, OH; 1/47 Sec Jr Cls; Chrs; Chrh Wkr; Cmnty Wkr; Hon Rl; Hosp Ade; Sch Mus; Sch Pl; Rptr Yrbk; Rptr Sch Nwsp; Brigham Young Univ.

DRIGGERS, TROY; Carey HS; Carey, OH; Aud/Vis; Hon Rl; Sch Pl; Drama Clb; Mth Clb; Spn Clb; Letter Glf; Letter Trk; GAA; Schlrshp 76 78; Schlstc Achvmnt Schlrshp 76; Univ; Elec.

DRISCOL, CLARA; Buchtel HS; Akron, OH; Chrh Wkr; Hosp Ade; VICA; Chrldng; Ohio St Univ.

DRISCOL, JUNE; Indiana Acad; Columbus, IN; VP Frsh Cls; Chrs; Hon Rl; NHS; Stu Cncl; Sch Nwsp; Andrews Univ; Phys Ther.

DRISCOLL, LINDA; Union HS; Losantville, IN; 37/80 Band; Hon Rl; Yrbk; Sch Nwsp; FHA; Gym; 4-H Awd; ITT; Photog.

DRISCOLL, PATRICK; Moeller HS; Cincinnati, OH; Cl Rep Jr Cls; Cls Rep Sr Cls; Letter Swmmng; Letter Ten; Coach Actv; College; Bus Mgmt.

DRISTAS, REBECCA; Andrean HS; Hobart, IN; 65/251 Chrh Wkr; Girl Scts; Hon Rl; GAA; DAR Awd; College; Nursing.

DRIVER, BARBARA; Bridgman HS; Bridgman, MI; Chrs; Chrh Wkr; Hon Rl; Yth Flsp; FHA; Sci Clb; Bsbl; Ten; Lake Michigan Coll; Legal Sec.

DRIVER, JULIA; Kalamazoo Central HS; Kalamazoo, MI; Lat Clb; Spn Clb; Natl Merit Ltr; Schlrshp From Kalamazoo Ed Assn For Grad In Top 20 Of Cl 79; 1st Pl In Free Enterprise Essay Contest 79; Michigan St Univ; Archaelogy.

DRIVER, MELISSA; St Ursula Academy; Maumee, OH; Yrbk; IM Sprt; La Federation Des Alliances Fran Caises Aux Etats Unis 76; Univ Of Dayton; Cmnctn Arts.

DRIVER, TAMMY; Midview HS; Grafton, OH; 18/267 Bus.

DROBINA, MICHAEL; Morgan HS; Malta, OH; Am Leg Boys St; Hon Rl; Lbry Ade; NHS; Off Ade; 4-H; Spn Clb; VICA; 4-H Awd; Ohio Univ; Elec Engr.

DROESCH, TIMOTHY L; Marion Local HS; Chickasaw, OH; Chrh Wkr; Cmnty Wkr; Hon Rl; Pep Clb; VICA; IM Sprt; Wright St Univ; Data Proc.

DROLL, LISA; St Wendelin HS; Fostoria, OH; 18/81 Band; Chrs; Hon Rl; JA; NHS; Sch Pl; Drama Clb; Pep Clb; Spn Clb; JA Awd; Vocational School.

DROME, DEBORAH; Whitmer HS; Toledo, OH; 6/910 Hon Rl; NHS; Rptr Yrbk; FTA; Am Leg Awd; V P Of French Honorary 78 79; Acad Letter 79; Univ; Acctg.

DROPIEWSKI, DAVID; Armada HS; Richmond, MI; 20/100 Cls Rep Frsh Cls; NHS; Sch Pl; Stu Cncl; Mth Clb; Letter Ftbl; Natl Merit Ltr; Whos Who 77; Adrain Coll; Pre Med.

DROPIEWSKI, MARIANNE; Ernest W Seaholm HS; Birmingham, MI; Cl Rep Jr Cls; Cls Rep Sr Cls; Band; Hon Rl; Jr NHS; Mod UN; Swmmng; Mic State Univ; Pre Med.

DROSKI, MARGARET; Union HS; Grand Rapids, MI; Trs Jr Cls; Band; JA; JA Awd; Tech School.

DROTAR, KAREN; Campbell Memorial HS; Campbell, OH; Chrh Wkr; Hon Rl; Natl Forn Lg; NHS; Rptr Sch Nwsp; Drama Clb; Fr Clb; Key Clb; Mth Clb; Chrldng; Youngstown State; Pre Med.

DROZ, STEPHEN B; Franklin HS; Westland, MI; Cls Rep Frsh Cls; Am Leg Boys St; Debate Tm; Lit Mag; Sct Actv; Sci Clb; Letter Bsbl; Letter Ftbl; Coach Actv; IM Sprt; Publications 78; Activities 78; Univ; Drafting.

DROZD, RENEE; Whitehall HS; Whitehall, MI; 51/156 Chrs; Girl Scts; Hon Rl; Off Ade; 4-H; 4-H Awd; Muskegon Comm Coll.

DROZDOWSKI, KATRINA; Pinckney HS; Pinckney, MI; Am Leg Aux Girls St; Hon Rl; Hosp Ade; Lbry Ade; Off Ade; Yrbk; Natl Merit SF; Michigan St Univ; Acctg.

DRUCKER, DEBBIE; Clarenceville HS; Livonia, MI; Cls Rep Frsh Cls; Cls Rep Soph Cls; Cl Rep Jr Cls; Cls Rep Sr Cls; Cmnty Wkr; Debate Tm; Drm Mjrt; Hon Rl; Natl Forn Lg; NHS; Michigan St Univ.

DRUMM, ELISA; Old Trail HS; Akron, OH; Cls Rep Frsh Cls; Cls Rep Soph Cls; VP Jr Cls; Sec Jr Cls; Trs Jr Cls; Chrh Wkr; Stu Cncl; Yrbk; Spn Clb; Hockey; Graphic Design.

DRUMMOND, KAREN; Fremont Ross HS; Fremont, OH; 34/456 Band; Girl Scts; Hon Rl; Jr NHS; NHS; 4-H; Pep Clb; Sci Clb; Bowling Green St Univ; Psych.

DRUMMOND, MAUREEN H; Lake Orion Commun HS; Lake Orion, MI; Pres Jr Cls; Girl Scts; Hon Rl; Jr NHS; Stu Cncl; Pep Clb; Mgrs; MSU; Poli Sci.

DRUMMOND, MICHELE; Bridgeport HS; Bridgeport, WV; Chrs; Hon Rl; Jr NHS; Yrbk; Sch Nwsp; Pres 4-H; Pep Clb; Spn Clb; 4-H Awd; College; Law.

DRUMMOND, RHONDA; Shady Spring HS; Daniels, WV; 6/180 Band; Hon Rl; NHS; Orch; Pep Clb; Spn Clb; Most Accomplished Musician Awd; Honor Letters; All County Hand; Marshall Univ.

DRURY, JANE; Upper Arlington HS; Columbus, OH; 42/619 Am Leg Aux Girls St; Hon Rl; Natl Forn Lg; NHS; Yrbk; Fr Clb; Ger Clb; Letter Crs Cntry; Letter Swmmng; Letter Trk; College; Medicine.

DRUSHEL, RICHARD; Liberty HS; Girard, OH; Am Leg Boys St; Band; Hon Rl; NHS; Sch Nwsp; Natl Merit SF; College; Pre Med.

DRWICK, LUANN; Mc Comb HS; Mccomb, OH; 5/83 VP Sr Cls; Band; Hon Rl; NHS; Sch Pl; Stu Cncl; 4-H; Pep Clb; Letter Trk; 4-H Awd; College; Medical.

DRYER, NANCY; Holly HS; Holly, MI; Pres Soph Cls; Cl Rep Jr Cls; Hon Rl; NHS; Stu Cncl; Pep Clb; Chrldng; PPFtbl; Eastern Michigan Univ; Nursing.

DRZEWIECKI, CATHY; Glen Lake HS; Cedar, MI; 1/71 Val; Band; Hon Rl; NHS; Quill & Scroll; Ed Yrbk; Sch Nwsp; Letter Bsbl; Letter Bsktbl; Letter Trk; Mich Tech Univ; Bio Sci.

DUAS, BONNIE; Hamady HS; Flint, MI; 10/145 Band; Girl Scts; Hon Rl; NHS; Capt Bsktbl; Trk; Twrlr; Lion Awd; Central Michigan Univ.

DUBAY, CHRISTOPHER; Valley Forge HS; Parma Hgts, OH; Cls Rep Sr Cls; Cmnty Wkr; Hon Rl; Yth Flsp; Letter Swmmng; College; Engr.

DUBAY, THOMAS W; Douglas Mac Arthur HS; Saginaw, MI; 43/300 Hon Rl; Jr NHS; NHS; Squires Club; Fresh & T V Bsbl; Michigan Tech Univ; Mech Engr.

DUBBERLY, STEVEN; East Liverpool HS; E Liverpool, OH; 56/360 Hon Rl; Lbry Ade; Sch Nwsp; Fr Clb; Spn Clb; IM Sprt; Achvmnt Awrd; Univ; Foreign Lang.

DUBBERT, FREDERICK R; Port Clinton HS; Port Clinton, OH; Boy Scts; Cmnty Wkr; Hon Rl; Sct Actv; DECA; Letter Ftbl; Letter Trk; Kiwan Awd; 2nd Pl Ohio Serv Industry Manuel DECA Trophy; Penn State Univ; Aeronautics.

DUBBINK, BRUCE H; Hamilton HS; Hamilton, MI; Band; Boy Scts; Hon Rl; Sct Actv; Yth Flsp; Pres 4-H; Ger Clb; Letter Bsbl; Letter Ftbl; Wrstlng; Univ; Data Proc.

DUBBINK, DOUGLAS; Hamilton HS; Hamilton, MI; 3/131 Girl Scts; NHS; FFA; Spn Clb; Chmn Ftbl; Letter Trk; Letter Wrstlng; Central Mic Univ.

DUBETZ, DIANNE; Rootstown HS; Ravenna, OH; Pres Soph Cls; Cls Rep Soph Cls; Cl Rep Jr Cls; Cls Rep Sr Cls; Am Leg Aux Girls St; Girl Scts; Hon Rl; Lbry Ade; NHS; Off Ade; Ohio St Univ; Engr.

DUBININ, PETER; Goshen HS; Goshen, IN; 40/269 Boy Scts; Pres Chrh Wkr; Hon Rl; Sct Actv; Stu Cncl; Yth Flsp; Rptr Yrbk; Ftbl; Letter Swmmng; Trk; Grace Coll; Theol.

DUBITES, THOMAS; Ripley HS; Ripley, WV; Chrh Wkr; Cmnty Wkr; Hon Rl; Sch Pl; Stg Crw; Drama Clb; 4-H; Fr Clb; Mth Clb; VICA; Univ; Engr.

DU BOIS, CAROL A; Lapeer East HS; Attica, MI; Debate Tm; Central Mic Univ; Journalism.

DU BOIS, DAVID; Talawanda HS; Oxford, OH; 9/321 Treas AFS; Hon Rl; NHS; Yth Flsp; Letter Ten; IM Sprt; Natl Merit Ltr; College; Soc Sci.

DU BOIS, DWAYNE; Moeller HS; Cincinnati, OH; Band; Hon Rl; Sch Mus; Sch Pl; Bsbl; Ftbl; Trk; IM Sprt; Univ; Bus.

DU BOIS, JULIA; Clay HS; South Bend, IN; Hon Rl; Quill & Scroll; Rptr Yrbk; Yrbk; Univ; Advert.

DU BOIS, MICHAEL; Elkhart Mem HS; Elkhart, IN; Hon Rl; Fr Clb; Bsbl; Ftbl; Swmmng; Wrstlng; Coach Actv; IM Sprt; Mgrs; Univ; History.

DUBOVSKY, JAMES; Tawas Area HS; E Tawas, MI; 2/155 Sal; Hon Rl; NHS; Letter Bsbl; Letter Bsktbl; Mich State Univ; Eng.

DUBY, PETER; Arthur Hill HS; Saginaw, MI; Hon Rl; NHS; Sci Clb; Ftbl; Mgrs; Natl Merit Ltr; Mich State Univ; Engr.

DUCA, MARIANNE; Campbell Mem HS; Campbell, OH; 1/210 Cls Rep Soph Cls; Trs Jr Cls; Hon Rl; NHS; Off Ade; Pol Wkr; Key Clb; Mth Clb; Sci Clb; Spn Clb; Youngstown St Univ; Comp Sci.

DUCEY, JAMES; Belleville HS; Belleville, MI; Boy Scts; Chrh Wkr; Hon Rl; Sct Actv; Lat Clb; Sci Clb; Capt Ftbl; Trk; IM Sprt; Natl Merit Schl; Michigan St Univ; Med.

DUCH, TERRI; James A Garfield HS; Garrettsville, OH; Hon Rl; Sch Mus; Sch Pl; Fr Clb; Pep Clb; Sci Clb; Swmmng; Letter Chrldng; Pom Pon; 4-H Awd; Kent State Univ; Architecture.

DUCH, TRACEY; Highland HS; Hinckley, OH; 94/207 Chrs; Chrh Wkr; Off Ade; Stg Crw; Pres Y-Teens; Lat Clb; Pep Clb; Natl Merit SF; Mt Saint Joseph Coll; Nurse.

DU CHAINE, JULIE; Escanaba Area Pub HS; Escanaba, MI; Hon Rl; Rptr Yrbk; Bay De Noc Comm Coll; Communication.

DUCHAK, ANNE; Archbishop Alter HS; Dayton, OH; Letter Socr; Ten; Letter Trk; Coach Actv; GAA; IM Sprt; Kiwan Awd; Pres Awd; Coll; Phys Educ.

DUCHNOWSKI, HELEN; St Andrews HS; Detroit, MI; 32/109 Chrh Wkr; Hon Rl; IM Sprt; Wayne St Univ; Nursing.

DUCIC, RENEE; Nordonia HS; Northfield, OH; Band; VP Chrh Wkr; Sch Mus; Sch Pl; Drama Clb; Letter Ten; Capt Twrlr; Bowling Green Tiffin Univ; Bus.

DU CILLE, ROBERT H; Redford HS; Detroit, MI; Band; Chrs; Chrh Wkr; Cmnty Wkr; Debate Tm; FCA; JA; Sct Actv; Alma College; Elec Engr.

DUCK, TERRI; Southern Local HS; Wellsville, OH; Hst Jr Cls; Chrh Wkr; Hon Rl; 4-H; FHA; OEA; Bsktbl; Busns Schl; Busns Admin.

DUCKER, CINDY; Perrysburg HS; Perrysburg, OH; Girl Scts; Sch Pl; Sct Actv; 4-H; Commercial Art.

DUCKRO, DON; Carroll HS; Dayton, OH; 10/290 Chrh Wkr; Hon Rl; Y-Teens; Treas Civ Clb; Trk; Natl Merit SF; Univ; Mech Engr.

DUCO, MICHAEL P; Steubenville Cath Cntrl HS; Steubenvll, OH; 23/204 Boy Scts; FCA; Hon Rl; NHS; Spn Clb; Ftbl; Soph Soc Studies Awd; Coll Prep Math III Awd; VP Of Natl Hnr Soc; Ohio St Univ; Law.

DUDA, KATHRYN M; Mt De Chantal Visitation Acd; Shadyside, OH; 7/31 Cls Rep Frsh Cls; VP Jr Cls; Pres Sr Cls; Band; Chrs; Hon Rl; NHS; Pres Orch; Sch Mus; Sch Pl; Bethany Coll; Cmnctns.

DUDDLES, KIMBERLY; Lake Orion HS; Pontiac, MI; 27/435 Band; Hon Rl; Jr NHS; NHS; All C ounty Varsity Sftbl 77; Oakland Univ; CPA.

DUDDLES, LISA; Benzie Central HS; Beulah, MI; 11/150 Trs Frsh Cls; Trs Soph Cls; Trs Jr Cls; Trs Sr Cls; Hon Rl; NHS; Stu Cncl; Rptr Yrbk; Rptr Sch Nwsp; Pep Clb; College.

DUDDLESON, DAWN; Baldwin HS; Baldwin, MI; 1/65 VP Jr Cls; Val; Band; Chrh Wkr; Girl Scts; Hon Rl; NHS; Sch Pl; Spn Clb; IM Sprt; Harvard Univ.

DUDECK, KAREN; St Joseph HS; So Bend, IN; Cls Rep Sr Cls; Cmnty Wkr; Off Ade; Pep Clb; Mgrs; Am Leg Awd; Ball St Univ; Spec Ed.

DUDEK, CINDY; Beaver Local HS; Calcutta, OH; Sch Pl; DECA; Eng Clb; Fr Clb; Lat Clb; Mat Maids; Mount Union Coll; Sci.

DUDEK, DAVID; Bishop Donahue HS; Wheeling, WV; Key Clb; Bsktbl; College.

DUDEK, DENISE; Richmond HS; Richmond, MI; 4/174 Chrs; Chrh Wkr; Hon Rl; NHS; Sec Stu Cncl; Rptr Yrbk; Rptr Sch Nwsp; Pres 4-H; IM Sprt; 4-H Awd; St Of Mi Comp Schlrshp 79; Daughter Of Yr Church Awd 78; Organic Chem 79; Geometry & Advncd Bio Awd 77; Ferris St Coll; Radiolgc Tech.

DUDEK, JANICE; Cardinal Ritter HS; Indianapolis, IN; Hon Rl; Pep Clb; Spn Clb; Chrldng; Coach Actv; IM Sprt; PPFtbl; College.

DUDEK, KAREN; North Royalton HS; N Royalton, OH; Fr Clb; Bsbl; Bsktbl; GAA; Lion Awd; Ohio St Univ; History.

DUDEK, MITCHELL; Sidney HS; Sidney, OH; Pres Sr Cls; Boy Scts; Chrh Wkr; FCA; Hon Rl; Stu Cncl; Key Clb; Ftbl; Trk; Wrstlng; Bluffton Coll; Busns Admin.

DUDLEY, DANIEL; Lima HS; Lima, OH; 1/500 Cl Rep Jr Cls; Band; Chrs; Hon Rl; Sch Mus; Stu Cncl; Yth Flsp; Letter Ten; College; Computer Science.

DUDLEY, GREGORY; Pontiac Central HS; Pontiac, MI; Cls Rep Frsh Cls; Hon Rl; NHS; Boys Clb Am; Fr Clb; Letter Bsktbl; Letter Ten; Oakland Univ; Engr.

DUDLEY, ONNAKA; Randolph Southern HS; Lynn, IN; Sch Pl; VP Yth Flsp; Yrbk; Drama Clb; 4-H; Lat Clb; Trk; Scr Kpr; 4-H Awd; College; Journalism.

DUDLEY, PAMELA; Willow Run HS; Ypsilanti, MI; 13/161 Cls Rep Soph Cls; Cl Rep Jr Cls; Cls Rep Sr Cls; Am Leg Aux Girls St; Band; Hon Rl; NHS; Off Ade; Ed Sch Nwsp; Tmr; Oakland Univ; Cmnctns Arts.

DUDLEY, TODD; Franklin Central HS; Indianapolis, IN; 1/260 Am Leg Boys St; Hon Rl; NHS; Letter Bsktbl; Trk; Am Leg Awd; Cit Awd; Attend U S Army Jr Sci & Humanities Symp 79; Butler Univ; Pre Med.

DUDZIK, HELEN; St Clement HS; Warren, MI; Hon Rl; Mic State Univ; Engr.

DUDZINSKI, MAREK; St Marys Prep; Hamtramck, MI; 12/25 Socr; Letter IM Sprt; Henry Ford Comm College; Mech Draft.

DUELLEY, DENISE; Keystone HS; La Grange, OH; Cls Rep Frsh Cls; Cls Rep Soph Cls; Cl Rep Jr Cls; Cls Rep Sr Cls; Chrs; Stu Cncl; FTA; Pep Clb; Chrldng; Tmr; Bus Schl; Bus.

DUEMMEL, CHRISTINA; Dublin HS; Dublin, OH; 49/157 Chrs; Hon Rl; Lit Mag; PAVAS; Sch Mus; 4-H; Spn Clb; Letter Trk; Univ.

DUEMMEL, TERESA; Dublin HS; Dublin, OH; 3/153 Hon Rl; Lit Mag; PAVAS; Sch Mus; Rptr Sch Nwsp; Drama Clb; 4-H; Spn Clb; Natl Merit Ltr; Univ.

DUERR, CRAIG; Carson City Crystal HS; Carson City, MI; 16/128 Cls Rep Frsh Cls; Am Leg Boys St; Hon Rl; Off Ade; Stu Cncl; Letter Crs Cntry; Letter Trk; Coach Actv; IM Sprt; Mgrs; Central Michigan Univ; Bus Admin.

DUERSTOCK, ROSE; Immaculate Conception Acad; Batesville, IN; 42/68 Girl Scts; Work.

DUFF, ANN; Kent Roosevelt HS; Kent, OH; Band; Cmp Fr Grls; Chrs; Chrh Wkr; Hon Rl; Lbry Ade; Yth Flsp; Pep Clb; Spn Clb; Bsbl; Univ; Sci.

DUFF, GIL; Deer Park HS; Cincinnati, OH; Cls Rep Frsh Cls; Boy Scts; Chrh Wkr; Off Ade; PAVAS; Sch Pl; Sct Actv; Yth Flsp; Sch Nwsp; Ftbl; Intl Thespian Soc; University; Performing Arts.

DUFF, KIM; Muskegon HS; Muskegon, MI; Cls Rep Soph Cls; Cl Rep Jr Cls; Hst Sr Cls; Cls Rep Sr Cls; Chrs; Hon Rl; Treas Stu Cncl; Fr Clb; Swmmng; Grand Valley State Coll; Soc Work.

DUFF, KIMBERLY; Muskegon Sr HS; Muskegon, MI; Cls Rep Soph Cls; Cl Rep Jr Cls; Hst Sr Cls; Cls Rep Sr Cls; Hon Rl; Treas Stu Cncl; Fr Clb; Swmmng; Mgrs; Muskegon Cmnty Coll; Soc Wrk.

DUFF, ROBERT; Walnut Ridge HS; Columbus, OH; Band; Boy Scts; Chrh Wkr; Hon Rl; NHS; Orch; Quill & Scroll; Sch Mus; VP Stu Cncl; Yth Flsp; Outstanding Journalist Newspaper; Announcer Bs ktbl Games; Ohio Univ; Broadcast Journalism.

DUFF, SHERYL; Frankenmuth HS; Frankenmuth, MI; 4/185 Band; Chrh Wkr; Debate Tm; Hon Rl; Hosp Ade; Natl Forn Lg; VP NHS; Sch Mus; Sch Pl; 4-H; Concordia Univ; Elem Educ.

DUFF, VALERIE; Stonewall Jackson HS; Charleston, WV; Chrs; Girl Scts; Hon Rl; Jr NHS; Lbry Ade; NHS; Stu Cncl; Y-Teens; Rptr Yrbk; Yrbk; Spanish Hnr Soc 78; Marshall Univ; Bus.

DUFFETT, PAULA; Grosse Ile HS; Grosse Ile, MI; 60/230 Cls Rep Frsh Cls; Chrh Wkr; Girl Scts; Hon Rl; Off Ade; Stu Cncl; Yth Flsp; Yrbk; GAA; IM Sprt; Michigan St Univ; Bus Admin.

DUFFEY, ERIN; John Adams HS; So Bend, IN; 103/395 Cls Rep Frsh Cls; Cls Rep Soph Cls; Chrs; Cmnty Wkr; Hon Rl; Off Ade; Sprt Ed Sch Nwsp; Rptr Sch Nwsp; Civ Clb; Drama Clb; College; Communications.

DUFFEY, KATHY; Stow Sr HS; Munroe Fl, OH; 157/564 Chrh Wkr; FCA; Letter Hockey; Letter Trk; Mgrs; Univ; Bio.

DUFFEY, RICHARD; Lakeview HS; Howard City, MI; Cls Rep Frsh Cls; Pres Sr Cls; Band; Debate Tm; Hon Rl; NHS; Sch Pl; Kalamazoo College; Philosophy.

DUFFIELD, PETER; Clearview HS; Lorain, OH; 10/130 Hon Rl; NHS; Sch Nwsp; Ftbl; Trk; Top 10 Of The Clss 77 79; LCCC; Archt.

DUFF JR, WALTER; Little Miami HS; Morrow, OH; Cls Rep Soph Cls; Cl Rep Jr Cls; Boy Scts; Hon Rl; Pep Clb; Ftbl; IM Sprt; Voice Dem Awd; College; Engr.

DUFFORD, A DIANE; Waterloo HS; Atwater, OH; 19/135 Cls Rep Soph Cls; Cl Rep Jr Cls; Band; Chrs; Hosp Ade; Stu Cncl; Fr Clb; Medcl Careers Progr 78; Young Citzns Awd 78; Whos Who In Foreign Lang 77; Univ; Med.

DUFFY, KIMBRA; New Albany HS; New Albany, IN; Chrs; Chrh Wkr; Hon Rl; Hosp Ade; NHS; Fr Clb; Pep Clb; College; Phys Therapist.

DUFFY, MARGARET; Oakwood Sr HS; Dayton, OH; Girl Scts; JA; Lbry Ade; Off Ade; Sch Mus; Sch Pl; Capt Bsbl; Trk; Chrldng; IM Sprt; E New Mexico Univ; Public Relations.

DUFFY, MARGARET; Tallmadge HS; Hatboro, PA; 41/351 Cls Rep Sr Cls; Treas Chrs; Mdrgl; NHS; Sch Mus; Sch Pl; Pres Drama Clb; IM Sprt; Temple Univ; Nurse.

DUFFY, NANCY; Evart HS; Evart, MI; Chrs; Girl Scts; Hon Rl; Natl Forn Lg; NHS; Sch Pl; Yth Flsp; Yrbk; Sch Nwsp; 4-H; Judson; Eng.

DUFFY, PATRICIA; Sandusky HS; Sandusky, OH; 49/404 Hon Rl; Lbry Ade; NHS; Sch Pl; Treas Drama Clb; Firelands Campus Coll; Busns.

DUFORD, KATHERYN; Reed City HS; Reed City, MI; Cls Rep Soph Cls; Cl Rep Jr Cls; Hon Rl; Stu Cncl; Rptr Sch Nwsp; Letter Bsktbl; GAA; Pres Awd; College; Rec & Sports Admin.

DUGA, TERRI; Bexley HS; Bexley, OH; 15/186 Band; Cmnty Wkr; Hon Rl; NHS; Quill & Scroll; Sch Mus; Sch Pl; Rptr Sch Nwsp; Am Leg Awd; Ohio St Univ; Pharm.

DU GAN, GEORGE; Otsego HS; Otsego, MI; 18/200 Band; Hon Rl; Pep Clb; Crs Cntry; Trk; IM Sprt; Lion Awd; Michigan St Univ; Pre Med.

DU GAN, JUDY; East Palestine HS; E Palestine, OH; Am Leg Aux Girls St; Cmp Fr Grls; Chrs; Hon Rl; Sch Pl; Sec Yth Flsp; Letter Bsbl; Letter Bsktbl; Letter Ten; Univ; Dentistry.

DU GAN, SUE; Clay HS; Oregon, OH; VP Frsh Cls; Band; Hon Rl; NHS; Stu Cncl; Rptr Yrbk; Ohio Univ; Bus Admin.

DUGAS, MARGARET; Newton HS; Laura, OH; Hon Rl; Lbry Ade; Sch Pl; Rptr Yrbk; 4-H; FFA; Bsktbl; Kettering Med Coll; Lab Tech.

DUGGAN, JOAN K; Briggs HS; Columbus, OH; 37/213 Am Leg Aux Girls St; DECA; 3rd Pl Dist Awd For Public Speaking; Stu Of Yr For DECA For Briggs;.

DUGGAN, MAUREEN; L Anse Creuse North HS; Mount Clemens, MI; 2/300 Hon Rl; MMM; Treas NHS; Sch Pl; Trk; Chrldng; JETS Awd; Michigan St Univ; Pre Vet Med.

DUGGER, DENNIS; Benton Harbor HS; Benton Hrbr, MI; Chrs; CAP; JA; MMM; Sch Mus; Sch Pl; Mgrs; College; Mngmnt.

DUGUID, ROBERT; Vandercook Lake HS; Jackson, MI; Trs Soph Cls; Trs Jr Cls; Chrh Wkr; Hon Rl; NHS; Mth Clb; Letter Glf; Cit Awd; College; Chem.

DUGUID, STEVE; Garrett HS; Garrett, IN; Aud/Vis; Boy Scts; Stg Crw; Yth Flsp; Rptr Sch Nwsp; Wrstlng; Mgrs; Purdue Univ; Comp Engr.

DU HAMEL, KATHRYN L; Rochester Sr HS; Rochester, MI; Chrh Wkr; Girl Scts; Hon Rl; NHS; Pol Wkr; VP Stu Cncl; Letter Glf; Capt Swmmng; Capt Scr Kpr; Capt Tmr; Rochester Area Youth Guidance Com Otstndng Teen Awrd 77; Swim Tm Coachs Awrd Most Spirited 76; Univ Of Michigan; Law.

DUIBLEY, PATTY; Belmont HS; Dayton, OH; Cls Rep Soph Cls; Am Leg Aux Girls St; Chrh Wkr; Off Ade; Rptr Yrbk; Rptr Sch Nwsp; Pep Clb; Bsbl; Bsktbl; Mgrs; Univ Of Dayton; Law.

DUJANOVIC, GEORGE; St Vincent St Mary HS; Barberton, OH; Chrh Wkr; JA; Sch Mus; Sci Clb; Am Leg Awd; JA Awd; VFW Awd;.

DUKE, CHRISTINE; Badin HS; Hamilton, OH; 40/223 Chrh Wkr; Cmnty Wkr; Hon Rl; NHS; Sch Mus; Sch Pl; Stg Crw; Ed Sch Nwsp; Drama Clb; Ger Clb; Miami Univ; Elem Educ.

DUKE, JAMES F; Milton Sr HS; Culloden, WV; Cls Rep Frsh Cls; Cls Rep Soph Cls; Cl Rep Jr Cls; Hon Rl; Jr NHS; Stu Cncl; DECA; Bsktbl; Crs Cntry; Trk; 2nd Pl Finnc & Certd Manual Of Wv; West Virginia Univ; Med.

DUKE, KATHLEEN; Western HS; Parma, MI; 1/175 NHS; Pol Wkr; Spn Clb; Letter Bsktbl; Coach Actv; Scr Kpr; Mich State Univ; Comp Sci.

DUKE, LISA A; Roosevelt Wilson HS; Nutter Frt, WV; Am Leg Aux Girls St; Band; Chrh Wkr; Hon Rl; Yth Flsp; Y-Teens; 4-H; FHA; Ten; Tmr; Fairmont St Coll; Med Lab Tech.

DUKE, ROBERT A; Winston Churchill HS; Livonia, MI; Aud/Vis; Band; Chrs; Chrh Wkr; Cmnty Wkr; Lbry Ade; Mdrgl; MMM; Orch; PAVAS; Eastman Schl Of Music; Vocation.

DUKE, VALLEN; Floyd Ctrl HS; Floyds Knobs, IN; 19/358 Hon Rl; JA; NHS; Off Ade; Pep Clb; VP Spn Clb; Univ.

DUKELOW, SCOTT R; Holt HS; Holt, MI; Boy Scts; Sct Actv; Letter Bsbl; Ftbl; Capt Swmmng; Mgrs; Univ; Fish & Wildlife.

DUKES, BARBARA; Ben Davis HS; Indianapolis, IN; 39/850 Hon Rl; NHS; Stu Cncl; Ger Clb; Letter Swmmng; IM Sprt; Indiana Univ; Acctg.

DUKRO, DAVID; Wapakoneta Sr HS; Wapakoneta, OH; 4/304 Cl Rep Jr Cls; NHS; Quill & Scroll; Red Cr Ade; VP Stu Cncl; Ed Yrbk; Rptr Sch Nwsp; Drama Clb; Pres Fr Clb; Mgrs; Ohio Tests Of Schlstc Ach Hnrbl Mention; Excel Awd Sci Day; St Andrews Choir; Coll; Math.

DULA, JEFFREY J; Solon HS; Solon, OH; 23/300 Chrs; Hon Rl; NHS; Pol Wkr; Key Clb; Letter Socr; Ten; Letter Wrstlng; IM Sprt; Natl Sci Foundation Schl Partr In Summer Sci Trang Prog 1978; Mvp Soccer Team All Conference Team In Scr 19; Univ; Med Research.

DULA, THOMAS; Clio HS; Clio, MI; Ftbl; Trk; IM Sprt; College.

DU LANEY, EMMETT; Daleville HS; Yorktown, IN; Rptr Yrbk; Rptr Sch Nwsp; Spn Clb; Coll; Journalist.

DU LANEY, KEVIN D; John Marshall HS; Moundsville, WV; Am Leg Boys St; Boy Scts; Hon Rl; VICA; Ftbl; IM Sprt; Am Leg Awd; Belmont Tech Coll.

DULAR, JANET; Kirtland HS; Kirtland, OH; 9/123 VP Sr Cls; AFS; Hon Rl; Jr NHS; NHS; Stg Crw; Drama Clb; Spn Clb; Scr Kpr; Natl Merit Ltr; College.

DULBERGER, KEHLEY; Park Tudor HS; Indianapolis, IN; Pres Frsh Cls; Pres Soph Cls; Girl Scts; Pol Wkr; Stu Cncl; Yrbk; Ed Sch Nwsp; Fr Clb; Hockey; IM Sprt; Youth Leadershp Prog 1978; Duke Univ; Law.

DULIN, CHERYL; Fountain Central HS; Veedersburg, IN; 5/118 Band; Hon Rl; NHS; Sec FSA; Indiana St Univ; Spec Ed.

DULING, MARGARET J; Ottawa Glandore HS; Ottawa, OH; Band; Drm Bgl; Hon Rl; NHS; Orch; Sch Mus; 4-H; Sci Clb; Spn Clb; Trk; Univ; Eng.

DULKOSKI, JODY; Jewett Scio HS; Jewett, OH; Trs Jr Cls; Band; Hon Rl; NHS; Off Ade; Sch Mus; Yth Flsp; Yrbk; Spn Clb; Spanish Acad Awd; Altrurian Clb Awd; Univ.

DULL, JONI; Eastlake North HS; Eastlake, OH; 150/750 Hon Rl; Sch Pl; Stu Cncl; Rptr Sch Nwsp; Spn Clb; Letter Trk; Chrldng; Letter IM Sprt; College; Speech.

DULL, RICHARD; John F Kennedy HS; Taylor, MI; 38/500 Aud/Vis; Hon Rl; Lbry Ade; Off Ade; Sch Pl; Stg Crw; Drama Clb; Comm Coll Of The Air Force; Aviation.

DULL, T; Van Wert HS; Van Wert, OH; Hon Rl; Spn Clb; Letter Bsktbl; Letter Crs Cntry; Univ Of Toledo; Phys Ed.

DULLE, JOYCE; Four County Jt Voc HS; Edon, OH; Sec Jr Cls; Chrs; Hon Rl; FHA; OEA; Northwest Tech Coll; Legal Sec.

DULWORTH, CRAIG; Western HS; Jackson, MI; Band; Chrh Wkr; FCA; Hon Rl; Pol Wkr; Letter Glf; IM Sprt; Mgrs; College.

DUMAIS, KATHERINE; Romeo HS; Romeo, MI; 18/405 Girl Scts; Hon Rl; NHS; Fr Clb; Capt Trk; Letter GAA; PPFtbl; Oakland Univ; Bio.

DUMAS, MICHELLE; Mason Cnty Ctrl HS; Ludington, MI; Cl Rep Jr Cls; Hon Rl; Jr NHS; Stu Cncl; Spn Clb; Trk; Chrldng; 4-H Awd; Univ.

DUMBACK, KIM; Sault Area HS; Slt Ste Maire, MI; Chrh Wkr; Hon Rl; 4-H; FFA; Lat Clb; Bsktbl; Coach Actv; IM Sprt; Scr Kpr; 4-H Awd; Univ Of Michigan; Phys Ther.

DUMBOLA, JOHN; Wintersville HS; Steubenvll, OH; Chrh Wkr; Lat Clb; Bsbl; Ohio Univ; Dentistry.

DUMFORD, DIANNA; Hagerstown Jr Sr HS; Hagerstown, IN; 18/175 Band; Drl Tm; Drm Bgl; Hon Rl; Y-Teens; Fr Clb; Twrlr; Cert Of Proficiency Acctg 1; Indiana Univ; Acctg.

DUMKE, KIMBERLY; Our Lady Of The Elms HS; Stow, OH; AFS; VP Chrs; Girl Scts; Hon Rl; Sch Mus; Sch Pl; 4-H Awd; Lion Awd; Univ; Dance Drama.

DUMMER, CATHERINE; North Farmington HS; Farmington Hls, MI; 14/390 Cls Rep Frsh Cls; Girl Scts; Hon Rl; Lbry Ade; NHS; Sch Pl; Treas Spn Clb; Chrldng; Michigan Tech Univ; Geology.

DU MOULIN, ROBERT; Ida HS; Monroe, MI; Band; 4-H; Ftbl; IM Sprt; Univ Of Michigan; Bus Mgmt.

DUNAWAY, BARRY; Coventry HS; Akron, OH; Cl Rep Jr Cls; Hon Rl; Rptr Sch Nwsp; Crs Cntry; Scr Kpr; Ohio State Univ; Physical Ther.

DUNAWAY, DENISE L; Rogers HS; Toledo, OH; 13/412 Cls Rep Frsh Cls; Cls Rep Soph Cls; Cl Rep Jr Cls; Hon Rl; NHS; Rptr Yrbk; Lat Clb; Trk; GAA; PPFtbl; Bowling Green State Univ; Accounting.

DUNAWAY, JOEL; Brookville HS; Brookville, IN; Cls Rep Frsh Cls; Pres Soph Cls; Cls Rep Soph Cls; Pres Jr Cls; Cl Rep Jr Cls; Chrs; Stu Cncl; Rptr Sch Nwsp; Key Clb; Ftbl; Stud Council VP 79; Hi Y 76 79; Bus Schl.

DUNAWAY, PATRICK; Connersville Sr HS; Connersville, IN; 80/384 Hon Rl; Drama Clb; Ger Clb; Sci Clb; U S Navy; Adv Elec.

DUNBAR, THERESA; Ben Davis HS; Indianapolis, IN; 21/835 Cls Rep Soph Cls; Am Leg Aux Girls St; Sec Chrs; Sec Natl Forn Lg; NHS; Stu Cncl; Sec Drama Clb; VP Lat Clb; Ten; C of C Awd; Amer Legion Outstanding Stu Awd; Winner Of Indiana St Speak Contest; Counselor Position Culver Military Acd; Harvard Brown Univ; Law.

DUNBECK, MARGARET; Marion HS; Marion, IN; Hon Rl; NHS; Quill & Scroll; Rptr Yrbk; Drama Clb; Ger Clb; Bsktbl; Letter Ten; College.

DUNCAN, BRETT; Princeton Community HS; Princeton, IN; 19/203 Boys Clb Am; Mth Clb; VICA; Bsktbl; Crs Cntry; Coach Actv; Vincennes Univ; Machine Trades.

DUNCAN, CASEY E; Waldo J Wood Memorial HS; Oakland City, IN; Pres Frsh Cls; Cls Rep Frsh Cls; Am Leg Boys St; Band; Chrs; Chrh Wkr; Capt Debate Tm; Drm Bgl; Drm Mjrt; Hon Rl; Lugar Symposium For Future Amr Leaders 78; Math Awd 79; Chem Awd 79; Univ Of S Florida; Pre Med.

DUNCAN, DONALD; Lincoln Consolidated HS; Belleville, MI; Band; Hon Rl; NHS; Eastern Michigan Univ; Acctg.

DUNCAN, JEAN; St Ursula Acad; Toledo, OH; Trs Jr Cls; Stu Cncl; Drama Clb; Spn Clb; College; Bus.

DUNCAN, JILL; Rensselaer Central HS; Rensselaer, IN; 7/180 Band; Chrs; Chrh Wkr; Capt Drl Tm; Hon Rl; Sch Mus; Sch Pl; Fr Clb; Capt Pom Pon; Purdue; Pharmacy.

DUNCAN, JULIE; Anderson HS; Anderson, IN; Cl Rep Jr Cls; Cls Rep Sr Cls; Band; FCA; Girl Scts; JA; Stu Cncl; Fr Clb; Letter Bsktbl; Letter Trk; Univ Of S Illinois.

DUNCAN, KIMBERELY; Withrow HS; Cincinnati, OH; 42/512 Hon Rl; VICA; Univ Of Cincinnati; Bus Admin.

DUNCAN, LINDA; Hundred HS; Hundred, WV; 2/45 Cls Rep Soph Cls; Band; Hon Rl; NHS; Sch Pl; Stg Crw; VP Stu Cncl; Ed Yrbk; Sec Drama Clb; West Virginia Univ; Med Lab Tech.

DUNCAN, LOUISE; Mathews HS; Vienna, OH; JA; Lbry Ade; Y-Teens; Yrbk; 4-H; Pep Clb; Spn Clb; Scr Kpr; 4-H Awd; JA Awd; Bus Schl; Bus.

DUNCAN, SANDY; Peterstown HS; Ballard, WV; Band; Chrs; Chrh Wkr; Cmnty Wkr; Hon Rl; Sch Pl; Yth Flsp; Fr Clb; FTA; Mth Clb; Art Typing & Amer Stds Awd 79; Univ; Bio Chem.

DUNCAN, SHARON; Parkersburg South HS; Washington, WV; Chrh Wkr; Hon Rl; Typing Clb 2 Yrs 76; Coll.

DUNCAN, SHERRY D; Shaw HS; East Cleveland, OH; 21/490 Cls Rep Frsh Cls; Cls Rep Soph Cls; Cl Rep Jr Cls; Chrh Wkr; Hon Rl; Jr NHS; Rptr Sch Nwsp; Capt Bsktbl; Capt Trk; Univ; Chem Engr.

DUNCAN, STEVEN; Garden City East HS; Garden City, MI; 61/450 Band; Chrh Wkr; Ger Clb; IM Sprt; Wayne St Univ; Pre Med.

DUNCAN, TIMOTHY; Athens HS; Princeton, WV; 2/75 Cls Rep Sr Cls; Sal; Hon Rl; Stu Cncl; Fr Clb; Bsbl; Capt Bsktbl; Crs Cntry; Trk; DAR Awd; Wv Univ; Med.

DUNGY, DAWN; Andrean HS; Gary, IN; Chrs; Chrh Wkr; Cmnty Wkr; Girl Scts; Yth Flsp; Bsbl; Bsktbl; Coach Actv; GAA; IM Sprt; Purdue Univ; Bus.

DUNHAM, DENISE; Winchester Community HS; Winchester, IN; 14/200 Am Leg Aux Girls St; Drm Mjrt; Hon Rl; NHS; Stu Cncl; Yrbk; 4-H; Univ Of Evansville; Legal Admin.

DUNHAM, MICHAEL; Arthur Hill HS; Saginaw, MI; Boy Scts; Sct Actv; Ftbl; Michigan St Univ.

DUNHAM, SHELLEY; Van Wert HS; Van Wert, OH; Cls Rep Frsh Cls; Cls Rep Soph Cls; Cl Rep Jr Cls; Cls Rep Sr Cls; Band; Chrs; Chrh Wkr; Hon Rl; Red Cr Ade; Stu Cncl; Whos Who In Music 78; Dist Band 78; Northwestern Bus Coll; Med Asst.

DUNIGAN, DANETTE; Pike Central HS; Petersburg, IN; Cl Rep Jr Cls; Band; Hon Rl; NHS; Sch Pl; Stu Cncl; Drama Clb; FHA; Pep Clb; Twrlr; Perfect Attnd 1976; Jobs Daughters Jr Princess 1978; Indiana St Univ; Optometry.

DUNKEL, ERIKA; Berea HS; Berea, OH; 70/551 Band; Chrh Wkr; Drm Mjrt; Hon Rl; Hosp Ade; NHS; Letter Gym; Letter Swmmng; Twrlr; Baldwin Wallace Coll; Bus Admin.

DUNKELBARGER, SHARON; North Posey HS; Evansville, IN; 11/186 Hon Rl; NHS; Off Ade; Quill & Scroll; Rptr Yrbk; Rptr Sch Nwsp; 4-H; Pep Clb; GAA; Pom Pon; Indiana St Univ; Elem Educ.

DUNKIN, LAURA; Monrovia HS; Mooresville, IN; 10/134 Cls Rep Frsh Cls; Band; Cmp Fr Grls; Chrs; Chrh Wkr; Girl Scts; Hon Rl; Lit Mag; Off Ade; Stu Cncl;.

DUNLAP, DEBORAH L; Fairmont Sr HS; Charleston, WV; 4/230 Trs Sr Cls; Chrs; Chrh Wkr; Hon Rl; Mdrgl; NHS; Stu Cncl; FBLA; Keyettes; Mth Clb; West Virginia Univ; Engr.

DUNLAP, DENNIS C; Parkersburg HS; Walker, WV; 1/740 Cls Rep Frsh Cls; Am Leg Boys St; Band; Chrh Wkr; Cmnty Wkr; Hon Rl; Yth Flsp; 4-H; Pep Clb; Bsbl; Univ; Engr.

DUNLAP, JILL; Claymont HS; Uhrichsville, OH; 27/200 Band; Hon Rl; Jr NHS; Sch Mus; Sch Pl; Drama Clb; FTA; Sec Lat Clb; Trk; Kent State Univ; Psych.

DUNLAP, LLOYD; Whitmore Lake HS; Whitmore Lk, MI; Band; Hon Rl; NHS; Sch Mus; Sch Pl; Stg Crw; Sch Nwsp; Rdo Clb; Cert Of Recognition State Of Mich Competitive Schlrsp 79; St Camp In Intermediate & Jr Open Dance; U S Air Force; Elec Cmnctns.

DUNLAP, RANAE G; Clear Fork HS; Bellville, OH; 17/170 Cls Rep Frsh Cls; Cls Rep Soph Cls; Chrs; Chrh Wkr; Hon Rl; NHS; Sch Mus; Stu Cncl; Yth Flsp; Fr Clb; Coll; Music.

DUNLAP, TERRY; Richmond HS; Richmond, IN; 1/522 Cls Rep Frsh Cls; Cls Rep Sr Cls; Val; Chrs; Hon Rl; Treas JA; Mdrgl; Ind Univ; Bus.

DUNLAP, VALERIE; Admiral King HS; Lorain, OH; 208/413 Cls Rep Frsh Cls; Cls Rep Soph Cls; Cl Rep Jr Cls; Band; Chrs; Chrh Wkr; Cmnty Wkr; Drl Tm; Drm Bgl; Girl Scts; 1st Black Majorette; 1st Runner Up Homecoming Queen; Rare Young Black Womens Sorority; Livingston Coll; Nursing.

DUNLEALY, MICHAEL; Cabrini HS; Allen Pk, MI; Cls Rep Frsh Cls; Cls Rep Soph Cls; Cl Rep Jr Cls; Pres Sr Cls; Boy Scts; Quill & Scroll; Red Cr Ade; Sch Pl; Stg Crw; Stu Cncl; Eastern Michigan Univ.

DUNLEVY, MARCIA; Fairless HS; Brewster, OH; 29/220 VP Soph Cls; Trs Jr Cls; Chrh Wkr; Hon Rl; NHS; Stu Cncl; VP Y-Teens; College.

DUNLEVY, STEVEN; Oak Glen HS; New Cumberland, WV; Ftbl; Ten; West Liberty.

DUNLOP, LINDA; Southfield HS; Southfield, MI; Natl Forn Lg; NHS; Sch Mus; Sch Pl; Yth Flsp; Drama Clb; Mi State Univ.

DUNN, BRENDA; Ft Hayes Career Ctr HS; Columbus, OH; Chrs; Chrh Wkr; Jr NHS; Sch Mus; Yth Flsp; 4-H; Crs Cntry; Scr Kpr; 4-H Awd; Univ; Dance.

DUNN, BRIAN; Van Wert HS; Van Wert, OH; Cl Rep Jr Cls; Am Leg Boys St; Hon Rl; Lbry Ade; VP NHS; Stu Cncl; Yth Flsp; Spn Clb; Letter Bsbl; Letter Bsktbl; College; Science.

DUNN, CARLA; Fort Frye HS; Lowell, OH; Pres Frsh Cls; Band; Hon Rl; Red Cr Ade; Sec Stu Cncl; FBLA; Pep Clb; Letter Chrldng; GAA; Pres Awd; Marietta Coll; Med Sec.

DUNN, CAROLYN; Marion HS; Marion, MI; 9/62 Chrs; Hon Rl; Pres NHS; Sch Mus; Stg Crw; Andrews Univ; Behavioral Sci.

DUNN, DAVE; Elizabeth Ann Johnson HS; Davison, MI; Boy Scts; Hon Rl; Jr NHS; NHS; ROTC; Letter Crs Cntry; Letter Trk; IM Sprt; Scr Kpr; Tmr; History Awd 78; Univ; Elec.

DUNN, JANICE; Adelphian Acad; Holly, MI; 35/43 Chrs; Chrh Wkr; Hon Rl; Rptr Yrbk; Sprt Ed Sch Nwsp; Capt Bsbl; Capt Bsktbl; Capt Hockey; Capt IM Sprt; Kettering Coll.

DUNN, JEFF; Norwood HS; Norwood, OH; 27/350 Band; Hon Rl; Orch; Sch Mus; College; Musical Instr.

DUNN, JONI J; North Knox HS; Bicknell, IN; 14/150 Band; Chrh Wkr; Girl Scts; Hon Rl; NHS; Stu Cncl; Yth Flsp; 4-H; FHA; Vincennes Bus Coll; Sec.

DUNN, LORI; East Clinton HS; Sabina, OH; Sec Soph Cls; Trs Soph Cls; Cl Rep Jr Cls; VP Sr Cls; Hon Rl; NHS; Off Ade; Stu Cncl; Rptr Yrbk; Pep Clb; Var Vllybl 76079; MVP Vllybl 77 79; All Lg Vllybl 78; Var Sftbl 76 78 & 79; All Lg Sftbl 79; MPV 79; Eastern Kentucky Univ; Exec Sec.

DUNN, LOU ANN; Bullock Creek HS; Midland, MI; 18/156 Chrh Wkr; Cmnty Wkr; Hon Rl; NHS; Yth Flsp; 4-H; Pep Clb; Sci Clb; Spn Clb; Natl Merit Ltr; Saginaw Vly St Coll; Nursing.

DUNN, MARGARET; Midview HS; Elyria, OH; 23/287 Band; Chrs; Hon Rl; JA; Jr NHS; Lit Mag; NHS; Sch Pl; Stg Crw; Yrbk; Jr Coll; Sec Sci.

DUNN, NANCY; Norwood HS; Norwood, OH; 33/300 Chrs; Chrh Wkr; Cmnty Wkr; Hon Rl; Jr NHS; Lbry Ade; NHS; Sch Mus; Sch Pl; #1 Rating In Solo Vc 79; Schlrshp From Norwood Tchrs Assoc 79; Northern Kentucky Univ; Music Educ.

DUNN, PATRICE; Clio HS; Clio, MI; Band; Girl Scts; Hosp Ade; Jr NHS; NHS; Sch Mus; Sct Actv; Spn Clb; Trk; Univ Of Michigan; Med Tech.

DUNN, P JEFFERY; Anderson HS; Anderson, IN; Lat Clb; Letter Bsbl; DAR Awd; Univ; Med.

DUNN, RAYMOND; Saginaw HS; Saginaw, MI; Boy Scts; Chrh Wkr; FCA; Hon Rl; Off Ade; Sct Actv; Letter Bsbl; Cit Awd; Coll; Acctg.

DUNN, ROBERT; Admiral King HS; Lorain, OH; Band; Hon Rl; Orch; Key Clb; Letter Ftbl; Letter Trk; Coll; Pre Law.

DUNN, SANDRA; Brookville HS; Brookville, IN; 93/193 Sch Pl; Yrbk; Ball State Univ.

DUNN, SHERRIE; Crispus Attucks HS; Indpls, IN; Cls Rep Frsh Cls; Cls Rep Soph Cls; Pres Jr Cls; Cls Rep Sr Cls; Am Leg Aux Girls St; Chrs; Cmnty Wkr; Girl Scts; Hon Rl; JA; Tennessee St Univ; Youth Cnslr.

DUNN, TRACY; Northwest HS; Canal Fulton, OH; Chrs; Chrh Wkr; Hon Rl; NHS; Fr Clb; Pep Clb; Letter Trk; Kent St Univ; Bio.

DUNNAVANT, CYNTHIA; Stonewall Jackson HS; Chrlstn, WV; Cls Rep Soph Cls; Cl Rep Jr Cls; Hon Rl; NHS; Stu Cncl; Spn Clb; Dnfth Awd; Univ; Elem Ed.

DUNNE, DEBORAH A; Grosse Ile HS; Grosse Ile, MI; Hosp Ade; Sch Mus; Sch Pl; Drama Clb; Trk; Univ; Engr.

DUNNEBACKE, ANNE; Lansing Catholic Ctrl HS; Lansing, MI; Hon Rl; NHS; Bsbl; Ten; Lansing Cmnty Coll; Soc Work.

DUNNIGAN, KAY; Bedford HS; Temperance, MI; Chrh Wkr; FCA; Hon Rl; Lit Mag; NHS; Rptr Sch Nwsp; Mat Maids; Michigan St Univ; Med.

DUNNING, LAURA; West Ottawa HS; Holland, MI; Band; Cmp Fr Grls; Hon Rl; Lit Mag; Mod UN; Pep Clb; PPFtbl;.

DUNNING, MARK; Switzerland Cnty Jr Sr HS; Vevay, IN; 9/118 Boy Scts; NHS; Sch Pl; Sct Actv; Stg Crw; Rptr Sch Nwsp; Drama Clb; Pres Fr Clb; Hanover Coll; Geology.

DUNNING, SALLY; Hamilton Community HS; Holland, MI; 1/131 Cls Rep Sr Cls; Val; NHS; Ed Yrbk; Rptr Sch Nwsp; 4-H; GAA; Ctrl Mic Univ; Eng.

DUNNINGTON, LEE ANN; Buffalo HS; Huntington, WV; Chrs; Chrh Wkr; Hon Rl; Lbry Ade; PAVAS; Letter Bsktbl; Letter Trk; GAA; IM Sprt; Mgrs; Hon Roll Stndt 78; Marshall Univ; Phys Educ.

DUNOYER, FRANCOIS; Alma HS; Alma, MI; 12/270 Hon Rl; NHS; Orch; Sch Pl; Bsktbl; Trk; College; Eng.

DUNSETH, COLLEEN; Eisenhower HS; Utica, MI; Band; Chrh Wkr; Cmnty Wkr; Hon Rl; Yth Flsp; VP 4-H; Bsbl; Bsktbl; Capt Trk; Coach Actv; Michigan St Univ; Vet.

DUNSMOOR, BETH; Point Pleasant HS; Pt Pleasant, WV; 1/220 Band; Chrh Wkr; Drm Mjrt; Pres Girl Scts; NHS; Stu Cncl; Yth Flsp; Pres Keyettes; Scr Kpr; Cit Awd; Wv Univ; Pharmacy.

DUNSMORE, PAULA; Memphis HS; Goodells, MI; Sec Soph Cls; Sec Jr Cls; Band; Cmnty Wkr; Girl Scts; Hon Rl; JA; Off Ade; Ed Yrbk; Yrbk; Port Huron Schl Of Bus; Bus.

DUNST, ALAN; West Catholic HS; Grand Rapids, MI; Band; Hon Rl; JA; NHS; Orch; Sch Mus; Rptr Sch Nwsp; Sch Nwsp; JA Awd; Natl Merit SF; Aquinas Coll; Soc.

DUNTEN, DAVID; Carroll HS; Ft Wayne, IN; 9/251 VP Frsh Cls; VP Soph Cls; Band; Chrs; Chrh Wkr; Hon Rl; NHS; Pol Wkr; Sch Mus; Sch Pl; Indiana Univ; Comp Prog.

DUNWELL, JULIE; E Grand Rapids HS; Grand Rapids, MI; Letter Gym; Letter Trk; Letter Chrldng; PPFtbl; Tmr; Univ; Med.

DUNWIDDIE, MARCIA; Bluffton HS; Bluffton, IN; Band; Yth Flsp; Y-Teens; OEA; Spn Clb; Letter Socr; Univ; Bus.

DUPERON, TAMMY; Reese HS; Saginaw, MI; Pres Frsh Cls; Pres Soph Cls; Pres Jr Cls; Hon Rl; NHS; Stu Cncl; Bsbl; Chrldng; Flint U Of M; Law.

DUPLER, BRENDA; Sheridan HS; Somerset, OH; 3/178 Chrs; Sec Chrh Wkr; Drl Tm; Hon Rl; Jr NHS; NHS; Off Ade; Sec Yth Flsp; Rptr Sch Nwsp; Pres 4-H; MATC Voc Tech Coll; Med.

DUPLER, DIANE; Frankfort Sr HS; Frankfort, IN; Cls Rep Frsh Cls; Cls Rep Soph Cls; Cl Rep Jr Cls; Cl Rep Jr Cls; Trs Sr Cls; Band; Chrs; Chrh Wkr; NHS; Orch; Butler Univ; Performing Arts.

DUPLER, MICKE; Frankfort Sr HS; Frankfort, IN; Band; Orch; Sch Mus; Yth Flsp; PPFtbl; Band Contest Medals As Lead Trumpet; College; Psych.

DU PREE, DEBORAH; Dowagiac Union HS; Dowagiac, MI; 45/208 Chrs; Hon Rl; NHS; Sch Mus; Basic Educ Opportunity Grant 79; MHEAA 79; Lake Michigan Coll; Radiologic Tech.

DU PREE, ROMI; The Andrews HS; Mayfld Hts, OH; 8/56 Band; Chrs; Girl Scts; Hon Rl; Yrbk; Swmmng; IM Sprt; Tmr; College; Engr.

DURAKO, KATHLEEN; Notre Dame Acad; Toledo, OH; Hon Rl; NHS; Fr Clb; Bsktbl; Ten; IM Sprt; College; Engr.

DURANCE, DWYANE; Tawas Area HS; Tawas, MI; Rdo Clb; Air Force; Gen Aviation Pilot.

DU RANT, CINDY; Buckeye N HS; Brilliant, OH; 26/106 Pres Frsh Cls; VP Jr Cls; Am Leg Aux Girls St; Hon Rl; NHS; Off Ade; Sch Mus; Sch Pl; Stu Cncl; Yth Flsp; Jefferson Tech Coll; Mgmt.

DU RANT, DEBRA; Watkins Memorial HS; Pataskala, OH; 3/201 Sal; Band; Hon Rl; Jr NHS; NHS; Off Ade; Yth Flsp; Yrbk; Letter Trk; PPFtbl; St Bd Awd Of Distnctn 79; Oh Bd Of Regnst Recgntn Cert 79; Cls Bst Ctzn & Slttrn 79; Stephens Coll; Fshn Design.

DURBAN, CYNTHIA; Marysville HS; Marysville, OH; Cls Rep Frsh Cls; Cls Rep Soph Cls; Am Leg Aux Girls St; Band; Chrs; Chrh Wkr; Hon Rl; NHS; Sch Mus; Stu Cncl; Berea Coll; Elem Ed.

DURBIN, BETH; St Marys Cntrl Catholic HS; Sandusky, OH; Cls Rep Frsh Cls; Cls Rep Soph Cls; Cl Rep Jr Cls; Chrs; GAA; Univ Of Toledo; Bus.

DURBIN, KAREN; Lehman HS; Sidney, OH; 1/93 Chrs; Chrh Wkr; Girl Scts; Hon Rl; NHS; Off Ade; Sch Mus; Wright State; Tchr.

DURBIN, KELLY; Piketon HS; Piketon, OH; 13/110 Chrs; Hon Rl; NHS; Sch Mus; Stg Crw; Yrbk; Rptr Sch Nwsp; FTA; Letter Bsbl; Letter Bsktbl; Ohio St Univ; Agri.

DURBIN, LORI; Winchester Community HS; Winchester, IN; 7/180 FCA; Hon Rl; NHS; Yth Flsp; Rptr Yrbk; FBLA; Pres FHA; FTA; Spn Clb; GAA; Olivet Nazarene Coll; Elem Educ.

DURBIN, MICHAEL G; Walsh Jesuit HS; Stow, OH; 8/167 Band; Chrh Wkr; Cmnty Wkr; Hon Rl; Bsktbl; Mgrs; Scr Kpr; Tmr; Loyola Univ; Dentistry.

DURCANIN, CYNTHIA; Firestone HS; Akron, OH; Cls Rep Sr Cls; JA; Quill & Scroll; Yth Flsp; Sprt Ed Yrbk; Yrbk; Sch Nwsp; Pep Clb; Letter Trk; Tmr; Ind Univ; Journalism.

DUREMDES, GENE B; Princeton HS; Princeton, WV; 31/360 Sec Soph Cls; Trs Soph Cls; Sec Jr Cls; Trs Jr Cls; Pres Sr Cls; Am Leg Boys St; Sec FCA; Hon Rl; Jr NHS; NHS; Stu Body Pres 79; Co Capt Footbl Team 79; Univ; Med.

DURESS, SCOTT; Upper Sandusky HS; Upper Sandusky, OH; 49/197 Band; Hon Rl; Sch Mus; Spn Clb; Ten; Ohi State.

DURHAM, CHRISTI; Marietta HS; Marietta, OH; Band; Drl Tm; Hon Rl; Hosp Ade; Off Ade; Fr Clb; Ger Clb; Spn Clb; Foreign Languages.

DURHAM, DAWN; Napoleon HS; Napoleon, OH; Hon Rl; Lbry Ade; NHS; Ger Clb; Officer In German Club 78; North West Tech Univ; Acctg.

DURHAM, ELAINE; Wauseon HS; Wauseon, OH; Hon Rl; NHS; Y-Teens; Rptr Sch Nwsp; Sch Nwsp; Fr Clb; Northern Arizona Univ; Optometrist.

DURHAM, GREGORY; Coloma HS; Coloma, MI; Cl Rep Jr Cls; Hst Sr Cls; Band; Debate Tm; Pol Wkr; Sch Nwsp; FSA; Ger Clb; Sci Clb; Lcrss; Lake Michigan Coll.

DURHAM, KELLY; Orchard View HS; Muskegon, MI; Chrs; Girl Scts; Hon Rl; Sch Pl; Gym; Swmmng; Wrstlng; Chrldng; PPFtbl; Scr Kpr; MCC; Nurse.

DURHAM, RHONDA; Loveland Hurst HS; Loveland, OH; 3/280 Cls Rep Frsh Cls; Cls Rep Soph Cls; Sec Jr Cls; Cl Rep Jr Cls; Hon Rl; NHS; Stu Cncl; Spn Clb; Letter Socr; Trk; Univ; Bio.

DURHAM, RONDA; Pike Delta York HS; Delta, OH; 22/133 Band; Chrs; Chrh Wkr; Girl Scts; Lbry Ade; 4-H; FHA; 4-H Awd; Vocational School; Business.

DURIAK, JOSEPH; Padna Franciscan HS; Hickley, OH; 113/265 Kent St Univ; Vet.

DURICEK, BETH A; Notre Dame Academy; Rossford, OH; Chrh Wkr; Cmnty Wkr; Hon Rl; Lbry Ade; NHS; FBLA; Pres Of St Mary Magdalene CYO 79; Univ Of Toledo.

DURICK, THOMAS; Struthers HS; Struthers, OH; 1/276 Pres Frsh Cls; Pres Soph Cls; Val; Am Leg Boys St; Debate Tm; Jr NHS; Pres NHS; Stu Cncl; Ed Yrbk; Rptr Yrbk; Youngstown St Univ; Chemistry.

DURICY, MICHAEL; John F Kennedy HS; Niles, OH; 1/192 Am Leg Boys St; Chrs; Debate Tm; Hon Rl; Lit Mag; Natl Forn Lg; NHS; Stu Cncl; Yrbk; FSA; Youngstown State; Elec Engr.

DURIGA, JODENE; West Branch HS; Salem, OH; Band; Orch; Sch Mus; Spn Clb; Indiana Univ; Music.

DURIVAGE, FRANCES; Franklin HS; Livonia, MI; 85/605 Pres Sr Cls; Chrs; Natl Forn Lg; Pl; Stu Cncl; Y-Teens; Drama Clb; Letter Bsktbl; Coach Actv; DAR Awd; Kalamazoo Coll; Admin Soc Work.

DURKIN, TIM; Jefferson HS; Monroe, MI; Jr NHS; Pres Stu Cncl; Bsbl; Capt Bsktbl; Capt Ftbl; Univ; Bus Mgmt.

DURKOS, DUANE M; Pike HS; Lebanon, IN; 410281 Boy Scts; Hon Rl; NHS; Mth Clb; Letter Bsbl; Purdue Univ; Engr.

DURKOVIC, MARK; Jefferson Area HS; Jefferson, OH; 9/200 Band; Chrs; Chrh Wkr; Sch Mus; Fr Clb; Eastern Coll; Bus Admin.

DURLING, DAVID; Waldron HS; Hudson, MI; 5/52 Band; Chrs; Chrh Wkr; Hon Rl; NHS; Sch Pl; Treas FFA; Grand Rapids Baptist Univ; Religion.

DURLING, RUTH; Waldron HS; Hudson, MI; 2/39 Sal; Band; VP Chrs; NHS; Sch Pl; VP Stu Cncl; VP Spn Clb; VP GAA; Dnfth Awd; Pres Awd; Moody Bible Inst; Music.

DURLING, RUTH; Waldron Area HS; Hudson, MI; 3/39 Cls Rep Soph Cls; Sal; Band; VP Chrs; Chrh Wkr; Hon Rl; NHS; Sch Pl; VP Stu Cncl; VP Spn Clb; Grand Rapids Baptist Coll; Music.

DURM, ANTHONY; Marlington HS; Alliance, OH; 23/320 Am Leg Boys St; Boy Scts; Treas NHS; FFA; Letter Crs Cntry; Letter Trk; Letter Wrstlng; Univ Of Akron; Mech Engr.

DUROCHER, CAROL; Plymouth Canton HS; Plymouth, MI; Chrs; Hon Rl; Off Ade; Trk; Madonna College; Marketing Mgmt.

DURR, MARK; Marion Adams HS; Sheridan, IN; 4/100 Hon Rl; Jr NHS; Natl Forn Lg; Stu Cncl; 4-H; Crs Cntry; IM Sprt; Purdue Univ.

DURR, MARSHA; Marion Adams HS; Sheridan, IN; 16/100 Lbry Ade; 4-H; FHA; Pep Clb; Bsktbl; GAA; Bus Schl; Office Work.

DURR, TRACY; Bucyrus HS; Bucyrus, OH; Cls Rep Frsh Cls; Pres Soph Cls; Cl Rep Jr Cls; Band; Drm Mjrt; Hon Rl; Sch Mus; Sch Pl; Stu Cncl; College; Nutrition.

DURRWACHTER, DARLEN; Walled Lake Central HS; Union Lake, MI; 11/360 Chrs; Hon Rl; NHS; PAVAS; Sch Mus; Sch Pl; Stg Crw; Drama Clb; Ger Clb; Voice Dem Awd; Mich State Univ; Music.

DURSO, THERESA; St Ursula Acad; Covington, KY; Cmnty Wkr; Girl Scts; Hon Rl; Hosp Ade; JA; Mod UN; NHS; Sct Actv; Trk; Chrldng; Univ Of Kentucky; Recreation.

DURST, DUANE; Lakota HS; Burgoon, OH; 51/144 Hon Rl; 4-H; FFA; Letter Ftbl; Letter Trk; Letter Wrstlng; Wrstlng 4 Yr Lttr 3 Yrs Capt & St Competitor 78; Univ; Bus Admin.

DURST, SANDRA; Ripley HS; Cottageville, WV; 5/320 Chrs; Chrh Wkr; Cmnty Wkr; Hon Rl; Hosp Ade; JA; Natl Forn Lg; NHS; Sch Pl; Sct Actv; Modrn Woodman Civic Oration Awd 1975; Womens Clb Hnrs Group 1976; Scholastic Lttr 1977; St Marys Schl Of Nursing; R N.

DURST, WILLIAM; Brookfield HS; Masury, OH; Boy Scts; Ftbl; Letter Trk; Usaf Acad; Civil Engr.

DURY, DONALD; Huntington St Josephs HS; Huntington, WV; Chrh Wkr; FCA; Hon Rl; Lit Mag; Yrbk; Glf; Socr; Coach Actv; Georgia Tech Univ; Elec Engr.

DUSENBERY, JANNINE; Roscommon HS; Roscommon, MI; Band; Chrs; Off Ade; Sch Mus; 4-H; Crs Cntry; Trk; Chrldng; GAA; IM Sprt; MSU; Bus Fields.

DUSKA, GERALYN; Catholic Central HS; Mingo Junction, OH; 3/226 Cl Rep Jr Cls; Am Leg Aux Girls St; Chrh Wkr; Hon Rl; NHS; Sch Mus; Sch Pl; Drama Clb; Spn Clb; Bsktbl; Ohio Academic Schlrsh 79; Ohio St Univ Fresh Schlr 79; Oh Brd Of Ed Awd Of Distinction 79; Ohio St Univ; Pre Vet Med.

DUSKEY, TERRI; Smithville HS; Smithville, OH; Band; FCA; Girl Scts; 4-H; Ger Clb; GAA; Twrlr; 4-H Awd; Tiffin U Bus Schl; Clerical Admin.

DUSSEL, KATHLEEN; Field HS; Kent, OH; 15/350 Cl Rep Jr Cls; Cls Rep Sr Cls; Hon Rl; NHS; Stu Cncl; 4-H; Letter Bsktbl; Gym; Coach Actv; 4-H Awd; Vllybl 3 Letterman & Sftbl Letter 79; Hon Mention All Metro In Vllybl 77; All Suburban Bsktbl 77; Kent St Univ; Spec Educ Instructor.

DUSSELJEE, MARY; Holland Christian HS; Holland, MI; 28/257 VP Jr Cls; Chrs; Hon Rl; NHS; Letter Swmmng; Grand Rapids Jr Coll; Elem Ed.

DUSTHIMER, LYNN; Elkhart Ctrl HS; Elkhart, IN; 2/400 Cls Rep Frsh Cls; Chrs; Cmnty Wkr; Hon Rl; Sec NHS; Stu Cncl; Letter Ten; Chrldng; Mgrs; Univ.

DUSZYNSKI, ARLINE; Notre Dame Academy; Toledo, OH; 4/164 Hon Rl; Jr NHS; NHS; Univ; Bus Educ.

DUSZYNSKI, JANET M; Notre Dame Academy; Toledo, OH; 1/134 Cl Rep Jr Cls; Cls Rep Sr Cls; Sch Pl; Stg Crw; Stu Cncl; Mgrs; Natl Merit SF; Univ; Med Tech.

DUTCHER, ALLEN; Hillman HS; Hillman, MI; 6/60 Boy Scts; Chrh Wkr; Hon Rl; Sec NHS; Sct Actv; Bsbl; Letter Ftbl; Central Mic Univ; Pre Engr.

DUTCHER, JOHN; West Branch HS; Salem, OH; Chrs; Lbry Ade; Sch Mus; Stg Crw; 4-H; FFA; Lat Clb; Ohio St Univ; Ag.

DU TIEL, SUZANNE; Alexander HS; Amesville, OH; Band; Chrs; Chrh Wkr; Hon Rl; Sch Pl; Yth Flsp; Sch Nwsp; Fr Clb; FHA; Mth Clb; Concours Natl De Francais Cert De Merite; Concours Natl De Francais Cert De Honneur; Ohio Univ; Law.

DUTKA, DAWN; Loudonville HS; Loudonville, OH; 2/134 Hon Rl; NHS; Stg Crw; Yth Flsp; Rptr Yrbk; Rptr Sch Nwsp; Drama Clb; Pres Lat Clb; Spn Clb; Natl Merit Ltr; Dist Honorable Mention In Eng II Ohio Test Of Schlstc Ach; Statistician Boys Varsity & Reserve Bsktbl; Lees Mc Rae Coll; Eng.

DUTRY, BARB; South Amerst HS; S Amherst, OH; Band; Chrs; Chrh Wkr; Sch Mus; Sch Pl; Sch Nwsp; FHA; Pep Clb; Bsbl; Coach Actv; LCC; Tchr.

DUTTLINGER, MARGARET; Kankakee Valley HS; Wheatfield, IN; Sec Jr Cls; Cls Rep Sr Cls; Chrs; Hon Rl; NHS; Off Ade; Sch Pl; Drama Clb; 4-H; OEA; Ball State Univ; Acctg.

DUTTON, JILL; Washington HS; Massillon, OH; Chrs; Off Ade; Quill & Scroll; Sec Stu Cncl; Spn Clb; Swmmng; Chrldng; IM Sprt; Scr Kpr; Univ; Sci.

DUTTON, MICHAEL; Marion Harding HS; Marion, OH; 18/450 Hon Rl; NHS; Stu Cncl; Y-Teens; Spn Clb; Ftbl; IM Sprt; Natl Hon Soc Crissenger Schlrshp 79; Oh St Univ Schlrshp 79; Ohio St Univ; Engr.

DUTY, MARY; Scott HS; Madison, WV; 6/175 Cl Rep Jr Cls; Chrh Wkr; Debate Tm; Hon Rl; NHS; Stu Cncl; Rptr Yrbk; Drama Clb; Univ; Bus Mgmt.

DUTY, ROGER; Allegan Sr HS; Allegan, MI; Chrh Wkr; Hon Rl; Yth Flsp; Letter Bsbl; Kalamazoo Vly Cmnty Coll; Pre Law.

DU VALL, DENNIS; Monroe HS; Monroe, MI; 14/586 Chrs; Hon Rl; NHS; Spn Clb; Elk Awd; Monroe Cnty Cmnty Coll; Art.

DU VALL, GREGORY; Greenville Sr HS; Greenville, OH; 19/380 Hon Rl; Boys Clb Am; Letter Trk; Ohio St Univ; Engr.

DU VALL, ROBIN; Bedford HS; Lambertvill, MI; 44/432 Chrs; Drl Tm; Hon Rl; NHS; Sch Pl; Stg Crw; Sch Nwsp; Drama Clb; Central Mic Univ; Tele Engr.

DUVELIUS, ROSE; Little Miami HS; Loveland, OH; Cl Rep Jr Cls; Hon Rl; Lit Mag; NHS; Off Ade; Sct Actv; Stg Crw; Stu Cncl; Yrbk; Ohio Visual Art Inst; Bus Art.

DUWEL, ANNE M; Ursuline Acad; Loveland, OH; 34/115 Cmnty Wkr; Sch Pl; Stg Crw; Drama Clb; 4-H; 4-H Awd; Columbus Coll; Arts.

DVORAK, JOSEPH; Breckenridge Community HS; Breckenridge, MI; Cls Rep Frsh Cls; Cmnty Wkr; Stu Cncl; Letter Bsbl; Letter Bsktbl; Letter Crs Cntry; Delta Coll; Amer History.

DVORAK, RADKA; Franklin HS; Livonia, MI; Trs Sr Cls; Hon Rl; NHS; Sct Actv; Sprt Ed Yrbk; Ger Clb; Socr; Alma; Med.

DVORSCAK, ANDREA; Highland HS; Muncie, IN; 6/494 Hon Rl; NHS; Ger Clb; Ball St Univ; Nursing.

DVORSCAK, ROBERT; George Rogers Clark HS; Whiting, IN; Cls Rep Frsh Cls; Cls Rep Soph Cls; Pres Jr Cls; Stu Cncl; Spn Clb; Bsbl; Spn Clb; Capt Crs Cntry; IM Sprt; Indiana Univ; Dent.

DWAN, NANCY; Petoskey HS; Petoskey, MI; 1/267 Val; Hon Rl; Jr NHS; NHS; Off Ade; Trk; Pres Awd; Lake Superior St Coll.

DWYER, EILEEN; Ursuline Academy; Loveland, OH; 13/105 Chrs; Cmnty Wkr; Sch Pl; Stg Crw; Xavier Univ; Bus.

DWYER, JULIE; Fraser HS; Fraser, MI; Hon Rl; Spn Clb; Scr Kpr; College; Med.

DWYER, SALLY; Douglas Mac Arthur HS; Saginaw, MI; 34/300 Cl Rep Jr Cls; Am Leg Aux Girls St; Hon Rl; NHS; Stu Cncl; Rptr Sch Nwsp; Lat Clb; Pep Clb; Letter Crs Cntry; Trk; College; Commercial Art.

DYBEN, TERRY; New Haven Sr HS; New Haven, IN; Aud/Vis; Boy Scts; Hon Rl; Lbry Ade; Ger Clb; Lat Clb; Sci Clb; Wrstlng; Coll; Med.

DYCH, DEBBIE; Mt Clemens HS; Mt Clemens, MI; Chrs; Chrh Wkr; Hon Rl; Jr NHS; Off Ade; Sch Mus; Letter Ten; Mgrs; Univ; Dent Hygnst.

DYE, CYNTHIA; Big Walnut HS; Sunbury, OH; Cls Rep Frsh Cls; Cls Rep Soph Cls; Chrs; Chrh Wkr; Cmnty Wkr; Debate Tm; Hon Rl; Sch Mus; Sch Pl; Sct Actv; College.

DYE, DAVE; Norton HS; Norton, OH; Lat Clb; Trk; Wrstlng; Coll; Optometry.

DYE, DOUG; West Branch Local HS; Alliance, OH; Hon Rl; NHS; FFA; Mgrs;.

DYE, JOHN; Bay HS; Bay Vill, OH; 37/373 Am Leg Boys St; Chrs; FCA; Hon Rl; Lit Mag; NHS; Sch Mus; College.

DYE, JOHN; Riverside HS; De Graff, OH; Band; Chrs; Stg Crw; Yrbk; 4-H; Rdo Clb; PPFtbl; 4-H Awd; Clark Tech Inst; Real Estate.

DYE, JULIE; Franklin Hgts HS; Grove City, OH; Drl Tm; Band; Chrs; Chrh Wkr; Hon Rl; VP NHS; Sch Mus; Sec 4-H; Sec FFA; Treas Key Clb; Ohio St Univ; Music Educ.

DYE, KEITH; Hannan HS; Glenwood, WV; Cls Rep Soph Cls; Cl Rep Jr Cls; Band; Boy Scts; Chrh Wkr; FCA; Hon Rl; Off Ade; Stu Cncl; Yth Flsp; Marshall Univ; Computer Prog.

DYE, LISA; Alexander HS; Pomeroy, OH; 1/120 Band; Chrs; Chrh Wkr; Hon Rl; Lbry Ade; Yrbk; Rptr Sch Nwsp; 4-H; Pres Fr Clb; Mth Clb; Ohio St Univ; Social Work.

DYE, MARK A; Parkersburg HS; Vienna, WV; Cls Rep Frsh Cls; Cls Rep Soph Cls; Cl Rep Jr Cls; Am Leg Boys St; Chrs; FCA; Hon Rl; Stu Cncl; Letter Ftbl; IM Sprt; Jr High All Cnty In Ftbl & Bsktbl; Cls Triple A Ftbl Champ; Univ.

DYE, PAMELA J; Triway HS; Wooster, OH; Chrs; Hon Rl; Sch Mus; Sch Pl; Stg Crw; Rptr Sch Nwsp; Drama Clb; Spn Clb; Letter Trk; Chrldng; Univ Of Akron; Psych.

DYE, SHERRY; Stanton HS; Salineville, OH; Band; Chrs; FCA; Girl Scts; Hon Rl; Lbry Ade; Sch Pl; Sct Actv; Yth Flsp; Rptr Sch Nwsp; Tech Coll; Med Sec.

DYE, VICKIE; Frontier HS; Newport, OH; 1/120 VP Sr Cls; Val; Band; Hon Rl; NHS; Sch Pl; Rptr Yrbk; OEA; Chrldng; GAA;.

DYER, D; Lexington Attendance Ctr HS; Lexington, MS; 10/121 VP Soph Cls; Cls Rep Sr Cls; Hon Rl; Rptr Sch Nwsp; Bsbl; Bsktbl; Chrldng; GAA; Twrlr; Btty Crckr Awd; Southern Univ; Poli Sci.

DYER, DEBORAH; Summerfield HS; Petersburg, MI; Band; Hon Rl; 4-H; Sec.

DYER, LOUNETTE; Orchard View HS; Muskegon, MI; 1/200 Val; Band; Hon Rl; NHS; Orch; Sch Mus; Mth Clb; Natl Merit SF; Perfect Scores On Mi St Solo Fest Proficiency Exams 77 78 & 79; Grand Rapids Symph Orch 78; Western Michigan Univ; Music Perf.

DYER, PATTY; Meigs HS; Bidwell, OH; Band; Hon Rl; Jr NHS; Lbry Ade; NHS; Off Ade; Stg Crw; VP 4-H; VP FFA; Pep Clb; FFA Star Greenhand Star Chapt Farmer Swine Prod & Public Speakg 1975; Cnty Jr Fair Bd Publicity Chrmn; Ohio St Univ; Agri.

DYER, SHARON; Margaretta HS; Castalia, OH; Sec Sr Cls; Chrh Wkr; GAA; Coll; Art.

DYER, SHARRON; Belleville HS; Belleville, MI; Cmnty Wkr; Girl Scts; Hon Rl; Univ; Child Dvlmnt.

DYER, THOMAS; Washington Irving HS; Clarksburg, WV; 1/200 Pres Sr Cls; Am Leg Boys St; Hon Rl; Yth Flsp; Key Clb; Lat Clb; Letter Bsktbl; Letter Glf; Letter Ten; Natl Merit Ltr; Univ; Med.

DYGERT, SALLY; Meadowdale HS; Dayton, OH; 2/239 Sal; Hon Rl; VP NHS; Sch Pl; Univ Of Mich Frosh Scholar Schlrshp; Cand For Honors Seminars Of Univ Of Dayton; NEDT Test Score Cert; Univ Of Michigan; Math.

DYHOUSE, VALERIE; Lincoln HS; Vincennes, WI; 10/282 Cls Rep Frsh Cls; Cls Rep Soph Cls; Cl Rep Jr Cls; Cls Rep Sr Cls; Boy Scts; Hon Rl; Fr Clb; IM Sprt; Natl Merit Ltr; Univ.

DYKA, SAMUEL M; Divine Child HS; Dearborn Hts, MI; 21/200 Pres Frsh Cls; Chrs; Chrh Wkr; Cmnty Wkr; Hon Rl; Sch Mus; Stg Crw; Wayne State Univ; Pre Med.

DYKAS, GLEN; Chadsey HS; Detroit, MI; Aud/Vis; Boy Scts; Hon Rl; Jr NHS; NHS; Off Ade; Boys Clb Am; Letter Bsktbl; Cit Awd; Eastern Univ.

DYKEMA, DEB; Hudsonville HS; Hudsonville, MI; Chrh Wkr; Debate Tm; FCA; Hon Rl; Stu Cncl; Pres Yth Flsp; Accounting.

DYKEMA, SUSAN J; Holland HS; Holland, MI; Chrs; Chrh Wkr; Stg Crw; Yrbk; Univ; Sci.

DYKEMA, TOM; Holland Christian HS; Holland, MI; Spn Clb; Glf; Letter Ten; IM Sprt; Davenport College; Data Proc.

DYKES, G; Solon HS; Solon, OH; Hon Rl; NHS; VP Mth Clb; Letter Crs Cntry; Letter Ten; Univ; Med Arts.

DYKES, KATRINA; Shady Spring HS; Daniels, WV; Band; Chrs; Chrh Wkr; Cmnty Wkr; Hon Rl; Lbry Ade; Off Ade; Yth Flsp; Rptr Yrbk; Pep Clb; Beckley Coll; Legal Sec Sci.

DYKSTRA, ALBERT; Hudsonville Public HS; Hudsonville, MI; Chrh Wkr; Ferris St Coll; Air Condtng.

DYKSTRA, DENNIS; Covenant Christian HS; Walker, MI; Hon Rl; Ger Clb; Letter Bsktbl; Letter Crs Cntry; IM Sprt; Mgrs; Davenport Coll; Acctg.

DYKSTRA, DOUG; Holland Christian HS; Holland, MI; 13/261 Hon Rl; Jr NHS; NHS; Yrbk; Bsbl; Letter Bsktbl; Letter Glf; Letter Ten; Letter Trk; Davenport College; Data Proc.

DYKSTRA, DUANE; Flathead HS; Kalispell, MT; Chrs; Mdrgl; Rptr Sch Nwsp; Spn Clb; Mgrs; Univ; History.

DYKSTRA, LAURA; Hopkins HS; Wayland, MI; 6/111 VP Sr Cls; Band; Hon Rl; NHS; Sch Pl; FHA; Natl Merit Ltr; Mercy Central Schl Of Nrsng; Nrse.

DYKSTRA, TIMOTHY; La Ville HS; Plymouth, IN; 8/200 Am Leg Boys St; NHS; Fr Clb; Bsktbl; Ftbl; Glf; Am Leg Awd; Coll.

DYSERT, DEANNA; Wellsville HS; Wellsville, OH; Cls Rep Frsh Cls; Cl Rep Jr Cls; Sec Chrs; Sch Pl; Stg Crw; Stu Cncl; Y-Teens; Yrbk; FTA; Pep Clb; State Vocal Competition Solo Excellent Rating; Oberlin Coll; Music.

DYWASUK, GERALD; Lake Orion HS; Lake Orion, MI; Cl Rep Jr Cls; Hon Rl; Pol Wkr; Stu Cncl; Rptr Yrbk; Natl Merit SF; Mich State Univ.

DZAPO, KYLE; Howland HS; Warren, OH; 33/432 Cls Rep Frsh Cls; Cls Rep Soph Cls; Band; Chrh Wkr; Hon Rl; Jr NHS; NHS; Y-Teens; Letter Bsktbl; Trk; Univ; Music Educ.

DZARNOWSKI, JANET; West Iron County HS; Gasstra, MI; Cls Rep Sr Cls; Chrh Wkr; Hon Rl; NHS; VP Stu Cncl; Capt Bsktbl; Gym; Trk; IM Sprt; College; Art.

DZIABA, IRENE S; La Porte HS; Laporte, IN; 38/530 Chrh Wkr; Hon Rl; Hosp Ade; NHS; Fr Clb; Univ; Physn.

DZIADOSZ, KAREN; Merrillville HS; Merrillville, IN; 69/596 Hon Rl; Off Ade; Ind Voc Tech College; Med Assistant.

DZIATKOWICZ, RICHARD; Madonna HS; Weirton, WV; Hon Rl; Letter Trk; IM Sprt; Voc Cert Of Carpentry 77 &78;.

DZIECIEHOWICZ, MARY; Nicholas County HS; Mt Nebo, WV; 42/215 Chrs; Chrh Wkr; Girl Scts; Hon Rl; Sch Mus; Sct Actv; Yth Flsp; 4-H; Pres FHA; Treas FTA Home Ec Awd 79; Choral Awd; Beckley Coll; Real Est.

DZIEDZIC, DANIEL; Carney Nadeau Public School; Carney, MI; Cls Rep Frsh Cls; Cls Rep Soph Cls; Cl Rep Jr Cls; Am Leg Boys St; Band; Boy Scts; Chrh Wkr; Hon Rl; Sch Pl; Sct Actv; Voc Schl; Master Craftsman.

DZIEPAK, DAMIEN; Sts Peter & Paul HS Sem; Newark, OH; 1/11 Sec Frsh Cls; Trs Soph Cls; VP Jr Cls; Hon Rl; Jr NHS; NHS; Sprt Ed Yrbk; Socr; Ten; Univ Of Detroit.

DZIEPAK, DAMIEN; St Peter & Paul Seminary; Oak Park, MI; 1/11 Sec Frsh Cls; Sec Soph Cls; Trs Soph Cls; Hon Rl; Jr NHS; NHS; Sch Pl; Stg Crw; Yrbk; Socr; Maryglade College; Foreign Lang.

DZIEPAK, PAUL; St Peter & Paul Seminary HS; Oak Park, MI; Cls Rep Frsh Cls; Cls Rep Soph Cls; Trs Jr Cls; Pres Sr Cls; Chrs; Chrh Wkr; Hon Rl; Jr NHS; NHS; Sch Pl; Mary Glade Coll.

DZIEPAK, PAUL; Sts Peter & Paul Smnry HS; Oak Park, MI; 3/4 Cls Rep Frsh Cls; Sec Soph Cls; Trs Jr Cls; Pres Sr Cls; Chrs; Chrh Wkr; Cmnty Wkr; Hon Rl; Jr NHS; Sch Pl; Mary Glade College; History.

DZIEWIT, GREGORY; Chadsey HS; Detroit, MI; Cl Rep Jr Cls; Hon Rl; Lbry Ade; Wayne State Univ; Med.

DZIEWIT, KATHY; St Florian HS; Hamtramck, MI; 7/76 Treas Chrs; Hon Rl; Natl Forn Lg; NHS; Sch Mus; Sch Pl; Macomb Cnty Comnty; Gen Educ.

DZIUBEK, RANDY; John Glenn HS; Westland, MI; Cls Rep Frsh Cls; Band; Chrh Wkr; Hon Rl; Jr NHS; NHS; Stu Cncl; Trk; Cit Awd; Univ Of Michigan; Math.

DZIUBINSKI, DAVID; John Adams HS; So Bend, IN; 17/400 VP Frsh Cls; Cls Rep Soph Cls; NHS; Ftbl; Capt Hockey; Trk; College; Biology.

DZMURA, MARK R; Linsly Military Institute; Wheeling, WV; 1/45 Band; Chrs; Chrh Wkr; Drm Bgl; Lbry Ade; Sch Pl; Stg Crw; Stu Cncl; Ed Sch Nwsp; Rptr Sch Nwsp; Carnegie Mellon Univ; Electrical.

DZUGAN, PAUL; Crestline HS; Crestline, OH; Chrh Wkr; Cmnty Wkr; Hon Rl; Rptr Yrbk; Rptr Sch Nwsp; Bsktbl; Trk; Coach Actv; Boston Coll; Cmnctns.

DZURKO, MARY L; Lumen Cordium HS; Solon, OH; Chrs; Chrh Wkr; Cmnty Wkr; Drl Tm; Girl Scts; Hon Rl; Lit Mag; Red Cr Ade; Sch Mus; Sch Pl; Akron St Univ; Jrnlsm.

E

EADEH, KATHY; Bishop Foley HS; Troy, MI; 30/196 Cls Rep Frsh Cls; Am Leg Aux Girls St; Hon Rl; NHS; Pol Wkr; IM Sprt; Am Leg Awd; Kiwan Awd; Univ Of Michigan; Law.

EADES, DIANE; Greenfield Ctrl HS; Greenfield, IN; Chrh Wkr; Hon Rl; NHS; Yth Flsp; 4-H; Pep Clb; Spn Clb; Mat Maids; Ball St Univ; Dietetics.

EADS, DANETTE; Fergus HS; Lewistown, MT; Chrs; Chrh Wkr; Hon Rl; Sch Mus; Sch Pl; Montana Inst Of The Bible; Music.

EADS, KENNETH; Princeton Comm HS; Princeton, IN; Boy Scts; Yth Flsp; Boys Clb Am; Letter Bsbl; Letter Ftbl; College; Electrical Engineer.

EADS, VICKY; Bedford North Lawrence HS; Bedford, IN; Aud/Vis; Chrs; Chrh Wkr; Hon Rl; Hosp Ade; NHS; Pol Wkr; Sec Yth Flsp; Beta Clb; VP OEA; N L Area Vo Tech Ctr.

EAGEN, PAMELA; Marysville HS; Smith Creek, MI; Band; Drl Tm; Hon Rl; NHS; Sct Actv; Stg Crw; Pep Clb; Trk; Pom Pon; Scr Kpr; Med.

EAGLE, CHARLES E; Newark Sr HS; Newark, OH; Jr NHS; Lit Mag; NHS; Eng Clb; Fr Clb; Ger Clb; Key Clb; Mth Clb; Sci Clb; Natl Merit SF; College; Chemistry.

EAGLES, MARC; Douglas Mac Arthur HS; Saginaw, MI; Chrh Wkr; JA; Yth Flsp; IM Sprt; Univ; Missionary.

EAKEN, DONNA; Bishop Nol Institute; Griffith, IN; 19/321 Hon Rl; Mth Clb; Pep Clb; Scr Kpr; Tmr; Natl Bus Hon Soc 79; 2nd Pl Winner In St Hist Day Contst 79; Univ; Child Psych.

EAKINS, BRYAN; Penn HS; Osceola, IN; Cls Rep Frsh Cls; Boy Scts; Chrh Wkr; FCA; Hon Rl; 4-H; Ger Clb; Letter Bsbl; Letter Ftbl; Pres Awd; Private Pilot License 1979; PHM All Sport Awd 1977; Univ; Aviation Flight Tech.

EAKINS, ROGER; La Brae HS; Southington, OH; 6/180 Cl Rep Jr Cls; Cls Rep Sr Cls; Am Leg Boys St; NHS; Stu Cncl; Rptr Yrbk; Spn Clb; Kent St Univ; Math.

EAKINS, SHARON; Rushville Consolidated HS; Rushville, IN; 35/290 Chrh Wkr; Cmnty Wkr; Hon Rl; Off Ade; Yth Flsp; Lat Clb; Pep Clb; Spn Clb; PPFtbl; Gov Hon Prg Awd; Anderson Coll; RN.

EARBY, BARRY E; Robichaud HS; Inkster, MI; Band; Boy Scts; Chrh Wkr; Drl Tm; ROTC; Ten; Am Leg Awd; DAR Awd; Ferris St Coll; Pharm.

EARHART, CYNTHIA; Lincoln West HS; Cleveland, OH; Hon Rl; Cit Awd; Univ; Vet.

EARICH, CANDI; Morgan HS; Malta, OH; Am Leg Aux Girls St; Chrh Wkr; Girl Scts; Hon Rl; NHS; Off Ade; 4-H; FBLA; Capt Bsktbl; PPFtbl;.

EARICK, SCOTT A; Bellefontaine HS; Bellefontaine, OH; 92/245 Am Leg Boys St; Band; Boy Scts; Debate Tm; Orch; Sch Pl; Sct Actv; Stg Crw; Ger Clb; Key Clb; College; Law.

EARL, ANNETTE; Buffalo HS; Kenova, WV; Chrs; Girl Scts; Hon Rl; Lbry Ade; Mdrgl; Y-Teens; Mth Clb; Spn Clb; Letter Bsktbl; Letter Trk; Ohio St Univ; Comp Progr.

EARL, BETHANY; Reading HS; Reading, MI; 6/95 Sec Sr Cls; Chrs; Chrh Wkr; Hon Rl; NHS; Stu Cncl; Yth Flsp; Rptr Yrbk; 4-H; Fr Clb; Kellogg Cmnty Coll; Nursing.

EARL, ERIC; Marshall HS; Marshall, MI; 6/300 Pres Frsh Cls; Cls Rep Soph Cls; Cl Rep Jr Cls; Cls Rep Sr Cls; Hon Rl; NHS; Letter Bsbl; Am Leg Awd; JA Awd; Univ; Law.

EARL, LAURA; Bluefield HS; Bluefield, WV; Cls Rep Frsh Cls; Cls Rep Soph Cls; Cl Rep Jr Cls; Hon Rl; Stu Cncl; FHA; Ger Clb; Pep Clb; Spn Clb; Gym; Univ; Spec Ed.

EARL, MARY; Mannington HS; Mannington, WV; Off Ade; Y-Teens; West Virginia Univ; Nursing.

EARL, TERRI; Mannington HS; Mannington, WV; Hon Rl; Bsktbl; IM Sprt; Univ; Phys Educ.

EARLEY, DANITA; Jane Addams Vocational HS; Cleveland, OH; Cls Rep Frsh Cls; Cls Rep Soph Cls; Cl Rep Jr Cls; Aud/Vis; Chrs; Drl Tm; Hon Rl; Jr NHS; Lbry Ade; NHS; Dyke Bus Coll; Sec.

EARLEY, DAVID; Washington HS; Massillon, OH; FCA; Spn Clb; Letter Ftbl; Trk; Univ; Mgmt.

EARLEY, PAM; N Putnam Jr Sr HS; Greencastle, IN; 17/155 Trs Soph Cls; Trs Jr Cls; Cmnty Wkr; FCA; Hon Rl; Jr NHS; NHS; Off Ade; Stu Cncl; 4-H; Mbr Of Honor Group 4 H Home Environment; 4 H Demonstration Contest Winner; College.

EARLL, CHERYL; Bentley HS; Livonia, MI; Pom Pon; College; Mech Engr.

EARLS, MARNEE; Shadyside HS; Bellaire, OH; Chrs; Debate Tm; Hon Rl; Sch Mus; Y-Teens; Spn Clb; Univ; Law.

EARLS, SCOTT; Rossford HS; Rossford, OH; 5/150 Hon Rl; Bsktbl; Glf; Ten; Univ Of Toledo; Computer Sci.

EARNEST, CINDY; Montcalm HS; Rock, WV; 2/59 VP Jr Cls; Cls Rep Sr Cls; Sal; Chrs; Chrh Wkr; Hon Rl; NHS; Stu Cncl; FHA; Bluefield St Univ; Nursing.

EARNEST, WILLIAM; Western Reserve HS; Wakeman, OH; 6/110 Cls Rep Frsh Cls; Cls Rep Soph Cls; Cl Rep Jr Cls; Cls Rep Sr Cls; Band; NHS; Sch Pl; Stu Cncl; Drama Clb; College; Comp Sci.

EARP, DAVID K; Washington Irving HS; Clarksburg, WV; Chrh Wkr; FCA; Hon Rl; Rptr Sch Nwsp; Fr Clb; Letter Crs Cntry; Letter Trk; Wv Univ.

EASH, BEVERLY; Pettisville HS; Wauseon, OH; Chrs; Chrh Wkr; Cmnty Wkr; Hon Rl; Hosp Ade; Sch Pl; Yth Flsp; 4-H; FHA; Goshen College; Nurse.

EASH, LISA; Fostoria HS; Fostoria, OH; 71/177 Band; Chrs; VP JA; Lbry Ade; Yth Flsp; Y-Teens; Fr Clb; VP JA Awd; Bowling Green St Univ; Bus Educ.

EASLEY, BETH; William A Wirt HS; Gary, IN; VP Frsh Cls; Pres Jr Cls; Hon Rl; Pep Clb; Spn Clb; Letter GAA; PPFtbl; Tmr; College; Nursing.

EASLEY, DANIEL; Okemos HS; Okemos, MI; Boy Scts; Bsktbl; Glf; Coach Actv; IM Sprt; Miami Univ; Bus Econ.

EASLY, JANET L; Whitmer HS; Toledo, OH; 18/810 Hon Rl; Lbry Ade; Sct Actv; Fr Clb; Natl Merit SF; Univ; Pre Vet Med.

EASON, FARAH; Portsmouth HS; Portsmouth, OH; 78/230 Cls Rep Frsh Cls; Cls Rep Soph Cls; Cl Rep Jr Cls; Cls Rep Sr Cls; Chrh Wkr; Cmnty Wkr; Sch Pl; Spn Clb; Am Leg Awd; Univ Of Cinn; Broadcasting.

EAST, JEFF; Port Huron Northern HS; Port Huron, MI; 101/460 Bsbl; Ftbl; Ferris St Coll; Busns.

EAST, KIMBERLY S; North Posey Jr Sr HS; Poseyville, IN; Cls Rep Frsh Cls; Cl Rep Jr Cls; Hon Rl; Lbry Ade; Yth Flsp; Pep Clb; Trk; GAA; Pom Pon; Pres Awd; Lockyear Busns Coll.

EAST, LINDA; Bedford North Lawrence HS; Bedford, IN; Off Ade; Sch Mus; Sch Pl; Yrbk; Rptr Sch Nwsp; Sch Nwsp; Drama Clb; Mth Clb; OEA; Pep Clb; College; Busns.

EASTER, SUSAN P; Monroe HS; Monroe, MI; Band; Cmp Fr Grls; Hon Rl; Jr NHS; NHS; Ten; Trk; Chrldng; Varsity Letter In Volleyball; College.

EASTER, TERRY; Athens HS; Princeton, WV; Pres Soph Cls; VP Jr Cls; Band; Chrh Wkr; Hon Rl; Lbry Ade; Off Ade; Yth Flsp; Ed Yrbk; Sec Key Clb; Tennessee Temple Univ.

EASTERBROOK, KIRK; Mancelona HS; Alden, MI; Band; Boy Scts; Hon Rl; Jr NHS; Sct Actv; Letter Ftbl; Letter Trk; Wrstlng; Michigan St Univ; Med.

EASTERDAY, CRAIG; Wadsworth HS; Wadsworth, OH; 60/367 Chrs; NHS; Sch Mus; Spn Clb; Bsbl; Letter Bsktbl; Letter Ftbl; Mgrs; Scr Kpr; Tmr; Akron Univ; Commcts.

EASTERDAY, CRAIG; Medina HS; Medina, OH; 5/350 VP Soph Cls; Am Leg Boys St; Hon Rl; NHS; Key Clb; Lat Clb; Letter Ftbl; Letter Trk; Natl Merit Ltr; Voice Dem Awd; College; Pre Med.

EASTERDAY, TED; Delaware Hayes HS; Delaware, OH; AFS; Band; Cmnty Wkr; Hon Rl; Yth Flsp; FTA; Key Clb; Ftbl; Trk; Wrstlng;.

EASTERLIN, COLLEEN; De Sales HS; Columbus, OH; Cls Rep Frsh Cls; Sec Soph Cls; Cl Rep Jr Cls; Pres Sr Cls; Stu Cncl; Gym; PPFtbl; Bus Schl.

EASTERLY, D; Perry HS; Massillon, OH; Chrh Wkr; Hon Rl; Jr NHS; Off Ade; IM Sprt; Univ Of Akron; Science.

EASTIN, WILLIAM; Carsonville Pt Sanilac HS; Pt Sanilac, MI; Aud/Vis; Hon Rl; Lbry Ade; Off Ade; Sprt Ed Yrbk; Rptr Yrbk; Yrbk; Sprt Ed Sch Nwsp; Rptr Sch Nwsp; Sch Nwsp; Alma Coll; Bus Admin.

EASTLING, ROBIN; Orchard View HS; Muskegon, MI; Cls Rep Frsh Cls; Cls Rep Soph Cls; Cl Rep Jr Cls; Hon Rl; Sch Pl; Rptr Yrbk; Chrldng; Mat Maids; Meskegon Bus Coll; Bus.

EASTMAN, AMY; River Valley HS; Caledonia, OH; 41/204 Cls Rep Frsh Cls; JA; Sec Stu Cncl; Rptr Sch Nwsp; Sec 4-H; Fr Clb; Swmmng; Letter Wrstlng; Letter Chrldng; Ltr In Volleyball; Univ; Psych.

EASTMAN, CHRISTINE; Southwestern HS; Flint, MI; Band; Hon Rl; NHS; Quill & Scroll; Yrbk; Rptr Sch Nwsp; Mic State Univ; Journalism.

EASTMAN, DAWN; North Union HS; W Mansfield, OH; Cls Rep Sr Cls; Aud/Vis; Band; Debate Tm; Hon Rl; Sch Pl; Stu Cncl; Yth Flsp; 4-H; Lat Clb; Univ; Med.

EASTMAN, JOHN; Ashtabula HS; Ashtabula, OH; 19/249 Hon Rl; NHS; Sch Mus; Rptr Yrbk; Drama Clb; Letter Ftbl; Swmmng; Trk; Wrstlng; Univ; Engr.

EASTMAN, TAMMY; Everett HS; Lansing, MI; Sch Nwsp; Mi Stdnts For Safer Hghway 77 79; Michigan St Univ; Vet Med.

EASTWOOD, CAROL; Medina Sr HS; Medina, OH; 4/380 Band; Chrh Wkr; Hon Rl; VP NHS; Orch; Sch Mus; Yth Flsp; Ed Sch Nwsp; Letter Crs Cntry; Stdnt Of Month 79; Akron Beacon Journl Staffer Of Yr 79; Grove City Coll.

EASTWOOD, RONALD; Medina Sr HS; Medina, OH; Cl Rep Jr Cls; Am Leg Boys St; Boy Scts; Chrs; Chrh Wkr; Cmnty Wkr; Sch Mus; Stu Cncl; Drama Clb; Pres Key Clb; Geneva Coll; Civil Engr.

EATER, DOUG; Madison Comprehensive HS; Mansfield, OH; Boy Scts; Chrs; Lbry Ade; Off Ade; Yth Flsp; Fr Clb; Mgrs; College.

EATON, BRUCE; Portage Northern HS; Portage, MI; Chrh Wkr; Pres Yth Flsp; Western Michigan Univ; Comp Sci.

EATON, JAMES; Central HS; Evansville, IN; Pol Wkr; Stu Cncl; Fr Clb; FSA; Sci Clb; Letter Bsbl; Coach Actv; Bucyrus Erie Schlrshps; Indiana Univ; Marine Bio.

EATON, JOHN; Maumee Valley Cntry Day HS; Perrysburg, OH; Cmnty Wkr; Hon Rl; Hosp Ade; Pol Wkr; Red Cr Ade; Boys Clb Am; Ftbl; Rice Univ; Bus Mgmt.

EBBERT, KELLEY; Bishop Donahue HS; Moundsville, WV; Cls Rep Soph Cls; Band; Girl Scts; Hon Rl; Stu Cncl; VP 4-H; Pep Clb; Scr Kpr; 4-H Awd; Scott Beauty Schl; Cosmetologist.

EBBESKOTTE, JANET; Delphos St Johns HS; Delphos, OH; 13/156 Cl Rep Jr Cls; Hon Rl; NHS; Stu Cncl; Sch Nwsp; 4-H; Bsktbl; Trk; Mia Oxford Univ; Social Worker.

EBBESMIER, RHONDA; Ottawa Glandorf HS; Ottawa, OH; Trs Sr Cls; Band; Girl Scts; Hon Rl; Orch; Treas Stu Cncl; Pres DECA; GAA; Capt IM Sprt; Scr Kpr; ATI; Botany.

EBBING, LYNETTE; Stephen T Badin HS; Hamilton, OH; 13/223 Drl Tm; Hon Rl; Jr NHS; NHS; Sch Mus; Treas Fr Clb; FHA; Natl Merit Ltr; Miami Univ; Systems Analysis.

EBE, BILL; Owosso HS; Owosso, MI; 113/460 Boy Scts; Pres FFA; Vocational Schl; Diesel Mech.

EBELL, MARK; Douglas Mac Arthur HS; Saginaw, MI; 1/300 Val; Band; Hon Rl; NHS; Pol Wkr; Sch Nwsp; Lat Clb; Capt Trk; Natl Merit Schl; Rotary Awd; Kalamazoo Coll; Med.

EBELS, JULIANN; N Michigan Christian HS; Falmouth, MI; VP Frsh Cls; Hon Rl; Lbry Ade; Sch Mus; Stg Crw; Rptr Yrbk; 4-H; Letter Bsktbl; 4-H Awd; Calvin Coll.

EBELS, MARY; Mc Bain N Christian HS; Falmouth, MI; 4/38 Sec Frsh Cls; Sec Soph Cls; Trs Soph Cls; Sec Jr Cls; Trs Jr Cls; Trs Sr Cls; Chrs; Chrh Wkr; Hon Rl; Sch Mus; Mercy Schl; Nursing.

EBERHARD, LAURA; Wheeling Park HS; Wheeling, WV; 2/700 Trs Jr Cls; Band; Chrh Wkr; Hon Rl; NHS; Stu Cncl; 4-H; Letter Trk; Mat Maids; 4-H Awd; George Stifel Endowment Fund Awd For Acad Exc; W Liberty St Coll Sci Fair 1st Pl Jr Engr 3rd Pl Sr Engr; W Virginia Univ; Genetics.

EBERHARD, LISA; Bay City All Saints Ctrl HS; Bay City, MI; Sec Jr Cls; Hon Rl; Mdrgl; Natl Forn Lg; VP NHS; Sch Mus; Rptr Sch Nwsp; Lake Superior St Coll; Geology.

EBERHARD, MARK; Lutheran E HS; Detroit, MI; Cls Rep Frsh Cls; Cls Rep Soph Cls; Pres Jr Cls; Cl Rep Jr Cls; Pres Sr Cls; Cls Rep Sr Cls; Boy Scts; Chrh Wkr; Hon Rl; NHS; Underclassmen Ath Of Yr; 2nd Team All Conf Ftbl; Michigan St Univ; Vet.

EBERHARDT, BARRY; Inkster HS; Inkster, MI; Band; Chrh Wkr; Debate Tm; Hon Rl; NHS; Orch; Letter Ten; Cit Awd; College.

EBERHARDT, KAREN; La Salle HS; South Bend, IN; 17/500 Band; Girl Scts; Hon Rl; Sch Nwsp; Drama Clb; Pep Clb; Sci Clb; Letter Swmmng; Purdue Univ; Acctg.

EBERHART, JAMES R; East Liverpool HS; East Liverpool, OH; 27/340 Band; Boy Scts; Chrs; Chrh Wkr; Cmnty Wkr; Lbry Ade; Key Clb; Lat Clb; Wrstlng; Latin Awrd 78; Metz Harper Shclrshp 78; St Bd Of Educ Basic Studies Awrd 78; Mount Union Coll; Psych.

EBERHART, MARY; Wylie E Groves HS; Birmingham, MI; 24/530 Chrs; Hon Rl; Jr NHS; Off Ade; Stu Cncl; Sprt Ed Yrbk; Socr; Swmmng; IM Sprt; Vllybl Team Capt 79; Univ; Bio.

EBERLE, LINDA; Upper Arlington HS; Columbus, OH; 30/650 AFS; Band; Hon Rl; NHS; Orch; Ger Clb; Natl Merit Ltr; Ohio State Univ; Electrical Engr.

EBERLE, LORI; Seeger HS; Pine Village, IN; 11/125 Cl Rep Jr Cls; Pres Sr Cls; Cls Rep Sr Cls; Hon Rl; NHS; Stu Cncl; 4-H; Fr Clb; Pep Clb; Chrldng; Purdue Univ; Home Ec.

EBERLE, MARY; Leetonia HS; Leetonia, OH; Hon Rl; Youngstown Coll; Bus.

EBERLEIN, LYNN; Unionville Sebewaing Sr HS; Sebewaing, MI; Chrs; Hon Rl; Ed Yrbk; Sec FHA; Univ; Home Ec.

EBERLY, EDWIN; Petoskey HS; Petoskey, MI; Band; Hon Rl; NHS; Natl Merit SF; Michigan Tech Univ; Math.

EBERLY, KEITH J; Norwalk HS; Norwalk, OH; 73/198 JA; Fr Clb; Bsbl; Bsktbl; Ftbl; Mgrs; JA Awd; Bowling Green St Univ; Admin Mgmt.

EBERLY, STEVEN S; Manchester HS; Akron, OH; Cls Rep Sr Cls; Stu Cncl; Yth Flsp; Key Clb; Pep Clb; Ftbl; Letter Trk; Wrstlng; Coach Actv; Mgrs; College.

EBERST, MARY E; Westerville N HS; Westerville, OH; 1/411 AFS; Am Leg Aux Girls St; Girl Scts; Hon Rl; Hosp Ade; JA; NHS; Red Cr Ade; Key Clb; Mth Clb; Kiwanis Acad Varsity Awd; Selected As Outstndng Sr Sci Stu; Univ Of Dayton Pres Schlrshp; Univ Of Dayton; Med.

EBERT, KATE; River Valley HS; Waldo, OH; 1/200 Cls Rep Frsh Cls; Am Leg Aux Girls St; Band; FCA; NHS; Sch Mus; Sec Stu Cncl; 4-H; Letter Crs Cntry; Letter Trk; Coll; Busns Mgmt.

EBLIN, SCOTT; Unioto HS; Chillicothe, OH; 23/117 Cls Rep Frsh Cls; Hon Rl; Fr Clb; Letter Bsbl; Capt Bsktbl; Am Leg Awd; Univ Of Cincinnati; Engr.

EBLIN, SCOTT; Huntington East HS; Huntington, WV; 33/360 Pres Jr Cls; Am Leg Boys St; Boy Scts; NHS; Sch Pl; Yth Flsp; Rptr Sch Nwsp; Drama Clb; Key Clb; SAR Awd; Davidson College; Humanities.

EBNER, LAURA; Beaumont Schl For Girls; Cleve Hts, OH; Chrs; Chrh Wkr; Cmnty Wkr; Girl Scts; Hosp Ade; Sct Actv; Stg Crw; Y-Teens; Socr; Swmmng; Miami Univ; Acctg.

EBRAT, ABDOL; Howe Military HS; Ann Arbor, MI; 1/33 Sec Jr Cls; Sec Sr Cls; NHS; ROTC; Ftbl; Trk; Wrstlng; Mic State Univ; Engr.

EBRIGHT, LORI; Brookhaven HS; Columbus, OH; Drl Tm; Hon Rl; Spn Clb; Trk; Treas Pom Pon; Scr Kpr; Tmr; Achvmnt Hon Roll 74 79; Super Achvmnt Hon Roll 74 & 79; Whos Who Awd 77; Columbus Bus Univ; Fshn Mdse.

EBRIGHT, ROXANNE; Ithaca HS; Ashley, MI; 10/132 Hon Rl; Spn Clb; Pom Pon; Mic State Math.

EBSCH, MICHAEL; Memominee HS; Menominee, MI; Cmnty Wkr; Hon Rl; Pol Wkr; Boys Clb Am; Ftbl; Ten; Scr Kpr; Tmr; Mic Tech; Med Tech.

EBY, DOUGLAS D; Baldwin Community Schools; Baldwin, MI; Band; Chrh Wkr; Hon Rl; Orch; Yth Flsp; Univ.

ECHARD, BEN; Washington Sr HS; Washington C H, OH; AFS; Am Leg Boys St; VP Band; Chrs; Chrh Wkr; Sch Mus; Ohio St Univ; Music.

ECHARD, SUSAN; Union Scioto HS; Chillicothe, OH; 17/125 Drl Tm; Hon Rl; Rptr Sch Nwsp; 4-H; FTA; Univ; Learning Disability.

ECHELBERGER, MATTHEW; St Francis HS; Traverse City, MI; 7/140 Hon Rl; Mod UN; NHS; Bsktbl; Ftbl; College Civil Engr.

ECHELBERGER, PAM; Loudonville HS; Perrysville, OH; Band; Girl Scts; Hon Rl; Sch Pl; 4-H; Bsktbl; Trk; Chrldng; Voc Schl; Animal Care.

ECHELBERGER, RONNY; Lucas HS; Mansfield, OH; Trs Jr Cls; Band; Chrs; Hon Rl; Lbry Ade; Sch Pl; Yrbk; Letter Trk; Mgrs; Tmr;.

ECK, BRIAN; Whitehall Sr HS; Whitehall, MI; 9/154 Band; Boy Scts; NHS; Sch Mus; Sch Pl; Ed Sch Nwsp; Drama Clb; Ger Clb; Wrstlng; Kalamazoo Coll; Physician.

ECKART, JULIE; Union County HS; Liberty, IN; 1/135 VP Frsh Cls; Aud/Vis; Hon Rl; Red Cr Ade; 4-H; Fr Clb; FFA; Letter Bsktbl; Scr Kpr; 4-H Awd; Sr Sci Fair Wnnr 78; Eng Awd 79; Star Greenhand Awd 78; Univ; Law Enforcement.

ECKART, KAREN; Copley HS; Akron, OH; Band; Hon Rl; NHS; Yth Flsp; Pep Clb; Spn Clb; College; Art.

ECKENRODE, SUSAN; Bishop Watterson HS; Columbus, OH; Chrs; Cmnty Wkr; Hosp Ade; Sch Pl; Sct Actv; Stg Crw; Rptr Yrbk; Rptr Sch Nwsp; Ohi State Univ; Journalism.

ECKENSWILLER, DIANA; Ubly Comm HS; Argyle, MI; 6/125 Hon Rl; Jr NHS; Sch Pl; Sec Stu Cncl; 4-H; Letter Bsktbl; 4-H Awd; Voice Dem Awd; 4 H St Rep For 4 H Natl Conf; 4 H St Rep Rabbit Natl 4 H Congress; 4 H St Rep Citizenship Shortcourse Trip; Michigan St Univ; Vet.

ECKER, KIMBERLY; Forest Park HS; Cincinnati, OH; 33/356 Band; Chrs; Chrh Wkr; Girl Scts; Hon Rl; NHS; Yth Flsp; Letter Socr; Letter Trk; Coach Actv; Bowling Green Univ; Phys Educ.

ECKERLE, SHEILA; Jasper HS; Jasper, IN; 42/200 Hon Rl; Pres JA; Pep Clb; Letter Trk; GAA; JA Awd; J A Sales Clb Achiever Awd 78; Gavel Awd 78; Jamco 78 & 79; NAJAC 78; Hairdresser.

ECKERMAN, ROBERT C; Swan Valley HS; Saginaw, MI; Letter Crs Cntry; Socr; Letter Swmmng; Letter Trk; Coach Actv; Natl Merit SF; Albion Univ; Med.

ECKERT, CHRIS A; Dominican HS; Detroit, MI; Chrh Wkr; Cmnty Wkr; Girl Scts; Hon Rl; Lbry Ade; Pres NHS; Off Ade; Orch; Sct Actv; Stu Cncl; Wayne St Univ; Spec Ed.

ECKERT, DEBRA A; Princeton Community HS; Princeton, IN; 19/203 Cl Rep Jr Cls; Debate Tm; Sch Pl; DECA; Drama Clb; Mth Clb; Spn Clb; GAA; Mat Maids; Parlimentary Proc Team St Wnr 1979; Vincennes Univ; Acctg.

ECKERT, JACQUELINE R; Milford HS; Milford, OH; 81/396 Girl Scts; Hon Rl; Sct Actv; FHA; Gym; Cit Awd; Chatham Coll; Math.

ECKERT, JULIE; Rochester Community HS; Rochester, IN; 22/176 Sec Jr Cls; Am Leg Aux Girls St; Chrs; Hon Rl; NHS; Stu Cncl; Pres Fr Clb; Ball State; Music.

ECKHART, ALICIA; Grandview Heights HS; Columbus, OH; 13/133 Band; Cmp Fr Grls; Chrs; Hon Rl; Jr NHS; NHS; Yth Flsp; Letter Bsktbl; Letter Trk; GAA; Varsity Vllybl 77 80; MVP Vllybl 79; Ohio St Univ; Rec.

ECKHART, BARBARA; Parkersburg South HS; Parkersburg, WV; VP Frsh Cls; VP Soph Cls; Cl Rep Jr Cls; Am Leg Aux Girls St; Band; Girl Scts; Hon Rl; Hosp Ade; Sch Pl; Stu Cncl; Parkersburg Cmnty Coll; Nursing.

ECKLEY, JOSEPH P; Stivers Patterson Co Op HS; Dayton, OH; 4/428 Cls Rep Soph Cls; Cl Rep Jr Cls; Chrh Wkr; NHS; Ed Yrbk; VICA; Crs Cntry; Trk; JA Awd; Natl Merit Ltr; Univ; Indust Design.

ECKMAN, DENISE; Lansing Christian HS; Lansing, MI; Chrs; Chrh Wkr; Hosp Ade; Sch Mus; Yth Flsp; Yrbk; Mi Dept Of Educ Comp Schlrshp 79; Lansing Cmnty Coll; Nursing.

ECKRICH, ELIZABETH; Roncalli HS; Indianapolis, IN; 11/202 Chrs; Hosp Ade; JA; Sec Mod UN; NHS; Sch Mus; JA Awd; Indiana Univ; Bio.

ECKSTEIN, ERIC; Crestview HS; Mansfield, OH; 3/121 Hst Frsh Cls; Pres Soph Cls; Band; Chrh Wkr; Hon Rl; Treas NHS; Treas 4-H; Bowling Green College; Biology.

ECKSTEIN, GLORIA; Terre Haute South Vigo HS; Terre Haute, IN; 43/650 Cls Rep Soph Cls; Cl Rep Jr Cls; Cls Rep Sr Cls; Hon Rl; NHS; Stu Cncl; Y-Teens; PPFtbl; Indiana St Univ.

ECKSTEIN, JOHN; Interlochen Arts Acad; Larsen, WI; Debate Tm; Hon Rl; Orch; Trk; IM Sprt; College; Physical Science.

ECKSTEIN, KENNETH G; Brunnerdale HS; Coldwater, OH; Sec Jr Cls; Trs Jr Cls; Pres Sr Cls; Chrs; Chrh Wkr; Hon Rl; NHS; Sch Mus; Sch Pl; Stu Cncl; St Josephs Coll; Sociology.

ECKSTEIN, PAULA; Buckeye Ctrl HS; New Washington, OH; Cls Rep Frsh Cls; Cls Rep Soph Cls; Cl Rep Jr Cls; Cls Rep Sr Cls; Band; Chrs; Chrh Wkr; Cmnty Wkr; Drl Tm; Hon Rl; OSU; Acctg.

ECKSTEIN, PEGGY; Immaculate Conception Acad; Batesville, IN; 5/69 Pres Jr Cls; Hon Rl; NHS; Sch Pl; Pres Stu Cncl; Purdue Univ; Psych.

ECONOMOU, JENNIFER; Turpin HS; Cincinnati, OH; 12/357 AFS; Chrs; NHS; Scr Kpr; Tmr; Univ Of Cincinnati; Accounting.

EDDS, BOB; Little Miami HS; Morrow, OH; Hon Rl; IM Sprt; Univ; Comp Progr.

EDDY, BRENDA; Parkersburg HS; Vienna, WV; Hon Rl; Hosp Ade; Off Ade;.

EDDY, DEANN; Saranac HS; Saranac, MI; VP Jr Cls; Cls Rep Sr Cls; Band; Chrh Wkr; Hon Rl; Sch Mus; Yth Flsp; Coach Actv; College; Phys Educ.

EDDY, DEBRA; Frontier HS; Reno, OH; 5/94 VP Jr Cls; Cl Rep Jr Cls; Cls Rep Sr Cls; Am Leg Aux Girls St; Chrh Wkr; Hon Rl; NHS; Sch Pl; Stu Cncl; Ed Yrbk; 1st Pl In Phys Educ 78; 1st Pl In Bus Math Eng & Jrnlsm 79; Marietta Coll; Acctg.

EDDY, JASON; Madison Comprehensive HS; Mansfield, OH; 150/470 Band; Boy Scts; Orch; Sct Actv; Ger Clb; IM Sprt; N Central Ohio Tech Schl; Bus Mgmt.

EDDY, JEFFREY S; Anderson HS; Anderson, IN; 91/415 Cls Rep Frsh Cls; Aud/Vis; Boy Scts; Chrs; FCA; Hon Rl; Sch Mus; Fr Clb; Glf; Swmmng; Univ; Genrl Mgmt.

EDDY, JOSEPH; Sistersville HS; Friendly, WV; 4/60 Pres Soph Cls; VP Jr Cls; Pres Sr Cls; Am Leg Boys St; Hon Rl; NHS; Pres Stu Cncl; Rptr Yrbk; FFA; Pep Clb; Marietta Coll; Petroleum Engr.

EDDY, NANCY; C A Beard Mem Schl Corp; Knightstown, IN; 9/154 Cls Rep Frsh Cls; Cls Rep Soph Cls; Trs Jr Cls; Cl Rep Jr Cls; Chrs; Hon Rl; Sch Mus; Stu Cncl; Yth Flsp; FBLA; Busns Schl; Legal Sec.

EDDY, REBECCA; Clay Battelle HS; Cassville, WV; Cls Rep Sr Cls; Chrs; Chrh Wkr; Hon Rl; Jr NHS; Sch Pl; Stu Cncl; Yth Flsp; Rptr Sch Nwsp; FHA; West Virginia Univ; Dent Hygnst.

EDDY, STEVE; Springport Sr HS; Springport, MI; VP Soph Cls; Aud/Vis; Chrh Wkr; Hon Rl; Lbry Ade; Natl Forn Lg; NHS; Sch Pl; Stg Crw; Drama Clb; Air Force Academy; Navigator.

EDDY, THOMAS; Clinton HS; Tipton, MI; Hon Rl; Rptr Sch Nwsp; Bsktbl; Letter Glf; Pro Bowler.

EDEN, CAREY; Milton HS; Milton, WV; Band; Cmnty Wkr; Hon Rl; Off Ade; Rptr Yrbk; VP 4-H; FBLA; Huntington Bus Schl; Legal Sec.

EDEN, PAULA; Solon HS; Solon, OH; 42/288 Hon Rl; Bowling Green St Univ; Health.

EDEN, ROBERT E; Fairfield HS; Fairfield, OH; 75/650 Pres Soph Cls; VP Jr Cls; Hon Rl; Ftbl; Hockey;.

EDENS, JEFF; Peterstown HS; Ballard, WV; Band; Chrh Wkr; Hon Rl; NHS; FFA; Mth Clb; Pep Clb; Bsktbl; Coach Actv; Scr Kpr; Sponsor Schl At Camp Horseshoe 79; Pres Of Delta Club 79; Check For Selling Fruit FFA 79; Store Mgr.

EDENS, TAMARA; Eastwood HS; Stony Ridge, OH; Chrh Wkr; Hon Rl; Off Ade; Stg Crw; Spn Clb; College; Art.

EDENS, WILLIAM; Marion Harding HS; Marion, OH; Cls Rep Soph Cls; Cl Rep Jr Cls; Boy Scts; Sct Actv; Fr Clb; Trk; God Cntry Awd; Armed Serv; Aviation.

EDER, B; South Charleston HS; S Charleston, WV; Cmnty Wkr; Hon Rl; Yth Flsp; Spn Clb; Letter Ftbl; Trk; Univ; Dent.

EDERER, MARY; Catholic Central HS; Grand Rapids, MI; Hon Rl; NHS; Rptr Sch Nwsp; Pres Spn Clb; Mat Maids; Grand Rapids Jr College.

EDGAR, JOHN; Monsignor John R Hackett HS; Kalamazoo, MI; Pres Soph Cls; Cmnty Wkr; Sch Pl; Stg Crw; Bsktbl; Socr; Coach Actv; IM Sprt;.

EDGAR, TERRY; Pontiac Central HS; Pontiac, MI; Hon Rl; NHS; Ferris St Coll; Data Proc.

EDGAR, TIM; Wadsworth Sr HS; Wadsworth, OH; Ed Sch Nwsp; Rptr Sch Nwsp; Ohio Univ; Jrnlsm.

EDGECOMB, JULIE; Yale HS; Yale, MI; Cl Rep Jr Cls; Girl Scts; Hon Rl; Off Ade; Stu Cncl; 4-H; Pep Clb; Chrldng; Univ; Real Estate.

EDGEWORTH, EILEEN; East Detroit HS; E Detroit, MI; Chrh Wkr; Girl Scts; Hon Rl; Hosp Ade; NHS; Red Cr Ade; Sct Actv; Letter Swmmng; Tmr; Natl Merit Ltr; Univ Of Mia; Nursing.

EDGEWORTH, THOMAS; St Clement HS; Warren, MI; 6/130 Hon Rl; NHS; Rptr Yrbk; Sprt Ed Sch Nwsp; Capt Bsbl; Bsktbl; Ftbl; Pres Northwood Inst; Bus Admin Mgmt.

EDGINGTON, DALE; Jonesville HS; Jonesville, MI; VP Jr Cls; Hon Rl; FFA; Capt Bsktbl; Letter Trk; Michigan St Univ; Soc Sci.

EDIE, THOMAS L; Port Huron Central HS; Port Huron, MI; 7/222 Boy Scts; Hon Rl; Sct Actv; Rptr

Sch Nwsp; Crs Cntry; Ftbl; Letter Trk; IM Sprt; Ferris State College; Sci.

EDINGFIELD, WAYNE; White Oak HS; Hillsboro, OH; Band; Chrh Wkr; Debate Tm; Hon Rl; Sch Mus; Sch Pl; Stg Crw; Yth Flsp; Sch Nwsp; 4-H; Lincoln Tech Schl; Farm Mgmt.

EDINGTON, BARBARA; Crispus Attucks HS; Indianapolis, IN; 24/250 Girl Scts; Hon Rl; Rptr Yrbk; Rptr Sch Nwsp; Ten; Indiana Univ; Nursing.

EDKINS, JAMES; West Catholic HS; Grand Rapids, MI; Debate Tm; Hon Rl; JA; NHS; Spn Clb; Letter Ten; Univ; Engr.

EDLUND, LAURIE; Mona Shores HS; Muskegon, MI; Band; NHS; Rptr Sch Nwsp; Sci Clb; Mic St U niv; Vet Med.

EDLY, LINDA; Carroll HS; Dayton, OH; 65/285 Band; Drl Tm; Hon Rl; Hosp Ade; Lbry Ade; Orch; Stu Cncl; Yrbk; Pep Clb; Spn Clb; College.

EDMOND, JEFFREY; Buckhannon Upshur HS; Buckhannon, WV; Cit Awd; Univ Of Morgantown; Pharm.

EDMOND, RANDI; Morgantown HS; Morgantwn, WV; Hon Rl; Jr NHS; Sct Actv; Mth Clb; Spn Clb; IM Sprt; Mat Maids; Foreign Lang Festv Honorable Mention Poster; Ship Of St Cert From Sec Of St; Letterman Awd For Mat Maids; West Virginia Univ; Medicine.

EDMOND, STEVEN; North Marion HS; Monongah, WV; Am Leg Boys St; Band; Hon Rl; NHS; Rptr Yrbk; Fr Clb; Bsktbl; Fairmont St Coll.

EDMOND, TIM; Tiffin Columbian HS; Tiffin, OH; Pres Frsh Cls; Girl Scts; JA; Fr Clb; Letter Bsbl; Letter Bsktbl; JA Awd; Univ; Cmnctns.

EDMONDS, CHRISTOPHER; Thomas A De Vilbiss HS; Toledo, OH; 11/237 Boy Scts; Cmnty Wkr; Hon Rl; Jr NHS; NHS; Pol Wkr; Quill & Scroll; Yrbk; NCTE; Hnrble Mention In English For The Ohio Tests Of Schlstc Achv; 5th In Pl In The City For The Half Mile Run; Univ Of Toledo; Social Work.

EDMONDS, DENA; Lincoln HS; Vincennes, IN; 63/308 Sec Soph Cls; Sec Jr Cls; Sec Sr Cls; Pres FHA; FNA; FTA; VP Pep Clb; DAR Awd; Vincennes Univ; Nursing.

EDMONDS, JONATHAN; Ravenna City HS; Ravenna, OH; Band; Boy Scts; Chrh Wkr; Hon Rl; Lbry Ade; Sct Actv; Yth Flsp; Sch Nwsp; 4-H; Ger Clb; Kent St Univ; Sci.

EDMONDS, KATHY; Riverside HS; Dearborn Hts, MI; Aud/Vis; Girl Scts; Hon Rl; Lbry Ade; Bsbl; Ten; Michigan St Univ; Vet.

EDMONDSON, JAMES A; Manistee Catholic Cntrl HS; Manistee, MI; VP Frsh Cls; Pres Soph Cls; Hon Rl; Stu Cncl; Bsbl; Bsktbl; Univ; Engr.

EDMONDSON, REBECCA; Monroe HS; Monroe, MI; 90/500 Sec Sr Cls; Chrs; Chrh Wkr; Hon Rl; Orch; Sch Mus; Yrbk; Adrian Coll.

EDMONDSON, THERESA; Winamac HS; Star City, IN; Chrh Wkr; Girl Scts; Hon Rl; Hosp Ade; Lbry Ade; Sch Mus; Sch Pl; Stg Crw; Yth Flsp; Drama Clb; Ivy Tech; Business.

EDMUNDSON, JAY D; Loogootee HS; Sarasota, FL; 8/150 Trs Jr Cls; Am Leg Boys St; Band; Boy Scts; Orch; Sch Mus; Sch Pl; College; Vet.

EDWARDS, ALBERT; Canfield HS; Canfield, OH; 111/275 Cls Rep Soph Cls; Cl Rep Jr Cls; Pres Sr Cls; Chrs; Hon Rl; Lit Mag; Sch Mus; Sch Pl; Sct Actv; Stg Crw; Youngstown St Univ; Indus Mgmt.

EDWARDS, ANGELA; Immaculata HS; Detroit, MI; Rptr Sch Nwsp; Sch Nwsp; Pep Clb; Vocational; Med.

EDWARDS, ANTOINETTE; Southfield HS; Southfield, MI; Cmp Fr Grls; Hon Rl; Red Cr Ade; Drama Clb; Fr Clb; Rus Clb; Spn Clb; Socr; Cit Awd; 4-H Awd; Purdue Univ; Aviation.

EDWARDS, BECKY; Barr Reeve HS; Loogootee, IN; 24/49 Band; Drl Tm; Hon Rl; 4-H; FHA; Vincennes Univ; Data Processing.

EDWARDS, BRIAN; Wapakoneta HS; Wapakoneta, OH; Band; Chrs; Hon Rl; Sch Mus; Stg Crw; Yth Flsp; Rdo Clb; Glf; Univ Of Cincinnati; Math.

EDWARDS, BRUCE; Dekalb HS; Auburn, IN; Boy Scts; Chrs; NHS; Sch Pl; Stg Crw; Yth Flsp; Y-Teens; Ger Clb; College; Teaching.

EDWARDS, BRUCE D; Huron HS; Ann Arbor, MI; 1/604 Band; Boy Scts; Hon Rl; Mth Clb; Letter Crs Cntry; Letter Trk; NCTE; Dartmouth Coll; Medicine.

EDWARDS, CYNTHIA; Roy C Start HS; Toledo, OH; Hosp Ade; Off Ade; Sch Pl; Fr Clb; Pep Clb; Letter Trk; Var Athletic Awd In Dance Grp Spartanettes 77; Voc Schl; Comp Prog.

EDWARDS, DANICE; South Lyon HS; So Lyon, MI; Hon Rl; NHS; Sch Mus; Stg Crw; Drama Clb; Fr Clb; Pep Clb; S Lyon HS Ski Clb 77; Intl Thespian Soc Troupe 1231 Treas 78; Youth Rcgntn Awrd Cmnty Serv & Acdmc Achvmnt; Hope Coll; Nuclear Engr.

EDWARDS, DANIEL B; Woodrow Wilson HS; Beckley, WV; Boy Scts; Hon Rl; NHS; Sct Actv; Yth Flsp; Natl Merit SF; College; Civil Engr.

EDWARDS, DEAN; Winchester Cmnty HS; Winchester, IN; Sec Chrh Wkr; VP NHS; FBLA; Letter Bsbl; Letter Bsktbl; Letter Ftbl; Bus Schl; Bus.

EDWARDS, DEBBIE; Bradford HS; Bradford, OH; Chrs; Lbry Ade; Spn Clb; College; Artist.

EDWARDS, DOUGLAS; Pike Central HS; Petersburg, IN; Band; Chrh Wkr; FCA; Hon Rl; Sch Pl; Key Clb; Sci Clb; Bsbl; David Lipscomb Coll; Sci.

EDWARDS, ELIZABETH; Bedford N Lawrence HS; Bedford, IN; 5/438 Hon Rl; NHS; Beta Clb; Ger Clb; Pep Clb; Letter Bsktbl; Letter Glf; Bausch & Lomb Awd; Kiwan Awd; Natl Merit Ltr; Exchange Clb Stu Of The Month; Admission With Distinction To Butler Univ; Academic Schlrshp From Butler; Butler Univ; Pharmacy.

EDWARDS, ELIZABETH; East Catholic HS; Detroit, MI; Girl Scts; Hon Rl; Univ Of Detroit; Spec Educ.

EDWARDS, GERALD; Hurricane HS; Hurrican, WV; Boy Scts; Hon Rl; Pep Clb; Rdo Clb; Bsktbl; Ftbl; West Virginia Tech Univ; Elec Engr.

EDWARDS, JESSICA; Hampshire County HS; Slanesville, WV; 8/232 AFS; Band; Chrs; Chrh Wkr; Hon Rl; Jr NHS; NHS; Yrbk; Drama Clb; Pres 4-H; Political Science.

EDWARDS, JOHN; Greenfield Central HS; Greenfield, IN; Yth Flsp; Boys Clb Am; Letter Bsbl; Letter Bsktbl; Letter Ftbl; University; Eng.

EDWARDS, KENNETH; Bloomfield HS; Bloomfield, IN; 9/95 Band; Boy Scts; Chrh Wkr; FCA; Hon Rl; NHS; Sct Actv; Yth Flsp; Lat Clb; Sci Clb; Basic Educ Opportnty Grant 79; St Stud Asst Commssn Of In 79; Indiana Univ; Microbio.

EDWARDS, LYNNE; Kenston HS; Chagrin Fls, OH; Drl Tm; Red Cr Ade; Letter Crs Cntry; Letter Trk; Mat Maids; PPFtbl; MVP In Cross Country; Honor Awd For Outstndng Schlstc Achvmnt In Soviet Union Class; College.

EDWARDS, MARILYN; Chesapeake HS; Chesapeake, OH; Cls Rep Frsh Cls; Sec Soph Cls; Cls Rep Soph Cls; Sec Jr Cls; Cl Rep Jr Cls; Cls Rep Sr Cls; Hon Rl; Off Ade; Stu Cncl; Sprt Ed Yrbk; Schlrshp Team; Homecoming Queen Cand; Rio Grande Coll.

EDWARDS, MARK; Greenville HS; Sheridan, MI; Band; Boy Scts; Chrh Wkr; Cmnty Wkr; Hon Rl; Sct Actv; Stu Cncl; FTA; Mth Clb; Spn Clb; Ctrl Mich Univ; Math.

EDWARDS, MARY; Anderson HS; Anderson, IN; 71/430 Cls Rep Soph Cls; Cl Rep Jr Cls; Cmnty Wkr; Girl Scts; Hon Rl; Hosp Ade; Trk; 4-H Awd; Pres Awd; Purdue Univ; Acctg.

EDWARDS, MARY B; Cardinal Mooney HS; Youngstown, OH; 70/288 Cmp Fr Grls; Cmnty Wkr; Hon Rl; Hosp Ade; Off Ade; Red Cr Ade; Sch Pl; Lat Clb; Pep Clb; Ten; Bowling Awd 1st Pl 78; Univ Of Virginia; Sci.

EDWARDS, MONICA; Covington HS; Covington, IN; 2/115 Sec Band; Chrh Wkr; Hon Rl; Fr Clb; Pep Clb; Letter Trk; Chrldng; Flute Soloist Dist & State 1st; French Awd; Honor Jacket; Purdue Univ; Engr.

EDWARDS, PAMELA; Yale HS; Goodells, MI; 5/162 Am Leg Aux Girls St; Hon Rl; NHS; Off Ade; Rptr Sch Nwsp; 4-H; Pep Clb; Letter Bsbl; Letter Chrldng; 4-H Awd;.

EDWARDS, PERCOLA; Cass Tech HS; Detroit, MI; Chrh Wkr; Hon Rl; NHS; Off Ade; FBLA; OEA; St Bus Offc Educ Club V Pres 1978; Jr Offc Trng Soc Treas 1978; Soc Of Cass Offc Trng Stus Prlmntrn 1978; Univ Of Michigan; Bus Admin.

EDWARDS, REBECCA; Eastern Local HS; Long Bottom, OH; 2/64 Band; Cmnty Wkr; Girl Scts; Hon Rl; Lbry Ade; NHS; Off Ade; Sch Mus; Sct Actv; Rptr Sch Nwsp; St 4 H Exch Delegate; Ohio St Conservation Camp Cnty Delegate; Coll.

EDWARDS, RICHARD; Triad HS; Cable, OH; Band; Chrs; Hon Rl; Sch Pl; 4-H; Twrlr; 4-H Awd; Clark Tech Coll; Exec Sec.

EDWARDS, RICKY; Greenfield Central HS; Greenfield, IN; Chrs; Yth Flsp; 4-H; FFA; Bsktbl; Ftbl; Trk; 4-H Awd; Pur Univ; Agri.

EDWARDS, SALLY; Carman Sr HS; Flint, MI; Letter Band; Hon Rl; Off Ade; OEA; Bsktbl; Crs Cntry; Trk; Chrldng; GAA; PPFtbl; Mott Cmnty Coll; Criminal Justice.

EDWARDS, STEVE; Pinconning HS; Pinconning, MI; 5/254 Pres Jr Cls; Band; Hon Rl; NHS; Stu Cncl; Coach Actv; DAR Awd; Bsbl All Confrnc Regnl Champs 77 78 & 79; Bsktbl Captn Dist Champs 78; Ftbl Captn All Confrnc 77 78 & 79; Michigan Tech Univ.

EDWARDS, SUSAN J; Wahama HS; New Haven, WV; Pres Frsh Cls; Cls Rep Frsh Cls; Cls Rep Soph Cls; Hon Rl; Lbry Ade; NHS; Off Ade; Ed Yrbk; FHA; Pep Clb; Coll.

EDWARDS, SUZANNE; Struthers HS; Struthers, OH; Pres Soph Cls; Band; Drm Mjrt; Drama Clb; FNA; Pep Clb; Spn Clb; Univ; Law.

EDWARDS, VERNA; John Adams HS; Cleveland, OH; VP Sr Cls; Band; Chrs; Chrh Wkr; Hon Rl; Jr NHS; NHS; Orch; Sch Pl; Gov Hon Prg Awd; Coll; Med.

EFAW, MATTHEW; North Marion HS; Mannington, WV; Am Leg Boys St; Aud/Vis; Hon Rl; NHS; Letter Bsktbl; Ftbl; IM Sprt; Am Leg Awd; DAR Awd; Wv Univ.

EFAW, TIMOTHY; Mannington HS; Mannington, WV; Hon Rl; 4-H; FFA; Air Force.

EFFINGER, MICHAEL; William Henry Harrison HS; Evansville, IN; Boy Scts; Hon Rl; Sct Actv; Ger Clb; Letter Wrstlng; Cit Awd; JETS Awd; Univ.

EFTA, THOMAS; Bishop Watterson HS; Columbus, OH; 17/249 Chrh Wkr; Hon Rl; Sch Nwsp; IM Sprt; Ohio St Univ; Engr.

EGAN, KATHLEEN E; Morton Sr HS; Hammond, IN; 8/436 Pres Frsh Cls; Pres Soph Cls; Hon Rl; Natl Forn Lg; Chmn NHS; Pres Quill & Scroll; Pres Stu Cncl; Ed Yrbk; Tmr; Dnfth Awd; Univ; Engr.

EGAN, ROY; Anderson HS; Cincinnati, OH; Aud/Vis; Hon Rl; Rptr Sch Nwsp; Ger Clb; College; Elec.

EGAN, THERESA M; Carl Brablec HS; Roseville, MI; Band; Hon Rl; Stu Cncl; Sci Clb; Trk; Chrldng; Michigan St Univ; Fine Arts.

EGBERT, DALE; Valley HS; Lucasville, OH; Band; Boy Scts; Sct Actv; Univ; Agri Tech.

EGBERT, LOIS; Valley HS; Lucasville, OH; Band; Chrs; Hon Rl; NHS; FHA; Mas Awd; E Kentucky Univ; Nursing.

EGELER, DAVE; Leland Public HS; Leland, MI; 8/34 Cls Rep Sr Cls; NHS; Red Cr Ade; Treas Stu Cncl; Rptr Yrbk; Rptr Sch Nwsp; Bsbl; Univ Of Michigan; Medicine.

EGERT, DEBBIE; Genoa Area HS; Millbury, OH; Cl Rep Jr Cls; Band; Chrh Wkr; Drl Tm; Hon Rl; Sch Pl; Stu Cncl; Yrbk; Rptr Sch Nwsp; Chrldng; Mercy Schl Of Nursing; RN.

EGG, LAURA; Marion Harding HS; Marion, OH; 10/450 FCA; Lit Mag; NHS; Sprt Ed Yrbk; Pep Clb; Mgrs; PPFtbl; Oh Bd Of Regents Hon For Otstndng Acad Achvmnt 79; Miami Univ; Eng.

EGGEMAN, CATHERINE; Delphos St John HS; Delphos, OH; 50/140 Hon Rl; Stg Crw; Rptr Sch Nwsp; FTA; Leo Clb; Trk; Coach Actv; IM Sprt; The Hauss Helms Schlrshp 79; Basic Educ Opportunity Grant 79; Northwestern Bus Coll; Acctg.

EGGERT, SCARLETT; Alter HS; Dayton, OH; Chrs; Chrh Wkr; Drl Tm; Girl Scts; Sch Mus; Spn Clb; Columbus Symphony Orch Concerto Comttn Winner 78; Amer Music Schslhp Asst Piano Natl Winner 72 73 & 74; Cincinnati Univ; Music.

EGGERT, SUSAN; Vly Forge Sr HS; Parma Hgts, OH; 177/777 Chrs; Girl Scts; Hon Rl; Sct Actv; Yth Flsp; Spn Clb; Coll; Spanish.

EGLOFF, JEFFREY H; Van Buren HS; Carbon, IN; 6/94 Band; Hon Rl; NHS; Yth Flsp; Key Clb; Mth Clb; Pep Clb; Sci Clb; Spn Clb; Crs Cntry; Purdue Univ; Elec Engr Tech.

EGNEW, TERESA; Central HS; Evansville, IN; Chrs; Drl Tm; NHS; 4-H; Lat Clb; Pep Clb; Letter Gym; Pom Pon; Excllnc In Schlshp 75 79; Purdue Univ; Vet Med.

EGOLF, CHRIS; Columbia City Joint HS; Columbia City, IN; Boy Scts; Sct Actv; Sci Clb; Purdue Univ; Forestry.

EGOLF, LISA; West Geauga HS; Novelty, OH; Band; Chrs; Chrh Wkr; Hon Rl; Yth Flsp; Rptr Sch Nwsp; Pep Clb; IM Sprt; PPFtbl; Twrlr; College; Elem Educ.

EGTVEDT, RICHARD T; Comstock Park HS; Comstock Pk, MI; Am Leg Boys St; Boy Scts; Chrs; NHS; Pol Wkr; Sch Mus; Letter Trk; Mic State Univ; Intl Relations.

EHINGER, LIANE; Bishop Dwenger HS; Ft Wayne, IN; Band; Chrs; Girl Scts; Hosp Ade; JA; Orch; Sch Mus; Sch Nwsp; 4-H; Twrlr; Mc Connel School Inc; Airln Stwrdss.

EHINGER, RAND; Fremont HS; Fremont, IN; 10/75 Hon Rl; Ftbl; Wrstlng;.

EHMER, CHRIS; Fairless HS; Beach City, OH; Pres Jr Cls; Am Leg Aux Girls St; Chrs; Girl Scts; Hon Rl; NHS; Y-Teens; Rptr Yrbk; Pres 4-H; FHA; 4 H St Ldrshp Camp 78; Stark Tech Bus Schl; Sec.

EHMER, JOAN M; Tuslaw HS; N Lawrence, OH; 20/180 Cls Rep Frsh Cls; Cls Rep Soph Cls; Sec Jr Cls; VP Sr Cls; Hon Rl; Jr NHS; NHS; Stu Cncl; Y-Teens; FHA; Vocational Schl; Nursing.

EHMKE, SHEILA A; Parkersburg HS; Parkersburg, WV; 22/715 AFS; Chrs; Chrh Wkr; Cmnty Wkr; Hon Rl; Mdrgl; Quill & Scroll; Sch Pl; Ed Sch Nwsp; Drama Clb; Parkersburg Comm Coll; Sec.

EHN, GARY; Engadine Consolidated HS; Gould City, MI; Hon Rl; Pres Stu Cncl; Yrbk; Sch Nwsp; Ftbl; Natl Merit Schl; Lake Superior St Coll; Bus Mgmt.

EHR, THOMAS; Bishop Foley HS; Troy, MI; Pres Sr Cls; Hon Rl; Stu Cncl; Rptr Sch Nwsp; Rdo Clb; Spn Clb; Bsktbl; Ftbl; Univ Of Mic; Bus Admin.

EHRET, JOAN; Perry HS; Canton, OH; Am Leg Aux Girls St; Chrh Wkr; Girl Scts; Hon Rl; Hosp Ade; Lit Mag; NHS; Off Ade; Fr Clb; Pep Clb; Nursing Schl; Nursing.

EHRET, KARRE; Canton South HS; Canton, OH; Chrs; Hon Rl; NHS; Sch Mus; Sch Pl; Drama Clb; Rdo Clb; Ursuline College; Fine Arts.

EHRHART, JEFFREY; Salem Sr HS; Salem, OH; 1/300 Hon Rl; Treas Mth Clb; Spn Clb; Brooks Contest Writing Awd; Hi Tri Hnr Soc; Coll; Comp Sci.

EHRMAN, BRIAN; Buckeye Central HS; New Washington, OH; 3/88 Band; Chrs; Chrh Wkr; Hon Rl; NHS; Sch Mus; Stg Crw; IM Sprt; Cit Awd; Natl Merit Ltr; All Oh St Fair Band 79; 4th Pl BGSU Dist & Hon Mention St Of Oh 79; Chem Div 3 In Oh Test Of Schlst Achvmt; Univ; Dent.

EHRMAN, JOANNE; Nordonia HS; Macedonia, OH; 40/412 Chrh Wkr; Hosp Ade; Jr NHS; Pres NHS; Pep Clb; Capt Chrldng; Pride Awrd Of Nordonia HS 78; Letter In Cheerldr 79; Homerm Rep 78; Mt St Joseph Univ; Nursing.

EHRMAN, JODY; Col Crawford HS; Galion, OH; Chrs; FCA; Hon Rl; Stu Cncl; Yth Flsp; Sprt Ed Yrbk; FHA; Pep Clb; Letter Trk; Letter Chrldng; Spring Arbor Coll; Phys Ed.

EHRNSBERGER, MARK; Margaretta HS; Bay View, OH; Boy Scts; Hon Rl; Opt Clb Awd; Eagle Scout 76; Youth Of The Month Optimist 77; Terra Tech Coll; Elec.

EHRSAM, CATHY L; Robert S Rogers HS; Toledo, OH; 2/412 Cls Rep Sr Cls; Chrs; Hon Rl; Jr NHS; NHS; Stu Cncl; VP Mth Clb; Sci Clb; Spn Clb; Chrldng; Ohio State Univ.

EHRSAM, ERIC; Cascade HS; Danville, IN; 130138 FBLA; Spn Clb; Ftbl; Letter Wrstlng; IUPUI; Dent.

EIB, LARRY; Springfield HS; Springfield, MI; Cl Rep Jr Cls; Pres Sr Cls; Am Leg Boys St; Chrs; Hon Rl; JA; Sch Mus; Sch Pl; Stg Crw; Treas Stu Cncl; Dale Carnegie Grad Schlrshp From Jr Ach; Natl Jr Ach Conf; Suomi Coll; Acctg.

EICH, KIM; Plymouth HS; Plymouth, IN; Band; Drl Tm; Yth Flsp; Drama Clb; Gym; Swmmng; Pom Pon; Tmr; Coll; Sci.

EICHELBERGER, JULIE; Seton HS; Cinti, OH; 30/300 Hon Rl; Jr NHS; Sch Mus; Fr Clb; Pep Clb; Cit Awd; Univ.

EICHELBERGER, KAY; Wynford HS; Bucyrus, OH; 4/140 Chrh Wkr; Hon Rl; Lbry Ade; NHS; Off Ade; Sch Pl; Rptr Sch Nwsp; VP FHA; Sec Spn Clb; Am Leg Awd; Ohio St Univ; Elem Ed.

EICHENAUER, TODD; Sidney HS; Sidney, OH; Chrs; NHS; Orch; Sch Mus; Stu Cncl; Pres Yth Flsp; Bsbl; Univ; Civil Engr.

EICHENBERG, LINDA; Chippewa Hills HS; Mecosta, MI; Hon Rl; Rptr Sch Nwsp; Sch Nwsp; Chrldng; College; Fashion Design.

EICHENBERGER, WILLIAM; New Albany HS; New Albany, IN; 15/565 Aud/Vis; Boy Scts; Hon Rl; NHS; Sch Mus; Sch Pl; Sct Actv; Ger Clb; Sci Clb; U S Air Force Acad; Elec.

EICHER, MELISSA J; Catholic Central HS; Steubenvll, OH; Band; Girl Scts; Hosp Ade; NHS; Sch Mus; Rptr Yrbk; Fr Clb; Treas FDA; Typng Awd 78; Univ; Pre Med.

EICHHORN, DONALD; Taylor HS; Cincinnati, OH; Hon Rl; Carpenter.

EICHKORN, LINDA; Douglas Macarthur HS; Saginaw, MI; Band; Chrs; Hon Rl; NHS; Sch Nwsp; Trk; College; Engr.

EICHLER, REBECCA; Eau Claire HS; Eau Claire, MI; Band; Hon Rl; Red Cr Ade; Rptr Yrbk; Letter Crs Cntry; Letter Trk; Chrldng; IM Sprt; Pom Pon; Grand Valley State College; Spts Med.

EICHORN, CONNIE; Shepherd HS; Blanchard, MI; Chrs; Girl Scts; Hon Rl; Hosp Ade; Lbry Ade; Off Ade; Yrbk; Rptr Sch Nwsp;.

EICHORN, RICHARD; Harbor HS; Ashtabula, OH; 12/182 Boy Scts; FCA; Hon Rl; JA; NHS; Sch Mus; Stu Cncl; Fr Clb; Pres Mth Clb; Ohi State Univ; Arch.

EICHORST, JIM; Clay HS; South Bend, IN; 182/467 Boy Scts; Hon Rl; Off Ade; Lat Clb; Letter Hockey; Wrstlng; Coach Actv; College.

EICHORST, JOHN P; Clay HS; South Bend, IN; 6/409 Jr NHS; NHS; Lat Clb; Letter Ftbl; Letter Hockey; Capt Lcrss; Kiwan Awd; Natl Merit Ltr; Outstndng Sci Stu; Hoosier St Schlr; Grad Summa Cum Laude; Rose Hulman Inst Of Tech; Engr.

EICKENHORST, FRANK; William Mason HS; Mason, OH; Band; Chrh Wkr; Hon Rl; Sch Mus; Yth Flsp; IM Sprt; Pres Of Band 79; Univ; Pre Law.

EICKHOFF, EDWARD; Lincoln Sr HS; Warren, MI; 2/316 Trs Sr Cls; Am Leg Aux Girls St; Chrh Wkr; Cmnty Wkr; Hon Rl; Mdrgl; NHS; DAR Awd; Natl Merit Schl; Phi Beta Kappa; Oakland Univ; Busns Mgmt.

EICKHOFF, LESLIE A; Withrow HS; Cincinati, OH; Chrs; Lbry Ade; Conservatory Of Music; Vocal Music.

EICKHOLT, KEN; Clio HS; Clio, MI; Chrh Wkr; Hon Rl; Jr NHS; Letter Crs Cntry; Ftbl; Letter Glf; Letter Trk; IM Sprt; Aquinas College.

EIFERT, GREG; Bishop Dwenger HS; Ft Wayne, IN; Stu Cncl; Key Clb; Capt Bsktbl; Trk; Univ; Bus.

EIFERT, LAURA; Bishop Watterson HS; Worthington, OH; Chrs; Hon Rl; Jr NHS; Sch Pl; Fr Clb; Lat Clb; Capt Chrldng; Scr Kpr; Univ Of Dayton; Busns.

EIFRID, ANGELA; Bishop Luers HS; Ftwayne, IN; Chrh Wkr; Hon Rl; Bsktbl; Trk; IM Sprt; PPFtbl; Scr Kpr; Univ; Mktg.

EIKEN, AMY; West Carrollton HS; Dayton, OH; 17/418 Am Leg Aux Girls St; Hon Rl; Jr NHS; NHS; Orch; Sch Mus; Sch Pl; Vllybl Ltr 78; Sftbl Ltr 78 & 79; Univ; Zoology.

EIKENBERY, BARBARA J; Tri Village HS; New Paris, OH; 15/62 Am Leg Aux Girls St; Band; Chrs; Chrh Wkr; Hon Rl; Jr NHS; Lbry Ade; NHS; Off Ade; Sch Pl;.

EILE, LORE; Unionville Sebewaing HS; Bay Port, MI; Chrh Wkr; Hon Rl; Sch Nwsp; 4-H; FHA; Cit Awd; 4-H Awd; Univ; Drawing.

EILE, LORE; Unionvle Sebewaing Area HS; Bay Port, MI; Chrh Wkr; Hon Rl; NHS; Yrbk; Sch Nwsp; 4-H; FHA; 4-H Awd; Univ; Fshn Illustration.

EILERMAN, KIMBERLY; Delphos Saint Johns HS; Delphos, OH; 12/139 Hon Rl; Hosp Ade; Jr NHS; NHS; Sch Pl; Sch Nwsp; FTA; Coach Actv; Bowling Green Univ; Acctg.

EILSIZOR, BETH; Urbana HS; Urbana, OH; 20/225 Chrs; Chrh Wkr; Lit Mag; NHS; Sch Mus; Rptr Sch Nwsp; VP Fr Clb; Mth Clb; Pres Rdo Clb; DAR Awd; Wright State Univ; Communication.

EIMER, MARK; Carroll HS; Dayton, OH; 35/285 Hon Rl; Ftbl; Trk; College; Engr.

EING, AMY; Groveport Madison HS; Columbus, OH; Cls Rep Frsh Cls; Band; Cmp Fr Grls; Girl Scts; Hon Rl; NHS; Stg Crw; Stu Cncl; Sch Nwsp; 4-H; Airline Stwd.

EINSELE, MARK; Hammond Tech Voc HS; Hammond, IN; Aud/Vis; Purdue Univ.

EIPPERT, JEANINE; Bay HS; Bay Vill, OH; 43/400 AFS; Chrh Wkr; Hon Rl; NHS; Quill & Scroll; Sch Nwsp; Principia Coll; Bus Mgmt.

EISBRENNER, LAURA; Watervliet HS; Watervliet, MI; 6/90 VP Frsh Cls; Trs Sr Cls; Cls Rep Sr Cls; Band; Chrs; Hon Rl; NHS; Sch Mus; Stu Cncl; Rptr Yrbk; Frederic Chopin Piano Awd 79; Stud Rep To Wateruliet Schl Bd 78; Univ Of Mi Alumni Schlrshp 79; Michigan St Univ; Jrnlsm.

EISCH, CATHERINE; Arthur Hill HS; Saginaw, MI; 63/552 Hon Rl; NHS; Off Ade; Pep Clb; Sci Clb;

Natl Merit Ltr; Saginaw City Employees Schlrshp; Delta Comm Coll.

EISCHER, KAREN; Frankenmuth HS; Bridgeport, MI; 1/180 Sec Soph Cls; Trs Jr Cls; Trs Sr Cls; Val; Am Leg Aux Girls St; Chrs; Debate Tm; FCA; Hon Rl; Natl Forn Lg; Univ Of Michigan; Nursing.

EISEL, MICHELLE; Rossford HS; Rossford, OH; 3/147 Chrs; Chrh Wkr; Hon Rl; Hosp Ade; NHS; Rptr Yrbk; Drama Clb; Spn Clb; Dnfth Awd; Univ Of Toledo; Nursing.

EISELE, ELLEN; Fowlerville HS; Fowlerville, MI; 3/170 Hon Rl; NHS; Pres Yth Flsp; 4-H; Fr Clb; FFA; 4-H Awd; College; Sci.

EISELE, T; North Huron HS; Kinde, MI; Cls Rep Frsh Cls; Sec Soph Cls; Hon Rl; Stu Cncl; Mich Tech Univ; Math.

EISENACH, RANDALL; Northrop HS; Ft Wayne, IN; 6/589 Hon Rl; Mth Clb; Sci Clb; C of C Awd; Rose Hulman Inst Of Tech; Elec Engr.

EISENGRUBER, PETER; Grosse Pointe North HS; Harper Wds, MI; FCA; Lbry Ade; NHS; Letter Ten; Coach Actv; Univ.

EISENHOUR, GERALD; Keyser HS; Keyser, WV; 1/248 Chrh Wkr; NHS; Lat Clb; Mth Clb; Bausch & Lomb Awd; God Cntry Awd; E Mennonite Coll; Chem.

EISENLOFFEL, KAREN; Malabar HS; Mansfield, OH; 2/230 Sal; Chrh Wkr; Hon Rl; NHS; Yrbk; Mth Clb; NCTE; Natl Merit Ltr; Ohio St Univ; Archt.

EISENMAN, WILLIA; Marietta Sr HS; Marietta, OH; 24/430 Debate Tm; NHS; VP Ger Clb; Key Clb; Letter Ftbl; Natl Merit SF; Oh St Dept Of Ed Martin Essex Schl For The Gftd 78; Herfurth Schlrshp Univ Of Cin 79; Univ Of Cincinnati; Mech Engr.

EISENMANN, CHERYL; Summerfield HS; Petersburg, MI; 3/81 Band; Chrs; Chrh Wkr; Cmnty Wkr; Hon Rl; NHS; Stg Crw; Spn Clb; Bsktbl; Trk; Amer Literature Awd; Spring Arbor Coll; Social Worker.

EISENMANN, DEBORAH L; Summerfield HS; Petersburg, MI; 2/80 Band; Chrh Wkr; Hon Rl; Treas NHS; Sch Pl; Pres Yth Flsp; Rptr Yrbk; Spn Clb; Bsktbl; Trk; Spring Arbor Coll; Pre Med.

EISENSTEIN, DAVID; Bexley HS; Bexley, OH; Hon Rl; Mth Clb; Sci Clb; Capt Ten; Univ; Med.

EISENTROUT, SYLVIA J; University HS; Morgantown, WV; Pres Jr Cls; Band; Chrs; Hon Rl; Treas Jr NHS; NHS; Yrbk; FBLA; Pep Clb; Sci Clb; Trade Schl; Flight Attendt.

EISER, GARY E; Purcell HS; Cincinnati, OH; 1/164 Pres Soph Cls; VP Sr Cls; Am Leg Boys St; Hon Rl; NHS; Ed Yrbk; Sch Nwsp; Am Leg Awd; Natl Merit Ltr; Rotary Awd; Cleveland Inst Of Art; Graphic Dsgn.

EISER, TOM; Purcell HS; Cincinnati, OH; 4/180 Cls Rep Frsh Cls; Trs Soph Cls; Cl Rep Jr Cls; Hon Rl; Mod UN; Stu Cncl; Lat Clb; Mth Clb; Letter Crs Cntry; IM Sprt; Univ Of Dayton; Math.

EISINGER, TONI; South Lyon HS; New Hudson, MI; 66/265 Bsbl; Bsktbl; Ferris St Coll; Bio.

EISMEIER, LAURIE E; Greenville HS; Greenville, MI; Debate Tm; Girl Scts; Hon Rl; Natl Forn Lg; Sch Pl; Sct Actv; Stg Crw; Drama Clb; Fr Clb; Ten; W Mich Univ; Communications.

EISSLER, PAULA; Central HS; Evansville, IN; 31/528 Cls Rep Soph Cls; Chrh Wkr; Hon Rl; NHS; Off Ade; Stu Cncl; Ger Clb; Mth Clb; Scr Kpr; Univ Of Evansville; Comp Sci.

EITING, LINDA; Minster HS; Minster, OH; 42/80 Sec Jr Cls; Chrs; Chrh Wkr; Cmnty Wkr; Hon Rl; Sch Mus; Stg Crw; Sch Nwsp; 4-H; FHA; Bus Schl; Sec.

EITMAN, STEPHEN; William Henry Harrison HS; Evansville, IN; Sch Mus; Sch Pl; Yth Flsp; Rptr Sch Nwsp; Drama Clb; Pres Ger Clb; God Cntry Awd; Natl Merit Ltr;.

EITNIEAR, VICKI; Hesperia HS; Hesperia, MI; 9/79 Trs Jr Cls; Trs Sr Cls; Hon Rl; Rptr Sch Nwsp; Capt Bsktbl; Letter Trk; Sci Awd For Highest Grade In Class; Typing Awd; Softball; Muskegon Busns Coll; Legal Sec.

EITZMAN, KATHY; Edgerton HS; Edgerton, OH; 4/82 Chrs; Hon Rl; NHS; Sec Spn Clb; GAA; Capt Mat Maids; Busns Schl; Acctg.

EIX, LAURA; Northrop HS; Ft Wayne, IN; 81/581 Hon Rl; Hosp Ade; JA; Lbry Ade; Off Ade; Cit Awd; Summer Hnrs Seminary Awdsd Chem At ISU 79; Achvmnt Awd In 1st Yr Spch 79; Achvmnt Awd In Chem 79; Indiana Univ; Chem.

EKDOM, D; Cedar Springs HS; Cedar Spgs, MI; 1/189 Sec Jr Cls; Band; Hon Rl; Jr NHS; NHS; Yth Flsp; Yrbk; Coll.

EKLEBERRY, TINA; Mohawk HS; Sycamore, OH; Band; Chrs; Hon Rl; Sch Mus; Sch Pl; Y-Teens; Pep Clb; Trk; Chrldng; College; Chiropractor.

ELAM, ANDREA; Franklin HS; Franklin, OH; Chrs; Hon Rl; Hosp Ade; Jr NHS; NHS; Pep Clb; Bsktbl; Univ; Exec Sec.

ELAM, GARRETT J; Greencastle HS; Greencastle, IN; 60/170 Pres Jr Cls; VP Sr Cls; JA; Pres Key Clb; Pep Clb; Sci Clb; Bsbl; IM Sprt; Scr Kpr; Tmr; Univ; Bus.

ELAM, LISA; Warren County Joint Voc Schl; Centerville, OH; Sec Jr Cls; Trs Jr Cls; Rptr Yrbk; OEA; Bsktbl; PPFtbl; Stu Of The Mnth 1979; Schl Queen For OEA 1979; Bus Schl; Leg Sec.

ELAM, LISA L; Clay Rural HS; Portsmouth, OH; 2/70 Sec Jr Cls; Pres Sr Cls; Sal; Band; Chrs; Chrh Wkr; Cmnty Wkr; Hon Rl; Hosp Ade; Lbry Ade; Ohio St Univ; Pre Med.

ELBERT, FRED; Lexington HS; Mansfield, OH; 20/271 Boy Scts; NHS; Orch; Sct Actv; Ger Clb; Mth Clb; Elk Awd; College; Sci.

EL CAMPBELL, THERESA E; Hammond HS; Hammond, IN; Cls Rep Frsh Cls; Cls Rep Soph Cls; Cl Rep Jr Cls; Chrs; Girl Scts; Jr NHS; Sch Mus; Sch Pl; Stg Crw; Tmr; In Univ N W Hon Stud Study Abroad France 79; Univ; Math.

ELCHERT, BRENDA J; Calvert HS; Tiffin, OH; Cl Rep Jr Cls; Hon Rl; JA; Sch Pl; Sct Actv; Stu Cncl; JA Awd; Bus Schl.

ELCHERT, GERALD; Calvert HS; Tiffin, OH; Chrs; Sch Mus; Sch Pl; Letter Ftbl; Voc Sch; Bldr.

ELCHERT, J; Calvert HS; Tiffin, OH; Sec Sr Cls; Chrs; Hon Rl; Jr NHS; Sch Pl; Stg Crw; Stu Cncl; Mth Clb; Pep Clb;.

ELCHERT, THERESA; Tiffin Calvert HS; Tiffin, OH; Cls Rep Frsh Cls; Cls Rep Soph Cls; Pres Jr Cls; Pres Sr Cls; Chrs; NHS; Sch Mus; Stu Cncl; Pep Clb; Chrldng; Bowling Green Univ; Elem Educ.

ELDER, CHARLES R; Liberty HS; Youngstown, OH; 9/246 Band; Hon Rl; Hosp Ade; NHS; Sch Pl; Letter Ten; Am Leg Awd; Natl Merit SF; Pres Of Grtr Ohio Cncl Regn BBYO 1978; Chrmn Of Jewsh Fed Of Youngstown 1977; Univ; Med.

ELDER, DAVID; Washington HS; South Bend, IN; 114/355 Hon Rl; Pep Clb; Purdue Univ; Elec Engr.

ELDER, DIANNA; Churubusco HS; Churubusco, IN; Letter Chrs; FCA; Hon Rl; NHS; Sch Mus; Drama Clb; FTA; Lat Clb; Pep Clb; Chrldng; Spec Awrd For Part In Hello Dolly 79; Univ.

ELDER, DOREEN; South Bend Washington HS; South Bend, IN; 101/355 Hon Rl; Spn Clb; Univ; Nursing.

ELDER, PATRICE; Oak Hill HS; Oak Hill, WV; 32/250 Band; Chrh Wkr; Hon Rl; Yth Flsp; Drama Clb; 4-H; Fr Clb; Pep Clb; IM Sprt; 4-H Awd; Home Ec Awd 76; Univ; Bus Admin.

ELDON, KAREN; Anderson Sr HS; Anderson, IN; Chrh Wkr; Hon Rl; Off Ade; Spn Clb; Ball St Univ; Spec Ed.

ELDRED, DAVID; Cass Tech HS; Detroit, MI; Drl Tm; ROTC; Yrbk; Fr Clb; Mth Clb; Sci Clb; Univ Of Michigan; Physics.

ELDRED, DEBORAH; Seneca East HS; Willard, OH; 4/90 Cls Rep Frsh Cls; Sec Jr Cls; Chrh Wkr; Cmnty Wkr; Hon Rl; Lbry Ade; Treas NHS; Off Ade; Sch Pl; Stg Crw; Dist & St Sci Fair Superior Rating 76; Readng Cir Awd Stdnt; Amer Lgn Test Top Stdnt In Sr Cls & Schl 79; Ohio Northern Univ; Pharm.

ELDREDGE, DARE; Pontiac Central HS; Sylvan Lk, MI; NHS; Sct Actv; Stu Cncl; Yth Flsp; Glf; Ten; Mich State Univ; Engr.

ELDRIDGE, AMBRA; Van Buren HS; Brazil, IN; 4/90 Am Leg Aux Girls St; Hon Rl; NHS; Ed Sch Nwsp; Drama Clb; 4-H; Pres Fr Clb; FTA; Pep Clb; French Awd 79; Jrnlsm Awd 79; Univ; Jrnlsm.

ELDRIDGE, DEE; South Amherst HS; S Amherst, OH; Band; Hon Rl; Lbry Ade; Sch Pl; Stg Crw; Yrbk; Drama Clb; Bsbl; Bsktbl; Coach Actv; Lorain County Comm Coll; Lab Tech.

ELDRIDGE, KEVIN; Lakota HS; W Chester, OH; 10/464 Chrh Wkr; Hon Rl; NHS; FFA; Sci Clb; Univ Of Cincinnati; Pre Med.

ELDRIDGE, MICHAEL; St Johns HS; St Johns, MI; 6/325 Cl Rep Jr Cls; Band; Hon Rl; Orch; Sch Mus; Sch Pl; Pres Drama Clb; Northern Mic Univ.

ELECK, RICHARD; North Royalton HS; N Royalton, OH; 34/286 Aud/Vis; Band; Drm Bgl; Hon Rl; Orch; Rptr Sch Nwsp; Sch Nwsp; Ohio Univ; Music Educ.

ELEGREET, NANCY; Tri Twp HS; Rapid Rvr, MI; Cls Rep Frsh Cls; VP Soph Cls; Cl Rep Jr Cls; Pres Sr Cls; Am Leg Aux Girls St; Band; Girl Scts; Hon Rl; VP Stu Cncl; Rptr Yrbk; Univ; Dentistry.

ELEK, MARCIA; Midview HS; Elyria, OH; 18/250 Band; Girl Scts; Hon Rl; Jr NHS; Mod UN; NHS; Off Ade; Stu Cncl; Rptr Yrbk; Rptr Sch Nwsp; Spitzer Auto Stores Schlrshp 79 80; Schlstc M Awd 79; Lorain Cnty Cmnty Coll; Mdse.

ELENDT, ANNA; Delta Sr HS; Swanton, OH; Chrs; Girl Scts; Hosp Ade; Lbry Ade; Red Cr Ade; 4-H; FFA; Voc Schl; Ag.

ELEY, LINDA; Niles Sr HS; Niles, MI; 6/388 Band; Chrh Wkr; Debate Tm; Hon Rl; NHS; Yrbk; Letter Trk; Opt Clb Awd; Rotary Awd; Rensselaer Math & Sci Awd; W Mi Univ Acad Schlshp; St Of Mi Compttv Schslhp; Western Michigan Univ; Acctg.

ELFERS, MARY; Reading Community HS; Reading, OH; 37/220 Sec Jr Cls; Hon Rl; Spn Clb; Bsktbl; Trk; Raymond Walters; Accounting.

ELHARD, JAKOEB J; Bexley HS; Bexley, OH; Band; Chrs; Hon Rl; Lit Mag; Orch; Quill & Scroll; Sch Mus; Stg Crw; Alternate For Natl Sci Foundation Program; 2nd Prize For Upperclass Poetry In Literature; Superior Rating; Capital Univ; Medicine.

ELHART, RAYETTA; West Ottawa HS; Holland, MI; Cl Rep Jr Cls; Chrs; Girl Scts; NHS; Sch Mus; Stu Cncl; Fr Clb; Ten; Trk; PPFtbl; Univ; Bus.

ELIACHEVSKY, ANDREW; Paul K Cousino Sr HS; Warren, MI; 14/680 Cls Rep Frsh Cls; Band; Boy Scts; Chrs; Chrh Wkr; Hon Rl; Jr NHS; NHS; Stu Cncl; Mth Clb; Schslhp Univ Of Mi Regnts Alumni 79; Univ Of Mi Chancllr Schlshp 79; Univ Of Michigan; Bus Admin.

ELIAS, DAWN; Salem HS; Salem, OH; 15/260 Band; Drm Mjrt; Hon Rl; Off Ade; Sch Mus; Stg Crw; Yrbk; Art Inst Of Atlanta; Intr Dsgn.

ELIAS, JANET; Hoover HS; N Canton, OH; Hon Rl; NHS; Rptr Sch Nwsp; Fr Clb; Sci Clb; Wittenberg Univ; Radiation Med.

ELIAS, MONA; St Francis De Sales HS; Morgantown, WV; Am Leg Aux Girls St; Chrh Wkr; Cmnty Wkr; Hon Rl; NHS; Off Ade; Stg Crw; Treas Drama Clb; Sec Fr Clb; West Virginia Univ; Engr.

ELIAS, RITA; Wheeling Park HS; Wheeling, WV; 11/567 Hon Rl; Hosp Ade; NHS; Stu Cncl; 4-H; Fr Clb; Cit Awd; Dnfth Awd; 4-H Awd; Charting Pin 4 H 75; Stifle 74 & 77; Sociology 78; Univ; Med.

ELIASON, DALE; Brooklyn HS; Brooklyn, OH; Hon Rl; NHS; PAVAS; Eng Clb; Mth Clb; Spn Clb; Gym; Natl Merit Ltr; Kent State; Business Management.

ELIE, LAWRENCE; Escanaba Area Public HS; Escanaba, MI; 74/438 Hon Rl; Letter Crs Cntry; Trk; Letter Wrstlng; Coach Actv; Mst Imprvd Wrstlr 79; Univ; Physics.

ELIJAH, BRIDGET F; South Newton HS; Bloomington, IN; 11/119 Chrs; Chrh Wkr; Girl Scts; Hon Rl; NHS; Quill & Scroll; Sch Pl; Yrbk; Lat Clb; Pep Clb; Indiana Univ; Occup Ther.

ELIOPOULOS, JANET; Andrean HS; Cary, IN; Chrh Wkr; Hon Rl; Jr NHS; Pol Wkr; Treas Yth Flsp; GAA; Purdue Univ; Fashion Mdse.

ELIOPULOS, KATHY; Orchard View HS; Muskegon, MI; 25/217 Band; Chrs; Chrh Wkr; Hon Rl; Yth Flsp; Muskagon Community Coll; Soc Work.

ELKIN, ELIZABETH; Haworth HS; Kokomo, IN; Pres Frsh Cls; Pres Sr Cls; Jr NHS; NHS; Ger Clb; Letter Trk; Purdue Univ; Comp Prog.

ELKIN, LES; West Lafayette HS; West Lafayette, IN; 62/185 Hon Rl; JA; Letter Wrstlng; JA Awd; Purdue Univ; Bio.

ELKINS, ANGIE; Springs Valley HS; French Lick, IN; 8/97 Trs Jr Cls; Band; Hon Rl; Yth Flsp; VP FHA; Pep Clb; Chrldng; 4-H Awd; Sullivan Jr Coll; Legal Sec.

ELKINS, BOBBI; Spring Lake HS; Spring Lake, MI; Chrs; Chrh Wkr; Hon Rl; Hosp Ade; Yth Flsp; Muskegon Bus; Acctg.

ELKINS, DARLENE; Sherman HS; Ashford, WV; Trs Jr Cls; Chrh Wkr; Cmnty Wkr; Girl Scts; Hon Rl; JA; Sch Pl; Yth Flsp; 4-H; Pep Clb; College; Phys Therapy.

ELKINS, GARRY; Medora HS; Medora, IN; 7/20 VP Jr Cls; Boy Scts; Hon Rl; Sch Pl; Stg Crw; Sci Clb; Capt Bsktbl; Crs Cntry; Letter Trk; Coach Actv; Indust Arts Awd 78 79; Phys Educ Awd 77 78; Perfect Attndnc 78 79; Univ; Bsktbl Coach.

ELKINS, KAREN; Oak Hill HS; Kincaid, WV; 21/200 Hon Rl; NHS; 4-H; FHA; 4-H Awd; Business Schl; Business Admin & Mgt.

ELKINS, KAREN; Parma HS; Parma, OH; Treas Girl Scts; Jr NHS; Quill & Scroll; Sct Actv; Rptr Sch Nwsp; Sch Nwsp; Fr Clb; College; Journalism.

ELKINS, ROBERT E; Champmanville HS; Logan, WV; Cl Rep Jr Cls; Band; Hon Rl; Sct Actv; Beta Clb; Key Clb; Mth Clb; Spn Clb; IM Sprt; All Cnty Bnd; Marshall Univ; Pre Law.

ELKINS, SANDRA; Oak Hill HS; Oak Hill, WV; Band; Cmp Fr Grls; Girl Scts; Hon Rl; NHS; Sch Pl; Drama Clb; Fr Clb; Pep Clb; Sci Clb; College; Chem Engr.

ELKINS, VICKY; Oceana HS; Cyclone, WV; Hon Rl; Sec NHS; Sec Yth Flsp; Yrbk; Sch Nwsp; Letter Bsktbl; GAA; Letter College; Law Enforcement.

ELLER, DEVIN; Decatur Central HS; Indpls, IN; 20/310 Chrs; Cmnty Wkr; Hon Rl; VP JA; Mdrgl; NHS; Off Ade; Sch Mus; Sch Pl; Stg Crw; Ind Univ Purdue; Comp Sci.

ELLER, KATHY; Ashtabula HS; Ashtabula, OH; 78/240 Cls Rep Frsh Cls; Cls Rep Soph Cls; Cl Rep Jr Cls; Cls Rep Sr Cls; Pres AFS; Cmnty Wkr; Lit Mag; Off Ade; Pol Wkr; Sec Stu Cncl; Grand Daughter Of WWI 78; Mbr Of Stud Council Cabinet & Pres 76 80; Ed Of Amer Field Serv Newsletter; Ursuline Coll; Fshn Mdse.

ELLER, KEVIN; Belleville HS; Belleville, MI; 73/479 Band; Boy Scts; Hon Rl; NHS; Ger Clb; Rdo Clb; Frgn Lang Hnr Awd 79; Cert Of Recognitions St Of Mi Comptn Schlrshp Progr 79; Michigan St Univ; Public Rltns.

ELLER, TAMMY; Alcona HS; Hubbard Lake, MI; Band; Girl Scts; Hon Rl; Off Ade; Sch Pl; Stg Crw; 4-H; Pep Clb; Spn Clb; Trk; College; Business.

ELLERBROCK, C; Kalida HS; Columbus Grove, OH; Am Leg Aux Girls St; Band; Hon Rl; NHS; Sch Mus; Sec 4-H; Treas FHA; Pep Clb; Letter GAA; 4-H Awd; Bowling Green St Univ; Med Rec Admin.

ELLERBROCK, SHARON; Miller City HS; Leipsic, OH; VP Frsh Cls; Chrs; Hon Rl; Lbry Ade; NHS; Rptr Yrbk; FHA; 4-H Awd; Natl Merit SF; Tech Schl; Busns.

ELLERBROCK, TONY; Ottawa Glandorf HS; Ottawa, OH; Cls Rep Soph Cls; Chrs; Chrh Wkr; H S Talent Show Winner 76 77 & 78; Church Guitarist Soloist & Song Ldr 74 79; Guitar Instr Mbr Of Bbrshp Cr;.

ELLERBROOK, MIKE; Ottawa Glandorf HS; Glandorf, OH; Cl Rep Jr Cls; Hon Rl; Sci Clb; Spn Clb; Bsbl; Ftbl;.

ELLERSON, SHERRY A; Ypsilanti HS; Ypsilanti, MI; Chrs; Chrh Wkr; Off Ade; ROTC; Chrldng; Scr Kpr; Cleary College.

ELLERT, TED; De Kalb HS; Waterloo, IN; 24/292 Chrs; Chrh Wkr; FCA; Hon Rl; Jr NHS; NHS; Sch Mus; Sch Pl; Stg Crw; Yth Flsp; Luther Coll; Civil Engr.

ELLIFRITT, LAURIE; Washington Irving HS; Clarksburg, WV; Cls Rep Sr Cls; Band; Hon Rl; NHS; Sch Pl; Stu Cncl; Yth Flsp; Leo Clb; West Virginia Univ; Acctg.

ELLIG, JERRY R; St Xavier HS; Cincinnati, OH; 12/264 Cls Rep Soph Cls; Cl Rep Jr Cls; Cls Rep Sr Cls; Hon Rl; Mod UN; NHS; Pol Wkr; Stu Cncl; Rptr Sch Nwsp; Xavier Univ; Econ.

ELLINGER, JOHN; Celina Sr HS; Celina, OH; Band; Hon Rl; Wright St Univ; Engr.

ELLINGTON, JEFFERY; Wilbur Wright HS; Dayton, OH; Aud/Vis; Chrh Wkr; Ftbl; Mgrs; Scr Kpr; Phys Ed 2 Awrd 78; Earth Sci Awrd 79; Elec Engr.

ELLINGTON, JOSALYN; Cedarville HS; Cedarville, OH; VP Chrs; Hon Rl; NHS; Off Ade; Sch Pl; Yth Flsp; Rptr Yrbk; Ed Sch Nwsp; Drama Clb; FBLA; Cedarville Coll; Sec.

ELLIOTT, BARBARA C; Morgan HS; Mc Connelsville, OH; 15/260 Pres Jr Cls; Am Leg Aux Girls St; Hon Rl; Jr NHS; NHS; 4-H; Spn Clb; Coll.

ELLIOTT, CONNIE; Delta HS; Albany, IN; Chrs; DECA; Rdo Clb; Letter Ftbl; Letter Gym; Letter Trk; Chrldng; Univ; Stewardess.

ELLIOTT, DANIEL; Traverse City Sr HS; Traverse City, MI; Hon Rl; Lit Mag; NHS; Rptr Sch Nwsp; Letter Trk; Natl Merit Ltr; Michigan Tech Univ; Engr.

ELLIOTT, DOUGLAS; Van Buren HS; Brazil, IN; 3/85 Band; Hon Rl; Pres NHS; Stu Cncl; VP Key Clb; Pres Spn Clb; Letter Crs Cntry; Letter Trk; College; Med.

ELLIOTT, ERIC; Center Line HS; Warren, MI; Band; Hon Rl; Orch; Michigan Tech Univ; Diesel Mech.

ELLIOTT, GREGORY; Garfield HS; Akron, OH; VP Jr Cls; Drl Tm; Hon Rl; Drama Clb; Ger Clb; OEA; Mas Awd; Bowling Green Univ; Data Proc.

ELLIOTT, JENNIFER; Ashtabula Harbor HS; Ashtabula, OH; 15/197 Pep Clb; Shorthand Awd 78; Econ Awd 79; Hon Mntn In Cmnty Essay Contst 79; Univ; Bus.

ELLIOTT, JOHN; Riverside HS; Degraff, OH; 13/85 Band; Boy Scts; Chrs; Hon Rl; NHS; Sch Pl; Stg Crw; Pep Clb; Spn Clb; Ftbl; College; Math.

ELLIOTT, JON; Cardington Lincoln HS; Cardington, OH; 9/78 Am Leg Boys St; Chrh Wkr; Capt FCA; Hon Rl; NHS; Stg Crw; Stu Cncl; Yth Flsp; Fr Clb; Letter Bsktbl; West Point; Army Officer.

ELLIOTT, KAREN S; Bellefontaine HS; Bellefontaine, OH; 69/250 Chrs; FCA; Hon Rl; Sch Mus; Sch Pl; Drama Clb; Treas OEA; Office Ed Assn Exec Awd; College; Computer Prog.

ELLIOTT, KIM; Northwood HS; Northwood, OH; Am Leg Aux Girls St; Band; Chrs; Girl Scts; Hon Rl; Stu Cncl; Rptr Yrbk; Ed Sch Nwsp; Bsktbl; GAA; Univ; Phys Ed.

ELLIOTT, KIM; Clio HS; Clio, MI; Band; Chrh Wkr; Girl Scts; Sct Actv; Yth Flsp; 4-H; Spn Clb; Concordia College; Deaconess.

ELLIOTT, KIMBERLY; Fountain Ctrl HS; Veedersburg, IN; Bible Coll; Psych.

ELLIOTT, LAURA E; Solon HS; Solon, OH; 88/288 Chrs; Chrh Wkr; Capt Drl Tm; FCA; Hon Rl; Hosp Ade; Sec MMM; Pol Wkr; Sch Mus; Stu Cncl; Univ; Art.

ELLIOTT, LESLEY; Sidney HS; Sidney, OH; Hon Rl; Off Ade; Orch; Stu Cncl; Rptr Yrbk; Letter Trk; Chrldng; Univ; Bus Admin.

ELLIOTT, LORI; West Washington HS; Fredericksburg, IN; 16/99 Band; Hon Rl; Sch Mus; Sch Pl; Drama Clb; Pep Clb; Trk; Chrldng; Twrlr; Univ; Med Tech.

ELLIOTT, MICHAEL; Washington HS; E Chicago, IN; Band; Wrstlng; Purdue Univ; Indus Engr.

ELLIOTT, PAMELA; Wapakoneta HS; Wapakoneta, OH; 78/332 Cl Rep Jr Cls; Chrs; Chrh Wkr; Sch Mus; Stg Crw; 4-H; Pep Clb; Letter Bsktbl; Coach Actv; GAA; Wright State Univ; Special Educ.

ELLIOTT, PATRICIA; Van Buren HS; Findlay, OH; 27/84 Trs Sr Cls; Band; Chrs; Hon Rl; NHS; Sch Mus; Sch Pl; Stg Crw; Yrbk; Sch Nwsp; Exclnt Rtg Sci Cntst 78; Solo Cntst I Rtg 75; Brigham Young Univ; Pblc Rltns.

ELLIOTT, PATRICIA; Central HS; Detroit, MI; 16/549 Chrh Wkr; Michigan St Univ; Engr.

ELLIOTT, ROBERT; Hamilton Taft HS; Hamilton, OH; 4/450 Hon Rl; Jr NHS; NHS; College; Acctg.

ELLIOTT, ROBIN; Crothersville HS; Crothersville, IN; 3/60 Am Leg Aux Girls St; FCA; Hon Rl; NHS; Off Ade; Stu Cncl; Yth Flsp; 4-H; Pep Clb; Letter Trk; College; Acctg.

ELLIOTT, SUZANNE; Valley Forge HS; Parma Hts, OH; 83/803 Band; Chrs; Girl Scts; Hon Rl; NHS; Orch; Stu Cncl; Lat Clb; God Cntry Awd; Kent St Univ; Nursing.

ELLIOTT, TARA; Salem HS; Salem, IN; Band; Chrs; Chrh Wkr; Yth Flsp; Drama Clb; Spn Clb; GAA; College; Gourmet Chef.

ELLIOTT, VALERIE; Loogootee HS; Loogootee, IN; Band; Chrh Wkr; Cmnty Wkr; Hon Rl; Off Ade; Sch Mus; Sch Pl; VP Sct Actv; Drama Clb; Pep Clb; Eng 3 & Spanish 3 Awds Loogootee HS Schlstc Awds Banquet 79; Whow Who In Midwestern HS Frgn Lang 79; Univ Of Evansville; Jrnlsm.

ELLIOTT, WM D; Liberty HS; Girard, OH; Chrh Wkr; Debate Tm; Hon Rl; NHS; Pol Wkr; Ftbl; Wrstlng; U S Air Force.

ELLIS, ALAN M; Washington HS; So Bend, IN; 10/337 Hon Rl; NHS; Letter Bsbl; Merit Awd Eng & Math 77; Coll; Bus Admin.

ELLIS, BRYAN R; Buffalo HS; Kenova, WV; Band; Chrh Wkr; Hon Rl; NHS; Sch Pl; Sprt Ed Sch Nwsp; Sch Nwsp; 4-H; Mth Clb; Sci Clb; Marshall Univ; Chemistry.

ELLIS, CAROLYN; Peru HS; Peru, IN; 35/296 Band; Debate Tm; Hon Rl; Natl Forn Lg; Fr Clb; Indiana Univ; Interpreter.

ELLIS, COURTENAY F; Seven Hills HS; Lexington, KY; 3/55 Hon Rl; Beta Clb; Natl Merit Ltr; Fr Natl Hnr Soc 76 78; Jr Natl Champ 77; Natl Comptn 77 79; Intl Comptn 78 & 79; Univ; Bio.

ELLIS, CYNTHIA K; Springs Valley HS; West Baden, IN; 11/97 Band; Pep Clb; Coach Actv; IM Sprt; Indiana Univ; Pre Med.

ELLIS, DAPHNE; Morgan HS; Mc Connelsville, OH; 35/232 4-H; VP FHA; Bsktbl; IM Sprt; PPFtbl; Twrlr; 4-H Awd; Muskingum Area Tech Coll; Child Dev.

ELLIS, DAVID; Norton HS; Norton, OH; Hon Rl; Akron Univ; Bus Mgmt.

ELLIS, DAVID; Carey HS; Carey, OH; FCA; Hon Rl; Drama Clb; Sci Clb; Bsbl; Letter Ftbl; Letter Socr; Coach Actv; IM Sprt; Outstndng Sales Leader For Courier; Superior Rating In Sci Fair; Ohio St Univ.

ELLIS, DAVID; Farmington HS; Farmington, MI; Ed Yrbk; Rptr Sch Nwsp; Sch Nwsp; Cal State Univ; Journalism.

ELLIS, DEBBIE; Eastbrook HS; Upland, IN; Chrs; FCA; Hon Rl; Off Ade; Stg Crw; Yth Flsp; VP Fr Clb; Pep Clb; Ctrl Wesleyan Coll; Med Tech.

ELLIS, DOREEN; Wintersville HS; Wintersville, OH; Sec Soph Cls; Sec Jr Cls; Band; Drl Tm; Hon Rl; NHS; Sch Mus; Sch Pl; Rptr Yrbk; Drama Clb; College; Dental Hygiene.

ELLIS, ELLA; Pike Central HS; Spurgeon, IN; Chrs; Chrh Wkr; Off Ade; Sch Pl; Stg Crw; Yth Flsp; Drama Clb; FHA; Ten; GAA; Univ; Nurse.

ELLIS, JAMES; Lawrence Central HS; Indianapolis, IN; Am Leg Boys St; Boy Scts; Stg Crw; Letter Trk; College; Acctg.

ELLIS, JANA; Chesapeake HS; Chesapeake, OH; VP Soph Cls; Pres Sr Cls; Band; Drm Mjrt; NHS; Sch Nwsp; Beta Clb; Trk; Vocational School.

ELLIS, JEFF; Holt HS; Holt, MI; 49/322 Letter Bsbl; Letter Ftbl; Coach Actv; IM Sprt; College; Acctg.

ELLIS, KELLI; Houghton Lake HS; Houghton Lk, MI; 19/160 Hon Rl; Jr NHS; NHS; Off Ade; Fr Clb; FHA; Pep Clb; Twrlr; Northern Mic; Nursing.

ELLIS, KELLY; Chesaning Union HS; Chesaning, MI; Band; Hon Rl; Off Ade; FHA; Pom Pon; Ferris State College; Cosmotology.

ELLIS, KIMBERLY; Southmont HS; Crawfordsville, IN; 23/167 Chrs; Hon Rl; Jr NHS; NHS; Stg Crw; Rptr Sch Nwsp; Drama Clb; Sec 4-H; FHA; College; Bus.

ELLIS, LESLIE J; Spring Lake HS; Spring Lake, MI; Chrs; Chrh Wkr; Girl Scts; Lbry Ade; Off Ade; Sch Mus; Sch Pl; Yth Flsp; Spn Clb; Trk; Ambassador Coll; Stewardess.

ELLIS, LINDA; Niles Mc Kinley HS; Niles, OH; 24/342 Band; Chrh Wkr; Capt Debate Tm; Girl Scts; Hon Rl; Natl Forn Lg; NHS; Sch Mus; Sch Pl; Sct Actv; General Motors Inst; Mech Engr.

ELLIS, LISA; Norwalk HS; Norwalk, OH; 11/200 VP Soph Cls; Drl Tm; Hon Rl; Sch Pl; Yth Flsp; Pom Pon; Scr Kpr; College; Physics.

ELLIS, LORRIE; Mattawan HS; Kalamazoo, MI; 4/120 Band; Hon Rl; NHS; Fr Clb; Pep Clb; Letter Chrldng; College; French.

ELLIS, LYNN; Jeffersonville HS; Jeffersonville, IN; Cls Rep Frsh Cls; Band; Drl Tm; FCA; Hon Rl; JA; Yth Flsp; 4-H; Letter Bsktbl; Letter Trk; Purdue Univ; Mech Engr.

ELLIS, MARSHALL; John F Kennedy HS; Taylor, MI; VP Frsh Cls; Trs Frsh Cls; VP Soph Cls; Univ.

ELLIS, MITCHELL F; Bishop Gallagher HS; Detroit, MI; Cls Rep Frsh Cls; Cls Rep Soph Cls; Am Leg Boys St; FCA; Stu Cncl; Bsbl; Bsktbl; Ftbl; Am Leg Awd; Pres Awd; Univ; Acctg.

ELLIS, PATRICK; Msgr John R Hackett HS; Kalamazoo, MI; Boy Scts; Sct Actv; IM Sprt; Natl Merit SF; Western Mic Univ; Ind Engr.

ELLIS, REBECCA; Twin Lakes HS; Monticello, IN; 7/214 Am Leg Aux Girls St; Natl Forn Lg; NHS; Stu Cncl; Mth Clb; Treas Rdo Clb; Letter Bsktbl; Letter Ten; Letter Mgrs; Kiwan Awd; Local 1000.

ELLIS, RONALD E; Okemos HS; Okemos, MI; 1/304 Val; Band; Boy Scts; Drl Tm; Treas NHS; Sch Mus; Yth Flsp; Kiwan Awd; Natl Merit SF; College; Physical Sci.

ELLIS, SALLY; Struthers HS; Struthers, OH; 10/270 Chrs; Hon Rl; Sch Pl; Sprt Ed Yrbk; VP Drama Clb; FTA; Lat Clb; Scr Kpr; Univ; Engr.

ELLIS, SUSAN; Eastern HS; Sardinia, OH; Band; Chrh Wkr; Hon Rl; Sec NHS; Sch Pl; Stu Cncl; Sprt Ed Yrbk; 4-H; VP Fr Clb; Twrlr; Morehead; Design.

ELLIS, TERESA; Morgan HS; Chesterhill, OH; 64/265 Band; Chrh Wkr; Girl Scts; Hon Rl; Off Ade; Stu Cncl; Yth Flsp; Rptr Yrbk; 4-H; Spn Clb; Sec.

ELLIS, TERESA; Man HS; Hunt, WV; 14 VP Sr Cls; Am Leg Aux Girls St; Hon Rl; Off Ade; Sch Pl; Sch Nwsp; Keyettes; Marshall Univ.

ELLIS, THERESA; Michigan Ctr HS; Michigan Center, MI; Cls Rep Soph Cls; Cl Rep Jr Cls; Band; Chrh Wkr; Girl Scts; Hon Rl; Bsktbl; Chrldng; Mgrs; Eastern Michigan Univ; Acctg.

ELLIS, VERNON; Sheridan HS; Somerset, OH; 5/194 Band; Hon Rl; Jr NHS; 4-H; FFA; Ten; IM Sprt; Top Swine Prod FFA 1977; Acctg Awd FFA 1977; Stage Band 1978; Capital Univ; Acctg.

ELLIS, VICTOR; Whitmer HS; Toledo, OH; Stg Crw; Boys Clb Am; DECA; Spn Clb; Letter Trk; IM Sprt; Ohi St; Bus Admin.

ELLIS, WILLIAM; Park Hills HS; Wp Afb, OH; 66/365 Hon Rl; Stu Cncl; Yth Flsp; Letter Glf; Mgrs; U S Air Force Acad; Comp Sci.

ELLISON, BRENDA; Madison Heights HS; Anderson, IN; Lbry Ade; Stu Cncl; Yrbk; OEA; Gym; Trk; Chrldng; Am Leg Awd; Ball St Univ; Tchr.

ELLISON, CHERYL; Immaculata HS; Detroit, MI; 4/100 Chrs; Chrh Wkr; Cmnty Wkr; Hon Rl; NHS; Fr Clb; Cit Awd; Univ Of Michigan; Med.

ELLISON, CHERYL; Evansville Central HS; Evansville, IN; Sec Jr Cls; Am Leg Aux Girls St; NHS; Pol Wkr; Sch Mus; Sch Pl; Stu Cncl; Drama Clb; Vanderbilt Univ; Pre Med.

ELLISON, DEANNE L; Spencer HS; Spencer, WV; 2/153 Sal; Band; Chrh Wkr; Cmnty Wkr; Hon Rl; Hosp Ade; Jr NHS; NHS; Sch Pl; Yth Flsp; SHS Honor Awd; Southwestern Univ; Medicine.

ELLISON, PATRICIA S; Hoover HS; North Canton, OH; 123/422 Cls Rep Frsh Cls; Band; Girl Scts; Hon Rl; Sct Actv; Letter Bsbl; Letter Bsktbl; Univ; Engr.

ELLISON, RUTH; Clinton Prairie HS; Mulberry, IN; 30/90 VP Jr Cls; Hon Rl; Bsktbl; Tmr; Acctg.

ELLISON, THERESA; Linden Mc Kinley HS; Columbus, OH; Hon Rl; JA; FHA; Pep Clb; Nursing.

ELLISTON, CINDY; Maple Valley HS; Nashville, MI; 30/121 Chrh Wkr; Cmnty Wkr; Girl Scts; Hon Rl; Off Ade; Rptr Sch Nwsp; 4-H; Bsbl; Letter Bsktbl; Letter Ten; Mi Bus Schls Assoc Schlrshp 79; Gregg Shorthand Penmanship Awd 78 & 79; Lester Hill On The Job Training Awd; Argubright Bus Coll; Legal Sec.

ELLITHORPE JR, ROBERT; Port Clinton HS; Port Clinton, OH; 65/280 Cls Rep Frsh Cls; Cl Rep Jr Cls; Cls Rep Sr Cls; FCA; Hon Rl; Stu Cncl; Letter Ftbl; Mech Engr.

ELLSWORTH, COLIN M; G P North HS; Grosse Pt Wds, MI; Chrs; FCA; Sch Mus; Yth Flsp; Ger Clb; Ten; Univ.

ELLSWORTH, JANE; Cuyahoga Falls HS; Cuyahoga Falls, OH; 27/807 Band; Chrs; Hon Rl; NHS; Sch Mus; Letter Swmmng; Natl Merit Schl; Univ Of Akron; Music.

ELLSWORTH, JANE E; Cuyahoga Falls HS; Cuyahoga Falls, OH; Band; Chrs; Chrh Wkr; Hon Rl; NHS; Sch Mus; Letter Swmmng; Natl Merit SF; Univ Of Akron; Elem Music Educ.

ELLSWORTH, STEVE; Clio HS; Clio, MI; 75/396 Hon Rl; Sprt Ed Yrbk; Rptr Yrbk; Sprt Ed Sch Nwsp; Rptr Sch Nwsp; Letter Bsktbl; Letter Glf; Natl Merit Schl; Central Michigan Univ; Bus Educ.

ELLWOOD, LIANE; Loy Norrix HS; Kalamzoo, MI; Hon Rl; Fr Clb; Cit Awd; Opt Clb Awd; Univ; Med.

ELMAN, JEFFREY; Timken HS; Canton, OH; Fr Clb; Crs Cntry; Letter Ftbl; College.

ELMORE, HEATHER; Buckhannon Upshur HS; Buckhannon, WV; Am Leg Aux Girls St; FCA; Girl Scts; NHS; Sec Yth Flsp; Bsktbl; Letter Trk; College; Social Sciences.

ELMORE, RHONDA; Jefferson HS; Newport, MI; 56/170 Rptr Sch Nwsp; Michigan St Univ; Journalism.

ELO, PHILIP J; Morton Sr HS; Hammond, IN; 69/485 Pres Soph Cls; Pres Jr Cls; Hon Rl; Sch Nwsp; Letter Bsbl; Letter Bsktbl; IM Sprt; PPFtbl; College; Archt Engr.

ELOWSKY, BETH; Bay City Western HS; Bay City, MI; 41/456 Band; Chrs; Hon Rl; NHS; Sch Mus; Sch Pl; Yth Flsp; Drama Clb; Sec 4-H; IM Sprt; St Of Mi Schlrshp 79; Grad With Hon 79; Concordia Coll; Spanish Tchr.

ELPERS, ALICE A; Central HS; Evansville, IN; 99/480 Cls Rep Soph Cls; Hon Rl; 4-H; Ind State Univ Evansville.

ELPERS, JANE; Logansport HS; Logansport, IN; Hon Rl; Sch Pl; VP OEA; Univ; Bus.

ELPERS, KAREN; North Posey HS; Poseyville, IN; Chrs; Chrh Wkr; Cmnty Wkr; Treas Debate Tm; Hon Rl; Hosp Ade; Treas Natl Forn Lg; Sch Mus; Sch Pl; Stg Crw; Coll; Med Tech.

ELROD, BRAD; Warren Central HS; Indpls, IN; 65/788 Cls Rep Soph Cls; Cl Rep Jr Cls; Cls Rep Sr Cls; Am Leg Boys St; Hon Rl; NHS; Stu Cncl; Key Clb; Pres Pep Clb; Natl Merit Ltr; Purdue; Electrical Engineering.

ELROD, BRENDA; Northfield HS; Wabash, IN; Band; Chrh Wkr; Hon Rl; Natl Forn Lg; NHS; Sch Mus; Sch Pl; Drama Clb; 4-H; Pep Clb; Sec.

ELSASS, TIM; North Canton Hoover HS; North Canton, OH; Chrs; Hon Rl; Stu Cncl; Trk; Had 1 Story & 2 Poem Pub In Mag Such As Free Spirit 79; 5 Time St Medl Awd Champ In Bwling 77 79; Akron Univ; Pro Bowler.

ELSASSER, KATHERINE; Lehman HS; Piqua, OH; 1/97 Sec Soph Cls; Val; Am Leg Aux Girls St; Band; Hon Rl; NHS; Treas 4-H; Bsktbl; Ohio St Univ; Animal Sci.

ELSASSER, THOMAS B; Pleasant HS; Marion, OH; Cls Rep Frsh Cls; VP Jr Cls; FCA; Stu Cncl; Ftbl; Trk; IM Sprt; Bus Schl; Bus Admin.

ELSBURY, CHRISTINE; Warsaw Community HS; Warsaw, IN; 8/400 Band; Hon Rl; Sch Mus; Pep Clb; Spn Clb; Lion Awd; Natl Merit Ltr; College.

ELSEA, JACKIE; Fostoria HS; Fostoria, OH; 10/200 Cls Rep Soph Cls; Cl Rep Jr Cls; Band; Hon Rl; Jr NHS; NHS; Stu Cncl; Y-Teens; Fr Clb; Letter Ten; Ohi State; Dent Hygiene.

ELSENHEIMER, GUY; Pewamo Westphalia Cmnty HS; St Johns, MI; Aud/Vis; Band; Chrs; Chrh Wkr; Hon Rl; Lbry Ade; Orch; PAVAS; Sch Mus; Sch Pl; Lansing Cmnty Coll; Elec.

ELSNER, LAURA; Henryville HS; Borden, IN; 8/70 Cl Rep Jr Cls; Band; Chrh Wkr; Hon Rl; NHS; Off Ade; Red Cr Ade; VP Stu Cncl; Yrbk; Rptr Sch Nwsp; Indiana Univ; Law.

ELSON, ANGELA; Greenville Sr HS; Greenville, OH; 26/360 Chrh Wkr; Hon Rl; NHS; Pol Wkr; Spn Clb; Sinclair Comm Coll; Med Sec.

ELSTEN, BRIAN; Madison Heights HS; Anderson, IN; 7/367 Cl Rep Jr Cls; Am Leg Boys St; Chrh Wkr; Hon Rl; NHS; VP Yth Flsp; Univ; Pharm.

ELSTON, CARMEN; Kearsley HS; Flint, MI; VP Sr Cls; Debate Tm; Hon Rl; Natl Forn Lg; Sch Pl; Pep Clb; Spn Clb; Letter Gym; Mic State; Pre Law.

ELSTON, CYNTHIA; Unionville Sebewaing HS; Unionville, MI; 5/113 Trs Frsh Cls; Cls Rep Soph Cls; Chrs; Chrh Wkr; Hon Rl; NHS; Stu Cncl; Yth Flsp; 4-H; FHA; Univ; Elem Ed.

ELSTON, CYNTHIA; Unionville Sebewaing Sr HS; Unionville, MI; Trs Frsh Cls; Cls Rep Soph Cls; Chrs; Chrh Wkr; Hon Rl; NHS; Stu Cncl; Yth Flsp; 4-H; FHA; College; Elem Ed.

ELSTON, DONNA; Eau Claire HS; Riverside, MI; 3/105 Girl Scts; Hon Rl; NHS; Yth Flsp; Lake Michigan Coll; Commercial Art.

ELSTON, TERESA; Delphi Cmnty HS; Bringhurst, IN; 26/150 Band; Hon Rl; Spn Clb; Letter Bsktbl; Ten; Pres Awd; Univ; Acctg.

ELSWICK, ALAN; Midview HS; Grafton, OH; Hon Rl; Wrstlng; Lorain Cnty Comm College; Accntg.

ELSWICK, JOETTA; St Francis Cabrini HS; Ecorse, MI; Cls Rep Frsh Cls; Band; Off Ade; Trk; IM Sprt; 2 Awd Of Activities 77; Univ Of Michigan; Med.

ELTON, JODY; Norton HS; Clinton, OH; Band; Capt Drl Tm; Girl Scts; NHS; Off Ade; Trk; Univ Of Akron; Comp Sci.

ELTZROTH, CYNTHIA; Peru HS; Peru, IN; 32/260 Hon Rl; JA; Off Ade; GAA; Natl Merit Ltr; Amer Educ Essay Winner 75; Journal Gazette Spelling Bee Winner 78; Purdue Schl Of Sci; Bio Chem.

ELTZROTH, VICKIE; Southwood HS; Wabash, IN; 24/131 Sec Sr Cls; Band; FCA; Hon Rl; Pres Stu Cncl; Yth Flsp; Rptr Sch Nwsp; 4-H; Trk; Capt Pom Pon; Purdue Univ; Vet Tech.

ELVEY, RONALD; Kenowa Hills HS; Grand Rapids, MI; Band; Hon Rl; NHS; College; Engineering.

ELWELL, SANDY; Fowlerville HS; Fowlerville, MI; 6/124.

ELWOOD, ANGELA; Hardin Northern HS; Dunkirk, OH; Chrs; Drm Bgl; Yrbk; FHA; Univ.

ELY, ELIZABETH; Arthur Hill HS; Saginaw, MI; 17/552 NHS; Sch Mus; Sec Stu Cncl; Pres Yth Flsp; Pep Clb; Chrldng; PPFtbl; Cit Awd; Opt Clb Awd; Central Mic Univ; Engr.

ELY, JENNIFER; Fulton Middleton HS; St Johns, MI; 7/98 Rptr Yrbk; 4-H; Letter Bsbl; Bsktbl; Chrldng; Michigan St Univ.

ELY, JON; Charleston HS; Charleston, WV; Am Leg Boys St; Hon Rl; Jr NHS; NHS; Sch Pl; Drama Clb; Sec Lat Clb; Ftbl; Scr Kpr; Natl Merit Ltr; Univ.

ELYA, LORI; High School; Emmett, MI; Girl Scts; Hon Rl; Off Ade; Yrbk; Gym; Chrldng; PPFtbl; Airlines Schl; Transportation.

ELYA, WENDY; William G Mather HS; Munising, MI; Band; Hon Rl; Lbry Ade; Day De Noc; Business.

ELYEA, JANET; Cheboygan Area HS; Cheboygan, MI; 20/108 Hon Rl; Hosp Ade; Off Ade; Red Cr Ade; Sch Pl; Rptr Yrbk; Rptr Sch Nwsp; Fr Clb; Lake Superior St Univ; Med.

ELZINGA, DARRYL; West Ottawa HS; Holland, MI; 2/325 Sal; Band; Hon Rl; Jr NHS; NHS; 4-H; Spn Clb; Letter Swmmng; Letter Ten; Natl Merit Ltr; Hope Coll; Pre Med.

ELZINGA, LORENE S; Holland Christian HS; Zeeland, MI; Band; Chrs; Chrh Wkr; Hosp Ade; Lbry Ade; Off Ade; Ger Clb; Calvin College; Music.

EMBLAD, RITA; L Anse HS; Skanee, MI; 13/103 Hon Rl; NHS; Bsktbl; Trk; Metropolitan St Coll; Acctg.

EMBREY, DAVID; Farwell HS; Farwell, MI; 6/112 Band; Hon Rl; Pol Wkr; Sch Mus; Sch Pl; Stg Crw; Drama Clb; Letter Ftbl; Central Michigan Univ; Comp Sci.

EMELANDA, JAMES; Hudsonville HS; Hudsonville, MI; Band; Univ.

EMELANDER, RONALD; Unity Christian HS; Jenison, MI; Boy Scts; Hon Rl; IM Sprt; Natl Merit Schl; Davenport Coll Of Bus; Acctg.

EMENS, ROBERT; Canfield HS; Canfield, OH; Band; Hon Rl; NHS; Fr Clb; IM Sprt; College; Bus Admin.

EMERICK, DEBBIE; Traverse City HS; Traverse City, MI; Hon Rl; Hosp Ade; FNA; Bsbl; Letter Trk; Nowestern Mic College; Nursing.

EMERICK, WILLIAM; John F Kennedy HS; Taylor, MI; Boy Scts; Chrh Wkr; Hon Rl; Rptr Sch Nwsp; Sch Nwsp; Bsktbl; IM Sprt; Central Michigan Univ; Jrnlsm.

EMERINE, KENNETH R; Arcadia Local HS; Fostoria, OH; 10/62 Band; Hon Rl; NHS; Stg Crw; 4-H; Wrstlng; 4-H Awd;.

EMERSON, JAMES; Moeller HS; Cincinnati, OH; Hon Rl; Lat Clb; Xavier Univ; Accounting.

EMERSON, KATHLEEN; Nitro HS; Nitro, WV; 1/285 Cl Rep Jr Cls; Val; Band; Hon Rl; Jr NHS; NHS; Mth Clb; Sec Sci Clb; Sec Spn Clb; Cit Awd; Marshall Univ; Pre Med.

EMERSON, PAULA; Caledonia Cmnty HS; Caledonia, MI; 20/140 Chrs; Hon Rl; NHS; Glf; Coach Actv; Mgrs; Aquinas Coll; Sci.

EMERSON, SANDRA; Wapakoneta Sr HS; Wapakoneta, OH; Band; Chrh Wkr; Hon Rl; NHS; Sec 4-H; VP Lat Clb; College; Medicine.

EMERY, JANE K; Hagerstown Jr Sr HS; Hagerstown, IN; 8/172 Hon Rl; NHS; Y-Teens; Rptr Yrbk; Fr Clb; FHA; Ball State Univ; Child Care.

EMERY, MARY; Roscommon HS; Roscommon, MI; Hst Frsh Cls; Band; Sch Mus; Stg Crw; Bsbl; Bsktbl; Coach Actv; GAA; Mas Awd; Bsktbl All Confernc 78; Coaching Spec Olympics Bsktbl Cert 78; Masonic Hon Queen Jobs Daughters 78; Univ Of S Florida; Educ For Mental.

EMERY, SANDY; Central HS; Switz City, IN; 3/48 Pres Band; Hon Rl; Lbry Ade; Lit Mag; NHS; Treas 4-H; Treas FHA; Pep Clb; Spn Clb; 4-H Awd; Univ; Nursing.

EMIGH, KEVIN D; Elisabeth Johnson HS; Mt Morris, MI; Chrs; Chrh Wkr; Hon Rl; NHS; Sch Mus; Sch Pl; Univ.

EMINGTON, DOUGLAS; Alcona Community HS; Lincoln, MI; Boy Scts; Chrh Wkr; Cmnty Wkr; Hon Rl; Jr NHS; NHS; Sct Actv; Yth Flsp; Y-Teens; FFA; Adrian Coll; P E.

EMMANOELIDES, DEMETRIOS; Washington HS; E Chicago, IN; Pres Chrh Wkr; FCA; Hon Rl; NHS; Fr Clb; FBLA; FHA; Ftbl; Capt Socr; JA Awd; Sci Fair; Art Awrd; Indiana St Univ; Acctg.

EMMEL, SHANNON; Lincoln HS; Gypsy, WV; Band; Boy Scts; Chrh Wkr; Girl Scts; Hon Rl; Yth Flsp; Y-Teens; Fr Clb; Pep Clb; Spn Clb; WVU; Pre Med.

EMMENDORFER, BRYCE; Ubly Community Schools; Ubly, MI; 6/111 Cls Rep Frsh Cls; Trs Sr Cls; Hon Rl; Jr NHS; NHS; Sch Pl; Stu Cncl; Letter Bsbl; Letter Ftbl; Letter Mgrs; Univ; Acctg.

EMMENDORFER, TIM; Ubly Community Schools; Ubly, MI; 17/103 VP Sr Cls; Hon Rl; NHS; Sch Pl; Letter Bsbl; Letter Bsktbl; Letter Mgrs; Ferris St Coll; Archt.

EMMERICH, CHRIS; Purcell HS; Cincinnati, OH; 3/185 Cls Rep Soph Cls; Cl Rep Jr Cls; Debate Tm; Hon Rl; Mod UN; Rptr Yrbk; Rptr Sch Nwsp; Sec Mth Clb; Trk; IM Sprt; Univ; Law.

EMMERS, THERESA; Carroll HS; Dayton, OH; 23/291 AFS; Chrh Wkr; Hon Rl; Lbry Ade; NHS; Sch Pl; Ed Sch Nwsp; Rptr Sch Nwsp; Pres Ger Clb; Mth Clb; Xavier Univ; Jrnlsm.

EMMERT, KAREN; Zanesville HS; Zanesville, OH; Chrs; Hon Rl; NHS; Stg Crw; Rptr Yrbk; Lat Clb; Sci Clb; Rotary Awd; Ohio St Univ; Landscape Archt.

EMMONS, DONNA; New Albany HS; New Albany, OH; Chrs; Chrh Wkr; Girl Scts; JA; Off Ade; Stu Cncl; Yth Flsp; 4-H; 4-H Awd; JA Awd; Asbury Coll; Soc Work.

EMMONS, MONICA R; Springfield South HS; Springfield, OH; 26/396 Sec Frsh Cls; VP Jr Cls; Band; Chrs; Hon Rl; Jr NHS; Natl Forn Lg; Off Ade; Orch; PAVAS; Two 2000 Schlrshp To Ashland Coll Essay Winner Twice; Ohio St Ideal Miss Harvest Queen Valentine Queen; Berkeley Univ; Medicine.

EMMONS, RITA A; Springs Valley HS; West Baden, IN; 12/80 Band; Chrh Wkr; Drl Tm; Hon Rl; Rptr Yrbk; Rptr Sch Nwsp; Lat Clb; Pep Clb; Indiana St Univ.

EMOND, MARBETH; South Charleston HS; Dunbar, WV; 38/296 Cls Rep Sr Cls; Chrh Wkr; Hon Rl; Jr NHS; Stu Cncl; Rptr Yrbk; Pres FBLA; FHA; Spn Clb; Scr Kpr; Mt Vernon Nazarene Coll; Acctg.

EMRICH, JOHN; Ottawa Hills HS; Grand Rapids, MI; Hon Rl; NHS; Grand Vly Univ; Law.

EMRICK, LAURIE; Warren Woods HS; Warren, MI; Hon Rl; NHS; Tmr; College.

EMSWILER, JACQUELINE; Charleston HS; Charleston, WV; Band; Hon Rl; Jr NHS; GAA; Concord Coll.

ENDEL, BARBARA; Waynesfield Goshen HS; Wapakoneta, OH; Band; Chrs; Drl Tm; Hon Rl; Stg Crw; Bsktbl; Trk; IM Sprt; Capt PPFtbl; Am Leg Awd; College; Physical Educ.

ENDELMAN, JULIE; Algonac HS; Algonac, MI; Band; Pres Chrh Wkr; Hon Rl; NHS; Sec OEA; Voice Dem Awd; Mi Bus Schls Assoc Schlrshp 900.

ENDELMAN, KAREN; Marysville HS; Marysville, MI; Cls Rep Frsh Cls; Cls Rep Soph Cls; Cmp Fr Grls; Chrh Wkr; Hon Rl; NHS; Sch Pl; Letter Bsktbl; Letter Trk; Michigan St Univ; Med.

ENDER, TERRY; North Huron HS; Kinde, MI; 2/55 Trs Soph Cls; Sal; Hon Rl; NHS; Orch; 4-H; Letter Bsktbl; Coach Actv; DAR Awd; Natl Merit SF; Delta Coll; Leg Sec.

ENDERLE, ALLISON; Columbus North HS; Columbus, OH; 6/300 VP Sr Cls; Am Leg Aux Girls St; Hon Rl; Jr NHS; NHS; Off Ade; Sch Pl; Stu Cncl; Rptr Sch Nwsp; Drama Clb; Univ.

ENDERS, LISA; Reeths Duffer HS; Muskegon, MI; 98/450 Chrh Wkr; Girl Scts; Hon Rl; Spn Clb; Univ; Tch Deaf.

ENDERS, MICHAEL; Western Brown Sr HS; Williamsbrg, OH; 1/170 Am Leg Boys St; Hon Rl; Treas NHS; Spn Clb; Univ.

ENDRES, GERALD; Suttons Bay Area Schl; Suttons Bay, MI; Band; Boy Scts; Hon Rl; Sch Mus; Sch Pl; Univ; Music.

ENDRES, LUCY; Talawanda HS; Oxford, OH; Band; Drl Tm; Girl Scts; Hon Rl; Off Ade; Sct Actv; 4-H; Pep Clb; Chrldng; IM Sprt; Cheerldng 77; Drill Tm 79; Miami Univ; Sci.

ENDRIS, MARCI; Bloomington North HS; Bloomington, IN; Hon Rl; Rptr Sch Nwsp; Gym; Trk; Chrldng; Opt Clb Awd; Pres Awd; Indiana Univ.

ENDRIS, SARAH; Providence HS; New Albany, IN; Hon Rl; Pep Clb; Letter Chrldng; College.

ENDRIS, TARA; New Albany HS; New Albany, IN; 35/565 Chrs; VP Debate Tm; Hon Rl; Jr NHS; NHS; Orch; Quill & Scroll; Sch Mus; Yrbk; Ger Clb; Univ.

ENDSLEY, JAY; Canal Winchester HS; Carroll, OH; Pres 4-H; Spn Clb; 4-H Awd; Natl Merit Ltr; Ohio State Univ; Chem Eng.

ENGEBRECHT, LINDA; John Glenn HS; Bay City, MI; Cls Rep Sr Cls; Chrh Wkr; Hon Rl; NHS; Stu

Cncl; Letter Trk; Pom Pon; Natl Merit SF; Delta Coll; Engr.

ENGEBRECHT, SUSAN; Concordia Lutheran HS; Ft Wayne, IN; 1/181 Chrs; Girl Scts; Hon Rl; 4-H; FBLA; Ger Clb; Bsktbl; Ten; GAA; 4-H Awd; Ball St Univ; Math.

ENGEL, BRIAN; Grosse Pointe North HS; Grosse Pt Wds, MI; Chrh Wkr; Cmnty Wkr; FCA; Hon Rl; NHS; Spn Clb; Letter Bsbl; Letter Bsktbl; Letter Ftbl; College; Med.

ENGEL, JANA; Carlisle HS; Carlisle, OH; 3/200 Trs Frsh Cls; Cls Rep Soph Cls; Trs Sr Cls; Chrs; Chrh Wkr; Cmnty Wkr; Hon Rl; Jr NHS; Ohio State Univ; Biochem.

ENGEL, LISA; John Adams HS; South Bend, IN; Hon Rl; Sec NHS; Quill & Scroll; Ed Yrbk; Yrbk; Sch Nwsp; 4-H; Natl Merit Ltr; Rotary Awd; College.

ENGEL, PENELOPE; Holgate HS; Holgate, OH; VP Sr Cls; Hon Rl; NHS; Yrbk; Spn Clb; Bsktbl; Ftbl; Scr Kpr; Dnfth Awd; BGSU; Nurse.

ENGELBACH, KIRK; Timken Sr HS; Canton, OH; Boy Scts; Chrs; Chrh Wkr; Hon Rl; Sch Mus; Sct Actv; Stg Crw; Drama Clb; Ger Clb; Cit Awd; Rotary Serv Awd 75; Univ; Math.

ENGELHARDT, DAVID; Arthur Hill HS; Saginaw, MI; Chrh Wkr; Hon Rl; NHS; Sci Clb; Awd For Academic Excellence From Mich St Univ; Michigan St Univ; Envir Bio.

ENGELMAN, ROGER; Northfield Jr Sr HS; Wabash, IN; 1/115 Band; Boy Scts; Hon Rl; NHS; Yth Flsp; 4-H; Bsbl; Crs Cntry; Letter Wrstlng; IM Sprt; Univ; Math.

ENGELS, SHELLEY; Montpelier HS; Montpelier, OH; Am Leg Aux Girls St; Band; Boy Scts; Chrs; Hon Rl; NHS; Sch Mus; Yth Flsp; 4-H; Fr Clb; Ohio State Univ; Pre Veterinary.

ENGH, DONALD; Fraser HS; Mt Clemens, MI; Hon Rl; Letter Trk; IM Sprt; Univ.

ENGLAND, ANDREW; Wabash HS; Wabash, IN; Chrs; Chrh Wkr; Cmnty Wkr; Debate Tm; Hon Rl; Off Ade; Sch Mus; Park College; Psych.

ENGLAND, BEN; Whitko HS; Pierceton, IN; 11/151 FFA; Indiana Univ; Law.

ENGLAND, BRIAN; Heath HS; Heath, OH; Chrs; Cmnty Wkr; Hon Rl; Mdrgl; Sch Mus; Sch Pl; Stg Crw; Rptr Yrbk; Drama Clb; College; Vet.

ENGLAND, CYNTHIA; Heath HS; Newark, OH; 9/151 Chrs; Girl Scts; Hon Rl; Jr NHS; NHS; Sch Mus; Sch Pl; Stg Crw; Rptr Yrbk; Drama Clb; Educ Awrd 100.

ENGLAND, ELIZABETH C; Marlington HS; Louisville, OH; Chrs; Hon Rl; Sct Actv; FFA; FTA; Letter Ten; Letter Trk; Wooster Ag Tech Inst; Landscape Dsgn.

ENGLAND, JANET; Wayne HS; Dayton, OH; Hst Sr Cls; Band; Chrh Wkr; Jr NHS; Sch Mus; Yth Flsp; OEA; Pep Clb; IM Sprt; Sinclair Cmnty Coll; Med.

ENGLAND, JULIE; Manchester HS; Manchester, MI; 6/106 Hst Soph Cls; Trs Jr Cls; Trs Sr Cls; Band; Chrs; Chrh Wkr; Cmnty Wkr; Drm Mjrt; Hon Rl; NHS; Schlrshp For Women In Engr 78; Schlrshp Yth For Understanding 77; Miss United Teenage Pageant 78; Michigan Tech Univ; Engr.

ENGLAND, LORI; Manchester HS; Manchester, MI; 3/106 Pres Jr Cls; Pres Sr Cls; Band; Chrs; Chrh Wkr; Hon Rl; Jr NHS; NHS; Orch; Sch Mus; Schlrshp For Women In Engr 78; Schlrshp For Yth Understanding Exchange; St Fnlst Miss Untd Teenage Pageant; Michigan Tech Univ; Engr.

ENGLAND, SHARON; Princeton HS; Cincinnati, OH; Chrh Wkr; Hon Rl; OEA; GAA; Scarlet Oaks Voc Schl; Data Proc.

ENGLAND, TERRI; Herbert Hoover HS; Elkview, WV; Band; Chrh Wkr; Girl Scts; Hon Rl; Sct Actv; Yth Flsp; 4-H; Fr Clb; 4-H Awd; God Cntry Awd; Univ Of Charleston; Radio Brdcstng.

ENGLANDER, TODD; Bloomington HS; Bloomington, IN; 7/325 Cl Rep Jr Cls; Cls Rep Sr Cls; Hon Rl; Hosp Ade; Jr NHS; Treas NHS; Pol Wkr; Red Cr Ade; Stu Cncl; Letter Ten; Valparaiso Univ; Pre Med.

ENGLE, ANNETTE; Hanover Central HS; Cedar Lake, IN; 10/137 Girl Scts; Hon Rl; Jr NHS; NHS; Sch Mus; Sch Pl; Sct Actv; Stg Crw; Stu Cncl; Drama Clb; College; Drama.

ENGLE, CATHERINE; Tri Central HS; Sharpsville, IN; 10/70 Chrs; Chrh Wkr; Hon Rl; NHS; Yth Flsp; Drama Clb; Pres Fr Clb; Pep Clb; Pom Pon; PPFtbl; Taylor Univ; Elem Ed.

ENGLE, MELINDA; Bellmont HS; Decatur, IN; Sec Sr Cls; Band; Hon Rl; Stu Cncl; Rptr Yrbk; Rptr Sch Nwsp; Spn Clb; Bsktbl; Ten; Univ.

ENGLE, NATHAN W; Floyd Central HS; New Albany, IN; Mod UN; Ed Sch Nwsp; Rptr Sch Nwsp; Natl Merit Ltr; Hoosier Scholr 1979; Floyd Ctrl Math Awd 1979; Indiana Univ; Comp Sci.

ENGLE, SHEILA; Centerville HS; Richmond, IN; JA; Y-Teens; IM Sprt; Purdue Univ; Interior Decort.

ENGLE, TERRI; Thomas Carr Howe HS; Indianapolis, IN; 9/568 Girl Scts; Hon Rl; Lit Mag; Treas NHS; Quill & Scroll; Sch Nwsp; Spn Clb; Univ; Sci.

ENGLEHART, CATHY; Avon HS; Avon, OH; 14/152 Hon Rl; Jr NHS; NHS; College; Allied Health Sci.

ENGLEKA, JENNIFER; Garfield HS; Akron, OH; Cls Rep Frsh Cls; Chrs; Chrh Wkr; Off Ade; Sch Pl; Stg Crw; Yth Flsp; Pep Clb; Gym; Akron Univ.

ENGLEMAN, SCOTT; Lakeview HS; Battle Creek, MI; 1/400 Hon Rl; NHS; Letter Ten; Univ; Math.

ENGLER, JAMES; Washington HS; Massillon, OH; 15/459 Chrh Wkr; Hon Rl; Jr NHS; Off Ade; Pres Stu Cncl; Pres Yth Flsp; Ger Clb; Letter Crs Cntry; Letter Trk; Cit Awd; St Qualifier 79; Univ; Foreign Lang.

ENGLERT, MICHAEL; Shenandoah HS; Middletown, IN; 19/118 Band; Rptr Yrbk; Mth Clb; Letter Glf; Mgrs; Am Leg Awd; Archt Model Home Awd; All Conf Golf; Most Inproved Golfer; Purdue Univ; Archt.

ENGLISH, BILL; Heritage Christian HS; Indianapolis, IN; 31/63 VP Soph Cls; Band; Hon Rl; Sch Pl; Stg Crw; Stu Cncl; Yrbk; Drama Clb; Letter Bsktbl; Grace Coll; Bible.

ENGLISH, DONETTA; Eastern HS; Bloomfield, IN; 13/78 Hon Rl; Hosp Adg; NHS; 4-H; FHA; 4-H Awd; Ivy Tech Univ; Acctg.

ENGLISH, ELAINE; Holy Name Nazareth HS; Parma, OH; Band; Hon Rl; Hosp Ade; NHS; Orch; Sch Mus; Sch Pl; Stg Crw; Drama Clb; Spn Clb; Univ; Med Records Admin.

ENGLISH, ELIZABETH; Nitro HS; Charleston, WV; Cls Rep Frsh Cls; Cls Rep Sr Cls; Chrs; Hon Rl; Stg Crw; Pep Clb; Swmmng; College; Sci.

ENGLISH, GARY; Anderson HS; Anderson, IN; 26/420 Band; Drm Bgl; Hon Rl; Jr NHS; NHS; Orch; Spn Clb; C of C Awd; Purdue Univ; Elec Engr.

ENGLISH, KATHIE; Turpin HS; Cincinnati, OH; 19/371 Off Ade; Bsktbl; Socr; Ten; PPFtbl; Miami Univ; Systems Analysis.

ENGLISH, MATT; Turpin HS; Cincinnati, OH; 90/357 Capt Socr; Letter Ten;.

ENGLISH, ROBERT; Marietta HS; Marietta, OH; 54/460 NHS; Fr Clb; Letter Ten; Col Land & Mines; Petro Engring.

ENGLISH, TRACI; Meadowbrook HS; Cambridge, OH; Sec Jr Cls; Cl Rep Jr Cls; Band; Hon Rl; Stu Cncl; Yth Flsp; Sec 4-H; Treas Fr Clb; VP FHA; Scr Kpr; Ohio State Univ; Computer Sci.

ENGSTROM, TERRI; Hubbard HS; Hubbard, OH; 32/365 Chrs; Girl Scts; Hon Rl; NHS; Off Ade; Red Cr Ade; Capt Bsktbl; Letter Trk; GAA; Youngstown St Univ; Acctg.

ENIS, KIM; Ursuline Acad; Cincinnati, OH; Natl Forn Lg; Pol Wkr; Sch Pl; Ed Sch Nwsp; Drama Clb; Fordam Univ; Journalism.

ENNEKING, KAREN; Minster HS; Minster, OH; Am Leg Aux Girls St; Chrs; Girl Scts; Hon Rl; Sec NHS; Sch Mus; Drama Clb; FTA; Pep Clb; Spn Clb; Ohio St Univ; Occupational Therapy.

ENNEKING, SALLY; Mother Of Mercy HS; Cincinnati, OH; 9/250 Chrs; Girl Scts; Hon Rl; NHS; Sct Actv; Fr Clb; College; Engr.

ENNIS, KAREN; Madeira HS; Cincinti, OH; 15/170 Chrs; Chrh Wkr; Hon Rl; Off Ade; Northland Bapt Bible Coll; Missn Wrk.

ENNIS, LAUREN; Bishop Dwenger HS; Ft Wayne, IN; Chrs; Hon Rl; Sch Mus; Sch Pl; Stg Crw; 4-H; Fr Clb; Westfield College; Spe Educ.

ENNIS, PAMELA; Yellow Springs HS; Yellow Sprg, OH; Chrs; Cmnty Wkr; Drl Tm; Girl Scts; Orch; Red Cr Ade; Stu Cncl; Yrbk; 4-H; Pep Clb; Ohio Univ; Communications.

ENNIS, PHILLIP; Northport Public HS; Northport, MI; 3/27 VP Jr Cls; Boy Scts; Hon Rl; NHS; Rptr Yrbk; Rptr Sch Nwsp; Letter Bsktbl; Letter Socr; Letter Trk; Natl Merit SF; Univ; Nuclear Engr.

ENOCH, SHERRI; Washington HS; Massillon, OH; Cls Rep Soph Cls; Band; Chrs; Hon Rl; NHS; Y-Teens; Drama Clb; Fr Clb; Pep Clb; Kent State; Commerical Art.

ENOCH, TERRI; Washington HS; Massillon, OH; Cl Rep Jr Cls; Band; Chrs; Chrh Wkr; Hon Rl; Hosp Ade; NHS; Off Ade; Sch Mus; Drama Clb; Univ; Advertising.

ENOS, BETH; Greensburg Community HS; Greensburg, IN; 7/193 Letter Band; Letter Chrs; Chrh Wkr; VP JA; NHS; Y-Teens; JA Awd; Butler Univ; Pblc Cmnctns.

ENRIETTO, JOHN; Bishop Dwenger HS; Ft Wayne, IN; Cl Rep Jr Cls; Aud/Vis; Boy Scts; JA; Sch Pl; Sct Actv; Y-Teens; Lat Clb; Ten; Letter Wrstlng; Ball St Univ; Archt.

ENRIGHT, BRIAN; Hammond HS; Hammond, IN; 35/375 Boy Scts; Hon Rl; Jr NHS; Mth Clb; Bsbl; Ftbl; JA Awd; Natl Art Inst Schlshp 75; 1st Pl Natl Math Exam 77; 3rd Pl Natl Math Exam 79; Univ; Math.

ENRIGHT, TAMMY; Emmerich Manual HS; Indianapolis, IN; Chrs; Hon Rl; Lbry Ade; Off Ade; Stu Cncl; Y-Teens; Pom Pon; Treas Twrlr; Top 25% Of Cl Fresh Soph & Jr 77 79; Blue Rbbns For A Fnls In Cl 77 79; Clark Bus Coll; Legal Sec.

ENRIQUE, MARICHELLE; Holy Name Nazareth HS; Brecksville, OH; Drl Tm; Hon Rl; Hosp Ade; Yth Flsp; Fr Clb; Pep Clb; Pom Pon; Univ; Pre Med.

ENSIGN, JAMES L; Lima Sr HS; Lima, OH; Band; Chrs; Hon Rl; Sch Mus; Sch Pl; Letter Swmmng; Letter Ten; Natl Merit SF; Miami Univ; Architect.

ENSIGN, MARK; Austin Town Fitch HS; Youngstown, OH; Key Clb; Bsktbl; Ftbl; Trk; Youngstown St Univ; Pro Ftbl.

ENSINGER, BECKY; River HS; Sardis, OH; Sec Frsh Cls; Sec Soph Cls; Sec Jr Cls; Chrh Wkr; Cmnty Wkr; Hon Rl; Off Ade; 4-H; Fr Clb; FTA; College; Secondary Ed.

ENSLEY, EDNA; Collinwood HS; Cleveland, OH; Hon Rl; Jr NHS; Lbry Ade; PAVAS; Sch Mus; Stg Crw; Drama Clb; Fr Clb; Cit Awd; Baldwin Wallace; Communications.

ENSMAN, LISA; Edgewood HS; Bloomington, IN; 1/180 Chrh Wkr; Hon Rl; NHS; Stg Crw; Drama Clb; Ger Clb; Natl Merit SF; Indiana Univ; Astro Physics.

ENTINGH, KAREN; Dayton Christian HS; Dayton, OH; 8/130 Cls Rep Soph Cls; Chrs; Hon Rl; NHS; Sec Stu Cncl; Socr; Cedarville; Computer Programming.

ENYART, DIANE K; Celina Sr HS; Celina, OH; 23/240 Am Leg Aux Girls St; Band; Chrh Wkr; Drl Tm; Hon Rl; NHS; Sch Mus; Fr Clb; FTA; Natl Merit SF; Findlay Coll; Bio.

ENYART, JEFFERY; Loveland Hurst HS; Loveland, OH; Trs Jr Cls; Trs Sr Cls; Band; Boy Scts; Drm Bgl; Hon Rl; Sch Mus; 4-H; Key Clb; Spn Clb; Univ Of Cincinnati; Acctg.

ENZWEILER, CYNTHIA; Seton HS; Cincinnati, OH; 12/267 Hon Rl; Jr NHS; NHS; Off Ade; Red Cr Ade; Rptr Sch Nwsp; College Of Mt St Joseph; Marketing.

EPLER, ANGIE; Brown County HS; Morgantown, IN; Hon Rl; NHS; Quill & Scroll; Sch Pl; Stg Crw; Ed Yrbk; Yrbk; Drama Clb; Pep Clb; Spn Clb; Hanover; Scndry Educ.

EPLEY, KRISTIN M; Our Lady Of Mercy HS; Detroit, MI; Sec Frsh Cls; Chrs; Chrh Wkr; Girl Scts; Sch Mus; Sch Pl; Sct Actv; Stg Crw; Drama Clb; Univ; Psych.

EPLIN, CHANE; Ellet HS; Akron, OH; 15/343 Cl Rep Jr Cls; Cls Rep Sr Cls; Chrs; Chrh Wkr; FCA; Hon Rl; Jr NHS; Mdrgl; NHS; Orch; Kent St Univ; Flight Tech.

EPLING, SCOT A; Spencer HS; Spencer, WV; 1/152 Am Leg Boys St; Band; Drm Bgl; Jr NHS; NHS; Stu Cncl; Sch Nwsp; Pres Drama Clb; Am Leg Awd; Wv Univ; Law.

EPLING, WILLIAM; Williamson HS; Williamson, WV; 1/80 Cl Rep Jr Cls; Cls Rep Sr Cls; Val; Am Leg Boys St; Band; Treas NHS; Stu Cncl; W Wv Univ; Engr.

EPPERSON, TERRY; Covington HS; Covington, IN; 5/117 Boy Scts; Chrs; Hon Rl; 4-H; Lat Clb; 4-H Awd; Honor Jacket; Latin I & II Awds; Danville Jr Coll; Science.

EQUIHUA, LORRAINE; West Side HS; Gary, IN; 28/650 Cls Rep Frsh Cls; Cmnty Wkr; Hon Rl; JA; NHS; Off Ade; Sch Pl; OEA; Pom Pon; JA Awd; Communications.

ERBECK, SUE; William Mason HS; Mason, OH; Cls Rep Frsh Cls; Cls Rep Soph Cls; VP Jr Cls; Stu Cncl; Yth Flsp; 4-H; Fr Clb; Sci Clb; Spn Clb; Ten; Ohio St Univ; Dental Hygiene.

ERBSKORN, ARTHUR; Morenci Area HS; Morenci, MI; Am Leg Boys St; Band; Boy Scts; Letter Bsktbl; Letter Glf; Letter Trk; Siena Hgts College; Med Tech.

ERCOLINE, LAURA; Bluefield HS; Bluefield, WV; 2/230 Chrs; Chrh Wkr; Hon Rl; Jr NHS; NHS; Ed Yrbk; Yrbk; Sec Civ Clb; VP Fr Clb; Pep Clb; 2 French Awds; Eng Awd; Math Awd; Laurel Leaves Awd For Eng; Univ Of Virginia; Speech Path.

ERDMANN, LISA; Linton Stockton HS; Linton, IN; Cl Rep Jr Cls; Am Leg Aux Girls St; Cmnty Wkr; Hon Rl; NHS; Pol Wkr; Stu Cncl; Ger Clb; Purdue Univ; Med.

ERDOS, JOSEPH; Cadiz HS; New Athens, OH; Chrs; Hon Rl; NHS; Sch Mus; Sch Pl; Rptr Sch Nwsp; Spn Clb; Bsbl; Bsktbl; Ftbl; Most Improved Player Bsbl; 1st Team All Dist Bsbl; 2nd Team All Eastern Buckeye Ohio Bsbl; West Liberty St Coll; Busns.

EREBIA, FEDERICO; Port Clinton HS; Port Clinton, OH; 19/289 FCA; Hon Rl; NHS; Orch; Red Cr Ade; VP FDA; Mth Clb; Spn Clb; Crs Cntry; Trk; Univ; Med.

EREHART, STEVE; Anderson HS; Anderson, IN; Hon Rl; NHS; Lat Clb; Swmmng; Coach Actv; Am Leg Awd; College.

EREKSON, CAMERON; Adams Central HS; Decatur, IN; 19/100 Trs Frsh Cls; Am Leg Boys St; NHS; Sct Actv; Ed Sch Nwsp; Drama Clb; Pres Ger Clb; Mth Clb; Letter Glf; JETS Awd; College; Nuclear Engr.

EREON, TERESA; Ludington HS; Ludington, MI; Pres Frsh Cls; Cl Rep Jr Cls; Am Leg Aux Girls St; Hon Rl; NHS; Treas Stu Cncl; Trk; Grand Valley St Coll; Poli Sci.

ERHARDT, JULIE; Spring Lake HS; Spring Lake, MI; 4/184 Hon Rl; Treas NHS; Off Ade; Spn Clb; Bsktbl; IM Sprt; Scr Kpr; C of C Awd; Elk Awd; Kiwan Awd; 2 Yr Letter Winnter Team Capt & All Cnfrnce Hnrble Mention In Jr Yr; Michigan St Univ; Acctg.

ERHART, PATRICIA; West Bloomfield HS; W Bloomfield, MI; 4/445 Trs Jr Cls; Sal; Hon Rl; NHS; Sch Mus; Pep Clb; Spn Clb; Letter Chrldng; PPFtbl; Scr Kpr; Mich State Univ; Med.

ERICH, JANET; Willoughby South HS; Will Hills, OH; 12/416 Band; NHS; Letter Bsbl; Letter Bsktbl; Amer Assoc Of Univ Women 76; Inducted Into Natl Hon Soc 78; German 2 Awd 78; Bowling Green Univ; Nutrition.

ERICHSEN, JOHN; Penn HS; Granger, IN; Band; NHS; Orch; Sch Mus; History Dist Cntst 2nd 77; Hist Dist Cntest 2nd 78;.

ERICKSEN, KURT; Forest Park HS; Forest Park, OH; 17/380 Boy Scts; Cmnty Wkr; Hon Rl; Glf; College; Law.

ERICKSEN, MARK B; Turpin HS; Cincinnati, OH; Chrs; Chrh Wkr; FCA; Yth Flsp; Letter Crs Cntry; Letter Socr; Mgrs; PPFtbl; Natl Merit Ltr; Miami Univ.

ERICKSEN, MATTHEW J; Turpin HS; Cincinnati, OH; 12/358 Cl Rep Jr Cls; Cls Rep Sr Cls; NHS; Glf; Natl Merit SF; Univ; Economics.

ERICKSON, BETH; Clinton HS; Tipton, MI; Hon Rl; Off Ade; Sch Mus; Sch Pl; Stg Crw; Stu Cncl; Rptr Yrbk; Ed Sch Nwsp; Rptr Sch Nwsp; Drama Clb; Michigan St Univ; Eng.

ERICKSON, JEANNE; North Muskegon HS; N Muskegon, MI; 49/110 Hon Rl; Treas 4-H; PPFtbl; College; Psychology.

ERICKSON, JUDY; Pine River HS; , ; Band; Chrs; Drm Mjrt; Hon Rl; Off Ade; Yrbk; 4-H; Letter Bsktbl; Chrldng; College.

ERICKSON, KAREN; Polaris Voc Center; Strongsville, OH; Girl Scts; Hon Rl; FFA; Twrlr; Polaris Voc Center; Horticulture.

ERICKSON, KATHY J; Reed City HS; Reed City, MI; Band; Hon Rl; NHS; Sch Pl; Stu Cncl; Rptr Sch Nwsp; Pep Clb;.

ERICKSON, KENNETH W; Eastlake North HS; Willowick, OH; 9/676 Chrh Wkr; FCA; Hon Rl; Jr NHS; NHS; Letter Bsktbl; Letter Ftbl; Kiwan Awd; College; Engr.

ERICKSON, LAURA; Farmington HS; Farmington, MI; Band; Hon Rl; Jr NHS; NHS; Stu Cncl; Natl Merit Ltr; Natl Merit SF; College.

ERICKSON, MARCIA; Pinckney HS; Pinckney, MI; Cls Rep Frsh Cls; Cls Rep Soph Cls; Chrh Wkr; NHS; Yrbk; Fr Clb; Bsbl; Bsktbl; Grand Rapids Baptist College; Speech.

ERICKSON, RONDENE; Luther L Wright HS; Ironwood, MI; 33/176 Pres Band; Hon Rl; 4-H; GAA; 4-H Awd; Gogebic Comm Coll; Acctg.

ERICKSON, SARAH; Marquette Sr HS; Marquette, MI; Band; Chrh Wkr; Cmnty Wkr; Hosp Ade; Orch; N Michigan Univ; Nursing.

ERICKSON, SHELLY; Pine River Jr Sr HS; Tustin, MI; Chrh Wkr; Hon Rl; Pres NHS; Rptr Yrbk; 4-H; Letter Bsktbl; Letter Chrldng; Kellogg Comm Coll; Phys Therapy.

ERISMAN, JEFFREY; Valley View HS; Frmrsvl, OH; Pres Band; Red Cr Ade; Sch Mus; Pep Clb; IM Sprt; Scr Kpr; Tmr; Marching Band Jazz Band Pep Band & Concert Band 78; Solo & Ensemble Comp Awd Superior Rating 77 78 & 79; Fire Fighting Schl; Paramedic.

ERJAVAC, STANLEY; Bishop Gallagher HS; Harper Wds, MI; 23/333 Boy Scts; Chrh Wkr; Cmnty Wkr; FCA; Hon Rl; NHS; Sct Actv; Mth Clb; Ftbl; Coach Actv; Univ Of Michigan; Law.

ERK, LISA; Harper Creek HS; East Le Roy, MI; Trs Frsh Cls; Trs Soph Cls; Cl Rep Jr Cls; VP Sr Cls; Hon Rl; NHS; Pol Wkr; Stu Cncl; Sch Nwsp; Fr Clb; Michigan St Univ; Child Psych.

ERKFRITZ, LISA; Clarkston HS; Clarkston, MI; Chrs; Girl Scts; Hon Rl; Lbry Ade; Ed Sch Nwsp; 4-H; Mth Clb; Oakland Univ; Comp Acctg.

ERKSA, DEBBIE; Wadsworth Sr HS; Wadsworth, OH; Hon Rl; NHS; Off Ade; Sch Pl; Drama Clb; Pep Clb; Spn Clb; College; English.

ERNEST, TAMMY; Brooke HS; Wheeling, WV; 62/532 Hon Rl; Yrbk; 4-H; Letter Gym; Mat Maids; 4-H Awd; Bus Schl; Sec.

ERNST, BARBARA; Western Brown Sr HS; Bethel, OH; 2/185 Cls Rep Frsh Cls; Cls Rep Soph Cls; VP Jr Cls; Chrs; Hon Rl; NHS; Off Ade; Stu Cncl; FHA; Spn Clb; Univ; Engr.

ERNST, D; Sidney HS; Sidney, OH; Chrs; Hon Rl; Key Clb; Pep Clb; Letter Ftbl; Letter Trk; Letter Wrstlng; IM Sprt; College; Engr.

ERNST, JACKIE; Upper Valley JVS; Sidney, OH; Cls Rep Sr Cls; Hon Rl; Sch Pl; Drama Clb; FHA; OEA; DAR Awd; Acad Ltr Achvmnt At Sch L79; Ambssdr Awd OEA 79; Stateswomn Awd OEA 79; Edison St Univ; Bus.

ERNST, KATRINA; Cloverdale HS; Cloverdale, IN; 4/84 Pres Jr Cls; Chrs; Hon Rl; NHS; Off Ade; Sch Mus; Stg Crw; Stu Cncl; Yrbk; Treas Drama Clb; Univ.

ERNST, LISA; Archbishop Alter HS; Centerville, OH; 26/277 Hon Rl; NHS; Ger Clb; Mgrs; 1st Hon 77 79; Fundamntl Algbr II & Trig Awd 79; Miami Univ; Guidance Cnslr.

ERNST, MICHAEL; Reading Comm HS; Reading, OH; Am Leg Boys St; Hon Rl; Jr NHS; Letter Crs Cntry; Letter Trk; Miami Univ; Zoology.

ERNSTHAUSEN, DAVE; Eastwood HS; Pemberville, OH; Band; Hon Rl; Stu Cncl; Treas Yth Flsp; FFA; Key Clb; Letter Bsktbl; Letter Ftbl; Bowling Green St Univ; Bio.

ERNSTHAUSEN, JACKIE; Elmwood HS; Bloomdale, OH; 20/105 Band; Chrs; Girl Scts; Hon Rl; MMM; Sch Pl; Rptr Yrbk; FTA; OEA; Chrldng;.

ERSKIN, LISA; Vestaburg Cmnty School; Vestaburg, MI; 10/74 Band; Chrs; Chrh Wkr; Hon Rl; NHS; Off Ade; Sch Mus; Sch Pl; Yth Flsp; Letter Bsbl; Montcalm Cmnty Coll.

ERSKINE, DEBBIE; Athens HS; East Leroy, MI; Hon Rl; Jr NHS; NHS; Off Ade; Sch Pl; Kellogg Community Coll; Eng.

ERTEL, DACE J; Chelsea HS; Chelsea, MI; Cls Rep Frsh Cls; Debate Tm; Sch Pl; Yrbk; Kalamazoo Univ; Health.

ERTEL, PAM; Brookville HS; Cedar Grv, IN; 6/200 Hon Rl; NHS; Treas Stu Cncl; Ed Yrbk; Rptr Sch Nwsp; Letter Bsktbl; Trk; Chrldng; Cincinnati Tech Coll; Med Asst.

ERTEL, PAM; Brookville HS; Cedar Grove, IN; 6/200 Cls Rep Sr Cls; Hon Rl; NHS; Treas Stu Cncl; Rptr Yrbk; Rptr Sch Nwsp; Bsktbl; Ten; Trk; Chrldng; Cincinnati Tech Coll; Med Asst.

ERTL, MARY; High School; Ionia, MI; 56/273 Cls Rep Frsh Cls; Cls Rep Soph Cls; Hon Rl; Hosp Ade; NHS; Stu Cncl; Spn Clb; Letter Bsktbl; Letter Trk; Letter Chrldng; Aquinas Coll; Health Related Area.

ERTLE, KARL; St Ignatius HS; Lakewood, OH; Cl Rep Jr Cls; Cls Rep Sr Cls; Chrh Wkr; Cmnty Wkr; Hon Rl; Hosp Ade; NHS; Stu Cncl; Yrbk; Rptr Sch Nwsp; Borromeo Coll; Liberal Arts.

ERTLE JR, JOHN B; St Edward HS; Lakewood, OH; 10/370 Jr NHS; Lit Mag; Yrbk; Ftbl; Univ.

ERVANS, MICHELE; Franklin HS; Livonia, MI; Cls Rep Soph Cls; Aud/Vis; Chrh Wkr; Cmnty Wkr; Lbry Ade; Off Ade; Sch Mus; Stu Cncl; Bsktbl; Swmmng; College; Social Work.

ERVIN, DANIEL; Teays Valley HS; Ashville, OH; Cls Rep Frsh Cls; Sec Soph Cls; Pres Jr Cls; Am Leg Boys St; Band; FCA; Hon Rl; NHS; Trk; Mas Awd; College.

ERVIN, DONALD S; Teays Valley HS; Ashville, OH; Sec Frsh Cls; Pres Soph Cls; Cl Rep Jr Cls; Band; FCA; Drama Clb; Key Clb; Ten; Dnfth Awd; 4-H Awd; College; Drama.

ERVIN, DOUGLAS; Father Joseph Wehrle Mem HS; Columbus, OH; Cls Rep Frsh Cls; Pres Sr Cls; Hon Rl; Jr NHS; NHS; Off Ade; Sch Pl; Stu Cncl; Rptr Sch Nwsp; Ftbl; Order Of De Molay; Coll; Law.

ERVIN, HEATHER; Bridgeport HS; Bridgeport, WV; Band; Chrs; Drm Mjrt; Girl Scts; Hon Rl; Jr NHS; NHS; Ten; Mgrs; College; Nuclear Physics.

ERVIN, L; Mason HS; Mason, MI; Girl Scts; Hon Rl; Treas Jr NHS; NHS; Treas Stu Cncl; Sci Clb; Natl Merit Ltr; Outstndng 1st Yr Draftsperson; Outstndng Soph Math Stu; Independent Research Sci; Univ; Archt.

ERVIN, LAURA; Miami Trace HS; Wash C H, OH; AFS; Band; Hon Rl; Off Ade; Sch Mus; Stg Crw; Yt h Flsp; Y-Teens; Rptr Sch Nwsp; 4-H; Miami Univ; Med.

ERWIN, DONALD; Owen Valley HS; Spencer, IN; Cls Rep Sr Cls; Hon Rl; Stu Cncl; VICA; Voc Schl.

ERWIN, HOLLY; Harrison HS; Harrison, MI; Lbry Ade; Rptr Sch Nwsp; Gym; Trk; Coach Actv; IM Sprt; Pres Awd; College.

ERWIN, JODIE; North Union HS; Richwood, OH; Hon Rl; Sch Nwsp; 4-H; Bsktbl; IM Sprt; PPFtbl; Univ.

ERWIN, LINDA; Bellefontaine Sr HS; Bellefontaine, OH; 13/241 Am Leg Aux Girls St; Band; Chrh Wkr; Hon Rl; Sch Pl; Pres Yth Flsp; Y-Teens; Treas FTA; Univ; Bus.

ERWIN, RICHARD; Walled Lake Central HS; Union Lake, MI; Chrs; Chrh Wkr; Cmnty Wkr; Hon Rl; NHS; Sch Mus; Sch Pl; Y-Teens; Ger Clb; IM Sprt; Univ; Pre Med.

ERWIN, RON; Lakeville Memorial HS; Columbiaville, MI; Band; Boy Scts; Hon Rl; Orch; Sch Mus; Trk; Rotary Awd; College; Architecture.

ESBENSHADE, CHERYL; Crestview HS; Shiloh, OH; Chrh Wkr; Hon Rl; Off Ade; Yth Flsp; FHA;.

ESBER, JIM; Valley Forge Sr HS; Parma Hts, OH; 7/704 Chrs; Hon Rl; Jr NHS; NHS; Sch Pl; Yth Flsp; Letter Trk; Cit Awd; Cleveland Inst Of Art; Art.

ESCH, CAROLYN; Grand Ledge HS; Grand Ledge, MI; Hon Rl; 4-H; 4-H Awd; Univ; Acctg.

ESCHLEMAN, MICHAEL; Wintersville HS; Bloomingdale, OH; Spn Clb; Letter Ftbl; IM Sprt; Coll; Broadcasting.

ESHELMAN, JAMES; Dearborn HS; Dearborn Hts, MI; Band; Boy Scts; Chrh Wkr; Hon Rl; NHS; Yth Flsp; Letter Swmmng; Tmr; Natl Merit Ltr; Michigan Tech; Chem Engr.

ESKEW, KATHY; Athens HS; Athens, WV; Chrh Wkr; Hon Rl; Yth Flsp; Yrbk; Fr Clb; Keyettes; Pep Clb; DAR Awd; Concord Coll; Cmnctns.

ESKIN, DIANE; Armada HS; Armada, MI; 7/114 Trs Jr Cls; Trs Sr Cls; Am Leg Aux Girls St; Band; Chrs; Cmnty Wkr; Hon Rl; NHS; Off Ade; Sch Mus; Central Michigan Univ; Spec Ed.

ESKINS, CYNTHIA; Huntington East HS; Huntington, WV; Cls Rep Frsh Cls; Letter Band; Hon Rl; Sci Clb; Letter Trk; College; Science.

ESKRIDGE, MARLA; Andrews Acad; Berrien Spring, MI; Cmnty Wkr; Rptr Yrbk; Rptr Sch Nwsp; Bsbl; Gym; Trk; IM Sprt; Andrews Univ; Physical Educ.

ESLINGER, TAMMY; Kingsford HS; Kingsford, MI; Band; Hon Rl; Letter Bsktbl; Letter Trk; Letter Coach Actv; College.

ESMONDE, KLAUDIA; Mendon Union HS; Mendon, OH; 1/33 Val; Band; Chrs; Hon Rl; NHS; Stu Cncl; Yrbk; Pep Clb; Bsktbl; Capt Chrldng; Univ; Food Sci.

ESON, ANNE; Eaton HS; Eaton, OH; 16/180 Am Leg Aux Girls St; Hon Rl; NHS; Treas Stu Cncl; Capt Pep Clb; Trk; Chrldng; GAA; Capt PPFtbl; Am Leg Awd; Miami Univ; Acctg.

ESPARZA, DAVID; Holy Redeemer HS; Detroit, MI; Chrh Wkr; Hon Rl; Spn Clb; Lawrence Inst Of Tech; Cntrctn Engr.

ESPER, LAURA; Clarenceville HS; Livonia, MI; 7/235 Cls Rep Frsh Cls; Cls Rep Soph Cls; Cls Rep Sr Cls; Treas Chrs; Girl Scts; Hon Rl; Sec Jr NHS; NHS; Sch Mus; Sch Pl; Dollars For Schlrs Schlrshp 79; Mi Comptn Schlrshp 79; Eastern Mi Univ Regional HS Awd 79; Michigan St Univ; Bus.

ESPER, LINDA; Miami Trace HS; Washington Ch, OH; Cmp Fr Grls; Chrs; Hon Rl; Jr NHS; Sch Mus; Sch Pl; Stg Crw; Drama Clb; 4-H; FNA; Nursing Schl; Nursing.

ESPICH, BENJAMIN; Columbia City Joint HS; Columbia City, IN; Aud/Vis; Band; Boy Scts; JA; Sct Actv; Boys Clb Am; Sci Clb; Swmmng; JA Awd; Ivy Tech Schl; Carpentry.

ESPINOSA, PAUL A; Jefferson HS; Charles Town, WV; 11/356 Am Leg Boys St; Boy Scts; Chrh Wkr; Cmnty Wkr; Hon Rl; NHS; Pol Wkr; Sct Actv; Stu Cncl; Pres Yth Flsp; St Of Wv Golden Horseshoe Awd Recpnt 76; Chrmn Of St Sen At Yth In Govt Conf 78; Univ; Bio.

ESPINOZA, DIANE; William A Wirt HS; Valparaiso, IN; VP Sr Cls; Band; Girl Scts; Hon Rl; Rptr Yrbk; Pep Clb; Trk; Chrldng; Valparaiso Univ; Bus Admin.

ESPOSITO, CARMELA; Fenwick HS; Middletown, OH; Am Leg Aux Girls St; Chrs; Cmnty Wkr; Capt Drl Tm; Hon Rl; NHS; Sch Mus; Pres Stu Cncl; Mgrs; Twrlr; Pres Of Mission Clb 79; Choreographer Of Anything Goes Musical 77; Stud Tchr At Mary Hiatts Dance Studio 75; Univ; Med.

ESSELSTEIN, BOB; St Francis De Sales HS; Columbus, OH; 60/250 Chrh Wkr; Cmnty Wkr; Letter Bsbl; Letter Bsktbl; Letter Ftbl; Gym; Am Leg Awd; C of C Awd; Cit Awd; Pres Awd; Capital Univ; Bus Admin.

ESSENBERG, LINDA; Adlai Stevenson HS; Sterling Height, MI; Trs Soph Cls; Cmnty Wkr; Debate Tm; Hon Rl; NHS; Sch Pl; Stg Crw; 4-H; FFA; Mgrs; Michigan State Univ; Agriculture.

ESSENMACHER, ANDREW; Carsonville HS; Carsonville, MI; 12/79 Band; Hon Rl; FDA; Fr Clb; Sci Clb; Ftbl; Trk; Cit Awd; 4-H Awd;.

ESSENMACHER, JEFF; Ubly Community HS; Ruth, MI; 13/114 Trs Jr Cls; Sec Band; Hon Rl; NHS; Letter Bsktbl; Letter Trk; IM Sprt; Delta College; Comp Oper.

ESSER, BRYAN; Anna HS; Anna, OH; 19/84 Band; Chrs; Debate Tm; Hon Rl; NHS; Orch; Sch Mus; Sch Pl; Drama Clb; Sci Clb; Ohio State Univ; Med Tech.

ESSER, TIMOTHY; Fraser HS; Fraser, MI; Hon Rl; Jr NHS; NHS; Letter Bsbl; Bsktbl; Letter Ftbl; Coach Actv; Univ Of Michigan; Dentistry.

ESSEX, ALICIA; Walnut Ridge HS; Columbus, OH; Band; Chrs; Drl Tm; Girl Scts; Hon Rl; Jr NHS; Off Ade; Sch Pl; Fr Clb; Sec Of Explorers Post #891 Comp Prog 78; General Motors Inst; Mech Engr.

ESSEX, BECKY E; Swan Valley HS; Saginaw, MI;

ESSEX, CINDY; Lakewood HS; Buckeye Lake, OH; Chrh Wkr; Hon Rl; Jr NHS; Stu Cncl; Yth Flsp; Yrbk; Rptr Sch Nwsp; Trk; Chrldng; GAA; Central Ohio Tech Coll.

ESSEX, DAVID; Walnut Ridge HS; Columbus, OH; 118/432 Band; Boy Scts; Chrs; Chrh Wkr; Orch; Sch Mus; Yth Flsp; Mas Awd; Bowling Green St Univ; Comp Prog.

ESSEX, DORENE; Wauseon HS; Wauseon, OH; Sec Frsh Cls; Trs Frsh Cls; Trs Sr Cls; Band; Drl Tm; Hon Rl; Sch Mus; Chrldng; Coll; Optometry.

ESSEX, SUE; Franklin Comm HS; Franklin, IN; 24/300 Cl Rep Jr Cls; Hon Rl; Hosp Ade; NHS; Rptr Sch Nwsp; 4-H; Lat Clb; Pep Clb; Sci Clb; Letter Swmmng; Purdue Univ.

ESSIG, SHELLEY; Theodore Roosevelt HS; Wyandotte, MI; Chrs; Girl Scts; Drama Clb; Swmmng; Trk; Henry Ford Communtiy College; Nurse.

ESTADT, MICHAEL; Zanesville Rosecrans HS; Zanesville, OH; 3/90 Chrh Wkr; Hon Rl; Pres NHS; Sprt Ed Yrbk; Rptr Yrbk; Pres 4-H; Key Clb; Lat Clb; Letter Trk; Rotary Awd; Joe Berg Sci & Math Seminar 78; Oh Schlstc Test Winner Bio 78; Univ; Bus Admin.

ESTELL, JOHN; Maumee HS; Maumee, OH; 1/316 Hon Rl; NHS; Exhibitor Intl Sci & Engr Fair; Ohio Schlstc Invitational Chess Tourn; Univ; Comp Engr.

ESTELLE, GERRY; Albion HS; Albion, MI; Hon Rl; NHS; Sch Pl; Letter Bsktbl; Letter Ftbl; Ten; Purdue Univ; Mech Eng.

ESTEP, DIANE; Ontario HS; Mansfield, OH; 27/176 Sec Sr Cls; AFS; Lbry Ade; Stu Cncl; DECA; Spn Clb; Chrldng; GAA; Scr Kpr; Volleyball Team 78; De Paul Univ; Bus Admin.

ESTEP, LORA; Oceana HS; Kopperston, WV; Cls Rep Soph Cls; Trs Jr Cls; Cl Rep Jr Cls; Cls Rep Sr Cls; Band; Hon Rl; VP NHS; College; Pre Med.

ESTEP, TAMARA; Marsh Fork HS; Whitesville, WV; VP Sr Cls; Am Leg Aux Girls St; Chrs; NHS; Stu Cncl; Yrbk; Sch Nwsp; Drama Clb; Dnfth Awd; Rotary Awd; Raleigh Cnty Voc Tech Ctr; Med Asst.

ESTER, HEIDI; South Dearborn HS; Moores Hill, IN; 32/230 Band; Chrs; Hon Rl; Jr NHS; NHS; Sec Stu Cncl; Yrbk; Letter Bsktbl; GAA; Ball State; Nursing.

ESTERLINE, DAWN; N Central HS; Pioneer, OH; Chrs; Chrh Wkr; Hon Rl; Sch Pl; Yth Flsp; FHA; Bsbl; Bsktbl; Coll; Nursing.

ESTERLINE, TODD; Dublin HS; Dublin, OH; 8/160 Hon Rl; NHS; Spn Clb; IM Sprt; Natl Merit Ltr; Ohi State Univ; Law.

ESTERLY, PAUL J; East Palestine HS; E Palestine, OH; Sch Nwsp; Key Clb; Glf; Merit Roll; Incentive Schlrshp; Youngstown St Univ; Mech Engr.

ESTERWOOD, CYNTHIA; St Agustine Acad; Cleveland, OH; Cls Rep Soph Cls; Cl Rep Jr Cls; Chrs; Hon Rl; Sch Mus; Stu Cncl; Drama Clb; IM Sprt; Akron Univ; Spec Ed.

ESTES, PAMELA; Central Hower HS; Akron, OH; 6/400 Cls Rep Sr Cls; Band; Hon Rl; NHS; Orch; Pol Wkr; Yth Flsp; Fr Clb; Crs Cntry; Letter Trk; Hnrbl Mntn In Kent St Univ Dstrct 77; Otstndng Stdnt Poet Of N E OH Ptry Fstvl 78; Univ; Intl Rltns.

ESTILL, DARLA; Parkersburg HS; Parkersburg, WV; 30/790 Am Leg Aux Girls St; Hon Rl; Capt Hosp Ade; Lit Mag; Stg Crw; Yth Flsp; Rptr Sch Nwsp; Sci Clb; Ohio St Univ; Vet.

ESTLACK, FRED; High School; Southington, OH; Pres Jr Cls; Am Leg Boys St; Beta Clb; Sci Clb; Bsktbl; Crs Cntry; Ftbl; Trk; Tmr; Univ.

ESTLER, KATHY; Barboursville HS; Barboursville, WV; VP Jr Cls; VP Sr Cls; Hon Rl; NHS; Stu Cncl; Mth Clb; Pep Clb; Spn Clb; Letter Glf; Letter Chrldng; Marshall Univ.

ESTRADA, LORETTA; Buena Vista HS; Saginaw, MI; Band; Chrh Wkr; Hon Rl; Hosp Ade; Sec NHS; Sct Actv; Treas Sci Clb; Spn Clb; Letter Bsktbl; Trk; College; Nursing.

ETCHISON, KEVIN; Alexandria Monroe HS; Alexandria, IN; 29/169 Am Leg Boys St; Band; Hon Rl; NHS; Ger Clb; Bsktbl; Ftbl; Mas Awd; Purdue Univ; Engr.

ETELAMAKI, TIMOTHY; Negaunee HS; Palmer, MI; Boy Scts; Hon Rl; Coll; Physics.

ETHERIDGE, BRET; Calumet HS; Gary, IN; 5/300 Hon Rl; Jr NHS; NHS; Off Ade; Pres Fr Clb; Pep Clb; Pres Sci Clb; Letter Wrstlng; Bausch & Lomb Awd; Purdue Univ; Horticulture.

ETIENNE, PAMELA; Perry Central HS; Tell City, IN; 1/90 Chrh Wkr; Cmnty Wkr; Hon Rl; NHS; 4-H; Fr Clb; Pep Clb; Ind Univ; Pre Med.

ETTENHOFER, JANELL; Franklin HS; Franklin, OH; 28/302 Chrs; Chrh Wkr; Girl Scts; Hon Rl; Sch Mus; Yth Flsp; 4-H; Pep Clb; Spn Clb; Univ; Religion.

ETTENSOHN, JOAN; Tell City HS; Tell City, IN; Sch Pl; Yth Flsp; Yrbk; Drama Clb; Western Kentucky Univ; Speech Ther.

ETZEL, MARGARET; Rivet HS; Vincennes, IN; Sec Jr Cls; Chrh Wkr; Hon Rl; Lbry Ade; Rptr Sch Nwsp; FHA; Pep Clb; Ten; Trk; Chrldng; Univ; Phys Ed Tchr.

ETZKORN, NANCY; Delphos St John HS; Spencerville, OH; 1/140 Val; Band; Chrs; Hon Rl; NHS; Orch; Sch Mus; Sch Nwsp; 4-H; Chrldng; Univ Of Toledo; Music.

EUBANK, GLENDA; Addison HS; Addison, MI; 23/136 Cls Rep Sr Cls; Band; Chrs; Chrh Wkr; Debate Tm; Hon Rl; Pol Wkr; Sch Mus; Stu Cncl; Yth Flsp; Michigan St Univ; Med Tech.

EUBANK, MARVIN; Admiral King HS; Lorain, OH; Aud/Vis; Stg Crw; Yrbk; VICA; Bell & Howell Inst; Indus Elec.

EUBANKS, LYNDA; Monrovia HS; Monrovia, IN; Band; Drm Mjrt; Hon Rl; Rptr Yrbk; Chrldng; GAA; Mgrs; PPFtbl; Business School.

EUBANKS, PHILIP; Redford History HS; Detroit, MI; Chrh Wkr; Cmnty Wkr; Hon Rl; JA; NHS; Off Ade; Sch Pl; Yth Flsp; Sch Nwsp; Bsbl; Hnr Awd 79; Univ Of Detroit; Acctg.

EU BANKS, TRACI; Richmond Sr HS; Richmond, IN; Band; Chrh Wkr; Hon Rl; Stu Cncl; Y-Teens; Pep Clb; Chrldng; IM Sprt; PPFtbl; Indiana Univ; Fashion Retailing.

EUCKER, DAVID T; Northland HS; Columbus, OH; Am Leg Boys St; Band; Boy Scts; Hon Rl; NHS; Orch; Pol Wkr; Sch Mus; Lat Clb; Spn Clb; Ohio St Univ; Law.

EUCKER, JEFFREY; Fairview HS; Fairview Park, OH; 5/268 Hon Rl; NHS; Sch Nwsp; Crs Cntry; Swmmng; Trk; Natl Merit Ltr; Miami Univ; Math.

EULER, BENNY; Jennings County HS; No Vernon, IN; Band; Chrh Wkr; Pres 4-H; Spn Clb; Bsktbl; IM Sprt; 4-H Awd; College; Bus Admin.

EULER, TINA M; Otsego HS; Bowling Green, OH; Pres Frsh Cls; Sec Soph Cls; Trs Soph Cls; VP Jr Cls; Sec Sr Cls; Cls Rep Sr Cls; Am Leg Aux Girls St; Hon Rl; Jr NHS; NHS; Univ.

EURICH, DAWN; Arthur Hill HS; Saginaw, MI; Chrh Wkr; Hon Rl; Sch Pl; Drama Clb; Spn Clb; Cit Awd; God Cntry Awd; Saginaw Valley St Coll; History.

EUSTICE, ROBERT; Norwood HS; Norwood, OH; Hon Rl; Vocational School; Elec.

EVANGELISTA, MARK A; North Farmington HS; Farmington Hls, MI; Hon Rl; Bsbl; Ftbl; IM Sprt; Mgrs; Mich Univ; Med.

EVANOSKY, DEBORAH; Ursuline HS; Youngstown, OH; 1/320 Trs Jr Cls; Am Leg Aux Girls St; Girl Scts; Hon Rl; JA; NHS; Sct Actv; FTA; Key Clb; Keyettes; Kent State Univ; Architecture.

EVANOWSKI, LETITIA; St Francis Cabrini HS; Allen Park, MI; Cmp Fr Grls; Drl Tm; Hon Rl; Yth Flsp; Pep Clb; Pom Pon; Pres Awd; Honor Roll Ltr 1976; Drill Varsity Ltr 1977; Varsity Drill Pines 1978; Univ Of Michigan.

EVANS, BELINDA; S Ripley HS; Versailles, IN; 10/104 Band; Chrs; Hon Rl; NHS; Quill & Scroll; Sch Pl; Yth Flsp; Yrbk; Rptr Sch Nwsp; Drama Clb; Marriage.

EVANS, BETH; Westlake HS; Westlake, OH; Pres AFS; Band; Hon Rl; Mod UN; Civ Clb; 4-H; Spn Clb; IM Sprt; 4-H Awd; Univ; Math.

EVANS, BEVERLY; Bruceton HS; Bruceton Mls, WV; Chrs; Chrh Wkr; Drl Tm; Hon Rl; Yrbk; 4-H; FHA; 4-H Awd; College; Elem Educ.

EVANS, BILLY; George Washington HS; Indianapolis, IN; 36/288 Am Leg Boys St; Hon Rl; NHS; Fr Clb; Bsbl; Letter Bsktbl; Capt Ftbl; Kiwan Awd; Kansas Wesleyan Univ; Bus Admin.

EVANS, CINDY; Harrison Community HS; Harrison, MI; Band; Capt Drl Tm; Drm Bgl; Hon Rl; Sch Pl; Drama Clb; Mid Michigan Cmnty Coll.

EVANS, D; Triway HS; Wooster, OH; Aud/Vis; Band; Chrs; Chrh Wkr; Hon Rl; Sch Mus; Sch Pl; Stg Crw; Yth Flsp; Pres Drama Clb; Kent St Univ; Telecmnctns.

EVANS, DANNY; Chesterton HS; Chesterton, IN; 99/413 Letter Ftbl; Letter Trk; Wrstlng; Purdue Univ; Mech Engr.

EVANS, DAVID; East Canton HS; E Canton, OH; Band; Yrbk; Fr Clb; Crs Cntry; Letter Trk; Letter Mgrs; Anapolis Naval Acad; Bio Sci.

EVANS, DAVID; Lincolnview HS; Delphos, OH; 18/80 Pres FFA; Bsbl; Bsktbl; Crs Cntry; Trk; Coach Actv; Bowling Green; Tchr.

EVANS, DINA; Wheeling Central Cath HS; Wheeling, WV; 22/132 Cls Rep Frsh Cls; Cls Rep Soph Cls; Cl Rep Jr Cls; Chrh Wkr; Hon Rl; Sch Mus; Stu Cncl; Rptr Yrbk; Rptr Sch Nwsp; Bsktbl; Marshall Univ; Med Tech.

EVANS, GARY; Concordia Lutheran HS; Ft Wayne, IN; Chrh Wkr; Pol Wkr; Rptr Sch Nwsp; Ger Clb; Treas Sci Clb; IM Sprt; College; Poli Sci.

EVANS, JACQULINE; James Addams Vocational HS; Cleveland, OH; Cmp Fr Grls; Drl Tm; Girl Scts; Lbry Ade; Y-Teens; FHA; Trk; Cit Awd; JA Awd; Bus Schl; Fshn Dsgn.

EVANS, JAMES; Goshen HS; Goshen, IN; 1/259 Cls Rep Frsh Cls; Cls Rep Soph Cls; Cls Rep Sr Cls; Val; FCA; Hon Rl; NHS; Yth Flsp; Fr Clb; Sci Clb; Manchester Coll; Acctg.

EVANS, JAMI; Brandon HS; Ortonville, MI; 1/239 Cls Rep Frsh Cls; Cls Rep Soph Cls; Cl Rep Jr Cls; Cls Rep Sr Cls; Band; Chrs; Debate Tm; Girl Scts; Hon Rl; NHS; Oakland Cnty 4 H Ldrshp Awd 1978; 1st R U Century Ldrs Schlrshp 1978; Alumni Dist Schlrshp Msu 1979; Michigan St Univ; Vet.

EVANS, JANA; West Side Sr HS; Gary, IN; Sec Band; Sec Chrh Wkr; Hon Rl; Jr NHS; NHS; Tmr; Cit Awd; Univ; Jrnlsm.

EVANS, JANE; Newark Sr HS; Newark, OH; Cl Rep Jr Cls; Drl Tm; Hon Rl; Off Ade; Stu Cncl; DECA; FHA; OEA; Mas Awd; Dist Miss Ohio Deca 1978; Demolay Sweetheart Runnerup 1977; Univ; Own Dance Studio.

EVANS, JANET; Turpin HS; Cincinnati, OH; Band; Chrh Wkr; Yth Flsp; College; Accounting.

EVANS, JOHN; Oak Hill HS; Oak Hill, OH; Pres Sr Cls; Chrh Wkr; Hon Rl; NHS; Stu Cncl; Rptr Sch Nwsp; 4-H; Lat Clb; 4-H Awd; Univ.

EVANS, JOHN; Kearsley HS; Burton, MI; Debate Tm; Hon Rl; Natl Forn Lg; Stg Crw; Spn Clb; Michigan St Univ; Vet.

EVANS, JOYCE; Turpin HS; Cincinnati, OH; Chrs; Cmnty Wkr; Hon Rl; Jr NHS; NHS; Spn Clb; Scr Kpr; Tmr; Thomas Moore Coll; Busns Admin.

EVANS, JULIE; Marysville HS; Saint Clair, MI; 1/178 Sec Frsh Cls; Cl Rep Jr Cls; Pres Sr Cls; Val; Am Leg Aux Girls St; Hon Rl; VP NHS; St Clair County Comm Coll; Vet Med.

EVANS, KAREN; Monroe HS; Monroe, MI; 14/650 Cmp Fr Grls; Hon Rl; Treas NHS; Capt Swmmng; Capt Ten; Chrldng; State Champ Synchronized Swimming 1979; City Champ In Tennis 2 Yrs 1976; Stdnt Of Yr In Jr High 1976; Eastern Michigan Univ; Bus.

EVANS, KATHI; Pennfield HS; Battle Creek, MI; 5/150 Cls Rep Frsh Cls; Sec Soph Cls; VP Jr Cls; VP Sr Cls; Am Leg Aux Girls St; Girl Scts; Hon Rl; Jr NHS; Pol Wkr; Stu Cncl; Ferris St Coll; Pharm.

EVANS, KELLY; Dunbar HS; Dunbar, WV; 1/170 Chrh Wkr; Cmnty Wkr; Hon Rl; JA; Jr NHS; Mod UN; NHS; Sch Mus; Stu Cncl; Y-Teens; Hugh O Brian Otstndng Soph 77; Wv Educ Assoc Citizen Of Yr 77; Ga Inst Of Tech MITE Prog 79; Univ; Med.

EVANS, KIM; South Ripley HS; Versailles, IN; 7/104 Trs Frsh Cls; Sec Sr Cls; Band; Chrs; Chrh Wkr; Drl Tm; Hon Rl; Mdrgl; NHS; Quill & Scroll; Bus Schl.

EVANS, KIMBERLY; Philo HS; Blue Rock, OH; Sec Jr Cls; Pres Sr Cls; Band; Chrs; Hon Rl; Hosp Ade; Red Cr Ade; Yth Flsp; 4-H; Fr Clb; Ohio Univ; RN.

EVANS, KRISTINA; Reed City HS; Reed City, MI; 40/160 Band; Hon Rl; Sch Pl; Trk; GAA; Mat Maids; PPFtbl; Scr Kpr; Rotary Awd; Ferris State; Cosmetology.

EVANS, LAURA E; Van Wert HS; Van Wert, OH; 19/201 Band; Chrs; Hon Rl; Hosp Ade; NHS; Y-Teens; 4-H; Lat Clb; Pep Clb; Bsbl; Univ; Pre Med.

EVANS, LAUREL; Benzie Central HS; Frankfort, MI; Chrh Wkr; Hon Rl; Stu Cncl; Yrbk; Sch Nwsp; 4-H; Pep Clb; Bsktbl; Letter Trk; 4-H Awd; Cntrl Michigan Univ; Comp Sci.

EVANS, LESLIE; Heath HS; Heath, OH; 9/151 Cls Rep Frsh Cls; Cls Rep Soph Cls; Cl Rep Jr Cls; Am Leg Aux Girls St; Chrs; Hon Rl; NHS; Stu Cncl; Letter Bsktbl; Letter Trk; Coll; Poli Sci.

EVANS, LISA; Chesterton HS; Chesterton, IN; 38/435 Cls Rep Frsh Cls; Sec Soph Cls; Cls Rep Soph Cls; Cl Rep Jr Cls; Chrs; Girl Scts; Hon Rl; Stu Cncl; Pep Clb; GAA; Purdue Univ; Math.

EVANS, L TANYA C; Newark Sr HS; Newark, OH; Cls Rep Frsh Cls; Hst Soph Cls; Cls Rep Soph Cls; Cl Rep Jr Cls; Band; Chrs; Chrh Wkr; Drl Tm; Girl Scts; Hon Rl; U S Air Force Acdy; Pediatrics.

EVANS, MALENA; Willow Run HS; Ypsilanti, MI; Hosp Ade; JA; Off Ade; Rptr Yrbk; Eastern Michigan Univ; Bus Mgmt.

EVANS, MARGARET; Bluefield HS; Bluefield, WV; 13/285 Chrs; Girl Scts; Hon Rl; Jr NHS; NHS; Quill & Scroll; Yth Flsp; Yrbk; Fr Clb; Keyettes; Laurel Leaves Awd Theme Writing; Curriculum Fair Awd 2nd Pl Typing; College.

EVANS, MARY; Union County HS; Liberty, IN; 6/128 Chrs; Chrh Wkr; Drl Tm; Hon Rl; Sch Mus; Pep Clb; Coach Actv; Pom Pon; Univ; Med.

EVANS, MICHAEL; Clarkston Sr HS; Clarkston, MI; Aud/Vis; Band; Boy Scts; Drm Bgl; Hon Rl; Sct Actv; Rptr Sch Nwsp; Sch Nwsp; Spn Clb; Scr Kpr; Varsity Ski Tm Capt & Letter; Rep To Civitan Yth Seminar; Eagle Scout; Michigan St Univ; Engr.

EVANS, NINA; R Nelson Snider HS; Ft Wayne, IN; 11/550 Sec Sr Cls; Band; Hon Rl; JA; Sch Mus; 4-H; Spn Clb; C of C Awd; Natl Merit Ltr; Ball St Univ.

EVANS, NORA; Manistique HS; Manistique, MI; 13/190 Band; Drl Tm; Hon Rl; Off Ade; Sch Pl; Stg Crw; Rptr Sch Nwsp; Trk; Chrldng; Natl Merit SF; Central Michigan Univ; Psych.

EVANS, PAM; Southport HS; Indianapolis, IN; VP Soph Cls; Sec Jr Cls; Cmnty Wkr; Girl Scts; Hon Rl; Pres JA; Pol Wkr; Stu Cncl; Sprt Ed Yrbk; Sch Nwsp; Homecomg Queen Candidate 1978; IUPUI; Law.

EVANS, PATRICIA A; Nordonia Sr HS; Northfield, OH; 130/412 Band; Cmnty Wkr; Off Ade; Yrbk; Ftbl; PPFtbl; Cit Awd; Span Awd 77; Pride Awd 78; Bus Schl; Bus.

EVANS, RANDAL; Fountain Central HS; Veedersburg, IN; 24/135 Sec Soph Cls; Aud/Vis; Chrh Wkr; Hon Rl; NHS; 4-H; FFA; Bsbl; Bsktbl; Letter Trk; Purdue Univ; Agri.

EVANS, ROBERT; Woodrow Wilson HS; Dunbar, WV; 111/483 Am Leg Boys St; Boy Scts; Hon Rl; Ftbl; Trk; Black Belt In Judo Natl Rank; Whos Who Among HS Stndts 77; Univ Of Charleston; Dr Of Chiroprctc.

EVANS, ROBERTA; Springboro HS; Centerville, OH; Band; Cmp Fr Grls; Drm Bgl; Hon Rl; JA; Stu Cncl; Yth Flsp; 4-H; Letter Bsbl; Letter Trk; Miami Univ; RN.

EVANS, SALLY; Chardon HS; Chardon, OH; 11/255 Chrh Wkr; Hon Rl; NHS; Yth Flsp; Pres OEA; OEA Prep Verbal Cmnctns I Reg St Nat 1st Pl 1978; Cmnctns II Reg St 1st Pl 1979; OEA Ambsr Torch 1979; Lakeland Cmnty Coll; Bus Mgmt.

EVANS, SUSIE; North Union HS; Marysville, OH; 13/140 Sec Sr Cls; Trs Sr Cls; Band; Chrs; Hon Rl; Lit Mag; NHS; Ohi State Univ; Veterinarian.

EVANS, SUZANNE M; Vassar HS; Millington, MI; Girl Scts; Quill & Scroll; Sct Actv; Rptr Yrbk; Rptr Sch Nwsp; Fr Clb; Spn Clb; College; Phys Therapy.

EVANS, TERESA; Allen E HS; Harrod, OH; Cmnty Wkr; Lbry Ade; Sch Nwsp; 4-H; Pep Clb; Trk; GAA; Track Awds; Spelling Bee; College.

EVANS, TINA; Galion HS; Galion, OH; Am Leg Aux Girls St; Band; Chrh Wkr; Hon Rl; Hosp Ade; NHS; Orch; VP Fr Clb; 4-H Awd; Ohi St Univ; Med.

EVANS, TODD; Newbury HS; Newbury, OH; Hon Rl; Jr NHS; NHS; Sch Pl; Pres Stu Cncl; Sci Clb; Spn Clb; Letter Bsbl; Letter Bsktbl; Letter Ftbl; Univ; Radio Cmnctns.

EVANS, TODD; Martinsburg HS; Martinsburg, WV; Pres Frsh Cls; Cls Rep Soph Cls; Hon Rl; Boys Clb Am; Key Clb; Ftbl; Trk; Fairmont State Coll; Drafting.

EVANS, VALERIE; Lakeview Sr HS; St Clair Shores, MI; Cls Rep Frsh Cls; Cls Rep Soph Cls; Band; Chrs; Hon Rl; Mdrgl; Off Ade; Orch; Sch Pl; Stu Cncl; Mi Natl Comp Schslhp 78; Jr Arion Musicl Awd In Orch 78; Awd Of Accptnc For Poetry Pub Essay Anthology 77; Michigan St Univ; Vet Med.

EVANS, VICKY; Ontonagon Area HS; Ontonagon, MI; Chrh Wkr; Girl Scts; Hon Rl; NHS; Off Ade; Yrbk; Drama Clb; 4-H; OEA; Trk; Muskegon Bus Coll; Soc Work.

EVANS, WILLIAM; Fayetteville Perry Local HS; Fayetteville, OH; 1/50 Val; Boy Scts; Chrs; Chrh Wkr; Cmnty Wkr; Debate Tm; Hon Rl; Jr NHS; NHS; Sch Mus; Xavier Univ; Bus.

EVANS, WILLIAM S; Cadiz HS; Cadiz, OH; Chrs; Hon Rl; Off Ade; Sch Mus; Sch Pl; Drama Clb; Trk; College; Law.

EVANS, ZARINA; Bristol HS; Bristolville, OH; 6/65 Pres Jr Cls; Chrs; Hon Rl; Jr NHS; NHS; Stu Cncl; Bsktbl; Trk; Ohi State; Sci.

EVARD JR, JOSEPH; North Ridgeville HS; N Ridgeville, OH; 117/400 Band; Boy Scts; Chrh Wkr; Hon Rl; Sct Actv; Kent St Univ; Med.

EVELAND, CATHY; Hilligard HS; Hilliard, OH; 42/367 Girl Scts; Hon Rl; NHS; Red Cr Ade; Kiwan Awd; Mt Carmel Schl Of Nursing; Nursing.

EVENS, DAVID; North Putnam HS; Fillmore, IN; Band; Chrh Wkr; Cmnty Wkr; FCA; Pres Yth Flsp; VP 4-H; Letter Bsbl; Letter Ftbl; 4-H Awd; Counselor For St Jr Leader Camp; Counselor For 4 H Camp; Honor Group For Natl 4 H Conf; College; Education.

EVENS, DAVID; North Putnam Jr Sr HS; Fillmore, IN; Band; Chrh Wkr; FCA; Yth Flsp; VP 4-H; Letter Bsbl; Letter Ftbl; 4-H Awd; Purdue Coll; Bio Sci.

EVENS, LYNNE; Reeths Putter HS; Muskegon, MI; Chrh Wkr; Cmnty Wkr; Girl Scts; JA; Talented Stud Schlrshp 79; Univ Of Michigan; Psych.

EVENS, MARK A; Lewis County HS; Weston, WV; Am Leg Boys St; Chrh Wkr; Hon Rl; Jr NHS; NHS; Pres Yth Flsp; Mgrs; Univ; Chem Engr.

EVERAGE, MIKE; Borden HS; Pekin, IN; Hon Rl; NHS; Bsbl; Bsktbl; Trk; Am Leg Awd;.

EVEREST, STACEY; Athens HS; Battle Crk, MI; Band; Cmp Fr Grls; Hon Rl; 4-H; Pep Clb; 4-H Awd; Receptionist.

EVERETT, BARBARA; David Anderson HS; Lisbon, OH; Band; Cmp Fr Grls; Chrs; NHS; Sch Mus; Yth Flsp; Y-Teens; Yrbk; Sci Clb; Trk; Kent St Univ; Home Ec.

EVERETT, CAMILLE; Chesapeake HS; Cheaspeake, OH; Chrh Wkr; Hon Rl; Yth Flsp; 4-H; FHA; Pep Clb; Bsktbl; Letter Trk; Scr Kpr; 4-H Awd; Univ; RN.

EVERETT, ELIZABETH; Saginaw HS; Saginaw, MI; Chrs; Chrh Wkr; Hosp Ade; JA; Jr NHS; Sch Mus; Sch Pl; JC Awd; Natl Merit Ltr; Delta College; Regist Nurse.

EVERETT, JULIE; Lumen Christi HS; Jackson, MI;

EVERETT, RODNEY; Bellmont HS; Decatur, IN; 18/244 Band; Drl Tm; Hon Rl; Jr NHS; Sci Clb; Purdue Univ; Engr.

EVERETT, SCOTT; Kent Roosevelt HS; Kent, OH; Boy Scts; Chrs; Hon Rl; Bsbl; Ftbl; Ten; College; Math.

EVERETT, STEPHEN E; Lumen Christi HS; Jackson, MI; Hon Rl; Fr Clb; Bsktbl; Letter Ftbl; Trk; IM Sprt; Natl Merit SF; College.

EVERHART, DWAIN; Waverly HS; Waverly, OH; Pres Jr Cls; Pres Sr Cls; Am Leg Boys St; Debate Tm; Hon Rl; NHS; Stu Cncl; Spn Clb; Am Leg Awd; Natl Merit Schl; Miami Univ; Pulp Paper Making.

EVERHART, RENEE; Coshocton HS; Coshocton, OH; Band; Hon Rl; Stu Cncl; Trk; Chrldng; GAA; PPFtbl; Ohio St Univ.

EVERINGHAM, MICHAEL; Perkins HS; Sandusky, OH; 39/265 Boy Scts; Chrh Wkr; Hon Rl; NHS; Red Cr Ade; ROTC; Yth Flsp; Bsbl; Ftbl; Chmn Swmmng; Miami Univ; System Analysis.

EVERLOVE, MARY A; Trenton HS; Trenton, MI; Hon Rl; NHS; Red Cr Ade; Stu Cncl; Sec Pep Clb; Chrldng; Tmr; Hillsdale Coll; Law.

EVERMAN, DIANA L; East Clinton HS; Sabina, OH; Cls Rep Sr Cls; Chrh Wkr; Cmnty Wkr; Girl Scts; Hon Rl; Lbry Ade; Off Ade; Yth Flsp; FTA; Pep Clb; Miami Univ; Secondary Ed.

EVERMAN, JAN M; Celina Sr HS; Celina, OH; Sec Frsh Cls; Pres Jr Cls; Girl Scts; Hon Rl; Jr NHS; NHS; Off Ade; Sct Actv; Ed Sch Nwsp; Rptr Sch Nwsp; Univ Of S Florida; Mktg.

EVERMAN, KELLY; Norwalk HS; Norwalk, OH; Drl Tm; Hon Rl; Jr NHS; NHS; Off Ade; Rptr Sch Nwsp; Lat Clb; Letter Ten; PPFtbl; Univ; Bio.

EVERS, ANDREW B; Charlestown HS; Charlestown, IN; 37/170 Band; Boy Scts; Orch; Yth Flsp; Yrbk; 4-H; Pep Clb; Glf; IM Sprt; 4-H Awd; Purdue Univ; Forestry.

EVERS, DIANN; St Henry HS; St Henry, OH; Band; Hon Rl; FHA; OEA; Pep Clb; Bus School; Sales.

EVERSMAN, GEORGE; St Ignatius HS; Pepper Pike, OH; 5/309 Boy Scts; Chrh Wkr; Hosp Ade; NHS; Sprt Ed Sch Nwsp; Rptr Sch Nwsp; Ten; IM Sprt; Natl Merit Ltr; College; Premedicine.

EVERSMAN, SHARON; New Knoxville Local HS; New Knoxville, OH; 6/42 Cls Rep Sr Cls; Am Leg Aux Girls St; Chrh Wkr; Girl Scts; NHS; Sch Pl; Stu Cncl; Rptr Yrbk; Rptr Sch Nwsp; Pres 4-H; Univ Of Cincinnati; German.

EVERSOLE, ANDREW; Fort Jennings HS; Ft Jennings, OH; 1/30 Sec Soph Cls; Val; Am Leg Boys St; Band; Chrs; Hon Rl; NHS; Sch Mus; Yrbk; Glf; Univ Of Dayton; Elec Engr.

EVERSOLE, CAROL; Fairless HS; Brewster, OH; Cmp Fr Grls; Chrh Wkr; Girl Scts; Hon Rl; Hosp Ade; Stu Cncl; Yth Flsp; Y-Teens; FHA; Pep Clb; Ohio St Univ; Bus.

EVERSOLE, DONALD; Allen East HS; Lafayette, OH; 14/107 Band; Chrs; Hon Rl; Sch Mus; 4-H; FFA; Pep Clb; Ohio Inst Of Tech; Comp Tech.

EVERSOLE, JAMI; Franklin HS; Franklin, OH; Chrs; Hon Rl; Sch Mus; Sch Pl; Drama Clb; Pep Clb; Trk; Capt Chrldng; Miami Univ.

EVERSOLE, JANICE; Tuslaw HS; Massillon, OH; 32/180 Band; Hon Rl; NHS; Orch; Stu Cncl; Yth Flsp; Malone; Bio.

EVERSOLE, REGINA; Withrow HS; Cincinnati, OH; Chrs; Cmnty Wkr; Girl Scts; Hon Rl; Cit Awd; Housng Opprtnts Made Equal Poster Awrd 79; Merit Achvmnt Awrd 79; Univ Of Cincinnati; Pharm.

EVERSON, GLENDA; Wayne HS; Dayton, OH; Hon Rl; NHS; Mgrs;.

EVERSON, MARY; T L Handy HS; Bay City, MI; 12/265 Trs Frsh Cls; Band; Drm Mjrt; NHS; Stu Cncl; Ger Clb; Ten; Natl Merit SF; Univ Of Michigan; Psych.

EVERTS, DUANA; North Putnam Jr Sr HS; Greencastle, IN; Lat Clb; Mth Clb; Sci Clb; Purdue Univ; Vet Med.

EVERTS, MIKE; Comstock Park HS; Comstock Pk, MI; Chrh Wkr; Hon Rl; Jr NHS; Natl Forn Lg; NHS; Off Ade; Pol Wkr; Stg Crw; Yth Flsp; Spn Clb; Northern Michigan Univ; Pre Med.

EVETT, TAMMY; Coloma HS; Coloma, MI; Sec Frsh Cls; Sec Soph Cls; Sec Jr Cls; Sec Sr Cls; Hon Rl; NHS; Stu Cncl; Fr Clb; Letter Bsbl; Ten; Univ Of Michigan; Law.

EVICK, JODI; St Clairsville HS; St Clairsville, OH; Sec Sr Cls; Chrs; Chrh Wkr; Hon Rl; Off Ade; Stu Cncl; Yth Flsp; Y-Teens; Rptr Yrbk; 4-H; Muskingum Coll; Elem Educ.

EVINGER, ROBERT; West Vigo HS; W Terre Haute, IN; 23/194 Aud/Vis; FCA; Hon Rl; Orch; Rdo Clb; Ind St Univ; Electronics.

EVOLA, JUDY; Lakeland HS; Union Lake, MI; Hon Rl; Natl Forn Lg; Rptr Yrbk; Rptr Sch Nwsp; Pep Clb; Spn Clb; Central Michigan Univ; Jrnlsm.

EVOY, KERRY; Marion Adams HS; Sheridan, IN; 1/99 Pres Soph Cls; Cls Rep Soph Cls; Cl Rep Jr Cls; Cls Rep Sr Cls; Hon Rl; Jr NHS; NHS; Stu Cncl; Letter Crs Cntry; Purdue Univ; Comp Prog.

EVRINGHAM, KARLA; Graham HS; De Graff, OH; Trs Jr Cls; Trs Sr Cls; Chrs; Off Ade; Sch Mus; Sch Pl; Stu Cncl; Rptr Yrbk; FHA; Chrldng;.

EVSANIO, MIKE; Woodrow Wilson HS; Youngstwn, OH; 44/341 Hon Rl; Youngstown St Univ.

EWALD, LYNN; Unionville Sebewaing HS; Unionville, MI; Bsbl; Bsktbl; Ftbl; Am Leg Awd;.

EWART, GLENN; Springfield Township HS; Akron, OH; Band; Boy Scts; Chrs; Debate Tm; Hon Rl; Lbry Ade; MMM; Natl Forn Lg; NHS; Fr Clb; Whos Who In Music 78; Spartanaires 78; Oh Forestry Assoc 76; Close Up 78; Univ Of Akron; Engr.

EWART, KATHLEEN; London HS; London, OH; Band; Hon Rl; Lit Mag; NHS; Yth Flsp; Rptr Yrbk; 4-H; College.

EWELL, TIMOTHY; Concordia Lutheran HS; Ft Wayne, IN; 5/187 Am Leg Boys St; Hon Rl; Jr NHS; Quill & Scroll; Ed Sch Nwsp; Pres Ger Clb; IM Sprt; Editor In Chief Schl Newspaper 79 80; Schlrshp For 2 Wk HS Jrnlsm Inst 78 & 79; Runner Up Dst Prog; Coll; Poli Sci.

EWEN, ROBIN; La Crosse HS; La Crosse, IN; Chrs; Chrh Wkr; Hon Rl; Jr NHS; Lbry Ade; NHS; Yth Flsp; Ger Clb; Leo Clb; Univ; Machinist.

EWERS, STEVE; Montpelier HS; Montplier, OH; Chrh Wkr; Hon Rl; 4-H; Letter Wrstlng; Coach Actv; Mgrs; Scr Kpr; Tmr; Univ; Bus Mgmt.

EWIN, KAREN; Boonville HS; Boonville, IN; 27/210 Trs Soph Cls; Trs Jr Cls; Band; Hon Rl; Stu Cncl; Pep Clb; Bsktbl; Trk; Chrldng; Pom Pon; MVP Frsh Track 1977; Indiana Univ; Phys Educ.

EWING, AMY; Greenfield Cntrl HS; Greenfield, IN; 15/303 FCA; Hon Rl; Fr Clb; Ten; Mgrs; Tmr; British Gymnastics Awds; Lahr Sr Schl Outstndng Intramural Awd; Pres Phys Fitness Awd; Purdue Univ; Dentistry.

EWING, JAMES B; Northwestern HS; Burbank, OH; Aud/Vis; Chrs; Hon Rl; NHS; Sch Mus; Drama Clb; 4-H; Pep Clb; Letter Ftbl; Letter Trk; Ohio St Univ; Engr.

EWING, KELLY; Scott HS; Toledo, OH; Bsbl; Letter Bsktbl; Coach Actv; Scr Kpr; Vllybl 79; Bowling Green St Univ.

EWING, KEVIN; Traverse City Sr HS; Traverse City, MI; 102/790 Cls Rep Frsh Cls; Hon Rl; Sprt Ed Sch Nwsp; Hockey; Capt Socr; Capt Ten; Michigan Tech Univ; Engr.

EWING, LORI; Midland Trail HS; Hico, WV; Chrs; Chrh Wkr; Hon Rl; NHS; Yrbk;.

EWING, ROBERT L; Brebeuf Preparatory HS; Indianapolis, IN; 79/145 Hon Rl; Letter Bsktbl; Trk; Natl Merit SF; Lttrd Var Basketbl 1976; Capt Of Var Basketbl Tm 1978; Univ; Engr.

EWING, SCOTT; Lawton HS; Lawton, MI; Band; Chrs; Hon Rl; Sch Mus; Ftbl; Trk; Wrstlng; Coach Actv; Tmr; Band Dept Awd Winner 79; Mi St Comptv Schlhsp 79; Ferris St Coll; Auto Serv.

EWING, SUZANNE; Maumee HS; Maumee, OH; 2/316 Hon Rl; Lit Mag; NHS; Treas Orch; Rptr Yrbk; Fr Clb; Natl Merit SF; College.

EWING, TAMARA; Point Pleasant HS; Pt Pleasant, WV; Girl Scts; Y-Teens; Civ Clb;.

EWING, THOMAS; South Range HS; Salem, OH; Pres Jr Cls; Hon Rl; Lbry Ade; NHS; 4-H; Ger Clb; Letter Crs Cntry; Letter Trk; Univ; Agri Engr.

EWY, KRISTEN; Elston HS; Mich City, IN; Sec Jr Cls; Sec Sr Cls; Hon Rl; Stu Cncl; Rptr Yrbk; Fr Clb; Pep Clb; Chmn Mat Maids; Scr Kpr; Ind Univ; Journalism.

EXLINE, WILLIAM; Marysville HS; Marysville, OH; 7/236 NHS; Sch Pl; Stg Crw; Key Clb; Lat Clb; Bsbl; IM Sprt; Natl Merit Ltr; Ohio St Univ; Comp Engr.

EXNER, ELLEN; Avondale HS; Bloomfield Hil, MI; 13/260 Cl Rep Jr Cls; NHS; Sch Mus; Sch Pl; Stu Cncl; Ed Sch Nwsp; VP Fr Clb; PPFtbl; Natl Merit SF; Opt Clb Awd; Wayne St Merit Schlrshp 79; Avondale Yth Invlmnt Awd 78; 2nd Pl Optimst Spch Contst 77; Wayne St Univ; Lib Arts.

EXNER, SUSAN; Brandywine HS; Niles, MI; AFS; Band; Girl Scts; JA; Sct Actv; 4-H; Pep Clb; Spn Clb; S W Michigan Coll; Nursing.

EXUM, MARC H; William A Wirt HS; Gary, IN; Band; Hon Rl; Orch; Pep Clb; Spn Clb; Bst Plyr In Sect Of Band; Valparaiso Tech Inst; Comp Sci.

EXUM, VANESSA; Warrensville Hts Sr HS; Warrensville, OH; Cmp Fr Grls; Hosp Ade; Off Ade; Cit Awd; Merit Schlrshp Awd In Bio & Algebra; Serv Awd As An Office Helper; Coll; Med.

EYEN, KEVIN; Cambridge HS; Cambridge, OH; 52/270 Key Clb; Capt Bsbl; Capt Ftbl; Coach Actv; Miami Univ; Archt.

EYINK, DIANE; Coldwater HS; Coldwater, OH; 19/147 Band; Chrs; Chrh Wkr; Hon Rl; NHS; Sch Mus; Rptr Sch Nwsp; Drama Clb; Ger Clb; Letter Gym; Miami Univ; Spec Ed.

EYINK, NANCY A; Celina Sr HS; Celina, OH; 1/240 Chrh Wkr; Hon Rl; NHS; Yrbk; FTA; Lat Clb; Natl Merit Ltr; Univ; Math.

EYMAN, CINDY; Fairfield Union HS; Lancaster, OH; 6/150 Sec Frsh Cls; Sec Band; Chrh Wkr; Drl Tm; Hon Rl; NHS; Sch Pl; Treas Stu Cncl; Yth Flsp; VP FTA; Sec.

EYNON, NEIL; St Edward HS; Westlake, OH; 50/400 Boy Scts; Chrs; Chrh Wkr; Debate Tm; Hon Rl; Jr NHS; NHS; PAVAS; Sch Mus; Dayton College; Drama.

EYSTER, JEFFREY; Northwest HS; Indianapolis, IN; 65/565 Hon Rl; Jr NHS; Lit Mag; NHS; Quill & Scroll; Sct Actv; Sprt Ed Yrbk; Rptr Yrbk; Yrbk; IM Sprt; Purdue Univ; Mech.

EYSTER, MARK; Williamston HS; Williamstown, MI; Boy Scts; Jr NHS; Rptr Yrbk; 4-H; Crs Cntry; Trk; 4-H Awd; College.

EZELL, GINA; John Adams HS; Cleveland, OH; Trs Frsh Cls; Cls Rep Frsh Cls; Cls Rep Soph Cls; Off Ade; Stg Crw; Stu Cncl; Drama Clb; Rdo Clb; Univ.

EZZO, DAWN; Liberty HS; Hubbard, OH; Cl Rep Jr Cls; Band; Hon Rl; Orch; Sch Mus; Sch Pl; Drama Clb; VP Fr Clb; Swmmng; Chrldng; Hon Prog 77 78 & 79; Univ; Pre Med.

F

FABER, DAVID; Beal City HS; Weidman, MI; Chrs; Hon Rl; FFA; Voc Schl.

FABER, DEBRA; Holgate HS; New Bavaria, OH; 10/58 Sec Soph Cls; Trs Jr Cls; Sec Sr Cls; Trs Sr Cls; Hon Rl; Jr NHS; NHS; Yrbk; Trk; Chrldng;.

FABER, DEBRA A; Holgate HS; New Bavaria, OH; 10/58 Sec Soph Cls; Trs Jr Cls; Sec Sr Cls; Trs Sr Cls; Hon Rl; NHS; Yrbk; Associated Schls Inc; Arilines.

FABER, STEVE; Ida Public HS; Ida, MI; Crs Cntry; Trk; 4-H Awd; Madonna Coll; Paramedic.

FABER, TIMOTHY; St Philip Cath Ctrl HS; Battle Creek, MI; Boy Scts; Chrs; Hon Rl; NHS; Sct Actv; Stu Cncl; 4-H; Lat Clb; Letter Ftbl; Am Leg Awd; Univ; Jrnlsm.

FABIAN, HENRY; Lutheran HS West; Clveland, OH; 1/97 Trs Soph Cls; Pres Jr Cls; Band; Chrh Wkr; Debate Tm; FCA; Hon Rl; Lit Mag; Mod UN; NHS; U S Naval Acad; Ocean Engr.

FABIAN, LISA; Bishop Dwenger HS; Ft Wayne, IN; Sec Soph Cls; VP Sr Cls; Hon Rl; NHS; Stg Crw; Key Clb; Mat Maids; Natl Merit Ltr; Eng Schlrshp For Poetry; Latin Awd Summa 76; Gld Mdl For Natl Ltin Exam; Bio Awd 77; Kappa Kappa Kappa; Univ; Pre Med.

FABIAN, MARGARET; Villa Angela Academy; Euclid, OH; 1/170 Boy Scts; Cmp Fr Grls; Hon Rl; Lbry Ade; NHS; Off Ade; Red Cr Ade; Sch Mus; IM Sprt; Natl Merit Ltr; 100.

FABIAN, MARY B; Campbell Memorial HS; Campbell, OH; Cls Rep Frsh Cls; Chrh Wkr; Hon Rl; Natl Forn Lg; Sch Pl; Stg Crw; Rptr Sch Nwsp; Drama Clb; FNA; Mth Clb; Youngstown State; Conmputer Science.

FABIAN, SUSAN; Warren Western Reserve HS; Warren, OH; 49/436 Band; Hon Rl; JA; Y-Teens; FTA; Sci Clb; Kent State Univ; Med.

FABIEN, ELIZABETH; John Glenn HS; Westland, MI; Aud/Vis; Chrh Wkr; Girl Scts; Hon Rl; Jr NHS; Orch; Fr Clb; Sci Clb; Univ; Psychology.

FABINY, LARRY; Canfield HS; Canfield, OH; Aud/Vis; Hon Rl; NHS; Ger Clb; Spn Clb; Natl Merit Ltr; College; Computer Science.

FABRIZIO, J; Niles Mckinley HS; Niles, OH; Letter Bsbl; Youngstown State; Chem Engr.

FABYAN, LINDA; Jackson Milton HS; Lake Milton, OH; 5/108 Am Leg Aux Girls St; Band; Cmp Fr Grls; Hon Rl; Hosp Ade; Red Cr Ade; Sch Mus; Sch Pl; Rptr Yrbk; Yrbk; Univ Of Pittsburgh; Nursing.

FABYAN, PETER; Bad Axe HS; Bad Axe, MI; Hon Rl; Capt Bsbl; Letter Bsktbl; Letter Ftbl; Coach Actv; Ferris St Coll; Tchr.

FACCENDA, SUSAN; St Josephs HS; South Bend, IN; 8/260 Hon Rl; NHS; Quill & Scroll; Sch Pl; Rptr Yrbk; Drama Clb; Spn Clb; DAR Awd; Univ Of Notre Dame; Law.

FACEMYER, DIANA L; Spencer HS; Spencer, WV; 1/150 Sec Chrs; Hon Rl; Sch Pl; Sch Nwsp; Drama Clb; 4-H; Ten; Chrldng; IM Sprt; 4-H Awd; Arch A Moore Vo Tech; Sec.

FACKLER, CHERYL; Lutheran HS East; Cleveland Hts, OH; Chrs; Girl Scts; Hon Rl; Off Ade; Sch Pl; Ed Yrbk; Rptr Sch Nwsp; Drama Clb; Letter Bsbl; Letter Bsktbl; Univ; Lang.

FACKLER, DEBORAH J; Concordia Lutheran HS; Ft Wayne, IN; 6/173 Chrh Wkr; Cmnty Wkr; Hon Rl; VP JA; NHS; Quill & Scroll; Yth Flsp; Ed Yrbk; Lat Clb; Natl Merit SF; College; Law.

FACKLER, JACKIE; Waldron Area HS; Camden, MI; 1/39 Trs Jr Cls; Trs Sr Cls; Chrh Wkr; Hon Rl; NHS; Off Ade; Sch Pl; Yth Flsp; FHA; Pep Clb; Olivet Nazarene Univ; Pre Med.

FACKLER, JACQUELINE; Waldron Area HS; Camden, MI; Trs Jr Cls; Trs Sr Cls; Hon Rl; NHS; Off Ade; Sch Pl; Bsktbl; Trk; Chrldng; GAA; Univ; Pre Med.

FACKNITZ, TAMMY; Kalkaska HS; Kalkaska, MI; Hon Rl; GAA; Univ; Child Care.

FACKS, LINDA; Columbia City Joint HS; Columbia City, IN; 6/247 Cls Rep Frsh Cls; Cls Rep Soph Cls; Cl Rep Jr Cls; Cls Rep Sr Cls; Chrh Wkr; Girl Scts; Hon Rl; Off Ade; Yrbk; 4-H; Carleton Coll.

FADELL, ALICIA; Andrean HS; Valparaiso, IN; 3/272 Hon Rl; Sec NHS; Sec Mth Clb; VP Spn Clb; Univ Of Denver; Physics.

FADELL, PATRICIA; Chesterton HS; Valparaiso, IN; Cls Rep Sr Cls; Chrh Wkr; Debate Tm; Drl Tm; Hon Rl; Sec NHS; Off Ade; Sch Pl; Stu Cncl; Pep Clb; Univ; Pre Law.

FADERO, STEPHEN; Bluefield HS; Bluefield, WV; 20/285 Am Leg Boys St; Band; Hon Rl; NHS; Fr Clb; Pep Clb; Most Otstndng Band Mbr 78; North Carolina St Univ; Aero Engr.

FADIL, GARY; St Edward HS; Middleburg Hts, OH; 24/360 Hon Rl; Jr NHS; Off Ade; Yrbk; Ftbl; Wrstlng; IM Sprt; Harvard Univ; Law.

FADOOL, DENISE; St Alphonsus HS; Dearborn, MI; 15/180 Cls Rep Soph Cls; Trs Jr Cls; Hon Rl; NHS; Sch Mus; Stu Cncl; Pep Clb; Chrldng; Univ Of Mich; Phys Ther.

FAFLICK, LORI; Fairview HS; Fairview Pk, OH; AFS; Hon Rl; NHS; Letter Trk; Chrldng; IM Sprt; Scr Kpr; Cit Awd; Kiwan Awd; Pres Awd; Purdue Univ; Engineering.

FAGAN, ANN; West Lafayette HS; W Lafayette, IN; 72/185 Chrs; Girl Scts; Sch Mus; Sch Pl; Sch Nwsp; Treas Drama Clb; Ten; Purdue Univ; Aero Engr.

FAGAN, JAMES; Hagerstown Jr Sr HS; Cambridge City, IN; Treas Band; Hon Rl; NHS; Pres 4-H; Pres FFA; FFA Hoosier Farmer Awd; FFA Star Chptr Farmer; Mbr St FFA Band; Kentucky Christian Coll; Ag.

FAGAN, KATHLEEN; Magnificat HS; Rocky River, OH; Pres Frsh Cls; Cl Rep Jr Cls; NHS; Stu Cncl;

Rptr Sch Nwsp; IM Sprt; Univ Of Notre Dame; Chem Engr.

FAGEN, PEGGY; Lake Central HS; Dyer, IN; 114/612 Cl Rep Jr Cls; Chrh Wkr; FCA; Hon Rl; Off Ade; Sch Mus; Ger Clb; Pep Clb; Chrldng; Coach Actv; Creighton Univ; Educ.

FAGER, STEVEN; Gwinn HS; Sawyer Afb, MI; Boy Scts; Hon Rl; Ftbl; Voc Schl; Const Elec.

FAGER, STEVEN; Gwinn HS; K I Sawyer AFB, MI; Boy Scts; Hon Rl; Ftbl; Voc Schl; Construction Elec.

FAGER, SUSAN; Gwinn HS; K I Sawyer, MI; Hon Rl; Sct Actv; Bsktbl; Crs Cntry; Trk; Mic Technological Univ; Forestry.

FAGERLUND, MARCIA; Mt Pleasant HS; Mt Pleasant, MI; Chrs; Hon Rl; Mdrgl; NHS; Off Ade; Sch Mus; Sch Pl; Yth Flsp; Pep Clb; Chrldng; Internatl Thespian Soc 79; Univ; Music.

FAGERMAN, MICHAEL; Cadillac HS; Cadillac, MI; Hon Rl; Letter Bsktbl; Letter Ftbl; Gm Inst Of Tech; Mech Engr.

FAGERMAN, SHERRI; Cadillac HS; Cadillac, MI; Cls Rep Soph Cls; NHS; Bsktbl; Trk; Pres GAA; Mich State.

FAGG, RODNEY; Clay City HS; Cory, IN; Pres Frsh Cls; Pres Soph Cls; Band; Chrh Wkr; Treas NHS; 4-H; Fr Clb; Olivet Nazarene Coll; Music.

FAGULA, GEORGE A; University HS; Jere, WV; Ftbl; IM Sprt; College; Phys Educ.

FAHERTY, TIM; Bishop Watterson HS; Columbus, OH; 37/241 Aud/Vis; Hon Rl; NHS; Sch Mus; Sch Pl; Stg Crw; Lat Clb; Ftbl; Ohio St Univ; Engr.

FAHEY, DIANE; Normandy HS; Parma, OH; 35/657 Chrs; Hon Rl; Yth Flsp; Fr Clb; Pep Clb; Trk; College; Med.

FAHEY, JOHN; Carson City Crystal HS; Muir, MI; Hon Rl; NHS; Pres Stu Cncl; 4-H; Crs Cntry; Trk; IM Sprt; College; Chemistry.

FAHLSING, STACY; Shawnee HS; Lima, OH; Cls Rep Frsh Cls; Girl Scts; Hon Rl; Off Ade; Spn Clb; Bsktbl; Trk; IM Sprt; PPFtbl; Scr Kpr; Ohio N Univ; Phys Ed.

FAHRER, DAVID E; Springfield HS; Holland, OH; Chrh Wkr; Hon Rl; Sprt Ed Yrbk; Sch Nwsp; Fr Clb; Bowling Green St Univ; Broadcasting.

FAHRIG, STEPHEN; Archbishop Alter HS; Centerville, OH; 5/325 NHS; Ger Clb; Key Clb; IM Sprt; College.

FAHRION, JOSEPH B; Lakeview HS; Cortland, OH; Aud/Vis; Socr; Trk; IM Sprt; Varsity Bsktbl Letter; Track & Ftbl Letter; Chess Clb; Marietta Univ; Math.

FAHRNER, SUZANNE; Grosse Pointe North HS; Grosse Pte Wds, MI; Chrh Wkr; Hon Rl; NHS; OEA; Spn Clb; PPFtbl; Mercy Coll; Med Tech.

FAHRNI, MICHELLE; Tuslaw HS; Massillon, OH; 13/177 Hon Rl; NHS; Stu Cncl; Y-Teens; Chmn FHA; Sec OEA; Stark Tech Coll; Comp Progr.

FAIDIGA, POLLY; Eastlake North HS; Eastlake, OH; Hon Rl; Off Ade; Sch Pl; Stg Crw; Stu Cncl; VICA; Letter Crs Cntry; Letter Trk; Scr Kpr; Univ; Enviro Sci.

FAIR, ELAINE; Beechcroft Sr HS; Columbus, OH; Chrs; Girl Scts; Hon Rl; Jr NHS; NHS; Off Ade; Sch Pl; Pres Ger Clb; OEA; Scholstc Achvmnt Awd For Above 3.60 Averg 1978; Prednt Of Germn Clb 1974; German Singing Soc 1972; Bus Schl; Court Reporter.

FAIR, EUGENE; Federal Hocking HS; Athens, OH; Chrh Wkr; Hon Rl; Yth Flsp; Perfect Attndnc Awd 76; Hocking Tech Coll; Acctg.

FAIR, JO; Sidney HS; Sidney, OH; Girl Scts; Hon Rl; NHS; Orch; Drama Clb; Pep Clb; Bsktbl; Letter Crs Cntry; Letter Ten; Letter Trk; Ohio St Univ; Vet Med.

FAIR, TERRI; Elkhart Central HS; Elkhart, IN; Chrs; Hon Rl; NHS; PAVAS; Sch Mus; Sch Pl; Stg Crw; Stu Cncl; Sec Drama Clb; Purdue Univ; Pharm.

FAIRBANKS, ERIC; Hampshire HS; Kirby, WV; 37/212 AFS; Hon Rl; NHS; Letter Bsktbl; Letter Crs Cntry; Letter Glf; Letter Trk; Wv Univ; Comp Sci.

FAIRBANKS, JEFFERY; Brethren HS; Irons, MI; Cls Rep Frsh Cls; Trs Soph Cls; Cls Rep Soph Cls; Cl Rep Jr Cls; Band; Hon Rl; Sch Mus; Stu Cncl; Y-Teens; Drama Clb;.

FAIRBANKS, RONALD; Lakota HS; Bradner, OH; 2/160 Am Leg Boys St; Hon Rl; NHS; Stu Cncl; Capt Ftbl; Ohio Northern Univ; Engineering.

FAIRCHILD, DARLA; Alpena HS; Alpena, MI; Band; Gym; Central Michigan Univ; Elem Ed.

FAIRCHILD, DEBBIE; Belmont HS; Dayton, OH; Cls Rep Soph Cls; Band; Drl Tm; Hon Rl; NHS; Orch; Yrbk; FHA; Univ Of Cincinnati; Art.

FAIRCHILD, GLENDA; Riverside HS; Degraff, OH; Chrs; Hon Rl; Lbry Ade; Sch Pl; Stg Crw; Stu Cncl; Yrbk; Sch Nwsp; Pep Clb; Spn Clb; Bus Schl; Bus.

FAIRCHILD, GREG; Hesperia HS; Hesperia, MI; VP Soph Cls; VP Jr Cls; Hon Rl; Natl Forn Lg; Sch Pl; Stg Crw; Drama Clb; Letter Bsbl;.

FAIRCHILD, JOHN; Green HS; Uniontown, OH; Cls Rep Frsh Cls; Chrh Wkr; Cmnty Wkr; FCA; Letter Bsktbl; IM Sprt; MVP Bsbl 74; Letter In Bsktbl 77; Coll; Law Enfrcmnt.

FAIRCHILD, LINDA; Mother Of Mercy HS; Cincinnati, OH; Band; Chrs; Hon Rl; Orch; Chrldng; Cit Awd; Awrd For Participtn In Bicentennial Parade 76; Univ.

FAIRCHILD, NATHAN R; Adrian HS; Adrian, MI; Chrs; Hon Rl; Sch Mus; Lat Clb; Mth Clb; Michigan St Univ; Sci.

FAIRE, MICHELLE; Merrillville Sr HS; Merrillville, IN; Chrs; Girl Scts; Hon Rl; Stu Cncl; Chrldng; Pom Pon; Scholastic Ach Awd; Purdue Univ; English.

FAIRES, JAY; Trimble Local HS; Glouster, OH; 7/95 Hst Soph Cls; Boy Scts; Hon Rl; NHS; Sct Actv; Stu Cncl; Spn Clb; Bsktbl; Ftbl; IM Sprt; Coll.

FAIRFIELD, HOLLY; Western Boone Jr Sr HS; Thorntown, IN; 6/163 Am Leg Aux Girls St; FCA; Girl Scts; Hon Rl; Lbry Ade; NHS; Off Ade; 4-H; VP Fr Clb; Pep Clb; Treas Of Star Club For Ltrman 78; Homcmng Queen Crt 79; Ball St Univ; Acctg.

FAIRFULL, HAROLD; Western Reserve Academy; Mountain View, CA; 45/86 Cmnty Wkr; Lit Mag; Off Ade; Orch; IM Sprt; 2 Yr Full Schslhp From Britsh Amer Educ Fdn 79; Harvard Univ; Bus.

FAIRHURST, CHRIS; Summerfield HS; Petersburg, MI; Pres Frsh Cls; Pres Soph Cls; Pres Jr Cls; Pres Sr Cls; Am Leg Aux Girls St; Band; Hon Rl; NHS; Sch Pl; 4-H; College; Public Relations.

FAIRHURST, KAREN; Meadowbrook HS; Buffalo, OH; Cls Rep Frsh Cls; Chrs; Hon Rl; Jr NHS; NHS; PAVAS; Stu Cncl; Rptr Yrbk; Rptr Sch Nwsp; VP 4-H; Ohio Univ; Photog.

FAIRLIE, PATRICIA; Lorain Catholic HS; Avon Lake, OH; 8/134 VP Band; Girl Scts; Hon Rl; NHS; Orch; Sch Pl; Rptr Sch Nwsp; Crs Cntry; Letter Trk; College; Data Processing.

FAIVOR, MARGARET; St Johns HS; St Johns, MI; Hon Rl; 4-H; Letter Bsktbl; IM Sprt; Mgrs; 4-H Awd; Ferris St Coll; Bus.

FAJACK, MARK S; Mentor HS; Mentor, OH; VP Jr Cls; Am Leg Boys St; Hon Rl; NHS; Pres Stu Cncl; Key Clb; Spn Clb; Crs Cntry; College; Bus Law.

FAKNER, THOMAS; Campbell Memorial HS; Campbell, OH; 96/212 Hon Rl; Sch Pl; Stg Crw; Sci Clb; Spn Clb; Capt Ftbl; Capt Trk; Coach Actv; IM Sprt; Kansas Wesleyan Univ; Comp Sci.

FALBO, CHRISTOPHER; Calvin M Woodward HS; Toledo, OH; Cl Rep Jr Cls; Boy Scts; Hon Rl; Jr NHS; Lbry Ade; Sch Mus; Sch Pl; Stg Crw; Stu Cncl; Drama Clb; Intl Thespian Soc; Hero Gourmet Grill; Owens Tech Coll; Food Sci.

FALCONBERRY, WADE; Lockland HS; Cincinnati, OH; Boy Scts; Hon Rl; NHS; Fr Clb; VICA; Ten; Cit Awd; SAR Awd; Diesel Mech.

FALCONE, LILIANA; Madonna HS; Weirton, WV; Chrs; Chrh Wkr; Hon Rl; Lit Mag; NHS; Pep Clb; Socr; Swmmng; Ten; Mat Maids; Mert Achvmnt Awd 78; Univ; Psych.

FALCONE, MARY T; Riverside HS; Mentor, OH; Cls Rep Soph Cls; Cl Rep Jr Cls; Hon Rl; NHS; Fr Clb; OEA;.

FALECKI, SANDRA; Memphis HS; Smith Crk, MI; Cls Rep Soph Cls; Hon Rl; Stu Cncl; Rptr Sch Nwsp; Sch Nwsp; 4-H; 4-H Awd; Univ; Bus.

FALER, RANDY; Coshocton HS; Coshocton, OH; Am Leg Boys St; Hon Rl; Lbry Ade; NHS; Red Cr Ade; Stg Crw; Key Clb; Sci Clb; Spn Clb; Bsktbl; Univ; Engr.

FALES, ANGIE; Memorial HS; Elkhart, IN; Patricia Stevens Schl; Modeling.

FALIN, DAVID W; Mt View HS; Welch, WV; Ten; Marshall Univ; Bus.

FALK, SUSAN; Northrop HS; Fort Wayne, IN; 90/580 Letter Band; Drm Bgl; Hon Rl; Pol Wkr; Gym; Letter Ten; Letter Trk; PPFtbl; Purdue Univ; Math.

FALLEN, ROBIN; Wirt County HS; Palestine, WV; Hon Rl; 4-H; FHA; Pep Clb; Bsktbl; Chrldng; PPFtbl; 4-H Awd; Bus Schl.

FALLER, SHELLY; Cuyahoga Falls HS; Cuyahoga Fls, OH; 99/807 Hon Rl; NHS; Pres OEA; Coach Actv; Public Reltns.

FALLON, ANN; St Joseph Academy; Cleveland, OH; Girl Scts; Hosp Ade; Sch Pl; Rptr Sch Nwsp; VP Fr Clb; 3rd Pl Level 4 In Diocesan For Lang Assn Contst For Poetry Recitation 79; Univ; Spec Educ.

FALLON, MAUREEN; St Joseph Acad; Lakewood, OH; 23/230 Sec Sr Cls; Stu Cncl; Sprt Ed Sch Nwsp; Coach Actv; PPFtbl; John Carroll Univ; Acctg.

FALLONE, FRANK; Allen Park HS; Allen Park, MI; Hon Rl; Stg Crw; Spn Clb; Natl Merit Ltr; R E T S Elect Sch; Electronics.

FALLS, RALPH L; Ironton HS; Ironton, OH; 15/200 Band; Boy Scts; NHS; Yth Flsp; Ger Clb; Letter Bsbl; Letter Crs Cntry; IM Sprt; God Cntry Awd; Sup Oh Dist Sci Fair 78; Univ; Engr.

FALOR, JOHN; Delta HS; Delta, OH; Cl Rep Jr Cls; Chrh Wkr; 4-H; FFA; Northwest Tech Collge.

FALOR, JOHN E; Delta HS; Delta, OH; 39/121 Chrh Wkr; 4-H; FFA; Northwest Tech College.

FALOR, LESTER A; Delta HS; Delta, OH; Sec Jr Cls; Pres Sr Cls; Chrh Wkr; Yth Flsp; FFA; De Kalb Awrd FFA & Acctg Awrd & Crop Prod Awrd 79; Star Chaptr Farmer FFA & Ag Mech Awrd 78; Star Greenhn; Northwest Technical Univ; Elec Engr.

FALSTAD, TODD; Quincy HS; Quincy, MI; Cls Rep Frsh Cls; Cls Rep Soph Cls; Cl Rep Jr Cls; Trs Sr Cls; Band; Boy Scts; Chrh Wkr; Cmnty Wkr; FCA; Hon Rl; Mi Yth Chaplin In Lansing Mi 79; Univ; Optometry.

FALTER, MARILYN; Seneca East HS; Bellevue, OH; Chrh Wkr; Hon Rl; Mbr Of Natl Assn Of Pastoricl Musicn 79; OMTA Buckeye Audtns In N Cntrl Dist 79; Orgnst At Church 75 79; Conservatory Of Music; Concert Orgns.

FALZON, MICHAEL; Crestwood HS; Dearborn Hts, MI; 1/400 Cl Rep Jr Cls; Val; Hon Rl; Treas NHS; Stu Cncl; Sprt Ed Yrbk; Rptr Yrbk; Yrbk; Ed Sch Nwsp; Rptr Sch Nwsp; Univ Of Michigan Regents Schlrshp Alumni Club 79; Univ Of Michigan; Acctg.

FANCHER, SCOTT; Floyd Central HS; Floyd Knobs, IN; Cl Rep Jr Cls; Cls Rep Sr Cls; Sch Mus; Sch Pl; Stg Crw; Treas Stu Cncl; Drama Clb; Rdo Clb; Opt Clb Awd; College; Pre Law.

FANKHAUSER, KARLA A; Robert S Rogers HS; Toledo, OH; 9/412 Cls Rep Frsh Cls; Cls Rep Soph Cls; Trs Jr Cls; Trs Sr Cls; Band; Jr NHS; NHS; Sch Mus; Sci Clb; Chrldng; Univ Of Michigan; Engr.

FANNIN, JANET; Gulf Comprehensive HS; New Port Richey, OH; Pres Frsh Cls; Pres Jr Cls; VP Sr Cls; Hon Rl; NHS; Sch Pl; Keyettes; Trk; Mgrs; PPFtbl; St Petes Jr Coll.

FANNIN, LISA; Kings HS; Loveland, OH; 14/180 Chrs; Hon Rl; NHS; Off Ade; Sch Mus; Sch Pl; Voc Schl; Acting.

FANNIN, VICKIE; Ainsworth HS; Flint, MI; FCA; Hon Rl; Off Ade; Bsbl; Bsktbl; Grand Rapids Bapt Bible Coll; Sec.

FANT, LINNEA; Chesterton HS; Chesterton, IN; 8/454 Am Leg Aux Girls St; Chrh Wkr; Cmnty Wkr; Hon Rl; Lbry Ade; NHS; Fr Clb; IM Sprt; Purdue Univ; Comp Sci.

FANTOZZI, LINA; Father Joseph Wehrle Mem HS; Columbus, OH; 1/112 Pres Jr Cls; Hon Rl; Hosp Ade; NHS; Stu Cncl; Ed Sch Nwsp; Mat Maids; Dnfth Awd; Ohio Dominican Coll; Early Child Ed.

FANTOZZI, NINA; Father Joseph Wehrle Mem HS; Columbus, OH; 6/115 Sec Jr Cls; Hon Rl; Kiwan Awd; Busns Schl; Vocation.

FANUKA, MARY; Sts Peter & Paul Area HS; Saginaw, MI; Chrs; Hon Rl; Chrldng; PPFtbl; College; Bus.

FARAGHER, PATRICIA; Beaumont HS; So Euclid, OH; Cmp Fr Grls; Chrh Wkr; Cmnty Wkr; FCA; Girl Scts; Hon Rl; Hosp Ade; IM Sprt; Univ; Advertising.

FARANSKI, SUSAN; West Catholic HS; Grand Rapids, MI; Cls Rep Sr Cls; Chrs; Hon Rl; NHS; Sch Mus; Rptr Sch Nwsp; Spn Clb; Swmmng; Chrldng; GRJC; Meteorology.

FARGO, GINA; Jefferson HS; Charles Town, WV; Pres Frsh Cls; VP Soph Cls; VP Jr Cls; Cls Rep Sr Cls; Hon Rl; Ten; Chrldng; Pres Awd; Shepherd Univ; Photog.

FARGUAHERSON, JANE; Mc Comb HS; Hoytville, OH; Cls Rep Frsh Cls; Treas Band; Chrh Wkr; Hon Rl; Sec NHS; Pres Yth Flsp; Pres 4-H; Capt Mat Maids; 4-H Awd; College; Elem Educ.

FARHAT, JANET; Our Lady Of Mercy HS; Livonia, MI; Chrs; Girl Scts; Hosp Ade; Michigan St Univ; Nursing.

FARHAT, MICHAEL; West Catholic HS; Grand Rapids, MI; Band; Chrh Wkr; Hon Rl; Sch Mus; Sch Pl; Univ; Pre Law.

FARHOOD, THOMAS; Clarence M Kimball HS; Royal Oak, MI; 17/604 Hon Rl; Mgrs; Scr Kpr; Tmr; Rochester Inst Of Tech; Printing.

FARINACCI, DENISE; Garfield Heights Sr HS; Garfield Hts, OH; 54/346 Girl Scts; Hosp Ade; OEA; Natl Merit Schl; Bus.

FARIS, KIMBERLY; Indiana Academy; Duluth, GA; Pres Soph Cls; Cl Rep Jr Cls; Band; Chrs; Chrh Wkr; Hon Rl; NHS; Sct Actv; Sch Nwsp; Pres Awd; Southern Missionary Coll; Nursing.

FARIS, SUSAN; Loogootee HS; Loogootee, IN; Band; Chrh Wkr; Drl Tm; Hon Rl; Yrbk; Fr Clb; Pep Clb; Trk; Pom Pon; Vincennes Univ; Nursing.

FARISON, DOUGLAS; Mt Pleasant HS; Mt Pleasant, MI; Chrs; Hon Rl; Mdrgl; NHS; Sch Mus; Sch Pl; Drama Clb; Ftbl; IM Sprt; Western Mic Univ; Printing Mgmt.

FARKAS, DAVID; Barberton HS; Barberton, OH; VP Frsh Cls; Cls Rep Soph Cls; Pres Jr Cls; VP Sr Cls; Boy Scts; Chrh Wkr; Hon Rl; NHS; Sct Actv; Stu Cncl; Eagle Scout; Most Improved Swimmer; Ohio St Univ; Bio.

FARKAS, SUSAN L; William A Wirt HS; Gary, IN; 2/230 Sal; Am Leg Aux Girls St; Sec Chrh Wkr; Drm Mjrt; Girl Scts; Hon Rl; Hosp Ade; Jr NHS; Sec NHS; Stu Cncl; Butler Univ; Pharm.

FARKAS, TIM; Ellet HS; Akron, OH; 8/361 Chrs; FCA; Hon Rl; Jr NHS; Mdrgl; NHS; Sch Mus; Stu Cncl; Sprt Ed Yrbk; Sprt Ed Sch Nwsp; Kent St Univ; Jrnlsm.

FARLEE, LENNY; Brown Cnty HS; Nashville, IN; 1/230 Cls Rep Frsh Cls; Cls Rep Soph Cls; Cl Rep Jr Cls; Cls Rep Sr Cls; Chrh Wkr; FCA; NHS; Stu Cncl; Sprt Ed Yrbk; 4-H; Coll; Conservation Career.

FARLER, MARCELLA; Brown County HS; Nashville, IN; 30/204 College; Secretarial Business.

FARLEY, AMY; Hoover HS; North Canton, OH; Hon Rl; NHS; Orch; Sct Actv; Ger Clb; Sci Clb; Letter Swmmng; Mgrs; Tmr; Natl Merit Ltr; College; Vet.

FARLEY, CATHY; Princeton HS; Princeton, WV; Hon Rl; Hosp Ade; Stu Cncl; Pep Clb; Bluefield St Univ; Nursing.

FARLEY, DEBBIE; Mahoning Cnty Jnt Voc Schl; Poland, OH; Chrs; Chrh Wkr; Cmnty Wkr; Hon Rl; Lbry Ade; Yth Flsp; DECA; St Comp In Bus Math 1979; Univ; Mrktng.

FARLEY, DONNA; Greenbrier East HS; Alderson, WV; 12/414 Band; MMM; NHS; Pres Yth Flsp; FTA; West Virginia Wesleyan Univ; Bio.

FARLEY, ROGER; Princeton HS; Princeton, WV; 46/345 Debate Tm; Hon Rl; Jr NHS; Pol Wkr; Yth Flsp; Spn Clb; DAR Awd; Gold Horseshoe Awd 76; Woodmen Of World Amer Hist Awd 77; Top 20 Stdnt 76; Henry Ford Cmnty Coll; Crmnl Justice.

FARLEY, TAMMY; Spanishburg HS; Kegley, WV; 1/42 Val; Band; Drm Mjrt; Hon Rl; Hosp Ade; VP NHS; Sec FBLA; FHA; Am Leg Awd; DAR Awd; Concord Coll; Med Tech.

FARLEY, TRACI; Marsh Fork HS; Arnett, WV; Hon Rl; Stu Cncl; 4-H; Bsktbl; Beckley College; Social Work.

FARLIE, BRENDA; Garden City West Sr HS; Gardencity, MI; Band; Hon Rl; Jr NHS; NHS; Sch Pl; VP Boys Clb Am; Socr; Scr Kpr; Cert Of Recgntn St Of MI Comptn Schlrshp 78; Schlrshp From Lake Superior St Coll & N MI Univ 78; Lake Superior St Coll; Forestry.

FARLOW, DAVID; Huntington N HS; Huntington, IN; Aud/Vis; Band; Boy Scts; Chrs; Chrh Wkr; Cmnty Wkr; Orch; Sch Mus; Sch Pl; Sct Actv; Yth Conservation Corps; St Police Career Camp; Anderson Coll; Law.

FARMER, ANNE; Lemon Monroe HS; Monroe, OH; 4/276 Band; Drl Tm; Hon Rl; NHS; Sch Mus; Stu Cncl; 4-H; Capt Chrldng; Cit Awd; 4-H Awd; Univ; Nurse.

FARMER, BETSY; Mathews HS; Cortland, OH; 10/156 Chrs; Hon Rl; NHS; Y-Teens; Ed Yrbk; Rptr Yrbk; 4-H; Spn Clb; Bsktbl; 4-H Awd; Ohio Univ; Bus.

FARMER, DAVID; Cathedral HS; Indianapolis, IN; 6/158 Hon Rl; IM Sprt; Purdue Univ; Elec Engr.

FARMER, DWIGHT; Terre Haute South Vigo HS; Terre Haute, IN; Sec Frsh Cls; Trs Sr Cls; Chrh Wkr; FCA; Hon Rl; Yth Flsp; DECA; Bsktbl; Crs Cntry; Letter Trk; Purdue Univ; Agri.

FARMER, ED; New Haven HS; New Haven, MI; 4/95 Cl Rep Jr Cls; Cls Rep Sr Cls; Boy Scts; Chrs; Chrh Wkr; Hon Rl; NHS; Sch Pl; Sct Actv; Stu Cncl; Michigan St Univ; Geol Engr.

FARMER, JEANMARIE; Brooke HS; Follansbee, WV; 18/460 Sec Soph Cls; FCA; Hon Rl; Jr NHS; Lit Mag; Pol Wkr; Y-Teens; Drama Clb; 4-H; Spn Clb; Univ; Bus Mgmt.

FARMER, KATHRYN; Gods Bible HS; Huntington, WV; VP Jr Cls; Trs Sr Cls; Chrs; Chrh Wkr; Hon Rl; Jr NHS; NHS; Sch Pl; Rptr Yrbk; Rptr Sch Nwsp; Algebra Home Ec & Math Awd; Marshall Univ; Nursing.

FARMER, LYDIA; Matoaka HS; Rock, WV; Chrs; Hon Rl; Sch Pl; Yth Flsp; FHA; Spn Clb; Bluefield State College; Nursing.

FARMER, MARK; Niles HS; Niles, MI; 4-H; Pres Spn Clb; Ambassador College; Spanish.

FARMER, MARY; Mount View HS; Pageton, WV; Sec Soph Cls; Chrs; Hon Rl; NHS; Quill & Scroll; Red Cr Ade; Yth Flsp; Sch Nwsp; Pres Of Stdnt Advisory 79; Pres Of Sub Debs 77 79; Bluefield St Univ; Bus.

FARMER, NANCY; Rogers HS; Wyoming, MI; 8/255 Hon Rl; Jr NHS; NHS; Ed Sch Nwsp; Rptr Sch Nwsp; Key Clb; Grand Rapids Jr Coll; Jrnlsm.

FARMER, PATRICIA; Lake Central HS; Dyer, IN; 77/468 Band; Chrh Wkr; Hon Rl; Hosp Ade; Orch; Sch Mus; Sch Pl; Stg Crw; Pom Pon; Campbellsville College.

FARMER, PAUL J; Immaculata HS; Detroit, MI; Cls Rep Sr Cls; Cmnty Wkr; Hon Rl; Sch Pl; Stg Crw; Stu Cncl; Fr Clb; Lat Clb; Univ Of Michigan.

FARMER, SUSAN; John Adams HS; S Bend, IN; Cls Rep Soph Cls; Cl Rep Jr Cls; Hon Rl; Off Ade; Stu Cncl; Chrldng; PPFtbl; Indiana Univ; Bus.

FARNALCHER, TERESA; Marysville HS; Marysville, OH; Cls Rep Soph Cls; Cl Rep Jr Cls; Chrs; Chrh Wkr; Girl Scts; Hon Rl; Mdrgl; Natl Forn Lg; NHS; Sch Mus; Finalist For Ms Teen Oh 79; Degree Of Excell In Speech 78; Univ; Hstry Tchr.

FARNAN, EVA M; Sacred Heart Academy; Shepherd, MI; 2/50 Jr NHS; 4-H; Spn Clb; Scr Kpr; 4-H Awd; Volleyball Tm; College; Psych.

FARNELL, DAVID; Stevenson HS; Livonia, MI; Hon Rl; Schoolcraft Coll; Bus Admin.

FARNER, TAMMY; Cloverdale HS; Gosport, IN; Hon Rl; Stu Cncl; 4-H; Bsktbl; Vet.

FARNO, DAWN; Upper Valley JVS; Pleasant Hill, OH; Pres Soph Cls; Pres Jr Cls; Pres Sr Cls; Cmnty Wkr; Girl Scts; Hon Rl; Lbry Ade; NHS; Off Ade; FHA; Volleybll Capt; Count All Star 2nd Volleybl Team 1979; Softball Capt All Star Team 1975; JVS Miss Jr Med; Paralegal Sec.

FARNSLEY, ARTHUR E; New Albany HS; New Albany, IN; 41/576 Am Leg Boys St; Hon Rl; Stu Cncl; Fr Clb; Natl Merit SF; Wabash Coll; Soc Sci.

FARNSWORTH, BILL; Marysville HS; Marysville, MI; Cls Rep Soph Cls; Cl Rep Jr Cls; Capt Bsbl; Bsktbl; Capt Ftbl; Coach Actv; College; Phys Education.

FARNSWORTH, JEWELL; Buckhannon Upshur HS; Buckhannon, WV; Cl Rep Jr Cls; Band; Chrs; Hosp Ade; Stu Cncl; Yth Flsp; Pres 4-H; Fr Clb; Pep Clb; Trk; Business Schl.

FARNUM, BRUCE; Vassar HS; Vassar, MI; 9/157 Cls Rep Frsh Cls; Hon Rl; NHS; Letter Ftbl; Trk; Scr Kpr; Central Mic Univ; Comp Sci.

FARR, ABIGAIL; Martinsville HS; Mooresville, IN; 1/390 Am Leg Aux Girls St; Girl Scts; NHS; Trk; GAA; Natl Merit Ltr; Butler Univ; Chemistry Pre Med.

FARR, SCOTT; Hamilton Southeastern HS; Noblesville, IN; 19/136 Chrh Wkr; Hon Rl; NHS; Quill & Scroll; Sch Pl; Ed Sch Nwsp; Drama Clb; Sci Clb; Bsktbl; Letter Glf; Ball St Univ Jrnlsm Workshops Best Layout 79; Ball St Univ Jrnlsm Workshops Excllnc In Photog 79; Western Kentucky Univ; Jrnlsm.

FARR, VALERIE; Mc Bain Rural Ag HS; Mc Bain, MI; 5/67 Sec Sr Cls; Chrh Wkr; Drl Tm; Hon Rl; NHS; Off Ade; Sch Mus; Stu Cncl; 4-H; Letter Trk; Univ; Sec.

FARRAH, MARK; Schafer HS; Southgate, MI; Band; Hon Rl; Bsbl; Ftbl; Wrstlng; Cit Awd; Central Michigan Univ; Broadcasting.

FARRAND, BILL; Sts Peter & Paul Seminary; Newark, OH; 5/11 Boy Scts; Chrs; Chrh Wkr; Cmnty Wkr; Yrbk; Maryglade Coll Seminary; History.

FARRAR, BRIAN; Franklin HS; Franklin, OH; Sec Jr Cls; Band; Debate Tm; Hon Rl; Stu Cncl; Ten; Trk; Letter Wrstlng; Univ; Math.

FARRAR, LINDA; Cheboygan Area HS; Cheboygan, MI; 17/199 Boy Scts; Chrh Wkr; Hon Rl; Off Ade; Sch Pl; Stg Crw; Chrldng; Grand Rapids Baptist; Data Processin.

FARRAR, LISA; Midview HS; Elyria, OH; Cls Rep Soph Cls; Band; Girl Scts; Hon Rl; Hosp Ade; Jr NHS; Lbry Ade; Stg Crw; Yth Flsp; 4-H; Lorain Cnty Comm Coll; Chem Tech.

FARRELL, CHRISTOPHER; St Xavier HS; Cincinnati, OH; 3/296 Cl Rep Jr Cls; Cls Rep Sr Cls; Chrh Wkr; Hon Rl; NHS; Sch Pl; Stu Cncl; Sch Nwsp; NCTE; Natl Merit SF; Univ Of Notre Dame; Bio.

FARRELL, DIANNE; South Newton Jr Sr HS; Kentland, IN; 10/117 Am Leg Aux Girls St; Chrh Wkr; VP NHS; Sch Pl; Rptr Yrbk; FHA; Lat Clb; PPFtbl; Tmr; Advanced Biology Awd; Purdue Univ; Science.

FARRELL, JAMES; Bishop Watterson HS; Upr Arlington, OH; 5/241 Hon Rl; JA; Yrbk; Sch Nwsp; Natl Merit Ltr; Univ; Econ.

FARRELL, JEANETTE; Summit Cntry Day HS; Park Hills, KY; 1/42 Cmnty Wkr; Hon Rl; NHS; Sch Pl; Sdlty; Ed Yrbk; Yrbk; Sch Nwsp; IM Sprt; Natl Merit Schl; Georgetown Univ.

FARRELL, JEANNE; South Newton Jr Sr HS; Kentland, IN; 3/100 Chrs; Girl Scts; Hon Rl; NHS; Off Ade; Sch Mus; Yrbk; FBLA; PPFtbl; DAR Awd; Purdue Univ; Mgmt.

FARRELL, JENNI; Boonville HS; Boonville, IN; 10/185 Band; Chrh Wkr; Hon Rl; Jr NHS; Natl Forn Lg; NHS; Sch Mus; Sch Pl; Pres Drama Clb; Pom Pon; Hanover Coll; Bio.

FARRELL, KATHY; Magnificat HS; Bay Village, OH; Cls Rep Frsh Cls; Cls Rep Soph Cls; VP Jr Cls; Chrs; Chrh Wkr; FCA; NHS; Stu Cncl; Spn Clb; Bsktbl; College.

FARRELL, MARY; Elyria Catholic HS; Elyria, OH; 20/200 Am Leg Aux Girls St; Chrs; Hon Rl; Jr NHS; Bsktbl; College; Child Psych.

FARRELL, MICHAEL; Brebeuf Prep; Indianpolis, IN; Band; Boy Scts; Chrh Wkr; Hon Rl; Sct Actv; Yth Flsp; Ger Clb; Crs Cntry; IM Sprt; Gov Hon Prg Awd; Univ; Dentistry.

FARRELL, PATRICIA; Northwood HS; Northwood, OH; Band; Chrs; Hon Rl; Hosp Ade; Treas JA; Jr NHS; Lbry Ade; Red Cr Ade; Rptr Yrbk; Fr Clb; Bowling Green Univ; Acctg.

FARRELL, RHONDA; Pennsboro HS; Pennsboro, WV; VP Frsh Cls; Cls Rep Soph Cls; Hon Rl; Natl Forn Lg; Off Ade; Sch Pl; Stu Cncl; Rptr Yrbk; Drama Clb; Fr Clb; Glenville St Univ; Bus.

FARRENS, CANDY; East Canton HS; E Canton, OH; Cls Rep Frsh Cls; Girl Scts; Stu Cncl; FHA; Pep Clb; Sci Clb; Spn Clb; Bsktbl; Trk; Scr Kpr; College; Sociology.

FARRER, ANN; Columbia City Joint HS; Columbia City, IN; Am Leg Aux Girls St; Pres Chrs; Natl Forn Lg; Sec NHS; Sch Mus; VP Stu Cncl; Drama Clb; Sec FTA; GAA; 4-H Awd; Eisenhower Shclrshp 79; Hanover Admissions Schlrshp 79; Hanover Coll.

FARRER, THOMAS; Anderson HS; Anderson, IN; Pres Frsh Cls; Chrh Wkr; Hon Rl; NHS; Off Ade; Pol Wkr; Fr Clb; College; Mech Engr.

FARRIER, SARAH; St Johns HS; St Johns, MI; Chrh Wkr; Cmnty Wkr; Girl Scts; Hon Rl; Orch; 4-H; 4-H Awd; Univ; Vet.

FARRIS, BRUCE; Reading HS; Reading, OH; 2/180 Hon Rl; Letter Ten; Univ; Chem Engr.

FARRIS, DAVID; George Washington HS; Charleston, WV; Cls Rep Frsh Cls; Am Leg Boys St; Band; Cmnty Wkr; Hon Rl; Jr NHS; Stu Cncl; Drama Clb; Cit Awd; Elk Awd; Wv Univ; Engr.

FARRIS, JOHN; West Lafayette HS; W Lafayette, IN; 94/185 Ftbl; Wrstlng; Purdue Univ; Engr.

FARRIS, SCOTT; Bloomfield HS; Bloomfield, IN; 30/96 VP Frsh Cls; Am Leg Boys St; Band; Hon Rl; Pres Stu Cncl; Sprt Ed Yrbk; DECA; Glf; Trk; Drum Major HS Band 79; Prew Fellwshp Of Chrstn Athletes 79; Jr Var Bsktbl Awds 78; Var Bsktbl Awd Awds 79; Marian Coll; Bus Admin.

FARRIS, TINA; West Washington HS; Campbellsburg, IN; Cls Rep Frsh Cls; Cls Rep Soph Cls; Band; Hon Rl; Stu Cncl; Drama Clb; Pep Clb; Chrldng; Spencerian Bus Coll; Exec Sec.

FARROW, FREEMAN L; Cranbrook HS; Highland Park, MI; Band; Boy Scts; Hon Rl; PAVAS; Sct Actv; Boys Clb Am; Key Clb; Letter Swmmng; Trk; Wrstlng; Univ; Med.

FARROW, GARY L; Benton Carroll Salem HS; Oak Harbor, OH; 5/193 Am Leg Boys St; Boy Scts; Chrh Wkr; Hon Rl; Letter Bsbl; Ftbl; Am Leg Awd; Univ; Archt.

FARROW, GREG; North Putnam HS; Roachdale, IN; Cls Rep Frsh Cls; Cls Rep Soph Cls; Band; FCA; Orch; Stg Crw; Stu Cncl; Spn Clb; Letter Bsktbl; Letter Crs Cntry; Vincennes Univ; Bldg Materials Tech.

FARROW, LINDA; Dominican HS; Detroit, MI; Cls Rep Frsh Cls; Cls Rep Soph Cls; Sec Jr Cls; Sec Sr Cls; Band; Orch; Stu Cncl; Swmmng; Chrldng; College; Med.

FARROW, MICHAEL; Brookville HS; New Trenton, IN; Band; Lbry Ade; Sct Actv; Y-Teens; Yrbk; Sch Nwsp; 4-H; Bsbl; Mgrs; Scr Kpr; Model Building 77 78; Lincoln Tech Coll; Diesel Mech.

FARRUGGIA, MARY; Independence HS; Rhodell, WV; 10/149 Drl Tm; Hon Rl; NHS; Stu Cncl; Rptr Yrbk; Beta Clb; Sec FBLA; Pep Clb; Soroptimist; Spn Clb; Know Your St Government Day; Univ Of Charleston; Sec Sci.

FARRUGIA, RENEE; Ferndale HS; Oak Park, MI; Hon Rl; NHS; College; Comp Sci.

FARSON, ROBERT; River Valley HS; Waldo, OH; 21/193 Chrh Wkr; Cmnty Wkr; FCA; Hon Rl; JA; Sct Actv; Yth Flsp; Spn Clb; Letter Wrstlng; Ohio St Univ; Acctg.

FASBENDER, MICHELLE; Oscoda HS; Oscoda, MI; Cl Rep Jr Cls; Band; Drl Tm; Hon Rl; Trk; Central Mic Univ.

FASKO, STEPH; St Joseph Acad; Lakewood, OH; Hon Rl; Bsktbl; College; Bio.

FASOL, JOANNA; Northfork HS; Keystone, WV; 10/123 Girl Scts; Hon Rl; Hosp Ade; Jr NHS; Yrbk; FHA; FTA; Wv Univ; Rn.

FASOLO, THOMAS; Benedictine HS; Cleveland, OH; 5/110 Hon Rl; Jr NHS; Off Ade; Stg Crw; Pres Yth Flsp; Rptr Sch Nwsp; Sch Nwsp; Fr Clb; IM Sprt; Scr Kpr; Univ; Pharmacy.

FASSBENDER, JOHN; Marquette Sr HS; Marquette, MI; Cls Rep Soph Cls; Band; Boy Scts; Hon Rl; Stu Cncl; Yrbk; Ger Clb; Pep Clb; Glf; Ten; Univ Of Michigan; Archt.

FASSLER, CURTIS; Pleasant HS; Marion, OH; Hon Rl; Fr Clb; Bsbl; IM Sprt; Amer Hist Schlr Tm; Sci Fair; Coll; Busns.

FAST, STEPHEN H; Cuyahoga Vlly Chrstn Acad; Akron, OH; 5/60 Pres Chrh Wkr; Hon Rl; Letter Bsktbl; Socr; Letter Trk; DAR Awd; Natl Merit SF; Opt Clb Awd; Wheaton Univ; Med.

FATHEREE, LARRY; Donald E Gavit HS; Hammond, IN; 17/244 Hon Rl; Jr NHS; NHS; Yth Flsp; Mth Clb; Letter Ftbl; Chrldng; Scr Kpr; Purdue Univ; Electrical Eng.

FATUTE, ALBERT; Little Miami HS; Maineville, OH; Aud/Vis; Boy Scts; Chrs; Chrh Wkr; Cmnty Wkr; Sch Mus; Sch Pl; Sct Actv; Boys Clb Am; Drama Clb; College; Law Enforcement.

FAUGHT, KIMBERLY; Roosevelt Wilson HS; Stonewood, WV; Letter Trk;.

FAULKENS, ROBERT; South Bend La Salle HS; South Bend, IN; 94/499 Cls Rep Frsh Cls; Cls Rep Soph Cls; VP Jr Cls; Am Leg Boys St; Chrh Wkr; JA; Jr NHS; NHS; Sch Nwsp; Pep Clb; Coll; Law.

FAULKER, SHELLEY; Perry HS; Perry, MI; Hon Rl; Sprt Ed Yrbk; Fr Clb; Bsktbl; Gym; Chrldng; Coach Actv; Coll; Human Bio.

FAULKNER, BETH; Wayne HS; Ft Wayne, IN; Sch Pl; Stg Crw; Rptr Yrbk; Yrbk; Sch Nwsp; OEA; Pep Clb; Gym; Trk; Mgrs; OEA Regnl Contst Recptnst 3rd Pl 79; COE VP;.

FAULKNER, CHERYL; Gavit Jr Sr HS; Hammond, IN; 29/218 Cls Rep Frsh Cls; Drl Tm; Hon Rl; Stu Cncl; Rptr Yrbk; Pep Clb; Spn Clb; Gym; GAA; Pom Pon; Purdue Univ; Nursing.

FAULKNER, DAVE; Highland HS; Highland, IN; 87/506 Am Leg Boys St; Boy Scts; Chrh Wkr; Hon Rl; NHS; Letter Ftbl; Letter Wrstlng; St Josephs Coll; Acctg.

FAULKNER, PAMELA; Brownsburg HS; Brownsburg, IN; 34/300 Cls Rep Frsh Cls; VP Soph Cls; VP Jr Cls; Girl Scts; Hon Rl; Lbry Ade; Off Ade; Stu Cncl; Pep Clb; Spn Clb; Otstndng Recogntn 79; Indiana Univ; Law.

FAURE, MARY; Upper Arlington HS; Columbus, OH; Chrs; Girl Scts; Sch Pl; Sct Actv; Drama Clb; Ger Clb; Ohio Univ; Natural Res.

FAUROTE, BETH; Bellmont HS; Decatur, IN; Trs Frsh Cls; Cls Rep Soph Cls; Hon Rl; Stu Cncl; DECA; Spn Clb; PPFtbl; Bus Schl; Bus Admin.

FAUST, AMY; Seton HS; Cincinnati, OH; Chrs; Drl Tm; Girl Scts; Sch Mus; Stg Crw; Pep Clb; Spn Clb; Trk; Chrldng; Mgrs; Cincinnati Tech College; Real Estate.

FAUST, JEANNE M; New Albany HS; New Albany, IN; 40/561 Hon Rl; NHS; VP 4-H; FTA; Natl Merit SF; Indiana Univ; Poli Sci.

FAUST, JEFFREY; Fredericktown HS; Fredericktown, OH; 15/113 Pres FCA; Hon Rl; Sct Actv; Yth Flsp; Spn Clb; Letter Ftbl; Letter Trk; IM Sprt; Scr Kpr; Tmr; Ohio St Univ.

FAUST, KATHLEEN; Peru Sr HS; Peru, IN; 14/300 Debate Tm; Hon Rl; JA; NHS; Fr Clb; Natl Merit Ltr; Hoosier Schlr 79; Indiana Univ; Humanities.

FAUSTIN, DAVID; Garber HS; Essexville, MI; 3/185 Pres Frsh Cls; Cls Rep Soph Cls; Boy Scts; Cmnty Wkr; Hon Rl; Letter Bsbl; Letter Bsktbl; Letter Trk; Coach Actv; Natl Merit SF; Coll; Civil Engr.

FAUVER, COLE; Lake Ridge Acad; Elyria, OH; 3/20 VP Frsh Cls; Cls Rep Soph Cls; VP Jr Cls; AFS; NHS; Stu Cncl; Yrbk; Lcrss; Socr; Natl Merit Ltr; Brown Univ; Law School.

FAUVER, ED; Bridgeport HS; Saginaw, MI; 19/350 Cl Rep Jr Cls; Band; Drl Tm; Hon Rl; Lbry Ade; Lit Mag; MMM; NHS; Orch; PAVAS; Michigan Tech Univ; Elec Engr.

FAUVER, EDWARD; Bridgeport Spaulding HS; Saginaw, MI; 15/330 Cl Rep Jr Cls; Band; Drl Tm; Hon Rl; NHS; Stu Cncl; Michigan Tech Univ; Elec Engr.

FAUX, PRISCILLA; Maderia HS; Cincinnati, OH; Trs Soph Cls; Trs Jr Cls; Pres Sr Cls; Cmnty Wkr; Off Ade; Sch Mus; Rptr Sch Nwsp; Drama Clb; OEA; Univ; Spec Ed.

FAVARO, ANGELA; Redford Union HS; Redford, MI; Hon Rl; Trk; Chrldng; IM Sprt; Univ; Marine Bio.

FAVETTI, SONYA; Richmond Hts HS; Richmond Hts, OH; Lbry Ade; NHS; Letter Gym; Ten; Trk; Kent St Univ; Interior Dsgn.

FAVORITE, ELIZABETH; Springport HS; Springport, MI; Pres Frsh Cls; Cls Rep Soph Cls; Trs Jr Cls; Band; Hon Rl; JA; Lit Mag; NHS; Off Ade; Sch Pl; Coll; Nursing.

FAWCETT, JULIE; Timken HS; Canton, OH; Chrs; Hon Rl; Jr NHS; Natl Forn Lg; NHS; Sch Mus; Stg Crw; Sch Nwsp; College; Vet.

FAWCETT, MELODY; James Ford Rhodes HS; Cleveland, OH; Cls Rep Frsh Cls; Pres Soph Cls; Pres Jr Cls; Cls Rep Sr Cls; Chrs; Chrh Wkr; Stu Cncl; Ger Clb; Trk; Cleveland St Univ; Elem Ed.

FAWLEY, KATHY; Warsaw Community HS; Warsaw, IN; Sec Debate Tm; Hon Rl; Natl Forn Lg; Off Ade; Rptr Yrbk; 4-H; Spn Clb; College.

FAY, DEBBY; Hubbard HS; Hubbard, OH; Girl Scts; Hon Rl; Off Ade; Stu Cncl; Trk; Choffin School Of Nursing; R N.

FAY, WILLIAM; Roscommon HS; Roscommon, MI; VP Frsh Cls; Pres Soph Cls; Band; Off Ade; Orch; Stu Cncl; Rptr Sch Nwsp; 4-H; 4-H Awd; JC Awd; College; Bus.

FAYNE, PRISCILLA; East HS; Cleveland, OH; Cls Rep Frsh Cls; Cl Rep Jr Cls; AFS; Chrh Wkr; Cmnty Wkr; Hon Rl; JA; Jr NHS; Lbry Ade; Lit Mag; Natl Merit Ltr 77 79; Natl Merit Schlrshp 77 79; Betty Crocker 76 79; Univ; Mach Oper.

FAZEKAS, WILLIAM; Strongsville HS; Strongsville, OH; Hon Rl; Lbry Ade; Rptr Yrbk; Fr Clb; JETS Awd; Natl Merit Ltr; Cleveland Inst Of Music; Comp.

FAZENBAKER, CHERYL A; Keyser HS; Keyser, WV; 1/250 AFS; Drl Tm; Hon Rl; NHS; Pep Clb; Natl Merit Ltr; College; Engr.

FAZIO, ANN M; Bishop Gallagher HS; Detroit, MI; 11/332 Cls Rep Sr Cls; Chrs; Girl Scts; Hon Rl; Sch Pl; Sch Nwsp; Chrldng; PPFtbl; University; Chem Engr.

FAZIO, FRANK; Cloverleaf HS; Seville, OH; Chrs; Hon Rl; NHS; Yrbk; Spn Clb; Lion Awd; Rotary Awd; Sales Awd Yrbk 78; Oh Univ Seminar Bus 79; Univ; Law.

FAZIO, SUE; Rogers HS; Toledo, OH; 51/412 Hon Rl; JA; DECA; Spn Clb; JA Awd; Owens Tech Coll; Bus Admin.

FEALY, KATHLEEN; Andrean HS; Merrillville, IN; 12/272 Cmnty Wkr; Hon Rl; NHS; Rptr Sch Nwsp; Drama Clb; Mth Clb; Voice Dem Awd; Marquette Univ; Brdcstng.

FEAR, WILLIAM; Reed City HS; Salem, OR; Hon Rl; Jr NHS; NHS; Yrbk; Sci Clb; Cit Awd; Oregon St Univ; Vet.

FEASEL, CATHERINE; Mohawk HS; Tiffin, OH; 1/126 Val; Hon Rl; Lit Mag; NHS; FTA; Spn Clb; Cit Awd; Bowling Green Univ; Education.

FEASEL, JEFFREY; Mohawks HS; Sycamore, OH; Pres Frsh Cls; VP Soph Cls; VP Jr Cls; Band; Boy Scts; Cmnty Wkr; Hon Rl; Orch; Stu Cncl; Bsbl;.

FEASEL, NICK; Elmwood HS; Bloomdale, OH; 30/120 Boy Scts; Chrs; Chrh Wkr; Hon Rl; Off Ade; Sch Mus; Sch Pl; Sct Actv; Stg Crw; VP Yth Flsp; Phys Ed Clb; College; Marketing.

FEATHERS, KAREN; Jefferson HS; Delphos, OH; Band; Chrs; Hon Rl; Sch Mus;.

FEATHERS, PAUL; Delphos Jefferson HS; Delphos, OH; Chrs; Chrh Wkr; Hon Rl; Red Cr Ade; Sch Mus; Fr Clb; Ftbl; Honor Roll; Ftbl; Chorus; Ohio St Univ; Biology.

FEAZEL, CINDY; Madison Comp HS; Mansfield, OH; Chrs; Orch; Sch Pl; Yth Flsp; 4-H; Spn Clb; Trk; Mgrs; 4-H Awd; Nyack Coll; Gnrl Educ.

FECHNER, SUZANNE; Adrian HS; Adrian, MI; 18/386 Chrh Wkr; Hon Rl; NHS; Yth Flsp; Ger Clb; Pres Swmmng; Natl Merit Ltr; Pres Awd; Kalamazoo Coll; Psych.

FEDDERS, ANDY; Fenwick HS; Franklin, OH; 29/95 Hon Rl; Ftbl; Wrstlng; IM Sprt; Miami Univ; Acctg.

FEDERICO, DARCY; Grand Haven Sr HS; Grand Haven, MI; Band; Hon Rl; NHS; Sch Mus; Drama Clb; Swmmng; Michigan St Univ; Audiology.

FEDERSPIEL, HOLLY; Arthur Hill HS; Saginaw, MI; Sct Actv; Sci Clb; S Intermediate Schl Best Artist; Cert Of Merit Roll & Perfect Attendence; Saginaw Valley St Coll; Med Lab Tech.

FEDEWA, MARY; St Johns HS; De Witt, MI; Ten; Trk; MSU.

FEDOR, CHRISTIAN; Bay HS; Bay Vill, OH; Cmnty Wkr; Hon Rl; Bsbl; Bsktbl; Coach Actv; All S W Conf Pitcher 79; Acad Acvhmtn Awd 77 79; Univ; Psych.

FEDOR, JEFF; Negaunee HS; Palmer, MI; Chrs; Debate Tm; Hon Rl; Lbry Ade; Mdrgl; Ed Sch Nwsp; Coll; Psych.

FEDORCHAK, BRAD; Canfield HS; Canfield, OH; Aud/Vis; Hon Rl; NHS; Letter Bsbl; Letter Ftbl; Natl Merit Ltr; Univ; Civil Engr.

FEDORKE, KATHIE; Guernsey Catholic Cntrl HS; Cambridge, OH; 11/27 Chrs; Chrh Wkr; Cmnty Wkr; Hon Rl; Sch Pl; Yrbk; 4-H; Pep Clb; Chrldng; DAR Awd; College; Nursing.

FEDORKO, JOSEPH A; St Joseph HS; Cleveland, OH; 22/243 Trs Frsh Cls; Cls Rep Soph Cls; VP Jr Cls; Band; Debate Tm; Hon Rl; JA; Natl Forn Lg; NHS; Orch; Cul Inst Of America; Culinary Arts.

FEDROFF, MARC S; St Xavier HS; Cincinnati, OH; 15/289 Hon Rl; NHS; Sch Mus; Sch Pl; Stu Cncl; Ed Yrbk; Drama Clb; Fr Clb; Natl Merit SF; College; Medicine.

FEDYNA, JOANNE; Bellevue HS; Bellevue, OH; 1/240 Cls Rep Sr Cls; Val; Treas Chrs; Hon Rl; NHS; Stu Cncl; Spn Clb; Ohi Univ; Chem.

FEECE, B; Laville HS; Lakeville, IN; 9/130 NHS; Pol Wkr; Ger Clb; Earlham Coll; Interpreting German.

FEECE, BETH; Laville HS; Lakeville, IN; 9/130 NHS; Pol Wkr; Ger Clb; Earlham College; German.

FEEHAN, MIKE; Patrick Henry HS; Deshler, OH; Hon Rl; Civ Clb; 4-H; FFA; Bsbl; 4-H Awd; Univ; Engr.

FEELEY, NANCY; Lorain Cath HS; Lorain, OH; Hon Rl; Sch Nwsp; Letter Bsbl; Letter Bsktbl; Lorain Cnty Cmnty Coll.

FEENEY, TERESA; Port Clinton HS; Port Clinton, OH; 1/280 Chrs; Hon Rl; Sec NHS; Mth Clb; Pep Clb; Spn Clb; Ten; Chrldng; Pom Pon; Dnfth Awd; Ohio Northern Univ; Pharmacy.

FEGAN, MACHELL; Norton HS; Norton, OH; NHS; Off Ade; Lat Clb; Bsbl; Bsktbl; Cit Awd; Band; College; Sci.

FEIBUSCH, EDNA; Berkley HS; Oak Park, MI; Hon Rl; Off Ade; Pol Wkr; Bsbl; IM Sprt; JC Awd; Michigan St Univ; Optometry.

FEIERSTEIN, BRYAN; Greenville HS; Greenville, OH; 1/380 VP Band; Chrs; Hon Rl; NHS; Orch; Sch Mus; Sch Pl; Sec Drama Clb; Lat Clb; VP Sci Clb; Ohio N Univ; Pharm.

FEIETSTEIN, BRYAN; Greenville HS; Greenville, OH; 1/380 Am Leg Boys St; VP Band; Hon Rl; NHS; Orch; Sch Mus; Sch Pl; Drama Clb; Ohio Northern Univ; Pharmacy.

FEIGEL, DONNA; Perry Meridian HS; Indianapolis, IN; 91/513 Chrh Wkr; Cmnty Wkr; Hon Rl; Off Ade; Pol Wkr; Yth Flsp; OEA; Pep Clb; Spn Clb; Mat Maids; Placed 6th In Comp Prog Dist Contest; Indiana Central Univ; Comp Tech.

FEIGEL, RENEE; Engadine Consolidated Schls; Engadine, MI; Band; Chrh Wkr; Hon Rl; 4-H; PPFtbl;.

FELAN, CAROLYN; Stevenson HS; Sterling Hts, MI; 105/529 Band; Girl Scts; Hon Rl; JA; Michigan Tech Univ; Geologist.

FELBER, KIM; Port Clinton HS; Port Clinton, OH; 3/268 Cls Rep Frsh Cls; Cls Rep Soph Cls; Cl Rep Jr Cls; Band; Hon Rl; Hosp Ade; NHS; Swmmng; Natl Merit SF; Awd Of Excellence; 5 Hr Summer Scholarship To Ohio Univ; Miami Univ; Busns.

FELBER, MICHAEL; Heritage Christian HS; Indianapolis, IN; Pres Frsh Cls; Pres Soph Cls; Pres Jr Cls; Pres Sr Cls; Band; Chrs; Hon Rl; Orch; Sch Mus; Stu Cncl; Bob Jones Univ; Religion.

FELBER, MICHAEL; Heritage Christian School; Indianapolis, IN; 13/63 Pres Frsh Cls; Pres Soph Cls; Pres Jr Cls; Pres Sr Cls; Hon Rl; NHS; Sch Mus; Stu Cncl; Socr; Trk; Bob Jones Univ; Bible.

FELCYN, WENDY; Dwight D Eisenhower HS; Rochester, MI; 41/602 Cls Rep Soph Cls; Sec Jr Cls; Chrh Wkr; Hon Rl; NHS; Sch Mus; Pres Spn Clb; Oakland Univ; Elem Ed.

FELD, JOHN C; Richmond Sr HS; Richmond, IN; Cls Rep Frsh Cls; Cls Rep Soph Cls; Cl Rep Jr Cls; Chrs; Chrh Wkr; FCA; Hon Rl; JA; Mdrgl; Sch Mus; Univ; Music.

FELD, MICHAEL; L C Mohr HS; South Haven, MI; Hon Rl; Stg Crw; IM Sprt; Ferris State College; Business Admin.

FELDHAUS, GREGORY A; Lockland HS; Lockland, OH; 20/64 Am Leg Boys St; Spn Clb; Bsktbl; Ftbl; Swmmng; Trk; Wrstlng; Univ Of Cincinnati.

FELDHISER, MARK; Alcona Comm HS; Lincoln, MI; VP Frsh Cls; Pres Soph Cls; Hon Rl; Bsbl; Bsktbl; Trk; Ferris Coll; Pharm.

FELDMAN, BECKY; Waldo J Wood Memorial HS; Oakland City, IN; 3/120 Band; Girl Scts; Hon Rl; Off Ade; Pol Wkr; Sch Nwsp; OEA; Pep Clb; PPFtbl; Am Leg Awd; Tri Kappa Schlrshp 79; Sr Eng Awrd 79; OEA Ambassador Awrd 79; ISUE; Keypunch Oper.

FELDMAN, DAVE; Elder HS; Cinn, OH; Cls Rep Sr Cls; Boy Scts; Chrh Wkr; Hon Rl; Sct Actv; Stu Cncl; Sch Nwsp; Pep Clb; Letter Wrstlng; Chrldng; Univ Of Cincinnati; Elec Tech.

FELDMAN, GREGORY; Hamilton Southeastern HS; Indianapo Is, IN; Hon Rl; Ger Clb; Sci Clb; Ftbl; Letter Wrstlng; IM Sprt; College; Mechanical Engineer.

FELDPAUSCH, FRANCIS; Cath Central HS; Grand Rpds, MI; 7/224 Boy Scts; Hon Rl; JA; NHS; Sch Pl; Rptr Sch Nwsp; Ger Clb; Mic State Univ; Engr.

FELDPAUSCH, GARY; Pewamo Westphalia HS; Fowler, MI; Cls Rep Sr Cls; Band; Drl Tm; Hon Rl; Sch Pl; Stg Crw; Twrlr; Univ Of Mich; Law.

FELDPAUSCH, KAREN; Kenowa Hills HS; Grand Rapids, MI; Band; Bsktbl; Trk; PPFtbl; College; Lab Tech.

FELDT, CHARLES; Mona Shores HS; Muskegon, MI; Boy Scts; NHS; Sch Pl; Sct Actv; Stg Crw; Drama Clb; Fr Clb; IM Sprt; Mi Comp Schlrshp 79; French Awd Top Stud In Schl; Michigan Tech Univ; Pre Med.

FELDT, JEFFERY; Arthur Hill HS; Saginaw, MI; 42/560 Hon Rl; JA; NHS; Bsbl; Capt Ftbl; Capt Glf; Coach Actv; IM Sprt; JA Awd; Michigan Tech Univ; Elec Engr.

FELDWISCH, JULIE; Memorial HS; Mendon, OH; 1/240 Am Leg Aux Girls St; Chrs; Girl Scts; Hon Rl; NHS; Sch Mus; Sch Pl; Sct Actv; Stg Crw; Y-Teens; Univ; Math.

FELGER, MARK; Garrett HS; La Otto, IN; 15/140 Hon Rl; Treas FFA; Trk; Natl Merit Ltr; Cert Of Recognition Outstndng Schlstc Ach; FFA Awds Of Merit; Purdue Univ; Agri.

FELICE, MICHELLE; Douglas Mac Arthur HS; Saginaw, MI; Hon Rl; Hosp Ade; NHS; Pep Clb; PPFtbl; Delta College.

FELICE, RITA; Normandy HS; Parma, OH; 20/635 Jr NHS; NHS; Orch; Sch Mus; Sch Pl; Stg Crw; Drama Clb; Pep Clb; Spn Clb; Letter Bsktbl; College; Sciences.

FELICIANO, ELIEZER; Admiral King HS; Lorain, OH; Chrh Wkr; JA; Lbry Ade; DECA; Crs Cntry; Trk; Tmr; Univ.

FELIX, DAWN; William Henry Harrison HS; W Lafayette, IN; Band; Chrh Wkr; Girl Scts; Hon Rl; Natl Forn Lg; Sch Mus; Yth Flsp; 4-H; Fr Clb; Keyettes; Service Awd In Music; Purdue Univ; Music Therapy.

FELIX, JEFFREY A; Taylor HS; N Bend, OH; Am Leg Boys St; Band; Hon Rl; Jr NHS; NHS; Key Clb; Letter Bsktbl; Letter Crs Cntry; Letter Ten; Univ; Bus.

FELL, LESLIE; Hubbard HS; Hubbard, OH; 29/350 Band; Chrh Wkr; Girl Scts; Hon Rl; JA; Spn Clb; Youngstown St Univ; Child Care.

FELL, REGINA; Libbey HS; Toledo, OH; Trs Jr Cls; Chrh Wkr; JA; Off Ade; Red Cr Ade; Pep Clb; VICA; IM Sprt; Natl Merit Ltr; Owens Tech; Medical Lab Asst.

FELL, RONNIE; Fairfield Union HS; Lancaster, OH; 15/150 VP Frsh Cls; VP Jr Cls; Chrs; Hon Rl; NHS; Sch Pl; Stu Cncl; Yth Flsp; Rptr Yrbk; Rptr Sch Nwsp; Community Nursing Schl.

FELL, VERONICA A; Fairfield Union HS; Lancaster, OH; VP Frsh Cls; VP Jr Cls; Chrs; Hon Rl; NHS; FTA; VP Spn Clb; Bsktbl; Trk; Chrldng; Cmnty Hosp Schl Of Nursing.

FELLAND, RUTH; Fairless HS; Wilmot, OH; 1/218 Val; Am Leg Aux Girls St; Band; Chrs; Hon Rl; Jr NHS; NHS; 4-H; Mth Clb; Sci Clb; Miami Univ.

FELLER, JAMES; Brookville HS; Brookville, IN; 11/190 Hon Rl; Sch Nwsp; Key Clb; Letter Bsbl; Letter Bsktbl; Letter Ftbl; Univ; Acctg.

FELLERHOFF, BECKY; Ursuline Academy; Cincinnati, OH; Chrh Wkr; Cmnty Wkr; Girl Scts; Lbry Ade; Pol Wkr; Quill & Scroll; Red Cr Ade; Sct Actv; Stg Crw; Yth Flsp; Coll; Law Enforcement.

FELLOWS, CHRIS; Anchor Bay HS; New Baltimore, MI; Sec Frsh Cls; Hon Rl; Jr NHS; NHS; Stu Cncl; Rptr Yrbk; OEA; Chrldng; Off Educ Assoc 2nd Pl St Comp 79; Off Educ Assoc Fnlst In Typng 79; Michigan St Univ; Bus.

FELTEN, BRIAN; New Haven HS; New Have, IN; Pres Frsh Cls; Cls Rep Frsh Cls; Cls Rep Soph Cls; Cl Rep Jr Cls; Band; Chrh Wkr; Pres JA; Natl Forn Lg; Sch Pl; Sct Actv; College; Civil Engr.

FELTES, SUSAN; Holy Name HS; Independence, OH; Hon Rl; Off Ade; Fr Clb; Pep Clb; IM Sprt; Pom Pon; Univ; Bus.

FELTMAN, JOHN W; Shepherd Public HS; Shepherd, MI; 23/119 Band; Hon Rl; Wrstlng; Natl Merit SF; 1st All Conf Wrstlng At 105 Lb 77; Dist Wrstlng At 105 2nd 77; Sclshp From N Mi; Northern Michigan Univ; Comp.

FELTNER, RICK; Floyd Central HS; Floyd Knobs, IN; Chrs; Hon Rl; Rptr Yrbk; Univ.

FELTON, KIMBERLY; Huntington North HS; Huntington, IN; 10/605 Cls Rep Frsh Cls; Cls Rep Soph Cls; Cl Rep Jr Cls; Cls Rep Sr Cls; Band; Drl Tm; Jr NHS; Yth Flsp; 4-H; Huntington Coll; Acctng.

FELTON, MELISSA; Bloomfield HS; Bloomfield, IN; 12/100 Pres Jr Cls; Sec Sr Cls; Chrs; Chrh Wkr; Girl Scts; Hon Rl; Hosp Ade; NHS; Sch Mus; Sch Pl; IUPUI; Nursing.

FELTON, MICHAEL; Linsly Inst; Wheeling, WV; Sec Jr Cls; Trs Jr Cls; Cls Rep Sr Cls; Boy Scts; Chrh Wkr; FCA; Rptr Yrbk; VP Fr Clb; Sci Clb; Letter Ftbl; College; Engr.

FELTY, JOHN; Lake Catholic HS; Cleveland Hts, OH; 13/360 Chrh Wkr; Hon Rl; NHS; Bsbl; Ftbl; John Carroll Univ; Comp Sci.

FELUMLEE, NANCY; Licking Valley HS; Newark, OH; Band; Chrh Wkr; Hon Rl; Yth Flsp; 4-H; Univ; Elem Educ.

FENDER, ANDY; Bloomington HS; Bloomington, IN; 109/389 Pres Frsh Cls; Chrs; Off Ade; Sch Pl; Stu Cncl; Ind Univ; Comp Science.

FENDER, MARY B; Hobart Sr HS; Hobart, IN; 1/400 Pres Frsh Cls; Sec Jr Cls; Trs Sr Cls; VP AFS; Am Leg Aux Girls St; Chrs; Cmnty Wkr; Girl Scts; Hon Rl; Hosp Ade; Indiana Coll; Language.

FENDERSON, AUDREY; Malabar HS; Mansfield, OH; 74/216 VP Frsh Cls; VP Sr Cls; Chrs; Pep Clb; Homecoming Queen Malabar 78; 1st Tm Au Cardinal Conference Selectn 78; MVP & Capt Vllybll 78; Bowling Green St Univ; RN.

FENDERSON, MARY; Rocky River HS; Rocky River, OH; Girl Scts; Hon Rl; NHS; Orch; Letter Chrldng; Univ; Sci.

FENDT, LISA; Hartland HS; Brighton, MI; 14/250 Band; Hon Rl; Treas NHS; Sch Pl; Drama Clb; Spn Clb; Northern Michigan Univ; Comp Sci.

FENECK, ANGELA; Merrillville HS; Merrillville, IN; 21/596 Chrh Wkr; Cmnty Wkr; Hon Rl; Hosp Ade; NHS; Fr Clb; FTA; Mgrs; PPFtbl; Univ Of Evansville; Chem.

FENIC, KAREN; Oakwood HS; Dayton, OH; 3/152 Cmp Fr Grls; Cmnty Wkr; Hosp Ade; NHS; Spn Clb; Natl Merit SF; Chemistry.

FENIMORE, CHERI; Highland HS; Anderson, IN; 24/408 Am Leg Aux Girls St; NHS; Sec Stu Cncl; Drama Clb; Fr Clb; Pep Clb; Letter Gym; PPFtbl; Indiana University; Accounting.

FENNELL, ANDREW; Gladwin HS; Gladwin, MI; Pres Frsh Cls; Cls Rep Soph Cls; Cl Rep Jr Cls; Band; Boy Scts; Hon Rl; NHS; Sch Pl; Sct Actv; Stg Crw; Various Scouting Awds; Marksman Awd Natl Rifle Assoc 76; Bus.

FENNELL, CARL D; Lincoln HS; Cambridge Cy, IN; 23/85 VP Frsh Cls; Cls Rep Soph Cls; Am Leg Boys St; Boy Scts; Hon Rl; Stu Cncl; Key Clb; Bsktbl; Trk; Am Leg Awd; Butler Univ; Pharm.

FENNELL, JAMES C; Pleasant Local HS; Marion, OH; 13/137 Chrh Wkr; Lbry Ade; IM Sprt; Natl Merit SF; State Scholastic Achievement Test; 8th In Gen Sci; U S Naval Academy; Elec Engr.

FENNELL, MARGARET; Warren Woods HS; Warren, MI; 76/348 Band; Chrs; Drl Tm; Hon Rl; Hosp Ade; NHS; Sch Mus; Stg Crw; Wayne State Univ; Allied Health.

FENNELL, SCOTT; Norwood HS; Norwood, OH; Am Leg Boys St; Hon Rl; Jr NHS; NHS; Crs Cntry; Trk; Wrstlng; College; Engineering.

FENNEMA, DAWN; South Christian HS; Moline, MI; Band; Cmnty Wkr; Debate Tm; Hon Rl; Yrbk; 4-H; Trk; 4-H Awd; Calvin Univ.

FENOGLIO, ANNA; South Vermillion HS; Clinton, IN; 12/180 Cls Rep Frsh Cls; Cls Rep Soph Cls; Cl Rep Jr Cls; Am Leg Aux Girls St; Hon Rl; NHS; Quill & Scroll; Sch Pl; Stu Cncl; Sprt Ed Yrbk; De Pauw Univ; Communications.

FENOGLIO, DENISE; Bishop Loers HS; Ft Wayne, IN; Trs Frsh Cls; Pres Soph Cls; Pres Jr Cls; Pres Sr Cls; Hon Rl; PPFtbl; Purdue Univ; Food Sci.

FENSKE, CAROL; Holland HS; Holland, MI; Band; Chrs; Chrh Wkr; Hon Rl; Orch; Yth Flsp; Ger Clb; Lat Clb; Pep Clb; Swmmng; Northern Mic Univ; Med.

FENSTER, ROBERT; Southfield Sr HS; Southfield, MI; Cl Rep Jr Cls; Pres Chrh Wkr; Yrbk; Lois Goode Schlrshp 79; Southfield Youth Guidance Awd 79; Mert Achvmnt Awd 79; Univ; Bus Admin.

FENSTERMACHER, BRUCE; Edwardsburg HS; Edwardsburg, MI; Boy Scts; Hon Rl; College.

FENSTERMAKER, JOYCE; Bristol Local HS; Bristolville, OH; Chrs; Chrh Wkr; Sch Mus; Sch Pl; Bsbl; Letter Bsktbl; Letter Trk; Southeastern Acad; Fashion Mdse.

FENSTERMAKER, KRISTIN; Broad Ripple HS; Indianapolis, IN; Cmp Fr Grls; Hon Rl; NHS; Off Ade; Quill & Scroll; Sch Pl; Yrbk; Drama Clb; Fr Clb; Glf; Purdue Univ.

FENTON, DEANNA; Avon HS; Avon, OH; 52/147 Band; Chrs; Hon Rl; Hosp Ade; JA; Sch Mus; Stg Crw; 4-H; Spn Clb; 4-H Awd; Voc Schl; Registered Nurse.

FENTON, JERILYN; St Marys Centrl Cath HS; Sandusky, OH; 3 Cmp Fr Grls; Chrs; Drl Tm; Spn Clb; GAA; College; Bus.

FENTON, KIM; Bloom Local HS; So Webster, OH; 3/85 Trs Soph Cls; Trs Jr Cls; Band; Chrs; Hon Rl; Jr NHS; NHS; Sch Pl; Sec Stu Cncl; Sec Yth Flsp; Shawnee St Univ; Educ.

FENTON, PATTY; Bloom Local HS; Scioto Furnace, OH; VP Soph Cls; VP Jr Cls; Band; Chrs; Chrh Wkr; Hon Rl; Sch Pl; Stu Cncl; FHA; Spn Clb; Shawnee St Univ; Nursing.

FENTON, PAUL; Bay Village HS; Bay Vill, OH; Cl Rep Jr Cls; VP Sr Cls; NHS; Stu Cncl; Yrbk; Letter Hockey; Letter Socr; Kiwan Awd; Univ.

FENTON, T; Roscommon HS; Roscommon, MI; Pres Frsh Cls; VP Sr Cls; Band; NHS; Orch; Sch Mus; 4-H; Bsbl; Bsktbl; Ftbl; College; Anthropology.

FENTON, TODD; Roscommon HS; Roscommon, MI; Pres Frsh Cls; Band; NHS; Sch Mus; Stu Cncl; 4-H; Letter Bsbl; Letter Bsktbl; Letter Ftbl; College; Anthropology.

FENTRESS, MARK; Detroit Country Day HS; Detroit, MI; Cls Rep Frsh Cls; Cls Rep Soph Cls; Cl Rep Jr Cls; Cls Rep Sr Cls; Band; Chrs; Chrh Wkr; Sch Mus; Stu Cncl; Spn Clb; Brown Univ; Law.

FENWICK, JOHN; Sycamore HS; Montgomery, OH; Sch Mus; Yth Flsp; Letter Swmmng;.

FERAN, EDWARD; St Edward HS; Lakewood, OH; Chrh Wkr; Cmnty Wkr; Hon Rl; Crs Cntry; Trk; IM Sprt; Cert Of Outstndg Schlrshp 78; Univ.

FERANCHAK, CATHERINE; Trinity HS; Youngstown, OH; 30/150 Drl Tm; Hon Rl; Pom Pon; Schlshp Cert Of Hon 78; Ohio Univ; Engl.

FERBER, CINDY; Munster HS; Munster, IN; 1/435 AFS; Hon Rl; NHS; Fr Clb; Tmr; Kiwan Awd; Univ Of Notre Dame; Chem Engr.

FERBER, MARK; Edison HS; Berlin Heights, OH; Band; 1st Place Erie Cnty Consrvtn League Rifle Team; College; Conservation.

FERDINAND, VICTOR; Jackson HS; Canal Fulton, OH; 45/409 Band; FCA; Hon Rl; NHS; Yth Flsp; Treas Ger Clb; Sci Clb; Ohio State Univ; Engr.

FERGUSON, AMY; Waverly HS; Waverly, OH; 1/157 Band; Chrh Wkr; Hon Rl; NHS; Stu Cncl; 4-H; FTA; Pep Clb; Am Leg Awd; 4-H Awd; Univ.

FERGUSON, BARBARA; Perry Meridian HS; Indianapolis, IN; 150/550 Chrs; Chrh Wkr; Hon Rl; Sch Mus; Rptr Sch Nwsp; 4-H; Fr Clb; 4-H Awd; Indiana Univ; Nursing.

FERGUSON, BELINDA; Clare HS; Clare, MI; Band; Cmp Fr Grls; FCA; Hon Rl; Hosp Ade; Fr Clb; Bsktbl; Mgrs; Univ; Law.

FERGUSON, BETH I; Coldwater HS; Quincy, MI; Chrs; Yth Flsp; DECA; 4-H; IM Sprt; 4-H Awd;.

FERGUSON, BROOK; Ridgedale HS; Marion, OH; 17/90 Am Leg Boys St; Band; Boy Scts; FCA; Hon Rl; Sct Actv; Yth Flsp; 4-H; Leo Clb; Ftbl; Bowling Green State Univ; Bus Admin.

FERGUSON, CHERYL; Central HS; Evansville, IN; 53/650 Sec Frsh Cls; Cls Rep Frsh Cls; Cls Rep Soph Cls; Cl Rep Jr Cls; Cls Rep Sr Cls; Am Leg Aux Girls St; Chrs; Hon Rl; Hosp Ade; JA; Univ; Sci.

FERGUSON, CHRIS; East Kentwood HS; Tempe, AZ; Hon Rl; JA; Jr NHS; Fr Clb; Spn Clb; Grand Rapids Jr Coll; Dent Tech.

FERGUSON, CYNTHIA; Wintersville HS; Wintrsvl, OH; Band; Chrh Wkr; Drl Tm; Lbry Ade; Off Ade; Sch Mus; Yth Flsp; Fr Clb; Letter Trk; Oh State Sch Of Cosm; Cosm.

FERGUSON, DARLA; Goshen HS; Goshen, IN; Am Leg Aux Girls St; Band; Chrh Wkr; JA; Natl Forn Lg; Sch Mus; Sch Pl; Stu Cncl; Rptr Sch Nwsp; Spn Clb; Indiana Univ; Jrnlsm.

FERGUSON, DEENA; London HS; London, OH; Cls Rep Frsh Cls; Cls Rep Soph Cls; Cl Rep Jr Cls; Am Leg Aux Girls St; Band; Chrs; Chrh Wkr; Cmnty Wkr; Hon Rl; NHS; Ohio Univ; Jrnlsm.

FERGUSON, GREGG; Dunbar HS; Institute, WV; Hon Rl; NHS; Y-Teens; Rptr Sch Nwsp; Mth Clb; Spn Clb; Voice Dem Awd; Univ; Med.

FERGUSON, JAMES; Bloomfield HS; Bloomfield, IN; 35/185 Chrs; Hon Rl; Sch Mus; Sch Pl; Stg Crw; Stu Cncl; Drama Clb; Lat Clb; Won 2 1st Plc Awd At Jr Classical League Convnt 76; Won Spec Merit Awd & 1st Plc At Jr Classical 77; Univ; Music.

FERGUSON, JENNIFER; Buffalo HS; Kenova, WV; Cl Rep Jr Cls; Band; Hon Rl; 4-H; FHA; Mth Clb; Trk; Marshall Univ; Sci.

FERGUSON, JILL; Sebring Mc Kinley HS; Sebring, OH; Chrs; Lbry Ade; Off Ade; Y-Teens; Rptr Yrbk; Ger Clb; Pep Clb; Scr Kpr; Reserve Vlybl Co Captain Jr Yr; Univ; X Ray Tech.

FERGUSON, JULI; Brownstown Central HS; Freetown, IN; 5/145 Chrs; Chrh Wkr; Girl Scts; Hon Rl; Lbry Ade; NHS; VP Quill & Scroll; VP Sch Mus; Sec Yth Flsp; Y-Teens; Indiana Univ.

FERGUSON, KENTON; Wayne HS; Dayton, OH; Hon Rl; Jr NHS; NHS; Univ; Pre Law.

FERGUSON, KIM; Ft Frye HS; Beverly, OH; Cl Rep Jr Cls; Trs Sr Cls; Band; Off Ade; Quill & Scroll; Rptr Sch Nwsp; Pres FTA; Scr Kpr; Twrlr; Pres 4-H Awd; Homecoming Queen 1979; FFA Queen Cand 1979; Twirling Comp 1st Div 1978; Washington Co Tech Coll; Real Estate.

FERGUSON, L; Catholic Central HS; Steubenvll, OH; 7/203 Hon Rl; NHS; Rptr Yrbk; Fr Clb; College Of Stuebenville.

FERGUSON, L; Eastbrook HS; Van Buren, IN; Am Leg Aux Girls St; Girl Scts; Hon Rl; 4-H; Fr Clb; FHA; Coach Actv; Am Leg Awd; Lion Awd; Univ; Bio.

FERGUSON, LANA; Warsaw Community HS; Warsaw, IN; 136/404 OEA; Schlstc Awd; Ball St Univ; Bus.

FERGUSON, MARIANNE; Graham HS; St Paris, OH; VP Frsh Cls; Pres Soph Cls; Chrs; Chrh Wkr; Cmnty Wkr; Off Ade; Sch Mus; Yth Flsp; FHA; OEA; Bus Schl; Sec.

FERGUSON, MARY; Ravenna HS; Ravenna, OH; Band; Treas Girl Scts; Hon Rl; JA; Fr Clb; College.

FERGUSON, MARY; Sts Peter And Paul Area HS; Saginaw, MI; Chrs; Chrh Wkr; Cmnty Wkr; Hon Rl; NHS; Pol Wkr; GAA; College; Math.

FERGUSON, MELODIE; Fredericktown HS; Mtvernon, OH; Chrs; Drl Tm; Girl Scts; Hon Rl; NHS; Sch Mus; Rptr Sch Nwsp; Pep Clb; Univ; Nursing.

FERGUSON, NORMAN; Maumee HS; Maumee, OH; 90/300 Glf; Univ; Engr.

FERGUSON, PAMELA; Tri West Hendricks HS; Pittsboro, IN; 26/118 Cmp Fr Grls; Hon Rl; Off Ade; Sch Pl; Sec Pep Clb; Spn Clb; Letter Trk; IM Sprt; Mgrs; Pom Pon; Univ Of Colorado; Acctg.

FERGUSON, PERRY L; Doddridge Cnty HS; West Union, WV; VICA; Capt Ftbl; Trk; Wrstlng; Salem Univ; Masonry.

FERGUSON, ROBERT; Columbus Brookhaven HS; Columbus, OH; Boy Scts; Hon Rl; Sct Actv; Bsktbl; Ftbl; Trk; IM Sprt; Scr Kpr; Tmr; College; Bus.

FERGUSON, ROBIN S; Mt Healthy HS; Cincinnati, OH; 11/542 Drl Tm; Hon Rl; NHS; Yth Flsp; Beta Clb; Treas Fr Clb; GAA; Cit Awd; College.

FERGUSON, SHERRY; Ironton HS; Ironton, OH; Band; Chrs; Pres Chrh Wkr; Cmnty Wkr; Hon Rl; JA; PAVAS; Sch Mus; Sch Pl; Sct Actv; Mt Vernon Nazarene Coll; Sociology.

FERGUSON, THOMAS; Algonac HS; Fair Haven, MI; CAP; Hon Rl; Sch Nwsp; 4-H; 4-H Awd; U S Air Force Academy; Aero Engr.

FERGUSON, TOM; North HS; Eastlake, OH; Boy Scts; Chrh Wkr; Hon Rl; Sct Actv; Letter Crs Cntry; Letter Trk; Engr.

FERGUSON, VALERIE; Peterstown HS; Lindside, WV; Band; Chrs; Capt Drl Tm; Hon Rl; NHS; Drama Clb; Fr Clb; FTA; Mth Clb; Pep Clb; Concord Coll; Psych.

FERGUSON, V WAYNE; Alcona HS; Hubbard Lake, MI; 9/121 Chrh Wkr; Jr NHS; Stu Cncl; Rptr Sch Nwsp; Pres FFA; Pep Clb; Capt Bsbl; Letter Bsktbl; Letter Ftbl; Benghauser Award Winner 74; Northwestern Univ; Bus Econ.

FERGUSON, WILLIAM; Put In Bay HS; Put In Bay, OH; 4/13 Am Leg Boys St; Boy Scts; Chrh Wkr; Cmnty Wkr; Debate Tm; Hon Rl; Sct Actv; Capt Bsbl; Capt Ftbl; Am Leg Awd; Bowling Green St Univ; Educ.

FERGUSON III, FRED E; Benedictine HS; Detroit, MI; Hon Rl; Univ Of Michigan; Engr.

FERIA, ALFONSO; Trenton HS; Pontiac, MI; Chrh Wkr; Hon Rl; NHS; IM Sprt; Natl Merit SF; Univ Of Mich.

FERIS, LESLIE; Worthington Jefferson HS; Worthington, IN; 2/40 Trs Soph Cls; Sec Jr Cls; Cls Rep Sr Cls; Drl Tm; Hon Rl; NHS; Stu Cncl; Beta Clb; 4-H; Pep Clb; Purdue Univ; Mgmt.

FERKANY, JAMES; Grand Blanc HS; Grand Blanc, MI; 74/679 Hon Rl; Letter Bsbl; Letter Socr; IM Sprt; Cntrl Mi Univ Bd Of Trustees Hon Schlrshp 79; Central Michigan Univ; Pre Med.

FERKINS, JILL; Mt Healthy HS; Cincinnati, OH; 146/572 Hon Rl; Private Sec.

FERLOTTI, MARK; Saint Thomas Aquinas HS; Alliance, OH; Business Schl; Busns Mgmt.

FERM, CAROLYN; Brookfield HS; Brookfield, OH; 17/160 Pres Jr Cls; Band; Drl Tm; Hon Rl; Jr NHS; NHS; Quill & Scroll; Treas Stu Cncl; Sprt Ed Yrbk; Treas Lat Clb; Bowling Green St Univ; Med Tech.

FERNANDEZ, A; Warren HS; Warren, MI; Cls Rep Soph Cls; Cl Rep Jr Cls; Hon Rl; Fr Clb; Letter Bsbl; Michigan St Univ; Soc Work.

FERNANDEZ, ANA; St Hedwig HS; Detroit, MI; Sec Jr Cls; Band; NHS; Rptr Yrbk; Michigan St Univ; English.

FERNANDEZ, DONNA; Liberty HS; Clarksburg, WV; 2/227 Cls Rep Sr Cls; Band; Hon Rl; Jr NHS; NHS; Stg Crw; Drama Clb; Pres FHA; Mth Clb; VP Spn Clb; Fairmont St Univ; Bus.

FERNANDEZ, EDUARDO B; Zeeland HS; Zeeland, MI; Pres Jr Cls; Am Leg Boys St; Jr NHS; Natl Forn Lg; NHS; Letter Bsbl; Letter Ftbl; IM Sprt; Mayor Pro Tem Schl 79; Michigan Univ; T V Brdcstng.

FERNANDEZ, MILDRED; Adelphian Academy; Flint, MI; Chrs; Hon Rl; Off Ade; Sct Actv; Yth Flsp; Andrews Univ; Mass Communications.

FERNANDEZ, MIRIAM; Adelphian Academy; Flint, MI; Chrs; Chrh Wkr; Hon Rl; Sch Nwsp; Bsbl; Bsktbl; Univ; Med Dr.

FERNATT, SHERRY; Pineville HS; Welch, WV; Hon Rl; IM Sprt;.

FERNEDING, DANIEL; Archbishop Alter HS; Dayton, OH; Cls Rep Soph Cls; Cl Rep Jr Cls; Pres Sr Cls; Chrs; Hon Rl; Sch Mus; Sch Pl; Stu Cncl; Sch Nwsp; VP Drama Clb; Boston Coll; Bus.

FERNETT, LARRY K; Stonewall Jackson HS; Charleston, WV; Chrh Wkr; Cmnty Wkr; FCA; Hon Rl; Yth Flsp; Sch Nwsp; Berkshire Chrstn College; X Ray Tech.

FERNSTRUM, ERIC; Grosse Pointe North HS; Grosse Pt Wds, MI; Univ; Criminal Justice.

FERRARA, JOSEPH; North Central HS; Indianapolis, IN; Hon Rl; NHS; Socr; College; Architecture.

FERRARE, MICCI; South Vermillion HS; Clinton, IN; 1/180 Cls Rep Frsh Cls; Cls Rep Soph Cls; Cl Rep Jr Cls; Am Leg Aux Girls St; FCA; Hon Rl; Off Ade; Stu Cncl; Eng Clb; Fr Clb; Who Who In Foreign Language; Schlstc C Pin; Schlstc S V Pin; Indiana Univ; Med Tech.

FERRARI, MARIANN; Madonna HS; Weirton, WV; 43/100 Cmp Fr Grls; Cmnty Wkr; Hon Rl; Lit Mag; Pep Clb; Chrldng; Mat Maids; Marian Medal 1976; Steele Mark Olympics 1976; West Virginia Univ; Acctg.

FERRARO, SANDRA; Cadiz HS; Cadiz, OH; 28/104 Sec Frsh Cls; Cls Rep Soph Cls; Band; Chrs; Hon Rl; NHS; Sch Pl; Stu Cncl; Ed Yrbk; Fr Clb; Bus Schl; Stenography.

FERRELL, GREGORY; Poca HS; Poca, WV; 15/250 Hon Rl; Sch Pl; Bsktbl; Crs Cntry; IM Sprt; West Vir State Univ; Indust Tech.

FERRELL, JEFFREY; Muskegon HS; Muskegon, MI; Cls Rep Frsh Cls; Band; Cmnty Wkr; Hon Rl; Stu Cncl; Rptr Sch Nwsp; Drama Clb; College; Engineer.

FERRELL, KIM; Ogemaw Heights HS; West Branch, MI; Chrs; NHS; Stu Cncl; Gym; Trk; Chrldng; PPFtbl; Univ Of Michigan; Medicine.

FERRELL, KRIS; Sandy Valley HS; Magnolia, OH; Chrs; Sch Mus; Bsbl; Ftbl; IM Sprt;.

FERRELL, LESLIE; Mc Comb Local HS; Deshler, OH; 5/82 Sec Soph Cls; Band; Chrs; Chrh Wkr; Hon Rl; Jr NHS; NHS; Off Ade; Yth Flsp; 4-H; Acad Hon Awds; Homecoming Crt Attndt; Univ; Med.

FERRELL, NATALIE; Fayetteville Perry Local HS; Fayetteville, OH; Band; Chrs; Girl Scts; Orch; Sch Pl; Fr Clb; Ger Clb; ORU; Teacher.

FERRELL, SHAWN; Southeastern HS; Richmondale, OH; Cls Rep Sr Cls; Boy Scts; Hon Rl; NHS; Sct Actv; Stu Cncl; Lat Clb; Letter Bsbl; Mgrs; Cit Awd; Eagle Scout Troop 39; Jr Councilor; 30 Times Trophy Winner World Karting Assn; Various Race Tracks; Ohio St Coll; Elec Engr.

FERRELL, SHERRY; Fairless HS; Beach City, OH; Girl Scts; Stu Cncl; Yth Flsp; Y-Teens; Rptr Yrbk; Pep Clb; Trk; Chrldng; Univ; CPA.

FERRELL, TAMMY; Grove City HS; Orient, OH; 73/449 Cl Rep Jr Cls; Band; Hon Rl; Stu Cncl; Yth Flsp; Nationwide Beauty Acad; Hair Stylst.

FERRELLI, CARLA L; Brooke HS; Follansbee, WV; 54/460 Cl Rep Jr Cls; Sec Sr Cls; Chrh Wkr; Cmnty Wkr; Jr NHS; Lit Mag; NHS; Quill & Scroll; Stu Cncl; Fr Clb; Bethany Coll; Health.

FERRELLI, MONICA; Catholic Central HS; Steubenville, OH; 34/227 Sec Frsh Cls; Hon Rl; NHS; Stu Cncl; Fr Clb; Pep Clb; IM Sprt; Youngstown State Univ.

FERRELL II, JAMES; Logan HS; Logan, WV; 23/296 Band; Boy Scts; Chrh Wkr; Hon Rl; Jr NHS; NHS; Sct Actv; Yth Flsp; Key Clb; Univ Of Ken; Civil Engr.

FERRERI, ANTHONY M; Chaney HS; Youngstown, OH; Hon Rl; NHS; Cert Of Mert 78; Gold C Pin 79; Cert Of Profcncyt 79; Univ; Acctg.

FERRI, BARBARA; Mifflin Sr HS; Columbus, OH; 1/216 Cls Rep Frsh Cls; Cl Rep Jr Cls; Val; Cmnty Wkr; Drl Tm; Girl Scts; Hon Rl; Hosp Ade; VP NHS; Quill & Scroll; Ohio Bd Of Regents Schlrshp

79; Ohio PTA Schlrshp 79; Ohio Stg Alumni Schlrshp 79; Ohio St Univ.

FERRIER, PATRICK; Oakridge HS; Muskegon, MI; 28/163 Boy Scts; Debate Tm; Hon Rl; Jr NHS; Michigan St Univ; Law.

FERRIER, VICTORIA; St Marys HS; St Marys, WV; 18/122 Chrh Wkr; Hon Rl; Lbry Ade; Off Ade; Sch Pl; Yth Flsp; Drama Clb; Bsktbl; Sec GAA; Scr Kpr; Sec Of Stdnt Coucnl 79; Univ.

FERRIOLO, NANCY; Pontiac Cath HS; Troy, MI; Trs Soph Cls; Val; Hon Rl; NHS; Sch Pl; Yth Flsp; Sch Nwsp; Fr Clb; Oakland Univ; Sociology.

FERRIS, KAREN; Benjamin Franklin HS; Livonia, MI; VP Soph Cls; VP Jr Cls; VP Sr Cls; Am Leg Aux Girls St; Chrs; Mdrgl; Sch Mus; Mercy College; Nursing.

FERRIS, LISA A; Kingswood Cranbrook HS; W Bloomfield, MI; Trs Jr Cls; Band; Chrs; Cmnty Wkr; Hon Rl; Orch; Sch Mus; College; Comp Sci.

FERRIS, TAMARA; Ionia HS; Lyons, MI; 40/272 Band; NHS; Yth Flsp; Rptr Yrbk; Rptr Sch Nwsp; 4-H; Fr Clb; Mgrs; 4-H Awd; OMHEAA 79; Central Mi Univ Brd Of Trustees Hnr Schlrshp 79; Alpha Upsilon Schlrshp 79; Central Michigan Univ; Spec Ed.

FERRO, JOHN; Clay HS; S Bend, IN; 185/430 Band; Hon Rl; Spn Clb; Letter Ftbl; Trk; Purdue Univ; Engr.

FERRO, PATRICK; Bedford Sr HS; Temperance, MI; 1/500 Val; FCA; NHS; Crs Cntry; Trk; IM Sprt; Natl Merit SF; Univ.

FERRONE, JUDI; Brooklyn HS; Brooklyn, OH; 23/173 Band; Hon Rl; NHS; Orch; Sch Mus; Drama Clb; Eng Clb; Treas Fr Clb; Letter Trk; IM Sprt; Univ Of Utah; Chem Engr.

FERRY, CAROLE; Theodore Roosevelt HS; Kent, OH; Pres Soph Cls; Pres Jr Cls; Chrs; Hon Rl; Pol Wkr; Sch Mus; Treas Stu Cncl; Rptr Sch Nwsp; Drama Clb; Pep Clb; Finlst Miss Teen Oh Pgnt 79; Cuy Falls Voc Schl; Med.

FERRY, MELISSA A; Liberty HS; Younstown, OH; 145/214 Band; Hon Rl; Orch; Fr Clb; Swmmng; Univ.

FERRY, RENEE; Bishop Ready HS; Columbus, OH; Am Leg Aux Girls St; Chrh Wkr; Hon Rl; NHS; Sch Mus; Rptr Sch Nwsp; Sec Fr Clb; Ohi Univ; Communications.

FERRY, TOM; Linton Stockton HS; Linton, IN; VP Frsh Cls; Am Leg Boys St; Hon Rl; Pol Wkr; Stu Cncl; FSA; Sci Clb; Capt Glf; Capt Ten; Cit Awd; Hoosier Boys St Amer Lgn 79; Purdue Univ; Sci Research.

FERTAL, FRANCIS; Padua Franciscan HS; Brunswick, OH; Hon Rl; 4-H; IM Sprt; College; Aviation.

FERTIG, RENEE; Pocahontas County HS; Dunmore, WV; 20/116 Band; Chrh Wkr; Hon Rl; 4-H; FFA; 4-H Awd; Fairmont Bus College.

FESENMYER, PATRICIA; Pleasant HS; Marion, OH; Cls Rep Soph Cls; Chrs; Hon Rl; Hosp Ade; Jr NHS; Lbry Ade; Off Ade; Spn Clb; Swmmng; Trk; Univ.

FESMIRE, ROY; Marquette Sr HS; Marquette, MI; Yth Flsp; Letter Crs Cntry; Letter Trk; IM Sprt; College; Sci.

FESSLER, J; Richmond D Sr HS; Richmond, IN; Aud/Vis; Hon Rl; JA; Purdue Univ; Elec Engr.

FESSLER, RENEE; South Dearborn HS; Aurora, IN; 76/263 Chrs; Drama Clb; Pep Clb; Letter Ten; GAA; IM Sprt; Indiana Univ; Engr.

FESSLER, SARAH; Berea HS; Berea, OH; AFS; Girl Scts; Hon Rl; NHS; Sct Actv; Stg Crw; Natl Merit Ltr; Univ.

FESTER, MIKE; Lasalle HS; Cincinnati, OH; Cls Rep Sr Cls; Boy Scts; Cmnty Wkr; FCA; Hon Rl; JA; Stg Crw; Bsbl; Ftbl; Wrstlng; Uc; Mach Engr.

FETHER, KATHY; Waldron Area HS; Waldron, MI; 2/41 Cl Rep Jr Cls; Sal; Chrh Wkr; Hon Rl; NHS; Off Ade; Sch Mus; Treas Stu Cncl; Pep Clb; Treas Spn Clb; Huntington Coll.

FETHER, KATHY; Waldron HS; Waldron, MI; 2/39 Cl Rep Jr Cls; Sal; Chrh Wkr; Hon Rl; NHS; Off Ade; Sch Pl; Treas Stu Cncl; Sec Spn Clb; Trk; College.

FETHERLING, PEGGY; North Central HS; Farmersburg, IN; 14/100 VP Band; Chrh Wkr; Drl Tm; Hon Rl; Sch Pl; Sec Drama Clb; FSA; FTA; Pep Clb; Pom Pon; Ind State; Elem Educ.

FETHEROFF, ROBIN E; Eastlake North HS; Willowick, OH; 72/669 Chrh Wkr; Hon Rl; Jr NHS; NHS; Off Ade; Ed Sch Nwsp; Pep Clb; Letter Chrldng; Scr Kpr; Univ; Tchr.

FETROW, BRENDA; Washington HS; Massillon, OH; Rptr Yrbk; OEA; Model.

FETT, LINDA; Lutheran East HS; St Clair Shores, MI; Chrs; Chrh Wkr; Hon Rl; NHS; Sch Mus; Yth Flsp; Rptr Yrbk; Rptr Sch Nwsp; Ger Clb; Pom Pon; E Michigan Univ; Spec Ed.

FETTE, MARY; St Ursula Academy; Cincinnati, OH; Univ; Soc Work.

FETTER, BARBARA; Barberton HS; Barberton, OH; Band; Chrh Wkr; Hon Rl; Jr NHS; Off Ade; Yth Flsp; Ed Yrbk; Ed Sch Nwsp; FTA; IM Sprt; Akron Univ; Bus.

FETTERS, ANNE; Arcadia Local Schl; Findlay, OH; 3/63 Sec Jr Cls; VP Band; Chrs; Chrh Wkr; NHS; Sch Mus; Ed Yrbk; 4-H; 4-H Awd; Univ; Floral Designer.

FETTERS, ANNE; Arcadia HS; Findlay, OH; 3/63 VP Frsh Cls; Sec Jr Cls; VP Band; Chrs; Hon Rl; Off Ade; Sch Mus; Ed Yrbk; Pres 4-H; FHA; J W White Floral Dsgn Schl.

FETTERS, MARCIA; Mason Sr HS; Mason, MI; Chrh Wkr; Hon Rl; Jr NHS; NHS; Pres 4-H; St Of Mi Comp Schlrshp 79; Va Elliott Awd 79; Lyman Briggs Univ; Bio.

FETTERS, MIKE; Hilliard HS; Lexington, OH; VP AFS; Jr NHS; NHS; Sch Pl; Rptr Sch Nwsp; Drama Clb; Spn Clb; Ftbl; Wrstlng; Cit Awd; AFS Schlrashp Exchange Stu To Japan 78; AFS Host Bros AFS Stu 77; Engr For A Day 78; Purdue Univ; Engr Sci.

FETTIG, BRIAN; Sacred Heart Academy; Mt Pleasant, MI; 5/54 NHS; Drama Clb; Lat Clb; Letter Bsbl; Letter Bsktbl; Letter Ftbl; Dnfth Awd; Lion Awd; Natl Merit Ltr; Rotary Awd; Michigan Tech Univ; Elec Engr.

FETTIG, LYNN; Tipton HS; Elwood, IN; 19/180 Pres Frsh Cls; Pres Soph Cls; Cls Rep Soph Cls; Cl Rep Jr Cls; Am Leg Aux Girls St; Chrs; Hon Rl; Stu Cncl; Pep Clb; Sci Clb; Ind Univ; Bus.

FETTIG, MAUREEN; Cadillac HS; Cadillac, MI; Chrs; Chrh Wkr; Cmnty Wkr; Hon Rl; Sch Mus; Trk; GAA; Pom Pon; PPFtbl;.

FETTIG, TERESA; Walled Lake Central HS; Union Lake, MI; Hon Rl; PAVAS; Yrbk; Sch Nwsp; Michigan State College; Comm Art.

FETTMAN, BETSEY; Timken HS; Canton, OH; Cls Rep Soph Cls; Chrs; Chrh Wkr; Girl Scts; Hon Rl; Natl Forn Lg; NHS; Sch Mus; College.

FETTY, CANDY; East Liverpool HS; E Liverpool, OH; Cls Rep Frsh Cls; Cls Rep Soph Cls; Cl Rep Jr Cls; Cls Rep Sr Cls; Band; Chrs; Drm Mjrt; Hon Rl; Lbry Ade; NHS;.

FETTY, ERIC; Buckeye South HS; Yorkville, OH; Cls Rep Soph Cls; Am Leg Boys St; Cmnty Wkr; NHS; Off Ade; Sch Mus; Sch Pl; Stg Crw; Drama Clb; Spn Clb; Ohio St Univ; History.

FETTY, MARGARET; Buckhannon Upshur HS; Buckhannon, WV; Band; Hon Rl; NHS; Rptr Yrbk; Pres 4-H; VP FBLA; 4-H Awd; Mbr St Winning 4 H Mini Band; 4 H Cnty Awds In Sweing Public Speaking & Hobbies; Coll; Elem Ed.

FETZER, KARL; Dayton Christian HS; Dayton, OH; Trs Soph Cls; Cls Rep Soph Cls; Pres Jr Cls; Cl Rep Jr Cls; Chrh Wkr; FCA; Hon Rl; Spn Clb; Letter Socr; IM Sprt; Cedarville College; Airline Pilot.

FEUER, SCOTT; Garden City West HS; Garden City, MI; CAP; Hon Rl; NHS; Pol Wkr; Ed Sch Nwsp; Sprt Ed Sch Nwsp; Rptr Sch Nwsp; Coach Actv; IM Sprt; Natl Merit SF; Cntrl Michigan Univ; Jrnlsm.

FEUERSTEIN, DAVID; Nordonia HS; Sagamor Hls, OH; 37/480 Boy Scts; Bsbl; Ftbl; Trk; Wrstlng; IM Sprt; Bowling Green St Univ; Bus Admin.

FEUTZ, DOUGLAS; Eminence Consolidated HS; Quincy, IN; 9/44 VP Frsh Cls; VP Jr Cls; Hon Rl; NHS; Off Ade; Rptr Yrbk; Bsbl; Gov Hon Prg Awd; Vincennes Univ; Mech Engr.

FEW, BETH; Wadsworth Sr HS; Wadsworth, OH; 55/367 Cls Rep Sr Cls; Chrs; Girl Scts; Hon Rl; Hosp Ade; NHS; PAVAS; Red Cr Ade; Sch Nwsp; Drama Clb; Voc Schl; Fashn Desgn.

FIACABLE, MARCIA; Merrillville HS; Merrillville, IN; 16/587 Chrs; Hon Rl; NHS; Spn Clb; Chrldng; IM Sprt; PPFtbl; Tmr; Purdue Univ; Natural Resources.

FIBER, CHARLES; Lincoln HS; Lumberport, WV; VP Frsh Cls; Cls Rep Frsh Cls; Am Leg Boys St; Hon Rl; NHS; Sch Pl; Stu Cncl; Letter Bsbl; Bsktbl; Letter Ftbl; Bsbl 2nd Tm All County 77 79; Bsbl Spec Hnrbl Mentn All St 79; Ftbl Hnrbl Mentn Al Big Ten 79;auth Of Yr 77; Univ; Bus Mgmt.

FICHTNER, JANE; Univ HS; Morgantown, WV; Trs Frsh Cls; Cls Rep Frsh Cls; Cls Rep Soph Cls; Trs Jr Cls; Band; Lbry Ade; Sch Mus; Sch Pl; Stu Cncl; Drama Clb; Bauder Bus Schl; Fshn Mdse.

FICK, JOHN; Timken HS; Canton, OH; Hon Rl; Stg Crw; Gym; Trk; College; Math.

FICK, MIKE; Barberton HS; Barberton, OH; Chrh Wkr; Hon Rl; Jr NHS; NHS; Letter Bsbl; Letter Bsktbl; Univ Of Akron; Chem Engr.

FICK, VICKIE; Colerain Sr HS; Cincinnati, OH; 24/693 Girl Scts; Hon Rl; Sct Actv; Ger Clb; Mth Clb; Sci Clb; Letter Bsbl; Ohio St Univ; Engr.

FICKERT JR, DONALD; Celina HS; Celina, OH; 50/242 Hon Rl; Jr NHS; NHS; FFA; Bsbl; IM Sprt; College; Acctg.

FICKLE, ROBERT; Clinton Prairie HS; Frankfort, IN; Band; Boy Scts; Off Ade; Yrbk; 4-H; FFA; IM Sprt; 4-H Awd; Photog.

FIDDLER, MARY E; Carmel HS; Carmel, IN; 258/685 Band; Hon Rl; Yth Flsp; Letter Bsktbl; Letter Trk; Var Vlybl Ltrd 78; In St Talent & Aptitude Grant 78; All Cnty Tm In Vlybl & Bsktbl 78; Indiana St Univ; Phys Educ.

FIDDLER, RON; Edgewood HS; Ellettsville, IN; Hon Rl; Letter Ftbl; Letter Trk; Capt Wrstlng; Ind Univ.

FIDLER, RANDY; East HS; Akron, OH; Aud/Vis; Lbry Ade; Orch; Sch Mus; Spn Clb; IM Sprt; Cit Awd; Akron Univ; Criminology.

FIEBELKORN, BONNIE; Almont Cmnty HS; Almont, MI; 1/98 Trs Frsh Cls; Sec Soph Cls; Sec Jr Cls; Trs Sr Cls; Val; Band; Debate Tm; Hon Rl; NHS; Sch Mus; Wayne St Univ; Phys Ther.

FIEBERKORN, KARLA; Burr Oak HS; Sturgis, MI; 8/30 Trs Soph Cls; Trs Jr Cls; Trs Sr Cls; Hon Rl; Off Ade; Letter Bsktbl; Letter Trk; GAA; Vllybl 77 80; Apher Fitness Awd 2 Yrs; Voc Schl; Stewardess.

FIEDELDEY, CAROLYN; South Dearborn HS; Aurora, IN; Sal; Chrs; Hon Rl; NHS; Sci Clb; Thomas More Coll; Bio.

FIEDLER, KIM; Logansport HS; Logansport, IN; Band; Indiana Univ; Acctg.

FIEDLER, ROY W; Vermilion HS; Vermilion, OH; 100/266 Hon Rl; Lbry Ade; DECA; Key Clb; Spn Clb; Bsktbl; C of C Awd; Kiwan Awd; Lion Awd; DECA Comp Dist 1st Pl St 4th Pl 19th Pl Natl Genl Mdse; Recipient Peter & Leah Full Meml Schlrshp; Bowling Green St Univ; Distr Ed.

FIEDOR, JAMES; St Alphonsus HS; Dearborn, MI; Chrs; Hon Rl; Spn Clb; Bsbl; Bsktbl; Ftbl; Trk; Mgrs; Tmr; Coll; Med.

FIEGER, BARBARA A; Canfield HS; Canfield, OH; Band; Chrs; Hon Rl; NHS; Sch Mus; Pep Clb; Univ.

FIELD, ELIZABETH A; Lawrence N HS; Indianapolis, IN; 1/400 Val; Am Leg Aux Girls St; NHS; Sch Mus; Stu Cncl; Letter Gym; Letter Swmmng; Letter Chrldng; Kiwan Awd; Natl Merit SF; College; Medicine.

FIELD, LAURA; Lawrence Central HS; Indianapolis, IN; Girl Scts; NHS; Quill & Scroll; Yth Flsp; Ed Yrbk; Beta Clb; Key Clb; Pep Clb; Mgrs; PPFtbl; Univ; Bus.

FIELDER, JACQUELINE; Onsted HS; Onsted, MI; 54/123 Sec Sr Cls; Girl Scts; Hon Rl; Lit Mag; Off Ade; Stg Crw; Sprt Ed Sch Nwsp; Sch Nwsp; 4-H; Pep Clb; Mass Comm.

FIELDS, BYRON; Decatur Central HS; Indnpls, IN; 23/302 Hon Rl; IM Sprt; Univ; Archt.

FIELDS, DANIEL; Pickerington HS; Pickerington, OH; Boy Scts; Chrs; Hon Rl; Lbry Ade; Bsbl; Ohio State Univ; Photo Journalism.

FIELDS, DEBRA; Highland Sr HS; Hinckley, OH; 56/202 Band; Chrs; Quill & Scroll; Sch Mus; Sch Pl; Rptr Sch Nwsp; Ger Clb; Lat Clb; Trk; Ohio St Univ; Health.

FIELDS, DENISE; John Hay HS; Cleveland, OH; 1/200 Cl Rep Jr Cls; Chrs; Chrh Wkr; Hon Rl; Pres Jr NHS; NHS; Stu Cncl; Yth Flsp; Rptr Sch Nwsp; OEA; John Carroll; Bus.

FIELDS, EDWARD D; Madison Comprehensive HS; Mansfield, OH; Fr Clb; Trk; Univ.

FIELDS, GAIL; Walton HS; Walton, WV; 1/40 Cls Rep Frsh Cls; Pres Soph Cls; Cl Rep Jr Cls; Val; Band; Debate Tm; Hon Rl; VP Jr NHS; NHS; Off Ade; Marshall Univ; Bus Admin.

FIELDS, GREGORY; Grosse Pte North HS; Grosse Pt Wds, MI; Aud/Vis; Band; Boy Scts; Cmnty Wkr; JA; Sch Pl; Sct Actv; Spn Clb; Ftbl; Trk; Michigan St Univ; Engr.

FIELDS, JAY; Dundee HS; Britton, MI; 2/110 Hon Rl; NHS; Yth Flsp; Bsbl; Oakland Univ; Engr.

FIELDS, JO; Acad Of The Immclt Cncptn; Batesville, IN; Chrs; Chrh Wkr; Hosp Ade; Stg Crw; Yrbk; Sch Nwsp; 4-H; Spn Clb; Bsbl; Herron Schl Of Art; Cmmrcl Artist.

FIELDS, JODY; Eastern HS; Owensburg, IN; Hon Rl; NHS; Quill & Scroll; Ed Yrbk; 4-H; Pep Clb; Voc Schl; Fash Merch.

FIELDS, KATHY; Kouts HS; Kouts, IN; Hon Rl; Lbry Ade; NHS; Stu Cncl; FHA; Pep Clb; Bsktbl; Trk; Chrldng; GAA; Comp Repairs Serv.

FIELDS, KIM; Anderson HS; Anderson, IN; Chrs; Chrh Wkr; Hon Rl; Lit Mag; NHS; Quill & Scroll; Yth Flsp; Y-Teens; Rptr Sch Nwsp; Spn Clb; Indiana Univ; Jrnlsm.

FIELDS, LORRI; Marion HS; Marion, IN; 192/650 Chrh Wkr; Girl Scts; JA; Drama Clb; Pep Clb; Summer Honors Seminar Indiana St Univ 79; Asst Bus Mgr For Drama Club; Purdue Univ; Home Ec.

FIELDS, MICHAEL; Mt View HS; Welch, WV; 139/250 Hon Rl;.

FIELDS, PAMELA; John Hay HS; Cleveland, OH; Band; Chrh Wkr; FCA; Hon Rl; Pol Wkr; Stu Cncl; Ed Yrbk; Rptr Yrbk; Pep Clb;.

FIELDS, RICK; Liberty Benton HS; Findlay, OH; Pres Soph Cls; Chrs; Hon Rl; Sch Mus; Sch Pl; Drama Clb; Letter Bsbl; Letter Bsktbl; Letter Ftbl; Letter Trk; Univ; Health.

FIELDS, ROCKY; Jennings County HS; No Vernon, IN; Chrs; Mdrgl; Sch Mus; Stg Crw;.

FIELDS, S; New Washington HS; Nabb, IN; 10/50 Trs Frsh Cls; Sec Soph Cls; Sec Jr Cls; Trs Sr Cls; Chrs; Chrh Wkr; Lbry Ade; Rptr Yrbk; Sch Nwsp; 4-H; Danville Cmnty Coll; Nursing.

FIELDS, TERESA L; Austin HS; Austin, IN; 17/100 Sec Jr Cls; Chrs; Chrh Wkr; Sch Pl; Yth Flsp; FTA; Lat Clb; Pep Clb; Sci Clb; Bsktbl; Girls State Alternate; Madison Schl Of Dance; Dance.

FIELEK, DIANE; Hartland HS; Hartland, MI; Band; Hon Rl; Spn Clb; Busns Schl; Acctg.

FIELSTRA, MIKE; Reeths Puffer HS; Muskegon, MI; Boy Scts; Hon Rl; Sct Actv; Bsbl; Trk; Muskegon Cmnty Coll; Bus.

FIELY, TED; Greenville Sr HS; Greenville, OH; 75/360 Cls Rep Frsh Cls; Cls Rep Soph Cls; Pres Jr Cls; Cl Rep Jr Cls; Pres Sr Cls; Cls Rep Sr Cls; NHS; Off Ade; Stu Cncl; Key Clb; Bowling Green St Univ; Optomtry.

FIEST, JAYNE; Mathews HS; Cortland, OH; Trs Soph Cls; Trs Jr Cls; Band; Girl Scts; Hon Rl; Stu Cncl; Y-Teens; Yrbk; Key Clb; Pep Clb;.

FIFER, WALTER; Thomas Carr Howe HS; Indianapolis, IN; 4/600 Hon Rl; Jr NHS; Pres NHS; Am Leg Awd; Univ; Vet.

FIGG, KARL; Grand Ledge HS; Mulliken, MI; Boy Scts; Fr Clb; Capt Swmmng; Letter Trk; Coach Actv; Michigan St Univ; Comp Sci.

FIGG, LYNETTE; Douglas Mac Arthur HS; Saginaw, MI; 36/300 Cl Rep Jr Cls; Cmnty Wkr; Drl Tm; Hon Rl; NHS; 4-H; Lat Clb; Letter Trk; 4-H Awd; MSU; Vet Sci.

FIGGINS, BARBARA; Gorham Fayette HS; Fayette, OH; Hon Rl; NHS; Stg Crw; Rptr Sch Nwsp; Letter Bsktbl; Letter Trk;.

FIGGINS, BEVERLY; Gorham Fayette HS; Fayette, OH; Band; Hon Rl; Stg Crw; Rptr Sch Nwsp; Bsktbl;.

FIGGS, BECKY; Carl Brablec HS; Roseville, MI; Band; Cmp Fr Grls; Chrs; Hon Rl; JA; Off Ade; Pom Pon; 1 Yr Punctual & Reg Attend 76; Schslrshp For Strght A 76; 3 Second Div Mdls For Solo & Ensmbl Fest; Wayne St Univ; Eng.

FIGGS, RENEE; Jefferson Union HS; Toronto, OH; Cls Rep Frsh Cls; Cls Rep Soph Cls; Cl Rep Jr Cls; Band; Hon Rl; Jr NHS; NHS; Treas Stu Cncl; Beta Clb; Ohi State; Biomed Engr.

FIGLAR, EDWARD; St Edward HS; Lakewood, OH; 1/330 VP Frsh Cls; Sec Soph Cls; VP Jr Cls; Pres Sr Cls; Val; Cmnty Wkr; Hon Rl; Cornell Univ; Phys Sci.

FIGLER, JENNIFER; Munster HS; Munster, IN; 14/406 AFS; Hon Rl; NHS; Sch Mus; Sch Pl; Drama Clb; Trk; Mat Maids; Ind Univ; Law.

FIGURACION, ANGELI; L C Mohr HS; South Haven, MI; Trs Soph Cls; Trs Jr Cls; Hon Rl; Pres NHS; Stg Crw; Sec Stu Cncl; Rptr Yrbk; Pep Clb; Letter Ten; Trk; Board Of Education Awds; University; Busns.

FIGY, MARSHA; Wauseon HS; Wauseon, OH; Sec Jr Cls; Chrh Wkr; Cmnty Wkr; Hon Rl; NHS; Off Ade; Yth Flsp; Y-Teens; FHA; Mat Maids; Anderson Coll.

FIKE, DEBORAH; Holland HS; Holland, MI; 4/280 Chrh Wkr; Hon Rl; NHS; Orch; Yth Flsp; Lat Clb; Hope Coll.

FIKE, JANICE; Parkersburg HS; Parkersburg, WV; Band; Chrh Wkr; Cmnty Wkr; Hon Rl; Hosp Ade; Yth Flsp; Brigham Young Univ; Phys Ther.

FILBY, MARLENE; Eastlake North HS; Willowick, OH; 162/650 Hon Rl; Hosp Ade; Jr NHS; Off Ade; Rptr Sch Nwsp; Sch Nwsp; Pep Clb; IM Sprt; Dent.

FILE, STEVEN; Garfield HS; Akron, OH; Band; Hon Rl; NHS; Off Ade; Orch; Fr Clb; Sci Clb; Univ Of Akron; Math.

FILER, DALE; Walled Lake Western HS; Walled Lake, MI; 90/450 Hon Rl; Letter Pep Clb; Letter Trk; IM Sprt; Pres Awd; Michigan St Univ; Med.

FILICCIA, BARRI; Holy Redeemer HS; Detroit, MI; Chrs; Hon Rl; Lbry Ade; Lit Mag; Off Ade; Fr Clb; FDA; Cit Awd; Marygrove Coll; Education.

FILICKY, MARILYN; Northwest HS; Canal Fulton, OH; Chrs; Hon Rl; Fr Clb; FHA; Pep Clb; Chrldng; Akron Univ; Nurse.

FILION, RENEE; Aquinas HS; Romulus, MI; Band; Hon Rl; Sch Pl; Drama Clb; College; Music.

FILIPOVSKA, LIDIJA; Franklin HS; Westland, MI; Hon Rl; Hosp Ade; Stu Cncl; Fr Clb; Sci Clb; Cit Awd; Univ Of Michigan; Dentistry.

FILIPPI, DOUGLAS; Buckeye North HS; Smithfield, OH; 19/141 Band; Boy Scts; Chrh Wkr; FCA; Hon Rl; NHS; Ftbl; Letter Wrstlng;.

FILISZNOWSKI, DEBRA; Grafton HS; Clarksburg, WV; Band; Chrs; Drl Tm; FCA; Hon Rl; Hosp Ade; Lbry Ade; Off Ade; Stu Cncl; Y-Teens; Tourn Bsktbl 2nd Pl Girls Tm 79; Fairmont Bus Coll; Clerical.

FILL, CHRIS TINA; Southridge HS; Huntingburg, IN; Band; Chrs; Hon Rl; Hosp Ade; Sch Mus; Yth Flsp; FHA; Swmmng; IM Sprt; Tmr; Beaconess Hosp Schl Of Nursing; RN.

FILLION, THERESE; Walled Lake Western HS; Walled Lake, MI; Aud/Vis; Chrh Wkr; Hon Rl; NHS; Letter Bsktbl; IM Sprt; Scr Kpr; Rotary Awd; Oakland Cmnty Coll; Chef.

FILSON, KAREN; Greenfield Central HS; Greenfield, IN; 97/300 Band; Yth Flsp; Bsktbl; GAA; College; Elementary Education.

FILSON, LORAN; Greenfield Central HS; Greenfield, IN; 51/301 Band; Boy Scts; Chrh Wkr; Hon Rl; Sch Pl; Yth Flsp; Letter Bsktbl; Letter Crs Cntry; Letter Trk; Chrldng; Univ; Radio.

FINAZZO, CHARLES; Clawson HS; Clawson, MI; Band; Letter Bsbl; College; Chemistry.

FINCEL, DAVID A; Lakota Sr HS; Middletown, OH; 20/446 Aud/Vis; Hon Rl; Lbry Ade; Off Ade; Kiwan Awd; Bernrd Munstrn Memrl Schsp Miami Univ Omert Almn Shcsp 79; Miami Univ; Systems Analysis.

FINCH, CATHY; Evansville Central HS; Evansville, IN; 14/528 Hon Rl; NHS; OEA; VP Sci Clb; Letter Mgrs; Univ Of Evansville; Comp Sci.

FINCH, FELICIA; White Pigeon HS; White Pigeon, MI; 1/94 Val; Am Leg Aux Girls St; Band; Lit Mag; NHS; Sch Pl; Yth Flsp; 4-H; Fr Clb; FHA; Glen Oaks Community Coll.

FINCH, JEFFREY; Nitro HS; Nitro, WV; Chrh Wkr; Hon Rl; Sch Pl; Stg Crw; Drama Clb; 4-H; Mth Clb; Mgrs; Scr Kpr; Gifted Prog; Work In TEC Weekends; Marshall Univ; Medicine.

FINCH, ROBYN; Salem Sr HS; Salem, OH; Band; Yth Flsp; Y-Teens; Twrlr; Stage Band 79; Sci Aid; Prom Chrmn; Univ; Phys Ther.

FINCH, TERRI; Nitro HS; Nitro, WV; 10/285 Pres AFS; Band; Chrs; Hon Rl; NHS; Sch Pl; Drama Clb; Sci Clb; Letter Crs Cntry; Voice Dem Awd; Bob Jones Univ; Med.

FINCH, TOD; Holt Sr HS; Lansing, MI; Ftbl; Lansing Cmnty Coll; Drafting.

FINCHIO, LILLIAN; Jenison HS; Jenison, MI; 48/350 Girl Scts; Hon Rl; JA; Rptr Yrbk; Pep Clb; St Of Mi Competetive Schlrshp 79; Stu Aid Grant For MSU 79; Basic Educ Opportunity Grant 79; Michigan St Univ; Pre Vet.

FINDERS, JANICE; Calumet HS; Goodland, KS; Pres Jr Cls; Cmp Fr Grls; Chrs; Hon Rl; Hosp Ade; NHS; Stu Cncl; FNA; IM Sprt; Univ; Med.

FINDLAY, THOMAS; Lake Catholic HS; Mentor, OH; Wrstlng; IM Sprt; College; Mech.

FINDLEY, BOB; La Salle HS; Cincinnati, OH; 18/270 Band; Boy Scts; Hon Rl; Orch; Sch Mus; Pep Clb; Bsbl; Letter Socr; College; Accounting.

FINDLEY, JEFFREY; Lorain Catholic HS; Lorain, OH; 43/160 Chrs; Chrh Wkr; Cmnty Wkr; Hon Rl; Sch Mus; Sch Pl; Stg Crw; Rptr Sch Nwsp; Letter Ten; NEDT Awd 75; Ohio St Univ; Comp Sci.

FINE, TERESA; Grand Ledge Acad; Grand Ledge, MI; Sec Frsh Cls; Band; Chrs; Hon Rl; Off Ade; IM Sprt; Scr Kpr; College; Acctg.

FINEGOLD, MARSHALL; Novi HS; Novi, MI; Hon Rl; Texas Tech; Computer Science.

FINERAN, MARCELLA; Lewis County HS; Ireland, WV; 13/272 Cls Rep Frsh Cls; Cl Rep Jr Cls; Cls Rep Sr Cls; Am Leg Aux Girls St; Band; Chrs; Hon Rl; NHS; Stu Cncl; Rptr Yrbk; Fairmont St Coll; Piano.

FINFROCK, GREGORY; Martinsburg HS; Martinsburg, WV; 1/200 Cls Rep Frsh Cls; Val; Am Leg Boys St; Band; Chrh Wkr; Hon Rl; NHS; Orch; Sch Mus; Sch Pl; Pres Scholar Finalist; Univ Of Virginia Honor Awd Schlrshp; Outstanding Sr Boy Alumni Assn Awd; Univ Of Virginia; Elec Engr.

FINGER, JON; Elston HS; Michigan City, IN; 71/313 Cls Rep Frsh Cls; Aud/Vis; Boy Scts; Hon Rl; NHS; Sch Mus; Sch Pl; Stg Crw; Coast Guard Acad; Marine Engr.

FINK, CAROLYN; Seeger Memorial HS; Williamsport, IN; 6/145 Am Leg Aux Girls St; Girl Scts; Hon Rl; Lbry Ade; NHS; Yrbk; Pres 4-H; FTA; Pep Clb; Indiana St Univ.

FINK, DEBRA L; Seeger Memorial HS; Williamsport, IN; 5/126 Band; Pres Chrh Wkr; Girl Scts; Lbry Ade; NHS; Sch Pl; Yrbk; 4-H; Fr Clb; Pres FTA; Indiana St Univ; Elem Ed.

FINK, JANE; Riverdale HS; Mt Blanchard, OH; 3/100 Chrs; Hon Rl; NHS; Sch Mus; Sch Pl; Rptr Yrbk; Rptr Sch Nwsp; FTA; Chrldng; IM Sprt; Ohio St Univ.

FINK, KAREN A; Norwalk HS; Norwalk, OH; Sec Soph Cls; Drl Tm; Hon Rl; Pep Clb; Spn Clb; Letter Ten; GAA; Pom Pon; Scr Kpr; College; Nursing.

FINK, LORIE E; Washington HS; Massillon, OH; Cls Rep Soph Cls; Sec Sr Cls; Band; Hon Rl; Orch; Drama Clb; Pep Clb; Spn Clb; Oherbien College; Nursing.

FINKBEINER, CYNTHIA; Mcnicholas HS; Cincinnati, OH; Chrs; Drl Tm; Hon Rl; Pep Clb; Gym; Socr; Ten; Chrldng; IM Sprt; Pom Pon; Zavier; Phys Edc.

FINKE, BROOKE; Hauser Jr Sr HS; Hope, IN; 3/103 VP Jr Cls; Band; Hon Rl; Lbry Ade; Mod UN; NHS; Sch Pl; Stu Cncl; 4-H; Pep Clb; Purdue Univ; Pre Vet.

FINKE, ELLEN; Chaminade Julienne HS; Dayton, OH; JA; Stg Crw; Ed Yrbk; Rptr Yrbk; College; Bio.

FINKE, KEVIN; St Xavier HS; Cincinnati, OH; 52/264 Band; Boy Scts; Sct Actv; Univ; Comp Sci.

FINKE, MARILEE; Our Lady Of Angels HS; Cincinnati, OH; 14/117 Girl Scts; Hon Rl; Hosp Ade; JA; NHS; Yrbk; Am Leg Awd; SAR Awd; Raymond Walters; X Ray Tech.

FINKEN, DEB; Archbold HS; Archbold, OH; Chrs; Hon Rl; Letter Sch Mus; VP Soph Cls; Rptr Yrbk; Rptr Sch Nwsp; Pep Clb; Bowling Green State Univ.

FINLEY, BRIAN; Jefferson Union HS; Richmond, OH; Ftbl; Akron Univ; Mechanical Engineering.

FINLEY, JEAN; East Clinton HS; Leesburg, OH; Hon Rl; NHS; Off Ade; VP FTA; Pep Clb; Bsktbl; Capt Chrldng; GAA; E Kentucky Univ; Acctg.

FINLEY, JON; Greensburg Community HS; Greensburg, IN; 11/215 Pres Jr Cls; Pres Band; VP Chrs; FCA; Hon Rl; Pres JA; Mdrgl; NHS; Sch Mus; Sch Pl; College; Medicine.

FINLEY, KIMBERLY; Dublin HS; Dublin, OH; 25/157 Band; Debate Tm; Hon Rl; PAVAS; Sci Clb; Spn Clb; Otterbein Coll; Fine Arts.

FINLEY, LEE; Sandy Valley HS; E Sparta, OH; 5/140 VP Soph Cls; Pres Band; Hon Rl; NHS; Sch Mus; Yrbk; Ger Clb; Ten; Mert Notice For Exclln In Band 78; West Liberty St Coll; Music.

FINLEY, LEONARD; Calumet HS; Gary, IN; 49/361 Cls Rep Frsh Cls; Cls Rep Soph Cls; Cl Rep Jr Cls; Trs Sr Cls; Cls Rep Sr Cls; Jr NHS; NHS; Stu Cncl; Bsktbl; Trk; Woodbury Coll; Int Design.

FINLEY, TAMMY; Clio HS; Clio, MI; 1/300 Trs Frsh Cls; Trs Soph Cls; Trs Jr Cls; Sec Sr Cls; Band; Hosp Ade; Jr NHS; NHS; Off Ade; Stu Cncl; Univ Of Michigan; Law.

FINLEY, TREL; Dublin HS; Dublin, OH; 36/155 Chrs; Debate Tm; Hon Rl; Off Ade; Sch Pl; Stg Crw; Drama Clb; Fr Clb; Sci Clb; Ohi Wesleyan Univ; Law.

FINLEY, VALERIE; Bloom Carroll HS; Lancaster, OH; 6/158 Chrh Wkr; Girl Scts; NHS; Fr Clb; Lat Clb; Letter Bsbl; Mt Vernon Nazarene College; Comp Sci.

FINN, CATHY; Archbishop Alter HS; Centerville, OH; Cls Rep Frsh Cls; Cls Rep Soph Cls; Cl Rep Jr Cls; Cmnty Wkr; Hosp Ade; Stu Cncl; Rptr Yrbk; Spn Clb; GAA; Natl Merit Ltr; College; Special Education.

FINN, CHRISTOPHER; Wadsworth HS; Wadsworth, OH; Chrh Wkr; Hon Rl; NHS; Mth Clb; Spn Clb; Bsktbl; Ftbl; Glf; Coach Actv; Ohio Univ; Mech Engr.

FINN, ERIN; Big Walnut HS; Sunbury, OH; Hon Rl; Bliss Coll; Fshn Mdse.

FINN, GRANT; Water Ford Kettering HS; Drayton Plains, MI; IM Sprt; Cert Of Recog St Of Mich Schlrshp; St MHEAA Schlrshp; Western Michigan Univ; Psych.

FINN, LORI; Cheboygan Catholic HS; Cheboygan, MI; 15/33 Cls Rep Soph Cls; Chrh Wkr; Cmnty Wkr; Hon Rl; Hosp Ade; Off Ade; Pol Wkr; Sch Mus; Sch Pl; Stg Crw; Ferris St Coll; Soc Serv.

FINNERAN, MARK; Boardman HS; Youngstown, OH; 70/580 Hon Rl; NHS; Quill & Scroll; Rptr Sch Nwsp; Sch Nwsp; Sci Clb; Crs Cntry; Trk; IM Sprt; Youngstown State; English.

FINNESSY, LYNN M; Northwestern HS; West Salem, OH; Cmp Fr Grls; Chrs; Girl Scts; Hon Rl; Off Ade; 4-H; FTA; Pep Clb; Letter Bsktbl; Letter Trk; Iowa State; Business.

FINNEY, DEVENIA; Lutheran HS East; Cleveland, OH; 12/40 VP Sr Cls; Chrh Wkr; Cmnty Wkr; Girl Scts; Lbry Ade; Pol Wkr; Sct Actv; Stu Cncl; Rptr Yrbk; Wittenberg Univ; Nursing.

FINSEL, JEANINE; Edgewood HS; N Kingsville, OH; 119/320 AFS; Boy Scts; Chrs; Hon Rl; Lat Clb; Sci Clb; Swmmng; College; Acctg.

FINSTROM, KATHLEEN; Cadillac Sr HS; Cadillac, MI; Band; Hon Rl; NHS; Yth Flsp; PPFtbl; Univ; Chem.

FINTA, SUSAN; Warren Western Reserve HS; Warren, OH; 28/478 Girl Scts; Hon Rl; NHS; Red Cr Ade; Sch Mus; Y-Teens; Fr Clb; Sci Clb; Swmmng; Hiram College; Bio.

FINTEL, LANNA; Patrick Henry HS; Hamler, OH; 13/121 Band; Chrs; Hon Rl; Orch; Rptr Sch Nwsp; Spn Clb; GAA; Bowling Green St Univ; Speech.

FINTON, DAVID; E Kentwood HS; Grand Rapids, MI; 1/400 Val; Band; Boy Scts; Debate Tm; Hon Rl; VP NHS; Orch; God Cntry Awd; Natl Merit Schl; Michigan St Univ; Math.

FINTON, DAVID J; East Kentwood HS; Grand Rapids, MI; 1/400 Val; Debate Tm; Hon Rl; VP NHS; Orch; God Cntry Awd; Natl Merit Schl; Mic State Univ; Math.

FINZER, STEVE; Turpin HS; Cincinnati, OH; 20/350 Off Ade; Letter Bsbl; Capt Socr; College; Accounting.

FIORAVANTE, PHILIP L; Kimball HS; Royal Oak, MI; Boy Scts; Cmnty Wkr; Hon Rl; Jr NHS; NHS; FSA; Sci Clb; Spn Clb; Letter Socr; Letter Univ Of Mic; Mech Engr.

FIORE, MARIA; Clay HS; S Bend, IN; 7/436 VP Soph Cls; Cl Rep Jr Cls; Hon Rl; VP Jr NHS; Stu Cncl; Fr Clb; Bsktbl; Crs Cntry; Trk; DAR Awd; Notre Dame; Engr.

FIORE, TRACY; Newark Catholic HS; Newark, OH; Chrs; Hon Rl; Sch Mus; Sch Pl; Stg Crw; Drama Clb; Fr Clb; Univ; Home Ec.

FIORILLI, ROBERT; St Ignatius HS; S Euclid, OH; 37/309 Cls Rep Soph Cls; Hon Rl; NHS; Lat Clb; Bsbl; IM Sprt; College; Bus Admin.

FIRALIO, SUE; High School; Bay Vill, OH; 34/350 Sec Jr Cls; Sec Sr Cls; Chrs; Girl Scts; Hon Rl; Hosp Ade; Jr NHS; NHS; Off Ade; Rptr Yrbk; Univ; Nursing.

FIREBAUGH, R TODD; Harrison HS; Evansville, IN; 1/465 Cls Rep Frsh Cls; Cls Rep Soph Cls; Cl Rep Jr Cls; Hon Rl; NHS; Stu Cncl; Letter Bsbl; Bsktbl; Letter Ftbl; IM Sprt; Univ.

FIREHAMMER, PAUL W; Buchanan HS; Niles, MI; 1/152 Band; Hon Rl; NHS; Orch; Sch Mus; Sch Pl; Cit Awd; Natl Merit SF; Univ Of Michigan; Elec Engr.

FIRESTINE, CONNIE L; Van Buren HS; Findlay, OH; 12/92 Band; Chrs; Hon Rl; NHS; Off Ade; Sch Mus; Rptr Yrbk; Yrbk; Rptr Sch Nwsp; C of C Awd; Findlay Coll; Acctg.

FIRESTONE, DEBORAH; Pathfinder HS; Northport, MI; Band; Hon Rl; NHS; Quill & Scroll; Yrbk; Rptr Sch Nwsp; 4-H; 4-H Awd; Mi Schlrshp; Adrian Coll Grant; Adrian Univ; Chem.

FIRSICH, ROBERT; Scecina Mem HS; Indianapolis, IN; 30/194 Hon Rl; Ger Clb; Ball St Univ; Acctg.

FIRST, ROBERTA; Lumen Cordium HS; Bedford, OH; Cl Rep Jr Cls; Chrs; Girl Scts; Hon Rl; Lit Mag; Sct Actv; Stu Cncl; Rptr Yrbk; Yrbk; Rptr Sch Nwsp; Case Western Reserve Univ; Chem Engr.

FISCHBACH, JOHN; Ottoville Local HS; Ft Jennings, OH; VP Jr Cls; Band; Chrh Wkr; Hon Rl; Sch Mus; Stg Crw; 4-H; Bsbl; IM Sprt; 4-H Awd; Univ; Acctg.

FISCHBACH, LESLIE; Nazareth Acad; Parma, OH; Chrh Wkr; Pol Wkr; Sch Pl; Bsbl; Swmmng; Coach Actv; Awd Of Merit Natl Math Exam; Coll; Intl Law.

FISCHBACH, VIRGINIA; Ottoville Local HS; Ft Jennings, OH; 4/70 Trs Frsh Cls; Pres Sr Cls; Sec Band; Hon Rl; NHS; Stg Crw; Rptr Sch Nwsp; Sec 4-H; Letter Bsktbl; Trk; Ohio Univ; Chem Engr.

FISCHER, CAROL; The North Royalton HS; N Royalton, OH; Chrs; Chrh Wkr; Sch Mus; Sch Pl; Drama Clb; Lat Clb; OEA; Opt Clb Awd; Cuyahoga Cmnty Coll; Bus Admin.

FISCHER, DEBBIE J; Waldron Jr Sr HS; Waldron, IN; 2/72 Pres Jr Cls; Band; Drm Mjrt; FCA; Hon Rl; FCA; Jr NHS; Red Cr Ade; Stu Cncl; Yrbk; Univ.

FISCHER, DOUGLAS; Newark Catholic HS; Newark, OH; VP Cmnty Wkr; Hon Rl; Letter Ftbl; Letter Trk; College.

FISCHER, HENRY; Homestead HS; Ft Wayne, IN; 3/385 Hon Rl; NHS; Beta Clb; Mth Clb; Natl Merit Ltr; Natl Merit SF; MIT; Physics.

FISCHER, JANINE; Delphos St Johns HS; Delphos, OH; Band; Chrh Wkr; Hon Rl; Hosp Ade; Stu Cncl; FTA; Gym; Trk; College; Occup Ther.

FISCHER, JANIS; Forest Park HS; Crystal Falls, MI; 5/90 Band; Chrs; Chrh Wkr; Cmnty Wkr; Girl Scts; Hon Rl; Sch Pl; Yth Flsp; Rptr Yrbk; Drama Clb; Univ; Med Lab Tech.

FISCHER, KENNETH; Bentley HS; Livonia, MI; Hon Rl; U Of M Dearborn; Engr.

FISCHER, KIMBERLY; Tell City HS; Tell City, IN; 8/249 Band; Chrh Wkr; Hon Rl; Hosp Ade; NHS; Sch Pl; Stu Cncl; Yth Flsp; Yrbk; VP Drama Clb; Indiana Univ; Optometry.

FISCHER, LINDA; William Henry Harrison HS; Evansville, IN; 11/450 Chrs; Hon Rl; Rptr Yrbk; Rptr Sch Nwsp; Sch Nwsp. Letter Ten; Cit Awd; Schlshp H 76 79; Indiana Univ; Pre Optometry.

FISCHER, LORI; Brandon HS; Ortonville, MI; 22/240 Cls Rep Frsh Cls; Sec Sr Cls; Chrs; NHS; Yrbk; Bsbl; Chrldng; Univ.

FISCHER, PAM; Marion Harding HS; Marion, OH; Hon Rl; Lit Mag; Sch Nwsp; Pep Clb; Sci Clb; JC Awd; Tri Rivers Voc Schl; Jrnlsm.

FISCHER, THOMAS; Wayne Memorial HS; Westland, MI; Hon Rl; NHS; Orch; Stu Cncl; Ger Clb; Hockey; Ten; Univ Of Michigan; Sci.

FISCHER, WILLIAM; Purcell HS; Norwood, OH; 40/179 Band; Hon Rl; Orch; Stu Cncl; Sprt Ed Yrbk; Yrbk; Rptr Sch Nwsp; Swmmng; Univ Of Cincinnati; Ecology.

FISCHHABER, JANICE S; Marshall HS; Marshall, MI; 23/258 Hon Rl; NHS; Sch Pl; Stg Crw; 4-H; 4-H Awd; Natl Merit SF; Michigan St Univ; Vet.

FISER, PAMELA; Clyde Sr HS; Clyde, OH; Am Leg Aux Girls St; Chrs; Hon Rl; NHS; Sch Mus; Sch Pl; Drama Clb; Ten; Trk; Chrldng; Findlay Coll; Theatre.

FISH, DEBORAH; Rochester Cmnty HS; Rochester, IN; 22/163 Cls Rep Soph Cls; Chrs; FCA; Hon Rl; Mdrgl; NHS; PAVAS; Sch Mus; Sch Pl; Stg Crw; Best One Act & Best Minor Actress Drama Clb; Most Improved Jr In Choir; Best Actress In Miracle Worker; Ball St Univ; Theatre.

FISH, KENNETH; Jackson County Western HS; Parma, MI; Band; Letter Crs Cntry; Letter Trk; IM Sprt; Michigan St Univ; Engr.

FISH, RHONDA; Brownstown Central HS; Brownstown, IN; Cls Rep Frsh Cls; Cls Rep Soph Cls; Cl Rep Jr Cls; Band; Chrs; Hon Rl; Sch Mus; Stu Cncl; 4-H; FTA; Univ; Comp Sci.

FISH, ROY; North HS; Columbus, OH; 25/300 Band; Chrs; Hon Rl; Jr NHS; NHS; Orch; Sch Mus; Bsbl; College; Music.

FISHBOUGH, KRISTEN; Westerville South HS; Westerville, OH; Pres Soph Cls; Pres Jr Cls; Am Leg Aux Girls St; Chrs; Chrh Wkr; Girl Scts; Hon Rl; PAVAS; Sch Mus; Sch Pl; Principia Univ; Marine Bio.

FISHEL, SUZANNE; Willoughby South HS; Willoughby, OH; 30/416 Hon Rl; JA; NHS; Sch Nwsp; Lakeland Cmnty Coll; Acctg.

FISHER, ALLEN; Gilmour Academy; Lyndhurst, OH; 22/80 Hon Rl; NHS; Yrbk; Sch Nwsp; Bsbl; Capt Glf; Wrstlng; IM Sprt; Mgrs; Bowling Captn Lttrd; Univ Of Notre Dame; Acctg.

FISHER, AMY; Salem HS; Salem, OH; Band; Chrs; Girl Scts; Hon Rl; Lbry Ade; Y-Teens; Fr Clb; FSA; Ger Clb; Heidelberg College; Music.

FISHER, ANNA; Corydon Ctrl HS; Corydon, IN; 1/182 Cl Rep Jr Cls; Val; Am Leg Aux Girls St; Chrh Wkr; Cmnty Wkr; Hon Rl; NHS; Mth Clb; Spn Clb; Cit Awd; Hanover Coll; Pre Med.

FISHER, BARBARA; Bluffton HS; Bluffton, OH; Drama Clb; Heidelberg; Archeology.

FISHER, BARBARA; Ishpeming HS; Ishpeming, MI; 2/125 Sal; Band; Debate Tm; Hon Rl; NHS; Yrbk; Fr Clb; Mic Tech Univ; Comp Sci.

FISHER, BRENDA; Mendon Union HS; Mendon, OH; Sec Frsh Cls; Trs Soph Cls; Sec Jr Cls; Band; Sec Chrs; Hon Rl; Off Ade; Sch Pl; Pep Clb; Capt Chrldng; Vantage Joint Voc Schl.

FISHER, BRIAN; Cascade HS; Clayton, IN; Pres Soph Cls; Letter Bsbl; Letter Ftbl; Ind State Univ; Printing.

FISHER, C DAVID; Loogootee HS; Loogootee, IN; 12/144 Trs Jr Cls; Am Leg Boys St; Band; Boy Scts; Chrh Wkr; Hon Rl; Spn Clb; Letter Crs Cntry; Trk; IM Sprt; Rose Hulman Inst Of Tech; Engr.

FISHER, DANIEL; De La Salle Collegiate; Detroit, MI; Hon Rl; Sch Pl; Stg Crw; Yrbk; Eng Clb; Fr Clb; Natl Merit SF; Univ Of Detroit; English.

FISHER, DANIEL; Whitmer HS; Cape Coral, FL; Boy Scts; Chrh Wkr; FCA; Hon Rl; Off Ade; Sct Actv; Yth Flsp; College; Sci.

FISHER, DAVE; Stryker Local HS; Stryker, OH; 21/50 Am Leg Boys St; Band; Chrs; Drm Bgl; Sch Pl; Rptr Yrbk; Sprt Ed Sch Nwsp; 4-H; Rdo Clb; 4-H Awd; Bowling Green State Univ; Music.

FISHER, DEBBIE; Belpre HS; Little Hockng, OH; Hon Rl; Pres Yth Flsp; Rptr Yrbk; Pres 4-H; Fr Clb; Gym; Pres Awd; Ideal Jobs Daughter Of The Year Bethel #65; College; Social Work.

FISHER, DEBRA; Troy HS; Troy, MI; 21/290 Band; Chrh Wkr; Hon Rl; NHS; Sch Pl; Stg Crw; Drama Clb; Univ Of Mic; Med.

FISHER, DENVER S; Dunbar HS; Dunbar, WV; Cls Rep Frsh Cls; Cls Rep Soph Cls; Boy Scts; Chrh Wkr; Hon Rl; JA; Mod UN; Sct Actv; Stu Cncl; Yth Flsp; Coll; Busns Admin.

FISHER, DIANA; Olentangy HS; Powell, OH; 48/140 Chrh Wkr; Drl Tm; Off Ade; Yth Flsp; Pres 4-H; FHA; PPFtbl; Tmr; 4-H Awd; Sec.

FISHER, DIANE; Carson City Crystal HS; Carson City, MI; Cls Rep Frsh Cls; Cls Rep Soph Cls; Hon Rl; NHS; Stu Cncl; Rptr Yrbk; GAA; IM Sprt; PPFtbl; Univ.

FISHER, GARY; Northeast Dubois HS; Dubois, IN; 15/78 Chrh Wkr; Cmnty Wkr; Hon Rl; PAVAS; FFA; Crs Cntry; Glf; Trk; IM Sprt; Scr Kpr; Eastern Kentucky Univ; Herd Mgr.

FISHER, GUY R; Pike HS; Indianapolis, IN; Hon Rl; FTA; Wrstlng; Aviation Elec.

FISHER, JACKIE; Martinsville HS; Martinsville, IN; 69/391 Chrs; Girl Scts; Hon Rl; Mdrgl; Sch Mus; Sec Yth Flsp; Rptr Yrbk; Rptr Sch Nwsp; VP DECA; Drama Clb; Indiana Central Univ; Mgmt.

FISHER, JEFFREY B; Princeton Community HS; Princeton, IN; 28/203 Aud/Vis; Band; Chrh Wkr; Orch; Stg Crw; Yth Flsp; Mth Clb; In St Univ Summer Hon Seminar 79; Indiana St Univ; Tech.

FISHER, JOSEPH; Amelia HS; Amelia, OH; 15/280 Hon Rl; Jr NHS; Lbry Ade; NHS; Fr Clb; College; Artist.

FISHER, KATHLEEN; Lawrence Central HS; Indianapolis, IN; 119/350 Mdrgl; Orch; Sch Mus; Yth Flsp; Key Clb; College; Medicine.

FISHER, KELLI; Chillicothe HS; Chillicothe, OH; Chrs; Hon Rl; Off Ade; 3yr Hnr Stu Awd 77; Univ; Elec Engr.

FISHER, KEN; Richmond HS; Richmond, IN; Cmnty Wkr; Hon Rl; Jr NHS; NHS; IM Sprt; Purdue Univ.

FISHER, KIMBERLEY; Lewis Cnty HS; Weston, WV; Cmnty Wkr; Hon Rl; Off Ade; Fr Clb; Pep Clb; West Virginia Univ; X Ray Tech.

FISHER, LAURA; Rutherford B Hayes HS; Delaware, OH; Hon Rl; Red Cr Ade; Y-Teens; Rptr Sch Nwsp; Pres 4-H; Key Clb; Lat Clb; Letter Chrldng; Dnfth Awd; 4-H Awd; Schlrshp 2nd Runner Up Natl Mk It With Wool Cont; Ohio Wnr 4 H Natl Comp In Public Speaking; OH Jersey Qn; Denison Univ; Communications.

FISHER, LOMAN T; Warren County Joint Voc HS; Franklin, OH; 28/302 Pres Jr Cls; Am Leg Boys St; Aud/Vis; Band; Hon Rl; NHS; Rdo Clb; Spn Clb; VICA; Ftbl; VICA Skilld Olympics 78; Elec Tchr Aid 78; Demnstrtns Of High Voltg Vidio Tae & Comp For Stdnt P Tchrs 78; Univ Of Cincinnati.

FISHER, LORA; Woodsfield HS; Woodsfield, OH; Band; Chrs; Drm Mjrt; Girl Scts; Sch Mus; Sch Pl; Sct Actv; Drama Clb; 4-H; Fr Clb; Ohio St Univ; Nursing.

FISHER, LYNDA; Big Bay De Noc HS; Manistique, MI; Chrs; Chrh Wkr; Hon Rl; Hosp Ade; Sch Pl; Sch Nwsp; 4-H; FHA; Gym; 4-H Awd; Coll; Music.

FISHER, MADONNA; Henry Ford II HS; Sterling Hgts, MI; 19/460 Trs Frsh Cls; Trs Soph Cls; Trs Jr Cls; Trs Sr Cls; Hon Rl; NHS; Stu Cncl; Bsbl; Letter Bsktbl; PPFtbl; Adrian Coll; Earth Sci.

FISHER, MALISSA; Dover HS; Dover, OH; Girl Scts; Hosp Ade; Lbry Ade; Fr Clb; Trk; Cert From West Liberty St Coll For Art Show; College; Fash Merch.

FISHER, MARCY; Fulton HS; Perrinton, MI; 5/94 Cls Rep Soph Cls; Cl Rep Jr Cls; Cls Rep Sr Cls; Hon Rl; Stu Cncl; Ed Sch Nwsp; Rptr Sch Nwsp; FSA; Mic Tech Univ; Chem Engr.

FISHER, MARIAN; East Palestine HS; Negley, OH; Univ; Bus.

FISHER, MARK; Grove City HS; Grove City, OH; 1/500 Cls Rep Soph Cls; Cl Rep Jr Cls; Cls Rep Sr Cls; Am Leg Boys St; Hon Rl; Jr NHS; VP NHS; VP Stu Cncl; Pep Clb; Letter Bsbl; Univ; Pre Dentistry.

FISHER, MARY; Canal Winchester HS; Canal Winch, OH; 14/90 Chrs; Chrh Wkr; Cmnty Wkr; Hon Rl; NHS; FHA; Spn Clb; Ohio Univ; Sec.

FISHER, MARY BETH; Bishop Luers HS; Ft Wayne, IN; Girl Scts; Hon Rl; Off Ade; Red Cr Ade; Sct Actv; Rptr Yrbk; PPFtbl; Cit Awd; 1st Class Girl Sct 77; St Marys Of Notre Dame Univ; Nurse.

FISHER, MATT; Cadiz HS; Cadiz, OH; VP Frsh Cls; VP Soph Cls; Hon Rl; Off Ade; Stg Crw; Stu Cncl; Yth Flsp; Lat Clb; Letter Bsbl; Letter Ftbl; Univ; Resp Ther.

FISHER, MAUREEN; Bishop Watterson HS; Columbus, OH; Band; Girl Scts; Hon Rl; Lbry Ade; Pep Clb; College; Communications.

FISHER, MICHAEL; Mason HS; Erie, MI; 34/119 Cls Rep Frsh Cls; Cls Rep Soph Cls; Debate Tm; Hon Rl; JA; Jr NHS; NHS; Sct Actv; Stu Cncl; 4-H; ACT Grants; BEOG; Northern Michigan Univ; Conservation.

FISHER, MICHELE; Our Lady Of Mercy HS; Southfield, MI; Cls Rep Soph Cls; Cl Rep Jr Cls; Cls Rep Sr Cls; Chrh Wkr; Girl Scts; Sch Mus; Sch Pl; Mic State Univ; Interior Design.

FISHER, MICHELLE; Miffin HS; Columbus, OH; Pres Chrh Wkr; Ftbl; Trk; Nursing School.

FISHER, MIKE; Breckenridge Jr Sr HS; Wheeler, MI; 2/110 Trs Frsh Cls; Cls Rep Soph Cls; Cl Rep Jr Cls; Stu Cncl; Pres FFA; Letter Bsbl; Michigan St Univ; Crop Prod.

FISHER, REBECCA; Tippecanoe Vly HS; Mentone, IN; 28/170 Chrs; Hon Rl; Lbry Ade; Drama Clb; FHA; Pep Clb; Ball St Univ; Home Ec.

FISHER, RICHARD; Malabar HS; Mansfield, OH; Boy Scts; Chrs; Hon Rl; Off Ade; Sec Yth Flsp; Ger Clb; Letter Glf; Mgrs; Ohio St Coll.

FISHER, ROBERT; Waterford Mott HS; Pontiac, MI; 13/347 Yth Flsp; Letter Crs Cntry; Letter Trk; Univ Of Mich; Computer Eng.

FISHER, ROLAND K; Spencer HS; Spencer, WV; Chrh Wkr; Cmnty Wkr; Hon Rl; Jr NHS; Sch Pl; Stg Crw; Yth Flsp; 4-H; Letter Bsktbl; Ftbl; West Virginia Univ; Civil Engr.

FISHER, S; Northeastern HS; Richmond, IN; Drl Tm; Hon Rl; Off Ade; Yth Flsp; Treas 4-H; Spn Clb; GAA; PPFtbl; 4-H Awd; Ind Univ East; Computer Programming.

FISHER, SANDRA; Immaculate Conception Acad; Batesville, IN; 23/75 Chrs; Hon Rl; JA; Stg Crw; Yth Flsp; IM Sprt;.

FISHER, SCOTT; Columbian HS; Tiffin, OH; 70/340 Aud/Vis; Boy Scts; Chrh Wkr; Hosp Ade; Sct Actv; Drama Clb; Ger Clb; Rdo Clb; Sci Clb; Cleveland St Univ; Phys Ther.

FISHER, SHAWN A; St Martin De Porres HS; Detroit, MI; 10/76 Trs Sr Cls; Hon Rl; NHS; Stu Cncl; Pep Clb; Capt Bsktbl; Coach Actv; Leadership Serv Govt Physics English Christian Sociology; Oakland Univ; Comp Sci.

FISHER, SHERRY; Elgin HS; Prospect, OH; 3/152 Treas Band; Jr NHS; Mod UN; Stu Cncl; VP Yth Flsp; FFA; Letter Trk; PPFtbl; Twrlr; 4-H Awd; College; Agriculture.

FISHER, SONIE; Notre Dame HS; Portsmouth, OH; 1/56 Pres Frsh Cls; Hon Rl; Rptr Sch Nwsp; 4-H; Bsktbl; Trk; Chrldng; 4-H Awd; Univ.

FISHER, STEVE; Park Hills HS; Fairborn, OH; 1/346 Val; Hon Rl; NHS; Ftbl; IM Sprt; Scr Kpr; Louisiana Tech; Engr.

FISHER, TAMELA; Tecumseh Sr HS; Adrian, MI; VP Soph Cls; Am Leg Aux Girls St; NHS; Pres Stu Cncl; Ed Yrbk; Pres FFA; Michigan St Univ.

FISHER, THOMAS; New Lexington Sr HS; New Lexington, OH; 15/150 Cls Rep Frsh Cls; Cls Rep Soph Cls; Cl Rep Jr Cls; Cls Rep Sr Cls; Chrs; Hon Rl; NHS; Stu Cncl; Y-Teens; Yrbk; Ohio St Univ.

FISHER, TOM; New Lexington Sr HS; New Lexington, OH; 15/170 Cls Rep Frsh Cls; Cls Rep Soph Cls; Cl Rep Jr Cls; Cls Rep Sr Cls; Chrs; Chrh Wkr; Hon Rl; NHS; Stu Cncl; Yrbk; Ohio St Univ.

FISHER, WILLIAM R; East Fairmont HS; Fairmont, WV; Am Leg Boys St; NHS; Yth Flsp; FBLA; Pres Key Clb; Mth Clb; Sci Clb; Trk; Fairmont St Univ; Elec.

FISHER JR, LYLE; Dunbar HS; Dunbar, WV; 1/180 Band; VP Jr NHS; NHS; Pres Fr Clb; Letter Wrstlng; Voice Dem Awd; Univ; Chem.

FISHPAW, DEANN; Bucyrus HS; Bucyrus, OH; 5/208 Am Leg Aux Girls St; Band; Hon Rl; Pres NHS; Sch Mus; Stu Cncl; Pres 4-H; VP FTA; Am Leg Awd; Cit Awd; Coll Of Steubenville; Bus Admin.

FISTLER, ELIZABETH; Royal Oak Dondero HS; Traverse City, MI; 10/423 Aud/Vis; Girl Scts; Hon Rl; NHS; Yrbk; Fr Clb; Bsbl; Bsktbl; GMI; Engr.

FITCH, CAROLINE; Mc Auley HS; Cinti, OH; Girl Scts; Sct Actv; Spansih Medl 79; St Bd Of Educ Awd Of Distnctn 79; Ohio St Univ; Intl Bus Admin.

FITCH, DIRK; Bellaire HS; Bellaire, OH; VP Sr Cls; Cls Rep Sr Cls; Boy Scts; Chrh Wkr; FCA; Hon Rl; Stu Cncl; Beta Clb; Fr Clb; Ftbl; Bowling Green St Univ; Educ.

FITCH, LAURA; Warren HS; Sterling Hts, MI; 1/500 Hon Rl; Jr NHS; Pres NHS; Fr Clb; Letter Ten; Scr Kpr; College; Health Sci.

FITCH, MARCY A; Medina Sr HS; Medina, OH; Cmp Fr Grls; Chrs; Hon Rl; Sch Mus; Bsktbl; IM Sprt; Pres Awd; Bowling Green Univ; Bus Mgmt.

FITCH, MARK; David Anderson HS; Lisbon, OH; Trs Soph Cls; Sec Key Clb; Bsktbl; Capt Ftbl; Scr Kpr; Coll.

FITCH, THOMAS; West Branch HS; Salem, OH; VP Jr Cls; VP Sr Cls; Am Leg Boys St; Band; NHS; Ten; Natl Merit Ltr; Hon Mention Oh Test Of Schlstc Achvmnt 77; Univ; Engr.

FITCHETT, PAMELA; R B Chamberlin HS; Aurora, OH; AFS; Girl Scts; NHS; College; Engr.

FITTLER, LORI; Clyde Sr HS; Clyde, OH; Am Leg Aux Girls St; Band; Hon Rl; Off Ade; Sch Mus; 4-H; IM Sprt; 4-H Awd; Hnr Roll Awd; Reserve Bsktbl Track; Terra Tech Schl; Comp Prog.

FITTRO, MELISSA; Olivet HS; St Petersburg, FL; Chrs; Drl Tm; Hon Rl; PAVAS; Sch Mus; Rptr Sch Nwsp; Drama Clb; Spn Clb; Barbizon Modeling Schl; Modeling.

FITZ, DAVID; Sandusky HS; Sandusky, OH; AFS; Band; Hon Rl; Fr Clb; Bowling Green State Univ; Accounting.

FITZ, GERALD; Benton Harbor HS; Benton Hbr, MI; Band; Chrh Wkr; Hon Rl; College; Elec Tech.

FITZ, GRANT; Traverse City HS; Traverse City, MI; 57/780 Cls Rep Frsh Cls; Cls Rep Soph Cls; Cl Rep Jr Cls; Hon Rl; NHS; Stu Cncl; Ftbl;.

FITZ, JANET; East Grand Rapids HS; Grand Rapids, MI; 49/289 Band; Chrs; Chrh Wkr; Hon Rl; Stg Crw; Pep Clb; Spn Clb; Letter Bsbl; PPFtbl; Western Michigan Univ; Engr.

FITZ, SANDRA; Watervliet HS; Watervliet, MI; 3/95 Cls Rep Frsh Cls; Chrs; Hon Rl; Mdrgl; NHS; Sch Mus; Stu Cncl; Yth Flsp; Spn Clb; Mgrs; Stdnt Councl Sec 78; Outstndng Soc Std Stdnt 79; St Of Mi Schslhp 820 79; Western Michigan Univ; Acctg.

FITZGERALD, CHARLES; Wintersville HS; Wintersville, OH; Jr NHS; Letter Ftbl; IM Sprt; Ohio Univ; Bus Admin.

FITZGERALD, CRAIG; Shepherd HS; Mt Pleasant, MI; Cl Rep Jr Cls; Band; Debate Tm; Drm Bgl; Hon Rl; Sch Mus; Yth Flsp; FTA; Pep Clb; Ftbl; Central Michigan Univ; Bus Mgmt.

FITZGERALD, JONI; Ann Arbor Pioneer HS; Ann Arbor, MI; Letter Bsktbl; Crs Cntry; Capt Trk; PPFtbl; Univ; Engr.

FITZGERALD, JOSEPH; Cathedral HS; Indianapolis, IN; 50/150 Hon Rl; Crs Cntry; Trk; IM Sprt; Butler Univ.

FITZGERALD, KELLEE; Poland Seminary HS; Poland, OH; Hon Rl; Hosp Ade; NHS; Stg Crw; Sch Nwsp; Drama Clb; Univ; Bus Admin.

FITZGERALD, PAMELA L; Washington HS; Washington, IN; 16/207 Chrs; Chrh Wkr; Hon Rl; NHS; DECA; 4-H; 4-H Awd; Oakland City Coll; Acctg.

FITZGERALD, PATRICK; St Ignatius HS; Bay Village, OH; 27/303 Cl Rep Jr Cls; Hon Rl; NHS; Stu Cncl; IM Sprt; Univ; Engr.

FITZ GERALD, SEAN; Bishop Borgess HS; Detroit, MI; Pres Sr Cls; Natl Forn Lg; NHS; Stg Crw; Univ Of Michigan; Poli Sci.

FITZGIBBON, BRENDA; Monroe HS; Monroe, MI; VP Chrs; Hon Rl; NHS; Sch Mus; Drama Clb; Letter Bsktbl; Chrldng; Monroe Comm Coll; Bus.

FITZPATRICK, ANN; Mc Auley HS; Cincinnati, OH; 30/259 Cls Rep Sr Cls; Aud/Vis; Chrh Wkr; Hon Rl; Sch Mus; Sch Pl; Drama Clb; Coach Actv; Natl Merit Schl; Pres Awd; Xavier Univ; Intl Affairs.

FITZPATRICK, BARRY; Bridgeport HS; Bridgeport, MI; 42/365 Band; Hon Rl; NHS; Mic Tech Univ; Engineering.

FITZPATRICK, CHRISTOPHER; Muskegon Mona Shores HS; Muskegon, MI; VP Soph Cls; VP Jr Cls; Stu Cncl; Yrbk; Rptr Sch Nwsp; Sci Clb; Letter Bsktbl; Notre Dame; Bus Admin.

FITZPATRICK, ELLEN; Charles F Brush HS; S Euclid, OH; 126/595 Sec Frsh Cls; Cls Rep Soph Cls; VP Jr Cls; Trs Sr Cls; Chrs; Girl Scts; Hosp Ade; Stu Cncl; Yrbk; Ed Sch Nwsp; Bowling Green St Univ.

FITZPATRICK, JACKIE; Carson City Crystal HS; Fowler, MI; Band; Hon Rl; NHS; Chrldng; Twrlr; Pres Awd; St Of Mi Comp Schlrshp 79; W Mi Univ Of Acad Schrlshp 79; Ferris St Coll; Pharm.

FITZPATRICK, KEVIN; Bishop Noll Inst; Griffith, IN; 74/360 Boy Scts; Hon Rl; Mth Clb; Spn Clb; Bsbl; Ftbl; Wrstlng; Purdue; Engr.

FITZPATRICK, KIM; James Ford Rhodes HS; Cleveland, OH; Jr NHS; NHS; Treas OEA; Cleveland St Univ.

FITZPATRICK, PENNY; North Union Sr HS; Marysville, OH; Drl Tm; Hon Rl; Lbry Ade; NHS; Off Ade; Rptr Yrbk; 4-H; FHA; Spn Clb; Letter Trk; Findlay Coll; Equestrian.

FITZPATRICK, PENNY; North Union HS; Marysville, OH; NHS; Rptr Yrbk; 4-H; FHA; Bsktbl; Crs Cntry; Trk; Findlay College; Equestrian.

FITZPATRICK, TERRI; Southeastern HS; Detroit, MI; Chrh Wkr; Girl Scts; Hon Rl; Lbry Ade; Off Ade; FTA; OEA; Pres Sci Clb; Letter Bsbl; Scr Kpr; Univ; Med.

FITZSIMMONS, JAMES; Chelsea HS; Gregory, MI; Pres Jr Cls; Natl Forn Lg; Yth Flsp; Drama Clb; Crs Cntry; Trk; Am Leg Awd; Drama.

FITZWATER, CHERYL; Fairless HS; Wilmot, OH; Chrs; 4-H; FHA;.

FITZWATER, JIMMY; Gilmer County HS; Glenville, WV; VP Jr Cls; Band; Chrs; Chrh Wkr; Cmnty Wkr; Hon Rl; Sch Pl; Drama Clb; Pep Clb; Univ; Music.

FITZWATER, MARGARET; Philip Barbour HS; Philippi, WV; VP Soph Cls; Sec Jr Cls; Band; Drm Mjrt; Girl Scts; Hon Rl; VP NHS; Sch Mus; Alderson Broaddus College.

FIX, LUCINDA J; Shelbyville Sr HS; Shelbyville, IN; 73/300 Girl Scts; Hon Rl; JA; Rptr Yrbk; Pep Clb; Outstndng Grl Of Yr Grls Club 1978; Gldn Grl Optmst Clb 1979; Cmps Lf Stdnt Drctr 1978; Indiana St Univ; Recreatn Directr.

FIX, MICHAEL; Bishop Borgess HS; Dearborn Hts, MI; Band; IM Sprt; Univ; Sci.

FIX, RICHARD; Rossford HS; Perrysburg, OH; Cls Rep Frsh Cls; Chrh Wkr; Hon Rl; Off Ade; Stu Cncl; Spn Clb; Bsbl; Bsktbl; Amer Lgn Boys St 79; Univ; Dent.

FLACK, DANNY; Greenbrier East HS; Lewisburg, WV; Chrh Wkr; FCA; Hon Rl; Lbry Ade; IM Sprt; Baptist Bible Coll; Christian Ed.

FLACK, DAVID; Pymatuning Vly HS; Williamsfield, OH; 16/135 Band; Boy Scts; Hon Rl; NHS; Sch Pl; Yrbk; Rptr Sch Nwsp; 4-H; Fr Clb; 4-H Awd; College; Computer Engr.

FLACK, PHILIP; Springfield Local HS; N Middletown, OH; Aud/Vis; Band; Hon Rl; Lbry Ade; Pep Clb; College; Math.

FLAGEL, BETTY; Les Cheneaux Comm HS; Cedarville, MI; 7/54 VP Sr Cls; Chrs; Chrh Wkr; Hon Rl; Lbry Ade; NHS; Off Ade; Sch Pl; Yth Flsp; Rptr Yrbk; Ferris State College;.

FLAGEL, S; Miami Valley HS; Dayton, OH; Sch Nwsp; Letter Socr; College; Sci.

FLAGG II, JAMES P; Fenwick HS; Middletown, OH; Band; Hon Rl; JA; Orch; Stg Crw; IM Sprt; Univ Of Cincinnati; Architec.

FLAHERTY, BRIAN; High School; Trenton, MI; Chrs; Hon Rl; NHS; Sch Mus; Drama Clb; Natl Merit SF; College.

FLAHERTY, ELLEN; St Francis De Sales HS; Columbus, OH; Girl Scts; Hon Rl; Rptr Sch Nwsp; Drama Clb; Lat Clb; Letter Gym; Ten; Univ.

FLAHERTY, JANE; West Geauga HS; Chesterland, OH; Chrs; Cmnty Wkr; Hon Rl; NHS; Off Ade; Sch Mus; Yth Flsp; IM Sprt; PPFtbl; Cit Awd; Cleveland St Univ; Law.

FLAHERTY, MARY; Lomen Cordium HS; Bedford, OH; 2/91 Trs Frsh Cls; Cls Rep Soph Cls; Val; Hon Rl; Lit Mag; Stg Crw; Stu Cncl; Rptr Yrbk; GAA; IM Sprt; Univ Of Evansville; Radio Tech.

FLAHERTY, MARY V; Liberty HS; Clarksburg, WV; Band; Chrs; Chrh Wkr; Cmnty Wkr; Hon Rl; Red Cr Ade; Sch Mus; Stg Crw; Sch Nwsp; Drama Clb; Glenville St Coll; Soc Worker.

FLAHERTY, SUSAN; Lumen Cordium HS; Bedford, OH; Hon Rl; Stg Crw; Chrldng; Coach Actv; Treas GAA; IM Sprt; Akron Univ; Legal Sec.

FLAHERTY, TAMMY; Ben Davis HS; Indianapolis, IN; Off Ade; PPFtbl; Opt Clb Awd; Ball St Univ; Acctg.

FLAHIFF, JOSEPH; Gibsonburg HS; Gibsonburg, OH; Hon Rl; DECA; 4-H; Trk; Terra Tech Coll; Graphic Cmnctns.

FLAITZ, JACQULINE; Notre Dame Acad; Whitehouse, OH; Chrh Wkr; Orch; Sch Mus; Spn Clb; College; Med.

FLAKE, JAMES; Portsmouth East HS; Portsmouth, OH; Chrs; Hon Rl; Rptr Sch Nwsp; Spn Clb; Letter Bsbl; Bsktbl; Ftbl; IM Sprt; Attended Rio Grande Coll Free Interprise System Wrkshp Earnd 2 Credits Hours 79; Eastern Kentucky Univ; Bus Admin.

FLAMM, LOUIS; La Salle HS; Cheviot, OH; 34/249 Hon Rl; NHS; Sch Mus; Sch Pl; Sct Actv; Rptr Yrbk; Rptr Sch Nwsp; SAR Awd; Univ Of Cincinnati; Engr.

FLANAGAN, COLLEEN; Bishop Foley HS; Troy, MI; 2/200 Sal; Chrs; Cmnty Wkr; Hon Rl; Lit Mag; NHS; Pol Wkr; Ed Sch Nwsp; Natl Merit Ltr;.

FLANAGAN, GARY; Fraser HS; Fraser, MI; Aud/Vis; Spn Clb; Bsbl; Ftbl; IM Sprt; Tmr; College.

FLANDERS, DONNA J; Hamilton Heights HS; Noblesville, IN; 1/110 Sec NHS; VP Yth Flsp; VP 4-H; Lat Clb; VP Mth Clb; Pep Clb; Sec Sci Clb; 4-H Awd; Natl Merit SF; Purdue Univ; Engr.

FLANDERS, JOHN; Perry HS; Canton, OH; Band; Boy Scts; Hon Rl; Jr NHS; NHS; Sch Mus; College; Med.

FLANDERS, LAUREN L; Federal Hocking HS; Guysville, OH; 15/135 Band; Hon Rl; Yth Flsp; Spn Clb; Letter Bsktbl; Letter Trk; All Oh St Fair Bnd 77 79; Ohio St Univ; Bio.

FLANDERS, LEE; Deer Park HS; Cincinnati, OH; Cls Rep Frsh Cls; Band; Chrh Wkr; CAP; Hon Rl; JA; Stu Cncl; Yth Flsp; Coach Actv; Ohi State Univ; Law Prof.

FLANIGAN, DANA; Lawrence Central HS; Indianapolis, IN; Band; JA; Red Cr Ade; Beta Clb; 4-H; Cert Superior Perf Natl Ed Dev Test 77; Bus Schl; Acctg.

FLANNERY, CELIA; Immaculate Conception Acad; Cincinnati, OH; Chrs; Chrh Wkr; Cmnty Wkr; Girl Scts; Hon Rl; JA; Orch; Quill & Scroll; Sch Mus; Sch Pl; Univ Of Cincinnati; Cmmrcl Art.

FLANNERY, JILL; Bad Axe HS; Bad Axe, MI; Trs Soph Cls; Hon Rl; Jr NHS; Natl Forn Lg; NHS; Sch Pl; Yrbk; Fr Clb; Sci Clb; God Cntry Awd; Michigan St Univ; Sci.

FLANNERY, KELLY; Summit Country Day HS; Batavia, OH; Pres Frsh Cls; Band; Chrh Wkr; Hon Rl; NHS; Pol Wkr; Stu Cncl; Yth Flsp; Pep Clb; Spn Clb; Soph Yr Straight A Schslhp Awd 77; Univ; Geol.

FLANNERY, PATRICK O; Hamilton Taft HS; Hamilton, OH; Band; Chrh Wkr; Cmnty Wkr; FCA; Spn Clb; Letter Bsbl; Letter Glf; Coach Actv; IM Sprt; Mgrs; Lttrs In Golf & Bsbll; Hnrs For Extra Class Activities; Miami Univ; Law Enforcement.

FLANNERY, ROBERT; Marietta Sr HS; Reno, OH; Boy Scts; Chrh Wkr; NHS; Sct Actv; Fr Clb; Key Clb; Rus Clb; Brigham Young Univ; Chem Engr.

FLANNERY, SHARON; Glen Este HS; Cincinnati, OH; Band; Chrh Wkr; Hon Rl; Pres Yth Flsp; Fr Clb; Pep Clb; Mary Rowe Moore Admin With Distinction To Univ Of Cincinnati 79; Univ Of Cincinnati; Exec Legal Sec.

FLASPOHLER, JEAN; Immaculate Conception Acad; Batesville, IN; 15/68 Hon Rl; 4-H;.

FLATTERY, DENISE; Arthur Hill HS; Saginaw, MI; Cl Rep Jr Cls; Cls Rep Sr Cls; Band; NHS; Orch; Fr Clb; VP Pep Clb; Central Mic Univ; Music.

FLAUGHER, ROGER; Beal City HS; Weidman, MI; Cls Rep Soph Cls; Cl Rep Jr Cls; Off Ade; Sch Pl; Stu Cncl; FFA; Sci Clb; Capt Bsbl; Bsktbl; Capt Ftbl; ACT Schslhp 79; MV Sr Ahlt 79; CMU; Athltc Trainer.

FLECK, DAVID; Celina Sr HS; Celina, OH; Hon Rl; NHS; Letter Crs Cntry; Letter Trk; IM Sprt; Natl Merit Ltr; Coll; Comp Sci.

FLECK, DEBORAH; Celina Sr HS; Celina, OH; Trs Sr Cls; NHS; FBLA; Ger Clb; Pep Clb; Bsktbl; GAA; PPFtbl; VFW Awd;.

FLECK, DEBRA A; Celina Sr HS; Celina, OH; Hon Rl; NHS; VICA; Bsktbl; GAA; IM Sprt; 8th In WBL Free Throw Percentg 1977; Earned Bsktbl Letter 1976;.

FLECK, LAUREN; South Knox HS; Vincennes, IN; 9/110 Chmn Drl Tm; Hon Rl; NHS; Quill & Scroll; Ed Yrbk; 4-H; FNA; Pep Clb; Ind Univ; Med Tech.

FLECK, PAMELA; Daleville HS; Anderson, IN; 5/59 Chrs; Chrh Wkr; Hon Rl; NHS; Yth Flsp; Rptr Yrbk; Sch Nwsp; OEA; Anderson College; Acctg.

FLECK, SANDRA; Celing Sr HS; Celina, OH; Chrs; Chrh Wkr; Hon Rl; Mdrgl; Treas NHS; Yth Flsp; Sec FBLA; Lat Clb; VP OEA; Pep Clb; Wright St Univ; Music.

FLECK, TONY; Liberty Benton HS; Findlay, OH; Boy Scts; Hon Rl; NHS; FFA; Ftbl; Trk; Letter Wrstlng; Mgrs; Bowling Green Univ; Elec.

FLEDDERMAN, JODY; Milan HS; Sunman, IN; 5/125 VP Frsh Cls; FCA; Hon Rl; Jr NHS; Off Ade; Stg Crw; Stu Cncl; Drama Clb; Lat Clb; Spn Clb; Voc Schl.

FLEDDERMAN, RONDA; Milan HS; Sunman, IN; 17/79 NHS; Ed Yrbk; Ohio Mech Inst; Shop Math.

FLEEGLE, JON; Arcadia Local HS; Arcadia, OH; 23/60 VP Soph Cls; Cl Rep Jr Cls; Chrs; Chrh Wkr; Debate Tm; Hon Rl; Lbry Ade; Sch Mus; Stu Cncl; Yth Flsp; Bowling Green St Univ; Bus Admin.

FLEENER, ROBERT; Dwight D Eisenhower HS; Saginaw, MI; 100/330 Cls Rep Frsh Cls; Cls Rep Soph Cls; C! Rep Jr Cls; Cls Rep Sr Cls; Am Leg Boys St; Hon Rl; Natl Forn Lg; Red Cr Ade; Stu Cncl; Rptr Yrbk; Coll; Bio.

FLEENER, TODD; Martinsville HS; Martinsville, IN; Hon Rl; Letter Crs Cntry; Coll.

FLEENOR, DAVID L; St Francis De Sales HS; Toledo, OH; 24/223 Debate Tm; Hon Rl; Natl Forn Lg; NHS; Stu Cncl; Capt Bsktbl; Natl Merit SF; Cornell Univ; History.

FLEENOR, PAULA; Chalker HS; Southington, OH; Cl Rep Jr Cls; Cls Rep Sr Cls; Band; Girl Scts; Off Ade; Y-Teens; Rptr Yrbk; Pep Clb; Spn Clb; Bsbl; Best Class Salesman Awd 10th Grd 78; Best Class Salesman Awd 11th Grd 79; Spanish.

FLEER, LIANE; Maysville HS; Zanesville, OH; Hon Rl; Hosp Ade; Jr NHS; NHS; Off Ade; Red Cr Ade; Stu Cncl; Sch Nwsp; Bsktbl; Swmmng; Univ; Med Dr.

FLEES, PAULA; Northport Public HS; Northport, MI; 4/26 Band; Chrh Wkr; Girl Scts; Hon Rl; NHS; 4-H; Pep Clb; Coll; Legal Sec.

FLEETWOOD, LINDA; Portage Northern HS; Kalamazoo, MI; Hon Rl; NHS; Lat Clb; Sci Clb; Natl Merit Ltr; Kalamazoo College; Pre Med.

FLEGEL, RICHARD; Ithaca HS; Ithaca, MI; Hon Rl; Letter Bsktbl; Capt Ftbl; Bus Schl; Auto Diesel Mech.

FLEISCHER, DAVID; Withrow Sr HS; Cincinnati, OH; Hon Rl; NHS; Natl Tech Inst For Deaf.

FLEISCHMAN, RENEE; Bishop Luers HS; Fort Wayne, IN; Hon Rl; Fr Clb; IM Sprt; PPFtbl; 4-H Awd; Univ; Bus.

FLEISHNER, KIMBERLE; Ontario HS; Mansfield, OH; 55/175 College; Lab Technologists.

FLEMING, AGGIE; Olivet HS; Olivet, MI; 9/81 Cmnty Wkr; Hon Rl; Eng Clb; Chrldng; Olivet College; Psychology.

FLEMING, BETH; Cuyahoga Valley Christian Ac; Cuyahoga Falls, OH; Hon Rl; NHS; Chrldng; Akron Univ; Exec Sec.

FLEMING, CHERYL L; Calhoun County HS; Arnoldsburg, WV; Cls Rep Soph Cls; Cl Rep Jr Cls; Pres Band; Chrs; Chrh Wkr; Cmnty Wkr; Drm Mjrt; Hon Rl; NHS; Off Ade; West Virginia Univ; Bus Admin.

FLEMING, CHRIS; Gull Lake HS; Augusta, MI; 5/240 Hon Rl; Jr NHS; NHS; Pres Sci Clb; Capt Crs Cntry; Ftbl; Capt Trk; Coach Actv; Natural Sci Schlrshp 79 83; Hope Coll; Chem.

FLEMING, DAWN; Lansing Everett HS; Lansing, MI; Band; Boy Scts; Hon Rl; Cit Awd; Michigan St Univ; Dent.

FLEMING, JUDITH; Onekama HS; Onekama, MI; Hon Rl; Off Ade; Sch Pl; Stg Crw; Rptr Yrbk; Drama Clb; Letter Trk; Pres Awd; Northwestern Cmnty Coll; Legal Sec.

FLEMING, KATHY; Bedford North Lawrence HS; Bedford, IN; Band; Chrs; Chrh Wkr; Cmnty Wkr; Hon Rl; Mdrgl; NHS; Ind Univ; Med Tech.

FLEMING, MINDY; River Valley HS; Waldo, OH; Cl Rep Jr Cls; Hon Rl; Stu Cncl; Yth Flsp; 4-H; Spn Clb; Trk; PPFtbl; Scr Kpr; College; Social Work.

FLEMING, NANCY; Bellmont HS; Decatur, IN; Trs Jr Cls; Cmnty Wkr; Girl Scts; Hon Rl; Stu Cncl; DECA; Swmmng; Ten; PPFtbl; IU Pu; Bus Mgmt.

FLEMING, PATRICK M; Franklin Hts HS; Grove City, OH; VP Soph Cls; Am Leg Boys St; Chrs; NHS; Quill & Scroll; Sch Pl; Stu Cncl; Sch Nwsp; Drama Clb; VP Key Clb; Jr Yr Awd The I Dare You Awd; Soph Yr Attended Annual Ohio Teenage Inst On Alchol & Other Drugs; Columbus Tech Inst; Bus.

FLEMING, ROBERT L; William Henry Harrison HS; Evansville, IN; 5/466 Cls Rep Soph Cls; Cl Rep Jr Cls; Band; Boy Scts; Chrh Wkr; Debate Tm; Hon Rl; Pres Natl Forn Lg; Pres NHS; Orch; HS Sci Stdnt Inst 79; St Hist Day 1st Pl Winner In 79; Culver Mitry Acad Summer Schlh Co Commander 73 78; Indiana Univ; Med.

FLEMING, T; Sidney HS; Sidney, OH; Chrs; Debate Tm; Hon Rl; Orch; Sch Mus; Pres 4-H; Mia Univ; Music Ed.

FLEMING, THERESA; Breckenridge Jr Sr HS; Breckenridge, MI; Chrs; Hon Rl; Sch Mus; Stu Cncl; Drama Clb; 4-H; Pep Clb; Chrldng; PPFtbl; 4-H Awd; Ferris St Univ; Dental.

FLEMING, TIM; Grand Ledge Academy; Grand Ledge, MI; Cls Rep Soph Cls; Cl Rep Jr Cls; Cls Rep Sr Cls; Sal; Hon Rl; Sch Nwsp; Bsbl; Bsktbl; Ftbl; Coach Actv; Michigan St Univ; Law.

FLEMING, WILLIAM; Grosse Pointe North HS; Gs Pte Wds, MI; Debate Tm; Hon Rl; NHS; Pol Wkr; Letter Ftbl; Letter Wrstlng; Coach Actv; Natl Merit Ltr; Natl Merit Schl; Univ; Law.

FLEMISTER, SANDRA; Withrow Sr HS; Cincinnati, OH; Hon Rl; Jr NHS; Stu Cncl; Civ Clb; FHA; Mth Clb; Pep Clb; Bsbl; Chrldng; C of C Awd; Dux Femina Withrow Women Hon Club 80; Upwrd Bound Univ Of Cincinnati 78 80; Head Pony Tap Dancing 80; Tuskegee Inst; Elec Engr.

FLEMMINGS, KIMBERLY; St Ursula Acad; Toledo, OH; Chrs; Chrh Wkr; Cmnty Wkr; FCA; Hosp Ade; Lbry Ade; Off Ade; Stg Crw; Yth Flsp; Drama Clb; College; Bus Admin.

FLENNOY, LALAH; Immaculata HS; Detroit, MI; Cls Rep Frsh Cls; Cls Rep Sr Cls; Hon Rl; Sprt Ed Sch Nwsp; Rptr Sch Nwsp; Pep Clb; Typing Awd; Spanish; Michigan St Univ; Busns Admin.

FLESCH, TERESA M; Whitehall Yearling HS; Whitehall, OH; 16/280 Cls Rep Frsh Cls; VP Soph

Cls; Cls Rep Soph Cls; Pres Jr Cls; Cl Rep Jr Cls; Girl Scts; Hon Rl; NHS; Off Ade; Red Cr Ade; Univ.

FLESHER, CONNIE; Lewis Cnty HS; Weston, WV; Band; Hon Rl; 4-H; Univ; Elem Ed.

FLESHER, KYLE; Garrett HS; Auburn, IN; Band; Chrs; Hon Rl; Sch Mus; Sch Pl; Drama Clb; Letter Ftbl; Ball State Univ; Music.

FLESHER, MARSHA; River Valley HS; Edison, OH; 22/215 Chrs; Girl Scts; Hon Rl; Hosp Ade; Lbry Ade; NHS; Sch Mus; Stg Crw; Rptr Yrbk; Rptr Sch Nwsp;.

FLESHMAN, GARY; Brookhaven HS; Columbus, OH; OSU.

FLETCHER, CAROL; Forest Hills Central HS; Grand Rapids, MI; 59/250 Band; Chrh Wkr; Sch Mus; Sch Pl; Stg Crw; Sch Nwsp; Drama Clb; Mic State Univ; Theatre.

FLETCHER, JOHN; East HS; Akron, OH; Cls Rep Frsh Cls; Chrh Wkr; FCA; Lbry Ade; Red Cr Ade; Sch Pl; Yth Flsp; Drama Clb; Sci Clb; Ftbl; Univ.

FLETCHER, KAREN; Cameron HS; Glen Easton, WV; 22/104 Band; Chrh Wkr; Drm Mjrt; Hon Rl; Mdrgl; NHS; Sch Pl; College; Med.

FLETCHER, LARRY; Crothersville Cmnty HS; Crothersville, IN; Boy Scts; Hon Rl; Off Ade; Sct Actv; 4-H; Letter Trk; Voc Schl; Carpentry.

FLETCHER, LISA; Batavia HS; Batavia, OH; Hon Rl; Spn Clb;.

FLETCHER, RHONDA; Grant HS; Grant, MI; Cls Rep Sr Cls; Chrs; Chrh Wkr; Hon Rl; Mdrgl; NHS; Sch Pl; Sec Stu Cncl; 4-H; FBLA; Spring Arbor Coll; Eng.

FLETCHER, ROBERT; Walkerville Rural Cmnty Schl; Walkerville, MI; 2/43 Pres Soph Cls; Hon Rl; NHS; Stu Cncl; 4-H; Bsbl; Bsktbl; Crs Cntry; Mgrs; 4-H Awd; Central Michigan Univ.

FLETCHER, TINA; North White HS; Monon, IN; 11/79 Hon Rl; NHS; Rptr Sch Nwsp; VP Ger Clb; Pep Clb; Ball State Univ; Elem Educ.

FLETCHER, TOM; Wylie E Groves HS; Southfield, MI; Letter Bsbl; Letter Bsktbl; Alma College; Physical Educ.

FLEWELLING, THOMAS; Niles Sr HS; Niles, MI; Off Ade; Cit Awd; Chess Club; Nursing Asst/orderly; Red Cross Volunteer; Univ Of Michigan; Medicine.

FLICK, MINDY; Kankakee Vly HS; Rensselaer, IN; Girl Scts; Stg Crw; Yrbk; OEA; Sci Clb; Spn Clb; PPFtbl;.

FLICK, RENEE; Mother Of Mercy HS; Cincinnati, OH; 65/231 Hon Rl; Fr Clb; Pep Clb; Capt Bsktbl; Socr; Letter Trk; GAA; IM Sprt; Mt St Joseph Univ; Dietetics.

FLICKINGER, DEBBIE; W Branch HS; Alliance, OH; 9/260 Sec Frsh Cls; Sec Soph Cls; Band; Hon Rl; NHS; Orch; Sch Mus; FTA; Akron Univ; Nursing.

FLING, TAMMY L; Big Walnut HS; Westerville, OH; 7/215 Band; Girl Scts; Off Ade; Stu Cncl; 4-H; Fr Clb; Trk; Chrldng; Scr Kpr; Pres Awd; Math.

FLINN, ANNE; Grandview Heights HS; Columbus, OH; Sec Soph Cls; Cls Rep Soph Cls; Cl Rep Jr Cls; Drl Tm; Sec FCA; Hon Rl; Jr NHS; Stu Cncl; Fr Clb; Letter Hockey; Univ.

FLINN, CAROL; Schoolcraft HS; Schoolcraft, MI; Girl Scts; Lbry Ade; NHS; Univ; Cmmrcl Art.

FLINT, DIANE; Pine River Jr Sr HS; Cadillac, MI; Sec Soph Cls; Band; Chrh Wkr; Hon Rl; NHS; Pres Stu Cncl; Fr Clb; DAR Awd; Kiwan Awd; North Park Coll; Med Tech.

FLINT, LINDA; Pine River Jr Sr HS; Cadillac, MI; Cl Rep Jr Cls; Band; Chrs; NHS; FHA; Spn Clb; Chrldng; College.

FLIS, DANIEL; St Francis De Sales HS; Toledo, OH; 20/200 Hon Rl; NHS; Bsbl; Bsktbl; IM Sprt; Univ; Acctg.

FLOATE, MICHELLE; Fulton HS; Maple Rapids, MI; 3/100 Pres Soph Cls; Pres Jr Cls; Cls Rep Sr Cls; Band; Girl Scts; Hon Rl; Sct Actv; Stu Cncl; 4-H; Mth Clb; Michigan Tech Univ; Chem.

FLOCKENHAUS, MICHAEL; Rossford HS; Rossford, OH; Band; Hon Rl; JA; Sch Mus; Sch Pl; Drama Clb; Fr Clb; FDA; Ten; Scr Kpr; Depauw Univ; Pre Med.

FLONOURY, ROWENA; Central HS; Detroit, MI; Chrh Wkr; Hon Rl; Wayne State Univ; Acctng.

FLOOD, ANGIE; Tri Vly HS; Trinway, OH; Band; Girl Scts; Hon Rl; Jr NHS; NHS; FHA; VP Spn Clb; GAA; Ohio Univ; Nursing.

FLOOD, ANGIE; Tri Valley HS; Trinway, OH; Band; Girl Scts; Hon Rl; FHA; VP Spn Clb; GAA; Univ; Nursing.

FLOOD, DIANA; Roy C Start HS; Toledo, OH; Treas Chrs; Girl Scts; Sch Mus; Stg Crw;.

FLOOD, JENNIFER; Howland HS; Warren, OH; 60/440 Sec Frsh Cls; Sec Jr Cls; Hon Rl; Hosp Ade; NHS; Stu Cncl; Ger Clb; PPFtbl; Univ Of Toledo; Pharm.

FLORA, TRACY; Twin Valley North HS; Brookville, OH; 1/120 VP Jr Cls; Val; Am Leg Aux Girls St; Drl Tm; NHS; Pres Stu Cncl; Chrldng; Natl Merit Ltr; Voice Dem Awd; Ohio St Univ; Biomed Engr.

FLORA, VALERIE; Graham HS; Urbana, OH; Chrs; Hon Rl; Jr NHS; Sch Mus; Sch Pl; Yth Flsp; 4-H; FFA; OEA; Trk; Sec.

FLOREA, RICHARD W; Elwood Cmnty HS; Elwood, IN; 22/284 Cls Rep Frsh Cls; Pres Soph Cls; VP Jr Cls; Cls Rep Sr Cls; Hon Rl; Jr NHS; Lbry Ade; Mod UN; Pol Wkr; Stg Crw; YMCA Brd Of Dir Mbr 77; Univ; Bus Admin.

FLORENCE, JENNIFER; Flushing HS; Flushing, MI; Drl Tm; Fr Clb; Mgrs; Univ Of Michigan; Psych.

FLORENCE, KIMBERLY; Goshen HS; Goshen, OH; Band; Chrs; Chrh Wkr; Girl Scts; Hon Rl; Off Ade; Sch Mus; Sch Pl; Sct Actv; Stg Crw; Flag Corps 1st Plc At Camp Crescendo Co Captn 78; 3 Yrs In Flags; Univ; Psych.

FLORENCE, WALTER T; Worthington HS; Worthington, OH; Trs Soph Cls; Cl Rep Jr Cls; Am Leg Boys St; Chrh Wkr; FCA; Hon Rl; NHS; Pol Wkr; Stu Cncl; Yrbk; Harding Univ; Bus Admin.

FLORENSKI, CATHERINE; Alba Pub HS; Alba, MI; Trs Frsh Cls; Trs Sr Cls; Chrs; Hon Rl; Lbry Ade; Sch Pl; Stg Crw; Rptr Yrbk; Yrbk; Rptr Sch Nwsp;.

FLORES, MILAGROS; Jane Addams HS; Cleveland, OH; Cl Rep Jr Cls; Cls Rep Sr Cls; Chrh Wkr; Hon Rl; Jr NHS; Scr Kpr; Cit Awd; 4-H Awd; Cleveland St Univ.

FLORIDIS, JOHN; Snider HS; Ft Wayne, IN; 80/565 Hon Rl; Orch; Sch Mus; Sprt Ed Yrbk; Ftbl; Trk; Univ; Music.

FLORIO, KATHRY; Fairfield HS; Hamilton, OH; 38/602 VP Soph Cls; Cls Rep Soph Cls; Cl Rep Jr Cls; Cls Rep Sr Cls; Sec Chrs; Stu Cncl; 4-H; Fr Clb; Lat Clb; Ten; Colorado St Univ.

FLORIO, MARY B; Howland HS; Warren, OH; 40/500 Cmnty Wkr; Hon Rl; Hosp Ade; Off Ade; Pol Wkr; Red Cr Ade; Y-Teens; Rptr Yrbk; Fr Clb; FNA; Nursing.

FLORY, JEFFREY; Ypsilanti HS; Ypsilanti, MI; Am Leg Boys St; Band; Drm Mjrt; Hon Rl; Pres NHS; Off Ade; Sch Pl; Spn Clb; Letter Gym; Socr; Eastern Mich Univ; Music.

FLORYJANSKI, VICKIE; Struthers HS; Struthers, OH; 83/269 Spn Clb; Bsktbl; Glf; Trk; IM Sprt; Youngstown St Univ; Art.

FLOWERS, BARRY; Frankfort HS; Ft Ashby, WV; 5/160 Hon Rl; NHS; Mth Clb; Ftbl; Mu Alpha Theta 79; Attendance Awd 79; Univ.

FLOWERS, DEBBY; River Rouge HS; River Rouge, MI; Hon Rl; Wayne St Univ; Comp Tech.

FLOWERS, KAREN M; Horace Mann HS; Gary, IN; Trs Frsh Cls; Trs Soph Cls; Hon Rl; NHS; Off Ade; Stu Cncl; Fr Clb; Letter Trk; Letter Mgrs; Cit Awd; Recvd Awd In Acctg Class 77; Recvd Letter Vllybl & Captn 78; Indiana St Univ; Acctg.

FLOWERS, KENNETH; Cass Technical HS; Detroit, MI; Chrh Wkr; Cmnty Wkr; Hon Rl; Pol Wkr; OEA; Coach Actv; Mgrs; Morehouse Coll Partila Tuition Schlshp 1979; Highst Hon Diploma 1979; Morehouse Coll; Psych.

FLOWERS, KEVIN; Groveport Madison HS; Groveport, OH; 10/580 Hon Rl; Stg Crw; Eng Clb; Spn Clb; Ftbl; Wrstlng; Notre Dame Univ; Phys Sci.

FLOWERS, LORI; Buckeye West HS; Adena, OH; 8/80 Pres Sr Cls; Am Leg Aux Girls St; Band; Chrs; Hon Rl; Hosp Ade; Lbry Ade; NHS; Stg Crw; Yrbk; Mercy Hosp Schl; Nursing.

FLOWERS, LORI K; Buckeye West HS; Adena, OH; 8/84 Pres Sr Cls; Am Leg Aux Girls St; Band; Chrs; Hon Rl; Hosp Ade; Lbry Ade; NHS; Yrbk; Drama Clb; Mercy Nursing Schl; RN.

FLOWERS, MELINDA; Eau Claire HS; Eau Claire, MI; Band; Chrh Wkr; FCA; Hon Rl; Sch Mus; Sch Pl; Bsktbl; Patricia Stevens Career College;modl.

FLOYD, CANDACE; Brooke HS; Follansbee, WV; 91/403 FCA; Hon Rl; 4-H; Spn Clb; Letter Trk; Mat Maids; 4-H Awd; Runner Up Free Enterprs Spch Contst 78; Camp Horseshoe 79; Fairmont St Coll; Hist.

FLOYD, ELANA; Salem HS; Salem, IN; Chrs; Chrh Wkr; Cmnty Wkr; Hon Rl; NHS; Sch Mus; Sch Pl; Yth Flsp; Drama Clb; Fr Clb; Indiana Central Univ; Nursing.

FLOYD, HOLLY; Shortridge HS; Indianapolis, IN; FCA; Hon Rl; Stu Cncl; 4-H; FDA; Mth Clb; Bsbl; Bsktbl; Trk; Coach Actv; Mi State; Med.

FLOYD, JAMES M; Greenbrier East HS; Lewisbrg, WV; Chrh Wkr; Hon Rl; Yth Flsp; Letter Ftbl; Engr.

FLOYD, KATHY; Eastmoor Sr HS; Columbus, OH; 38/290 Cls Rep Frsh Cls; Chrh Wkr; Hon Rl; Jr NHS; Stu Cncl; Trk; Chrldng; Scr Kpr; Tmr; ABC Schlrshp; Natl Jr Honor Society; Ohio House Of Rep Awd; Capital Univ; Medicine.

FLOYD, KIMBERLY; Highland Park Comm HS; Highland Pk, MI; Band; Chrh Wkr; Cmnty Wkr; Hon Rl; Lbry Ade; Off Ade; Yth Flsp; Drama Clb; FHA; Cit Awd; Christian Debutante Metro Dist Bapt Assn; Coll; Hotel Mgmt.

FLOYD, ROSALIND; Highland Park Comm HS; Highland Pk, MI; VP Frsh Cls; Cl Rep Jr Cls; Chrs; Chrh Wkr; Hon Rl; Sch Mus; Sch Pl; Drama Clb; Rdo Clb; Pom Pon; Interlocin Music Camp Schlrshp; College; Nursing.

FLOYD, WENDY; Glen Este Sr HS; Cincinnati, OH; Sec Frsh Cls; Cls Rep Soph Cls; Sec Jr Cls; Sec Sr Cls; Am Leg Aux Girls St; Girl Scts; Hon Rl; NHS; Stu Cncl; Pep Clb; Amer Lgn Amer Awd Soph; Univ; Retail Buying.

FLUCUS, SHARON; Andrean HS; Merrillville, IN; 84/251 VP Frsh Cls; Drl Tm; Hon Rl; Stg Crw; Mth Clb; OEA; Spn Clb; Chrldng; IM Sprt; Pom Pon; Univ.

FLUECKIGER, DEBORAH; Chardon HS; Chardon, OH; 2/150 Sec Frsh Cls; Chrs; Natl Forn Lg; NHS; Yth Flsp; Rptr Sch Nwsp; Drama Clb; 4-H; FHA; Pep Clb; Univ.

FLUEGEMANN, SHARON A; Seton HS; Cincinnati, OH; 21/271 Am Leg Aux Girls St; Chrs; Girl Scts; Hon Rl; Jr NHS; Pres NHS; FBLA; Am Leg Awd; Night Schl; Sec.

FLUEGGE, VERONICA; Michigan Lutheran Seminary; Elkton, MI; Chrs; Sec Chrh Wkr; 4-H; Letter Trk; IM Sprt; Pom Pon; 4-H Awd; Travlng Singing Show Grp 78 80; Piano Std 69 78; Univ; Tchr.

FLUHARTY, KIMBERLY J; Fairview HS; Fairview, WV; Cls Rep Soph Cls; Cl Rep Jr Cls; Band; Hon Rl; Y-Teens; Rptr Yrbk; Rptr Sch Nwsp; Treas FHA; Chrldng; Fairmont St Coll; Sec.

FLUHARTY, LISA; Mannington HS; Mannington, WV; 3/130 VP Soph Cls; Chrh Wkr; Girl Scts; Hon Rl; Y-Teens; Rptr Yrbk; FHA; Chrldng; IM Sprt; Twrlr; Fairmont St Coll; Nursing.

FLUHARTY, REBECCA; Lincoln HS; Wallace, WV; 17/158 Cl Rep Jr Cls; Pres NHS; Sch Pl; Stu Cncl; Treas Drama Clb; VICA; Bsktbl; Mas Awd; Natl Merit SF; Wv Univ; Aero Engr.

FLUHARTY, REBECCA A; Lincoln HS; Wallace, WV; 18/168 Cl Rep Jr Cls; Hon Rl; Pres NHS; Sch Mus; Stu Cncl; Treas Drama Clb; VP VICA; Bsktbl; Natl Merit SF; West Virginia Univ; Engr.

FLURY, JENNIFER L; Perry HS; Massillon, OH; Sec Jr Cls; Sec Sr Cls; Band; Chrs; Chrh Wkr; Drl Tm; Girl Scts; Hosp Ade; Natl Forn Lg; Off Ade; Akron Univ; Nurse.

FLYNN, CHRISTOPHER; Yorktown HS; Yorktown, IN; 15/190 Hon Rl; Jr NHS; NHS; Spn Clb; Bsbl; Ftbl; Purdue Univ; Engr.

FLYNN, DANIEL; Douglas Mac Arthur HS; Saginaw, MI; 85/350 Cls Rep Soph Cls; Cl Rep Jr Cls; Hon Rl; Stu Cncl; Swmmng; College.

FLYNN, DEIRDRE; Escanaba Area Public HS; Escanaba, MI; 22/438 Cls Rep Frsh Cls; Cls Rep Soph Cls; Band; Girl Scts; Hon Rl; Jr NHS; Rptr Yrbk; Gym; Letter Ten; Trk; Michigan St Univ.

FLYNN, FRANK; Heath HS; Heath, OH; 5/150 Trs Soph Cls; Trs Jr Cls; Trs Sr Cls; Pres Band; Debate Tm; Natl Forn Lg; NHS; Sch Pl; Pres Fr Clb; Treas Sci Clb; Amer Lgn Amer & Gov Tst Awd 77 & 78; Oh Test Of Schlstc Achvmnt Bio 13th Pl 77; Regnl Wnnr In St Art Contst; Univ; Engr.

FLYNN, JEFFREY J; Genoa HS; Genoa, OH; Boy Scts; Chrs; Sct Actv; Key Clb; Crs Cntry; Trk; Univ Of Toledo; Bus Admin.

FLYNN, JEROME; Tekonsha HS; Tekonsha, MI; 1/60 Pres Frsh Cls; Trs Soph Cls; Hon Rl; Stu Cncl; Lat Clb; Bsbl; Letter Ftbl; Letter Wrstlng; Coach Actv; Mgrs; Kalamazoo Coll; Mech Engr.

FLYNN, KATHLEEN; Marian HS; Troy, MI; Cmnty Wkr; Lit Mag; NHS; Bsbl; Bsktbl; GAA; Scr Kpr; College; Advertising.

FLYNN, KELLY; Central HS; Switz City, IN; Trs Jr Cls; Am Leg Aux Girls St; VP NHS; Ed Yrbk; Scr Kpr; Vincennes Univ; Sec.

FLYNN, MARRA; Springfield Catholic HS; London, OH; 4/144 Chrh Wkr; Hon Rl; NHS; Red Cr Ade; Yrbk; Fr Clb; Kiwan Awd; Cert Of Awds For Part In Typng 1 Bus Sklls Olympics 78; Spec Rec Awd In Typng 79; Spec Rec Awd In Psych 79; Wright St Univ; Psych.

FLYNN, PAMELA; Lincoln Park HS; Lincoln Pk, MI; Girl Scts; Hon Rl; Lbry Ade; Off Ade; Red Cr Ade; Rptr Sch Nwsp; Literary Club Awd; Cert Of Schlrshp; College; Nursing.

FLYNN, VICKI; Flushing HS; Mt Morris, MI; Girl Scts; Hon Rl; Lbry Ade; Sct Actv; Unif Of Mic Flint; Marine Bio.

FOCHT, BRYAN; Graham HS; St Paris, OH; Cls Rep Frsh Cls; Cls Rep Soph Cls; Am Leg Boys St; NHS; Sch Mus; Stu Cncl; Rptr Yrbk; 4-H; Miami Univ; Bus Acctg.

FOCHT, MARJORIE; Southfield Christian HS; Farmington Hill, MI; 1/75 Chrs; Hon Rl; Yth Flsp; Drama Clb; Ger Clb; Chrldng; Calvin Coll; Medical.

FOCKE, JULIE; Archbishop Alter HS; Kettering, OH; Cmnty Wkr; Hon Rl; Fr Clb; Gym; Pres Awd; College.

FODDRILL, D LEANNE; Edgewood HS; Bloomington, IN; Band; Sch Mus; Sch Pl; Stg Crw; Yth Flsp; Drama Clb; Pep Clb;.

FOERSTER, LAURIE; Lutheran East HS; St Clair Shores, MI; 23/147 Chrs; NHS; Rptr Yrbk; Ger Clb; Bsktbl; Univ; Educ.

FOGARTY, DEIRDRE; Our Lady Of The Elms HS; Cuyahoga Falls, OH; Chrs; Hon Rl; Ed Sch Nwsp; Notre Dame College; Fash Desi.

FOGARTY, KAREN; East HS; Akron, OH; Band; Chrs; Drm Bgl; Drm Mjrt; Hon Rl; VP NHS; Orch; Sch Mus; Rptr Yrbk; Pep Clb; Whos Who Amng Amer HS Stu 77; Acadmc Schlrshp Univ Of Akron 79; Univ Of Akron; Bus Admin.

FOGELSONGER, KURT; Bay City Central HS; Bay City, MI; 68/513 Hon Rl; Boys Clb Am; Crs Cntry; Trk; Lawrence Inst Of Tech; Archt.

FOGLE, BETH; North Putnam Jr Sr HS; Greencastle, IN; Hon Rl; Rptr Yrbk; Rptr Sch Nwsp; 4-H; OEA; Pep Clb; Spn Clb; Vincennes Univ; Bus Admin.

FOGLE, DE LYNN; Southfield Christian HS; Orchard Lake, MI; 4/75 Cls Rep Frsh Cls; Sec Jr Cls; Chrh Wkr; Hon Rl; Stu Cncl; DAR Awd; College; Med Tech.

FOGLE, S; Perry HS; Massillon, OH; 6/450 Cmnty Wkr; FCA; Hon Rl; NHS; Sch Pl; Stg Crw; Spn Clb; Bsktbl; Am Leg Awd; Coll; Sci.

FOGLE, TAMMY L; Dayton Christian HS; Dayton, OH; Chrh Wkr; Drl Tm; Hon Rl; Lbry Ade; Rptr Yrbk; Trk; Kettering Med Schl; Reg Nurse.

FOGLEMAN, GARY; Woodrow Wilson HS; Beckley, WV; 140/512 Cls Rep Frsh Cls; Cls Rep Soph Cls; Cl Rep Jr Cls; Pres Jr Cls; Pres Chrh Wkr; Debate Tm; Hon Rl; JA; Natl Forn Lg; Off Ade; Key Club Pres; Wv Oratory Champion; Thespian Pres; Univ Of Dayton; Poli Sci.

FOGT, ELDON G; Madison Heights HS; Anderson, IN; Boy Scts; VICA; Ftbl; Trk; Wrstlng; Most Pins Trophy In Wrestling; College; Elec Engr.

FOGT, JEFFREY; West Carrollton HS; W Carrollton, OH; 20/418 Band; Boy Scts; Chrh Wkr; Cmnty Wkr; Hon Rl; Jr NHS; Natl Forn Lg; College; Optometrist.

FOIST, TONY; Jennings County HS; Scipio, IN; 5/325 Cl Rep Jr Cls; Hon Rl; NHS; Sch Pl; Stu Cncl; Spn Clb; Architecture.

FOJAS, JOSEPH; Wintersville HS; Steubenville, OH; Boy Scts; Sch Pl; Sprt Ed Yrbk; Yrbk; Sprt Ed Sch Nwsp; Rptr Sch Nwsp; Sch Nwsp; Spn Clb; Trk; Miami Univ.

FOLAND, SHEILA; Mississinewa HS; Marion, IN; 24/200 Hon Rl; NHS; Sch Pl; Stg Crw; Yrbk; Drama Clb; 4-H; Pep Clb; Spn Clb; Purdue Univ; Psych.

FOLDEN, CYNTHIA; Maysville HS; Zanesville, OH; 5/217 Band; Hon Rl; JA; NHS; Sch Pl; Yth Flsp; Rptr Yrbk; Ohio Northern Univ; Chem.

FOLEY, ANNE; Bishop Borgess HS; Detroit, MI; Hon Rl; NHS; Stu Cncl; Yrbk; Pep Clb; Letter Bsbl; Letter Bsktbl; GAA; IM Sprt; Univ.

FOLEY, CHRISTINE; Msgr John R Hackett HS; Kalamazoo, MI; 5/130 Band; Drm Mjrt; Hon Rl; NHS; Orch; Sch Mus; Sch Pl; Stg Crw; VP Spn Clb; Univ; Pre Law.

FOLEY, CLAIRE; Peck Commun HS; Melvin, MI; 2/61 VP Frsh Cls; Hon Rl; NHS; Stu Cncl; 4-H; FHA; Letter Bsbl; Bsktbl; Letter Trk; Coach Actv; Univ.

FOLEY, EILEEN; Allen Park HS; Allen Park, MI; Cls Rep Frsh Cls; Cls Rep Soph Cls; Cl Rep Jr Cls; Cmp Fr Grls; Chrs; Gym; Cit Awd; Fashion Inst Of America; Fashionmdse.

FOLEY, KAREN; Stephen T Badin HS; Fairfield, OH; 28/240 Chrs; Chrh Wkr; Hon Rl; Pres JA; NHS; FBLA; Spn Clb; Southern Ohi College; Exe Sec.

FOLEY, MICHELLE; Caro HS; Caro, MI; Cls Rep Frsh Cls; Cls Rep Soph Cls; Pres Jr Cls; Cl Rep Jr Cls; Trs Sr Cls; Cls Rep Sr Cls; Chrs; Chrh Wkr; FCA; Hon Rl; Northeastern Schl Of Commerce; Acctg.

FOLEY, ROSEMARY B; Clay HS; South Bend, IN; 148/495 Sec Sr Cls; Hosp Ade; Off Ade; Indiana Univ; Nursing.

FOLEY, STEVE; Millington HS; Millington, MI; VP Jr Cls; Hon Rl; Stu Cncl; Capt Ftbl; Wrstlng; Kansas St Univ; Agri.

FOLEY, TERRESA; Williamsburg HS; Batavia, OH; Cls Rep Soph Cls; Stu Cncl; Yth Flsp; Yrbk; Spn Clb; Letter Bsktbl; Letter Trk; Univ.

FOLIO, RICHARD; Brooke HS; Wellsburg, WV; 81/403 Rptr Yrbk; Rptr Sch Nwsp; Sci Clb; Carnegie Mellon.

FOLK, MARY; Lima Sr HS; Lima, OH; 56/500 Band; Chrs; Chrh Wkr; Hon Rl; Orch; Sec Yth Flsp; Univ; Music Ther.

FOLKERTH, ANDREW; Upper Arlington HS; Columbus, OH; 1/620 Hon Rl; NHS; Stu Cncl; FDA; Spn Clb; Ten; College; Law.

FOLKERTH, ANNE; Oakwood HS; Dayton, OH; 35/140 Chrs; Chrh Wkr; CAP; Cmnty Wkr; FCA; Hon Rl; Hockey; Trk; Chrldng; College; Dental Hygienist.

FOLLETT, DOUGLAS; Ross Beatty HS; Cassoplis, MI; 4/150 Chrh Wkr; Hon Rl; NHS; Yth Flsp; Ten; Mgrs; Scr Kpr; Univ.

FOLTA, TIMOTHY B; West Lafayette HS; W Lafayette, IN; 78/190 Am Leg Boys St; Boy Scts; FCA; Hon Rl; Lit Mag; Sch Mus; Sch Nwsp; Letter Ftbl; IM Sprt; Univ; Bus Mgmt.

FOLTZ, CHRIS; Southern Wells HS; Geneva, IN; Am Leg Boys St; Hon Rl; NHS; FFA; Rotary Awd; Univ; Elec Engr.

FOLTZ, DONALD; Mathias HS; Mathias, WV; 2/28 Boy Scts; Hon Rl; Jr NHS; NHS; Crs Cntry; Lcrss; Air Force; Physics.

FOLTZ, TIMOTHY C; South Vermillion HS; Clinton, IN; 15/165 Band; Boy Scts; Hon Rl; Sct Actv; 4-H; Lat Clb; Mth Clb; Crs Cntry; Letter Swmmng; God Cntry Awd; 4 H Conservation Trophies; Eagle Scout; Latin Honor Soc; Purdue Univ; Agric.

FOLZ, ROBERT; Reitz Memorial HS; Evansville, IN; 6/223 Cls Rep Frsh Cls; Cls Rep Soph Cls; Cl Rep Jr Cls; Hon Rl; NHS; Stg Crw; Ftbl; IM Sprt; Illinois Univ; Comp Sci.

FONNER, THOMAS; Magnolia HS; New Martinsvle, WV; Pres Soph Cls; Am Leg Boys St; Band; NHS; Sch Mus; Sch Pl; Stu Cncl; Letter Ten; Am Leg Awd; JC Awd; College; Music.

FONTAINE, MARK; Greenfield Central HS; Greenfield, IN; 4-H; Bsbl; Ftbl; IM Sprt; Mgrs; 4-H Awd; Purdue; Construction.

FONTANA, BOB; Grosse Pt North HS; Grosse Pt Shore, MI; 3/535 Cls Rep Frsh Cls; Cls Rep Soph Cls; Cl Rep Jr Cls; FCA; Hon Rl; NHS; PAVAS; Pol Wkr; Sch Pl; Stg Crw; Wayne St Univ; Dr.

FONTE, LEISA; Sandy Valley HS; Magnolia, OH; 12/172 Trs Frsh Cls; Chrs; Cmnty Wkr; NHS; Stu Cncl; Spn Clb; Letter Bsktbl; Letter Trk; Letter Ohio State Univ.

FOODY, HELEN; Divine Child HS; Dearborn Ht, MI; Chrs; Hon Rl; Hosp Ade; Sch Pl; Yrbk; Fr Clb; Letter Crs Cntry; Letter Trk; GAA; Univ.

FOOR, CHARLES; Archbold Area HS; Archbold, OH; Band; Boy Scts; Chrs; Chrh Wkr; Hon Rl; Sch Mus; Stg Crw; Yrbk; 4-H; IM Sprt; Univ; History Ed.

FOOR, JEFF; Gladwin HS; Gladwin, MI; Chrh Wkr; FCA; Hon Rl; JA; Stu Cncl; Bsbl; Bsktbl; Ftbl; Coach Actv; Lion Awd; Central Michigan Univ; Bus.

FOOS, KAREN; Cardington Lincoln HS; Cardington, OH; 3/79 Am Leg Aux Girls St; Band; Hon Rl; NHS; Sch Pl; Rptr Yrbk; Rptr Sch Nwsp; Marion Tech College; Med Sec.

FOOS, KATHY; Ridgedale HS; Marion, OH; 18/96 VP Sr Cls; Band; Drl Tm; Hon Rl; Pres Yth Flsp; Pres 4-H; Spn Clb; Letter Bsbl; Letter Tech Schl; Respiratory Ther.

FOOS, LYNN; St Joseph Central Cath HS; Fremont, OH; Cls Rep Soph Cls; Hon Rl; Stu Cncl; 4-H; 4-H Awd; Tech Schl; Art.

FOOSE, JEANNE; Vinson HS; Huntington, WV; 1/100 Val; Am Leg Aux Girls St; Band; Drm Mjrt; Hon Rl; Hosp Ade; NHS; Stu Cncl; Keyettes; Trk; Coll; Med.

FOOSE, JOYCE; Central Cath HS; Wheeling, WV; Cmnty Wkr; Hon Rl; Yrbk; Sch Nwsp; West Liberty St Coll; Med Tech.

FOOTE, DAVID; Bay HS; Bay Village, OH; 119/330 Band; Boy Scts; Sch Mus; Sct Actv; Wrstlng; Miami Univ; Law.

FOOTE, WILLIAM; Cuyahoga Heights HS; Vllyvw, OH; 2/72 Cls Rep Soph Cls; VP Jr Cls; Hon Rl; Sch Pl; Stu Cncl; Yth Flsp; Sch Nwsp; Fr Clb; Ftbl; Trk; College; Comp Engr.

FORBES, BRUCE A; Hesperia Sr HS; Hesperia, MI; 12/80 Cls Rep Soph Cls; Band; Hon Rl; Stu Cncl; 4-H; Letter Ftbl; Capt Trk; Letter Wrstlng; Central Mich Univ; Accounting.

FORBES, LANCE; South Vigo HS; Terre Haute, IN; Boy Scts; Hon Rl; Mod UN; Univ; Engr.

FORBUSH, DONNA; Keystone HS; La Grange, OH; 15/130 Cl Rep Jr Cls; Sec Chrs; Hon Rl; Off Ade; Stu Cncl; Yrbk; Rptr Sch Nwsp; Pep Clb; Capt Chrldng; Scr Kpr; Elyria Acad; Cosmetology.

FORBUSH, PENCY; Goodrich HS; Goodrich, MI; Chrs; Chrh Wkr; Hon Rl; Hosp Ade; Lbry Ade; Red Cr Ade; Sch Mus; Sch Pl; Stg Crw; Marion Coll; Nursing.

FORCHE, SHARON; Deerfield HS; Blissfield, MI; Sec Jr Cls; Band; Girl Scts; Hon Rl; Hosp Ade; Rptr Yrbk; Yrbk; Rptr Sch Nwsp; Letter Chrldng; Lenewee Vo Tech; Bus.

FORD, A; Rensselaer Ctrl HS; Rensselaer, IN; 29/162 Band; Chrs; Chrh Wkr; Drm Mjrt; Hon Rl; NHS; Sch Mus; Drama Clb; Fr Clb; Butler Univ.

FORD, ALICE; Fraser HS; Fraser, MI; Band; Chrs; Chrh Wkr; Drm Mjrt; Mdrgl; NHS; Sch Mus; Sch Pl; Stg Crw; Hope College; Music Educ.

FORD, CHRIS; Lakeshore HS; St Clair Shrs, MI; Cls Rep Sr Cls; Band; Boy Scts; Hon Rl; Jr NHS; Orch; Stu Cncl; Rptr Sch Nwsp; Sci Clb; Tmr; Univ Of Michigan; Atmospheric Engr.

FORD, DARLENE M; Immaculata HS; Detroit, MI; Chrs; Chrh Wkr; Cmnty Wkr; Hon Rl; Yth Flsp; Boys Clb Am; Spn Clb; Ten; Cit Awd; Natl Merit Ltr; Honor Cert & Merit Awd; Univ; Jrnlsm.

FORD, DAVID; Harper Creek HS; Battle Creek, MI; Debate Tm; Hon Rl; Spn Clb; Coll; Conservation.

FORD, EUGENE; Monroe HS; Monroe, MI; 2/560 Cls Rep Sr Cls; Sal; Hon Rl; Treas JA; Jr NHS; NHS; Pres Stu Cncl; Pres Fr Clb; Crs Cntry; Trk; Co Salutatorian 78; Schlrshp Prest Univ Of Miami 79; All Egl Hurdler 79; Michigan St Univ; Pre Med.

FORD, GARLAND; Shortridge HS; Indianapolis, IN; Chrh Wkr; Hon Rl; Mth Clb; Ind Univ; Med.

FORD, GREGORY; Madison HS; Madison, OH; Boy Scts; Hon Rl; Spn Clb; Bsktbl; Ftbl; Trk; College; Architecture.

FORD, ILLICE; Highland Park Community HS; Highland Park, MI; Drl Tm; Hon Rl; ROTC; Cit Awd; Ldrshp Ribbon 79; Outsdng Ldrshp Ribbon 79; Longevity Drill Tm Ribbon 79; US Air Force; Meteorology.

FORD, KEVIN; Pike Delta York Sr HS; Delta, OH; Band; Boy Scts; Chrs; Stg Crw; Drama Clb; 4-H; Wrstlng; Mgrs; Indepndt Order Of Odd Fellows Delegate To The Youth Pilgrimage To U S 78; Military Serv; Sales.

FORD, KIMBERLY; Kenowa Hills HS; Grand Rapids, MI; Girl Scts; NHS; Yth Flsp; Letter Ten; Letter Trk; Michigan St Univ; Vet.

FORD, LISA; Licking Valley HS; Newark, OH; 15/147 Trs Jr Cls; Trs Sr Cls; Chrh Wkr; Hon Rl; Hosp Ade; NHS; Off Ade; Stu Cncl; Y-Teens; Yrbk; Ohio St Univ; Nursing.

FORD, LULA; Federal Hocking HS; Amesville, OH; 38/101 Chrs; Chrh Wkr; Cmnty Wkr; FCA; Girl Scts; Hon Rl; JA; Pol Wkr; Sch Mus; Sct Actv; Eng Schlshp 77; Star Green Hand FFA 77; Top Salesman 77 78 & 79; Tri Cnty Voc Schl; Agri Bus.

FORD, MATTHEW; Moeller HS; Cincinnati, OH; NHS; Letter Bsbl; Coach Actv; IM Sprt; Alumni Merit Schlshp 79; Enquirer Schlrshp 79; Kenwood Womens Club 79; Miami Univ; Pulp & Paper Tech.

FORD, RAMONA; Benton Harbor Sr HS; Benton Hrbr, MI; VP Soph Cls; Pres Jr Cls; Band; Chrh Wkr; Hon Rl; Scr Kpr; Oakwood Coll; Psych.

FORD, RANDY; Champion HS; Warren, OH; Cls Rep Frsh Cls; Am Leg Boys St; Hon Rl; Off Ade; Sch Pl; Ed Sch Nwsp; Letter Bsktbl; Letter Ten; Bowling Green St Univ; Jrnlsm.

FORD, RHONDA; Northfield HS; Lagro, IN; Hon Rl; JA; Red Cr Ade; Stg Crw; 4-H; FHA; Mat Maids; Ind Univ; Art.

FORD, RICK; Huntington North HS; Huntington, IN; 33/160 VP Jr Cls; Hon Rl; Jr NHS; NHS; Stg Crw; Stu Cncl; Lat Clb; Letter Crs Cntry; Letter Trk; IM Sprt; Ball State; Arch.

FORD, SELENA; Gladwin HS; Gladwin, MI; Chrh Wkr; Lit Mag; NHS; Sch Pl; Yrbk; College; English.

FORD, STEPHEN; Clinto Massie HS; Wilmington, OH; Band; Chrs; Hon Rl; 4-H; Pep Clb; Wright State; Drafting.

FORDHAM, STEPHEN; South Haven Sr HS; South Haven, MI; Chrs; Hon Rl; Pres 4-H; Pep Clb; Cit Awd; 4-H Awd; Univ; Elec Engr.

FORDICE, JAN; North Putnam Jr Sr HS; Russellville, IN; 12/103 FCA; Hon Rl; NHS; 4-H; Lat Clb; OEA; GAA; Mat Maids; Pom Pon; 4-H Awd; Indiana St Univ; Bus Ed.

FOREMAN, BRAD; Maumee HS; Maumee, OH; Boy Scts; Chrh Wkr; FCA; Hon Rl; Sct Actv; Yth Flsp; Key Clb; Letter Ftbl; Trk; Capt Wrstlng; Ftb Lplayer Of Wk 78; 1st Team All NLL Wrstlng 79; Excelnnt Rating For Sci Fair 79; Univ Of Cincinnati; Chem Engr.

FOREMAN, CECILIA; Nettie Lee Roth HS; Dayton, OH; Band; Debate Tm; Girl Scts; Hon Rl; NHS; Orch; Sch Pl; Drama Clb; Pep Clb; Cit Awd; AKA Schlrshp Awrd For Yng Lds 76; Thomas & Hochwalt Awrd Comp For HS Chem Stud Hnrble Mntn 79; Ohio St Univ; Chem Engr.

FOREMAN, DAVE; Southern HS; Portland, OH; Hon Rl; NHS; 4-H; Letter Bsktbl; Coll.

FOREMAN, DAVID; Southern HS; Portland, OH; Hon Rl; NHS; 4-H; Letter Bsktbl; College.

FOREMAN, LINDA; Buckeye Vly HS; Delaware, OH; 19/185 Cls Rep Frsh Cls; Cls Rep Soph Cls; Cl Rep Jr Cls; Cls Rep Sr Cls; Band; Chrs; Hon Rl; NHS; Orch; Sch Mus; Mt Carmel Schl; Nursing.

FOREMAN, THERESA; Van Wert HS; Van Wert, OH; Band; Chrs; Hon Rl; Off Ade; Ger Clb; Swmmng; Letter Trk; Chrldng; Ohio Univ.

FOREMAN, THOMAS; Clinton HS; Tecumsen, MI; VP Jr Cls; Hon Rl; Ed Sch Nwsp; Bsktbl; Natl Merit SF; Univ; Life Sci.

FORESTER, ROBERT L; Kenmore HS; Akron, OH; Cls Rep Frsh Cls; Cls Rep Soph Cls; Cl Rep Jr Cls; Boy Scts; Yth Flsp; OEA; Bsktbl; Ftbl; Chrldng; College; Accountant.

FORGACS, STEVEN; Divine Child HS; Dearborn Hts, MI; Stg Crw; Coach Actv; IM Sprt; Michigan St Univ; Geology.

FORGETTE, KRISTA; Menominee HS; Menominee, MI; Chrh Wkr; Girl Scts; Hon Rl; Jr NHS; Off Ade; N Michigan Univ; Public Relations.

FORINASH, LISA; Roosevelt Wilson HS; Nutter Fort, WV; 18/122 Band; Chrs; Drm Mjrt; Hon Rl; NHS; Off Ade; Sch Pl; Y-Teens; Fairmont Comm Coll; Med Tech.

FORKEL, SUSAN; Salem Sr HS; Salem, OH; Hon Rl; Yrbk; FSA; Ger Clb; Mth Clb; Coll.

FORKEL, SUSAN; Salem HS; Salem, OH; Hon Rl; Yrbk; FSA; Ger Clb; Mth Clb; College.

FORKER, BRAD; Garrett HS; Garrett, IN; VP Band; Chrs; FCA; Hon Rl; Mdrgl; NHS; Sch Mus; Sch Pl; Letter Bsbl; Crs Cntry; Purdue Univ; Pharm.

FORKERT, RICHARD; Elmhurst HS; Ft Wayne, IN; 7/400 Am Leg Boys St; Band; Trs Frsh Cls; VP JA; Purdue Acad Leadrshp Seminar 78; In St Univ Summer Hon Seminars For Math & Comp & Elec 79; Univ; Elec.

FORMAN, ANGELA; Hopewell Loudon HS; Fostoria, OH; 17/95 Cl Rep Jr Cls; Chrs; Hon Rl; NHS; Red Cr Ade; Sch Mus; Stu Cncl; Rptr Sch Nwsp; Cit Awd; Pres Awd; Trainee With Toledo Ballet Co 79; Univ; Dance.

FORMAN, MINDY; Oak Hill HS; Oak Hill, WV; Pres Frsh Cls; Am Leg Aux Girls St; Band; NHS; Sch Pl; Fr Clb; Letter Trk; Chrldng; West Virginia Univ; Med.

FORMICA, ROBERT W; Euclid HS; Euclid, OH; Cl Rep Jr Cls; Hon Rl; Hosp Ade; Treas JA; Off Ade; Stu Cncl; Pep Clb; JA Awd; College; Bus.

FORNEY, MYRNA; Regina HS; Cleveland Hts, OH; Sec Sr Cls; Chrs; Chrh Wkr; Cmnty Wkr; Hon Rl; JA; Pep Clb; Bsktbl; Trk; IM Sprt; Univ; Pre Law.

FORNI, CHARLES; Magnolia HS; New Martinsvle, WV; Hon Rl; Sci Clb; Crs Cntry; IM Sprt; Univ; Sci.

FORREST, L ARICK; Dublin HS; Columbus, OH; 32/157 Hon Rl; NHS; PAVAS; Letter Ftbl; Letter Ten; Coach Actv; IM Sprt; 3 Pt 75 GPA Awd; Art Awd; Most Valuable Player On HS Tennis Team; Kent St Univ; Fine Arts.

FORREST, MARY J; Montabella HS; Edmore, MI; 13/106 VP Jr Cls; Pres Sr Cls; Hon Rl; NHS; Stu Cncl; Chrldng; PPFtbl; Montcalm Cmnty Coll.

FORREST, MICHAEL; Chalker HS; Southington, OH; 14/75 Chrh Wkr; Off Ade; Sct Actv; Stu Cncl; Yrbk; Pep Clb; Spn Clb; Bsbl; Bsktbl; Ftbl; Kent State Univ; Criminal Justice.

FORRESTER, TERESA A; Wayne HS; Ft Wayne, IN; VP Sr Cls; Cmp Fr Grls; Chrs; Drl Tm; Girl Scts; Lbry Ade; OEA; Pom Pon; PPFtbl; Dgts; Bus.

FORRESTER, THOMAS; Strongsville Sr HS; Strongsville, OH; Cls Rep Frsh Cls; Hon Rl; Jr NHS; Bsbl; Bsktbl; Glf; Ten; Natl Merit Ltr; Ohio St Univ; Med Engr.

FORRY, SANDRA; L C Mohr HS; S Haven, MI; Band; Cmp Fr Grls; Chrs; Sch Mus; Stg Crw; Pep Clb; Bd Of Educ Awd 79; Bnd Lttr & Key Choral Pin 78; Perf Attnd Awd 79; Lake Michigan Coll; Legal Sec.

FORSHEY, L; Pike Delta York HS; Delta, OH; Band; Chrs; Stu Cncl; Yrbk; 4-H; Fr Clb; FTA; Bsbl; Twrlr; 4-H Awd; OSU; Spec Ed Tech.

FORSHEY, RALPH; Woodsfield HS; Woodsfield, OH; 14/63 Sch Pl; Stg Crw; Yrbk; 4-H; Fr Clb; Kiwan Awd; Voice Dem Awd; Tech School; Elec.

FORSMARK, DAVID; Genesee Christian HS; Flint, MI; 2/9 Pres Sr Cls; Sal; Letter Bsbl; Letter Bsktbl; Letter Socr; Northwood Inst; Bus Mgmt.

FORSTHOEFEL, JOHN; Carroll HS; Dayton, OH; Hon Rl; Univ Of Dayton; Elec Engr.

FORSTHOFFER, JOSEPH; Northwest HS; Canal Fulton, OH; Band; Chrh Wkr; Hon Rl; NHS; Quill & Scroll; Stg Crw; Yrbk; Sch Nwsp; Rdo Clb; Natl Merit Ltr; Ohio Univ; Journalism.

FORSYTH, GREGORY; Howe Military HS; Belelville, MI; 1/45 Chrh Wkr; Drl Tm; FCA; Hon Rl; Natl Forn Lg; NHS; Stu Cncl; Rptr Sch Nwsp; Spn Clb; Opt Clb Awd; U S Air Force Academy; Comp Sci.

FORSYTHE, STEVEN L; Genoa Area HS; Millbury, OH; 2/190 Cls Rep Soph Cls; Sec Band; Hon Rl; NHS; Orch; Sch Mus; Sct Actv; Stg Crw; Stu Cncl; Pres Mth Clb; Ariz State Univ; Astrophysics.

FORTE, PAM; Thomas W Harvey HS; Painesville, OH; Trs Frsh Cls; Trs Jr Cls; Trs Sr Cls; Band; Hon Rl; NHS; FBLA; Spn Clb; Bsktbl; Trk; Bowling Green St Univ; Bus Admin.

FORTELKA, SANDRA; Manistee Catholic Ctrl HS; Manistee, MI; Hon Rl; Mgrs; Univ; Elem Ed.

FORTELL, JACKIE; Chillicothe HS; Chillicothe, OH; Band; Chrh Wkr; CAP; Drl Tm; Hon Rl; Jr N HS; Natl Forn Lg; NHS; Lat Clb; St Champ Of Natl Drill Team Assn; Forensics League Awd Degree Of Honor Degree Of Merit; Ohio St Univ.

FORTENBERRY, DENNIS; Kearsley HS; Samson, AL; 67/375 Band; Chrh Wkr; Hon Rl; JA; Natl Forn Lg; Sch Pl; Rptr Sch Nwsp; Swmmng; Ten; JA Awd; Enterprize St Jr College; Business.

FORTH, LAURA; Dawson Bryant HS; Coal Grove, OH; 5/122 Band; Hon Rl; NHS; Sch Mus; Yrbk; Pep Clb; Top In Acctg II; 2nd In Shorthand II; 2nd In Busns Eng; Sr Popularity Hardes Wrkr; Quiz Bowl Schlrshp; Shawnee St Coll; Acctg.

FORTHEY, VICTORIA; Highland HS; Hinckley, OH; Trs Sr Cls; Band; Girl Scts; Hon Rl; Treas NHS; Sch Mus; Stu Cncl; Sec Y-Teens; 4-H; Key Clb; Ohio St Univ; Vet Med.

FORTIER, VIRGINIA; Davison Sr HS; Davison, MI; Chrs; Cmnty Wkr; Hon Rl; Orch; Red Cr Ade; Sch Mus; Sch Pl; Stg Crw; Drama Clb; Hon Mbr Of Thespian Soc Trp 698 77 78 & 79; Regnl HS Awd From Eastern Mi Univ 79; Schlrshp 79; Eastern Michigan Univ; Occptnl Ther.

FORTIN, COLETTE; Clarkston Sr HS; Clarkston, MI; Cls Rep Frsh Cls; Cls Rep Soph Cls; Sec Jr Cls; Cls Rep Sr Cls; Chrh Wkr; Hon Rl; NHS; Off Ade; Red Cr Ade; Stu Cncl; Oakland Univ; Sociology.

FORTINE, MICHAEL; Cardinal Mooney HS; Poland, OH; 1/293 Cls Rep Soph Cls; Cl Rep Jr Cls; Cls Rep Sr Cls; Val; Hon Rl; JA; Jr NHS; Natl Forn Lg; NHS; Sch Mus; Columbia Univ; Econ.

FORTINO, KIM; Sacred Heart HS; Mt Pleasant, MI; 17/52 Trs Frsh Cls; Cls Rep Soph Cls; Cmnty Wkr; Girl Scts; Hon Rl; Lbry Ade; Off Ade; Rptr Yrbk; Eng Clb; Pep Clb; Central Mic Univ; Physical Educa.

FORTMAN, THOMAS S; The Columbus Academy; Westerville, OH; Hon Rl; Sch Pl; Rptr Sch Nwsp; Fr Clb; Letter Socr; Letter Wrstlng; Capt Chrldng; Natl Merit SF; Harvard Cup 76; Univ; Aerospace Engr.

FORTNER, BARBARA; Henry Ford HS; Detroit, MI; 4-H; Sci Clb; Letter Swmmng; Coach Actv; GAA; Mgrs; Scr Kpr; Tmr; 4-H Awd; Univ Of Michigan; Animal Sci.

FORTNER, GUY R; Western Hills HS; Cincinnati, OH; 400/800 Hon Rl; Pres DECA; Bsktbl; Ftbl; Gym; Capt Trk; Pres Awd;.

FORTNEY, JAMES; Cameron HS; Cameron, WV; 22/107 Chrs; Hon Rl; NHS; Lat Clb; Sci Clb; Mgrs; Coll; Fish Culture Tech.

FORTNEY, ROBERT; Fairmont Sr HS; Fairmont, WV; Am Leg Boys St; Hon Rl; NHS; Bsktbl; Letter Wrstlng; Elk Awd; Fairmont St Coll; Dent.

FORTON, JENNIFER; Lanse Creuse HS; Mt Clemens, MI; Pres Frsh Cls; Pres Soph Cls; Trs Sr Cls; Hon Rl; Jr NHS; Lit Mag; Pres NHS; PAVAS; Sch Mus; Sch Pl; Schlstc Mag Inc Natl Hon Mention Creative Writing 78; Schlstc Mag Natl Hon Mention Art Pringmaking 79; Hope Coll; Cmnctns.

FORTSON, AARON; Bridgman HS; Bridgman, MI; 15/95 Band; CAP; Hon Rl; NHS; Sch Pl; Sct Actv; Stu Cncl; Ger Clb; Sci Clb; Trk; Embry Riddle Univ; Aerospace Engr.

FORTUNA, NANCY; Perry Meridian HS; Indianpolis, IN; Chrs; FCA; Hon Rl; Sch Mus; Yth Flsp; Fr Clb; Pep Clb; Chrldng; Univ.

FORTUNATO, M; Catholic Central HS; Steubenvll, OH; 7/204 Band; Hon Rl; NHS; Sch Pl; Drama Clb; Spn Clb; Univ; Nursing.

FORTUNATO, MICHELLE; Woodrow Wilson HS; Youngstown, OH; Off Ade; VP Ger Clb; Keyettes; Pep Clb; Trk; Capt Chrldng; Tri Hi Y; Coll; Comp Studies.

FORWARD, SHERYL; Western HS; Jackson, MI; Band; Chrs; Sch Mus; Gym; Coll; Physics.

FOSBRINK, KARLA; Brownstown Central HS; Brownstown, IN; 29/145 Am Leg Aux Girls St; Band; Chrs; Chrh Wkr; Girl Scts; Quill & Scroll; Sch Mus; Ed Sch Nwsp; 4-H; 4-H Awd; College; Music.

FOSDICK, KAREN; St Marys Cathedral HS; Gaylord, MI; Band; Drl Tm; Girl Scts; Hon Rl; Red Cr Ade; Sct Actv; Yrbk; Rptr Sch Nwsp; 4-H; Pep Clb; Ski Racing CUSSA Finals Minnesota; Amer & Me Essay Contest; Adrian Coll; Sociology.

FOSHEIM, LISA; Fairborn Baker HS; Fairborn, OH; Chrs; Hon Rl; Pres Stu Cncl; Rptr Sch Nwsp; Homecoming Queen 1978; Univ; Educ.

FOSNIGHT, ELISE; Ravenna HS; Ravenna, OH; 17/327 AFS; Chrh Wkr; Cmnty Wkr; Hon Rl; Hosp Ade; NHS; Yth Flsp; Pres 4-H; Fr Clb; Cit Awd; Univ; Phys Ther.

FOSS, JOHN; Delton Kellog HS; Delton, MI; 38/160 Pres Band; Chrh Wkr; Sch Nwsp; Capt Crs Cntry; Capt Trk; Western Mic Univ; Bus.

FOSS, ROBERT; Mason HS; Mason, MI; Hon Rl; Jr NHS; NHS; Rptr Sch Nwsp; 4-H; Spn Clb; Ftbl; College; Pre Med.

FOSS, WENDY; Maumee HS; Maumee, OH; Girl Scts; JA; Spn Clb; Owens Tech Schl; Sec.

FOSSNOCK, DOREEN; Clinton Prairie HS; Frankfort, IN; 16/96 Girl Scts; NHS; Yth Flsp; Yrbk; Sch Nwsp; Pres 4-H; FHA; Pep Clb; Spn Clb; Mat Maids; Girl Scout Natl Convention Candidate 78; Purdue Univ; Tchr.

FOSTER, ADRIAN; Urbana HS; Urbana, OH; 33/240 Chrs; Hon Rl; Lit Mag; Off Ade; Letter Bsktbl; GAA; Butler Univ; Phys Educ.

FOSTER, AMY; Little Miami HS; Morrow, OH; Cls Rep Frsh Cls; Cls Rep Sr Cls; Chrh Wkr; Hon Rl; Stu Cncl; Yrbk; Fr Clb; Pep Clb; Letter Ten; Trk; Busniess School; Secretarial.

FOSTER, ANGELA R; Redford HS; Detroit, MI; Cl Rep Jr Cls; Chrs; Hon Rl; NHS; Michigan St Univ; Med.

FOSTER, AUDREY; New Haven HS; New Haven, MI; 16/105 Chrs; Girl Scts; Hon Rl; NHS; Sch Nwsp; OEA; Pep Clb; Letter Bsktbl; Letter Trk; Coach Actv; Oakland Univ; Busns.

FOSTER, CAROL; Southgate HS; Southgate, MI; 29/250 Band; Hon Rl; NHS; Pol Wkr; Yrbk; Pep Clb; Natl Merit Ltr; Univ Of Mic; Psych.

FOSTER, CATHERINE; Toronto HS; Toronto, OH; Sec Frsh Cls; Cls Rep Soph Cls; Hon Rl; Sch Mus; Stu Cncl; Rptr Sch Nwsp; Spn Clb; Chrldng; Cit Awd; Univ Of Akron; Medical Tech.

FOSTER, CATHY; Beaumont Girls HS; Clevelnd Hts, OH; Cmnty Wkr; Hon Rl; Pol Wkr; Spn Clb; Swmmng; Ohio Univ; Spanish.

FOSTER, CONNIE S; Attica Jr Sr HS; Attica, IN; 7/76 Pres Frsh Cls; Pres Soph Cls; Hon Rl; ISU; Art.

FOSTER, CRYSTAL; Lima Sr HS; Lima, OH; Cls Rep Frsh Cls; Band; Girl Scts; Hon Rl; Lbry Ade; Off Ade; Sct Actv; Sch Nwsp; Pep Clb; Spn Clb; Cosmetology.

FOSTER, DANIEL; Divine Child HS; Garden City, MI; Cls Rep Frsh Cls; Hon Rl; Letter Bsbl; Letter Ftbl; IM Sprt; Voice Dem Awd; Univ; Bus Admin.

FOSTER, DWAINE; Benedictine HS; Cleveland, OH; Cls Rep Frsh Cls; Cls Rep Soph Cls; Cl Rep Jr Cls; Chrh Wkr; Cmnty Wkr; JA; Lbry Ade; Stg Crw; Rptr Yrbk; Yrbk; College; Architect.

FOSTER, JILL; Cadiz HS; Cadiz, OH; 34/134 Cls Rep Frsh Cls; Chrs; Cmnty Wkr; Hon Rl; NHS; Off Ade; Sch Mus; Sch Pl; Stg Crw; Yth Flsp; Kent St Univ; Theater Ed.

FOSTER, JOHN; Brownsburg HS; Pittsboro, IN; Chrh Wkr; Sec Ger Clb; Mas Awd; Univ; Educ.

FOSTER, KAREN; Wheelersburg HS; Wheelersburg, OH; 16/162 Trs Soph Cls; Trs Jr Cls; Band; Chrs; Girl Scts; Sch Mus; Stu Cncl; Lat Clb; Pep Clb; Chrldng; Marshall Univ; Legal Sec.

FOSTER, KATHARINE; Maumee Valley Cntry Day HS; Perrysburg, OH; Cl Rep Jr Cls; Girl Scts; Hon Rl; Letter Bsktbl; Letter Hockey; Letter Socr; Letter Trk; Coach Actv; Scr Kpr; Tmr; Coll; Natural Sci.

FOSTER, KATHY; Kenowa Hills HS; Grand Rapids, MI; Chrs; Chrh Wkr; Cmnty Wkr; Girl Scts; Sch Pl; Sct Actv; Yth Flsp; Rptr Sch Nwsp; 4-H; Pep Clb; JV Bsktbl Record For Rebounds; Grand Rapids Jr Coll; Crim Justice.

FOSTER, KEVIN N; Robert S Rogers HS; Toledo, OH; 20/400 Boy Scts; Chrs; Cmnty Wkr; Hon Rl; JA; Jr NHS; NHS; Sch Mus; Sch Pl; Stg Crw; College; Medicine.

FOSTER, KIM; George Washington HS; E Chicago, IN; 36/292 Cls Rep Frsh Cls; Cls Rep Soph Cls; Cl Rep Jr Cls; Cls Rep Sr Cls; Hon Rl; Off Ade; Stu Cncl; Bsktbl; Chrldng; GAA; Ind State.

FOSTER, KRISTIN; Warren Central HS; Indianapolis, IN; 28/850 Hon Rl; Jr NHS; Mdrgl; NHS; Stu Cncl; IM Sprt; Scr Kpr; Purdue Univ; Premed.

FOSTER, LEANN; Jimtown HS; Elkhart, IN; 3/100 Cls Rep Frsh Cls; Cls Rep Soph Cls; Pres Jr Cls; VP NHS; Pres Stu Cncl; Drama Clb; FHA; Pep Clb; Manchester Coll; Accounting.

FOSTER, LESLIE; Lewis Cnty HS; Weston, WV; Hon Rl; Jr NHS; NHS; Stu Cncl; 4-H; 4-H Awd; Davis & Elkins Univ; Comp Sci.

FOSTER, LINDA; Madison Comp HS; Mansfield, OH; Chrh Wkr; Girl Scts; Red Cr Ade; Stu Cncl; Rptr Sch Nwsp; Pep Clb; VICA; Bsbl; Bsktbl; Gym; North Central Tech Schl; RN.

FOSTER, LINETTE; Brown City HS; Brown City, MI; 4/90 Hon Rl; Lbry Ade; Treas NHS; Off Ade; Stu Cncl; Rptr Sch Nwsp; 4-H; FHA; Pres FTA; Pom Pon;.

FOSTER, MARK; Oak Hill HS; Oak Hill, WV; Hon Rl; NHS; 2nd Pl Fayette Co Math Fiedl Day 79; Mbr Wv Regnl 4 Math Team To Wv St Math Field Day 79; West Virginia Inst Of Tech; Elec Enr.

FOSTER, MIKE; Wilmington HS; Wilmington, OH; Boy Scts; Hon Rl; Stg Crw; 4-H; Spn Clb; Letter Bsbl; Awd From Clinton Cnty Sheriffs Dept 78; Univ; Engr.

FOSTER, PAUL; St Francis HS; Morgantown, WV; Cls Rep Frsh Cls; Cls Rep Soph Cls; Am Leg Boys St; Hon Rl; NHS; Stu Cncl; Drama Clb; Fr Clb; Sci Clb; Bsktbl; Univ.

FOSTER, REGINA; Gauley Bridge HS; Gauley Bridge, WV; 13/82 Trs Frsh Cls; Cls Rep Soph Cls; Trs Jr Cls; Trs Sr Cls; Am Leg Aux Girls St; Band; Chrs; Potomac State; Pharmacology.

FOSTER, RICHARD; All Saints Central HS; Bay City, MI; Rdo Clb; Central Michigan Univ; Elec Engr.

FOSTER, SHELLEY; Fountain Cntrl HS; Hillsboro, IN; 19/135 Chrs; Drl Tm; Girl Scts; Hon Rl; Sch Mus; Sct Actv; Rptr Yrbk; Rptr Sch Nwsp; Fr Clb; FHA; 1st Class Girl Scout Highest Awd; Pin For Honor Roll; Medal For Winning Spelling Bee; Busns Schl; Sec.

FOSTER, STEPHANIE; Erieview Catholic HS; Cleveland, OH; 17/130 Chrs; Chrh Wkr; Drl Tm; Hon Rl; NHS; Stu Cncl; IM Sprt; Case Western Reserve Univ; Bio Sci.

FOSTER, STEVE; Ithaca HS; Ithaca, MI; Pres Frsh Cls; Pres Soph Cls; Pres Jr Cls; Am Leg Boys St; Hon Rl; NHS; Yth Flsp; Sprt Ed Sch Nwsp; Letter Ten; College; Engineering.

FOSTER, SUSAN; Columbiana HS; Columbiana, OH; Band; Cmp Fr Grls; Chrs; Chrh Wkr; Hon Rl; Yth Flsp; Spn Clb; South Eastern Acad; Travel Ind.

FOSTER, TIMOTHY; Lockland HS; Lockland, OH; 26/80 Chrh Wkr; Rptr Yrbk; Sprt Ed Sch Nwsp; Letter Bsbl; Letter Bsktbl; Letter Crs Cntry; Scr Kpr; Tmr; Cit Awd; SAR Awd; Univ.

FOSTER, TINA; Greeneview HS; Jamestown, OH; 29/112 Chrh Wkr; FHA; Sci Awd 76; Clark Tech Coll; Med Sec Tech.

FOSTER, YVONNE; South Central HS; Union Mls, IN; Cmp Fr Grls; Chrh Wkr; 4-H; FHA; Pep Clb; Spn Clb; 4-H Awd; Univ; Criminology.

FOSTER III, GEORGE A; Elkhart Central HS; Elkhart, IN; Boy Scts; Orch; Boys Clb Am; Swmmng; Purdue Univ; Forestry.

FOTI, SAM; Charles F Brush HS; Lyndhurst, OH; Cls Rep Frsh Cls; Cls Rep Soph Cls; Cl Rep Jr Cls; Cls Rep Sr Cls; Band; Treas Stu Cncl; Univ; Engr.

FOTIEO, PETER; Grand Rapids Central HS; Grand Rapids, MI; 12/300 Hon Rl; Jr NHS; NHS; Ed Sch Nwsp; Ten; Univ Of Michigan.

FOUGEROUSSE, DIANNE; Reading HS; Reading, MI; 3/97 VP Band; Hon Rl; NHS; Stu Cncl; Yrbk; Ed Sch Nwsp; Pres Fr Clb; PPFtbl; Natl Merit Ltr; Univ Of Michigan; Bus Admin.

FOUNDS, BRIAN; John Glenn HS; Chandlersville, OH; Chrh Wkr; Hon Rl; NHS; Stu Cncl; Pres Yth Flsp; VP 4-H; Sec FFA; Letter Ftbl; Ohio St Univ; Agri.

FOUNTAIN, CAROL; Ida HS; Ida, MI; 26/140 Band; Chrs; Drl Tm; Yth Flsp; Ed Yrbk; Ed Sch Nwsp; Pres Drama Clb; Central Mic Univ; Music.

FOUNTAIN, CRAIG; Vassar HS; Vassar, MI; 14/150 Hon Rl; Quill & Scroll; Stg Crw; Rptr Yrbk; Rptr Sch Nwsp; Ctrl Mich Univ; Math.

FOURNIER, SERGE; John Glenn HS; Canton, MI; Aud/Vis; Hon Rl; JA; Pep Clb; Bsbl; Hockey; Swmmng; IM Sprt; JA Awd; Pres Awd; Bus Schl.

FOUST, ALICE; Parkside HS; Jackson, MI; Cls Rep Frsh Cls; Cls Rep Soph Cls; Cl Rep Jr Cls; Band; Cmnty Wkr; Girl Scts; Hon Rl; Mic State; Soc Work.

FOUST, CINDY; Poland Seminary HS; Poland, OH; Cmnty Wkr; Hon Rl; Lbry Ade; Lit Mag; Off Ade; Quill & Scroll; Y-Teens; Rptr Sch Nwsp; Sch Nwsp ; Drama Clb; Chosen For Children Intl Village To Gustamaea 77; All Star Awd For Tennis 78; Photog Edit For Schl Newspaper; Brown Univ; Photog.

FOUST, SHERYL; Bloomington HS North; Greenwood, IN; Band; Chrh Wkr; CAP; Debate Tm; Girl Scts; Natl Forn Lg; Ger Clb; Pep Clb; Natl Forensic League Degree Of Merit 79; Natl Forensic League Degree Of Hon 79; Civil Air Patrol 78; Indiana Univ; Juvenile Law.

FOUT, ERIC; Hobart Sr HS; Hobart, IN; 1/390 Boy Scts; Chrh Wkr; Hon Rl; NHS; Rdo Clb; Pres Sci Clb; Wrstlng; Article Publ Ill History Magazine; Outstanding Spanish Stu; Schlrshp Nominee; College; Anthropology.

FOUT, WILLIAM; Riverdale HS; Forest, OH; 51/104 VP Frsh Cls; Cl Rep Jr Cls; Hon Rl; Sch Mus; Sch Pl; Stg Crw; Stu Cncl; Drama Clb; FTA; Bsktbl; Univ.

FOUTS, DEBBIE; N Miami HS; Deedsville, IN; 5/115 Band; Chrs; Sec Chrh Wkr; FCA; Hon Rl; MMM; NHS; Off Ade; Yth Flsp; Drama Clb; Manchester Coll; Sec Sci.

FOUTS, DEBRA; North Miami HS; Deedsville, IN; 5/115 Chrs; Sec Chrh Wkr; MMM; NHS; Pres 4-H; Pres FHA; OEA; Mgrs; Dnfth Awd; 4-H Awd; Manchester Coll; Sec Sci.

FOUTS, KATHY; Turpin HS; Cincinnati, OH; Cls Rep Frsh Cls; VP Soph Cls; VP Jr Cls; Chrs; Sch Pl; Stu Cncl; VP Drama Clb; Letter Chrldng; PPFtbl; Univ; Psych.

FOUTY, ANGELINA; Jackson HS; Jackson, OH; 28/250 Hon Rl; Hosp Ade; NHS; Quill & Scroll; Sch Pl; Stg Crw; Ed Yrbk; Yrbk; Pep Clb; Trk; Univ; Cmnctns.

FOUTY, DOUGLAS; Columbia Central HS; Clark Lake, MI; VP Frsh Cls; Cls Rep Soph Cls; Cl Rep Jr Cls; Cls Rep Sr Cls; Band; Lbry Ade; Sch Mus; Stu Cncl; Letter Bsktbl; Letter Ftbl; All St Ftbl 77; All Amer Ftbl 78; Ftbl Schlrshp To Univ Of Wi 79; Univ Of Wisconsin.

FOUTY, TERRIA; Spencer HS; Spencer, WV; Hon Rl; Hosp Ade; Off Ade; DECA; 4-H; FHA; Pep Clb; Sec.

FOUTY, TIMOTHY; Vandercook Lake HS; Jackson, MI; 7/90 Band; Hon Rl; Bsbl; Bsktbl; Ftbl; Cit Awd; Natl Merit Schl; Univ.

FOUTZ, BRYAN; Washington HS; Massillon, OH; 46/480 Aud/Vis; Chrs; Hon Rl; NHS; Sch Mus; Spn Clb; Television Broadcasting.

FOUTZ, JEFF; Washington HS; Massillon, OH; Chrs; Chrh Wkr; Hon Rl; Sch Mus; Sch Pl; Stg Crw; Sprt Ed Yrbk; Yrbk; Drama Clb; Ger Clb;.

FOUTZ, JIM; Greenville Sr HS; Greenville, OH; Cls Rep Soph Cls; Cl Rep Jr Cls; Chrs; Hon Rl; Rptr Sch Nwsp; DECA; Coach Actv; Cit Awd; VFW Awd; Voice Dem Awd; Pub Spkng Awd Dist Compttn 3rd Pl 77; VFW Voice Of Dem 1st Pl City 1st Cnty 3rd Dist 78; Wilburforce Univ; Poli Sci.

FOWLER, ANITA; North Putnam HS; Bainbridge, IN; 1/150 Cmnty Wkr; Drl Tm; FCA; Hon Rl; NHS; Off Ade; 4-H; OEA; Pep Clb; Spn Clb; O/S First Yr Spanish Awd; Mbr Natl Hnr Soc; Hanover Coll; Math.

FOWLER, ANTHONY; John R Buchtel Univ HS; Akron, OH; Sch Nwsp; Ftbl; Capt Wrstlng; Univ.

FOWLER, CYNTHIA; Philip Barbour HS; Philippi, WV; Chrh Wkr; Hon Rl; NHS; Stu Cncl; Yth Flsp; Drama Clb; Sec Keyettes; Alderson Broaddus College; Educ.

FOWLER, CYNTHIA; Castle HS; Newburgh, IN; Hon Rl; Lbry Ade; Lat Clb; Purdue Univ; Med.

FOWLER, DAWN; Chelsea HS; Dexter, MI; Chrs; Hon Rl; JA; Fr Clb; College; Journalism.

FOWLER, DEBBIE; Washington Catholic HS; Washington, IN; 5/40 Sec Frsh Cls; Sec Soph Cls; VP Jr Cls; Sec Sr Cls; Am Leg Aux Girls St; Girl Scts; Hon Rl; Jr NHS; NHS; Stg Crw; Indiana Univ; Sociology.

FOWLER, EDWARD; Lakeview HS; Cortland, OH; 3/184 Pres Frsh Cls; Am Leg Boys St; Chrh Wkr; Cmnty Wkr; Hon Rl; NHS; Sch Pl; Ohi State Univ; Dent.

FOWLER, GARY; Mt Healthy HS; Cincinnati, OH; 29/579 Chrh Wkr; Hon Rl; Beta Clb; Spn Clb; Oh Test Of Schlstc Achvmtn Spanish II 76; Oh Test Of Schlstc Acvhmtn Amer Hist 14th Pl 78; Univ; Hist.

FOWLER, JOSEPH; Barr Reeve HS; Montgomery, IN; 18/43 Cmnty Wkr; Lbry Ade; 4-H; FFA; Bsktbl; Crs Cntry; Trk; IM Sprt; 4-H Awd; Vincennes Univ; Aviation.

FOWLER, KAREN; Point Pleasant HS; Pt Pleasant, WV; Chrh Wkr; Cmnty Wkr; Hon Rl; Yth Flsp; Sprt Ed Sch Nwsp; Rptr Sch Nwsp; Sch Nwsp; 4-H; FHA; Lat Clb; Marshall Univ; Psych.

FOWLER, MARGARET; Reitz Memorial HS; Evansville, IN; 1/210 Chrh Wkr; Cmnty Wkr; Hon Rl; NHS; Red Cr Ade; Indiana St Univ; Med Tech.

FOWLER, MARK; Woodward HS; Cincinnati, OH; Bsbl; Ftbl; Letters & Trophy; Bar Trophy; Univ.

FOWLER, MASON; Cadiz HS; Hopedale, OH; Cls Rep Soph Cls; Hon Rl; Stg Crw; Bsbl; Glf; Univ.

FOWLER, MELODY; Hicksville HS; Hicksville, OH; Cls Rep Frsh Cls; Aud/Vis; Chrs; Girl Scts; Hon Rl; Sch Mus; Sch Pl; Sch Nwsp; Lat Clb; Pep Clb; De Fiance Coll; Comprehensive Busns.

FOWLER, NINA; South Vigo HS; Terre Haute, IN; Band; Hon Rl; Lbry Ade; Off Ade; Stu Cncl; Y-Teens; Pep Clb; Trk; Pom Pon; PPFtbl; Jr Adv Exec Comm; Jr Prom Attnd; MSA & ASA Sftbl League; Nominated For Ms Teen USA; ISU; Eng Prof.

FOWLER, TIMOTHY R; John R Buchtel Sr HS; Akron, OH; 85/452 Cls Rep Frsh Cls; Cls Rep Soph Cls; Cl Rep Jr Cls; Hon Rl; Stu Cncl; FBLA; Letter Ftbl; Letter Socr; Letter Trk; Letter Wrstlng; Co llege; Busns Admin.

FOWLER, TRACEY; Coventry HS; Akron, OH; Band; Chrs; Girl Scts; Sch Mus; Stu Cncl; Rptr Sch Nwsp; Spn Clb; Trk; GAA; Bus Schl; Lgl Sec.

FOWLER, WILLIAM R; Highland Park Comm HS; Highland Park, MI; 19/243 Cmnty Wkr; Hon Rl; NHS; Off Ade; Yth Flsp; Stu Cncl; Rptr Yrbk; OEA; Cranbrook Horizons Upward Bound; Soc Studies Eng; Highland Park Caucas Clb Awd; NAACP Act So Part Awd; Kalamazoo Coll; Poli Sci.

FOWLKES, RONDA M; Immaculata HS; Detroit, MI; Chrs; Cmnty Wkr; Pol Wkr; Pres Stu Cncl; Ed Yrbk; Sch Nwsp; IM Sprt; Cent Iii Leaders Letter Of Commend For Runner Up 1978; Criminal Justice Progr.

FOWLKES, TONYA; Immaculata HS; Detroit, MI; Cls Rep Soph Cls; Cl Rep Jr Cls; Hon Rl; Pol Wkr; Rptr Sch Nwsp; Sch Nwsp; Fr Clb; Bsktbl; Trk; Texas El Paso Univ; Chem Engr.

FOX, ALICE; Capac Jr Sr HS; Capac, MI; Hon Rl; OEA; Letter Trk; GAA; Bus Schl; Data Processing.

FOX, ALICE; St Marys HS; Belmont, WV; Band; Girl Scts; PPFtbl;.

FOX, ANNETTE; Ida HS; Monroe, MI; 5/132 Cls Rep Sr Cls; Am Leg Aux Girls St; Pres NHS; Stu Cncl; Letter Bsktbl; Capt Trk; GAA; Michigan St Univ; Bio Chem.

FOX, BETH; Lansing Catholic Ctrl HS; Lansing, MI; 6/140 Cls Rep Frsh Cls; Sec Soph Cls; Sec Jr Cls; Sec Sr Cls; Hon Rl; Hosp Ade; Jr NHS; NHS; Off Ade; Sch Mus; Acad Schlrshp For Western Univ 79; Michigan St Univ; Acctg.

FOX, BETH; West Carrollton Sr HS; W Carrollton, OH; 19/420 Band; Capt Drl Tm; Hon Rl; Treas Jr NHS; NHS; Off Ade; Sch Pl; Drama Clb; Pep Clb; Swmmng; Univ; Lib Art.

FOX, BRENDA; Buckeye Central HS; Bloomville, OH; 5/90 Pres Soph Cls; Hon Rl; Sec Spn Clb; Am Leg Awd; Cit Awd; Univ.

FOX, C; Grand Ledge HS; Lansing, MI; Band; Debate Tm; Lat Clb; Michigan St Univ; Rehab Counseling.

FOX, CHRISTI; Alexandria Monroe HS; Alexandria, IN; Hosp Ade; Y-Teens; Pres Ger Clb; Pep Clb; Mgrs; Univ; Nursing.

FOX, CONNIE J; Attica Jr Sr HS; Attica, IN; 3/84 Band; Chrh Wkr; Hon Rl; NHS; Sch Pl; Stg Crw; Ed Yrbk; Sec Drama Clb; Fr Clb; De Paun Univ; Comp Math.

FOX, DAVID; West Geavga HS; Novelty, OH; 5/353 Debate Tm; Hon Rl; NHS; Letter Bsbl; Socr; IM Sprt; Ohi State Univ; Liberal Arts.

FOX, DEBORAH; Kirtland HS; Kirtland, OH; 1/110 Trs Sr Cls; Val; Am Leg Aux Girls St; Pres NHS; Capt Bsktbl; Letter Trk; Am Leg Awd; Bausch & Lomb Awd; Elk Awd; Voice Dem Awd; Notre Dame Coll; Pre Pharm.

FOX, DIANE; Lakeview HS; Cortland, OH; 80/145 Band; Hon Rl; PAVAS; Sch Pl; Yth Flsp; Rptr Sch Nwsp; Sec 4-H; Letter Trk; Twrlr; 4-H Awd; Class Of Yr Awd By Dance Teacher; News Story Voted By Fellow Classmates As Best Article In Paper; Coll; Journalism.

FOX, ELAINE; Otsego HS; Tontogany, OH; 5/158 Band; Chrs; Chrh Wkr; Girl Scts; Hon Rl; Jr NHS; NHS; Orch; Yth Flsp; 4-H; Univ Of Toledo; Pharm.

FOX, FRANK; Lake Michigan Catholic HS; Sodus, MI; 30/105 Cls Rep Soph Cls; Chrh Wkr; Hon Rl; Sch Pl; Stg Crw; Yth Flsp; Yrbk; Drama Clb; Cit Awd; Kiwan Awd; Univ; Bus Admin.

FOX, FRED; Bishop Noll Inst; Hammond, IN; 111/321 Band; Hon Rl; Orch; Mth Clb; Sportsmanship Awd In Track 77; Music Awds 77 79; St Josephs Univ; Finance.

FOX, GRACE; Eastern HS; Beaver, OH; Chrs; Drl Tm; Hon Rl; Sch Mus; Sch Pl; Drama Clb; FTA; Pep Clb; Pom Pon; Shawnee St Cmnty Coll; X Ray Tech.

FOX, HEATHER; Greenville HS; Greenville, MI; Cls Rep Frsh Cls; Band; Cmnty Wkr; Hon Rl; Stu Cncl; Letter Ten; Kalamazoo Coll; Pre Med.

FOX, JANET; Doddridge Cnty HS; West Union, WV; Band; Hon Rl; Lbry Ade; NHS; Stu Cncl; Pres Mth Clb; Pep Clb; Univ; Nursing.

FOX, JOYCE; Field HS; Mogadore, OH; 33/300 Cmp Fr Grls; Chrs; Hon Rl; NHS; Off Ade; Sch Mus; Sch Pl; Rptr Yrbk; Drama Clb; Sci Clb; Akron Univ; Data Proc.

FOX, KATHY; Franklin Community HS; Franklin, IN; 45/280 Chrh Wkr; Cmnty Wkr; Indiana Central Univ; R N.

FOX, KIMBERLY A; Independence HS; Sophia, WV; 7/145 VP Soph Cls; Cmnty Wkr; Hon Rl; VP JA; Pres NHS; Ed Sch Nwsp; Beta Clb; Pep Clb; Pres Sci Clb; JA Awd; Sally Hatfield Memorial Schlrshp 1979; Pinecrest Hosp Schlrshp 1979; Laurence E Tierney Schlrshp 1979; Concord Coll; Med Tech.

FOX, LORRAINE A; Plymouth HS; Plymouth, IN; 1/225 Val; Band; Hon Rl; MMM; NHS; Eng Clb; Pres Fr Clb; VP Mth Clb; DAR Awd; Natl Merit Ltr; Univ Of Notre Dame; Languages.

FOX, LYNDA; Galion Sr HS; Galion, OH; 40/275 Am Leg Aux Girls St; Hosp Ade; Off Ade; Capt Bsktbl; Ohio St Univ; Med.

FOX, MATTHEW; Greenville HS; Greenville, MI; 33/238 Cls Rep Soph Cls; Chrh Wkr; Hon Rl; Stu Cncl; Fr Clb; Ten; IM Sprt; Montcalm Comm Coll; Criminal Justice.

FOX, MELISSA; Westerville North HS; Westerville, OH; 189/429 Ed Yrbk; Sec DECA; Letter Bsbl; Coach Actv; GAA; PPFtbl; Volleyball Letter; Inter Club Council; Ohio St Univ; Acctg.

FOX, MIKE; Bellbrook HS; Spring Valley, OH; 27/150 Cls Rep Frsh Cls; Cls Rep Soph Cls; Band; Chrh Wkr; Hon Rl; NHS; Stu Cncl; Yth Flsp; Spn Clb; College; Computer Sci.

FOX, MIKE; Bishop Donahue HS; Wheeling, WV; 3/50 Pres Frsh Cls; Cls Rep Frsh Cls; Chrh Wkr; VP NHS; Key Clb; Capt Bsbl; Capt Bsktbl; Ftbl; Cit Awd; DAR Awd; West Virginia Univ; Elec Engr.

FOX, MIKE; Bishop Donohue HS; Wheeling, WV; Pres Frsh Cls; Cls Rep Frsh Cls; VP NHS; Stu Cncl; Key Clb; Bsbl; Bsktbl; Ftbl; Cit Awd; DAR Awd; Wv Univ; Elec Engr.

FOX, PATRICK; Fisher Catholic HS; Lancaster, OH; Am Leg Boys St; Debate Tm; Hon Rl; NHS; 4-H; Key Clb; Letter Crs Cntry; Letter Trk; 4-H Awd; Univ; Elec Engr.

FOX, RICHARD; Kirtland HS; Kirtland, OH; Trs Jr Cls; AFS; Hon Rl; NHS; Bsbl; Bsktbl; Lakeland Cmnty Coll; Bus.

FOX, ROBERTA; Midland Trail HS; Hico, WV; Hon Rl; NHS; Stg Crw; Drama Clb; Fr Clb; VICA; IM Sprt; Cosmetology Schl; Cosmetologist.

FOX, SARAH; Troy HS; Troy, MI; 11/280 Trs Soph Cls; Sec Jr Cls; Am Leg Aux Girls St; Band; Girl Scts; Hon Rl; NHS; Capt Bsktbl; Capt Trk; Mgrs; Univ Of Michigan; Comp Sci.

FOX, SHERRI; Twin Valley North HS; Lewisburg, OH; Chrs; Drl Tm; Hon Rl; NHS; Stu Cncl; Pep Clb; Crs Cntry;.

FOX, STEVEN; Douglas Mac Arthur HS; Saginaw, MI; 65/310 Cl Rep Jr Cls; Trs Sr Cls; Cls Rep Sr Cls; Hon Rl; Jr NHS; NHS; Stu Cncl; Yth Flsp; Pep Clb; Ftbl; Natl Hon Soc Pres 79; People To People Stud Ambassador Prog 79; Saginaw Gun Clb Small Bore Rifle Tm 74 80; Univ; Law.

FOX, THOMAS; St Johns HS; St Johns, MI; Hon Rl; NHS; Coll.

FOXWORTH, MARY; Northwestern HS; Flint, MI; Hon Rl; Sec NHS; Rptr Yrbk; St Of Mi Comp Cert Of Merit 78; Univ Of Mi Grant St Of Mi Comp Exam 79; Univ Of Michigan; Pre Med.

FOXWORTHY, LISA; Marion Adams HS; Sheridan, IN; Cl Rep Jr Cls; FCA; Hon Rl; JA; Jr NHS; NHS; Off Ade; Stu Cncl; Yth Flsp; Rptr Sch Nwsp; Indiana Univ; Flight Attendant.

FOXX, DEBORAH; Bay HS; Bay Vill, OH; Chrs; Girl Scts; Gym; Chrldng; IM Sprt; Miami Univ; Elem Ed.

FOY, LINDA; Calumet HS; Calumet, MI; Hon Rl; Yrbk; Pep Clb; Bsktbl; IM Sprt; Twrlr; College.

FOY, LISA; St Johns HS; Dewitt, MI; 21/298 Band; Hon Rl; NHS; Orch; Sch Mus; Sch Pl; Drama Clb; 4-H; Ten; 4-H Awd; Ferris State Coll; Pre Med.

FOY, MARY; Holt HS; Holt, MI; Cmnty Wkr; Red Cr Ade; Fr Clb; Letter Bsktbl; Coach Actv; Univ; Occupt Ther.

FOY, MARY B; Ursuline Acad; Cincinnati, OH; Cl Rep Jr Cls; Cls Rep Sr Cls; Chrs; Hon Rl; Sch Pl; Stu Cncl; College.

FOY, SUE; Van Buren HS; Brazil, IN; Sec Soph Cls; Band; Girl Scts; Hon Rl; Rptr Yrbk; 4-H; Fr Clb; FHA; Pep Clb; Trk; Ind State Univ.

FRAAS, HENRY C; Bexley HS; Columbus, OH; Cl Rep Jr Cls; Chrs; Hon Rl; Stu Cncl; Rptr Yrbk; IM Sprt; College; Law.

FRADE, M; Our Lady Of Mercy HS; Birmingham, MI; NHS; Mth Clb; Sci Clb; Spn Clb; Oakland Univ; Sci.

FRADL, CYNTHIA; Yale HS; Goodells, MI; Chrs; Cmnty Wkr; Hon Rl; Sch Pl; 4-H; Pep Clb; Spn Clb; Trk; Pom Pon; PPFtbl; Univ; Pre Law.

FRADL, KATHLEEN; Yale HS; Goodells, MI; 16/168 Cl Rep Jr Cls; Sec Sr Cls; Band; Hon Rl; NHS; Sch Pl; Stg Crw; Stu Cncl; 4-H; Bsktbl; St Clair County Comm Coll; Vet Asst.

FRAENKEL, PETER; Upper Arlington HS; Columbus, OH; 26/610 Chrs; Hon Rl; Jr NHS; Fr Clb; Sci Research.

FRAGALE, LOUISE; Morgantown HS; Morgantown, WV; Cl Rep Jr Cls; Girl Scts; Hon Rl; Lbry Ade; NHS; Stu Cncl; Pres 4-H; Mth Clb; Spn Clb; College; Engr.

FRAGALE, SAM; Notre Dame HS; Clarksburg, WV; Cls Rep Frsh Cls; Cls Rep Soph Cls; Cl Rep Jr Cls; VP Sr Cls; Am Leg Boys St; Chrh Wkr; NHS; Stu Cncl; Key Clb; Ftbl; WVU; Engr.

FRAGOMENIC, GINA; John Adams HS; South Bend, IN; 59/415 Hon Rl; Coach Actv; College.

FRAHM, DAVE J; Celina Sr HS; Celina, OH; 19/241 Hon Rl; Jr NHS; NHS; 4-H; FFA; IM Sprt; 4-H Awd; State Officer Future Farmer Of Amer 1978; State F F A Degree; Ohio St Univ; Agri.

FRAIN, KAREN; Sylvania Northview HS; Sylvania, OH; Hon Rl; Red Cr Ade; Sch Nwsp; Pep Clb; Gym; Chrldng; IM Sprt; PPFtbl; Miami Univ; Elem Ed.

FRALEY, ANITA; Shady Spring HS; Shady Spring, WV; 1/155 Cls Rep Frsh Cls; Cls Rep Soph Cls; Val; Band; Chrs; Chrh Wkr; Pres FCA; Hon Rl; NHS; Sch Pl; Radford Coll; Psych.

FRALEY, CHARLES; Fort Gay HS; Ft Gay, WV; VP Jr Cls; Hon Rl; Sch Pl; Stu Cncl; Pep Clb; Rdo Clb; Spn Clb; Letter Bsbl; Letter Ftbl; Marshall Univ; Marine Bio.

FRALEY, CYNTHIA; Perrysburg HS; Perrysburg, OH; 22/251 Cls Rep Frsh Cls; Trs Soph Cls; Sec Jr Cls; VP Sr Cls; Am Leg Aux Girls St; Hon Rl; JA; NHS; Sch Mus; Sch Pl; Bowling Green St Univ; Jrnlsm.

FRALEY, ED; Rock Hill HS; Ironton, OH; Hon Rl; Beta Clb; Sci Clb; Ftbl; College.

FRALEY, JENNIFER; Moorefield HS; Moorefield, WV; 4/88 Band; Chrs; Cmnty Wkr; Hon Rl; Treas Jr NHS; Pres NHS; Pol Wkr; Marshall Univ; Med.

FRALEY, JENNIFER; Wauseon HS; Wauseon, OH; Chrs; Hon Rl; Lbry Ade; Sch Mus; Y-Teens; Fr Clb; Pep Clb; Gym; GAA; BGSU; Pre Law.

FRALEY, KATHLEEN D; Clear Fork HS; Dorothy, WV; 8/48 Band; Chrs; Girl Scts; Hon Rl; Jr NHS; NHS; Pep Clb; Bsktbl; Trk; IM Sprt; Eng Awd 77; Glenville St Coll; Sec.

FRALICH, REBECCA; Beecher HS; Flint, MI; 4/275 Band; Chrs; Chrh Wkr; Hon Rl; NHS; Orch; Pres Yth Flsp; Rptr Yrbk; Chrldng; DAR Awd; Spring Arbor Coll.

FRALICK, BRAD; Cheboygan Area HS; Cheboygan, MI; Hon Rl; Sch Pl; Stu Cncl; Fr Clb; Trk; Univ Of Mic.

FRAMBAUGH, JENNIE; Stow HS; Munroe Fls, OH; 93/595 Chrs; Hon Rl; NHS; Off Ade; Lat Clb; Lion Awd; Univ; Vet Med.

FRAMBES, DONNA; Marian HS; Norwood, OH; Chrh Wkr; Cmnty Wkr; Hon Rl; Hosp Ade; JA; Fr Clb; GAA; IM Sprt; Mgrs; Scr Kpr; Sci Awd 75; Xavier Univ; Psych.

FRAME, DAVID; Anderson HS; Anderson, IN; 33/425 Am Leg Boys St; Band; Chrs; Chrh Wkr; Drm Bgl; Hon Rl; NHS; Sch Mus; Fr Clb; Indiana St Univ; Communications.

FRAME, DEBBIE; Morgantown HS; Morgantwn, WV; Cls Rep Soph Cls; Chrs; Stu Cncl; Ten; IM Sprt; Univ.

FRAME, DENISE M; Northeastern HS; Williamsburg, IN; 41/121 Band; Hon Rl; Sch Mus; Sch Pl; Drama Clb; Sec 4-H; FHA; Key Clb; Cit Awd; 4-H Awd; Housing Kitchen Planning Awd; St 4 H Band; Musical Exclinc In Choir Band;.

FRAME, K; Calhoun County HS; Millstone, WV; Cls Rep Frsh Cls; Cls Rep Soph Cls; Band; Sch Mus; Drama Clb; Chrldng; Coach Actv; Psych.

FRAME, TED; North Central HS; Pioneer, OH; Cls Rep Soph Cls; Am Leg Boys St; Boy Scts; Hon Rl; NHS; Sct Actv; Stu Cncl; FFA; Trk; Wrstlng; Most Improved Wrestler; Most Pins; 2nd Year Varsity; Captain 3rd Yr Varsity; College.

FRAMPTON, TRACEY; Culver Girls Academy; Columbus, OH; 11/191 Band; Girl Scts; Hon Rl; Orch; Drama Clb; Fr Clb; Pep Clb; Letter Bsktbl; Letter Swmmng; Letter Trk; Blue Key Soc Jr Class Hon Soc For Culver Stud; Univ; Bio Sci.

FRANCE, LISA; Plymouth HS; Plymouth, IN; Chrs; Chrh Wkr; Sch Mus; Stg Crw; Yth Flsp; Drama Clb; Fr Clb; Gym; Hanover College; Elementary Ed.

FRANCE, NORMA J; Eastern HS; Waverly, OH; Chrs; Sec Chrh Wkr; Hon Rl; Lbry Ade; Sch Mus; Sec Yth Flsp; Rptr Yrbk; Rptr Sch Nwsp; Pep Clb; Spn Clb; Shawnee St Coll; Jrnlsm.

FRANCEL, PAUL; St Francis De Sales HS; Toledo, OH; 1/223 Trs Frsh Cls; Pres Jr Cls; Pres Sr Cls; Boy Scts; Pres Chrh Wkr; Cmnty Wkr; VP Debate Tm; FCA; Hon Rl; Jr NHS; College; Medicine.

FRANCEL, PETER; St Francis De Sales HS; Toledo, OH; 17/210 Pres Frsh Cls; Cls Rep Frsh Cls; Pres Soph Cls; Trs Soph Cls; Pres Jr Cls; Boy Scts; Chrs; Chrh Wkr; Cmnty Wkr; Debate Tm; Ldrshp & Serv Awrd 77; Youth Grp Rep 78; Univ.

FRANCHI, CHRISTIE; North Farmington HS; Farmington Hls, MI; Cls Rep Frsh Cls; Cls Rep Sr Cls; Hon Rl; Hosp Ade; Stu Cncl; Yth Flsp; Yrbk; Fr Clb; Sci Clb; Capt Chrldng; Univ Of Michigan; Med.

FRANCHINA, ANTHONY; Carroll HS; Xenia, OH; Aud/Vis; Cmnty Wkr; JA; PAVAS; Sch Mus; Sch Pl; Stg Crw; Ed Sch Nwsp; Drama Clb; Eng Clb; Univ Of Dayton; Pre Law.

FRANCIS, BOB; Martins Ferry HS; Martins Ferry, OH; 13/214 VP Frsh Cls; Cls Rep Soph Cls; Hon Rl; NHS; Sch Pl; Stu Cncl; Yth Flsp; Bsktbl; Ftbl; Ohio Univ; Acctg.

FRANCIS, CATHY; Wintersville HS; Wintersville, OH; Girl Scts; Lbry Ade; Fr Clb; GAA;.

FRANCIS, CYNTHIA; Petoskey HS; Petoskey, MI; Girl Scts; Sct Actv; Fr Clb; Mic Tech Univ; Comp Sci.

FRANCIS, DAVE; Martins Ferry HS; Moundville, WV; Cls Rep Frsh Cls; Boy Scts; Hon Rl; Sct Actv; Stu Cncl; Sci Clb; Bsbl; Mgrs; Univ.

FRANCIS, DEBORAH; Liberty HS; Clarksburg, WV; 63/227 Chrh Wkr; Girl Scts; Hon Rl; Lbry Ade; NHS; Off Ade; Sct Actv; Stu Cncl; Yth Flsp; Y-Teens; Honors Eng Progrm 1978; French I Tchr Aide; Fairmont St Coll; Elem Educ.

FRANCIS, DEBORAH M; Liberty HS; Clarksburg, WV; Chrh Wkr; Hon Rl; Lbry Ade; Stu Cncl; Yth Flsp; Fr Clb; Pep Clb; Chrldng; Mas Awd; Fairmont St Univ; Elem Educ.

FRANCIS, DEBRA K; Logan HS; Rockbridge, OH; 25/310 Chrh Wkr; Hon Rl; NHS; Off Ade; Stu Cncl; Yth Flsp; Y-Teens; Pep Clb; Chrldng; PPFtbl; Capital Univ; Bus.

FRANCIS, JAMES E; Belmont HS; Dayton, OH; Trs Frsh Cls; VP Soph Cls; Pres Jr Cls; Pres Sr Cls; Boy Scts; Off Ade; Stu Cncl; Y-Teens; Fr Clb; Pep Clb; Morehouse Coll.

FRANCIS, LAWRENCE; Flint Southwestern HS; Flint, MI; Quill & Scroll; Rptr Sch Nwsp; Letter Crs Cntry; Letter Hockey; IM Sprt; W Mi Univ Acad Schlshhp; Western Michigan Univ; Pre Chiroprct.

FRANCIS, MARTHA E; Tipton HS; Tipton, IN; 23/175 Band; Chrs; Hon Rl; Sch Mus; Sec Yth Flsp; Ed Yrbk; Ed Sch Nwsp; 4-H; 4-H Awd; Ball St Univ; Jrnlsm.

FRANCIS, PATTY; Brandon HS; Ortonville, MI; Trs Sr Cls; Band; Chrs; Girl Scts; NHS; Sch Mus; VP Stu Cncl; Sprt Ed Yrbk; Capt Chrldng; Alma Coll; Elem Ed.

FRANCIS, VICKI; Zane Trace HS; Chillicothe, OH; 7/127 Cls Rep Frsh Cls; Band; Chrs; Girl Scts; Hon Rl; Sec Stu Cncl; Rptr Sch Nwsp; Sec 4-H; Pep Clb; Spn Clb; Miss Geranium Festvl Queen 78; 1st Runner Up Miss Crescendo 78; Ohio Univ.

FRANCISCO, DIANE; Creston HS; Grand Rapids, MI; 1/395 Cls Rep Frsh Cls; Cls Rep Sr Cls; Val; Band; Hosp Ade; Sec NHS; Sch Mus; Trk; Am Leg Awd; DAR Awd; Ctrl Mich Univ; Math.

FRANCISCO, JAMES; Hauser Jr Sr HS; Hope, IN; 3/90 Band; Hon Rl; NHS; Sec FFA; Rose Hulman Univ; Engr.

FRANCK, KRISTINE; St Augustine Acad; Lakewood, OH; Cmp Fr Grls; Chrh Wkr; Drl Tm; Hon Rl; Hosp Ade; Drama Clb; Fr Clb; Keyettes; Pep Clb; IM Sprt; Marion Coll; Psych.

FRANCKOWIAK, PHILIP; Boyne Falls Public HS; Boyne Falls, MI; Cls Rep Frsh Cls; Pres Soph Cls; Cls Rep Sr Cls; Val; Chrh Wkr; Hon Rl; Stu Cncl; Ed Yrbk; Rptr Sch Nwsp; Lion Awd; Muskegon Bus Coll; Acctg.

FRANCOEUR, ANNE; Adrian HS; Adrian, MI; Chrh Wkr; Hon Rl; NHS; Red Cr Ade; Pep Clb; Sci Clb; Trk; Natl Merit Ltr; Univ; Pharm.

FRANK, BARBARA; Kimball HS; Royal Oak, MI; Chrs; Mdrgl; NHS; Orch; General Motors Inst; Bus Admin.

FRANK, BILL; Perry HS; Massillon, OH; Chrs; Natl Forn Lg; NHS; Sch Mus; Sch Pl; Stg Crw; Rptr Sch Nwsp; Key Clb; Scr Kpr; Ohio St Univ; Law.

FRANK, CARRIE; Traverse City Sr HS; Traverse City, MI; Girl Scts; VP Orch; Sch Mus; Pep Clb; GAA; Mat Maids; Kiwan Awd; Natl Merit Ltr; St Hon Orch 79; St Police Kiwanis Law Enforcmnt Career Camp 79; Vc Pres Explorers Law Enfrcmnt 78; Ferris St Univ; Law Enfrcmnt.

FRANK, CATHERINE; Bluffton Harrison HS; Bluffton, IN; Chrs; Chrh Wkr; Hon Rl; Lbry Ade; Sec Pol Wkr; Stg Crw; Y-Teens; Pep Clb; Spn Clb; IM Sprt; Coll.

FRANK, DENISE E; Stryker HS; Stryker, OH; 16/50 VP Soph Cls; Pres Jr Cls; Pres Sr Cls; Band; Chrs; NHS; Rptr Yrbk; Rptr Sch Nwsp; Gym; Trk; Whos Who Amer HS Student 1977; Capt Varsity Cheerldrs 1978; Bowling Green St Univ; Elem Educ.

FRANK, GREGORY R; Edon HS; Edon, OH; Band; Hon Rl; Stg Crw; Spn Clb; Bsktbl; Letter Crs Cntry; Letter Trk; IM Sprt; K Of C Pro Life Essay Contst 2nd Pl 79;.

FRANK, KATHY; Canton South HS; Canton, OH; Band; Hon Rl; Lit Mag; NHS; Sec 4-H; OEA; Akron Univ; Exec Sec.

FRANK, LINDA; Marian HS; Troy, MI; Cmnty Wkr; Girl Scts; Hon Rl; Mod UN; Rptr Yrbk; IM Sprt; St Of Michigan Comp Schlrshp Prog 79; Advanced Placemnt Hist 79; Univ; Intr Design.

FRANK, LORI; Goodrich HS; Goodrich, MI; Chrh Wkr; Hon Rl; Yth Flsp; 4-H; Fr Clb; Twrlr; 4-H Awd;.

FRANK, LYNN; Southfield Christian HS; Birmingham, MI; 3/60 Cmp Fr Grls; Chrs; Girl Scts; Hon Rl; NHS; Yrbk; Letter Bsktbl; MVP Sftbl; Volleyball Letter; Skib Club; Hope Coll; Chem.

FRANK, MARTHA; Ursuline Acad; Madeira, OH; Chrs; Sec Stu Cncl; Xavier Univ; Business Admin.

FRANK, PHILLIP; Franklin HS; Livonia, MI; Band; Swmmng; Michigan St Univ; Vet Med.

FRANK, RANDALL; Bridgman HS; Bridgman, MI; Band; Chrs; Hon Rl; NHS; Sch Mus; Sch Pl; Stg Crw; Bsktbl; Letter Trk; Coach Actv; U S Army; Welder.

FRANK, ROBERT M; Euclid Sr HS; Euclid, OH; 9/703 Chrs; Hon Rl; NHS; Quill & Scroll; Rptr Yrbk; Ten; IM Sprt; Natl Merit SF; Finalist Ohio Univ Amer Hstry Cntst; College; Bio.

FRANK, SHARON; Elkhart Mem HS; Elkhart, IN; 86/520 Hon Rl; Rptr Sch Nwsp; VP Fr Clb; JA Awd; Kiwan Awd; Lion Awd; Univ; Vet.

FRANK, TERESA; Marlington HS; Louisville, OH; 6/265 Cls Rep Soph Cls; Am Leg Aux Girls St; Band; Chrs; Hon Rl; Jr NHS; NHS; Orch; Sch Mus; Sch Pl; Univ Of Akron; Med Asst.

FRANK, WILLIAM E; Perry HS; Massillon, OH; Chrs; Hon Rl; Natl Forn Lg; Sch Mus; Sch Pl; Stg Crw; Sch Nwsp; Drama Clb; Scr Kpr; Superior Speaker H R NFL East Ohio Stu Congress; Finalist Extemp Speaking Ohio St Tournament; Ohio St Univ; Law.

FRANKFURTH, THOMAS; Revere HS; Akron, OH; Hon Rl; Glf; Univ; Law.

FRANKHALL JR, BILL; Athens HS; E Leroy, MI; 40/85 Cls Rep Frsh Cls; Boy Scts; Chrh Wkr; Cmnty Wkr; FCA; Hon Rl; JA; Sch Pl; Sct Actv; Stu Cncl; College; Industrial Machines.

FRANKLIN, BETH; Harding HS; Marion, OH; AFS; Band; Chrs; Chrh Wkr; Girl Scts; Hon Rl; Mdrgl; Orch; Sch Mus; VP Fr Clb; Univ; HS Tchr.

FRANKLIN, BOBBY; Mount View HS; Big Sandy, WV; 63/232 Sec Jr Cls; Chrh Wkr; VP Jr NHS; Pol Wkr; Sch Pl; Stu Cncl; 4-H; Pres FBLA; College; Sec.

FRANKLIN, GREGORY; Bosse HS; Evansville, IN; Chrh Wkr; FCA; Hon Rl; Red Cr Ade; Pep Clb; Ftbl; Glf; Swmmng; Wrstlng; IM Sprt; Univ Of Evansville; Acctg.

FRANKLIN, HARRIET; Point Pleasant HS; Pt Pleasant, WV; Girl Scts; Hon Rl; NHS; Stu Cncl; Y-Teens; Keyettes; Pep Clb; Capt Bsktbl; Trk; College.

FRANKLIN, JACYNTHIA; River Rouge HS; River Rouge, MI; Cls Rep Frsh Cls; Cls Rep Soph Cls; Chrs; Hon Rl; Stu Cncl; Trk; Scr Kpr; Cit Awd; Univ; Phys Ther.

FRANKLIN, JOHN; Brookfield HS; Brookfield, OH; Band; Boy Scts; Cmnty Wkr; Hon Rl; Sct Actv; Yth Flsp; Coach Actv; General Mtrs Inst; Elec Engr.

FRANKLIN, KALON; Mac Kenzie HS; Detroit, MI; Hon Rl; NHS; Off Ade; FDA; Cit Awd; College.

FRANKLIN, KATHERINE E; Middletown HS; Middletown, OH; Hosp Ade; Natl Forn Lg; NHS; Ed Yrbk; Rptr Sch Nwsp; Drama Clb; Spn Clb; Letter Chrldng; Natl Merit SF; Univ; Jrnlsm.

FRANKLIN, LINDA; Blue River Valley Jr Sr HS; New Castle, IN; 18/95 Band; Drl Tm; Hon Rl; JA; NHS; Off Ade; Yth Flsp; OEA; Spn Clb; Trk; Ball St Univ; Bus.

FRANKLIN, SHARON; Wheeling Park HS; Wheeling, WV; 51/590 Cls Rep Sr Cls; AFS; Chrh Wkr; Hon Rl; Jr NHS; NHS; VP Stu Cncl; Drama Clb; Fr Clb; Chmn Ten; Univ Of Cincinnati; Art.

FRANKLIN, STANLEY E; Brookfield HS; Brookfield, OH; Pres Soph Cls; Band; Boy Scts; Hon Rl; NHS; Stu Cncl; Beta Clb; Lat Clb; Letter Wrstlng; JETS Awd; Hugh O Brian Youth Foundtn Leadrshp; Martin W Essex Schl For Gifted Oh St Univ 79; US Militay Workshop 79; Univ; Math.

FRANKLIN, WILLIAM; Medina Sr HS; Medina, OH; 34/359 Hon Rl; NHS; Letter Hockey; IM Sprt; Ohio St Univ; Archt.

FRANKO, MARY BETH; Hubbard HS; Hubbard, OH; 3/350 Band; Hon Rl; Lit Mag; NHS; Rptr Yrbk; Pres Fr Clb; Capt Bsktbl; Trk; Rotary Awd; Univ; Bio Sci.

FRANKS, BARBIE; Tiffin Columbian HS; Tiffin, OH; Hon Rl; 4-H; Ger Clb; Trk; Kent St Univ; Archt.

FRANKS, DONNA; Hillsdale HS; Jeromesville, OH; 5/100 Chrs; Chrh Wkr; Girl Scts; Hon Rl; NHS; Yth Flsp; 4-H; Fr Clb; FHA; Crs Cntry; Findlay Coll; Elem Ed.

FRANKS, JIM; Smithville HS; Smithville, OH; Cls Rep Sr Cls; Pres Chrs; Hon Rl; NHS; Stu Cncl; Sprt Ed Sch Nwsp; Ger Clb; Letter Bsbl; Letter Ftbl; Wrstlng; Ohi Univ; Comp Sci.

FRANKS, JOYCE; Southmont Jr Sr HS; Ladoga, IN; Band; Cmp Fr Grls; Chrh Wkr; Cmnty Wkr; Girl Scts; Hosp Ade; PAVAS; Yth Flsp; FHA; Pep Clb; Eleventh Florence Schultz Crtv Wrtng Awrd 1st Pl.

FRANKS, LAURA; Frankfort Sr HS; Frankfort, IN; Orch; Sch Mus; Sch Pl; 4-H; Ball St Univ; Drama.

FRANKS, LAURIE; Liberty Benton HS; Findlay, OH; 1/54 Am Leg Aux Girls St; Chrs; Hon Rl; NHS; Yrbk; Letter Trk; Ohio Tests Of Scholastic Achvmnt In Algebra II 15th In Dist & Bio 20th In State; Ohio St Univ; Sci.

FRANKS, MELANIE; Olivet HS; Olivert, MI; VP Sr Cls; Band; Drm Mjrt; Hon Rl; 4-H; VICA; Trk; Chrldng; Twrlr; 4-H Awd; Proof Encoder.

FRANKS, PAM; Corunna HS; Owosso, MI; 9/220 Sec Jr Cls; Drl Tm; Hon Rl; NHS; Off Ade; Yrbk; Pres 4-H; Trk; 4-H Awd; Cntrl Michigan Univ; Lab Tech.

FRANKS, RICHARD; Columbia City Joint HS; Columbia City, IN; 36/256 Chrh Wkr; Pres Yth Flsp; Spn Clb; Christian Coll; Bus.

FRANKS, RONALD; Traverse City HS; Traverse City, MI; 43/780 Hon Rl; NHS; Letter Bsbl; Letter Glf; Am Leg Awd; Ferris St Coll; Pharm.

FRANSSEN, PATTY; Concord Cmnty HS; Concord, MI; Drl Tm; Hon Rl; Jr NHS; Lbry Ade; NHS; Sch Mus; Sch Pl; Stg Crw; Stu Cncl; Rptr Yrbk; Jackson Community Coll; Dent Hygnst.

FRANTZ, JULIA; Lehman HS; Sidney, OH; Cls Rep Frsh Cls; Cls Rep Soph Cls; Band; Chrs; Girl Scts; Sch Mus; Sch Pl; Sct Actv; Stg Crw; Stu Cncl; Ohio Northern Univ; Pharmacy.

FRANTZ, LARRY; Central Catholic HS; Massillon, OH; 50/247 Hon Rl; IM Sprt; Univ Of Dayton; Chemistry.

FRANTZ, NEAL; Whitko HS; Sidney, IN; Cls Rep Frsh Cls; Pres Soph Cls; Cl Rep Jr Cls; Chrs; Chrh Wkr; Pres FCA; NHS; College.

FRANTZ, WENDY; Eaton HS; Eaton, OH; 5/195 Drl Tm; Hon Rl; Jr NHS; Lbry Ade; 4-H; Fr Clb; Pep Clb; GAA; 4-H Awd; College; Journalism.

FRANZ, BLAINE; Edgerton HS; Edgerton, OH; 4/70 Pres Frsh Cls; Pres Jr Cls; VP Sr Cls; Am Leg Boys St; Hon Rl; NHS; Bsbl; Ftbl; Wrstlng; College; Forestry.

FRANZ, ERIC; Black River HS; W Salem, OH; Hon Rl; NHS; Treas 4-H; Ger Clb; 4-H Awd; College.

FRANZ, JOANNE; Andrean HS; Schererville, IN; 50/272 Cls Rep Frsh Cls; Hon Rl; Off Ade; Univ Of Evansville; Paralgl Std.

FRANZ, MILLIE; Kenton Sr HS; Kenton, OH; Hon Rl; Ohio St Univ; Foreign Lang.

FRANZ, TONI; Chippewa Hills HS; Stanwood, MI; Band; Debate Tm; Hon Rl; Orch; Spn Clb; Chrldng; Ferris St Coll; Radiolgc X Ray Tech.

FRANZ, TONY; Mackinaw City HS; Mackinaw City, MI; 5/25 Trs Frsh Cls; Trs Soph Cls; Cls Rep Soph Cls; Cl Rep Jr Cls; Cls Rep Sr Cls; Aud/Vis; Band; Hon Rl; Sch Pl; Stg Crw; Saginaw Vly St Coll; Bus Mgmt.

FRANZE, JEFF; Bellmont HS; Decatur, IN; Cls Rep Soph Cls; Pres Jr Cls; Stu Cncl; Rptr Sch Nwsp; DECA; Spn Clb; Letter Wrstlng; Coach Actv; NEIAC All Conf In Wrstlng 77 79; IHSAA Particpnt Awd For Outstndg Achvmnt In Wrstlng 77 79; Iowa Univ; Tchr.

FRANZE, LINDA; East HS; Akron, OH; 13/344 Chrs; Hon Rl; Hosp Ade; Mat Maids; Natl Merit Ltr; Ladies Aux For Essay Citation 77; Fine Art Achvmnt 75 & 76; Univ; Nursing.

FRANZEN, GARY; Beavercreek HS; Dayton, OH; 1/702 Val; AFS; Debate Tm; Hon Rl; NHS; Ed Sch Nwsp; Capt IM Sprt; Natl Merit SF; Univ; Aero Engr.

FRASCELLO, MARIANN; Barberton HS; Barberton, OH; Band; Hosp Ade; JA; Ger Clb; Ohio State; Mech Engr.

FRASER, ANGELA; Franklin HS; Westland, MI; Hon Rl; JA; Cit Awd; Mic State Univ; Osteopathy.

FRASER, ELIZABETH; Washington Irving HS; Clarksburg, WV; 7/139 Cl Rep Jr Cls; Sec Sr Cls; Am Leg Aux Girls St; Boy Scts; Hon Rl; NHS; Pol Wkr; VP Yth Flsp; Yrbk; Sch Nwsp; College.

FRASER, LISA; Melvindale HS; Melvindale, MI; 5/400 Band; Chrh Wkr; Drl Tm; Girl Scts; Hon Rl; NHS; Mth Clb; Pep Clb; Alma Coll.

FRASIER, CHERI; Reading HS; Montgomery, MI; Cls Rep Soph Cls; Cls Rep Sr Cls; Band; Hon Rl; Off Ade; Stu Cncl; Yth Flsp; Yrbk; Rptr Sch Nwsp; 4-H; Truck Driver.

FRASSINELLI, JANE; Bluefield HS; Bluefield, WV; 41/300 Cls Rep Frsh Cls; Chrh Wkr; Hon Rl; Jr NHS; Rptr Yrbk; Yrbk; Gym; Pres Awd; College; Religion.

FRASUR, TERRY; Union County HS; Liberty, IN; 14/128 Chrs; Hon Rl; Rptr Yrbk; Pep Clb; Bsktbl; Trk; Mgrs; Tech Coll; Architectural Engr.

FRASURE, LISA D; Fairfield Union HS; Bremen, OH; 10/158 Band; Chrh Wkr; Drl Tm; Girl Scts; Hon Rl; Jr NHS; Orch; Rptr Yrbk; Rptr Sch Nwsp; 4-H; Spanish Schlrshp Team; College; Medicine.

FRASURE, SHARON; Walkerville HS; Walkerville, MI; 2/31 Pres Frsh Cls; Sec Sr Cls; NHS; Bsktbl; Chrldng; Northern Michigan Univ; Nursing.

FRATE, CHRIS; Gilmour Academy; Shaker Hts, OH; Hon Rl; Lit Mag; NHS; Sch Nwsp; Univ.

FRATE, DANIEL; Benedictine HS; S Euclid, OH; Boy Scts; Hon Rl; Jr NHS; NHS; Fr Clb; Ftbl; Cleveland St Univ; Pre Law.

FRATINO, PHILIP; Lake Catholic HS; Willoughby, OH; Cls Rep Sr Cls; Chrh Wkr; Hon Rl; Wrstlng; IM Sprt; Lakeland Cc & Garfield College; Acct.

FRATTER, R; Griffith HS; Griffith, IN; 21/300 Band; Hon Rl; Sch Pl; Ind Univ; Psych.

FRATUS, MARK; Heath HS; Heath, OH; FCA; Hon Rl; Letter Ftbl; Univ; Law.

FRAVEL, DAVID; Groveport Madison HS; St Paul, MN; 37/353 Chrh Wkr; Fr Clb; Sheaves For Christ Schlrshp To Apostolic Bible Inst 79; Awd By United Pentecostal Church Internatl; Apostolic Bible Inst.

FRAY, CAROLYN; Pymatuning Valley HS; Andover, OH; 25/130 Am Leg Aux Girls St; Chrs; Rptr Sch Nwsp; Am Leg Awd; Kent State Univ; Public Relations.

FRAZER, BRENDA; Seton HS; Cincinnati, OH; Hst Jr Cls; Hon Rl; Hosp Ade; Red Cr Ade; FBLA; OEA; Bus Schl; Bus.

FRAZER, ROBIN; Benton Harbor HS; Benton Hbr, MI; Band; Hon Rl; NHS; Rptr Yrbk; Sec Mth Clb; Univ.

FRAZIER, BEVERLY; Amelia HS; Amelia, OH; 34/300 Am Leg Aux Girls St; Band; Chrs; Hon Rl; Sch Mus; Yth Flsp; Drama Clb; Pep Clb; Merit Choir Awd; Superior Accomplishment Awd Amer Lit; Superior Rating I Solo Voice Contest; Malone Univ; Music.

FRAZIER, CRAIG; Muskegon Sr HS; Muskegon, MI; Cl Rep Jr Cls; Band; NHS; Stu Cncl; 1st Pl Schl Art Show Most Creative; 1st Pl Dist Solo Ensemble A Duet; 2nd Pl St Solo Ensemble A Duet; Univ Of Michigan; Med Research.

FRAZIER, DEBRA; Greencastle HS; Greencastle, IN; Hon Rl; JA; Drama Clb; Pep Clb; Sci Clb; Spn Clb; Scr Kpr; Tmr; De Pauw Univ; Math.

FRAZIER, DONNA; Hilliard HS; Columbus, OH; Cls Rep Frsh Cls; AFS; Chrs; Hon Rl; Jr NHS; Orch; Sch Mus; Stu Cncl; Drama Clb; FDA; Tex Womens Univ; Nurse.

FRAZIER, DOZITA L; Oak Park HS; Oak Park, MI; Chrh Wkr; Lbry Ade; Off Ade; Red Cr Ade; OEA; VICA; Cit Awd; Detroit Coll Of Bus; Legal Sec.

FRAZIER, FAYE; Withrow HS; Cincinnati, OH; Cl Rep Jr Cls; Band; Hon Rl; Pep Clb; VICA; Chrldng; Coll; Exec Sec.

FRAZIER, FRANKIE; Wapakoneta HS; Wapakoneta, OH; Band; Girl Scts; Gym;.

FRAZIER, HAROLD; Engadine Consolidated HS; Naubinway, MI; Trs Soph Cls; Band; Boy Scts; Hon Rl; Sch Pl; Bsbl; Bsktbl; Trk; Univ.

FRAZIER, JAMI; Malabar HS; Mansfield, OH; 22/280 Cl Rep Jr Cls; Cls Rep Sr Cls; Am Leg Aux Girls St; NHS; Treas Stu Cncl; Rptr Yrbk; Mth Clb; Ten; Chrldng; Cit Awd; Univ; Nursing.

FRAZIER, JULIE A; Watervliet HS; Watervliet, MI; 14/91 Cls Rep Soph Cls; Trs Jr Cls; Chrs; Girl Scts; Hon Rl; Lbry Ade; NHS; Off Ade; Sch Mus; Sct Actv; St Of Mi Compt Schlhp 79; Div Sclshp In Eng 79; Lake Michigan Coll; Lib Art.

FRAZIER, LAVONNA; Lockland HS; Cincinnati, OH; 1/65 VP Sr Cls; Capt Drl Tm; Hon Rl; NHS; Pres Stu Cncl; Rptr Yrbk; Pep Clb; Spn Clb; Trk; GAA; Psych.

FRAZIER, LEANNE; Olentangy HS; Delaware, OH; Chrs; Girl Scts; Hon Rl; Sch Mus; Sct Actv; Columbus Coll; Interior Dsgn.

FRAZIER, RAYMOND; West Side Sr HS; Gary, IN; 8/650 Cls Rep Frsh Cls; Cls Rep Soph Cls; Pres Jr Cls; Cls Rep Sr Cls; Aud/Vis; Boy Scts; Chrh Wkr; Cmnty Wkr; Hon Rl; JA; Purdue Univ; Mgmt.

FRAZIER, SHERRIE; Miami Trace HS; New Holland, OH; 26/234 AFS; Hon Rl; Jr NHS; NHS; Sch Pl; Drama Clb; VP FHA; Sci Clb; Capt GAA; Bookkeeping.

FRAZIER, STEPHANIE R; Hughes HS; Cincinnati, OH; Sec Jr Cls; Cl Rep Jr Cls; Hon Rl; Sch Pl; Pep Clb; IM Sprt; Cit Awd; Univ Of Cincinnati.

FRAZIER, STEPHANIE; Carmel HS; Carmel, IN; Cls Rep Frsh Cls; Trs Jr Cls; Cls Rep Sr Cls; Chrs; Hon Rl; Hosp Ade; NHS; Sch Mus; Stg Crw; Stu Cncl; Univ; Nursing.

FREA, DIANE E; Bishop Ready HS; Orient, OH; 5/150 Hon Rl; Jr NHS; NHS; Quill & Scroll; Rptr Yrbk; Rptr Sch Nwsp; Sch Nwsp; College; Psychiatry.

FREBIS, RAY; Ripley Union Lewis HS; Ripley, OH; 1/96 VP NHS; Sch Pl; Treas Stu Cncl; Letter Bsbl; Letter Bsktbl; Am Leg Awd; Rio Grande Coll.

FRECH, ANNETTE; Stow HS; Stow, OH; 10/500 Chrh Wkr; Cmnty Wkr; Hon Rl; Hosp Ade; Lbry Ade; NHS; Stu Cncl; Fr Clb; Sec Pep Clb; IM Sprt; College; Medicine.

FRECK, JANET; Lumen Cordium HS; Bedford, OH; Cls Rep Sr Cls; Hon Rl; Stu Cncl; Spn Clb; GAA; IM Sprt; John Carroll Univ; Psych.

FREDEKING, WILLIAM; Princeton HS; Princeton, WV; 46/327 Chrh Wkr; Cmnty Wkr; FCA; Hon Rl; Jr NHS; Stu Cncl; Sch Nwsp; Fr Clb; Key Clb; Bsktbl; Schlrshp Awd 77; Concord Coll; Pharm.

FREDENBURG, CATHERINE; Mason Sr HS; Mason, MI; Hon Rl; NHS; 4-H; VICA; Letter Crs Cntry; IM Sprt; 4-H Awd; Pres Awd; Michigan St Univ; Agri.

FREDERICK, ANGELA; Charleston HS; Charleston, WV; Pres Frsh Cls; Cls Rep Soph Cls; Cl Rep Jr Cls; Hon Rl; Jr NHS; NHS; Chrldng; Univ Of Ken; Med.

FREDERICK, BETH; Admiral King HS; Lorain, OH; Chrs; Hon Rl; Off Ade; Sch Mus; Gym; Ohio St Univ; Bus Mgmt.

FREDERICK, BILL; Notre Dame HS; Anmoore, WV; Hst Jr Cls; Chrh Wkr; Cmnty Wkr; FCA; Hon Rl; Bsktbl; Ftbl; Glf; Ltr Mn Club; Bus Schl; Bus Mgmt.

FREDERICK, CARLIE; Theodore Roosevelt HS; Wyandotte, MI; 48/425 Cl Rep Jr Cls; Sec Sr Cls; Pres Band; Hon Rl; Treas NHS; Pres Yth Flsp; JA Awd; Natl Merit Schl; Certf Of Good Citizenship 78 & 79; Band Sweetheart 79; Wayne St Univ; Pre Nursing.

FREDERICK, CHARLENE; Mc Auley HS; Cincinnati, OH; Chrs; Chrh Wkr; Rptr Sch Nwsp; Univ; Spec Educ.

FREDERICK, CHRIS; Parkway HS; Rockford, OH; 4/85 Trs Jr Cls; Trs Sr Cls; Pres Band; Hon Rl; VP NHS; Pep Clb; Treas Sci Clb; Pres Spn Clb; PPFtbl; Luthern Schl Of Nursing; RN.

FREDERICK, CHRISTINE; Parkway HS; Rockford, OH; 5/82 Trs Soph Cls; Trs Jr Cls; Trs Sr Cls; Pres Band; Hon Rl; VP NHS; Treas Sci Clb; Pres Spn Clb; PPFtbl; Dnfth Awd; Lutheran Schl Of Nursing; RN.

FREDERICK, CURTIS; Lebanon HS; Lebanon, OH; Boy Scts; Hon Rl; Letter Bsbl; Letter Ftbl; Letter Trk; IM Sprt; Pres Awd; Univ; Conservation.

FREDERICK, KAREN; Lumen Christi HS; Jackson, MI; 22/239 Band; Chrs; Chrh Wkr; Cmnty Wkr; Drm Mjrt; Hon Rl; JA; NHS; PAVAS; Sch Mus; Titan Times Newsppr Cert Of Recngtn 79; Mi Dept Of Educ Schslhp 79; Michigan St Univ; Vet Med.

FREDERICK, KARLA; Crestline HS; Crestline, OH; Cls Rep Frsh Cls; Sec Soph Cls; Sec Jr Cls; Chrs; Hon Rl; Off Ade; Sch Mus; Stu Cncl; Sch Nwsp; Bsktbl; Ohio St Coll; Elem Ed.

FREDERICK, KATHLEEN; Bloomfield Hills Andover HS; Bloomfieldhls, MI; 158/441 Chrs; Chrh Wkr; Drl Tm; Off Ade; Sch Mus; Albion Coll Music Schlrshp 79; Albion Coll; Music.

FREDERICK, MARK; Port Clinton HS; Pt Clinton, OH; Chrs; Hon Rl; College; Bus.

FREDERICK, NINA; Calhoun County HS; Nobe, WV; Band; Chrs; Chrh Wkr; Cmnty Wkr; Drl Tm; Hon Rl; Sch Mus; Stu Cncl; Yth Flsp; 4-H; Voc Schl; Sec.

FREDERICK, SUZANNE; Ann Arbor Huron HS; Ann Arbor, MI; Cls Rep Sr Cls; Chrs; FCA; Pep Clb; Capt Crs Cntry; Letter Gym; Capt Trk; VP GAA; Cit Awd; Opt Clb Awd; Univ Of Michigan; Social Work.

FREDERICKS, RONALD A; Campbell Memorial HS; Campbell, OH; Boy Scts; Chrh Wkr; FCA; Bsktbl; Ftbl; IM Sprt; Univ.

FREDERICKSON, SYDNEY; Nordonia HS; Northfield, OH; PPFtbl; COE 79; Cuyahoga Cmnty Coll; Court Rprtng.

FREDERKING, GINNIE; Euclid HS; Euclid, OH; 30/703 AFS; Band; Chrs; Chrh Wkr; Hon Rl; NHS; Sch Mus; Baldwin Wallace; Elem Educ.

FREDLINE, KAREN; Haslett HS; Haslett, MI; 46/154 Chrs; Chrh Wkr; JA; Mdrgl; Sch Mus; Sch Pl; Brigham Young Univ; Elem Ed.

FREDLOCK, CARLA; Brooke HS; Wellsburg, WV; 1 8/466 Cls Rep Frsh Cls; Cls Rep Soph Cls; Chrs; Chrh Wkr; Hon Rl; Mdrgl; NHS; Orch; Quill & Scroll; Sch Mus; West Virginia Wesleyan Coll; Music.

FREDRICK, PAUL; Terre Haute North HS; Terre Haute, IN; 20/640 Cl Rep Jr Cls; Cls Rep Sr Cls; Am Leg Boys St; Hon Rl; NHS; Off Ade; Stu Cncl; Fr Clb; Key Clb; Ten; De Pauw Univ; Law.

FREDRICKSON, PAULA; Luther L Wright HS; Ironwood, MI; 2/176 Sal; Band; Chrh Wkr; Hon Rl; NHS; Rptr Sch Nwsp; Pep Clb; Ten; Kiwan Awd; Gogebic Comm Coll; Chem Engr.

FREDRICKSON, PETER; Luther L Wright HS; Ironwood, MI; 53/176 Aud/Vis; Boy Scts; Chrh Wkr; Drl Tm; Hon Rl; ROTC; Sch Pl; Sct Actv; Yth Flsp; Yrbk; Gogebic Comm Coll; Multi Media Comm.

FREE, ALMENA; Rogers HS; Michigan City, IN; 25/524 Band; Chrh Wkr; Hon Rl; Hosp Ade; Jr NHS; NHS; Spn Clb; VICA; Ind Univ; Bio Med.

FREE, ANNE; Saint Ursula Acad; Toledo, OH; Hon Rl; Sch Pl; Drama Clb; Fr Clb; Lat Clb; College; History.

FREE, MITCH; Edgerton HS; Edgerton, OH; 5/62 Pres Soph Cls; Sec Sr Cls; Hon Rl; NHS; Spn Clb; Bsbl; Bsktbl; Ftbl; Otterbein Coll.

FREE, PATRICK; Douglas Mac Arthur HS; Saginaw, MI; Band; Boy Scts; Chrh Wkr; Cmnty Wkr; Orch; Sct Actv; Stu Cncl; Rptr Sch Nwsp; Lat Clb; IM Sprt; Mic State; Microbiology.

FREED, DOUGLAS; Redford HS; Detroit, MI; Chrh Wkr; NHS; Univ.

FREED, PAMELA; Ithaca HS; Sumner, MI; 12/133 Band; Hon Rl; Jr NHS; NHS; Stg Crw; Pep Clb; Chrldng; Natl Merit SF; Rotary Awd; Michigan St Univ; Sci.

FREEH, JULIE; Margaretta HS; Castalia, OH; 6/138 Am Leg Aux Girls St; Chrs; Hon Rl; NHS; Off Ade; Stu Cncl; Letter Bsbl; Letter Trk; GAA; Cit Awd; Columbus Tech Inst; Med Lab Tech.

FREEHLING, DONNA; Au Gres Sims HS; Au Gres, MI; Trs Frsh Cls; Trs Jr Cls; Band; Chrh Wkr; Hon Rl; Sprt Ed Yrbk; 4-H; Letter Bsbl; Letter Bsktbl; Letter Trk; USCA Natl Chrldr Champion 79; Ferris St Coll; Cosmetology.

FREELAND, DAVE; East Preston Jr HS; Hopemont, WV; Trs Soph Cls; Pres Jr Cls; Chrh Wkr; Jr NHS; 4-H; Pres FFA; Letter Ftbl; 4-H Awd; St Farmers Degree FFA 79; Coal Miner.

FREELAND, GERARD; Atlanta HS; Atlanta, MI; 2/65 Trs Soph Cls; Hon Rl; NHS; Sch Pl; Stg Crw; Yrbk; Letter Trk; Cit Awd; Univ Of Michigan; Marine Bio.

FREELAND, LEAH; Northeastern HS; Richmond, IN; Hon Rl; Sprt Ed Sch Nwsp; Letter Bsktbl; GAA; IM Sprt; PPFtbl; College; Physical Educ.

FREELAND, LINDA; Benton Central HS; Fowler, IN; 67/232 Cls Rep Soph Cls; Hon Rl; Lbry Ade; Stu Cncl; OEA; Pep Clb; Ten; GAA; Mgrs; Mat Maids; Varsity Vllybl Tm 77; St Officer For Office Educ Assoc Of In 78; Ball St Univ; Voc Educ.

FREELS, JED; Northrop HS; Ft Wayne, IN; 133/582 Boy Scts; Chrs; Chrh Wkr; Cmnty Wkr; PAVAS; Sch Mus; Sch Pl; Stg Crw; Drama Clb; Letter Ftbl; Music Letter 79; Univ; Tchr Of Fine Arts.

FREEMAN, CHRISTIE; Hamilton Southeastern HS; Noblesville, IN; Chrs; Girl Scts; JA; Sec 4-H; Fr Clb; OEA; 4-H Awd; Ball St Univ; Spec Educ.

FREEMAN, COLLEEN; Arthur Hill HS; Saginaw, MI; Hon Rl; NHS; Orch; Sch Mus; Ger Clb; Ten; Delta College; Med.

FREEMAN, DELL; South Point HS; South Point, OH; Band; Chrs; Chrh Wkr; Hon Rl; Stu Cncl; Rptr Sch Nwsp; Beta Clb; FTA; Spn Clb; Ohi Valley College.

FREEMAN, DENISE A; Celina Senior HS; Celina, OH; 45/240 Hon Rl; NHS; OEA; GAA; Scr Kpr;.

FREEMAN, DOUGLAS; Clyde Sr HS; Fremont, OH; Boy Scts; Hon Rl; Sct Actv; Trk; Schlstc Awrd 77 & 79; Air Force; Aero Engr.

FREEMAN, DOUGLAS J; Creston HS; Grand Rapids, MI; Chrh Wkr; Cmnty Wkr; Hon Rl; Jr NHS; NHS; Stu Cncl; Spn Clb; Ftbl; Trk; Am Leg Awd; 1st Pl Winner Writing 1975; PSAT Comm Student 1978; Scholarshop Finlst; Univ; Archt.

FREEMAN, IRVIN; Cadiz HS; Cadiz, OH; Boy Scts; Chrs; Hon Rl; Lbry Ade; Sch Pl; Drama Clb; 4-H; Letter Ftbl; US Army.

FREEMAN, L; Triway HS; Wooster, OH; 40/170 Chrs; Sch Mus; Sch Pl; Drama Clb; 4-H; Chrldng; GAA; 4-H Awd; Univ Of Dayton; Communications.

FREEMAN, LOUISE A; William Henry Harrison HS; W Lafayette, IN; Letter Band; Hon Rl; Rptr Yrbk; 4-H; Fr Clb; Pep Clb; Ten; 4-H Awd; French Hnr Soc 78; Univ.

FREEMAN, MARIE; Scott HS; Madison, WV; Hon Rl; Stg Crw; Pep Clb; Letter Bsktbl; Letter Trk; Honorable Mentn In Bsktbll 78; Honor Banquet 78; Marshall Univ; Parks Mgmt.

FREEMAN, M SUSAN; South Bend St Josephs HS; S Bend, IN; 12/240 Hon Rl; NHS; Quill & Scroll; Yrbk; Drama Clb; Fr Clb; Pep Clb; Spn Clb; Univ Of Notre Dame; Bus.

FREEMAN, RENEE; Tippecanoe HS; Tipp City, OH; 18/196 Cls Rep Frsh Cls; Cls Rep Soph Cls; Cl Rep Jr Cls; Cls Rep Sr Cls; Hon Rl; NHS; Stu Cncl; Ed Sch Nwsp; Wright State Univ; Bus Admin.

FREEMAN, STEVE; Huntington HS; Huntington, WV; Cls Rep Frsh Cls; Am Leg Boys St; Hon Rl; Red Cr Ade; Sprt Ed Yrbk; Key Clb; Ftbl; Trk; Wrstlng; IM Sprt; Univ; Dentistry.

FREEMAN, SUZANNE; Lehman HS; Sidney, OH; Girl Scts; Hon Rl; NHS; Sch Pl; Yrbk; Rptr Sch Nwsp; Drama Clb; FHA; FTA; Univ Of Dayton; Bus.

FREEMAN, TERESA; Avondale Sr HS; Pontiac, MI; 13/255 Cls Rep Frsh Cls; Cls Rep Soph Cls; Cl Rep Jr Cls; Band; Hon Rl; Hosp Ade; Jr NHS; Lbry Ade; NHS; Quill & Scroll; Michigan St Univ; Journalism.

FREEMAN, TINA; Arsenal Tech HS; Indianapolis, IN; Hon Rl; Home Ec Dept Awd Given By The Schl 79; Butler Univ; Home Ec.

FREEMON, DOUG; The Miami Valley Schl; Kettering, OH; Cls Rep Frsh Cls; Band; JA; Orch; Fr Clb; Bsktbl; Scr Kpr; Tmr; Bsktbll Most Improved Plyr 77 78; Boston Coll; Pre Law.

FREER, JANET; Eaton Rapids Sr HS; Eaton Rapids, MI; Band; Chrs; Hon Rl; Lbry Ade; NHS; Sch Mus; Sch Pl; Stg Crw; Yrbk; Regnst Schlsp 79; Vomberg Scslhp 79; Eastern Michigan Univ; Bus Admin.

FREER, JENNIFER; Fairview Area HS; Curran, MI; Fr Clb; College; Med.

FREER, MARK; Memorial HS; St Marys, OH; 32/220 Boy Scts; Chrh Wkr; Hon Rl; Hosp Ade; Sch Mus; Sch Pl; Sct Actv; Stg Crw; Pres Yth Flsp; Drama Clb; Univ; Pre Med.

FREER, REBECCA; Muskegon HS; Muskegon, MI; Cmnty Wkr; JA; PAVAS; Stg Crw; Rptr Sch Nwsp; Sch Nwsp; Letter Bsbl; Letter Ten; JA Awd; Cmnty Mental Health Serv Cert Of Appreciation 77; Michigan Tech Univ; Forestry.

FREES, DEBBIE; Cambridge HS; Cambridge, OH; Cls Rep Frsh Cls; Cls Rep Soph Cls; Capt Band; Chrs; Chrh Wkr; Cmnty Wkr; Hon Rl; Sec NHS; Pres Yth Flsp; Coll; Spec Ed.

FREESE, CAROLYN; Washington Irving HS; Clarksburg, WV; 9/139 Y-Teens; Fr Clb; Lat Clb; West Virginia Univ; Computer Sci.

FREEZE, JOHN; Peebles HS; Peebles, OH; Band; Chrs; Cmnty Wkr; Hon Rl; Lbry Ade; Sch Mus; Sch Pl; Stg Crw; Sch Nwsp; Drama Clb; Ohio State Univ; Photog.

FREGONARA, JOAN; Allen Park HS; Allen Pk, MI; Band; Chrs; Hon Rl; Jr NHS; Orch; Sch Mus; Sch Pl; Stg Crw; Drama Clb; Ten; Univ Of Michigan; Med.

FREIBURGER, JULIE; Bishop Dwenger HS; Ft Wayne, IN; Chrs; Chrh Wkr; Cmnty Wkr; Hon Rl; Yth Flsp; Eng Cert Of Hon; French & Bio Cert Of Hom & Amer Lit Awd; Chem Cert Of Hon Hon Rol Med; Univ; Chem Engr.

FREIER, RENEE; Ann Arbor Pioneer HS; Ann Arbor, MI; Chrs; Chrh Wkr; Girl Scts; Hon Rl; Sch Mus; Sch Pl; Sct Actv; Yrbk; Sch Nwsp; Drama Clb; Univ Of Michigan; Law.

FREIRE, MICHAEL; St Ignatius HS; Parma, OH; Chrh Wkr; Cmnty Wkr; Hon Rl; Pres Mod UN; Natl Forn Lg; Pol Wkr; Treas Yth Flsp; IM Sprt; Scr Kpr; Tmr; Kenyon College; Intrntl Reltns.

FRELLO, ROBERT; A D Johnston HS; Bessemer, MI; Trs Soph Cls; Trs Jr Cls; Letter Bsbl; Letter Bsktbl; Letter Ftbl; Letter Ten; Gogebic; Acctg.

FREMGEN, SUE; Archbishop Alter HS; Kettering, OH; 28/331 Girl Scts; Hon Rl; NHS; Stu Cncl; Drama Clb; Fr Clb; Pep Clb; Letter Trk; GAA; Mgrs; Univ Of Dayton; Math.

FRENCH, BRENDA; Cardington Lincoln HS; Cardington, OH; Am Leg Aux Girls St; Chrs; Drm Bgl; FCA; Marion Tech Coll; Leg Sec.

FRENCH, BRETT; Ouid Elsie HS; Owosso, MI; Band; Boy Scts; Hon Rl; Sct Actv; Yth Flsp; 4-H; FFA; Crs Cntry; Ftbl; Wrstlng; Michigan St Univ; Vet.

FRENCH, CURTIS; Edwardsburg HS; Edwardsburg, MI; Cls Rep Frsh Cls; Cls Rep Soph Cls; Band; Boy Scts; Drm Bgl; Hon Rl; Sct Actv; Letter Bsbl; Wrstlng; Purdue Univ; Engr.

FRENCH, CYNTHIA; Malabar HS; Mansfield, OH; 50/287 Cls Rep Sr Cls; Band; Chrs; Cmnty Wkr; Girl Scts; Hon Rl; JA; Red Cr Ade; Sch Mus; Stu Cncl; College; History.

FRENCH, DEBORAH; Richmond HS; Richmond, IN; 14/550 Chrh Wkr; Hon Rl; Jr NHS; NHS; Quill & Scroll; VP Y-Teens; DAR Awd; Oral Roberts Univ; Med.

FRENCH, DONNA; Schoolcraft HS; Schoolcraft, MI; Band; Chrh Wkr; Hon Rl; NHS; Red Cr Ade; Yth Flsp; 4-H; Fr Clb; 4-H Awd; Olivet Nazarene Coll; LPN.

FRENCH, GREGORY; Shortridge HS; Indianapolis, IN; 4/450 Boy Scts; Chrh Wkr; Hon Rl; Treas NHS; Sct Actv; Yth Flsp; 4-H; Mth Clb; DAR Awd;.

FRENCH, STEVEN; Gladwin HS; Gladwin, MI; Cls Rep Frsh Cls; Cls Rep Soph Cls; Pres Sr Cls; Hon Rl; NHS; Stu Cncl; Bsbl; Central Mic Univ.

FRENCH, TERESA; Connersville Sr HS; Connersville, IN; Cls Rep Frsh Cls; Cls Rep Soph Cls; Cl Rep Jr Cls; Cls Rep Sr Cls; Hon Rl; Stu Cncl; Spn Clb; Bsktbl; IM Sprt; 4-H Awd; Honorary Hoosier Schlrshp Awd; Indiana Univ; Comp Sci.

FRENCH JR, BARRY; Clio HS; Montrose, MI; 14/400 Cls Rep Sr Cls; Band; NHS; Pol Wkr; Sch Pl; Stu Cncl; Drama Clb; Pres Spn Clb; Univ Of Michigan; Pre Law.

FRENS, GREGORY; Fremont Public HS; Newaygo, MI; 40/235 Hon Rl; Lbry Ade; Sch Pl; Rptr Yrbk; Yrbk; Sch Nwsp; Natl Merit SF; Natl Merit Schl; Gerger Baby Food Schlrshp; Paris Studio Of Photog Schlrshp; Mi Interschlstc Press Assoc Awd; Lansing Cmnty Coll; Photog.

FRERICHS, DONALD J; East Kentwood HS; Hudsonville, MI; CAP; Hon Rl; Lbry Ade; Grank Rapids Jr College; Data Proc.

FRESHWATER, MICHAEL; Brooke HS; Wellsburg, WV; 23/403 Boy Scts; Hon Rl; Lit Mag; Off Ade; Sch Mus; Stu Cncl; Ger Clb; Pres Key Clb; Kiwan Awd; Univ; Med.

FREUDENBERG, JANA K; Princeton Community HS; Princeton, IN; Cl Rep Jr Cls; Girl Scts; Stu Cncl; 4-H; Mth Clb; Pep Clb; Spn Clb; 4-H Awd; College; Radio Tech.

FREUDENBERG, RACHEL; Kingswood Schl; Lathrup Vlg, MI; Chrs; Hon Rl; Jr NHS; Lbry Ade; Mdrgl; Sch Mus; Sch Pl; Rptr Yrbk; Rptr Sch Nwsp; Drama Clb; Univ; Natural Sci.

FREUDENSCHUSS, H; Belmont HS; Dayton, OH; Trs Jr Cls; Trs Sr Cls; Band; Drl Tm; Hosp Ade; NHS; Off Ade; Orch; Red Cr Ade; Ed Yrbk; Wright St Univ.

FREY, ANDY; Purcell HS; Cincinnati, OH; 14/200 Cl Rep Jr Cls; Hon Rl; Bsktbl; Chrldng; IM Sprt; Ohio State Univ; Electrical Engr.

FREY, CAROL; Acad Of The Immaculate Conce; Cincinnati, OH; VP Frsh Cls; Sec Soph Cls; Sec Jr Cls; Chrs; Girl Scts; Hon Rl; Hosp Ade; NHS; Sch Mus; VP Stu Cncl; Univ Of Cincinnati; Art.

FREY, DEBI; Heritage Christian HS; Indianapolis, IN; Band; Chrh Wkr; Hon Rl; Stg Crw; Yth Flsp; Rptr Yrbk; Bsktbl; Socr; Trk; GAA; Univ; Sci.

FREY, JANE T; Brookville HS; Cedar Grv, IN; 5/200 Sec Frsh Cls; Hon Rl; NHS; Pres 4-H; Ger Clb; Mgrs; 4-H Awd; Coll Of Mt St Joseph; Med Lab Tech.

FREY, JANET; Bishop Fenwick HS; Middletown, OH; 3/89 Trs Sr Cls; Sec Band; Hon Rl; NHS; Stu Cncl; Fr Clb; Coll Of Mt St Joseph; Elem Ed.

FREY, JOHN; Purcell HS; Cincinnati, OH; Hon Rl; Yrbk; Sch Nwsp; Spn Clb; Glf; IM Sprt; Univ; Graphic Design.

FREY, KELLY; Franklin Monroe HS; Bradford, OH; 16/76 Cls Rep Soph Cls; Am Leg Aux Girls St; Sec Band; Chrs; Hon Rl; Off Ade; Sch Pl; Stu Cncl; Rptr Yrbk; Rptr Sch Nwsp; Univ Of Cincinnati; Acctg.

FREY, LINDA; Colerain HS; Cincinnati, OH; Chrs; Chrh Wkr; Hon Rl; Sch Mus; Sch Pl; Drama Clb; FTA; Ger Clb; Pep Clb; Univ Of Cincinnati; Tchr.

FREY, LINDA; Michigan Lutheran HS; Battle Crk, MI; Aud/Vis; Band; Chrs; Chrh Wkr; Hon Rl; Off Ade; Orch; Trk; Dr Martin Lutheran College; Teach.

FREY, NYLA; Dayton Christian HS; New Carlisle, OH; 16/92 Hon Rl; NHS; Spn Clb; Trk; Goshen Coll; Education.

FREY, RUSSELL; Napoleon HS; Jackson, MI; Hon Rl; Mgrs; Univ; Marine Sci.

FREY, VICTOR; Brookville HS; Cedar Grove, IN; 10/200 Hon Rl; NHS; Sch Nwsp; 4-H; FFA; Crs Cntry; Trk; 4-H Awd; Purdue; Agri.

FREYBERGER, JEAN; Houghton HS; Houghton, MI; 1/115 Treas Girl Scts; Hon Rl; Ed Yrbk; Letter Swmmng; PPFtbl; Macalester College.

FREYGANG, W; Elmhurst HS; Ft Wayne, IN; 17/320 Boy Scts; Chrh Wkr; FCA; Hon Rl; Mth Clb; Ftbl; Socr; Wrstlng; Cit Awd; Purdue Univ; Aeronautical Engr.

FREY JR, JOHN; St Xavier HS; Cincinnati, OH; 204/264 Pres Sr Cls; Cmnty Wkr; Hon Rl; Bsbl; Bsktbl; Ftbl; IM Sprt; Natl Merit Ltr; Natl Merit Schl; Miami Univ; Acctg.

FRICHTEL, LINDA; Woodrow Wilson HS; Youngstown, OH; 32/334 Hon Rl; Hosp Ade; Lbry Ade; NHS; Red Cr Ade; Y-Teens; Key Clb; Keyettes; Pom Pon; Kiwan Awd; Youngstown State; Physical Therapy.

FRICHTL, KATHLEEN; Bishop Noll Institute; Calumet City, IL; 111/321 Chrs; Chrh Wkr; Cmnty Wkr; Drl Tm; Girl Scts; Hon Rl; Sch Mus; Sct Actv; Civ Clb; Letter Swmmng; Univ; Bus.

FRICK, ANITA; Philo HS; Zanesville, OH; Chrs; Chrh Wkr; Hon Rl; Sch Mus; Sec Yth Flsp; Ger Clb; GAA; Muskingum Area Tech Coll; Sec Sci.

FRICK, PAUL E; Brandon HS; Ortonville, MI; Chrh Wkr; Hon Rl; Sch Pl; Yth Flsp; Glf; Ten; Trk; Scr Kpr; Tmr; Univ Of Michigan; Law.

FRICK, STEPHEN; Sacred Heart Acad; Mt Pleasant, MI; Val; Boy Scts; Hon Rl; NHS; Lat Clb; Mth Clb; Natl Merit SF; Natl Merit Schl; Houghton Mic; Math.

FRICKE, DAVE; Northwest HS; Canal Fulton, OH; 15/181 Am Leg Boys St; Hon Rl; NHS; Lat Clb; Crs Cntry; Wrstlng; College; Bio.

FRICKE, JOHN; Fulton HS; Middleton, MI; 20/89 Boy Scts; 4-H; FFA; Mth Clb; Bsktbl; Letter Ftbl; Michigan St Univ; Agri.

FRICKE, WADE M; Westlake HS; Westlake, OH; 6/287 Cls Rep Frsh Cls; Pres Soph Cls; Cls Rep Soph Cls; Pres Jr Cls; Cl Rep Jr Cls; Am Leg Boys St; Chrs; Hon Rl; Jr NHS; NHS; Coaches Awd 76; Univ; Med.

FRICKER, TRACY; Libbey HS; Toledo, OH; Band; Hon Rl; JA; NHS; Ohio State; Veterinary Medicine.

FRIDDLE, KEVIN; Alcona HS; Barton City, MI; Band; Boy Scts; Chrh Wkr; Hon Rl; Rptr Yrbk; 4-H; Ftbl; Trk; Cit Awd; Received Schlrshp Thrue St Of Mich; Ath Of Yr Awd From Alcona High; Received Duke Sterling Awd From Alcona; Lake Superior St Univ; CPA.

FRIDLEY, KATHY; Groveport Madison HS; Groveport, OH; Band; Chrh Wkr; Cmnty Wkr; Hon Rl; NHS; Orch; Sch Mus; Drama Clb; Fr Clb; 4-H Awd; Ohio St Univ; Theatre.

FRIEDEMAN, DAN; Lutheran East HS; St Clair Shores, MI; Band; Hon Rl; Univ; Elec.

FRIEDMAN, AMIE; Southfield HS; Southfield, MI; Chrh Wkr; Hon Rl; Lbry Ade; Off Ade; Fr Clb; College; Med.

FRIEDMAN, JILL; Firestone HS; Akron, OH; 44/365 Band; Chrs; Drl Tm; Hon Rl; NHS; Sch Mus; Pep Clb; Twrlr; Univ.

FRIEDMAN, MITCH; Malabar HS; Mansfield, OH; 18/283 Cls Rep Soph Cls; Trs Jr Cls; Trs Sr Cls; Hon Rl; Jr NHS; NHS; Rptr Yrbk; Mth Clb; College.

FRIEDMAN, TOD; North Farmington HS; W Bloomfield, MI; Chrh Wkr; Hon Rl; Brandeis Univ Mich State; Bus Admin.

FRIEDRICHS, NECIA M; Wheeling Park HS; Wheeling, WV; Debate Tm; Hon Rl; Yth Flsp; Beta Clb; 4-H; Pep Clb; Bsbl; Swmmng; Tmr; Univ Of Georgia; Biology.

FRIEL, GREG; Pocohontas County HS; Marlinton, WV; 1/125 Cl Rep Jr Cls; Hon Rl; NHS; Quill & Scroll; Rptr Yrbk; Rptr Sch Nwsp; Klassrm Kwuz T V Quiz Show Team; Quiz A Matic News Bowl T V Quiz Show Team; Univ; Med.

FRIEND, CARLA; Warren Western Reserve HS; Warren, OH; 48/477 Chrh Wkr; Hon Rl; JA; Jr NHS; NHS; Treas Stu Cncl; Pres Yth Flsp; Y-Teens; Rptr Yrbk; Fr Clb; Ohio St Univ.

FRIEND, DARIN; Quincy HS; Coldwater, MI; Trs Frsh Cls; Trs Soph Cls; Trs Jr Cls; Hon Rl; Jr NHS; NHS; 4-H; Letter Bsbl; Letter Bsbl; Letter Ftbl;.

FRIEND, LAURA; Brookville HS; Connersville, IN; Hon Rl; Indiana Tech Univ; Comp Sci.

FRIEND, MELINDA; Keyser HS; Keyser, WV; Hon Rl; Stu Cncl; Pres Lat Clb; VICA; Scndry Enrchmnt Progr 78; Potomac St Coll; History.

FRIERSON, ALLISON; Our Lady Of Mercy HS; Detroit, MI; Cls Rep Sr Cls; Pol Wkr; Sch Nwsp; Univ Of S Calif; Psych.

FRIERSON, FRANCES; John May HS; Cleveland, OH; 32/251 Cls Rep Sr Cls; Off Ade; Rptr Yrbk; Cit Awd; Kent St Univ; Soc Work.

FRIES, DOUG; Ada HS; Ada, OH; 5/94 Cmnty Wkr; Hon Rl; Jr NHS; NHS; Sch Pl; Fr Clb; Bsbl; Bsktbl; Crs Cntry; College; Busns.

FRIES, JOEL; Monroeville HS; Monroeville, OH; Am Leg Boys St; Hon Rl; FFA; Bsbl; Ftbl; Agri Mech.

FRIES, MARY M; Columbia City Jt HS; Columbia City, IN; Band; Chrh Wkr; Hon Rl; NHS; Stu Cncl; Yrbk; 4-H; FFA; FNA; Pep Clb; Purdue Univ; Animal Sci.

FRIESEN, ANNE; Gladwin HS; Gladwin, MI; 15/146 VP Sr Cls; Band; Chrh Wkr; Hon Rl; NHS; Stu Cncl; N Cntrl Michigan Coll; Resprtry Ther.

FRIESENBORG, TRUDY; Fairmont West HS; Kettering, OH; 7/468 Aud/Vis; Band; Chrh Wkr; Hon Rl; Orch; Stg Crw; Yth Flsp; Fr Clb; Mth Clb; Pep Clb; Dragon Bell Awd In Foreign Lang French; Natl French Test 3rd In St 7th In Region; Coll; Law.

FRIESS, BRENT; Corunna HS; Corunna, MI; Am Leg Boys St; Boy Scts; Hon Rl; Letter Bsbl; Bsktbl; Letter Ftbl; Swmmng; Trk; All Confrnc In Bsbl 79; Lansing Cmnty Coll; Truck Driver.

FRIIHAUF, DAVID; Berkshire HS; Burton, OH; 24/132 AFS; Band; Chrs; Hon Rl; Pres MMM; Off Ade; PAVAS; Sch Pl; Stg Crw; Drama Clb; Bowling Green St Univ; Brdcstng.

FRINK, CARLA; Fountain Central HS; Kingman, IN; 28/135 Cls Rep Soph Cls; Band; Drl Tm; Hon Rl; NHS; Stu Cncl; Rptr Sch Nwsp; Lat Clb; Bsktbl; Trk; Miss Cngnlty Fountaincnty Fair 78; Butler Univ; Psych.

FRISBEE, SUSAN; Lexington HS; Mansfield, OH; 8/260 Trs Soph Cls; Trs Jr Cls; Jr NHS; NHS; Stu Cncl; Y-Teens; Fr Clb; Key Clb; Trk; Chrldng; Univ Of Toledo; Educ.

FRISCHKORN, MARGARET; Madison Heights HS; Anderson, IN; Band; Hon Rl; NHS; Gym; Trk; College; Engr.

FRISCHKORN, MARY; Anderson HS; Anderson, IN; 24/433 Cl Rep Jr Cls; Treas Boy Scts; FCA; Hon Rl; NHS; Ger Clb; Pep Clb; Letter Bsktbl; Trk; College.

FRIST, JEFFREY; Marion HS; Gas City, IN; Hon Rl; Orch; Sch Mus; Sch Pl; Drama Clb; Fr Clb; Sci Clb; Ind Univ; Pre Med.

FRISTICK, CHERYL; John Glenn HS; Westland, MI; Chrs; Hon Rl; Fr Clb; Univ Of Michigan; Pharm.

FRITCH, RANDALL; River Valley HS; Marion, OH; 43/193 Chrs; Chrh Wkr; Stg Crw; Stu Cncl; Yth Flsp; 4-H; Fr Clb; Bsktbl; Capt Ftbl; Ohi State Univ; Agri Bus.

FRITH, RODNEY; Brown County HS; Nineveh, IN; Hon Rl; College; Engr.

FRITINGER, AMY; Lake Catholic HS; Pnsvl, OH; Chrs; Hon Rl; Hosp Ade; Lit Mag; NHS; Sch Mus; Sch Pl; Stg Crw; PPFtbl; Univ; Comp Sci.

FRITSCH, JULIE; River Valley HS; Three Oaks, MI; Hon Rl; Spn Clb; Bus Schl; Acctg.

FRITTS, JOHN; Mount View HS; Gary, WV; 34/248 Cls Rep Frsh Cls; Am Leg Boys St; Chrh Wkr; Hon Rl; Jr NHS; NHS; Sch Pl; Key Clb; Letter Ftbl; Letter Trk; Marshall Unvi; Pre Architecture.

FRITZ, BETH; Beaver Local HS; E Liverpool, OH; Cls Rep Sr Cls; Am Leg Aux Girls St; Band; Chrs; NHS; Sch Mus; Yrbk; College; Med Tech.

FRITZ, CELIA; Whitehall Yearling HS; Whitehall, OH; Cls Rep Frsh Cls; Cls Rep Soph Cls; Cl Rep Jr Cls; Cls Rep Sr Cls; Off Ade; Stu Cncl; Bsbl; Capt Bsktbl; Capt Ten; Capital Univ; Bus Admin.

FRITZ, CONSTANCE; Olivet HS; Olivet, MI; Aud/Vis; Cmp Fr Grls; Chrs; Hon Rl; Lbry Ade; Off Ade; JA Awd; Pres Awd;.

FRITZ, JAMES; Medina Sr HS; Medina, OH; 19/359 Cls Rep Frsh Cls; Am Leg Boys St; Chrs; Cmnty Wkr; Hon Rl; Jr NHS; NHS; Sch Mus; Sch Pl; Stu Cncl; USAFA; Engr.

FRITZ, JAN; Garden City West HS; Garden City, MI; Band; Drl Tm; Girl Scts; Hon Rl; JA; Sct Actv; 4-H; 4-H Awd; College; Writing.

FRITZ, JIM; Rensselaer Central HS; Rensselaer, IN; 12/170 Coll; Operations Research.

FRITZ, KATHY S; Clyde Sr HS; Clyde, OH; 5/213 Hon Rl; NHS; Sch Mus; Ed Sch Nwsp; FBLA; OEA; IM Sprt;.

FRITZ, KAYE; Centennial HS; Columbus, OH; 1/213 Hst Sr Cls; Val; Am Leg Aux Girls St; Chrs; Chrh Wkr; Hon Rl; Hosp Ade; Jr NHS; Lbry Ade; Lit Mag; Stu Advisor Of Newspaper & Yrbk; Academic Achvmtn Awd; Humanitarian Awd; College; Journalism.

FRITZ, NANCY; Waterford Township HS; Pontiac, MI; Cls Rep Frsh Cls; Cls Rep Soph Cls; Chrs; Cmnty Wkr; Girl Scts; Hon Rl; NHS; Off Ade; Pol Wkr; Sch Mus; Central Michigan Univ.

FRITZ, PAULA; Inland Lakes HS; Indian River, MI; Hon Rl; Bsktbl; Trk; GAA; College; Science.

FRITZ, TINA; Garden City West HS; Garden City, MI; Cl Rep Jr Cls; Girl Scts; NHS; Stu Cncl; Drama Clb; Ger Clb; Bsbl; Bsktbl; Tmr; Univ Of Michigan; Phys Ther.

FRITZINGER, J STEVEN; Parkway HS; Celina, OH; 17/96 Boy Scts; Debate Tm; Hon Rl; Sec Yth Flsp; Sci Clb; Univ; Comp Sci.

FRITZINGER, STEVEN; Parkway HS; Celina, OH; 17/98 Am Leg Boys St; Chrh Wkr; Sci Clb; Univ; Comp Sci.

FRITZSCHE, APRIL; Green HS; Akron, OH; 10/325 Drl Tm; Hon Rl; Drama Clb; Pres Fr Clb; Pep Clb; Gym; IM Sprt; Pom Pon; College; Fashion Mdse.

FRITZSCHE, DANA; Hamilton Taft HS; Hamilton, OH; 35/350 AFS; Band; Hon Rl; JA; Lit Mag; Ger Clb; Pep Clb; Swmmng; GAA; College.

FRIZZELL, JEFF; Portage Northern HS; Portage, MI; Hon Rl; Mod UN; NHS; Ger Clb; Univ Of Michigan; Busns.

FRIZZELL, REGINA; Eastern HS; Pekin, IN; Chrh Wkr; Cmnty Wkr; Lbry Ade; Sch Pl; Yth Flsp; Yrbk; Drama Clb; 4-H; GAA; 4-H Awd; Sunshine 4 Yr Pin 79; Cincinnati Bible Coll; Voice.

FRIZZELL, SUE; Hammond Baptist HS; Hammond, IN; 4/73 Chrs; Chrh Wkr; Hon Rl; NHS; Sch Mus; Yth Flsp; Ger Clb; Pep Clb; Coopertn Awrd 1976; Hyles Anderson Coll; Elem Educ.

FROEDGE, ERIC; Southmount HS; Crawfordsville, IN; 34/175 Am Leg Boys St; FCA; Hon Rl; Jr NHS; Pep Clb; Spn Clb; Bsktbl; Univ; Hist.

FROEHLICH, J; East Palestine HS; E Palestine, OH; Cls Rep Sr Cls; Band; Chrs; Sec Cmnty Wkr; Off Ade; Sch Pl; Stu Cncl; Spn Clb; Ten; Ohi State; Airlines.

FROEHLICH, PAUL M; Barnesville HS; Barnesville, OH; 35/125 Cls Rep Sr Cls; Hon Rl; NHS; Stg Crw; Pres Stu Cncl; Drama Clb; Fr Clb; VP FFA; De Kalb Awd Achvmnt In Agri 78; Star Chaptr Farmer Awd 78 & 79; Ohio St Univ; Voc Agri Educ.

FROEHLICH, WILLIAM; Tell City HS; Tell City, IN; 38/231 Hon Rl; Spn Clb; Univ; Chem Sci.

FROHMADER, JUDY; Sault Area HS; Slt Ste Marie, MI; Chrs; Chrh Wkr; Hon Rl; Hosp Ade; Mdrgl; NHS; Lat Clb; Lake Superior State College; Nursing.

FROHRIEP, DENISE C; Colon HS; Colon, MI; 10/85 VP Soph Cls; VP Jr Cls; VP Sr Cls; Band; Chrh Wkr; Drm Mjrt; Girl Scts; Hon Rl; NHS; Sch Mus; Univ; Bus Admin.

FROMAN, PAUL D; Marlington HS; Minerva, OH; 24/284 Boy Scts; Hon Rl; Sct Actv; Yth Flsp; 4-H; Spn Clb; Letter Ten; Cornell Coll; Engr.

FROMME, CAROL; Central Catholic HS; Toledo, OH; 1/306 Val; Chrh Wkr; Cmnty Wkr; Girl Scts; Hon Rl; Jr NHS; NHS; Univ Of Toledo; Math.

FRONCZEK, ANDREW; Eastlake North HS; Eastlake, OH; Pres Jr Cls; Am Leg Boys St; Pres NHS; Pol Wkr; Ger Clb; Letter Socr; Letter Trk; Am Leg Awd; Bausch & Lomb Awd; Cit Awd; Century III Alternate Sr; Academic Challenge Team Sr; St Sec Ohio Fed Students German Jr; NEDT 10%; Univ; Med.

FRONING, CHARLES; Sidney HS; Sidney, OH; Cl Rep Jr Cls; Chrs; Chrh Wkr; Cmnty Wkr; FCA; Hon Rl; NHS; Bsbl; Bsktbl; Ftbl; Univ.

FRONING, CHUCK; Sidney HS; Sidney, OH; Chrs; Chrh Wkr; Cmnty Wkr; FCA; Hon Rl; NHS; Letter Bsbl; Letter Bsktbl; Letter Ftbl; Coach Actv; Coll; Civil Engr.

FRONT, MARY E; Wheeling Cntrl Catholic HS; Wheeling, WV; 15/137 Chrh Wkr; Hon Rl; JA; NHS; Sch Mus; Sch Pl; Stg Crw; Drama Clb; FNA; JA Awd; Wheeling Coll; Nursing.

FRONTIERO, ROSE; Fraser HS; Fraser, MI; Cls Rep Soph Cls; Band; Girl Scts; Hon Rl; Stu Cncl; Sci Clb; Wayne St Univ; Math.

FRONTZ, GREG; Meadowbrook HS; Byesville, OH; 34/151 Aud/Vis; Hon Rl; Pep Clb; Sci Clb; Letter Ftbl; Trk; Univ; Bio Sci.

FROSSAR, JOE; Anderson HS; Anderson, IN; Hon Rl; Letter Bsbl; Letter Ftbl; Am Leg Awd; Pres Awd; Univ; Indus Mgmt.

FROSSARD, THERESA; Bennett HS; Marion, IN; 3/30 Sec Soph Cls; Trs Soph Cls; Sec Jr Cls; Trs Jr Cls; Hon Rl; NHS; Sch Pl; Stu Cncl; Drama Clb; Fr Clb; College.

FROST, ANN E; Timken Sr HS; Canton, OH; Band; Hon Rl; VP NHS; Stu Cncl; Treas 4-H; IM Sprt; 4-H Awd; Meredith Manor; Riding Instr.

FROST, DEBBIE; Lutheran West HS; Middleburg, OH; Girl Scts; Yrbk; Ger Clb; Pep Clb; Trk; IM Sprt; Cuyahoga Cmnty Coll.

FROST, DEBBIE; Oxford West Campus HS; Leonard, MI; Chrs; Girl Scts; Hon Rl; Sch Mus; Sch Pl; DECA;.

FROST, JAMES; Noui HS; Detroit, MI; 20/250 Cls Rep Frsh Cls; Cl Rep Jr Cls; Aud/Vis; Hon Rl; Sprt Ed Sch Nwsp; Bsbl; Ftbl; Glf; Hockey; Pres Awd; U Of M; Phys Educa.

FROST, SUSAN; Norton HS; Norton, OH; Band; Cmnty Wkr; Drl Tm; Girl Scts; Hon Rl; Jr NHS; Lbry Ade; Off Ade; PAVAS; Sch Pl; Outstndng Math Stu 76; Perfct Attnd 76 76; Univ; Marine Bio.

FROUNFELKER, PAULA; Archbishop Alter HS; Centerville, OH; Hon Rl; NHS; Spn Clb; Letter Bsbl; Letter Bsktbl; Univ Of Dayton; Dental Hygiene.

FRUIT, DEBORAH; Henry Ford II HS; Sterlng Hts, MI; Band; Chrs; Drm Bgl; Girl Scts; VP JA; Off Ade; Sct Actv; Yth Flsp; Sec Eng Clb; Spn Clb; Macomb Cmnty Coll; Psych.

FRUM, MICHELE; Flemington HS; Rosemont, WV; 11/48 Band; Chrs; Hon Rl; NHS; Yth Flsp; Yrbk; 4-H; Fr Clb; FBLA; Pep Clb;.

FRUSH, CANDACE; South Harrison HS; W Milford, WV; 1/86 Val; Band; Hon Rl; Jr NHS; NHS; Sch Pl; Letter Bsktbl; Letter Trk; Bausch & Lomb Awd; Cit Awd; W Virginia Inst Of Tech; Civil Engr.

FRUSH, SANDRA; South Harrison HS; W Milford, WV; Hst Frsh Cls; Hst Jr Cls; Band; Hon Rl; Jr NHS; NHS; Sch Pl; Stu Cncl; Drama Clb; FHA; Comp Sci.

FRUTH, TERESA; Indiana Acad; Arcadia, IN; 5/54 Chrs; Hon Rl; NHS; Sch Nwsp; Southern Missionary Coll.

FRY, CHARLES; Springboro HS; Springboro, OH; Band; Chrs; Hon Rl; NHS; Orch; Ohio Scholastic Test In Amer History 14th Pl Regional; College; Biological Sci.

FRY, DEBBIE; Springboro HS; Franklin, OH; Hon Rl; NHS; 4-H; Chrldng; 4-H Awd; Pres Awd; Pres Of Warren Co Beet Club; Miss Ohio United Teenager Photogenic; Ohio Honey Bee Festival Queens Court;.

FRY, JAMES E; Ceredo Kenova HS; Kenova, WV; Am Leg Boys St; Hon Rl; NHS; Sch Pl; Sprt Ed Yrbk; Drama Clb; Mth Clb; Spn Clb; Bsktbl; Crs Cntry; Marshall Univ; Law.

FRY, JOHN J; Wickliffe Sr HS; Wickliffe, OH; Hon Rl; NHS; Am Leg Awd; Natl Merit Ltr; Case Western Reserve Univ; Elec Engr.

FRY, JUNE; Four Cnty Joint Voc School; Edon, OH; Band; Hon Rl; NHS; VICA; Trade Schl; Cosmetology.

FRY, LINDA; Columbia City Joint HS; Columbia City, IN; Pres Frsh Cls; Cls Rep Soph Cls; Cl Rep Jr Cls; FCA; Pres Natl Forn Lg; NHS; Sch Mus; Sch Pl; Stu Cncl; Rptr Yrbk; Coll; Eng.

FRY, LISA; High School; Toledo, OH; 17/810 Am Leg Aux Girls St; Chrs; Hon Rl; JA; NHS; Sch Mus; Stg Crw; Pep Clb; Letter Socr; PPFtbl; Bowling Green St Univ; Bio.

FRY, MARY; Heritage HS; Monroeville, IN; 25/187 Band; Cmnty Wkr; Girl Scts; Hon Rl; Off Ade; Stu Cncl; 4-H; Gym; IM Sprt; PPFtbl; St Josephs Coll; Sociology.

FRY, MELISSA K; Edon Northwest HS; Edon, OH; 6/69 Am Leg Aux Girls St; Band; Chrs; Hon Rl; NHS; FHA; OEA; Trk; Busns Schl; Exec Sec.

FRY, PAULA; Timken Sr HS; Canton, OH; Letter Band; Chrh Wkr; Girl Scts; Hon Rl; Treas Yth Flsp; IM Sprt; Tmr; Aultman Schl Of Nursing; R N.

FRY, SHARI; Columbiana HS; Columbiana, OH; Cl Rep Jr Cls; Chrh Wkr; Cmnty Wkr; Hon Rl; Jr NHS; Lbry Ade; NHS; Off Ade; Sec.

FRY, SUSAN; Mississinewa HS; Marion, IN; 12/200 Am Leg Aux Girls St; Chrh Wkr; Hon Rl; Jr NHS; NHS; Sch Pl; Stg Crw; Yth Flsp; Drama Clb; 4-H; Univ; Bus.

FRYDLEWICZ, LAURA; North Huron HS; Port Austin, MI; 3/25 Pres Frsh Cls; Hon Rl; Stu Cncl; Treas FHA; Letter Bsbl; Bsktbl; Scr Kpr; Coll; Bus.

FRYE, ABIGAIL; Potterville HS; Potterville, MI; 5/66 Trs Frsh Cls; Trs Soph Cls; Trs Jr Cls; NHS; Univ; Nursing.

FRYE, CINDI; Walnut Ridge Sr HS; Columbus, OH; Hon Rl; Fr Clb; Ger Clb; Natl French Contest Awd Of Merit 79; Whos Who Amer HS Stud 78; PTA Awd Of Merit For French 79; Ohio St Univ; Lang.

FRYE, DEE; L And M HS; Lyons, IN; 8/35 Am Leg Aux Girls St; Band; Chrh Wkr; Beta Clb; 4-H; FHA; Pep Clb; Bsktbl; Pom Pon; 4-H Awd; Univ Of Ind; Data Proc.

FRYE, DIANA; Land M HS; Lyons, IN; 8/35 Am Leg Aux Girls St; Band; Chrh Wkr; Beta Clb; 4-H; FFA; FHA; Letter Bsktbl; Pom Pon; 4-H Awd; Ind State Univ; Data Proc.

FRYE, KAREN; Frankfort Sr HS; Frankfort, IN; 10/280 Band; Chrs; Cmnty Wkr; NHS; Orch; Sch Mus; Stu Cncl; Drama Clb; Fr Clb; Lat Clb; Univ.

FRYE, KENDYL; Chardon HS; Chardon, OH; 31/235 Girl Scts; Jr NHS; NHS; Sch Mus; Sch Pl; Stg Crw; PPFtbl; Cit Awd; DAR Awd; Bowling Green St Univ; Health.

FRYE, KRISTOFER D; Elwood Community HS; Elwood, IN; 30/262 Cls Rep Soph Cls; Cl Rep Jr Cls; Mth Clb; Sci Clb; Mgrs; Ball State; Architecture.

FRYE, RODGER; Cloverdale Clovers HS; Poland, IN; 39/85 Chrs; Sch Mus; Spn Clb; Crs Cntry; Glf; Trk; Coach Actv; Mgrs; Indiana St Univ; US Air Force.

FRYE, SHERRI A; Carey HS; Carey, OH; Hon Rl; NHS; Sch Pl; Yrbk; Drama Clb; Trk; Chrldng; GAA; Univ; Bio.

FRYER, BRENDA; Lakeview HS; Cortland, OH; 15/180 VP Frsh Cls; VP Soph Cls; Sec Jr Cls; Sec S r Cls; Am Leg Aux Girls St; Band; Girl Scts; Hon Rl; VP NHS; Y-Teens; Kent St Univ; Early Chldhd Educ.

FRYER, DOUGLAS; Alma HS; Alma, MI; 5/250 Cls Rep Frsh Cls; Boy Scts; Hon Rl; NHS; Orch; Stu Cncl; Letter Bsktbl; Letter Ftbl; Letter Trk; College; Law.

FRYER, SALLI; Jewett Scio HS; New Rumley, OH; Cmnty Wkr; Hosp Ade; Spn Clb; Gov Hon Prg Awd; Jefferson Tech Schl; Sec.

FRYLING, DEVIN; Mount Vernon Acad; Mt Vernon, OH; Band; Chrs; Chrh Wkr; Hon Rl; Orch; Socr; IM Sprt; Southern Missionay College; Comp Tec.

FRYMAN, ANGELIA; Gods Bible School & College; Burlington, KY; Band; Chrs; Chrh Wkr; Cmnty Wkr; Orch; Sch Mus; Sch Pl; Mth Clb; VICA; Univ Of Kentucky; RN.

FRYMAN, CHRIS; Bellbrook HS; Bellbrook, OH; 8/162 Cls Rep Frsh Cls; Cls Rep Soph Cls; Cl Rep Jr Cls; VP Sr Cls; Hon Rl; NHS; Stg Crw; Ftbl; IM Sprt; Miami Of Ohio Univ; Systms Anlyst.

FRYMIER, MARK; London HS; London, OH; 33/153 Cl Rep Jr Cls; Cls Rep Sr Cls; Am Leg Boys St; Band; Boy Scts; Cmnty Wkr; Hon Rl; Lit Mag; Quill & Scroll; Sch Mus; King Fool Of Jr Class 79; Kathidee Assoc Schlrshp Awd 79; Univ.

FUCHS, ANDREA; Wayne Memorial HS; Westland, MI; Chrs; Cmnty Wkr; Hon Rl; JA; Lbry Ade; Off Ade; Sch Mus; Sec Ger Clb; VP Mth Clb; Bsktbl; Eastern Univ; German.

FUCHS, B; Northeastern HS; Richmond, IN; 16/139 Cls Rep Frsh Cls; Cls Rep Soph Cls; Drl Tm; Hon Rl; NHS; Sch Mus; Stu Cncl; IM Sprt; Coll; Bus.

FUCHS, KEVIN; Southwestern HS; Edinburgh, IN; Band; Chrh Wkr; Cmnty Wkr; Lbry Ade; Off Ade; Yth Flsp; Yrbk; Rptr Sch Nwsp; Drama Clb; 4-H; Bus Schl; Bus Admin.

FUCHS, MARY; Mater Dei HS; Evansville, IN; Cls Rep Frsh Cls; Cls Rep Soph Cls; Cl Rep Jr Cls; Sec Sr Cls; Band; Hon Rl; Stg Crw; Stu Cncl; Indiana St Univ.

FUERST, ANN; Waynesfield Goshen HS; New Hampshire, OH; Pres Frsh Cls; Capt Drl Tm; Hon Rl; NHS; Off Ade; Spn Clb; PPFtbl; Sec.

FUERST, GARY; St Edward HS; Cleveland, OH; 27/309 Hon Rl; IM Sprt; Scr Kpr; Tmr;.

FUERST, JUDY; Delphos St John HS; Delphos, OH; Band; Hon Rl; NHS; Rptr Sch Nwsp; FTA; IM Sprt; Northwestern Bus Coll; Legal Sec.

FUGATE, ANDREW; Parkside HS; Jackson, MI; Chrs; Chrh Wkr; Hon Rl; Sch Pl; Stu Cncl; Letter Ftbl; SAR Awd; Mic Christian College; Comp Oper.

FUGATE, DAVID; Springfield North HS; Springfield, OH; College.

FUGIEL, DAWN; St Ladislaus HS; Detroit, MI; Cls Rep Frsh Cls; Cl Rep Jr Cls; Sec Sr Cls; Chrh Wkr; Cmnty Wkr; Hon Rl; Sch Mus; Sch Pl; Stg Crw; Stu Cncl; Americana Inst; Optician.

FUGO, ALAN; Benedictine HS; Cleveland, OH; Chrs; Hon Rl; MMM; Orch; PAVAS; Sch Pl; Stg Crw; Drama Clb; FBLA; FDA; Cleveland St Univ.

FUHR, NANCY; Sandusky HS; Sandusky, OH; 17/410 Cls Rep Frsh Cls; Cls Rep Soph Cls; Chrs; VP Chrh Wkr; Hon Rl; NHS; Sct Actv; Bowling Green State Univ; Bus Admin.

FUHRHOP, BRENDA; Patrick Henry HS; Hamler, OH; 27/117 Am Leg Aux Girls St; Band; Chrs; Chrh Wkr; Hon Rl; Sch Mus; Bsktbl; Trk; GAA; Dedication Awd In Bsktbl; Outstndng Soph Band Awd; Sr Band Awd; Northwest Tech Univ; Acctg.

FUHRMAN, JOHN; Port Hope Community Schls; Port Hope, MI; Cls Rep Frsh Cls; Cls Rep Soph Cls; Cl Rep Jr Cls; Cls Rep Sr Cls; Boy Scts; Hon Rl; Stu Cncl; Rptr Yrbk; Beta Clb; Rotary Awd; Ctrl Michigan Univ; Acctg.

FUHRMAN, KEN; Northrop HS; Ft Wayne, IN; Band; Hon Rl; Purdue; Agri.

FUHRMAN, MICHAEL; Ionia HS; Ionia, MI; Band; Boy Scts; Hon Rl; Gym; CMU; Bus.

FUHS, CONNIE; Wood Memorial HS; Fort Branch, IN; Chrh Wkr; Cmnty Wkr; FCA; Off Ade; Pol Wkr; OEA; Letter Bsktbl; Trk; Mgrs; Scr Kpr; Vllybl Co Capt Ltr MVP & Mentl Attd Awd; Athltc Schlshp To Oakland City Coll; Phys Educ Stdnt Leadr 3 Yrs; Oakland City Coll; Elem Educ.

FUJAWA, MICHELE; Mishawaka HS; Mishawaka, IN; 29/469 Chrs; Hon Rl; Sch Mus; Fr Clb; Mgrs; DAR Awd; St Marys Coll; Eng.

FUKUNAGA, NINA; West Lafayette Sr HS; W Lafayette, IN; 18/185 Band; Hon Rl; Pep Clb; Letter Bsktbl; Letter Trk; IM Sprt; Purdue Univ; Pre Med.

FULCHER, MIKE; Clay HS; Oregon, OH; Ed Sch Nwsp; Sch Nwsp; Univ; Jrnlsm.

FULEKI, SHARI; Canal Winchester HS; Canal Winch, OH; 27/101 Band; Chrs; Hon Rl; Jr NHS; NHS; Pres Stu Cncl; Drama Clb; Spn Clb; Treas GAA; Rifle Squad Mbr; Vlybl; Miami Univ; Music.

FULK, GINA C; Martinsburg HS; Martinsburg, WV; Cls Rep Frsh Cls; VP Soph Cls; Cls Rep Soph Cls; VP Jr Cls; Band; Hon Rl; Stu Cncl; Keyettes; Chrldng; Univ.

FULK, KIMBERLY; Columbian HS; Tiffin, OH; 11/342 Band; Hon Rl; NHS; Ed Sch Nwsp; 4-H; Bsktbl; Ohio St Univ; Jrnlsm.

FULKERSON, CHRISTINE; Fairview HS; Fairview Park, OH; 35/286 Cmp Fr Grls; Girl Scts; Hon Rl; Off Ade; IM Sprt; College; Acctg.

FULKS, LORI; South Point HS; Chosapeake, OH; Band; Chrh Wkr; Cmnty Wkr; Hon Rl; Hosp Ade; JA; Pol Wkr; Yth Flsp; Rptr Sch Nwsp; Drama Clb; Hugh O Brian Youth Found Awd; College; Psych.

FULKS, MARJORIE; Hardin Northern HS; Dunkirk, OH; 1/65 Cls Rep Frsh Cls; Band; Chrh Wkr; Hon Rl; Stu Cncl; Yth Flsp; Rptr Sch Nwsp; 4-H; Bsktbl; Letter Trk;.

FULKS, MARY; Chalker HS; Southington, OH; Band; Chrs; Chrh Wkr; Cmnty Wkr; Off Ade; Y-Teens; Sch Nwsp; Sci Clb; 1st Alt To Buckeye Girls St; Band Sec & Tres; Y Teens V P; Kent St Univ; Nursing.

FULL, RENEE; Waterloo HS; Atwater, OH; Hon Rl; Off Ade; Pep Clb; IM Sprt; PPFtbl; Scr Kpr;.

FULLENKAMP, JANE; Marion Local HS; Maria Stein, OH; Band; Hon Rl; NHS; 4-H; Pep Clb; Sci Clb; Trk; IM Sprt; 4-H Awd; College; Bus.

FULLENKAMP, STEVE; Jay County HS; Portland, IN; 9/450 Am Leg Boys St; Jr NHS; NHS; Boys Clb Am; Ftbl; Trk; Wrstlng; Am Leg Awd; Catholic Youth Organiz; Ball St Univ; Finance.

FULLER, CHERI; Union HS; Grand Rapids, MI; Chrs; Hon Rl; JA; Cit Awd; JA Awd; College; Comp Progr.

FULLER, DANIEL; Padua Franciscan HS; Broadview Hts, OH; Cmnty Wkr; Hon Rl; Ftbl; Trk; Coach Actv; Ftbll Schlrshp 79; American HS Athlete 78; Ashland Univ; Sports Psych.

FULLER, DARLENE; Reed City HS; Reed City, MI; 14/170 Cls Rep Soph Cls; Am Leg Aux Girls St; Hon Rl; NHS; Sch Mus; Sch Pl; Treas Stu Cncl; Ed Sch Nwsp; 4-H; FHA; Ferris State Coll; Aas Court.

FULLER, GINA; Westerville South HS; Westerville, OH; 20/281 Hon Rl; Off Ade; Sch Mus; Stu Cncl; OEA; Pep Clb; Letter Swmmng; Chrldng; PPFtbl; Scr Kpr; Airline Work.

FULLER, JILL; Lincoln HS; Vincennes, IN; Chrs; Sec FCA; Lbry Ade; Sch Mus; Sch Pl; Drama Clb; FHA; Pres Pep Clb; Letter Ten; Chrldng; Vincennes Univ.

FULLER, KAREN; Bay HS; Bay Village, OH; 4/360 Cls Rep Frsh Cls; Chrh Wkr; Hon Rl; Lit Mag; NHS; Sch Pl; Ed Sch Nwsp; Letter Bsktbl; IM Sprt; PPFtbl; Otstndng Math Stud 76; Teenage Inst On Alcohol & Other Drugs 79; Univ; Finance.

FULLER, LES; Gwinn HS; Skandia, MI; Band; Boy Scts; Hon Rl; Sct Actv; IM Sprt; Mic Tech Univ; Forestry.

FULLER, LISA; Maysville HS; Zanesville, OH; 1/200 Am Leg Aux Girls St; Hon Rl; NHS; Stu Cncl; Yth Flsp; Rptr Yrbk; Sch Nwsp; Trk; Univ; Speech Pathologist.

FULLER, LISA; Withrow HS; Cincinnati, OH; 94/567 Chrs; Chrh Wkr; Hon Rl; JA; Sch Mus; FHA; Ger Clb; Pep Clb; Univ Of Cin; Comp Progr.

FULLER, MICHAEL; Olivet HS; Olivet, MI; 2/96 Hon Rl; NHS; Pres Yth Flsp; FFA; Letter Trk; Kiwan Awd; College; Mech Drafting.

FULLER, T; Clinton HS; Manchester, MI; Band; Hon Rl; NHS; Stg Crw; Spn Clb; Letter Trk; IM Sprt; College.

FULLER, TRACY; Clinton HS; Manchester, MI; Band; NHS; Stg Crw; Spn Clb; Letter Trk; GAA; IM Sprt; PPFtbl; Scr Kpr; Tmr; Most Imprvd Runner In Track 77; Most Valuable Runner In Track 78; 3 Yr Awrd In Track 79; Univ.

FULLERTON, MARILYN; Washington Irving HS; Clarksburg, WV; Treas Band; Hon Rl; Y-Teens; Fr Clb; Wv Univ; Landscape Architecture.

FULLGRAF, DENISE; Griffith HS; Griffith, IN; 59/320 Chrs; Hon Rl; Jr NHS; DECA; Pep Clb; GAA; Scr Kpr; Acctg.

FULLIE, WILLIAM; Richmond Sr HS; Richmond, IN; Cls Rep Soph Cls; Cl Rep Jr Cls; Chrs; Hon Rl; Stg Crw; Stu Cncl; Sch Nwsp; Ftbl; Univ; Bus.

FULLIN, MARGARET; Bishop Watterson HS; Columbus, OH; 23/250 Cls Rep Soph Cls; Chrs; Hon Rl; Jr NHS; Sch Mus; Stu Cncl; Rptr Yrbk; Mth Clb; Mt St Joseph; Chem.

FULMER, CYNTHIA; Green HS; Uniontown, OH; 43/328 Trs Jr Cls; Chrs; Hon Rl; JA; NHS; Y-Teens; Pep Clb; IM Sprt; JA Awd; Akron Univ; Bus Admin.

FULMER, LISA; Danville HS; Danville, IN; Band; Hon Rl; Lbry Ade; Rptr Sch Nwsp; 4-H; Ger Clb; Trk; Purdue Univ; Sci.

FULPER, SEAN; Warren Central HS; Indianapolis, IN; 114/875 Hon Rl; NHS; Pres OEA; Univ Of Indiana; Computer Prog.

FULTE, JANET; Gavit Jr Sr HS; Hammond, IN; 6/250 Cmnty Wkr; Hon Rl; Jr NHS; NHS; Off Ade; Y-Teens; Pres Spn Clb; Hoosier St Schlrshp 79; N Cntrl Cmm 78; Honor Society 79; Indiana Univ N W; Dent Hygn.

FULTON, BENJAMIN; Dayton Christian HS; Troy, OH; Pres Sr Cls; Sch Pl; Crs Cntry; Letter Trk; Mgrs; Michigan St Univ; Horticulture.

FULTON, BRIAN; Terre Haute North HS; Terre Haute, IN; 79/583 Cls Rep Sr Cls; Am Leg Boys St; Chrh Wkr; Hon Rl; Mod UN; Natl Forn Lg; Stu Cncl; Key Clb; Letter Bsbl; Ind State Univ; Industrial Tech.

FULTON, CHERYL L; Defiance Sr HS; Defiance, OH; 23/295 Chrs; Chrh Wkr; Hon Rl; Jr NHS; Sch Mus; Sch Pl; Stg Crw; Yth Flsp; Sci Clb; Spn Clb; Toledo Univ; Medicine.

FULTON, DAVID; Theodore Roosevelt HS; Kent, OH; 28/370 AFS; Hon Rl; Hosp Ade; Quill & Scroll; Yrbk; Spn Clb; Capt Ten; Coll; Med.

FULTON, DAVID; Scott HS; Madison, WV; Cls Rep Frsh Cls; Boy Scts; Hon Rl; Jr NHS; Sct Actv; Stu Cncl; Yth Flsp; VICA; Bsktbl; Marshall Univ.

FULTON, DORIS; Four County Joint Voc HS; Berkey, OH; Trs Jr Cls; Band; Chrs; Hon Rl; Lbry Ade; NHS; Sch Mus; OEA; GAA; Perfect Attendance Awd;.

FULTON, DOUGLAS; Jefferson HS; Jefferson, OH; Cmnty Wkr; Sprt Ed Sch Nwsp; Spn Clb; Bsbl; Bsktbl; Ftbl; Coach Actv; IM Sprt; Scr Kpr; Tmr; Coll; Jrnlsm.

FULTON, EUNICE; Union Bible Seminary; Westfield, IN; Cls Rep Soph Cls; VP Jr Cls; Chrs; Chrh Wkr; Cmnty Wkr; Hon Rl; Hosp Ade; Orch; Stu Cncl; Yth Flsp; Vocl Schl; Nursing.

FULTON, JENNY; Shelby Sr HS; Shelby, OH; Band; Hon Rl; Treas 4-H; Lat Clb; 4-H Awd; Coll; Busns Admin.

FULTON, JULIE; Brookhaven HS; Columbus, OH; Am Leg Aux Girls St; Band; Hon Rl; Jr NHS; Lit Mag; NHS; 4-H; Am Leg Awd; Natl Merit Ltr; College; Behavioral Sci.

FULTON, KAREN; Peebles HS; Peebles, OH; Sec Frsh Cls; Sec Soph Cls; Sec Jr Cls; Band; Chrs; Hon Rl; Ed Yrbk; Drama Clb; FHA; FTA; Morehead Univ; Med.

FULTON, MICHAEL; St Paul HS; Norwalk, OH; 4/58 Am Leg Boys St; Hon Rl; Fr Clb; Mth Clb; Coll; Petroleum Engr.

FULTON, SHARON K; Perry Meridian HS; Indianapolis, IN; 1/567 Cls Rep Frsh Cls; Val; Am Leg Aux Girls St; Band; Chrh Wkr; Drl Tm; Drm Mjrt; Girl Scts; Hon Rl; Jr NHS; De Pauw Univ; Physician.

FULTZ, BETTY; Dodd Ridge Cnty HS; Salem, WV; Lbry Ade; FHA; Pep Clb; VICA; Salem Coll; Nursing.

FULTZ, DEANN; Clyde Sr HS; Clyde, OH; 12/143 Chrs; Hon Rl; Sec NHS; OEA; Wrstlng; Mgrs; Scr Kpr; Mbr Scholastic Soc; 1st Girl Manager For Wrestling; College; Acctg.

FUNG, ALICE; Bishop Watterson HS; Oberlin, OH; Chrs; Chrh Wkr; Hon Rl; JA; NHS; Sch Nwsp; Fr Clb; JA Awd; Oberlin Coll; Archt.

FUNG, LUCY; Stephen T Badin HS; Hamilton, OH; 22/236 Sec Frsh Cls; Cls Rep Soph Cls; Cl Rep Jr Cls; Cls Rep Sr Cls; Hon Rl; NHS; Stu Cncl; Y-Teens; Spn Clb; Opt Clb Awd; Rochurst Univ; Respirtory Therapy.

FUNK, CAROL; Terre Haute N Vigo HS; Terre Haute, IN; Chrs; Drl Tm; Hon Rl; Off Ade; Y-Teens; 4-H; Fr Clb; Sec OEA; Busns Schl.

FUNK, CAROLYN L; N Central HS; Indianapolis, IN; 21/1065 Trs Soph Cls; Hon Rl; NHS; Sch Nwsp; Pep Clb; Swmmng; Coll.

FUNK, DIANE; Frankfort HS; Ft Ashby, WV; Pres AFS; Band; Drl Tm; Hon Rl; Lbry Ade; NHS; Stu Cncl; Mth Clb; Mat Maids; Potomac State; Accntg.

FUNK, J; Belleville HS; Ypsilanti, MI; Cls Rep Frsh Cls; Hon Rl; Rptr Sch Nwsp; Drama Clb; Spn Clb; Eastern Michigan Univ; Bus Admin.

FUNK, KIMBERLY; Crooksville HS; Corning, OH; 13/92 Chrh Wkr; Hon Rl; Sch Pl; Yth Flsp; Bookkeeper.

FUNK, LAURIE; Fayetteville HS; Fayetteville, WV; 45/85 Hon Rl; Off Ade; Rptr Yrbk; Ed Sch Nwsp; Rptr Sch Nwsp; FBLA;.

FUNK, NANCY; Comstock Park HS; Comstock Park, MI; Am Leg Aux Girls St; Hon Rl; Jr NHS; Natl Forn Lg; NHS; Ed Yrbk; Pep Clb; Am Leg Awd; Cit Awd; Opt Clb Awd; Central Michigan Univ; Law.

FUNK, RICHARD; Rossford HS; Rossford, OH; 4/1 47 Am Leg Boys St; Band; Chrh Wkr; NHS; Letter Glf; College; Engr.

FUNKE, MELANIE A; Tipton HS; Tipton, IN; Sec Soph Cls; 4-H; Gym; Chrldng; 4-H Awd; Purdue Univ; Horticulture.

FUNKHOUSER, VICKI; William Henry Harrison HS; Lafayette, IN; 91/281 JA; Pol Wkr; Sec DECA; 4-H; Capt Glf; 1st Place Dist Contest Finance & Credit DECA; 6th Place St Overall Finance & Credit DECA; Franklin College; Law.

FUNNELL, ELIZABETH; Fremont Public HS; White Cloud, MI; Band; Girl Scts; Hon Rl; NHS; Sch Mus; Sct Actv; 4-H; Spn Clb; Michigan St Univ; Vet.

FUNNELL, LUCINDA; Whitehall HS; Whitehall, MI; 34/150 Cls Rep Frsh Cls; Cls Rep Soph Cls; Am Leg Aux Girls St; Band; Chrh Wkr; Girl Scts; Hon Rl; Muskegon Bus College; Data Proc.

FUNTA, JANET; James Ford Rhodes HS; Cleveland, OH; Chrs; Hon Rl; Hosp Ade; NHS; Orch; Ger Clb; IM Sprt; Pom Pon; Cit Awd; Butler Univ; Pharm.

FUQUA, LYNDA; Terre Haute North Vigo HS; Terre Haute, IN; Cls Rep Frsh Cls; Cls Rep Soph Cls; Cl Rep Jr Cls; Cls Rep Sr Cls; Hon Rl; NHS; Off Ade; Sch Pl; Pres DECA; Drama Clb; Hoosier Schlshp 1979; Acad Schlshp In St Univ 1979; 2nd Pl DECA Girl Stdnt Of Yr St Contst 1978; Indiana St Univ; Industrial Tech.

FURBEE, KENNETH; Linsly Inst; Shadyside, OH; ROTC; Ger Clb; Ftbl; IM Sprt; Coll; Hist.

FURBEE, PAM; Bishop Donahue HS; Moundsville, WV; 3/64 Band; Chrs; Chrh Wkr; Hon Rl; Pep Clb; Spn Clb; West Virginia Univ; Civil Engr.

FURBEE, RICHARD; Southern HS; Racine, OH; Pres Jr Cls; Band; Chrh Wkr; Stu Cncl; Rptr Yrbk; Drama Clb; Fr Clb; Sci Clb; Cit Awd; 4-H Awd; Perfect Attendance Awd; Chess Club; Schlrshp Team; College; Math.

FURBEE, RICHARD L; Southern HS; Racine, OH; Pres Jr Cls; Am Leg Boys St; Band; NHS; Stu Cncl; Rptr Yrbk; Drama Clb; Fr Clb; Sci Clb; VICA; Ohio Univ; Elec Engr.

FUREY, SCOTT; Centreville HS; Centreville, MI; Chrs; Hon Rl; Sch Pl; Bsbl; Ftbl; Capt Wrstlng; Drafting.

FURGASON, MARY; Hackett HS; Kalamazoo, MI; Hon Rl; NHS; Yth Flsp; Spn Clb; Bsktbl; Mgrs; PPFtbl; Univ Of Michigan; Phys Therapy.

FURLICH, STEPHAN; A D Johnston HS; Bessemer, MI; Hon Rl; Rptr Sch Nwsp; Letter Ftbl; Trk; IM Sprt; College; Eng.

FURLONG, CHERYL; Royal Oak Dondero HS; Royal Oak, MI; 7/453 Hon Rl; Jr NHS; Lit Mag; NHS; Sec Orch; Sch Mus; Sch Nwsp; Fr Clb; Univ; Acctg.

FURLONG, JANET L; Seton HS; Cincinnati, OH; 41/255 Chrs; Girl Scts; Sch Mus; Rptr Yrbk; VP Spn Clb; Tmr; College; Language.

FURLOW, GERALD; Washington HS; Massillon, OH; Hon Rl; Spn Clb; Univ Of Akron; Md Of Kids.

FURMAN, DINA; Crestview HS; Shelby, OH; Hon Rl; Spn Clb; Mat Maids; Scr Kpr;.

FURNESS, MYRNA; Lake Fenton HS; Fenton, MI; 12/170 Chrh Wkr; Girl Scts; Hon Rl; NHS; Yth Flsp; 4-H; Trk; 4-H Awd; Adrian Coll; Acctg.

FURROW, DONNA S; Shady Spring HS; Shady Spring, WV; Chrh Wkr; Cmnty Wkr; Girl Scts; Lbry Ade; Off Ade; 4-H; FFA; Bsktbl; Trk; Horse Proficiency Medal; Ham Bacon & Egg Show; College.

FURRY, JODI A; North Ridgeville Sr HS; N Ridgeville, OH; 2/350 Pres Chrs; Chrh Wkr; Hon Rl; Mdrgl; Pres NHS; Letter Ten; Whos Who Amg Amer H S Stu 1977; Whos Who In Music 1977; Univ; Organ.

FURST, GWENDOLYN; Andrews Acad; Berrien Spring, MI; Aud/Vis; Kettering College; Nursing.

FURSTENAU, GAYLE; Ovid Elsie HS; Elsie, MI; Sec Frsh Cls; Cls Rep Soph Cls; Cl Rep Jr Cls; Trs Sr Cls; Chrs; Hon Rl; NHS; Sch Mus; Yth Flsp; 4-H; Univ; Med.

FURTAW, MARY E; Rogers City HS; Rogers City, MI; Band; Drl Tm; Hon Rl; Drama Clb; Pep Clb; Trk; Chrldng; Cit Awd; 4-H Awd; Pres Awd; College; Social Work.

FURTO, TONI; Bishop Noll Institute; Hammond, IN; 69/321 Hon Rl; Mth Clb; Knight Of Columbus Awd 76; Ctznapprcntcshp Progr 79; Univ; Lab Tech.

FURTWENGLER, BRET; Loveland Hurst HS; Loveland, OH; 7/251 Cls Rep Sr Cls; Chrh Wkr; Cmnty Wkr; FCA; Hon Rl; Jr NHS; NHS; Stu Cncl; Ed Yrbk; Key Clb; Miami Univ; Finance.

FUSCO, JOHN; St Alphonsus HS; Dearborn, MI; Cls Rep Frsh Cls; Cls Rep Soph Cls; Cl Rep Jr Cls; Chrs; Hon Rl; Jr NHS; Sch Pl; Stu Cncl; Letter Crs Cntry; Letter Trk; Univ; Engr.

FUSCO, PAULA; St Alphonsus HS; Dearborn, MI; 9/181 Cls Rep Frsh Cls; Cls Rep Soph Cls; Trs Jr Cls; VP Sr Cls; Chrs; Hon Rl; NHS; Orch; Sch Mus; Sch Pl; Univ Of Michigan; Engr.

FUSILIER, MIKE; Pinckney HS; Pinckney, MI; Am Leg Boys St; Letter Band; Hon Rl; Pres NHS; Yth Flsp; 4-H; Cit Awd; 4-H Awd; Natl Merit Ltr; Botany & Zoology Awd 77; Univ; Sci.

FUSON, CYNTHIA; Terre Haute North Vigo HS; Terre Haute, IN; 99/583 Chrs; Hon Rl; Sec JA; Pol Wkr; Y-Teens; OEA; JA Awd; Indiana St Univ.

FUSON, MELISSA; Franklin HS; Franklin, OH; 21/559 Chrs; Hon Rl; Ed Yrbk; OEA; Miami Univ; Acctg.

FUSSELMAN, ROBIN; Farmington Local HS; W Farmington, OH; 1/24 VP Jr Cls; Hon Rl; NHS; Beta Clb; FTA; Pep Clb; Scr Kpr; Kent St Univ.

FUSSNER, LARRY; Rocky River HS; Rocky Rvr, OH; Socr; IM Sprt; College; Dentistry.

FUTHEY, TRACY; Wheeling Park HS; Wheeling, WV; 4/579 Hon Rl; NHS; Letter Bsktbl; 8th In Regnl Math Day Part In St Math Day 79; Awd For Otstndng Achvmnt In Math & Sci Summer Prog 79; Univ; Archt.

FUTO, DEBORAH; Nordonia HS; Sagamore Hls, OH; 1/450 Cls Rep Frsh Cls; Cls Rep Soph Cls; Cl Rep Jr Cls; Cls Rep Sr Cls; Val; Chrs; Girl Scts; Hon Rl; Lbry Ade; NHS; John Carroll Univ; Bus Admin.

G

GAABO, ARLENE; Calumet HS; Mohawk, MI; 27/146 Band; Chrs; Hon Rl; NHS; Rptr Yrbk; FTA; Pep Clb; Western Mic Univ; Spec Ed.

GAABO, MARTTI; Waterford Township HS; Union Lake, MI; 1/414 Girl Scts; Hon Rl; Letter Bsbl; Ten; Mic State Univ; Architecture.

GAAR, DIANA; Anderson Highland HS; Anderson, IN; 50/478 Yth Flsp; 4-H; Univ; Acctg.

GABALA, M; Hopkins HS; Hopkins, MI; 13/95 Hon Rl; Bsbl; Bsktbl; Trk; Scr Kpr; Tmr; Univ; Bus Admin.

GABALA, MARK; Hopkins Public HS; Hopkins, MI; 10/100 Hon Rl; Letter Bsbl; Ten; Coach Actv; IM Sprt; Scr Kpr; Tmr; Bus Schl; Bus Admin.

GABANY, SHEILA; Warren HS; Sterling Hts, MI; Cls Rep Soph Cls; Cl Rep Jr Cls; VP Sr Cls; Cls Rep Sr Cls; Hon Rl; NHS; Letter Ten; GAA; Univ Of Michigan; Phys Ther.

GABAY, LILLIAN; East HS; Akron, OH; 1/300 Val; Am Leg Aux Girls St; Natl Forn Lg; Pres NHS; Sch Nwsp; VP Fr Clb; Capt Gym; Letter Trk; Opt Clb Awd; Oberlin College.

GABBARD, BRAD; Celina HS; Celina, OH; Hon Rl; NHS; FTA; Letter Bsbl; Letter Bsktbl; College; Communications.

GABBARD, MARTIN; Kings Mills HS; S Lebanon, OH; Hon Rl;.

GABEL, SARAH; Port Clinton HS; Port Clinton, OH; 10/230 VP Sr Cls; Am Leg Aux Girls St; Chrs; Hon Rl; Jr NHS; NHS; Lat Clb; Ten; Chmn Chrldng; Miami Univ; Comp Sci.

GABELL, MICHAEL; Negaunee HS; Palmer, MI; Boy Scts; Lbry Ade; Rptr Sch Nwsp; Cit Awd; Mich Tech; Electrical Engr.

GABET, LEISA; Bishop Luers HS; New Haven, IN; Hon Rl; 4-H; IM Sprt; PPFtbl; 4-H Awd; Lion Awd; Bus Schl.

GABLE, JOHN; New Lexington HS; New Lexington, OH; 42/170 Pres Jr Cls; Pres Sr Cls; Am Leg Boys St; Aud/Vis; Boy Scts; Chrs; Chrh Wkr; Hon Rl; NHS; Stg Crw; Best Off Lineman 79; Ohio St Univ; Bus Admin.

GABLE, PATRICIA; Harry S Truman Sr HS; Taylor, MI; Drm Bgl; Girl Scts; Hon Rl; NHS; Drama Clb; Bsktbl; Gym; Trk; Mgrs; Tmr; Univ Of Michigan; Sci.

GABLE, PATTI; Glen Este HS; Cincinnati, OH; 16/285 Cls Rep Soph Cls; Cl Rep Jr Cls; Sec Sr Cls; Am Leg Aux Girls St; Band; Hon Rl; NHS; VP Pep Clb; Spn Clb; Univ Of Cincinnati; Nurse.

GABLE, SUSAN; Avon HS; Danville, IN; Am Leg Aux Girls St; Band; Cmp Fr Grls; Hon Rl; NHS; Sch Mus; Ger Clb; Ten; Purdue; Vet Med.

GABLE, TERESA; Whitko HS; So Whitley, IN; FCA; Stu Cncl; 4-H; Bsktbl; Trk; Univ; Phys Ther.

GABOR, SUSAN; Ontario HS; Mnsfld, OH; 15/200 Girl Scts; Hon Rl; Jr NHS; NHS; Rptr Sch Nwsp; Sch Nwsp; Pep Clb; Scr Kpr; Bus Schl; Bus.

GABREK, MARK; Bishop Luers HS; Ft Wayne, IN; Cls Rep Frsh Cls; Cls Rep Soph Cls; Cl Rep Jr Cls; Band; Hon Rl; Orch; Stg Crw; Crs Cntry; College; Music.

GABRIC, JODY T; Marlington HS; Alliance, OH; Am Leg Aux Girls St; Chrs; Yth Flsp; Pres 4-H; VP FFA; 4-H Awd; Ohio State Univ; Horticulture.

GABRIEL, ANNE M; Nordonia HS; Northfield, OH; 44/440 Chrs; Hon Rl; Hosp Ade; Akron Univ; Nutrition.

GABRIEL, JASMINE; Penn HS; Mishawaka, IN; Band; Chrh Wkr; Hon Rl; PPFtbl; Notre Dame Univ; Pre Med.

GABRIEL, JULIE; Bishop Watterson HS; Columbus, OH; Cls Rep Soph Cls; Girl Scts; Hon Rl; Jr NHS; NHS; Sch Mus; Sch Pl; Stu Cncl; Fr Clb; Lat Clb; College; Poli Sci.

GABRIEL, JULIE; Wayne Twp HS; Dayton, OH; Treas AFS; Fr Clb; Girl Scts; Hon Rl; Jr NHS; NHS; Sct Actv; Ed Yrbk; VP 4-H; VP Fr Clb; Pep Clb; Ohio St Univ; Intl Busns.

GABRIEL, KIM; Franklin Heights HS; Columbus, OH; Cls Rep Frsh Cls; Cls Rep Soph Cls; Cl Rep Jr Cls; Hosp Ade; Stu Cncl; Sch Nwsp; Key Clb; OEA; Bsktbl; Gym; 1st Runner Up In Schl Dist OEA Queens Cont; Clark Tech Coll; Court Reporter.

GABRIS, JOSEPH; Muskegon HS; Muskegon, MI; Band; Hon Rl; Jr NHS; NHS; Yth Flsp; Hockey; Trinity Lutheren Coll; Bus.

GABROSEK, JOE; Barberton HS; Wadsworth, OH; Am Leg Boys St; Chrh Wkr; FCA; Hon Rl; Jr NHS; NHS; Spn Clb; Bsktbl; Crs Cntry; Univ.

GACETTA, JAMI; Archbishop Alter HS; Centervll, OH; 79/305 Cmp Fr Grls; Cmnty Wkr; Hon Rl; Key Clb; Gym; Letter Socr; Trk; GAA; Bowling Green Univ; Busns.

GACH, SUSAN M; Elyria Catholic HS; Elyria, OH; 14/188 Treas Chrs; Hon Rl; Stg Crw; Yrbk; Sch Nwsp; Drama Clb; Pep Clb; Spn Clb; Letter Ten; Letter Chrldng; College; Commercial Art.

GADACZ, AGNES; Washington HS; South Bend, IN; 20/355 Chrs; Chrh Wkr; Girl Scts; Hon Rl; VP JA; Treas NHS; Sch Pl; Yrbk; Fr Clb; College; Photog.

GADACZ, BARBARA; Washington HS; South Bend, IN; 37/355 Chrs; Chrh Wkr; Girl Scts; Hon Rl; Yrbk; Fr Clb; College; Educ Of Deaf.

GADACZ, CARMEN; Washington HS; South Bend, IN; 13/355 Chrs; Chrh Wkr; Hon Rl; NHS; Stu Cncl; Rptr Yrbk; Fr Clb; College; Sci.

GADD, AMY; Farmington Local HS; W Farmington, OH; 8/24 Sec Soph Cls; Band; Girl Scts; Hosp Ade; Beta Clb; 4-H; FTA; Pep Clb; Bsbl; Chrldng; Runner Up For Girls Buckeye St; Univ.

GADD, REBECCA; Webster County HS; Cowen, WV; Chrh Wkr; Cmnty Wkr; Hon Rl; Y-Teens; 4-H; Pep Clb; VICA; 4-H Awd; Glenville State; Commputer Science.

GADDES, TOMI; Columbia Central HS; Brooklyn, MI; 21/180 Cls Rep Frsh Cls; Cls Rep Soph Cls; Sec Jr Cls; Sec Sr Cls; Chrs; Chrh Wkr; Hon Rl; NHS; Stu Cncl; Chrldng; Jackson Comm Coll; CPA.

GADDIS, JULAINE; Henry Ford HS; Detroit, MI; Band; Hon Rl; NHS; Off Ade; Mth Clb; Sci Clb; Bsktbl; Swmmng; Cit Awd; Univ Of Michigan; Math.

GADZINSKI, ELIZABETH; St Ladislaus HS; Detroit, MI; 6/90 Cls Rep Frsh Cls; Chrs; Hon Rl; Sch Pl; Drama Clb; Fr Clb; Pep Clb; Wayne St Univ; Medicine.

GAEBEL, TAMMY; Danville HS; Danville, IN; Hon Rl; Off Ade; College; Vet.

GAERTNER, BARBARA; Trenton HS; Trenton, MI; Hon Rl; NHS; Letter Ten; Michigan St Univ; Phys Educ.

GAETH, LORI; Owendale Gagetown HS; Owendale, MI; 2/42 Trs Soph Cls; Cl Rep Jr Cls; Trs Sr Cls; Sal; Am Leg Aux Girls St; Girl Scts; Hon Rl; NHS; Off Ade; Sch Pl; Central Mi Univ; Business.

GAFF, SHERRI; Waterford Kettering HS; Waterford, MI; 1/400 Val; Jr NHS; NHS; Letter Trk; PPFtbl; Natl Merit SF; Natl Merit Schl; Hope Coll; Med.

GAFF, TERRI; Waterford Kettering HS; Waterford, MI; Cmp Fr Grls; Debate Tm; Hon Rl; NHS; Sch Mus; Sch Pl; Stg Crw; Stu Cncl; Scr Kpr; Tmr; Bus.

GAFILL, MARY; Culver Girls Academy; South Bend, IN; 50/198 Hon Rl; Lit Mag; Sch Mus; Sch Pl; Stg Crw; IM Sprt; Cit Awd; Univ; Theatre.

GAGE, DANA; Archbishop Alter HS; Dayton, OH; Chrs; Cmnty Wkr; Hosp Ade; Pol Wkr; Quill & Scroll; Red Cr Ade; ROTC; Civ Clb; Spn Clb; Bsktbl; Ohi State Univ; Law.

GAGE, JULIET; Galion HS; Galion, OH; 12/275 Cls Rep Frsh Cls; Cls Rep Soph Cls; Cl Rep Jr Cls; Cls Rep Sr Cls; Am Leg Aux Girls St; Pres NHS; Stu Cncl; 4-H; Columbus Bus Univ; Fashion Mdse.

GAGE, RON; Bellmont HS; Decatur, IN; 21/244 Chrs; Chrh Wkr; Cmnty Wkr; Hon Rl; NHS; Spn Clb; Mgrs; Bus Schl; Finance.

GAGER, MICHAEL; Greenville Sr HS; Rockford, MI; Boy Scts; FFA; Michigan St Univ; Dairy Sci.

GAGERMEIER, DIANE; Sidney HS; Sidney, OH; Chrs; Girl Scts; Hosp Ade; Lbry Ade; Orch; Sch Mus; Sct Actv; Stg Crw; 4-H; IM Sprt; Edison State; Elem Educ.

GAGERN, MARTIN; Lutheran HS; Dearborn, MI; Band; Chrh Wkr; Hon Rl; NHS; Sch Mus; Sch Pl; Drama Clb; Letter Trk; Coach Actv; Natl Merit Ltr; Wayne St Univ; Pre Med.

GAGGIN, KEVIN; Allen Park Public HS; Allen Park, MI; Chrh Wkr; Hon Rl; Yth Flsp; Ftbl; Northern Michigan Univ; Archt.

GAGLE, CINDY; Jay County HS; Portland, IN; 15/400 Am Leg Aux Girls St; Band; Debate Tm; Hon Rl; Natl Forn Lg; NHS; Quill & Scroll; Sch Pl; Opt Clb Awd; Voice Dem Awd; College; Tv Broadcasting.

GAGLE, KELLY; Perrysburg HS; Perrysburg, OH; Chrs; Chrh Wkr; Girl Scts; Hon Rl; Jr NHS; Sch Mus; Sch Pl; Drama Clb; Ger Clb; Sec Leo Clb; Univ; Bus Admin.

GAGLE, MARK; Celina HS; Celina, OH; Letter Bsbl; Letter Glf; IM Sprt; College; Comp Progr.

GAGNE, CHARLES; Troy HS; Troy, MI; 60/300 Am Leg Boys St; Hon Rl; NHS; Capt Swmmng; Mgrs; Natl Merit Ltr; Opt Clb Awd; Michigan St Univ.

GAGNON, JANET; Wayne Memorial HS; Wayne, MI; Hon Rl; Scr Kpr; Wayne Cnty Cmnty Coll Trstee Schlrshp 79; St Of Mi Dept Of Ed Comp Hnry Awd Frm Hse Of Rep Of St Of Mi 79; Wayne Cnty Cmnty Coll; Animal Hlth.

GAHM, LISA; Valley Local HS; Lucasville, OH; Sec Frsh Cls; Trs Soph Cls; Band; Hon Rl; Sec NHS; Off Ade; Sch Pl; Yrbk; FHA; FTA;.

GAICH, SHARON; Genoa Area HS; Curtice, OH; VP Frsh Cls; Chrs; Chrh Wkr; Hon Rl; Hosp Ade; Sch Mus; Sch Pl; Chmn Stu Cncl; Rptr Sch Nwsp; Sec FTA; Univ Of Toledo; Elem Educ.

GAIER, D; Versailles HS; Versailles, OH; Band; Lbry Ade; 4-H; 4-H Awd; Voca Schl; Elec.

GAIER, DEBBIE; London HS; London, OH; 1/130 Am Leg Aux Girls St; Hon Rl; NHS; Quill & Scroll; Stu Cncl; Yth Flsp; Rptr Yrbk; Fr Clb; C of C Awd; Kiwan Awd; Wittenberg; Life Sciences.

GAIER, DONNA; London HS; London, OH; 3/130 Am Leg Aux Girls St; Hon Rl; Lit Mag; NHS; Quill & Scroll; Yth Flsp; Rptr Yrbk; Fr Clb; C of C Awd; Wittenberg Univ; Math.

GAIER, TONY; Versailles HS; Versailles, OH; 40/130 Band; Chrh Wkr; FCA; Hon Rl; 4-H; Mth Clb; Sci Clb; Letter Ftbl; Tmr; 4-H Awd; Voc Schl; Mgmt.

GAINER, EDWARD C; Heritage Christian HS; Indianapolis, IN; VP Soph Cls; Band; Chrs; Sch Pl; Yrbk; Drama Clb; Fr Clb; Socr; Trk; Psychology.

GAINER, PATTY; Heath HS; Heath, OH; 55/155 Chrs; Cmnty Wkr; Hon Rl; Hosp Ade; Pol Wkr; Sch Mus; Stg Crw; Yth Flsp; Rptr Yrbk; Drama Clb; Ohio St Univ; Communications.

GAINER, RICK; Parkersburg HS; Parkersburg, WV; Hon Rl; Bus Schl; Cpa.

GAINES, CYNTHIA; Loudonville HS; Loudonville, OH; 2/128 Band; Chrs; Chrh Wkr; Hon Rl; Jr NHS; NHS; Stg Crw; Treas Stu Cncl; Rptr Sch Nwsp; 4-H; Art Club Tres; College; Busns Mgmt.

GAINES, MICHELE; Dominican HS; Detroit, MI; Cls Rep Soph Cls; Cls Rep Sr Cls; Chrh Wkr; Hon Rl; Ed Yrbk; Coach Actv; PPFtbl; Natl Merit Ltr; Natl Merit Schl; Miss Nu Dawn Gamma Phi Delta Sorority Delta Nu Chapter; Michigan St Univ; Bio Med Engr.

GAINEY, WESLEY; John Marshall HS; Indianapolis, IN; 6/611 Am Leg Boys St; Boy Scts; Hon Rl; NHS; Sch Mus; Stu Cncl; Key Clb; Spn Clb; Ten; Notre Dame; Law.

GAINEY, WESLEY R; John Marshall HS; Indianapolis, IN; 6/611 Cls Rep Sr Cls; Am Leg Boys St; Boy Scts; Hon Rl; NHS; Sch Mus; Sct Actv; Stu Cncl; Key Clb; Spn Clb; Dist Key Club Pres 1979; 2nd Pl J F Conover 1979; Wabash Coll; Corp Law.

GAINOK, CONSTANCE J; Wellington Sr HS; Wellington, OH; 14/130 Am Leg Aux Girls St; Band; Chrs; Chrh Wkr; Hon Rl; Mdrgl; NHS; Quill & Scroll; Yth Flsp; Rptr Sch Nwsp; Bowling Green St Univ; Speech.

GAINOK, KATHY; South Amherst HS; S Amherst, OH; 2/60 Pres Soph Cls; Trs Jr Cls; Band; Hon Rl; Lbry Ade; NHS; Stu Cncl; Rptr Yrbk; Fr Clb; Pep Clb; Univ.

GAISER, DIANE K; Marshall HS; Marshall, MI; Girl Scts; Hon Rl; Orch; 4-H; IM Sprt; Mgrs; Univ; Bus.

GAJ, JAMES; Highland HS; Hinckley, OH; 13/207 Trs Frsh Cls; Trs Soph Cls; Trs Jr Cls; Trs Sr Cls; Band; Chrs; Hon Rl; NHS; Letter Crs Cntry; Letter Trk; Akron Univ; Math.

GAJDA, BARBARA; Holy Name HS; Garfield Hts, OH; 38/350 Hon Rl; Jr NHS; Rptr Yrbk; Rptr Sch Nwsp; Fr Clb; IM Sprt; Univ.

GAL, ALYSON B; Plainwell HS; Plainwell, MI; 1/247 Band; Cmnty Wkr; Girl Scts; Hon Rl; NHS; Orch; Pol Wkr; Sch Pl; Stg Crw; Drama Clb; Knox Coll; Law.

GALA, CHETAN; Bloomington North HS; Bloomington, IN; College; Bio.

GALANIC, PETER; Admiral King HS; Lorain, OH; Cls Rep Frsh Cls; Cls Rep Soph Cls; Band; Hon Rl; Orch; Stu Cncl; Letter Bsbl; Ohio St Univ; Vet.

GALANT, CRAIG; Washington HS; Massillon, OH; Boy Scts; Cmnty Wkr; Hon Rl; Sct Actv; Stu Cncl; Sci Clb; Spn Clb; Ftbl; Ten; Univ; Pre Med.

GALASSO, MICHAEL J; Jimtown HS; Elkhart, IN; Hst Sr Cls; Pol Wkr; DECA; Fr Clb; Pep Clb; Letter Ftbl; Letter Glf; St DECA 2nd Pl Sales 1978; Pepsi Learn & Earn 2nd Pl 1979; Ball St Univ; Bus.

GALBAUGH, BRYANT; Princeton HS; Sharonville, OH; 27/731 Hon Rl; NHS; Quill & Scroll; Rptr Yrbk; Sprt Ed Sch Nwsp; Ger Clb; Bsbl; Natl Merit Commended Stu; Outstanding Journalism Stu; Miami Univ.

GALBRAITH, KAREN; Forest Park HS; Crystal Falls, MI; 1/79 Val; Band; Chrs; Girl Scts; Hon Rl; Yth Flsp; Bsktbl; IM Sprt; Northern Mich Univ; Acctng.

GALE, TODD; Owesso HS; Owosso, MI; 39/406 Band; Hon Rl; NHS; Lat Clb; Michigan St Univ; Law.

GALE, VINCENT; Redford Union HS; Redford, MI; Boy Scts; Chrs; Hon Rl; JA; NHS; Sch Mus; Sch Pl; Stu Cncl; Rptr Yrbk; Spn Clb; Univ; Advertising.

GALEA JR, JOSEPH; Elyria Catholic HS; Elyria, OH; Pres Frsh Cls; Chrs; Cmnty Wkr; Hon Rl; PAVAS; Sch Mus; Sch Pl; Stg Crw; Stu Cncl; College; Bus.

GALFORD, TAMARA; Piketon HS; Lucasville, OH; 7/115 Chrs; Girl Scts; Hon Rl; Pres MMM; Sch Mus; 4-H; Pres FHA; VP FTA; Pres OEA; Am Leg Awd; Voc.

GALFORD, TOM; Harrison HS; Gladwin, MI; Band; Boy Scts; Hon Rl; Sct Actv; Stg Crw; 4-H; 4-H Awd; Consrvtn Awd 75; Ferris St Coll; Diesel Mech.

GALIA, JOSEPHINE; Centerline Sr HS; Warren, MI; 63/423 Hon Rl; Jr NHS; Natl Forn Lg; Sch Mus; Sch Pl; Drama Clb; Spn Clb; Gym; Opt Clb Awd; VFW Awd; Oakland Univ; Communications.

GALIDA, STEPHANIE; Struthers HS; Struthers, OH; 18/285 Hon Rl; NHS; Pep Clb; Spn Clb; IM Sprt; Youngstown St Univ; Comp Sci.

GALKO, PATTY; Trenton HS; Trenton, MI; Girl Scts; Hon Rl; Jr NHS; Sct Actv; Spn Clb; Michigan St Univ; Cmmrcl Art.

GALL, VINCENT; Lincoln HS; Shinnston, WV; 38/149 Am Leg Boys St; Boy Scts; Hon Rl; Lbry Ade; NHS; Sch Pl; Sci Clb; Natl Merit SF; 4 Yr Consol Schlrshp; West Virginia Inst Of Tech; Physics.

GALLA, JUDY; St Marys HS; Lake Leelanau, MI; Sec Frsh Cls; Sec Soph Cls; Sec Jr Cls; Hon Rl; Yrbk; 4-H; Pep Clb; Bsbl; Chrldng; IM Sprt; Northwestern Univ; Acctg.

GALLAGHER, ANDREA; Monroe HS; Monroe, MI; VP Jr Cls; Cmnty Wkr; Hon Rl; Jr NHS; NHS; Sch Pl; Stu Cncl; Yrbk; FSA; Pep Clb; Univ; Art.

GALLAGHER, ANN; Ursuline Academy; Loveland, OH; 2/106 Cmnty Wkr; Mod UN; Univ; Chem Engr.

GALLAGHER, COLLEEN; Madonna HS; Weirton, WV; Chrh Wkr; Cmnty Wkr; Hon Rl; Lit Mag; Rptr Yrbk; Yrbk; Sch Nwsp; Drama Clb; Pep Clb; Ten; Pittsburgh Inst; Int Dsgn.

GALLAGHER, COLLEEN; Badin HS; Fairfield, OH; Chrh Wkr; Cmnty Wkr; Hon Rl; Sch Pl; Stu Cncl; Sch Nwsp; Drama Clb; Natl Merit Ltr; College; Journalism.

GALLAGHER, DOROTHY; Fisher Catholic HS; Lancaster, OH; Sec Frsh Cls; Trs Frsh Cls; Sec Soph Cls; Trs Soph Cls; Sec Jr Cls; Trs Jr Cls; Hon Rl; NHS; FDA; Pep Clb; Ohio State Univ; Pshychology.

GALLAGHER, EVERETT E; Chillicothe HS; Chillicothe, OH; 1/366 Val; Am Leg Boys St; Band; Boy Scts; Chrh Wkr; Debate Tm; Hon Rl; Natl Forn Lg; Pres NHS; Stu Cncl; Bowling Green St Univ; Med.

GALLAGHER, JEFFREY; Bishop Gallagher HS; Detroit, MI; 124/333 Band; Boy Scts; Chrh Wkr; Hon Rl; Sch Mus; Sch Pl; Rptr Yrbk; College; Business Mgnt.

GALLAGHER, JIM; Ursuline HS; Youngstown, OH; Letter Trk; Youngstown State Univ; Engr.

GALLAGHER, KATHLEEN; Dominican HS; Detroit, MI; Band; Cmnty Wkr; Hon Rl; Hosp Ade; Sec NHS; Sch Pl; IM Sprt; PPFtbl; Univ Of Michigan; Poli Sci.

GALLAGHER, MAGGIE; Ursuline HS; Youngstown, OH; 112/350 Cmp Fr Grls; Girl Scts; Hon Rl; Sct Actv; Drama Clb; Pep Clb; Spn Clb; Trk; Coll; Communications.

GALLAGHER, MARK J; Big Walnut HS; Sunbury, OH; 6/237 Cls Rep Frsh Cls; Cls Rep Soph Cls; Cl Rep Jr Cls; Cls Rep Sr Cls; Am Leg Boys St; Band; Boy Scts; Hon Rl; NHS; Sct Actv; Univ; Bio.

GALLAGHER, PATRICIA; Barnesville HS; Barnesville, OH; Sec Frsh Cls; Sec Soph Cls; Cls Rep Sr Cls; Am Leg Aux Girls St; Band; Debate Tm; Girl Scts; Hon Rl; Muskingum College.

GALLAGHER, RICH; De Kalb HS; Auburn, IN; 33/300 NHS; Ten; IM Sprt; Hoosier Schlr; St Schlrshp; NELAC All Conf Tennis; Indiana Univ; Acctg.

GALLAGHER, ROSE; Flat Rock HS; Flat Rock, MI; FCA; Yrbk; Letter Bsbl; Letter Trk; Chrldng; GAA; PPFtbl; Coll; Phys Educ.

GALLAGHER, TIMOTHY; Eastlake North HS; Willowick, OH; 70/706 Hon Rl; Spn Clb; John Caroll Univ.

GALLAHER, BRENDA; South Point HS; South Point, OH; Cls Rep Frsh Cls; Cls Rep Soph Cls; Cl Rep Jr Cls; Band; Stu Cncl; FTA; Pep Clb; Chrldng; Costal Carolina Coll; Law.

GALLAHER, DEBBIE; Grafton HS; Grafton, WV; Cls Rep Frsh Cls; Trs Soph Cls; Cl Rep Jr Cls; Band; Hon Rl; Hosp Ade; Stu Cncl; Fr Clb; Keyettes; Fairmont State College; Nurse.

GALLAHER, WANDA; Beaver Local HS; Lisbon, OH; Fr Clb; GAA; Univ; Bio.

GALLARDO, JOHN D; Williamson HS; Williamson, WV; 30/120 Boy Scts; Hon Rl; Sct Actv; Stu Cncl; Pres FBLA; Spn Clb; Proficiency Awd Typewriting 1 79; FBLA Econ Awd 79; 2nd Pl S W Va Sci Fair 79; George Washington Univ; Bus Admin.

GALLATIN, BOBBI; South Vermillion HS; Clinton, IN; 10/150 Cls Rep Soph Cls; Am Leg Aux Girls St; FCA; Hon Rl; VP JA; Stu Cncl; Fr Clb; Pep Clb; Letter Trk; Letter Chrldng; Indiana St Univ; Med Tech.

GALLAWAY, BARBARA; Howell HS; Howell, MI; 52/395 Hon Rl; NHS; 4-H; Crs Cntry; GAA; 4-H Awd; Mich State Univ.

GALLAWAY, COLLEEN; Lawrence Central HS; Indianapolis, IN; 73/375 Cmp Fr Grls; Natl Forn Lg; Off Ade; Sch Pl; Drama Clb; Pep Clb; Part In Lily Endwmnt Progr 79; Upper 10% NEDT 76; Spch Team Sec 78; Univ; Psych.

GALLE, CINDY; Immaculate Conception Acad; Oldenburg, IN; 22/68 Chrs; Chrh Wkr; Girl Scts; Hon Rl; Orch; Sch Mus; Sch Pl; 4-H; Spn Clb; 4-H Awd; Indiana Univ; Music.

GALLENSTEIN, ANN; Archbishop Alter HS; Kettering, OH; Hosp Ade; Coach Actv; Univ; Speech Path.

GALLIGHER, CHARLES; Bluefield HS; Bluefield, WV;.

GALLIMORE, LECIA L; Princeton HS; Princeton, WV; Pres Soph Cls; Cmnty Wkr; NHS; Off Ade; Stu Cncl; Ed Sch Nwsp; Pep Clb; Letter Chrldng; DAR Awd; Bluefield St Univ; Busns Sec.

GALLINA, GARY; Chippewa Valley HS; Mt Clemens, MI; Cls Rep Frsh Cls; Hon Rl; Sch Pl; Drama Clb; Spn Clb; Western Michigan; CPA.

GALLION, SHAUNI; Brownstown Central HS; Brownstown, IN; 19/140 Sec Sr Cls; Band; Chrh Wkr; Girl Scts; Hon Rl; 4-H; Pep Clb; Spn Clb; GAA; IM Sprt; Olivet Nazarene College; Legal Assnt.

GALLITTO, ROBYN; Boardman HS; Youngstown, OH; 29/558 NHS; Spn Clb; Letter Gym; Scr Kpr; Wittenberg; Bio.

GALLO, LAURIE D; Our Lady Of The Lakes HS; Waterford, MI; Sec Soph Cls; VP Jr Cls; Hon Rl; NHS; Spn Clb; Letter Bsbl; Letter Bsktbl; GAA; IM Sprt; PPFtbl; College.

GALLO, MARIE; Catholic Central HS; Steubenville, OH; 18/226 Cls Rep Frsh Cls; Am Leg Aux Girls St; Hon Rl; Jr NHS; NHS; Sch Mus; Sch Pl; Stu Cncl; Univ Of Dayton; Comm Arts.

GALLOGLY, JACKIE; Philo HS; Chandlersville, OH; 12/207 VP Frsh Cls; VP Sr Cls; VP NHS; Rptr Yrbk; Rptr Sch Nwsp; Pres 4-H; Letter Trk; Chrldng; VP GAA; 4-H Awd; Ohio Univ.

GALLOGLY, JANICE; Linden HS; Fenton, MI; Band; Chrh Wkr; Hon Rl; Rptr Yrbk; Letter Bsbl; Spring Arbor Coll; Music.

GALLOGLY, THOMAS; Adams Cntrl HS; Decatur, IN; Chrh Wkr; Hon Rl; NHS; Yth Flsp; 4-H; 4-H Awd; Univ.

GALLOWAY, BRIAN; Portsmouth HS; Portsmouth, OH; 12/235 Hon Rl; NHS; Sch Pl; Ten; Denison Univ.

GALLOWAY, CYNTHIA L; University HS; Morgantown, WV; Band; Drm Mjrt; Hon Rl; Jr NHS; Twrlr; JFK Phys Fitness Awd 1st In Jr Hgh For 3 Consectv Yrs 74 76; Outstndg Jr Typist Awd 77; West Virginia Univ; Legal Sec.

GALLOWAY, GREG; Franklin Hts HS; Grove City, OH; 37/315 Cl Rep Jr Cls; Chrs; Hon Rl; NHS; Stu Cncl; Letter Bsbl; Letter Ftbl; Pres Of Natl Hon Soc 78; 1 Of Top Athlts Of S W Schl Dist 78; High Awd In Bsbl 78; Univ.

GALLOWAY, JINNY; Brunswick HS; Brunswick, OH; Chrh Wkr; FCA; Lbry Ade; Off Ade; Sec Yth Flsp; 4-H; FTA; Pep Clb; Spn Clb; Elk Awd; Asbury Coll; Elem Ed.

GALLOWAY, LAURA; Tecumseh HS; Tecumseh, MI; 29/235 Am Leg Aux Girls St; Hon Rl; Sch Pl; Ger Clb; PPFtbl; N Michigan Univ; Busns Admin.

GALLOWAY, SANDRA; Jesup W Scott HS; Toledo, OH; 17/400 Cls Rep Frsh Cls; Band; Drl Tm; Hon Rl; Jr NHS; NHS; Stu Cncl; Chrldng; Twrlr; Bowling Green State Univ; Phys Ther.

GALLUP, BARB; Evergreen HS; Lyons, OH; Cls Rep Frsh Cls; Trs Sr Cls; Band; Hon Rl; NHS; Sch Pl; Rptr Yrbk; Drama Clb; 4-H; Fr Clb; Univ; Engr.

GAMBELLIN, EARNEST; Brooke HS; Follansbee, WV; 150/450 Boy Scts; Cmnty Wkr; FCA; Hon Rl; Sct Actv; Sci Clb; Spn Clb; Bsktbl; Trk; IM Sprt; West Virginia Univ; Bus.

GAMBLE, ALLEN; Bendle HS; Flint, MI; 1/100 Pres Frsh Cls; Cls Rep Frsh Cls; Cl Rep Jr Cls; Cls Rep Sr Cls; Val; Hon Rl; NHS; Stu Cncl; Letter Bsbl; Mich State Univ; Financial Admin.

GAMBLE, JANET; Pine River HS; Reed City, MI; Girl Scts; Hon Rl; NHS; Off Ade; 4-H; Spn Clb; Letter Bsktbl; Letter Trk; IM Sprt; 4-H Awd; Alma Coll; Phys Ed.

GAMBLE, JEFF; Riverside HS; Degraff, OH; Band; Chrs; Hon Rl; Sch Pl; Stg Crw; Yth Flsp; 4-H; Rdo Clb; Mgrs; 4-H Awd; Urbana Coll; Mortuary Sci.

GAMBLE, LYDIA; Carrollton HS; Carrollton, OH; 23/259 Hon Rl; NHS; Spn Clb; Kent St Univ; Busns Admin.

GAMBLE, STEVE A; Riverside HS; De Graff, OH; 7/80 Cls Rep Soph Cls; Cl Rep Jr Cls; Hon Rl; NHS; Sch Pl; VP Stu Cncl; Rdo Clb; Spn Clb; Letter Ftbl; Voice Dem Awd; Bowling Green St Univ; Eng.

GAMELIN, ARLENE; Bendle Sr HS; Burton, MI; 3/96 Girl Scts; Hon Rl; JA; NHS; Off Ade; Sct Actv; PPFtbl; Univ Of Michigan; Comp Sci.

GAMES, KATHY; Brookville HS; Brookville, OH; Hon Rl; Off Ade; Sch Pl; Stu Cncl; Rptr Yrbk; VP Pep Clb; Chrldng; PPFtbl; Bowling Green St Univ; Bus Admin.

GAMMON, ANNE; Bosse HS; Evansville, IN; Hon Rl; VICA; Cit Awd; Univ; Bio.

GAMPEL, CARL; Bridgman HS; Bridgman, MI; 38/91 Band; Boy Scts; Chrh Wkr; Hon Rl; Orch; Sct Actv; VP Yth Flsp; Boys Scouts Of Amer Order Of The Arrow; Lake Michigan Coll; Acctg.

GAMPONIA, JESSICA; Spencer HS; Spencer, WV; Cls Rep Frsh Cls; Cl Rep Jr Cls; Band; Jr NHS; 4-H; VP Pep Clb; Letter Trk; Chrldng; Mat Maids; 4-H Awd; All Tourney Bsktbll Chrldr 78; Univ; Med.

GANDEE, DAVID L; Walton HS; Gandeeville, WV; Pres Frsh Cls; Pres Soph Cls; Pres Jr Cls; Am Leg Boys St; Band; Boy Scts; Hon Rl; Jr NHS; NHS; Stu Cncl; Outstndg Band Mbr 78; Univ; Music.

GANDER, VAN; Cambridge HS; Cambridge, OH; 15/200 Cls Rep Frsh Cls; Cls Rep Soph Cls; Cl Rep Jr Cls; Hon Rl; Stu Cncl; Sprt Ed Sch Nwsp; Key Clb; Spn Clb; Glf; Ten; Coll; Pre Law.

GANDOLF, LANA; Northwest HS; Colorado Spring, CO; 62/506 Hon Rl; Jr NHS; Pol Wkr; Mth Clb;.

GANDY, RAYMOND; St Albans HS; St Albans, WV; 14/403 Chrh Wkr; Hon Rl; Jr NHS; NHS; Soroptimist; Capt Swmmng; Clarion St Coll; CPA.

GANG, DAVID; St Francis De Sales HS; Toledo, OH; 66/223 Band; Boy Scts; Hon Rl; Orch; Sch Mus; Rptr Yrbk; Rptr Sch Nwsp; IM Sprt; Univ Of Toledo; Bus Admin.

GANG, LESA; Perry HS; Canton, OH; Girl Scts; NHS; Sch Pl; Pep Clb; Letter Chrldng; 1st Pl Ohio St Dist Grange Sewing 79; Speech Club; Univ; Fshn Dsgn.

GANGIDINE, JEFFREY; St Ignatius HS; N Olmsted, OH; 60/300 Chrh Wkr; Hon Rl; Stg Crw; Y-Teens; Yrbk; Bsbl; Bsktbl; Letter Socr; Coach Actv; IM Sprt; Univ; Bus.

GANGLER, CHRIS; Caro Cmnty HS; Caro, MI; Band; Debate Tm; Hon Rl; NHS; Off Ade; DAR Awd;.

GANNAWAY, ANNE; Hurricane HS; Hurricane, WV; Hon Rl; Pep Clb; VICA;.

GANNON, ALFRED; Oak Hill HS; Oak Hill, WV; Am Leg Boys St; Hon Rl; NHS; Sch Pl; Drama Clb; Fr Clb; Pep Clb; Pres Of Natl Hon Soc 79; Chair Of Coll Day 78; Mbr Of Winning Tm At WVIT Eng Bowl 78; Duke Univ; Med.

GANNON, E MICHAEL; University Liggett School; Detroit, MI; Aud/Vis; Band; Hon Rl; Lbry Ade; Off Ade; Sch Nwsp; Crs Cntry; Univ Of Detroit; Bus Admin.

GANNON, JIM; Fairview HS; Fairview Pk, OH; Boy Scts;.

GANNON, KAREN; Immaculate Conception Acad; Batesville, IN; 3/70 Pres Sr Cls; Chrh Wkr; Girl Scts; Hon Rl; NHS; Sch Pl; Stg Crw; Spn Clb; Swmmng; Univ; Acctg.

GANNON, LAURA; Rock Hill Sr HS; Ironton, OH; 1/142 VP Jr Cls; Pres Sr Cls; Val; Band; Debate Tm; Hon Rl; Jr NHS; NHS; Stu Cncl; Yrbk; Ohio Univ; Chem Engr.

GANNON, LESLIE; Rock Hill Sr HS; Pedro, OH; Sec Soph Cls; Cls Rep Soph Cls; Sec Jr Cls; Chrh Wkr; Drl Tm; Hon Rl; Stu Cncl; Yth Flsp; 4-H; Spn Clb; Rio Grande Univ; Primary Tchr.

GANNON, RHONDA; Rock Hill Sr HS; Ironton, OH; Cls Rep Sr Cls; Band; Chrs; Chrh Wkr; Hon Rl; NHS; Stu Cncl; Beta Clb; Fr Clb; Mth Clb; Cincinnati Conserv; Music.

GANS, R; Northville HS; Northville, MI; Hon Rl; Lbry Ade; NHS; Yth Flsp; Ger Clb; Bsbl; Bsktbl; Letter Ftbl; Letter Swmmng; Trk; College.

GANSHORN, REBECCA; La Ville Jr Sr HS; Warsaw, IN; Chrs; Off Ade; FHA; Pep Clb; Spn Clb; Chrldng; Am Leg Awd;.

GANT, MARIAN; John Adams HS; Cleveland, OH; Sec Frsh Cls; Cls Rep Soph Cls; Hon Rl; JA; NHS; Stu Cncl; FNA; Cit Awd; Gov Hon Prg Awd; Natl Merit SF; Univ.

GANTERT, LAURA; Marysville Sr HS; Marysville, OH; Chrs; Chrh Wkr; Girl Scts; Lbry Ade; Sch Pl; Rptr Sch Nwsp; Drama Clb; 4-H; Univ Of Cincinnati; Sociology.

GANTHIER, STANLEY; St Francis De Sales HS; Toledo, OH; 1/203 Hon Rl; NHS; Fr Clb; IM Sprt; Algebra II French II Religion Amer Hstry Awards; Soc Dstngshd Amer HS Stu; University; Engr.

GANTZ, JILL; Webberville Comm HS; Webberville, MI; 4/72 Trs Soph Cls; Am Leg Aux Girls St; Chrh Wkr; Hon Rl; NHS; Sch Pl; Yth Flsp; Rptr Sch Nwsp; 4-H; FFA; Grand Rapids Baptist Coll; Psych.

GANZEL, PETE; St Francis De Sales HS; Toledo, OH; Cls Rep Frsh Cls; Cls Rep Soph Cls; Cl Rep Jr Cls; Cls Rep Sr Cls; Chrs; Chrh Wkr; Cmnty Wkr; PAVAS; Pol Wkr; Sch Mus; CYO Pres 77 & 78; CYO Exec Cntl For Diocese 79; Univ Of Cincinnati; Tchr.

GAPCZYNSKI, JULIE; Rogers City HS; Rogers City, MI; 17/156 Sec Frsh Cls; Sec Soph Cls; AFS; Band; Hon Rl; NHS; Sch Pl; Stg Crw; Drama Clb; 4-H; Lake Superior State Coll; Crim Just.

GARABELLI, LINDA M; Swan Valley HS; Saginaw, MI; 18/188 Cls Rep Frsh Cls; Boy Scts; Jr NHS; NHS; Sch Pl; Sct Actv; Stg Crw; Stu Cncl; 4-H; DAR Awd; Univ Of Michigan; Phys Therapy.

GARARD, TERESA; Columbia City Joint HS; Columbia City, IN; Chrs; Girl Scts; JA; Lbry Ade; 4-H; 4-H Awd; Beauty & Fashion Coll; Modeling.

GARAVAGLIA, MARTIN; Notre Dame HS; Detroit, MI; Hon Rl; Jr NHS; NHS; Rptr Yrbk; Yrbk; Letter Ten; Coach Actv; IM Sprt; Natl Merit Ltr; Natl Merit SF; Michigan St Univ; Psych.

GARBE, CONNIE; Norton HS; Norton, OH; 33/300 Cmnty Wkr; Girl Scts; Hon Rl; Lbry Ade; NHS; Sch Pl; Sct Actv; Stg Crw; Stu Cncl; Fr Clb; Norton Fam & Tchr Schlrshp Assn 79; Schlrshp Awd 73; March Of Dimes Teenage Rep Ldrshp Awd 78; Univ Of Akron; Acctg.

GARBER, JO; Bishop Ready HS; Galloway, OH; Drl Tm; Hosp Ade; Pol Wkr; Sch Mus; Sch Pl; Rptr Sch Nwsp; Drama Clb; Spn Clb; GAA; Mat Maids; Ohio St Univ; Pre Law.

GARBERICH, STEVE; Ontario HS; Mansfield, OH; 27/189 Bsbl; Bsktbl; Crs Cntry;.

GARBRANDT, VICKY; Hilliard HS; Hilliard, OH; AFS; Girl Scts; Lbry Ade; Orch; Sch Mus; Sct Actv; Yth Flsp; FHA; Treas OEA; Gym; Ohio St Univ; Busns Ed.

GARBRECHT, THOMAS P; Marysville HS; Marysville, OH; Am Leg Boys St; Band; Chrh Wkr; Cmnty Wkr; Debate Tm; Hosp Ade; Jr NHS; Lbry Ade; Sch Mus; Sec Yth Flsp; Ohio Coll; Library Sci.

GARCHA, NINA; Kent Roosevelt HS; Kent, OH; Cls Rep Frsh Cls; Cl Rep Jr Cls; Cls Rep Sr Cls; Hon Rl; NHS; Stu Cncl; Fr Clb; Pep Clb; Letter Hockey; IM Sprt; Kent State Univ; Bus Acctng.

GARCIA, CARLOS; Arthur Hill HS; Saginaw, MI; Chrh Wkr; Hon Rl; DECA; Sci Clb; Spn Clb; Univ; Law.

GARCIA, CARMEN; Pike Delta York HS; Delta, OH; Band; Chrs; Spn Clb; Letter Trk; Univ; Art Educ.

GARCIA, CATHY; Lakota HS; Burgeon, OH; 3/133 Trs Jr Cls; Cls Rep Sr Cls; Hon Rl; NHS; Sch Mus; Sch Pl; Stu Cncl; Rptr Yrbk; Rptr Sch Nwsp; Drama Clb; Bowling Green St Univ; Psych.

GARCIA, DAWN; Lake Orion Sr HS; Oxford, MI; Hon Rl; Lit Mag; NHS; Treas Stu Cncl; Rptr Yrbk; Yrbk; Rptr Sch Nwsp; Oakland Comm Coll; Med Tech.

GARCIA, DOMINGO G; Walsh Jesuit HS; Pepper Pike, OH; Hon Rl; Hosp Ade; Crs Cntry; IM Sprt; Natl Merit Ltr; Academic Scholarship; MVP Walsh Jesuit Jr High Chess Team; Case Western Reserve Univ; Engr.

GARCIA, LINDA; Saginaw HS; Saginaw, MI; Chrh Wkr; Hon Rl; Cert Of Proficiency For Typing 62 Wds Minute 79; Awd A Tuition Grant For 1200.

GARCIA, MAURICIO J; Chaminade Julienne HS; Dayton, OH; Bsktbl; Scr Kpr; College.

GARCIA, NELLY; Lincoln West HS; Cleveland, OH; Chrs; Girl Scts; Hon Rl; Pres Jr NHS; Off Ade; Stu Cncl; Gym; Chrldng; Baldwin Wallace Coll; Soc Work.

GARCIA, NORA; Bishop Noll Institute; Hammond, IN; Chrh Wkr; Cmnty Wkr; Debate Tm; Hon Rl; Natl Forn Lg; Sch Mus; Drama Clb; Sci Clb; Spn Clb; Natl Forensic Lge Awd 78; Amherst Coll; Poli Sci.

GARCIA, RAQUEL; Horace Mann HS; Gary, IN; 35/306 Hon Rl; Rptr Yrbk; OEA; Spn Clb;.

GARCIA, TERRY; Bishop Ready HS; Columbus, OH; VP Jr Cls; Chrs; Chrh Wkr; Girl Scts; VICA; Ten; Btty Crckr Awd; Capital Univ; Nursing.

GARD, MARY; La Salle HS; South Bend, IN; 4/490 Am Leg Aux Girls St; Hon Rl; NHS; Rptr Sch Nwsp; 4-H; Swmmng; DAR Awd; 4-H Awd; Univ.

GARD, PAM; Clay City HS; Cory, IN; Trs Jr Cls; Trs Sr Cls; Band; Drl Tm; VP NHS; Yth Flsp; 4-H; Pep Clb; Letter Trk; Chrldng; Oliver Nazarene Coll; Psych.

GARDELLA, GAIL C; Forest Park HS; Cincinnati, OH; 19/350 Cls Rep Frsh Cls; Chrs; Girl Scts; Hon Rl; Quill & Scroll; Sch Mus; Stu Cncl; Rptr Sch Nwsp; Pep Clb; Chrldng; Univ Of Cincinnati; Marketing.

GARDINER, DUKEANA; Escanaba Area Public HS; Escanaba, MI; 156/438 Chrs; Stg Crw; Drama Clb; Fr Clb; Northern Michigan Univ.

GARDNER, AMY; Olentangy HS; Galena, OH; 20/150 VP Frsh Cls; Cls Rep Frsh Cls; Pres Soph Cls; Pres Jr Cls; Chrh Wkr; FCA; Hon Rl; Lbry Ade; Sch Mus; Sch Pl; Univ; Recreation Dir.

GARDNER, CAROL; Bishop Noll Institute; Chicago, IL; 35/321 Hon Rl; Pep Clb; Scr Kpr; Natl Bus Honor Soc 79; Prest Serv Club 79; Illinois St Univ; Bus.

GARDNER, CATHY JO; Maplewood Area Joint Voc Sch; Ravenna, OH; 1/24 Sec Soph Cls; Pres Jr Cls; Hst Sr Cls; Hon Rl; JA; Stu Cncl; Yrbk; DECA; Ger Clb; Pep Clb; Kent St Univ; Distributive Educ.

GARDNER, CHERYL; Central HS; Grand Rapids, MI; Chrs; Cmnty Wkr; Girl Scts; Hon Rl; Key Clb; USC; Law.

GARDNER, DAVID; West Jefferson HS; W Jefferson, OH; Sal; Hon Rl; NHS; Fr Clb; Ftbl; Ten; Trk; Kiwan Awd; Columbus Tech Inst; Comp Prog.

GARDNER, DAVID; La Salle HS; Cincinnati, OH; 108/249 Hon Rl; Ftbl; IM Sprt; Univ Of Cincinnati; Architecture.

GARDNER, DON; Orrville HS; Orrville, OH; 37/166 Aud/Vis; Chrh Wkr; Cmnty Wkr; Hon Rl; Lbry Ade; Stg Crw;.

GARDNER, EDWARD T; Indian Valley South HS; Gnadenhutten, OH; Hon Rl; Yth Flsp; Pep Clb; Bsktbl; Ftbl;.

GARDNER, JAN; Riverview Commun HS; Riverview, MI; Band; Chrs; Chrh Wkr; Girl Scts; Hon Rl; Jr NHS; Chrldng; Cit Awd; Univ Of Michigan; Bus Admin.

GARDNER, JANE; Waldron HS; Shelbyville, IN; 4/75 Sec Frsh Cls; Sec Jr Cls; Band; Chrs; FCA; Hon Rl; NHS; Sch Pl; Yth Flsp; Ed Yrbk; Univ; Psych.

GARDNER, JANE E; Waldron HS; Shelbyville, IN; Sec Frsh Cls; Sec Jr Cls; Band; Chrs; Chrh Wkr; FCA; Hon Rl; Yth Flsp; Ed Yrbk; 4-H; Univ; Sociology.

GARDNER, JENNY; Loudonville HS; Loudonville, OH; Am Leg Aux Girls St; Band; Chrs; Jr NHS; NHS; Stu Cncl; Sprt Ed Yrbk; Rptr Sch Nwsp; Letter Trk; Cit Awd; College.

GARDNER, JULIE; New Albany HS; New Albany, IN; 41/565 Cls Rep Frsh Cls; Cl Rep Jr Cls; Am Leg Aux Girls St; Chrh Wkr; Debate Tm; Hon Rl; NHS; Stg Crw; Stu Cncl; Yth Flsp; Ball St Univ; Psych.

GARDNER, LYNN; Green HS; Akron, OH; 48/320 Band; Chrs; Chrh Wkr; Hon Rl; JA; Mdrgl; Off Ade; Stg Crw; Yrbk; Drama Clb; Akron Univ; Psych.

GARDNER, MARK; David Anderson HS; Lisbon, OH; 14/96 VP Soph Cls; VP Jr Cls; Am Leg Boys St; Chrh Wkr; NHS; Stu Cncl; Key Clb; Ftbl; Trk; Scr Kpr; R L Leggett Schlrshp 79; Jr Sr Prom King 78 & 79; Teenager Of The Mnth For Schl & Dist 79; Slippery Rock St Colll.

GARDNER, MARTY; Lawrenceburg HS; Lawrncbrg, IN; Cls Rep Soph Cls; Hon Rl; Stu Cncl; Rptr Yrbk; Key Clb; Spn Clb; Bsbl; Letter Ftbl; Letter Wrstlng; IM Sprt; Univ.

GARDNER, NORMAN; North Ridgeville HS; N Ridgeville, OH; Cls Rep Frsh Cls; Hon Rl; Leo Clb; Spn Clb; Bsbl; Ftbl; Scr Kpr; Lion Awd; Univ Of Michigan; Forestry Engr.

GARDNER, RANDALL; Buckeye Central HS; New Washington, OH; 2/80 Band; Letter Ftbl; IM Sprt; North Central Tech Coll; Mech Engr.

GARDNER, STEVEN; Columbus Academy; Westerville, OH; 6/45 Pres Jr Cls; Val; Sec Am Leg Boys St; Hon Rl; Sch Pl; Pres Yth Flsp; Rptr Sch Nwsp; Drama Clb; Socr; Chrldng; Duke Univ.

GARDNER, WAYNE; Pine River Jr Sr HS; Le Roy, MI; Hon Rl; NHS; Rptr Yrbk; Pep Clb; Letter Crs Cntry; Capt Trk; Letter Wrstlng; Michigan St Univ; Pre Law.

GARDNER, WENDY; Westfield Washington HS; Westfield, IN; Cls Rep Soph Cls; VP Jr Cls; Hon Rl; NHS; Stu Cncl; Yth Flsp; Pep Clb; Spn Clb; Trk; Chrldng; Univ; Comp Sci.

GAREIS, KELLEE; Brookfield HS; Brookfield, OH; 18/160 Chrs; Hon Rl; NHS; Quill & Scroll; Sch Pl; Yrbk; Treas Beta Clb; Spn Clb; Kent State Univ; Speech & Hearngpath.

GAREN, MARCIA D; Defiance Sr HS; Defiance, OH; Band; Hon Rl; JA; NHS; Stg Crw; Stu Cncl; Rptr Yrbk; Pep Clb; Mat Maids; Univ.

GAREY, LORY; Miller HS; Crooksville, OH; Trs Jr Cls; Band; Hon Rl; Lbry Ade; Treas NHS; Sch Pl; Stu Cncl; Sec Yth Flsp; 4-H; FBLA; Spec Serv Awrd 79; Univ.

GAREY, TRACI; Upper Valley Joint Voc HS; Covington, OH; Hon Rl; Lbry Ade; Yrbk; 4-H; FHA; FTA; OEA; Pep Clb; Legal Sec.

GARFIELD, RONALD; St Agatha HS; Detroit, MI; 60/160 Aud/Vis; Boy Scts; Chrh Wkr; Sct Actv; Rptr Yrbk; Spn Clb; Letter Bsbl; Letter Ftbl; Hope Coll; Chem.

GARGANO, ANNE; Holland HS; Holland, MI; Chrh Wkr; Hon Rl; Off Ade; Yth Flsp; Fr Clb; Mgrs; Hope College; Engl.

GARGANO, PATRICIA; St Mary Academy; Monroe, MI; 12/131 Cmp Fr Grls; Cmnty Wkr; Hon Rl; Hosp Ade; NHS; Stu Cncl; FNA; Pep Clb; Bsbl; Bsktbl; Four Year Honor Roll; Student Faculty Board 78; St Vincents Hosp; Radiology Tech.

GARING, KEVIN; Broad Ripple HS; Indianapolis, IN; Band; Hon Rl; Sch Mus; Mth Clb; Sci Clb; College; Chem.

GARLAND, AMANDA; Garfield HS; Akron, OH; Chrs; Cmnty Wkr; Drl Tm; Hosp Ade; JA; Off Ade; Fr Clb; Lat Clb; Pep Clb; JA Awd; College; Psych.

GARLAND, JEFF; Eau Claire HS; Sodus, MI; Boy Scts; Hon Rl; VP NHS; Pres Stu Cncl; Yrbk; Sch Nwsp; Bsktbl; Ten; Frsh Phys Sci Awd; Jr Eng Awd & Phys Educ Awd; Lansing Cmnty Coll; Photog.

GARLAND, JOHN; Switzerland County HS; Vevay, IN; Sch Mus; Sch Pl; Stg Crw; Drama Clb; 4-H; FFA; Sci Clb; Trk; IM Sprt; Tmr; Univ.

GARLAND, KIMBERLY; Zanesville HS; Zanesville, OH; 20/400 Chrh Wkr; Drl Tm; Girl Scts; Hon Rl; Jr NHS; NHS; Off Ade; Yth Flsp; Lat Clb; Sci Clb; Ohio Northern Univ; Pharm.

GARLAND, VALERIE J; John J Pershing HS; Detroit, MI; Chrs; Hon Rl; NHS; ROTC; Sch Pl; Drama Clb; Am Leg Awd; Dnfth Awd; DAR Awd; Superior Jr Cadet 1977; Volleyball 3 Ltrs; Univ; Poli Sci.

GARLICK, JOSEPH; Richmond HS; Richmond, MI; Pres Soph Cls; Band; NHS; Letter Ftbl; Richmond Ed Assoc Schlrshp 79; St Of Mi Comp Schlrshp 79; Sr Ath Awd 79; Oakland Univ; Med Tech.

GARLICK, MICHAEL T; Arthur Hill HS; Saginaw, MI; Boy Scts; Chrh Wkr; Drm Bgl; Sct Actv; Stg Crw; Drama Clb; Pep Clb; Sci Clb; Elk Awd; Mic State; Chem Engr.

GARMAN, RONALD; Howland HS; Warren, OH; 8/440 Cls Rep Sr Cls; Boy Scts; NHS; Stu Cncl; Letter Crs Cntry; Trk; Natl Merit SF; College; Engr.

GARMATTER, SCOTT; Bluffton HS; Col Grv, OH; Capt Ftbl;.

GARMON, ALVIN; Libbey HS; Toledo, OH; 38/285 Cmnty Wkr; Hon Rl; NHS; Boys Clb Am; Pep Clb; Bsktbl; Coach Actv; IM Sprt; Mgrs; Scr Kpr; College; Bus Admin.

GARMON, CINDY; Sand Creek HS; Adrian, MI; Cmp Fr Grls; Chrh Wkr; Cmnty Wkr; Rptr Yrbk; FHA; Univ; Elem Educ.

GARN, DIANNE; E Liverpool HS; E Liverpool, OH; 24/342 Band; Cmp Fr Grls; Chrh Wkr; Lit Mag; FTA; Spn Clb; Kent St Univ; Nutrition.

GARN, KATHRYN; Saint Ursula Acad; Toledo, OH; Cls Rep Soph Cls; Sec Jr Cls; Hon Rl; Sch Pl; Drama Clb; Fr Clb; Bowling Green Univ.

GARNCZARSKI, WIESIA; St Ladislaus HS; Detroit, MI; Chrh Wkr; Hon Rl; Drama Clb; Fr Clb; Pep Clb; Trk; Mercy Coll; Dietetics.

GARNER, CAROL; Fulton HS; Middleton, MI; 13/109 Trs Soph Cls; Cls Rep Sr Cls; Hon Rl; Stu Cncl; 4-H; FHA; Mth Clb; Trk; Chrldng; Pom Pon; College; Computer Progr.

GARNER, DEBBIE; Centerville HS; Centerville, OH; OEA; Mgrs; Bus Schl; Clerical.

GARNER, DEBRA; Benjamin Bosse HS; Evansville, IN; Chrh Wkr; Girl Scts; Hon Rl; Hosp Ade; Sct Actv; Fr Clb; Letter Gym; Chrldng; Cit Awd; Pres Awd; City Math Champ; Univ; Med.

GARNER, GREGORY; Deer Park HS; Cincinnati, OH; 40/220 Band; Boy Scts; Drm Bgl; Hon Rl; Stg Crw; Yth Flsp; Sch Nwsp; Nom To Natl Hon Soc 79; In AP Hon Math Class Calculus 79; Univ; Bus Admin.

GARNER, JENNIFER; Alexandria Monroe HS; Alexandria, IN; Band; Drl Tm; Girl Scts; Hon Rl; Hosp Ade; NHS; Off Ade; Sch Mus; Pep Clb; Spn Clb; Soc Work.

GARNER, LANA; Mason Consolidated HS; La Salle, MI; 30/125 Band; Chrs; Chrh Wkr; Hon Rl; NHS; Sch Pl; FHA; Monroe Cnty Comm College; Bus Admin.

GARNER, STUART; Seven Hills HS; Cincinnati, OH; 11/50 VP Frsh Cls; Cls Rep Soph Cls; VP Jr Cls; Chrs; Hon Rl; Stu Cncl; Mth Clb; Bsbl; Letter Socr; Coach Actv; Univ; Aero Space Engr.

GARNER, TAMMIE; Meadowdale HS; Dayton, OH; Cls Rep Frsh Cls; Cls Rep Soph Cls; Sch Pl; Stu Cncl; Pep Clb; Gym; Hndbl; Trk; Chrldng; Pom Pon; Coll; Sci.

GARNER, TRACY; Freeland HS; Freeland, MI; Band; Chrh Wkr; Hon Rl; Yth Flsp; Pep Clb; Natl Merit Schl; Delta College; Bus Mgmt.

GARNES, DAVID; Marion Harding HS; Marion, OH; Drm Bgl; Sci Clb; College; Architecture.

GARNES, GREGORY; East HS; Columbus, OH; Off Ade; Spn Clb; College; Dentistry.

GARNETT, LISA; Hebron HS; Hebron, IN; Band; Hon Rl; Rptr Sch Nwsp; Drama Clb; FHA; OEA; Pep Clb; Spn Clb; Bsbl; Gym;.

GARNETT, ROBERT F; Reitz Memorial HS; Evansville, IN; 2/220 Pres Soph Cls; Hon Rl; NHS; Stu Cncl; Rptr Sch Nwsp; Sch Nwsp; Letter Crs Cntry; Letter Trk; St Seme Finlst In Optimist Oratorical Contst; Math Dept Awd; Univ; Law.

GARNETT, VALERIE; Garden City East HS; Garden City, MI; 1/375 Cls Rep Soph Cls; Cl Rep Jr Cls; Val; Band; Sec Jr NHS; Stu Cncl; Ten; Chrldng; Wayne St Merit Schlrshp 79; Mi Competitive Schlrshp Awd 79; Western Mi Univ Schlrshp 79; Wayne St Univ; Radiation Ther Tech.

GARNICA, MAGDALENA; Bishop Noll Inst; E Chicago, IN; Cls Rep Frsh Cls; Cls Rep Soph Cls; Cl Rep Jr Cls; Hon Rl; Stu Cncl; Spn Clb; Mat Maids; Scr Kpr; Purdue Univ; Political Science.

GARNICK, STEPHEN; Toronto HS; Toronto, OH; Am Leg Boys St; Hon Rl; Univ; Optometry.

GARNICK, STEVE; Toronto HS; Toronto, OH; Am Leg Boys St; Hon Rl; Optometry.

GARNO, CARL; Utica Sr HS; Newark, OH; Hon Rl; Off Ade; Spn Clb; Whos Who Among Amer HS Stu 77; Voc Schl.

GAROFALO, JULIE; Solon HS; Solon, OH; Chrs; Hon Rl; Hosp Ade; NHS; Rptr Yrbk; Yrbk; Pep Clb; IM Sprt; Hnr Mention In Amer Hist Div 1; Awd Pin 100 Hrs Of Volunteer Hosp Work; Hnr Roll Stu; Kent St Univ; Med Rec.

GAROZZO, JOHN; De La Salle Collegiate HS; East Detroit, MI; Hon Rl; Sch Pl; Stg Crw; Bsbl; IM Sprt; Macomb Cnty Cmnty Coll; Elec Engr.

GARR, WILLIAM; Notre Dame HS; Detroit, MI; Debate Tm; Hosp Ade; NHS; Sch Mus; Stg Crw; Yrbk; Ed Sch Nwsp; Mic State Univ.

GARRABRANT, TERRI; Northridge HS; Johnstown, OH; Hon Rl; Lbry Ade; Stu Cncl; Pres Yth Flsp; FHA; VP FTA; Spn Clb; Acad Schlrshp Tm In Eng 78; Acad Awd For Lib Work 79; Ohio Dominican Univ; Lib Sci.

GARRARD, CHRISTIE; Centerville HS; Centerville, OH; 47/687 Cls Rep Soph Cls; Cl Rep Jr Cls; Chrs; Chrh Wkr; Hon Rl; Jr NHS; NHS; Sch Mus; Pep Clb; Letter Chrldng; Wright St Univ; Educ.

GARREN, MIKE; Barberton HS; Barberton, OH; Hon Rl; Univ Of Akron; Engr.

GARRETSON, REGGIE; Guyan Valley HS; Branchland, WV; 18/100 Cl Rep Jr Cls; Pres Sr Cls; Boy Scts; Hon Rl; NHS; Stu Cncl; 4-H; Sci Clb; Bsktbl; Ftbl; Football Schlrshp W Va Inst Of Tech; Sr Superlatives Mr Guyan Valley Most Athletic; Class A All Tourn Team; W Virginia Inst Of Tech; Mining Engr.

GARRETT, AMY; Hastings HS; Dowling, MI; Sec Soph Cls; Trs Soph Cls; Cl Rep Jr Cls; Band; Hon Rl; NHS; Stu Cncl; Beta Clb; Bsktbl; Letter Trk; Mich Tech Univ; Engineering.

GARRETT, ANITA; The Flint Academy; Flint, MI; Chrs; Chrh Wkr; Hon Rl; Lbry Ade; Off Ade; Capt Bsktbl; Chrldng; Scr Kpr; Baker Jr Coll; Sec.

GARRETT, BECKY; Philo HS; Zanesville, OH; Band; Hon Rl; Lit Mag; NHS; Off Ade; Orch; Sch Mus; Sch Pl; Yrbk; Tech College; Data Proc.

GARRETT, BOBBIE; Sandusky HS; Sandusky, OH; 145/500 Chrs; Chrh Wkr; Hon Rl; Lbry Ade; Off Ade; OEA; Trk; Ohio St Univ; Eng.

GARRETT, DEBORAH; Pontiac Central HS; Pontiac, MI; Cls Rep Frsh Cls; Cls Rep Soph Cls; Cl Rep Jr Cls; Sch Nwsp; Pep Clb; Bsktbl; Trk; Coach Actv; PPFtbl; Perfct Attndnc Awd 75; Univ Of Detroit; Nursing.

GARRETT, DEBRA; Davison Sr HS; Davison, MI; Girl Scts; Hon Rl; Sct Actv; Yrbk; Rptr Sch Nwsp; Sci Clb; Capt Chrldng; Michigan Competitive Schlrshp; Cheerleading Comp 8th In Nation 3rd In Mich; Awd Key To City St Bskblt Champ; Michigan St Univ.

GARRETT, GORDON; John R Buchtel Univ HS; Akron, OH; Cls Rep Frsh Cls; Cls Rep Soph Cls; Cl Rep Jr Cls; Cls Rep Sr Cls; Aud/Vis; Band; Hon Rl; Sch Pl; Stu Cncl; Sch Nwsp; Univ Of Akron; Elec Tech.

GARRETT, JON; Culver Military Academy; Lacon, IL; 125/200 Band; Chrs; Hon Rl; ROTC; Glf; Ten; Trk; IM Sprt; Cit Awd; Colorado St Univ; Law.

GARRETT, JULIE; Shenandoah HS; Middletown, IN; 11/118 Cls Rep Frsh Cls; NHS; Mth Clb; Coach Actv; Mat Maids; Coll; Nursing.

GARRETT, LAURA; Port Austin Public HS; Port Austin, MI; Sec Soph Cls; Pres Jr Cls; Chrs; Hon Rl; Sch Mus; Sch Pl; Stu Cncl; Yth Flsp; Drama Clb; FHA; Spring Arbor Coll; Christian Music.

GARRETT, MARIBETH; Eaton HS; Camden, OH; 57/171 Hon Rl; Kettering Coll; RN.

GARRETT, PAM; Tecumseh HS; New Carlisle, OH; 58/344 Cls Rep Frsh Cls; Hon Rl; Jr NHS; NHS; VP FBLA; Bsktbl; Mgrs; Scr Kpr; Sinclair Comm Coll; Elec Data Procs.

GARRETT, RICK; Niles HS; Niles, MI; Treas Chrs; Hon Rl; Sch Mus; Sch Pl; Stu Cncl; Drama Clb; Lion Awd; Vocational; Architecture.

GARRETT, RYAN; Stockbridge HS; Stockbridge, MI; 13/133 Am Leg Boys St; Pres Band; Cmnty Wkr; Drm Mjrt; Hon Rl; NHS; Sch Mus; Sci Clb; Bsbl; Bsktbl; Outstndg Ath Awd Stockbridge HS 79; Mi Comptn Schlrshp Awd 79; Olivet Trustees Schlrshp 79; Olivet Coll; Elem Ed.

GARRETT, SHERRY; Bedford HS; Bedford, OH; Cl Rep Jr Cls; Band; Chrs; Chrh Wkr; Spn Clb; Univ; Bus Admin.

GARRETT, STEVAN; Kimball HS; Royal Oak, MI; 288/609 Band; Boy Scts; Hon Rl; JA; Sct Actv; Yth Flsp; Northern Michigan Univ; Math Tchr.

GARRETT, SUSAN; Williamstown HS; Williamstown, WV; Yth Flsp; Y-Teens; Pep Clb; Letter Trk; Mgrs; College; Dental Asst.

GARRETT, TIM; Reynoldsburg HS; Reynoldburg, OH; Ohio St Univ; Bus Mgmt.

GARRINGER, LAYNE; Miami Trace HS; Jamestown, OH; AFS; Band; Chrh Wkr; Hon Rl; Jr NHS; NHS; Orch; Sch Mus; Drama Clb; FFA; Abilene Christian Univ; Agri.

GARRIOTT, DONNA; Salem HS; Scottsburg, IN; Aud/Vis; Band; Chrh Wkr; Hon Rl; NHS;.

GARRISON, DAVID; Southwestern HS; Edinburg, IN; 7/63 Aud/Vis; Band; Chrs; Chrh Wkr; Cmnty Wkr; Hon Rl; Sch Mus; Drama Clb; 4-H; FFA; Natl Math Contest Awd 1979; Purdue Univ; Agri.

GARRISON, DENISE R; Hillsboro HS; Hillsboro, OH; Pres Frsh Cls; Cls Rep Soph Cls; Band; Chrs; Chrh Wkr; Cmnty Wkr; Sch Mus; Stg Crw; Stu Cncl; Trk; Homecoming Attendant 1978; Miami Jacobs Univ; Fashion Mdse.

GARRISON, KRYSTAL; Hillsdale HS; Ashland, OH; 7/120 Cls Rep Soph Cls; VP Sr Cls; Sec Band; Chrs; Hon Rl; Sec NHS; Sch Mus; Sch Pl; Stg Crw; Drama Clb; North Central Tech Coll; X Ray Tech.

GARRISON, LAURA; William Henry Harrison HS; W Laf, IN; Cmp Fr Grls; FFA; Pres Spn Clb; Univ.

GARRISON, VIRGINIA; Seeger Memorial HS; Boswell, IN; Chrh Wkr; Hon Rl; Hosp Ade; Lbry Ade; Stg Crw; Yrbk; Drama Clb; 4-H; Mas Awd; Busns Schl; Busns.

GARRITANO, ANN MARIE L; Divine Child HS; Dearborn Hgts, MI; 1/200 Chrs; Cmnty Wkr; Hon Rl; Pres NHS; Sci Clb; Trk; IM Sprt; Natl Merit SF; City Of Dearborn Environmntl Agncy Commissioner; Detroit Regional Sci Fair Winner; College; Medicine.

GARROD, PAUL F; Lawrence HS; Lawrence, MI; 15/51 Cls Rep Soph Cls; Band; Chrh Wkr; Off Ade; Sch Mus; Sch Pl; Yth Flsp; Ed Sch Nwsp; Sprt Ed Sch Nwsp; 4-H; Western Michigan Univ; Radio Telecom.

GARROD, SCOTT; Lawrence HS; Lawrence, MI; Cl Rep Jr Cls; Pres Sr Cls; Treas Band; Hon Rl; Pres NHS; Sch Pl; Pres Stu Cncl; VP Yth Flsp; 4-H; Capt Ftbl; Michigan St Univ; Comp Sci.

GARSTECK, CHRISTINE; Strongsville HS; Strongsville, OH; Cl Rep Jr Cls; Jr NHS; Quill & Scroll; Stu Cncl; 4-H; FHA; GAA; PPFtbl; Scr Kpr; 4-H Awd; Cuyahoga Comm Coll; Aviation.

GARTHWAITE, SCOTT; Escanaba Area Public HS; Greenville, MI; 26/423 Band; Boy Scts; Chrh Wkr; JA; NHS; Pol Wkr; Yth Flsp; Rptr Sch Nwsp; JA Awd; Mic Tech Univ; Chem Eng.

GARTNER, LORA; Hammond HS; Hammond, IN; Chrs; Hon Rl; Jr NHS; Sch Mus; Rptr Yrbk; Indinan Univ; Arts.

GARTON, MARTY; Lewis County HS; Weston, WV; Chrh Wkr; Cmnty Wkr; Hon Rl; Letter Bsbl; Crs Cntry; Ftbl; Letter Trk; Voc Schl; Construction.

GARULA, LAURA; William Mason HS; Mason, OH; 12/189 AFS; Am Leg Aux Girls St; Girl Scts; Hon Rl; NHS; Fr Clb; Sci Clb; Scr Kpr; Schlstc Acvhtn Test French I 77; Schlstc Achvmtn Tst French II 78; Schlstc Acvmtn Test Algbr II 79; Univ; Med Tech.

GARVER, KIM; Northwestern HS; W Salem, OH; Chrs; Girl Scts; Sch Pl; Yth Flsp; Drama Clb; FTA; Lat Clb; Pep Clb; Capt Chrldng; Scr Kpr; College; Elem Ed.

GARVERICK, HANNAH; Cardington Lincoln HS; Cardington, OH; Pres Frsh Cls; Chrs; Hon Rl; NHS; Off Ade; Sch Pl; Yrbk; Bowling Green Univ; Vet Assist.

GARVERICK, RUTH; Eastmoor Sr HS; Columbus, OH; 31/290 Band; Chrh Wkr; Hon Rl; Yth Flsp; Pres OEA; College; Personnel Admin.

GARVEY, JAMES; Padua Franciscan HS; Parma, OH; 28/270 Cls Rep Frsh Cls; Cls Rep Sr Cls; Hon Rl; Jr NHS; Pres NHS; Stu Cncl; Key Clb; Capt Crs Cntry; Trk; Letter Wrstlng; John Carroll Univ; Acctng.

GARVEY, PATRICIA; Marietta HS; Marietta, OH; Band; Girl Scts; Hon Rl; Yth Flsp; Fr Clb; GAA; IM Sprt; Scr Kpr; College.

GARVIN, JAMES; Tecumseh HS; Pt Clinton, OH; 61/245 Chrh Wkr; Pres Yth Flsp; 4-H; Crs Cntry; Letter Trk; IM Sprt; Scr Kpr; Tmr; Pres Awd; Mi Compt Schlshp 7.; Michigan St Univ; Bus Mgmt.

GARVIN, LARRY T; Oak Park HS; Oak Park, MI; 20/360 Cmnty Wkr; Lit Mag; Mod UN; Pol Wkr; Stu Cncl; FDA; Coach Actv; Natl Merit SF; Honors Convocation Service Awards 77; Explorers Post 77; Michigan Mathematics Prize Competiton Semi Finslis; Univ; Pre Med.

GARVIN, PAUL; Clyde HS; Clyde, OH; Am Leg Boys St; Boy Scts; Chrh Wkr; Hon Rl; NHS; Sct Actv; Letter Trk; Ohi State Univ; Natural Resource.

GARWOOD, HELEN; Hazel Park HS; Hazel Park, MI; 6/306 Hon Rl; NHS; Twrlr; Mas Awd; Pres Awd; Alma Coll; Acctg.

GARWOOD, JENNIFER; Fairmont West HS; Kettering, OH; Chrs; Chrh Wkr; Girl Scts; Hon Rl; Orch; Sch Mus; Pep Clb; Letter Bsktbl; Warren Wilson Coll; Tchr.

GARY, DEBORAH; Dearborn HS; Dearborn, MI; Hon Rl; Ten; IM Sprt; College; Bus.

GARY, KENNETH; Fremont HS; Fremont, IN; 17/70 Band; Hon Rl; Sch Mus; Sch Pl; Stg Crw; Drama Clb; 4-H; Spn Clb; Capt Crs Cntry; Letter Trk; Mech Drawng Awd 77; Gold Medl In All St Solo Ensmbl 79; Univ; Elec Engr.

GARY, SHERI; Perry HS; Lima, OH; VP Frsh Cls; Cls Rep Soph Cls; Hon Rl; Sch Pl; Stu Cncl; Rptr Sch Nwsp; Trk; Ohi State Beauty Acad; Beautician.

GARY, VANESSA; Henry Ford HS; Detroit, MI; 24/496 Chrh Wkr; Hon Rl; NHS; Yrbk; Lat Clb; Mercy Coll; Nursing.

GARZA, DONNA; Tiffin Columbian HS; Bloomville, OH; Band; Chrs; Chrh Wkr; Girl Scts; Hon Rl; Lbry Ade; Off Ade; Sct Actv; 4-H; Pep Clb; Regnl History Day Superior Jr 79; Oh St History Day Contest Excellnt Jr 79; Solo & Ensemble Contst 3; Voc Schl; Acctg.

GARZA, LORI A; Wayne Memorial HS; Westland, MI; Hon Rl; Spn Clb; Letter Trk; Univ; RN.

GARZA, MICHELLE; Divine Child HS; Dearborn Hts, MI; Chrs; Drl Tm; Hon Rl; Lit Mag; Sch Mus;

Sch Pl; Stg Crw; Drama Clb; Spn Clb; Letter Trk; Univ Of Michigan; Cosmetology.

GARZA, MIKE; Loy Norrix HS; Kalamazoo, MI; Boy Scts; Hon Rl; Michigan St Univ; Mech Engr.

GARZA, RACHEL C; Port Clinton HS; Pt Clinton, OH; Hon Rl; NHS; FHA; Coll; Chiropractic.

GARZA, ROSANNE; Bishop Noll Inst; Hammond, IN; 61/337 Band; Hon Rl; NHS; Tmr; St Mary Of The Woods; Pre Dent.

GARZELLONI, TINA; Mona Shores HS; Muskegon, MI; Hon Rl; NHS; Sch Pl; Rptr Yrbk; Rptr Sch Nwsp; Muskegon Community College; Bus.

GASCHO, LONNIE; Fairview Area Schools; Fairview, MI; 2/47 Sal; Am Leg Boys St; Hon Rl; Sprt Ed Sch Nwsp; Letter Bsbl; Bsktbl; Letter Crs Cntry; Letter Glf; Letter Trk; Pres Awd; Best Sr Athlete 78; Alma Coll; Acctg.

GASE, STEPHEN; Tiffin Calvert HS; Tiffin, OH; 8/96 Chrs; Hon Rl; Treas JA; Sch Mus; Ftbl; Ten; IM Sprt; Scr Kpr; Tmr; Cit Awd; Bowling Green St Univ; Math.

GASIECKI, MICHAEL J; Bishop Noll Inst; Chicago, IL; 29/363 Bsktbl; Letter Ftbl; IM Sprt; Univ Of Illinois; Vet Med.

GASKELL, KENNETH; Winston Churchill HS; Livonia, MI; Cls Rep Frsh Cls; Cls Rep Soph Cls; Cl Rep Jr Cls; Cls Rep Sr Cls; Band; Boy Scts; Pol Wkr; Stu Cncl; Mth Clb; OEA; 17th Plc Office Educ Clb Comp Data Proc 79; Eagle Sct Boy Sct 77; Michigan St Univ; Comp Design.

GASKINS, CHARLES R; Point Pleasant HS; Point Pleasant, WV; 15/270 Am Leg Boys St; Band; Chrs; Chrh Wkr; Drl Tm; Hon Rl; NHS; Pres Yth Flsp; VP 4-H; Key Clb; Univ; Pharm.

GASPAR, TERESA; Parchment HS; Parchment, MI; Chrs; Girl Scts; Hon Rl; NHS; Sch Mus; Sch Pl; Glf; Natl Merit Schl; Michigan St Univ.

GASPAR, TROY; Carman HS; Flint, MI; Chrs; Sch Mus; Sch Pl; Stg Crw; Drama Clb; Mic Tech; Math.

GASPAROVIC, DEBORAH; Owosso HS; Owosso, MI; 18/406 Chrs; Hon Rl; NHS; 4-H; Lat Clb; 4-H Awd; Natl Merit Ltr; Lansing Cmnty Coll; Comp Progr.

GASPER, DARLENA; Greenville HS; Greenville, OH; 97/332 Band; Chrs; Drl Tm; Hon Rl; Sch Mus; Business School; Secretarial.

GASPER, MARK; Fairport Harding HS; Fairport, OH; 4/53 Trs Soph Cls; Hon Rl; NHS; Sch Mus; Sch Pl; Stg Crw; Capt Bsktbl; Marquette Univ; Business.

GASPER, SHARON; Clay HS; South Bend, IN; Cls Rep Soph Cls; Cl Rep Jr Cls; Cls Rep Sr Cls; Cmnty Wkr; Hon Rl; Lbry Ade; Off Ade; PAVAS; Sch Pl; Stg Crw; Summ Hon Theatre Sem Awd 79; Northwestern Univ; Theatre.

GASPER, SUSAN; Martinsburg HS; Martinsburg, WV; 38/220 Girl Scts; Hon Rl; Hosp Ade; Lbry Ade; NHS; 4-H; Sci Clb; Coll; Nursing.

GASS, KARL; Miami Trace HS; Washington Ch, OH; 5/275 Am Leg Boys St; Band; Chrh Wkr; Hon Rl; NHS; Drama Clb; Treas Sci Clb; Trk; Am Leg Awd; College; Optical Engineering.

GASSER, CINDY; Salem HS; Scottsburg, IN; Am Leg Aux Girls St; VP Chrs; NHS; Stu Cncl; Ed Yrbk; Rptr Sch Nwsp; Drama Clb; Spn Clb; PPFtbl; Jurnlsm Summer Workshp At In Univ For Ed 78; Awd For Bst Featr Story Wrter On Schl Newsppr 79; Indiana Univ S E; Psych.

GASSER, PATTY; Ottoville Local HS; Delphos, OH; Hon Rl; Lbry Ade; Yrbk; FHA; Business School; Sec.

GASSMAN, R; St Clement HS; Warren, MI; Aud/Vis; Boy Scts; Chrh Wkr; Hon Rl; JA; Stg Crw; Sch Nwsp; Bsbl; Letter Bsktbl; Ftbl; Michigan St Univ; Busns.

GAST, GREGORY; Withrow HS; Cincinnati, OH; 63/554 Cmnty Wkr; Debate Tm; Hon Rl; Natl Forn Lg; Off Ade; PAVAS; Pol Wkr; Sch Mus; Sch Pl; Stg Crw; Ohio Univ; Poli Sci.

GASTEL, PATTI; St Joseph Cntrl Catholic HS; Fremont, OH; 10/85 Hon Rl; NHS; FTA; Letter Bsktbl; Am Leg Awd; Bowling Green St Univ; Comp Sci.

GASTIAN, JON; Springfield HS; Springfield, MI; Band; Hon Rl; Bsbl; Bsktbl; Ftbl; Mgrs;.

GASTINEAU, EDWARD A; Stonewall Jackson HS; Charleston, WV; Am Leg Boys St; Aud/Vis; Boy S cts; Chrh Wkr; Cmnty Wkr; FCA; Hon Rl; Sct Actv; Yth Flsp; Key Clb; Eagle Scout 77; Od Of Arrow 75; Lodge Chief Of Od Of Arrow 78; West Virginia Univ; Med.

GASTINEAU, JEFF; Tecumseh HS; New Carlisle, OH; 18/402 Band; FCA; Hon Rl; Pres Jr NHS; Pres NHS; Sch Mus; Letter Bsbl; Bsktbl; Ftbl; Miami Central Conf Scholar Athlete Awd; College; Music.

GASTINEAU, TERESA; Central HS; Switz City, IN; 1/48 Val; Sec NHS; Red Cr Ade; Purdue Univ; Acctg.

GASTON, BARBARA; South Harrison HS; Lost Creek, WV; Sec Frsh Cls; Chrs; Jr NHS; NHS; FBLA; Fairmont Comm Coll; Data Proc.

GASTON, KATHRYN M; Lordstown HS; Warren, OH; Band; Chrs; Hon Rl; VP Lbry Ade; Yth Flsp; OEA; Trk; Scr Kpr; College; Nursing.

GASTON, LOU; Buckhannon Upshur HS; Buckhannon, WV; Cls Rep Frsh Cls; Pres Soph Cls; Pres Jr Cls; Chrs; Girl Scts; Hon Rl; Sch Mus; Stu Cncl; 4-H; Pep Clb; Buckhannon Comm Theatre;.

GASTON, SHARON; Chaminade Julienne HS; Dayton, OH; VP Soph Cls; Hon Rl; NHS; Dnfth Awd; Otstndng Stud Serv Awd 78; Howard Univ; Bus.

GASTON, VICKY; Weir HS; New Cumberland, WV; 54/343 Band; Chrh Wkr; Yth Flsp; Pres 4-H; Spn Clb; Twrlr; 4-H Awd; Glenville St Coll; Elem Educ.

GATES, BETSY; Columbia City Joint HS; Columbia City, IN; 1/273 Cls Rep Frsh Cls; Cls Rep Soph Cls; Pres Jr Cls; Cl Rep Jr Cls; Pres Sr Cls; Cls Rep Sr Cls; Am Leg Aux Girls St; Band; Chrs; Chrh Wkr; Whos Who In Frgn Lang In In & Ky 78; Historian Of Th Yr 79;.

GATES, DEEANN; Brooke HS; Follansbee, WV; 2/461 Cls Rep Frsh Cls; Sal; Chrs; Chrh Wkr; Lit Mag; Mdrgl; Quill & Scroll; Drama Clb; Spn Clb; Trk; Jefferson Tech Coll; Elec Engr.

GATES, DIANA; Bedford North Lawrence HS; Bedford, IN; 84/450 Hon Rl; Fr Clb; Mth Clb; Bedford North Lawrence Oakland; Sec.

GATES, DONNA; Parkside HS; Jackson, MI; 15/348 Chrs; Debate Tm; Hon Rl; Mdrgl; Natl Forn Lg; Pol Wkr; Sch Mus; Rptr Sch Nwsp; Sch Nwsp; Capt Swmmng; Jackson Cmnty Coll; Bus Admin.

GATES, DONNA; Brooke HS; Follansbee, WV; 1/461 Cl Rep Jr Cls; Val; VP Chrs; Chrh Wkr; Debate Tm; Pres FCA; Hon Rl; Lit Mag; Mdrgl; VP NHS; Bethany Coll; Math.

GATES, INDIA; Libbey HS; Toledo, OH; Chrh Wkr; Hon Rl; JA; Stu Cncl; Fr Clb; Spn Clb; Chrldng; Elk Awd; JA Awd; Ohio State Univ; Sci.

GATES, KAREN MARIE; Seton HS; Cincinnati, OH; 12/271 VP Soph Cls; Cl Rep Jr Cls; Cls Rep Sr Cls; Hon Rl; Jr NHS; NHS; Ed Sch Nwsp; Rptr Sch Nwsp; Spn Clb; IM Sprt; Xavier Univ; Comm Broadcasting.

GATES, LAWRENCE M; Moeller HS; Cincinnati, OH; 131/272 Letter Bsbl; Letter Bsktbl; Letter Ftbl; Letter Glf; IM Sprt; Purdue Univ; Bus Mgmt.

GATES, LORI; Brownsburg HS; Brownsburg, IN; Hon Rl; NHS; 4-H; Ger Clb; Lat Clb; 4-H Awd; Indiana Univ; Bio.

GATES, ROSALIND; Cass Technical HS; Detroit, MI; Cmp Fr Grls; Girl Scts; Hon Rl; Jr NHS; Lbry Ade; Sch Mus; Sch Pl; Stu Cncl; Rptr Yrbk; Rptr Sch Nwsp; Spelman; Chem Engr.

GATEWOOD, KAREN; North Newton HS; Lake Village, IN; Hon Rl; Lbry Ade; Sec NHS; Sch Pl; Drama Clb; 4-H; Purdue Univ; Comp Sci.

GATHERS, GARTH N; Harrison HS; W Lafayette, IN; Rptr Yrbk; Drama Clb; Wrstlng; Purdue Univ.

GATIAN, DAVID R; North Ridgeville HS; N Ridgeville, OH; 32/400 Cls Rep Sr Cls; Hon Rl; Sch Pl; Stg Crw; Stu Cncl; Drama Clb; Capt Wrstlng; Bus.

GATIAN, KATHI; Stow HS; Stow, OH; Cls Rep Frsh Cls; Cls Rep Soph Cls; Cl Rep Jr Cls; Sal; Girl Scts; Hon Rl;.

GATIAN, SHERRIE; Morgantown HS; Morgantown, WV; Sec Jr Cls; Cl Rep Jr Cls; Chrs; Girl Scts; Hon Rl; Stu Cncl; Rptr Yrbk; 4-H; Chrldng; GAA; West Virginia Univ; Bsns Mgmt.

GATICA, MARK; Michael Hamady Comm HS; Flint, MI; 4/165 Cls Rep Frsh Cls; Cls Rep Soph Cls; Debate Tm; Hon Rl; Natl Forn Lg; NHS; Stu Cncl; Rptr Yrbk; Rptr Sch Nwsp; VP Key Clb; Speech Awd; Univ Of Michigan; Poli Sci.

GATIEN, DENISE; North Central Area HS; Spalding, MI; 9/62 Yrbk; Bay De Noc Community College; Wat Te.

GATIO, MICHAEL; Mcnicholas HS; Cincinnati, OH; VP Frsh Cls; Hon Rl; NHS; Stu Cncl; Sprt Ed Sch Nwsp; Bsbl; Coach Actv; IM Sprt; College.

GATTA, GERRI; Niles Mc Kinley HS; Niles, OH; Cls Rep Soph Cls; Am Leg Aux Girls St; Hon Rl; Jr NHS; Stu Cncl; DECA; Drama Clb; PPFtbl; Univ; Sci.

GATTE, PAMELA; Brownstown Central HS; Brownstown, IN; 34/138 Trs Jr Cls; Cls Rep Sr Cls; Chrs; Chrh Wkr; Hon Rl; Sch Mus; Sec Stu Cncl; FTA; Pep Clb; VP Spn Clb; Indiana Univ; Elem Educ.

GATTON, C; Elmhurst HS; Ft Wayne, IN; 17/346 AFS; Am Leg Aux Girls St; Hon Rl; Natl Forn Lg; NHS; Pol Wkr; Twrlr; C of C Awd; St Francis Coll; Med Tech.

GATTON, JACQUELINE; Columbian HS; Tiffin, OH; Hon Rl; Lbry Ade; Rhema Bible Coll.

GATZ, LAURA; Mt Clemens HS; Mt Clemens, MI; 34/314 Hon Rl; NHS; Off Ade; Stg Crw; Natl Merit Schl; Michigan St Univ; Forestry.

GATZEK, PAULA; Richmond Sr HS; Richmond, IN; 8/575 Band; Hon Rl; NHS; GAA; Purdue Univ; Med Tech.

GAUCK, BRIAN; Milan HS; Milan, IN; 7/89 Band; Chrs; Hon Rl; NHS; Sch Mus; Sch Pl; Drama Clb; 4-H; FFA; Pep Clb; Purdue Univ; Agriculture.

GAUER, MICHELE; Terre Haute South Vigo HS; Terre Haute, IN; 1/630 Val; Am Leg Aux Girls St; Girl Scts; Hon Rl; JA; NHS; Y-Teens; Ger Clb; Kiwan Awd; Indiana St Univ; Acctg.

GAUG, DARRELL; Copley Sr HS; Fairlwan, OH; 30/350 Pres Frsh Cls; Chrs; Chrh Wkr; Hon Rl; Sch Mus; Stu Cncl; Sprt Ed Yrbk; Sch Nwsp; Spn Clb; Ftbl;.

GAUKER, BRIAN; Lincoln HS; Cambridge City, IN; 12/137 Pres Frsh Cls; VP Jr Cls; NHS; Yrbk; Capt Bsbl; Bsktbl; Ftbl; Am Leg Awd; Cit Awd; Butler Univ; Bus.

GAUKER, VIKKI; Richmond HS; Richmond, IN; Am Leg Aux Girls St; Chrs; Girl Scts; Hon Rl; Hosp Ade; JA; Treas Orch; PAVAS; Pol Wkr; Sch Mus; Univ; Comp Sci.

GAUL, NANCY; Berrien Springs HS; Berrien Springs, MI; 13/111 Hon Rl; NHS; 4-H; Pep Clb; Spn Clb; Trk; 4-H Awd; St Of Mi Competitive Schlrshp 79; Western Michigan Univ.

GAULT, TOYNIA; Jennings Co HS; No Vernon, IN; Chrs; Chrh Wkr; Girl Scts; Sch Mus; Pep Clb; Spn Clb; Mas Awd; Worthy Advisor N Vernon Assembly #84; Grand Rep Intl Order Rainbow For Girls In In; Indiana Univ; Psych.

GAULTIER, CHRISTINA; Traverse City HS; Traverse City, MI; Hon Rl; NHS; Orch; Stg Crw; 4-H; Pep Clb; Cit Awd; Alma College; Art.

GAUNT, MITCHELL; Point Pleasant HS; Pt Pleasant, WV; Chrh Wkr; NHS; Yth Flsp; DECA; Key Clb; Letter Ten; W Virginia Inst Of Tech; Elec Engr.

GAUNT, RICHARD; Malabar HS; Mansfield, OH; 30/233 Boy Scts; NHS; Sch Pl; Key Clb; Mth Clb; Crs Cntry; Swmmng; God Cntry Awd; Natl Merit Ltr; Univ Of Cincinnati; Ind Design.

GAURONSKAS, MARY L; Lamphere HS; Madison Ht, MI; 2/320 Hon Rl; Treas NHS; Off Ade; Fr Clb; College; Chemical Engr.

GAUSMAN, LINDA; Tippecanoe HS; Tipp City, OH; 17/190 Cmnty Wkr; Hon Rl; Off Ade; Yrbk; Trk; Scr Kpr; Univ.

GAUTHIER, JAMES; St Xavier HS; Cincinnati, OH; 101/270 Cls Rep Soph Cls; Cls Rep Sr Cls; Cmnty Wkr; Hon Rl; Stu Cncl; Boys Clb Am; Letter Ftbl; Capt Glf; Letter Trk; IM Sprt; Univ; Bus Admin.

GAVANDITTI, PATRICIA; Solon HS; Solon, OH; Cls Rep Frsh Cls; Cls Rep Soph Cls; Cl Rep Jr Cls; Cls Rep Sr Cls; Chrs; Hon Rl; Red Cr Ade; Stu Cncl; Scr Kpr; Univ; Nursing.

GAVENDA, JULIE; Fulton HS; Ithaca, MI; 4-H; FHA; Mth Clb; Davenport Bus Schl; Bus.

GAVIGAN, KIM; Rochester HS; Rochester, MI; 20/500 Cls Rep Frsh Cls; Band; Chrh Wkr; Hon Rl; Jr NHS; NHS; 4-H; Gym; Trk; Chrldng; Gym Trophy MVP; Best Horsewoman Trophy; Outstndng Awds In All Subjects; Michigan Tech Univ; CPA.

GAVIN, JULIE L; Seton HS; Cincinnati, OH; 28/283 Cls Rep Frsh Cls; Cls Rep Soph Cls; Cls Rep Sr Cls; Chrs; Hon Rl; Jr NHS; NHS; Fr Clb; Univ Of Cincinnati; Nursing.

GAVIN, M LISA; Seton HS; Cincinnati, OH; 40/255 Pres Frsh Cls; Cls Rep Soph Cls; Cl Rep Jr Cls; Hon Rl; Jr NHS; NHS; Pol Wkr; Red Cr Ade; Stu Cncl; Rptr Sch Nwsp; College; Journalism.

GAVRUN, ANDREA; Hopkins HS; Hopkins, MI; Band; Chrh Wkr; Cmnty Wkr; Girl Scts; Hon Rl; Jr NHS; Off Ade; Yth Flsp; 4-H; Calvin Coll; Elem Spec Educ Tchr.

GAW, JOHN; Sycamore HS; Cincinnati, OH; Boy Scts; Red Cr Ade; Socr; Swmmng; IM Sprt; College; Bus Mgmt.

GAWART, CHRIS; Harper Creek HS; Battle Creek, MI; 2/244 Sal; Am Leg Boys St; Boy Scts; VP Chrs; Hon Rl; Sch Mus; Drama Clb; Pres Spn Clb; Am Leg Awd; Opt Clb Awd; College; Busns Admin.

GAWEDZINSKI, LAURIE; Archbishop Alter HS; Dayton, OH; Red Cr Ade; Stu Cncl; Yrbk; Bsktbl; GAA; First Honors 77; Univ; Pre Med.

GAWELEK, JOHN; Padua Franciscan HS; N Royalton, OH; 112/258 CAP; Hon Rl; Socr; Cleveland State Univ; Aero Elec.

GAWNE, DAVE; Maplewood HS; Cortland, OH; Am Leg Boys St; Hon Rl; NHS; Off Ade; Beta Clb; FTA; Bskbtbl Trainer 78; Univ; Phys Ther.

GAWNE, SHERYL; Ovid Elsie HS; Henderson, MI; Band; Girl Scts; 4-H; FHA; 4-H Awd; College; Nursing.

GAWRON, MARY L; Technical Voc HS; Hammond, IN; 4/180 Pres Soph Cls; Cl Rep Jr Cls; Am Leg Aux Girls St; Girl Scts; Hon Rl; NHS; Sch Mus; Sch Pl; Stg Crw; Stu Cncl; Veterans Of Foreign Wars Speech Contest; Internatl Thespian Soc Outstanding Participation In The Theatre; Indiana Univ; Medicine.

GAWRON, SANDRA; Warrensville Hts HS; Warrensvle, OH; Girl Scts; Hon Rl; Jr NHS; Lbry Ade; NHS; Ursuline Univ; Med.

GAY, BRENDA; Augres Sims HS; Au Gres, MI; Hon Rl; Lbry Ade; Rptr Sch Nwsp; Jrnlsm I Awrd 79; Hnrbl Mention In Typng Ii 79; US Navy; Intellignc Operator.

GAY, CATHERINE; Douglas Mac Arthur HS; Saginaw, MI; Hon Rl; NHS; Pep Clb; PPFtbl; Michigan St Univ; Pub Relations.

GAY, EMMA; South HS; Youngstown, OH; Chrs; Chrh Wkr; CAP; Hon Rl; JA; Spn Clb; Bsktbl; College; Prof Law.

GAY, JAMES; Lutheran East HS; Detroit, MI; Pres Soph Cls; Pres Jr Cls; Pres Sr Cls; Hon Rl; NHS; Stu Cncl; Sch Nwsp; Letter Bsbl; Letter Ftbl; Michigan Tech Univ; Bus Admin.

GAY, KATHLEEN; Kenowa Hills HS; Grand Rapids, MI; Hon Rl; NHS; 4-H; Pom Pon; PPFtbl; Univ; Comp Prog.

GAY, LISA; Milan HS; Milan, IN; 12/80 Band; Hon Rl; NHS; Sch Pl; Drama Clb; FTA; Crs Cntry; Swmmng; Letter Trk; Lettermens Club; Chess Club & Tres Of Jr High Club; Ball St Univ; Psych.

GAY, MICHELLE; Canfield HS; Canfield, OH; 5/258 Pres Jr Cls; Band; Drl Tm; Girl Scts; Hon Rl; Natl Forn Lg; NHS; Y-Teens; Ger Clb; Key Clb; Univ; Med.

GAY, TIMOTHY; Petoskey HS; Petoskey, MI; Yth Flsp; FFA; Great Lakes Maritime Acad; Ship Engr.

GAYDE, PAMELA; Shortridge HS; Indianapolis, IN; 16/440 Cls Rep Frsh Cls; Trs Soph Cls; Cl Rep Jr Cls; Girl Scts; Hon Rl; NHS; Sch Mus; Fr Clb; Mth Clb; Butler Univ; Pharm.

GAYDOS, MARY R; Holy Name Nazareth HS; Parma, OH; Hon Rl; Lat Clb; Received Hnrbl Merit Of Cum Laude In Natl Latin Exam; Received Cum Laude In Latin Studies; Univ; Bus.

GAYDOSH, JUDY; Lorain Catholic HS; Lorain, OH; Aud/Vis; Chrh Wkr; Cmnty Wkr; Hon Rl; NHS; Pol Wkr; Sch Nwsp; DECA; Ashland College; Radio Television.

GAYDOSH, MARY L; Lordstown HS; Warren, OH; 10/53 Band; Chrs; Hon Rl; JA; Sch Mus; Yth Flsp; Drama Clb; Pep Clb; Chrldng; Society Distinguished Amrcn HS Studnts 1978; Berklee Coll; Music.

GAYLE, DONNA; East HS; Columbus, OH; Drl Tm; Girl Scts; Hon Rl; Sch Pl; OEA; Cit Awd; Ohio State Univ; Photography.

GAYLE, KELLI; Switzerland County Jr Sr HS; Bennington, IN; 8/136 Sec Soph Cls; Hon Rl; Off Ade; Stg Crw; Stu Cncl; Drama Clb; Pep Clb; Spn Clb; Chrldng; Vincennes Univ; Phys Ther.

GAYLE, KELLY; Anderson HS; Anderson, IN; Hon Rl; Fr Clb; Ball St Univ; Business.

GAYLORD, HEIDI; Whitmer HS; Toledo, OH; 110/910 Chrs; Off Ade; Sch Pl; Concert Chr VP 78; Concert Chr Varsity Ltr 78; Univ Toledo; Interpreter.

GAYLORD, J ERIC; Cardinal Ritter HS; Indianapolis, IN; Band; Boy Scts; Chrs; Hon Rl; Orch; Sch Mus; Sch Pl; Sct Actv; Indiana Univ; Archt Drafting.

GAYNOR, CARLA E; Liberty HS; Reynoldsville, WV; 20/226 Cls Rep Frsh Cls; Cls Rep Soph Cls; Cl Rep Jr Cls; Band; Chrs; Cmnty Wkr; Girl Scts; Hon Rl; Jr NHS; Off Ade; Fairmont St Univ; Eng.

GAYNOR, JENNIFER; Lincoln HS; Shinnston, WV; 34/158 Am Leg Aux Girls St; Band; Boy Scts; Chrs; Chrh Wkr; Hon Rl; Yth Flsp; Glenville St Coll; Sec Sci.

GAYNOR, MARK; Philip Barbour HS; Philippi, WV; Am Leg Boys St; Band; Chrh Wkr; Hon Rl; Stu Cncl; Yth Flsp; Key Clb; Trk; West Vir Univ; Forestry.

GAYNOR, SUSAN; Stephen T Badin HS; Hamilton, OH; 44/222 Chrh Wkr; Drl Tm; Sch Mus; Sch Pl; Stg Crw; Drama Clb; Key Clb; Spn Clb; Gym; S wmmng; Univ; Drama.

GAZIA, GUY; Madonna HS; Weirton, WV; Chrh Wkr; Hon Rl; Jr NHS; NHS; Sci Clb; Letter Ten; IM Sprt; West Virginia Univ; Chem Eng.

GBUR, GEORGE; Wellsville HS; Wellsville, OH; 1/108 Treas Band; Hon Rl; Sec NHS; Stg Crw; Sec Key Clb; Am Leg Awd; Dnfth Awd; Estelle Elton Awd For Excllnc In Eng 78; Ruth Kerr Memrl For Excllnc In Amer History 79; Univ.

GEAGAN, THOMAS; Ross Beatty HS; Dawagiac, MI; 1/125 Cls Rep Sr Cls; NHS; Sch Pl; Ed Sch Nwsp; Sprt Ed Sch Nwsp; Drama Clb; Ten; College; Law.

GEARHART, K; Windham HS; Windham, OH; 18/90 Hon Rl; Rptr Yrbk; Spn Clb; Bsbl; Bsktbl; Letter Ftbl; Letter Trk; College.

GEARHART, KAREN; Bluefield HS; Bluefld, WV; Chrh Wkr; Treas Girl Scts; Hon Rl; Sct Actv; Yth Flsp; Drama Clb; Fr Clb; FHA; Pep Clb; GAA; Concord Coll.

GEARHART, LESLIE J; Eastlake North HS; Eastlake, OH; Off Ade; Sch Mus; Sch Pl; Stg Crw; Ed Yrbk; Rptr Sch Nwsp; Drama Clb; Pep Clb; Rdo Clb; Sci Clb; St Bd Of Educ Basic Std Awd 79; Univ; Drama.

GEARHEART, GARY; Bluefield HS; Bluefield, WV; FCA; Stu Cncl; Pres Yth Flsp; Letter Bsktbl; Letter Ftbl; Letter Trk; Coach Actv; Concord College; Phy Educ.

GEARY, SHELLY; Marcellus HS; Decatur, MI; Band; Chrs; Trk; Letter Chrldng; College; Drama.

GEARY, TERESA; Holland HS; Holland, MI; Cmp Fr Grls; Chrh Wkr; Cmnty Wkr; Debate Tm; Stg Crw; Ger Clb; Univ; Nursing.

GEASON, DEBRA; Sandusky St Marys Centrl HS; Sandusky, OH; GAA; Providence Schl; Practical Nurse.

GEBERS, DEB; Tinora HS; Defiance, OH; Off Ade; 4-H; Bsktbl; Trk; GAA; Dnfth Awd; Northwest Tech Sch; Acctg.

GEBERT, DAWN; Griffith HS; Griffith, IN; 7/289 Chrh Wkr; Girl Scts; Hon Rl; Jr NHS; NHS; Sct Actv; Yth Flsp; Pep Clb; Sweatergirl 78 79 & 80; Earned Major Letter 78; Booster Clb Spec Serv Awd 77 78 & 79; Wheaton Univ; Sci.

GEBERT, ED; Whitko HS; Pierceton, IN; Band; Chrs; Hon Rl; Natl Forn Lg; Sch Pl; Sprt Ed Sch Nwsp; Drama Clb; Sci Clb; Letter Bsbl; Letter Ten; College; Music.

GEBHARDT, DANIEL; Wynford HS; Bucyrus, OH; 1/125 Pres Frsh Cls; Cls Rep Soph Cls; AFS; Band; Hon Rl; NHS; 4-H; Spn Clb; Am Leg Awd; 4-H Awd; Univ; Art.

GEBHARDT, SAMUEL L; Cedar Springs HS; Cedar Spgs, MI; 2/155 Trs Sr Cls; Band; Hon Rl; Jr NHS; NHS; Glf; Ten; Salutatorian Of Sr Class; Michigan St Univ; Vet.

GECOWETS, LINDA; Westerville South HS; Westerville, OH; Chrs; Letter Swmmng; Ohio St Univ.

GEDDA, GLEN; A D Johnston HS; Bessemer, MI; Michigan Tech Univ; Med Tech.

GEDDES, DENISE; Chelsea HS; Chelsea, MI; 85/265 Hon Rl; Spn Clb; PPFtbl; Univ Of S Calif; Retail Sales Mgr.

GEDERT, SUE; Unionville Sebewaing Area H; Unionville, MI; Cl Rep Jr Cls; Band; Hon Rl; Stu Cncl; FHA; Letter Bsbl; Letter Bsktbl; Scr Kpr; Western Michigan Univ; Med.

GEDRA, JIM; Central Catholic HS; Canton, OH; Ftbl; Trk; Ohio St Univ.

GEDVILA, LISA; West Catholic HS; Grand Rapids, MI; Hon Rl; Spn Clb; Natl Merit Schl.

GEDVILLAS, SHIRLEY; Westwood HS; Champion, MI; 33/108 Hon Rl; OEA; Trk; Mgrs; Northern Mich Univ; Acctg.

GEE, LORI; Southgate HS; Southgate, MI; CAP; Drl Tm; Hon Rl; Jr NHS; Mic Tech.

GEE, MELISSA; Greenbrier East HS; Trout, WV; 11/325 VP Frsh Cls; Cl Rep Jr Cls; Hon Rl; NHS;

Sch Pl; Yrbk; Rptr Sch Nwsp; 4-H; Letter Bsktbl; College; Vet Med.

GEE, ROBERT; Trenton HS; Trenton, MI; Chrs; Chrh Wkr; Hon Rl; Lbry Ade; Cit Awd; Univ.

GEERINCK, KATHRYN M; Richmond Sr HS; Richmond, IN; Chrh Wkr; Hon Rl; Jr NHS; NHS; Pol Wkr; Y-Teens; Spn Clb; Free Enterprise Essay Competition 1st Pl City & Reg; Diploma Of Merit Exc In Spanish; Coll; Busns Admin.

GEERS, LAUREL; Lutheran HS West; N Olmsted, OH; Chrs; Hon Rl; Hosp Ade; NHS; Yth Flsp; Rptr Yrbk; Drama Clb; Spn Clb; Natl Merit Ltr; Calvin Coll.

GEESE, RONDA; Cambridge HS; Cambridge, OH; 48/270 Cl Rep Jr Cls; Cls Rep Sr Cls; Chmn Cmnty Wkr; Hon Rl; NHS; Off Ade; Stu Cncl; FTA; Pep Clb; Tmr; Muskingum Coll; Psych.

GEESEY, EMILY; Montpelier HS; Montpelier, OH; 1/109 Val; Band; Hon Rl; NHS; Sch Mus; Pres Yth Flsp; Chrldng; DAR Awd; Natl Merit Ltr; Ohio St Univ; Math.

GEESEY, KELLEY; Montpelier HS; Montpelier, OH; Sec Chrh Wkr; Sch Mus; Nursing Schl; Reg Nurse.

GEESLING, MICHELE; Miami Trace HS; Washington Ch, OH; 9/261 AFS; Am Leg Aux Girls St; Hon Rl; Jr NHS; NHS; Rptr Yrbk; Rptr Sch Nwsp; 4-H; FTA; Mat Maids; Tech Schl; Comp Prog.

GEGENHEIMER, ALAN; Goodrich HS; Goodrich, MI; Band; Boy Scts; Hon Rl; Sct Actv; Ger Clb; Bsktbl; Ftbl; Ten; Univ.

GEHEB, JANET M; Rivet HS; Vincennes, IN; Chrs; Hon Rl; Trk; IM Sprt; Vincennes Univ; Respitory Ther.

GEHLMANN, GREGORY; Lorain Catholic HS; Lorain, OH; 14/132 Band; NHS; Sch Pl; Stu Cncl; Sprt Ed Yrbk; Letter Bsbl; Letter Crs Cntry; College; Math.

GEHRES, LYNDIA L; Castle HS; Chandler, IN; 12/333 Band; Chrh Wkr; Hon Rl; Jr NHS; Yth Flsp; 4-H; Sci Clb; JETS Awd; Natl Merit Ltr; Univ Of Evansville; Mech Engr.

GEHRET, DORIS; Versailles HS; New Weston, OH; Chrh Wkr; Cmnty Wkr; JA; FHA; Voc Schl; Nursing.

GEHRING, KELLY; Perry HS; Massillon, OH; Band; Hon Rl; Jr NHS; NHS; OEA; Bsktbl; Jr Acct Stu Of The Yr 1979; Hist Of Voc Acctg Class 1979; Coll; Comp Prog.

GEHRINGER, THOMAS; Ovid Elsie HS; Elsie, MI; 4-H; Distributive Educ Prog; Adrian Univ; Busns.

GEHRKE, TIMOTHY; Greenville HS; Greenville, MI; Chrh Wkr; Hon Rl; Capt Bsbl; Ftbl; IM Sprt; E Mic Univ; Crim Justice.

GEIB, CONNIE; Waterloo HS; Atwater, OH; Hon Rl; Sch Pl; Beta Clb; Bsktbl; IM Sprt; Radiology.

GEICK, TIMOTHY; Port Huron HS; Marysville, MI; 25/330 Hon Rl; NHS; Letter Glf; St Clair Cnty Comm Coll; Elec Tech.

GEIER, KATHY; Saint Johns HS; Delphos, OH; 10/150 Band; Girl Scts; Hon Rl; NHS; Sch Nwsp; 4-H; Gym; 4-H Awd; Ohio State; Physica Therapy.

GEIGER, CHRISTINE; East Canton HS; E Canton, OH; Chrs; Chrh Wkr; Hon Rl; Jr NHS; Yth Flsp; FTA; Spn Clb; Echoes 78 79; Cosmotologist.

GEIGER, JEANNE; John F Kennedy HS; Cortland, OH; 7/178 Sec Frsh Cls; Sec Soph Cls; Sec Sr Cls; Am Leg Aux Girls St; Hon Rl; Sec Stu Cncl; Am Leg Awd; Miami Univ; Systems Analyst.

GEIGER, KIMBERLY; Munster HS; Munster, IN; 93/409 Band; Chrs; Chrh Wkr; Off Ade; Sch Mus; Pep Clb; IM Sprt; Mat Maids; PPFtbl; Tmr; Indiana Univ; Nursing.

GEIGER, MARY A; Magnificat HS; Brook Park, OH; Sec Soph Cls; Pres Jr Cls; Pres Sr Cls; Chrs; NHS; Stu Cncl; Dnfth Awd; Jane Addams Voc Schl; Nursing.

GEIGER, PAMELA; Bishop Dwenger HS; Ft Wayne, IN; Chrs; Pol Wkr; Bishop Dwenger Rep 4th Congressional Stu Prog; NISBOVA Vocal & Ensembles Contest 1st Pl 2nd 3rd Div Vocal; Univ; Govt.

GEIGER, RONALD; Mohawk HS; Tiffin, OH; Aud/Vis; Chrh Wkr; Lbry Ade; Yth Flsp; 4-H; FTA; Spn Clb; Bsktbl; Crs Cntry; Ftbl; Ohio St Univ; Aviation.

GEIGER, STEVE; Clermont Northeastern HS; Batavia, OH; Chrh Wkr; Hon Rl; Pres Yth Flsp; Pep Clb; Spn Clb; Crs Cntry; Trk; Mgrs; College; Pre Med.

GEIGER, VIVIAN; Delta Sr HS; Delta, OH; Cmp Fr Grls; Chrs; Chrh Wkr; Cmnty Wkr; Girl Scts; Hosp Ade; Lbry Ade; Red Cr Ade; Sch Mus; Sch Pl; Univ; Nurse.

GEIL, REBECCA L; W Geauga HS; Novelty, OH; 40/350 Band; Chrs; Hon Rl; Mdrgl; NHS; Sch Mus; Sch Pl; Stg Crw; Drama Clb; Natl Merit SF; Univ; Mgmt.

GEIS, ELLEN; Connersville HS; Connersville, IN; 8/400 Am Leg Aux Girls St; Hon Rl; Jr NHS; NHS; Ger Clb; IM Sprt; Tmr; Elk Awd; Indiana Univ; Nursing.

GEIS, LAURA; Brookville HS; Brookville, IN; 6/196 Hon Rl; Yrbk; Sch Nwsp; Spn Clb; Ten; St Marys Univ; Art.

GEISE, DAVE; Coldwater HS; Coldwater, OH; Trs Frsh Cls; Cls Rep Soph Cls; Pres Jr Cls; VP Sr Cls; Chrs; Hon Rl; Stu Cncl; Spn Clb; Letter Bsbl; Ftbl; Wright St Univ; Bio.

GEISE, MELINDA; Coldwater HS; Coldwater, OH; 1/140 Trs Frsh Cls; VP Soph Cls; VP Jr Cls; VP Band; Hon Rl; Jr NHS; Drama Clb; Pres FTA; Bsktbl; Chrldng;.

GEISE, SANDY; Paul Harding HS; Ft Wayne, IN; 19/247 Drl Tm; FCA; Hon Rl; OEA; Letter Ten; Chrldng; Pom Pon; Prof Tennis.

GEISELMAN, TRACY; Sycamore HS; Cincinnati, OH; Hon Rl; Red Cr Ade; Key Clb; Pep Clb; Letter Swmmng; Tmr; Mst Imprvd Var Swimmer 79; Art Show Awd 78; Miami Univ; Enviro Sci.

GEISER, JOSEPH G; Mc Clain HS; Chase Mills, NY; Pres Frsh Cls; Pres Jr Cls; FCA; Quill & Scroll; Sch Pl; Ed Sch Nwsp; Bsbl; Bsktbl; Capt Socr; JA Awd; St Joseph Coll; Poli Sci.

GEISER, KAREN E; Anderson HS; Cincinnati, OH; 55/377 Cls Rep Frsh Cls; Cls Rep Soph Cls; Sec Jr Cls; Girl Scts; Hon Rl; Yth Flsp; Fr Clb; Gym; Trk; Chrldng; Univ.

GEISERT, CHRYSTINE; Meridian HS; Sanford, MI; 9/150 Hon Rl; Pep Clb; Spn Clb; Bsktbl; Scr Kpr; College; Oceanographer.

GEISHARK, CAROL; Columbian HS; Tiffin, OH; Hosp Ade; JA; Yrbk; Spn Clb; IM Sprt; JA Awd; Univ; Nursing.

GEISMAN, GAIL; Upper Arlington HS; Columbus, OH; 1/610 AFS; Girl Scts; Hon Rl; NHS; Sct Actv; Yth Flsp; Rptr Yrbk; Spn Clb; GAA; College.

GEISS, GLORIA; Reitz Memorial HS; Evansville, IN; 33/220 Cls Rep Soph Cls; Sec Jr Cls; Sec Sr Cls; Treas Chrs; Girl Scts; Hon Rl; JA; Pol Wkr; Stu Cncl; Rptr Yrbk; Semi Finlst Optmst Oratrcl Contst 78; Univ Of Evansville; Math.

GEISS, LAURIE; Strongsville Sr HS; Strongsville, OH; Cls Rep Frsh Cls; Cls Rep Soph Cls; Sec Jr Cls; Cl Rep Jr Cls; VP Sr Cls; Cls Rep Sr Cls; Hon Rl; Sec Jr NHS; NHS; Stu Cncl; Univ; Acctg.

GELDERSMA, DOUGLAS K; Belding HS; Belding, MI; Band; Hon Rl; Sch Pl; Stg Crw; Drama Clb; FFA; Rdo Clb;.

GELDRICH, MARIE; Lemon Monroe HS; Middletown, OH; Hon Rl; Rptr Sch Nwsp; Drama Clb; FHA; Pep Clb; Spn Clb; Ten; Trk; GAA; JA Awd; Ohi Univ; Bus Admin.

GELIOS, DAVE; Archbold HS; Archbold, OH; Trs Frsh Cls; Pres Jr Cls; Pres Sr Cls; Am Leg Boys St; Chrs; Pres NHS; Sch Mus; Stu Cncl; Bsktbl; Voice Dem Awd; Amer Leg Amer Contest 77; Outstnding Soph Awd By Hugh O Brien Yth Fndtn 77; Univ Of Toledo Honor Choir Mbr; Univ Of Toledo; Music.

GELLERT, LINDA; Bridgman HS; Bridgman, MI; Hon Rl; Jr NHS; NHS; 4-H; Trk; IM Sprt; 4-H Awd; Kalamazoo Coll; Law.

GELLNER, GREGORY A; John Marshall HS; Wheeling, WV; Cls Rep Soph Cls; Cl Rep Jr Cls; Sal; Am Leg Boys St; Hon Rl; Jr NHS; NHS; Stu Cncl; Crs Cntry; Trk; Top Schlstc Awd 76; Frank Taylor Jr Law Awd Mountainer Boys St 79; Part In Moto Cross Racing 78 & 79; Univ; Law.

GELLNER, WENDY; Wheeling Park HS; Wheeling, WV; Trs Sr Cls; Hon Rl; NHS; Off Ade; Letter Ten; Capt Chrldng; College; Engr.

GELNETT, MELODY R; Ross Beatty HS; Dowagiac, MI; 5/135 Trs Frsh Cls; Cl Rep Jr Cls; Cls Rep Sr Cls; Hon Rl; Sec NHS; Quill & Scroll; Sch Mus; Sch Pl; Stg Crw; Stu Cncl; Western Michigan Univ; Math.

GELPI, JEFFREY A; West HS; Columbus, OH; Am Leg Boys St; Band; Boy Scts; Hon Rl; Off Ade; Orch; PAVAS; Red Cr Ade; Sch Pl; Stg Crw; Ohio St Univ; Pre Med.

GELUSO, MARY; Union HS; Grand Rapids, MI; Hon Rl; NHS; Spn Clb; Gym; Swmmng; Chrldng; Kiwan Awd; Voc Schl; Bus.

GEMELAS, FAYE; Brooklyn HS; Brooklyn, OH; 24/180 Chrs; Hon Rl; Hosp Ade; Lbry Ade; NHS; Off Ade; Eng Clb; Mth Clb; Spn Clb; Cuyahoga Comm Coll; Art.

GEMMEL, DEBORAH; West Branch HS; Salem, OH; 15/230 Chrh Wkr; Lbry Ade; NHS; VP Lat Clb; Univ; Comp Sci.

GEMMER, TERRY; Wilmington HS; Wilmington, OH; Debate Tm; FFA; Lat Clb; Letter Ftbl; 4-H Awd; Ohio St Univ.

GENAUTIS, PAMELA; Northview HS; Grand Rapids, MI; Hon Rl; JA; Spn Clb; PPFtbl; Michigan St Univ.

GENDRON, PAMLA M; Kingsford HS; Iron Mtn, MI; Chrs; Chrh Wkr; Sch Mus; Sch Pl; Sec Yth Flsp; 4-H; 4-H Awd; Coll; Eng.

GENDT, BART; Big Walnut HS; Sunbury, OH; 5 9/238 Am Leg Boys St; Boy Scts; Chrh Wkr; Yth Flsp; Fr Clb; Letter Bsktbl; Letter Glf; Letter Trk; Col Tech Inst; Structural Draftsman.

GENET, CAROL; Washington HS; Massillon, OH; 50/459 Chrs; Hon Rl; Sch Mus; Pep Clb; Swmmng; Nusing School; Nursing.

GENGNAGEL, SUSAN; Dekalb HS; Auburn, IN; 18/285 Chrs; Hon Rl; NHS; Sch Mus; Sch Pl; Rptr Yrbk; Rptr Sch Nwsp; FTA; Pep Clb; Spn Clb; Depauw Univ; Elem Educ.

GENSCH, HERBERT; Shenandoah HS; Middletown, IN; 25/118 Am Leg Boys St; Band; Chrs; Chrh Wkr; Pres Ger Clb; Letter Trk; Co Mst Imprvd Runner In Track 79; Univ; Med.

GENSLER, DIANA R; Robert S Rogers HS; Toledo, OH; 3/412 Chrs; Sec Chrh Wkr; VP Cmnty Wkr; Girl Scts; Hon Rl; NHS; Pol Wkr; Sct Actv; Stg Crw; Sec Yth Flsp; College; Genetic Engr.

GENTILE, DAVE; James Ford Rhodes HS; Clevel and, OH; Cls Rep Frsh Cls; Cls Rep Soph Cls; Cl Rep Jr Cls; Cls Rep Sr Cls; Chrs; Hon Rl; Off Ade; Sch Mus; Stu Cncl; Rptr Yrbk; Miami Univ; Cmnctns.

GENTILE, MICHELLE; Sturgis HS; Sturgis, MI; Sec Soph Cls; Trs Jr Cls; Trs Sr Cls; Sch Pl; Stu Cncl; Drama Clb; PPFtbl; Grand Valley St Coll; Spec Ed.

GENTILE, TRISH; Bishop Dwenger HS; Fort Wayne, IN; Cls Rep Frsh Cls; Cls Rep Soph Cls; Chrs; Hon Rl; NHS; Sch Mus; Yrbk; Pep Clb; Capt Pom Pon; Coll; Dent.

GENTILLE, MARY; St Peters HS; Mansfield, OH; Chrh Wkr; Cmnty Wkr; Hon Rl; Lbry Ade; NHS; Red Cr Ade; Sch Mus; Sch Pl; Stg Crw; Rptr Yrbk; Univ; Forestry.

GENTIS, RHONDA; Southern Wells HS; Bluffton, IN; 11/96 Chrh Wkr; Hon Rl; NHS; Yth Flsp; 4-H; Pep Clb; Letter Bsktbl; Letter Gym; Letter Trk; Capt Chrldng; Purdue Univ; Phys Ed.

GENTNER, VICTOR; North College Hill HS; Cincinnati, OH; Cls Rep Frsh Cls; Cls Rep Soph Cls; Hon Rl; Sch Mus; Sch Pl; Stu Cncl; Rptr Sch Nwsp; Drama Clb; OEA; Univ Of Cincinnati; Accounting.

GENTRY, CHET; Center Line HS; Warren, MI; 10/415 Cls Rep Frsh Cls; Pres Jr Cls; Cl Rep Jr Cls; Pres Sr Cls; Cls Rep Sr Cls; Band; Boy Scts; Chrs; Chrh Wkr; Hon Rl; Wayne St Univ Merit Schlrshp; Wayne St Univ; Med.

GENTRY, DENISE; Northwestern HS; Wooster, OH; Hosp Ade; JA; Sch Pl; 4-H; Trk; IM Sprt;.

GENTRY, KIMBERLY; Southmont Jr Sr HS; New Market, IN; 11/151 Am Leg Aux Girls St; Band; Cmp Fr Grls; Chrh Wkr; Cmnty Wkr; Hon Rl; Jr NHS; NHS; Off Ade; Orch; I Dare You Awd 79; South Mont Royal Ambssdr 79; Achvmnt Awd 79; Univ Of Kentucky; Foreign Lang.

GENTRY, MICHAEL L; Greenfield Central HS; Greenfield, IN; 24/275 Hon Rl; NHS; Pres 4-H; Treas FFA; IM Sprt; 4-H Awd; Purdue Univ; Animal Sci.

GENTRY, VIRGINIA; John F Kennedy HS; Cleveland, OH; Chrh Wkr; Yth Flsp; Cit Awd; Ohio St Univ; Bus Admin.

GENTZ, CHRISTINE; Lutheran HS North; Fraser, MI; 2/110 Sal; Band; Hon Rl; NHS; Sch Pl; Yth Flsp; Letter Bsbl; Outsdng Christ Fem Ath Of The Yr Awd 79; Pres Schlrshp Fr Concordia 79; Vllbl 1st Tm All Conf Hon Ment 79; Concordia Teachers Coll; Elem Tchr.

GENWRIGHT, RAUL; Buena Vista HS; Saginaw, MI; Band; Chrh Wkr; Cmnty Wkr; Hon Rl; Jr NHS; Yth Flsp; 4-H; Bsktbl; Coach Actv; Cit Awd; Schlrshp Dow Summer Engr Mi St Univ 78; Schlstc Hon Buena Vista HS 79; Genrl Motors Inst; Mech Engr.

GEORG, TERESA; Reynoldsburg HS; Reynoldsburg, OH; Chrs; Hon Rl; Trk; IM Sprt; Ohi State; Nurse.

GEORGAKIS, DIANE; Kankakee Vly Jr Sr HS; De Motte, IN; 69/180 Chrs; Girl Scts; Hon Rl; Off Ade; Pom Pon; PPFtbl; Indiana Univ.

GEORGE, ANTHONY; Clinton Massie HS; Wilmington, OH; Cls Rep Soph Cls; Cl Rep Jr Cls; Chrh Wkr; Cmnty Wkr; Hon Rl; Hosp Ade; NHS; Stu Cncl; Rptr Yrbk; 4-H; Univ; Sports Med.

GEORGE, BENNY; Memphis Comm HS; Smith Crk, MI; Hon Rl; 4-H; Letter Bsktbl; Letter Trk; Coll; Automotive Design.

GEORGE, CAROLE L; Zanesville HS; Zanesville, OH; VP Frsh Cls; Band; Chrh Wkr; Drm Mjrt; Girl Scts; Hon Rl; NHS; Rptr Yrbk; Pres 4-H; Sci Clb; Busns Schl; CPA.

GEORGE, CHARLES E; Tyler Cnty HS; Middlebourne, WV; 2/90 Pres Jr Cls; Jr NHS; Sec Mth Clb; Letter Bsbl; Letter Bsktbl; Letter Ftbl; Letter Trk; IM Sprt; Univ; Med.

GEORGE, CHRISTOPHER; Franklin Community HS; Franklin, IN; Cls Rep Frsh Cls; Cls Rep Soph Cls; Pres Jr Cls; Trs Sr Cls; Cls Rep Sr Cls; Am Leg Boys St; Jr NHS; NHS; Stg Crw; Stu Cncl; Purdue Univ; Commercial Aviation.

GEORGE, DON; Moeller HS; Cincinnati, OH; Hon Rl; Coach Actv; IM Sprt; Univ Of Cincinnati; Indus Dsgn.

GEORGE, JIM; Unioto HS; Chillicothe, OH; 3/100 Cls Rep Frsh Cls; Pres Soph Cls; Cl Rep Jr Cls; FCA; Hon Rl; NHS; Stu Cncl; Ed Yrbk; Capt Bsbl; Capt Ftbl; Coll; Civil Engr.

GEORGE, JOHN; Henry Ford II Sr HS; Utica, MI; 36/438 Chrh Wkr; Hon Rl; Ten; Univ Of Michigan; Orthodntst.

GEORGE, JULIE; Otsego HS; Kalamazoo, MI; Hon Rl; Hosp Ade; Lbry Ade; Mod UN; Rptr Sch Nwsp; Spn Clb; Yout For Understndng Yr Exchng Stdnt To Spain 79; Kalamazoo Coll; For Lang.

GEORGE, KEITH; Liberty HS; Clarksburg, WV; Boy Scts; Chrh Wkr; Hon Rl; Jr NHS; Yth Flsp; 4-H; Fr Clb; Elk Awd; West Virginia Univ.

GEORGE, KENNETH; Arthur Hill HS; Saginaw, MI; Boy Scts; Sch Pl; Sct Actv; Stg Crw; Yth Flsp; Sci Clb; Spn Clb; Univ Of Michigan; Chem.

GEORGE, KIM; Elmwood HS; Bloomdale, OH; Trs Frsh Cls; Sec Soph Cls; Sec Jr Cls; Band; Sct Actv; Girl Scts; Hon Rl; NHS; Sprt Ed Sch Nwsp; Sch Nwsp; Coll.

GEORGE, KRISTIE; Washington Irving HS; Clarksburg, WV; Band; Sct Actv; Yth Flsp; Yrbk; Sch Nwsp; 4-H; Lat Clb; 4-H Awd; Ohio Inst Of Photog; Photog.

GEORGE, MARTIN; Connersville HS; Connersville, IN; 67/400 Chrh Wkr; Cmnty Wkr; Hon Rl; JA; Sch Pl; Drama Clb; Spn Clb; Coach Actv; IM Sprt; Ball St Univ; Elem Educ.

GEORGE, MOLLY; Pleasant HS; Caledonia, OH; Band; Hon Rl; Orch; Mat Maids; Scr Kpr; Tmr; Columbus Coll Of Art; Fine Arts.

GEORGE, MONYCA L; Tri Village HS; New Madison, OH; Trs Jr Cls; Sec Band; Chrs; Hon Rl; Pep Clb; Bsktbl; Trk; Chrldng; Pres Awd; Miami Valley Nursing Schl; R N.

GEORGE, PAM; Buckeye West HS; Harrisville, OH; Chrh Wkr; Hon Rl; NHS; Off Ade; Yth Flsp; Rptr Yrbk; 4-H; FHA; OEA; Chrldng; Jeff Tech Voc Schl; Sec.

GEORGE, REGINA; St Francis Desales HS; Columbus, OH; 98/197 Girl Scts; Hosp Ade; Red Cr Ade; Sct Actv; Voc Schl; Med.

GEORGE, SANDI; West Vigo HS; W Terre Haute, IN; 5/193 Band; Drl Tm; Hon Rl; JA; NHS; Sch Pl; Stu Cncl; Pres Y-Teens; Sec FTA; Rotary Awd; Purdue Univ; Psych.

GEORGE, SANDY; Penn Harris Madison HS; Mishawaka, IN; Cmp Fr Grls; Chrh Wkr; Hon Rl; Sch Pl; Ger Clb; Ball St Univ; Busns Admin.

GEORGE, SUSAN; Woodward HS; Cincinnati, OH; 44/398 Hon Rl; Off Ade; Univ Of Cincinnati; Nursing.

GEORGE, SUSAN M; Thomas A De Vilbiss HS; Toledo, OH; 16/300 Trs Jr Cls; Trs Sr Cls; Chrs; Chrh Wkr; Hon Rl; Jr NHS; Mdrgl; NHS; Quill & Scroll; Ed Yrbk; Univ Of Toledo; Corp Law.

GEORGE, TERRI L; South Knox HS; Vincennes, IN; 12/125 VP Jr Cls; Band; Cmp Fr Grls; Hon Rl; NHS; Stu Cncl; Yrbk; Fr Clb; FHA; Mth Clb; Vincennes Univ; Phys Ther.

GEORGE, VICTORIA; Utica HS; Newark, OH; Cls Rep Frsh Cls; Pres Soph Cls; Cls Rep Soph Cls; Cl Rep Jr Cls; Pres Sr Cls; Cls Rep Sr Cls; Hon Rl; NHS; Ohi State Univ; Phys Sci.

GEORGEPHY, LORI; Green HS; Akron, OH; Chrs; Chrh Wkr; Sch Mus; Sch Pl; Y-Teens; Sch Nwsp; Drama Clb; Pep Clb; Akron Univ; English Typography.

GEORGIO, LYNN; Nordonia HS; Macedonia, OH; Cls Rep Frsh Cls; Cls Rep Soph Cls; Cl Rep Jr Cls; JA; Sct Actv; Drama Clb; 4-H; Fr Clb; Pep Clb; Swmmng; Bus Schl; Model.

GEORGIOU, ELECTRA; Kearsley HS; Burton, MI; Hon Rl; Lbry Ade; Yth Flsp; OEA; Merit Achvmnt Awd 79; Univ Of Michigan; Bus Admin.

GEOZEFF, JERILYN; New Castle Chrysler HS; New Castle, IN; Chrs; Girl Scts; Hon Rl; Lbry Ade; Off Ade; Yth Flsp; 4-H; Attendance; Sports; Math; College.

GEPFORD, ANDREA; John Glenn HS; New Concord, OH; Trs Jr Cls; Trs Sr Cls; Band; Chrs; Drl Tm; Drm Bgl; Drm Mjrt; Hon Rl; Off Ade; Sch Mus; Miami Univ.

GEPFORD, LUANNE; Shepherd HS; Mt Pleasant, MI; 9/117 Trs Sr Cls; Hon Rl; NHS; FTA; Pep Clb; Chrldng; PPFtbl; Central Mic Univ; Clercial Work.

GEPHART, JAYNE; Ashtabula HS; Ashtabula, OH; 7/354 AFS; Chrs; Hon Rl; JA; NHS; Off Ade; Rptr Yrbk; Fr Clb; Ger Clb; Kent State Univ; Nursing.

GERACI, MARK; Moeller HS; Cincinnati, OH; 1/230 Cmnty Wkr; Hon Rl; NHS; Sch Pl; Stg Crw; Rptr Sch Nwsp; Swmmng; Natl Merit Ltr; Acad Schlrshp Pepperdine Univ 79; Spanish Hon Soc 78; Univ Of Colorado; Psych.

GERAKIS, MAGDALENE; Brooklyn Sr HS; Brooklyn, OH; 49/169 Chrs; Hosp Ade; Stu Cncl; Rptr Sch Nwsp; Ger Clb; Kent St Univ; Tele Cmnctns.

GERARD, PATTY; Anderson HS; Cincinnati, OH; Girl Scts; NHS; Off Ade; Yrbk; FBLA; OEA; Spn Clb; Ohi Univ; Acctg.

GERARD, TWILA; Grafton HS; Grafton, WV; Band; Hon Rl; Hosp Ade; Lbry Ade; Fr Clb; IM Sprt; PPFtbl; Twrlr; All Fest Band 78; Fairmont St Coll; Courtroom Stenog.

GERARDOT, CHRIS; Woodlan HS; New Haven, IN; 3/133 Am Leg Boys St; Hon Rl; Natl Forn Lg; NHS; Yrbk; FFA; Ftbl; Letter Wrstlng; Dnfth Awd; Opt Clb Awd; Univ; Law.

GERARDOT, ERNEST; Heritage HS; Monroeville, IN; Band; Hon Rl; Orch; Sch Mus; IM Sprt; Band Serv Awd 79; Univ; Archt.

GERARDOT, PAUL J; Bishop Luers HS; Ft Wayne, IN; Chrh Wkr; Cmnty Wkr; Pol Wkr; Stg Crw; Stu Cncl; Sch Nwsp; Key Clb; IM Sprt; Kiwan Awd; BLHS Key Clb Otstndng Serv Awd 76 79; BLHS Key Clb Otstndng Officer Awd 79; Univ; Soc Work.

GERARDOT, REYNE L; Heritage HS; Monroeville, IN; 79/178 Cmnty Wkr; Drl Tm; Sch Pl; Stg Crw; 4-H; Lat Clb; Pom Pon; 4-H Awd; Purdue Univ; Science.

GERBER, CATHERINE; Margaretta HS; Castalia, OH; 11/148 Band; Chrs; Chrh Wkr; Hon Rl; NHS; FHA; Providence Hosp Schl; Nursing.

GERBER, CHERYL L; Adams Central HS; Decatur, IN; 17/113 Trs Soph Cls; Band; Chrs; Chrh Wkr; Hon Rl; JA; NHS; Off Ade; Sch Mus; Yrbk;.

GERBER, CYNTHIA F; Shenandoah HS; Middletown, IN; 14/124 Girl Scts; Drama Clb; VP FHA; Mgrs; Univ; Acctg.

GERBER, GLADYS; Jackson Center HS; Jackson Center, OH; 10/42 Band; Hon Rl; Quill & Scroll; Ed Sch Nwsp; Rptr Sch Nwsp; Univ; Photog.

GERBER, JAN; Forest Park HS; Ferdinand, IN; Sec Band; Quill & Scroll; Sch Mus; Sch Nwsp; Beta Clb; Letter Trk; Capt Chrldng; Fresh Attendant On Bsktbl Queens Court; Sr Bsktbl Queen Candidate;.

GERBER, JILL; Clay City HS; Clay City, IN; 8/52 Sec Soph Cls; Band; Hon Rl; NHS; Yth Flsp; 4-H; FHA; Pep Clb; Sci Clb; Letter Bsktbl; Job.

GERBER, JOSEPH; Jasper HS; Jasper, IN; Ftbl; Trk; College.

GERBER, MARY; Fairview HS; Fariview Park, OH; AFS; Hon Rl; Hosp Ade; Yth Flsp; Sci Clb; Letter Bsktbl; Letter Trk; Coach Actv; IM Sprt; College; Medicine.

GERBER, VICTORIA L; Adams Central HS; Decatur, IN; 2/113 Cls Rep Frsh Cls; Band; Chrs; Chrh Wkr; Cmnty Wkr; Capt Drl Tm; Hon Rl; NHS; Orch; Sch Mus; Indiana Univ; Dental Assistant.

GERBIC, JAMES; Padua Franciscan HS; Parma, OH; Band; Boy Scts; Hon Rl; JA; Orch; Ger Clb; Bsktbl; Ftbl; JA Awd; Ohio State; Pharmacy.

GERBIG, DON; Barberton HS; Barberton, OH; 14/500 Boy Scts; Chrs; Hon Rl; Jr NHS; Sct Actv; VP Ger Clb; Akron Univ; Bio Sci.

GERBRACHT, JEFFREY; South Newton HS; Brook, IN; Boy Scts; Hon Rl; Yth Flsp; 4-H; Ger Clb; Sci Clb; Letter Crs Cntry; Glf; College; Wildlife.

GERCKE, MARCIA; Edison HS; Berlin Hts, OH; Am Leg Aux Girls St; Aud/Vis; Band; Girl Scts; Hon Rl; Natl Forn Lg; NHS; College; Medicine.

GERDEMAN, ANN; North Baltimore HS; N Baltimore, OH; Cls Rep Soph Cls; Cl Rep Jr Cls; Cls Rep Sr Cls; Chrs; Chrh Wkr; Girl Scts; Hon Rl; Lbry Ade; Pol Wkr; Toledo Univ; Natural Sciences.

GERDEMAN, FRANKLIN; Baker HS; Dayton, OH; 40/309 Trs Soph Cls; Aud/Vis; Band; Chrs; Hon Rl; Jr NHS; NHS; Orch; Sch Mus; Sch Pl; Hugh O Brien Ldrshp Awrd 78; Thesbians 79; Tulane Univ; Poli Sci.

GERDEMAN, LYNN; Delphos St Johns HS; Delphos, OH; Band; Girl Scts; Hon Rl; NHS; Sch Nwsp; 4-H; FTA; Pep Clb; 4-H Awd; God Cntry Awd; Univ; Spch Pathology.

GERDICH, THOMAS; Donald E Gavit Jr Sr HS; Hammond, IN; Bsktbl; Capt Ftbl; Capt Trk; Indiana Univ; Dent.

GERDINK, JAMES E; Terre Haute North Vigo HS; Terre Haute, IN; 1/650 Cls Rep Frsh Cls; Cls Rep Soph Cls; Cl Rep Jr Cls; Stu Cncl; Letter Crs Cntry; Trk; JETS Awd; Natl Merit Ltr; Rose Hulman Inst; Engr.

GERDT, STEVEN; Munster HS; Munster, IN; Am Leg Boys St; Hon Rl; Sct Actv; Stu Cncl; Ger Clb; Mth Clb; IM Sprt; College.

GERENCER, THOMAS; Grant HS; Bailey, MI; Cls Rep Frsh Cls; VP Soph Cls; Cl Rep Jr Cls; Pres Sr Cls; Band; Stu Cncl; 4-H; Sci Clb; Bsktbl; Trk; Emergency Med Tech.

GERFEN, DARRELL; Elgin HS; Prospect, OH; 49/137 Chrs; Chrh Wkr; Pres Yth Flsp; 4-H; FFA; 4-H Awd; Marion Tech School; Bus Mgmt.

GERFEN, LORRI; Elgin HS; Prospect, OH; Chrh Wkr; Cmnty Wkr; Hon Rl; NHS; Yth Flsp; 4-H; Sec FFA; Sec Lat Clb; PPFtbl; Scr Kpr; Marion Co Pork Queen & Dist Pork Queen 78; Oh Poland Chira Queen 78; FFA Public Speaking 79; Ohio St Univ; Agri Educ.

GERHAN, MARTHA; Warren Central HS; Indianapolis, IN; 34/873 Pres Frsh Cls; Cls Rep Soph Cls; Cl Rep Jr Cls; Am Leg Aux Girls St; Chrh Wkr; FCA; Hon Rl; NHS; Stu Cncl; Fr Clb; College.

GERHARD, SCOTT; Pickerington HS; Pickerington, OH; Band; Chrs; Chrh Wkr; Cmnty Wkr; Hon Rl; VP JA; Jr NHS; NHS; College; Med.

GERICKE, JENNIFER; Dover HS; Dover, OH; 40/243 Band; Chrs; Girl Scts; Hon Rl; Sch Mus; Sct Actv; FNA; FTA; Natl Merit Schl; Spanish Outstanding Ach Awd; 2 Yr Band Letter; 1st Chair Flutist In Symphonic Band; College; Elem Ed.

GERKE, MICHAEL; New Haven HS; New Haven, IN; Trs Frsh Cls; Boy Scts; Hon Rl; Fr Clb; Letter Bsbl; Mgrs; Amer French Tchrs Cert 77 79; Indiana Univ; Dent.

GERKEN, ALAN; Napoleon HS; Napoleon, OH; 4-H; 4-H Awd; Univ; Archt.

GERKEN, BETHANN; Napoleon HS; Napoleon, OH; Am Leg Aux Girls St; Yth Flsp; 4-H; Spn Clb; Northwest Tech Coll; Sec.

GERKEN, COLLEEN; Notre Dame HS; Portsmouth, OH; Chrs; Chrh Wkr; Hon Rl; Pol Wkr; Sch Pl; Sprt Ed Yrbk; Rptr Yrbk; Yrbk; Drama Clb; 4-H; Ohio St Univ; Bus Admin.

GERKEN, DARLENE; Archbold HS; Archbold, OH; 7/130 Am Leg Aux Girls St; Hon Rl; NHS; Yrbk; Rptr Sch Nwsp; Pep Clb; Letter Bsbl; GAA; Am Leg Awd; Voice Dem Awd; Bowling Green St Univ.

GERKEN, JILL; Delta HS; Delta, OH; Sec Jr Cls; Chrs; NHS; Sch Nwsp; FHA; FTA; Letter Bsbl; Letter Trk; Letter Mat Maids; Bowling Green St Univ; Fshon Design.

GERKEN, KATHY; Napoleon HS; Napoleon, OH; Girl Scts; Hon Rl; FHA; Lat Clb; PPFtbl; Coll; Sec.

GERKEN, MARY A; Holgate HS; New Bavaria, OH; 2/48 Band; Chrh Wkr; Hon Rl; NHS; VP Yth Flsp; Pres 4-H; FHA; Mth Clb; Pep Clb; Sci Clb; Placed 7th In Maumee Vlly Math Cont 79; Placed 9th In 1st Yr Chem In BGSU Dist In Oh Test 79; Del To 4 H C; Univ.

GERKEN, PAM; Patrick Henry HS; Malinta, OH; 8/100 Band; Chrs; VP Chrh Wkr; Girl Scts; Hon Rl; Sch Mus; Sec 4-H; Sci Clb; VP Spn Clb; 4-H Awd; Univ; Med Tech.

GERKER, JIM; Ottoville Local HS; Cloverdale, OH; Hon Rl; Sch Mus; Sch Nwsp; Univ; Bus.

GERKIN, TODD M; Parkersburg HS; Vienna, WV; 3/800 VP Sr Cls; Am Leg Boys St; Boy Scts; Chrh Wkr; FCA; Hon Rl; Sct Actv; Yth Flsp; Boys Clb Am; Pres Pep Clb; Univ Of Virginia; Chemistry.

GERKS, RICHARD C; Lakewood HS; Sunfield, MI; 26/235 Hon Rl; Lbry Ade; Sprt Ed Sch Nwsp; Rptr Sch Nwsp; Sch Nwsp; Pres 4-H; Ger Clb; Letter Bsbl; Mgrs; Letter Mat Maids; Michigan St Univ; Jrnlsm.

GERLACH, M B; Trenton HS; Trenton, MI; Band; Hon Rl; NHS; Orch; Ger Clb; Univ.

GERLAND, ROBERT; Mentor HS; Mentor, OH; Cmnty Wkr; Hon Rl; Natl Merit Ltr; Oh Basic Studies Awd Of Distinction; Ohio St Univ; Optometry.

GERLINE, JILL; South Wern HS; Edinburg, IN; 2/65 Pom Pon; Scr Kpr; Cit Awd; Gov Hon Prg Awd; Natl Merit SF; Natl Merit Schl; Opt Clb Awd; Univ Of Evansville; Pre Med.

GERMAN, M; Delphos Jefferson HS; Delphos, OH; 12/120 Sec Soph Cls; Band; Hon Rl; Hosp Ade; Pres NHS; Sch Mus; Stu Cncl; Sci Clb; College; Registered Nurse.

GERMAN, NANCY A; Ottawa Glandorf HS; Ottawa, OH; Lbry Ade; Off Ade; DECA; Drama Clb; FHA; Ten; GAA; Scr Kpr; Business Schl; Exec Sec.

GERMANN, BEN; Ripley Union Lewis HS; Ripley, OH; Sch Pl; Ed Yrbk; Yrbk; Pres Spn Clb; Univ; Engr.

GERMANN, GAYLE L; Lincolnview HS; Delphos, OH; 1/81 Val; Am Leg Aux Girls St; Pres Band; Pres Chrs; Chrh Wkr; Hosp Ade; NHS; Sch Mus; Sch Pl; Sch Nwsp; Roger K Thompson Self Reliance Awd; Black Inc Sec Awd; Black Inc Outstanding Sr In Van Wert County Awd; College; Sec.

GERMANN, NEIL; Penn HS; Wyatt, IN; Hon Rl; 4-H; Letter Mgrs; 4-H Awd; Carrier Of Month Awd S Bend Trib 77; Kodak Photog Awd 77; Voc Schl; Mech.

GERMANO, DAVE; John Adams HS; S Bend, IN; 2/500 Hon Rl; Lit Mag; NHS; Quill & Scroll; Rptr Yrbk; Lcrss; Ten; Natl Merit Ltr; Natl Merit SF; Natl Merit Schl; College.

GERMANO, GINA M; John Adams HS; South Bend, IN; 30/415 Hon Rl; Lit Mag; NHS; Orch; Quill & Scroll; Sch Mus; Ed Yrbk; Yrbk; Natl Merit Ltr; Indiana Univ; Social Work.

GERNS, EDWARD; West Lafayette HS; W Lafayette, IN; 45/190 Band; Hon Rl; Crs Cntry; Swmmng; Trk; IM Sprt; Ball St Univ; Archt.

GEROLD, LARRY; Sandusky HS; Sandusky, OH; Chrh Wkr; Letter Ftbl; Letter Wrstlng; IM Sprt; Scr Kpr; Ohio St Univ; Busns.

GERREN, DAVID; Hoover HS; North Canton, OH; Band; Chrs; Chrh Wkr; Hon Rl; Orch; Sch Mus; Sch Pl; Yth Flsp; Univ Of Akron; Electrical Eng.

GERRITS, LINDA; Holland Christian HS; Holland, MI; Trs Frsh Cls; Chrh Wkr; 4-H; Ger Clb; Bsbl; IM Sprt; 4-H Awd; Dutchdanie 78 & 79; J V Vllybl Team 77; Davenport Coll; Acctg.

GERSHANOFF, JENNIE; Mooresville HS; Mooresville, IN; Chrs; Hon Rl; NHS; FFA; Ger Clb; Trk; GAA; Indiana Univ; Nursing.

GERST, STEVEN; Lowell Sr HS; Lowell, IN; 170/250 Band; Boy Scts; VICA; Ftbl; Purdue Univ; Indus Engr.

GERSTENBERGER, BARBARA; Sandusky HS; Sandusky, OH; Hon Rl; NHS; Yth Flsp; Rptr Yrbk; Rptr Sch Nwsp; 4-H; Pep Clb; Chrldng; 4-H Awd; Natl Merit SF; Central Michigan Univ; Acctg.

GERULSKI, MICHAEL; Bay City Western HS; Auburn, MI; Natl Merit SF; Michigan Tech Univ; Chem Engr.

GERWIG, MARK; Bellmont HS; Decatur, IN; Chrs; Cmnty Wkr; Mdrgl; Sch Mus; Sch Pl; Drama Clb; Lat Clb; Sci Clb; Swmmng; Ball St Univ; Dent.

GERWIN, JOSEPH; Reading Community HS; Reading, OH; 3/217 Am Leg Boys St; Hon Rl; Jr NHS; NHS; Rdo Clb; Ten; Am Leg Awd; Northwestern Univ; Bio Med Engr.

GERZEN, SANDRA; Negaunee HS; Negaunee, MI; Band; Hon Rl; Sci Clb; IM Sprt; PPFtbl; Univ; Nursing.

GESAMAN, RON; United Local HS; Salem, OH; FCA; Quill & Scroll; Stg Crw; Yth Flsp; Rptr Sch Nwsp; Fr Clb; Ftbl; Trk; Woster Coll; Jrnlsm.

GESCHKE, MARY; Cuyahoga Vly Jt Voc HS; Northfield, OH; Band; Chrs; Chrh Wkr; Pep Clb; Moody Bible Inst; Sec.

GESCHWIND, PAMLA; Cedar Lake Acad; Gobles, MI; Chrs; Hon Rl; NHS; Stg Crw; Yth Flsp; Yrbk; Sch Nwsp; Pres Beta Clb; Andrews Univ; Counciling.

GESING, RICHARD G; Boardman HS; Youngstown, OH; 97/601 Band; FCA; Hon Rl; NHS; Treas Mth Clb; Capt Gym; Whos Who Among Amer HS Stud 77; All Amer In Gymnastics 77; U S Military Acad; Elec Engr.

GESING, ROBERT G; Boardman HS; Boardman, OH; 30/601 FCA; Hon Rl; NHS; Quill & Scroll; Yrbk; VP Mth Clb; Wrstlng; Sr Art Awd; 175 Lb Tm Eastern Ohio All St Tm; Art Comp Schlrshp Syracuse Univ; Columbus Coll Of Art Design; Syracuse Univ; Art.

GESINSKI, TIMOTHY; Southfield Lathrop HS; Southfield, MI; Hon Rl; Letter Bsbl; Letter Ftbl; Letter Wrstlng; IM Sprt; Mic State Univ; Vet.

GESSEL, DEBBIE; Waynedale HS; Wooster, OH; 1/122 Band; Hon Rl; NHS; Yth Flsp; FTA; Trk; Chrldng; Bausch & Lomb Awd; Dnfth Awd; Gov Hon Prg Awd; N Cntrl Tech Coll; Nursing.

GESSLER, CAROL; Euclid Sr HS; Euclid, OH; 61/728 Hon Rl; JA; OEA; Cit Awd; OEA Busns Math 2nd Pl Regional Comp; Lakeland Comm Coll; Legal Tech.

GESWEIN, BEV; Benton Central HS; Fowler, IN; 76/235 Cls Rep Frsh Cls; Cls Rep Soph Cls; Trs Jr Cls; Cls Rep Sr Cls; Band; Chrh Wkr; Hon Rl; Lbry Ade; Off Ade; 4-H; OEA Awds Diplmnt Stswmn & Amb Awds 78; Golf Awds 4 Yr Awd Hoosier Conf & Mst Vlble 78; Indiana St Univ; Bus Admin.

GETTEL, DEBORAH; Owen Gage HS; Sebewaing, MI; Trs Soph Cls; Cl Rep Jr Cls; Sec Sr Cls; Hon Rl; NHS; Stu Cncl; 4-H; FHA; Letter Bsktbl; College.

GETTY, THOMAS; Bishop Luers HS; Ft Wayne, IN; Hon Rl; Key Clb; Ftbl; College; Pre Med.

GETZ, C; Elmhurst HS; Ft Wayne, IN; 52/400 Boy Scts; Fr Clb; Coll; Sci.

GETZ, CARLA; Coloma HS; Coloma, MI; Chrs; Girl Scts; Hon Rl; Sct Actv; Fr Clb; Pep Clb; Trk; JA Awd; Western Mich Univ; Psych.

GEURINK, STEVEN; Allendale Public HS; West Olive, MI; Cls Rep Soph Cls; Cl Rep Jr Cls; VP Sr Cls; Cls Rep Sr Cls; Band; Chrh Wkr; FCA; Hon Rl; NHS; PAVAS; Kalamazoo Coll; Art.

GEVAS, BRYAN; Parkersburg HS; Parkersburg, WV; Chrs; Sch Mus; Sci Clb; W Va Wesleyan College;.

GEYER, JANICE; Western HS; Kokomo, IN; 8/204 Chrs; Hon Rl; Jr NHS; Lit Mag; NHS; Sch Mus; Yth Flsp; Ball State; Music.

GEYER, LORE; Parma Sr HS; Parma, OH; 2/782 Chrs; NHS; Orch; Natl Piano Playing Audtn Dist Mbr Of Natl Frat Of Stdnt Musicn 77 79; Adv Plcmnt Progr Coll Bd Amer Hist 79; Baldwin Wallace Coll; Hist.

GHAPHERY, NICK; Linsly HS; Wheeling, WV; Chrh Wkr; Debate Tm; Hosp Ade; ROTC; Spn Clb; Bsktbl; Capt Socr; Letter Ten; Coach Actv; JA Awd; Hon Jr Achvmnt Awd 79; Awd Foul Shotting Champ Of Linsly Bsktbl Team 79; West Virginia Univ; Med.

GHEARING, LARRY L; Jackson HS; Jackson, OH; 1/230 Am Leg Boys St; Band; Hon Rl; NHS; Sch Mus; Sci Clb; Letter Bsbl; Letter Bsktbl; Crs Cntry; Ohio Test Of Schlstc Ach Algebra I & II Geometry; Ohio St Univ; Elec Engr.

GHERING, AMY; Chadsey HS; Detroit, MI; Hon Rl; Pol Wkr; Sch Pl; Stg Crw; Stu Cncl; Drama Clb; Univ Of Mich; Chem.

GHILONI, DIANE; Newark Catholic HS; Newark, OH; Girl Scts; Hon Rl; NHS; PAVAS; Fr Clb; Lat Clb; Rotary Awd; Essay Printed In Young Amer Speaks Natl Press & Essay Bk 77; Sec & Treas Of Latin Clb 78; Univ; Performing Arts.

GHODOOSHIM, SEPTEMBER; West Geauga HS; Chesterland, OH; Cls Rep Soph Cls; Chrs; Hon Rl; Sch Mus; Sch Nwsp; Exc In Journalism; Honorable Mention In Englsh In Kent St Dist & State Of Ohio; Ohio St Univ; Comp Programming.

GHOLSON, JILL; West Washington HS; Salem, IN; 6/97 Hon Rl; NHS; Rptr Yrbk; Yrbk; Drama Clb; Pres 4-H; VP FHA; Sullivan Bus College; Bus.

GIACOBBI, JODDI; Cadiz HS; Cadiz, OH; 7/138 Cl Rep Jr Cls; VP Sr Cls; Hon Rl; Jr NHS; NHS; 4-H; OEA; Letter Bsktbl; Wrstlng; GAA; Jeff Tech College; Computer Prog.

GIACONIA, JOSEPH; Kirtland HS; Kirtland, OH; Cl Rep Jr Cls; Am Leg Boys St; Chrs; Hon Rl; Pres Jr NHS; Sec NHS; Stu Cncl; Yth Flsp; Pres Key Clb; Sci Clb; Case Western Reserve Univ; Med.

GIANCOLA, DANIEL E; Springfield Local HS; N Middletown, OH; Cls Rep Soph Cls; Hon Rl; Stu Cncl; Sprt Ed Sch Nwsp; Fr Clb; Bsbl; Bsktbl; Youngstown St Univ; Health.

GIANGRANDE, JOHN; Cleveland Central Cathlc HS; Cleveland, OH; Cls Rep Frsh Cls; Cls Rep Soph Cls; Cl Rep Jr Cls; Boy Scts; Chrh Wkr; Drm Bgl; Mod UN; Sch Pl; Stu Cncl; Honors Awd Wnr I Art 79; Honors Field Of Soc Studies 79; Cleveland St Univ; Bus.

GIANNAMORE, PAUL; Wintersville HS; Steubenville, OH; 13/283 Am Leg Boys St; Sch Pl; Spn Clb; Mgrs; Univ; Metalurgical Engr.

GIANOTTO, CATHERINE; Wooster HS; Wooster, OH; Fr Clb; Univ; Acctg.

GIASSON, SUSAN; St Annes Warren HS; Warrem, MI; Cls Rep Frsh Cls; Cls Rep Soph Cls; Cl Rep Jr Cls; Chrs; Chrh Wkr; Off Ade; Trk; Voc Schl; Advertising.

GIBB, JIM; Ridgedale HS; Morral, OH; 45/110 VP Soph Cls; Chrh Wkr; Hon Rl; Yrbk; Spn Clb; Letter Bsbl; Letter Bsktbl; Glf; IM Sprt; Univ.

GIBBON, LISA; Madison HS; Madison, OH; Girl Scts; Hon Rl; Univ.

GIBBONEY, BRIAN; Bradford HS; Bradford, OH; 1/59 Val; Hon Rl; Lbry Ade; NHS; Lion Awd;.

GIBBONEY, JAMES; Ben Davis HS; Indianapolis, IN; Chrs; Hon Rl; Natl Forn Lg; NHS; Sch Mus; Sch Pl; Stg Crw; Yrbk; Drama Clb; 4-H; Univ; Sci Research.

GIBBONEY, LORI; Brownsburg HS; Brownsbg, IN; Chrh Wkr; Hon Rl; NHS; Stg Crw; Fr Clb; Sci Clb; PPFtbl; College; Bio Chem.

GIBBONS, DONALD; Howell HS; Howell, MI; Boy Scts; Hon Rl; Sct Actv; Trk; Coach Actv; Spanish Awd 78; Michigan St Univ; Pre Law.

GIBBONS, DOUGLAS; Taylor HS; Cleves, OH; Pres Sr Cls; Am Leg Boys St; Band; Hon Rl; Lbry Ade; Sch Pl; Stu Cncl; Drama Clb; Ftbl; Trk; Hon For Its Acad Tm Mbr 78; Univ; Comp Engr.

GIBBONS, LEIGH; Martins Ferry HS; Martins Ferry, OH; 21/205 Chrs; Girl Scts; Hon Rl; Sci Clb; Bsktbl; Swmmng; GAA; Univ.

GIBBONS, MARY C; Cathedral HS; Indianapolis, IN; 11/150 Chrs; Chrh Wkr; Girl Scts; Hon Rl; Lbry Ade; Sch Mus; Sch Pl; Sct Actv; 4-H; Univ Of San Diego; Bus.

GIBBONS, MAUREEN; St Joseph Acad; Cleveland, OH; Cls Rep Frsh Cls; Pres Soph Cls; Chrh Wkr; Hon Rl; NHS; Sch Pl; Stu Cncl; College; Med.

GIBBONS, PATRICK; Archbishop Alter HS; Kettering, OH; 110/330 Cls Rep Soph Cls; Pres Jr Cls; Cls Rep Sr Cls; Chrs; Hon Rl; Sch Mus; Pres Stu Cncl; Key Clb; Univ Of Cincinnati; Indust Design.

GIBBONS, PHIL B; Granville HS; Granville, OH; 2/136 Sal; NHS; Pres Yth Flsp; Drama Clb; VP Key Clb; Sci Clb; Bsktbl; Capt Crs Cntry; Letter Trk; Natl Merit SF; Univ.

GIBBONS, TAMMY; Buckeye West HS; Smithfield, OH; 10/84 Hon Rl; NHS; 4-H; OEA; 4-H Awd; Vocational School.

GIBBS, BILL; Calumet HS; Hobart, IN; 1/300 Cls Rep Frsh Cls; Cl Rep Jr Cls; Cls Rep Sr Cls; Hon Rl; Jr NHS; NHS; Stu Cncl; Fr Clb; FSA; Pep Clb; Florida Inst Of Tech; Marine Bio.

GIBBS, CINDY; Solon HS; Solon, OH; Chrs; FCA; Hon Rl; NHS; Sch Mus; Sch Pl; Stg Crw; Drama Clb; College; Acct.

GIBBS, DOUGLAS F; Arthur Hill HS; Saginaw, MI; 2/544 Band; Debate Tm; Hon Rl; NHS; Orch; Sch Pl; Sct Actv; Sci Clb; Natl Merit SF; Rotary Awd; Outstanding Soph Boy 1977; Outstanding Jr Boy 1978; Recepient Regents Alumni Schlrshp Univ Of Michigan 1979; Univ Of Michigan; Pre Med.

GIBBS, JOE; High School; Rockport, IN; VP Frsh Cls; VP Soph Cls; Pres Jr Cls; Service.

GIBBS, JOHN; Dover HS; Dover, OH; 17/245 Hon Rl; Jr NHS; Capt Crs Cntry; Letter Trk; IM Sprt; Univ; Archt.

GIBBS, JUDY; Milton HS; Ona, WV; Cls Rep Soph Cls; Cl Rep Jr Cls; Chrs; Chrh Wkr; Hon Rl; Sch Mus; Sch Pl; Yth Flsp; Sprt Ed Sch Nwsp; FBLA; Marshall Coll; Banking.

GIBBS, KEVIN; Allen Park HS; Allen Park, MI; Univ Of Mich.

GIBBS, LORA; Avon Jr Sr HS; Danville, IN; 11/181 VP Frsh Cls; VP Soph Cls; VP Jr Cls; Chrs; Chrh Wkr; Mdrgl; 4-H; Pep Clb; Spn Clb; Gym; IUPUI; Elect.

GIBBS, MARK; Jay County HS; Redkey, IN; Band; Boy Scts; Drl Tm; Hon Rl; Jr NHS; Fr Clb; Swmmng; Ball State; Counsling.

GIBBS, PETE; Fairmont West HS; Blacksburg, VA; 125/498 Debate Tm; Hon Rl; Natl Forn Lg; Sch Pl; Yth Flsp; Ed Yrbk; Drama Clb; Lat Clb; JC Awd; Natl Merit SF; Univ Of Vir; Philosophy.

GIBBS, RICK; Otsego HS; Haskins, OH; 5/130 Sec Jr Cls; Am Leg Boys St; Hon Rl; NHS; Spn Clb; Bsktbl; Letter Crs Cntry; College; Med Tech.

GIBBS, TAMMY; R B Chamberlin HS; Twinsburg, OH; Trs Sr Cls; FCA; Hon Rl; NHS; Stu Cncl; HS Schlrshp Banquet 77 & 79; Nursing Schl; RN.

GIBLER, MISTY; Kingsford HS; Kingsford, MI; Chrs; Hon Rl; Off Ade; Sch Mus; Stg Crw; Chrldng; Swing Choir Camp Schlrshp; College; Nursing.

GIBLIN, CLARE; St Augustine Academy; Lakewood, OH; 40/150 Chrs; Girl Scts; Hon Rl; Sch Mus; Sch Pl; Rptr Sch Nwsp; Sch Nwsp; Drama Clb; Pep Clb; Gym; Editor St Augustine Impress Newspaper For Schl Yr; Participant Irish Way Prog; Baldwin Wallace Coll; Theater Arts.

GIBLIN, CORNELIUS J; Culver Military Academy; Yardley, PA; 73/195 ROTC; Ftbl; Wrstlng; IM Sprt; Culver Woodcraft Camp Regmntl Commdnr 76; Honor Council Rep 79; Mbr Of Culver Ranger Unit 78 79 80; Univ Of Pennsylvania; MBA.

GIBNEY, PATTY; Grosse Pointe South HS; Grss Pte Pk, MI; Cmp Fr Grls; Hosp Ade; Sch Mus; Sch Pl; Stu Cncl; PPFtbl; Tmr; Ferris State Coll; Dental Asst.

GIBSON, BRIAN; Aquinas HS; Allen Pk, MI; Cls Rep Soph Cls; VP Jr Cls; VP Sr Cls; Hon Rl; Stu Cncl; Bsktbl; Trk; IM Sprt; Univ; Engr.

GIBSON, BRUCE; Matewan HS; Meador, WV; Hon Rl; Jr NHS; Sec NHS; 4-H; Letter Bsbl; Bsktbl; Letter Ftbl; IM Sprt; Blue Ribbon In Sci Fair 77; 2 Yrs French Lang 77; Marshall Univ.

GIBSON, CAROL; Scott HS; Foster, WV; Cls Rep Frsh Cls; Cls Rep Soph Cls; Cl Rep Jr Cls; Band; Hon Rl; Jr NHS; Stg Crw; Rptr Yrbk; 4-H; Pep Clb; Marshall Cmnty Coll; Leg Asst.

GIBSON, CATHERINE; Lakota HS; Rising Sun, OH; Sec Jr Cls; VP Sr Cls; Hon Rl; Sec Stu Cncl; Drama Clb; Crs Cntry; Trk; Chrldng; Cit Awd; Home St Attndt & Wrstlng Queen 78; Home Soph Attndt 76; Soc Stud Awd 78; Bowling Green St Univ; Recrtn.

GIBSON, CYNTHIA; Vinson HS; Huntington, WV; 5/110 Band; Chrs; Hon Rl; Pres NHS; Ed Sch Nwsp; Marshall Univ Huntington; Sec Ed.

GIBSON, DEWEY; Williamsburg HS; Virginia Beach, VA; 20/79 Chrs; Hon Rl; Jr NHS; NHS; Sci Clb; Spn Clb; Bsktbl; Mgrs; Community Coll; Law.

GIBSON, DON; Southfield Christian HS; Pontiac, MI; 5/65 Cl Rep Jr Cls; VP Sr Cls; Band; Hon Rl; NHS; Stu Cncl; Yth Flsp; Crs Cntry; Socr; Trk; Albion Coll; Medicine.

GIBSON, GLORIA; Springfield HS; Springfield, MI; Band; Chrs; Chrh Wkr; Hon Rl; JA; FHA; Ten; Trk; JA Awd; 3rd Pl In Schl Art Show 79; Kellogg Community Coll; Data Proc.

GIBSON, JOHNIE; Union HS; Grand Rapids, MI; Boy Scts; Hon Rl; NHS; Sct Actv; Capt Crs Cntry; Capt Trk; Wrstlng; Jr College; Architecture.

GIBSON, JOYCE; Ontario HS; Crestline, OH; 17/198 Chrs; Chrh Wkr; Girl Scts; Hon Rl; JA; NHS; FHA; VP OEA; Trk; Cit Awd; Bowling Green St Univ; Education.

GIBSON, KAREN; Richmond HS; Richmond, IN; Hon Rl; NHS; Letter Swmmng; Letter Mgrs; College.

GIBSON, KEN; Norwood HS; Norwood, OH; 8/350 Chrh Wkr; Hon Rl; Jr NHS; NHS; Rptr Sch Nwsp; Key Clb; Spn Clb; Ten; Am Leg Awd; Spanish Natl Hnr Soc 78; Univ; Bus Admin.

GIBSON, KIM; Climax Scotts HS; Climax, MI; Hon Rl; Spn Clb; Letter Chrldng; PPFtbl; Univ; Bus.

GIBSON, LAURA; Northmont Sr HS; Dayton, OH; Band; Chrs; Drl Tm; Girl Scts; Hon Rl; Univ; Nursing.

GIBSON, LINDA; Mother Of Mercy HS; Cincinnati, OH; 6/235 Cmp Fr Grls; Hon Rl; NHS; Sch Pl; Yth Flsp; Civ Clb; Drama Clb; VP Spn Clb; GAA; IM Sprt; College; Medicine.

GIBSON, LISA; Garden City East HS; Garden City, MI; Chrs; Hon Rl; PAVAS; Sch Pl; Drama Clb; Eastern Mic; Comm Art.

GIBSON, LORI; John Glenn Sr HS; New Concord, OH; Chrs; Hon Rl; Yth Flsp; Muskingum Area Tech Coll.

GIBSON, LUCY; Solon HS; Solon, OH; Hon Rl; Fr Clb; Sci Clb; Natl Merit Ltr; Univ; Bio.

GIBSON, MARK; Mooresville HS; Mooresville, IN; 21/277 Hon Rl; Lit Mag; NHS; Rptr Sch Nwsp; Ger Clb; Sci Clb; Socr; Butler Univ; Pre Vet Med.

GIBSON, MARK W; St Charles Preparatory HS; Westerville, OH; Hon Rl; NHS; Glf; Socr; Letter Wrstlng; Univ; Acturial Sci.

GIBSON, REGINA; Ansonia HS; Ansonia, OH; Sal; Pres Band; Chrs; Sec NHS; Sec Yth Flsp; FHA; OEA; Edison State Community Coll; Acctg.

GIBSON, ROBIN; Garfield HS; Hamilton, OH; Chrs; Chrh Wkr; Hon Rl; Jr NHS; Lbry Ade; NHS; Sch Mus; Southern Ohio College.

GIBSON, SANDRA; Liberty HS; Bristol, WV; Chrh Wkr; Cmnty Wkr; Hon Rl; Jr NHS; Yth Flsp; VP DECA; Drama Clb; Real Est.

GIBSON, SHARON; Mt Vernon Academy; Wakeman, OH; Cl Rep Jr Cls; Hon Rl; Southern Missionary Coll; Psych.

GIBSON, TERESA; Lakeview HS; St Clair Shores, MI; 21/546 Chrh Wkr; Hon Rl; Jr NHS; NHS; Orch; Univ Of Michigan; Physical Therapy.

GIBSON, TIMOTHY D; Sidney HS; Sidney, OH; Hon Rl; Key Clb; George Washington Univ; Engr.

GIBSON, TRACY L; Cadiz HS; Cadiz, OH; 17/103 Am Leg Aux Girls St; Band; Chrh Wkr; Hon Rl; NHS; Off Ade; Yth Flsp; Lat Clb; Great Lakes Bible Coll; Christn Educ.

GIBSON, VICKY; Oceana HS; Cyclone, WV; Cl Rep Jr Cls; Chrh Wkr; Hon Rl; NHS; Off Ade; Yth Flsp; Yrbk; Sch Nwsp; FBLA; FNA; Southern W Virginia Coll; Exec Sec.

GIBSON, WAYNE; Cambridge HS; Cambridge, OH; Aud/Vis; Chrs; Hon Rl; Key Clb; Wrstlng; Coach Actv; Cin Univ; Engr.

GIBSON, WILLIAM; Willard HS; Willard, OH; Hon Rl; Jr NHS; NHS; Glf; Letter Trk; IM Sprt; C of C Awd; College; Medicine.

GICK, DEBBIE; Clinton Prairie HS; Colfax, IN; 19/90 Band; Chrh Wkr; Girl Scts; VP NHS; Off Ade ; Sct Actv; VP 4-H; Sec FHA; Lat Clb; Sec Sci Clb; Purdue Univ; Vet.

GIDDINGS, DEBORAH; Everett HS; Lansing, MI; Jr NHS; NHS; Letter Chrldng; PPFtbl; Natl Merit SF; Central Mic Univ; Chem.

GIDLEY, DONNA; Calumet HS; Gary, IN; Mod UN; Off Ade; Sch Pl; Y-Teens; Drama Clb; OEA; Pep Clb; Pom Pon; Bus Schl; Model.

GIDOW, LINDA; West Muskingum HS; Zanesville, OH; Band; Chrs; Hosp Ade; Sch Mus; Y-Teens; 4-H; FHA; 4-H Awd; Univ; Comp Sci.

GIEBNER, DEBBIE; Brush HS; Lyndhurst, OH; Cl Rep Jr Cls; Girl Scts; Off Ade; Trk; GAA; PPFtbl; Scr Kpr; College.

GIERA, JAMES; St Frances Cabrini HS; Dearborn, MI; Chrh Wkr; Hon Rl; NHS; Spn Clb; Trk; Kiwan Awd; Univ Of Detroit; Dent.

GIERAK, KAREN; Romulus Sr HS; Romulus, MI; Trs Soph Cls; Cl Rep Jr Cls; Hon Rl; NHS; Stu Cncl; Spn Clb; Trk; Mgrs; Mat Maids; Scr Kpr; Michigan St Univ; Animal Tech.

GIERE, KEN; Coldwater HS; Coldwater, OH; Pres Frsh Cls; Pres Soph Cls; Pres Jr Cls; Pres Sr Cls; Cmnty Wkr; Hon Rl; Jr NHS; NHS; Ger Clb; Letter Wrstlng; College.

GIERKE, JOHN; Sault Area HS; Sault Ste Marie, MI; 18/314 Hon Rl; NHS; IM Sprt; Lake Superior State Coll; Engr.

GIERSCHICK, ROBERT; West Bloomfield HS; W Bloomfield, MI; 160/480 Boy Scts; Chrs; Cmnty Wkr; Sch Mus; Stg Crw; Yrbk; Swmmng; Trk; Oakland Univ; Bus Mgmt.

GIES, EDWARD C; Lumen Christi HS; Jackson, MI; Cl Rep Jr Cls; Cls Rep Sr Cls; Am Leg Aux Girls St; Hon Rl; NHS; Stu Cncl; Rptr Sch Nwsp; Crs Cntry; Opt Clb Awd; Univ; Engr.

GIES, JANE; Western HS; Bay City, MI; Band; Chrs; Chrh Wkr; Cmnty Wkr; Hon Rl; 4-H; Key Clb; Bsbl; Cit Awd; 4-H Awd; College; Sec.

GIESE, MARIO; Ross HS; Hamilton, OH; 1/177 Val; Am Leg Boys St; Hon Rl; Pres NHS; Rptr Sch Nwsp; Capt Bsbl; Ftbl; Trk; Miami Univ Oxford; Engr.

GIESSLER, JAMES; Fairless HS; Navarre, OH; 13/217 Chrs; Chrh Wkr; Hon Rl; NHS; Sch Mus; Sch Pl; Drama Clb;.

GIFFORD, ALLEN; Bloom HS; Wheelersburg, OH; Boy Scts; Chrh Wkr; Hon Rl; Lbry Ade; Off Ade; Stg Crw; Earl Ham Univ; Nuclear Physicist.

GIFFORD, DAVID; Buckhannon Upshur HS; Buckhannon, WV; Trs Soph Cls; Trs Jr Cls; Chrh Wkr; Cmnty Wkr; Hon Rl; Sprt Ed Yrbk; Sch Nwsp; 4-H; Mgrs; 4-H Awd; George Sharpe Land Judging Awd 78; Camp Minawanea 79; Mbr Of St Champ Land Judging Tm 78; West Virginia Univ; Med.

GIFFORD, JAMIE; Griffith Sr HS; Griffith, IN; Chrs; Chrh Wkr; Hon Rl; Off Ade; Yth Flsp; Y-Teens;.

GIFFORD, SHARON; Liberty HS; Poland, OH; 69/238 Chrs; JA; Lbry Ade; Off Ade; Yth Flsp; Sch Nwsp; Fr Clb; FTA; JA Awd; Youngstown St Univ; Psych.

GIGLIO, C ANDREW; Our Lady Of Lakes HS; Pontiac, MI; Hon Rl; Yrbk; Fr Clb; Univ Of Michigan; Sci.

GILB, PRISCILLA; South Dearborn HS; Aurora, IN; 21/265 Chrs; Chrh Wkr; Hon Rl; NHS; Ind Univ; Bus.

GILBERT, CHARLOTTE; Gabriel Richard HS; Trenton, MI; Hon Rl; Sch Mus; Sch Pl; Stg Crw; Stu Cncl; Pres Drama Clb; Fr Clb; Xavier Univ; Psych.

GILBERT, CHERYL; Jefferson Area HS; Dorset, OH; Cls Rep Frsh Cls; Aud/Vis; Chrs; Hon Rl; Drama Clb; FTA; Gym; Trk; Wrstlng; Chrldng; Kent St Univ; Phys Educ.

GILBERT, CYNTHIA A; Turpin HS; Cincinnati, OH; 1/358 NHS; Off Ade; Sch Pl; Rptr Sch Nwsp; Drama Clb; PPFtbl; Scr Kpr; Tmr; Natl Merit SF; Third In State Ohio Tests Of Scholastic Achievement Eng; Second In State Ohio Tests Of Scholastic Achievmnt; Univ; Poli Sci.

GILBERT, CYNTHIA J; Comstock Park HS; Comstock Park, MI; Cmp Fr Grls; Girl Scts; Hon Rl; Lbry Ade; NHS; Off Ade; Sch Pl; Rptr Yrbk; Ed Sch Nwsp; 4-H; Spelling Bee Awds 78 & 79; Grand Rapids Jr Coll; Data Proc.

GILBERT, DANIEL; Holy Rosary HS; Flint, MI; Pres Jr Cls; Yrbk; Sch Nwsp; Letter Bsbl; Letter Bsktbl; Letter Ftbl; Hon Roll 76; Univ Of Michigan; Law.

GILBERT, DANITA; Coshocton HS; Coshocton, OH; Cls Rep Frsh Cls; VP Soph Cls; Cl Rep Jr Cls; Hon Rl; Sec Stu Cncl; Ed Sch Nwsp; Sec Key Clb; Ten; IM Sprt; PPFtbl; Univ; Psych.

GILBERT, DANYA; Big Rapids HS; Big Rapids, MI; Pres Sr Cls; Jr NHS; NHS; Stu Cncl; 4-H; Gym; IM Sprt; Mat Maids; MSU; Pre Vet.

GILBERT, DAVID; De Witt HS; Dewitt, MI; Boy Scts; Sct Actv; Eagle Scout Awd 76; Michigan St Univ; Pre Law.

GILBERT, DAWN; Clarence M Kimball HS; Royal Oak, MI; Chrs; Hon Rl; Sch Mus; Drama Clb; Spn Clb; Gym; Tmr; Univ.

GILBERT, DONNA; Owosso HS; Owosso, MI; Chrs; Hon Rl; Mdrgl; Pep Clb; Letter Chrldng; College; Advertising.

GILBERT, LISA; Valley HS; Minford, OH; 1/112 Band; Chrs; Hon Rl; NHS; Sch Pl; FTA; Pep Clb; Twrlr; Ohio Northern Univ; Pharm.

GILBERT, LOUISE; Glen Oak Schl; Aurora, OH; Chrs; Hon Rl; Sch Pl; Stg Crw; Fr Clb; Swmmng; Scr Kpr; Tmr; Mc Gill Univ; Law.

GILBERT, MARGARET; Shellyville HS; Shelbyville, IN; Hon Rl; Lat Clb; Pep Clb; IM Sprt; Ball State Univ; Bus.

GILBERT, NINA M; Westland HS; Columbus, OH; Cls Rep Frsh Cls; Cls Rep Soph Cls; Chrs; Hon Rl; NHS; Sch Mus; Sch Pl; Stu Cncl; Drama Clb; Mat Maids; Ohio St Univ; Music.

GILBERT, PAM; Anthony Wayne HS; Whitehouse, OH; 26/287 Pres Frsh Cls; Chrs; NHS; Sch Mus; Sch Pl; Pres Stu Cncl; Rptr Yrbk; Spn Clb; Letter Bsktbl; Letter Crs Cntry; Univ; Drama.

GILBERT, PATRICIA; New Washington HS; Marysville, IN; VP Sr Cls; Am Leg Aux Girls St; Debate Tm; Hon Rl; Pres NHS; Pres Stu Cncl; Rptr Sch Nwsp; Sch Nwsp; FFA; Pres Pep Clb; Outstndng Young Amer 79; Hoosier Schlr 79; Grtr Clark Cnty Schl Assoc Of Educ Sec 79; Sullivan Jr Coll Of Bus; Exec Sec.

GILBERT, PAUL; Orchard View HS; Muskegon, MI; 4/210 Hon Rl; NHS; Letter Bsbl; Letter Bsktbl; Letter Crs Cntry; Capt IM Sprt; Muskegon Community College; Engr.

GILBERT, PAULA; Weir HS; Weirton, WV; 97/385 Band; Hon Rl; NHS; Sch Mus; Yth Flsp; 4-H; Spn Clb; GAA; Mat Maids; Twrlr; Alderson Broaddus Univ; Nurse.

GILBERT, SCOTT; Bellaire HS; Bellaire, OH; 40/238 Band; Chrh Wkr; Hon Rl; NHS; Sch Pl; Stg Crw; Sch Nwsp; Drama Clb; Rdo Clb; God Cntry Awd; Took Coll Courses While In HS; Wheeling Coll; Med.

GILBERT, SUSAN; W V Fisher Catholic HS; Lancaster, OH; 17/74 Chrs; Hon Rl; OUL; Bus.

GILBERT, SUSAN; Richmond Sr HS; Richmond, IN; 8/600 Hon Rl; JA; NHS; Orch; Y-Teens; JA Awd; Purdue Univ; Indus Engr.

GILBERT, VIRGINIA; Muskegon Sr HS; Muskegon, MI; Hon Rl; NHS; Natl Merit SF; Harry E Brown & Clara H Brown Schslhp; Muskegon Cmnty Coll; Occupt Ther.

GILBERT, WILLIAM; Willow Run HS; Ypsilanti, MI; 13/250 Hon Rl; Mth Clb; Glf; JETS Awd; Wastenaw Jr College; Comp Progr.

GILBOE, GERARD; Southgate HS; Southgate, MI; 16/325 Hon Rl; Jr NHS; NHS; Ten; Michigan St Univ.

GILBOY, MARGIE; Hoover HS; North Canton, OH; Band; Chrs; Girl Scts; Hon Rl; Orch; Yrbk; Pep Clb; Spn Clb; Trk; IM Sprt; Akron; Legal Secretary.

GILBREATH, CINDY; Theodore Roosevelt HS; Wyandotte, MI; Hon Rl; NHS; Bus Schl; Bank.

GILBREATH, JUDITH; Big Rapids HS; Paris, MI; 2/194 Cls Rep Soph Cls; Trs Jr Cls; Chrs; Hon Rl; Treas NHS; Sch Mus; Stu Cncl; Letter Bsbl; Letter Bsktbl; Letter Trk; Ferris St Coll; Dent Hygnst.

GILBRIDE, NANCY L; North HS; Willowick, OH; 55/650 Am Leg Aux Girls St; Drl Tm; Hon Rl; NHS; Sch Mus; Sch Pl; Sec Stu Cncl; Ed Sch Nwsp; Rptr Sch Nwsp; Sec Drama Clb; John Carroll Univ; Commnctns.

GILDE, ED; Kenowa Hills HS; Marne, MI; 2/225 Cls Rep Frsh Cls; Cls Rep Soph Cls; VP Jr Cls; NHS; Stu Cncl; Bsbl; Ftbl; Wrstlng; IM Sprt; Grand Rapids Jr Coll; Bus.

GILDEA, LARRY A; Schoolcraft HS; Schoolcraft, MI; Boy Scts; Hon Rl; Sct Actv; Letter Bsbl; Letter Bsktbl; Crs Cntry; Ftbl; Glf; Letter Ten; Univ; Elec Engr.

GILDEA, ROBERT; Portage Central HS; Portage, MI; Hon Rl; Letter Wrstlng; Mic State Univ; Physics.

GILDERSLEEVE, MARILYN; Dollar Bay HS; Dollar Bay, MI; 2/28 Trs Frsh Cls; Pres Soph Cls; Pres Jr Cls; Cls Rep Sr Cls; Sal; Hon Rl; Jr NHS; NHS; Stu Cncl; Michigan Tech Univ; Bio Sci.

GILDERSLEEVE, TAMMIE; Harbor HS; Ashtabula, OH; Yth Flsp; Rptr Yrbk; Rptr Sch Nwsp; Pep Clb; Chrldng; Kent State Univ.

GILES, DANIEL P; Brebeuf Preparatory School; Zionsville, IN; Cmnty Wkr; Hon Rl; Sch Nwsp; Pep Clb; Letter Ftbl; Letter Wrstlng; IM Sprt; Purdue Univ; Physics.

GILES, GREGORY S; Jefferson Union HS; Steubenville, OH; 30/150 Cl Rep Jr Cls; Am Leg Boys St; Band; Chrh Wkr; Cmnty Wkr; Hon Rl; Sch Mus; Stu Cncl; Rptr Yrbk; Yrbk;.

GILES, LINDA; Berkley HS; Huntington Wood, MI; Band; Stu Cncl; MSU; Bus.

GILES, SHANNON; Wirt Cnty HS; Leroy, WV; Cls Rep Frsh Cls; Cls Rep Soph Cls; Cl Rep Jr Cls; Cmp Fr Grls; Chrh Wkr; Cmnty Wkr; Girl Scts; Stu Cncl; Yrbk; 4-H;.

GILES, STEPHEN; Webster Cnty HS; Cowen, WV; Cls Rep Sr Cls; Chrh Wkr; Cmnty Wkr; Sch Pl; Stu Cncl; Yth Flsp; Pep Clb; Rdo Clb; Bsktbl; Coach Actv; Cumberland Coll; Phys Ed.

GILES, VALERIE; Cass Technical HS; Detroit, MI; 81/893 Cls Rep Soph Cls; Cmp Fr Grls; Chrh Wkr; Cmnty Wkr; FCA; Hon Rl; NHS; Off Ade; Orch; Pol Wkr; Mi Comp Awd 79; Univ Of Detroit; Religious Studies.

GILFILEN, T; Hurricane HS; Hurrican, WV; Aud/Vis; Boy Scts; Chrh Wkr; Cmnty Wkr; Hon Rl; Sct Actv; Cls Rep Sr Cls; Charleston Univ; Med.

GILKERSON, KAREN; Greenbrier East HS; Renick, WV; Chrs; Chrh Wkr; Hon Rl; NHS; Yth Flsp; Y-Teens; 4-H; Alderson Broaddus Coll; Nursing.

GILKERSON, MISTY L; Huntington E HS; Huntington, WV; Cls Rep Frsh Cls; VP Soph Cls; Sec Jr Cls; Chrs; Hon Rl; Mdrgl; Off Ade; Sch Mus; Stu Cncl; Chrldng; Music Awd; Outstndng Cheerleading Awd; Capt Of Cheerleading Squad Awded Letter & Bar; Marshall Univ; History.

GILKESON, SARAH; Hathaway Brown HS; Shaker Hgts, OH; VP Sr Cls; AFS; Chrs; Hon Rl; PAVAS; Sch Mus; Sch Pl; Rptr Yrbk; Univ.

GILKEY, MICHAEL J; St Xavier HS; Cincinnati, OH; JA; NHS; Sch Mus; Sch Pl; Stg Crw; IM Sprt; JETS Awd; Purdue Univ; Elec Engr.

GILL, MAJEL; Stonewall Jackson HS; Charleston, WV; Chrh Wkr; Girl Scts; Hon Rl; NHS; Y-Teens; Rptr Yrbk; Spn Clb; Mgrs; Univ; Sci.

GILL, MARY; All Saints Central HS; Bay City, MI; 4/167 Hon Rl; Hosp Ade; NHS; Pres Stu Cncl; Bsktbl; Pom Pon; Opt Clb Awd; Stdnt Councl Awd 79; Al St HS Acad Awd 79; Mi Compttv Schlshp Awd 79; St Marys Coll; Med Tech.

GILL, RANDY; Cass Tech; Detroit, MI; 2/898 Sal; NHS; Beta Clb; Fr Clb; Mth Clb; Kalamazoo College; Heart Surgeon.

GILL, REBECCA; Berrien Springs HS; Berrien Spgs, MI; 3/140 Cls Rep Soph Cls; Band; Drl Tm; Hon Rl; NHS; Sch Mus; Sch Pl; Stu Cncl; Yth Flsp; Yrbk; Western Univ.

GILL, ROBIN; Memorial HS; St Marys, OH; Chrs; Hon Rl; Hosp Ade; Sch Nwsp; West Branch Ohio Univ; X Ray Tech.

GILL, STEPHEN; Corunna HS; Owosso, MI; Band; Cmnty Wkr; Hon Rl; Pol Wkr; Sch Mus; Sct Actv; Rdo Clb; Trk; JA Awd; Delta Coll; Elec Tech.

GILL, STEVE; Shelbyville HS; Shelbyville, IN; 46/289 Hon Rl; NHS; Sprt Ed Sch Nwsp; Boys Clb Am; Spn Clb; IM Sprt; Ball State; Radio.

GILL, TRACEY; Yale HS; Yale, MI; Band; Hon Rl; Sci Clb; St Clair Cnty Cmnty Coll; Educ.

GILL, WANDA; Schoolcraft HS; Schoolcraft, MI; Girl Scts; Hon Rl; Lbry Ade; Off Ade; Bsbl; Letter Bsktbl; Letter Trk; Bsktbl Schlshp W Bskbl Camp 77; Bsktbl Schsp Hoosier Bsktbl Camp 78; Kalamazoo Vly Cmnty Coll; Phys Educ.

GILLASPY, BETH L; Bellbrook HS; Bellbrook, OH; 7/160 Cls Rep Sr Cls; Capt Drl Tm; Hon Rl; NHS; Stu Cncl; Yth Flsp; Rptr Yrbk; Pep Clb; Spn Clb; GAA; Ohio Univ; Interpersonal Commun.

GILLAUGH, SHARON; Cedarville HS; Cedarvl, OH; Band; Chrs; Drl Tm; FCA; Yth Flsp; 4-H; Letter Bsktbl; Letter Trk; Twrlr; 4-H Awd; Clark Tech Coll; Sec.

GILLELAND, JUDITH; Northmont HS; Dayton, OH; Cls Rep Sr Cls; Band; Drl Tm; Hon Rl; Stu Cncl; Yrbk; Drama Clb; Bsktbl; Scr Kpr; Miami Univ; Chemistry.

GILLEN, JOHN; Parma Sr HS; Parma, OH; Boy Scts; Chrh Wkr; JA; Boys Clb Am; Law Enfrcmnt.

GILLEN, TRACY; Washington HS; Washington, IN; 10/194 Chrs; Chrh Wkr; Hon Rl; NHS; Sch Pl; Stg Crw; Treas Yth Flsp; Drama Clb; 4-H; Fr Clb; Univ Of Evansville; Spec Ed.

GILLENWATER, THOMAS; Matoaka HS; Lashmeet, WV; Am Leg Boys St; Band; Boy Scts; Hon Rl; NHS; Stu Cncl; 4-H; Key Clb; Coll; Engr.

GILLENWATER, THOMAS S; Matoaka HS; Lashmeet, WV; 5/60 Am Leg Boys St; Band; Boy Scts; Hon Rl; NHS; Stu Cncl; 4-H; Key Clb; Ctznshp Given By Sheriff Of Mercer Co 76; Bluefield St Univ; Elec.

GILLEROTH, KRISTINA; Mt Vernon Academy; Mt Vernon, OH; Cl Rep Jr Cls; Band; Chrs; Chrh Wkr; Hon Rl; Orch; Sch Pl; Bsktbl; Mt Vernon Nazarene Coll; Elem Ed.

GILLES, CHERYL; William Wirt HS; Gary, IN; Hon Rl; Jr NHS; Lbry Ade; Rptr Sch Nwsp; Excellence In Journalism; College; Journalism.

GILLES, CHERYL; William A Wirt HS; Gary, IN; Hon Rl; Jr NHS; Sec Lit Mag; NHS; Rptr Sch Nwsp; Univ; Jrnlsm.

GILLES, JAMES; Central HS; Evansville, IN; Ftbl; IM Sprt; Voc Schl; Auto Mech.

GILLES, JENNIFER; Reitz Memorial HS; Evansville, IN; Hon Rl; Ger Clb; Capt Pep Clb; Capt Sci Clb; Mgrs; Indiana Univ;.

GILLES, MICHELE M; Waldron HS; Shelbyville, IN; 1/59 Sal; Am Leg Aux Girls St; Chrs; VP Stu Cncl; Treas 4-H; Pres Lat Clb; Pres Pep Clb; Cit Awd; DAR Awd; Natl Merit Ltr; Purdue Univ; Engineering.

GILLESPIE, ANN; Walter E Stebbins HS; Dayton, OH; Band; Chrh Wkr; Girl Scts; Hon Rl; NHS; Yth Flsp; Capt Chrldng; Ohio St Univ; Comp Progr.

GILLESPIE, CAROLYN K; George A Dovdero HS; Royal Oak, MI; 10/429 Band; Pres Chrs; Cmnty Wkr; Hon Rl; Mdrgl; NHS; Orch; PPFtbl; NCTE; Natl Merit SF; Univ; Elem Educ.

GILLESPIE, CRYSTAL; Oak Glen HS; Chester, WV; Band; Boy Scts; Girl Scts; Fr Clb; Pep Clb; Bus Schl; CPA.

GILLESPIE, DAVID; Danville Community HS; Danville, IN; 21/188 Chrs; VP FCA; Hon Rl; PAVAS; Sch Mus; Stg Crw; Drama Clb; Pep Clb; Bsbl; IM Sprt; Indiana Univ; Chem.

GILLESPIE, ELAINE; Calvert HS; Tiffin, OH; 24/99 Cls Rep Frsh Cls; Cls Rep Soph Cls; Cl Rep Jr Cls; VP Sr Cls; NHS; Sch Mus; Stu Cncl; Yrbk; Chrldng; Cit Awd; Miami Univ; Sociology.

GILLESPIE, JEANNE; Greenfield Central HS; Greenfield, IN; 2/300 Chrs; FCA; Hon Rl; NHS; Pol Wkr; Red Cr Ade; Sch Mus; Sch Pl; Stg Crw; Drama Clb; Purdue Univ; Engr.

GILLESPIE, JEREMY; Mariemont HS; Cincinnati, OH; 8/146 Pres Frsh Cls; Cls Rep Frsh Cls; Cls Rep Soph Cls; Trs Jr Cls; Cl Rep Jr Cls; Pres Band; NHS; Orch; Sch Mus; Pres Stu Cncl; Peer Counselor; Capt Of Its Acad Team; John Philip Sousa Band Awd; US Naval Acad; Naval Archt.

GILLESPIE, MARGO; Bloomington HS; Bloomington, IN; 126/393 Band; Girl Scts; Quill & Scroll; Sct Actv; Yrbk; VP 4-H; Trk; Mgrs; 4-H Awd; Indiana Univ; Journalism.

GILLESPIE, MARK; Brown County HS; Nineveh, IN; 81/229 Am Leg Boys St; Aud/Vis; Lbry Ade; Mod UN; Quill & Scroll; Sch Mus; Sch Pl; Stg Crw; Sprt Ed Sch Nwsp; Sch Nwsp; Pres In HS Press Assoc 78; Natl Hnrbl Mntn Quill & Scroll Current Events Quiz 78; Indiana Univ; Telecmnctns.

GILLESPIE, TERRY; Garfield HS; Hamilton, OH; Boy Scts; Hon Rl; Jr NHS; NHS; Socr; Capt Wrstlng; Ohio St Univ; Math.

GILLESPIE, TODD; Jay County HS; Portland, IN; Pres Sr Cls; Am Leg Boys St; Chrh Wkr; FCA; Hon Rl; Jr NHS; NHS; Pres Yth Flsp; Letter Swmmng; Letter Ten; Univ; Pre Med.

GILLETT, CHRISTOPHER; Harrison Cmnty HS; Harrison, MI; 21/170 Band; Hon Rl; Natl Forn Lg; NHS; Engr Schl; Comp Dsgn Engr.

GILLETT, LORI; Onaway Area HS; Onaway, MI; 2/99 VP Frsh Cls; Sec Sr Cls; Sal; Band; Girl Scts; Pres Stu Cncl; Pep Clb; Trk; Chrldng; IM Sprt; Alpena Cmnty Coll; Bus.

GILLETTE, LINDA; Perrysburg HS; Perrysburg, OH; 4/251 Sec Band; Girl Scts; Hon Rl; Pres NHS; Ger Clb; Pres Mth Clb; Sci Clb; Crs Cntry; Trk; Natl Merit SF; Univ; Bio Sci.

GILLEY, GREG; St Martin HS; Ocean Springs, MS; Hon Rl; PAVAS; Sch Pl; Stg Crw; Beta Clb; Drama Clb; Fr Clb; Ftbl; Ten; Trk; Univ Of Mississippi; Computer Sci.

GILLHAM, RANDALL; Lakewood HS; Newark, OH; 13/170 Boy Scts; Hon Rl; Jr NHS; NHS; Bsbl; Bsktbl; Capt Ftbl; Capt IM Sprt; Ohi St Univ; Acctg.

GILLIAM, ANTOINETTE; Mt Hope HS; Mt Hope, WV; Pres Frsh Cls; Cls Rep Soph Cls; Cl Rep Jr Cls; Cmnty Wkr; Hon Rl; Off Ade; Stu Cncl; College; Nursing.

GILLIAM, LAURA; Wadsworth Sr HS; Wadsworth, OH; 49/367 Chrs; Chrh Wkr; FCA; Hon Rl; NHS; Stu Cncl; Yth Flsp; Pep Clb; Spn Clb; Chrldng; Wittenberg Univ; Med.

GILLIAM, MACRINA; Groveport Madison Sr HS; Groveport, OH; 1/357 Sec Band; Cmp Fr Grls; Hon Rl; NHS; Orch; Sch Mus; Rptr Sch Nwsp; Ohio St Univ; Eng.

GILLIAM, SARAH J; William Mason HS; Mason, OH; 3/200 Trs Jr Cls; AFS; Band; Chrs; Drl Tm; Girl Scts; Hon Rl; Lbry Ade; NHS; Sct Actv; Sun Schl Attendance Pin; Schl Perfect Attendance; Schlstc Ach Tm; Coll; Art.

GILLIAN, NORAN; Donald E Gavit Jr Sr HS; Hammond, IN; 9/214 Treas Band; Hon Rl; Jr NHS; Pres MMM; NHS; Stg Crw; Ger Clb; Trk; Mgrs; Calumet Regnl Sci Fari Silver Medl 78; NISBOVA Const Sax Duet 1st Pl 79; Purdue Univ; RN.

GILLICH, BONNIE; Ashtabula HS; Ashtabula, OH; 5/256 Hon Rl; Sec NHS; VP Fr Clb; Univ Of Toledo; Nurse.

GILLIGAN, ANN; Bishop Donahue HS; Wheeling, WV; Chrh Wkr; Hon Rl; Jr NHS; Stu Cncl; Rptr Sch Nwsp; Spn Clb; Bsktbl; GAA; Marietta College; Educ.

GILLIGAN, JANET; Lawrence Central HS; Indianapolis, IN; 10/390 Chrs; Chrh Wkr; Girl Scts; Hon Rl; Pres Yth Flsp; Pep Clb; College; Bus Adm.

GILLIGAN, JOHN; St Xavier HS; Cincinnati, OH; 77/268 Cmnty Wkr; Hon Rl; Fr Clb; Letter Crs Cntry; Letter Trk; IM Sprt; Univ; Med.

GILLIGAN, TOM; Madeira HS; Cinciqnati, OH; 47/160 Spn Clb; Capt Bsbl; Letter Bsktbl; Capt IM Sprt; Scr Kpr; Tmr; Univ; Elec.

GILLILAND, BRENDA A; Prairie Heights HS; Wolcottville, IN; 3/136 Band; Hon Rl; NHS; Orch; 4-H; FTA; Pep Clb; Bsktbl; Cit Awd; 4-H Awd; College; Home Ec.

GILLILAND, KIMBERLEY; Memorial HS; St Marys, OH; Chrs; Hon Rl; Y-Teens; Pep Clb; GAA; IM Sprt; Kiwan Awd; Bus Schl; Acctg.

GILLILAND, PAMELA; North Union HS; Raymond, OH; Band; Hon Rl; NHS; Sec 4-H; Spn Clb;.

GILLIN, DAWN; Adrian HS; Adrian, MI; 22/365 Chrs; Chrh Wkr; Hon Rl; Hosp Ade; NHS; Sec Orch; Sch Mus; Yth Flsp; Lat Clb; Adrian College; Child Psych.

GILLIS, BARBARA; Morton HS; Hammond, IN; 21/436 Chrs; Hon Rl; Hosp Ade; NHS; Quill & Scroll; Stu Cncl; Sch Nwsp; FTA; Pep Clb; PPFtbl; Univ; Nursing.

GILLISON, FRANK; Ursuline HS; Youngstown, OH; Chrh Wkr; Hon Rl; Pres JA; Fr Clb; Gym; Coach Actv; JA Awd; Univ; Elec Engr.

GILLISON, JILL; Benzie County Central HS; Arcadia, MI; 7/136 Band; Chrs; Chrh Wkr; Hon Rl; Jr NHS; NHS; Sch Mus; Yth Flsp; 4-H; Letter Bsktbl; Ferris St Coll; Med Lab Tech.

GILLISPIE, DEBBIE; Southeastern Indiana Voc HS; Milan, IN; Cl Rep Jr Cls; Chrs; Hon Rl; NHS; Stu Cncl; DECA; Bus Mgmt.

GILLISPIE, GREGORY; Montpelier HS; Montpelier, OH; Cmnty Wkr; Hon Rl; Sch Mus; Sch Pl; Stg Crw; Ed Yrbk; Fr Clb; Ger Clb; Bsbl; Capt Swmmng; US Marine Corps; Arcrft Mech.

GILLMAN, ANNETTE; Immaculate Conception Acad; Brookville, IN; 11/75 VP Soph Cls; Trs Jr Cls; Chrs; Chrh Wkr; Girl Scts; Hon Rl; Orch; Sch Mus; Stu Cncl; 4-H; College; Nursing.

GILMAN, ANDREW; Lake Ridge Acad; Lorain, OH; Hon Rl; NHS; Sch Pl; Yrbk; Letter Ten; Univ; Med.

GILMAN, ROBIN; Eastern Pulaski Cmnty HS; Star City, IN; Band; Chrh Wkr; Hon Rl; Jr NHS; Rptr Yrbk; Drama Clb; 4-H; Pep Clb; Spn Clb; JA Awd; Univ; Tchr.

GILMER, LAURA; Jackson Milton HS; Lake Milton, OH; Band; Hon Rl; Lbry Ade; Ger Clb; Mrch Band Flag Line; Kent St Univ; Ancient History.

GILMORE, BRENT; Elkhart Memorial HS; Elkhart, IN; 56/500 Letter Chrs; Hon Rl; Letter Natl Forn Lg; Stu Cncl; Yth Flsp; IM Sprt; Purdue Univ; Med.

GILMORE, CARL; Indian Valley South HS; Gnadenhutten, OH; 1/95 Cls Rep Frsh Cls; Trs Soph Cls; Trs Jr Cls; Trs Sr Cls; Am Leg Boys St; Hon Rl; NHS; Sch Pl; Stu Cncl; Yrbk; Alderson Broaddus Univ; Bus Admin.

GILMORE, DANIEL; Western Reserve Acad; Hudson, OH; 20/89 Band; Boy Scts; Hon Rl; Lbry Ade; Orch; Sch Mus; Rptr Sch Nwsp; Lat Clb; Ftbl; Duke ; Bus.

GILMORE, JACK; Princeton HS; Princeton, WV; Boy Scts; Chrs; Chrh Wkr; Cmnty Wkr; Mdrgl; Ed Sch Nwsp; Drama Clb; 4-H; Key Clb; Pep Clb; Natl Quilt Scroll Hnry Cayear Recpt 78; Bluefield Coll; Law.

GILMORE, JAMES F; Centerville Sr HS; Centerville, IN; 12/170 Band; Chrh Wkr; Debate Tm; FCA; Hon Rl; JA; Jr NHS; NHS; Sch Pl; Stu Cncl; Achiever Awd Jr Exec Awd Exec Awd Twice Mbr & 100 Sales Club & 1000 Co Jr Achvmnt; Chess Team Pres; Purdue Univ; Engr.

GILMORE, JOHN; Tygarts Valley HS; Dailey, WV; 5/500 Am Leg Boys St; Hon Rl; NHS; 4-H; Letter Ftbl; Mgrs;.

GILMORE, KIMBERLEE A; Briggs HS; Columbus, OH; Pol Wkr; Stu Cncl; Sch Nwsp; Drama Clb; Spn Clb; Chrldng; Cheerleading Squad 3rd Pl 1978; Comp At Camp; Ohio St Univ; Fashn Mdse.

GILMORE, LINDA; Pleasant HS; Marion, OH; Hon Rl; Y-Teens; Rptr Yrbk; Trk; Chrldng; Mgrs; OSU; Speech Hearing Therapy.

GILMORE, LIONEL B; Kyger Creek HS; Cheshire, OH; VP Frsh Cls; Pres Soph Cls; Fr Clb; Key Clb; Bsbl; Bsktbl; Ftbl; Trk; Elect Apprentice.

GILMOUR, KAREN; Franklin HS; Westland, MI; Chrh Wkr; Girl Scts; Hon Rl; Sct Actv; Letter Trk; Chrldng; Pom Pon; Cit Awd; College.

GILREATH, RODNEY P; Aquinas HS; Inkster, MI; 10/200 Chrs; Chrh Wkr; Hon Rl; Jr NHS; NHS; Sch Mus; Sch Pl; Yrbk; Sch Nwsp; Natl Merit SF; Univ Of Michigan; Med.

GILREATH, STEPHEN W; Bethel Local HS; Tipp City, OH; 2/100 Am Leg Boys St; Am Leg Aux Girls St; Chrs; Hon Rl; Jr NHS; Stu Cncl; Boys Clb Am; Fr Clb; VP Spn Clb; Letter Bsbl; AATSP Natl Span Awd 77 78 & 79; Ohio Test Of Schlstc Achiev Span 77; Ohio Test Of Schlstc Achiev Chem 78; Wright St Univ; Chem.

GILROY, TIMOTHY; Saint Ignatius HS; So Euclid, OH; Boy Scts; IM Sprt; Bus.

GILSON, LESLIE; Triway HS; Wooster, OH; Boy Scts; Chrh Wkr; Hon Rl; Sct Actv; Yth Flsp; 4-H; FFA; Wrstlng; IM Sprt; 4-H Awd; 4th Yr In St Timber Cruising 76; 9 Yr 4 H Mbr; Agri Tech Schl; Sheep Prod.

GILSON, ROBIN; Delta Sr HS; Delta, OH; 15/150 Aud/Vis; Boy Scts; Hon Rl; NHS; PAVAS; Drama Clb; 4-H; Bsktbl; Letter Ftbl; Trk; Univ; Lib Arts.

GILVARY, CLAIRE; Archbishop Alter HS; Kettering, OH; Chrs; Girl Scts; Hon Rl; Hosp Ade; NHS; Off Ade; Off Ade; Sch Mus; Sch Pl; Sct Actv; Eng Departmental Awds 1977; Univ; Econ.

GILYON, SUE; Midpark HS; Middleburg Hts, OH; 30/664 Cmp Fr Grls; Chrh Wkr; Hon Rl; NHS; Sprt Ed Yrbk; Letter Bsbl; College.

GINDER, KIMBERLY; Hudson HS; Hudson, OH; 39/287 Cls Rep Soph Cls; Cls Rep Sr Cls; Am Leg Aux Girls St; Hon Rl; NHS; Stu Cncl; Capt Chrldng; PPFtbl; Am Leg Awd; Stephen F Austin St Univ.

GINDERSKE, GERALD W; Swan Valley HS; Saginaw, MI; Band; Boy Scts; Cmnty Wkr; Jr NHS; NHS; Pol Wkr; Stu Cncl; Socr; Wrstlng; Geometry Awrd; Algebra Awrd; Chemistry Awrd; Albion Coll; Medicine.

GINDLESBERGER, ANNE; Northwest HS; Canal Fulton, OH; 33/184 Band; Chrh Wkr; Girl Scts; Hon Rl; NHS; Red Cr Ade; Pres Y-Teens; Rptr Yrbk; Rptr Sch Nwsp; Fr Clb; College; Medical Lab Asst.

GINDLESBERGER, SUE; Northwest HS; Canal Fulton, OH; 1/174 Cls Rep Soph Cls; Cl Rep Jr Cls; Cls Rep Sr Cls; Hon Rl; NHS; Sch Mus; Sec Stu Cncl; Sec Y-Teens; Letter Bsktbl; Nursing School; Nurse.

GINEMAN, TAMARA; Liberty Center HS; Liberty Cntr, OH; Trs Soph Cls; Band; Chrs; Hon Rl; NHS; Sch Mus; Sec Stu Cncl; Yth Flsp; Yrbk; Sec FTA; Recipient Of 78 79 Outstanding Jr Serv; College; Nursing.

GINGERY, MARY; Garrett HS; Garrett, IN; 13/130 Band; Chrs; Hon Rl; Natl Forn Lg; NHS; Orch; Sch Mus; Sch Pl; Stg Crw; Rptr Sch Nwsp; Indiana Purdue Univ; Comp Progr.

GINGO, DAVID J; Archbishop Hoban HS; Uniontown, OH; 3/148 Hon Rl; NHS; Yrbk; Ed Sch Nwsp; Rptr Sch Nwsp; Beta Clb; Boys Clb Am; Natl Merit Ltr; Natl Merit SF; Voice Dem Awd; Stanford Univ; Med.

GINGO JR, A; Western Reserve Acad; Stow, OH; 22/90 Hon Rl; Off Ade; Letter Swmmng; Ten; Trk; Coach Actv; IM Sprt; Tmr; Univ; Med.

GINGRICH, JEFFREY; Bad Axe HS; Bad Axe, MI; 1/138 Cls Rep Sr Cls; Val; Aud/Vis; Pres NHS; Stg Crw; Fr Clb; Sci Clb; Letter Ftbl; Letter Ten; Spring Arbor Coll; Bio.

GINGRICH, MITCHELL; Bluffton HS; Bluffton, OH; 5/93 Chrh Wkr; Cmnty Wkr; Hon Rl; Stg Crw; Yth Flsp; Rptr Sch Nwsp; Lat Clb; Univ; Med.

GINLEY, PATRICK E; Padua Fransican HS; Brook Pk, OH; Hon Rl; Letter Bsbl; Letter Ftbl; College.

GINLEY, TODD; Bishop Borgess HS; Redford, MI; IM Sprt; College; Pharmacy.

GINN, DUANE A; Bluffton Harrison HS; Bluffton, IN; Yth Flsp; Ger Clb; Taylor Univ; Music.

GINNINGS, LISA S; Wadsworth HS; Wadsworth, OH; Chrs; Chrh Wkr; Cmnty Wkr; Girl Scts; Hon Rl; Hosp Ade; NHS; Yth Flsp; Fr Clb; Tmr; AAU Comptv Swimming 73 76; Univ; Psych.

GINOP, CLAY; Cheboygan Catholic HS; Levering, MI; Boy Scts; 4-H; Letter Bsbl; Letter Bsktbl; Letter Ftbl; 4-H Awd; Natl Merit Ltr; Merit Achievement Awd; Alpena Schl; Farming.

GINTER, KEN; Washington HS; S Bend, IN; 16/355 Band; Hon Rl; NHS; Sch Mus; Lat Clb; Pep Clb; Bsbl; Scr Kpr; Ball St Univ; Bus.

GINTHER, LESILE; Harbor Beach Comm HS; Ruth, MI; Chrs; NHS; Sch Pl; Rptr Sch Nwsp; Pres 4-H; VP FFA; Crs Cntry; Letter Ftbl; Trk; Cit Awd; Tech Schl; Computer Tech.

GINTHER, RONALD; Washington HS; Massillon, OH; Boy Scts; Chrh Wkr; Hon Rl; Pol Wkr; Sct Actv; Rptr Sch Nwsp; Ger Clb; Sci Clb; Letter Swmmng; Scr Kpr; Univ; Bio.

GIOIA, PAMELA; Rogers HS; Wyoming, MI; 19/350 Hon Rl; NHS; Key Clb; Gym; Grand Valley St Coll; English.

GIORDANO, JACKIE; North Vermillion HS; Hillsdale, IN; 1/59 Cls Rep Frsh Cls; Sec Jr Cls; Trs Sr Cls; Band; Hon Rl; NHS; 4-H; OEA; DAR Awd; St Mary Of The Woods Univ; Acctg.

GIORLANDO, JOANNE; Baker HS; Dayton, OH; 6/335 Pres AFS; Am Leg Aux Girls St; Hon Rl; Quill & Scroll; Rptr Sch Nwsp; Drama Clb; Fr Clb; New Mexico St Univ; Comp Sci.

GIPSON, REBECCA; Decatur Jr Sr HS; Decatur, MI; Hon Rl; Lbry Ade; Eng Clb; Mth Clb; Sci Clb; Univ Of Michigan; Neurologist.

GIRARD, CAROL; Gladstone Area HS; Gladstone, MI; Band; Chrs; Girl Scts; Hon Rl; NHS; Sch Mus; Sec 4-H; 4-H Awd; Natl Merit SF; Natl Merit Schl; Bay De Noc Community Coll; Sec.

GIRARD, ERIC; Stow HS; Stow, OH; Cls Rep Frsh Cls; Trs Soph Cls; Trs Jr Cls; VP Sr Cls; Chrs; Debate Tm; Sch Pl; Stu Cncl; Lat Clb; Hndbl; Univ; Med.

GIRARD, GLORIA; Magnificat HS; Brook Park, OH; Chrs; Chrh Wkr; Akron Univ; Nursing.

GIRARDOT, JEFFREY; St Philip Catholic Ctrl HS; Battle Crk, MI; 1/60 Cls Rep Frsh Cls; Cls Rep Soph Cls; Cl Rep Jr Cls; Cls Rep Sr Cls; Hon Rl; NHS; Stg Crw; Fr Clb; Letter Bsbl; College; Premed.

GIRBERT, KAREN; Loveland Hurst HS; Loveland, OH; 12/250 Cl Rep Jr Cls; Am Leg Aux Girls St; Hon Rl; NHS; Ger Clb; Key Clb; SAR Awd; Band; Jr NHS; College; Elem Educ.

GIRIMONT, J; Bluefield HS; Bluefld, WV; 18/256 Chrs; Hon Rl; Jr NHS; NHS; Rptr Sch Nwsp; Lat Clb; Pep Clb; Mgrs; College; Commercial Art.

GIROUX, JOHN; Servite HS; Grosse Pointe, MI; 3/92 VP Jr Cls; VP Sr Cls; Hon Rl; NHS; Letter Bsktbl; Michigan St Univ; Engr.

GIRTON, RENEE; Randolph Southern HS; Lynn, IN; 2/80 Sal; Am Leg Aux Girls St; Hon Rl; NHS; Sch Pl; Stg Crw; Rptr Yrbk; Drama Clb; Lat Clb; Spn Clb; Indiana Univ; Bio.

GIRTZ, LISA; North White HS; Monticello, IN; Cls Rep Frsh Cls; Trs Jr Cls; Sec Sr Cls; Band; Chrs; Chrh Wkr; Hon Rl; Sch Mus; Sch Pl; Stg Crw; Hoosier Schlr; Purdue Univ Band Camp Awd; Purdue Univ; Photog.

GISH, JIM; Lexington HS; Mansfield, OH; 29/248 NHS; Stu Cncl; Key Clb; Glf; Eastern Ken Univ; Acctg.

GISONDI, DONNA; Beavercreek HS; Xenia, OH; 113/653 Cls Rep Frsh Cls; Cls Rep Soph Cls; Cl Rep Jr Cls; Sal; Hon Rl; Off Ade; Sch Pl; Gym; Trk; Chrldng; Indiana St Univ; Biology.

GISSINGER, JACQUELINE; Norton HS; Clinton, OH; Girl Scts; Hon Rl; NHS; Off Ade; Sct Actv; Lat Clb; Mgrs; Scr Kpr; Merit Achvmnt Awd 77; Ohio St Univ; Med.

GISSY, MARIE; Woodsfield HS; Woodsfield, OH; Chrh Wkr; Sch Pl; Yth Flsp; Yrbk; Drama Clb; 4-H; Fr Clb; Pep Clb; Voice Dem Awd; Univ; Speech.

GITTINGER, TODD; Sturgis HS; Sturgis, MI; Aud/Vis; NHS; IM Sprt; Michigan St Univ; Elec Engr.

GIUDICI, SANDRA A; Adlai E Stevenson HS; Sterling Hts, MI; 1/531 Sec Soph Cls; Val; Am Leg Aux Girls St; Chrh Wkr; Cmnty Wkr; Hon Rl; Natl Forn Lg; VP NHS; Off Ade; Pol Wkr; Exclince In Psych Award 1979; Outstndng Bus Stdnt 1978; Outstndng Shrthnd Ii Stdnt 1979; Univ; Bus Admin.

GIULIANO, EDWARD T; Peck HS; Melvin, MI; Sec Soph Cls; Cls Rep Sr Cls; Band; Hon Rl; Off Ade; Stu Cncl; Rptr Yrbk; Rptr Sch Nwsp; St Of Mi Compttv Schlshp 79; Photog Awd 79; Michigan St Univ; Jrnlsm.

GIVAN, GARRY; South Dearborn HS; Moores Hill, IN; 8/265 VP Frsh Cls; Trs Soph Cls; Am Leg Boys St; Band; Chrh Wkr; Hon Rl; NHS; Yth Flsp; Capt Crs Cntry; Letter Trk; Univ; Lab Tech.

GIVEN, MARK D; Braxton Co HS; Frametown, WV; Band; Chrs; Chrh Wkr; Hon Rl; Jr NHS; NHS; Orch; Alderson Broaddus College; Music.

GIVENS, CAROLYNN; Muskegon Heights HS; Muskegon Ht, MI; 9/200 Trs Frsh Cls; Cls Rep Soph Cls; Cl Rep Jr Cls; Band; Debate Tm; Hon Rl; NHS; Off Ade; Stu Cncl; Y-Teens; Grambling St Univ; Bio.

GIVENS, REGINALD; Washington HS; South Bend, IN; 64/355 Band; Chrh Wkr; Cmnty Wkr; Hon Rl; NHS; Orch; Sch Mus; Sch Pl; Sch Nwsp; Ftbl; College; Math.

GIVENS, TIMOTHY W; East Canton HS; Louisville, OH; Cl Rep Jr Cls; Am Leg Boys St; Aud/Vis; Hon Rl; Jr NHS; Natl Forn Lg; NHS; Sch Pl; Stg Crw; Stu Cncl; 4 H Demonstration Talk At Ohio St Fair; Ohio St Univ; Agri.

GIZZI, ZANE; Howland HS; Warren, OH; 25/440 Am Leg Boys St; Band; Chrh Wkr; Capt Debate Tm; Hon Rl; Natl Forn Lg; Pres NHS; Treas Yth Flsp; Rptr Yrbk; Ftbl; College.

GLAAB, CHRISTOPER; South Dearborn HS; Dillsboro, IN; Band; Chrs; Sch Pl; Stg Crw; Drama Clb; Spn Clb; Univ; Music.

GLADEN, RENEE; Elmhurst HS; Ft Wayne, IN; 123/346 Chrs; Hon Rl; Pol Wkr; Sch Pl; Health; Home Ec; Indiana Univ; Lib Arts.

GLADWIN, SUSAN; Upper Arlington HS; Columbus, OH; Chrs; Chrh Wkr; Cmnty Wkr; Drl Tm; Girl Scts; Hon Rl; Lbry Ade; Sch Mus; Stg Crw; Yth Flsp; Coll; Sci.

GLANCY, LINDA; Little Miami HS; Morrow, OH; 13/195 Cls Rep Sr Cls; Hon Rl; NHS; Off Ade; Stu Cncl; Rptr Yrbk; VP Fr Clb; PPFtbl; E Ferguson Mem Schlrshp 79; MVP Varsity Vlybl 79; Selected For 1st Team FAVC Lg Vlybl 79; Cumberland Coll; Acctg.

GLAROS, GEORGE; Jackson HS; Massillon, OH; Cls Rep Frsh Cls; Band; Chrh Wkr; Hon Rl; Sch Mus; Stu Cncl; 4-H; Spn Clb; 4-H Awd; College; Optometry.

GLASCOCK, JANE; Fountain Central HS; Kingman, IN; 31/118 Band; Chrh Wkr; Hon Rl; Lbry Ade; Off Ade; Yth Flsp; Pres 4-H; Treas FBLA; FHA; Lat Clb;.

GLASER, MICHAEL; Wheeling Central Cath HS; Wheeling, WV; 8/130 Cls Rep Frsh Cls; Cls Rep Soph Cls; Pres Jr Cls; Chrh Wkr; Hon Rl; Sch Nwsp; Letter Ten; Univ; Engr.

GLASGOW, REBECCA; Buckeye South HS; Dillonvale, OH; Hon Rl; NHS; Y-Teens; 4-H; Pep Clb; Jefferson Cnty Tech Coll; Drafting.

GLASPIE, DALE; Leslie HS; Leslie, MI; Band; Girl Scts; Hon Rl; Off Ade; Sct Actv; Rptr Sch Nwsp; Bsktbl; Trk; Mgrs; Larsing Community College; Soc Work.

GLASS, CARLA; Ben Davis HS; Indianapolis, IN; Cl Rep Jr Cls; Aud/Vis; Chrs; Cmnty Wkr; Hon Rl; Pres JA; Stg Crw; Stu Cncl; Pres Fr Clb; Mat Maids;.

GLASS, ELAINE; Bishop Ready HS; Grove City, OH; Hon Rl; NHS; DECA; Letter Chrldng; Franklin Univ; CPA.

GLASS, EUGENIA; Marion HS; Marion, IN; Hon Rl; Quill & Scroll; Rptr Yrbk; Ithica Coll; Phys Therapy.

GLASS, JANICE; Eastbrook HS; Upland, IN; 12/187 Sec Jr Cls; Sec Sr Cls; Band; Chrs; Chrh Wkr; Drl Tm; Hon Rl; Sch Mus; Sch Pl; Pres Yth Flsp; Indiana Central Univ; Religion.

GLASS, JOE; Sanford Meridian HS; Sanford, MI; VP Soph Cls; Pres Jr Cls; Band; Hon Rl; NHS; Stu Cncl; Sch Nwsp; Spn Clb; Letter Bsbl; Letter Ftbl; Michigan St Univ; Educ.

GLASS, KARL; De Kalb HS; Waterloo, IN; 15/278 VP Soph Cls; Cls Rep Sr Cls; Am Leg Boys St; Natl Forn Lg; NHS; Sch Pl; Ger Clb; Univ; Psych.

GLASS, LESA; Jane Addams HS; Cleveland, OH; Chrh Wkr; Cmnty Wkr; Drl Tm; Hon Rl; NHS; Stu Cncl; Rptr Yrbk; FDA; FNA; Mth Clb; Attendance Awd; Geografical Filing Awd; Shorthand Gregg Awd; College; Nursing.

GLASS, MICHAEL; Seaholm HS; Birmingham, MI; Cls Rep Frsh Cls; Hon Rl; Stu Cncl; Yrbk; ROTC; Rdo Clb; Cls Rep Sr Cls; Univ Of Michigan.

GLASS, TODD; Yorktown HS; Yorktown, IN; 4/200 Cls Rep Soph Cls; Cl Rep Jr Cls; Pres Sr Cls; Am Leg Boys St; Band; Drm Mjrt; FCA; MMM; NHS; VP Ger Clb; Hanover Univ; Poli Sci.

GLASSCO, JEANIE; Bedford N Lawrence HS; Williams, IN; 55/450 Hon Rl; Lbry Ade; Off Ade; Sch Mus; Sch Pl; Beta Clb; Cit Awd; Bedford N Lawrence Voc; Bus.

GLASSFORD, SANDY; Benjamin Franklin HS; Westland, MI; Hon Rl; Orch; Sch Mus; Socr; Coach Actv; Cit Awd; Univ Of Mich; Dent.

GLASSFORD, SKIP; Otsego HS; Grand Rapids, OH; Cl Rep Jr Cls; Boy Scts; Hon Rl; Jr NHS; Sct Actv; Stu Cncl; Fr Clb; Letter Bsbl; Letter Crs Cntry; College; Medicine.

GLATT, CHERI; Merrillville HS; Merrillville, IN; Girl Scts; Sct Actv; Pep Clb; Letter Chrldng; Pom Pon; PPFtbl; Scr Kpr; Tmr; Natl Merit Ltr; Bus Schl; Bus.

GLAUB, KENNETH; Yorktown HS; Yorktown, IN; Hndbl; Wrstlng; Pepperdine Coll; Archt.

GLAUS, NANCY; Minerva HS; Minerva, OH; Am Leg Aux Girls St; Band; Hon Rl; Lbry Ade; Pres Natl Forn Lg; NHS; Sch Pl; Stg Crw; Rptr Yrbk; Pres Drama Clb; Miami Univ; Diplomacy.

GLAUSER, GUY; Cardinal Stritch HS; Northwood, OH; 27/210 Debate Tm; Hon Rl; NHS; Sch Mus; Stu Cncl; Sprt Ed Sch Nwsp; Bsbl; Bsktbl; Ftbl; Mgrs; Toledo Univ; Politics.

GLAZA, MARK; Adlai E Stevenson HS; Sterling Hts, MI; Band; Lit Mag; Sch Pl; Stg Crw; Drama Clb; Natl Merit Schl; Cntl Mic Univ; Music.

GLAZE, CLAUDIA S; South Central HS; Elizabeth, IN; 7/67 Sec Frsh Cls; Trs Soph Cls; Hon Rl; Rptr Yrbk; 4-H; FHA; Mth Clb; Pep Clb; Spn Clb; Chrldng; Indiana Univ S E.

GLAZE, DOLLETTA; Ross Beatty HS; Cassopolis, MI; 14/130 Sec Jr Cls; Pres Sr Cls; Band; Drm Mjrt; Hon Rl; NHS; Stg Crw; Stu Cncl; Rptr Yrbk; 4-H; Sportsmn Big 10 Outstndng Girl Atht 79; Michigan St Univ; Engr.

GLAZIER, SCOTT; Indian Valley North HS; New Phila, OH; Band; Hon Rl; NHS; Ger Clb; Otterbein College; Chemistry.

GLEASN, CYNTHIA; Bluffton HS; Bluffton, OH; Chrs; Drl Tm; Hon Rl; 4-H; FHA; PPFtbl; 4-H Awd; Northwestern Bus Coll.

GLEASON, JOHN; Washington HS; Massillon, OH; Am Leg Boys St; Debate Tm; Hon Rl; Boys Clb Am; Spn Clb; Letter Glf; College; Poli Sci.

GLEASON, PENNY; Danville HS; Danville, IN; 36/152 Hon Rl; Lbry Ade; Pep Clb; Spn Clb; Phys Achvmnt Awd 77; Page For The Senate 77; Bus Schl; Sec.

GLEASON, ROBERT; Franklin HS; Livonia, MI; Hon Rl; Rptr Sch Nwsp; Cit Awd; College; Medicine.

GLEASON, SUSAN L; Hathaway Brown HS; Cleveland, OH; Trs Sr Cls; AFS; Chrs; Hon Rl; Rptr Sch Nwsp; Drama Clb; Bsktbl; Natl Merit SF; College; Bio.

GLEASON, THERESA; Berkley HS; Berkley, MI; Chrs; NHS; Gym; Letter Trk; Capt Chrldng; GAA; Sienna Hts Coll; Sociology.

GLEASON, THOMAS D; East Grand Rapids HS; Grand Rapids, MI; Trs Sr Cls; Hon Rl; NHS; Letter Crs Cntry; Letter Wrstlng; Natl Merit Ltr; College; Sci Resr.

GLEASON, TIMOTHY; Lehman HS; Sidney, OH; Cl Rep Jr Cls; Band; Chrs; Sch Mus; Stu Cncl; Spn Clb; Bsktbl; Crs Cntry; Ten; Trk; Univ; Bus Admin.

GLEAVES, PAUL; Jackson HS; Jackson, OH; 23/228 Am Leg Boys St; Boy Scts; Hon Rl; NHS; Yrbk; Pep Clb; Sci Clb; Univ; Geol.

GLEDHILL, DEBORAH; Lakeview HS; St Clair Shores, MI; Hon Rl; Hosp Ade; NHS; OEA; Pres Wayne State Univ.

GLEI, DAN; North Adams HS; Hillsdale, MI; 2/65 Band; Boy Scts; Chrh Wkr; Cmnty Wkr; Debate Tm; Hon Rl; Lit Mag; NHS; Sch Pl; Drama Clb; Michigan St Univ; Horticulture.

GLEISINGER, DAN; Barberton HS; Barberton, OH; 72/500 Band; Hon Rl; Coll; Engr.

GLEITZ, ELLEN; Niles Sr HS; Niles, MI; Sec Sr Cls; Chrs; Hon Rl; NHS; Pol Wkr; Ushers Club; Honors Choir; Prom Decorating Chairman; Indiana Univ; Nursing.

GLENDENING, JEFFREY; Lake Michigan Catholic HS; St Joseph, MI; Hon Rl; JA; Off Ade; Stg Crw; Bsbl; Letter Glf; JA Awd; Natl Merit SF; Jr Achvmnt Officer VP Mfg; Jr Achvmnt Production Wrkr Of The Yr; Golf Most Valuable Player; Western Michigan Univ; Accounting.

GLENN, CATHY; Rutherford B Hayes HS; Delaware, OH; Band; Chmn Drl Tm; Girl Scts; Hon Rl; Sch Nwsp; 4-H; Bus Schl.

GLENN, JOHN; Washington HS; Massillon, OH; Boy Scts; Chrs; Chrh Wkr; Hon Rl; Stu Cncl; Yth Flsp; Ed Yrbk; Sprt Ed Yrbk; Spn Clb; Ftbl; College; Marine Bio.

GLENN, MARGARET; Howell Sr HS; Howell, MI; 6/395 Sec Soph Cls; Cl Rep Jr Cls; Cls Rep Sr Cls; Band; Chrs; Chrh Wkr; Hon Rl; NHS; Sch Mus; Sec Stu Cncl; Eastern Michigan Univ; Spec Educ.

GLICK, CATHERINE; Washington HS; East Chicago, IN; 1/270 Hon Rl; NHS; Sch Pl; Stg Crw; Drama Clb; Fr Clb; FTA; Key Clb; Pep Clb; Univ.

GLICK, LOVETA; Hauser Jr Sr HS; Hope, IN; Cls Rep Frsh Cls; Cls Rep Soph Cls; Cl Rep Jr Cls; Cmnty Wkr; Off Ade; Stu Cncl; Pep Clb; Letter Bsktbl; GAA; MIP Vllybll 78; Stu Cncl Pres 80; Coord Comm Heritage Of Hope 80; Ball St Univ.

GLIDDEN, JODY; Eastern HS; Solsberry, IN; Band; Hon Rl; NHS; Off Ade; Stu Cncl; Pep Clb; Vocational School.

GLIDDEN, STEVE; Brownsburg HS; Brownsburg, IN; 14/350 Hon Rl; IM Sprt; Purdue Univ; Engr.

GLIEBE, MARK J; Lake Catholic HS; Euclid, OH; 32/315 Cls Rep Frsh Cls; VP Soph Cls; Cl Rep Jr Cls; Cls Rep Sr Cls; Hon Rl; Lit Mag; Ger Clb; Bsktbl; Ftbl; IM Sprt; Bowling Green St Univ; Comp Sci.

GLIME, REBECCA; Fraser HS; Fraser, MI; 21/592 Hon Rl; NHS; Rptr Sch Nwsp; Sci Clb; Swmmng; IM Sprt; PPFtbl; Albion Coll; Psych.

GLINIECKI, MARY; Ubly HS; Ruth, MI; Band; Hon Rl; Jr NHS; Sch Pl; 4-H; FFA; PPFtbl; 4-H Awd; Michigan St Univ; Vet.

GLISTA, JIM; West Branch HS; Salem, OH; 50/260 Cls Rep Frsh Cls; Chrs; Debate Tm; Hon Rl; NHS; Stg Crw; Stu Cncl; Rptr Sch Nwsp; Sch Nwsp; Treas 4-H; Ohio St Univ; Pblc Relations.

GLOCK, DAVID; Wauseon HS; Wauseon, OH; Hon Rl; Northwest Tech Coll; Comp Sci.

GLODEN, SHAWN; Climax Scotts HS; Battle Creek, MI; 5/54 Cls Rep Frsh Cls; Hon Rl; NHS; Letter Bsbl; Capt Bsktbl; Capt Ftbl; Am Leg Awd; Dnfth Awd; Natl Merit Ltr; Rotary Awd; Western Michigan Univ; Engr.

GLOECKLER, DORIS A; Stow Lakeview HS; Stow, OH; Chrh Wkr; Cmnty Wkr; Girl Scts; Hosp Ade; JA; Off Ade; Sch Pl; Ger Clb; Pep Clb; IM Sprt; Bus Sch; Sec.

GLOGOZA, EVA T; Cathedral HS; Indianapolis, IN; 35/152 Girl Scts; Lbry Ade; NHS; Sch Mus; Sch Nwsp; OEA; Capt Chrldng; Exec Sec.

GLOVA, KAREN; Struthers HS; Struthers, OH; Cmp Fr Grls; Hon Rl; Spn Clb; Voice Dem Awd;.

GLOVA, PAUL; Struthers HS; Struthers, OH; 3/196 Cl Rep Jr Cls; Hon Rl; Jr NHS; FSA; Spn Clb; Letter Bsbl; Letter Crs Cntry; Letter Ten; Natl Merit Ltr; Youngstown Univ; Engr.

GLOVER, CLINTON; Bethel HS; New Carlisle, OH; Cl Rep Jr Cls; Band; Boy Scts; Chrs; Chrh Wkr; Drm Bgl; Hon Rl; Orch; Sch Mus; Sct Actv; All Ohio St Band; Scouting Gold Awd For Special Achv; College; Music.

GLOVER, DAVID; Washington Irving HS; Clarksburg, WV; Cls Rep Frsh Cls; Am Leg Boys St; Yth Flsp; Rptr Yrbk; Sprt Ed Sch Nwsp; Sch Nwsp; Lat Clb; Sci Clb; Ftbl; Glf; West Virginia Univ; Acctg.

GLOVER, MISCHELLE; Reeths Puffer HS; Muskegon, MI; 15/370 Band; Hon Rl; NHS; Chrldng; PPFtbl; Muskegon Cmnty Coll.

GLOVER, RICK; Clawson HS; Clawson, MI; Band; Sch Mus; Univ Of Mich; Organic Chem.

GLOWACKI, KEVIN T; St Joseph Preparatory Semina; Grand Rapids, MI; 1/8 Cls Rep Frsh Cls; Pres Sr Cls; Chrh Wkr; Hon Rl; Pres NHS; Pres Stu Cncl; Yrbk; Capt Bsktbl; IM Sprt; Natl Merit SF; Loyola Of Chicago; Classics.

GLOWACKI, PAUL; Bishop Luers HS; Ft Wayne, IN; Hon Rl; Sec Key Clb; Kiwan Awd; Purdue Univ; Engr.

GLOWER, JACOB; Upper Arlington HS; Columbus, OH; 92/692 Debate Tm; Hon Rl; Trk; IM Sprt; Natl Merit SF; Ohio State Univ; Elec Engr.

GLOWSKI, CATHERINE M; Bishop Noll Institute HS; Chicago, IL; 5/370 Cls Rep Frsh Cls; Cls Rep Soph Cls; Chrh Wkr; Hon Rl; NHS; Quill & Scroll; Rptr Sch Nwsp; Bsbl; IM Sprt; St Xavier Coll; Nursing.

GLOYD, DOUGLAS; Meigs HS; Dexter, OH; Hon Rl; Letter Wrstlng; Rio Grande Coll; Biology.

GLOYD, ROBERT; Paw Paw HS; Paw Paw, WV; Trs Frsh Cls; Cls Rep Frsh Cls; Cl Rep Jr Cls; Debate Tm; Hon Rl; NHS; Stu Cncl; Bsbl; Bsktbl; Pres Awd; Coll; Acctg.

GLUGLA, CELESTE; St Florian HS; Detroit, MI; 1/115 Pres Jr Cls; Debate Tm; Hon Rl; Treas Natl Forn Lg; NHS; Pres Stu Cncl; Treas Fr Clb; Sci Clb; VFW Awd; Voice Dem Awd; Science Fair & Air Force Awds; Cert Of Merit; Wayne State Univ; Medicine.

GLUVNA, MARY ANN; St John HS; Ashtabula, OH; Am Leg Aux Girls St; Band; Girl Scts; Hon Rl; Hosp Ade; Pres Lbry Ade; NHS; Rptr Yrbk; Pres Fr Clb; Sec Sci Clb; Kent St Univ; Med.

GLYNN, ROBERT; Tri Village HS; New Madison, OH; Band; Hon Rl; Yth Flsp; 4-H; Fr Clb; FFA; Mgrs; Natl Merit SF; Outstndg Fresh FFA 77; Attend Case Inst Of Tech Smmr Sci Symposium 79; General Mtrs Inst; Mech Engr.

GLYNN, SARA; Dansville Agricultural Schl; Webberville, MI; Sec Frsh Cls; Chrh Wkr; Cmnty Wkr; Hon Rl; JA; NHS; Off Ade; 4-H; FHA; Letter Bsktbl; March Of Dimes Redog 78; Michigan St Univ; Bio.

GNEGAN, ELIZABETH; High School; Muncie, IN; Hon Rl; NHS; Sch Mus; FHA; Pep Clb; Spn Clb; Crs Cntry; Ten; Chrldng; Tmr; Univ Of Ill; Acctg.

GOAD, ELIZABETH; St Josephs HS; Huntington, WV; 6/40 Cls Rep Frsh Cls; Cls Rep Soph Cls; Cmp Fr Grls; Cmnty Wkr; Hon Rl; Lbry Ade; Sch Pl; Rptr Yrbk; Rptr Sch Nwsp; FBLA; Marshall Univ.

GOAD, EMILY; Rensselaer Central HS; Rensselaer, IN; 12/164 Band; Chrs; Chrh Wkr; Hon Rl; NHS; Sch Mus; 4-H; Fr Clb; Lion Awd; Purdue Univ; Comp Sci.

GOAD, JACQUELINE; William Henry Harrison HS; Evansville, IN; 79/459 Cls Rep Soph Cls; Cl Rep Jr Cls; Stu Cncl; Pep Clb; Pom Pon; PPFtbl; Cit Awd; Coll; Phys Therapy.

GOAR, CINDA; Hagerstown Jr Sr HS; Hagerstown, IN; 2/242 Sec Chrh Wkr; Girl Scts; Hon Rl; VP Yth Flsp; FHA; Bus Schl; Sec.

GOATLEY, JAMES; Haslett HS; Haslett, MI; 17/154 Cl Rep Jr Cls; Band; Cmnty Wkr; NHS; Sch Mus; Sch Pl; Stg Crw; Stu Cncl; Univ.

GOBERT, TERRY; Greencastle HS; Greencastle, IN; Pres FCA; Hon Rl; Sct Actv; FTA; Pres Key Clb; Pep Clb; Sci Clb; Capt Bsbl; Letter Bsktbl; Capt Ftbl; Indiana Univ; Bus.

GOBLE, C JANE; O A Carlson HS; Gibraltar, MI; 97/239 Chrh Wkr; Cmnty Wkr; Hon Rl; Off Ade; Trk; GAA; Natl Merit SF; Resltn From Gibraltar City Councl In Recgntn Of Serv As Actng City Clerk Of Gibraltar 79; Henry Ford Cmnty Coll; Bus Admin.

GOBLE, KEVIN; West Jefferson HS; Galloway, OH; Am Leg Boys St; Lat Clb; Spn Clb; Bsktbl; Capt Ftbl; Trk; Univ; Pharm.

GOBLE, ROBIN A; Columbia City Joint HS; Columbia City, IN; 2/249 Sal; Chrh Wkr; Hon Rl; NHS; Pres Spn Clb; Letter Bsktbl; Crs Cntry; Letter Trk; NCTE; Indiana Cntrl Univ; Pre Med.

GOBLE, SARA; Park Hills HS; Fairborn, OH; Chrs; Lit Mag; Pres NHS; Quill & Scroll; Stu Cncl; Sch Nwsp; Hockey; Trk; Miami Univ; Micro Bio.

GOBOL, JOHN A; Oak Glen HS; Newell, WV; Cls Rep Frsh Cls; Am Leg Boys St; Hon Rl; Jr NHS; Bsktbl; Univ; Engr.

GOBROGGE, DEB; Otsego HS; Weston, OH; Am Leg Aux Girls St; Band; Chrh Wkr; Hon Rl; Jr NHS; NHS; Drama Clb; 4-H; Scr Kpr; 4-H Awd; College; Elem Ed.

GOBS, MICHAEL; Mohawk HS; Sycamore, OH; Cls Rep Frsh Cls; Cls Rep Soph Cls; Cmnty Wkr; Lit Mag; Stg Crw; Stu Cncl; Colorado Schl; Gunsmith.

GOCHNEAUR, TERRIE; Harbor Sr HS; Ashtabula, OH; AFS; JA; Off Ade; Rptr Yrbk; Pep Clb; Sec Spn Clb; JA Awd; Kent St Univ; Bus.

GOCKE, KAREN; Cascade HS; Coatesville, IN; Cl Rep Jr Cls; Hon Rl; Off Ade; Stu Cncl; 4-H; FBLA; Pep Clb; Spn Clb; Bsbl; Chrldng; Hmcmng Princess; Treas Stu Council; College.

GOCSIK, AMY; Cardinal Stritch HS; Toledo, OH; Cls Rep Frsh Cls; Cls Rep Soph Cls; Cl Rep Jr Cls; Chrh Wkr; NHS; Stg Crw; Stu Cncl; Fr Clb; Scr Kpr; VFW Awd; Univ.

GODBY, M; Greenbrier East HS; Lewisburg, WV; Chrh Wkr; College; Electronic Engr.

GODDARD, CHRIS; North Union HS; Marysville, OH; Band; Drl Tm; Girl Scts; Hon Rl; Lbry Ade; Off Ade; Red Cr Ade; Sct Actv; Rptr Yrbk; 4-H; Slvr Home Ec Mdl 77; Ohio St Univ; Police Officer.

GODDARD, DAVE; Harrison HS; Lafayette, IN; 8/290 Pres Frsh Cls; Band; Drm Bgl; Hon Rl; Jr NHS; NHS; Sch Mus; Ed Yrbk; Mth Clb; Rotary Awd; Purdue Univ; Engr.

GODDARD, DAVE; William Henry Harrison HS; Lafayette, IN; 10/304 Band; Jr NHS; NHS; Orch; Sch Mus; Pres Stu Cncl; Ed Yrbk; Rptr Yrbk; Yrbk; Mth Clb; Purdue Univ; Engr.

GODDARD, DAVID; Woodridge HS; Cuyahoga Fls, OH; 44/126 Chrs; Ger Clb; Sci Clb; Jr Vrsty Trak 77; Jr Vrsty Golf 78; Ohio St Univ; Acctg.

GODDARD, JILL R; Howell HS; Howell, MI; 100/400 Cmp Fr Grls; Chrh Wkr; Hon Rl; JA; Off Ade; Yth Flsp; Ger Clb; Lansing Cmnty Coll; Photg.

GODDARD, PAMELA; Wheeling Park HS; Wheeling, WV; 18/600 Cmnty Wkr; Hon Rl; Stifel Awrd 77; Univ; Tchr.

GODDEYNE, MARY; Essexville Hampton HS; Essexville, MI; 10/195 Cls Rep Soph Cls; Cl Rep Jr Cls; Trs Sr Cls; Cls Rep Sr Cls; Am Leg Aux Girls St; Chrs; Chrh Wkr; Debate Tm; Hon Rl; Sch Mus; Ctrl Michigan Univ; Psych.

GODFREY, ANGELA; Matooka HS; Rock, WV; Band; Drm Mjrt; Girl Scts; Hon Rl; NHS; Yrbk; Rptr Sch Nwsp; 4-H; FHA; Treas Keyettes; WVU; Arts.

GODFREY, JANET; South Amherst HS; S Amherst, OH; Band; Chrs; Hon Rl; Sch Mus; Rptr Yrbk; Drama Clb; Pep Clb; PPFtbl; College; Teacher.

GODFREY JR, RAY; Glen Este HS; Batavia, OH; Boy Scts; FCA; Hon Rl; Spn Clb; Letter Bsbl; Letter Bsktbl; Letter Ftbl; Wrstlng; Wilmington College; Bus.

GODGLUCK, CHRISTINE; St Joseph Ctrl Cath HS; Huntington, WV; Chrs; Chrh Wkr; Hon Rl; Drama Clb; Pep Clb; Glf; Mgrs; Coll; Med.

GODLEW, SCOTT; Bangor HS; Bangor, MI; Trs Frsh Cls; Trs Soph Cls; Trs Jr Cls; Am Leg Boys St; Band; Boy Scts; Hon Rl; Stu Cncl; Yth Flsp; Key Clb; Michigan Tech Univ; Astrophsics.

GODLEWSKI, BENJAMIN; Manistique HS; Manistique, MI; Boy Scts; Letter Bsktbl; Letter Ftbl; Letter Trk; Coach Actv; Scr Kpr; Tmr; Us Air Force Academy; Computers.

GODLEWSKI, KATHY; Admiral King HS; Lorain, OH; VP Sr Cls; Chrh Wkr; Hon Rl; Lbry Ade; Yrbk; Key Clb; Ten; IM Sprt; Scr Kpr; Univ; Acctg.

GODLEWSKI, RANDY; Escanaba Area Public HS; Cornell, MI; 200/438 Band; Chrh Wkr; Quill & Scroll; Rptr Sch Nwsp; Sch Nwsp; Ftbl; 4-H Awd; Univ; Phys Educ.

GODMER, VICKI; St Charles HS; St Charles, MI; Chrs; Cmnty Wkr; Girl Scts; Sch Mus; Sch Pl; Sct Actv; Trk; Twrlr; Mic State; Sociology.

GODOWN, RENEE; Greenville HS; Greenville, OH; Orch; Art Inst Of Pittsburg; Interior Desg.

GOE, BRYAN; Yorktown HS; Yorktown, IN; 12/180 Hon Rl; NHS; Fr Clb; Glf; Letter Swmmng; College; Engr.

GOEBEL, BRENDA; Montpelier HS; Montpelier, OH; Band; Chrh Wkr; Tmr; Business Schl; Comp Progr.

GOEBEL, DAVID; Padua Franciscan HS; Parma, OH; Boy Scts; FCA; Capt Hockey; Coach Actv; JA Awd; Univ; Bus.

GOEBEL, DEBBIE; Clermont Northeastern HS; Goshen, OH; Band; Hon Rl; NHS; VP Fr Clb; Pep Clb; Xavier Univ; Math.

GOEBEL, EVELYN; Federal Hocking HS; Coolville, OH; Trs Frsh Cls; VP Soph Cls; Cls Rep Soph Cls; Hon Rl; NHS; Sch Pl; Stu Cncl; Rptr Yrbk; 4-H; Spn Clb; Univ.

GOEBEL, JULIE; Ovid Elsie HS; Ovid, MI; Chrh Wkr; Hon Rl; NHS; Sec Stu Cncl; Ed Yrbk; Rptr Sch Nwsp; Treas Pep Clb; Mgrs; Scr Kpr;.

GOEBEL, KATHY; Hillman Community HS; Hillman, MI; Trs Soph Cls; Band; Chrs; Chrh Wkr; Hon Rl; Lbry Ade; NHS; Off Ade; Sch Pl; 4-H; Bethany Lutheran Coll.

GOEBEL, KURT; Hillman HS; Hillman, MI; 7/60 Chrh Wkr; Hon Rl; NHS; Stg Crw; Treas FFA; Letter Bsktbl; Letter Trk; 4-H Awd; Bethany Lutheran Coll.

GOEBEL, ROBERT; Mt Vernon Sr HS; Mt Vernon, IN; Chrh Wkr; Cmnty Wkr; Debate Tm; Drl Tm; Hon Rl; FFA; Indiana Tech Schl; Construction.

GOEDDE, STEVE; Mater Dei HS; Evansville, IN; 12/175 Trs Jr Cls; Trs Sr Cls; Hon Rl; Jr NHS; NHS; Bsktbl; Ftbl; Trk; IM Sprt; Kiwan Awd; Purdue; Engr.

GOEDERT, CHARLES; Ferndale HS; Ferndale, MI; 30/500 Debate Tm; Hon Rl; Mod UN; Natl Forn Lg; Pol Wkr; Rotary Awd; Wayne State Univ; Poli Sci.

GOEGOR, CYNTHIA; Brooklyn HS; Brooklyn, OH; Cls Rep Soph Cls; Cl Rep Jr Cls; Band; Chrs; Chrh Wkr; Hosp Ade; Stu Cncl; College; Engr.

GOEHLER, MARK; Norton HS; Norton, OH; 31/291 Cmnty Wkr; FCA; Hon Rl; NHS; Off Ade; Bsbl; Letter Ftbl; Univ.

GOEPPNER, CHERYL; Jasper HS; Jasper, IN; 8/321 Am Leg Aux Girls St; Hon Rl; Ed Sch Nwsp; VP Civ Clb; Pep Clb; Univ Of Evansville; Nursing.

GOERGE, SANDRA; Brighton HS; Brighton, MI; Girl Scts; Hon Rl; Voc Schl; Cosmtlgy.

GOERING JR, GENE; Pittsford Area HS; Hudson, MI; 1/50 Cls Rep Sr Cls; Band; Hon Rl; NHS; Sch Pl; Stu Cncl; Drama Clb; 4-H; FFA; Letter Bsktbl; Young Peoples Citizenship Seminar Albion Coll; FFA Outstanding Jr Awd; Camp Miniwanea Leadership Conf; Michigan St Univ; Vet Medicine.

GOERLICH, LINDA; Anchor Bay HS; New Baltimore, MI; 2/250 Hon Rl; NHS; OEA; Oakland Univ.

GOERS, SUSAN; Meadowdale HS; Dayton, OH; Band; Chrh Wkr; Hon Rl; Pep Clb; Scr Kpr; Sec.

GOERSS, MATTHEW; Hartland Consolidated School; Fenton, MI; Boy Scts; Hon Rl; Sprt Ed Yrbk; Spn Clb; Capt Bsktbl; Ftbl; Trk; Univ; Engr.

GOETTEMOELLER, CHERYL; Versailles HS; Versailles, OH; Band; Chrs; Hon Rl; Lbry Ade; Drama Clb; 4-H; VP FHA; Trk; Twrlr; 4-H Awd; Eastern Kentucky Univ; Art.

GOETTEMOELLER, LORI; Marion Local HS; Maria Stein, OH; 14/88 Chrs; Hon Rl; NHS; Pep Clb; Sci Clb; IM Sprt; Letter Mgrs; Scr Kpr; Tmr; Univ; Sec.

GOETZ, AL; Brookside HS; Sheffield Lake, OH; 16/173 Hon Rl; Letter Bsbl; Letter Glf; Air Force.

GOETZ, BERNARD; Whiteford HS; Ottawa Lk, MI; Cls Rep Frsh Cls; Chrh Wkr; Cmnty Wkr; Hon Rl; NHS; 4-H; Spn Clb; Bsktbl; Glf; Cit Awd; Univ Of Toledo; Engr.

GOETZ, GERALD; Cardinal Stritch HS; Oregon, OH; 11/178 Cls Rep Sr Cls; Am Leg Boys St; Debate Tm; Hon Rl; NHS; Pol Wkr; Stu Cncl; Y-Teens; Rptr Sch Nwsp; Fr Clb; Univ Of Toledo; Acctg.

GOETZ, MARGARET; North Farmington HS; Farm Hills, MI; Chrh Wkr; Girl Scts; Hon Rl; NHS; Pres Yth Flsp; Ger Clb; Natl Merit SF; Univ; Bio.

GOETZ, ROBERT; Tri Valley HS; Dresden, OH; 28/230 Am Leg Boys St; Hon Rl; Crs Cntry; Trk; Ohio State; Mech Engr.

GOETZ, VICKI; New Richmond HS; New Richmond, OH; 13/192 Band; Hon Rl; JA; Lbry Ade; NHS; Quill & Scroll; Sch Pl; Rptr Yrbk; Rptr Sch Nwsp; Sch Nwsp; Bst News Story Of Yr 79; Serv Awd Jrnslm 79; Mst Conscients Staffers Aqwd 78; Univ Of Cincinnati; Fshn Design.

GOFF, JAMES; Northfield HS; Wabash, IN; Boy Scts; Chrs; Chrh Wkr; Hon Rl; Treas Lbry Ade; Sch Mus; 4-H; Mth Clb; Sci Clb; Spn Clb; Univ; Engr.

GOFF, JEFFREY; Fredericktown HS; Fred, OH; Cls Rep Frsh Cls; Cls Rep Soph Cls; Cl Rep Jr Cls; Chrs; Chrh Wkr; Hon Rl; Mdrgl; Quill & Scroll; Sch Mus; Sch Pl; Tennessee Temple Univ; Brdcst Minsty.

GOFF, KENNETH; Hudsonville HS; Hudsonville, MI; Letter Trk; Michigan St Univ; Acctg.

GOFF, MICHELLE; Bedford North Lawrence HS; Bedford, IN; Hon Rl; NHS; Beta Clb; Pep Clb; Spn Clb; Bsktbl; Glf; Butler Univ; Accounting.

GOFF, NATALIE; Philip Barbour HS; Belington, WV; Cl Rep Jr Cls; Band; Treas Chrh Wkr; Hon Rl; NHS; Keyettes; Mat Maids; Bus Schl.

GOFF, TIMOTHY; Waldron HS; Shelbyville, IN; Cls Rep Soph Cls; Cl Rep Jr Cls; Cls Rep Sr Cls; FCA; Ed Sch Nwsp; Boys Clb Am; Drama Clb; Key Clb; Lat Clb; Letter Bsbl; Military.

GOFORTH, CHRISTINA; Avondale HS; Pontiac, MI; 78/270 Chrs; Mdrgl; PAVAS; Sch Mus; Stu Cncl; Am Leg Awd; God Cntry Awd; Oakland Univ; Music.

GOGGIN, JOHN; Benedictine HS; Shaker Hts, OH; Cls Rep Frsh Cls; Cls Rep Soph Cls; Cl Rep Jr Cls; Hon Rl; Stu Cncl; Key Clb; Ftbl; Wrstlng; Coach Actv; Mgrs; Work.

GOGGIN, KATHERINE; Bishop Luers HS; Ft Wayne, IN; Chrs; Chrh Wkr; Girl Scts; Hon Rl; Sch Mus; Sch Pl; Ed Sch Nwsp; VP 4-H; Fr Clb; 4-H Awd; Univ; Marine Bio.

GOGGIN, MICHAEL; Padua Fransican HS; Parma, OH; 107/262 Boy Scts; Hon Rl; JA; IM Sprt; Mgrs; Scr Kpr; Cuyahoga Comm Coll; Pol Sci.

GOGOLA, SUSAN; Trenton HS; Trenton, MI; Band; Hon Rl; Off Ade; Orch; Rptr Sch Nwsp; Hnrd By Eastern Mi Univ For Outstndg Achvmnt In Math 76; Michigan Tech Univ; Elec Engr.

GOGOLIN, HEIDI; Reed City HS; Reed City, MI; 6/159 VP Sr Cls; Hon Rl; Jr NHS; NHS; Stu Cncl; Letter Trk; Chrldng; Calvin.

GOHR, DEBRA; Bay City Central HS; Bay City, MI; 55/464 Girl Scts; Hon Rl; NHS; Sct Actv; PPFtbl; Cit Awd; Pres Awd; Bus Schl; Bus.

GOING, MARK; Gods Bible School; Greenfield, IN; Band; Boy Scts; Chrs; Chrh Wkr; Hon Rl; Orch; Sct Actv; Mth Clb; Spn Clb; Mbr Of HS Quartet 78; Univ; Music.

GOING, THOMAS; Arsenal Technical HS; Indianapolis, IN; Cls Rep Frsh Cls; Cl Rep Jr Cls; Am Leg Boys St; Chrh Wkr; Hosp Ade; NHS; Key Clb; Purdue; Air Traffic Control.

GOINGS, JENNIFER; Walnut Hills HS; Cincinnati, OH; Chrs; Chrh Wkr; Cmnty Wkr; Hon Rl; Hosp Ade; Off Ade; Sch Mus; Sch Pl; Yth Flsp; Pep Clb; Univ; Comp Tech.

GOINS, CLARINE; William Henry Harrison HS; Lafayette, IN; Girl Scts; Hon Rl; Off Ade; Fr Clb; Letter Bsktbl; Swmmng; PPFtbl; Univ; Archt.

GOINS, MARK; Valley View HS; Germantown, OH; Pres Chrh Wkr; Hon Rl; 4-H; 4-H Awd; Free Gospel Bible Inst; Preacher.

GOINS, SUE; North Union HS; Richwood, OH; Hon Rl; Lbry Ade; NHS; Yth Flsp; Treas DECA; Pres 4-H; Trk; IM Sprt; 4-H Awd; Marion Tech Coll; Acctg.

GOLBA, DENISE; Adams HS; So Bend, IN; Cls Rep Frsh Cls; Cls Rep Soph Cls; Cmp Fr Grls; Chrh Wkr; Hon Rl; Lbry Ade; 4-H; Pep Clb; Capt Trk; College; Fash Mdse.

GOLBA, TIM; Chaminade Julienne HS; Dayton, OH; Hon Rl; Rptr Sch Nwsp; IM Sprt; Univ Of Cinn; Architecture.

GOLBESKY, LISA; Andrean HS; Merrillville, IN; Hon Rl; Stu Cncl; Rptr Sch Nwsp; In St Schlsp; Indiana Univ; Paralegal.

GOLBINEC, KATHLEEN; Notre Dame Academy; Toledo, OH; Chrs; Chrh Wkr; Cmnty Wkr; Girl Scts; Hosp Ade; PAVAS; Sch Mus; Sch Pl; Stg Crw; Drama Clb; Univ; Opera.

GOLDBERG, DANIEL P; Hawken HS; Hunting Valley, OH; 20/110 Cmnty Wkr; Hon Rl; PAVAS; Sch Pl; Ed Sch Nwsp; Key Clb; Bsbl; Ftbl; Wrstlng; Natl Merit SF; Acad Honors 75 76 76 77 77 78; Med.

GOLDBERG, LISA; Jefferson HS; Lafayette, IN; 3/570 Cls Rep Frsh Cls; Sec Soph Cls; Trs Soph Cls; Sec Jr Cls; Trs Jr Cls; VP Sr Cls; Hon Rl; NHS; Orch; Fr Clb; Purdue Univ; Engr.

GOLDBERG, PETER R; Wapakoneta HS; Wapakoneta, OH; College.

GOLDEN, MARCHELL; Hamilton Township HS; R A F B, OH; Chrs; Girl Scts; Hon Rl; Mdrgl; Stu Cncl; Fr Clb; Sci Clb; Trk; GAA; Natl Merit Ltr; Univ; Music.

GOLDEN, ROCHELLE; Clio HS; Clio, MI; 52/396 Band; Hon Rl; NHS; Off Ade; Sch Mus; Yth Flsp; Gulf Coast Bible Coll; Psych.

GOLDEN, ROY; Bethel Tate HS; Bethel, OH; 12/230 Am Leg Boys St; Boy Scts; Sch Nwsp;.

GOLDEN, SALLY; River Valley HS; Sawyer, MI; 7/150 Hon Rl; NHS; Ger Clb; Davenport College; Bus.

GOLDEN, SARAH; Henry Ford HS; Detroit, MI; Cls Rep Frsh Cls; Sec Soph Cls; Cl Rep Jr Cls; Hon Rl; FNA; Pep Clb; Spn Clb; Pom Pon; Cit Awd; Detroit Coll Of Busns; CPA.

GOLDEN, VICKIE; Firelands HS; Amherst, OH; Trs Frsh Cls; Cls Rep Soph Cls; Cl Rep Jr Cls; Stu Cncl; Chrldng; Scr Kpr;.

GOLDER, GEORGE; Big Rapids HS; Big Rpds, MI; Hon Rl; Natl Forn Lg; NHS; Sch Pl; Drama Clb; Fr Clb; Dnfth Awd; DAR Awd; Elk Awd; Natl Merit SF; Univ Of Mich; Law.

GOLDER, JEFFREY; Brownsburg HS; Brownsbg, IN; 48/300 Chrh Wkr; Hon Rl; NHS; Quill & Scroll; Sch Nwsp; Ger Clb; Sci Clb; Ten; IUPUI; Dent.

GOLDEY, ELLEN; Talawanda HS; Oxford, OH; Am Leg Aux Girls St; Cmp Fr Grls; VP Chrs; Hon Rl; Jr NHS; NHS; Stu Cncl; 4-H; Hockey; GAA; College; Medicine.

GOLDIE, WENDY; Garrett HS; Garrett, IN; 1/141 Chrh Wkr; Cmnty Wkr; Girl Scts; Hon Rl; NHS; Quill & Scroll; Sct Actv; Yth Flsp; Ed Sch Nwsp; FFA; Headliner Awd Overall Perf At HS; Amer Guild Of Music Outstndng Awd; Indiana Univ Journalism Inst; College; Journalism.

GOLDMAN, BRUCE N; Berkley HS; Royal Oak, MI; 1/487 Cls Rep Frsh Cls; Cls Rep Soph Cls; Cl Rep Jr Cls; Jr NHS; NHS; Sct Actv; Stu Cncl; Am Leg Awd; Cit Awd; Natl Merit SF; Univ Of Mic; Corporate Law.

GOLDSBERRY, LISA; South Spencer Rebels HS; Newburgh, IN; 36/160 Cls Rep Soph Cls; Hon Rl; Lbry Ade; Stu Cncl; Sch Nwsp; Lib Awd 79; Beauty Schl.

GOLDSBERRY, MARTHA; Ripley Union Lewis HS; Rd, OH; 2/89 Am Leg Aux Girls St; Pres NHS; Off Ade; Sch Pl; Yth Flsp; Yrbk; Treas 4-H; FHA; DAR Awd; 4-H Awd; Maysville Cmnty Coll; Bus Mgmt.

GOLDSBURY, SUE; Bishop Ready HS; Columbus, OH; 25/135 VP Frsh Cls; Pres Jr Cls; Hon Rl; Jr NHS; NHS; Sch Pl; Rptr Yrbk; Chrldng; Mat Maids; Scr Kpr; Ohio State; Law.

GOLDSBY, TERESA; Mitchell HS; Mitchell, IN; Band; Hst Frsh Cls; Hon Rl; 4-H; 4-H Awd; Arionawd Mst Outstndng Jr Bandsmn 79; All Amer Hall Of Fame Band Hon 79; Part In U S Coll Wind Bwl 79; Univ; Music.

GOLDSMITH, BECKY; Doddridge County HS; Greenwood, WV; Hon Rl; Jr NHS; Fr Clb; FBLA; FHA; Pep Clb; United Career Center; Bus.

GOLDSMITH, EVELYN; Edison HS; Lake Station, IN; Chrh Wkr; Hon Rl; Jr NHS; Mod UN; Off Ade; DECA; Pep Clb; Flor Coll.

GOLDSMITH, JULIE; Delta Sr HS; Swanton, OH; Chrs; Sch Pl; 4-H; Mat Maids; 4-H Awd; Univ; Stenographer.

GOLDSTEIN, ANDREW; West Geauga HS; Chesterland, OH; 13/352 Cls Rep Frsh Cls; Cls Rep Soph Cls; Cl Rep Jr Cls; Band; Hon Rl; Jr NHS; Pres NHS; Stu Cncl; Ten; IM Sprt; Leroy Spahr Galvin Memrl Schlrshp 79; Miami Univ; Econ.

GOLDSTEIN, BARBARA; Carman HS; Flint, MI; Hon Rl; NHS; Univ; Sci.

GOLDSTEIN, JAY; West Bloomfield HS; W Bloomfield, MI; 57/439 Hon Rl; NHS; Sprt Ed Sch Nwsp; Rptr Sch Nwsp; Bsbl; IM Sprt; Mgrs; Mic St Univ; Health.

GOLDY, RICHARD; Ogemaw Hts HS; Midland, MI; Hon Rl; NHS; Key Clb; Sci Clb; VICA; Bsbl; Trk; Kiwan Awd; Michigan Tech Univ; Aero Engr.

GOLEM, ELAINE; Lutheran HS; Parma, OH; 17/105 Chrs; Girl Scts; Hosp Ade; NHS; Spn Clb; College; Internatl Business.

GOLENZ, DOUG; Archbishop Alter HS; Bellbrook, OH; 100/278 Cl Rep Jr Cls; Stg Crw; Yth Flsp; Yrbk; Univ; Graphics Engr.

GOLEY, SHARON; Covington HS; Covington, IN; 7/110 Band; Chrh Wkr; Hon Rl; Jr NHS; Sch Pl; Stu Cncl; Pep Clb; Trk; GAA; Mgrs; College; Business.

GOLIAS, DAVID; Trinity HS; Garfield Hts, OH; 30/150 Hon Rl; IM Sprt; College; Acctg.

GOLIAS, KAREN; Stow HS; Munroe Fls, OH; 46/600 Girl Scts; Hon Rl; Off Ade; Bsktbl; Letter Trk; IM Sprt; College; Nursing.

GOLL, STACEY; Ferndale HS; Pleasant Ridge, MI; 9/393 Sec Soph Cls; Hon Rl; Jr NHS; NHS; Rptr Yrbk; Rptr Sch Nwsp; Ger Clb; Trk; GAA; IM Sprt; Phi Beta Kappa Awd 79; Northern Michigan Univ; Acctg.

GOLLEHON, VIRGINIA; W E Stebbins HS; Dayton, OH; Band; Hon Rl; ROTC; Beta Clb; Spn Clb; Univ Of Colorado; Comp Sci.

GOLLIHER, DIANA; Pendleton Heights HS; Anderson, IN; 12/305 Sec Band; Drl Tm; Hosp Ade; Off Ade; Pep Clb; Sec Spn Clb; Mgrs; Ball State Univ; Rn.

GOLLNAST, KARL R; Bridgman HS; Bridgman, MI; Band; Drm Mjrt; Hon Rl; NHS; Sch Mus; Stg Crw; Sci Clb; Swmmng; Coach Actv; Ferris State Univ; Tool & Die.

GOLOBICH, MICHAEL; Northwest HS; Indianapolis, IN; Am Leg Boys St; Hon Rl; Pres NHS; Stg Crw; Letter Ten; IM Sprt; DAR Awd; College; Law.

GOLTZ, JAMES; Lawrenceburg HS; Lawrenceburg, IN; 8/160 Hon Rl; NHS; Sci Clb; Bausch & Lomb Awd; Natl Merit Ltr; College; Comp Progr.

GOMEZ, JOSEPH; Madonna HS; Weirton, WV; 35/100 Hon Rl; NHS; Key Clb; Bsktbl; Ftbl; IM Sprt; College; Business.

GOMEZ, REBECCA; Andrean HS; Merrillville, IN; 85/261 Sec Soph Cls; Pres Sr Cls; Hon Rl; NHS; Stu Cncl; Sch Nwsp; Drama Clb; Columbia Univ; Communication.

GOMOLUCH, BRENDA; Laura F Osborn HS; Detroit, MI; Cl Rep Jr Cls; Aud/Vis; Chrs; Hon Rl; Natl Forn Lg; NHS; Sch Nwsp; Drama Clb; Spn Clb; Swmmng; Mercy Coll; Nursing.

GONDA, LORI; Imlay City Cmnty HS; Attica, MI; Girl Scts; Hon Rl; NHS; FFA; Michigan St Univ; Vet.

GONGWER, CAMERON; Anderson HS; Anderson, IN; Am Leg Boys St; Chrh Wkr; Hon Rl; Jr NHS; NHS; Yth Flsp; Letter Crs Cntry; Letter Trk; College; Medicine.

GONGWER, MELODY; Eastbrook HS; Upland, IN; 8/200 Hon Rl; Jr NHS; Lbry Ade; Sch Pl; Ger Clb; Lat Clb; Univ; Pre Med.

GONOS, AUDREY; South Amherst HS; S Amherst, OH; Band; Girl Scts; Hon Rl; Lbry Ade; Pres NHS; Stg Crw; Stu Cncl; 4-H; Ger Clb; Sci Clb; Superior Rating St Sci Fair; Presentation Of Sci Fair Proj At Ohio Acad Of Sci Meeting; Ohio St Univ; Med.

GONSER, TODD; Olivet HS; Olivet, MI; 19/80 Band; Hon Rl; Drama Clb; Spn Clb; Bsbl; Letter Bsktbl; Letter Ftbl; Ten; Letter Trk; Mgrs; Coll; Tchr.

GONYEA, DAVE; Delphos Jefferson HS; Delphos, OH; Pres Soph Cls; Band; Chrh Wkr; Hon Rl; Sch Mus; Stu Cncl; Sci Clb; Spn Clb; Glf; Cugahoga Community College; Physasst.

GONYEA, DAVID; Delphos Jefferson Sr HS; Delphos, OH; Pres Frsh Cls; Pres Soph Cls; Band; Boy Scts; Chrs; Chrh Wkr; Hon Rl; Sch Mus; Stu Cncl; Sci Clb; Cuyahoga Cmnty Coll; Med Asst.

GONYER, CARLA; Otsego HS; Weston, OH; 3/125 Sec Chrs; Hon Rl; Hosp Ade; Sec JA; NHS; Sch Pl; VP Yth Flsp; Drama Clb; 4-H; College; Nursing.

GONYER, DARLA; Otsego HS; Weston, OH; 6/125 Chrs; Hon Rl; Jr NHS; NHS; Sch Pl; Sec Yth Flsp; Drama Clb; Sec 4-H; 4-H Awd; Owens Tech Schl; Sec.

GONYER, LORI; Manchester HS; Manchester, MI; Band; Chrh Wkr; Hon Rl; Orch; Sch Mus; Northern Michigan Univ; Comp Sci.

GONZALES, CARMEN; Wayland Union HS; Wayland, MI; Girl Scts; Hon Rl; Sch Mus; IM Sprt; Natl Merit Ltr; Western Michigan Univ; Exec Sec.

GONZALES, CRISTELLA; Defiance Sr HS; Defiance, OH; Cls Rep Frsh Cls; Hon Rl; JA; Lbry Ade; Off Ade; Stg Crw; Stu Cncl; Rptr Sch Nwsp; Sch Nwsp; Chrldng; Var Cheerldr Rcvd J V & Var Ltr 77 79; Ohio St Univ; Physn.

GONZALES, DAN; Munster HS; Munster, IN; 189/414 Cls Rep Soph Cls; Cl Rep Jr Cls; Hon Rl; Ten; De Pauw Univ; Psych.

GONZALES, GILBERT; Patrick Henry HS; Hamler, OH; Band; Chrs; Hon Rl; Sch Mus; Boys Clb Am; Trk; Univ.

GONZALES, LESLEY; Oak Hill HS; Oak Hill, WV; Am Leg Aux Girls St; Band; Chrs; Hon Rl; NHS; Sch Pl; Drama Clb; Fr Clb; Pep Clb; Ten; West Virginia Univ; Educ.

GONZALES, PATRICIA; Washington HS; E Chicago, IN; 42/250 Sec Soph Cls; VP Jr Cls; Sch Mus; Sch Pl; Pres Stu Cncl; Yrbk; Drama Clb; Fr Clb; Spn Clb; College; Theater Arts.

GONZALES, RANDY; Merrillville HS; Merrillville, IN; VP Frsh Cls; Boy Scts; Stu Cncl; Letter Ftbl; Letter Trk; IM Sprt; College; Bus.

GONZALES JR, RONALD; Douglas Mac Arthur HS; Saginaw, MI; Cls Rep Sr Cls; Boy Scts; Chrh Wkr; Hon Rl; Treas NHS; Lat Clb; Letter Ftbl; Trk; Coach Actv; Pres Awd; MVP Track; MVP JV Ftbl; MVP Bsktbl; Univ; Health.

GONZALEZ, CYNTHIA; Carroll HS; Flora, IN; Chrs; FCA; Girl Scts; Jr NHS; NHS; Stg Crw; Pres Drama Clb; Spn Clb; Univ.

GONZALEZ, DAVID; Theodore Roosevelt HS; E Chicago, IN; 5/199 VP Soph Cls; Am Leg Boys St; VP Band; Orch; Stu Cncl; Rptr Yrbk; Rptr Sch Nwsp; Fr Clb; Mth Clb; Ftbl; Latino Schlr Awd From ALMA In IU Bloomington; College; Law.

GONZALEZ, DIANA; Boardman HS; Canfield, OH; Hon Rl; Jr NHS; Lbry Ade; VP NHS; Pep Clb; Spn Clb; Letter Ten; Capt Chrldng; Schlrshp To Youngstown St Univ 79; Won Awd Form Kent St Univ In Lang Declamation Contest 77; Grove City Coll; Acctg.

GONZALEZ, EMILIO R; Clay HS; Oregon, OH; Hon Rl; Sch Pl; Stg Crw; Boys Clb Am; Hockey; Apprenticeship As Machinist.

GONZALEZ, KAREN; Merrillville Sr HS; Merrillville, IN; 108/596 Cl Rep Jr Cls; Cls Rep Sr Cls; Chrh Wkr; Cmnty Wkr; Hon Rl; Lbry Ade; Stu Cncl; Yth Flsp; FTA; Pep Clb; Whos Who Among Amer HS Stud 77; Hoosier Schlr 79; Hon Spanish Awd 77; Manchester Coll; Bus Admin.

GONZALEZ, MILAGRIN; Horace Mann HS; Gary, IN; Hon Rl; Jr NHS; NHS; Spn Clb; College;.

GONZALEZ, THERESA; W Carrollton Sr HS; W Carrollton, OH; 54/418 Drm Bgl; Hon Rl; Sec JA; Jr NHS; Rptr Yrbk; Rptr Sch Nwsp; Spn Clb; Trk; Mat Maids; Univ Of Dayton; Busns Admin.

GOOCH, LISA; Princeton HS; Princeton, WV; 12/350 Chrh Wkr; Hon Rl; Jr NHS; NHS; Sch Nwsp; Keyettes; Spn Clb; Letter Bsbl; GAA; Univ; Law.

GOOCH, REBECCA; Wellsville HS; Wellsville, OH; Sec Soph Cls; Band; Chrh Wkr; Y-Teens; Sch Nwsp; FTA; Pep Clb; Chrldng; VFW Awd; NAACP Sec & V Pres; Bowling Green St Univ; Vet.

GOOD, DANNY; Clermont N E HS; Batavia, OH; Trs Jr Cls; Band; FCA; NHS; Sch Pl; Stu Cncl; Drama Clb; Pres Fr Clb; Ftbl; Stu Cncl Pres; Ftbl Tm Capt; Clermont Co Gifted & Talented Prog; Ohio Univ; Communications.

GOOD, DAVID L; Pike HS; Indianapolis, IN; 52/324 Band; Hon Rl; NHS; ROTC; Mth Clb; Ten; Natl Merit SF; Wabash Univ; Chemistry.

GOOD, DIANE; La Ville Jr Sr HS; Lakeville, IN; 3/131 Pres Soph Cls; Cls Rep Soph Cls; Cl Rep Jr Cls; Cls Rep Sr Cls; Sal; Am Leg Aux Girls St; NHS; Stu Cncl; 4-H; Fr Clb; Michiana Coll Of Commerce; Acctg.

GOOD, DIANE; La Ville HS; Lakeville, IN; 3/131 Pres Soph Cls; Cls Rep Soph Cls; Cl Rep Jr Cls; Cls Rep Sr Cls; Sal; Am Leg Aux Girls St; Pres NHS; Off Ade; VP Stu Cncl; Drama Clb; Michiana Coll Of Commerce; Acctg.

GOOD, PHILIP R; Highland HS; Medina, OH; 13/260 VP Frsh Cls; Pres Soph Cls; Am Leg Boys St; Band; Hon Rl; NHS; Stu Cncl; 4-H; Ger Clb; Crs Cntry; Univ.

GOOD, PHILLIP; St Johns HS; Saint Johns, MI; 23/325 Boy Scts; Hon Rl; Jr NHS; NHS; Sct Actv; Spn Clb; Natl Merit Ltr; Lansing Community College; Elec Engr.

GOOD, THOMAS; West Ottawa HS; Holland, MI; Hon Rl; Western Coll; Acctg.

GOOD, TODD; Western HS; Parma, MI; Boy Scts; Chrh Wkr; Hon Rl; Yth Flsp; Crs Cntry; Trk; Most Valuable Cross Cntry 77; All Cnty Cross Cntry 77; Eastern Michigan Univ; Comp Sci.

GOODARD, MICHAEL; Marietta HS; Marietta, OH; 40/406 Letter Band; NHS; Orch; Stg Crw; Yth Flsp; Rptr Sch Nwsp; Ger Clb; Crs Cntry; Kent State Univ; Communications.

GOODE, AMY; Wadsworth Sr HS; Wadsworth, OH; 20/367 VP Jr Cls; Cl Rep Jr Cls; Pres Sr Cls; Sal; Girl Scts; Hon Rl; Hosp Ade; VP Yth Flsp; Rptr Sch Nwsp; Fr Clb; Ohio St Univ; Elem Educ.

GOODE, DEBORAH; Kearsley HS; Flint, MI; Chrs; Girl Scts; Hon Rl; Spn Clb;.

GOODE, L TONYA; Emerson Sr HS; Gary, IN; Hon Rl; Y-Teens; Pep Clb; Capt Chrldng; Miss Sophmore 1977; Univ.

GOODEARLE, CLARK; Meadowbrook HS; Byesville, OH; Mth Clb; Spn Clb; Ftbl; Trk; Wrstlng; Mgrs;.

GOODEN, DARNELL; Buchtel Univ HS; Akron, OH; Cls Rep Frsh Cls; Hon Rl; Ftbl; Trk; Wrstlng; Univ; Bus.

GOODENOUGH, BETH; Paulding HS; Paulding, OH; 14/198 Band; Hon Rl; NHS; Sch Mus; Pres Y-Teens; Ed Yrbk; 4-H; Treas FHA; Sci Clb; IM Sprt; Univ; Med.

GOODENOUGH, CHRISTINE; Faith Bapt Acad; Portage, MI; Chrs; Chrh Wkr; Hon Rl; Lbry Ade; Off Ade; Yth Flsp; Rptr Yrbk; Bsbl; Bsktbl; Socr; Grand Rapids Bapt Coll; Elem Ed.

GOODGION, TONI; Lincoln HS; Cambridge, IN; 17/135 Band; Chrh Wkr; Drl Tm; Girl Scts; Hon Rl; Sct Actv; Yth Flsp; 4-H; OEA; Spn Clb; Indiana Univ; Acctg.

GOODHALL, PATRICK; West Iron Cnty HS; Iron River, MI; Hon Rl; NHS; Letter Bsbl; Natl Merit Schl; Michigan Tech Univ; Chem Engr.

GOODHEW, JANICE; Penn HS; South Bend, IN; Band; Pom Pon; Kendall School Of Design; Int Design.

GOODIN, LAURA; Thomas Carr Howe HS; Indianapolis, IN; Chrs; Chrh Wkr; Girl Scts; Hosp Ade; NHS; Yth Flsp; Cit Awd;.

GOODIN, LISA; Austin HS; Austin, IN; 6/75 VP Jr Cls; Hon Rl; Jr NHS; NHS; Sch Pl; Stu Cncl; FTA; Chrldng; Coach Actv; Cit Awd; College; Elem Educ.

GOODIN, RITA; Henryville HS; Memphis, IN; Hon Rl; NHS; Spn Clb; Charles Allen Prosser Schl; Sec.

GOODING, DEBORAH; St Albans HS; St Albans, WV; 17/400 AFS; Chrs; Chrh Wkr; JA; Jr NHS; NHS; Fr Clb; Mth Clb; Michigan Tech Univ; Civil Engr.

GOODMAN, CHERYL; Brookville HS; Brookville, IN; 46/200 VP Soph Cls; VP Jr Cls; Am Leg Aux Girls St; Drl Tm; Hon Rl; Quill & Scroll; Y-Teens; Ed Sch Nwsp; Rptr Sch Nwsp; Letter Trk; Indiana St Univ; Art.

GOODMAN, JAYNE; West Washington HS; Fredericksbg, IN; Cls Rep Frsh Cls; Cls Rep Soph Cls; Band; Drl Tm; Hon Rl; NHS; Stu Cncl; Yrbk; FFA; Pep Clb; Vincennes Univ; Horticulture.

GOODMAN, JUDY; Greensburg HS; Greensburg, IN; 45/209 Sec Jr Cls; Am Leg Aux Girls St; Chrs; Chrh Wkr; Cmnty Wkr; FCA; Girl Scts; Hon Rl; Mdrgl; Off Ade; Univ Of Evansville; Poli Sci.

GOODMAN, KENNETH C; Tippecanoe Valley HS; Mentone, IN; 2/180 Band; Chrs; Hon Rl; NHS; Sch Mus; Sch Pl; Stg Crw; Yth Flsp; Pres Y-Teens; Chmn Drama Clb; Le Tourneau Univ; Pre Med.

GOODMAN, LOUISE; Gladstone Area HS; Gladstone, MI; VP Frsh Cls; Pres Soph Cls; Pres Jr Cls; Chrh Wkr; Hon Rl; Off Ade; Quill & Scroll; Stg Crw; Rptr Sch Nwsp; Drama Clb; Univ Of Michigan; Pharmacy.

GOODMAN, MARK; Muskegon HS; Muskegon, MI; Hon Rl; NHS; PAVAS; Sch Pl; Drama Clb; Spn Clb; Letter Ten; Tmr; Ferris State Coll; Pharmacy.

GOODMAN, MARK; Goshen HS; Goshen, IN; Band; Sch Mus; Crs Cntry; Purdue Univ; Pharmacist.

GOODMAN, ROBERT A; Warren G Harding HS; Warren, OH; Cls Rep Frsh Cls; Cls Rep Soph Cls; Cl Rep Jr Cls; Am Leg Boys St; FCA; Hon Rl; Lit Mag; NHS; Stu Cncl; Ftbl;.

GOODMAN, SHARON; Bishop Gallagher HS; Detroit, MI; Chrh Wkr; Hon Rl; Hosp Ade;.

GOODNIGHT, KEVIN; Frankfort Sr HS; Frankfort, IN; 86/205 Boy Scts; Chrs; Chrh Wkr; MMM; Yth Flsp; Wrstlng; Tmr; Mas Awd; Pres Awd; Western Kentucky Univ; Music Comp.

GOODNITE, JUDY; Point Pleasant HS; Point Pleasant, WV; 18/250 Cls Rep Frsh Cls; Sec Girl Scts; Hon Rl; NHS; Y-Teens; Rptr Yrbk; 4-H; Keyettes; Letter Scr Kpr; 4-H Awd; Home Ec Awd 76; 1 Of 4 Winner To Go To St Comptn To Model My Sewing 77; Top Winner St Comttn For Sewng 79; Univ; CPA.

GOODPASTER, CYNTHIA; Union HS; Economy, IN; Band; FHA; Pep Clb; Spn Clb; Letter Gym; Letter Chrldng; GAA; Twrlr; Art Schl; Cmmrcl Art.

GOODREAU, KRISTEN; Coldwater HS; Coldwater, MI; 5/300 Chrs; Mdrgl; Sec NHS; Sch Mus; Pep Clb; Letter Bsktbl; Letter Gym; GAA; IM Sprt; Michigan St Univ; Vet.

GOODREAU, LINDA; Franklin HS; Livonia, MI; Chrs; Hosp Ade; Ed Sch Nwsp; Rptr Sch Nwsp; College; Nurse.

GOODRICH, ANITA L; Walnut Hills HS; Cincinnati, OH; Sch Mus; Yth Flsp; Chrldng; Natl Merit SF; Chem Pre Med.

GOODRICH, DARCI; Danville Community HS; Santa Fe, NM; FCA; Quill & Scroll; Sprt Ed Yrbk; Capt Trk; College.

GOODRICH, DEBRA; Chagrin Falls HS; Chagrin Falls, OH; Girl Scts; Hon Rl; Sprt Ed Sch Nwsp; Gym; Chrldng; Mat Maids; PPFtbl; Hillsdale College.

GOODRICH, PATRICIA; Harbor Springs HS; Harbor Springs, MI; Girl Scts; Hon Rl; Lbry Ade; Yrbk; Northern Michigan Univ.

GOODRID, LINDA; Pike Central HS; Petersburg, IN; 16/192 Hon Rl; Lbry Ade; NHS; FHA;.

GOODWILL, RICHARD; Washington HS; Massillon, OH; 82/492 AFS; Chrh Wkr; Hon Rl; NHS; VP Yth Flsp; Sci Clb; Bowling Green Univ; Comp Sci.

GOODWILLIE, ROBERT; Grandview Heights HS; Columbus, OH; Boy Scts; Chrh Wkr; Ftbl; Letter Trk; Brigham Young Univ; Tech Illistrator.

GOODWIN, ANNE; Kingswood HS; Birmingham, MI; Cls Rep Soph Cls; Cl Rep Jr Cls; Pres Sr Cls; Hon Rl; Hosp Ade; Jr NHS; Mdrgl; Sch Mus; Sch Pl; Sch Nwsp; College; Med.

GOODWIN, BERNADETTE; Father J Wehrle Memorial HS; Columbus, OH; 28/115 Hon Rl; NHS; Technical College; Animal Husbandry.

GOODWIN, DEBORAH; Western HS; Detroit, MI; Band; Hon Rl; NHS; DECA; Chrldng; Mic State; Acctg.

GOODWIN, MARK; George Washington HS; Charleston, WV; Band; Hon Rl; Mod UN; Sct Actv; Univ; Hstry.

GOODWIN, R; Snyder HS; Ft Wayne, IN; 150/565 CAP; Hon Rl; Letter Ftbl; Trk; Univ Of South Carolina; Marine Sci.

GOODWIN, REGINALD; Cass Technical HS; Detroit, MI; Boy Scts; Chrs; Hon Rl; Sct Actv; Boys Clb Am; Letter Ftbl; IM Sprt; College; Elec.

GOODWIN, ROBERT; Bishop Dwenger HS; Ft Wayne, IN; Band; Boy Scts; Chrs; Chrh Wkr; Orch; Sch Mus; Ivy Tech Voc Schl.

GOODWIN, STEVEN; Warren Ctrl HS; Indianapolis, IN; Boy Scts; Chrs; Sct Actv; Yth Flsp; Sci Clb; Letter Gym; Purdue Univ; Forestry.

GOODWIN, THOMAS; Liberty Benton HS; Mc Comb, OH; Cls Rep Sr Cls; Aud/Vis; Boy Scts; Hon Rl; NHS; Sch Mus; Stu Cncl; Yrbk; Letter Crs Cntry; Letter Trk; Bowling Green St Univ; Communication.

GOODYEAR, DAVID; Flint Southwestern Cmnty HS; Flint, MI; Band; NHS; Orch; Sct Actv; Ferris St Coll; Pharm.

GOOLSBY, DARRELL; Southeastern HS; Detroit, MI; 2/255 Sal; Aud/Vis; Band; Hon Rl; NHS; Stg Crw; Cit Awd; Pres Awd; The Detroit Police Depart Yth Awd 79; The Region 8 Brd Of Ed Awd 79; Pres Of First Engr Club In Det Schl 79; Cntr For Creative Studies; Inds Dsgn.

GOOLSBY, DEREK; Patterson Cooperative HS; Dayton, OH; Boy Scts; Boys Clb Am; Wv Inst Of Tech; Draftsman.

GOOLSBY, ROSALYN; Scott HS; Toledo, OH; Cl Rep Jr Cls; Hon Rl; Jr NHS; Off Ade; Stu Cncl; College; Sec.

GOOLSBY, SARAH; Union HS; Losantville, IN; Hon Rl; Lbry Ade; NHS; Ed Yrbk; Rptr Yrbk; 4-H; FHA; Pep Clb; Voc Schl.

GOONEN, KATHY; Avon HS; Plainfld, IN; 15/192 Drl Tm; Hon Rl; Off Ade; Rptr Yrbk; VP Pep Clb; Spn Clb; Bsktbl; Letter Trk; Pom Pon; Univ.

GOOSMAN, DAVID; Dunbar HS; Dunbar, WV; Aud/Vis; Band; Hon Rl; NHS; Orch; Sch Mus; VP Fr Clb; Mth Clb; Pep Clb; Wv St Univ; Restraunt Mgmt.

GOOTS, TINA; Notre Dame HS; Clarksburg, WV; FCA; Stg Crw; Bsktbl; IM Sprt; Fairmont St Univ; Comm Arts.

GORANSON, ANN; Mona Shores HS; Muskegon, MI; Chrh Wkr; Girl Scts; NHS; 4-H; 4-H Awd; Pres Awd; Mic State Univ; Med.

GORBETT, LISA; Brownstown Central HS; Freetown, IN; Trs Soph Cls; Band; Chrh Wkr; FTA; GAA; IM Sprt; Mgrs; Ball State; Social Studies.

GORBY, BARBARA; Tyler County HS; Middlebourne, WV; 2/97 Pres Frsh Cls; Cls Rep Soph Cls; Cl Rep Jr Cls; Sal; Band; Hon Rl; NHS; Sch Pl; Stu Cncl; Dnfth Awd; Fairmont St College; Nursing.

GORBY, DENISE; Crestview Local HS; New Waterford, OH; Hon Rl; Sch Mus; Sch Pl; Stg Crw; Drama Clb; Spn Clb; College; Cummunications.

GORBY, KATHY; Fairland HS; Proctorville, OH; 40/153 Band; Chrh Wkr; Hon Rl; Jr NHS; Yrbk; Mth Clb; Pep Clb; Bsbl; Bsktbl; 4-H Awd; Shawnee St Coll; Retail Mrktng.

GORBY, YURI; Brooke HS; Bethany, WV; 15/466 Chrs; FCA; Hon Rl; Mdrgl; NHS; Sch Mus; Stu Cncl; Yth Flsp; Drama Clb; 4-H; Bethany Coll; Marine Bio.

GORCZYCA, ROBERT; James Ford Rhodes HS; Cleveland, OH; Hon Rl; NHS; Ger Clb; IM Sprt; Univ; Math.

GORDAN, ELIAS; East Chicago Washington HS; East Chicago, IN; 1/292 Cls Rep Sr Cls; Val; Chrh Wkr; Debate Tm; Hon Rl; JA; NHS; Orch; Stu Cncl; FTA; Univ; Med.

GORDLEY, BETH; Brookville HS; Brookville, OH; 23/160 Cls Rep Frsh Cls; Cls Rep Soph Cls; Cl Rep Jr Cls; Cls Rep Sr Cls; Chrs; Hon Rl; NHS; Sch Mus; Stu Cncl; Rptr Yrbk; Ohio Inst Of Photography; Photog.

GORDON, BARBARA; Jonesville HS; Jonesville, MI; Band; Cmnty Wkr; Girl Scts; Hon Rl; Red Cr Ade; Sct Actv; Rptr Sch Nwsp; 4-H; Pep Clb; IM Sprt; Band Boosters Schorshp Music; Blue Lake Fine Arts Schlrshp; Individualized Reading Awd Pin; N Carolina Schl Of Arts; Music.

GORDON, BONNIE; Central Catholic HS; Wheeling, WV; 3/140 Cl Rep Jr Cls; Hon Rl; NHS; Sch Mus; Sch Pl; Stg Crw; Stu Cncl; Drama Clb; Wheeling Coll; Education.

GORDON, BRIAN; Bethesda Christian HS; Lebanon, IN; Chrs; Chrh Wkr; Hon Rl; Yth Flsp; 4-H; Sci Clb; Letter Bsbl; Letter Bsktbl; 4-H Awd; Wabash Univ; Sci.

GORDON, BRIAN; Wheeling Cntrl Catholic HS; Wheeling, WV; 11/140 Cls Rep Soph Cls; Cl Rep Jr Cls; Chrh Wkr; Hon Rl; NHS; Sch Mus; Sch Pl; Stg Crw; Stu Cncl; Drama Clb; Wheeling Coll; Communications.

GORDON, CHERYL L; Ontario HS; Mansfield, OH; 6/200 Hon Rl; NHS; Spn Clb; Bsktbl; Scr Kpr; Am Leg Awd; Natl Merit Ltr; Natl Merit SF; Univ; English.

GORDON, CHRISTINE; Wayne HS; Ft Wayne, IN; Orch; Coop Off Educ 1979; Outstanding Coe Awd 1979; Perf Attndnc Awd 1977 & 1978; Purdue Univ; Bus.

GORDON, D; Elmhurst HS; Ft Wayne, IN; 18/413 AFS; Letter Band; Hon Rl; Yrbk; PPFtbl; Univ; Interior Dsgn.

GORDON, DARYL M; Euclid Sr HS; Euclid, OH; 47/746 Debate Tm; Hon Rl; NHS; Rptr Yrbk; FDA; Natl Merit Ltr; Univ; Bio.

GORDON, DIANA; Chelsea HS; Chelsea, MI; Chrs; Hon Rl; Sch Nwsp; Mich Univ; Social Work.

GORDON, DON; Wadsworth Sr HS; Wadsworth, OH; 116/349 VP Sr Cls; Stu Cncl; Key Clb; Spn Clb; Wrstlng; SAR Awd; Univ.

GORDON, DORINDA; Wayne HS; Dayton, OH; Sec Sr Cls; Treas Chrs; Girl Scts; PAVAS; Sch Pl; Stu Cncl; N W Jr HS Achvmtn In Soc Std Awd 76; Foldsingers Sweethert Awd 76; Notre Dame Schsl Cls Fvrt Awd 77; Univ; Soc Work.

GORDON, GLENN; Grand Haven HS; Grand Haven, MI; Band; Chrs; Chrh Wkr; Hon Rl; Jr NHS; NHS; Yth Flsp; College.

GORDON, KEITH; Van Wert HS; Van Wert, OH; 15/280 Trs Jr Cls; Pres Sr Cls; Chrs; Hon Rl; Sprt Ed Yrbk; Lat Clb; Spn Clb; Letter Bsktbl; Letter Glf; Rotary Awd; Univ; Dent.

GORDON, LINNE; Quincy HS; Quincy, MI; Hon Rl; Off Ade; 4-H; Fr Clb; Trk; Chrldng; 4-H Awd; W Michigan Univ; Acctg.

GORDON, LORI L; North Putnam Jr Sr HS; Roachdale, IN; Band; FHA; OEA; Pep Clb; Bsktbl; GAA; Exec Diplomat Sateswoman & Ambassador Awds OEA 78; Pblc Rltns.

GORDON, RAE JEAN; Cuyahoga Vlly Christian Acad; Akron, OH; 5/68 Chrh Wkr; Hon Rl; Rptr Yrbk; Letter Hockey; Univ; Phys Ther.

GORDON, RODNEY; Federal Hocking HS; Coolville, OH; Trs Jr Cls; Hon Rl; Sprt Ed Yrbk; Spn Clb; Bsktbl; Letter Ftbl; Trk; Univ.

GORDON, SHERI; Pittsford Area HS; Osseo, MI; VP Frsh Cls; Pres Soph Cls; Cl Rep Jr Cls; Band; Hon Rl; Lbry Ade; NHS; Off Ade; Sch Pl; Stu Cncl; Ferris St Coll; Lab Tech.

GORDON, SHERI; Pittsford HS; Osseo, MI; Pres Frsh Cls; Cls Rep Soph Cls; Cl Rep Jr Cls; Band; Hon Rl; Lbry Ade; NHS; Ferris State College; Lab Tech.

GORDON, SHERMAN; Sandusky HS; Sandusky, OH; JA; Yrbk; 4-H; Trk; Wrstlng; JC Awd; Ohio State Univ; Tech Drawing.

GORDON, SHERRY; Dowagiac Union HS; Dowagiac, MI; Cls Rep Sr Cls; Band; Chrh Wkr; Hon Rl; NHS; Stu Cncl; Drama Clb; 4-H; 4-H Awd; Sw Mich College.

GORDON, STEPHEN; Zionsville Comm HS; Zionsville, IN; 7/148 Chrh Wkr; FCA; Hon Rl; Stg Crw; Y-Teens; 4-H; VP Spn Clb; Trk; Am Leg Awd; JC Awd; General Motors Inst; Mech Engr.

GORDON, TERRANCE G; South Spencer HS; Rockport, IN; 45/145 Boy Scts; Chrh Wkr; Cmnty Wkr; Hon Rl; Sct Actv; Pres Yth Flsp; Letter Crs Cntry; Letter Trk; Letter Mgrs; Univ.

GORDON, THOMAS; St Edwards HS; N Olmsted, OH; 253/400 Cls Rep Frsh Cls; Cls Rep Soph Cls; Cl Rep Jr Cls; Cmnty Wkr; Debate Tm; FCA; Stu Cncl; Rptr Yrbk; Spn Clb; Ftbl; Kent St Oh Trainers Prog 79; Volntr Psychiatric Inst 79; Bay Village Trianers Prog 78; Notre Dame Univ; Bus.

GORDON, THOMAS; Clarence M Kimball HS; Royal Oak, MI; Hon Rl; Ger Clb; IM Sprt; Univ; Bus.

GORE, JEFF; Richmond Sr HS; Richmond, IN; 72/565 Hon Rl; Jr NHS; Sch Pl; Treas Spn Clb; Letter Ten; Trk; PPFtbl; Univ; Dentistry.

GORE, NATALIE; Arsenal Technical HS; Indianapolis, IN; Am Leg Aux Girls St; Hon Rl; Lbry Ade; Natl Forn Lg; Off Ade; Drama Clb; Treas Ger Clb; Key Clb; Mgrs; Cit Awd; German Awd 77 & 78; Math Awd 78; Howard Univ; Pre Med.

GORENC, DEBORAH; Bedford HS; Bedford, OH; Chrs; Hon Rl; Hosp Ade; NHS; Sch Pl; Drama Clb; Spn Clb; Dyke College.

GOREY, KELLY; Bexley HS; Bexley, OH; 55/186 Cl Rep Jr Cls; Drl Tm; Hon Rl; Sch Mus; Yrbk; Fr Clb; Rus Clb; Swmmng; Pom Pon; Miami Univ; Political Science.

GORGAS, CAROL; Bay HS; Bay Vill, OH; Band; Chrh Wkr; Drm Bgl; Girl Scts; Orch; Sch Mus; Yth Flsp; Pep Clb; Letter Trk; Scr Kpr; Univ.

GORGAS, STEVEN; Churchill HS; Livonia, MI; Cls Rep Sr Cls; Boy Scts; Cmnty Wkr; ROTC; Sct Actv; Sci Clb; Letter Swmmng; Tmr; Michigan St Univ; Engr.

GORGES, SUZANNE; Loveland Horst HS; Loveland, OH; Hon Rl; NHS; Fr Clb; Pep Clb; Silver Schlrshp Pin 78 & 79; Univ.

GORGONIO, SUZANNE C; Notre Dame HS; Clarksburg, WV; 13/53 Chrs; Chrh Wkr; Cmnty Wkr; NHS; Off Ade; Fr Clb; Mth Clb; Pep Clb; Bsktbl; IM Sprt; 2nd Pl WV St Ability Counts Essay Contest 1979; Honorable Mention All County In Girls Basktbl 1978; Fairmont St Coll.

GORHAM, DENISE; Clearview HS; Lorain, OH; VP Sr Cls; Cls Rep Sr Cls; Band; Chrh Wkr; Hon Rl; JA; NHS; Orch; Yrbk; Bsktbl; Ohio Univ; Radio TV Communications.

GORHAM, ELIZABETH; Goshen HS; Goshen, IN; 43/270 Pres Frsh Cls; Cls Rep Soph Cls; Cl Rep Jr Cls; Band; Hon Rl; NHS; Natl Forn Lg; Stu Cncl; Rptr Yrbk; Pep Clb; Purdue Univ; Nursing.

GORJANC, CATHY; Lake Catholic HS; Mntr, OH; Band; Hon Rl; Rptr Yrbk; Letter Bsbl; Letter Bsktbl; PPFtbl; Coll; Acctg.

GORKOWSKI, CATHY; De Vilbiss HS; Toledo, OH; 1/400 Sec Jr Cls; Cl Rep Jr Cls; Chrs; Chrh Wkr; Girl Scts; Hon Rl; Lbry Ade; Quill & Scroll; Ed Yrbk; Yrbk; Univ; Bus.

GORMAN, CYNTHIA; Akron E HS; Akron, OH; Band; Chrs; Girl Scts; Lbry Ade; Off Ade; Yrbk; Pep Clb; Akron Univ.

GORMLEY, MAURA; John F Kennedy HS; Warren, OH; 55/180 Cls Rep Soph Cls; Chrh Wkr; Hon Rl; JA; Red Cr Ade; Stu Cncl; Fr Clb; Pep Clb; Bsktbl; College; Social Welfare.

GORNEY, GREGORY; Saint Francis De Sales HS; Toledo, OH; 49/193 Hon Rl; Sch Mus; Rptr Sch Nwsp; Letter Swmmng; IM Sprt; College; Journalism.

GORNIE, BERNADETTE; Grosse Pointe North HS; Grosse Pt Wds, MI; Chrh Wkr; Hon Rl; Ctr For Creative Studies; Art.

GORNOWICZ, LAURA; Ubly HS; Ubly, MI; Hon Rl; Hosp Ade; NHS; Off Ade; Stg Crw; Rptr Yrbk; Yrbk; Mgrs; Univ; RN.

GORNY, KATHLEEN; T Roosevelt HS; E Chiacgo, IN; 7/196 Chrs; Univ.

GORONZY, TAMY; Mt Vernon Acad; Mt Vernon, OH; Cls Rep Frsh Cls; Cls Rep Soph Cls; Sec Jr Cls; Trs Jr Cls; Hon Rl; JA; Gym; JA Awd; Pres Awd; Kettering Med Coll; Nursing.

GORRELL, LISA; Strongsville HS; Zionsville, IN; Girl Scts; Hon Rl; Hosp Ade; Jr NHS; NHS; Red Cr Ade; Rptr Sch Nwsp; Lat Clb; Pres Sci Clb; Butler Univ; Phys.

GORRELL, ROBIN; Washington Irving HS; Clarksburg, WV; 3/161 Cls Rep Frsh Cls; Chrh Wkr; FCA; Hon Rl; NHS; Stg Crw; Yth Flsp; Lat Clb; Pep Clb; Univ; Bio.

GORSKI, JEFFREY; St Francis Desales HS; Toledo, OH; 55/200 Cls Rep Frsh Cls; Hon Rl; Sch Nwsp; Capt Ftbl; Letter Trk; Capt Wrstlng; IM Sprt; Alternate Elite Freestyle Wrstlng Wrld Champ Team 78; 2nd Multi Sprt Jr Olympics 220 Lb Greco Roman Div 78; Univ; Bus.

GORSKI, JOSEPH; Cody HS; Detroit, MI; Hon Rl; Letter Bsbl; Bausch & Lomb Awd; Cert Of Tecgntn Fro Being Shlshp Comp 79; Awd Of Mert For Outstndng Achtn In Spansih 79; Michigan St Univ; Mech Engr.

GORSKI, RICHARD; Cardinal Mooney HS; Poland, OH; 83/274 Band; Chrh Wkr; Hon Rl; JA; Lbry Ade; Natl Forn Lg; Yth Flsp; Drama Clb; Spn Clb; Ohio St Univ; Law.

GORSUCH, LINDA; Corydon Central HS; Corydon, IN; 4/160 Am Leg Aux Girls St; Band; Drl Tm; Yth Flsp; Rptr Sch Nwsp; 4-H; Fr Clb; Pep Clb; Letter Ten; College.

GORSUCH, PAM; Carroll HS; Ft Wayne, IN; Cmp Fr Grls; Chrs; Chrh Wkr; Cmnty Wkr; Girl Scts; Hon Rl; Girl Scts; Jr NHS; NHS; Off Ade; Indiana Voc Tech Coll; Bus.

GORSUCH, PAMELA; Corydon Central HS; Corydon, IN; Band; Capt Drl Tm; NHS; Pres Yth Flsp; Drama Clb; Fr Clb; FTA; Pep Clb; Otterbein; Art Educ.

GORT, KATHY; Hudsonville HS; Hudsonville, MI; Chrh Wkr; FCA; Hon Rl; Off Ade; Pep Clb; Chrldng; Hon Cords 79; St Competitive Schlrshp 79; Bus Tchr Asst Sec 78; Bus Educ.

GORT, ROBERTA; Rockford Sr HS; Rockford, MI; 32/400 Band; Chrh Wkr; Hon Rl; NHS; 4-H; 4-H Awd; Natl Merit Ltr; Grand Rapids Jr Coll; RN.

GORTE, DAWN; Taylor Ctr HS; Taylor, MI; Girl Scts; Hon Rl; Lbry Ade; Off Ade; Bus Schl; Med Sec.

GORTON, CATHY; Britton Macon HS; Britton, MI; Hon Rl; Yrbk; Rptr Sch Nwsp; Bsbl; Bsktbl; Coll; Busns Mgmt.

GORTSEMA, DOUG; South Christian HS; Grand Rapids, MI; VP Frsh Cls; Trs Jr Cls; Band; Chrh Wkr; Debate Tm; Hon Rl; Jr NHS; NHS; Yth Flsp; Letter Ftbl; College; Meteorology.

GORWITZ, RACHEL; Interlochen Arts Academy; Oshkosh, WI; Orch; Fr Clb; Natl Merit Ltr; Music.

GORYL, MICHAEL; West Bloomfield HS; Orchard Lake, MI; 79/440 Hon Rl; IM Sprt; Mic State Univ; Mech Engr.

GORZELANCZYK, CHERYL; Lumen Cordium HS; Bedford, OH; Trs Sr Cls; Cmp Fr Grls; Drl Tm; Hon Rl; Sch Mus; Stu Cncl; GAA; IM Sprt; Univ; Soc.

GORZELANCZYK, CHESTER; Chanel HS; Bedford, OH; Cls Rep Sr Cls; Chrs; Hon Rl; NHS; Sch Mus; Ed Yrbk; IM Sprt; Miami Univ; Archt.

GOSHAY, MONICA; West Side Sr HS; Gary, IN; Band; Chrh Wkr; Cmnty Wkr; Girl Scts; Lbry Ade; Off Ade; Pep Clb; Mat Maids; Scr Kpr; Tmr; Univ; Math.

GOSHEN, JANETTA; John Hay HS; Cleveland, OH; Band; Chrs; Chrh Wkr; Drl Tm; Girl Scts; Off Ade; Stu Cncl; OEA; Cit Awd; Cleveland St Univ; Med Sec.

GOSHMAN, GRETCHEN; Vassar HS; Vassar, MI; 10/143 Trs Jr Cls; Band; Hon Rl; Natl Forn Lg; NHS; Ed Sch Nwsp; Drama Clb; Mic State Univ; Music Therapy.

GOSHORN, MARK; Alma HS; Alma, MI; 60/256 Michigan Comp Schlrshp; Cntrl Michigan Univ; Busns Admin.

GOSLEE, MICHAEL; North Posey Sr HS; Poseyville, IN; 19/162 Hon Rl; NHS; Pep Clb; Letter Ftbl; IM Sprt; Univ; Aero.

GOSLIN, DUANE; Unionville Sebewaing HS; Unionville, MI; Aud/Vis; Band; Cmnty Wkr; Hon Rl; Letter Crs Cntry; Letter Trk; Coach Actv; Ferris St Coll; Archt Drafting.

GOSS, DIANA J; Eastern HS; Salem, IN; Chrs; Chrh Wkr; Hon Rl; NHS; Sch Mus; Pep Clb; Indiana Univ; Bus.

GOSS, GUY; A D Johnston HS; Bessemer, MI; Am Leg Boys St; Hon Rl; Ftbl; Trk; IM Sprt; Am Leg Awd; College; Law.

GOSSARD, PAIGE; Allen East HS; Harrod, OH; Cl Rep Jr Cls; Chrs; Sch Mus; Stu Cncl; Rptr Yrbk; Yrbk; Rptr Sch Nwsp; Pres 4-H;.

GOSSETT, DEAN; Oscar A Carlson HS; Rockwood, MI; 6/236 Hon Rl; NHS; FTA; Crs Cntry; Coach Actv; Natl Merit Schl; Minerals Indust Educ Foundtn Schlrshp 79; Otstndng Sci & Soc Studies Stud 75 79; Manga Cum Laude Grad 79; Michigan Tech Univ; Metal Engr.

GOSSETT, RANDI; Ben Davis HS; Indianapolis, IN; 20/834 Sec Chrs; Chrh Wkr; Debate Tm; Hon Rl; Orch; Pol Wkr; Pom Pon; Anderson Coll; Spanish.

GOSSMAN, KAREN; New Albany HS; Westerville, OH; 2/92 Cls Rep Soph Cls; Cl Rep Jr Cls; Cls Rep Sr Cls; Band; NHS; Off Ade; Stu Cncl; 4-H; Ger Clb; Trk; Scholarship Awd; Business School; Legal Sec.

GOSSMAN, MARY; Bishop Borgess HS; Detroit, MI; 19/485 Hon Rl; NHS; Fr Clb; IM Sprt; Kalamazoo Coll; English.

GOSSWEILER, TIM; Brownsburg HS; Brownsburg, IN; Am Leg Boys St; NHS; Crs Cntry; Ten; IM Sprt; Pres Awd; Univ.

GOTCH, KATHRYN; Beavercreek HS; Xenia, OH; 38/702 FCA; Hon Rl; NHS; Sct Actv; Letter Ten; Letter Trk; IM Sprt; Scr Kpr; U S Air Force Prep Schl; Sci.

GOTCHALL, JOHN; Sandy Valley HS; Waynesburg, OH; Boy Scts; Chrh Wkr; FCA; Hon Rl; Lbry Ade; Sct Actv; Yth Flsp; VICA; Bsktbl; IM Sprt; Univ; Acctg.

GOTHA, MARY; Ida HS; Ida, MI; 38/159 Hon Rl; Monroe County Comm College.

GOTSCHALL, DAVID; Minerva HS; Minerva, OH; Band; Boy Scts; Hon Rl; NHS; Yth Flsp; Yrbk; Pres Lat Clb; Univ Of Cincinnati; Pre Med.

GOTSCHALL, JANESE; Minerva HS; Minerva, OH; 1/241 Sec Jr Cls; Am Leg Aux Girls St; Band; Chrh Wkr; Hon Rl; Hosp Ade; Yth Flsp; Lat Clb; Pep Clb; Vocational Schl; Nursing.

GOTSHALL, JAMES; East Canton HS; E Canton, OH; Hon Rl; Jr NHS; NHS; Sch Pl; Drama Clb; Bsktbl; Coach Actv; IM Sprt; Scr Kpr; Tmr; Math.

GOTTBERG, MATTHEW; David Anderson HS; Lisbon, OH; Chrs; Hon Rl; Sch Mus; Stg Crw; Ftbl; Ohio St Univ; Agri.

GOTTCHALK, BETTY; Brown City HS; Brown City, MI; 22/89 Band; Chrh Wkr; Hon Rl; Lbry Ade; Off Ade; Yth Flsp; 4-H; Fr Clb; FHA; Twrlr; Bus Schl; Med Sec.

GOTTFRIED, LYLE; Upper Sandusky HS; Upper Sandusky, OH; Band; Hon Rl; NHS; Stg Crw; Sec 4-H; Am Leg Awd; 4-H Awd; Tiffin Univ; Acctg.

GOTTLER, DAWN; Brandon HS; Oxford, MI; 6/220 Sec Jr Cls; VP Sr Cls; Band; Hon Rl; Lbry Ade; NHS; Gym; Trk; IM Sprt; Coll; Med.

GOTTLIEB, GAYLE; St Ursula Acad; Cincinnati, OH; Chrs; Hon Rl; Mod UN; Sch Pl; Fr Clb; College; Phys Ther.

GOTTMER, BARBARA; Lockland HS; Cincinnati, OH; 4/75 Drl Tm; Hon Rl; NHS; Stu Cncl; Univ; Nursing.

GOTTRON, JEFF; Fremont St Joseph Cath HS; Fremont, OH; Cls Rep Frsh Cls; Cls Rep Soph Cls; Cl Rep Jr Cls; Cls Rep Sr Cls; Chrh Wkr; Jr NHS; NHS; Stu Cncl; Key Clb; Bsbl; College; Dentistry.

GOTTRON, JON; Fremont Ross HS; Fremont, OH; Cls Rep Sr Cls; Boy Scts; Chrh Wkr; Cmnty Wkr; Hon Rl; Mod UN; Quill & Scroll; Red Cr Ade; Sct Actv; Rptr Yrbk; Ball St Univ; Elem Ed.

GOTTSCHALK, ELLEN; Thomas A Devilbiss HS; Toledo, OH; 9/320 Girl Scts; Hon Rl; Pres Jr NHS; NHS; Off Ade; Pol Wkr; Ger Clb; Awd Of Merit For Outstndng Achvmnt In German; 11th In Ohio Test Of Schlstc Achvmnt In Bowling Green St Univ; College; Foreign Language.

GOTTSCHALK, INGO; Zeeland HS; Hudsonville, MI; Band; Hon Rl; Jr NHS; Wrstlng; Univ.

GOTTSCHALK, NANCY; Harrison HS; Farmington Hs, MI; 73/367 Cls Rep Frsh Cls; Sec Soph Cls; Cls Rep Soph Cls; Sec Jr Cls; Hon Rl; Jr NHS; NHS; Ger Clb; Twrlr; Natl Merit SF; Western Mich Univ; Psych.

GOTTSCHALT, PENNIE; Scecina Memorial HS; Indinapolis, IN; Chrs; Hon Rl; NHS; Pol Wkr; Sch Mus; Yrbk;.

GOTTSCHE, JULIE; Central HS; Switz City, IN; 1/27 Sec Frsh Cls; Trs Soph Cls; Chrs; Hon Rl; NHS; Orch; Sec Pep Clb; Letter Bsktbl; Indiana St Univ; Phys Educ.

GOTTSHALL, MICHAEL; Timken Sr HS; Canton, OH; Boy Scts; Hon Rl; OEA; Am Leg Awd; Kent St Univ; Law Enforcement.

GOUBEAUX, MICHAEL; Harmon Drive HS; Greenville, OH; 4/320 Hon Rl; Jr NHS; NHS; Sch Pl; Drama Clb; Spn Clb; Natl Merit SF; Miami Univ; Chem Engr.

GOUBEAUX, MIKE; Russia Local HS; Versailles, OH; 12/34 Hon Rl; Sch Pl; Sdlty; Stg Crw; Stu Cncl; Sci Clb; Dnfth Awd; Ohio Northern Univ; Med.

GOUDREAU, MARY; Manistique HS; Gulliver, MI; VP Frsh Cls; Drm Mjrt; Hon Rl; Natl Forn Lg; Rptr Sch Nwsp; Capt Bsktbl; Trk; Mgrs; Twrlr; Natl Merit SF; Northern Michigan Univ; Elem Ed.

GOUER, PAMELA; Philip Barbour HS; Philippi, WV; 50/200 Band; Chrs; Chrh Wkr; Hon Rl; Sec 4-H; Sec FFA; VICA; Letter Bsktbl; Letter Trk; Mat Maids; Equestrian Tm High Point Eng Hunt Seat Awd; Jr Bowling High Game; Potomac St Coll; Agri.

GOUGH, AUSTIN R; Licking Cnty Joint Voc HS; Newark, OH; Am Leg Boys St; Hon Rl; VP VICA; Am Leg Awd; Lincoln Tech; Auto Mech.

GOUGH, GARY R; Hubbard HS; Hubbard, OH; 22/330 Hon Rl; Key Clb; College; Math.

GOUGH, JAMES; Connersville HS; Connersville, IN; 6/400 Am Leg Boys St; Hon Rl; Jr NHS; NHS; Y-Teens; Civ Clb; Pep Clb; Spn Clb; Ftbl; IM Sprt; Ind Univ; Optometry.

GOUGH, ROBERT; Carsonville Port Sanilac HS; Applegate, MI; Band; Chrh Wkr; Hon Rl; NHS; PAVAS; Stu Cncl; Ed Yrbk; Rptr Sch Nwsp; Drama Clb; Mic State Univ; Studio Art.

GOULD, DWAYNE; Rogers Sr HS; Michigan City, IN; 57/508 Cl Rep Jr Cls; Band; Hon Rl; Jr NHS; NHS; Off Ade; Stu Cncl; VICA; Natl Merit Schl; PNC; Archt.

GOULD, GREGORY; Whitmer Sr HS; Toledo, OH; Boy Scts; Hon Rl; JA; Jr NHS; Spn Clb; Mbr Of Spanish Hon Society 78; Cert Of Part Awd In Atlantic Pacific 78; Annual Math Contest Of Ohio Cncl; Ball St Univ; Engr.

GOULD, MARTHA; Northwestern HS; Polk, OH; 15/160 Chrs; Hon Rl; Sch Pl; Stg Crw; Drama Clb; Pres 4-H; Pres FHA; FTA; Lat Clb; 4-H Awd; Busns Schl.

GOULD, SANDY; Grandview Hts HS; Columbus, OH; Drl Tm; Capt Bsktbl; Chrldng; Univ.

GOULDING, GREG; Yale HS; Yale, MI; 87/160 Cls Rep Sr Cls; Hon Rl; Sct Actv; Stu Cncl; Bsktbl; Ftbl; Trk;.

GOULDING, JAMES; Otsego HS; Otsego, MI; Boy Scts; Cmnty Wkr; Hon Rl; Lat Clb; Pep Clb; Spn Clb; Ftbl; Trk; Scr Kpr; Tmr; Michigan St Univ; Comp Sci.

GOULDSHERRY, ALICE; David Anderson HS; Columbiana, OH; 22/100 Cmp Fr Grls; Hon Rl; Off Ade; Sch Mus; Trs Soph Cls; Rptr Sch Nwsp; Pres Soph Cls; Cls Rep Frsh Cls; Bsktbl; Letter Trk; Mbr Of 5 Mbr Bio Olymp Tm 79; Awd Of Dstnghsd St Bd Of Educ Crs Of Basic Std 79; Sr Hon Awd 79; Hiram Univ; Pre Med.

GOULET, BRIGETTE; John Carroll HS; Fairborn, OH; 11/285 Chrh Wkr; Hon Rl; Jr NHS; Stu Cncl; Drama Clb; Ger Clb; Key Clb; IM Sprt; Mgrs; College; Acctg.

GOULET, MARK; Bay City Western HS; Kawkawlin, MI; 10/438 Band; Hon Rl; NHS; Delta Coll; Pharm.

GOULET, MIKE; Western HS; Kawkawlin, MI; 14/438 Band; Hon Rl; NHS; IM Sprt; Western Michigan Univ; Sci.

GOULET, RUSSELL; Clay HS; Oregon, OH; 60/340 Boy Scts; NHS; Pres Yth Flsp; Sprt Ed Yrbk; Sprt Ed Sch Nwsp; College; Journalism.

GOUNDRILL, DALE; High School; Battle Crk, MI; Band; Boy Scts; Work.

GOURDIE, CHERYL; Traverse City HS; Traverse City, MI; Hon Rl; NHS; Pres Orch; Sch Mus; Pep Clb; Mich State Univ; Civil Engr.

GOURDOUZE, LORI; Terre Haute North Vigo HS; Terre Haute, IN; 33/700 Cls Rep Frsh Cls; Cls Rep Soph Cls; Sec Jr Cls; Cl Rep Jr Cls; Sec Sr Cls; Aud/Vis; Chrs; Drl Tm; Ind State; Elem Educ.

GOURLAY, TIM; Niles Sr HS; Niles, MI; Pres Frsh Cls; Cls Rep Soph Cls; Chrs; Cmnty Wkr; Hon Rl; Sch Mus; Sch Pl; Stu Cncl; Letter Bsbl; Letter Bsktbl; Ftbl Plyr Of Week 77 & 78; Outstng Male Stdnt 77; Univ.

GOVITZ, LORI; Beaverton HS; Beaverton, MI; 11/154 Sec Frsh Cls; Sec Soph Cls; Sec Jr Cls; Sec Sr Cls; Cls Rep Sr Cls; Girl Scts; Hon Rl; NHS; Sct Actv; Stu Cncl; Mid Michigan Cmnty Coll; Comp Sci.

GOWER, DENISE; Coalton HS; Ellamore, WV; 7/33 Band; Chrh Wkr; Drm Mjrt; Hon Rl; NHS; Off Ade; Ed Yrbk; 4-H; Letter Bsktbl; 4-H Awd; Fairmont St Coll; Educ.

GOWRIGHT, TANYA J; Middletown HS; Middletown, OH; 182/500 Cl Rep Jr Cls; Band; Chrs; Chrh Wkr; Cmnty Wkr; Drl Tm; Girl Scts; Hon Rl; Sch Pl; Stu Cncl; Central St Univ; Child Devplmnt Tech.

GOYMERAC, JAMES; Escanaba Area Public HS; Wells, MI; 50/442 Chrh Wkr; Hon Rl; NHS; Bsktbl; Ftbl; Letter Trk; IM Sprt; Mich Tech Univ; Elec Engr.

GRABB, CHRISTA; Bishop Flaget HS; Chillicothe, OH; 5/37 Girl Scts; Hon Rl; NHS; Sch Pl; Treas Fr Clb; Spn Clb; Scr Kpr; DAR Awd; Univ Of Cincinnati; Criminal Justice.

GRABER, BOB; Barr Reeve HS; Cannelburg, IN; Cls Rep Frsh Cls; Cls Rep Soph Cls; Cl Rep Jr Cls; Hon Rl; Stu Cncl; FFA; Bsbl; Bsktbl; Glf; Perfct Attndnc 68 77; Purdue Univ; Archt Engr.

GRABER, BRET N; Barr Reeve HS; Montgomery, IN; 20/49 Band; Chrh Wkr; Cmnty Wkr; Hon Rl; Sch Mus; Sch Pl; Yth Flsp; Rptr Sch Nwsp; Eng Clb; Fr Clb; Bnd Awd For Being Bst Jr Drmmr 78; Prom Prince 78; Indiana St Univ; Bsbl.

GRABER, KIM; Northrop HS; Ft Wayne, IN; 79/587 FCA; Hon Rl; Treas JA; Gym; Trk; Chrldng; Purdue Univ; Phys Ed.

GRABER, MARK; Rittman HS; Rittman, OH; 18/118 Hon Rl; Bsbl; Bsktbl; Ftbl; Scr Kpr; Tmr; Muskingum Coll; Busns Mgmt.

GRABER, TERRY; Jonathon Alder HS; Plain City, OH; 11/99 Pres Frsh Cls; Cl Rep Jr Cls; Am Leg Boys St; Hon Rl; NHS; Pres Stu Cncl; Pres FFA; Letter Bsbl; Letter Ftbl; Bluffton College; CPA.

GRABHAM, JILL; Zionsville Community HS; Zionsville, IN; Cls Rep Frsh Cls; Cls Rep Soph Cls; Cl Rep Jr Cls; Chrs; FCA; Hon Rl; Sch Mus; Fr Clb; Chrldng; IM Sprt; Purdue Univ; Soc Wrkr.

GRABLE, K; Marshall HS; Marshall, MI; Am Leg Aux Girls St; Debate Tm; Hon Rl; Natl Forn Lg; Sch Mus; Stg Crw; 4-H; Fr Clb; Jones Madison Resid College; Law.

GRABNER, D; Heritage HS; Ft Wayne, IN; 34/177 Hon Rl; Letter Ftbl; Letter Glf; College; Mech Engr.

GRABNER, L; Bishop Watterson HS; Columbus, OH; Cmp Fr Grls; Chrh Wkr; Hon Rl; NHS; Sct Actv; Bsktbl; Ohi State Univ; Languages.

GRABOW, PENNY; New Haven HS; Mt Clemens, MI; Hon Rl; Lbry Ade; 4-H; 4-H Awd; Natl Merit Schl; Macomb Comm Coll; Nursing.

GRACE, BOU Y; Brooklyn HS; Brooklyn, OH; Chrs; Girl Scts; Fr Clb; Bsktbl; Gym; Swmmng; Ten; Trk; Tri C Univ; Interior Dsgn.

GRACE, EDWIN K; Jesup W Scott HS; Toledo, OH; 5/200 Band; Chrs; Chrh Wkr; Hon Rl; NHS; Orch; Sch Pl; Treas Stu Cncl; Boys Clb Am; Fr Clb; College; Music.

GRACE, JEFF; South Range HS; Columbiana, OH; Cls Rep Soph Cls; Cls Rep Sr Cls; Am Leg Boys St; Hon Rl; NHS; Stu Cncl; Letter Crs Cntry; Letter Trk; Coll; Law.

GRACE, KATHLEEN; Yale HS; Emmett, MI; 2/180 Val; Chrs; Chrh Wkr; Hon Rl; NHS; Off Ade; 4-H; Spn Clb; IM Sprt; 4-H Awd; John Carroll Univ; Bus.

GRACZYK, JENNIFER; Clay HS; Granger, IN; 147/382 Off Ade; Quill & Scroll; Rptr Sch Nwsp; Sch Nwsp; Bsktbl; Swmmng; Capt Trk; Indiana Univ.

GRADER, AMY; Northside HS; Muncie, IN; Am Leg Aux Girls St; Debate Tm; Hon Rl; Hosp Ade; NHS; Stu Cncl; 4-H; Lat Clb; Mth Clb; Sci Clb; Purdue Univ; Chem Engr.

GRADERT, MARK; Maple Hts Sr HS; Maple Hgts, OH; Band; Bsbl; Bsktbl; Vet.

GRADISEK, E; Lorain Catholic HS; Lorain, OH; Hon Rl; Ed Yrbk; Sprt Ed Yrbk; Rptr Yrbk; Yrbk; Sch Nwsp; FDA; IM Sprt; PPFtbl; Ohio State; Pre Veterinary Med.

GRADY, EILEEN; St Joseph Acad; N Olmsted, OH; Cls Rep Frsh Cls; Cls Rep Soph Cls; VP Jr Cls; Hon Rl; Hosp Ade; NHS; Stu Cncl; Rptr Yrbk; Fr Clb; Bsbl; Univ; Nursing.

GRADY, PHILIP L; Solon HS; Solon, OH; Band; Chrs; Hon Rl; MMM; Orch; Pol Wkr; Sct Actv; 4-H; Treas OEA; 4-H Awd; Top 10 Awrd Forestry Cmp; All Ohio St Fair Bnd; Advanced Math & Sci Prgrms; John Carroll Univ; Cpa.

GRADY, SHELLIE; Sault Area HS; Slt Ste Marie, MI; Cls Rep Frsh Cls; Cls Rep Soph Cls; VP Chrs; Hon Rl; Stu Cncl; Mth Clb; Spn Clb; Lake Superior State Coll; Elem Educ.

GRAEBERT, PAUL; Carl Brablec HS; Roseville, MI; 72/398 Hon Rl; Adrian Coll; Earth Sci.

GRAEF, GRETCHEN; Oakwood HS; Dayton, OH; AFS; Chrs; Cmnty Wkr; FCA; Hon Rl; JA; NHS; Off Ade; Sch Mus; Sch Pl; Univ; Dietetics.

GRAESSLE, VINCENT; Bishop Ready HS; Columbus, OH; Val; Am Leg Boys St; Hon Rl; NHS; Pol Wkr; Stg Crw; Stu Cncl; Bsbl; Wake Forest Univ; Dentistry.

GRAF, BART; Wauseon HS; Wauseon, OH; 10/150 VP Frsh Cls; VP Jr Cls; Am Leg Boys St; FCA; Hon Rl; NHS; Stu Cncl; College; Engr.

GRAFFIN, ERICA S; Port Clinton HS; Pt Clinton, OH; Band; Chrh Wkr; Cmnty Wkr; Lbry Ade; Off Ade; Yth Flsp; FHA; Pep Clb; Crs Cntry; Trk;.

GRAFFIUS, JUDY; Canfield HS; Canfield, OH; Cls Rep Soph Cls; Cl Rep Jr Cls; Hon Rl; Stu Cncl; Y-Teens; Fr Clb; Ger Clb; GAA; Ohio St Univ; Sci.

GRAFTON, ELLEN; Jefferson Union HS; Steubenville, OH; 1/145 Am Leg Aux Girls St; Band; Chrh Wkr; Hon Rl; Jr NHS; Orch; Stu Cncl; Rptr Sch Nwsp; Beta Clb; Ohio Valley Schl Of Nursing; Nurse.

GRAFTON, LAURIE; Celina HS; Celina, OH; Hon Rl; Off Ade; 4-H; Cit Awd;.

GRAGIDO, JACQUELINE; Kankakee Valley HS; Wheatfield, IN; 5/125 Pres Jr Cls; Band; Drm Bgl; Drm Mjrt; Hon Rl; NHS; Sch Pl; 4-H; Pep Clb; Sci Clb; Otstndng Jr Band Mbr 79; Otstndng 2nd Yr Spanish Stud 78; Math Achvmnt Awds 75 78; Valparaiso Univ; Med Tech.

GRAHAM, ALICE J; Southern Wells Jr Sr HS; Keystone, IN; 10/96 Trs Soph Cls; Chrh Wkr; Hon Rl; NHS; Y-Teens; 4-H; Key Clb; Spn Clb; 4 H Tenure Awd Cnty Record Book Awd; Home Furnishing Awd; Soc Dstngshd Amer HS Stu; Bible College ; Busns Ed.

GRAHAM, BETTY; Bishop Ready HS; Columbus, OH; Cmnty Wkr; Hon Rl; Spn Clb; Coach Actv; IM Sprt; Mat Maids; Ohio St Univ; Phys Ther.

GRAHAM, BRENDA; University HS; Morgantown, WV; Chrs; Hon Rl; Jr NHS; Mdrgl; Sch Mus; Sch Pl; Stg Crw; Rptr Sch Nwsp; Drama Clb; FBLA; West Virginia Univ; Bus.

GRAHAM, BRENDA L; University HS; Albright, WV; Chrs; Hon Rl; Jr NHS; Mdrgl; NHS; Quill & Scroll; Rptr Sch Nwsp; Drama Clb; FBLA; Sci Clb; Wheeler Bus Schl; Exec Sec.

GRAHAM, CAROL; Charles F Kettering; Detroit, MI; Chrs; Chrh Wkr; Girl Scts; Hon Rl; Hosp Ade; JA; Jr NHS; Lbry Ade; Off Ade; Pep Clb; Mercey Schl Of Nursng; Nurse.

GRAHAM, CHERYL; Western HS; Kokomo, IN; Sec Band; Pres Chrs; Sec JA; Mdrgl; NHS; Stu Cncl; PPFtbl; Attended Jr Ach Midwest Conference; College; Social Work.

GRAHAM, CRYSTAL L; Lawrence County Jt Voc Schl; Chesapeake, OH; 14/129 Band; Hon Rl; NHS; Rptr Sch Nwsp; Sch Nwsp; 4-H; OEA;.

GRAHAM, CYNDEE; North HS; Timberlake, OH; Band; Chrs; Chrh Wkr; Cmnty Wkr; Girl Scts; 4-H; Swmmng; Coach Actv; Scr Kpr; 4-H Awd; Univ; Bio.

GRAHAM, DEBORAH; Pineville HS; Pineville, WV; Chrh Wkr; Hon Rl; Jr NHS; NHS; Pep Clb; Bus.

GRAHAM, DEBORAH B; Bellbrook HS; Bellbrook, OH; 6/158 Sec Soph Cls; Sec Sr Cls; Band; Chrh Wkr; Hon Rl; Mod UN; VP NHS; Sch Pl; Drama Clb; Lat Clb; Ohio Univ; Music Ed.

GRAHAM, DIANNE; Morgan HS; Mc Connelsville, OH; Trs Sr Cls; Am Leg Aux Girls St; Chrh Wkr; Hon Rl; Sec NHS; Off Ade; Drama Clb; 4-H; FTA; Sci Clb; Ohio St Univ; Educ.

GRAHAM, DION; Walnut Hills HS; Cincinnati, OH; Cls Rep Sr Cls; Capt Debate Tm; Sch Mus; Sch Pl; Pres Yth Flsp; Rptr Sch Nwsp; Pres Drama Clb; Miami Univ; Law.

GRAHAM, GENE; Williamston HS; Williamston, MI; Chrs; Hon Rl; Jr NHS; Off Ade; Stu Cncl; Rptr Sch Nwsp; 4-H; FFA; Mic State Univ; Agri.

GRAHAM, JACQUELINE; Hughes HS; Cincinnati, OH; FFA; Bsbl; Bsktbl;.

GRAHAM, JODI; Ursuline Acad; Cincinnati, OH; 50/108 Cls Rep Frsh Cls; Cmnty Wkr; Stu Cncl; Chrldng; College.

GRAHAM, JOHN; St Annes HS; Warren, MI; Cls Rep Frsh Cls; Cls Rep Soph Cls; Cl Rep Jr Cls; JA; Stg Crw; Stu Cncl; Yrbk; Letter Ten; JA Awd;.

GRAHAM, JOHN; St Ignatius HS; Hudson, OH; Chrh Wkr; Hon Rl; JA; Lit Mag; Rdo Clb; John Carroll; Accountant.

GRAHAM, JOHN; Tipton HS; Tipton, IN; 20/167 Cls Rep Frsh Cls; Cls Rep Soph Cls; VP Jr Cls; Cl Rep Jr Cls; Cls Rep Sr Cls; Treas Stu Cncl; Pres FBLA; Univ; Bus Admin.

GRAHAM, JULIANA; Bishop Hartley HS; Columbus, OH; 48/175 Cls Rep Frsh Cls; Sec Soph Cls; Sec Jr Cls; Cl Rep Jr Cls; Pres Sr Cls; Cls Rep Sr Cls; Girl Scts; Hon Rl; Hosp Ade; Pol Wkr; Nominted To Attend Girls St 78; Spirt Spreader For The Oh Assoc Of Stu Coun 78; 3rd Pl Homemkr Of Yr 79; Ohio Dominican Coll; Soc Sci.

GRAHAM, KATHLEEN J; St Francis De Sales HS; Columbus, OH; 19/189 Drl Tm; Hon Rl; Fr Clb; Univ Of Dayton; Comp Sci.

GRAHAM, LEEANNE; Marysville Sr HS; Marysville, OH; Chrs; Chrh Wkr; Cmnty Wkr; Girl Scts; Hon Rl; Hosp Ade; 4-H; Spn Clb; Coll; Comp Prog.

GRAHAM, LISA; Flushing Sr HS; Flushing, MI; Band; Chrh Wkr; Drl Tm; PAVAS; Yth Flsp; Twrlr; Coll; Fash Merch.

GRAHAM, LORI; St Louis HS; Alma, MI; 14/130 Band; Hon Rl; NHS; Sch Pl; Chrldng; Central Michigan Univ; Art.

GRAHAM, LORI; Matoaka HS; Rock, WV; 4/66 Am Leg Aux Girls St; Hon Rl; VP NHS; Off Ade; Pres Stu Cncl; Yrbk; Pres FHA; Pres Keyettes; Pep Clb; Bsktbl; Concord Univ; Elem Ed.

GRAHAM, MARK; A D Johnston HS; Bessemer, MI; College; Engineering.

GRAHAM, MARSHA; Portland HS; Winchester, KY; Lbry Ade; PPFtbl; DAR Awd; College; Business.

GRAHAM, MARY L; Archbishop Alter HS; Dayton, OH; Chrs; Hon Rl; NHS; Ed Sch Nwsp; GAA; IM Sprt; Ohio St Univ.

GRAHAM, MONICA D; Norwalk HS; Norwalk, OH; Trs Sr Cls; Chrs; Chrh Wkr; Hon Rl; 4-H; Bsktbl; Letter Trk; Outstndng HS Jr; Coll; Acctg.

GRAHAM, R; Frontier HS; New Matamoras, OH; Pres Sr Cls; Am Leg Boys St; Hon Rl; NHS; Rptr Yrbk; Bsktbl; Am Leg Awd; Bowling Galen; Comp Sci.

GRAHAM, SANDY; Sault Area HS; Slt Ste Marie, MI; 3/350 VP Frsh Cls; Cls Rep Soph Cls; Cl Rep Jr Cls; Band; Cmp Fr Grls; Chrh Wkr; Cmnty Wkr; Hon Rl; Jr NHS; Lbry Ade; Lake Superior St Coll; Med Tech.

GRAHAM, SHERRY; Charles F Kettering Sr HS; Detroit, MI; Pres Soph Cls; Chrs; Chrh Wkr; Girl Scts; Hon Rl; JA; Lbry Ade; NHS; FHA; Pep Clb;.

GRAHAM, SUSAN; Andrean HS; Merrillville, IN; 32/254 Cls Rep Frsh Cls; Hon Rl; NHS; Pep Clb; Capt Chrldng; GAA; Univ; Psych.

GRAHAM, SUSAN; Beavercreek HS; Dayton, OH; 17/702 Sec Frsh Cls; VP Soph Cls; VP Jr Cls; Cls Rep Sr Cls; Chrh Wkr; Drl Tm; Hon Rl; NHS; Ed Yrbk; Scr Kpr; Eastern Ky Univ; Law.

GRAHAM, SUSAN; Climax Scotts HS; Climax, MI; Hon Rl; FHA; Bus Schl.

GRAHAM, TAMMY; Sebring Mc Kinley HS; Sebring, OH; 33/91 VP Frsh Cls; VP Soph Cls; Chrs; Chrh Wkr; Hon Rl; Yrbk; Rptr Sch Nwsp; Sch Nwsp; 4-H; Pep Clb; Hannah & Mullins Schl; Nursing.

GRAHAM, THOMAS; New Buffalo HS; New Buffalo, MI; Hon Rl; Sprt Ed Sch Nwsp; Rptr Sch Nwsp; 4-H; VICA; Trk; JETS Awd; Southwestern Mic; Engr.

GRAHAM, TRESA; Matoaka HS; Matoaka, WV; 16/63 Cls Rep Frsh Cls; Cls Rep Soph Cls; Cl Rep Jr Cls; Hon Rl; Rptr Sch Nwsp; FHA; Pep Clb; Bsktbl; Concord Coll; Elem Tchr.

GRAHAM, WILLIAM F; Musselman HS; Inwood, WV; 10/126 Am Leg Boys St; Capt Band; Hon Rl; Orch; Am Leg Awd; West Virginia Univ; Music Educ.

GRAHN, TONYA; Heritage Christian Schl; Indianapolis, IN; 5/63 Band; Hon Rl; Letter Bsktbl; Bob Jones Univ; Elem Ed.

GRAINGER, PATRICIA; Fenton Sr HS; Fenton, MI; Chrs; Girl Scts; Hon Rl; Off Ade; Sch Mus; Sch Pl; Stg Crw; Trk; Scr Kpr; Tmr; Michigan St Univ; Tchr.

GRALAK, SHERRY; St Ursula Academy; Toledo, OH; Cls Rep Frsh Cls; Hon Rl; Letter Bsktbl; Awd In Shorthand For 3 Min Transcription At 60 WPM; College; Sec.

GRAM, WENDY; Claymont HS; Uhrichsville, OH; 10/206 Am Leg Aux Girls St; Girl Scts; Hon Rl; Jr NHS; NHS; Yth Flsp; Drama Clb; FTA; Lat Clb; Akron Univ; Bio.

GRAMIGNA, KAREN; Harry S Truman HS; Taylor, MI; Cls Rep Frsh Cls; Cls Rep Soph Cls; Am Leg Aux Girls St; Drl Tm; Girl Scts; Hon Rl; Rptr Yrbk; Letter Crs Cntry; Letter Trk; Univ; Comp Sci.

GRAMLING, LINDA; Eaton Rapids HS; Eaton Rapids, MI; Hon Rl; NHS; Yth Flsp; Spn Clb; Letter Swmmng; Tmr; Univ Of Michigan; Lib Arts.

GRAMMES, VIRGINIA; St Joseph Academy; Cleveland, OH; Cls Rep Soph Cls; Cl Rep Jr Cls; Cls Rep Sr Cls; Girl Scts; Hosp Ade; Stu Cncl; GAA; St Vincen Charity Hosp; Nursing.

GRAMS, MICHAEL; Isaac C Elston HS; Mich City, IN; Hon Rl; Jr NHS; NHS; Sch Mus; Fr Clb; Glf; Hockey; Ten; Cit Awd; College; Medicine.

GRAMS, ROBIN; Highland HS; Highland, IN; 33/494 Band; Chrh Wkr; Cmnty Wkr; Hosp Ade; NHS; Sec FHA; Sci Clb; C of C Awd; Tri St Univ; Aero Engr.

GRANATA, KEVIN; St Francis De Sales HS; Toledo, OH; 28/200 Debate Tm; Hon Rl; Natl Forn Lg; Sch Mus; Stg Crw; Sch Nwsp; Lat Clb; Ftbl; College; Physics.

GRAND, JULIE; Perry HS; Massillon, OH; Chrs; Girl Scts; Hon Rl; NHS; Off Ade; Fr Clb; Univ; Micro Bio.

GRANDBERRY, SYBIL M; Immaculata HS; Detroit, MI; Hon Rl; Hosp Ade; Pol Wkr; Yth Flsp; Rptr Yrbk; Ed Sch Nwsp; Rptr Sch Nwsp; Sch Nwsp; Letter Trk; Oakland Univ; Busns Admin.

GRANDY, DIANA; St Joseph HS; St Joseph, MI; Cls Rep Frsh Cls; Cls Rep Soph Cls; Cl Rep Jr Cls; Chrs; FCA; Hon Rl; NHS; Sch Mus; Sch Pl; Yth Flsp; College.

GRANGER, GREG; Littlefield Public HS; Alanson, MI; Cls Rep Soph Cls; Trs Jr Cls; Boy Scts; Sct Actv; Stu Cncl; Yrbk; Crs Cntry; Trk; North Central Michigan Coll; Chem.

GRANGER, TAMARA; Washington HS; Washington, IN; Hon Rl; Fr Clb; Pep Clb; Letter Bsktbl; Natl Merit Ltr; Indiana St Univ; Busns Mgmt.

GRANICH, JODI; Bloomington HS South; Bloomington, IN; 3/385 Trs Frsh Cls; Am Leg Aux Girls St; Hon Rl; Jr NHS; NHS; Treas Stu Cncl; Treas OEA; 1st Pl Regnl Acctg; OEA Contst 2nd & 3rd Pl Job Intervw; Univ; Bus.

GRANITTO, JEFFREY; Cardinal Mooney HS; Youngstown, OH; 139/295 Boy Scts; Glf; IM Sprt; Bus.

GRANNAN, JEALYN; Franklin Central HS; Indianapolis, IN; Band; Girl Scts; Sch Pl; Sct Actv; Pep Clb; Ind Univ; Accounting.

GRANSTRA, SHAWN; Traverse City HS; Traverse City, MI; Hon Rl; Jr NHS; NHS; Trk; Natl Merit SF; Northwestern Mich Coll; Nurse.

GRANT, CARY; Lamphere HS; Madison Hts, MI; 32/340 Chrs; Hon Rl; Mdrgl; Sch Mus; Sch Pl; Drama Clb; Wayne State Univ; Comp Pro.

GRANT, GERALDINE; Arthur Hill HS; Saginaw, MI; Girl Scts; JA; Orch; Ten; Wayne St Univ; Mass Communications.

GRANT, J KEVIN; Roosevelt Wilson HS; Stonewood, WV; Chrs; Leo Clb; VICA; Ftbl; Glf; Scr Kpr; Natl Piano Playing Auditions Div Of The Amer College Of Musicians; Fairmont State Univ; CPA.

GRANT, MARSHALL; Bloomington South HS; Bloomington, IN; 6/385 Chrs; Hon Rl; Jr NHS; Mdrgl; NHS; Sch Mus; Sch Pl; Drama Clb; Best Performance In Drama; Best Supporting Actor; Freshman Honors Prog Schlrshp Univ Of Deleware; College; Engr.

GRANT, MONIQUE A; Dayton Christian HS; Dayton, OH; Chrs; Drl Tm; Hon Rl; Y-Teens; Sprt Ed Sch Nwsp; Rptr Sch Nwsp; Trk; Pres Awd; Susannah Ross Schlshp Awd 1975; Bible Verses Schl 1977 78; 1st Runner Up In Ms Edority 1978; UCLA; English.

GRANT, TARYN; Roosevelt HS; Gary, IN; Band; Hon Rl; Jr NHS; NHS; Off Ade; FHA; FTA; Cit Awd; Purdue Univ; Pharm.

GRANT, TOM; Jefferson Union HS; Toronto, OH; VP Frsh Cls; VP Jr Cls; Boy Scts; Chrs; Chrh Wkr; Cmnty Wkr; Sch Mus; Sch Pl; Letter Ftbl; Letter Wrstlng; Univ; Law.

GRANT, VALORIE A; Aiken HS; Cincinnati, OH; Pres Frsh Cls; Pres Jr Cls; Girl Scts; Yth Flsp; Socr; Chrldng; Am Leg Awd; Cit Awd; Univ Of Washington; Busns Admin.

GRANTHAM, ANGELA; Bloomington HS; Bloomington, IN; Aud/Vis; Band; Hosp Ade; Sch Mus; Voc Schl; Tech Hlth Serv.

GRANTHAM, HOWARD E; Garfield HS; Akron, OH; Boy Scts; Chrh Wkr; VICA; Kent St Coll; Drafting.

GRANTHAM, JOHN S; R Nelson Snider HS; Ft Wayne, IN; 186/564 Aud/Vis; Hon Rl; Purdue Univ; Radio Cmnctns.

GRANTHEN, MARY; Fraser HS; Sterling Hts, MI; NHS; Sci Clb; Macomb Cnty Comm Coll; Comp.

GRANTONIC, A; Steubenville Catholic HS; Mingo Jct, OH; Am Leg Aux Girls St; Chrh Wkr; Hon Rl; Hosp Ade; NHS; Sch Mus; Stu Cncl; Drama Clb; FHA; Pres Pep Clb; College; Art Ther.

GRANZOW, JO ELLEN; Upper Arlington HS; Upper Arlington, OH; 96/648 Cmp Fr Grls; Girl Scts; Hon Rl; NHS; Stu Cncl; Ger Clb; Pep Clb; Chrldng; Letter GAA; Tmr; Ohio St Univ; Busns.

GRASER, GEORGANNE; Garfield HS; Akron, OH; Hon Rl; Treas JA; Off Ade; JA Awd; Akron Univ; Bus Admin.

GRASS, TONYA; Shelby Sr HS; Shelby, OH; Band; Chrs; Chrh Wkr; Cmnty Wkr; Girl Scts; Hon Rl; NHS; Pol Wkr; Rptr Sch Nwsp; Drama Clb; Bowling Green St Univ; Law.

GRASSMAN, DEANNE; Wooster HS; Wooster, OH; 12/364 Cls Rep Soph Cls; Trs Sr Cls; Drm Mjrt; JA; NHS; FHA; Spn Clb; Chrldng; Alternate To Buckeye Girls State; Sr Attendant Homecoming Ct; Stu Of Month; Ohio Northern Univ; Pharmacy.

GRASSMAN, JACKIE; Loudonville HS; Loudonville, OH; 20/130 Band; Chrs; Girl Scts; Hon Rl; NHS; Sch Pl; Stg Crw; Yrbk; Sch Nwsp; 4-H; Coll.

GRASSMAN, PATRICIA; Wooster HS; Wooster, OH; Chrs; Natl Forn Lg; Sch Mus; Sch Pl; Drama Clb; Fr Clb; Ger Clb; Spn Clb; Trk; Chrldng; Montery Inst Of Frgn Std; Lngustcs.

GRATA, KAREN; Wm A Wirt HS; Gary, IN; Pres Frsh Cls; Hon Rl; Jr NHS; Sch Pl; Stu Cncl; Rptr Yrbk; 4-H; Fr Clb; 4-H Awd; Part Student Ldrshp Inst Indiana Univ 1978; Gifted & Talented Program 1977; Purdue Univ; Art.

GRATE, RUTH; United Local HS; Salme, OH; 19/127 Chrh Wkr; Hon Rl; Lbry Ade; Spn Clb; Voice Dem Awd; Mt Vernon Nazarene Coll; Nursing.

GRATE, STEVEN; New Hope Christian School; Camden, MI; 1/4 Cls Rep Sr Cls; Val; Chrs; FFA; Capt Bsktbl; Letter Crs Cntry; Capt Socr; Pres Phys Fitness Awd 78 79; New Hope Schl Athletic Sportsmen Of Yr 79; Letourneau Coll; Mech Engr.

GRATER, CYNTHIA; Fairview HS; Fairview Pk, OH; 41/256 Girl Scts; Hon Rl; Letter Bsktbl; Letter Trk; IM Sprt; Vlybl Ltr & Defense Awd 78; Bsktbl Hustle Awd 78; Sci Fair Awd 2nd Pl 79; Cincinnati Univ; Nursing.

GRAUBNER, MICHAEL; Vassar HS; Vassar, MI; 6/150 Band; Hon Rl; Stg Crw; Fr Clb; Alma College.

GRAVELY, KATHY; Southwestern HS; Shelbyville, IN; 1/60 VP Frsh Cls; VP Soph Cls; VP Jr Cls; Am Leg Aux Girls St; Band; NHS; Yth Flsp; Rptr Yrbk; Rptr Sch Nwsp; Drama Clb; Purdue Univ; Wildlife Sci.

GRAVES, BASCOM W; Glen Este HS; Cincinnati, OH; Hon Rl; Spn Clb; Bsktbl; Ftbl; Univ; Dent.

GRAVES, BRENDA; Columbia City Joint HS; Ft Wayne, IN; Chrh Wkr; Hon Rl; NHS; Fr Clb; Pep Clb; Mat Maids; Coll; Home Ec.

GRAVES, CHERRIE; Bexley Sr HS; Bexley, OH; Cmp Fr Grls; Drl Tm; Hon Rl; Pol Wkr; Stg Crw; Fr Clb; Lat Clb; Pom Pon; Mbr Of Phi Alpha Chi Sorority; Coll; Intl Busns.

GRAVES, DOUGLAS M; Rockford HS; Rockford, MI; Boy Scts; JA; Mic State Univ; Acctg.

GRAVES, JANICE E; Perry Central HS; Tell City, IN; 6/93 VP Soph Cls; VP Jr Cls; Am Leg Aux Girls St; Hon Rl; Lbry Ade; NHS; Sch Pl; Stg Crw; VP Y-Teens; Drama Clb; College.

GRAVES, KATHY; Matoaka HS; Matoaka, WV; 3/45 Pres Frsh Cls; Pres Jr Cls; Am Leg Aux Girls St; Chrs; Chrh Wkr; Hon Rl; NHS; Sch Pl; Yrbk; Pres Keyettes; West Virginia Univ; Eng.

GRAVES, SHANNON; Lewis County HS; Jane Lew, WV; Trs Frsh Cls; Band; Drm Mjrt; Hon Rl; Off Ade; Sch Pl; Stu Cncl; Yth Flsp; Y-Teens; Drama Clb; Prom Committee; 1st Pl Field Commander Awd At Competition; Fairmont St Coll; Biology.

GRAVES, SUSAN; Bloomington HS North; Bloomington, IN; Band; Hon Rl; Hosp Ade; 4-H; IM Sprt; 4-H Awd; Indiana Univ; Bus.

GRAVINO, NICK; Trinity HS; Maple Hts, OH; 30/150 Band; Boy Scts; Chrh Wkr; Hon Rl; NHS; Sch Mus; Capt Ftbl; Univ; Pre Med.

GRAVIT, LOIS; Bethesda Christian HS; Crawfordsville, IN; 1/25 Chrs; Chrh Wkr; Hon Rl; Univ.

GRAY, ADELE; Farmington HS; Farmington Hls, MI; Cl Rep Jr Cls; Band; Hon Rl; Natl Forn Lg; NHS; Orch; Stu Cncl; Fr Clb; Univ; Dent.

GRAY, BRIAN; Wilmington Sr HS; Wilmington, OH; 31/280 Aud/Vis; Boy Scts; Chrh Wkr; Red Cr Ade; Sct Actv; Yth Flsp; Rptr Yrbk; Yrbk; 4-H; Cit Awd; Univ; Family Med.

GRAY, DWAYNE; Garfield HS; Hamilton, OH; 5/300 Pres Jr Cls; Am Leg Boys St; Band; Boy Scts;

Hon Rl; Jr NHS; Mod UN; NHS; Sch Pl; Stg Crw; Univ; Engr.

GRAY, ELIZABETH; Holland HS; Holland, MI; 42/297 Trs Jr Cls; Band; Pres Cmp Fr Grls; Cmnty Wkr; Hon Rl; Hosp Ade; Treas JA; NHS; Yrbk; Sec Ger Clb; Northwood Inst; Bus Mgmt.

GRAY, FREDONNA; Fayetteville HS; Fayetteville, WV; Am Leg Aux Girls St; Band; Chrs; Chrh Wkr; Cmnty Wkr; Girl Scts; Hon Rl; Pol Wkr; Sch Mus; Sct Actv; Hon Mntn Gov Awd Abilties Counts Essay Contst M9; Centry 21 Typing Awd 78; Intl Od Of Rainbw Gilf Advsr 79; Univ; Dent Hygnst.

GRAY, GWENDOLYN R; Attica Jr & Sr HS; Attica, IN; 20/83 Pres Soph Cls; Chrh Wkr; Cmnty Wkr; Hon Rl; Off Ade; Pep Clb; Gym; Swmmng; Capt Chrldng; Voc Schl.

GRAY, HELEN; Shortridge HS; Indianapolis, IN; 14/549 AFS; Pres Aud/Vis; Chrs; Hon Rl; Treas JA; Jr NHS; NHS; Stg Crw; Stu Cncl; Rptr Yrbk; Se Acad Fl; Travel Career Training.

GRAY, JAMES; Elk Rapids HS; Kewadin, MI; 1/110 Aud/Vis; Boy Scts; Debate Tm; Hon Rl; Natl Forn Lg; NHS; Sct Actv; Yrbk; 4-H; Glf; West Point; Science.

GRAY, JAMES H; Dublin HS; Plain City, OH; Aud/Vis; Band; Chrs; Hon Rl; NHS; Sch Mus; Stg Crw; Fr Clb; Socr; Univ; Pro Musician.

GRAY, JULIE; Westland HS; Grove City, OH; 110/496 Girl Scts; Hon Rl; DECA; 4-H; Pres OEA; IM Sprt; 4-H Awd;.

GRAY, JULIE; Columbia HS; Columbia Sta, OH; VP Jr Cls; Chrs; Girl Scts; Stu Cncl; FHA; Pep Clb; Letter Bsbl; Bsktbl; Univ.

GRAY, KEVIN; Rossford HS; Perrysburg, OH; 1/165 Val; Chrs; Hon Rl; VP NHS; Sch Pl; Pres Stu Cncl; Drama Clb; Fr Clb; Ftbl; Trk; Ohio State Univ; Engr.

GRAY, KIM; Pike Central HS; Otwell, IN; Band; Chrh Wkr; Hon Rl; NHS; Sch Mus; Sch Pl; Drama Clb; Pep Clb; Chrldng; DAR Awd; College; Therapy.

GRAY, KIMBERLY; St Mary Academy; Monroe, MI; 6/117 Hon Rl; NHS; Sch Pl; Sci Clb; Monroe County Comm Coll.

GRAY, KIMBERLY J; St Mary Academy; Monroe, MI; 6/117 Hon Rl; NHS; Sch Pl; Sci Clb; Michigan St Univ.

GRAY, LILLIE; Timken Sr HS; Canton, OH; 37/569 Cls Rep Frsh Cls; Cls Rep Soph Cls; Cl Rep Jr Cls; Am Leg Aux Girls St; Chrs; Chrh Wkr; Hon Rl; Jr NHS; VP MMM; Natl Forn Lg; Heidalberg Coll; Busns Admin.

GRAY, LINDA; Rogers HS; Michigan City, IN; 50/498 Chrs; Debate Tm; Hon Rl; NHS; Quill & Scroll; Sch Mus; Sch Pl; Stg Crw; Rptr Yrbk; Drama Clb; Weber Coll For Lang Awd 76; Univ Of Indiana; Intl Bus Admin.

GRAY, LONORA; Kettering HS; Detroit, MI; Cl Rep Jr Cls; Cls Rep Sr Cls; Chrs; Chrh Wkr; Hon Rl; NHS; Sch Pl; Ed Sch Nwsp; Drama Clb; Cit Awd; College; Child Psych.

GRAY, LORI; Gull Lake HS; Battle Creek, MI; 55/228 Chrs; DECA; Drama Clb; 4-H; Fr Clb; Pep Clb; 4-H Awd; Univ; Bus Mgmt.

GRAY, LORI; Franklin Heights HS; Columbus, OH; 59/301 Chrh Wkr; Drl Tm; Sch Pl; Stg Crw; Drama Clb; Key Clb; Mat Maids; Scr Kpr; Univ; Pediatrician.

GRAY, MARSHA A; Attica HS; Attica, IN; 37/70 Girl Scts; Pep Clb; Air Force; Mech.

GRAY, MIKE; Greenfield Central HS; Greenfield, IN; Band; Jr NHS; Sci Clb; Univ; Astrophysics.

GRAY, PAMELA; Green HS; Uniontown, OH; Cls Rep Frsh Cls; Girl Scts; Hon Rl; Stu Cncl; Yth Flsp; Y-Teens; Drama Clb; Crs Cntry; Trk; Wrstlng; College; Psych.

GRAY, PATRICIA; Green HS; Akron, OH; 30/325 Chrs; Chrh Wkr; Hon Rl; Off Ade; Yth Flsp; Y-Teens; Pep Clb; Bus Schl.

GRAY, PENELOPE; Norwood HS; Norwood, OH; Chrs; Chrh Wkr; Hon Rl; VP Jr NHS; Sec NHS; Stu Cncl; Pep Clb; Univ Of Cincinnati; Med.

GRAY, RICHARD; Montabella HS; Edmore, MI; 1/106 Val; Am Leg Boys St; Boy Scts; Chrs; Chrh Wkr; Hon Rl; NHS; Sch Pl; Sct Actv; Drama Clb; Marion Coll; Law.

GRAY, ROBIN; Eastern HS; Pekin, IN; Band; Chrh Wkr; Drl Tm; Hon Rl; 4-H; Pep Clb; 4-H Awd; Bible College.

GRAY, ROBIN; Point Pleasant Sr HS; Leon, WV; Chrh Wkr; NHS; Univ; Nursing.

GRAY, SCOTT A; Woodmore HS; Pemberville, OH; 5/142 VP Frsh Cls; Cls Rep Soph Cls; Cl Rep Jr Cl s; Am Leg Boys St; Band; Boy Scts; Hon Rl; NHS; Pres Stu Cncl; Letter Bsbl; Recd Eagle Scout Awd; Elected To Order Of Arrow BSA; Univ; Parks/rec.

GRAY, SHARON; Stow HS; Stow, OH; Hon Rl; Letter Bsktbl; Letter Crs Cntry; Letter Socr; Letter Trk; Coach Actv; GAA; IM Sprt; JA Awd; College; Phys Educ.

GRAY, SHARON I; Celina Sr HS; Celina, OH; 7/240 Girl Scts; Hon Rl; Sec NHS; Stu Cncl; Fr Clb; VP FBLA; Treas Pep Clb; Trk; Chrldng; Treas GAA; Univ; Acctg.

GRAY, STEVEN; Huntington North HS; Andrews, IN; Bsbl; Coach Actv; Voc Schl; Cons Officer.

GRAY, STEVEN; Kearsley HS; Flint, MI; Orch; Bsktbl; Glf; Huntington Coll; Sci.

GRAY, TRINA; South Dearborn HS; Aurora, IN; VP Soph Cls; Hon Rl; Pep Clb; Letter Swmmng; Letter Trk; Chrldng; GAA; IM Sprt; Scr Kpr; Tmr; College; Comp Progr.

GRAYBILL, JOHN; Central Christian HS; Leola, PA; 10/70 Chrs; Rptr Sch Nwsp; Bsktbl; Socr; Hesston College.

GRAYBILL, JOHN; Big Rapids HS; Big Rapids, MI; Band; Chrs; Hon Rl; Mdrgl; NHS; Sch Mus; Spring Arbor College; Ministries.

GRAYSON, LYNN; Whiteland Community HS; Whiteland, IN; 22/235 Band; Hon Rl; NHS; Stu Cncl; DECA; FHA; FTA; Pep Clb; Trk; Mgrs; IUPUI; Poli Sci.

GRAYSON, MELISSA; Quitman HS; Quitman, MS; Cls Rep Frsh Cls; Chrs; Lbry Ade; FHA; College; Clerical Worker.

GRAYSON, PATRICIA; Cody HS; Detroit, MI; 10/400 Band; Chrs; Hon Rl; Hosp Ade; Off Ade; ROTC; Univ Of Mic.

GRAYSON, STEPHEN; George Washington HS; Charleston, WV; Boy Scts; JA; Key Clb; IM Sprt; Univ Of Tenn; Nuclear Engr.

GRAYZAR, TRACY; Buckeye North HS; Dillonvale, OH; 1/118 Hon Rl; VP NHS; Off Ade; Sec Stu Cnc l; Yrbk; Pep Clb; Sci Clb; Spn Clb; West Liberty State College.

GRAYZAR, TRACY L; Buckeye N HS; Dillonvale, OH; 1/119 Band; Chrs; Hon Rl; NHS; Off Ade; Stu Cncl; Yrbk; Pep Clb; Sci Clb; Spn Clb; Univ Of Pittsburgh.

GRCEVIC, ELIZABETH; Struthers HS; Struthers, OH; 34/276 Chrs; Debate Tm; Hon Rl; Rptr Yrbk; Yrbk; Rptr Sch Nwsp; DECA; Lat Clb; Rdo Clb; Youngstown St Univ; Busns Admin.

GRCEVICH, STEPHEN; Boardman HS; Boardman, OH; 40/597 Natl Forn Lg; NHS; Treas Stu Cncl; Ger Clb; Mth Clb; Am Leg Awd; DAR Awd; Natl Merit SF; N E Ohio Univ; Med.

GREAL, JACQUELINE; Walled Lake Central HS; Union Lake, MI; Chrs; Chrh Wkr; Girl Scts; Hon Rl; Mod UN; NHS; Sch Mus; Stg Crw; Ger Clb; Michigan St Univ; Criminal Justice.

GREASER, F CHRISTOPHR; St Josephs Prep Sem; Tunnelton, WV; 3/9 Pres Frsh Cls; Pres Soph Cls; Chrs; Hon Rl; Stu Cncl; Lat Clb; Mth Clb; Spn Clb; Letter Bsktbl; Letter Wrstlng; Golden Horseshoe Winner W V Hstory; Coached Intermural Bsktbl 79; Marshall Univ; Geological Engr.

GREATHOUSE, MICHAEL; East HS; Columbus, OH; Cmnty Wkr; Hon Rl; Boys Clb Am; 4-H; Spn Clb;.

GREATHOUSE, REBECCA; Brownstown Central HS; Seymour, IN; 23/142 Cmnty Wkr; Hon Rl; Stg Crw; Rptr Sch Nwsp; 4-H; VP FTA; Pep Clb; Vincennes Univ; Distributive Marketg.

GREATHOUSE, REGINA; West Preston Sr HS; Masontown, WV; Sec Soph Cls; Capt Drl Tm; Hon Rl; Stu Cncl; Rptr Yrbk; VICA; Chrldng; West Virginia Univ; Nursing.

GREATHOUSE, SHERRY; Austintown Fitch HS; Austintown, OH; Trs Jr Cls; Off Ade; DECA; OEA; Mahoning Cnty Joint Voc Schl; Photog.

GREATHOUSE, WILLIAM; Flemington HS; Rosemont, WV; 1/42 Sec Jr Cls; Band; Boy Scts; Hon Rl; NHS; Orch; Sch Mus; Sch Pl; Sct Actv; Rptr Yrbk; West Virginia St VICA Pres; West Virginia Golden Horseshoe Awd; All State Band; Mass Inst Of Tech; Elec Engr.

GREAVES, JAMES; Theodore Roosevelt HS; Kent, OH; Chrs; Hon Rl; Sch Mus; Stu Cncl; Drama Clb; Sci Clb; Bsktbl; Crs Cntry; Socr; Trk; Northwestern; Physics.

GRECO, J; Archbishop Alter HS; Bellbrook, OH; 20/331 Boy Scts; Chrs; Hon Rl; NHS; Sec Spn Clb; Univ Of Dayton.

GRECO, JAMES; Weirton Madonna HS; Weirton, WV; Pres Frsh Cls; Chrh Wkr; VP Stu Cncl; Letter Ftbl; Letter Ten; Letter Wrstlng; IM Sprt; Mgrs; Coll; Busns.

GRECO, MARY; Madonna HS; Weirton, WV; Chrs; Hon Rl; Yrbk; FNA; Pep Clb; Prncssin Mountain St Forest Fest 79; West Virginia Univ; Pharm.

GRECULA, MICHAEL J; Mingo HS; Mingo Jct, OH; 1/132 Cls Rep Soph Cls; Am Leg Boys St; Aud/Vis; Band; Boy Scts; Chrh Wkr; Cmnty Wkr; Hon Rl; NHS; Sct Actv; Coll; Chem.

GREEGOR, CYNTHIA; Northwestern HS; Wooster, OH; Hon Rl; NHS; Sch Pl; Drama Clb; 4-H; Bsbl; Chrldng; IM Sprt; PPFtbl; Scr Kpr; Ohi State Univ; Sci.

GREEK, ANDREA; Adlai Stevenson HS; Sterling Hgts, MI; 72/530 Chrs; Chrh Wkr; Cmnty Wkr; Hon Rl; NHS; Red Cr Ade; Yth Flsp; Easter; Spec Educ.

GREEN, ALAN H; Valley View HS; Germantown, OH; Band; Chrh Wkr; NHS; Sci Clb; Spn Clb; Ten; Air Force.

GREEN, BARBARA K; Marlington HS; Louisville, OH; 116/280 Cl Rep Jr Cls; Cls Rep Sr Cls; Chrs; Lbry Ade; Off Ade; Sec Stu Cncl; Yth Flsp; 4-H; FHA; OEA; Stark Tech Coll; Sec.

GREEN, BECKY; David Anderson HS; Lisbon, OH; Hon Rl; Lbry Ade; Sch Mus; Treas Y-Teens; Rptr Sch Nwsp; VP Fr Clb; Letter Trk; Univ.

GREEN, BEVERLY; Buckeye North HS; Brilliant, OH; 25/119 Trs Frsh Cls; Band; Chrs; Hon Rl; Lbry Ade; NHS; Off Ade; Sch Pl; Yrbk; Ohi State Univ; Journalism.

GREEN, BRENDA; Jesup W Scott HS; Toledo, OH; 9/272 Cls Rep Frsh Cls; Cls Rep Soph Cls; Cl Rep Jr Cls; Hon Rl; NHS; Stu Cncl; Fr Clb; Mth Clb; Ohio St Univ; Engr Tech.

GREEN, CONNIE; North Putnam HS; Roachdale, IN; Treas FCA; Hon Rl; Pres Stu Cncl; Rptr Yrbk; Sch Nwsp; Sec Spn Clb; Bsktbl; Trk; Vincennes Univ; Law Enforcement.

GREEN, DE ANN; Philip Barbour HS; Philippi, WV; Band; Chrh Wkr; Girl Scts; Hon Rl; Hosp Ade; Stu Cncl; Sec Yth Flsp; Drama Clb; Pres 4-H; Keyettes; Vocational Schl; Fash Design.

GREEN, DEBRA; Caldwell HS; Caldwell, OH; 4/105 Chrs; Hon Rl; Lbry Ade; Treas 4-H; Sec FFA; FHA; Lat Clb; Pep Clb; Letter Bsbl; Scr Kpr; Ohio St Univ; Farm Mgr.

GREEN, DEBRA; Harper HS; Harper Woods, MI; FCA; Hon Rl; Sch Nwsp; Chrldng; GAA; IM Sprt; College; Veterinarian.

GREEN, DIANA; Pine River HS; Le Roy, MI; Band; Chrs; Chrh Wkr; Hon Rl; 4-H; Fr Clb; Bsbl; Pom Pon; College; Sec.

GREEN, DIANA; Peebles HS; Sinking Spring, OH; Hst Soph Cls; Hst Jr Cls; Pres 4-H; Treas FHA; FTA; Bsktbl; Capt Chrldng; Shawnee State Tech Coll; Nursing.

GREEN, DIANA L; Mc Cutcheon HS; Lafayette, IN; 23/261 Band; Girl Scts; Hon Rl; JA; Natl Forn Lg; NHS; Fr Clb; Letter Trk; Letter Wrstlng; Natl Achievmnt Comnd Student 1978; Univ; Engr.

GREEN, GERALD; Henry Ford HS; Detroit, MI; 3/496 Cls Rep Sr Cls; Hon Rl; Letter Bsbl; Letter Bsktbl; Letter Crs Cntry; Opt Clb Awd; Harvard Univ; Elec Engr.

GREEN, GREGORY; Jennings County HS; No Vernon, IN; 26/351 Chrs; Chrh Wkr; Hon Rl; Jr NHS; NHS; Sch Mus; Yth Flsp; FSA; Mth Clb; Sci Clb; Perfct Attndnc 72 79; Air Force Acad; Math.

GREEN, JEFFERY; Kaukakee Valley Jr Sr HS; Rensselaer, IN; Hon Rl; FFA; Letter Ftbl; Trk; Purdue Univ; Mech Engr.

GREEN, JERRI; Portsmouth East HS; New Boston, OH; 8/81 Hon Rl; NHS; Off Ade; Stu Cncl; Bsbl; Bsktbl; Chrldng;.

GREEN, JOANN; Hilltop HS; W Unity, OH; Chrs; Hon Rl; Lbry Ade; Rptr Sch Nwsp; Chrldng; Univ; Vet Asst.

GREEN, JUDY; Madison Plains HS; London, OH; 24/156 Hst Sr Cls; Am Leg Aux Girls St; Band; Chrh Wkr; Hon Rl; Hosp Ade; Yth Flsp; 4-H; Spn Clb; IM Sprt; Century 21 Bookkeeping Awd 78;.

GREEN, JULIE; North White HS; Monon, IN; 2/80 Pres Jr Cls; Chrs; Hon Rl; NHS; Sch Mus; Yrbk; Drama Clb; Ger Clb; Mth Clb; Chrldng; Univ.

GREEN, KAREN; Springfield Local HS; New Middletown, OH; Hon Rl; Yrbk; FTA; Pep Clb; Trk; Capt Chrldng; Youngstown State; Business.

GREEN, KATHLEEN; Toronto HS; Toronto, OH; Girl Scts; Hosp Ade; Spn Clb; Ohio Vly Hosp; Nursing.

GREEN, KEVIN; Dearborn HS; Dearborn, MI; Chrh Wkr; Hon Rl; Rptr Yrbk; Rptr Sch Nwsp; Wrstlng; IM Sprt; Natl Merit Ltr; Mic Tech Univ; Elec Engr.

GREEN, LANCE; Coloma HS; Coloma, MI; VP Jr Cls; Band; Hon Rl; Stu Cncl; 4-H; Pep Clb; Letter Bsktbl; Letter Trk; Coach Actv; IM Sprt; College.

GREEN, LAURA; Marion HS; Marion, IN; Chrs; Chrh Wkr; Hon Rl; Sch Mus; Sch Pl; Drama Clb; College; Theology.

GREEN, LESLIE; Champion HS; Warren, OH; Stg Crw; Scr Kpr; Col Univ; Ind Arts.

GREEN, LICIA; Indian Hill HS; Cincinnati, OH; VP Frsh Cls; Cls Rep Frsh Cls; Trs Soph Cls; Cls Rep Soph Cls; Cmnty Wkr; Pol Wkr; Stu Cncl; Sch Nwsp; Pep Clb; IM Sprt; Outstndng Stdnt Cncl Member 77; Howard Univ; Cmnctns.

GREEN, LINDA; Central HS; Detroit, MI; Chrh Wkr; Drl Tm; Hon Rl; Sch Pl; Stu Cncl; Bsktbl; Cit Awd; College.

GREEN, LINDA; Morgantown HS; Morgantown, WV; Girl Scts; Hon Rl; Mth Clb; IM Sprt; Mat Maids; Scr Kpr; Tmr; Wv Univ; Med.

GREEN, LORI; Granville HS; Granville, OH; Cls Rep Sr Cls; Lit Mag; Off Ade; Sch Pl; Rptr Yrbk; Rptr Sch Nwsp; Fr Clb; Spn Clb; Chrldng; Sec GAA; Place Natl Federation Of St Poetries; Ohio St Univ; Stewardess.

GREEN, LORINDA; Cass Tech HS; Detroit, MI; Cmp Fr Grls; Chrs; Chrh Wkr; Hon Rl; Off Ade; Bsbl; Bsktbl; Socr; Swmmng; Ten; City Of Detroit Bd Of Educ Awd 79; 1st Pl Bowling 78 & 79; Mbr Of Co Op; Mbr Of Computer Club; Univ Of Michigan; Cmnctns.

GREEN, MARION; South Harrison HS; Jane Lew, WV; Band; Hon Rl; Jr NHS; NHS; Stg Crw; Stu Cncl; FHA; FTA; Pep Clb; Bsktbl; West Va Univ; Psych.

GREEN, MARK A; Oak Hills HS; Cincinnati, OH; 17/875 Hon Rl; Mod UN; NHS; Ger Clb; Natl Merit SF; Pres Of German Club; College; Biology.

GREEN, MARKLIN; Mt Vernon Acad; Gallipolis, OH; Band; Boy Scts; Chrs; Chrh Wkr; Trk; IM Sprt; Columbia Union College; Church Organ.

GREEN, MATT; Cadillac HS; Cadillac, MI; Band; Orch; Sch Pl; Crs Cntry; Trk; Wrstlng; Mich State Univ; Poli Sci.

GREEN, MIKE; Westerville North HS; Westerville, OH; 11/480 Band; Boy Scts; Chrs; Hon Rl; NHS; Orch; PAVAS; Sch Mus; Sch Pl; Sct Actv; All Ohio State Yth Choir; Buckey All Star Bnd; Musical Hnrs; College; Accounting.

GREEN, PAMELA; Lawrenceburg HS; Lawrenceburg, IN; Cls Rep Frsh Cls; VP Soph Cls; Band; Drl Tm; Hon Rl; Stu Cncl; Pep Clb; Ten; Pres Awd; Indiana Univ; Comp Prog.

GREEN, RANDY; Marion Harding HS; Marion, OH; 85/450 Chrs; Chrh Wkr; Cmnty Wkr; Sch Mus; Sch Pl; Stg Crw; Rptr Yrbk; Yrbk; Drama Clb; Spn Clb; Marion Tech College; Bus Adm.

GREEN, REBECCA L; De Kalb HS; Ashley, IN; 8/283 Am Leg Aux Girls St; Band; Chrs; Natl Forn Lg; NHS; Sch Mus; Sch Pl; Drama Clb; Sec 4-H; FTA; Tri Kappa Annual Honors Banquet; Ball St Univ; Math.

GREEN, REED M; Liberty HS; Bolt, WV; Cls Rep Frsh Cls; Pres Soph Cls; Cls Rep Soph Cls; Am Leg Boys St; Cmnty Wkr; Stu Cncl; Ftbl; Trk; Wrstlng; Coach Actv; Univ.

GREEN, ROBERT; Hartland HS; Brighton, MI; Chrh Wkr; College; Sci.

GREEN, ROBERT; Urbana HS; Urbana, OH; Band; Hon Rl; Yth Flsp; Ten; Cit Awd; Univ; Sci.

GREEN, ROBERT; East Kentwood HS; Kentwood, MI; Chrs; Stg Crw; Spn Clb; Letter Ftbl; Letter Trk; IM Sprt; Two All Confrnc Awd In Track 79; Michigan St Univ; Bus Mgmt.

GREEN, ROBERT; Central HS; Evansville, IN; 80/465 VP Frsh Cls; Hon Rl; NHS; Stu Cncl; Ed Yrbk; Letter Bsktbl; Letter Glf; Letter Ten; IM Sprt; Cit Awd; Univ Of Evansville; Acctg.

GREEN, ROBIN C; Marlington HS; Alliance, OH; Chrs; Lbry Ade; Off Ade; Sch Mus; Stu Cncl; 4-H; FHA; OEA; Pep Clb; Stark Tech Coll; Sec.

GREEN, ROGER J; Rochester Cmnty HS; Rochester, IN; 60/166 Pep Clb; Bsbl; Ten; Coach Actv; Voc Schl.

GREEN, SCOTT; Fowlerville HS; Howell, MI; Band; Hon Rl; Glf; Letter Trk; Mich State; Chem Engr.

GREEN, SHERRY; Withrow HS; Cincinnati, OH; Hon Rl; Jr NHS; Stu Cncl; Bsbl; Trk; Chrldng; GAA; Ten State; Cpa.

GREEN, STEPHANIE; South Ripley HS; Versailles, IN; 5/112 Band; Hon Rl; Stu Cncl; 4-H; Sec Spn Clb; Cit Awd; 4-H Awd; Lion Awd; Sunshine Soc Vice Pres; Luther League Pres; Univ; Bus Admin.

GREEN, STEVEN; John Adams HS; So Bend, IN; 112/395 Voc Schl; Drafting.

GREEN, SUSAN; Richmond Sr HS; Richmond, IN; 199/549 Cl Rep Jr Cls; Cls Rep Sr Cls; Chrs; Girl Scts; Hosp Ade; Sct Actv; Stu Cncl; VP Spn Clb; Letter Gym; Mgrs; Indiana Univ East; Nursing.

GREEN, SUSAN; Maumee HS; Maumee, OH; 6/316 Hon Rl; NHS; Quill & Scroll; Y-Teens; Yrbk; Sch Nwsp; PPFtbl; Natl Merit Ltr; Ohio State; Vet.

GREEN, VERONICA M; Buena Vista HS; Saginaw, MI; 42/137 Cmp Fr Grls; Girl Scts; Hon Rl; Lbry Ade; Off Ade; Stu Cncl; Yth Flsp; Rptr Yrbk; Pom Pon; Pres Awd; Delta Coll; Busns.

GREEN, VICKY; Lake Central HS; Schererville, IN; Cls Rep Frsh Cls; Cls Rep Soph Cls; Cl Rep Jr Cls; Chrh Wkr; Hon Rl; NHS; Y-Teens; Yrbk; Pep Clb; Tmr; Indiana Univ.

GREEN, VICTORIA; Pineville HS; Pineville, WV; Pres Jr Cls; Am Leg Aux Girls St; Hon Rl; Jr NHS; Off Ade; Sch Pl; Stu Cncl; Rptr Yrbk; Yrbk; Drama Clb; Univ.

GREEN, WILIAM; Penn HS; Mishawaka, IN; Boy Scts; Hon Rl; 4-H; Capt Swmmng; IM Sprt; College; Law.

GREEN, W R; Culver Military Acad; Rushville, IN; 20/191 Boy Scts; Debate Tm; Natl Forn Lg; ROTC; Yth Flsp; Boys Clb Am; Ftbl; Wrstlng; IM Sprt; Natl Merit Ltr; College; Pre Med.

GREENAN, JOSEPH; John Marshall HS; Moundsville, WV; Am Leg Boys St; Aud/Vis; Chrs; Cmnty Wkr; Sch Mus; Sch Pl; Drama Clb; IM Sprt; Natl Merit Ltr; John Marshall Most Versatile Male Perf 78; Intramurals Best Bowler 78; Amer Jr Bowling Con 78; West Virginia Univ; Psych.

GREENAWALT, LORI; Jackson Milton HS; North Jackson, OH; 1/111 Chrs; Chrh Wkr; Hon Rl; NHS; Off Ade; Cedarville Coll; Accounting.

GREENE, BECKY; Lemon Monroe HS; Monroe, OH; Cls Rep Soph Cls; Sec Jr Cls; Band; Chrs; Chrh Wkr; Girl Scts; Hon Rl; NHS; Orch; Sch Mus; Flag Unit Co Captn 79; Univ; Dent.

GREENE, BRENDA; Marysville HS; Marysville, OH; Chrh Wkr; Stu Cncl; Yth Flsp; Bethany Nazarene Univ; Child Psych.

GREENE, DANIEL; Allen Park HS; Allen Park, MI; Cls Rep Frsh Cls; Cls Rep Soph Cls; Cl Rep Jr Cls; Pres Sr Cls; Boy Scts; Stu Cncl; Yth Flsp; FBLA; Spn Clb; Ftbl; Wayne St Univ.

GREENE, DONNA; Parma HS; Parma, OH; Cl Rep Jr Cls; Cls Rep Sr Cls; Hon Rl; Rptr Sch Nwsp; Swmmng; Cleveland State Univ; English.

GREENE, GEROGIA; Jackson HS; Jackson, OH; 26/230 Chrh Wkr; Hon Rl; NHS; Off Ade; Yth Flsp; 4-H; Capt PPFtbl; 4-H Awd; Ohio Univ; Educ.

GREENE, HOLLY; Reynoldsburg HS; Reynoldsburg, OH; Cmp Fr Grls; Chrs; Chrh Wkr; Girl Scts; Hon Rl; NHS; Scr Kpr; Univ; Eng.

GREENE, LEATRICE; Cass Technical HS; Detroit, MI; Hon Rl; NHS; Off Ade; Y-Teens; FDA; Mth Clb; Spn Clb; Gnrl Exclinc Awrd 76; Metroplitan Detroit Youth Awrd 79; St Of MI Crtfct Of Merit 79; Univ Of Michigan; Doctor.

GREENE, LINDA; Hurricane HS; Hurricane, WV; Trs Soph Cls; Pres Jr Cls; Chrs; Girl Scts; Hon Rl; Stu Cncl; Y-Teens; Yrbk; Marshall Univ.

GREENE, LISA; Northwest HS; Clinton, OH; Chrs; Chrh Wkr; Cmnty Wkr; Hon Rl; NHS; Fr Clb; Pep Clb; Chrldng; Univ; Soc Work.

GREENE, MARY; Washington Irving HS; Clarksburg, WV; Trs Soph Cls; Trs Jr Cls; Hon Rl; NHS; Pol Wkr; Quill & Scroll; Sch Pl; Stu Cncl; Yth Flsp; Rptr Yrbk; West Virginia Univ; Bio.

GREENE, MICHAEL; Warren Western Reserve HS; Warren, OH; FCA; Hon Rl; Red Cr Ade; Ger Clb; Pep Clb; Capt Wrstlng; IM Sprt; College; Law.

GREENE, MIKE; Springboro HS; Lebanon, OH; Am Leg Boys St; Hon Rl; Pres NHS; Letter Ftbl; Letter

Trk; Am Leg Awd; Natl Merit SF; Miami Of Ohio; Business.

GREENE, MISSY; Rensselaer Central HS; Rensselaer, IN; Cl Rep Jr Cls; Band; Hon Rl; Yth Flsp; Fr Clb; FDA; Keyettes; Pep Clb; Letter Bsktbl; Letter Trk; Univ; Marine Bio.

GREENE, PATRICIA; Tell City HS; Tell City, IN; 10/226 Chrh Wkr; Girl Scts; Hon Rl; NHS; Spn Clb; Indiana Univ; Comp Sci.

GREENE, REBECCA; Webster Co HS; Cowen, WV; Cmnty Wkr; 4-H; Pep Clb; Trk; Chrldng; Twrlr; 4-H Awd;.

GREENE, RICHARD; St Francis De Sales HS; Toledo, OH; 19/200 Boy Scts; Hon Rl; Ten; IM Sprt; Coll; Bus Law.

GREENE, TERRY; East Fairmont HS; Fairmont, WV; 80/263 Cls Rep Frsh Cls; Cls Rep Soph Cls; Trs Jr Cls; Chrh Wkr; Hon Rl; Off Ade; Stu Cncl; DECA; Drama Clb; FBLA; Fairmont St Coll; Elem Ed.

GREENE JR, EVERETT; Shortridge HS; Indianapolis, IN; 10/326 Cls Rep Sr Cls; FCA; NHS; Rptr Yrbk; DECA; Mth Clb; Letter Ftbl; Letter Trk; Kiwan Awd; Natl Merit Ltr; Indiana Univ; Architecture.

GREENFIELD, TERRI L; Flemington HS; Bridgeport, WV; Sch Nwsp; Fr Clb; FHA; Pep Clb; VICA; Letter Bsktbl; Chrldng; Interior Dsgn.

GREENHAM, JOHN H; Port Huron HS; Port Huron, MI; 22/327 Cls Rep Soph Cls; Band; Debate Tm; Hon Rl; NHS; Mth Clb; Mic Tech Univ; Engr.

GREENHILL, KERRY; Admiral King HS; Lorain, OH; Band; Chrh Wkr; Hon Rl; FHA; Pep Clb; Univ; Health Admin.

GREENHOE, AMY; Marysville HS; Marysville, MI; 3/174 Pres Frsh Cls; Cls Rep Soph Cls; Cl Rep Jr Cls; Cls Rep Sr Cls; NHS; Quill & Scroll; Sch Mus; Stg Crw; Stu Cncl; Ferris State College; Med Tech.

GREENHUT, BARRY J; Clay HS; Granger, IN; 3/406 Band; Chrs; Hon Rl; JA; Treas NHS; Pol Wkr; Sch Mus; Stu Cncl; Fr Clb; Natl Merit SF; University; Physics.

GREENHUT, SAUL; Ferndale HS; Oak Park, MI; 19/375 NHS; Ten; Rotary Awd; Univ Of Mic; Med.

GREENIDGE, JAN; Andrews Acad; Berrien Spgs, MI; Chrs; Spn Clb; Andrews Univ; Bio.

GREENING, ERIC; Alma HS; Alma, MI; Band; Chrh Wkr; Sch Mus; Sch Pl; Stg Crw; Yth Flsp; Drama Clb; Rotary Awd; Mic State Univ.

GREENING, ROBERT C; Reese HS; Reese, MI; Hon Rl; FFA; Mth Clb; Letter Trk; Mgrs; Tmr; Cit Awd; Bus Schl; Bus Mgmt.

GREENLAND, CAROL; John Marshall HS; Cleveland, OH; Red Cr Ade; Rptr Sch Nwsp; VP OEA; Chrldng; Coach Actv; Cit Awd; Natl Jr Tennis League Indiv Sportsmanship Trophy; College; Computer Prog.

GREENLEAF, DEBRA; Geneva Secondary HS; Geneva, OH; Cl Rep Jr Cls; JA; Lit Mag; Yrbk; JA Awd; Coll; Acctg.

GREENLEAF, ORLAND K; Spencer HS; Reedy, WV; Cls Rep Soph Cls; Band; Cmnty Wkr; Orch; Stu Cncl; Yth Flsp; Pres 4-H; VP FFA; Pres VICA; IM Sprt; Arch Moore Voc Schl; Carpentry.

GREENLEE, CYNTHIA; High School; Bluffton, IN; Gym; Trk; Bus Schl; Sec.

GREENLEE, EDWARD; Wintersville HS; Wintrsvll, OH; 12/282 Hon Rl; Spn Clb; Letter Glf; Bowling Green State Univ.

GREENLEE, JENNIFER; East Noble HS; Kendallville, IN; 2/260 Trs Jr Cls; Trs Sr Cls; Sal; FCA; NHS; Drama Clb; Letter Gym; Letter Swmmng; Letter Ten; Chrldng; Miami Univ.

GREENLEE, KAREN; Union Scioto HS; Chillicothe, OH; 20/124 Trs Sr Cls; Band; Hon Rl; Sec NHS; Sch Mus; Pres Stu Cncl; VP Stu Clb; Bsktbl; Capital Univ; Nursing.

GREENLEE, LISA; Lakeview HS; Cortland, OH; Band; Chrs; Hon Rl; Y-Teens; Beta Clb; Fr Clb; Letter Trk; Hiram Coll; Soc Wrkr.

GREENMAN, BOB; Carmel HS; Carmel, IN; 36/685 Band; Boy Scts; Hon Rl; NHS; Sct Actv; Pres Ger Clb; Pres Key Clb; Indiana Univ; Medicine.

GREENOP, JULIE; Belding HS; Belding, MI; Chrh Wkr; Hon Rl; NHS; Rptr Yrbk; 4-H; Fr Clb; Spn Clb; Cit Awd; 4-H Awd; College; Comp Sci.

GREENOUGH, DEBORAH; Lansing Everett HS; Lansing, MI; 2/454 Trs Frsh Cls; Cls Rep Frsh Cls; Sal; Hon Rl; Jr NHS; Lbry Ade; NHS; Stu Cncl; Yth Flsp; Civ Clb; St Of Mi Competitive Schlrshp Progr 79; Natl Jr Civilian Awd 76; Awd Of Acad Excell Fr Mi St Univ 79; Michigan St Univ; Med Tech.

GREENWALD, MARGARET; Stow HS; Stow, OH; Cmnty Wkr; JA; Rptr Sch Nwsp; Sch Nwsp; OEA; Pep Clb; Offc Educ.

GREENWALD, MARY; Creston HS; Grand Rapids, MI; 16/395 Trs Sr Cls; Chrs; Hon Rl; Mdrgl; NHS; Sch Mus; Spn Clb; Hope College; Psych.

GREENWALD, SALLIE; West Geavga HS; Chesterland, OH; Cls Rep Frsh Cls; Band; Chrs; Hon Rl; Off Ade; Stu Cncl; Pep Clb; Spn Clb; Bsbl; IM Sprt; Freshman Serv Awd ; Serv Awds For Gym Leading ; Declamation Awd In Spanish Participation; Univ; Lang.

GREENWALT, MARSHA; Logan Elm HS; Kingston, OH; 32/185 Band; FCA; Hon Rl; NHS; 4-H; GAA; 4-H Awd; Capital Univ; Nursing.

GREENWALT, PAMELA; Ursuline HS; Youngstown, OH; 51/289 Cmnty Wkr; Hon Rl; Off Ade; FTA; Pep Clb; IM Sprt; St Finalist In Miss United Teenager Pageant 79; Whos Who In Amer HS 78; Plcd 9th In St Comp For Typing 78; Youngstown Coll Of Bus; Sec.

GREENWAY, KATHERINE; Howell HS; Howell, MI; 67/398 Drl Tm; Hon Rl; NHS; 4-H; Key Clb; Pom Pon; PPFtbl; 4-H Awd; Western Michigan Univ; Bus.

GREENWELL, TERESA; Bishop Fenwick HS; Middletown, OH; VP Sr Cls; Drl Tm; Hon Rl; NHS; Sch Mus; Sch Pl; Fr Clb; Chrldng; Univ; Jrnlsm.

GREENWOOD, BARBARA; Earnest W Seaholm HS; Bloomfield Hill, MI; Cls Rep Sr Cls; Band; PAVAS; Sch Mus; Stg Crw; Univ Of Michigan.

GREENWOOD, JANE; Frontier HS; Newport, OH; 43/135 Sec Jr Cls; Band; Sch Pl; Yrbk; Letter Bsktbl; Twrlr; Ohio Valley Med Center; Nursing.

GREENWOOD, KEVIN L; Bellaire HS; Bellaire, OH; 1/223 Am Leg Boys St; Chrh Wkr; Hon Rl; Lit Mag; NHS; Sec Quill & Scroll; Rptr Yrbk; Yrbk; Rptr Sch Nwsp; Sch Nwsp; Top Hnrs For Overall Perfrmnce HS Jrnlsm Inst In Univ 78; Appoinnnt To The M W Essex Schl For Giftd 79; Univ; Cmmrcl Art.

GREENWOOD, RODNEY A; Coshocton HS; Coshocton, OH; Chrh Wkr; Hon Rl; Key Clb; Sci Clb; Letter Ten; IM Sprt; College; Math.

GREER, DOUG; Glen Este HS; Cincinnati, OH; 10/272 Hon Rl; NHS; Fr Clb; Pep Clb; Letter Bsbl; Letter Bsktbl; Univ; Med.

GREER, GREGORY; Indiana Acad; Indianapolis, IN; 4/54 Trs Frsh Cls; Trs Soph Cls; Band; Chrs; Hon Rl; Off Ade; Ed Yrbk; Rptr Sch Nwsp; IM Sprt; Natl Merit Ltr; Andrews Univ; Biology.

GREER, GREGORY; Valley Local HS; Lucasville, OH; 2/110 Pres Frsh Cls; Cls Rep Frsh Cls; Cls Rep Soph Cls; Cl Rep Jr Cls; Band; Chrs; VP Stu Cncl; Crs Cntry; Trk; Dnfth Awd; Med.

GREER, JEFF; Jennings County HS; No Vernon, IN; Band; Pol Wkr; FFA; Pep Clb; Spn Clb; Univ; Allied Health.

GREER, JOHN C; Marian HS; South Bend, IN; 6/150 Am Leg Boys St; Hon Rl; Treas NHS; Capt Bsbl; Letter Ftbl; IM Sprt; JETS Awd; Natl Merit SF; Univ Of Notre Dame; Engr.

GREER, MARK; Richwood HS; Richwood, WV; 5/200 VP Soph Cls; Am Leg Boys St; NHS; Stu Cncl; Pep Clb; Capt Glf; Am Leg Awd; Cit Awd; Century III Ldrshp Awd; West Virginia Univ; Optometry.

GREER, RUDENIA; Jane Addams Vocational HS; Cleveland, OH; Hosp Ade; Off Ade; Red Cr Ade; Stu Cncl; Y-Teens; OEA; IM Sprt; College; Medical.

GREER, SUSAN; Ben Davis HS; Indianapolis, IN; Band; Hst Frsh Cls; Cmnty Wkr; Girl Scts; Hon Rl; JA; Lbry Ade; NHS; Sch Mus; Bus Schl; Bus Admin.

GREER, THOMAS; Oakwood HS; Dayton, OH; Band; Hon Rl; NHS; Off Ade; Orch; Sch Mus; Ftbl; Ten; Natl Merit Ltr; College; Medicine.

GREER, VICTOR; West Side Sr HS; Gary, IN; Cls Rep Frsh Cls; Band; Boy Scts; Hon Rl; Jr NHS; NHS; Sct Actv; Letter Bsktbl; Letter Ftbl; Letter Trk; Arizona St Univ; Cmrcl Art.

GREGERSEN, RENEA; Western HS; Parma, MI; Girl Scts; 4-H; GAA; Michigan St Univ; Animal Resrch.

GREGG, CHERYL A; Bellbrook HS; Bellbrook, OH; 20/168 Cls Rep Frsh Cls; Chrh Wkr; Hon Rl; Lbry Ade; NHS; Stg Crw; Stu Cncl; Lat Clb; Pep Clb; Letter Trk; Varsity Ltr Club; Finalist Miss June Jamboree; Finalist Miss Teen Ohio Pageant; Univ.

GREGG, DEBRA; Zanesville HS; Zanesville, OH; 4/350 Band; Chrs; Chrh Wkr; Hon Rl; NHS; Sch Mus; Yth Flsp; Yrbk; Lat Clb; Natl Merit Ltr; Rotary Club Of Zanesville Schslhp Recgntn Bangqt 78 & 79; Oh Test Of Schlstc Achvmnt Hon Mntn In Eng 78; Univ; Math.

GREGG, JENNIFER; Triad HS; Cable, OH; 4/75 Band; Hon Rl; NHS; Rptr Yrbk; Sec 4-H; Trk; Letter Chrldng; GAA; Scr Kpr; Twrlr; Wittenberg Univ; Elem Educ.

GREGG, JOY; Columbiana HS; Columbiana, OH; 21/98 Trs Soph Cls; Trs Jr Cls; Trs Sr Cls; Chrs; Hon Rl; NHS; Yrbk; Pep Clb; Chrldng; PPFtbl; Harding Univ; Acctg.

GREGG, MARY; Yellow Springs HS; Yellow Sprg, OH; 18/80 Orch; Pol Wkr; Sch Mus; Rptr Yrbk; Letter Socr; Spanish 2 Achvmnt Awd 77; Rating 1 For Violin Solo; Solo & Ensemble Contest Class A 79; Violin Tchr 77 80; Univ; Zoology.

GREGG, MARY; John Adams HS; S Bend, IN; 17/405 Band; Chrh Wkr; Drm Bgl; Hon Rl; NHS; Orch; Quill & Scroll; Sch Mus; Sch Pl; Yth Flsp; Indiana Univ; Jrnlsm.

GREGG, PAULA; Fairview HS; Bryan, OH; Chrs; Hon Rl; 4-H; FTA; Pep Clb; VP Spn Clb; Mgrs; 4-H Awd; Toledo Univ; Speech Ther.

GREGG, PETER E; Princeton HS; Cincinnati, OH; 2/651 Sal; Chrs; Hon Rl; NHS; Sch Mus; Sch Pl; Drama Clb; Socr; NCTE; Natl Merit SF; Univ; Bio Med Engr.

GREGG, SANDRA; Trinity HS; Garfield Hts, OH; 6/143 Cls Rep Soph Cls; Chrh Wkr; Hon Rl; Pres JA; Stu Cncl; Cleveland State; Bus Admin.

GREGORICH, GLORIA; Westfield Washington HS; Carmel, IN; Chrh Wkr; Hon Rl; Lbry Ade; Quill & Scroll; Sch Mus; Sch Pl; Stg Crw; Rptr Sch Nwsp; Drama Clb; Ball State; Drama.

GREGORY, CHERYLYNN; Rutherford B Hayes HS; Delaware, OH; Chrs; Cmnty Wkr; Girl Scts; Natl Forn Lg; Orch; Sch Mus; Sec Yth Flsp; 4-H; Treas Spn Clb; Opt Clb Awd; Miami Univ; Elem Educ.

GREGORY, DAVID; Wood Memorial HS; Evansville, IN; Boy Scts; Voc Schl.

GREGORY, DOUG; Ridgedale HS; Marion, OH; Band; Hon Rl; Treas Yth Flsp; Univ; Archt.

GREGORY, JOHN; Hurricane HS; Hurricane, WV; VP Jr Cls; FCA; Stu Cncl; Letter Ftbl; Letter Trk; Scr Kpr; 4-H Awd; Pres Comedy Club 78; West Virginia Univ; Archt.

GREGORY, JOHN; Belding HS; Belding, MI; Chrh Wkr; Hon Rl; Yth Flsp; Fr Clb; Michigan Competitive Schlrshp; Suomi Coll; Acctg.

GREGORY, JONORA; Wheelersburg HS; Wheelersburg, OH; 10/150 Hon Rl; Marshall Univ; Phys Ther.

GREGORY, JULIE; Utica Sr HS; Newark, OH; 19/196 Band; Pres Chrs; Hon Rl; NHS; Pol Wkr; Sch Pl; Yth Flsp; Drama Clb; OSU Schl Of Music; Accmpnst.

GREGORY, LOIS J; Rocky River HS; Rocky River, OH; 40/307 Cl Rep Jr Cls; Hon Rl; Hosp Ade; Jr NHS; Lit Mag; NHS; Stu Cncl; Fr Clb; NCTE; Homecoming Qn Of Rock Rvr; Highest Honor Roll ; Kiwanis Club Schlrshp; St Marys Coll; Busns Admin.

GREGORY, LYNN; Kimball HS; Royal Oak, MI; Chrs; Hon Rl; Jr NHS; NHS; Off Ade; Sch Mus; Drama Clb; Letter Swmmng; PPFtbl; Tmr; Hillsdale Coll; Med.

GREGORY, MARK; Petoskey HS; Petoskey, MI; 50/215 Lat Clb; Letter Bsbl; Letter Crs Cntry; Ferris St College; Nuclear.

GREGORY, PAMELA; Glen Oak HS; Cleveland, OH; Jr NHS; Lbry Ade; Sch Mus; Sprt Ed Yrbk; Chrldng; CAP; Coll; Photo Journalism.

GREGORY, STEPHANIE; Field HS; Suffield, OH; 48/240 VP Frsh Cls; VP Sr Cls; Chrh Wkr; Cmnty Wkr; Girl Scts; Hon Rl; NHS; Off Ade; FHA; Pep Clb; 300.

GREGORY, TERRAN; Glen Oak School; Cleveland, OH; VP Soph Cls; Cls Rep Sr Cls; Chrh Wkr; Cmnty Wkr; Jr NHS; Stu Cncl; Yth Flsp; Vassar Coll.

GREGORY JR, JOHN; Mooresville HS; Mooresville, IN; 11/225 Chrh Wkr; FCA; Hon Rl; Jr NHS; NHS; Off Ade; Pres 4-H; Pres FFA; Letter Crs Cntry; Purdue Univ; Agri.

GREIB, CHRISTINE; Marine City HS; Marine City, MI; 2/200 Sec Frsh Cls; Cls Rep Frsh Cls; Cl Rep Jr Cls; Hon Rl; NHS; Sch Pl; Stu Cncl; Rptr Sch Nwsp; Sch Nwsp; Drama Clb; Univ; Comm Art.

GREIER, MARY A; Leetonia HS; Leetonia, OH; 4/86 Am Leg Aux Girls St; Band; Hon Rl; JA; NHS; Rptr Yrbk; 4-H; 4-H Awd; JA Awd; Cert Of Honor; Journalism Awd Cert; Band Awds Cert Gold Bar Letter & Pin; Kent St Univ; Journalism.

GREIVENKAMP, GREGG A; La Salle HS; Cincinnati, OH; 5/275 Sec Band; Hon Rl; NHS; Orch; Sch Mus; Yrbk; Rptr Sch Nwsp; Mth Clb; Thomas More Univ; Bus Admin.

GREIWE, DIANE; Colerain HS; Cincinnati, OH; Cl Rep Jr Cls; Hon Rl; Jr NHS; Sch Mus; Stu Cncl; Drama Clb; Ger Clb; Letter Chrldng; Miami Univ; Bus.

GREIWE, DONNA; Norwood HS; Norwood, OH; Hon Rl; Jr NHS; Stg Crw; Fr Clb; Pep Clb; GAA; Mgrs; Scr Kpr; Tmr; Univ Of Cincinnati; Lang.

GREIWE, DOUGLAS; Purcell HS; Cincinnati, OH; 55/189 Cls Rep Soph Cls; Cl Rep Jr Cls; Pres Sr Cls; Cls Rep Sr Cls; Stu Cncl; Bsktbl; Ftbl; Glf; Chrldng; Was Voted Pres Of My Sr Class 78; Univ Of Cincinnati; Interior Dsgn.

GREKOWICZ, CHRIS; Harbor Beach Cmnty HS; Harbor Beach, MI; Aud/Vis; Hon Rl; Pres 4-H; VP FFA; Pep Clb; Trk; 4-H Awd; Michigan St Univ; Farmer.

GREMBOWICZ, VICTORIA; Lasalle HS; South Bend, IN; Cls Rep Soph Cls; Cl Rep Jr Cls; Cmp Fr Grls; Hon Rl; Hosp Ade; Off Ade; Sch Pl; Chrldng; College; Nursing.

GREMEL, LORI; Unionville Sebewaing HS; Sebewaing, MI; 9/109 Band; Chrs; Yrbk; Chrldng; Mic State Univ.

GREMLING, CHRIS; Chaminade Julienne HS; Oakwood, OH; Boy Scts; Hon Rl; Red Cr Ade; Sch Pl; Sct Actv; Y-Teens; Bsktbl; Socr; IM Sprt; Univ Of Dayton; Mechanical Engineer.

GRENER, CYNTHIA L; Newark Sr HS; Newark, OH; Cls Rep Frsh Cls; Cls Rep Soph Cls; Cl Rep Jr Cls; Cmp Fr Grls; Chrs; Drl Tm; Hon Rl; Jr NHS; NHS; Sch Mus; College.

GRENERT, NANCY; Laville Jr Sr HS; Lakeville, IN; Cmp Fr Grls; Hon Rl; NHS; Fr Clb; FHA; Sci Clb; Trk; Goshen Coll; Bus.

GRENKE, LYNNE; Gaylord HS; Gaylord, MI; Band; Hon Rl; NHS; 4-H; Ferris St Coll; Med Rec Admin.

GRENN, JOSEPH; St Alphonsus HS; Dearborn, MI; 37/171 Debate Tm; Hon Rl; Bsktbl; Crs Cntry; Swmmng; Trk; Tmr; General Motors Inst; Bus.

GRESAK, TOM; Bishop Donahue HS; Wheeling, WV; 10/64 Pres Frsh Cls; Cls Rep Frsh Cls; Trs Soph Cls; Boy Scts; Hon Rl; Stu Cncl; Treas Key Clb; Spn Clb; Bsbl; Ftbl; College; Busns Mgmt.

GRESHAM, BERNICE; East Technical HS; Cleveland, OH; Cls Rep Soph Cls; Band; Cmnty Wkr; Hon Rl; Hosp Ade; Off Ade; Orch; Civ Clb; Fr Clb; FNA; Juvenile Justice Fair 1st Prize 79; Western Reserve Educ Fund 79; Hon Roll 79; Atlanta Univ; Nursing.

GRESHAM, SHERRI; Warrensville Heights HS; Warrensville Hg, OH; 3/211 Sec Frsh Cls; Sec Soph Cls; Sec Jr Cls; Sec Sr Cls; Aud/Vis; Drl Tm; Hon Rl; Sec Jr NHS; Sec NHS; Stg Crw; Univ.

GRESHAM, SUSAN; Brookhaven HS; Columbus, OH; Cmp Fr Grls; Chrs; Chrh Wkr; Hon Rl; Hosp Ade; Lit Mag; Treas NHS; Yth Flsp; Rptr Sch Nwsp; Spn Clb; Natl Fed Of Music Club Three Awds In Piano 75; Mbr Of Natl Frater Of Stu Mus 72 79; Mbr Of Sat Mus Clb 72; Univ; Nurse.

GRESHAM, SUSAN; North Farmington HS; Farmington Hls, MI; Hon Rl; Gym; Michigan St Univ; Med Tech.

GRESSEL, MICHAEL; Lakota HS; W Chester, OH; 20/500 Hon Rl; NHS; Univ Of Cincinnati; Chem Engr.

GRESSEL, STEPHEN C; Fairfield Sr HS; Hamilton, OH; 7/598 Hon Rl; NHS; Fr Clb; Natl Merit SF; Univ; Math.

GRESZCZUK, K; Andrean HS; Crown Pte, IN; Lat Clb; Mth Clb; IM Sprt; Purdue Univ; Chem Engr.

GREUEL, MELANIE; Gahanna Lincoln HS; Gahanna, OH; 41/448 Trs Jr Cls; Band; Chrh Wkr; Hon Rl; NHS; Treas Yth Flsp; Treas DECA; Treas Spn Clb; Capt Chrldng; Columbus Tech Inst; Comp Prog.

GREVE, JOAN; Manistee Catholic Cntrl HS; Manistee, MI; 10/65 Sec Sr Cls; Band; Hon Rl; Sch Pl; Drama Clb; Bus Mgmt.

GREVER, MATT; Mc Nicholas HS; Cincinnati, OH; 61/240 Hon Rl; Sch Pl; Ftbl; IM Sprt; Coll; Accntg.

GREVING, ELLEN; Loudonville HS; Perrysville, OH; Hosp Ade; NHS; Off Ade; Rptr Yrbk; Rptr Sch Nwsp; FHA; FNA; Ten Temple Univ; Audiology.

GREWE, SHANNON; Marlington HS; Alliance, OH; 14/267 Am Leg Aux Girls St; Chrs; Cmnty Wkr; Hon Rl; Sct Actv; Drama Clb; 4-H; Fr Clb; Pep Clb; Bowling Green Univ; Cpa.

GREY, DAVID S; Cranbrook HS; West Bloomfield, MI; 7/115 Hon Rl; Red Cr Ade; Rptr Yrbk; IM Sprt; Natl Merit SF; College; Medicine.

GREY, DELANNA; New Lexington HS; Lancaster, OH; 11/165 Chrs; Hon Rl; NHS; Pol Wkr; Sch Mus; Sch Pl; Stg Crw; Rptr Sch Nwsp; Drama Clb; OEA; Whos Who Among Amer HS Stdnt 77; St Bd Mbr Of Intl Thespian Soc 78; Bst Thespian Awd 78; Ohio Univ; Theater.

GREY, JULIANA; Benton Harbor HS; Benton Hbr, MI; Chrh Wkr; Cmnty Wkr; Debate Tm; Sch Pl; Stg Crw; Spn Clb; IM Sprt; Scr Kpr; Andrews Univ; Med.

GREYERBIEHL, DONNA; Hartland HS; Milford, MI; Hon Rl; Off Ade; Spn Clb; Letter Mgrs; Scr Kpr; Emu; Soc Work.

GRIBBEN, JULIE; Hurricane HS; Hurricane, WV; Girl Scts; Hon Rl; Y-Teens; Pep Clb; Letter Bsktbl; IM Sprt; W Virginia Plce Acad; St Police Prg.

GRIBBLE, TRACI; Loudonville HS; Loudonville, OH; Chrs; Chrh Wkr; Hon Rl; NHS; Sch Mus; VP Stu Cncl; Pres Yth Flsp; Rptr Yrbk; Sch Nwsp; Drama Clb; Heidelberg Coll; Opera Singer.

GRICEWICH, MARK; Bridgeport HS; Bridgeport, WV; 35/200 Pres Frsh Cls; Pres Soph Cls; Band; Chrh Wkr; Cmnty Wkr; Hon Rl; Jr NHS; Sec NHS; VP Stu Cncl; Pres Yth Flsp; College; Busns.

GRIDER, CHRISTINE; Henryville HS; Henryville, IN; Chrh Wkr; Cmnty Wkr; Hon Rl; Ed Sch Nwsp; Treas Sch Nwsp; FHA; Trk; College; Modeling.

GRIEBENOW, M GRANT; Parkside HS; Jackson, MI; 15/360 Stu Cncl; Rptr Yrbk; Ger Clb; Capt Crs Cntry; Capt Trk; Orm Roberts Univ; Med.

GRIECO, KAREN; Wickliffe HS; Wickliffe, OH; AFS; Hon Rl; PPFtbl; 4-H Awd; Lakeland Comm College; Bus.

GRIEP, LYNNEA; North Central HS; Indianapolis, IN; Chrs; Chrh Wkr; Girl Scts; Yth Flsp; Natl Merit Ltr; Univ.

GRIER, DANIELE M; East HS; Columbus, OH; 61/272 Cl Rep Jr Cls; Cls Rep Sr Cls; Hon Rl; NHS; Off Ade; Stu Cncl; Rptr Sch Nwsp; Trk; Ohio St Univ; Law.

GRIER, KAREN L; Washington HS; Massillon, OH; Cl Rep Jr Cls; Band; Chrs; Chrh Wkr; Cmnty Wkr; Hosp Ade; Orch; Sch Mus; Pep Clb; Spn Clb; Univ; Med.

GRIER, KATHLEEN; South Haven Public HS; South Haven, MI; 15/230 Cmp Fr Grls; FCA; Hon Rl; NHS; Sch Pl; Pres Yth Flsp; Rptr Yrbk; 4-H; 4-H Awd; Michigan St Univ; Spec Ed.

GRIESELHUBER, DIANE; Stephen T Badin HS; Hamilton, OH; 1/225 VP Frsh Cls; Pres Soph Cls; Hon Rl; Hosp Ade; NHS; Sec Stu Cncl; Treas 4-H; Fr Clb; Swmmng; Ten; Univ; Math.

GRIESEMER, MARY; North Knox HS; Vincennes, IN; 11/173 Chrh Wkr; Hon Rl; NHS; Yth Flsp; FHA; Pep Clb; Vincennes Univ; Nursing.

GRIESER, BETH; Pettisville HS; Wauseon, OH; Sec Frsh Cls; Sec Sr Cls; Chrs; Chrh Wkr; Hon Rl; NHS; Yth Flsp; GAA; College; Nursing.

GRIESER, LINDA; Stryker HS; Stryker, OH; Band; Chrs; Hon Rl; Stu Cncl; Ed Yrbk; Rptr Sch Nwsp; 4-H; FHA; Bsktbl; Northwest Tech Voc Schl; Exec Sec.

GRIESINGER, BARRY; Taylor Ctr HS; Taylor, MI; 1/400 Hon Rl; NHS; Bsktbl; Trk; Univ.

GRIESINGER, BRIAN; Taylor Center HS; Taylor, MI; 5/400 Pres Jr Cls; Pres Sr Cls; Hon Rl; NHS; Letter Bsktbl; Letter Trk; Univ.

GRIESINGER, JEANNE; Adrian HS; Adrian, MI; 48/386 Chrs; Chrh Wkr; FCA; Hon Rl; NHS; Sch Mus; Lat Clb; Letter Bsktbl; Cert Of Regntn St Of Mi Comptty Schlshp 79; ITT Tech Schl; Elec.

GRIESMER, CATHY; Beaumont HS; Cleve Hts, OH; Hon Rl; Rptr Yrbk; Trk; Natl Merit Ltr; College.

GRIFFIN, ANGELA; Gallia Acad HS; Gallipolis, OH; Band; Chrs; Cmnty Wkr; Orch; Sch Pl; Yrbk; Sch Nwsp; Ohi Univ; Speech Sciences.

GRIFFIN, BONNIE; Lake Orion HS; Pontiac, MI; 90/425 Chrs; Chrh Wkr; Hon Rl; Jr NHS; Grand Rapids Baptist College; Educ.

GRIFFIN, CHRISTOPHER; Andrean HS; Gary, IN; 20/274 Hon Rl; NHS; Pres Lat Clb; VP Mth

Clb; Pres Sci Clb; Mass Inst Of Tech; Food & Nutrition.

GRIFFIN, DWYANE; Central HS; Grand Rapids, MI; Pres Sr Cls; Sch Pl; Swmmng; Ten; Wrstlng; Univ.

GRIFFIN, ERNEST; Les Cheneaux Cmnty HS; Cedarville, MI; Boy Scts; Lbry Ade; Sct Actv; Univ; Comp Sci.

GRIFFIN, GIGI; North HS; Springfield, OH; Chrs; Hon Rl; Fr Clb; Swmmng; Ten; Chrldng; College; Bus.

GRIFFIN, GLEN; Holt HS; Holt, MI; 25/345 Hon Rl; NHS; Letter Ten; IM Sprt; Mgrs; Cit Awd; Natl Merit Ltr; Mgr Of The Holt HS Store; Pepperdine Univ; Busns.

GRIFFIN, GRANT; Watervliet Public Schools; Watervliet, MI; Cls Rep Frsh Cls; Cls Rep Soph Cls; Cl Rep Jr Cls; Pres Sr Cls; Cls Rep Sr Cls; Am Leg Boys St; Band; Drm Bgl; Hon Rl; VP NHS; Otstndng Sr Boy Schl Awd 79; Natl Schl Choral Awd 79; Captn Schl Quiz Bowl Tm 78; Cert Of Recogntn 79; Michigan St Univ; Dent.

GRIFFIN, JILL; Wickliffe HS; Wickliffe, OH; AFS; Band; Boy Scts; Hon Rl; Hosp Ade; Mod UN; Sch Mus; Rptr Sch Nwsp; Euclid Gnerl Hostp Resp Ther 750 79; Akron Univ; Resp Ther.

GRIFFIN, JOHN; Carman HS; Flint, MI; 2/380 Cls Rep Sr Cls; Sal; Chrs; Hon Rl; NHS; Letter Bsbl; Mgrs; Natl Merit Ltr; Hope Coll; Chem.

GRIFFIN, JOSEPH P; St Xavier HS; Cincinnati, OH; 77/264 Cls Rep Soph Cls; Cl Rep Jr Cls; Boy Scts; Chrh Wkr; Hon Rl; Stu Cncl; Yrbk; Rptr Sch Nwsp; Pep Clb; IM Sprt; College; Pre Med.

GRIFFIN, JULIA; Our Lady Of Mercy HS; Farmington Hls, MI; Cls Rep Frsh Cls; Cmnty Wkr; Yth Flsp; Michigan St Univ; Bus.

GRIFFIN, LAURA; Niles HS; Niles, MI; 43/388 Hon Rl; Hosp Ade; Stu Cncl; Bsbl; Mic St; Journalism.

GRIFFIN, MARGO; Shelby HS; Shelby, MI; Hon Rl; Off Ade; Rptr Sch Nwsp; Sch Nwsp; FHA; Spn Clb; Scr Kpr; Muskegon Busns Schl; Med Asst.

GRIFFIN, RUTH E; Scecina Mem HS; Indianapolis, IN; 90/194 Chrs; Chrh Wkr; Cmnty Wkr; Bsbl; Letter Bsktbl; Trk; GAA; IM Sprt; Vlybl Varsity Letter Jr Varsity Medal 2 Varsity Medals; Table Tennis Singles 1st & 2nd Doubles 1st & 2nd; College; Professional Sports.

GRIFFIN, S; Taylor HS; Kokomo, IN; 7/186 Girl Scts; Hon Rl; NHS; Fr Clb; Bsbl; Letter Gym; Wrstlng; Chrldng; PPFtbl; College.

GRIFFIN, STACIE; Field HS; Kent, OH; Hon Rl; OEA; Ten; Kiwan Awd; Reg State & Natl Placement For Info Communications;.

GRIFFIN, STEVEN; Benedictine HS; Cleveland, OH; 14/99 Hon Rl; NHS; Sch Nwsp; Fr Clb; IM Sprt; Cleveland State Univ; Math.

GRIFFIN, THOMAS; St Edward HS; Rocky River, OH; 2/370 Chrs; Hon Rl; Lit Mag; Mod UN; NHS; Sch Mus; Med.

GRIFFIN, WILLIAM; Wayland HS; Dorr, MI; 16/193 Hon Rl; NHS; Orch; Sch Pl; Sct Actv; Ed Sch Nwsp; Letter Ftbl; Trk; Natl Merit Ltr; Albion Coll Schlstc Schlrshp 79; Eng Soc Studies & Drama Awd 79; Albion Coll; Bio.

GRIFFIN, WILLIAM; Edwardsburg HS; Edwardsburg, MI; Band; Boy Scts; Chrs; NHS; Sch Mus; Yrbk; Sch Nwsp; Fr Clb; Wrstlng;.

GRIFFING, KATHLEEN; Plymouth Canton HS; Plymouth, MI; 1/412 Val; Band; Girl Scts; Jr NHS; Mod UN; NHS; Sch Mus; Yth Flsp; Fr Clb; Natl Merit Finalist 79; Capt Of Soccer; Stanford Univ.

GRIFFIN III, HERBERT E; Bedford North Lawrence HS; Bedford, IN; 8/380 Chrs; Cmnty Wkr; Letter Debate Tm; NHS; Beta Clb; VP Drama Clb; Spn Clb; Kiwan Awd; Voice Dem Awd; Stu Of Month; Honor Bar Thespian; Indiana Univ; Theatre.

GRIFFIS, LISA M; Madison Comprehensive HS; Mansfield, OH; Cls Rep Frsh Cls; VP Soph Cls; Cl Rep Jr Cls; Chrs; Drl Tm; Stu Cncl; Fr Clb; Pom Pon;.

GRIFFITH, AMY; Madeira HS; Madeira, OH; 2/165 Band; Chrs; Girl Scts; Hon Rl; JA; NHS; Sch Mus; Stg Crw; Drama Clb; Lat Clb; Raymond G Seifert Awd; Academic Ach Awd; Involved In Teen Counseling; College; Liberal Arts.

GRIFFITH, BRIAN; Robert S Rogers HS; Toledo, OH; 10/412 Cl Rep Jr Cls; Band; Hon Rl; Pres NHS; Orch; Sch Mus; Sch Pl; Stg Crw; Stu Cncl; Sci Clb;.

GRIFFITH, CASSANDRA; Buchtel HS; Akron, OH; 121/465 Lbry Ade; Lit Mag; Ed Sch Nwsp; Rptr Sch Nwsp; Swmmng; Natl Merit SF; Univ; Envrnmntl Sci.

GRIFFITH, CHARLES; South Vermillion HS; St Bernice, IN; Boy Scts; Hon Rl; Sct Actv; Boys Clb Am; FBLA; JC Awd; Cert Of Awd Eng & Sci 76; Best Boy Stud Awd 76; Louisiana St Univ.

GRIFFITH, DAWN; East HS; Akron, OH; Band; Hon Rl; Off Ade; Sci Clb; Spn Clb; Heidelberg Coll; Psychology.

GRIFFITH, DEREK; Brooke HS; Colliers, WV; 92/403 Hon Rl; Univ; Chem.

GRIFFITH, DONNA; Crestwood HS; Hiram, OH; Cl Rep Jr Cls; Cls Rep Sr Cls; Cmnty Wkr; Girl Scts; Hon Rl; Off Ade; Stu Cncl; Pep Clb; Gym; Capt Chrldng; Ohio State; Physical Therapy.

GRIFFITH, JONATHAN; South Charleston HS; S Charleston, WV; Hon Rl; Jr NHS; Ftbl; Letter Trk; College; Chem.

GRIFFITH, KATHLEEN M; Flushing HS; Flushing, MI; Band; Hon Rl; Rptr Yrbk; Rptr Sch Nwsp; Lat Clb; Michigan St Univ; Psych.

GRIFFITH, KATHRYN; Walnut Hills HS; Cincinnati, OH; Sec Band; Hon Rl; Off Ade; Natl Merit Schl; Procter & Gamble Schlrshp 4 Yrs 79; Ohio St Univ; Finance.

GRIFFITH, KYLE; Wilmington HS; Wilmington, OH; Sec Chrs; Treas Cmnty Wkr; Treas Hon Rl; NHS; Sch Mus; Yth Flsp; Treas 4-H; Pep Clb; Chrldng; Scr Kpr; Ohio Wesleyan Univ; Nursing.

GRIFFITH, LAURA; Bluefield HS; Bluefield, WV; Chrs; Girl Scts; Hon Rl; Yrbk; Mgrs; Univ; Math.

GRIFFITH, MARLENE; Marysville HS; Marysville, OH; 3/230 Cmnty Wkr; Hon Rl; Lbry Ade; NHS; Off Ade; Sch Pl; 4-H; Mth Clb; Chrldng; GAA; Ohio St Univ; Psych.

GRIFFITH, PAUL; Greenfield Central HS; Greenfield, IN; 52/350 Pres Jr Cls; Am Leg Boys St; Band; Chrh Wkr;.

GRIFFITH, SCOTT; Shortridge HS; Indianapolis, IN; Hon Rl; Lit Mag; NHS; Mth Clb; Crs Cntry; Trk; Ind Univ; Liberal Arts.

GRIFFITH, SHARI; Chippewa Hills HS; Remus, MI; 11/208 Hon Rl; NHS; 4-H; Trk; 4-H Awd; Ferris St Coll; Pre Vet.

GRIFFITH, SHARON S; Terre Haute North Vigo HS; Terre Haute, IN; 54/637 Cls Rep Frsh Cls; Hon Rl; Off Ade; Orch; Sch Mus; Stu Cncl; Y-Teens; Lat Clb; Tmr; Mst Outstntnd Orchr Stdnt 77; Univ Of S Florida; Chem.

GRIFFITH, TARI BETH; Madison HS; Madison, OH; Chrs; Hon Rl; NHS; Off Ade; Sch Pl; Drama Clb; Spn Clb; Baldwin Wallace Univ; Law.

GRIFFITH, TIM; Groveport Madison HS; Columbus, OH; Chrh Wkr; Hon Rl; Trk; Ohio State Univ.

GRIFFITH, TRACI; Smithville HS; Marshallvl, OH; Band; NHS; Sch Pl; Yth Flsp; Fr Clb; Ger Clb; Trk; GAA; Miami Univ; Speech.

GRIFFITHS, JANA; Oak Hill HS; Oak Hill, OH; Am Leg Aux Girls St; Band; Chrs; Hon Rl; NHS; Sch Mus; Sch Pl; Yth Flsp; Yrbk; Beta Clb; Ohio Univ; Med Tech.

GRIFFITHS, PATRICIA; Danbury HS; Marblehead, OH; 3/62 Trs Frsh Cls; Cls Rep Frsh Cls; Pres Soph Cls; Pres Sr Cls; Girl Scts; Hon Rl; NHS; Sch Pl; Rptr Yrbk; FHA; Marblehead Bank Schlshp; Norton Awd; Firelands Univ; Bus Educ.

GRIGEREIT, TODD; Hammond HS; Hammond, IN; 3/3 Am Leg Boys St; Aud/Vis; Hon Rl; Jr NHS; Natl Forn Lg; NHS; Capt Swmmng; Trk; DAR Aw d; Pres Awd; College.

GRIGG, JOANNA; Stow HS; Stow, OH; 12/595 Chrs; Chrh Wkr; NHS; Orch; Mth Clb; Trk; Univ; Sci.

GRIGGS, MARY; Clay HS; South Bend, IN; 56/459 Hon Rl; JA; Lit Mag; NHS; Univ Of Ind; Comm Artist.

GRIGGS, SHARON; Lakeview HS; St Clair Shores, MI; 4/550 Hon Rl; NHS; Quill & Scroll; Ed Sch Nwsp; Fr Clb; Capt Gym; Letter Swmmng; Central Michigan Univ.

GRIGGS, SUSAN; Decatur Jr Sr HS; Decatur, MI; Band; Hon Rl; Lbry Ade; Softball Varsity Letter; Softball Selected To 1st Team All Conf; Coll; Busns Admin.

GRIGSBY, DONNA; Amelia HS; Batavia, OH; Chrh Wkr; Hon Rl; Lbry Ade; Yth Flsp; Drama Clb; College; Art Ed.

GRIGSBY, SANDRA; Wayland Union HS; Dorr, MI; 23/193 Cls Rep Soph Cls; Cl Rep Jr Cls; Band; Cmp Fr Grls; Debate Tm; Hon Rl; Sch Pl; Stu Cncl; PPFtbl; Mi Comptn Schlrshp 79; Michigan St Univ; Vet Med.

GRILL, DEBRA A; Lakeview HS; St Clair Shores, MI; Hon Rl; NHS; Letter Ten; Mic State; Zoology.

GRIM, ARLENE; Federal Hocking HS; Stewart, OH; Chrs; Cmnty Wkr; Hon Rl; Off Ade; FBLA; Sec FFA; GAA; Hocking Tech College.

GRIM, TERRI; New Albany Sr HS; New Albany, IN; 208/565 Chrs; Debate Tm; Girl Scts; Off Ade; Orch; Stg Crw; Sch Nwsp; Ger Clb; Sci Clb; Trk; Purdue Univ; Engr.

GRIM, THOMAS; Black River HS; Homerville, OH; 11/100 Band; Boy Scts; Chrs; Chrh Wkr; Hon Rl; Sch Pl; Beta Clb; 4-H; Ger Clb; Sci Clb; Ohio St Univ; Engr.

GRIME, PENNY; Liberty Center HS; Liberty Center, OH; Girl Scts; Sct Actv; FHA; OEA; GAA; PPFtbl;.

GRIMES, DANA; Elwood Comm HS; Elwood, IN; 14/186 Cls Rep Sr Cls; Band; Chrh Wkr; Hon Rl; Jr NHS; NHS; Sch Mus; Yrbk; Spn Clb; Rotary Awd; Memphis St Univ; Music.

GRIMES, GLENDA; Wintersville HS; Winterwvl, OH; 97/288 Girl Scts; Lbry Ade; Off Ade; Spn Clb; Jefferson Tech Schl; Med.

GRIMES, JANE; Cambridge HS; Cambridge, OH; Am Leg Aux Girls St; Pres Band; Chrs; Chrh Wkr; Hon Rl; NHS; Yth Flsp; Evangel Coll.

GRIMES, JOHN S; Hagerstown HS; Hagerstown, IN; 8/160 Band; Hon Rl; NHS; Rptr Sch Nwsp; Sch Nwsp; Fr Clb; Sci Clb; Opt Clb Awd; Ind Univ.

GRIMES, LAURIE; Negaunee HS; Negaunee, MI; Chrs; Chrh Wkr; Drm Bgl; Hon Rl; Rptr Yrbk; Yrbk; PPFtbl; Voice Dem Awd; Univ; Archt.

GRIMES, MARGARITA; Nettie Lee Roth HS; Dayton, OH; Cls Rep Frsh Cls; Cls Rep Soph Cls; Cl Rep Jr Cls; Cmnty Wkr; Hon Rl; Lbry Ade; Stu Cncl; DECA; FHA; Cit Awd; Univ; Mgmt.

GRIMM, ALISA; Keystone HS; La Grange, OH; 2/135 Chrh Wkr; Drl Tm; Hon Rl; NHS; Sch Pl; Yrbk; Drama Clb; FTA; Pep Clb; Trk; Univ Of Toledo; Engr.

GRIMM, DIANA; Fowlerville HS; Fowlerville, MI; 7/150 Band; Chrh Wkr; Hon Rl; NHS; 4-H; Key Clb; Mth Clb; Twrlr; 4-H Awd; Nazareth Coll; Nursing.

GRIMM, DIANE; Blanchester HS; Midland, OH; 8/165 Hon Rl; NHS; Sch Pl; Eng Clb; FHA; FTA; Spn Clb; Am Leg Awd; College.

GRIMM, MARY B; Sistersville HS; Sistersville, WV; Chrs; Chrh Wkr; Hon Rl; Sch Pl; Stg Crw; Drama Clb; FHA; VP Pep Clb; Mt Vernon Nazarene College.

GRIMM, RANDY; Cardington Lincoln HS; Cardington, OH; Cls Rep Frsh Cls; Band; Chrh Wkr; Hon Rl; Sch Pl; 4-H; VP FFA; IM Sprt; 4-H Awd; Ohio St Univ; Ag.

GRIMM, STEPHANIE; Springboro HS; Springboro, OH; 3/195 Am Leg Aux Girls St; Band; Hon Rl; NHS; Sch Pl; Stg Crw; Sec Stu Cncl; Ed Yrbk; Bowling Green State Univ; Comunictns.

GRIMM, STEPHEN; Lawton HS; Lawton, MI; VP Frsh Cls; Trs Sr Cls; Hon Rl; Sch Mus; Stu Cncl; Pres Sci Clb; Bsbl; Letter Ftbl; Capt Wrstlng; IM Sprt; Schls Dept Awd In Sci 78; Mi Comp Schlrshp 78; W Mi Univ Acad Schlrshp 78; Kalamazoo Coll; Organic Chem.

GRIMM, STEVEN; Whitmer HS; Toledo, OH; 41/810 Hon Rl; NHS; Fr Clb; Ftbl; Bowling Green St Univ; Comp Sci.

GRIMM, VICTOR; Washington HS; Massillon, OH; Band; Hon Rl; Orch; Boys Clb Am;.

GRIMMER, LESLIE; Sycamore HS; Mont, OH; 100/450 Chrs; Hon Rl; JA; Lit Mag; Rptr Yrbk; Yrbk; Rptr Sch Nwsp; Sch Nwsp; College; Law.

GRIMMETT, DONALD; Lenore HS; Dingess, WV; Beta Clb; College; Mining Engr.

GRIMMETT, MELVIN; Crooksville HS; Crooksville, OH; 3/95 Boy Scts; Hon Rl; Sch Pl; Stg Crw; Sci Clb; Spn Clb; Trk; Marietta Coll; Petroleum Engr.

GRIMSHAW, RHONDA; Grosse Pointe South HS; Grss Pte Park, MI; Chrh Wkr; Cmnty Wkr; Girl Scts; Hon Rl; NHS; PAVAS; Sch Pl; Yth Flsp; Trk; Tmr; Univ Of Michigan; Bio.

GRIMSKI, LINDA; Lincoln HS; Warren, MI; Val; Hon Rl; Jr NHS; NHS; Ed Yrbk; Ed Sch Nwsp; College.

GRIMSLID, TAMI; Penn HS; Mishawaka, IN; Girl Scts; Hon Rl; Off Ade; Yrbk; Pep Clb; PPFtbl; Tmr; Purdue; Fashion.

GRINDSTAFF, MITZI; Schafer HS; Southgate, MI; Cls Rep Frsh Cls; Pres Sr Cls; Band; Girl Scts; Hon Rl; Off Ade; Sct Actv; OEA;.

GRINER, PEGGY; Minster HS; Minster, OH; 21/80 Chrh Wkr; Girl Scts; Hon Rl; Sch Pl; Drama Clb; FTA; Pep Clb; VP Spn Clb; Bsktbl; Letter Trk; Good Samaratin Hosp; Nursing.

GRINER, SHIRLEY; Brownsburgh HS; Brownsburg, IN; 13/297 Cl Rep Jr Cls; Am Leg Aux Girls St; Cmnty Wkr; Hon Rl; Lbry Ade; NHS; Off Ade; Y-Teens; 4-H; Pep Clb; Ball St Univ; Busns Admin.

GRINONNEAU, LEE; Rogers HS; Toledo, OH; Chrh Wkr; Hon Rl; FDA; Letter Ftbl; Letter Trk; PPFtbl; Univ Of Tol; Pre Med.

GRINS, NORA; Normandy Sr HS; Lake Jackson, TX; 31/660 Chrs; Hon Rl; NHS; Ger Clb; Univ.

GRISE, G; Snider HS; Ft Wayne, IN; Chrh Wkr; Hon Rl; Bsktbl; Trk; Purdue Univ; Engr.

GRISE, KAREN; Niles HS; Niles, MI; 4/403 Band; Chrh Wkr; Girl Scts; Hon Rl; Orch; Stu Cncl; Yth Flsp; Sch Nwsp; 4-H; Pres Awd; Ferris State Coll; Pharmacy.

GRISSOM, GARY; Union Cnty HS; Liberty, IN; Aud/Vis; Chrs; Hon Rl; Lbry Ade; Yth Flsp; Pres FFA; Gym;.

GRISSOM, NORMAN D; St Xavier HS; Lawrenceburg, IN; 63/301 Cls Rep Frsh Cls; Cl Rep Jr Cls; Hon Rl; Stu Cncl; Glf; IM Sprt; Natl Merit Ltr; Pres Awd; Mich; Law.

GRISSOM, RUTH; Cass Tech HS; Detroit, MI; Band; Hon Rl; Lbry Ade; Sch Mus; Butler Univ; Med Tech.

GRISSOM, SUSAN; Clinton Prairie HS; Frankfort, IN; 22/91 Trs Sr Cls; Chrs; Chrh Wkr; Girl Scts; Hon Rl; JA; Yth Flsp; Y-Teens; 4-H; FBLA; Vocation School; Horse Trainer.

GRIT, JONATHAN; Willard HS; Willard, OH; 1/200 FCA; NHS; Orch; Sch Mus; Sprt Ed Sch Nwsp; Ten; Coach Actv; IM Sprt; Calvin Univ; Dent.

GRIT, PAMELA K; Hudsonville HS; Hudsonville, MI; 3/188 Band; Hon Rl; NHS; Grand Vly St Coll; Nursing.

GRITEMAN, KARIN; Liberty Center HS; Napoleon, OH; Hst Sr Cls; Am Leg Aux Girls St; Band; Chrs; Chrh Wkr; Cmnty Wkr; Hon Rl; NHS; Sch Mus; Sch Pl; Bowling Green St Univ.

GRITMAN, MELISSA; Medina Sr HS; Medina, OH; 32/380 Cls Rep Sr Cls; Chrs; NHS; Sch Mus; Sch Pl; Stg Crw; Stu Cncl; Drama Clb; Pep Clb; PPFtbl; Muskingum Coll Schlrshp; Drama Tech Awd; Muskingum Coll; Biology.

GROCE, ANGEL; Crothersville Cmnty HS; Crothersville, IN; 2/70 Hon Rl; 4-H; Bsktbl; Trk; Univ; Tchr.

GROCHOLSKI, GREGORY; Bay City Western HS; Kawkawlin, MI; 140/438 Band; Chrs; Chrh Wkr; Hon Rl; Orch; Sch Mus; Rdo Clb; Northwood Inst; Bus Admin.

GROEN, MARY; Marquette HS; Michigan City, IN; 8/66 Hon Rl; NHS; Stu Cncl; Rptr Yrbk; Fr Clb; Chrldng; College; Busns Admin.

GROEN, PHYLLIS; Marquette HS; Rochester, MI; Sec Frsh Cls; Sec Soph Cls; Cmnty Wkr; Hon Rl; Sch Mus; Drama Clb; Fr Clb; Swmmng; College; Dietician.

GROEN, RONALD D; Calvin Christian HS; Grand Rapids, MI; Band; Hon Rl; Stu Cncl; Bsktbl; Crs Cntry; IM Sprt; Univ; Acctg.

GROENINK, STEVE; Grand Rapids Central HS; Grand Rapids, MI; Chrh Wkr; Hon Rl; Mod UN; NHS; Sch Mus; Pep Clb; Ten; Am Leg Awd; Coll; Law.

GROESSER, JANELLE; Portland HS; Portland, MI; Band; Girl Scts; Hon Rl; Capt Chrldng; PPFtbl; Michigan St Univ; Nursing.

GROEWA, ERIC; Solon HS; Solon, OH; Chrh Wkr; Hon Rl; Yth Flsp; Letter Ten; IM Sprt; 2nd Honor Roll Frshmn & Soph Yrs; College; Engr.

GROEWA, LORI M; Solon HS; Solon, OH; Chrh Wkr; Yth Flsp; Pep Clb; Frsh 1st Honor Roll; Jr Perfect Attendance; College; Busns Mgmt.

GROF, SHIRLEY; Portage Lakes Jt Voc HS; Akron, OH; 123/203 Hst Jr Cls; Hst Sr Cls; Chrs; Cmnty Wkr; Girl Scts; Hon Rl; Off Ade; Sct Actv; Yth Flsp; OEA; 3rd Pl Historian OOEA Contest; Stark Tech Schl; Court Steno.

GROFF, KEN; Bellbrook HS; Bellbrook, OH; 50/200 Chrh Wkr; Cmnty Wkr; FCA; Yth Flsp; Yrbk; Fr Clb; Bsbl; Capt Bsktbl; Ftbl; Glf; Taylor Univ; Art.

GROGAN, KATHY; Upper Arlington HS; Columbus, OH; 177/645 Chrs; Drl Tm; Hon Rl; Pol Wkr; Sch Mus; Pep Clb; GAA; Honor Awd 77; Champion Synchronized Swimmer 78; Ohio St Univ; Engr.

GROGG, DEBRAH; Tecumseh HS; Donnelsville, OH; 48/344 Cls Rep Frsh Cls; AFS; Band; Drl Tm; Hon Rl; Jr NHS; NHS; FBLA; FHA; Pep Clb; Outstndng Jr BOE Awd; Sinclair Comm Coll; Marketing.

GROH, KEVIN; Fairless HS; Navarre, OH; Band; Chrs; Chrh Wkr; Hon Rl; NHS; Sch Mus; Stu Cncl; Pres Yth Flsp; Drama Clb; VP Mth Clb; Univ Of Akron; RN.

GROHER, WILLIAM; New Albany HS; Borden, IN; Cmnty Wkr; Hon Rl; Sch Nwsp; IM Sprt; Mgrs; Ivy Tech; Fire Fighter.

GROLEAU, DEAN; Big Bay De Noc HS; Nahma, MI; Chrh Wkr; Hon Rl; 4-H; 4-H Awd; Air Force.

GROLEAU, PHILLIP; Big Bay De Noc HS; Rapid River, MI; Cls Rep Soph Cls; Cl Rep Jr Cls; Chrh Wkr; Hon Rl; Stu Cncl; 4-H; Bsktbl; Ftbl; IM Sprt; Scr Kpr; Spch Awd HS 77; Bio Awd 76; Stu Coun & Prom Court 78;.

GROLEAU, VICKI; Big Bay De Noc HS; Rapid River, MI; 4/52 Sec Frsh Cls; Pres Soph Cls; Pres Jr Cls; Am Leg Aux Girls St; Band; Chrs; Chrh Wkr; Cmnty Wkr; Hon Rl; Lbry Ade; Awd For Sci Outstndng Stdtn 77;outstndng Stndt Awd In Agri 77; Awd Chr Outstndng Stdnt 78; Univ; Jrnlsm.

GROLLE, KAREN; Otsego HS; Bowling Green, OH; Chrh Wkr; Cmnty Wkr; Girl Scts; Hon Rl; Jr NHS; NHS; Yth Flsp; Yrbk; 4-H; Mth Clb; Bowling Green St Univ; Info Systems.

GROMACKI, GAIL; Cedarville HS; Cedarville, OH; 2/63 Sal; Chrs; Chrh Wkr; Hon Rl; NHS; Sch Pl; Ed Yrbk; Drama Clb; FBLA; FTA; Cedarville Coll.

GRONE, ANNE; Delphos St Johns HS; Delphos, OH ; 8/150 Hon Rl; NHS; Rptr Yrbk; 4-H; College; Journalism.

GRONER, JOHN; Ursuline HS; Girard, OH; 9/286 Hon Rl; NHS; Ger Clb; Coach Actv; Scr Kpr; Tmr; Youngstown St Univ Schlrshp; Schlrshp From St Rose Parish To Ursuline; Athletic Trophies Bsbl & Bsktbl; Youngstown St Univ.

GRONOSTAJ, VERONICA; James Ford Rhodes HS; Cleveland, OH; Chrs; Hon Rl; NHS; Ger Clb; Cit Awd; Univ Of Arizona; Astronomy.

GROOME, STEVEN; Indian Hill HS; Cincinnati, OH; Band; Boy Scts; Chrh Wkr; Hon Rl; Mod UN; Sch Pl; Sct Actv; College.

GROOMER, ANN E; Brownsburg HS; Brownsburg, IN; 1/316 Cls Rep Frsh Cls; Cls Rep Soph Cls; Cl Rep Jr Cls; Cls Rep Sr Cls; Val; Band; Chrh Wkr; Cmnty Wkr; Drm Mjrt; Girl Scts; Chrldr St Chmp 76; Cnty Chmp 76; Best Supp Act Of The Yr 77; Brn Gm & Ky To Cty Ind 77; Fin In Ms Teen 77; Indi ana Univ; Micro Bio.

GROOMS, CAROL; Erieview Catholic HS; Cleveland, OH; VP Jr Cls; Hon Rl; NHS; Pres Stu Cncl; Bsbl; Univ; Phys Ther.

GROOMS, ROBERT; Western HS; Peebles, OH; 1/76 VP Jr Cls; Hon Rl; NHS; Fr Clb; OSU; Civil Engr.

GROOMS, SUSAN; West Union HS; W Union, OH; 15/118 Trs Soph Cls; Sec Jr Cls; Band; Chrs; Chrh Wkr; Cmnty Wkr; Girl Scts; Hon Rl; Hosp Ade; NHS; Shawnee St Cmnty Coll; Nursing.

GROOT, TRACY; Fremont Ross HS; Fremont, OH; 85/450 VP Natl Forn Lg; NHS; Off Ade; Sch Mus; Sch Pl; Stg Crw; Stu Cncl; Pres Drama Clb; Letter Trk; Findlay Coll; Speech.

GROOTHUIS, PETER; Battle Creek Central HS; Battle Crk, MI; Boy Scts; Chrs; Sch Mus; Sct Actv; Yth Flsp; Ftbl; IM Sprt; Kellogg Comm Coll.

GROOVER, DAVID A; Elwood Community HS; Elwood, IN; 4/246 Hon Rl; Jr NHS; NHS; Off Ade; Yth Flsp; Lat Clb; Mth Clb; Sci Clb; Ball St Univ; Acctg.

GROPP, THERESA; W Vigo HS; W Terre Haute, IN; 19/208 Chrs; Chrh Wkr; Hon Rl; Jr NHS; Lbry Ade; NHS; Off Ade; Sch Mus; Y-Teens; Indiana St Univ; Acctg.

GROSCHKE, CHRISTINA; Flat Rock HS; Flat Rock, MI; Band; FCA; Hon Rl; Off Ade; VICA; Bsbl; GAA; PPFtbl; Ferris State College; Avionic Elec.

GROSE, JENNIFER; Liberty Benton HS; Findlay, OH; Pres Frsh Cls; Band; Chrs; Chrh Wkr; Hon Rl; Jr NHS; NHS; Sch Mus; Yth Flsp; Yrbk; Univ; Soc Work.

GROSE, KIM; Woodhaven HS; Woodhaven, MI; 46/218 Band; Chrs; Girl Scts; Sch Pl; Stu Cncl; Letter Swmmng; Tmr; College; Busns.

GROSE, MELANIE; Lewis County HS; Weston, WV; Sec Soph Cls; Cl Rep Jr Cls; Chrh Wkr; Hon Rl; Jr NHS; NHS; Stu Cncl; Pep Clb; Mat Maids; Morgantown Bus Schl; Cosmotlgst.

GROSKLAS, PATSY; Frontier HS; Marietta, OH; Hon Rl; Off Ade; FHA; OEA; GAA;.

GROSKLOS, S; Fort Frye HS; Coal Run, OH; 6/126 Pres Jr Cls; Hon Rl; Sch Pl; Spn Clb;.

GROSS, ALLISON; Medina HS; Medina, OH; AFS; Hosp Ade; Red Cr Ade; Ohio U; Psych.

GROSS, CARA; East Noble HS; Laotto, IN; 65/259 Band; Chrs; Hon Rl; Yth Flsp; Yrbk; 4-H; Mgrs; 4-H Awd; Most Improved Flag Awd Flag Corp Band; Flag Corp Capt Honor Flag Corp Band; Indiana Univ; Commercial Art.

GROSS, DEBRA; Penn HS; S Bend, IN; 25/487 Hon Rl; NHS; Spn Clb; Letter Ten; IM Sprt; PPFtbl; Univ; Bus.

GROSS, DIANE; Calvert HS; Tiffin, OH; 19/99 Chrs; Hon Rl; JA; Sch Mus; JA Awd; Tiffin Univ; Med Sec.

GROSS, ELAINE; Stephen T Badin HS; Fairfield, OH; 58/222 Chrs; Hon Rl; 4-H; 4-H Awd; Purdue Univ; Forestry.

GROSS, GARY; St Pauls HS; Norwalk, OH; 6/57 Am Leg Boys St; Band; Hon Rl; JA; NHS; 4-H; Lat Clb; Ftbl; Wrstlng; JA Awd; Univ.

GROSS, GEOFFREY; Elmhurst HS; Ft Wayne, IN; Boy Scts; JA; Sct Actv; Stg Crw; Trk; Scr Kpr; JA Awd; Eagle Scout 77; Od Of Arrow 76; Indiana Univ; Law.

GROSS, GORDON K; Pontiac Central HS; Pontiac, MI; Cls Rep Frsh Cls; Cls Rep Soph Cls; Cl Rep Jr Cls; Hon Rl; Boys Clb Am; 4-H; Bsbl; Mgrs; Cit Awd; 4-H Awd; Univ; Law.

GROSS, JAMES D; Mooresville HS; Mooresville, IN; 17/280 Am Leg Boys St; Boy Scts; Chrh Wkr; NHS; Sct Actv; Yrbk; Sci Clb; Crs Cntry; Trk; Varsity Letter Cross Cnty & Track; Most Improved In Cross Cntry; Rose Hullman Inst Of Tech; Chem Engr.

GROSS, JULIE; Berkshire HS; Garrettsville, OH; Cl Rep Jr Cls; Trs Sr Cls; Drl Tm; Stu Cncl; 4-H; Bowling Green Univ; Business.

GROSS, KATHLEEN; Waterford Mott HS; Pontiac, MI; 18/400 VP Soph Cls; Hon Rl; Sec Stu Cncl; Rptr Sch Nwsp; Oakland Univ; Poli Sci.

GROSS, KATHY; Douglas Mac Arthur HS; Rochester, MI; 8/300 Cls Rep Frsh Cls; Chrs; Cmnty Wkr; Girl Scts; Hon Rl; MMM; NHS; Pol Wkr; Sch Mus; Sch Pl; Whos Who In Midwestern Foriegn Lang Stud 79; Otstnding Stud In Hon Eng 78; Otstnding Stud In Spanish 3 79; Univ; Bio.

GROSS, LAURA; Rockford HS; Belmont, MI; Cls Rep Frsh Cls; Cls Rep Soph Cls; Sec Jr Cls; Cls Rep Sr Cls; Boy Scts; Cmnty Wkr; Hon Rl; NHS; Alma; Dentistry.

GROSS, LAUREL; Chesaning HS; St Charles, MI; VP Frsh Cls; Trs Soph Cls; VP Jr Cls; Sec Sr Cls; Hon Rl; Jr NHS; Rptr Sch Nwsp; Letter Trk; Chrldng; Coll; Photog.

GROSS, LISA; Elk Rapids HS; Elk Rapids, MI; Band; Hon Rl; Bsktbl; Terris State; Pharmacy.

GROSS, MARGARET; Owosso HS; Owosso, MI; Chrh Wkr; Hon Rl; Hosp Ade; Lat Clb; Capt Bsktbl; GAA; Cit Awd; Central Michigan; Pre Med.

GROSS, MARY J; Notre Dame Academy; Toledo, OH; Girl Scts; Mod UN; Lat Clb; IM Sprt; Letter IM Sprt; Univ; Nursing.

GROSS, MISSY; Andrean HS; Gary, IN; 7/272 Am Leg Aux Girls St; Girl Scts; Hon Rl; Jr NHS; NHS; Mth Clb; Sci Clb; Spn Clb; Ten; Indiana Univ; Bio.

GROSS, M RYAN; Shelbyville SR HS; Shelbyville, IN; 4/288 Chrh Wkr; NHS; Lat Clb; Coll; Natural Sci.

GROSS, NATHAN; Columbia Central HS; Brooklyn, MI; 68/150 Cls Rep Frsh Cls; Cls Rep Soph Cls; Cl Rep Jr Cls; VP Sr Cls; Boy Scts; Sch Mus; Sch Pl; Sct Actv; Stg Crw; VP Stu Cncl; Ftbl Schsp Univ Of Toledo 79; All Amer Wrstlng 79; All Cnty All Conf 3 Yrs MVP Wrstlgn; Univ Of Toledo; Scndry Educ.

GROSS, RICHARD; Elwood Community HS; Elwood, IN; Stu Cncl; Lat Clb; Ftbl; Wrstlng; Indiana Central Univ; Dentistry.

GROSS, ROSETTA; Liberty HS; Salem, WV; 70/231 Chrh Wkr; Cmnty Wkr; Hon Rl; Lbry Ade; Sch Pl; Stg Crw; Drama Clb; Pres 4-H; FBLA; FHA; Recognition For Wrk Awd Given FBLA 79; 1st Pl Trophy 4 H Saftey Poster Cntst 77; Ohio Valley Coll; RN.

GROSS, SHERRI; Fairborn Baker HS; Fairborn, OH; Chrh Wkr; Debate Tm; Hon Rl; Lit Mag; Natl Forn Lg; NHS; Off Ade; Quill & Scroll; Rptr Sch Nwsp; Drama Clb; Georgetown Coll; Communication Arts.

GROSS, SHERYL; Sandy Vly HS; Magnolia, OH; 1/160 Cls Rep Frsh Cls; Cls Rep Soph Cls; VP Jr Cls; Am Leg Aux Girls St; Chrs; Hon Rl; Jr NHS; Lbry Ade; Natl Forn Lg; NHS; Univ; Med.

GROSS, STEPHEN J; St Xavier HS; Hamilton, OH; 3/264 Band; Cmnty Wkr; Hon Rl; NHS; Rptr Yrbk; Mth Clb; Trk; IM Sprt; JETS Awd; University; Medicine.

GROSS, WILLIAM; Fraser HS; Fraser, MI; 143/609 Ftbl; Wrstlng; Coll; History.

GROSSE, BEVERLEY; Ravenna HS; Ravenna, OH; 4/327 Band; Cmnty Wkr; Hon Rl; Hosp Ade; NHS; PAVAS; Rptr Yrbk; Baldwin Wallace College; German.

GROSSMAN, M; Triton HS; Bourbon, IN; 10/96 Hon Rl; NHS; Spn Clb; Letter Bsktbl; Trk; Univ.

GROSSMAN, MARSHA; Madeira HS; Cincinnati, OH; 29/165 Sec Soph Cls; Sec Jr Cls; Sec Sr Cls; Hon Rl; Stu Cncl; Fr Clb; Chrldng; IM Sprt; Univ; Health & Sciences.

GROSSMAN, TONY; Lawrenceburg HS; Lawrenceburg, IN; Boy Scts; Chrh Wkr; Sct Actv; 4-H; Lat Clb; Bsktbl; Capt Swmmng; Purdue Univ; Forestry.

GROTE, GRETCHEN; Culver Girls Academy; Madison, IN; 30/191 VP Frsh Cls; FCA; Hon Rl; Lbry Ade; Red Cr Ade; Yth Flsp; Pep Clb; Capt Swmmng; IM Sprt; Cit Awd; Univ.

GROTH, BARBARA; Saint Annes HS; Warren, MI; 4/70 Cls Rep Frsh Cls; Chrh Wkr; Hon Rl; Hosp Ade; NHS; Yrbk; Ed Sch Nwsp; Spn Clb;.

GROTHAUSE, PEGGY; St John HS; Delphos, OH; 7/150 Cls Rep Frsh Cls; Cls Rep Soph Cls; Cl Rep Jr Cls; Cls Rep Sr Cls; Am Leg Aux Girls St; Band; Hon Rl; Jr NHS; Stu Cncl; College.

GROTHAUSE, TRACI; Celina Sr HS; Celina, OH; Chrh Wkr; Hon Rl; NHS; Stg Crw; Ed Sch Nwsp; Sch Nwsp; Letter Trk; Letter GAA; Mgrs; Univ; Home Economics.

GROTHMAN, JULIE; Escanaba Area Public HS; Escanaba, MI; 20/425 Hon Rl; 4-H; Natl Merit SF; Michigan St Univ; Bus.

GROTHOUSE, MARK; Chaminade Julienne HS; Dayton, OH; Sec Jr Cls; FCA; Sch Pl; Letter Crs Cntry; Letter Trk; JA Awd; Univ; Med.

GROTT, THOMAS A; Purcell HS; Cincinnati, OH; 8/179 Cls Rep Sr Cls; Hon Rl; Stu Cncl; Rptr Sch Nwsp; IM Sprt; Univ Of Cincinnati; Civil Engr.

GROUDLE, TIMOTHY; Holy Name Nazareth HS; Independence, OH; Hon Rl; Letter Bsktbl; Letter Glf; Scr Kpr; College; Engrng.

GROULX, JUDI; Holy Rosary Educ Ctr HS; Flint, MI; VP Frsh Cls; Pres Soph Cls; Bsktbl; Trk; Univ Of Michigan; Eng.

GROUNDS, LORI; Bloomington HS South; Bloomington, IN; 73/399 Band; Chrs; Chrh Wkr; Hon Rl; Hosp Ade; Mdrgl; Sch Mus; Sch Pl; 4-H; OEA; Outstndng Pianist Awrd For BHSS Choral Dept 79; Schlrshp To The In Summer Choral Music Clinic 76; Profssnl Careers Inst; Paramed Offc.

GROUS, ALBIN; St Marys Preparatory HS; Philadelphia, PA; 6/27 Cls Rep Frsh Cls; Cls Rep Soph Cls; Cl Rep Jr Cls; Cls Rep Sr Cls; Chrh Wkr; Hon Rl; NHS; Stu Cncl; Ed Sch Nwsp; Mr Sr Of Class 79; Cert Of Recogntn St Of Mi Comp Schlrshp Prog 79; St Marys Coll; Philosophy.

GROVE, DEB; Vantage Voc Paulding HS; Oakwood, OH; 6/162 Hon Rl; NHS; Drama Clb; 4-H; Mth Clb; C of C Awd; 4-H Awd; Sec.

GROVE, DEBRA E; Springfield Local HS; New Middletown, OH; 1/160 Cls Rep Frsh Cls; Val; AFS; Hon Rl; Fr Clb; FTA; Pep Clb; Trk; Twrlr; Natl Merit SF; Univ; Pre Med.

GROVE, JUNE; Berkeley Springs HS; Berkeley Spg, WV; 8/130 Cl Rep Jr Cls; Cls Rep Sr Cls; Band; Chrs; Chrh Wkr; Cmnty Wkr; Hon Rl; Jr NHS; NHS; Off Ade; Fairmont St Coll; Rsptry Ther.

GROVE, SALLY; Frankfort Sr HS; Frankfort, IN; Am Leg Aux Girls St; Band; Chrs; Chrh Wkr; Drm Bgl; Girl Scts; Hon Rl; NHS; Orch; Sch Mus; Dist & State Music Awds 1975; All State Choir 1978; IU Music Clinic 1975; Indiana Univ; Music.

GROVE, SHELLY; Van Wert HS; Van Wert, OH; 5/209 Am Leg Aux Girls St; Chrs; Chrh Wkr; Hon Rl; NHS; Yth Flsp; Y-Teens; Fr Clb; Pep Clb; Scshp Team; Ohio Northern Univ; Pharm.

GROVE, TIM; Washington Catholic HS; Washington, IN; 6/52 VP Frsh Cls; Chrs; Chrh Wkr; Hon Rl; Key Clb; Lat Clb; Pep Clb; Mgrs; Am Leg Awd; Indiana Univ; Law.

GROVE, TODD W; Northwood HS; Nappanee, IN; 91/207 Boy Scts; Chrh Wkr; FCA; Hon Rl; Red Cr Ade; Sch Nwsp; 4-H; Bsktbl; Trk; College; Criminology.

GROVENOR, SHELDON; North Muskegon HS; Whitehall, MI; Band; Cmnty Wkr; Hon Rl; Sch Mus; Fr Clb; Pep Clb; Rdo Clb; IM Sprt; Scr Kpr; Cit Awd; Coll; Electronics.

GROVER, LAURA; Ferndale HS; Ferndale, MI; Debate Tm; Hon Rl; NHS; Pol Wkr; Lat Clb; Natl Merit SF; Rotary Awd; Wayne State Univ; Physiopsych.

GROVER, MARK; Ravenna HS; Ravenna, MI; 21/103 Hon Rl; NHS; Letter Bsktbl; Letter Ftbl; Letter Trk; Muskegon Cmnty Coll; Comp Prog.

GROVES, CONNIE; White Pigeon HS; White Pigeon, MI; Chrs; JA; Yrbk; Fr Clb; FHA; Pep Clb; Bsktbl; Gym; Trk; Chrldng; Glen Oaks Cmnty Coll; Cosmetology.

GROVES, DIANA; St Clair HS; Marine City, MI; 1/214 Cls Rep Soph Cls; Cl Rep Jr Cls; Trs Sr Cls; Cls Rep Sr Cls; Val; Chrs; Chrh Wkr; Pres NHS; Sch Pl; Stg Crw; Oakland Univ; Medicine.

GROVES, JANA; Avon HS; Danville, IN; Cls Rep Soph Cls; Trs Jr Cls; Cl Rep Jr Cls; Pres Sr Cls; Cls Rep Sr Cls; Chrs; Off Ade; Stu Cncl; Rptr Yrbk; Pep Clb; Best Reporting Notebook Jrnlsm Camp Ball St Univ 78; Indiana Univ.

GROVES, JENNIFER; Malabar HS; Mansfield, OH; Cls Rep Soph Cls; Cls Rep Sr Cls; Band; Girl Scts; Hon Rl; Jr NHS; NHS; Sct Actv; Stu Cncl; Yth Flsp; Univ.

GROVES, KEITH; Meadowbrook HS; Pleasant City, OH; 8/179 Am Leg Boys St; Band; Chrs; Chrh Wkr; Cmnty Wkr; Debate Tm; Hon Rl; Jr NHS; NHS; Sch Pl; Ohio St Univ; Archt.

GROVES, LORI; Louisville HS; Louisville, OH; 1/360 Pres Soph Cls; Sec Jr Cls; Cls Rep Sr Cls; Val; Treas Natl Forn Lg; NHS; Treas Stu Cncl; Capt Chrldng; Am Leg Awd; Mas Awd; Georgetown Univ; Foreign Serv.

GROVES, S; Northville HS; Northville, MI; FCA; PAVAS; Drama Clb; Fr Clb; Bsktbl; GAA; Bus Schl; Fshn Mdse.

GROVES, WILLIAM; Barnesville HS; Barnesville, OH; 14/127 Hon Rl; NHS; Sct Actv; FTA; Key Clb; Letter Bsktbl; Letter Ftbl; Letter Trk; Mgrs; Belmont Tech Coll; Civil Const Engr.

GROW, RAYMOND; Struthers HS; Struthers, OH; Chrh Wkr; FCA; JA; Yrbk; 4-H; Spn Clb; Bsktbl; Glf; Coach Actv; IM Sprt; Youngstown St Univ; Brdcstng.

GROWCOCK, DIANA; Staunton HS; Birnamwood, WI; Band; Chrh Wkr; Cmnty Wkr; Drl Tm; NHS; Sprt Ed Sch Nwsp; Pep Clb; Chrldng; Pom Pon; Ricks Coll; Acrobatic.

GROZA, LOUIS J; Berea HS; Berea, OH; 35/530 Hon Rl; Jr NHS; NHS; Bsktbl; Ftbl; Trk; Coach Actv; College; Bus Communications.

GRUBAUGH, HEIDI; Kent Roosevelt HS; Kent, OH; Chrs; Chrh Wkr; Girl Scts; Hosp Ade; Off Ade; DECA; Pep Clb; Gym; Swmmng; IM Sprt; Kent St Univ; Fash Merch.

GRUBAUGH, KATHY; North Knox HS; Oaktown, IN; Chrs; Chrh Wkr; Girl Scts; Hon Rl; Hosp Ade; 4-H; Univ; Med.

GRUBB, ANTHONY D; Newark Sr HS; Newark, OH; Debate Tm; Jr NHS; Natl Forn Lg; NHS; Pol Wkr; Eng Clb; Key Clb; Letter Crs Cntry; Univ; Pre Law.

GRUBB, GAY; Covington HS; Covington, IN; Band; Chrh Wkr; Hon Rl; NHS; Sch Pl; Yth Flsp; Fr Clb; FHA; Pep Clb; PPFtbl; Indiana Ctrl Univ; Bus Mgmt.

GRUBB, GREGG; Galesburg Augusta HS; Galesburg, MI; 2/109 Boy Scts; Hon Rl; Sct Actv; Bsbl; Letter Ftbl; Trk; Paperboy Of Yr Kalamazoo Gazette 74 77; 3rd Plc Mi Press Assoc 77; Univ; Engr.

GRUBB, JENNY; Pickaway Ross Joint Voc Ctr; Waverly, OH; Band; Hon Rl; 4-H; FBLA; Pep Clb; VICA; Trk; Chrldng; Scr Kpr; 4-H Awd; Tech Coll; X Ray Tech.

GRUBB, JENNY; Huntington Local HS; Waverly, OH; Band; Hon Rl; VP Chrs; Pep Clb; VICA; Trk; Chrldng; Scr Kpr; 4-H Awd; Natl Merit Ltr; Univ; Phys Educ.

GRUBB, KATHERINE; John Adams HS; S Bend, IN; 69/425 Am Leg Aux Girls St; Chrh Wkr; Hon Rl; Lit Mag; Quill & Scroll; Yth Flsp; Rptr Sch Nwsp; Sch Nwsp; Drama Clb; Mas Awd; Purdue Univ; Jrnlsm.

GRUBB, KIM; Mc Comb HS; Mccomb, OH; Band; Chrh Wkr; Cmnty Wkr; Lbry Ade; Off Ade; Yth Flsp; 4-H; FTA; Pep Clb; Gym; Univ; Phys Educ.

GRUBB, NANCY; Oceana HS; Oceana, WV; Girl Scts; Hon Rl; Pep Clb; Spn Clb; Bus Schl.

GRUBBA, PAULA; Southfield HS; Southfield, MI; Cl Rep Jr Cls; Band; PAVAS; Pol Wkr; Sch Mus; Sch Pl; Stu Cncl; Rptr Sch Nwsp; Spn Clb; Twrlr; College; Journalism.

GRUBBS, DEBORAH; Warsaw Community HS; Warsaw, IN; Girl Scts; Lbry Ade; Off Ade; Sct Actv; DECA; FBLA; Trk; Pres Awd; Vocational School.

GRUBBS, MARCIA; Adelphian Acad; Holly, MI; Chrs; Hon Rl; Lbry Ade; Off Ade; Sch Mus; Sch Pl; Bsktbl; Gym; IM Sprt; PPFtbl; Andrews Univ; Cosmot.

GRUBBS, SANDRA; David Anderson HS; Lisbon, OH; 8/115 Sec Cmp Fr Grls; Hon Rl; Lbry Ade; Y-Teens; Fr Clb; FNA; Sci Clb; Am Leg Awd; Ohio St Univ; Vet Sci.

GRUBE, DAVE; Kankakee Valley HS; De Motte, IN; Hon Rl; Yth Flsp; Chmn Bsktbl; Glf; College.

GRUBE, KATHLEEN; Kankakee Valley HS; Wheatfield, IN; Am Leg Aux Girls St; Chrs; Hon Rl; NHS; OEA; Sci Clb; Treas Spn Clb; Am Leg Awd; Geom Awd 78; Typing Awd 78; Spanish Awd 78; Acctg Awd 79; Purdue Univ.

GRUBER, CHRIS; Hackett HS; Kalamazoo, MI; 4/130 Hon Rl; Letter Bsktbl; Letter Mgrs; PPFtbl; Michigan Univ; Acctg.

GRUBER, DAVID J; Columbus West HS; Columbus, OH; 3/350 Cls Rep Sr Cls; Am Leg Boys St; Aud/Vis; VP Band; Boy Scts; Chrh Wkr; Hon Rl; Jr NHS; NHS; Pres Orch; Urban HS Renewal Cncl Stu Rep; Columbus Public Schl Seminiar For Outstndng HS Jr; Ohio St Univ; Audio Engr.

GRUBER, DAWN; Reese HS; Richville, MI; Am Leg Aux Girls St; Chrs; Chrh Wkr; Girl Scts; Yth Flsp; Ger Clb; Bsktbl; Trk; PPFtbl; Am Leg Awd; Univ; Law.

GRUBER, DEBRA; Copley HS; Akron, OH; Trs Jr Cls; Sec Sr Cls; Chrs; Hon Rl; NHS; Off Ade; Rptr Yrbk; Pep Clb; Spn Clb; Crs Cntry; Bowling Green Univ; Educ.

GRUBER, JOSEPH; Moeller HS; Cincinnati, OH; 8/250 VP Frsh Cls; Cl Rep Jr Cls; VP Sr Cls; Hon Rl; Lit Mag; NHS; Stu Cncl; Rptr Sch Nwsp; Lat Clb; Letter Bsbl; Joe Quinn Awd Schlr Ath; Archbishop Nc Nicholas Awd; Gold Shield Awd; Man Of Moeller Best Defensive Back; Notre Dame Univ; Law.

GRUBER, KAREY; Reese HS; Reese, MI; Band; Hon Rl; Yth Flsp; Trk; Chrldng; PPFtbl; Univ; Med Lab Tech.

GRUELL, TODD; Union County HS; Liberty, IN; 44/128 Chrs; Cmnty Wkr; Hon Rl; Sch Mus; Letter Ftbl; Coach Actv; Indiana State Univ; Us History.

GRUEN, TAMI; West Lafayette Sr HS; West Lafayette, IN; 66/185 Chrs; Chrh Wkr; Hon Rl; Sch Mus; Sch Pl; Stu Cncl; Yth Flsp; Rptr Yrbk; Drama Clb; Pep Clb; St Finlst In Miss Teen In Pgnt 79; Purdue Univ.

GRUENEMIER, PEGGY; Fairfield Sr HS; Fairfield, OH; Chrs; Chrh Wkr; Girl Scts; Hon Rl; Lbry Ade; Off Ade; Sct Actv; Stu Cncl; Fr Clb; Trk; Deaconess Univ; Tchr.

GRUESSNER, MICHELE; Marion L Steele HS; Amherst, OH; Sec Jr Cls; NHS; Off Ade; Pol Wkr; Ger Clb; Sci Clb; Letter Crs Cntry; Letter Trk; IM Sprt; PPFtbl; Miami Univ; Psych.

GRUETZ, ERIC; Robert Rogers HS; Toledo, OH; 5/450 Hon Rl; NHS; Mth Clb; Letter Glf; Letter Socr; College; Math.

GRUHL, TAMI; Zionsville Comm HS; Zionsville, IN; Cmnty Wkr; Girl Scts; Sct Actv; Sprt Ed Yrbk; Yrbk; 4-H; Pep Clb; Spn Clb; Bsbl; Trk; Hmcmng Queen 1978; Butler Univ; Fshn Mdse.

GRUMERETZ, MIKE; St Philip Catholic Ctrl HS; Battle Creek, MI; Hon Rl; Ftbl; College; Civil Engineer.

GRUMERETZ, PAUL; Lakeview HS; Battle Creek, MI; Hon Rl; Ftbl; Coach Actv; IM Sprt; Oakland Univ; Comp Sci.

GRUMERETZ, S; St Philip HS; Battle Crk, MI; NHS; PPFtbl; Am Leg Awd; Bus Schl; Sec.

GRUMMAN, TERESA A; Westland HS; Columbus, OH; 89/404 Girl Scts; Hon Rl; Orch; Sch Mus; Sec OEA; Trk; GAA; Clark Tech Schl; Court Reporter.

GRUN, G; Menominee HS; Menominee, MI; Cl Rep Jr Cls; Band; Hon Rl; Stu Cncl; Trk; Coach Actv; IM Sprt; College; Phys Ther.

GRUNDAS, CONNIE; Douglas Mac Arthur HS; Saginaw, MI; 15/300 Band; Chrh Wkr; Hon Rl; NHS; Yrbk; Pom Pon; Kiwan Awd; College; Architecture.

GRUNDER, SHELLY; Minerva HS; Minerva, OH; 6/210 Chrh Wkr; Cmnty Wkr; Girl Scts; Hon Rl; Hosp Ade; Treas Spn Clb; Scr Kpr; Coll Of Wooster; Tchr.

GRUNDTISCH, DEBBIE; Upper Sandusky HS; Upper Sandusky, OH; Am Leg Aux Girls St; Band; Girl Scts; Hon Rl; NHS; Yth Flsp; Bsktbl; Swmmng; Trk; Am Leg Awd; College.

GRUNER, CRAIG; Forest Hills Ctrl HS; Grand Rapids, MI; Band; Sch Mus; Sch Pl; Yth Flsp; Crs Cntry; Trk; Grand Rapids Jr Coll; Bus.

GRUNWALD, GAIL; Charles F Brush HS; Lyndhurst, OH; Cls Rep Frsh Cls; Cls Rep Soph Cls; Stu Cncl; Letter Ten; IM Sprt; Tmr; College; Wildlife Mgmt.

GRUPE, KEN; Oakwood HS; Dayton, OH; Boy Scts; FCA; NHS; Stu Cncl; Socr; College.

GRUSCINSKI, THOMAS; Catholic Central HS; Grand Rapids, MI; 8/225 Pres Jr Cls; Pres Sr Cls; Am Leg Boys St; Band; Hon Rl; NHS; Yrbk; Univ Of Notre Dame; Law.

GRUSENMEYER, RON; Chaminade Julienne HS; Dayton, OH; Boy Scts; Chrh Wkr; Cmnty Wkr; Hon Rl; JA; Pres 4-H; Wrstlng; IM Sprt; 4-H Awd; JA Awd; Ohio St Univ; Agri.

GRUSKIEWICZ, JACKIE; Pymatuning Valley HS; Williamsfield, OH; 16/144 Sec Jr Cls; Sec Sr Cls; Am Leg Aux Girls St; Chrs; NHS; Ed Yrbk; VP FFA; Scr Kpr; Kent St Univ; Lab Tech.

GRYGIER, BARBARA; Capac Jr Sr HS; Emmett, MI; 26/110 Band; Hon Rl; 4-H; Letter Trk; GAA; 4-H Awd; Univ; Dent Ofc Asst.

GRYGIER, KATHLEEN; Capac Jr Sr HS; Emmett, MI; 5/123 Sec Soph Cls; Sec Sr Cls; Band; Hon Rl; Hosp Ade; NHS; 4-H; FNA; League Honord Band 76 78; Michigan St Univ; Vet Med.

GRYS, GREGORY; Trinity HS; Garfield Hts, OH; 30/143 Chrs; Cmnty Wkr; Hon Rl; NHS; Mth Clb; Trk; Mgrs; Scr Kpr; Trinity Academic Schlrshp 79; Univ; Math.

GRYWALSKI, AIMEE; Garfield HS; Akron, OH; Chrh Wkr; Hon Rl; Hosp Ade; NHS; Red Cr Ade; VP Stu Cncl; Yth Flsp; Rptr Sch Nwsp; Sci Clb; Letter Ten; Univ Of Akron; Nursing.

GRZECHOWSKI, RAYMOND; St Alphonsus HS; Detroit, MI; 145/177 Off Ade; PAVAS; Rptr Sch Nwsp; Letter Trk; Chrstms Show Intertnr; Mastor Of Muppets; Henry Ford Cmnty Coll; Pre Med.

GRZELAK, CHRISTINE M; Barberton HS; Barberton, OH; 47/620 Chrs; Chrh Wkr; Hon Rl; Hosp Ade; Jr NHS; Lbry Ade; NHS; Off Ade; Rptr Yrbk; FNA; Akron Univ; Nursing.

GRZELAK, KEITH; Houghton HS; Dollar Bay, MI; Band; Boy Scts; Drm Bgl; Hon Rl; Sct Actv; Spn Clb; Letter Crs Cntry; Ftbl; Trk; Natl Merit Ltr; Michigan Tech Univ; Pre Med.

GRZYBOWSKI, JANESE; Union HS; Grand Rapids, MI; Cmp Fr Grls; Chrh Wkr; Hon Rl; JA; NHS; Crs Cntry; Ten; Junior College; Pre Med.

GRZYBOWSKI, PAULA; Divine Child HS; Dearborn, MI; Chrs; Hon Rl; Ed Sch Nwsp; Ger Clb; Pep Clb; Univ; Nursing.

GUADIANA, JESUS; Washington HS; East Chicago, IN; 3/300 Pres Soph Cls; Cl Rep Jr Cls; NHS; Orch; Boys Clb Am; Bsbl; Wrstlng; College; Engr.

GUARASCI, CARLA; Bishop Watterson HS; Columbus, OH; Cls Rep Frsh Cls; Cls Rep Soph Cls; Am Leg Aux Girls St; Chrs; Chrh Wkr; Hon Rl; NHS; Sch Mus; Sch Pl; Stg Crw; College; Pharmacy.

GUARINO, CATHERINE; Royal Oak Dondero HS; Berkley, MI; Band; Hon Rl; Lit Mag; NHS; Sch Mus; Pep Clb; Spn Clb; Natl Merit SF; Oakland Univ; Human Res.

GUBA, PHIL; Bloomington HS South; Bloomington, IN; 3/350 Hon Rl; NHS; Sci Clb; Letter Crs Cntry; Letter Trk; Bausch & Lomb Awd; Kiwan Awd; Rotary Awd; Indiana Univ; Dent.

GUCKENBERGER, SHIRLEY; Oscoda Area HS; Oscoda, MI; 24/359 Trs Jr Cls; Am Leg Aux Girls St; Hon Rl; Jr NHS; NHS; Off Ade; Stu Cncl; Keyettes; Letter Chrldng; Northwood Institute; Public Rel.

GUCKER, JIM; Mohawk HS; Mc Cutchenville, OH; 5/115 Am Leg Boys St; Chrs; NHS; Sch Pl; VP Yth Flsp; Pres 4-H; Spn Clb; Letter Bsbl; Bsktbl; Letter Ftbl; Law.

GUDAITIS, JAMES J; Perry HS; Massillon, OH; NHS; Univ; Aero Engr.

GUDE, BROOK; Loveland Hurst HS; Loveland, OH; Band; Hon Rl; Ger Clb; Lat Clb; Mth Clb; Natl Latin Honor Soc 76 78; Awd 76; Top Eng Student Awd For Yr 76; Silver Schlrshp Awd 78 79; Univ Of Cincinnati; Med.

GUDORF, KEITH; Minster Local HS; Minster, OH; Pres Frsh Cls; Am Leg Boys St; Boy Scts; Chrs; Chrh Wkr; Hon Rl; NHS; Sch Mus; Sch Pl; Sct Actv; Coll; Social Work.

GUENTERBERG, BRIAN; Adelphian Acad; Plymouth, MI; VP Soph Cls; Aud/Vis; Band; Chrs; Ed Yrbk; Sch Nwsp; Tmr; Univ; Anesthesiologist.

GUENTHER, CAROL; Michigan Lutheran Seminary; Monroe, MI; Cmp Fr Grls; Chrs; Chrh Wkr; Hon Rl; Pol Wkr; Sch Pl; Yth Flsp; Trk; Chrldng; IM Sprt; Dr Martin Luther Coll; Schl Tchr.

GUENTHER, JAMES; Yellow Springs HS; Yellow Sprg, OH; 4/75 Chrs; Debate Tm; Natl Forn Lg; NHS; Orch; Sch Mus; Letter Crs Cntry; Trk; Univ.

GUENTHER, JENNIE; Northwestern HS; Wooster, OH; Chrs; Off Ade; Yrbk; Sch Nwsp; Drama Clb; 4-H; FTA; Scr Kpr; Business School; Secretary.

GUENTHER, KATHY; Hoover HS; North Canton, OH; Cls Rep Frsh Cls; Chrs; Hon Rl; Jr NHS; Sch Mus; College.

GUERARD, MICHELE; Redford Union HS; Redford, MI; 9/550 Hon Rl; Jr NHS; NHS; Bsktbl; Crs Cntry; Letter Trk; GAA; Larwence Inst Of Tech; Architect.

GUERINCY, JANET E; Augres Sims HS; Augres, MI; Band; Hon Rl; Natl Forn Lg; 4-H; Bsktbl; 4-H Awd; College.

GUERNSEY, BRIAN; Henryville HS; Henryville, IN; Chrh Wkr; Cmnty Wkr; Letter Bsbl; Letter Bsktbl; Am Leg Awd; Indiana Univ; Bus.

GUERNSEY, PAMELA; Southport HS; Indianapolis, IN; Am Leg Aux Girls St; Band; Hon Rl; NHS; Off Ade; Stu Cncl; Drama Clb; Letter Crs Cntry; Letter Trk; GAA; Purdue Univ; Sociology.

GUERRA, CYNTHIA; Allen Park HS; Allen Park, MI; Ed Yrbk; Univ Of Michigan; Journalism.

GUERRA, LUCIA; Maplewood HS; Mexico, OH; Cmp Fr Grls; Chrh Wkr; Girl Scts; NHS; Sch Pl; Beta Clb; Drama Clb; FTA; Spn Clb; Crs Cntry; College; Communication.

GUERRA, REGINA; Malabar HS; Mansfield, OH; Chrs; Chrh Wkr; Hon Rl; JA; Stu Cncl; Univ; Micro Bio.

GUERRIERI JR, RONALD; Lowellville HS; Lowellville, OH; 5/41 VP Sr Cls; Chrh Wkr; Cmnty Wkr; Hon Rl; NHS; Yrbk; Lat Clb; Thiel College; Med Tech.

GUERRIERO, CAROLYN; Regina HS; Cleveland, OH; Aud/Vis; Chrh Wkr; Cmnty Wkr; Hon Rl; Cleveland State; Bus.

GUERTAL, ELIZABETH A; Whitehall Yearling HS; Whitehall, OH; Am Leg Aux Girls St; Band; NHS; Off Ade; Orch; Sch Nwsp; Crs Cntry; Capt Trk; Univ.

GUERTAL, WILLIAM; Whitehall Yearling HS; Whitehall, OH; 15/300 Cls Rep Frsh Cls; Cl Rep Jr Cls; Cls Rep Sr Cls; Am Leg Boys St; Band; Hon Rl; NHS; Ohio St Univ; Engr.

GUERTIN, JUDY; Mt Healthy HS; Mt Healthy, OH; Cmnty Wkr; Girl Scts; Off Ade; Sch Pl; Fr Clb; Pep Clb; Bsktbl; Mgrs; Scr Kpr;.

GUEST, JOHN; Onsted HS; Brooklyn, MI; 18/123 Hon Rl; Sch Pl; Rptr Yrbk; Rptr Sch Nwsp; Natl Merit Ltr; Oakland Univ; Comp Sci.

GUEST, LORI; Jackson Memorial HS; Canton, OH; Am Leg Aux Girls St; Stu Cncl; Y-Teens; Yrbk; Sec Ger Clb; Letter Swmmng; Mat Maids; Tmr; Ohi State; Dental Hygiene.

GUEST, LORI; West Muskingum HS; Mt Perry, OH; Hon Rl; Jr NHS; NHS; Sci Clb; Spn Clb; Letter Bsktbl; GAA; Mgrs; Am Leg Awd; Vsty Ltr Vlybl 78; Most Const Sttr Vlybl Co Champs 78; Univ; Phys Educ.

GUFFEY, CHARLOTTE; Union HS; Losantville, IN; Cls Rep Soph Cls; Cl Rep Jr Cls; Trs Sr Cls; Band; Chrh Wkr; Hon Rl; Off Ade; Treas Stu Cncl; Sch Nwsp; 4-H; Indiana Bus Coll.

GUFFY, PATRICIA; Lumen Christi HS; Jackson, MI; Hon Rl; IM Sprt; Horthand I Awd 79; Central Michigan Univ; Tchr.

GUFREDA, TIMOTHY; St Joseph HS; Cleveland, OH; 60/320 Aud/Vis; Hon Rl; Lit Mag; Sch Mus; Stu Cncl; Rptr Sch Nwsp; IM Sprt; Scr Kpr; Cleveland St Univ; Mech Engr.

GUGALA, CAROLYN; Adlai E Stevenson HS; Sterling Hts, MI; 9/525 Hon Rl; NHS; OEA; Natl Merit Ltr; Wayne State Univ; Bus.

GUGGINO, TANIA; Buckeye HS; Litchfield, OH; Pres Jr Cls; Sch Mus; VICA; Univ; Archt.

GUGINO, LESLIE; Douglas Mac Arthur HS; Saginaw, MI; 14/350 Cls Rep Soph Cls; Cl Rep Jr Cls; Sec Sr Cls; Chrh Wkr; Girl Scts; Hon Rl; JA; NHS; Sch Pl; Stu Cncl; Mi Intrschlstc Press Awrds 1st Pl Interview Hon Ment Feature Column; Spec Recgntn In Honors Engr; Eastern Coll; Theatre Arts.

GUGLE, SCOT; Reed City HS; Reed City, MI; Am Leg Boys St; Chrh Wkr; Hon Rl; Pres Yth Flsp; Trk; Schstc Achvmnt Awdx 77 79; Natl Hon Soc Cert Of Hon 79; All Star Algbr Awd; Univ; Bus Admin.

GUGLIEMATTO, TINA; Groveport Madison HS; Groveport, OH; VP Frsh Cls; VP Soph Cls; Drl Tm; Stu Cncl; Rptr Sch Nwsp; Mat Maids; PPFtbl; Scr Kpr; Ohio State Univ; Education.

GUICE, BETTINA; Washington Irving HS; Clarksburg, WV; Letter Band; Hon Rl; Sch Mus; Y-Teens; Fr Clb; Pep Clb; Letter Chrldng; College.

GUIDA, JOE; West Geauga HS; Novelty, OH; Boy Scts; Chrs; Chrh Wkr; FCA; Hon Rl; Off Ade; Sch Pl; Yrbk; Pep Clb; Bsbl; Cmnty Bsbl All St 77; Bsktbl Awd; CVC J N Champ Ftbl & Bsktbl; Univ; Phys Educ.

GUIDEN, DIANE; George Rogers Clark HS; Whiting, IN; 19/218 Am Leg Aux Girls St; Band; Chrs; Drm Mjrt; Jr NHS; Orch; Sch Mus; Bsbl; Trk; Indiana State Univ; Accountant.

GUIDER, GEOFF; West Geauga HS; Chesterland, OH; Hon Rl; Stu Cncl; Bsbl; Bsktbl; Glf; IM Sprt; College.

GUIDI, TERRY; Morgantown HS; Westover, WV; Yrbk; Letter Ftbl; Letter Wrstlng; Coach Actv; IM Sprt; Scr Kpr; Tmr; JA Awd; WV St Wrstlng Trounmnt 4th Pl 79; Brooke Cnty Inv & Big 10 2(d Pl 79; Wnnr Of Univ HS Tournmnt 79; Univ; Phys Educ.

GUIKEMA, SUSAN; Clay HS; South Bend, IN; Hon Rl; NHS; 4-H; Ger Clb; Lat Clb; Crs Cntry; Trk; 4-H Awd; Calvin Coll; Pre Med.

GUILBAULT, DEBBIE; Center Line HS; Centerline, MI; Hon Rl; Lbry Ade; Coll; Cosmetology.

GUILD, RANDALL J; Ithaca HS; Ithaca, MI; 10/139 Band; Boy Scts; Chrs; Hon Rl; Mdrgl; NHS; Sch Mus; Treas Stu Cncl; Ten; Rotary Awd; Michigan St Univ; Comp Sci.

GUILFOYLE, DONALD; Springfield HS; Springfield, MI; 11/80 VP Sr Cls; Hon Rl; Jr NHS; Pep Clb; Letter Bsbl; Bsktbl; Capt Wrstlng; Am Leg Awd; Kellogg Community & Ferris; Acctg.

GUILLIAM, TY; Tinora HS; Defiance, OH; Cls Rep Frsh Cls; Chrs; Hon Rl; Sch Mus; Stg Crw; Letter Bsktbl; Letter Crs Cntry; Coach Actv; Univ.

GUILLOZET, SUE; Russia Local HS; Russia, OH; 6/34 VP Frsh Cls; VP Soph Cls; VP Jr Cls; Chrs; Hon Rl; Pres NHS; Sch Pl; Yrbk; Drama Clb; Pep Clb; College; Phys Ed.

GUINTO, PATRICIA A; Highland HS; Brunswick Hls, OH; 6/242 Cls Rep Frsh Cls; Cls Rep Soph Cls; Cl Rep Jr Cls; Cls Rep Sr Cls; Chrs; Hon Rl; Pres NHS; Off Ade; Sch Mus; Sec Stu Cncl; Univ; Engr.

GUIRE, BARBARA; Coalton HS; Mabie, WV; Cls Rep Frsh Cls; Cls Rep Soph Cls; VP Jr Cls; Pres Band; Hon Rl; Sch Pl; Stg Crw; Stu Cncl; Ed Sch Nwsp; Pres 4-H; Univ; English.

GUIRE, JAMES A; Coalton HS; Norton, WV; 7/32 Am Leg Boys St; Chrh Wkr; Cmnty Wkr; Hon Rl; Lbry Ade; Stg Crw; Yrbk; Sch Nwsp; Drama Clb; 4-H; Univ; Bio.

GUIRLINGER, CHRISTOHER; Pleasant HS; Marion, OH; Band; Hon Rl; JA; Orch; Sch Pl; Sprt Ed Yrbk; Yrbk; Drama Clb; Univ; Elec Engr.

GUISGAND, RAYMOND; Brighton Area HS; Brighton, MI; Cls Rep Frsh Cls; Chrs; Cmnty Wkr; Sch Pl; Stg Crw; Stu Cncl; Bsbl; Bsktbl; College; Interior Design.

GUITAR, EMILY; Lorain County Joint Voc Schl; Wellington, OH; Pres Jr Cls; Hon Rl; Stu Cncl; OEA; Chrldng; IM Sprt; Scr Kpr; Kent St Univ; Acctg.

GULAJSKI, LISA; Cuyahoga Falls HS; Silverlake, OH; Cl Rep Jr Cls; Am Leg Aux Girls St; Hon Rl; VP JA; NHS; Sec Stu Cncl; Sec Fr Clb; Pep Clb; Chrldng; JA Awd; College; Optometry.

GULAN, RICHARD J; Catholic Central HS; Steubenville, OH; 41/205 Am Leg Boys St; FCA; Hon Rl; NHS; Letter Bsbl; Letter Ftbl; IM Sprt; Univ.

GULAS, CHARLES; Struthers HS; Poland, OH; 65/275 Hon Rl; Voice Dem Awd; Univ.

GULEFF, CANDI; Washington HS; Massillon, OH; Band; Off Ade; Pep Clb; Swmmng; Twrlr; Marshall Univ.

GULICK, DAVID; Breckenridge HS; Merrill, MI; 10/130 Hon Rl; NHS; Stu Cncl; Yth Flsp; 4-H; FFA; Letter Bsktbl; Letter Trk; 4-H Awd; Rotary Awd; Michigan St Univ; Ag.

GULICK, THOMAS; Byron HS; Byron, MI; Band; Hon Rl; Sch Pl; Stu Cncl; 4-H; FFA; Letter Bsktbl; Letter Ftbl; Letter Trk; 4-H Awd; Western Michigan Univ; Communication.

GULIEK, DAVE; Breckenridge Jr Sr HS; Merrill, MI; 10/109 Hon Rl; NHS; Stu Cncl; 4-H; Pres FFA; Letter Bsktbl; Letter Trk; 4-H Awd; Rotary Awd; Michigan State Univ; Agri.

GULLETT, LISA; Union City Community HS; Union City, IN; 2/90 Trs Frsh Cls; Trs Soph Cls; VP Jr Cls; Hon Rl; NHS; Sch Mus; Sch Pl; 4-H; OEA; Spn Clb; Purdue Univ; Pre Vet Med.

GULLEY, WILLIAM R; St Marys Of Redford HS; Detroit, MI; Boy Scts; Hon Rl; NHS; Sch Pl; Sct Actv; God Cntry Awd; Univ Of Michigan; Eng.

GULLIKSEN, JE MAE; Northrop HS; Fort Wayne, IN; 8/646 Chrs; Chrh Wkr; Cmnty Wkr; Hon Rl; Natl Forn Lg; Sch Mus; Sch Pl; C of C Awd; St Olaf College; Family Study.

GULLING, LISA; West Branch HS; Beloit, OH; 1/249 Band; Chrs; Hon Rl; Jr NHS; NHS; Sch Mus; Rptr Yrbk; FTA; Pep Clb; GAA; Univ Of Akron; Nursing.

GULLION, LISA; Warren Woods HS; Warren, MI; Hon Rl; JA; Sch Pl; Drama Clb; JA Awd; Wayne St; Law.

GULU, DIANNE; Memorial HS; Campbell, OH; 1/210 Val; Drm Mjrt; Hon Rl; NHS; Yth Flsp; Drama Clb; FNA; Sec Key Clb; Mth Clb; Youngstown State Univ; Med.

GULUTZ, ANNALISA; East Liverpool HS; E Liverpool, OH; 33/366 Cls Rep Soph Cls; Am Leg Aux Girls St; Sec Chrs; Chrh Wkr; Hon Rl; Treas NHS; Sch Mus; Sec Eng Clb; Pep Clb; Spn Clb; Chosen For St Achievmnt Test In Spanish; Sec Of NIKE & Hi Tri Clbs; College; Busns Mgmt.

GUM, DANIAL W; Sandusky HS; Sandusky, OH; Cl Rep Jr Cls; Boy Scts; Chrh Wkr; JA; Sct Actv; Treas VICA; JA Awd; Science.

GUMINSKI, KAREN; Aquinas HS; Dearborn Hts, MI; Girl Scts; Hon Rl; NHS; Mic Tech Univ; Engr.

GUMKOWSKI, JOHN; La Salle HS; South Bend, IN; 78/488 Hon Rl; Treas JA; Pep Clb; Univ; Bus.

GUMMERE, PEGGY; Van Buren HS; Brazil, IN; 5/84 Chrs; Chrh Wkr; Girl Scts; Hon Rl; NHS; Sch Mus; Fr Clb; FHA; FTA; Pep Clb; Algebra 1 Awd 77; Bio Awd 78; French 2 Awd 79; St Finalist Miss United Tn 79; Hon Queen Jobs Daughters 79; Purdue Univ; Math.

GUMOWSKI, ALEX B; George Washington HS; Charleston, WV; Cls Rep Frsh Cls; Cls Rep Soph Cls; Am Leg Boys St; Treas JA; Jr NHS; Stu Cncl; Sprt Ed Sch Nwsp; FBLA; Key Clb; Letter Ten; Univ Of Va Jefferson Schlr Awd 79; 1st Pl Kanawha County Math Field Day 77; Helen Barnett Awd For Top Eng; Univ.

GUMP, KATHY; Lincoln HS; Wallace, WV; Cl Rep Jr Cls; Chrs; Hon Rl; Treas NHS; Sch Mus; 4-H; FHA; Pep Clb; VICA; Military Serv.

GUNDER, JOAN; Henry Ford II HS; Sterling Hts, MI; 8/453 Chrh Wkr; Hon Rl; NHS; Bsbl; Bsktbl; GAA; Natl Merit SF; Wayne St Univ; Acctg.

GUNDLE, DOREEN; North Farmington HS; Farm Hills, MI; Cls Rep Frsh Cls; Chrh Wkr; Hon Rl; JA; Jr NHS; Natl Forn Lg; NHS; Off Ade; Sch Pl; Stu Cncl; Univ Of Michigan; Eng.

GUNDLER, MONICA; Badin HS; Hamilton, OH; 35/226 VP Soph Cls; Hon Rl; NHS; Stu Cncl; Rotary Awd; Coll Of Mt St Joseph; Soc Work.

GUNDY, KIMBERLY; Reeths Puffer HS; Muskegon, MI; 82/284 Band; Chrs; Chrh Wkr; Hon Rl; St Of Mi Competitive Schlrshp 79; Muskegon Cmnty Coll; Clerical.

GUNN, BELINDA; Benedictine HS; Detroit, MI; Cmp Fr Grls; Chrs; Girl Scts; Hon Rl; JA; Sch Pl; Pe p Clb; Cert Of Mert In Music 74; Bio Awd 77; Chem Awd 78; Michigan St Univ; Eng.

GUNN, DAVID; Utica HS; Utica, OH; 50/195 Band; Chrs; Chrh Wkr; Cmnty Wkr; Sch Mus; Drama Clb; Bsbl; Capt Bsktbl; Ftbl; Coll; Acctg.

GUNN, EDMUND; Horace Mann HS; Gary, IN; Band; Hon Rl; Sch Mus; Letter Bsbl; Ftbl; Purdue Univ; Elec Engr.

GUNN, JEFFREY; N Central HS; Alvordton, OH; Am Leg Boys St; Boy Scts; Hon Rl; Off Ade; Sct Actv; Sprt Ed Sch Nwsp; Bsktbl; Capt Glf; Trk; JETS Awd; Tri State Coll; Mech Engr.

GUNN, LESLYE; Brown City HS; Brown City, MI; Sec Frsh Cls; Sec Sr Cls; Band; Chrs; Chrh Wkr; Cmnty Wkr; Hon Rl; Stu Cncl; FHA; FTA; 1st & 2nd Rating Dist & St Solo & Ensemble Band; FTA Schlrshp; Central Michigan Univ; Journalism.

GUNN, MICHELLE; Immaculate Conception Acad; Dayton, OH; VP Jr Cls; Chrs; Chrh Wkr; Hon Rl; Sch Pl; Sec Stu Cncl; Rptr Yrbk; Rptr Sch Nwsp; Sch Nwsp; Yth Flsp; College; Creative Writing.

GUNN, ROGER; Benjamin Bosse HS; Evansville, IN; 10/329 Hon Rl; NHS; Lat Clb; Bsbl; Cit Awd; Rcvd Invitation To Univ Of Evansville Tri St Hnrs Dinner 79; Univ.

GUNNER, JAMES; Clay HS; Oregon, OH; 1/366 Hon Rl; NHS; College; Chemical Engr.

GUNNING, HENRY; Paw Paw HS; Paw Paw, WV; 1/26 Am Leg Boys St; Hon Rl; NHS; Sch Pl; Letter Bsktbl; West Virginia Inst Of Tech; Physics.

GUNNING, MARY SUE; Cowell Sr HS; Lowell, IN; Chrh Wkr; Girl Scts; Hon Rl; Off Ade; Sch Pl; Rptr Sch Nwsp; Pep Clb; Swmmng; Chrldng; GAA; All Amer HS 77; Qualfd For Ball St Swim Schlrshp 77; Girls HS Swim Sect Champ 78; Univ.

GUNNOE, DONNA; Meadow Bridge HS; Danese, WV; 1/61 Sec Jr Cls; Val; Chrs; Chrh Wkr; Hon Rl; NHS; Sch Pl; Stu Cncl; Yth Flsp; Rptr Sch Nwsp; Eng Achvmnt Awd 79; Know Your Cnty Govt Delgt 78; Marshall Univ; Nursing.

GUNNOE, MARSHA; H H Dow HS; Midland, MI; 106/422 Cmnty Wkr; Hon Rl; Sct Actv; Stu Cncl; Ed Yrbk; Rptr Sch Nwsp; Pres DECA; Letter Swmmng; PPFtbl; Sci Lab Asst 75; 2nd Pl Awd In DECA Comp 78; 1st Pl Awd Indisplay Cntst Mrktng 79; Ferris St Coll; Acctg.

GUNRISCO, KAREN; Marcellus HS; Marcellus, MI; Cl Rep Jr Cls; FCA; Hon Rl; Rptr Yrbk; Bsktbl; Gym; Letter Chrldng; Elk Awd; Mic State Univ; Vet Med.

GUNSELL, DEBRA; Durand Area HS; Swartz Crk, MI; Chrs; Drl Tm; Sch Pl; Rptr Sch Nwsp; Letter Ten; Mat Maids; PPFtbl; Hurley School; Radiology Tech.

GUNTER, LORI; Eastern HS; Greentown, IN; 12/130 Cls Rep Sr Cls; Hon Rl; Off Ade; Sec Stu Cncl; FHA; Pep Clb; Sec Chrldng; Natl Merit Ltr; Univ; Psych.

GUNTER, WILLIAM; St Albans HS; St Albans, WV; Rptr Sch Nwsp; Journalism.

GUNTHER, CONNIE; Dexter HS; Dexter, MI; Treas Girl Scts; Hon Rl; Hosp Ade; Lbry Ade; Sct Actv; Stu Cncl; Drama Clb; Ger Clb; Pep Clb; Pres Awd; Cgirl Scout Acknwldgmnt Awd 79; Michigan St Univ; Bus Admin.

GUNTHER, DAVID; Sts Peter & Paul Area HS; Saginaw, MI; 13/117 Chrs; Hon Rl; NHS; Sch Mus; Stg Crw; Bsbl; Capt Glf; Mgrs; Nation Hnr Soc Hnr Roll; Math Awd Bus Awd 76; Natl Hon Soc Hnr Roll Math Awd 77; Michigan Tech Univ; Indstrl Engr.

GUNTHER, MARGARET; De Vilbiss HS; Toledo, OH; Girl Scts; Hon Rl; Hosp Ade; Lbry Ade; Quill & Scroll; Stg Crw; Rptr Yrbk; Fr Clb; Toledo Univ; Bus Admin.

GUNYULA, KATHY; Mineral Ridge HS; Mineral Ridge, OH; 5/70 Band; Hon Rl; Quill & Scroll; Stu Cncl; Rptr Sch Nwsp; Beta Clb; Ger Clb; Key Clb; Pom Pon; PPFtbl; Youngstown St Univ; Med Tech.

GUPTA, LATHA; Bluefield HS; Bluefield, WV; 38/250 Chrs; Hon Rl; Jr NHS; Rptr Yrbk; Fr Clb; Pep Clb; Honros Eng Prog 79 80; Univ; Psych.

GURA, MARY LOU; St Clement HS; Detroit, MI; Hon Rl; Jr NHS; NHS; Letter Bsbl; GAA; Scr Kpr; Univ; Bus.

GURGALL, LORI; North Central Area HS; Hermansville, MI; Sec Jr Cls; Band; Sch Mus; Sch Pl; Drama Clb; FHA; Bsktbl; Chrldng; IM Sprt; Pom Pon; Voc Schl; Health Careers.

GURGOS, MICHELE; Boardman HS; Youngstown, OH; 22/600 Girl Scts; Hon Rl; Y-Teens; Spn Clb; Mat Maids; Scr Kpr; Martion Awd 76; Univ; Elec Engr.

GURISKO, CATHRYN; Finney HS; Detroit, MI; Hon Rl; NHS; Letter Glf; Letter Swmmng; Mgrs; Tmr; Am Leg Awd; Cit Awd; College; Marine Bio.

GURNEY, DAWN; Cloverdale HS; Cloverdale, IN; Chrs; Cmnty Wkr; Debate Tm; Girl Scts; Lbry Ade; Sch Mus; Y-Teens; Eng Clb; FBLA; FSU; Math.

GURNIK, SUSAN; Scecina Memorial HS; Indianapolis, IN; 8/216 Cls Rep Frsh Cls; Cls Rep Soph Cls; Cmnty Wkr; Hon Rl; NHS; Off Ade; Stu Cncl; Letter Ten; IM Sprt; Purdue; Engr.

GURSAL, JIHAN D; Fairview HS; Fairview Park, OH; Cls Rep Frsh Cls; Sec Soph Cls; Cl Rep Jr Cls; AFS; Girl Scts; Hon Rl; Lit Mag; Orch; Red Cr Ade; Stu Cncl; Musical Awd 1st Pl Trombone Solo 77; Ohio St Univ; Pharm.

GURSKI, MICHAEL; St Peters HS; Mansfield, OH; Trs Frsh Cls; Trs Jr Cls; Cmnty Wkr; Hon Rl; Sch Pl; Stg Crw; Stu Cncl; Yrbk; Drama Clb; Sci Clb; Univ.

GURTNER, JOLENNA; Vantage Joint Voc HS; Van Wert, OH; Cls Rep Sr Cls; Hon Rl; Hosp Ade; JA; Stu Cncl; VP DECA; 4-H; Lat Clb; JA Awd; Mas Awd;.

GUSEMAN, JOHN F; Fairfield Union HS; Bremen, OH; Hon Rl; Jr NHS; Key Clb; College.

GUSHEN, GLENDA; Ithaca HS; Ithaca, MI; Trs Frsh Cls; Sec Soph Cls; Sec Jr Cls; Girl Scts; Hon Rl; OEA; Pep Clb; Scr Kpr; Lansing Bus Inst; Legal Sec.

GUSHMAN, PATRICIA; St Agatha HS; Detroit, MI; 10/131 Hon Rl; Treas NHS; Sch Pl; Ed Yrbk; Yrbk; Capt Trk; Natl Merit SF; Mercy Coll; Nursing.

GUSHMAN, PATRICIA; St Agatha HS; Redford, MI; Hon Rl; Treas NHS; Sch Pl; Ed Yrbk; Drama Clb; Capt Trk; Natl Merit SF; Mercy Coll Of Detroit; Reg Nurse.

GUSLER, TIMOTHY O; Bedford North Lawrence HS; Bedford, IN; 69/420 Am Leg Boys St; Band; Chrh Wkr; Hon Rl; NHS; Pol Wkr; Yth Flsp; Letter Bsktbl; Letter Trk; Voice Dem Awd; Univ; Math.

GUSSE, HOLLIE; Nordonia HS; Macedonia, OH; Band; Yth Flsp; Capt Twrlr; Cit Awd; Mas Awd; Kent St Univ; Home Ec.

GUST, JAMES; Muskegon HS; Muskegon, MI; Band; Boy Scts; Hon Rl; Pres JA; NHS; Stu Cncl; Pres JA Awd; Mich State Univ; Acctg.

GUST, LAWRENCE; Ironwood Catholic HS; Ironwood, MI; 2/25 VP Soph Cls; Chrs; Chrh Wkr; Hon Rl; NHS; Sch Pl; Cit Awd; Dnfth Awd; Mic Tech Univ; Bus Mgmt.

GUSTAFSON, DALE A; Bishop Noll Inst; Chicago, IL; 10/360 Boy Scts; Drm Bgl; Hon Rl; Bsbl; Coach Actv; Mgrs; United Air Forc ROTC 4 Ys Federl Schlshp Alternt 1979; Il St Scholr 1979; Jr Hon Guard 1977; Purdue Univ; Meteorology.

GUSTAFSON, DARRYL; Mount Vernon Acad; Mt Vernon, OH; Pres Soph Cls; Pres Jr Cls; Aud/Vis; Hon Rl; Lbry Ade; IM Sprt; Scr Kpr; Tmr; College; Law.

GUSTAFSON, GREGG; Negaunee HS; Negaunee, MI; Cmnty Wkr; Hon Rl; Bsbl; Letter Bsktbl; Letter Ftbl; Letter Ten; Mi Com Pschlshp 79; Mi Athtc Assn Upper Peninsula 1st Pl Champ Tennis Doubles 79; All Conf Bsktbl Team; N Michigan Univ; Psych.

GUSTAFSON, ROSEMARY; La Salle HS; St Ignace, MI; Sec Jr Cls; Band; Drl Tm; Hon Rl; Sch Pl; Stg Crw; Rptr Yrbk; Drama Clb; Trk; Letter Chrldng; Lake Superior Univ; RN.

GUSTAFSON, TERRIE; Brighton HS; Brighton, MI; Hon Rl; Rptr Sch Nwsp; Ferris Univ; Pharm.

GUSTER, RODNEY; Cass Technical HS; Chelsea, MI; Aud/Vis; Boy Scts; Cmnty Wkr; Hon Rl; Ftbl; Trk; Capt IM Sprt; Cit Awd; Mi Compt Schslhp 78; Eastern Michigan Univ; Indust Tech.

GUT, DIANNE; Erieview Cath HS; Parma, OH; Cls Rep Sr Cls; Chrs; Hon Rl; Mod UN; NHS; Coll; Phys Therapy.

GUTER, HANS; St Charles Prep HS; Columbus, OH; Trs Sr Cls; Boy Scts; Hon Rl; NHS; Sch Pl; Stu Cncl; Ftbl; Trk; Wrstlng; College; Med.

GUTERBA, CHERYL; Springfield Local HS; Poland, OH; 19/145 Chrh Wkr; Girl Scts; Hon Rl; NHS; Off Ade; Sct Actv; OEA; Trk; Youngstown St Univ; Crt Reporting.

GUTHRIDGE, CHERYL; Warrensville Heights HS; Warrensville, OH; Cls Rep Frsh Cls; Band; Chrs; Hon Rl; NHS; Cit Awd; Univ; Sec.

GUTHRIE, JULIE; Springboro HS; Miamisburg, OH; 3/200 Band; Chrh Wkr; Hon Rl; NHS; Orch; Sch Pl; Ed Yrbk; Capt Chrldng; GAA; PPFtbl; Ohio St Univ; Pre Med.

GUTHRIE, PAUL; Centreville Public HS; Centreville, MI; Band; Hon Rl; NHS; Glen Oaks Comm College; Scic.

GUTHRIE, SCOTT; Marlette HS; Marlette, MI; 16/158 Chrs; Debate Tm; Hon Rl; NHS; Sch Pl; Drama Clb; Letter Bsbl; IM Sprt; Michigan St Univ; CPA.

GUTHRIE, SUE; Monroe HS; Monroe, MI; Aud/V-is; Lbry Ade; Monroe Cmnty Coll; Child Care.

GUTMANN, ANNE; Lehman HS; Piqua, OH; 14/87 Hon Rl; VP NHS; Stg Crw; Yrbk; Letter Bsktbl; Crs Cntry; Letter Trk; Chr Club Pres; Jr Cnslr Chldlrn Intl Summer Vly Camp In Norway; Univ.

GUTMANN, BECKY; Bexley HS; Columbus, OH; 5/186 Band; Hon Rl; NHS; Rptr Sch Nwsp; Fr Clb; Letter Ten; IM Sprt; Univ Of Mic; Sci.

GUTOWSKI, KENNETH; Manistee Catholic Cntrl HS; Manistee, MI; 20/64 Hon Rl; West Shore Cmnty Coll; Mech.

GUTOWSKI JR, WALTER; West Catholic HS; Grand Rapids, MI; Band; Hon Rl; Mdrgl; NHS; Sch Mus; Letter Crs Cntry; Letter Swmmng; Letter Trk; College; Printing.

GUTRIDGE, DEBRA; East Knox HS; Howard, OH; 3/66 Am Leg Aux Girls St; Chrs; Chrh Wkr; Treas Girl Scts; Treas NHS; Quill & Scroll; Sch Pl; Sct Actv; Sec Yth Flsp; Ed Yrbk; Ohio State Univ; Elem Educ.

GUTRIDGE, MICHELE R; Licking Valley HS; Newark, OH; 1/158 VP Jr Cls; Am Leg Aux Girls St; VP Band; Chrh Wkr; Drl Tm; Hon Rl; Pres NHS; VP Stu Cncl; Yrbk; Pres Pep Clb; Ohio State Univ; Health Sci.

GUTSCHENRITTER, VICTORIA M; St Josephs HS; South Bend, IN; Chrs; Hon Rl; Mdrgl; Quill & Scroll; Sch Mus; Rptr Yrbk; Ger Clb; ExclInc In German I II & III 76 77 & 78; Exclinc In Bio 77; Univ; Lib.

GUTTENBERG, DEMA; Kenton HS; Kenton, OH; 9/204 Band; Chrh Wkr; Girl Scts; Hon Rl; NHS; Yth Flsp; FHA; Bluffton College; Med Tech.

GUTWEIN, JANICE; West Central HS; Francesville, IN; Band; Chrs; Chrh Wkr; Cmnty Wkr; Hon Rl; Jr NHS; Lbry Ade; NHS; Sch Mus; Sch Pl; Purdue Univ; Psych.

GUTZWILLER, KIRK W; East Central HS; Harrison, OH; 3/230 Hon Rl; NHS; Yth Flsp; Letter Glf; Letter Ten; Letter Wrstlng; JETS Awd; Top Math Stu Grades 7 11 1979; Tied For Highest Score Natl Math Exam 1979; Highest PSAT Score Verb & Math; Purdue Univ; Engr.

GUY, CHARLES; Madison HS; Madison, OH; Band; Boy Scts; Chrh Wkr; Hon Rl; Sct Actv; Pres Yth Flsp; Rptr Yrbk; Sci Clb; Univ Of Dayton; Anthropology.

GUY, DONALD G; Northrop HS; Ft Wayne, IN; 2/584 Hon Rl; Orch; Rdo Clb; Tri Kappa Awd 78; Univ; Elec Engr.

GUY, GERI; Columbiana HS; Columbiana, OH; 35/102 Band; Chrh Wkr; Drm Mjrt; Hon Rl; Off Ade; Y-Teens; Yrbk; Sch Nwsp; OEA; Pep Clb; Exec Dplmt & States Womn Awds 78; Ambssdr Awd 79; Skills Compt 79; Youngstown St Univ; Criminology.

GUY, LORI; St Charles HS; Saginaw, MI; 2/130 Sec Jr Cls; Hon Rl; Stu Cncl; Trk; Chrldng; GAA; IM Sprt; Univ; Cmnctns.

GUY, PATTY; Maplewood HS; Cortland, OH; 3/89 Cls Rep Frsh Cls; Cls Rep Soph Cls; Band; Chrs; Hon Rl; NHS; Sch Pl; Pres Stu Cncl; Ed Yrbk; Rptr Sch Nwsp; Kent St Univ; Psych.

GUY, SUSAN; Andrews Acad; Berrien Spring, MI; Chrh Wkr; Hon Rl; NHS; Off Ade; Stu Cncl; Rptr Yrbk; Yrbk; Rptr Sch Nwsp; Loma Linda Univ; Eng.

GUYER, CHERYL; Hubbard HS; Hubbard, OH; Band; Chrh Wkr; Sch Mus; Yth Flsp; Youngstown St Univ; Music.

GUYER, CHERYL; Peru HS; Peru, IN; 23/283 Trs Frsh Cls; Trs Soph Cls; Trs Jr Cls; Trs Sr Cls; Band; Chrs; Chrh Wkr; Ball State; Spec Ed.

GUYER, DAWN; Linden HS; Linden, MI; Chrs; Chrh Wkr; Girl Scts; Hon Rl; NHS; Off Ade; Sch Mus; Sch Pl; Drama Clb; GAA; Baker Jr Coll; Sec.

GUYER, JULIA A; Munster HS; Munster, IN; 30/402 Chrs; Sec Chrh Wkr; Girl Scts; Hon Rl; Jr NHS; Lbry Ade; Sch Mus; Sct Actv; Sch Nwsp; In Univ Hnrs Progr In Frgn Lang For HS Stu 79; Olivet Nazarene Coll; Foreign Serv.

GUYER, MICHELLE; Peru HS; Peru, IN; 5/283 Band; Chrs; Hon Rl; MMM; NHS; Sch Pl; Elk Awd; Butler Univ; Music.

GUYETTE, LAWRENCE; Traverse City HS; Traverse City, MI; 3/108 Sec Frsh Cls; Hon Rl; Mod UN; NHS; Stu Cncl; Letter Ftbl; IM Sprt; Univ Of Mic; Law.

GUYTON, KENNETH; Southeastern HS; Detroit, MI; Boy Scts; Cmnty Wkr; Hon Rl; Sct Actv; OEA; Bsktbl; Cit Awd; Detroit Coll Of Business; Acctg.

GUYTON, KIMBERLY; Mt Vernon Acad; Akron, OH; Chrh Wkr; Hon Rl; Hosp Ade; Lbry Ade; Sch Pl; Stu Cncl; Spn Clb;.

GUZA, NANCY; Lake Shore HS; St Clair Shores, MI; Band; Hon Rl; Systems Analysis.

GUZDIAL, MARK; Bishop Foley HS; Royal Oak, MI; 3/190 Hon Rl; Lit Mag; NHS; Rptr Sch Nwsp; Eng Clb; Sci Clb; Crs Cntry; Trk; College; Comp Design.

GUZZETTA, ROBERT; Lemon Monroe HS; Monroe, OH; 26/292 Band; Hon Rl; Pol Wkr; Glf; Ten;.

GUZZO, LISA; Columbus Bishop Ready HS; Columbus, OH; Cls Rep Soph Cls; Sec Jr Cls; Girl Scts; Hon Rl; Jr NHS; NHS; Stg Crw; OEA; Chrldng; Barbizon Voc Schl; Interior Dec.

GWEN, JUSTICE; Willow Run HS; Ypsilanti, MI; Band; Chrh Wkr; Hon Rl; NHS; Letter Bsbl; Cit Awd; College.

GWIN, RIC; Gahanna Lincoln HS; Gahanna, OH; VP Frsh Cls; Pol Wkr; IM Sprt; Notre Dame Univ; Acctg.

GWIRTZ, KATHLEEN; Shelby HS; Shelby, OH; Chrh Wkr; Hon Rl; Quill & Scroll; Stg Crw; 4-H; FHA; Lat Clb; 4-H Awd; College; Phys Ther.

GWIZDALA, MARLENE; Bay City Central HS; Munger, MI; Cls Rep Sr Cls; Sal; Hon Rl; Lbry Ade; NHS; Stu Cncl; Eng Clb; PPFtbl; Natl Merit SF; Delta Coll; Med.

GWOZDZ, DAVID; Rossford HS; Rossford, OH; Chrh Wkr; Hon Rl; Spn Clb; Chess Team; Ohio St Univ; Vet.

GYORGYI, SANDRA; John Adams HS; So Bend, IN; 60/405 Pres Sr Cls; Cls Rep Sr Cls; Hon Rl; Stu Cncl; Sch Nwsp; Lat Clb; Capt Ten; Kiwan Awd; Jr Wightman Cup Tennis Northern In 78; Univ; Bus.

GYORKOS, DERRICK; John F Kennedy HS; Taylor, MI; Hon Rl; Rptr Yrbk; Sprt Ed Sch Nwsp; Bsktbl; Trk; Scr Kpr; Tmr; Acctg.

GYSAN, FLORENCE; Margaretta HS; Castalia, OH; 3/156 Chrs; Chrh Wkr; Girl Scts; Hon Rl; Sec NHS; Pres 4-H; VP FHA;.

H

HAACK, MARK; Clarence M Kimball HS; Royal Oak, MI; Band; Chrh Wkr; Hon Rl; Yth Flsp; IM Sprt; Univ Of Michigan; Archt.

HAAG, BRIGITT; St Alphonsus HS; Dearborn, MI; 25/126 Hst Frsh Cls; Hon Rl; Pres JA; Off Ade; Sch Mus; Swmmng; College; Business.

HAAGSMA, TIM; S Christian HS; Grand Rapids, MI; Band; Chrs; Hon Rl; Pres JA; NHS; Yth Flsp; Bsktbl; Letter Crs Cntry; Letter Trk; JA Awd; Calvin Coll; Pro Engr.

HAAK, C; Holland Christian HS; Holland, MI; Cls Rep Frsh Cls; Am Leg Aux Girls St; Band; Chrs; Chrh Wkr; Cmnty Wkr; Drm Mjrt; Hon Rl; Lit Mag; Stu Cncl; 1st Div In Solo & Ensemble Flute; Calvin Coll; Eng.

HAAMID, BAHIR G; Warrensville Hts HS; Warrensville, OH; 18/207 Pres Frsh Cls; Cls Rep Soph Cls; Stu Cncl; Yrbk; DECA; Wrstlng; IM Sprt; JETS Awd; Ohio St Univ; Industrl Engr.

HAAN, LORI; Gahanna Lincoln HS; Gahanna, OH; 98/440 Trs Soph Cls; Chrs; FCA; Hon Rl; Off Ade; Sch Pl; Stu Cncl; DECA; Drama Clb; Pep Clb; Ohio Univ; Cmnctns.

HAAN, MICHELLE; Kelloggsville HS; Wyoming, MI; 11/158 Hon Rl; Sch Pl; Letter Bsktbl; Univ; Nursing.

HAAR, CONNIE; Woodmore HS; Elmore, OH; Chrs; Chrh Wkr; Girl Scts; Hon Rl; Jr NHS; Lbry Ade; NHS; Sch Mus; Yth Flsp; Bowling Green St Univ; Spec Ed.

HAAR, DAVE; Sandusky St Marys Ctrl HS; Sandusky, OH; Cls Rep Frsh Cls; VP Jr Cls; Cls Rep Sr Cls; Treas NHS; Ger Clb; Capt Bsbl; Capt Ftbl; Lion Awd; Natl Merit Ltr; Bluffton Coll; Acctg.

HAAR, LORI; Michigan Lutheran Seminary; Saginaw, MI; 18/62 Sec Sr Cls; Cls Rep Sr Cls; Chrs; Chrh Wkr; Hon Rl; Sec Stu Cncl; Pep Clb; Letter Chrldng; Capt IM Sprt; PPFtbl; Delta Coll Brd Of Trustee Schlrshp 79; Delta Coll.

HAAS, BETH; Edgewood HS; Bloomington, IN; 2/235 Hon Rl; Hosp Ade; NHS; Sch Pl; Stu Cncl; Yrbk; Drama Clb; Spn Clb; Lion Awd; Ind Univ; Psych.

HAAS, BETHANY S; Arenac Eastern HS; Omer, MI; 1/38 Trs Sr Cls; Val; Band; Chrs; Chrh Wkr; Debate Tm; Hon Rl; NHS; Yth Flsp; Rptr Yrbk; Acad Excellence Schlrshp; Mich Competitive Schlrshp; Sftbl 3 Letters; Michigan St Univ; Math.

HAAS, BETH E; Edgewood HS; Bloomington, IN; Cls Rep Frsh Cls; Cl Rep Jr Cls; Cmnty Wkr; Hon Rl; Hosp Ade; Sch Mus; Sch Pl; Stg Crw; Stu Cncl; Drama Clb; Indiana Univ; Clinical Psych.

HAAS, DANIEL; Standish Sterling Cntrl HS; Standish, MI; Cls Rep Frsh Cls; Cls Rep Soph Cls; Trs Sr Cls; Hon Rl; Stu Cncl; 4-H; Letter Ftbl; IM Sprt; Scr Kpr; Mi St Distingshd; MSU Hon Coll Alumni Schlshp Test 79; Mi Compttv Awd; Michigan St Univ.

HAAS, DARLENE; Standish Sterling Centrl HS; Standish, MI; 9/152 Band; Chrs; Chrh Wkr; Girl Scts; Hon Rl; Hosp Ade; Sch Pl; Alma College; Music.

HAAS, DAVID; Saint Xavier HS; Ft Mitchell, KY; 65/265 NHS; Letter Swmmng; IM Sprt; Xavier Univ; Pre Med.

HAAS, EDWIN; Muskegon HS; Muskegon, MI; Band; Chrh Wkr; Hon Rl; NHS; Stu Cncl; Yth Flsp; Univ Of Michigan.

HAAS, JEANNE; St Francis Central HS; Morgantown, WV; 2/70 Pres Soph Cls; Pres Jr Cls; Band; Chrs; Hon Rl; NHS; Sch Mus; Sch Pl; Sec Drama Clb; Fr Clb; Univ; Early Childhood Ed.

HAAS, JIMMY; Dunbar HS; Charleston, WV; Sec Jr Cls; Am Leg Boys St; Chrs; Chrh Wkr; Hon Rl; NHS; Stu Cncl; Beta Clb; Letter Ftbl; Letter Wrstlng; College; Comp Sci.

HAAS, LAURIE; Marietta Sr HS; Lowell, OH; Hon Rl; Hosp Ade; NHS; OEA; Parkersburg Cmnty Coll; Bank Mgmt.

HAAS, MICHELE; St Joseph Acad; Fairview Pk, OH; Chrh Wkr; Girl Scts; Hon Rl; Y-Teens; Rptr Yrbk; Rptr Sch Nwsp; Fr Clb; Crs Cntry; Chrldng; College; Nursing.

HAAS, RETTA; Regina HS; Cleveland Hts, OH; Cl Rep Jr Cls; Hon Rl; Jr NHS; Bsbl; Bsktbl; College.

HAAS, RICHARD; Padua Franciscan HS; Parma, OH; Boy Scts; Hon Rl; JA; JA Awd; Univ.

HAATAJA, GERRIE; Ewen Trout Creek HS; Bruce Crossing, MI; 5/43 Band; Chrh Wkr; Treas Debate Tm; Hon Rl; Lbry Ade; Lit Mag; Natl Forn Lg; Yth Flsp; Yrbk; 4-H; Northern Michigan Univ; Spch Cmnctn.

HABERMAN, MARK; Port Clinton HS; Pt Clinton, OH; Am Leg Boys St; Boy Scts; Hon Rl; Rptr Yrbk; Rptr Sch Nwsp; 4-H; Ger Clb; Letter Bsbl; Letter Bsktbl; Ftbl; Ohio St Univ; Journalism.

HABERMAS, JAMES; Grand River Acad; Canton, MI; 3/23 Cls Rep Soph Cls; Trs Jr Cls; Hon Rl; NHS; Stu Cncl; Socr; Wrstlng; Scr Kpr; Tmr; Eastern Michigan Univ; Data Proc.

HABERMAS, RONALD; South Lake HS; St Clair Shore, MI; 20/450 Hon Rl; Ger Clb; Rdo Clb; Ten; Trk; Wrstlng; Univ Of Mic; Acctg.

HABIAN, GEORGE; Rocky River HS; Rocky River, OH; Band; Boy Scts; Chrs; Chrh Wkr; Hon Rl; Jr NHS; Orch; Sch Mus; Sch Pl; Stg Crw; Case Western Reserve Univ; Med.

HABIBI, SOHRAB; Floyd Central HS; New Albany, IN; NHS; Stu Cncl; Ftbl; Socr; Capt Wrstlng; Coll; Vet.

HABICHT, DAVE; Mount Clemens HS; Mt Clemens, MI; Air Force Community Coll; Pilot.

HABIG, TODD; De Kalb Central United HS; Auburn, IN; 1/287 FCA; Jr NHS; NHS; Yth Flsp; Ger Clb; Letter Bsktbl; Letter Glf; Coach Actv; Lion Awd; Penfield Est Schlrshp; Zeke Young Athletic Schlrshp; Assoc Tri Kappa Awd For Top Schlr; Butler Univ.

HABJANIC, SYLVIA; Cleveland Ctrl Catholic HS; Cleveland, OH; 35/180 Cls Rep Frsh Cls; Chrs; Drm Bgl; Hon Rl; Off Ade; Sch Mus; Stu Cncl; Schiller College; French.

HACKATHORN, ANGELA; St Paul HS; Norwalk, OH; 6/82 Sec Frsh Cls; Am Leg Aux Girls St; Band; Hon Rl; NHS; Fr Clb; Pep Clb; Cit Awd; Bowling Green St Univ; Sec Ed.

HACKENBERGER, RANAE; Edison HS; Norwalk, OH; Band; Chrh Wkr; Hon Rl; NHS; Orch; Yth Flsp; Drama Clb; FTA; College.

HACKENBRACHT, JEFFREY; Marion Harding HS; Marion, OH; Yrbk; Spn Clb; Capt Glf; Ohio St Univ; Civil Engr.

HACKENBRACHT, THOMAS; Ridgewood HS; W Lafayette, OH; Hon Rl; 4-H; Letter Crs Cntry; 4-H Awd; Ohio St Univ; Natural Resources.

HACKER, BEVERLY; Centerville HS; Dayton, OH; 7/687 Band; NHS; Pep Clb; PPFtbl; Miami Univ; Finance.

HACKER, KEVIN; Decatur Central HS; Camby, IN; 3/305 Band; Hon Rl; NHS; Sct Actv; Stu Cncl; 4-H; 4-H Awd; College; Art.

HACKER, RICHARD; Sandusky HS; Sandusky, OH; Hon Rl; DECA; Voc Schl.

HACKETT, ANNETTE; Frankfort Sr HS; Frankfort, IN; 11/260 Am Leg Aux Girls St; Band; Chrs; Girl Scts; NHS; Sch Mus; Sch Pl; Lat Clb; Pom Pon; Pres Awd; Ivy Tech Schl; Comp Sci.

HACKETT, IRIS E; Northwestern HS; Detroit, MI; Band; Chrh Wkr; Cmnty Wkr; Hon Rl; JA; Jr NHS; MMM; NHS; Sch Mus; Cit Awd;.

HACKETT, JANE; Pontiac Central HS; Pontiac, MI; Band; Drm Mjrt; Hon Rl; NHS; Orch; Rptr Yrbk; Rptr Sch Nwsp; Gym; Swmmng; Central Mich Coll; Psych.

HACKETT, LINDA; John F Kennedy Sr HS; Taylor, MI; Band; Hon Rl; Letter Ten; IM Sprt; PPFtbl;.

HACKETT, MATTHEW; Avondale Sr HS; Rochester, MI; 6/257 Treas AFS; Chrs; Chrh Wkr; Hon Rl; Mdrgl; Sch Mus; Spn Clb; Wayne St Univ; Lib Arts.

HACKETT, PAMELA; Our Lady Of Mercy HS; Detroit, MI; Chrs; Chrh Wkr; Cmnty Wkr; Hon Rl; Pol Wkr; Sch Mus; Sci Clb; Spn Clb; Univ Of Michigan; Chem Engr.

HACKETT, SUSAN; Bishop Fenwick HS; Middletown, OH; 4/87 Band; Hon Rl; NHS; Fr Clb; Univ Of Dayton; Acctg.

HACKMAN, DARLA; Brownstown Central HS; Brownstown, IN; 26/147 Cl Rep Jr Cls; Am Leg Aux Girls St; Hon Rl; Yth Flsp; Sec Civ Clb; Pres 4-H; Pres FFA; FTA; Pep Clb; GAA; FFA St Farmer Degree; Indiana Miss Teen U S A Pageant; VP Of Indiana Jr Horticulture Assn; Purdue Univ; Law.

HACKMANN, LESLI; Carroll HS; South Bend, IN; Band; Cmnty Wkr; Hon Rl; NHS; Orch; Ger Clb; Key Clb; Spn Clb; IM Sprt; St Bd Of Educ Awd Of Distinction 79; German 2 Achvmnt Awd 79; International World Series Dog Show Showman Awd; St Marys Coll; Engr.

HACKNEY, CASSANDRA; West Jefferson HS; W Jefferson, OH; 8/98 Cls Rep Soph Cls; Sec Jr Cls; Cl Rep Jr Cls; Sec Sr Cls; Cls Rep Sr Cls; Am Leg Aux Girls St; Band; Chrh Wkr; Hon Rl; Miami Univ; Med.

HACKNEY, ROGER; Lapeer East HS; Lapeer, MI; Band; Boy Scts; Girl Scts; JA; Stu Cncl; 4-H; Crs Cntry; IM Sprt; Cit Awd; 4-H Awd; Univ Of Michigan; Bus Admin.

HACKNEY, SANDRA; West Jefferson HS; W Jefferson, OH; 9/98 VP Jr Cls; Sec Sr Cls; Chrh Wkr; Sec NHS; Letter Bsktbl; Capt Trk; Kiwan Awd; Letter Miami Univ; Medicine.

HACKWORTH, MICHAEL; London HS; London, OH; 33/133 Chrh Wkr; Hon Rl; Sct Actv; Letter Ftbl; College.

HADDAD, GREGG; Sylvania Northview HS; Sylvania, OH; 11/296 VP Debate Tm; Hon Rl; Natl Forn Lg; NHS; Treas Quill & Scroll; Sch Mus; Sch Pl; Ed Sch Nwsp; IM Sprt; College.

HADDAD, KIMBERLY; Potterville HS; Dimondale, MI; 7/70 Trs Sr Cls; Chrh Wkr; Girl Scts; Hon Rl; NHS; Yth Flsp; Sprt Ed Yrbk; Crs Cntry; PPFtbl; Bus Schl.

HADDEN, KIM; Ashley HS; Ithaca, MI; Hon Rl; Lbry Ade; Off Ade; FTA; Mgrs;.

HADDEN, TERESA; Chatard HS; Indianapolis, IN; 56/195 Girl Scts; Hon Rl; Jr NHS; NHS; Sch Mus; Stg Crw; Letter Mgrs; Mat Maids; Purdue Univ.

HADDING, SANDRA K; Wapakoneta Sr HS; Cridersvll, OH; Off Ade; Rptr Yrbk; FBLA; OEA; Spn Clb; Ohio St Univ; Legal Sec.

HADDIX, CRISTINA; Buckhannon Upshur HS; Buckhannon, WV; Cls Rep Frsh Cls; Sec Soph Cls; Cls Rep Soph Cls; Cl Rep Jr Cls; Am Leg Aux Girls St; Chrs; Chrh Wkr; Cmnty Wkr; Drl Tm; Hon Rl; Study Tour France & Switzerland 79; Univ; Phys Ther.

HADDIX, SHERI; Philip Barbour HS; Philippi, WV; 32/200 Trs Frsh Cls; VP Soph Cls; Sec Sr Cls; Hon Rl; Stu Cncl; Keyettes; Capt Chrldng; Marshall Univ; Psych.

HADDON, PAMELA; Staunton HS; Brazil, IN; 4/47 Sec Frsh Cls; Pres Soph Cls; Pres Jr Cls; Chrs; Chrh Wkr; Hon Rl; NHS; Off Ade; Sch Pl; Stu Cncl; Indiana St Univ; Bus Admin.

HADDOW, WILLIAM; Woodridge HS; Peninsula, OH; 22/130 Chrh Wkr; Hon Rl; Yth Flsp; Fr Clb; Spn Clb; Letter Bsktbl; IM Sprt; Univ.

HADINGER, MICHAEL; Green HS; Akron, OH; 43/365 Band; Chrs; Cmnty Wkr; Mdrgl; Off Ade; Orch; Yth Flsp; Sprt Ed Sch Nwsp; Rptr Sch Nwsp; Bsbl; Univ.

HADLEY, JOHN; Lawrenceburg HS; Lawrncbrg, IN; Am Leg Boys St; Hon Rl; NHS; Sci Clb; Letter Trk; Letter Wrstlng; St Johns Univ.

HADLEY, LAURA; Bridgman HS; Bridgman, MI; Am Leg Aux Girls St; Chrh Wkr; Hon Rl; NHS; Sci Clb; Ten; Partcptd In Europn Tour With Amer Inst For Foreign Std 79; Ferris St Coll; Data Proc.

HADLEY, LEE A; Mooresville HS; Mooresville, IN; 22/265 Band; Hon Rl; VP NHS; Sch Nwsp; 4-H; Sci Clb; Capt Bsktbl; Ten; Franklin Coll; Vet Med.

HADLEY, TRELA; Monrovia HS; Mooresville, IN; Chrh Wkr; Hon Rl; Rptr Yrbk; Rptr Sch Nwsp; Spn Clb; Mgrs; Mat Maids; Busns Schl; Sec.

HADORN, JANET; Bridgeport HS; Bridgeport, WV; Sec Soph Cls; Sec Jr Cls; Hon Rl; NHS; Stu Cncl; Y-Teens; Pep Clb; Chrldng; Univ.

HAFER, C; Wheelersburg HS; Sciotovll, OH; 33/135 Band; Chrs; Girl Scts; Hon Rl; Hosp Ade; Pep Clb; Sec.

HAFERD, WILLIAM; Galvon Sr HS; Galion, OH; Debate Tm; Hon Rl; Off Ade; Sch Nwsp; Bsktbl; Ftbl; IM Sprt; Scr Kpr; Tmr; DAR Awd; Univ; Elec Engr.

HAFFNER, BECKY J; South Side HS; Fort Wayne, IN; 5/429 Cls Rep Sr Cls; Band; Chrh Wkr; Hon Rl; NHS; Lat Clb; Bsktbl; C of C Awd; Cit Awd; JETS Awd; Whos Who In HS Forgn Lng 1977; Tri Kappa Schlstc Achvmnt Awd 1978; Purdue Merit For Wmns In Engr 1979; Purdue Univ; Chem Engr.

HAFFNER, DENEEN; Perry HS; Canton, OH; Pres Frsh Cls; VP Soph Cls; VP Jr Cls; Chrs; Natl Forn Lg; Off Ade; Quill & Scroll; Stg Crw; Stu Cncl; Rptr Sch Nwsp; Ohio St Univ.

HAFFNER, SANDI; Merrill HS; Merrill, MI; Chrs; Hon Rl; NHS; FFA; Pom Pon; Star Greenhand FFA 1977; Scholarship FFA 1977; Central Michigan Univ; Tchr.

HAFFNER, TERESA; Jay County HS; Portland, IN; 1/490 VP AFS; Am Leg Aux Girls St; Band; Chrs; Drl Tm; Hon Rl; Jr NHS; NHS; Quill & Scroll; Y-Teens; In Cultural Ed And Fine Arts Found Schlrshp 78; Math Sci Inst At IU 79; Univ; Med.

HAFLER, DAVID; Westfall HS; Orient, OH; 10/135 Band; Boy Scts; NHS; Orch; Yrbk; Fr Clb; Sci Clb; French II Awd 78; Oh Schlstc Achvmnt Test In French I 77 French II 78; Univ; Math.

HAFNER, BOB; Griffith Sr HS; Griffith, IN; Aud/V-is; Band; Cmnty Wkr; Hon Rl; Jr NHS; Sch Mus; Stg Crw; Crs Cntry; Swmmng; Trk; Purdue Univ; Dent.

HAFNER, DEBORAH; Millersport HS; Millersport, OH; 7/54 Cls Rep Frsh Cls; Am Leg Aux Girls St; Band; Chrs; Girl Scts; Hon Rl; Lbry Ade; NHS; Sch Pl; Stu Cncl; 5th Grd Spanish Tutor 78; Open Door Stu Exchange Progr In Costa Rica 78; Marching Bnad Field Commander 79; Ohio St Univ; Dent Hygnst.

HAFNER, JUDITH; Fitzgerald HS; Warren, MI; Cl Rep Jr Cls; Hon Rl; Jr NHS; NHS; Quill & Scroll; Yrbk; Fr Clb; Pep Clb; Letter Ten; Natl Merit Schl; Michigan St Univ; Psych.

HAFNER, MARILYN; Chelsea HS; Chelsea, MI; 12/250 Hon Rl; NHS; Sch Nwsp; Univ; Spanish.

HAFNER, MARK; Rogers HS; Toledo, OH; 36/420 Cls Rep Frsh Cls; Cls Rep Sr Cls; Hon Rl; Spn Clb; College; Law.

HAFNER, ROBERT; Sandusky HS; Sandusky, OH; Boy Scts; Hon Rl; NHS; Letter Ftbl; Trk; Letter Wrstlng; IM Sprt; College; Busns.

HAGAN, DEBBIE; Capac HS; Capac, MI; Trs Frsh Cls; Cls Rep Frsh Cls; Hon Rl; Stu Cncl; Yrbk; Sch Nwsp; 4-H; Bsktbl; Trk; GAA; Cosmetology Coll.

HAGAN, DONNA; Beallsville HS; Jerusalem, OH; 4/79 Sec Soph Cls; Trs Soph Cls; Band; Chrh Wkr; FCA; Hon Rl; NHS; Letter Chrldng; Letter Tmr; Am Leg Awd; Marietta Coll; Forestry.

HAGAN, DONNA; Archbishop Alter HS; Centerville, OH; 30/350 Band; Hon Rl; NHS; Orch; Sch Pl; Key Clb; Spn Clb; Capt Gym; Purdue Univ; Engr.

HAGAN, KATHLEEN M; Clay HS; Granger, IN; Band; Chrs; Chrh Wkr; Girl Scts; Hon Rl; Sch Mus; Sct Actv; 4-H; Fr Clb; 4-H Awd; 1s Pl Sci Fair 76; Indiana Univ; Med Tech.

HAGAN, KEELAN; Fairmont West HS; Kettering, OH; 1/480 Hon Rl; Hosp Ade; Lbry Ade; Fr Clb; Pep Clb; Bsktbl; Hockey; Trk; PPFtbl; Dragon Bell Awd 79; Otstndng Foreign Lang Awd 78; Schlrshp Awd 77; Univ.

HAGAN, KERRY; Centennial HS; Worthington, OH; Aud/Vis; Lit Mag; NHS; PAVAS; Sch Pl; Ed Yrbk; Rptr Yrbk; Rptr Sch Nwsp; Bsktbl; Gov Hon Prg Awd; Univ; Graphic Design.

HAGAN, MARY E; Bloomington S HS; Bloomington, IN; 17/315 Hon Rl; Lit Mag; Orch; Sch Mus; Yrbk; Sch Nwsp; Natl Merit SF; Purdue Univ; Chem Engr.

HAGAN, RUTHANN; Berea HS; Berea, OH; Stu Cncl; Mas Awd; College; Archt.

HAGAR, MAURICE; Clio HS; Clio, MI; 64/387 Chrh Wkr; Cmnty Wkr; Hon Rl; VP Yth Flsp; Sch Nwsp; Treas DECA; Fr Clb; IM Sprt; Hope Coll; Poli Sci.

HAGEDORN, PAULA; Gibson Southern HS; Ft Branch, IN; 55/198 Cls Rep Sr Cls; Stu Cncl; Letter Trk; IM Sprt; PPFtbl; JC Awd; Univ Of Evansville; Nursing.

HAGEE, MAUREEN; Ursuline Acad; Cincinnati, OH; Cmnty Wkr; Coll; Computer Science.

HAGELGANS, LA NEL; Centreville HS; Centreville, MI; 1/80 VP Frsh Cls; Pres Soph Cls; Am Leg Aux Girls St; NHS; Stu Cncl; Ed Yrbk; Twrlr; Eckerd Coll; Chem.

HAGELGANS, LA NEL L; Centreville HS; Centreville, MI; 1/75 VP Frsh Cls; Pres Soph Cls; Am Leg Aux Girls St; Hon Rl; NHS; Stu Cncl; Ed Yrbk; Bsktbl; Trk; Twrlr; Univ; Nutrition.

HAGEMANN, KURT; John Glenn HS; Westland, MI; Hon Rl; Ftbl; Trk; IM Sprt; Natl Merit Schl; Central Michigan Univ; Busns Admin.

HAGEMEYER, KATHRYN; Elmwood HS; Wayne, OH; 1/130 Chrs; NHS; Rptr Yrbk; 4-H; FHA; Chrldng; IM Sprt; Dnfth Awd; 4-H Awd; Outstanding Jr Of Yr 79; Teen Volunteer Of Yr For Ohio 76; Miss Ohio FHA; HERO St Finalist 79; Univ; Art Ther.

HAGEN, JULIE; Valley HS; Mt Carbon, VA; Cls Rep Frsh Cls; Girl Scts; Hon Rl; NHS; Stu Cncl; Chrldng; West Virginia Tech Coll; Sec.

HAGEN, LAURIE; Pt Huron Northern HS; Marysville, MI; Cls Rep Frsh Cls; Cls Rep Soph Cls; Cl Rep Jr Cls; Hon Rl; Stu Cncl; Ed Sch Nwsp; Ger Clb; Cls Rep Soph Cls; St Of Mi Comt Schlshp 79; Michigan St Univ; Jrnlsm.

HAGEN, ROBIN; Garfield HS; Akron, OH; Stu Cncl; Spn Clb; Akron Univ.

HAGEN, SUSANNE; Lake Orion Comm HS; Lake Orion, MI; Girl Scts; Hon Rl; Jr NHS; Ten; Letter Trk; Chrldng; College.

HAGENBUCH, CLU; Ross Beatty HS; Cassopolis, MI; Band; Hon Rl; Bsbl; Glf; Western Michigan Univ; X Ray Tech.

HAGENBUCH, JON; Mendon Jr Sr HS; Three Rivers, MI; VP Soph Cls; Pres Jr Cls; Pres Sr Cls; Hon Rl; NHS; Stu Cncl; Sprt Ed Yrbk; Sch Nwsp; Pep Clb; Bsktbl; I Dare You Awd 79; Univ; Bus Mgmt.

HAGER, BRAD; Boardman HS; Youngstown, OH; 80/607 FCA; Hon Rl; Boys Clb Am; Mth Clb; Sci Clb; Letter Crs Cntry; Letter Trk; IM Sprt; Miami Univ; Business Acct.

HAGER, GLENDA; Marlette HS; Brown City, MI; 5/130 Hon Rl; NHS; Stu Cncl; Yth Flsp; Treas Ger Clb; Bausch & Lomb Awd; Cedarville College;.

HAGER, JAN; Whitehall HS; Whitehall, MI; 16/150 Band; Chrh Wkr; Cmnty Wkr; Hon Rl; Sch Mus; Stg Crw; Spn Clb; Ten; Chrldng; Muskegon Cmnty Coll.

HAGER, ROBERT; Padva Franciscan HS; Burnswick, OH; 64/258 Cls Rep Soph Cls; Cl Rep Jr Cls; Hon Rl; Fr Clb; Letter Ftbl; IM Sprt; Univ.

HAGER, RONALD; Hartland HS; Howell, MI; Cls Rep Soph Cls; Boy Scts; Hon Rl; Rptr Yrbk; Yrbk; Bsktbl; Ftbl; Mic State College; Art.

HAGER, SCOTT A; Streetsboro HS; Streetsboro, OH; Boy Scts; Hon Rl; JA; Sct Actv;.

HAGER, TERESA; Scott HS; Foster, WV; Cls Rep Soph Cls; Am Leg Aux Girls St; Chrh Wkr; Debate Tm; Hon Rl; Jr NHS; Sch Pl; Stu Cncl; Yth Flsp; Ed Yrbk; Univ; Med.

HAGERTY, ANNE T; Immaculata HS; Detroit, MI; 1/93 Cls Rep Soph Cls; Val; Hon Rl; Mod UN; NHS; Stu Cncl; Drama Clb; Fr Clb; Letter Bsbl; Letter Bsktbl; Univ; Econ.

HAGERTY, BRIAN; Steub Catholic Central HS; Steubenville, OH; Boy Scts; Cmnty Wkr; Debate Tm; Sch Mus; Sch Pl; Sct Actv; Stg Crw; Sch Nwsp; Drama Clb; Key Clb; College; Pro Umpire.

HAGEY, KAY; North HS; Columbus, OH; 4/325 Am Leg Aux Girls St; Band; Cmp Fr Grls; Chrs; Chrh Wkr; Drm Mjrt; Hon Rl; Jr NHS; NHS; Orch; Ohio State Univ; Bio Engr.

HAGGERTY, ZARMELL; Erieview Catholic HS; Cleveland, OH; Chrh Wkr; Cmnty Wkr; Girl Scts; Hon Rl; Mod UN; Sct Actv; Stg Crw; Schlrshp To Erieview Coll 76; Mbr Of Jr Council On World Affairs 79; Bsbl For Lakewood League 78; Bus Schl; Exec Sec.

HAGLE, B; North Huron HS; Kinde, MI; Boy Scts; Sct Actv; Yrbk; Saginaw Valley State College; Bus.

HAGLER, SUSAN; Holy Rosary HS; Burton, MI; 3/41 Sec Frsh Cls; Sec Soph Cls; Sec Jr Cls; Hon Rl; NHS; Sch Pl; Rptr Yrbk; Glf; Chrldng; Univ Of Michigan.

HAGMAN, ELIZABETH A; Marian Heights Academy; Hawesville, KY; 3/20 Trs Sr Cls; Hon Rl; Treas NHS; VP Sdlty; Stu Cncl; Rockhurst Coll; Pre Law.

HAGMAN, ELIZABETH; Marian Heights Academy; Hawesville, KY; 3/20 Trs Sr Cls; Cls Rep Sr Cls; Hon Rl; Treas NHS; VP Sdlty; Stu Cncl; Bausch & Lomb Awd; Cit Awd; Rockhurst Coll; Sociology.

HAGOOD, CATHY; Flat Rock HS; Flat Rock, MI; 6/130 Band; Chrs; Chrh Wkr; Girl Scts; Hon Rl; NHS; Sct Actv; Yth Flsp; Letter Bsbl; GAA; Univ Of Michigan; Pre Med.

HAGUE, LUCRETIA; Prairie Heights HS; Angola, IN; 12/136 Band; Hon Rl; NHS; Stg Crw; Stu Cncl; Yth Flsp; Drama Clb; 4-H; Pep Clb; College.

HAGUE, THOMAS; Earnest W Seaholm HS; Bloomfield Hls, MI; 28/630 Cls Rep Frsh Cls; Chrs; Hon Rl; NHS; Letter Bsbl; Bsktbl; Letter Ftbl; Alcoa Fdn Schslp 4 Yrs 79; Michigan St Univ; Engr.

HAGY, JOHN; Davison HS; Davison, MI; 41/490 Aud/Vis; Chrh Wkr; Hon Rl; Fr Clb; Mich State Univ; Vet.

HAHN, BARBARA; Benjamin Bosse HS; Evansville, IN; Hon Rl; Rptr Yrbk; Yrbk; Rptr Sch Nwsp; Sch Nwsp; Cit Awd; Indiana Voc Tech Coll.

HAHN, CARLA; Eau Claire HS; Eau Claire, MI; 2/98 Sal; Hon Rl; Sec NHS; Bsbl; Bsktbl; Jackson Comm Coll; Busns.

HAHN, DAVID; Terre Haute North Vigo HS; Terre Haute, IN; 137/600 Hon Rl; Pol Wkr; Notre Dame Coll; Acctg.

HAHN, DAVID; Bridgeport HS; Saginaw, MI; Boy Scts; Jr NHS; NHS; Delta Coll; Engr.

HAHN, JOE; Caro HS; Caro, MI; Pres Soph Cls; Chrs; Hon Rl; Stg Crw; Fr Clb; Letter Bsbl; Pres Awd; Univ; Jrnlst.

HAHN, JOY E; Meadowdale HS; Dayton, OH; 10/239 Cmnty Wkr; Girl Scts; Hosp Ade; Lbry Ade; NHS; Orch; Sch Pl; IM Sprt; Mgrs; Medals & Trophy For Fencing; Hocking Tech Coll; Conservation.

HAHN, KARLA; Greensburg Cmnty HS; Greensburg, IN; Chrs; Drl Tm; FCA; Hosp Ade; Off Ade; Sch Mus; Mat Maids; Pom Pon; Tmr; JA Awd; Univ Of Evansville; Nursing.

HAHN, MICHAEL; Greensburg Comm HS; Greensburg, IN; Cls Rep Sr Cls; FCA; Pep Clb; Spn Clb; Bsbl; Ftbl; Wrstlng; Kiwan Awd; Natl Merit Ltr; Univ Of Evans; Elec Engr.

HAHN, MONICA; Galien Township HS; Buchanan, MI; 1/53 Cls Rep Frsh Cls; Cls Rep Soph Cls; Cl Rep Jr Cls; Pres Sr Cls; Cls Rep Sr Cls; Val; Am Leg Aux Girls St; Band; Debate Tm; Girl Scts; Michigan Tech Univ; Busns Admin.

HAHN, PHILIP; Holy Name HS; Garfield Hts, OH; 8/329 Hon Rl; Jr NHS; IM Sprt; Univ; Elec Engr.

HAHN, RUTH; Bullock Creek HS; Midland, MI; Band; Girl Scts; Hon Rl; JA; Yth Flsp; Pep Clb; Trk; GAA; JA Awd; Northern Michigan Univ; Acctg.

HAHN, SHARON; Northside HS; Muncie, IN; FCA; NHS; Yth Flsp; Lat Clb; Gym; Chrldng; College.

HAID, JOHN; Taft Sr HS; Hamilton, OH; Aud/Vis; Debate Tm; Rptr Sch Nwsp; Fr Clb; Letter Socr; IM Sprt; Denison Univ; Busns.

HAIN, KIM; Mason HS; Holt, MI; Cls Rep Soph Cls; Cl Rep Jr Cls; Hon Rl; Pres Jr NHS; Stu Cncl; Rptr Sch Nwsp; 4-H; Mgrs; Scr Kpr; Mich State Univ; Med.

HAINAULT, KATHY; Cedar Lake Academy; Escanaba, MI; Chrh Wkr; Hon Rl; NHS; Off Ade; Rptr Yrbk; Rptr Sch Nwsp; IM Sprt; Cit Awd; Andrews Univ; Nursing.

HAINES, ANDY; Purcell HS; Cincinnati, OH; 26/180 Band; Hon Rl; Orch; IM Sprt; Cin Tech College; Real Estate.

HAINES, BEVERLY; Miami Trace HS; Bloomingburg, OH; Band; Hon Rl; DECA; Mgrs; Scr Kpr; Ohio State Univ; Psych.

HAINES, CAROL; Euclid Sr HS; Euclid, OH; 114/705 Girl Scts; Hosp Ade; Treas OEA; Cit Awd;.

HAINES, DIANE; Arthur Hill HS; Saginaw, MI; Trs Soph Cls; Trs Jr Cls; Trs Sr Cls; Hon Rl; NHS; Yth Flsp; Fr Clb; Pep Clb; Swmmng; Spring Arbor Coll; Elem Ed.

HAINES, L ANNE; John Adams HS; South Bend, IN; 5/415 Hon Rl; Lit Mag; NHS; Sch Pl; Drama Clb; Natl Merit SF; Indiana Univ; Writing.

HAINES, LAURENCE; Ashtabula HS; Ashtabula, OH; Hon Rl; Sch Pl; Stg Crw; Yrbk; Letter Ftbl; Letter Trk; College; Communications.

HAINES, MARY L; High School; Sabina, OH; Trs Sr Cls; Band; Girl Scts; Hon Rl; 4-H; OEA; IM Sprt; 4-H Awd; Parliamentary Procedures 77 79; Columbus Bus Univ; Bus Admin.

HAINES, MONICA; Lapeer East HS; Lapeer, MI; Band; Chrh Wkr; Yth Flsp; Yrbk; Bsbl; Bsktbl; PPFtbl;.

HAINES, SARAH; Munster HS; Munster, IN; Hon Rl; Lit Mag; Case Western Reserve Univ; Civilengr.

HAINES, SUSAN; Lincolnview HS; Van Wert, OH; 9/70 Pres Band; Treas Sct Actv; 4-H; Pep Clb; Letter Bsktbl; Letter Trk; Sftbl All Star Tm 3 Yrs; Vllybl Letter; Univ; Phys Educ Tchr.

HAINES, TERRI; Huntington Local HS; Chillicothe, OH; 2/92 VP Jr Cls; Sal; Am Leg Aux Girls St; Drm Mjrt; Fr Clb; Bsktbl; Trk; Chrldng; Am Leg Awd; Natl Merit SF; Ohio Univ; Elem Educ.

HAINES, TRACY; Greenville HS; Greenville, OH; Orch; Letter Bsktbl; Capt Glf; Letter Trk; Ball State Univ; Business Admin.

HAINLINE, NORA M; Marian HS; Redford, MI; Chrh Wkr; Cmnty Wkr; Hon Rl; Letter Ten; IM Sprt; Notre Dame Univ; Home Ec.

HAIP, RENEE; Lexington Sr HS; Lexington, OH; Cls Rep Frsh Cls; Cl Rep Jr Cls; Hon Rl; Jr NHS; NHS; Ten; Univ; Bus Mgmt.

HAIR, RUTH; Colerain Sr HS; Cincinnati, OH; Cmp Fr Grls; Chrs; Hon Rl; Sch Mus; Sch Pl; Stg Crw; Drama Clb; Pres Ger Clb; German Hnr Soc; Intl Thespian Soc; Cert Of Recog Outstanding Ach; Coll; Foreign Lang.

HAIRSTON, CRAIG; Muskegon HS; Muskegon, MI; Cls Rep Frsh Cls; Hon Rl; Sch Nwsp; FNA; Spn Clb; Bsktbl; Ftbl; Letter Trk; IM Sprt; C of C Awd; Notre Dame Univ; Bus Mgmt.

HAIRSTON, DENISE; Warrensville Heights HS; Warrensville, OH; 25/230 Cls Rep Sr Cls; Jr NHS; NHS; Stu Cncl; Pep Clb; Mat Maids; Pom Pon; Tmr; Kent State; Architecture.

HAIRSTON, DONALD G; Williamson HS; Williamson, WV; Cls Rep Frsh Cls; Am Leg Boys St; Hon Rl; NHS; Key Clb; Letter Bsbl; Letter Bsktbl; Letter Ftbl; Rotary Bsktbl Awd 78; All Area Ftbl All Area Bsktb; Univ.

HAIRSTON, TANYA; Chadsey HS; Detroit, MI; Sec Sr Cls; Chrs; Chrh Wkr; Hon Rl; Stu Cncl; Pep Clb; Wayne St Univ; Health.

HAIRSTON, VANESSA A; Bluefield HS; Bluefield, WV; Sec Frsh Cls; Cls Rep Soph Cls; Hst Jr Cls; Band; Hon Rl; Off Ade; Stu Cncl; Yth Flsp; Y-Teens; 4-H; Atlanta Univ; Bus Admin.

HAIST, BETH; Unionville Sebewaing HS; Sebewaing, MI; Hon Rl; Fr Clb; Bsktbl; Trk; Coach Actv; Tmr; Am Leg Awd; Bus Sch; Bus.

HAJSKI, SHARLENE; North Ridgeville Sr HS; N Ridgeville, OH; 34/334 Cls Rep Soph Cls; Drl Tm; Hon Rl; NHS; Off Ade; Stu Cncl; Pep Clb; Spn Clb; Tmr;.

HAKALA, CHRIS; Negaunee HS; Negaunee, MI; Hon Rl; IM Sprt; Northern Mic Univ.

HAKE, LISA; Morgantown HS; Morgantwn, WV; Sec Am Leg Aux Girls St; Chrs; Girl Scts; Hon Rl; Sch Nwsp; Fr Clb; Mth Clb; Swmmng; Am Leg Awd; College; Medicine.

HAKE, PHILIP; Eaton HS; Eaton, OH; Boy Scts; FFA; Spn Clb; Ftbl; Trk; Ohio State Univ; Chemical Engr.

HAKE, REBECCA; Eaton HS; Eaton, OH; Girl Scts; Hon Rl; JA; Off Ade; Yrbk; GAA; Miami Univ; Bus.

HAKER, HEATHER; Solon HS; Solon, OH; 12/288 AFS; Band; Chrs; Hon Rl; Mdrgl; VP MMM; NHS; Sch Mus; Yth Flsp; Mth Clb; Kent St Univ; Pre Vet.

HALCOMB, DARLENE G; Adena HS; Frankfort, OH; 20/86 Cls Rep Sr Cls; Chrs; Hon Rl; Lbry Ade; NHS; Off Ade; Stg Crw; Stu Cncl; Y-Teens;.

HALDEMAN, DIANA; Fredericktown HS; Fred, OH; 29/130 Band; Chrs; Hon Rl; Orch; 4-H; FHA; Pep Clb; Spn Clb; 4-H Awd; Univ.

HALDEMAN, DUANE; Dondero HS; Royal Oak, MI; Band; Drm Bgl; Orch; Red Cr Ade; Sch Mus; Sch Pl; Yrbk; Sch Nwsp; Brooks Inst Of Photog; Pro Model.

HALE, BECKIE; Pike Central HS; Petersburg, IN; Band; FCA; Hon Rl; NHS; Stu Cncl; Yth Flsp; Sci Clb; Letter Swmmng; Trk; 4-H Awd; Indiana Univ; Sci.

HALE, CAROLINE M; Decatur Central HS; Indpls, IN; 9/306 Am Leg Aux Girls St; Boy Scts; Chrs; Chrh Wkr; Hon Rl; Mdrgl; NHS; Off Ade; Yth Flsp; FTA; Scholastic Letter; Thespian Letter Choral; Reserve Volleyball Letter; Indiana Central Univ; Medicine.

HALE, CYNTHIA; Briggs HS; Columbus, OH; 54/213 VP Sr Cls; Chrs; Chrh Wkr; DECA; Drama Clb; Spn Clb; Ten; GAA; Ohio State Univ; Drama.

HALE, DAWN; Ashtabula HS; Ashtabula, OH; Chrs; Hon Rl; JA; NHS; PAVAS; Sch Pl; Stu Cncl; Yrbk; Drama Clb; Mat Maids; Univ; Drama.

HALE, JOHN; Toronto HS; Toronto, OH; Hon Rl; Letter Bsbl; Letter Bsktbl; Trk; Schlrshp Test Biology; Akron Univ; Engr.

HALE, KAREN; Sandusky HS; Sandusky, MI; 4/114 Chrh Wkr; Hon Rl; NHS; Letter Bsktbl; Letter Trk; Coach Actv; Natl Merit Ltr; Albion Coll; Mgmt.

HALE, KEVIN; Shelby Sr HS; Shelby, OH; 15/253 Band; Chrs; Hon Rl; Lat Clb; Sci Clb; Letter Glf; Letter Ten; Mbr Of U S Of Amer Schl Band 79; Golf Tm Ranked 4th In St 78; Boys St Alternate 163 Earnd Superior S & E 79; Coll; Math.

HALE, KIMBERLY; Piketon HS; Piketon, OH; 16/96 Trs Frsh Cls; Sec Soph Cls; Trs Soph Cls; VP Sr Cls; Pres Band; MMM; NHS; Ohi Univ; Speech And Hearing.

HALE, LISA; Charleston Catholic HS; Charleston, WV; Band; Drl Tm; Drm Mjrt; Girl Scts; Hon Rl; JA; Off Ade; Stu Cncl; Twrlr; JA Awd; Tchers Art Awrd 78; Univ Of Dallas; Art.

HALE, REGINA; Flint Central HS; Flint, MI; Drl Tm; Hon Rl; NHS; Off Ade; Univ Of Mi Regnst Almni Schlshp 79; Grad With High Dstnctn 79; Univ Of Michigan; Health Sci.

HALE, ROBIN; Independence HS; Coal City, WV; 1/159 Pres Frsh Cls; Pres Jr Cls; Pres Sr Cls; Val; Am Leg Aux Girls St; NHS; Stu Cncl; Beta Clb; Chrldng; Twrlr; Raleigh Countys Jr Miss; 1st Runner Up To All American Girl; Beckley Coll; Hotel Mgmt.

HALE, SANDRA; Buffalo HS; Huntingtn, WV; 13/141 Band; Chrs; Drm Mjrt; Hon Rl; Mod UN; Sch Mus; Sch Pl; Stg Crw; Yth Flsp; Drama Clb; All Area Band 78; All St Chorus 79; Drum Major Awrd 78; Univ.

HALE, TAMMY; William Henry Harrison HS; W Lafayette, IN; Girl Scts; Hon Rl; Sct Actv; Sch Nwsp; 4-H; Mgrs; Purdue Univ; Art.

HALE, WENDY; Zanesville HS; Zanesville, OH; Chrs; Chrh Wkr; Hon Rl; NHS; Orch; Sch Mus; Drama Clb; Capt Pep Clb; Tmr; Vllybl Letter 2nd Yr Varsity Awd & Sportsmanship Awd 76 79; Univ; Archt.

HALEY, GEORGE; Saint Josephs HS; S Bend, IN; Hon Rl; Letter Wrstlng; Natl Merit Ltr; Notre Dame Univ; Acctg.

HALEY, JOHN; Northrop HS; Ft Wayne, IN; Boy Scts; Hon Rl; JA; Off Ade; Sch Nwsp; Spn Clb; Cit Awd; Indiana Univ; Dent.

HALFACRE, VINCENT; Patterson Cooperative HS; Dayton, OH; 12/626 Aud/Vis; Band; Chrs; Drm Bgl; Hon Rl; JA; Orch; Sch Pl; Stg Crw; Boys Clb Am; Music Educ Assoc Awrds Solo & Ensmbl 1977; Outstndg Sophmr Band Awrd 1977; Straight A Basebl Tickets 1977; Univ; Elec Spec.

HALKIDES, CHRIS; Lake Central HS; St John, IN; 1/480 Band; Debate Tm; Lit Mag; Stu Cncl; Natl Merit SF; Voice Dem Awd; Wabash College; Economics.

HALKOSKI, JACKIE; St Ladislaus HS; Detroit, MI; Chrh Wkr; Gacomb College; Acctg.

HALL, BONNIE; Jackson HS; Jackson, OH; 114/298 Band; Chrs; Capt Drl Tm; Lat Clb; Rio Grande College; Phys Ther.

HALL, BRAD; Washington Irving HS; Clarksburg, WV; VP Sr Cls; Am Leg Boys St; Hon Rl; NHS; 4-H; Keyettes; Lat Clb; Sci Clb; Glf; College; Doctor.

HALL, BRENDA; Emerson HS; Gary, IN; Hon Rl; ROTC; Busns Schl.

HALL, BRIAN; Glenoak HS; N Canton, OH; 1/700 Val; Band; Chrs; Hon Rl; Jr NHS; NHS; Sch Mus; Sch Nwsp; College; Bus Admin.

HALL, CATHERINE A; New Haven HS; New Haven, IN; 9/282 Band; Chrs; Hon Rl; Stu Cncl; Pres Lat Clb; Whos Who In For Lang In In & Ky HS 78; David Lipscomb Coll; Med.

HALL, CATHERINE; Nordonia HS; Northfield, OH; NHS; Off Ade; Yrbk; Akron Univ; Nursing.

HALL, CHERYL; Attica HS; Attica, IN; 14/70 Hon Rl; Spn Clb; Capt Bsktbl; Capt Ten; Trk; College; Physical Educ.

HALL, CHRISTINA; Adelphian Academy; Troy, MI; Chrs; Hon Rl; Off Ade; VP Stu Cncl; Rptr Yrbk; Rptr Sch Nwsp; Fr Clb; Socr; Andrews Univ; Bus Admin.

HALL, CHRISTINE; Bremen HS; Bremen, IN; 2/102 Trs Soph Cls; Trs Jr Cls; Am Leg Aux Girls St; Chrh Wkr; FCA; Hon Rl; Sec NHS; Pep Clb; Concordia College; Educ.

HALL, CINDY M; Corydon Central HS; Central, IN; 20/164 Chrs; Girl Scts; Hon Rl; Stu Cncl; 4-H; Pep Clb; Spn Clb; GAA; IM Sprt; PPFtbl; Sullivan Bus College; Sec.

HALL, CYNTHIA; Bridgeport Sr HS; Bridgeport, WV; Band; Chrh Wkr; Hon Rl; Jr NHS; NHS; Yth Flsp; Y-Teens; Mth Clb; VICA; Coll; Med Offc Asst.

HALL, DARCY; Madison HS; Adrian, MI; 2/57 Trs Frsh Cls; Pres Soph Cls; Pres Jr Cls; Pres Sr Cls; Sal; Am Leg Aux Girls St; Hon Rl; Mdrgl; NHS; Sch Pl; Eastern Michigan Univ; Mktg.

HALL, DARRELL R; Buffalo HS; Kenova, WV; Chrh Wkr; Hon Rl; NHS; Mth Clb; Letter Bsbl; Letter Bsktbl; Letter Ftbl; Trk; Mbr Of TAG Prgrm; Capt Of Bsktbl Team; Marshall Univ.

HALL, DAVID; Covington HS; Covington, OH; Val; Sec Band; Hon Rl; VP NHS; Off Ade; Sch Pl; FTA; Sci Clb; Am Leg Awd; Voice Dem Awd; College; Computer Science.

HALL, DEBI LYNN; Williamsburg HS; Williamsburg, OH; Trs Soph Cls; Cl Rep Jr Cls; Chrs; Girl Scts; Hon Rl; Hosp Ade; Jr NHS; Sch Pl; FNA; Sci Clb; Univ; Med.

HALL, DEBORA; Parkside HS; Jackson, MI; Hon Rl; Bsbl; Bsktbl; Ferris St Univ; Mech Engr.

HALL, DEBRA; West Union HS; West Portsmouth, OH; 5/118 Chrs; Hon Rl; Hosp Ade; NHS; Ed Sch Nwsp; Drama Clb; Eng Clb; Shawnee State College; Med.

HALL, EDWARD; Fruitport HS; Muskegon, MI; 10/281 Band; Boy Scts; NHS; Sct Actv; Eagle Scout Awd 79; Lions Ofmi All St Band 79; Bd Of Trustees Schlp 79; John Phillip Sousa Band Aw D79; Muskegon Cmnty Coll; Music.

HALL, GAIL; Firelands HS; Wellington, OH; Pres Soph Cls; Trs Jr Cls; Chrs; Girl Scts; Hon Rl; NHS; 4-H; OEA; Pep Clb; Letter Bsktbl; Business Schl; Stenography.

HALL, GREGORY; University HS; Cleveland, OH; Band; Lbry Ade; Off Ade; Orch; Sch Pl; Stg Crw; Sch Nwsp; Drama Clb; Trk; IM Sprt; Williams Coll; Pre Med.

HALL, GREGORY A; Winfield HS; Scott Depot, WV; Boy Scts; Hon Rl; NHS; Sct Actv; Sprt Ed Yrbk; Beta Clb; VICA; JA Awd; Univ Of Florida; Aero Engr.

HALL, J; Mason HS; Mason, MI; Sec Sr Cls; Girl Scts; Jr NHS; NHS; Sct Actv; Letter Gym; Letter Chrldng; Scr Kpr; Mich State Univ.

HALL, JACQUALINE M; S Newton Jr Sr HS; Goodland, IN; Chrs; Off Ade; Sch Pl; Ed Sch Nwsp; FTA; Lat Clb; Pep Clb; Sci Clb; Letter Swmmng; Scr Kpr; Indiana Univ; Journalism.

HALL, JAMES; Spring Lake Sr HS; Spring Lake, MI; 55/186 Boy Scts; Hon Rl; Mod UN; Pol Wkr; Sch Mus; Sct Actv; Stg Crw; Sprt Ed Yrbk; Sprt Ed Sch Nwsp; Rptr Sch Nwsp; Oakland Univ; Comp Sci.

HALL, JAMIE; R Nelson Snider HS; Ft Wayne, IN; Cls Rep Frsh Cls; Cls Rep Soph Cls; Cl Rep Jr Cls; Cls Rep Sr Cls; Chrs; Hon Rl; Sch Mus; Sch Pl; Fr Clb; Purdue Univ; Indus Mgmt.

HALL, JANET L; Switzerland County HS; Vevay, IN; Sec Frsh Cls; VP Jr Cls; Hon Rl; Off Ade; Sch Pl; Stu Cncl; Rptr Sch Nwsp; Drama Clb; FHA; Pep Clb; Ball St Univ; Phys Ther.

HALL, JEFFREY; Yorktown HS; Yorktown, IN; 17/200 Cls Rep Frsh Cls; Cls Rep Sr Cls; Chrs; FCA; Hosp Ade; NHS; Stu Cncl; Purdue Univ; Acctg.

HALL, JENNIFER; Shelby Sr HS; Shelby, OH; Cl Rep Jr Cls; AFS; Am Leg Aux Girls St; Band; Chrs; Drl Tm; Girl Scts; Hon Rl; Sch Pl; Treas Yth Flsp; Vlybl Letter; Univ; Math.

HALL, JENNY; Morgan HS; Mc Connelsville, OH; Hon Rl; NHS; Off Ade; Drama Clb; 4-H; 4-H Awd; Barber Schl; Beautician.

HALL, JILL; Perry Central HS; Derby, IN; 1/96 Pres Sr Cls; Val; Band; Girl Scts; Hon Rl; VP NHS; Sct Actv; Stu Cncl; Fr Clb; Indiana Univ; Acct.

HALL, JILL A; Perry Cntrl Comm Schl Corp; Derby, IN; 1/96 Pres Sr Cls; Val; Band; Hon Rl; NHS; VP Sct Actv; Fr Clb; Mgrs; DAR Awd; Natl Merit SF; Indiana Univ; Psych.

HALL, JOEL J; Clay HS; South Bend, IN; 150/500 Aud/Vis; Boy Scts; Hon Rl; Sch Pl; Stg Crw; Yrbk; Fr Clb; Swmmng; Eagle Scout Awd 79; Schlstc Art Awd Photg Gold Key 77 & 78; Univ; Marine Bio.

HALL, JOEY J; Coshocton HS; Coshocton, OH; 56/178 Am Leg Boys St; Sch Nwsp; Pres Key Clb; Bsbl; Bsktbl; Letter Ftbl; Wrstlng; IM Sprt; Univ.

HALL, JULIUS; Jefferson Area HS; Jefferson, OH; Univ; Math.

HALL, KAREN; Inland Lakes HS; Indian River, MI; 4/79 VP Sr Cls; Hon Rl; Stu Cncl; Capt Bsktbl; Trk; GAA; Scr Kpr; Lion Awd; Hillsdale Coll.

HALL, KATHIE; Firelands HS; Wellington, OH; 1/146 Val; Band; Hon Rl; NHS; Off Ade; 4-H; Chrldng; Pom Pon;.

HALL, KAYE; Canton South HS; Canton, OH; Cls Rep Frsh Cls; Am Leg Aux Girls St; Band; Hon Rl; Trk; Mercy Schl Of Nursing; Nursing.

HALL, KELLY; Edison HS; Milan, OH; Band; Mat Maids; Scr Kpr; 4-H Awd; College.

HALL, KENNETH; Pike Central HS; Winslow, IN; Sec Band; Hon Rl; NHS; Sch Pl; Pres Drama Clb; Univ; Acctg.

HALL, KENNETH; Onaway Community Schl; Onaway, MI; 4/98 Pres Sr Cls; Band; Boy Scts; Chrh Wkr; Hon Rl; NHS; Sch Pl; Stu Cncl; 4-H; Bsktbl; Michigan Tech Univ; Geol Engr.

HALL, KRISTINE; South Haven HS; S Haven, MI; Cls Rep Frsh Cls; Trs Soph Cls; Band; FCA; Hon Rl; Hosp Ade; Jr NHS; NHS; Stu Cncl; Swmmng; Univ; Med.

HALL, LEACY; Charles E Chadsey HS; Detroit, MI; Hon Rl; Lbry Ade; Off Ade; Stu Cncl; Sch Nwsp; Cit Awd; Wayne St Univ; Engr.

HALL, LINDA; John F Kennedy Sr HS; Cleveland, OH; 8/400 Hon Rl; Treas NHS; Off Ade; Cit Awd; Cleveland St Univ; Engr.

HALL, LISA; South HS; Columbus, OH; 31/342 Hon Rl; OEA; CTI Tech Coll; Photog.

HALL, LISA; East HS; Akron, OH; 4/300 Cl Rep Jr Cls; Cls Rep Sr Cls; Band; Hon Rl; Jr NHS; NHS; Sch Mus; Sec Stu Cncl; Pep Clb; Univ Of Akron; Bus.

HALL, LORI; Newton Falls HS; Newton Falls, OH; Chrh Wkr; Girl Scts; Hon Rl; Hosp Ade; NHS; Stu Cncl; Y-Teens; Sprt Ed Sch Nwsp; FTA; Pres Spn Clb; Liberty Bapt College; Education.

HALL, LORI; Parkersburg HS; Vienna, WV; Chrs; Chrh Wkr; Hon Rl; Hosp Ade; Mdrgl; Sch Mus; Yth Flsp; GAA; Parkersburg Cmnty Coll; RN.

HALL, LORI; Norton HS; Clinton, OH; 10/315 Chrh Wkr; Hon Rl; Hosp Ade; Jr NHS; NHS; Off Ade; Lat Clb; Univ Of Akron; Nurse.

HALL, LYNNETTE; Elyria Cath HS; Fairview Park, OH; Band; Hon Rl; Yrbk; Drama Clb; Spn Clb; Trk; Natl Merit Ltr; VP Of Band Sr Jr Yr; Chosen To Attend The Women In Engr; Workshop At Michigan Tech Univ; Coll; Med.

HALL, MARTI; Ross Sr HS; Hamilton, OH; Letter Chrldng; Univ; Pre Law.

HALL, MARY; East HS; Akron, OH; 45/329 Hon Rl; Off Ade; DECA; Letter Bsktbl; Trk; Pres Of DECA Club 78; 4.0 Av In Soph Yr; Univ; Law.

HALL, PAULA D; South Amherst HS; South Amherst, OH; 14/64 Sec Frsh Cls; Sec Jr Cls; Off Ade; Stg Crw; Drama Clb; Gym; Letter Chrldng; Mgrs; 1st Yr J V Cheerleader & Hmcmng Attendant; Lorain County Comm Coll; Home Ec.

HALL, PENELOPE; Rock Hill HS; Ashland, KY; 37/162 Band; Hon Rl; Beta Clb; Pep Clb; Sci Clb; Ashland Comm College; Soc Work.

HALL, RICK V; Cowan HS; Muncie, IN; Hon Rl; NHS; Sci Clb; Bsbl; Letter Club; College; History.

HALL, ROBERT; Davison HS; Davison, MI; Band; Chrs; Hon Rl; Orch; Sch Mus; Sch Pl; Sct Actv; Stg Crw; OEA; Delgt For IOOF UN Pilgramage For Youth 79; Outstndngjr In Var Chr; Univ; Mortuary Sci.

HALL, ROGER; Eastern HS; Beaver, OH; Chrs; Chrh Wkr; Cmnty Wkr; Debate Tm; Hon Rl; Sch Mus; Sch Pl; Stg Crw; Drama Clb; Pep Clb; College; Data Processing.

HALL, SARAH; Northwestern HS; Detroit, MI; 19/279 Hon Rl; NHS; Sci Clb; Cit Awd; Acctg Awd; Tennis Awd; Wayne St Univ; Acctg.

HALL, SHARON; Yale HS; Goodells, MI; 11/162 Chrs; Chrh Wkr; Girl Scts; Hon Rl; Sct Actv; Letter Bsbl; Letter Bsktbl; IM Sprt; St Clair Comm Coll; Elem Education.

HALL, SHELLEY; Lexington HS; Lexington, OH; Cls Rep Soph Cls; Cls Rep Sr Cls; Band; Chrs; Drl Tm; Off Ade; Sch Pl; Stu Cncl; Y-Teens; Rptr Yrbk; Ohio St Univ; Bus Admin.

HALL, SHIRLEY; Struthers HS; Struthers, OH; 26/275 Hon Rl; FNA; Lat Clb; Pep Clb; Voc Sch; Nursing.

HALL, SHOYNA; Amelia HS; Amelia, OH; 29/287 Chrs; Chrh Wkr; Hon Rl; NHS; Univ Of Cincinnati; Elem Ed.

HALL, STEPHANIE; Turpin HS; Cincinnati, OH; 26/371 Chrs; Lat Clb; Gym; Univ; Vet.

HALL, STEPHEN J; Gibson Southern HS; Fort Branch, IN; 1/189 Val; Beta Clb; 4-H; Key Clb; Pres Sci Clb; JETS Awd; Natl Merit Ltr; Rose Hullman Inst Of Tech; Elec Engr.

HALL, STEVEN; High School; Weirton, WV; 38/466 Chrs; Chrh Wkr; Hon Rl; Mdrgl; NHS; Stu Cncl; Key Clb; Elec Contrctng.

HALL, SUSAN; Knightstown HS; Knightstown, IN; Cls Rep Frsh Cls; Am Leg Aux Girls St; Chrh Wkr; Girl Scts; Hon Rl; NHS; Off Ade; Sct Actv; Stu Cncl; Ed Yrbk; Ball St Univ; Acctg.

HALL, T; Federal Hocking HS; Coolville, OH; Band; Girl Scts; Hon Rl; 4-H; FBLA; Pep Clb; Trk; Chrldng; GAA; IM Sprt; Math Awd; Athletic Awd; Typing Awd; Hocking Tech Coll; Sec.

HALL, TAMMY J; Frankton HS; Frankton, IN; 5/185 Band; Drl Tm; FCA; Girl Scts; Hon Rl; NHS; Off Ade; 4-H; FBLA; Pep Clb; Ball St Univ; Bus.

HALL, TERESA; Lenore HS; Williamson, WV; Am Leg Aux Girls St; Band; Chrh Wkr; Cmnty Wkr; Hon Rl; Orch; Beta Clb; Pep Clb; Mgrs; Scr Kpr; Chosen Out Of Jr Class To Go To St Capital; Chosen To Attend The Close Up Prog; Slctd For Mingo Al Cnty Bnd; Univ Of Cincinnati; Retailing.

HALL, TERESA; Austin HS; Austin, IN; 13/130 Chrs; Hon Rl; Jr NHS; Stu Cncl; Lat Clb; Sci Clb; Bsktbl; Chrldng; Univ; Sales Mgr.

HALL, TERESA; Maysville HS; S Zanesville, OH; Chrs; Girl Scts; Yth Flsp; Muskingum Area Tech Coll; Radiology.

HALL, TERRILYN; Lake Fenton HS; Grand Blanc, MI; 49/170 Girl Scts; Hon Rl; Sch Mus; Sch Pl; Sct Actv; Jobs Daughters Schlrshp; Adrian Coll; Acctg.

HALL, THERESA; Oxford Area Cmnty HS; Oxford, MI; 2/225 Trs Frsh Cls; Cls Rep Frsh Cls; Trs Soph Cls; Cls Rep Soph Cls; Sec Jr Cls; Cl Rep Jr Cls; Sec Sr Cls; Cls Rep Sr Cls; Sal; AFS; Frnch Awd 78 & 79; Stu Coun Serv Awd 79; EMU Regnets Schrlshp 79; Oakland Co Comm Trust Schlrshp 79; Eastern Michigan Univ; Comp Sci.

HALL, TRACI; David Anderson HS; Lisbon, OH; Sec Soph Cls; Pres Jr Cls; Cmp Fr Grls; Chrh Wkr; Hon Rl; NHS; Quill & Scroll; Y-Teens; Rptr Yrbk; Ed Sch Nwsp; College; Biology.

HALL, VALERIE; Marion Harding HS; Marion, OH; 9/450 Lit Mag; NHS; Stu Cncl; Rptr Sch Nwsp; 4-H; Spn Clb; 4-H Awd; Ohio State Univ; Psych.

HALL, VICKI; South HS; Columbus, OH; Chrs; Hon Rl; Lbry Ade; OEA; Bus Schl.

HALL, WILLIAM L; Linsly Inst; Wheeling, WV; Hon Rl; NHS; Fr Clb; Trk; IM Sprt; Natl Merit Ltr; College.

HALL, WILLIAM P; Huntington East HS; Huntington, WV; 30/300 Am Leg Boys St; Chrs; Chrh Wkr; Hon Rl; Mdrgl; Sch Mus; Yth Flsp; Fr Clb; VP Key Clb; Mth Clb; Marshall Univ; Math.

HALLADAY, LAURIE; Reed City HS; Reed City, MI; VP Jr Cls; Letter Bsktbl; Univ.

HALLBERT, CHRIS; Grant HS; Grant, MI; Chrs; Chrh Wkr; Cmnty Wkr; Girl Scts; Hon Rl; Sch Pl; 4-H; Pep Clb; Letter Trk; Coll; Counseling.

HALLER, BARBARA; Wyoming Park HS; Wyoming, MI; 22/225 Band; Hon Rl; NHS; Sch Pl; Plyr Of Week Awd From The Newspaper For Ok White League 79; Var Athletic Ltr For Softball & Volleyball; Kendall Schl Of Design; Cmmrcl Art.

HALLER, JOHN G; Bloomfield Hills Andover HS; West Bloomfield, MI; 12/240 Off Ade; Sch Mus; Yth Flsp; Ger Clb; Ten; Delta Epsilon Phi German Hon Soc 79; High Math Awd 77; Univ; Aero Engr.

HALLER, MARY; Huron HS; Ann Arbor, MI; 13/600 Treas Band; Hon Rl; Orch; Univ Of Mich.

HALLETT, CINDY; Whiteland Community HS; Greenwood, IN; 14/297 Sec Chrs; Hon Rl; Sch Mus; FBLA; Pep Clb; Business Schl; Legal Sec.

HALLIBURTON, MARK S; Northern HS; Detroit, MI; Cls Rep Frsh Cls; Cls Rep Soph Cls; Cl Rep Jr Cls; Chrs; Cmnty Wkr; Debate Tm; Hon Rl; Lbry Ade; NHS; Off Ade; Wayne State Univ; Bus Admin.

HALLIDAY, BRENDA; Bloomington North HS; Bloomington, IN; Band; Drl Tm; Girl Scts; Hon Rl; Sch Mus; 4-H; Fr Clb; Pom Pon; 4-H Awd; Indiana Univ; Med.

HALLIDAY, JENNIFER; Heath HS; Heath, OH; Cls Rep Frsh Cls; Bsktbl; Trk; Lion Awd; Univ Of Cincinnati.

HALLINEN, DIANE; Franklin HS; Livonia, MI; MSU; Vet Med.

HALLMARK, LESLIE; Staunton HS; Brazil, IN; 5/65 Boy Scts; Chrh Wkr; Hon Rl; Jr NHS; Stu Cncl; Mth Clb; Sci Clb; Glf; Purdue; Mech Engr.

HALLOCK, JEFFERY; Owendale Gagetown HS; Owendale, MI; Band; Boy Scts; Sch Pl; Stg Crw; Pep Clb; Bsbl; Bsktbl; Ftbl; Trk; Tmr;.

HALLORAN, ANNE; Holy Name Nazareth HS; Parma Hts, OH; Cls Rep Frsh Cls; Cls Rep Soph Cls; Chrs; Hon Rl; NHS; Stu Cncl; Spn Clb; Coach Actv; GAA; IM Sprt; Coll.

HALLQUIST, NANCY; Waterford Township HS; Pontiac, MI; Band; Debate Tm; Hon Rl; Jr NHS; Lbry Ade; NHS; Ten; Alma College; Acctg.

HALLS, DAVID; Ferndale HS; Plsnt Rdg, MI; Chrh Wkr; FCA; NHS; Quill & Scroll; Sprt Ed Sch Nwsp; Spn Clb; Bsktbl; Letter Ftbl; Letter Ten; Natl Merit SF; College; Engr.

HALMAN, SANDRA; Ashtabula Harbor HS; Ashtabula, OH; 35/200 Cls Rep Frsh Cls; Cls Rep Soph Cls; Cl Rep Jr Cls; AFS; Band; Chrh Wkr; Hosp Ade; Kent St Univ; Nursing.

HALOSKI, MICHELE L; Oregon Davis HS; Grovertown, IN; 10/58 Chrh Wkr; Hon Rl; Rptr Yrbk; 4-H; Pep Clb; Gym; Chrldng; IM Sprt; Pom Pon; 4-H Awd; Univ; Law.

HALPIN, ANN; Fairmont West HS; Kettering, OH; Treas AFS; Hon Rl; Off Ade; Pol Wkr; Quill & Scroll; Ed Sch Nwsp; Spn Clb; Scr Kpr; International Communications.

HALSEY, MARY; West Muskingum HS; Hopewell, OH; Cls Rep Frsh Cls; Sec Soph Cls; Girl Scts; Hon Rl; Jr NHS; Sct Actv; Stu Cncl; Y-Teens; FHA; Pep Clb; Cincinnati Univ; Fshn Dsgn.

HALSEY, MIKE; Bluefield HS; Bluefield, WV; Hon Rl; Key Clb; Bsbl; Pres Awd; Univ; Bus Admin.

HALSEY, SCOTT; Valley View HS; Germantown, OH; Letter Bsbl; Capt Bsktbl; Letter Ftbl; IM Sprt; Voc Schl; Electrician.

HALSTEAD, DANIEL; St Johns HS; Saint Johns, MI; Hon Rl; NHS; Orch; 4-H; Gym; IM Sprt; Mich State Univ; Chem Engr.

HALSTEAD, MARK; Marsh Fork HS; Montcoal, WV; Boy Scts; Hon Rl; Sch Nwsp; Bsbl; Bsktbl; IM Sprt;.

HALSTEAD, SCOTT; Dublin HS; Powell, OH; 51/157 Chrs; Hon Rl; Spn Clb; Otterbein Coll; Equine Sci.

HALTER, MIKE; Sandy Valley HS; Magnolia, OH; Cls Rep Soph Cls; Cl Rep Jr Cls; Hon Rl; Stu Cncl; Spn Clb; Trk; Vocational School; Math.

HALUSKA, BRIAN; Benedictine HS; Cleve Hts, OH; 10/100 Band; Boy Scts; Hon Rl; Sch Pl; Stg Crw; Ed Sch Nwsp; Drama Clb; Univ; Advrtsng.

HALVERSON, PAUL; North Muskegon HS; N Muskegon, MI; 7/108 Cmp Fr Grls; Chrh Wkr; FCA; Hon Rl; NHS; Sct Actv; Ger Clb; Mth Clb; Ten; IM Sprt; Michigan Tech Univ; Mech Engr.

HALWES, SUZANNE; Wood Memorial HS; Elberfeld, IN; 1/96 Am Leg Aux Girls St; Band; Chrh Wkr; Hon Rl; Off Ade; Sch Mus; Yth Flsp; Ed Sch Nwsp; Pep Clb; Geom Awd 78; Adv Bio Awd 78; Fresh Bio Cett Of Mrt 77; Chem Cert Of Mrt 79; Adv Algebra Awd 79; Hnr Roll; Univ Of Evansville.

HAM, DOUGLAS K; Bridgeprt Spauldng Cmnty HS; Bridgeport, MI; 25/355 Band; Chrh Wkr; Hon Rl; Jr NHS; NHS; Orch; Sch Mus; Sch Pl; Stg Crw; VP Ger Clb; Ferris St Coll; Pre Optometry.

HAM, ELIZABETH V; Marquette HS; Michigan City, IN; 8/81 Cls Rep Frsh Cls; Hon Rl; Off Ade; Pol Wkr; Sch Mus; Chmn Stu Cncl; Sch Nwsp; Fr Clb; Pep Clb; Ten; Univ Of Notre Dame; Law.

HAM, GILDA; Marian HS; Mishawaka, IN; 7/155 Trs Sr Cls; Hon Rl; JA; NHS; Rptr Yrbk; Rptr Sch Nwsp; Pep Clb; Trk; JA Awd; Univ Of Notre Dame; Engr.

HAM, LINDA; Flushing Sr HS; Flushing, MI; 168/570 Chrh Wkr; Cmnty Wkr; Hon Rl; Natl Forn Lg; Red Cr Ade; Sch Mus; Sch Pl; Drama Clb; Opt Clb Awd; C S Mott Cmnty Coll; Nursing.

HAMAD, CAMILLE; St Vincent St Mary HS; Akron, OH; Treas Chrh Wkr; Hon Rl; Sch Pl; Yrbk; Sch Nwsp; Pep Clb; Ten; Univ; Sprt; PPFtbl; Natl Merit Ltr; Airline; Travel Agnt.

HAMAD, MARY; St Ursula Academy; Cincinnati, OH; Hon Rl; Mod UN; Univ; Engr.

HAMADE, JAMAL; Frank Cody Sr HS; Detroit, MI; Hon Rl; NHS; Drama Clb; Mth Clb; Sci Clb; Spn Clb; Mi Tuition Schlshp 79; Western Michigan Univ; Law.

HAMAIDE, CINDY; Genoa Area HS; Genoa, OH; Hon Rl; FHA; Spn Clb; Gym; GAA; College; Architect.

HAMANN, HEINZ; Culver Military Acad; Susanville, CA; Trs Frsh Cls; Boy Scts; Hon Rl; ROTC; Rptr Sch Nwsp; 4-H; Rus Clb; Bsbl; Ftbl; Cit Awd; Univ Of California; Envir Engr.

HAMANN, JULIE; Adrian Sr HS; Adrian, MI; 40/385 Cls Rep Frsh Cls; Sec Soph Cls; Cls Rep Soph Cls; Sec Band; Capt Drl Tm; Hon Rl; Lbry Ade; NHS; Stu Cncl; Rptr Yrbk; Mi Merit Schlrshp Cert 79; Central Michigan Univ; Med.

HAMAR, HEIDI; Calumet HS; Calumet, MI; 23/148 VP Band; Chrs; Chrh Wkr; NHS; Sch Mus; Pres Stu Cncl; VP Pep Clb; Bsktbl; Trk; Chrldng; Alma Coll.

HAMATY, JOHN; Hastings HS; Hastings, MI; Cls Rep Soph Cls; VP Jr Cls; Am Leg Boys St; Band; Hon Rl; Jr NHS; NHS; Stu Cncl; Y-Teens; Fr Clb; Coll; Busns Mgmt.

HAMBERG, JAMES; Marion Local HS; Saint Henry, OH; 5/93 Am Leg Boys St; Chrh Wkr; Hon Rl; NHS; Off Ade; FTA; Mth Clb; Pep Clb; Sci Clb; Bsbl; Ohio St Univ; Chem Engr.

HAMBERG, JAMES; Marion Local HS; St Henry, OH; 5/93 Am Leg Boys St; Chrh Wkr; Hon Rl; NHS; FTA; Mth Clb; Pep Clb; Sci Clb; Bsbl; Bsktbl; Ohio St Univ; Chem Engr.

HAMBERGER, DAVID; Andrews Academy; Berrien Spring, MI; Cl Rep Jr Cls; VP Sr Cls; Aud/Vis; Chrs; Cmnty Wkr; Stu Cncl; Yrbk; Fr Clb; Ftbl; Letter IM Sprt; Andrews Univ; History Tchr.

HAMBLY, MELISSA; Brookside HS; Sheffield Lke, OH; 18/234 Chrs; Lorain County Comm Coll; Bus.

HAMBRIGHT, JOY; Lamphere HS; Madison Hgts, MI; 19/340 Hon Rl; Lbry Ade; Red Cr Ade; Fr Clb; Swmmng; PPFtbl; Tmr; Natl Merit SF; Detroit Coll Of Busns; CPA.

HAMBURGER, DEBBIE; Waynesfield Goshen HS; Lakeview, OH; Sec Jr Cls; Drl Tm; Hon Rl; Stg Crw; 4-H; FHA; Bsktbl; Trk; Chrldng; PPFtbl; Northwestern Bus Schl; Sec.

HAMBY, DENNIS; South Dearborn HS; Aurora, IN; 37/259 Hon Rl; Yrbk; Trk; College; Elec Engineer.

HAMBY, JOAN; Solon HS; Solon, OH; 31/288 Hon Rl; NHS; Ed Yrbk; Ed Sch Nwsp; Gym; College; English.

HAMDEN, CHARLES; Adlai Stevenson HS; Sterling Hts, MI; 120/538 Bsktbl; Capt Crs Cntry; Letter Trk; Tmr; Rittenmeyer Schlrshp Sheet Metal Loc 79; All Macomb Cnty Crss Cntry 78; All East Mi League 77; Macomb Cnty Cmnty Coll; Mgmt.

HAMEL, JOSEPH; Washington HS; Massillon, OH; Aud/Vis; Chrh Wkr; Hon Rl; College; Aeronautics.

HAMEL, SHARON; Domincan HS; St Clair Shrs, MI; Band; PAVAS; Sch Mus; Drama Clb; Michigan St Univ; Park & Rec Mgmt.

HAMER, LISA M; Greensburg Cmnty HS; Greensburg, IN; 38/200 Band; Chrs; Girl Scts; NHS; Off Ade; Orch; Sch Mus; Sch Pl; Mat Maids; Pom Pon; Bus Schl; Sec.

HAMER, TINA; Franklin HS; Franklin, OH; Chrs; Hon Rl; Sch Mus; Univ; Art.

HAMIL, KEVIN; Mona Shores HS; Muskegon, MI; Chrh Wkr; Hon Rl; NHS; IM Sprt; Muskegon Cmnty Coll; Bus Admin.

HAMILTON, AIMEE; Hobart Sr HS; Hobart, IN; 2/390 VP Soph Cls; Am Leg Aux Girls St; Hon Rl; Sec Jr NHS; NHS; Sch Mus; Sch Pl; Stu Cncl; Drama Clb; Fr Clb; College.

HAMILTON, BARBARA; Clear Fork Valley HS; Mansfield, OH; 5/164 Band; Hon Rl; Hosp Ade; NHS; Off Ade; Stu Cncl; Yrbk; Fr Clb; FHA; Scr Kpr; Ohio St Univ.

HAMILTON, BARBARA S; Lincoln HS; Shinnston, WV; 10/158 Am Leg Aux Girls St; Girl Scts; Hon Rl; NHS; Sci Clb; Spn Clb; West Virginia Univ; Animal Sci.

HAMILTON, BETH; Cedarville HS; Cedarvl, OH; Cls Rep Soph Cls; Cls Rep Sr Cls; Band; Chrs; Drl Tm; FCA; Girl Scts; Sct Actv; Stu Cncl; Yth Flsp; Clark Tech Coll; Nursing.

HAMILTON, CALEB; Hampshire HS; Romney, WV; 5/210 AFS; Am Leg Boys St; Band; Hon Rl; NHS; Sprt Ed Sch Nwsp; Letter Crs Cntry; Letter Trk; Univ; Engr.

HAMILTON, CALLIE; Elk Rapids HS; Kewadin, MI; 2/90 VP Frsh Cls; Pres Jr Cls; Trs Sr Cls; Sal; Chrh Wkr; Girl Scts; Hon Rl; Lbry Ade; Natl Forn Lg; NHS; Ferris St Coll; Bus Admin.

HAMILTON, CAROL; Clay Battelle HS; Fairview, WV; Aud/Vis; Treas Girl Scts; Hon Rl; Sch Pl; Stg Crw; Monogalia Voc Tech Ctr; Bus.

HAMILTON, CHRISTINA; North HS; Akron, OH; 12/342 Band; Hon Rl; JA; NHS; Orch; Sch Pl; Yth Flsp; VICA; Trk; Ferris State College; Accounting.

HAMILTON, CHRISTOPHER; Culver Military Academy; Ft Wayne, IN; 25/191 Boy Scts; Chrh Wkr; Hon Rl; Pol Wkr; ROTC; Yth Flsp; Sch Nwsp; Drama Clb; Fr Clb; Inducted To Blue Key Society 79; Univ; Med.

HAMILTON, CYNTHIA; Howland HS; Warren, OH; 22/430 Debate Tm; Hon Rl; Natl Forn Lg; Spn Clb; Natl Merit SF; Univ; Intrnl Relations.

HAMILTON, ELIZABETH L; North Central HS; Indianapolis, IN; Pres Chrs; Hon Rl; Jr NHS; Lit Mag; Mod UN; NHS; Sch Mus; Stu Cncl; Pres Yth Flsp; NCTE; Univ.

HAMILTON, HOLLY; William A Wirt HS; Gary, IN; 13/230 Sec Frsh Cls; Band; Chrh Wkr; Cmnty Wkr; Hon Rl; NHS; Off Ade; Pol Wkr; Sch Pl; Stu Cncl; Univ; Bio.

HAMILTON, JULIANA; Central HS; Evansville, IN; 54/480 Cls Rep Frsh Cls; Cls Rep Soph Cls; Cl Rep Jr Cls; Cls Rep Sr Cls; Cmnty Wkr; NHS; Off Ade; Pol Wkr; Red Cr Ade; Stu Cncl; Acad Awd Murray St Univ 79; Murray St Univ; Acctg.

HAMILTON, KIM; Indian Creek HS; Morgantown, IN; Sec Jr Cls; Chrs; FCA; Hon Rl; Sch Mus; FFA; Treas Pep Clb; Chrldng; PPFtbl; Butler Univ; Psych.

HAMILTON, KRISTINA; Onekama HS; Kaleva, MI; Cls Rep Frsh Cls; Cl Rep Jr Cls; Chrs; Hon Rl; Sch Pl; Stu Cncl; Drama Clb; Pres 4-H; FHA; Pep Clb; Homcmng Rep Jr & Sr Yr; MVP Skier Top 10 In Conf 78; 4 H Sent To St Horse Show Brnz Medl 76; Cntrl Michigan Univ.

HAMILTON, MARGARET; West Carrollton Sr HS; W Carrollton, OH; 3/400 Hon Rl; Jr NHS; NHS; Orch; Sch Mus; Sch Pl; Rptr Sch Nwsp; VP Fr Clb; Univ; Engr.

HAMILTON, MARY; La Ville Jr Sr HS; Lakeville, IN; 1/135 Chrs; Sec NHS; Stu Cncl; Pres Yth Flsp; Pres 4-H; Treas Ger Clb; Sci Clb; Letter Ten; IM Sprt; Mgrs; Var Ltr In Vllybl; Grand Champ In Cnty 4 H Dress Revue 77; Mental Attitude Trophy In Tennis 78; Purdue Univ; Pharm.

HAMILTON, MINDY; Cadillac Sr HS; Cadillac, MI; Letter Band; Hon Rl; Wrstlng; Mgrs; Mat Maids; Scr Kpr; Tmr; Albion Univ; Psych.

HAMILTON, PAUL; Carman HS; Flint, MI; 49/312 Cls Rep Frsh Cls; Hon Rl; Rptr Sch Nwsp; Bsktbl; Coach Actv; IM Sprt; Mat Maids; Scr Kpr; Tmr; Univ; Acctg.

HAMILTON, ROD; Whiteoak HS; Mowrystown, OH; 1/55 Pres Jr Cls; Pres Band; Chrs; Hon Rl; Fr Clb; Glf; Univ.

HAMILTON, SCOTT; Canton South HS; Canton, OH; Cls Rep Frsh Cls; Pres Soph Cls; Cls Rep Soph Cls; Cl Rep Jr Cls; Aud/Vis; VP FCA; Hon Rl; Pres JA; Natl Forn Lg; NHS; Univ Of Cin; Mech Engr.

HAMILTON, TERI; South Newton HS; Kentland, IN; 9/120 Cls Rep Frsh Cls; Cl Rep Jr Cls; Am Leg Aux Girls St; Band; Drl Tm; Girl Scts; Hon Rl; NHS; Off Ade; Sch Pl; Intrntl Fine Arts Coll; Fashion Byer.

HAMIT, C; Perry HS; Massillon, OH; Pres Frsh Cls; Cls Rep Frsh Cls; Cls Rep Soph Cls; Boy Scts; FCA; Sct Actv; Stu Cncl; Yth Flsp; Ftbl; Swmmng; College; Bio.

HAMLIN, BOB; Admiral King HS; Lorain, OH; Cmnty Wkr; Hon Rl; Off Ade; Sch Pl; Sch Nwsp; Fr Clb; Key Clb; Ten; General Motors Inst; Corp Law.

HAMLIN, CAROL; Andrews Acad; Berrien Spgs, MI; Yrbk; IM Sprt; Andrews Univ; Med.

HAMLIN, ELIZABETH; Chesapeake HS; Chesapeake, OH; 17/140 Band; Cmp Fr Grls; Chrh Wkr; Girl Scts; Hon Rl; Orch; Beta Clb; Quiz Bowl 1977; Ohio St Univ; Soc Sci.

HAMLIN, GARY; Barberton HS; Barberton, OH; Cls Rep Sr Cls; Boy Scts; Chrh Wkr; Hon Rl; Stu Cncl; Letter Wrstlng; Case Western Reserve; Mech Engr.

HAMLIN, JILL; Norwalk HS; Norwalk, OH; Chrh Wkr; Cmnty Wkr; Hon Rl; Off Ade; Yth Flsp; Rptr Yrbk; Pep Clb; Letter Trk; Letter Chrldng; GAA; Toccoa Falls Bible Coll; Trvl Guide.

HAMLIN, LINDA; East Kentwood HS; Kentwood, MI; Chrs; Hon Rl; Swmmng; Davenport Coll Of Bus; Acctg.

HAMLIN, MIKE; Garfield HS; Hamilton, OH; 29/330 Cls Rep Sr Cls; Chrh Wkr; Hon Rl; Jr NHS; Off Ade; Rptr Yrbk; Ed Sch Nwsp; Rptr Sch Nwsp; Sch Nwsp; 4-H; Univ; Bookkeeping.

HAMLIN, MISTY; Crestwood HS; Mantua, OH; 79/238 4-H; Capt Bsktbl; All Portg Cnty Lg In Bsktbl 79; Awd Of Distnctn From St Bd Of Educ 79; Kent St Univ; Bus Admin.

HAMLY, ROBERT; Grand Ledge HS; Grand Ledge, MI; 111/418 Hon Rl; Ftbl; Wrstlng; IM Sprt; Mich St Univ; Bus Admin.

HAMM, RHONDA; Spanishburg HS; Rock, WV; 2/34 Sec Soph Cls; Cl Rep Jr Cls; Band; Chrs; Chrh Wkr; Hon Rl; Sch Mus; Stu Cncl; Yrbk; FHA; Kentucky Univ; Computer Prog.

HAMM, TAMRA; Mariemont HS; Cincinnati, OH; AFS; Chrs; Hosp Ade; Stg Crw; Yth Flsp; Yrbk; Drama Clb; 4-H; Fr Clb; Pep Clb; Univ Of Cincinncitti; Airlines.

HAMMAN, MITCH; De Kalb HS; Auburn, IN; 10/287 Am Leg Boys St; Hon Rl; NHS; Ger Clb; VP Sci Clb; Bsbl; Ftbl; Dollars For Schlrs Schlrshp 79; Purdue Univ; Chem.

HAMMAR, JAMES; James A Garfield HS; Garrettsville, OH; 5/114 Boy Scts; Chrh Wkr; Hon Rl; Treas NHS; Off Ade; Sch Mus; Treas Stu Cncl; Drama Clb; Pres Spn Clb; Am Leg Awd; Ohio State Univ; Optometry.

HAMMEL, JANE; North HS; Bloomington, IN; Band; Chrh Wkr; FCA; Jr NHS; Treas NHS; 4-H; Fr Clb; Ten; 4-H Awd; 4 H Child Care Grand Champ 78 & 79; Indiana Univ; Occupt Ther.

HAMMEL, VANA; Huntington North HS; Huntington, IN; 26/603 Chrs; Chrh Wkr; Sch Mus; 4-H; Pep Clb; Letter Trk; 4-H Awd; Purdue Univ; Vet Science.

HAMMER, BLAINE A; Indian Hill Sr HS; Cincinnati, OH; Chrs; Girl Scts; Hon Rl; Sch Mus; Sch Pl; Drama Clb; Fr Clb; Pep Clb; PPFtbl; Pres Israeli Progr Yty Comm 78; Gnrl Bd Of United Synagogue Yth 78; Univ; Pre Law.

HAMMER, DORIS; Lutheran HS West; Southgate, MI; 3/157 Band; Pres Chrs; Sec NHS; Off Ade; Sch Mus; Sch Pl; Drama Clb; Pom Pon; Pres Schlrshp Awd 79; Homecoming Queen 78; Otstndng Female Vocalist 79; Concordia Univ.

HAMMER, J; Muncie Central HS; Muncie, IN; Hon Rl; Off Ade; Lat Clb; Sci Clb; Spn Clb; Univ; Physics.

HAMMER, JEFFREY; Wintersville HS; Wintersville, OH; Cls Rep Frsh Cls; Cls Rep Soph Cls; Boy Scts; Stg Crw; Fr Clb; IM Sprt; Univ; Med.

HAMMER, KAREN; Springfield Local HS; New Middletown, OH; 15/152 Trs Jr Cls; Girl Scts; Lbry Ade; NHS; Yrbk; Pom Pon; Warren Wilson College.

HAMMER, RITA; Magnificat HS; Bay Village, OH; Chrh Wkr; Cmnty Wkr; Girl Scts; Sch Mus; Sch Pl; Stg Crw; Crs Cntry; Trk; Chrldng; IM Sprt; Univ Of Akron; Engr.

HAMMER, SUSAN; Taylor Center HS; Taylor, MI; 25/385 Chrs; Hon Rl; Treas NHS; Sch Mus; Stg Crw; Wayne St Univ; Engr.

HAMMERBACHER, NEIL; Sts Peter & Paul HS; Saginaw, MI; 29/116 Cls Rep Frsh Cls; Cls Rep Soph Cls; Chrs; Sch Mus; Bsbl; Bsktbl; Ftbl; Wrstlng; Co Chrmn Stdnt Councl; Saginaw Vly St Coll; Crmnl Justc.

HAMMES, ROBIN; South Newton HS; Brook, IN; 5/105 Band; Chrh Wkr; Girl Scts; Hon Rl; Hosp Ade; NHS; Sch Pl; Ind State Univ; Rn.

HAMMON, JEFF; Defiance Sr HS; Defiance, OH; Am Leg Boys St; Boy Scts; Chrh Wkr; Cmnty Wkr; Hon Rl; Lbry Ade; Sct Actv; Pres DECA; Spn Clb; Mgrs; DECA Stu Of Yr; Attendend Jr Cadet Week At St Highway Patrol Grad; Placed 1st In Free Enterprise; Univ Of Oklahoma; Business Mgmt.

HAMMON, SHERRI; Woodlan HS; Hicksville, OH; Chrs; Natl Forn Lg; Sch Mus; Stg Crw; Stu Cncl; Yth Flsp; Drama Clb; Pres 4-H; FFA; FHA; Purdue Univ; Fash Retailing.

HAMMOND, DAVE; Cambridge HS; Cambridge, OH; 60/318 Am Leg Boys St; Hon Rl; Letter Bsbl; Letter Bsktbl; IM Sprt; Runner Up In Oh Vly Atholtc Conf Soph Of Yr 78; Univ.

HAMMOND, FAITH; Clio HS; Clio, MI; Hon Rl; Jr NHS; NHS; Mott Comm College; Accgt.

HAMMOND, JENNIFER E; Covert HS; Sodus, MI; 3/35 Hon Rl; Lbry Ade; Mod UN; NHS; Off Ade; Red Cr Ade; Sch Pl; Ed Yrbk; Ed Sch Nwsp; 4-H; Kalamazoo Coll; Photojournalism.

HAMMOND, KAREN; Lincoln HS; Cambridge, IN; 12/140 Trs Frsh Cls; Trs Sr Cls; Band; Hon Rl; NHS; Off Ade; Sch Pl; Stg Crw; Yth Flsp; Y-Teens; Indiana Univ; Bus.

HAMMOND, KELLY; Coshocton HS; Coshocton, OH; Cls Rep Frsh Cls; Cls Rep Soph Cls; Cl Rep Jr Cls; Cls Rep Sr Cls; Am Leg Aux Girls St; Chrs; Cmnty Wkr; Hon Rl; Stu Cncl; Rptr Sch Nwsp; Bowling Green St Univ.

HAMMOND, MARGARET; High School; Interlocken, MI; Cl Rep Jr Cls; Band; Girl Scts; Hon Rl; JA; Jr NHS; Lbry Ade; NHS; Sct Actv; Stg Crw; Univ; Fine Arts.

HAMMOND, RUSS; Canfield HS; Canfield, OH; 18/258 Chrh Wkr; NHS; Yth Flsp; Fr Clb; Letter Wrstlng; Univ; Comp Progr.

HAMMOND, TERESA; Kyger Creek HS; Gallipolis, OH; Hst Soph Cls; Band; Chrs; Chrh Wkr; Drl Tm; Hosp Ade; Sec NHS; FHA; Pres Keyettes; Lat Clb; Univ.

HAMMOND, TONYA; Huntington North HS; Huntington, IN; Chrs; Lbry Ade; Sch Mus; Stu Cncl; Pep Clb; Soph Ct Hmcmng; St Finalist Miss United Teen Pageant; Coll.

HAMMONS, JEANETTE; Keyser HS; Keyser, WV; 51/248 Hon Rl; Sec FBLA; Pep Clb; Mineral County Vo Tech Cntr; Med Sec.

HAMMONS, R; Decatur Central HS; Indnpls, IN; 28/305 Hon Rl; 4-H; Clark College; Comp Tech.

HAMMONTREE, PATRICIA; Wauseon HS; Wauseon, OH; Chrs; Drl Tm; Sch Mus; Yth Flsp; Y-Teens; Drama Clb; 4-H; Fr Clb; Cincinnati Univ; Interior Design.

HAMON, PAULA; Ripley HS; Ripley, WV; Band; Chrs; Girl Scts; Hon Rl; Stg Crw; Yth Flsp; FNA; Pom Pon; College.

HAMPSHIRE, LARRY D; Versailles HS; Versailles, OH; 14/150 Band; Chrs; Chrh Wkr; Sch Mus; Sch Pl; Treas Yth Flsp; Drama Clb; Natl Merit SF; Dist Biology Test; All Cnty Band; All Cnty State Band; Bowling Green Univ; Music.

HAMPSHIRE, NANCY; Wilmington HS; Wilmington, OH; Cls Rep Frsh Cls; Cl Rep Jr Cls; Band; Cmnty Wkr; Hon Rl; NHS; Stg Crw; Pep Clb; IM Sprt; Univ; Bus.

HAMPTON, CECILLIA; West Side HS; Gary, IN; 32/650 Hst Jr Cls; VP Sr Cls; Chrs; Hon Rl; Hosp Ade; Jr NHS; Red Cr Ade; FDA; Lat Clb; Ind Univ; Med.

HAMPTON, DONNA; North HS; Columbus, OH; 4/325 Band; Hon Rl; Jr NHS; NHS; Orch; 4-H; Lat Clb; 4-H Awd; Ohio St Univ; Bio Sci.

HAMPTON, GRAY W; Huntington HS; Huntington, WV; 1/300 VP Sr Cls; Am Leg Boys St; Chrs; Chrh Wkr; Debate Tm; Hon Rl; Jr NHS; Pres NHS; Stu Cncl; Yth Flsp; College.

HAMPTON, JOY; B H Sr HS; Benton Hbr, MI; Chrh Wkr; Girl Scts; Jr NHS; Sch Pl; Stg Crw; Stu Cncl; Drama Clb; Pres Spn Clb; Michigan St Univ; Public Relations.

HAMPTON, KATHY; New Palestine HS; New Palestine, IN; 20/172 Band; Treas Chrh Wkr; Pres Girl Scts; Hosp Ade; NHS; Sct Actv; Stu Cncl; Treas Yth Flsp; Yrbk; Spn Clb; Indiana Univ; RN.

HAMPTON, SHERMAN; Big Creek HS; Bishop, VA; 22/115 VP Frsh Cls; Pres Sr Cls; Band; Chrh Wkr; Cmnty Wkr; Hon Rl; Pep Clb; Capt Bsbl; Letter Bsktbl; Letter Ftbl; West Vir Univ; Ind Engr.

HAMPTON, WILLIAM; Greenbrier East HS; Lewisburg, WV; Hon Rl; Rptr Sch Nwsp; Sch Nwsp; Trk; Bus Schl; Drftng.

HAMRICK, ANDREW; Jefferson HS; Charlestown, WV; Am Leg Boys St; Chrs; Chrh Wkr; Hon Rl; Stg Crw; Yrbk; Rptr Sch Nwsp; Stage Mgr Jefferson Pop Sngrs 77 80; Pres Jr Civitn 79; Spec Olympcs Wkr 78; West Virginia Univ; Pediatrics.

HAMRICK, KAREN; George Washington HS; Charleston, WV; Band; Drm Mjrt; Hon Rl; Jr NHS; Keyettes; College; Fine Arts.

HAMRICK, MARVIN; Parkway HS; Willshire, OH; 13/96 Hst Jr Cls; Chrh Wkr; Hon Rl; Yth Flsp; Yrbk; Treas 4-H; FFA; 4-H Awd; JA Awd; Jr Fair Board Jr Advisior; Campus Life; College.

HAMRICK, PEGGY; Roosevelt Wilson HS; Stonewood, WV; Chrs; Chrh Wkr; Hon Rl; Pres Yth Flsp; Y-Teens; 4-H; Leo Clb; Mth Clb; Pep Clb; Chrldng; Bsns Schl; Sec.

HAMRICK, ROBERT; Coalton HS; Norton, WV; 14/33 Hon Rl; Drama Clb; Sci Clb; VICA; Bsbl; Constr.

HAMROCK, GERARD; Chaney HS; Youngstown, OH; Ed Sch Nwsp; Univ Of Cincinnati; Aero Engr.

HAMSTRA, CHRISTINE L; Edgewood HS; Bloomington, IN; 8/194 Trs Jr Cls; Chrs; Chrh Wkr; Drl Tm; FCA; Hon Rl; NHS; Off Ade; Sch Mus; Yrbk; Ivy Tech Voc Schl; Nursing.

HAMSTRA, CORINNA; Kouts HS; Kouts, IN; VP Soph Cls; Cls Rep Soph Cls; Pres Jr Cls; Cl Rep Jr Cls; Cls Rep Sr Cls; Sec NHS; Off Ade; Sch Pl; Sec Stu Cncl; 1st Pl Regional Sci Fair 77; Voc Schl; Dent Asst.

HAMSTRA, SHARI; Kankakee Vly HS; Wheatfield, IN; NHS; 4-H; OEA; PPFtbl; Bus Schl.

HAN, JON; Rutherford B Hayes HS; Delaware, OH; Cls Rep Frsh Cls; Pres Sr Cls; Am Leg Boys St; Chrs; Chrh Wkr; Cmnty Wkr; Hon Rl; Lbry Ade; NHS; P ol Wkr; Soc Of Distinguished Amer HS Students; Honorable Mention In Dist English; Superior At Dist Sci Fair; College; English.

HANAHAN, THOMAS; Triton Central HS; Boggstown, IN; 3/145 NHS; Sch Pl; VP Stu Cncl; Yrbk; Drama Clb; Sec Key Clb; Pres Spn Clb; Capt Bsktbl; Capt Ten; DAR Awd; Univ Of Notre Dame; Business.

HANAWAY, MALISSA; Hammond Tech Voc HS; Hammond, IN; 15/235 Cl Rep Jr Cls; Debate Tm; Girl Scts; Natl Forn Lg; PAVAS; Sch Mus; Sch Pl; Stg Crw; Stu Cncl; Rptr Yrbk; Purdue Univ; Acctg.

HANCOCK, AMY; Amelia Sr HS; Amelia, OH; 31/280 Chrh Wkr; Hon Rl; Lbry Ade; NHS; Yrbk; IM Sprt; Cedarville Univ; Med Lab Tech.

HANCOCK, BRENDA; Houghton Lake HS; Houghton Lk, MI; 23/120 Letter Band; Chrh Wkr; Hon Rl; NHS; Sec Yth Flsp; Pep Clb; Letter Bsbl; Letter Gym; Letter Chrldng; Letter Mgrs; Ferris; Dent Hygiene.

HANCOCK, LISA; N Posey Jr Sr HS; Griffin, IN; Girl Scts; Hon Rl; Rptr Sch Nwsp; 4-H; Pep Clb; GAA; IM Sprt; 4-H Awd; Coll; Elem Ed.

HANCOCK, MARTIN; St Francis De Sales HS; Toledo, OH; 15/186 Cls Rep Soph Cls; Hon Rl; Sprt Ed Sch Nwsp; Fr Clb; Scr Kpr; Tmr; Ohio Univ; Jrnlsm.

HANCOCK, ROBERT; Bluffton HS; Beaverdam, OH; Band; Boy Scts; Chrs; Sch Mus; Sct Actv; Letter Scr Kpr; Bus Schl.

HANCOCK, TIMOTHY; Bethel Christian Schl; Walled Lake, MI; Chrh Wkr; Sch Pl; Ed Yrbk; Sch Nwsp; Letter Socr; Trk; Natl Merit Ltr; St Of Michigan Comp Schlrshp; Ferris St Coll; Sci.

HAND, DAWN; Margaretta HS; Castalia, OH; 15/180 Chrs; Hon Rl; Pep Clb; Chrldng; IM Sprt; Mas Awd; Bus Schl; Bus Mgmt.

HAND, RICHARD; Quincy HS; Quincy, MI; Boy Scts; Chrs; Chrh Wkr; Hon Rl; Sch Mus; Sct Actv; Boys Clb Am; 4-H; 4-H Awd; Adrian Coll; Dentistry.

HAND, TERRI; Reading HS; Montgomery, MI; Hon Rl; Yth Flsp; 4-H; Fr Clb; 4-H Awd; Bus Schl.

HANDLER, ROBIN; Monroe HS; Monroe, MI; 22/594 Hon Rl; NHS; Stu Cncl; OEA; Coach Actv; Mgrs; VFW Awd; Thrift Shop Schlrshp; Cert For Excellence Of Schlrshp In Acctg & Sec Lab; Cleary Coll; Stenographer.

HANDLEY, CARL F; Hurricane HS; Hurricane, WV; Letter Bsktbl; Letter Ftbl; Letter Trk; AA All Sthrn 3rd Team; Virginia Tech Univ; Accounting.

HANDLEY, DEBORAH; Lebanon HS; Lebanon, OH; Chrs; Chrh Wkr; Hon Rl; Pres Yth Flsp; Fr Clb; Pep Clb; Univ; RN.

HANDLEY, EILEEN; Plainwell HS; Plainwell, MI; Girl Scts; Hon Rl; Hosp Ade; NHS; Sch Pl; Pep Clb; Spn Clb; Ten; Nazareth College; Surgical Nurse.

HANDMACHER, VICKI; Beavercreek HS; Dayton, OH; 68/702 AFS; Hon Rl; NHS; Mat Maids; Scr Kpr; Tmr; Ohi State Univ; Bio Sci.

HANDORF, JULIE; Seton HS; Cincinnati, OH; 13/266 Pres Girl Scts; Jr NHS; NHS; Sct Actv; Drama Clb; Treas Fr Clb; Mth Clb; Capt IM Sprt; Miami Univ; Systems Analysis.

HANDORF, JULIE A; Seton HS; Cincinnati, OH; 13/271 Pres Girl Scts; Hon Rl; Jr NHS; NHS; Treas Sct Actv; Drama Clb; Treas Fr Clb; Socr; Miami Univ; Comp Sci.

HANDORF, PHILIP C; St Xavier HS; Xenia, OH; Boy Scts; Cmnty Wkr; NHS; Rptr Sch Nwsp; Fr Clb; VP Mth Clb; Cit Awd; Natl Merit SF; Univ; Comp.

HANDWERK, ALICIA M; Fredericktown HS; Fredericktown, OH; 3/118 Am Leg Aux Girls St; Chrs; Chrh Wkr; Debate Tm; Hon Rl; NHS; Quill & Scroll; Sch Nwsp; Sch Pl; Yth Flsp; College; Law.

HANDWORK, LAWRENCE; Austintown Fitch HS; Canfield, OH; 1/750 VP NHS; Key Clb; Bsktbl; Letter Ftbl; Letter Trk; NCTE; Natl Merit Ltr; Ohio Schlst Achv Test Hnrble Mention; College; Medicine.

HANEL, MARY J; Our Lady Of The Lakes HS; Drayton Plains, MI; Hon Rl; Lbry Ade; NHS; Off Ade; Rptr Yrbk; Drama Clb; Fr Clb; PPFtbl; Oakland Comm Coll; Legal Sec.

HANELT, DIANA; Catholic Central HS; Salt Lake City, UT; Hon Rl; Lbry Ade; NHS; Sch Mus; Sch Pl; Yrbk; Sch Nwsp; Pep Clb; VP Spn Clb; Univ Of Utah; Art.

HANER, BARON; Gallia Acad; Gallipolis, OH; Pres Frsh Cls; Cls Rep Soph Cls; Chrh Wkr; Cmnty Wkr; FCA; Stu Cncl; Spn Clb; Bsbl; Ftbl; Trk; Marshall; Real Estate.

HANES, HAROLD; Richmond HS; Richmond, IN; 100/600 Boy Scts; Orch; Sch Nwsp; College; Jrnlsm.

HANES, KIMBERLY; Bloom Local HS; South Webster, OH; Am Leg Aux Girls St; Band; Chrs; Hon Rl; Off Ade; Sch Pl; 4-H; FHA; OEA; Letter Chrldng; Univ; Med Sec.

HANES, R; Heath HS; Heath, OH; Hon Rl; Key Clb; College.

HANES, RONALD; Holton HS; Holton, MI; 11/95 Hon Rl; NHS; IM Sprt; Talented Youth Schlhsp 79; Notre Dame Univ; Bus Admin.

HANES, TINA; Grant HS; Sand Lk, MI; Hon Rl; College; Sec.

HANEY, CURT; Belding HS; Belding, MI; Sprt Ed Yrbk; Mic State; Criminal Justice.

HANEY, JODI; Maumee HS; Toledo, OH; 21/316 Trs Frsh Cls; Pres Sr Cls; Am Leg Aux Girls St; Hon Rl; Jr NHS; NHS; Y-Teens; Sch Nwsp; 4-H; Capt Bsktbl; Cmnctns.

HANEY, KELLY; St Augustine Acad; Cleveland, OH; 16/130 Chrs; Hon Rl; Rptr Yrbk; Fr Clb; Cls Rep Sr Cls; Bowling Green State Univ; Bus Admin.

HANEY, KIM; Clarkston HS; Drayton Pln, MI; Chrs; Girl Scts; Hon Rl; Off Ade; Sct Actv; Stg Crw; Drama Clb; IM Sprt; PPFtbl; Western Univ; Psych.

HANEY, MARY; Ravenna HS; Ravenna, OH; 27/313 Band; Chrh Wkr; Girl Scts; Hon Rl; Hosp Ade; NHS; Fr Clb; Coll; Dentistry.

HANEY, PENNY; Tippecanoe Valley HS; Mentone, IN; Cls Rep Frsh Cls; Pres Jr Cls; Pres Sr Cls; Hon Rl; NHS; Stu Cncl; OEA; Pep Clb; Spn Clb; Letter Chrldng; Work At Akron Exch St Bank.

HANEY, SUSAN; Goshen HS; Goshen, IN; 1/269 Cls Rep Soph Cls; Am Leg Aux Girls St; Treas FCA; NHS; Pres 4-H; Letter Bsktbl; Letter Trk; Coach Actv; Dnfth Awd; 4-H Awd; Purdue Univ; Pre Vet.

HANEY, TIM; Franklin HS; Franklin, OH; Letter Bsbl; Letter Bsktbl; Georgetown Coll.

HANEY, WILLIAM; Huntington HS; Huntington, WV; 1/299 Hon Rl; NHS; Sct Actv; Fr Clb; Mth Clb; Natl Merit Ltr; Marshall Univ; Pre Med.

HANEY JR, DALE; Westfall HS; Orient, OH; 2/135 Cls Rep Frsh Cls; Cls Rep Soph Cls; Am Leg Boys St; Band; Boy Scts; NHS; Stg Crw; Stu Cncl; Rptr Yrbk; Fr Clb; Ohio State Univ; Law.

HANGE, ELIZABETH; Black River HS; Spencer, OH; 15/130 Sec Frsh Cls; Band; Chrs; Hon Rl; NHS; Sch Pl; Stu Cncl; Y-Teens; Rptr Yrbk; Yrbk; 5th Pl St FFA Public Speaking; Medina Cnty Dairy Princess; Ohio St Univ; Vet.

HANGER, LOIS; Hinton HS; Wayside, WV; Chrs; Hon Rl; Off Ade; Yth Flsp; 4-H; FHA; Lat Clb; Btty Crckr Awd; Dnfth Awd; 4-H Awd; W Virginia Univ; Human Resources.

HANIS, RITA; Kimball HS; Royal Oak, MI; Girl Scts; Hon Rl; NHS; Orch; Letter GAA; Acctg.

HANKE, DONALD; Central HS; Bay City, MI; Band; Hon Rl; Mic Tech Univ; Elec Engr.

HANKE, GREGG; Harper Creek HS; Ceresco, MI; Boy Scts; Hon Rl; Stg Crw; Letter Bsbl; Letter Swmmng; Coach Actv; Scr Kpr; Tmr; Univ; Comp Sci.

HANKENHOF, JANE; Notre Dame Academy; Toledo, OH; Pres Jr Cls; Cmnty Wkr; Stu Cncl; Spn Clb; Trk; Coach Actv; Track Ribbons 79; Univ; Clinical Psych.

HANKISON, KARLA; Valley HS; Lucasville, OH; Chrh Wkr; Girl Scts; Hon Rl; Treas NHS; Sch Pl; Pres Stu Cncl; Yth Flsp; Rptr Yrbk; FHA; FTA; Asbury Coll; Child Psych.

HANKO, JOE; Eau Claire HS; Bangor, MI; 12/100 Cmnty Wkr; Debate Tm; Drl Tm; Hon Rl; JA; Sch Mus; Sch Pl; Stg Crw; Capt Wrstlng; IM Sprt; Sci.

HANKS, PAM; Portage Lakes Joint Voc Schl; North Canton, OH; 16/328 Hon Rl; Off Ade; OEA; IM Sprt; Dnfth Awd; Exec Sec.

HANLEY, CATHARINE; Southern Local HS; Salineville, OH; 1/110 Pres Frsh Cls; Val; Hon Rl; NHS; Stu Cncl; Lat Clb; Chrldng; Miami Univ Of Ohi.

HANLEY, JOHN; Garden City W HS; Garden City, MI; 50/416 Band; Hon Rl; NHS; Letter Trk; IM Sprt; Natl Merit SF; Natl Merit Schl; Michigan Tech Univ; Chem Engr.

HANLEY, SCOTT; Heritage HS; Monroeville, IN; Band; Chrh Wkr; Hon Rl; JA; Purdue Univ; Archt Drafting.

HANLIN, FRANK; Weirton Madonna HS; Slovan, PA; 33/99 Hon Rl; NHS; Pres Key Clb; Bsktbl; Trk; Univ Of Hawaii; Med.

HANLON, MICHAEL K; North Putnam HS; Coatesville, IN; Chrs; Cmnty Wkr; Sct Actv; Ftbl; Mas Awd; Pres Awd;.

HANN, MARY; Holland HS; Holland, MI; 10/330 Band; Cmp Fr Grls; Hon Rl; NHS; Yth Flsp; Rptr Yrbk; Drama Clb; 4-H; FNA; 4-H Awd; Michigan Univ; Law.

HANNA, BECKY; South Charleston HS; S Charleston, WV; FCA; Girl Scts; Hon Rl; Yth Flsp; Pep Clb; Bsktbl; Gym; Swmmng; Chrldng; Coll; Soc Work.

HANNA, CHRISTY; David Anderson HS; Lisbon, OH; Sec Jr Cls; Am Leg Aux Girls St; Hon Rl; Cl Rep Jr Cls; NHS; Yth Flsp; Y-Teens; Treas Fr Clb; Trk; Muskingum Coll.

HANNA, CRAIG; Ursuline HS; Lowellville, OH; 100/326 Debate Tm; Hon Rl; Capt Natl Forn Lg; Ed Sch Nwsp; Rptr Sch Nwsp; Lat Clb; Mth Clb; Natl Forensic Lg Awd Of Hon & Awd Of Mert & Awd Of Excllnc 79; Kent St Univ; Tele Cmnctns.

HANNA, HUGH D; Bloomington HS; Bloomington, IN; Sch Mus; Sch Pl; Drama Clb; College; Theatrics.

HANNA, JULIE M; Western Reserve Academy; Peninsula, OH; Chrs; Hon Rl; Sch Mus; Letter Bsktbl; Hockey; Letter Trk; Univ; Eng.

HANNA, MAGED; Bellbrook HS; Bellbrook, OH; Aud/Vis; Boy Scts; Hon Rl; Sct Actv; Fr Clb; Socr; College; Med Biological.

HANNA, MARY; Our Lady Star Of The Sea HS; Detroit, MI; Chrh Wkr; Hon Rl; Sch Mus; Rptr Yrbk; Yrbk; Rptr Sch Nwsp; Sch Nwsp; GAA; Natl Merit Schl; Mich State Univ; Journalism.

HANNA, PATRICIA; Warren Woods HS; Warren, MI; Cls Rep Soph Cls; Cl Rep Jr Cls; Cls Rep Sr Cls; Hosp Ade; NHS; Stu Cncl; Bsktbl; Trk; Mgrs; Natl Merit Schl; Michigan St Univ; Vet.

HANNAH, CHARLENE; Tipton HS; Tipton, IN; Chrs; Cmnty Wkr; Hon Rl; Sch Pl; 4-H; Pep Clb; Sci

Clb; GAA; IM Sprt; 4-H Awd; Purdue Univ; Wildlife Sci.

HANNAH, DAVID A; Western Reserve Acad; Hudson, OH; 50/89 Band; Chrs; Hon Rl; Off Ade; Sch Mus; Sch Pl; Stg Crw; Lcrss; Socr; IM Sprt; College; Music.

HANNAH, GARY; High School; Blacklick, OH; 22/435 Am Leg Boys St; Hon Rl; Jr NHS; NHS; Sch Mus; Letter Bsbl; Capt Ftbl; Letter Socr; Akron Univ; Business Admin.

HANNAH, MARK; Fairview HS; Fairview Pk, OH; Hon Rl; Off Ade; Yth Flsp; Sch Nwsp; VICA; Mas Awd; West Shore Voc; Graphic Arts.

HANNAHS, KEVIN; Newcomerstown HS; Newcomerstown, OH; VP Frsh Cls; Am Leg Boys St; Aud/Vis; FCA; Hon Rl; Sch Pl; Stg Crw; Sprt Ed Yrbk; Capt Bsbl; Letter Ftbl; Hocking Tech Coll; Park Ranger.

HANNAHS, KRISTIN A; Rosecrans HS; Zanesville, OH; 1/95 Hon Rl; NHS; Ed Sch Nwsp; Sci Clb; Natl Merit SF; Univ; Chem.

HANNAMAN, STEVEN K; Winfield HS; Scott Depot, WV; Boy Scts; Hon Rl; JA; Jr NHS; Sct Actv; Fr Clb; Mth Clb; Univ; Math.

HANNAN, RANDAL; Onsted HS; Manitou Bch, MI; Hon Rl; Sch Pl; Ed Yrbk; Yrbk; Rptr Sch Nwsp; Sch Nwsp; Natl Merit Ltr; Michigan St Univ; Bio.

HANNEMAN, BERNICE A; Kalida HS; Columbus Grove, OH; Pres Band; Chrs; Hon Rl; Orch; Sch Mus; Ed Sch Nwsp; 4-H; Sec FHA; GAA; Scr Kpr; Univ; Geol.

HANNER, GREGORY; Brownstown Central HS; Norman, IN; Hon Rl; Stg Crw; Yth Flsp; Pep Clb; Spn Clb; IM Sprt; Bio Hnr; Monetary St Schlrshp; Purdue Univ; Mech Engr.

HANNETT, LAURA; Muskegon Sr HS; Muskegon, MI; Cls Rep Frsh Cls; VP Soph Cls; VP Jr Cls; Band; Chrh Wkr; Hon Rl; Hosp Ade; JA; Lbry Ade; Red Cr Ade; Awana Hnr Awd 76; Exploring Activity Awd 78; Detroit Univ; Respiratory Ther.

HANNUM, LISA M; Cathedral HS; Indianapolis, IN; 3/150 Trs Soph Cls; Cls Rep Sr Cls; Hon Rl; NHS; Off Ade; Sch Pl; Stu Cncl; Yrbk; Rptr Sch Nwsp; 4-H; Univ Of Notre Dame; Engr.

HANNUM, TERESA; Meadowbrook HS; Pleasant City, OH; Cls Rep Frsh Cls; Cls Rep Soph Cls; Pres Jr Cls; Band; Chrh Wkr; Hon Rl; Lbry Ade; Stu Cncl; Yth Flsp; Ed Yrbk; Jr Fair Bd VP 1978; Fife & Drum Corp; Algebra Achievement Test 1977; Ohio St Univ; Comp Sci.

HANOOD, VICKI; Magnolia HS; New Martinsvle, WV; 32/170 Band; Girl Scts; Hon Rl; Sct Actv; Letter Trk; Letter Chrldng; College; Busns Admin.

HANS, JANET; Tuslaw HS; Massillon, OH; 17/185 Band; Chrs; Girl Scts; Hon Rl; NHS; Orch; 4-H; 4-H Awd; Akron Univ; Respiratory Therapy.

HANS, JUDITH; Loudonville HS; Loudonville, OH; Band; Chrs; Cmnty Wkr; Hon Rl; Stg Crw; Yrbk; Trk; College; Horticulture.

HANSBARGER, JOHN H; Princeton HS; Princeton, WV; Hon Rl; Key Clb; Spn Clb; Bsktbl;.

HANSBROUGH, BETH; Memorial HS; St Marys, OH; 1/222 Band; Sec Chrs; Chrh Wkr; Cmnty Wkr; Hon Rl; NHS; Yth Flsp; Y-Teens; Sec Sci Clb; IM Sprt; Univ; Zoology.

HANSEL, TODD; West Muskingum HS; Zanesville, OH; 1/175 Pres Frsh Cls; Am Leg Boys St; Chrs; Chrh Wkr; Hon Rl; NHS; Sch Mus; Yth Flsp; Pep Clb; Spn Clb; Oh Test Of Schlstc Achvmnt Aglbr I 5th In St 2nd In Dist 77; Oh Test Schltc Achvmnt Geom H M St 4th Dist 78; Univ Of Cincinnati; Engr.

HANSELL, SAUL; Roeper City & Country HS; Detroit, MI; Aud/Vis; Mod UN; Sch Pl; Stg Crw; Ed Sch Nwsp; Univ.

HANSELMAN, LAUREY; Ubly Community School; Minden City, MI; 2/130 Sal; Band; Cmnty Wkr; Girl Scts; Hon Rl; Pres NHS; FHA; Whos Who Among Amer HS Stndt 78; Bio II Chem Amer Hist & Band Awds 78; Genr Sci Eng 9 Home Ec Awd 76; Michigan St Univ; Med.

HANSEN, BARBARA; Adrian HS; Adrian, MI; 23/386 Cmp Fr Grls; Chrs; Chrh Wkr; Hon Rl; Off Ade; Stg Crw; Fr Clb; Mth Clb; Northern Michigan Univ; Art.

HANSEN, BRUCE; Port Clinton HS; Port Clinton, OH; 4/270 Boy Scts; Chrh Wkr; Hon Rl; Natl Forn Lg; NHS; Orch; Y-Teens; Lat Clb; Bsbl; Capt Ten; College; Computer Sci.

HANSEN, CHRISTINE E; William A Wirt HS; Gary, IN; VP Jr Cls; Hon Rl; Pres Jr NHS; Pep Clb; Spn Clb; GAA; Mat Maids; Tmr; Cit Awd; College; Comp Sci.

HANSEN, ERIC; Perrysburg HS; Perrysburg, OH; 5/251 Hon Rl; Jr NHS; Sch Mus; Sch Pl; Stg Crw; Yth Flsp; Beta Clb; Drama Clb; Sci Clb; Crs Cntry; College; Engr.

HANSEN, GREGORY D; Grand Ledge HS; Grnd Ledge, MI; Cls Rep Frsh Cls; Cls Rep Soph Cls; Aud/Vis; Band; Pres Boy Scts; Chrh Wkr; Hon Rl; NHS; Sct Actv; Stu Cncl; Univ; Engr.

HANSEN, HOLLI; Indian Hill HS; Cincinnati, OH; Chrs; Chrh Wkr; Cmnty Wkr; Girl Scts; Hon Rl; Lbry Ade; Off Ade; Stu Cncl; Yth Flsp; Mth Clb; Hnr Roll; Hnr Roll Spanish Natl Hnr Soc; Miami Univ; Busns.

HANSEN, HOPE; Lebanon Sr HS; Lebanon, IN; Sec Frsh Cls; Sec Jr Cls; Sec Sr Cls; Am Leg Aux Girls St; Chrs; Hon Rl; Jr NHS; NHS; Sch Mus; Stg Crw; Depaw Univ; Visual Art.

HANSEN, K; Western Reserve Acad; Hudson, OH; 30/100 Cl Rep Jr Cls; Chrs; Cmnty Wkr; Hon Rl; Off Ade; PAVAS; Sch Mus; Sch Pl; Drama Clb; Hockey; Univ; Music.

HANSEN, LISA; Whitko HS; Columbia City, IN; Hon Rl; Sch Pl; Rptr Sch Nwsp; Drama Clb; 4-H; Fr Clb; FFA; Trk; Purdue Univ; Vet Med.

HANSEN, MARK; Flushing HS; Flushing, MI; 1/524 Band; Boy Scts; Chrs; NHS; Orch; Sch Mus; Lion Awd; Opt Clb Awd; College; Comp Sci.

HANSEN, MICHAEL; Montabella HS; Edmore, MI; 4/115 Boy Scts; Chrh Wkr; Hon Rl; NHS; Spn Clb; Bsktbl; Ftbl; Trk; Central Michigan Univ; Elec Engr.

HANSEN, MICHELLE; Lakeview HS; Coral, MI; VP Frsh Cls; VP Soph Cls; Letter Band; Hon Rl; NHS; Rptr Sch Nwsp; 4-H; FTA; Spn Clb; Capt Chrldng; College; Health.

HANSEN, RANDALL; Mason County Central HS; Ludington, MI; 17/125 VP Frsh Cls; Pres Soph Cls; Band; Chrh Wkr; Hon Rl; NHS; Pres Yth Flsp; 4-H; Bsbl; Letter Bsktbl; Mich Comp Schlrshp; Schlrshp & The Corwill & Margie Jackson Fndtn Schlrshp 79; 4 Yr Hnr Stdnt 75 79; Aquinas Coll; Bus.

HANSEN, RAYMOND; North Central HS; Hermansville, MI; Hon Rl; JA; NHS; Stg Crw; Yth Flsp; Natl Merit Schl; Vocational Schl; Auto Mech.

HANSEN, RENEE; Hopkins HS; Dorr, MI; Pres Frsh Cls; Hon Rl; Off Ade; Rptr Sch Nwsp; Western Univ; Counseling.

HANSEN, RICK; Greenville Sr HS; Gowen, MI; Chrh Wkr; Hon Rl; Yth Flsp; Alma Univ; Pre Med.

HANSEN, SCOTT; North Muskegon HS; N Muskegon, MI; Aud/Vis; Hon Rl; NHS; Bsktbl; Ftbl; Scr Kpr; Tmr; Univ Of Michigan.

HANSEN, VANESSA; Montabella HS; Edmore, MI; Letter Band; Chrh Wkr; Drl Tm; Girl Scts; Hon Rl; Yrbk; 4-H; Letter Trk; Ferris St Coll; Data Processing.

HANSERD, ANDREA; Southeastern HS; Detroit, MI; Sec Frsh Cls; Cl Rep Jr Cls; Girl Scts; Hon Rl; JA; Off Ade; Sch Pl; Drama Clb; Rdo Clb; Cit Awd; Univ; Law.

HANSHUE, SCOTT; Grant HS; Grant, MI; 10/125 Band; Boy Scts; Hon Rl; Sch Pl; Stu Cncl; FSA; Sci Clb; Ftbl; Trk; IM Sprt; Sci Club Sci Fair Winner 1st Pl 79; 225 Schshp For Oceanog 79; Michigan Tech Univ; Bio Oceanog.

HANSMAN, MARK; Glen Este HS; Cincinnati, OH; Am Leg Boys St; Chrh Wkr; Cmnty Wkr; Hon Rl; Spn Clb; IM Sprt; Univ; Bus.

HANSON, BONNIE S; Cheboygan Area HS; Cheboygan, MI; 3/180 Band; Chrh Wkr; Cmnty Wkr; Girl Scts; Hon Rl; Hosp Ade; Yth Flsp; Letter Trk; Capt Chrldng; Lake Superior St Coll; Health.

HANSON, DAVID; Alpena HS; Alpena, MI; 80/744 Hon Rl; Stu Cncl; 4-H; Lat Clb; 4-H Awd; Mich Tech Univ; Chem Engr.

HANSON, DENNIS; T L Handy HS; Bay City, MI; 26/431 Hon Rl; Jr NHS; NHS; Spn Clb; Bsktbl; Natl Merit Ltr; Univ Of Michigan; Pre Law.

HANSON, JANINE; Our Lady Of The Lakes HS; Pontiac, MI; 1/45 Trs Frsh Cls; Cls Rep Frsh Cls; Val; Hon Rl; NHS; Sch Mus; Fr Clb; Chrldng; Natl Merit SF; Michigan State Univ.

HANSON, LISA; Pendleton Heights HS; Pendleton, IN; Quill & Scroll; Yrbk; Sch Nwsp; Ger Clb; Ten; Mat Maids; Ball State Univ; Printing.

HANSON, LORI; Cheboygan Area HS; Cheboygan, MI; Band; Sec Chrh Wkr; Hon Rl; NHS; Sch Pl; Yth Flsp; Sec Fr Clb; College.

HANSON, MARK; Chardon HS; Chardon, OH; 3/250 Sal; Am Leg Boys St; Sec FCA; Hon Rl; Pres NHS; Stg Crw; Letter Bsbl; Letter Bsktbl; Mat Maids; Elk Awd; Allegheny Coll; Bus.

HANSON, MOLLY; Newark Sr HS; Newark, OH; D rl Tm; Hon Rl; Stg Crw; Fr Clb; Pom Pon; Mas Awd; Pittsburgh Art Inst; Cmmrcl Dsgnr.

HANSON, RANDY; Mt Healthy HS; Cincinnati, OH; Band; Hon Rl; NHS; Red Cr Ade; Coll Conservatory Of Music; Music.

HANSON, ROBERT; Morgan Local HS; Malta, OH; 6/249 Am Leg Boys St; Hon Rl; NHS; VICA; Bsbl; IM Sprt; Rotary Awd; Washington Tech Coll; Auto Mech.

HANSON, SHARON; Beavercreek HS; Xenia, OH; 306/702 Cls Rep Sr Cls; Chrs; Drl Tm; Off Ade; Yth Flsp; Sch Nwsp; Pep Clb; IM Sprt; Pom Pon; Natl Merit Ltr; Bowling Greene Univ; Fashion Mdse.

HANT, GREGORY; Hicksville HS; Hicksville, OH; Hon Rl; NHS; Lat Clb; Ftbl; Trk; Ohio State Univ; Acctg.

HANTZIS, CHARLES W; Northwest HS; Indianapolis, IN; 3/530 Am Leg Boys St; Hon Rl; NHS; Quill & Scroll; Ed Yrbk; Rptr Yrbk; Yrbk; Fr Clb; Cit Awd; DAR Awd; Natl Chrstns & Jews Human Relations Awd; Physics Student Awd; Purdue Univ; Physics.

HANUS, DAN; Morrison R Waite HS; Toledo, OH; 79/265 Cls Rep Frsh Cls; Cls Rep Soph Cls; Cl Rep Jr Cls; Cls Rep Sr Cls; Hon Rl; Off Ade; Sch Pl; Stg Crw; Pep Clb; Bsbl; Univ Of Toledo; Educ.

HANUS, NANCY; Warren Woods HS; Warren, MI; 3/370 Cmnty Wkr; Girl Scts; Hon Rl; NHS; Ed Yrbk; Rptr Yrbk; Yrbk; Ed Sch Nwsp; Sprt Ed Sch Nwsp; Rptr Sch Nwsp; Ohio St Univ; Jrnlsm.

HAP, TONIA; Union City Comm HS; Union City, IN; 2/120 Chrs; Cmnty Wkr; Capt Drl Tm; Hon Rl; NHS; Sch Mus; VP Stu Cncl; Yth Flsp; Eng Clb; Fr Clb; Delegte To Sen Lugars Sympsm For Tomorrws Ldrs; Foreign Languages Outstndg Frnch Stu; Ind Unv Stu Ldrshp In; Butler Univ; Pharmacy.

HAPP, ORA L; St Francis De Sales HS; Columbus, OH; Chrh Wkr; Hon Rl; Sch Pl; Lat Clb; Gym; College; Cmmrcl Photog.

HAPPEL, KATHY; Castle HS; Newburgh, IN; 52/375 Hon Rl; Pol Wkr; Sch Mus; Sch Pl; Ind State Univ; English.

HARADEM, DAVID P; Lorain Catholic HS; Avon, OH; Cls Rep Soph Cls; Am Leg Boys St; VP Band; Boy Scts; Chrh Wkr; Hon Rl; NHS; College; Law.

HARBACHECK, MARK; Lexington HS; Lexington, OH; 54/217 Cls Rep Frsh Cls; Cl Rep Jr Cls; Stu Cncl; Letter Trk; Univ.

HARBAUGH, JON; Highland HS; Wadsworth, OH; Cmnty Wkr; Hon Rl; Key Clb; Letter Ftbl; Coach Actv; IM Sprt; Mgrs; Scr Kpr; Schlstc Art Awrd Gold Key & Blue Ribbon 77; Univ; Engr.

HARBER, RONALD G; Bishop Dwenger HS; Fort Wayne, IN; 1/268 Val; Aud/Vis; Chrh Wkr; Hon Rl; Lbry Ade; NHS; Treas Sch Pl; JETS Awd; Purdue Univ; Elec Engr.

HARBERT, KELLYANN; Grafton HS; Grafton, WV; Band; Chrs; Hon Rl; Jr NHS; Sch Mus; Sch Pl; VP Drama Clb; Letter Trk; IM Sprt; PPFtbl; Wv Univ; Business.

HARBICK, MARK; Marquette Sr HS; Marquette, MI; 49/425 Trs Sr Cls; Am Leg Boys St; Band; Hon Rl; Orch; Sch Mus; Yrbk; Ger Clb; John Phillip Sousa Band Awd 79; Exchng Stdnt To W Germny 79; Whos Who In Music 79; Univ Of Kentucky; Archt.

HARBIN, JULIE; North Knox HS; Freelandville, IN; 17/173 Band; FCA; NHS; Yth Flsp; 4-H; Pep Clb; Letter Bsktbl; Letter Trk; 4-H Awd; Vincennes Univ; Med Tech.

HARBISON, ROGER; Floyd Central HS; New Albany, IN; 69/347 Boy Scts; Hon Rl; NHS; Pol Wkr; Stu Cncl; 4-H; Ftbl; Univ Of Louisville; Engr.

HARBOLD, BETH; Canton South HS; E Sparta, OH; Chrh Wkr; Girl Scts; Hon Rl; JA; Lbry Ade; Sch Pl; Rptr Yrbk; Drama Clb; Pep Clb; Univ; Med.

HARBOUR, PAULA; Milton HS; Milton, WV; Pres Frsh Cls; VP Soph Cls; Band; Jr NHS; Sct Actv; Stu Cncl; Sch Nwsp; Spn Clb; Art Work & Photography Exhibited At Huntington Galleries Wv; Schlrshp To Huntington Galleries Classes; Columbus Coll; Interior Design.

HARBOUR, STEPHEN; Washington HS; E Chicago, IN; 33/368 Chrh Wkr; Cmnty Wkr; Bsbl; Letter Ftbl; College; Eng.

HARCLERODE, KRIS; La Brae Sr HS; Leavittsburg, OH; 7/180 Am Leg Aux Girls St; Hon Rl; Sec NHS; Rptr Sch Nwsp; JETS Awd; Ohio Schlrshp Team Test Taken In Chem; Univ; Bus Admin.

HARDACRE, CRYSTAL; Canton South HS; Canton, OH; Cls Rep Frsh Cls; Chrs; Chrh Wkr; Hon Rl; Lbry Ade; Off Ade; Sch Nwsp; Fr Clb; Pep Clb; Kent St Univ; CPA.

HARDAWAY, RICKIE; Central HS; Detroit, MI; Wayne St Univ; Chem.

HARDBARGER, JILL; Big Walnut HS; Galena, OH; 23/223 Band; Hon Rl; Yrbk; Mt Carmel Schl Of Nursing; RN.

HARDBARGER, ROBIN; Licking County Joint Voc HS; Newark, OH; 9/196 Hon Rl; NHS; OEA; College; Sec.

HARDEN, CHERYL; Shaw HS; E Cleveland, OH; Pres Jr Cls; Band; Hon Rl; Off Ade; OEA; College; Busns Admin.

HARDEN, JOSEPH G; Berea HS; Berea, OH; Am Leg Boys St; Debate Tm; Natl Forn Lg; NHS; Rptr Yrbk; Natl Merit SF; College.

HARDEN, PAM; Southern Local HS; Racine, OH; Chrs; Chrh Wkr; Hon Rl; Yth Flsp; Yrbk; Busns Schl; Busns.

HARDEN, RANDY; Haslett HS; Williamston, MI; 70/162 Letter Bsbl; Letter Bsktbl; Letter Ftbl; Letter Trk; Coach Actv; Tmr; College; Communications.

HARDEN, RUTH; Concord HS; Concord, MI; Band; Chrs; Sch Mus; Sch Pl; Stu Cncl; FHA; Jackson Comm College; Nursing.

HARDER, NOREEN; Washington HS; Massillon, OH; Cls Rep Sr Cls; Hon Rl; Jr NHS; NHS; Stu Cncl; Fr Clb; Lat Clb; Pep Clb; College; Nursing.

HARDER, SHELLY; Tuslaw HS; Massillon, OH; Band; Hon Rl; Jr NHS; Stu Cncl; Y-Teens; Pep Clb; Chrldng; X Ray Tech.

HARDESTY, ILANA; Hampshire HS; Augusta, WV; 2/212 Sal; Hon Rl; Jr NHS; NHS; Sch Pl; Sch Nwsp; Drama Clb; Harvard; Physics.

HARDESTY, KIMBERLY; Edgewood HS; Bloomington, IN; 60/250 Sec Frsh Cls; Sec Soph Cls; Band; Chrs; Chrh Wkr; FCA; Girl Scts; Sch Mus; Sch Pl; Stg Crw; Indiana Univ; Busns.

HARDESTY, THERESA J; Stow HS; Stow, OH; Band; Chrs; Cmnty Wkr; Girl Scts; Hon Rl; Jr NHS; PAVAS; Sch Mus; Lat Clb; Cit Awd; Kent St Univ; Geol.

HARDIEK, TERI; Fremont HS; Fremont, IN; 6/77 Pres Frsh Cls; Trs Jr Cls; Hon Rl; Rptr Sch Nwsp; Fr Clb; Bicentenial Essay Contest 1976; Univ; Psych.

HARDIES, KAREN; Goshen HS; Goshen, IN; Cls Rep Frsh Cls; Cl Rep Jr Cls; Cmnty Wkr; Hon Rl; Stu Cncl; Y-Teens; Letter Ten; Letter Chrldng; Univ.

HARDIN, DAWN; Upper Arlington HS; Columbus, OH; AFS; Chrs; Cmnty Wkr; Hon Rl; Rptr Sch Nwsp; Ger Clb; Pep Clb; Mat Maids; Scr Kpr; Tmr; Ohio St Univ; Bus Admin.

HARDIN, JIM; Negaunee HS; Negaunee, MI; Hon Rl; Bsktbl; Ten; Trk; Natl Merit Ltr; Mic Technological Univ; Engr.

HARDIN, REGINA; Magnolia HS; Matewan, WV; Band; Chrs; Hon Rl; NHS; Bsktbl; Trk; GAA; S West Virginia Cmnty Coll.

HARDIN, THOMAS; Central HS; Evansville, IN; Chrh Wkr; FCA; Hon Rl; MMM; Natl Forn Lg; Hanover; Foreign Languages.

HARDING, ALPHONSE; Evansville Day Schl; Evansville, IN; Trs Frsh Cls; Trs Soph Cls; Cl Rep Jr Cls; Trs Sr Cls; Hon Rl; Sch Mus; Sch Nwsp; Crs Cntry; Indiana AAU All St Swim Team 78; Indiana AAU Swimming Travel Team; Univ; Law.

HARDING, BARBARA; Zionsville Community HS; Zionsville, IN; 49/150 Girl Scts; Hon Rl; Indiana St Univ; Tchr.

HARDING, BONNIE K; Arsenal Technical HS; Indianapolis, IN; 7/625 Cmp Fr Grls; Chrs; Hon Rl; Sch Mus; Cit Awd; DAR Awd; 7.0 Avr Or Highr Grd Pt Avr 77 79; Spanish Awd Math Awd 77 79; Te Chr Contst Chrs 1st Ratng 78; Univ.

HARDING, CATHY; Lowell Sr HS; Lowell, IN; 49/272 VP Soph Cls; VP Jr Cls; Cls Rep Sr Cls; Hon Rl; Sch Mus; Stu Cncl; Drama Clb; 4-H; VICA; Letter Bsktbl; 4 H Indiana St Clothing Champion; 4 H Noble Awd; Lake Cnty Indian Trail Grange Achvmnt Awd; Purdue Univ; Youth Extension Agent.

HARDING, CHERYL; West Side HS; Gary, IN; 14/680 Trs Sr Cls; Hon Rl; Off Ade; Stu Cncl; FBLA; Sci Clb; Mat Maids; Scr Kpr; Tmr; Indiana Univ; Bus.

HARDING, ERIC; Unioto HS; Chillicothe, OH; 30/114 Am Leg Boys St; Boy Scts; FCA; Hon Rl; Letter Ftbl; College.

HARDING, JANE R; Garaway HS; Sugarcreek, OH; Am Leg Aux Girls St; Band; Chrh Wkr; Hon Rl; NHS; Off Ade; Yth Flsp; 4-H; FHA; Ger Clb; College; Nursing.

HARDING, JEANNE; Clearview HS; Lorain, OH; 1/97 Trs Sr Cls; Val; Am Leg Aux Girls St; VP Band; Hon Rl; NHS; Off Ade; Sch Pl; Yrbk; Drama Clb; Lorain Cty Community Coll; Sec Sci.

HARDING, JOHN G; Bristol Local HS; Bristolville, OH; Am Leg Boys St; Aud/Vis; Boy Scts; Hon Rl; NHS; Stg Crw; Bsktbl; Glf; Trk; College.

HARDING, MELODY; Concord HS; Hanover, MI; 8/95 VP Soph Cls; Am Leg Aux Girls St; Chrh Wkr; Hon Rl; Hosp Ade; NHS; Stu Cncl; Jackson Community College; Nursing.

HARDING, MICHAEL; Amelia HS; Cincinnati, OH; Hon Rl; Yrbk; IM Sprt; Military Service; Nuclear Power.

HARDMAN, BELINDA; Liberty HS; Clarksburg, WV; Chrs; Hon Rl; Off Ade; Y-Teens; Drama Clb; 4-H; Pep Clb; Spn Clb; Cmnty Coll; Music.

HARDMAN, CLARICE; Washington HS; Massillon, OH; Chrs; Hon Rl; Jr NHS; NHS; Sch Mus; Fr Clb; Pep Clb; Aultman Hosp Schl; Nursing.

HARDMAN, KAREN; Newbury HS; Chardon, OH; Chrs; Chrh Wkr; Hon Rl; Jr NHS; NHS; Sch Mus; Sch Pl; Drama Clb; Spn Clb; Univ; HS Eng Tchr.

HARDMAN, PAGE L; Charleston HS; Charleston, WV; Chrs; Hon Rl; JA; Off Ade; Stu Cncl; Yth Flsp; Y-Teens; Civ Clb; Drama Clb; Pep Clb; Libbey Owensford Natl Bicentennial Essay Contest 3rd Pl 1976; Amer Inst Foreign Study; DAR Hon Partic Awd; Univ Of Kentucky; Med.

HARDWICK, FRANK; Pennfield HS; Battle Creek, MI; Boy Scts; Pres JA; Sch Pl; JA Awd; Top 4% Of Mi Math Comp 78; KCC; Elec Engr.

HARDWICK, SUSAN; Washington HS; Massillon, OH; Am Leg Aux Girls St; Chrs; Hon Rl; Jr NHS; NHS; Sch Mus; Yth Flsp; Drama Clb; Lat Clb; Buckeye Girls St; Ohio Honors Chorale; Ohio All State Choir; Ohio St Univ; Law.

HARDWRICK, CYNTHIA; Highland Park Cmnty HS; Highland Pk, MI; Hon Rl; JA; Pep Clb; Univ Of Milwaukee; Psych.

HARDY, ELIZABETH; Oakwood HS; Dayton, OH; Chrs; Chrh Wkr; FCA; Girl Scts; Hon Rl; NHS; Stu Cncl; Y-Teens; College.

HARDY, FREDERICK; Southeastern HS; Detroit, MI; Pres Chrs; NHS; Pres Stu Cncl; OEA; Letter Ten; Cit Awd; Opt Clb Awd; Coll; Busns Admin.

HARDY, KEVIN D; Stonewall Jackson HS; Charleston, WV; Boy Scts; Chrs; Chrh Wkr; Hon Rl; Mdrgl; Stu Cncl; All County Chorus; All State Chorus; College; Music.

HARDY, LEIGH; Witko HS; Pierceton, IN; Aud/Vis; Boy Scts; Chrh Wkr; Drl Tm; Y-Teens; Boys Clb Am; Ger Clb; Letter Ftbl; Hockey; Trk; Coll; Agri.

HARDY, PAM; Hillsdale HS; Jeromesville, OH; 22/130 Sec Frsh Cls; Sec Sr Cls; Am Leg Aux Girls St; Yth Flsp; FHA; Lat Clb; Sci Clb; Bsbl; GAA; IM Sprt; North Cntrl Tech Univ; Rsprtry Ther.

HARDY, PHILIP D; North HS; Youngstown, OH; 9/115 Cl Rep Jr Cls; Cls Rep Sr Cls; Hon Rl; NHS; Sch Pl; Drama Clb; Letter Bsktbl; Capt Ftbl; Letter Trk; Univ Of Pittsburg; Engr.

HARDY, TERRY; Fremont HS; Fremont, MI; 8/238 Cls Rep Sr Cls; Band; Hon Rl; NHS; Orch; Pol Wkr; Sch Pl; Stu Cncl; Ger Clb; Letter Bsbl; Gerber Baby Food Fund Schlrshp 79; Mi Competitive Schlrshp 79; Michigan St Univ; Chem Engr.

HARE, JANE; Howland HS; Warren, OH; 10/400 Sec Soph Cls; Cls Rep Sr Cls; Band; Hon Rl; Natl Forn Lg; NHS; Stu Cncl; Y-Teens; Ed Yrbk; Ed Sch Nwsp; Kent St Univ; Radio TV Brdcstng.

HARE, JOHN M; Carmel HS; Carmel, IN; 112/678 Cls Rep Frsh Cls; Cls Rep Soph Cls; Cl Rep Jr Cls; Cls Rep Sr Cls; Hon Rl; NHS; Lat Clb; Ftbl; Trk; C of C Awd; 3rd Pl IN St Bench Press Contest 79; 3rd Pl IN Best Built HS Boy 78; Mbr Of St Champ AAA Ftbl Team 78; Purdue Univ; Engr.

HARE, NANCY; Alexander HS; Athens, OH; 4/142 VP Frsh Cls; Band; Chrh Wkr; Cmnty Wkr; Drl Tm; Hon Rl; NHS; Rptr Yrbk; Spn Clb; Warren Wilson Coll; Elem Ed.

HARGER, JULIE; Port Clinton HS; Pt Clinton, OH; Cls Rep Sr Cls; Chrs; Hosp Ade; Stu Cncl; Fr Clb; Swmmng; GAA; Tmr; Bauder Of Atlanta; Fshn Merch.

HARGER, KIMBERLEY; Buckeye Valley HS; Delaware, OH; Cmp Fr Grls; Girl Scts; Hon Rl; Yth Flsp; IM Sprt; College; Psych.

HARGER, KIRK; Munising HS; Munising, MI; Band; Hon Rl; Sct Actv; Stg Crw; Capt Crs Cntry; Capt Trk; Univ; Wildlife.

HARGETT, ANITA; Crothersville HS; Crothersville, IN; 12/80 Sec Frsh Cls; Band; Chrh Wkr; Drl Tm; FCA; Hon Rl; Off Ade; Yth Flsp; Bsktbl; Trk; Computer Programing.

HARGETT, DIANE; Southeast HS; Rootstown, OH; Chrs; Chrh Wkr; Hon Rl; Rptr Sch Nwsp; Pep Clb; Am Leg Awd; Malone Coll; Soc Work.

HARGETT, RAYMOND; Glen Este HS; Cincinnati, OH; Hon Rl; NHS; Sch Mus; Miami Univ; Jrnlsm.

HARGIS, RICK; West Vigo HS; W Terre Haute, IN; 1/193 Trs Frsh Cls; Trs Sr Cls; Val; FCA; Mod UN; Natl Forn Lg; NHS; Off Ade; Pres Stu Cncl; Drama Clb; Purdue Univ; Comp Sci.

HARGITT, MACY; Ben Davis HS; Indianapolis, IN; 45/864 FCA; NHS; Spn Clb; Capt Gym; Swmmng; Trk; Univ Of New Mexico; Teacher.

HARGO, TARAH; Madison Comprehensive HS; Mansfield, OH; Band; JA; Sch Pl; Stu Cncl; Rptr Sch Nwsp; Fr Clb; Trk; JA Awd; Opt Clb Awd; Jr Achvmnt Miss J A Of Ohio Keynote Spkr 78 79; Church 1st Pl Wnr Oratorical Cntst 78; French 1st Runner Up; Univ; Radio & TV Brdcstng.

HARIG, SUZAN; South Dearborn HS; Sunman, IN; 89/225 Band; Girl Scts; Hon Rl;.

HARING, STEVE; Mansfield Christian HS; Bellville, OH; Cls Rep Sr Cls; Chrs; Capt Socr; Judson College.

HARIS, DAPHINE; Monrovia HS; Mooresville, IN; Cls Rep Frsh Cls; Cls Rep Soph Cls; Cl Rep Jr Cls; Hon Rl; Sch Pl; Stu Cncl; Spn Clb; Letter Gym; Letter Trk; GAA; Gym Most Dedicated Awd 78; Gym MVP Awd 79; Univ; Acctg.

HARKENRIDER, KRISTI; Bishop Dwenger HS; Ft Wayne, IN; Trs Sr Cls; Chrh Wkr; Cmnty Wkr; Hon Rl; Ger Clb; Letter Ten; Trk; Biology Schlrshp Jeff Walker Mem Awd; German Awd; Typing Awd; College; Banking.

HARKER, PENNY; Zane Trace HS; Chillicothe, OH; 6/95 Pres Soph Cls; Hon Rl; Sch Pl; Yth Flsp; Drama Clb; FHA; Pep Clb; Sci Clb; Spn Clb; DAR Awd; Natl Hon Soc 1977; Otterbein Coll; Pre Med.

HARKINS, EILEEN; Our Lady Of Mercy HS; Farmington, MI; Chrh Wkr; Hon Rl; Off Ade; Stu Cncl; Yrbk; Spn Clb; Bsktbl; Scndry Educ.

HARKNESS, GERALD A; Lumen Christi HS; Jackson, MI; Boy Scts; Letter Ftbl; Letter Hockey; Univ; Lib Arts.

HARLAN, TERRI; Fremont Ross HS; Fremont, OH; 50/500 Cls Rep Sr Cls; Band; Cmp Fr Grls; Hon Rl; JA; Jr NHS; NHS; Stu Cncl; FHA; Capt Pom Pon; Voc Schl; Cosmetology.

HARLESS, DAVID; Greenville Sr HS; Greenville, OH; 25/380 Chrh Wkr; Hon Rl; Drama Clb; Treas Sci Clb; Spn Clb; Coll; Elec Engr.

HARLESS JR, JIM; Jackson HS; Jackson, OH; 30/240 Cl Rep Jr Cls; Aud/Vis; Boy Scts; Hon Rl; NHS; Rptr Sch Nwsp; Lat Clb; Pep Clb; Sci Clb; College; Architect.

HARLEY, JOHN; Monongah HS; Idamay, WV; Hon Rl; Bsktbl; Letter Ftbl; Trk; Coll.

HARLOS, JEAN A; Lebanon HS; Lebanon, IN; 8/265 Am Leg Aux Girls St; Chrs; Girl Scts; Hon Rl; Off Ade; Sch Mus; Stg Crw; Yrbk; 4-H; Pep Clb; Bauder Coll; Fashion Mdse.

HARLOW, DALE; Lockland HS; Cincinnati, OH; 7/70 Trs Soph Cls; Band; Chrh Wkr; Hon Rl; NHS; Yth Flsp; Letter Bsbl; Letter Ftbl; Letter Trk; Letter Wrstlng; Univ Of Cincinnati; Acctg.

HARLOW, JEFF; Maumee HS; Maumee, OH; 42/315 Hon Rl; Bsktbl; Ten; Toledo Univ; Comp Progr.

HARLOW, KEVIN; Fulton HS; Perrinton, MI; Band; Boy Scts; Hon Rl; Boys Clb Am; 4-H; Mth Clb; Ferr is State Coll.

HARM, CAROL; Lutheran HS East; Detroit, MI; Cls Rep Soph Cls; Chrs; Hon Rl; Off Ade; Sct Actv; Rptr Sch Nwsp; Lat Clb; Pep Clb; Scr Kpr; Michigan St Univ; Bus Mktng.

HARMAN, DEBORAH; Farmington HS; Farmington, MI; Cls Rep Frsh Cls; Pres Soph Cls; Hon Rl; JA; Stu Cncl; JA Awd; Kalamazoo College; Psych.

HARMAN, GINA; Belpre HS; Belpre, OH; Band; Girl Scts; Hon Rl; Rptr Yrbk; Twrlr; Pres Awd; Parkersburg Comm College; Bus Admin.

HARMAN, REBECCA; Portsmouth East HS; Sciotoville, OH; 4/81 Chrh Wkr; Hon Rl; Hosp Ade; Jr NHS; Lbry Ade; VP NHS; Fr Clb; Sec FTA; Pep Clb; Voice Dem Awd; Olivet Nazarene Coll; Nursing.

HARMAN, RHONDA; South Central HS; Wanatah, IN; Hon Rl; NHS; Letter Bsktbl; Letter Trk; College; Athletic Training.

HARMAN, RICK; Warsaw Community HS; Claypool, IN; Boy Scts; Chrs; Chrh Wkr; Debate Tm; Natl Forn Lg; 4-H; Da Lite Screen Schskhp Aw; Bell Howell Univ; Aero Engr.

HARMAN, SHERRY; Princeton HS; Princeton, WV; 18/347 Chrh Wkr; Hon Rl; Lbry Ade; Sec NHS; Yth Flsp; Pres Fr Clb; Treas Keyettes; Concord College; Elem Educ.

HARMER, GWENDOLYN; Lincoln HS; Shinnston, WV; Trs Jr Cls; Am Leg Aux Girls St; Band; Drm Mjrt; Hon Rl; Jr NHS; NHS; Stu Cncl; Sec Fr Clb; Pep Clb; Univ.

HARMEYER, JACKIE; Reading Community HS; Reading, OH; 75/210 Band; Hon Rl; Lbry Ade; Pep Clb; Spn Clb; Wrstlng; Mat Maids; Tmr; Univ Of Cincinniti; Pharm.

HARMON, ANNA; Big Creek HS; Warriormines, WV; Hon Rl; Lbry Ade; FHA; Pep Clb; Sci Clb; Chrldng; Concord Coll; Bus.

HARMON, B; Hastings HS; Hastings, MI; Band; Hon Rl; NHS; Trk; Olivet Nazarene Coll; Acctg.

HARMON, CYNTHIA; Arcanum HS; Greenville, OH; Cls Rep Frsh Cls; Chrs; Off Ade; Yrbk; College; Math.

HARMON, GARY; Ida HS; Monroe, MI; 4/135 Pres Frsh Cls; Chrh Wkr; Hon Rl; NHS; Yth Flsp; IM Sprt; Univ Of Michigan; Pre Med.

HARMON, KAREN; Champion HS; Warren, OH; Hon Rl; NHS; Off Ade; Stg Crw; Yrbk; Scr Kpr; Kent State Branch; Acct.

HARMON, KEVIN; Mather HS; Au Train, MI; Band; Hon Rl; Letter Ftbl; Capt Trk; IM Sprt; Northern Michigan Univ.

HARMON, PAMELA; Marion Franklin HS; Columbus, OH; 29/312 Chrs; Drl Tm; Hon Rl; Off Ade; Stu Cncl; OEA; Pom Pon; Ohio St Univ; Elem Ed.

HARMON, TAMMY; Waldron HS; Waldron, MI; 1/50 Trs Frsh Cls; Trs Soph Cls; Trs Jr Cls; Band; Hon Rl; NHS; Sch Pl; Spn Clb; GAA; Mgrs; Phys Ed Awd; Treasurers Awd;.

HARMS, ARTHUR; Merrillville HS; Merrillville, IN; 42/642 NHS; Coll; Med.

HARMS, NOREEN; Chippewa Valley HS; Mt Clemens, MI; Sec Chrh Wkr; Hon Rl; NHS; College.

HARNER, DIANNE; La Porte HS; La Porte, IN; 11/500 MMM; Orch; Pol Wkr; Sch Mus; Ed Sch Nwsp; 4-H; Fr Clb; Pep Clb; Cert Of Academic Excellence; College; Comp Sci.

HARNER, DIANNE; Laporte HS; La Porte, IN; Cmnty Wkr; Hon Rl; MMM; Sec NHS; Orch; Pol Wkr; Treas 4-H; Fr Clb; GAA; IM Sprt; College; Bus.

HARNETT, MARY BETH; Archbishop Alter HS; Kettering, OH; 16/289 Cls Rep Soph Cls; Cl Rep Jr Cls; Drl Tm; Hon Rl; NHS; Stu Cncl; Rptr Sch Nwsp; Sec Drama Clb; Fr Clb; Miami Univ; Communications.

HAROLD, DEEDREA; Spencer HS; Newton, WV; Chrh Wkr; Cmnty Wkr; Debate Tm; Hon Rl; Jr NHS; Off Ade; Sec FFA; IM Sprt; Glenville St Coll; Agri.

HARP, TERRI; Jefferson Sr HS; Delphos, OH; 2/12 0 Am Leg Aux Girls St; Band; Chrs; Hon Rl; NHS; Sch Mus; Sch Pl; Stu Cncl; Y-Teens; Leo Clb; Lima Tech Coll; Comp Progr.

HARP, TERRI; Delphos Jefferson HS; Delphos, OH; 2/120 Am Leg Aux Girls St; Band; Chrs; Hon Rl; NHS; Sch Pl; Stu Cncl; Y-Teens; Leo Clb; Sci Clb; Lima Tech Coll; Comp Progr.

HARP, TODD; Talawanda HS; Oxford, OH; Boy Scts; Hon Rl; Jr NHS; Key Clb; Crs Cntry; Trk; Miami Univ; Officer U S Navy.

HARPER, ANGLEA; Walton HS; Walton, WV; VP Soph Cls; Sec Jr Cls; Trs Jr Cls; Am Leg Aux Girls St; Hon Rl; Jr NHS; Sec NHS; Sch Pl; Marshall Univ; Art Educ.

HARPER, BOB; Norwood HS; Norwood, OH; 130/345 Am Leg Boys St; Chrh Wkr; Pol Wkr; Sec Lat Clb; Letter Ftbl; Letter Trk; Natl Merit Ltr; Univ; Pre Med.

HARPER, BRIDGETTE; Whitko HS; S Whitley, IN; Chrs; Chrh Wkr; Hon Rl; Lbry Ade; Off Ade; Drama Clb; OEA; Bus Schl; Exec Sec.

HARPER, BRIGETTE; Whitko HS; So Whitley, IN; Chrs; Chrh Wkr; Hon Rl; Lbry Ade; OEA;.

HARPER, CENETHIA; Kettering HS; Detroit, MI; Chrh Wkr; Hon Rl; Jr NHS; Bsktbl; Cit Awd; Univ; Pediatrics.

HARPER, CYNTHIA S; Rock Hill Sr HS; Pedro, OH; Cls Rep Frsh Cls; Sec Soph Cls; Trs Jr Cls; Cl Rep Jr Cls; Hon Rl; Stu Cncl; Spn Clb; Bus Schl; Legal Sec.

HARPER, ELIZABETH A; Circleville HS; Riverton, WV; 8/30 Sec Frsh Cls; Cls Rep Frsh Cls; Sec Soph Cls; Cls Rep Soph Cls; Sec Jr Cls; Cls Rep Sr Cls; Band; Chrs; Chrh Wkr; Hon Rl; South Branch Voc Ctr; Bus.

HARPER, FREDERICK B; Seaholm HS; Birmingham, MI; Aud/Vis; Band; Boy Scts; Hon Rl; Mod UN; Fr Clb; Cit Awd; Natl Merit SF; Cornell Univ; Engr.

HARPER, JEFFREY; Carrollton HS; Carrollton, OH; Pres Chrs; Chrh Wkr; Treas FCA; Hon Rl; NHS; Sch Mus; VP Stu Cncl; Letter Bsbl; Letter Bsktbl; Muskingum College; Communications.

HARPER, KIM; Our Lady Of The Lakes HS; Ortonville, MI; 16/47 Hon Rl; Lbry Ade; NHS; Off Ade; Red Cr Ade; Rptr Yrbk; Fr Clb; Chrldng; PPFtbl; Central Michigan Univ; Bus Admin.

HARPER, LYNN; Moorefield HS; Moorefield, WV; Cls Rep Frsh Cls; Cls Rep Soph Cls; Cl Rep Jr Cls; Am Leg Aux Girls St; Chrh Wkr; Hon Rl; Jr NHS; NHS; Sch Pl; Stu Cncl; Adv Placement Progr At Cncl Univ 79; Univ; Anim Sci.

HARPER, PAM; Centerville HS; Centerville, OH; 27/687 Hon Rl; NHS; Pep Clb; Capt Chrldng; PPFtbl; Bowling Green St Univ; Intntl Bus.

HARPER, RANDALL; South Harrison HS; Lost Creek, WV; Band; Chrs; Chrh Wkr; Lbry Ade; Sch Pl; Yth Flsp; Fr Clb; Mgrs; Creative Writing Awd Womans Club; Stu Action In Ed Club; Theology Club Pres 78 79 Sec 77; Alderson Broaddus Coll.

HARPER, RICHARD; Western Reserve HS; Collins, OH; Band; Boy Scts; Hon Rl; Yth Flsp; Ftbl; Voc Schl; Elec.

HARPER, ROBERT; West Side HS; Gary, IN; 58/650 Cls Rep Sr Cls; Hon Rl; NHS; Ftbl; Wrstlng; Coach Actv; Sc State College; Bus Admin.

HARPER, ROSEMARY; Mt Healthy HS; Cincinnati, OH; 1/470 Val; Band; Chrh Wkr; Hon Rl; NHS; Beta Clb; Fr Clb; Edgecliff Coll; Poli Sci.

HARPER, SCOTT; Fountain Central HS; Veedersburg, IN; 8/106 Cls Rep Frsh Cls; Cls Rep Soph Cls; Cl Rep Jr Cls; Cls Rep Sr Cls; Am Leg Boys St; Band; Boy Scts; FCA; Hon Rl; Mod UN; Ball St Univ; Bus.

HARPER, SHARON; Northern Sr HS; Detroit, MI; Cmnty Wkr; Girl Scts; Hon Rl; Stu Cncl; DECA; FTA; Bsktbl; Trk; Cit Awd; 4-H Awd; Alcorn St Univ; Food Serv.

HARPER, STEPHANIE; Tri Valley HS; Dresden, OH; 13/216 Sec Soph Cls; Sec Jr Cls; Cls Rep Sr Cls; Y-Teens; Hon Rl; Pres NHS; Sch Pl; Stg Crw; Stu Cncl; Pres Drama Clb; Ohio State Univ; Child Psych.

HARPER, STEVEN; Creston HS; Grand Rpds, MI; Band; Hon Rl; Jr NHS; Wrstlng; Natl Merit Ltr; Univ.

HARPER, VALERIE M; New Palestine HS; Finley, IN; Sec Soph Cls; Sec Jr Cls; Sec Sr Cls; Drl Tm; Hon Rl; Stg Crw; Yrbk; 4-H; Pep Clb; Spn Clb; Engr.

HARPER, VINCENT P; Lawrence North HS; Indianapolis, IN; Cmnty Wkr; FCA; Hon Rl; Pol Wkr; Quill & Scroll; Sprt Ed Sch Nwsp; Sch Nwsp; Bsktbl; Letter Ftbl; Letter Trk; Butler Univ; Journalism.

HARPEST, ROSALIE; Greenville Sr HS; Greenville, OH; 61/320 Chrh Wkr; Hon Rl; Off Ade; Yth Flsp; Rptr Sch Nwsp; Sch Nwsp; Fr Clb; OEA; Pres Of Coop Off Educ Club 78; Church Organist & Pianist 79; Soloist 79; Fort Wayne Bible Coll; Clerical Wrk.

HARPOLD, PATTI; Montezuma HS; Rockville, IN; 2/32 Trs Jr Cls; Sal; Chrs; Drm Mjrt; Hon Rl; Yrbk; 4-H; FHA; Pep Clb; Bsktbl; Voc Schl; Beautician.

HARPRING, JULIE A; Seton HS; Cincinnati, OH; 18/255 Pres Soph Cls; Girl Scts; Hon Rl; NHS; Sch Pl; Sct Actv; Stg Crw; Stu Cncl; Pep Clb; Spn Clb; College; Sci.

HARPSTER, DAYNA; Huron HS; Huron, OH; 3/220 Cls Rep Soph Cls; Cl Rep Jr Cls; Cls Rep Sr Cls; Chrh Wkr; Cmnty Wkr; Hon Rl; NHS; Sec Stu Cncl; Chrldng; Mgrs; Miami Univ Of Ohio; Pre Law.

HARR, J; Lumen Christi HS; Jackson, MI; Pep Clb; IM Sprt; Univ; Bus.

HARRAND, LINDA; Imlay City HS; Imlay City, MI; Cmp Fr Grls; Hon Rl; Rptr Yrbk; 4-H; Fr Clb; Sci Clb; Bsbl; IM Sprt; 4-H Awd; College; Bio Sci.

HARREL, MARYJANE; Jackson HS; Jackson, OH; 60/250 Chrs; Chrh Wkr; Rptr Yrbk; FHA; OEA; Pep Clb; College; Sec.

HARRELL, BRENDA; London HS; London, OH; Cmp Fr Grls; Hon Rl; Hosp Ade; Jr NHS; Univ; Acctg.

HARRELL, DAVID; Northfield HS; Wabash, IN; Hon Rl; VICA; Ftbl; Hon Roll 78 & 79; Perfct Attndnc 79; Ivy Tech Voc Schl; Tool Maker.

HARRELL, JERRY; Warsaw Cmnty HS; Warsaw, IN; 63/394 Band; Hon Rl; Yth Flsp; Y-Teens; Sch Nwsp; Swmmng; Mgrs; Tmr; Univ.

HARRELL, TERRI; Mt Healthy HS; Mt Healthy, OH; 110/522 Cls Rep Frsh Cls; Drl Tm; Hon Rl; Lbry Ade; Off Ade; Pep Clb; GAA; Univ Miami;comp Progr.

HARRIETT, JEANNETTE; Howland HS; Warren, OH; 8/418 Hon Rl; Y-Teens; Pep Clb; Univ.

HARRIGAN, DIANA; Taylor Center HS; Taylor, MI; 6/400 Am Leg Aux Girls St; Hon Rl; NHS; Ed Yrbk; Chrldng; Mgrs; PPFtbl; Scr Kpr; Tmr; Univ Of Michigan; Phys Ther.

HARRIGAN, MOLLY; Midland HS; Midland, MI; Hon Rl; Swmmng; Trk; Northern Mich; Physical Ed.

HARRIMAN, KELLY; Mount Clemens HS; Mt Clemeb, MI; Pres Frsh Cls; Cl Rep Jr Cls; Cls Rep Sr Cls; Chrs; Hon Rl; Jr NHS; NHS; Rptr Sch Nwsp; Sch Nwsp; DAR Awd; College; Journalist.

HARRING, RAYMOND; North Adams HS; Hillsdale, MI; Hon Rl; Stg Crw; Drama Clb; Ftbl; Trk; Univ; Electrician.

HARRINGTON, CAROL; Richmond Sr HS; Richmond, IN; 171/628 FCA; Hon Rl; Off Ade; Letter Ten; Arizona St Univ; Bus.

HARRINGTON, JANICE; Theodore Roosevelt HS; Kent, OH; Cls Rep Frsh Cls; Band; Cmp Fr Grls; Chrs; Chrh Wkr; Cmnty Wkr; Drl Tm; Hon Rl; Orch; Sch Mus; Schlrshp Awd; Part Of Group Which Broke Guinness Bok Record For Twirling; Various St & Natl Twirling Awds; College; Psych.

HARRINGTON, JEFFREY; St Francis De Sales HS; Toledo, OH; 10/200 Cls Rep Frsh Cls; Chrs; Chrh Wkr; Debate Tm; Hon Rl; Natl Forn Lg; NHS; Sch Mus; Stg Crw; Stu Cncl; College; Journalism.

HARRINGTON, KIM; Newbury HS; Novelty, OH; Sec Frsh Cls; Pres Soph Cls; Cl Rep Jr Cls; Pres Chrs; Sch Mus; Sch Pl; Drama Clb; Ger Clb; Letter Crs Cntry; Letter Trk; Univ; Drama.

HARRINGTON, LORI; Camden Frontier HS; Camden, MI; 1/43 Trs Frsh Cls; Band; Chrs; Hon Rl; NHS; Sch Pl; Yth Flsp; Rptr Sch Nwsp; Sec Fr Clb; Trk; Oral Roberts Univ; Music.

HARRINGTON, ROBERT; Michigan Lutheran Seminary; Adrian, MI; 22/62 Cls Rep Sr Cls; Chrs; Chrh Wkr; Hon Rl; Sch Pl; Drama Clb; Bsbl; Ftbl; Glf; IM Sprt; Northwestern College; Ministerial.

HARRINGTON, SUSAN; Canfield HS; Canfield, OH; 47/256 Band; Hon Rl; Lit Mag; Stg Crw; Rptr Sch Nwsp; Fr Clb; Univ; Bus Admin.

HARRINGTON, TONY; Anderson HS; Anderson, IN;

HARRIOTT, DAN; Britton Macon Area HS; Britton, MI; Hon Rl; Rptr Yrbk; Sci Clb; Bsktbl;.

HARRIS, ALAN; Cuyahoga Falls HS; Cuyahoga Fls, OH; 21/731 Hon Rl; Jr NHS; NHS; Capt IM Sprt; Rotary Schoolar 2 Yrs 78; J V Bsktbl 78; Cert In CPR 79; Univ Of Akron; Engr.

HARRIS, ALAN; Cardington Lincoln HS; Cardington, OH; Cls Rep Soph Cls; Cl Rep Jr Cls; VP Band; Chrh Wkr; Hon Rl; VP NHS; Sch Pl; Stg Crw; VP Stu Cncl; Treas FFA; Ohio State Univ; Production Ag.

HARRIS, ANGIE; Cardinal Stritch HS; Toledo, OH; 11/215 Pres Frsh Cls; Pres Soph Cls; Pres Jr Cls; VP Sr Cls; Band; Hon Rl; NHS; Off Ade; Red Cr Ade; Sch Mus; Lions Store Teen Board; Univ Of Toledo; Legal Sec.

HARRIS, APRIL; Yellow Springs HS; Yellow Sprg, OH; Chrs; Chrh Wkr; Letter Trk; Chrldng; Coll.

HARRIS, ARVANDERS; John Hay HS; Cleveland, OH; Cmp Fr Grls; Girl Scts; Hon Rl; Off Ade; Pom Pon; Air Force; Elec Engr.

HARRIS, BARBARA; Johnstown HS; Johnstown, OH; 30/140 Band; Chrs; Cmnty Wkr; Hon Rl; Off Ade; Orch; Pol Wkr; Sch Mus; Mat Maids; Scr Kpr; Findlay College; Social Work.

HARRIS, BECKY; N Vigo HS; Terre Haute, IN; Cls Rep Soph Cls; Cl Rep Jr Cls; Chrs; Drl Tm; Hon Rl; Stu Cncl; Y-Teens; Pom Pon; Twrlr; Natl Order Of Jobs Daughters; College; Cosmetology.

HARRIS, BERNARD; South HS; Youngstown, OH; 5/327 Band; Boy Scts; Chrh Wkr; Debate Tm; Hon Rl; Yth Flsp; Boys Clb Am; Trk; Scr Kpr; Plane Geometry Awd; Ohio State Univ; Medicine.

HARRIS, BEVERLY; Benzie Central HS; Beulah, MI; Hon Rl; Good Citizenship Awd;.

HARRIS, BILL; Ursuline HS; Girard, OH; Cls Rep Soph Cls; Stu Cncl; Spn Clb; Wrstlng; Scr Kpr; Marines.

HARRIS, BRIDGETTE; Jane Addams Voc HS; E Cleveland, OH; Cmp Fr Grls; JA; Sch Pl; Cit Awd;.

HARRIS, CAMILLE A; Osborn HS; Detroit, MI; Cmnty Wkr; Drl Tm; Hon Rl; NHS; Off Ade; ROTC; Drama Clb; Spn Clb; Ten; Trk; Superio Jr Cadet Medal ROTC; Expert Marksmanship Badge ROTC; Best Female Cadet Placque ROTC Summer Camp; College; Wildlife Conservation.

HARRIS, CATHERINE; St Joseph HS; Lakewille, IN; Chrs; Drl Tm; Hon Rl; Pres 4-H; Ger Clb; 4-H Awd; Coll.

HARRIS, CHARLES; Parkersburg HS; Parkersburg, WV; Boy Scts; Hon Rl; Pol Wkr; Letter Bsktbl; Glf; IM Sprt; Elk Awd; Univ; Poli Sci.

HARRIS, CHERYL; Bexley HS; Bexley, OH; Chrh Wkr; Drl Tm; Off Ade; Orch; Sch Mus; Stg Crw; VP Yth Flsp; GAA; Pom Pon; Vocational School.

HARRIS, CHERYL; Southern Wells Jr Sr HS; Bluffton, IN; 17/88 Sec Sr Cls; Chrs; Hon Rl; NHS; Off Ade; 4-H; Pep Clb; Ball St Univ; Bus Admin.

HARRIS, CHERYL; Brown County HS; Nineveh, IN; 11/149 Letter Bsktbl; Ten; Letter Trk; IM Sprt; Franklin College; Math.

HARRIS, CRAIG L; Grand Ledge Academy; Napoleon, MI; Pres Jr Cls; Chrs; Chrh Wkr; Hon Rl; Yrbk; IM Sprt;.

HARRIS, CYNTHIA E; North Montgomery HS; Crawfordsville, IN; 6/205 Band; Cmnty Wkr; Hosp Ade; Jr NHS; NHS; Yth Flsp; Ger Clb; Mgrs; Natl Merit SF; College; Pediatrician.

HARRIS, DAN; Highland HS; Marengo, OH; 12/130 NHS; Sch Mus; Pres 4-H; Bsktbl; Capt Ftbl; Trk; Wrstlng; Am Leg Awd; College; Industrial Art.

HARRIS, DEBBIE; Wirt Cnty HS; Elizabeth, WV; Band; Drm Bgl; Girl Scts; Hon Rl; Y-Teens; 4-H; Pres FTA; Letter Bsktbl; GAA; PPFtbl; Mountain St Coll; Stenographer.

HARRIS, DEBORAH; Galion HS; Galion, OH; Girl Scts; Hon Rl; Treas JA; NHS; Off Ade; Treas Pep Clb; God Cntry Awd; Ohio State Univ; Elem Tchr.

HARRIS, DEBRA; Arsenal Tech HS; Indianapolis, IN; 42/657 Chrs; Chrh Wkr; Hon Rl; Ger Clb; Mth Clb; Gov Hon Prg Awd; Marian College; Secondary Special Ed.

HARRIS, DENISE; Berrien Spgs HS; Berrien Spgs, MI; 34/141 Hon Rl; Off Ade; Rptr Yrbk; Ger Clb; Trk; Lake Michigan Coll; Bus.

HARRIS, DIANNA; Olivet HS; Olivet, MI; Chrh Wkr; Hon Rl; 4-H; FHA; Scr Kpr; 4-H Awd; Lansing Comm College; Legal Sec.

HARRIS, DONNA; Ecorse HS; Ecorse, MI; Band; Hon Rl; Chrldng; Twrlr; Wayne St Univ; Nursing.

HARRIS, E STEVEN; Westfall HS; Mt Sterling, OH; Sec Frsh Cls; Band; Chrs; Orch; Sch Mus; Sch Pl; 4-H; Ohi St Univ; Music Educ.

HARRIS, EVELYN; Roosevelt HS; Gary, IN; Band; Sch Mus; Indiana Bloomington Univ; Poli Sci.

HARRIS, FELICIA A; Murray Wright HS; Detroit, MI; VP Jr Cls; VP Sr Cls; Cmnty Wkr; Hon Rl; Jr NHS; Stu Cncl; Chrldng; Am Leg Awd; Natl Honor Soc; W J I B Soul Teen Reporter; Michigan St Univ; Computer Sci.

HARRIS, GARY; John Glenn HS; Westland, MI; Band; Hon Rl; Univ; Geography.

HARRIS, GERALDINE; East Tech HS; Cleveland, OH; Lbry Ade; Off Ade; Cit Awd; Ashland Coll; Drama.

HARRIS, GREG; Cuyahoga Falls HS; Cuyahoga Falls, OH; Band; Chrs; Cmnty Wkr; Hon Rl; Orch; Sch Mus; IM Sprt; Bst Trng Sqd Awd Mrchng Band 1976; Bst New Bandsman Awd 1976; Most Outstndng Bandsman Awd 1978; Univ Of Cinncinati; Music.

HARRIS, GREG; Terre Haute North Vigo HS; Terre Haute, IN; Band; Chrh Wkr; Hon Rl; Stu Cncl; Rptr Sch Nwsp; VP DECA; Mgrs; 4-H Awd; Natl Merit Ltr; Fith Pl Awd In Food Serv Are Of DECA 1979; Univ; Bus.

HARRIS, HUBERT D; Saginaw HS; Saginaw, MI; 13/331 Band; Chrh Wkr; Cmnty Wkr; Hon Rl; NHS; Sch Nwsp; 4-H; Crs Cntry; Michigan St Univ; Fin Admin.

HARRIS, JACKIE; Patterson Coop HS; Dayton, OH; Cls Rep Frsh Cls; Cls Rep Soph Cls; Cl Rep Jr Cls; Chrs; OEA; Letter Chrldng; Coach Actv; Coll; Law.

HARRIS, JACQUELINE; Marian HS; Cincinnati, OH; Sec Jr Cls; Cl Rep Jr Cls; Pres Sr Cls; Girl Scts; Hon Rl; Jr NHS; NHS; Yrbk; IM Sprt; Coll.

HARRIS, JAVONNE; Northern HS; Detroit, MI; Chrs; Cmnty Wkr; Hon Rl; NHS; Sch Mus; Bsbl; Bsktbl; GAA; Cit Awd; Schlrshp For High Point Avg 77 & 78; Recvd Hon Awd 77; Michigan St Univ; Psych.

HARRIS, JEFF; W H Harrison HS; W Lafayette, IN; 41/308 Boy Scts; Natl Forn Lg; Sch Pl; Yth Flsp; Rptr Yrbk; Drama Clb; College; Med.

HARRIS, JEFF; Jeffrey Duane Leroy Harris; Muskegon, MI; Band; Boy Scts; Chrs; Hon Rl; Orch; Sch Mus; Sch Pl; Letter Bsbl; Letter Ftbl; Muskegon Community Coll; Arch.

HARRIS, JEFF; Seaholm HS; Birmingham, MI; 64/654 Cls Rep Frsh Cls; Cls Rep Sr Cls; NHS; Letter Bsbl; Letter Bsktbl; Letter Ftbl; Letter Trk; Coach Actv; Natl Merit Schl; Univ Of Michigan; Law.

HARRIS, JEFFREY L; Moeller HS; Silverton, OH; 65/280 Band; Hon Rl; JA; Jr NHS; Lit Mag; Crs Cntry; Ken State; Bio.

HARRIS, JESSE; Walnut Hills HS; Cincinnati, OH; Chrh Wkr; Cmnty Wkr; Hon Rl; Civ Clb; Bsktbl; Math.

HARRIS, JO; Oceana HS; Clear Fork, WV; Trs Soph Cls; Cmp Fr Grls; Chrh Wkr; Debate Tm; Hon Rl; Off Ade; Pol Wkr; Pep Clb; Spn Clb; Marshall Univ; Math.

HARRIS, JUDY; Tecumseh HS; Tecumseh, MI; Band; Hon Rl; NHS; Spn Clb; Letter Gym; Letter Chrldng; College; Nursing.

HARRIS, KEITH L; Lancaster HS; Lancaster, OH; 18/567 Cls Rep Sr Cls; Pres Band; Boy Scts; Chrh Wkr; Debate Tm; Hon Rl; Jr NHS; Lit Mag; Natl Forn Lg; Pres NHS; Purdue Univ; Mech Engr.

HARRIS, KELLE; Northwest HS; Indianapolis, IN; 4/450 Am Leg Aux Girls St; Hon Rl; Hosp Ade; Lit Mag; NHS; Quill & Scroll; Ed Sch Nwsp; IM Sprt; NCTE; Natl Merit Schl; Wellesley Coll; Eng.

HARRIS, KEVIN; Meadow Bridge HS; Elton, WV; 3/61 Hon Rl; VP NHS; Sch Pl; Yrbk; Sec Fr Clb; West Virginia Univ.

HARRIS, KEVIN; Jewett Scio HS; Jewett, OH; 7/78 Band; Boy Scts; Hon Rl; Rptr Yrbk; 4-H; Spn Clb; 4-H Awd; College; Bus Admin.

HARRIS, KIMBERLEE; Morgantown HS; Morgantwn, WV; Chrh Wkr; Hon Rl; NHS; Pres Yth Flsp; Mth Clb; College; Petroleum Engr.

HARRIS, LANNY L; Henry Ford II HS; Sterling Hghts, MI; 46/473 Band; Chrs; Chrh Wkr; Hon Rl; NHS; Sch Mus; Sch Pl; Evangel Coll; Music.

HARRIS, LIBBY; North Central HS; Indpls, IN; Chrs; Stu Cncl; Pep Clb; Letter Chrldng; GAA; IM Sprt; Ball State Univ; Home Ec.

HARRIS, LISA; Kewanna HS; Kewanna, IN; Pres Jr Cls; Cls Rep Sr Cls; Chrs; Hon Rl; Stu Cncl; Pep Clb; Bsbl; Bsktbl; Chrldng; Kokomo Univ; Nursing.

HARRIS, LISA; Woodlan HS; New Haven, IN; 1/150 Chrs; Chrh Wkr; Girl Scts; Hon Rl; NHS; Stg Crw; Drama Clb; 4-H; FHA; Lat Clb; Tri Kappa Schlrshp Awd 78; Purdue Univ.

HARRIS, LORI; Inkster HS; Westland, MI; Band; Chrs; Chrh Wkr; Hon Rl; Lbry Ade; Off Ade; Sch Pl; Eastern Mic Univ.

HARRIS, LYNETTE; East HS; Columbus, OH; 19/300 Band; Chrs; Cmnty Wkr; Drm Mjrt; Hon Rl; Hosp Ade; Jr NHS; NHS; Off Ade; Sch Nwsp; Capital Univ; Pre Law.

HARRIS, MARCUS; Buchtel HS; Akron, OH; Band; Off Ade; Sch Mus; Sch Pl; Stu Cncl; Drama Clb; IM Sprt; College; Accounting.

HARRIS, MARIE; Floyd Central HS; Greenville, IN; Hon Rl; Off Ade; Lat Clb; PPFtbl; Indiana Univ; Nursing.

HARRIS, MARTIN; Beachwood HS; Beachwood, OH; 1/150 Debate Tm; Mod UN; Natl Forn Lg; NHS; College; Law; Political Sci; Math.

HARRIS, MARY; Delphos Jefferson HS; Delphos, OH; Band; Chrs; Hon Rl; Lbry Ade; NHS; Sch Mus; Y-Teens; Fr Clb; Trk; IM Sprt; College; Art.

HARRIS, MARY; Park Hills HS; Fairborn, OH; Chrs; Chrh Wkr; Drm Bgl; Hon Rl; Jr NHS; NHS; College; Med.

HARRIS, MICHAEL; Kearsley HS; Flint, MI; Boy Scts; Chrs; Lbry Ade; Mdrgl; Yth Flsp; Univ Of Michigan; Acctg.

HARRIS, NORMAN; Calumet HS; Merrillville, IN; VICA; College; Agircultre.

HARRIS, PAMELA; East Kentwood HS; Kentwood, MI; 4 Pres Frsh Cls; Cl Rep Jr Cls; VP Sr Cls; Chrs; Debate Tm; Hon Rl; Lbry Ade; Kalamazoo College; Pol Sci.

HARRIS, PAUL; Wilbur Wright HS; Dayton, OH; Band; Orch; Sct Actv; Letter Trk; Wrstlng; Univ; Math.

HARRIS, PHRONDA; Philip Barbour HS; Century, WV; Chrh Wkr; Hon Rl; Lbry Ade; 4-H; Pep Clb; Safe Driver Awd 78; Fairmont St Coll; Acctg.

HARRIS, REGINALD; John F Kennedy HS; Cleveland, OH; Chrh Wkr; Ftbl; IM Sprt; Cit Awd; Mert Roll Perfct Attndnc 78 & 79; MVP Bsbl 75; Ftbl Wd; Ohio Univ; Comp Tech.

HARRIS, ROBBIE; Chesapeake HS; Chesapeake, OH; 14/140 Cl Rep Jr Cls; Hon Rl; Stu Cncl; Beta Clb; Capt Crs Cntry; Capt Trk; Univ.

HARRIS, ROBERT; Midland HS; Midland, MI; Band; Boy Scts; Hon Rl; Sct Actv; Crs Cntry; Trk; Eagle Scout 76; Od Of Arrow 76; Engr Explrer Post 79; Univ; Med.

HARRIS, ROBERT; Chesapeake HS; Chesapeake, OH; 14/140 Cl Rep Jr Cls; Cls Rep Sr Cls; Hon Rl; Beta Clb; Chmn Crs Cntry; Chmn Trk; Marshall Univ.

HARRIS, ROBIN; Bristol Local HS; Bristolville, OH; Am Leg Aux Girls St; Band; Chrs; NHS; Sch Mus; 4-H; Letter Bsktbl; College; Forestry.

HARRIS, RODNEY; East HS; Columbus, OH; Band; Debate Tm; Hon Rl; Lbry Ade; Lit Mag; NHS; Stu Cncl; Sch Nwsp; VICA; Ten; Barbizon Schl Of Fshn; Fshn Mdse.

HARRIS, ROGER; Northern Sr HS; Detroit, MI; Drl Tm; Hon Rl; ROTC; E Michigan Univ; Elec Engr.

HARRIS, RON; Southport HS; Southport, IN; 29/425 Hon Rl; Yth Flsp; OEA; Pep Clb; IM Sprt; 1st Pl OEAI Data Processing Computer Test; OEA Chapter VP; Purdue Univ; Data Processing.

HARRIS, SCOTT; Orleans HS; Orleans, IN; VP Frsh Cls; Band; Hon Rl; Yth Flsp; 4-H; Bsbl; Bsktbl; Glf; 4-H Awd; De Moley Bars In Athletics Regligion Schlstcs 77; Purdue Univ; Engr.

HARRIS, STEWART L; Rochester Adams HS; Rochester, MI; Am Leg Boys St; Chrs; Hon Rl; NHS; PAVAS; Sch Mus; Sch Pl; Sct Actv; Stg Crw; Drama Clb; Honor Thespian; College; Liberal Arts.

HARRIS, SUSAN; Martin Luther King Jr Sr HS; Detroit, MI; 1/200 Val; Chrs; Chrh Wkr; Cmnty Wkr; Hon Rl; Lbry Ade; NHS; Pol Wkr; Sch Mus; FTA; Univ Of Michigan; Comp Engr.

HARRIS, TAMRA; Muskegon Sr HS; Muskegon, MI; Chrh Wkr; Hon Rl; Yrbk; Letter Swmmng; Mgrs; Muskegon Cmnty Coll.

HARRIS, TEANDRE; William A Wirt HS; Gary, IN; Cls Rep Frsh Cls; Sec Soph Cls; Sec Sr Cls; Chrs; Hon Rl; JA; Jr NHS; NHS; Off Ade; Orch; Spelman Univ; Pharm.

HARRIS, THERESA; Ewen Trout Creek Cnsldtd HS; Trout Creek, MI; 6/43 Hon Rl; Chrldng; N Mic Univ; Sec.

HARRIS, TRACY; Jefferson Union HS; Steubenville, OH; 24/150 VP Soph Cls; VP Jr Cls; VP Sr Cls; Chrs; Hosp Ade; Stu Cncl; Y-Teens; Beta Clb; Treas Pep Clb; PPFtbl; Jefferson Tech College; Lpn.

HARRIS, TRACY; Greenville HS; Greenville, OH; 8/380 Cls Rep Soph Cls; Girl Scts; Hon Rl; Ed Sch Nwsp; Rptr Sch Nwsp; Spn Clb; Ten; Ball St Univ; Jrnlsm.

HARRIS, TRINA; Chesaning Union HS; Chesaning, MI; 14/251 Chrh Wkr; Hon Rl; NHS; VP Stu Cncl; 4-H; Fr Clb; Trk; Treas Chrldng; 4-H Awd; Voice Dem Awd; Part Of St Champnshp Cheerldng Sqd 79; Michigan St Univ; Med.

HARRIS, VALERIE; Martin Luther King Sr HS; Detroit, MI; 13/200 Hon Rl; Hosp Ade; Jr NHS; NHS; Y-Teens; Letter Glf; Wayne St Univ; Psych.

HARRIS, VALETTA; Horace Mann HS; Gary, IN; Chrh Wkr; Hon Rl; JA; DECA; FHA; Spn Clb; Cit Awd; Sec JA Awd; Gary Career Ctr Schl; Cosmetology.

HARRIS, WENDI; Madison Comprehensive HS; Mansfield, OH; Treas Band; Lbry Ade; Orch; Sch Pl; Ger Clb; Cincinnati Cons Of Music; Music.

HARRIS JR, CLYDE A; Central Hower HS; Akron, OH; Cl Rep Jr Cls; Hon Rl; Red Cr Ade; Rptr Yrbk; Bsbl; IM Sprt; Univ; Chem Engr.

HARRISON, AMY; Elmwood HS; Rising Sun, OH; Sec Frsh Cls; Cl Rep Jr Cls; Chrs; Sch Mus; Stu Cncl; 4-H; FHA; Sci Clb; Letter Trk; Letter Chrldng; Univ; Med.

HARRISON, BETHALYN; Chardon HS; Chardon, OH; Boy Scts; Chrs; Girl Scts; Hosp Ade; Lbry Ade; Lit Mag; MMM; NHS; Off Ade; Sch Mus; Hiram Coll; Med.

HARRISON, BRENT; Croswell Lexington HS; Jeddo, MI; Am Leg Boys St; Band; Chrh Wkr; Hon Rl; NHS; Stu Cncl; Pres Yth Flsp; Letter Bsbl; Coach Actv; Rotary Awd; Nominated For Schlrshp ACT 79; Player Of Yr Babe Ruth Bsbll 78; Michigan St Univ; Comp Sci.

HARRISON, CHRISTINE; Whetstone HS; Columbus, OH; Chrs; Hon Rl; NHS; Letter Ten; Univ; Pro Tennis.

HARRISON, CYNTHIA; Pontiac Northern HS; Pontiac, MI; Band; Cmp Fr Grls; Chrh Wkr; Drl Tm; Hon Rl; Chrldng; Cit Awd; Michigan St Univ.

HARRISON, DAVID; Wapakoneta HS; Wapakoneta, OH; 2/350 Cmnty Wkr; Hon Rl; NHS; Yth Flsp; IM Sprt; Natl Merit Ltr; College; Psych.

HARRISON, DEBBIE; Central Hower HS; Akron, OH; 95/435 Band; Orch; Lat Clb; Akron Univ; Diplomacy.

HARRISON, DEBRA; Chelsea HS; Chelsea, MI; Hon Rl; NHS; Off Ade; 4-H; FFA; Chrldng; 4-H Awd; Mic State Univ; Vet Med.

HARRISON, GREGORY; Wapakoneta Sr HS; Wapakoneta, OH; 19/332 Hon Rl; NHS; Spn Clb; IM Sprt; Natl Merit Ltr; Spanish Natl Hnr Soc 78 79; Spirit Awd 78 79; Ohio Bd Of Regents Acad Achvmnt 78 79; Bowling Green St Univ; Pre Law.

HARRISON, JOSEPH; Jewett Scio HS; Scio, OH; Hon Rl; NHS; Stu Cncl; 4-H; 4-H Awd; College; Vet.

HARRISON, KARLENE; Riverview Community HS; Riverview, MI; 18/253 Hon Rl; NHS; Yth Flsp; Fr Clb; Cert Of Recognitn For Otstndng Acad Achvmnt In St Of Mi Schlrshp Comp 79; Oakland Univ; Psych.

HARRISON, KEITH; Flint Northern HS; Flint, MI; 20/500 Chrh Wkr; Hon Rl; NHS; Letter Crs Cntry; Letter Trk; Mic Tech Univ; Physics.

HARRISON, KELLEY; Bishop Donahue HS; Mc Mechen, WV; Treas Chrs; Chrh Wkr; Cmnty Wkr; Hon Rl; Hosp Ade; Mdrgl; Sch Pl; Sec Stu Cncl; Pres Yth Flsp; Rptr Yrbk; Stdnt Of Month 76; Youthdelgt To Wv Annl Confrnc Unitd Metholdist Church 78; Teen Bd Nominee 79; West Virginia Wesleyan Univ; Psych.

HARRISON, KEVIN; Martin Luther King Jr HS; Detroit, MI; 9/176 Chrs; Drl Tm; Hon Rl; NHS; ROTC; Rptr Sch Nwsp; Sch Nwsp; Pep Clb; Ten; Cit Awd; Washington Univ; Archt.

HARRISON, KEVIN; Lockland HS; Cincinnati, OH; 2/80 Chrs; Hon Rl; NHS; Sch Mus; Sch Pl; Stg Crw; Fr Clb; Letter Ftbl; Letter Ten; Mgrs; Univ Of Cincinnati; Elec Engr.

HARRISON, LARRY; Kyger Creek HS; Gallipolis, OH; Band; Hon Rl; Sch Pl; Key Clb; Lat Clb; Bsbl; Letter Ftbl; Ten; College.

HARRISON, LISA; Little Miami HS; Maineville, OH; Cls Rep Soph Cls; Cl Rep Jr Cls; Hon Rl; Off Ade; Sec Stu Cncl; Spn Clb; Letter Trk; PPFtbl; Univ; Archt.

HARRISON, LISA; Philo HS; Zanesville, OH; Band; Chrs; Cmnty Wkr; Drm Bgl; Girl Scts; Hon Rl; Hosp Ade; Lit Mag; Off Ade; 4-H; Muskingum Area Joint Voc Schl; Med.

HARRISON, LORI; St Clement HS; Centerline, MI; Pres Sr Cls; Chrh Wkr; Hon Rl; Jr NHS; Treas NHS; Off Ade; Pol Wkr; Civ Clb; Capt Chrldng; Coach Actv; Service; Sociology; Michigan St Univ; Busns Admin.

HARRISON, MARK; Lawrence Central HS; Lawrence, IN; College.

HARRISON, MELANIE; Kettering Senior HS; Detroit, MI; Hon Rl; JA; NHS; Off Ade; Cit Awd; Ctr For Creative Studies; Cmmrcl Art.

HARRISON, MELANIE; Heritage Christian HS; Indianapolis, IN; 18/63 Bsktbl; Mgrs; Pensacola Christian Coll; Bus Admin.

HARRISON, MICHAEL; Thornapple Kellogg HS; Middleville, MI; Band; Hon Rl; Glf; Wrstlng; Comptv Schlrshp 79; Thornapple Kellogg Sci Schlrshp 79; Michigan St Univ; Math.

HARRISON, MISTY; Brown County HS; Nashville, IN; 4-H; Spn Clb; 4-H Awd; Busns Schl; Sec.

HARRISON, ROBIN; Oak Hill HS; Oak Hill, OH; 8/100 Cls Rep Frsh Cls; Cls Rep Soph Cls; Pres Jr Cls; Cls Rep Sr Cls; Band; Chrs; Girl Scts; Hon Rl; VP NHS; Sch Mus; Voc Schl; Cosmetology.

HARRISON, SHERRY; Kyger Creek HS; Gallipolis, OH; 1/63 Trs Soph Cls; Trs Jr Cls; Band; Chrs; Hon Rl; Pres NHS; Sch Mus; College; Math.

HARRISON, SHERRY; Kyger Creek HS; Cheshire, OH; Chrs; Hon Rl; Lbry Ade; NHS; 4-H; FHA; Pep Clb; Bsktbl; 4-H Awd; Columbus Bus Univ; Mgr Of Fshn Store.

HARRISON, TAMI; Clay Sr HS; Oregon, OH; Band; Girl Scts; Hon Rl; Hosp Ade; VP JA; Sch Mus; Fr Clb; FTA; Band Marcher Of The Week; Band Jr & Sr Squad Ldr; Voc Schl; RN.

HARRISON, THOMAS L; Northwest HS; Indianapolis, IN; 3/506 Capt Band; Boy Scts; Hon Rl; NHS; Orch; Sch Mus; U S Collegiate Wind Band Distinguished Serv Awd 78; Superior Rating In St Solo Contest 78; Otstndg Math 77; Ball St Univ; Archt.

HARRISON, TODD; Davison Sr HS; Davison, MI; Fr Clb; Mth Clb; OEA; Won 1st Pl Trophy In Acctg II At BOEC Reg Tourn; Univ; CPA.

HARRISON, YVONNE; Watkins Mem HS; Pataskala, OH; 6/226 Hon Rl; NHS; Off Ade; Fr Clb; Trk; Scr Kpr; Tmr; Bus Schl.

HARRITOS, BARB; Mt Gilead HS; Mt Gilead, OH; Pres Frsh Cls; Band; Chrs; Hon Rl; Lbry Ade; Orch; 4-H; Spn Clb; Bsktbl; GAA; Mt St Joseph Univ; Med Lab Tech.

HARROD, SHERRI; Austin HS; Austin, IN; 12/111 Band; Chrh Wkr; Girl Scts; Pol Wkr; Sch Pl; Yth Flsp; 4-H; FTA; Pep Clb; 4-H Awd; Purdue Univ; Natural Resources.

HARROD, SHERRI; Austin HS; Scottsburg, IN; Band; Chrh Wkr; Girl Scts; NHS; Sch Pl; Pres 4-H; Treas FTA; Pep Clb; 4-H Awd; Purdue Univ; Natural Resources.

HARROD, THERESE; Memorial HS; St Marys, OH; Chrs; Hon Rl; Sec Lbry Ade; 4-H; Spn Clb; Trk; Mgrs; Scr Kpr; College; Art Stu.

HARROLD, MARK; Crestview HS; Columbiana, OH; 15/84 Hon Rl; Scr Kpr; Kiwan Awd; Hocking Tech Voc Schl.

HARRY, JILL A; North Central HS; Indianapolis, IN; Cls Rep Frsh Cls; Cls Rep Sr Cls; Hon Rl; NHS; Natl Achievement Scholarship Commended Student 78; Indiana Univ; Bus Admin.

HARRY, TINA; Flushing HS; Flushing, MI; 14/514 Band; Hon Rl; NHS; Orch; Sch Mus; Drama Clb; Fr Clb; Mich St Univ; Vet Medicine.

HARSAR, ALBERT; Admiral King HS; Lorain, OH; Hon Rl; Orch; Yrbk; Fr Clb; Key Clb; Ten; Coll; Busns Admin.

HARSBARGER, LARRY; Van Buren HS; Ctr Pnt, IN; Boy Scts; Chrs; Chrh Wkr; Cmnty Wkr; Hon Rl; Sch Pl; Sct Actv; Stg Crw; Yth Flsp; Sprt Ed Sch Nwsp; Indiana St Univ; Radio.

HARSH, BRADLEY; Tecumseh HS; Tecumseh, MI; 64/265 Band; Drm Bgl; Hon Rl; Eastern Mic Univ; Acctg.

HARSHA, WILLIAM; Plymouth Salem HS; Plymouth, MI; 90/541 FCA; Hon Rl; NHS; Yth Flsp; Letter Bsbl; St Of Mi Comp Schlrshp Awd 79; Univ Of Michigan; Bus.

HARSHBARGER, STEVE; Tecumseh HS; Medway, OH; 26/401 Cl Rep Jr Cls; Hon Rl; Jr NHS; Stu Cncl; VP Fr Clb; Univ.

HARSHE, DARLA; Liberty Benton HS; Findlay, OH; Trs Jr Cls; Am Leg Aux Girls St; Band; Chrs; Hon Rl; NHS; Sch Mus; Dent Assistant.

HARSHMAN, DANIEL; North Miami HS; Roann, IN; 6/122 Am Leg Boys St; Chrh Wkr; NHS; Sprt Ed Sch Nwsp; Drama Clb; Military.

HARSHMAN, HOLLY; Howland HS; Warren, OH; Band; Hon Rl; Orch; Yrbk; Findlay Coll; Psych.

HARSHMAN, LAURA J; Southern Wells HS; Keystone, IN; 15/97 Chrh Wkr; Hon Rl; NHS; Pep Clb; Chrldng; PPFtbl; Am Leg Awd; Ball St Univ; Acctg.

HARSHMAN, TODD A; Muncie Central HS; Muncie, IN; Cls Rep Frsh Cls; Aud/Vis; JA; DECA; Spn Clb; IM Sprt; JA Awd; Ball State Univ; Advertising.

HARSIN, JEFF; Switzerland Cnty HS; Vevay, IN; 8/128 Pres Jr Cls; Pres Sr Cls; Band; Chrs; Hon Rl; MMM; NHS; Off Ade; Pol Wkr; Sch Mus; Indiana Univ; Bus Mgmt.

HART, AIMEE; St Ursula Acad; Cincinnati, OH; Cls Rep Frsh Cls; Cls Rep Soph Cls; Cl Rep Jr Cls; Hon Rl; Jr NHS; NHS; Stu Cncl; Spn Clb; Ohi State Univf Pharmacy.

HART, BRIAN; Jefferson Township HS; Dayton, OH; 1/135 Band; Hon Rl; NHS; Orch; Sch Nwsp; Spn Clb; Cit Awd; Natl Merit Ltr; Slctd Hnrs Semnr Of Met Dayton 78 80; Part In Martin Essex Schl For Gftd 79; Rcvd Cert From Natl Ed Dvlpmnt; Univ; Bio.

HART, CAROLYN; Barr Reeve HS; Cannelburg, IN; 2/49 Pres Frsh Cls; Pres Soph Cls; VP Jr Cls; Am Leg Aux Girls St; Hon Rl; Stu Cncl; Beta Clb; 4-H; FHA; Pep Clb; Univ; Soc Work.

HART, CHRISTINE; West Wood Heights HS; Flint, MI; 2/160 Pres Soph Cls; Pres Jr Cls; Sal; Debate Tm; Hon Rl; Natl Forn Lg; NHS; 4-H; Gym; Ten; Univ Alumni Schlrshp 79; What Amer Means To Me Essay Contest 3rd 79; Gold Chords At Grad 79; Univ Of Michigan; Law.

HART, DANIEL; John R Buchtel HS; Akron, OH; 8/452 Hon Rl; College; Bio.

HART, DENNIS; Barr Reeve HS; Cannelburg, IN; 11/55 Chrh Wkr; Hon Rl; Beta Clb; 4-H; FFA; Pep Clb; Bsbl; IM Sprt; 4-H Awd; Purdue Univ; Agri.

HART, DREW; Whitehall Yearling HS; Whitehall, OH; Aud/Vis; Band; Drm Bgl; Trk; College; Music Educ.

HART, ERIC S; Circleville HS; Circleville, OH; AFS; Hon Rl; NHS; Sprt Ed Yrbk; Sec Key Clb; Pres Lat Clb; Natl Merit SF; Univ; Chem Engr.

HART, GAYNELLE; Revere HS; Richfield, OH; Band; Hon Rl; Univ Of Akron; Vet.

HART, HOPE; Union Local HS; Belmont, OH; 1/147 Val; Chrh Wkr; Sec NHS; Stu Cncl; Pres 4-H; Treas FHA; Treas GAA; 4-H Awd; Ohio Univ; Nutrition.

HART, JOAN E; Vermilion HS; Vermilion, OH; 1/255 Band; Hon Rl; Lit Mag; Orch; Quill & Scroll; Sch Nwsp; Key Clb; Spn Clb; IM Sprt; PPFtbl; Knights Of Columbus Outstanding Sr Marching Bnd Mbr; Reporter Of The Yr; Century III Ldrs Prog Winner; Miami Univ; Systems Analysis.

HART, JOHN; Winfield HS; Winfield, WV; 1/130 Cls Rep Frsh Cls; VP Jr Cls; Pres Sr Cls; Val; Am Leg Boys St; Hon Rl; NHS; VP Beta Clb; Mth Clb; Pres Pep Clb; Mass Inst Of Tech; Engr.

HART, KEVIN R; Newcomerstown HS; Guernsey, OH; 2/100 Am Leg Boys St; Band; Hon Rl; Lbry Ade; NHS; Sch Mus; Sch Pl; 4-H; Trk; Univ; Chem.

HART, LAURA; Salem Sr HS; Salem, OH; 50/245 Cls Rep Soph Cls; Cl Rep Jr Cls; Sec Sr Cls; Cmp Fr Grls; Off Ade; Stu Cncl; Fr Clb; Key Clb; Pep Clb; GAA; Kent St Univ; Fshn Mdse.

HART, LESTER; Fairless HS; Navarre, OH; Crs Cntry; Trk; IM Sprt; Univ; Comp.

HART, MELANIE; Greensburg Cmnty HS; Greensburg, IN; 37/208 Cls Rep Frsh Cls; Band; Chrs; Chrh Wkr; Girl Scts; Hon Rl; JA; Mdrgl; Sch Mus; Sch Pl; Whos Who In Amer HS Stu 77; Whos Who In Foreign Lang In Indiana 77; Indiana Central Univ; Nursing.

HART, MIKE; North Daviess Jr Sr HS; Plainville, IN; 32/89 Trs Frsh Cls; Band; Chrs; FCA; Lbry Ade; Sch Mus; 4-H; Spn Clb; Glf; Ten; Indiana Univ; History.

HART, NORMAN; De Kalb HS; Waterloo, IN; 5/287 Aud/Vis; Hon Rl; NHS; Ger Clb; Sci Clb; KAPPA Schlrshp; A Hoosier Schlr Awd; Purdue Univ Cert Of Recognition; Purdue Univ; Physics.

HART, PATRICK; Algonac HS; Algonac, MI; Aud/Vis; Band; Boy Scts; Hon Rl; Jr NHS; NHS; Boys Clb Am; Ftbl; Trk; Northwestern Michigan Coll; Engr.

HART, PEGGY; Switzerland County HS; Canaan, IN; Sch Mus; Sch Pl; Stg Crw; Farming.

HART, RANDY; Westland HS; Columbus, OH; Band; Boy Scts; Sct Actv; Undecided.

HART, RANDY; Cheboygan Area HS; Cheboygan, MI; Band; Boy Scts; Hon Rl; Sch Mus; Ftbl; Trk; Central Mic Univ.

HART, REBECCA A; Berea HS; Berea, OH; Hon Rl; Jr NHS; NHS; Off Ade; Ohio St Univ; Vet.

HART, RIAN; Pickens HS; Pickens, WV; Trs Frsh Cls; VP Soph Cls; Cl Rep Jr Cls; Boy Scts; Cmnty Wkr; Sch Pl; Sct Actv; Stu Cncl; Yth Flsp; 4-H; Page In House Of Delegates For Julia Petsenberger 77; Mbr Of Helvetia Folk Dance Grp; Coll; Civil Engr.

HART, RON; Wadsworth Sr HS; Wadsworth, OH; Chrs; Chrh Wkr; Cmnty Wkr; Pol Wkr; Sch Mus; Stg Crw; Bsktbl; Scr Kpr; Tmr; Coll.

HART, ROXANNE; Greenville Sr HS; Greenville, OH; 2/360 Sal; Chrs; Chrh Wkr; Hosp Ade; Lit Mag; NHS; Rptr Yrbk; Treas Drama Clb; Lat Clb; VP Sci Clb; Rotary Exchange Stu To Brazil; Sertoma Natl Heritage Essay Contest Dist Winner; Univ Of Toledo; Medicine.

HART, SANDRA; Franklin HS; Franklin, OH; VP Frsh Cls; Hosp Ade; Off Ade; GAA; Mbr Of Future Secretaries; Univ; Psych.

HART, SEAN; Salem HS; Salem, OH; 51/360 Cls Rep Frsh Cls; Cls Rep Soph Cls; VP Jr Cls; Cl Rep Jr Cls; Cls Rep Sr Cls; Am Leg Boys St; Band; FCA; Hon Rl; Off Ade; College; Health.

HART, STEVEN; Highland Park HS; Highland Pk, MI; Pres Sr Cls; Band; Boy Scts; Chrs; Chrh Wkr; Quill & Scroll; Stu Cncl; Yrbk; Rptr Sch Nwsp; Boys Clb Am; Morehouse Univ; Radio & T V.

HART, TINA; Athens HS; East Leroy, MI; 27/84 VP Jr Cls; Cmp Fr Grls; Hon Rl; NHS; Pep Clb; Gym; Trk; Chrldng; PPFtbl; Scr Kpr; Perfect Attendance For One Year 1977 78;.

HART, TINA; Tuslaw HS; Massillon, OH; VP Frsh Cls; VP Soph Cls; VP Jr Cls; Chrh Wkr; Hon Rl; Jr NHS; Stu Cncl; Y-Teens; Pep Clb; Chrldng; Ohio State Univ; Phys Ther.

HART, TRACY; Beauercreek HS; Xenia, OH; 3/702 Cls Rep Soph Cls; Cl Rep Jr Cls; Hon Rl; NHS; Pep Clb; Letter Bsktbl; Letter Socr; Cit Awd; College; Sci.

HARTE, BRIAN; West Bloomfield HS; Westbloomfield, MI; 100/430 Hon Rl; Mi Comptn Schlrshp 79; Stu Aid Grant 79; Michigan St Univ; Engr.

HARTE, JENNIFER; North Farmington HS; Farm Hills, MI; Hon Rl; Jr NHS; NHS; VP Fr Clb; Univ Of Mic; Engr.

HARTENSTEIN, MARK; Firelands HS; Wakeman, OH; 18/175 Aud/Vis; Hon Rl; NHS; Pres 4-H; FBLA; FFA; IM Sprt; Mgrs; Scr Kpr; 4-H Awd; Univ; Comp Sci.

HARTER, CINDY; Cuyahoga Hts HS; Valley View, OH; Band; Drm Mjrt; Spn Clb; Twrlr; Cuyahoga Cmnty Coll; Acctg.

HARTER, GARY D; Valley HS; Smithfield, WV; 1/90 VP Frsh Cls; Cls Rep Soph Cls; Band; Boy Scts; Hon Rl; Treas NHS; Quill & Scroll; Sch Mus; Sch Pl; Stu Cncl; Inlt Thespian Soc Treas 79; U S Naval Acad; Chem.

HARTER, JAMES A; Ruthaford B Hayes HS; Delaware, OH; Boy Scts; Pol Wkr; Key Clb; Letter Bsktbl; Letter Ftbl; Trk; Coach Actv; Tmr; 4-H Awd; Miami Univ; Law.

HARTER, KRIS; Clear Fork HS; Bellville, OH; 11/160 Trs Soph Cls; Trs Jr Cls; Chrs; Cmnty Wkr; Girl Scts; Hon Rl; Lbry Ade; NHS; Red Cr Ade; Sch Mus; Univ; Osteopath.

HARTER, LYNDA; Northside HS; Muncie, IN; Chrs; Hon Rl; Treas JA; Mdrgl; Sch Mus; Sct Actv; Stg Crw; JA Awd; Ball State.

HARTER, MAUREEN; New Albany HS; New Albany, OH; 5/98 Cls Rep Frsh Cls; Band; Hon Rl; Stu Cncl; Rptr Sch Nwsp; Letter Bsktbl; IM Sprt; Sftbl 2 Var Ltr Coachs Awd 77; Vllybl 1 Var Ltr 78; Univ; Radio.

HARTER, THOMAS; Elder HS; Cinn, OH; Quill & Scroll; Rptr Sch Nwsp; Thomas More College; Bus Admin.

HARTESVELT, JANET; Suttons Bay HS; Suttons Bay, MI; VP Soph Cls; Pres Jr Cls; Am Leg Aux Girls St; Chrh Wkr; Girl Scts; Hon Rl; Lbry Ade; Yrbk; Sch Nwsp; Letter Bsktbl; Univ Of Michigan.

HARTESVELT, JANET C; Suttons Bay HS; Sutton Bay, MI; VP Soph Cls; Pres Jr Cls; Am Leg Aux Girls St; Girl Scts; Hon Rl; Lbry Ade; Sct Actv; Stu Cncl; Yrbk; Letter Bsktbl; Univ Of Michigan; Solar Dsgn.

HARTFORD, CHERYL; Catholic Ctrl HS; Wyoming, MI; Cmp Fr Grls; Chrh Wkr; Girl Scts; Hon Rl; Davenport Bus Schl; Acctg.

HARTFORD, STEVE; Clay Sr HS; Oregon, OH; 51/354 Lbry Ade; NHS; Fr Clb; Ftbl; Natl Merit Ltr; Toledo Univ; Law.

HARTH, SHARON; Euclid Sr HS; Euclid, OH; Hon Rl; JA; Cit Awd; Univ; Spec Ed.

HARTINGS, CAROLYN A; Celina Sr HS; Celina, OH; 25/241 Cls Rep Soph Cls; Cl Rep Jr Cls; Cls Rep Sr Cls; Hon Rl; NHS; Stu Cncl; 4-H; Fr Clb; FBLA; Pep Clb; Univ; Bus Retail.

HARTLE, LORI; Fountain Central Jr & Sr HS; V eedersburg, IN; Chrh Wkr; Lbry Ade; Yth Flsp; 4-H; 4-H Awd; Vocational Schl; Blacksmith.

HARTLEROAD, MELANIE; Lewis County HS; Weston, WV; 30/287 Band; Chrh Wkr; Girl Scts; Hon Rl; Jr NHS; NHS; Sch Mus; Sch Pl; Stg Crw; Treas Y-Teens; West Virginia Univ; Comp Prog.

HARTLEY, CHERYL; New Palestine HS; New Palestine, IN; Band; Chrs; Chrh Wkr; Cmnty Wkr; Girl Scts; Hon Rl; Sct Actv; Yrbk; 4-H; Spn Clb; Indiana Univ; Nursing.

HARTLEY, DEBBIE; Madison Hts HS; Anderson, IN; 56/289 Band; Chrs; Hon Rl; Pres OEA; Spn Clb; Ball St Univ; Busns.

HARTLEY, JON; Pendleton Heights HS; Anderson, IN; 61/303 FCA; Quill & Scroll; Beta Clb; Rdo Clb; Scr Kpr; Cit Awd; Kiwan Awd; Ball State Univ; Radio Broadcasting.

HARTLEY, TIMOTHY; Butler HS; Vandalia, OH; Band; NHS; Sch Pl; Drama Clb; Mbr Of Schl Match Wits Panel For Butler On TV; Private Pilot; Ohio St Univ; Law.

HARTLEY, WILLIAM; Wylie E Groves HS; Birmingham, MI; Boy Scts; Chrs; Chrh Wkr; Bsbl; Bsktbl; Coach Actv; IM Sprt; Mgrs; Mic State; Phy Educa.

HARTLINE, TOM; Bridgman HS; Baroda, MI; Cmnty Wkr; Hon Rl; Off Ade; Ger Clb; Letter VICA; Bsktbl; IM Sprt; Lake Michigan Coll; Mgmt.

HARTMAN, ANNETTE; Bishop Luers HS; Ft Wayn E, IN; VP Am Leg Aux Girls St; Chrs; Hon Rl; VP JA; NHS; Sch Pl; Rptr Sch Nwsp; Univ; Math.

HARTMAN, BRIAN; Rockville HS; Rockville, IN; 20/86 Am Leg Boys St; FCA; Hon Rl; NHS; Red Cr Ade; Sch Pl; Stu Cncl; Letter Bsbl; Letter Bsktbl; Letter Ftbl; De Pauw Univ; Bus.

HARTMAN, CHERYL; Bishop Dwenger HS; Ft Wayne, IN; Cl Rep Jr Cls; Girl Scts; Hon Rl; Sct Actv; Stg Crw; Stu Cncl; 4-H; Pep Clb; VICA; Mat Maids; Ball State.

HARTMAN, DEBRA; Ionia HS; Ionia, MI; 16/273 NHS; 4-H; 4-H Awd; Edmond & Mary Chapin Shclshp 79; MHEAA 79; Hon In Geom & Bio 77; Michigan St Univ; Vet Med.

HARTMAN, DIANE; Vicksburg HS; Vicksburg, MI; Cls Rep Frsh Cls; Cls Rep Soph Cls; Girl Scts; Hon Rl; NHS; Stg Crw; Stu Cncl; 4-H; FTA; Pep Clb; Math Awd 76; Projects For March Of Dimes 77; Univ; Elem Schl Tchr.

HARTMAN, GAYLE; Northeastern Jr Sr HS; Fountain Cty, IN; 8/121 Pres Soph Cls; Pres Jr Cls; Trs Sr Cls; Chrh Wkr; Hon Rl; NHS; Stu Cncl; Letter Bsktbl; PPFtbl; Am Leg Awd; Indiana Univ; Acctg.

HARTMAN, JEANNE; Rockville HS; Rockville, IN; 3/97 Band; Chrh Wkr; FCA; Girl Scts; Hon Rl; NHS; Red Cr Ade; Sct Actv; Ind State Univ.

HARTMAN, JERRY; Plymouth HS; Plymouth, OH; Rptr Sch Nwsp; Crs Cntry; Capt Ten; IM Sprt; Am Leg Awd; Ohio St Univ; Jrnlsm.

HARTMAN, JILL; Wawasee HS; Syracuse, IN; Hon Rl; DECA;.

HARTMAN, JODIE R; Roosevelt Wilson HS; Nutter Frt, WV; Cls Rep Frsh Cls; Cls Rep Soph Cls; Am Leg Aux Girls St; Band; Chrh Wkr; Hon Rl; NHS; Stu Cncl; Yth Flsp; Y-Teens; West Virginia Univ; Engr.

HARTMAN, JOHN; Rocky River HS; Rocky Rvr, OH; Hon Rl; Lit Mag; Sch Nwsp; Ger Clb; Crs Cntry; Ftbl; Capt Wrstlng; Capt IM Sprt; Pl Of Hon At R R HS For Excellnc In Art W Shore Rotary Art Contst 78; Work In Paintng Shop Learn Tricks; Cleveland Inst Of Art; Fine Arts.

HARTMAN, JOY; Dublin HS; Galena, OH; 26/152 Cls Rep Frsh Cls; Cmp Fr Grls; Hon Rl; Lat Clb; Pep Clb; Chrldng; Ohio St Univ; Law.

HARTMAN, KAREN; Immaculate Conception Acad; Batesville, IN; 2/68 Chrs; Chrh Wkr; Girl Scts; Hon Rl; Off Ade; Sch Mus; Sch Pl; Yrbk; 4-H; Spn Clb; Ballstate; Nursing.

HARTMAN, KATHY; Whitko HS; So Whitley, IN; Chrs; Chrh Wkr; Hon Rl; Sch Mus; Yth Flsp; Drama Clb; 4-H; OEA; Cit Awd; 4-H Awd; Univ; Dentistry.

HARTMAN, KELLY L; Fairmont West HS; Kettering, OH; 62/471 Chrs; Drl Tm; Hon Rl; Lbry Ade; Sch Mus; Rptr Yrbk; Fr Clb; Pep Clb; Letter Gym; Trk; Scholar Athlete; Natl French Test; College.

HARTMAN, KEVIN; North Putnam Jr Sr HS; Bainbridge, IN; Am Leg Boys St; Chrh Wkr; FCA; NHS; Yth Flsp; Spn Clb; Bsktbl; Letter Crs Cntry; Socr; Letter Trk; Univ; Bus Mgmt.

HARTMAN, KIM; R Nelson Snider HS; Ft Wayne, IN; 142/564 Chrs; Chrh Wkr; Girl Scts; Hon Rl; Hosp Ade; Yth Flsp; Sch Nwsp; Fr Clb; Pom Pon; PPFtbl; Purdue Univ; Nursing.

HARTMAN, LODEMA; Norton HS; Norton, OH; Chrs; Chrh Wkr; FCA; Treas Yth Flsp; Y-Teens; Trk; Ohio St Univ; Vet.

HARTMAN, RANDY; Richmond Sr HS; Richmond, IN; 39/602 Hon Rl; NHS; 4-H; Key Clb; Lat Clb; IM Sprt; Dnfth Awd; 4-H Awd; Hoosier Schlr 79; Indiana Univ; Chem.

HARTMAN, SHERRY; North Wood HS; Elkhart, IN; 13/196 Band; Chrh Wkr; Hon Rl; NHS; Yth Flsp; Ger Clb; Goshen Coll; Nursing.

HARTMAN, STEVEN; St Joseph Sr HS; Saint Joseph, MI; VP Mth Clb; Letter Bsbl; Letter Ftbl; Coach Actv; IM Sprt; Kalamazoo Coll; Engr.

HARTMAN, THERESA; Trinity HS; Maple Hts, OH; 3/120 Sec Soph Cls; Chrs; Hon Rl; Pep Clb; Spn Clb; Mat Maids; Bowling Green Univ; Accounting.

HARTMANN, GREGORY A; Park Tudor HS; Indianapolis, IN; Sch Pl; Stg Crw; Letter Socr; Natl Merit SF; College.

HARTMANN, JEFFERY; La Salle HS; Cincinnati, OH; 76/252 Hon Rl; Coach Actv; IM Sprt; Mgrs; Scr Kpr; Notre Dame Univ; CPA.

HARTNELL, LORETTA; Farwell Area HS; Farwell, MI; 2/115 Cl Rep Jr Cls; VP Sr Cls; Cls Rep Sr Cls; Sal; Band; Chrs; Chrh Wkr; Debate Tm; Drm Mjrt; Hon Rl; Natl Hnr Soc Schlrshp Frm The Natl Assn Of Prncpls 79; MI Comp Schlrshp 79; Outstndg Teen Ldr Awd 4 H 77; Mid Michigan Cmnty Coll; Bus Admin.

HARTNETT, CATHY; Fr Joseph Wehrle Mem HS; Columbus, OH; Hon Rl; NHS; Mgrs; Coll Of Mt St Joseph; Nursing.

HARTNETT, PATRICK; Riverside HS; Dearborn Hts, MI; Am Leg Boys St; Band; Hon Rl; Fr Clb; Ten; Univ Of Michigan; Comp Oper.

HARTSELL, KAREN; North Adams HS; N Adams, MI; VP Soph Cls; Pres Jr Cls; Cl Rep Jr Cls; Chrh Wkr; Hon Rl; Lbry Ade; NHS; Sch Pl; Stu Cncl; Yth Flsp; Hillsdale Coll.

HARTSELL, LISA; Wayne Memorial HS; Westland, MI; NHS; Orch; Ger Clb; Germ Club Schlrshp To Study In Germ 79; Univ Of Michigan; Nurse.

HARTSHORN, AMY; Northridge HS; Johnstown, OH; 2/124 Band; Chrs; Hon Rl; NHS; Orch; Y-Teens; Treas Spn Clb; Whos Who In Foreign Lang In Oh HS Spanish 79; Oh Tests Eng 5th Plc In Dist M9; NEDT 77 78; Tech Schl; Dent Lab.

HARTSHORN, JACQUELINE; Watkins Mem Plum HS; Pataskala, OH; 63/203 Chrs; Hon Rl; Off Ade; Trk; Bus Schl; Acctg.

HARTSHORN, SUE; Wauseon HS; Wauseon, OH; Chrs; CAP; Hon Rl; Red Cr Ade; Sch Mus; Stu Cncl; Rdo Clb; Mat Maids; Am Leg Awd; VFW Awd; Mert Acvhtmnt Awd 79; Bus Schl; Mgmt.

HARTSING, DELORES; Cardinal Stritch HS; Genoa, OH; Hon Rl; Owens Tech Coll; Archt Drafting.

HARTSOCK, BELINDA; Lincoln HS; Cambridge, IN; 42/148 Chrh Wkr; Hon Rl; FHA; Berea; Home Ec Tchr.

HARTSOUGH, DEBORA; Chillicothe HS; Chillicothe, OH; Band; Drl Tm; Hon Rl; Lbry Ade; NHS; Rptr Sch Nwsp; Superstar Awd Ashland Coll Firebird Drill Team Camp; Band Letter & Bars; Ohio St Univ; Cmnctns.

HARTSOUGH, SCOTT; Colerain Sr HS; Cincinnati, OH; Chrs; Hon Rl; VP Jr NHS; Mdrgl; NHS; Off Ade; Sch Mus; Sch Pl; Drama Clb; Ger Clb; Thespian Hon Progr Vc Pres 79; N W Cincinnati Boy Of Month 78; Perfct Attndnc 5 Yrs; Univ Of Kentucky; Acctg.

HARTWELL, SAMUEL S; University HS; Shaker Hts, OH; Pres Frsh Cls; AFS; Hon Rl; Ed Sch Nwsp; Sch Nwsp; Natl Merit SF; Yale Univ.

HARTWICK, TONYA; Kewanna HS; Kewanna, IN; Trs Soph Cls; Cl Rep Jr Cls; Hon Rl; Off Ade; Rptr Yrbk; Ed Sch Nwsp; Pep Clb; College.

HARTWIG, DEEANNA; Rapid River HS; Rapid River, MI; 1/70 Cls Rep Soph Cls; Cl Rep Jr Cls; Girl Scts; Hon Rl; Sct Actv; Stu Cncl; Letter Bsktbl; Letter Trk; Scr Kpr; Tmr; Lake Superior St Coll; Psych.

HARTZELL, DANNETTE; Mannington HS; Rachel, WV; 6/114 Chrs; Hon Rl; Hosp Ade; NHS; Off Ade; Pres Yth Flsp; Y-Teens; 4-H; Treas Mth Clb; Letter Bsktbl; West Virginia Univ; Genrl Engr.

HARTZELL, JAMIE; Triton HS; Etna Green, IN; Sec Jr Cls; Band; Hon Rl; 4-H; Pep Clb; Letter Ten; GAA; IM Sprt; DAR Awd; Pres Awd; Business School; Secretarial.

HARTZELL, JOHN; Bridgeport HS; Bridgeport, WV; Am Leg Boys St; Hon Rl; Jr NHS; Key Clb; Letter Bsbl; St Champ In Babe Ruth Bsbl 76 & 78; Univ; Sci.

HARTZELL, SUSAN; Buckeye West HS; Adena, OH; 6/87 Band; Drl Tm; Hon Rl; NHS; Orch; Stg Crw; Yth Flsp; Drama Clb; 4-H; FTA; Scolarship Team 78; Science Club Award 78; Univ; Psych.

HARTZKE, DEBBIE; Penn HS; Granger, IN; VP Frsh Cls; Sec Soph Cls; Trs Jr Cls; Cmnty Wkr; Hon Rl; Hosp Ade; Orch; Pep Clb; PPFtbl; Opt Clb Awd; S W Michigan Univ; Nursing.

HARTZLER, CINDY; Bethany Christian HS; Goshen, IN; VP Frsh Cls; Cls Rep Frsh Cls; Pres Soph Cls; Chrs; Hon Rl; Sch Pl; Pres Stu Cncl; Rptr Sch Nwsp; Ger Clb; Pep Clb; Goshen Coll; Soc Work.

HARTZLER, ROB; Warsaw Comm Sr HS; Warsaw, IN; Cls Rep Frsh Cls; PAVAS; Letter Ftbl; John Herron Art Inst; Ox Bow Summer Workshop; John Herron Inst; Fine Arts.

HARTZOG, CHRISTOPHER; Bishop Luers HS; Ft Wyane, IN; Band; Boy Scts; Chrs; Chrh Wkr; Hon Rl; JA; Orch; Trk; Cit Awd; Indiana Univ; Music Ed.

HARTZOG, JOSEPH; Bluefield HS; Bluefield, WV; 50/300 Pres Frsh Cls; Cls Rep Soph Cls; Cl Rep Jr Cls; FCA; Hon Rl; Jr NHS; Pres Stu Cncl; Ed Sch Nwsp; Key Clb; Spn Clb; Ftbl Best Around; Pres Builders Clb; Univ Of Kentucky; Med.

HARVAN, MARYELLEN; Regina HS; Cleveland, OH; 4/200 Chrh Wkr; Hon Rl; NHS; Stg Crw; Natl Merit Ltr; Illinois Inst Of Tech; Chem Engr.

HARVAN, MICHELE; Holy Name Nazareth HS; Cleveland, OH; Chrh Wkr; Hon Rl; Sch Pl; Sdlty; Spn Clb; Gym; Trk; Chrldng; K Of C Schlrshp 76; 3rd Pl Ping Pong Trophy 78; Vllybl Trophy 78; Cuyahoga Cmnty Coll; Art.

HARVATH, JIM; Clio HS; Clio, MI; Aud/Vis; Hon Rl; NHS; Stg Crw; Univ Of Michigan; Elec Dsgn Engr.

HARVEY, AMY; James A Garfield HS; Garrettsville, OH; Cls Rep Soph Cls; VP Band; NHS; Sch Mus; Yth Flsp; Y-Teens; Rptr Yrbk; Pres 4-H; Spn Clb; Bsktbl; Bsns Schl.

HARVEY, AMY L; Whitko HS; S Whitley, IN; 15/151 Chrh Wkr; Hon Rl; NHS; Yth Flsp; Rptr Yrbk; Letter Trk; GAA; Taylor Univ.

HARVEY, CYNDRA; Magnolia HS; New Martinsvle, WV; 7/200 Band; Chrs; Chrh Wkr; Capt Debate Tm; Hon Rl; Mdrgl; Natl Forn Lg; NHS; Sch Mus; Sch Pl; Best Affirmative Awd For Jr Town Meeting Debate 79; All Fest Bands 77; Natls In Lincoln Douglass Debate 79; Univ; Music Composition.

HARVEY, D; Terre Haute North Vigo HS; Terre Haute, IN; Cls Rep Frsh Cls; Aud/Vis; Hon Rl; Stu Cncl; Spn Clb; Ind Univ; Chem.

HARVEY, DARREL; Lake Ville Memorial HS; Otisville, MI; Chrh Wkr; Hon Rl; Sch Mus; Sch Pl; Rptr Sch Nwsp; Letter Bsbl; Letter Bsktbl; Letter Ftbl; Univ.

HARVEY, DAVE; Cardington Lincoln HS; Cardington, OH; 1/79 Am Leg Boys St; Band; Chrh Wkr; FCA; Hon Rl; NHS; Orch; Stg Crw; Stu Cncl; Rptr Yrbk; Ohio St Univ; Agri Econ.

HARVEY, DEBRA; Gull Lake HS; Richland, MI; 15/256 Band; Chrs; Chrh Wkr; Cmnty Wkr; FCA; Hon Rl; NHS; Sch Mus; Sch Pl; Pres Yth Flsp; Hope Coll.

HARVEY, DOROTHY M; Lake Catholic HS; Mentor, OH; Chrs; Chrh Wkr; Treas Girl Scts; Hon Rl; Jr NHS; Lbry Ade; Lit Mag; PAVAS; Sch Mus; Sch Pl; College; Medicine.

HARVEY, JAMES B; Logan Sr HS; Chauncey, WV; Cls Rep Soph Cls; Cl Rep Jr Cls; Am Leg Boys St; Boy Scts; Cmnty Wkr; Hon Rl; NHS; Sct Actv; Rptr Sch Nwsp; Ealge Scout Awd 79; Voc Schl; Carpentry.

HARVEY, JEFFREY; Stow Sr HS; Stow, OH; Hon Rl; Lat Clb; Socr; Trk; Mbr Of Jr Classical Lg 78; Univ; Archt.

HARVEY, KIM; North Vermillion HS; Dana, IN; 1/97 Trs Frsh Cls; Band; Chrs; Sec Chrh Wkr; Hon Rl; Lbry Ade; NHS; Pres Spn Clb; Bsktbl; Mgrs; Purdue Univ; Chem Engr.

HARVEY, LISA; Dunbar HS; Dunbar, WV; Cmnty Wkr; Rptr Sch Nwsp; FBLA; Pep Clb; Chrldng; Mgrs; Cit Awd; West Virginia Univ; Law.

HARVEY, MARCIA; Notre Dame HS; Salem, WV; 2/54 Am Leg Aux Girls St; Pres Band; NHS; Sch Pl; Rptr Yrbk; VP Fr Clb; Pres Sci Clb; Chrldng; Univ; Med.

HARVEY, PATRICIA; Buena Vista HS; Saginaw, MI; 12/157 Chrh Wkr; Cmnty Wkr; Girl Scts; Hosp Ade; Lbry Ade; NHS; Red Cr Ade; Sch Pl; Stu Cncl; Rptr Yrbk; Malcolm X Awrd 79; Honors Awrd 79; Wolverine St Batpist Convntn Oretoiral Contst 79; Michigan St Univ; Jrnlsm.

HARVEY, SCOTT; Maumee HS; Maumee, OH; 50/325 Hon Rl; NHS; Bsbl; Ftbl; Glf; IM Sprt; Mgrs; Univ Of Miami; Engr.

HARVEY, STEPHEN B; Walnut Ridge HS; Columbus, OH; Chrh Wkr; Fr Clb; Letter Bsktbl; Letter Ftbl; Letter Trk; College; Bio Sci.

HARVEY, TINA; New Albany HS; New Albany, OH; Girl Scts; Hon Rl; NHS; Pep Clb; Spn Clb; Trk; College.

HARVEY, VIRGINIA; Brown City Community HS; Brown City, MI; Band; Hon Rl; Fr Clb; FHA;.

HARWAT, TRENA; Brooke HS; Wellsburg, WV; 147/466 Band; Drl Tm; Hon Rl; Lit Mag; Stu Cncl; Yrbk; FNA; Lat Clb; Pep Clb; Mat Maids; Ohio Valley Gen Hosp Schl Of Nursing.

HARWOOD, DAWN; Brookside HS; Sheffield Lke, OH; Band; Hon Rl; NHS; Treas FTA; Chrldng; Lorain Community; Elem Educ.

HARWOOD, DEAN R; Brookside HS; Sheffield Lke, OH; Hon Rl; NHS; Sprt Ed Sch Nwsp; Bsktbl; Capt Glf; Letter Trk; Lorain Comm Coll; Comp Sci.

HARWOOD, NANETTE; Les Cheneaux Community HS; Cedarville, MI; Hon Rl; Sch Pl; Northern Michigan Univ; Acctg.

HASECUSTER, TRACY; Waldron HS; St Paul, IN; Band; Chrh Wkr; Girl Scts; Sct Actv; Yth Flsp; Rptr Sch Nwsp; Pep Clb; Ball St Univ; Phys Ther.

HASELSCHWARDT, SARAH; Chelsea HS; Chelsea, MI; 9/250 VP Jr Cls; Am Leg Aux Girls St; NHS; Off Ade; Sch Mus; Yrbk; Letter Ten; Capt Chrldng; Coll.

HASELTON, PAMELA; Walter E Stebbins HS; Dayton, OH; Girl Scts; Hon Rl; Hosp Ade; Sch Mus; Sch Pl; Sct Actv; Drama Clb; Cit Awd; God Cntry Awd; Univ; Eng.

HASHIMOTO, NAOMI; Yellow Springs HS; Yellow Sprg, OH; 17/76 Ed Yrbk; Yrbk; Fr Clb; Dartmouth Univ.

HASKAMP, RONALD; Greensburg Community HS; Greensbrg, IN; 1/203 Val; Am Leg Boys St; FCA; Hon Rl; NHS; Sch Pl; Lat Clb; Sci Clb; Purdue Univ; Engr.

HASKELL, JODY; Penn HS; Granger, IN; 5/457 Cls Rep Frsh Cls; Chrh Wkr; Hon Rl; NHS; Sch Pl; Yth Flsp; Fr Clb; Pep Clb; Butler Univ; Bus.

HASKETT, PATRICIA; Newbury HS; Chagrin Falls, OH; Chrs; Hon Rl; Jr NHS; NHS; Drama Clb; Ger Clb; Capt Bsktbl; Capt Crs Cntry; Capt Trk; JC Awd; Univ; Educ.

HASKETT, SHELLEY; John Marshall HS; Indianapolis, IN; 76/467 Hon Rl; Off Ade; Sch Mus; Sch Pl; Stu Cncl; Key Clb; Spn Clb; Chrldng; PPFtbl; Ball St Univ; Pre Law.

HASKINS, AUDREY; Edgewood HS; Trenton, OH; 12/294 Capt Drl Tm; Girl Scts; Hon Rl; JA; Sec Frsh Cls; Stg Crw; Rptr Sch Nwsp; Sch Nwsp; Drama Clb; Miami Univ; Elem Educ.

HASKINS, DAVID; Lowell HS; Lowell, IN; 4-H; Bsbl; Ball State Univ; Architecture.

HASKINS, DIANE; Maumee HS; Maumee, OH; 17/341 VP Chrs; Hon Rl; NHS; Quill & Scroll; Pres Yth Flsp; Sprt Ed Sch Nwsp; Letter Bsbl; Letter Bsktbl; Letter Ten; Ohi Univ; Journalism.

HASKINS, JODI; Harper Creek HS; Ceresco, MI; 1/244 Cls Rep Soph Cls; Trs Jr Cls; Am Leg Aux Girls St; Hon Rl; Jr NHS; NHS; Pol Wkr; Stu Cncl; 4-H; Spn Clb; Michigan St Univ.

HASKINS, LORI; Midland HS; Midland, MI; 65/486 Treas Band; Hon Rl; NHS; Pol Wkr; Pres Ger Clb; PPFtbl; Receve Awd For 4th Highest Bsktbl Avg In City; Nazareth Coll; Nursing.

HASKINS, PAMELA; Catholic Central HS; Steubenvll, OH; 10/204 Sec Frsh Cls; Sec Soph Cls; Sec Jr Cls; Pres Sr Cls; Am Leg Aux Girls St; Hon Rl; NHS; College; Elem Educa.

HASKINS, TAMMY; Greenwood Community HS; Indianapolis, IN; 21/255 Chrh Wkr; Hon Rl; NHS; Stg Crw; Pres Drama Clb; Letter Ten; Soc Of Dist Amer HS Stu 78; Taylor Univ; Bio.

HASLINGER, KIMBERLY; Old Trail School; Bath, OH; Trs Frsh Cls; Pres Soph Cls; Pres Jr Cls; Hon Rl; Lit Mag; Stu Cncl; Ed Yrbk; Rptr Yrbk; Rptr Sch Nwsp; Letter Bsktbl; Univ; Bus.

HASS, JULIE; Milford HS; Highland, MI; Band; Cmnty Wkr; Hon Rl; NHS; 4-H; Ger Clb; IM Sprt; Mic State Univ; Vet Med.

HASSAN, RONALD G; Brooke HS; Bethany, WV; 5/403 Am Leg Boys St; Boy Scts; Hon Rl; NHS; Sct Actv; 4-H; Key Clb; Spn Clb; Wrstlng; Coach Actv; Eagle Scout 78; Univ Of Maryland; Fire Sci.

HASSEL, THOMAS; Purcell HS; Cincinnati, OH; Sec Frsh Cls; Sec Soph Cls; Sec Jr Cls; Hon Rl; Sct Actv; Capt Ftbl; Letter Trk; Chrldng; IM Sprt; College; Engr.

HASSELBACH, LAURA A; L M Powers Educ Ctr; Flushing, MI; 4/250 Cmp Fr Grls; Pres Debate Tm; Hon Rl; Natl Forn Lg; Sec NHS; Letter Trk; Natl Merit SF; Univ Of Michigan; Med Doctor.

HASSELBECK, THERESA; Houston HS; Houston, OH; Hon Rl; Sch Pl; Stg Crw; Rptr Sch Nwsp; Sch Nwsp; 4-H; Pep Clb; Trk; Mgrs; Scr Kpr; Voc Schl; Bookkeeping.

HASSELL, VICKI; Plymouth HS; Plymouth, IN; 20/250 AFS; Cmp Fr Grls; Hon Rl; Red Cr Ade; Stu Cncl; Ed Yrbk; Rptr Yrbk; Drama Clb; Spn Clb; Hanover; Elem Ed.

HASSEN, ROBERT; Chippewa Hills HS; Chippewa Lake, MI; Band; Debate Tm; Hon Rl; Sch Mus; Sch Pl; Stg Crw; Central Mic Univ; Writing.

HASSER, MONICA; Benton Central Jr Sr HS; Earl Park, IN; 27/232 Hon Rl; NHS; VP OEA; IM Sprt; OEA Stenographic I Winner; Typing I Awd Intensive Ofc Lab Sec Awd;.

HASSEVOORT, STEVEN; West Ottowa HS; Holland, MI; 12/313 Band; Chrh Wkr; Hon Rl; NHS; Orch; Yth Flsp; Natl Merit Ltr; Hope College; Architecture.

HASSINGER, RODNEY; Howell HS; Howell, MI; Hon Rl; NHS; Michigan St Univ.

HAST, DONNA; Edison HS; Berlin Heights, OH; Band; Hon Rl; NHS; 4-H; FTA; Bsktbl; Trk; GAA; Mgrs; 4-H Awd; Bowling Green State Univ; Phys Ed.

HASTEDT, CHARLENE; Fairview HS; Mark Ctr, OH; 1/125 Val; Am Leg Aux Girls St; Hon Rl; Pres NHS; 4-H; FHA; Mth Clb; Spn Clb; Mgrs; DAR Awd; Univ Of Toledo.

HASTEDT, VICTORIA; Fairview HS; Mark Center, OH; 1/110 Cls Rep Frsh Cls; Cls Rep Soph Cls; Am Leg Aux Girls St; Hon Rl; NHS; Sec 4-H; Mth Clb; Spn Clb; Gym; Top 10% In NEDT 78; Awd In Physiology Anatomy Algbr II 79; Univ; Zoology.

HASTILOW, DEBORAH; New Albany HS; New Albany, OH; Band; Chrh Wkr; Hon Rl; Off Ade; Ger Clb; Bsktbl; Trk; IM Sprt; Cit Awd; Pres Awd; Columbus Tech Schl; EMT.

HASTINGS, CANDY; Lutheran HS West; Rocky River, OH; Chrh Wkr; Girl Scts; Pres Sct Actv; Yth Flsp; Rptr Sch Nwsp; Treas Sci Clb; Twrlr; God Cntry Awd; Rep To Ireland Expermnt In Internatl Living 79; Rep For Oh Leadrshp Seminar 78; Sr Achvmnt Awd 78; Allan Hancock Coll; Forestry.

HASTINGS, DARLENE; Marion L Steele HS; Elyria, OH; 114/353 Band; Letter Chrs; Hon Rl; Hosp Ade; Sch Mus; Stg Crw; Yrbk; Drama Clb; Fr Clb; FTA; Lorain Cnty Community Coll; Data Pro.

HASTINGS, KARIS; Garber HS; Essexville, MI; 1/178 Cls Rep Frsh Cls; Cls Rep Soph Cls; Cls Rep Sr Cls; Am Leg Aux Girls St; Band; Debate Tm; Natl Forn Lg; Sch Mus; Sch Pl; Stu Cncl; Univ; Poli Sci.

HASTINGS, KATHY; Kenton Sr HS; Kenton, OH; 31/193 Hon Rl; NHS; Quill & Scroll; Ed Sch Nwsp; Bowling Green St Univ; Nursing.

HASTINGS, LAURIE; Chelsea HS; Chelsea, MI; AFS; Hon Rl; Jr NHS; 4-H; Trk; 4-H Awd; Michigan St Univ; Med.

HASTINGS, MARK; Greene County Central HS; Newberry, IN; 10/30 VP Frsh Cls; Chrh Wkr; Hon Rl; Stu Cncl; Pres Yth Flsp; Rptr Yrbk; FFA; Pep Clb; Capt Bsktbl; Crs Cntry; Ivy Tech Schl; Computer.

HASTINGS, MICHELLE; Buckeye W HS; Mt Pleasant, OH; 5/83 Band; Chrs; Chrh Wkr; Cmnty Wkr; Girl Scts; Hon Rl; Sch Mus; Sch Pl; Sct Actv; Stg Crw; Oral Roberts Univ; Ministry.

HASTINGS, SHARON; Highland HS; Medina, OH; Cl Rep Jr Cls; Cls Rep Sr Cls; Band; Chrs; Drl Tm; Hon Rl; Jr NHS; NHS; Off Ade; Sch Mus; Univ; Math.

HASTON, CINDY; Carme HS; Carmel, IN; Aud/Vis; Hon Rl; NHS; DECA; Radio Disc Jockey.

HASTON, DOUGLAS; Shenandoah HS; Middletown, IN; 34/118 Am Leg Boys St; Sch Nwsp; Letter Wrstlng; Univ; Sci.

HASTREITER, TIM; Memorial HS; St Marys, OH; 42/212 NHS; Rptr Sch Nwsp; Letter Bsbl; Letter Bsktbl; Capt Ftbl; IM Sprt; Ohio St Univ; Busns Admin.

HATALA, CHERYL L; Springfield Local HS; Poland, OH; Trs Frsh Cls; Trs Soph Cls; Cl Rep Jr Cls; AFS; Chrh Wkr; Cmnty Wkr; Drl Tm; Girl Scts; Hon Rl; Hosp Ade; Univ; Cler Work.

HATALA, GLENN; Streetsboro HS; Streetsboro, OH; Band; Boy Scts; Hon Rl; Orch; Letter Ftbl; Letter Trk; Wrstlng; Air Force Acad; Tech Engr.

HATCH, DEBBIE; Van Buren HS; Findlay, OH; 6/90 Sec Sr Cls; Band; Chrs; Hon Rl; NHS; Sch Mus; Yth Flsp; Ed Yrbk; Chrldng; Bowling Green State Univ.

HATCH, GREER; Whitehall HS; Whitehall, MI; 67/150 Drama Clb; Central Michigan Univ; Acctg.

HATCH, NANCY; Center Line Sr HS; Center Line, MI; 36/427 Trs Sr Cls; Band; Sec Jr NHS; NHS; Sch Pl; Stu Cncl; Fr Clb; OEA; Chrldng; Twrlr; Central Michigan Univ; Bus Educ.

HATCH, NANCY R; Center Line Sr HS; Center Line, MI; 37/417 Trs Sr Cls; Hon Rl; Sec Jr NHS; Lit Mag; NHS; Sch Pl; Stu Cncl; Fr Clb; OEA; Swmmng; Central Michigan Univ; CPA.

HATCH, STANLEY W; Ann Arbor Pioneer HS; Ann Arbor, MI; Am Leg Boys St; Band; Boy Scts; Hon Rl; Sct Actv; Sprt Ed Yrbk; Sprt Ed Sch Nwsp; Letter Crs Cntry; Trk; Kiwan Awd; Univ; Natural Resources.

HATCHER, GREG; Albion HS; Albion, MI; Band; FCA; Hon Rl; Sch Pl; Stg Crw; Letter Bsbl; Letter Crs Cntry; Letter Wrstlng; Tmr; Rotary Awd; Alma Coll; Bus.

HATCHER, HERBERT; Garrett HS; Churubuseo, IN; FCA; Hon Rl; Pep Clb; Spn Clb; Letter Ftbl; Letter Trk; St Hon Schlrshp 79; Hoosier Schlr Awd 79; Span Hon Soc Pres Jr Yr Sec Tres Sr Yr 77 78 & 79; Univ; Acctg.

HATER, BETTE; Mt Healthy HS; Cincinnati, OH; Cl Rep Jr Cls; Lbry Ade; Bsbl; Bsktbl; Ten; IM Sprt; Mgrs; College.

HATFIELD, ANN; Belding HS; Belding, MI; Lbry Ade; Sch Pl; Stg Crw; Yth Flsp; Rptr Sch Nwsp; Drama Clb; FFA; Trk; Olivet Nazerene Coll; Cmnctns.

HATFIELD, BARRY; Streetsboro HS; Streetsboro, OH; 9/194 Chrh Wkr; Hon Rl; NHS; Rptr Sch Nwsp; Sch Nwsp; Ohio Test Of Schlstc Achiev Amer History 79; Univ; Acctg.

HATFIELD, CHRISTOPHER; Bishop Dwenger HS; Fort Wayne, IN; Trs Frsh Cls; Am Leg Boys St; Boy Scts; Hon Rl; NHS; Pres Stu Cncl; Letter Ten; Coach Actv; Natl Merit SF; Notre Dame Univ; Government.

HATFIELD, DIANNE; Franklin Comm HS; Franklin, IN; 15/285 AFS; Band; Chrh Wkr; Girl Scts; NHS; Orch; Sch Mus; Sch Pl; Stu Cncl; Lat Clb; Ball St Univ; Chemistry.

HATFIELD, GREGORY J; Bishop Dwenger HS; Ft Wayne, IN; 2/270 Pres Frsh Cls; VP Soph Cls; Cl Rep Jr Cls; Am Leg Boys St; Boy Scts; Hon Rl; NHS; Stu Cncl; Wrstlng; Notre Dame; Political Science.

HATFIELD, JAMES; Clay Sr HS; Curtice, OH; Chrs; Chrh Wkr; Hon Rl; JA; Univ; Psych.

HATFIELD, JOE D; Hurricane HS; Hurrican, WV; Hon Rl; Letter Crs Cntry; Letter Trk; IM Sprt; Univ.

HATFIELD, KATHY; Unioto HS; Chillicothe, OH; 10/125 Band; Chrs; Hon Rl; NHS; Fr Clb; Letter Bsktbl; Letter Trk; Coach Actv; Univ; Acctg.

HATFIELD, MARK; Mansfield Malabar HS; Mansfield, OH; 13/37 Cl Rep Jr Cls; Cls Rep Sr Cls; Am Leg Boys St; Band; Hon Rl; NHS; Ed Sch Nwsp; Crs Cntry; Ten; Trk; College.

HATFIELD, MICHAEL; Willard HS; Willard, OH; Band; Boy Scts; Hon Rl; Orch; Yth Flsp; Ftbl; Letter Wrstlng; Univ.

HATFIELD, NANCY; Xenia HS; Xenia, OH; 33/518 Cls Rep Sr Cls; Am Leg Aux Girls St; Hon Rl; NHS; Stu Cncl; Fr Clb; Trk; Natl Hnr Soc Awd 79; Schlstc Awd Vlybl 78; Vlybl 2 Yr Varsity; Miami Univ; Office Admin.

HATFIELD, PHILLIP; Williamson HS; Williamson, WV; Am Leg Boys St; Hon Rl; NHS; Sci Clb; College; Engr.

HATFIELD, ROBERT; Bishop Flaget HS; Chillicothe, OH; 2/40 Hon Rl; NHS; Spn Clb; Bsbl; Bsktbl; Trk; Ohio St Univ; Law.

HATHAWAY, ANN; Whitko HS; Pierceton, IN; Am Leg Aux Girls St; Chrs; Hon Rl; MMM; Sch Mus; Sch Pl; Rptr Sch Nwsp; Glf; GAA; Ball State Univ; Music.

HATHAWAY, DAVID; De Kalb HS; Auburn, IN; FCA; NHS; Bsktbl; Trk; College; Math.

HATHAWAY, HOPE; Wintersville HS; Steubenville, OH; Band; Chrh Wkr; Hon Rl; Jr NHS; NHS; Orch; Sch Pl; Stg Crw; Drama Clb; Fr Clb; Youngstown St Univ; Bio.

HATHAWAY, JONATHAN; Liberty HS; Salem, WV; 6/231 Am Leg Boys St; Band; Boy Scts; Chrs; Hon Rl; Jr NHS; NHS; Sch Mus; Mth Clb; Ten; Wv Univ Achvmnt Schlrshp 79; Masonic Schlrshp 79; West Virginia Univ; Elec Engr.

HATHAWAY, KATHRYN; Otsego HS; Kalamazoo, MI; 2/216 Cls Rep Soph Cls; Sec Jr Cls; Cl Rep Jr Cls; Sec Sr Cls; Sal; Chrs; Chrh Wkr; Cmnty Wkr; Drl Tm; Hon Rl; Voted Most Likely To Succeed By Classmates; Reg & St Honors Choir; Yng Peoples Ctznshp Seminar Schlrshp Rec; Grace Coll; Educ.

HATHAWAY, NANCY; New Haven HS; New Have, IN; Cls Rep Frsh Cls; Cls Rep Soph Cls; Pres Jr Cls; Cl Rep Jr Cls; Hon Rl; Stu Cncl; Letter Bsktbl; Trk; PPFtbl; Univ.

HATHAWAY, NANCY; Hurricane HS; Hurricane, WV; Band; Cmnty Wkr; Girl Scts; Hon Rl; Sct Actv; Yth Flsp; Y-Teens; FBLA; West Virginia Univ; Legl Asst.

HATHAWAY, PAMELA; Garfield HS; Akron, OH; 6/450 Hon Rl; Treas JA; NHS; OEA; Spn Clb; Cit Awd; JA Awd; Busns Schl; Busns Admin.

HATHAWAY, RHEA A; Groveport Madison Sr HS; Columbus, OH; Band; Drl Tm; Girl Scts; Hon Rl; NHS; PPFtbl; Scr Kpr; Busns Schl; Data Processing.

HATHAWAY, ROBYN; Glen Este HS; Batavia, OH; Hon Rl; Off Ade; Drama Clb; Pep Clb; Univ Of Cincinnati.

HATHCOCK, LISA A; Interlochen Arts Academy; Ft Smith, AR; Cls Rep Frsh Cls; Band; Chrs; Girl Scts; Hon Rl; Jr NHS; NHS; Stu Cncl; Sec Fr Clb; Univ.

HATHORN, TAMARA; Watkins Memorial HS; Balt, OH; 8/226 Cmnty Wkr; Girl Scts; Hon Rl; 4-H; Lat Clb; Trk; 4-H Awd; Awd Of Distinction By St Of Oh 79; Hon Roll 4 Semestrs 78; Hon Roll 6 Semestrs 77; Ohio Univ; Vet Med.

HATLEY, MITZI; Wellston HS; Wellston, OH; 17/148 Sec Jr Cls; Band; Chrs; Hon Rl; VP Stu Cncl; Bsktbl; Sftbl Letter & All League Hon Mention; Tri Hi Y; Schlrhsp Tm; Univ.

HATT, SHELLY; Chelsea HS; Chelsea, MI; 13/210 Hon Rl; Lbry Ade; NHS; 4-H; FFA; PPFtbl; Scr Kpr; Jackson Cmnty Coll; Data Proc.

HATTEN, LISA; Buffalo HS; Kenova, WV; Cl Rep Jr Cls; Band; Chrh Wkr; Hon Rl; Sch Pl; Yth Flsp; Rptr Yrbk; Yrbk; Drama Clb; 4-H; Typing II Awd 78; All Area Band 79; Annual Yearbk Bus Mgr; Bus Schl; Sec.

HATTEN, TAMMY; Buffalo HS; Kenova, WV; 12/103 VP Sr Cls; Band; Chrs; Hon Rl; NHS; Off Ade; Sch Mus; Sch Pl; Sprt Ed Yrbk; Drama Clb; Frederick Chopin Pianist Awd; Typing II Awd; All St Pianist Accompanist;.

HATTEN, TERRI; Whetstone HS; Columbus, OH; Am Leg Aux Girls St; Band; Hon Rl; Jr NHS; NHS; Stu Cncl; Spn Clb; Capt Chrldng; PPFtbl; C of C Awd; Semi Finalist & Then Finalist In Miss Teenage Pageant In 77; Ernd Excel By Oh Acad Of Sci For Sci Proj 77; Univ; Mrktng.

HATTER, MIKE; Whetstone HS; Columbus, OH; Boy Scts; Drama Clb; Lat Clb; Letter Crs Cntry; Letter Trk; Ohi State Univ; Educ.

HATTERY, HALANA; La Ville Jr Sr HS; South Bend, IN; 5/130 Chrs; NHS; Stg Crw; Rptr Yrbk; Yrbk; Sch Nwsp; Sec Drama Clb; Fr Clb; FHA; Twrlr; Ball St Univ; Jrnlsm.

HATTIG, T; Brandon HS; Oxford, MI; 20/190 Hon Rl; Crs Cntry; Trk; IM Sprt; Scr Kpr; Oakland Cmnty Coll; Bus Mgmt.

HATTLE, JIMMY; Eastern HS; Lucasville, OH; Hon Rl; Stu Cncl; Rptr Yrbk; Rptr Sch Nwsp; 4-H; Pep Clb; Bsbl; Bsktbl; Algebra 1 Schlrshp Tm 76; Sci Schlrshp 77; Univ.

HATTON, LADONNA; Worthington HS; Columbus, OH; 1/575 Val; Band; Natl Forn Lg; NHS; Orch; Sch Mus; Ed Yrbk; Case Western Reserve Univ; Law.

HATTON, STEPHEN; Loveland Hurst HS; Loveland, OH; 15/290 Hon Rl; VP JA; Ger Clb; Key Clb; Pep Clb; Letter Socr; Dnfth Awd; Univ; Brdcstng.

HATZELL, JULIE; Jay County HS; Redkey, IN; Am Leg Aux Girls St; Cmnty Wkr; Hon Rl; NHS; Chmn Stu Cncl; Pres Yth Flsp; Y-Teens; Sci Clb; Letter Gym; Chrldng; Holds Shcl Record For Optional 1978; Ball State Univ; Phys Ther.

HAUBENSTRICKER, TIM; Frankenmuth HS; Frankenmuth, MI; 1/180 Am Leg Boys St; Band; Chrh Wkr; Hon Rl; NHS; Sct Actv; Letter Trk; Ferris St Univ; Comp Sci.

HAUBERT, MAXINE; New Riegel HS; Alvada, OH; 3/51 VP Frsh Cls; Trs Jr Cls; VP Sr Cls; VP Band; Chrs; Hon Rl; NHS; Sch Pl; FHA; FTA; Elkhart Inst Of Tech; Med Lab Tech.

HAUBERT, PHILIP C; Kimball HS; Royal Oak, MI; 20/597 Boy Scts; Chrs; Hon Rl; NHS; Sch Mus; Sct Actv; Rptr Yrbk; Mth Clb; Letter Crs Cntry; Trk; Michigan St Univ; Phys Sci.

HAUDENSCHILD, ERIC; Loudonville HS; Lakeville, OH; Am Leg Boys St; Chrh Wkr; Hon Rl; Jr NHS; NHS; Rptr Yrbk; Rptr Sch Nwsp; Bsbl; Bsktbl; Capt Ftbl; Univ.

HAUENSTEIN, GENNA; Clay Battelle HS; Burton, WV; Pres Band; Hon Rl; Jr NHS; Lbry Ade; NHS; Stu Cncl; Sprt Ed Sch Nwsp; College; Med Assist.

HAUER, DEE; Brownstown Central HS; Vallonia, IN; 1/140 Trs Jr Cls; Pres Sr Cls; Hon Rl; NHS; FFA; Sci Clb; Spn Clb; Letter Trk; GAA; IM Sprt; College; Soc Work.

HAUER II, D; Hurricane HS; Hurricane, WV; Boy Scts; Chrh Wkr; Sct Actv; Yth Flsp; Ten; IM Sprt; God Cntry Awd; College; Aeronautical.

HAUETER, GEORGIA; Smithville HS; N Lawrence, OH; Am Leg Aux Girls St; Chrs; Hon Rl; Sch Pl; Pres Yth Flsp; Drama Clb; Fr Clb; Fairmont St Univ; Bus Admin.

HAUG, DENISE; William Henry Harrison HS; Evansville, IN; Hon Rl; Hosp Ade; JA; Cit Awd; JA Awd; Tri St Beauty Coll; Cosmetology.

HAUGAARD, KRISTINE; Lawrence HS; Lawrence, MI; Sec Frsh Cls; VP Soph Cls; Cl Rep Jr Cls; Band; Hon Rl; Sch Pl; Stu Cncl; Rptr Yrbk; Chrldng; GAA; Michigan St Univ.

HAUGHN, JAMES; Wabash HS; Wabash, IN; 2/200 Hon Rl; NHS; Sch Mus; Sch Pl; Ftbl; Wrstlng; Mbr Of Hnr Progr For Frgn Lang Stu IU 78; Gridiron Awd Var Ltr & Hghst GPA 77; Rcptnt Of Ruth M Schrlshp; Carleton Coll.

HAUGHT, JEFFERY; North Marion HS; Farmington, WV; Boy Scts; Chrh Wkr; FCA; Hon Rl; Sch Mus; Sct Actv; Yth Flsp; Bsktbl; Ftbl; IM Sprt; Mt Vernon Nazarene Coll.

HAUGHT, KENNETH; Lincoln HS; Lumberport, WV; Hst Frsh Cls; Chrh Wkr; Hon Rl; VICA; Bsktbl; Law.

HAUGHT, LORI; Valley HS; Reader, WV; Sec Jr Cls; Band; Drm Mjrt; Girl Scts; Hon Rl; Sch Pl; Yth Flsp; Sprt Ed Yrbk; Sec Bsktbl; WVU; Math.

HAUGHT, MICHAEL W; Marietta HS; Marietta, OH; Debate Tm; Hon Rl; 4-H; Ohio State Univ; Engr.

HAUGHT, TERRY; Mannington HS; Mannington, WV; 1/114 Pres Sr Cls; Val; Am Leg Boys St; Pres Aud/Vis; NHS; Stg Crw; Mth Clb; Am Leg Awd; Elk Awd; Fairmont St Coll; Engr Tech.

HAUGUEL, NANCY; Washington HS; So Bend, IN; 2/355 Cmp Fr Grls; Chrs; Hon Rl; NHS; Sch Mus; Sch Pl; Stg Crw; Yrbk; Drama Clb; Fr Clb; Univ; Acctg.

HAUHT, SUSAN; Coloma HS; Coloma, MI; 11/220 Hon Rl; NHS; Off Ade; Sch Pl; Stg Crw; Sec Drama Clb; VP 4-H; Mic State Univ; Bus Admin.

HAUKE, JANET; Ripley Union Lewis HS; Ripley, OH; Cl Rep Jr Cls; Am Leg Aux Girls St; Girl Scts; Hon Rl; NHS; Sch Pl; Sct Actv; Sdlty; Stg Crw; Stu Cncl; Yrbk; Univ Of Dayton; Interior Dsgn.

HAUMESSER, SCOTT; Medina Sr HS; Medina, OH; Sch Mus; Sch Pl; Stg Crw; Key Clb; Sci Clb; Tech Schl; Elec Engr.

HAUN, JOETTA; University HS; Morgantown, WV; 20/160 Cls Rep Frsh Cls; Cls Rep Soph Cls; Cl Rep Jr Cls; Chrs; Hon Rl; Jr NHS; Pol Wkr; Sch Mus; Sch Pl; Stu Cncl; WVU; Dent Hygnst.

HAUPRICH, DENA; Morton Sr HS; Hammond, IN; 63/499 Cls Rep Frsh Cls; Cls Rep Soph Cls; Cl Rep Jr Cls; Cls Rep Sr Cls; Girl Scts; Hon Rl; Jr NHS; Pol Wkr; Quill & Scroll; Stu Cncl; Indiana Univ; Nursing.

HAUPT, ERIC K; Bentley HS; Livonia, MI; 4/659 Band; Boy Scts; Chrh Wkr; Cmnty Wkr; Hon Rl; Sct Actv; Elk Awd; Univ Of Mic; Engr.

HAUSBECK, MARY; Bridgeport HS; Saginaw, MI; 4/360 Cls Rep Soph Cls; Cl Rep Jr Cls; Cls Rep Sr Cls; Band; Chrh Wkr; Cmnty Wkr; Hon Rl; Hosp Ade; NHS; Quill & Scroll; W Mc Nally Schlrshp 79; News Corrspndnt Saginaw News 79; Membr Of Homecmng Court 79; Michigan St Univ; Horticltr.

HAUSE, GREGORY; Elgin HS; La Rue, OH; 20/155 VP Soph Cls; Chrs; Hon Rl; Lat Clb; Letter Ftbl; Letter Trk; College; Law.

HAUSER, FRANK J; Steubenville Cath Cntrl HS; Steubenville, OH; 50/200 Pres Band; Boy Scts; Chrh Wkr; Hon Rl; Spn Clb; Trk; Univ; Econ.

HAUSER, MARY; Oak Hills HS; Cincinnati, OH; 35/854 VP AFS; Hon Rl; NHS; Crs Cntry; Trk; Tmr; Univ Of Cincinnati; Lang.

HAUSFELD, MICHAEL A; R Nelson Snider HS; Ft Wayne, IN; 63/585 Chrh Wkr; Hon Rl; Letter Bsbl; IM Sprt; Cit Awd; Distngsh Schlr 77 & 78; Miami Univ; Acctg.

HAUT, WILLIAM; Elkhart Central HS; Elkhart, IN; Band; Hon Rl; Ten; IM Sprt; Univ.

HAUTANEN, SUSAN; Roosevelt HS; Marenisco, MI; VP Soph Cls; VP Jr Cls; Band; Chrs; Hon Rl; Natl Forn Lg; Rptr Yrbk; Sch Nwsp; Pep Clb; College.

HAUTER, KAY; Crestview HS; Van Wert, OH; Chrh Wkr; Lbry Ade; Rptr Sch Nwsp; 4-H; FHA; Pep Clb; 4-H Awd; St Homemaker;.

HAUTMAN, GERALD; Bishop Foley HS; Detroit, MI; 25/200 Aud/Vis; Hon Rl; Natl Forn Lg; NHS; Rptr Sch Nwsp; Crs Cntry; Trk; IM Sprt; Mic State Univ; Pre Vet.

HAVANAS, JOHN; Chamberlin HS; Twinsburg, OH; Letter Ftbl; Univ Of Akron.

HAVELY, ROD; Hamilton Southeastern HS; Noblesville, IN; Cl Rep Jr Cls; Cls Rep Sr Cls; Chrh Wkr; FCA; Hon Rl; Sch Mus; Sch Pl; Stu Cncl; Yth Flsp; Pep Clb; Purdue Univ; Elec Engr.

HAVEMAN, JAN; S Christian HS; Grand Rapids, MI; 4/173 Sec Frsh Cls; Band; Boy Scts; Chrs; Chrh Wkr; Hon Rl; Letter Bsktbl; Letter Trk; IM Sprt; Mgrs; Univ; Med.

HAVEN, DARLA; Lebanon HS; Franklin, OH; 17/300 Band; Cmp Fr Grls; Chrs; Drl Tm; Hon Rl; NHS; Sch Pl; Stg Crw; Drama Clb; Fr Clb; Cincinnati Univ; Comm Art.

HAVENS, JANE; Fairview Park HS; Fairview Pk, OH; Band; Cmnty Wkr; Drm Mjrt; FCA; Hosp Ade; Pol Wkr; Sct Actv; College; Law.

HAVENS, KEVIN; Madison Plains HS; Mt Sterling, OH; Boy Scts; Cmnty Wkr; Hon Rl; Pres FFA; Ftbl; St Farmer Awd; Star Agri Busns Man; Outstndng Youth In Madison Co In Swine Production; Laurel Oaks Voc Schl; Ag.

HAVENS, LINDA; Belding HS; Belding, MI; Band; Hon Rl; NHS; Off Ade; Sch Mus; Stg Crw; VP Pep Clb; Letter Mgrs; Pom Pon; Coll; Busns.

HAVENS, SHARON; Zane Trace HS; Kingston, OH; 7/95 Am Leg Aux Girls St; NHS; Rptr Yrbk; Rptr Sch Nwsp; Sec 4-H; FHA; Pres Pep Clb; Spn Clb; Ross Cnty Jr Fairboard Mbr 77 & 78; Chillicothe Municpl Ct Stu Bailiff 78; FHH Queen; Ohio St Univ; Human Serv Tech.

HAVENSTEIN, PAUL; Flat Rock Sr HS; Flat Rock, MI; Band; Hon Rl; Jr NHS; Sch Mus; Sch Pl; Drama Clb; Sci Clb; Top 5 Acad Awd 77; Soroptimist Schlrshp 77; Interlochen All Stater 76 77 & 78; Univ Of Michigan; Forensic Med.

HAVERLAND, DOUG; Linsly Institute; Steubenville, OH; Chrh Wkr; Hon Rl; ROTC; Ger Clb; Capt Swmmng; Top German Stdnt 3 Yrs; Univ; Pre Med.

HAVERLAND, JENI; Carey HS; Carey, OH; 10/86 Cls Rep Sr Cls; Am Leg Aux Girls St; Hon Rl; NHS; Sch Mus; Sch Pl; Stu Cncl; Y-Teens; Ohio Wesleyan Univ; Law.

HAVERLAND, MICHAEL; Forest Park HS; Forest Pk, OH; 91/385 Am Leg Boys St; Boy Scts; Chrs; Chrh Wkr; Cmnty Wkr; Pol Wkr; Sch Mus; Sct Actv; Yth Flsp; Letter Bsktbl; College; Bus Marketing.

HAVERLAND, TERESA; Mc Auley HS; Cincinnati, OH; Stg Crw; Bsbl; Gym; Swmmng; Coach Actv; GAA; IM Sprt; Mgrs; Univ Of Cincinnati; Comp Prog.

HAVERSPERGER, STEVEN; Jennings County HS; No Vernon, IN; Boy Scts; Hon Rl; NHS; Rptr Sch Nwsp; Pep Clb; Bsktbl; Coach Actv; Ball State; Carpentry.

HAVEY, GLENNA S; Kalkaska HS; Kalkaska, MI; 11/135 Band; Chrh Wkr; Girl Scts; Hon Rl; NHS; Sch Pl; GAA; College; Acctg.

HAVLIK, CAROL; Clay HS; S Bend, IN; Cl Rep Jr Cls; Chrh Wkr; Stu Cncl; Pep Clb; Coll; Zoology.

HAWARNY, AMY; Milan HS; Milan, MI; Band; Girl Scts; Hon Rl; Orch; Sch Mus; Sch Pl; Stg Crw; Sprt Ed Yrbk; Drama Clb; St Of Michigan Comp Schlrshp Awd; Eastern Michigan Univ; Spec Ed.

HAWBAKER, LYNN; South Adams HS; Geneva, IN; 44/125 Chrh Wkr; Yth Flsp; 4-H; Pres FFA; Star Greenhand FFA; 2nd In Dist Crop Production; 2nd In Dist Reports Scrapbook; Purdue Univ; Agri.

HAWES, GLENDA; Salem HS; Salem, IN; Band; Chrs; Chrh Wkr; PAVAS; Sch Mus; Sch Pl; Y-Teens; Drama Clb; Pep Clb; Spn Clb; Miss Ideal Jobs Daughter 76; Division 1 Solo At ISMA Vocal 79; Bakers Dozen Vocal Grp 78; Indiana Univ; Speech.

HAWES, GREGORY; Reitz Memorial HS; Evansville, IN; 140/230 Chrh Wkr; Hon Rl; Stu Cncl; Yth Flsp; Ed Sch Nwsp; Rptr Sch Nwsp; Sci Clb; Crs Cntry; Trk; IM Sprt; Ind Univ; Bus.

HAWES, LAURA; Huntington HS; Huntington, WV; 21/252 Hon Rl; NHS; Sch Pl; Y-Teens; Drama Clb; Fr Clb; Lat Clb; Pep Clb; Mat Maids; Vanderbilt Univ; Molecular Biology.

HAWK, ANDREW; Fairmont West HS; Kettering, OH; Hon Rl; NHS; Fr Clb; Mth Clb; Capt Bsbl; Letter Bsktbl; Capt Socr; Depauw Univ; Sci.

HAWK, MARSHA; Beavercreek HS; Xenia, OH; Chrh Wkr; Hon Rl; Hosp Ade; NHS; Off Ade; Kettering Coll Of Med Arts; R N.

HAWK, MICHAEL; Chillicothe HS; Chillicothe, OH; Hon Rl; Drama Clb; Lat Clb; Trk; Ohi St Univ; English.

HAWK, SHERYL; West Carrollton HS; W Carrollton, OH; Orch; Sch Mus; Ger Clb; Bsktbl; Nalt Hon Soc 79; 5 Th Yr Awd In ERA 79; Highst Ineng Segment Of PSAT Incls 79; Univ; Comp Sci.

HAWK, STEVEN; Jefferson HS; Kearneysville, WV; Hon Rl; Sec Spn Clb; IM Sprt; Military.

HAWK, VICKI; Parkway HS; Rockford, OH; Trs Frsh Cls; Band; Hon Rl; Lbry Ade; 4-H; FTA; Lat Clb; Pep Clb; Sci Clb; Spn Clb; Lima Tech Coll; Comp Sci.

HAWKEY, BARBARA; Arcanum Butler HS; Arcanum, OH; 27/99 Aud/Vis; Hon Rl; Sec FHA; Scr Kpr; Ohi State; Comp Prog.

HAWKEY, THOMAS; Clawson HS; Clawson, MI; Boy Scts; Chrh Wkr; Hon Rl; Sct Actv; Trk; Air Force Acad.

HAWKINS, CASSANDRA; Alter HS; Centerville, OH; 53/350 Cls Rep Sr Cls; Chrs; Drl Tm; Hon Rl; Sch Mus; Sch Pl; Drama Clb; Fr Clb; GAA;.

HAWKINS, CRYSTAL L; Bridgeport Sr HS; Bridgeport, WV; Band; Hon Rl; Jr NHS; NHS; Y-Teens; Pep Clb; Awd Cert Of Merit For Natl Ed Deve Test; West Virginia Univ; Medicine.

HAWKINS, DARLA; Central Preston HS; Kingwood, WV; Band; Chrs; Chrh Wkr; Hon Rl; Yth Flsp; 4-H; FTA; Gym; Swmmng; Chrldng; Beauty School; Beaut.

HAWKINS, DEB; Westerville North HS; Westerville, OH; 81/447 Aud/Vis; Band; Chrs; Girl Scts; Hon Rl; Orch; Fr Clb; 1st Pl Medal Ohio Music Ed Assn Choral; Ohio St Univ; English.

HAWKINS, GWENDOLYN; Henry Ford HS; Detroit, MI; 48/432 Chrs; Hon Rl; Capt Bsktbl; Letter Trk; Volleyball Letter; All City Track & Field High Jump; All City Basketball; Univ Of Michigan; Computer Sci.

HAWKINS, JEANINE L; Mason Sr HS; Mason, MI; Band; Chrs; Hon Rl; Jr NHS; Off Ade; Sch Mus; Sch Pl; Yrbk; Pres 4-H; Sec FFA; Schlrshp Awd FFA 77 79; 4th Pl Essay Contest Ingham Co Lawyers Wives 77; Univ; Bus Admin.

HAWKINS, JEFFREY F; Edgewood HS; Ellettsville, IN; 14/223 Band; Boy Scts; Chrh Wkr; Hon Rl; Sct Actv; Yth Flsp; Boys Clb Am; Elk Awd; Indiana Univ; Accounting.

HAWKINS, JOHN; Lima Sr HS; Lima, OH; 75/500 Aud/Vis; Band; Boy Scts; Chrs; Hon Rl; Lbry Ade; Orch; Sch Mus; Pep Clb; Chess Club; Purdue Univ; Elec Engr.

HAWKINS, KAREN; Buckhannon Upshur HS; Buckhannon, WV; Hon Rl; Lbry Ade; NHS; Ed Yrbk; Rptr Sch Nwsp; Sch Nwsp; 4-H; Coll.

HAWKINS, KATRINA; Tipton HS; Tipton, IN; 36/169 Cl Rep Jr Cls; Cls Rep Sr Cls; Band; Chrs; Sch Mus; Sec Stu Cncl; 4-H; Sci Clb, Bsktbl; Letter Trk; Univ.

HAWKINS, LYNDA; North Miami HS; Peru, IN; Chrs; Hon Rl; Lbry Ade; Sec MMM; VP 4-H; 4-H Awd; Ind State Univ; Legal Sec.

HAWKINS, MEREDITH; Marian HS; South Bend, IN; Hon Rl; PAVAS; Sch Mus; Stg Crw; Rptr Yrbk; Yrbk; Rptr Sch Nwsp; Mth Clb; Swmmng; Trk; Antioch Univ; Art.

HAWKINS, MICHAEL; Covert HS; South Haven, MI; 2/40 Trs Frsh Cls; Cls Rep Frsh Cls; Cls Rep Soph Cls; Band; Boy Scts; Chrs; Chrh Wkr; Hon Rl; Jr NHS; Mod UN; Mic State; Law.

HAWKINS, MICHAEL W; Decatur Central HS; Indianapolis, IN; Chrh Wkr; Hon Rl; Pol Wkr; Yth Flsp; FFA; Coach Actv; Cit Awd; JA Awd; Tomlinson Coll; Minister.

HAWKINS, PAM; Monsignor John Hackett HS; Kalamazoo, MI; Red Cr Ade; Spn Clb; Glf; Western Michigan Univ; Occup Ther.

HAWKINS, PAMELA; Princeton HS; Princeton, WV; Trs Jr Cls; Band; Cmnty Wkr; Hon Rl; Jr NHS; Quill & Scroll; Stu Cncl; Ed Sch Nwsp; Rptr Sch Nwsp; Fr Clb; West Virginia Univ; Law.

HAWKINS, REBECCA; Cadiz HS; Hopedale, OH; Am Leg Aux Girls St; Chrs; Chrh Wkr; Hon Rl; Sch Pl; Yth Flsp; Drama Clb; 4-H; Lat Clb; Grand Rep To La Of Of Rainbow 78; Jefferson Tech Schl; LPN.

HAWKINS, REBECCA; Continental HS; Continental, OH; Chrs; Chrh Wkr; Hon Rl; Lbry Ade; NHS; Off Ade; Sch Pl; Stu Cncl; Yth Flsp; Fredericks Beauty College; Cosmetolo.

HAWKINS, TODD; Washington HS; Massillon, OH; Hon Rl; Boys Clb Am; Fr Clb; Ftbl; Natl Merit Ltr; College.

HAWKINS, VERNEDA; Lumen Cordium HS; Cleveland, OH; 5/94 Sec Sr Cls; Cls Rep Sr Cls; Hon Rl; Hosp Ade; JA; Sec Jr NHS; NHS; Off Ade; Stu Cncl; FNA; Univ Of Cincinnati; Pharm.

HAWKINS, WILLIAM B; William Henry Harrison HS; W Lafayette, IN; 50/350 Cl Rep Jr Cls; Band; Chrh Wkr; Cmnty Wkr; Drm Bgl; Hon Rl; NHS; Sch Mus; Stu Cncl; Yrbk; Univ; Pre Law.

HAWLEY, THERESA; Brookhaven HS; Zanesfield, OH; 28/434 Chrs; Girl Scts; Hon Rl; Jr NHS; NHS; Off Ade; Sch Mus; Sct Actv; Yth Flsp; Pres OEA; Brookhaven HS Academy Of Schlrs; Reg Finalist In Office Ed Assoc St Contest; Western Carolina Univ; Ag Mgmt.

HAWN, JENNY; Columbia City Joint HS; Columbia City, IN; 12/272 Girl Scts; Hon Rl; Pres NHS; Yth Flsp; 4-H; FTA; Spn Clb; 4-H Awd; Univ; Scndry Educ.

HAWN, JOAN; Manistique HS; Manistique, MI; Sec Jr Cls; Treas Stu Cncl; 4-H; Bsktbl; Trk; Mgrs; 4-H Awd; N Michigan Univ; Med Tech.

HAWN, JOHN; St Ignatius HS; University Hts, OH; Hon Rl; IM Sprt; College; Law.

HAWORTH, JEFFREY; Gaylord HS; Gaylord, MI; Hon Rl; NHS; Stu Cncl; Sch Nwsp; Pres FFA; Letter Crs Cntry; Letter Trk; IM Sprt; Lake Superior St Coll; Fish Bio.

HAWORTH, LORI; Winchester Community HS; Winchester, IN; Treas Girl Scts; Hon Rl; Lbry Ade; Stu Cncl; Fr Clb; FHA; Letter Bsktbl; Chrldng; Mas Awd; Reid Memorial Hosp; Lab Tech.

HAWROT, DIANE; Madonna HS; Weirton, WV; 3/100 Am Leg Aux Girls St; Chrs; Hon Rl; Pres NHS; Sch Mus; Stg Crw; Treas Stu Cncl; Yrbk; Rptr Sch Nwsp; Letter Ten; West Virginia Univ; Pharm.

HAWTHORNE, DALVIN; Chesapeake HS; Proctorville, OH; 23/140 Chrs; Hon Rl; Beta Clb; VICA;.

HAWTHORNE, SYDNA; Plainwell HS; Plainwell, MI; Chrh Wkr; Hon Rl; Off Ade; Yth Flsp; Yrbk; Rptr Sch Nwsp; Sch Nwsp; Spn Clb; PPFtbl; Taylor Univ; Eng.

HAY, ANGIE; Anderson HS; Anderson, IN; Cls Rep Frsh Cls; Cls Rep Soph Cls; Cl Rep Jr Cls; Girl Scts; Hon Rl; Stu Cncl; Y-Teens; Letter Gym; Letter Trk; Varsity Letter Jacket; Ball St Univ; Busns.

HAY, DONNA M; Beaver Local HS; E Liverpool, OH; 16/242 Band; Girl Scts; Hon Rl; Jr NHS; NHS; Yrbk; OEA; Kent St Univ; Busns Mgmt.

HAY, KATHLEEN; Morley Stanwood HS; Morley, MI; Chrs; NHS; Stu Cncl; Letter Ten; St Of Mi Comptty Schlshp 79; Northern Michigan Univ; Law Enfrcmnt.

HAYDEN, GERALYNN; Washington HS; East Chicago, IN; Hon Rl; NHS; Off Ade; FTA; Key Clb; Spn Clb; Purdue Univ; Comp Sci.

HAYDEN, HOLLY; Fairview HS; Fairvw Pk, OH; 36/279 AFS; Drl Tm; Hon Rl; Rptr Yrbk; Ten; IM Sprt; Univ Of Arizona.

HAYDEN, LISA; Wood Memorial HS; Francisco, IN; Chrs; Hon Rl; Lit Mag; 4-H; Pep Clb; 4-H Awd; Univ; Bus.

HAYDEN, REBECCA; Pike Central HS; Winslow, IN; Girl Scts; Hon Rl; Lit Mag; NHS; Off Ade; Rptr Sch Nwsp; Sch Nwsp; Pep Clb; Chrldng; Univ.

HAYDEN, ROBIN; Cuyahoga Falls HS; Cuahoga Fls, OH; Cl Rep Jr Cls; Cls Rep Sr Cls; Chrs; Chrh Wkr; Hon Rl; Off Ade; Y-Teens; Pep Clb; Vllybl 76 79; Attended Teenage Inst On Alcohol & Other Drugs 79; Univ Of Akron; Chem.

HAYDEN, SCOTT; Lowell Sr HS; Lowell, IN; Aud/Vis; Hon Rl; Sch Nwsp; FDA; FFA; 4-H Awd; Purdue Univ; Electr.

HAYDEN, SHARON; Avon HS; Danville, IN; 7/181 Cls Rep Frsh Cls; Cl Rep Jr Cls; Cls Rep Sr Cls; Band; Hon Rl; NHS; Stu Cncl; Pep Clb; Spn Clb; Letter Trk;.

HAYDEN, STEVE; Cuyahoga Falls HS; Cuyahoga Fls, OH; Hon Rl; JA; Ftbl; Rotary Awd; Univ; Chem Engr.

HAYE, DAWN; Millington HS; Millington, MI; Trs Soph Cls; Hon Rl; NHS; Rptr Yrbk; Rptr Sch Nwsp; Treas Fr Clb; Letter Bsbl; Bsktbl; Letter Gym; Capt Chrldng; Schlstc M Clb 77; Arizona St Univ; Bus.

HAYE, ERIN; Bluefield HS; Bluefld, WV; Band; Chrh Wkr; Hon Rl; Jr NHS; NHS; Yth Flsp; FHA; Spn Clb; Capt Bsktbl; Emory G Henry Coll; Soc Wrk.

HAYES, BRENT; Federal Hocking HS; Guysville, OH; Hon Rl; Sprt Ed Yrbk; Rptr Sch Nwsp; 4-H; VP FFA; Bsbl; Bsktbl; Coach Actv; Am Leg Awd; 4-H Awd; Prom Prince; Jr Marshall Graduation; Grand Champ Dairy Cow Meigs Co Fair; College; Phys Ed.

HAYES, BRIAN D; Hauser HS; Columbus, IN; 1/95 Pres Soph Cls; Aud/Vis; Band; Hon Rl; Mod UN; NHS; Orch; Spn Clb; Letter Trk; Purdue Univ; Aeronautical Engineer.

HAYES, BRIAN D; Westview HS; Shipshewana, IN; 1/90 Val; Band; Pres Chrs; Chrh Wkr; Hon Rl; NHS; Sch Mus; Pres Yth Flsp; Letter Ten; Natl Merit SF; Fort Wayne Bible Coll; Music.

HAYES, CHRISTINE; Westerville North HS; Westerville, OH; 8/450 Cl Rep Jr Cls; Am Leg Aux Girls St; Chrs; Drl Tm; Girl Scts; Hon Rl; NHS; Sec Stu Cncl; FHA; Spn Clb; Perf Attn Awrd 78; 1st Class Girl Scout Awrd 75; Miami Univ; Scndry Educ.

HAYES, CHRISTINE; Bishop Foley HS; Clawson, MI; 16/196 Hon Rl; Hosp Ade; Sch Mus; Sch Pl; Letter Trk; Capt Chrldng; Pom Pon; PPFtbl; Natl Merit SF; College; Nursing.

HAYES, DIANA; North Posey Sr HS; Wadesville, IN; Chrh Wkr; Cmnty Wkr; 4-H; Fr Clb; OEA; Ten; 4-H Awd; 450 Schlhsp From Oakland City Coll 79; Attndnc Awd 71 72 & 74; 2nd Pl In St Wendel Mth Contst 75; IVY Tech Coll; Acctg.

HAYES, DONALD; Walnut Ridge HS; Columbus, OH; 45/429 Boy Scts; Chrs; Hon Rl; Sct Actv; Letter Trk; Ohio St Univ; Med.

HAYES, DOUG; Westview Jr Sr HS; Shipshewana, IN; 1/84 Val; Band; Pres Chrs; Hon Rl; NHS; Sch Mus; Pres Yth Flsp; Letter Ten; Fort Wayne Bible Coll.

HAYES, FORREST; Harry S Truman HS; Taylor, MI; NHS; Univ Of Michigan; Astronomy.

HAYES, HEIDI; Salem HS; Salem, OH; 14/290 Rotary Awd; Univ Of Cincinnati; Econ.

HAYES, JAMES; Plainwell HS; Plainwell, MI; Cls Rep Sr Cls; Aud/Vis; Cmnty Wkr; Debate Tm; Sch Pl; Sprt Ed Yrbk; Yrbk; Sch Nwsp; Fr Clb; Letter Bsktbl; Homecoming King Sr Yr 79; Nazareth Coll; Tchr.

HAYES, JEFFREY; Cambridge HS; Cambridge, OH; Hon Rl; Rptr Sch Nwsp; Key Clb; Letter Bsbl; Letter Bsktbl; Ohio Univ; Bus.

HAYES, JO L; Monrovia HS; Monrovia, IN; 5/134 Am Leg Aux Girls St; Band; Chrs; Girl Scts; Hon Rl; NHS; Rptr Yrbk; Spn Clb; College; Communications.

HAYES, KATHLEEN; William G Mather HS; Munising, MI; Band; Girl Scts; Hon Rl; Lbry Ade; Sch Pl; Stu Cncl; Rptr Sch Nwsp; PPFtbl; Lake Superior St Univ; Child Dev.

HAYES, LATONYA; Jane Addams Voc HS; Cleveland, OH; Drl Tm; Girl Scts; Capt Bsktbl; Trk; IM Sprt; Bsktbl Capt; Most Outstndng Track Woman Trophy; Intramural Sports Participation Awd; Coll; Med Sec.

HAYES, LISA; George A Dondero HS; Sterling Hts, MI; 40/425 Aud/Vis; Chrs; Pres Chrh Wkr; Cmnty Wkr; Girl Scts; Hon Rl; Lbry Ade; NHS; PAVAS; Sct Actv; Michigan State Univ; Major Soc Work.

HAYES, LISA K; Wahama HS; New Haven, WV; Cl Rep Jr Cls; Hon Rl; Capt Chrldng; Univ; Dent Hygn.

HAYES, LOU; Milton HS; Culloden, WV; Letter Band; Off Ade; Sch Mus; FBLA; Pep Clb; Gym; GAA;.

HAYES, MICHAEL; Fisher Catholic HS; Lancaster, OH; Sec Jr Cls; Cmnty Wkr; FCA; Key Clb; Bsktbl; Crs Cntry; Ten; John Carroll Univ; Purchasing.

HAYES, MICHELLE; Northville HS; Northville, MI; Band; Hon Rl; NHS; Letter Crs Cntry; Letter Trk; Most Valuable In Track; Most Valuabe In Cross Country; Schoolcraft Comm Coll; Vet.

HAYES, REGGIE; Southern Wells HS; Liberty Center, IN; 10/95 Hon Rl; NHS; Bsktbl; Letter Ftbl; Trk; Am Leg Awd; Univ; Radio Announcer.

HAYES, SHERRIE; Pike Central HS; Petersburg, IN; Chrs; Chrh Wkr; Hon Rl; Lbry Ade; NHS; Pol Wkr; Sch Pl; Yth Flsp; Y-Teens; FHA; Univ.

HAYES, SUSAN; Herbert Henry Dow HS; Midland, MI; Sec Band; Chrs; Drl Tm; Hon Rl; Hosp Ade; NHS; Orch; Sch Pl; Stg Crw; Yth Flsp; Dow Corning Schlrshp For Yth For Understanding Summer Prog; Stu Of Yr In German II & Drama; Coll; Med.

HAYES, TAMMY; East HS; Akron, OH; 30/334 Chrs; Cmnty Wkr; Drm Mjrt; Hon Rl; Lbry Ade; Off Ade; Red Cr Ade; Ed Sch Nwsp; 1st Pl In Vandalism Speech Cont 77; Bus.

HAYES, TERRI; Franklin Comm HS; Franklin, IN; 10/286 Sec Sr Cls; Cmnty Wkr; Hon Rl; NHS; Stu Cncl; FHA; Sec Pep Clb; Sci Clb; Spn Clb; PPFtbl; Purdue Univ; Nursing.

HAYES, THERESA J; Fairland HS; Scottown, OH; 15/152 Cls Rep Frsh Cls; Sec Soph Cls; Trs Soph Cls; Cls Rep Soph Cls; Cl Rep Jr Cls; Cls Rep Sr Cls; Band; Hon Rl; NHS; Stu Cncl; Ohi State; Phys Ther.

HAYFORD, KATHY; Springfield HS; Battle Crk, MI; Band; Stg Crw; Drama Clb; FHA; Pep Clb; Yth Talent Exhibit Awd Fshn Design 79; Yth Talent Exhibit Awd Sewing 78; Band Awds 77 79; Univ; Elem Educ.

HAYGOOD, GARY; John Adams HS; So Bend, IN; 56/396 Hon Rl; Letter Bsbl; Letter Ftbl; Letter Wrstlng; PPFtbl; College; Math.

HAYGOOD, NORMA; Woodward HS; Cincinnati, OH; 2/3 Cl Rep Jr Cls; Pres Sr Cls; Cls Rep Sr Cls; Hon Rl; JA; Jr NHS; NHS; Off Ade; Ohio Univ; Acctg.

HAYHOW, AMANDA; Chillicothe HS; Chill, OH; 100/366 Chrs; Chrh Wkr; Hon Rl; Lbry Ade; Natl Forn Lg; Sch Pl; Stg Crw; Heidelberg College;bio Psych.

HAYHURST, CONNIE; Perrysburg HS; Perrysburg, OH; AFS; Girl Scts; Hon Rl; Hosp Ade; JA; Jr NHS; NHS; Fr Clb; Bowling Green St Univ; Eng.

HAYHURST, RITA; Mannington HS; Mannington, WV; Hon Rl; Quill & Scroll; Stu Cncl; Yth Flsp; Rptr Sch Nwsp; Sec 4-H; Letter Bsktbl; Letter Trk; Elk Awd; 4-H Awd; Fairmont St Coll; Art.

HAYNAL, LOIS; Indiana Academy; Washington, DC; VP Soph Cls; Band; Hon Rl; NHS; Pacific Union Coll; Occuptnl Therp.

HAYNE, MICHAEL; Buffalo HS; Kenova, WV; Boy Scts; Hon Rl; Mod UN; Sct Actv; Sch Nwsp; 4-H; Mth Clb; 4-H Awd; W Virginia Tech Univ; Organic Chem.

HAYNES, AMY; Kenston HS; Chagrin Fls, OH; Band; Chrs; Drl Tm; Pres Girl Scts; Hon Rl; Sch Mus; Sch Pl; Stg Crw; Stu Cncl; Drama Clb; Univ; Intl Bus.

HAYNES, DENISE; Center Line HS; Warren, MI; Band; Chrh Wkr; Drm Mjrt; Hon Rl; Rptr Yrbk; Spn Clb; Twrlr; NCTE; Macomb Univ; Psych.

HAYNES, GREGORY H; George Washington HS; Charleston, WV; Pres Sr Cls; Am Leg Boys St; Chrh Wkr; FCA; Sec Jr NHS; Mod UN; Pres FBLA; VP Key Clb; Letter Trk; IM Sprt; Modular System Scheduling Tm Captn 78; Univ.

HAYNES, KAREN; Morgantown HS; Morgantown, WV; Chrs; Cmnty Wkr; Yth Flsp; Rptr Sch Nwsp; Monangulea Cnty Voc Tec; Lpn.

HAYNES, NANCY; Dayton Christian HS; Dayton, OH; 40/120 Band; Chrs; Cmnty Wkr; Drl Tm; Hon Rl; Sch Mus; Capt IM Sprt; JC Awd; Voice Dem Awd; Natl Spanish Exam Awd 79; Drama Tm Awd 79; Bible Memorization Awd 79; Univ; Theatre Arts.

HAYNES, RICK; Turpin HS; , ; 64/357 Letter Bsktbl; Letter Ftbl; PPFtbl; College; Education.

HAYNES, STEPHAN; Warren Local HS; Little Hocking, OH; 1/220 Val; Am Leg Boys St; Chrh Wkr; Hon Rl; NHS; Fr Clb; Mth Clb; Mgrs; Scr Kpr; Am Leg Awd; Natl Honor Soc Student Of The Yr 78; TV Honor Soc Schlrshp 79; Harding Univ; Comp Sci.

HAYNES, STEVE; Jackson HS; Jackson, OH; 1/230 Hon Rl; Pres NHS; Y-Teens; Lat Clb; Sci Clb; Letter Glf; Yth In Government 79; Various Awds In Arts Festivals 77; Schlrshp In Algebra 77; Univ; Acctg.

HAYNES, VORAS; Tygarts Vly HS; Valley Bend, WV; Cls Rep Frsh Cls; VP Soph Cls; Cl Rep Jr Cls; Am Leg Boys St; Hon Rl; Pres NHS; Letter Bsbl; Letter Bsktbl; Letter Ftbl; IM Sprt; Named To All Trnmnt Team W Virginia St Bsbl Playoffs; Lettered On 2 St Championship Bsbl Teams; Coll; Poli Sci.

HAYS, CHERYL; Flushing HS; Flushing, MI; 34/522 Chrh Wkr; Hon Rl; Hosp Ade; NHS; Off Ade; Sec Yth Flsp; Spn Clb; Univ Of Mic; Registered Nurse.

HAYS, DEBRA; Hanover Central HS; Cedar Lake, IN; 16/137 Chrh Wkr; FCA; Girl Scts; Hon Rl; Jr NHS; Lbry Ade; NHS; Stu Cncl; Pep Clb; Mgrs; Purdue Extension Coll; Nursing.

HAYS, MARK; St Marys HS; St Marys, WV; 14/250 Aud/Vis; Boy Scts; Chrh Wkr; Cmnty Wkr; FCA; Hon Rl; Sch Pl; Stu Cncl; Mth Clb; Ftbl; Bell & Howell Inst Of Elec; Elec.

HAYSLETT, SHERIE; Winfield HS; Scott Depot, WV; Girl Scts; Hon Rl; Letter Bsktbl; Marshall Univ; Phys Educ.

HAYWARD, RICHARD; Romeo HS; Leonard, MI; Boy Scts; Hon Rl; Ger Clb; Wrstlng; Mich State Univ; Comp Sci.

HAYWOOD, LISA; Meadow Brook HS; Byesville, OH; VP Soph Cls; Cl Rep Jr Cls; Hon Rl; Stu Cncl; Fr Clb; Pep Clb; Letter Chrldng; College; X Ray Tech.

HAYWOOD, LISA; Meadowbrook HS; Byesville, OH; VP Soph Cls; Cl Rep Jr Cls; Hon Rl; Stu Cncl; Yrbk; Fr Clb; Pep Clb; Chrldng; College; Medicine.

HAZAGA, ROBERT; Andrean HS; Crown Pt, IN; 33/254 Hon Rl; Lat Clb; Purdue Univ; Engr.

HAZARD, VERN P; Vicksburg HS; Scotts, MI; 67/240 Hon Rl; NHS; Sch Pl; Bsbl; Bsktbl; Ftbl; Rotary Awd; Olivet Coll; Phys Ed.

HAZEL, BETTY; Eastwood HS; Luckey, OH; 33/185 Cls Rep Soph Cls; Cl Rep Jr Cls; Hst Sr Cls; Cls Rep Sr Cls; Hon Rl; Off Ade; Sch Pl; Stu Cncl; Rptr Sch Nwsp; Pep Clb;.

HAZEL, BRENDA; Northmont HS; Clayton, OH; 2/486 Sal; Chrh Wkr; Yth Flsp; Ten; Eastern Ken Univ; Computer Science.

HAZEL, JULIEE; Harper Creek HS; Battle Creek, MI; 34/244 Cls Rep Frsh Cls; Pres Soph Cls; Pres Jr Cls; Pres Sr Cls; Am Leg Aux Girls St; Cmp Fr Grls; VP VP Frsh Cls; Drama Clb; Pres Fr Clb; Student Of The Month; B C Exchange Club; NCA Superstar Awd; Outstanding French Club Mbr; Eastern Mich Univ; Intl Trade.

HAZEL, KAREN; Columbiana HS; Columbiana, OH; 19/105 Hon Rl; Spn Clb; Trk; Univ; Special Ed.

HAZEL, LISA; Anderson HS; Anderson, IN; Cls Rep Frsh Cls; Off Ade; Swmmng; Trk; Scr Kpr; Tmr; Twrlr; Pres Awd; Ind Univ; Phys Educ.

HAZELETT, SONYA; West Side HS; Gary, IN; 60/650 Cls Rep Frsh Cls; Chrs; Chrh Wkr; Cmnty Wkr; Hon Rl; Jr NHS; Lbry Ade; Stu Cncl; Yrbk; Indiana St Univ; Spanish Tchr.

HAZELMAN, MICHELLE; Yalc HS; Emmett, MI; Hon Rl; 4-H; 4-H Awd; St Clair Community Coll; Real Estate.

HAZELTINE, WANDA; Monroe Sr HS; Monroe, MI; Chrh Wkr; Cmnty Wkr; Hon Rl; Off Ade; Yth Flsp; Sprt Ed Sch Nwsp; VP Spn Clb; IM Sprt; Scr Kpr; Tmr; Eastern Michigan Univ; Spec Ed.

HAZELWOOD, ATHENA J; East HS; Columbus, OH; Drl Tm; Hon Rl; Jr NHS; Cit Awd;.

HAZELWOOD, GAYLE; Cambridge HS; Cambridge, OH; 100/281 Pres Frsh Cls; VP Jr Cls; Letter Bsktbl; Tmr; Twrlr; Ohio Univ; Comp Prog.

HAZEN, DEAN; Walnut Ridge HS; Columbus, OH; 42/429 Chrs; Hon Rl; NHS; Sct Actv; Florida State Univ; Meteorology.

HAZLE, JUDY; Fremont Ross HS; Lindsey, OH; Chrs; Hon Rl; Off Ade; GAA; IM Sprt;.

HAZLE, LESLIE; St Johns HS; St Johns, MI; Cls Rep Frsh Cls; Am Leg Aux Girls St; Chrs; Chrh

Wkr; FCA; Hon Rl; Hosp Ade; Sch Mus; Stg Crw; Stu Cncl; Bronson Schl Of Nursing; Nursing.

HAZLETT, BOB; Buckeye North HS; Smithfield, OH; 8/130 Pres Sr Cls; FCA; NHS; Pep Clb; Letter Bsbl; Letter Ftbl; IM Sprt; Western Michigan Univ; Elec Engr.

HAZLETT, LAURA M; Decatur Central HS; Indnpls, IN; Chrh Wkr; Hon Rl; Natl Hnr Soc 79; Whos Who In Frgn Lang In Mid W 79; Brigham Young Univ.

HAZLEWOOD, ATHENA J; East HS; Columbus, OH; Drl Tm; Hon Rl; Jr NHS; Cit Awd;.

HAZLEWOOD, MIKE; Princeton HS; Princeton, WV; 123/360 FCA; Bsbl; Letter Ftbl; Letter Glf; Wrstlng; Marshall Univ; Optometry.

HAZZARD, RODNEY; Deerfield HS; Deerfield, MI; 7/43 Am Leg Boys St; Band; Boy Scts; Hon Rl; Sct Actv; Bsbl; Bsktbl; Letter Ftbl; Letter Trk; Coach Actv; E Mich Univ; Comp Tech.

HEAD, DANA; Providence HS; Lanesville, IN; Cls Rep Frsh Cls; Cls Rep Soph Cls; Hon Rl; Off Ade; Stu Cncl; Beta Clb; Civ Clb; Chrldng; Purdue Univ; Animal Sci.

HEAD, LORI; Milan HS; Milan, MI; Hon Rl; Cleary Coll; Bus Mgmt.

HEAD, MARY; New Richmond HS; New Richmond, OH; 46/197 Band; Chrh Wkr; Drm Mjrt; Hon Rl; JA; NHS; Off Ade; Sch Mus; Yrbk; Fr Clb; Our Land Of Great Honor Band 76 79; Dst 14 Honor Band 78; Bob Jones Univ; Music.

HEAD, PATRICIA; South Spencer HS; Rockport, IN; 4-H; Ger Clb; OEA; Trk; IM Sprt; Letter Mgrs; Owensboro Bus Coll; Acctg.

HEAD, ROBERT; Airport HS; Monroe, MI; 30/207 Band; Lawerence Inst Of Tech; Architecture.

HEADLEE, CURTIS; University HS; Morgantown, WV; Jr NHS; Lbry Ade; FFA; West Virginia Univ; Forestry.

HEADLEY, KIM; Lebanon HS; Mason, OH; ROTC; Fr Clb; Columbia Sch Of Brdcstng; Brdcstr.

HEADMAN, CATHY; Ashtabula HS; Ashtabula, OH; 1/208 Val; Band; Chrh Wkr; Girl Scts; Jr NHS; NHS; Sec Off Ade; Sch Mus; Pres Yth Flsp; Ed Yrbk; Akron Univ; R N.

HEADRICK, MELISSA; Flushing Sr HS; Flushing, MI; 5/532 Hon Rl; NHS; Yth Flsp; Gym; Letter Ten; Letter Trk; IM Sprt; Natl Merit Ltr; Michigan St Univ; Engr.

HEADWORTH, KIMBERLY; Clermont Northeastern HS; Batavia, OH; 9/210 Band; Chrs; Chrh Wkr; Cmnty Wkr; FCA; Girl Scts; Hon Rl; Mod UN; Ohi Univ; Communications.

HEADY, TOM; Avon HS; Plainfield, IN; 620198 Hon Rl; Hosp Ade; Ger Clb; Sci Clb; Bsbl; Scr Kpr; Purdue Univ; Vet Med.

HEADY, WARREN; Hammond Baptist HS; Dyer, IN; Band; Chrs; Chrh Wkr; Hon Rl; Sch Mus; Sch Pl; Capt Bsktbl; Socr; Ten; Trk; Hyles Anderson Coll; Music.

HEALD, PHILIP; Ironton HS; Ironton, OH; Band; JA; Ger Clb; IM Sprt; Univ; Med.

HEALEY, RHONDA; De Kalb HS; Ashley, IN; 18/281 Chrs; FCA; Girl Scts; Ger Clb; Pep Clb; Bsbl; Gym; Chrldng; Tri Kappa Scholastic Awd; Manchester Coll; Medicine.

HEALY, GEORGIA; Marian HS; Birmingham, MI; Cl Rep Jr Cls; Hon Rl; Lit Mag; Mod UN; Fr Clb; Letter Trk; Mic State Univ; French.

HEALY, JEAN; Saint Josephs HS; Granger, IN; Cls Rep Frsh Cls; Cls Rep Soph Cls; Sec Jr Cls; Jr NHS; Stu Cncl; Drama Clb; Ten; Trk; IM Sprt; PPFtbl; College; Sci.

HEALY, KATHRYN E; Mt Notre Dame HS; Cincinnati, OH; 4/165 Hon Rl; Lbry Ade; Sch Mus; Sch Nwsp; JA Awd; Univ Of Cincinnati; Chemistry.

HEALY, RICHARD; John Marshall HS; Glen Dale, WV; 91/443 Aud/Vis; Rptr Yrbk; Sch Nwsp; Rdo Clb; Dr David Ealy Schlrshp 79; Govt Action Prog 79; Whos Who Among Amer HS Stud 78; West Liberty St Coll; Bus Admin.

HEALY, VICKIE; Gladstone HS; Gladstone, MI; 110/230 Band; Chrs; Chrh Wkr; Girl Scts; Quill & Scroll; Ed Yrbk; Rptr Yrbk; Yrbk; 4-H; FHA; Bay De Noc Comm Coll; Tchr.

HEAP, HEIDI; South Lyon HS; So Lyon, MI; Band; Chrs; Hon Rl; NHS; Quill & Scroll; Sch Mus; Sch Pl; Drama Clb; Twrlr; Youth Recgntn Awd 79; Univ; Math.

HEARD, ANITA; Jane Addams Vocational HS; Cleveland, OH; Stu Cncl; Central St Univ; R N.

HEARD, BRYAN; John Hay HS; Cleveland, OH; Band; Boy Scts; Cmnty Wkr; Univ; Cmmrcl Pilot.

HEARD, KAREN M; Roosevelt HS; Gary, IN; Hon Rl; NHS; FTA; Tennessee St Univ; Nursing.

HEARN, DANNY; Pine River HS; Le Roy, MI; Boy Scts; Hon Rl; Sch Pl; Spn Clb; Ftbl; 4-H Awd; Ferris St Coll; Avionics.

HEARNS, KRISTI; Ludington HS; Ludington, MI; Chrs; Hon Rl; Sch Mus; Drama Clb; Ten; Trk; Chrldng; Central Mic Univ; Bus Mrktng.

HEARST, STEVEN; East Technical HS; Cleveland, OH; Hon Rl; Hosp Ade; NHS; Stu Cncl; Yrbk; Cit Awd; Cleveland St Univ; Acctg.

HEARY, TRACY; Elmwood HS; N Baltimroe, OH; Boy Scts; Chrs; Mgrs; Chess Tourn 4th Pl 76; Chess Club Mst Imprvd 77; Navy; Elect.

HEATER, KAREN; Flemington HS; Bridgeport, WV; 7/46 Band; Hon Rl; NHS; Rptr Yrbk; Rptr Sch Nwsp; 4-H; Fr Clb; FBLA; FHA; Pep Clb; W Va All State Bank; Fairmont St Coll; Acctg.

HEATH, BRENDA; Kettering HS; Detroit, MI; Cls Rep Sr Cls; Hon Rl; Jr NHS; NHS; Off Ade; Stu Cncl; Sch Nwsp; Chrldng; Univ Of Michigan; Accounting.

HEATH, DAN; Mineral Ridge HS; Mc Donald, OH; 10/65 Aud/Vis; Band; Boy Scts; Chrs; Lbry Ade; Yrbk; Beta Clb; Bsktbl; Trk; IM Sprt; Univ; Comp Progr.

HEATH, DEBORAH A; Mendon Community School; Mendon, MI; Trs Frsh Cls; Cls Rep Soph Cls; Band; Hon Rl; NHS; Stu Cncl; Fr Clb; Pep Clb; Chrldng; PPFtbl; Univ; Legal Research.

HEATH, JAN; Graham HS; Springfield, OH; 62/185 Chrs; Hosp Ade; Lbry Ade; Sch Mus; Sch Pl; Yrbk; Sch Nwsp; Scr Kpr; Bowling Green Univ; Nursing.

HEATH, KARYN; Pymatuning Valley HS; Andover, OH; Band; Chrs; NHS; Sch Pl; Stu Cncl; Ed Sch Nwsp; Drama Clb; 4-H; Pres 4-H Awd; Univ; Cmnctn Art.

HEATH, LISA; Lincolnview HS; Van Wert, OH; Band; Chrs; JA; Sch Mus; Yth Flsp; 4-H; FHA; Business School.

HEATH, ROBERT M; Walter E Stebbins HS; Kettering, OH; 30/453 Band; MMM; ROTC; FSA; Sci Clb; W E Stebbins Soc For Academic Excel; Master Hnr Carrier Awd Dayton Daily Newspr; Karate Purple Belt; Florida Inst Of Tech; Oceanogrpher.

HEATH, SALLY; Black River HS; Sullivan, OH; Band; Girl Scts; Stu Cncl; 4-H; Fr Clb; VP FHA; Sci Clb; Letter Trk; Mgrs; 4-H Awd;.

HEATH, THERESA; Clarence M Kimball HS; Royal Oak, MI; Band; Hon Rl; NHS; Michigan St Univ; Nursing.

HEATON, DIANE; East Knox HS; Howard, OH; Chrs; Hon Rl; Quill & Scroll; Sch Pl; Stg Crw; Rptr Sch Nwsp; Sch Nwsp; Drama Clb; FHA; Pep Clb; Ohio St Univ; Psych.

HEATON, JOY; Watkins Memorial HS; Pataskala, OH; Cls Rep Frsh Cls; Cls Rep Soph Cls; Cl Rep Jr Cls; Band; VP Chrs; Drl Tm; Sec FCA; Off Ade; Sch Mus; Sch Pl; Mt Vernon Coll; Public Relations.

HEATON, RHONDA; Dansville Agri HS; Dansville, MI; VP Frsh Cls; Hon Rl; Off Ade; Rptr Sch Nwsp; 4-H; Bsktbl; Chrldng; IM Sprt; Mgrs; 4-H Awd; Joan Jewett Bus Schl; Travel Agent.

HEATON, SARAH; Elwood Cmnty HS; Elwood, IN; Hon Rl; Jr NHS; NHS; Lat Clb; Mth Clb; Sci Clb; Natl Merit Ltr; Kappa Delta Phi Schlrshp 79; Purdue Univ; Bio.

HEATON, VANESSA; Bloomfield HS; Bloomfield, IN; Hon Rl; Pep Clb; Spn Clb; Univ; Cosmetology.

HEATOR, GREGORY; Coldwater HS; Coldwater, MI; 73/290 Crs Cntry; Trk; Tri State; Bus.

HEATWOLE, DAVID; Hampshire HS; Romney, WV; 15/200 Cls Rep Frsh Cls; Cls Rep Soph Cls; AFS; Band; Hon Rl; Stg Crw; Drama Clb; Spanish Awrd 76; West Virginia Univ.

HEAVENER, DONNA; Jewett Scio HS; Scio, OH; 7/84 Sec Soph Cls; Hon Rl; NHS; Sch Mus; Ed Sch Nwsp; Spn Clb; Schl Of Nursing; RN.

HEAVENER, SUE; Hampshire HS; Romney, WV; 30/213 Sec Frsh Cls; Cls Rep Soph Cls; Sec Jr Cls; Sec Sr Cls; Treas AFS; Am Leg Aux Girls St; Chrh Wkr; Shepherd College; Phys Ed.

HEAVENRIDGE, RUTH; Waverly HS; Waverly, OH; 9/167 Am Leg Aux Girls St; Band; Hon Rl; NHS; Rptr Yrbk; Rptr Sch Nwsp; 4-H; Fr Clb; 4-H Awd; Blair Cumm Schl For Jrnlsm 79; Pike Cntry Jr Fairboard Tres 77; Ohio St Univ; Jrnlsm.

HEAVILIN, BROOKE; Cadiz HS; Cadiz, OH; Chrs; Chrh Wkr; Hon Rl; Off Ade; Sch Mus; Rptr Sch Nwsp; Drama Clb; 4-H; Fr Clb; 4-H Awd; Natl Clb Congress In Chicago 4 H 79; Citznshp Wa Focus 79; Winner At St Fair Nutrition Show 4 H 78; Youngstown St Univ; Bus Admin.

HEAVNER, GWYN; Buckhannon Upshur HS; French Creek, WV; Am Leg Aux Girls St; Band; Chrs; Chrh Wkr; Girl Scts; Hon Rl; NHS; Sct Actv; Yth Flsp; IM Sprt; Wesleyon College.

HEBBLE, MARY; Bishop Watterson HS; Worthington, OH; 9/250 Chrh Wkr; Cmnty Wkr; Hon Rl; Jr NHS; NHS; Sct Actv; PPFtbl; Ohio St Univ; Spec Ed.

HEBDEN, KENNETH; Central Lake Public HS; Central Lake, MI; Am Leg Boys St; Boy Scts; Hon Rl; Sct Actv; Letter Bsbl; Letter Bsktbl; Letter Ftbl; IM Sprt; Mgrs; Scr Kpr; Davenport Coll; Bus Mgmt.

HEBDEN, PAMELA; Central Lake Public HS; Central Lake, MI; 3/46 VP Sr Cls; Val; Cmnty Wkr; Hon Rl; Lbry Ade; NHS; Sprt Ed Yrbk; Rptr Sch Nwsp; 4-H; Pep Clb; Sfrbl 2nd Team All Confrnc 77 79; Davenport Coll; Acctg.

HEBEL, CHRISTOPHER; Ogemaw Hts HS; Alger, MI; Aud/Vis; Band; Cmnty Wkr; Lbry Ade; Lit Mag; Sch Pl; Stg Crw; Sprt Ed Yrbk; Rptr Yrbk; Yrbk; Delta Coll; Radio Tv Brdcstng.

HEBEL, SCOTT R; North Central HS; Indianapolis, IN; 219/999 Band; Hon Rl; Sch Pl; Stu Cncl; Key Clb; Sci Clb; IM Sprt; Mgrs; Natl Merit Ltr; Natl Merit SF; Yth Sci Camp Cnslr 77; Rugby Tm 78; Marching Band 78; Purdue Univ; Meteorology.

HEBERER, SUE; Bishop Foley HS; Clawson, MI; 14/196 Cls Rep Sr Cls; Girl Scts; Hon Rl; NHS; Sch Pl; Capt Bsktbl; Univ; Phys Ther.

HEBERER, SUSAN; Bishop Foley HS; Clawson, MI; 14/193 Cls Rep Sr Cls; Girl Scts; Hon Rl; NHS; Sch Mus; Spn Clb; Capt Bsktbl; IM Sprt; Natl Merit SF; Oakland Univ; Phys Ther.

HEBERLIE, SUSAN; Erieview Catholic HS; Cleveland, OH; 25/101 Cls Rep Frsh Cls; Cls Rep Soph Cls; Chrs; Chrh Wkr; Drl Tm; Hon Rl; Stu Cncl; Y-Teens; Chrldng; Kent St Univ; Public Relations.

HEBERT, BETH; Bishop Watterson HS; Columbus, OH; Hon Rl; NHS; Bsbl; Bsktbl; Natl Merit Ltr; College; Law.

HEBERT, JOHN; Saint Clement HS; Centerline, MI; Boy Scts; Chrh Wkr; Hon Rl; Letter Ftbl; Letter Trk; College; Ftbl.

HEBNER, CAROLYN; Pine River Jr Sr HS; Tustin, MI; Band; Girl Scts; Hon Rl; Sch Mus; Yth Flsp; 4-H; College; Data Processing.

HECHLER, ERIN; William Mason HS; Mason, OH; 29/194 Drl Tm; Hon Rl; Off Ade; Sch Pl; 4-H; Gym; Chrldng; IM Sprt; PPFtbl; 4-H Awd; Christ Hosp Schl Of Nrsng; Rn.

HECHLER, KIMBERLY; Upper Arlington HS; Columbus, OH; 111/625 AFS; Cmnty Wkr; Drl Tm; Hon Rl; Sch Nwsp; VP Fr Clb; Ten; GAA; Mas Awd; Ohio Univ; Intl Communications.

HECHT, ELIZABETH; Hoover HS; North Canton, OH; Am Leg Aux Girls St; Hon Rl; Hosp Ade; NHS; Stg Crw; Y-Teens; Rptr Yrbk; Ed Sch Nwsp; Rptr Sch Nwsp; Pres Ger Clb; Univ; Comp Sci.

HECK, JEFFREY; Hamilton Southeastern HS; Noblesville, IN; FCA; Hon Rl; Sch Pl; Sprt Ed Yrbk; Rptr Yrbk; Rptr Sch Nwsp; Drama Clb; Ger Clb; Spn Clb; Ten; College; Rad Tel.

HECK, JILL; Milton HS; Milton, WV; Trs Sr Cls; Band; Pres Chrs; Hon Rl; Treas Jr NHS; NHS; Sch Mus; Yth Flsp; Yrbk; Sch Nwsp; 9th Grd Music Awrd 76; Eng 2 Awrd 78; Wv HS Writing Comp Feature Finalist 79; Marshall Univ; Eng.

HECKATHORN, M ROBERT; Wellsville HS; Wellsville, OH; 21/154 Am Leg Boys St; Hon Rl; Pep Clb; Ftbl; Trk; Wrstlng; Varsity W Club 78; The St Bd Of Educ Awd Of Distinction 79; Youngstown St Univ; Elec Engr.

HECKATHORNE, DARLYS; Galion Sr HS; Galion, OH; Am Leg Aux Girls St; Chrs; Chrh Wkr; Hon Rl; JA; Lbry Ade; NHS; Off Ade; Yth Flsp; Voice Dem Awd; Univ; Jrnlsm.

HECKER, DAVE; West Carrollton HS; West Carrollton, OH; Band; Hon Rl; Red Cr Ade; OEA; Sinclair; Comp Prog.

HECKER, JENNIFER; Springboro HS; Miamisburg, OH; Band; Hon Rl; NHS; FTA; Rotary Awd; Ohio St Univ; Optometry.

HECKERD, BARRY; Port Clinton HS; Port Clinton, OH; 6/280 Boy Scts; Chrs; Ftbl; Letter Trk; Univ; Engr.

HECKMAN, LORI; Upper Valley Joint Voc HS; Piqua, OH; Trs Jr Cls; Girl Scts; Hon Rl; Lbry Ade; Y-Teens; DECA; Pep Clb; Spn Clb; Univ Of Southern Cal; Brdcstng.

HECKMAN, MARY; Mentor HS; Mentor, OH; 72/733 Am Leg Aux Girls St; Chrs; Hon Rl; 4-H; Coach Actv; IM Sprt; PPFtbl; Am Leg Awd; 4-H Awd; Natl Merit Ltr; Bus Schl; Bus.

HECTOR, BECKY; Cory Rawson HS; Findlay, OH; Chrs; Chrh Wkr; Cmnty Wkr; Hon Rl; Fr Clb; Pep Clb; Bsktbl; Scr Kpr; Bowling Green St Univ; Cmnctns.

HEDGE, LINDA; Windham HS; Windham, OH; Band; Chrs; Girl Scts; Hon Rl; NHS; Sch Pl; Sct Actv; Drama Clb; Spn Clb; Univ; Bus Admin.

HEDGE, THERESA; Southmont HS; Ladoga, IN; 8/178 Am Leg Aux Girls St; Chrs; FCA; Hon Rl; Jr NHS; NHS; Ger Clb; Letter Bsktbl; Letter Ten; Purdue Univ; Vet Med.

HEDGES, DEIRDRE; Sheridan HS; Thornville, OH; Chrs; Hon Rl; Jr NHS; NHS; IM Sprt;.

HEDGES, RUTH; Lima HS; Lima, OH; 14/483 Chrs; Chrh Wkr; Hon Rl; JA; Sch Mus; Yth Flsp; Bluffton Coll; Elem Educ.

HEDINGTON, TINA; Warsaw Community HS; Warsaw, IN; Band; Off Ade; 4-H; Key Clb; 4-H Awd;.

HEDL, DOUGLAS A; Leetonia HS; Leetonia, OH; Am Leg Boys St; Chrh Wkr; Stg Crw; Rptr Sch Nwsp; Spn Clb; Bsbl; Bsktbl; Ftbl; Coach Actv; IM Sprt; Bowling Green St Univ; Educ.

HEDL, MARGIE; Leetonia HS; Leetonia, OH; Band; Cmp Fr Grls; Chrs; Hon Rl; Sch Mus; Sch Pl; Rptr Sch Nwsp; Drama Clb; Pep Clb; Spn Clb; College; Nursing.

HEDLUND, KAREN; Whitehall HS; Whitehall, MI; Band; Hon Rl; NHS; Stg Crw; Letter Ten; Muskegon Cmnty Coll; Bus.

HEDRICK, ALAN CRAIG; Winfield HS; Scott Depot, WV; Band; Hon Rl; JA; Jr NHS; Yth Flsp; Ten; JA Awd; Univ Of Cincinnati; Architecture.

HEDRICK, DIANE J; Greencastle HS; Greencastle, IN; 8/180 Cls Rep Frsh Cls; Cls Rep Soph Cls; Cl Rep Jr Cls; FCA; Treas Yth Flsp; 4-H; Pep Clb; Sci Clb; Swmmng; Chrldng; College; Interior Design.

HEDRICK, GARY; Jackson HS; Massillon, OH; Boy Scts; Chrs; FCA; JA; Yth Flsp; Crs Cntry; Trk; Miami Univ; Pre Law.

HEDRICK, JASON; Northwestern HS; Kokomo, IN; Cmnty Wkr; Hon Rl; NHS; Lat Clb; Sci Clb; Ftbl; Trk; Wrstlng; Purdue Univ; Mech Engr.

HEDRICK, PRECIOUS; Tucker Cnty HS; Thomas, WV; 10/126 Band; Chrh Wkr; Hon Rl; NHS; Off Ade; FBLA; Potomac St Coll; Data Processing.

HEEG, MARK A; Springfield North HS; Springfield, OH; Trs Frsh Cls; Chrs; Hon Rl; NHS; Orch; Stu Cncl; Pres Ger Clb; Lat Clb; Pres Sci Clb; Latin Awd Top Schlshp Trophy; Outstndng Stdnt Awd Math Bio Eng Germn HPE & Amer Histry; Wittenberg Univ; Concert Pianist.

HEERSPINK, DONNA; Holland Christian HS; Holland, MI; Cmp Fr Grls; Chrs; Pres Chrh Wkr; Sch Pl; Drama Clb; Ger Clb; Gym; Trk; Northwestern College; Christian Educ.

HEETHUIS, EDWIN; Jackson Parkside HS; Jackson, MI; VP Frsh Cls; Band; Hon Rl; Quill & Scroll; Rptr Sch Nwsp; Ger Clb; Hndbl; Mic Tech Univ; Mech Engr.

HEFFELMIRE, POLLY; Marion Adams HS; Sheridan, IN; 7/100 Band; Hon Rl; Jr NHS; NHS; GAA; College.

HEFFERNAN, BETH; St Joseph Academy; N Olmsted, OH; Chrh Wkr; Hosp Ade; Y-Teens; Sci Clb; Letter Bsktbl; College; Social Sci.

HEFFERNAN, JULIA; Washington Catholic HS; Washington, IN; Girl Scts; Hon Rl; Y-Teens; 4-H; Pep Clb; Spn Clb; YMCA Aquatic Cert For Aquatic Ldrshp 78; YMCA Swmmng Sportmnshp Awd; Vincennes Univ; Pharm.

HEFFERNAN, PAUL; Catholic Central HS; Farmington, MI; Hon Rl; NHS; Wayne State Univ; Bio.

HEFFNER, JEFF; Memorial HS; St Marys, OH; 20/232 Band; Chrh Wkr; Hon Rl; Yth Flsp; Ftbl; Wrstlng; Mgrs; U Of Cincinnati; Archt Drafting.

HEFFNER, JEFFREY; Memorial HS; St Marys, OH; 20/222 Band; Hon Rl; Yth Flsp; Ftbl; Wrstlng; Mgrs; Univ Of Cincinnati; Archt.

HEFFROM, M; Grand Ledge HS; Eagle, MI; Natl Forn Lg; Yth Flsp; Ger Clb; Michigan St Univ.

HEFKE, SUSAN; Everett Sr HS; Lansing, MI; Chrh Wkr; 4-H; Rcvd Var Ltr For Schlrst Achvcmnt 79; Sec.

HEFLIN, FRANK; Southwestern HS; Edinburg, IN; Pres Sr Cls; Aud/Vis; Band; Chrh Wkr; Sch Mus; 4-H; FFA; VP Key Clb; Treas Sci Clb; 4-H Awd; Indiana St Univ; Bus.

HEFLIN, GREG; St Marys HS; Bens Run, WV; Sprt Ed Sch Nwsp; Ftbl; Trk; Wrstlng; Vocational School.

HEFNER, DEBORAH; Medina HS; Medina, OH; 3/341 Trs Frsh Cls; Trs Soph Cls; Trs Jr Cls; Band; Drl Tm; NHS; Orch; Pep Clb; GAA; Miami Univ; Comp Sci.

HEFNER, JILL; Spencerville HS; Spencerville, OH; 2/100 Hon Rl; NHS; Stg Crw; FHA; Letter Bsktbl; Letter Trk; Treas GAA; IM Sprt; Mgrs; Univ; Educ.

HEFNER, KAMMI; Bridgeport Sr HS; Bridgeport, WV; Band; Chrs; Chrh Wkr; Cmnty Wkr; Girl Scts; Hon Rl; Jr NHS; Pres NHS; Orch; PAVAS; West Virginia Univ; Vet.

HEFNER, RUSTY; Moorefield HS; Moorefield, WV; Trs Jr Cls; Hon Rl; NHS; Rptr Yrbk; Ed Sch Nwsp; Marshall Univ; Marketing.

HEFT, DEBORAH; Skyvue HS; Lewisville, OH; 1/59 Pres Sr Cls; Chrs; Hon Rl; Lbry Ade; Sec NHS; Yth Flsp; Yrbk; Pres 4-H; Am Leg Awd; 4-H Awd; Ohio St Univ; Finance.

HEGEDUS, AMY; Jenison HS; Jenison, MI; Band; Chrh Wkr; Hon Rl; Hosp Ade; JA; OEA; Ten; Natl Merit Ltr; Grand Vly St Coll; Comp Prog.

HEGEDUS, GERALD; Wehrle HS; Columbus, OH; Boy Scts; Letter Ftbl; College; Liberal Arts.

HEGEDUS, GREGORY A; Norwood HS; Norwood, OH; Trs Jr Cls; Band; Boy Scts; Hon Rl; Treas Lat Clb; Letter Ftbl; Letter Trk; College; Engineering.

HEGEDUS, JILL; Reeths Puffer HS; N Muskegon, MI; Band; Girl Scts; Hon Rl; Trk; Pom Pon; PPFtbl; Michigan St Univ.

HEGEDUS, NADINE; N Royalton HS; Broadview Hts, OH; Hon Rl; NHS; OEA; College; Paralegal.

HEGER, TOM; Menominee HS; Menominee, MI; 6/275 Am Leg Boys St; Band; Boy Scts; Hon Rl; Jr NHS; NHS; Ger Clb; Natl Merit Ltr; Michigan St Univ; Marketing Research.

HEGLIN, ED; Croswell Lexington HS; Croswell, MI; 21/187 Band; NHS; Sch Mus; Sch Pl; Letter Trk; Mic State Univ; Physics.

HEHRER, JODI; Ovid Elsie HS; Ovid, MI; Trs Soph Cls; Girl Scts; Hon Rl; Hosp Ade; Bsktbl; Crs Cntry; Letter Trk; Mic State Univ; Registered Nurse.

HEIBEL, MARIAN; Hopkins HS; Dorr, MI; 15/111 Jr NHS; NHS; Rptr Sch Nwsp; Sch Nwsp; Spn Clb; Michigan St Univ.

HEIBY, GAYLE; Jay County HS; Portland, IN; 23/435 Aud/Vis; Chrh Wkr; Hon Rl; Jr NHS; Lbry Ade; Lit Mag; NHS; Quill & Scroll; Sch Mus; Stg Crw; Univ; Lib Sci.

HEIDEBRINK, PAM; Lake HS; Millbury, OH; 5/190 Cl Rep Jr Cls; Hon Rl; NHS; Stu Cncl; Yth Flsp; 4-H; Pep Clb; Spn Clb; Letter Bsktbl; Letter Trk; Bowling Green St Univ; Bus.

HEIDEL, SUE; New Richmond HS; New Richmond, OH; 38/197 Hon Rl; Hosp Ade; NHS; Sch Mus; Sch Pl; Drama Clb; Pres 4-H; Fr Clb; VP Pep Clb; Ten; Univ; Med Tech.

HEIDEN, JAMES J; Britton Macon Area HS; Britton, MI; Cls Rep Sr Cls; Am Leg Boys St; Hon Rl; Stu Cncl; Yrbk; Letter Bsktbl; Trk; 4-H Awd; Monroe Cmnty Univ; Math.

HEIDENREICH, GRETCHEN; Hamilton Southeastern HS; Noblesville, IN; 61/150 Hon Rl; Stg Crw; Drama Clb; 4-H; VP OEA; VP Spn Clb; Letter Swmmng; Ten; Tmr; Purdue Univ; Bus.

HEIDENREICH, JEANEN; Marshall HS; Marshall, MI; 10/250 Cmnty Wkr; Debate Tm; Hon Rl; NHS; Sch Pl; Ed Sch Nwsp; Ten; Chrldng; Cit Awd; VFW Awd; Albion Coll; Eng.

HEIDGER, SALLY; Douglas Mac Arthur HS; Saginaw, MI; 33/300 Cls Rep Soph Cls; Cl Rep Jr Cls; Sec Sr Cls; Chrh Wkr; Drl Tm; Hon Rl; Lit Mag; NHS; Orch; Sch Pl; Varsity Track Most Improved; Best Camper; College; Social Work.

HEIDISCH, JENNIFER; East Detroit HS; Warren, MI; Band; Chrs; Hon Rl; Lbry Ade; Wayne St Univ; Nursing.

HEIDLEBAUGH, CAROL A; Liberty Benton HS; Findlay, OH; 2/52 Pres Soph Cls; Band; Chrs; Hon Rl; NHS; Off Ade; Pres Stu Cncl; Yrbk; 4-H; Letter Trk; Bowling Green St Univ; Elem Educ.

HEIDORN, KATHY; South Ripley Jr Sr HS; Milan, IN; Band; Hon Rl; Lbry Ade; Stu Cncl; Pres 4-H; Sci Clb; Spn Clb; 4-H Awd; College; Home Ec.

HEIDORN, MARK; Flushing Sr HS; Flushing, MI; Hon Rl; Sch Mus; Sch Pl; Stg Crw; Stu Cncl; Drama Clb; Pres Fr Clb; Natl Merit Ltr; Kalamazoo Coll; Poli Sci.

HEIER, CHRISTINA; Jeffersonville HS; Jeffersonville, IN; FCA; Ger Clb; PPFtbl; Univ; Soc Sci.

HEIERMAN, AMY; Chillicothe HS; Chillicothe, OH; 9/365 Trs Sr Cls; AFS; Band; Chrh Wkr; Debate Tm; Hon Rl; Natl Forn Lg; NHS; Colgate Univ; Pre Med.

HEIGEL, KIMBERLY; Centerville HS; Dayton, OH; 11/680 NHS; Off Ade; Quill & Scroll; Yrbk; Pep Clb; Natl Merit Ltr; Univ Of Dayton; Engr.

HEIKA, MICHAEL; Traverse City HS; Traverse City, MI; Cls Rep Frsh Cls; Aud/Vis; Hon Rl; Stu Cncl; Ftbl; IM Sprt; NMC; Law.

HEIL, ANN; Gabriel Richard HS; Ann Arbor, MI; 1/75 Cls Rep Frsh Cls; Hon Rl; NHS; Stu Cncl; Sch Nwsp; Fr Clb; Natl Merit SF; Univ Of Mic; Aeronautical Engr.

HEIL, BARB; Ridgedale HS; Nevada, OH; 20/96 Chrs; Hon Rl; Sch Mus; Spn Clb; Letter Letter Ohio State Univ; Education.

HEIL, DAN; Lehman HS; Piqua, OH; Bsbl; Chmn Ftbl; Trk; Wrstlng; Winona Minn.

HEIL, JANICE; Father J Wehrle Memrl HS; Columbus, OH; 20/115 Cl Rep Jr Cls; Aud/Vis; Band; Chrh Wkr; Drl Tm; Girl Scts; Hon Rl; Stu Cncl; Yth Flsp; GAA; Ohio State Univ; Photo Journalism.

HEIL, JOAN; Gabriel Richard HS; Ann Arbor, MI; 1/82 Sec Jr Cls; Val; Chrs; Hon Rl; NHS; Sch Pl; Stg Crw; Drama Clb; Pres Fr Clb; Michigan Tech Univ; Engr.

HEIL, KAREN; Morral Ridgedale HS; Marion, OH; 1/73 Cl Rep Jr Cls; Val; Band; Chrs; Chrh Wkr; Hon Rl; Jr NHS; Lit Mag; NHS; Off Ade; Altrvsa Schshp 79; Top Girl Athlr Of Ridgedale High 79; Miami Univ; Psych.

HEILAND, JAN; Anna HS; Anna, OH; 10/73 Sec Jr Cls; Band; Chrh Wkr; NHS; Sch Mus; Yrbk; 4-H; F HA; Trk; Pres Awd; Bus Schl.

HEILE, JULIE; Reading HS; Reading, OH; 57/228 Trs Soph Cls; Cl Rep Jr Cls; VP Sr Cls; Girl Scts; Hosp Ade; Off Ade; Pep Clb; Spn Clb; Trk; Chrldng; Bowling Green Univ; Hosp Admin.

HEILERS, JOLENE; Anna Local HS; Anna, OH; 7/69 Band; Cmnty Wkr; Drm Bgl; Drm Mjrt; Hon Rl; Rptr Yrbk; Drama Clb; 4-H; FHA; GAA; Edison State; Accounting.

HEILIG, JENNINGS; Plainwell HS; Plainwell, MI; Band; Hon Rl; Sch Mus; Stg Crw; Fr Clb; Embry Riddle Aero Univ.

HEILMAN, DAVID; Grove City HS; Grove City, OH; 87/509 Cl Rep Jr Cls; Cls Rep Sr Cls; Sch Pl; Stu Cncl; Yth Flsp; Pres Drama Clb; Pres Pep Clb; Coach Actv; Opt Clb Awd; Drama Clb Schlshp 1979; Stdnt Councl Fellowshp Awd 197; Firelands Coll; Drama.

HEILMAN, LAURIE; Carrollton HS; Carrollton, OH; Chrs; Chrh Wkr; Cmnty Wkr; Sch Mus; 4-H; FHA; 4-H Awd; Jefferson Tech Coll; Busns Mgmt.

HEILMAN, MELINDA; Black River HS; Spencer, OH; Chrs; Sch Mus; 4-H; FHA; Bus Schl; Law Enforcement.

HEILMAN, TED; Saranac HS; Saranac, MI; Cls Rep Frsh Cls; Boy Scts; Hon Rl; Lbry Ade; NHS; Sct Actv; Stu Cncl; Pres Spn Clb; Letter Bsbl; Letter Bsktbl; Letters & Senate Resolution To St Champ Bsbl Team; Letter & Resolution Of Tribute To Semi Finalist Basketbl; College; Nuclear Fussion.

HEIM, KATHY; Woodrow Wilson HS; Youngstwn, OH; Sec Jr Cls; JA; Off Ade; Sch Pl; Yth Flsp; Sch Nwsp; Drama Clb; Pep Clb; VICA; JA Awd; Youngstown St Univ; Nursing.

HEIM, LISA; Heath HS; Heath, OH; Band; Chrs; Hon Rl; Sch Mus; OEA; Bus Schl; Sec.

HEIM, TINA; Nordonia HS; Northfield, OH; Hon Rl; Bus Schl; Insurance.

HEIMACH, JULIE A; De Kalb HS; Auburn, IN; 60/349 Cls Rep Soph Cls; Cl Rep Jr Cls; Cls Rep Sr Cls; Pol Wkr; Stu Cncl; Yth Flsp; Rptr Yrbk; Ger Clb; Pep Clb; Chrldng; Ravenscroft Bty Coll; Cosmetology.

HEIMANN, BRENT; Washington HS; Massillon, OH; 1/482 Val; Am Leg Boys St; Boy Scts; Hon Rl; Jr NHS; NHS; Stu Cncl; Pres Spn Clb; Letter Crs Cntry; Univ Of Cin; Chem Engr.

HEIMBACH, CYNTHIA; Norton HS; Norton, OH; 25/275 Sec Soph Cls; Sec Sr Cls; Chrs; Hon Rl; Jr NHS; NHS; Sch Mus; Sec Lat Clb; Treas Pep Clb; Sec Sci Clb; Coll; Sci.

HEIMLICH, LORI; River Valley HS; Waldo, OH; Cls Rep Soph Cls; Band; Chrs; Chrh Wkr; Hon Rl; NHS; Sch Mus; Stu Cncl; Yth Flsp; Rus Clb; College; English.

HEIN, CARL; Mason Sr HS; Mason, MI; Cls Rep Frsh Cls; Cls Rep Soph Cls; Hon Rl; Jr NHS; Rptr Sch Nwsp; Bsktbl; Univ; Law Enforcement.

HEIN, NATALIE; Adlai E Stevenson HS; Sterling Hts, MI; 104/487 Hon Rl; Hosp Ade; Sct Actv; Cit Awd; Natl Merit Schl; Arts Club 76; Perfect Attdn 75 77; Instructor Aide 75 78; Oakland Univ; Med Tech.

HEIN, TIM; Marquette HS; Marquette, MI; Sch Nwsp; Sci Clb; Spn Clb; Ftbl; IM Sprt; Scr Kpr; Mas Awd; College; Bus.

HEINDEL, ALLEN W; Celina Sr HS; Celina, OH; 33/240 Band; NHS; Pres Yth Flsp; Pres 4-H; 4-H Awd; Fort Wayne Bible Coll; Pastoral Mini.

HEINEKING, KAREN; Theodore Roosevelt HS; Kent, OH; Band; Cmp Fr Grls; Chrh Wkr; Drl Tm; Swmmng; Kent St Univ; Med.

HEINEMAN, KENNETH; Williamston HS; Williamston, MI; Am Leg Boys St; Capt Debate Tm; Natl Forn Lg; Sch Pl; Ed Sch Nwsp; Sch Nwsp; Am Leg Awd; Michigan St Univ; Jrnlsm.

HEINEMAN, LEE ANN; Mc Clain HS; Leesburg, OH; 27/150 Drama Clb; FTA; Letter Trk; 13th Plc In Oh Tests Of Schlstc Achvmnt 76; Whos Who In Foreign Langs 79; Cmnty Hosptl Schl; RN.

HEINEMANN, NORMA; Coldwater HS; Coldwater, MI; Band; Cmp Fr Grls; Hosp Ade; Pol Wkr; Sch Mus; Stg Crw; Yrbk; 4-H; 4-H Awd; Kellogg Comm Coll.

HEINEN, LISA; Seton HS; Cincinnati, OH; Hon Rl; Univ Of Cincinnati; Dent Hygiene.

HEINER, BETH; Huntington HS; Huntington, WV; Cls Rep Frsh Cls; Cls Rep Soph Cls; Cl Rep Jr Cls; Chrs; Chrh Wkr; Cmnty Wkr; Hon Rl; Yth Flsp; Drama Clb; Pep Clb; Second Alternate Miss Teenage Huntington Pageant; Finalist Miss Teenage Huntington Pageant; College; Equestrian.

HEINGARTNER, GORDON; Rutherford B Hayes HS; Delaware, OH; Chrs; Chrh Wkr; Hon Rl; Yth Flsp; Sci Clb; Socr; Trk; Pres Awd; Coll; Sci.

HEINL, JENNIFER; Crestwood HS; Mantua, OH; 66/238 VP Sr Cls; Pres Chrs; Chrh Wkr; Sch Mus; Stu Cncl; Yrbk; Pep Clb;.

HEINLEIN, DANIEL; Indiana Academy; Plymouth, IN; 8/65 VP Frsh Cls; Trs Soph Cls; Chrh Wkr; Cmnty Wkr; Hon Rl; NHS; Stg Crw; Mth Clb; Bsbl; Capt Bsktbl; Andrews Univ; Auto Mech.

HEINO, TINA; Gladstone Area HS; Gladstone, MI; 1/203 Val; Hon Rl; Lbry Ade; NHS; Natl Merit Ltr; Bay De Noc Cmnty Coll; Pre Law.

HEINOLD, TAMMY; Whitko HS; Pierceton, IN; Trs Jr Cls; Band; FCA; NHS; Yrbk; Pres 4-H; Pep Clb; Bsktbl; Letter Mgrs; Scr Kpr; College; Acctg.

HEINRICH, JACKIE; Augres Sims HS; Au Gres, MI; Debate Tm; Hon Rl; Lbry Ade; Sch Pl; Rptr Yrbk; Rptr Sch Nwsp; Bsktbl; College; Bus Mgmt.

HEINRICHS, LISE; Seneca E HS; Ahica, OH; Band; Chrs; Chrh Wkr; Cmnty Wkr; Hon Rl; Hosp Ade; Lbry Ade; Off Ade; Red Cr Ade; Sch Pl; Univ Of Toledo; Educ.

HEINS, DONNA J; Morton Sr HS; Hammond, IN; Sec Sr Cls; NHS; Quill & Scroll; Stu Cncl; Rptr Sch Nwsp; Sch Nwsp; Pep Clb; PPFtbl; Indiana Univ; Busns Admin.

HEINS, WILLIAM A; Firestone HS; Eau Claire, WI; Band; Debate Tm; Natl Forn Lg; NHS; Trk; NCTE; Wharton Schl Of Bus; Law.

HEINTSCHEL, GREGORY; Central Catholic HS; Toledo, OH; 30/350 Cls Rep Frsh Cls; Cl Rep Jr Cls; Hon Rl; Lit Mag; NHS; Stu Cncl; Sch Nwsp; Univ Of Toledo; Pre Med.

HEINTZ, DAVID; Lake Central HS; Schererville, IN; 2/519 Sal; Boy Scts; Chrh Wkr; Cmnty Wkr; Hon Rl; NHS; Sch Pl; Stg Crw; Fr Clb; Pres Leo Clb; Tri Kappa Schlrshp; 4 Yr Perfect Attendance; 1st Plc In NHS Quiz Bowl Tournament & MVP; Purdue Univ; Elec Engr.

HEINTZ, DOUGLAS; Brookfield HS; Brookfield, OH; Cl Rep Jr Cls; Band; Boy Scts; Hon Rl; NHS; Sct Actv; Stu Cncl; Yth Flsp; Beta Clb; Lat Clb; Univ; Engr.

HEINTZELMAN, JUDITH; Chagrin Falls HS; Chagrin Fl, OH; Chrs; Cmnty Wkr; Girl Scts; Hon Rl; Lit Mag; Sch Mus; Sct Actv; Sch Nwsp; College; Bio Sci.

HEINY, JANET; Lapel HS; Lapel, IN; 7/100 Band; Chrs; Hon Rl; NHS; Sch Mus; Sch Nwsp; Pep Clb; Mgrs; Purdue Univ; Business Mgmt.

HEINY, LYNNETTE; Lapel HS; Lapel, IN; Chrs; Cmnty Wkr; Hon Rl; NHS; Sch Mus; Yrbk; Pep Clb; College; Comm Art.

HEINZ, KATHERINE M; Jeffersonville HS; Jeffersonville, IN; 1/650 Sec Frsh Cls; Sec Soph Cls; Sec Jr Cls; Hon Rl; NHS; Key Clb; Chrldng; PPFtbl; Am Leg Awd; College.

HEINZ, LORI; Howell HS; Howell, MI; Hon Rl; Rptr Sch Nwsp; Sch Nwsp; IM Sprt; Scr Kpr; Univ; Jrnlsm.

HEINZ, SHERRI; Manistique HS; Manistique, MI; VICA; Letter Trk; Elec.

HEINZEL, LAURIE; Rogers City HS; Rogers City, MI; 1/142 Val; AFS; Band; Hon Rl; NHS; Pep Clb; Letter Bsktbl; Letter Trk; IM Sprt; Central Mich Univ; Comp Progrm.

HEINZL, ANNIE; Windham HS; Windham, OH; 2/109 Trs Jr Cls; Hon Rl; Sch Pl; Stg Crw; Ed Sch Nwsp; Drama Clb; Spn Clb; Bsktbl; Trk; Chrldng; Volleyball; Hostess Club; Ohio Univ; Phys Therapy.

HEIRONIMUS, DON; Miami Trace HS; Washington Ch, OH; Sec Jr Cls; Am Leg Boys St; Chrs; Chrh Wkr; FSA; Sci Clb; Letter Ftbl; Letter Trk; College; Geology.

HEIS, ALLEN; Mc Nicholas HS; Cincinnati, OH; Band; Sch Nwsp; Letter Ftbl; Voc Schl; Comm Art.

HEISEL, AMY L; Seton HS; Cincinnati, OH; 6/255 Girl Scts; Hon Rl; Jr NHS; NHS; Sch Pl; Sprt Ed Sch Nwsp; Fr Clb; Pep Clb; Coach Actv; College; Science.

HEISEL, JOHN; Ridgedale HS; New Bloomington, OH; Band; VP Chrs; Hon Rl; Quill & Scroll; Sch Mus; Pres Yth Flsp; Rptr Sch Nwsp; 4-H; Crs Cntry; Trk; Ohio St Univ; Music.

HEISELMAN, KELLY; Deer Park HS; Cincinnati, OH; Cls Rep Soph Cls; Cl Rep Jr Cls; Band; Chrh Wkr; Cmnty Wkr; Hon Rl; NHS; Stu Cncl; Sch Nwsp; College; Art.

HEISER, CHAD; Ashtabula HS; Ashtabula, OH; 26/208 AFS; Boy Scts; Chrh Wkr; Hon Rl; JA; Sct Actv; Ger Clb; JA Awd; Kent State; Bus Mgmt.

HEISHMAN, KATHY; Hurricane HS; Hurricane, WV; Chrh Wkr; Girl Scts; Hon Rl; Lbry Ade; NHS; Sct Actv; Sec Stu Cncl; 4-H; Pep Clb; Letter Ten; Marshall Univ; Nursing.

HEISHMAN, MARK; Hurricane HS; Hurricane, WV; 1/200 Pres Frsh Cls; Pres Soph Cls; Am Leg Boys St; FCA; NHS; Stu Cncl; Letter Bsktbl; Letter Crs Cntry; Letter Trk; Dnfth Awd; College; Chemistry.

HEISHMAN, MARK; Hurricane HS; Hurrican, WV; 2/200 Am Leg Boys St; Chrh Wkr; VP NHS; Stu Cncl; Letter Bsktbl; Letter Crs Cntry; Letter Trk; Dnfth Awd; God Cntry Awd; West Virginia Tech Univ; Chem Engr.

HEISLER, CINDY; Edgerton HS; Edgerton, OH; 10/81 Hon Rl; NHS; Ed Yrbk; Treas Fr Clb; IM Sprt; Mat Maids; Univ; Psych.

HEISS, CATHERINE; Warren Local HS; Marietta, OH; Trs Frsh Cls; Band; Chrs; Sch Mus; Treas Stu Cncl; Drama Clb; Fr Clb; Pep Clb; Bowling Green State Univ; Chemistry.

HEISS, MARY ANN; Lake Catholic HS; Wickliffe, OH; 25/305 Band; Hon Rl; Lit Mag; NHS; Miami Univ; Poli Sci.

HEIST, MELINDA; Greenville HS; Greenville, OH; Cmnty Wkr; Girl Scts; 4-H; Swmmng; Tmr; College; Math.

HEISTAND, DAN; Oakridge HS; Twin Lk, MI; Cls Rep Frsh Cls; Pres Soph Cls; Pres Jr Cls; Am Leg Boys St; Band; Boy Scts; Hon Rl; NHS; Pep Clb; IM Sprt; Univ; Comp Systems.

HEITHAUS, DAVID E; Richmond Sr HS; Richmond, IN; Hon Rl; Sch Nwsp; Letter Swmmng; DAR Awd; Univ; Engr.

HEITJAN, THOMAS; Servite HS; Detroit, MI; 1/90 Cls Rep Frsh Cls; Hon Rl; Pres NHS; Univ.

HEITKAMP, BETTY; Marion Local HS; Minster, OH; Hon Rl; Pep Clb; Scr Kpr;.

HEITKAMP, DEBRA; Minster HS; Minster, OH; 6/80 Band; Chrs; Chrh Wkr; Girl Scts; Hon Rl; NHS; FTA; Pep Clb; College; Bus Admin.

HEITKAMP, KENNETH; Minster HS; Minster, OH; Chrh Wkr; Hon Rl; Bsbl; Letter Bsktbl; Letter Ftbl; Univ; Bus.

HEITZ, LINDA; Shawe Memorial HS; Madison, IN; Cls Rep Frsh Cls; Trs Soph Cls; Trs Jr Cls; Trs Sr Cls; Hosp Ade; Rptr Yrbk; Sch Nwsp; Pep Clb; Chrldng; Ind Univ.

HEITZ, TIMOTHY; Notre Dame HS; Clarksburg, WV; 9/52 Key Clb; Wv Univ; Engr.

HEITZMAN, DEBRA; Continental HS; Cloverdale, OH; Band; Hon Rl; Treas Stu Cncl; Yth Flsp; Yrbk; Spn Clb; Bus Schl; Acctg.

HEJDUK, DONNA; Bedford Sr HS; Bedford Hts, OH; Hon Rl; Jr NHS; NHS; OEA; Scr Kpr;.

HELD, DOROTHY; Wehrle HS; Columbus, OH; 6/115 Cls Rep Soph Cls; Hon Rl; Stu Cncl; Chrldng; Ohio St Univ; Vet Med.

HELD, JENNIFER; Rutherford B Hayes HS; Delaware, OH; 10/325 Cl Rep Jr Cls; AFS; Cmnty Wkr; Hon Rl; Jr NHS; NHS; Sch Mus; Stg Crw; Stu Cncl; Y-Teens; Hanover Admissions Schlrshp; Hayes Academic Awds; Pres Schlrshp; Hanover Coll; Biology.

HELD, KATHLEEN; Walnut Ridge HS; Columbus, OH; Chrs; Cmnty Wkr; Hon Rl; Jr NHS; NHS; Off Ade; Trk; Scr Kpr; Columbus Tech Inst; Acctg.

HELD, MIKE; Wadsworth Sr HS; Wadsworth, OH; Boy Scts; Chrs; Chrh Wkr; Cmnty Wkr; FCA; Hon Rl; Sct Actv; Stu Cncl; Yth Flsp; Key Clb; Univ; Pharmacy.

HELD, SANDRA; Edon HS; Edon, OH; 1/72 Sec Soph Cls; Sec Sr Cls; NHS; Sec Stu Cncl; Rptr Yrbk; Sec FHA; Spn Clb; Letter Bsktbl; Dnfth Awd; DAR Awd; Bowling Green State Univ; Acctg.

HELD, SANDY; Edon HS; Edon, OH; 1/68 Sec Soph Cls; Cl Rep Jr Cls; Sec Sr Cls; Val; Chrs; Hon Rl; Sec NHS; Sch Mus; Sec Stu Cncl; Rptr Yrbk; College.

HELDRETH, NANCY; Dunbar HS; Charleston, WV; Cls Rep Frsh Cls; Hon Rl; Jr NHS; Lbry Ade; Stu Cncl; Sec 4-H; FBLA; Pep Clb; IM Sprt; 4-H Awd; W Virginia St Coll; Acctg.

HELESKI, MARGO; Ubly HS; Bad Axe, MI; FFA;.

HELFRICH, CHERRI; Mater Dei HS; Evansville, IN; Gym; Chrldng; IM Sprt; College.

HELFRICH, KURT; Austintown Fitch HS; Youngstown, OH; 13/655 Am Leg Boys St; Band; Boy Scts; Hon Rl; NHS; Stg Crw; Sci Clb; Am Leg Awd; JA Awd; Natl Merit SF; Univ; Aerospace Engr.

HELFRICH, KURT A; Austintown Fitch HS; Youngstown, OH; 13/655 Am Leg Boys St; Band; NHS; Yth Flsp; Sci Clb; JA Awd; Natl Merit SF; Rotary Awd; College; Aero Engr.

HELGE, LYNN; Upper Sandusky HS; Upper Sandusky, OH; 17/205 Cls Rep Frsh Cls; Pres Soph Cls; Sec Jr Cls; Band; Chrs; Chrh Wkr; Girl Scts; Hon Rl; Sch Mus; Sch Pl; Columbus Tech Inst; Med Lab Tech.

HELLEMS, GERI; Litchfield HS; Allen, MI; Cls Rep Soph Cls; Band; Letter Debate Tm; Girl Scts; Hon Rl; Lbry Ade; Sch Pl; Stu Cncl; Letter Trk; Mgrs; Ferris State; Vet.

HELLER, CATHI; Elgin HS; Larue, OH; 11/150 Chrh Wkr; Hon Rl; Sch Mus; Sch Pl; Stg Crw; Yth Flsp; 4-H; FHA; Bsbl; Trk; College; Fashion Mdse.

HELLER, CHARLES; Washington HS; Washington, IN; 54/197 Band; Boy Scts; Pres Chrh Wkr; Cmnty Wkr; Pol Wkr; Yth Flsp; VP DECA; Pep Clb; Capt IM Sprt; Bowling Letter 1976; Vincennes Univ; Bus Admin.

HELLER, SUE; Galien HS; Buchanan, MI; 2/52 Pres Jr Cls; Sal; VP NHS; Ed Yrbk; Capt Bsktbl; College.

HELLINE, TRACEY; Washington HS; Massillon, OH; Chrs; Hon Rl; Sch Mus; Y-Teens; Ger Clb; Pep Clb; Letter Swmmng; IM Sprt; Letter Mgrs; Scr Kpr; Univ; Phys Ed.

HELLMER, MELANIE; Cabrini HS; Taylor, MI; Hon Rl; Fr Clb; Ger Clb; Pom Pon; College; Med.

HELLOW, PAUL; Soo Area HS; Sault Ste Mari, MI; Debate Tm; Drl Tm; Hon Rl; NHS; Capt ROTC; Crs Cntry; Trk; Rotary Awd; Lake Superior St Univ.

HELLOW, PAUL; Soo Area HS; Sault Ste Marie, MI; Debate Tm; Drl Tm; Hon Rl; Jr NHS; NHS; Capt ROTC; Crs Cntry; Lake Superior State College; Engr.

HELLSTERN, ANN; Our Lady Of The Elms HS; Becksville, OH; Cmnty Wkr; Hon Rl; Lbry Ade; Off Ade; Bsbl; College; Nursing.

HELLSTERN, ANN; Our Lady Of The Elms HS; Brecksville, OH; 6/36 Chrh Wkr; Cmnty Wkr; Hon Rl; Lbry Ade; Off Ade; Bsbl; College; Med.

HELLWEGE, PATRICIA; Concordia Lutheran HS; Ft Wayne, IN; Band; Hon Rl; NHS; FBLA; Letter Bsktbl; Letter Trk; Oral Roberts Univ; Math.

HELM, CATHY; Brownsburg HS; Brownsburg, IN; 10/270 Cls Rep Soph Cls; Cl Rep Jr Cls; Hon Rl; NHS; Stu Cncl; Sch Nwsp; Mat Maids; Natl Merit Ltr; Certf For Superior Perf On NEDT Tests 77; Indiana St Univ; Cmnctns.

HELM, GUSTAVIA; Thomas Carr Howe HS; Indianapolis, IN; Girl Scts; Hon Rl; Chmn Bsktbl; Ten; Trk; Air Force Acad; Elec Engr.

HELM, STEVEN; Andrews Academy; Berrien Spring, MI; Sch Pl; Spn Clb; IM Sprt; Andrews Univ.

HELM, STEVEN; Andrews Acad; Berrien Spgs, MI; Sch Pl; Spn Clb; IM Sprt; Andrews Univ.

HELM, TONYA R; East HS; Columbus, OH; Cl Rep Jr Cls; Chrh Wkr; Cmnty Wkr; Hon Rl; Jr NHS; NHS; Sch Pl; Stu Cncl; Pep Clb; Spn Clb; Outstanding History & Math Awd; Dancing Scholarship; College; Comp Prog.

HELMAN, CAROL; Houston HS; Sidney, OH; 4/67 Band; Chrs; NHS; Sch Pl; Yth Flsp; Ed Yrbk; 4-H; FHA; VP OEA; 4-H Awd; Edison St Coll; Exec Sec.

HELMER, CAMILLE; Parkway HS; Rockford, OH; 1/97 Chrs; Chrh Wkr; Hon Rl; NHS; Yth Flsp; VP FHA; VP FTA; Sci Clb; Trk; NEDT Cert; College.

HELMER, JAN; Harper Creek HS; Battle Creek, MI; 23/244 Hon Rl; Jr NHS; NHS; Stg Crw; Yth Flsp; Drama Clb; Spn Clb; Calvin Coll; Art.

HELMER, KATHRYN; Bishop Dwenger HS; Ft Wayne, IN; Cls Rep Soph Cls; Chrs; Hon Rl; NHS; Sch Mus; Sch Pl; Stu Cncl; Fr Clb; Indiana Univ; Phys Ther.

HELMICK, HOWARD; Mannington HS; Mannington, WV; 21/114 Band; Boy Scts; Chrs; Chrh Wkr; Hon Rl; Mgrs; Scr Kpr; Tmr; Fairmont St Univf Mining Engr.

HELMICK, LISABETH; Pennsboro HS; Ellenboro, WV; Chrh Wkr; Girl Scts; Hon Rl; FHA; FTA; Chrldng; 4-H Awd; Parkersburg Cmnty Coll; Nursing.

HELMICK, SHERRY; Berrien Springs HS; Berrien Spgs, MI; 22/110 Hon Rl; Lbry Ade; NHS; Sch Mus; Sch Pl; Stg Crw; Sec Drama Clb; 1st Pl Sculpture 79; 3rd Pl Sculpture 79; Thespian Soc Honor Bar 79; Ctr For Creative Stds; Sculpture.

HELMIG, JANET; Oakwood HS; Dayton, OH; Hon Rl; Letter Chrldng; Letter Mgrs; Univ; Elem Ed.

HELMKAMP, ELAINE; East Noble HS; Kendallville, IN; 44/273 Band; Hon Rl; Hosp Ade; NHS; Drama Clb; 4-H; OEA; Pep Clb; Sci Clb; Ten; Pur due Univ; Home Ec.

HELMKE, LYNN; National Trail HS; Eaton, OH; Band; Chrs; Girl Scts; Hon Rl; NHS; Orch; Sct Actv; Stg Crw; Sec 4-H; FTA; 1st Class Girl Scout 77; All Oh Youth Band Oh St Fair 79; Oh N Music Camp 76 79; 2 Yrs Hon Band; Univ; Music.

HELMKE, TODD; Woodlan HS; Woodburn, IN; FCA; Hon Rl; Letter Bsbl; Ftbl; IM Sprt; Natl Merit Ltr; College; Physical Education.

HELMS, ATHENA; Western HS; Russiaville, IN; 6/222 Cls Rep Frsh Cls; Cls Rep Soph Cls; Cl Rep Jr Cls; Chrs; Chrh Wkr; FCA; Hon Rl; NHS; Off Ade; Stu Cncl; College; Special Ed.

HELMS, DAVE A; Buckeye South HS; Tiltonsville, OH; Am Leg Boys St; Chrh Wkr; Hon Rl; Jr NHS; NHS; Pol Wkr; Spn Clb; Letter Ftbl; Scr Kpr; Ohi State Univ; Dentistry.

HELMS, MARGARET; Yorktown HS; Muncie, IN; 4/200 Am Leg Aux Girls St; Band; Hon Rl; Jr NHS; MMM; NHS; Rptr Sch Nwsp; Fr Clb; Swmmng; Ball State Univ; Music Educ.

HELMS, STEPHANIE M; Southern Wells Jr Sr HS; Warren, IN; 15/96 Band; Chrs; Hon Rl; NHS; Bus Schl; Bus.

HELMUTH, DONNA; Fairfield Union HS; Rushville, OH; 2/158 Chrh Wkr; Hon Rl; Hosp Ade; Jr NHS; Sec Yth Flsp; 4-H; FNA; 4-H Awd; English; Columbus Tech Inst; Animal Health.

HELMUTH, MOLLYE; Orrville HS; Orrville, OH; Sec Soph Cls; Sec Jr Cls; Sec Sr Cls; Am Leg Aux Girls St; Band; Chrh Wkr; FCA; FTA; Pep Clb; Letter Trk; Bowling Green St Univ; Elem Deaf Ed.

HELMUTH, RON; Findlay HS; Findlay, OH; 65/686 Boy Scts; Pres JA; NHS; Quill & Scroll; Sch Mus; Sch Pl; Stg Crw; Sch Nwsp; Drama Clb; Rdo Clb; Eagle Scout Award 1977; Antl Jr Achvmnt Conf Delegate 1978; Ohio Univ; Commctns.

HELSINGER, JENNIFER; Little Miami HS; Morrow, OH; Band; Hon Rl; Lit Mag; NHS; Off Ade; Yrbk; 4-H; Spn Clb; Twrlr; Coll.

HELSTEIN, LISA; Negaunee HS; Negaunee, MI; Chrs; Hon Rl; Y-Teens; Pep Clb; Sci Clb; Letter Bsktbl; Letter Trk; Univ.

HELT, DAVID R; Highland Sr HS; Highland, IN; Am Leg Boys St; Hon Rl; NHS; ROTC; Sch Pl; Stg Crw; Drama Clb; Key Clb; Sci Clb; Letter Socr; Purdue Univ; Aeronautical.

HELT, RANDY; Mt Gilead HS; Mt Gilead, OH; 30/125 Am Leg Boys St; FCA; Hon Rl; Yth Flsp; Pres 4-H; Pres FFA; Bsbl; Crs Cntry; IM Sprt; 4-H Awd; Ohio St Univ; Agri.

HELT, REGINA; Rockville HS; Rockville, IN; Sec Jr Cls; Sec Sr Cls; Chrh Wkr; Hon Rl; NHS; Yth Flsp; Bsktbl; Letter Trk; PPFtbl; Tmr; College; Medical.

HELTON, ALESIA; Madison HS; Madison Hts, MI; Hon Rl; Off Ade; Spn Clb; Trk; IM Sprt; Wayne State Univ; Law.

HELTON, ANDREA L; Zane Trace HS; Chillicothe, OH; Band; Chrh Wkr; Hosp Ade; Sch Pl; Yth Flsp; 4-H; Key Clb; Spn Clb; 4-H Awd; Univ; Wildlife Mgmt.

HELTON, TERESA; Greenfield Central HS; Greenfield, IN; 19/300 Chrs; Chrh Wkr; Hon Rl; Lbry Ade; Mdrgl; NHS; Sch Mus; Rptr Sch Nwsp; 4-H; Covenant Foundation Coll; Nursing.

HEMBRUCH, JOHN; Carman Sr HS; Flint, MI; 14/430 Boy Scts; Chrs; Hon Rl; NHS; Pol Wkr; Yth Flsp; Ftbl; Univ; Acctg.

HEMINGER, LAURIE; Clay HS; Oregon, OH; Cls Rep Sr Cls; Hon Rl; Jr NHS; NHS; Stu Cncl; 4-H; Pep Clb; Trk; Chrldng; Pom Pon; Bowling Green; Medical Tech.

HEMINGWAY, D; Flushing HS; Flushing, MI; Band; FCA; IM Sprt; Mgrs; Scr Kpr; Tmr; College; Math.

HEMKER, DEBRA; Delphos St John HS; Delphos, OH; 15/146 Band; Hon Rl; VP NHS; Sch Nwsp; Trk; Chrldng; Voc Schl; Nursing Schl.

HEMLEIN, KATHRYN; Chagrin Falls HS; Chagrin Falls, OH; AFS; Band; Chrs; Girl Scts; Hon Rl; Lit Mag; Pres NHS; Sch Mus; Sch Nwsp; Pres Fr Clb; Ohio Test Of Scholastic Ach French Ii; Cleveland Press Spelling Contest Jr Div Champion; College; Bio Sci.

HEMMELGARN, JULIE; Centerville HS; Centerville, OH; 59/687 Girl Scts; NHS; Sch Mus; Sch Pl; Sct Actv; DECA; Wright St Univ; Acctg.

HEMMER, TAMELA; Warsaw Community HS; Warsaw, IN; 74/405 Chrs; Hon Rl; JA; Lbry Ade; Sch Pl; DECA; JA Awd; Kappa Kappa Kappa Hon Awd 79; Univ; Psych.

HEMMER, TRACY; Seton HS; Cincinnati, OH; Chrh Wkr; Hon Rl; Hosp Ade; Pol Wkr; Sch Mus; Letter Ten; GAA; IM Sprt; Am Leg Awd; SAR Awd; Natl Federtn Of Music Club Supr 73 79; Univ; History.

HEMMERICH, LYNDA; Morton Sr HS; Hammond, IN; 12/436 Band; Hon Rl; NHS; Orch; Stg Crw; FTA; Sci Clb; Band Contest Awrd; Purdue Univ; Bio.

HEMMING, CHARLES; Logan Elm HS; Circleville, OH; Chrh Wkr; FCA; Hon Rl; Sch Pl; Mth Clb; Bsktbl; Letter Trk; Hocking Tech School; Comp Sci.

HEMMINGER, KAREN; New Riegel HS; New Riegel, OH; 6/51 Sec Jr Cls; Band; Chrs; Hon Rl; NHS; Sch Mus; 4-H; FHA; Pep Clb; Chrldng; Tiffin Univ; Acctg.

HEMMINGER, KATHY M; New Riegel HS; New Riegel, OH; 5/48 Chrs; Hon Rl; NHS; Sch Mus; Sch Pl; 4-H; FHA; Pep Clb; Spn Clb; IM Sprt; Toledo Coll; Psych.

HEMPFLING, ANITA; Liberty Benton HS; Findlay, OH; Pres Jr Cls; Band; Chrh Wkr; Hon Rl; NHS; FHA; Letter Trk; Twrlr; Outstndng Jr 79; Schlshp Team 77 79; FHA Cnty Offc 7; Univ; Bus.

HEMPFLING, CHARLES; Delphos St Johns HS; Delphos, OH; 29/150 Hon Rl; FFA; IM Sprt; College; Agric.

HEMPHILL, DAN; Parkersburg Catholic HS; Parkersburg, WV; Hon Rl; Pol Wkr; Rptr Yrbk; Rptr Sch Nwsp; Bsbl; IM Sprt; West Virginia Univ; Bio.

HEMPHILL, KEMBERLEE; Gallia Academy; Northup, OH; 33/222 Band; Chrh Wkr; NHS; Sec Yth Flsp; Sch Nwsp; 4-H; FTA; 4-H Awd; Tennessee Temple Univ; Elem Ed.

HEMPSTED, YVONNE; Haslett HS; Haslett, MI; Band; Chrs; Hon Rl; Lbry Ade; Off Ade; Orch; 4-H; Pep Clb; Letter Chrldng; Mic State Univ; Bus.

HENADY, TODD; South Newton Jr Sr HS; Goodland, IN; FFA; Letter Bsbl; Ftbl; Letter Wrstlng; Scr Kpr; Lincoln Tech Schl; Mechanic.

HENAGAN, PATRICK; Douglas Mac Arthur HS; Saginaw, MI; 20/375 Cmnty Wkr; Hon Rl; Lbry Ade; NHS; Orch; Red Cr Ade; Sct Actv; Sch Nwsp; Ger Clb; Outstndng Chem & German Ach Awds; Coll; Chem.

HENCKE, FRED; James A Garfield HS; Garrettsville, OH; 8/110 VP Sr Cls; Hon Rl; Jr NHS; Ed Sch Nwsp; Letter Bsbl; Bsktbl; Letter Glf; Wrstlng; Hiram Coll; Comp Sci.

HENCRICKS, GRETCHEN; Manistee Cath Central HS; Manistee, MI; Hon Rl; Rptr Sch Nwsp; Bsktbl; West Shore Cmnty Coll.

HENDERSHOT, FRANCHESKA; Licking Valley HS; Frazeysburg, OH; Pres Soph Cls; Cls Rep Soph Cls; Band; Chrs; Hon Rl; Sch Mus; 4-H; Letter Bsktbl; Letter Trk; Letter Chrldng; College; Medical.

HENDERSHOT, JEFF; Meadowbrook HS; Senecaville, OH; 15/185 Cls Rep Soph Cls; Aud/Vis; Band; Chrh Wkr; Hon Rl; JA; Lbry Ade; Orch; Stu Cncl; Ohi State Univ; Archit.

HENDERSHOT, JULIE; Bexley HS; Columbus, OH; Cls Rep Frsh Cls; Band; Girl Scts; Hon Rl; Stu Cncl; Yth Flsp; Drama Clb; Sci Clb; Spn Clb; Letter Bsbl; Best Athlete; Varsity Basketball Co Captain; Pres Of Presbyteens; College; Psychology.

HENDERSON, BETH; Rochester Cmnty HS; Rochester, IN; Cls Rep Frsh Cls; Trs Jr Cls; Chrs; FCA; Hon Rl; Off Ade; Sch Mus; Sch Pl; Yth Flsp; Pep Clb; Voc Schl; Bio Sci.

HENDERSON, BRIAN; Norton HS; Norton, OH; 4/342 Pres Frsh Cls; Pres Soph Cls; VP Jr Cls; Cmnty Wkr; Hon Rl; NHS; Mth Clb; Bsktbl; Letter Ftbl; Letter Trk; College; Math.

HENDERSON, CHERRYL; Buena Vista HS; Saginaw, MI; Cls Rep Soph Cls; Cl Rep Jr Cls; Band; Girl Scts; Hon Rl; Sch Pl; Stu Cncl; Drama Clb; 4-H; Pep Clb; Howard Univ; Sci.

HENDERSON, CYNTHIA; Wakefield HS; Wakefield, MI; Trs Frsh Cls; Band; Chrh Wkr; Hon Rl; 4-H; FHA; Ger Clb; Pep Clb; Voice Dem Awd; Amer Lg Police Cadet Progr 79; Op Bentalgy Participnts 79; Gld Mdl In Dist Comptns Of Mi Forensics 79; Northland Coll; Psych.

HENDERSON, DOUGLAS L; Lake Orion Cmnty HS; Lake Orion, MI; Boy Scts; Hon Rl; Jr NHS; NHS; Bsbl; Capt Ftbl; Wrstlng; Univ.

HENDERSON, ERIC S; Genoa Area HS; Genoa, OH; 3/168 Am Leg Boys St; Chrh Wkr; Hon Rl; NHS; 4-H; IM Sprt; Mgrs; 4-H Awd; Natl Merit Ltr; Univ; Astronomy.

HENDERSON, GREGGORY; Delaware Hayes HS; Delaware, OH; Cls Rep Frsh Cls; AFS; Boy Scts; Cmnty Wkr; FCA; Hon Rl; VP Pol Wkr; Sct Actv; Stu Cncl; Yth Flsp; Cand For Boys St 79; VP Of The De Cnty Teen Age Rep 78; Miami Univ; Tchr.

HENDERSON, JACQUELINE; Southwestern HS; Detroit, MI; Sec Frsh Cls; Sec Soph Cls; Sec Jr Cls; Sec Sr Cls; Hon Rl; NHS; Off Ade; Pep Clb; Chrldng; Mic State Univ; Med.

HENDERSON, JAMES; Pt Pleasant HS; Henderson, WV; Pres 4-H; Fr Clb; FFA; Trk; Letter Wrstlng; 4-H Awd; FFA Grennhnd Awd 76; FFA Dairy Profcncy Awd 77; FFA Dairy Profcnct 2nd In St On Wv 78; Potomac St Coll; Agri Tech.

HENDERSON, JEFFREY; Dunbar HS; Dayton, OH; Cls Rep Frsh Cls; VP Soph Cls; VP Jr Cls; VP Sr Cls; Band; JA; MMM; Stu Cncl; Rptr Yrbk; Rptr Sch Nwsp; Jarvis Christian Coll; Economics.

HENDERSON, JOY; Yorktown HS; Muncie, IN; 4/172 Am Leg Aux Girls St; Chrh Wkr; Hon Rl; Hosp Ade; NHS; Sec Yth Flsp; FBLA; Ball State Univ.

HENDERSON, KAREN; Rochester Community HS; Rochester, IN; 16/159 Cls Rep Frsh Cls; Chrs; Hon Rl; Jr NHS; Sch Nwsp; Drama Clb; Pep Clb; Letter Ten; Pom Pon; Purdue Univ; Comp Sci.

HENDERSON, KAY; Brownsburg HS; Indianapolis, IN; 45/314 Cls Rep Soph Cls; Cl Rep Jr Cls; Hon Rl; NHS; Quill & Scroll; Yrbk; Rptr Sch Nwsp; Fr Clb; PPFtbl; Univ; Mass Cmmnctns.

HENDERSON, KEITH; Our Lady Of Providence HS; Charlestown, IN; 69/175 Sch Mus; Letter Ftbl; Letter Trk; Letter Wrstlng; Coach Actv; Opt Clb Awd; Valparaiso Univ; Criminal Justice.

HENDERSON, LORI; Brooke HS; Weirton, WV; 31/495 Chrh Wkr; Cmnty Wkr; Debate Tm; Hon Rl; NHS; Quill & Scroll; Pres Stu Cncl; Yrbk; Spn Clb; IM Sprt; West Liberty St Coll; Cmnctns.

HENDERSON, M; Trenton HS; Trenton, MI; Hon Rl; Jr NHS; Sprt Ed Sch Nwsp; Letter Ftbl; Trk; Wrstlng; Univ; Psych.

HENDERSON, MARY; Sheridan HS; Somerset, OH; 16/180 Chrs; Chrh Wkr; Hon Rl; Lbry Ade; NHS; FHA; IM Sprt; Muskingnum Tech.

HENDERSON, MYRA; Henry Ford HS; Detroit, MI; Chrh Wkr; Hon Rl; Lbry Ade; Off Ade; Cit Awd; Wayne State; Phys Therapist.

HENDERSON, PAT; Bishop Watterson HS; Worthington, OH; Band; Sch Pl; Wrstlng; St A A 126 Lb St Champ 79; HS All Amer 79; Sclhsp Kent St Univ 79; Ohio Coahces Assoc Schlsp 79; Kent St Univ.

HENDERSON, PAUL; Tiffin Columbian HS; Tiffin, OH; Cls Rep Frsh Cls; Cls Rep Soph Cls; Pres Jr Cls; Band; Chrs; Hon Rl; Sch Mus; Sch Pl; Stg Crw; Stu Cncl; Slctn To Choristers Top 20 Vocalst In Schl 78; Slctd Membr Of The Natl Thespian Soc 78; Slctd Publcty Staff; Univ; Drama.

HENDERSON, PETER; Lake Michigan Catholic HS; St Joseph, MI; Boy Scts; Chrh Wkr; FCA; Hon Rl; Lbry Ade; Off Ade; Yth Flsp; Sprt Ed Yrbk; Rptr Yrbk; Sprt Ed Sch Nwsp; Univ; Old World Hist.

HENDERSON, PIPPA; Glen Oak School; Cleveland, OH; Chrs; PAVAS; Y-Teens; Sprt Ed Sch Nwsp; Rptr Sch Nwsp; Drama Clb; Bsbl; Bsktbl; Ten; Social Comm 77; Stdnt Affairs 77; Univ; Poli Law.

HENDERSON, RACHEL; Ogemaw Heights HS; West Branch, MI; 25/177 Chrs; Chrh Wkr; Girl Scts ; Hon Rl; Lbry Ade; Sch Mus; Stg Crw; Yth Flsp; Davenport College Of Bus; Acct.

HENDERSON, RONALD; Salem HS; Salem, IN; 3/156 Pres Sr Cls; JA; NHS; Sch Nwsp; Pep Clb; Spn Clb; Mgrs; JA Awd; Natl Merit Ltr; Opt Clb Awd; Kappa Kappa Kappa Gen Schlrshp Awd; Schl Newspaper Contribution Awd; Hoosier Schlr; Univ Of Notre Dame; Archt.

HENDERSON, SHARI; Walnut Hills HS; Cincinnati, OH; Cls Rep Frsh Cls; Chrs; Chrh Wkr; Drl Tm; Sch Mus; FDA; Awd For Sci Fair Superior Rating 76 77; Univ Of Cincinnati; Med.

HENDERSON, SUSAN; Upper Arlington HS; Columbus, OH; 20/600 Sec Sr Cls; Hon Rl; NHS; Sec Quill & Scroll; Stu Cncl; Ed Sch Nwsp; Rptr Sch Nwsp; Fr Clb; Univ Of N Carolina; Journalism.

HENDERSON, TERRI; Gull Lake HS; Augusta, MI; Band; Hon Rl; NHS; Capt Bsbl; Capt Bsktbl; Coach Actv; Western Michigan Univ; Ther.

HENDERSON, TIMOTHY; Brooke HS; Wellsburg, WV; 125/403 Cls Rep Sr Cls; Boy Scts; Hon Rl; Lat Clb; Letter Bsbl; Letter Ftbl; Trk; IM Sprt; Mass Coll; Pharmacist.

HENDERSON, TONY D; Bangor HS; Bangor, MI; Am Leg Boys St; Hon Rl; Bsbl; Letter Bsktbl; Letter Ftbl; Adrian College; Acctg.

HENDERSON, VICTOR; R Nelson Snider HS; Ft Wayne, IN; Boy Scts; Hon Rl; Letter Trk; Univ; Bus.

HENDERSON, WALTER; Elkhart Memorial HS; Elkhart, IN; 27/514 Pres Frsh Cls; Trs Frsh Cls; Cls Rep Frsh Cls; Cls Rep Soph Cls; Chrs; Hon Rl; Jr NHS; Mdrgl; NHS; Sch Mus; Art Instructn Schls Schlrshp 76; Hon Roll 3 Yrs 76; Sport Major Trophy 76; Univ.

HENDREN, GREG; Reading HS; Reading, OH; Univ Of Cincinnati; Engr.

HENDRICKS, BETH; Mansfield Malabar HS; Mansfield, OH; 12/271 Girl Scts; Hon Rl; NHS; Mth Clb; Univ.

HENDRICKS, CARL; Fenton Sr HS; Fenton, MI; Cmnty Wkr; Stg Crw; Bsbl; Bsktbl; Ftbl; Coach Actv; IM Sprt; Opt Clb Awd; Ferris St Coll; Pharm.

HENDRICKS, DEBORAH; New Richmond HS; Cincinnati, OH; 1/194 Val; Hon Rl; NHS; Pres Quill & Scroll; Treas Stu Cncl; Rptr Yrbk; Ed Sch Nwsp; Fr Clb; Pep Clb; Swmmng; Miami Univ; Med Tech.

HENDRICKS, GRETCHEN; Manistee Catholic Ctrl HS; Manistee, MI; Hon Rl; Sprt Ed Sch Nwsp; Rptr Sch Nwsp; Bsktbl; West Shore; Social Service.

HENDRICKS, JOHN; Lake Ridge Academy; N Olmsted, OH; Letter Lcrss; Letter Socr; Cleveland Press Outstndng Carrier 77; Univ Of Toledo; Physics.

HENDRICKS, LEANN; Hamilton Southeastern HS; Noblesville, IN; Pres Soph Cls; Cls Rep Soph Cls; Hon Rl; Sec Quill & Scroll; Stu Cncl; Rptr Yrbk; OEA; Pep Clb; Letter Sci Clb; Mgrs; Bus Schl; Bus Admin.

HENDRICKS, LORRAINE; Van Wert HS; Van Wert, OH; Band; Chrs; Girl Scts; Hon Rl; NHS; Y-Teens; Pep Clb; Spn Clb; Twrlr; Univ; Med Tech.

HENDRICKS, MICHAEL; Sparta Sr HS; Sparta, MI; 4/191 Chrh Wkr; Hon Rl; NHS; Sec Sci Clb; Rotary Awd; MI St Univ Academic Achvmnt Schlrshp 79; MI Comptn Schlrshp Awd 79; Grad Top Ten In Cl; Michigan St Univ; Vet.

HENDRICKS, PAMELA; Indiana Acad; So Bend, IN; Chrs; Hon Rl; Stu Cncl; 4-H; Gym; Coach Actv; 4-H Awd; Andrews Univ; Law.

HENDRICKS, RICHARD; Breckenridge Jr Sr HS; Breckenridge, MI; Cls Rep Frsh Cls; Cls Rep Soph Cls; Cl Rep Jr Cls; Hon Rl; Sch Mus; Stu Cncl; Yth Flsp; Rptr Yrbk; Rptr Sch Nwsp; 4-H; Cntrl Michigan Univ; Acctg.

HENDRICKSON, AUDREY; Hammond Christian Academy; East Gary, IN; Cls Rep Frsh Cls; Cls Rep Soph Cls; Cl Rep Jr Cls; Sec Sr Cls; Cls Rep Sr Cls; Sal; Chrs; Chrh Wkr; FCA; Hon Rl; Indiana Univ; Nursing.

HENDRICKSON, DEAN; Forest Park HS; Crystal Falls, MI; 12/79 Band; Hon Rl; Ed Sch Nwsp; Glf; Trk; IM Sprt; Mic Tech Univ; Bus Admin.

HENDRICKSON, JAY; Gwinn HS; Gwinn, MI; Boy Scts; Hon Rl; Sct Actv; 4-H; VICA; Mgrs; 4-H Awd;.

HENDRICKSON, R; North Union HS; Richwood, OH; Chrs; Cmnty Wkr; Girl Scts; Hon Rl; Hosp Ade; Lbry Ade; Bus Schl; Meteorologist.

HENDRICKSON, TERRI; Napoleon HS; Brooklyn, MI; Chrh Wkr; Hon Rl; NHS; Jackson Community College; Comp Sci.

HENDRIX, CINDY; Waterloo HS; Atwater, OH; Letter Band; Chrs; Chrh Wkr; Girl Scts; Hon Rl; NHS; Sct Actv; Pres Beta Clb; Sci Clb; Spn Clb; Oh State Univ; Physics.

HENDRIX, JANET; Walnut Ridge HS; Columbus, OH; 76/429 Chrh Wkr; Drl Tm; Hon Rl; Jr NHS; Yth Flsp; Rptr Yrbk; Fr Clb; Pom Pon; Denison Univ; Math.

HENDRIX, LORIAN; Edgewood HS; Bloomington, IN; Chrs; Hon Rl; Stg Crw; Yth Flsp; Drama Clb; Ger Clb; Indiana Univ; Tele Cmnctns.

HENDRIX, RHEA; Springs Vly HS; French Lick, IN; 1/71 Val; Band; Drm Mjrt; Hon Rl; NHS; Off Ade; Sch Pl; Stu Cncl; Fr Clb; Lat Clb; Indiana St Univ; Psych.

HENDRIX, RHEA; Springs Valley HS; French Lick, IN; 1/74 Val; Band; Drm Mjrt; Hon Rl; NHS; Off Ade; Stu Cncl; Yth Flsp; Fr Clb; Lat Clb; Indiana St Univ.

HENEGAR, LEE; Frontier HS; Nw Mtmrs, OH; Sec Sr Cls; Chrs; Girl Scts; Hon Rl; Sch Pl; Sec Stu Cncl; VP Yth Flsp; College; Engr.

HENEHAN, MATTHEW; Hackett HS; Kalamazoo, MI; Boy Scts; Chrs; Hon Rl; Sch Mus; Sch Pl; Sct Actv; Stg Crw; Drama Clb; Bsbl; IM Sprt; Univ; Soc Sci.

HENEHAN, MATTHEW G; Hackett HS; Kalamazoo, MI; Boy Scts; Chrs; Hon Rl; NHS; Sch Pl; Stg Crw; Drama Clb; Bsbl; IM Sprt; Scr Kpr; Univ; Sociology.

HENEISEN, LILY; Calumet HS; Gary, IN; Band; JA; Sch Pl; Sch Nwsp; Drama Clb; Natl Merit Ltr; Indiana Univ; English.

HENEXSON, KAY; Pickerington HS; Pickerington, OH; Rptr Yrbk; Bus Schl.

HENGSTEBECK, ELIZABETH; St Agatha HS; Redford, MI; 11/131 Am Leg Aux Girls St; Hon Rl; VP NHS; Stu Cncl; Treas Drama Clb; Fr Clb; Capt Bsktbl; Letter Trk; Coach Actv; Central Mic Univ; Bio.

HENGY, SANDRA; St Clement HS; Detroit, MI; 10/115 Cls Rep Frsh Cls; Hon Rl; NHS; Stu Cncl; IM Sprt; Wayne St Univ; Nursing.

HENISA, SEAN; North Side HS; Ft Wayne, IN; Boy Scts; Chrs; JA; Pol Wkr; Sct Actv; Rptr Yrbk; Rptr Sch Nwsp; Sch Nwsp; DECA; Crs Cntry; Purdue Univ; Motel Admin.

HENKE, BRAD; Sidney HS; Sidney, OH; Chrh Wkr; NHS; Ger Clb; Bsktbl; Glf; Coach Actv; IM Sprt; Miami Univ Ohi; Chem.

HENKEL, DOUG; Port Clinton HS; Pt Clinton, OH; Chrs; College; Bus Mgmt.

HENKENBERNS, CATHERINE A; Seton HS; Cincinnati, OH; 54/273 Hon Rl; NHS; Sprt Ed Sch Nwsp; Pep Clb; Capt Bsktbl; Mgrs; Scr Kpr; Mt St Joseph Coll; Phys Ed.

HENKENER, ELIZABETH; Anderson HS; Cincinnati, OH; 19/377 Cls Rep Soph Cls; VP Band; VP Chrs; Girl Scts; Hon Rl; Yth Flsp; Ger Clb; Bsktbl; Swmmng; Ten; Kiwanis Music Schlrshp 1978; Girl Scouts First Class 1976; Univ; Sci.

HENKLE, CHERI; Union Scioto HS; Chillicothe, OH; 31/121 Cl Rep Jr Cls; Am Leg Aux Girls St; Chrs; Off Ade; Stu Cncl; Spn Clb; Letter Trk; Letter Chrldng; Scr Kpr; Bus Schl; Acctg.

HENKLE, KENNETH C; London HS; S Vienna, OH; Hon Rl; Sch Mus; Sch Pl; Stg Crw; Rptr Yrbk; Sch Nwsp; Drama Clb; VP 4-H; Pres FFA; Pep Clb; Vocational Schl; Welding.

HENLEY, CRAIG; Buena Vista HS; Saginaw, MI; 29/185 Cls Rep Frsh Cls; Cls Rep Soph Cls; Cl Rep Jr Cls; Band; Pres Chrs; Chrh Wkr; Cmnty Wkr; Hon Rl; Stu Cncl; Rptr Sch Nwsp; Michigan St Univ; Pre Med.

HENN, MARTY; Shortridge HS; Indianapolis, IN; Girl Scts; Hon Rl; NHS; Rptr Yrbk; Rptr Sch Nwsp; Mth Clb; College.

HENNE, HEATHER; Napoleon HS; Napoleon, OH; Band; Girl Scts; Hon Rl; Lbry Ade; Orch; Red Cr Ade; Stg Crw; 4-H; Spn Clb; Ten; Univ; Spec Ed.

HENNE, TRACY; Poca HS; Poca, WV; 20/152 Sec Sr Cls; Chrh Wkr; Hon Rl; NHS; Off Ade; Stu Cncl; Treas FBLA; IM Sprt; Univ; Acctg.

HENNEGAN, LISA; Lapel HS; Lapel, IN; Cls Rep Frsh Cls; Cls Rep Soph Cls; Cl Rep Jr Cls; Cls Rep Sr Cls; Chrs; Chrh Wkr; Cmnty Wkr; Girl Scts; Hon Rl; Lbry Ade; Chrldg Ltr 78; Sec.

HENNEN, JANET; Wirt County HS; Elizabeth, WV; Chrh Wkr; Hon Rl; NHS; Yth Flsp; 4-H; Treas FHA; Pep Clb; Parkensburg Cmnty Coll.

HENNEN, KENNY; Wirt County HS; Palestine, WV; 33/99 Yth Flsp; 4-H; FFA; Ftbl; 4-H Awd; College; Construction.

HENNESSEE, EMILY; Dayton Christian HS; Enon, OH; Sec Chrh Wkr; Chrh Wkr; Hon Rl; Hosp Ade; Pres Yth Flsp; Pres 4-H; Bsktbl; Cit Awd; 4-H Awd; Varsity Vlbyl; Homecoming Ct; Total Person Awd; Pensacola Christian Univ; Nursing.

HENNEY, BONNIE; Burr Oak HS; Burr Oak, MI; FCA; Hon Rl; Hosp Ade; Sch Mus; Sch Pl; Yth Flsp; Letter Chrldng; GAA; Univ; Dent Asst.

HENNIG, WENDY; Michigan Lutheran Seminary; Williamston, MI; Trs Sr Cls; Band; Chrs; Chrh Wkr; Hon Rl; Stu Cncl; Letter Trk; Chrldng; IM Sprt; PPFtbl; Michigan St Univ; Med Tech.

HENNING, DENISE; St Johns HS; St Johns, MI; Chrh Wkr; FCA; Hon Rl; JA; Jr NHS; NHS; Letter Bsbl; Letter Bsktbl; Western Mic Univ; Acct.

HENNING, JONATHAN; Minerva HS; Paris, OH; 1/218 Pres Soph Cls; Hon Rl; NHS; Yth Flsp; VP FFA; Spn Clb; Am Leg Awd; Natl Merit SF;.

HENNING, JULIE; Ridgedale HS; Morral, OH; 10/85 Sec Chrs; Hon Rl; Yth Flsp; Sec 4-H; Spn Clb; Trk; 4-H Awd; Ohi State; Accounting.

HENNING, MICHAEL; Memorial HS; St Marys, OH; Band; Boy Scts; Chrh Wkr; Hon Rl; Sch Mus; Sch Pl; Sct Actv; Stg Crw; Stu Cncl; Yth Flsp; Univ; Geol.

HENNIS, JODY; Jewett Scio HS; Jewett, OH; Band; Sec Girl Scts; Hon Rl; Off Ade; Sch Mus; Sct Actv; 4-H; FHA; Pres Spn Clb; 4-H Awd; 4 State Library Reading Awds; Perfect Attendance Awd; Ohio Pupils Reading Circle Awd; Dover Cosmetology Schl; Beautician.

HENNIS, STEVEN; Walnut Ridge HS; Columbus, OH; 151/526 Band; Chrs; Hon Rl; NHS; Bsktbl; Crs Cntry; Trk; Columbus Tech Inst; Data Proc.

HENNON, BETH; North Putnam Jr Sr HS; Roachdale, IN; 10/104 Cls Rep Soph Cls; Cl Rep Jr Cls; Cls Rep Sr Cls; Band; Drl Tm; NHS; Sch Mus; VP Stu Cncl; Rptr Yrbk; Rptr Sch Nwsp; De Pauw Coll; Speech.

HENNON, BETH A; North Putnam Jr Sr HS; Roachdale, IN; 10/110 Am Leg Aux Girls St; Band; Drl Tm; NHS; Sch Mus; Stu Cncl; Rptr Yrbk; Rptr Sch Nwsp; Pep Clb; DAR Awd; Ball St Univ; Speech Pathology.

HENRI, VALERIE; Cabrini HS; Allen Park, MI; Drl Tm; Hon Rl; Trk; Pom Pon; PPFtbl; Cit Awd; Nazareth Univ; Nursing.

HENRICHS, BRENDA; Kankakee Valley HS; De Motte, IN; 7/290 Band; Chrh Wkr; Hon Rl; NHS; Yth Flsp; OEA; Hoosier Shclr Awd 79; Whos Who 78; Shorthand 120 WPM 79; Internatl Bus Coll; Acctg.

HENRICKS, JAN; Trenton HS; Trenton, MI; Chrh Wkr; Hon Rl; Orch; Sch Mus; Fr Clb; Pep Clb; Univ; Aeronautical Engr.

HENRY, BEVERLY; Woodward HS; Toledo, OH; Girl Scts; Off Ade; FFA; Bsbl; Bsktbl; Scr Kpr; Univ; Zoology.

HENRY, BRENDA; Western Boone Jr Sr HS; Jamestown, IN; 40/150 Band; Drl Tm; Hon Rl; Rptr Sch

Nwsp; 4-H; Pep Clb; Trk; Chrldng; GAA; 4-H Awd; Ivy Tech Voc Schl; Phys Therapy.

HENRY, CAROLYN; Highland Park Community HS; Highland Pk, MI; Chrh Wkr; Spn Clb; Hndbl; Trk; Scr Kpr; Cit Awd; Wayne State Univ; R N.

HENRY, CARRIE; Olivet HS; Olivet, MI; Chrs; Chrh Wkr; Hon Rl; NHS; Off Ade; Sch Mus; Yrbk; Rptr Sch Nwsp; Pep Clb; Chrldng; Fine Arts Awds; Journalism Awd; Home Ec Awd; Kellogg Comm Coll; Busns.

HENRY, COLLEEN; Magnificat HS; Rocky River, OH; Cls Rep Frsh Cls; Band; Chrh Wkr; Girl Scts; Red Cr Ade; Sch Pl; Sct Actv; Stg Crw; Sch Nwsp; Fr Clb; Awd The Opportunity To Attnd Amer Red Cross Ldrshp Wrksp 78; Bowling Green St Univ; Law.

HENRY, DARLA; Nitro HS; Nitro, WV; Cls Rep Frsh Cls; Cls Rep Soph Cls; Cl Rep Jr Cls; Cls Rep Sr Cls; Band; FCA; Hon Rl; JA; Sch Mus; Stu Cncl; W Virginia St Coll.

HENRY, DENISE; Meadowbrook HS; Cumberland, OH; Cmp Fr Grls; Chrs; Drl Tm; Rptr Sch Nwsp; 4-H; FHA; Pep Clb; 4-H Awd; Bank Teller.

HENRY, GARY; Bishop Dwenger HS; Ft Wayne, IN; 13/245 Cls Rep Soph Cls; VP Jr Cls; Cls Rep Sr Cls; Am Leg Boys St; CAP; Hon Rl; NHS; Rptr Sch Nwsp; Ger Clb; Civil Air Patrol GLR Flight Schlrshp; Civil Air Patrol Wings Pilot; CAP Mitchell & Earhart Awds & Cadet; U S Air Force Academy; Astro Engr.

HENRY, HAROLD; Malabar HS; Mansfield, OH; Band; Hon Rl; NHS; Yth Flsp; Mth Clb; Letter Trk; Scr Kpr; Tmr; College; Mechanical Engr.

HENRY, HOLLY; Seton HS; Cincinnati, OH; 36/255 Chrs; Girl Scts; Hon Rl; Jr NHS; NHS; Sch Mus; Sct Actv; Rptr Sch Nwsp; Lat Clb; Univ; Jrnlsm.

HENRY, JEFF; Marshall HS; Marshall, MI; Band; Hon Rl; Orch; College; Comp Sci.

HENRY, JEFFREY L; Hilliard HS; Hilliard, OH; 273/450 Chrs; JA; Sch Mus; Sch Pl; Stg Crw; JA Awd; Ohio State Univ; Computer Science.

HENRY, JOSEPH C; Central HS; Detroit, MI; Band; Drm Bgl; Hon Rl; Off Ade; Orch; Sch Mus; Sch Pl; Fr Clb; Swmmng; Trk; Kentucky St Univ; Music.

HENRY, KRIS; Greenville HS; Greenville, OH; Chrs; Drl Tm; Hon Rl; Sinclair Comm Coll; Commrcl Art.

HENRY, LAUREN; Reese HS; Reese, MI; Band; Chrh Wkr; Debate Tm; Girl Scts; Hon Rl; Stu Cncl; Yth Flsp; 4-H; Ger Clb; Trk; Saginaw Vly St Coll; Med Lab Tech.

HENRY, LE ANNE; Central Catholic HS; Canton, OH; 15/249 Hon Rl; Off Ade; IM Sprt; Grad Hon Cords 79; Akron Univ; Psych.

HENRY, MARK; Northrop HS; Ft Wayne, IN; Chrh Wkr; Hon Rl; Orch; Sch Mus; Sct Actv; Yrbk; Letter Ten; Cit Awd; Indiana Univ; Med.

HENRY, MICHAEL; Chagrin Falls HS; Chagrin Falls, OH; Lit Mag; Rptr Sch Nwsp; College; Mass Communications.

HENRY, NANCY; Caro HS; Caro, MI; Am Leg Aux Girls St; Chrh Wkr; Debate Tm; Hon Rl; NHS; Off Ade; Yth Flsp; Fr Clb; Pep Clb; Chrldng; Frnch Class Awd 79; Debate Awd 77; Spec Olympic Volunteer 79; Univ; Frgn Lang.

HENRY, SANDRA; Bedford HS; Toledo, OH; Sec Jr Cls; Chrs; NHS; Pol Wkr; Lat Clb; Bsktbl; Trk; Chrldng; Central Michigan Univ.

HENRY, SHARON R; Martinsburg Sr HS; Martinsburg, WV; Hosp Ade; Sch Mus; Yth Flsp; College; Music.

HENRY, THOMAS; Northrop HS; Ft Wayne, IN; 79/587 Boy Scts; Chrs; Hon Rl; Bsbl; Coll.

HENRY, THOMAS; Bellbrook HS; Bellbrook, OH; Hon Rl; Spn Clb; Letter Glf; IM Sprt; Univ; Elec Engr.

HENSEL, BRYAN; Ridgedale HS; Morral, OH; Hon Rl; Letter Bsbl; Letter Bsktbl; College.

HENSEL, KATHLEEN; Eastlake North HS; Eastlake, OH; Cls Rep Frsh Cls; Hon Rl; Sch Pl; Stu Cncl; Yrbk; Chrldng; Mgrs; Natl Merit Ltr; Ohio St Univ; Nursing.

HENSIL, CHRISTINA; Elkins HS; Elkins, WV; 9/240 Sec Soph Cls; Cl Rep Jr Cls; Cls Rep Sr Cls; Am Leg Aux Girls St; Band; Hon Rl; NHS; Stu Cncl; Sch Nwsp; Keyettes; Bsktbll MVP 76; Bsktbll Co Capt 78; Jr Attendant In Homecoming Ct 78; Univ; Law.

HENSLER, DAVID; Michigan Lutheran Seminary; Saginaw, MI; 20/63 Letter Trk; IM Sprt; Voc Schl; Travel Bus.

HENSLER, JOAN; Mother Of Mercy HS; Cincinnati, OH; Cl Rep Jr Cls; Hon Rl; Fr Clb; Spn Clb; Bsktbl; Socr; Swmmng; GAA; Univ; Criminal Admin.

HENSLER, MARK; Mt Healthy HS; Cincinnati, OH; 35/550 Band; Hon Rl; Sch Mus; Yth Flsp; Rptr Sch Nwsp; Beta Clb; Ger Clb; Pro Music.

HENSLEY, BRENDA; Vinson HS; Huntington, WV; Band; Chrs; Girl Scts; Hon Rl; Ten; Tigerette; Stu Govt; Majorett; Girls Sftbl; Social Studies Fair 1st Pl Cnty 2nd Pl State; Marshall Univ; Psych.

HENSLEY, CHRISTINA; Northmont Sr HS; Dayton, OH; Cls Rep Frsh Cls; Chrs; Hon Rl; Fr Clb; Pep Clb; Wright St Univ; Elem Ed.

HENSLEY, CHRISTOPHER; St Francis Cabrini HS; Allen Pk, MI; Hon Rl; Trk; IM Sprt; Henery Ford; Banking.

HENSLEY, JAN; Green HS; Akron, OH; 60/319 Chrs; Hosp Ade; Off Ade; Pep Clb; Univ; Bus Admin.

HENSLEY, JEAN; Chesapeake HS; Chesapeake, OH; 6/140 Chrs; Hon Rl; Marshall Univ; Intl Affairs.

HENSLEY, MARILYN; Eastbrook HS; Van Buren, IN; 5/181 Cls Rep Frsh Cls; Pres Sr Cls; Am Leg Aux Girls St; Chrs; Hon Rl; Hosp Ade; NHS; Off Ade; Sch Pl; Stu Cncl; Intl Bus Schl; Med Sec.

HENSLEY, RANDALL T; Central Baptist HS; Addyston, OH; VP Frsh Cls; Cls Rep Frsh Cls; Trs Soph Cls; Boy Scts; Chrh Wkr; Cmnty Wkr; Vocational School; Small Eng Repair.

HENSLEY, SHERRI; Eastern HS; Salem, IN; 15/80 Pres Frsh Cls; Trs Soph Cls; Pres Sr Cls; Band; Hon Rl; Stu Cncl; 4-H; Pep Clb; Spn Clb; Letter Bsktbl; College; Phys Educ.

HENSLEY, TERESA; Winfield HS; Winfield, WV; Cls Rep Frsh Cls; Cls Rep Soph Cls; Cl Rep Jr Cls; Band; Drm Mjrt; Jr NHS; 4-H; Pep Clb; Bsktbl; 4-H Awd; College; Elementary Education.

HENSON, CHARLES; Pt Pleasant HS; Pt Pleasant, WV; 30/260 Cls Rep Frsh Cls; Cls Rep Soph Cls; Boy Scts; Chrh Wkr; Hon Rl; NHS; Sct Actv; Pres Yth Flsp; Key Clb; VICA; World Conservtn Awd 78; Bus Schl; Comp Oper.

HENSON, KIMBERLY; Franklin HS; Franklin, OH; 151/295 Sec Jr Cls; Sec Sr Cls; Hosp Ade; JA; Off Ade; Stu Cncl; OEA; JA Awd; Miami Univ; Elem Educ.

HENTGES, DEANNE; Eastwood HS; Bowling Green, OH; 2/180 Band; Hon Rl; Jr NHS; NHS; Sch Mus; Stu Cncl; Pres 4-H; Lat Clb; Pep Clb; Letter Trk; Bowling Green St Univ; Phys Educ.

HENTHORN, DANIEL M; Magnolia HS; New Martinsvle, WV; Am Leg Boys St; Chrs; Chrh Wkr; Hon Rl; Natl Forn Lg; Sch Mus; Sch Pl; Drama Clb; Letter Ftbl; Letter Trk; Wv All St Cast Aciting 78; Hon Thespian 79; Univ.

HENTHORN, JOHN; Shadyside HS; Shadyside, OH; VP Frsh Cls; VP Soph Cls; Cl Rep Jr Cls; Cls Rep Sr Cls; Am Leg Boys St; Chrs; Hon Rl; Stu Cncl; Letter Ftbl; Trk; Schl Minstrel Musicl Solo; Schl Var Show Musicl Solo;.

HENTHORNE, GERALD; Valley HS; Jacksonburg, WV; Hon Rl; Sct Actv; Rptr Yrbk; FFA; Trk; College.

HENTOSH, GINA; Hubbard HS; Hubbard, OH; Girl Scts; Hon Rl; Lit Mag; Quill & Scroll; Ed Yrbk; Rptr Sch Nwsp; FDA; Lat Clb; Trk; GAA; Tri Cnty Journalism Assn; West Minster Math Tms; Chaplain Of Tri Hi Y Club; Ohio St Univ; Psych.

HENZE, BRYAN; Clay HS; South Bend, IN; 173/320 Band; Boy Scts; Chrh Wkr; Cmnty Wkr; Hon Rl; Hosp Ade; Letter Ftbl; Socr; Trk; Purdue; Elec Eng.

HEPFER, DOUGLAS A; Mason Sr HS; Mason, MI; Aud/Vis; Boy Scts; Hon Rl; Jr NHS; Sct Actv; Yrbk; Rptr Sch Nwsp; Sch Nwsp; Sci Clb; God Cntry Awd; MSU; Photog.

HEPLER, DIANA; Orchard View HS; Muskegon, MI; Letter Bsbl; Letter Bsktbl; Muskegon Cmnty Coll.

HEPP, BRIAN; Southfield Lathrup Sr HS; Southfield, MI; Boy Scts; Chrh Wkr; Hon Rl; MMM; NHS; Orch; Sch Mus; Sct Actv; Bsbl; 1st Rating In Area Solo Ensemble; 2nd Rating In St Solo Ensemble; Univ; Pre Med.

HEPWORTH, LINDA; Whitehall HS; Whitehall, MI; Chrh Wkr; Hon Rl; Lbry Ade; Off Ade; Muskegon Bus College; Sec.

HERALD, JOY; New Richmond HS; New Richmond, OH; Chrs; Chrh Wkr; Cmnty Wkr; Hon Rl; Lbry Ade; NHS; PAVAS; Quill & Scroll; Sch Mus; Yth Flsp; Univ Of Kentucky; Math.

HERBER, KENT; Fremont HS; Fremont, IN; 11/80 Hon Rl; NHS; Bsktbl; Ftbl; Univ; Bus Mgmt.

HERBER, KEVIN; Fremont HS; Fremont, IN; Hon Rl; NHS; Stg Crw; Spn Clb; Bsktbl; Ftbl; Glf; Trk; College.

HERBER, ROBERT P; Bishop Dwenger HS; Ft Wayne, IN; Band; Chrh Wkr; Hon Rl; NHS; Stu Cncl; Mgrs; St Gregorys Seminary; Philosophy.

HERBST, PEGGY; Seton HS; Cincinnati, OH; 11/283 Hon Rl; JA; Jr NHS; NHS; Fr Clb; FBLA; Pep Clb; GAA; IM Sprt; Univ Of Cincinnati; Acctg.

HERCAMP, THEODORE D; Indian Creek HS; Nineveh, IN; 6/148 Hon Rl; Jr NHS; NHS; Lat Clb; Sci Clb; Ftbl; Wrstlng; Univ.

HERCZEG, JOHN; Trenton HS; Trenton, MI; 37/537 Hon Rl; Jr NHS; NHS; Ftbl; Trk; IM Sprt; Natl Merit SF; Albion Univ; Pre Engr.

HERDIECH, ANN MARIE; Cabrini HS; Allen Pk, MI; 5/162 Natl Forn Lg; NHS; Sch Pl; Stg Crw; Drama Clb; Pres Ger Clb; Letter Trk; Univ; Indst Engr.

HERDMAN, HEATHER; Marietta Sr HS; Marietta, OH; 69/412 Trs Frsh Cls; VP Chrs; Hon Rl; Mdrgl; PAVAS; Red Cr Ade; Sch Pl; Stg Crw; Rptr Yrbk; Drama Clb; Ohio Wesleyan Univ; Music.

HERDMAN, LINDA; Waterford Kettering HS; Drayton Plains, MI; Trs Frsh Cls; Girl Scts; Hon Rl; Hosp Ade; Rptr Yrbk; Rptr Sch Nwsp; Pom Pon; Oakland Univ; Phys Ther.

HERENDEEN, CATHERINE; Clay HS; S Bend, IN; Cl Rep Jr Cls; Cls Rep Sr Cls; Aud/Vis; Band; Cmp Fr Grls; Chrs; Hon Rl; Jr NHS; Orch; Sch Mus; Ca Schlrshp Fdn; Univ; Jrnlsm.

HERENE, JACQUELINE; Valley Forge Sr HS; Parma, OH; 27/777 Am Leg Aux Girls St; Hon Rl; Jr NHS; Yrbk; Fr Clb; Ger Clb; Coll; RN.

HERGENRATHER, KEN; Roy C Start HS; Toledo, OH; 104/400 Quill & Scroll; Stu Cncl; Rptr Yrbk; Yrbk; DECA; Socr; Univ Of Toledo; Acctg.

HERGENRODER, MARILYN; Salem HS; Salem, OH; Cmp Fr Grls; Chrs; Hon Rl; Orch; Sch Mus; Sch Pl; Y-Teens; Ger Clb; OEA; Vocational School.

HERINGTON, BARBARA; Madeira HS; Madeira, OH; 10/165 Chrs; Girl Scts; Hon Rl; Sch Mus; Sch Pl; Stg Crw; Drama Clb; Ger Clb; Natl Merit Ltr; Coll.

HERION, BETH; Chagrin Falls HS; Chagrin Falls, OH; 17/167 Pres Frsh Cls; Sec Soph Cls; VP Jr Cls; Chrs; NHS; Sch Mus; Sch Pl; Mth Clb; Wake Forest Univ.

HERKERT, GREG; St Xavier HS; Cincinnati, OH; 78/264 Boy Scts; Hon Rl; Hockey; Univ Of Southern Florida; Med.

HERLIHY, LORI; Butler HS; Vandalia, OH; Chrs; Girl Scts; Hon Rl; Off Ade; DECA; Letter Bsbl; Coach Actv; Wright State; Flight Attendent.

HERM, VALERIE; Douglas Mac Arthur HS; Saginaw, MI; Hon Rl; Jr NHS; NHS; Univ; Dent Asst.

HERMAN, ANITA; Lakeview HS; Stow, OH; 15/550 Hon Rl; JA; NHS; Rptr Sch Nwsp; OEA; KSU.

HERMAN, CHARLENE; Bryan HS; Bryan, OH; 3/200 Am Leg Aux Girls St; Sec Chrs; Hon Rl; VP JA; NHS; Sec Stu Cncl; Rptr Sch Nwsp; VP Lat Clb; GAA; JA Awd; Parkview Methdst Schl Nrsng; RN.

HERMAN, GLEN; Riverside HS; Dearborn Hts, MI; Cls Rep Soph Cls; Band; Chrh Wkr; Cmnty Wkr; Hon Rl; NHS; Sch Mus; Stu Cncl; Yth Flsp; Fr Clb; Band Ltr 78; Athltc Part Awd 79; Univ; Physics.

HERMAN, LORNA; Niles HS; Niles, MI; Band; Hon Rl; Sec JA; Off Ade; Pol Wkr; Fr Clb; Lat Clb; Pep Clb; Pom Pon; Northern Mic Univ; Psych.

HERMAN, MARK; Unionville Sebewaing HS; Sebewaing, MI; Boy Scts; Chrh Wkr; Hon Rl; Yth Flsp; Sch Nwsp; 4-H; Bsbl; Ten; Coach Actv; Am Leg Awd; MSU; Architectural Drafting.

HERMAN, MARY; La Salle HS; South Bend, IN; 7/488 Hon Rl; NHS; Pep Clb; Chrldng; Hnr Roll All 3yrs Of HS; Coll; Busns.

HERMAN, MELISSA B; Interlochen Arts Academy; Alexandria, VA; Band; Cmnty Wkr; Hon Rl; Univ Of Virginia.

HERMAN, RICHARD; Beachwood HS; Beachwood, OH; AFS; PAVAS; Sch Pl; Stg Crw; Letter Ftbl; Trk; Wrstlng; Univ; Bus.

HERMAN, TERESA; Spencerville HS; Spenverville, OH; 10/100 VP Soph Cls; Band; Chrh Wkr; Hon Rl; Sch Mus; Sch Pl; Stg Crw; Yth Flsp; Rptr Yrbk; Spn Clb; Ohio St Univ.

HERMAN, TERESA; Quincy HS; Quincy, MI; 15/118 Pres Jr Cls; Sec Band; Capt Drl Tm; NHS; Sec Rptr Yrbk; Rptr Sch Nwsp; FTA; Letter Bsktbl; Letter Trk; Lansing Cmnty Coll; Lgl Asst.

HERMANCE, ROBIN; R Nelson Snider HS; Ft Wayne, IN; 48/585 Fr Clb; Purdue Univ; Comp Sci.

HERMES, DAVID; Port Clinton HS; Pt Clinton, OH; 22/260 Chrs; Hon Rl; Swmmng; 4-H Awd; Ohio St Univ; Pharm.

HERMES, DAVID; Port Clinton HS; Port Clinton, OH; Chrs; Hon Rl; Red Cr Ade; 4-H; Terra Tech Voc Schl; Law Enfrcmnt.

HERMES, KIM; St Agatha HS; Detroit, MI; Lbry Ade; NHS; Aquinas Coll; Bus.

HERNAN, NOREEN; Euclid Sr HS; Euclid, OH; Capt Drm Mjrt; Hon Rl; Tmr; Twrlr; Coll; Communications.

HERNANDEZ, LISA K; E C Washington HS; E Chicago, IN; 13/280 Hon Rl; NHS; Coll; Optometry.

HERNANDEZ, NORMA; Bishop Foley HS; Warren, MI; Chrs; Hon Rl; Spn Clb; College; Nursing.

HERNDON, NICHOLAS; Wadsworth HS; Wadsworth, OH; Band; Chrh Wkr; FCA; Key Clb; Ftbl; Wrstlng; Univ Of Cincinnati; Archt.

HERNDON, STEVE; Wadsworth Sr HS; Wadsworth, OH; FCA; Hon Rl; Pol Wkr; Letter Bsktbl; Letter Ftbl; Wrstlng; College; Psych.

HERNLY, ELAINE; Union HS; Williamsburg, IN; Sec Frsh Cls; Sec Soph Cls; Trs Jr Cls; Band; Hon Rl; NHS; Pres 4-H; FHA; Treas Lat Clb; Spn Clb; College; Medicine.

HERON, PATRICK; Onaway HS; Millersburg, MI; Sch Pl; 4-H; 4-H Awd; Univ; Indus Construction.

HERPORT, TINA; Clinton Central HS; Frankfort, IN; Band; Chrh Wkr; Girl Scts; Hon Rl; Sch Mus; Pep Clb; Spn Clb; Miss United Teenager Contest Finals 77; Bus Schl; Bus.

HERR, SHARI; Bluffton HS; Pandora, OH; VP Frsh Cls; Band; Chrs; Chrh Wkr; Hon Rl; Off Ade; Sch Mus; VP Stu Cncl; Drama Clb; Pres 4-H; Office Work.

HERRALA, LAURE; Mona Shores HS; Muskegon, MI; Hon Rl; Crs Cntry; Letter Gym; Letter Trk; Letter Chrldng; College; Med.

HERRE, JOHN C; Sycamore HS; Cincinnati, OH; 28/470 Hon Rl; Mod UN; Natl Merit SF; College.

HERREMA, BRIAN; Calvin Christian HS; Wyoming, MI; Aud/Vis; Chrs; Yrbk; Bsbl; Ftbl; Trk; Wrstlng; Mgrs; Mich State; Engr.

HERRERA, KAREN A; Park Hills HS; Fairborn, OH; Band; Chrs; Hon Rl; Red Cr Ade; Spn Clb; Trk; IM Sprt; Acad Ach Awd Natl Honor Soc; Cert Of Athletic Recognition Track; Ohio St Univ; Vet.

HERRGORD, DEANN; Reeths Putter HS; Muskegon, MI; Trs Soph Cls; Trs Jr Cls; Trs Sr Cls; Chrh Wkr; Hon Rl; Stu Cncl; Yth Flsp; Rptr Sch Nwsp; Chrldng; PPFtbl; Hmcmng Chairperson; Trinity Univ; Soc Work.

HERRICK, JERYL; Chelsea HS; Chelsea, MI; Band; Hon Rl; NHS; Rptr Yrbk; Bsktbl; Forensic Tm Went To St Finals; Michigan St Univ; Spch Ther.

HERRICK, KARLA; Loy Norrix HS; Kalamazoo, MI; Debate Tm; Rdo Clb; Wrstlng; Western Michigan Univ; Cmnctns.

HERRICK, L; Hillman Cmnty HS; Hillman, MI; 2/60 Sec Soph Cls; VP Jr Cls; VP Sr Cls; Hon Rl; VP NHS; Sch Pl; Yrbk; Bsbl; Bsktbl; Central Michigan Univ; Sec.

HERRICK, PAT; Reading Jr Sr HS; Reading, MI; Boy Scts; Chrh Wkr; Sprt Ed Sch Nwsp; Bsktbl; IM Sprt; Natl Merit SF; Univ Of Nebraska; Criminology.

HERRICK, STEVE; Toronto HS; Toronto, OH; Boy Scts; Hon Rl; Ftbl; Natl Merit Schl; Kent St Univ; Mech Engr.

HERRIMAN, DAN; Howland HS; Warren, OH; 1/430 Cls Rep Soph Cls; Cl Rep Jr Cls; Band; Cmnty Wkr; Hon Rl; Natl Forn Lg; Stu Cncl; Yth Flsp; Rptr Yrbk; Univ; Pre Med.

HERRING, BRUCE L; Arsenal Technical HS; Indianapolis, IN; Cls Rep Frsh Cls; JA; Mth Clb; Natl Merit Ltr; Purdue Univ; Chem Engr.

HERRING, CINDY; Mississinewa HS; Jonesboro, IN; 62/200 Hon Rl; Hosp Ade; Pol Wkr; Pres 4-H; FHA; Pres OEA; Pep Clb; IM Sprt; College; Bus Admin.

HERRING, DELANA; Fr Joseph Wehrle Memrl HS; Colum Bus, OH; Bsktbl; Rotary Awd; Central St Univ; Soc Work.

HERRING, DENNIS; Columbus North HS; Columbus, OH; Cls Rep Sr Cls; Hon Rl; NHS; Pol Wkr; Ed Sch Nwsp; Ger Clb; Socr; Natl Merit SF; Esquire Awd For Achvmnt 1976; Ohio St Univ; Aero Engr.

HERRING, JANINA; Tipton HS; Tipton, IN; 48/173 Chrh Wkr; Hon Rl; 4-H; Pep Clb; Sci Clb; 4-H Awd; Marion Coll.

HERRING, KEVIN; Mt Vernon Academy; Worthington, OH; Cls Rep Sr Cls; Band; Chrs; Chrh Wkr; FCA; Stu Cncl; Capt Bsktbl; IM Sprt; Scr Kpr; Tmr; Otterbein Coll; Bus Admin.

HERRING, LORI; Shelby HS; New Era, MI; Girl Scts; Hosp Ade; 4-H; Fr Clb; Muskeon Community College; Sec.

HERRING, MICHAEL; Greenville HS; Greenville, OH; Hon Rl; Spn Clb; Ten; College; Sci.

HERRING, SHEILA; Crispus Attucks HS; Indianapolis, IN; Chrs; VP Chrh Wkr; Hon Rl; Sch Mus; Spn Clb; Acctg 1 & 2 Awd 78; Univ; Public Acctg.

HERRINGTON, SHEILA; Glen Este HS; Cincinnati, OH; Chrh Wkr; Girl Scts; Sch Mus; Sch Pl; Stu Cncl; Yth Flsp; Drama Clb; Fr Clb; Texas A & M Univ; Med Research.

HERRINTON, ELIZABETH; George Washington HS; Charleston, WV; Cls Rep Soph Cls; Cl Rep Jr Cls; Trs Sr Cls; Band; Drl Tm; Girl Scts; Hon Rl; Jr NHS; Sct Actv; Stu Cncl; 1st Class Girl Scout Awd 76; William & Mary Univ; Acctg.

HERRIOTT, BETTY; Marion Harding HS; Marion, OH; Sec AFS; Drl Tm; Girl Scts; Hon Rl; Treas JA; Orch; VP Yth Flsp; Pep Clb; Trk; PPFtbl;.

HERRMAN, JENNIFER; Tyler Cnty HS; Middlebourne, WV; 13/97 Band; Drl Tm; Hon Rl; Treas JA; Pres NHS; Off Ade; Sch Pl; Treas Stu Cncl; Drama Clb; FTA; Fairmont St Coll; Drafting.

HERRMANN, CYNTHIA; St Ursula Acad; Toledo, OH; Chrh Wkr; Girl Scts; Hon Rl; Orch; Rptr Sch Nwsp; Ger Clb; Univ Of Toledo; Business Admin.

HERRMANN, JENNIFER; Tyler Co HS; Middlebourne, WV; 13/102 Band; Drl Tm; Hon Rl; JA; Pres NHS; Off Ade; Treas Stu Cncl; Drama Clb; FTA; Pep Clb; Fairmont St Coll; Drafting.

HERRMANN, KARYN; Riverview Community HS; Riverview, MI; 1/250 Val; Chrh Wkr; Hon Rl; Jr NHS; NHS; Rptr Sch Nwsp; Fr Clb; FTA; Kiwan Awd; Univ Of Mich; Engr.

HERRON, DENISE; Salem Sr HS; Salem, OH; 1/300 Am Leg Aux Girls St; Band; Cmp Fr Grls; Hon Rl; Rptr Yrbk; Ger Clb; Pep Clb; Hi Tri High Schlstc Standards; Sec Salem Jr Music Clb; Brooks Writing Awd; Coll; Med Sci.

HERRON, DOLLIE; Decatur HS; Decatur, MI; VP Jr Cls; Chrh Wkr; Hon Rl; Stu Cncl; 4-H; Capt Bsktbl; Letter Trk; Chrldng; PPFtbl; Mic State Univ; Communications.

HERRON, DONNA; Black River HS; Sullivan, OH; 9/100 Sec Band; Hon Rl; Sch Pl; Rptr Sch Nwsp; Treas Drama Clb; VP Fr Clb; Ger Clb; Sec Sci Clb; Case Western Reserve Univ; Sci.

HERRON, LISA; Madonna HS; Follansbee, WV; 5/95 Hon Rl; NHS; Stg Crw; 4-H; Pep Clb; Bsktbl; GAA; Mat Maids; 4-H Awd; West Virginia Univ; Busns.

HERRON, LYNN; Triton Central HS; Fairland, IN; 10/175 FCA; Hon Rl; Drama Clb; 4-H; Spn Clb; 4-H Awd; Univ; Math.

HERRON, PATRICK; Revere HS; Richfield, OH; Band; Boy Scts; Orch; Sch Mus; Sct Actv; Univ Of Colorado; Dent.

HERRON, TOBY; Conotton Valley HS; Sherrodsville, OH; Cls Rep Frsh Cls; VP Sr Cls; Band; Chrh Wkr; Hon Rl; Sch Mus; Stg Crw; Stu Cncl; Rptr Yrbk; Yrbk; Rio Grand Coll.

HERRON JR, ROBERT; Carrollton HS; Carrollton, OH; 60/250 Cl Rep Jr Cls; Cls Rep Sr Cls; FCA; Letter Ftbl; Capt Trk; West Liberty State Coll; Bus.

HERRYGERS, RITA; Catholic Central HS; Grand Rapids, MI; Hon Rl; Stg Crw; Drama Clb; Trk; Univ Of Michigan; Med.

HERSCHBERGER, CHRIS; Northridge HS; Goshen, IN; 7/145 Chrs; Hon Rl; Hosp Ade; NHS; Sch

Mus; Yth Flsp; Rptr Yrbk; Pep Clb; Trk; Univ; Nursing.

HERSCHER, ANNA; George Washington HS; Charleston, WV; Girl Scts; Hon Rl; NHS; Letter Trk; Univ Of Tennessee; Archt Design.

HERSEY, TOMMIJUANA; Lake Michigan Catholic HS; Benton Hrbr, MI; Pres Band; Chrs; Hon Rl; JA; Sch Mus; Gym; Letter Trk; Mgrs; Capt Pom Pon; Tmr; Arizona St Univ; Law.

HERSHBERGER, JANE; Newton HS; Pleasant Hl, OH; 1/60 Band; Chrs; Chrh Wkr; Cmnty Wkr; Hon Rl; Lbry Ade; NHS; Yth Flsp; FHA; Scr Kpr; Oh Univ Summer Schlrshp Prog 79; Math Recognition Awrd 78 & 79; FHA Parliamentary Procedure Tm Chrwmn 78; Univ; Child Psych.

HERSHBERGER, SUSAN; Wadsworth HS; Wadsworth, OH; Cls Rep Frsh Cls; Girl Scts; Sct Actv; Stu Cncl; 4-H; Trk; 4-H Awd; Univ; Comm Art.

HERSHEY, SANDRA; Crestview HS; Leetonia, OH; Treas Chrs; Chrh Wkr; Girl Scts; Hon Rl; Off Ade; Sch Mus; Sec Yth Flsp; 4-H; Pep Clb; Bsktbl; Goshen Coll; Nurse.

HERSHISER, MICHAEL; Sandusky HS; Sandusky, OH; Band; Hon Rl; JA; VICA; Ohio State; Vet.

HERSHNER, KIMBERLY; Ontario HS; Msnfld, OH; 2/176 Sec Frsh Cls; Sec Soph Cls; Cl Rep Jr Cls; AFS; Am Leg Aux Girls St; Band; Hon Rl; Jr NHS; NHS; Stu Cncl; Miami Univ; Acctg.

HERSOM, BEVERLY; Shady Spring HS; Beaver, WV; 14/155 Hon Rl; NHS; Sch Pl; Stg Crw; Sch Nwsp; Drama Clb; Alderson Broaddus Coll; Educ.

HERSTAD, CYNTHIA; Elmhurst HS; Ft Wayne, IN; AFS; Band; Hon Rl; Y-Teens; Bsktbl; Mgrs; PPFtbl; Cit Awd; Drake Univ; Psych.

HERTEL, BETH; Van Wert HS; Van Wert, OH; Band; Chrh Wkr; Hon Rl; Treas JA; NHS; VP Off Ade; Yth Flsp; Y-Teens; Pres Yrbk; 4-H; Jr Achievmnt Bus Wm Of The Yr 1979; Off Educ Assoc Stateswoman Awd 1979; 4 H Fd Nutr & Cons Educ Awd 1977; Acctg.

HERTEL, FRANK; Rutherford B Hayes HS; Delaware, OH; 24/340 Chrh Wkr; Hon Rl; ROTC; Fr Clb; Socr; Ten; Am Leg Awd; Natl Merit Ltr; SAR Awd; Univ; Aero Engr.

HERTEL, JAY; Leetonia HS; Leetonia, OH; 1/94 Pres Jr Cls; Am Leg Boys St; Band; Boy Scts; Chrh Wkr; Hon Rl; NHS; Sch Mus; Sch Pl; Stu Cncl; College; Medicine.

HERTENSTEIN, STEVE; Lynchburg Clay HS; Lynchburg, OH; Boy Scts; Stg Crw; IM Sprt; Voice Dem Awd; Railroad.

HERTENSTEIN, TERESA; Carroll HS; Camden, IN; 6/120 Chrs; Chrh Wkr; Hon Rl; NHS; 4-H; Fr Clb; Vincennes Univ; Law Enforcement.

HERTLEIN, DAVE; Springfield Local HS; Poland, OH; Boy Scts; Fr Clb; Bsktbl; Univ.

HERTLEIN, DAVID; Springfield Local HS; Poland, OH; 1/130 Am Leg Boys St; NHS; Pres Stu Cncl; Sch Nwsp; Fr Clb; Bsktbl; Univ; Engr.

HERZER, WILLIAM A; Gavvett HS; Garrett, IN; VP Jr Cls; Am Leg Boys St; Chrh Wkr; Pres FCA; Hon Rl; NHS; Yth Flsp; Bsktbl; Crs Cntry; Fellowship Of Christian Athlete Awd; 2nd All Conf Bsktbl Team; All Sectional Bsktbl Team; College; Math.

HERZOG, DEBBIE; Port Clinton HS; Pt Clinton, OH; AFS; Band; Hon Rl; Orch; Treas Ger Clb; Bsktbl; GAA; Asst Coordinator Of Annual Govt Day 79; Bowling Green St Univ.

HERZOG, LUANN; Reading HS; Reading, OH; 55/225 Chrs; Girl Scts; Sct Actv; Yth Flsp; Ed Yrbk; Sprt Ed Yrbk; Rptr Yrbk; Yrbk; Sch Nwsp; College; Nursing.

HESCH, CRHISTINE; Pickerington HS; Pickeringtn, OH; Band; Chrh Wkr; Girl Scts; Hon Rl; NHS; Y-Teens; Rptr Sch Nwsp; Ger Clb; God Cntry Awd; Outstndng Band Mbr 77; Ohio St Univ; Hist.

HESCOTT, MARK; Kearsley HS; Burton, MI; 52/375 Boy Scts; Hon Rl; IM Sprt; Scr Kpr; Tmr; Univ Of Michigan; Bus Admin.

HESEMAN, J BRAD; North Central HS; Bloomington, IN; Boy Scts; Cmnty Wkr; Hon Rl; NHS; Red Cr Ade; Sct Actv; Stg Crw; Stu Cncl; Pres Key Clb; Kiwan Awd; Indiana Univ; Law.

HESEMANN, JAMES F; Rogers HS; Toledo, OH; Hon Rl; Sci Clb; Socr; Toledo Univ; Science.

HESHELMAN, ANGIE; N Daviess Jr Sr HS; Plainville, IN; 17/94 Band; Girl Scts; Hon Rl; Rptr Sch Nwsp; Sch Nwsp; 4-H; FHA; Pep Clb; GAA; Home Ec Awd; Flag Carrier; Vincennes Univ; Computer Tech.

HESKITT, MICHAEL; De Witt HS; Dewitt, MI; 8/150 Aud/Vis; Boy Scts; Hon Rl; Sct Actv; Wrstlng; Michigan Tech Univ; Mech Engr.

HESLIN, BRUCE; West Lafayette HS; W Lafayette, IN; 13/185 VP Jr Cls; Am Leg Boys St; Boy Scts; FCA; Hon Rl; NHS; Yth Flsp; Sprt Ed Yrbk; Bsbl; Letter Ten; Prom Board Charman 78; Research Grant Amer Heart Assoc 77; 1st Pl Sr Bio Div Kokomo Regnl Sci Fair 77; Univ; Chem Engr.

HESS, DANA; Urbana HS; Urbana, OH; Clark Tech Coll; Comp Prog.

HESS, DAVID; Bishop Watterson HS; Columbus, OH; Hon Rl; Wrstlng; College; Architecture.

HESS, DEBBIE; Graham HS; De Graff, OH; Band; Chrh Wkr; Hon Rl; Yth Flsp; 4-H; OEA; 4-H Awd; Sinclair Coll; Acctg.

HESS, GAIL; Morton Sr HS; Hammond, IN; 36/436 Cls Rep Soph Cls; Cl Rep Jr Cls; Hon Rl; NHS; VP FTA; Spn Clb; Trk; PPFtbl; In St Schlrshp 79; Purdue Univ; Spanish.

HESS, GREGORY; Stonewall Jackson HS; Charleston, WV; Hon Rl; Jr NHS; Sch Pl; Mth Clb; Spn Clb; College; Acctg.

HESS, JAMES C; Shenandoah HS; Middletown, IN; 13/124 Pres Sr Cls; Am Leg Boys St; Band; Chrh Wkr; Cmnty Wkr; Hon Rl; Mth Clb; Letter Bsbl; Letter Ftbl; Littl Lg Sportmns Awd 74; Natl Babe Ruth Athltc Of Yr 76; Math Assoc Of Amer Awd 79; Univ; Math.

HESS, KELLY; Elmwood HS; Wayne, OH; Chrs; Hon Rl; Off Ade; Rptr Yrbk; Pep Clb; Kiwan Awd; Most Acad Sci Stud 76; Most Acad Eng Stud 76; Univ; Soc Work.

HESS, LINDA; North Putnam HS; Bainbridge, IN; Chrs; Drl Tm; Girl Scts; Hon Rl; NHS; 4-H; Pep Clb; Spn Clb; Chrldng; Pom Pon;.

HESS, LINDA; Howland HS; Warren, OH; 12/418 Cls Rep Frsh Cls; Cls Rep Soph Cls; Hon Rl; Natl F orn Lg; Yth Flsp; Y-Teens; 4-H; Pep Clb; Trk; IM Sprt; Univ; Law.

HESS, LORA; Lemon Monroe HS; Middletown, OH; 14/278 Band; NHS; Orch; PAVAS; Sch Mus; Pres Sct Actv; Mth Clb; Bsktbl; Cit Awd; Univ; Engr.

HESS, MARK; Chaminade Julienne HS; Dayton, OH; Trs Jr Cls; Chrh Wkr; Stu Cncl; Rptr Sch Nwsp; Letter Bsbl; Glf; IM Sprt; Wright St Univ; Real Estate.

HESS, MARY; Vassar HS; Vassar, MI; 14/200 Sec Jr Cls; Sec Sr Cls; Hon Rl; Off Ade; Sch Mus; Sch Pl; Stg Crw; Yrbk; Sch Nwsp; Drama Clb; Michigan St Univ; Psych.

HESS, PAM; Northwest HS; Clinton, OH; 18/186 Band; Drm Mjrt; Hon Rl; NHS; Off Ade; Sch Pl; Yrbk; Treas Fr Clb; Twrlr; Bowling Green; Nursing.

HESS, PATRICK; Bellmont HS; Decatur, IN; 72/244 Spn Clb; Univ; Acctg.

HESS, PAUL; Centerville HS; Centerville, OH; 1/680 Val; Debate Tm; Natl Forn Lg; NHS; VP Ger Clb; Ten; Elk Awd; NCTE; Rotary Awd; Univ Of Mi Schlr 78; Univ Of Michigan; Econ.

HESS, RICK; Elizabeth A Johnson Mem HS; Mt Morris, MI; Cls Rep Frsh Cls; Band; Letter Ftbl; Letter Hockey; Letter Swmmng; Michigan St Univ; Med.

HESS, SHERYL; North White HS; Monon, IN; 8/68 Hon Rl; Sch Mus; Sch Pl; Stu Cncl; Drama Clb; 4-H; Ger Clb; Bsktbl; Trk; GAA; Univ; Acctg.

HESS, TAMMY; Washington HS; Washington, IN; Chrs; FCA; Hon Rl; Yth Flsp; 4-H; Pep Clb; Bsktbl; Trk; Univ; Comp Sci.

HESSEL, HOLLY; Andrews Academy; Berrien Spring, MI; Chrh Wkr; NHS; Fr Clb; Dnfth Awd; Andrews Univ; Behavioral Sci.

HESSION, MARY; Cathedral HS; Indianapolis, IN; 22/150 Hon Rl; Jr NHS; NHS; Letter Bsktbl; Letter Glf; IM Sprt; Rcvd The Al Feeney Awrd For Otstndng Athlete 79; Rcvd A Golf Schlrshp To La St Univ 79; Capt Of Golf Tm 79; Louisiana St Univ; Genrl Bus.

HESSLER, CHRIS; Bishop Foley HS; Royal Oak, MI; Boy Scts; Chrh Wkr; Cmnty Wkr; Hon Rl; Sch Pl; Sct Actv; Ftbl; Coach Actv; IM Sprt; Am Leg Awd; Univ; Chef.

HESSMAN, JERI; Woodrow Wilson HS; Youngstown, OH; 41/357 Cls Rep Soph Cls; Seton Hill Coll; Poli Sci.

HESTER, JULIE G; New Buffalo HS; New Buffalo, MI; Hon Rl; Hosp Ade; Lbry Ade; Nurses Aide.

HESTING, VONDA; Columbia City Joint HS; Columbia City, IN; 11/260 Cl Rep Jr Cls; Chrh Wkr; FCA; Hon Rl; Yth Flsp; 4-H; FTA; Pep Clb; Ball St Univ; Spec Ed.

HESTON, JEFFREY; Niles Mc Kinley HS; Niles, OH; 17/420 Band; Hon Rl; NHS; Sch Mus; 4-H; 4-H Awd; Univ; Engr.

HESTON, R E; Cambridge HS; Kimbolton, OH; Cl Rep Jr Cls; Band; Chrs; Chrh Wkr; Cmnty Wkr; Hon Rl; Yth Flsp; 4-H; 4-H Awd; VFW Awd; College; Sci.

HESTWOOD, JEFFEREY; Parkside HS; Jackson, MI; Letter Swmmng; Tmr; College Engr.

HETHERINGTON, ANNA; Gladwin HS; Gladwin, MI; 13/147 Cls Rep Frsh Cls; Cls Rep Soph Cls; Band; Chrh Wkr; Hon Rl; NHS; Off Ade; Stu Cncl; Yth Flsp; Scr Kpr; Spring Arbor Coll; Law.

HETRICK, DANA; Vicksburg HS; Vicksburg, MI; Band; Ed Yrbk; Rptr Yrbk; Rptr Sch Nwsp; FTA; Ferris State; Med Lab Tech.

HETRICK, THOMAS P; Defiance Sr HS; Defiance, OH; Am Leg Boys St; Band; Boy Scts; Chrs; Chrh Wkr; Hon Rl; NHS; Sct Actv; Mth Clb; Letter Ten; Univ.

HETSON, GREG; Hubbard HS; Hubbard, OH; 31/330 Band; Hon Rl; Capt Swmmng; Scr Kpr; Tmr; Youngstown State Univ; Mech Engr.

HETTINGA, KIM; Lapel HS; Anderson, IN; 19/100 Chrs; Hon Rl; Off Ade; Sch Mus; VP Yth Flsp; Sec Pep Clb; Sci Clb; Ind State Univ; Psych.

HETTINGHOUSE, MICHAEL; South Bend La Salle HS; S Bend, IN; 43/488 Cls Rep Frsh Cls; Hon Rl; Treas JA; Pol Wkr; IM Sprt; Mgrs; Univ.

HETZEL, JOEL R; Mohawk HS; Sycamore, OH; Boy Scts; Chrs; Sct Actv; Sprt Ed Yrbk; Letter Wrstlng; Chrldng; Cit Awd; Armed Forces; Radio Cmnctns.

HETZEL, KARL; Bexley HS; Bexley, OH; 1/186 Val; Hon Rl; NHS; Miami Univ; Engr Tech.

HETZEL, NANCY; Lakota HS; W Chester, OH; 12/450 Hon Rl; NHS; Off Ade; Socr; Trk; Mgrs; Kiwan Awd; Wittenberg Univ.

HETZLER, DAVID; Sidney HS; Sidney, OH; Hon Rl; Univ; Aviation.

HETZLER, PHIL; Ansonia HS; Rossburg, OH; 17/80 Chrs; FCA; JA; Sprt Ed Yrbk; FFA; OEA; Letter Bsbl; Letter Bsktbl; Letter Crs Cntry; College; Acctg.

HETZLER, SCOTT D; Franklin HS; Franklin, OH; Pres Jr Cls; Band; Drm Mjrt; Hon Rl; Pol Wkr; Stu Cncl; VP Spn Clb; Bsbl; Gym; C of C Awd; Ltr St Champ & All Amer Team Gymnastics 78; Govrnors Recngtn Awd For Gymnastics 78; Miami Univ; Psysn.

HEURING, THOMAS; Chatard HS; Indianapolis, IN; 25/195 Hon Rl; Bsbl; Ball St Univ; Archt.

HEUSCHELE, JANE; Douglas Mac Arthur HS; Saginaw, MI; Hon Rl; Jr NHS; NHS; Ger Clb; Pep Clb; Cit Awd; Saginaw Valley St Coll; CPA.

HEWETT, LISA; West Carrollton Sr HS; W Carrollton, OH; Chrs; Hon Rl; Hosp Ade; Sec Off Ade; VP FBLA; Pep Clb; Hosptl Wrk Awd; Academic Recogntn Hnrs Ltr; ERA Awd Educ Recogntn Assoc; Mgmt.

HEWITT, CHRISTINE A; Westerville North HS; Westerville, OH; 19/427 Cls Rep Frsh Cls; Chrs; Drl Tm; Girl Scts; Hon Rl; NHS; Sec Yth Flsp; Miami Univ; Nursing.

HEWITT, EILEEN; Jackson Milton HS; Lk Milton, OH; Trs Frsh Cls; Band; Rptr Yrbk; 4-H; Ger Clb; Letter Bsktbl; Crs Cntry; Letter Trk; Bausch & Lomb Awd; Pres Awd; Youngstown St Univ; Bio.

HEWITT, JAY; Cameron HS; Cameron, WV; 37/110 Cls Rep Frsh Cls; Cls Rep Soph Cls; Cl Rep Jr Cls; Cls Rep Sr Cls; Aud/Vis; Boy Scts; Cmnty Wkr; Hon Rl; Sch Pl; Sct Actv; Belmont Tech Schl; Metallurgist.

HEWITT, SCOTT; Saint Edward HS; N Olmsted, OH; 5/350 Debate Tm; Hon Rl; Lit Mag; Natl Forn Lg; NHS; Rptr Sch Nwsp; Key Clb; Socr; College; Chem Engr.

HEWITT, SUSAN; Logansport HS; Logansport, IN; Band; Chrs; Sch Mus; Sch Pl; Stu Cncl; Drama Clb; Ger Clb; Univ; Nursing.

HEY, BOBBI; Bluffton HS; Bluffton, OH; 1/93 Am Leg Aux Girls St; Band; Hon Rl; NHS; Rptr Sch Nwsp; VP FTA; Treas Lat Clb; Letter Trk; GAA; PPFtbl; Univ.

HEYD, DELVITA; J A Garfield HS; Garrettsville, OH; Cls Rep Frsh Cls; Cls Rep Soph Cls; Trs Sr Cls; Cls Rep Sr Cls; Hon Rl; Stu Cncl; Pep Clb; Bsbl; Chrldng; IM Sprt; Gnrl Bus; Univ.

HEYD, LINDA E; Fairfield Union HS; Bremen, OH; 5/158 Chrh Wkr; Cmnty Wkr; Girl Scts; Hon Rl; Jr NHS; Lbry Ade; Sct Actv; Yth Flsp; 4-H; FHA; Ohio Univ; Acctg.

HEYDE, ROBERT; Crestview HS; Shelby, OH; Hon Rl; Yrbk; Rptr Sch Nwsp; Rdo Clb; Hockey; Wrstlng; Univ; Natural Resources.

HEYDEN, PAM; Lumen Christi HS; Jackson, MI; Chrh Wkr; Hon Rl; PAVAS; Stg Crw; Rptr Sch Nwsp; Spn Clb; Trk; Spanish Cert 76; JCC Dept Schlshp 79; Univ; Med.

HEYER, SUSAN; Monroe HS; Monroe, MI; 13/586 Chrh Wkr; Cmnty Wkr; Hon Rl; NHS; Yth Flsp; Ferris St Coll; Bus Admin.

HEYKOOP, MELINDA; Fostoria HS; Fostoria, OH; 11/177 Sec Frsh Cls; Trs Frsh Cls; VP Soph Cls; VP Jr Cls; Cls Rep Sr Cls; Hon Rl; NHS; Stu Cncl; Y-Teens; Rptr Yrbk; Univ; Sci.

HEYL, JENNIFER A; Ursuline Academy; Cincinnati, OH; 8/138 Cl Rep Jr Cls; Cls Rep Sr Cls; NHS; Stu Cncl; Ten; Tmr; Cit Awd; Natl Merit SF; Pre Med.

HEYMAN, DIANA; Eastmoor HS; Columbus, OH; 41/290 Chrs; Sch Pl; Y-Teens; Spn Clb; Swmmng; Cert Of Merit For Participation In Swim Team; Miami Univ; Psych.

HIATT, DEBRA; Danville Community HS; Danville, IN; 31/152 Chrh Wkr; Cmnty Wkr; Girl Scts; Rptr Yrbk; 4-H; FHA; Swmmng; Ten; Pom Pon; Tmr; Butler Univ; Interior Design.

HIATT, GERALD; Traverse City Sr HS; Traverse City, MI; Boy Scts; Cmnty Wkr; Sct Actv; Natl Merit Ltr; Ferris St Coll; Optometry.

HIATT, MARGIE; Churubusco HS; Churubusco, IN; 7/125 Cl Rep Jr Cls; Cls Rep Sr Cls; Am Leg Aux Girls St; Band; Hon Rl; NHS; Stu Cncl; Ed Yrbk; FNA; Spn Clb; Indiana Univ; Med.

HIATT, MELISSA; Eastbrook HS; Upland, IN; 1/180 Am Leg Aux Girls St; Band; Drl Tm; Drm Mjrt; Hon Rl; NHS; Sch Mus; Ind Univ; Phys Ther.

HIATT, SANDY; Madison Hts HS; Anderson, IN; 21/376 Chrs; Hon Rl; NHS; 4-H; Bsktbl; 4-H Awd; Kiwan Awd; Ball St Univ; Acctg.

HIBBARD, ELISABETH; Fowlerville HS; Howell, MI; Chrh Wkr; Girl Scts; Lbry Ade; Sct Actv; Rptr Sch Nwsp; 4-H; Mgrs; Scr Kpr; Univ.

HIBBARD, KRISTINE; Millington HS; Millington, MI; 30/170 Am Leg Aux Girls St; Sch Pl; Rptr Sch Nwsp; Fr Clb; Bus Schl; Acctg.

HIBNER, JILL; Richmond Sr HS; Richmond, IN; Band; Hon Rl; Fr Clb; Indiana Univ.

HICE, CYNTHIA; Van Buren HS; Brazil, IN; Cl Rep Jr Cls; Chrh Wkr; Hosp Ade; Lbry Ade; FHA; Music And Art.

HICHMAN, DAVID; St Alphonsus HS; Dearborn Hts, MI; Chrh Wkr; Hon Rl; Univ; Law.

HICKENBOTTOM, KAREN; St Clairsville HS; St Clairsville, OH; Girl Scts; Hon Rl; Off Ade; Yth Flsp; Y-Teens; Rptr Yrbk; 4-H; Pep Clb; GAA; IM Sprt; Fshn Mdse.

HICKERSON, LINDA; Mt Vernon HS; Mt Vernon, OH; Chrh Wkr; Girl Scts; Hon Rl; NHS; Off Ade; OEA; Diplomat Awd; 1st Pl In Prepared Speech II Reg OEA; Academic Awd;.

HICKEY, KATHRYN; Ravenna HS; Ravenna, OH; Chrs; Girl Scts; Hon Rl; Lbry Ade; Ed Yrbk; Yrbk; Sch Nwsp; Fr Clb; Pep Clb; Bsktbl; Ohio State; Md.

HICKEY, MICHAEL; Meadowdale HS; Dayton, OH; Chrh Wkr; Hon Rl; Yth Flsp; Ftbl; IM Sprt; Dentist.

HICKEY, TOM; Deer Park HS; Cincinnati, OH; Boy Scts; Hon Rl; Sch Nwsp; Ftbl; College; Art.

HICKEY, TOM; Black River HS; Chippewa, OH; Boy Scts; 4-H; Pep Clb; Spn Clb; Wrstlng; Tmr; 4-H Awd; JC Awd; USJC Awd; Akron Univ; Legal.

HICKMAN, CHRISTINE L; Beaver Local HS; E Liverpool, OH; 25/238 Band; Drl Tm; Hon Rl; NHS; Off Ade; Stg Crw; Yrbk; OEA;.

HICKMAN, DWAYNE; Milton HS; Milton, WV; Chrh Wkr; Hon Rl; FFA; Ftbl; Voc Schl; Machines.

HICKMAN, JANE; Rosedale HS; Rosedale, IN; VP Jr Cls; Drl Tm; Hon Rl; Mod UN; Civ Clb; Pep Clb; Chrldng; Mgrs; Pom Pon; Tmr; Indiana Univ; CPA.

HICKMAN, JASON; Champion Sr HS; Warren, OH; Boy Scts; Chrs; Mdrgl; Off Ade; Sch Mus; Sct Actv; Pres Awd; U S Marine Corp Mert Serv 78; Outsntndg Chrl Mbr 78; Marine Corps.

HICKMAN, JOHN; Eaton HS; Eaton, OH; 19/190 Bsbl; Bsktbl; Ftbl; Miami Univ; Ind Educ.

HICKMAN, SANDRA; Pt Pleasant HS; Pt Pleasant, WV; Chrh Wkr; Girl Scts; Hon Rl; Lbry Ade; NHS; Yth Flsp; 4-H; Spn Clb; 4-H Awd; West Virginia Univ; Bio.

HICKMAN, TERESA; Teays Valley HS; Ashville, OH; 6/182 Hon Rl; NHS; Spn Clb; Scr Kpr; Ohio Univ; Archaeology.

HICKMAN, TRACEY; Dwight D Eisenhower HS; Rochester, MI; Chrldng; Tmr; Western Michigan Univ; X Ray Tech.

HICKMAN, TRACIE; Liberty HS; Clarksburg, WV; Chrs; Hon Rl; Lbry Ade; NHS; Sch Pl; Stg Crw; Pep Clb; Sci Clb; Spn Clb; Fairmont St Coll; Theatre.

HICKOK, RHONDA; North Union HS; Richwood, OH; Chrs; Cmnty Wkr; Drl Tm; Hon Rl; Jr NHS; Lbry Ade; NHS; Pep Clb; Gym; Letter Trk; Marion Tech Schl; Bus.

HICKOK, SARAH; Olivet HS; Olivert, MI; Band; Drm Mjrt; Hon Rl; Sch Mus; Stu Cncl; Drama Clb; Trk; Chrldng; Central Mic; Sociology.

HICKS, ANITA; Garfield HS; Akron, OH; Band; Hon Rl; Hosp Ade; Jr NHS; NHS; Off Ade; Stu Cncl; OEA; Dnfth Awd; College; Comp Sci.

HICKS, ANN E; Greenbrier West HS; Alderson, WV; 3/148 Band; Chrs; Chrh Wkr; Debate Tm; Hon Rl; Sec NHS; Sch Pl; Ed Sch Nwsp; Drama Clb; Fr Clb; Marshall Univ; Journalism.

HICKS, BARBARA; Ashtabula HS; Ashtubula, OH; Band; Girl Scts; Kent State; Nurse.

HICKS, BELINDA; Garaway HS; Sugarcreek, OH; 13/95 Sec Sr Cls; Am Leg Aux Girls St; Band; Lbry Ade; NHS; Off Ade; Sch Pl; Drama Clb; Pep Clb; Twrlr; Stark Tech Coll; Marketing.

HICKS, CATHY; Du Pont HS; Charleston, WV; Chrs; Hon Rl; Lat Clb; Mth Clb; Ten; Univ; CPA.

HICKS, DAVID; Shady Spring HS; Cool Ridge, WV; Band; Chrh Wkr; Hon Rl; JA; Pep Clb; Musician.

HICKS, DONNA; Indian Valley North HS; New Philad, OH; Hon Rl; Univ; Lit.

HICKS, DUANE; St Joseph HS; Willowick, OH; Boy Scts; Chrs; Hon Rl; Sch Mus; Sct Actv; Stg Crw; Swmmng; Trk; Bowling Green State Univ; Marine Bio.

HICKS, FELICIA; Lakota HS; W Chester, OH; 77/459 VP Chrs; Hon Rl; Sch Mus; Fr Clb; Pep Clb; Chrldng; Health Awd 76; Univ Of Cincinnati; Nursing.

HICKS, GLORIA; Muskegon HS; Muskegon, MI; Hon Rl; JA; Off Ade; 4-H; Cit Awd; Natl Merit Ltr; Michigan Bus Schls Schlrshp 79 80 & 80 81; Michigan Tuition Grant 79 80; Muskegon Bus Coll; Bus Mgmt.

HICKS, HENRY W; Pickens HS; Pickens, WV; 1/13 Trs Soph Cls; Cls Rep Sr Cls; Am Leg Boys St; Hon Rl; NHS; Stu Cncl; Rptr Yrbk; Rptr Sch Nwsp; Bsktbl; Cit Awd; Typing Awd 1978; Acctg Awd 1978; Davis & Elkins Coll; Philosophy.

HICKS, JOANNE E; Firestone HS; Akron, OH; Yth Flsp; Hockey; Letter Swmmng; Tmr; College; Psych.

HICKS, JON E; Memorial HS; Elkhart, IN; 29/455 Band; Chrh Wkr; Debate Tm; Hon Rl; Natl Forn Lg; Orch; Letter Glf; Natl Merit Fnlst 1979; Natl Engr Tst Top 10% 1979; John Hopkins Univ; Pre Law.

HICKS, JOYCE; Rogers HS; Toledo, OH; Band; Drm Mjrt; JA; Off Ade; Fr Clb; Ohio State; Sci.

HICKS, KENNETH; Indian Creek Sr HS; Trafalgar, IN; 26/163 Boy Scts; Hon Rl; Sct Actv; Sprt Ed Yrbk; Yrbk; Fr Clb; Sci Clb; Univ.

HICKS, KENNETH L; U S Grant Joint Vocl Schl; Bethel, OH; 55/125 Trs Jr Cls; Cl Rep Jr Cls; Trs Sr Cls; Cls Rep Sr Cls; Chrs; Hon Rl; Treas JA; Off Ade; Sch Mus; Sch Pl; Perfect Attendance For Past Six Yrs 1973; 3rd Pl At OOEA Regnl Comp In Genrl Cler 1977; V P Of Mfg Jr Ach; Univ Of Cincinnati; Bus.

HICKS, MARK; Cheboygan Area HS; Cheboygan, MI; Hon Rl; Fr Clb; Sci Clb; Letter Ftbl; Letter Trk; IM Sprt; Natl Merit Ltr; Michigan St Univ; Bus Mgmt.

HICKS, MICHELLE; Westerville S HS; Westerville, OH; Cls Rep Frsh Cls; Cls Rep Soph Cls; Cl Rep Jr Cls; Cls Rep Sr Cls; Cmp Fr Grls; FCA; Stu Cncl; Pep Clb; Letter Chrldng; PPFtbl; All Star Cheerleader At Franklin Hts Ohio St Lrgst Cheerldng Competition; Nom For Sertcoma Chrstms Queen; Ohio State Univ; Special Ed.

HICKS, ROBERT; Wayne Mem HS; Westland, MI; Hon Rl; Lbry Ade; Red Cr Ade; Sch Mus; Stg Crw; Spn Clb; Univ Of Michigan; Indus Elec.

HICKS, SHARON; Amanda Clearcreek HS; Lancaster, OH; Cmnty Wkr; Hon Rl; Jr NHS; NHS; Off Ade; Yrbk; FTA; Ohio Univ; Comp Sci.

HICKS, SHARON; Greenville HS; Greenville, OH; 1/350 Val; Hon Rl; NHS; Pres Yth Flsp; FHA; Sec VICA; Taylor Univ; Pre Engr.

HICKS, SUSAN; Wyoming Park HS; Wyoming, MI; Hon Rl; Pres NHS; Off Ade; 4-H; Fr Clb; IM Sprt; 4-H Awd; Michigan St Univ; Med.

HICKS, TAMMIA A; Marshall HS; Marshall, MI; 11/280 Chrs; Chrh Wkr; Hon Rl; NHS; Sch Mus; Stg Crw; 4-H; Fr Clb; Trk; 4-H Awd; College.

HICKS, TERRY; Jefferson HS; Ranson, WV; Chrs; Cmnty Wkr; Girl Scts; Hon Rl; Lbry Ade; FBLA; Univ; Soc Sci.

HICOK, CHESTER; Roosevelt HS; Wyandotte, MI; Chrs; Hon Rl; Fr Clb; Bsbl; Bsktbl; Crs Cntry; Letter Swmmng; Natl Merit Ltr; Natl Merit SF; Natl Merit Schl; Mic Tech Univ; Mech Engr.

HIDALGO, ANA; St Ursula Academy; Cincinnati, OH; 35/101 Cls Rep Soph Cls; Pres Jr Cls; Chrh Wkr; Cmnty Wkr; Girl Scts; NHS; Sch Pl; Stu Cncl; Spn Clb; Dnfth Awd; 1st In City For Excllnce In Spanish Amer Assn Of Tchrs Of Spanish; Girl Scout Wider Opprotunity To Hawaii; Univ Of Cincinnati.

HIDDE, MIKE; Lincoln HS; Vincennes, IN; 1/282 Boy Scts; Chrh Wkr; Cmnty Wkr; FCA; Hon Rl; Sct Actv; Ftbl; Trk; Wrstlng; Univ; Geology.

HIDER, JAMES; St Vincent St Mary HS; Akron, OH; Chrs; Mdrgl; Sch Mus; Sch Pl; Yrbk; Mth Clb; Ftbl; Univ Of Dayton; Acctg.

HIEBER, JEFFREY; Byron Area HS; Byron, MI; 14/78 Band; Boy Scts; Quill & Scroll; Sprt Ed Sch Nwsp; 4-H; Letter Bsbl; Letter Bsktbl; Letter Ftbl; Natl Merit SF; Natl Merit Schl; Ferris State Coll; Architecture.

HIESTAND, MICHELE; Eaton HS; Eaton, OH; 10/171 VP Jr Cls; Am Leg Aux Girls St; Band; Chrs; Girl Scts; Hon Rl; Jr NHS; Lbry Ade; NHS; Sch Mus; Hanover Coll; Archt.

HIETALA, ROBERT; Harvey HS; Painesville, OH; Hon Rl; NHS; DECA; Bsbl; Ftbl; Trk; Lake Erie Coll; Bus Mgmt.

HIETT, BARBARA; S Vermillion HS; Clinton, IN; Band; Off Ade; Stg Crw; Drama Clb; 4-H; Pep Clb; Letter Trk; Letter Chrldng; GAA; IM Sprt; Homecoming Canidated Queen; Vermillion County Queen; Sec Of Letterman Club; Vocational Schl; Cosmetology.

HIGAR, JAMIE; Metropolitan Schl; Linton, IN; 12/83 Chrh Wkr; Hon Rl; Jr NHS; NHS; Quill & Scroll; Sch Pl; Sch Nwsp; Drama Clb; FHA; Univ; Legal Sec.

HIGBEA, CHERYL A; Delphos Jefferson Sr HS; Delphos, OH; 4/116 Pres Jr Cls; Pres Sr Cls; Am Leg Aux Girls St; Band; Chrs; Drl Tm; Girl Scts; Hon Rl; NHS; Orch; Typing Pin For Fastest Typist 59 WAM 79; Cert Of Schlrstc Achvmnt Hon Roll 77 78 & 79; Bowling Green Univ; Music.

HIGENDORF, ALLAN; Orchard View HS; Muskegon, MI; 3/250 Chrh Wkr; Debate Tm; Hon Rl; Lbry Ade; NHS; Ten; Cit Awd; Olivet Nazarene Coll; Christn Educ.

HIGGINBOTHAM, ANNETTE; Henryville HS; Henryville, IN; 4/70 Cls Rep Soph Cls; Cl Rep Jr Cls; Cls Rep Sr Cls; Am Leg Aux Girls St; Band; Girl Scts; NHS; Treas Stu Cncl; FHA; Spn Clb; Ind Univ Southport; Medicine.

HIGGINBOTHAM, KATINA; East HS; Columbus, OH; Cls Rep Soph Cls; Chrs; Hon Rl; Y-Teens; JC Awd; Ohio St Univ; Engr.

HIGGINBOTHAM, REBECCA; Poca HS; Nitro, WV; 19/152 Band; Hon Rl; NHS; Fr Clb; VICA; Putnam Cnty All Cnty Band 78; Cmmrcl Art.

HIGGINBOTHAM, ROBIN; Noblesville HS; Noblesville, IN; Chrh Wkr; Hon Rl; Red Cr Ade; Pres Yth Flsp; Pres 4-H; Sec FFA; PPFtbl; Scr Kpr; Tmr; 4-H Awd; FFA Schlrshp Awd; Honor Group In 4 H Fashion Review; Business Schl; Court Reporter.

HIGGINBOTTOM, BARBARA; Bluffton HS; Bluffton, IN; Hon Rl; Off Ade; VP Y-Teens; Pep Clb; Letter Bsktbl; Univ.

HIGGINS, ANN; Trimble Local HS; Glouster, OH; 7/103 Sec Frsh Cls; Cls Rep Soph Cls; Cl Rep Jr Cls; Band; Girl Scts; Hon Rl; NHS; Pres Stu Cncl; Yrbk; Letter Bsktbl; Univ Of Denver; Lawyer.

HIGGINS, CINDY L; Centerburg HS; Centerburg, OH; 15/64 Sec Jr Cls; Sec Sr Cls; Hon Rl; NHS; Sec Stu Cncl; Sec Yth Flsp; Rptr Yrbk; Ed Sch Nwsp; 4-H; FHA; Sec Work.

HIGGINS, DAVID; Austintown Fitch HS; Youngstown, OH; 80/700 Chrs; NHS; Sch Mus; Stg Crw; Youngstown State Univ; Computer Sci.

HIGGINS, DAWN; Shelbyville HS; Shelbyville, IN; Am Leg Aux Girls St; JA; NHS; Yth Flsp; Spn Clb; Letter Ten; Indiand Univ; Criminal Justice.

HIGGINS, GENE; Heath HS; Heath, OH; Hon Rl; Spn Clb; Embry Riddle Univ; Aviation.

HIGGINS, JOHN A; Northville HS; Northville, MI; Am Leg Boys St; Boy Scts; Chrh Wkr; Hon Rl; NHS; Sch Mus; Stg Crw; Rptr Yrbk; Ger Clb; Hockey; Univ; Engr.

HIGGINS, JUDY; New Albany HS; Westerville, OH; 4/98 Trs Soph Cls; Trs Jr Cls; Band; Chrs; Chrh Wkr; Hon Rl; Sec Ger Clb; College.

HIGGINS, KENDRA; William Henry Harrison HS; Evansville, IN; Cmnty Wkr; Hon Rl; VICA; Cit Awd; Shclrshp H 77; Indiana Univ; Med.

HIGGINS, KEVIN; Ludington HS; Ludington, MI; Hon Rl; NHS; Letter Swmmng; Trk; Elk Awd; Grand Valley State Colleges; Engr.

HIGGINS, LINDA; Switzerland County Jr Sr HS; Bennington, IN; 6/120 Hon Rl; Lbry Ade; NHS; Off Ade; Sch Pl; Drama Clb; Sec FHA; Vincennes Jr Coll.

HIGGINS, SCOTT; Madison Plains HS; Mt Sterling, OH; Am Leg Boys St; Boy Scts; Debate Tm; Hon Rl; Mod UN; 4-H; Spn Clb; Bsbl; Ftbl; Wrstlng; Ohio St Univ; Chem.

HIGGINS, SUZANNE; Lawrence Ctrl HS; Indianapolis, IN; 127/437 Girl Scts; Sct Actv; Pep Clb; Letter Swmmng; Capt Mat Maids; PPFtbl; Indiana Univ; Dentistry.

HIGGINS, WILLIAM; Struthers HS; Struthers, OH; Pres Jr Cls; Chrs; Sch Mus; Sch Pl; Stg Crw; Stu Cncl; Drama Clb; Lat Clb; IM Sprt; Mgrs; Mst Promising New Mbr Drama 76; Ohio St Univ; Pharm.

HIGGS, LINDA; Martins Ferry HS; Martins Ferry, OH; Band; Chrs; Girl Scts; Hon Rl; Lbry Ade; Sch Mus; Stg Crw; Yth Flsp; Spn Clb; Univ; Forestry.

HIGGS, MAUREEN; Wayne Memorial HS; Wayne, MI; Cls Rep Sr Cls; FCA; Hon Rl; Ger Clb; Mth Clb; Letter Trk; Tmr; Western Mich; Spec Educ.

HIGH, PAMELA S; Lexington HS; Lexington, OH; 126/245 Sec Soph Cls; Chrh Wkr; Stg Crw; Stu Cncl; Yth Flsp; 4-H; FHA; Spn Clb; Trk; IM Sprt; Ohio State Univ; Home Ec.

HIGH, ROBERT; Dublin HS; Dublin, OH; Aud/Vis; Boy Scts; Chrs; JA; Lbry Ade; Off Ade; Sct Actv; Stg Crw; Rptr Yrbk; Rptr Sch Nwsp; 3rd In Sales V P Of Yr 79; Ohio St Univ; Mgmt Consultant.

HIGH, STEVE; William Henry Harrison HS; W Lafayette, IN; Boy Scts; Cmnty Wkr; Hon Rl; Sch Pl; Sct Actv; Stg Crw; Fr Clb; Letter Ftbl; Letter Wrstlng; IM Sprt; Purdue Univ; Bus Mgmt.

HIGHHOUSE, TRACI; Olmsted Falls HS; Olmsted Falls, OH; Chrs; Drl Tm; Gym; Trk; Modeling.

HIGHLANDER, PAM; Margaretta HS; Castalia, OH; Cls Rep Sr Cls; Chrs; Chrh Wkr; FCA; Hon Rl; Stu Cncl; Yth Flsp; Pres FHA; OEA; GAA; Miss Oh Office Educ Assoc 78; Ehove Jt Voc Schl; Soc Sec Admin.

HIGHMILLER, DEBBIE; Tri Jr Sr HS; Spiceland, IN; Band; Lbry Ade; Drama Clb; FHA; Ten; 4-H Awd; Univ; Phys Ther.

HIGHT, DURAY; Southeastern HS; Detroit, MI; Cmnty Wkr; Hon Rl; JA; DECA; Cit Awd; College; Comp Sci.

HIGHT, MICHELLE; Adelphian Academy; Vassar, MI; Band; Chrh Wkr; FCA; Hon Rl; Yth Flsp; Beta Clb; Gym; Scr Kpr; Saginaw Bus Inst; Sec.

HIGHTOWER, WHITNEY; River Rouge HS; River Rouge, MI; Aud/Vis; Band; Boy Scts; Hon Rl; NHS; Off Ade; Sch Pl; Sct Actv; Boys Clb Am; Spn Clb; Control Data Inst; Comp Programmer.

HIGLE, AMY; Troy HS; Troy, MI; 23/286 Hon Rl; NHS; Swmmng; Tmr; Mic State Univ.

HIGLEY, CAROL; Danbury Twp Local HS; Marblehead, OH; 1/62 VP Soph Cls; Cl Rep Jr Cls; Cls Rep Sr Cls; Val; Band; Hon Rl; NHS; Off Ade; Sch Pl; Pres Stu Cncl; Bowling Green St Univ; Bus Admin.

HILBERT, THOMAS; Jonathan Alder HS; Plain City, OH; Am Leg Boys St; Band; Letter Bsktbl; Letter Ftbl; Capt Trk; IM Sprt; Am Leg Awd; Bowling Green Univ; Law.

HILBRANDT, TRACI; Douglas Mac Arthur HS; Saginaw, MI; Chrs; Chrh Wkr; Cmnty Wkr; Hon Rl; Hosp Ade; NHS; Yth Flsp; Spn Clb; Univ.

HILDEBRANDT, ROBERT; Moeller HS; Reading, OH; Hon Rl; Rptr Sch Nwsp; Letter Crs Cntry; Letter Ten; IM Sprt; Ohio Coll Applied Sci; Elec Engr.

HILDERBRAND, KIM; Dowagiac Union HS; Dowagiac, MI; Cl Rep Jr Cls; Cls Rep Sr Cls; Chrh Wkr; Hon Rl; Pres Yth Flsp; Rptr Yrbk; Fr Clb; Central Mic Univ; Public Health Educ.

HILDRETH, DEBBIE; Winchester Community HS; Winchster, IN; VP Chrh Wkr; FCA; Hon Rl; Jr NHS; Treas NHS; Yth Flsp; FBLA; Letter Ten; College.

HILE, MARCIA; Columbia City Joint HS; Columbia City, IN; 69/279 Girl Scts; Hon Rl; JA; Ger Clb; Manchester Coll; Acctg.

HILE, SUSAN; Ansonia HS; Rossburg, OH; Trs Frsh Cls; Cls Rep Sr Cls; Chrs; Chrh Wkr; Cmnty Wkr; Hon Rl; Hosp Ade; Lbry Ade; Sch Mus; Sch Pl; Reid Mem Hosp; Radiological Tech.

HILEMAN, DEBORAH; Parkway HS; Rock Ford, OH; 11/82 Am Leg Aux Girls St; Hon Rl; Lat Clb; Pep Clb; Pres Sci Clb; Spn Clb; Bsktbl; Pres Trk; PPFtbl; Purdue Univ; Bio Sci.

HILEMAN, MAGGIE; Norton HS; Norton, OH; 25/338 Band; Chrh Wkr; Hon Rl; Jr NHS; Orch; 4-H; GAA; IM Sprt; Scr Kpr; 4-H Awd; Univ; Nursing.

HILENSKI, SCOTT; Admiral King HS; Lorain, OH; Boy Scts; FCA; Hon Rl; Letter Ftbl; Ohio St Univ; Archt.

HILER, KATHY; Ross Sr HS; Okeana, OH; 10/265 Am Leg Aux Girls St; Chrh Wkr; Hon Rl; NHS; Sec Yth Flsp; VP Spn Clb; Letter Bsbl; Letter Bsktbl; IM Sprt; JA Awd; Univ.

HILES, REBECCA; Frankfort Adena HS; Frankfort, OH; 2/85 VP AFS; Sec Band; Chrs; Pres NHS; Pres Yth Flsp; Rptr Yrbk; Rptr Sch Nwsp; Bsktbl; Univ Of Cincinnati; Criminal Justice.

HILES, REBECCA J; Frankfort Adena HS; Frankford, OH; 2/80 Sec AFS; Sec Band; Chrs; Hon Rl; Pres NHS; Sch Pl; Stu Cncl; Pres Yth Flsp; Rptr Yrbk; Rptr Sch Nwsp; Univ Of Cincinnati; Criminal Justice.

HILFINGER, JOHN; Thomas A De Vilbiss HS; Toledo, OH; 1/285 Sal; Am Leg Boys St; Cmnty Wkr; Hon Rl; Jr NHS; NHS; VP Stu Cncl; Rptr Sch Nwsp; Pres Ger Clb; Letter Ten; Cornell Univ; Economics.

HILK, SCOTT; Prineton HS; Sharonville, OH; 100/700 Hon Rl; Rus Clb; Crs Cntry; Swmmng;.

HILL, ALAN; West Side HS; Gary, IN; 63/650 Hon Rl; Jr NHS; Bsbl; Purdue Univ; Comp Tech.

HILL, BARBARA; Scott HS; Chapmanville, WV; Am Leg Aux Girls St; Chrh Wkr; Cmnty Wkr; Jr NHS; Pol Wkr; Pres Stu Cncl; Yrbk; Wv S Community College; Rn.

HILL, BARBARA; Crown Point HS; Crown Point, IN; 11/479 Chrh Wkr; Hon Rl; Lbry Ade; Lit Mag; Treas NHS; Quill & Scroll; Yrbk; Lat Clb; Valparaiso Univ; Acctg.

HILL, BRENDA; Southeastern HS; Detroit, MI; Girl Scts; Hon Rl; JA; Stu Cncl; Rdo Clb; Sci Clb; Swmmng; Cit Awd; Michigan St Univ; Med.

HILL, CARRIE; Kearsley HS; Davison, MI; 108/400 Hon Rl; Sch Pl; Letter Crs Cntry; Letter Glf; Letter Ten; Letter Trk; Letter Chrldng; Mott Cmnty Coll.

HILL, CHERYL; Marquette HS; Marquette, MI; Am Leg Aux Girls St; Chrh Wkr; Debate Tm; Fr Clb; Am Leg Awd; College; Poli Sci.

HILL, CINDY; Continental Local HS; Continental, OH; Band; Chrh Wkr; Hon Rl; Yth Flsp; 4-H; FFA; Am Leg Awd; Bus Schl; Acctng.

HILL, CYNTHIA E; Cass Tech HS; Detroit, MI; Aud/Vis; Girl Scts; Stg Crw; Fr Clb; Swmmng; Natl Merit Ltr; Pres Awd; Coll; Photog.

HILL, DALE; Winchester Community HS; Winchester, IN; Hon Rl; Bsbl; Ten; Wrstlng; Mgrs;.

HILL, DAMITA J; Madison Heights HS; Anderson, IN; 31/376 Sec Frsh Cls; Cls Rep Soph Cls; Sec Jr Cls; Band; Girl Scts; Hon Rl; Hosp Ade; Lbry Ade; Off Ade; Pep Clb; Cand For Miss Teen USA; Page For House Of Rep; Prom Qn Cand; Ball St Univ; Elem Ed.

HILL, DAVID; Williamstown HS; Williamstown, WV; 1/119 Cls Rep Frsh Cls; Cls Rep Soph Cls; Cl Rep Jr Cls; Cls Rep Sr Cls; Am Leg Boys St; Hon Rl; Treas NHS; Letter Bsktbl; Letter Ftbl; College; Engr.

HILL, DAVID; Lutheran East HS; Roseville, MI; Chrh Wkr; Hon Rl; Stg Crw; Yth Flsp; Lat Clb; Spn Clb; Bsbl; Bsktbl; Ftbl; MCCC; Architect.

HILL, DEAN; Richmond Sr HS; Richmond, IN; Cls Rep Soph Cls; Cl Rep Jr Cls; Hon Rl; Stu Cncl; Lat Clb; Letter Ftbl; Purdue Univ; Mech Engr.

HILL, DEBORAH; Princeton HS; Princeton, WV; Cls Rep Soph Cls; Chrh Wkr; Hon Rl; Jr NHS; Stu Cncl; Yth Flsp; Pep Clb; Spn Clb; Letter Ten; Concord Coll; Sociology.

HILL, DEBORAH; Rockville HS; Rockville, IN; 1/98 Am Leg Aux Girls St; Band; Hon Rl; NHS; FHA; Pep Clb; Gym; Trk; College.

HILL, DEBRA; Montrose Hill Mc Cloy HS; Montrose, MI; Cmnty Wkr; Hon Rl; Lit Mag; NHS; Sch Pl; Rptr Yrbk; Sch Nwsp; Pres Drama Clb; Spn Clb; Cit Awd; Bst Supporting Actess 78;.

HILL, DEBRA; Adena HS; Frankfort, OH; 13/85 Pres AFS; Chrs; Drl Tm; Hon Rl; Jr NHS; Sec NHS; Stu Cncl; Yrbk; Pres 4-H; Ohio Univ; Human Ser Tech.

HILL, DENISE; Peck Cmnty HS; Peck, MI; Hon Rl; Bsktbl; Univ; Comp Sci.

HILL, DENNIS; High School; Lapeer, MI; Pres Jr Cls; Sal; Pres NHS; Sch Mus; Pres Stu Cncl; Yrbk; Letter Ftbl; Letter Trk; Natl Merit Schl; Univ Of Mich; Engr.

HILL, DONNA; Mount Notre Dame HS; Reading, OH; 1/180 Sec Frsh Cls; Sec Soph Cls; Cl Rep Jr Cls; Cls Rep Sr Cls; Val; Chrh Wkr; Hon Rl; NHS; Stu Cncl; Fr Clb; Univ Of Cinn; Bus.

HILL, FAYE; Wood Memorial HS; Oakland, IN; Hon Rl; Off Ade; Sch Nwsp; OEA; Pep Clb; Chrldng; PPFtbl; Bus Schl; Bus.

HILL, GENA; Decatur Central HS; Indnpls, IN; Chrs; Hon Rl; JA; Off Ade; Ed Sch Nwsp; Pep Clb; Swmmng; IM Sprt; Indiana Bus Coll; Typist.

HILL, HEIDI H; Lewis Cnty HS; Camden, WV; Band; Chrh Wkr; Hon Rl; Jr NHS; Y-Teens; Ed Yrbk; 4-H; Am Leg Awd; 4-H Awd; Voice Dem Awd; West Virginia Univ; Chem.

HILL, JAMES; Springfield Local HS; New Middletown, OH; Hon Rl; Jr NHS; NHS; Fr Clb; Mgrs; Youngstown State Unive; Computer Sci.

HILL, JEFFREY; Alma HS; Sumner, MI; Pol Wkr; Alma Coll; Law.

HILL, JEFFREY; Everett HS; Lansing, MI; Lansing Community College; Radio.

HILL, JOANNA; Scott HS; Turtle Ck, WV; Cls Rep Frsh Cls; Trs Soph Cls; Cls Rep Soph Cls; VP Jr Cls; Cl Rep Jr Cls; Chrs; Chrh Wkr; Hon Rl; Sch Pl; Stu Cncl; Marshall Univ; Law.

HILL, JOHN A; Moeller HS; Silverton, OH; Boy Scts; Chrh Wkr; Cmnty Wkr; Hon Rl; Stg Crw; Yth Flsp; IM Sprt; Scr Kpr; Tmr; Univ; Bus Admin.

HILL, JOHN L; South Point HS; South Point, OH; Chrh Wkr; Rptr Sch Nwsp; Spn Clb; Letter Ftbl; Wrstlng; Marshall Univ; Cmnctns.

HILL, JULIA; Philip Barbour HS; Philippi, WV; Chrs; Chrh Wkr; Hon Rl; Yrbk; Rptr Sch Nwsp; Drama Clb; 4-H; Fr Clb; Keyettes; 4-H Awd; Honor West Virginia Strawberry Festv Princess; Marshall Univ; Busns Admin.

HILL, KAREN; Green HS; Akron, OH; 10/315 Hon Rl; NHS; Y-Teens; Rptr Sch Nwsp; VP OEA; Sec GAA; Akron Univ; Sec.

HILL, KAREN; Marquette HS; Marquette, MI; 5/420 Hon Rl; Orch; 4-H; 4-H Awd; Mich State Univ; Vet Med.

HILL, KAREN; Portage Lakes Joint Voc Schl; Akron, OH; 10/215 Akron Univ; Bus Admin.

HILL, KIM; Ripley HS; Sandyville, WV; VP Jr Cls; Band; Chrs; Pres Jr NHS; Pres Stu Cncl; VP 4-H; Letter Trk; Chrldng; 4-H Awd; Alderson Broaddus Univ; Phys Asst.

HILL, LA; Cass Technical HS; Detroit, MI; Chrs; Chrh Wkr; Cmnty Wkr; Hon Rl; Off Ade; Cit Awd; Career Recrtmnt In Tele Cmnctns Indust 79; Hon Recmndtn Rose Carrier WJR Radio Sttn 79; Univ Of Michigan; Acctg.

HILL, LINDA; Edgewood HS; Bloomington, IN; Hon Rl; Letter Bsktbl; Letter Trk; Univ.

HILL, LISA; Dunbar HS; Dunbar, WV; Chrs; Hon Rl; NHS; Stg Crw; VP Stu Cncl; Pep Clb; Bsktbl; Letter Ten; Letter Mat Maids; Marshall Univ; Sci.

HILL, LISA; Federal Hocking HS; Amesville, OH; Cl Rep Jr Cls; Hon Rl; Stu Cncl; Rptr Yrbk; Fr Clb; FBLA; Pep Clb; Art.

HILL, LLOYD; Warrensville Hts HS; Warrensville, OH; Cls Rep Frsh Cls; Yrbk; Sch Nwsp; Bsbl;.

HILL, LORI; Bradford HS; Bradford, OH; Trs Frsh Cls; Pres Jr Cls; VP Jr Cls; Cls Rep Sr Cls; Drl Tm; Hon Rl; Sec NHS; 4-H; FHA; OEA;.

HILL, LORI; Ithaca HS; Ithaca, MI; Girl Scts; Hon Rl; FHA; Letter Bsktbl; Chrldng; Pom Pon; M J Murphy Bty Schl; Cosmetology.

HILL, LORRAINE M; Columbus East HS; Columbus, OH; 2/272 Cls Rep Frsh Cls; Cls Rep Soph Cls; Cl Rep Jr Cls; Cls Rep Sr Cls; Sal; Band; Chrh Wkr; Hon Rl; Jr NHS; NHS; Ohio St Univ; Optometry.

HILL, LORRAINE M; Columbus E HS; Columbus, OH; 2/272 Sal; Band; Hon Rl; Jr NHS; Lbry Ade; NHS; Off Ade; Orch; Stu Cncl; Rptr Yrbk; Ohio St Univ; Optometry.

HILL, MARK A; Jackson HS; Canton, OH; Pres Frsh Cls; Band; Hon Rl; JA; Stu Cncl; Boys Clb Am; Spn Clb; Ten; College; Med.

HILL, MELANIE; Washington Irving HS; Clarksburg, WV; Band; Hon Rl; Yth Flsp; Lat Clb; West Virginia Univ; Pharm.

HILL, MICHAEL; Inland Lakes HS; Indian River, MI; 5/90 Sec Frsh Cls; Trs Soph Cls; Sec Jr Cls; Trs Jr Cls; Sec Sr Cls; Trs Sr Cls; Hon Rl; Ed Sch Nwsp; Cit Awd; VFW Awd; Ferris State; Optometry.

HILL, MYNA; Southeastern HS; Londonderry, OH; Hon Rl; Off Ade; DECA; Lat Clb; Pep Clb; Chrldng; Ohio Univ; Amer Hist Tchr.

HILL, NANCY; West Catholic HS; Grand Rapids, MI; Hon Rl; Letter Bsktbl; Univ; Bus Admin.

HILL, NATALIE; Lakota HS; Risingsun, OH; VP Frsh Cls; VP Soph Cls; Pres Jr Cls; Am Leg Aux Girls St; NHS; Stu Cncl; Drama Clb; Mercy Schl Of Nursing; RN.

HILL, PAT; Jackson Milton HS; North Jackson, OH; 8/108 Hon Rl;.

HILL, PETER; Parkersburg South HS; Washington, WV; Boy Scts; Chrh Wkr; Hon Rl; Stg Crw; Yth Flsp; Trk; West Virginia Univ; Elec Engr.

HILL, RANDALL J; Hamilton HS; Holland, MI; 35/131 Cls Rep Soph Cls; Cl Rep Jr Cls; Band; Hon Rl; Stg Crw; Stu Cncl; Ger Clb; Letter Ftbl; Letter Trk; Letter Wrstlng; Central Michigan Univ; Bus Admin.

HILL, REBECCA; Becky Hill HS; Warren, OH; Cmnty Wkr; Hosp Ade; JA; Lit Mag; Quill & Scroll; Sch Mus; Stu Cncl; Rptr Sch Nwsp; Fr Clb; Trk; North Carolina Schl Of Arts; Dance.

HILL, RICHARD; Northrop HS; Ft Wayne, IN; Chrs; Jr NHS; Mdrgl; Sch Mus; Sch Pl; Professional Magician.

HILL, ROBERT; Pike HS; Indianapolis, IN; Band; Jr NHS; VP NHS; VP Mth Clb; Letter Crs Cntry; Trk; Dnfth Awd; College; Engr.

HILL, RONALD; Solon HS; Solon, OH; Aud/Vis; Boy Scts; Chrh Wkr; Sct Actv; VP Yth Flsp; Letter Swmmng; Vocational School; Illustration.

HILL, RUSTY; New Albany HS; New Albany, IN; Cls Rep Frsh Cls; Capt Wrstlng; IM Sprt;.

HILL, SANDRA; South Charleston HS; S Charleston, WV; Cls Rep Frsh Cls; Hon Rl; Jr NHS; Off Ade; VP Stu Cncl; Pep Clb; Spn Clb; Swmmng; Letter Ten; Marshall Univ; Med.

HILL, SHELIA; Princeton HS; Kellysville, WV; Chrs; Chrh Wkr; Sch Pl; Rptr Sch Nwsp; Letter Bsktbl; Coach Actv; IM Sprt; Bluefield St Coll; Phys Ed.

HILL, STANLEY; Libbey HS; Toledo, OH; Chrh Wkr; FCA; Hon Rl; NHS; Yth Flsp; 4-H; Bsbl; Ftbl; Trk; Wrstlng; Univ; Law.

HILL, TAMMY; Bellbrook HS; Cookeville, TN; 15/165 NHS; Hndbl; Admin Mgmt Soc; Natl Honor Society; Gymnastics; Tennessee Tech Univ; Busns Admin.

HILL, TERI; Winfield HS; Winfield, WV; 11/123 Chrs; Hon Rl; Jr NHS; NHS; Sch Pl; Stg Crw; Drama Clb; FHA; Bsktbl; Letter Ten; Soc Of Dist Amer HS Stu; West Virginia St Coll; Bus.

HILL, TERRY J; Calumet HS; Copper City, MI; 37/143 Band; Chrs; Hon Rl; Sch Mus; Sch Pl; Stg Crw; Ed Yrbk; Fr Clb; FTA; Mic State Univ; Art.

HILL, TINA; Mt Vernon Academy; Orlando, FL; Band; Chrs; Hon Rl; Letter Bsktbl; Gym; Letter Socr; Letter Trk; 200 Schlshp From Mt Vernon 78; Univ; Lab Tech.

HILL, VATA C; Lutheran HS E; Cleveland, OH; 11/44 Girl Scts; Orch; Pep Clb; Med Schl; Med.

HILL, YVONNE; E Technical HS; Cleveland, OH; 4/302 Hon Rl; Jr NHS; NHS; OEA; Trk; Tmr; Cit Awd; Baldwin Wallace; Acctg.

HILLEBRAND, DEBBIE; Dominican HS; Detroit, MI; Cls Rep Frsh Cls; Cls Rep Soph Cls; VP Jr Cls; Band; Chrs; Mdrgl; Orch; Sch Mus; Sch Pl; Stu Cncl; Univ.

HILLIARD, BONITA; Warrensville Hts HS; Warrensville, OH; Lbry Ade; Spn Clb; Bsktbl; Mgrs; Eng Awd 76 77; Honor Roll 78 79; Merit Roll 78 79; Univ; Acctg.

HILLIARD, MARLA; Northwest HS; Canal Fulton, OH; Cls Rep Sr Cls; Chrs; Girl Scts; Hon Rl; Sch Mus; Stu Cncl; Yth Flsp; Pres Y-Teens; Bowling Green State Univ; Vocal Musi.

HILLIARD, MICHAEL; Bishop Foley HS; Hazel Pk, MI; Boy Scts; Hon Rl; Capt Bsktbl; Letter Ftbl; Acad Letter; Univ Of Michigan; Forestry.

HILLIKER, DAVID; Lake Fenton HS; Grand Blanc, MI; 25/179 Band; Boy Scts; Hon Rl; NHS; Glf; Michigan St Univ; Engr.

HILLIN, SUZANNE; Ripley HS; Ripley, WV; 3/257 Cmnty Wkr; Hon Rl; Hosp Ade; Jr NHS; NHS; Stg Crw; Sec Mth Clb; Sci Clb; DAR Awd; West Virginia Univ; Elec Engr.

HILLMAN, MARY L; Archbishop Alter HS; Dayton, OH; 30/294 Chrs; Hon Rl; Rptr Sch Nwsp; Sch Nwsp; Fr Clb; Chrldng; IM Sprt; College; Fashion Merch.

HILLMAN, TRACEY; Clarkston HS; Clarkston, MI; Cls Rep Soph Cls; Boy Scts; Chrs; Drm Bgl; Hon Rl; Lbry Ade; Sch Pl; Stg Crw; Drama Clb; Mth Clb; Electrician.

HILLS, LISA; Jane Addams HS; Cleveland, OH; Drl Tm; FTA; Ten; Trk; Voc Schl; Designing.

HILLSTEAD, STEVEN; Muskegon Sr HS; Muskegon, MI; Chrh Wkr; Hon Rl; NHS; VP Orch; Capt Ftbl; Cit Awd; Mi Press Assn Outstndng Carrier Of Yr Awd 78; Blue Lk Fine Art Camp Intl Symphony Orch Eurpn Tour 78; Michigan St Univ; Civil Engr.

HILLYARD, JULIE; Philip Barbour HS; Junior, WV; 2/200 Hon Rl; NHS; Off Ade; Sch Pl; Mth Clb; Am Leg Awd; Sec Of Art Club 78 79; Acad Schlrshp To Davis & Elkins Coll 79; Synod Of Trinity Schlrshp 79; Davis & Elkins Coll; Sec Sci.

HILOW, ELEANORE E; St Augustine Acad; Lakewood, OH; 31/133 Chrs; Mod UN; Sch Mus; Sch Pl; Stg Crw; Stu Cncl; Yrbk; Drama Clb; Key Clb; Coach Actv; Miami Univ; Bus.

HILTBRAND, DONNA; Glen Este HS; Batavia, OH; 2/255 Trs Soph Cls; Trs Jr Cls; Trs Sr Cls; Band; Chrh Wkr; Sch Mus; Sec Pep Clb; Spn Clb; Ohi State Univ; Fashion Mdsg.

HILTBRAND, ROBERT; Jackson HS; North Canton, OH; Band; Boy Scts; Hon Rl; NHS; Sct Actv; Yth Flsp; Spn Clb; Spanish II Schlrshp Team 78; Univ; Engr.

HILTON, DENISE; Churubusco HS; Churubusco, IN; 7/132 Sec Jr Cls; Trs Jr Cls; Am Leg Aux Girls St; Band; Chrs; Cmnty Wkr; Hon Rl; Purdue Univ; Micro Bio.

HILTON, DENISE; Morton Sr HS; Hammond, IN; 22/401 VP Jr Cls; Cls Rep Sr Cls; Girl Scts; Hon Rl; Jr NHS; NHS; Orch; Pol Wkr; Pep Clb; Trk; Purdue Lafayette Univ; Vet Med.

HILTY, JACQUELINE; Wintersville HS; Wintersville, OH; 19/282 Pres Frsh Cls; VP Soph Cls; Cl Rep Jr Cls; Band; Chrh Wkr; Stu Cncl; Yth Flsp; Rptr Yrbk; Spn Clb; Letter Trk; College; Psychology.

HILTZ, LINDA; Lapeer East HS; Lapeer, MI; Band; Hon Rl; Sch Mus; Yth Flsp; Univ; Math Tchr.

HILTZ, RAYMOND; Servite HS; Detroit, MI; Trs Frsh Cls; Trs Soph Cls; Trs Jr Cls; Trs Sr Cls; Hon Rl; NHS; Letter Bsktbl; IM Sprt; Natl Merit Schl; Detroit College Of Bus; Acctg.

HILTZ, VALERIE; Kenowa Hills HS; Comstock Park, MI; 14/230 Cl Rep Jr Cls; Am Leg Aux Girls St; Chrs; Debate Tm; NHS; Sch Mus; Sch Pl; Treas Stu Cncl; Drama Clb; Grand Valley State College; Advtsng.

HILVERS, MARIA; Ottoville Local HS; Ft Jennings, OH; Chrs; Girl Scts; Hon Rl; Off Ade; Sch Mus; Sch Pl; Rptr Yrbk; Drama Clb; Eng Clb; Bus Schl.

HILVERS, MELINDA; Pennsboro HS; Pennsboro, WV; Band; Chrh Wkr; Hon Rl; NHS; Letter Bsktbl; Trk; Capt Chrldng; GAA; PPFtbl; Glenville St Univ; Tchr.

HIMEBROOK, RUTH; Switz City Central HS; Linton, IN; Band; Chrs; Hon Rl; NHS; Orch; Yrbk; Pep Clb; Spn Clb; Bsbl; Bsktbl; Modeling.

HIMELRICK, JULIE; Lewis County HS; Jane Lew, WV; Pres Frsh Cls; Band; Chrs; Hon Rl; NHS; Stu Cncl; Vocational School; Fashion Design.

HIMES, DEBRA; Roy C Start HS; Toledo, OH; Chrs; Chrh Wkr; Girl Scts; FHA; Bowling Green Start; Home Ec.

HIMSEL, ANGELA; Jasper HS; Jasper, IN; Chrs; Debate Tm; Hon Rl; Natl Forn Lg; Pol Wkr; Sch Mus; Sch Pl; Ed Sch Nwsp; Drama Clb; Opt Clb Awd; Indiana Univ.

HINA, BRAD; Philo HS; Roseville, OH; Hon Rl; Fr Clb; Letter Bsbl; Letter Bsktbl; Univ; Surveyor.

HINA, SUSAN; W Muskingum HS; Hopewell, OH; Chrs; Girl Scts; Hon Rl; Lbry Ade; NHS; Off Ade; Sch Mus; Yth Flsp; Rptr Sch Nwsp;.

HINDERBERGER, REGAN; Brookville HS; Brookville, IN; 60/200 Chrh Wkr; Girl Scts; Hon Rl; 4-H; Spn Clb; Letter Trk; IM Sprt; 4-H Awd; Univ; Bus.

HINDERS, JULIA; Celina HS; Celina, OH; Cl Rep Jr Cls; Cls Rep Sr Cls; Am Leg Aux Girls St; Chrs; Hon Rl; Jr NHS; NHS; Sch Mus; Sch Pl; Stg Crw; Miami Univ; Education.

HINDI, MICHAEL; Clay Sr HS; Oregon, OH; 23/350 Chrs; Hon Rl; Jr NHS; Off Ade; Sch Mus; Sch Pl; Drama Clb; Fr Clb; Mth Clb; Sci Clb; Toledo Univ Summr Research Sympsm 78; Tech Soc Of Toledo T U Research Presentation 78; Univ; Physics.

HINDMAN, FRED; Magnolia HS; New Martinsvle, WV; Hon Rl; Crs Cntry; Ftbl; Trk; Am Leg Awd; Top Schltc Boy 77; To P 10% Acad Avchvmnt 77 & 78; Westminster Coll; Med Research.

HINDMAN, LOREEN; Morgantown HS; Morgantwn, WV; Chrs; Chrh Wkr; Sch Pl; Trk; Chrldng; West Virginia Univ; Med.

HINDS, JENNIFER; All Gres Sims HS; Au Gres, MI; Chrs; Cmnty Wkr; Hon Rl; Pol Wkr; Rptr Sch Nwsp; Special Olympic Vlntr 77; Dance Marathon 78; Music Awrd & Preforming Arts Awrd Cnty Fair Awrds; Performing Arts.

HINEBAUGH, KATHY; Willard HS; Willard, OH; Band; Chrs; Girl Scts; Jr NHS; Sch Mus; Rptr Yrbk; 4-H; Bsbl; IM Sprt; Scr Kpr; Univ; Med Tech.

HINEN, LAURA; Columbia City Jt HS; Ft Wayne, IN; Chrs; Sch Mus; Sch Pl; Drama Clb; Ger Clb; GAA; Pom Pon; Health Careers Clb Pres 77 78 & 79; Manchester Coll; Pre Med.

HINES, DONNA; Clarkston HS; Clarkston, MI; 12/500 Chrs; Girl Scts; Hon Rl; Lbry Ade; NHS; Sch Mus; Drama Clb; 4-H; 4-H Awd; Michigan St Univ; Veterinarian.

HINES, ELLEN; Stephen T Badin HS; Fairfield, OH; 23/223 Cls Rep Frsh Cls; Cl Rep Jr Cls; Cls Rep Sr Cls; Am Leg Aux Girls St; Chrh Wkr; Hon Rl; Hosp Ade; NHS; Sch Pl; Stu Cncl; College; Aero Engr.

HINES, GREGORY; Pleasant HS; Prospect, OH; 1/150 Cls Rep Frsh Cls; Am Leg Boys St; Hon Rl; NHS; Pol Wkr; Quill & Scroll; Sch Pl; Stg Crw; Ed Yrbk; Drama Clb; Schl Geom Team 1st In Dust 13th In St 78; Schl Algbr I Team Lth In Dist Hon Mntn In St 77; Univ; Bus Admin.

HINES, JACQUELINE; East HS; Columbus, OH; Chrh Wkr; Lbry Ade; Off Ade; Columbus Tech Inst; Exec Sec.

HINES, JAMES L; Benton Harbor HS; Benton Harbor, MI; 6/638 Cl Rep Jr Cls; Boy Scts; Chrh Wkr; Hon Rl; JA; NHS; 4-H; Key Clb; Mth Clb; Spn Clb; Southwestern Fastest Human 1979; Athletic Of Year 1979; Univ; Engr.

HINES, JOE; East High HS; Cleveland, OH; Band; Hon Rl; Hosp Ade; JA; NHS; Fr Clb; Ftbl; Trk; IM Sprt; Rotary Awd; Engineering.

HINES, MARTHA; Cabrini HS; Lincoln Park, MI; VP Soph Cls; VP Jr Cls; Chrs; Drl Tm; Girl Scts; Hon Rl; Sch Mus; Capt Pom Pon; Bus Schl; Sec.

HINES, PATRICIA; Mendon HS; Three Rivers, MI; Pres Frsh Cls; Sec Sr Cls; Band; Hon Rl; NHS; Yth Flsp; Letter Trk; Letter Chrldng; PPFtbl; Univ; Dent Asst.

HINES, SARON; Beecher HS; Flint, MI; Cls Rep Soph Cls; Cl Rep Jr Cls; Boy Scts; Hon Rl; JA; Jr NHS; NHS; Spn Clb; Chrldng; C of C Awd; Morehouse College; Med.

HINES, STEVEN; John Glenn HS; Westland, MI; Hon Rl; Bsbl; IM Sprt; Univ; Law.

HINES, TIMOTHY; Bishop Luers HS; Ft Wayne, IN; 86/186 Boy Scts; Chrh Wkr; Sprt Ed Yrbk; Rptr Yrbk; Yrbk; Sprt Ed Sch Nwsp; Rptr Sch Nwsp; Fr Clb; Letter Bsbl; Bsktbl; Coll.

HINGA, CLARK; Hackett HS; Kalamazoo, MI; Sch Mus; Sch Pl; Stg Crw; Yrbk; Drama Clb; Sci Clb; Spn Clb; Letter Bsbl; IM Sprt; Michigan St Univ; Agri.

HINGSON, RAY; Kenton HS; Kenton, OH; Hon Rl; Ger Clb; Am Leg Awd; Brigham Young Univ; Acctg.

HINKLE, CYNTHIA; Yorktown HS; Muncie, IN; Hon Rl; FBLA; Sec OEA; Pep Clb; Spn Clb; Trk; Chrldng; Ball St Univ; Busns.

HINKLE, JAMES; Cody HS; Detroit, MI; Band; Boy Scts; JA; Sct Actv; Rptr Yrbk; Rptr Sch Nwsp; Pep Clb; Univ; Law Schl.

HINKLE, KATHY; Moorefield HS; Old Fields, WV; 6/88 Cls Rep Frsh Cls; Am Leg Aux Girls St; Band; Chrs; Hon Rl; Sec Jr NHS; VP NHS; Sch Pl; Stg Crw; Ed Yrbk; Shepherd Coll; Pre Vet Med.

HINKLE, LAURIE; Calumet HS; Gary, IN; 12/320 Sec Frsh Cls; Sec Soph Cls; Sec Jr Cls; Sec Sr Cls; Hon Rl; JA; Off Ade; Sch Pl; Stg Crw; Stu Cncl; D Roberts Csmtlgy Schl; Makeup Artst.

HINKLE, MARY; Teays Valley HS; Circleville, OH; Am Leg Aux Girls St; Chrs; Chrh Wkr; Hon Rl; NHS; Sch Mus; Sch Pl; Rptr Yrbk; Rptr Sch Nwsp; Drama Clb; Capitol Univ; Poli Sci.

HINKLE, NANCY; Centerville HS; Dayton, OH; Key Clb; Swmmng; Trk; Miami Jacobs Jr Coll; Med Asst.

HINKLEY, KIMBERLY K; Pershing HS; Detroit, MI; Hon Rl; NHS; FBLA; Wayne State Univ; Cpa.

HINMAN, BRIAN; Manton Consolidated Schools; Manton, MI; 5/100 Hon Rl; 4-H; FFA; FTA; Letter Bsktbl; Letter Crs Cntry; Letter Ftbl; Letter Trk; 4-H Awd; Band Awd 74 79; Schlrshp Awd 77 & 78; Attendance Awd 77; Voc Schl; Woodwork.

HINMAN, TAMARA; Vicksburg HS; Vicksbrg, MI; 3/230 Chrh Wkr; Hon Rl; NHS; Rptr Yrbk; Sprt Ed Sch Nwsp; Spn Clb; Bsbl; Bsktbl; College; Journalism.

HINNEGAN, PATRICIA; Wayne HS; Dayton, OH; 30/525 AFS; Band; NHS; Rptr Yrbk; Pres FBLA; Spn Clb; 1st Pl In Econ In Ohio Future Busns Ldrs Of Amer; 3rd Pl In Acctg In FBLA Dist Comp; Recv Honor Cord; Wright St Univ; Busns Admin.

HINOJOSA, LYDIA; Hammond Tech HS; Hammond, IN; Off Ade; Bsbl; Ten; Bus Schl.

HINOJOSH, CATHERINE; Hammond Technical Vocational; Hammond, IN; 6/250 Chrs; Girl Scts; Hon Rl; Lbry Ade; NHS; Off Ade; Sch Mus; Sch Pl; Lat Clb; Trk; Purdue Univ; Pharmacy.

HINRICHSEN, HELGA C; Solon HS; Solon, OH; Hon Rl; Lbry Ade; NHS; Sch Nwsp; Pep Clb; Letter Bsktbl; Ten; Letter Trk; Coach Actv; Mgrs; Univ; Med.

HINSHAW, B; Northeastern HS; Richmond, IN; 22/148 VP Chrs; Hon Rl; Sch Mus; Drama Clb; Pres 4-H; 4-H Awd; Ball State Univ; Music.

HINSHAW, TRACY; Carmel HS; Carmel, IN; 99/722 Cls Rep Frsh Cls; Chrh Wkr; Hon Rl; Off Ade; Stu Cncl; Pep Clb; Letter Chrldng; C of C Awd; Ind Univ; Bus.

HINSKY, DOUG; Bellmont HS; Decatur, IN; Pres Frsh Cls; Cls Rep Soph Cls; VP Jr Cls; Cls Rep Sr Cls; Am Leg Boys St; Hon Rl; NHS; Quill & Scroll; Stu Cncl; Sprt Ed Sch Nwsp; Ball St Univ; Cmmrcl Art.

HINSLEY, MARTIN; Charles F Brush HS; Lyndhurst, OH; Aud/Vis; Boy Scts; Hon Rl; Sct Actv; Fr Clb; Sci Clb; Coll; Busns Mgmt.

HINSMAN, MATTHEW; William Henry Harrison HS; W Lafayette, IN; 1/300 Band; Pres NHS; Stg Crw; Letter Crs Cntry; Letter Trk; IM Sprt; Opt Clb Awd; Purdue Univ; Sci.

HINTON, CATHY; Waverly HS; Waverly, OH; Chrh Wkr; Hon Rl; NHS; Off Ade; Fr Clb; FTA; Bus Schl.

HINTON, JANE; Delphos Jefferson HS; Delphos, OH; Sec Jr Cls; Band; Chrs; Hon Rl; Lbry Ade; NHS; Off Ade; Sch Mus; Y-Teens; Chrldng; College.

HINTON, KAY; Huron HS; Huron, OH; Chrs; Cmnty Wkr; Hon Rl; JA; Mdrgl; Sch Mus; Sch Pl; Pep Clb; Spn Clb; Bsbl; Kent State Univ.

HINTON, REGINA; Madison Comprehensive HS; Mansfield, OH; Chrs; Girl Scts; VP 4-H; Business School.

HINTZ, GWENDOLYN A; Marian HS; South Bend, IN; Hon Rl; JA; Stu Cncl; Yrbk; 4-H; 4-H Awd; Indiana Univ; Special Ed.

HINZ, PAUL; Port Hope Comm HS; Edina, MN; Sch Nwsp; Letter Ftbl; Concordia Coll; Lib Arts.

HINZ JR, LEON; Grand River Academy; Detroit, MI; 1/24 Cls Rep Frsh Cls; Cls Rep Soph Cls; Cl Rep Jr Cls; Hon Rl; NHS; Stu Cncl; Letter Bsktbl; Letter Socr; Letter Ten; Outstndng Student In Class; Headmasters Cup; Schl Chess Champ; College.

HINZMAN, BRENDA K; Mt Vernon Sr HS; Mt Vernon, OH; Chrh Wkr; Drl Tm; Lit Mag; Sch Mus; Pom Pon; College; Dance.

HINZMAN, DEBRA; Gilmer Co HS; Troy, WV; 1/97 Cls Rep Frsh Cls; Sec Soph Cls; Val; Debate Tm; Hon Rl; NHS; Stu Cncl; Yth Flsp; 4-H; FHA; West Virginia Univ; Bio.

HIPKISS, LAURI; Brooke HS; Wellsburg, WV; 30/470 Debate Tm; Hon Rl; Jr NHS; NHS; Quill & Scroll; Y-Teens; Yrbk; Pep Clb; Sci Clb; Spn Clb; W Liberty State College; Phys Ther.

HIPP, DAVID C; St Johns HS; Toledo, OH; 3/210 Boy Scts; Hon Rl; Sct Actv; Spn Clb; Ohio St Univ; Dentistry.

HIPP, STEVEN; Calvert HS; Tiffin, OH; 1/100 Cls Rep Soph Cls; Cl Rep Jr Cls; Chrh Wkr; Debate Tm; Hon Rl; JA; VP NHS; Stu Cncl; College; Math.

HIPPLE, JACQUELINE S; Howland Sr HS; Warren, OH; 30/450 Hon Rl; Jr NHS; NHS; Y-Teens; Yrbk; Sch Nwsp; Ger Clb; Sec Pep Clb; Trk; Letter Chrldng; College; Art.

HIPPLEHEUSER, ALAN; Terre Haute North Vigo HS; Terre Haute, IN; 7/600 Band; Pres Chrs; Hon Rl; JA; Mdrgl; Mod UN; Natl Forn Lg; Off Ade; Orch; Sch Mus; Jr Achvmnt Natl Personnel Finalist 50.

HIRE, WENDY; Edison HS; Milan, OH; 18/164 Band; Chrs; Chrh Wkr; Hon Rl; NHS; Drama Clb; Mgrs; Scr Kpr; Firelands Coll; Exec Secretary.

HIRSCH, DON; Kankakee Valley HS; Wheatfield, IN; 28/200 Band; Drm Bgl; NHS; Stu Cncl; Mth Clb; Sci Clb; Crs Cntry; Trk; Wrstlng; 4-H Awd; College; Math.

HIRSCH, PAULA; Kenton Ridge HS; Springfield, OH; 31/170 Off Ade; Rptr Yrbk; Boy Scts; FHA; Trk; Chrldng; GAA; Pom Pon; Univ; Sec.

HIRSCH, PETREA; Adena HS; Frankfort, OH; 19/82 Band; Hon Rl; Jr NHS; NHS; Off Ade; Y-Teens; Yrbk; Rptr Sch Nwsp; 4-H; 4-H Awd; Ohi Univ; Elementary Ed.

HIRSCH, SARAH; North Posey HS; Poseyville, IN; Am Leg Aux Girls St; Hon Rl; Red Cr Ade; Pep Clb; Bsktbl; Trk; GAA; IM Sprt; Mgrs; Univ Of Evansville; Early Child Dev.

HIRSCHINGER, CHARLES; Muncie Northside HS; Muncie, IN; Ger Clb; Swmmng; Purdue Univ; Civil Engr.

HIRTH, CATHY; Seton HS; Cincinnati, OH; Girl Scts; Hon Rl; Sct Actv; Spn Clb; Letter Gym; Socr; Chrldng; Xavier Thomas Moore Univ; Med Tech.

HIRZEL, BARBARA; Whitehall Yearling HS; Columbus, OH; Cls Rep Frsh Cls; Cls Rep Soph Cls; Letter Bsktbl; Letter Chrldng; PPFtbl; Scr Kpr; Tmr; Ohio St Univ; Psych.

HIRZEL, KATHY; Northwood HS; Nothwood, OH; Sec Jr Cls; Band; Chrs; Girl Scts; Hon Rl; Stu Cncl; Rptr Yrbk; Ger Clb; Bsbl; Bsktbl; Girls Varsity Bsktbl MVP; Head Majorette; Coll.

HISE, JOE; Lincoln HS; Wallace, WV; Aud/Vis; Boy Scts; Chrh Wkr; Cmnty Wkr; Hon Rl; NHS; VICA; VP Of Voc Ind Clubs Of Amer 78; 3rd Pl Contstnt In The Radio T V Repair Cntst Hld At United Career Cntr 78; Engr.

HISEK, THOMAS; Padua Franciscan HS; Seven Hls, OH; 20/280 Hon Rl; Lat Clb; Glf; Coach Actv; IM Sprt; Natl Merit Ltr; St Columokille Schlrshp 76; Marquette Univ; Jrnlsm.

HISER, JODINE; Adena HS; Clarksburg, OH; Chrs; Hon Rl; Off Ade; Sch Pl; Y-Teens; Yrbk; Rptr Sch Nwsp; Drama Clb; 4-H; Capt Chrldng; Ohio St Univ; Elem Ed.

HISER, KATHY A; Morgantown HS; Morgantown, WV; 28/500 Pres Hosp Ade; NHS; Rptr Yrbk; Mth Clb; Pep Clb; IM Sprt; DAR Awd; Natl Merit SF; Tri Hi Y Club; W Va Univ Semi Final Scholarshp; West Virginia Univ; Speech Pathlgy.

HISER, NANCY; Newton HS; Bradford, OH; 10/50 Band; Chrs; Chrh Wkr; Hon Rl; Lbry Ade; Stg Crw; 4-H; FHA; 4-H Awd; College; Interior Decorating.

HISHON, CHRIS; Anchor Bay HS; Anchorville, MI; Boy Scts; Hon Rl; Pol Wkr; Sct Actv; Stg Crw; Ftbl; Trk; Mgrs; Scr Kpr; Tmr; Eagle Sct 79; Coll.

HISLE, GREGORY C; Williamsburg HS; Williamsburg, OH; 6/97 Pres Band; Pres Chrs; Hon Rl; Lbry Ade; MMM; NHS; Sch Mus; Sch Pl; Stu Cncl; Sch Nwsp; Cumberland Coll; Commrcl Art.

HISLIP, BRENT; North Knox HS; Freelandville, IN; Chrh Wkr; Cmnty Wkr; FCA; Hon Rl; NHS; Yth Flsp; 4-H; Bsbl; Bsktbl; Ftbl; Vincennes Univ; Drafting.

HISSOM, ERIC; Defiance HS; Defiance, OH; 23/300 Chrs; Chrh Wkr; Debate Tm; Hon Rl; NHS; Sch Mus; Sch Pl; Stg Crw; Drama Clb; Gym; Dist Rep For Nazarene Yth Intl 78; Mt Vernon Nazarene Univ; Cmnctns.

HISSOM, MIKE; Woodshield HS; Woodsfield, OH; Cls Rep Frsh Cls; Band; Chrs; Chrh Wkr; Hon Rl; Sch Pl; Stu Cncl; Rptr Yrbk; Drama Clb; Fr Clb; Ohio State Univ; Aeronautical Engr.

HITCHCOCK, JUDI; Covington HS; Covington, OH; VP Frsh Cls; Band; Drm Mjrt; Hon Rl; NHS; Fr Clb; Letter Trk; Chrldng; PPFtbl; Club Tri Hi Y 77 80; Head Majorette 78; Edison St Cmnty Coll; Sales.

HITCHCOCK, KELLY; Madison Comprehensive HS; Mansfield, OH; Band; Girl Scts; Orch; Yth Flsp; VFW Awd; Voice Dem Awd; College; Accounting.

HITCHCOCK, KIMBERLY; Heath HS; Heath, OH; Hon Rl; Hosp Ade; Spn Clb; Letter Gym; Chrldng; Lion Awd; Rotary Awd; Spanish Awd; Newarks Rotary Club Camp Enterprise; Received Most Dedicated For Gymnastics; College; Comp Sci.

HITCHCOCK, LYNDA; Columbia HS; Columbia St, OH; Pres Band; Hon Rl; NHS; Off Ade; Sprt Ed Yrbk; 4-H; Fr Clb; Pep Clb; Trk; Chrldng; Lorain Cnty Cmnty Coll.

HITCHCOCK, NANCY; Triway HS; Shreve, OH; Band; Chrs; FCA; Girl Scts; Hon Rl; Off Ade; Stg Crw; Drama Clb; 4-H; Spn Clb; Eastern Kentucky Univ; Spec Educ.

HITCHCOCK, PATRICIA; Hazel Park HS; Hazel Park, MI; 1/306 Cls Rep Frsh Cls; Cls Rep Soph Cls; VP Jr Cls; Val; Am Leg Aux Girls St; Band; Hon Rl; Alma College; Bus.

HITCHCOCK, SALENE; Holy Redeemer HS; Detroit, MI; Pres Frsh Cls; Pres Soph Cls; Pres Jr Cls; Hon Rl; NHS; Eng Clb; Capt Crs Cntry; Univ.

HITCHCOCK, STEPHEN; Heath HS; Heath, OH; Band; Hon Rl; Sch Pl; Stg Crw; Drama Clb; Ohio State; Engr.

HITCHENS, JOSEPH; Mt Clemens HS; Mt Clemens, MI; Chrh Wkr; Hon Rl; JA; Jr NHS; NHS; Schlstc Awd 79; Western Michigan Univ; Math.

HITCHENS, RICHARD; Shaker Hts HS; Shaker Hts, OH; 5/470 Chrs; Bsktbl; Ten; Early Exposure To Engr Progr At Case W Reserve Univ 77; Ashlnd Coll Bsktbl Camp Foul Shtng Champ 78; Univ Of Cincinnati; Acctg.

HITCHINS, MICHAEL; Ypsilanti HS; Ypsilanti, MI; Hon Rl; NHS; Sch Mus; Sch Pl; Stg Crw; Stu Cncl; Drama Clb; Ftbl; Capt Swmmng; Tmr; E Mich Univ; Law.

HITE, DALE; Whiteland Community HS; Franklin, IN; Band; Boy Scts; FCA; Hon Rl; VP NHS; Sct Actv; Yth Flsp; 4-H; Key Clb; VP OEA; IUPUI; Comp Sci.

HITE, DANIEL; Centerville HS; Richmond, IN; 8/175 Pres Jr Cls; Band; Hon Rl; NHS; Pol Wkr; Sch Mus; Pres Stu Cncl; Spn Clb; Letter Crs Cntry; Letter Trk; Ind Univ; Ancient History.

HITE, JERRY; Greenville HS; Greenville, OH; Cls Rep Soph Cls; Cl Rep Jr Cls; Hon Rl; Bsktbl; Ftbl; Bluffton Coll; Elem Educ.

HITE, MIKE; Plymouth HS; Plymouth, IN; Hon Rl; Stg Crw; Fr Clb; Letter Bsbl; Letter Bsktbl; Letter Ftbl; Coach Actv; JC Awd; Pres Awd; Univ; Law.

HITE, REBECCA; Lakeview HS; Cortland, OH; Chrs; Chrh Wkr; CAP; Girl Scts; Hon Rl; Yth Flsp; Y-Teens; Pep Clb; Mas Awd; Chrl Mst Imprbd Singer 76; Outstndng Jr Female Chrl 78; Youngstown St Univ; Music Educ.

HITE, SHERRI H; Buffalo HS; Huntington, WV; 3/150 Band; Hon Rl; Off Ade; Sch Pl; Yth Flsp; Yrbk; FHA; Mth Clb;.

HITE, SHERRI; Buffalo HS; Huntington, WV; 3/150 Band; Hon Rl; NHS; Sch Pl; Yth Flsp; Yrbk; Drama Clb; FHA; OEA; College; Sec.

HITE, STEPHEN; Columbian HS; Tiffin, OH; 1/342 Band; Boy Scts; Chrs; Hon Rl; Sch Mus; Drama Clb; Natl Merit Ltr; 12th In Oh St Div 1 Oh Tst Of Schlstc Achvmnt In Chem 79; Outstndg Sci Stu E Jr HS 77; Univ; Bio.

HITE, TREVA; Gwinn HS; Gwinn, MI; Band; Hon Rl; Letter Swmmng; Mgrs; Northern Mic Univ; Acctg.

HITE, TY; Greenfield Central HS; Greenfield, IN; 112/318 Cls Rep Soph Cls; Drama Clb; 4-H; Bsbl; Bsktbl; Crs Cntry; Ftbl; Glf; Trk; Chrldng; Univ.

HITES, THOMAS; Madison HS; Madison, OH; 35/298 Cls Rep Frsh Cls; Aud/Vis; Chrs; Hon Rl; Stu Cncl; Letter Bsbl; Akron Univ; Poli Sci.

HITESHEW, M; Lewis County HS; Weston, WV; Cls Rep Frsh Cls; Aud/Vis; Band; Chrs; Jr NHS; VP Stu Cncl; Y-Teens; Sch Nwsp; Pres Drama Clb; Wv Univ; Elem Educ.

HITI, FRANK; Lake Catholic HS; Euclid, OH; 30/330 Cls Rep Frsh Cls; Cls Rep Soph Cls; Hon Rl; Stu Cncl; Rptr Sch Nwsp; Letter Trk; College; Science.

HITOW, TOBI; Southfield Lathrup Sr HS; Southfield, MI; Hon Rl; Pol Wkr; Michigan St Univ; Law.

HITSELBERGER, CHARLES; Sandusky St Mary Cath HS; Bay City, MI; Aud/Vis; Drl Tm; Ger Clb; Key Clb; Sci Clb; Trk; Natl Merit Ltr; Univ Of Michigan; Comp Sci.

HITT, RAY; Stryker HS; Stryker, OH; 1/50 Val; Band; Hon Rl; NHS; Bausch & Lomb Awd; Schlrshp Oh Acad 79; Math Awd Otstndng Musician Awd 79; Best All Around Boy Awd 79; Univ Of Cincinnati; Elec Engr.

HITTIE, DEANNE; Struthers HS; Struthers, OH; Trs Soph Cls; Trs Jr Cls; Trs Sr Cls; Cmp Fr Grls; Treas Chrs; Treas JA; Sch Mus; Sch Pl; Treas Stu Cncl; Y-Teens; Youngstown St Univ; Acctg.

HITTLE, BONNIE; Tri Valley HS; Dresden, OH; Trs Soph Cls; Pres Jr Cls; Cl Rep Jr Cls; Pres Sr Cls; Band; Chrh Wkr; Treas Yth Flsp; Pres 4-H Awd; Newark State; Home Ec.

HITTLE, CARRIE; Kankakee Valley HS; Wheatfield, IN; 13/250 Cl Rep Jr Cls; Band; Chrh Wkr; Cmnty Wkr; Drl Tm; Drm Bgl; Hon Rl; NHS; 4-H; Pep Clb; Natl 4 H Achvmnt Records 79; Alternate For Hoosier Girls St 79; Alternate For St Public Speaking Contest 79; Univ.

HITTLE, GARY; Greenville Sr HS; Greenville, OH; Band; Chrs; Hon Rl; Orch; Sch Mus; Sct Actv; Yth Flsp; Pep Clb; Spn Clb; Ftbl; Ohio St Univ; Policeman.

HITTLER, JOAN M; Our Lady Of Mercy HS; Lathrup Village, MI; VP Boy Scts; NHS; Sch Pl; Stu Cncl; Rptr Yrbk; Ger Clb; Sci Clb; Natl Merit SF; Suma College; Psych.

HITTNER, DAVID; Vandalia Butler Sr HS; Dayton, OH; 18/380 Band; Boy Scts; Hon Rl; Lbry Ade; NHS; Stg Crw; Boys Clb Am; Drama Clb; Fr Clb; Natl Merit Ltr; De Pauw Univ; Sci.

HIVELY, DARLA; Meadowbrook HS; Pleasant City, OH; 25/179 Hon Rl; Lbry Ade; NHS; Off Ade; Sch Pl; Rptr Yrbk; Pres FBLA; Pep Clb; Trk; Capt Chrldng; Sec.

HIXON, DEBORAH; Lincoln HS; Shinnston, WV; Cl Rep Jr Cls; Cls Rep Sr Cls; Hon Rl; Lbry Ade; Sch Pl; Stg Crw; Stu Cncl; Ed Sch Nwsp; Rptr Sch Nwsp; Drama Clb; 3rd Pl Poetry Contst; Co Fnd & Treas Chrstn Stdnt Club; Comp Tech Schl; Comp Tech.

HIXON, PAUL; Ironton HS; Ironton, OH; Hon Rl; Sci Clb; Spn Clb; Letter Ten; IM Sprt; Ohio St Univ; Acctng.

HIZA, JENNIFER; Muskegon HS; Muskegon, MI; Hon Rl; Hosp Ade; Lbry Ade; College; Architect.

HJORTSBERG, FREDERICK; Maumee HS; Maumee, OH; 45/300 IM Sprt; Natl Merit Ltr; Ohio St Univ; Dent.

HLAD, SANDY; Morton Sr HS; Hammond, IN; 2/419 Hon Rl; Quill & Scroll; Sprt Ed Sch Nwsp; Rptr Sch Nwsp; Fr Clb; Pep Clb; Letter Bsktbl; PPFtbl; College; Lib Arts.

HLUCK, GEORGE; Padua Franciscan HS; N Royalton, OH; 9/258 Hon Rl; NHS; Ger Clb; Mth Clb; Sci Clb; Letter Crs Cntry; Socr; Trk; West Point Acad; Sci.

HLYNSKY, VERA; Perry HS; Canton, OH; Hon Rl; NHS; Fr Clb; College.

HO, PAMELA; Niles Sr HS; Niles, MI; Girl Scts; Hon Rl; Off Ade; Yrbk; 4-H; FBLA; Pep Clb; 4-H Awd; Western Michigan Univ; Spec Ed.

HOADLEY, REGINA; Hammond HS; Hammond, IN; 35/333 Band; Girl Scts; Hon Rl; Jr NHS; Orch; Fr Clb; Purdue Univ; Elem Ed.

HOAG, JOHN; Ida HS; Monroe, MI; 19/160 Band; Chrs; NHS; 4-H; Vocational School.

HOAG, JOHN C; Wadsworth Sr HS; Wadsworth, OH; 1/367 Val; Am Leg Boys St; Boy Scts; Yth Flsp; Key Clb; Mth Clb; Trk; Ohio Board Of Regents Schlrshp; Medina Cnty Stu Of Yr; Case Academic Schlrshp; Case Western Reserve Univ.

HOAG, LINDA; Marysville HS; St Clair, MI; Chrh Wkr; Girl Scts; Hon Rl; Lbry Ade; Sct Actv; 4-H; Scr Kpr; Cit Awd; 4-H Awd; Bus Schl; Bus.

HOAG, MELISSA; L C Mohr HS; South Haven, MI; 8/230 Chrs; NHS; Orch; Pep Clb; Am Leg Awd; Kiwan Awd; Central Michigan Univ.

HOAG, STEVEN; Springport HS; Springport, MI; Band; Hon Rl; Lbry Ade; Off Ade; Sch Pl; Bsktbl; Duke Univ; Economics Bus.

HOAGLIN, RUSSELL; Concord Community HS; Concord, MI; Hon Rl; Jackson Community College; Data Proc.

HOAGLUND, TERRI; Pine River HS; Tustin, MI; Chrs; Chrh Wkr; Hon Rl; Natl Forn Lg; NHS; Yth Flsp; Nursing Schl; Nursing.

HOAGLUND, TERRI; Pine River Jr Sr HS; Tustin, MI; 2/90 Sal; Chrs; Chrh Wkr; Hon Rl; Natl Forn Lg; NHS; Stg Crw; Yth Flsp; Butler Worth Schl Nursing; Nurse.

HOALT, TRACEE; North Knox HS; Bicknell, IN; 25/154 Trs Sr Cls; Chrh Wkr; Girl Scts; Hon Rl; Off Ade; Stu Cncl; 4-H; Pep Clb; Chrldng; Ivy Tech Coll; Med Lab Asst.

HOAR, MIKE; Tiffin Columbian HS; Tiffin, OH; Aud/Vis; Chrs; Hon Rl; Sprt Ed Yrbk; Sch Nwsp; Spn Clb; Bsbl; Ftbl; Glf; IM Sprt; Bowling Green St Univ; Pre Med.

HOARD, BRUCE; Ithaca Public HS; Ithaca, MI; Band; Hon Rl; Rptr Sch Nwsp; Sch Nwsp; Letter Ftbl; Mi State Univ; Chemistry.

HOARD, STEVE; Breckenridge Jr Sr HS; St Louis, MI; 5/100 Hon Rl; NHS; Yth Flsp; 4-H; FFA; Bsbl; Letter Ftbl; 4-H Awd; Michigan St Univ; Ag.

HOARD, STEVEN F; Breckenridge Jr Sr HS; St Louis, MI; 5/110 Hon Rl; NHS; Pres Yth Flsp; 4-H; FFA; Letter Ftbl; 4-H Awd; FFA State Skills Contest Gold Awd; Attended HS Engr Inst Michigan St Univ; Michigan State Univ; Agri.

HOARD, VERONICA; Shepherd HS; Shepherd, MI; Band; Girl Scts; Hon Rl; FTA; Letter Bsktbl; Letter Trk; Coach Actv; PPFtbl; Outstndng Frsh Band; High Pt Jr Track; Ctrl Michigan Univ; Photog.

HOBART, STEPHEN; Bishop Watterson HS; Columbus, OH; 40/289 Boy Scts; Hon Rl; Letter Trk; Letter Wrstlng; Univ Of Cincinnati; Engr.

HOBAUGH, JAMES O; Seeger Memorial HS; West Lebanon, IN; 2/145 Pres Frsh Cls; Pres Soph Cls; Pres Jr Cls; Am Leg Boys St; Hon Rl; NHS; Stg Crw; Pres Stu Cncl; Pep Clb; Letter Ftbl; Indiana St Univ; Accounting.

HOBBA, HOLLY; Green HS; Akron, OH; Band; Chrs; Girl Scts; Hon Rl; Hosp Ade; NHS; Sch Mus; Stu Cncl; Bsktbl; Trk; Akron Univ; Acctg.

HOBBA, WILLIAM J; Green HS; Akron, OH; 1/320 Val; Boy Scts; Chrs; VP FCA; Pres NHS; Sct Actv; Stg Crw; Yth Flsp; Ed Yrbk; Letter Wrstlng; Case Western Reserve Univ; Elec Engr.

HOBBS, ALICIA; Richmond HS; Richmond, IN; Band; Chrs; Hon Rl; Hosp Ade; Jr NHS; Lbry Ade; NHS; FBLA; Y-Teens; Spn Clb; College; Bus.

HOBBS, GREGORY; Western HS; Russiaville, IN; 25/220 Hon Rl; NHS; Sch Nwsp; Sec FFA;.

HOBBS, JACQUELINE; Father Joseph Wehrle Mem HS; Columbus, OH; Drl Tm; Hon Rl; JA; Lat Clb; Natl Merit Ltr; Ohio St Univ; Engr.

HOBBS, JEFFREY; Salem HS; Salem, IN; 50/168 Aud/Vis; JA; Ball St Univ.

HOBBS, JODY; Madison Hts HS; Anderson, IN; 23/407 Band; Drm Bgl; Girl Scts; Hon Rl; NHS; Off Ade; Sct Actv; 4-H; Fr Clb; OEA; Ofc Educ Assoc Ach Awd; Ball St Univ; Busns Ed.

HOBBS, KATHY; Morgantown HS; Morgantown, WV; Band; Hon Rl; Jr NHS; Sch Pl; Stu Cncl; Yrbk; Drama Clb; Pep Clb; IM Sprt; Twrlr; West Virginia Univ; Bus.

HOBBS, LISA; Douglas Mac Arthur HS; Saginaw, MI; Cls Rep Soph Cls; Band; Hon Rl; NHS; Sch Mus; Stu Cncl; Yth Flsp; Pom Pon; Collegef Medical Technology.

HOBBS, MARK; Clinton Massie HS; Clarksville, OH; Chrs; Chrh Wkr; Hon Rl; Sch Pl; Sct Actv; Spn Clb; Crs Cntry; Ftbl; Trk; Coach Actv; 9th In Oh St Crss Cntry Meet 77; Univ; Cmmrcl Pilot.

HOBBS, MELISSA; Brookhaven HS; Columbus, OH; Sec Frsh Cls; Trs Sr Cls; Chrs; Girl Scts; Hon Rl; Sct Actv; Fr Clb; OEA; Pep Clb; Bsbl; Southeast Career Center; Admin.

HOBBS, TARA; Robert S Rogers HS; Toledo, OH; Trs Frsh Cls; Trs Soph Cls; Cl Rep Jr Cls; Band; JA; Off Ade; Orch; Spn Clb; IM Sprt; PPFtbl; College; Social Science.

HOBBS, THERESA M; Edgewood HS; Bloomington, IN; Chrs; Hon Rl; Off Ade; PAVAS; Sch Mus; Pep Clb; Letter Chrldng; Indiana Univ; Music.

HOBBS, VARNA M; Patterson Co Op HS; Dayton, OH; Chrs; Chrh Wkr; JA; VICA; IM Sprt; Psychtrst.

HOBLER, MELINDA; Memorial HS; St Marys, OH; 4-H; FHA; Pep Clb; Wright St Univ; Art.

HOBRLA, SHARON; Lansing Everett HS; Lansing, MI; Aud/Vis; Girl Scts; JA; Jr NHS; NHS; Pep Clb; Letter Crs Cntry; Trk; Univ; Engr.

HOBSON, DOUG; New Richmond HS; New Richmond, OH; Am Leg Boys St; FCA; NHS; Quill & Scroll; Yth Flsp; Drama Clb; Glf; Am Leg Awd; Kiwan Awd; Natl Merit SF; Ohio State Univ; Dentistry.

HOBSON, LORI; Eastern HS; Pekin, IN; VP Frsh Cls; Trs Soph Cls; Band; Drl Tm; Stu Cncl; 4-H; Pep Clb; Spn Clb; Bsktbl; Trk;.

HOBSON, MARK; Orleans HS; Orleans, IN; 20/70 Cl Rep Jr Cls; Band; Chrh Wkr; Drm Mjrt; Hon Rl; 4-H; Crs Cntry; Letter Trk; Coach Actv; 4-H Awd; Ball St Univ; Archt.

HOCHENDONER, MICHELE H; Jackson Milton HS; Lake Milton, OH; Pres Soph Cls; Band; Girl Scts; Hon Rl; Off Ade; Orch; Sch Mus; Sct Actv; Stu Cncl; Key Clb; College.

HOCHSTETLER, KAREN; Northwestern HS; West Salem, OH; 17/97 Treas Chrs; Hon Rl; Sch Mus; Yth Flsp; Sch Nwsp; 4-H; Pres FHA; Pep Clb; Ashland Coll; Fashion Mdse.

HOCHSTETLER, KATHYRN; Bethany Christian HS; Goshen, IN; Sec Soph Cls; Trs Sr Cls; Chrs; Chrh Wkr; Hon Rl; Orch; Ed Sch Nwsp; 4-H; Ger Clb; Ten; College; Journalism.

HOCK, LISSIE; Otsego HS; Bowling Green, OH; 17/110 Am Leg Aux Girls St; Band; Hon Rl; Jr NHS; Off Ade; Orch; Sch Pl; Stg Crw; Drama Clb; Fr Clb; All Oh St Fair Band 78; All Cnty Band 77; Bowling Green St Univ; Music Educ.

HOCK, TERESA; Freeland HS; Freeland, MI; 5/118 Sec Frsh Cls; Pres Jr Cls; Hon Rl; Jr NHS; NHS; Letter Bsbl; Capt Bsktbl; Chrldng; Natl Merit Schl; Schlstc Feml Athlt 79; N Mi Univ Bd Of Controls 79; Drafgng Hist & Govt Awd 78; Northern Michigan Univ; Archt.

HOCKER, ALITA; Greenfield Central HS; Greenfield, IN; Band; Drl Tm; Jr NHS; NHS; Spn Clb; Mat Maids; Ind State Ball State; Life Sci Bio.

HOCKER, DARREL; Bellaire HS; Bellaire, OH; Trs Frsh Cls; Hon Rl; Ftbl; Letter Trk; IM Sprt; College; Law.

HOCKER, RICHARD; Franklin Monroe HS; Greenville, OH; 21/77 VP Frsh Cls; Pres Soph Cls; Cl Rep Jr Cls; FCA; Hon Rl; NHS; Sch Pl; Stu Cncl; Rptr Sch Nwsp; FFA; Wilmington Coll; Agriculture Ec.

HOCKER, RICK; Southeastern HS; Richmondale, OH; 4/93 Pres Jr Cls; Pres Sr Cls; Band; Chrs; Chrh Wkr; Hon Rl; Jr NHS; NHS; Orch; Sch Pl; Ohio Northern Univ; Eng.

HOCTEL, CINDY; Van Buren HS; Findly, OH; Sec Frsh Cls; Band; Cmp Fr Grls; Chrs; Hon Rl; Lbry Ade; Sch Mus; Yth Flsp; Rptr Yrbk; Mat Maids; Anderson College; Bus Admin.

HODAK, KURT; Washington HS; Massillon, OH; Am Leg Boys St; Band; Hon Rl; NHS; Orch; Ger Clb; College; Bus Admin.

HODDER, TANYA; Sault Area HS; Slt Ste Marie, MI; 35/280 Chrh Wkr; Hon Rl; NHS; Treas Lat Clb; IM Sprt; Lion Awd; St Of Mi Compt Shclhsp 79; Hon Of Achvmnt In Latin 79; Lake Superior St Coll; Comp Progr.

HODGE, BRUCE; Cleveland Cntrl Catholic HS; Cleveland, OH; Cls Rep Frsh Cls; Cls Rep Soph Cls; Cl Rep Jr Cls; Sal; Am Leg Boys St; Hon Rl; Mod UN; NHS; Stu Cncl; Ftbl; Blackburn College; Law.

HODGE, DEBBIE; Greenbrier East HS; Ronceverte, WV; 18/413 Band; Chrs; Chrh Wkr; FCA; Hon Rl; Orch; Pep Clb; Chrldng; Twrlr;.

HODGE, DENISE; East Kentwood HS; Kentwood, MI; Chrs; Chrh Wkr; Spn Clb; Trk; PPFtbl; Michigan St Univ; Law.

HODGE, JANET E; Peru HS; Peru, IN; VP Jr Cls; Chrs; Cmnty Wkr; Hon Rl; Sch Mus; Stu Cncl; Yth Flsp; Rptr Sch Nwsp; Pep Clb; Bsktbl; Univ Of California; Foreign Language.

HODGE, JENNIFER; Warrensville Hts HS; Warrensvl Hts, OH; Cmp Fr Grls; Chrs; Chrh Wkr; Hosp Ade; JA; Off Ade; Stu Cncl; FHA; Pep Clb; Rdo Clb; Kent St Univ; Acctg.

HODGE, LAURIE; West Lafayette HS; West Lafayette, IN; Cls Rep Frsh Cls; FCA; Hon Rl; Stu Cncl; Yth Flsp; Keyettes; Pep Clb; Trk; Chrldng; Univ; Dent Hygn.

HODGE, NICOLE; Cody HS; Detroit, MI; Hon Rl; Wayne State; Psychology.

HODGE, PAUL; Allegan HS; Allegan, MI; 6/193 VP Sr Cls; Hon Rl; NHS; Stu Cncl; Bsktbl; Letter Crs Cntry; Letter Trk; Rotary Awd; Dollars For Schlrs Schlrshp; St Of Michigan Schlrshp; Ferris St Coll Merit Schlrshp; Ferris St Coll; Optometry.

HODGE, STEPHEN; Princeton HS; Princeton, WV; 134/370 Pres Soph Cls; Boy Scts; Chrs; FCA; Sch Pl; Sct Actv; Stu Cncl; Yth Flsp; Fr Clb; Key Clb; Life Scout 78; Tennis Regnl Winner 79; West Virginia Univ; Bus.

HODGES, CYNTHIA; William Henry Harrison HS; W Lafayette, IN; Trs Frsh Cls; Hst Jr Cls; VP Sr Cls; Cls Rep Sr Cls; Band; Hon Rl; Off Ade; 4-H; Keyettes; Pep Clb; Purdue.

HODGES, DAVID B; Aquinas HS; Southgate, MI; Hon Rl; Letter Wrstlng; Central Mic College; Gen Bus.

HODGES, LAURA; Belding HS; Belding, MI; Band; Chrh Wkr; FCA; Hon Rl; NHS; Sch Mus; Yth Flsp; 4-H; Pep Clb; Bsktbl; Grand Rapids Baptist Coll; Psych.

HODGES, LORI; Seton HS; Cincinnati, OH; 25/270 Hon Rl; Pep Clb; Bsktbl; Socr; Coach Actv; Capt IM Sprt; Edgecliff; Art.

HODGES, MARY; Hastings HS; Hastings, MI; Chrs; Hon Rl; NHS; PAVAS; Sch Mus; Sch Pl; Stg Crw; Ed Sch Nwsp; Rptr Sch Nwsp; Sch Nwsp; Michigan St Univ; Acctg.

HODGES, NORELL; Buchtel University HS; Akron, OH; Band; Chrs; Chrh Wkr; Cmnty Wkr; Drm Bgl; Hon Rl; Orch; Sch Mus; Sch Nwsp; DECA; Univ Of Akron; Bus Admin.

HODGES, TERESA; Hastings HS; Hastings, MI; Chrs; Ferris St Coll; Respiratory Ther.

HODGES, TIM D; Carmel HS; Carmel, IN; 14/680 Hon Rl; NHS; Letter Ftbl; Letter Trk; IM Sprt; JETS Awd; Natl Merit Ltr; Wabash Honor Schlrshp; Firestone Corp Schlrshp; Indiana St Commission Schlrshp; Wabash Coll; Medicine.

HODGESON, NANCY; Northwestern HS; Wooster, OH; Band; Chrs; Hon Rl; Sch Mus; Drama Clb; Lat Clb; Pep Clb; Bsktbl; Trk; PPFtbl;.

HODIL, LISA; Brush HS; Lyndhurst, OH; 52/650 Girl Scts; Hon Rl; Lbry Ade; NHS; Rptr Yrbk; IM Sprt; Ohio State Univ; Math.

HODNICKI, LINDA; Our Lady Of Mt Carmel HS; Lincoln Park, MI; 8/62 Aud/Vis; Chrs; Chrh Wkr; Hon Rl; NHS; Off Ade; Sch Mus; Pep Clb; College; Special Ed.

HODOVAL, JODI; Marshall HS; Marshall, MI; 16/258 Chrh Wkr; Cmnty Wkr; Hon Rl; Jr NHS; NHS; Off Ade; Yth Flsp; IM Sprt; Natl Merit Ltr; Marshall Jr Miss 78; Pres Schslhp From Hillsdale Coll 79; Hillsdale Coll.

HODSDON, JONI; Ottawa Hills HS; Grand Rapids, MI; Cls Rep Soph Cls; Chrh Wkr; Hon Rl; Jr NHS; Natl Forn Lg; NHS; Drama Clb; FDA; College; Theatre.

HODSON, DEENA K; Triton Central HS; Fairland, IN; 3/163 Chrs; Chrh Wkr; Capt Drl Tm; FCA; NHS; Off Ade; Sec Sch Pl; Sec Stu Cncl; Sec Drama Clb; Pres 4-H; Indiana Univ; Phys Ther.

HODSON, KAREN; Shenandoah HS; Shirley, IN; 3/124 Am Leg Aux Girls St; Hon Rl; NHS; VP Spn Clb; JETS Awd; Ball St Univ; Acctg.

HOEDEMAN, MICHAEL; Mason HS; Mason, MI; Band; Boy Scts; Chrh Wkr; Cmnty Wkr; Hon Rl; Jr NHS; Sch Mus; God Cntry Awd; Lion Awd; Natl Merit Ltr; Michigan St Univ; Acctg.

HOEFEL, EUGNE; Adlai Stevenson HS; Sterling Hts, MI; Hon Rl; NHS; Lawerence Inst Of Tec; Architecture.

HOEFEL, ROSEANNE; Buchtel Univ HS; Akron, OH; 8/452 Chrs; Hon Rl; Jr NHS; NHS; Off Ade; Sch Mus; Mth Clb; Scr Kpr; Tmr; Awds Of Excellence In Hlth & Earth Sci 1978; Mu Alpha Theta Mbrshp & Plcmnt In French Aptitude Tst 1978; Univ Of Akron; Math.

HOEFENER, JUDSON; Shelbyville HS; Shelbyville, IN; Hosp Ade; Glf; IM Sprt; Ind Univ; Commerical Art.

HOEFERLIN, MICHELLE; Ursuline HS; Hubbard, OH; Chrs; Hon Rl; Natl Forn Lg; Stg Crw; Pres Drama Clb; Fr Clb; Pep Clb; Scr Kpr; Univ Of Michigan; Pre Med.

HOEFFEL, CYNTHIA; Napoleon HS; Napoleon, OH; Chrs; Hon Rl; Jr NHS; NHS; 4-H; Fr Clb; FHA; College; Business Admin.

HOEFFLER, CHRIS; Reading HS; Cincinnati, OH; Cls Rep Frsh Cls; Off Ade; Pep Clb; Scr Kpr; Univ; Acctg.

HOEFFOER, CHRISTINE; Warren HS; Warren, MI; Hon Rl; NHS; Sch Mus; Stg Crw; Ten; Univ Of Mic; Engr Architect.

HOEFLICH, ANNE; Greenville Sr HS; Greenville, OH; 30/360 Chrs; Chrh Wkr; Hon Rl; NHS; Sch Mus; Sch Pl; Stg Crw; Yth Flsp; Drama Clb; Perfect Attendance Awd;.

HOEFLICH, LORRI; New Richmond HS; New Richmond, OH; Band; Orch; Sch Mus; Sch Pl; Yrbk; VP Fr Clb; IM Sprt; Scr Kpr; Univ Of Cinn; Tchr.

HOEFLICH, NANCY; Clear Fork HS; Butler, OH; 2/164 Hon Rl; NHS; FHA; Treas Spn Clb; Sec VICA; GAA; Univ; Dent Hygnst.

HOEFLINGER, SU ELLEN; Flint Christian HS; Clio, MI; VP Jr Cls; Pres Sr Cls; Chrs; Chrh Wkr; Hon Rl; Hosp Ade; VP Yth Flsp; Yrbk; Rptr Sch Nwsp; Letter Bsktbl; Christian Character Awd; MVP Defensive Girls Bsktbll; Varsity Clb Pres; Sports Awds; College; Nursing.

HOEFT, ROBERTA; Pioneer HS; Ann Arbor, MI; Chrh Wkr; Girl Scts; Hon Rl; Off Ade; Drama Clb; Pep Clb; Mat Maids; Concordia Coll; Psych.

HOEFT, SCOTT; Adrian HS; Adrian, MI; Hon Rl; Jr NHS; NHS; Mth Clb; Sci Clb; Ftbl; Natl Merit Ltr; Univ; Pre Med.

HOEGEMAN, STEVEN R; Taylor HS; Cleves, OH; Chrh Wkr; Letter Bsbl; Bsktbl; Ftbl; Scr Kpr; College.

HOEH, MARY; Brethren HS; Kaleva, MI; Cl Rep Jr Cls; Trs Sr Cls; Chrs; Hon Rl; Lbry Ade; Rptr Yrbk; Sch Nwsp; Drama Clb; FHA; Bsbl; Central Mich Univ; Library Sci.

HOEHN, DEBRA A; Ottawa Glandorf HS; Ottawa, OH; Band; Sch Mus; Stg Crw; Sprt Ed Yrbk; Sprt Ed Sch Nwsp; Drama Clb; Sci Clb; GAA; Bowling Green Area School; Nursing.

HOEHNE, BRENDA K; Russia Local School; Houston, OH; 7/44 Sec Frsh Cls; Sec Soph Cls; Band; Chrs; Hon Rl; Stu Cncl; OEA;.

HOEHNER, PAUL J; North Lutheran HS; Rochester, MI; 1/115 Washington Univ; Medicine.

HOEKSEMA, LORI L; Imlay City HS; Imlay City, MI; 2/185 Sal; Chrh Wkr; Hon Rl; Natl Forn Lg; NHS; Yrbk; Sprt Ed Sch Nwsp; Rptr Sch Nwsp; Sch Nwsp; Letter Bsktbl; Ferris St Coll; Adv.

HOEKSTRA, STEVE; Timothy Christian HS; Elmhust, IL; 15/92 Hon Rl; NHS; Sch Mus; Sch Nwsp; Drama Clb; IM Sprt; Trinity Christian Univ; Med.

HOENE, JEFF; Archbishop Alter HS; Kettering, OH; Hon Rl; NHS; Key Clb; Natl Merit Ltr; College; Natural Science.

HOENIE, JANE; Carroll HS; Dayton, OH; 14/285 Sec Frsh Cls; Chrh Wkr; Drl Tm; Hon Rl; NHS; Sch Nwsp; Ger Clb; Rus Clb; Trk; Pres Awd; College; Political Science.

HOENIE, JOANN; Celina HS; Celina, OH; Band; Chrh Wkr; Hon Rl; Jr NHS; NHS; Orch; Sch Mus; College; Med.

HOEPPNER, THERESA; Douglas Mac Arthur HS; Saginaw, MI; 14/300 Hon Rl; NHS; Pep Clb;.

HOERSTEN, STEPHEN A; Parkway HS; Rockford, OH; 17/85 Am Leg Boys St; Boy Scts; FCA; Rptr Yrbk; 4-H; Letter Ftbl; Letter Trk; Mgrs; Univ; Arch.

HOESS, FRANCIS; Bishop Noll Inst; Hammond, IN; 37/343 Hon Rl; Mth Clb; Letter Socr; Purdue Univ; Chem Engr.

HOESS, HEIDI; New Richmond HS; Bethel, OH; Band; Hon Rl; NHS; Stu Cncl; 4-H; Fr Clb; Pep Clb; Chrldng; Am Leg Awd; 4-H Awd; Univ; Zoology.

HOETING, DEBORAH A; Seton HS; Cincinnati, OH; 11/255 Chrs; Cmnty Wkr; Hon Rl; Jr NHS; NHS; Pep Clb; Socr; Trk; Coach Actv; GAA; College; Grahic Artist.

HOEVEL, KURT; Bishop Luers HS; Ft Wayne, IN; 7/200 Hon Rl; Jr NHS; NHS; Glf; College.

HOFACKER, JULIE; St Paul HS; Norwalk, OH; 26/84 Girl Scts; Hon Rl; Hosp Ade; Sch Pl; Sprt Ed Yrbk; Rptr Sch Nwsp; 4-H; Pep Clb; 4-H Awd; Firelands Coll; Early Chldhd Educ.

HOFACKER, MICKEY; Monroeville HS; Monroeville, OH; 2/95 Chrh Wkr; NHS; Letter Bsbl; Letter Bsktbl; Capt Ftbl; Coach Actv; College; Horticulture.

HOFACKER, VELDA; St Vincent St Mary HS; Akron, OH; 8/263 Cls Rep Soph Cls; Cl Rep Jr Cls; Cls Rep Sr Cls; Am Leg Aux Girls St; Chrh Wkr; Cmnty Wkr; Debate Tm; Hon Rl; Lbry Ade; Lit Mag; Univ Of Akron; Pre Law.

HOFACKER _II, GERALD; Bluffton HS; Bluffton, OH; 4/93 Chrs; Chrh Wkr; Hon Rl; NHS; Sch Mus; Sch Pl; VP Yth Flsp; Drama Clb; FTA; Lat Clb; Lima Tech College; Comp Prog.

HOFER, CATHIE; Menomineo HS; Menominee, MI; Girl Scts; Hon Rl; Jr NHS; Capt Trk; College; Pre Med.

HOFER, DEBORAH; Anderson HS; Anderson, IN; 100/463 Girl Scts; Hon Rl; Hosp Ade; Lbry Ade; Quill & Scroll; Yth Flsp; Y-Teens; Yrbk; Sch Nwsp; 4-H; Ball St Univ; Dietician.

HOFER, KENNETH A; Elwood Community HS; Elwood, IN; Boy Scts; Sch Pl; Stg Crw; Drama Clb; Lat Clb; Bsbl; Bsktbl; Ind Inst Of Tech; Mech Engr.

HOFER, KRISTINE; East Detroit HS; East Detroit, MI; 15/650 Hon Rl; NHS; Rptr Yrbk; Leo Clb; Mat Maids; Home Ec Department Awd 79; Adrian Coll; Fshn Mdse.

HOFER, STEVEN R; Warren Central HS; Indianapolis, IN; 78/840 Sch Mus; Drama Clb; IM Sprt; Natl Merit SF; Univ; Sci.

HOFF, BRIAN; Midland HS; Midland, MI; 25/480 Boy Scts; Chrh Wkr; Hon Rl; NHS; Pres PAVAS; Sch Pl; Sct Actv; Pres Yth Flsp; Drama Clb; 4-H; Hope Coll; Bio Chem.

HOFF, KEVIN; Washington HS; South Bend, IN; Hon Rl; Ten; Patrol Capt & Outstndng Patrol Bay 75; Charles F Sonneborn Sportmnshp Awd 77; 9 Yr Schslhtc Awd 76; Univ; Acctg.

HOFF, MARY E; Immaculate Conception Acad; Brookville, IN; 7/48 Cls Rep Frsh Cls; Chrs; Chrh Wkr; Cmnty Wkr; Girl Scts; Hon Rl; Pres NHS; Orch; Sch Mus; Sch Pl; Vincennes Univ; Agribusns.

HOFF, MICHAEL A; Buena Vista HS; Saginaw, MI; Band; Boy Scts; Hon Rl; 4-H; Sci Clb; Engineering.

HOFF, RICHARD; Marietta Sr HS; Marietta, OH; 34/408 Hon Rl; Bsbl; Marietta Coll; Acctg.

HOFF, TINA; Michigan Center HS; Munith, MI; Sec Jr Cls; Cls Rep Sr Cls; Hon Rl; NHS; Stg Crw; Bsktbl; Jackson Community College; Acctg.

HOFFENBERGER, KIRSTEN; Unionvil Sebewaing Area HS; Unionville, MI; Am Leg Aux Girls St; Band; Chrh Wkr; Cmnty Wkr; Girl Scts; Hon Rl; Sch Mus; Yth Flsp; Lat Clb; Bsbl; North Park Coll; Psych.

HOFFER, CLAIRE; Edwardsburg Sr HS; Edwardsbrg, MI; 3/150 Band; Chrs; Sch Mus; Pep Clb; Chrldng; Univ; Oceanography.

HOFFER, JOSEPH; Bishop Luers HS; Ft Wayne, IN; Boy Scts; Hon Rl; Sct Actv; Ger Clb; Bsktbl; Hockey; Socr; Univ.

HOFFER, THERESA; Guernsey Catholic Cntrl HS; Cambridge, OH; 8/27 VP Frsh Cls; VP Soph Cls; VP Jr Cls; Pres Sr Cls; Hon Rl; NHS; Sch Pl; Stu Cncl; Sec Key Clb; Capt Bsktbl; John Carroll Univ.

HOFFERBERT, HOLLY; Adlai E Stevenson HS; Sterling Hts, MI; 9/525 Band; Chrh Wkr; NHS; OEA; Central Mich Univ; Elem Educ.

HOFFMAN, AMY; Bellevue HS; Bellevue, OH; 17/224 Chrs; VP Chrh Wkr; Girl Scts; Hon Rl; NHS; FHA; FTA; OEA; Bowling Green State Univ; Bus Adm.

HOFFMAN, AMY; Van Wert HS; Van Wert, OH; Trs Frsh Cls; Trs Soph Cls; Am Leg Aux Girls St; Chrs; Girl Scts; Hon Rl; Treas NHS; College; French.

HOFFMAN, ANDREW; East Noble HS; Wolcottville, IN; 4/259 Chrh Wkr; NHS; Yth Flsp; 4-H; Letter Bsbl; Bsktbl; Letter Ftbl; Ten; Trk; Wrstlng; College; Chiropractor.

HOFFMAN, BARBARA; North Side HS; Ft Wayne, IN; 2/495 VP Jr Cls; Trs Sr Cls; Sal; Am Leg Aux Girls St; NHS; Stu Cncl; Trk; Dnfth Awd; Indiana Univ; French.

HOFFMAN, BETH; Bay Village HS; Bay Vill, OH; Trk; Univ; Wildlife Mgmt.

HOFFMAN, CARL; Indiana Academy; Cicero, IN; Cls Rep Frsh Cls; Cl Rep Jr Cls; Chrh Wkr; Red Cr Ade; Stu Cncl; Sch Nwsp; Bsktbl; Capt Ftbl; Gym; IM Sprt; Andrews Univ.

HOFFMAN, CARRIE; Hastings HS; Hastings, MI; Band; Yth Flsp; Yrbk; Beta Clb; Fr Clb; PPFtbl; Michigan St Univ; Music.

HOFFMAN, CHERYL ANN; Triton HS; Etna Green, IN; Band; Hon Rl; FHA; Pep Clb; Bus Schl; Acctg.

HOFFMAN, CRAIG; Chagrin Falls HS; Chagrin Falls, OH; Ftbl; Wrstlng; IM Sprt; College; Bus Mgmt.

HOFFMAN, D; Heritage HS; Monroeville, IN; 10/176 Band; Chrs; Chrh Wkr; Cmnty Wkr; Hon Rl; Off Ade; Orch; Sch Mus; FTA; Univ; Med.

HOFFMAN, DANIEL; Shaker Hts HS; Cupertino, OH; 35/575 Band; Hon Rl; Sch Mus; Rptr Sch Nwsp; Capt Socr; Coach Actv; Natl Merit Ltr; United Synagogue Yth Pres; All N E Ohio Soccer Team; Key Awd Schlstc Achvmnt; Univ Of California; Engr.

HOFFMAN, DAWN; Pontiac Central HS; Pontiac, MI; Cls Rep Frsh Cls; Cls Rep Soph Cls; Band; Girl Scts; NHS; Sch Nwsp; Letter Ten; PPFtbl; Cit Awd; Oakland Cmnty Coll; Dent Hygnst.

HOFFMAN, DEBBIE; Martinsville Sr HS; Eminence, IN; Cls Rep Frsh Cls; Chrs; Hon Rl; Stu Cncl; Treas DECA; 4-H; Spn Clb;.

HOFFMAN, DEBORAH; Eastmoor Sr HS; Columbus, OH; 18/290 Cls Rep Sr Cls; Chrh Wkr; Hon Rl; Jr NHS; NHS; Yth Flsp; Yrbk; Fr Clb; Ten; College.

HOFFMAN, E JULIANNE; Jeffersonville HS; Jeffersonville, IN; Chrs; Chrh Wkr; Cmnty Wkr; FCA; Girl Scts; Hon Rl; Jr NHS; Sch Mus; Yth Flsp; Pep Clb; Typing Profcncy Awd 79; Jeffersonvile Invt Yth Chr 78; Revival Singng Grp 78; Univ; Early Child Educ.

HOFFMAN, ERIC; Fenwick HS; Middletown, OH; Boy Scts; Chrh Wkr; Hon Rl; Sch Mus; Sct Actv; Univ Of Dayton; Engr.

HOFFMAN, GATHA; Philip Barbour HS; Galloway, WV; Hon Rl; Yth Flsp; Drama Clb;.

HOFFMAN, JOELLEN; Bishop Dwenger HS; Ft Wayne, IN; Hon Rl; Hosp Ade; JA; Rptr Yrbk; JA Awd; College; Med Tech.

HOFFMAN, JOHN; Lake Fenton HS; Fenton, MI; 6/170 Hon Rl; NHS; Bsktbl; Crs Cntry; Trk; Michigan St Univ; Engr.

HOFFMAN, KAREN; Edison HS; Berlin Hts, OH; Band; Yrbk; Rptr Sch Nwsp; Sch Nwsp; FFA; Trk; College.

HOFFMAN, KAREN S; Eastern Greene County HS; Bloomfield, IN; 11/80 Trs Jr Cls; Chrs; Chrh Wkr; Hon Rl; NHS; Off Ade; Sch Mus; 4-H; Pep Clb; 4-H Awd; Indiana Univ; Optometry.

HOFFMAN, KEVIN S; Malabar HS; Mansfield, OH; Cls Rep Frsh Cls; Band; Chrh Wkr; FCA; Hon Rl; NHS; Stu Cncl; Yth Flsp; Sch Nwsp; Ger Clb; Univ; Archt.

HOFFMAN, LISA; Holgate HS; Holgat4, OH; Trs Frsh Cls; Trs Soph Cls; Trs Jr Cls; Trs Sr Cls; Band; NHS; Yth Flsp; Chrldng; Am Leg Awd; Voice Dem Awd; College.

HOFFMAN, LORI; Griffith Sr HS; Griffith, IN; 48/281 Chrh Wkr; Girl Scts; Hon Rl; Jr NHS; Univ; Radiologic Tech.

HOFFMAN, MARLENE; Father Joseph Wehrle Mem HS; Columbus, OH; 1/105 Hon Rl; Cit Awd; Soc Dstngshd Amer HS Stu; Natl HS Awd For Excellence; Schlstc Ach Awd; Ohio St Univ; Medicine.

HOFFMAN, MARLIN; Southfield HS; Southfield, MI; Aud/Vis; Band; Hon Rl; Lbry Ade; Off Ade; Sch Pl; Stg Crw; Michigan St Univ; Acctg.

HOFFMAN, MARY; Harper Creek Sr HS; Battle Creek, MI; Cls Rep Soph Cls; Cl Rep Jr Cls; Am Leg Aux Girls St; Hon Rl; NHS; Fr Clb; Capt Trk; College.

HOFFMAN, MELINDA; Maumee HS; Maumee, OH; 94/316 Band; Hon Rl; Bowling Green State; Spec Educ.

HOFFMAN, MICHELLE; Van Wert HS; Van Wert, OH; 10/210 Am Leg Aux Girls St; Chrs; Cmnty Wkr; Girl Scts; Hon Rl; NHS; Sch Pl; Stg Crw; Y-Teens; Rptr Yrbk; Valparaiso Univ; History.

HOFFMAN, MICHELLE; Lebanon HS; Lebanon, OH; 55/296 Drl Tm; Hon Rl; ROTC; 4-H; Spn Clb; Mgrs; Scr Kpr; 4-H Awd; Natl Soujners Awd For Mst Amerism In Corp 79; Outstndng Cadet In Oh 771st AFJROTC 78; Grad 6 Out 100 79; Florida Southern Coll; Child Psych.

HOFFMAN, PATTI; Newcomerstown HS; Newcomerstown, OH; 1/105 Cls Rep Soph Cls; Cl Rep Jr Cls; Cls Rep Sr Cls; Val; Aud/Vis; Treas FCA; Hon Rl; VP NHS; Pres Stu Cncl; Malone College; Acctg.

HOFFMAN, ROBERT; Garber HS; Essexville, MI; Hon Rl; Natl Forn Lg; Bsktbl; IM Sprt; Cit Awd; Natl Merit Ltr; Natl Merit SF; College; Bio.

HOFFMAN, ROBYN; Herbert Hoover HS; Charleston, WV; Band; Chrh Wkr; Hon Rl; Off Ade; Yth Flsp; Rptr Sch Nwsp; Fr Clb; Bsktbl; Letter Ten; Trk; Florida Univ; Interior Design.

HOFFMAN, ROXANNE; Crooksville HS; Crooksville, OH; Trs Frsh Cls; Trs Soph Cls; Pres Jr Cls; Chrh Wkr; Drl Tm; Hon Rl; Hosp Ade; Lbry Ade; Sch Pl; Stu Cncl; Ohio Univ; Soc Work.

HOFFMAN, SAMUEL; Winamac Cmnty HS; Winamac, IN; Cl Rep Jr Cls; Hon Rl; Jr NHS; NHS; Stu Cncl; 4-H; Letter Glf; Dnfth Awd; Purdue Univ; Aeronautical Engr.

HOFFMAN, STEVE; Madeira HS; Cincinnati, OH; Hon Rl; Stu Cncl; Boys Clb Am; Letter Ftbl; PPFtbl; Cit Awd; USJC Awd; College; Med.

HOFFMAN, STEVEN; Flushing HS; Flushing, MI; NHS; Bsktbl; Ftbl; Coach Actv; Opt Clb Awd; Univ; Mech Engr.

HOFFMAN, THERESA; North Farmington HS; Frmngtn Hls, MI; Chrs; Hon Rl; Lbry Ade; Univ; Math.

HOFFMANN, DAVID; Cathedral HS; Indianapolis, IN; 2/150 Sal; Capt Band; Hon Rl; NHS; Orch; Sch Mus; Rptr Yrbk; Ed Sch Nwsp; Fr Clb; Mth Clb; Lawrence Univ; Math.

HOFFMANN, DONNA; Colerain Sr HS; Cincinnati, OH; Chrh Wkr; Hon Rl; Stg Crw; Drama Clb; Fr Clb; Flager Univ; Bus.

HOFFMANN, HAROLD; West Ottawa HS; Holland, MI; Trs Sr Cls; Aud/Vis; Hon Rl; JA; Jr NHS; Yth Flsp; 4-H; Fr Clb; Letter Crs Cntry; Socr; Univ.

HOFFMANN, K; North Central HS; Indianapolis, IN; 80/1060 Band; Cmp Fr Grls; Drm Mjrt; Hon Rl; NHS; Ten; Twrlr; College; Vet.

HOFFMANN, KAREN; Traverse City Sr HS; Traverse City, MI; 70/750 Hon Rl; NHS; Kiwan Awd; Traverse City Sr HS Foreign Language Awd; St Of Mich Acad Schlrshp; Univ Of Michigan; Bio Chem.

HOFFMANN, LINDA; North Royalton HS; N Royalton, OH; 53/286 Aud/Vis; Lbry Ade; Off Ade; Sch Pl; Stg Crw; Stu Cncl; Drama Clb; Pep Clb; Spn Clb; Trk; College.

HOFFMANNER, ALAN; Watterson HS; Worhtington, OH; 15/250 Am Leg Boys St; Chrh Wkr; Cmnty Wkr; Hon Rl; Jr NHS; Sdlty; Fr Clb; Letter Crs Cntry; Univ Of Mia; Law.

HOFFMASTER, ANNE; Wynford HS; Bucyrus, OH; 1/140 Val; Band; Chrh Wkr; Hon Rl; NHS; Stg Crw; Stu Cncl; Yth Flsp; Rptr Yrbk; Letter Trk; Univ Of Toledo; Pharmacy.

HOFFMEISTER, BRUCE; Purcell HS; Cincinnati, OH; 3/189 VP Soph Cls; VP Sr Cls; Am Leg Boys St; Hon Rl; Mod UN; NHS; Yrbk; Sch Nwsp; Letter Bsbl; Letter Wrstlng; Ohio St Univ; Biology.

HOFFMEYER, RHONDA; Hagerstown HS; Hagerstown, IN; 14/142 Chrs; FCA; Hon Rl; 4-H; Fr Clb; Sci Clb; Chrldng; Univ; Dent Asst.

HOFFSTETTER, SUSAN; Winfield HS; Scott Depot, WV; Sec Frsh Cls; Trs Frsh Cls; Hon Rl; Jr NHS; Stu Cncl; Yth Flsp; Fr Clb; FHA; Pep Clb; Chrldng; Univ; Math.

HOFMAN, NANCY; Zeeland HS; Zeeland, MI; Chrs; PPFtbl; Beauty College; Cosmetology.

HOFMANN, CYNTHIA; Scecina Mem HS; Indianapolis, IN; 17/194 Cl Rep Jr Cls; Hon Rl; NHS; Chrldng; IM Sprt; Mgrs; Indiana St Univ; Journalism.

HOFMANS, FRAN; St Clement HS; Warren, MI; Pres Frsh Cls; Cmnty Wkr; Hon Rl; NHS; Sch Pl; Ed Yrbk; Rptr Sch Nwsp; GAA; Univ.

HOFMEISTER, KURT; Sandusky HS; Sandusky, OH; 17/393 Hon Rl; NHS; Off Ade; Sct Actv; College; Mech Engr.

HOFMEYER, MARY; Holland HS; Holland, MI; Band; Chrs; Chrh Wkr; Hon Rl; Yth Flsp; Lat Clb; Calvin Coll; Bus.

HOFSTETTER, SUSAN L; Winfield HS; Scott Depot, WV; Sec Frsh Cls; Trs Frsh Cls; Hon Rl; Jr NHS; Stu Cncl; Fr Clb; FHA; Pep Clb; Ten; Chrldng; West Virginia Coll; Math.

HOGAN, ALAN; Washington Catholic HS; Washington, IN; 9/59 Pres Frsh Cls; Pres Soph Cls; Pres Jr Cls; Am Leg Boys St; Chrh Wkr; Cmnty Wkr; Hon Rl; Jr NHS; NHS; Off Ade; Notre Dame Univ; Law.

HOGAN, ANDREW; Saint Xavier HS; Cincinnati, OH; 74/279 Chrh Wkr; Pol Wkr; Y-Teens; Bsbl; Coach Actv; IM Sprt; Harvard College; Bus.

HOGAN, CINDY; Terre Haute North Vigo HS; Terre Haute, IN; Cls Rep Frsh Cls; Cls Rep Soph Cls; Cl Rep Jr Cls; Band; Cmnty Wkr; Drl Tm; Girl Scts; Hon Rl; Off Ade; Sch Mus; Jr Attndnt Ftbll Queen 1978; Best Gymnst Awrd 1978; Membr Gymnstcs Team Won Sectnl Champnshp 1977; Indiana St Univ; Elem Tchr.

HOGAN, MARTIN; Sandusky St Marys Ctrl HS; Sandusky, OH; 2/119 Am Leg Boys St; Hon Rl; JA; NHS; Red Cr Ade; Ger Clb; Sci Clb; Sec JA Awd; Scotts Hi Q Team; Ohio Jr Sci & Human Symp Bd Of Dir; Superior In Ohio Sci Fair; Univ; Engr.

HOGAN, MICHAEL; Pocahontas County HS; Dunmore, WV; 6/125 Cls Rep Frsh Cls; NHS; Off Ade; Sch Pl; Stu Cncl; Yth Flsp; Drama Clb; FFA; VICA; Am Leg Awd; West Virginia Inst; Mech Engr.

HOGAN, MIKE; Brebeuf Prep School; Indianapolis, IN; Cls Rep Soph Cls; Hon Rl; Natl Forn Lg; Pol Wkr; Sch Mus; Sch Pl; Stu Cncl; Drama Clb; Ten; IM Sprt; Purdue Univ; Engr.

HOGAN, ROBERT; Bishop Gallagher HS; Detroit, MI; 34/333 Cls Rep Frsh Cls; Cls Rep Soph Cls; Cl Rep Jr Cls; Hon Rl; Natl Forn Lg; NHS; Stu Cncl; Letter Bsbl; Letter Crs Cntry; Capt IM Sprt; Hnrs Roll Recog 4 Qtrs 77 78 & 79; Univ; Aero.

HOGANSON, EDWARD D; Calumet HS; Laurium, MI; Boy Scts; Chrh Wkr; Debate Tm; Hon Rl; NHS; Pol Wkr; Yth Flsp; Ed Sch Nwsp; Letter Crs Cntry; Letter Trk; Harvard; Law.

HOGG, MS; Dansville Agri HS; Webberville, MI; Trs Soph Cls; Hon Rl; Rptr Sch Nwsp; Bsktbl; Lansing Comm Coll; Nurse.

HOGGE, MICHELE; Franklin Hts HS; Columbus, OH; Cls Rep Frsh Cls; Quill & Scroll; Stg Crw; Sch Nwsp; Drama Clb; Gym; Ten; Chrldng; College.

HOGHE, TRACY; Lincolnview HS; Middle Pt, OH; Chrs; Off Ade; VP Yth Flsp; Rptr Sch Nwsp; Sch Nwsp; Pres 4-H; OEA; GAA; Scr Kpr; International Bus College; Legalsecr.

HOGLE, KARLA; Olivet HS; Springport, MI; 10/80 Band; Hon Rl; Off Ade; Drama Clb; FHA; Kellogg Cmnty Coll; Acctg.

HOGLE, TAMARA; Charlotte HS; Charlotte, MI; 8/304 Sec Sr Cls; Band; Cmp Fr Grls; Chrh Wkr; Hon Rl; NHS; Sch Mus; Stu Cncl; Yth Flsp; 4-H; CHS Acctg Awd 78; Northern Michigan Univ; Acctg.

HOGNE, TRACY; Lincolnview HS; Middle Point, OH; Band; Chrs; Chrh Wkr; Off Ade; VP Yth Flsp; Rptr Sch Nwsp; Pres 4-H; GAA; Scr Kpr; 4-H Awd; Bus Schl; Sec.

HOGREFE, JAYNE; Lorain Catholic HS; Lorain, OH; Sec Frsh Cls; Cls Rep Soph Cls; Sec Jr Cls; Cls Rep Sr Cls; Chrs; Chrh Wkr; Hon Rl; Hosp Ade; NHS; Stu Cncl; Cert Of Merit From The State; E Michigan Univ; Occup Therapy.

HOGREFE, PAULA; Liberty Center Local HS; Liberty Cntr, OH; Band; Chrs; Chrh Wkr; Cmnty Wkr; Hon Rl; JA; Off Ade; Sch Mus; Stu Cncl; Yth Flsp; Bowling Green St Univ; Bus.

HOGSTEN, THOMAS; Brecksville HS; Brecksville, OH; Am Leg Boys St; Boy Scts; NHS; Quill & Scroll; Sch Mus; Stu Cncl; Ed Yrbk; Sch Nwsp; Drama Clb; Mth Clb; Univ; Engr.

HOGUE, KRISSE; Perry HS; Massillon, OH; Hon Rl; Jr NHS; NHS; Off Ade; Trk; Bus Schl; Sec.

HOGUE, MELINDA L; Warren Central HS; Indianapolis, IN; 67/873 Chrh Wkr; Cmnty Wkr; Hon Rl; Treas JA; Lbry Ade; NHS; Off Ade; Orch; Drama Clb; OEA; Daughter Of The Term Jobs Daughters; College; Busns Admin.

HOGUE, PATRICK R; Jackson HS; Massillon, OH; 120/409 Band; Chrh Wkr; Hon Rl; Rptr Yrbk; FFA; Am Leg Awd; College; Busns Mgmt.

HOGUE, SHARON; Tri Valley HS; Adamsville, OH; 6/215 Sec Band; Treas Chrs; Girl Scts; Hon Rl; NHS; Off Ade; Sch Pl; Stg Crw; Treas Stu Cncl; Rptr Yrbk; Muskingum Area Tech Coll; Sec.

HOH, ROBERT; New Richmond HS; New Richmond, OH; Cmnty Wkr; NHS; IM Sprt; College; Computer Programming.

HOHE, ELLEN; Huntington Catholic HS; Huntington, IN; Pres Frsh Cls; Pres Soph Cls; Cls Rep Sr Cls; Hon Rl; NHS; Stg Crw; Stu Cncl; Rptr Yrbk; Chrldng; Gov Hon Prg Awd; Internatl Busns Coll; Admin Asst.

HOHEISEL, ERIC J; Bishop Watterson HS; Worthington, OH; 45/283 Pres Sr Cls; Am Leg Boys St; Hon Rl; NHS; Sch Mus; Stu Cncl; Fr Clb; Capt Bsktbl; JC Awd; Univ; Advertising.

HOHL, CHERYL; Redford Union HS; Redford, MI; Chrh Wkr; Hon Rl; Fr Clb; Pep Clb; Trk; Chrldng; Coach Actv; College.

HOHL, CHRISTOPHER; Fairmont West HS; Kettering, OH; 82/478 Chrs; FCA; Hon Rl; Letter Ftbl; Letter Trk; IM Sprt; Bowling Green St Univ; Acctg.

HOHLBAUGH, DONNA; Springfield HS; Akron, OH; Band; Chrh Wkr; Hon Rl; Y-Teens; Chmn OEA; Spn Clb; Bsktbl; Trk; College; Law.

HOHLBEIN, JOYCE A; Springfield HS; Toledo, OH; 2/250 Trs Frsh Cls; Cls Rep Soph Cls; Am Leg Aux Girls St; Hon Rl; Off Ade; Stu Cncl; Pep Clb; Letter Trk; Sec GAA; VP Mat Maids; College.

HOHLER, MOLLY; Monroeville HS; Norwalk, OH; Band; Hon Rl; Hosp Ade; 4-H; Spn Clb; Drama Clb; Pep Clb; Bsktbl; GAA; 4-H Awd; Capt Of The Flag Corp 79; Capt Of Jr Varsity Bsktbll Tm 77; Univ; Med.

HOHMAN, DONNA; Edison HS; Milan, OH; Sec Frsh Cls; Chrs; Girl Scts; Hon Rl; NHS; Sch Mus; Sch Pl; Sec Drama Clb; FTA; Fireland Campus Coll; Sec.

HOHMAN, R; Calvert HS; Tiffin, OH; Band; Wrstlng;.

HOHOLIK, PATRICIA; Manistique HS; Manistique, MI; Band; 4-H; FHA; Bsbl; Letter Bsktbl; Trk; Lake Superior State Coll; Pharmacy.

HOJNACKI, ROBERT; Notre Dame HS; East Detroit, MI; 30/218 Hon Rl; NHS; Spn Clb; IM Sprt; Natl Merit Ltr; Mich State; Petro Geology.

HOKE, SHARON; Versailles HS; Versailles, OH; 1/133 Pres Frsh Cls; Pres Soph Cls; Val; Band; Chrs; FCA; Hon Rl; NHS; Sch Mus; Sch Pl; Univ Of Dayton; Engr.

HOKE, TIM; Terre Haute South Vigo HS; Terre Haute, IN; 160/550 Cl Rep Jr Cls; Hon Rl; Mod UN; Natl Forn Lg; Sch Pl; Stg Crw; Rptr Sch Nwsp; Drama Clb; Lat Clb; Hoosier Schlr 79; Indiana Univ; Theatre.

HOLALY, SUSAN; Flushing HS; Flushing, MI; 1/523 Val; Girl Scts; Hon Rl; NHS; Rptr Yrbk; Fr Clb; Glf; Chrldng; IM Sprt; PPFtbl; Western Mich Univ; Dance.

HOLBEN, CHARITY; Wm V Fisher Catholic HS; Lancaster, OH; Cmnty Wkr; Hon Rl; NHS; Red Cr Ade; Fr Clb; Letter Bsktbl; Chrldng; Bus Schl; Sec.

HOLBEN, S; Grand Ledge HS; Lansing, MI; Chrh Wkr; Hosp Ade; 4-H; Spn Clb; Letter Ten; 4-H Awd; College.

HOLBERT, JULIE A; Pellston HS; Brutus, MI; Sec Frsh Cls; Trs Soph Cls; Trs Jr Cls; Sec Sr Cls; Band; Hon Rl; NHS; Sch Pl; Bsbl; Pom Pon;.

HOLBORN, DEBBIE; Vanderbilt Area HS; Vanderbilt, MI; 3/27 Sec Jr Cls; Trs Jr Cls; Hon Rl; Rptr Yrbk; Rptr Sch Nwsp; Natl Merit SF; Alma Coll; Eng.

HOLBROOK, ALISA; Valley View HS; Germantown, OH; Chrs; Girl Scts; Hon Rl; 4-H; FHA; Letter Trk; Mat Maids; Scr Kpr; Tmr; College; Photography.

HOLBROOK, BOBBIE; Willow Run HS; Ypsilanti, MI; Girl Scts; Hon Rl; Yrbk; Soc Std Awd 77; Prom Princess Ct; Std Of Week; Eastern Michigan Univ; Acctg.

HOLBROOK, DOUGLAS R; Pleasant HS; Marion, OH; 11/145 Cls Rep Soph Cls; Cl Rep Jr Cls; Pres Band; Treas JA; Lbry Ade; NHS; Rptr Yrbk; Treas JA Awd; College; Finance.

HOLBROOK, GREG; Cowan HS; Muncie, IN; 9/70 Boy Scts; Hon Rl; NHS; Sch Pl; Stg Crw; Yth Flsp; 4-H; 4-H Awd; General Motors Inst; Engr.

HOLBROOK, JEANIE; Lynchburg Clay HS; Lynchburg, OH; 16/98 Pres Soph Cls; Pres Band; Chrs; Hon Rl; Sch Pl; Stu Cncl; Yrbk; Sch Nwsp; Sec 4-H; Pep Clb; Business School; Secretarial.

HOLBROOK, LISA; Martins Ferry HS; Martins Ferry, OH; Band; Chrh Wkr; Hon Rl; VP Stu Cncl; Y-Teens; Rptr Yrbk; Sec Fr Clb; Letter Ten;.

HOLCOMB, DORA; Buckhannon Upshur HS; Crawford, WV; 50/291 Hon Rl; NHS; Busns Schl; Sec.

HOLCOMB, JAY M; George Washington HS; Charleston, WV; 10/353 Sec Jr Cls; VP Sr Cls; Am Leg Boys St; Boy Scts; Hon Rl; Jr NHS; Mod UN; Sct Actv; Stu Cncl; FBLA; 2nd Pl In Mr FBLA Comp At St Confrnv 79; Leadrshp Awd 79; Univ; Pre Law.

HOLCOMB, LU; Ridgedale HS; Morral, OH; 4/97 Band; Chrs; Chrh Wkr; FCA; Hon Rl; Sch Mus; Yth Flsp; Yrbk; 4-H; Leo Clb; Univ; Bio.

HOLCOMB, RICHARD; North Muskegon HS; N Muskegon, MI; 27/108 Cls Rep Frsh Cls; Hon Rl; NHS; Sch Mus; Stg Crw; Stu Cncl; Letter Ftbl; Letter Trk; Letter Wrstlng; IM Sprt; Coll; Bio.

HOLCOMBE, SUE; West Geavga HS; Chagrin Falls, OH; AFS; Band; Chrs; Hon Rl; Jr NHS; MMM; Orch; Cornell; Vet.

HOLD, WENDY M; Lasalle HS; South Bend, IN; 14/488 Band; Chrs; Sch Mus; 4-H; 4-H Awd; College.

HOLDBURG, LINDA; Cass City HS; Cass City, MI; 27/150 Band; Chrh Wkr; Hon Rl; Jr NHS; Lbry Ade; Orch; Pres Yth Flsp; 4-H; FTA; Olivet Nazarene College; Special Ed.

HOLDEMAN, KAREN; Mishawaka HS; Mishawaka, IN; 118/358 Hon Rl; Indiana Univ; Eng.

HOLDEMAN, VICKIE; Plymouth HS; Plymouth, IN; 37/275 Band; Girl Scts; Yth Flsp; Lat Clb; Bsktbl; Coach Actv; PPFtbl; 4-H Awd; College; Science, Veterinarian.

HOLDEN, ANITA; Lexington HS; Mansfield, OH; 24/272 Band; Y-Teens; FNA; Mth Clb; College; Pharmacy.

HOLDEN, ANITA; Lexington Sr HS; Mansfield, OH; Band; Drl Tm; Hon Rl; Y-Teens; Ger Clb; Mth Clb; Univ; Pharmacy.

HOLDEN, DEBRA; Edgewood Sr HS; Andover, OH; Sec Soph Cls; Cl Rep Jr Cls; Chmn AFS; Band; Chrs; Chrh Wkr; Girl Scts; NHS; Sch Pl; Sct Actv; Coll; Educ.

HOLDEN, KAREN; Lynchburg Clay HS; Lynchburg, OH; Band; Chrs; Chrh Wkr; Cmnty Wkr; Hon Rl; Lbry Ade; FHA; Pep Clb; VFW Awd; Univ; Art.

HOLDER, ANGELA C; Park Tudor HS; Indianapolis, IN; Hon Rl; Mod UN; Rptr Sch Nwsp; Civ Clb; Fr Clb; IM Sprt; Natl Merit Ltr; Exchng Stu With Indiana Univ Hnrs Prgrm For HS Stu; Steinway Piano Orchestra; Medical Explorers; College.

HOLDER, SUSAN; Switzerland County HS; Patriot, IN; 23/150 Chrs; Off Ade; Fr Clb; Pep Clb; Trk; Ball State.

HOLDERBAUM, RICHARD; Bremen HS; Wakerusa, IN; Hon Rl; Yth Flsp; 4-H; FFA; 4-H Awd;.

HOLDERBAUM, TRUDY; Henry Ford II HS; Sterling Hts, MI; 23/423 Treas Chrs; Chrh Wkr; Hon Rl; Hosp Ade; NHS; Sch Mus; Sch Pl; Pres Ger Clb; Key Clb; Central Michigan Univ; Spec Ed.

HOLDERFIELD, BELINDA; Green HS; Uniontown, OH; 31/320 Chrs; Hon Rl; Off Ade; Y-Teens; Pep Clb; Kent St Univ; Acctg.

HOLDERMAN, PATRICIA; Colon HS; Colon, MI; 12/72 Sec Frsh Cls; Trs Frsh Cls; Band; Chrs; Chrh Wkr; Drl Tm; Drm Bgl; Hon Rl; Lbry Ade; NHS; Dr Awd Trophy For All Schl Play 79; Cert Of Acad Achvmnt 78; Cert Of Dramatics Activities In Schl Musical; Grand Rapids Baptist Univ; Educ.

HOLDGREVE, MARIA; Delphos St Johns HS; Delphos, OH; 7/154 Pres Band; Hon Rl; NHS; Ed Sch Nwsp; FTA; Letter Gym; Univ; Educ.

HOLDREN, DALE; Marietta HS; Marietta, OH; 1/450 Val; AFS; Boy Scts; Natl Forn Lg; NHS; Sch Pl; Ed Sch Nwsp; Fr Clb; Key Clb; Dnfth Awd; Univ Of Was; Bio Engr.

HOLDREN, TODD; Zane Trace HS; Chillicothe, OH; Pres Sr Cls; Band; NHS; Pres Stu Cncl; Pres Drama Clb; Pres 4-H; Capt Ftbl; 4-H Awd; Natl Merit Ltr; Voice Dem Awd; PTO Schlrshp 79; 4 H Schlrshp 79; Pres Classroom; Morehead Univ; Pre Law.

HOLDRIETH, PATRICK; Oakwood HS; Dayton, OH; Hon Rl; Sch Mus; Sch Pl; Stg Crw; Drama Clb; Univ; Bus Admin.

HOLDSWORTH, SCOTT; Newcomerstown HS; Newcomerstown, OH; 14/111 Pres Sr Cls; Am Leg Boys St; Pres FCA; NHS; Sch Pl; FTA; Bsktbl; Capt Ftbl; Trk; Natl Merit Ltr; Ohio Northern Univ; Bus.

HOLEN, KATHY; Saint Joseph Acad; Cleveland, OH; Girl Scts; Hon Rl; Rptr Sch Nwsp; FDA; Sci Clb; Pres Awd; Accepted Into Hnr Eng I Of 35 Girls Chosen; Rollerskating Working For Gold Metal In Dance; Univ Of Cincinnati; Pre Med.

HOLEY, LORI; Hill Comm HS; Lansing, MI; 15/369 Debate Tm; Hon Rl; Jr NHS; NHS; Bsktbl; IM Sprt; Natl Merit Ltr; Concordia Teachers Coll; Sec Educ.

HOLFINGER, K; Versailles HS; Versailles, OH; 4/126 Band; Chrs; Chrh Wkr; FCA; Hon Rl; Sch Pl; Sch Nwsp; FDA; Letter Bsktbl; Letter Trk; Miami Univ.

HOLFINGER, MARK; Madison Comprehensive HS; Mansfield, OH; Chrs; Chrh Wkr; Fr Clb; Bsbl; Mgrs; Cit Awd; SAR Awd; Univ; Crime Detection.

HOLIDAY, STEVE; New Albany HS; New Albany, IN; Chrh Wkr; FCA; Letter Crs Cntry; Letter Trk; Ind Univ; Pharmacy.

HOLIHAN, CAROL; Bridgeport HS; Saginaw, MI; 47/352 Cl Rep Jr Cls; Cls Rep Sr Cls; Boy Scts; Hon Rl; Hosp Ade; NHS; Sec Stu Cncl; Ger Clb; John & Flornce Goll Mem Schlrshp 79; Gilbert Vasquez Schlrshp 79; Saginaw Valley St Univ; Soc Wrk.

HOLIHAN, CORENE; Swan Valley HS; Saginaw, MI; Sec Sr Cls; Val; Chrh Wkr; Sch Pl; Spn Clb; Lion Awd; Natl Merit Schl; Michigan St Univ; Engr.

HOLIK, ROBIN; Maplewood Jr Sr HS; Cortland, OH; 7/80 Girl Scts; Hon Rl; Hosp Ade; Sec NHS; Off Ade; Sch Pl; Rptr Yrbk; Rptr Sch Nwsp; VP Beta Clb; Treas Drama Clb; Univ.

HOLL, BLAIR; Talawanda HS; Oxford, OH; 58/320 Capt Swmmng; IM Sprt; Capt Of Swim Tm 79; Hon Roll 77 78 & 79; Miami Univ; Bus.

HOLLADAY, CHRIS; Madison Hts HS; Anderson, IN; 25/360 Cl Rep Jr Cls; VP Band; Boy Scts; Hon Rl; NHS; Indiana Univ; Med.

HOLLAND, ANNE; Culver Girls Acad; Sandwich, IL; Cls Rep Sr Cls; Band; Chrs; Girl Scts; Hon Rl; Lbry Ade; Ger Clb; Pep Clb; IM Sprt; Tmr; Univ; Bus.

HOLLAND, ANNE; Middletown HS; Middletown, OH; 1/550 VP Frsh Cls; Pres Soph Cls; Cls Rep Soph Cls; Cl Rep Jr Cls; FCA; Hon Rl; Jr NHS; Off Ade; Beta Clb; Mth Clb; Purdue Univ; Chem Engr.

HOLLAND, BARBARA; Grand Ledge Acad; Sunfield, MI; Hosp Ade; Lbry Ade; Yrbk; Andrews Univ; Pre Law.

HOLLAND, CAROLYN; Allegan Sr HS; Allegan, MI; Band; Hon Rl; Natl Forn Lg; NHS; Sch Pl; Stg Crw; Lat Clb; Pep Clb; Letter Bsktbl; Trk; Northern Michigan Univ; Med Tech.

HOLLAND, CONNIE; Portsmouth East HS; Portsmouth, OH; 2/55 Pres Frsh Cls; Sec Jr Cls; Cmnty Wkr; Hon Rl; Jr NHS; NHS; Stu Cncl; Rptr Yrbk; Univ Of Cincinnati; Med.

HOLLAND, DAVID; Columbus Acad; Columbus, OH; VP Sr Cls; Sch Nwsp; Fr Clb; Letter Crs Cntry; Letter Trk; Natl Merit SF; Ohio St Univ; Comp Sci.

HOLLAND, GARY A; Newark Sr HS; Newark, OH; 154/600 Cls Rep Frsh Cls; Cls Rep Sr Cls; Chrs; Chrh Wkr; Hon Rl; NHS; Stu Cncl; Yth Flsp; DECA; Lat Clb; U S Air Force Acad; Law.

HOLLAND, ISABEL B; Seaholm HS; Troy, MI; Cls Rep Soph Cls; Cl Rep Jr Cls; Cls Rep Sr Cls; Girl Scts; Hon Rl; Jr NHS; NHS; Pol Wkr; Sch Mus; Stg Crw; 1st Prz Grtr San Diego Sci & Engr Fair 76; Chrmn Of My HS Chapt Of Amer Cancer Soc 79; Univ; Med.

HOLLAND, JENNIFER; Clinton Massie HS; Waynesville, OH; Hon Rl; PPFtbl; Cincinnati Tech College; Data Proc.

HOLLAND, JOHN; Hazel Park HS; Hazel Park, MI; Hon Rl; NHS; Quill & Scroll; Ed Yrbk; Rptr Yrbk; Ed Sch Nwsp; Rptr Sch Nwsp; Mth Clb; Cit Awd; Natl Merit Schl; Univ; Comp Progr.

HOLLAND, JOHN; Bexley HS; Bexley, OH; 25/184 Boy Scts; Chrh Wkr; Cmnty Wkr; NHS; Yth Flsp; Sch Nwsp; Mth Clb; Sci Clb; Spn Clb; Capt Ftbl; U S Naval Acad; Engineering.

HOLLAND, KIM; Creston HS; Grand Rpds, MI; Cls Rep Frsh Cls; Cls Rep Soph Cls; Sec Jr Cls; VP Sr Cls; Band; Chrs; Chrh Wkr; Cmnty Wkr; Hon Rl; Jr NHS; Michigan St Univ; Med.

HOLLAND, LEONA; Watervliet HS; Watervliet, MI; Band; Chrh Wkr; Hon Rl; Yth Flsp; FFA; Pres Spn Clb; Rcvd An Awd For Bus 79; Rcvd An Awd For Sewing 77; Lake Michigan Coll; Bus.

HOLLAND, MARTIN C; Seaholm HS; Troy, MI; Boy Scts; Cmnty Wkr; Hon Rl; JA; Pol Wkr; Crs Cntry; Letter Swmmng; Trk; Wrstlng; Coach Actv; Finalist In Mich Math Comp; Qualified For St A Swim Champ; Coll; Med.

HOLLAND, MICHAEL; Cadillac HS; Cadillac, MI; Aud/Vis; Hon Rl; Ftbl; Letter Ten; Mic State Univ; Bus.

HOLLAND, RAYMOND; Aquinas HS; Westland, MI; Drl Tm; Hon Rl; Yth Flsp; Bsktbl; Univ Of Mich; Engr.

HOLLANDBECK, MIKE; Warren Central HS; Indianapolis, IN; 11/768 Aud/Vis; Band; Boy Scts; Chrs; Chrh Wkr; Cmnty Wkr; Hon Rl; Jr NHS; NHS; Orch; Whos Who In Bio; Bus; Eng & Math 76; 1st In Dist Solo & Ensemble Contest 76 79; Natl Math Exam 76; Univ; Bus.

HOLLANDSWORTH, ROGER; Roosevelt Wilson HS; Clarksburg, WV; Band; Cmnty Wkr; Drm Bgl; Hon Rl; Orch; Sch Pl; Stg Crw; Pres Fr Clb; Mth Clb; Sci Clb; Univ Of South Carolina; Mech Engr.

HOLLAR, JEFFERY; Lima HS; Lima, OH; 49/500 Boy Scts; Chrs; Hon Rl; JA; Sch Pl; Drama Clb; Fr Clb; Spn Clb; JA Awd; College; Languages.

HOLLAR, PAM; Miami Trace HS; Washington C H, OH; Band; Drl Tm; Hon Rl; Sch Mus; Sch Pl; Sch Nwsp; Drama Clb; Pres 4-H; FHA; FSA; Bsns Schl; Acctg.

HOLLEMAN, ERIC; St Francis De Sales HS; Columbus, OH; Chrh Wkr; Spn Clb; Bsktbl; Ftbl; Trk; Univ; Bus Admin.

HOLLEN, JAMES; Madison Heights HS; Anderson, IN; .

HOLLEWA, NANCY; Dominican HS; Detroit, MI; Jr NHS; Off Ade; Sch Pl; FTA; Bsbl; Letter Bsktbl; Bus Schl; Sec.

HOLLEY, ANGELA; Metropolitan Schl Dist; Jasonville, IN; 33/86 Chrs; Drl Tm; Drm Bgl; Hon Rl; Quill & Scroll; Sch Nwsp; FHA; Pep Clb; Pom Pon; ISU; Sec.

HOLLEY, BOB; Hauser HS; Clifford, IN; 32/110 FFA; Crs Cntry; Trk; College; Engineering.

HOLLEY, BRIAN; Brookside HS; Sheffield Lke, OH; Hon Rl; Ja; Jr NHS; NHS; Letter Trk; JA Awd; Top 10 Percent 79; Lorain County Cmnty Coll; Bus Admin.

HOLLEY, RUSSELL W; Grosse Ile HS; Grosse Ile, MI; Chrh Wkr; Cmnty Wkr; Hon Rl; NHS; Yth Flsp; Letter Bsbl; Letter Glf; Coach Actv; IM Sprt; Most Improved Player Bsbl; Coll; Archt.

HOLLEY, SCOTT; Evansville Central HS; Evansville, IN; Jr NHS; NHS; Letter Ten; Chrldng; Univ; Vet.

HOLLIBAUGH, KATHLEEN; Logansport HS; Logansport, IN; 14/343 Sec Frsh Cls; Chrs; Girl Scts; Hon Rl; Jr NHS; NHS; Pres Natl Forn Lg; NHS; Off Ade; Sch Mus; Sch Pl; Ball St Univ; Eng.

HOLLIDAY, ISABEL; Dublin HS; Powell, OH; 39/153 Cls Rep Frsh Cls; Chrs; Cmnty Wkr; FCA; Hon Rl; Lbry Ade; Lit Mag; Off Ade; Sch Mus; Civ Clb; Ohio Univ; Phys Ed.

HOLLINGER, BETH; Garrett HS; Garrett, IN; 7/130 Debate Tm; Hon Rl; NHS; Yth Flsp; Rptr Sch Nwsp; 4-H; FHA; GAA; Pom Pon; 4-H Awd; Purdue Univ; Social Work.

HOLLINGER, NATHAN; Fairless HS; Beach City, OH; Am Leg Boys St; Boy Scts; Sct Actv; Letter Bsbl; Letter Bsktbl; Letter Ftbl; Univ; Med.

HOLLINGSHEAD, CINDY; Lima HS; Lima, OH; 50/438 Cls Rep Frsh Cls; Cls Rep Soph Cls; Cl Rep Jr Cls; VP Sr Cls; Chrs; Cmnty Wkr; Hon Rl; Hosp Ade; Mdrgl; S Methodist Univ; Advertising.

HOLLINGSWORTH, DOUGLAS; Kokomo HS; Kokomo, IN; Boy Scts; Chrs; Mdrgl; Off Ade; Sch Mus; Sch Pl; Sct Actv; Stg Crw; OEA;.

HOLLINGSWORTH, KEITH; West Geauga HS; Chesterland, OH; Cls Rep Frsh Cls; Chrs; FCA; Hon Rl; Jr NHS; NHS; Letter Bsktbl; Letter Ftbl; Coach Actv; Natl Merit Ltr; College; Med.

HOLLINS, RICHARD; Zanesville HS; Zanesville, OH; Cls Rep Frsh Cls; Cls Rep Soph Cls; Cl Rep Jr Cls; Boy Scts; FCA; Hon Rl; Stu Cncl; Boys Clb Am; Spn Clb; Letter Ftbl; Top 10 Stdnt Of Frsh Yr 76; Univ; Pro Ftbl.

HOLLIS, CORINNE; Fordson; Dbn Hgts, MI; Sch Pl; Drama Clb; Hockey; Trk; IM Sprt; HFCC; Bus.

HOLLIS, DANNY; Boonville HS; Boonville, IN; 12/220 Chrh Wkr; Hon Rl; Sci Clb; Indiana St Univ; Cmnctns.

HOLLIS, MARK; Croswell Lexington HS; Lexington, MI; Pres Frsh Cls; Pres Soph Cls; Hon Rl; NHS; Sch Mus; Sch Pl; Stg Crw; Rptr Sch Nwsp; Drama Clb; Sci Clb; Michigan St Univ; Med.

HOLLIS, THOMAS; Bishop Flaget HS; Chillicothe, OH; Hon Rl; Stg Crw; Bsktbl; Crs Cntry; Trk; College; Law.

HOLLISTER, DEBORAH; Jefferson Union HS; Irondale, OH; 3/150 Trs Frsh Cls; Band; Cmnty Wkr; Hon Rl; Hosp Ade; Orch; Beta Clb; Oceanography.

HOLLISTER, ROBIN; Niles Sr HS; Niles, MI; 17/402 Sec Band; Hon Rl; Pres Yth Flsp; VP 4-H; 4-H Awd; Indiana Voc Tech Coll; Comp Prog.

HOLLMAN, MARTHA; Concordia Lutheran HS; Ft Wayne, IN; 70/187 Band; Chrh Wkr; JA; Off Ade; Bsbl; Ten; GAA; PPFtbl; Stage Band 78; Lib For Var Band 79; Workd For Youth Conservtn Corps Camp 79; Univ; Phys Educ.

HOLLON, MARY; Lexington HS; Mansfield, OH; 70/280 Trs Sr Cls; Band; Drl Tm; Sch Pl; Stu Cncl; Y-Teens; Drama Clb; Swmmng; Coach Actv; GAA; Univ; Psych.

HOLLOWAY, ANDRE; William A Wirt HS; Gary, IN; Band; Boy Scts; Hon Rl; Boys Clb Am; Fr Clb; Pep Clb; Letter Bsktbl; Letter Ftbl; Letter Trk; Ind Univ.

HOLLOWAY, DEBRA; Harding HS; Marion, OH; AFS; Chrs; Hon Rl; Ohio St Univ; Nursing.

HOLLOWAY, JAMES; Green HS; Uniontown, OH; 49/321 JA; Fr Clb; Ftbl; College; Political Science.

HOLLOWAY, MARK; Miami Trace HS; Bloomingburg, OH; Cls Rep Frsh Cls; Cmnty Wkr; Hon Rl; JA; Lbry Ade; Off Ade; Stg Crw; 4-H; FFA; 4-H Awd; Ohio St Univ; Swine Herdsmen.

HOLLOWAY, TERRI; Douglas Mac Arthur HS; Saginaw, MI; Cls Rep Frsh Cls; Trs Soph Cls; VP Jr Cls; Am Leg Aux Girls St; Hon Rl; NHS; Sch Pl; Pres Stu Cncl; Pep Clb; Pom Pon; Competition Plays Best Actress Awd; Michigan St Univ; Busns Admin.

HOLLOWAY, WILLIAM; River Valley HS; Caledonia, OH; Boy Scts; Chrs; Hon Rl; Lbry Ade; Off Ade; Clb; Bus.

HOLLOWELL, BONNIE; Snider HS; Ft Wayne, IN; Band; Hon Rl; Lbry Ade; Orch; Sch Mus; Fr Clb; Med.

HOLLOWELL, LORI; Gwinn HS; Skandia, MI; 1/206 Val; Hon Rl; NHS; Capt Bsktbl; Capt Trk; Coach Actv; Natl Merit SF; Pres Awd; Michigan Tech Univ.

HOLM, JACQUELYN; Bremen HS; Bremen, IN; 1/122 Sec Frsh Cls; Trs Sr Cls; Val; Hon Rl; VP NHS; Stu Cncl; Pres Spn Clb; Mgrs; Mat Maids; Indiana Univ; Physics.

HOLM, MELODY J; Paw Paw HS; Paw Paw, MI; 12/187 Chrs; Chrh Wkr; Hon Rl; NHS; Sec Stu Cncl; Yth Flsp; Rptr Yrbk; Hope College; Phys Educ.

HOLM, RUTH; Arthur Hill HS; Saginaw, MI; Chrh Wkr; Lbry Ade; NHS; Orch; Sch Mus; Ger Clb; Cit Awd; Natl Merit Schl; Spring Arbor Coll; Music.

HOLMAN, JAMES; Wauseon HS; Wauseon, OH; 23/113 VP Frsh Cls; VP Soph Cls; VP Jr Cls; Am Leg Boys St; Chrs; Debate Tm; Hon Rl; Sch Pl; Pres Stu Cncl; 4-H; Toledo Univ; Mech Engr.

HOLMES, A; Greenbrier East HS; Whte Slphr Spgs, WV; Cmnty Wkr; Hon Rl; Rptr Yrbk; FHA; FTA; West Va Univ; Social Worker.

HOLMES, AARON; John Hay HS; Cleveland, OH; 6/251 Cls Rep Sr Cls; Debate Tm; Hon Rl; Lbry Ade; NHS; Capt Ftbl; Capt Trk; Cit Awd; Wilmington College; Art.

HOLMES, COLLEEN; Forest Hills Central HS; Grand Rapids, MI; Pres Sr Cls; Chrs; Hon Rl; Mdrgl; Sch Mus; Stu Cncl; PPFtbl; Mich State Univ; History.

HOLMES, GREG; Schoolcraft HS; Schoolcraft, MI; 5/85 VP Soph Cls; Cls Rep Soph Cls; Pres Sr Cls; Band; Boy Scts; Hon Rl; JA; NHS; Sch Pl; Sct Actv; Michigan Tech Univ; Engr.

HOLMES, JAMES A; J W Sexton HS; Lansing, MI; 74/359 Band; Chrs; JA; Mdrgl; Sch Mus; Socr; Concordia; Eng.

HOLMES, JEFFREY; Salem HS; Salem, IN; Cls Rep Soph Cls; Cl Rep Jr Cls; Trs Sr Cls; Cls Rep Sr Cls; Boy Scts; Hon Rl; NHS; Sch Pl; Sct Actv; Stu Cncl; Outstndng Achvmnt In Soc Std 74; Hon Mntn In UN Pelgrimg For Youth 78; Amer Legn Boys St Altern t; Indiana Univ; Comp Sci.

HOLMES, JOHN; George Washington HS; Charleston, WV; IM Sprt; Marshall Univ.

HOLMES, LISA; Durand Area HS; Durand, MI; 19/221 Pres Soph Cls; Cls Rep Soph Cls; Pres Jr Cls; Cl Rep Jr Cls; Pres Sr Cls; Cls Rep Sr Cls; Am Leg Aux Girls St; Band; Chrs; Drm Bgl; Baker Jr College; Data Proc.

HOLMES, MIKE; Ida HS; Ida, MI; Band; Boy Scts; Chrh Wkr; Yth Flsp; IM Sprt; Scr Kpr; Mic Tech; Forestry Mang.

HOLMES, PAM; Madison Comprehensive HS; Mansfield, OH; Fr Clb; Letter Bsktbl; Letter Trk; Ohio St Univ; Vet Med.

HOLMES, PATRICK; Woodrow Wilson HS; Youngstown, OH; 78/368 Cls Rep Frsh Cls; Trs Jr Cls; Aud/Vis; Boy Scts; Chrs; Debate Tm; Hon Rl; JA; Off Ade; PAVAS; Youngstown Univ; Bus Admin.

HOLMES, SCARLET; Jonesville HS; Jonesville, MI; 10/100 Am Leg Aux Girls St; Chrs; Cmnty Wkr; Sch Mus; Sch Pl; Rptr Sch Nwsp; Sch Nwsp; College; Dance.

HOLMES, TOM; Bishop Dwenger HS; Ft Wayne, IN; Hon Rl; Ftbl; Trk; College; Marine Biology.

HOLMES JR, GERRY; Vestaburg Cmnty HS; Blanchard, MI; 4/75 Cls Rep Soph Cls; Chrh Wkr; Hon Rl; Lbry Ade; Sch Pl; Stu Cncl; Mgrs; Park Coll; Acctg.

HOLMES JR, JOHN F; Grosse Ile HS; Grosse Ile, MI; Band; Cmnty Wkr; Hon Rl; NHS; Letter Crs Cntry; Letter Trk; Dnfth Awd; Natl Merit Ltr; College.

HOLMES JR, RICHARD; Bellbrook HS; Bellbrook, OH; Band; Chrs; Sch Mus; Ten; Am Leg Awd; Amer Lgn Govt & Ctznshp Awd 79; Congrsmn Clarence Brown Yth Advsr Council 79; Law Schl; Finance.

HOLMSTROM, SANDRA; Howland HS; Warren, OH; 4/400 Band; Girl Scts; Hon Rl; Hosp Ade; Y-Teens; Yrbk; Rptr Sch Nwsp; Spn Clb; Letter Glf; Ten; College.

HOLOHAN, COLETTE; Immaculate Conception Acad; Cabery, IL; 49/68 Chrs; Orch; Sch Pl; Stg Crw; Rptr Sch Nwsp; Pres 4-H; Kankakee Cmnty Coll; Sec.

HOLOVACS, CAROLE; Firelands HS; Amherst, OH; Pres Frsh Cls; VP Soph Cls; Chrs; Hon Rl; PAVAS; Chrldng; Communications.

HOLOWELL, ANDREW; Zanesville HS; Zanesville, OH; Debate Tm; Hon Rl; Sci Clb; USAF Acad; Physical Sciences.

HOLQUIST, ROBERT C; Springfield Local HS; New Middletown, OH; AFS; Aud/Vis; Chrh Wkr; Hon Rl; Lbry Ade; Univ Of Arizona; Astronomy.

HOLSAPPLE, MICHAEL R; Salem HS; Salem, IN; 8/150 Band; Hon Rl; NHS; Lat Clb; Ind Univ Southeast.

HOLSAPPLE, MISTY; Greenville Sr HS; Greenville, OH; 47/380 VP Frsh Cls; Cls Rep Soph Cls; Cl Rep Jr Cls; Cls Rep Sr Cls; Chrh Wkr; Drl Tm; Stu Cncl; Yth Flsp; Spn Clb; Letter Pom Pon; Cedarville Coll; Elem Ed.

HOLSCHER, BRENDA; South Knox HS; Vincennes, IN; 41/106 Hon Rl; Off Ade; 4-H; Pep Clb; Letter Trk; IM Sprt; Whos Who Among Amer HS Stu; Vincennes Univ Awd; Vincennes Univ; Agri Bus.

HOLSCLAW, CHRIS; Floyd Central HS; Floyd Knobs, IN; Chrs; Hon Rl; Letter Bsktbl; Letter Trk; Purdue Univ; Bus Mgmt.

HOLSINGER, LISA; Newton HS; Pleasant Hill, OH; Sec Band; VP Chrs; Chrh Wkr; Drl Tm; Drm Mjrt; Hon Rl; Hosp Ade; Sch Mus; Sch Pl; FHA; Univ Of Cincinnati; Nursing.

HOLSINGER, SHERRY; Covington HS; Covington, OH; Sec Frsh Cls; Pres Soph Cls; Pres Jr Cls; Pres Sr Cls; Chrs; Hon Rl; Lbry Ade; Sch Pl; Sch Nwsp; Fr Clb; Miami Univ; Vocal Music.

HOLSO, DONALD; L Anse HS; L Anse, MI; 2/96 Sal; Am Leg Boys St; Band; Chrs; Hon Rl; Sch Pl; Ed Yrbk; Sprt Ed Yrbk; Rptr Yrbk; Mic Tech Univ; Elec Engr.

HOLSTEIN, ALICIA; Shady Spring HS; Beaver, WV; Band; Chrh Wkr; FCA; Hon Rl; Sec NHS; Cit Awd; Appalachian Bible Coll; Tchr.

HOLSWORTH, DANIEL; Meridian HS; Sanford, MI; 28/133 Hon Rl; Glf; Saginaw Valley State College; Chem.

HOLT, CYNTHIA; Matoaka HS; Matoaka, WV; Trs Jr Cls; Stu Cncl; Yrbk; Keyettes; Pep Clb; Chrldng; Bluefield State College; Law.

HOLT, DENISE; Chaminade Julienne HS; Dayton, OH; Chrs; Chrh Wkr; Cmnty Wkr; JA; Pep Clb; 3rd In Jr Olympics In Judo; Soc Dir Of Al Ka Pals; V P Of Resurrection Teen Club; Howard Univ; Busns Mgmt.

HOLT, KAREN; Smithville HS; Smithville, OH; Band; Hon Rl; Yrbk; Rptr Sch Nwsp; 4-H; FHA; GAA; 4-H Awd; Perfect Attendance 8 Yrs; 3.25 GPA; Home Ecology Awd; College; Comp Sci.

HOLT, KAREN; Firelands HS; Wellington, OH; 3/180 Chrs; Chrh Wkr; Cmnty Wkr; Hon Rl; NHS; Sch Mus; Yth Flsp; 4-H; FHA; College; Home Ec.

HOLT, KELLY; Cardinal Mooney HS; Youngstown, OH; 54/300 Hon Rl; Off Ade; Spn Clb; Swmmng; Natl Merit SF; Marie & Frank Bowers Trust 77 80; Irish Way Schlrshp Finalist 79; Univ.

HOLT, KIMBERLY R; Rogers HS; Toledo, OH; Band; Hon Rl; Pres JA; Off Ade; Orch; JA Awd; College; Music.

HOLT, MARK; Tippecanoe Valley HS; Warsaw, IN; 5/160 Chrh Wkr; Pres NHS; 4-H; FFA; Spn Clb; Letter Bsbl; Capt Ftbl; Letter Wrstlng; IM Sprt; Purdue Univ; Pre Vet.

HOLT, MARK; Rutherford B Hayes HS; Delaware, OH; 2/250 Sal; Am Leg Boys St; Hon Rl; NHS; Pres Spn Clb; Letter Ftbl; Letter Trk; Univ Of Toledo; Pre Med.

HOLT, ROBERT; Kalamazoo Central HS; Kalamazoo, MI; Cls Rep Frsh Cls; Boy Scts; NHS; Stu Cncl; Fr Clb; Letter Hockey; Capt Socr; Univ; Law.

HOLT, ROGER D; Temple Christian School; Canton, MI; Am Leg Boys St; Chrs; Hon Rl; Sch Pl; Stu Cncl; Letter Bsbl; Capt Bsktbl; Crs Cntry; Letter Socr; IM Sprt; Cert From St Of MI Comp Schlshp Prog 79; Henry Ford Cmnty Coll; Sci.

HOLT, VICKI; Seton HS; Cincinnati, OH; Girl Scts; Hon Rl; Letter Bsktbl; Socr; GAA; Coll; Eng.

HOLTER, EDWARD; Eastern Meigs HS; Pomeroy, OH; Band; Pres 4-H; Pres FFA; Letter Trk; 4-H Awd; State P Natl Delegate FFA; County Achvmnt Awd; Ohio St Winner In Diary 4 H; Ohio State Winner In Ag; Vocational Schl; Agri.

HOLTFORTH, JOHN; Owosso HS; Owosso, MI; 135/406 Hon Rl; Mas Awd; Michigan Tech Univ; Elec Engr.

HOLTHOUSE, RENE; Richmond Sr HS; Richmond, IN; 22/650 Band; Drl Tm; Hon Rl; NHS; Fr Clb; Pep Clb; Gym; Pom Pon; Scr Kpr; Dnfth Awd; St Marys Coll.

HOLTMAN, DAVID; Northwest HS; Indianapolis, IN; 27/513 Band; Boy Scts; Hon Rl; Orch; General Motors Inst; Mech Engr.

HOLTSCHULTE, JOSEPH; Upper Sandusky HS; Upper Sandusky, OH; Band; Chrs; Chrh Wkr; Sch Mus; Yth Flsp; Bsktbl; Trk; IM Sprt; Marion Tech College; Bus Mgmt.

HOLTVOIGT, JAMES; Archbishop Alter HS; Miamisbrg, OH; Boy Scts; Chrh Wkr; Hon Rl; Red Cr Ade; Sct Actv; Rptr Sch Nwsp; Sch Nwsp; Drama Clb; FFA; Lat Clb; Optmst Oratrcl Awd 76; Natl Hon Soc 78; Emory Univ; Pre Med.

HOLTZ, PAUL; Rogers HS; Toledo, OH; Hon Rl;.

HOLTZ, TAMI; Morral Ridgedale HS; Marion, OH; 9/108 Cls Rep Frsh Cls; Cls Rep Soph Cls; Cl Rep Jr Cls; Band; Hon Rl; NHS; Stu Cncl; FHA; Chrldng; IM Sprt; College; Tchr.

HOLTZ, VIRGINIA; Lutheran HS; Detroit, MI; 8/158 VP Soph Cls; Band; Hon Rl; NHS; Sch Mus; Sch Pl; Stg Crw; Valparaiso Univ; Bus.

HOLTZAPFEL, KEN; Ironton HS; Ironton, OH; Pres Frsh Cls; VP Jr Cls; Hon Rl; JA; Ger Clb; Ohi St Univ; Business Acct.

HOLTZHAUER, CHIP; Memorial HS; St Marys, OH; Cls Rep Frsh Cls; Am Leg Boys St; Stu Cncl; Letter Bsbl; Letter Ftbl; Rotary Awd; All Dist Hon Mention Ftbl 78; Notre Dame Univ; Archt Design.

HOLUB, DON; Solon HS; Solon, OH; Boy Scts; Chrh Wkr; Hon Rl; NHS; Yth Flsp; Fr Clb; Letter Bsbl; IM Sprt; Oh Test Of Schslhp Achvmnt 14th Pl Dist Hon Mntn St 78; Univ; Acctg.

HOLUB, MELISSA; Gull Lake HS; Battle Creek, MI; Band; Hon Rl; Sch Nwsp; Sci Clb; Capt Trk; Capt PPFtbl; Michigan St Univ; Animal Husbandry.

HOLUP, THERESA; Whiteford HS; Ottawa Lake, MI; Hon Rl; NHS; Rptr Yrbk; Rptr Sch Nwsp; Natl Merit Ltr;.

HOLWERDA, MICHAEL; South Christian HS; Byron Center, MI; Boy Scts; Chrs; Natl Forn Lg; Sch Mus; Sch Pl; Ger Clb; Univ; Actor.

HOLYCROSS, BETH; Tri West Hendricks HS; Jamestown, IN; 1/120 Cls Rep Soph Cls; Sec Jr Cls; Cmp Fr Grls; FCA; Hon Rl; NHS; Off Ade; Stu Cncl; 4-H; Fr Clb; College.

HOLYCROSS, KIM; Tri West Hendricks HS; Jamestown, IN; 4/120 Cl Rep Jr Cls; Cls Rep Sr Cls; Am Leg Aux Girls St; Cmp Fr Grls; FCA; Hon Rl; NHS; Off Ade; Sec Stu Cncl; 4-H; De Pauw Univ; Elem Educ.

HOLZINGER, WILLIAM; Padua Franciscan HS; Parma, OH; Val; Hon Rl; Jr NHS; NHS; Yrbk; Fr Clb; FTA; Cit Awd; JA Awd; Natl Merit Schl; Quincy College; Religious Studies.

HOLZMER, LUCY; Hobart Sr HS; Hobart, IN; 17/395 Am Leg Aux Girls St; Chrh Wkr; Girl Scts; Hon Rl; Pres NHS; PAVAS; Sch Mus; Sch Pl; Stg Crw; Drama Clb; St Francis Coll; Commcl Art.

HOLZMEYER, CAROL; Gibson Southern HS; Ft Branch, IN; 77/200 Trs Sr Cls; Hosp Ade; JA; Sch Pl; Stu Cncl; 4-H; FHA; Pep Clb; Sci Clb; 4-H Awd; Univ Of Evansville; Nursing.

HOLZSCHUH, SHERYL; Hale HS; S Branch, MI; Chrh Wkr; Hon Rl; Off Ade; Grand Rapids Bible Inst; Stenography.

HOM, DIANE; Eastlake North HS; Eastlake, OH; Off Ade; Stu Cncl; Sch Nwsp; Cleveland St Univ; Med.

HOM, HAROLD; Fairview Park HS; Fairview Pk, OH; Band; Hon Rl; Mod UN; NHS; Sci Clb; Spn Clb; Academic Challenge Tv Progr 76; Spanish Hnr Society 77; Ohio Schlstc Test On US Hstry 8th Pl 78; Univ; Med.

HOM, HAROLD; Fairview HS; Fairview Park, OH; Cls Rep Frsh Cls; Hon Rl; Mod UN; NHS; Sci Clb; Spn Clb; Univ.

HOMAN, CATHY; Fort Recovery HS; Ft Recovery, OH; 3/75 VP Frsh Cls; Pres Jr Cls; Am Leg Aux Girls St; Chrs; Chrh Wkr; Hon Rl; NHS; Stu Cncl; FHA; OEA; Schlrshp Team Mem;.

HOMAN, CINDY; Memorial HS; St Marys, OH; 15/252 Am Leg Aux Girls St; Hon Rl; Y-Teens; Yrbk; FNA; FTA; Ohio St Univ; Phys Therapy.

HOMAN, DONALD; Marion Local HS; Celina, OH; Chrh Wkr; NHS; Stu Cncl; Pres FFA; Pep Clb; Sci Clb; VFW Awd;.

HOMAN, EARL; Coldwater HS; Coldwater, OH; 35/158 Hon Rl; FFA; Farming.

HOMAN, JOSEPH V; Marion Local HS; Maria Stein, OH; 3/93 Chrh Wkr; Hon Rl; Treas NHS; Treas Stu Cncl; Pres FFA; Pep Clb; Sci Clb; Am Leg Awd; Miami Univ; Chem Engr.

HOMAN, LINDA; Marion Local HS; Celina, OH; Chrs; Cmnty Wkr; Hon Rl; Jr NHS; NHS; Sch Mus; Yrbk; Business.

HOMCO, J; George Washington HS; E Chicago, IN; 33/264 Bsktbl; Purdue Univ.

HOMEISTER, RAYMOND; Grosse Ile HS; Grosse Ile, MI; Band; Chrs; Chrh Wkr; Cmnty Wkr; Hon Rl; Mdrgl; Orch; Pol Wkr; Sch Mus; Sch Pl; Downriver Citizens Office Hnr 94 Volunteer 79; Michigan Democratic Party Camp Worker 78; Poli Sci.

HOMER, CAMERON; Northeastern HS; Fountain City, IN; 31/180 Band; Boy Scts; Treas JA; Most Imprvd Player Band 78; Best Actor LDS Rd Shows 78; Univ; Archt.

HOMER, CYNTHIA; Berea HS; Brook Pk, OH; Sec Frsh Cls; Chrh Wkr; Cmnty Wkr; Hon Rl; NHS; Stu Cncl; Yth Flsp; Pep Clb; Letter Chrldng; IM Sprt; Bowling Green Univ; Acctg.

HOMME, KEVIN; St Alphonsus HS; Detroit, MI; Chrs; Hon Rl; Sprt Ed Sch Nwsp; Rptr Sch Nwsp; Letter Trk; College.

HONAKER, ARTHUR; South Charleston HS; S Charleston, WV; Chrh Wkr; Jr NHS; Spn Clb; Crs Cntry; Letter Trk; Military; Educ.

HONAKER, DENNY E; Big Creek HS; English, WV; 5/125 Am Leg Boys St; Aud/Vis; Band; Pres Of Natl Soc 79; Master Of Cermns Of Annl Miss Owl Contst 78; Awd For Bst Musicn 75 79; Marshall Univ; Lab Tech.

HONAKER, PERRY; Marlington HS; Alliance, OH; 8/256 Am Leg Boys St; Band; Chrh Wkr; Hon Rl; NHS; Yth Flsp; FFA; Lat Clb; Sci Clb; Mount Union College; Biology.

HONBAUM, DEBBIE; Chelsea HS; Chelsea, MI; Cls Rep Frsh Cls; Pres Soph Cls; Cls Rep Soph Cls; VP Jr Cls; Cl Rep Jr Cls; Band; Hon Rl; Stu Cncl; Yth Flsp; 4-H; Blue Lake Fine Arts Camp Schlrshp 76; Univ; Bus.

HONCHUL, GREGORY; Oak Hill HS; Oak Hill, OH; Hon Rl; NHS; Stg Crw; Military Service; Aero Engr.

HONECK, JILL; Patrick Henry HS; Malinta, OH; 9/115 Cls Rep Soph Cls; Cl Rep Jr Cls; Band; Chrs; Chrh Wkr; Hon Rl; Sch Mus; Stu Cncl; VP Sci Clb; Letter Gym; Math Schlr Team 1976; Toledo Hosp Schl Nursing; Rn.

HONER, AMY; Kingswood HS; Jackson, MI; VP Soph Cls; Sec Jr Cls; Sch Pl; Stu Cncl; Fr Clb; Pep Clb; Letter Glf; Letter Ten; IM Sprt; Mgrs; Univ; Bus.

HONESS, MARY; Cathedral HS; Indianapolis, IN; 5/148 Sec Sr Cls; Chrh Wkr; Cmnty Wkr; Hon Rl; NHS; Sec Stu Cncl; Yth Flsp; Rptr Yrbk; Yrbk; Bsktbl; Georgetown Univ; Law.

HONEYCUTT, DAVID; Buckhannon Upshur HS; Buckhannon, WV; VICA; AM VICA Clb Chaplain; 3rd Pl At Upshur Cnty Math Field Day; Teen Disc Jockey At WBUC Radio; College; Construction.

HONEYCUTT, JAMES R; Comstock Park HS; Comstock Pk, MI; 3/147 Trs Frsh Cls; Trs Soph Cls; Cl Rep Jr Cls; Cls Rep Sr Cls; Am Leg Boys St; Hon Rl; NHS; Off Ade; Pol Wkr; Sch Mus; Grand Rapids Jr Coll; Engr.

HONEYWILL, KATHY; Fairborn Baker HS; Dayton, OH; Hon Rl; Hosp Ade; Off Ade; Quill & Scroll; Stu Cncl; Sch Nwsp; Beta Clb; Pep Clb; Trk; Capt Chrldng; Wright State Univ; Bsns.

HONIGFORD, DIANE; Ottoville Local HS; Ft Jennings, OH; Band; Cmp Fr Grls; Chrs; Girl Scts; Hon Rl; Off Ade; Sch Mus; Yrbk; GAA; College; Barbering.

HONIGFORD, TOM; Coldwater HS; Coldwater, OH; Boy Scts; Hon Rl; Sch Pl; Sct Actv; Spn Clb; Bsbl; Letter Bsktbl; Ftbl; Coach Actv; IM Sprt; Coll.

HONIGFORT, PAMELA; Ottawa Glandorf HS; Ottawa, OH; Drl Tm; Hon Rl; NHS; Off Ade; Sch Pl; Ger Clb; GAA; Univ.

HOOBER, LORA; Union HS; Modoc, IN; Hon Rl; Off Ade; Ed Sch Nwsp; Rptr Sch Nwsp; 4-H; FHA; Chmn Bsbl; Ind Business College; Receptionist.

HOOCK, JENNIFER; William A Wirt Sr HS; Gary, IN; 1/230 Val; Band; Debate Tm; Girl Scts; Hon Rl; Hosp Ade; Jr NHS; NHS; Rptr Yrbk; Mth Clb; Obarlin Coll; Psych.

HOOD, CHARLES C; Andover HS; Birmingham, MI; 74/443 Aud/Vis; Hon Rl; Lbry Ade; Ger Clb; Letter Socr; IM Sprt; Hope College; Pre Med.

HOOD, DAVID W; Robert S Rogers HS; Toledo, OH; Boy Scts; Chrs; FCA; Sct Actv; Yth Flsp; College.

HOOD, JILL; South Haven HS; South Haven, MI; 40/230 Band; Chrs; Girl Scts; Hon Rl; Hosp Ade; 4-H; Swmmng; Trk; Cit Awd; 4-H Awd; Northern Michigan Univ; Nursing.

HOOD, LLOYD; Martins Ferry HS; Martins Ferry, OH; 40/215 Pres Frsh Cls; Cls Rep Soph Cls; VP Sr Cls; Hon Rl; Stu Cncl; Capt Bsktbl; Letter Ftbl; Letter Trk; College.

HOOD, ROBERT; Gallia Academy HS; Gallipolis, OH; Cls Rep Frsh Cls; Chrs; Chrh Wkr; Lbry Ade; Sch Mus; Stu Cncl; Yth Flsp; Letter Bsktbl; Letter Ftbl; Mgrs; Univ; Bus.

HOOK, LINDA; Bridgeport HS; Bridgeport, WV; 10/200 Am Leg Aux Girls St; Chrs; Hon Rl; NHS; Letter Bsktbl; Letter Trk; Natl Merit Ltr; West Virginia Univ; Engr.

HOOK, SHEILA; Gwinn HS; Oscoda, MI; Girl Scts; Hon Rl; NHS; Sct Actv; OEA; Trk; U S Army; Law Enfrcmnt.

HOOKER, CLAIRE; Immaculata HS; Detroit, MI; Girl Scts; Hon Rl; JA; Sct Actv; Cit Awd; Univ; Cmnctns.

HOOKER, JILL; Gladwin HS; Gladwin, MI; 7/168 Chrh Wkr; Cmnty Wkr; NHS; Letter Ten; College; Acct.

HOOKER, KEVIN; Madison HS; Adrian, MI; 16/59 Trs Sr Cls; Band; Hon Rl; Sch Pl; Stu Cncl; Ed Sch Nwsp; Key Clb; Letter Bsktbl; Letter Trk; Fine Arts Sr Of Yr 79; Siena Heights Univ; Commercial Art.

HOOKER, TIM; Scecina Memorial HS; Indianapolis, IN; JA; Sch Mus; Fr Clb; Spn Clb; Bsbl; Ari State Univ; Pro Baseball.

HOOKS, SHANE; North Newton HS; Lake Village, IN; Aud/Vis; Boy Scts; Chrh Wkr; Hon Rl; Sch Pl; Stu Cncl; Sprt Ed Yrbk; Sprt Ed Sch Nwsp; Drama Clb; 4-H; St Jophes Rensslaer Coll; Tchr.

HOOPER, DENISE; Ashtabula HS; Ashtabula, OH; Cmnty Wkr; Girl Scts; Hon Rl; Off Ade; Yth Flsp; Yrbk; Tmr; Bus Schl; Spec Educ.

HOOPER, KLAYTON; Tri Valley HS; Dresden, OH; 10/230 Hon Rl; NHS; Sch Pl; Yrbk; Sch Nwsp; Drama Clb; 4-H; Pres FFA; VP Lat Clb; Mgrs; Ohio St Univ.

HOOPER, LISA J; Monroeville HS; Monroeville, OH; Cls Rep Frsh Cls; Cls Rep Soph Cls; Cl Rep Jr Cls; Band; Drm Bgl; Drm Mjrt; Girl Scts; Hon Rl; Sch Mus; Sch Pl; Vocational Schl; X Ray Tech.

HOOPER, LORRY; Ashtabula HS; Ashtabula, OH; 40/230 Cls Rep Frsh Cls; Cls Rep Soph Cls; Chrh Wkr; Cmnty Wkr; Girl Scts; Hosp Ade; Sdlty; Stu Cncl; Yth Flsp; Akron Univ; Nursing.

HOOPER, SANDRA; Westland HS; Columbus, OH; Chrh Wkr; Yth Flsp; 4-H; Am Leg Awd; Cit Awd; DAR Awd; Gov Hon Prg Awd; JA Awd; Natl Merit Ltr; Natl Merit SF; Computer Techn.

HOOPES, ROBERT; West Branch Local HS; Beloit, OH; Band; Boy Scts; Chrh Wkr; Hon Rl; Orch; Sch Mus; Sch Pl; Treas Lat Clb; Youngstown St Univ; Music.

HOOPS, CHRIS; Meadowbrook HS; Pleasant City, OH; Band; Hon Rl; Lbry Ade; Off Ade; 4-H; FTA; Pep Clb; Sci Clb; Spn Clb; FTA Awd 79; Univ; Elem Educ.

HOOPS, RUSTY; Napoleon HS; Napoleon, OH; Chrh Wkr; Letter Glf; Bus Schl; Radio Brdcstng.

HOOPS, VICKI; Holgate HS; Holgate, OH; 2/59 Sec Frsh Cls; Trs Soph Cls; Sec Jr Cls; Band; Hon Rl; Jr NHS; NHS; Off Ade; Sch Pl; Yrbk; Univ Of Virginia; Math.

HOORMAN, JAMES; Ottawa Glandorf HS; Ottawa, OH; Cls Rep Sr Cls; Am Leg Boys St; Band; Chrs; Hon Rl; NHS; Stu Cncl; 4-H; Spn Clb; Ohi St Univ; Agriculture.

HOOSE, TROY; Hill Mc Cloy HS; Montrose, MI; Band; Chrh Wkr; Cmnty Wkr; Hon Rl; Rptr Sch Nwsp; Sch Nwsp; Letter Crs Cntry; Cit Awd; Olivet Nazarene Coll; Marine Biology.

HOOTON, KAREN; Bridgeport Sr HS; Bridgeport, WV; VP Soph Cls; Sec Sr Cls; Band; Hon Rl; Sch Pl; Stu Cncl; Y-Teens; Spn Clb; Chrldng; West Virginia Univ; Speech Pathology.

HOOVER, AMY; Defiance HS; Defiance, OH; Band; Hon Rl; Jr NHS; Rptr Sch Nwsp; Spn Clb; Bsktbl; Mgrs; Columbus Schl Of Art; Artist.

HOOVER, ANTHONY C; Marlington HS; Louisville, OH; 25/300 Am Leg Boys St; Chrh Wkr; Hon Rl; Letter Crs Cntry; Letter Trk; Tmr; College; Electrical Engineering.

HOOVER, DEBBIE; Marion Harding HS; Marion, OH; 3/449 Cl Rep Jr Cls; Sal; Lit Mag; NHS; Sch Mus; Sch Pl; Rptr Yrbk; Fr Clb; Tmr; Ohio Univ; Busns.

HOOVER, EVAN; Northwood HS; Goshen, IN; 25/191 Chrh Wkr; Hon Rl; NHS; Sch Pl; Pres Yth Flsp; Drama Clb; 4-H; Ger Clb; 4-H Awd; Ivy Tech Coll; Comp Progr.

HOOVER, LAURA; Anderson HS; Anderson, IN; 97/350 Chrh Wkr; Girl Scts; Hon Rl; Hosp Ade; Lbry Ade; Sch Mus; FHA; Sec Ger Clb; Mth Clb; Indiana Bus Coll; Admin.

HOOVER, LA VONDA; Imlay City Community HS; Imlay City, MI; 3/161 Band; Chrs; Chrh Wkr; Hon Rl; NHS; Sch Mus; Fr Clb; Eatern Mennonite College; Soc Work.

HOOVER, LINDA; Green HS; Uniontown, OH; 4/335 Band; Chrs; Girl Scts; Hon Rl; NHS; Y-Teens; Rptr Sch Nwsp; Lat Clb; Sec OEA; GAA; Akron Univ; Med.

HOOVER, MARILYN; Climax Scotts HS; Climax, MI; 10/70 Band; Chrs; Hon Rl; Natl Forn Lg; Sct Actv; Sch Pl; Trk; Univ.

HOOVER, MARK; Summerfield HS; Petersburg, MI; Hon Rl; Girl Scts; Jr NHS; NHS; Coach Actv; JA Awd; Toledo Univ 78; Hnrs Awd 77; High Schlstc Achvmnt Awd 79; Univ; Vet Med.

HOOVER, MARTY; Kent Theodore Roosevelt HS; Kent, OH; Hon Rl; Kent State Univ; Art.

HOOVER, NANCY E; Rensselaer Central HS; Rensselaer, IN; 23/162 Band; Hon Rl; NHS; Sch Mus; Fr Clb; Keyettes; Swmmng; Purdue Univ; Pharmacy.

HOOVER, RICHARD G; Lewis County HS; Weston, WV; 30/273 Cls Rep Frsh Cls; Cls Rep Soph Cls; Sec Jr Cls; Cl Rep Jr Cls; Cls Rep Sr Cls; Am Leg Boys St; Band; Boy Scts; Chrh Wkr; FCA; Winner In 2 Math Contests In Co; Won All 3 Of Co Contests 1st Pl; Co Math Awd; W Virginia Univ; Engr.

HOOVER, TANYA; Penn HS; Oceola, IN; 8/499 Cmp Fr Grls; Chrh Wkr; FCA; Hon Rl; Hosp Ade; Yth Flsp; Top 10 Bible Quizzers 77 78 & 79; Anderson Univ; Acctg.

HOOVER, TRACY; Seneca East HS; Republic, OH; Trs Frsh Cls; Sec Soph Cls; Cl Rep Jr Cls; Band; Chrs; Stu Cncl; Trk; Chrldng; Scr Kpr; Tmr; Technical Schl; Stewardess.

HOOVER, VALERIE; Belpre HS; Belpre, OH; 46/204 Band; Chrs; Chrh Wkr; Cmnty Wkr; Drm Bgl; Drm Mjrt; Girl Scts; Hon Rl; Hosp Ade; JA; Consvty Of Music Univ Cincnti; Music.

HOOVERMAN, MELISSA; James A Garfield HS; Garrettsville, OH; Band; Sch Mus; Yrbk; 4-H; Sci Clb; Bsktbl; Chrldng; Area Tech Inst; Equestrian.

HOPE, SANDY; Fraser HS; Fraser, MI; Chrh Wkr; Girl Scts; Hon Rl; NHS; Red Cr Ade; Sct Actv; Yrbk; Rptr Sch Nwsp; Sci Clb; IM Sprt; Michigan St Coll.

HOPF, MARLA; Jasper HS; Jasper, IN; 5/275 Girl Scts; Hon Rl; Hosp Ade; Sct Actv; 4-H; Pep Clb; IM Sprt; 4-H Awd; Jr Cvtn 77; Univ; Bus.

HOPKINS, CYNTHIA; Carroll HS; Flora, IN; 11/103 Chrs; Hon Rl; NHS; Stg Crw; Drama Clb; Eng Clb; Fr Clb; Ten; PPFtbl; Bus Schl; Sec.

HOPKINS, ERIC; Warren Central HS; Indpls, IN; 14/800 Chrh Wkr; Hon Rl; Jr NHS; Key Clb; Bsbl; Wrstlng; IM Sprt; Art Awd For Good Perfrmnc 78; Univ; Engr.

HOPKINS, ERIC; Libbey HS; Toledo, OH; 39/376 Pres Sr Cls; Am Leg Boys St; Aud/Vis; Hon Rl; JA; Boys Clb Am; Fr Clb; Mth Clb; Bsktbl; Trk; Univ; Acctg.

HOPKINS, JOHN; Eau Claire HS; Eau Claire, MI; Cls Rep Frsh Cls; FCA; Hon Rl; Ftbl; Trk; Wrstlng; IM Sprt; JA Awd; Univ; Law Enforcement.

HOPKINS, JO LYNN; Morgan HS; Mc Connelsville, OH; Am Leg Aux Girls St; Hon Rl; NHS; Off Ade; Sch Pl; Rptr Yrbk; Rptr Sch Nwsp; Drama Clb; 4-H; Pep Clb; Coll; Social Work.

HOPKINS, JULIE; Samel HS; Salem, IN; 13/265 Sec Frsh Cls; Sec Soph Cls; Sec Jr Cls; Sec Sr Cls; Hon Rl; FHA; Pep Clb; Spn Clb; IUS; Soc Work.

HOPKINS, JULIET; Whitmer Sr HS; Toledo, OH; Boy Scts; Girl Scts; JA; FHA; Ger Clb; Mgrs; Scr Kpr; Univ; German.

HOPKINS, KAREN; William Henry Harrison HS; Harrison, OH; 32/203 Band; Chrh Wkr; Pres Girl Scts; Hon Rl; Hosp Ade; VP JA; Lbry Ade; Georgetown College; Tchr.

HOPKINS, LISA C; Howland HS; Warren, OH; 1/430 Band; Chrs; Cmnty Wkr; Debate Tm; Hon Rl; Hosp Ade; VP JA; Natl Forn Lg; NHS; Y-Teens; Univ.

HOPKINS, NANCY; Port Clinton HS; Port Clinton, OH; Trs Frsh Cls; Trs Soph Cls; Sec Sr Cls; Trs Sr Cls; Hon Rl; Hosp Ade; Off Ade; DECA; Letter Trk; C of C Awd; 1st Pl St General Merch DECA; 1st Pl Dist For Job Interview Contest DECA; Homecoming Attendant; Kent State Univ.

HOPKINS, NATALIE; Union Cnty HS; Liberty, IN; 9/135 Cls Rep Soph Cls; Cl Rep Jr Cls; Cls Rep Sr Cls; Am Leg Aux Girls St; Chrh Wkr; Drl Tm; Hon Rl; NHS; VP Stu Cncl; Pep Clb; Univ; Bus.

HOPKINS, SELDEN T; Lemon Monroe HS; Middletown, OH; 51/263 Boy Scts; Chrh Wkr; Hon Rl; Rptr Sch Nwsp; Letter Bsbl; Letter Wrstlng; IM Sprt; Scr Kpr; Tmr; Morehead St Univ; Eng.

HOPKINS, SERRETHA; Horace Mann HS; Gary, IN; VP Soph Cls; Band; Chrh Wkr; Drm Mjrt; Hon Rl; JA; Jr NHS; NHS; Off Ade; Red Cr Ade; Tuskegee Inst; Bio.

HOPKINS, WILLIAM E; Libbey HS; Toledo, OH; 39/376 Pres Sr Cls; Am Leg Boys St; Aud/Vis; Hon Rl; JA; NHS; Boys Clb Am; Fr Clb; Letter Bsktbl; Trk; Univ; Acctg.

HOPMA, SUZANNE; Reeths Puffer HS; Muskegon, MI; 26/361 Band; Hon Rl; JA; Letter Chrldng; Mgrs; PPFtbl; Pres Awd; Univ; Bus.

HOPMAN, BARBARA; Our Lady Star Of The Sea HS; Grosse Pt Shrs, MI; 1/51 Val; Hon Rl; NHS; Sch Mus; Sch Pl; Rptr Yrbk; Ed Sch Nwsp; Spn Clb; GAA; IM Sprt; Univ Of Detroit; Acctg.

HOPP, PATRICIA; Elk Rapids HS; Elk Rapids, MI; 5/86 Band; Debate Tm; Girl Scts; Hon Rl; Stu Cncl; Sch Nwsp; Pres 4-H; 4-H Awd; Lion Of Mi All St Band 79; Music Educ.

HOPP, RON S; Cheboygan Area HS; Mullett Lake, MI; VP Soph Cls; Trs Jr Cls; Trs Sr Cls; Am Leg Boys St; Band; Hon Rl; Sch Pl; Stu Cncl; Sci Clb; Ferris State Coll; Pharmacy.

HOPPE, DOMINIQUE; Dearborn HS; Dearborn, MI; Cls Rep Frsh Cls; Cls Rep Soph Cls; Trs Jr Cls; AFS; Hon Rl; NHS; Sch Mus; Sch Pl; Stu Cncl; Swmmng; Univ Of Michigan; Intl Relations.

HOPPE, RONALD; St Francis Cabrini HS; Detroit, MI; Cls Rep Frsh Cls; Sch Pl; Stu Cncl; Letter Ftbl; Letter Trk; IM Sprt; Kiwan Awd; Univ; Law.

HOPPER, CHRISTIE; Olentangy HS; Delaware, OH; Sec Frsh Cls; Cls Rep Soph Cls; VP Jr Cls; Hon Rl; Stu Cncl; Sec 4-H; Sec Spn Clb; 4-H Awd; Delegate To Oh 4h Clb Congress 79; Natl Make It Yoursif With Wool Contst 78; Outstndg Of The Day Oh St Fair; Bus Schl.

HOPPER, HOWARD; Highland HS; Hinckley, OH; 74/28 Boy Scts; Hon Rl; Sch Pl; Lat Clb; Crs Cntry; Trk; IM Sprt; Higland Honsoc Ltr 79; Univ.

HOPPER, KAREN; Whetstone HS; Columbus, OH; Chrs; Hon Rl; Hosp Ade; Lit Mag; NHS; Off Ade; VP 4-H; Ohio St Univ; Hosp Admin.

HOPPER, KENT; Northwest HS; Indianapolis, IN; 1/506 Hon Rl; NHS; Natl Merit SF; Learn About Busns Prog Wabash Coll; General Motors Inst; Indus Mgmt.

HOPPER, LISA; Springs Valley HS; French Lick, IN; 19/97 Band; Chrs; Chrh Wkr; Girl Scts; Hon Rl; Pol Wkr; Sch Pl; Yth Flsp; Pep Clb; IM Sprt; Indiana Univ S E; Med Tech.

HOPPER, MARY; Crispus Attucks HS; Indianapolis, IN; Sec Jr Cls; Am Leg Aux Girls St; Hon Rl; NHS; Stg Crw; Stu Cncl; Ed Sch Nwsp; Lat Clb; Ten; Natl Merit Ltr; College; Educ Tchr.

HOPPER, MICHAEL D; Plymouth HS; Plymouth, IN; Chrs; Chrh Wkr; Natl Forn Lg; NHS; ROTC; Stu Cncl; Yth Flsp; Yrbk; Eng Clb; Mth Clb; Rose Hulman Coll; Chem Engr.

HOPPER, PAT; Seeger Memorial HS; Pine Village, IN; 10/126 Band; Hon Rl; Hosp Ade; NHS; Sch Mus; Sch Pl; Drama Clb; Pep Clb; Hoosier Schlr; Best Soph Marcher; Best Marching Squad; Indiana Univ; Nursing.

HOPPES, CHRISTINE; Tiffin Columbian HS; Tiffin, OH; Band; Chrs; Hon Rl; Lbry Ade; Yth Flsp; Sec 4-H; Fr Clb; 4-H Awd; College; Acctg.

HOPPING, BRADLEY M; Madeira HS; Madeira, OH; 8/178 Hon Rl; Lbry Ade; NHS; Pol Wkr; Rptr Yrbk; Pres Lat Clb; Letter Socr; Outstndg Latin III Stu 78; Outstndg Amer Hstry Stu 78; Purdue Univ; Aero Engr.

HOPPING, LOUISE; South Dearborn HS; Aurora, IN; 21/250 Band; Chrs; Hon Rl; Hosp Ade; NHS; Pep Clb; Ftbl; Gym; Letter Trk; Letter Wrstlng; Purdue Univ; Engr.

HOPPS, KATHLEEN; All Saints HS; Bay City, MI; Chrh Wkr; Hon Rl; Mdrgl; Natl Forn Lg; NHS; Sch Mus; Sch Pl; Bsktbl; Coach Actv; Pom Pon; Univ Of Michigan; Psych.

HOPPS, KEITH; University HS; Cleveland, OH; Aud/Vis; Off Ade; Rptr Sch Nwsp; Capt Bsktbl; Trk; Williams Univ.

HOPSON, TIMOTHY; South Greene HS; Greeneville, TN; Pres Sr Cls; Hon Rl; NHS; Stu Cncl; Pres Sci Clb; IM Sprt; Kiwan Awd; Tennessee Tech Univ; Entomology.

HOPTON, DENNIS L; Flushing Sr HS; Flushing, MI; 18/495 Boy Scts; Chrs; NHS; Yth Flsp; Mgrs; Scr Kpr; Anderson Coll; Comp Sci.

HOPTRY, DAVID; Lexington HS; Lexington, OH; Cls Rep Frsh Cls; Boy Scts; Sct Actv; Ger Clb; Mth Clb; Ftbl; Trk; Mgrs; Univ.

HORAN, WILLIAM; Greensburg Community HS; Greensburg, IN; 16/195 FCA; Hon Rl; Pres NHS; 4-H; Sci Clb; Spn Clb; Letter Ftbl; Letter Wrstlng; Purdue Univ; Vet.

HORANYI, ANNA; Belmont HS; Dayton, OH; Cls Rep Soph Cls; Cmnty Wkr; Drl Tm; Hon Rl; Sch Pl; Yth Flsp; Rptr Yrbk; Rptr Sch Nwsp; Drama Clb; Chrldng; Mbr Jr Cncl On World Affairs; College; Law.

HORCHNER, JEFFERY; Rapid River HS; Rapid Rvr, MI; VP Sr Cls; Am Leg Boys St; Chrh Wkr; Cmnty Wkr; Hon Rl; Letter Bsktbl; Michigan Tech Univ; Comp Sci.

HORDYK, DARLENE; Creston HS; Grand Rpds, MI; Cmp Fr Grls; Chrs; Hosp Ade; Aquinas Coll; Nursing.

HORESOVSKY, GREG; Cheboygan Area HS; Cheboygan, MI; Band; Boy Scts; Hon Rl; Orch; Sch Pl; Blue Lake Intl Band 79; Dist II Hon Band 77 & 78; Mc Donald All Amer HS Band 79; Univ Of Michigan; Physn.

HORGAN, CHRISTINE; Swanton HS; Swanton, OH; Band; Chrs; Hon Rl; Mdrgl; NHS; Orch; Sch Mus; Yth Flsp; FTA; Spn Clb; Univ Of Toledo; Elem Ed.

HORLOCKER, JACKI; Westerville South HS; Westerville, OH; Chrs; Off Ade; Rptr Yrbk; Pep Clb; VP Mat Maids; PPFtbl; Scr Kpr; Edgecliff Coll; Elem Ed.

HORMAN, JENNY; Edison HS; Milan, OH; 15/162 Am Leg Aux Girls St; Chrs; Girl Scts; Hon Rl; NHS; Sch Mus; Sch Pl; Stg Crw; Treas Drama Clb; Pres FTA; Miami Univ; Special Educ.

HORMANN, AMY; Wapakoneta Sr HS; Wapakoneta, OH; 25/350 Am Leg Aux Girls St; Band; Hon Rl; Red Cr Ade; Yrbk; Lat Clb; Univ Of Cincinnati; Med Tech.

HORMUTH, SARAH; William Henry Harrison HS; Evansville, IN; Band; Hon Rl; Civ Clb; Ger Clb; Letter Glf; PPFtbl; Cit Awd; College; Bus.

HORN, BRIDGET; Lumen Christi HS; Jackson, MI; 13/240 Hon Rl; Jr NHS; NHS; Off Ade; Jackson Cmnty Coll; Sec.

HORN, DAVID; Moellen HS; Cincinnati, OH; Aud/Vis; Chrs; Chrh Wkr; Hon Rl; Mdrgl; Off Ade; Stg Crw; FBLA; Bsbl; Ftbl; Xavier Univ; Busns Admin.

HORN, DENISE; Heath HS; Heath, OH; 1/125 Cls Rep Frsh Cls; Cls Rep Soph Cls; FCA; Girl Scts; Hon Rl; Natl Forn Lg; NHS; Stu Cncl; Univ; Bus Mgmt.

HORN, DIANA; Warsaw Cmnty HS; Warsaw, IN; 12/400 Chrh Wkr; FCA; Hon Rl; Yth Flsp; 4-H; Fr Clb; Trk; GAA; 4-H Awd; Kiwan Awd; Univ.

HORN, GEORGE; Sturgis HS; Sturgis, MI; Boy Scts; Cmnty Wkr; Jr NHS; NHS; Sct Actv; Letter Bsbl; Bsktbl; Glen Oaks Comm College; Bus Mgmt.

HORN, GLENDA; Ithaca HS; Ithaca, MI; Band; Chrs; Hon Rl; 4-H; Fr Clb; 4-H Awd; Lion Awd;.

HORN, JAY; Waynesfield HS; Wapakoneta, OH; 1/60 VP Frsh Cls; Cls Rep Soph Cls; Cl Rep Jr Cls; Band; Chrs; Hon Rl; Jr NHS; NHS; Orch; Sch Mus; Case Western Reserve Univ; Comp Engr.

HORN, JAY; Waynesfield Goshen HS; Wapakonata, OH; 1/60 VP Frsh Cls; Band; Chrs; Hon Rl; Jr NHS; NHS; Sch Mus; Sch Pl; Stu Cncl; Yrbk; Univ; Comp Engr.

HORN, JOHN; Pineville HS; Pineville, WV; Am Leg Boys St; Hon Rl; Jr NHS; NHS; Stu Cncl; Yth Flsp; Drama Clb; Pep Clb; Sci Clb; Letter Bsbl; Math Field Day Winner 2nd Pl In Countu 9thj Grd 77; Univ; Drafting.

HORN, JUDY; North White HS; Monon, IN; Band; Hon Rl; NHS; Off Ade; FBLA; GAA; IM Sprt;.

HORN, KIRSTIE; North Adams HS; N Adams, MI; 34/49 Hon Rl; Lbry Ade; NHS; Off Ade; 4-H; Treas FTA; Mgrs; Spartan Bus Acad; Keypunch Oprtr.

HORN, LORI S; Talawanda HS; Hamilton, OH; Pres Frsh Cls; Cl Rep Jr Cls; Hosp Ade; Stu Cncl; Sec 4-H; Fr Clb; Pep Clb; Capt Chrldng; 4-H Awd; Mas Awd; Univ Of Kentucky; Jrnlsm.

HORNBROOK, SAMUEL; Watkins Memorial HS; Kirkersville, OH; 23/236 Band; Chrs; Chrh Wkr; Hon Rl; Orch; IM Sprt; Grand Rapids Baptist Coll; Bible.

HORNE, GAIL; Bexley HS; Columbus, OH; Cls Rep Soph Cls; Chrs; Hon Rl; Red Cr Ade; Drama Clb; Fr Clb; Rus Clb; Univ Of Pennsylvania; Bus.

HORNE, LAURA; Liberty Benton HS; Findlay, OH; Chrs; Hon Rl; Off Ade; Letter Swmmng; St Beauty Acad; Cosmetologist.

HORNE, NANCY D; Cassopolis Ross Beatty HS; Cassopolis, MI; Cls Rep Frsh Cls; Cls Rep Sr Cls; Band; Drm Mjrt; Hon Rl; NHS; Sch Mus; Sch Pl; Stg Crw; Stu Cncl; Univ Of Florida; Archt.

HORNE, PATRICIA; Charles Stewart Mott HS; Warren, MI; 79/650 NHS; Mgrs; Natl Merit SF; Macomb Cnty Cmnty Coll; Gen Bus.

HORNER, CHRISTINE; Our Lady Of Mt Carmel HS; Wyandotte, MI; Pep Clb; Spn Clb; Bsbl; College; Vet.

HORNER, DAWN E; Loudonville HS; Loudonville, OH; Am Leg Aux Girls St; Band; Chrh Wkr; Hon Rl; Jr NHS; Sch Pl; VP Yth Flsp; Rptr Yrbk; Sch Nwsp; Drama Clb; Jrnlsm Assoc Of Oh Scl Awd Of Excllncy 78; Ohio St Univ; Tch Handicpd.

HORNER, ELIZABETH; Magnolia HS; Proctor, WV; Cls Rep Frsh Cls; Cls Rep Soph Cls; Am Leg Aux Girls St; Band; Hon Rl; Yrbk; Fr Clb; Script Comm For Magnolia Day 78; Co Chrmn For Homecoming Parade Dance 78; Co Chrmn For Prom 79; Univ; Bus Mgmt.

HORNER, LINDA; Mt Clemens HS; Mt Clemens, MI; 19/200 Band; Girl Scts; Hon Rl; Hosp Ade; NHS; Pol Wkr; Sct Actv; Letter Gym; IM Sprt; Mgrs; Central Michigan Univ; Spec Educ.

HORNER, NORMAN; Cardinal Stritch HS; Walbridge, OH; Chrs; Hon Rl; JA; NHS; Letter Crs Cntry; JA Awd; Univ; Archt.

HORNER, REBECCA J; Marysville HS; Marysville, MI; Chrs; Hon Rl; PAVAS; Sch Mus; Sch Pl; Stg Crw; Drama Clb; Fr Clb; Pep Clb; St Clair Cnty Cmnty Coll; Chem Engr.

HORNES, BRENDA; Benton Harbor HS; Benton Hrbr, MI; Hon Rl; Off Ade; Parsons; Sec.

HORNEY, BYRON; Wilmington HS; Wilmington, OH; 22/286 Boy Scts; Chrh Wkr; FCA; Hon Rl; Sct Actv; Yth Flsp; 4-H; Spn Clb; Wrstlng; Mgrs; Univ; Math Statistics.

HORNEY, CAROL; Colerain Sr HS; Cincinnati, OH; Band; Hon Rl; Jr NHS; NHS; Mth Clb; Spn Clb; Xavier Univ; X Ray Tech.

HORNING, CHRIS; Ferndale HS; Pleasant Ridge, MI; Chrs; Stg Crw; Rdo Clb; VICA; Crs Cntry; Trk; Gov Hon Prg Awd; Oakland Comm College; Architecture.

HORNING, MARK; Lake View HS; Stow, OH; Hon Rl; Bsbl; Bsktbl; Ftbl; Coach Actv; Lion Awd; College; Business.

HORNING, MIKE; Sebring Mckinley HS; Sebring, OH; 27/94 Chrh Wkr; Bsbl; Bsktbl; Coach Actv; IM Sprt; College; Marketing.

HORNOR, BARBARA; Roosevelt Wilson HS; Nutterfort, WV; 2/130 Hon Rl; Yth Flsp; Y-Teens; Yrbk; 4-H; Fr Clb; FTA; Leo Clb; Cit Awd; 4-H Awd; Fairmont St Coll; Education.

HORNOR, J TIM; Bay HS; Bay Village, OH; Cls Rep Soph Cls; Cl Rep Jr Cls; Band; Chrs; Orch; Sch Mus; Stu Cncl; Crs Cntry; Rotary Awd; Univ; Orch Mbr.

HORNUNG, JUDITH A; Eudid Sr HS; Euclid, OH; Chrs; Stg Crw; Stu Cncl; Mth Clb; Hndbl; Letter Swmmng; GAA; Tmr; Mbr Of Eudid Varsity Ch orale; Coll; Public Relations.

HORNYAK, MARGARET; Cardinal Stritch HS; Oregon, OH; Cls Rep Frsh Cls; Trs Soph Cls; Am Leg Aux Girls St; Chrh Wkr; Debate Tm; Drl Tm; Girl Scts; Hon Rl; College; Med.

HORRALL, GREGORY; Princeton Cmnty HS; Princeton, IN; 1/210 NHS; Letter Crs Cntry; Letter Trk; U S Air Force Academy; Airline Pilot.

HORRIGAN, TIMOTHY J; Trenton HS; Trenton, MI; 6/550 Hon Rl; Ger Clb; Natl Merit SF; Univ Of Michigan; Pre Med.

HORSCH, SHIRLEY; Parkside HS; Jackson, MI; 29/344 Cls Rep Sr Cls; Chrs; Hon Rl; Hosp Ade; PAVAS; Sch Pl; Yth Flsp; Letter Gym; Cert Of Recognition St Of Mi Comptn Schlrshp Progr 79; Departmntl Awd Bus Ed 79; Schlstc Hnr Awd 76 79; Ferris St Coll; Acctg.

HORSEFIELD, NANCY; Licking Heights HS; Reynoldsburg, OH; Band; Girl Scts; Hon Rl; VP OEA; Licking County JVS; Bus Admin.

HORSFALL, PATRICIA; Climax Scotts HS; Scotts, MI; Sec Frsh Cls; Sec Jr Cls; Chrh Wkr; Hon Rl; NHS; Sch Pl; Yth Flsp; FHA; College; Nursing.

HORSFORD, JULIE; Jackson County Western HS; Jackson, MI; VP Frsh Cls; Trs Jr Cls; VP Sr Cls; Chrs; Cmnty Wkr; Mdrgl; NHS; Eastern Mic Syracuse; Drama.

HORSLEY, CHERYL; Midland HS; Midland, MI; 64/486 Cmp Fr Grls; Chrs; Hon Rl; Jr NHS; NHS; Yth Flsp; DECA; Mic State; Acctg.

HORSLEY, KAREN; William Henry Harrison HS; Harrison, OH; 19/218 Band; Girl Scts; Hon Rl; Jr NHS; PAVAS; Sch Pl; Sct Actv; Stg Crw; Drama Clb; Scr Kpr; Miami Univ; Anthropologist.

HORSLEY, LISA; Columbus North HS; Columbus, OH; 18/325 Cls Rep Soph Cls; Cl Rep Jr Cls; Cls Rep Sr Cls; Pres Boy Scts; Chrs; Drl Tm; Girl Scts; Hon Rl; Hosp Ade; Jr NHS; 1st Place Art Show 1974; Ohio St Univ; Med.

HORSLEY, MIKE; Mt Healthy HS; Cincinnati, OH; 8/500 NHS; Ger Clb; Univ.

HORSLEY, R; Terre Haute HS; Terre Haute, IN; Chrs; Hon Rl; Mgrs;.

HORST, JANE; South Range HS; Columbiana, OH; Trs Frsh Cls; Trs Soph Cls; Trs Sr Cls; Chrh Wkr; Hon Rl; NHS; Off Ade; Yth Flsp; Rptr Yrbk; S Range Sci Fair 2nd In Bio 77; Goshen Coll; Bus.

HORST, PAUL; South Range Local HS; North Lima, OH; 10/140 Chrh Wkr; Hon Rl; Lbry Ade; NHS; Bsktbl; Embry Riddle; Aeronautical Engr.

HORSTMAN, NANCY; Ottoville Local Schl; Cloverdale, OH; 14/68 Sec Soph Cls; Hon Rl; Sch Mus; Sch Pl; Yrbk; Drama Clb; Sec FHA; Sec OEA; Intl Bus Coll; Acctg.

HORSTMAN, REBECCA; Ottoville HS; Cloverdale, OH; Chrs; Hon Rl; Off Ade; Sch Mus; Ed Yrbk; Drama Clb; 4-H; Trk; 4-H Awd; Univ; Comp Progr.

HORTON, CYNTHIA; Walled Lake Western HS; Walled Lk, MI; Hon Rl; Natl Forn Lg; Pres Yth Flsp; Yrbk; OEA; Mas Awd; Oakland Cmnty Coll; Acctg.

HORTON, DALE; Benedictine HS; Cleveland, OH; NHS; Letter Ftbl; Trk; IM Sprt; Coll; Busns.

HORTON, DAVID; F J Reitz HS; Evansville, IN; Sec Am Leg Boys St; Chrs; Pol Wkr; Stu Cncl; DECA; Spn Clb; Cit Awd; DECA St & Dist Awds; College; Busns.

HORTON, JEFF; Portsmouth East HS; Portsmouth, OH; Cls Rep Frsh Cls; Cl Rep Jr Cls; Aud/Vis; Band; Chrs; Hon Rl; Lbry Ade; Mdrgl; Sch Mus; Sch Pl; Eng Schlrshp Tm 79; Otstndng Vocal Jr Stud 79; Morehead St Univ; Music.

HORTON, JERRY; Greenville Sr HS; Greenville, MI; Hon Rl; 4-H; Letter Bsbl; Letter Bsktbl; Ftbl; Letter Trk; 4-H Awd; Have Been Considered For St Of Mi Comptn Schlrshp Progr 79; Was Accptd To Camp Retupmoc Comp Seminar 79; General Mtrs Inst; Auto Engr.

HORTON, LAVERNE; Washington HS; E Chicago, IN; 7/279 Band; Chrh Wkr; Hon Rl; NHS; Stu Cncl; 4-H; Pres Fr Clb; Cit Awd; Univ; Bus Mgmt.

HORTON, LORI; Mooresville HS; Camby, IN; Chrs; Hon Rl; Mdrgl; NHS; Sch Mus; Drama Clb; Fr Clb; Pres FHA; Ten; PPFtbl; Ind Univ Bloomington; Marketing.

HORTON, MARNITA; Wirt HS; Gary, IN; Girl Scts; Hon Rl; Pep Clb; Spn Clb; GAA; Sumr Hon At In St Univ 79; Indiana St Univ.

HORTON, SANDEE; Champion HS; Warren, OH; 15/260 Band; Drm Mjrt; Hon Rl; Hosp Ade; Orch; Sch Pl; Yth Flsp; Rptr Sch Nwsp; Drama Clb; Spn Clb; Univ.

HORTON, SHERRIE; Clare HS; Clare, MI; Chrs; Chrh Wkr; Hon Rl; Off Ade; Yth Flsp; Fr Clb; College; Corporate Law.

HORTON, YOLANDA; Jane Addams Vocational HS; Cleveland, OH; Sec Jr Cls; Cmp Fr Grls; Chrh Wkr; Drl Tm; Girl Scts; Hon Rl; JA; Jr NHS; Cit Awd; JA Awd; Kent St Univ; Clerical.

HORVAT, DIANE M; Fairmont West HS; , ; Trs Frsh Cls; Trs Soph Cls; Trs Jr Cls; Cmp Fr Grls; Girl Scts; NHS; ROTC; Stg Crw; OEA; Wright St Univ; Bus Admin.

HORVAT, KIM; Bloomfield Mespo Local HS; N Bloomfield, OH; 5/28 Cls Rep Frsh Cls; Cls Rep Soph Cls; Cl Rep Jr Cls; Cls Rep Sr Cls; Band; Hon Rl; Off Ade; Sch Mus; Sch Pl; Stg Crw; Kent St Univ; Phys Ed.

HORVATH, ANGIE; Waite HS; Toledo, OH; 19/269 Hon Rl; NHS; Off Ade; Red Cr Ade; Sdlty; Sec Stu Cncl; Yrbk; Rptr Sch Nwsp; DECA; Ger Clb; Toledo Univ; Busns Admin.

HORVATH, JAMES; Stow Sr HS; Kent, OH; Letter Ftbl; Trk; IM Sprt; Big Dog Awd Ftbl 78; Sec Of Var S Club 79; Univ; Dent.

HORVATH, KATHLEEN A; Lake Catholic HS; Eastlake, OH; 35/340 Cls Rep Frsh Cls; Cls Rep Soph Cls; Cl Rep Jr Cls; VP Sr Cls; Girl Scts; Hon Rl; Hosp Ade; Sch Pl; Stu Cncl; Rptr Sch Nwsp; Cleveland St Univ; Phys Ther.

HORVATH, KIMBERLEY; Bellbrook HS; Bellbrook, OH; Band; Drm Bgl; FFA; Letter College; Medicine.

HORVATH, ROB; Haslett HS; E Lansing, MI; 5/162 Cls Rep Soph Cls; Cl Rep Jr Cls; Chrs; NHS; Bsbl; Crs Cntry; Letter Wrstlng; HS All Amer Hon Progr 78; Mi HS St Finals Wrestling Qualifier 77; Mi HS St Finals Wrstlng 4th Pl 78; Univ; Human Sci.

HORVATH, SUZANNE; Buckeye South HS; Rayland, OH; Hon Rl; FHA; OEA; Bus Sch1; Data Proc.

HORWATT JR, WILLIAM; Eastlake North Rangers HS; East Lake, OH; 176/670 Aud/Vis; Band; Boy Scts; Hon Rl; Crs Cntry; Letter Socr; Letter Trk; Cleveland St Univ; Med.

HOSAFLOOK, THEODORE; Buckhannon Upshur HS; Buckhannon, WV; Boy Scts; CAP; Sct Actv; Sci Clb; Trk; Regnl Sci & Engr Fair Physics 1st 76; U S Air Force Awd 76; St Sci & Engr Fair Physics 1st Pl 78; Univ; Astro Engr.

HOSE, MARK; Ovid Elsie HS; Ovid, MI; Cl Rep Jr Cls; Hon Rl; NHS; Sch Pl; Pres Stu Cncl; Ed Sch Nwsp; Bsbl; Bsktbl; Glf; Coach Actv; Univ; Archt.

HOSE, MARK R; Ovid Elsie HS; Ovid, MI; Cl Rep Jr Cls; Hon Rl; NHS; Off Ade; Sch Pl; Stu Cncl; Ed Sch Nwsp; Bsbl; Glf; Univ; Archt.

HOSEA, LOVELLA; Henry Ford HS; Detroit, MI; VP Frsh Cls; Trs Soph Cls; Hon Rl; Lbry Ade; Spn Clb; Trk; Cit Awd; Wayne St Univ; Acctg.

HOSEY, JOSEPH; North HS; Youngstown, OH; Pres Sr Cls; VP Sr Cls; Cmnty Wkr; Hon Rl; Jr NHS; NHS; Pol Wkr; Rptr Yrbk; Ed Sch Nwsp; College.

HOSINSKI, KAREN; Marian HS; Mishawaka, IN; 26/145 Chrs; Hon Rl; Sch Mus; IM Sprt; Mgrs; Scr Kpr; Tmr; Univ.

HOSKEN, WENDI; Reeths Puffer Sr HS; No Muskegon, MI; Band; Stg Crw; Rptr Sch Nwsp; Spn Clb; Trk; Peggy White Schl; Cosmetology.

HOSKIN, HOLLY; High School; Sandusky, OH; Band; Chrs; Hon Rl; Sch Mus; FNA; Spn Clb; Gym; Kiwan Awd;.

HOSKINS, REBECCA; North HS; Columbus, OH; 18/325 Trs Sr Cls; Chrs; Chrh Wkr; Drl Tm; Girl Scts; Hon Rl; Hosp Ade; Jr NHS; Sec NHS; Off Ade; Ohio State Univ; Medicine.

HOSKINS, SUE; Clermont Northeastern HS; Willamsburg, OH; Chrs; Hon Rl; Rptr Yrbk; Rptr Sch Nwsp; Pep Clb; Chrldng; Scr Kpr; Live Oaks Voc Schl; Cosmetology.

HOSKINS, TINA; Pontiac Northern HS; Pontiac, MI; Cls Rep Sr Cls; Cmp Fr Grls; Chrh Wkr; Cmnty Wkr; Girl Scts; Hon Rl; Hosp Ade; Jr NHS; NHS; Off Ade; Mi Comp Schlrshp Univ Of Mi; Navy; Ocean Systm Tech.

HOSKINS, VICKI; Hamilton S E HS; Noblesville, IN; Girl Scts; OEA; Pep Clb; Spn Clb; Chrldng; Mgrs; ISU; CPA.

HOSKINS, WILLIAM; St Xavier HS; Cincinnati, OH; Boy Scts; Chrh Wkr; Hon Rl; NHS; Pol Wkr; Sct Actv; Rptr Yrbk; Trk; IM Sprt; Natl Merit Ltr; Boy Scouts Ad Altare Dei Awrd 77; Univ.

HOSKINSON, DONNA; Morgan HS; Mc Connelsville, OH; VP Soph Cls; Am Leg Aux Girls St; Hon Rl; Lbry Ade; NHS; Off Ade; Rptr Sch Nwsp; Spn Clb; Letter Bsbl; Univ; Phys Educ Tchr.

HOSKINSON, MARGARET E; Shadyside HS; Shadyside, OH; Cl Rep Jr Cls; Band; Hon Rl; NHS; Off Ade; Sch Mus; Stu Cncl; Y-Teens; Spn Clb; IM Sprt;.

HOSLER, BOB; Loudonville Perrysville HS; Perrysville, OH; Hon Rl; NHS; Pol Wkr; Yrbk; Sec Lat Clb; Spn Clb; Adv Spanish Stu Mexico Trip; 1 Yr Hnr/merit Roll Cert; Ohio Test Of Schlstc Ach Sr Soc Studies; Arizona Univ; Intl Trade.

HOSMER, RICK; Elmwood HS; Cygnet, OH; Hon Rl; 4-H; FFA; Letter Ftbl; IM Sprt; 4-H Awd;.

HOSTELLEY, GREG; St Ignatius HS; Parma Hts, OH; 31/251 Sec Soph Cls; JA; Pol Wkr; Yrbk; Rptr Sch Nwsp; Rdo Clb; Scr Kpr; J A Cleveland St Univ 400 Scshp & Area Treas Of Yr & Area Outstndng Young Busmn 79; Cleveland St Univ; Bus Mgmt.

HOSTETER, PATTI; Wyoming Park HS; Wyoming, MI; 5/227 Band; Hon Rl; NHS; Stg Crw; Pep Clb; Spn Clb; Letter Ten; Michigan St Univ; Engr.

HOSTETLER, CHERYL; Westview Jr Sr HS; La Grange, IN; 9/83 Hon Rl; NHS; Pep Clb; Letter Gym; Letter Trk; Chrldng; GAA; Harding Univ; Phys Educ.

HOSTETLER, CRISTINE; Merrillville HS; Merrillville, IN; Band; Chrh Wkr; Girl Scts; Hon Rl; Stu Cncl; College; Bus.

HOSTETLER, GAIL; Warren Central HS; Indianapolis, IN; Chrs; Chrh Wkr; Hosp Ade; Sch Mus; Yth Flsp; IUPUI; Nursing.

HOSTETLER, JONDA; Lynchburg Clay HS; Lynchburg, OH; 11/100 Sec Jr Cls; Band; Chrs; Chrh Wkr; Hon Rl; Stu Cncl; Chrldng; Voice Dem Awd; Miami Valley Schl Of Nursing; Nrsng.

HOSTETLER, LEE A; Buckeye West HS; Mt Pleasant, OH; Hon Rl; NHS; 4-H; Pep Clb; Sci Clb; Chrldng; Scr Kpr; 4-H Awd; College; Accounting.

HOSTETLER, LOIS; Smithville HS; Marshallvl, OH; Band; Chrs; Chrh Wkr; FCA; Hon Rl; NHS; 4-H; Fr Clb; GAA; 4-H Awd; Wright State Univ; Nursing.

HOSTETLER, MARGARET; Andrean HS; Merrillville, IN; 40/296 Pres Band; Drm Mjrt; Girl Scts; Hon Rl; NHS; Orch; Sch Mus; Rptr Yrbk; GAA; College; Music.

HOSWELL, LORRAINE M; Belmont HS; Datyon, OH; Drl Tm; Girl Scts; Lbry Ade; Off Ade; Stu Cncl; Spn Clb; Socr; Chrldng; Vocational Schl; Dance.

HOTCHKISS, CATHY; Our Lady Of The Lakes HS; Drayton Plains, MI; 15/45 Trs Soph Cls; Cl Rep Jr Cls; Chrh Wkr; Girl Scts; Hon Rl; Sct Actv; Stu Cncl; Eng Clb; Fr Clb; VICA; Wayne St Univ; Med Asst.

HOTT, DENISE; Hampshire HS; Augusta, WV; Hon Rl; Off Ade; Yrbk; Drama Clb; FBLA; Trk; Letter Pom Pon; Shepherd College; Bus Admin.

HOTT, LORETTA; North HS; Columbus, OH; Cls Rep Frsh Cls; Cls Rep Soph Cls; Cl Rep Jr Cls; Hon Rl; Stu Cncl; OEA; Chrldng; Mat Maids; PPFtbl; Scr Kpr; Ohio St Univ; Exec Sec.

HOTT, MITSI; Hampshire HS; Bloomery, WV; 4/213 Cl Rep Jr Cls; AFS; Chrs; Chrh Wkr; Hon Rl; Jr NHS; NHS; Stg Crw; Stu Cncl; Drama Clb; Shepherd Coll; Pharm Sci.

HOTT, RHONDA; Hampshire HS; Augusto, WV; AFS; Chrs; Hon Rl; Hosp Ade; Sch Pl; Stu Cncl; D rama Clb; 4-H; Twrlr; College; Registered Nurse.

HOTT, TIMOTHY; Hampshire HS; Kirby, WV; 60/218 AFS; Treas Am Leg Boys St; Chrs; Pres Chrh Wkr; Hon Rl; Pres Yth Flsp; Treas FFA; Potomac St Coll.

HOTTEL, ANNA; Avon Jr Sr HS; Indianpls, IN; 31/192 Hon Rl; Lbry Ade; Sch Pl; Drama Clb; Fr Clb; Cedarville Univ; Scndry Educ.

HOTTOIS, MICHAEL; Normandy HS; Parma, OH; 15/654 Band; Boy Scts; Cmnty Wkr; Hon Rl; Natl Forn Lg; Stu Cncl; Key Clb; Lat Clb; Univ.

HOTTOIS, ROBERT; Parma Franciscan HS; Seven Hls, OH; Chrh Wkr; Hon Rl; NHS; Key Clb; Letter Swmmng; 4-H Awd; Bowling Green Univ; Bus Admin.

HOUCHINS, DEBORAH; Shady Spring HS; Daniels, WV; 23/155 Cls Rep Sr Cls; Band; Chrh Wkr; Drm Mjrt; FCA; Hon Rl; NHS; Sch Pl; Stu Cncl; Drama Clb; Beckley Coll; Acctg.

HOUCHINS, MARK; Pike Central HS; Winslow, IN; Hon Rl; NHS; Purdue Univ; Engr.

HOUCK, BONNIE; Alma HS; Riverdale, MI; 35/244 Bsktbl; Univ Of Mic; Ve.

HOUCK, DEBORAH; Holgate HS; Holgate, OH; 14/38 Band; Drm Mjrt; Hon Rl; Sch Pl; Rptr Sch Nwsp; Ger Clb; Twrlr; Voice Dem Awd; Northwest Tech; Acctg.

HOUCK, TOM; Hicksville HS; Hicksville, OH; Aud/Vis; Boy Scts; Hon Rl; Sct Actv; Spn Clb; Ftbl; IM Sprt; Tmr; Pres Awd; Washington Univ; Engr.

HOUGH, LISA; Rutherford B Hayes HS; Delaware, OH; Chrs; Drl Tm; Hon Rl; Yth Flsp; 4-H; Ohi State; Ed.

HOUGH, WHITNEY; Rochester HS; Rochester, MI; AFS; Band; Chrs; Pres Chrh Wkr; Cmnty Wkr; Hon Rl; Mod UN; NHS; Pol Wkr; Sch Mus; College; Medicine.

HOUGH, WILLIAM J; Upper Arlington HS; Upper Arlington, OH; 1/610 Hon Rl; Fr Clb; French Natl Hnr Soc 78 79; Univ; Law.

HOUGHAWOUT, PAM; Elmwood HS; Bloomdale, OH; Band; Treas Chrs; Hon Rl; MMM; Sch Pl; Yth Flsp; VP FTA; Sci Clb; IM Sprt; M J Owens Tech Schl; Optemetry Asst.

HOUGHTALING, RETTA; Grand Ledge HS; Grand Ledge, MI; 25/416 Band; Hon Rl; NHS; Orch; Voice Dem Awd; Lansing Comm College; Comp Progr.

HOUGHTON, ANNETTE; Cedar Spring HS; Sand Lake, MI; Band; Hon Rl; FFA; Grand Rapids Baptist College; Social.

HOUGLAND, DEBBIE; Western HS; Peebles, OH; 9/76 Band; Chrs; Hon Rl; 4-H; Fr Clb; FHA; 4-H Awd;.

HOULDIESON, BRAD; Griffith Sr HS; Griffith, IN; Stu Cncl; Sprt Ed Sch Nwsp; Rptr Sch Nwsp;.

HOUMARD, CHARLES; Green HS; Akron, OH; 4/250 Band; Hon Rl; NHS; Coll; Music.

HOUMARD, JOSEPH; Green HS; Akron, OH; 28/317 JA; NHS; VP Yth Flsp; Letter Crs Cntry; Letter Trk; Capt IM Sprt; Manchester Coll; Pre Med.

HOUMES, PATTI; Fountain Central Jr & Sr HS; Veedersburg, IN; 6/146 Cls Rep Soph Cls; Band; Hon Rl; Hosp Ade; NHS; Quill & Scroll; Sch Pl; Rptr Sch Nwsp; Sch Nwsp; Purdue Univ; Nursing.

HOUNSHELL, ROSALIE; Dayton Christian HS; Dayton, OH; Hon Rl; NHS; Sch Mus; Yrbk; Chrldng; Tmr; Ach Awd For Bible Memorization; Outstndng Speech Stu Awd; Recognition For Excellence In French; Ivy League Schl; Fine Arts.

HOUPT, LOWELL; Owen Vly HS; Spencer, IN; 3/200 Pres Jr Cls; Val; Band; Chrh Wkr; Capt FCA; NHS; Sch Mus; Letter Ftbl; Mgrs; Univ; Music.

HOUSE, JANET; St Joseph HS; Niles, MI; Cls Rep Frsh Cls; Chrh Wkr; Girl Scts; Hon Rl; Stu Cncl; Yth Flsp; Key Clb; Letter Swmmng; Trk; Michigan St Univ; Bus Admin.

HOUSE, KAY; Shenandoah HS; New Castle, IN; 5/118 Hon Rl; NHS; Sch Nwsp; Mth Clb; Sci Clb; College; Math.

HOUSE, MARY J; Cascade HS; Clayton, IN; 13/136 Cl Rep Jr Cls; Band; Hon Rl; Stu Cncl; 4-H; FBLA; FHA; Pep Clb; Gym; Trk; Purdue Univ; Elem Educ.

HOUSE, SONYA; North HS; Columbus, OH; 23/325 Hon Rl; Jr NHS; NHS; Fr Clb; Ohio St Univ; Psych.

HOUSEHOLDER, CHARLES; Sebring Mc Kinley HS; Sebring, OH; Chrs; Lbry Ade; PAVAS; Sch Mus; Yrbk; Trk; Akron Barber Coll; Cosmetology.

HOUSENGA, TODD; Houghton Lake HS; Prudenville, MI; Hon Rl; NHS; Bsbl; Bsktbl; Coach Actv; Univ.

HOUSER, KRIS; Bloom Carroll HS; Lancaster, OH; 8/155 Band; Hon Rl; NHS; Off Ade; Stu Cncl; Capt Chrldng; Scr Kpr; Tmr; Am Leg Awd; Baldwin Wallace Coll; Acctg.

HOUSER, SUSAN; Kearsley HS; Flint, MI; 54/380 Cls Rep Soph Cls; Cl Rep Jr Cls; Cls Rep Sr Cls; Band; Hon Rl; Natl Forn Lg; Off Ade; Sct Actv; Stu Cncl; Letter Trk; Bst All Round Feml 79; Mst Outstndng Chrldr 79; Univ Of Michigan; Med Tech.

HOUSER, TAMMY; Chaney HS; Youngstown, OH; 43/370 Cmp Fr Grls; Hon Rl; Off Ade; Pol Wkr; Rptr Sch Nwsp; Spn Clb; PPFtbl; Youngstown St Univ; Comp Tech.

HOUSEWORTH, KIM; Martinsville HS; Martinsville, ID; Sec Frsh Cls; Cls Rep Frsh Cls; Sec Soph Cls; Cls Rep Soph Cls; Sec Jr Cls; Cl Rep Jr Cls; Stu Cncl; Gym; Swmmng; Chrldng; Rcvd Letter In Diving 1977; Univ Of Miami; Dent Asst.

HOUSKA, RONDA; Highland HS; Hinckley, OH; Cls Rep Soph Cls; Cl Rep Jr Cls; Sch Mus; Stu Cncl; Ed Yrbk; Key Clb; Pep Clb; Ten; Letter Chrldng; College; Criminal Justice.

HOUSMAN, BRENDA; Midland Trail HS; Hico, WV; Drm Mjrt; Hon Rl; DECA; Fr Clb; Pep Clb; VICA; Twrlr; West Virginia Tech.

HOUSTON, CRAIG; Rensselaer Central HS; Rensselaer, IN; Hon Rl; 4-H; FFA; IM Sprt; Scr Kpr; 4-H Awd; Hoosier Schlr Awd 79; Sigma Alpha Chi Schlrshp 79; Sr Grd Champ Swine Showmn In St Fair 77; ITT Tech Inst; Elec Engr.

HOUSTON, ERIC; Lima Sr HS; Lima, OH; Cls Rep Frsh Cls; Boy Scts; Chrh Wkr; DECA; Glf; Trk; IM Sprt; Bowling Green St Univ; Art.

HOUSTON, JOYCE; Brookville HS; Brookville, IN; Band; 4-H; Pep Clb; Scr Kpr; Band Awd; Coll; Nursing.

HOUSTON, KAY A; Swan Valley HS; Saginaw, MI; Cls Rep Frsh Cls; Cls Rep Soph Cls; Cls Rep Sr Cls; Hosp Ade; Jr NHS; NHS; Sch Pl; Pres Stu Cncl; Drama Clb; Spn Clb; Homecoming Court; Michigan State Univ; Med Asst.

HOUSTON, LILLIAN; East Technical HS; Cleveland, OH; 9/304 Cls Rep Frsh Cls; Cls Rep Soph Cls; Cl Rep Jr Cls; Cls Rep Sr Cls; AFS; Chrs; Chrh Wkr; Alliance College; Bus Admin.

HOUSTON, LISA; Pontiac Ctrl HS; Pontiac, MI; Chrs; Chrh Wkr; Hon Rl; Sch Mus; Sch Pl; Drama Clb; Capt Crs Cntry; Trk; Cit Awd; Tennessee St Univ; Occup Ther.

HOUSTON, MELANIE; Bishop Noll Institute; E Chicago, IN; 64/321 Cls Rep Frsh Cls; Cls Rep Soph Cls; Cl Rep Jr Cls; Drl Tm; Hon Rl; Y-Teens; Spn Clb; Pom Pon; Arizona St Univ; Archt.

HOUTMAN, LYNDA S; Plainwell HS; Kalamazoo, MI; 1/225 Chrs; Chrh Wkr; Hon Rl; NHS; PAVAS; Sch Mus; Yth Flsp; Beta Clb; 4-H; Fr Clb; Univ.

HOUTS, RANDAL; Boardman HS; Boardman, OH; 38/558 Hon Rl; JA; NHS; Spn Clb; IM Sprt; JA Awd; Jr Achvmnt Delegate To NAJAC 78; Jr Achvmnt VP Of Youngstown Chamber 79; Jr Achvmnt Officer Of Yr 78; Univ Of Cincinnati; Archt.

HOVANEC, JAMES; Croswell Lexington HS; Crosell, MI; Hon Rl; FFA; Letter Ftbl; Letter Trk; Coll; Profsnl Welder.

HOVANEC, MIKE; Hubbard HS; Hubbard, OH; Letter Swmmng; Coach Actv; IM Sprt; Tmr; Cit Awd; Opt Clb Awd; Perfect Attnd 76; Univ.

HOVANIC, BARBARA; Warren Western Reserve HS; Warren, OH; 32/432 Band; Bowling Green Univ; Marine Bio.

HOVARTER, CARLA; East Noble HS; Kendallvile, IN; 123/269 Band; Stg Crw; Drama Clb; Mat Maids; PPFtbl; Ari W College; Radio Tv Commnctn.

HOVARTER, SHARI; De Kalb HS; Corunna, IN; 33/284 Chrs; Girl Scts; VP JA; NHS; Sct Actv; Ger Clb; Pep Clb; JA Awd; College; Med Tech.

HOVATER, ALISON; Chelsea HS; Chelsea, MI; Chrs; Chrh Wkr; FCA; Mdrgl; Sch Mus; 4-H; Sci Clb; Capt Bsbl; Swmmng; Evangel Coll; Music Mnstry.

HOVE, JEFF; Crown Point HS; Crown Point, IN; 13/600 Cls Rep Frsh Cls; Cls Rep Soph Cls; Hon Rl; Jr NHS; NHS; Stu Cncl; Letter Bsbl; Letter Ftbl; Wrstlng; JETS Awd; Purdue Univ; Engr.

HOVEN, MARY J; Saint Augustine Acad; Cleveland, OH; Lbry Ade; Orch; Sch Mus; Sch Pl; Rptr Sch Nwsp; Sch Nwsp; Cleveland State; Ecological Area.

HOVEN, MATT; Wapakoneta Sr HS; Wapakoneta, OH; 2/330 Hon Rl; NHS; Fr Clb; Letter Bsbl; Letter Bsktbl; Natl Merit Ltr; Natl Merit SF; Univ; Bus Admin.

HOVERMAN, DANIEL; Midland HS; Midland, MI; Band; Hon Rl; Sct Actv; Stg Crw; Michigan Tech Univ; Chemistry.

HOVEY, KYLE; Aurora HS; Aurora, OH; VP Chrs; Hon Rl; Sec NHS; Sch Mus; VP Mth Clb; Pep Clb; Letter Bsktbl; PPFtbl; Scr Kpr; Cincinnati; Nursing.

HOVING, KATHERINE; Seven Hills HS; Cincinnati, OH; Debate Tm; Hon Rl; Hosp Ade; Rptr Yrbk; Ten; IM Sprt; Smith College; International.

HOVINGA, JOY; Calvin Christian HS; Grand Rapids, MI; Band; Chrh Wkr; Cmnty Wkr; Hon Rl; Hosp Ade; Yth Flsp; Drama Clb; 4-H; Pep Clb; IM Sprt; Michigan State Univ; Physical Ther.

HOVIS, GREGG; Washington HS; Massillon, OH; Chrs; Chrh Wkr; Sch Mus; Stg Crw; Spn Clb; College; Hotel Motel Mgmt.

HOWALD, JANICE; Buckeye Valley HS; Delaware, OH; Hon Rl; Yth Flsp; 4-H; Letter Ten; Mgrs; Scr Kpr; Ohio State Univ; Dent Asst.

HOWARD, ARTHUR; John Hay HS; Cleveland, OH; Hon Rl; Jr NHS; NHS; Rptr Sch Nwsp; Fr Clb; Cit Awd; Michigan St Univ; Engr.

HOWARD, BARBARA; Our Lady Of Mercy HS; Detroit, MI; Aud/Vis; Chrs; Chrh Wkr; Cmnty Wkr; Girl Scts; Off Ade; Sct Actv; Yth Flsp; Cit Awd; Mic State; Psych.

HOWARD, BERTHA; East HS; Columbus, OH; 27/256 Chrh Wkr; Hon Rl; NHS; 4-H; 4-H Awd; Franklin Univ; Bus Admin.

HOWARD, BRENT T; Athens HS; Athens, OH; Cl Rep Jr Cls; Am Leg Boys St; Chrh Wkr; NHS; Pol Wkr; Stu Cncl; Yth Flsp; Fr Clb; Key Clb; Rotary World Affairs Inst; Univ; Pre Law.

HOWARD, CARRIE L; Springfield Local HS; Poland, OH; Chrs; Hon Rl; Lbry Ade; Off Ade; Rptr Sch Nwsp; 4-H; Pep Clb; Spn Clb; Letter IM Sprt; 4-H Awd; Bus Schl.

HOWARD, DAVID; Clintondale HS; Mt Clemens, MI; 14/290 NHS; Capt Ftbl; Letter Trk; Wayne St Univ; Bus Admin.

HOWARD, ELIZABETH; Little Miami HS; Morrow, OH; 1/195 VP Frsh Cls; Cl Rep Jr Cls; Val; Hon Rl; Lit Mag; VP NHS; Pol Wkr; Pres Fr Clb; Ger Clb; Sci Clb; Outstndng Stdnt In Chem Calculus & Analyitc Geom 79; Whos Who In For Lang French Germn & Spansih 79; Wright St Univ; Physics.

HOWARD, FRANK; Garfield HS; Hamilton, OH; Cls Rep Sr Cls; Am Leg Boys St; Hon Rl; JA; NHS; Off Ade; Stu Cncl; Spn Clb; Letter Ftbl; Wrstlng; Ohio Univ; Med Tech.

HOWARD, HEATHER L; Three Rivers HS; Sturgis, MI; 2/245 Pres Sr Cls; Cls Rep Sr Cls; Sal; Am Leg Aux Girls St; Chrs; Debate Tm; Hon Rl; Natl Forn Lg; Sec NHS; Stu Cncl; Albion Coll; Med.

HOWARD, JAMES; Mt Hope HS; Mt Hope, WV; 7/86 Band; Chrs; Hon Rl; Jr NHS; NHS; Rptr Sch Nwsp; Spn Clb; Bsktbl; Ftbl; IM Sprt; Wva Inst Of Tech; Comp Mgmt.

HOWARD, JEFFREY; East Grand Rapids HS; Grand Rapids, MI; Hon Rl; Grand Rapids Junior College.

HOWARD, JILL; Hubbard HS; Hubbard, OH; 9/350 Chrh Wkr; Hon Rl; Off Ade; Sch Mus; Y-Teens; Yrbk; Rptr Sch Nwsp; Treas Lat Clb; Voice Dem Awd; College; Medicine.

HOWARD, JOHN; John F Kennedy HS; Taylor, MI; Cls Rep Frsh Cls; Cls Rep Soph Cls; Cl Rep Jr Cls; Pres Sr Cls; Boy Scts; Rptr Yrbk; Bsktbl; Letter Ftbl; Letter Trk; All League All Area 2nd Team Track; College; Drafting.

HOWARD, JOSEPH; Woodrow Wilson HS; Youngstown, OH; Boy Scts; Cmnty Wkr; JA; Pol Wkr; Sct Actv; VICA; Bsbl; Trk; Stdnt Of Yr 79; 3rd Pl Brnz Trophy Regnl VICA Olympics 79; Choffin Career Schl; Law Enfrcmnt.

HOWARD, JOSEPH; Whitko HS; Pierceton, IN; VP Soph Cls; Chrs; Chrh Wkr; FCA; Sch Mus; Sch Pl; Bsbl; Letter Ftbl; Trk; IM Sprt; Kosciusko County Youth Rep For Farm Bureau 77; 1st Recipient Of Annual Pierceton Serv Awd 76; Ohio St Univ; Rotogravure Printing.

HOWARD, JULIE; High School; Livonia, MI; Chrs; Sch Mus; Sch Pl; Stg Crw; Central Michigan Univ.

HOWARD, K; Gwinn HS; Skandia, MI; Cmnty Wkr; Hon Rl; Sch Nwsp; VICA; Wrstlng; Cit Awd; Natl Merit Ltr; Natl Merit SF; Voc Schl; Elec.

HOWARD, KAREN; Madison Plains HS; London, OH; Band; Chrh Wkr; Off Ade; Sch Pl; Yth Flsp; Rptr Yrbk; 4-H; FFA; FHA; Spn Clb; Greenhand Degree; Business Skill Olympics; Citizenship Awd; Bliss Busns Schl; Exec Law Sec.

HOWARD, KATHY; Huntington East HS; Huntington, WV; Cls Rep Frsh Cls; Hon Rl; Jr NHS; Lit Mag; Rptr Yrbk; Letter Bsktbl; Marshall Univ; Art.

HOWARD, KATHY; Laurel HS; Laurel, IN; Chrs; Drl Tm; Hon Rl; NHS; Ed Sch Nwsp; Rptr Sch Nwsp; Pep Clb; Bsktbl; Trk; Mgrs; Indiana Central Univ; RN.

HOWARD, KEITH; Hamilton HS; Hamilton, IN; 5/55 Pres Sr Cls; Am Leg Boys St; Band; Boy Scts; Chrh Wkr; Pres NHS; Stu Cncl; Letter Ftbl; Mgrs; DAR Awd; Depauw Univ; Poli Sci.

HOWARD, KEN; Guinn HS; Skandia, MI; Hon Rl; Sch Nwsp; Wrstlng; Cit Awd; Natl Merit Ltr; NMU Skill Ctr; Electricity.

HOWARD, LA DONNA; Covington HS; Covington, IN; Band; Hon Rl; Stg Crw; Yth Flsp; 4-H; Bsktbl; 4-H Awd; Univ; Bio.

HOWARD, MARK; Princeton HS; Princeton, WV; 3/330 Chrs; NHS; Quill & Scroll; Rptr Sch Nwsp; Key Clb; Bsktbl; Capt Crs Cntry; Capt Trk; Am Leg Awd; Kiwan Awd; Virginia Polytech Inst; Comp Sci.

HOWARD, MICHAEL; Castle HS; Newburgh, IN; 17/222 Band; Hon Rl; Treas Yth Flsp; 4-H; NEDT Cert 77; Jr Dance Comm 78; Univ; Chem.

HOWARD, MIKE; Harbor Beach Cmnty HS; Harbor Beach, MI; 14/141 Boy Scts; Chrh Wkr; Cmnty Wkr; Hon Rl; NHS; Sct Actv; Mth Clb; Letter Ftbl; Letter Trk; Scr Kpr;.

HOWARD, NANCY; Whitehall Yearling HS; Whitehall, OH; Cls Rep Frsh Cls; Cl Rep Jr Cls; Band; Girl Scts; Hon Rl; Stu Cncl; Sch Nwsp; Ohi State Univ; Interior Design.

HOWARD, PAUL; Hubbard HS; Hubbard, OH; 19/350 Hon Rl; FBLA; Key Clb; Lat Clb; Bsktbl; Letter Ftbl; Youngstown State Univ; Comp Sci.

HOWARD, RANDY; Inland Lakes HS; Indian River, MI; Trs Soph Cls; Trs Jr Cls; Trs Sr Cls; Aud/Vis; Boy Scts; Cmnty Wkr; Hon Rl; Mth Clb; Letter Bsbl; Letter Bsktbl; College; Math.

HOWARD, RHONDA; Wyoming Park HS; Wyoming, MI; 32/227 Band; Chrh Wkr; FCA; NHS; Sch Mus; Spn Clb; Letter Mgrs; Grand Rapids Jr Coll; Child Psych.

HOWARD, ROBERT; Central Preston Sr HS; Kingwood, WV; Hon Rl; FFA; VICA; Letter Bsbl; Bsktbl; IM Sprt; Mgrs; Voc Schl; Bldg Construction.

HOWARD, ROBERT; Avon Jr Sr HS; Danville, IN; Hon Rl; Ger Clb; IM Sprt; Univ.

HOWARD, ROGER; Jewett Scio HS; Jewett, OH; 11/90 Band; Hon Rl; Orch; Sch Mus; Sprt Ed Yrbk; Ed Sch Nwsp; Letter Bsbl; Letter Ftbl; Coach Actv; Scr Kpr; Kent St Univ; Psych.

HOWARD, SANDRA; St Johns HS; St Johns, MI; Girl Scts; Hon Rl; Lbry Ade; Yth Flsp; 4-H;.

HOWARD, TERESA; Wehrle HS; Columbus, OH; Letter Bsbl; Mgrs; Captial Univ; Social Work.

HOWARD, TRIANDOS; East HS; Columbus, OH; Hon Rl; DECA; Bsbl; Busns Schl; Mechanics.

HOWARD, TUANA; Marion Harding HS; Marion, OH; Band; Chrs; JA; Fr Clb; Chrldng; Spanish Club Cert Of Mert Awd 78; Ohio St Univ; Med.

HOWDYSHELL, CAROLYN; Pickerington HS; Pickerington, OH; 1/210 Pres Sr Cls; Am Leg Aux Girls St; Hon Rl; NHS; Stu Cncl; Lat Clb; Mth Clb; PPFtbl; Cedarville Coll; Sec.

HOWDYSHELL, LORI A; New Lexington Sr HS; New Lexington, OH; Am Leg Aux Girls St; Chrs; Hon Rl; NHS; Off Ade; Ed Yrbk; 4-H; Trk; GAA; Muskingum Tech Coll; Retail Mktg.

HOWE, AMY; Napoleon HS; Napoleon, OH; Cl Rep Jr Cls; Am Leg Aux Girls St; Band; Chrh Wkr; Hon Rl; JA; Lbry Ade; Sch Mus; Sch Pl; Stu Cncl; Schlrshp Team; Math Contests GTCHTM & Maumee Valley; Univ; Brdcstng.

HOWE, ANN; Meridian Sr HS; Sanford, MI; 8/126 Pres Jr Cls; VP Jr Cls; Cmnty Wkr; Hon Rl; Jr NHS; NHS; Sch Mus; Drama Clb; Fr Clb; Pep Clb; Farm Bureaus Young Peoples Smnr Elctd Prcnct Delgt 79; Vrsty Lttr In Vllybll 77 Foregin Lang Ski Clb Pres; Central Michigan Univ; Brdcstng.

HOWE, DAVID; Barberton HS; Barberton, OH; Sch Mus; Sch Pl; Drama Clb; Sci Clb; Trk; Akron Univ; Civil Engr.

HOWE, DEBRA; Prairie Heights HS; Hudson, IN; 27/136 Band; Chrh Wkr; Hon Rl; Lbry Ade; Off Ade; 4-H; FTA; Bsktbl; Intl Bus College; Accrg.

HOWE, JAMES F; Fairmont East HS; Kettering, OH; 11/502 Am Leg Boys St; FCA; Hon Rl; NHS; Letter Bsbl; Letter Ftbl; IM Sprt; Univ; Petroleum Engr.

HOWE, LORI; West Carrollton HS; W Carrollton, OH; Chrs; Girl Scts; Pep Clb; Chrldng; GAA; College; Bus.

HOWE, SHELLY; Tri County HS; Howard City, MI; 2/88 Sec Frsh Cls; Pres Soph Cls; Sec Sr Cls; Hon Rl; NHS; Treas Stu Cncl; Chrldng; Ferris State College; Bus.

HOWELL, ANN; Hedgesville HS; Shepherdstown, WV; Chrh Wkr; 4-H; FHA; Coll; RN.

HOWELL, BETH; Elmhurst HS; Ft Wayne, IN; 16/400 Chrh Wkr; Hon Rl; Kettering Coll Of Med Arts; Med Asst.

HOWELL, DAWN; Union HS; Parker City, IN; Band; Chrh Wkr; Hon Rl; NHS; 4-H; Sec Lat Clb; VICA; Letter Bsktbl; 4-H Awd; Univ; History.

HOWELL, DE WAYNE; Goshen HS; Pleasant Plain, OH; Boy Scts; Chrs; Chrh Wkr; Hon Rl; NHS; Crs Cntry; Trk; Univ Of Cincinnati; Chem.

HOWELL, MARCIA; Robert S Rogers HS; Toledo, OH; Cls Rep Frsh Cls; Band; Girl Scts; Hon Rl; Hosp Ade; Jr NHS; Orch; Sch Mus; Sch Pl; Sct Actv; College.

HOWELL, MARILYN; Hobart Sr HS; Hobart, IN; 2/450 Cls Rep Frsh Cls; Cls Rep Soph Cls; Cmnty Wkr; Hon Rl; Jr NHS; Pol Wkr; Sec Stu Cncl; Ger Clb; Pep Clb; Gym; Indiana Univ; Law.

HOWELL, PATRICIA; Marion Harding HS; Marion, OH; Cls Rep Sr Cls; Band; Girl Scts; Orch; Sch Mus; Stg Crw; Stu Cncl; Fr Clb; Bsktbl; Trk; Band Pres; Jazz Pep & Marching Bands; Band Rep & Sec; Heidelberg Coll; Medicine.

HOWELL, RHONDA; Marion HS; Marion, IN; Chrs; Hon Rl; NHS; Sch Mus; Sch Pl; Drama Clb; Whos Who In Foregin Lang 79; Acad Letter Of Achvmnt 79; In St Schlrhsp Hon 79; Indiana Univ; Sociology.

HOWELL, RHONDA; Cedarville HS; Cedarville, OH; Lbry Ade; Sch Pl; Stg Crw; Rptr Sch Nwsp; Sch Nwsp; Drama Clb; Spn Clb; Dnfth Awd;.

HOWELL, ROBERT; Heath HS; Heath, OH; 22/158 FCA; Hon Rl; Bsbl; Bsktbl; IM Sprt; Coll; Educ.

HOWELL, ROBERT; Midland Trial HS; Lookout, WV; Boy Scts; Chrs; Hon Rl; NHS; Fr Clb; Bsbl; Letter Bsktbl; Letter Ftbl; Letter Trk; College; Educ.

HOWELL, ROJEUNA; Beaumont Girls HS; Cleve Hts, OH; Chrs; Chrh Wkr; Hon Rl; Lit Mag; Orch; Bsktbl; Trk; Coach Actv; GAA; Cuyahoga Cmnty Coll; Educ.

HOWELL, SOPHIA; Perry HS; Massillon, OH; Chrh Wkr; Cmnty Wkr; Debate Tm; Drm Mjrt; Lbry Ade; Off Ade; Orch; Pol Wkr; Twrlr; Kent St Univ; Spec Educ.

HOWELL, STEVEN; River Valley HS; Three Oaks, MI; Rdo Clb; Mgrs; DAR Awd; Perfct Attndnc; Univ; Comp Sci.

HOWELL, TAMMY; Watkins Mem HS; Pataskala, OH; Chrs; Hon Rl; Ger Clb; IM Sprt; Kiwan Awd; Tech Schl; Comp Prog.

HOWELL, TERESA; Port Clinton HS; Pt Clinton, OH; Chrs; Girl Scts; Hon Rl; Sct Actv; VP 4-H; Ger Clb; Scr Kpr; 4-H Awd; College; Educ.

HOWELLS, BRONWEN; North Royalton HS; Broadview Ht, OH; Cl Rep Jr Cls; Band; Chrh Wkr; Hon Rl; NHS; Orch; Sch Mus; Sch Pl; Yrbk; Rptr Sch Nwsp; Miami Univ; Cmnctns.

HOWERTON, NANCY; Princeton HS; Princeton, WV; Cl Rep Jr Cls; Chrh Wkr; Jr NHS; Sch Pl; Stu Cncl; Drama Clb; Fr Clb; Keyettes; Mbr Natl Thespian Soc; Univ.

HOWERY, JEFF; Petoskey HS; Petoskey, MI; Band; Orch; Letter Ftbl; Letter Trk; IM Sprt; Bus Schl; Mgmt.

HOWES, ANN; Morgantown HS; Morgantwn, WV; Yrbk; Spn Clb; West Virginia Univ; Phys Ther.

HOWES, CINDY; Licking Valley HS; Newark, OH; 3/147 Am Leg Aux Girls St; Band; Chrh Wkr; Hon Rl; NHS; Rptr Yrbk; Sch Nwsp; Pep Clb; Sci Clb; Letter Trk; Ohio State Univ; Archt.

HOWES, GREGORY; Onekama Consolidated Schls; Brethren, MI; Band; Boy Scts; Hon Rl; Yth Flsp; Fr Clb; Mth Clb; Ftbl; IM Sprt; Michigan St Univ.

HOWETT, MARK; Fostoria HS; Fostoria, OH; Chrs; Lbry Ade; Natl Forn Lg; Sch Pl; Stg Crw; Sch Nwsp; Drama Clb; Fr Clb; Lat Clb; Ten; Ohi St; Law.

HOWEY, SARA; Peru HS; Peru, IN; 15/275 Cls Rep Soph Cls; Cl Rep Jr Cls; Pres Sr Cls; Chrh Wkr; Hon Rl; NHS; Off Ade; Stu Cncl; Yth Flsp; Rptr Yrbk; Butler.

HOWIE, KIMBERLY; East HS; Columbus, OH; Hon Rl; OEA; Fort Horks Career Cntr; Word Proc.

HOWISON, REBECCA; J W Sexton HS; Lansing, MI; Chrs; Chrh Wkr; Mdrgl; NHS; Sch Mus; Stu Cncl; Yth Flsp; Letter Bsbl; Capt Swmmng; Chrldng; Mi Comp Schlrshp Prog Cert 79; Athletic Achvmnt Cert 79; Vocal Music Medal 79; Michigan St Univ.

HOWLAND, BILL; Clay Sr HS; Oregon, OH; Univ Of Toledo.

HOWLETT, JOHN E; Minerva HS; Minerva, OH; 44/241 Am Leg Boys St; Chrs; Hon Rl; Sch Mus; 4-H; 4-H Awd; West Va Univ; Wildlife.

HOWLETT, JULIE; Flushing Sr HS; Flushing, MI; Band; Hon Rl; NHS; Orch; Sch Mus; Sch Pl; Stg Crw; Drama Clb; Fr Clb; Letter Trk; Michigan St Univ; Pre Med.

HOWLETT, MARY H; Marian HS; Bloomfield Hls, MI; Cls Rep Frsh Cls; Girl Scts; Stg Crw; Michigan Tech Univ; Engr.

HOWLEY, MARY; Jefferson Area HS; Rock Creek, OH; 1/196 Val; AFS; Chrs; Lbry Ade; NHS; Sch Mus; Sch Pl; Pres Stu Cncl; Scr Kpr; Rotary Awd; Ohio St Univ; Phys Ther.

HOWLEY, THOMAS; Ross Beatty HS; Cassopolis, MI; Cl Rep Jr Cls; Band; Hon Rl; NHS; Sch Mus; Sch Pl; Yth Flsp; Rptr Sch Nwsp; Letter Bsbl; Letter Crs Cntry; Central Michigan Univ; Drama.

HOWSARE, LOIS; Chesterton Sr HS; Valpariso, IN ; 68/399 Chrs; Hosp Ade; Sch Mus; Sch Pl; 4-H; 4-H Awd; Indiana Univ; Nursing.

HOWSON, CAROLYN; Reeths Puffer HS; Muskegon, MI; 13/287 NHS; Rptr Sch Nwsp; Letter Trk; Capt Chrldng; PPFtbl; Muskegon Community Coll; Teach.

HOXSIE, JULIE; Cedar Springs HS; Cedar Spgs, MI; Band; Chrs; Hon Rl; Jr NHS; NHS; 4-H; Sci Clb; Spn Clb; Cit Awd; 4-H Awd; Washington Short Course 79; St Forestry Rep 79; Michigan St Univ; Lymnology.

HOY, COLLEEN; Windham HS; Windham, OH; Sec Frsh Cls; Hon Rl; Stg Crw; Spn Clb; Vlybl Team Letter; College; Busns.

HOY, DAVE; Father Wehrle HS; Columbus, OH; 7/110 Cls Rep Frsh Cls; Cls Rep Soph Cls; Cl Rep Jr Cls; Am Leg Boys St; Hon Rl; NHS; Pres Stu Cncl; Rptr Sch Nwsp; Capt Bsktbl; Ftbl; John Carroll Univ; Math.

HOY, MARY J; Whetstone HS; Columbus, OH; 41/320 Chrs; Hon Rl; Off Ade; Sch Mus; Fr Clb; Lat Clb; OEA; OEA Reg Typing I 1st Place; St Typing I 2nd Place; Natl Typing I 16th Place; Ohio St Univ; Acctg.

HOY, MELODEE; Upper Sandusky HS; Upper Sandusky, OH; 19/213 Chrh Wkr; Hon Rl; Off Ade; Drama Clb; 4-H Awd; Ohio State.

HOY, RUSSELL; Riverdale HS; Forest, OH; 18/104 Cmnty Wkr; Hon Rl; Spn Clb; Letter Crs Cntry; Trk; 1st Hardin Cnty Chem 79; Pl 154 Out Of 347 In Finals Of GTCTM; Lima Tech Univ; Comp Progr.

HOYER, KEVIN; Barboursville HS; Huntington, WV; Am Leg Boys St; Hon Rl; NHS; Marietta Coll; Ind Engr.

HOYH, DAVID; Benton Harbor HS; Benton Hbr, MI; Cls Rep Soph Cls; Cl Rep Jr Cls; Band; Boy Scts; Hon Rl; JA; NHS; Sct Actv; Ed Yrbk; Rptr Yrbk; Mich St.

HOYING, JACQUELINE; Russia Local HS; Covington, OH; 10/34 Sec Frsh Cls; Sec Jr Cls; Sec Sr Cls; Band; Chrs; Girl Scts; Hon Rl; Hosp Ade; NHS; Off Ade; Capital Univ; Nursing.

HOYING, SUSAN; St Henry HS; St Henry, OH; Chrs; Hon Rl; NHS; Yrbk; Rptr Sch Nwsp; Drama Clb; OEA; Pep Clb; Chrldng; GAA;.

HOYING, TIM; Oakwood HS; Dayton, OH; Capt Band; Hon Rl; Pres NHS; Sch Mus; Sch Pl; Yrbk; Drama Clb; Ten; Natl Merit Ltr; College.

HOYLE, DAWN; Brighton HS; Brighton, MI; 2/388 Sal; Pres Boy Scts; Hon Rl; NHS; Pres FHA; Letter Ten; GAA; PPFtbl; Natl Merit SF; Bd Of Control Distinguished Schlrshp 79; Public Serv Awd 79; Lake Superior St Coll; Law.

HOYLE, MOLLY; Our Lady Of The Elms HS; Akron, OH; Gym; Miami Univ; Pre Law.

HOYNG, DOUGLAS; Celina HS; Celina, OH; Chrs; NHS; Letter Bsbl; IM Sprt; Natl Merit Ltr; Univ Of Dayton; Computer Engineering.

HOYO, LISA; St Clairsville HS; St Clairsville, OH; 20/225 Band; Hon Rl; NHS; Off Ade; Yrbk; Sprt Ed Sch Nwsp; FTA; Pep Clb; Chrldng; College; Elem Ed.

HOYT, JANET; Eastern HS; Lansing, MI; 6/350 Sec Jr Cls; Trs Sr Cls; Band; Boy Scts; Chrs; Chrh Wkr; Debate Tm; Girl Scts; Oakland Univ; Music.

HOYT, LAURA; South Central HS; Hanna, IN; 35/95 Aud/Vis; Cmnty Wkr; Lbry Ade; 4-H; FHA; Cit Awd; 4-H Awd; Working; Dietary Aide.

HOYT, RALPH; Little Miami HS; Morrow, OH; Chrs; Hon Rl; Pres JA; Fr Clb; Pep Clb; Capt Ftbl; Trk; Wrstlng; IM Sprt; JA Awd; USAF Academy; Engr.

HOYT, RANDELL; Meridian HS; Sanford, MI; VP Frsh Cls; Hon Rl; Bsktbl; Ftbl; Trk; Capt Ferris State College; Tech Draft.

HOYT, ROBERT; Otsego HS; Otsego, MI; Band; Mod UN; Spn Clb; Bsbl; IM Sprt; St Of Mi Compt Scslhp 78; Western Michigan Univ; Comp Progr.

HOYT, ROBIN; White Pine HS; White Pine, MI; Band; Cmp Fr Grls; Chrs; Chrh Wkr; Hon Rl; NHS; Univ; Foreign Languages.

HOYT, SUSAN; Zanesville HS; Zanesville, OH; VP Jr Cls; VP Sr Cls; Chrs; Cmnty Wkr; Hon Rl; Hosp Ade; Stu Cncl; Rptr Yrbk; Mgrs; Bowling Green State Univ.

HOZA, ANDREA; Saint Vincent Saint Mary HS; Akron, OH; Chrs; Chrh Wkr; Cmnty Wkr; JA; Lbry Ade; Drama Clb; FBLA; Business School; Bus.

HRADEK, DAVID; Benedictine HS; Garfield Hts, OH; 8/102 Sec Jr Cls; Hon Rl; NHS; Sprt Ed Sch Nwsp; Spn Clb; Bsbl; IM Sprt; College; Archt.

HRANKO, BETH; Shadyside HS; Shadyside, OH; Band; Hon Rl; Y-Teens; Spn Clb; GAA; Vocational School, Secretarial.

HRDLICKA, LEIGH A; Bellaire HS; Bellaire, OH; Chrs; Girl Scts; Hon Rl; Yth Flsp; Y-Teens; Spn Clb; Bsktbl; Chrldng; IM Sprt; Btty Crckr Awd; Wheeling Beauty Coll; Cosmetology.

HREBEC, JOHN; Andrean HS; Merrillville, IN; 6/272 Hon Rl; Sch Pl; Stg Crw; Rptr Yrbk; Drama Clb; Mth Clb; IM Sprt; Natl Merit SF; Indiana St Schlrshp; Univ Of Notre Dame; Busns.

HREHA, STEVEN J; Ashtabula St John HS; N Kingsville, OH; 1/120 Cl Rep Jr Cls; Cls Rep Sr Cls; Am Leg Boys St; Hon Rl; NHS; Stu Cncl; Lat Clb; Sci Clb; Letter Crs Cntry; Letter Trk; Jacksonville Univ; Engr.

HRICOVSKY, MARIANNE; Rossford HS; Rossford, OH; 13/147 Hon Rl; GAA; Home Econ Awrd 1977; Membr Exploer Club 1977; St Vincents Hosp Schl Of Nrsng; RN.

HRITSKO, BOB; Admiral King HS; Lorain, OH; Cmnty Wkr; Hon Rl; Yrbk; Letter Ten; Univ; Math.

HRIVNAK, MARY; Berea HS; Berea, OH; 90/600 Band; Chrh Wkr; Hon Rl; NHS; Orch; Yrbk; Ten; Trk; IM Sprt; 4-H Awd; College; Bus.

HROMETZ, JANET; East Canton HS; E Canon, OH; Band; Chrs; Chrh Wkr; Girl Scts; Sct Actv; 4-H; Fr Clb; FHA; Pep Clb; Chrldng; Stark Tech Coll; CPA.

HRUSKOCY, MARYCOLETTE; Bishop Noll Inst; Whiting, IN; Cls Rep Frsh Cls; VP Soph Cls; Cl Rep Jr Cls; NHS; Quill & Scroll; Stu Cncl; Ed Yrbk; Sch Nwsp; Mth Clb; Ind State Univ; Chem.

HRVATIN, DIANE; Salem Sr HS; Salem, OH; Chrh Wkr; Off Ade; Yth Flsp; Drama Clb; FSA; Pep Clb; Sci Clb; VICA; DAR Awd; Gregg Shorthand Awd 78; Univ; Photog.

HRVATIN, MARY; North HS; Willowick, OH; 77/773 Cls Rep Soph Cls; Cl Rep Jr Cls; Chrh Wkr; Hon Rl; NHS; Off Ade; Stu Cncl; Rptr Sch Nwsp; Spn Clb; Letter Chrldng; Univ; Phys Ed.

HSI, JEFFREY; Loy Norrix HS; Kalamazoo, MI; 24/450 Band; Treas Chrs; Hon Rl; NHS; Orch; Sch Mus; Letter Ten; Kalamazoo Coll; Chemistry.

HUANG, JACKSON; Bishop Watterson HS; Columbus, OH; Hon Rl; JA; Jr NHS; Fr Clb; JA Awd; Univ Of Columbus; Pre Med.

HUASER, KIM; Kenston HS; Chagrin Fls, OH; Chrs; Drl Tm; Hon Rl; Sch Mus; Yrbk; College; Busns.

HUBBARD, ANDREA; Collinwood HS; Cleveland, OH; Cls Rep Soph Cls; Cl Rep Jr Cls; Hst Sr Cls; Cls Rep Sr Cls; Cmp Fr Grls; Cmnty Wkr; Debate Tm; Girl Scts; Hon Rl; Jr NHS; Allegheny Univ; Med.

HUBBARD, CYNTHIA; Walton HS; Walton, WV; 8/40 Hon Rl; Jr NHS; Sch Pl; Treas Stu Cncl; Drama Clb; VP FBLA; Letter Bsktbl; Trk; GAA;.

HUBBARD, DANIEL K; Union County HS; Liberty, IN; 25/128 Am Leg Boys St; Aud/Vis; Band; Chrh Wkr; Cmnty Wkr; Hon Rl; Sch Mus; Stg Crw; Yth Flsp; Ed Sch Nwsp; In Boy St Fair Schl 78; St Jr Leadr Confrnc 79; Univ; Finance.

HUBBARD, DAVID; Jimtown HS; Elkhart, IN; 2/90 Hon Rl; NHS; Sch Mus; Sch Pl; Stg Crw; Drama Clb; Univ; Art Tchr.

HUBBARD, ROBYN; Fostoria HS; Fostoria, OH; Cmp Fr Grls; Chrh Wkr; Hon Rl; JA; Lbry Ade; 4-H; FHA; Spn Clb; GAA; 4-H Awd; Univ; Dent Asst.

HUBBARD, SONIA; South Dearborn HS; Moores Hl, IN; 18/270 Chrh Wkr; Hon Rl; NHS; Sch Pl; Yth Flsp; Drama Clb; 4-H; Pep Clb; GAA; IM Sprt; Purdue; Nurse.

HUBBARD, TROY; Salem HS; Salem, IN; Cls Rep Frsh Cls; Cls Rep Soph Cls; Cl Rep Jr Cls; Cls Rep Sr Cls; Band; Boy Scts; Chrh Wkr; JA; Lit Mag; Sct Actv; Evansville Univ; Cmnctns.

HUBBARD, VICKI; Washington HS; Massillon, OH; Drama Clb; Ger Clb; Swmmng; Massillon Cmnty Hosp Schl; Nursing.

HUBBELL, BRADLEY; Mattawan HS; Kalamazoo, MI; 36/144 VP Sr Cls; Hon Rl; Natl Forn Lg; Stu Cncl; Yrbk; Rptr Sch Nwsp; Fr Clb; Natl Merit Schl; Hon Awd For Sr Of Yr 79; Hon Of Degree Of Hon Natl Forencis 79; Almn Schlsp 79; Michigan St Univ; Politics.

HUBBELL, BRYAN; North Muskegon HS; Whitehall, MI; Aud/Vis; Hon Rl; Lit Mag; NHS; Yrbk; Sch Nwsp; Bsbl; Natl Merit Ltr; U S Air Force Academy; Aero Engr.

HUBBELL, REBECCA; Hicksville HS; Hicksville, OH; 24/108 Band; Chrs; Hon Rl; Hosp Ade; Sch Mus; Ed Yrbk; Sch Nwsp; Fr Clb; Spn Clb; College; Major Course.

HUBBELL, TIM; Turpin HS; Cincinnati, OH; NHS; VP Lat Clb; Natl Merit SF; State Of Ohio Dept Of Educ Awd; Georgia Inst Of Tech; Bio Chem.

HUBBELL JR, ANDREW; Onsted Cmnty HS; Adrian, MI; 29/120 Aud/Vis; Boy Scts; Hon Rl; Lbry Ade; Sct Actv; Rptr Yrbk; 4-H; Rdo Clb; Michigan St Univ; Comp Sci.

HUBBS, KAREN; Cameron HS; Cameron, WV; 23/105 Am Leg Aux Girls St; Hon Rl; 4-H; FFA; FHA; Pep Clb; 4-H Awd;.

HUBER, DANA; Green HS; Uniontown, OH; Cls Rep Soph Cls; Trs Jr Cls; Cls Rep Sr Cls; Hon Rl; Off Ade; Stu Cncl; Y-Teens; Yrbk; Pep Clb; Scr Kpr; Univ.

HUBER, DOUGLAS; Normandy Sr HS; Parma, OH; 22/649 Chrs; Debate Tm; Hon Rl; Natl Forn Lg; Spn Clb; College; Accounting.

HUBER, KATHY; Brookville HS; Harrison, OH; 9/200 Chrs; Chrh Wkr; Hon Rl; Lbry Ade; NHS; Yrbk; Ger Clb; Bsktbl; Ten; IM Sprt; College.

HUBER, LORI; Bluffton HS; Bluffton, OH; 6/100 Am Leg Aux Girls St; Chrs; Chrh Wkr; Hon Rl; NHS; Sch Mus; Rptr Sch Nwsp; Drama Clb; Pres Eng Clb; VP Lat Clb; Ohio St Univ; Psych.

HUBER, MARK; Floyd Central HS; New Albany, IN; Band; Chrh Wkr; Cmnty Wkr; Hon Rl; 4-H; IM Sprt; 4-H Awd; Purdue; Elec Engr.

HUBER, MARY; Archbishop Alter HS; Dayton, OH; Cmnty Wkr; NHS; Rptr Sch Nwsp; Ohio Univ.

HUBER, MARY; Patrick Henry HS; Malinta, OH; 1/118 Cls Rep Sr Cls; Am Leg Aux Girls St; Hon Rl; NHS; Off Ade; Y-Teens; Stu Cncl; Rptr Sch Nwsp; Sch Nwsp; Bsktbl; Defiance Coll; Elem Educ.

HUBER, MELISSA; Northridge HS; Middlebury, IN; 33/150 Band; Cmnty Wkr; Hon Rl; NHS; 4-H; Pep Clb; Letter Bsktbl; Criminal Justice.

HUBER, PHILLIP; Greenfield Central HS; Greenfield, IN; Aud/Vis; Hon Rl; Jr NHS; NHS; Boys Clb Am; Ger Clb; Mth Clb; Swmmng; Hancock Bank & Trust Awrd 76 78; Purdue Univ; Engr.

HUBER, RICHARD; Woodlan HS; New Haven, IN; Boy Scts; FFA; Letter Crs Cntry; Trk; Mgrs; JA Awd; Purdue.

HUBER, ROB; Mt Healthy HS; Cincinnati, OH; VP Stu Cncl; Glf; Ten; Bowling Green Univ; Archt.

HUBER, SANDRA; Brownstown Central HS; Brownstown, IN; 1/140 Sec Frsh Cls; Drm Mjrt; Pres NHS; Quill & Scroll; VP Stu Cncl; Yth Flsp; FFA; Pres Lat Clb; VP Sci Clb; DAR Awd; Indiana Univ.

HUBER, TAMARA J; Buena Vista HS; Saginaw, MI; 11/175 Hon Rl; Ctrl Michigan Univ; Comp.

HUBER, THERESA; Ursuline Acad; Cincinnati, OH; 15/110 Cls Rep Frsh Cls; Pres Soph Cls; Cl Rep Jr Cls; Cls Rep Sr Cls; Chrs; Cmnty Wkr; Hon Rl; Hosp Ade; Pol Wkr; Sch Pl; Miami Univ; Med.

HUBER, WANDA; Brown Cnty HS; Columbus, IN; Am Leg Aux Girls St; Rptr Yrbk; DECA; Pres 4-H; FHA; Pep Clb; Sci Clb; Spn Clb; Sec Pom Pon; Ivy Tech Univ; Nursing.

HUBERS, JEFFREY; Wyoming Park HS; Wyoming, MI; Grand Rapids Jr College; Data Proc.

HUBERT, JULIE; Reitz Memorial HS; Evansville, IN; 8/226 Cmnty Wkr; Hon Rl; Hosp Ade; NHS; Sch Pl; Trk; Coach Actv; IM Sprt; Cit Awd; DAR Awd; Coll.

HUBERT, ROBERT; South Dearborn HS; Aurora, IN; Hon Rl; NHS; 4-H; Purdue; Mechanical Engineering.

HUBHARD, TROY; Salem HS; Salem, IN; Cls Rep Frsh Cls; Cls Rep Soph Cls; Cl Rep Jr Cls; Cls Rep Sr Cls; Band; Boy Scts; Chrh Wkr; FCA; Hon Rl; JA; STUCO Pres; Troop Patrol Leador Boy Scouts; College; Communications.

HUBLEIN, JULIE; Hartland HS; Howell, MI; 9/253 Band; Chrh Wkr; Girl Scts; Hon Rl; NHS; Pol Wkr; Yth Flsp; Fr Clb; Univ Of Michigan; History.

HUBLEY, MATTHEW; Huntington North HS; Andrews, IN; Hon Rl; NHS; Letter Ftbl; Letter Wrstlng; Scr Kpr; Ind Univ; Med.

HUBLY BROWN, JEANETTE; Harper Creek HS; Battle Creek, MI; Hon Rl; VP JA; NHS; Sch Mus; Drama Clb; 4-H; Fr Clb; JA Awd; College; Hlth Sci.

HUCK, R; Sault Area HS; Slt Ste Marie, MI; Hon Rl; Sch Mus; Sch Pl; Rptr Sch Nwsp; 4-H; Pep Clb; IM Sprt; DAR Awd; 4-H Awd; College.

HUCK, STAN; Waterford HS; Vincent, OH; 2/68 Sal; Am Leg Boys St; Chrs; Hon Rl; NHS; Spn Clb; Letter Crs Cntry; Letter Trk; Am Leg Awd; DAR Awd; Ohio Univ; Soc Std.

HUCK, STANLEY; Waterford HS; Vincent, OH; 2/67 Am Leg Boys St; Chrs; NHS; Sch Pl; Sci Clb; Spn Clb; Crs Cntry; Trk; Wrstlng; Am Leg Awd; Ohio Univ; Eng.

HUCK, WM; Soo Area HS; Sault Ste Marie, MI; 100/300 Sal; CAP; FCA; Sprt Ed Yrbk; Mth Clb; VICA; Bsktbl; Ftbl; Wrstlng; 4-H Awd; Devery Inst Of Tech; Elec Engr.

HUCKABY, BRIAN; Jefferson HS; Harpers Ferry, WV; Hon Rl; Spn Clb; College.

HUCKLEBERRY, JAMIE; New Albany HS; New Albany, IN; 101/565 Cl Rep Jr Cls; Band; Debate Tm; Hon Rl; NHS; Stu Cncl; Ger Clb; IM Sprt; PPFtbl; 4-H Awd; Purdue Univ; Aeronautical Engr.

HUCKSTEP, BRUCE; Western Boone Jr Sr HS; Jamestown, IN; 3/142 Am Leg Boys St; Hon Rl; Butler Univ; Pharm.

HUDACHEK, JOE; Wierton Madonna HS; Weirton, WV; 13/109 Cls Rep Frsh Cls; Boy Scts; Hon Rl; Jr NHS; NHS; Sct Actv; Pep Clb; Trk; Natl Merit SF; West Virginia Univ; Engr.

HUDAK, MARK; Timken Sr HS; Canton, OH; Am Leg Boys St; Chrh Wkr; Hon Rl; NHS; Ftbl; Letter Trk; Coll; Sci.

HUDDILSTON, JULIE; Medina HS; Medina, OH; 44/341 Cls Rep Frsh Cls; Cls Rep Soph Cls; VP Jr Cls; VP Sr Cls; Chrs; Sec Cmnty Wkr; Hon Rl; NHS; Stu Cncl; Letter Ten; College; Law.

HUDDLESTON, GARY; Yorktown HS; Muncie, IN; 1/225 Am Leg Boys St; Hon Rl; NHS; Stu Cncl; Pres Ger Clb; Bsbl; Bsktbl; Ftbl; College; Sci.

HUDDLESTON, KELLIE; Bethesda Christian HS; Indianapolis, IN; 2/25 Sal; Chrs; Chrh Wkr; Girl Scts; Hon Rl; Pol Wkr; Sch Pl; Yth Flsp; Ed Yrbk; Rptr Yrbk; College; Secondary Ed.

HUDEPOHL, LOIS; South Dearborn HS; Milan, IN; Chrh Wkr; Cmnty Wkr; Hon Rl; Lbry Ade; Sch Pl; Y-Teens; Civ Clb; Drama Clb; Pres Awd; College; Nursing.

HUDGINS, LINDA; Mohawk HS; Sycamore, OH; 13/129 Band; Chrs; Chrh Wkr; Cmnty Wkr; Hon Rl; Hosp Ade; Lit Mag; Respiratory Ther; Pespiratory Ther.

HUDIK, RON; Evergreen HS; Berkey, OH; 7/132 Am Leg Boys St; Hon Rl; Rptr Sch Nwsp; Fr Clb; Letter Bsbl; Bsktbl; Capt Ftbl; Coach Actv; Univ; Engr.

HUDNALL, JONATHAN; Poca HS; Poca, WV; 1/155 VP Band; Chrs; Chrh Wkr; Hon Rl; NHS; Johnson Bible Coll; Music.

HUDNALL, KAY; Nitro HS; Nitro, WV; 17/276 AFS; Band; Hon Rl; NHS; Yth Flsp; Yrbk; VP Sci Clb; West Virginia St Coll; Busns.

HUDNALL, LISA; Nitro HS; Nitro, WV; AFS; Band; Hon Rl; JA; Jr NHS; Sch Pl; College; Pyssical Therapist.

HUDNALL, TINA; Carlisle Sr HS; Miamisburg, OH; Chrs; Chrh Wkr; Girl Scts; Hosp Ade; Lbry Ade; Off Ade; OEA; Mgrs; Scr Kpr; Miami Jacobs Bus Schl; Bus.

HUDOCK, LINDA; Lake Orion HS; Lake Orion, MI; 40/300 Hon Rl; Jr NHS; Lbry Ade; Off Ade; Drama Clb; Ten; Speech Cont 2nd Pl; MFP Varsity Tennis; Oakland Univ; Law.

HUDOK, ELLEN; Schafer HS; Southgate, MI; Letter Band; Hon Rl; OEA; Bsbl; Hockey; GAA; Detroit Bus Inst; Bus.

HUDOK, JANET; Toronto HS; Toronto, OH; FCA; Hon Rl; Fr Clb; Pep Clb; Spn Clb; Bsktbl;.

HUDSON, ALLEN; South Range HS; Canfield, OH; Hon Rl; Sch Mus; Stg Crw; Drama Clb; Ger Clb; Scr Kpr; College; Interpreter.

HUDSON, BETH; Eastern HS; Solsberry, IN; 6/90 Band; Chrh Wkr; Hon Rl; NHS; Off Ade; Pep Clb; IV Tech; Sec.

HUDSON, DEBORAH; South Range HS; Canfield, OH; Chrs; Chrh Wkr; Girl Scts; Hon Rl; NHS; Off Ade; Yth Flsp; Mgrs; Scr Kpr; Univ; Poli Law.

HUDSON, DIANA; Pleasant HS; Prospect, OH; Band; Hon Rl; Lit Mag; Off Ade; Sch Pl; Stg Crw; Yrbk; Rptr Sch Nwsp; Drama Clb; IM Sprt; Marion Tech Coll; Med Sec.

HUDSON, EARL; West Side Sr HS; Gary, IN; 52/650 Cl Rep Jr Cls; Band; Hon Rl; NHS; Pres Of Natl Hon Soc 78; Arkansas Univ; Music.

HUDSON, JAMES; Richmond HS; Richmond, IN; Cls Rep Frsh Cls; Cls Rep Soph Cls; Cl Rep Jr Cls; Trs Sr Cls; Band; Hosp Ade; Sch Mus; Sch Pl; Stu Cncl; Lat Clb; College; Med.

HUDSON, JULIA; Lapel HS; Lapel, IN; 3/100 Chrs; Hon Rl; Jr NHS; NHS; Sch Mus; Rptr Yrbk; Lat Clb; Pep Clb; Sci Clb; Ftbl; Univ.

HUDSON, KATHERINE; Reed City HS; Reed City, MI; Cls Rep Sr Cls; Chrh Wkr; Debate Tm; Hon Rl; Natl Forn Lg; NHS; Off Ade; Sch Mus; Sch Pl; Stg Crw; HS Math Team Ferris St Coll Math Field Day Relay Team 1st Pl 78; Univ.

HUDSON, LINDA; Nordonia HS; Northfield, OH; 141/440 Sch Mus; Sch Pl; Stg Crw; Yrbk; Drama Clb; PPFtbl; Ohio State.

HUDSON, MARSHALL D; Garfield Sr HS; Hamilton, OH; 16/376 Cmnty Wkr; Hon Rl; Mod UN; NHS; Off Ade; Rptr Yrbk; Rptr Sch Nwsp; IM Sprt; Miami Univ; English.

HUDSON, NANCY; Byron Area HS; Byron, MI; 6/78 Cl Rep Jr Cls; Cls Rep Sr Cls; Band; Chrh Wkr; Cmnty Wkr; Girl Scts; Hon Rl; Hosp Ade; NHS; Sch Pl; Eastern Michigan Univ; Soc Work.

HUDSON, PAUL; Marysville HS; Marysville, MI; Boy Scts; Sch Pl; Univ.

HUDSON, RITA; Springs Valley HS; Paoli, IN; 5/73 Sal; Sec Frsh Cls; Hon Rl; NHS; Sch Pl; Rptr Yrbk; 4-H; OEA; Pep Clb; 4-H Awd; Ind Univ; Bus.

HUDSON, TONI; Southern Local HS; Racine, OH; 7/92 Chrs; Hon Rl; Yth Flsp; Drama Clb; Fr Clb; Univ; Interior Dsgn.

HUDSPETH, JENNIFER; Hanover Ctrl HS; Cedar Lake, IN; Cls Rep Sr Cls; NHS; Pres Stu Cncl; Pom Pon; Am Leg Awd; Louisiana St Univ; Acctg.

HUDSPETH, JENNIFER; Hanover Central HS; Cedar Lake, IN; 15/126 Cls Rep Sr Cls; Drl Tm; NHS; Pres Stu Cncl; Pom Pon; PPFtbl; Indiana Univ; Acctg.

HUEBERT, MARIE; Huntington North HS; Huntington, IN; 133/548 Cls Rep Sr Cls; Band; Girl Scts; Off Ade; Sch Mus; Stu Cncl; Fr Clb; Pep Clb; Ten; Chrldng; IUPU; Acctg.

HUEBLER, JOHN; Arthur Hill HS; Saginaw, MI; Band; Chrh Wkr; Hon Rl; JA; Quill & Scroll; Stu Cncl; Rptr Yrbk; Ed Sch Nwsp; Univ; Jrnlsm.

HUEBNER, KELLY; Stephen T Badin HS; Faithfield, OH; Drl Tm; Hosp Ade; Lat Clb; Gym; Letter Trk; Univ; Nursing.

HUEBNER, KENNETH; Streetsboro HS; Streetsboro, OH; Hon Rl; Sch Mus; Sch Pl; Rptr Yrbk; Ed Sch Nwsp; Drama Clb; FTA; C of C Awd; Kent St Univ; Educ.

HUEFNER, JULIE; Rosecrans HS; Zanesville, OH; 11/81 Hon Rl; JA; Jr NHS; Treas NHS; Sch Nwsp; Lat Clb; Bsktbl; Swmmng; Trk; Rotary Awd; Numerous Trophies & Awds In Horsemanship & Showmanship 76 79; Went To Italy With Latin Club 77; Ohio St Univ; Orthodontics.

HUELSKAMP, RUTH; Holy Rosary HS; Flint, MI; 6/57 Hon Rl; Letter Bsktbl; Letter Trk; Univ Of Michigan.

HUELSKAMP, SHARON K; Ft Recovery HS; Ft Recovery, OH; 11/73 Band; Chrh Wkr; Hon Rl; NHS; Sec FHA; VP OEA; Pres GAA; Twrlr; Bus Schl; Sec.

HUELSMAN, FRED; Sidney HS; Maplewood, OH; Pres Frsh Cls; Chrh Wkr; Hon Rl; Pres Stu Cncl; Drama Clb; 4-H; Bsbl; Letter Ftbl; Letter Wrstlng; Univ; Law.

HUETTNER, MARY; Bishop Dwenger HS; Ft Wayne, IN; 10/253 Sec Frsh Cls; Cl Rep Jr Cls; Chrh Wkr; Hon Rl; Hosp Ade; NHS; Sch Mus; Fr Clb; Gym; Chrldng; Coll; Corporate Law.

HUEY, ERIC; La Salle HS; Cincinnati, OH; 30/250 Hon Rl; NHS; Crs Cntry; Trk; Notre Dame Univ; Aeronautics.

HUEY, SHIRLEY; Marlington HS; Alliance, OH; 65/273 Chrs; Girl Scts; Sch Mus; Stg Crw; Ed Yrbk; Rptr Yrbk; Yrbk; FTA; Kent State Univ; Eng.

HUFF, BRUCE A; Gods Bible HS; Robinson, IL; Chrs; Chrh Wkr; Cmnty Wkr; Hon Rl; Red Cr Ade; Yth Flsp; Spn Clb; Ftbl; Gods Bible Coll; Ministry.

HUFF, CAROL A; Cadillac Sr HS; Cadillac, MI; 1/325 Trs Sr Cls; Val; Am Leg Aux Girls St; Girl Scts; Hon Rl; Natl Forn Lg; NHS; Stg Crw; Rptr Yrbk; Drama Clb; Regents Alumni Awrd Univ Of Michigan 1979; Univ Of Michigan; Phys Ther.

HUFF, CORINNA; Belleville HS; Belleville, MI; Chrs; Chrh Wkr; Cmnty Wkr; Debate Tm; Mdrgl; Yth Flsp; Yrbk; Detroit Bible Coll.

HUFF, DAVE; Cambridge HS; Cambridge, OH; Cls Rep Frsh Cls; Cls Rep Soph Cls; Cl Rep Jr Cls; Hon Rl; Letter Bsbl; Bsktbl; Letter Glf; College; Bus.

HUFF, DENISE; East Palestine HS; E Palestine, OH; Band; Drm Mjrt; Hon Rl; FHA; Letter Bsktbl; Coach Actv; Mgrs; Twrlr; Bus Schl; Horse Training.

HUFF, KIM; West Washington HS; Salem, IN; Sec Sr Cls; Chrs; Chrh Wkr; Hon Rl; Lbry Ade; Off Ade; Sch Mus; Sch Pl; Stg Crw; Stu Cncl; Ball St Univ; Bus.

HUFF, LAURA; South Point HS; South Point, OH; Band; Rptr Sch Nwsp; Drama Clb; Fr Clb; Chrldng; Marshall Univ.

HUFF, MARSHA; Union Local HS; Flushing, OH; 9/143 Am Leg Aux Girls St; Hon Rl; Stu Cncl; Yth Flsp; Yrbk; Sch Nwsp; Lat Clb; Pres Pep Clb; Pres Soroptimist; Chrldng; Wooster College; Psych.

HUFF, PATRICK; Hampshire HS; Romney, WV; 47/215 AFS; Hon Rl; Yth Flsp; Letter Ftbl; Letter Ten; Univ.

HUFF, REBECCA; Greenbrier East HS; Whte Slphr Spgs, WV; VP Frsh Cls; Band; Chrh Wkr; Hon Rl; VP Jr NHS; NHS; Stu Cncl; Sec Civ Clb; Letter Chrldng; Univ; Bus Admin.

HUFF, STEVEN; Wayne HS; Dayton, OH; ROTC; Am Leg Awd; Univ.

HUFF, TERESA; Vinson HS; Huntington, WV; 1/120 Val; Am Leg Aux Girls St; Chrh Wkr; Hon Rl; Jr NHS; NHS; FBLA; Mth Clb; Ashland Schlr Awd 79; R C Byrd Schlstc Recognition Awd 79; Amer Soc Of Wmns Acctg Awd 79; Marshall Univ; Acctg.

HUFF, TROY; Valley Local HS; Lucasville, OH; 5/110 Band; Boy Scts; Hon Rl; NHS; Bsktbl; Ftbl; Trk; Univ Of Cincinnati; Medicine.

HUFFER, BRETT; Clinton Central HS; Forest, IN; 2/109 Am Leg Boys St; FCA; Hon Rl; NHS; Sci Clb; Bsktbl; Letter Crs Cntry; Trk; Scr Kpr; Tmr; Won Womens Christian Temperance League Poster Contest 3rd In St 78; 1st Pl In Art Show Water Color 78; IUK; Elec Engr.

HUFFER, KATHY; Clinton Prairie HS; Frankfort, IN; 11/90 Chrs; Hon Rl; NHS; Yth Flsp; Ed Sch Nwsp; Rptr Sch Nwsp; FHA; Bsbl; Letter Bsbl; Coach Actv; Ivy Tech; Resp Therapy.

HUFFMAN, BETH; Southern Local HS; Racine, OH; Chrs; Sch Mus; VP Stu Cncl; Pep Clb; Chrldng; Hocking Tech Schl; Sec.

HUFFMAN, DEBBIE; Morgan HS; Stockport, OH; 10/250 Cl Rep Jr Cls; Chrh Wkr; Girl Scts; Hon Rl; Lbry Ade; NHS; Sct Actv; Stu Cncl; 4-H; Spn Clb; Washington Tech Voc Schl; Bus.

HUFFMAN, DEBORAH; St Ursula Academy; Cincinnati, OH; Hon Rl; JA; Sch Pl; Sch Nwsp; Letter Bsbl; Letter Bsktbl; IM Sprt; Scr Kpr; Schlrshp Awd Pin From Summit 78; MVP For Sftbl From Summit 77; Univ; Acctg.

HUFFMAN, DIANA; Carrollton HS; Dellroy, OH; 73/255 Aud/Vis; Girl Scts; Hon Rl; Sch Pl; Stg Crw; Rptr Yrbk; Yrbk; Ohi State; Home Ec.

HUFFMAN, DONNA; Sherman HS; Seth, WV; VP Jr Cls; Band; Drm Mjrt; Sch Pl; VP Stu Cncl; Golden Horseshoe Awd 75; All Fest Band Mbr 78 79; Know Your St Govt Rep 79; Coll.

HUFFMAN, ELIZABETH; Edwardsburg HS; Edwardsbg, MI; 11/147 Debate Tm; Girl Scts; NHS; Rptr Sch Nwsp; Ger Clb; Letter Trk; Sw Mic College; Acctg.

HUFFMAN, ERICKA; Delta HS; Albany, IN; 25/295 Am Leg Aux Girls St; Girl Scts; Hon Rl; Jr NHS; NHS; 4-H; FHA; Lat Clb; Sci Clb; 4-H Awd; Ball State Univ; Sci.

HUFFMAN, GARY; Staunton HS; Brazil, IN; 2/50 Chrh Wkr; Hon Rl; Stu Cncl; Key Clb; Bsbl; Mgrs; Indiana St Univ.

HUFFMAN, JOYCE; Tri Jr Sr HS; Lewisville, IN; Chrs; Drl Tm; Hon Rl; Lbry Ade; NHS; Sec FHA; Pep Clb; Trk; GAA; IM Sprt; Delta Kappa Gamma Awd 79; Soc Std Awd 79; Ball St Univ; Elem Educ Tchr.

HUFFMAN, LINDA; Whiteland Cmnty HS; New Whiteland, IN; 19/219 NHS; Spn Clb; Coll; Nursing.

HUFFMAN, LINDA; Whiteland Community HS; New Whiteland, IN; 19/229 NHS; Spn Clb; College; Nursing.

HUFFMAN, LISA; Fairfield Union HS; Hide A Way Hls, OH; 12/158 Band; Drl Tm; Hon Rl; Jr NHS; Orch; 4-H; Crs Cntry; Trk; IM Sprt; Pom Pon; All County Band; Miami Univ; Busns Admin.

HUFFMAN, LISA K; Gahanna Lincoln HS; Gahanna, OH; Lbry Ade; Off Ade; Yth Flsp; DECA; Mgrs; PPFtbl; Univ; Optometric Prog.

HUFFMAN, MARY; Milton Union HS; Ludlow Fl, OH; 13/250 Band; Hon Rl; Off Ade; Pol Wkr; Stu Cncl; FBLA; FTA; Letter Trk; St Marys College; Government.

HUFFMAN, PAMELA; Spanishburg HS; Kegley, WV; 5/42 Sec Frsh Cls; Cls Rep Sr Cls; Band; VP Chrs; Hon Rl; NHS; Sch Pl; Pres Stu Cncl; Yrbk; FBLA; 1979 Homecoming Queen 1979; To Oklahoma With WVU Band 1979; All Tournament Basketball Tm 1979; Bluefield St Coll; Reg Nurse.

HUFFMAN, PATRICIA; Roosevelt Wilson HS; Clarksburg, WV; 24/122 Band; Chrs; Girl Scts; Hon Rl; Sch Pl; Sct Actv; Y-Teens; FBLA; Leo Clb; Pep Clb; Busns Schl; Busns.

HUFFMAN, RENE; La Salle HS; South Bend, IN; Chrs; Cmnty Wkr; Girl Scts; Hon Rl; Sch Mus; Sch Pl; 4-H; Pep Clb; Trk; 4-H Awd; Coll; Nurse.

HUFFMAN, ROBERT S; Fairfield Union HS; Hide A Way Hill, OH; 4/150 Chrs; Hon Rl; Jr NHS; NHS; Sch Pl; Stg Crw; Stu Cncl; 4-H; Fr Clb; Key Clb; U S Naval Academy; Nuclear Engr.

HUFFMAN, SHARON; Upper Sandusky HS; Upper Sandusky, OH; 3/216 Band; Chrs; Chrh Wkr; NHS; Sch Mus; Yrbk; 4-H; FNA; Univ Of Toledo; Nursing.

HUFFMAN, STEVE; Arcanum Butler HS; Arcanum, OH; 76/122 Swmmng; IM Sprt; Morehead; Industrial Arts.

HUFFMAN, TERRA K; Barboursville HS; Huntington, WV; Trs Jr Cls; Band; Drm Mjrt; Girl Scts; Hon Rl; Hosp Ade; Off Ade; Sch Pl; Y-Teens; Rptr Sch Nwsp; Marshall Univ.

HUFFMAN, VICKI; South Harrison HS; Clarksburg, WV; 15/100 Trs Frsh Cls; VP Jr Cls; Am Leg Aux Girls St; Band; Chrh Wkr; Hon Rl; Jr NHS; NHS; Stg Crw; Stu Cncl; Best Sr High Cheerldr 78; 1st Team All St Bsktbll 78; Modern Wv St Record Most Pts In Bsktbll Game 78; Univ.

HUFFORD, BETH; Holland HS; Holland, MI; Hon Rl; Orch; PPFtbl; Hope College.

HUFFORD, HOWARD L; Milan HS; Milan, MI; Boy Scts; Hon Rl; Sct Actv; Letter Bsbl; Bsktbl; Ftbl; Wrstlng; IM Sprt; Army; Bio Engr.

HUFFORD, JILL; Eastwood HS; Perrysburg, OH; Band; Hon Rl; Hosp Ade; JA; Fr Clb; College; Vet Med.

HUFNAGEL, NANCY; Seton HS; Cincinnati, OH; Hon Rl; NHS; Pres Orch; Sch Mus; Fr Clb; Pep Clb;.

HUFSTETLER, GUY; Perry HS; Massillon, OH; Am Leg Boys St; Chrs; Chrh Wkr; Hon Rl; Natl Forn Lg; VP NHS; PAVAS; Quill & Scroll; Sch Mus; Sch Pl; Jr Most Likely To Succeed In Sr Yr; Eckelberry Awd; Outstanding Freshman Candidate; College; Optometry.

HUGGINS, BRUCE P; West Preston HS; Reedsville, WV; Pres Jr Cls; Am Leg Boys St; Hon Rl; Jr NHS; Treas NHS; Stu Cncl; Mth Clb; Letter Glf; Wv Univ; Educ.

HUGHART, MARY; Dupont HS; Belle, WV; Lat Clb ; Univ.

HUGHBANKS, BOB; Scecina Memorial HS; Indianapolis, IN; Mgrs; IUPUI Indpls.

HUGHES, AMY; Oak Hills HS; Cincinnati, OH; DECA; Univ Of Cincinnati; Acctg.

HUGHES, ANNE; Magnificat HS; Rocky River, OH; Chrh Wkr; Cmnty Wkr; Mod UN; Off Ade; Red Cr Ade; Yth Flsp; Rptr Sch Nwsp; Key Clb; Spn Clb; Greater Cleveland Chapter Ldrshp Candidate Amer Red Cross; Coll; Public Relations.

HUGHES, BARTT; Jackson HS; Massillon, OH; Band; Boy Scts; Hon Rl; Boys Clb Am; Univ; Archt.

HUGHES, CATHERINE; W V Fisher Catholic HS; Lancaster, OH; Cmp Fr Grls; Chrs; Chrh Wkr; Cmnty Wkr; Hon Rl; Sch Pl; Stg Crw; Sch Nwsp; Drama Clb; Swmmng; College; Drama.

HUGHES, CHERYL; Luther L Wright HS; Ironwood, MI; 17/175 Hon Rl; Sch Pl; Gym; College; Dental Hygiene.

HUGHES, CONSTANCE; North HS; Willowcik, OH; Cls Rep Frsh Cls; Hon Rl; Stu Cncl;.

HUGHES, DARSI; Greenville Sr HS; Greenville, OH; 47/360 Band; Hon Rl; Lbry Ade; Rptr Sch Nwsp; Miami Univ; Eng Educ.

HUGHES, DEE; Union Cnty HS; Liberty, IN; Chrs; Drl Tm; Letter Trk; Voc Schl; Nursing.

HUGHES, DONALD L; Parkway HS; Rockford, OH; 21/83 FCA; Hon Rl; Sch Pl; Yth Flsp; Lat Clb; Sci Clb; Bsktbl; Letter Ftbl; Letter Trk; Manchester Coll; History.

HUGHES, ELIZABETH; North Farmington HS; Farmington Hls, MI; Band; Hon Rl; Natl Forn Lg; Orch; Sch Mus; Sch Pl; Stg Crw; Rptr Yrbk; Yrbk; Rdo Clb; Univ Of Mich; English.

HUGHES, GINA; Harbor HS; Ashtabula, OH; AFS; Chrs; Off Ade; Rptr Yrbk; Yrbk; Rptr Sch Nwsp; Lat Clb; Ohio Univ; Broadcasting.

HUGHES, JAMES J; Columbus Alternative HS; Columbus, OH; Cls Rep Frsh Cls; CAP; Pol Wkr; Sch Mus; Yth Flsp; Ed Sch Nwsp; Rptr Sch Nwsp; Natl Merit SF; Telluride Assoc Summer Prog Schlr 78; Univ; Soc Sci.

HUGHES, JEFF; R Nelson Snider HS; Ft Wayne, IN; 280/585 Hon Rl; Letter Ftbl; Hockey; Bowling Green St Univ.

HUGHES, JENNIE; Northwood HS; Goshen, IN; 98/205 Cls Rep Frsh Cls; Band; Chrh Wkr; Hon Rl; Sch Pl; Drama Clb; Ten; GAA; JA Awd; Pres Soph Cls; S W Michigan Coll; Interpreter.

HUGHES, JERRY; Frontier HS; Chalmers, IN; Am Leg Boys St; Boy Scts; Hon Rl; Sct Actv; 4-H; FFA; Crs Cntry; Trk; 4-H Awd; Purdue Univ; Agriculture.

HUGHES, JOAN; Jonesville HS; Jonesville, MI; Hon Rl; NHS; Rotary Awd; Coll; Dent Hygiene.

HUGHES, JOHN; Du Pont HS; Belle, WV; Band; Boy Scts; Chrs; Chrh Wkr; Orch; Sch Mus; Stg Crw; 4-H; Letter Wrstlng; 4-H Awd; West Virginia Univ; Music.

HUGHES, JOHN; Oak Hill HS; Oak Hill, OH; 1/90 Val; Hon Rl; NHS; Pres Stu Cncl; Ed Yrbk; Ed Sch Nwsp; Bsbl; Ohi N Univ; Pharmacy.

HUGHES, JOY; Tri Valley HS; Nashport, OH; Band; Hon Rl; Off Ade; Yth Flsp; Sec 4-H; FTA; VP Spn Clb; Bsktbl; Univ; Elem Educ.

HUGHES, KAREN; Nordonia HS; Northfield, OH; Cls Rep Sr Cls; Chrs; Girl Scts; Off Ade; Stu Cncl; IM Sprt; Mgrs; PPFtbl; Bus School.

HUGHES, KAREN; Onaway HS; Ocqueoc, MI; 18/96 Hon Rl; Lbry Ade; Off Ade; Sch Pl; Stg Crw; Sprt Ed Yrbk; Yrbk; 4-H; 4-H Awd; Ferris St Univ; Dent.

HUGHES, KAREN F; Cass Technical HS; Detroit, MI; Hon Rl; Jr NHS; Sch Pl; Drama Clb; College; Drama.

HUGHES, KATHERINE; Immaculata HS; Highland Pk, MI; Band; Drl Tm; Hon Rl; JA; Orch; Central Michigan Univ; Dent.

HUGHES, KEITH G; Lake Orion Comm HS; Lake Orion, MI; Aud/Vis; Chrh Wkr; Capt CAP; Cmnty Wkr; Drl Tm; Jr NHS; Lit Mag; Yrbk; Sch Nwsp; Pres Fr Clb; Oakland Comm Coll; Med Tech.

HUGHES, KIM; Parkway HS; Rockford, OH; 10/97 Hon Rl; FHA; Pep Clb; PPFtbl;.

HUGHES, LAURA; Mc Auley HS; Cincinnati, OH; Chrh Wkr; Cmnty Wkr; Stg Crw; GAA; IM Sprt; Univ; Comm Art.

HUGHES, LISA; Spencer HS; Spencer, WV; Sec Frsh Cls; Band; Chrh Wkr; Drm Mjrt; Girl Scts; Hon Rl; Lbry Ade; Off Ade; Sch Pl; Yth Flsp; Univ; Chem Engr.

HUGHES, LISA; Wayne HS; Dayton, OH; 25/635 Sec Soph Cls; VP Jr Cls; FCA; Hon Rl; Jr NHS; Sec NHS; Stu Cncl; Pres DECA; Chrldng; Stdn Tof Yr Awd 79; 4th Pl Free Enterprs Awd InDECA St Compttn 78; Miami Univ; Educ.

HUGHES, MARK; Kirtland HS; Chesterland, OH; Sec Frsh Cls; VP Soph Cls; Cmnty Wkr; Key Clb; Capt Bsbl; Capt Bsktbl; Ten; IM Sprt; Mgrs; Miami Univ; Pro Baseball.

HUGHES, MARY; Nicholas County HS; Summersville, WV; 26/214 Cl Rep Jr Cls; Band; Chrh Wkr; Hon Rl; Sch Pl; Stu Cncl; Yth Flsp; FBLA; FTA; GAA; Concord Coll; Acctg.

HUGHES, MARY; Sebring Mckinley HS; Sebring, OH; Chrs; Cmnty Wkr; Lbry Ade; Yrbk; 4-H; Fr Clb; FHA; Pep Clb; Chrldng; College; Sec.

HUGHES, MIKE; Shady Spring HS; Daniels, WV; 45/160 Chrh Wkr; FCA; Hon Rl; Lbry Ade; Yth Flsp; VICA; Crs Cntry; Ftbl; Letter Wrstlng; 4-H Awd; Appalachian Bible Coll; Engr.

HUGHES, PATRICK; Baker HS; Fairborn, OH; Boy Scts; Hon Rl; Yrbk; Bsktbl; Ftbl; Wrstlng; Miami Univ; Cmctns.

HUGHES, PHILIP; London HS; London, OH; 25/160 VP Frsh Cls; Cls Rep Frsh Cls; Pres Soph Cls; Cls Rep Soph Cls; Pres Jr Cls; Cl Rep Jr Cls; Hon Rl; College; Bus.

HUGHES, RANDY; Benton Harbor HS; Benton Hrbr, MI; .

HUGHES, ROBERT; Clay Battelle HS; Fairview, WV; Cl Rep Jr Cls; Cls Rep Sr Cls; Band; Chrs; Chrh Wkr; Orch; Sch Mus; Sch Pl; FFA; Trk; Forest Mgmt Awd; United Nations Pilgrimage For Youth Awd; Valley Forge Bible Coll; Music.

HUGHES, ROBERTA; Edgewood HS; Hamilton, OH; 14/253 Band; Chrh Wkr; Hon Rl; NHS; Off Ade; Orch; Rptr Sch Nwsp; Fr Clb; Scr Kpr; Special 3 Yr French Awd; Recognized In Whos Who; Miss Hemisphere Southern Ohio; Middletown Miami Univ; Lib Arts.

HUGHES, SUE E; Lake Orion HS; Lake Orion, MI; Trs Frsh Cls; Cls Rep Soph Cls; Sec Jr Cls; Cl Rep Jr Cls; Band; Cmnty Wkr; Off Ade; Sch Mus; Stg Crw; Stu Cncl; Business Schl.

HUGHES, WHITNEY; Cambridge HS; Cambridge, OH; Am Leg Aux Girls St; Band; Cmp Fr Grls; Hon Rl; Hosp Ade; Sch Pl; Yth Flsp; 4-H; Fr Clb; Univ.

HUGUENARD, JEANNETTE; Bishop Luers HS; Ft Wayne, IN; Chrs; Hon Rl; Sch Mus; Sch Pl; Sch Nwsp; Fr Clb; IUPU; Music.

HUGUENIN, MICHELE; Galion Sr HS; Galion, OH; Am Leg Aux Girls St; Band; Chrh Wkr; Girl Scts; Hon Rl; Hosp Ade; NHS; Off Ade; Sec Yth Flsp; Gym; Ohio Northern Univ; Pharm.

HUGULEY, KEITH; Inkster HS; Inkster, MI; 1/250 Pres Frsh Cls; Hst Soph Cls; Cl Rep Jr Cls; Band; Debate Tm; Hon Rl; NHS; Orch; Stu Cncl; Bsbl; Highest Ranking Stdnt In Class 76 78; Purdue Univ; Indstl Engr.

HUHN, ANTHONY; Bishop Dwenger HS; Grabill, IN; Boy Scts; Hon Rl; College; Sci.

HUHTA, JUDITH M; Zeeland HS; Zeeland, MI; Am Leg Aux Girls St; Chrs; Chrh Wkr; Hon Rl; Mdrgl; NHS; Stg Crw; Yth Flsp; Letter Ten; IM Sprt; Grand Rapids Baptist Coll.

HUIBRECHTS, MARION; Orchard View HS; Muskegon, MI; Hon Rl; NHS; Red Cr Ade; Stu Cncl; Rptr Yrbk; Sch Nwsp; Bsbl; Mgrs; Pom Pon; Scr Kpr; College; History.

HUIBREGTSE, JON; Plymouth Canton HS; Plymouth, MI; Band; Hon Rl; Orch; Univ Of Michigan; Pre Med.

HUISINGH, JACK; Holland HS; Holland, MI; Cls Rep Frsh Cls; Pres Jr Cls; Cls Rep Sr Cls; Band; Pres Chrh Wkr; Pres JA; Yth Flsp; Civ Clb; FBLA; Letter Swmmng; Hope Coll; Bus Admin.

HUISMANN, CHRIS; Grand Haven HS; Spring Lake, MI; 43/389 Band; Boy Scts; Hon Rl; Jr NHS; NHS; Sch Mus; Sch Pl; Central Mic Univ; Law.

HUIZENGA, CAROL; Grand Rapids Cath Ctrl HS; Grand Rapis, MI; Trs Frsh Cls; Trs Soph Cls; Trs Jr Cls; Trs Sr Cls; Hon Rl; Stu Cncl; Rptr Sch Nwsp; Lat Clb; IM Sprt; Univ; Bus.

HUKARI, FRED; James A Garfield HS; Garrettsville, OH; Cls Rep Frsh Cls; Cls Rep Soph Cls; Cl Rep Jr Cls; Cls Rep Sr Cls; Band; Hon Rl; Coach Actv; Kent State Univ; Bus Admin.

HUKARI, TERRI; James A Garfield HS; Garrettsville, OH; Sec Frsh Cls; Sec Soph Cls; Girl Scts; Hon Rl; Sch Pl; Pres Stu Cncl; Fr Clb; Pep Clb; Bsktbl; Chrldng; Art Awd; Tri St Univ; Comp Sci.

HULBERT, HEIDI; Westerville North HS; Columbus, OH; Sec Band; Cmp Fr Grls; Chrs; Chrh Wkr; Hon Rl; NHS; Pres Orch; Sch Mus; Yth Flsp; Crs Cntry; College; Nursing.

HULBERT, LYNN; Edgewood Sr HS; Ashtabula, OH; 12/250 Band; Chrs; Pres NHS; Sch Mus; Sch Pl; Drama Clb; Sci Clb; Spn Clb; Twrlr; Cit Awd; Univ.

HULIN, CYNTHIA; Whitehall Sr HS; Whitehall, MI; 14/150 Sch Mus; Rptr Yrbk; Drama Clb; Intl Hair Dsgn Coll Schlrshp; Magna Cum Laude; Outstndng Schlstc Ach Awd; Intl Hair Dsgn Coll; Cosmetology.

HULING, CATHERIN; Summerfield HS; Petersburg, MI; Chrs; Chrh Wkr; Girl Scts; Hon Rl; Stg Crw; Pep Clb; Trk; PPFtbl; OMEA Solo & Ensmbl Comp 76; 3 Yr Choir Pin 78; Dramatics Awrd 79; Eastern Univ.

HULING, DAVID; Springfield HS; Springfield, MI; Cls Rep Frsh Cls; Cls Rep Soph Cls; Hon Rl; Jr NHS; Michigan St Univ; Elec Engr.

HULL, AMY; Stephen T Badin HS; Hamilton, OH; 38/219 Cmnty Wkr; Hon Rl; Lit Mag; Tmr; Univ.

HULL, BRENDA; East Knox HS; Howard, OH; Cls Rep Frsh Cls; Sec Sr Cls; Cls Rep Sr Cls; Hon Rl; Sch Pl; Stu Cncl; FHA; Pep Clb; Typing II; Bookkeeping Shorthand I Gen Busns Ofc & Painting I; Business Schl; Busns Admin.

HULL, CHRISTINE; Brown City HS; Brown City, MI; Sec Jr Cls; Chrs; Drl Tm; Hon Rl; NHS; Off Ade; Stu Cncl; Rptr Sch Nwsp; 4-H; FHA; St Clair Cnty Cmnty Coll; Lgl Sec.

HULL, DAVID; Big Rapids HS; Big Rapids, MI; Hon Rl; IM Sprt; College.

HULL, DEANNA; St Charles HS; Saginaw, MI; Chrs; Girl Scts; Hon Rl; Baker Jr Coll Of Flint; Sec.

HULL, DENISE; Lewis Co HS; Jane Lew, WV; Band; Chrh Wkr; FCA; Hon Rl; NHS; Bsktbl; Mat Maids; PPFtbl; Stonewall Jackson Memrl Hosp; Radlgc.

HULL, JEAN; Bridgeport HS; Bridgeport, WV; 48/189 Girl Scts; Hon Rl; Jr NHS; Y-Teens; DECA; Drama Clb;.

HULL, JOHN; Greenwood Comm HS; Greenwood, IN; 16/230 Pres Sr Cls; Hon Rl; NHS; Quill & Scroll; Yrbk; Key Clb; Letter Crs Cntry; Letter Trk; IM Sprt; JA Awd; Recipient Indiana Univ Merit Schlrshp & Krannert Mem Schlrshp; Indiana Univ; Dentistry.

HULL, JUDITH L; Grandview Heights HS; Columbus, OH; 4/130 Cls Rep Frsh Cls; Chrs; Girl Scts; Hon Rl; Jr NHS; NHS; Stu Cncl; Sci Clb; Spn Clb; Mgrs; Ohio St Univ; Acctg.

HULL, MATTHEW; Ursuline HS; Youngstown, OH; Boy Scts; Sct Actv; Crs Cntry; College; Marine Sci.

HULL, PHYLLIS; South Ripley HS; Holton, IN; 10/113 Chrs; Chrh Wkr; Cmnty Wkr; Hon Rl; Quill & Scroll; Sch Mus; Sch Pl; Yth Flsp; Yrbk; Sch Nwsp; Marian Coll; Elem Educ.

HULL, SUSAN; Athens HS; Troy, MI; 14/500 Sec Frsh Cls; Pres Soph Cls; Cl Rep Jr Cls; Am Leg Aux Girls St; Band; Cmnty Wkr; Hon Rl; NHS; Red Cr Ade; Stu Cncl; College.

HULL, TIMOTHY; North Central Area HS; Hermansville, MI; Pres Frsh Cls; Pres Soph Cls; Pres Jr Cls; Am Leg Boys St; Aud/Vis; VP Stu Cncl; Letter Bsktbl; Letter Ftbl; Letter Trk; Dnfth Awd; Univ.

HULLIHEN, SAMUEL; Lakeview HS; Warren, OH; Cls Rep Sr Cls; Boy Scts; Hon Rl; Lbry Ade; Sct Actv; Boys Clb Am; VFW Awd; Voice Dem Awd; Youngstown St Univ; Broadcasting.

HULLINGER, ROBIN; Lima Sr HS; Lima, OH; Cls Rep Frsh Cls; Cl Rep Jr Cls; Girl Scts; Sch Pl; Stg Crw; Stu Cncl; Drama Clb; Spn Clb; Chrldng; Univ; Drama.

HULSE, GREGORY; Anderson HS; Anderson, IN; Hon Rl; Spn Clb; Letter Wrstlng; Mas Awd; Purdue Univ; Engr.

HULTEEN, CHERYL; Westerville North HS; Westerville, OH; 13/420 Cls Rep Sr Cls; Am Leg Aux Girls St; Cmp Fr Grls; Chrs; Chrh Wkr; Hon Rl; NHS; Sch Mus; Sch Pl; Stg Crw; Heidelberg Univ; Music.

HULTQUIST, STEPHEN S; Flushing HS; Flushing, MI; Chrs; Hon Rl; Mdrgl; NHS; Natl Merit Schl; Mich State Univ; Engr.

HULVERSON, SCOTT; Croswell Lexington HS; Croswell, MI; Cls Rep Soph Cls; Band; Hon Rl;

NHS; Orch; Sch Mus; Stg Crw; Stu Cncl; Letter Ten; IM Sprt; Michigan St Univ; Mrktng.

HUM, AMY; Columbiana HS; Columbiana, OH; Cls Rep Soph Cls; Sec Jr Cls; Cl Rep Jr Cls; Sec Sr Cls; Chrs; Hon Rl; Stu Cncl; Fr Clb; OEA; Pep Clb; Bus Schl; Legal Sec.

HUMBARGER, CONSTANCE; North Central HS; Montpelier, OH; Band; Chrs; Chrh Wkr; Girl Scts; Hon Rl; Off Ade; Sch Mus; Sch Pl; Stg Crw; Yth Flsp; Otterbein Univ; Sociology.

HUMBARGER, GARY; Clay HS; Oregon, OH; 2/366 Band; Boy Scts; Hon Rl; VP JA; Jr NHS; NHS; Sch Mus; VP Yth Flsp; Sch Nwsp; JA Awd; College; Engr.

HUMBAUGH, KRAIG E; Washington HS; Washington, IN; 1/207 Sec Sr Cls; Cls Rep Sr Cls; Val; Boy Scts; NHS; Sch Pl; Stu Cncl; Beta Clb; Drama Clb; VP 4-H; Univ.

HUMBLE, KELLY; Jewett Scio HS; Scio, OH; Am Leg Aux Girls St; Hon Rl; NHS; Spn Clb; Letter Bsktbl; Univ Of Akron.

HUME, M; St Philip Cath Ctrl HS; Battle Crk, MI; Cls Rep Frsh Cls; Cls Rep Soph Cls; Cmp Fr Grls; Hon Rl; NHS; Stu Cncl; Lat Clb; Pep Clb; Chrldng; PPFtbl; Michigan St Univ; Sec.

HUME, MAGGIE; St Philip Cath Central HS; Battle Creek, MI; 4/70 Cls Rep Frsh Cls; Cls Rep Soph Cls; Cmp Fr Grls; Hon Rl; NHS; Stu Cncl; Lat Clb; OEA; Pep Clb; Chrldng; Kellogg Comm Coll; Sec.

HUME, MELODY; Dayton Christian HS; Dayton, OH; Trs Sr Cls; Band; Chrs; Chrh Wkr; Hon Rl; Hosp Ade; NHS; Sch Mus; Yth Flsp; Cit Awd; Bible Memorztn Awd 78; Southeastern Coll; Music.

HUME, THOMAS R; Wood Memorial HS; Oakland City, IN; Chrh Wkr; Hon Rl; Pol Wkr; Univ; Elect Engr.

HUML, KAREN; New Haven HS; New Have, IN; 21/351 Band; Girl Scts; Hon Rl; Yth Flsp; Drama Clb; Ger Clb; Sci Clb; Trk; Coll; Dentistry.

HUMM, TAMMY; North Farmington HS; Farm Hills, MI; Chrs; Chrh Wkr; Hon Rl; Natl Forn Lg; NHS; Fr Clb; College; Spec Educ.

HUMMEL, AMY; Chippewa HS; Doylestown, OH; Cls Rep Sr Cls; Am Leg Aux Girls St; Band; Hon Rl; Sch Pl; Stu Cncl; Rptr Yrbk; Pep Clb; Pres Spn Clb; Bsktbl; Univ; Bus.

HUMMEL, DEBRA; Elmwood HS; Bloomdale, OH; Chrs; Sec Chrh Wkr; Hon Rl; Yth Flsp; 4-H; Bsktbl; IM Sprt; Ohi State Univ; Acctg.

HUMMEL, NAN; Penn HS; Bremen, IN; 1/450 Cls Rep Frsh Cls; Am Leg Aux Girls St; Sec Chrh Wkr; Hon Rl; Sec NHS; 4-H; IM Sprt; PPFtbl; College; Law.

HUMMEL, PHIL; Cadillac Sr HS; Cadillac, MI; Cl Rep Jr Cls; Hon Rl; NHS; Stu Cncl; Capt Ftbl; Trk; Pres Awd; Michigan St Univ; Bus.

HUMPERT, REGINA; St John HS; Delphos, OH; Band; Chrh Wkr; 4-H; Gym; C of C Awd; 4-H Awd; God Cntry Awd; College; Health Prof.

HUMPHRESS, SONJIA; Danville Community HS; Danville, IN; 3/155 Chrs; FCA; Hon Rl; Hosp Ade; Lbry Ade; NHS; Sch Mus; Stg Crw; Rptr Sch Nwsp; Fr Clb; French Awd 77 & 78; Pres Tri Hi Y 79; Hon Queen Jobs Daughter 79; Univ; Pre Med.

HUMPHREY, DEBRA; Seton HS; Cincinnati, OH; Am Leg Aux Girls St; Cmnty Wkr; Hon Rl; Lit Mag; Yth Flsp; Rptr Sch Nwsp; Pep Clb; IM Sprt; Univ.

HUMPHREY, DENNIS; Hardin Northern HS; Dunkirk, OH; 16/65 Band; Sec Chrh Wkr; Orch; Treas FFA; Ohio State Univ; Agri.

HUMPHREY, JILL; Wylie E Groves HS; Birmingham, MI; 1/500 Val; Chrs; Hon Rl; Jr NHS; NHS; Sch Mus; Sch Pl; Stg Crw; Letter Bsktbl; Letter Trk; Michigan St Univ; Agri.

HUMPHREY, JIM; Terre Haute North Vigo HS; Terre Haute, IN; Sec Soph Cls; Sec Jr Cls; Cl Rep Jr Cls; VP Sr Cls; Aud/Vis; Band; Boy Scts; Chrh Wkr; Hon Rl; Sch Mus; Indiana Univ; Dentistry.

HUMPHREY, MEEGHAN; Grand River Academy; Ashtabula, OH; 1/23 Val; Drm Bgl; Hon Rl; JA; NHS; PAVAS; Drama Clb; Wrstlng; Mgrs; Cit Awd; Oberlin Coll; Liberal Arts.

HUMPHREY, MELANIE S; Loudonville Perrysville HS; Loudonville, OH; Band; Chrs; Lbry Ade; Off Ade; Sch Pl; Yth Flsp; 4-H; FFA; Spn Clb; Chrldng; College; Lawyer.

HUMPHREY, MELISSA; Hale Area HS; Hale, MI; 8/60 Band; Chrs; Chrh Wkr; Hon Rl; Sch Pl; Drama Clb; Letter Trk; College; Nursing.

HUMPHREY, RANDY; East Liverpool HS; East Liverpool, OH; Boy Scts; Lbry Ade; Sct Actv; Univ Of Akr; Military Srvc.

HUMPHREY, THOMAS; Elston HS; Mich City, IN; Band; Boy Scts; Chrs; Chrh Wkr; Hon Rl; Off Ade; Sct Actv; Socr; ISU; Math.

HUMPHREYS, KATHY; Heath HS; Heath, OH; Cls Rep Soph Cls; Cl Rep Jr Cls; Cls Rep Sr Cls; Hon Rl; Off Ade; Treas Stu Cncl; Letter Trk; Scr Kpr; Central Ohio Tech Coll; Sec.

HUMPHREYS, SHIRLEE L; Walton HS; Walton, WV; Band; Hosp Ade; Rptr Sch Nwsp; Sch Nwsp; FHA; VICA; St Finalist In Miss Wv Natl Teenager Pageant 79; Awd For Being In Band All In HS 79; Univ Of Charleston; Nursing.

HUMPHREYS, STEPHEN; Bethany Christian HS; Warren, MI; 5/50 Pres Jr Cls; Pres Sr Cls; Hon Rl; Sch Pl; Rptr Sch Nwsp; Letter Bsbl; Letter Bsktbl; Letter Socr; Scr Kpr; Cit Awd; College; Business.

HUMPHREYS, THOMAS; Hinton HS; Hinton, WV; Hon Rl; Lbry Ade; FBLA; Key Clb; Letter Bsbl; Bsktbl; Ftbl; Concord Coll; Bus.

HUMPHRIES, BRENDA; Cass Tech HS; Detroit, MI; Cls Rep Frsh Cls; Chrs; Chrh Wkr; Cmnty Wkr; Hon Rl; Off Ade; Rptr Sch Nwsp; Eng Clb; OEA; Swmmng; Marygrove Coll; Bus Admin.

HUMPHRIES, PEGGY; Cloverdale HS; Cloverdale, IN; Chrs; Sch Mus; 4-H; FTA; OEA; Spn Clb; Mgrs; Scr Kpr; ISU; Radio Communication.

HUMPHRIES, VENITA; Alexandria Monroe HS; Alexandria, IN; 53/159 Sec Jr Cls; Chrs; Chrh Wkr; Cmnty Wkr; Yth Flsp; Pep Clb; IM Sprt; College; Phy Ed Teacher.

HUMSTON, ELLEN; Valley Local HS; Lucasville, OH; 1/107 VP Frsh Cls; Chrh Wkr; Hon Rl; Pres NHS; Off Ade; Stu Cncl; Yth Flsp; FHA; Letter Bsktbl; Asbury Coll; Psychology.

HUNE, LAURA; Fowlerville HS; Fowlerville, MI; Chrs; Hon Rl; Off Ade; PPFtbl; Lansing Comm Coll; Public Relations.

HUNE, SUSANNE; West Muskingum HS; Zanesville, OH; Chrs; Cmnty Wkr; Girl Scts; Hon Rl; Sch Mus; Sch Pl; Stg Crw; Y-Teens; Rptr Yrbk; Yrbk; Sftbl Champ Tm Mbr 77; Bowling Green St Univ; Retail Mktg.

HUNGER, DONNA; South Ripley HS; Versailles, IN; Band; Chrh Wkr; Hon Rl; Quill & Scroll; Fr Clb; Pep Clb; Spn Clb; Univ Of Evansville; Phys Ther.

HUNGERFORD, JOEL; Tippecanoe HS; Tipp City, OH; Cl Rep Jr Cls; Hon Rl; Stu Cncl; Ftbl; Wrstlng; College.

HUNGERFORD, MARY; Euclid Sr HS; Euclid, OH; 5/703 AFS; Band; Hon Rl; Jr NHS; NHS; Sch Mus; Rptr Sch Nwsp; Natl Merit Ltr; Syracuse Univ; Dietetics.

HUNGERMAN, MARGARET; Our Lady Of Mercy HS; Farmingtonhill, MI; Chrs; FTA; Rdo Clb; Spn Clb; Trk; Mary Grove Coll; Foreign Language.

HUNGERMAN, TOM; Elyria Catholic HS; Elyria, OH; Hon Rl; Lorain County Community College;bus.

HUNGLER, ANNA M; Seton HS; Cincinnati, OH; 5/274 Treas Girl Scts; Hon Rl; Jr NHS; Lbry Ade; NHS; Sct Actv; Sec Lat Clb; Univ Of Cincinnati; Chem Engr.

HUNKINS, MARY; Vassar HS; Vassar, MI; Band; Hon Rl; FHA; Spn Clb;.

HUNKLER, PAT; Barnesville HS; Barnesville, OH; 19/130 VP Frsh Cls; VP Soph Cls; Hon Rl; Lbry Ade; NHS; Yrbk; FTA; Key Clb; Ftbl; Trk; Kenyon College.

HUNLEY, JOHN; Bexley HS; Columbus, OH; 13/185 Hon Rl; NHS; Orch; Yth Flsp; Rptr Sch Nwsp; Fr Clb; Natl Merit Ltr; Merit Schlrshp From Indiana Univ; Cum Laude Soc; Indiana Univ; Busns Finance.

HUNLEY, PEGGY; N Knox HS; Oaktown, IN; 12/150 Pres Jr Cls; FCA; Girl Scts; Hon Rl; NHS; Stu Cncl; FHA; Pep Clb; Chrldng; Cheerleading Awd Of Excellence; 1st Place At Cheerldng Cmp; 3rd & 1st Pl Trphy For Cheerleading; Indiana Business College; Sec.

HUNSANGER, DAVID; Ubly Comm HS; Ruth, MI; Hon Rl; NHS; FHA; IM Sprt; Coll; Geol.

HUNSINGER, HEIDI; Madison Comprehensive HS; Mansfield, OH; Band; NHS; FHA; Ger Clb; Ohio St Univ; Engr.

HUNSUCKER, KEITH; Mogadore HS; Mogadore, OH; Cl Rep Jr Cls; Band; Pres Chrs; Hon Rl; VP NHS; Orch; Sch Mus; Sch Pl; Stu Cncl; Rptr Sch Nwsp; Attnd Engr Sci Semnr At US Naval Acad 79; Top 1% On ACT Score Of 30 79; Univ.

HUNT, AMY; Northrop HS; Ft Wayne, IN; 31/586 Girl Scts; Hon Rl; Lbry Ade; Stg Crw; Drama Clb; Spn Clb; Univ; Soc Work.

HUNT, ANGELA; Connersville Sr HS; Milton, IN; 5/401 Hon Rl; Natl Forn Lg; Treas NHS; Pres 4-H; FFA; Key Clb; IM Sprt; Elk Awd; 4-H Awd; Amer & Indiana Jr Angus Assn; Purdue Univ; Vet.

HUNT, BARBARA; Bexley HS; Bexley, OH; Chrh Wkr; Hon Rl; Stg Crw; Drama Clb; Lat Clb; Letter Trk; Cum Laude Soc 79; Univ.

HUNT, BECKY; Philip Barbour HS; Buckhannon, WV; Hon Rl; Stu Cncl; FBLA; FHA; Pep Clb; Bus Schl.

HUNT, BRENDA; Wirt Cnty HS; Elizabeth, WV; Band; Bsktbl; Letter Trk; Chrldng; GAA; Voc Schl; Cosmetology.

HUNT, BRENDA; Jefferson HS; Monroe, MI; 22/211 Band; Cmp Fr Grls; Hon Rl; Hosp Ade; Jr NHS; Red Cr Ade; Stu Cncl; Fr Clb; FHA; Western Univ; Fshn Mdse.

HUNT, CHUCK; Oceana HS; Oceana, WV; Band; Chrh Wkr; Hon Rl; Treas Yth Flsp; Sch Nwsp; Sci Clb; Delegate To United Meth Annual Conf 78; West Virginia Univ; Soc Work.

HUNT, C JOY; East Kentwood HS; Grand Rapids, MI; Lbry Ade; Stu Cncl; Yth Flsp; Lat Clb; Chrldng; PPFtbl; Cit Awd; Grace Bible Coll; Nursing.

HUNT, CONNIE; Martinsville HS; Martinsville, IN; 52/385 Chrs; Hon Rl; Sch Mus; Drama Clb; Spn Clb; ITT; Exec Sec.

HUNT, CRYSTAL; Lincoln HS; Shinnston, WV; 49/150 Trs Frsh Cls; Sec Jr Cls; Cls Rep Sr Cls; VP Chrs; Hon Rl; Stu Cncl; Treas Fr Clb; Bsktbl; Fairmont State; Elec.

HUNT, DAMON; Southwestern HS; Detrit, MI; Hon Rl; NHS; Letter Trk; Am Leg Awd; Cit Awd; Lawrence Inst Of Tech; Elec.

HUNT, DAVID; Davison HS; Davison, MI; Boy Scts; Hon Rl; Jr NHS; Sec Spn Clb; College; Med Tech.

HUNT, DUANE A; Bear Lake HS; Bear Lake, MI; 2/35 VP Frsh Cls; Pres Soph Cls; Chrs; Hon Rl; NHS; Crs Cntry; Trk; Univ; Poli Sci.

HUNT, HELEN; Roy C Start HS; Toledo, OH; 15/400 Girl Scts; Hon Rl; Hosp Ade; Pres NHS; Off Ade; Quill & Scroll; Stu Cncl; Sch Nwsp; Eng Clb; Pres Fr Clb; Univ Of Toledo; Jrnlsm.

HUNT, JANE; Adrian HS; Adrian, MI; 49/500 Cls Rep Frsh Cls; Sal; Chrh Wkr; Cmnty Wkr; Hon Rl; JA; NHS; Pol Wkr; Stu Cncl; Ed Sch Nwsp; Univ Of Michigan.

HUNT, JEFF; Spencer HS; Spencer, WV; Chrh Wkr; Hon Rl; Jr NHS; NHS; Sprt Ed Yrbk; Drama Clb; Letter Bsktbl; Letter Ftbl; Letter Glf; Coach Actv; Univ; Law.

HUNT, JEFFERY A; Hesperia HS; Hesperia, MI; 8/79 Cmnty Wkr; Hon Rl; Sch Pl; Stg Crw; Drama Clb; Key Clb; Letter Glf; Trk;.

HUNT, JENNIFER; Paulding Exempted Vlg Schl; Paulding, OH; 18/198 Band; Chrs; Chrh Wkr; Hon Rl; Sch Mus; Sch Pl; Stg Crw; Rptr Sch Nwsp; Sch Nwsp; Drama Clb; Dist III Fest Band 78; ONU Band Camp Outstnndng In Theory 78; Ohio St Univ; Eng.

HUNT, JOCELYN; Murray Wright HS; Detroit, MI; Band; Girl Scts; Hon Rl; Lbry Ade; Sch Mus; FHA; Sci Clb; Cit Awd; College; Mntl Hlth.

HUNT, JOHN; Cadillac HS; Cadillac, MI; Hon Rl; Sch Nwsp; Ger Clb; Letter Ten; Rotary Awd; College.

HUNT, KEVIN; Hastings Area HS; Hastings, MI; Band; Boy Scts; Chrs; Chrh Wkr; Cmnty Wkr; Hon Rl; Orch; Sch Pl; Sct Actv; Western Mic Univ; Secondary Educ.

HUNT, KIMBERLY A; Van Buren Local HS; Findlay, OH; 21/92 Band; Chrs; Chrh Wkr; Girl Scts; Hon Rl; Lbry Ade; NHS; Off Ade; Red Cr Ade; Sch Mus; Bst Actrss Awd Drama Club 78; 1/th In Dist On Oh Schlstc Achvmnt Test 77; 4th In Oh St Eng 78; Bowling Green Univ; Theatre.

HUNT, MARLA; Hesperia HS; Hesperia, MI; 8/77 Sec Soph Cls; Sec Jr Cls; Hon Rl; Sch Pl; Drama Clb; FHA; Crs Cntry; Trk; Chrldng; PPFtbl; Muskegon Comm Coll; Acctg.

HUNT, MARLEY J; Eastern HS; Pekin, IN; Hon Rl; NHS; College.

HUNT, MICHAEL; Jay Cnty HS; Bryant, IN; Cls Rep Frsh Cls; FCA; Hon Rl; Jr NHS; NHS; Stu Cncl; Yth Flsp; Letter Bsbl; Letter Bsktbl; Letter Ftbl; Purdue Univ; Engr.

HUNT, MONICA; Upper Scioto Valley HS; Kenton, OH; Trs Frsh Cls; VP Soph Cls; Chrh Wkr; Hon Rl; Stu Cncl; Yrbk; Beta Clb; 4-H; Bsktbl; Chrldng; Wittenberg Coll; Nursing.

HUNT, PAMELA; Waverly HS; Waverly, OH; 2/166 Chrs; Hon Rl; NHS; Sch Pl; Yth Flsp; Fr Clb; Rising Sr Progr Berea Coll Berea Ky Wldlfe Bio 79; Schlrshp Tm Frnch 1st Yr Eng 2nd Yr Amer Hstry 3rd Yr 77; Univ; Nurse.

HUNT, REBECCA; Meridian Sr HS; Sanford, MI; Band; Chrh Wkr; Girl Scts; Hon Rl; Sch Mus; Stu Cncl; Yth Flsp; Pep Clb; Univ; Tchr.

HUNT, RHONDA; Fairmont HS; Fairmont, WV; 60/300 Chrs; Chrh Wkr; Hon Rl; Natl Forn Lg; Off Ade; Yth Flsp; FBLA;.

HUNT, SUSAN; R Nelson Snider HS; Ft Wayne, IN; Cls Rep Soph Cls; Chrh Wkr; Hon Rl; Pol Wkr; Stu Cncl; Fr Clb; Letter Ten; Letter Chrldng; PPFtbl; Purdue Univ; Psych.

HUNT, TERESA; Floyd Central HS; Floyd Knobs, IN; 5/343 Chrh Wkr; Hon Rl; Jr NHS; NHS; Pol Wkr; Ger Clb; Bsktbl; Crs Cntry; Trk; Scr Kpr; Indiana Univ; Elem Ed.

HUNT, TERRENCE; St Ignatius HS; Rocky River, OH; 65/352 Lat Clb; Crs Cntry; Trk; IM Sprt; College; Med.

HUNT, WILLIAM; Parkside HS; Jackson, MI; Chrh Wkr; 4-H; Bsktbl; Cit Awd; Univ Of Mic;.

HUNTER, ANGELA; Warrensville Hts HS; Warrensville, OH; Cl Rep Jr Cls; JA; Off Ade; Stu Cncl; Rptr Yrbk; Sch Nwsp; Pep Clb; Voc Schl; Fshn Dsgn.

HUNTER, BEV; Mitchell HS; Mitchell, IN; 9/151 Am Leg Aux Girls St; Hon Rl; Jr NHS; Treas NHS; Quill & Scroll; Yrbk; 4-H; Capt Bsktbl; Purdue Univ; Pre Vet.

HUNTER, BRADLEY; Brownsburg HS; Brownsbrg, IN; Cls Rep Frsh Cls; Cls Rep Soph Cls; Aud/Vis; Hon Rl; Lbry Ade; Off Ade; Stu Cncl; Spn Clb; Bsktbl; Ten; Most Improved Plyr Awd Trophy For Tennis 78; Butler Univ; Archt.

HUNTER, BRIAN; Franklin Central HS; Indianapolis, IN; 32/265 Letter Bsbl; IM Sprt; Univ; Acctg.

HUNTER, CHRISTOPHER; Chaminade Julienne HS; Dayton, OH; Cls Rep Frsh Cls; Cls Rep Sr Cls; Boy Scts; Chrh Wkr; Sct Actv; Stu Cncl; Boys Clb Am; Spn Clb; Letter Bsktbl; Scr Kpr; Univ Of Cincinnati; Architecture.

HUNTER, CONNIE; Morrison R Waite HS; Toledo, OH; Hon Rl; Hosp Ade; NHS; FHA; OEA; 3 Awrds For High Spd In Shrthnd; High Achvmnt In Intensive Offc Educ; 1st Plc For Prfrdng In Rgnl Comp; Michael Owens Tech Coll; Sec.

HUNTER, DAVID; Clawson HS; Clawson, MI; 4/298 JA; NHS; JA Awd; Univ Of Mic; Zoology.

HUNTER, DEANA; Zionsville Comm HS; Zionsville, IN; 8/150 Band; Cmnty Wkr; Girl Scts; Hon Rl; VP NHS; Drama Clb; Pep Clb; Ind Univ; Computer Sci.

HUNTER, DON; Chillicothe HS; Chillicothe, OH; 14/365 Cls Rep Sr Cls; Am Leg Boys St; Hon Rl; JA; Sch Pl; Stg Crw; DECA; Mgrs; Am Leg Awd; Ohio Univ; Acting.

HUNTER, DONNIE; Greenbrier East HS; Alderson, WV; 70/430 Chrh Wkr; Cmnty Wkr; FCA; Hon Rl; Pol Wkr; Yth Flsp; Rptr Yrbk; Rptr Sch Nwsp; Bsbl; Ftbl; All Coalfield Conference Ftbl; Athletic Schlrshp; Whos Who 77; Concord Coll; Phys Ther.

HUNTER, FRANCIS; Anderson HS; Anderson, IN; Cl Rep Jr Cls; Boy Scts; Chrh Wkr; Hon Rl; Sct Actv; Stu Cncl; Letter Swmmng; Chrldng; Tmr; Purdue Univ; Pre Dent.

HUNTER, GREGORY; Morgantown HS; Morgantown, WV; 98/410 Quill & Scroll; Rptr Yrbk; Sprt Ed Sch Nwsp; Rptr Sch Nwsp; Ger Clb; Capt Ftbl; IM Sprt; DAR Awd; West Virginia Univ; Journalism.

HUNTER, JAMES; Chesapeake HS; Chesapeake, OH; 13/180 Hon Rl; NHS; Letter Bsbl; Letter Wrstlng; Univ; Med.

HUNTER, JAMES; Inkster HS; Westland, MI; 4/200 Chrh Wkr; Debate Tm; Hon Rl; NHS; Off Ade; Sch Pl; Stu Cncl; College; Civil Engr.

HUNTER, JAMES E; Chesapeake HS; Chesapeake, OH; Hon Rl; NHS; Letter Wrstlng; Univ; Med Pathlgst.

HUNTER, JOYCE; Valley View HS; Germantown, OH; Drl Tm; Girl Scts; Hon Rl; Jr NHS; Mat Maids; PPFtbl; Tmr; Univ.

HUNTER, KENNETH; Lutheran West HS; Redford Twp, MI; 15/157 Hon Rl; Lbry Ade; NHS; Rptr Yrbk; Ger Clb; Natl Merit Ltr; Mich State Univ; Astronomy.

HUNTER, KIMBERLY; Garfield HS; Akron, OH; Sec JA; Lbry Ade; DECA; Drama Clb; Pom Pon; UCLA; Med.

HUNTER, MARY; Carrollton HS; Saginaw, MI; Hon Rl; NHS; Off Ade; PAVAS; Sch Mus; Sch Pl; Stg Crw; Drama Clb; Sci Clb; Univ.

HUNTER, MICHAEL; Gladwin HS; Gladwin, MI; Hon Rl; Davenport; Accgt.

HUNTER, SARAH; Rutherford B Hayes HS; Delaware, OH; 15/300 AFS; Chrh Wkr; Girl Scts; Hon Rl; VP JA; Orch; Sch Mus; Yth Flsp; Fr Clb; Letter Trk; Univ; Sci.

HUNTER, SHERRY; Fairfield Sr HS; Fairfield, OH; 152/541 Chrs; Chrh Wkr; Hon Rl; Hosp Ade; Lbry Ade; Four Yr Chorus Awd; D R Lee Vocational Schl; Nursing.

HUNTER, VALERIA; Cass Tech HS; Detroit, MI; Cls Rep Sr Cls; Cmp Fr Grls; Hon Rl; Lbry Ade; VP NHS; Off Ade; Pres Y-Teens; Rptr Sch Nwsp; FTA; Ger Clb; Spelman Coll; Chem Engr.

HUNTER, VALERIA L; Cass Tech HS; Detroit, MI; Cls Rep Sr Cls; Cmp Fr Grls; Hon Rl; VP NHS; Off Ade; Pres Y-Teens; Rptr Sch Nwsp; FTA; Ger Clb; Mth Clb; Sewing Club; Sewing Awd; College; Chem Engr.

HUNTER, VERONICA; Corydon Central HS; Corydon, IN; Band; Cmnty Wkr; 4-H; Pep Clb; Univ; Elem Tchr.

HUNTINE, MIKE; Bishop Luers HS; Ft Wayne, IN; Hon Rl; Key Clb; Letter Glf; Letter Ten; IM Sprt; PPFtbl; Pres Awd; Indiana Univ; Bus.

HUNTING, AMBER; Guyan Valley HS; Branchland, WV; 5/98 Cls Rep Frsh Cls; Cls Rep Soph Cls; Cl Rep Jr Cls; Chrh Wkr; Hon Rl; NHS; Stu Cncl; Ed Yrbk; Rptr Sch Nwsp; Trk;.

HUNTINGTON, JOYCE; Northeastern HS; Fountain Cy, IN; Hon Rl; 4-H; GAA; 4-H Awd;.

HUNT JR, EDMOND; Roscommon HS; Higgins Lk, MI; Lawrence Inst Of Tech; Architecture.

HUNTLEY, MARTY; W Union HS; W Union, OH; 10/150 Pres Jr Cls; Hon Rl; NHS; Yrbk; Pep Clb; Bsbl; Bsktbl; Busns Schl; Busns Mgmt.

HUNTMAN, BRET; Flushing HS; Flushing, MI; Trs Frsh Cls; Cls Rep Soph Cls; Band; Boy Scts; Debate Tm; Hon Rl; Natl Forn Lg; Stu Cncl; Ftbl; Letter Trk; Univ Of Michigan; Bus.

HUNTOON, JULIE; Grand Ledge HS; Grand Ledge, MI; Band; Yth Flsp; 4-H; Lat Clb; LCC.

HUNTSMAN, B; Perry HS; Navarre, OH; Aud/Vis; Chrs; Sch Mus; Sch Pl; Stg Crw; Rptr Sch Nwsp; Ftbl; Trk; JA Awd; Pres Awd; College; Civil Engineer.

HUNTSMAN, BOB; Zanesville HS; Zaneville, OH; Chrs; Debate Tm; Hon Rl; NHS; Sch Mus; Stg Crw; Ftbl; Muskingum Area Tech Coll; Accts.

HUNTZINGER, JO; Lapel HS; Anderson, IN; 17/79 Sec Soph Cls; Sec Jr Cls; Sec Sr Cls; Yrbk; 4-H; Lat Clb; Pep Clb; Bsktbl; 4-H Awd; Purdue Univ; Home Ec.

HUNTZINGER, MARIA; Nitro HS; Charleston, WV; Chrs; Rptr Yrbk; Beta Clb; Drama Clb; Spn Clb; West Virginia St Coll; Law.

HUNYOR, ROBIN; Clay Sr HS; Oregon, OH; Band; Hon Rl; Lbry Ade; Fr Clb; Pep Clb; VICA; GAA; Univ; Dent Asst.

HUNZIKER, RAYMOND E; Lake Catholic HS; Wickliffe, OH; 40/320 Boy Scts; Lit Mag; NHS; Pol Wkr; Cleveland St Univ; Marine Bio.

HUPP, CHRIS; Northrop HS; Fort Wayne, IN; Letter Ftbl; Trk; Wrstlng; Cit Awd; Univ; Bus.

HUPP, DOYLE; Calhoun County HS; Grantsville, WV; Cls Rep Frsh Cls; Cls Rep Soph Cls; Boy Scts; FCA; Hon Rl; NHS; Sct Actv; Stu Cncl; FFA; Bsbl; Glenville St Coll; Land Surveying.

HUPP, LEISE; Lutheran North HS; Mount Clemens, MI; Band; Chrs; Hon Rl; Letter Bsktbl; Letter Trk; Macomb County Comm College; Med Tech.

HUPP, LINDA; Coldwell HS; Caldwell, OH; Cmp Fr Grls; Chrh Wkr; Cmnty Wkr; Girl Scts; Hon Rl; Sch Pl; Sct Actv; FHA; Pep Clb;.

HUPP, MICHAEL; Clear Fork HS; Bellville, OH; 1/160 Band; Boy Scts; NHS; Spn Clb; Crs Cntry; Trk; Engr Summer Cnfrnce Ohio St Univ; Ohio St Univ; Aero Engr.

HUPP, PATRICK; Logan Elm HS; Kingston, OH; Chrh Wkr; Hon Rl; NHS; Pres Yth Flsp; Pres FFA; IM Sprt; Agriculture Tech Inst.

HUPP, TERESA; Logan Elm HS; Laurelville, OH; 24/185 Band; Jr NHS; NHS; Off Ade; 4-H; Ohio St Univ; Acctg.

HURA, DOUGLAS; Ursuline HS; Youngstown, OH; 77/345 Boy Scts; Chrh Wkr; Cmnty Wkr; Hon Rl; VP FDA; Key Clb; Spn Clb; History Day Contest 1st Plc Regnl 1st Plc St 76; Hiram Coll; Pre Med.

HURD, AMY; David Anderson HS; Lisbon, OH; 210115 Chrs; Hon Rl; Sch Mus; Yth Flsp; Y-Teens; Fr Clb; IM Sprt; Baldwin Wallace Coll; Elem Educ.

HURD, KATHLEEN; Lakeview HS; Cortland, OH; Band; Drm Mjrt; Hon Rl; Hosp Ade; Lbry Ade; Rptr Sch Nwsp; Pres Soph Cls; FTA; Sec Ger Clb; Twrlr; Kent State; Sec.

HURD, STEVEN; Crestwood HS; Mantua, OH; 8/214 Sec Chrs; Chrh Wkr; Hon Rl; NHS; Sch Mus; Beta Clb; 4-H; 4-H Awd; Kent State Univ; Media.

HURD, VANCE; Norwayne HS; Creston, OH; Pres Frsh Cls; Pres Sr Cls; Band; Chrh Wkr; Hon Rl; Yth Flsp; Bsktbl; Crs Cntry; Ftbl; Trk; College.

HURLEY, JEREMIAH L; Elder HS; Cincinnati, OH; 26/400 Cls Rep Frsh Cls; Cls Rep Soph Cls; Cl Rep Jr Cls; Sec Sr Cls; Am Leg Boys St; Hon Rl; Pol Wkr; Sct Actv; Stu Cncl; Sprt Ed Sch Nwsp; Youth In City Govt Progr 79; Scripps Howard St Govt Day 79; Teen Alchl & Drug Inst 79; Univ; Pre Law.

HURON, ROBERT A; Chesapeake HS; Chesapeake, OH; 1/144 Band; Boy Scts; Hon Rl; Mod UN; NHS; Sct Actv; Pol Wkr; Beta Clb; Bsbl; Bsktbl; Ohio State Univ; Entomology.

HURSEY, ROBERT; Amanda Clearcreek HS; Lancaster, OH; Band; Boy Scts; Drm Bgl; Hon Rl; Capt Ftbl; Trk; IM Sprt; Univ; Foreign Lang Spnsh.

HURSH, SHARON; Malabar HS; Mansfield, OH; 34/261 Band; Hon Rl; NHS; Off Ade; Orch; Red Cr Ade; Gym; Swmmng; Trk; Coach Actv; Univ; Phys Ther.

HURSONG, LISA; Mt Healthy HS; Cincinnati, OH; Cl Rep Jr Cls; Hon Rl; Off Ade; Sec Stu Cncl; Ed Sch Nwsp; Rptr Sch Nwsp; Beta Clb; Fr Clb; Univ; Cmnctns.

HURST, ANDREW; Benton Harbor HS; Benton Harbor, MI; Cls Rep Sr Cls; Chrh Wkr; Cmnty Wkr; FCA; Hon Rl; Jr NHS; 4-H; Bsktbl; Ftbl; Trk; Indiana Ctrl Univ; Bus Mgmt.

HURST, ANN; Western Reserve HS; Wakeman, OH; 15/100 Band; Chrs; Hon Rl; Hosp Ade; Lbry Ade; NHS; Yth Flsp; Ohio St Univ.

HURST, BONITA; Port Clinton HS; Port Clinton, OH; Sec Jr Cls; Hst Sr Cls; Cls Rep Sr Cls; Hon Rl; Lbry Ade; Rptr Yrbk; Rptr Sch Nwsp; OEA; Chrldng; GAA; Terra Tech Coll; Comp Progr.

HURST, CLARA; Laingsburg HS; Laingsburg, MI; 3/79 Hon Rl; NHS; Off Ade; Rptr Yrbk; Rptr Sch Nwsp; Sec FHA; Capt Trk; Capt Chrldng; GAA; PPFtbl; Lansing Cmnty Coll; Bus.

HURST, DEBORAH S; Terre Haute North Vigo HS; Terre Haute, IN; Hon Rl; Natl Forn Lg; Sch Pl; Drama Clb; Univ; Theatre.

HURST, JULIE; Sycamore HS; Cincinnati, OH; 32/470 Hon Rl; JA; NHS; Yth Flsp; Ger Clb; Pep Clb; Mgrs; Mat Maids; Duke Univ; Psychology.

HURST, JULIE; Wauseon HS; Wauseon, OH; Sec Soph Cls; Am Leg Aux Girls St; Hon Rl; Hosp Ade; Stu Cncl; Pres Y-Teens; Ed Sch Nwsp; Sec DECA; Treas FHA; Am Leg Awd; Ohio State Univ.

HURST, KATHERINE; Aurora HS; Aurora, OH; 1/162 AFS; Hon Rl; NHS; Sch Mus; Sch Pl; Stg Crw; Sec Drama Clb; Mth Clb; Natl Merit Schl; Allegheny Coll; Med.

HURST, MARCIA; Fowlerville HS; Fowlerville, MI; 9/170 Band; Chrs; Girl Scts; Hon Rl; NHS; Bsktbl; Letter Crs Cntry; Letter Trk; IM Sprt; PPFtbl; College; Coach.

HURST, MATTHEW K; Morgan HS; Mc Connelsville, OH; Am Leg Boys St; Boy Scts; Chrh Wkr; H on Rl; NHS; Pres Yth Flsp; Rptr Sch Nwsp; Spn Clb; Ohi St Univ; Comp Sci.

HURST, SCOTT M; Logan Sr HS; Logan, WV; Am Leg Boys St; Boy Scts; FCA; Hon Rl; Lbry Ade; NHS; Sct Actv; Yth Flsp; Key Clb; Sci Clb; Johns Hopkins Univ; Med.

HURT, BERTRAM; Parkside HS; Jackson, MI; Cls Rep Frsh Cls; Cls Rep Soph Cls; Hon Rl; Ger Clb; Ftbl; Univ Of Michigan; German.

HURT, DORA; Columbian HS; Tiffin, OH; Cls Rep Frsh Cls; Band; Hon Rl; 4-H; IM Sprt; 4-H Awd; Terra Tech College; Law Sec.

HURT, JUDITH; Big Rapids HS; Big Rpds, MI; Cl Rep Jr Cls; Chrh Wkr; Sch Pl; Stu Cncl; Fr Clb; Letter Trk; Chrldng; IM Sprt; Ferris St Univ; Vet.

HURT, SHERRY; Cedar Lake Academy; Berrien Spgs, MI; Sec Soph Cls; Chrs; Hon Rl; Mdrgl; Off Ade; Ftbl; Andrews Univ; Business Admin.

HURTH, JENNI; High School; Gladstone, MI; Cls Rep Soph Cls; Band; Chrs; Chrh Wkr; Hon Rl; Mdrgl; NHS; Stu Cncl; Univ; Sci.

HURTIG, TERRY; Wayne HS; Dayton, OH; Hon Rl; Letter Ftbl; ITT Tech Inst; Tool Desgn Engr.

HURTUBISE, LARRY; Bishop Ready HS; Columbus, OH; 52/250 Crs Cntry; Letter Wrstlng; Univ Of Minnesota.

HUSBAND, LINDA; Adrian Sr HS; Adrian, MI; 47/386 Am Leg Aux Girls St; Hon Rl; NHS; FTA; Ten; Trk; GAA; Adrian Coll; Enviro Engr.

HUSE, LORI; Madison Hts HS; Anderson, IN; 23/450 Chrs; FCA; Hon Rl; Lbry Ade; NHS; Sch Mus; 4-H; Gym; 4-H Awd; IUPUI; Med Tech.

HUSER, MICHAEL; Zionsville Community HS; Zionsville, IN; AFS; Boy Scts; Chrh Wkr; Cmnty Wkr; Hon Rl; Sch Pl; Spn Clb; Crs Cntry; Marquette; Pre Law.

HUSK, MARTHA; East HS; Akron, OH; Chrs; Hon Rl; Hosp Ade; Cit Awd; Coll; Nursing.

HUSK, NANCY R; Fort Frye HS; Beverly, OH; Band; Chrs; Chrh Wkr; Girl Scts; Stg Crw; Yth Flsp; FFA; Spn Clb; Ohio St Univ; Vet Med.

HUSMAN, DAVID W; Walnut Hills HS; Cincinnati, OH; 83/453 Chrs; Hon Rl; Pol Wkr; Sch Mus; Yth Flsp; Cit Awd; Mas Awd; SAR Awd; St Vocal Solo Contst Spr 79; Supr Rtg Ensembel 79; H S Schlrshp Music Excell 79; Ohio St Univ; Sci.

HUSS, CRAIG; Fremont HS; Fremont, IN; Cls Rep Soph Cls; Band; Chrh Wkr; Hon Rl; Orch; Sch Mus; Sch Pl; Stu Cncl; Yth Flsp; 4-H; Univ; Elec Engr.

HUSS, CRAIG; Fremont Comm HS; Fremont, IN; 6/75 Hon Rl; Sch Mus; Sch Pl; Stu Cncl; Yth Flsp; Mth Clb; Pep Clb; Bsktbl; Crs Cntry; Trk; College.

HUSSAR, SUSAN; St Thomas Aquinas HS; Canton, OH; Cl Rep Jr Cls; Cls Rep Sr Cls; Am Leg Aux Girls St; Girl Scts; Hon Rl; Sch Mus; Sch Nwsp; FNA; Spn Clb; Gym; Walsh Coll; Nursing.

HUSSELL, STEVE; Bedford HS; Bedford Hts, OH; Pres Band; Hon Rl; Jr NHS; Orch; Spn Clb; Letter Trk; College; Bus.

HUSSUNG, LISA; Lanesville HS; Lanesville, IN; Sec Jr Cls; Chrs; Chrh Wkr; Sec FCA; Hon Rl; NHS; Sch Mus; Yth Flsp; Yrbk; Pres 4-H; Univ; Med.

HUSTER, PETE; Moeller HS; Cincinnati, OH; 34/295 Cls Rep Sr Cls; Hon Rl; Jr NHS; NHS; PAVAS; Sdlty; Stu Cncl; Pep Clb; Socr; Chrldng; Univ Of Cincinnati; Graphic Dsgn.

HUSTON, RHEA; Dunbar HS; Dunbar, WV; 1/165 Val; Band; Chrh Wkr; NHS; Sch Mus; Sch Pl; Sch Nwsp; Spn Clb; Chrldng; Lion Awd; Senator R Byrd Recogn Awd 79; Capt Of Ship Of State 79; Mt Vernon Nazarene Coll; Comp Sci.

HUSTON, WAYNE; Madeira HS; Madeira, OH; Band; Chrs; Sch Mus; Bsktbl; Mgrs; Univ; Chem Engr.

HUTCHINGS, KARLA; Dexter HS; Dexter, MI; 6/160 Band; Chrs; Girl Scts; Hon Rl; NHS; Yth Flsp; Ed Yrbk; Yrbk; 4-H; FFA; Stanley M Henes Sci Awd 79; Washtenaw Cnty 4 H Queen 77; 4 ' Natl Horse Judgng Ind Pl 6th 6th & 8th 77; Michigan St Univ; Vet Med.

HUTCHINGS, LEEANN; Stow Sr HS; Stow, OH; Off Ade; Y-Teens; OEA; Pep Clb; Scr Kpr; Univ.

HUTCHINGS, PATRICIA; Upper Arlington HS; Columbus, OH; 34/610 Sec AFS; Band; Hon Rl; Jr NHS; NHS; Sch Pl; Yrbk; Drama Clb; Ger Clb; Univ.

HUTCHINS, DONNA; Harding HS; Marion, OH; 33/470 Chrh Wkr; NHS; Orch; Sch Mus; Rptr Sch Nwsp; Sch Nwsp; FTA; Ohio St Univ; Educ.

HUTCHINS, KALLA; Marion Harding HS; Marion, OH; 22/460 Chrh Wkr; Cmnty Wkr; Hon Rl; Lit Mag; NHS; VP Yth Flsp; Sch Nwsp; Sec FTA; Univ Of Cincinnati; Graphic Design.

HUTCHINSON, BRENT; Indian River Inland Lake HS; Topinabee, MI; 3/75 VP Frsh Cls; Aud/Vis; Chrh Wkr; Debate Tm; Hon Rl; Sci Clb; Bsbl; Capt Bsktbl; Capt Ftbl; Trk; NWMC; Pet Tech.

HUTCHINSON, CAROLYN; Roscommon HS; Roscommon, MI; Trs Jr Cls; Cl Rep Jr Cls; Trs Sr Cls; Cls Rep Sr Cls; Sal; Band; Chrs; Mdrgl; NHS; Orch; General Motore Institute; Indu Engin.

HUTCHINSON, JEFF; Williamsburg HS; Marathon, OH; Hon Rl; 4-H; Spn Clb; VICA; Letter Bsktbl; Letter Ftbl; Letter Ten; Tech Drafting.

HUTCHINSON, JEFF; Watkins Memorial HS; Granville, OH; Boy Scts; Sch Mus; 4-H; FFA; Pep Clb;.

HUTCHINSON, J S; Culver Military Academy; Columbus, OH; ROTC; Bsktbl; Chrldng; Gold A For A GPA Of 3.5 Or Over 77; Silver A For GPA Of 3.0 Or Over 77; Univ; Bus.

HUTCHINSON, JUDY; Northview Public HS; Grand Rapids, MI; 95/290 Chrh Wkr; Hon Rl; Sch Pl; Drama Clb; Pres Spn Clb; Bsktbl; Aquinas Coll; Spanish.

HUTCHINSON, LAURIE; Brown City HS; Brown City, MI; Band; Hon Rl; Sec NHS; Treas Stu Cncl; FTA; Pep Clb; Chmn Chrldng;.

HUTCHINSON, PATRICIA; Reed City HS; Reed City, MI; 36/172 Hon Rl; NHS; Stu Cncl; FHA; PPFtbl; Ferris St Coll; Bus Admin.

HUTCHINSON, RONALD; Reed City HS; Reed City, MI; Band; Chrh Wkr; Debate Tm; Hon Rl; NHS; Sch Mus; Sch Pl; Stu Cncl; Sch Nwsp; 4-H; Albion Coll; Dentistry.

HUTCHINSON, ROSE A; Richwood HS; Tioga, WV; Band; Chrh Wkr; Hon Rl; NHS; Sch Nwsp; Treas 4-H; 4 H Awd & Charting Pin; Marshall Univ; Journalism.

HUTCHINSON, TIM; Buffalo HS; Kenova, WV; 7/112 Am Leg Boys St; Band; Chrs; Chrh Wkr; Cmnty Wkr; Drm Mjrt; Hon Rl; Pres NHS; Orch; Sch Pl; Whos Who In Music 78; Outstndg Acadmc Stu In Amer HS 79; Ashland St Voc Tech Schl; Elec Tech.

HUTCHISON, ALICIA; Ripley HS; Ripley, WV; Am Leg Aux Girls St; Band; Chrs; Drl Tm; Hon Rl; Off Ade; Sch Pl; Stg Crw; Drama Clb; FBLA; West Virginia Univ; Vet.

HUTCHISON, J; Frontier HS; Newport, OH; Pres Frsh Cls; Cls Rep Soph Cls; Band; Chrh Wkr; NHS; Chrldng; Schooling.

HUTCHISON, JAMES R; East Liverpool HS; E Liverpool, OH; Boy Scts; Chrs; Chrh Wkr; Spn Clb; God Cntry Awd; Natl Merit SF; Eagle Scout 1975;.

HUTCHISON, KEITH; Tri Village Local HS; New Madison, OH; Band; Chrs; Hon Rl; NHS; Sch Pl; Stg Crw; Fr Clb; Glf; Wright State Univ; Pre Med.

HUTCHISON, THOMAS E; Brighton Area HS; Brighton, MI; Cls Rep Soph Cls; Boy Scts; Cmnty Wkr; Red Cr Ade; Stu Cncl; Letter Swmmng; Michigan Competitive Schlrshp Awd; Michigan St Univ; Marketing.

HUTCHISON JR, R; Perry HS; Canton, OH; Boy Scts; FCA; Hon Rl; JA; NHS; Ftbl; Letter Ten; Wrstlng; Akron; Engineering.

HUTFILZ, JULIE; Michigan Lutheran Seminary; Merrill, MI; Trs Soph Cls; Hon Rl; Letter Trk; Homcmng Piano Queens Ct 77; Vllybll Lttrd; Crtfct Of Honor For Excllnc In Schlrshp 78; Alma Coll; Med.

HUTKO, MARLENE; Bishop Gallagher; Detroit, MI; 62/333 Hon Rl; Yrbk; Trk; PPFtbl; Cit Awd; Univ.

HUTSON, FERNE; Chagrin Falls HS; Chagrin Falls, OH; AFS; Band; Sec Chrs; Drl Tm; Hon Rl; Lit Mag; Sch Mus; Stu Cncl; Pres Yth Flsp; Oberlin Consrvtry Of Music; Music.

HUTSON, MIKE; Franklin HS; Franklin, OH; Chrh Wkr; Sch Pl; Stg Crw; Pep Clb; Spn Clb; Bsbl; Letter Bsktbl; Crs Cntry; College; Broadcasting.

HUTSON, TERRI; Chagrin Falls HS; Chagrin Falls, OH; AFS; Chrs; Hon Rl; Hosp Ade; Sch Mus; Stg Crw; Yth Flsp; Letter Trk; Centre Coll; Language.

HUTSON, WILLIAM; Houghton Lake Shs; Houghton Lk, MI; 9/149 Trs Jr Cls; Pres Sr Cls; Am Leg Boys St; Hon Rl; Jr NHS; NHS; Stu Cncl; Bsbl; Trk; Pres Awd; Ferris St Univ; Busns Admin.

HUTTER, NANCY; Martinsville HS; Martinsville, IN; Cl Rep Jr Cls; Cmp Fr Grls; Girl Scts; Hon Rl; Jr NHS; NHS; Off Ade; Stu Cncl; Sprt Ed Sch Nwsp; Sch Nwsp; 4-H; Indiana Univ; Phys Ed.

HUTTO, MELISSA; Interlochen Arts Academy; Brutus, MI; Band; Girl Scts; Hon Rl; Lbry Ade; Sct Actv; Letter Trk; Western Michigan Univ; Med Librarian.

HUTTON, DAVID; Mount Ellis Academy; College Place, WA; Pres Frsh Cls; Band; Chrs; Hon Rl; Stg Crw; Stu Cncl; Ftbl; IM Sprt; Scr Kpr; Tmr; Walla Walla Coll; Medicine.

HUTTON, JAMES; South Haven HS; South Haven, MI; Hon Rl; Treas NHS; Capt Bsbl; Mic State Univ; Forestry.

HUTTON, KATHY; Euclid Sr HS; Euclid, OH; Hon Rl; Jr NHS; NHS; Red Cr Ade; Sch Mus; Bsbl; PPFtbl; Bus Schl.

HUTTON, SHELIA; Emerson HS; Gary, IN; Cls Rep Soph Cls; Cl Rep Jr Cls; Chrh Wkr; Girl Scts; Hon Rl; Jr NHS; Off Ade; Stu Cncl; Y-Teens; College; Nurse.

HUTZEL, BARRY; Reading Cmnty HS; Reading, OH; Hon Rl; Ftbl; Trk; Wrstlng; Univ Of Cincinnati; Indus Dsgn.

HUVER, TODD; Catholic Ctrl HS; Grand Rpds, MI; Aud/Vis; Boy Scts; Lbry Ade; Letter Ftbl; Coach Actv; IM Sprt; Univ.

HUVLER, BRENDA; Northmor HS; Lexington, OH; VP Band; Chrs; Chrh Wkr; Cmnty Wkr; FCA; Sch Mus; Sec 4-H; Chmn Bsktbl; Trk; 4-H Awd; Ohio State Univ; Floriculture.

HUYCK, ANGELA; Hamilton Heights HS; Arcadia, IN; Chrh Wkr; Hon Rl; Univ; Educ.

HUYCK, JENNIFER; Lakewood HS; Sunfield, MI; 70/169 Cls Rep Frsh Cls; Chrs; Hon Rl; Lit Mag; DECA; Pep Clb; Trk; Chrldng; Grand Valley St Coll; Spec Ed.

HUYGHE, STEVE; Mathews HS; Vienna, OH; 30/146 Band; Boy Scts; Cmnty Wkr; Hon Rl; Sct Actv; Yth Flsp; Rptr Yrbk; Fr Clb; Key Clb; Pep Clb; Youngstown St Univ; Bus Admin.

HYATT, CHARLES W; Brebeuf Prep HS; Zionsville, IN; 3/145 Boy Scts; Hon Rl; Lit Mag; NHS; Ed Sch Nwsp; Mth Clb; Capt Swmmng; Univ; Lit.

HYATT, DIANE; Brandon HS; Ortonville, MI; Chrs; Hon Rl; NHS; Sch Pl; Outstndng Ach Awd For Music & Soc Studies; Outstndng Ach Awd For Speech Drama; Awd For Chorus Pin; Suomi Coll; Lib Arts.

HYDE, DANIEL R; Meridian HS; Edenville, MI; 5/128 Band; Chrs; Hon Rl; NHS; Sch Mus; Stg Crw; Drama Clb; Rdo Clb; Univ Of Mic; Comp Engr.

HYDE, DEBBIE; Fulton HS; Middleton, MI; Band; Chrh Wkr; Hon Rl; Off Ade; Yth Flsp; Rptr Sch Nwsp; 4-H; FHA; Scr Kpr; 4-H Awd; Central Michigan Univ; Bus Educ.

HYDE, DEBBIE; Wintersville HS; Bloomingdale, OH; Band; Cmp Fr Grls; Girl Scts; Hon Rl; Off Ade; Orch; Y-Teens; Spn Clb; Bsktbl; GAA; Ohio State; Phys Educ.

HYDE, GENA; Pine River Jr Sr HS; Tustin, MI; 2/98 Pres Frsh Cls; Cls Rep Soph Cls; Band; Chrs; Chrh Wkr; Hon Rl; NHS; Stu Cncl; Capt Bsbl; College; Music.

HYDE, RONDA; Center Grove HS; Greenwood, IN; 10/288 Cls Rep Soph Cls; Cl Rep Jr Cls; Cls Rep Sr Cls; Hon Rl; NHS; Treas OEA; Pep Clb; Acctg.

HYDE, RUTH; Yale HS; Emmett, MI; Hon Rl; Yrbk; Univ; Psych.

HYDER, PERRY; Green HS; Akron, OH; 14/317 Band; Hon Rl; NHS; Univ Of Akron; Mechanical Engr.

HYLDAHL, CAROL; Davison HS; Davison, MI; Cls Rep Frsh Cls; Band; Treas Boy Scts; Cmnty Wkr; Girl Scts; Hon Rl; Treas Fr Clb; Mth Clb; St Of Mi Schlshp 79; Notre Dame Univ; Law.

HYLER, DAVID; Ottawa Hills HS; Grand Rapids, MI; Band; Hon Rl; NHS; ROTC; Am Leg Awd; Univ; Med.

HYLL, DONA; Belmont HS; Dayton, OH; Band; Chrs; Hon Rl; Stg Crw; Drama Clb; Sec Fr Clb; IM Sprt; Wright St Univ; Theater Arts.

HYMA, LORRAINE; Grant HS; Grant, MI; Band; Girl Scts; Hon Rl; Yth Flsp; FBLA; FTA; Pep Clb; Bsbl; PPFtbl; Hope College; Elem Educ.

HYMAN, LYNN; Lake Ridge Academy; Elyria, OH; Cls Rep Soph Cls; Pres Jr Cls; Cl Rep Jr Cls; Hon Rl; Stu Cncl; Ed Yrbk; Yrbk; Fr Clb; Hockey; Ten; Univ.

HYMAN, MARK; Bexley HS; Bexley, OH; Sci Clb; VICA; Wrstlng; College; Machinist.

HYMAN, MERLENE; Erieview Catholic HS; Cleveland, OH; Trs Sr Cls; Chrs; Chrh Wkr; Hon Rl; Lbry Ade; Mod UN; NHS; Sch Mus; Stu Cncl; Yth Flsp; Univ; Med.

HYMES, BARBARA; East HS; Columbus, OH; Cls Rep Soph Cls; Chrs; Chrh Wkr; Hon Rl; Jr NHS; Lbry Ade; Stu Cncl; FHA; Pep Clb; Spn Clb; Natl Jr Honor Soc Awd; College; Social Work.

HYNDMAN, BRIAN E; Jimtown HS; Elkhart, IN; 1/125 Pres Frsh Cls; Pres Soph Cls; Pres Jr Cls; Band; Hon Rl; Stu Cncl; Rptr Yrbk; Capt Bsbl; Letter Ten; Letter Wrstlng; Univ; Bus Mgmt.

HYNDMAN, CATHERINE J; St Thomas Aquinas HS; Atwater, OH; 4/175 Cls Rep Frsh Cls; Band; Chrs; Chrh Wkr; Girl Scts; Natl Forn Lg; NHS; Sch Mus; Sct Actv; Stg Crw; Univ; Chem.

HYNEMAN, SUSAN; Princeton Community HS; Patoka, IN; 35/203 Sec Jr Cls; Hosp Ade; Pep Clb; Univ Of Evansville; Phys Ther Asst.

HYNES, CYNTHIA; Ben Davis HS; Indianapolis, IN; 13/850 Band; Cmnty Wkr; Hon Rl; NHS; Spn Clb; Bsktbl; Mgrs; Attended Senator Richard Lugars Symposium Tomorrows Leaders; Purdue Univ; Vet.

HYNES, JULIE; Dexter HS; Dexter, MI; Sec Soph Cls; Pres Jr Cls; Band; Hon Rl; NHS; Red Cr Ade; Yth Flsp; Ger Clb; Western Mich Univ; Health Ed.

HYNES, VERNON; Bridgeport HS; Bridgeport, OH; Hon Rl; Spn Clb; Bsbl; Glf; Belmont Tech; Mfg.

HYPES, BOBBY E; Charleston HS; Charleston, WV; Am Leg Boys St; Boy Scts; Hon Rl; Jr NHS; Ftbl; Trk; Wrstlng; Mgrs; Cit Awd; College; Law.

HYPES, PAMELA; Johnstown Monroe HS; Johnstown, OH; 1/140 Val; NHS; VP Stu Cncl; Pres Yth Flsp; Ed Sch Nwsp; Pres 4-H; Cit Awd; Bowling Green Su; Deaf Educ.

HYRE, GAIL L; Tri Village HS; New Madison, OH; Band; Chrs; Hon Rl; Sec OEA; College; Health.

HYSELL, ERIC; Lakota HS; Middletown, OH; Band; Boy Scts; Hon Rl; Sch Nwsp; 4-H; Spn Clb; 4-H Awd; Univ; Conservation.

HYSLOP, DAVID B; Marine City HS; Marine City, MI; 3/160 Chrs; Chrh Wkr; Hon Rl; NHS; Sch Pl; Stu Cncl; Yth Flsp; Cedarville Coll; Chem.

HYSLOP, THOMAS; Marquette Sr HS; Marquette, MI; Debate Tm; Natl Forn Lg; Natl Merit Ltr; Univ; Law.

HYTEN, STEPHANIE; Greencastle HS; Greenncastle, IN; Band; FCA; Hon Rl; JA; Yth Flsp; 4-H; Fr Clb; Pep Clb; Letter Swmmng; Trk; College; Psychology.

I

IACOBELLI, ANGELA; Cousino Sr HS; Warren, MI; Cls Rep Soph Cls; Cl Rep Jr Cls; Hon Rl; Hosp Ade; Jr NHS; NHS; VP Mth Clb; Sci Clb; PPFtbl; Natl Merit Ltr; Univ Of Detroit; Med.

IACOBUCCI, MARIE; Boardman HS; Canfield, OH; Chrh Wkr; Girl Scts; Hon Rl; JA; Y-Teens; DECA; Sci Clb; JA Awd; Younstown State Univ; Bio.

IAFELICE, ROBERT; St Edward HS; Cleveland, OH; 41/340 Band; Hon Rl; NHS; Sch Mus; College.

IAGULLI, MARGIE; Austintown Fitch HS; Younstown, OH; 100/700 Cls Rep Frsh Cls; Cls Rep Soph Cls; Cl Rep Jr Cls; Band; Hon Rl; Hosp Ade; Trk; Chrldng; PPFtbl; Scr Kpr; Ohio St Univ; Med Asst.

IAMES, DONNA M; Seton HS; Cincinnati, OH; 28/268 Hon Rl; NHS; Treas Stu Cncl; Fr Clb; Pep Clb; Swmmng; Coach Actv; IM Sprt; Mgrs; Xavier Univ; Consumer Sci.

IANNANTUONO, DOUGLAS; Calvert HS; Tiffin, OH; Natl Merit Ltr; College; Bus.

IANNONE, JIM; St Francis De Sales HS; Toledo, OH; Dayton; Engineering.

IANNUCCI, JOHN; Warren John F Kennedy HS; Warren, OH; Hon Rl; JA; Lit Mag; NHS; Pol Wkr; Quill & Scroll; Rptr Yrbk; Rptr Sch Nwsp; JA Awd; Georgetown Univ; Bus Law.

IATRIDES, HELEN; Hammond HS; Hammond, IN; 10/300 Trs Jr Cls; Cl Rep Jr Cls; Trs Sr Cls; Am Leg Aux Girls St; Chrs; Hon Rl; Jr NHS; Mdrgl; Natl Forn Lg; NHS; Purdue Univ; Engr Mgmt.

ICE, BILLIE; Calhoun County HS; Grantsville, WV; Cl Rep Jr Cls; Am Leg Aux Girls St; Chrs; Hon Rl; Lbry Ade; NHS; Ed Yrbk; Rptr Yrbk; FHA; Glenville State; Business Admin.

ICE, DAWN; Lincoln HS; Lumberport, WV; Cl Rep Jr Cls; Band; NHS; Sec Stu Cncl; VP Yth Flsp; Yrbk; FTA; Letter Chrldng; Air Transportation.

ICE, JEFFREY K; Madison Heights HS; Anderson, IN; Band; Boy Scts; Chrh Wkr; Cmnty Wkr; JA; MMM; Sct Actv; Yth Flsp; 4-H; 4-H Awd; Univ.

ICE, RICHARD J; Madison Hts HS; Anderson, IN; Cls Rep Frsh Cls; Cl Rep Jr Cls; AFS; Boy Scts; Chrh Wkr; Cmnty Wkr; Debate Tm; Hon Rl; Hosp Ade; MMM; Hoosier Schlr Indiana St Schlrshp; Outstndng Ach Life Sci; IHSA Forensic Dist & Adv To Sec Competition; Wabash Coll; Med.

ICE, WILLIAM; Wellsville HS; Wellsville, OH; Boy Scts; Hon Rl; Letter Ftbl; Letter Trk; Jefferson Tech Coll; Civ Engr.

ICKES, CHRISTOPHER; Washington HS; Massillon, OH; Band; Boy Scts; Chrs; Sct Actv; Boys Clb Am; Lat Clb; Plumber.

ICKES, GREG L; Northwestern HS; West Salem, OH; Hon Rl; Sch Pl; Rptr Yrbk; Rptr Sch Nwsp; VP Drama Clb; FTA; Bsbl; IM Sprt; Univ.

IDDINGS, BARBARA; Crown Point HS; Crown Point, IN; Band; Hon Rl; Pep Clb; Sci Clb; Spn Clb; Valporaiso; Soc Work.

IDE, JEANNE; Greenbrier West HS; Smoot, WV; 2/137 Cls Rep Soph Cls; Band; Chrs; Chrh Wkr; Hon Rl; NHS; Sch Mus; Stu Cncl; Fr Clb; FHA; Jr Rep For Know Your St Govt Day 1979; All County Band & Chorus 1977; Tri Hi Y Club 1978; Univ; Sec.

IDE, TONY; Cadillac HS; Cadillac, MI; Chrs; Hon Rl; Sch Mus; Sch Pl; Hockey; W Mich Univ; Psych.

IDEN, PAMELA; Zanesville HS; Zanesville, OH; Band; Chrh Wkr; Hon Rl; Sch Pl; Yth Flsp; Lat Clb; Capt Bsbl; Letter Bsktbl; Vllybl Capt 76; Vllyb Ltr 2nd Yr Var Awd 77; Univ; Sci.

IDLEMAN, JUDY; Union HS; Mt Storm, WV; 2/24 Pres Jr Cls; Chrs; Hon Rl; Stu Cncl; Beta Clb; Fr Clb; Bsktbl; Scr Kpr; 4-H Awd; Potomac St Coll; Vet.

IEZZI, JULIE; Olentangy HS; Galena, OH; 3/139 Hon Rl; NHS; Spn Clb; Antioch College.

IGEL, JOAN; Upper Arlington HS; Columbus, OH; Hon Rl; Sch Pl; Stu Cncl; Fr Clb; Pep Clb; Capt Chrldng; Tmr; College; Busns.

IGNATOSKI, DEBBIE; Hopkins HS; Dorr, MI; Hon Rl; Sch Pl; Rptr Sch Nwsp; Fr Clb; FHA; Trk; Chrldng; College; Counseling.

IGNAZZITTO, GINA; Valley Forge HS; Parma, OH; Band; Hon Rl; Sch Pl; Rptr Sch Nwsp; Drama Clb; Fr Clb; VICA; Pantomine Co; Morning Announcmnts; Ohio Univ; Cmnctns.

IHLE, KATHY; Ironton HS; Ironton, OH; 22/184 Chrs; Chrh Wkr; Hon Rl; JA; Off Ade; Ger Clb; Sci Clb; Letter Trk; GAA; IM Sprt; Morehead St Univ; Bus Admin.

IHLE, LAURIE; Austintown Fitch HS; Youngstown, OH; Cls Rep Frsh Cls; Cls Rep Soph Cls; VP Jr Cls; VP Sr Cls; Girl Scts; Hon Rl; NHS; Sct Actv; Stu Cncl; Youngstown State; Vet Med.

IHRMAN, CLAIRE; Holland HS; Holland, MI; Hon Rl; NHS; Rptr Sch Nwsp; Spn Clb; Letter Ten; Twrlr; Hope College.

IKER, TERESA; Central Baptist HS; Cincinnati, OH; 4/20 Pres Frsh Cls; Cls Rep Frsh Cls; Pres Soph Cls; Chrs; Hon Rl; Sch Mus; Sch Pl; Stg Crw; Stu Cncl; Fr Clb; 3.75 Avg 77; Cincinnati Tech Coll; Acctg.

IKINS, CATHERINE; Parkside HS; Jackson, MI; Band; FCA; Hon Rl; Rptr Sch Nwsp; Spn Clb; Letter Trk; Univ.

ILCONICH, LINDA; Rossford HS; Rossford, OH; 11/147 Cls Rep Frsh Cls; Band; Cmnty Wkr; Univ Of Toledo; Med Tech.

ILER, BRAIN; Charles F Brush HS; S Euclid, OH; Hon Rl; Glf; Univ; Engr.

ILER, CONNIE; Garber HS; Essexville, MI; Hst Soph Cls; Cmnty Wkr; Hon Rl; Hosp Ade; Red Cr Ade; Cit Awd; College; Graphic Arts.

ILES, LINDA; Northwood HS; Northwood, OH; Band; Chrs; Chrh Wkr; Hon Rl; Orch; Bsktbl; Mgrs; Scr Kpr; Owens Bus Schl; Bus.

ILES, RHONDA; Quincy Cmnty Schl; Quincy, MI; Band; Chrh Wkr; Hon Rl; Off Ade; 4-H; Fr Clb; Trk; IM Sprt; 4-H Awd; Achvmnt Awd 4 H 76; Beef Awd 4 H 76; French Awd 79; Michigan St Univ.

ILES, WILLIAM; Stivers Patterson Coop HS; Dayton, OH; Boy Scts; Chrs; Hon Rl; JA; Sct Actv; Boys Clb Am; OEA; Glf; IM Sprt; U S Air Force Acad.

ILKKA, GREG; Goodrich HS; Goodrich, MI; Band; Chrh Wkr; Hon Rl; Sct Actv; Pep Clb; Trk; Mgrs; Michigan Tech Univ; Engr.

ILLENCIK, THOMAS; Ursuline HS; Girard, OH; 47/300 Aud/Vis; Chrh Wkr; Hon Rl; Stg Crw; Trk; Youngstown State; Computer Progrmng.

ILLES, B; Solon HS; Solon, OH; Bsbl; Coach Actv; IM Sprt; College.

ILLES, MARY; Archbishop Alter HS; Dayton, OH; 35/290 Sec Chrs; Chrh Wkr; Drl Tm; Hon Rl; NHS; PAVAS; Sch Mus; Sch Pl; Rptr Sch Nwsp; Drama Clb; English & Religion Departmental Awds; College; Theatre.

ILSTRUP, THOMAS G; Calvin M Woodward HS; Toledo, OH; Pres Jr Cls; VP Sr Cls; Am Leg Boys St; Chrs; Chrh Wkr; Hon Rl; NHS; Sch Mus; Sch Pl; Stg Crw; Harvard Bk Awd From Harvard Club Of Toledo 79; Sammy Awd For Perfrmnce In Schl Musical Godspell On Stage 79; Univ; Vet.

IMBER, THOMAS; Wadsworth HS; Wadsworth, OH; Pres Sr Cls; Boy Scts; Hon Rl; Off Ade; Stu Cncl; DECA; FBLA; Bsbl; Glf; Swmmng; College; Business Admin.

IMBODY, DENYSE; River Valley HS; Marion, OH; Band; Chrs; Girl Scts; JA; Orch; Sch Mus; Fr Clb; Rdo Clb; JA Awd; A Rating Of Superior At Cnty & Dist Sic 75 76 & 79; Jr Achvmnt Sales Club; 100% Attend; Ohio St Univ; Bus.

IMBROGNO, P; Lorain Catholic HS; Lorain, OH; Cls Rep Soph Cls; Band; Chrs; Hon Rl; Rptr Sch Nwsp; Civ Clb; Drama Clb; Intl Fine Arts College; Fashion Mdse.

IMBUS, KAREN; Mc Nicholas HS; Batavia, OH; Pres Frsh Cls; Cls Rep Soph Cls; Pres Jr Cls; VP Sr Cls; Hon Rl; NHS; GAA; Univ; Med.

IMEL, BRIAN; Clinton Prairie HS; Frnkfrt, IN; 16/90 Aud/Vis; Hon Rl; Stg Crw; VP FFA; Purdue Univ; Farming.

IMEL, DIANA; George Washington HS; Indianapolis, IN; Cl Rep Jr Cls; Band; Chrh Wkr; NHS; Orch; Drama Clb; 4-H; Letter Gym; Chrldng; Opportunities To Learn About Bus 79; Univ; Dent Asst.

IMFELD, STEVE; Bishop Fenwick HS; Middletown, OH; 5/92 Chrh Wkr; Cmnty Wkr; Hon Rl; NHS; Letter Crs Cntry; Letter Trk; Letter Wrstlng; IM Sprt; Univ Of Cin; Engr.

IMGRUND, THEODORE; Three Rivers HS; Three Rivers, MI; Am Leg Boys St; Chrs; Debate Tm; Mdrgl; Sch Mus; Sch Pl; Stg Crw; Rptr Sch Nwsp; Crs Cntry; Trk; Eastern Michigan Univ; Mktg.

IMHOFF, BRIDGET; Lakeview HS; Lakeview, MI; Hon Rl; NHS; Stu Cncl; Yth Flsp; Yrbk; Rptr Sch Nwsp; FTA; Ten; Chrldng; GAA; Vocational Schl; Interior Design.

IMHOFF, JUDITH; Clay HS; Oregon, OH; Band; FCA; Hon Rl; Fr Clb; Bsktbl; Trk; College; Phys Educ.

IMHOFF, REBECCA; Talawanda HS; Hamilton, OH; 56/321 Trs Jr Cls; Chrs; Hon Rl; Fr Clb; OEA; Miami Univ; Nursing.

IMHOFF, SUE; Clay HS; Oregon, OH; 97/317 Girl Scts; Hon Rl; Fr Clb; FTA; Pep Clb; Scr Kpr; Univ; Bus Admin.

IMHOFF, SUSAN; Clay Sr HS; Oregon, OH; 97/350 Hon Rl; Fr Clb; Pep Clb; Swmmng; Ten; Scr Kpr; Univ; Bus Admin.

IMINSKI, MARIA; Wayne Memorial HS; Westland, MI; Chrs; Chrh Wkr; Hon Rl; Jr NHS; Natl Forn Lg; NHS; Ger Clb; Western Mic College; Air Plane Piolt.

IMLER, CHRISTAL; Marysville HS; Marysville, MI; 20/180 Pres Soph Cls; Chrh Wkr; Hon Rl; NHS; Sch Pl; Stg Crw; VP Stu Cncl; Drama Clb; Sec Fr Clb; OEA; St Finalist For Piano Michigan Music Tchrs Comp 76; Gold Cup In Achvmnt Testing; Med Gold Cup In Achvmnt; Michigan St Univ.

IMMARINO, THOMAS; Ledgemont HS; Thompson, OH; AFS; Aud/Vis; Band; Boy Scts; Hon Rl; Sct Actv; Stg Crw; Boys Clb Am; Drama Clb; Spn Clb; Kent State Coll; Business.

IMMEL, DAVE; Jackson HS; Massillon, OH; Boy Scts; Chrs; Sct Actv; Yrbk; Spn Clb; Swmmng; Ten; Electrician.

IMRAY, DINA; Cardinal Stritch HS; Perrysburg, OH; 14/212 Chrs; Hon Rl; NHS; Stu Cncl; Sch Nwsp; Pres Spn Clb; College; Dent Hygiene.

IMWALLE, ANGELA; Marion Local HS; Maria Stein, OH; 2/89 VP Band; Hon Rl; VP NHS; Stu Cncl; Pres 4-H; Mth Clb; Sci Clb; Bsktbl; Scr Kpr; College.

IMWALLE, JAY; Marion Local HS; Maria Stein, OH; 15/90 Chrs; Chrh Wkr; Cmnty Wkr; Hon Rl; Jr NHS; NHS; Sch Pl; 4-H; Pep Clb;.

INBODY, LISA; Cory Rawson HS; Mt Cory, OH; Hon Rl; NHS; Sch Pl; Ed Yrbk; Rptr Sch Nwsp; Capt Bsktbl; Letter Trk; Bowling Green St Univ; Acctg.

INCORVIA, ANNEMARIE; Eastlake North HS; Willowick, OH; 21/639 Hon Rl; Sch Pl; Pep Clb; Trk; Univ Of Los Angeles.

INCROPERA, TERRI; Harrison HS; W Laf, IN; 14/340 Girl Scts; Hon Rl; Ger Clb; Bsktbl; Swmmng; Ten; Purdue Univ; Engr.

INFANTE, CARL; John F Kennedy HS; Niles, OH; Chrs; Chrh Wkr; Cmnty Wkr; Hon Rl; Lit Mag; Quill & Scroll; Sch Pl; Stg Crw; Sch Nwsp; Drama Clb; Youngstown St Univ; Indus Psych.

INFIELD, JAMES; High School; Sugarcreek, OH; Aud/Vis; Boy Scts; Hon Rl; NHS; Yth Flsp; Ger Clb;.

INGALLS, MARK; Petoskey HS; Petoskey, MI; Yth Flsp; Spn Clb; Letter Crs Cntry; Trk; IM Sprt; N Ctrl Michigan Coll; Bus Mgmt.

INGER, TRACY; Lutheran East HS; E Detroit, MI; Pres Frsh Cls; Cls Rep Soph Cls; Cl Rep Jr Cls; Band; Hon Rl; Letter Bsbl; Capt Ftbl; Lawrence Inst Of Tech; Mech Engr.

INGERSOLL, DENISE; Edison HS; Milan, OH; 15/282 Hst Soph Cls; Chrh Wkr; Hon Rl; NHS; Quill & Scroll; Rptr Yrbk; Yrbk; Rptr Sch Nwsp; Sci Clb; Mat Maids; Jacobs Bus Schl.

INGHAM, CHARLOTTE; Huntington HS; Chillicothe, OH; 20/94 Trs Sr Cls; Chrh Wkr; Hon Rl; Lbry Ade; NHS; Stg Crw; Yth Flsp; FTA; Bsktbl; Cit Awd; Perfect Attndnc 77;.

INGHAM, LAURA; Galion HS; Galion, OH; 3/300 Trs Frsh Cls; Band; Chrs; Girl Scts; Hon Rl; Hosp Ade; Jr NHS; Lbry Ade; NHS; Sch Pl; College; Science.

INGLE, CATHERINE; Jasper HS; Jasper, IN; 59/300 Am Leg Aux Girls St; Band; Chrs; Chrh Wkr; Girl Scts; Hon Rl; Hosp Ade; Red Cr Ade; Civ Clb; Pep Clb; Indiana Univ; German Lang.

INGLE, DEBORAH; Lincoln West HS; Cleveland, OH; 119/300 Pres Yth Flsp; OEA; Cit Awd; Amer Soc Of Wmns Acctg Merit Awd 1979; Data Proc.

INGLIS, ROBERT; Arthur Hill HS; Saginaw, MI; Hon Rl; College; Conservation.

INGOLD, JANE; Goshen HS; Goshen, IN; 40/269 Chrh Wkr; Hon Rl; Yth Flsp; Pres 4-H; Fr Clb; FHA; Glf; Ten; Goshen Coll.

INGRAHAM, SALLY; Mason County Central HS; Scottville, MI; 11/150 Cls Rep Frsh Cls; Cls Rep Soph Cls; Band; Girl Scts; Hon Rl; Yth Flsp; 4-H; Letter Bsktbl; Capt Trk; C of C Awd; Spgs Arbor Acad Schlrshp 79; Acad Excell Awd 79; Track Hon All Conf 4th Pl St Finals Mile Relay 79; Spring Arbor Coll; Nurse.

INGRAHAM, SUSAN; Rockford HS; Muskegon, MI; 45/390 Band; Drm Mjrt; Hon Rl; Orch; Sch Mus; Stg Crw; Drum Major Awd 79; Michigan St Univ; Med Tech.

INGRAM, DAVID; Mt Hope HS; Mt Hope, WV; 2/83 Pres Soph Cls; Val; Am Leg Boys St; Band; Boy Scts; Chrs; Hon Rl; Pres NHS; Pres FBLA; Bausch & Lomb Awd; Interpreter Arabic Syrian Language.

INGRAM, KADEEJAH W; Immaculata HS; Detroit, MI; Cls Rep Soph Cls; Cl Rep Jr Cls; Chrs; Cmnty Wkr; PAVAS; Red Cr Ade; Sch Mus; Sch Pl; Stg Crw; Yrbk; Honor Awd City Of Detroit; History Contest 2nd Pl; Equiestrian Ribbon 1st Pl; Jumping Ribbon 2nd Pl; Cornell Univ; Vet Med.

INGRAM, PAMELA; Jennings Co HS; Butlerville, IN; 5/340 Cls Rep Soph Cls; Cl Rep Jr Cls; Cls Rep Sr Cls; Sec NHS; Sec Stu Cncl; Pres Spn Clb; Awds English Spanish Typing Algebra Composition; Honor Homecoming Queen; Schlrshp In St Univ Academic; Indiana St Univ; Elem Ed.

INGRAM, STEVEN; Midland Trail HS; Ansted, WV; Hon Rl; NHS; VICA; Fayette Plateau Voc Tech; Carpentry.

INGRAM, TINA; Bishop Borgess HS; Detroit, MI; 10/475 Cmp Fr Grls; Cmnty Wkr; Girl Scts; Hon Rl; NHS; Sct Actv; Stg Crw; Natl Merit Ltr; Schlstc Art Awd 79; Univ; Fine Art.

INGRAM, TORI L; Newark Sr HS; Newark, OH; VP Soph Cls; Cls Rep Soph Cls; Trs Jr Cls; Cl Rep Jr Cls; Cls Rep Sr Cls; Chrs; Chrh Wkr; Drl Tm; Jr NHS; Lbry Ade; Univ Of Akron; Chem.

INHERST, MARTHA; Barnesville HS; Jerusalem, OH; 16/126 Chrh Wkr; Hon Rl; Hosp Ade; Lbry Ade; Sch Pl; Rptr Yrbk; Drama Clb; Pres 4-H; Fr Clb; FHA; Ohio Valley Genrl Hosp; Nursing.

INMAN, BARBARA; Westlake HS; Westlake, OH; Cls Rep Frsh Cls; Band; Cmp Fr Grls; Chrh Wkr; Drm Mjrt; FCA; Stu Cncl; GAA; IM Sprt; Univ; Phys Ther.

INMAN, BRET; Berkley HS; Berkley, MI; Cls Rep Soph Cls; Pres Jr Cls; Pres Sr Cls; Am Leg Boys St; Stu Cncl; Ger Clb; Am Leg Awd; Central Michigan Univ; Brdcstng.

INMAN, KIM; Jay County HS; Portland, IN; Cls Rep Frsh Cls; Cls Rep Soph Cls; Cl Rep Jr Cls; Sec JA; Off Ade; Stg Crw; Y-Teens; Sec.

INMAN, MATTHEW; East Palestine HS; E Palestine, OH; Cls Rep Frsh Cls; Cls Rep Soph Cls; Pres Jr Cls; Cl Rep Jr Cls; Boy Scts; Sch Pl; Stu Cncl; Key Clb; Ftbl; God Cntry Awd; Incentive Schlrshp Fresh; Eagle Scout; President Fresh Soph Hi Y Soph Yr; College; Anthropology.

INMAN, SHELLY; Jefferson Area HS; Jefferson, OH; 20/230 Cls Rep Frsh Cls; Cls Rep Soph Cls; AFS; Band; Chrs; Chrh Wkr; Cmnty Wkr; College; Nursing.

INNIS, CAMY; East Detroit HS; Warren, MI; Hon Rl; Off Ade; Rptr Yrbk; Mat Maids; PPFtbl; Scr Kpr; Tmr; Macomb Cmnty Coll; Law Enforcement.

INSCO, JEANNIE; Buffalo HS; Kenova, WV; Trs Soph Cls; VP Jr Cls; Trs Sr Cls; NHS; Sch Pl; Yrbk; Mth Clb; Trk; Chrldng; DAR Awd; Marshall Univ.

INSKEEP, ANDREA L; Rensselaer Central HS; Rensselaer, IN; 30/165 Cls Rep Frsh Cls; Cls Rep Soph Cls; Cl Rep Jr Cls; Cls Rep Sr Cls; Cmnty Wkr; Hon Rl; Off Ade; Sch Mus; Sch Pl; Stu Cncl; Purdue Univ; Elem Tchr.

INTAGLIATA, KENT; Cardinal Stritch HS; Oregon, OH; 33/230 Trs Frsh Cls; Cls Rep Soph Cls; Hon Rl; NHS; Stg Crw; Boys Clb Am; Drama Clb; Fr Clb; Wrstlng; Coach Actv; Arkansas Univ; Cmnctns.

INWOOD, JOHN; Mishawaka Marian HS; South Bend, IN; 3/156 Cls Rep Soph Cls; Cl Rep Jr Cls; Hon Rl; NHS; Stu Cncl; Pep Clb; Letter Glf; Notre Dame Univ; Med.

IOAS, SUZANNE; Fairmont West HS; Kettering, OH; 9/500 Cmnty Wkr; FCA; Hon Rl; VP Stu Cncl; Fr Clb; Hockey; Coll; Intl Relations.

IORGULESCU, DANIELA; Pleasant HS; New Berlin, WI; 6/146 Chrs; Hon Rl; Stg Crw; Yrbk; Drama Clb; Sci Clb; IM Sprt; Jr Marshall At Grad Exerceses; Oh Yth Sci Sympsm; Oh Sci & Math Conf; Eng Schlsp Team; Univ; Archt.

IOTT, REGINA; Kalkaska HS; Kalkaska, MI; 4/140 Chrh Wkr; Hon Rl; NHS; Sch Pl; Yrbk; 4-H; Bus Schl; Bus.

IOVALDI, ANN; Bishop Gallagher HS; Detroit, MI; 9/330 Trk; Mgrs; Univ Of Detroit; Archt.

IRBY, CAROL; Roosevelt HS; Gary, IN; Pres Soph Cls; Trs Jr Cls; Band; Chrh Wkr; Hon Rl; JA; Y-Teens; Fr Clb; Trk; Twrlr; Schlrshp Awd 77 78 & 78 79; Honors Orch 77 78 & 78 79; Univ; Bus Mgmt.

IRBY, SHERYL; Emerson HS; Gary, IN; 21/149 Hon Rl; JA; NHS; Off Ade; 4-H; Fr Clb; FBLA; OEA; Chrldng; Cit Awd; Miss Emerson & Fashion Trophey 1978; Data Processing Cert 1979; Purdue Calumet Univ; Comp Sci.

IRELAN, TOM; Delta HS; Muncie, IN; Cl Rep Jr Cls; Cls Rep Sr Cls; Hon Rl; NHS; Stu Cncl; Lat Clb; Sci Clb; Letter Glf; Cit Awd; Rotary Awd; Univ; Med.

IRELAND, JIM; St Francis De Sales HS; Toledo, OH; Band; Boy Scts; Hon Rl; Off Ade; Stg Crw; IM Sprt; Michigan Univ; Med.

IRELAND, KEVIN M; Cass Technical HS; Detroit, MI; 2/950 Pres Soph Cls; Band; Pres NHS; Treas Stu Cncl; Rptr Sch Nwsp; Fr Clb; Mth Clb; Letter Swmmng; DAR Awd; Natl Merit SF; Massachusetts Inst Of Tech; Comp Eng.

IRELAND, PATRICK R; Fremont HS; Fremont, MI; 3/250 Band; Boy Scts; Hon Rl; Pres NHS; Pol Wkr; Stu Cncl; Drama Clb; Pres Ger Clb; Sci Clb; Pres Spn Clb; Univ Of Notre Dame; Languages.

IRELAND, WESLEY; Fremont HS; Fremont, IN; 6/50 Band; Hon Rl; NHS; Orch; Bsbl; Bsktbl; Ball St Univ; Music.

IRETON, MICKEY; Shenandoah HS; Shirley, IN; 17/149 Chrh Wkr; Hon Rl; Mth Clb; Sci Clb; Letter Crs Cntry; Letter Trk; IM Sprt; College; Engr.

IRISH, DEBRA; Ovid Elsie HS; Ovid, MI; Chrh Wkr; Girl Scts; Hon Rl; Mdrgl; Sch Pl; Yth Flsp; Rptr Sch Nwsp; FHA; PPFtbl; Lansing Cmnty Coll; Soc Work.

IRISH, LEE; Hartland HS; Howell, MI; Band; Cmnty Wkr; Hon Rl; MMM; Fr Clb; College; Med Tech.

IRISH, PATRICK; Chippewa Hills HS; Barryton, MI; 52/212 Boy Scts; Debate Tm; Hon Rl; JA; Spn Clb; Wrstlng; IM Sprt; Mgrs; Dnfth Awd; Natl Merit Ltr; MUCC Conservation Camp Schlrshp; Univ; Engr.

IRISH, THOMAS; Kakaska HS; Fife Lake, MI; 6/100 NHS; Bsbl; Air Force; Aero Engr.

IRMEN, MICHELLE; Theodore Roosevelt HS; Wyandotte, MI; Cls Rep Soph Cls; Cl Rep Jr Cls; Band; Cmp Fr Grls; Hon Rl; NHS; Orch; Stu Cncl; Letter Bsktbl; Letter Swmmng; Coll; Geol Engr.

IRONS, JENNIFER; Columbiana HS; Columbiana, OH; 2/107 Sec Band; Cmp Fr Grls; Chrh Wkr; Hon Rl; Mdrgl; VP NHS; Treas Yth Flsp; Univ Of Cin; Chem Engr.

IRVEN, STEVE; Northrop HS; Fort Wayne, IN; 40/577 Hon Rl; 4-H; Cit Awd; 4-H Awd; Natl Merit Ltr; Indiana Purdue Univ; Acctg.

IRVIN, BONNIE; Zanesville HS; Zanesville, OH; Band; Chrs; Drl Tm; Hon Rl; NHS; Sec Yrbk; Pres Sci Clb; GAA; Natl Merit SF; 3.5 Club; Univ; Educ.

IRVIN, MARIAN; Oscar A Carlson HS; Trenton, MI; 17/243 Rptr Sch Nwsp; FTA; GAA; IM Sprt; Natl Merit SF; Michigan St Univ; Acctg.

IRVINE, ANNE; Dominican HS; Detroit, MI; Cmnty Wkr; NHS; Sch Pl; Crs Cntry; Letter Trk; Coach Actv; Natl Merit SF; College; Architecture.

IRVINE, DEBORAH; New Albany HS; New Albany, OH; Rptr Yrbk; Pep Clb; Univ; Photog.

IRVINE, ROBERT; Norwood HS; Norwood, OH; 24/348 Band; Hon Rl; Orch; Sch Mus; Key Clb; Mth Clb; Univ; Music.

IRVINE, ROBERT S; Norwood HS; Norwood, OH; 24/343 Band; Hon Rl; Orch; Sch Mus; Key Clb; Mth Clb; Univ; Music.

IRVING, PRICE; Greenfield Central HS; Greenfield, IN; 129/300 4-H; Spn Clb; Letter Bsbl; Bsktbl; Mgrs; Univ; Phys Educ.

IRVING, WILLIAM; Aquinas HS; Riverview, MI; Fr Clb; Mic State Univ; Law.

IRWIN, CATHY S; Garfield Sr HS; Hamilton, OH; 6/376 Chrh Wkr; Hon Rl; Jr NHS; NHS; Stu Cncl; Y-Teens; Rptr Yrbk; 4-H; OEA; Tmr; Newspaper Art Editor; S W Ohio Appaloosa Youth Assoc Sec; Mbr Of The Appaloosa Horse Club;.

IRWIN, CHRIS; Clay Sr HS; South Bend, IN; 99/430 Girl Scts; Hon Rl; Sct Actv; 4-H; Trk; IM Sprt; Tmr; 4-H Awd; Purdue Univ; Vet.

IRWIN, KATHRYN; Decatur HS; Decatur, MI; Cls Rep Sr Cls; Hon Rl; Sch Pl; Stu Cncl; Yth Flsp; Rptr Sch Nwsp; 4-H; Letter Trk; 4-H Awd; Kalamazoo Vally Comm Coll; Psych.

IRWIN, KENT; Terre Haute South Vigo HS; Terre Haute, IN; Cls Rep Frsh Cls; Pres Jr Cls; Hon Rl; JA; Yrbk; Rdo Clb; Glf; Meis Purchs Prz Awd Art 79; U S Sen Page 79; Univ; Bus.

IRWIN, MARY; Holt Sr HS; Holt, MI; 24/350 Cls Rep Frsh Cls; Trs Soph Cls; Cl Rep Jr Cls; VP Sr Cls; Chrs; Chrh Wkr; Girl Scts; Hon Rl; Natl Forn Lg; NHS; Univ; Med Tech.

IRWIN, MICHAEL D; Padua HS; Strongsville, OH; Boy Scts; Chrs; Chrh Wkr; Sct Actv; Univ; Aero Engr.

ISAAC, GREGORY; Charlestown HS; Otisco, IN; 34 Chrh Wkr; Cmnty Wkr; Hon Rl; Off Ade; 4-H; Sci Clb; Spn Clb; IM Sprt; 4-H Awd; Ind Univ; Comp Science.

ISAACS, DWAYNE; Connersville HS; Connersville, IN; Cls Rep Sr Cls; Hon Rl; Letter Ftbl; Letter Wrstlng; Ind Univ.

ISAACS, GREGORY B; Gallia Academy HS; Vinton, OH; 11/256 Cls Rep Frsh Cls; Boy Scts; Chrs; Chrh Wkr; Cmnty Wkr; Hon Rl; NHS; Sch Mus; Sch Pl; Sct Actv; Schlrshp From Buckeye Rural Elec Co Op 79; Schlrshp From St Emblm Club 79; Schlrshp From Natl Suprm Emb Clb; Asbury Coll; Engr.

ISAACS, JANICE; Laurel HS; Laurel, IN; 4/29 Sec Frsh Cls; Trs Frsh Cls; Hon Rl; NHS; Rptr Sch Nwsp; Spn Clb; Scr Kpr; Soc Std.

ISAACS, THOMAS; Garfield HS; Hamilton, OH; Chrs; Hon Rl; Jr NHS; Mod UN; NHS; Pol Wkr; Yth Flsp; Spn Clb; Miami Univ; Chiropractor.

ISAACS, WENDY; Hillman Community HS; Hillman, MI; Band; Chrs; Girl Scts; Hon Rl; Sch Pl; 4-H; FHA; Letter Trk; Twrlr; 4-H Awd; College.

ISAACSON, LAURIE; Summerfield HS; Dundee, MI; Cmp Fr Grls; Chrs; Chrh Wkr; Hon Rl; Off Ade; Sch Pl; Yrbk; 4-H; Pep Clb; Trk; College; Interior Decorating.

ISABELLA, MARK; Flemington HS; Flemington, WV; 7/42 Pres Soph Cls; Hon Rl; Treas NHS; Sch Pl; Sprt Ed Yrbk; Rptr Yrbk; Ed Sch Nwsp; Rptr Sch Nwsp; Pres Fr Clb; Pres FTA; Fairmont St Coll; Broadcasting.

ISABELLA, MARK S; Notre Dame HS; Bridgeport, WV; 6/54 Pres Frsh Cls; Pres Soph Cls; Band; Chrs; Cmnty Wkr; Treas Stu Cncl; Key Clb; Mth Clb; Bsktbl; Trk; Superior Rating In Natl Fraternity Of Musicians; West Virginia Univ; Medicine.

ISBELL, EILEEN; Hammond HS; Hammond, IN; 35/330 Chrs; Chrh Wkr; Jr NHS; Letter Bsktbl; Pom Pon; Coll.

ISENBARGER, LARRY; Bethel HS; New Carlisle, OH; Pres Jr Cls; Band; Chrs; Hon Rl; Jr NHS; Orch; Sch Mus; Stu Cncl; Singing Ensemble 79;.

ISENBARGER, TIM; Jimtown HS; Osceola, IN; 14/120 Hon Rl; Rptr Yrbk; Yrbk; DECA; Fr Clb; Pep Clb; Ten; PPFtbl; Scr Kpr; Indiana Univ; Busns.

ISENBERG, ROBERT; Jefferson Area HS; Jefferson, OH; Univ; Cmmrcl Art.

ISENNAGLE, JOHN; Whitehall Yearling HS; Whitehl, OH; 1/300 Val; Hon Rl; NHS; Pres Yth Flsp; Rptr Yrbk; C of C Awd; Lion Awd; Natl Merit Ltr; Ohio State Univ; Acctg.

ISENNAGLE, T; High School; Whitehall, OH; Yth Flsp; Y-Teens; Fr Clb; Ohio St Univ; Educ.

ISHERWOOD, ANN; St Augustine Acad; Cleveland, OH; Hon Rl; Hosp Ade; Pep Clb; Sci Clb;.

ISLE, PENNY; Whitmore Lake HS; Whitmore Lk, MI; 4/90 Hon Rl; Jr NHS; NHS; Sch Pl; Fr Clb; College; Artist.

ISLER, CAROLYN; Stephen T Badin HS; Okeana, OH; 4/220 Cl Rep Jr Cls; Cls Rep Sr Cls; Hon Rl; VP NHS; Stu Cncl; Rptr Sch Nwsp; Sec 4-H; IM Sprt; 4-H Awd; Kiwan Awd; Chosen To Give Speech Presntn At Optimist Club 77; Natl Hnr Soc Sec 78; Univ; Comp Sci.

ISLER, WILLIAM P; Windham HS; Windham, OH; Pres Frsh Cls; Pres Soph Cls; Cls Rep Soph Cls; Cl Rep Jr Cls; Cls Rep Sr Cls; Am Leg Boys St; Hon Rl; Lit Mag; Pres NHS; Pres Stu Cncl; March Of Dimes Rep; Univ; Pre Law.

ISLEY, BRENDA; Clear Fork HS; Mansfield, OH; 9/164 Cls Rep Soph Cls; Trs Jr Cls; Chrh Wkr; Cmnty Wkr; Drl Tm; Girl Scts; Hosp Ade; NHS; Yrbk; Opt Clb Awd; The Defiance Coll; Soc Work.

ISMAILOGLU, MEHMET; Harper Creek HS; Battle Crk, MI; Cls Rep Frsh Cls; Hon Rl; Fr Clb; Letter Ten; Albion Coll; Medicine.

ISNER, JEFFREY; Grafton Sr HS; Grafton, WV; Band; FCA; Hon Rl; Orch; Sch Mus; Key Clb; Letter Ftbl; Swmmng; IM Sprt; West Virginia Univ; Dentistry.

ISOLA, DANIEL J; Bishop Gallagher HS; Harper Woods, MI; 5/328 Hon Rl; Bsbl; IM Sprt; Univ Of Michigan; Chemistry.

ISOM, TINA; Nordonia Sr HS; Macedonia, OH; VP Jr Cls; Chrs; Chrh Wkr; Debate Tm; Girl Scts; Hosp Ade; Lbry Ade; Off Ade; Sct Actv; Stg Crw; Akron Univ; Radiology.

ISON, JOY; Highland HS; Anderson, IN; 11/426 Chrs; Hon Rl; NHS; Pep Clb; Spn Clb; PPFtbl; Comp Sci & Appld Math Worksp For HS Stdnt At Ball St Univ 79; Outstndng Achvmntineng 76; Purdue Univ; Comp Sci.

ISON, LINDA; Westerville South HS; Westerville, OH; Am Leg Aux Girls St; Girl Scts; Hon Rl; Stu Cncl; Pep Clb; Gym; Letter Chrldng; PPFtbl; Scr Kpr; Tmr; College.

ISON, SCOTT; Clermont Northeastern HS; Batavia, OH; Cls Rep Frsh Cls; Cls Rep Soph Cls; Pres Jr Cls; Pres Sr Cls; Chrh Wkr; FCA; Sct Actv; Stu Cncl; Yth Flsp; 4-H; Univ; Educ.

ISON, THERESA; Eastern HS; Lucasville, OH; Chrs; Hon Rl; Hosp Ade; Yrbk; College; Phys Ther.

ISONHOOD, ROBIN; F J Reitz HS; Evansville, IN; 33/435 Hon Rl; JA; Jr NHS; NHS; Orch; Sch Mus; Sch Pl; Stg Crw; Stu Cncl; Drama Clb; Honorary Scholarship St Of Indiana 1980; Scholarship Indiana St Univ 1979; Indiana St Univ; Acctg.

ISPHORDING, MARY; Ursuline Acad; Cincinnati, OH; 2/108 Cls Rep Frsh Cls; Cls Rep Soph Cls; Cl Rep Jr Cls; Sec Sr Cls; Hon Rl; Jr NHS; NHS; Sch Pl; Stg Crw; Stu Cncl; Coll; Med.

ISRAEL, CAROLYNE; Mt Vernon Academy; Worthington, OH; Pres Frsh Cls; Chrs; Chrh Wkr; Hon Rl; Sch Mus; Stu Cncl; Cert For Highst Score In Amer Govt 77; A Sec Treas 77; S A Vc Pres 79; Andrews Univ; Sci.

ISTRABADI, FEISAL A; Bloomington HS South; Bloomington, IN; 36/389 NHS; Orch; Sch Mus; Sch Pl; Gold Music Hnr Awd For Orch 79; Best Supporting Performance In Drama 78; Med Schl.

ITAMURA, JAN; Terre Haute South Vigo HS; Terre Haute, IN; 100/630 Cls Rep Soph Cls; Cl Rep Jr Cls; Cls Rep Sr Cls; Chrs; Chrh Wkr; Cmnty Wkr; FCA; Hon Rl; Mod UN; Off Ade; College; Elem Ed.

ITSON, CINDY; Black River HS; Spencer, OH; Chrs; Girl Scts; Sch Pl; Sct Actv; Rptr Yrbk; Rptr Sch Nwsp; Drama Clb; Capt 4-H; Spn Clb; Scr Kpr; Navy; Registered Nursing.

ITTER, MARK; Michigan Lutheran Seminary; Bay City, MI; Chrs; Chrh Wkr; Ftbl; Mgrs; Northwestern Coll; Tchr.

IVANAC, LYDIA; Andrean HS; Lake Station, IN; Hon Rl; Off Ade; Calumet Coll; Sec.

IVANOVICH, DAVE; Turpin HS; Cincinnati, OH; 7/342 Chrh Wkr; Hon Rl; Sch Pl; Rptr Sch Nwsp; Drama Clb; Oberlin Univ; English.

IVANOVICH, ROCCO; Jackson County Western HS; Albion, MI; Trs Frsh Cls; NHS; Fr Clb; Mth Clb; Letter Bsktbl; Letter Ftbl; Acad Schslp From St Of Mi 79; All St Ftbl 77; Cntrl Michigan Univ; Systm Analysis.

IVANYE, ROSEMARY; Charles F Brush HS; Lyndhst Mayfld, OH; 2/627 Am Leg Aux Girls St; Band; CAP; Hon Rl; NHS; Sch Mus; Sch Pl; Yth Flsp; Rptr Sch Nwsp; Drama Clb; Kent St Univ; Art.

IVEN, BERNIE; Lima Ctrl Cath HS; Elida, OH; Cls Rep Soph Cls; Boy Scts; Hon Rl; NHS; Sch Pl; Sct Actv; Stu Cncl; Trk; Wrstlng; The Ohio St Univ; Bus Admin.

IVENS, KEITH; Dowagiac Union HS; Dowagiac, MI; 11/215 Pres Frsh Cls; Hon Rl; NHS; Pres Stu Cncl; Drama Clb; VP Sci Clb; Capt Ten; Elk Awd; Lion Awd; Natl Merit Schl; Schlrshp 79; Sportsmans Big 10 Awd 79; Michigan St Univ; Pre Med.

IVENS, SANDRA K; Marcellus HS; Marcellus, MI; Sec Chrs; Hon Rl; Lbry Ade; Off Ade; Sch Mus; Yth Flsp; Pep Clb; Letter Bsktbl; Letter Trk; Letter Chrldng; Southwestern Cmnty Coll; Bus.

IVERS, REBECCA; Amelia HS; Cincinnati, OH; Hon Rl; Off Ade; Fr Clb; Lat Clb; IM Sprt; Univ Of Cincinnati; Bus.

IVERSON, BEVERLY K; Culbertson HS; Culbertson, MI; 1/28 VP Soph Cls; Sec Jr Cls; Val; Pres Band; Chrs; Drm Mjrt; Hon Rl; Pres NHS; Trk; Capt Chrldng; E Montana Coll; Acctg.

IVES, GWENDOLYN; Fowlerville HS; Fowlerville, MI; Chrh Wkr; Hon Rl; Hosp Ade; PPFtbl; Univ; Phys Ther.

IVES, LISA; Tecumseh HS; Tecumseh, MI; 2/255 Sal; Band; Chrh Wkr; Hon Rl; NHS; Off Ade; FBLA; Adrian College; Acctg.

IVEY, DAWN; Frankenmuth HS; Frankenmuth, MI; 5/196 Cls Rep Frsh Cls; Cls Rep Sr Cls; Chrs; Chrh Wkr; Debate Tm; Hon Rl; Natl Forn Lg; Sec NHS; Red Cr Ade; Sch Mus; Concordia Teachers Coll; Spec Ed.

IVEY, SHERI; Belpre HS; Belpre, OH; 20/200 Chrs; Chrh Wkr; Cmnty Wkr; Girl Scts; Hon Rl; Hosp Ade; Mdrgl; NHS; Off Ade; Sch Mus; Reg OEA Contest 1st 1979; Reg OEA Contest 2nd 1979; St OEA Contest 3rd 1979; Ohio Univ; Bus.

IVEY, SUSAN; Parma HS; Parma, OH; Hon Rl; Off Ade; Fr Clb; Lat Clb; Pep Clb; Letter Ten; College; Oceanography.

IVORY, AUDREY; George Washington HS; E Chicago, IN; 9/270 Chrh Wkr; Drl Tm; Hon Rl; JA; Sec NHS; Fr Clb; VP FHA; Key Clb; Pep Clb; Twrlr; Natl Hon Society 78; Purdue Univ; Archt.

IVORY, CORNELIA D; Northeastern HS; Detroit, MI; Cmp Fr Grls; Chrs; Girl Scts; Fr Clb; Bsbl; Bsktbl; Chrldng; GAA; Pom Pon; Univ; Eng.

IVORY, LORETTA; East Tech HS; Cleveland, OH; Hon Rl; Rptr Sch Nwsp; Drama Clb; Cit Awd; Univ; Law.

IWEN, BRENDA; Chesaning Union HS; Burt, MI; Cmp Fr Grls; Chrs; Hon Rl; Chrldng; Delta Univ.

IZOR, SANDRA K; Valley View HS; Farmersville, OH; Hst Soph Cls; Hon Rl; Lbry Ade; FHA; Business School; Executive Secretary.

IZZARD, KENNETH; Northridge HS; Newark, OH; Hon Rl; Fr Clb; Sci Clb; Bsktbl; Trk; 4-H Awd; Ohi State Univ; Sci.

J

JABARA, JANINE; Mancelona HS; Mancelona, MI; 1/79 Cls Rep Soph Cls; Pres Jr Cls; Band; Chrh Wkr; Hon Rl; NHS; Sch Mus; Yth Flsp; Hope Coll; Music.

JABBARPOUR, JADOLLAH; Point Pleasant HS; Pt Pleasant, WV; Am Leg Boys St; Band; Boy Scts; Hon Rl; VP NHS; Pres Stu Cncl; Fr Clb; Key Clb; College; Med.

JABBARPOUR, YAD; Point Pleasant HS; Point Pleasant, WV; Boy Scts; Hon Rl; NHS; Stu Cncl; Key Clb; Pep Clb; Letter Ten; Letter Wrstlng; Am Leg Awd; Univ.

JABBARPOUR, YADOLLAH; Point Pleasant HS; Point Pleasant, WV; Am Leg Boys St; Band; Boy Scts; VP NHS; Pres Stu Cncl; Key Clb; Fr Clb; Letter Ten; Letter Trk; Letter Wrstlng; University; Med.

JABBUSCH, SCOTT; Admiral King HS; Lorain, OH; Off Ade; Bsbl; Glf; Scr Kpr; College; Architecture.

JABS, SUSAN; Elkhart Memorial HS; Elkhart, IN; 19/496 Band; Hon Rl; Hosp Ade; NHS; Sch Nwsp; Ger Clb; Mth Clb; Letter Swmmng; Univ; Engr.

JACHIMIAK, JIM; S Ripley Jr Sr HS; Versailles, IN; Hon Rl; NHS; Quill & Scroll; Rptr Yrbk; Rptr Sch Nwsp; Drama Clb; Fr Clb; Mth Clb; Sci Clb; Lion Awd; Univ; Journalism.

JACHMAN, MATTHEW; St Marys Of Redford HS; Detroit, MI; 4/165 Aud/Vis; Hon Rl; Sec NHS; Pol Wkr; Quill & Scroll; Sch Pl; Stg Crw; Ed Sch Nwsp; Sch Nwsp; Marquette Univ.

JACK, CAROL; Medina Sr HS; Medina, OH; 7/340 Hon Rl; NHS; Red Cr Ade; Rptr Yrbk; Pep Clb; Natl Merit Ltr; Univ; Pre Med.

JACK, PHILIP; Manistique HS; Germfask, MI; Hon Rl; 4-H; Scr Kpr; 4-H Awd; Univ Of Idaho; Engr.

JACKANICH, PAUL; Cardinal Mooney HS; Youngstown, OH; Hon Rl; Youngstown St Univ; Archt.

JACKARD, MICHELLE; Bloomington HS; Bloomington, IN; Cl Rep Jr Cls; Girl Scts; Hon Rl; NHS; Sct Actv; Stu Cncl; Fr Clb; Pep Clb; Swmmng; Mgrs; Univ; Pre Med.

JACKETT, DANIEL; Pinconning HS; Linwood, MI; Hon Rl; NHS; Letter Bsktbl; Letter Ftbl; Trk; IM Sprt; Michigan St Univ; Acctg.

JACKO, JIM; Solon HS; Solon, OH; 28/280 Cls Rep Frsh Cls; Cls Rep Soph Cls; Cl Rep Jr Cls; Cls Rep Sr Cls; Hon Rl; Jr NHS; NHS; Key Clb; Pep Clb; Marietta Univ; Petroleum Engr.

JACKSON, BETH; Rensselaer Central HS; Rensselaer, IN; 28/166 Band; Chrh Wkr; Drl Tm; Hon Rl; NHS; 4-H; FNA; Lat Clb; Pom Pon; De Pauw Univ; Nursing.

JACKSON, BETH; Rensselaer Central HS; Rensselier, IN; Chrh Wkr; Drl Tm; Hon Rl; NHS; FNA; Lat Clb; Pom Pon; De Pauw Univ; Nursing.

JACKSON, BETSY; Bexley HS; Columbus, OH; 32/185 AFS; Debate Tm; Hon Rl; Sch Pl; Rptr Sch Nwsp; Drama Clb; Pres Spn Clb; Miami Univ; Theater.

JACKSON, BRADLEY D; Parchment HS; Parchment, MI; 33/150 Am Leg Boys St; Boy Scts; Chrh Wkr; Hon Rl; Sch Mus; Sch Pl; Spn Clb; Letter Ten; Natl Merit SF; Pores Of Yr J A 79; Outstndng Young Busmn J A 79; Full Need J A Schlshp For Frsh Yr 79; Kalamazoo Coll; Pre Law.

JACKSON, BRIAN; Cardington Lincoln HS; Cardington, OH; VP Jr Cls; Hon Rl; Stg Crw; Sprt Ed Sch Nwsp; Rptr Sch Nwsp; VP 4-H; Sec FFA; Letter Bsbl; Bsktbl; Letter Ftbl; Ohio St Univ; Vet.

JACKSON, CHARLETTA; Buena Vista HS; Saginaw, MI; Trs Frsh Cls; Cls Rep Soph Cls; Hon Rl; Y-Teens; Rptr Sch Nwsp; Pep Clb; Trk; 4-H Awd; JA Awd; Natl Merit Ltr; Bus Schl; Bus Admin.

JACKSON, CHECITA V; East HS; Columbus, OH; Band; Drm Mjrt; Jr NHS; Off Ade; Stu Cncl; 4-H; Spn Clb; Letter Trk; Twrlr; Pres Awd; Ohio St Univ; Bio Chem.

JACKSON, CHRISTINE; Sebring Mckinley HS; Sebring, OH; Sec Band; Drm Mjrt; Sch Mus; Rptr Sch Nwsp; Sch Nwsp; Drama Clb; Sec Ger Clb; Pep Clb; Twrlr; College; Music.

JACKSON, CRAIG; Elgin HS; La Rue, OH; .

JACKSON, CYNTHIA; Orange HS; Chagrin Falls, OH; 7/250 Trs Frsh Cls; Cl Rep Jr Cls; Cls Rep Sr Cls; AFS; Hon Rl; Sec Stu Cncl; Sprt Ed Sch Nwsp; Letter Gym; Capt Hockey; Swmmng; Miami Univ; Orthodontics.

JACKSON, DALE; Terre Haute South Vigo HS; Terre Haute, IN; Band; Chrh Wkr; Indiana St Univ; Criminology.

JACKSON, DAVID; Edwardsburg HS; Edwardsburg, MI; Hon Rl; Letter Bsbl; Acad Awd A Aver Or Better For The Yr 77; Perfect Attendance 78; Univ.

JACKSON, DAVID; Northview HS; Grand Rapids, MI; 28/291 Hon Rl; JA; NHS; Fr Clb; JA Awd; Aquinas Coll; Acctg.

JACKSON, DEANNA; Athens HS; Princeton, WV; Chrs; Hon Rl; Rptr Sch Nwsp; Fr Clb; Keyettes; Chrldng; Pensacola Christian Coll; Elem Educ.

JACKSON, DEBORAH; Franklin Hts HS; Columbus, OH; 3/247 Trs Sr Cls; Cls Rep Sr Cls; Am Leg Aux Girls St; Cmp Fr Grls; Chrs; Girl Scts; Hon Rl; NHS; Sch Mus; Sct Actv; Acctg Centur 21 Office Ed Assn; Typing Filing; Prepared Verbal Communications Awd; College; Mgmt.

JACKSON, DEBRA; Leslie HS; Leslie, MI; Cl Rep Jr Cls; Band; Hon Rl; NHS; Sch Mus; Stu Cncl; Yth Flsp; Pres 4-H; PPFtbl; 4-H Awd; College.

JACKSON, DEBRA L; Oregon Davis Jr Sr HS; Walkerton, IN; 7/69 Treas Drm Mjrt; Hon Rl; Lbry Ade; NHS; Yrbk; Sec FHA; VP Pep Clb; Letter Bsktbl; Letter Gym; Letter Trk; Coll; Busns Admin.

JACKSON, DELIA; Holland HS; Holland, MI; Band; Hon Rl; Orch; Davenport Bus College; Legal Sec.

JACKSON, DENISE; Mifflin HS; Columbus, OH; Cl Rep Jr Cls; Chrh Wkr; Lbry Ade; Ohi State Univ; Pediatrican.

JACKSON, DIANNA L; Bloomfield HS; Bloomfield, IN; Band; Chrh Wkr; Hon Rl; Coll; Art.

JACKSON, ELLEN; Western Hills HS; Cincinnati, OH; 149/867 Chrs; Chrh Wkr; Girl Scts; Hon Rl; Sch Mus; Stu Cncl; Yth Flsp; Mgrs; Cedarville College; Education.

JACKSON, GLORIA; Inkster HS; Inkster, MI; Sec Sr Cls; Chrh Wkr; Cmnty Wkr; Hon Rl; Lbry Ade; Off Ade; Stu Cncl; FBLA; OEA; Pep Clb; Coll Of Bus; Exec Sec.

JACKSON, GLORIA; Pocahontas County HS; Marlinton, WV; 11/125 Band; Chrs; Chrh Wkr; Cmnty Wkr; Girl Scts; Hon Rl; JA; Lbry Ade; NHS; Off Ade; W Virginia Inst Of Tech; Med Rec.

JACKSON, GLORY; Southwestern HS; Detroit, MI; Girl Scts; Hon Rl; Hosp Ade; JA; NHS; Stu Cncl; Rptr Sch Nwsp; FTA; Pep Clb; Cit Awd; Schlshp Awd 76 79; New Detroit Progr 79; Cnslr Aid Awd 77 79; Pres Of Ladies Quartrly 79; Coll; Fshn Buyer.

JACKSON, GREGORY S; Mc Kinley Sr HS; Canton, OH; Pres Jr Cls; Am Leg Boys St; Band; Chrs; Hon Rl; Off Ade; Sch Mus; Pres Stu Cncl; Drama Clb; FTA; Whos Who Among Amer Music Stdnt 76; Martin Essex Schls For Gifted 79; Stdnt Talent Serv Recgntn 79; Univ Of Cincinnati; Music Educ.

JACKSON, H WARN; Parkside HS; Jackson, MI; Cls Rep Frsh Cls; Cls Rep Soph Cls; Cl Rep Jr Cls; VP Sr Cls; Stu Cncl; Ten; Univ Of Michigan; Engr.

JACKSON, J; London Public HS; London, OH; Am Leg Boys St; Sch Pl; Rptr Sch Nwsp; Drama Clb; Fr Clb; Ftbl; Ten; Trk; Ohi Univ; Journalism.

JACKSON, JAMES; Western Boone Jr Sr HS; Jamestown, IN; Pres Frsh Cls; Band; Drm Bgl; Sch Mus; Sch Pl; Stg Crw; Key Clb; Swmmng; Wrstlng; Opt Clb Awd; Outstndg Percussionist 2 Yrs 78; ISU; Pro Musician.

JACKSON, JAY; Roosevelt Wilson HS; Nutter Fort, WV; Am Leg Boys St; Band; Chrh Wkr; Hon Rl; Treas NHS; Orch; Sch Pl; Pres Stu Cncl; Pres Yth Flsp; VP Leo Clb; West Virginia Univ; Chem Engr.

JACKSON, JEANNINE; West Ottawa HS; Holland, MI; Cls Rep Frsh Cls; Cls Rep Soph Cls; Cl Rep Jr Cls; Am Leg Aux Girls St; Chrs; Debate Tm; Girl Scts; NHS; Stu Cncl; Lat Clb; Close Up Prog 79; Univ; Law.

JACKSON, JEFF B; Roosevelt Wilson HS; Nutter Fort, WV; Cl Rep Jr Cls; Am Leg Boys St; Band; Chrh Wkr; Hon Rl; Pres Stu Cncl; Treas Yth Flsp; Drama Clb; Leo Clb; Letter Ftbl; Univ; Sci.

JACKSON, JO; Huntington North HS; Warren, IN; Pep Clb; Bsktbl; GAA; Ball St Univ; Spec Ed.

JACKSON, JODI; Atherton HS; Burton, MI; 1/185 Cl Rep Jr Cls; Trs Sr Cls; Val; Hon Rl; NHS; Sch Pl; Letter Bsktbl; Letter Trk; Voice Dem Awd; Ltr In Vlybl; Recieved Hon Mention Recognition 78; Univ Of Michigan; Med.

JACKSON, JODI; Oak Glen HS; Chester, WV; Band; Drm Mjrt; Fr Clb; Pep Clb; Bus Schl; Stewardess.

JACKSON, JOHN; Lincoln HS; Enterprise, WV; 43/150 Am Leg Boys St; Hon Rl; Yrbk; Fr Clb; Sci Clb; Am Leg Awd; Fairmont St Univ; Med.

JACKSON, JUDITH L; North Ridgeville Sr HS; N Ridgeville, OH; Chrs; Hon Rl; Sch Pl; Spn Clb; Lorain Comm Coll; Busns Ed.

JACKSON, JUNE; Newton Local HS; Covington, OH; Hst Sr Cls; Band; Chrs; Chrh Wkr; Capt Drl Tm; Off Ade; Sch Pl; Miami Valley School Of Nursing; Rn.

JACKSON, KAREN; Brookhaven HS; Columbus, OH; Cl Rep Jr Cls; Girl Scts; Hon Rl; Jr NHS; Off Ade; Sch Pl; Stu Cncl; Yth Flsp; Fr Clb; Mia College; Spec Educ.

JACKSON, KAREN G; Warrensville Hts HS; Warrensville, OH; Cmp Fr Grls; Cmnty Wkr; Drl Tm; Univ; RN.

JACKSON, KARL; Buena Vista HS; Saginaw, MI; 9/185 Cls Rep Soph Cls; VP Jr Cls; Pres Sr Cls; Hon Rl; Pres NHS; Sci Clb; Ftbl; Ten; Rotary Awd; MSU; Pre Med.

JACKSON, KATHLEEN; Mount Clemens HS; Mt Clemens, MI; 13/350 Hon Rl; NHS; Stg Crw; Rptr Sch Nwsp; Spn Clb; Chrldng; Tmr; W Michigan Univ; Fshn Mdse.

JACKSON, KELLY; Paul L Dunbar HS; Dayton, OH; Band; Chrh Wkr; Hon Rl; NHS; Sch Pl; Y-Teens; Drama Clb; Pep Clb; JA Awd; Bauder Fashion Coll; Modeling.

JACKSON, KENNETH; John F Kennedy Sr HS; Cleveland, OH; IM Sprt; Indstrl Tech.

JACKSON, KIMBERLY; Dayton Christian HS; Dayton, OH; 8/95 Chrh Wkr; Hon Rl; NHS; Ed Sch Nwsp; Spn Clb; Scr Kpr; Cit Awd; Volleyball Jr Varsity 78; Softball Varsity 79; Spanish Natl Honor Soc 77; Wright St Univ; Jrnlsm.

JACKSON, LISA A; Brooke HS; Colliers, WV; 40/467 Cls Rep Frsh Cls; Cls Rep Soph Cls; Trs Jr Cls; Cl Rep Jr Cls; Cls Rep Sr Cls; Chrh Wkr; Hon Rl; Jr NHS; NHS; Off Ade; Jefferson Tech Coll; Data Processing.

JACKSON, LORI; Merrillville HS; Merrillville, IN; 202/610 Hon Rl; Stu Cncl; Pom Pon; Indiana Univ; Dental Hygiene.

JACKSON, LORI; Sebring Mc Kinley HS; Sebring, OH; Sec Jr Cls; Band; Chrs; Hon Rl; Off Ade; Yth Flsp; Rptr Yrbk; Sec Drama Clb; Fr Clb; Fshn.

JACKSON, LYNDA B; Jesup W Scott HS; Toledo, OH; Cls Rep Soph Cls; Cl Rep Jr Cls; VP Sr Cls; Band; Chrs; Chrh Wkr; Hon Rl; Pres JA; NHS; 4-H; Owens Tech Schl; Comp Prog.

JACKSON, LYNN D; Mogadore HS; Mogadore, OH; Sec Frsh Cls; Hon Rl; NHS; Fr Clb; Pom Pon; PPFtbl; Akron Univ; Social Work.

JACKSON, MARK; Coldwater HS; Coldwater, OH; Chrs; Hon Rl; Sch Nwsp; Natl Merit Ltr; Ohio State Univ; Comp Sci.

JACKSON, MARKIE; Prairie Hts Cmnty School; Orland, IN; 18/136 Girl Scts; Hon Rl; Rptr Yrbk; 4-H; FBLA; FHA; Pep Clb; Spn Clb; Wrk With Small Chldrn.

JACKSON, MARY; Stonewall Jackson HS; Charleston, WV; Hon Rl; Stu Cncl; Pep Clb; Letter Gym; Letter Chrldng; Cit Awd;.

JACKSON, MARY; Pioneer HS; Ann Arbor, MI; Chrs; Hon Rl; Ger Clb; Letter Swmmng; Western Mich; Bio.

JACKSON, MAXINE; Benedictine HS; Detroit, MI; 15/120 Cls Rep Frsh Cls; Cls Rep Soph Cls; Cl Rep Jr Cls; Hon Rl; JA; Off Ade; Pol Wkr; Pep Clb; College; Phys Therapy.

JACKSON, MELANIE; Roosevelt Wilson HS; Mt Clare, WV; Hon Rl; Hosp Ade; Sch Pl; FNA; VICA; Mbr Of Nalt Latin Honsoc 78; Schslp From U S Hosp Aux 78; West Virginia Univ; Med Tech.

JACKSON, MELVIN; Madison Plains HS; Mt Sterling, OH; Cls Rep Soph Cls; Pres Jr Cls; Pres Sr Cls; Am Leg Boys St; Hon Rl; NHS; Quill & Scroll; Sch Pl; Stu Cncl; Yrbk; Univ.

JACKSON, MICHAEL; Laville HS; Lakeville, IN; Am Leg Boys St; Band; Chrh Wkr; Yth Flsp; Fr Clb; Mth Clb; Sci Clb; Glf; Ball St Univ; Archt.

JACKSON, MICHELE; United Local HS; Medina, OH; 14/145 Sec Frsh Cls; Cls Rep Soph Cls; Chrs; Chrh Wkr; Hon Rl; NHS; Stu Cncl; Yth Flsp; Fr Clb; USJC Awd; Malone College; Education.

JACKSON, MORGANN; Buena Vista HS; Saginaw, MI; Pres Frsh Cls; Cls Rep Soph Cls; Cl Rep Jr Cls; Trs Sr Cls; Hon Rl; NHS; Rptr Sch Nwsp; Sci Clb; Capt Bsktbl; Trk; Univ Of Michigan; Bio Chem.

JACKSON, PATRICIA; Theodore Roosevelt HS; Gary, IN; Aud/Vis; Chrs; Chrh Wkr; Debate Tm; Hon Rl; NHS; Fr Clb; FTA; Rdo Clb; College; Criminal Justice.

JACKSON, PAULA J; Southwestern HS; Hanover, IN; Cls Rep Frsh Cls; Cls Rep Soph Cls; Cl Rep Jr Cls; Cls Rep Sr Cls; Hon Rl; NHS; Stu Cncl; FHA; Chrldng; Ball St Univ; Interior Dsgn.

JACKSON, PENNY; Hazel Park HS; Hazel Pk, MI; Sch Pl; Stg Crw; Fr Clb; Pep Clb; Mas Awd; Lawence Tech; Elec Eng.

JACKSON, RICHARD; Harding HS; Marion, OH; Pres Frsh Cls; Pres Soph Cls; Band; Hon Rl; NHS; Sch Pl; Spn Clb; Bsbl; Letter Bsktbl; Letter Ftbl; Crissinger Awd 79; Schlrshp Ohio Wesleyan Univ For 4 Yrs; Ohio Wesleyan Univ; Admin Bus.

JACKSON, RICHARD; Elk Garden HS; Elk Garden, WV; Cls Rep Frsh Cls; Cl Rep Jr Cls; Am Leg Boys St; Hon Rl; Sch Pl; Stu Cncl; Bsktbl; Mgrs;

Cross Cntry Awd For Mst Imprved Runner 78; Potomac St Univ; Dr.

JACKSON, RICHARD; Highland HS; Anderson, IN; 13/407 Cmnty Wkr; Hon Rl; Jr NHS; NHS; Letter Bsbl; Ftbl; C of C Awd; Purdue Univ; Vet.

JACKSON, RICK; Gallia Acad; Gallipolis, OH; Sci Clb; Spn Clb; Ohi Univ; Civil Engr.

JACKSON, ROBERT; Edwardsburg HS; Edwardsburg, MI; Hon Rl; Letter Bsbl; College.

JACKSON, ROCHELLE; Highland HS; Anderson, IN; Band; Chrh Wkr; Sec Girl Scts; Hon Rl; NHS; 4-H; Fr Clb; PPFtbl; 4-H Awd; Pres Awd; Band Awd Flute 2 Solo Awds 76; Purdue Univ; Engr.

JACKSON, RUBY; Tipton HS; Tipton, IN; Sec FBLA; Sec OEA; Pep Clb; Ball St Univ; Bus.

JACKSON, RUSSELL; Jefferson HS; Lafayette, IN; 1/560 Cls Rep Frsh Cls; Cls Rep Sr Cls; Val; Am Leg Boys St; Band; Chrh Wkr; Hon Rl; Jr NHS; Natl Forn Lg; VP NHS; Youth Of Month 1978; Honored By Rotary Club; Elk Club Most Imprtnt Stdnt 1978; De Pauw Univ; Foreign Corrspndt.

JACKSON, RUTH; Oakwood HS; Dayton, OH; FCA; Hon Rl; JA; NHS; Ed Yrbk; Letter Bsktbl; Capt Hockey; Capt Chrldng; IM Sprt; JA Awd; Univ; Psych.

JACKSON, SANDRA E; Muskegon Hts Sr HS; Muskegon Hts, MI; Pres Frsh Cls; Cls Rep Soph Cls; Cl Rep Jr Cls; Cls Rep Sr Cls; Band; Hon Rl; NHS; Stu Cncl; Trk; Mgrs; Muskegon Cmnty Coll; Resp Ther.

JACKSON, SANDY; Bluefield HS; Bluefld, WV; 66/285 Capt Drl Tm; Hon Rl; Stu Cncl; Pep Clb; Sec Spn Clb; East Tenn State Univ; Spec Ed.

JACKSON, SHELIA; Regina HS; Cleveland, OH; Chrh Wkr; JA; Coll; Med.

JACKSON, SONYA; Meadowdale HS; Dayton, OH; 19/274 Pres Sr Cls; Cmnty Wkr; Hon Rl; Off Ade; OEA; Pep Clb; Chrldng; Univ Of Cincinnati; Comp Sci.

JACKSON, SUSAN R; Theodore Roosevelt HS; Kent, OH; 11/400 Band; Chrs; Hon Rl; NHS; Orch; Yth Flsp; Drama Clb; Pep Clb; Hockey; Natl Merit SF; Univ; Piano.

JACKSON, SYLVIA; Alpena HS; Ossineke, MI; Hon Rl; Sch Mus; Sch Pl; Stg Crw; Drama Clb; Ger Clb; Alpena Comm Coll; Flight Attndnt.

JACKSON, TAMARA; East HS; Columbus, OH; Pres Sr Cls; Am Leg Aux Girls St; Chrs; Chrh Wkr; Drl Tm; Girl Scts; Hon Rl; Jr NHS; NHS; Off Ade; Vllybl Letter 78; Reporter At Ft Hayes Optical Class 78; Stud Council Rep 78; Ft Hayes Career Cntr; Optometry.

JACKSON, TAMMY; Tyler County HS; New Martinsvl, WV; 5/90 Am Leg Aux Girls St; Hon Rl; Sec JA; Stu Cncl; Yrbk; VP FHA; FTA; Pep Clb; Salem Coll; Elem Ed.

JACKSON, TARA; Ridgemont HS; Mt Victory, OH; 12/39 Cls Rep Soph Cls; Cl Rep Jr Cls; Trs Sr Cls; Girl Scts; Hon Rl; NHS; Stu Cncl; Pres FHA;.

JACKSON, TERESA; Rutherford B Hayes HS; Delawre, OH; Chrh Wkr; Cmnty Wkr; Girl Scts; Off Ade; Scr Kpr; Tmr; Ohio State; Law.

JACKSON, THOMAS; Eaton HS; Camden, OH; Stu Cncl; Yth Flsp; 4-H; Pres FFA; Lat Clb; Pep Clb; Ftbl; Trk; Cit Awd; 4-H Awd; Washington D C Ldrshp Cnfnrce; Ohio St Univ; Ag.

JACKSON, TINA; Brooke HS; Weirton, WV; 178/403 Trs Frsh Cls; Sec Soph Cls; Sec Jr Cls; Chrh Wkr; Hon Rl; Lit Mag; Stu Cncl; Spn Clb; Swmmng; IM Sprt; West Virginia Univ; Dietetics.

JACKSON, TOM; Spencer HS; Spencer, WV; Sch Pl; Stg Crw; Bsbl; Bus Schl.

JACKSON, VALARIE; Northern Sr HS; Detroit, MI; Cmp Fr Grls; Hon Rl; JA; Jr NHS; NHS; Off Ade; FDA; FTA; Pep Clb; Spn Clb; Univ Of Michigan; Med.

JACKSON, VALERIE; Chadsey HS; Detroit, MI; Chrs; Chrh Wkr; Hon Rl; Red Cr Ade; Sct Actv; Yth Flsp; Boys Clb Am; FBLA; Swmmng; Ten; Wayne State Univ; Acctg.

JACKSON, VENAS; Lakeview HS; Howard City, MI; Cls Rep Sr Cls; Chrs; Hon Rl; Stu Cncl; Yrbk; FTA; Spn Clb; Capt Chrldng; GAA; IM Sprt; Schlrshp Cert; Achvmnt Awd; College; Law.

JACOB, KENT; Walnut Hills HS; Cincinnati, OH; Boy Scts; Debate Tm; Hon Rl; Hosp Ade; Natl Forn Lg; Sch Mus; Sch Pl; Stg Crw; Swmmng; Awd & Recgntn For Debt Team 78; MIP For Swimming 76; Bar Assoc Debt In Explore 77; Univ; Pre Law.

JACOBON, TAMMY; Sparta Sr HS; Sparta, MI; Hon Rl; Pom Pon;.

JACOBONI, FRANK; St Agatha HS; Farmington Hill, MI; Hon Rl; Spn Clb; Coach Actv; Univ Of Michigan.

JACOBS, AMY; Durand Area HS; Durand, MI; 33/221 Cls Rep Frsh Cls; Cls Rep Soph Cls; Band; Chrs; Chrh Wkr; Cmnty Wkr; Hon Rl; Mdrgl; NHS; Off Ade; Stu Of The Wk 78; ACT Schlrshp 79; Jobs Daughter Schlrshp 79; Univ Of Michigan; Bus.

JACOBS, DAVE; Fredericktown HS; Fred, OH; FCA; Hon Rl; Drama Clb; Pep Clb; Spn Clb; Letter Bsbl; Bsktbl; Ftbl; IM Sprt; Scr Kpr; Univ.

JACOBS, DIANE; Yellow Springs HS; Yellow Sprg, OH; 3/79 Trs Frsh Cls; Trs Soph Cls; Trs Jr Cls; NHS; Sch Pl; Drama Clb; Letter Bsktbl; Letter Trk; College; Comm Art.

JACOBS, DIANNA; Philip Barbour HS; Flemington, WV; Band; Hon Rl; NHS; Yth Flsp; 4-H; 4-H Awd; College; Elementary Education.

JACOBS, JAMES; Tri HS; New Lisbon, IN; 1/84 Aud/Vis; Hon Rl; NHS; Red Cr Ade; Stg Crw; FFA; Rdo Clb; Dnfth Awd; JETS Awd; Univ; Engr.

JACOBS, JAMES L; Tri Jr Sr HS; New Lisbon, IN; 1/84 Aud/Vis; Hon Rl; NHS; Red Cr Ade; Stg Crw; Rdo Clb; Dnfth Awd; JETS Awd; Natl Merit Ltr; Purdue Univ; Elec Engr.

JACOBS, JULI; Revere HS; Hinckley, OH; Pres Soph Cls; Band; Chrs; Gov Hon Prg Awd; Akron Univ; Comp Engr.

JACOBS, JULIE; Arcadia HS; Findlay, OH; Band; Girl Scts; Hon Rl; NHS; Yth Flsp; Yrbk; FHA; Trk; Chrldng; Scr Kpr; College.

JACOBS, KIM; Huntington HS; Chillicothe, OH; Band; Chrh Wkr; NHS; Yrbk; 4-H; Fr Clb; FTA; Sec OEA; Trk; Chrldng; Ohio Univ; Journalism.

JACOBS, LAURENCE; Essexville Garber HS; Essexville, MI; 53/185 Trs Frsh Cls; Trs Soph Cls; Trs Jr Cls; Chrs; Natl Forn Lg; Sch Mus; Sch Pl; Pep Clb; Delta Coll; Brdcstng.

JACOBS, LINETTE; St Johns HS; St Johns, MI; Band; Hon Rl; Hosp Ade; Sch Mus; Sch Pl; 4-H; 4-H Awd; Elem Tchrs Aide Houghton Miflan Tutorial Prog 78; Lake Superior St Coll; Med.

JACOBS, LORI; Algonac HS; Algonac, MI; Cls Rep Frsh Cls; Cls Rep Sr Cls; Hon Rl; NHS; Stu Cncl; Rptr Sch Nwsp; OEA; 1st Plc St 8th Plc Natl Bus Office Educ Clb Stenographic 2 Comp 79; Bus Educ Dept Awd For Stud Excllnc 79; St Clair Cnty Cmnty Coll; Exec Sec.

JACOBS, MARK; Marquette HS; Marquette, MI; Sal; Am Leg Boys St; Sch Mus; Stg Crw; Yrbk; Mic Tech Univ; Engr.

JACOBS, MARK W; Marquette Sr HS; Marquette, MI; 4/500 Am Leg Boys St; Sch Mus; Sct Actv; Sprt Ed Yrbk; Natl Merit SF; Natl Merit Schl; Michigan Tech Univ; Engr.

JACOBS, MICHAEL; Rockford Sr HS; Rockford, MI; 3/400 Cls Rep Sr Cls; Am Leg Boys St; Band; Hon Rl; NHS; Lat Clb; Keyettes; Letter Bsktbl; Letter Crs Cntry; Letter Trk; St Pres Of Jr Classical League 77 78 & 79; Athlete Of Yr 78; Top 10 Schlrshp 79; Central Michigan Univ; Scndry Educ.

JACOBS, MICHAEL D; Bedford N Lawrence HS; Bedford, IN; 3/400 Cls Rep Soph Cls; Cls Rep Sr Cls; Sal; Boy Scts; Chrs; Debate Tm; Hon Rl; Natl Forn Lg; NHS; FTA; Indiana Univ; Accounting.

JACOBS, MOLLY; Rossford HS; Rossford, OH; Chrs; Hon Rl; Sch Mus; Sch Pl; Rptr Yrbk; Drama Clb; Fr Clb; Letter Crs Cntry; Ohio St Univ; Medicine.

JACOBS, RANDALL S; South Range HS; North Lima, OH; VP Frsh Cls; Chrs; Hon Rl; Lbry Ade; NHS; Sch Mus; Stu Cncl; Rptr Sch Nwsp; Drama Clb; Letter Bsktbl; Univ; Bus Admin.

JACOBS, ROGER; Springs Valley HS; West Baden, IN; Hst Frsh Cls; Cls Rep Soph Cls; Pres Jr Cls; Band; Hon Rl; Stu Cncl; Letter Bsbl; Letter Bsktbl; Letter Ftbl; Coach Actv; Perfect Attendance Awrd; College; Computer Sci.

JACOBS, SHARON; Barr Reeve HS; Loogootee, IN; 5048 Hon Rl; Lbry Ade; Rptr Yrbk; Beta Clb; FHA; Pep Clb; Pres Spn Clb; Univ; Elem Educ Tchr.

JACOBS, TAMRA J; Circleville HS; Circleville, OH; 13/231 AFS; Band; Cmp Fr Grls; Chrh Wkr; Girl Scts; Hon Rl; NHS; Sch Pl; Pres Yth Flsp; Drama Clb; English Merit Society 1976; Jerry Lewis Tel 1975; Jr Classical League 1979; Univ Of Tennessee; Deaf Educ.

JACOBSEN, NANCY; Zeeland HS; W Olive, MI; Band; Hon Rl; Rptr Yrbk; 4-H; 4-H Awd; Spec Educ.

JACOBSON, DAN; Madison HS; Madison, OH; 120/290 Cls Rep Sr Cls; Hon Rl; Stu Cncl; Crs Cntry; Wrstlng; Ohi State; Landscape Design.

JACOBSON, LORI; Luther L Wright HS; Ironwood, MI; 3/179 Pres Frsh Cls; Chrs; Chrh Wkr; NHS; Off Ade; Sch Mus; Stu Cncl; Yth Flsp; Gogebic Comm College; Court Reporter.

JACOBSON, MARK; Leelanau HS; Glen Arbor, MI; Cls Rep Soph Cls; Pres Jr Cls; Boy Scts; Chrs; Hon Rl; Sch Pl; Stu Cncl; Yth Flsp; Ed Sch Nwsp; Sch Nwsp; Cornell Univ; Hotel Admin.

JACOBSON, MARSHA; Rayen HS; Youngstown, OH; 9/220 Band; Hon Rl; Sch Pl; Stu Cncl; Key Clb; Lat Clb; Gym; College; Pediatrician.

JACOBSON, TAMMY; Sparta Sr HS; Sparta, MI; Hon Rl; Pom Pon; Receptnst.

JACOBSON, THOMAS R; Heritage Christian HS; Indianapolis, IN; Band; Chrs; Chrh Wkr; FCA; Sch Mus; Sch Pl; Stg Crw; Grace College; Engr.

JACONETTE, MARK; St Francis De Sales HS; Columbus, OH; 54/182 Aud/Vis; Chrh Wkr; Hon Rl; Lbry Ade; Bsbl; Ftbl; Wrstlng; Rotary Awd; College; Comp Studies.

JACOSKY, LENNY; Flat Rock HS; Flat Rock, MI; 2/112 Sal; Hon Rl; Treas NHS; Bsktbl; Capt Ftbl; Capt Trk; College; Busns.

JACQUAY, JUSTINA; Northrop HS; Ft Wayne, IN; 79/587 Girl Scts; Off Ade; OEA; Trk; Mgrs; Scr Kpr; Tmr; Cit Awd; VP St Francis College; Comp.

JACQUOT, KEN; Sycamore HS; Cincinnati, OH; Boy Scts; Hon Rl; NHS; Sch Pl; Sct Actv; Stg Crw; Drama Clb; Trk; Wrstlng; Ohio St Univ; Med.

JADACH, NELLA E; Bishop Foley HS; Royal Oak, MI; 1/200 Am Leg Aux Girls St; Chrs; Debate Tm; Hon Rl; NHS; Pol Wkr; Sch Mus; Rptr Sch Nwsp; Chrldng;.

JAEB, MIKE; East Canton HS; E Canton, OH; 4/107 Pres Soph Cls; Cls Rep Soph Cls; VP Jr Cls; Am Leg Boys St; Hon Rl; Jr NHS; NHS; Sprt Ed Yrbk; Letter Ftbl; College; Comm Art.

JAEGER, JEANNE; Escanaba HS; Escanaba, MI; 102/450 Trs Frsh Cls; Sec Soph Cls; Sec Jr Cls; Sec Sr Cls; Chrs; Hon Rl; Sch Nwsp; Letter Ten; Mich State Univ.

JAFFE, CARRIE; Oak Hill HS; Jackson, OH; 16/112 Hon Rl; Lbry Ade; Sch Nwsp; Beta Clb; Mbr Of Flag Corps 78; Schlshp Fro 3 Yrs & Pl In Dist 2 Of Those 3 Yrs 76 79; Ohio Univ; Psych.

JAGER, CHARLES; Lakeshore HS; Stevensville, MI; 17/295 Cl Rep Jr Cls; Cls Rep Sr Cls; Band; NHS; Quill & Scroll; Stu Cncl; Sprt Ed Sch Nwsp; Ger Clb; Bsktbl; Am Leg Awd; Kalamazoo Coll.

JAGERS, ANGELA; Lumen Cordium HS; Cleveland, OH; Cmp Fr Grls; Chrs; Pres Chrh Wkr; Drl Tm; FCA; Hon Rl; Pres JA; Bsbl; Swmmng; Univ Of Cincinnati; Nursing.

JAGGER, TRUDY; Defiance HS; Defiance, OH; 71/295 Band; Chrh Wkr; Drl Tm; Girl Scts; Hon Rl; JA; Stg Crw; Yth Flsp; Spn Clb; Letter Trk; College.

JAGGERS, SANDRA; Edon HS; Edon, OH; Band; Chrs; Sch Mus; Sch Pl; 4-H; Pep Clb; 4-H Awd;.

JAGGERS, STEVEN; Frankfort Sr HS; Frankfort, IN; 6/245 NHS; Sprt Ed Sch Nwsp; Drama Clb; FBLA; Key Clb; Pres Spn Clb; Outstndng Soph Spnsh Stu 77; High Life Staff Awd HS Ppr 78; Spanish Awd 78; St Band Cntst 1st Pl 76; Taylor Univ; Painting.

JAGGI, DONN; Fenton Sr HS; Fenton, MI; Am Leg Boys St; Cmnty Wkr; Quill & Scroll; Sprt Ed Sch Nwsp; Bsbl; Glf; Wrstlng; Natl Merit Ltr; Spirit & Hustle Awd For Wrtlng 78; Annl Law Day Part 79; Schl Newsppr 77 80; Michigan St Univ; Jrnlsm.

JAGLOWSKI, CHARLES; West Catholic HS; Grand Rapids, MI; 1/290 Hon Rl; JA; NHS; Sch Mus; Fr Clb; IM Sprt; Univ; Law.

JAGOSZ, ROBINN; Fraser HS; Fraser, MI; Pres Frsh Cls; Band; Chrs; Hon Rl; NHS; Stu Cncl; Pep Clb; Spn Clb; College; Bookkeeping.

JAHN, KATHI; Ubly Community HS; Ruth, MI; 1/101 Cls Rep Soph Cls; NHS; Red Cr Ade; Pres Stu Cncl; Ed Sch Nwsp; 4-H; FHA; Emp Ruth State Bank; Bank Teller.

JAHRMAN, CHRISTOPHER; Carroll HS; Cutler, IN; Cls Rep Frsh Cls; Cls Rep Soph Cls; Hst Jr Cls; Hon Rl; Off Ade; Stu Cncl; Yth Flsp; Yrbk; Rptr Sch Nwsp; Sch Nwsp; John Butler Editorial Awd From Ball St Univ; Dist Staff Awd From HS Paper; Indiana St Coll; Journalism.

JAJE, STEPHEN; Garden City West Sr HS; Garden City, MI; 14/405 Hon Rl; NHS; Bsbl; Capt Ftbl; IM Sprt; Scr Kpr; MHEAA Schlr 79; Edward Clery Schlrshp Prog 79; Bio Awd 79; Wayne St Univ; Bio.

JAKACKI, PETER A; Bishop Borgess HS; Livonia, MI; Band; Hon Rl; Jr NHS; NHS; Orch; Sch Mus; Sch Pl; Stg Crw; Fr Clb; Bsbl; Natl Hon Soc Gold Cord 79; Kalamazoo Coll; Med.

JAKARY, SUSAN; John Glenn HS; Westland, MI; Hon Rl; Spn Clb; PPFtbl; College; Foreign Lang.

JAKEE, KEITH; Lutheran East HS; Detroit, MI; 29/156 Hon Rl; Pol Wkr; Stu Cncl; Crs Cntry; Ftbl; Trk; Letter Wrstlng; Schlrshp To Operation Bentley Govt Simulation; Michigan St Univ; Science.

JAKES, LORI; Douglas Mac Arthur HS; Saginaw, MI; 3/302 Am Leg Aux Girls St; Chrh Wkr; Hon Rl; NHS; Ger Clb; Trk; Natl Merit Ltr; Outsndng Chem Physics & Govt; Michigan St Univ.

JAKLIC, KIM; Ferndale HS; Ferndale, MI; Chrh Wkr; Cmnty Wkr; Girl Scts; Hon Rl; Stg Crw; Bsbl; Bsktbl; Hon Bio Stdnt 77; Hon Stdnt Trainer For Ferndale Ftbl Team 78; Univ Of Mississippi; Med Tech.

JAKSE, GREGORY; Wickliffe HS; Wickliffe, OH; 25/330 Aud/Vis; Hon Rl; NHS; Cleveland State Univ; Engr.

JAKSETIC, DANIEL; Cardinal Stritch HS; Toledo, OH; 13/172 Hon Rl; NHS; Sprt Ed Yrbk; Sch Nwsp; Bsbl; Crs Cntry; Wrstlng; Univ Of Toledo; Acctg.

JAKUBEK, JOSEPH; Campbell Memorial HS; Campbell, OH; 15/210 Hon Rl; NHS; Mth Clb; Sci Clb; Spn Clb; Glf; Scr Kpr; Youngstown State Univ; Pre Med.

JAKUBIK, PAUL; Catholic Central HS; Northville, MI; 10/205 Boy Scts; NHS; Pol Wkr; Sci Clb; Glf; IM Sprt; Gabriel Richard Awd 76; Metro Detroit Sci Fair Awd 78; MI Outstndng Achvmnt Awd 78; Kalamazoo Coll; Dent.

JAMBE, SUZANNE; Huntington HS; Huntington, WV; 10/280 Hon Rl; NHS; Stu Cncl; Fr Clb; Mth Clb; Pep Clb; Univ Of Vir; Bus.

JAMES, ANGELA; Dominican HS; Detroit, MI; Band; Chrs; Chrh Wkr; Girl Scts; JA; Orch; Sch Mus; Trk; Pom Pon; PPFtbl; Siena Hts Coll; Bio.

JAMES, ANGIE; Loudonville HS; Lakeville, OH; 1/135 Chrs; Hon Rl; Jr NHS; NHS; Stg Crw; Pres Yth Flsp; Yrbk; Rptr Sch Nwsp; 4-H; 4-H Awd; College.

JAMES, ANTHONY; Robichaud HS; Inkster, MI; 3/300 Hst Jr Cls; Boy Scts; Debate Tm; Hon Rl; Boys Clb Am; Bsktbl; Coach Actv; Tmr; Cit Awd; Coll.

JAMES, BEVERLY; Chalker HS; Southington, OH; Am Leg Aux Girls St; Band; Chrh Wkr; Yth Flsp; Ed Sch Nwsp; Rptr Sch Nwsp; Pres Beta Clb; Ohi State Univ; Agri.

JAMES, CAROLYN L; Winfield HS; Winfield, WV; 10/120 Band; Drl Tm; Girl Scts; Hon Rl; Jr NHS; NHS; Off Ade; 4-H; Mth Clb; 4-H Awd; Univ; Lab Tech.

JAMES, CELESTE; Big Creek HS; Caretta, WV; Hon Rl; Rptr Sch Nwsp; Modeling Schl.

JAMES, CYNTHIA; Warren Central HS; Indianapolis, IN; Hon Rl; Lit Mag; Rptr Yrbk; Rptr Sch Nwsp; VP FHA; US Navy; Personnelman.

JAMES, DEBBIE; Champion HS; Warren, OH; Hon Rl; NHS; Off Ade; Sch Pl; Sch Nwsp; OEA; Pep Clb; Letter Trk; Kent St Univ; Office Mgmt.

JAMES, DEBORAH; Floyd Central HS; Georgetown, IN; 48/340 Trs Soph Cls; Cls Rep Soph Cls; Trs Jr Cls; Cl Rep Jr Cls; Trs Sr Cls; Cls Rep Sr Cls; Chrs; Chrh Wkr; Hon Rl; Pol Wkr; Hoosier Schlr 79; Purdue Univ; Bio Med Engr.

JAMES, DEBRA S; Winfield HS; Winfield, WV; Band; Drl Tm; Girl Scts; Hon Rl; Jr NHS; NHS; 4-H; Mth Clb; Spn Clb; 4-H Awd; College; Math.

JAMES, GEORGE; Walter P Chrysler Memrl HS; New Castle, IN; Cmnty Wkr; DECA; Cit Awd; Otstndng Schlrshp For 4 Semesters 78; Industrial Arts Awrd 76; 1st Plc Trophy For Dist 9 Decca Mkt Test 79;.

JAMES, GWEN; Jane Addams HS; Cleveland, OH; Chrs; Chrh Wkr; Off Ade; Yth Flsp; 4-H; Bsbl; Cit Awd; 4-H Awd; Kent State Univ; Architecture.

JAMES, JEFF; Prairie Hts HS; Wolcottville, IN; 21/137 Cls Rep Frsh Cls; Cls Rep Soph Cls; Cl Rep Jr Cls; Cls Rep Sr Cls; Pres Band; Chrs; Chrh Wkr; Hon Rl; Sch Pl; Stg Crw; Hoosier Farmer Awd; FFA Parlimentary Procedure Team; Outstndng Club Mbr 4 H; Purdue Univ; Vet.

JAMES, JOHN; Mt Healthy HS; Cincinnati, OH; 110/508 Boy Scts; Sch Pl; Stg Crw; Rptr Sch Nwsp; VP Drama Clb; Weber St Univ; Film Production.

JAMES, JOSEPH; Kent City HS; Bailey, MI; 15/95 Band; Boy Scts; Hon Rl; NHS; Sci Clb; Letter Bsbl; Letter Ftbl; Scr Kpr; Tmr; Ferris St Univ; Indus Chem.

JAMES, KARLOS; Martin Luther King Jr Sr HS; Detroit, MI; Band; Chrs; Chrh Wkr; Cmnty Wkr; Hon Rl; Lbry Ade; Orch; Sch Pl; Stu Cncl; Drama Clb; Univ; Bio.

JAMES, KATRINA; Central HS; Detroit, MI; Girl Scts; Hon Rl; Michigan St Univ; Med.

JAMES, KENNY; Waynesfield Goshen HS; Waynesfield, OH; 3/46 Pres Frsh Cls; Pres Sr Cls; Am Leg Boys St; Band; Hon Rl; Jr NHS; NHS; Spn Clb; Bsktbl; Letter Ftbl; College; History.

JAMES, LORI; Benjamin Logan HS; Rushsylvania, OH; Band; Chrs; Hon Rl; Sch Mus; Yth Flsp; 4-H; FHA; Am Leg Awd; DAR Awd; 4-H Awd; Lima Tech Coll; Dent Hygiene.

JAMES, LORREEN; Eau Claire HS; Eau Claire, MI; Band; Cmnty Wkr; FCA; Hon Rl; 4-H; Pep Clb; Bsktbl; Chrldng; Ferris St Coll; Acctg.

JAMES, MAUREEN T; Seton HS; Cincinnati, OH; 49/310 Pres Frsh Cls; Cls Rep Soph Cls; Sec Jr Cls; Chrs; Chrh Wkr; NHS; VP Stu Cncl; Socr; Letter Swmmng; Cit Awd; Xavier Univ.

JAMES, MICHAEL; Hampshire HS; Augusta, WV; Hon Rl; Off Ade; Berea Coll; Indstrl Arts.

JAMES, ROBERT; Miami Trace HS; Greenfield, OH; 8/256 Am Leg Boys St; Boy Scts; Hon Rl; NHS; 4-H; FFA; Sci Clb; Letter Ftbl; Letter Trk; Letter Wrstlng; Ohio St Univ; Voc Agri.

JAMES, ROBERT; Fayetteville HS; Fayetteville, WV; 1/80 Hon Rl; Treas NHS; Fr Clb; W V Institute Of Tech; Chemical Engr.

JAMES, TIM; Champion HS; Warren, OH; Val; FCA; Hon Rl; NHS; Stu Cncl; Letter Bsbl; Glf; Scr Kpr; Cit Awd; Natl Merit Schl; Arizona St Univ; Acctg.

JAMESON, ANDY; Napoleon HS; Napoleon, OH; Band; Chrs; Chrh Wkr; Hon Rl; Sch Pl; 4-H; Lat Clb; Pep Clb; Swmmng; Ohio Northern Univ; Sci.

JAMESON, MARK A; Goshen HS; Goshen, IN; Hon Rl; JA; Stu Cncl; Fr Clb; Letter Swmmng; IM Sprt; Indiana Univ; Law.

JAMESON, MARY; Tippecanoe Valley HS; Rochester, IN; 9/180 Pres Frsh Cls; Pres Soph Cls; Chrs; Chrh Wkr; NHS; 4-H; Pep Clb; Gym; Swmmng; Trk; Univ; Bus.

JAMEYSON, JULIE; Medina Sr HS; Medina, OH; 14/359 Girl Scts; Hon Rl; NHS; Red Cr Ade; Drama Clb; 4-H; Ger Clb; Pep Clb; GAA; PPFtbl; Bowling Green St Univ.

JAMIESON, SCOTT; Andrean HS; Gary, IN; 52/251 Chrs; Hon Rl; Jr NHS; Stg Crw; Drama Clb; Spn Clb; Letter Trk; Univ; Agri.

JAMIOT, MARILYN; Cleveland Cntrl Cath HS; Cleveland, OH; Girl Scts; Hon Rl; Sct Actv; Stg Crw; GAA; IM Sprt; Twrlr; Cleveland St Univ; Personnel Mgmt.

JAMISON, CRAIG; Freeland HS; Freeland, MI; Aud/Vis; Band; Hon Rl; Rptr Yrbk; Saginaw Valley St College.

JAMISON, RODGER; John Hay HS; Cleveland, OH; Chrh Wkr; Debate Tm; Graduate Of Andover Summer Session Phillips Acad; Louis Stokes Honor For Exc; Awd Of Distinction; Univ Of Cincinnati; Engr.

JAMISON, VANESSE; Jane Addams Voc HS; Cleveland, OH; Sch Pl; Sct Actv; Drama Clb; Swmmng; Trk; IM Sprt; Cit Awd; Natl Merit Ltr; 2nd Pl Awd Trophy Bike Rodeo; Perfect Attend; San Jose St Univ; Comp Analyst.

JAMMER, BRENDA; Bay City Western HS; Auburn, MI; Chrh Wkr; Hon Rl; NHS; Lk Superior St U; Natural Resources.

JAMNICK, TAMMY; Milan HS; Ypsilanti, MI; VP Jr Cls; Pres Sr Cls; Hon Rl; Jr NHS; Rptr Sch Nwsp; Spn Clb; Bsbl; Chrldng; PPFtbl;.

JAMROS, ROBERT; William G Mather HS; Shingleton, MI; Aud/Vis; NMU; Civil Engr.

JANDA, SCOTT; Gilmour Acad; Chagrin Fls, OH; 12/82 Trs Jr Cls; Pres Sr Cls; Mdrgl; Chrh Wkr; Hon Rl; NHS; Yth Flsp; Yrbk; Sch Nwsp; IM Sprt; Univ; Bus.

JANECZEK, DENISE; Madison HS; Madison, OH; 34/250 VP Boy Scts; Chrs; Hon Rl; Hosp Ade; NHS; Drama Clb; Sec Ger Clb; Crs Cntry; Scr Kpr; Tmr; College; Nursing.

JANEK, JEAN; United Local HS; Winona, OH; 37/130 Band; Girl Scts; Hon Rl; Sch Pl; Rptr Yrbk; Fr Clb; Pep Clb; Letter Bsktbl; Letter Trk; GAA; Univ Of Akron; Acctg.

JANES, BRIAN; Grand Rapids Union HS; Grand Rapids, MI; 1/350 Cls Rep Frsh Cls; Cl Rep Jr Cls; VP Sr Cls; Cls Rep Sr Cls; Val; Hon Rl; Jr NHS; NHS; Pol Wkr; Stu Cncl; Gustave Wolf Awd 78; Hope Acad Schlsp Gold Key Athltc Key 7.; Hope Univ; Psych.

JANES, CHARLIE; West Geauga HS; Novelty, OH; Chrs; Hon Rl; Sprt Ed Yrbk; Ftbl; Letter Trk; Letter Coach Actv; IM Sprt; Mgrs; Scr Kpr; Tmr; Univ; Cmnctns.

JANES, DUANE; University HS; Morgantown, WV; Band; Boy Scts; Chrs; Chrh Wkr; Debate Tm; Hon Rl; Jr NHS; Sct Actv; Drama Clb; West Virginia Univ; Vet.

JANES, JUDITH; Morgan HS; Stockport, OH; 13/250 Hon Rl; NHS; Pol Wkr; FHA; Scr Kpr;.

JANES, KIM; Triton HS; Bourbon, IN; 3/90 Trs Frsh Cls; Sec Soph Cls; Am Leg Aux Girls St; Sec Chrh Wkr; Hon Rl; Pres NHS; 4-H; FBLA; VP FHA; Pep Clb; Ball St Univ; Acctg.

JANEZIC, PATRICIA; Streetsboro HS; Streetsboro, OH; Cls Rep Soph Cls; Cl Rep Jr Cls; Hon Rl; Jr NHS; Pres Stu Cncl; Rptr Yrbk; FTA; OEA; Trk; Univ; Ct Steno.

JANG, EDWARD; High School; Cincinnati, OH; 18/264 Band; Cmnty Wkr; Hon Rl; Hosp Ade; NHS; Socr; IM Sprt; College; Pre Med.

JANICZEK, NANCY; St Florian HS; Detroit, MI; 1/75 Sec Frsh Cls; Sec Soph Cls; Sec Jr Cls; Sec Sr Cls; Hon Rl; Natl Forn Lg; NHS; Rptr Yrbk; Letter Bsktbl; Univ Of Michigan; Chemistry.

JANIEC, SHERRY; St Hedwig HS; Detroit, MI; Sec Frsh Cls; Sec Soph Cls; Sec Jr Cls; Chrs; Hon Rl; Off Ade; Rptr Yrbk; Chrldng; 1st Honors Historical Speech; Class Sec Ach; Wayne St Univ; Drama.

JANINI, CHARLES; Green Senior HS; Akron, OH; Boy Scts; Hon Rl; NHS; Sct Actv; Crs Cntry; Ftbl; Trk; Wrstlng; IM Sprt; College.

JANIS, LINDA; Lumen Cordium HS; Solon, OH; Cls Rep Frsh Cls; VP Soph Cls; Drl Tm; Hon Rl; Stg Crw; Stu Cncl; IM Sprt; Stdnt Advisory Bd Awd 77; Univ; Cmnctns.

JANISZEWSKI, KAREN; Northrop HS; Ft Wayne, IN; Chrs; Hon Rl; Sch Mus; PPFtbl; IUPU; Dental Hygenist.

JANITOR, LISA A; Cuyahoga Hts HS; Brooklyn Hts, OH; 1/70 Girl Scts; Hon Rl; Lit Mag; Fr Clb; Pep Clb; Trk; IM Sprt; PPFtbl; Natl Merit Ltr; Schl Spllng Champ 75 79; Chem Corp Cert Of Mert 79; St In Oh Test Of Schlstc Achvmnt 77 79; Case Western Reserve Univ; Math.

JANJANIN, DAN; Ursuline HS; Youngstown, OH; 66/350 Cmnty Wkr; Hon Rl; Wrstlng; College; Chem.

JANK, CARRIE; Grosse Ile HS; Grosse Ile, MI; Debate Tm; Girl Scts; Hon Rl; Natl Forn Lg; Sch Pl; Stg Crw; Drama Clb; Spn Clb; Swmmng; Univ; Elec Engr.

JANKE, MATTHEW; Parma Sr HS; Parma, OH; 110/800 Letter Ftbl; Letter Hockey; Coll.

JANKE, MICHAEL; Medina HS; Medina, OH; 39/341 Band; Hon Rl; Lit Mag; NHS; Yth Flsp; Key Clb; Letter Crs Cntry; Trk; College; Advertising.

JANKOWIAK, KATHY; Manistee HS; Manistee, MI; 28/186 Girl Scts; Hon Rl; Jr NHS; NHS; Sch Pl; Yrbk; Sch Nwsp; Drama Clb; Sec Fr Clb; Editor In Chief At Michigan Yth In Govt 79; Pres Of Schl Tri Hi Y Clb; Central Michigan Univ; Jrnlsm.

JANKOWSKI, JEFFERY J; St Francis De Sales HS; Toledo, OH; 29/180 Chrh Wkr; Hon Rl; Hosp Ade; Sch Mus; Stg Crw; Stu Cncl; Latin Honor Society; Univ Of Toledo; Health.

JANMEY, DIANE; Lutheran West HS; N Olmsted, OH; Hon Rl; NHS; Yrbk; Sci Clb; Spn Clb; Crs Cntry; Letter Trk; Letter Mgrs; Tmr;.

JANNECK, KARLA; Danville HS; Danville, IN; 6/155 Am Leg Aux Girls St; Band; Girl Scts; Hon Rl; Lbry Ade; NHS; Quill & Scroll; Sch Mus; Sch Pl; Stg Crw; Purdue Univ; Sci.

JANNING, DOUG; Alter HS; Dayton, OH; Band; Hon Rl; NHS; Orch; IM Sprt; Natl Merit SF; Univ Of Dayton; Comp Sci.

JANNING, J; Our Lady Of Angels HS; Cincinnati, OH; Letter Socr; GAA; Univ Of Cincinnati; Law Enforcement.

JANOS, CYNTHIA; Lake Catholic HS; Painesville, OH; Chrs; Chrh Wkr; Cmnty Wkr; FCA; Hon Rl; Yrbk; Sch Nwsp; Pep Clb; Letter Bsbl; Coach Actv; Gregg Typing Awd; Cert Of Merit Typing I; GCC-GAC All St Sftbl Tm; College; Horticulture.

JANOSKO, STEPHAN; Keystone HS; La Grange, OH; 4/133 Band; Boy Scts; Chrh Wkr; Hon Rl; NHS; Sct Actv; Ed Yrbk; Rptr Yrbk; Pres Drama Clb; Pep Clb; Keystone PTA Schlrshp 79; Eng For A Day 79; Ohio St Univ; Bio Med Engr.

JANOTA, LORRIE; Nordonia HS; Northfield, OH; Cls Rep Frsh Cls; Cls Rep Soph Cls; Cl Rep Jr Cls; NHS; Sch Mus; Trk; IM Sprt; Mgrs; College; Sci.

JANOVEC, JOHN; Norton HS; Norton, OH; 1/370 Aud/Vis; Chrh Wkr; Hon Rl; Jr NHS; NHS; Stu Cncl; VP Lat Clb; Mbr Of Schls Tm That Took Oh Schlstc Acvmnt Test Bio 78; Mbr Of Tm Appeared On TV Show Acad Challenge 79; Univ; Acctg.

JANOWSKI, GREGG; Bay City All Saints HS; Bay City, MI; 1/167 Val; Band; Hon Rl; NHS; Sch Mus; Glf; Natl Merit SF; Michigan Tech Univ; Mech Engr.

JANSEN, GREG; Bishop Ready HS; Columbus, OH; 34/142 Cls Rep Soph Cls; Hon Rl; Stu Cncl; Crs Cntry; Wrstlng; Ohio St Univ; Bus Admin.

JANSMA JR, DAVID; Calvin Christian HS; Grandville, MI; 2/120 Hon Rl; Crs Cntry; Swmmng; Trk; IM Sprt; Scr Kpr; Natl Merit Ltr; Univ; Pre Med.

JANSON, RAYMOND; Canton South HS; Canton, OH; Band; Boy Scts; Chrh Wkr; Hon Rl; Natl Forn Lg; NHS; VP Stu Cncl; Sch Nwsp; Drama Clb; 4-H; Univ; Law.

JANSON, TERRI; Richmond HS; Richmond, IN; 32/550 Cl Rep Jr Cls; Chrs; Hon Rl; NHS; Letter Swmmng; College.

JANSSEN, PAM; A D Johnston HS; Bessemer, MI; Cl Rep Jr Cls; Band; Hon Rl; Sch Mus; Pep Clb; Bsktbl; Trk; Chrldng; Michigan St Univ; Bio.

JANUS, JON; Newton Falls HS; Newton Falls, OH; Chrs; Hon Rl; Sch Pl; Pep Clb; Spn Clb; Bsbl; Bsktbl; Ftbl; Coach Actv; Univ.

JANUSH, RACHELLE; Bishop Foley HS; Detroit, MI; Cls Rep Frsh Cls; Am Leg Aux Girls St; Chrs; Chrh Wkr; Hon Rl; Lbry Ade; Mod UN; Natl Forn Lg; NHS; Pol Wkr; 5th Plc Forensics Det Metro Catholic Forensic League 76; Natl Sci Foundation Schlrshp 79; Wayne St Univ; Med.

JANZ, ROBERT; Clinton Prairie HS; Frankfort, IN; Hon Rl; Stg Crw; Sci Clb; Spn Clb; Bsbl; Crs Cntry; Glf; IM Sprt; Ball State Univ; Pre Den.

JANZ, ROGER; Clinton Prairie HS; Frankfort, IN; 14/91 Hon Rl; Lbry Ade; Sci Clb; Spn Clb; Letter Bsbl; Crs Cntry; Wrstlng; Coach Actv; IM Sprt; Univ; Law.

JAPCZYNSKI, J; Catholic Central HS; Steubenvll, OH; Boy Scts; Chrh Wkr; Hon Rl; Sct Actv; Key Clb; Lat Clb; Wrstlng; USC; Bus.

JAPCZYNSKI, JOSEPH C; Catholic Ctrl HS; Steubenville, OH; Boy Scts; Chrh Wkr; Hon Rl; Sct Actv; Key Clb; Lat Clb; Wrstlng; OSC; Bus.

JAPES, LISA M; Adlai Stevenson HS; Livonia, MI; 32/813 Hon Rl; Natl Merit SF; Univ Of Michigan; Phys Ther.

JA QUAY, ANITA; Dayton Christian HS; Kettering, OH; 12/92 Chrh Wkr; Girl Scts; Hon Rl; NHS; Sch Mus; Chrldng; GAA; IM Sprt; Cedarville College; Registered Nurse.

JAQUAY, J; Bishop Watterson HS; Columbus, OH; 64/280 Cls Rep Frsh Cls; Trs Soph Cls; Cl Rep Jr Cls; Band; Chrs; Chrh Wkr; Cmnty Wkr; FCA; Girl Scts; Hon Rl; Univ; Bus Mgmt.

JAQUAYS, JOLENE; Jackson Cnty Western HS; Spring Arbor, MI; 12/171 Band; Girl Scts; NHS; Yth Flsp; Pres 4-H; Pres Pep Clb; Spn Clb; 4-H Awd; Central Michigan Univ.

JARA, JULIE; Austintown Fitch HS; Youngstown, OH; 30/662 Cls Rep Frsh Cls; Cls Rep Soph Cls; Sec Sr Cls; Hon Rl; NHS; Off Ade; Stu Cncl; Pres Y-Teens; Treas DECA; Winner Ohio St DECA Competition Genl Merch Series; Youngstown Ed Foundation Schlrshp; Youngstown State Univ; Acctg.

JARABEK, CHRIS; Charlotte HS; Charlotte, MI; Hon Rl; Letter Bsktbl; Letter Crs Cntry; Letter Ftbl; Letter Trk; Coach Actv; Cit Awd; Aquinas College; Bus Admin.

JARC, CHRISTOPHER; Willoughby South HS; Eastlake, OH; 25/454 Pres Jr Cls; Pres Sr Cls; Am Leg Boys St; Boy Scts; Hon Rl; NHS; Stu Cncl; Rptr Yrbk; Bsktbl; Am Leg Awd; Ohio St Univ; Med.

JARDING, LISA M; Peru HS; Peru, IN; Cls Rep Frsh Cls; Cls Rep Soph Cls; Cl Rep Jr Cls; Am Leg Aux Girls St; Hon Rl; Stu Cncl; Pep Clb; Chrldng; GAA; Mgrs; Univ; Sci.

JARECKI, FRANK L; St Andrew HS; Detroit, MI; Pres Frsh Cls; Pres Jr Cls; Chrs; Hon Rl; NHS; Stg Crw; Rptr Yrbk; Ten;.

JARMAN, JILL; Buckeye North HS; Mingo Junction, OH; Trs Frsh Cls; Girl Scts; Hon Rl; Sch Pl; Drama Clb; 4-H; Pep Clb; Sci Clb; Spn Clb; VICA; Florida State; Biology.

JAROSICK, BARBARA; North Royalton HS; N Royalton, OH; 5/265 Hon Rl; Jr NHS; NHS; Fr Clb; C of C Awd; Lion Awd; Ohio Univ; Art.

JAROSINSKI, MARK; John Marshall HS; Indianapolis, IN; 32/610 Hon Rl; Sci Clb; Bsbl; Letter Ftbl; Letter Wrstlng; Butler Univ; Pharm.

JARRELL, CLAUDIA; Huntington E HS; Huntington, WV; Band; Drm Mjrt; Hon Rl; Jr NHS; FBLA; Spn Clb; College.

JARRELL, DONALD; Sylvania Northview HS; Toledo, OH; 12/176 AFS; Boy Scts; Cmnty Wkr; Hon Rl; NHS; Pol Wkr; Quill & Scroll; Sct Actv; Spn Clb; Letter Bsktbl; Univ; Med.

JARRELL, EUNICE; Crum HS; Dunlow, WV; VP Jr Cls; Chrs; Hon Rl; Jr NHS; Beta Clb; FHA; Marshall Univ; Tchr.

JARRELL, P; Marsh Fork HS; Rock Crk, WV; Hon Rl; Letter Ftbl; Dnfth Awd; Beckley Coll.

JARRELL, PAULA; Marsh Fork HS; Rock Creek, WV; Chrh Wkr; Hon Rl; Jr NHS; Eng Clb; 4-H; Pep Clb; Bsktbl; Trk; Beckley Coll.

JARRELL, SARA; Milton HS; Ona, WV; 6/300 Sec Soph Cls; Hon Rl; Jr NHS; NHS; Sch Pl; Stu Cncl; Spn Clb; Trk; GAA; IM Sprt; Marshall Univ; Pre Law.

JARRETT, ANNETTE; Fayetteville HS; Fayetteville, WV; Chrh Wkr; Hon Rl;.

JARRETT, DEBRA A; West Side Sr HS; Gary, IN; Cl Rep Jr Cls; Hon Rl; Mdrgl; NHS; Y-Teens; DECA; FHA; GAA; Busns Schl; Marketing.

JARRETT, GARY; Winchester Community HS; Winchester, IN; 40/170 Pres Frsh Cls; Am Leg Boys St; Boy Scts; FCA; Hon Rl; Fr Clb; Bsbl; Bsktbl; Ftbl; DAR Awd; Ball State; Elec Engr.

JARRETT, JAMES; Southfield Lathrup Sr HS; Southfield, MI; Hon Rl; IM Sprt; Natl Merit Schl; Univ Of Michigan; Math.

JARRETT, TAMARA; Worthington HS; Worthington, OH; 55/565 Cls Rep Frsh Cls; Cl Rep Jr Cls; Pres Sr Cls; Cls Rep Sr Cls; Am Leg Aux Girls St; Hon Rl; Jr NHS; NHS; Stu Cncl; Pep Clb; Columbus Coll Of Art; Art.

JARVEY, JANET; L Anse HS; Lanse, MI; 13/105 Band; Chrs; Hon Rl; Hosp Ade; NHS; Stg Crw; VI CA; Gym; Trk; PPFtbl; Univ; Nursing.

JARVI, JILL; Ashtabula Harbor HS; Austinburg, OH; 35/189 Cl Rep Jr Cls; VP Sr Cls; AFS; JA; Off Ade; Stu Cncl; Yrbk; 4-H; Fr Clb; GAA; Univ; Public Relations.

JARVIE, DAVID; Ironton HS; Ironton, OH; Band; Boy Scts; JA; NHS; Sch Pl; Drama Clb; Crs Cntry; Ten; College; Chem Engr.

JARVIS, CARLITA A; Hurricane HS; Hurricane, WV; Hon Rl; JA; Pep Clb; IM Sprt; Bus Schl; Data Proc.

JARVIS, DANIEL; Cheboygan Area HS; Cheboygan, MI; Hon Rl; Sch Pl; Yth Flsp; Ftbl; Trk; IM Sprt; Univ; Bus Admin.

JARVIS, EUGENE; Benton Harbor HS; Millburg, MI; Cl Rep Jr Cls; Aud/Vis; Band; Boy Scts; Hon Rl; JA; Lbry Ade; NHS; Sch Mus; Sct Actv; Univ.

JARVIS, GREGORY A; Liberty HS; Youngstown, OH; Boy Scts; Cmnty Wkr; Stg Crw; Letter Bsbl; Letter Bsktbl; Letter Ftbl; Trk; Coach Actv; Natl Merit Ltr; Pres Awd; Univ Of Cincinnati; Pathology.

JARVIS, KATHY; Immaculate Conception Acad; Waldron, IN; Chrs; Chrh Wkr; Girl Scts; Hon Rl; Hosp Ade; NHS; Orch; Quill & Scroll; Sch Pl; Stu Cncl; Univ Of Notre Dame; Pre Med.

JARVIS, RACHEL; Southeast HS; Rootstown, OH; 3/176 Hon Rl; Sec NHS; Off Ade; Yth Flsp; 4-H; FSA; Pres Sci Clb; 4-H Awd; NCTE; OH Rep To AAAS Annual Meeting 1979; Outstndng Sci Stu Awd 1976; Pres Of Health Careers In Amera Clb; Kent St Univ; Bio Chem.

JARZAB, SHAWN; High School; Maple Hgts, OH; Cls Rep Frsh Cls; Cls Rep Sr Cls; Stu Cncl; Letter Bsbl; Letter Ftbl; Letter Trk; Cit Awd; Bowling Green Univ; Astronomy.

JASKOT, JEFF; John Glenn HS; Westland, MI; Hon Rl; Lit Mag; NHS; Orch; Lawrence Inst Of Tech Summer Sci Inst; Acad Pin; Hnrble Mention Short Story In Schlstc Writing Awds; Coll; Comp Sci.

JASPER, CONNIE; Aiken HS; Cincinnati, OH; Cls Rep Frsh Cls; Chrs; Girl Scts; Hon Rl; Sch Mus; Sch Pl; Pres FTA; Pep Clb; Chrldng; Univ; Jrnlsm.

JASSO, SUSAN; Melvindale HS; Melvindale, MI; Cls Rep Sr Cls; Hon Rl; Jr NHS; NHS; Stu Cncl; Rptr Yrbk; Spn Clb; Univ Of Mic; Chem Engr.

JASURA, JOANNE; Pinconning Area HS; Pinconning, MI; Sec Jr Cls; Chrh Wkr; Hon Rl; Hosp Ade; NHS; Yrbk; FTA; Bsbl; PPFtbl; Univ; Health.

JASZCZAK, MICHAEL; Parma Sr HS; Parma, OH; 8/782 Chrs; Hon Rl; Lit Mag; Sch Mus; Sch Pl; Stu Cncl; Drama Clb; Sci Clb; Schsltc Art Awd 77& 79; Natl Hon Soc 79; Univ; Art.

JAWORSKI, DIANE; Admiral King HS; Lorain, OH; Cls Rep Frsh Cls; Cls Rep Soph Cls; Cl Rep Jr Cls; Trs Sr Cls; Cls Rep Sr Cls; Band; Hon Rl; JA; Off Ade; Stu Cncl; Lorain Cnty Com; Bus.

JAWORSKY, ANNA M; Corunna HS; Corunna, MI; 56/112 Band; Hon Rl; Yrbk; Mich Tech Univ; Land Survey.

JAY, ANNE MARIE; Marian Heights Academy; Washburn, IL; Sec Frsh Cls; Cls Rep Frsh Cls; Cls Rep Soph Cls; Pres Jr Cls; Cl Rep Jr Cls; Hon Rl; NHS; Sdlty; Stu Cncl; Fr Clb; Hist Day Reg Comp Hist Paper 1st Pl 1979; Music Contst 1st Flute Solo 1978; Univ; Psych.

JAY, DAVID; Milton Union HS; W Milton, OH; Band; Boy Scts; Hon Rl; NHS; Wrstlng; Univ Of Dayton; Mech Engr Tech.

JAYANTHI, VENKATA; St Francis De Sales HS; , ; 9/233 Hon Rl; NHS; Stg Crw; Rptr Sch Nwsp; Capt Socr; Coach Actv; IM Sprt; Mgrs; College; Medicine.

JAYNE, LEAH; Oak Hill HS; Oak Hill, OH; Band; Chrs; Chrh Wkr; NHS; Sch Pl; Pres 4-H; VP Fr Clb; Pep Clb; Letter Bsktbl; Chrldng; Tennessee Temple Univ; Eng.

JAYNES, DAVID; Wapakoneta HS; Wapakoneta, OH; 4-H; FFA; Bsbl; Mgrs; 4-H Awd; Northwestern Bus College.

JAYNES, DENNIS; Switzerland Co HS; Vevay, IN; 6/126 Band; Chrs; MMM; NHS; Sch Mus; Pres 4-H; Sec Sci Clb; Spn Clb; 4-H Awd; Voice Dem Awd; Tech Inst; Archt Engr.

JAYNES, DENNIS; Switzerland Cnty HS; Vevay, IN; 6/134 Band; Chrs; Chrh Wkr; Drm Mjrt; Hon Rl; MMM; NHS; Pres 4-H; Dnfth Awd; 4-H Awd; ITT; Architecture.

JAYNES, LOIS; Rushville Consolidated HS; Rushville, IN; Band; Chrh Wkr; Hon Rl; Hosp Ade; Stu Cncl; Yth Flsp; 4-H; FHA; Pres Lat Clb; 4-H Awd; Ball St Univ; Nursing.

JAZAK, ALAN; Trinity HS; Garfield Hts, OH; Boy Scts; Chrs; Hon Rl; Rptr Yrbk; Fr Clb; Schsltc Awd Cert From Union Of Poles In Amer 76; 200 Cert Of Schslhp From Holy Name Soc 76; Cert Of Hon 79; Ohio St Univ; Archt.

JAZDZYK, LINDA; Ravenna HS; Ravenna, MI; 2/101 Cls Rep Frsh Cls; Sal; Hon Rl; Pres NHS; Off Ade; Sch Pl; Stu Cncl; Ed Yrbk; Bsbl; Chrldng; Adrian Coll; Chem.

JEANMARIE, TONYIA; Our Lady Of Mercy HS; Detroit, MI; Cls Rep Frsh Cls; Hosp Ade; NHS; Pep Clb; Sci Clb; Bell Creatvty Awd 79; Sci Fair Awd 79; U S Air Force Awd 79; Univ Of Michigan; Med.

JEANMOUGIN, PAUL; La Salle HS; Cincinnati, OH; 6/270 Cls Rep Frsh Cls; Cls Rep Soph Cls; Pres Jr Cls; Trs Sr Cls; Boy Scts; NHS; Stu Cncl; Rptr Sch Nwsp; Trk; Kiwan Awd; Jr Womens Club Schlrshp; Catholic Youth Organization Pres; Univ Of Dayton; Chem Engr.

JEANNERO, DENISE; Riverside HS; Dearborn Hts, MI; Trs Soph Cls; VP Sr Cls; Chrs; Girl Scts; Hon Rl; JA; NHS; Drama Clb; Fr Clb; Natl Merit SF; Michigan St Univ; Jrnlsm.

JEFFERIES, MARK K; Lincoln HS; Shinnston, WV; Boy Scts; Ftbl; Voc Schl; Elec.

JEFFERIES, WILLIAM T; William Henry Harrison HS; Cleves, OH; 13/250 Am Leg Boys St; Debate Tm; Hon Rl; Jr NHS; Lbry Ade; NHS; Sch Mus; Yth Flsp; 4-H; Univ Of Cincinnati; Engr.

JEFFERIS, BECKY J; Barnesville HS; Barnesville, OH; Am Leg Aux Girls St; Band; Drm Mjrt; Hon Rl; NHS; FHA; FTA; Bsktbl; Trk; VP GAA; College; Fash.

JEFFERS, AARON; Gallia Acad; Gallipolis, OH; Cls Rep Soph Cls; Cl Rep Jr Cls; Glf; College.

JEFFERS, MARY J; James Ford Rhodes HS; Cleveland, OH; Hosp Ade; Stu Cncl; IM Sprt; Scr Kpr; Natl Merit Schl; Bus Schl; Bus.

JEFFERS, PAMELA; Terre Haute North Vigo HS; Terre Haute, IN; Band; Chrh Wkr; Girl Scts; Hon Rl; Orch; Quill & Scroll; Y-Teens; Yrbk; 4-H; GAA; Indiana St Univ; Tchr.

JEFFERS, VICKI; Hinton HS; Jumping Branch, WV; Rptr Sch Nwsp; FBLA; Mth Clb; Spn Clb; Bsktbl; Chrldng; GAA; Marshall Univ; Biology.

JEFFERSON, ANN; John R Buchtel High Univ; Akron, OH; 104/412 Chrh Wkr; Hon Rl; Hosp Ade; VICA; Awd Of Merit For Outstndng VICA 76; Club Class Prss; Pres Of Med VICA Class; Ohio St Univ; RN.

JEFFERSON, ANTHONY; Lincoln HS; Centervll, IN; 20/145 Boy Scts; Hon Rl; JA; Yth Flsp; Letter Bsktbl; Trk; Mgrs; C of C Awd; Cit Awd; Coll; Comp Sci.

JEFFERSON, DEBORAH; Southwestern HS; Detroit, MI; Hon Rl; NHS; Mich State Univ; Nursing.

JEFFERSON, MARC T; Cincinnati Country Day Schl; Cincinnati, OH; Chrs; Hon Rl; Mod UN; Sch Mus; Drama Clb; Fr Clb; Mth Clb; Trk; IM Sprt; Univ; Engr.

JEFFERY, DENNIS; Lebanon HS; Lebanon, OH; 27/300 Capt Band; Drm Bgl; Hon Rl; Orch; ROTC; Sch Mus; Sch Pl; Bsktbl; IM Sprt; Most Otstndng Musician 78; Dayton Jazz Artists Soc 77; Lebanon Band Stud Dir 78; Univ Of Cincinnati; Music.

JEFFERY, JAMES; Center Line HS; Centerline, MI; Aud/Vis; Band; Chrh Wkr; Hon Rl; Jr NHS; Lbry Ade; NHS; Sch Mus; Univ Of Mic; Comp Engr.

JEFFERY, SALLY; Center Line HS; Centerline, MI; 36/425 Chrh Wkr; Hon Rl; Pres Jr NHS; NHS; Ed Sch Nwsp; Fr Clb; Sci Clb; Ferris State College; Tech Ilus.

JEFFREY, ROBYNE; Warren Western Reserve HS; Warren, OH; 3/497 Band; Hon Rl; Hosp Ade; NHS; Quill & Scroll; Red Cr Ade; Sch Mus; Y-Teens; Ed Yrbk; Yrbk; General Motors Inst; Engr.

JEFFRIES, BONNIE; Salem HS; Salem, IN; Aud/Vis; Hon Rl; Lbry Ade; Sch Mus; Sch Pl; Stg Crw; Drama Clb; Spn Clb; Indiana Univ; Spec Ed.

JEFFRIES, BRYAN; Catholic Central HS; Wintersville, OH; 73/204 Pres Frsh Cls; Pres Soph Cls; Cl Rep Jr Cls; Pres Sr Cls; FCA; Hon Rl; Sch Mus; Sch Pl; Pres Stu Cncl; Pres Drama Clb; Miami Univ; Politics.

JEFFRIES, CHAUNCEY; Mckinley HS; Canton, OH; 12/586 Cls Rep Frsh Cls; VP Sr Cls; Am Leg Boys St; Jr NHS; NHS; Yrbk; Fr Clb; Letter Bsktbl; Yale; Pre Law.

JEFFRIES, GARY; Northrop HS; Ft Wayne, IN; Letter Crs Cntry; IM Sprt; Mgrs; Scr Kpr; Univ.

JEFFRIES, GLENN; Escanaba Area Public HS; Escanaba, MI; Band; JA; NHS; Sch Nwsp; Ftbl; Trk; Mich Tech Univ; Engr.

JEFFRIES, JILL R; Roosevelt Wilson HS; Clarksburg, WV; Hon Rl; DECA; Leo Clb; Pep Clb; Farimont State; Psych.

JEFFRIES, JOHN; Reed City Sr HS; Reed City, MI; Hon Rl; Crs Cntry; Trk; Medal Winner In Old Kent River Bank Run; Medal Winner In White Cloud Summer Fest Run; Voc Schl; Machine.

JEFFRIES, LARRY; Northrop HS; Ft Wayne, IN; Letter Ftbl; Coach Actv; Scr Kpr; College.

JEFFRIES, PAUL; South Vigo HS; Terre Haute, IN; 41/630 Band; Hon Rl; Mod UN; NHS; Orch; 4-H; Lat Clb; 4-H Awd; Washington Univ; Medicine.

JEFFRIES, RITA; North Putnam HS; Roachdale, IN; Pres Soph Cls; Pres Jr Cls; Am Leg Aux Girls St; NHS; 4-H; Pep Clb; Spn Clb; Letter Bsktbl; Letter Trk; Chrldng;.

JEFFRIES, TERI; Vinson HS; Huntington, WV; Cls Rep Frsh Cls; Band; Chrs; Chrh Wkr; Capt Drl Tm; Hon Rl; Y-Teens; Rptr Sch Nwsp; Pep Clb; Coll; Journalism.

JELLIS, PAULA; Davison Sr HS; Davison, MI; Hon Rl; Sch Pl; Stg Crw; Drama Clb; Ger Clb; Letter Bsbl; Bsktbl; Univ Of Michigan; Psych.

JELTES, DAVID; Grandville HS; Grandville, MI; 11/322 Am Leg Boys St; Band; Boy Scts; Hon Rl; JA; NHS; Sct Actv; Letter Glf; Letter Ten; JA Awd; Mich Tech Univ; Chem Engr.

JEN, DAVID H; Morton Sr HS; Hammond, IN; 3/419 Debate Tm; Hon Rl; Indiana Univ.

JENCELESKI, BARBARA; Dominican HS; Detroit, MI; Band; Chrh Wkr; Cmnty Wkr; Girl Scts; Hon Rl; Hosp Ade; Sch Pl; Stg Crw; Ed Yrbk; Univ; Bio.

JENDER, LINDA; George Rogers Clark HS; Whiting, IN; 1/218 Cls Rep Frsh Cls; Pres Soph Cls; Cls Rep Soph Cls; Trs Jr Cls; Cl Rep Jr Cls; Jr NHS; Sct

Actv; Spn Clb; Letter Trk; GAA; NEDT Top 10% Awd 79; Calumet Coll Bk Awd 79; Purdue Calumet Univ; Comp Sci.

JENDER, N; Our Lady Of Mercy HS; Ann Arbor, MI; Lat Clb; College; Philosophy.

JENKIN, DAVE L; Bloomington HS South; Bloomington, IN; 9/310 VP Jr Cls; FCA; Hon Rl; Pres NHS; Quill & Scroll; Stu Cncl; Yrbk; Mgrs; Am Leg Awd; Rotary Club Sacslhp 79; In Ky All Star Gam Bsktbl Statstcn 79; Prom King 78; Clemson Univ; Financial Mgmt.

JENKINS, BRIAN; Ironton HS; Ironton, OH; Boy Scts; Chrh Wkr; Cmnty Wkr; Hon Rl; NHS; Sct Actv; Yth Flsp; Letter Ftbl; Trk; God Cntry Awd; Bench Press Meet Awd 79; Ealge Scout & Asst Scout Master 79; Univ; Med.

JENKINS, C; Belmont HS; Dayton, OH; Band; Gym; Chrldng; College.

JENKINS, C; Sidney HS; Sidney, OH; Trs Jr Cls; Band; Hon Rl; Sec NHS; Orch; Sch Mus; Yth Flsp; Crs Cntry; College; French Educ.

JENKINS, CASANDRA; Ridgedale HS; Marion, OH; 2/96 Letter Band; Chrs; Girl Scts; Hon Rl; Quill & Scroll; Sch Mus; Rptr Sch Nwsp; Spn Clb; Gym; Trk; Cnty Sci Fair Superior Rnkng 77; Schlrshp Team 77 & 79; Univ; Elem Educ.

JENKINS, CHRIS; Our Lady Of Providence HS; Clarksville, IN; Am Leg Boys St; Chrs; Hon Rl; Sch Mus; Sch Pl; Indiana Univ; Psych.

JENKINS, CORNELLA; Barberton HS; Barberton, OH; 56/499 GAA; Rotary Awd; Sec.

JENKINS, DEBRA; John Adams HS; So Bend, IN; Chrs; Chrh Wkr; Hon Rl; Lit Mag; Pep Clb; Univ; Sociology.

JENKINS, ELAINE; Breckenridge Jr Sr HS; Wheeler, MI; 4/105 Cls Rep Soph Cls; Cl Rep Jr Cls; Band; Chrh Wkr; Girl Scts; Hon Rl; Mdrgl; NHS; Off Ade; Sch Mus; Univ; R N.

JENKINS, ELAINE C; Breckenridge Jr Sr HS; Wheeler, MI; 3/100 Cls Rep Soph Cls; Cl Rep Jr Cls; Band; Chrh Wkr; Girl Scts; Hon Rl; Lbry Ade; Mdrgl; NHS; Sch Mus; College.

JENKINS, EUGENIA; Jane Addams Voc HS; Cleveland, OH; Pres Jr Cls; Pres Sr Cls; Cls Rep Sr Cls; Debate Tm; JA; Lbry Ade; Red Cr Ade; Stu Cncl; Gym; Kiwan Awd; Notre Dame Coll; Poli Sci.

JENKINS, JAMES R; Bishop Hartley HS; Whitehall, OH; 63/180 Bsbl; Ftbl; IM Sprt; Otterbein Coll; Chem.

JENKINS, JENNIE; Breckenridge Jr Sr HS; Wheeler, MI; Sec Frsh Cls; VP Soph Cls; Cl Rep Jr Cls; Pres Sr Cls; Pres Band; Hon Rl; Pres NHS; Stu Cncl; Treas Drama Clb; Spn Clb; Delta Coll; Drafting.

JENKINS, KATE; Rock Hill Sr HS; Ironton, OH; Band; Bsktbl; Trk; GAA; Morehead Univ; Phys Therapy.

JENKINS, KELLY; Watkins Memorial HS; Pataskala, OH; Trs Soph Cls; Cls Rep Sr Cls; Band; Chrs; Girl Scts; Hon Rl; Jr NHS; NHS; Red Cr Ade; Sch Mus; College; Aptomitrist.

JENKINS, KELLY; Heritage Christian HS; Indianapolis, IN; Band; Chrs; Girl Scts; Hon Rl; NHS; Sch Mus; Stg Crw; Rptr Yrbk; Rptr Sch Nwsp; Letter Trk; College; Physiology.

JENKINS, KEVIN; Rochester Adams HS; Rochester, MI; Boy Scts; Chrh Wkr; Debate Tm; Hon Rl; Natl Forn Lg; NHS; Ger Clb; Albion Coll; Med.

JENKINS, KIMBERLY; Regina HS; Cleveland, OH; Cmp Fr Grls; Chrs; Chrh Wkr; Drl Tm; Girl Scts; Hon Rl; Jr NHS; Orch; Stu Cncl; Ger Clb; Ranked 7th In Fresh Class; Earlham Coll; English.

JENKINS, LISA; Highland HS; Fredericktown, OH; 1/127 FCA; NHS; Rptr Sch Nwsp; Bsktbl; Trk; Ohio Univ; Art.

JENKINS, LOU ANN; Concord HS; Elkhart, IN; Hon Rl; JA; Jr NHS; NHS; Orch; Pep Clb; Cit Awd; JA Awd; Ivy Tech Schl; Comp Progr.

JENKINS, LOURA; Eastern HS; Waverly, OH; Band; Chrs; Drl Tm; Girl Scts; Hon Rl; Sch Pl; Yrbk; Drama Clb; Rdo Clb; Ohi Northern Univ; Law.

JENKINS, LUCINDA; Van Buren HS; Knightsvl, IN; 1/85 Chrh Wkr; Hon Rl; Hosp Ade; NHS; Off Ade; 4-H; FHA; FTA; Pep Clb; 4-H Awd; Indiana St Univ; Dietetics.

JENKINS, MARK; Jackson HS; Jackson, OH; Hon Rl; Letter Bsbl; Bsktbl; Letter Ftbl; Coach Actv; Univ; Hist.

JENKINS, ROBIN D; Liberty HS; Clarksburg, WV; 10/228 VP Frsh Cls; Cls Rep Frsh Cls; Cl Rep Jr Cls; Band; Chrs; Hon Rl; NHS; Sch Pl; Sec Stu Cncl; Y-Teens; Fairmont St Coll; Soc Work.

JENKINS, SHEILA; Western Hills HS; Cincinnati, OH; Cls Rep Frsh Cls; Cls Rep Soph Cls; Cl Rep Jr Cls; Chrh Wkr; Cmnty Wkr; Drl Tm; Girl Scts; Hon Rl; JA; Off Ade; Ohio State Univ; Phys Ther.

JENKINS, STEPHEN; Vinson HS; Huntington, WV; 7/115 Sec Frsh Cls; Trs Frsh Cls; Sec Soph Cls; Trs Soph Cls; Sec Jr Cls; Trs Jr Cls; Sec Sr Cls; Trs Sr Cls; Am Leg Boys St; Chrh Wkr; Marshall Univ; Forestry.

JENKINS, STEVEN R; Frankfort HS; Ridgeley, WV; Hon Rl; Mth Clb; Potomac State; Math.

JENKINS, TAMI; Woodrow Wilson HS; Youngstown, OH; 168/307 Cl Rep Jr Cls; Hst Sr Cls; Chrh Wkr; Stg Crw; Stu Cncl; Yth Flsp; Y-Teens; Ed Sch Nwsp; Drama Clb; OEA; Youngstown St Univ; Exec Sec.

JENKINS, TIMOTHY; Tekonsha HS; Tekonsha, MI; VP Frsh Cls; VP Soph Cls; Cl Rep Jr Cls; Hon Rl; Stu Cncl; Rptr Yrbk; Rptr Sch Nwsp; Letter Bsbl; Letter Bsktbl; Letter Ftbl.

JENKINSON, DENISE; Fraser HS; Fraser, MI; Band; Hon Rl; Stu Cncl; IM Sprt; Univ; Spanish.

JENKS, JEFF; Sexton HS; Lansing, MI; 15/365 Hon Rl; Jr NHS; Stu Cncl; Letter Bsktbl; Letter Ftbl; Letter Trk; IM Sprt; SAR Awd; General Motors Inst; Engr.

JENKS, NAN; Xenia HS; Xenia, OH; 66/516 Cl Rep Jr Cls; VP Sr Cls; Chrs; Hon Rl; Stu Cncl; 4-H; Capt Chrldng; 4-H Awd; College; Dental Hygiene.

JENKS, TODD; Comstock Park HS; Comstock Pk, MI; 12/160 Cls Rep Sr Cls; Boy Scts; Hon Rl; NHS; Stu Cncl; Ftbl; Trk; Gen Mtrs Inst; Elec Engr.

JENNINGS, BETH; Muncie Northside HS; Muncie, IN; 11/241 Pres Band; Girl Scts; NHS; Sch Mus; Sch Pl; Pres Yth Flsp; Rptr Yrbk; Purdue Univ; Home Ec.

JENNINGS, BURTON K; Brooke HS; Wellsburg, WV; 12/390 Cmnty Wkr; Hon Rl; Lit Mag; Lat Clb; Sci Clb; IM Sprt; Univ; Engr.

JENNINGS, CHRIS; Colon HS; Colon, MI; 4/63 Chrh Wkr; Hon Rl; NHS; Sch Mus; Sch Pl; DECA; Drama Clb; Crs Cntry; Trk; Busns Schl.

JENNINGS, DANIEL; Philo HS; Philo, OH; Debate Tm; Hon Rl; Stu Cncl; VICA; Coll; Forestry.

JENNINGS, DAWN; Rensselaer Central HS; Rensselaer, IN; Hon Rl; Sch Mus; Stu Cncl; Drama Clb; Spn Clb; Swmmng; Trk; College; Drama.

JENNINGS, DEREK; Amelia HS; Cincinnati, OH; Am Leg Boys St; Hon Rl; Jr NHS; NHS; Letter Crs Cntry; Letter Trk; Ach In Spanish I & II Bio & Chem; Univ; Chem Engr.

JENNINGS, ERIC; Athens HS; Athens, OH; Chrs; Chrh Wkr; NHS; Pol Wkr; Sch Mus; Sch Pl; Rptr Sch Nwsp; Ftbl; Letter Ten; IM Sprt; Univ; Jrnlsm.

JENNINGS, JANEEN; Johnstown Monroe HS; Johnstown, OH; Band; Hon Rl; NHS; FTA; Ohio St Univ; Psych.

JENNINGS, LAURA; Our Lady Of Providence HS; Jeffersonville, IN; Chrs; Hon Rl; Sch Mus; Natl Merit SF; Univ Of Del.

JENNINGS, LLOYD; Brownsburg HS; Brownsbrg, IN; 64/314 Voc Schl; Mech Engr.

JENNINGS, LORI A; Shelbyville HS; Shelbyville, IN; Cls Rep Soph Cls; Band; Chrs; Drl Tm; Girl Scts; Hon Rl; Off Ade; Rptr Yrbk; Rptr Sch Nwsp; Drama Clb; Hnr Queen Of Jobs Daughtrs Bethel 37 78; Whos Who Amng HS Stu 77; IUPUI; Real Estate.

JENNINGS, MARK; Centerville HS; Centerville, OH; Chrh Wkr; Hosp Ade; Jr NHS; NHS; Sch Pl; Ten; Natl Merit SF; Oberlin.

JENNINGS, TAMMI; Terre Haute N Vigo HS; Terre Haute, IN; Chrs; Girl Scts; Hon Rl; Off Ade; Y-Teens; DECA; 4-H; 4-H Awd;.

JENNINGS, WALTER; North HS; Youngstown, OH; 3/130 Hon Rl; JA; Sci Clb; N E Ohio Coll Of Med; Med.

JENSEN, CHARLES; Negaunee HS; Negaunee, MI; 35/149 Hon Rl; Mi Higher Educ Asst Authority Comp Schlrshp 79; Basic Educ Opport Grant 79; Michigan Tech Univ; Mech Engr.

JENSEN, CINDY; Montabella HS; Six Lakes, MI; Pres Soph Cls; VP Sr Cls; Chrh Wkr; Letter Chrldng; PPFtbl; Delta Univ Ctr; Dent Hygnst.

JENSEN, DAN; Ottawa Mills HS; Grand Rapids, MI; Band; Chrh Wkr; Hon Rl; Jr NHS; NHS; Orch; Fr Clb; Pep Clb; MSU; Chem Engr.

JENSEN, GREGORY A; Midland HS; Midland, MI; Boy Scts; Natl Merit SF; Michigan State Univ; Comp Sci.

JENSEN, HEIDI; Port Clinton HS; Pt Clinton, OH; Cls Rep Frsh Cls; Sec Soph Cls; Cl Rep Jr Cls; Am Leg Aux Girls St; Chrs; Hon Rl; NHS; College; Educ.

JENSEN, HEIDI J; Port Clinton HS; Pt Clinton, OH; 24/290 Cls Rep Frsh Cls; Sec Soph Cls; Cl Rep Jr Cls; Am Leg Aux Girls St; Chrs; Hon Rl; NHS; Stu Cncl; Fr Clb; Scr Kpr; Coll; Early Childhood Educ.

JENSEN, KARREN; Canfield HS; Canfield, OH; Chrs; Chrh Wkr; Girl Scts; Hon Rl; Lit Mag; Sch Mus; Stg Crw; Y-Teens; Rptr Sch Nwsp; Drama Clb; College; Business.

JENSEN, PHILIP; Midland HS; Midland, MI; Band; Hon Rl; Univ; Wildlife Mgmt.

JENSEN, STEVEN; St Xavier HS; Cincinnati, OH; Cls Rep Frsh Cls; Cls Rep Soph Cls; Cl Rep Jr Cls; Band; Boy Scts; Chrh Wkr; Cmnty Wkr; Hon Rl; JA; Mod UN; College; Law.

JEREMY, DAN; Clay Sr HS; Oregon, OH; Hon Rl; Univ; Acctg.

JERGE, MARTIN; St Joseph Prep Seminary; St Clairsville, OH; 6/19 Sec Frsh Cls; Boy Scts; Chrh Wkr; Cmnty Wkr; Hosp Ade; NHS; Rptr Sch Nwsp; Capt Bsktbl; Coach Actv; IM Sprt; W Tap Tele Hom Soc Nat Spanish Hon Soc 1979; Basketball Awds 1979; Prep Invt All Tourney 1978; Marietta Coll; Eng.

JERGER, JAN; Montpelier HS; Montpelier, OH; 6/107 Pres Jr Cls; Am Leg Aux Girls St; Hon Rl; Lbry Ade; Off Ade; Yth Flsp; Fr Clb; OEA; Bsktbl; Four Cnty Joint Voc Schl; Sec.

JERIC, JOAN M; Lumen Cordium HS; Northfield, OH; 12/90 Sec Soph Cls; Sec Jr Cls; Hon Rl; Stu Cncl; Bsbl; Letter Bsktbl; GAA; IM Sprt; Miami Of Ohio; Accounting.

JERINA, LOIS; Jane Addams Voc HS; Cleveland, OH; Boy Scts; Cmp Fr Grls; Chrs; CAP; Hon Rl; Med Lab Asst.

JERLES, MARILYN; Goshen HS; Goshen, IN; Letter Band; Drm Mjrt; Bsktbl; Letter Trk; Indiana St Univ; Retail Mrktng.

JERNIGAN, JOAN; Pleasant HS; Marion, OH; Band; Chrh Wkr; Lbry Ade; Sch Pl; Yth Flsp; Rptr Yrbk; Rptr Sch Nwsp; Drama Clb; College; Soc Work.

JERNSTADT, HONEY; Fulton HS; Maple Rapids, MI; Lbry Ade; Off Ade; Yth Flsp; Ed Sch Nwsp; Rptr Sch Nwsp; FHA; Ferris State Coll; Architecture.

JEROME, GREGORY A; Barberton HS; Barberton, OH; 77/474 Cls Rep Frsh Cls; Hon Rl; Jr NHS; Ger Clb; Bsbl; Crs Cntry; IM Sprt; Principals Hon Roll 76 79; Univ; Bus Mgmt.

JEROME, JOY; Van Wert HS; Van Wert, OH; Cls Rep Frsh Cls; Cls Rep Soph Cls; Cl Rep Jr Cls; Cls Rep Sr Cls; Am Leg Aux Girls St; Band; Chrs; Chrh Wkr; Hon Rl; NHS; Parkview Sch Of Nursing; Nursing.

JEROME, LORI; Pymatuning Valley HS; Jefferson, OH; 6/134 Band; Hon Rl; NHS; Sch Pl; Ed Sch Nwsp; Drama Clb; 4-H; FTA; Spn Clb; 4-H Awd; Local Spanish Declamation Contest; Poster Contest For One Act Plays 1st Place; Wilma Boyd Career Schl; Airlines.

JERRED, RICHARD; Clare HS; Clare, MI; 4-H; Letter Trk; Capt IM Sprt; Cit Awd; 4-H Awd; Mi Comp Schlrshp Awd 79; Adrian Univ; Pre Law.

JERVIS, ROBERT D; Wayne HS; Wayne, WV; NHS; Yth Flsp; Natl Merit SF; Univ; Nuclear Sci.

JESIONOWSKI, KAREN; Sts Peter And Paul Area HS; Reese, MI; Band; Girl Scts; Hosp Ade; NHS; Letter Trk; College; Industrial Engr.

JESITUS, ROBERT; Maple Hts Sr HS; Maple Hgts, OH; 1/500 Hon Rl; Jr NHS; Cit Awd; Ohio Scholastic Achievmnt Tests Algebra I Div I 4th Dist 16th St; CYO Bsktbl; 1st Pl Math Olympiad; Case Coll; Math.

JESKE, RICK; Ewen Trout Creek HS; Trout Creek, MI; 10/50 Pres Soph Cls; Bsbl; Bsktbl; Capt Ftbl; Wrstlng; Scr Kpr; Tmr; Michigan St Univ; Phys Educ.

JESKO, J; Grand Ledge HS; Grnd Ledge, MI; Cls Rep Frsh Cls; Band; Hon Rl; Sec NHS; Lat Clb; Ferris St Coll; Legal Asst.

JESS, CAROL; Washington HS; Massillon, OH; Band; Chrh Wkr; Hon Rl; Quill & Scroll; Sec Fr Clb; Bsktbl; Trk; IM Sprt; Cleveland Inst; Music.

JESSE, PEG; Margaretta HS; Castalia, OH; 1/115 Trs Soph Cls; Am Leg Aux Girls St; Band; Drm Mjrt; Hon Rl; JA; NHS; Scr Kpr; Tmr; Twrlr; Bowling Green St Univ; Acctg.

JESSMORE, JANET; Douglas Mac Arthur HS; Saginaw, MI; 34/300 Chrh Wkr; Hon Rl; NHS; Ger Clb; Mathematics.

JESSUP, SUE; Madison Hts HS; Anderson, IN; 2/350 Am Leg Aux Girls St; FCA; Lit Mag; NHS; Off Ade; Orch; 4-H; Fr Clb; Bsktbl; Ten; St Sectional Tennis Trnmnt Semi Finals; College; Liberal Arts.

JESUE, KATHY; High School; Lincoln Pk, MI; Chrs; Girl Scts; Hon Rl; Rptr Sch Nwsp; Sch Nwsp; Drama Clb; Spn Clb; Natl Merit Ltr; Henry Ford Univ; Dent Hygnst.

JETER, CHRIS; Mississinewa HS; Gas City, IN; 10/189 Band; Chrh Wkr; Hon Rl; NHS; IM Sprt; Purdue Univ; Comp Sci.

JETER, JENNIFER K; Central Hower HS; Akron, OH; 74/400 Cl Rep Jr Cls; Chrs; Hon Rl; Pres JA; Jr NHS; NHS; Lit Mag; Natl Forn Lg; Stu Cncl; JA Awd; Voice Dem Awd; Ohio Univ; Drama.

JETER, MARTHA A; Whetstone HS; Columbus, OH; 78/322 CAP; Hon Rl; Jr NHS; OEA; Pep Clb; PPFtbl; Ohio State Univ; Aeronautical Engr.

JETT, BETHANY; Dupont HS; Cedar Grv, WV; Cmnty Wkr; Mth Clb; Pep Clb; Swmmng; Coll.

JETT, BRIAN; Mona Shores HS; Muskegon, MI; Cls Rep Frsh Cls; Band; Chrh Wkr; Sch Mus; Stu Cncl; Yth Flsp; Ftbl; College; Bio.

JETT, PAULA D; Batavia HS; Batavia, OH; Band; Chrh Wkr; Hon Rl; Pres Yth Flsp; Fr Clb; Pep Clb; Scr Kpr; Mas Awd; Ltr In Vllybl 78; Univ; Psych.

JETT, R; Calhoun County HS; Minnora, WV; Boy Scts; Hon Rl; VICA; College; Engineering.

JEWEL, DOUGLAS L; De Kalb Central HS; Auburn, IN; Chrs; NHS; Drama Clb; 4-H; St Pres Ind Hist Soc 1979; Awd Soc Pioneers Of Ind 1979; Ind Jr Hist Soc Awd 1975; Vincennes Univ; Auto Mech.

JEWELL, LISA; North Central HS; Shelburn, IN; 25/100 Hon Rl; Sch Pl; Drama Clb; 4-H; FSA; FTA; Lat Clb; Pep Clb; Bsktbl; GAA; Franklin Coll; Phys Ed.

JEWELL, WILLIAM; Dowagiac Union HS; Dowagiac, MI; Am Leg Boys St; Boy Scts; Hon Rl; VP NHS; Sch Nwsp; Treas Fr Clb; Letter Bsbl; Hillsdale College; Pre Med.

JEZDIMIR, THERESA; Fitzgerald HS; Warren, MI; Hon Rl; Off Ade; Cit Awd;.

JEZERINAC, REBECCA; Elgin HS; Prospect, OH; 2/155 Band; Girl Scts; Hon Rl; NHS; Fr Clb; Scr Kpr; Univ; Bio.

JHA, GYAN; Walnut Hills HS; Cincinnati, OH; Hon Rl; Letter Bsbl; University; Pre Med.

JIMENEZ, CHRISTINE; Holy Redeemer HS; Detroit, MI; 11/131 Cl Rep Jr Cls; Cls Rep Sr Cls; Chrs; Hon Rl; NHS; Sch Mus; Yrbk; Drama Clb; Wayne State Univ; Med Tech.

JIMENEZ, MICHELLE; Holy Name Nazareth HS; Middleburg Ht, OH; Hon Rl; NHS; Stg Crw; VP Spn Clb; Spanish Hon Soc 79; Univ; Sci.

JINN, MEE; Stow HS; Stow, OH; Ohi State Univ; Dentist.

JIRA, JAY; Padua Franciscan HS; Parma, OH; 15/300 Band; Hon Rl; NHS; Orch; Pep Clb; Swmmng; Dayton Univ; Engr.

JIRA, PAUL; N Royalton HS; N Royalton, OH; Aud/Vis; Band; College; Aviation Pilot.

JIVIDEN, KIMBERLY; Gallia Academy; Gallipolis, OH; Pres Frsh Cls; Trs Soph Cls; Sec Jr Cls; Chrs; Chrh Wkr; Cmnty Wkr; FCA; Hon Rl; Hosp Ade; Lbry Ade; Ohio St Univ; Nursing.

JOACHIM, RAIF; Bridgman HS; Bridgman, MI; Hon Rl; NHS; Letter Bsktbl; Ftbl; IM Sprt; Am Leg Awd; Coll; Engr.

JOBE, KIMBERLY; Dunbar HS; Dunbar, WV; Chrs; Hon Rl; Jr NHS; Off Ade; Stg Crw; Pep Clb; Letter Bsktbl; Letter Trk; Letter IM Sprt; Triple A All St In Bsktbl 1st Team All KVC 1st Team 77; All KVC 1st Team 78; Sftbl Team Fast Pitch 4 Yrs; Univ; Athltc Trng.

JOBE, WILLIAM; Grand Blanc HS; Grand Blanc, MI; 125/635 Hon Rl; Univ Of Michigan; Engr.

JOBE JR, JACK; Wellsville HS; Wellsville, OH; Cls Rep Frsh Cls; Cls Rep Soph Cls; Cl Rep Jr Cls; Cls Rep Sr Cls; Stu Cncl; FTA; Letter Ftbl; Letter Trk; Letter Wrstlng; Mount Union; Phys Ed.

JOBES, JON; Arcanum HS; Arcanum, OH; Band; Boy Scts; Chrs; Yrbk; Civ Clb; 4-H; Fr Clb; IM Sprt; Mgrs; 4-H Awd; Univ Of Dayton; Teacher.

JOCHEM, VICTOR; Upper Arlington HS; Columbus, OH; 36/645 Boy Scts; Hon Rl; Ger Clb; Socr; Coach Actv; Denison.

JOCHEN, MARSHA; Hill Community HS; Lansing, MI; Band; Chrh Wkr; Hon Rl; JA; Lbry Ade; NHS; Trk; Mi Comp Schlhsp; Northern Michigan Univ; Nursing.

JOCHUM, FRANCIS E; Euclid Sr HS; Euclid, OH; 99/691 Cls Rep Frsh Cls; Cls Rep Soph Cls; Cl Rep Jr Cls; Cls Rep Sr Cls; Chrh Wkr; Cmnty Wkr; Hon Rl; NHS; Pol Wkr; Pres Stu Cncl; Mbr Natl Athltc Schlshp Soc Of Scndry Schl 78; Bessie Wells Schlshp Recpnt 79; John Carroll Univ; Pre Dent.

JOCIUS, JERROLD; Wirt HS; Gary, IN; Hon Rl; Purdue Univ; Chem Engr.

JODOCY, STEPHANIE; Mid Peninsula HS; Rock, MI; Band; Chrh Wkr; Hon Rl; Mt Senario Coll; Music.

JODREY, KEVIN; Eastern HS; Decatur, OH; Chrs; Hon Rl; Sch Mus; VICA; Univ; Comp Sci.

JOELSON, HARLAN; Sylvania Southview HS; Toledo, OH; Boy Scts; Hon Rl; Quill & Scroll; Sch Pl; Sprt Ed Sch Nwsp; Rptr Sch Nwsp; Letter Ten; Univ; Bus.

JOEST, CINDY; Reitz Memorial HS; Newburgh, IN; Band; Girl Scts; Hon Rl; Univ Of Evansville; Nursing.

JOEST, RALPH A; Triton Central HS; Fairland, IN; 1/185 NHS; Ftbl; Univ; Comp Sci.

JOHANNES, GREG; Climax Scotts Cmnty HS; Climax, MI; Band; Hon Rl; Yth Flsp; 4-H; Bsbl; Michigan St Univ; Ag.

JOHANNESEN, JENNIE; Lasalle HS; South Bend, IN; 34/488 Chrh Wkr; Hon Rl; NHS; Quill & Scroll; Yth Flsp; Rptr Yrbk; Sch Nwsp; College.

JOHANNIGMAN, JEFFREY D; St Xavier HS; Cincinnati, OH; 16/289 Cls Rep Frsh Cls; Cls Rep Soph Cls; Cl Rep Jr Cls; Cls Rep Sr Cls; Cmnty Wkr; Mod UN; NHS; Stu Cncl; Rptr Sch Nwsp; Mth Clb; Purdue Univ; Comp Sci.

JOHANNINSMEIER, JO; Lincoln HS; Vincennes, IN; 27/290 Band; Drm Mjrt; FTA; Pep Clb; College; Engineering.

JOHANNSEN, LYNDA; Port Clinton Sr HS; Pt Clinton, OH; 13/244 Band; Chrs; Girl Scts; NHS; Orch; 4-H; Univ Of Toledo; Nurse.

JOHANSEN, JEFFREY; High School; South Haven, MI; Capt Swmmng; IM Sprt; Scr Kpr; Tmr; MSU; Pre Vet.

JOHANSEN, SUE; St Augustine Academy; Cleveland, OH; Chrs; Hon Rl; Hosp Ade; Sch Pl; Stu Cncl; Rptr Yrbk; Drama Clb; Fr Clb; Key Clb; Pres Sci Clb; Univ; Public Rel.

JOHN, JEFFREY; Hilliard HS; Hilliard, OH; Hon Rl; Jr NHS; Vocational Schl; Field Engr.

JOHN, LAUER; Hammond HS; Hammond, IN; 14/333 Debate Tm; Hon Rl; Jr NHS; Natl Forn Lg; NHS; PAVAS; Quill & Scroll; Sch Pl; Sct Actv; Ed Yrbk;.

JOHN, MARGARET; Regina HS; Mt Clemens, MI; FCA; Hon Rl; NHS; Letter Bsktbl; Mic Univ; Dental Hygiene.

JOHN, SHARON; Waldron Jr Sr HS; Shelbyville, IN; Band; Drl Tm; Girl Scts; Hosp Ade; Off Ade; Treas 4-H; Pep Clb; Pom Pon; 4-H Awd; Mas Awd; Page For House Of Rep Of Indiana 77; Ball St Univ; Bus.

JOHN, THOMAS A; Olentangy HS; Powell, OH; 23/200 Band; Hon Rl; JA; Jr NHS; Orch; Sch Pl; Stg Crw; Drama Clb; 4-H; Mth Clb; Ohio St Univ; Mech Engr.

JOHNCOX, ROBERT; Waterford Township HS; Pontiac, MI; 6/397 Hon Rl; NHS; Lawrence Inst Of Tech; Mech Engr.

JOHNROCK, RONDA; Hastings HS; Hastings, MI; Chrs; Hon Rl; Rptr Sch Nwsp; Beta Clb; Fr Clb; Letter Gym; Chrldng; Univ; Jrnlsm.

JOHNS, ALICE; Crown Point HS; Cedar Lake, IN; 12/365 Band; Hon Rl; NHS; Bausch & Lomb Awd; Purdue Univ; Vet.

JOHNS, CHRISTOPHER; Pontiac Central HS; Pontiac, MI; Band; Hon Rl; NHS; Orch; Red Cr Ade; Sch Mus; Yrbk; Wayne St Univ; Phys Ther.

JOHNS, COURTNEY; Grandview Hts HS; Columbus, OH; Boy Scts; FCA; Hon Rl; Sct Actv; Bsktbl; Ftbl; Ten; Cit Awd; Ohio St Univ; Bus.

JOHNS, DAVID A; Dover HS; Dover, OH; 20/250 Cls Rep Frsh Cls; Cls Rep Soph Cls; Am Leg Boys St; Hon Rl; Stu Cncl; Letter Bsbl; Letter Bsktbl; Letter Ftbl; Am Leg Awd; College; Elem Ed.

JOHNS, LEAH; Wakefield HS; Wakefield, MI; 2/62 Sal; Chrh Wkr; Hon Rl; Natl Forn Lg; Sch Pl; Ed Yrbk; Drama Clb; Crs Cntry; Trk; Rotary Awd; Gogebic Cmnty Coll; Soc Work.

JOHNS, MARJORIE; White Pine HS; White Pine, MI; 5/35 Cls Rep Frsh Cls; Sec Soph Cls; Sec Jr Cls; Sec Sr Cls; Chrs; Chrh Wkr; Cmnty Wkr; Girl Scts; Hon Rl; Hosp Ade; Northern Michigan Univ; Sec.

JOHNS, SHERRI; Salem HS; Salem, OH; Sec Soph Cls; Sec Jr Cls; Band; Cmp Fr Grls; Hon Rl; Off Ade; Sch Mus; Stu Cncl; Yrbk; Mth Clb; Lewis Weinberger & Hill; Cosmetology.

JOHNS, STUART; Kirtland HS; Kirtland, OH; Cl Rep Jr Cls; Cls Rep Sr Cls; Hon Rl; Off Ade; Stu Cncl; Rptr Sch Nwsp; Treas Key Clb; Capt Socr; Letter Ten; Coach Actv; College; Engr.

JOHNS, TERRI; Philip Barbour HS; Philippi, WV; Band; Hon Rl; NHS; Color Guard Bnd; Univ; Sci.

JOHNS, TERRI; Salem Sr HS; Salem, OH; 50/252 Trs Soph Cls; Cls Rep Soph Cls; Band; Cmp Fr Grls; Hon Rl; Sch Mus; Stu Cncl; Key Clb; Mth Clb; Pep Clb; Univ Of Akron; Acctg.

JOHNS, WHITNEY; Grandview Heights HS; Columbus, OH; Boy Scts; Hon Rl; Jr NHS; Spn Clb; Letter Bsktbl; Letter Ftbl; Letter Ten; IM Sprt; College; Acctg.

JOHNSON, ALTHEA; Southwestern HS; Detroit, MI; 10/210 Cls Rep Frsh Cls; Cls Rep Soph Cls; Cl Rep Jr Cls; Cls Rep Sr Cls; Band; Chrs; Chrh Wkr; Drm Mjrt; Hon Rl; Mod UN; Michigan St Univ.

JOHNSON, A LYNN; Girard HS; Girard, OH; VP Sr Cls; AFS; Am Leg Aux Girls St; Chrs; Debate Tm; Jr NHS; Mdrgl; NHS; Pol Wkr; Sch Mus; Rep For Natl Acad Of Sci 1979; Miss Teenage Amer Natl Cand 1979; Girls Nation Alt 1978; Ohio St Univ; Bio Med Engr.

JOHNSON, AMY; Attica HS; Attica, IN; Band; Chrh Wkr; Girl Scts; Hon Rl; NHS; Orch; Sch Pl; Sct Actv; Yth Flsp; Drama Clb; De Pauw Univ; Soc Work.

JOHNSON, AMY; Grand Ledge HS; Eagle, MI; 2/416 Sal; Band; Hon Rl; NHS; Ger Clb; Letter Gym; Letter Ten; Mic Tech Univ; Chem Eng.

JOHNSON, ANNE; Spring Lake HS; Spring Lake, MI; 10/183 Hon Rl; Hosp Ade; NHS; IM Sprt; 4-H Awd; Natl Merit SF; Western Michigan Univ; Med.

JOHNSON, ANNE T; Bexley HS; Columbus, OH; Hon Rl; Hosp Ade; Lit Mag; Sch Nwsp; Pep Clb; Spn Clb; Ten; GAA; Hollins Coll; Creatv Writng.

JOHNSON, ANNETTE; Alma HS; Elwell, MI; Band; Girl Scts; Hon Rl; NHS; Sprt Ed Sch Nwsp; Eng Clb; Pep Clb; Sci Clb; Trk; Michigan St Univ; Acctg.

JOHNSON, BARBARA; East HS; Cleveland, OH; 26/228 VP Frsh Cls; Band; Hon Rl; Y-Teens; Lat Clb; Cit Awd; Baldwin Wallace Coll; Clinical Psych.

JOHNSON, BELINDA; Greensburg Comm HS; Greensburg, IN; Chrs; Hon Rl; Mdrgl; Sch Mus; Yth Flsp; Yrbk; Pres 4-H; Pep Clb; 4-H Awd; Univ; Med.

JOHNSON, BERNIE; Big Creek HS; Coalwood, WV; 1/90 Pres Frsh Cls; Pres Soph Cls; Val; Am Leg Boys St; Chrh Wkr; NHS; Stu Cncl; Sprt Ed Yrbk; Key Clb; Spn Clb; GA Pacific Schlrshp 79; Senator Byrd Schlstc Recognition Awd 79; W Virginia Inst Of Tech; Elec Engr.

JOHNSON, BRENDA; Washington Irving HS; Clarksburg, WV; Chrs; Hosp Ade; Lbry Ade; Sch Nwsp; Pep Clb; Trk; Tmr; Fairmont St Coll; Acctg.

JOHNSON, BRENDA; Michigan Center HS; Michigan Center, MI; Band; Drm Mjrt; Hon Rl; Sci Clb; Mgrs; Twrlr; Univ Of Michigan; Acctg.

JOHNSON, BRIAN; Reynoldsburg HS; Reynoldsburg, OH; Band; Boy Scts; Chrh Wkr; JA; Lbry Ade; Off Ade; Sch Mus; Sch Pl; Sct Actv; Stg Crw; Univ; Bus Admin.

JOHNSON, BRIAN; Southern Local HS; Portland, OH; Band; Chrs; Hon Rl; NHS; Fr Clb; Marietta College.

JOHNSON, BRIDGET; Belleville HS; Belleville, MI; NHS; Gym; Mic State; Bus.

JOHNSON, BURLEY W; West Preston HS; Kingwood, WV; Hon Rl; Mth Clb; VICA; Typing Awd 78; Fairmont St Coll; Elec Engr.

JOHNSON, C; Immaculata HS; Detroit, MI; Cmp Fr Grls; Hon Rl; NHS; Stu Cncl; Yth Flsp; Lat Clb; Bsbl; Coach Actv; College; Computer Engr.

JOHNSON, CALVIN; Elmhurst HS; Ft Wayne, IN; Bsktbl; Cit Awd; Univ; Electronics.

JOHNSON, CARL; Chesterton HS; Chesterton, IN; Letter Swmmng; Purdue Univ; Bio Sci.

JOHNSON, CAROL R; Pioneer HS; Ann Arbor, MI; 29/611 Girl Scts; Hon Rl; Red Cr Ade; Sct Actv; Sch Nwsp; Fr Clb; Ten; Letter Trk; NCTE; Univ Of Michigan; Archt.

JOHNSON, CAROLYN; Warrensville HS; Warrensvl Hts, OH; Cl Rep Jr Cls; Sec Sr Cls; Chrh Wkr; Cmnty Wkr; Girl Scts; Sch Pl; Stg Crw; Stu Cncl; Case Western Reserve; Pediatrician.

JOHNSON, CAROLYN; Hardin Northern HS; Ada, OH; Cls Rep Sr Cls; Band; Chrs; Cmnty Wkr; Hon Rl; Ed Yrbk; Rptr Yrbk; 4-H; Treas FHA; Trk; Schl shp Awd In FHA 79; Bowling Green Univ.

JOHNSON, CATHY; La Ville Jr Sr HS; Plymouth, IN; 42/135 Cls Rep Frsh Cls; Cls Rep Soph Cls; Cl Rep Jr Cls; Cls Rep Sr Cls; Band; 4-H; IM Sprt; 4-H Awd; Wilma Boyd Career Schl; Travel.

JOHNSON, CHERYL; Adlai Stevenson HS; Sterling Hts, MI; 113/530 Band; Orch; Sch Mus; Fr Clb; Pres Awd; Alma College.

JOHNSON, CHRIS; Chesapeake HS; Proctorville, OH; 40/150 Crs Cntry; Ftbl; Univ; Pre Law.

JOHNSON, CHRISTINE M; John R Buchtel Univ HS; Akron, OH; 6/462 Hon Rl; Jr NHS; NHS; Sprt Ed Yrbk; Sprt Ed Sch Nwsp; Capt Bsktbl; Ftbl; GAA; Bausch & Lomb Awd; Natl Merit Ltr; West Point Academy; Medicine.

JOHNSON, CONNIE; Lake Linden Hubbell HS; Lake Linden, MI; Trs Frsh Cls; Band; Chrh Wkr; Hon Rl; Hosp Ade; Lbry Ade; Off Ade; Sch Pl; Stu Cncl; Yth Flsp; N Michigan Univ; Nursing.

JOHNSON, CORRINA; Eminence HS; Paragon, IN; 7/45 Drl Tm; Hon Rl; Off Ade; Rptr Sch Nwsp; Sci Clb; Pom Pon; Ind Univ; Telecommunications.

JOHNSON, CURT; Northmont HS; Dayton, OH; Boy Scts; Chrh Wkr; Sct Actv; Yth Flsp; Letter Bsbl; Letter Ftbl; IM Sprt; VP Of Varsity N Club 79; Mst Imprvd Ftbl Plyr Awd 78; CIT Financl Serv Awd For Outstndg Player Of Week; Univ Of Wyoming; Bus Admin.

JOHNSON, CYNTHIA; Carroll HS; Dayton, OH; Band; Chrh Wkr; Rptr Sch Nwsp; Fr Clb; 1st Chair Flute In Band 79; Superior Awd In Piano From Natl Piano Plyng Audtns 77 79; French I Awd 79; Univ; Music Educ.

JOHNSON, CYNTHIA; Marion HS; Marion, IN; Chrh Wkr; Girl Scts; Hon Rl; NHS; Sch Pl; Sct Actv; Yth Flsp; Drama Clb; Spn Clb; Mgrs; Taylor Univ; Chrstn Educ.

JOHNSON, CYNTHIA; Emerson HS; Gary, IN; Chrs; Chrh Wkr; Cmnty Wkr; JA; Red Cr Ade; ROTC; Drama Clb; Cit Awd; Invocational Tech Coll.

JOHNSON, CYNTHIA; South Dearborn HS; Aurora, IN; Chrs; JA; Sch Pl; Drama Clb; Pep Clb; IM Sprt; Spencerian Coll; Fshn Sales.

JOHNSON, CYNTHIA R; London HS; London, OH; 1/145 Val; Am Leg Aux Girls St; Hon Rl; Pres NHS; Treas Stu Cncl; Sec Drama Clb; Letter Trk; Chrldng; Am Leg Awd; Capital Univ; Nursing.

JOHNSON, DANIEL; West Ottawa HS; Holland, MI; 2/300 Cls Rep Frsh Cls; VP Jr Cls; Band; Hon Rl; NHS; Orch; VP Stu Cncl; Pres Yth Flsp; Drama Clb; Ten; Univ; Engr.

JOHNSON, DANIEL; Field HS; Kent, OH; Boy Scts; Hon Rl; Red Cr Ade; Sct Actv; Kent State Univ; Business.

JOHNSON, DANIEL R; Cuyahoga Vly Christian Acad; Stow, OH; 2/80 VP Soph Cls; Stu Cncl; Ger Clb; Letter Socr; Letter Trk; College; Civil Engr.

JOHNSON, DARCY; Caro HS; Caro, MI; Band; Debate Tm; Hon Rl; NHS; Letter Crs Cntry; Letter Trk; 4-H Awd; Mas Awd; Central Univ; Science.

JOHNSON, DAVID; La Porte HS; Laporte, IN; 39/700 Cls Rep Frsh Cls; Chrs; Chrh Wkr; Debate Tm; Natl Forn Lg; NHS; Stu Cncl; Spn Clb; Univ.

JOHNSON, DAVID; Benedictine HS; Detroit, MI; Hon Rl; Capt Bsbl; Letter Bsktbl; Letter Crs Cntry; College; Mech Engr.

JOHNSON, DAVID; Western HS; Spring Arbor, MI; Boy Scts; Debate Tm; Natl Forn Lg; Sct Actv; 4-H; 4-H Awd; Elec Engr.

JOHNSON, DAVID A; Belmont HS; Dayton, OH; 8/350 Cl Rep Jr Cls; VP Sr Cls; Hon Rl; Pres NHS; Off Ade; Orch; Letter Ftbl; Letter Ten; Trk; Natl Merit SF; Baylor Univ; Pre Law.

JOHNSON, DAWN; T Roosevelt HS; E Chicago, IN; 52/215 Cls Rep Frsh Cls; Cls Rep Soph Cls; Cl Rep Jr Cls; Cls Rep Sr Cls; Band; Cmnty Wkr; Hon Rl; Off Ade; Yrbk; Sch Nwsp; Fisk Univ; Psych.

JOHNSON, DEAN; High School; Crothersville, IN; FCA; Sch Pl; Pep Clb; Letter Bsbl; College; Bus.

JOHNSON, DEBORAH; Hackett HS; Kalamazoo, MI; Girl Scts; Spn Clb; Letter Swmmng; GAA; IM Sprt; PPFtbl; Scr Kpr; Tmr; Sftbl 3 Letters 77 78 & 79; Vllybl Letter 78; Univ; Bus Admin.

JOHNSON, DEBORAH; Lumen Gordium HS; Cleveland, OH; 10/100 Sec Jr Cls; Cl Rep Jr Cls; Chrs; Chrh Wkr; Hon Rl; Lit Mag; Pres NHS; Stu Cncl; Rptr Yrbk; Rptr Sch Nwsp; Coll; Spec Ed.

JOHNSON, DEBORAH J; Crispus Attucks HS; Indpls, IN; 4/218 Cls Rep Sr Cls; Band; Chrs; Hon Rl; Sch Mus; Fr Clb; Spn Clb; Butler Univ; Forgien Languages.

JOHNSON, DEBRA; Sparta HS; Comstock Park, MI; Pres Sr Cls; Chrs; Hon Rl; Jr NHS; NHS; Stu Cncl; Bsktbl; Trk; Am Leg Awd; Ferris State College; Cosmetology.

JOHNSON, DEIDRA; Roosevelt HS; Gary, IN; Hon Rl; JA; Fr Clb; Ind State Univ; Cpa.

JOHNSON, DEIRDRA; Southwestern HS; Detroit, MI; Chrh Wkr; Debate Tm; Hon Rl; JA; Jr NHS; MMM; NHS; Off Ade; Yth Flsp; Yrbk; Univ; Med Asst.

JOHNSON, DENISE; Washington HS; South Bend, IN; Cls Rep Frsh Cls; Cls Rep Soph Cls; Cl Rep Jr Cls; Chrh Wkr; Cmnty Wkr; Debate Tm; Hon Rl; Stu Cncl; Rptr Yrbk; Fr Clb; Univ; Tele Cmnctns.

JOHNSON, DEREK V; Wayne HS; Dayton, OH; Cls Rep Soph Cls; Cls Rep Sr Cls; FCA; Hon Rl; Stu Cncl; Yth Flsp; Letter Ftbl; IM Sprt; Oh Indust Arts Exclint Cert 79; W Point Military Acad Recogntn 79; U S Air Force Acad Recogntn 79; Univ; Elec.

JOHNSON, DEVONA; Patterson Coop HS; Dayton, OH; 65/455 Cls Rep Frsh Cls; Cls Rep Soph Cls; Cl Rep Jr Cls; Hon Rl; VICA; IM Sprt; 1st Pl Section 1 Dental Arts Table Clinic; Sinclair Comm Coll; Dent Hygiene.

JOHNSON, DIANA; Norwalk HS; Norwalk, OH; 6/207 Sec Jr Cls; Sec Sr Cls; Band; Cmp Fr Grls; Chrh Wkr; Drl Tm; Girl Scts; Hon Rl; Off Ade; Yth Flsp; Univ; Spec Educ.

JOHNSON, DIANE; North Dickinson County HS; Channing, MI; VP Soph Cls; Band; Cmp Fr Grls; Chrh Wkr; Hon Rl; Sch Pl; Stu Cncl; Drama Clb; Eng Clb; Pep Clb; College; Acgt.

JOHNSON, DIANE; Nitro HS; Charleston, WV; Chrh Wkr; Hon Rl; NHS; Sec 4-H; FBLA; Mth Clb; Pep Clb; Spn Clb; Mgrs; 4-H Awd; West Virginia Inst Of Tech; Comp Sci.

JOHNSON, DWAYNE; Redford HS; Detroit, MI; Cl Rep Jr Cls; Chrh Wkr; Cmnty Wkr; Debate Tm; NHS; ROTC; C of C Awd; Univ; Bus Admin.

JOHNSON, ELIZABETH; Concord HS; Albion, MI; 2/75 Sal; Hon Rl; NHS; Rptr Sch Nwsp; Bsktbl; Trk; Dnfth Awd; Natl Merit Ltr; Michigan State Univ; Social Science.

JOHNSON, ELLEN; Bellevue HS; Vermontville, MI; 6/80 Hon Rl; Pres NHS; Yrbk; 4-H; Spn Clb; Crs Cntry; Kellogg Comm Coll; Med Lab Tech.

JOHNSON, ELLEN; Seton HS; Cincinnati, OH; Girl Scts; Hon Rl; Hosp Ade; Jr NHS; NHS; Kiwan Awd; Xavier Univ.

JOHNSON, ELLEN; Chillicothe HS; Chillicothe, OH; Band; Chrh Wkr; Drl Tm; Hon Rl; NHS; Sch Mus; Sch Pl; Stu Cncl; Ohio State Univ.

JOHNSON, ENOCH; Central Preston HS; Tunnelton, WV; Hon Rl; Fr Clb; Coll.

JOHNSON, ERIC; William V Fisher Cath HS; Logan, OH; 1/75 Am Leg Boys St; Hon Rl; NHS; Quill & Scroll; Yrbk; Sch Nwsp; Fr Clb; FDA; DAR Awd; Natl Merit Ltr; College; Medicine.

JOHNSON, ERIK J; Swan Valley HS; Saginaw, MI; 6/190 Boy Scts; Hon Rl; Jr NHS; NHS; Stu Cncl; Ftbl; Socr; Swmmng; Wrstlng; Mgrs; Navy ROTC Schlrshp; Soc Dist Amer HS Stu; Michigan Univ; Nuclear Engr.

JOHNSON, GARY R; Wayne Memorial HS; Wayne, MI; Chrh Wkr; Debate Tm; Hon Rl; JA; Jr NHS; NHS; Rptr Sch Nwsp; Sch Nwsp; Ger Clb; JA Awd; Center For Creative Studies; Adv Des.

JOHNSON, GEORGIA A; Hammond Tech Voc HS; Hammond, IN; Chrs; Red Cr Ade; Sch Mus; 4-H; 4-H Awd; College; Auto Mech.

JOHNSON, GINA; Taft Senior HS; Hamilton, OH; 43/444 Trs Soph Cls; Chrs; Chrh Wkr; Drl Tm; Sch Pl; Y-Teens; Drama Clb; Spn Clb; Pom Pon; JC Awd; Miami Univ; Systems Analysis.

JOHNSON, GORDON; Chippewa Vly HS; Mt Clemens, MI; Boy Scts; Hon Rl; Glf; Hockey; IM Sprt; W Michigan Univ; Flight Tech.

JOHNSON, GREG; Park Hills HS; Fairborn, OH; 1/350 Val; Am Leg Boys St; Band; Boy Scts; Chrs; NHS; Sch Mus; Pres Stu Cncl; Mth Clb; Wrstlng; MIT; Math.

JOHNSON, HEIDI; Gull Lake HS; Galesburg, MI; 2/250 Band; Girl Scts; NHS; Orch; Sch Mus; Fr Clb; Sci Clb; Trk; PPFtbl; Univ.

JOHNSON, JACQUELINE; Coloma HS; Coloma, MI; Trs Soph Cls; Band; Hon Rl; Stu Cncl; 4-H; Letter Trk; Chrldng; Lake Michigan Coll; X Ray Tech.

JOHNSON, JACQUELINE; A D Johnston HS; Bessemer, MI; VP Frsh Cls; VP Soph Cls; VP Jr Cls; Chrh Wkr; Yrbk; Rptr Sch Nwsp; Pep Clb; Capt Bsktbl; Letter Trk; Natl Merit SF; Univ.

JOHNSON, JAMES; Kingsford HS; Quinnesec, MI; Aud/Vis; Boy Scts; Chrs; Hon Rl; Red Cr Ade; Sch Pl; Rptr Yrbk; Drama Clb; Capt Swmmng; Cit Awd; Swim Team Capt; Order Of Arrow 78; Eagle Scout Awd 79; NMU; State Trooper.

JOHNSON, JAMES; Big Walnut HS; Galena, OH; 34/218 Band; Boy Scts; Sct Actv; VP Yth Flsp; FFA; Sci Clb; Trk; God Cntry Awd; Ohi St Univ; Agri Engr.

JOHNSON, JANE; Mt Pleasant HS; Mt Pleasant, MI; Hon Rl; NHS; Treas Spn Clb; Letter Trk; Central Mic Univ.

JOHNSON, JANET; Escanaba Area Public HS; Escanaba, MI; 64/435 Band; Cmp Fr Grls; Chrh Wkr; Hon Rl; Lbry Ade; Sch Pl; Yth Flsp; 4-H; Trk; IM Sprt; Michigan St Univ; Horticulture.

JOHNSON, JANICE; George Roger Clark HS; Hammond, IN; 31/218 Band; Cmp Fr Grls; Chrs; Chrh Wkr; Drl Tm; Girl Scts; Yrbk; Sch Nwsp; Fr Clb; PPFtbl; ISU; Psych.

JOHNSON, JANICE; Hamilton HS; Holland, MI; 6/140 Band; Cmp Fr Grls; Chrh Wkr; Debate Tm; Hon Rl; NHS; Sch Mus; Sch Pl; Stg Crw; Yrbk; Hope Coll; Psych.

JOHNSON, JAY; Parkersburg HS; Vienna, WV; Chrs; Chrh Wkr; Sch Mus; Yth Flsp; Pep Clb; Bsbl; Letter Ftbl; Ftbl; Wrstlng; IM Sprt; Univ.

JOHNSON, JAY; Baptist Academy; Indianapolis, IN; 3/20 Trs Jr Cls; Trs Sr Cls; Am Leg Boys St; Band; Chrs; Chrh Wkr; Hon Rl; Mdrgl; Orch; Sch Mus; Indiana State Music Contest 3 Yrs 1st Pl; Trade School; Archt Drafting.

JOHNSON, JAY; Hamilton Southeastern HS; Noblesvle, IN; 44/137 Chrh Wkr; Hon Rl; Sch Mus; Sch Pl; Stg Crw; Treas DECA; VP Sci Clb; Letter Wrstlng; Scr Kpr; Tmr; Univ Of Florida; Physics.

JOHNSON, JEANINE; Huntington North HS; Huntington, IN; 20/603 Hon Rl; Sec 4-H; Ger Clb; Pep Clb; 4-H Awd; Natl Educ Development Test 78; Univ; Bus.

JOHNSON, JEANNIE; Mt Vernon Sr HS; Mt Vernon, IN; 3/300 Trs Jr Cls; Trs Sr Cls; AFS; Am Leg Aux Girls St; Hon Rl; Jr NHS; NHS; Stu Cncl; Fr Clb; OEA; Murray St Univ; Bus.

JOHNSON, JEFF; Adrian HS; Adrian, MI; 80/386 Aud/Vis; Boy Scts; Chrh Wkr; Hon Rl; NHS; Off Ade; Sct Actv; Yth Flsp; Mic State Univ.

JOHNSON, JEFFERY; Crispus Attucks HS; Indianapolis, IN; Hon Rl; Fr Clb; Outstanding 2nd Yr French Stu; Coll; Meteorology.

JOHNSON, JEFF L; Goshen HS; Goshen, IN; 12/256 Chrs; Hon Rl; Natl Forn Lg; Sch Mus; Sch Pl; Drama Clb; Spn Clb; Indiana Univ; Bus.

JOHNSON, JEFFREY; Heritage Christian School; Carmel, IN; 6/63 Band; Chrh Wkr; Hon Rl; Yth Flsp; Ger Clb; Pep Clb; Natl Merit Ltr; Pres Of Yty Group 78; Bob Jones Univ; Mech Engr.

JOHNSON, JEFFREY; Miami Trace HS; Washington Ch, OH; AFS; Chrh Wkr; Cmnty Wkr; Treas Lbry Ade; Off Ade; Stg Crw; Treas Yth Flsp; Drama Clb; 4-H; FSA; St Alternate Elec Awd 4 H 79;.

JOHNSON, JEFFREY; Western Boone Jr Sr HS; Thorntown, IN; Cls Rep Frsh Cls; Cls Rep Soph Cls; Am Leg Boys St; Band; Boy Scts; Cmnty Wkr; FCA; Hon Rl; Red Cr Ade; Sch Mus; Thesbian Soc 79; Cert Emergency Med Tech 79; Indiana St Univ; Sci.

JOHNSON, JEFFREY; Gwinn HS; Gwinn, MI; 3/200 Boy Scts; Chrs; Hon Rl; Natl Merit Ltr; Little League All Stars; Michigan Tech Univ; Elec Engr.

JOHNSON, JENNIFER; Anderson HS; Anderson, IN; Girl Scts; Hon Rl; Yth Flsp; Fr Clb; Pep Clb; Bsktbl; Mgrs; Univ; Early Chldhd Educ.

JOHNSON, JENNIFER; Eastmoor HS; Columbus, OH; JA; Pep Clb; Capt Chrldng; JA Awd; Ohio St Univ; Comp Operator.

JOHNSON, JILL; Greenville Sr HS; Greenville, OH; Band; Chrs; Girl Scts; Hon Rl; Off Ade; Sch Mus; 4-H; Southeastern Acad; Travel.

JOHNSON, JOANNA J; Southfield Christian HS; Hazel Park, MI; Cls Rep Frsh Cls; Trs Jr Cls; Trs Sr Cls; Chrs; Hon Rl; NHS; Stu Cncl; Drama Clb; Letter Bsbl; Letter Chrldng; Wayne State Coll; Phys Therapy.

JOHNSON, JOANNE; Wadsworth Sr HS; Wadsworth, OH; Chrs; Chrh Wkr; Cmnty Wkr; Hon Rl; Pep Clb; Spn Clb; Trk; Univ Of Akron; Elem Ed.

JOHNSON, JOHN; Waynesfield Goshen HS; Lakeview, OH; 2/51 Cls Rep Frsh Cls; Pres Jr Cls; Band; Chrs; Hon Rl; Jr NHS; NHS; Stu Cncl; 4-H; Pep Clb; Bowling Green St Univ; Acctg.

JOHNSON, JOHN; Heritage Christian School; Indianapolis, IN; Band; Boy Scts; Chrh Wkr; Hon Rl; Pol Wkr; Stg Crw; Ger Clb; Trk; Bob Jones Univ.

JOHNSON, JOHN K; Walnut Hills HS; Cincinnati, OH; Band; Boy Scts; Hon Rl; Sch Mus; Sct Actv; Yth Flsp; Pep Clb; Ftbl; Letter Wrstlng; IM Sprt; Univ Of Cincinnati Minority Schlr Prog; College; Medicine.

JOHNSON, JOSEPH; Cadillac Sr HS; Cadillac, MI; Cmnty Wkr; Hon Rl; Michigan St Univ; Hotel Mgmt.

JOHNSON, JUANITA; Prairie Heights HS; Pleasant Lk, IN; Chrh Wkr; Hon Rl; Jr NHS; NHS; Yth Flsp; FTA; Bus Schl; Bus.

JOHNSON, JULIANN; Marquette HS; Michigan City, IN; 1/69 Cls Rep Frsh Cls; Cls Rep Soph Cls; VP Jr Cls; Hon Rl; Sch Mus; Stu Cncl; Fr Clb; Capt Chrldng; Letter Scr Kpr; Univ.

JOHNSON, JULIE; Turpin HS; Cincinnati, OH; 18/320 Hon Rl; Jr NHS; NHS; Capt Bsktbl; Capt Socr; Swmmng; Capt PPFtbl; College; Finance.

JOHNSON, JULIE; Midland Trail HS; Ansted, WV; Hon Rl; NHS; College; Soc Work.

JOHNSON, JULIE; Bangor HS; Bangor, MI; 17/94 Band; Cmp Fr Grls; Hon Rl; Key Clb; Pep Clb; Bsbl; Bsktbl; Kiwan Awd; Hope College; Math.

JOHNSON, JULIE; Okemos HS; Okemos, MI; 50/350 Pol Wkr; Letter Ten; Alma Coll.

JOHNSON, JULIE; Republic Michigamme HS; Republic, MI; VP Frsh Cls; Band; Girl Scts; Hon Rl; Stu Cncl; Fr Clb; Trk; Univ; Music.

JOHNSON, JULIE; Holt HS; Holt, MI; 4/275 Natl Forn Lg; NHS; Pol Wkr; Sch Pl; Sec Yth Flsp; Fr Clb; Swmmng; IM Sprt; Tmr; Lion Awd; Mic St Univ; Comp.

JOHNSON, JULIET; Negaunee HS; Negaunee, MI; Band; Chrs; Hon Rl; Hosp Ade; Natl Forn Lg; PAVAS; Pep Clb; Sci Clb; Letter Ten; PPFtbl; Mic State; Jrnlsm.

JOHNSON, K; Dansville Agricultural HS; Leslie, MI; Cmnty Wkr; Hon Rl; Bus.

JOHNSON, KAREN; Brownstown Central HS; Brownstown, IN; 23/150 Band; Chrh Wkr; Hon Rl; Sch Mus; FTA; Lat Clb; Pep Clb; Ten; GAA; IM Sprt; Indiana Univ; Music.

JOHNSON, KAREN; Clawson HS; Clawson, MI; 24/298 Hon Rl; Spn Clb; Swmmng; Oakland Cmnty Coll; Acctg.

JOHNSON, KAREN; Laingsburg HS; Laingsburg, MI; 2/80 Cls Rep Sr Cls; Sal; Band; Hon Rl; NHS; Coach Actv; PPFtbl; Western Mic Univ; Speech.

JOHNSON, KAREN; Cuyahoga Falls HS; Cuyahoga Fls, OH; 1/750 Band; Hon Rl; Hosp Ade; NHS; Bsktbl; Rotary Awd; NCTC Writing Compttn 78; Oh St Math Contst 78; Univ; Comp Sci.

JOHNSON, KAREN; Meadowbrook HS; Cumberland, OH; Sch Nwsp; Marrieta College; Art Commrcl.

JOHNSON, KAREN; Belmont HS; Dayton, OH; Band; Chrs; Chrh Wkr; Hon Rl; Lbry Ade; Pres NHS; Pres Yth Flsp; College.

JOHNSON, KARIN; Shelby HS; New Era, MI; Band; Chrh Wkr; Hon Rl; Off Ade; Sch Pl; Ed Yrbk; Drama Clb; Fr Clb; Chrldng; Coll; Cmnctns.

JOHNSON, KARL; Buffalo HS; Prichard, WV; Boy Scts; Hon Rl; NHS; Sct Actv; 4-H; Ftbl; 4-H Awd; College; Elec.

JOHNSON, KATHY M; North Ridgeville HS; N Ridgeville, OH; 21/373 Cmp Fr Grls; Chrh Wkr; Cmnty Wkr; Hon Rl; Lbry Ade; NHS; Spn Clb; Cuyahoga Comm Coll; Reg Nursing.

JOHNSON, KATRYNA; Ravenna HS; Ravenna, OH; 9/315 Band; Girl Scts; Hon Rl; NHS; Sch Mus; Sch Pl; Rptr Sch Nwsp; Sch Nwsp; Drama Clb; 4-H; Univ; Jrnlsm.

JOHNSON, KEITH E; Thomas M Cooley HS; Detroit, MI; Hon Rl; Rptr Yrbk; Rptr Sch Nwsp; Univ; Jrnlsm.

JOHNSON, KELLIE; Edgerton HS; Bryan, OH; 3/86 VP Soph Cls; VP Jr Cls; Am Leg Aux Girls St; Hon Rl; NHS; Sci Clb; Spn Clb; Letter Bsktbl; Letter Trk; Coach Actv; College.

JOHNSON, KELLY; North Daviess HS; Odon, IN; Sec Chrs; Chrh Wkr; Drl Tm; Hon Rl; Mdrgl; Sch Mus; 4-H; FHA; Pep Clb; Trk; Bus Schl; Legal Sec.

JOHNSON, KELLY; Whitehall Yearling HS; Columbus, OH; Chrh Wkr; Girl Scts; Lbry Ade; Tech Schl; Mental Health.

JOHNSON, KEVIN; Bosse HS; Evansville, IN; Cls Rep Frsh Cls; Cls Rep Soph Cls; Chrs; Hon Rl; Pol Wkr; Sch Pl; Stu Cncl; Murray State; Med.

JOHNSON, KEVIN; Grand Rapids Forest HS; Grand Rapids, MI; 3/136 Sch Pl; Sct Actv; Stg Crw; Letter Ftbl; Grand Rapids Jr Coll; Jrnlsm.

JOHNSON, KIM; Central Preston HS; Kingwood, WV; Band; Hon Rl; NHS; Pep Clb; Chrldng; W Vir Univ; Bio.

JOHNSON, KIM; Collinwood HS; Cleveland, OH; Cl Rep Jr Cls; Trs Sr Cls; Hon Rl; Stu Cncl; Rptr Sch Nwsp; Sch Nwsp; DECA; Martha Holden Jennings Motvtnl Schlshp Awd 77; Anthrops Motvtnl Schlshp Awd 78; Dyke Coll; CPA.

JOHNSON, KIMBERLY; Heath HS; Heath, OH; Hon Rl; Hosp Ade; VP Sci Clb; Letter Gym; GAA; Most Improved Gym 77; 3rd All Around Class 2 Dist 78; 200 Hrs Candy Stripper 79; Ohio Northern Univ; Pharm.

JOHNSON, KIMBERLY; Arthur Hill HS; Saginaw, MI; 89/490 Cls Rep Frsh Cls; Band; Drm Bgl; Hosp Ade; Sch Pl; Treas Yth Flsp; Sec Fr Clb; Pep Clb; Michigan Competitive Schlrshp; BEOG; Lake Superior St Coll; Coll.

JOHNSON, KIMBERLY; Newton Falls HS; Newton Falls, OH; Pres Frsh Cls; Trs Soph Cls; Sec Jr Cls; Band; Hosp Ade; NHS; Sch Pl; Y-Teens; Yrbk; FNA; Univ.

JOHNSON, KIRK; David Anderson HS; Lisbon, OH; 12/111 VP Frsh Cls; Am Leg Boys St; Aud/Vis; Band; Boy Scts; Chrh Wkr; FCA; Hon Rl; Jr NHS; Sch Mus; Univ; Elec Engr.

JOHNSON, KIRK E; David Anderson HS; Lisbon, OH; Am Leg Boys St; Band; Boy Scts; FCA; Hon Rl; VP NHS; Stu Cncl; Ed Yrbk; Pres Key Clb; Crs Cntry; Ohio State; Engineering.

JOHNSON, KORREE; Allegan HS; Allegan, MI; 29/193 Band; Hon Rl; NHS; Orch; Stg Crw; Schlrshp St Of Mich Competitive Schlrshp Prog; Coll; Drafting.

JOHNSON, LANA; Peterstown HS; Peterstown, WV; Sec Jr Cls; Trs Jr Cls; Drl Tm; Hon Rl; NHS; Yrbk; Sch Nwsp; Sec Fr Clb; VP FHA; VP Pep Clb; Bluefield St Coll; Acctg.

JOHNSON, LANCE L; Horace Mann HS; Gary, IN; Band; Hon Rl; Sch Pl; Stg Crw; Boys Clb Am; Mgrs; Character Awd; Indiana Univ.

JOHNSON, LANDY; Holt HS; Lansing, MI; Hon Rl; Sch Pl; Civ Clb; Fr Clb; Letter Bsbl; Letter Swmmng; Coach Actv; Cit Awd; Pres Awd; USC; Lib Arts.

JOHNSON, LAURA; Wilmington HS; Wilmington, OH; 14/279 Sec Frsh Cls; Cls Rep Soph Cls; Cls Rep Sr Cls; Am Leg Aux Girls St; Sec Chrs; Drl Tm; Girl Scts; Miami Jacobs College Of Bus; Fas Adm.

JOHNSON, LAUREN J; Highland HS; Anderson, IN; Band; Chrh Wkr; Cmnty Wkr; Girl Scts; Hon Rl; Sct Actv; Yth Flsp; Rptr Yrbk; Pep Clb; Sci Clb; Competed Natl Explorer Olympics; 5 Varsity Letters; College; Public Relations.

JOHNSON, LEANN; Bellefontaine Sr HS; Bellefontaine, OH; 9/240 Am Leg Aux Girls St; Band; Chrs; Chrh Wkr; Girl Scts; Hon Rl; NHS; Sch Mus; Sch Pl; Stg Crw; Natl Ach Semi Finalist; Anitz Oglesbee Awd; Harold Kerr Legion Post Schlrshp; Princeton Univ; Medicine.

JOHNSON, LEISHA; Groveport Madison HS; Groveport, OH; Band; Chrs; Chrh Wkr; Cmnty Wkr; Hon Rl; Orch; Lat Clb; Whos Who Among Amer HS Stu 78; Columbus Yth Symphony 76 79; Lab Asst Horticulture 79; Ohio St Univ; Law.

JOHNSON, LEONARD; Catholic Central HS; Grand Rpds, MI; 10/211 Band; Boy Scts; Chrh Wkr; Hon Rl; Orch; Sch Pl; Rptr Sch Nwsp; Drama Clb; Swmmng; Mbr Of MSBOA Dist 10 Hon Band 77; Mbr Of Class B Champ Quiz Bowl Tm 79; Univ Of Michigan; Pre Med.

JOHNSON, LIBBY; Wadsworth HS; Wadsworth, OH; FCA; Hon Rl; NHS; Yth Flsp; Fr Clb; FTA; Capt Crs Cntry; Capt Gym; Letter Trk; Kiwan Awd; Marietta Coll; Elem Educ.

JOHNSON, LISA; Henry Ford II HS; Sterling Hts, MI; 83/432 Hon Rl; Univ; Sci.

JOHNSON, LISA; Parkersburg HS; Parkersburg, WV; Cmnty Wkr; Stg Crw; Scr Kpr; Parkersburg Cmnty Coll; Child Psych.

JOHNSON, LISA; Whitehall HS; Whitehall, MI; Band; Chrh Wkr; Girl Scts; Hon Rl; PAVAS; Rptr Yrbk; 4-H; Ten; Mgrs; 4-H Awd; Western Univ; Art.

JOHNSON, LISA; Lexington HS; Mansfield, OH; 41/271 Chrs; Drl Tm; Hosp Ade; Mdrgl; Sch Nwsp; Fr Clb; College; Music.

JOHNSON, LORI; Bridgeport HS; Bridgeport, WV; Hosp Ade; Lbry Ade; NHS; Sch Pl; Fr Clb; Spn Clb; WVU; Pre Nursing.

JOHNSON, LORI; Decatur Central HS; Indpls, IN; 1/300 Hon Rl; NHS; Quill & Scroll; Stu Cncl; Rptr Sch Nwsp; 4-H; OEA; Pep Clb; Mat Maids; Scr Kpr; Indiana Central Univ; Sec Sci.

JOHNSON, LORI; Forest Park HS; Crystal Falls, MI; 17/79 Hon Rl; Lbry Ade; Yth Flsp; Sprt Ed Sch Nwsp; 4-H; FNA; Bsktbl; Trk; IM Sprt; Northern Michigan Univ; Health Educ.

JOHNSON, LORIN; Republic Michigamme HS; Republic, MI; Band; Chrh Wkr; Hon Rl; Fr Clb; Bsktbl; Trk; 4-H Awd; Michigan Tech Univ; Med.

JOHNSON, LORRI; Jane Addams Vocational HS; Cleveland, OH; Aud/Vis; Cmp Fr Grls; Chrs; Chrh Wkr; JA; Lbry Ade; Sch Mus; Sch Pl; Sawyer College Of Bus; Fashion Buyer.

JOHNSON, LORYN; Smithville HS; Smithville, OH; Cl Rep Jr Cls; Sec Sr Cls; VP Band; Chrs; FCA; Hon Rl; VP NHS; Ed Yrbk; GAA; Scr Kpr; Oh Univ; Music.

JOHNSON, LUANN; Orekama Consolidated HS; Bear Lk, MI; Cls Rep Frsh Cls; Band; Girl Scts; Hon Rl; Sch Pl; Yrbk; Drama Clb; 4-H; FHA; Pep Clb; West Shore Cmnty Coll.

JOHNSON, LYNN; Vanburen HS; Harmony, IN; 20/96 Drl Tm; Hon Rl; FBLA; Pres Pep Clb; VP Spn Clb; GAA; Pom Pon; Ind St Univ; Bus.

JOHNSON, LYNN; Marion HS; Marion, IN; Band; Drl Tm; Hon Rl; NHS; Sct Actv; Yth Flsp; Sec 4-H; Sci Clb; Pom Pon; 4-H Awd; Indiana Univ; Dent Hygnst.

JOHNSON, LYNNE; Shadyside HS; Shadyside, OH; Band; Sec Chrs; Hon Rl; NHS; Sch Pl; Y-Teens; Letter Bsbl; Letter Bsktbl; Pres GAA; IM Sprt; West Liberty St Coll; Music.

JOHNSON, M; Decatus Central HS; Indnpls, IN; 40/340 Boy Scts; Cmnty Wkr; Hon Rl; JA; Natl Forn Lg; Pol Wkr; Sct Actv; Drama Clb; Lat Clb; Rep De Molay Of Demolay; Coll; Comp Prog.

JOHNSON, M; Fairland HS; Proctorvll, OH; Boy Scts; Hon Rl; Sct Actv; Rptr Yrbk; Boys Clb Am; Fr Clb; Mth Clb; Pep Clb; Bsbl; Ftbl; Univ Of Southern Cal; Dentistry.

JOHNSON, MARCUS; Padua Franciscan HS; Seven Hills, OH; 47/276 Cls Rep Frsh Cls; Boy Scts; Y-Teens; Rptr Yrbk; Key Clb; Swmmng; Natl Merit SF; Wright St Univ; Systems Analysis.

JOHNSON, MARGE; Wm G Mather HS; Munising, MI; Cl Rep Jr Cls; Band; Chrh Wkr; Girl Scts; Hon Rl; Sch Pl; Stu Cncl; Rptr Sch Nwsp; FHA; Crs Cntry; P Stevens Career College; Fashn Mdse.

JOHNSON, MARIA; Our Lady Of Providence HS; New Albany, IN; Ind Univ Southeast.

JOHNSON, MARILYN; Marysville HS; Marysville, MI; Band; Cmp Fr Grls; Chrs; Chrh Wkr; Drl Tm; FCA; Hon Rl; College; Handicapped Teacher.

JOHNSON, MARK; Algonac HS; Algonac, MI; Hon Rl; Jr NHS; NHS; Letter Bsbl; Letter Bsktbl; Bd Of Trustees Schslp 80; Mi Higher Educ Schslhp 80; St Clair Cnty Cmnty Coll; Acctg.

JOHNSON, MARK C; Crown Point HS; Crown Point, IN; 25/500 Hon Rl; NHS; Yth Flsp; Natl Merit SF; Purdue Univ; Elec Engr.

JOHNSON, MARK R; Brandon HS; Ortonville, MI; Cls Rep Frsh Cls; Chrh Wkr; Hon Rl; Pres 4-H; Mi St 4 H Tool Awd Conservation 78; Ferris St Coll; Archt Engr.

JOHNSON, MARSHA L; Indiana Academy; Alexandria, IN; 8/57 Chrs; Chrh Wkr; Hon Rl; Lbry Ade; NHS; Off Ade; Ger Clb; IM Sprt; Andrews Univ; Acctg.

JOHNSON, MARTHA; St Frances Cabrini HS; Allen Pk, MI; 1/170 Hon Rl; NHS; Sch Mus; Sch Pl; Stg Crw; Drama Clb; Sec Ger Clb; Trk; Mgrs; Univ Of Michigan; Chem.

JOHNSON, MARY; Rutherford B Hayes HS; Delaware, OH; JA; Off Ade; Y-Teens; 4-H; FFA; Pep Clb; Bsktbl; Socr; Trk; Mgrs; Univ; Horticulture.

JOHNSON, MELISSA; Mc Comb HS; Hoytville, OH; 13/80 Am Leg Aux Girls St; Chrs; Chrh Wkr; Hon Rl; Jr NHS; NHS; Sch Mus; Pres Yth Flsp; Pep Clb; Chrldng; Univ; Music.

JOHNSON, MICHAEL; Deer Park HS; Deer Park, OH; Boy Scts; Hon Rl; NHS; SAR Awd; Ohio State Univ; Chemical Eng.

JOHNSON, MICHAEL T; Minerva HS; Minerva, OH; Cmnty Wkr; Hon Rl; Lbry Ade; NHS; Rptr Yrbk; Lat Clb; Letter Glf; Univ; Math.

JOHNSON, MITCHELL; Loogootee HS; Loogootee, IN; Stu Cncl; Letter Trk; Indiana HS Rodeo Mbr; Murray St Univ; Mech Engr.

JOHNSON, NORBERT; Gahanna Lincoln HS; Gahanna, OH; Aud/Vis; Boy Scts; Chrh Wkr; Cmnty Wkr; Hon Rl; PAVAS; Sct Actv; Ger Clb; Rdo Clb; Trk; Univ Of Cincinnati; Archt.

JOHNSON, PAM; Posen Consolidated HS; Posen, MI; Chrh Wkr; Lbry Ade; 4-H; FHA; 4-H Awd; Alpena Cmnty Coll; Photog.

JOHNSON, PAMELA; Benton Central HS; Fowler, IN; Band; Chrs; Chrh Wkr; Girl Scts; Hon Rl; FHA; Sci Clb; Spn Clb; GAA; Univ; HS Hist Tchr.

JOHNSON, PATRICIA; A D Johnston HS; Bessemer, MI; Pres Frsh Cls; Pres Soph Cls; Pres Jr Cls; Band; Hon Rl; Stu Cncl; Pep Clb; Letter Bsktbl; Letter Trk; Univ.

JOHNSON, PATRICIA; Sturgis HS; Sturgis, MI; Band; Drm Bgl; Hon Rl; NHS; Orch; Sch Mus; Sch Pl; Stg Crw; PPFtbl; Acad Schlrshp Central Michigan Univ; Rotary Hnr Stu Awd; Central Michigan Univ; Comp Sci.

JOHNSON, PHILLIP; Woodhaven HS; Flat Rock, MI; Hon Rl; VICA; Letter Ten; Ferris State College; Elec.

JOHNSON, PHYLLIS; W Preston Sr HS; Masontown, WV; Chrs; Chrh Wkr; Yth Flsp; Ed Yrbk; Pep Clb; West Virginia St Univ.

JOHNSON, POLLY A; Marion Adams HS; Sheridan, IN; 8/93 Cls Rep Soph Cls; Cl Rep Jr Cls; Cls Rep Sr Cls; Hon Rl; Jr NHS; Treas NHS; Stu Cncl; Pep Clb; Capt Chrldng; Twrlr; Ball State Univ; Soc Work.

JOHNSON, R; Lakota HS; W Chester, OH; 110/484 Band; Boy Scts; Chrs; Chrh Wkr; CAP; Hon Rl; Off Ade; Sch Mus; Sch Pl; Stg Crw; New Mexico St Univ; Chem Engr.

JOHNSON, RALPH; Grand Rapids Cath Cntrl HS; Grand Rpds, MI; Cl Rep Jr Cls; Cls Rep Sr Cls; Band; Pres Chrh Wkr; JA; Pres Stu Cncl; Yrbk; Sch Nwsp; Coach Actv; JA Awd; Stdnt Councl Serv Awd 79; GMI; Indust Engr.

JOHNSON, RANDY; Marquette Sr HS; Marquette, MI; 7/420 VP Frsh Cls; Trs Soph Cls; Cl Rep Jr Cls; Trs Sr Cls; Am Leg Boys St; Band; Drm Bgl; Orch; PAVAS; Sch Mus; Michigan St Univ; Law.

JOHNSON, RENEA; Saint Joseph Acad; Cleveland, OH; Cmp Fr Grls; Chrs; Hon Rl; Sci Clb; Gym; Ohi State; History Teacher.

JOHNSON, REX; Northwood HS; Wakarusa, IN; Am Leg Boys St; Band; Chrh Wkr; Cmnty Wkr; Hon Rl; Sch Pl; Stg Crw; Drama Clb; Pep Clb; IM Sprt; Indiana Univ.

JOHNSON, RICHARD; New Albany HS; New Albany, IN; Aud/Vis; Chrh Wkr; Bsktbl; Bus.

JOHNSON, RICK; Lincoln HS; Vincennes, IN; 27/280 Band; Boy Scts; Hon Rl; Yth Flsp; Rptr Sch Nwsp; 4-H; Letter Crs Cntry; Letter Trk; Natl Merit Ltr; Purdue Univ; Chem Engrg.

JOHNSON, RICKY; Vinson HS; Huntington, WV; Hon Rl; FHA; Bsktbl; Ftbl; Marshall Univ; Engr.

JOHNSON, ROBERT; Anderson HS; Anderson, IN; 25/402 Am Leg Boys St; Chrs; FCA; Hon Rl; NHS; Spn Clb; Bsktbl; Ftbl; C of C Awd; Gov Hon Prg Awd; Purdue Univ; Comp Prog.

JOHNSON, ROBERT B; Huntington HS; Huntington, WV; Am Leg Boys St; Boy Scts; Chrs; Hon Rl; Jr NHS; NHS; Red Cr Ade; Sch Pl; Stu Cncl; Key Clb; Univ; Eng.

JOHNSON, ROBIN; Howell HS; Howell, MI; Trs Frsh Cls; Band; Girl Scts; Hon Rl; Stu Cncl; IM Sprt; PPFtbl; Univ; Engr.

JOHNSON, RUSSELL E; New Haven HS; Fort Wayne, IN; 17/259 Band; Boy Scts; Hon Rl; JA; NHS; Lat Clb; Rdo Clb; Natl Merit SF; Eagle Scout Awd; Yth Oppor United Delegate; College; Elec Engr.

JOHNSON, S; Perry HS; Canton, OH; Chrs; Chrh Wkr; NHS; College.

JOHNSON, SALLI; Northridge HS; Johnstown, OH; 20/130 Girl Scts; Hon Rl; Off Ade; Sch Nwsp; 4-H; Spn Clb; Trk; Chrldng; Mgrs; Scr Kpr; Vocational Schl; Broadcasting.

JOHNSON, SALLY; Hartford HS; Hartford, MI; Cls Rep Soph Cls; Cl Rep Jr Cls; Cls Rep Sr Cls; Band; Sch Pl; Sec Stu Cncl; Pep Clb; Letter Trk; Chrldng; PPFtbl; Bus Schl; Bus Mgmt.

JOHNSON, SANDRA; Horace Mann HS; Gary, IN; Cls Rep Frsh Cls; Band; Girl Scts; Hon Rl; Jr NHS; Treas NHS; Trk; GAA; Pom Pon; Math Awd In Geom 78; IVY Tech Voc Univ; Analyst Progr.

JOHNSON, SANDRA; Cass Tech HS; Detroit, MI; Chrh Wkr; Girl Scts; Hon Rl; Lbry Ade; Off Ade; Stu Cncl; Y-Teens; Eng Clb; FDA; Cit Awd; Univ Of Detroit; Psych.

JOHNSON, SARA; Jane Addams Voc HS; Cleveland, OH; Hosp Ade; JA; Rptr Sch Nwsp; Cit Awd; Perfect Attend Awd 79; Happy Awd From Principal For News Article 77; Univ; Marketing.

JOHNSON, SCOTT; Maple Heights HS; Maple Heights, OH; Crs Cntry; Trk; Kent St Univ.

JOHNSON, SCOTT; London HS; London, OH; 23/133 Hon Rl; Ftbl; Trk; Clark Tech College; Computer Prog.

JOHNSON, SEAN; Scecina Memorial HS; Indianapolis, IN; Chrs; Sch Mus; Sch Pl; Ind Univ; English.

JOHNSON, SHANE; Maysville HS; Zanesville, OH; Boy Scts; Chrh Wkr; Hon Rl; Lbry Ade; Sct Actv; Yth Flsp; Southeastern Bible Coll; Minister.

JOHNSON, SHANNON; Northrop HS; Ft Wayne, IN; 17/587 Hon Rl; Ed Yrbk; Sch Nwsp; New Sentinel Kodak Newspr Snapshot Awd 1st Pl 78; 1st Pl In Emotion Category Photog 79; Otstndng Jrnlm Stud; Ball St Univ; Photojrnlsm.

JOHNSON, SHARON; St Frances Cabrini HS; Allen Pk, MI; Cmnty Wkr; Girl Scts; Hon Rl; Lat Clb; Spn Clb; Bsbl; Univ.

JOHNSON, SHAWN; Calhoun County HS; Grantsville, WV; Am Leg Aux Girls St; Chrs; Chrh Wkr; Cmnty Wkr; Drl Tm; Off Ade; Red Cr Ade; Pep Clb; Sci Clb; Fairmont State College; Mortuary Sci.

JOHNSON, SHERRY; Decatur Central HS; Indnpls, IN; 31/302 Pres Frsh Cls; Girl Scts; Hon Rl; Mod UN; Quill & Scroll; Stu Cncl; Yrbk; Rptr Sch Nwsp; Pep Clb; Letter Glf; Indiana Univ; Bus.

JOHNSON, STACY; West Ottawa HS; Holland, MI; Cls Rep Frsh Cls; Cls Rep Soph Cls; Cl Rep Jr Cls; Band; Chrs; Chrh Wkr; Mdrgl; MMM; Sch Mus; Sch Pl; Berklee College; Prof Performance.

JOHNSON, STEPHANIE; Emerson HS; Gary, IN; Band; Hon Rl; Off Ade; Stu Cncl; Trk; Chrldng; Awrd Achvmnt Rbbn For Typng 78; Awrd Merit Outstndng Achvmnt In French I 78; Awrd Achvmnt Rbbn For Chem 78; Indiana Univ; X Ray Tech.

JOHNSON, STEVEN; Orleans HS; Orleans, IN; 5/63 Hon Rl; NHS; Stu Cncl; Letter Bsbl; Letter Bsktbl; Schl Tchr.

JOHNSON, STEVEN; Lapeer East Sr HS; Lapeer, MI; Yrbk; Trk;.

JOHNSON, SUSAN; Carroll HS; Bringhurst, IN; 33/120 Chrs; Chrh Wkr; Sch Mus; Sch Pl; Stg Crw; Yth Flsp; Drama Clb; Fr Clb; Oral Robert Univ; Music.

JOHNSON, SUSAN A; North Central HS; Indianapolis, IN; Hon Rl; NHS; Indiana Univ; Creative Writer.

JOHNSON, SUSAN J; Jackson Milton HS; North Kackson, OH; 11/117 Sec Frsh Cls; VP Soph Cls; Pres Jr Cls; Chrs; Girl Scts; Hon Rl; NHS; Off Ade; Sch Pl; Stu Cncl; Univ.

JOHNSON, SUSIE; Webster County HS; Camden N Gauley, WV; Hon Rl; NHS; Yth Flsp; Yrbk; 4-H; Fr Clb; Pep Clb; Trk; Chrldng; GAA; Fairmont St Coll; Airline Stewardess.

JOHNSON, TAMI; N Dickinson Cnty HS; Iron Mtn, MI; Band; Chrs; Cmnty Wkr; Hon Rl; Lbry Ade; Sch Mus; Rptr Sch Nwsp; Pep Clb; Spn Clb; Trk; Concert Band Metal Earned; Y F U Exchange Stu To Mexico; Y F U Rep Of The Upper Pennisula; Ferris St Coll; X Ray Tech.

JOHNSON, TENNA; Clay Battelle HS; Pentress, WV; Band; Girl Scts; Orch; Stg Crw; Yrbk; Mth Clb; Pep Clb; Sci Clb; Bsktbl; Trk; Archt Drafting Awd St Contest; Miss United States Teenager; Univ; Archt.

JOHNSON, TERESA; Bluefield HS; Bluefield, WV; Chrs; Hon Rl; NHS; Sch Mus; Stu Cncl; Yrbk; Civ Clb; Spn Clb; Soc Studies Awd 77; Hon Stud 77; Stud Of Ne Eng 74 79; Bluefield St Coll; Bus.

JOHNSON, TERESSA; Du Pont HS; Shrewsbury, WV; Hon Rl; Jr NHS; FBLA; Pep Clb; Carver Career Voc Schl; Sec.

JOHNSON, TERRI; Huntington Catholic HS; Huntington, IN; Chrs; Girl Scts; Hon Rl; Sch Pl; Stg Crw; Rptr Yrbk; Pep Clb; Letter Trk; Capt Chrldng; GAA; Who Whos Among Amer HS Cheerleaders 1977; Intl Bus Coll; Sec.

JOHNSON, THERESA; Memphis HS; Emmett, MI; 20/87 Cls Rep Frsh Cls; Cls Rep Soph Cls; VP Jr Cls; Girl Scts; Hon Rl; Off Ade; Stu Cncl; 4-H; Bsbl; Trk; St Clair Cmnty Coll; Advertising.

JOHNSON, THURSTON; Union HS; Losantville, IN; Band; Chrh Wkr; Hon Rl; NHS; Rptr Yrbk; Olivet Nazarene Coll; Cmnctns.

JOHNSON, TIMOTHY; Harry S Truman HS; Taylor, MI; Bsbl; IM Sprt; Natl Merit Ltr; St Of Mi Schlrshp 78; Alma Pres Schlrshp 78; Alma Coll; Pre Med.

JOHNSON, TIMOTHY; Bedford N Lawrence HS; Bedford, IN; 80/420 Hon Rl; Jr NHS; NHS; Beta Clb; Lat Clb; Mth Clb; Pep Clb; Bsktbl; Glf; Mgrs; Indiana Univ; Bus.

JOHNSON, TOM; A D Johnston HS; Ramsay, MI; Band; Drm Bgl; Hon Rl; Natl Merit SF; Univ.

JOHNSON, TRACY; Harbor Springs HS; Hrbr Spgs, MI; Sec Frsh Cls; Sec Soph Cls; Sec Jr Cls; Hon Rl; Bsbl; Bsktbl; Trk; Chrldng; Coach Actv; Mich State Univ; Fashion.

JOHNSON, VANNIECE; Cass Technical HS; Detroit, MI; PAVAS; Rptr Yrbk; Rptr Sch Nwsp; Univ Of Detroit; Marine Bio.

JOHNSON, VIRGINIA; Northridge HS; Bristol, IN; Chrs; Drl Tm; Hon Rl; Yrbk; Sch Nwsp; 4-H; Pep Clb; Voc Schl; Vet Tech.

JOHNSON, VIRGINIA F; Marion HS; Marion, IN; 209/710 Am Leg Aux Girls St; Chrs; Hon Rl; 4-H; Capt Bsktbl; Gym; Trk; Chrldng; GAA; 4-H Awd; Recvd Exchg Club Awd In Vlybl 1978; Who Who Among Amer HS Stu; Indiana Univ; Phys Educ.

JOHNSON, WENDY; Jesup W Scott HS; Toledo, OH; Chrh Wkr; Hon Rl; NHS; Y-Teens; Fr Clb; OEA; Fisk Univ; Comp Prog.

JOHNSON, WENDY; Gladstone Area HS; Gladstone, MI; Chrh Wkr; Hon Rl; Sch Pl; Yrbk; Drama Clb; Spn Clb; Trk; Chrldng; Mgrs; PPFtbl; Ferris St Coll; Med Lab Tech.

JOHNSON, ZAVAAN; Grove City HS; Urbancrest, OH; Band; Chrs; Orch; Am Leg Awd; Natl Merit Ltr; Opt Clb Awd; Soc Dstngshd Amer HS Stu; Sr Class Exe Committee; Bowling Green St Univ; Music.

JOHNSON JR, JAMEY; Cameron HS; Cameron, WV; 4/115 Hon Rl; NHS; Y-Teens; 4-H; FFA; Pep Clb; PPFtbl; Wv Univ; Educa.

JOHNSON JR, ROBERT A; R Nelson Snider HS; Ft Wayne, IN; Chrs; Hon Rl; Spn Clb; Indiana St Univ; Aviation.

JOHNSTON, CARRIE; Fairfield Union HS; Bremen, OH; 1/150 Cls Rep Soph Cls; Cl Rep Jr Cls; Sec Sr Cls; Band; Chrh Wkr; Cmnty Wkr; Drm Mjrt; Hon Rl; Jr NHS; NHS; Shawnee St Cmnty Coll; Dent Hygiene.

JOHNSTON, CHERYL; Pike HS; Indianapolis, IN; 2/287 Sal; Am Leg Aux Girls St; Band; Chrh Wkr; Girl Scts; Hon Rl; Pres Jr NHS; Lbry Ade; Pres NHS; Orch; Math & Sci Awd Rensselaer Poly Inst Mdl 79; ISEF Miss Technology 79; J Sanford Mem For Outstndg Stu 76; Purdue Univ; Metallurgical Engr.

JOHNSTON, CHERYL; Logan Elm HS; Circleville, OH; Band; Chrh Wkr; Hon Rl; NHS; Yth Flsp; Pres 4-H; Trk; 4-H Awd;.

JOHNSTON, DAVID; St Francis De Sales HS; Toledo, OH; 5/200 Boy Scts; Hon Rl; NHS; Yrbk; Sch Nwsp; Univ.

JOHNSTON, DAVID; North Posey HS; Poseyville, IN; Hon Rl; Ger Clb; Bsktbl; Letter Ftbl; IM Sprt; ISUE; German.

JOHNSTON, DENISE; Tuscarawas Central Cath HS; New Phila, OH; Cls Rep Frsh Cls; Hon Rl; Yrbk; Sch Nwsp; Pep Clb; Bsktbl; Ten; Stark Tech Coll; Acctg.

JOHNSTON, D LANCE; Columbia City Joint HS; Columbia City, IN; Cls Rep Frsh Cls; Cls Rep Soph Cls; Cl Rep Jr Cls; Band; Boy Scts; Stu Cncl; Sprt Ed Sch Nwsp; Spn Clb; DAR Awd; Univ; Cmnctns.

JOHNSTON, GAINES; Tell City HS; Tell City, IN; Sct Actv; Spn Clb; Letter Crs Cntry; Letter Trk; Western Kentucky Univ; Acctg.

JOHNSTON, J; Western Reserve Acad; Hudson, OH; 55/86 Chrs; Hon Rl; Ftbl; Capt Lcrss; Letter Swmmng; College; Pre Dent.

JOHNSTON, JANET; Martinsville HS; Martinsville, IN; Chrh Wkr; Girl Scts; Orch; Sch Mus; Yrbk; 4-H; Letter Glf; GAA; Pom Pon; Mas Awd; College; A rchitecture.

JOHNSTON, JEANIE; North Adams HS; North Adams, MI; 6/48 Band; Hon Rl; Sch Pl; Drama Clb; Pres 4-H; Jackson Comm Coll.

JOHNSTON, JILL; Celina Sr HS; Celina, OH; Cls Rep Frsh Cls; Cls Rep Soph Cls; Cl Rep Jr Cls; Chrs; Hon Rl; Stu Cncl; Fr Clb; FBLA; Ger Clb; Chrldng; Chem Bowl Tm 1979; Univ.

JOHNSTON, JILL; Davison HS; Davison, MI; Cls Rep Soph Cls; Am Leg Aux Girls St; Band; Chrs; Chrh Wkr; Cmnty Wkr; Drl Tm; Girl Scts; Hon Rl; Mdrgl; Outstndng Jr In Chr 78; Perfct Attndnc; Active In Jobs Daughter & Chr Church; Univ Of Michigan; Tchr.

JOHNSTON, JOSEPH; Milton HS; Ona, WV; Boy Scts; Hon Rl; FBLA; Ten; West Virginia Univ; Engr.

JOHNSTON, KATHI; Mc Comb HS; Mccomb, OH; 7/80 Hst Sr Cls; Band; Chrs; Girl Scts; Hon Rl; Lbry Ade; NHS; Sch Mus; Stg Crw; Yth Flsp; Wooster Univ; Optometry.

JOHNSTON, LAURA; Milton HS; Ona, WV; Chrs; Hosp Ade; NHS; Red Cr Ade; Ed Sch Nwsp; Rptr Sch Nwsp; Fr Clb; FHA; Lat Clb; Miss Teenage Hunt Finalist; Berea Coll; Nursing.

JOHNSTON, LELIA; Wirt County HS; Elizabeth, WV; 2/102 VP Jr Cls; Band; Chrh Wkr; Hon Rl; Pres NHS; Off Ade; Pres FHA; College; Elem Ed.

JOHNSTON, LYDIA; Wilbur Wright HS; Dayton, OH; 18/240 Chrs; Chrh Wkr; Hon Rl; Lbry Ade; NHS; Sch Mus; Sch Pl; Stg Crw; Stu Cncl; Treas Yth Flsp; John Hall Awd; Ohio Univ; Lab Tech.

JOHNSTON, MARI; Servite HS; Detroit, MI; Sec Jr Cls; Chrs; Hon Rl; NHS; Trk; Mgrs; Univ Of Michigan; Jrnlsm.

JOHNSTON, MARLENE; Lake Orion HS; Lake Orion, MI; Chrh Wkr; Cmnty Wkr; Girl Scts; Hon Rl; Sch Pl; Sct Actv; Yrbk; Rptr Sch Nwsp; Sch Nwsp; Bowling Team Capt & Awds; Good Conduct Honor; Univ Of Michigan; Med Lab Tech.

JOHNSTON, MATT; Sebring Mc Kinley HS; Sebring, OH; 15/93 Trs Frsh Cls; Trs Soph Cls; Trs Sr Cls; Am Leg Boys St; Aud/Vis; Hon Rl; NHS; Off Ade; Letter Bsktbl; Letter Ftbl; College; Business Admin.

JOHNSTON, MAURA; Immaculata HS; Detroit, MI; Chrs; Hon Rl; NHS; Sch Pl; Stg Crw; Fr Clb; Univ; Engr.

JOHNSTON, MERRI J; Sparta HS; Sparta, MI; Band; Pres Chrs; Chrh Wkr; Girl Scts; Hon Rl; Hosp Ade; Mdrgl; Pres Fr Clb; Gym; GAA; Grand Rapids Baptist Coll; Tchr.

JOHNSTON, MICHAEL; Alma HS; Alma, MI; 9/240 Chrh Wkr; Sec NHS; Letter Bsbl; Letter Bsktbl; Univ Of Notre Dame; Pre Med.

JOHNSTON, STEPHEN A; Walnut Hills HS; Cincinnati, OH; Band; Boy Scts; Hon Rl; Coll; Elec Dsgn.

JOHNSTON, TERRY J; Jackson Center HS; Maplewood, OH; 3/41 Am Leg Boys St; Aud/Vis; Letter Band; Boy Scts; Chrh Wkr; Cmnty Wkr; Hon Rl; Lbry Ade; NHS; Orch; As Schls Match Wits T V & Academia Tm 76 80; St Schlshp Test 1st Tm Cnty Eng 6th Dist; Ohio Northern Univ; Hstry.

JOHOSKE, DANE; Roscommon HS; Roscommon, MI; 4/130 Cls Rep Soph Cls; Pres NHS; Sch Mus; Sprt Ed Yrbk; Capt Bsbl; Bsktbl; Ftbl; Coach Actv; Natl Merit SF; Natl Merit Schl; Univ Of Michigan; Aero Engr.

JOINER, FREDERICK; Waterford Township HS; Pontiac, MI; 18/380 Hon Rl; IM Sprt; Mi St Univ Awd For Acad Exclnc 79; St Of Mi Schlrshp & Grant Prog Hon & Monetary Awd 79; Summa Cum Laude; Michigan St Univ; Vet Med.

JOKELA, JENNIFER; Mid Peninsula HS; Rock, MI; 1/44 Trs Frsh Cls; VP Soph Cls; Pres Jr Cls; Cl Rep Jr Cls; VP Sr Cls; Val; Am Leg Aux Girls St; N Mic Univ; Photo.

JOKIK, SHELLY; Kenowa Hills HS; Grand Rapids, MI; VP Soph Cls; Jr NHS; NHS; Sch Pl; Yth Flsp; 4-H; Trk; Chrldng; Pom Pon; PPFtbl; Grand Rapids College; Soc Work.

JOLES, CARA; Cheboygan Area HS; Cheboygan, MI; Band; Drm Mjrt; Hon Rl; NHS; Sch Mus; Sch Pl; Fr Clb; College; Piano.

JOLLY, DAVID; Chippewa Valley HS; Mt Clemens, MI; Aud/Vis; Hon Rl; NHS; Stg Crw; Ed Sch Nwsp; Rptr Sch Nwsp; Capt Bsbl; Capt Bsktbl; Alpena Jr Coll; Criminal Justice.

JOMJULIO, BILL; Mayfield HS; Gates Mills, OH; Cl Rep Jr Cls; Cls Rep Sr Cls; Pol Wkr; Sch Mus; Sch Pl; Stu Cncl; Bsktbl; Ftbl; Trk; Coll; Dentistry.

JONAITIS, BARBARA; Kenowa Hills HS; Grand Rapids, MI; 18/225 JA; NHS; Rptr Yrbk; Rptr Sch Nwsp; JA Awd; Aquinas College; Acctg.

JONAS, WILLIAM; Parkersburg HS; Vienna, WV; 86/740 Pres Frsh Cls; Chrs; Chrh Wkr; Hon Rl; Sch Mus; Sch Pl; Stu Cncl; Yth Flsp; Lat Clb; Bsktbl; Fresh Bsktbl Picked Captian Of All Cnty Team By Area Bsktbl Coaches; Soph Bsktbl Leading Scorer & Rebounder; Coll; Chem Engr.

JONAUS, MARY C; Grand Haven Sr HS; Grand Haven, MI; Cls Rep Frsh Cls; Cl Rep Jr Cls; Cls Rep Sr Cls; Band; Girl Scts; Hon Rl; Jr NHS; NHS; PAVAS; Sch Mus; Univ Of Michigan; Jrnlsm.

JONES, AL; Al Jones HS; Dunbar, WV; VP Frsh Cls; VP Soph Cls; VP Jr Cls; Hon Rl; JA; Stg Crw; Fr Clb; College; Phy Ed.

JONES, ALISA; Robert S Rogers HS; Toledo, OH; Hon Rl; Jr NHS; FHA; Treas OEA; PPFtbl; Honorable Mention Spanish Contest; Toledo Univ; Busns.

JONES, ANDREA; Fennville HS; Fennville, MI; Cls Rep Frsh Cls; Cls Rep Soph Cls; Cl Rep Jr Cls; Cls Rep Sr Cls; Band; Chrs; Cmnty Wkr; Girl Scts; Hon Rl; Lbry Ade; Natl Campers & Hikers Assoc Schlrshp 79; St Of Mi Comp Schlrshp 79; Nominatd For Natl Safety Council Awd 79; William James Coll; Rec Gerontology.

JONES, ANDREW; Gladstone Area HS; Gladstone, MI; JA; Lbry Ade; Sch Pl; Drama Clb; Northern Mich Univ; Dramatics.

JONES, ANGELA; Carlisle HS; Franklin, OH; 11/200 Chrs; Hon Rl; Jr NHS; NHS; Sch Mus; Carlisle HS Honor Awd For Acctg I 1979; Carlisle Educ Rcgntn Assc 1979; Univ; Fshn Buying.

JONES, ANITA; Shady Spring HS; Shady Spring, WV; 30/155 Chrh Wkr; FCA; JA; NHS; Sch Pl; Stu Cncl; Pep Clb; Mat Maids; JA Awd; Berea Coll; Med Asst.

JONES, ANITA; South Central Jr Sr HS; Corydon, IN; 6/60 Am Leg Aux Girls St; Band; Drm Mjrt; Hon Rl; Yrbk; Spn Clb; Letter Bsktbl; IM Sprt; Univ; Nursing.

JONES, ANNA; Calumet HS; Gary, IN; 23/293 Chrh Wkr; NHS; Quill & Scroll; Rptr Yrbk; Rptr Sch N wsp; Pres Fr Clb; OEA; Pres Spn Clb; Quill & Scroll Winner Calumet 1979; 3rd Pl Gen Cler Reg Off Edu 1979; Indiana Univ; Speech Ther.

JONES, ANTOINETTE; East Catholic HS; , ; 3/64 Trs Frsh Cls; Sec Soph Cls; NHS; Off Ade; Univ; Photography.

JONES, BERTHA; Olentangy HS; Delaware, OH; FHA; Spn Clb; PPFtbl; Bluffton Univ; Pre Med.

JONES, BEVERLY; Van Wert HS; Van Wert, OH; Band; Chrs; Hon Rl; Sec NHS; Sch Pl; Y-Teens; Rptr Sch Nwsp; Pep Clb; Spn Clb; Ohio Univ; Chem.

JONES, BRENDA; Monroe HS; Monroe, MI; 12/550 Cls Rep Soph Cls; Cl Rep Jr Cls; Cls Rep Sr Cls; Chrh Wkr; Hon Rl; Lit Mag; Sec NHS; Off Ade; Sch Pl; Stu Cncl; Univ Of Toledo; Nurse.

JONES, BRENDA; Jimtown HS; Elkhart, IN; 11/96 Chrs; Chrh Wkr; Hon Rl; Off Ade; Sch Nwsp; Pep Clb; VICA; Bsktbl; Trk; JA Awd; College; Cosmetol ogy.

JONES, BRUCE; Marquette Sr HS; Marquette, MI; Aud/Vis; Chrh Wkr; Hon Rl; Lbry Ade; Yth Flsp; Letter Ten; Univ.

JONES, CAROL; Fountain Central HS; Wingate, IN; 1/120 Val; Am Leg Aux Girls St; Capt Drl Tm; Hon Rl; NHS; Sch Pl; Rptr Yrbk; Sch Nwsp; VP Fr Clb; Natl Merit Ltr; Indiana St Univ; Math.

JONES, CAROL; Tecumseh HS; New Carlisle, OH; 18/300 AFS; Band; Chrs; Chrh Wkr; FCA; Hon Rl; Jr NHS; NHS; Sch Mus; Sch Pl;.

JONES, CASSANDRA; Willow Run HS; Ypsilanti, MI; Cls Rep Soph Cls; Off Ade; Stu Cncl; Rptr Sch Nwsp; Pep Clb; Letter Bsktbl; Chrldng; Coach Actv; Bowling Green St Univ; Acctg.

JONES, CASSANDRA K; Elmhurst Sr HS; Ft Wayne, IN; 19/430 Hon Rl; Off Ade; Sch Pl; Stg Crw; Drama Clb; Purdue Univ; Acting.

JONES, CATHY; Withrow HS; Cincinnati, OH; Girl Scts; Hon Rl; JA; FHA; Girls Week Mother Daug Banq 76; Honor Roll 78; Edgecliff Coll; Bus Admin.

JONES, CHARLOTTE; Jefferson Twp HS; Dayton, OH; Cls Rep Frsh Cls; Chrs; Chrh Wkr; Cmnty Wkr; Hon Rl; JA; Sch Pl; Pres College; Med.

JONES, CHERYL L; Atherton Sr HS; Burton, MI; Cls Rep Frsh Cls; Sec Sr Cls; Chrh Wkr; Hon Rl; Hosp Ade; JA; Lbry Ade; Red Cr Ade; Sch Pl; Stu Cncl; Harvard Univ; Pre Med.

JONES, CHRIS; Archbishop Alter HS; Dayton, OH; Drama Clb; Fr Clb; Purdue Univ; Nuclear Engr.

JONES, CHRISTOPHER; Garber HS; Essexville, MI; Letter Swmmng; Letter Ten; Albion Univ; Sci.

JONES, CINDY; Greensburg Community HS; Greensburg, IN; 14/203 Letter Band; Letter Chrs; Chrh Wkr; Hon Rl; Hosp Ade; Mdrgl; NHS; Sch Mus; Sch Pl; Indiana Voc Tech Coll; Acctg.

JONES, COLLEEN; Floyd Central HS; Georgetown, IN; Hon Rl; JA; Orch; Bsbl; Pennsylvania St Univ; Nursing.

JONES, CURTIS; North HS; Lowellville, OH; 5/126 Chrs; Chrh Wkr; Hon Rl; JA; NHS; Yth Flsp; Rptr Sch Nwsp; Sci Clb; JA Awd; Howard Univ; Pre Med.

JONES, DAREK; Marine City HS; Marine City, MI; Cls Rep Soph Cls; Cl Rep Jr Cls; Band; Boy Scts; Hon Rl; Spn Clb; Letter Ftbl; Letter Trk; Wrstlng; IM Sprt; Natl Jr Sci Awd; Michigan St Univ; Acctg.

JONES, DARRELENE; New Albany HS; New Albany, IN; 99/565 Chrs; Hon Rl; Hosp Ade; Stu Cncl; Pep Clb; Rdo Clb; Chrldng; Indiana Univ; Phys Educ.

JONES, DEANNA; Bridgman HS; Bridgman, MI; Am Leg Aux Girls St; NHS; Sch Mus; Sch Pl; Sci Clb; Letter Bsktbl; IM Sprt; Mgrs; Pom Pon; Am Leg Awd; College.

JONES, DEBBIE; Wintersville HS; Wintersville, OH; Cls Rep Soph Cls; Cl Rep Jr Cls; Hon Rl; Stu Cncl; Spn Clb; GAA; Ohio State; Computer Sci.

JONES, DEBORAH; Carson City Crystal Area HS; Carson City, MI; Band; Hon Rl; NHS; Sch Pl; Yth Flsp; Rptr Yrbk; Rptr Yrbk; Capt Trk; Grand Rapids Baptist College; Forest.

JONES, DEBORAH; Piqua Central HS; Piqua, OH; Band; Chrs; Girl Scts; Hon Rl; Orch; Sch Mus; Sch Pl; Drama Clb; 4-H; Fr Clb; Music Awd 77 78 & 79; Univ; Nurse.

JONES, DEBORAH; Marion HS; Marion, IN; Chrh Wkr; Hon Rl; NHS; OEA; Univ; Bus Mgmt.

JONES, DENISE; Cass Tech HS; Detroit, MI; Sec Sr Cls; Debate Tm; Hon Rl; PAVAS; Stu Cncl; Howard Univ; Bus.

JONES, DENISE; Springfield HS; Battle Crk, MI; Cmp Fr Grls; Stu Cncl; Letter Bsktbl; PPFtbl; College; Acctg.

JONES, DENISE; Clio HS; Clio, MI; 2/450 Chrs; Chrh Wkr; Girl Scts; Hon Rl; Jr NHS; NHS; Sct Actv; Letter Bsktbl; Letter Crs Cntry; Letter Trk; Central Michigan Univ; Comp Sci.

JONES, DENNIS; Garaway HS; Dundee, OH; 5/86 Am Leg Boys St; Boy Scts; Chrs; Chrh Wkr; Debate Tm; Hon Rl; NHS; Sch Pl; Stg Crw; Yth Flsp; All Oh St Fair Yth Chr 78; Schlrshp Mdl 79; Schl Masco Mr Pirate 79; Kent St Univ; Music.

JONES, DENNIS; Princeton Community HS; Hazelton, IN; 17/222 Cl Rep Jr Cls; Pres Sr Cls; Chrh Wkr; Treas NHS; Treas Stu Cncl; Pres DECA; C of C Awd; Indiana St Univ; Dstrbtv Educ.

JONES, DIANA; Houghton HS; Houghton, MI; 29/114 Band; Chrs; Hon Rl; Sch Pl; Rptr Yrbk; 4-H; Trk; Capt Chrldng; PPFtbl; Michigan Tech Univ.

JONES, DIANA; Patrick Henry HS; Deshler, OH; Chrh Wkr; Hon Rl; Pres Spn Clb; College; Med Tech.

JONES, DIANE; Muskegon HS; Muskegon, MI; Chrh Wkr; Hon Rl; Rptr Sch Nwsp; College; Broadcasting.

JONES, DONALD; Battle Creek Central HS; Battle Creek, MI; 9/500 Band; Hon Rl; NHS; Orch; Sch Mus; Letter Ten; Natl Merit SF; Natl Merit Schl; Mich Stae Univ; Computer Sci.

JONES, DONNIE; Crispus Attucks HS; Indpls, IN; Band; Hon Rl; JA; Boys Clb Am; Lat Clb; Trk; JA Awd; Ball State; Music.

JONES, DWAYNE K; Greenville Sr HS; Greenville, OH; Band; Boy Scts; Chrh Wkr; Hon Rl; Orch; Sch Mus; Sch Pl; Sci Clb; Band Achvmnt Awd; Orchestra Achvmnt; Music Awd; College; Law.

JONES, EARL; Washington HS; Massillon, OH; Boy Scts; Chrs; Hon Rl; Sct Actv; Ger Clb; Tech Schl; Computers.

JONES, ELEANOR; Bloomington North HS; Bloomington, IN; Band; Chrh Wkr; Girl Scts; Hosp Ade; Fr Clb; Sci Clb; Cottey Coll; Bus.

JONES, ELIZABETH; Msgr John R Hackett HS; Kalamazoo, MI; Boy Scts; Hon Rl; IM Sprt; 4-H Awd; Natl Merit Ltr; Western Michigan Univ; Lib Arts.

JONES, ELIZABETH; Greencastle HS; Greencastle, IN; Band; FCA; Hon Rl; JA; NHS; Yth Flsp; Fr Clb; Pep Clb; Letter Swmmng; JA Awd; College.

JONES, ERIC; Rutherford B Hayes HS; Delaware, OH; Aud/Vis; Band; 4-H; FFA; Trk; Mgrs; 4-H Awd; Hocking Tech Inst.

JONES, ERIC D; Linden Mc Kinley HS; Columbus, OH; 10/268 Hon Rl; NHS; VICA; Franklin Univ; Computer Tech.

JONES, ERNIE; South Spencer HS; Richland, IN; Hon Rl; Pol Wkr; Rptr Sch Nwsp; Ftbl; Trk; IM Sprt; Mgrs; Victor Mohr Sclshp 79; Indiana St Univ; Bus.

JONES, FRED; Zane Trace HS; Kingston, OH; 9/98 Cmnty Wkr; Hon Rl; Jr NHS; NHS; Y-Teens; Fr Clb; Letter Bsbl; Letter Bsktbl; Crs Cntry; Coach Actv; Miami Univ; Acctg.

JONES, GABRIELLE; Bellaire HS; Bellaire, OH; Hst Jr Cls; Chrs; Hon Rl; JA; Sch Mus; Y-Teens; Fr Clb; OEA; Pep Clb; Mgrs; Akron Univ; Bus Admin.

JONES, GAIL; East HS; Cleveland, OH; Band; JA; Ger Clb; Trk; Cit Awd; JA Awd; College; Architecture.

JONES, GEOFFREY; Talcott HS; Hinton, WV; Chrh Wkr; Hon Rl; FBLA; Letter Bsbl; Scr Kpr;.

JONES, GREGORY; Kearsley HS; Usaf Academy, CO; 5/400 Band; Boy Scts; Hon Rl; JA; Natl Forn Lg; NHS; Orch; Sch Pl; Sct Actv; Air Frc Acad; Astrntcl Engr.

JONES, GREGORY; Glen Este HS; Cincinnati, OH; Hon Rl; NHS; Fr Clb; Pep Clb; Ftbl; Trk; Am Leg Awd; Univ.

JONES, HENRY; Bluefield HS; Bluefield, WV; 6/313 Hon Rl; Jr NHS; NHS; Rptr Sch Nwsp; Key Clb; Pep Clb; Sec Spn Clb; Ftbl; Trk; U S Military Acad.

JONES, JAMES; Union County HS; Liberty, IN; 12/125 Band; Chrs; Hon Rl; NHS; Sch Mus; Sch Pl; Yth Flsp; Drama Clb; 4-H; 4-H Awd; Purdue Univ; Agri.

JONES, JAMI; Edward Lee Mc Clain HS; Greenfield, OH; 7/143 Am Leg Aux Girls St; Band; Chrs; Chrh Wkr; Debate Tm; FCA; Girl Scts; Jr NHS; NHS; Off Ade; Ohio St Univ; Broadcast Journalism.

JONES, JAN; Hudson HS; Hudson, OH; 27/300 Cmnty Wkr; Pep Clb; Chrldng; PPFtbl; Ohio St Univ; Bus Mgmt.

JONES, JANE; Shepherd HS; Mt Pleasant, MI; Band; Chrs; Lbry Ade; Orch; Sch Pl; Yth Flsp; DECA; Ten; Mgrs; Michigan Christian Coll.

JONES, JANET; Chapmanville HS; Harts, WV; Cls Rep Soph Cls; Cl Rep Jr Cls; Am Leg Aux Girls St; Girl Scts; Pres Jr NHS; Rptr Yrbk; Rptr Sch Nwsp; Pres Beta Clb; Keyettes; Pep Clb; Ms Sftbl Amer Leag Played For 7 Yrs Min Leag All Star 2yrs; Maj Leag All Star 2yrs & Went To Rich Va; Univ; Eng.

JONES, JEFF; Washington Irving HS; Clarksburg, WV; 12/131 Cls Rep Soph Cls; Cl Rep Jr Cls; Chrh Wkr; Hon Rl; Stu Cncl; Yth Flsp; Rptr Yrbk; Sprt Ed Sch Nwsp; Key Clb; Lat Clb; All St Rnng Bck & Big Ten 78; Player Of The Week 78; Harrison Cnty Trck Hi Pnt 77; Univ; Jrnlsm.

JONES, JEFF; West Geavga HS; Chesterland, OH; FCA; Hon Rl; Letter Ftbl; PPFtbl; Fresh Schlrshp Awd For Hghst Grd Pt Av 77; Was On Cleveland Plain Dlr Drm Tm For Ftbl 78; Univ; Bio.

JONES, JEFFERY W; Detroit Northern Sr HS; Detroit, MI; Pres Jr Cls; Debate Tm; Hon Rl; NHS; Stu Cncl; Letter Bsbl; Ftbl; Capt Glf; Letter Trk; Coach Actv; Mbr Of Awrd Winning Debate Tm 79; HS Engr Inst Schlrshp Recipient 79; Univ; Law.

JONES, JENNIE; Fremont HS; Grant, MI; Cmp Fr Grls; Girl Scts; Hon Rl; Sch Pl; DECA; 4-H; Gym; PPFtbl; C of C Awd; 4-H Awd; Muskegon Bus Coll; Mktg.

JONES, JENNIFER; Canfield HS; Canfield, OH; 25/258 Chrs; Hon Rl; NHS; Sch Mus; Y-Teens; Ger Clb; Trk; Ohio St Univ; RN.

JONES, JEREMY; Stow HS; Stow, OH; VP Soph Cls; Treas Band; Chrs; VP Debate Tm; Natl Forn Lg; Sch Pl; VP Stu Cncl; Lat Clb; IM Sprt; Akron Univ; Engineer.

JONES, JESSE J; New Haven HS; New Haven, MI; Bsktbl; Ftbl; Trk; St Of Mi Comptn Schlrshp 79; Michigan St Univ; Pre Law.

JONES, JOAN; Taft Sr HS; Hamilton, OH; 45/412 Chrs; Jr NHS; Sch Mus; Sch Pl; Y-Teens; Drama Clb; Ger Clb; Cumberland Coll; Music.

JONES, JOHN; Arthur Hill HS; Saginaw, MI; Band; Drm Bgl; Hon Rl; JA; Orch; Quill & Scroll; Sprt Ed Sch Nwsp; Michigan St Univ; Elec Engr.

JONES, JOSEPH; Rochester Comm HS; Rochester, IN; 16/163 Cls Rep Frsh Cls; FCA; Hon Rl; NHS; Yth Flsp; Letter Bsktbl; Letter Ten; Letter Trk; Charles & Elizabeth Babcock Schlrshp Mem Fund; Honorary Indinana St Schlrshp; Rose Hulman Inst Of Tech; Civil Engr.

JONES, JULIE; Hartland HS; Milford, MI; Band; Hon Rl; Lit Mag; NHS; Yrbk; Rptr Sch Nwsp; Sec Fr Clb; Mgrs; Honorable Mention In Youth Talent Exhibit In Poetry; Selected To Take The Alumni Dstngshd Schlrshp Test; Michigan St Univ; English.

JONES, KAREN; Green HS; Akron, OH; NHS; Sch Pl; Ed Sch Nwsp; Sprt Ed Sch Nwsp; Rptr Sch Nwsp; Drama Clb; Letter Bsktbl; Letter Ten; Carnegie Mellon Univ.

JONES, KAREN; Eastlake North HS; Willowick, OH; 120/706 Cls Rep Frsh Cls; Hon Rl; Stg Crw; Stu Cncl; Pep Clb; Spn Clb; Crs Cntry; Socr; Trk; Chrldng; Lakeland Coll; Int Design.

JONES, KAREN; Reed City HS; Reed City, MI; 48/150 Cls Rep Sr Cls; Band; Chrs; Chrh Wkr; Girl Scts; Hon Rl; Off Ade; Sch Pl; Stu Cncl; Yth Flsp; Ferris State College; Reading Spec.

JONES, KARLA; Hillsboro HS; Hillsboro, OH; 9/170 Sec Soph Cls; Sec Sr Cls; Am Leg Aux Girls St; NHS; Sci Clb; Letter Bsktbl; Chrldng; Coach Actv; DAR Awd; Natl Merit Schl; Bowling Green St Univ; Chemistry.

JONES, KATHERINE; Shelbyville Sr HS; Shelbyville, IN; 27/300 Hon Rl; NHS; Off Ade; Sch Pl; Drama Clb; Fr Clb; Pep Clb; Treas Sci Clb; Spn Clb; PPFtbl; Purdue Univ; Intl Bus.

JONES, KATHLEEN; Clio HS; Clio, MI; 41/375 OEA; College; Busns Admin.

JONES, KELLY; Bremen HS; Bremen, IN; 13/98 FCA; Hon Rl; Hosp Ade; NHS; Rptr Sch Nwsp; Sch Nwsp; Letter Bsktbl; Trk; College; Elementary Educ.

JONES, KELLY; Middletown HS; Middletown, OH; Hon Rl; NHS; Pol Wkr; 4-H; FHA; Miami Univ; Bus Admin.

JONES, KELLY; Coleman HS; Coleman, MI; 3/100 Hon Rl; Bsktbl; Pres Phys Fitness 77; Jack Pinea Confrnc Girls Bsktbl 1st Tm 78; Girls Sfgbl 75 78; Cntrl Michigan Univ; Genrl.

JONES, KERRY; Cheboygan Catholic HS; Cheboygan, MI; Cls Rep Frsh Cls; Cls Rep Soph Cls; Sec Jr Cls; Boy Scts; Drl Tm; Pol Wkr; Red Cr Ade; Sct Actv; Stu Cncl; Bsbl; Ferris St Univ; Paramedic.

JONES, KIMBERLY; Elkins HS; Elkins, WV; Chrh Wkr; Girl Scts; Hosp Ade; Yth Flsp; FHA; Pep Clb; Gym; Trk; A B College; Nursing.

JONES, KIMBERLY; Shortridge HS; Indianapolis, IN; Trs Soph Cls; Chrs; Hon Rl; Lbry Ade; Sch Pl; Stg Crw; Yth Flsp; Bsbl; Letter Trk; Coach Actv; Indiana Univ; Math.

JONES, KIP; Springs Valley HS; French Lick, IN; NHS; Yrbk; Fr Clb; Hoosier Boys St Delegate 79; U S History Awd 79; Natl Honor Soc 79; College; Law.

JONES, KRISTEN; Redford HS; Detroit, MI; Cls Rep Frsh Cls; Cls Rep Soph Cls; Cl Rep Jr Cls; Chrh Wkr; Cmnty Wkr; Girl Scts; Hon Rl; JA; Off Ade; Pol Wkr; Metro Detroit Yth Awd 79; Natl Exchange Stu Of The Mnth 79; Univ; Psych.

JONES, LARRY; Dansville HS; Leslie, MI; VP Jr Cls; Hon Rl; NHS; MSU.

JONES, LARRY P; Centerline HS; Warren, MI; Boy Scts; Chrh Wkr; Hon Rl; Jr NHS; Sci Clb; Letter Crs Cntry; Letter Trk; Letter Wrstlng; Mic State Univ; Aeronautical Engr.

JONES, LAURA; Huntington East HS; Huntington, WV; 51/314 Sec Band; Chrs; Chrh Wkr; Girl Scts; Hon Rl; Hosp Ade; Mdrgl; NHS; Off Ade; Sch Mus; Marshall Univ; Music.

JONES, LAURA B; East HS; Youngstown, OH; 4/181 Debate Tm; Hon Rl; Jr NHS; NHS; Off Ade; Sch Pl; Stu Cncl; OEA;.

JONES, LEIGH; Firestone HS; Akron, OH; 8/365 Hon Rl; NHS; Stu Cncl; Yth Flsp; Rptr Yrbk; Rptr Sch Nwsp; Letter Bsktbl; Perfect Attendance 79; Univ; Archt.

JONES, LENNETTE; Our Lady Of Providence HS; New Albany, IN; Cls Rep Frsh Cls; Chrh Wkr; Girl Scts; Hon Rl; Stu Cncl; Eng Clb; Fr Clb; Pep Clb; Trk; Letter Chrldng; Purdue Univ; Psych.

JONES, LES; James A Garfield HS; Garrettsville, OH; Hon Rl; Sch Nwsp; Capt Ftbl; Tri St Univ; Aero Engr.

JONES, LISA; Schafer HS; Southgate, MI; Band; Chrs; Girl Scts; Hon Rl; NHS; Sch Mus; Sct Actv; Stg Crw; Drama Clb; Fr Clb; Travel Academy; Stewardess.

JONES, LISA; Covert HS; Covert, MI; Band; Hon Rl; NHS; Bsktbl; Chrldng; Band; Cheerleading; National Honor Soc; Western Michigan Univ; Spec Ed.

JONES, LOIS; Eastbrook HS; Van Buren, IN; 3/200 Hon Rl; NHS; Off Ade; Ed Sch Nwsp;.

JONES, LORI; Cardington Lincoln HS; Marengo, OH; VP Soph Cls; Trs Sr Cls; Am Leg Aux Girls St; FCA; Hon Rl; NHS; Off Ade; Stg Crw; Rptr Yrbk; Fr Clb; Muskingum Coll.

JONES, LUANNE; Meadowdale HS; Dayton, OH; Drl Tm; Hosp Ade; Lbry Ade; NHS; Orch; OEA; Pep Clb; Wright State Univ; Psych.

JONES, LYNDON; William H Harrison Sr HS; Harrison, OH; Band; Hon Rl; JA; NHS; Sch Mus; Sch Pl; Stu Cncl; Yth Flsp; Drama Clb; Lat Clb; 1st Pl Chem Awd In 78 Schl Sci Fair 79; Part In Operation Yth At Xavier Univ In June 78; Ohio St Univ; Elec Engr.

JONES, LYNN A; Weirton HS; Weirton, WV; Sec Frsh Cls; Hst Soph Cls; Hst Jr Cls; Cls Rep Sr Cls; Chrh Wkr; Cmnty Wkr; Hon Rl; NHS; Y-Teens; 4-H; Jefferson Tech Inst; Comp Prog.

JONES, LYNNE; Rutherford B Hayes HS; Delaware, OH; AFS; Debate Tm; Hon Rl; NHS; Orch; Yth Flsp; VP Key Clb; Natl Merit Ltr; College; English.

JONES, M; Mississinewa HS; Gas City, IN; Hon Rl; NHS; Yrbk; Fr Clb; OEA; Voc Schl; Bus.

JONES, MARGARET; Greencastle HS; Greencastle, IN; FCA; Hon Rl; VP JA; NHS; Fr Clb; Pep Clb; Letter Swmmng; Ten; Univ.

JONES, MARGOT; The Miami Valley HS; Dayton, OH; Pres Frsh Cls; Hon Rl; Off Ade; Sch Pl; Yrbk; Hockey; GAA; Art.

JONES, MARK; Patrick Henry HS; Grelton, OH; 14/100 Cls Rep Soph Cls; Cl Rep Jr Cls; Aud/Vis; Hon Rl; Stu Cncl; Yth Flsp; 4-H; Sci Clb; Ftbl; Capt Wrstlng; Univ; Chiropractor.

JONES, MARK; Huntington North HS; Warren, IN; Band; Boy Scts; Hon Rl; Ball State; Architecture.

JONES, MARK E; Washington HS; Washington, IN; 11/194 Am Leg Boys St; Band; Chrh Wkr; NHS; Yth Flsp; Beta Clb; 4-H; FFA; Purdue Univ; Agri.

JONES, MARLENA; Flint Open Schl; Flint, MI; Cls Rep Soph Cls; Band; Chrs; Chrh Wkr; Girl Scts; Sch Mus; Sch Pl; Bsbl; Elk Awd; Opt Clb Awd; Received Awd In Phi Delta Sorrity Poetry Contst 1979; Trophy In Elks Oretorical Contst 1979; Univ Of Michigan; Psych.

JONES, MARSHA; Carrollton HS; Carrollton, OH; 12/229 Hon Rl; NHS; 4-H; Treas FHA; Lat Clb; Ohio St Univ; Phys Therapy.

JONES, MARTY; Gladwin HS; Gladwin, MI; Chrs; Chrh Wkr; Yth Flsp; DECA; VICA; Delta College; Physical Therapy.

JONES, MARY; Eastern HS; Bloomfield, IN; 25/86 Cl Rep Jr Cls; Am Leg Aux Girls St; Chrs; Chrh Wkr; Drl Tm; Girl Scts; Hosp Ade; Lbry Ade; Off Ade; Yth Flsp; College; Nursing.

JONES, MARY; Loy Norrix HS; Kalamzoo, MI; 20/426 Chrs; Debate Tm; Girl Scts; Hon Rl; NHS; Off Ade; Orch; Sch Mus; Sct Actv; Bsktbl; Beloit Coll; Bio.

JONES, MARYELLEN; Anderson HS; Anderson, IN; 2/443 Am Leg Aux Girls St; Band; Drl Tm; Drm Mjrt; Hon Rl; NHS; Pol Wkr; Y-Teens; 4-H; FHA; Jr Cls Salutatorn 78; Pres Clsrm In Wa Dc 80; Outstndng Frsh & Soph Latin Stdnt 77; Indiana Univ; Acctg.

JONES, MEREDITH; North HS; Springfield, OH; Band; Chrs; Hon Rl; NHS; Stg Crw; Pol Wkr; Ed Yrbk; Spn Clb; Trk; Chrldng; Coll.

JONES, MICHAEL; Beaver Local HS; E Liverpool, OH; Sch Mus; Sch Pl; Drama Clb; Eng Clb; Bsbl; Coach Actv; Letter Mgrs; Kent St Univ; Scndry Educ.

JONES, MICKEY; Madison HS; N Madison, OH; 16/260 Cls Rep Frsh Cls; Cls Rep Soph Cls; Stu Cncl; 4-H; Keyettes; Pep Clb; Bsbl; Bsktbl; Twrlr; 4-H Awd; Coll; Interior Decorating.

JONES, MIKE; Continental Local HS; Continental, OH; 13/58 Boy Scts; VP NHS; Spn Clb; Crs Cntry; Trk; Am Leg Awd; Cit Awd; Ohi State Univ; Mech Engr.

JONES, MINDY; Everett HS; Lansing, MI; Trk; Michigan St Univ; Pre Med.

JONES, MONA; Solon HS; Solon, OH; Cls Rep Frsh Cls; Chrs; Drl Tm; Hon Rl; Rptr Sch Nwsp; Sch Nwsp; Letter Bsktbl; Letter Trk; Pom Pon; PPFtbl; 2nd Runner Up Solon Homedays Queen Cntst; Bowling Green Univ; Horticulture.

JONES, PAMELA; Deckerville Community School; Deckerville, MI; Pres Band; Chrs; Girl Scts; Hon Rl; Sch Mus; 4-H; OEA; Trk; Univ; Music.

JONES, PATRICIA; Adena HS; Frankfort, OH; Pres Jr Cls; AFS; Band; Chrs; Hon Rl; Jr NHS; NHS; Stu Cncl; VP 4-H; Letter Mgrs; Ohio St Univ; Nursing.

JONES, PATRICIA; East HS; Columbia, OH; Chrs; Chrh Wkr; Hosp Ade; Lbry Ade; Sch Nwsp; Fr Clb; FHA; Pep Clb; Swmmng; Voc Schl; Child Care.

JONES, PATRICIA; Norwood HS; Norwood, OH; Band; Chrh Wkr; Drm Bgl; Hon Rl; Orch; Univ; Art.

JONES, PATTI; New Riegel HS; New Riegel, OH; 6/48 Sec Frsh Cls; Hon Rl; NHS; Sch Pl; Stg Crw; Rptr Yrbk; Treas 4-H; FHA; Pep Clb; Treas Spn Clb; Bowling Green Univ; Elem Ed.

JONES, PENNY; Douglas Macarthur HS; Saginaw, MI; Hon Rl; Letter Ten; College; Veterinary Med.

JONES, PHILIP; London HS; London, OH; 18/133 Band; Boy Scts; Chrh Wkr; Hon Rl; Sct Actv; Fr Clb; Univ.

JONES, PRISCELLA; Cleveland Central Cath HS; Cleveland, OH; Chrh Wkr; Pres JA; Off Ade; Bsbl; Coll; Med.

JONES, RALPH; Central Lake Public School; East Jordon, MI; Band; Chrs; Cmnty Wkr; Hon Rl; Stg Crw; St Schlsp 79; Adrian Coll; Psych.

JONES, RALPH; Salem Sr HS; Salem, OH; Aud/Vis; Band; Hon Rl; Key Clb; Spn Clb; Trk; Youngstown St Univ; Chem.

JONES, RHONDA; Mannington HS; Mannington, WV; Pres Frsh Cls; Hon Rl; Hosp Ade; Stu Cncl; VP Y-Teens; FHA; Letter GAA; IM Sprt; Fairmont St Univ; Nursing.

JONES, RICHARD; Pennsboro HS; Pennsboro, WV; FFA; Mgrs; Triangle Tech; Air Conditioning.

JONES, RONDA; Little Miami HS; Loveland, OH; Chrh Wkr; Hon Rl; Lit Mag; NHS; Off Ade; Sct Actv; Fr Clb; Univ; Math.

JONES, RONELLE; Shortridge HS; Indianapolis, IN; 46/327 VP Soph Cls; Pres Jr Cls; Off Ade; Orch; Quill & Scroll; Rptr Yrbk; Rptr Sch Nwsp; Boys Clb Am; 4-H; Fr Clb; Indiana Univ; Physics.

JONES, SANDRA; Southwestern HS; Edinburgh, IN; Band; Hon Rl; NHS; Sch Mus; Sch Pl; Yth Flsp; Yrbk; Sch Nwsp; Drama Clb; Pep Clb; Franklin Coll.

JONES, SANDRA; Argos Community School; Argos, IN; Hon Rl; NHS; Sec Stu Cncl; Ed Yrbk; FHA; FTA; Pep Clb; Manchester Coll; Home Ec.

JONES, SANDY; Springs Valley HS; French Lick, IN; 4/97 Girl Scts; Hon Rl; Stu Cncl; DECA; FHA; OEA; Pep Clb; Trk; Vincennes Univ; Bus Mgmt.

JONES, SANDY; Wapakoneta HS; Buckland, OH; Band; Chrs; Hon Rl; Spn Clb; Twrlr; Univ.

JONES, SCOTT; Ontario HS; Mnsfld, OH; 1/175 Am Leg Boys St; Chrh Wkr; Hon Rl; Pres NHS; Orch; Fr Clb; Letter Crs Cntry; Letter Swmmng; Letter Trk; Coll; Chem.

JONES, SCOTT; Indian Creek HS; Morgantown, IN; 4/161 Am Leg Boys St; FCA; Hon Rl; VP NHS; Off Ade; Spn Clb; Letter Bsbl; Bsktbl; Letter Ftbl; Univ; CPA.

JONES, SHARLENE; Yorktown HS; Muncie, IN; 43/180 Chrs; Hon Rl; 4-H; FBLA; Sec Spn Clb; 4-H Awd; College; Interpretor.

JONES, SHELLI; Continental Local HS; Continental, OH; Chrh Wkr; Cmnty Wkr; Hon Rl; Off Ade; FHA; Voc Schl; Home Econ.

JONES, SHERRY; Our Lady Of Angels HS; Cincinnati, OH; 20/30 Cmp Fr Grls; Chrh Wkr; Girl Scts; Off Ade; Sch Pl; Stg Crw; Drama Clb; Fr Clb; Sci Clb; Wittenberg Univ; Corp Law.

JONES, SHIRLEY; Oscoda HS; Gwinn, MI; 28/298 Boy Scts; Cmnty Wkr; Hon Rl; Hosp Ade; Lbry Ade; NHS; Off Ade; Mich State Univ; Nursint.

JONES, STEPHEN; Northwest HS; Indianapolis, IN; Cmnty Wkr; Hon Rl; NHS; Off Ade; IU PUI Dental Schl; Dent.

JONES, STEPHEN E; Wellston HS; Wellston, OH; 14/145 Band; Boy Scts; Chrs; Chrh Wkr; Hon Rl; NHS; Sch Mus; Sct Actv; Stg Crw; Ohi Univ.

JONES, STEVE; Niles Mc Kinley HS; Niles, OH; 66/421 AFS; Jr NHS; NHS; Keyettes; VP Lat Clb; Letter Glf; IM Sprt; Youngstown St Univ; Bus.

JONES, STEVIE; Glen Oak School; Shaker Hts, OH; Cls Rep Frsh Cls; Chrs; Cmnty Wkr; Off Ade; Stu Cncl; Yrbk; Sch Nwsp; Bsbl; Bsktbl; Chrldng; Stephens Coll; Intr Dsgn.

JONES, SUSAN; Decatur HS; Decatur, MI; Pres Soph Cls; Hon Rl; Stg Crw; Stu Cncl; Rptr Sch Nwsp; Pep Clb; Chrldng; PPFtbl; Scr Kpr; Western Mic Univ; Public Relations.

JONES, SUSAN; Tekonsha HS; Tekonsha, MI; 2/36 Chrs; Girl Scts; Hon Rl; Sch Pl; Sct Actv; Stg Crw; Stu Cncl; Drama Clb; 4-H; Ger Clb; Yth For Understanding Exchange Stu To Germany 77; Class Salutatorian 79; CISO Futuristic Schl Rep 79; Olivet Coll; Bio Chem.

JONES, SUSAN; Centerville HS; Centerville, OH; Cmp Fr Grls; Sch Mus; Fr Clb; Pom Pon; Point Park Coll; Dance.

JONES, TAMMY; Streetsboro HS; Streetsboro, OH; Hon Rl; Off Ade; OEA; College; Office Educ.

JONES, TANDRA; Du Pont HS; Charleston, WV; Cl Rep Jr Cls; Chrs; Hon Rl; JA; Jr NHS; Lbry Ade; Quill & Scroll; Sch Mus; Stu Cncl; Rptr Sch Nwsp; Thespians 77; Univ; Bus Admin.

JONES, TEENA; Lakeview HS; Lakeview, MI; 24/130 Band; Chrs; Chrh Wkr; Hon Rl; Sch Mus; Spn Clb; PPFtbl; 4-H Awd; Western Mich Univ; Music.

JONES, TERESA; Springboro HS; Springboro, OH; 26/199 Chrs; Girl Scts; Hon Rl; Sct Actv; Yth Flsp; Rptr Yrbk; 4-H; FTA; 4-H Awd; Mas Awd; Natl Sci Fdn Proj 79; Chosen For Warren County Youth Choir 76; Oh Wesleyan Fest Chorus 77 78 & 79; Heidelberg Coll; Forester.

JONES, TERESA; Milton Union HS; W Milton, OH; 72/230 Cmp Fr Grls; Off Ade; 4-H; FTA; Bsktbl; Trk; GAA; 4-H Awd; All Lg Vlybl 79; Honrbl Mention All Lg Bsktbl 79; Ohio St Univ.

JONES, TERESA; Switzerland Cnty Jr Sr HS; Canaan, IN; 10/122 Band; Hon Rl; Sec MMM; Sec NHS; Off Ade; Sch Pl; Drama Clb; FHA; Pep Clb; Spn Clb; Chrm Top 10 In Cls 1979; Sr Bnd Jckt 8 Yrs 1979; Crtfct Sys Hon Schlr 1979; Vincennes Univ; Secondary Educ.

JONES, TERRISITA; Warrensville Hts HS; Warrensville, OH; Cmp Fr Grls; Chrs; Drl Tm; Stu Cncl; Yrbk; Pres DECA; Letter Trk; Arizona St Univ; Bus Admin.

JONES, THOMAS; Mc Donald HS; Mc Donald, OH; 4/87 Am Leg Boys St; Aud/Vis; Hon Rl; NHS; Stg Crw; Trk; IM Sprt; Am Leg Awd; Youngstown St Univ; Comp Prog.

JONES, THOMAS D; Allen Park HS; Allen Park, MI; Cls Rep Sr Cls; Boy Scts; Chrs; Ferris State; Pharmacy.

JONES, TIM; Wadsworth Sr HS; Wadsworth, OH; Boy Scts; Cmnty Wkr; FCA; Hon Rl; Stu Cncl; Key Clb; Spn Clb; Bsktbl; Crs Cntry; Coach Actv; Univ; Bio.

JONES, TIMOTHY; Norwood HS; Norwood, OH; 29/348 Aud/Vis; Band; Chrs; Chrh Wkr; Hon Rl; Jr NHS; Natl Forn Lg; NHS; Drama Clb; Eng Clb; N Kentucky Univ; Music.

JONES, TINA; Buffalo HS; Huntington, WV; Hon Rl; Y-Teens; Spn Clb; Gym; Chrldng; Marshall Univ; Nursing.

JONES, TINKER; Philip Barbour HS; Belington, WV; Band; Hon Rl; NHS; Pres 4-H; Pres FFA; Univ; Drafting Engr.

JONES, TODD; West Branch HS; Alliance, OH; Boy Scts; Hon Rl; FFA; Bsbl; Letter Ftbl; Wrstlng; IM Sprt; Univ; Tele Cmnctns.

JONES, TONY; Springs Valley HS; W Baden, IN; 25/96 Hon Rl; Stu Cncl; 4-H; Fr Clb; Glf; Mgrs; 4-H Awd; Ind Univ; Law.

JONES, TRENT; Peebles HS; Peebles, OH; 1/100 Trs Jr Cls; Band; Boy Scts; Hon Rl; Sch Mus; Fr Clb; Letter Bsbl; Letter Bsktbl; Crs Cntry; Ftbl; College; Communications.

JONES, TRICIA; Indian Hill HS; Cincinnati, OH; 47/280 Pres Frsh Cls; VP Soph Cls; Sec Jr Cls; Cls Rep Sr Cls; Chrh Wkr; Girl Scts; Hon Rl; Lit Mag; Stu Cncl; Rptr Yrbk; Univ; Agri Cmnctns.

JONES, URSULA; Wehrle HS; Columbus, OH; 4/115 Chrh Wkr; Drl Tm; Girl Scts; Hon Rl; Soc Of Dist Amer HS Stu; Sci Awd For Biology; Columbus Coll Of Art; Fash Design.

JONES, VALERIE; John Hay HS; Cleveland, OH; 17/341 Cls Rep Sr Cls; Hon Rl; Jr NHS; Stu Cncl; Univ Of Cincinnati; Engr.

JONES, VALLI; Philip Barbour HS; Philippi, WV; Band; Cmp Fr Grls; Chrh Wkr; Girl Scts; Hon Rl; Hosp Ade; Sch Pl; Stu Cncl; Drama Clb; Fr Clb; West Virginia Univ; Social Work.

JONES, VERONICA; Immaculata HS; Detroit, MI; Hosp Ade; Orch; Sch Mus; Sch Pl; Sct Actv; Yth Flsp; Y-Teens; Fr Clb; FTA; Pep Clb; Cert Of Appreciation From Henry Ford Hosp; Cert For Participation In Natl Youth Sports Prog; Cert Phys Ed; Michigan St Univ; Medicine.

JONES, VICKI; Lakeview Sr HS; Stow, OH; Chrs; Chrh Wkr; Hosp Ade; JA; Stu Cncl; Lat Clb; JA Awd; Univ; Nursing.

JONES, VICKI S; Waterford Kettering HS; Drayton Plains, MI; 1/388 Chrh Wkr; Sec NHS; Letter Bsbl; Capt Chrldng; Cit Awd; DAR Awd; Natl Merit Ltr; General Motors Inst; Engr.

JONES, WELLIAM; Henry Ford Ii HS; Sterling Hts, MI; 111/444 Boy Scts; Ftbl; Trk; Wrstlng; Mich; U S Navy.

JONES, WESLEY P; Redford HS; Detroit, MI; Pres Jr Cls; Chrh Wkr; FCA; VICA; Ftbl; Trk; Lawrence Inst Of Tech.

JONES, WILLIAM; Buchanan HS; Buchanan, MI; Cls Rep Frsh Cls; VP Soph Cls; Cls Rep Soph Cls; VP Jr Cls; VP Sr Cls; Boy Scts; Pres Chrh Wkr; Pol Wkr; Univ Of Hawaii; Med.

JONES, WILLIAM; Martins Ferry HS; Martins Ferry, OH; 25/214 Pres Soph Cls; Hon Rl; NHS; Capt Bsbl; Bsktbl; Ftbl; Rio Grande Coll; Acctg.

JONES, W TRENT; North Knox HS; Oaktown, IN; 17/150 Band; Boy Scts; Hon Rl; NHS; 4-H; College; Architect.

JONES JR, SAM; Park Tudor HS; Indianapolis, IN; Cls Rep Soph Cls; Chrs; Chrh Wkr; Hon Rl; Mdrgl; Sch Mus; Yth Flsp; Bsktbl; Socr; Natl Merit Schl; Duke Univ; Pre Law.

JONGEKRYG, BRIAN; Zeeland HS; W Olive, MI; 7/200 Hon Rl; Ger Clb;.

JONKER, CHARLES; Holland Christian HS; Holland, MI; Band; Chrh Wkr; Hon Rl; Jr NHS; NHS; Letter Bsktbl; Letter Socr; Hope Coll; Bio.

JOOSTBERNS, ANDREW; Maple Vly HS; Vermontville, MI; 17/150 Cls Rep Sr Cls; Hon Rl; NHS; Stu Cncl; Letter Bsbl; Bsktbl; Ftbl; W Michigan Univ; Bus.

JORDAN, BRETT; Portsmouth HS; Portsmouth, OH; Chrh Wkr; Hon Rl; Letter Ftbl; Letter Trk; Northeastern Univ; Envir Sci.

JORDAN, CATHERINE; Cass Technical HS; Detroit, MI; Chrs; Chrh Wkr; Debate Tm; Girl Scts; Hon Rl; Off Ade; Cit Awd; Eastern Michigan Univ; Bus Admin.

JORDAN, CHRYSTAL; Urbana HS; Urbana, OH; 20/220 Band; Chrs; Chrh Wkr; Hon Rl; Jr NHS; NHS; Yth Flsp; 4-H; Mth Clb; Spn Clb; Cmnty Hosp Schl Of Nursing; RN.

JORDAN, DALE; Coventry HS; Akron, OH; Band; Boy Scts; Chrh Wkr; Hon Rl; Quill & Scroll; Sch Pl; Ed Sch Nwsp; Lat Clb; Wrstlng; Case Western Reserve; Chemistry.

JORDAN, DENISE; Canfield HS; Youngstown, OH; 127/274 Chrs; Chrh Wkr; Hon Rl; Mdrgl; Off Ade; Sch Mus; Y-Teens; Spn Clb; IM Sprt; Airline School; Stewardess.

JORDAN, DENISE; Grant HS; Grant, MI; Chrs; Cmnty Wkr; Girl Scts; Hon Rl; 4-H; Pep Clb; IM Sprt; PPFtbl; Cit Awd; 4-H Awd; Certf For Completing 450 Hrs At Voc Cntr In Data Proc; Newaygo Cnty Area Voc Cntr; Progr.

JORDAN, DENISE; Euclid Sr HS; Euclid, OH; Cls Rep Soph Cls; Cl Rep Jr Cls; Hon Rl; Jr NHS; Off Ade; Pep Clb; Socr; Scr Kpr; Cit Awd; CEC Awd In Geometry 78; CEC Awd In Eng 79; Univ; Bus.

JORDAN, J; Richmond Sr HS; Richmond, IN; Cls Rep Frsh Cls; Cls Rep Soph Cls; Debate Tm; Hon Rl; Jr NHS; Pol Wkr; Stu Cncl; Y-Teens; Spn Clb; Mgrs; Ball St Univ; Foreign Lang.

JORDAN, JENNIFER; Notre Dame Academy; Toledo, OH; Hon Rl; NHS; Quill & Scroll; Sch Pl; Stu Cncl; Rptr Yrbk; Sch Nwsp; Ten; College; Communications.

JORDAN, JOHN R; Granville HS; Granville, OH; 14/136 Am Leg Boys St; Hon Rl; NHS; Lat Clb; Mth Clb; Sci Clb; Capt Ftbl; Natl Merit SF; Univ; Biochem.

JORDAN, KRIS; Concordia Lutheran HS; Ft Wayne, IN; 7/160 Cls Rep Frsh Cls; Cls Rep Soph Cls; Cl Rep Jr Cls; Cls Rep Sr Cls; Chrh Wkr; Cmnty Wkr; Hon Rl; Hosp Ade; Jr NHS; NHS; Wittenberg Univ; English.

JORDAN, LAURA; St Francis De Sales HS; Columbus, OH; Cls Rep Soph Cls; Hon Rl; Stu Cncl; Mat Maids; PPFtbl; Tmr; Business School.

JORDAN, LISA; Walled Lake Western Sr HS; Walled Lk, MI; Chrs; Chrh Wkr; Cmnty Wkr; Girl Scts; Hon Rl; Lbry Ade; Sct Actv; Rptr Sch Nwsp; Fr Clb; East Tennessee St Univ; Lit.

JORDAN, MAGGIE; St Joseph Academy; Cleveland, OH; Pres Jr Cls; Chrs; Hon Rl; Hosp Ade; Pres Stu Cncl; Rptr Yrbk; Mth Clb; John Carroll Univ; Bus Admin.

JORDAN, MARIE; Benton Harbor HS; Benton Hbr, MI; Band; JA; PAVAS; Sch Pl; Stg Crw; Drama Clb; 4-H; Fr Clb; Drama Activities Awrd 78; Univ; Law.

JORDAN, MARY; St Joseph Academy; Cleveland, OH; 13/230 Cls Rep Frsh Cls; Cls Rep Soph Cls; Pres Jr Cls; Pres Sr Cls; Hon Rl; Rptr Yrbk; Rptr Sch Nwsp; Drama Clb; DAR Awd; Voice Dem Awd; Georgetown Univ; Jrnlsm.

JORDAN, MELODY R; Du Pont HS; Charleston, WV; Girl Scts; Hon Rl; 4-H; Pep Clb; Chrldng; Univ Of Charleston; Bus.

JORDAN, MONIKA L; Immaculata HS; Detroit, MI; 16/93 Girl Scts; Hon Rl; Mod UN; NHS; Sct Actv; Stu Cncl; Spn Clb; Letter Bsbl; Letter Bsktbl; Mgrs; Michigan St Univ; Med.

JORDAN, QUINTIN; Woodward HS; Cincinnati, OH; Cls Rep Frsh Cls; Cls Rep Soph Cls; Cl Rep Jr Cls; Cls Rep Sr Cls; Band; Boy Scts; Chrh Wkr; Cmnty Wkr; Hon Rl; JA; Otstndng Marching Band Mbr 78; Otstndng Instrumentalist 76 79; St John Amezion Church Schlrshp 78; Baldwin Wallace Univ.

JORDAN, RALPH; Alexander HS; Pomeroy, OH; Hon Rl; Sch Pl; Stg Crw; Rptr Sch Nwsp; 4-H; Pep Clb; Spn Clb; Bsktbl; 4-H Awd; Bus Schl.

JORDAN, REBECCA L; Jennings County HS; No Vernon, IN; 2/420 Sec Chrh Wkr; Girl Scts; Hon Rl; NHS; Sch Pl; Sct Actv; Stg Crw; Lee College; Religion.

JORDAN, RICK; West Carrollton Sr HS; Dayton, OH; Hon Rl; NHS; Rptr Sch Nwsp; Fr Clb; Rdo Clb; Opt Clb Awd; Tennessee Temple Univ; Brdcstng.

JORDAN, ROGER; Davison HS; Davison, MI; Rptr Sch Nwsp; Univ Of Michigan; History.

JORDAN, STEVE; Tecumseh HS; New Carlisle, OH; Aud/Vis; Lbry Ade; NHS; Sch Mus; Sch Pl; Stg Crw; Rptr Sch Nwsp; Drama Clb; Fr Clb; Cit Awd; Wright St Univ; Acctg.

JORDAN, SUE; Revere HS; Akron, OH; Cl Rep Jr Cls; Cls Rep Sr Cls; Band; Stu Cncl; Pep Clb; Capt Trk; PPFtbl; Univ Of Akron.

JORDAN, SUSAN A; Jackson HS; Massillon, OH; 33/409 Hon Rl; NHS; Y-Teens; Fr Clb; OEA; Pep Clb; Letter Swmmng; Tmr; Vocational Stu Of Month; Sec Treas Varsity J Club; Bowling Green Univ; CPA.

JORDAN, ZELDA; Perry Baptist HS; Morrice, MI; 2/8 Chrs; Girl Scts; Hon Rl; Lbry Ade; Off Ade; Rptr Yrbk; Rptr Sch Nwsp; FHA; Univ; Conservation.

JORDON, BRENDA; Tecumseh HS; New Carlisle, OH; 27/450 VP Soph Cls; VP Jr Cls; AFS; FCA; Hon Rl; Jr NHS; Off Ade; Stu Cncl; Yrbk; Sch Nwsp; Worthy Advisor Of Rainbow For Girls; Bethel Twp Firemans Queen; Central Western Firemans Queen; Technical Schl; Dental Asst.

JORDON, LYNDA; Napoleon HS; Jackson, MI; 33/162 Band; Off Ade; Letter Bsbl; Letter Glf; Cert Of Recngnt 79; Confrnc Champ Of Sftbl 79; Acad All Confrnc Awd 79; Michigan St Univ; Engr.

JORGENSEN, LINDA; Wayne HS; Dayton, OH; 52/700 AFS; Hon Rl; Sec Jr NHS; Sec NHS; Rptr Yrbk; Spn Clb; Coll; Soc Sci.

JORGENSON, GARY; Calumet HS; Laurium, MI; Pres Chrh Wkr; Michigan Tech Univ; Law.

JORGENSON, JANET; New Lexington Sr HS; New Lexington, OH; 40/150 VP Soph Cls; Cl Rep Jr Cls; Cls Rep Sr Cls; Aud/Vis; Chrh Wkr; Hon Rl; Stu Cncl; 4-H; FHA; Pep Clb; Hocking Tech Coll; Nursing.

JOSEF, ERNEST; Ripley HS; Ripley, WV; 1/248 Hon Rl; Beta Clb; 4-H; Mth Clb; Sci Clb; Letter Ten; IM Sprt; 4-H Awd; Natl Merit Ltr; Dept Of Ed Golden Horse Shoe Awd; Natl HS & Jr Coll Math Clb; Cert Of Meritorious Awds; West Virginia Univ.

JOSEPH, CARLA; Onekama Consolidated HS; Onekama, MI; 1/60 Band; Hon Rl; NHS; Sch Pl; Yth Flsp; Drama Clb; Natl Merit Ltr; Manchester Coll.

JOSEPH, DAN; Ironton HS; Ironton, OH; Boys Clb Am; Ger Clb; Wrstlng; Frsh Awd 90% Av In All Cls 76; Univ; Archt.

JOSEPH, GREG; St Xavier HS; Cincinnat, OH; 75/280 Cls Rep Sr Cls; Cmnty Wkr; Hon Rl; Jr NHS; NHS; Swmmng; Trk; IM Sprt; Spnsh Hnr Soc 78; Co Chairmn Of Fresh Orientn 78 80; Bus.

JOSEPH, JENNIFER; Allen East HS; Lafayette, OH; 33/110 Trs Jr Cls; Band; Chrs; Chrh Wkr; Sch Pl; Yth Flsp; Yrbk; 4-H; Fr Clb; Univ.

JOSEPH, LYNN; Westerville North HS; Westerville, OH; Chrs; Drl Tm; Hon Rl; Stg Crw; 4-H; Letter Gym; Ohio St Univ; Philosophy.

JOSEPH, MARIA; Our Lady Of Mercy HS; W Bloomfield, MI; 1/300 Cls Rep Frsh Cls; Cls Rep Soph Cls; Cmnty Wkr; Hon Rl; NHS; Bsbl; IM Sprt; Natl Merit Ltr; Concours Natl De Francois Cert Of Merit 78; Cert For Excel In Art 77; Tutoring Elem Eng & Math; Fine Arts.

JOSEPH, STEVE; Bridgeport HS; Saginaw, MI; Sch Pl; Letter Ftbl; Letter Trk; Letter Wrstlng; Coach Actv; Central Michigan Univ; Jrnlsm.

JOSEPH, WILLIAM; Napoleon HS; Napoleon, OH; 24/275 Am Leg Boys St; Debate Tm; Hon Rl; Jr NHS; Natl Forn Lg; Orch; Lat Clb; Bsktbl; Crs Cntry; College; Law.

JOSEY, RICHARD; Highland Park Commty HS; Highland Park, MI; Cls Rep Frsh Cls; Hon Rl; NHS; Sch Pl; Pres Stu Cncl; Drama Clb; Pres Fr Clb; VP Lat Clb; Pep Clb; Trk; Univ Of Michigan; Communications.

JOSHUA, STACY; East Chicago Roosevelt HS; E Chicago, IN; Girl Scts; Hon Rl; Lbry Ade; Off Ade; FTA; Bus Schl; Sec.

JOSLEN, JULIE A; Big Rapids HS; Big Rapids, MI; NHS; Rptr Yrbk; Rptr Sch Nwsp; Chrldng; Ferris St Coll; Dent Hygnst.

JOSLIN, NANCY A; Northville HS; Northville, MI; 1/337 Cls Rep Soph Cls; Cl Rep Jr Cls; Am Leg Aux Girls St; Band; Natl Forn Lg; VP NHS; Stu Cncl; Ed Sch Nwsp; Rptr Sch Nwsp; Tmr; E Mi Univ Regnst Schslp For Outstndng HS Jrs 79; Gold Key From Detroit News Schlstc Writng Awd Featr 79; Univ; Pre Law.

JOSLYN, THOMAS; Athens HS; East Leroy, MI; Pres Soph Cls; Hon Rl; Quill & Scroll; Sch Pl; Pres Stu Cncl; Yrbk; Letter Bsbl; Letter Bsktbl; Trk; Coach Actv; Michigan State Univ; Communications.

JOST, TERRY; Calvin Christian HS; Grand Rapids, MI; Chrs; Ftbl; Wrstlng; Natl Merit SF; Univ.

JOURDAIN, CHRISTINE; Clare HS; Clare, MI; Cl Rep Jr Cls; Trs Sr Cls; Cls Rep Sr Cls; Band; Hon Rl; NHS; Stu Cncl; Yrbk; Sec 4-H; Fr Clb; Lansing Bus Inst; Legal Sec.

JOURILES, GREGORY; Cleveland Heights HS; University Hts, OH; 1/800 Ger Clb; Letter Bsktbl; Capt Socr; Coach Actv; NCTE; Natl Merit Ltr; Superior Achvmnt MAA Test 1978; Stanford Univ.

JOURNIC, STEVE; Streetsboro HS; Streetsboro, OH; Hon Rl; Rptr Sch Nwsp; Rdo Clb; Univ.

JOVANOVICH, RAY W; Hammond HS; Hammond, IN; 10/334 Cls Rep Soph Cls; Pres Jr Cls; Am Leg Boys St; Hon Rl; Jr NHS; Natl Forn Lg; NHS; FDA; Letter Trk; Calumet Coll Alumni Awrd 79; Cross Cntry 3 Yr Lttmn & All St Tm & Tm Capt 76; Swimming 3 Yr Lttrmn; Univ; Pre Dent Med.

JOVEN, ARIEL; Fruitport HS; Muskegon, MI; 10/281 Am Leg Boys St; Band; Hon Rl; NHS; Bsktbl; Ten; Muskegon Comm Coll; Engr.

JOY, BILL; Whitko HS; South Whitley, IN; 12/155 Am Leg Boys St; Hon Rl; Natl Forn Lg; NHS; Pol Wkr; Stg Crw; Drama Clb; Sci Clb; Ten; Coach Actv; Indiana Univ; Math.

JOY, JONI; North Branch HS; Fostoria, MI; Chrh Wkr; Hon Rl; NHS; Yth Flsp; 4-H; Pep Clb; PPFtbl; Alpena Cmnty Coll; Foreign Lang.

JOY, LAURA; Patrick Henry HS; Grelton, OH; 13/118 Cl Rep Jr Cls; Am Leg Aux Girls St; Treas Chrs; Sec NHS; Sch Mus; Sec Stu Cncl; Sec Spn Clb; GAA; Scr Kpr; Ohio Northern Univ; Elem Ed.

JOY, REBECCA; Vinson HS; Huntington, WV; VP Frsh Cls; VP Soph Cls; VP Jr Cls; VP Sr Cls; Chrs; Chrh Wkr; Hon Rl; Sec NHS; Y-Teens; Fr Clb; 3rd Highst Awd Acctg I 78; Marshall Univ; Acctg.

JOYCE, ANNE; Ursuline HS; Youngstown, OH; 13/350 Cls Rep Frsh Cls; Sec Jr Cls; Girl Scts; Hon Rl; Jr NHS; NHS; Stu Cncl; FTA; College; Nursing.

JOYCE, DALE; Highland HS; Anderson, IN; 41/400 Cls Rep Frsh Cls; Cls Rep Sr Cls; Am Leg Boys St; Band; Boy Scts; Chrh Wkr; Hon Rl; NHS; Pol Wkr; Stu Cncl; Indiana Univ; Business & Math.

JOYCE, DEBBIE; South Knox HS; Vincennes, IN; Girl Scts; Hon Rl; Red Cr Ade; FHA; FNA; Pres OEA; GAA; Outstndg Bus Stdnt Awd 1979; Oea Awd Sales 1979; Cert Of Reg 1979; Hoosier Schlr Awd 1979; Vincennes Univ; Bus Admin.

JOYCE, JEFFERY; Mount View HS; Thorpe, WV; Pres Frsh Cls; VP Soph Cls; Chrs; Chrh Wkr; Cmnty Wkr; Hon Rl; JA; Ohi Univ; Bus Admin.

JOYCE, MARY E; St Augustine Academy; Lakewood, OH; Cls Rep Frsh Cls; Cls Rep Soph Cls; Cl Rep Jr Cls; Hon Rl; Hosp Ade; Sch Mus; Sch Pl; Stu Cncl; FNA; Spn Clb; Music Awds Piano; College; Nursing.

JOYCE, ROBERT; Bishop Dwenger HS; Ft Wayne, IN; 19/245 CAP; Hon Rl; NHS; Sch Mus; Sch Pl; Stg Crw; Sch Nwsp; Letter Fr Clb; College; Aerospace Engr.

JOYCE, ROBERT K; Marquette HS; Michigan City, IN; 14/76 Cl Rep Jr Cls; VP Sr Cls; Am Leg Boys St; Band; Chrs; Hon Rl; NHS; Sch Mus; Rptr Sch Nwsp; Drama Clb; Univ Of Notre Dame; Archt.

JOYE, JAMES D; Rutherford B Hayes HS; Delaware, OH; Boy Scts; Chrh Wkr; Hon Rl; JA; Sct Actv; Yth Flsp; Ger Clb; Pres Key Clb; Lat Clb; Bsbl; Univ; Med.

JOYNER, ANGELA; Watkins Memorial HS; Pataskala, OH; Chrs; Hon Rl; NHS; Letter Gym;.

JOZWIAK, BERNARD; Clay Sr HS; S Bend, IN; 10/409 Cls Rep Sr Cls; Hon Rl; NHS; Stu Cncl; Capt Crs Cntry; Letter Trk; Kiwan Awd; Purdue Univ; Indust Engr.

JOZWIAK, JOHANNA; Midland HS; Midland, MI; 31/476 Hon Rl; Off Ade; Pol Wkr; Fr Clb; IM Sprt; Bd Of Control Schrlshp Mich Comp Schlrshp; Cert Of Recogn; Kalamazoo Coll Grant; Kalamazoo Coll; Law.

JROSOSKY, ROGER; Newbury HS; Newbury, OH; 10/63 Cls Rep Soph Cls; Hon Rl; Jr NHS; NHS; Stu Cncl; VICA; Letter Bsktbl; Ftbl; Voc School; Machinist.

JUDAY, DAVID; William G Mather HS; Wetmore, MI; 7/105 Pres Frsh Cls; Band; Hon Rl; NHS; Stg Crw; Bsktbl; Letter Trk; IM Sprt; Univ.

JUDD, ELLEN; Clio HS; Clio, MI; Band; Hon Rl; Jr NHS; NHS; Off Ade; Sch Mus; Sch Pl; Pep Clb; Ten; Un Flint; Bus.

JUDD, JACQUELINE; Norton HS; Norton, OH; Hon Rl; Hosp Ade; JA; NHS; Drama Clb; Pep Clb; Chrldng; JA Awd; Sec Rotary Awd; Akron Univ.

JUDD, JANET; St Joseph Academy; Parma, OH; Pres Girl Scts; Hon Rl; Hosp Ade; Sec JA; Lbry Ade; VP Orch; Sct Actv; JA Awd; Marian Awd Girls Scout 78; Cleveland St Univ; Comp.

JUDD, JOHN; Kiser HS; Dayton, OH; Cls Rep Frsh Cls; Cls Rep Soph Cls; Cl Rep Jr Cls; Cls Rep Sr Cls; Chrs; Lbry Ade; NHS; Sch Mus; Stu Cncl; OEA; Awrd For 5 Yrs Straights A; Univ; Music.

JUDD, JOSEPH B; Jennings County HS; No Vernon, IN; Band; Boy Scts; NHS; Sch Pl; Ger Clb; Rotary Awd; Ind Univ; German.

JUDD, MARSHA; West Catholic HS; Grand Rapids, MI; 10/265 Band; Hon Rl; NHS; Lat Clb; Natl Merit Ltr; Aquinas Coll; Acctg.

JUDE, BRENDA; Kermit HS; Kermit, WV; 5/28 Beta Clb; Drama Clb; FHA; Pep Clb; Spn Clb; Capt Bsktbl; Capt Chrldng; College.

JUDE, CATHY A; Kermit HS; Kermit, WV; 4/27 Sec Sr Cls; Band; Hon Rl; Beta Clb; FHA; Pep Clb; Spn Clb; Bsktbl; Capt Chrldng; Univ.

JUDE, CHARLES; Jesup W Scott HS; Toledo, OH; Hon Rl; Boys Clb Am; Letter Ftbl; Letter Trk; Letter Wrstlng; Univ; Comp Tech.

JUDGE, JOHN W; Bellmont HS; Decatur, IN; 5/231 Am Leg Boys St; Band; Chrh Wkr; Cmnty Wkr; Hon Rl; NHS; Orch; Sch Mus; Sct Actv; 4-H; Richard Lugar Symposium For Tomorrows Ldrs 78; Whos Who In Midwestern HS Foreign Lang 79; Coll; Bio.

JUDGE, MARY; North Farmington HS; Farm Hills, MI; Cls Rep Frsh Cls; Chrs; Girl Scts; Hon Rl; Off Ade; Sch Pl; Sct Actv; Stg Crw; Stu Cncl; Bsktbl; College; Display.

JUDGE, PATRICIA; Otsego HS; Bowling Gren, OH; 26/125 Cmp Fr Grls; Hon Rl; Natl Forn Lg; Pol Wkr; Sch Pl; Drama Clb; Ger Clb; Pep Clb; Gym; Trk; Awd Of Excellence Phys Fit; Recommendation Fo Commendation Speech; N W Reg Ohio Scholastic Art Awd; Ohio St Univ; Theatre.

JUDIS, JANET; Rockford Sr HS; Belmont, MI; Hon Rl; JA; Sch Pl; Gym; PPFtbl; Central Michigan Univ.

JUDIS, JEFFERY; Lakeview HS; Six Lakes, MI; 27/145 Hon Rl; FTA; Spn Clb; Letter Bsbl; Letter Bsktbl; Letter Glf; Central Michigan Univ.

JUDSON, TIMM; University HS; Gates Mills, OH; 4/90 Sec Frsh Cls; AFS; Hon Rl; Stu Cncl; Rptr Yrbk; Sprt Ed Sch Nwsp; Fr Clb; Key Clb; Letter Bsbl; Letter Ftbl; Highest Hnr Bracket Hnr Roll; MVP Runner Up Ftbl; Leading Rusher Ftbl; Bowdoin Coll; Busns.

JUDY, DEBBIE; Arcanum Butler HS; Arcanum, OH; 7/99 Chrs; Hon Rl; Pres 4-H; VP FHA; Scr Kpr; 4-H Awd; Voc Schl; Nurse.

JUDY, DINA; Harman School; Harman, WV; 2/18 VP Jr Cls; Pres Sr Cls; Val; Band; Chrs; Chrh Wkr; Hon Rl; NHS; Sch Pl; Ed Yrbk; Alderson Broaddus Coll; Med Sci.

JUDY, KATHLEEN; Big Walnut HS; Sunbury, OH; 42/253 Band; Cmnty Wkr; Drl Tm; Girl Scts; JA; Off Ade; Sch Mus; Sch Pl; Sct Actv; Stu Cncl; Univ; Sec.

JUDY, ROBERT; North Miami HS; Denver, IN; Hon Rl; Trk; Outsdng Stu Final & Voc Schl 79; US Marine Corps; Auto Mech.

JUDY, RONDA; Hopkins HS; Byron Ctr, MI; Chrs; Girl Scts; Hon Rl; NHS; Letter Trk; Letter Twrlr; Bus Schl; Sci.

JUECKSTOCK, DIANE; Kimball HS; Royal Oak, MI; 188/602 Chrs; Chrh Wkr; Cmnty Wkr; Hon Rl; Hosp Ade; NHS; Yth Flsp; Mercy Coll; Nursing.

JULIAN, ANNE; Mason HS; Mason, MI; Chrh Wkr; Jr NHS; Fr Clb; Swmmng; Trk; Chrldng; Outstndng Understndng & Comp Of Short Story 79; Ferris St Coll; Pharm.

JULIAN, DEBBIE; Valparaiso HS; Valparaiso, IN; 169/467 Chrs; Drl Tm; Girl Scts; Stg Crw; Y-Teens; DECA; 4-H; Vincennes Univ; Busns Admin.

JULIAN, GAIL; Jackson HS; North Canton, OH; 56/409 Band; Chrs; Chrh Wkr; Hon Rl; Hosp Ade; Sct Actv; Yth Flsp; Pep Clb; Spn Clb; Swmmng; Coll; R N.

JULYLIA, MICHELLE; Villa Angela Acad; Cleveland, OH; 1/189 Val; Band; Chrh Wkr; Girl Scts; Hon Rl; NHS; Orch; Sct Actv; Stu Cncl; Bausch & Lomb Awd; Cleveland St Univ; Chem Engr.

JUNAK, KAREN; Westwood HS; Ishpeming, MI; Cls Rep Frsh Cls; Band; Girl Scts; Hon Rl; Sct Actv; 4-H; OEA; Pep Clb; Bsktbl; Pres Awd; N Michigan Univ; Pub Relations.

JUNE, BARRY; Goodrich HS; Goodrich, MI; Pres Sr Cls; Band; Boy Scts; Hon Rl; College.

JUNG, BARBARA; Oak Hill HS; Converse, IN; 28/160 Am Leg Aux Girls St; Chrs; FCA; Girl Scts; Hon Rl; NHS; Stg Crw; FHA; Pep Clb; Spn Clb; Purdue Univ; Early Childhood Ed.

JUNG, CHRIS; Brush HS; S Euclid, OH; Boy Scts; Hon Rl; Sct Actv; Yth Flsp; Bsktbl; Glf; Letter Wrstlng; IM Sprt; College; Chem Engr.

JUNG, LORI; Centerville HS; Dayton, OH; 67/680 Chrs; NHS; OEA; GAA; IM Sprt; Scr Kpr; Tmr; Miami Univ; Math.

JUNG, YOOK J; West Technical HS; Cleveland, OH; 11/588 Hon Rl; NHS; Yth Flsp; OEA; Baldwin Wallace Coll; Acctg.

JUNGBLUT, MAUREEN C; Holland HS; Holland, MI; Cmnty Wkr; Hon Rl; Hosp Ade; NHS; Orch; Nazareth Coll; Nursing.

JUNGCLAS, DANIEL; Roseville HS; Roseville, MI; 1/451 Cls Rep Soph Cls; Val; Chrh Wkr; Hon Rl; NHS; Pol Wkr; Sch Mus; Sch Pl; Stg Crw; Stu Cncl; Schls Hall Of Fame Or Roseville HS 78; Phi Beta Kappa Awd; Ohio Univ; Theatre.

JUNGE, DANIEL; Napoleon HS; Napoleon, OH; College; Mechanical Engineering.

JUNGLAS, DANA; North Newton HS; Demotte, IN; 10/144 Hon Rl; NHS; FBLA; Bsbl; Bsktbl; Univ; Bus Admin.

JUNIET, KATHLEEN; Immaculate Conception Acad; Cincinnati, OH; 17/68 Chrs; Hon Rl; Orch; Sdlty; Stg Crw; Stu Cncl; Yrbk; Sch Nwsp; Ger Clb; GAA; Marian Coll; Art Therapy.

JUNK, CRAIG; Adena HS; Frankfort, OH; 12/80 VP Jr Cls; Chrs; Hon Rl; Jr NHS; Y-Teens; Rptr Sch Nwsp; Sch Nwsp; 4-H; Key Clb; Letter Bsbl; Ohio Inst Of Tech; Elec Engr.

JUNKENS, JAMIE; Hammond Baptist HS; Hammond, IN; Sec Frsh Cls; Trs Frsh Cls; Sec Jr Cls; Chrs; Chrh Wkr; Hon Rl; Jr NHS; NHS; Off Ade; Chrldng; Hyles Anderson Coll; Elem Ed.

JUNKER, KARI; Norwood HS; Norwood, OH; Am Leg Aux Girls St; Hon Rl; Lit Mag; Treas Stu Cncl; Treas Fr Clb; Pep Clb; Socr; Trk; Coach Actv; GAA; Xavier Univ; History.

JUNKINS, BRENDA; Liberty HS; Bristol, WV; Band; Chrh Wkr; Hon Rl; Lbry Ade; NHS; Sch Pl; Stg Crw; Yrbk; Sch Nwsp; FBLA; W Virginia Career Coll; Med Sec Asst.

JURACEK, TODD; Perry HS; Perry, MI; Cls Rep Frsh Cls; Cls Rep Soph Cls; Cl Rep Jr Cls; Cls Rep Sr Cls; Hon Rl; VP Stu Cncl; Capt Pep Clb; Letter Trk; Letter Wrstlng; Univ Of Michigan; Civil Engr.

JURASEK, CHARLENE; Concord HS; Concord, MI; 1/75 Pres Frsh Cls; Pres Jr Cls; Pres Sr Cls; Val; Treas NHS; Sch Pl; Yrbk; Capt Bsktbl; Letter Trk; Univ Of Mich; Engr.

JURASIN, PAUL; A D Johnston HS; Ramsay, MI; Cls Rep Frsh Cls; Trs Jr Cls; Letter Bsbl; Letter Ftbl; Letter Ten; IM Sprt; Univ.

JURATOVAC, EVANNE; Nordonia HS; Sagamore Hls, OH; 7/443 Cls Rep Frsh Cls; Cls Rep Soph Cls; Cl Rep Jr Cls; Chrh Wkr; Girl Scts; Hosp Ade; Jr NHS; NHS; Sch Mus; Yth Flsp; Ohio Schl Tests; Principals 9 11; Univ; Nursing.

JURCAK, RONALD; Padua Franciscan HS; Cleveland, OH; Hon Rl; Fr Clb; Bsbl; IM Sprt; Ohio St Univ; Optometry.

JURCENKO, SCOTT; Jefferson Area HS; Jefferson, OH; AFS; Band; Sch Mus; Stg Crw; Spn Clb; Glf; Trk; Ohio State Univ; Elec Engr.

JURCZYNSKI, DEBBIE; Admiral King HS; Lorain, OH; 16/413 Chrs; Cmnty Wkr; Girl Scts; Hon Rl; Hosp Ade; NHS; Off Ade; Treas Y-Teens; OEA; Univ Of Toledo; Legal Asst.

JUREK, CHRISTOPHER; St Francis De Sales HS; Toledo, OH; Boy Scts; Hon Rl; Sct Actv; Stu Cncl; Rptr Sch Nwsp; Trk; IM Sprt; University; Law.

JUREK, KENNETH; Washington HS; South Bend, IN; 90/350 Band; Orch; Busns Schl; CPA.

JURIK, KIMBERLY; Pine River Jr Sr HS; Luther, MI; Band; Chrs; Hon Rl; NHS; Sch Mus; 4-H; FHA; Pep Clb; Mgrs; 4-H Awd; 8th Grade Algebra Awd; Jr Varsity Volleyball; College; Social Work.

JUST, HOLLY; Field HS; Kent, OH; Band; Cmp Fr Grls; Chrh Wkr; Cmnty Wkr; Drm Bgl; Hon Rl; Jr NHS; NHS; Off Ade; Sec Stu Cncl; Gym Placed In Jr Olymp 76; Voted Soph Homecoming Attndnt 77; Pres Of Middle Schl Stu Cncl 75; Univ Of Akron; Acctg.

JUSTICE, DEBORAH; Adena HS; Clarksburg, OH; 3/85 Pres Frsh Cls; Pres Soph Cls; AFS; Am Leg Aux Girls St; Band; Chrs; Debate Tm; Hon Rl; Jr NHS; NHS; Banking.

JUSTICE, FRELON; Willow Run HS; Ypsilanti, MI; Boy Scts; Trk; JETS Awd; Willow Run HS Chess Champ; Univ; Aero Engr.

JUSTICE, GARY R; Nitro HS; Nitro, WV; Cls Rep Frsh Cls; Pres Soph Cls; Am Leg Boys St; Boy Scts; Hon Rl; Stg Crw; Stu Cncl; Yth Flsp; Spn Clb; Letter Bsbl; College; Cmmrcl Art.

JUSTICE, JACKIE; Crestview HS; Mansfield, OH; Cls Rep Soph Cls; Chrs; Chrh Wkr; Debate Tm; Girl Scts; Hon Rl; Hosp Ade; Lbry Ade; Sch Mus; Stu Cncl; Teens Action Prog 75; March Of Dimes 77; North Central Tech Univ; RN.

JUSTICE, LARRY; Oceana HS; Matheny, WV; Cl Rep Jr Cls; Cmnty Wkr; Debate Tm; Hon Rl; Sch Pl; Pep Clb; Bsbl; Letter Bsktbl; Letter Trk; Tmr; Marshall Univ; Mining Engr.

JUSTICE, LINDA; Sandusky HS; Sandusky, OH; 19/404 Band; Hon Rl; NHS; OEA; C of C Awd; Bowling Green St Univ; Bus Admin.

JUSTICE, ROBERT J; Dunbar Sr HS; Dunbar, WV; Cls Rep Soph Cls; Cl Rep Jr Cls; Cls Rep Sr Cls; Hon Rl; NHS; Off Ade; Stu Cncl; Rptr Yrbk; Yrbk; Rptr Sch Nwsp; Univ; Sci.

JUSTICE, RONNIE; Logan HS; West Logan, WV; Cls Rep Soph Cls; Band; Boy Scts; Chrh Wkr; Hon Rl; Pol Wkr; Sct Actv; Yth Flsp; Ed Sch Nwsp; Pres Beta Clb; Key Club Dist Board; Homeroom Officer; Prayer Club Council; West Virginia Univ; Poli Sci.

JUSTISON, GEORGE; East Palestine HS; E Palestine, OH; 4/142 Am Leg Boys St; Band; Boy Scts; Chrh Wkr; Debate Tm; Hon Rl; NHS; Ohi State Univ; Phys Ther.

JUSTO, EMILIO; Andrean HS; Crown Pt, IN; 1/272 Val; Boy Scts; Cmnty Wkr; Hon Rl; Hosp Ade; NHS; Stg Crw; Stu Cncl; Rptr Sch Nwsp; Drama Clb; Schl County & St Recipient Of Good Citizen Awd From Daughters Of Amer Revo & Eligible For Natl Awd 79; Univ Of Michigan; Med.

JUTTE, BECK; Coldwater HS; Coldwater, OH; Band; Chrs; Hon Rl; Stg Crw; Rptr Sch Nwsp; 4-H; Spn Clb; Letter Trk; IM Sprt;.

JUTTE, P; High School; Versailles, OH; 12/132 Band; Stg Crw; Drama Clb; Spn Clb; Univ.

K

KAAKE, LORI; Snider HS; Ft Wayne, IN; Girl Scts; Hon Rl; NHS; Yth Flsp; Pep Clb; Spn Clb; Trk; Ind Univ; Comp.

KAAKE, WENDY L; R Nelson Snider HS; Ft Wayne, IN; 21/500 Girl Scts; Hon Rl; Lbry Ade; Sch Pl; Rptr Yrbk; Yrbk; Drama Clb; Spn Clb; Univ.

KAATZ, INGRID; St Mary Academy; Newport, MI; 1/130 Hon Rl; NHS; Fr Clb; Ger Clb; Sci Clb; Univ; Ecol Resrch.

KABACINSKI, KEVIN; Lake Shore HS; St Clair Shore, MI; 125/583 Boy Scts; Hon Rl; Jr NHS; Sct Actv; Letter Crs Cntry; Letter Trk; Coach Actv; Scr Kpr; Univ Of Detroit; Civil Engr.

KABAT, SHELLY L; St Ursula Academy; Maumee, OH; 1/88 Hon Rl; Pres Fr Clb; Sci Clb; Natl Merit Ltr; Univ; Pre Med.

KABBANI, YOUSSEF; Cody HS; Detroit, MI; Hon Rl; NHS; FDA; Mth Clb; Sci Clb; Univ Of Mich.

KABLE, ALICIA; Wickliffe Sr HS; Wickliffe, OH; 31/320 AFS; Band; Chrs; Hon Rl; Mod UN; NHS; Off Ade; Sch Pl; Stg Crw; Treas Drama Clb; Akron Univ; Nursing.

KABLE, VICTOR; Bellmont HS; Decatur, IN; 61/244 Hon Rl; Letter Bsbl; Letter Ftbl; IM Sprt; Univ; Archt.

KABODIAN, ARMEN; Rochester Adams HS; Rochester, MI; 130/530 Cls Rep Sr Cls; JA; NHS; PAVAS; Sch Pl; Stg Crw; Stu Cncl; Drama Clb; Fr Clb; Socr; Oakland Univ.

KACENSKI, LYNDEL; Columbiana HS; Columbiana, OH; Cl Rep Jr Cls; Band; Drl Tm; Hon Rl; Sec JA; Stu Cncl; Y-Teens; Rptr Sch Nwsp; Sch Nwsp; Sec OEA; OEA Ambassador Statesman Diplomat & Exec; College; Exec Sec.

KACHILLA, AMY; Zanesville HS; Zanesville, OH; Am Leg Aux Girls St; Cmnty Wkr; Girl Scts; Hon Rl; Hosp Ade; Lit Mag; NHS; Orch; Sct Actv; Ohi State College.

KACHMARIK, TIM; Padua Franciscan HS; Parma, OH; Cmnty Wkr; Hon Rl; Letter Bsbl; Capt Bsktbl; Capt Ftbl; Scr Kpr; Tmr; Cleveland St Univ; Acctg.

KACHO, BRENDA; Greeneview HS; Jamestown, OH; 2/120 Sal; Chrs; Chrh Wkr; Hon Rl; NHS; Yrbk; 4-H; Treas OEA; Wright St Univ; Acctg.

KACHOVEC, PATRICIA; Jackson Milton HS; N Jackson, OH; Cl Rep Jr Cls; Cls Rep Sr Cls; NHS; Off Ade; Stu Cncl; Rptr Sch Nwsp; Key Clb; College; Computer Technology.

KACHUR, MICHAEL; Maplewood HS; Cortland, OH; Am Leg Boys St; Chrh Wkr; Hon Rl; NHS; Beta Clb; Bsktbl; Trk; Coach Actv; College.

KACIK, RICHARD; Morgantown HS; Morgantwn, WV; Cls Rep Frsh Cls; Boy Scts; Hon Rl; Jr NHS; NHS; Stu Cncl; Yrbk; Ger Clb; Mth Clb; Coach Actv; Most Artistic In Schl; Most Creative In Schl; German Awd; W Virginia Univ; Engr.

KACKLEY, GARY; Meadowbrook HS; Byesville, OH; VP FFA; Ftbl; Univ; Agri.

KACKLEY, JERRY; Meadowbrook HS; Byesville, OH; Pres Frsh Cls; Hon Rl; FFA; Lat Clb; Ftbl; College; Accounting.

KACSOR, DEBORAH; Northside HS; Ft Wayne, IN; Band; Chrs; Drl Tm; Hon Rl; Lbry Ade; NHS; Sch Mus; Rptr Sch Nwsp; Pep Clb; Pom Pon; St Francis; Teacher.

KACZANOWSKI, ROBERT; Wayland HS; Wayland, MI; Pres Frsh Cls; Pres Soph Cls; Pres Jr Cls; Am Leg Boys St; Debate Tm; Hon Rl; NHS; Sci Clb; Michigan St Univ.

KACZMAREK, DAVID A; Greenfield Central HS; Greenfield, IN; Boy Scts; Spn Clb; Eagle Scout; Chess Club; Natl Spanish Honor Soc; College; Medicine.

KACZMAREK, LORI; Manistee Public HS; Manistee, MI; 8/197 Cls Rep Soph Cls; Cl Rep Jr Cls; Pres Sr Cls; Hon Rl; NHS; Stu Cncl; Fr Clb; Capt Ten; Am Leg Awd; DAR Awd; Pres Of Natl Hon Soc 78; Sr Home Rep ;good Citizen Of The Yr 78; Dads

Club Girl Ath Of The Yr 78; Michigan St Univ; Psych.

KACZMAREK, LYNN; Lasalle HS; South Bend, IN; 11/488 Hon Rl; NHS; Bus Schl.

KACZMAREK, NICHOLAS E; All Saints Ctrl HS; Essexville, MI; Cl Rep Jr Cls; Cls Rep Sr Cls; Stg Crw; Letter Bsbl; Letter Ftbl; Letter Trk; Air Force Acad.

KACZOROWSKI, ERIKA; East Chicago Roosevelt HS; E Chicago, IN; 18/214 Am Leg Aux Girls St; Girl Scts; Hon Rl; NHS; Treas Fr Clb; Spn Clb; Purdue Univ; Soc Work.

KACZOWKA, JUDY; Boardman HS; Boardman, OH; 18/558 Chrh Wkr; Hon Rl; Jr NHS; NHS; Fr Clb; Youngstown St Univ; Educ.

KACZPERSKI, MARY; St Mary Acad; Romulus, MI; 17/129 Cl Rep Jr Cls; Sec Sr Cls; CAP; Debate Tm; Hon Rl; Mod UN; NHS; Mic State Univ; Journalism.

KACZPERSKI, MARY; St Mary Academy; Romulus, MI; 17/133 Cl Rep Jr Cls; Sec Sr Cls; CAP; Drl Tm; Hon Rl; Hosp Ade; Mod UN; NHS; Stu Cncl; Sci Clb; Michigan St Univ; Journalism.

KACZYNSKI, GARY; Madonna HS; Weirton, WV; 6/100 Hon Rl; NHS; Stg Crw; Drama Clb; Key Clb; Trk; IM Sprt; Scr Kpr; Univ; Elec Engr.

KADDATZ, MIKE; Lake Orion HS; Lake Orion, MI; Aud/Vis; Hon Rl; Ftbl; Lake Superior St Coll; Law Enforcmnt.

KADEL, KELLY; Elmhurst HS; Ft Wayne, IN; 32/400 Cls Rep Frsh Cls; Cls Rep Soph Cls; Cl Rep Jr Cls; Aud/Vis; Hon Rl; Red Cr Ade; Sch Mus; Sch Pl; Stg Crw; Stu Cncl;.

KADERABEK, PAUL; West Catholic HS; Grand Rapids, MI; Hon Rl; JA; Jr NHS; Lat Clb; Glf; Socr; IM Sprt; Univ; Bus Admin.

KADETZ, TAMMY; William Henry Harrison HS; Harrison, OH; VP Jr Cls; Pres Sr Cls; Cmnty Wkr; Hon Rl; Sec NHS; Letter Bsbl; Letter Bsktbl; Letter Ten; VP GAA; Hon H Jr Yr 78; Univ; Phys Ther.

KADIYALA, RAJENDRA K; West Lafayette Sr HS; W Lafayette, IN; Cls Rep Sr Cls; Am Leg Boys St; Band; Boy Scts; Debate Tm; Hon Rl; NHS; Orch; Sch Mus; Stu Cncl; IN Circulation Exec Assoc Aschlrshp 78; Underclassman Music Awd 78; B Ruth IN N S All Star Bsbl Team 78; Univ; Med.

KADROVICH, ANNE; Mona Shores HS; Muskegon, MI; Band; Chrs; Girl Scts; Mdrgl; Muskegon Community; Music.

KADUSKY, LORI; Lumen Cordium HS; Bedford, OH; Cls Rep Frsh Cls; Hon Rl; Jr NHS; NHS; Sch Pl; Stg Crw; Stu Cncl; Pep Clb; College; Law.

KADY, JEFF; Bishop Donahue HS; Mc Mechen, WV; Chrh Wkr; Cmnty Wkr; Hon Rl; Sch Mus; Sch Pl; Key Clb; Spn Clb; Bsbl; Bsktbl; Ftbl; College; Journalism.

KADY, SHARON; South Lake HS; St Clair Shore, MI; Chrh Wkr; Girl Scts; Hon Rl; Off Ade; Sct Actv; Letter Bsktbl; Coach Actv; GAA; IM Sprt; PPFtbl; Adrian Coll; Bus.

KAECHELE, LINDA; Thornapple Kellogg HS; Middleville, MI; 2/152 Sal; Hon Rl; NHS; Sch Pl; Aquinas College; Soc Work.

KAEHR, SHARYL; Adams Central HS; Bluffton, IN; Cls Rep Sr Cls; Chrs; Chrh Wkr; Hon Rl; Hosp Ade; Mdrgl; Off Ade; Stg Crw; Stu Cncl; Drama Clb; Univ.

KAELBER, MARK; Jackson HS; Massillon, OH; Band; Treas Chrh Wkr; Cmnty Wkr; Orch; Fr Clb; Malone Coll; Music Educ.

KAELBER, NANCY; River Vly HS; Waldo, OH; 21/207 Band; NHS; Sch Mus; VP Yth Flsp; Spn Clb; Malone Coll; Elem Ed.

KAFER, KAREN; Upper Arlington HS; Columbus, OH; 135/610 Band; Hon Rl; JA; Stg Crw; Spn Clb; GAA; IM Sprt; Mgrs; JA Awd; Vllybl 76; Ohio St Univ; Law.

KAFERLE, JACQUI; Harbor HS; Ashtabula, OH; 48/197 Band; VP Spn Clb; VP GAA; Scr Kpr; College; Veterinarian Medicine.

KAFILA, NANCY; Plymouth Canton HS; Plymouth, MI; Chrs; Cmnty Wkr; Hon Rl; Eastern Michigan Univ; Busns.

KAFKER, ROGER; Cincinnati Country Day Schl; Cincinnati, OH; 1/66 Cmnty Wkr; Hon Rl; Mod UN; NHS; VP Stu Cncl; Rptr Yrbk; Ed Sch Nwsp; Letter Bsktbl; Letter Socr; Letter Ten; Class Schl 79; Frech Lang Prize 79; Cntry Day Awd For Serv & Character 78 79; Univ.

KAFTON, JOYCE; Cameron HS; Cameron, WV; 29/103 Band; Hon Rl; Off Ade; Orch; Y-Teens; Sec Lat Clb; Recd Superior On Flute Duet By Music Educ Solo & Ensemble Fest 76; Awd At W Liberty St Coll For Duet Super; Hagerstown Bus Coll; Acctg.

KAGE, THERESA; Willard HS; Willard, OH; Chrs; Chrh Wkr; MMM; Sch Mus; Sch Pl; Stg Crw; Drama Clb; 4-H; 4-H Awd; Ohio St Univ; Drama.

KAHAL, ANDREA; Bath HS; Lima, OH; 23/191 Sec Band; Hon Rl; NHS; Orch; Sch Mus; Treas Yth Flsp; Yrbk; Spn Clb; Trk; IM Sprt; Ohio Univ; Television Broadcasting.

KAHL, SHERRI L; Austin HS; Austin, IN; 4/100 Hon Rl; Pol Wkr; 4-H; FTA; Pep Clb; Sec Spn Clb; Ten; Scholastic Trophy; Purdue Univ; Computer Tech.

KAHLE, LOIS; Kalida HS; Kalida, OH; Chrh Wkr; Hon Rl; NHS; Sch Mus; 4-H; Bsktbl; GAA; IM Sprt; 4-H Awd; College.

KAHLER, MICHAEL; Adelphian Academy; Minnetonka, MN; Band; Chrs; Hon Rl; Sch Pl; Rptr Yrbk; IM Sprt; Andrews Univ; Engineering.

KAHN, DAVID; Montpelier HS; Montpelier, OH; 4/102 VP Jr Cls; Cl Rep Jr Cls; Am Leg Boys St; Chrs; Chrh Wkr; Hon Rl; NHS; Orch; Sch Mus; Stu Cncl; Bowling Green St Univ; Theatre.

KAIDO, MARK; Maysville HS; Zanesville, OH; Pres Frsh Cls; VP Soph Cls; Sec Jr Cls; Cls Rep Sr Cls; FCA; NHS; Pol Wkr; Key Clb; Bsbl; Bsktbl; Marietta Coll; Pre Law.

KAIFESH, MARK; Mott Sr HS; Warren, MI; Hon Rl; Crs Cntry; Trk; Michigan Dept Of Educ Schlrshp To WSU; Wayne St Univ; Elec Engr.

KAIL, CONNIE; Canton South HS; E Sparta, OH; Band; Chrh Wkr; Hon Rl; NHS; Pres Yth Flsp; Mth Clb; Sci Clb; Spn Clb; 4-H Awd; Ohio Merit Algebra I Awrd 77; Ohio St Univ; Pharm.

KAIN, TAMARA; Owendale Gagetown HS; Owendale, MI; Girl Scts; Hon Rl; FHA; Letter Bsktbl; Trk; Letter Chrldng; College; Soc Work.

KAINULAINEN, MICHAEL; Negaunee HS; Negaunee, MI; Band; Hon Rl; Northern Mic Univ.

KAISER, ANNA; Bishop Ready HS; Grove City, OH; Hon Rl; Kiwan Awd; Columbus Tech Inst; Animal Tech.

KAISER, CHARLES R; North Knox HS; Bruceville, IN; 11/150 Hon Rl; NHS; Sec FFA; Voc Schl; Mech.

KAISER, DAVID; South Dearborn HS; Aurora, IN; 33/265 Cls Rep Sr Cls; Stu Cncl; Yrbk; Bsktbl; IM Sprt; Univ; Math.

KAISER, DEBRA; Pinckney Cmnty HS; Lakeland, MI; Band; Hon Rl; Hosp Ade; Sch Pl; Sct Actv; Stg Crw; Pep Clb; Ten; Coll; Acctg.

KAISER, DIANA; Rivet HS; Vincennes, IN; Trs Frsh Cls; Chrh Wkr; Cmnty Wkr; Girl Scts; Hon Rl; Stu Cncl; Y-Teens; Rptr Sch Nwsp; Sch Nwsp; 4-H; Univ; Bus.

KAISER, DIANE; Fort Recovery HS; Ft Recovery, OH; 7/90 Sec Frsh Cls; Pres Soph Cls; Sec Chrs; VP NHS; Sch Mus; Stu Cncl; FTA; Pep Clb; IM Sprt; Voice Dem Awd; Univ Of Dayton; Elementary Educ.

KAISER, JANICE; Sullivan HS; Carlisle, IN; Cl Rep Jr Cls; Cls Rep Sr Cls; Hon Rl; Stu Cncl; Yrbk; 4-H; Pep Clb; Chrldng; Pom Pon; College.

KAISER, KIMBERLY; Maple Heights HS; Maple Hgts, OH; 23/350 Sec Jr Cls; Cls Rep Sr Cls; Chrs; Hon Rl; Jr NHS; NHS; Stu Cncl; Capt Chrldng; Gold Awd 77; Univ; Med Tech.

KAISER, KIRK; Upper Valley J V S HS; Piqua, OH; Pres Sr Cls; Aud/Vis; DECA; Fr Clb; Letter Wrstlng; Announcr For Audio Visual Prod Publicising The JVS 79; Mbr Of Tm Plcd 1st In DECA St Brdcst Arts Series; Ohio Univ; Cmnctns.

KAISER, MICHAEL G; North Farmington HS; Farmington Hls, MI; Chrh Wkr; Hon Rl; Natl Merit Ltr; Univ; Comp Sci.

KAISER, PETER; Walnut Hills HS; Cincinnati, OH; Hon Rl; Jr NHS; Sch Pl; Rptr Yrbk; FDA; Bsbl; IM Sprt; Univ; Med.

KAISER, RUTH; Napoleon HS; Napoleon, MI; Girl Scts; Hon Rl; Off Ade; Sct Actv; Yth Flsp; Yrbk; Sch Nwsp; Sci Clb; Univ; Phys Ed.

KAISER, SUSAN; Our Lady Of Mercy HS; Northville, MI; 3/300 Cl Rep Jr Cls; NHS; Red Cr Ade; Letter Ten; Univ; Educ.

KAISER, SUSAN; Bremen HS; Bremen, IN; Chrs; FCA; Hon Rl; Sch Mus; Sch Pl; Stu Cncl; Yth Flsp; Drama Clb; Pep Clb; Spn Clb; College; Elem Educ.

KAISER, TODD; Triton HS; Etna Green, IN; 19/94 Cls Rep Frsh Cls; Cls Rep Soph Cls; Cl Rep Jr Cls; Pres Sr Cls; Am Leg Boys St; VP Chrs; Lit Mag; Sch Mus; Spn Clb; IM Sprt; De Pauw Univ; Law.

KAJI, REIKO; Rogers HS; Toledo, OH; 1/412 Val; Hon Rl; NHS; Sch Mus; Sec Mth Clb; VP Sci Clb; Spn Clb; College.

KALAMAROS, PHILIP; St Josephs HS; South Bend, IN; Cl Rep Jr Cls; Aud/Vis; Boy Scts; Hon Rl; Sct Actv; Yth Flsp; Letter Crs Cntry; Letter Trk; IM Sprt; Univ Of Notre Dame; Bus.

KALAYCIOGLU, MATT; Lincoln HS; Shinnston, WV; Pres Soph Cls; Am Leg Boys St; Boy Scts; Chrh Wkr; Hon Rl; Hosp Ade; Jr NHS; Pres NHS; Sch Mus; Pres Sct Actv; Univ; Bio.

KALB, BRENDA; Buckeye Ctrl HS; Bloomville, OH; 8/89 Band; Hon Rl; NHS; Yth Flsp; IM Sprt; Voice Dem Awd; Univ; Zoology.

KALCHIK, PATRICIA; Northport Public HS; Northport, MI; 7/26 Sec Frsh Cls; NHS; Yrbk; Natl Merit SF; Northwestern Mich Coll; Bus Mgmt.

KALCHIK, REBECCA; Northport Public School; Suttons Bay, MI; 10/26 Cmp Fr Grls; 4-H; Spn Clb; 4-H Awd; Western Michigan Univ; Comp Sci.

KALCHIK, REBECCA; Northport Public HS; Suttons Bay, MI; 10/26 Cmp Fr Grls; 4-H; Spn Clb; 4-H Awd; Western Univ; Comp Progr.

KALDUS, THERESA; Erieview Catholic HS; Cleveland, OH; Chrs; Chrh Wkr; Hon Rl; NHS; Ed Sch Nwsp; Rptr Sch Nwsp; Notre Dame Coll; Chem.

KALE, THOMAS; Rochester HS; Rochester, IN; 11/166 Band; Hon Rl; NHS; Sct Actv; Stg Crw; Yth Flsp; Drama Clb; FFA; Sci Clb; Letter Swmmng; Purdue Univ; Elec Engr.

KALE, TRACEY; North Union HS; Richwood, OH; 36/92 Band; Hon Rl; NHS; Off Ade; Yth Flsp; 4-H; Spn Clb; Gym; Trk; Chrldng; Univ; Phys Educ.

KALETHA, ANGEL; Elston HS; Michigan City, IN; Chrh Wkr; Chmn Drl Tm; Hon Rl; NHS; Sch Mus; Stu Cncl; Pep Clb; Spn Clb; Mat Maids; Chmn Pom Pon; Lee College.

KALIL, KIM; Magnificat HS; N Olmsted, OH; Cls Rep Frsh Cls; Trs Soph Cls; Sec Jr Cls; VP Sr Cls; Am Leg Aux Girls St; Chrs; Hosp Ade; JA; NHS; Bowling Green College.

KALININ, LYNN; Adlai Stevenson HS; Sterling Hts, MI; 30/528 Cls Rep Sr Cls; Band; Chrh Wkr; Hon Rl; JA; NHS; DECA; OEA; Detroit Coll Of Bus; C P A.

KALIS, PAM; Lakewood HS; Lakewood, OH; 107/863 Cls Rep Frsh Cls; Cls Rep Soph Cls; Sec Chrs; Girl Scts; Hon Rl; NHS; Rptr Sch Nwsp; OEA; Oh Offce Educ Assoc Reg 12, 3rd Pl Inf Cmmntns Ii 1979; Certfd Life Grd & Swm Inst; Cleveland State Univ; Cmmntns.

KALL, PHILIP F; Benedictine HS; Chesterland, OH; Boy Scts; NHS; Off Ade; Sct Actv; Stu Cncl; Rptr Yrbk; Rptr Sch Nwsp; Key Clb; Spn Clb; Letter Wrstlng; Univ; Bus Admin.

KALLANDER, SCOTT; Talawanda HS; Oxford, OH; 30/321 Hon Rl; NHS; Yth Flsp; IM Sprt; College; Forestry.

KALLAS, JAMES; Bloom Local School; Wheelersburg, OH; Trs Frsh Cls; Band; Boy Scts; Chrs; Hon Rl; Sch Pl; Stu Cncl; Drama Clb; 4-H; Bsbl; Shawnee St Coll; Elec.

KALLAY, BRADFORD; Riverside HS; Painesville, OH; Hon Rl; Letter Crs Cntry; Letter Trk; IM Sprt;.

KALLIMANI, HELEN; Jimtown HS; Elkhart, IN; 1/96 Chrh Wkr; Hon Rl; NHS; Off Ade; Yth Flsp; Treas 4-H; FHA; Pep Clb; VP Spn Clb; Mgrs; College.

KALLINKI, ANITA; Fairport Harding HS; Fairport Hrbr, OH; Rptr Yrbk; Pep Clb; GAA; Lakeland Comm College ; Photog.

KALLINSKI, EUGENE; Hale HS; Hale, MI; 7/55 NHS; Letter Bsbl; Univ; Mech Engr.

KALMAN, MICHELE; Buckeye South HS; Yorkville, OH; Cl Rep Jr Cls; Band; Hon Rl; NHS; Stu Cncl; Y-Teens; Rptr Yrbk; Rptr Sch Nwsp; Drama Clb; VP Pep Clb; Schlshp Team 77; Univ.

KALMBACH, ANNA; Cadillac Sr HS; Cadillac, MI; 1/300 Treas Chrs; Chrh Wkr; Hon Rl; Jr NHS; VP NHS; Sch Mus; Stg Crw; Yth Flsp; Rotary Awd; 1st Rating Piano Solo Local & St Mi Band Orch Assoc; Hope Coll; Pre Med.

KALONICK, CHRISTINE; Buckeye West HS; Adena, OH; 10/84 Am Leg Aux Girls St; Chrh Wkr; Hon Rl; Jr NHS; Lbry Ade; Sec NHS; Off Ade; Yrbk; Sch Nwsp; VP Sci Clb; Jefferson Tech Coll; Med Sec.

KALSEN, SUSAN; La Salle HS; S Bend, IN; 26/488 Chrh Wkr; Girl Scts; Hon Rl; Off Ade; Sch Mus; Sch Pl; Sct Actv; Rptr Yrbk; Rptr Sch Nwsp; Drama Clb; Indiana Univ; Bus.

KALT, LOREN; New Philadelphia HS; New Phila, OH; Chrh Wkr; Hon Rl; JA; DECA; Spn Clb; JA Awd; Univ; Bus Mgmt.

KALTENBACH, CAROL; Otsego HS; Weston, OH; Am Leg Aux Girls St; Band; Chrs; Hon Rl; Sch Pl; Drama Clb; Letter Trk; Coll.

KALTENBACH, CHERYL; Otsego HS; Weston, OH; Am Leg Aux Girls St; Band; Chrs; Hon Rl; Sch Pl; Drama Clb; Letter Trk; Univ.

KALUZA, ANNA; Canfield HS; Canfield, OH; Band; Girl Scts; JA; Yth Flsp; Bsktbl; Trk; PPFtbl; Saint Elizabeths Nursing Schl; Rn.

KAMBOURIS, ROSS; Campbell Memorial HS; Campbell, OH; Band; Orch; Pres Fr Clb; Mth Clb; Pep Clb; Sci Clb; College.

KAMER, KIM; Grant HS; Grant, MI; Sec Jr Cls; Hon Rl; Yth Flsp; Pres 4-H; FFA; Letter Bsktbl; GAA; Cit Awd; 4-H Awd; Michigan St Univ; Animal Tech.

KAMIDOI, KATHRYN; Capac HS; Capac, MI; Trs Frsh Cls; Sec Soph Cls; Cl Rep Jr Cls; Trs Sr Cls; Hon Rl; NHS; Stu Cncl; Ed Yrbk; Rptr Yrbk; Sch Nwsp; Law Schl; Law.

KAMINSKI, CINDY; St Andrew HS; Detroit, MI; 15/103 FCA; Hon Rl; Lbry Ade; NHS; Rptr Sch Nwsp; FBLA; Capt Bsbl; Capt Bsktbl; Coach Actv; IM Sprt; Univ Of Mich; Business Management.

KAMINSKI, CONNIE; Waterford Twp HS; Pontiac, MI; Band; Girl Scts; Hon Rl; Chrldng; Pom Pon; Lion Awd; Natl Merit Schl; Oakland Univ; Nursing.

KAMINSKI, KAROL; Magnificat HS; Middleburg Hts, OH; VP Sr Cls; Cmnty Wkr; NHS; Stg Crw; Yrbk; Letter Bsbl; Letter Bsktbl; GAA; Ath Of Yr 77; Schlstc Art Show Gld Key Wnnr 77; HS All Amer Ath & Miss Teen Oh Fnlst 78; Univ; Art.

KAMINSKI, LISA M; Marian HS; Royal Oak, MI; Aud/Vis; CAP; Hon Rl; Lit Mag; Mod UN; Stu Cncl; Ed Sch Nwsp; Fr Clb; Trk; Cit Awd; Serv Awd 76; Projct Close Up Awd 79; Nomination For Congrssnl Rage 79; Univ; Archt Engr.

KAMINSKI, PAUL; Troy HS; Troy, MI; Band; Chrh Wkr; Cmnty Wkr; Hon Rl; Jr NHS; NHS; Orch; Yth Flsp; Pep Clb; Bsbl; Michigan St Univ.

KAMINSKY, CARRIE; Beaumont Girls HS; University Hts, OH; Cls Rep Soph Cls; Hon Rl; Lit Mag; Stu Cncl; Sch Nwsp; Coach Actv; GAA; Miami Univ; Finance.

KAMINSKY, ED; Cuyahoga Hts HS; Valley View, OH; 9/72 Hon Rl; Fr Clb; Ftbl; Glf; Wrstlng; Gemologist.

KAMMANN, ELLEN; Bishop Gallagher HS; Detroit, MI; 20/332 Hon Rl; Michigan St Univ; Law.

KAMMERER, DENISE; Imlay City HS; Attica, MI; Band; Chrs; Girl Scts; Hon Rl; Chrldng; Pom Pon; Business Sch; Secretarial.

KAMODY, STEVE; Marion L Steele HS; Amherst, OH; Band; Hon Rl; Letter Bsktbl; IM Sprt; Kent St Univ; Acctg.

KAMP, ANDREA L; Dearborn HS; Dearborn Hts, MI; 10/528 Band; Chrh Wkr; Cmnty Wkr; Hon Rl; Lit Mag; NHS; Orch; Sch Mus; Sch Pl; Stg Crw; Phi Beta Kappa Cert 1979; Regents Schlrshp 1979; Univ Of Michigan; Eng.

KAMPE, KAREN; Defiance HS; Definace, OH; Cl Rep Jr Cls; Pres Sr Cls; Trs Sr Cls; Am Leg Aux Girls St; Girl Scts; Hon Rl; Jr NHS; Treas NHS; Off Ade; Pol Wkr; Bowling Green St Univ; Brdcst Jrnlsm.

KAMPE, KAREN; Williamston HS; Williamston, MI; 6/147 AFS; Band; Girl Scts; Jr NHS; Pres Stu Cncl; Mich Tech Univ; Engr.

KAMPHUIS, KEVIN; West Ottawa HS; Holland, MI; Hon Rl; Letter Bsbl; Letter Bsktbl;.

KAMPMAN, KIMBERLY A; Beaumont School For Girls; Chagrin Falls, OH; Trs Soph Cls; Cl Rep Jr Cls; Pres Sr Cls; Cmnty Wkr; Hon Rl; Lit Mag; NHS; Stu Cncl; Fr Clb; Univ; Vet Med.

KAMPRATH, PAUL H; Monroe HS; Monroe, MI; Band; Chrh Wkr; Hon Rl; Yth Flsp; Yrbk; 4-H; 4-H Awd; Northland Coll Schlrshp 79; Monroe HS Trap Shooting Tm 79; St Of Mi Comp Schlrshp 79; Northland Coll; Natural Resources.

KAMPS, KATHY; Calvin Christian HS; Wyoming, MI; Trs Soph Cls; Cls Rep Soph Cls; Sec Jr Cls; Band; Hon Rl; Sch Pl; College; Music.

KANAAN, JANATTE D; Pioneer HS; Ann Arbor, MI; Hosp Ade; Red Cr Ade; PPFtbl; Univ Of Michigan; Med.

KANAVEL, LINDA; Tri Valley HS; Frazeysburg, OH; 2/216 Band; Drm Mjrt; Hon Rl; NHS; Off Ade; Yrbk; Sec 4-H; Twrlr; Mt Carmel Schl Of Nursng; R N.

KANDAH, GHADA; Ursuline HS; Youngstown, OH; 8/286 Hon Rl; Walsh Coll; Sci.

KANDAH, TERESA; Ursuline HS; Youngstown, OH; 3/286 Hon Rl; Case Western Reserve Univ; Sci.

KANDEL, MARA; West Branch Local HS; Salem, OH; Hon Rl; 4-H; Sec FFA; Ger Clb; Trk; Star Chapter Farmer Awd; Ohio State Univ; Agri.

KANE, ANNEROSE; Austintown Fitch HS; Youngstown, OH; Hon Rl; Lbry Ade; Ger Clb; College; Education.

KANE, APRIL; N Coll Hill Jr Sr HS; Cincinnati, OH; Aud/Vis; Band; Pres Chrh Wkr; Hon Rl; Jr NHS; Sch Mus; Sch Pl; Yrbk; Sch Nwsp; Sec Drama Clb; Miami Univ; Spec Ed.

KANE, CARMEL; Immaculate Conception Acad; No Vernon, IN; 58/68 Chrs; Chrh Wkr; Cmnty Wkr; Orch; Sch Mus; Stg Crw; 4-H; Spn Clb; 4-H Awd; Cnty Rep In Girls 4 H St Fair Schl 79; Jr Leader Roundup Purdue Univ 75; Jr Leader Confrnc Purdue Univ 78; Bus Schl; Sec.

KANE, JOAN; Harbor HS; Ashtabula, OH; 35/183 Hst Jr Cls; Pres Sr Cls; AFS; JA; Jr NHS; NHS; Red Cr Ade; OEA; IM Sprt; Typing Awd 1975;.

KANE, MARY; John F Kennedy HS; Cortland, OH; 48/154 Band; Chrh Wkr; Hon Rl; NHS; VP FTA; Letter Bsbl; Letter Bsktbl; Business Schl; Sec Sci.

KANE, MARYBETH; Philo HS; Zanesville, OH; Chrs; Hon Rl; NHS; Sch Mus; Yrbk; Rptr Sch Nwsp; 4-H; Fr Clb; GAA; Ohio St Univ; Law.

KANE, PATRICIA; Oscar A Carlson HS; Gibralter, MI; 14/217 Hon Rl; Rptr Sch Nwsp; FTA; Letter Bsktbl; Trk; Western Michigan Univ; Pre Med.

KANE, SCOTT; Nordonia HS; Northfield, OH; Chrs; Stg Crw; Crs Cntry; Ftbl; Hndbl; Letter Trk; IM Sprt; Akron Univ; Mech Engr.

KANG, PETE; North Central HS; Indianapolis, IN; Boy Scts; Debate Tm; Hon Rl; Natl Forn Lg; Orch; Stg Crw; Stu Cncl; Yrbk; Sci Clb; Ten; Univ; Pre Med.

KANGAS, KARI; Calumet HS; Laurium, MI; Band; Chrh Wkr; Hon Rl; Pep Clb; Bsktbl; Trk; Chrldng; IM Sprt; Univ.

KANGAS, KELLY; Gwinn HS; Gwinn, MI; Chrh Wkr; Hon Rl; Fr Clb; Gym; Ten; Norther Mich Univ; Special Educ.

KANIA, DIANE; Bishop Borgess HS; Detroit, MI; 65/480 Cls Rep Frsh Cls; Cl Rep Jr Cls; Cls Rep Sr Cls; Chrs; Jr NHS; Natl Forn Lg; NHS; Wayne State Univ; Bio.

KANIEWSKI, KAREN; Clay HS; S Bend, IN; Hon Rl; Indiana Univ.

KANNAPEL, JERRY; New Albany HS; New Albany, IN; 262/565 Aud/Vis; Hon Rl; Letter Bsbl; Letter Ftbl; Trk; DAR Awd; Indiana Univ; Phys Ed.

KANNE, GREGG; Rensselaer Central HS; Fair Oaks, IN; 6/162 Pres Frsh Cls; Cls Rep Frsh Cls; Pres Soph Cls; Cls Rep Soph Cls; Cl Rep Jr Cls; Cls Rep Sr Cls; Chrs; Purdue Univ; Agri.

KANOTT, FRANCES; Oceana HS; Lynco, WV; 5/125 Sec Frsh Cls; Sec Soph Cls; Hon Rl; NHS; Rptr Yrbk; Pep Clb; Spn Clb; Bus Schl; Sec.

KANSMAN, ERIN R; Farmington HS; Farmington, MI; Cls Rep Frsh Cls; Cls Rep Sr Cls; Am Leg Aux Girls St; Girl Scts; Hon Rl; NHS; Off Ade; Stu Cncl; Pep Clb; Letter Bsktbl; Univ; Bus Admin.

KANTAK, GLENN R; Centennial HS; Worthington, OH; 1/225 Pres Frsh Cls; Pres Jr Cls; Cl Rep Jr Cls; Am Leg Boys St; Hon Rl; Jr NHS; Pol Wkr; Stu Cncl; Sch Nwsp; Ger Clb; College; Business Administration.

KANTNER, RONALD; Wapakoneta Sr HS; Wapakoneta, OH; Cls Rep Soph Cls; Band; Chrh Wkr; Stu Cncl; Yth Flsp; Letter Crs Cntry; Letter Ftbl; Letter Swmmng; Ten; Letter Trk; Univ.

KANTOR, SUSAN; Maplewood HS; Cortland, OH; Trs Soph Cls; Trs Jr Cls; Hon Rl; Hosp Ade; Red Cr Ade; Fr Clb; FTA; Bsbl; Letter Bsktbl; Akron Schl Of Nursing; Med.

KANTZ, DOROTHY D; Andrews School; Painesville, OH; Sec Frsh Cls; Chrs; Chrh Wkr; Hon Rl; Sch Mus; Stg Crw; Yth Flsp; Sprt Ed Yrbk; Rptr

Yrbk; Drama Clb; Thespian Soc 79; John Carroll Univ; Law.

KANTZER, KIM; Marion Pleasant HS; Marion, OH; Hon Rl; NHS; Quill & Scroll; Stu Cncl; Rptr Sch Nwsp; FHA; Letter Bsktbl; Letter Trk; IM Sprt; Tmr; Ltrin Vllybl; Ohio St Univ; Educ.

KAO, CHENG; Huron HS; Ann Arbor, MI; Cmnty Wkr; Hosp Ade; Sci Clb; Univ Of Michigan; Doctor.

KAPALCZYNSKI, RALPH; St Joseph HS; St Joseph, MI; Band; Boy Scts; Chrs; FCA; NHS; Sct Actv; Lat Clb; Letter Bsbl; Letter Ftbl; College; Sci.

KAPALKA, DAVID; Munster HS; Munster, IN; 18/403 Aud/Vis; Chrh Wkr; Hon Rl; NHS; Sch Mus; Sch Pl; Stg Crw; Drama Clb; Am Leg Awd; Thespian; Purdue Univ; Elec Engr.

KAPELKA, KATHLEEN; Tiffin Calvert HS; Tiffin, OH; Band; Girl Scts; Hon Rl; Hosp Ade; NHS; Sch Mus; Ten; Chrldng; Mgrs; Twrlr; Terra Tech Schl; Early Childhood Ed.

KAPES, MARK; Solon HS; Solon, OH; Band; Hon Rl; Letter Bsbl; IM Sprt; Ohio St Univ; Bio Sci.

KAPITAN, DAVID; Griffith HS; Griffith, IN; 90/300 Cls Rep Sr Cls; Hon Rl; Stu Cncl; Ftbl; Trk; College.

KAPLAN, BRADLEY; Walnut Ridge HS; Columbus, OH; Band; Hon Rl; NHS; Orch; Sch Mus; Indiana Univ; Mktg.

KAPLAN, DAVID R; Clarenceville HS; Livonia, MI; 1/220 Val; Aud/Vis; Pres NHS; Rptr Sch Nwsp; Letter Bsbl; Opt Clb Awd; Summa Cum Laude; Dept Awd Outstndng Ach In Creative Writing & Journalism; Phi Beta Kappa Awd Schlstc Ach; Michigan St Univ; Hotel Mgmt.

KAPLAN, KELLY M; Evergreen HS; Berkey, OH; Band; Stg Crw; Ed Sch Nwsp; Rptr Sch Nwsp; GAA; Toledo Univ.

KAPLAN, NANCY; George Rogers Clark HS; Whiting, IN; 7/218 Am Leg Aux Girls St; Pres JA; Jr NHS; Lbry Ade; Drama Clb; Fr Clb; GAA; JA Awd; Univ; Med.

KAPLAN, SHERI; North Farmington HS; Farm Hills, MI; Cmnty Wkr; Girl Scts; Hon Rl; Yrbk; Letter Bsktbl; Letter Swmmng; GAA; Natl Merit Ltr; Michigan St Univ; Pre Law.

KAPLE, KAREN; Buckeye Central HS; New Washington, OH; VP Sr Cls; Chrh Wkr; Hon Rl; Red Cr Ade; Fr Clb; Bsbl; Bsktbl; Swmmng; Chrldng; Univ Of Notre Dame; Archt.

KAPP, LISA; Alma HS; Alma, MI; 13/240 Pres Band; Drm Mjrt; NHS; Capt Bsktbl; Capt Trk; Lion Awd; Alma College; Envir Eng.

KAPPEL, GREGORY; Fairview HS; Fairview Pk, OH; 10/268 Hon Rl; NHS; VP Stu Cncl; Rptr Yrbk; Bsbl; Letter Bsktbl; Univ.

KAPPLER, RICHARD; Lake Linden Public HS; Hubbell, MI; 20/65 Pres Soph Cls; Sec Jr Cls; Cls Rep Sr Cls; Hon Rl; Lbry Ade; Natl Forn Lg; Sch Pl; Stu Cncl; Fr Clb; Pep Clb; Suomi Coll.

KAPSAL, CHRIS; Anderson Sr HS; Cincinnati, OH; Band; Boy Scts; Orch; Rptr Sch Nwsp; Ger Clb; Ten; Am Leg Awd; Natl Merit Ltr; Univ.

KAPUSTAR, MICHAEL; Clay HS; Oregon, OH; Hon Rl; Owens Voc Schl; Diesel Mech.

KAPUSTKA, KAREN; Carson City Crystal HS; Carson City, MI; Pres Soph Cls; Chrh Wkr; Hon Rl; NHS; Off Ade; Rptr Yrbk; Spn Clb; Capt Chrldng; IM Sprt; Scr Kpr; Univ Of Mic; Pre Med.

KARABEC, JOHN; R B Chamberlain HS; Twinsburg, OH; Cmnty Wkr; Off Ade; Sch Pl; Stg Crw; Letter Ten; Akron Univ; Bus Admin.

KARADEEMA, KEVIN; Taylor Center HS; Taylor, MI; 17/388 Cls Rep Frsh Cls; Boy Scts; Hon Rl; Jr NHS; NHS; Bsbl; Bsktbl; Ftbl; Coach Actv; Mic State Univ; Vet.

KARADIN, KIMBERLY; Our Lady Of The Elms HS; Akron, OH; Chrs; Chrh Wkr; Cmnty Wkr; Girl Scts; Hon Rl; Sch Pl; Univ Of Akron; Hist.

KARAM, BRIAN; Timken Sr HS; Canton, OH; Ohio St Univ; Vet Med.

KARANDOS, PAMELA; Warren Central HS; Indpls, IN; Hon Rl; Stg Crw; Stu Cncl; Drama Clb; Fr Clb; Pep Clb; Mat Maids; Scr Kpr; English Asst; Univ; Spec Ed.

KARANTONIS, TONEY; Clear Fork HS; Colcord, WV; 2/26 Trs Soph Cls; Sal; Am Leg Boys St; Band; Hon Rl; NHS; Ed Yrbk; Rptr Sch Nwsp; 4-H; FBLA; Morris Harvey Univ; Busns.

KARAS, ARTHUR; Carman HS; Flint, MI; Band; Chrs; Hon Rl; Sch Mus; Hofstra Univ.

KARAS, MARIA; Niles Mc Kinley HS; Niles, OH; Cl Rep Jr Cls; AFS; Hon Rl; Jr NHS; NHS; Stu Cncl; Yrbk; Drama Clb; Pep Clb; PPFtbl; Ohio St Univ.

KARAS, MARTHA; Rochester HS; Rochester, MI; Girl Scts; Hon Rl; NHS; Pol Wkr; Letter Swmmng; Univ; Animal Sci.

KARBOSKE, LETHA; Mason County Central HS; Ludington, MI; Sec Soph Cls; Sec Jr Cls; Band; Hon Rl; NHS; Spn Clb; College; Dance.

KARCH, LORI; St Francis De Sales HS; Gahanna, OH; Drl Tm; Hon Rl; Sch Pl; Stg Crw; Drama Clb; Univ; Jrnlsm.

KARIAINEN, CARLA; Ewen Trout Crk Cnsldtd HS; Trout Creek, MI; 5/44 Trs Sr Cls; Band; Hon Rl; Sch Nwsp; Trk; Mich Tech Univ; Nurse.

KARINEN, KIRA; Plymouth Salem HS; Canton, MI; 51/600 Band; Girl Scts; Hon Rl; Orch; Socr; Trk; Natl Merit SF; Univ Of California; Forestry.

KARKIEWICZ, PAUL; Washington HS; South Bend, IN; 6/355 Band; Hon Rl; NHS; Spn Clb; Coll; Envir Health.

KARL, R; Cardinal Stritch HS; Curtice, OH; Cls Rep Frsh Cls; Cls Rep Soph Cls; Band; Sch Mus; Yth Flsp; Fr Clb; Letter Swmmng; Letter Trk; College; Astronomy.

KARLICH, DARLENE; Linden Mc Kinley HS; Columbus, OH; 3/268 Hon Rl; Jr NHS; Lbry Ade; NHS; Off Ade; Gym; Columbus Tech Inst; Sec Sci.

KARMAN, ROBB T; The Leelanan HS; Hudson, OH; Pres Sr Cls; Hon Rl; Pol Wkr; Letter Socr; Elk Awd; Natl Merit SF; College; Medicine.

KARNACK, SANDRA; Forest Park HS; Crystal Falls, MI; 23/79 Cls Rep Frsh Cls; Cls Rep Soph Cls; Cl Rep Jr Cls; Trs Sr Cls; Band; Hon Rl; Off Ade; Stu Cncl; IM Sprt; Cit Awd; Michigan Tech Univ; Bus Admin.

KARNES, JAMES; St Joseph HS; Huntington, WV; Boy Scts; Letter Bsbl; Letter Socr; Letter Wrstlng; College.

KARNES, LINDA; Nitro Sr HS; Nitro, WV; Chrs; Chrh Wkr; Drl Tm; Hon Rl; Drama Clb; IM Sprt; Spanish Awd; W Virginia St Coll; Spec Ed.

KARNICKI, DONNA; St Mary Academy; Carleton, MI; 4/130 Cmnty Wkr; Hon Rl; NHS; Sch Nwsp; Pres Fr Clb; VP Sci Clb; Voice Dem Awd; Monroe County Cmnty Coll.

KARNOSH, M; New Philadelphia Sr HS; New Phila, OH; Chrs; Hon Rl; JA; NHS; Sch Mus; Stg Crw; Drama Clb; 4-H; Univ; Lib Sci.

KARNS, LESLIE; North Daviess HS; Odon, IN; 45/98 Sec Jr Cls; Trs Jr Cls; Band; FCA; Sprt Ed Sch Nwsp; Sec Pep Clb; Bsktbl; Trk; Chrldng; Coach Actv; 5 Finalists In WBAK 38 TV Contest For Writtin Essay 77; Captain Of Sftbl Team Also Pitcher; Indiana Univ; Athletic Trainer.

KAROLCHYK, MARY ANN; Aquinas HS; Lincoln Park, MI; Cls Rep Soph Cls; Girl Scts; Hon Rl; NHS; Stu Cncl; Rptr Yrbk; Rptr Sch Nwsp; Trk; Scr Kpr; Wayne St Univ; Nursing.

KARP, LYLE; Reese HS; Reese, MI; Am Leg Boys St; Hon Rl; Letter Bsbl; Letter Bsktbl; Letter Ftbl; Univ.

KARP, REBECCA E; Lewis Cnty HS; Horner, WV; Cls Rep Soph Cls; Chrs; Cmnty Wkr; Debate Tm; FCA; Hon Rl; Sch Pl; Stu Cncl; 4-H; Pep Clb; Glenville St Univ; Sec.

KARPER, TERRI; West Branch HS; Beloit, OH; Chrs; Chrh Wkr; Pep Clb; Bsktbl; Trk; Univ; Elem Ed.

KARPIAK, SHARON; Archbishop Alter HS; Kettering, OH; Drl Tm; Coll; Exec Sec.

KARR, DIANE; Edsel Ford HS; Dearborn, MI; Cls Rep Frsh Cls; Cls Rep Soph Cls; Cl Rep Jr Cls; Cls Rep Sr Cls; Cmnty Wkr; Hon Rl; Hosp Ade; NHS; Stu Cncl; Ger Clb; Michigan St Univ.

KARR, MICHAEL; Crown Point HS; Crown Point, IN; 10/509 Boy Scts; Hon Rl; Jr NHS; NHS; Trk; DAR Awd; Purdue Univ; Science.

KARRICK, MARK; Eastern Local HS; Beaver, OH; 14/70 Aud/Vis; Band; Boy Scts; Hon Rl; Sct Actv; Rptr Yrbk; Sci Clb; IM Sprt; Dnfth Awd; Became An Eagle Scout 77; U S Navy; Adv Elec.

KARRICK, MARK W; Eastern Local HS; Beaver, OH; 12/70 Aud/Vis; Band; Boy Scts; Hon Rl; Yrbk; Dnfth Awd; Eagle Scout; Mbr Of The Order Of The Arrow;.

KARSEN, JOHN C; Alcona Community HS; Lincoln, MI; 8/124 Hon Rl; Jr NHS; NHS; Off Ade; Yrbk; Cit Awd; Univ; Bus.

KARST, LARRY A; Marion Franklin HS; Columbus, OH; Am Leg Boys St; Hon Rl; Jr NHS; NHS; Sch Pl; Drama Clb; VICA; Am Leg Awd; Rotary Awd; 2 French Hnr Soc Awds 1 For St Another For Nation 77; OSU; Law.

KARST, PATRICK; Huntington North HS; Huntington, IN; 59/585 Pres Jr Cls; Pres Sr Cls; Am Leg Boys St; Boy Scts; Stu Cncl; Pres 4-H; Treas FFA; 4-H Awd; Purdue Univ; Agri.

KARSTEN, GERALD; Alpena HS; Alpena, MI; Pres FCA; Hon Rl; NHS; Pres Yth Flsp; Letter Ftbl; Letter Hockey; Alpena Comm Coll; Data Processing.

KARTHOLL, NANCY; Bishop Dwenger HS; Ft Wayne, IN; Chrs; Hon Rl; Sch Mus; Sch Pl; 4-H; Pom Pon; AATF Natl French Exam 2nd In State; College; Drama.

KARUS, JUDITH A; Ohio Hi Point Joint Voc Schl; West Liberty, OH; Hon Rl; Off Ade; Fr Clb; OEA; Clerk Typist.

KASAB, TONY; Fitzgerald HS; Warren, MI; Letter Bsbl; Univ; Chemistry.

KASAVAGE, SUZANNE; Groveport Madison HS; Obetz, OH; 32/632 Girl Scts; Hon Rl; Off Ade; Sch Pl; Stu Cncl; Yrbk; Rptr Sch Nwsp; Drama Clb; Pep Clb; Spn Clb; Ohio St Univ; Oceanography.

KASCHAK, JOHN; Normandy HS; Parma, OH; 57/649 Cls Rep Frsh Cls; NHS;.

KASCHALK, MICHAEL; East Detroit HS; East Detroit, MI; Pres Sr Cls; Hon Rl; NHS; Stu Cncl; Bsbl; Bsktbl; Crs Cntry; Trk; Wayne State Univ; Electrical Engr.

KASELONIS, TIMOTHY F; Euclid Sr HS; Euclid, OH; Hon Rl; U S Air Force Acad; Law.

KASER, JAMES; St Francis De Salls HS; Sylvania, OH; 42/200 Hon Rl; Letter Bsktbl; Letter Ftbl; Letter Trk; Univ; Engr.

KASKOCSAK, TERRI; Archbishop Alter HS; Kettering, OH; Cls Rep Soph Cls; Drl Tm; Sch Mus; Sch Pl; Rptr Sch Nwsp; Sch Nwsp; Drama Clb; IM Sprt; Univ; Psych.

KASMAR, JUDEE; Niles Mc Kinley HS; Niles, OH; 57/420 Univ; Nursing.

KASPER, KATHLEEN; Medina Sr HS; Medina, OH; Univ; Cmnctns.

KASPER, RAY; Benedictine HS; Cleve Hts, OH; 40/95 Cl Rep Jr Cls; Band; Chrh Wkr; Drm Mjrt; Orch; Sch Mus; Sch Pl; Rptr Sch Nwsp; Drama Clb; Pep Clb; Univ; Educ.

KASPERSKI, MIKE; Memphis HS; Memphis, MI; Cl Rep Jr Cls; Aud/Vis; Hon Rl; Rptr Yrbk; Yrbk; Univ.

KASPRYZYCKI, ELIZABETH; St Florian HS; Detroit, MI; 6/76 Sec Jr Cls; Hon Rl; Lbry Ade; Letter Natl Forn Lg; VP NHS; Treas Stu Cncl; Drama Clb; Sec Fr Clb; Mth Clb; Bsktbl; Stu Of The Month; Univ Of Detroit; Engr.

KASPRZAK, ROBERT; Catholic Central HS; Grand Rapids, MI; Chrh Wkr; Hon Rl; NHS; Lat Clb; Glf; IM Sprt; College; Attorney.

KASSEBAUM, JEANETTE; Hamilton S E HS; Noblesville, IN; 6/150 Am Leg Aux Girls St; Band; Hon Rl; Pres MMM; Treas NHS; Sch Mus; Sch Pl; VP Drama Clb; VP Ger Clb; College; Engr.

KASTELIC, JOHN; St Joseph HS; Euclid, OH; 2/285 Sal; Hon Rl; Lit Mag; Mod UN; NHS; Stu Cncl; Ed Yrbk; Ger Clb; IM Sprt; Natl Merit Ltr; Univ Of Notre Dame; Chem Engr.

KASTNER, MATT; Hopkins Public HS; Hopkins, MI; Band; Hon Rl; NHS; Stu Cncl; Spn Clb; Letter Bsktbl; Letter Ten; Mic State Univ; Sci.

KASTNER, MICHAEL; Tiffin Calvert HS; Tiffin, OH; Band; Chrs; Hon Rl; Lbry Ade; MMM; Off Ade; PAVAS; Red Cr Ade; Sch Mus; Sch Pl; Music Schslhp 500 79; Siena Hts Coll; Music.

KASUNIC, LISA; Tuslaw HS; Massillon, OH; 29/156 Band; Chrs; Hon Rl; Pres Lbry Ade; Orch; Rptr Yrbk; VP FTA; Chrldng;.

KASUNICK, STACIE; Washington HS; Massillon, OH; Chrs; Hon Rl; Jr NHS; Off Ade; Trk; Univ; Art.

KASZAR, JON; Jefferson Area HS; Dorset, OH; Band; Cmnty Wkr; Hon Rl; 4-H; Fr Clb; 4-H Awd; Ohio State Univ; Veterinarian.

KASZNIA, VICKY; Washington HS; South Bend, IN; Hon Rl; NHS; Off Ade; Stu Cncl; Rptr Yrbk; Fr Clb; Scr Kpr; Indiana Univ; Phys Ther.

KASZOWSKI, DEBBIE; Brookfield HS; Masury, OH; Chrs; Girl Scts; NHS; Off Ade; Beta Clb; Spn Clb; Trk; College.

KATERBA, LISA; Admiral King HS; Lorain, OH; Chrh Wkr; Debate Tm; Hon Rl; Sdlty; Rptr Yrbk; Yrbk; Letter Ten; Natl Ed Dev Test Cert Of Merit; Ohio Test Of Schlstc Ach Cert Of Merit In French 2nd Yr; Univ; Indus Engr.

KATERBERG, MIKE; South Christian HS; Caledonia, MI; Pres Frsh Cls; Band; Chrh Wkr; Debate Tm; Hon Rl; NHS; Sch Pl; Stg Crw; IM Sprt; General Motors Inst; Engr.

KATHMAN, PATTY; Oak Hills HS; Cincinnati, OH; Trs Sr Cls; Hon Rl; OEA; GAA; IM Sprt; Mgrs; Scr Kpr; Tmr; Diamond Oaks CDC; Acctg.

KATKIC, MARY B; Our Lady Of Mercy HS; Southfield, MI; Girl Scts; Hon Rl; Stg Crw; Rptr Yrbk; Mth Clb; Univ Of Michigan; Advertising.

KATLIN, MICKEY; Howell HS; Howell, MI; 118/395 Boy Scts; FCA; Hon Rl; Sct Actv; Coach Actv; IM Sprt; Mgrs; Cit Awd; 4-H Awd; Kiwan Awd; Lake Superior St Coll; Bus.

KATSCHKE, KAREN; Fitch HS; Youngstown, OH; 101/655 Chrh Wkr; Cmnty Wkr; Hon Rl; Hosp Ade; Jr NHS; Red Cr Ade; Y-Teens; Mgrs; PPFtbl; St Elizabeth Schl Of Nursing; RN.

KATTER, JULIA; Castle HS; Newburgh, IN; 30/333 Trs Jr Cls; Am Leg Aux Girls St; Band; Chrs; Chrh Wkr; Sch Mus; Stg Crw; Ball State; Dietitics.

KATTER, KAREN; Wilmington HS; Wilmington, OH; Cl Rep Jr Cls; Chrs; Sch Mus; Stu Cncl; 4-H; Bsktbl; 4-H Awd; Ohio 4 H Club Congress; 4 H Ach Awd; VP Jr Leadership 4 H Club; College; Phys Therapy.

KATTER, SHANA; Martinsville HS; Martinsville, IN; 14/425 Chrs; Chrh Wkr; Cmnty Wkr; Girl Scts; Hon Rl; Mdrgl; Sch Mus; Sct Actv; 4-H; Spn Clb; 1 Chrl Ad 77 & 78; 4 Chrl Awds 79; Purdue Univ; Vet.

KATTERMAN, HERBERT; Lapeer W Sr HS; Lapeer, MI; Cls Rep Sr Cls; Band; Chrh Wkr; Hon Rl; NHS; Stu Cncl; Fr Clb; Crs Cntry; Letter Trk; Natl Merit Schl; Michigan St Univ; Comp Sci.

KATTUS, TARA; Colerain Sr HS; Cincinnati, OH; Cls Rep Sr Cls; Hon Rl; Quill & Scroll; Ed Yrbk; Rptr Yrbk; Ger Clb; Bsbl; Sftbl; Socr; Letter Trk; German Honor Soc 77 78 & 78 79; Univ.

KATZ, HOWARD; Shaker Heights HS; Shaker Heights, OH; Hon Rl; Sch Nwsp; Pres DECA; Ohio Univ; Marketing.

KATZ, JILL; Reeths Puffer HS; Muskegon, MI; 69/281 Band; Hon Rl; Rptr Yrbk; Voc Schl; Photog.

KATZ, SUSAN; Ida HS; Toledo, OH; NHS; Ed Yrbk; Rptr Sch Nwsp; Ohio St Univ.

KATZER, SCOTT; Wilbur Wright HS; Dayton, OH; 7/262 Aud/Vis; Boy Scts; Hon Rl; NHS; Sch Pl; Stg Crw; Stu Cncl; Ger Clb; Am Leg Awd; Univ Of Chicago; Physics.

KAUBLE, SUSAN; Rutherford B Hayes HS; Delaware, OH; Band; Hon Rl; Y-Teens; FTA; Spn Clb; CTI; Data Proc.

KAUFFMAN, AUDREY; Columbiana HS; Columbiana, OH; 2/105 Sec Frsh Cls; Trs Soph Cls; Band; Chrh Wkr; Hon Rl; Jr NHS; Stu Cncl; Sch Nwsp; Fr Clb; College; Language Interp.

KAUFFMAN, CINDY; Franklin Monroe HS; Arcanum, OH; 2/80 Hst Soph Cls; Hst Jr Cls; VP Band; Chrs; VP NHS; Off Ade; Sch Pl; Pres Yth Flsp; FSA; FTA; Sinclair Comm Coll; Aviation Admin.

KAUFFMAN, DIANE; Milton Union HS; W Milton, OH; 12/217 Cmp Fr Grls; Chrs; Chrh Wkr; Hon Rl; Lbry Ade; NHS; Off Ade; FBLA; FTA; Sinclair Community College; Med.

KAUFFMAN, JEFF; Triton HS; Etna Green, IN; Cl Rep Jr Cls; Boy Scts; Chrh Wkr; VP FCA; Hon Rl; Stu Cncl; Letter Ftbl; Letter Trk; Letter Wrstlng; Mgrs; Voc Schl; Elec.

KAUFFMAN, KAREN; Taylor Center HS; Taylor, MI; 94/425 Chrh Wkr; Hon Rl; Lbry Ade; Red Cr Ade; Sch Pl; Yth Flsp; Rptr Yrbk; Drama Clb; Letter Gym; Trk; Mercy Coll; Nursing.

KAUFFMAN, KARLA; Columbia City Joint HS; Columbia City, IN; 1/290 VP Soph Cls; Pres Jr Cls; Pres Sr Cls; Val; Am Leg Aux Girls St; Chrh Wkr; Debate Tm; Northwestern Univ; Foreign Lang.

KAUFFMAN, LORA; Fredericktown HS; Fred, OH; 9/120 Hon Rl; Yth Flsp; Rptr Sch Nwsp; Sec 4-H; Scr Kpr; Tmr; 4-H Awd; Girls St Alt 79; 3 Yr Schlrshp Tm 79; Univ; Botany.

KAUFFMAN, MARY; Fairbanks HS; Marysville, OH; Hon Rl; Lbry Ade; Sch Nwsp; College; Sec.

KAUFMAN, KEITH; Norton HS; Clinton, OH; Boy Scts; Chrs; Hon Rl; JA; Jr NHS; Sch Mus; Sct Actv; Stu Cncl; Drama Clb; Lat Clb; Univ.

KAUFMAN, KENNETH; Cedarville HS; Cedarville, OH; Chrs; Cmnty Wkr; Lbry Ade; Yth Flsp; Sprt Ed Sch Nwsp; Rptr Sch Nwsp; FBLA; Crs Cntry; Trk; Mgrs; Cedarville Coll.

KAUFMAN, LISA; Mineral Ridge HS; Mineral Ridge, OH; Hon Rl; Off Ade; Y-Teens; Univ; Nursing.

KAUFMAN, SARAH; Quincy HS; Coldwater, MI; Chrs; Hon Rl; Fr Clb; College; Psych.

KAUFMAN, SCOTT; Ottoville HS; Ottoville, OH; Band; Cmnty Wkr; Drm Bgl; Hon Rl; Rptr Sch Nwsp; IM Sprt; College.

KAUFMANN, NANCY; Eastlake North HS; Willowick, OH; 1/700 Sec Sr Cls; Am Leg Aux Girls St; Hon Rl; Jr NHS; NHS; Sch Mus; Sch Pl; Yrbk; Drama Clb; Am Leg Awd; Univ; Anthropology.

KAUFMANN, PAUL E; Eastlake N HS; Willowick, OH; 42/670 Am Leg Boys St; Chrh Wkr; Hon Rl; Jr NHS; Treas NHS; Sch Mus; Sch Pl; Yth Flsp; Drama Clb; Ger Clb; Yale Univ; Archt.

KAUNTZ, EDMUND; North Royalton HS; N Royalton, OH; 3/278 Am Leg Boys St; Aud/Vis; Hon Rl; NHS; Rptr Sch Nwsp; Case Western Reserve Univ; Economics.

KAUP, MICHAEL R; Tippecanoe HS; Tipp City, OH; AFS; Am Leg Boys St; Boy Scts; Hon Rl; Bsktbl; Coach Actv; IM Sprt; Coll; Med.

KAUPPILA, TODD; Fairport Harding HS; Fairport Hbr, OH; 6/47 Hon Rl; NHS; Letter Bsktbl; Letter Ftbl; Letter Trk; Mgrs; Scr Kpr; Tmr; Am Leg Awd; Case Western Reserve Univ; Computer.

KAURICH, THOMAS; North HS; Columbus, OH; 1/300 Cls Rep Soph Cls; Cl Rep Jr Cls; Am Leg Boys St; Band; Boy Scts; Chrs; Hon Rl; Jr NHS; Mdrgl; NHS; Piano Accmpnst All Sngng Grps ; Oh Musc Tchrs Awrd ; Columbus Symphny Orch Wnnr; Julliard Univ; Concert Pianist.

KAUSS, ANDREA; Bay HS; Bay Vill, OH; Chrs; Girl Scts; Hon Rl; Off Ade; Sch Mus; Sch Pl; Yth Flsp; Scr Kpr; Tmr; Allegheny College; Bus.

KAUTZ, MARGARET G; Zanesville HS; Zanesville, OH; 21/383 Band; Cmnty Wkr; Hon Rl; NHS; Off Ade; Orch; Stg Crw; Yrbk; Sch Nwsp; Ten; Ohio Univ; Archt.

KAVA, CATHY J; Winston Churchill HS; Livonia, MI; Hon Rl; Fam Lfe Dept Awd 77; Schoolcraft Coll Trust Schlrshp Awd 79; Semi Final In Mi St Comp Schlrshp Progr 79; Schoolcraft Cmnty Coll; Acctg.

KAVANAUGH, ANNE; Hackett HS; Kalamazoo, MI; Hon Rl; JA; Ten; PPFtbl; JC Awd; Western Michigan Univ; Bus Admin.

KAVANAUGH, PETER; Cheboygan Area HS; Cheboygan, MI; Sec Frsh Cls; VP Sr Cls; Am Leg Boys St; Hon Rl; NHS; Sch Pl; Fr Clb; Bsktbl; Crs Cntry; Letter Trk; Univ Of Mic; Math.

KAVERMAN, SHARON; Delphos St Johns HS; Delphos, OH; Cls Rep Frsh Cls; Cls Rep Soph Cls; Cl Rep Jr Cls; Chrh Wkr; Cmnty Wkr; Hon Rl; Hosp Ade; NHS; Sch Pl; Rptr Yrbk; History Proj Awd 2nd Pl 1978; Typewriting Awd 1974; Sr Candy Striper 1977; Mbr Of Mission Soc 1976; Schl Of Nursing; Nurse.

KAWASAKI, AKI; Madison Heights HS; Anderson, IN; 3/350 Chrh Wkr; Jr NHS; NHS; Orch; Lat Clb; Ten; 4-H Awd; Indiana Univ; Med.

KAWSKY, MARY; Our Lady Star Of The Sea HS; Grosse Pt Wds, MI; Hon Rl; NHS; Sch Pl; Rptr Yrbk; Rptr Sch Nwsp; Drama Clb; GAA; IM Sprt; Univ Of Detroit; Dent Hygnst.

KAY, ANITA; Howland HS; Warren, OH; 125/430 Band; Hon Rl; JA; NHS; Off Ade; Y-Teens; Yrbk; FNA; Pep Clb; JA Awd; Youngstown St Univ; Psych.

KAY, DEBRA; Fenton HS; Fenton, MI; Chrs; Chrh Wkr; Cmnty Wkr; Girl Scts; PAVAS; Sch Mus; Rptr Yrbk; Yrbk; Sch Nwsp; College; Photog.

KAY, MARSHA; Beachwood HS; Beachwood, OH; 6/157 Cl Rep Jr Cls; Am Leg Aux Girls St; Pres Debate Tm; Natl Forn Lg; NHS; Stu Cncl; Sec Fr Clb; College; Pre Med.

KAY, MATTHEW; Gilmour Academy; University Hts, OH; Hon Rl; NHS; Ed Sch Nwsp; IM Sprt; Univ.

KAY, MIKE; St Ignatius HS; Lyndhurst, OH; Hon Rl; Stu Cncl; Lat Clb; Rdo Clb; Bsktbl; Crs Cntry; Glf; Trk; IM Sprt; College; Bus Admin.

KAY, SUSAN; Pleasant HS; Marion, OH; 7/160 Band; Chrh Wkr; Hon Rl; JA; NHS; Yth Flsp; FHA; Chrldng; Piano Guild Awd; Univ; Psych.

KAYAFAS, GUS; Wintersville HS; Wintersville, OH; Chrs; Chrh Wkr; Hon Rl; Sch Mus; Spn Clb; Trk; Wrstlng; Kent St Univ; Archt.

KAYE, THOMAS; Berea HS; Berea, OH; 9/527 Cl Rep Jr Cls; Boy Scts; Hon Rl; NHS; Sch Pl; Sct Actv; Drama Clb; Fr Clb; Swmmng; Ten; Univ Of S California; Cinema.

KAYI, LEYLA; Farmington Sr HS; Farmington Hls, MI; Cls Rep Frsh Cls; Chrs; Hon Rl; Mdrgl; Sec Pep Clb; Ten; Michigan St Univ; Drama.

KAYLA, DEBORAH; Lake HS; Uniontown, OH; Band; Chrs; Girl Scts; Hon Rl; Jr NHS; Y-Teens; Cit Awd; Univ Of Akron; Psych.

KAYLE, CORINNE; Lorain Catholic HS; Lorain, OH; Chrs; Hon Rl; Off Ade; Pol Wkr; Sprt Ed Sch Nwsp; Rptr Sch Nwsp; Sch Nwsp; Pep Clb; Lorain Cmnty Coll; Cmnctns.

KAYLOR, REBECCA; Martins Ferry HS; Martins Ferry, OH; 53/214 Hon Rl; Off Ade; Y-Teens; Bradford Schl; Exec Sec.

KAYS, CHRIS; Decatur Central HS; Indianapolis, IN; Sch Pl; Stg Crw; Drama Clb; Mas Awd; Indiana Univ; Child Psych.

KAYS, MARK; North Putnam HS; Bainbridge, IN; 28/115 Band; NHS; Sch Mus; Sch Pl; Crs Cntry; Swmmng; Ten; Ball State Univ; Bus.

KAYSON, MARY; Gabriel Richard HS; Rockwood, MI; Hosp Ade; Detroit Coll; Acctg.

KAZLAUSKY, JOANIE; Wehrle HS; Columbus, OH; 8/115 VP Sr Cls; Hon Rl; Stu Cncl; Trk; Scr Kpr; Bauder Fashion Coll; Fash Merch.

KAZMAIER, LISA; Glen Oak School; Mayfield, OH; Cmnty Wkr; Girl Scts; Off Ade; Sch Mus; Sch Pl; Sct Actv; Stg Crw; Y-Teens; Sch Nwsp; IM Sprt; Descriptive & Narrative Writing Awd 76 77; Univ; Fshn Design.

KAZMER, ANDREA; West Geauga HS; Chesterland, OH; Band; Chrs; Debate Tm; Girl Scts; Hon Rl; Lbry Ade; Stu Cncl; Ed Sch Nwsp; Chrldng; 4-H Awd; College.

KAZMIERSKI, JOSEPH; Bay City All Saints Ctrl HS; Bay City, MI; Capt Bsktbl; Delta Cmnty Coll; Bus Admin.

KAZMIERSKI, STEVEN; All Saints Central HS; Bay City, MI; Band; Chrh Wkr; Cmnty Wkr; Hon Rl; Sch Mus; Bsbl; Glf; IM Sprt; College; Engr.

KAZYAK, RONALD; Bay City Central HS; Bay City, MI; Hon Rl; Pol Wkr; Coach Actv; Delta College; Acctg.

KEAFFABER, JEFF; R Nelson Snider HS; Ft Wayne, IN; 34/602 Cls Rep Soph Cls; Hon Rl; JA; Stu Cncl; Rptr Yrbk; Rptr Sch Nwsp; Glf; Ind Purdue; Chemeistry.

KEAGGY, CAROLYN; Hubbard HS; Hubbard, OH; Chrs; Chrh Wkr; Hon Rl; Chrldng; College; Music.

KEALY, TERESA; Kalamazoo Central HS; Kalamazoo, MI; 30/435 Hon Rl; JA; NHS; Letter Crs Cntry; Letter Trk; Cit Awd; Western Michigan Univ; Lib Art.

KEAN, MEG; Yale HS; Yale, MI; 5/170 VP Soph Cls; Trs Jr Cls; Am Leg Aux Girls St; Hon Rl; NHS; Stu Cncl; Yrbk; Spn Clb; St Clair Cnty Community Coll; Bus.

KEAN, ROBERT; Yale HS; Avoca, MI; Hon Rl; 4-H; Letter Bsbl; Letter Bsktbl; 4-H Awd; Univ; Bus.

KEANE, DOUGLAS; Hackett HS; Kalamazoo, MI; Wrstlng; Michigan Univ; Engr.

KEANE, JIM; Wylie E Groves HS; Franklin, MI; 191/550 Chrh Wkr; Cmnty Wkr; Letter Trk; IM Sprt; Tmr; Opt Clb Awd; Michigan St Univ; Bus Admin.

KEARNEY, BEN; South Amherst HS; So Amherst, OH; Cls Rep Sr Cls; Boy Scts; Chrs; Chrh Wkr; Lbry Ade; Red Cr Ade; Stu Cncl; Am Leg Awd; Lorain Cnty Community; Ministry.

KEARNEY, BRYAN; James A Garfield HS; Garrettsville, OH; Cls Rep Frsh Cls; Chrh Wkr; Hon Rl; Sci Clb; College; Dent.

KEARNEY, JOAN; Gabriel Richard HS; Ann Arbor, MI; 8/82 Chrs; Girl Scts; Hon Rl; Lbry Ade; NHS; Fr Clb; Pres Pep Clb; Bsbl; Bsktbl; Natl Merit SF; Ctrl Michigan Univ; Spec Ed.

KEARNEY, JOHN; St Edward HS; Cleveland, OH; Cls Rep Frsh Cls; Cls Rep Soph Cls; Cl Rep Jr Cls; Chrh Wkr; Cmnty Wkr; Letter Glf; IM Sprt;.

KEARNEY, LORI; Marion Franklin HS; Columbus, OH; 51/350 Hon Rl; Pep Clb; GAA; Marion Franklin Voc Schl; Nursing.

KEARNS, KEVIN; Madison Comp HS; Mansfield, OH; Yrbk; Key Clb; Bsbl; Crs Cntry; IM Sprt; Univ.

KEARNS, MARK; Elgin HS; La Rue, OH; Cls Rep Frsh Cls; Cls Rep Soph Cls; Cls Rep Sr Cls; Hon Rl; Jr NHS; Mod UN; NHS; Stu Cncl; Yth Flsp; Lat Clb; Lettered As A Soph Ftbl & Bsktbl; Univ; Bio Med Engr.

KEARNS, MARY; Beaver Local HS; Lisbon, OH; Band; Chrs; NHS; Eng Clb; Fr Clb; Youngstown St Univ; Lang.

KEARNS, NANCY; Eastern HS; Russellville, OH; 1/92 Trs Sr Cls; Band; Chrh Wkr; Hon Rl; NHS; Sch Pl; Treas Rptr Yrbk; Treas Fr Clb; Univ Of Cin.

KEARNS, THOMAS; Padua Franciscan HS; Cleveland, OH; Letter Crs Cntry; Trk; Univ; Cmnctns.

KEASLING, B; Union County HS; Liberty, IN; 13/148 Band; Chrs; FCA; Hon Rl; Mdrgl; NHS; Sch Mus; Yth Flsp; Stdnt Athletic Trainer 7 Letters 77 78 & 79; Ball St Univ; Scndry Educ.

KEATING, CLIFFORD E; Fairview HS; Fairview Park, OH; Boy Scts; Hon Rl; Lbry Ade; Orch; Red Cr Ade; Sch Mus; Sct Actv; Sci Clb; College; Marine Bio.

KEATLEY, E; Talcott HS; Indian Mills, WV; Lbry Ade; DAR Awd; Marshall; Industrial Arts.

KEATLEY, MARY; Kirtland HS; Kirtland, OH; 5/120 Pres Jr Cls; Sec AFS; Am Leg Aux Girls St; Hon Rl; NHS; Pres Stu Cncl; Am Leg Awd; College; Business.

KEATON, KATHY; Iaeger HS; Ieager, WV; Chrh Wkr; Cmnty Wkr; Debate Tm; Hon Rl; Jr NHS; NHS; Fr Clb; Twrlr; Mc Dowell County Voc; Med.

KECK, ANDREW; Harrison HS; Evansville, IN; 7 490 Boy Scts; Chrh Wkr; Hon Rl; NHS; Sch Pl; Sct Actv; Stg Crw; Stu Cncl; Pres Yth Flsp; Ger Clb; College.

KECK, BETH; Ida HS; Ida, MI; VP Soph Cls; Band; Hon Rl; Off Ade; Stu Cncl; 4-H; Pep Clb; GAA; Mat Maids; 4-H Awd; College; Dental Ass.

KECK, MARY; Newark Catholic HS; Newark, OH; Am Leg Aux Girls St; Hon Rl; NHS; Sec Stu Cncl; Trk; Treas GAA; Ohio State Univ.

KECK, REBECCA; Jackson Milton HS; No Jackson, OH; Cl Rep Jr Cls; Sec Sr Cls; Am Leg Aux Girls St; Band; Girl Scts; Hon Rl; Hosp Ade; NHS; Off Ade; Red Cr Ade; Youngstown State Univ; Zoology.

KECK, STEPHEN; Akron North HS; Akron, OH; 90/343 Chrs; Sch Mus; Sch Pl; Stg Crw; FTA; Bsbl; IM Sprt; Akron Univ; Primary Educ.

KECZAN, JOHN; Bramwell HS; Nemours, WV; 3/29 Cls Rep Soph Cls; VP Jr Cls; Chrs; Hon Rl; NHS; Stu Cncl; Key Clb; Bsktbl; Crs Cntry; Trk; Univ; Elec Engr.

KEE, DIANE; St Agatha HS; Detroit, MI; Trs Jr Cls; Trs Sr Cls; Hon Rl; Hosp Ade; Jr NHS; NHS; Off Ade; Stu Cncl; Eng Clb; Fr Clb; College.

KEE, DONALD E; Green HS; Clinton, OH; Aud/Vis; Chrs; Treas JA; Lbry Ade; Sch Mus; Sch Pl; Drama Clb; Akron Univ; Elec Engr.

KEE, DONNA; Franklin HS; Franklin, WV; 3/85 Sec Jr Cls; Pres Sr Cls; Hon Rl; Hosp Ade; NHS; Sch Pl; Stu Cncl; Yth Flsp; 4-H; FHA; Pres Of FHA; Sec Of FHA; West Virginia Univ; Phys Therapy.

KEEBLER, CYNTHIA G; Loveland Hurst HS; Loveland, OH; 8/279 Chrh Wkr; Hon Rl; Hosp Ade; Mod UN; Sec NHS; Pres Yth Flsp; Yrbk; Sch Nwsp; Drama Clb; 4-H; Dope Stop Teen Cnslng 1979; Miami Univ; Intl Jrnlsm.

KEEFE, LISA; Niles HS; Niles, MI; 3/415 Band; Treas Girl Scts; Hon Rl; NHS; Sch Mus; Sch Pl; Sct Actv; Yth Flsp; Rptr Yrbk; Sch Nwsp; Natl Hon Soc Straight A Ltr 79; 3 Mus Schlrshp 76 77 & 78; Mbr Of Bluelake Fine Arts Cmp Intl Bnd 78; Univ; Jrnlsm.

KEEFE, MARIE; Medina Sr HS; Medina, OH; Cls Rep Frsh Cls; Cls Rep Soph Cls; Hon Rl; FTA; Pep Clb; Spn Clb; IM Sprt; Tmr; Kent St Univ; Fshn Mdse.

KEEFE, MICHAEL; St Ignatius HS; Shaker Hts, OH; 139/305 Chrh Wkr; JA; Socr; IM Sprt; College.

KEEFER, BOB; Akron East HS; Akron, OH; 23/334 Band; Chrh Wkr; Letter Swmmng; Akron Univ; Chem.

KEEGAN, JEANETTE; Felicity Franklin HS; Moscow, OH; 6/69 Pres Frsh Cls; VP Jr Cls; Hon Rl; NHS; Sch Pl; Stu Cncl; Ed Sch Nwsp; Treas 4-H; Capt Bsktbl; Chrldng; Univ Of Cincinnati; Exec Sec.

KEEGAN, KEVIN; Magnolia HS; New Martinsvle, WV; 12/200 Hon Rl; Letter Ten; Virginia Polytech Inst; Chem Engr.

KEEGAN, LISA; Ehove Joint Voc HS; Vickery, OH; Chrh Wkr; Cmnty Wkr; Girl Scts; JA; Off Ade; Sch Pl; Stg Crw; Stu Cncl; Yrbk; Pres Drama Clb; Best Actress; Best Thespian; Ambassador Awd OEA;.

KEELER, DEBORAH; Benzie Central HS; Benzonia, MI; Band; Debate Tm; Drm Mjrt; Hon Rl; Hosp Ade; Lbry Ade; NHS; Red Cr Ade; Sch Pl; Drama Clb; Univ; Nurse.

KEELER, ELAINE; Concord Community HS; Concord, MI; Band; Girl Scts; 4-H; Bsbl; Bsktbl; Chrldng; 4-H Awd; Jackson Cmnty Coll.

KEELER, JULIE; St Ursula Acad; Toledo, OH; Chrs; Chrh Wkr; Hon Rl; Jr NHS; NHS; Quill & Scroll; Sch Mus; Rptr Yrbk; Univ Of Toledo; Nursing.

KEELER, MARIAN; Withrow HS; Cincinnati, OH; Cls Rep Frsh Cls; Cls Rep Soph Cls; Cl Rep Jr Cls; Chrs; Chrh Wkr; Hon Rl; JA; Orch; Sch Mus; Sch Pl; Xavier Univ; Law.

KEELER, MARY; Milan HS; Milan, MI; Am Leg Aux Girls St; Band; Hon Rl; NHS; Univ Of Mic; History.

KEELER, REBECCA; Waterford Township HS; Pontiac, MI; 39/441 Band; Cmp Fr Grls; Hon Rl; Hosp Ade; Sch Pl; Stu Cncl; Yth Flsp; Rptr Sch Nwsp; Pep Clb; Natl Merit Schl; Grad Summa Cum Laude 79; Wayne St Univ; RN.

KEELING, ERIC; Fountain Central HS; Kingman, IN; Hon Rl; NHS; Sci Clb;.

KEELING, NORA; Danville Community HS; Danville, IN; 3/150 Band; Pres Chrh Wkr; Drl Tm; FCA; Hon Rl; VP Ger Clb; Pep Clb; Ten; Cit Awd; Delta Epsilon Phi Nat Ger Hnr Soc 78; In St Piano 2nd Div Mdl 79; Smith Walbridge Rifle Cmp Attitude Awd 78; Olivet Nazarene Coll.

KEELS, KIM; Mt Notre Dame HS; Cincinnati, OH; 31/181 Chrh Wkr; Cmnty Wkr; Girl Scts; Hon Rl; Sch Pl; Sct Actv; Bsktbl; Coach Actv; GAA; IM Sprt; Xavier Univ; Montessori Ed.

KEEN, ED; Gladwin HS; Gladwin, MI; Hon Rl; Trk; College; Mechanics.

KEEN, JEFFREY; River Rouge HS; River Rouge, MI; Hon Rl; Sct Actv; DECA; Bsbl; Ftbl; Trk; IM Sprt; Tmr; JC Awd; Coll.

KEEN, SANDI K; Mt Vernon Sr HS; Mt Vernon, OH; Chrh Wkr; Drl Tm; Girl Scts; Sch Pl; Yth Flsp; Pep Clb; Chrldng; Ohio St Univ; Legal Sec.

KEENA, BRIGID; Grandville HS; Grandville, MI; Hon Rl; Spn Clb; Chrldng; Univ; Engr.

KEENAN, TIMOTHY; George Washington HS; Charleston, WV; Band; Hon Rl; Sch Mus; Sch Pl; Stg Crw; Key Clb; Letter Bsbl; Univ Of Pittsburgh; Medicine.

KEENE, PEARL C; Iaeger Sr HS; Jolo, WV; Drm Mjrt; Hon Rl; Sec Jr NHS; Sch Pl; FHA; Mth Clb; Lit Awd; Blue Ribbon In Math Fair; Amer Studies Awd; VP Of Iaeger HS Reading Club; Little French Acad; Beautician.

KEENER, FRANCES; Holy Rosary HS; Burton, MI; VP Soph Cls; Pres Sr Cls; Girl Scts; Hon Rl; Sch Pl; Stu Cncl; Trk; Tmr; College; Bus Admin.

KEENER, KEVIN; Stow Sr HS; Stow, OH; Chrs; Hon Rl; Sch Mus; Stg Crw; 4-H; IM Sprt; Phys Educ Awd 78; Voc Schl; Indstrl Arts.

KEENER, TRICIA; Upper Arlington HS; Columbus, OH; 37/610 Chrh Wkr; Hon Rl; NHS; Sch Pl; Drama Clb; Ger Clb; Crs Cntry; Letter GAA; Ohio St Univ; Nutrition.

KEENEY, MARK; Park Hills HS; Fairborn, OH; Hon Rl; Jr NHS; Lit Mag; Quill & Scroll; Y-Teens; Rptr Sch Nwsp; Sch Nwsp; Drama Clb; Us Air Force; Electronic Computer.

KEERAN, CALVIN W; Hardin Northern HS; Dunkirk, OH; VP Sr Cls; Am Leg Boys St; Hon Rl; Pres FFA; Letter Ftbl; Letter Trk; Dnfth Awd; Ohi Nothern Univ; Engr.

KEERAN, REBECCA S; Euclid Sr HS; Euclid, OH; Red Cr Ade; Cerritos Jr Coll; Child Care.

KEES, LAURI; Portsmouth HS; Portsmouth, OH; 23/225 Chrh Wkr; Drl Tm; Girl Scts; NHS; Sch Pl; Stg Crw; Yth Flsp; Drama Clb; College; Arts.

KEESLAR, JAMES; Quincy HS; Quincy, MI; 3/120 Am Leg Boys St; NHS; Stu Cncl; Beta Clb; Letter Bsktbl; Letter Trk; Cit Awd; Cls Rep Frsh Cls; Cls Rep Soph Cls; Boy Scts; College; Bus Admin.

KEESLAR, PAUL; Hackett HS; Kalamazoo, MI; Boy Scts; Hon Rl; Letter Trk; IM Sprt; Awd In Earth Sci 77; Awd In Algbr 2 & Trig 79; Awd For Acad Achvmnt 79; Art.

KEESLER, SHARLA J; Gods Bible HS; Nebraska City, NE; 3/19 Chrh Wkr; Debate Tm; Hon Rl; NHS; Ed Sch Nwsp; 4-H; Mth Clb; Gods Bible Schl Coll; Sec.

KEESUCKER, KATHY; South Harrison HS; Jane Lew, WV; Cl Rep Jr Cls; Am Leg Aux Girls St; Band; Hon Rl; NHS; Stu Cncl; VP 4-H; VP FHA; Pep Clb; 4-H Awd; Fairmont St Coll; Acctg.

KEETON, BRENDA L; Quincy HS; Quincy, MI; Band; Cmp Fr Grls; Chrh Wkr; Hon Rl; Sch Mus; Pep Clb; Am Leg Awd; Lion Awd; Olivet Nazarene Coll; Child Psych.

KEETON, CATHLEEN L; Southwestern HS; Franklin, IN; 11/58 Sec Sr Cls; Chrs; Sch Pl; Sch Nwsp; Drama Clb; Pep Clb; Trk; Chrldng; Homecoming Queen; Drama Club Sec; Sunshine Soc Pres;.

KEETON, GARRY; Western Hills HS; Cincinnati, OH; 147/830 Cls Rep Frsh Cls; Cls Rep Soph Cls; Cl Rep Jr Cls; Cls Rep Sr Cls; Hon Rl; Stu Cncl; Spn Clb; Capt Bsbl; Southern Illinois Univ.

KEFALOS, JAMES; Barberton HS; Barberton, OH; Hon Rl; Jr NHS; Ger Clb; Akron Univ; Med.

KEGG, LAURA; Oak Hills HS; Cincinnati, OH; 7/850 Cls Rep Sr Cls; NHS; Quill & Scroll; Stu Cncl; Ed Sch Nwsp; Chrldng; Natl Merit Ltr; Univ Of Cincinnati; Bus.

KEHNER, THOMAS; Washington HS; Massillon, OH; AFS; Band; Hon Rl; Jr NHS; NHS; Ed Yrbk; Pres Spn Clb; Ten; Mgrs; College; Engr.

KEHRER, TERESA; Westfield Washington HS; Westfield, IN; Chrs; Chrh Wkr; Girl Scts; Hon Rl; Sch Mus; Sch Pl; Sct Actv; Yth Flsp; Spn Clb; Bus Schl; Legal Sec.

KEHRES, RENEE; Southeast HS; Diamond, OH; VP Soph Cls; Pres Jr Cls; Cl Rep Jr Cls; Am Leg Aux Girls St; Band; Hon Rl; Treas NHS; Quill & Scroll; Stu Cncl; Rptr Yrbk; Malone Coll; Bus Admin.

KEIFER, ROBERT; Rose D Warwick HS; Burlington, MI; Band; Hon Rl; Sch Pl; Drama Clb; Kellog Comm College.

KEIFFER, CAROLE; Danville Community HS; Danville, IN; Cls Rep Frsh Cls; Cls Rep Soph Cls; Cl Rep Jr Cls; Cls Rep Sr Cls; Chrs; Stu Cncl; Ten; Chrldng; Bus Schl; Bus.

KEIFFER, JACK; Dunbar HS; Dunbar, WV; 8/175 VP Frsh Cls; VP Soph Cls; Trs Jr Cls; Trs Sr Cls; Am Leg Boys St; Jr NHS; NHS; Ftbl; Vir Polytechnic Inst; Comp Sci.

KEILER, LESLIE; Upper Arlington HS; Columbus, OH; 136/610 Chrs; Chrh Wkr; Girl Scts; Hon Rl; Ger Clb; Swmmng; GAA; Mgrs; Tmr; Wittenberg; Psych.

KEILITZ, ROBERT; Caro Community HS; Caro, MI; 7/160 Band; Debate Tm; Hon Rl; NHS; Off Ade; Sct Actv; Letter Wrstlng; Drum Major 76 79; John Phillip Sousa Band Awd 79; Tri County Hnrs Band 77 79; Ctrl Michigan Univ; Music Educ.

KEILY, THERESA; Centerville HS; Westminster, CO; 36/690 Chrh Wkr; NHS; Off Ade; Pep Clb; IM Sprt; Univ Of Colorado; Busns Ed.

KEIM, KELLY; Ladywood HS; Livonia, MI; 5/79 VP Jr Cls; Girl Scts; Hon Rl; Hosp Ade; NHS; Quill & Scroll; Sch Mus; Stu Cncl; Rptr Sch Nwsp; FHA; Western Michigan Univ; Occup Ther.

KEINATH, WAYNE; Deerfield HS; Blissfield, MI; 3/32 Cl Rep Jr Cls; Hon Rl; NHS; Stu Cncl; Letter Crs Cntry; Ftbl; Letter Trk; Coll; Comp Sci.

KEISLER, MARK; North Newton HS; Demotte, IN; 21/300 Hon Rl; Quill & Scroll; Ed Sch Nwsp; Sprt Ed Sch Nwsp; FBLA; Letter Bsbl; Letter Swmmng; Purdue; Photojournalist.

KEISTER, MATTHEW; Churubusco HS; Albion, IN; Chrs; Chrh Wkr; Hon Rl; Yth Flsp; 4-H; Pres FFA; Purdue Univ; Agri.

KEISTER, ROBERT; Hampshire HS; Romney, WV; Band; Chrs; Chrh Wkr; Hon Rl; Yth Flsp; W Vir Univ; Comp Tech.

KEITH, BETTY; Charlestown HS; Charlestown, IN; 34/155 Chrs; Chrh Wkr; Hon Rl; JA; FHA; Pep Clb; Spn Clb; Bus Schl.

KEITH, DONALD; George Rogers Clark HS; Whiting, IN; 20/218 Cls Rep Frsh Cls; Cls Rep Soph Cls; Cl Rep Jr Cls; Cls Rep Sr Cls; Chrs; Chrh Wkr; Sch Mus; Stu Cncl; Socr; DAR Awd; College; Chem.

KEITH, DONNA; Switzerland Cnty HS; Bennington, IN; 13/126 Hon Rl; Pep Clb; Spn Clb; Bsktbl; Trk; Scr Kpr; Tmr; Ivy Tech Univ; Archt.

KEITH, GARY; Switzerland County HS; Bennington, IN; 2/118 Cls Rep Frsh Cls; Cl Rep Jr Cls; Sal; Hon Rl; VP NHS; Off Ade; Sch Mus; Stu Cncl; Pep Clb; Spn Clb; Wabash Coll.

KEITH, MICHELLE; Switzerland Co Jr Sr HS; Rising Sun, IN; 11/126 VP Jr Cls; Chrh Wkr; Off Ade; Sch Pl; Stg Crw; Stu Cncl; Drama Clb; Pep Clb; Bsktbl; Trk;.

KEITH, RICHARD; Peebles HS; Peebles, OH; Band; Boy Scts; Chrs; Chrh Wkr; Cmnty Wkr; Sch Mus; Sch Pl; Sct Actv; Stg Crw; Yth Flsp; All Ohio FFA Band; Chapt Farmer Degree; Electrification Awd; Univ Of Cincinnati; Photog.

KEITH, TODD; Medina Sr HS; Medina, OH; Red Cr Ade; 4-H; Letter Bsktbl; Letter Ftbl; Letter Trk; Letter Wrstlng; Mgrs; Kent St Univ; Sports Medicine.

KEIZER, GRETCHEN; Saint Joseph HS; Grand Rapids, MI; Treas Band; FCA; Quill & Scroll; Sch Mus; Sch Pl; Yth Flsp; Rptr Yrbk; Hope College.

KEIZER, JACKIE; Wayland HS; Wayland, MI; 12/193 Hon Rl; NHS; Off Ade; Rptr Yrbk; 4-H; Capt Bsktbl; PPFtbl; 4-H Awd; Harry Mutler Awd Top Female Athlete 77; All Amer Bkstbl Player 78; Mi St Comp Schlrshp 79; Kalamazoo Vly Cmnty Univ; Phys Educ.

KELADES, MARIE; Campbell Memorial HS; Campbell, OH; Cls Rep Frsh Cls; Cls Rep Soph Cls; Cl Rep Jr Cls; Cls Rep Sr Cls; Chrh Wkr; JA; Rptr Yrbk; Key Clb; Pep Clb; Youngstown Univ; Dietetics.

KELCH, LYNNE; Carrollton HS; Carrollton, OH; 14/230 Cls Rep Frsh Cls; Pres Soph Cls; Cl Rep Jr Cls; Band; Hon Rl; NHS; 4-H; Pres FHA; VP Lat Clb; 4-H Awd; Ohio State Univ; Nursing.

KELCHNER, CHARLOTTE; Bridgeport HS; Bridgeport, WV; Hon Rl; Jr NHS; NHS; Y-Teens; Trk; Natl Merit SF; Rotary Awd; College; Marine Biology.

KELL, JILL; North Central Area HS; Wilson, MI; 1/60 NHS; Stu Cncl; Ed Yrbk; 4-H; FHA; Pom Pon; Cit Awd; Brooks College; Int Design.

KELL, MOLLY; Bishop Foley HS; Madison Hgts, MI; Chrs; Hon Rl; Off Ade; Sch Mus; Sch Pl; Rptr Sch Nwsp; Chrldng; GAA; PPFtbl; Wayne St Univ; Spec Educ.

KELLACKEY, NORA; Holyname Nazareth HS; N Royalton, OH; Chrh Wkr; Hon Rl; Coach Actv; College; Engr.

KELLAM, MARK; Tri HS; Spiceland, IN; 9/83 Hon Rl; JA; NHS; Sch Pl; Ed Yrbk; Ed Sch Nwsp; Drama Clb; In Univ; Journalism.

KELLAR, DANIEL R; Uppr Valley Joint Voc School; Houston, OH; Chrs; Chrh Wkr; Cmnty Wkr; Hon Rl; Sch Pl; Sch Nwsp; DECA; Drama Clb; Mgrs; Art Schl; Cartoonist.

KELLAR, SHARON; Wintersville HS; Wintersville, OH; 28/267 Band; Girl Scts; Sch Mus; Sch Pl; Sct Actv; Yth Flsp; Fr Clb; GAA; Univ; Art.

KELLAS, GEORGE; Bridgeport HS; Barton, OH; VP Jr Cls; Pres Sr Cls; Boy Scts; Chrh Wkr; Hon Rl; Lbry Ade; Off Ade; Sct Actv; Stu Cncl; Pres OEA; Ohio St Univ; Comp Sci.

KELLAS, ROBERT; A D Johnston HS; Ramsay, MI; 8/80 Cls Rep Frsh Cls; Cl Rep Jr Cls; Cls Rep Sr Cls; Hon Rl; NHS; Stu Cncl; Rptr Yrbk; Sprt Ed Sch Nwsp; Rptr Sch Nwsp; Mic Tech Univ; Comp Sci.

KELLEHER, SHEILA; Magnificat HS; Rocky River, OH; Hosp Ade; Jr NHS; Mod UN; NHS; Red Cr Ade; Natl Merit Ltr; Natl Merit SF; Natl Merit Schl; Wellesley Coll; Chem.

KELLEHER, SHEILA M; Magnificat HS; Rocky River, OH; Hosp Ade; Jr NHS; Lbry Ade; Mod UN; NHS; Red Cr Ade; Rptr Sch Nwsp; Natl Merit SF; College; Medicine.

KELLENBERGER, LORI; Merrillville HS; Merrillville, IN; 60/604 Band; Chrs; Hon Rl; NHS; Sch Mus; Sch Pl; Stg Crw; Stu Cncl; Rptr Yrbk; Drama Clb; Band And Vocal Comptn Awd 76 79; Univ; Dvlpmnt Psych.

KELLER, ALISA; Bellevue Sr HS; Bellevue, OH; 3/230 Cl Rep Jr Cls; Cls Rep Sr Cls; Am Leg Aux Girls St; Chrs; Cmnty Wkr; Hon Rl; Hosp Ade; Jr NHS; VP NHS; Stu Cncl; Coll Of Mt St Joseph; Nursing.

KELLER, BETH; Sandusky HS; Sandusky, OH; 22/425 Hon Rl; NHS; Letter Gym; Treas Swmmng; Bowling Green Univ.

KELLER, BETH; Penna County HS; Holland, OH; Chrs; Girl Scts; Hon Rl; Off Ade; Stu Cncl; Y-Teens; 4-H; Pep Clb; Gym; Chrldng; Bus Schl; Typing.

KELLER, BETH; Lake HS; Perrysburg, OH; Band; Cmp Fr Grls; Chrs; Chrh Wkr; Sch Mus; Yth Flsp; Yrbk; Drama Clb; FBLA; Trk; Toledo Univ; Secretarial Work.

KELLER, BETH; Reed City HS; Reed City, MI; 16/147 Cls Rep Sr Cls; Chrh Wkr; Hon Rl; NHS; Pres Yrbk; Cit Awd; Ferris St Coll; Sci.

KELLER, CHRISTINE; Austintown Fitch HS; Youngstown, OH; 93/641 Hon Rl; Lbry Ade; Y-Teens; Pep Clb; Ten; Trk; PPFtbl; St Elizabeths Sch; Nursing.

KELLER, CONNIE; Bucyrus HS; Bucyrus, OH; Sch Mus; Drama Clb; 4-H; Letter Bsktbl; Letter Trk; Bowling Green St Univ; Elem Educ.

KELLER, DEBBIE; Fairfield Sr HS; Fairfield, OH; Chrs; Off Ade; Fr Clb; Sci Clb; Swmmng; Univ Of Cincinnati; Fshn Mdse.

KELLER, DEBORAH; Cadillac Sr HS; Cadillac, MI; Band; Chrh Wkr; Hon Rl; NHS; Sct Actv; Letter Bsbl; Bsktbl; GAA; PPFtbl; Northern Michigan Univ; Phys Ther.

KELLER, DONNA; Southgate HS; Southgate, MI; 11/255 Hst Sr Cls; Band; Hon Rl; VP NHS; Rptr Sch Nwsp; Sch Nwsp; Pres Mth Clb; Trk; St Of Mi Shclshp To UM; Awd Of Hon For Math; Awd Of Hon For Eng & Histrn; Univ Of Michigan; Psych.

KELLER, DUSTY; Father Wehrle Memorial HS; Columbus, OH; 5/114 Cl Rep Jr Cls; Hon Rl; JA; Orch; Stu Cncl; Rptr Sch Nwsp; Ftbl; College; Medicine.

KELLER, EILEEN; Boardman HS; Youngstown, OH; Cmnty Wkr; Hon Rl; Hosp Ade; Natl Forn Lg; Orch; Pol Wkr; Red Cr Ade; Spn Clb; Most Improved Violinist 78; Cert For Partcpt In Music Fest 77; Cert Of Honor In Profsnl Conf 79; Youngstown St Univ.

KELLER, GAIL S; Greenville Sr HS; Greenville, OH; 126/380 Pres Soph Cls; Pres Jr Cls; Chrh Wkr; Sch Mus; Yth Flsp; Rptr Sch Nwsp; Drama Clb; Spn Clb; Chrldng; Univ; Theatre.

KELLER, JEFF; Centerville HS; Centerville, IN; 17/150 Hon Rl; Crs Cntry; Trk; Univ; Archt.

KELLER, JUDY; Ashley Community HS; Ashley, MI; Sec Sr Cls; Band; Hon Rl; NHS; Off Ade; Rptr Yrbk; Drama Clb; Pep Clb; Twrlr; Office Wrk.

KELLER, LETIA A; Berkley HS; Oak Park, MI; Chrs; Chrh Wkr; Girl Scts; Hon Rl; Mdrgl; Pol Wkr; Yrbk; Letter Trk; GAA; 2nd Pl Awd Yth Fitness Ath Activities 78; Stanford Univ; Bus Admin.

KELLER, LISA; Northland HS; Columbus, OH; 5/393 Hon Rl; NHS; Sch Pl; Stg Crw; Yrbk; Drama Clb; Sec Ger Clb; Scholastic Achvmnt Awd; Bliss Coll; Court Reporter.

KELLER, LISA; Buckeye South HS; Rayland, OH; 23/120 Hst Soph Cls; Band; Debate Tm; Hon Rl; Lbry Ade; PAVAS; Y-Teens; Drama Clb; Pep Clb; Spn Clb; Tech Coll; Nursing.

KELLER, LOIS; Shakamak HS; Coalmont, IN; 6/98 Band; Chrh Wkr; Chmn Drl Tm; Hon Rl; NHS; Quill & Scroll; Ed Yrbk; Pep Clb; I S U;.

KELLER, MARY; Jennings County HS; Commiskey, IN; 82/358 Band; 4-H; Pep Clb; Cit Awd; Dnfth Awd; 4-H Awd;.

KELLER, NANCY; Millersport HS; Millersport, OH; Chrs; Hon Rl; Off Ade; Sch Pl; FHA; Key Clb; Pep Clb; Spn Clb; Chrldng; IM Sprt; Business Schl; Sec.

KELLER, NOLA; T L Handy HS; Bay City, MI; 3/369 Cmnty Wkr; Hon Rl; Treas NHS; Pol Wkr; Ger Clb; Suomi College; Law Enforcement.

KELLER, PAMELA; Clay Sr HS; Oregon, OH; Girl Scts; Hon Rl; Drama Clb; Fr Clb; FTA; Pep Clb; Mat Maids; Scr Kpr; Certf On Continuous Acad Achvmnt; Univ; Law.

KELLER, PAUL; Worthington Jefferson HS; Worthington, IN; Pres Frsh Cls; VP Soph Cls; Pres Jr Cls; Pres Band; Hon Rl; NHS; Stu Cncl; Beta Clb; Ger Clb; Trk; Cand For St Beta Club Pres; College; Medicine.

KELLER, RENEE; Memphi HS; Memphis, MI; Girl Scts; Hon Rl; Off Ade; 4-H; Letter Bsbl; Letter Bsktbl; PPFtbl; 4-H Awd; Bus Schl; Sec.

KELLER, RONDA; South Spencer HS; Rockport, IN; Band; Girl Scts; Hon Rl; Sch Pl; Sct Actv; Drama Clb; 4-H; DAR Awd; Bus.

KELLER, SANDRA; Andrews Acad; Stevensville, MI; 7/97 Cls Rep Frsh Cls; Cls Rep Soph Cls; Cl Rep Jr Cls; Sec Sr Cls; Band; Chrs; Chrh Wkr; Andrews Univ; Bus.

KELLER, STACY; Edon HS; Edon, OH; 4/70 Band; Chrh Wkr; Hon Rl; Lbry Ade; NHS; Off Ade; Sch Pl; Sch Nwsp; Spn Clb; Am Leg Awd; Univ Of Cincinnati; Vet.

KELLER, STEPHEN; Chesterton HS; Chesterton, IN; 51/434 Trs Sr Cls; Boy Scts; Chrh Wkr; Cmnty Wkr; Hon Rl; Sct Actv; Capt Swmmng; Scr Kpr; Tmr; MVP Duneland Conf Swimming 78; MVP Swin Team 77 & 78; Mst Imprvd 76 77 & 78; Univ; Comp Sci.

KELLER, SUSAN; West Geauga HS; Chesterland, OH; 11/352 Debate Tm; Hon Rl; Lbry Ade; Kent State Univ; Med Tech.

KELLER, VALERIE; Covington HS; Covington, IN; 16/107 Pres Frsh Cls; Band; Capt Drl Tm; Girl Scts; Hon Rl; Stu Cncl; Pep Clb; Pom Pon;.

KELLEY, ANNETTE; Central HS; Evansville, IN; JA; NHS; Off Ade; OEA; Ind State Univ.

KELLEY, AUDREY; Barnesville HS; Barneville, OH; Chrs; Hon Rl; Sch Mus; Sch Pl; Rptr Sch Nwsp; Drama Clb; 4-H; FHA; FTA; GAA; Ohio St Univ.

KELLEY, BARBARA; Galion Sr HS; Galion, OH; Sch Pl; Pres Drama Clb; Pres OEA; North Central Tech Coll.

KELLEY, BETH; Prairie Hts HS; Hudson, IN; 54/137 Drl Tm; Off Ade; Rptr Yrbk; FTA; Mat Maids; Pom Pon; Bus Schl; Receptionist.

KELLEY, CHRISTINE; South Harrison HS; Clarksburg, WV; Band; Hon Rl; Jr NHS; NHS; Pres Stu Cncl; Yth Flsp; Yrbk; 4-H; FBLA; FHA;.

KELLEY, CONNIE; Tyler County HS; Middlebourne, WV; 11/101 Sec Soph Cls; Hst Sr Cls; Am Leg Aux Girls St; Hon Rl; JA; Lbry Ade; NHS; Sch Pl; Drama Clb; FBLA; Most Outstanding Cheerleader 1977; Student Of The Week; Dist Amer HS Stud; Belmont Tech Coll; Exec Sec.

KELLEY, D; Adena HS; Clarksburg, OH; Chrs; Yth Flsp; Y-Teens; Yrbk; 4-H; FHA; Mgrs; 4-H Awd; Delicatessen Employee.

KELLEY, DARLA S; Elk Garden HS; Elk Garden, WV; VP Soph Cls; VP Jr Cls; Pres Stu Cncl; 4-H; FBLA; Bsktbl; Chrldng; Vocational Schl; Nursing.

KELLEY, DARLENE; Fairfield HS; Highland, OH; Chrs; Drl Tm; Sch Pl; Yrbk; Drama Clb; FHA; Pep Clb; Spn Clb; Capt Pom Pon; Rio Grande Univ.

KELLEY, DEBORAH; Mentor HS; Willoughby, OH; 269/761 Hon Rl; Treas DECA; Rotary Awd; 2nd Pl DECA Competition Team Mgmt; Mentor HS Sr Of Month; Chairman Of Advertising Committee; Lakeland Comm Coll; Busns Admin.

KELLEY, DENA; Wyoming Park HS; Wyoming, MI; Band; Drm Bgl; Hon Rl; Lbry Ade; Ed Yrbk; Rptr Yrbk; Yrbk; Ger Clb; Ten; IM Sprt; Michigan St Univ; Vet.

KELLEY, DIANA; Bloomfield HS; Bloomfield, IN; Chrs; Girl Scts; Hon Rl; JA; Lbry Ade; Pep Clb; Bsbl; Am Leg Awd; JA Awd; Beautician School.

KELLEY, JOSEPH; Cadiz HS; Cadiz, OH; 13/110 Cls Rep Frsh Cls; Cls Rep Soph Cls; VP Jr Cls; Aud/Vis; Hon Rl; NHS; Off Ade; Sch Pl; Stu Cncl; Lat Clb; Univ Of Miami; Bus.

KELLEY, JUDY L; Seton HS; Cincinnati, OH; 8/273 Hon Rl; Jr NHS; NHS; Off Ade; Fr Clb; Univ Of Cincinnati; Analyst.

KELLEY, K; Marshall HS; Marshall, MI; Band; Cmp Fr Grls; Chrh Wkr; Hon Rl; Orch; Univ; Child Psych.

KELLEY, KATHY; Eastern HS; Haslett, MI; Hon Rl; Jr NHS; NHS; Off Ade; Sci Clb; Michigan St Schlrshp; Michigan St Univ; Med.

KELLEY, KEVIN; Port Clinton HS; Pt Clinton, OH; Hon Rl; Stg Crw; Fr Clb; Letter Swmmng; Ten; Univ; Chem Engr.

KELLEY, LE ANNE; Franklin Community HS; Franklin, IN; 44/300 FCA; Hon Rl; JA; NHS; Treas Eng Clb; Sci Clb; Bsktbl; Glf; Ten; PPFtbl; Indiana Univ.

KELLEY, LORI; Willard Sr HS; Willard, OH; 77/175 Chrs; Chrh Wkr; Cmnty Wkr; Girl Scts; Hosp Ade; Sch Mus; Sch Pl; Sct Actv; Yth Flsp; Drama Clb; Sandusky Schl Of LPN; Nursing.

KELLEY, MARY; Heath HS; Heath, OH; Cls Rep Soph Cls; Cl Rep Jr Cls; VP Sr Cls; Cls Rep Sr Cls; Hon Rl; Stu Cncl; Key Clb; Spn Clb; Chrldng; Bus Schl.

KELLEY, MATTHEW; Walled Lake Central HS; Union Lake, MI; Hon Rl; Yth Flsp; Punctual Attdnce Awd 76 77; Michigan Tech Univ; Chem Engr.

KELLEY, MICHAEL; Kyger Creek HS; Gallipolis, OH; Sec Jr Cls; Band; Hon Rl; Sch Pl; Fr Clb; Key Clb; Lat Clb; VICA; Letter Ftbl; Letter Ten; Schlshp Team; Ohio St Univ; Archt.

KELLEY, MICHAEL; Baker HS; Fairborn, OH; Hon Rl; Lit Mag; Sch Nwsp; Boys Clb Am; 4-H; Letter Ftbl; Capt Wrstlng; Univ Of Tennessee; Pre Law.

KELLEY, MICHAEL; Mather HS; Shingleton, MI; 2/122 NHS; Letter Ftbl; Letter Wrstlng; Mic Tech Univ; Math.

KELLEY, MISCHEL; Timken HS; Canton, OH; Band; Hon Rl; NHS; 4-H; IM Sprt; Scr Kpr; Am Leg Awd; College; Rn.

KELLEY, NANCY; Hubbard HS; Hubbard, OH; 18/333 Girl Scts; Hon Rl; Hosp Ade; Lbry Ade; Off Ade; Red Cr Ade; Spn Clb; Trumbull Mem Hosp Schl; Nursing.

KELLEY, PEGGY; Thornapple Kellogg HS; Middleville, MI; Band; Chrs; Hon Rl; NHS; Ten; Grand Rapids Jr College; Interior Ds.

KELLEY, RONALD; Airport HS; Carleton, MI; 3/216 Am Leg Boys St; Hon Rl; 4-H; Fr Clb; Bsbl; Glf; IM Sprt; Mic Tech Univ; Elec Engr.

KELLEY, SCOTT; Cadiz HS; Cadiz, OH; 13/104 Cls Rep Frsh Cls; VP Soph Cls; VP Jr Cls; Aud/Vis; Hon Rl; NHS; Off Ade; Sch Pl; Stu Cncl; Lat Clb; Univ; Bus.

KELLEY, SHANNON; West Lafayette HS; W Lafayette, IN; 1/185 Cls Rep Soph Cls; Am Leg Aux Girls St; FCA; Hon Rl; NHS; Sch Nwsp; Keyettes; Pep Clb; Letter Ten; Univ; Bio Chem Engr.

KELLEY, SHIELA; Clarkston HS; Clarkston, MI; Cls Rep Frsh Cls; Cls Rep Soph Cls; Am Leg Aux Girls St; Band; Girl Scts; Hon Rl; Off Ade; Sct Actv; Stu Cncl; Pep Clb; Michigan St Univ; Psych.

KELLEY, WANDA; Bruceton HS; Bruceton Mills, WV; Cls Rep Frsh Cls; Cls Rep Soph Cls; Cl Rep Jr Cls; Chrs; Hon Rl; Sch Pl; Sec Stu Cncl; Pres FHA; Letter Bsktbl; GAA;.

KELLING, NANCY; Admiral King HS; Lorain, OH; 6/413 Hon Rl; Sec NHS; Kiwan Awd; Ohio Univ; Engineering.

KELLIS, KELLY; Reeths Puffer HS; Muskegon, MI; Chrs; Chrh Wkr; Hon Rl; Yth Flsp; Rptr Sch Nwsp; Sch Nwsp; PPFtbl; Oral Roberts Univ; Law.

KELLISON, PATRICIA L; Pocahontas County HS; Hillsboro, WV; Chrs; Hon Rl; Sch Pl; FHA; Pep Clb; Trk; Chrldng; Bus Schl; Sec.

KELLMAN, MARK; Tuslaw Local HS; Navarre, OH; Am Leg Boys St; Band; Boy Scts; Wrstlng; Univ; Wildlife Mgmt.

KELLNER, SANDY; Griffith HS; Griffith, IN; Hon Rl; Jr NHS; Chrldng; College; Nursing.

KELLOGG, RANDY; Southern Wells HS; Montpelier, IN; Cl Rep Jr Cls; Cls Rep Sr Cls; Hon Rl; NHS; Pres Stu Cncl; Letter Bsbl; Letter Bsktbl; Letter Ftbl; Kiwan Awd; Rotary Awd; Indiana Univ; Bus.

KELLOGG, SHEILA; Au Gres Sims HS; Au Gres, MI; 9/48 Chrh Wkr; Girl Scts; Hon Rl; Lbry Ade; Sch Pl; Rptr Yrbk; Rptr Sch Nwsp; Sch Nwsp; Mgrs; Cntrl Michigan Univ; Lib Art.

KELLOGG, THOMAS; Lakeview HS; Cortland, OH; Hon Rl; Lbry Ade; Stu Cncl; Rptr Yrbk; Fr Clb; Mth Clb; Letter Bsktbl; Letter Glf; Univ; Phys Educ.

KELLY, ADRIANNE; Cardinal HS; Huntsburg, OH; 20/103 Sec Soph Cls; Band; Cmp Fr Grls; Cmnty Wkr; Girl Scts; Sch Pl; Sct Actv; Stg Crw; Rptr Yrbk; 4-H; Kent St Univ; Eng.

KELLY, ANNE; Carroll HS; Xenia, OH; 26/276 Hon Rl; NHS; Spn Clb; IM Sprt; Natl Merit Ltr; Cincinnati Reds Straignt A Prog; Coll; Comp Sci.

KELLY, BARBARA; Cadillac HS; Cadillac, MI; 14/300 Hon Rl; NHS; Off Ade; Yth Flsp; Mi State Univ; International Affairs.

KELLY, BARBARA; East HS; Akron, OH; Band; Sch Mus; Fr Clb; Univ; Elem Ed.

KELLY, BETH A; St Agatha HS; Redford, MI; Sec Soph Cls; Hon Rl; NHS; Sec Stu Cncl; Fr Clb; Bsbl; Letter Bsktbl; Univ; Spec Educ.

KELLY, BEVERLY; Martin Luther King Sr HS; Detroit, MI; 11/201 Chrs; Chrh Wkr; Cmnty Wkr; Hon Rl; Lbry Ade; Off Ade; Rptr Yrbk; Fr Clb; Pom Pon; Cit Awd; Wayne St Univ; Bus Mgmt.

KELLY, BILL; Caseville HS; Caseville, MI; Hon Rl; Jr NHS; NHS; Stu Cncl; Letter Bsktbl; Letter Ftbl; Letter Trk; Scr Kpr; Industrial Arts Awd 79; Univ; Archt.

KELLY, BRENDA; Hardin Northern HS; Dola, OH; VP Jr Cls; Pres Sr Cls; Val; Am Leg Aux Girls St; Hon Rl; NHS; Stu Cncl; Ed Sch Nwsp; OEA; Bsktbl;.

KELLY, CAROL; Fayetteville HS; Fayetteville, WV; Chrs; Hon Rl; Sch Mus; Sch Pl; Stg Crw; Stu Cncl; Rptr Yrbk; Drama Clb; West Virginia Tech; Med Records.

KELLY, CHARLES T; Kenston HS; Chagrin Falls, OH; Boy Scts; Debate Tm; Sch Pl; Yrbk; Sch Nwsp; Fr Clb; Crs Cntry; Glf; Ten; IM Sprt; College; Hotel Mgmt.

KELLY, COLLEEN; Bloomfield Lahser HS; Blmfld Hills, MI; Chrs; Lit Mag; Sch Mus; Sch Pl; Stg Crw; Drama Clb; Sci Clb; Aquinas College.

KELLY, CYNTHIA; Wayne Memorial HS; Wayne, MI; Hon Rl; Jr NHS; NHS; Rptr Sch Nwsp; Fr Clb; Mth Clb; IM Sprt; Scr Kpr; Mic State; Vet Med.

KELLY, D; Sault Area HS; Slt Ste Marie, MI; 12/318 Hon Rl; Hosp Ade; Red Cr Ade; Treas OEA; Trk; IM Sprt; Lake Superior State College; Rn.

KELLY, DANIEL; St Thomas Aquinas HS; Southgate, MI; Hon Rl; Letter Bsktbl; Letter Glf; Eastern Mic Univ; Bus.

KELLY, DAVID; Maple Hts Sr HS; Maple Hgts, OH; Hon Rl; Jr NHS; Ed Sch Nwsp; Rptr Sch Nwsp; Univ.

KELLY, DAVID M; Chesterton HS; Porter, IN; 30/354 Band; Chrs; Debate Tm; Hon Rl; Mdrgl; Natl Forn Lg; NHS; Sch Mus; Sch Pl; Stg Crw; Natl Eagle Scout Assn; Drum Major Indi 500 All St Band Fest Of St Marching Bands Of Amer; CHS Sr Drama Awd; Purdue Univ; Engr.

KELLY, DENIS; Cardinal Ritter HS; Indianapolis, IN; Hon Rl; Crs Cntry; Ten; IM Sprt; College; Zoology.

KELLY, DONNA; Barberton HS; Barberton, OH; 46/520 Sch Nwsp; Treas OEA; GAA; Acctg 1st Pl In Reg Comp 1979; Acctg 9th Pl In State Comp 1979; AMS Bus Stdt Of The Year 1979; Univ Of Akron; CPA.

KELLY, JAMES; St Joseph Prep Seminary; Vienna, WV; 1/9 Chrs; Chrh Wkr; Cmnty Wkr; Jr NHS; NHS; Sch Pl; Stu Cncl; Ed Yrbk; Sch Nwsp; Scr Kpr; Natl Math Prof Awd; Natl Educ Devlpmnt Awd; Wheeling Coll; Philosophy.

KELLY, JANA; Riverside HS; De Graff, OH; Trs Soph Cls; Band; Chrs; Hon Rl; Lbry Ade; Treas Stu Cncl; 4-H; Pep Clb; Rdo Clb; Pres Spn Clb; Ohio Northern Univ; Pharm.

KELLY, JENNIFER; Hilliard HS; Columbus, OH; Chrs; FCA; Hon Rl; Sch Pl; Rptr Yrbk; Rptr Sch Nwsp; Drama Clb; Fr Clb; Bsktbl; Gym; Ohio St Univ; Retail Mdse.

KELLY, JOHN; Jackson Parkside; Jackson, MI; Band; Boy Scts; Debate Tm; Hon Rl; Sch Mus; Stu Cncl; Letter Glf; Jackson Comm College.

KELLY, JOHN; Princeton HS; Princeton, WV; Natl Merit Ltr; Coll; Comp Sci.

KELLY, KAREN; Traverse City St Francis HS; Trav City, MI; 15/106 NHS; Pep Clb; Trk; N W Michigan Coll; Lib Arts.

KELLY, KATHY; Miami Trace HS; Washington Ch, OH; 93/266 AFS; Band; Orch; FHA; FTA; Tmr; Amer Assn Of Univ Of Women Schlrshp; St Board Awd Of Distinction; Ohio Univ; Early Elem Ed.

KELLY, KATHY; John Glenn HS; Cambridge, OH; 1/200 Sec Frsh Cls; Sec Soph Cls; Sec Jr Cls; Sec Sr Cls; Band; Chrs; NHS; Off Ade; Sch Mus; Lat Clb; Ohio State Univ; Med Tech.

KELLY, KIM; Fremont Ross HS; Fremont, OH; Band; Cmp Fr Grls; Drl Tm; Hon Rl; Natl Forn Lg; Sch Pl; Stg Crw; Stu Cncl; Key Clb; Pep Clb; College; Acctg.

KELLY, LAURA; Fairview HS; Fairview Pk, OH; 101/262 Letter Band; Girl Scts; Hon Rl; Off Ade; Yth Flsp; Sci Clb; Spn Clb; Letter Trk; IM Sprt; Coll; Nursing.

KELLY, LISA; Dominican HS; Detroit, MI; Cmnty Wkr; Hosp Ade; Off Ade; Sch Pl; Stg Crw; 4-H; FBLA; FNA; Trk; Natl Merit Ltr; Michigan St Univ; Exec Sec.

KELLY, LISA; Cuyahoga Falls HS; Cuyahoga Fls, OH; Chrs; Chrh Wkr; Hon Rl; NHS; Stg Crw; Pep Clb; Chrldng; Akron Univ; Busns Mgmt.

KELLY, M; Our Lady Of Mercy HS; Southfield, MI; Cls Rep Frsh Cls; Cl Rep Jr Cls; Chrh Wkr; Hon Rl; NHS; Sch Pl; Stg Crw; Sci Clb; Spn Clb; Univ Of Mich; Med.

KELLY, MARK; Frontier HS; Chalmers, IN; Hon Rl; 4-H; FFA; Letter Bsbl; IM Sprt; Letter Mgrs; Farmer.

KELLY, MAUREEN; Cardinal Mooney HS; Youngstown, OH; 40/295 Am Leg Aux Girls St; Capt Debate Tm; Natl Forn Lg; NHS; Pol Wkr; Eng Clb; Lat Clb; Letter Swmmng; Letter Ten; Am Leg Awd; St Marys Coll; Pre Law.

KELLY, MAUREEN; Bishop Luers HS; Ft Wayne, IN; Chrs; Hon Rl; Stg Crw; Rptr Sch Nwsp; Fr Clb; GAA; IM Sprt; College; Math.

KELLY, MICHAEL; Franklin Heights HS; Grove City, OH; 2/300 Chrs; Hon Rl; Hosp Ade; JA; Red Cr Ade; Ten; Cit Awd; Columbus Tech Inst; Med Lab Tech.

KELLY, MIKE; W E Groves HS; Southfield, MI; Boy Scts; JA; Sct Actv; Sci Clb; College.

KELLY, PATRICIA; New Richmond HS; New Richmond, OH; Cls Rep Frsh Cls; Cls Rep Sr Cls; Sec NHS; VP Quill & Scroll; Stu Cncl; Rptr Yrbk; Rptr Sch Nwsp; Fr Clb; N Kentucky Univ.

KELLY, PATRICK; Coldwater HS; Coldwater, MI; 5/290 Hon Rl; Jr NHS; NHS; Key Clb; Bsbl; Ftbl; IM Sprt; DAR Awd; Kiwan Awd; Central Mich Univ; Bus Admin.

KELLY, PAULA; Saint Alphonsus HS; Dearborn, MI; 42/171 Chrs; Hon Rl; Sch Mus; Pep Clb; Bsbl; Bsktbl; GAA; PPFtbl; College; Phys Ther.

KELLY, PENNY; Houghton Lake HS; Houghton Lk, MI; Chrs; Hon Rl; NHS; FHA; Pep Clb; Central.

KELLY, ROBERT V; Lumen Christi HS; Jackson, MI; Cls Rep Frsh Cls; Boy Scts; Hon Rl; NHS; Sct Actv; Rptr Sch Nwsp; Sch Nwsp; Trk; Wrstlng; St Of Mi Cmptve Progr Semi Final 78; Univ Of Michigan; Bus.

KELLY, ROBIN; Lake Central HS; Schererville, IN; Cls Rep Frsh Cls; Cls Rep Soph Cls; Band; Chrs; Hon Rl; Sch Mus; Sch Pl; Drama Clb; OEA; Capt Pom Pon; Homecoming Queen; Ball State Univ; Communications.

KELLY, SAMUEL; Central Preston HS; Albright, WV; Band; Hon Rl; Sch Pl; Stu Cncl; 4-H; Mth Clb; VICA; Bsktbl; Wrstlng; 4-H Awd; Preston Cnty Ed Entr; Pwr Mech.

KELLY, SANDRA; Clinton Massie HS; Blanchester, OH; Hon Rl; NHS; Chrldng; PPFtbl; College; Park Management.

KELLY, SHAWN; Holly Sr HS; Holly, MI; Swmmng; US Air Force Acd; Aeronautical Engr.

KELLY, SUSAN; St Marys Cathedral HS; Gaylord, MI; Band; Drm Bgl; Hon Rl; Drama Clb; Letter Bsktbl; Letter Trk; Pom Pon; Ferris St Coll; Legal Investigator.

KELLY, SUZANNE; Fairmont West HS; Dayton, OH; 29/470 Cls Rep Frsh Cls; Boy Scts; Girl Scts; Hon Rl; Sct Actv; Stg Crw; Fr Clb; Mth Clb; Tmr; Univ; Engr.

KELLY, TAMMY; Maumee HS; Maumee, OH; Hon Rl; Lbry Ade; Off Ade; Bowling Green St Univ; Art.

KELLY, TERRI; St Peter & Paul Area HS; Saginaw, MI; Cl Rep Jr Cls; Cls Rep Sr Cls; Hon Rl; NHS; Stu Cncl; Civ Clb; Fr Clb; Univ; Med.

KELLY, WARREN; Henry Ford HS; Detroit, MI; 82/529 Chrh Wkr; Cmnty Wkr; Debate Tm; Sch Mus; Drama Clb; FDA; Mth Clb; Sci Clb; Kalamazoo Coll; Elec Engr.

KELM, JEANIE; Salem HS; Campbellsburg, IN; 20/168 Girl Scts; Indiana Univ; Nursing.

KELMAN, ADINA; Shaker Heights HS; Shaker Hts, OH; Chrh Wkr; Hon Rl; Rptr Sch Nwsp; Univ; History.

KELMAN, JACKIE; St Stephen Area HS; Saginaw, MI; Cls Rep Frsh Cls; Girl Scts; Hon Rl; Off Ade; Rptr Yrbk; Rptr Sch Nwsp; Fr Clb; Pep Clb; Letter Bsbl; Letter Bsktbl; Northern Mich Univ; Elem Educ.

KELNER, ANDREW; Merrillville HS; Merrillville, IN; Hon Rl; NHS; Univ.

KELP, ANDREW; Brown County HS; Nashville, IN; 9/200 Hon Rl; Sch Nwsp; 4-H; Coach Actv; 4-H Awd; College; Comp Tech.

KELP, BETSY; Brown County HS; Nashville, IN; 11/200 Band; Drl Tm; Treas FCA; NHS; Rptr Yrbk; Pres Pep Clb; Letter Bsktbl; Letter Ten; Pom Pon; Mas Awd; French Hon Soc 78; Univ; Sci.

KELSER, JANETTE; Loudonville HS; Loudonville, OH; Sec Frsh Cls; Cls Rep Soph Cls; Chrs; Jr NHS; Off Ade; Sch Pl; Stu Cncl; Pep Clb; Schlstc Achievement 76; Coll; Health.

KELSEY, CHRISTOPHER; Pike HS; Indpls, IN; Band; Boy Scts; Rptr Sch Nwsp; Univ; Indus Engr.

KELSEY, DARRELL; Western Boone Jr Sr HS; Lebanon, IN; Band; FCA; Hon Rl; Boys Clb Am; 4-H; Capt Ftbl; Letter Wrstlng; 4-H Awd; Univ; Mech Engr.

KELSEY, DOUG; Maumee HS; Maumee, OH; Letter Wrstlng; College; Advrtsng.

KELSEY, KEVIN; Arthur Hill HS; Saginaw, MI; Boy Scts; Hon Rl; NHS; Sct Actv; Elk Awd; Univ; Marine Bio.

KELSEY, RANDY; Whitko HS; South Whitley, IN; 1/150 Pres Sr Cls; Val; NHS; Rptr Sch Nwsp; Pres

4-H; Pres FFA; Ftbl; Wrstlng; Dnfth Awd; DAR Awd; Purdue Univ; Agri Engr.

KELSO, CRYSTAL; Ravenna HS; Ravenna, OH; 28/320 NHS; Civ Clb; Spn Clb; Ohio St Univ; Engr.

KELSO, JANE; Marietta Sr HS; Marietta, OH; 23/440 Cls Rep Soph Cls; AFS; Chrh Wkr; NHS; Yth Flsp; Spn Clb; Ohio Wesleyan Univ.

KEMBLE, JULIE; Mc Auley HS; Cincinnati, OH; Girl Scts; Hon Rl; JA; Lit Mag; Mod UN; Quill & Scroll; Sch Mus; Sch Pl; Ed Sch Nwsp; Drama Clb; Ohio State Univ; Jrnlsm.

KEMBLE, KATHERINE; Newaygo HS; Newaygo, MI; 3/94 NHS; 4-H; Letter Bsktbl; Letter Trk; Albion Coll; Pre Med.

KEMERLING, LYDIA; Walnut Ridge HS; Columbus, OH; Chrs; Hon Rl; Lbry Ade; NHS; Boys Clb Am; Spn Clb; Univ; Eng.

KEMME, MARIANNE; High School; Cinti, OH; Hon Rl; Bsbl; Ten; GAA; IM Sprt; Good Samaritan Schl Of Nursing.

KEMMER, SANDY; Ridgedale HS; Marion, OH; Hon Rl; Stu Cncl; Sec Spn Clb; Gym; IM Sprt; College; Psychology.

KEMMERER, PAM; Hedgesville HS; Hedgesville, WV; Chrs; Chrh Wkr; Hon Rl; Sch Mus; Sch Pl; Drama Clb; Frederick Comm; Orthodontic Asst.

KEMMERLIN, LAURA R; Watervliet HS; Watervliet, MI; 13/90 Chrs; NHS; FFA; Scr Kpr; Natl Merit Ltr; Mi State Univ; Retailing.

KEMNITZ, RUTH; John Marshall HS; Indpls, IN; 30/611 Hon Rl; Ger Clb; Trk; Ball State Univ; Architecture.

KEMP, BEVERLY; North Daviess HS; Odon, IN; Chrs; Cmnty Wkr; Hon Rl; Sch Pl; Yth Flsp; Rptr Sch Nwsp; Vocational School.

KEMP, DAVE; Culver Military Academy; Lk Oswego, OR; 43/206 Pres Jr Cls; Pres Sr Cls; Boy Scts; Chrs; Chrh Wkr; Cmnty Wkr; Drl Tm; FCA; ROTC; Sct Actv; Cert Ldrshp Instructor Mdl 79; Outstndg Proficiency Ribbon 79; The Slvr A For Academics 78; Stanford Univ; Archt.

KEMP, KIMBERLY; Washington HS; Massillon, OH; Am Leg Aux Girls St; Hon Rl; Hosp Ade; NHS; Stg Crw; Yrbk; Drama Clb; Sci Clb; Sec Spn Clb; IM Sprt; Top Teen Volunteer At Massillon Comm Hosp; Massillon Comm Hosp; Nursing.

KEMP, KIMBERLY K; Bainesville HS; Barnesville, OH; Band; Hon Rl; Hosp Ade; Sch Mus; 4-H; FHA; FTA; GAA; Mgrs; 4-H Awd; Belmont Tech Schl; Med Asst.

KEMP, LOREE; Elmhurst HS; Fort Wayne, IN; 28/346 Mat Maids; PPFtbl; Indiana Puedue; Accounting.

KEMP, PAUL; Unionvle Sebewaing Area HS; Sebewaing, MI; FFA; Bsktbl; College; Landscaping.

KEMP, RHONDA; Black River HS; Homerville, OH; 31/98 Am Leg Aux Girls St; Band; Off Ade; Rptr Yrbk; VP 4-H; Treas Fr Clb; FHA; Pres Sci Clb; Letter Gym; Scr Kpr; Tech Schl; Nursing.

KEMP, SCOTT; Concordia Lutheran HS; Ft Wayne, IN; 63/200 Chrh Wkr; Cmnty Wkr; Hockey; IM Sprt; PPFtbl; Univ; Bus.

KEMP, SHEILA; Loogootee Community HS; Loogootee, IN; 39/150 VP Soph Cls; VP Jr Cls; Band; Hon Rl; Stu Cncl; Sprt Ed Yrbk; Rptr Yrbk; Pep Clb; Purdue Univ; Comp Sci.

KEMP, TAMMY; West Washington HS; Campbellsburg, IN; Hon Rl; Sch Mus; Sch Pl; Yth Flsp; Yrbk; Drama Clb; FFA; Pep Clb; Spn Clb; Bsktbl; Indiana Univ; Hist.

KEMPER, KAREN; St Francis De Sales HS; Columbus, OH; Rptr Yrbk; Drama Clb; Fr Clb; Gym; Mat Maids; Tmr; Bliss Bus Coll; Court Steno.

KEMPER, RICKENA; Millersport HS; Thornville, OH; VP Jr Cls; Hon Rl; Hosp Ade; Lbry Ade; NHS; Sch Pl; Stg Crw; Rptr Yrbk; Yrbk; Rptr Sch Nwsp; Eng Schlrshp Team 77 78 & 79; Ohio Univ; Eng.

KEMPF, GERRI; Jasper HS; Jasper, IN; 5/290 Am Leg Aux Girls St; Hon Rl; Beta Clb; Pres 4-H; Pep Clb; Purdue Univ; Horticulture.

KEMPPAIENEN, PATRICK; Baraga HS; Pelkie, MI; Boy Scts; Hon Rl; 4-H; Letter Ftbl; Mich Tech Univ; Bus Admin.

KENCIK, DAVID; Troy HS; Troy, MI; 43/310 Aud/Vis; Chrs; Chrh Wkr; Hon Rl; Lbry Ade; Sch Mus; Mth Clb; Sci Clb; Act Cert Of Outsdng Perf 79; Michigan Tech Univ; Comp Sci.

KENDALL, JODI; Cannelton HS; Cannelton, IN; 2/35 Band; Drl Tm; Girl Scts; Hon Rl; NHS; Sch Pl; Rptr Yrbk; Drama Clb; Pep Clb; Letter Trk; Volleyball Letter; College.

KENDALL, KELLY; Marshall HS; Marshall, MI; 54/270 Cmnty Wkr; Hon Rl; NHS; VP Fr Clb; IM Sprt; Btty Crckr Awd; Western Mic Univ; Speech Pathology.

KENDALL, POLLY N; Fairborn Baker HS; Dayton, OH; Band; Chrs; Chrh Wkr; Drl Tm; Hon Rl; Lbry Ade; Off Ade; Sch Mus; Sch Pl; Stg Crw; Wright State Univ; Musical Theatre.

KENDALL, RICHARD; Spencer HS; Spencer, WV; Band; Drm Mjrt; Hon Rl; Jr NHS; NHS; Sch Pl; Stu Cncl; Ed Sch Nwsp; 4-H; 4-H Awd; Thespian Of Troupe 279; West Virginia Univ; Music.

KENDALL, RICK; Rushville Consolidated HS; Knightstown, IN; 6/292 Aud/Vis; Hon Rl; Jr NHS; NHS; Stu Cncl; Elk Awd; Ind State Univ; Chemistry.

KENDLE, TINA; Penn HS; Mishawaka, IN; Band; Girl Scts; Hon Rl; Off Ade; 4-H; 4-H Awd; College; Management.

KENDRA, ANN; St Augustine Acad; Lakewood, OH; Hon Rl; NHS; IM Sprt; Univ Of Dayton; Public Relations.

KENDRICK, ANN; Lake Michigan Cath HS; Benton Hrbr, MI; Hon Rl; Sci Clb; Letter Trk; Coll.

KENDRICK, MARY; Central Catholic HS; Lafayette, IN; 3/100 Cls Rep Frsh Cls; Cls Rep Soph Cls; Cl Rep Jr Cls; Cls Rep Sr Cls; Trs Frsh Cls; Hon Rl; JA; Jr NHS; NHS; Sch Mus; Xavier Univ; Intl Bus.

KENDRICK, TERESA; Albion Sr HS; Albion, MI; 5/200 Cls Rep Soph Cls; Pres Sr Cls; Cmp Fr Grls; Hon Rl; Jr NHS; Natl Forn Lg; NHS; Sch Mus; Sch Pl; Stu Cncl; 1st Place In Dist Forensics Trnmnt; 2nd Place Reg Forensics Trnmnt; 1st Place Natl Spanish Exam; Univ Of Michigan; Medicine.

KENDRICK, WILLIAM; Lake Michigan Cath HS; Bntn Hrbr, MI; 18/102 Boy Scts; Hon Rl; Sct Actv; Rptr Yrbk; Letter Trk; IM Sprt; Indiana Inst Of Tech; Comp Engr.

KENDRICKS, CAMILLE JO; Andrean HS; Gary, IN; Band; Chrh Wkr; Cmnty Wkr; Hon Rl; Hosp Ade; Sch Mus; Sec Drama Clb; Pep Clb; Pom Pon; Ball St Univ; Mass Cmnctns.

KENDZIOR, MICHAEL; Franklin HS; Livonia, MI; Am Leg Boys St; Chrs; Hon Rl; Pol Wkr; UFM.

KENERSON, JOHN E; Eastlake North HS; Willowick, OH; 11/670 Hon Rl; NHS; Letter Ftbl; Letter Trk; Natl Merit Ltr; College; Industrial Admin.

KENNARD, SCOTT A; Plymouth HS; Willard, OH; Band; Boy Scts; Hon Rl; Crs Cntry; Ten; Trk; College; Communications.

KENNE, DEBORAH; Alpena HS; Alpena, MI; 19/744 Cl Rep Jr Cls; Sec Sr Cls; Drl Tm; Hon Rl; Stu Cncl; Rptr Sch Nwsp; Sch Nwsp; Chrldng; Pom Pon; PPFtbl; Michigan St Univ; Soc Work.

KENNEALLY, BECKY; South Range HS; North Lima, OH; 10/180 Cl Rep Jr Cls; Chrh Wkr; Girl Scts; Hon Rl; NHS; Off Ade; Sch Mus; Sch Pl; Y-Teens; Drama Clb; Youngstown State Univ; History.

KENNEALLY, RICHARD W; Turpin HS; Cincinnati, OH; 1/357 Band; Stg Crw; Univ.

KENNEBECK, JOHN; Whitehall Sr HS; Whitehall, MI; Hon Rl; Ger Clb; Letter Bsbl; Letter Glf; Mgrs; JA Awd; Michigan St Univ; Dentistry.

KENNEDY, ANN; Breckenridge Jr Sr HS; Breckenridge, MI; 2/102 Trs Frsh Cls; Trs Soph Cls; Pres Jr Cls; Band; Chrh Wkr; Girl Scts; Hon Rl; NHS; Stu Cncl; 4-H; College; Computer Sci.

KENNEDY, BILLIE; Madison Plains HS; Mt Sterling, OH; Cl Rep Jr Cls; Am Leg Aux Girls St; Band; Sec Chrs; NHS; Sch Pl; Treas Yth Flsp; Ohi State Univ; Bus Admin.

KENNEDY, BILLIE JO; Madison Plains HS; Mt Sterling, OH; Cl Rep Jr Cls; Band; Sec Chrs; Hon Rl; Mod UN; Sch Mus; Treas Yth Flsp; Pres 4-H; Spn Clb; 4-H Awd; College; Acctg.

KENNEDY, BRIAN; Grosse Pointe North HS; Grosse Pte Wds, MI; 40/550 Chrh Wkr; Cmnty Wkr; FCA; Hosp Ade; Lbry Ade; NHS; Rptr Yrbk; Ger Clb; Letter Crs Cntry; Letter Trk; Univ Of Mich; Pre Med.

KENNEDY, CAROL; Dondero HS; Royal Oak, MI; 14/400 Hon Rl; NHS; Yrbk; 4-H; Fr Clb; Gym; Natl Merit SF; Oakland Univ; Bio.

KENNEDY, CATHY R; Iaeger HS; Powell, TN; Hon Rl; Sch Pl; Stu Cncl; FHA; Mth Clb; Pep Clb; Univ Of Tennessee.

KENNEDY, CHERYL; Wheelersburg HS; Wheelersburg, OH; 2/165 Sal; Band; Chrs; Girl Scts; Hon Rl; NHS; Orch; Sch Mus; Sch Pl; Lat Clb; 5th In Div II; Ohio Univ Dist 1T Jr Algebra; Natl Cert Of Merit On NEDT; Ohio St Univ; Biology.

KENNEDY, CHRISTOPHER; St Joseph Central HS; Huntington, WV; Boy Scts; Chrs; Hon Rl; Sch Mus; Sct Actv; Bsktbl; Capt Glf; Scr Kpr; Eagle Boy Scout Hnr 78; World Conservtn Awd 78; Marshall Univ; Med.

KENNEDY, DAN; Whitko HS; Columbia City, IN; Chrs; Natl Forn Lg; FFA; FTA; Wrstlng; Purdue Univ; Auto Mech.

KENNEDY, DENNIS; Belding Central HS; Belding, MI; Hon Rl; Letter Bsbl; Letter Ftbl; IM Sprt; Montcalm Cmnty Coll; Law Enforcement.

KENNEDY, DIANE; Tuslaw HS; Massillon, OH; 7/168 Drl Tm; Hon Rl; NHS; Sch Mus; Y-Teens; Pep Clb; Spn Clb; Bsktbl; Chrldng; Career School; Airline Stewardess.

KENNEDY, JAMES A; Talawanda HS; Oxford, OH ; 15/320 Am Leg Boys St; Chrs; Chrh Wkr; NHS; Pol Wkr; Yth Flsp; Rptr Sch Nwsp; Drama Clb; Letter Bsbl; Stanford; Science.

KENNEDY, JELANE; Greenville HS; Greenville, MI; Hon Rl; Lbry Ade; Yth Flsp; Pep Clb; Pres Spn Clb; Letter Trk; Mgrs; Alma College; Chem.

KENNEDY, JO LYNNE; Caro Community HS; Caro, MI; Trs Frsh Cls; Band; Drl Tm; FCA; Hon Rl; NHS; Off Ade; Yth Flsp; Bsbl; Achvmnt Awd For Piano 78; Hon Awd For Piano 79; Solo & Ensemble & Dist Band Medals 76 77 & 78; Ferris St Coll; Pharm.

KENNEDY, JOYCE; Herbert Hoover Sr HS; Clendenin, WV; Chrs; Chrh Wkr; Hon Rl; Jr NHS; Rptr Sch Nwsp; FHA; Letter Bsktbl; Letter Trk; IM Sprt; Voc Schl; LPN.

KENNEDY, JULIE; Arthur Hill HS; Saginaw, MI; Band; Girl Scts; Hon Rl; Hosp Ade; Sct Actv; Sci Clb; Delta State College; Radiology Tech.

KENNEDY, KAREN; Hubbard HS; Hubbard, OH; 48/350 Sec Frsh Cls; Sec Soph Cls; Sec Jr Cls; Sec Sr Cls; Band; Hon Rl; Jr NHS; Lit Mag; NHS; Orch; Youngstown St Univ; X Ray Tech.

KENNEDY, KENNY; Cloverdale Community Schools; Cloverdale, IN; 25/86 Chrs; Chrh Wkr; Debate Tm; Red Cr Ade; Sch Mus; Sch Pl; Yth Flsp; Yrbk; Drama Clb; Letter Bsbl; Tchr.

KENNEDY, KIRK; Harbor Springs HS; Hrbr Spgs, MI; Boy Scts; Hon Rl; Sch Pl; VP Stu Cncl; Yrbk; Drama Clb; Pep Clb; Rdo Clb; Spn Clb; Northern Mic College; Engr.

KENNEDY, LAURA; La Porte HS; La Porte, IN; 9/500 Cmp Fr Grls; Chrs; Chrh Wkr; Cmnty Wkr; Hon Rl; Mdrgl; MMM; NHS; Sch Mus; Sch Pl; Indiana Univ Honors In French 79; Univ.

KENNEDY, LEO; Breckenridge HS; Breckenridge, MI; 100/118 FFA; Capt Crs Cntry; Capt Ftbl; Trk; Wrstlng; Mgrs; Alma Coll; Bus Mgmt.

KENNEDY, MARK; Northwest HS; Lucasville, OH; Aud/Vis; Chrs; Chrh Wkr; Hon Rl; Quill & Scroll; Sch Pl; Yth Flsp; Rptr Yrbk; Rptr Sch Nwsp; 4-H; Shawnee St Univ; Optometrist.

KENNEDY, MARTHA J; Ironton HS; Ironton, OH; Band; Spn Clb; Ohio State Univ; Elem Educ.

KENNEDY, MATTHEW; Culver Military Academy; De Motte, IN; Cl Rep Jr Cls; Boy Scts; Drl Tm; FCA; Hon Rl; Lbry Ade; ROTC; Sct Actv; Ger Clb; Swmmng; Eagle Scout Awd With 3 Palms 75; Gunston Medal 79; Edward Taylor Tilley Mem Sabre 79; Univ; Sci.

KENNEDY, MAUREEN; Hoover HS; North Canton, OH; 128/422 Chrs; Chrh Wkr; Cmnty Wkr; Girl Scts; Hon Rl; Hosp Ade; Lbry Ade; Sct Actv; Pep Clb; Spn Clb; Yng Citizens Awd 78; 1st Class Girl Scout 77; Marion Awd Natl Cthlc Scouting Medal 75; Univ; Occptnl Ther.

KENNEDY, MAUREEN; Bishop Watterson HS; Worthington, OH; 13/250 Chrs; Chrh Wkr; Cmnty Wkr; Hon Rl; Hosp Ade; NHS; Sch Mus; Yrbk; Treas Lat Clb; Mth Clb; Miami Univ; Pre Med.

KENNEDY, MIKE; Indian Valley North HS; New Phila, OH; Cls Rep Frsh Cls; Trs Soph Cls; Am Leg Boys St; Hon Rl; Stu Cncl; Ger Clb; Sci Clb; Bsktbl; Letter Glf; Letter Trk; College; Physics.

KENNEDY, MIKE; Guernsey Noble Voc HS; Cambridge, OH; Pres Sr Cls; Boy Scts; Hon Rl; Sct Actv; DECA; FFA; Ftbl; Trk; Dnfth Awd; Muskingun Area Tech Coll; Law.

KENNEDY, PATRICIA; Bay HS; Bay Village, OH; Chrs; Pres Girl Scts; Hon Rl; NHS; Sch Mus; Sch Pl; Rptr Yrbk; Rptr Sch Nwsp; VP Drama Clb; Rdo Clb; Intl Thespian Soc; Girl Scout 1st Class Awd; High Schl Choraleers; Coll.

KENNEDY, PATTY; Austintown Fitch HS; Youngstown, OH; Chrs; Chrh Wkr; Yth Flsp; Y-Teens; Gym; Liberty Baptist Bible Coll; Missions.

KENNEDY, REBECCA; Walled Lake Western HS; Union Lake, MI; Girl Scts; Hon Rl; Fr Clb; Eastern Michigan Univ; Intl Lang.

KENNEDY, SHARI; Johnstown Monroe HS; Johnstown, OH; Hon Rl; NHS; Sch Pl; Pres 4-H; VP FHA; Mgrs; Ohi State Univ; Vet Med.

KENNEDY, SHAWN; West Geauga HS; Chesterland, OH; FCA; Hon Rl; Letter Ftbl; Letter Wrstlng; IM Sprt; Univ; Engr.

KENNEDY, STEPHEN; Culver Military Academy; Maumee, OH; 49/198 Cls Rep Frsh Cls; Cls Rep Soph Cls; Chrs; Debate Tm; Drl Tm; Hon Rl; Lbry Ade; ROTC; Sch Mus; Sch Pl; Plebe New Cadet Of Yr At CMA 78; Meritorious Serv Awd 77; Virginia Military Inst; Pre Law.

KENNEDY, STEVE; Princeton HS; Cincinnati, OH; 73/651 Band; NHS; Fr Clb; Kent State Univ; Acctg.

KENNEDY, THOMAS; Washington Irving HS; Clarksburg, WV; VP Frsh Cls; Hon Rl; Stu Cncl; Yth Flsp; Fr Clb; Key Clb; Univ; Engr.

KENNEDY, THOMAS; Padua Franciscan HS; Berea, OH; Hon Rl; Ftbl; Coach Actv; IM Sprt; College; Comp Sci.

KENNEDY, TIM; Griffith HS; Griffith, IN; 26/281 Hon Rl; Jr NHS; Letter Wrstlng; Most Improved Wreslter; Univ; Sci.

KENNEDY, TRACEY; Madeira HS; Cincinnati, OH; 42/170 Chrh Wkr; Girl Scts; Lit Mag; PAVAS; Sch Pl; Ed Sch Nwsp; Rptr Sch Nwsp; Drama Clb; Lat Clb; Spn Clb; Miami Univ; Law.

KENNELL, CAROLE; Maplewood HS; Cortland, OH; 4/86 Cls Rep Sr Cls; Hon Rl; NHS; Stu Cncl; Yrbk; Sec Beta Clb; Sec Drama Clb; Bsktbl; Scr Kpr; Trumbull Sch Of Nursing; Nurse.

KENNEY, BRAD; John Glenn HS; Cambridge, OH; 10/184 Pres Aud/Vis; Chrs; Hon Rl; Lbry Ade; Sec NHS; Yrbk; Sch Nwsp; Sec Fr Clb; Crs Cntry; Georgia Tech Univ; Indstrl Engr.

KENNEY, C; Regina HS; Mayfield Hts, OH; Cls Rep Frsh Cls; Cls Rep Soph Cls; Cl Rep Jr Cls; Cls Rep Sr Cls; Chrh Wkr; Hon Rl; Jr NHS; Stu Cncl; Yrbk; GAA; Univ; Marketing.

KENNEY, JAYNE; Hampshire HS; Levels, WV; 58/220 Trs Frsh Cls; Cls Rep Soph Cls; Trs Jr Cls; AFS; Band; Chrs; Drm Mjrt; Hon Rl; Sch Pl; Stu Cncl; Activity Ltr 78; Shenandoah Conserv Of Music; Music.

KENNEY, RICHARD; Highland HS; Marengo, OH; VP Jr Cls; Am Leg Boys St; VP Aud/Vis; Pres FFA; Ftbl; Am Leg Awd; Univ.

KENNY, JOHN; Rensselaer Central HS; Rsnsselaer, IN; 2/170 Sal; Band; Hon Rl; NHS; Rptr Sch Nwsp; Letter Bsbl; Letter Bsktbl; Coach Actv; Indiana Univ.

KENNY, KELLY; Henry Ford II HS; Sterling Hts, MI; 31/463 Hon Rl; NHS; Capt Bsbl; Capt Bsktbl; Coach Actv; Mgrs; Oakland Univ; Elem Ed.

KENSINGER, RANDY; Oregon Davis HS; Hamlet, IN; Sec Soph Cls; Hon Rl; 4-H; Pep Clb; Letter Bsbl; Letter Bsktbl; Letter Trk; Univ.

KENT, ANDRE; Cass Technical HS; Detroit, MI; Band; Cmnty Wkr; Debate Tm; PAVAS; Pol Wkr; Stu Cncl; FBLA; Bsktbl; Ten; IM Sprt; Wayne St Univ; Pre Med.

KENT, CURTIS; Edgewood HS; Bloomington, IN; 1/223 Hon Rl; Spn Clb; Indiana Univ.

KENT, DANI; R B Chamberlin HS; Twinsburg, OH; Chrs; Hon Rl; Univ; Med.

KENT, JAMES R; West Muskingum HS; Zanesville, OH; 1/180 Val; VP Band; Chrs; Chrh Wkr; NHS; VP Key Clb; Natl Merit SF; Ohio St Summer Piano Wrkshp 1978; Intrnl Thespian Soc 1978; Principals List 1975; Oberlin Consrv Music; Organ.

KENT, KARI; William Henry Harrison HS; Evansville, IN; 21/466 Cls Rep Frsh Cls; Cls Rep Soph Cls; Cl Rep Jr Cls; Chrh Wkr; Hon Rl; NHS; Stu Cncl; Yth Flsp; Rptr Sch Nwsp; Letter Glf; City Tite Lin Girls HS Golf 78; Univ.

KENT, LUCINDA; Galion HS; Galion, OH; Sec Soph Cls; Sec Jr Cls; AFS; Band; Sec Chrs; Chrh Wkr; Hon Rl; Jr NHS; NHS; Yth Flsp; Bowling Green St Univ; Home Ec.

KENT, STEVEN; Perry HS; Perry, MI; 13/170 Hon Rl; NHS; Treas Stu Cncl; Rptr Sch Nwsp; Spn Clb; Letter Bsbl; Letter Ftbl; Tmr; Acad Letter For 3 Consecutive Terms; 2nd Team All Conf In Bsbl; Hnr Mention On Lansing All Area Bsbl Team; Univ Of Michigan; Engr.

KENT, SUSAN; Walled Lake Western HS; Wixom, MI; Chrh Wkr; Hon Rl; Sch Mus; Sch Pl; Rptr Sch Nwsp; Sch Nwsp; Cit Awd; Bob Jones Univ; Acctng.

KENT, TERESA; Morrice HS; Bancroft, MI; 1/58 Val; Band; Girl Scts; Hon Rl; NHS; 4-H; 4-H Awd; Natl Merit Schl; Band Awd To Blue Lk Fine Arts Camp 76; Susan F Winegar Schlrshp 79; Drum Major Of Marching Orioles 75 77; Western Michigan Univ; Soc Work.

KENWORTHY, KELLY; Randolph Southern Jr Sr HS; Lynn, IN; 3/85 VP Soph Cls; Chrs; Girl Scts; Hon Rl; Jr NHS; NHS; Sch Mus; 4-H; FBLA; Pep Clb; Bus Clb; Acctg.

KENWORTHY, KEVIN; Eaton HS; Eaton, OH; 1/186 Cl Rep Jr Cls; Cls Rep Sr Cls; Band; Boy Scts; Hon Rl; Jr NHS; NHS; Stu Cncl; Univ Of Akron; Pre Med.

KENYON, BRAD; La Porte HS; Laporte, IN; Sch Pl; Stg Crw; U S Coast Guard; Gnrl Arts.

KENYON, JANE; Harper Creek HS; Ceresco, MI; 6/250 Cls Rep Frsh Cls; Cls Rep Soph Cls; Cl Rep Jr Cls; Cmnty Wkr; Hon Rl; NHS; Fr Clb; Capt Ten; Trk; PPFtbl; Albion Coll; Education.

KENYON, T; Corunna HS; Corunna, MI; 23/210 Sec Sr Cls; Hon Rl; Crs Cntry; Letter Trk; Chrldng; Coll.

KEOWN, BLAKE; Lexington HS; Lexington, OH; 31/250 Band; Hon Rl; Ohio Inst Of Tech; Electronics.

KEPLAR, KIM; Hamilton Twp HS; Lockbourne, OH; 12/214 Cls Rep Frsh Cls; Cls Rep Soph Cls; Band; Hon Rl; NHS; Chrldng; Voc Schl; Jrnlsm.

KEPNER, JONATHAN; Badger HS; Hartford, OH; Cl Rep Jr Cls; Am Leg Boys St; Off Ade; Yrbk; Beta Clb; 4-H; FFA; Pep Clb; Bsktbl; Capt Crs Cntry; Ohio St Univ.

KEPPLER, ROBERT; Strasburg Franklin HS; Strasburg, OH; Band; Boy Scts; Chrs; Sch Mus; Letter Trk; God Cntry Awd; Work; Desil Mech.

KEPREOS, JEFF; Martins Ferry HS; Martins Ferry, OH; VP Frsh Cls; Hon Rl; Letter Bsktbl; Letter Ftbl; Elk Awd; Univ.

KEPSHIRE, PATTIE; Merrillville Sr HS; Merrillville, IN; 135/618 Cls Rep Soph Cls; Cl Rep Jr Cls; Cls Rep Sr Cls; Sch Pl; Stg Crw; Stu Cncl; Drama Clb; Pep Clb; GAA; Pom Pon; Optician.

KERANEN, D; Calumet Public HS; Calumet, MI; Hon Rl; Hosp Ade; NHS; FNA; Voice Dem Awd; Northern Mic Univ; Nutrition.

KERBLESKI, GERARD; T L Handy HS; Bay City, MI; 35/322 Band; Cmnty Wkr; Hon Rl; NHS; Pol Wkr; Pres Stu Cncl; H Mackey Mem Schlrshp; St Of Mi Comp Schlrshp; Cert Of Hnr For Outstndg Achvmnt In Stu Govnmnt; Michigan St Univ; Sci.

KERBY, DEB; Barberton HS; Barberton, OH; 129/499 AFS; Letter Band; Girl Scts; Hon Rl; Lbry Ade; Sch Mus; Sec FHA; OEA; Spn Clb; Cit Awd; Akron Univ; Busns.

KERCE, DENISE; Wayne Mem HS; Westland, MI; Am Leg Aux Girls St; Chrs; Chrh Wkr; Hon Rl; NHS; Off Ade; Red Cr Ade; Sch Mus; Stg Crw; Ger Clb; Eastern Univ; Nursing.

KERCH, LORRAINE; Columbia City Joint HS; Columbia City, IN; Trs Jr Cls; Trs Sr Cls; Hon Rl; Sec NHS; VP Yth Flsp; VP 4-H; Sec FHA; Ger Clb; Trk; Pom Pon; Univ; Elem Tchr.

KERCHER, JANET; Goshen HS; Goshen, IN; 15/221 Band; Hon Rl; NHS; 4-H; Fr Clb; Sci Clb; Purdue Univ; Bio Sci.

KERCHER, JEFF; Goshen HS; Goshen, IN; 65/268 Hon Rl; Letter Ten; Coll; Art.

KERCHER, MICHELE; Mater Dei HS; Evansville, IN; 1/185 Val; Cmnty Wkr; Hon Rl; NHS; Sci Clb; Rotary Awd; VFW Awd; Voice Dem Awd; Purdue Univ; Chem Research.

KEREKES, RODNEY A; Bishop Donahue HS; Moundsville, WV; 13/52 Cls Rep Soph Cls; Cl Rep Jr Cls; Cls Rep Sr Cls; Boy Scts; Hon Rl; NHS; Pres Stu Cncl; 4-H; Key Clb; Spn Clb; Natl High Schl Awrd Excellnc 1977; Natl Honor Soc Nov Stdnt Of The Month 1978; All OVAC 1st Team Ftbl Sqd; Culinary Inst Of Amer; Chef.

KEREKES JR, RODNEY; Bishop Donahue HS; Moundsville, WV; 11/54 Cls Rep Soph Cls; Cl Rep Jr Cls; Cls Rep Sr Cls; Boy Scts; Hon Rl; NHS; Pres Stu Cncl; 4-H; Key Clb; Spn Clb; Culinary Inst; Culinary Arts.

KEREKGYARTO, SUSAN; Cardinal Stritch HS; Toledo, OH; 14/212 Chrs; Chrh Wkr; Hon Rl; Hosp Ade; NHS; Pres Sdlty; Fr Clb; Spn Clb; VFW Awd; Med Explorers Post 471; Young Life Of Toledo; CYO; Univ Of Toledo; Med.

KERG, SUE; Lehman HS; Sidney, OH; 9/87 Sec Soph Cls; Sec Jr Cls; Band; Hon Rl; Rptr Yrbk; Pep Clb; Spn Clb; Letter Trk; Chrldng; GAA; Kent St Univ; Spec Ed.

KERKER, ED; Northrop HS; Ft Wayne, IN; Elec.

KERKHOVE, KELLY; Attica Jr Sr HS; Attica, IN; 1/76 Cls Rep Frsh Cls; Cls Rep Soph Cls; Cl Rep Jr Cls; Band; Hon Rl; NHS; VP Stu Cncl; Pep Clb; Letter Bsktbl; Chrldng; Univ.

KERLEY _III, CHARLES B; Elder HS; Cincinnati, OH; 27/382 Chrs; Hon Rl; Ger Clb; Mth Clb; Letter Crs Cntry; Chrldng; IM Sprt; SAR Awd; Xavier Univ; Bus Acctg.

KERLIN, CHRIS; Rensselaer Central HS; Rensselaer, IN; Hon Rl; Letter Crs Cntry; Letter Swmmng; Purdue Univ; Landscape Archt.

KERN, BETH; Delta HS; Delta, OH; Band; 4-H; Voc Schl; Keypunch Operator.

KERN, CAMERON; Albion Sr HS; Albion, MI; Band; Boy Scts; Hon Rl; Natl Forn Lg; Pol Wkr; Sct Actv; Stg Crw; Yth Flsp; Yrbk; Sch Nwsp; College; Poli Sci.

KERN, CHRISTOPHER; Cardinal Ritter HS; Indianapolis, IN; 30/164 VP Jr Cls; Band; Boy Scts; Hon Rl; NHS; Sch Mus; Ftbl; Trk; Wrstlng; College.

KERN, GREGORY; Port Huron HS; Port Huron, MI; 23/200 Cl Rep Jr Cls; Cls Rep Sr Cls; Hon Rl; NHS; Red Cr Ade; Stu Cncl; Sprt Ed Sch Nwsp; Pres DECA; Capt Bsbl; Capt Ftbl; Saginaw Valley Univ; Bus Mgmt.

KERN, JEANNE; Muskegon Catholic Cntrl HS; Muskegon Hts, MI; 6/175 Band; Hon Rl; NHS; Pep Clb; Spn Clb; Trk; IM Sprt; Muskegon Community Coll.

KERN, JOHN G; Frankfort Sr HS; Frankfort, IN; 1/250 Band; Boy Scts; Chrh Wkr; Cmnty Wkr; Pres NHS; Pres Orch; Sch Mus; Sct Actv; Yth Flsp; Fr Clb; Purdue Univ; Engr.

KERN, KIMBERLY; Mitchell HS; Mitchell, IN; 7/143 Chrs; Drl Tm; FCA; Hon Rl; Sec NHS; Stu Cncl; Fr Clb; Pep Clb; Chrldng; Pom Pon; Indiana St Univ; Physical Education.

KERN, PAM; Vincennes Lincoln HS; Vincennes, IN; 42/289 Cls Rep Frsh Cls; Chrs; FCA; Hon Rl; Stu Cncl; Yth Flsp; DECA; Pep Clb; Sci Clb; Chrldng; Univ; Comp Sci.

KERN, STEVE; Lucas HS; Mansfield, OH; 1/65 Am Leg Boys St; Chrh Wkr; Hon Rl; NHS; Rptr Yrbk; Rptr Sch Nwsp; Bsktbl; Trk; IM Sprt; College.

KERNAN, BRIAN; Archbishop Alter HS; Centerville, OH; 40/335 Cls Rep Sr Cls; Chrs; Cmnty Wkr; Hon Rl; NHS; Sec Ger Clb; Key Clb; Bsbl; IM Sprt; Univ Of Dayton; Dentistry.

KERNER, DAVID; Solon HS; Solon, OH; 34/288 Band; Hon Rl; Orch; Mth Clb; IM Sprt; Bowling Green Univ; Acctg.

KERNER, JAMES; Reitz Memorial HS; Evansville, IN; 60/231 Boy Scts; Chrh Wkr; Cmnty Wkr; Hon Rl; Sct Actv; Stg Crw; Boys Clb Am; Wrstlng; IM Sprt; Univ Of Evansville; Bus.

KERNER, LOIS; Kalida HS; Kalida, OH; Hon Rl; Rptr Sch Nwsp; Treas FHA; GAA; Mgrs; Scr Kpr; OSU; Radiology.

KERNER, MELISSA; Lakeview HS; Cortland, OH; Hon Rl; NHS; Beta Clb; Lat Clb; Mth Clb; Bsktbl; Coach Actv; College; Comp Sci.

KERNER, PATRICIA; Medina Sr HS; Medina, OH; 82/381 AFS; Band; Chrh Wkr; VP Yth Flsp; Pres 4-H; Ger Clb; Pep Clb; Sec Sci Clb; Crs Cntry; Trk; Law.

KERNICKY, JANE L; North Farmington HS; Farmington Hls, MI; Cls Rep Frsh Cls; Sec Soph Cls; Pres Jr Cls; Am Leg Aux Girls St; Band; Cmnty Wkr; Hon Rl; Jr NHS; Natl Forn Lg; NHS; Eng Jrnlsm Orch French Offic Bsktbl & Stdnt Souncl Awds 77; Forencs 2 1st Pl 1 2nd Pl 2 3rd Imprmto Spkng; Kalamazoo Coll; Political.

KERNS, BECKY; Springs Vly Comm HS; French Lick, IN; 9/97 Cls Rep Soph Cls; Band; Hon Rl; Stu Cncl; 4-H; FHA; Pep Clb; Spn Clb; Twrlr; 4-H Awd; Soc Dstngshd Amer HS Stu; 753 Twirling Awds; Miss Orange County; College; Fashion Design.

KERNS, GARY; Lincoln HS; Clarksburg, WV; 23/158 Pres Jr Cls; Trs Sr Cls; Am Leg Boys St; NHS; VP Stu Cncl; Yrbk; Letter Ftbl; Glenville St Coll; Surveying.

KERNS, HUGH; North Putnam Jr Sr HS; Roachdale, IN; 42/152 Aud/Vis; FCA; Hon Rl; Lbry Ade; Stg Crw; Drama Clb; VICA; Mgrs; Indiana St Univ; Audio.

KERNS, MARK; Sebring Mc Kinley HS; Sebring, OH; 11/97 Hon Rl; Off Ade; Letter Bsbl; IM Sprt; Gulf Coast Comm Coll; Business.

KERNS, PATTY; University HS; Morgantown, WV; 21/166 Band; Chrh Wkr; Hon Rl; Lbry Ade; NHS; Quill & Scroll; Yrbk; Sch Nwsp; FFA; Letter Ten; College; Photography.

KERNS, RODNEY; Sidney HS; Sidney, OH; Aud/Vis; Chrh Wkr; Hon Rl; Sch Pl; Stg Crw; DECA; Mac Donalds Mgr.

KERNS, STEVEN; Versailles HS; Versailles, OH; 5/130 Band; Boy Scts; Chrs; FCA; Hon Rl; Sch Mus; Stg Crw; Drama Clb; Fr Clb; Letter Ftbl; Bd Of Dir Cmnty Youth Ctr 79; Univ.

KERNS, VICKY; Wirt County HS; Elizabeth, WV; Sec Soph Cls; Band; Chrs; Hon Rl; NHS; Sch Pl; FBLA; Chrldng; Marshall Univ; Bus.

KERNS, VICKY A; Indian Lake HS; Huntsville, OH; VP Sr Cls; Chrs; Hon Rl; Fr Clb; OEA; Sci Clb; Gym; 4 Tourch Awd In OEA 79; Outstnndg Stdnt Awd In Sr Cls 79; Oh St Bd Of Educ Awd Of Dstnctn 79;.

KERPER, CAROLE; John Glenn HS; Cambridge, OH; 48/200 Band; Chrs; Cmnty Wkr; Hon Rl; Sch Mus; Sch Pl; Drama Clb; Fr Clb; College; Art.

KERPSACK, HEIDI; Canfield HS; Canfield, OH; 24/268 Chrs; Hon Rl; NHS; Sch Mus; Rptr Sch Nwsp; Chrldng; PPFtbl; Scr Kpr; Univ Of Fla Miami; Business Admin.

KERR, ANN; Aquinas HS; Southgate, MI; Hon Rl; Univ Of Hawaii; Underwater Photo.

KERR, BARBARA; St Johns HS; St Johns, MI; Cmnty Wkr; Girl Scts; Hon Rl; Hosp Ade; FNA; 200 Hr Pin For Work At Hosp 79; Cert Of Hon For Wrk At Clinton Memrl Hosp 78; Lansing Cmnty Coll; RN.

KERR, KERRY; Alma HS; Elwell, MI; Trs Sr Cls; Chrs; Chrh Wkr; Hon Rl; NHS; Sch Mus; Sch Pl; Yth Flsp; 4-H; Spn Clb; Farm Bureau Citizenship Seminar; 4 H Dairy Awd Trip World Dairy Expo; Citizenship Shortcourse Washington Dc; Nazarene Olivet Coll; Psych.

KERRIGAN, MICHAEL J; Badin HS; Hamilton, OH; 43/219 VP Jr Cls; Am Leg Boys St; Hon Rl; NHS; Pres Stu Cncl; Sprt Ed Sch Nwsp; Rptr Sch Nwsp; Sch Nwsp; Ten; University; Communications.

KERSCHENSTEINER, DAWN R; Whitko HS; Claypool, IN; Band; Chrs; Chrh Wkr; FCA; Hon Rl; NHS; Sch Mus; Sch Pl; Drama Clb; OEA; College.

KERSHAW, CAROLYN; Kirtland HS; Kirtland, OH; Cl Rep Jr Cls; VP AFS; Cmp Fr Grls; Chrh Wkr; VP NHS; Sch Pl; Sec Stu Cncl; Letter Hockey; Natl Merit Ltr; College.

KERSHAW, DAVID; West Geauga HS; Novelty, OH; Cls Rep Soph Cls; Chrs; Chrh Wkr; Cmnty Wkr; FCA; Hon Rl; Yth Flsp; College; Pre Med.

KERSHAW, DAWN; Edison HS; Lake Station, IN; Off Ade; Rptr Sch Nwsp; Sch Nwsp; DECA; College; Dental Hygienists.

KERSHNER, TONYA; Elkhart Memorial HS; Elkhart, IN; 11/500 Chrs; Hon Rl; Sec Hosp Ade; Rptr Sch Nwsp; Sch Nwsp; Spn Clb; Kiwan Awd; Lion Awd; Opt Clb Awd; Rotary Awd; Part Awd For Jrnlsm 79; Ctznshp Awd 75; 2 Yr Part Awd Fron Elkhart Genrl Hosp Jr Aux 79; Univ; Sci.

KERSJES, JACK; Rockford Sr HS; Ada, MI; 23/350 Hon Rl; NHS; Michigan St Univ; Acctg.

KERSJES, TIMOTHY C; East Kentwood HS; Kentwood, MI; Chrs; Stu Cncl; JA; Sch Mus; Stg Crw; Coach Actv; IM Sprt; Mgrs; Scr Kpr; Tmr; 3 Yr Perfct Attend In HS 74 79; Bus Schl; Bus.

KERST, KINA; Ontario HS; Mansfield, OH; 7/176 Trs Sr Cls; Cls Rep Sr Cls; AFS; Cmnty Wkr; Hon Rl; Off Ade; Pol Wkr; Stu Cncl; Rptr Sch Nwsp; Spn Clb; Univ; Poli Sci.

KERSTEFF, KAREN; Merrillville HS; Merrillville, IN; 39/611 Hon Rl; Jr NHS; NHS; Stu Cncl; Ten; PPFtbl; St Josephs College; Banking.

KERSTEN, DEBRA; Portage Central HS; Portage, MI; 80/375 Girl Scts; Hon Rl; Sci Clb; Spn Clb; Michigan St Univ; Vet Med.

KERSTEN, LAURA; Ishpeming HS; Ishpeming, MI; Band; Hon Rl; Sec NHS; Sch Mus; Sch Pl; Pres Yth Flsp; Rptr Yrbk; Rptr Sch Nwsp; Treas FHA; PPFtbl; Taylor Univ; Bus Admin.

KERSTETTER, DAVID J; Garden City West Sr HS; Garden City, MI; Band; Boy Scts; Hon Rl; Jr NHS; Off Ade; Sct Actv; Rptr Sch Nwsp; Pep Clb; Crs Cntry; Trk; Art Club 76; Scout Of The Yr 76; Eagle Scout 77; Pres Awd 76; Univ; Comp Progr.

KERSTETTER, NED; Northwestern HS; West Salem, OH; Pres Jr Cls; Aud/Vis; Chrh Wkr; Hon Rl; NHS; Sch Pl; Stu Cncl; Yth Flsp; Drama Clb; VP FTA; Univ; Engr.

KERVIN, KELLY; South Dearborn HS; Cincinnati, OH; Hst Soph Cls; Hst Jr Cls; Cmp Fr Grls; Chrs; Cmnty Wkr; Hon Rl; Lbry Ade; Rptr Sch Nwsp; Trk; Chrldng; Us Army.

KERZICH, TERESA; Cadillac Sr HS; Harrietta, MI; Cls Rep Frsh Cls; Sec Jr Cls; Hon Rl; NHS; Stu Cncl; 4-H; Spn Clb; Chrldng; PPFtbl; Rotary Awd; Michigan St Univ; Law.

KESAR, MICHAEL; Lutheran E HS; Detroit, MI; Chrs; Chrh Wkr; Hon Rl; Mdrgl; NHS; Sch Pl; Yth Flsp; Yrbk; Drama Clb; Ger Clb; Concordia Coll; Music.

KESCHL, LISA; Bishop Gallagher HS; Detroit, MI; 4/332 Girl Scts; Hon Rl; Off Ade; Sch Mus; Am Leg Awd; Cit Awd; College.

KESECKER, LYNETTE; Berkeley Springs HS; Berkeley Spgs, WV; Chrh Wkr; Off Ade; Sch Nwsp; FBLA; FHA;.

KESECKER, SHELLY; Martinsburg Sr HS; Martinsburg, WV; Hon Rl; Jr NHS; NHS; Sch Pl; Stu Cncl; Yth Flsp; Yrbk; Rptr Sch Nwsp; Sch Nwsp; Keyettes; Most Spirited Chrldr Awd 1978; Homecoming Queen Cand 1978; Univ; Social Work.

KESHNER, GLENN; Oak Park HS; Oak Pk, MI; Hon Rl; Lbry Ade; Lit Mag; Off Ade; Rptr Sch Nwsp; Spn Clb; IM Sprt; Univ.

KESKENY, RHONDA; Aquinas HS; Lincoln Park, MI; Cls Rep Soph Cls; Cl Rep Jr Cls; Cls Rep Sr Cls; Cmp Fr Grls; Chrh Wkr; Hon Rl; Sec NHS; Orch; Stu Cncl; Sprt Ed Yrbk; Eastern Michigan Univ; Spec Ed.

KESLER, SCOTT B; Jay County HS; Dunkirk, IN; 1/402 Band; Hon Rl; NHS; Mth Clb; Sci Clb; Crs Cntry; Trk; Bausch & Lomb Awd; JETS Awd; Pres Awd; Purdue Univ; Engr.

KESLING, SCOTT; Springboro HS; Lebanon, OH; Cmnty Wkr; 4-H; IM Sprt; 4-H Awd; Armed Serv Aptitude Battory; Ohio St Univ; Med.

KESMODEL, AMY; Hamilton S E HS; Noblesville, IN; Hon Rl; Lbry Ade; NHS; Off Ade; Yth Flsp; Pep Clb; Beauty Coll; Cosmetology.

KESNER, BRENT; Petersburg HS; Petersburg, WV; 5/94 Am Leg Boys St; Band; NHS; Sch Mus; Sch Pl; Stg Crw; Drama Clb; Bsktbl; Ftbl; Letter Ten; Geo Washington Univ; Political Sci.

KESNER, TERESA; Keyser HS; Keyser, WV; 21/247 Chrs; Chrh Wkr; Hon Rl; NHS; Stu Cncl; FBLA; Pep Clb; Public Speaking 1st Pl Regnl Conv 79; Public Speaking 1st Pl St Conv 79; Public Speaking Natl Conv 79; Sec.

KESSEL, EMILY; Wellsville HS; Wellsville, OH; 3/125 Am Leg Aux Girls St; VP Band; Hon Rl; VP NHS; Treas Y-Teens; Rptr Yrbk; Am Leg Awd; Dnfth Awd; Math Assoc Of Amer Awd 78; Mbr Of Schl Camp Coll Bwl Team 77; Univ.

KESSEL, MELINDA J; Keyser HS; Keyser, WV; 1/180 AFS; Band; Drl Tm; Girl Scts; Hon Rl; Sch Mus; VP Stu Cncl; Yth Flsp; FBLA; Ten; NEDT Certificate 1978; Honorary Senate Page 1977; County Sci Fair Winner 1978; Potomac St Coll; Phys Ther.

KESSIE, JOE; Whitko HS; Columbia City, IN; AFS; Am Leg Boys St; Chrs; Hon Rl; FFA; Bsktbl; IM Sprt; Cit Awd; Purdue Univ; Agri Econ.

KESSLER, BARBARA; Perry HS; Canton, OH; 3/480 Pres Jr Cls; Hon Rl; NHS; Stu Cncl; Sci Clb; Spn Clb; C of C Awd; Univ Of Cincinnati; Metallurgy.

KESSLER, DEBORAH; Tri Valley HS; Nashport, OH; 5/220 Chrh Wkr; Hon Rl; Jr NHS; NHS; FHA; Spn Clb; OUZ; Med.

KESSLER, DEBORAH L; Tri Valley HS; Nashport, OH; Chrh Wkr; Hon Rl; FHA; Spn Clb; Ohio Univ; Med.

KESSLER, ELIZABETH; Mt Vernon Acad; Springfield, OH; 80/125 Chrs; Chrh Wkr; Hon Rl; Sch Mus; Yth Flsp; GAA; IM Sprt; Kettering Med Coll; Nursing.

KESSLER, FREDERICK; Trivalley HS; Dresden, OH; Hon Rl; Spn Clb; Letter Ftbl; Muskingum Area Tech College; Law.

KESSLER, HERBERT C; North Olmsted HS; North Olmsted, OH; Hon Rl; NHS; Eng Clb; Natl Merit SF; John Caroll Univ; Acctg.

KESSLER, JANET; Franklin Cmnty HS; Franklin, IN; Sec AFS; Band; Chrh Wkr; Girl Scts; Hon Rl; NHS; Sch Mus; Sct Actv; Stg Crw; Yth Flsp; Whos Who Inmidwstrn HS Frng Lang 79; Cert De Comp Spnsh Awd 79; Sci Bio 1 Awd 77; Univ.

KESSLER, LAURA; Archbishop Alter HS; Dayton, OH; Chrs; Girl Scts; Hosp Ade; Sec Lbry Ade; Pep Clb; Mt St Joseph On The Ohio; Dietetics.

KESSLER, MARY; Wellston HS; Wellston, OH; 16/97 Trs Jr Cls; Pres Sr Cls; Am Leg Aux Girls St; Band; Girl Scts; Jr NHS; NHS; Stu Cncl; Yrbk; 4-H; Sr Of Month Of March; Busns Schl.

KESSLER, MARY; Whitehall Yearling HS; Whitehall, OH; Am Leg Aux Girls St; Chrh Wkr; Girl Scts; Hon Rl; Sch Pl; Sct Actv; Stg Crw; OEA; Spn Clb; Ten; Univ.

KESSLER, PEGGY; Du Pont HS; Belle, WV; Chrs; Jr NHS; Off Ade; Sch Mus; Rptr Yrbk; Lat Clb; Univ; Interior Dsgn.

KESSLER, PENNY; William V Fisher Cath HS; Lancaster, OH; Sch Pl; Ed Yrbk; Sprt Ed Yrbk; Rptr Yrbk; Bsbl; Chrldng; Sec.

KESSLER, TAMMY; Buckeye North HS; Brilliant, OH; Band; Chrs; Drm Mjrt; Girl Scts; Hon Rl; Pep Clb; Spn Clb; Capt Bsbl; GAA; Twrlr; Ohio State.

KESSLER, TRACY; Greenfield Central HS; Greenfield, IN; 66/300 Girl Scts; Sct Actv; Sec Yth Flsp; 4-H; Ger Clb; Mth Clb; 4-H Awd; Purdue Univ; Science.

KESSLING, LINDA; Mc Auley HS; Cinti, OH; Aud/Vis; Hon Rl; Hosp Ade; JA; Sch Mus; Rptr Yrbk; Spn Clb; GAA; IM Sprt; Miami Univ; Marketing.

KESTELOOT, JO ANN; Grayling HS; Grayling, MI; 13/148 Aud/Vis; Debate Tm; Girl Scts; Hon Rl; L bry Ade; NHS; Sch Pl; Yth Flsp; Rptr Yrbk; Yrbk; Grayling Alumni Assoc Schlrshp 79; St Of Mi Schlrshp; Northern Michigan Univ; Math.

KESTERSON, J; Cambridge HS; Cambridge, OH; Cls Rep Frsh Cls; Cls Rep Soph Cls; Cl Rep Jr Cls; Cls Rep Sr Cls; Chrh Wkr; Cmnty Wkr; Hon Rl; Off Ade; Stu Cncl; Yrbk; Muskingum Coll; Sci.

KESTNER, JEFFREY; West Branch HS; Alliance, OH; 16/260 Band; VP Chrs; Hon Rl; NHS; Sch Mus; Sch Pl; Ed Yrbk; Univ Of Akron.

KETCHAM, SUZANNE; Fairfield Union HS; Lancaster, OH; 2/150 Chrs; Hon Rl; Jr NHS; NHS; Sch Pl; VP Stu Cncl; 4-H; FTA; Keyettes; Pres Pep Clb; Ohio St Univ; Educ.

KETCHAM, SUZANNE; Fairfield Union HS; Rushville, OH; 2/147 Sal; Chrs; Hon Rl; Jr NHS; NHS; Sch Pl; VP Stu Cncl; 4-H; FTA; Pres Pep Clb; Ohio St Univ; Phys Ed.

KETCHEM, MARK; Ishpeming HS; Ishpeming, MI; 39/125 Boy Scts; Hon Rl; Sct Actv; Ftbl; Glf; IM Sprt; Mgrs; Northern Michigan Univ; Med Lab Tech.

KETCHEN, GAVIN; Dayton Christian HS; Centerville, OH; Chrs; Hon Rl; Fr Clb; Letter Bsbl; Letter Bsktbl; Letter Socr; Univ Of Dayton; Med.

KETCHUM, BRENDA; Stanton HS; Hammondsville, OH; Band; Chrs; Hon Rl; NHS; Off Ade; Fr Clb; Pep Clb; IM Sprt; Band Solo St Contst Ratign Superior 79; Kent St Univ; Elem Educ.

KETCIK, GARY; Manistique Area HS; Manistique, MI; Boy Scts; Cmnty Wkr; Hon Rl; Sct Actv; Bsbl; Bsktbl; Ftbl; Trk; Scr Kpr; Elk Awd; Hoopshoot Cont Loc 1st Dist St 3rd 72; Punt Pass & Kick Loc 1st Dist 4th 75; Lake Superior St Coll; Cnstrctn.

KETELHUT, TAMMY; Pioneer HS; Ann Arbor, MI; Drl Tm; Sch Mus; Sch Pl; Stg Crw; Drama Clb; 4-H; Spn Clb; College; Vet.

KETNER, LISA; Anderson HS; Anderson, IN; 6/450 Cls Rep Frsh Cls; VP Jr Cls; Cl Rep Jr Cls; Cls Rep Sr Cls; Chrs; Hon Rl; NHS; VP Stu Cncl; Rptr Sch Nwsp; Sch Nwsp; Rotary Club Sportsmnshp Awd 79; Hugh O Brian Youth Fdn Awd 77; Spanish Hon Soc 78; Indiana Univ; Attorney.

KETTEL, KEITH; Ironton HS; Ironton, OH; 39/190 Band; Boy Scts; Chrh Wkr; Hon Rl; Yth Flsp; Ger Clb; Pep Clb; Pikeville College; Music.

KETTEN, ELIZABETH; Msgr John R Hackett HS; Richland, MI; Cls Rep Sr Cls; Hon Rl; NHS; Stu Cncl; Swmmng; French Hnry Awd 79; Soc Stu Hnr Awd 79; Phys Sci Awd 77; Kalamazoo Coll; Med.

KETTLER, MICHELLE; St Ursula Academy; Toeldo, OH; Fr Clb; Awd For Superior Performnc In NEDT 77; Superior Achvmnt Rating Sci Proj 76; Eastern Michigan Univ; Occuptnl Ther.

KEVORKIAN, ANDREW; Southwestern HS; Detroit, MI; Chrh Wkr; Jr NHS; Univ Of Mic; Biochemist Engineer.

KEVWITCH, ARRON; Rose D Warwich HS; Tekansha, MI; Hon Rl; 4-H; Bsktbl; Crs Cntry; Ftbl; Trk; Voc Tech Schl.

KEY, BARBARA A; Pike Central HS; Petersburg, IN; 1/192 Cl Rep Jr Cls; Cls Rep Sr Cls; Val; Chrh Wkr; Hon Rl; NHS; Sch Mus; Sch Pl; Stg Crw; Stu Cncl; Univ Of Evansville.

KEY, CRAIG; Mansfield Christian HS; Mansfield, OH; Aud/Vis; Band; Chrh Wkr; Sch Mus; Yth Flsp; Rdo Clb; Le Tourneau College; Elec Engin.

KEY, DEBRA; Andrean HS; Gary, IN; 33/251 Chrh Wkr; Hon Rl; Yth Flsp; Yrbk; Lat Clb; Mth Clb; Pep Clb; Univ; Anesthesiologist.

KEY, JEANINE; Martin Luther King Jr Sr HS; Detroit, MI; Chrh Wkr; Cmnty Wkr; Girl Scts; Hon Rl; VP DECA; St Of Mich Let It Be Known Spec Tribute; St Of Mich Cert Of Merit; MDYF Recog Of Comm Serv; Wayne St Univ; Communications.

KEYES, KATRINA; Keyser HS; Piedmont, WV; 30/250 Chrs; Hon Rl; Jr NHS; NHS; Capt ROTC; Sch Pl; Mth Clb; Trk; Capt Chrldng; VFW Awd; Potomac St Coll; Sociology.

KEYES, KRISTEN; John Glenn HS; Bay City, MI; 22/326 Cls Rep Frsh Cls; Cls Rep Soph Cls; Sec Jr Cls; VP Sr Cls; Band; Hon Rl; NHS; Sch Mus; Sch Pl; Stg Crw; Alma Coll; Eng.

KEYES, TANYA; Linden Mc Kinley Sr HS; Columbus, OH; 15/270 Trs Sr Cls; Band; Hon Rl; Jr NHS; NHS; Stu Cncl; Sch Nwsp; DECA; Bsktbl; Ftbl; Awd From Ohio St Univ Of Minority Affairs; Scholastic Ach; Career Recruitment Telecommunications; Ohio St Univ; Journalism.

KEYLOR, HYDE; East Palestine HS; Columbiana, OH; 23/148 Aud/Vis; Hon Rl; Sch Pl; 4-H; Key Clb; VICA; Bsktbl; Ftbl; Letter Ftbl; 4-H Awd; Industrial Arts Awd 79; Customizer Van & Car.

KEYS, BRENDA; Bluefield HS; Bluefld, WV; 29/285 Chrh Wkr; Hon Rl; Jr NHS; Natl Forn Lg; NHS; Sch Mus; Sch Pl; Stg Crw; Stu Cncl; Yth Flsp; Concord Coll Regnl HS Drama & Forensic Fest 79; Laurel Leaves 79; Jr Class Exec Comm 78; Univ; Real Estate.

KEYS, BRETT; Chesterton HS; Chesterton, IN; 27/454 Boy Scts; Hon Rl; NHS; 4-H; Bsbl; Ftbl; Wrstlng; Mgrs; Univ; Engr.

KEYS, KATHLEEN; Big Rapids HS; Big Rapids, MI; 20/175 Band; Chrh Wkr; Hon Rl; Natl Forn Lg; NHS; Sch Mus; 4-H; Fr Clb; Central Mich Univ; Chem.

KEYS, RAMONA; Chesaning HS; Oakley, MI; Band; Chrs; Chrh Wkr; Girl Scts; Hon Rl; NHS; Sch Pl; Yrbk; Drama Clb; 4-H; Grand Rapids Baptist Coll; Elem Educ.

KEYSER, DAVID; Portage Northern HS; Portage, MI; Band; Boy Scts; Chrs; Hon Rl; NHS; Orch; Sch Mus; Pres Sci Clb; Mic Tech U; Mech Engr.

KEYSER, PAMELA; Bremen HS; Bremen, IN; Hst Sr Cls; Sec Chrh Wkr; FCA; Hon Rl; Sch Mus; Sch Pl; Stu Cncl; Drama Clb; Pres Fr Clb; Pep Clb; Purdue Univ; Elem Educ.

KEYSER, STEPHANIE; Belleville HS; Belleville, MI; Sec NHS; Stg Crw; Yrbk; Mgrs; Tmr; Central Michigan Univ; Pre Engr.

KEYSER, TERRY; Bullock Creek HS; Midland, MI; Boy Scts; Chrh Wkr; Hon Rl; Sch Pl; Rptr Yrbk; Sci Clb; Crs Cntry; Trk; Coach Actv; Scr Kpr; Univ; Engr.

KHALIL, SHEREIF; Solon HS; Solon, OH; Aud/Vis; Hon Rl; Fr Clb; Bsktbl; Ftbl; Letter Socr; Trk; College; Med.

KHAN, AMY J; Lakeshore HS; Stevensville, MI; 3/275 Cls Rep Frsh Cls; Trs Soph Cls; Trs Jr Cls; Trs Sr Cls; Cmnty Wkr; Hon Rl; NHS; Off Ade; Sch Mus; Sch Pl; Albion Coll; Optometrist.

KHARBAS, VIJAY; Northrop HS; Ft Wayne, IN; 37/554 Aud/Vis; Boy Scts; Hon Rl; Boys Clb Am; Capt Wrstlng; Perfect Attendance Awd 74 79; Univ; Archt.

KHATRI, SUNITA; Clawson HS; Sterling Hts, MI; AFS; Chrs; Girl Scts; Hon Rl; JA; Sct Actv; Fr Clb; Mth Clb; Univ; Med.

KHAURI, PARISA; Howland HS; Warren, OH; Hon Rl; Akron Univ; Physician.

KHOURNY, ROSE; Our Lady Of Mt Carmel HS; Wyandotte, MI; 6/65 Sec Soph Cls; Sec Jr Cls; Hon

Rl; Jr NHS; Sch Mus; Stu Cncl; Y-Teens; Spn Clb; Letter Bsbl; Letter Bsktbl; Univ Of Michigan; Med.

KHOURY, RUBY; Mt Vernon Acad; Elyria, OH; Chrs; Chrh Wkr; Cmnty Wkr; FCA; Hon Rl; Lbry Ade; NHS; Off Ade; Sch Pl; Yth Flsp; Loma Linda Univ; Math.

KHOURY, RUBY; Mount Vernon Acad; Elyria, OH; Chrs; Chrh Wkr; Cmnty Wkr; Hon Rl; Lbry Ade; NHS; Off Ade; Sch Pl; Sct Actv; Drama Clb; Loma Linda Univ; Math.

KIBBE, DAVID; Manton Consolidated HS; Manton, MI; 2/50 Cl Rep Jr Cls; Pres Sr Cls; Sal; Band; Boy Scts; Chrh Wkr; Hon Rl; Hillsdale College; Poli Econ.

KIBBEY, MARTHA; Brookhaven HS; Columbus, OH; 12/434 Cls Rep Sr Cls; Chrs; Drl Tm; Hon Rl; Lbry Ade; NHS; Stu Cncl; Rus Clb; Chrldng; Rotary Awd; Acad Of Schlrs Diploma With Distinction 79; Girl St Runner Up 78; 500.

KIBBEY, NANETTE; Ludington HS; Ludington, MI; Band; Chrs; Girl Scts; Hon Rl; Hosp Ade; Lbry Ade; Mdrgl; Ftbl; JC Awd; Michigan St Univ; Music.

KIBBEY, WARREN; Ludington HS; Ludington, MI; Boy Scts; Chrh Wkr; Sct Actv; Yth Flsp; DECA; Basic Educ Opprtn Grant 79 80; Natl Direct Stdnt Loan 79 80; Supplement Educ Oppor Grant I 79 80; Ferris St Coll; Mech Drafting.

KIBELLUS, CARLTON; Concordia Lutheran HS; Ft Wayne, IN; Chrh Wkr; Drl Tm; Hon Rl; ROTC; FBLA; College; Sci.

KIBLER, L; Wellston HS; Wellston, OH; Band; Chrs; NHS; Sch Mus; Sch Pl; Stg Crw; Crs Cntry; Glf; Trk; Military Acad; Engr.

KIBLER, RICHARD; East Liverpool HS; E Liverpool, OH; 7/350 Chrs; Debate Tm; Lit Mag; NHS; Sch Mus; Sch Pl; Stg Crw; Yth Flsp; Drama Clb; Key Clb; Ohio St Univ; Theatre.

KICHAK, MICHELLE; Notre Dame HS; Clarksburg, WV; 3/54 Chrh Wkr; Cmnty Wkr; Hon Rl; Hosp Ade; Rptr Yrbk; Drama Clb; Mth Clb; Sci Clb; Bsktbl; Chrldng; West Virginia Univ; Med Tech.

KICK, CHERRI; Loudonville HS; Loudonville, OH; Chrh Wkr; Hon Rl; NHS; Sprt Ed Sch Nwsp; Letter Bsktbl; Letter Trk; Letter Chrldng; College.

KICK, VIRGINIA; Loundonville HS; Loudonville, OH; Band; Chrs; Chrh Wkr; Cmnty Wkr; Hon Rl; Hosp Ade; Jr NHS; NHS; Sch Pl; VP Yth Flsp; Delegate To Nazarene World Yth Cnfrnce; Mt Vernon Nazarene Coll; Religion.

KIDALOSKI, SUSAN; Northwest HS; Canal Fulton, OH; Cls Rep Frsh Cls; Cls Rep Soph Cls; Cl Rep Jr Cls; Am Leg Aux Girls St; Drm Mjrt; Girl Scts; Hon Rl; JA; NHS; Pres PAVAS; Akron Schl; Nursing.

KIDD, CHARLES; Gavit Jr Sr HS; Hammond, IN; 36/218 Boy Scts; Chrh Wkr; FCA; Hon Rl; Jr NHS; Bsktbl; Crs Cntry; Trk; Pres Awd; US Air Force Academy; Aero.

KIDD, JACQUELI; Lutheran HS; Detroit, MI; Chrh Wkr; Hon Rl; Yrbk; Trk; Concordia College; Eng Tchr.

KIDD, JANICE M; Withrow HS; Cincinnati, OH; 14/551 Hon Rl; Pep Clb; Univ Of Cincinnati; Legal Sec.

KIDD, LORI; Howland HS; Warren, OH; 7/476 Chrs; Chrh Wkr; Hon Rl; Sch Mus; Yth Flsp; Letter Glf; Ohio Tests Of Schlstc Achvmnts English Hnrble Mention; Soc Dstngshd Amer HS Stu; Publctn Natl Poetry Press; Youngstown State Univ; Psychology.

KIDD, MARY; Seeger HS; W Lebanon, IN; Hon Rl; Lbry Ade; Drama Clb; FTA; Business School; Secretary.

KIDD, ROBERT; Howland HS; Warren, OH; 1/430 Cls Rep Sr Cls; Am Leg Boys St; Boy Scts; Chrs; Hon Rl; Mdrgl; NHS; Sch Mus; Fr Clb; Letter Glf; Mass Inst Of Tech; Engr.

KIDD, STEPHANIE; Northrop HS; Ft Wayne, IN; Band; Hon Rl; Orch; Sch Mus; Rptr Sch Nwsp; Chrldng; Pom Pon; Indiana Univ; Med.

KIDD, STEVEN; Belmont HS; Dayton, OH; Cls Rep Frsh Cls; Pres Soph Cls; Cl Rep Jr Cls; Cls Rep Sr Cls; Boy Scts; Hon Rl; NHS; Wright State.

KIDDER, CYNTHIA; Bullock Creek HS; Midland, MI; Hon Rl; Jr NHS; Lbry Ade; NHS; Letter Swmmng; Letter IM Sprt; Helper Of Spec Olympics 79; Mbr Of Explorers Clb 79; Univ; Sec.

KIDMAN, D; Lumen Christi HS; Jackson, MI; Hon Rl; Sch Mus; Sch Pl; Y-Teens; Letter Ftbl; IM Sprt; Scr Kpr; Tmr; Natl Merit SF; Univ; Archt.

KIDWELL, DONNA; Berkeley Springs HS; Berkely Spg, WV; 20/125 Cls Rep Frsh Cls; Cls Rep Soph Cls; Chrs; Hon Rl; NHS; Stu Cncl; Drama Clb; Keyettes; Pres Pep Clb; Letter Scr Kpr; W Liberty State Coll; Dental Hygiene.

KIDWELL, MARY; Loogootee Community HS; Loogootee, IN; Am Leg Aux Girls St; Chrh Wkr; Hon Rl; Sch Mus; Sch Pl; Sct Actv; Sprt Ed Yrbk; Drama Clb; Fr Clb; Trk; College; Pre Med.

KIEFER, KAREN; South Knox HS; Vincennes, IN; 14/107 Am Leg Aux Girls St; Hon Rl; Lbry Ade; NHS; Red Cr Ade; Stu Cncl; 4-H; FHA; Treas FNA; Univ Of Evansville; Physical Ther.

KIEFER, KATHY; North Ridgeville HS; N Ridgeville, OH; 10/360 Hon Rl; NHS; Fr Clb; Sec OEA; Lorain Cnty Cmnty Coll; Engr.

KIEFER, TODD; Shelby Sr HS; Shelby, OH; Band; Boy Scts; Chrs; Hon Rl; JA; Sct Actv; Lat Clb; Sci Clb; Univ; Jrnlsm.

KIEFFER, KRISTY; Mohawk HS; Tiffin, OH; Band; Hon Rl; Lit Mag; NHS; Off Ade; Sch Pl; Y-Teens; Rptr Yrbk; Drama Clb; Treas FTA;.

KIEFFNER, DAN; Jasper HS; Jasper, IN; 45/280 Hon Rl; Mgrs; California Poly Tech Univ; Elec Engr.

KIEFT, CHERYL; Grand Haven HS; Grand Haven, MI; 36/385 Girl Scts; NHS; Yth Flsp; Trk; Nazareth College; Nursing.

KIEHL, DEBRA; Covington HS; Covington, OH; Band; Chrs; Chrh Wkr; Hon Rl; Stu Cncl; Ed Yrbk; 4-H; Fr Clb; 4-H Awd; Univ; Nursing.

KIEL, BRIAN; St Johns HS; St Johns, MI; 1/300 Hon Rl; NHS; VICA; Letter Crs Cntry; Trk; IM Sprt; Michigan Tech Univ Bd Of Control Schlrshp; MHEAA Schlrshp; Co Valedictorian Of 79 Class; Michigan Tech Univ; Elec Engr.

KIEL, NICOLE; Dunbar HS; Dunbar, WV; Cmp Fr Grls; Girl Scts; JA; Off Ade; Sch Pl; Sct Actv; Bsktbl; Hockey; Socr; Letter Trk; Marshall Univ; Dentist.

KIEL, SHERYL; Chelsea HS; Chelsea, MI; 5/230 Band; Girl Scts; Hon Rl; NHS; Capt Bsktbl; Univ.

KIELBASA, MARK; George Washington HS; E Chicago, IN; 20/285 Am Leg Boys St; Aud/Vis; Chrh Wkr; Hon Rl; NHS; Fr Clb; Key Clb; Bsktbl; Capt Glf; Mgrs; Wabash Coll; Busns.

KIEN, JOYCE; Lowell HS; Lowell, IN; Schlrshp To E Il Univ Music Camp 79; Univ; Musical Ther.

KIENLE, STEVE C; Grosse Pointe S HS; Grosse Pt Cy, MI; 22/600 Band; Drm Bgl; Hon Rl; NHS; Sch Mus; Yth Flsp; Chmn Lat Clb; Letter Swmmng; Natl Merit SF; Univ; Chem.

KIENTZ, THOMAS; Brownsburg HS; Brownsbrg, IN; 28/293 NHS; Glf; Purdue Univ; Ind Mgmt.

KIERAS, DAVID M; Creston HS; Grand Rapids, MI; 5/460 Pres Frsh Cls; Val; Am Leg Boys St; Treas FCA; Hon Rl; Pres NHS; Stu Cncl; Ftbl; Cit Awd; Natl Merit SF;.

KIERGAN, CHRISTOPHER; Brebeuf Prep; Indianapolis, IN; 12/145 Boy Scts; Cmnty Wkr; Hon Rl; NHS; Sct Actv; Sch Nwsp; Fr Clb; Mth Clb; Crs Cntry; Swmmng; U S Naval Acad; Aeronautical Engr.

KIERNAN, BARBARA; Dondero HS; Royal Oak, MI; Chrs; Chrh Wkr; Hon Rl; NHS; Sch Mus; Sch Pl; Stg Crw; Drama Clb; Fr Clb; Univ; Soc Sci.

KIERONSKI, LIZ; Annapolis HS; Dearborn Hgts, MI; Drl Tm; Hon Rl; Chrldng; Scr Kpr; Tmr; Cit Awd; Central Michigan Univ; CPA.

KIES, CATHY; Anna HS; Anna, OH; 5/69 Band; Chrs; Hon Rl; NHS; Sch Mus; Fr Clb; FTA; Spn Clb; GAA; Volcal Ensmbl 78; 1st In County In French II Schlshp Test 77; County Chrs 78; Univ; Music Educ.

KIESEL, JAMES; Bishop Gallagher HS; Detroit, MI; 124/333 Boy Scts; Hon Rl; Sch Pl; Scr Kpr; Tmr; Pres Awd; Univ Of Mich; Acctg.

KIESLER, THOMAS; Floyd Central HS; New Albany, IN; 30/380 Cl Rep Jr Cls; Cls Rep Sr Cls; Chrs; Hon Rl; Jr NHS; NHS; Fr Clb; Bsktbl; Crs Cntry; Trk; Univ; Engr.

KIESSEL, JEFFREY; St Joseph HS; St Joseph, MI; Cls Rep Frsh Cls; Boy Scts; Chrh Wkr; FCA; JA; NHS; ROTC; Letter Bsbl; Letter Bsktbl; Letter Ftbl; Mich State Univ; Bus Admin.

KIESSLING, ELAINE; Marshall HS; Marshall, MI; 37/258 Band; Chrh Wkr; Hon Rl; JA; Orch; Sch Mus; 4-H; 4-H Awd; Hillsdale Coll; Acctg.

KIFFMEYER, WILLIAM; Elder HS; Cincinnati, OH; 29/400 Boy Scts; Chrh Wkr; Hon Rl; Hosp Ade; Stg Crw; Yrbk; Ger Clb; Coach Actv; College; Medicine.

KIGAR, TREVA; Napoleon HS; Napoleon, OH; Chrh Wkr; Hon Rl; Natl Forn Lg; NHS; Lat Clb; Spn Clb; Tmr; Voice Dem Awd; Quiz Team; Bowling Green St Univ; Bus.

KIGER, DANIEL; Mineral Ridge HS; Mineral Ridge, OH; 13/76 VP Frsh Cls; Cls Rep Frsh Cls; Cls Rep Soph Cls; Cl Rep Jr Cls; Aud/Vis; Chrs; Hon Rl; Yrbk; Sch Nwsp; Beta Clb; Youngstown St Univ; Comp.

KIGER, MATTHEW; Doddridge County HS; Ctr Point, WV; 6/120 Boy Scts; Hon Rl; NHS; Stu Cncl; Yth Flsp; FFA; VP FTA; Pep Clb; Letter Bsbl; Letter Ftbl; Academic Schlrshp To Salem Coll 79; Schlastic Lttr Awd 79; Salem Coll; Bus.

KIGHT, KIM; Western Reserve HS; Wakeman, OH; Hon Rl; Hosp Ade; Jr NHS; NHS; Rptr Yrbk; Rptr Sch Nwsp; Ohio Univ.

KIHM, JEANNIE; Hackett HS; Kalamazoo, MI; Sec Frsh Cls; Trs Frsh Cls; Cls Rep Frsh Cls; VP Soph Cls; NHS; Stu Cncl; Letter Hockey; Ten; Chrldng; Mgrs; Michigan St Univ; Med.

KIHN, TAMYRA; North Posey HS; Poseyville, IN; Hon Rl; Natl Forn Lg; Sch Mus; Sch Pl; Stg Crw; 4-H; Pep Clb; GAA; IM Sprt; College; Design.

KILANO, SUE; Redford Union HS; Redford, MI; Trk; Scr Kpr; Tmr; Cit Awd; Univ Of California; Law.

KILAR, TOM; Hubbard HS; Hubbard, OH; Boy Scts; Cmnty Wkr; Hon Rl; Pol Wkr; Spn Clb; Bsbl; Ftbl; Wrstlng; Kent St Univ; Engr.

KILBOURNE, PAMELA; Wayne Memorial HS; Wayne, MI; Cls Rep Sr Cls; Hon Rl; Orch; Sch Pl; Sct Actv; Stg Crw; Sch Nwsp; Spn Clb; Swmmng; Wrstlng; Hon Soc Awd 77; Eastern Michigan Univ; Bus Mgmt.

KILBOURNE, WILLIAM G; Okemos HS; East Lansing, MI; 6/328 Band; Cmnty Wkr; Orch; Sch Mus; Letter Swmmng; Scr Kpr; Tmr; Natl Merit SF; Univ; Archt.

KILBURN, KRYSTA; Lebanon HS; Franklin, OH; 20/385 Chrh Wkr; Hon Rl; Hosp Ade; Lbry Ade; NHS; Off Ade; Sci Clb; Pres Spn Clb; Univ; Nursing.

KILBURN, LORI A; Anderson HS; Anderson, IN; 50/402 Chrs; Cmnty Wkr; Hon Rl; Sch Mus; Sch Pl; Drama Clb; 4-H; Fr Clb; Chrldng; Cit Awd; Miss Teenage Amer Semi Finalist; Swing Choir Choreographer; Best Actress Awd; Anderson Coll; Nursing.

KILE, CHARLENE; Franklin HS; Upper Tract, WV; Trs Frsh Cls; Cls Rep Frsh Cls; Cls Rep Soph Cls; Cls Rep Sr Cls; Chrs; Chrh Wkr; Cmnty Wkr; Hon Rl; Stu Cncl; Yth Flsp; Whos Who Among Amer HS Cheerleaders 78;.

KILE, SUSAN; Miami Trace HS; Sabina, OH; 41/249 Sec AFS; Treas Band; Chrs; Chrh Wkr; Sch Mus; Pres 4-H; Pres FNA; Sec FSA; Cit Awd; College; Nurse.

KILEY, JENNIFER; Whitehall HS; Whitehall, MI; Cls Rep Frsh Cls; VP Soph Cls; VP Jr Cls; VP Sr Cls; Chrh Wkr; Hon Rl; NHS; Stu Cncl; Gym; Chrldng; Michigan St Univ; Medicine.

KILFIAN, MARY; Marysville HS; Raymond, OH; Band; IM Sprt;.

KILFOYLE, KATHLEEN; Elyria Catholic HS; Elyria, OH; VP Soph Cls; Cl Rep Jr Cls; Am Leg Aux Girls St; Cmp Fr Grls; Chrs; Cmnty Wkr; Girl Scts; Hon Rl; Hosp Ade; Jr NHS; Ohio St Univ; Jrnlsm.

KILGORE, CAROLYN; Wheelersburg HS; Sciotoville, OH; Chrs; Hon Rl; Pep Clb; Spn Clb; Gym; Chrldng; Mas Awd; Ohio St Univ.

KILGORE, SHERRI; Alexandria Monroe HS; Anderson, IN; Band; Girl Scts; Hon Rl; Sch Pl; Spn Clb; Bsbl; Bsktbl; Bsktbl Symbolic Awd 76; Bsktbl Captn 77 78 & 79; Univ.

KILIAN, CAROL; Clay HS; S Bend, IN; Off Ade; 4-H; Pom Pon; 4-H Awd; Voc Schl; Fshn Mdse.

KILIAN, LORI; Southridge HS; Huntngbrg, IN; Sec Jr Cls; VP Sr Cls; Band; Drl Tm; Hon Rl; Pep Clb; Letter Swmmng; Huntingburg Study Club Awd 79; Membr Of Flag Corp Band; Indiana Univ; Dent Asst.

KILIMAS, MARIA; Bishop Gallagher HS; Detroit, MI; 17/328 Hon Rl; College.

KILL, REGINA; Delphos St Johns HS; Delphos, OH; Pres Soph Cls; Chrh Wkr; Hon Rl; Pol Wkr; Stu Cncl; Ed Yrbk; Fr Clb; Pres FTA; Letter Gym; Chrldng; Ohio St Univ; Elem Ed.

KILLIAN, MICHELLE; Alexandria Monroe HS; Alexandria, IN; Chrs; Sec Girl Scts; Hon Rl; NHS; Yth Flsp; Sec 4-H; Pep Clb; Spn Clb; Letter Bsktbl; 4-H Awd; Univ.

KILLINGBECK, BETHAN; Reed City HS; Reed City, MI; 12/160 VP Soph Cls; Cl Rep Jr Cls; Girl Scts; Hon Rl; Jr NHS; NHS; Stg Crw; Stu Cncl; Ed Sch Nwsp; Rptr Sch Nwsp; Ferris St Coll; Fshn Mdse.

KILLINGSWORTH, JULIE; South Haven HS; South Haven, MI; Cmp Fr Grls; Hon Rl; Bus Schl; Sec.

KILLION, SANDY; Bishop Dwenger HS; Ft Wayne, IN; Chrs; Girl Scts; Hon Rl; Red Cr Ade; Sch Pl; Y-Teens; Bsbl; Bsktbl; Trk; Chrldng; Ball St Univ.

KILLMON, DIANE; Indian Hill HS; Cincinnati, OH; Girl Scts; Treas JA; Sct Actv; Spn Clb; Univ; Bus Admin.

KILLOUGH, LISA; Talawanda HS; Oxford, OH; 69/321 Cmp Fr Grls; Hon Rl; 4-H; Fr Clb; College; Law.

KILMER, JEFFREY; Wadsworth Sr HS; Wadsworth, OH; Cls Rep Frsh Cls; Boy Scts; Chrs; Stu Cncl; Spn Clb; Letter Mgrs; Letter Scr Kpr; Univ Of Akron; Poli Sci.

KILPATRICK, MARIBETH; Claymont HS; Uhrichsville, OH; 6/212 Band; Hon Rl; Jr NHS; NHS; 4-H; Pres FTA; Pep Clb; Pom Pon; Univ Of Akron; Respiratory Therapy.

KILPATRICK, SHARON; John F Kennedy HS; Warren, OH; 54/168 Am Leg Aux Girls St; Debate Tm; Girl Scts; Hosp Ade; JA; Lit Mag; Natl Forn Lg; NHS; Off Ade; Quill & Scroll; Irish Way Schlrshp; Runner Up Volunteer Of The Yr; Newspaper Schlrshp; College; Law.

KILPATRICK, SHERRY; Claymont HS; Uhrichsville, OH; 39/206 Am Leg Aux Girls St; Band; Girl Scts; Hon Rl; Jr NHS; Off Ade; Quill & Scroll; Rptr Sch Nwsp; Pres Fr Clb; FTA; Akron Univ; Elem Educ.

KILPS, RHONDA D; Washington HS; Washington, IN; 37/194 Band; Girl Scts; Hon Rl; Hosp Ade; JA; Lbry Ade; Rptr Yrbk; DECA; Fr Clb; Pep Clb; Vincennes Univ; Computer Prog.

KILWAY, KAREN; Tallmadge HS; Tallmadge, OH; Cl Rep Jr Cls; Cls Rep Sr Cls; Am Leg Aux Girls St; Debate Tm; Hon Rl; Natl Forn Lg; Treas NHS; Sch Mus; VP Stu Cncl; Pep Clb; Akron Univ; Law.

KIM, BENEDICT; St Ignatius HS; N Olmsted, OH; 28/300 JA; Mod UN; NHS; FDA; Mth Clb; Cit Awd; College; Pre Med.

KIM, BENEDICT H; St Ignatius HS; N Olmstead, OH; Chrs; JA; Mod UN; NHS; FDA; Mth Clb; IM Sprt; College; Pre Med.

KIM, HYUN C; Fairview HS; Fariview Pk, OH; Letter Wrstlng; Univ; Archt.

KIM, JOE; Bishop Ready HS; Columbus, OH; 3/130 Cls Rep Sr Cls; Boy Scts; Hon Rl; Pol Wkr; Sct Actv; Stu Cncl; Bsbl; College; Copm Sciences.

KIM, PAUL E; Galion HS; Galion, OH; 1/270 Chrs; Chrh Wkr; Hon Rl; Sec NHS; Orch; Yth Flsp; Rptr Yrbk; Capt Crs Cntry; Letter Trk; DAR Awd; College; Medicine.

KIM, STEVE H; Maumee Valley Cntry Day HS; Maumee, OH; Hon Rl; Yrbk; Sprt Ed Sch Nwsp; Rptr Sch Nwsp; Socr; Ten; Natl Merit SF; College; Math.

KIMBALL, BOB; Bay HS; Bay Vill, OH; 20/325 Hon Rl; NHS; Letter Bsbl; Letter Bsktbl; Coach Actv; Miami Univ; Acctg.

KIMBALL, JANET; Cedarville HS; Yellow Spg, OH; 2/55 Cls Rep Frsh Cls; Cl Rep Jr Cls; Sec Sr Cls; Band; Hon Rl; NHS; Stu Cncl; Yrbk; 4-H; FTA; College; Tchr.

KIMBALL, SHERYL; Saranac HS; Saranac, MI; Band; Chrs; Chrh Wkr; Hon Rl; NHS; Sch Mus; Yth Flsp; Spn Clb;.

KIMBALL, WALTER C; Cadiz HS; Cadiz, OH; 7/104 Hon Rl; NHS; Lat Clb; JETS Awd; Amer Literature Awd; Biology Awd; Most Industrious Acctg 1 Stu; College; Physics.

KIMBLE, JANIS; Perry Meridian HS; Indianapolis, IN; 6/513 Hon Rl; NHS; Fr Clb; OEA; Placed 1st In Comp Prog At OEA St Cont; Placed 15th In Comp Prog At OEA Natl Cont; College; Comp Prog.

KIMBLE, KEVIN; Marysville HS; Marysville, OH; 4/250 Am Leg Boys St; Debate Tm; Hon Rl; JA; Natl Forn Lg; NHS; Off Ade; Pol Wkr; Stg Crw; Key Clb; Received 10 Varsity Debate Awds For Reaching Final Rounds At Natl Tourn; Mem Congressman Browns Yth Council; College; Criminal Law.

KIMBLE, TRACY; Fairless HS; Brewster, OH; 12/225 Cls Rep Frsh Cls; Cls Rep Soph Cls; Cl Rep Jr Cls; Cls Rep Sr Cls; Chrs; Chrh Wkr; Girl Scts; Hon Rl; Hosp Ade; Off Ade;.

KIMBROUGH, ROCHELLE; Beechcroft HS; Columbus, OH; Pres Jr Cls; Chrs; Jr NHS; Yth Flsp; OEA; Capt Trk; Chrldng; PPFtbl; Cit Awd; College; Law.

KIMBROUGH, VALERIE; Oak Park HS; Oak Park, MI; 64/340 Chrs; Chrh Wkr; Girl Scts; Hon Rl; Off Ade; Stu Cncl; Yth Flsp; OEA; Wayne St Univ; Mgmt Bus Admin.

KIME, PATRICIA A; Colon HS; Colon, MI; Band; Chrs; Chrh Wkr; Capt Drl Tm; Hon Rl; Sch Mus; Sch Pl; Drama Clb; Fr Clb; Pep Clb; Keybd Piano Solo 76 & 77; Area Compttn 78 & 79; Grand Rapids Bapt Univ; Music.

KIMES, JOY; Columbia City Joint HS; Columbia City, IN; Band; Chrh Wkr; Capt Drl Tm; Girl Scts; Hosp Ade; Sch Mus; Drama Clb; 4-H; Pep Clb; Spn Clb; Ball State Univ; Nurse.

KIMES, MARY L; Cardinal Mooney HS; Youngstown, OH; 6/300 Cls Rep Soph Cls; Cl Rep Jr Cls; Hon Rl; Natl Forn Lg; NHS; Stu Cncl; Lat Clb; College; Nursing.

KIMLER, ALICIA; St Joseph Central HS; Huntington, WV; Am Leg Aux Girls St; Hon Rl; PAVAS; Sec Stu Cncl; Keyettes; Pep Clb; Letter Swmmng; Chrldng; Opt Clb Awd; V Pres Med Exploring; Won Area 6 Public Speaking Contest; Miss Teenage Amer Huntington Finalist; Marshall Univ; Nursing.

KIMM, LORI; Wynford HS; Nevada, OH; 15/106 Band; Chrs; Chrh Wkr; Cmnty Wkr; Girl Scts; Hon Rl; Orch; Stg Crw; Pres Yth Flsp; 4-H; College; Pre Law.

KIMMEL, DAVE; Bishop Watterson HS; Columbus, OH; Cls Rep Frsh Cls; Cls Rep Soph Cls; Cl Rep Jr Cls; Cls Rep Sr Cls; Hon Rl; Stu Cncl; Lat Clb; Sci Clb; Letter Ftbl; Letter Trk; St Finalist Local & Zone Winner Optimist; Intl Oratorical Contest; Coll; Music.

KIMMEL, FRANK; Yale HS; Yale, MI; Chrs; NHS; Stu Cncl; 4-H; Letter Bsbl; Letter Bsktbl; Letter Ftbl; Univ.

KIMMEL, MARY; Cardinal Mooney HS; Boardman, OH; 9/310 Cl Rep Jr Cls; Cls Rep Sr Cls; Hon Rl; Natl Forn Lg; NHS; Stu Cncl; Trk; Capt Chrldng; Univ; Doctor.

KIMMELL, ANDREW; Columbia City Joint HS; Columbia City, IN; 66/279 Boy Scts; Sct Actv; Ger Clb; Ballstate; Comp Progr.

KIMPEL, BETH A; Columbiana HS; Columbiana, OH; 3/100 Trs Frsh Cls; Sec Soph Cls; Band; Cmp Fr Grls; Chrs; Chrh Wkr; Hon Rl; NHS; Youngstown State Univ; Phys Ther.

KIMPSON, APRIL; Martin Luther King HS; Detroit, MI; 20/200 Hon Rl; Spn Clb; Bsbl; Michigan St Univ; RN.

KIMURA, LORI; Euclid Sr HS; Euclid, OH; 97/747 Hon Rl; Off Ade; Univ; Acctg.

KIN, KAREN; Mohawk HS; Mc Cutchenville, OH; Band; Lit Mag; Y-Teens; Sprt Ed Yrbk; Drama Clb; 4-H; FTA; Lat Clb; Chrldng; St Vincients Schl Of Nursing; Nurse.

KIN, NANCY; Mohawk HS; Mc Cutchenville, OH; Band; Chrs; Hon Rl; Sch Mus; Sch Pl; 4-H; FTA; Lat Clb; Chrldng; Cit Awd; Toledo Hosp Schl; Nursing.

KINASZ, JULIE; Bridgeport Spaulding HS; Saginaw, MI; Band; Girl Scts; Hon Rl; Pep Clb; Spn Clb; Letter Bsbl; Letter Bsktbl; GAA; Delta; Nursing.

KINCADE, JILL; Nordonia HS; Northfield, OH; 11/412 Chrs; Cmnty Wkr; Girl Scts; Hon Rl; NHS; Sch Mus; Spn Clb; Hon Mention Dist For Oh Schlstc Achvmnt Tests In Spanish 1 77; Recvd Acad Awds For Spanish 3 79; Univ; Math.

KINCAID, BARBARA; Tipton HS; Tipton, IN; 19/185 Chrs; NHS; Sch Mus; Sch Pl; Rptr Sch Nwsp; Drama Clb; Acad Hnr Awd; Indiana Univ; Comp Sci.

KINCAID, BRIAN; Monsignor John R Hackett HS; Kalamazoo, MI; 11/134 VP Jr Cls; Band; Boy Scts; Hon Rl; NHS; Stu Cncl; Sci Clb; Letter Mgrs; College; Law.

KINCAID, DEAN; Columbia City Joint HS; Columbia City, IN; 46/253 Cl Rep Jr Cls; Cls Rep Sr Cls; Am Leg Boys St; Treas Chrh Wkr; Hon Rl; Treas FTA; Spn Clb; Amer Legion Citznshp Awd 75; Schlrshp Awd 75; Schl Citznshp Awd 75; Grace Coll; Elem Educ.

KINCAID, DONNA; Girard HS; Girard, OH; Hon Rl; NHS; Y-Teens; OEA; Letter Bsktbl; Mgrs; Busns Schl; Acctg.

KINCAID, GREGORY; Oak Hill HS; Kincaid, WV; Chrs; Chrh Wkr; Cmnty Wkr; Hon Rl; Yth Flsp; Fr Clb; WVIT; Chem.

KINCAID, JANET; Midland Trail HS; Ramsey, WV; Chrh Wkr; Cmnty Wkr; Hon Rl; NHS; Off Ade; FBLA; Fayette Plateau Vo Tech; Stenography.

KINCAID, KELLY; Dupont HS; Belle, WV; Band; Chrh Wkr; Rptr Sch Nwsp; Drama Clb; 4-H; Lat Clb; Pep Clb; Mgrs; Mat Maids; Scr Kpr; College.

KINCAID, LINDA; Clio HS; Clio, MI; Band; Chrh Wkr; NHS; Spring Arbor Coll; Psych.

KINCAID, LORI; John F Kennedy HS; Taylor, MI; 13/400 Band; Girl Scts; Hon Rl; Off Ade; Sch Mus; Sch Pl; Sct Actv; Stg Crw; VP Drama Clb; Swmmng; Univ.

KINCAID, QUOSETT Y; Kettering Sr HS; Detroit, MI; Hon Rl; NHS; FTA; Cit Awd; Michigan Univ; Computer Sci.

KINCAID, TERESA; Meadow Bridge HS; Danese, WV; 4/60 Pres Frsh Cls; Trs Soph Cls; Chrs; Chrh Wkr; Hon Rl; NHS; Sch Pl; Wv Univ; Pr Phys Ther.

KINCH, TERESA; Michigan Center HS; Jackson, MI; Band; Hon Rl; Lbry Ade; NHS; Off Ade; Eng Clb; Jackson Bus Univ; Exec Sec.

KINCHELOE, CHERI; Mott HS; Warren, MI; Hon Rl; Off Ade; Quill & Scroll; Gym; Detroit Creative Arts College; Photo.

KINDEL, SHELLY; Canfield HS; Canfield, OH; Band; Drl Tm; Hon Rl; Lbry Ade; PAVAS; Sch Pl; Stg Crw; Lat Clb; Spn Clb; Youngstown St Univ; Nursing.

KINDER, KEVIN; Stonewall Jackson HS; Charleston, WV; Aud/Vis; Chrh Wkr; Jr NHS; Lat Clb; Mth Clb; Sci Clb; Mgrs; Duke Univ; Med.

KINDERVATOR, JOHN; Rossford HS; Perrysburg, OH; 8/135 Cls Rep Frsh Cls; Cl Rep Jr Cls; VP Sr Cls; Cls Rep Sr Cls; Chrs; Hon Rl; Pres NHS; Sch Mus; Sch Pl; Stu Cncl; Adrain Coll; Sci.

KINDIG, TONY; Warsaw Cmnty HS; Warsaw, IN; Band; DECA; Indiana Univ; Acctg.

KINDINGER, MARY; Glenwood HS; New Boston, OH; Trs Frsh Cls; Trs Sr Cls; Band; Hon Rl; NHS; Off Ade; Sch Pl; Yth Flsp; 4-H; Letter VICA; Otterbein Coll; Phys Ed.

KINDINGER, MICHAEL; Crestline HS; Crestline, OH; Am Leg Boys St; Band; Boy Scts; Hon Rl; Sch Mus; Sch Pl; Stg Crw; Yth Flsp; Yrbk; Drama Clb; Univ; Math.

KINDL, LISA; Marshall HS; Marshall, MI; 1/280 Cls Rep Frsh Cls; Chrs; Hon Rl; NHS; Sch Mus; Sch Pl; Stg Crw; Ed Sch Nwsp; Rptr Sch Nwsp; Sch Nwsp; Univ; Law.

KINDLE, CHRIS; Hedgesville HS; Hedgesville, WV; Cls Rep Frsh Cls; Cls Rep Soph Cls; Chrh Wkr; Hon Rl; NHS; Sch Pl; Drama Clb; FBLA; Pep Clb; James Rumsey Vo Tech Schl; Bus Ed.

KINDLE, ROBIN; Upper Scioto Valley HS; Alger, OH; 4/65 VP Frsh Cls; VP Soph Cls; VP Jr Cls; Am Leg Aux Girls St; Hon Rl; NHS; Sch Pl; Sec Beta Clb; Drama Clb; Sci Clb; Vlybl Letterman Co Capt; Schlrshp Test Sr Soc Studies; College; English.

KINDRED, DON; Anderson HS; Anderson, IN; 61/415 Hon Rl; NHS; Ger Clb; Purdue Univ; Elec Engr.

KINDSVATTER, BRIAN; Wintersville HS; Wintersville, OH; 67/282 Cls Rep Soph Cls; Boy Scts; Sct Actv; Spn Clb; Bsbl; Bsktbl; Glf; IM Sprt; Scr Kpr; Bowling Green St Univ; Bio.

KINDT, JOHN; La Ville Jr Sr HS; Lakeville, IN; VP Sr Cls; Am Leg Boys St; VP NHS; VP Stu Cncl; 4-H; Mth Clb; Sci Clb; Spn Clb; Letter Crs Cntry; Letter Trk; Ball St Univ; Acctg.

KINDT, LISA; St Josephs HS; Fremont, OH; 10/87 Sec Band; Chrs; Hon Rl; NHS; Pep Clb; Bowling Green St Univ; Elem Art Tchr.

KINEMOND, TREVA; Minerva HS; Minerva, OH; 11/241 Chrs; Hon Rl; 4-H; FHA; Lat Clb; Pep Clb; 4-H Awd; Lion Awd; Savings Bond Spelling Contest; Busns Schl.

KINES, BECKY A; Philip Barbour HS; Philippi, WV; Band; Hon Rl; Yth Flsp; VP 4-H; Fr Clb; Spn Clb; 4-H Awd; College.

KING, ANDREW; Moeller HS; Reading, OH; Boy Scts; Hon Rl; Lit Mag; NHS; Sch Pl; Stg Crw; Northern Kentucky Univ; Bio Sci.

KING, ATMORE J; Rogers HS; Toledo, OH; Cls Rep Soph Cls; Chrs; JA; Sct Actv; Stu Cncl; Boys Clb Am; Bsktbl; Trk; Scr Kpr; Tmr; College; Law.

KING, BABETTE; Otsego HS; Plainwell, MI; 6/222 Cls Rep Frsh Cls; Cls Rep Soph Cls; Cl Rep Jr Cls; Cls Rep Sr Cls; Band; Hon Rl; Orch; Sch Mus; Sch Nwsp; Pres Awd; Albion Coll; Med Tech.

KING, BARBARA J; Linden Mc Kinley HS; Columbus, OH; VP Frsh Cls; Girl Scts; Hon Rl; Lbry Ade; NHS; Off Ade; Stu Cncl; Rptr Yrbk; Drama Clb; Legal Sec.

KING, BEVERLY; Princeton HS; Princeton, WV; 79/345 Chrs; Hon Rl; Sch Mus; FHA;.

KING, BEVERLY; Williamstown HS; Williamstown, WV; 41/120 Chrs; JA; Y-Teens; Drama Clb; Pep Clb; W Virginia Univ; Law.

KING, BRIAN; Vicksburg HS; Kalamazoo, MI; 64/246 Boy Scts; Cmnty Wkr; Hon Rl; Hosp Ade; NHS; Sct Actv; Ftbl; JA Awd; Western Mic; Elect Engr.

KING, BRIAN; Whitmer HS; Toledo, OH; 37/810 Band; Chrs; Chrh Wkr; Drm Bgl; Hon Rl; NHS; Sch Mus; Stg Crw; Spn Clb; Socr; Univ Of Toledo; Pahrmacy.

KING, CAROL; Redford Union HS; Redford, MI; Band; Chrs; Hon Rl; Pep Clb; Cit Awd; College; Acctg.

KING, CASSANDRA; Aurora HS; Mansfield, OH; Sec Band; NHS; Mth Clb; Gym; Trk; PPFtbl; Ohio St Univ; Med.

KING, CHARLOTTE; Wadsworth Sr HS; Wadsworth, OH; Band; Chrs; Girl Scts; Natl Forn Lg; Drama Clb; Fr Clb; OEA; Med.

KING, CHERYL; Broad Ripple HS; Indianapolis, IN; Cls Rep Frsh Cls; Cls Rep Soph Cls; Cl Rep Jr Cls; Am Leg Aux Girls St; Hon Rl; Hosp Ade; JA; Jr NHS; NHS; Off Ade; Purdue Univ; Bio.

KING, DAPHNE; Ripley HS; Evans, WV; Chrs; Chrh Wkr; Trs Frsh Cls; Univ; Med.

KING, DAVID; Avon HS; Plainfield, IN; 31/158 Band; Hon Rl; Boys Clb Am; Ger Clb; Letter Ten; Purdue Univ; Comp Sci.

KING, DAWN; Monroe Central Jr Sr HS; Farmland, IN; 3/92 Band; Chrh Wkr; FCA; Hon Rl; Hosp Ade; NHS; Off Ade; Sch Mus; FHA; Pep Clb; Ball St Univ; Nursing.

KING, DEBORAH; Terre Haute N Vigo HS; Terre Haute, IN; Cls Rep Soph Cls; Aud/Vis; Hon Rl; Quill & Scroll; Stu Cncl; Y-Teens; Ed Yrbk; Rptr Sch Nwsp; 4-H; Fr Clb; Indiana St Univ; Busns.

KING, DENNA; Corydon Central HS; Corydon, IN; Band; Drl Tm; Drm Mjrt; Hosp Ade; Yth Flsp; FHA; Pep Clb; Spn Clb; Pom Pon; 4-H Awd; Schl Of Modeling; Model.

KING, DENNIS; Princeton HS; Princeton, WV; 24/340 Chrh Wkr; Hon Rl; NHS; 4-H; Key Clb; Letter Crs Cntry; Letter Trk; 4-H Awd; Kiwan Awd; Bluefield Coll; Elec Engr.

KING, DERIK; Franklin HS; Franklin, OH; Letter Bsbl; Letter Ftbl; College; Psychology.

KING, DONALD; Thomas Carr Howe HS; Indianapolis, IN; 11/621 Hon Rl; NHS; Rptr Yrbk; College; Cpa.

KING, ERIC; Jackson HS; Jackson, OH; 70/230 Am Leg Boys St; Chrs; Hon Rl; 4-H; Elk Awd; 4-H Awd; College; Flying.

KING, HEIDE; Franklin HS; Westland, MI; Chrh Wkr; Cmnty Wkr; Hon Rl; Schoolcraft Coll; Med.

KING, J; Hurricane HS; Hurrican, WV; Hon Rl; Rptr Sch Nwsp; Pep Clb; Letter Trk; Army; Agriculture.

KING, JAMES; Eaton HS; Eaton, OH; 40/190 Trs Sr Cls; Am Leg Boys St; Band; Chrs; Hon Rl; Sch Mus; Stu Cncl; Yth Flsp; Pres Y-Teens; Sch Nwsp; Bluffton.

KING, JANETTE; Springs Valley HS; French Lick, IN; Chrs; Chrh Wkr; Sch Mus; Yth Flsp; FHA; Rego Voc Schl; Sec.

KING, JEFF; Wehrle HS; Columbus, OH; 1/115 Hon Rl; Bsbl; Bsktbl; Glf; Science Awd; Perfect Attendance Awd; All League Awd For Golf; College; Busns.

KING, JEFF; Union HS; Modoc, IN; 8/68 Cls Rep Sr Cls; Band; Hon Rl; NHS; Stu Cncl; Bsktbl; Letter Glf; Univ; Advertising Art.

KING, JEFFREY; Harrison HS; W Laf, IN; 31/308 Am Leg Boys St; Band; Boy Scts; Jr NHS; NHS; Bsktbl; Ftbl; Trk; Am Leg Awd; Cit Awd; College; Law.

KING, JOAN; Bishop Foley HS; Royal Oak, MI; 20/230 Hon Rl; NHS; Sch Mus; Stg Crw; Crs Cntry; Trk; Coach Actv; Tmr; Univ; Computer Science.

KING, JOAN; Upper Arlington HS; Columbus, OH; Cmnty Wkr; Hon Rl; Sch Pl; Sprt Ed Yrbk; Spn Clb; GAA; Univ; Math.

KING, KATHLEEN; Anderson Sr HS; Anderson, IN; 11/465 Cls Rep Frsh Cls; Trs Soph Cls; Sec Sr Cls; Hon Rl; NHS; Yth Flsp; Spn Clb; Letter Glf; Letter Ten; Chrldng; Univ; Bus Admin.

KING, KATHY; Field HS; Mogadore, OH; 19/245 Hon Rl; Jr NHS; NHS; Pep Clb; Chrldng; Kent State Univ.

KING, KATHY; Bristol Local HS; Bristolville, OH; Band; Hon Rl; Jr NHS; NHS; Sch Mus; Yrbk; Bsbl; Chrldng; Scr Kpr; Voice Dem Awd; Kent State Univ.

KING, KELLY; Hopewell Loudon HS; Alvada, OH; 2/90 Cls Rep Sr Cls; Sal; Aud/Vis; Band; Boy Scts; Hon Rl; NHS; Sch Mus; Sch Pl; VP Stu Cncl; Univ Of Toledo; Elec Engr.

KING, KELLY; Scacina Memorial HS; Indianapolis, IN; 8/194 Girl Scts; Hon Rl; JA; NHS; Off Ade; Sct Actv; Yrbk; IM Sprt; College; Pediatrician.

KING, KEVIN; Meigs HS; Middleport, OH; 6/200 VP Jr Cls; Am Leg Boys St; Band; Chrh Wkr; Cmnty Wkr; Hon Rl; NHS; Sch Mus; Sch Pl; Yrbk; Ohio Univ; Music.

KING, KEVIN; Clay HS; Oregon, OH; Band; Boy Scts; Cmnty Wkr; Hon Rl; Sch Pl; Yrbk; Sch Nwsp; IM Sprt; College; Behavioral Sci.

KING, KIMBERLY; Central HS; Detroit, MI; 23/519 Cmp Fr Grls; Girl Scts; Hon Rl; Yth Flsp; Wayne State Univ.

KING, LAURIE; Mendon HS; Three Rivers, MI; Cls Rep Frsh Cls; Hon Rl; Sch Mus; Stu Cncl; 4-H; Pep Clb; Trk; Letter Chrldng; PPFtbl; Scr Kpr; Univ.

KING, LAURITA; Pettisville HS; Archbold, OH; Trs Frsh Cls; Cls Rep Soph Cls; Cl Rep Jr Cls; Chrs; Hon Rl; NHS; Off Ade; Stu Cncl; Yth Flsp; Yrbk; Eastern Mennonite Coll; Soc Work.

KING, LESLIE; Warrensville Heights HS; Warrensville, OH; Aud/Vis; Band; Hon Rl; Jr NHS; Lbry Ade; Off Ade; Sch Mus; Sprt Ed Yrbk; Rptr Yrbk; Yrbk; All Confrnc 1st Tm In Sftbl Letter 78; Explorers Post #65 78; Univ; Chem Engr.

KING, LINDA; Terre Haute North Vigo HS; Terre Haute, IN; 45/647 Cls Rep Frsh Cls; Drl Tm; Hon Rl; Off Ade; Y-Teens; 4-H; FHA; Spn Clb; GAA; Pom Pon; Indiana St Univ; Foreign Lang.

KING, LISA; Sistersville HS; Sistersville, WV; 10/55 VP Frsh Cls; VP Soph Cls; Pres Jr Cls; Pres Sr Cls; Chrh Wkr; Hon Rl; Hosp Ade; NHS; Stu Cncl; Pep Clb; Ohio Vly Coll; Nursing.

KING, LISA; Green HS; Akron, OH; Chrs; Hon Rl; Off Ade; Sch Pl; Stg Crw; Yrbk; Rptr Sch Nwsp; Drama Clb; 4-H; Ward Clerk.

KING, LOU; Huntington HS; Chillicothe, OH; Band; Hon Rl; NHS; Fr Clb; VICA; Trk; Chrldng; IM Sprt; Pom Pon; Twrlr; Pickaway Ross Voc Schl; Health Occpn.

KING, MARTHLENA A; Lewis County HS; Alum Bridge, WV; Trs Jr Cls; Chrh Wkr; FCA; Stu Cncl; FHA; Pres Pep Clb; Letter Bsktbl; Letter Trk; Coach Actv; PPFtbl; Bus Schl.

KING, MARY; Clay Battelle HS; Burton, WV; Cl Rep Jr Cls; Chrs; Hon Rl; Jr NHS; NHS; Off Ade; Rptr Yrbk; FHA; Pep Clb; Chrldng; W Virginia Univ; Cosmetology.

KING, MARY; Frontier Local HS; Reno, OH; Cmnty Wkr; Hon Rl; FTA; PCC; Elem Ed.

KING, MICHAEL; Vicksburg Cmnty HS; Vicksburg, MI; Aud/Vis; Lbry Ade; Wrstlng; Univ; Comp Sci.

KING, MICHAEL D; Lewis County HS; Alum Bridge, WV; FCA; Hon Rl; Pep Clb; Capt Bsktbl; Capt Ftbl; Coach Actv; PPFtbl;.

KING, MICHELE; Fort Frye HS; Beverly, OH; Hst Soph Cls; VP Jr Cls; FHA; Bsktbl; Chrldng; GAA; Pres Awd; X Ray Tech.

KING, MICHELLE; Perry HS; Painesville, OH; 1/127 Sec Jr Cls; Trs Sr Cls; Val; Am Leg Aux Girls St; Band; Chrs; Hon Rl; Jr NHS; Lbry Ade; NHS; Oh St 4 H Fshn Bd 79; Lk County Jr Fair Bd; St Fair Rep With Sewing Proj 76 79; Hiram Coll; Med.

KING, MICHELLE; Bridgman Sr HS; Bridgman, MI; Cls Rep Frsh Cls; Cls Rep Soph Cls; Cl Rep Jr Cls; Band; Cmnty Wkr; Debate Tm; Hon Rl; NHS; Off Ade; Sch Mus; ACT/PSAT Test; Bnd Slvr Mdl; Michigan State Univ; Animal Sci.

KING, MICHELLE; Monroe Central HS; Parker City, IN; 10/92 Cls Rep Sr Cls; Am Leg Aux Girls St; Band; FCA; Hon Rl; NHS; Stu Cncl; VP FHA; Gym; Chrldng; Ball State Univ; Bus Admin.

KING, MICHELLE; Springboro HS; Springboro, OH; Chrs; Hon Rl; IM Sprt; Warren Cnty Voc Schl.

KING, MIKE; Mc Nicholas HS; Cincinnati, OH; 35/261 Hon Rl; Jr NHS; Letter Bsbl; Letter Bsktbl; Socr; Coach Actv; IM Sprt; Natl Merit Ltr; Mardi Gras Ct Schl Trad; Cls Pres; Natl Hon Soc; Notre Dame Univ; Coaching.

KING, MIKE; River Valley HS; Caledonia, OH; 15/207 Chrh Wkr; Hon Rl; Treas NHS; Lat Clb; Bsbl; IM Sprt; Ohio St Univ.

KING, NANCY; Richmond Sr HS; Richmond, IN; 24/827 Cls Rep Frsh Cls; Hon Rl; NHS; Stu Cncl; 4-H; Spn Clb; Bsktbl; 4-H Awd; Natl Merit Ltr; Indiana Univ; Sociology.

KING, NANCY G; University HS; Osage, WV; Sec Frsh Cls; Trs Frsh Cls; Hon Rl; Lbry Ade; Sch Mus; Stu Cncl; Letter Trk; Chrldng; IM Sprt; Cit Awd; West Virginia Univ.

KING, PAULA; Amelia HS; Amelia, OH; Chrs; Chrh Wkr; JA; Twrlr; JA Awd; Coll; Photog.

KING, PEGGY RUTH; Martinsburg Sr HS; Kearneysville, WV; 3/236 Chrs; Hon Rl; NHS; Natl Merit SF; Shepherd College.

KING, QUINTIN L; University HS; , ; Cls Rep Frsh Cls; Cls Rep Soph Cls; Cl Rep Jr Cls; Cls Rep Sr Cls; AFS; Aud/Vis; Boy Scts; Chrh Wkr; Cmnty Wkr; JA; Northwestern Univ; Busns Admin.

KING, RANDAL; Tiffin Calvert HS; Republic, OH; Pres Band; Chrh Wkr; Hon Rl; Stu Cncl; 4-H; Wrstlng; Cit Awd; 4-H Awd; Military.

KING, RENEE; Botkins HS; Botkins, OH; 13/50 Sec Frsh Cls; Band; Chrs; Hon Rl; NHS; Red Cr Ade; Sch Mus; Rptr Sch Nwsp; Sch Nwsp; 4-H;.

KING, S; Greenbrier East HS; Whte Slphr Spg, WV; Cls Rep Soph Cls; Cl Rep Jr Cls; Chrh Wkr; FCA; Jr NHS; Glf; West Va Univ; Politics.

KING, SANDY; Sisterville HS; Sistersville, WV; 10/58 Cl Rep Jr Cls; Trs Sr Cls; Am Leg Aux Girls St; Chrh Wkr; Hon Rl; NHS; Stu Cncl; FBLA; Pep Clb; Chrldng;.

KING, SARAH; Gull Lake HS; Richland, MI; 4/228 Cl Rep Jr Cls; Cls Rep Sr Cls; Girl Scts; Hon Rl; NHS; Stu Cncl; 4-H; Sci Clb; Spn Clb; Chrldng; Health Field.

KING, SCOTT; Sault Area HS; Sault Ste Marie, MI; 39/400 Hon Rl; NHS; Rptr Sch Nwsp; Letter Bsktbl; Ten; IM Sprt; Mgrs; Lake Superior St Univ; Sci.

KING, SHEILA; Columbus North HS; Columbus, OH; 6/325 Cls Rep Soph Cls; Cl Rep Jr Cls; Pres Sr Cls; Sec Band; Chrs; Hon Rl; Jr NHS; NHS; Stu Cncl; Key Clb; Ohio St Univ; Pre Med.

KING, SHERRY; Shenandoah HS; Middletown, IN; Hon Rl; Stu Cncl; FFA; VP Sci Clb; Pres Spn Clb; Letter Bsktbl; Letter Mgrs; Scr Kpr;.

KING, SHERRY; Henryville HS; Henryville, IN; Cl Rep Jr Cls; Cls Rep Sr Cls; Chrh Wkr; Hon Rl; Sch Pl; Stu Cncl; Yrbk; Sch Nwsp; FHA; Pep Clb; Prosse Voc Schl; Data Transcriber.

KING, SHERRY L; Lake Orion Community HS; Lake Orion, MI; 1/460 Val; Band; Chrs; Hon Rl; NHS; Sch Pl; Stg Crw; Yth Flsp; Treas Drama Clb; General Motors Inst; Mech Engr.

KING, SHERYL; Triton HS; Bourbon, IN; 16/95 Band; Chrh Wkr; Drl Tm; Hon Rl; NHS; Sch Pl; Yth Flsp; Yrbk; Drama Clb; FTA; Ball St Univ.

KING, STANLEY; Southridge HS; Huntingburg, IN; Am Leg Boys St; Hon Rl; Bsktbl; Trk;.

KING, SUANNE; Alexandria Monroe HS; Alexandria, IN; Chrs; Hon Rl; NHS; Off Ade; Pep Clb; Spn Clb; Ball St Univ; Speech Path.

KING, SUSAN J; Highland HS; Highland, IN; 1/494 Cls Rep Soph Cls; Cl Rep Jr Cls; Val; NHS; Sec Stu Cncl; FHA; Spn Clb; Elk Awd; Lion Awd; College; Bio Med Engr.

KING, SYLVIA; Dublin HS; Dublin, OH; 21/160 Cls Rep Frsh Cls; Trs Soph Cls; Cls Rep Soph Cls; Band; Cmp Fr Grls; Chrs; Drm Mjrt; Girl Scts; Hon Rl; NHS; Malone Coll; Christian Ed.

KING, TONI; Redford HS; Detroit, MI; Cls Rep Soph Cls; Cl Rep Jr Cls; Sal; Drm Mjrt; Hon Rl; Jr NHS; Lbry Ade; NHS; Off Ade; Sch Mus; Straight A Honor Pin; 1st Honor Awd; Accepted To Lawrence Inst Of Tech Summer Sci Prog; Michigan St Univ; Archt.

KING, TUESDAY; Northrop HS; Ft Wayne, IN; 17/581 Trs Sr Cls; Am Leg Aux Girls St; Band; Chrh Wkr; Hon Rl; Stu Cncl; Univ Of Chicago; Pre Med.

KING, VENICE LYNN; Bishop Hartley HS; Columbus, OH; Chrh Wkr; Hon Rl; Hosp Ade; Off Ade; Pep Clb; Trk; Chrldng; IM Sprt; Bus Admin.

KING, WILMER W; Adena HS; Clarksburg, OH; Cl Rep Jr Cls; Chrh Wkr; Hon Rl; Jr NHS; NHS; Stu Cncl; Yrbk; Mead Essay Winner 78; Ohio Univ; History.

KING II, DARRELL H; Tippecanoe Vly HS; Mentone, IN; 25/179 Band; Chrh Wkr; NHS; Pres 4-H; FFA; Letter Ftbl; 4-H Awd; Swine Judging Cont Winner; FFA Awds; College; Agri.

KINGMAN, LORENA; Andrews Academy; Berrien Spgs, MI; 3/85 Hon Rl; NHS; Orch; Andrews Univ; Math.

KINGREA, RODNEY; Greenfield Central HS; Greenfield, IN; CAP; Hon Rl; FSA; Mth Clb; Spn Clb; Purdue Univ; Meteorolgy.

KINGSTROM, DAVID R; Pontiac Northern HS; Pontiac, MI; Band; Boy Scts; Hon Rl; Orch; Michigan St Univ; Bus.

KINKEAD, BRENDA; Marion Adams HS; Sheridan, IN; 5/98 VP Sr Cls; Chrs; FCA; Hon Rl; Jr NHS; NHS; Sch Mus; Sch Pl; 4-H; Sec FHA; Univ; Bus.

KINKEAD, KATHY; Marion Adams HS; Sheridan, IN; 9/93 Sec Frsh Cls; Sec Jr Cls; Sec Sr Cls; Cls Rep Sr Cls; Am Leg Aux Girls St; Hon Rl; Jr NHS; NHS; Pres Stu Cncl; Pep Clb;.

KINKOPF, INGRID; Erieview Catholic HS; Brooklyn, OH; Cls Rep Soph Cls; VP Jr Cls; Cls Rep Sr Cls; Chrs; Hon Rl; Hosp Ade; JA; Stu Cncl; Yrbk; Univ; Nursing.

KINLEY, SCOTT; Douglas Mac Arthur HS; Saginaw, MI; Debate Tm; Hon Rl; Capt Socr; IM Sprt; Univ; Bus Admin.

KINLEY, TRACY; Lexington HS; Lexington, OH; Band; Drl Tm; Y-Teens; Fr Clb; College.

KINNEE, LISA; Notre Dame Acad; Toledo, OH; Girl Scts; JA; Sch Pl; FBLA; Ger Clb; IM Sprt; Bus Schl.

KINNETT, GAYLE; New Palestine HS; Greenfield, IN; Drl Tm; Hon Rl; Sch Pl; Yth Flsp; Yrbk; Drama Clb; 4-H; Pep Clb; Pom Pon; 4-H Awd; Hancock City Hostl Schl; X Ray Tech.

KINNEY, ANNETT; Kearsley HS; Flint, MI; Girl Scts; JA; Yrbk; Tmr; JA Awd; College; Dental Asst.

KINNEY, CHERI; Valley Forge Sr HS; Parma, OH; 69/704 Cls Rep Sr Cls; Hon Rl; Stu Cncl; Chrldng; Cuyahoga Cmnty Coll; Bus Admin.

KINNEY, CLINTON; Crothersville Community HS; Paris Crossing, IN; Pres Sr Cls; FCA; NHS; Off Ade; Yth Flsp; Bsbl; Bsktbl; Crs Cntry; College; Conservation.

KINNEY, MICHAEL; Liberty HS; Clarksburg, WV; 16/230 Band; Chrh Wkr; Hon Rl; Jr NHS; NHS; Orch; Sch Mus; Sch Pl; 4-H; Mth Clb; All St Band 79; John Phillip Sousa Awd 79; West Virginia Univ.

KINNEY, SHARON; New Lexington HS; New Lexington, OH; 8/147 Am Leg Aux Girls St; Hon Rl; Jr NHS; NHS; Stg Crw; Rptr Sch Nwsp; OEA;.

KINNUNEN, TARA; Peru HS; Peru, IN; 11/279 Sec Band; Chrs; Hon Rl; Mdrgl; MMM; NHS; Pres Fr Clb; Ivy Tech Univ; Int Design.

KINSELLA, DAVID; Adams HS; Rochester, MI; Hon Rl; Letter Bsbl; Michigan St Univ; Bio Sci.

KINSELLA, KAREN; Madeira HS; Cincinnat, OH; PAVAS; Sch Pl; Stg Crw; Drama Clb; Fr Clb; Key Clb; Swmmng; College; Psychology.

KINSER, ANGELA; Corydon Central HS; Corydon, IN; Cls Rep Frsh Cls; Hon Rl; Stu Cncl; Louisville Univ; Med.

KINSER, ELVIE; Spanishburg HS; Camp Creek, WV; 8/42 Chrs; Hon Rl; Jr NHS; Yrbk; FBLA; FHA; Bus Schl; Bus Ed.

KINSER, KATHY; Spanishburg HS; Camp Creek, WV; 8/33 Hon Rl; Sch Pl; Yth Flsp; FBLA; FHA; Pep Clb; Bluefield St Univ; Sec.

KINSER, SHIRLEY; Bloomington South HS; Bloomington, IN; Mat Maids;.

KINSEY, KAREN; Lemon Monroe HS; Monroe, OH; 3/290 Cls Rep Frsh Cls; Sec Soph Cls; Cls Rep Soph Cls; Cl Rep Jr Cls; Boy Scts; Chrs; Girl Scts; Hon Rl; Sch Mus; Sct Actv; College; Liberal Arts.

KINSEY, PAUL; St Clairsville HS; St Clairsville, OH; Hon Rl; Yth Flsp; Yrbk; Pres 4-H; Dnfth Awd; Natl Forestry Winner; Attend American Youth Foundation Camp; Outstndng Day In Electricty At Ohio St Fair; Miami Univ; Pulp & Paper Tech.

KINSINGER, DENISE; East Canton HS; E Canton, OH; Am Leg Aux Girls St; Band; Cmp Fr Grls; Chrs; Chrh Wkr; Girl Scts; Hon Rl; Hosp Ade; Lbry Ade; 4-H; Pres Of Band 79; Univ; Nurse.

KINSLEY, JANET; St Francis Central HS; Morgantown, WV; Chrs; Hon Rl; Pres Jr NHS; Rptr Yrbk; Rptr Sch Nwsp; Treas Sch Nwsp; Fr Clb; Pep Clb; French Awd 76; Univ; Psych.

KINSMAN, CAROLYN; Belding HS; Belding, MI; Cmp Fr Grls; Chrh Wkr; Hon Rl; Orch; Sch Pl; Yth Flsp; Central Mic Univ; Elem Educ.

KINTZELE, ANN; Marquette HS; Michigan City, IN; 1/72 Am Leg Aux Girls St; Hon Rl; Jr NHS; NHS; Pol Wkr; Stg Crw; Sprt Ed Yrbk; Pres Ger Clb; Sci Clb; Cit Awd; Drake Univ; Pharmacy.

KINZER, HOPE; Western HS; Peebles, OH; Sec Soph Cls; Trs Jr Cls; Trs Sr Cls; Hon Rl; Yrbk; Fr Clb; FHA; Pep Clb; Chrldng; Shawnee St Coll; Sec.

KINZIE, BETH; Andrean HS; Merrillville, IN; 100/250 Chrh Wkr; Cmnty Wkr; Girl Scts; Hon Rl; Sct Actv; Yrbk; Sch Nwsp; Pep Clb; St Joseph Univ; Art.

KINZLER, KAREN D; Harrison HS; Farmington Hill, MI; 1/376 Hon Rl; NHS; Ger Clb; Mgrs; Tmr; Natl Merit SF; College; Engineering.

KIOUSIS, SAM; Schafer HS; Southgate, MI; Bsktbl; Ftbl; Michigan Univ; Med.

KIPINA, MARTHA; Cedar Lake Academy; Houghton, MI; Chrs; Hon Rl; Lbry Ade; NHS; Yrbk; DAR Awd; Natl Merit Ltr; Andrews Univ; Behavioral Sci.

KIPP, DAVID; Cedar Lake Acad; Onaway, MI; Cmnty Wkr; Debate Tm; Hon Rl; Yrbk; Sch Nwsp; Andrews Univ; Bus.

KIPP, KATHY; Chesapeake HS; Chesapeake, OH; Hon Rl; Drama Clb; Bsktbl; Lettered In Vlybl; Marshall Univ; Sociology.

KIPP, KRISTOPHER M; Walsh Jesuit HS; Akron, OH; 15/131 Cls Rep Frsh Cls; Chrh Wkr; Cmnty Wkr; Hon Rl; Hosp Ade; Stg Crw; Stu Cncl; IM Sprt; College; Health Admin.

KIPP, T; Greenbrier East HS; Whte Slphr Spg, WV; Hon Rl; Stu Cncl; Yth Flsp; Ten; College.

KIPPOLA, CONNIE; Westwood HS; Ishpeming, MI; Band; Hon Rl; Pres NHS; OEA; Letter Bsktbl; 3rd Pl Trophy At OEA St Comptn For Ljob Mamual Unemployed 79; Cert For Membrshp In SOEC 79; Natl Hnr Soc; Gogebic Cmnty Coll; Court Reptr.

KIRACOFE, DEBBIE; Eaton HS; Eaton, OH; 38/165 Cls Rep Sr Cls; Hon Rl; Off Ade; Stu Cncl; 4-H; FFA; Pep Clb; Migmi Univ; Hme Ec.

KIRACOFE, DEBORAH; Eaton HS; Eaton, OH; 38/165 Cls Rep Sr Cls; Hon Rl; Off Ade; Stu Cncl; 4-H; Pep Clb; Letter Trk; Coach Actv; GAA; PPFtbl; Miami Univ; Home Ec.

KIRAY, KAREN; Centerville HS; Centerville, OH; 223/687 Cls Rep Frsh Cls; Drl Tm; Sch Mus; Sec OEA; Chrldng; Lion Awd; Ohio St Univ; Busns Ed.

KIRBITZ, CRAIG; Atherton HS; Davison, MI; Pres Soph Cls; Recvd Letters In Sports Ftbll Bsktbll Tennis & Track 76 79; Coll; Phys Ther.

KIRBY, JENNIFER; Franklin HS; Franklin, OH; 85/302 Cl Rep Jr Cls; Cls Rep Sr Cls; Off Ade; Stu Cncl; Rptr Sch Nwsp; Pep Clb; Spn Clb; Bsktbl; Letter Ten; Mgrs; Miami Univ; Nursing.

KIRBY, KATHY; Rochester HS; Rochester, IN; 7/174 Trs Frsh Cls; Chrs; Chrh Wkr; Drl Tm; FCA; Hon Rl; NHS; Sch Mus; Yth Flsp; Sch Nwsp; Purdue Univ; Psych.

KIRBY, KIMBERLY; Mullens HS; Mullens, WV; 14/85 Hon Rl; Jr NHS; NHS; Stu Cncl; Yth Flsp; Y-Teens; Rptr Yrbk; Rptr Sch Nwsp; Beta Clb; FBLA; West Virginia Univ.

KIRBY, LISA; John F Kennedy HS; Taylor, MI; 33/475 Band; Girl Scts; Hon Rl; Letter Gym; College; Nursing.

KIRBY, MELANIE; Waldron Area HS; Waldron, MI; 7/39 Band; Hon Rl; NHS; Sch Pl; Spn Clb; Letter Bsktbl; Chrldng; DAR Awd; Univ.

KIRBY, ROSE; Cleveland Ctrl Catholic HS; Brook Pk, OH; 20/130 Hon Rl; JA; NHS; Fr Clb; JA Awd; Case Western Reserve Univ; Psych.

KIRCHER, KONARAD; Fairmont West HS; Kettering, OH; 27/471 Pres Frsh Cls; Bsbl; Capt Ftbl; IM Sprt; Ski Club Offcr 79; Univ; Math.

KIRCHGESSER, ELLEN; East Grand Rapids HS; E Grand Rapids, MI; Cls Rep Soph Cls; Cl Rep Jr Cls; Trs Sr Cls; Hon Rl; Jr NHS; NHS; Stu Cncl; Pep Clb; Letter Swmmng; Mgrs; College; Chem Engr.

KIRCHHOFER, DIXIE; Whitehall HS; Whitehall, OH; 25/277 Boy Scts; Hon Rl; Spn Clb; Swmmng; Univ; Stewardess.

KIRCHHOFF, RICHARD; Lake Central HS; Dyer, IN; 25/510 Hon Rl; NHS; Ger Clb; Crs Cntry; Trk; Purdue Univ; Engr.

KIRCHMEIER, JEFF; Wilmington Sr HS; Wilmington, OH; Band; Lat Clb; Phi Delta Sigma Schlstc Hon Frat 77 78 & 79; Univ; Astronomy.

KIRCHNER, ANN M; Highland HS; Hinckley, OH; Band; Cmp Fr Grls; Chrh Wkr; Drl Tm; Girl Scts; Orch; Sct Actv; FHA; Lat Clb; College; Nursing.

KIRCHNER, DAVID; Anderson HS; Anderson, IN; 15/443 Hon Rl; Jr NHS; NHS; Spn Clb; Indiana Univ; Acctg.

KIRCHNER, RUTH; Caldwell HS; Caldwell, OH; Pres NHS; Off Ade; Trk; Marietta College; Marine Bio.

KIRCHOFF, YVETTE; North Knox HS; Bicknell, IN; 1/150 Chmn Drl Tm; FCA; Hon Rl; NHS; Yth Flsp; 4-H; FHA; Lat Clb; Letter Trk; Pom Pon; Univ.

KIRILCUK, TAMARA; Whetstone HS; Columbus, OH; 14/320 Sec Frsh Cls; Cls Rep Soph Cls; Cl Rep Jr Cls; Am Leg Boys St; Girl Scts; Hosp Ade; Jr NHS; NHS; Pol Wkr; Sch Pl; Case Western Res Univ.

KIRINCIC, HELEN A; Morton HS; Hammond, IN; Hon Rl; Jr NHS; NHS; Rptr Sch Nwsp; Pep Clb; Sci Clb; PPFtbl; Travel Club Pres; Citizens Apprenticeship Prgrm; College; Law.

KIRK, ABBIE; West Union HS; Otway, OH; Hon Rl; Drama Clb; 4-H; FFA; Lion Awd; Chatman Univ; Animal Sci.

KIRK, AMY; Henryville HS; Charleston, IN; Hon Rl; Lbry Ade; NHS; Pep Clb; Letter Bsktbl; Coach Actv; IM Sprt; Indiana Univ S E; Phys Educ.

KIRK, ANN; Beavercreek HS; Dayton, OH; Cls Rep Frsh Cls; Cls Rep Soph Cls; Cl Rep Jr Cls; Cls Rep Sr Cls; Hon Rl; Stu Cncl; Pep Clb; Trk; IM Sprt; Mgrs; Wright State Univ; Environmentals St.

KIRK, BRIAN; New Palestine HS; Morristown, IN; Chrs; Hon Rl; FFA; Spn Clb; Wrstlng; College; Lawyer.

KIRK, JANICE; North Knox HS; Bicknell, IN; 18/150 Hon Rl; NHS; Treas Yth Flsp; Treas 4-H; Fr Clb; FHA; Vincennes Univ; Accounting.

KIRK, LISA; Kankakee Vly HS; Demotte, IN; Girl Scts; NHS; Sci Clb; Spn Clb; PPFtbl; Purdue Univ; Pre Med.

KIRK, R; Decatur Central HS; Indnpls, IN; Hon Rl; Sch Nwsp; IM Sprt; College; Radio.

KIRK, RANDY; Caro HS; Caro, MI; Hon Rl; Lbry Ade; Yth Flsp; Rptr Sch Nwsp; Letter Glf; JC Awd; Ferris St Univ; Bus.

KIRK, SCOTT; Felicity Franklin HS; Felicity, OH; 8/69 Hon Rl; Sch Pl; Sprt Ed Sch Nwsp; Letter Bsbl; Bsktbl; Letter Glf; Coach Actv; IM Sprt; Univ; Recreation.

KIRKBRIDE, JACKIE; Washington HS; Massillon, OH; 56/459 Hon Rl; Off Ade; Spn Clb; Scr Kpr; Nursing Schl; Nurse.

KIRKENDALL, BETH; Western HS; Russiaville, IN; 7/196 Sec Frsh Cls; Sec Soph Cls; Sec Jr Cls; Sec Sr Cls; Am Leg Aux Girls St; Capt Drl Tm; FCA; Hon Rl; VP NHS; Pres Stu Cncl; Purdue Univ; Intr Dsgn.

KIRKENDALL, SUSAN; Sickerington HS; Pickerington, OH; Band; Chrs; Drl Tm; Hon Rl; NHS; Fr Clb; Chrldng; Otterbein Coll; Psychology.

KIRKHAM, KAY; Daleville HS; Daleville, IN; 2/78 Cls Rep Frsh Cls; Cls Rep Soph Cls; VP Jr Cls; VP Sr Cls; Drl Tm; Hon Rl; NHS; Off Ade; Sch Mus; Stu Cncl; Outstndng Sr High Majortt 78; Farm Bureau Ctznshp Semnr 79; 4 H Jr Leard Counlc 78 80; Purdue Univ; Fshn Retailer.

KIRKHOFF, AMY; Shaker Hts HS; Shaker Hts, OH; Band; Chrs; Chrh Wkr; Cmnty Wkr; Hon Rl; Mdrgl; Sch Mus; Yth Flsp; Rptr Yrbk; Univ; Bus Admin.

KIRKLAND, ELLEN; Northern HS; Detroit, MI; Hon Rl; Off Ade; Y-Teens; DECA; Pep Clb; Scr Kpr; Cit Awd; Univ; Phys Ther.

KIRKLAND, EUGENE A; Columbus East HS; Columbus, OH; Boy Scts; Hon Rl; Lbry Ade; Rptr Sch Nwsp; Boys Clb Am; 4-H; Wrstlng; 4-H Awd; 3rd Pl Sci Fair 8th Grade 1976; Art Coll; Cmmrcl Art.

KIRKLAND, MARK; Leetonia HS; Leetonia, OH; 2/87 Band; Hon Rl; Sch Mus; Sch Pl; Stu Cncl; Spn Clb; College; Math Engr.

KIRKMAN, SCOTT; Corunna HS; Corunna, MI; 17/207 Chrh Wkr; Hon Rl; NHS; FFA; Crs Cntry; Letter Trk; Saginaw Valley State Coll; Phys.

KIRKMAN, SHAREE; Inkster HS; Inkster, MI; Hon Rl; Off Ade; Pep Clb; Chrldng; Cit Awd; Bus Schl; Sec.

KIRKMAN, SUSAN; Northmont HS; Phillipsburg, OH; Girl Scts; Hon Rl; Orch; Red Cr Ade; Letter Bsktbl; College; Archaeology.

KIRKPATRICK, BRAD; Dayton Christian HS; New Carlisle, OH; Band; Boy Scts; Chrh Wkr; Hon Rl; Red Cr Ade; Yth Flsp; Letter Bsbl; Bsktbl; Cit Awd; Varsity Bsebl Mighty In Spirit; Total Person; Freshman Attendant Hmcmng Ct; College; Engr.

KIRKPATRICK, COLLEEN; William V Fisher Cath HS; Lancaster, OH; Hon Rl; Hosp Ade; Yrbk; Fr Clb; FDA; Trk; Univ; Med.

KIRKPATRICK, JAMES; Huntington North HS; Huntington, IN; 105/625 Jr NHS; Lbry Ade; Sprt Ed Sch Nwsp; 4-H; Crs Cntry; College; History.

KIRKPATRICK, KAY L; Wawasee HS; Syracuse, IN; 5/224 Hon Rl; Natl Forn Lg; NHS; Ed Sch Nwsp; Fr Clb; Pres Mth Clb; Letter Swmmng; DAR Awd; Natl Merit Ltr; Eng Dept Awd 1979; Most Valbl Staffer Awd 1979; Hon Stdnt Chords 197; Colorado Schl Of Mines; Chem Engr.

KIRKPATRICK, KIM; Turpin HS; Cincinnati, OH; Chrh Wkr; Univ; Math.

KIRKPATRICK, KIM; Bishop Watlerson HS; Columbus, OH; Aud/Vis; Hon Rl; NHS; Sch Mus; Sch Pl; Rptr Yrbk; Yrbk; Sch Nwsp; Lat Clb; Gov Hon Prg Awd; Art Schlrshp For Sat Classes At Columbus Coll Of Art & Design 78; OSU; Art.

KIRKPATRICK, LEE; Fountain Central HS; Veedersburg, IN; 3/120 Cls Rep Sr Cls; Am Leg Boys St; Pres Band; Hon Rl; NHS; Sch Pl; Stu Cncl; Rptr Yrbk; Drama Clb; Pres FSA; Butler Univ; Med.

KIRKPATRICK, LEE; Fountain Central Jr Sr HS; Veedersburg, IN; 3/125 Cl Rep Jr Cls; Band; Hon Rl; NHS; Off Ade; Sch Pl; Stu Cncl; Yrbk; Drama Clb; Fr Clb; College; Medicine.

KIRKPATRICK, SHERI; Frontier HS; Nw Mtmrs, OH; Girl Scts; Hon Rl; Off Ade; Sch Pl; OEA; GAA; Washington Tech Coll; Acctg.

KIRKPATRICK, TOM; Kimball HS; Royal Oak, MI; Chrs; NHS; Sch Mus; Crs Cntry; Teacher.

KIRKSEY, SUSAN; Wooster HS; Wooster, OH; 32/330 Band; Ohio State Univ; Psychiatrist.

KIRLIN, GLEN W; Univ Of Liggett HS; Grosse Pointe, MI; VP Frsh Cls; Trs Soph Cls; Pres Jr Cls; Pres Sr Cls; Boy Scts; Chrs; Cmnty Wkr; Hon Rl; Sch Mus; Sch Pl; Univ; Engr.

KIRSCH, ANDREA; Adrian HS; Adrian, MI; Hon Rl; NHS; Fr Clb; Letter Glf; GAA; Tmr; Ferris State College; Cmmrcl Art.

KIRSCH, BRIAN; Elyria Catholic HS; Sheffield Lke, OH; Aud/Vis; Chrh Wkr; Hon Rl; Sch Pl; Sch Nwsp; Kent St Univ; Archt.

KIRSCH, MATTHIAS J; Cousino Sr HS; Warren, MI; Hon Rl; NHS; Pol Wkr; Ger Clb; Mth Clb; Sci Clb; IM Sprt; Natl Merit Ltr; Mrt Schlrshp Wayne St Univ79; HS Validictorian 79; Phi Betta Kappa Mbr 79; Wayne St Univ; Chem.

KIRSCHENBAUER, ELIZABETH; St Johns HS; St Johns, MI; Chrh Wkr; FCA; Hon Rl; Jr NHS; Sec NHS; Sec Yth Flsp; Letter Ten; IM Sprt; Concordia Lutheran Coll; Tchr.

KIRSCHNER, MARK; Walnut Hills HS; Cincinnati, OH; Hon Rl; Hosp Ade; NHS; Sch Nwsp; Lat Clb; Mth Clb; Bsktbl; Coach Actv; IM Sprt; DAR Awd; Univ Of Michigan; Pre Med.

KIRTLEY, BEVERLY; High School; Brownsburg, IN; 24/350 Cls Rep Frsh Cls; Cls Rep Soph Cls; Cl Rep Jr Cls; Cmnty Wkr; Girl Scts; Hon Rl; JA; Off Ade; Stu Cncl; Pep Clb; Marriage.

KIRTS, KIM; Marion Harding HS; Marion, OH; 100/490 Am Leg Aux Girls St; Band; Chrs; Off Ade; Sch Mus; Sch Pl; Sprt Ed Yrbk; Ed Sch Nwsp; Pep Clb; Spn Clb; Ohio Univ; Jrnlsm.

KIRWAN, TIM; Marian HS; S Bend, IN; Band; Boy Scts; Hon Rl; Sct Actv; 4-H; Crs Cntry; Trk; IM Sprt; 4-H Awd; Univ; Engr.

KISAMORE, JACQUELINE A; Circleville HS; Onego, WV; Hst Sr Cls; Chrs; Chrh Wkr; Hon Rl; FHA; Spn Clb; Bsktbl; South Branch Voc Schl; Nursing.

KISER, DENISE; Canal Winchester HS; Cnl Winchester, OH; Cls Rep Frsh Cls; Cls Rep Soph Cls; Hon Rl; Off Ade; Stu Cncl; Drama Clb; Trk; Chrldng; Am Leg Awd; Ohio St Univ; Fashion Mdse.

KISER, KELLY; Frontier HS; Chalmers, IN; 4/80 Band; Chrh Wkr; Hon Rl; Sec NHS; 4-H; Pep Clb; Letter Trk; Capt Pom Pon; 4-H Awd; Purdue Univ; Spanish.

KISER, KELLY; Edison HS; Milan, OH; Am Leg Aux Girls St; Band; Chrh Wkr; Hon Rl; Lbry Ade; NHS; Drama Clb; 4-H; FTA; Chrldng; Firelands Bowling Green Univ; Speech.

KISER, KHRIS; Edison HS; Milan, OH; 16/164 Chrs; Chrh Wkr; Hon Rl; NHS; Pol Wkr; Stg Crw; Yth Flsp; 4-H; FHA; FTA; Firelands Coll; Phys Therapy.

KISER, SARA; Buffalo HS; Kenova, WV; Sec Soph Cls; Sec Jr Cls; Band; Drm Mjrt; Hon Rl; Red Cr Ade; Sch Pl; Stg Crw; Rptr Sch Nwsp; Sch Nwsp; Marshall Univ; Legal Asst.

KISH, BERNADETTE; La Salle HS; South Bend, IN; 52/477 Hon Rl; Hosp Ade; Fr Clb; Pep Clb; Univ; Psych.

KISH, GERALDINE; Normandy HS; Parma, OH; Hon Rl; Jr NHS; Lbry Ade; NHS; Orch; Yth Flsp; Fr Clb; FTA; Rdo Clb; Cit Awd; Elem Educ.

KISH, JANE; Hubbard HS; Hubbard, OH; Chrs; Chrh Wkr; Sch Pl; Yth Flsp; Lat Clb; Glf; Gym; Youngstown St Univ; Music.

KISH, JANET; Ctrl Catholic HS; Toledo, OH; 11/303 Chrs; Chrh Wkr; Cmnty Wkr; Hon Rl; Lbry Ade; NHS; Off Ade; PAVAS; Sch Mus; Sch Pl; Univ Of Toledo; Bus Admin.

KISH, SALLIE; Douglas Macarthur HS; Saginaw, MI; Chrh Wkr; Sch Pl; Stu Cncl; Yrbk; Trk; PPFtbl; JC Awd; College; Soc Work.

KISH, SANDRA J; Hubbard HS; Hubbard, OH; Chrs; Debate Tm; Hon Rl; NHS; Quill & Scroll; Sch Mus; Sch Nwsp; FDA; Pres Lat Clb; Letter Glf; Ashland Coll; Bio Chem.

KISNER, DONNA; Waldron Area Schools; Pittsford, MI; 1/52 Cls Rep Soph Cls; Band; Hon Rl; Hosp Ade; Sch Pl; Stu Cncl; Rptr Yrbk; Pep Clb; Bsktbl; Trk; Univ; Acctg.

KISNER, FLEETA; Grafton HS; Grafton, WV; 13/164 Chrh Wkr; Hon Rl; NHS; Sec 4-H; Fr Clb; 4-H Awd; Hon Stud Top 10% Of Class 78; 1st Plc French Creative Writing At Foreign Lang Fest 76; Nike Stud Of Mnth; Fairmont St Coll; Nursing.

KISS, ANNA; Hicksville HS; Hicksville, OH; 7/95 Sec Soph Cls; Trs Soph Cls; Band; Chrs; Chrh Wkr; Hon Rl; NHS; Oh State Univ; Journalism.

KISS, JANE; Martins Ferry HS; Martins Ferry, OH; Chrh Wkr; Cmnty Wkr; Girl Scts; Hon Rl; Sch Mus; Sch Pl; Y-Teens; Am Leg Awd; Ohio Test Of Schlstc Achvmnt 8th Pl; State VP Of Jr Cthlc Daughters; Barbizon Modeling Schl; Model.

KISSACK, T ALAN; Solon HS; Solon, OH; Chrh Wkr; Hon Rl; NHS; Sch Pl; Stg Crw; Yrbk; Sch Nwsp; Drama Clb;.

KISSANE, CHRISTINE; Fulton HS; Perrinton, MI; Band; Chrh Wkr; Cmnty Wkr; Hon Rl; Yth Flsp; Rptr Yrbk; Yrbk; Rptr Sch Nwsp; Sch Nwsp; Pres 4-H; Ferris St Coll; Med Tech.

KISSEE, KONNIE; Highland HS; Highland, IN; 132/521 Band; Hon Rl; NHS; Stu Cncl; Pep Clb; IM Sprt; Scr Kpr; Vllybl Var Ltr & Mst Imprvd 78; N W Indiana Univ; Acctg.

KISSEL, CARMEN; Reitz Memorial HS; Haubstadt, IN; Chrs; Chrh Wkr; Red Cr Ade; Bsbl; Bsktbl; Marian College; Health Field.

KISSEL, MARIE; Princeton Community HS; Princeton, IN; 4/222 Cls Rep Sr Cls; Am Leg Aux Girls St; Band; Chrs; Chrh Wkr; Jr NHS; Mdrgl; Univ Of Notre Dame.

KISSEL, MARY; Gibson Southern HS; Ft Branch, IN; 2/208 Chrs; Chrh Wkr; Cmnty Wkr; Girl Scts; Hon Rl; NHS; Sch Mus; Sch Pl; Beta Clb; Drama Clb; Indiana Univ; Journalism.

KISSEL, SHEILA; Gibson Southern HS; Ft Branch, IN; Chrs; Chrh Wkr; Cmnty Wkr; Girl Scts; Hon Rl; NHS; Sch Pl; Beta Clb; Drama Clb; Pres 4-H; Indiana Univ; Sci.

KISSELL, ANDREA; Robert S Rogers HS; Toledo, OH; Band; Hon Rl; Orch; Sch Mus; VP Lat Clb; Mas Awd; Various Musical Excmlb Awd & Band Awd 4 Yrs; Univ Of Toledo; Meteorology.

KISSICK, CINDY; Hagerstown Jr Sr HS; Hagerstown, IN; 15/172 VP Jr Cls; Band; Chrh Wkr; Hon Rl; NHS; 4-H; Sci Clb; Swmmng; Twrlr; 4-H Awd; Manchester Univ; Pre Med.

KISSICK, RICK; Manchester HS; Manchester, OH; Cls Rep Sr Cls; Stu Cncl; FFA; State Farmer Degree 1978;.

KISSING, KATHERINE; South Dearborn HS; Aurora, IN; Hon Rl; FFA; Letter Bsktbl; Letter Trk; Univ Of Cincinnati; Accounting.

KISTNER, JOHN; Delta Sr HS; Delta, OH; Chrs; Chrh Wkr; Sch Pl; Stg Crw; Rptr Sch Nwsp; Drama Clb; Tmr; Adrian Coll.

KISTNER, LAURIE; Anderson HS; Anderson, IN; 22/435 Hon Rl; Jr NHS; NHS; Yth Flsp; VP Fr Clb; College; Sci.

KITCHEN, LISA; Northfield HS; Andrews, IN; FCA; Hon Rl; Natl Forn Lg; NHS; Rptr Yrbk; Rptr Sch Nwsp; Pres 4-H; Pres FHA; Bsbl; 4-H Awd; Manchester Coll; Interior Design.

KITCHEN, TERESA; Alba Public HS; Elmira, MI; 1/15 Trs Jr Cls; Chrs; Hon Rl; Lbry Ade; NHS; Sch Mus; Pep Clb; Trk; Coll; Law.

KITCHIN, KRAIG; Troy HS; Troy, MI; 76/312 VP Frsh Cls; VP Soph Cls; VP Jr Cls; Pres Sr Cls; Am Leg Boys St; NHS; Sch Pl; Mich State Univ; Tele Bus Cmmnctns.

KITTEL, JEFF; Highland HS; Marengo, OH; 29/127 Pres FCA; NHS; Sch Mus; Sch Pl; Capt Ftbl; Trk; Wrstlng; University.

KITTELL, VICKEY L; Solon HS; Solon, OH; AFS; Aud/Vis; Band; Chrh Wkr; Cmnty Wkr; FCA; Girl Scts; Hon Rl; Jr NHS; Lbry Ade; Natl Presbyterian Schlshp 79; Coll Of Wooster; Foreign Lang.

KITTEN, GINA; Forest Park HS; Ferdinand, IN; 3/124 Hon Rl; Sec NHS; Beta Clb; Bsktbl; College; Nursing.

KITTLE, ANITA; Ross Sr HS; Hamilton, OH; Sec Frsh Cls; Cls Rep Frsh Cls; Pres Soph Cls; Cls Rep Soph Cls; Cls Rep Sr Cls; JA; Off Ade; Stu Cncl; Yrbk; Pep Clb; Eastern Kentucky Univ; Soc Work.

KITTLE, LAURA; Morrice HS; Morrice, MI; Band; Girl Scts; Hon Rl; Lbry Ade; Off Ade; Yrbk; Sch Nwsp; FHA; Pep Clb; Gym; Math Awd 76; Var Ltr In Sftbl 78; Var Ltr In Vlybl 78; Michigan St Univ; Bus.

KITTLE, PAMELA; Flat Rock HS; Flat Rock, MI; Chrs; Sch Mus; Sci Clb; Air Force; Law.

KITTLE, PHILIP; Cameron HS; Cameron, WV; Chrs; Hon Rl; 4-H; Belmont Tech; Welding.

KITTLE, RHONDA; Grafton HS; Flemington, WV; Letter Band; Chrh Wkr; Quill & Scroll; Rptr Yrbk; 4-H; FBLA; Pep Clb; Letter Bsktbl; Capt Ten; PPFtbl; Stu Of The Mnth For Feb 79; Runner Up In Tennis Regionals 79; Fairmont St Coll; Med Lab Tech.

KITTLE, TONYA K; Buffalo HS; Huntington, WV; 6/103 Pres Soph Cls; Hon Rl; Jr NHS; Lbry Ade; Mod UN; NHS; Off Ade; Y-Teens; Rptr Yrbk; Sch Nwsp; Outstanding Academic Stu In Amer HS; Sr Of Month; Marshall Univ; Acctg.

KITTLESON, LYNN; Cedar Lake Academy; Alpena, MI; Sec Jr Cls; Chrs; Hon Rl; Off Ade; Sch Pl; IM Sprt; Scr Kpr; Tmr; Pres Awd; Andrews Univ; Business Acctg.

KITZMILLER, JO ANN; West Branch HS; Alliance, OH; 8/260 Trs Soph Cls; Trs Sr Cls; Band; Chrs; Chrh Wkr; Cmnty Wkr; Hon Rl; Jr NHS; NHS; Orch; Akron Coll; Elem Ed.

KLAEREN, PATRICK J; Otsego HS; Otsego, MI; 2/245 Cl Rep Jr Cls; Am Leg Boys St; Hon Rl; Mod UN; NHS; Sch Mus; Sch Pl; Rptr Yrbk; Spn Clb; Univ; Soc Sci.

KLAFFKE, DORIS; Northrop HS; Ft Wayne, IN; Indiana Univ.

KLAIN, RONALD A; North Central HS; Indianapolis, IN; 30/1200 Pres Frsh Cls; VP Soph Cls; Pres Sr Cls; Debate Tm; Hon Rl; Mod UN; Natl Forn Lg; NHS; Pol Wkr; Stu Cncl; Outstanding Stu Awd; Stu Advocate To Twp Schl Bd; State Champ Congressional Debate; University; Poli Sci.

KLAMT, JOHN; Zeeland HS; Zeeland, MI; Capt Bsktbl; Capt Ftbl; Natl Merit Schl; Hope College; Bus Admin.

KLANN, KAREN; Nordonia HS; Macedonia, OH; 29/407 Chrs; Girl Scts; Hon Rl; Hosp Ade; NHS; VICA; Letter Mgrs; PPFtbl; Voc Schl Sr Cls Treas 78; Univ Of Akron; Bio.

KLAPHEKE, MARK; Bishop Dwenger HS; Ft Wayne, IN; Boy Scts; Sct Actv; Univ; Acctg.

KLAPKO, CHARLES; Hamady HS; Flint, MI; Letter Glf; Letter Ten; Mott Cmnty Coll; Art.

KLARQUIST, THOMAS; Cadillac HS; Cadillac, MI; 1/302 Val; Chrh Wkr; Cmnty Wkr; Hon Rl; NHS; Pol Wkr; Natl Merit Ltr; W Mich Univ; Pre Med.

KLASSEN, DEBBIE; Crown Point HS; Crown Point, IN; 14/570 Hon Rl; Hosp Ade; NHS; Mgrs; Kiwan Awd; Univ; Bus Admin.

KLATY, SARA; Carsonville Port Sanilac HS; Carsonville, MI; Chrs; Hon Rl; OEA; Schoolcraft Comm College; Acctg.

KLAUS, THERESA D; Thomas A De Vilbiss HS; Toledo, OH; 56/235 Girl Scts; Hon Rl; Hosp Ade; JA; Off Ade; DECA; Lat Clb; JA Awd; Univ Of Toledo; Busns.

KLAVINS, ANDIS; East Kentwood HS; Kentwood, MI; 4/418 Chrs; Chrh Wkr; Hon Rl; Jr NHS; Mod UN; NHS; Letter Bsktbl; Grand Rapids Jr College; Mech Engr.

KLAWINSKI, CHRIS; Colon HS; Colon, MI; Hon Rl; Lbry Ade; Rptr Sch Nwsp; FFA; Bsktbl; Ftbl; Trk; College; Electronics.

KLAY, JEANINE; Bluffton HS; Bluffton, OH; 13/95 Band; Chrh Wkr; Girl Scts; Hon Rl; NHS; Off Ade; Pres Yth Flsp; Fr Clb; Treas FTA; Letter Trk; Ohio Tests Of Schlstc Ach; 5th Pl Bowling Green St Univ Dist French II; Sel As Mbr Of Mission Encounter Tm; Ft Wayne Bible Coll; Educ.

KLEAR, EILEEN; Lorain Catholic HS; N Ridgeville, OH; Hon Rl; Coach Actv; IM Sprt; Univ; Art.

KLEAR, K; Miller City HS; Continental, OH; 5/53 Pres Jr Cls; Band; Chrs; Chrh Wkr; Hon Rl; NHS; Yrbk; FHA; IM Sprt; Dnfth Awd; College; Sci.

KLEBER, NANCY; Bishop Dwenger HS; Ft Wayne, IN; Chrh Wkr; Hosp Ade; Stu Cncl; Fr Clb; Gym; Trk; Pom Pon; Ball St Univ; Artist.

KLECK, RENEE; Pike Delta York Sr HS; Delta, OH; VP Frsh Cls; VP Soph Cls; VP Jr Cls; VP Sr Cls; Band; Chrs; Hon Rl; Jr NHS; NHS; Stu Cncl; Earlham Coll; Natural Sci.

KLECKA, ROBERT N; George Washington HS; E Chicago, IN; 117/263 Band; Boy Scts; Sch Mus; Sch Pl; Sct Actv; Stg Crw; Spn Clb; Crs Cntry; Socr; Mgrs; Med Tech.

KLECKNER, KATHI; Penn HS; Mishawaka, IN; Band; FCA; Girl Scts; Hon Rl; 4-H; Swmmng; Tmr; 4-H Awd; Ind Univ At Bloomington; Psychology.

KLEE, JACK; Perry HS; Morrice, MI; 17/169 Aud/Vis; Hon Rl; NHS; Rptr Yrbk; Rptr Sch Nwsp; Sch Nwsp; FFA; FFA Agri Elec Profcncy Awd 79; Voc Schl; Engr.

KLEE, JACQUELYN; Madonna HS; Weirton, WV; 23/98 Chrs; Hon Rl; NHS; Rptr Sch Nwsp; College; Med.

KLEE, JOHN; Bishop Watterson HS; Columbus, OH; 5/283 Boy Scts; Chrh Wkr; Cmnty Wkr; Hon Rl; NHS; Sct Actv; Lat Clb; Crs Cntry; Trk; Letter Wrstlng; Notre Dame Univ; Aeronautical Engr.

KLEEH, GREGORY; Cardinal Mooney HS; Youngstown, OH; 10/290 Aud/Vis; Hon Rl; Jr NHS; NHS; Spn Clb; Letter Bsktbl; Letter Glf; Letter Ten; IM Sprt; Univ; Dent.

KLEI, JAIMIE; Northwest HS; Cincinnati, OH; Hon Rl; NHS; Lat Clb; SAR Awd; College; Chem Engr.

KLEIMAN, DIANE; North Central Area HS; Wilson, MI; 11/65 Stg Crw; Yrbk; IM Sprt; Pom Pon; Community College; Secretary.

KLEIMAN, JANIS; Rushville Consolidated HS; Rushville, IN; 3/287 Am Leg Aux Girls St; Band; Hon Rl; NHS; Fr Clb; Mth Clb; Letter Bsktbl; Letter Glf; Ind Univ; Phys Educ.

KLEIN, ALAN; Brooke HS; Wellsburg, WV; Cls Rep Soph Cls; Boy Scts; Chrh Wkr; FCA; Sct Actv; Letter Bsbl; Ftbl; IM Sprt; West Virginia Univ; Masonry.

KLEIN, CYNTHIA; Westlake Sr HS; Westlake, OH; Chrs; Tmr; Kiwan Awd;.

KLEIN, DEBORAH; North HS; Eastlake, OH; 156/707 Chrh Wkr; Hon Rl; Spn Clb; Lake Erie Coll; Intl Bus.

KLEIN, FRANCINE; Our Lady Of The Lakes HS; Pontiac, MI; Hon Rl; NHS; Sch Pl; Spn Clb; Natl Merit Ltr; Oakland Univ; Language.

KLEIN, HEIDI; Marshall HS; Marshall, MI; 60/262 Cls Rep Sr Cls; Cmnty Wkr; NHS; Stu Cncl; Fr Clb; FFA; Chmn Ten; Alma College; Art.

KLEIN, HOWARD; Southfield HS; Southfield, MI; Aud/Vis; Hon Rl; Lbry Ade; Off Ade; Stg Crw; Sch Nwsp; Spn Clb; Wayne St Univ; Pharm.

KLEIN, JENNIFER; Tucker County HS; Parsons, WV; 6/126 Band; Hon Rl; NHS; Quill & Scroll; Y-Teens; Sch Nwsp; Bsktbl; IM Sprt; Kiwan Awd; Marshall Univ; Archt.

KLEIN, JON; Athens HS; E Leroy, MI; 30/89 Pres Frsh Cls; Band; Hon Rl; VICA; Michigan St Univ; Agri.

KLEIN, JUDY; Marcellus Comm HS; Marcellus, MI; VP Frsh Cls; Cls Rep Soph Cls; Cl Rep Jr Cls; Hon Rl; Stu Cncl; Rptr Yrbk; 4-H; Capt Bsktbl; Capt Chrldng; GAA; Southwestern Univ.

KLEIN, JULIE; Pewamo West Phalia HS; Pewamo, MI; 3/117 Band; Drl Tm; Hon Rl; NHS; PAVAS; Sch Pl; Letter Trk; Butterworth Hosp Schl; Nursing.

KLEIN, KAY; Sylvania Northview HS; Sylvania, OH; 4/350 Sec AFS; Hon Rl; VP NHS; VP Quill & Scroll; Ed Yrbk; Pep Clb; Letter Swmmng; DAR Awd; Natl Merit SF; Univ Of Wisconsin; Journalism.

KLEIN, KENT; Lakeview HS; Cortland, OH; 14/180 Am Leg Boys St; Chrs; NHS; Sch Mus; Sch Pl; Stu Cncl; Yrbk; Rptr Sch Nwsp; Beta Clb; Drama Clb; Kent State Univ; Telecommunications.

KLEIN, LAURIE; Southfield Lathrup Sr HS; Southfield, MI; Hon Rl; Stg Crw; Natl Merit Ltr; Natl Merit SF; Univ Of Michigan; Med.

KLEIN, MIKE; Patrick Henry HS; Napoleon, OH; 11/100 Band; Chrs; Chrh Wkr; Hon Rl; Orch; Stg Crw; Yth Flsp; Univ.

KLEIN, RICHARD; St Xavier HS; Cincinnati, OH; 43/264 Hon Rl; College; Architecture.

KLEIN, ROXANN; Lakeland HS; Highland, MI; 3 Drl Tm; Girl Scts; Off Ade; Pom Pon; Cit Awd; S W Oakland Voc Schl; Archt Drafting.

KLEIN, SANDY; Portage Northern HS; Portage, MI; Hon Rl; Hosp Ade; NHS; Gov Hon Prg Awd; Opt Clb Awd; Univ Of Mic; Rn.

KLEIN, SUSAN; St Alphonsus HS; Detroit, MI; Chrs; Hon Rl; Off Ade; Yrbk; VP GAA; PPFtbl; Michigan St Univ; Dietetics.

KLEIN, SUSAN; Colerain HS; Cincinnati, OH; Chrs; Treas Girl Scts; Hon Rl; Pres Stu Cncl; Pres Pep Clb; Pres Spn Clb; Cincinnati Tech; Med Tech.

KLEIN, TODD; Croswell Lexington HS; Lex, MI; Hon Rl; NHS; Capt Glf; Letter Glf; College; Engr.

KLEINBAUER, CHRIS; Bloomington HS; Bloomington, IN; 12/385 Pres Frsh Cls; VP Jr Cls; Cl Rep Jr Cls; Hon Rl; Pres Jr NHS; VP Stu Cncl; Socr; Ten; Coll; Chem.

KLEINE, HERMAN E; Turpin HS; Cincinnati, OH; Boy Scts; Chrh Wkr; Sct Actv; Bsktbl; Letter Socr; PPFtbl; Univ; Sys Analst.

KLEINHANS, KATHY; Pinconning Area HS; Rhodes, MI; Trs Soph Cls; Trs Jr Cls; Hon Rl; Ftbl; GAA; IM Sprt; PPFtbl; College; Med.

KLEINHELTER, JEAN; Frankfort Sr HS; Frankfort, IN; 2/250 Band; Chrs; NHS; Sch Mus; Sch Pl; Stu Cncl; Lat Clb; Pep Clb; Natl Merit Schl; Univ; Pre Med.

KLEINHENZ, MARY; Marion Local HS; Maria Stein, OH; VP Frsh Cls; Sec Soph Cls; Sec Jr Cls; Band; Chrs; Hon Rl; NHS; Orch; Treas Stu Cncl; Drama Clb; College; Bus Management.

KLEINJAN, EDWARD; Holland Sr HS; Holland, MI; Cls Rep Frsh Cls; Aud/Vis; Boy Scts; Hon Rl; Ger Clb; Natl Merit Ltr; Muskegon Cmnty Coll; Law Enforcement.

KLEINKE, FRANK; Stephenson HS; Wallace, MI; 8/104 Am Leg Boys St; Hon Rl; NHS; 4-H; Bsktbl; Ftbl; Trk; Coach Actv; IM Sprt; Tmr; Michigan Tech Univ; Elec Engr.

KLEINOW, TODD; Utica HS; Utica, MI; 5/379 Hon Rl; Treas NHS; Bsbl; Capt Bsktbl; Letter Ftbl; Univ; Law.

KLEINRICHERT, CAROLYN; New Haven HS; New Haven, IN; 49/350 Off Ade; Y-Teens; FSA; Sec Sci Clb; Trk; PPFtbl; Ind Purdue.

KLEINSMITH, DENNIS T; St Marys Prep HS; E Lansing, MI; Cls Rep Soph Cls; Cls Rep Sr Cls; Hon Rl; Sct Actv; Pres Stu Cncl; Sch Nwsp; Drama Clb; IM Sprt; Michigan St Univ; Psych.

KLEINSMITH, SUZANNE; Escanaba Area Public HS; Escanaba, MI; Sec Frsh Cls; Am Leg Aux Girls St; Pol Wkr; Letter Bsktbl; GAA; IM Sprt; Natl Merit Schl; Kalamazoo Coll; Public Policy.

KLEISMIT, KAREN; Vandalia Butler HS; Vandalia, OH; Girl Scts; Hon Rl; Off Ade; 4-H; 4-H Awd; College; Computer Science.

KLEJKA, JOHN; Lorain Catholic HS; Sheffield Lk, OH; Chrh Wkr; Hon Rl; Y-Teens; DECA; Bsbl; Univ; Bus Admin.

KLEKODA, RHONDA; Ottawa Hills HS; Grand Rapids, MI; Chrs; Hon Rl; Mdrgl; NHS; Orch; Sch Mus; Swmmng; Natl Merit Schl; Aquinas College; Music.

KLEM, CHRISTIE; Winchester Community HS; Winchester, IN; Chrh Wkr; Hon Rl; Fr Clb; FHA; Spn Clb; Glf; Trk; Chrldng; Evansville Univ; Photo Jrnlsm.

KLEM, JANE; Southridge HS; Huntingburg, IN; Chrs; Hon Rl; Hosp Ade; Sch Mus; Stg Crw; Sec FHA; Pep Clb; Spn Clb; Tmr; College; Radiologic Tech.

KLEM, SUZANNE; Redford HS; Detroit, MI; Pres Soph Cls; Pres Jr Cls; Pres Sr Cls; Hon Rl; Stu Cncl; Rptr Yrbk; Letter Hockey; Northern Univ; Forrestry.

KLEMAN, KAREN; Delphos St Johns HS; Delphos, OH; Band; Hon Rl; NHS; Sch Mus; Sch Pl; Rptr Sch Nwsp; FTA; Mth Clb; Trk; IM Sprt; Univ Of Dayton; Acctg.

KLEMKOWSKY, PETER J; Owendale Gagetown Area HS; Owendale, MI; 8/58 Trs Frsh Cls; Cls Rep Soph Cls; Pres Jr Cls; Pres Sr Cls; Band; Hon Rl; NHS; Sct Actv; Letter Bsbl; Letter Bsktbl; Univ; Pro Sports.

KLEMM, HAROLD; C S Mott HS; Warren, MI; Chrh Wkr; Ger Clb; Coach Actv; College; Engr.

KLEMME, STEVEN; Connersville HS; Connersville, IN; 15/250 Hon Rl; NHS; Boys Clb Am; Sci Clb; Spn Clb; Letter Trk; Purdue Univ; Zoology.

KLENK, DANIEL; Saints Peter & Paul HS; Saginaw, MI; Boy Scts; Chrs; Chrh Wkr; Mdrgl; Sch Mus; Sch Pl; Drama Clb; Bsbl; Ftbl; Trk; Soc Of Dist Amer HS Stu; Mem Of Stu Ambassador Prog; Saginaw Valley St Coll; Technology.

KLENK, DIANE; Bridgeport HS; Morris, IL; 1/202 Sec Frsh Cls; Trs Soph Cls; Trs Jr Cls; Pres Sr Cls; Am Leg Aux Girls St; Band; Girl Scts; Jr NHS; NHS; Stu Cncl; Univ Of Illinois; Biology.

KLENKE, JOYCE; Chaminade Julienne HS; Dayton, OH; Hon Rl; JA; Spn Clb; Coach Actv; Univ; Interior Decorating.

KLEPPER, BETH; Southwestern Community HS; Flint, MI; Chrh Wkr; Cmnty Wkr; Hon Rl; Hosp Ade; NHS; Letter Swmmng; Mic State Univ; Med.

KLEREKOPER, TOD M; Lakeland HS; Highland, MI; Hon Rl; Bsbl; Mic State Univ; Cpa.

KLETT, SHARI; Norwalk HS; Norwalk, OH; Girl Scts; Hon Rl; Hosp Ade; Lbry Ade; NHS; Off Ade; Orch; Sct Actv; Yth Flsp; 4-H; Coll; Med.

KLEWER, MARY; Van Wert HS; Van Wert, OH; Chrs; Chrh Wkr; Girl Scts; Hon Rl; Lbry Ade; Yth Flsp; Y-Teens; FHA; Pep Clb; Spn Clb; Vantage Voc Schl; Data Proc.

KLICK, BONNIE; Fairless HS; Navarre, OH; Band; Hon Rl; Sec NHS; VP 4-H;.

KLIEMANN, KAREN; John Glenn HS; Westland, MI; Band; NHS; Fr Clb; Univ Of Michigan; Acctg.

KLIMEK, BRAD; Lasalle HS; South Bend, IN; 102/500 Drama Clb; Bsbl; Univ.

KLIMEK, GARY; Terre Haute N Vigo HS; Terre Haute, IN; 1/675 Cls Rep Frsh Cls; Cls Rep Soph Cls; Cl Rep Jr Cls; Aud/Vis; Chrh Wkr; Hon Rl; Stu Cncl; Yrbk; Sch Nwsp; Boys Clb Am; Coll; Engr.

KLIMEK, TAMMY; St Josephs HS; South Bend, IN; 39/239 Cls Rep Soph Cls; Hon Rl; NHS; Sch Mus; Sch Pl; Pep Clb; Capt Pom Pon; Holy Cross Jr Coll; Bus Admin.

KLIMKE, SUE C; Father Joseph Wehrle HS; Columbus, OH; 3/115 Cls Rep Frsh Cls; Chrs; Chrh Wkr; Hon Rl; Lbry Ade; Off Ade; Sch Mus; Stg Crw; Yrbk; High School Awd For Excellance; Cert Of Merit For French; Art Awd; Univ Of Tampa; Marketing.

KLIMKO, CHARLES; Aiken Sr HS; Cincinnati, OH; 1/576 Hon Rl; Pres NHS; Pol Wkr; Sec Key Clb; Spn Clb; DAR Awd; Natl Merit Schl; Ohio St Univ; Industrial Engr.

KLIMKO, MARY; Aiken Sr HS; Cincinnati, OH; Hon Rl; Pol Wkr; Fr Clb; Lat Clb; Mat Maids; History Stu Of The Month; Foreign Language Stu Of The Month; Trea Foriegn Language Honor Soc; Univ Of Cincinnati; English.

KLINE, ANTHONY; East HS; Sciotoville, OH; 15/127 VP Frsh Cls; VP Soph Cls; VP Jr Cls; Band; Debate Tm; Hon Rl; Lbry Ade; Orch; Pol Wkr; Stu Cncl;.

KLINE, CAMILLE; Columbia City Joint HS; Columbia City, IN; 17/273 Chrh Wkr; FCA; Hon Rl; NHS; Yth Flsp; FTA; Pep Clb; Spn Clb; Bsktbl; Ten; Univ; Acctg.

KLINE, CATHY; De Kalb HS; Waterloo, IN; 40/292 Band; Capt Drl Tm; Sec JA; NHS; Sch Mus; Sec Yth Flsp; 4-H; Pep Clb; IM Sprt; John Phillip Sousa Band Awd; A Hoosier Scholar; Tri Kappa Scholastic Awd; Indiana St Univ; Busns.

KLINE, CHRIS A; Eastlake North HS; Willowick, OH; 14/669 FCA; Hon Rl; NHS; Sprt Ed Sch Nwsp; Rptr Sch Nwsp; Capt Ftbl; College; Education.

KLINE, CHRISTINE; Sycamore HS; Cincinnati, OH; Hon Rl; Key Clb; Trk; College; System Analysis.

KLINE, CONNIE; Heritage HS; New Haven, IN; 11/178 Girl Scts; Hon Rl; NHS; Stg Crw; Yrbk; OEA; Busns Schl; Sec.

KLINE, DON; Kalkaska HS; Alden, MI; 3/117 Hon Rl; Sch Pl; NEDT Natl Testing Awd; Farm Bureau Ins Grp Writing Awd; Mich Comp Schlrshp; N W Michigan Coll; Comp Progr.

KLINE, DOUGLAS; Fairview HS; Fairview Pk, OH; 1/270 VP Band; NHS; Orch; Rptr Yrbk; VP Drama Clb; Sci Clb; IM Sprt; Purdue Univ; Chemical Eng.

KLINE, JAMES; Lima Perry HS; Cridersville, OH; 5/67 Pres Jr Cls; Am Leg Boys St; Chrs; Hon Rl; Jr NHS; Stu Cncl; Pep Clb; Bsktbl; Ftbl; Am Leg Awd; BGSU; Comp Tech.

KLINE, JIM; Lima Perry HS; Lima, OH; Pres Jr Cls; Chrs; Hon Rl; Pep Clb; Spn Clb; Bsbl; Bsktbl; Ftbl; Univ Of Dayton; Education.

KLINE, JOHN; Kenston HS; Chagrin Falls, OH; Pres Frsh Cls; Pres Soph Cls; Chrs; Hon Rl; Lbry Ade; Off Ade; PAVAS; Sch Mus; Sch Pl; Stg Crw; College; Law.

KLINE, JULIE; Roscommon HS; Higgins Lake, MI; 2/141 Band; Chrs; Cmnty Wkr; Pres NHS; Sch Mus; Sch Pl; 4-H; Letter Bsktbl; Letter Trk; GAA; Varsity Letter Awd For Ski Team 78; St Of Michgian Competitivce Schlrshp Progr 79; Ferris St Coll; Cmmrcl Art.

KLINE, JULIE; Field HS; Kent, OH; Girl Scts; Hon Rl; NHS; Stu Cncl; 4-H; Pep Clb; Chrldng; Kent St College.

KLINE, KATHY; Greenville HS; Greenville, OH; 85/375 Cls Rep Soph Cls; Cl Rep Jr Cls; Cls Rep Sr Cls; Band; Drl Tm; Hon Rl; Stu Cncl; 4-H; Spn Clb; Trk; Columbus Tech Univ; Phys Ther.

KLINE, KEITH; Memorial HS; Bristol, IN; Hon Rl; Cert Of Achvmnt T V Prod 79; Otstndng Stud Schl Behavior 72; Univ; T V Prod.

KLINE, KELLY; Madison Comprehensive HS; Mansfield, OH; 4/470 Sec Jr Cls; Sec Sr Cls; Band; Chrh Wkr; Sec NHS; Sec Stu Cncl; Pres 4-H; Pres Fr Clb; Bsbl; Crs Cntry; Ohio N Univ; Elem Educ.

KLINE, KIMBERLY; Mc Comb HS; Deshler, OH; Cls Rep Sr Cls; Chrh Wkr; Hon Rl; Off Ade; Stu Cncl; Yth Flsp; FHA; Pep Clb; Trk; Chrldng; Bowling Green State Univ; Nursing.

KLINE, LAURA; West Catholic HS; Grand Rapids, MI; Chrh Wkr; Hon Rl; NHS; Spn Clb; Grand Rapids Jr Coll; Med Sec.

KLINE, LAURA; Huntington North HS; Huntington, IN; 85/603 Chrs; Chrh Wkr; Hosp Ade; Jr NHS; Red Cr Ade; Sch Mus; Stg Crw; Yth Flsp; Pep Clb; College; Nursing.

KLINE, LESLIE; Ontario HS; Mansfield, OH; 14/198 Pres Frsh Cls; Cls Rep Soph Cls; Sec AFS; ROTC; Stu Cncl; Fr Clb; Ten; Am Leg Awd;.

KLINE, LESLIE A; Ontario HS; Mansfield, OH; 19/199 Pres Frsh Cls; Cls Rep Soph Cls; AFS; Hon Rl; Pol Wkr; Red Cr Ade; Stg Crw; Stu Cncl; Fr Clb; Ten; Berkeley Univ; Politics.

KLINE, LORI; Lakota HS; Rising Sun, OH; Pres Soph Cls; Chrs; Girl Scts; Hon Rl; NHS; Yrbk; 4-H; Spn Clb; Scr Kpr; Bowling Green St Univ; Bus Admin.

KLINE, MARK; Elyria Catholic HS; Sheffield Lke, OH; Aud/Vis; Chrh Wkr; Hon Rl; Spn Clb; Mgrs; Military Acad; Dermatologist.

KLINE, MARTINE; Liberty Benton HS; Findlay, OH; 8/58 Cl Rep Jr Cls; Am Leg Aux Girls St; Band; Chrs; Hon Rl; NHS; Orch; Sch Mus; Stu Cncl; Yrbk; Bowling Green St Univ; Music Educ.

KLINE, MARY; Alpena HS; Posen, MI; Band; Chrh Wkr; Cmnty Wkr; PAVAS; Lat Clb; Natl Merit Schl; E Mich Univ; Soc Work.

KLINE, MARY; Huntington Catholic HS; Huntington, IN; 3/33 Sec Jr Cls; VP Sr Cls; Hon Rl; NHS; Red Cr Ade; Yrbk; 4-H; FNA; Swmmng; Purdue Univ; Nursing.

KLINE, MICHAEL; Grand Haven HS; Spring Lake, MI; Am Leg Boys St; Band; Chrh Wkr; FCA; Hon Rl; Jr NHS; NHS; Central Mic Univ; Bus Admin.

KLINE, NANCY; Crestwood HS; Dearborn Hts, MI; Trs Soph Cls; Trs Jr Cls; Hon Rl; Lbry Ade; NHS; Stu Cncl; Fr Clb; Ten; Chrldng; Mic State Univ; Horticulture.

KLINE, TIMOTHY; Perry HS; Painesville, OH; Band; Boy Scts; Stg Crw; Yrbk; Rptr Sch Nwsp; Sch Nwsp; Key Clb; Glf; Univ; Pro Photog.

KLINE, TRACEY; Madison Comprehensive HS; Mansfield, OH; Cl Rep Jr Cls; Band; Drl Tm; Off Ade; Stu Cncl; Rptr Yrbk; FHA; Ger Clb; IM Sprt; Ohio St Univ.

KLINE, WILLIAM; Grafton HS; Grafton, WV; 28/164 Cl Rep Jr Cls; Cls Rep Sr Cls; Chrs; Hon Rl; NHS; Sch Mus; Sch Pl; West Vir Univ; Optemetry.

KLINEFELT, ROBIN; Dominican HS; Detroit, MI; Cls Rep Soph Cls; Hon Rl; Stg Crw; Yrbk; Spn Clb; College; Tcher.

KLINESTIVER, DONALD; Milton HS; Milton, WV; Am Leg Boys St; Hon Rl; Jr NHS; NHS; Sch Mus; Stu Cncl; Spn Clb; Ftbl; Ten; Wrstlng; Coll.

KLING, T; Hartford HS; Watervliet, MI; Hon Rl; 4-H; FFA; Wrstlng; Carpenter.

KLINGBEIL, LINDA; Walled Lake Central HS; Union Lake, MI; Chrs; Hon Rl; Sch Mus; Stg Crw; Ger Clb; Swmmng; Mic State; Bus.

KLINGEL, GEOFFREY; Marion Harding HS; Marion, OH; Chrs; Sch Mus; Rptr Sch Nwsp; Rdo Clb; Spn Clb; Univ; Broadcast Jrnlsm.

KLINGENBERG, JANICE; Bedford HS; Temperance, MI; 1/460 Chrs; Chrh Wkr; Hon Rl; NHS; Sch Mus; Yth Flsp; Cedarville Coll; Comp Sci.

KLINGENBERG, KEITH; Upper Arlington HS; Columbus, OH; 284/610 Hon Rl; Ger Clb; Letter Crs Cntry; Letter Socr; Letter Trk; Univ; Archt Engr.

KLINGER, SHELLEY; Fort Frye HS; Lowell, OH; 10/129 Am Leg Aux Girls St; Band; Hon Rl; Jr NHS; NHS; Off Ade; Sch Mus; Yrbk; VP Pep Clb; Bsbl; Sinclair Comm Coll; Dental Hygiene.

KLINGLER, BETH; Groveport Madison HS; Columbus, OH; Band; Hon Rl; Lbry Ade; NHS; Spn Clb; Capt Chrldng; PPFtbl; Ohio St Univ; Nursing.

KLINGLER, DENISE; Groveport Madison HS; Columbus, OH; Hon Rl; NHS; Sch Mus; Drama Clb; Spn Clb; Mat Maids; PPFtbl;.

KLINGLER, MARK; St Charles Prep; Columbus, OH; Boy Scts; Hon Rl; NHS; Ger Clb; Letter Ftbl; Capt Trk; IM Sprt; College; Engr.

KLINK, MARY; Saint Alphonsus HS; Dearborn, MI; 39/177 Yrbk; Wayne State Univ; Journalism.

KLINKER, JANET; Heritage HS; Monroeville, IN; 52/187 Chrh Wkr; Hon Rl; Off Ade; Pep Clb; IM Sprt; PPFtbl; Cert Awd For Spanish 1 & 2 76; Awd For Eng 76; Awd For Spanish 76; Univ; Air Traffic Controller.

KLINKER, KIMBERLY; Central Catholic HS; W Lafayette, IN; 12/96 Capt Drl Tm; Hon Rl; Hosp Ade; Lbry Ade; NHS; VP Fr Clb; Pom Pon; Purdue Univ; Nursing.

KLINZING, CYNTHIA; Newberry HS; Newberry, MI; 7/112 VP Frsh Cls; Hon Rl; Hosp Ade; NHS; Sch Pl; Spn Clb; Chrldng; PPFtbl; Am Leg Awd; Northern Michigan Univ; Nursing.

KLISZ, ANN; Fremont Ross HS; Fremont, OH; 15/470 Cls Rep Soph Cls; Cl Rep Jr Cls; Cls Rep Sr Cls; AFS; Cmp Fr Grls; Chrs; Jr NHS; Hon Rl; Jr NHS; NHS; Ohio St Univ; Art.

KLITCH, TIMOTHY J; Grandview Hts HS; Columbus, OH; 3/130 Pres NHS; Rptr Sch Nwsp; Bsktbl; Capt Ten; Univ; Archt.

KLOC, STANLEY; Cass City HS; Cass City, MI; Yrbk; Sch Nwsp; JA Awd; Center For Creative Studies; Photog.

KLODZEN, KAY; Calumet HS; Gary, IN; 21/285 Hon Rl; NHS; OEA; Pom Pon; Purdue Univ; Nursing.

KLOECKNER, BLAINE; Grand Ledge HS; Eagle, MI; 43/418 Boy Scts; Chrh Wkr; Hon Rl; Jr NHS; NHS; Sct Actv; DECA; FDA; Spn Clb; Bsbl; St Of Mi Competitive Schlrshp Awd 79; Eagle Scout 77; Beloit Coll Grant 79; Beloit Coll; Doctor.

KLOEPFER, CYNTHIA; Vanlue Local HS; Carey, OH; Cl Rep Jr Cls; Band; Chrs; Debate Tm; Hon Rl; Off Ade; Sch Mus; Sch Pl; Stu Cncl; Yth Flsp; Bowling Green State Univ; Health.

KLOEPPING, ROBERT; Mater Dei HS; Evansville, IN; Chrh Wkr; Hon Rl; Jr NHS; NHS; Natl Forn Lg; Quill & Scroll; Sch Mus; Sch Pl; Rptr Sch Nwsp; Opt Clb Awd; College; Language.

KLOMPMAKER, ANITA; Holland Chr HS; Holland, MI; Cls Rep Frsh Cls; Band; Chrs; Chrh Wkr; Hon Rl; Jr NHS; NHS; Stu Cncl; Yth Flsp; Ed Sch Nwsp; Calvin Coll; Med.

KLOOCK, MARGO; Northwest HS; Jackson, MI; Cls Rep Soph Cls; Trs Jr Cls; Band; Hon Rl; Jr NHS; NHS; Stu Cncl; Yth Flsp; Pep Clb; Capt Gym; Michigan St Univ; Vet.

KLOOSTRA, KATHRYN; Howell HS; West Branch, MI; 2/395 Sal; Hon Rl; NHS; Yth Flsp; Ger Clb; Pom Pon; Butterworth Hospital Schl; Rn.

KLOPFENSTEIN, ANDREA; Crestline HS; Crestline, OH; Cls Rep Soph Cls; Trs Jr Cls; Trs Sr Cls;

Am Leg Aux Girls St; Chrs; Rptr Yrbk; Bsktbl; Ohio St Univ.

KLOPFENSTEIN, BETTY; Wayne Trace HS; Paulding, OH; 4/130 Chrh Wkr; Hon Rl; Hosp Ade; Jr NHS; NHS; OEA;.

KLOPFENSTEIN, JANE M; Hilltop HS; West Unity, OH; 7/65 Cls Rep Soph Cls; Sec Jr Cls; Sec Sr Cls; Band; Chrs; Drm Bgl; Hon Rl; NHS; Yrbk; 4-H; Bowling Green Univ; Elem Educ.

KLOPFENSTEIN, JOHN; Memorial HS; St Marys, OH; 30/225 Cls Rep Frsh Cls; Cls Rep Soph Cls; Am Leg Boys St; Hon Rl; Jr NHS; NHS; Pol Wkr; Stu Cncl; Sprt Ed Yrbk; Ed Sch Nwsp; Ohio St Univ; Journalism.

KLOPFENSTEIN, ROBIN; Washington HS; S Bend, IN; 53/452 Band; Hon Rl; Fr Clb; College.

KLOS, THAIS; Hartland HS; Fenton, MI; Hon Rl; Lit Mag; Ed Yrbk; Fr Clb; Ten; Cleary Coll; Stenographer.

KLOSEK, VICTORIA; Dublin HS; Dublin, OH; 43/154 Girl Scts; Hon Rl; Rptr Yrbk; Rptr Sch Nwsp; Letter Bsbl; Bsktbl; Letter Hockey; Letter Swmmng; Mgrs; Boys Swim Tm Mgr Letter; Coll; Med.

KLOSKA, ELIZABETH; Marian HS; South Bend, IN; Cls Rep Frsh Cls; Hon Rl; Hosp Ade; VP NHS; Sch Mus; Sch Pl; Yrbk; Pep Clb; Letter Ten; St Marys Coll; Medicine.

KLOSOWSKI, JULIE; All Saints Central HS; Bay City, MI; Cmnty Wkr; Girl Scts; Hon Rl; Hosp Ade; Mdrgl; VP NHS; Sch Mus; Treas Sct Actv; DAR Awd; Voice Dem Awd; Pres Of Bay Cnty Youth Council 78; All Sts Acad Awrd 79; Chosen To Join Engr Workshop 79; Univ; Elec Engr.

KLOSOWSKI, MARTIN; Mount Pleasant HS; Mount Pleasant, MI; Cls Rep Sr Cls; Hon Rl; Letter Bsbl; Letter Bsktbl; Letter Ftbl; Gym; IM Sprt; PPFtbl; Natl Merit Ltr; Central Mic Univ; Educ.

KLOSTERMAN, JAMES J; Bishop Fenwick HS; Middletown, OH; 2/90 Cl Rep Jr Cls; Am Leg Boys St; Band; Chrh Wkr; Hon Rl; Hosp Ade; JA; NHS; Sch Mus; College; Med.

KLOSTERMAN, LINDA; Mc Auley HS; Cincinnati, OH; Chrs; Girl Scts; Hon Rl; JA; Stg Crw; Yth Flsp; Swmmng; Ten; Trk; Cincinnati Tech Coll; Data Proc.

KLOSZEWSKI, LISA; W H Harrison HS; Harrison, OH; 6/208 Hon Rl; Jr NHS; NHS; Sch Pl; Drama Clb; Ten; Trk; GAA; Edinboro Coll.

KLOTZ, RONDA; Lakota HS; Rising Sun, OH; Chrs; Chrh Wkr; Cmnty Wkr; Girl Scts; Sch Mus; Ed Sch Nwsp; Rptr Sch Nwsp; 4-H; GAA; 4-H Awd; Terra Tech.

KLUDING, JUDI; Monroeville HS; Norwalk, OH; 1/75 Cls Rep Frsh Cls; Cls Rep Soph Cls; Pres Jr Cls; Cl Rep Jr Cls; VP Sr Cls; Val; Hon Rl; NHS; Off Ade; Quill & Scroll; Bowling Green St Univ.

KLUDING, MIKE; Monroeville HS; Norwalk, OH; 4-H; FFA; Bsktbl; Ftbl; 4-H Awd;.

KLUDY, KIMBERLY; Shelby HS; Shelby, MI; Band; Chrh Wkr; Girl Scts; Hon Rl; Hosp Ade; Sch Pl; 4-H; Fr Clb; Bsbl; Trk; Muskegon Comm College; Journalist.

KLUEG, SHELLY; Central HS; Evansville, IN; 140/482 Hon Rl; Hosp Ade; Off Ade; Red Cr Ade; Sch Nwsp; Pres 4-H; VP OEA; Voc Cert In Data Processing 78; Ambassador Awd Of OEA 78; 5th Pl Comp OEA Regional Contest 78; Acctg.

KLUG, BILL; Elmhurst HS; Ft Wayne, IN; Cls Rep Frsh Cls; Aud/Vis; Boy Scts; Hon Rl; Sct Actv; Rptr Yrbk; Rptr Sch Nwsp; Letter Wrstlng; Purdue Univ; Mech Engr.

KLUG, BRIAN; River Valley HS; Buchanan, MI; Hon Rl; 4-H; Pres FFA; 4-H Awd; Mich College; Dairy Science.

KLUG, GERARD; St Francis De Sales HS; Toledo, OH; 21/180 Cl Rep Jr Cls; NHS; Lourdes College; Art.

KLUG, JAMES; Reading Comm HS; Reading, OH; 5/219 Cls Rep Soph Cls; Chrh Wkr; Hon Rl; NHS; Sct Actv; Ger Clb; Glf; Ohio State Univ; Electrical Engring.

KLUG, VIVIAN; Fayetteville Perry HS; Fayetteville, OH; Chrs; Chrh Wkr; Hon Rl; Fr Clb; Bsktbl; College; Rn.

KLUISZA, MARK; Howell HS; Howell, MI; College; Paramedic.

KLUK, K; Our Lady Of Mercy HS; Farm Hls, MI; Cls Rep Soph Cls; Cmnty Wkr; Girl Scts; Hon Rl; Coach Actv; Mgrs; Scr Kpr; Tmr; Michigan St Univ; Nursing.

KLUMP, DONALD; St Peter & Paul Area HS; Saginaw, MI; Pres Frsh Cls; Cls Rep Soph Cls; Cl Rep Jr Cls; Cls Rep Sr Cls; Hon Rl; NHS; Yrbk; Ftbl; Coll.

KLUNK, ELIZABETH A; Seton HS; Cincinnati, OH; 75/291 Chrs; Hon Rl; Spn Clb; Mia Univ; Bus.

KLUSKOWSKI, PAUL; South Haven HS; South Haven, MI; 2/230 Hon Rl; NHS; Crs Cntry; Trk; Am Leg Awd; Kiwan Awd; Rotary Awd; VFW Awd; Ferris St Coll; Heavy Equip Serv.

KLUSMAN, DIANE; Laurel HS; Laurel, IN; Band; Chrs; Hon Rl; Lbry Ade; NHS; Yrbk; Pres 4-H; Trk; 4-H Awd;.

KMONK, JANET; Rossford HS; Rossford, OH; 7/156 Girl Scts; Hon Rl; Fr Clb; GAA; Bowling Green St Univ; Acctg.

KNABB, KATHLEEN; Glen Este HS; Batavia, OH; 2/255 Cls Rep Soph Cls; Cl Rep Jr Cls; Pres Sr Cls; Am Leg Aux Girls St; Band; Chrh Wkr; Cmnty Wkr; Xavier Univ; Educ.

KNAGGS, ANN C; Lamphere HS; Madison Hts, MI; 11/336 Hon Rl; JA; NHS; Ed Sch Nwsp; PPFtbl; Best 1st Yr Newspaper Stu; Best Editorial; Univ Of Michigan; Photography.

KNAP, ANDY; Charleston Catholic HS; Charleston, WV; 10/76 Boy Scts; Chrh Wkr; Pres JA; Sct Actv; Key Clb; Sci Clb; Bsktbl; IM Sprt; Cit Awd; Dnfth Awd; Univ Of Tenn; Industril Engr.

KNAPE, TRACY; Forest Hills Central Sr HS; Grand Rapids, MI; 32/240 Chrh Wkr; Hon Rl; JA; Mod UN; NHS; Sch Mus; Sch Pl; Stg Crw; Letter Ten; Scr Kpr; Awd In Mi Compttv Schslp Progr 79; Gold Tassel For Grad 79; Michigan St Univ; Fshn Mdse.

KNAPKE, DOROTHY; Marion Local HS; Chickasaw, OH; 9/90 Am Leg Aux Girls St; Hon Rl; NHS; Sch Nwsp; FTA; Pep Clb; Sci Clb; Univ Of Ten; Foresty.

KNAPKE, JUDITH; Versailles HS; Versailles, OH; FCA; Hon Rl; JA; NHS; 4-H; FTA; Chrldng; GAA; Tmr; JA Awd; Northwestern Busns Coll; Busns Admin.

KNAPKE, NANCY; Coldwater HS; Coldwater, OH; Band; Chrs; Cmnty Wkr; Hon Rl; Hosp Ade; Ger Clb; Trk; IM Sprt; Mgrs; Miami Vly Schl Of Nursing; RN.

KNAPKE, WAYNE; Williamsburg HS; Batavia, OH; 4/99 Band; Boy Scts; Hon Rl; JA; NHS; Stu Cncl; Pep Clb; Spn Clb; Glf; Ten; University.

KNAPP, ELESE; North Newton HS; De Motte, IN; Hon Rl; NHS; Spn Clb; PPFtbl; Perfect Attendance;.

KNAPP, ELIZABETH M; Highland HS; Hinckley, OH; 3/208 Hon Rl; NHS; FHA; Spn Clb; Wrstlng; Scr Kpr; Fairview Schl Of Nursing; Nurse.

KNAPP, JAMES; Saint Josephs HS; S Bend, IN; Boy Scts; Chrh Wkr; Cmnty Wkr; Boys Clb Am; Spn Clb; Letter Ftbl; Trk; College; Lasw.

KNAPP, JEANNINE; Monsgr John R Hackett HS; Kalamazoo, MI; 3/136 Girl Scts; Hon Rl; JA; Jr NHS; NHS; Bsbl; Western Michigan Univ; Aviation.

KNAPP, KAREN; Elwood Community HS; Elwood, IN; 11/269 Band; Chrs; Chrh Wkr; Girl Scts; Hon Rl; Jr NHS; Sch Pl; Stu Cncl; Drama Clb; Pep Clb; College; Music.

KNAPP, KRISTINA; Hilltop HS; W Unity, OH; 10/70 Cls Rep Soph Cls; Cl Rep Jr Cls; Cls Rep Sr Cls; Band; Chrs; Hon Rl; Off Ade; Sch Pl; Stg Crw; Stu Cncl; Northwest Tech; Exec Sec.

KNAPP, LAURA; Grant HS; Grant, MI; Hon Rl; 4-H; Bsktbl; GAA; Cit Awd; 4-H Awd; College.

KNAPP, LEIGH A; Margaretta HS; Castalia, OH; Band; Girl Scts; Lbry Ade; 4-H; Trk; Tmr; 4-H Awd; Youth In Gov; Ohio St Univ; Paralegal Tech.

KNAPP, MARY; Tri County HS; Howard City, MI; 7/89 Trs Soph Cls; Trs Jr Cls; Trs Sr Cls; Band; Chrh Wkr; Girl Scts; Hon Rl; NHS; Mic State Univ; Telecommunications.

KNAPP, MICHELLE; St Peters HS; Mansfield, OH; Girl Scts; Yth Flsp; Yrbk; Rptr Sch Nwsp; Drama Clb; Key Clb; IM Sprt; Univ; Retail Mgmt.

KNAPP, TIM; Little Miami HS; Morrow, OH; Hon Rl; Sct Actv; Y-Teens; Letter Bsbl; Letter Bsktbl; Letter Ftbl; Letter Trk; IM Sprt; Wright St Univ; Comp Sci.

KNAPP, TIMOTHY; Douglas Mac Arthur HS; Saginaw, MI; 10/350 Cls Rep Frsh Cls; Cls Rep Soph Cls; Cl Rep Jr Cls; Am Leg Boys St; Hon Rl; NHS; Fr Clb; Swmmng; Univ; Archt.

KNARR, FELICE; Scecina Memorial HS; Indianapolis, IN; Chrs; Girl Scts; Hon Rl; NHS; Marian College; English.

KNARR, RANDOLPH F; Spencer HS; Spencer, WV; Band; Hon Rl; Jr NHS; Mth Clb; IM Sprt; Rensselaer Polytech Inst; Engr.

KNAUTZ, JOSEPH; Newbury HS; Newbury, OH; FFA; Ger Clb; Bsktbl;.

KNECHT, MARY; Miami Trace HS; Washington, OH; AFS; Y-Teens; FBLA; FHA; Spn Clb; Ohi State Univ; Comp Progr.

KNEEBONE, JAMES; Yale HS; Yale, MI; 22/180 Am Leg Boys St; Band; Chrh Wkr; Hon Rl; 4-H; Letter Ftbl; Ten; Capt Wrstlng; 4-H Awd; Univ Of Michigan; Bus Mgmt.

KNEISLEY, JENNIFER; North Central HS; Indianapolis, IN; 12/1060 Chrs; Hon Rl; NHS; Stu Cncl; Yth Flsp; Bsktbl; Natl Merit Ltr; Natl French Contest 4th Pl & 3rd Pl; Natl Assoc Of Chemists Contest North Cntrl Rep; Peom Publishd; Univ.

KNELL, KONRAD; John F Kennedy HS; Taylor, MI; 1/500 Cl Rep Jr Cls; Band; Chrs; Chrh Wkr; Debate Tm; NHS; Orch; College; Med.

KNELLINGER, HEIDI; Martins Ferry HS; Martins Ferry, OH; Band; Chrs; Hon Rl; Stu Cncl; Y-Teens; Sci Clb; Spn Clb; Letter Bsktbl; Letter Trk; GAA; College; Medicine.

KNEPLEY, KEVIN; Napoleon HS; Napoleon, OH; FCA; Hon Rl; Spn Clb; Letter Bsktbl; Letter Crs Cntry; Letter Trk; Cincinatti; Engineering.

KNEPP, ROBERT; Grayling HS; Grayling, MI; Band; Hon Rl; Jr NHS; Lit Mag; NHS; Pep Clb; Scr Kpr; Tmr; Pres Awd; 1st Solo Ensmbl 79; Hon Bnd Interlochen 78; St Of Mi Cmptv Schlrshp 79; Pres Awd Alma Coll 79; Alma Coll; Pre Nuclear Engr.

KNEPP, TERRY; Northridge HS; Middlebury, IN; Band; Sec Chrh Wkr; Hon Rl; Pres Yth Flsp; 4-H; Letter Bsbl; 4-H Awd; Bus Schl.

KNEZETIC, JAMES; Admiral King HS; Lorain, OH; 120/413 Chrs; Chrh Wkr; Hon Rl; Sch Mus; Sch Pl; Ten; Art Inst Of Pittsburgh; Cmmrcl Art.

KNIAT, LISA; Spring Lake HS; Spring Lake, MI; Chrs; Hon Rl; Mod UN; Letter Swmmng; Mgrs; Tmr; Eva Covacs Acad; Bus Educ.

KNICELY, PAMELA; Gallia Academy HS; Gallipolis, OH; 9/234 Chrs; Chrh Wkr; VP NHS; Sch Pl; Rptr Yrbk; Sprt Ed Sch Nwsp; Drama Clb; FTA; Letter Trk; Hanover Coll.

KNICKEL, LINDA; Elgin HS; Prospect, OH; 3/129 Hon Rl; NHS; Stg Crw; Drama Clb; Pres FHA; Lat Clb; PPFtbl; Marion Tech Coll; Acctg.

KNICKERBOCKER, BETTY; Northwest HS; Canal Fulton, OH; Band; Hon Rl; Jr NHS; NHS; Pres 4-H; Rdo Clb; Spn Clb; Letter Trk; Scr Kpr; 4-H Awd; Univ Of Akron.

KNICKERBOCKER, BRAD; Chelsea HS; Chelsea, MI; Boy Scts; Chrh Wkr; Hon Rl; Sct Actv; Yth Flsp; Letter Bsbl; Letter Bsktbl; Letter Ftbl; IM Sprt; College; Law.

KNICKERBOCKER, JOHN A; Swartz Creek HS; Swartz Creek, MI; 20/418 Cls Rep Sr Cls; Jr NHS; NHS; Stu Cncl; Sch Nwsp; Mgrs; Voice Dem Awd; Cntrl Mi Univ Hon Schlshp 79; St Of Mi Compttv Schlshp 79; Cntrl Michigan Univ; Bus Admin.

KNICKERBOCKER, JULIE; Lakeville Memorial HS; Davison, MI; 49/189 Band; Chrh Wkr; Hon Rl; Sch Pl; Rptr Sch Nwsp; Spn Clb; Chrldng; Voice Dem Awd; Bryan Coll.

KNIES, BETH; Jasper HS; Jasper, IN; 11/300 Chrh Wkr; Cmnty Wkr; Treas Girl Scts; NHS; Sct Actv; Stg Crw; Civ Clb; Drama Clb; Mat Maids; College; Business.

KNIFFEN, MICHAEL; Houghton Lake HS; Merritt, MI; Letter Bsbl; Pres Phys Ftnss Awd 77 78 & 79; Michigan St Univ; Photog.

KNIGHT, BRAD; Inland Lakes HS; Afton, MI; 37/75 Hon Rl; Yrbk; Pres 4-H; Bsbl; 4-H Awd; Vocational Schl; Electronics.

KNIGHT, CORINNE; Maplewood HS; Cortland, OH; 26/87 Beta Clb; FHA; FTA; Voc Schl; Nursing.

KNIGHT, DEBORAH; Tawas Area HS; E Tawas, MI; Cls Rep Soph Cls; Band; Hon Rl; NHS; Stu Cncl; Pres Yth Flsp; Keyettes; Capt Chrldng; College; Law.

KNIGHT, DENISE; Huntington North HS; Warren, IN; Am Leg Aux Girls St; Chrs; Girl Scts; Sec 4-H; FFA; Letter GAA; 4-H Awd; Worthy Advisor Of Rainbow 79; Treas Of Sunshine Soc 79; Contestant In Miss Teen USA 79; Huntington Beauty Coll; Beautician.

KNIGHT, DONALD; Archbishop Moeller HS; Terrace Pk, OH; Aud/Vis; Band; Chrh Wkr; Hon Rl; Lit Mag; Sch Mus; Sch Pl; Yth Flsp; Rptr Sch Nwsp; Ohio Wesleyan Univ; Law.

KNIGHT, JOE; Cory Rawson HS; Jenera, OH; Aud/Vis; 4-H; FFA; Pep Clb; Wrstlng; 4-H Awd;.

KNIGHT, JOHN; Fairmont West HS; Kettering, OH; Cls Rep Frsh Cls; Band; Chrs; Chrh Wkr; Cmnty Wkr; Hon Rl; Sch Mus; Letter Ftbl; Trk; Wrstlng; Purdue; Engr.

KNIGHT, JOHN; West Bloomfield HS; Keego Harbor, MI; 264/422 Mgrs; Natl Merit SF; Oakland Univ; Engr.

KNIGHT, KELLEY; Western HS; Bay City, MI; 7/465 Band; Chrh Wkr; Debate Tm; Hon Rl; NHS; Sch Mus; PPFtbl; Valparaiso Univ; Med Tech.

KNIGHT, KIM; Mablewood Jr & Sr HS; N Bloomfield, OH; Chrs; NHS; Off Ade; Beta Clb; 4-H; Pres Fr Clb; Pep Clb; Chrldng; Dnfth Awd; Univ.

KNIGHT, MID; Northwestern HS; West Salem, OH; Cls Rep Frsh Cls; Cls Rep Soph Cls; Band; Chrs; NHS; VP Stu Cncl; VP Yth Flsp; FTA; Lat Clb; Bsbl; College.

KNIGHT, MIKKI; Doddridge Cnty HS; West Union, WV; Pres Soph Cls; Cls Rep Soph Cls; Pres Jr Cls; Band; Hon Rl; NHS; Pres Stu Cncl; Pep Clb; Bsktbl; Trk; West Virginia Univ; Vet.

KNIGHT, PHILLIP; Portage Central HS; Portage, MI; 10/360 Cls Rep Soph Cls; Pres Jr Cls; Chrs; Hon Rl; Capt Ftbl; Capt Trk; Natl Merit SF; Univ Of Michigan; Engr.

KNIGHT, REBECCA; Old Trail HS; Akron, OH; Chrs; Hon Rl; Sch Mus; Yrbk; Fr Clb; Spn Clb; Letter Hockey; Soc Of Distgh Amer Hs Stu 1978; Univ; Spanish.

KNIGHT, RICK; Elkins HS; Elkins, WV; Boy Scts; Chrs; Chrh Wkr; Sct Actv; Letter Trk; Athltc Achvmtn Ltr In Track 78; Christ For The Nations Inst; Ministr.

KNIGHT, ROBERT; Romulus HS; Romulus, MI; Am Leg Boys St; Hon Rl; Fr Clb; Letter Bsbl; Letter Ftbl; Eastern Michigan Univ; Comp Sci.

KNIGHT, SAM; Windham HS; Windham, OH; 65/82 Cls Rep Sr Cls; Band; Chrs; Lit Mag; Stu Cncl; Rptr Sch Nwsp; Bsktbl; Kent State Univ; Music.

KNIGHT, SHIRLEY K; Michigan Center HS; Mich Cntr, MI; Cl Rep Jr Cls; Band; Chrs; Chrh Wkr; Cmnty Wkr; Girl Scts; Hon Rl; JA; Lbry Ade; NHS; Univ Of Michigan; Phys Ther.

KNIGHT, THERESA; St Agatha HS; Detroit, MI; Pres Soph Cls; Hon Rl; NHS; VP Stu Cncl; Rptr Yrbk; Chrldng; Univ.

KNIGHTING, LORA; Gallia Acad; Bidwell, OH; Girl Scts; Hon Rl; Off Ade; Sct Actv; Yth Flsp; Y-Teens; FHA; Pep Clb; Sci Clb; Colorado St Univ; Law.

KNIOLA, JEFF; Marquette HS; Michigan City, IN; Boy Scts; Sch Pl; Sci Clb; Letter Socr; Trk; Opt Clb Awd; College; Science.

KNIPP, DEBRA; Rock Hill Sr HS; Pedro, OH; 44/142 Band; Drl Tm; Girl Scts; Hon Rl; Yth Flsp; 4-H; Pep Clb; Trk; GAA; Busns Schl; Clerical Busns.

KNIPPENBURG, TRACY; Grandview Heights HS; Columbus, OH; Drl Tm; Jr NHS; Off Ade; Sch Pl; Fr Clb; Bsktbl; Hockey; Mat Maids; Univ; Engl.

KNISELY, BARBARA; Sylvania Northview HS; Sylvania, OH; AFS; Off Ade; Sch Pl; Sch Nwsp; Sec Fr Clb; Bowling Green Univ; Journalism.

KNISELY, BRETT; Elmwood HS; Wayne, OH; 17/112 Hon Rl; NHS; Sci Clb; Letter Bsbl; Letter Bsktbl; Letter Ftbl; Univ.

KNISELY, SHERRI; Columbia City Joint HS; Columbia City, IN; Hon Rl; Lbry Ade; NHS; 4-H; Letter Bsktbl; Letter Trk; PPFtbl; Ball State; Conservation.

KNISKA, DAN; Parkersburg Catholic HS; Parkersburg, WV; 2/55 VP Frsh Cls; Cl Rep Jr Cls; Sal; Chrs; Cmnty Wkr; Pres NHS; Capt Bsbl; Bsktbl; Coach Actv; Elk Awd; Wv Univ; Industrial Engr.

KNISLEY, BRIGETTE; Paint Valley HS; Bainbridge, OH; Cls Rep Frsh Cls; Cls Rep Soph Cls; Cl Rep Jr Cls; Hon Rl; Stu Cncl; FHA; Bus Schl.

KNOBB, KIM; Washington HS; Massillon, OH; Girl Scts; Off Ade; 4-H; Spn Clb; Bsktbl; Gym; Trk; IM Sprt; Mat Maids; 4-H Awd; Univ.

KNOBLOCH, KIM; Hopkins Public HS; Hopkins, MI; Band; Hon Rl; NHS; Letter Bsktbl; Wrstlng; Army Reserve; Nursing.

KNOCH, JERRY; Woodhaven HS; Flat Rock, MI; Band; Hon Rl; Jr NHS; Treas NHS; Univ.

KNODEL, CYNTHIA; Walnut Hills HS; Cincinnati, OH; Chrs; Hon Rl; Sch Pl; Yth Flsp; Yrbk; VP Spn Clb; Trk; Univ; Bus.

KNODELL, LISA; Big Walnut HS; Sunbury, OH; 32/248 Chrs; Hon Rl; Fr Clb; FHA; Chrldng; Capital Univ; Nursing.

KNOEDLER, JUDY; Whitmore Lake HS; Whitmore Lake, MI; Trs Jr Cls; Band; Hon Rl; Treas Jr NHS; VP NHS; Sec Stu Cncl; Ed Yrbk; Ctrl Michigan Univ; Elem Ed.

KNOL, DAVID; Jenison Public HS; Jenison, MI; Band; Drm Bgl; Hon Rl; Orch; Pol Wkr; Bsbl; Glf; Music Schlrshp To Blue Lk Fine Arts Camp 78; Awd For Best Jazz Musician 78; St Of Mi Comp Schlrshp Awd 79; Grand Rapids Jr Coll; Music.

KNOL, SUSI; Jenison HS; Jenison, MI; Band; Chrs; Chrh Wkr; Drl Tm; Hon Rl; Sch Mus; Sch Pl; Stu Cncl; 4-H; OEA; Music Schlrshp Midwestern Music Camp Kansas St Univ; Jr Coll; Nursing.

KNOLL, KAREN; Niles HS; Niles, MI; 22/388 Band; Hon Rl; Chrldng; Mic State Univ; Criminal Justice.

KNOLL, KAY; Niles Sr HS; Niles, MI; VP Frsh Cls; Sec Soph Cls; VP Jr Cls; Hon Rl; NHS; Stu Cncl; Letter Chrldng; Outstndng 9th Grd Stnt; Stdnt Govt Day Party Co Leader; N Club For Var Ltr Earners 79; Ferris St Univ; Dent Hygnst.

KNOLL, KEVIN; Niles HS; Niles, MI; NHS; Capt Ftbl; Capt Wrstlng; Natl Merit SF; College.

KNOLL, MARTHA; Muskegon HS; Muskegon, MI; Band; Chrs; Chrh Wkr; Hon Rl; NHS; Off Ade; Yth Flsp; Pep Clb; Sec Spn Clb; St Comp Schlrshp 79; Muskegon Cmnty Coll Schlrshp 79; Natl Fed Bus Schlrshp 79; Whos Who H S 78; Muskegon Cmnty Coll; Music.

KNOLL, MICHAEL; Lanse HS; Lanse, MI; Hon Rl; NHS; Trk; IM Sprt; Mic State Univ; General.

KNOLLINGER, BERNARD; Wheeling Park HS; Triadelphia, WV; Pres Sr Cls; AFS; Natl Forn Lg; NHS; Quill & Scroll; Sprt Ed Sch Nwsp; Bsktbl; Letter Ftbl; Letter Trk; Georgetown Univ.

KNOOP, ANNETTE; Sidney HS; Sidney, OH; Pres Chrs; Hon Rl; Pres NHS; Off Ade; Sch Mus; Pres Drama Clb; Bsktbl; Scr Kpr; Stu Coun Stu Recognition Awd 78; Bowling Green St Univ; Phys Ther.

KNOOP, NORMA; Tippecanoe Valley HS; Mentone, IN; Trs Soph Cls; Trs Jr Cls; Band; Chrs; Drl Tm; Girl Scts; Hon Rl; NHS; Sch Mus; Yth Flsp; Volleyball Tm; Univ; Dent Hygn.

KNOOP, TRACY; Reed City Public HS; Reed City, MI; Cls Rep Soph Cls; Cl Rep Jr Cls; Band; Hon Rl; Jr NHS; NHS; Stu Cncl; Rptr Yrbk; Rptr Sch Nwsp; Sci Clb; Michigan St Univ; Agri.

KNOP, JULIE; Walled Lake Central HS; Union Lake, MI; Hon Rl; NHS; Off Ade; Ger Clb; OEA; St Of Mich Competitive Schlrshp; Lake Superior St Bd Of Ctrl Schlrshp; BEOG; Lake Superior St Univ; Chem Engr.

KNOPF, CHRIS; Kenston HS; Chagrin Fls, OH; 3/220 NHS; Bsktbl; Bst Fresh Eng Stu; Bst Adv Asian Studies Stu 76; Hnrbl Mentn In Kent St Dist Of Oh Test Of Schlstc Adchvmnt; Northwestern Univ; Pre Law.

KNOPF, ROBBI; Shaker Hts HS; Shaker Hts, OH; Chrs; Hon Rl; Sch Mus; Sch Pl; Stu Cncl; Univ; Foreign Lang.

KNOPP, BRIAN; St Joseph Central Cath HS; Fremont, OH; Cls Rep Frsh Cls; Chrh Wkr; Stu Cncl; Rptr Sch Nwsp; Key Clb; Bsktbl; Glf; IM Sprt; Ohio St Univ; Cmnctns.

KNOPP, KATHLEEN; Heritage Christian School; Fountaintown, IN; Band; Hon Rl; Yrbk; Pensacola Christian Coll; Bus.

KNOPP, LAURIE; S Range HS; Salem, OH; 51/133 VP Frsh Cls; Pres Jr Cls; Pres Sr Cls; Aud/Vis; Chrs; Stg Crw; Rptr Yrbk; Drama Clb; Spn Clb; Capt Bsktbl; HS All Amer Basketball; Inter Cnty League 1st Team Basketball; Inter Cnty League 2nd Team Basketball; Otterbein Coll; Phys Ed.

KNOPSNIDER, DANIEL S; Streetsboro HS; Streetsboro, OH; Boy Scts; Hon Rl; Ftbl; Letter Trk; Wrstlng; Armed Serv.

KNORR, KAMIE S; Davison Sr HS; Davison, MI; Hon Rl; Lbry Ade; Off Ade; IM Sprt; PPFtbl; Scr Kpr; Univ; CPA.

KNOTH, CONSTANCE; Celina HS; Coldwater, OH; Hon Rl; 4-H; Lat Clb; Lima Tech College; Social Work.

KNOTT, ANNA M; Westland HS; Darbydale, OH; 1/404 Cls Rep Frsh Cls; Hon Rl; Lbry Ade; Treas OEA; GAA; Busns Schl; Legal Sec.

KNOTT, KIM; De Kalb HS; Auburn, IN; 150292 Aud/Vis; Chrs; Chrh Wkr; Hon Rl; NHS; Yth Flsp; 4-H; Pep Clb; Spn Clb; Ten; Indiana Central Univ; Math.

KNOTTS, SUSAN; Arlington HS; Indianapolis, IN; Am Leg Aux Girls St; Chrs; Girl Scts; Hon Rl; NHS; Orch; Sch Mus; Stu Cncl; Yrbk; Pom Pon; Indiana St Univ; Busns Admin.

KNOUS, TOM; Memorial HS; St Marys, OH; 45/243 Pres Frsh Cls; Pres Soph Cls; Cl Rep Jr Cls; Cmnty Wkr; Stu Cncl; Letter Bsbl; Letter Ftbl; Mbr Of The Snaps Percussion Corps Natl Champs 78; Mbr Of The Sci Schlrshp Tm; Stu Cncl Pres For Upcmng Yr; Ohio Northern Univ; Pharm.

KNOUSE, TODD; Upper Arlington HS; Columbus, OH; 39/610 FCA; Hon Rl; Fr Clb; Capt Bsktbl; Coll; Acctg.

KNOWLAN, JEFF; Pittsford Area HS; Pittsford, MI; Pres Frsh Cls; Debate Tm; Hon Rl; Lbry Ade; FFA; Letter Bsktbl; Letter Ftbl; Letter Trk; Scr Kpr; Univ.

KNOWLES, PAULA; Orchard View HS; Muskegon, MI; 16/192 Chrs; Hon Rl; NHS; Off Ade; Rptr Yrbk; Rptr Sch Nwsp; Chrldng; Mushegon Business College; Acctg.

KNOWLES, ROBERT S; Charleston HS; Charleston, WV; Cls Rep Sr Cls; Am Leg Boys St; Boy Scts; Cmnty Wkr; Hon Rl; Jr NHS; NHS; Stg Crw; Stu Cncl; Lat Clb; Univ Of Kentucky; Mech Engr.

KNOWLTON, EDIE; Crestwood HS; Mantua, OH; Am Leg Aux Girls St; Jr NHS; NHS; Orch; Red Cr Ade; ROTC; Stu Cncl; Beta Clb; Spn Clb; Capt Bsktbl; Univ Of Miami; Phys Ther.

KNOWLTON, EDIE S; Crestwood HS; Mantua, OH; Sec Jr Cls; Am Leg Aux Girls St; Letter Band; Letter Drm Mjrt; NHS; Stu Cncl; Beta Clb; Chmn Bsktbl; Letter Trk; Univ Of Miami; Phys Ther.

KNOWLTON, SCOTT; Sistersville HS; Sistersville, WV; Hon Rl; Rptr Sch Nwsp; Sch Nwsp; Univ; Pharm.

KNOX, ARLENE; Inkster HS; Inkster, MI; Chrh Wkr; Hon Rl; JA; Trk; Chrldng; Cit Awd; Eastern Univ; Acctg.

KNOX, BETH; Wauseon HS; Wauseon, OH; Band; Chrs; Sch Mus; Yth Flsp; Bsktbl; Trk; Bowling Green Univ; Soc Work.

KNOX, JACK; East Noble HS; Kendalvile, IN; Hon Rl; Bsktbl; Ftbl; Trk; Wrstlng; Franklin Ferris State; Teacher.

KNOX, JENNI; Crawfordsville HS; Crawfordsville, IN; 23/223 Cmnty Wkr; Hon Rl; JA; NHS; Sch Pl; Stg Crw; Pres OEA; Pep Clb; Tmr; Schlrshp From Oakland City Coll; Ball St Univ; Spec Ed.

KNOX, JOHN S; Bishop Hartley HS; Columbus, OH; 3/190 Cls Rep Frsh Cls; Cls Rep Soph Cls; Cl Rep Jr Cls; Am Leg Boys St; Hon Rl; NHS; Stu Cncl; Letter Bsbl; Letter Bsktbl; Letter Glf; Univ; Engr.

KNOX, MARK; Wm G Mather HS; Munising, MI; Cls Rep Frsh Cls; Cls Rep Soph Cls; Aud/Vis; Band; Boy Scts; Hon Rl; Stu Cncl; Letter Trk; Michiga Tech; Engineering.

KNOX, PHYLLIS; Milan HS; Milan, MI; Chrs; Girl Scts; Hosp Ade; Off Ade; Stg Crw; Drama Clb; Fr Clb; VICA; Trk; Univ; Nursing.

KNOX, ROBBIE; Western HS; Detroit, MI; Chrh Wkr; Hon Rl; Wayne St Univ; Spec Ed.

KNOX, S E; Cameron HS; Cameron, WV; 1/103 Trs Sr Cls; Am Leg Boys St; Boy Scts; Hon Rl; NHS; Wrstlng; West Vir Univ; Science.

KNOX, SHERRY; Westfall HS; Mt Sterling, OH; 1/140 NHS;.

KNOX, TONYA L; Henry Ford HS; Detroit, MI; Aud/Vis; Chrs; Chrh Wkr; Cmnty Wkr; Girl Scts; Hon Rl; Lbry Ade; Mod UN; Off Ade; Pol Wkr; Phys Ftns Awd; Vlybl Tm Cptn; Florida A & M Univ; Pharm.

KNOX, VALERIE; Berkley HS; Berkley, MI; Sec Chrs; Debate Tm; Mdrgl; Pres Orch; Sch Mus; Sch Pl; Stu Cncl; Depauw Univ; Music.

KNOX, WILLIAM; Barnesville HS; Barnesville, OH; 18/130 Trs Frsh Cls; Cls Rep Soph Cls; VP Jr Cls; Cl Rep Jr Cls; VP Sr Cls; Debate Tm; Treas Stu Cncl; FTA; Key Clb; Letter Bsbl; Marietta Coll; Bus.

KNUE, PATRICIA A; Seton HS; Cincinnati, OH; 2/273 Hon Rl; Mod UN; NHS; Orch; DAR Awd; Kiwan Awd; College; Phys Therapy.

KNUE, SUSAN; Edinburgh HS; Edinburgh, IN; Fr Clb; Bsktbl; Am Leg Awd; Basic Educ Opptortunity Grant; Supplemental Educ Opportunity Grant; St Grant; Indiana Central Univ; Nursing.

KNUEVEN, DOUG; La Salle HS; Cincinnati, OH; 10/263 Hon Rl; Ohio St Univ; Vet.

KNUEVEN, DOUGLAS; La Salle HS; Cincinnati, OH; 10/257 Hon Rl; NHS; Ohio St Univ; Vet.

KNUEVEN, THOMAS E; William Mason HS; Mason, OH; 19/170 Cls Rep Sr Cls; Band; Boy Scts; Hon Rl; Orch; Stg Crw; Pep Clb; Sci Clb; Univ; Music.

KNUFF, CHRISTINE; Boardman HS; Boardman, OH; 65/595 Chrs; Hon Rl; NHS; Sch Mus; Stg Crw; Y-Teens; Mth Clb; Univ Of Akron; Econ.

KNUFF, EDWARD; Ursuline HS; Hubbard, OH; Band; Chrh Wkr; Orch; Sch Pl; Yrbk; Trk; Schlstc Art Awds Photog 76; Ireland Stdy Schlrshp 78; 1st Pl Photog Awd 79; Youngstown St Univ; Bus.

KNUPP, DEBORAH L; Hubbard HS; Hubbard, OH; 28/350 Cls Rep Frsh Cls; Band; Hon Rl; NHS; Off Ade; FTA; Youngstown Civics Day Representative; Sec Of Tri Hi Y; Sec Of Busns Club; Youngstown St Univ; Acctg.

KNUPP, DOROTHY; Hubbard HS; Hubbard, OH; Sec Band; Girl Scts; Sch Mus; Yth Flsp; Pres FBLA; Hubbard Cmnty Youth League Girls Sftbll 75; Tri Hi Y Pres 78; Youngstown St Univ; Acctg.

KNUST, BILLY; Princeton Community HS; Patoka, IN; 13/233 Aud/Vis; FCA; Hon Rl; Boys Clb Am; 4-H; VICA; Letter Wrstlng; In St Champ Motorcycle Racing 4 Yrs 72 76; S Il Champ Mortcyle Racng 75 & 76; Vincennes Univ; Mach.

KNUTEL, JANET; River Valley HS; Three Oaks, MI; 10/158 Band; Hon Rl; NHS; Sch Pl; Drama Clb; Ger Clb; Letter Trk; Northwestern Univ.

KNUTILLA, SUSAN; Williamston HS; Tampa, FL; 10/156 Sec AFS; Am Leg Aux Girls St; Band; Girl Scts; Jr NHS; Yth Flsp; Univ Of Florida; Phys Ther.

KNYCH, CAROL; Cathedral HS; Indianapolis, IN; Cls Rep Soph Cls; Sec Sr Cls; Am Leg Aux Girls St; Chrh Wkr; Cmnty Wkr; Hon Rl; NHS; Pep Clb; Chrldng; Letter Coach Actv; Yth Leadershp Progr Eili Lilly Endowment 1978; Indiana Stu Leadershp Inst 1978; Univ; Bus Admin.

KOBAK, JOSEPH J; Padua Franciscan HS; Brunswick, OH; Hon Rl; Sch Nwsp; Airforce; Cmmrcl Pilot.

KOBASIC, MARY; Escanaba Area Public HS; Escanaba, MI; 31/442 Chrh Wkr; Cmnty Wkr; Hon Rl; NHS; IM Sprt; Mic State Univ; Bus Admin.

KOBASKO, MIKE; Bishop Donahue HS; Moundsville, WV; Chrh Wkr; Hon Rl; JA; Key Clb; Bsbl; Bsktbl; Ftbl; JA Awd; Univ.

KOBBERDAHL, TRACY; Finneytown HS; Cincinnati, OH; 15/251 Hon Rl; NHS; Spn Clb; Socr; Chrldng; Mat Maids; Scr Kpr; Tmr; DAR Awd; Raymond Walters Coll; Dental Hygiene.

KOBELAK, NATALIE; Bethel HS; Tipp City, OH; 2/103 Trs Jr Cls; Hon Rl; Jr NHS; NHS; Off Ade; Treas Fr Clb; Trk; Chrldng; Coach Actv; IM Sprt; Ohio St Univ; Mech Engr.

KOBER, ANN; Hubbard HS; Hubbard, OH; 13/350 Cmp Fr Grls; Hon Rl; Spn Clb; Letter Glf; IM Sprt; Recognition For Being In Star Prog; Youngstown St Univ; Comp Sci.

KOBER, BRIAN J; Kenowa Hills HS; Grand Rpds, MI; Band; Debate Tm; NHS; Sch Pl; Sci Clb; Grand Rapids Jr College; Engr.

KOBERMANN, RAYMOND; St Francis De Sales HS; Columbus, OH; Cls Rep Soph Cls; Cl Rep Jr Cls; Aud/Vis; Sch Pl; Sct Actv; Stu Cncl; Drama Clb; Fr Clb; Key Clb; Pep Clb; Univ Of Dayton; Indus Engr.

KOBILARCSIK, DIANNE; Tuslaw HS; Massillon, OH; 28/160 Sec Soph Cls; Cl Rep Jr Cls; Chrs; Off Ade; Sch Pl; Stu Cncl; Y-Teens; FHA; Pep Clb; Capt Chrldng; College.

KOBISA, MARGARET; Meridian HS; Hope, MI; 6/125 Chrs; Girl Scts; Hon Rl; JA; Jr NHS; Lit Mag; NHS; Stu Cncl;.

KOBLIN, ANDREA; Oak Park HS; Huntington Wds, MI; 64/400 Spn Clb; Gym; Chrldng; IM Sprt; Mich State Univ; Soc Sci.

KOBOLD, LISA; North Liberty HS; South Bend, IN; 10/101 Chrs; Chrh Wkr; Hon Rl; Sch Pl; Stg Crw; Rptr Yrbk; Yrbk; Drama Clb; 4-H; Pep Clb; Purdue Univ; Interior Dsgn.

KOBYLARZ, LINDA; Howell HS; Howell, MI; 45/395 Cmnty Wkr; Hon Rl; Pres JA; Lit Mag; Rptr Sch Nwsp; Pres JA Awd; Michigan St Univ; Comp Sci.

KOCAK, KATHLEEN; Regina HS; Cleveland, OH; Cl Rep Jr Cls; Hon Rl; NHS; Bsbl; Bsktbl; Ohio Northern Univ; Pharm.

KOCH, ALAN; Ottawa Glandorf HS; Ottawa, OH; Am Leg Boys St; Boy Scts; Hon Rl; NHS; Sci Clb; Bsktbl; IM Sprt;.

KOCH, ELAINE; Northwestern HS; Wooster, OH; Cls Rep Frsh Cls; Pres Sr Cls; Band; Chrs; Chrh Wkr; Hon Rl; Jr NHS; NHS; Sch Pl; Stg Crw; Stu Cncl; College; Speech & Hearing Ther.

KOCH, HEIDI; Euclid Sr HS; Euclid, OH; Hon Rl; Ger Clb; Bus Schl; Legal Sec.

KOCH, JAMES; Owendale Gagetown HS; Gagetown, MI; 1/41 Val; Hon Rl; Lbry Ade; NHS; Stg Crw; Dnfth Awd; Natl Merit SF; Saginaw Valley State College; Chem E.

KOCH, JAY; Lima Sr HS; Lima, OH; 3/453 Band; Chrh Wkr; Hon Rl; Yth Flsp; IM Sprt; Bowling Green St Univ; Math.

KOCH, JOHN; Parkway HS; Rockford, OH; 5/120 Chrs; Hon Rl; NHS; FFA; Ftbl; Lincoln Tech; Farmer.

KOCH, JOSEPH; Rochester Cmnty HS; Rochester, IN; 19/166 Hon Rl; NHS; 4-H; FFA; Glf; Mgrs; 4-H Awd; Rfct Attndnc Awrd 77 79; Univ; Acctg.

KOCH, JULIA; Bay City Western HS; Midland, MI; Chrs; Hon Rl; Rptr Sch Nwsp; Zion Lutheran Yth Group Christian Growth Chrmn Soph; Zion Lutheran Yth Grp Historian & Sec; Delta Comm Coll; Busns.

KOCH, KENNETH; Springfield Local HS; Petersburg, OH; Band; Boy Scts; Chrh Wkr; Cmnty Wkr; Hon Rl; Sct Actv; Yth Flsp; Sprt Ed Sch Nwsp; Sch Nwsp; 4-H; Voc; Comp Sci.

KOCH, LISA; Edison Sr HS; Lake Sta, IN; 5/171 Girl Scts; Hon Rl; NHS; Sch Mus; Yth Flsp; Bsktbl; Ten; Letter Trk; Pom Pon; PPFtbl; Univ; Elec Engr.

KOCH, MIKE; Mc Comb HS; Mc Comb, OH; 1/62 Trs Sr Cls; Val; Am Leg Boys St; Band; Hon Rl; Pres NHS; Sch Pl; Stu Cncl; Spn Clb; Trk; Miami Univ; Archt.

KOCH, WALTER; Bryan HS; Bryan, OH; 8/200 Trs Jr Cls; Band; Chrs; Hon Rl; VP JA; Jr NHS; NHS; Rptr Yrbk; Yrbk; Rptr Sch Nwsp; Univ Of Toledo; Pharm.

KOCHANOWSKI, RONNIE; Elkhart Ctrl HS; Elkhart, IN; 67/400 Cls Rep Soph Cls; Cl Rep Jr Cls; Cls Rep Sr Cls; Chrs; Cmnty Wkr; Hon Rl; Stu Cncl; Cit Awd; Kiwan Awd; Lion Awd; Univ; Archt Tech.

KOCHENSPARGER, CYNTHIA; Berkley HS; Huntngtn Wds, MI; 2/400 Cls Rep Soph Cls; Trs Jr Cls; Band; Chrh Wkr; NHS; Stu Cncl; Yth Flsp; Harvard Book Awd 79; St Officer Od Of Rainbow For Girls In Mi 79; Univ; Med.

KOCHENSPARGER, KEVIN; New Lexington Sr HS; New Lexington, OH; 7/140 Am Leg Boys St; Band; Chrs; Chrh Wkr; Hon Rl; Jr NHS; NHS; Sch Pl; Treas Fr Clb; Pep Clb; Miami Univ; Systems Analyst.

KOCHER, KAREN; Brooke HS; Follansbee, WV; 124/403 Cmp Fr Grls; Chrh Wkr; Cmnty Wkr; JA; Pol Wkr; Lat Clb; Pep Clb; Mat Maids; JA Awd; West Virginia Univ; Law.

KOCHER, LINDA; William Henry Harrison HS; Cleves, OH; 1/218 VP AFS; Girl Scts; Hon Rl; NHS; Stu Cncl; FTA; Pres Spn Clb; Hon H Awd 5 Sem On Hon Roll 79; Amer Hist Algbr II Earth Sci Spanish 1 2 & 3 Awds 77 79; Frsn Schlhsp Awd; Miami Univ; Spec Educ Tchr.

KOCHHEISER, KAREN; Crestview HS; Mansfield, OH; Band; Hon Rl; Stu Cncl; FHA; Spn Clb; Bsktbl; Trk; Bowling Green Univ; Phy Educ.

KOCHIS, MIKE; Valley Forge HS; Parma, OH; 24/766 Cls Rep Sr Cls; Boy Scts; Hon Rl; Stu Cncl; Bsbl; Letter Bsktbl; Letter Ftbl; Letter Trk; Pres Awd; Hiram Coll; Medicine.

KOCHIS, PATTY; Valley Forge HS; Parma, OH; 184/704 Girl Scts; Hon Rl; Bsbl; Bsktbl; Coach Actv; Scr Kpr; Cleveland St Univ; Spec Ed.

KOCJAN, KATHLEEN; Lake Catholic HS; Eastlake, OH; 5/342 Chrs; Cmnty Wkr; Hon Rl; Lit Mag; Ger Clb; Univ.

KOCK, REX; Garrett HS; Garrett, IN; Aud/Vis; Yth Flsp; Indiana Univ; Pre Med.

KOCKS, CARL; Arthur Hill HS; Saginaw, MI; Boy Scts; Hon Rl; Letter Ten; Schlshp From UAW 668 79; Ferris St Coll; Optometry.

KOCON, ROBERT; Donald E Gavit Jr Sr HS; Hammond, IN; 23/274 Hon Rl; NHS; Letter Wrstlng; In St Schlsp 79; Purdue Univ; Mach.

KOCSIS, JEFF; Wyoming Park HS; Wyoming, MI; 14/240 VP Boy Scts; Chrh Wkr; Hon Rl; NHS; Stg Crw; Letter Wrstlng; Michigan St Univ; Civil Engr.

KOCSIS, RANDALL K; Fairmont Sr HS; Fairmont, WV; Am Leg Boys St; Chrh Wkr; Hon Rl; Spn Clb; Ftbl; Trk; Del To State Conservation Camp; Ches Club Treas; Univ; Law Enfrcmnt.

KOCUR, JANET; Morton Sr HS; Hammond, IN; Hon Rl; Rptr Sch Nwsp; Pep Clb; GAA; PPFtbl; Univ; Sec.

KOCZAT, DIANE; East Detroit HS; E Detroit, MI; Band; Girl Scts; Hon Rl; Sch Pl; DECA; Mat Maids; General Motors Inst; Sales.

KOCZWARA, DEBORAH; Struthers HS; Poland Twp, OH; Lbry Ade; Off Ade; 4-H; Spn Clb; Bsktbl; Trk; Tmr; 4-H Awd; Youngstown St Univ; Comp Sci.

KOECHLEY, MARTY; Ctrl Catholic HS; Toledo, OH; Hon Rl; Off Ade; Stg Crw; Letter Ftbl; Wrstlng; IM Sprt; Univ Of California; Sci.

KOEDYKER, DAWN; Calumet HS; Gary, IN; 25/297 Am Leg Aux Girls St; Hon Rl; Jr NHS; Y-Teens; OEA; Pep Clb; Trk; Pom Pon; 4-H Awd; College; Med Record Tech.

KOEHL, BEA; Bishop Dwenger HS; Avilla, IN; Cl Rep Jr Cls; Band; Hon Rl; JA; Sch Mus; Stu Cncl; College; Educ.

KOEHLER, CAROL; Mohawk HS; Sycamore, OH; Band; Drm Mjrt; Hon Rl; Pres NHS; Off Ade; Rptr Yrbk; Ed Sch Nwsp; Drama Clb; FTA; Mgrs; Heidelberg Coll; Elem Ed.

KOEHLER, GINA; Bishop Watterson HS; Columbus, OH; Hon Rl; Sch Pl; Fr Clb; Coach Actv; Miami; Eng.

KOEHLER, JACKIE; Washington HS; Massillon, OH; Band; Chrs; Stg Crw; Y-Teens; DECA; Drama Clb; Swmmng; Trk; Mgrs; Sec Of DECA I Class; Clinic Aid;.

KOEHLER, LYNN; Unionville Sebewaing HS; Sebewaing, MI; 1/105 Girl Scts; Hon Rl; NHS; Stu Cncl; Univ; Acctg.

KOEHLER, RICHARD K; New Albany HS; New Albany, IN; Cls Rep Frsh Cls; Cls Rep Soph Cls; Cl Rep Jr Cls; Band; Cmnty Wkr; Debate Tm; Hon Rl; NHS; Orch; Sch Mus; Indiana Univ; Med.

KOEHLER, SALLY; Upper Sandusky HS; Upper Sandusky, OH; 51/190 Chrs; Hon Rl; Stg Crw; Y-Teens; Yrbk; 4-H; Spn Clb; Letter Ten; Trk; Letter Mgrs; Univ.

KOEHM, LISA; Garrett HS; Garrett, IN; Cmp Fr Grls; Hon Rl; Ger Clb; Pep Clb; Spn Clb; Letter Bsktbl; Letter Trk; Coll; Phys Ed.

KOELER, ROBERT; Eastern HS; Russellville, OH; 3/92 Cls Rep Frsh Cls; Cls Rep Soph Cls; Cl Rep Jr Cls; Hst Sr Cls; Band; Hon Rl; Pres NHS; Stu Cncl; Fr Clb; Letter Bsbl; Cincinnati Tech Coll; Engr.

KOELSCH, JACKIE; Evergreen HS; Metamora, OH; Cls Rep Soph Cls; Cls Rep Sr Cls; Hon Rl; Sch Pl; Stu Cncl; Drama Clb; 4-H; Fr Clb; Chrldng; GAA; College; Public Relations.

KOELSCH, JACQUELINE; Evergreen HS; Metamora, OH; Cls Rep Soph Cls; Cls Rep Sr Cls; Hon Rl; Sch Pl; Stu Cncl; Drama Clb; Fr Clb; Chrldng; GAA; Am Leg Awd; Toledo Univ; Cmnctns.

KOELSCH, JAMES; South HS; Willoughby, OH; 47/416 Boy Scts; Jr NHS; NHS; Sct Actv; Cleveland State Univ; Math.

KOELZER, KATHLEEN; Aquinas HS; Canton, MI; Chrs; Chrh Wkr; Girl Scts; Hon Rl; Red Cr Ade; Pep Clb; Univ; Lib Arts.

KOELZER, THOMAS; West Catholic HS; Grand Rapids, MI; Band; Boy Scts; FCA; Hon Rl; Letter Swmmng; Letter Ten; IM Sprt; Tmr; Univ.

KOELZER, TIMOTHY; West Catholic HS; Grand Rapids, MI; Band; Boy Scts; FCA; Hon Rl; Jr NHS; NHS; Ftbl; Capt Swmmng; Ten; IM Sprt; Univ; Advertising.

KOENEMANN, CAROL; New Haven HS; New Haven, IN; Cls Rep Frsh Cls; Cls Rep Soph Cls; Band; Girl Scts; Hon Rl; Sch Pl; Stu Cncl; Drama Clb; Ger Clb; Sci Clb; College; Phys Ther.

KOENIG, CATHERINE; Elk Rapids HS; Williamsburg, MI; Girl Scts; Hon Rl; NHS; Spn Clb; Univ Of Missouri; Jrnlsm.

KOENIG, JAMES; Corunna HS; Corunna, MI; Trs Frsh Cls; Am Leg Boys St; Chrh Wkr; Hon Rl; Jr NHS; NHS; Bsktbl; Glf; Mgrs; Scr Kpr; Michigan St Univ; Med.

KOENIG, JAMES; St Charles Prep HS; Columbus, OH; 20/90 Boy Scts; Hon Rl; Jr NHS; NHS; Sct Actv; Stg Crw; Yrbk; Sch Nwsp; Spn Clb; Trk; Reserve Ltr In Soccer 77; Univ; Civil Engr.

KOENIG, L; Richmond HS; Richmond, IN; 90/650 Cls Rep Frsh Cls; Pres Soph Cls; Trs Jr Cls; Chrs; Debate Tm; Hon Rl; Yth Flsp; College; Acctg.

KOENIG, LORI; West Geauga HS; Chagrin Fls, OH; 18/354 Band; Chrs; Chrh Wkr; Hon Rl; Jr NHS; NHS; Orch; Stg Crw; PPFtbl; Scr Kpr; Case Western Reserve Univ; Vet Sci.

KOENIG, MATTHEW; Northville HS; Northville, MI; Band; Boy Scts; Chrh Wkr; Cmnty Wkr; Sch Mus; Stg Crw; Ger Clb; Michigan St Univ; Archt.

KOENIG, SCOTT; Lima Central Catholic HS; Lima, OH; 35/185 Pres Frsh Cls; Cls Rep Soph Cls; Cl Rep Jr Cls; Am Leg Boys St; Hon Rl; NHS; Lat Clb; Ftbl; Coach Actv; HS CYO Basketball; Univ.

KOENIG, SCOTT; Reading Cmnty HS; Reading, OH; Cls Rep Frsh Cls; Pres Soph Cls; Pres Jr Cls; Pres Sr Cls; Cmnty Wkr; Sch Pl; Stu Cncl; Letter Ftbl; Univ; Archt.

KOENIG, TERRI; Mineral Ridge HS; Niles, OH; 8/70 Trs Frsh Cls; Cls Rep Frsh Cls; Cls Rep Soph Cls; Cl Rep Jr Cls; Chrs; Hon Rl; JA; NHS; Sct Actv; Stu Cncl; Kent St Univ; Phys Ed.

KOENIG, TRACY; Wapakoneta Sr HS; Wapakoneta, OH; Chrs; Hon Rl; NHS; Sch Mus; Yth Flsp; Y-Teens; Rptr Yrbk; Rptr Sch Nwsp; Lat Clb; Univ; Comp Prog.

KOENIGSBERG, SUSAN; Northmont HS; Dayton, OH; Trs Frsh Cls; Trs Soph Cls; Hon Rl; Orch; Sec Stu Cncl; Rptr Sch Nwsp; Natl Merit SF; Wellesley College; Med.

KOEPELE, DEBBIE; Chelsea HS; Chelsea, MI; 15/200 Band; Debate Tm; Hon Rl; NHS; Orch; Sch Mus; Voice Dem Awd; MSU.

KOEPELE, JOHN C; Chelsea HS; Chelsea, MI; 3/200 Am Leg Boys St; Debate Tm; Hon Rl; NHS; Rptr Yrbk; Mich State Univ; Comp Sci.

KOEPFER, ALANA; Maumee HS; Maumee, OH; Orch; Fr Clb; Bowling Green St Univ; Engr.

KOERNER, COLLEEN; Southmont HS; Crawfordsville, IN; Band; Cmp Fr Grls; Chrh Wkr; Hon Rl; JA; Jr NHS; Off Ade; Sch Mus; Sch Pl; Stg Crw; Bus Schl; Acctg.

KOESTER, ANNE; Ottoville HS; Ottoville, OH; Hon Rl; Lbry Ade; Sch Mus; Stg Crw; Rptr Yrbk; Rptr Sch Nwsp; 4-H; Scr Kpr; Tmr; 4-H Awd; Bowling Green St Univ; Sec Ed.

KOESTER, BETTY; North Posey HS; Wadesville, IN; 3/162 Trs Sr Cls; Hon Rl; NHS; Off Ade; VP OEA; GAA; IM Sprt; College.

KOESTERS, DENISE; Coldwater HS; Coldwater, OH; 5/140 Chrs; Girl Scts; Hon Rl; Hosp Ade; Lbry Ade; Sch Mus; Stg Crw; Drama Clb; FTA; Pep Clb;.

KOEWLER, JAMES L; F J Reitz HS; Evansville, IN; 16/500 Band; Capt Debate Tm; Hon Rl; Jr NHS; VP Natl Forn Lg; NHS; Sch Pl; Ger Clb; Natl Merit SF; Opt Clb Awd; Participant In High Schl Science Student Inst At I U; College; Medicine.

KOHANSKI, KAREN; Medina HS; Medina, OH; 17/348 Am Leg Aux Girls St; Band; Chrs; Hon Rl; Hosp Ade; NHS; Orch; Sch Mus; PPFtbl; Bowling Green Univ; Bus.

KOHARKO, DAN; Bishop Noll Inst; Munster, IN; 54/321 Hon Rl; Letter Ftbl; Glf; Trk; Wrstlng; College; Aeronautical Engr.

KOHL, DEBBIE; Perrysburg HS; Perrysburg, OH; Trs Jr Cls; Girl Scts; Hon Rl; NHS; Stu Cncl; Yrbk; Sch Nwsp; Pep Clb; Spn Clb; Swmmng; Coll.

KOHL, KAREN; Grandville HS; Grand Rapids, MI; Hon Rl; Lbry Ade; Rptr Sch Nwsp; Sch Nwsp; Swmmng; Grand Rapids Jr Coll; Archt.

KOHL, SCOTT; Cambridge HS; Cambridge, OH; Hon Rl; NHS; 4-H; 4-H Awd; Drafting.

KOHLER, MICHAEL; Padua Franciscan HS; Parma, OH; 30/253 Cls Rep Frsh Cls; Hon Rl; NHS; Stu Cncl; Coach Actv; IM Sprt; Kent State Univ; Architecture.

KOHLER, SUZANNE; New Philadelphia HS; Nw Philadelphia, OH; Am Leg Aux Girls St; Chrs; Chrh Wkr; Hon Rl; JA; Pol Wkr; Yth Flsp; Pep Clb; Bsktbl; Trk;.

KOHLMEIER, JACKIE; Fairless HS; Navarre, OH; Off Ade; Pol Wkr; Stu Cncl; Y-Teens; FHA; Pep Clb; Letter Chrldng; GAA; Stark Tech; Computer Prog.

KOHLMEYER, LINDA; Broad Ripple HS; Indianapolis, IN; Mdrgl; Orch; Sch Mus; Fr Clb; Key Clb; Bsktbl; Glf; Trk; IM Sprt; Kiwan Awd; Indiana Univ; Dent.

KOHLS, MARTHA; Ft Jennings HS; Ft Jennings, OH; Trs Jr Cls; Band; Chrs; Hon Rl; Sch Mus; Sch

Pl; Yrbk; 4-H; Fr Clb; Chrldng; Bowling Green St Univ; Speech Path.

KOHLS, SHARON; St Ursula Academy; Cincinnati, OH; Girl Scts; Hon Rl; Spn Clb; Bsbl; Chrldng; IM Sprt; Right To Life Club 78; Univ.

KOHN, DAVID; Calumet HS; Calumet, MI; Chrs; ROTC; Ftbl; Superior Cadet Awd JROTC 78 & 79; Cadet Of Yr & Cadet Of Month 79; Michigan Tech Univ.

KOHN, PHILLIP; Grosse Ile HS; Grosse Ile, MI; Band; Hon Rl; Sch Mus; Sch Pl; Letter Crs Cntry; Letter Trk; College; Elec.

KOHRING, LOU A; Eastwood HS; Pemberville, OH; Band; Chrh Wkr; Girl Scts; Hon Rl; NHS; Sch Mus; Sch Pl; Stg Crw; Yrbk; VP 4-H; Ohio State Univ; Nursing.

KOHSEL, DEBORAH; Fennville HS; Fennville, MI; Cls Rep Frsh Cls; Trs Jr Cls; Band; Chrh Wkr; Hon Rl; Hosp Ade; NHS; Sch Pl; Stu Cncl; Rptr Sch Nwsp; Central Michigan Univ; Recreation.

KOHUTH, PEGGY; Holy Name HS; Parma, OH; Cmp Fr Grls; Chrs; Hon Rl; Hosp Ade; Stg Crw; Pep Clb; Univ.

KOIS, BARBARA; Lake Catholic HS; Mentor, OH; 13/330 Cl Rep Jr Cls; Hon Rl; NHS; Off Ade; Sch Mus; Stu Cncl; Chrldng; College; Med.

KOJAC, DIANA; Morgantown HS; Westover, WV; Chrs; Chrh Wkr; Hon Rl; Sch Mus; Sch Pl; Stg Crw; Pres Yth Flsp; Drama Clb; Ger Clb; Mrs Yedloskys Awd 76; History Awd Medal 77; Eng Awd Medal 77; West Virginia Univ; Acctg.

KOKALARI, SUSAN; Edwin Denby HS; Detroit, MI; 1/350 Val; Hon Rl; Jr NHS; Lbry Ade; NHS; Wayne St Univ; Chem.

KOKALY, CRAIG; Bay City All Sts Central HS; Bay City, MI; Hon Rl; Boys Clb Am; Eng Clb; Spn Clb; Ftbl; Letter Trk; IM Sprt; Cit Awd; Central Mic.

KOKENGE, DAWN J; Valley View HS; Farmersville, OH; Chrh Wkr; Cmnty Wkr; Capt Drl Tm; Hon Rl; NHS; Off Ade; Pres 4-H; 4-H Awd; All American HS Drill Tm Mbr 78; Best Cpt Of Tipp City Best Cpt Of Beavercreek; Drill Tm Comp; Best Cpt In;.

KOKER, KIMBERLY; Revere HS; Las Vegas, NV; 51/205 Chrs; Chrh Wkr; Hon Rl; Off Ade; Sch Mus; Music Team For Rex Humbard World Wide Ministries; Univ Of Nevada.

KOKOS, DENNIS; Lake Catholic HS; Mentor, OH; Boy Scts; Chrs; JA; Mth Clb; Sci Clb; Spn Clb; Bsbl; C of C Awd; JA Awd; Opt Clb Awd; College; Bus.

KOLAR, MARY; Ursuline HS; Austintown, OH; 144/350 Chrs; Girl Scts; Hon Rl; Off Ade; Sct Actv; FTA; Pres Pep Clb; Youngstown St Univ; Creative Writing.

KOLAR, RANDY; Henry Ford HS; Sterling Hts, MI; Hon Rl; Pol Wkr; Mich State Univ; Cpa.

KOLARIK, MATTHEW; Hoover HS; N Canton, OH; Boy Scts; Chrs; Chrh Wkr; Sct Actv; Univ Of Akron; Elec Engr.

KOLARIK, SHARON; Northport HS; Northport, MI; 7/26 Trs Frsh Cls; Cls Rep Sr Cls; Band; Chrs; Chrh Wkr; Hon Rl; NHS; Rptr Yrbk; Northwestern Michigan Coll.

KOLASA, ANN; Williamston HS; Williamston, MI; Pres Frsh Cls; Trs Soph Cls; Sec Sr Cls; AFS; Am Leg Aux Girls St; Band; Chrh Wkr; Cmnty Wkr; Debate Tm; Hon Rl; Michigan St Univ; Humanities.

KOLASA, MARY; Williamston HS; Williamston, MI; AFS; Band; Cmp Fr Grls; Chrh Wkr; Debate Tm; Hon Rl; Jr NHS; Stu Cncl; Yrbk; 4-H; Student Rep To Board Of Ed; Ski Club; College; Nursing.

KOLASKI, JUIANA T; Cheboygan Area HS; Cheboygan, MI; Band; Hon Rl; Orch; Sch Pl; Bsktbl; Mercy Coll; Dietetics.

KOLASKI, JULIANA; Cheboygan Area HS; Cheboygan, MI; 21/190 Band; Hon Rl; Orch; Sch Pl; Letter Bsktbl; Mercy College; Dietetics.

KOLB, BEVERLY; Brookville HS; Brookville, IN; 28/208 Chrs; Girl Scts; Hon Rl; NHS; Sch Nwsp; 4-H; Ger Clb; 4-H Awd; Natl Merit Schl; German Club Schlrshp 79; Art Club Treas 79; Manchester Coll; Pre Law.

KOLB, CARRIE; Castle HS; Chandler, IN; 7/388 Band; JA; NHS; Sci Clb; Natl Merit Ltr; Purdue Univ; Engr.

KOLB, LISA; Inland Lakes HS; Indian River, MI; 6/80 Pres Frsh Cls; Trs Soph Cls; Pres Jr Cls; Hon Rl; Stu Cncl; Chrldng; N W Michigan Coll; Psych.

KOLB, REBECCA; Central HS; Essexville, MI; 72/464 Band; Girl Scts; Hon Rl; Eng Clb; Cit Awd; College; Physical Ther.

KOLB, ROBIN; Union County HS; Liberty, IN; 41/135 Lbry Ade; College; Elem Educ.

KOLBERG, TOM; Coshocton HS; Coshocton, OH; Debate Tm; Red Cr Ade; Rptr Yrbk; Key Clb; Sci Clb; Spn Clb; Bsktbl; Swmmng; Ten; Chrldng; Hocking Tech Coll; Forestry.

KOLBUS, JEFFRY; Bishop Noll Institute; Hammond, IN; 28/337 Hon Rl; Jr NHS; NHS; VP Stu Cncl; Yth Flsp; Mth Clb; Letter Bsbl; Univ Of Notre Dame; Pre Dentistry.

KOLBUS, TAMMY; William G Mather HS; Munising, MI; 20/103 Cls Rep Frsh Cls; Girl Scts; Hon Rl; Stg Crw; Stu Cncl; Northern Michigan Univ; Vet Med.

KOLEAN, TIMOTHY; West Ottawa HS; Holland, MI; Boy Scts; Bsktbl; Crs Cntry; IM Sprt; Muskegon Busns Coll; Acctg.

KOLENIC, STACEY; Nordonia HS; Northfield, OH; Chrh Wkr; Sch Pl; Drama Clb; Pep Clb; PPFtbl; Scr Kpr; Univ; Interior Dsgn.

KOLESAR, EDWARD; Strongsville Sr HS; Strongsville, OH; Cls Rep Frsh Cls; Cls Rep Soph Cls; Pres Jr Cls; Cls Rep Sr Cls; Band; Cmnty Wkr; Jr NHS; NHS; Sch Mus; Stg Crw; Univ.

KOLETTIS, GEORGE J; Andrean HS; Merrillville, IN; Chrh Wkr; Hon Rl; Stu Cncl; Rptr Yrbk; Fr Clb; Mth Clb; Sci Clb; Capt Ten; Opt Clb Awd; Univ; Med.

KOLETTIS, GEORGIA; Andrean HS; Merrillville, IN; Cls Rep Sr Cls; Chrh Wkr; Cmnty Wkr; Hon Rl; Sch Pl; Stu Cncl; Drama Clb; Fr Clb; Mth Clb; Pep Clb; Hoosier Scholar 79; Northwestern Univ.

KOLIS, JEANNETTE; Lumen Cordium HS; Walton Hills, OH; Chrh Wkr; Hon Rl; Capt Stu Cncl; Yrbk; College; Art, Psychology, Or Med.

KOLISER, DARLA; Austintown Fitch HS; Austintown, OH; 59/655 Cls Rep Frsh Cls; Cl Rep Jr Cls; Hon Rl; NHS; Red Cr Ade; Treas Lat Clb; Letter Ten; Letter Trk; PPFtbl; Plaq Semi Fnlst Miss Teen Ohio Bty Cont 78; 2nd Pl Athlete 5 Mile Race 79; Amer Red Cross Volunteer 79; Youngstown St Univ; Med.

KOLISER, DARRA; Austintown Fitch HS; Youngstown, OH; 29/655 Hon Rl; Jr NHS; Red Cr Ade; Ten; Trk; PPFtbl; Youngstown State Univ; Med.

KOLLAR, KIMBERLY; W Branch HS; Salem, OH; 3/268 VP Frsh Cls; Trs Soph Cls; Pres Jr Cls; Am Leg Aux Girls St; Chrs; Hon Rl; Pres NHS; Sch Mus; Ed Yrbk; Mat Maids; Youngstown St Univ; Spec Ed.

KOLLASCH, KRISTEN; Lake Orion Cmnty HS; Lake Orion, MI; Cls Rep Frsh Cls; Sec Soph Cls; Hon Rl; Jr NHS; Stu Cncl; Rptr Yrbk; Rptr Sch Nwsp; Capt Chrldng; Opt Clb Awd; Highest G P A Natl Jr Honor Soc 1977; Univ; Med.

KOLLATH, DONNA J; Rocky River HS; Rocky River, OH; Chrh Wkr; Hon Rl; Hosp Ade; VP Yth Flsp; Chmn Gym; College.

KOLLENBERG, JUDITH; Southfield Lathrup Sr HS; Southfield, MI; Girl Scts; Hon Rl; Hosp Ade; Off Ade; Red Cr Ade; Ger Clb; Spn Clb; Lion Awd; Grant To Kalamazoo Coll 79; Stdnt In Hist Of HS To Take 3 Foreign Lang 79; Mi St High Sclstc Grant 79; Georgetown Univ; Spanish.

KOLLHOFF, SUSAN; Traverse City Sr HS; Traverse, MI; 106/800 Band; Pep Clb; Swmmng; Northwestern Michigan Coll; Dent Hyg.

KOLLING, TINA; Mother Of Mercy HS; Cincinnati, OH; Hon Rl; Fr Clb; Capt Ten; Miami Univ; Med Tech.

KOLLOUS, CHRISTINE; Bishop Noll Institute; Hammond, IN; 28/321 Girl Scts; Hon Rl; Off Ade; Sch Mus; Sct Actv; Mth Clb; Letter Swmmng; Pom Pon; Notre Dame Univ; Business.

KOLMETZ, JANE E; Center Line HS; Warren, MI; Band; Sec Chrh Wkr; Hon Rl; Jr NHS; Stu Cncl; Sec Yth Flsp; Sec Fr Clb; Sci Clb; Ltr Var Vllybl 78; Univ Of Michigan.

KOLNITYS, THEODORE M; Harry S Truman HS; Taylor, MI; Band; Hon Rl; Letter Crs Cntry; Univ Of Michigan; Mech Engr.

KOLODZIEJ, KENNETH B; O P Morton Sr HS; Hammond, IN; 31/436 Boy Scts; Chrh Wkr; Hon Rl; NHS; Sct Actv; Sch Nwsp; Fr Clb; Sci Clb; Letter Ftbl; Letter Socr; Indiana Univ; Accounting.

KOLOMIZEW, WLADIMIR; Brooklyn HS; Brooklyn, OH; NHS; Rptr Yrbk; Letter Hockey; Coach Actv; Scr Kpr; Tmr; College; Psych.

KOLONICH, LINDA; Aquinas HS; Southgate, MI; NHS; Rptr Yrbk; Univ; Pre Med.

KOLONICH, LINDA M; Aquinas HS; Southgate, MI; Hosp Ade; NHS; Rptr Sch Nwsp; Bsktbl; Univ Of Michigan; Sci.

KOLOPUS, ANN; Central Catholic HS; N Canton, OH; Chrs; Hon Rl; JA; Rptr Yrbk; Spn Clb; IM Sprt; Pres Awd; Hosp Nursing Schl.

KOLOSIONEK, MARK; James Ford Rhodes HS; Cleveland, OH; Cl Rep Jr Cls; Cls Rep Sr Cls; Hon Rl; Jr NHS; NHS; Fr Clb; Mth Clb; Bsktbl; Cit Awd; Case Western Reserve Univ; Dentistry.

KOLOSIUK, ANDREW; Charles Stewart Mott HS; Warren, MI; Hon Rl; NHS; College; Eng.

KOLPACKE, STEPHEN; Henry Ford Ii HS; Sterling Hts, MI; 31/424 NHS; VICA; Bsbl; Ftbl; Mich Tech; Mech Engr.

KOLSCHEFSKE, WENDY; Shelby HS; Shelby, MT; Pres Jr Cls; Hon Rl; NHS; Ed Sch Nwsp; Pep Clb; Trk; College.

KOLTHOFF, KIMBERLEY; Whiteland Community HS; Franklin, IN; 72/226 Band; Cmp Fr Grls; Chrs; JA; Stu Cncl; FHA; Pep Clb; Sci Clb; IM Sprt; Univ; Nursing.

KOLTUNSKI, PATRICIA; Notre Dame Academy; Toledo, OH; Cls Rep Frsh Cls; Sec Soph Cls; Trs Jr Cls; Pres Sr Cls; NHS; Stu Cncl; Univ; Med Tech.

KOLTYK, GREGORY; Adlai Stevenson HS; Livonia, MI; Band; Hon Rl; Orch; Univ; Music.

KOLTZ, DENNIS; St Peter & Paul Seminary; Pittsburgh, PA; 4/11 Boy Scts; Stg Crw; Yrbk; Letter Socr; Univ Of Detroit; Philosophy.

KOMAN, STEVE; Lincoln Park HS; Lincoln Park, MI; 144/553 Cls Rep Sr Cls; Am Leg Boys St; Boy Scts; Ftbl; Trk; Mgrs; All Area All League Letter Winner; All League All Area H M All Suburban; Most Valuabel Player H M All Metro; Univ Of Toledo; Law Enforcement.

KOMIS, AMY J; Jackson HS; Jackson, MI; 23/326 Hon Rl; NHS; Jackson Cmnty Coll.

KOMISARCIK, ED; Andrean HS; Merrillvle, IN; 15/251 Cls Rep Frsh Cls; Cls Rep Soph Cls; Chrh Wkr; Hon Rl; Stu Cncl; IM Sprt; Top Ten Schlrshp Awd 76; Photog Club; Purdue Univ; Comp Sci.

KOMMERS, CYNTHIA; St Joseph HS; South Bend, IN; 8/263 Hon Rl; Fr Clb; Gym; Univ; Dance.

KOMON, MELANIE; Evergreen HS; Metamora, OH; Chrs; Hon Rl; Lit Mag; Spn Clb; GAA; College; Acctg.

KOMPANIK, JILL; Mineral Ridge HS; Mcdonald, OH; 5/74 Trs Frsh Cls; Chrs; Hon Rl; Jr NHS; NHS; Yrbk; Beta Clb; Pep Clb; Letter Bsktbl; Trk; Bowling Green St Univ; Educ.

KONAL, CHRISTOPHER; Notre Dame HS; East Detroit, MI; Cls Rep Soph Cls; Cl Rep Jr Cls; Hon Rl; NHS; Pol Wkr; Rptr Sch Nwsp; Eng Clb; Letter Ftbl; Letter Gym; Letter Trk; Univ Of Detroit; Journalism.

KONCHEL, JAMES; Bishop Borgess HS; Dearborn Hts, MI; 83/475 Chrh Wkr; Hon Rl; NHS; Quill & Scroll; Ed Yrbk; Natl Merit SF; Univ Mich At Dearborn; Bus Admin.

KONCHESKY, MICHAEL; University HS; Morgantown, WV; 5/146 Aud/Vis; Band; Boy Scts; Hon Rl; Pres Jr NHS; Pres Lbry Ade; NHS; Sch Mus; Sct Actv; Stg Crw; Eagle Scout Awrd 1976; Outstndng 9th Grd Awrd 1977; Outstndng Bio I Stndnt Awrd 1978; West Virginia Univ; Elec Engr.

KONCZAL, JOSEPH C; Oxford Area Cmnty HS; Oxford, MI; 7/214 Band; Boy Scts; Hon Rl; Natl Merit Ltr; Rotary Awd; St Of Mi Comptn Schlrshp 79; Oxford HS Soc Studies Awd 79; Mst Imprvd Plyr Awd Varsity Band 78; Michigan St Univ; Chem.

KONDIK, DALE; Lake Catholic HS; Mentor, OH; Cls Rep Frsh Cls; Pres Soph Cls; Cl Rep Jr Cls; Cls Rep Sr Cls; Hon Rl; Rptr Yrbk; Rptr Sch Nwsp; Letter Ftbl; Letter Trk; IM Sprt; Christian Life 1977; I Dare You 1979; Univ; Sci.

KONDIK, NORMA; Bedford HS; Bedford Hts, OH; Hon Rl; Letter Bsbl; Letter Bsktbl; GAA; Zonta Awd 1979; FOE Outstndng Basketbl Plyr Awd 1979; COE Outstndng Achvmnt Awd 1979; Univ; Advrtsng Spec Counslr.

KONEY, THOMAS; Troy HS; Troy, MI; 7/300 Am Leg Boys St; Band; Boy Scts; Hon Rl; NHS; Ed Sch Nwsp; Crs Cntry; Trk; Natl Merit Ltr; College.

KONIECZNY, SHEILA; Catholic Central HS; Grand Rapids, MI; Chrh Wkr; Hon Rl; Sch Mus; Stg Crw; Yth Flsp; Drama Clb; Spn Clb; VICA; Ten; Aquinas Coll; Business.

KONKLER, VICKY; Sheridan HS; Somerset, OH; Band; Chrh Wkr; Girl Scts; Hon Rl; JA; Jr NHS; NHS; Sct Actv; Sec OEA; Sci Clb; Bus Schl; Legal Sec.

KONKOL, JEANNE; Washington HS; South Bend, IN; 4/355 Hon Rl; JA; NHS; Orch; Sch Mus; Stu Cncl; Lat Clb; Youth Consrvtn Corps Best Worker Awd 78; Jr Waltons Treas 78; Univ; Envrnl Studies.

KONNO, KATHRYN; Marian HS; Blmfld Hls, MI; Hon Rl; Fr Clb; Natl Merit Ltr; College; Acctg.

KONOVSKY, KELLI; Kankakee Valley HS; De Motte, IN; Band; Girl Scts; Hon Rl; Sct Actv; Yth Flsp; Yrbk; OEA; PPFtbl; Intl Bus Coll; Legal Sec.

KONOWITZ, STANELY; New Buffalo Area School; New Buffalo, MI; Boy Scts; Chrs; Hon Rl; Natl Forn Lg; Sch Mus; Sch Pl; Sct Actv; Stg Crw; Yrbk; Drama Clb; Thespian Troupe #532 4 Star Mbr 79; Thespian Troupe #532 Sec For 2 Terms 78; 3rd Pl In Cnty Frnscs Compet; Northwestern Univ; Costume Dsgn.

KONTIO, JAMES; Negaunee HS; Negaunee, MI; Am Leg Boys St; Band; Chrh Wkr; Debate Tm; Natl Forn Lg; NHS; Yth Flsp; Adrian College; Med Progr.

KONTONICKAS, CINDY; Western Hills HS; Cincinnati, OH; 386/866 Cls Rep Frsh Cls; Cls Rep Soph Cls; Cl Rep Jr Cls; Cls Rep Sr Cls; Chrldng; Ohio St Univ.

KONTONICKAS, LISA; Yellow Springs HS; Yellow Springs, OH; 21/71 Band; Chrs; Orch; Sch Mus; Yrbk; Letter Crs Cntry; Trk; Ohi Univ; Graphic Design.

KONTUR, JEANNE; Lumen Cordium HS; Bedford, OH; 12/92 Cls Rep Soph Cls; Pres Jr Cls; Chrs; Drl Tm; Hon Rl; Jr NHS; Lit Mag; NHS; Off Ade; Stu Cncl; Kent St Univ; Med.

KONWINSKI, LINDA; Catholic Ctrl HS; Wyoming, MI; 10/250 Hon Rl; Lbry Ade; Off Ade; Natl Merit Ltr; Aquinas Coll; Bio.

KOOI, DOUGLAS; Albion HS; Albion, MI; Debate Tm; Hon Rl; Ftbl; Trk; Rotary Awd; Eastern Mic Univ; Bus Admin.

KOOISTRA, KIMBERLY; Calvin Christian HS; Wyoming, MI; 3/160 Band; Hon Rl; Sch Pl; Letter Trk; Natl Merit SF; Univ; Bio.

KOOKER, MARTIN; Bluffton HS; Bluffton, OH; Pres Soph Cls; Cl Rep Jr Cls; Cls Rep Sr Cls; Aud/Vis; Band; Boy Scts; Chrs; Drm Mjrt; Sch Mus; Sch Pl; Ohio St Univ; Phys Ed.

KOOL, ERIC; Cedarville HS; Cedarville, OH; 1/63 Band; Hon Rl; VP NHS; Fr Clb; Capt Crs Cntry; Letter Trk; Natl Merit Ltr; Miami Univ; Science.

KOOLSTRA, GORDON; Mc Bain Rural Agri HS; Lake City, MI; Cls Rep Sr Cls; Chrs; Hon Rl; Stu Cncl; Yth Flsp; Rptr Sch Nwsp; 4-H; 4-H Awd; Ferris St Coll; Law Enfrcmnt Officer.

KOONCE, MELODY; Shadyside HS; Jacobsburg, OH; Band; Chrs; Hon Rl; Y-Teens; Spn Clb; GAA; Voc Schl; Sec.

KOONS, JEFF; North Canton Hoover HS; No Canton, OH; Chrs; Chrh Wkr; Cmnty Wkr; Hon Rl; Sch Pl; Y-Teens; Beta Clb; Letter Bsbl; Bsktbl; Liberty Baptist Coll; Bus Admin.

KOONTZ, CYNDI; Norwalk HS; Norwalk, OH; Sec Soph Cls; Cl Rep Jr Cls; Cls Rep Sr Cls; Drl Tm; Hon Rl; NHS; Treas Stu Cncl; Fr Clb; Pep Clb; Letter Ten; Ohio St Univ; Elem Ed.

KOONTZ, DAVID; Marian HS; Clearwater, FL; Hon Rl; Pol Wkr; Socr; IM Sprt; Hnrbl Mention In Bus Law 78; Outstndg In Earth Sci Awd 79; Tampa Coll; Bus Admin.

KOONTZ, DOUGLAS A; Warsaw Community HS; Warsaw, IN; 26/370 Band; Chrh Wkr; Hon Rl; Sch Mus; Eng Clb; Grace College; History.

KOONTZ, GARY; Tyler County HS; New Martinsvle, WV; 6/115 Trs Jr Cls; Hon Rl; VP JA; NHS; Sch Pl; Stu Cncl; FFA; Apprenticeship; Carpenter.

KOONTZ, GARY K; Tyler County HS; New Martinsvile, WV; 4/105 Trs Jr Cls; VP JA; NHS; Stu Cncl; FFA; Letter Ftbl; Letter Trk; IM Sprt; Carpentry.

KOONTZ, MARIANNE; Chaminade Julienne HS; Dayton, OH; Chrs; Hosp Ade; JA; Miami Valley Schl Of Nursing; RN.

KOOPMAN, ANTON; Floyd Ctrl HS; Floyds Knobs, IN; 7/359 Hon Rl; Natl Merit Ltr; Purdue Univ; Mech Engr.

KOOPMAN, MARGARET; Floyd Central HS; Floyds Knobs, IN; 30/352 Chrs; Hon Rl; NHS; PAVAS; Crs Cntry; Letter Trk; Scr Kpr; Tmr; Kiwan Awd; St Joseph Coll; Phys Ed.

KOOPS, PAULA; Holland Christian HS; Holland, MI; Chrh Wkr; Cmnty Wkr; Ger Clb; Gym; IM Sprt; Hope Coll; Elem Educ.

KOORS, CATHY; Bennett HS; Marion, IN; 2/30 Pres Frsh Cls; Pres Jr Cls; Hon Rl; NHS; Sch Pl; Stu Cncl; Drama Clb; Fr Clb; Pep Clb; Ten; Ball State Univ; Speech.

KOORS, JANNICE; Mc Auley HS; Harrison, OH; 8/280 Chrs; Chrh Wkr; Hon Rl; NHS; Sch Mus; Sch Pl; Stu Cncl; College; Bus.

KOORS, MARY; Bennett HS; Marion, IN; 2/25 Pres Frsh Cls; Pres Jr Cls; Am Leg Aux Girls St; Hon Rl; NHS; Stu Cncl; Fr Clb; Ten;.

KOOWTZ, CHARLES; Harbor Springs HS; Hoarbor Spgs, MI; Am Leg Boys St; Hon Rl; Letter Bsktbl; Letter Glf; Letter Trk; Univ.

KOPACZ, ROBERT; Kearsley HS; Davison, MI; 33/400 Hon Rl; Letter Bsbl; Letter Glf; Letter Hockey; Univ Of Michigan; Bus Admin.

KOPANEK, SHARON; Buena Vista HS; Saginaw, MI; Band; Chrh Wkr; Hon Rl; Sch Nwsp; 4-H; Sci Clb; Saginaw Valley State College; Bio.

KOPANKO, KATHY; Webster Cnty HS; Cleveland, WV; Band; Chrh Wkr; Hon Rl; NHS; 4-H; Pep Clb; Chrldng; 4-H Awd; WVU; Aviation.

KOPAS, CAROL; Berkley HS; Berkley, MI; 6/410 Band; Chrs; Chrh Wkr; Debate Tm; Jr NHS; Natl Forn Lg; NHS; Off Ade; Orch; Kalamazoo Coll; Lib Arts.

KOPCHAK, DENA M; Port Clinton HS; Port Clinton, OH; 14/289 Girl Scts; Hon Rl; Hosp Ade; 4-H; Ger Clb; 4-H Awd; Superior Ratings Local Dist & State Sci Fair; Stu Of The Month; Ohio State Univ; Medicine.

KOPCO, JAMES; Benedictine HS; Cleveland, OH; 2/100 Band; Hon Rl; NHS; Orch; Sch Mus; Drama Clb; Ger Clb; Bausch & Lomb Awd; Kiwan Awd; Case Inst Of Tech; Aerospace Engr.

KOPEA, DAWN; Nordonia HS; Northfield, OH; Cl Rep Jr Cls; Chrh Wkr; Hosp Ade; NHS; Stu Cncl; Drama Clb; Pep Clb; Letter Chrldng; Brecksville Voc Schl; Office Systems.

KOPERA, KAREN; East Detroit HS; East Detroit, MI; Hon Rl; Trk; Wayne State Univ; Psych.

KOPF, PAUL; Saint Johns HS; Toledo, OH; Band; Sch Nwsp; 2nd Honors For GPA; College; Psychology.

KOPF, RONALD; Forest Park HS; Crystal Falls, MI; Hon Rl; Lbry Ade; Letter Ftbl; Trk; IM Sprt; St Of Mi Schlrshp 79; Northern Michigan Univ; Water Sci.

KOPINSKY, GREG; Campbell Memorial HS; Campbell, OH; Chrh Wkr; Hon Rl; Stg Crw; Mth Clb; Bsktbl; Natl Merit Ltr; College; Carpenter.

KOPNICK, ANN; A D Johnston HS; Bessemer, MI; 2/81 Sal; Hon Rl; Letter Ten; IM Sprt; Michigan Tech Univ; Bio.

KOPNISKY, MARGARET; Woodrow Wilson HS; Youngstown, OH; Sec Band; Hon Rl; JA; Y-Teens; Treas Fr Clb; Key Clb; Lat Clb; Sci Clb; Twrlr; Bus Schl.

KOPP, DANIEL; Anderson HS; Anderson, IN; Hon Rl; Lit Mag; NHS; Treas Quill & Scroll; Lat Clb; Natl Merit Ltr;.

KOPP, NANCY A; Springfield HS; Holland, OH; Cls Rep Soph Cls; Cl Rep Jr Cls; Cls Rep Sr Cls; NHS; Stu Cncl; Drama Clb; Spn Clb; Letter Chrldng; Air National Guard.

KOPPENHOFER, LAURA; Oregon Davis HS; Grovertown, IN; 9/67 VP Sr Cls; Sec FCA; NHS; Sch Pl; Rptr Sch Nwsp; Drama Clb; Pres FHA; Mth Clb; Pres Pep Clb; Sci Clb; J V Vlybl; Homecoming Ct; Tres Varsity Club; De Pauw Univ; Elem Ed.

KOPPENHOFER, LORI A; Swan Valley HS; Saginaw, MI; 21/200 Drl Tm; Trk; Pom Pon; Michigan St Univ; Law.

KOPPES, K C; Wadsworth HS; Wadsworth, OH; 52/349 Letter Band; Chrs; Cmnty Wkr; Pres Natl Forn Lg; NHS; Off Ade; Sch Pl; Drama Clb; Pres 4-H; Spn Clb; 4 H Horse Prjct Achvmtn Medl For Outstndng Contrbtn 77 & 78; 4 H Achmvt Medl For Outstndng Contrvnt 78; Univ.

KOPRONICA, DONNA; Amherst Marion L Steele HS; Amherst, OH; Stu Cncl; Rptr Sch Nwsp; Fr Clb; Pep Clb; Trk; Chrldng; IM Sprt; PPFtbl; Scr Kpr; Bus Schl; Acctg.

KORCHYK, JEROME; Northrop HS; Ft Wayne, IN; 210/550 Aud/Vis; VP JA; Indiana Univ; Systems Analyst.

KOREN, GREGORY J; Rutherford B Hayes HS; Delawre, OH; Boy Scts; Chrh Wkr; Cmnty Wkr; Sch

Pl; Sct Actv; Stg Crw; Eng Clb; Key Clb; IM Sprt; Univ; Theatre.

KOREN, KATHLEEN; Struthers HS; Struthers, OH; 16/262 Am Leg Aux Girls St; Lbry Ade; Y-Teens; Drama Clb; Lat Clb; Glf; Youngstown State Univ.

KORMOS, GEORGENE; Euclid HS; Euclid, OH; Chrs; Hon Rl; Sch Mus; College; Psych.

KORNAK, JODI; Lumen Christi HS; Jackson, MI; 13/236 Sec Sr Cls; Hon Rl; NHS; Pep Clb; IM Sprt; Algebra 1 Medal 77; Spanish 3 Medl 79; Spanish 1 Cert 77; Chem Cert 79; Theology Cert 79; Univ; Med.

KORNEGAY, SIGHLE; Blanchester HS; Fayetteville, OH; 2/164 Hon Rl; NHS; Sch Pl; Stu Cncl; Ed Yrbk; Yrbk; Drama Clb; Fr Clb; Spn Clb; Univ.

KORNICK, JEFF; Padua Franciscan HS; Strongsville, OH; Cls Rep Frsh Cls; Hon Rl; Jr NHS; Yrbk; Sci Clb; Socr; IM Sprt; St Louis Univ; Sci.

KORNOWSKI, RONALD; Padua Franciscan HS; Brunswick, OH; Cls Rep Frsh Cls; Hon Rl; Lat Clb; Letter Ftbl; IM Sprt; 3 Consecutive Yrs Polish Falcon Athletic Assn Sr Track/field All Around Champion; College.

KORNS, STEPHEN; Eaton HS; Eaton, OH; 8/175 Boy Scts; Chrs; Hon Rl; Jr NHS; Sch Mus; Rptr Sch Nwsp; Letter Bsktbl; IM Sprt; Ohio St Univ; Aero Engr.

KORODAN, KATHERINE M; Memphis HS; Memphis, MI; Bsbl; College; Art.

KORONA, JOANNE; St Alphonsus HS; Detroit, MI; Rptr Yrbk; Henry Ford C College; Dental Tech.

KOROSEC, TIM; Solon HS; Lexington, KY; 15/300 Cls Rep Frsh Cls; Aud/Vis; Chrs; Hon Rl; Jr NHS; Lbry Ade; NHS; Off Ade; Sch Pl; Ten; Treas Natl Hnr Soc; Univ Of Kentucky; Busns.

KOROTKO, CHARLES; Bishop Foley HS; Warren, MI; Boy Scts; Chrh Wkr; Debate Tm; Hon Rl; Hosp Ade; NHS; Sch Mus; Sch Pl; Sct Actv; Stg Crw; Hon Awd In Latin 76 79; Hon Awd In Debate & Forensics 76; Acad Letter 76 79; Univ.

KORPI, DAVID; Negaunee HS; Negaunee, MI; Cls Rep Frsh Cls; Cls Rep Soph Cls; Cl Rep Jr Cls; Band; Hon Rl; Stu Cncl; Ten; Mgrs; Ferris State Univ; Optometry.

KORSON, JOZELL; St Mary HS; Lake Leelanau, MI; 1/14 VP Frsh Cls; Pres Soph Cls; Pres Sr Cls; Val; Chrs; Cmnty Wkr; Hon Rl; Sch Pl; Rptr Yrbk; Yrbk; Michigan St Univ; Communications.

KORSON, KAREN; St Marys HS; Suttons Bay, MI; Sec Sr Cls; Hon Rl; Lbry Ade; Off Ade; 4-H; 4-H Awd; Northwestern Mich Coll; Bus Mgmt.

KORTAS, FRAN; Theodore Roosevelt HS; Wyandotte, MI; Drl Tm; Drm Bgl; Hon Rl; Wayne Cnty Community; Nurse.

KORTE, VIRGINIA; Delphos St Johns HS; Delphos, OH; 16/139 Cl Rep Jr Cls; Cls Rep Sr Cls; Hon Rl; NHS; Sch Pl; Sch Nwsp; Pres FTA; Gym;.

KORTEPETER, SUZANNE; Franklin Cmnty HS; Franklin, IN; VP Jr Cls; FCA; Stu Cncl; Pep Clb; GAA; IM Sprt; PPFtbl; Scr Kpr; Marion Univ; Sci.

KORTGARDNER, KAREN; Oak Hills HS; Cincinnati, OH; 90/854 Pres AFS; Chrh Wkr; Hosp Ade; Lbry Ade; Red Cr Ade; Am Leg Awd; Xavier Univ; Nursing.

KORTHAUER, DANIEL; Hanover Central HS; Cedar Lake, IN; 31/147 Am Leg Boys St; Hon Rl; Pres Jr NHS; Letter Crs Cntry; Letter Trk; IM Sprt; Am Leg Awd; Cit Awd; Lion Awd; Valporaiso Univ; Acct.

KORTJOHN, KATHRYN; St Clement HS; Centerline, MI; Cls Rep Frsh Cls; Cls Rep Soph Cls; Hon Rl; NHS; Sch Pl; Stg Crw; Stu Cncl; Rptr Sch Nwsp; Drama Clb; Pep Clb; Central Mic Univ; Engl Major.

KORTZ, LAURA; Onekama Consolidated HS; Manistee, MI; Cls Rep Frsh Cls; Cl Rep Jr Cls; Cmp Fr Grls; Girl Scts; Hon Rl; Lbry Ade; Sch Pl; Stu Cncl; Ed Yrbk; Rptr Yrbk;.

KORTZ, TAMMIE; Vicksburg HS; Vicksburg, MI; 34/263 Hst Sr Cls; Band; Chrh Wkr; Hon Rl; NHS; Orch; Sch Mus; 4-H; Fr Clb; FTA; Michigan St Univ; Spec Educ.

KORYTKOWSKI, BARBARA; Bishop Borgess HS; Detroit, MI; Letter Debate Tm; Hon Rl; JA; Letter Natl Forn Lg; NHS; Pol Wkr; Sch Mus; Sch Pl; Drama Clb; Spn Clb; St Of Mi Comp Schlrshp 79; Kowalski Sausage Schlrshp 79; Forensic Debate Epitome Awd 79; Madonna Coll; Bio.

KORZI, STEVE; Brooke HS; Weirton, WV; 49/446 West Virginia Univ; Bio.

KOS, GREG; Niles Mc Kinley Sr HS; Niles, OH; 39/425 Band; Chrs; Debate Tm; Hon Rl; Natl Forn Lg; NHS; Sch Mus; Sch Pl; Stu Cncl; Drama Clb; PTA Schlrshp Awd; Various Spch Tm Comptn Awds; Major & Minor Lds In Phys; Kent St Univ; Chem.

KOSAK, LINDY; Marian HS; Bloomfield Hl, MI; Chrh Wkr; Lit Mag; Letter Glf; Letter Swmmng; Most Valuable Player Golf Team; College; Child Psych.

KOSAK, RAYMOND; St Philips Catholic HS; Battle Creek, MI; Cls Rep Frsh Cls; Cls Rep Soph Cls; Hon Rl; Stg Crw; Letter Bsktbl; Letter Ftbl; IM Sprt; College; Busns Mgmt.

KOSANKE, MARK; De La Salle Collegiate HS; Detroit, MI; Am Leg Boys St; Chrs; Chrh Wkr; Hon Rl; Sch Mus; Sch Pl; Y-Teens; Sch Nwsp; Drama Clb; Coach Actv; Univ Of Detroit; Bus Admin.

KOSAR, LEONARD; Ursuline HS; Youngstown, OH; 82/350 Hon Rl; Letter Bsbl; Letter Ftbl; Univ.

KOSARIK, JAMES; Brooke HS; Colliers, WV; 25/466 JA; Lit Mag; NHS; Quill & Scroll; Pres Stu Cncl; Fr Clb; Sci Clb; IM Sprt; Elk Awd; JA Awd; Pen Univ; Meterology.

KOSCH, BELINDA; Continental HS; Continental, OH; Cls Rep Frsh Cls; VP Soph Cls; Hon Rl; Lbry Ade; Off Ade; Stu Cncl; Rptr Yrbk; Am Leg Awd; Lima Tech Schl; Sec.

KOSCHMANN, NANCI; North Central HS; Indpls, IN; 254/999 Cls Rep Frsh Cls; Cls Rep Soph Cls; Cl Rep Jr Cls; Hon Rl; Chrldng; Indiana Univ; Nurse.

KOSCHUTNIK, MARGARET; Clearview HS; Lorain, OH; Hon Rl; NHS; Pres FHA; Dnfth Awd; DAR Awd; Lorain Cnty Comm Coll; Data Proc.

KOSCICA, DONNA; Crown Point HS; Crown Point, IN; 1/500 Am Leg Aux Girls St; Debate Tm; Hon Rl; Natl Forn Lg; NHS; Spn Clb; Kiwan Awd; College; Pol Sci.

KOSCIELNIAK, KIMBERLY; Frank Cody HS; Detroit, MI; Band; Girl Scts; Hon Rl; NHS; Orch; Sec Key Clb; Hon Mntn Detriot News Schlstc Writng Awd 78; Finlst Waynce St Creatv Writing Conttst 78; Univ Of Missouri; Bio.

KOSCIELNIAK, MARY; St Marys Cathedral HS; Gaylord, MI; 20/59 Cls Rep Soph Cls; Cl Rep Jr Cls; Cls Rep Sr Cls; Band; CAP; Hon Rl; NHS; Off Ade; Sch Mus; Ferris State; Advert.

KOSCIELNY, GARY; Normandy HS; Parma, OH; 5/650 Hon Rl; Spn Clb; Letter Bsbl; Letter Ftbl; IM Sprt; Natl Merit Ltr; Natl Merit SF; Harvard Univ; Medicine.

KOSCIOLKO, BERNADETTE; St Alphonsus HS; Dearborn, MI; 19/171 Cls Rep Sr Cls; Chrs; Lbry Ade; Hon Rl; Sch Mus; Sch Pl; Pep Clb; Univ; Tchr.

KOSEK, LYNN; Grosse Pointe North HS; Gs Pte Wds, MI; Hon Rl; NHS; Spn Clb; Letter Ten; Albion College; Science.

KOSEL, RUSTY; Sandusky HS; Sandusky, OH; Boy Scts; Chrh Wkr; Hon Rl; VP NHS; Treas Orch; Sct Actv; Stg Crw; Ftbl; Letter Wrstlng; Ohio State Univ; Engr.

KOSHI, JEFFREY; Battle Creek Central HS; Battle Crk, MI; Cls Rep Sr Cls; Hon Rl; Pol Wkr; Natl Merit Ltr; Michigan St Univ.

KOSHKO, CYNTHIA; Warren Woods HS; Warren, MI; 2/358 Sec Frsh Cls; Cls Rep Frsh Cls; Sal; Chrs; Debate Tm; NHS; Sch Mus; Wayne St Univ; Mass Comm.

KOSIARA, MICHAEL; Gaylord St Marys HS; Gaylord, MI; Hon Rl; Sch Nwsp; Ftbl; Letter Trk; Albion College; Educa.

KOSIAREK, CATHERINE S; Bishop Dwenger HS; Grabil, IN; Sec Sr Cls; Cmnty Wkr; Girl Scts; Hon Rl; Hosp Ade; JA; Jr NHS; Sch Pl; Rptr Yrbk; Rptr Sch Nwsp; Coll; Journalism.

KOSIBOSKI, JUANITE; Onekama HS; Manistee, MI; Trs Jr Cls; Hon Rl; Pep Clb; Letter Bsktbl; Letter Trk; Central Univ; Med.

KOSICH, TODD; Glen Oak HS; Canton, OH; Pres Sr Cls; Am Leg Boys St; Band; Boy Scts; Hon Rl; Jr NHS; NHS; Stu Cncl; Yrbk; Pep Clb; Miami Univ; Med.

KOSIK, KEITH; Akron Fairgrove HS; Reese, MI; Aud/Vis; Boy Scts; Hon Rl; Sct Actv; Yrbk; Bsbl; Ftbl; Univ; Archt.

KOSINSKI, MIKE; Holy Spirit Seminary; Toledo, OH; 1/4 Sec Soph Cls; Pres Sr Cls; Val; Chrs; Hon Rl; Pres NHS; VP Stu Cncl; Ed Yrbk; Xavier Univ; Psych.

KOSINSKI, SHERRY; Washington HS; South Bend, IN; 5/354 Chrs; Hon Rl; NHS; Sch Mus; 4-H; Ger Clb; Pom Pon; Cit Awd; 4-H Awd; Notre Dame Univ; Acctg.

KOSISKO, KENNETH; Padua Franciscan HS; Cleveland, OH; Business School; Computers.

KOSITS, KIMBERLY; Solon HS; Solon, OH; 25/288 Hon Rl; Hosp Ade; Lbry Ade; Off Ade; Pep Clb; Bsktbl; PPFtbl; Univ; Nursing.

KOSKELA, KEVIN; Marquette HS; Marquette, MI; 108/422 Hon Rl; Yrbk; Natl Merit SF; Univ Of Tex; Aerospace Engr.

KOSLOW, SCOTT; Franklin HS; Livonia, MI; 5/600 Hon Rl; VP JA; Lit Mag; Natl Forn Lg; Stu Cncl; Fr Clb; JA Awd; Univ Of Mic; Law.

KOSMIDER, JANA; Perrysburg HS; Perrysburg, OH; Spn Clb; Letter Ten; Cincinnati; Interior Decorating.

KOSNIK, DONALD J; Charles F Brush HS; S Euclid, OH; Aud/Vis; Band; Drl Tm; Orch; Sch Mus; College; Elec Engr.

KOSS, CRAIG; Oscoda Area HS; Oscoda, MI; 23/236 Am Leg Boys St; Band; Hon Rl; Lbry Ade; Red Cr Ade; Letter Swmmng; Letter Chrldng; Coach Actv; Scr Kpr; Ferris St Coll; Tech Illustration.

KOSS, TAMMIE; Owendale Gagetown HS; Gagetown, MI; 8/40 Band; Hon Rl; Jr NHS; NHS; Off Ade; Pep Clb; Spn Clb; Cit Awd; Sec.

KOST, BRIAN; Stow HS; Stow, OH; 1/559 Hon Rl; Pres Jr NHS; Pres NHS; Rptr Sch Nwsp; Mth Clb; IM Sprt; Ohio State Univ; Engr.

KOST, MARK; Southfield Lathrup Sr HS; Southfield, MI; Band; Hon Rl; Orch; Sch Mus; Letter Bsbl; IM Sprt; Michigan St Univ; Acctg.

KOSTA, MELISSA; John Glenn HS; Westland, MI; Band; Pres Jr Cls; Hon Rl; JA; Lbry Ade; Sct Actv; Oakland Univ; Dent.

KOSTAN, DANIEL; Euclid Sr HS; Euclid, OH; Hon Rl; Crs Cntry; Trk; Natl Merit Ltr; Univ; Meteorology.

KOSTECKI, JEFF; Theodore Roosevelt HS; Wyandotte, MI; Boy Scts; Hon Rl; Swmmng; Tmr; VFW Awd; Univ.

KOSTECKI, MARY; Madonna HS; Weirton, WV; 13/100 Cmnty Wkr; Hon Rl; JA; Lit Mag; NHS; Pep Clb; Mat Maids; JA Awd; College; Medicine.

KOSTER, DANIEL G; Ottawa Hills HS; Grand Rapids, MI; 2/500 Am Leg Boys St; Band; Chrh Wkr; Hon Rl; JA; Pres NHS; Orch; Sch Mus; Yth Flsp; Letter Hockey; Univ Of Michigan; Pre Med.

KOSTER, JENNIFER; Howell HS; Howell, MI; 51/385 Band; Chrh Wkr; Girl Scts; Hon Rl; NHS; Sct Actv; PPFtbl; Natl Merit Ltr; Central Mich Univ; Acctg.

KOSTOFF, CHRISTOPHER; Copley HS; Akron, OH; 12/310 Cls Rep Sr Cls; Treas Chrs; Chrh Wkr; Hon Rl; NHS; Sch Mus; Treas Yth Flsp; Rptr Yrbk; Pres Fr Clb; Univ Of Akron.

KOSTOHRYZ, DENICE; Brecksville HS; Broadview Hts, OH; 16/390 Hon Rl; Off Ade; Sch Pl; Rptr Yrbk; Drama Clb; Ger Clb; Trk; Ohio Univ; Comp Sci.

KOSTREVAGH, ELISABETH; Monsignor J R Hackett HS; Kalamazoo, MI; Cls Rep Frsh Cls; Cmnty Wkr; Hon Rl; IM Sprt; Natl Merit Ltr; Opt Clb Awd; Washington Workshop; Univ Of Michigan; Accounting.

KOSZALKA, MARIA; St Andrew HS; Dearborn, MI; 4/104 Trs Jr Cls; Sec Sr Cls; Chrh Wkr; Hon Rl; NHS; Pol Wkr; Rptr Yrbk; Yrbk; Rptr Sch Nwsp; Sch Nwsp; Wayne St Univ; Lab Tech.

KOSZUTA, LAUREEN; Flat Rock HS; Flat Rock, MI; Sec Frsh Cls; Trs Frsh Cls; Trs Sr Cls; Chrs; FCA; Hon Rl; Off Ade; Yth Flsp; Sci Clb; Coach Actv; College; Bus.

KOT, MARK; Valley Forge HS; Parma, OH; 23/704 Rptr Sch Nwsp; Bsbl; Bsktbl; Cornell Univ; Archt.

KOTAJARVI, MARK; Calumet HS; Laurium, MI; 20/149 Chrs; Hon Rl; NHS; Sch Mus; Rptr Yrbk; Univ Of Michigan; Archt.

KOTCHEROWSKI, JOYCE; St Ursula Acad; Toledo, OH; Cls Rep Soph Cls; Sec Jr Cls; VP Sr Cls; Chrs; Girl Scts; Stu Cncl; Fr Clb; Bowling Green St Univ; Bus Admin.

KOTEL, ROBIN; Gwinn HS; Gwinn, MI; Band; Hon Rl; Off Ade; 4-H; Crs Cntry; Trk; Voc Schl

KOTHERA, KELLY; Cardinal HS; Huntsburg, OH; 16/104 Girl Scts; Hon Rl; Lbry Ade; Off Ade; Stg Crw; Yrbk; 4-H; GAA; Scr Kpr; 4-H Awd;.

KOTILA, GREGG; Hancock Central HS; Hancock, MI; 18/95 Band; Hon Rl; NHS; Sch Pl; Stg Crw; Letter Crs Cntry; Natl Merit Schl; Mich Tech Univ; Elec Engineer.

KOTLARCZYK, MARK; Holy Spirit Seminary; Findlay, OH; 2/10 Sec Frsh Cls; VP Soph Cls; Cl Rep Jr Cls; Hon Rl; Hosp Ade; Treas NHS; Sch Pl; Stu Cncl; Drama Clb; Spn Clb; Pontifical Coll; Priesthood.

KOTLARSIC, FRANK; St Ignatius HS; Cleveland, OH; 137/311 Ftbl; Letter Wrstlng; IM Sprt; Cincinnati Tech College; Arch Eng.

KOTNIK, JOE; W Geavga HS; Chesterlands, OH; FCA; Hon Rl; Bsbl; Letter Crs Cntry; Letter Wrstlng; Ohio St Univ; Engr.

KOTSOL, EVIE J; Campbell Mem HS; Campbell, OH; Pres Jr Cls; Pres Sr Cls; Band; Chrh Wkr; Orch; Pep Clb; Sci Clb; Spn Clb; Scr Kpr; Univ; Marine Bio.

KOTTKE, DEBBIE; Belleville HS; Belleville, MI; Cls Rep Frsh Cls; Chrh Wkr; Hon Rl; Spn Clb; Bsktbl; GAA; Scr Kpr; E Michigan Univ; Psych.

KOTYUK, PATRICIA; Solon HS; Solon, OH; 1/288 Cl Rep Jr Cls; AFS; Chrh Wkr; FCA; Hon Rl; Treas NHS; Sch Mus; Sch Pl; Stg Crw; Stu Cncl; Univ; Sci.

KOUDELKA, DAWN; Nordonia HS; Northfield, OH; Cmnty Wkr; Girl Scts; JA; Off Ade; John Caroll; Law.

KOUDELKA, TERI; River Valley HS; Marion, OH; 3/200 Chrs; Chrh Wkr; Cmnty Wkr; Hon Rl; NHS; Off Ade; Sch Mus; Fr Clb; Sci Clb; Glf; Bowling Green St Univ; Spec Ed.

KOUNTOUPIS, SOPHIA; Henry Ford HS; Detroit, MI; Hon Rl; Quill & Scroll; Sch Pl; Stu Cncl; Rptr Yrbk; Fr Clb; Letter Glf; Univ Of Mic; Med.

KOUNTZ, MICHELLE; Hampshire County HS; Romney, WV; Girl Scts; Hon Rl; Lbry Ade; Sch Pl; Sct Actv; 4-H; DAR Awd; College; Art Tchr.

KOURTESIS, PETER; Lamphere HS; Madison Hts, MI; Cls Rep Frsh Cls; Band; Boy Scts; Chrh Wkr; Hon Rl; Orch; Sct Actv; Stu Cncl; Yth Flsp; Letter Swmmng; Law.

KOURY, KRISTIN; Notre Dame Academy; Lambertville, MI; Home Ec.

KOUSHIAFES, CARRIE; Highland HS; Highland, IN; 56/534 Cmp Fr Grls; Hon Rl; NHS; Pep Clb; Spn Clb; Ten; Pom Pon; Purdue Univ.

KOVAC, CLARA; Norton HS; Norton, OH; Cls Rep Frsh Cls; Am Leg Aux Girls St; Chrs; Chrh Wkr; Hon Rl; JA; Natl Forn Lg; NHS; Off Ade; Sch Mus; Bob Jones Univ; Physical Education.

KOVACEVIC, JOSEPH; Strongsville Sr HS; Strongsville, OH; Hon Rl; Ten; IM Sprt; Univ Of Akron; Bus Mgmt.

KOVACH, AUDREY; Aquinas HS; Southgate, MI; Cls Rep Soph Cls; Hon Rl; Off Ade; Stu Cncl; Pep Clb; Crs Cntry; Trk; Chrldng; College; Journalism.

KOVACH, CATHERINE; Regina HS; S Euclid, OH; Hon Rl; NHS; Stg Crw; Stu Cncl; GAA; IM Sprt; Univ.

KOVACH, JOHN; Indian Valley South HS; Newcomerstown, OH; 6/95 Chrs; Hon Rl; VP Yth Flsp; 4-H; Pep Clb; Bsktbl; Univ; Acctg.

KOVACH, JUDITH M; George Rogers Clark HS; Whiting, IN; 12/285 Hon Rl; Jr NHS; NHS; Sdlty; Pep Clb; Spn Clb; Bsktbl; Ten; IM Sprt; Vllybl 77 78 & 79; Art Club; St Marys Of Notre Dame Univ; Med.

KOVACH, MARIANNE; Shadyside HS; Shadyside, OH; Am Leg Aux Girls St; Hon Rl; NHS; Y-Teens; Spn Clb; Univ; Nursing.

KOVACH, MARJORIE L; Oakridge Sr HS; Muskegon, MI; 13/108 Band; Chrh Wkr; Hon Rl; Jr NHS; NHS; Stu Cncl; Yth Flsp; 4-H; Pep Clb; Scr Kpr; CMU Brd Of Trustee Hnr Schlrshp 79; Mi Comptn Schlrshp 79; BEOG 79; Cntrl Michigan Univ; Publc Hlth Educ.

KOVACH, STEVE; Stow HS; Stow, OH; Chrh Wkr; Rptr Sch Nwsp; Letter Ftbl; Voc Schl.

KOVACK, MIKE; Wadsworth HS; Wadsworth, OH; Cls Rep Frsh Cls; VP Soph Cls; Cl Rep Jr Cls; Aud/Vis; Band; Chrh Wkr; Cmnty Wkr; Debate Tm; Hon Rl; JA; Univ Of S Florida; Pre Law.

KOVACS, JEFFREY; Groveport Madison Frsh HS; Columbus, OH; Band; Chrh Wkr; Cmnty Wkr; Orch; Spn Clb; Ten; Ohio St Univ; Mech Engr.

KOVACS, MARLENE; Clay Sr HS; Oregon, OH; Chrs; Hon Rl; Off Ade; Pep Clb; Spn Clb; Soc Wrk.

KOVALCHICK, GREGORY; Warren Western Reserve HS; Warren, OH; Hon Rl; NHS; Ftbl; Kent St Univ; Pre Conservation.

KOVALCHIK, CAROL; Saint Francis De Sales HS; Columbus, OH; Girl Scts; Hon Rl; Red Cr Ade; GAA; PPFtbl; Columbus Tech Inst; Secretarial Sci.

KOVALCHIK, GARY; Meadowbrook HS; Pleasant City, OH; 21/179 Boy Scts; Hon Rl; 4-H; Mth Clb; Muskingum Coll; Med.

KOVALCIK, GINA; Erieview Catholic HS; Cleveland, OH; Cls Rep Frsh Cls; Chrs; Chrh Wkr; Cmnty Wkr; Hon Rl; Lit Mag; Pol Wkr; Yrbk; Bsbl; Hocking Tech College.

KOVELSKI, KATHLEEN; Buckeye West HS; Rayland, OH; 4/85 Sec Frsh Cls; VP Soph Cls; Pres Jr Cls; Am Leg Aux Girls St; Band; Drm Mjrt; Hon Rl; Lbry Ade; NHS; Off Ade; Jefferson County Tech Inst; Med Tech.

KOVERT, TERI; Crothersville HS; Crothersville, IN; Sec Frsh Cls; Sec Soph Cls; NHS; 4-H; Pep Clb; Chrldng; 4-H Awd;.

KOVIAK, CAROL J; Elyria Catholic HS; Elyria, OH; 1/190 Val; Band; Chrs; Chrh Wkr; Girl Scts; Hon Rl; Mdrgl; NHS; Orch; Sch Mus; Notre Dame Coll; Chem.

KOWAL, DANIEL; Port Clinton HS; Pt Clinton, OH; Hon Rl; Swmmng; Ten; Bowling Green St Univ; Bus Admin.

KOWAL, DANNY; Port Clinton HS; Pt Clinton, OH; Chrs; Hon Rl; Swmmng; Ten; Bowling Green St Univ; Bus Admin.

KOWAL, KAREN; Marian HS; Birmingham, MI; Chrh Wkr; Girl Scts; Hon Rl; Lbry Ade; Sec NHS; Off Ade; Stg Crw; Yth Flsp; Spn Clb; Swmmng; Univ; Bus.

KOWALESKI, JEAN; Our Lady Of Mercy HS; Farmington, MI; Lbry Ade; NHS; Sch Mus; Fr Clb; Treas Sci Clb; Univ; Respiratory Ther.

KOWALESKI, JOHN; Southgate HS; Southgate, MI; Hon Rl; Jr NHS; NHS; Sch Pl; Stg Crw; Trk; Wrstlng; JC Awd; Michigan St Univ; Indstrl Engr.

KOWALEWSKI, KAREN; Rochester HS; Rochester, MI; 31/382 Cls Rep Frsh Cls; Cls Rep Soph Cls; Band; Chrh Wkr; Hon Rl; Hosp Ade; Lit Mag; NHS; Letter Ten; Letter Trk; Acad Schlrshp W Mi Univ 79; Acad Schlrshp From St Of Mi 79; Western Michigan Univ; Spec Educ.

KOWALEWSKI, MICHAEL; Divine Child HS; Hamtramck, MI; Hon Rl; IM Sprt; Michigan St Univ; Acctg.

KOWALK, BRIAN; Eaton Rapids HS; Eaton Rapids, MI; Chrs; Chrh Wkr; Hon Rl; Yth Flsp; Spn Clb; Univ; Comp Sci.

KOWALSKI, BUTCH; Marquette HS; Michigan City, IN; Boy Scts; Hon Rl; Jr NHS; Lbry Ade; Sct Actv; Stu Cncl; Spn Clb; Crs Cntry; Trk; Univ.

KOWALSKI, DANIEL; Put In Bay HS; Put In Bay, OH; 1/6 Pres Frsh Cls; Hon Rl; Capt Bsbl; Bsktbl; Capt Ftbl; Am Leg Awd; Bowling Green St Univ; Educ.

KOWALSKI, DAVID A; South Bend Washington HS; South Bend, IN; 60/365 Pres Sr Cls; Am Leg Boys St; Band; Chrs; Chrh Wkr; Hon Rl; Jr NHS; NHS; Sch Mus; Stu Cncl; Univ; Med.

KOWALSKI, DENNIS; St Francis De Sales HS; Toledo, OH; Hon Rl; Ger Clb; IM Sprt; Univ; Med.

KOWALSKI, KENNETH P; Catholic Central HS; Redford, MI; Hon Rl; NHS; Pol Wkr; Stu Cncl; Ed Yrbk; Yrbk; Sci Clb; Trk; IM Sprt; Cert Of Honor St Of Mich Schlrshp Program 79; Aquinas Coll Presidental Ldrshp Schlrshp 79; Aquinas Coll; Bus Admin.

KOWALZYK, KATHY; All Saints Central HS; Bay City, MI; Cls Rep Frsh Cls; Cl Rep Jr Cls; Cls Rep Sr Cls; Hon Rl; NHS; Stu Cncl; Chrldng; Delta Comm College; Data Processing.

KOWATCH, LORI; Northwestern HS; West Salem, OH; Cls Rep Frsh Cls; Hon Rl; Off Ade; Stg Crw; Rptr Yrbk; Sprt Ed Sch Nwsp; Rptr Sch Nwsp; Drama Clb; Sec Fr Clb; Bsktbl; Serv Awd Frsh Yr; Ashland Coll; Elem Educ.

KOYANAGI, DOUGLAS; Bloomington South HS; Bloomington, IN; Pres Jr Cls; Pres Stu Cncl; Swmmng; College.

KOZAK, MARIE J; Dominican HS; Detroit, MI; Cls Rep Frsh Cls; Sec Soph Cls; Cmnty Wkr; Stu Cncl; Yrbk; Mgrs; Am Leg Awd; Univ; Soc Work.

KOZAN, FRANCES; Cass City HS; Cass City, MI; 13/157 Cls Rep Frsh Cls; Cls Rep Soph Cls; Cl Rep Jr Cls; Cls Rep Sr Cls; Pres Band; Chrs; Chrh Wkr; Cmnty Wkr; Debate Tm; Hon Rl; Honor Cord Grad; Regents Alumi Schlar Awd; St Of Mich Honorary

Schlrshp; AAUW Schlrshp; Univ Of Michigan; Speech Comm.

KOZAR, MICHAEL G; Eastlake North HS; Willowick, OH; 83/669 Hon Rl; NHS; Capt Ftbl; Univ; Geol.

KOZELEK, KAKI; Bexley HS; Bexley, OH; Chrh Wkr; Hon Rl; Fr Clb; Univ; Math.

KOZERSKI, DANNA; Our Lady Of Mercy HS; Farm Hls, MI; Cls Rep Frsh Cls; Chrh Wkr; Hon Rl; NHS; Stg Crw; Yrbk; Chrldng; Univ; Bus.

KOZICKI, KAREN; North Farmington HS; Farm Hills, MI; Chrs; Hon Rl; Fr Clb; Wrstlng; College.

KOZINSKI, MICHAEL E; Perry HS; Massillon, OH; 32/480 Band; Boy Scts; Hon Rl; Natl Forn Lg; NHS; Quill & Scroll; Sch Mus; Sch Pl; Sprt Ed Sch Nwsp; Drama Clb; Univ Of Akron; Acctg.

KOZIOL, SANDRA; Lincoln West HS; Cleveland, OH; Hon Rl; Jr NHS; Bsbl; Bsktbl; GAA; IM Sprt; Univ Of Dayton; Educational.

KOZLOWSKI, KATHLEEN; Our Lady Of Mercy HS; Detroit, MI; Chrs; Cmnty Wkr; Girl Scts; Lbry Ade; Mod UN; NHS; Sch Pl; Rptr Sch Nwsp; Sch Nwsp; Eng Clb; Univ Of Michigan; Eng.

KOZLOWSKI, LAURA; St Marys Cathedral HS; Gaylord, MI; Band; Chrs; Drl Tm; Hon Rl; NHS; Sch Mus; Sch Pl; Drama Clb; College.

KOZLOWSKI, LORI; Solon HS; Solon, OH; Cmp Fr Grls; Drl Tm; Hon Rl; Pep Clb; Shung Shi Club; Univ; Nutritionist.

KOZLOWSKI, PAUL; Hanover Central HS; Cedar Lake, IN; 2/126 Hon Rl; Jr NHS; NHS; Spn Clb; Ten; Coach Actv; Florida Inst Of Tech; Marine Bio.

KOZLOWSKI, TERESA; River Vly HS; Three Oaks, MI; Cls Rep Frsh Cls; Cls Rep Soph Cls; Cls Rep Sr Cls; Hon Rl; VP NHS; Treas Stu Cncl; Rptr Yrbk; Drama Clb; Spn Clb; Natl Merit Schl; Kalamazoo Coll; Dentistry.

KRAAI, CATHY; Maple Valley Jr Sr HS; Vermontville, MI; Trs Jr Cls; Band; Girl Scts; Hon Rl; NHS; Sch Mus; Sch Pl; Letter Bsktbl; Letter Trk; GAA; Lansing Cmnty Coll; Comm Art.

KRABBE, M; East Clinton HS; Sabina, OH; Hon Rl; Yth Flsp; 4-H; FFA; Ftbl; Voc Schl; Ag.

KRAEGEL, RANDY; Elida HS; Elida, OH; 4/255 Chrh Wkr; Hon Rl; NHS; Pres Yth Flsp; Rptr Yrbk; FTA; Lat Clb; Ohio Brd Of Ed Awd Of Distinct 79; Westinghse Sci Hon Inst 79; Acad Schlrshp To Rose Hulman Inst Of Tech 79; Rose Hulman Inst Univ; Elec Engr.

KRAEMER, CINDY M; Seton HS; Cincinnati, OH; 192/282 Pres Chrs; Hon Rl; Lbry Ade; Sch Mus; Pep Clb; Spn Clb; Thomas More Univ; Bus Mgmt.

KRAEMER, LORI; Marion L Steele HS; Amherst, OH; 50/369 Hon Rl; NHS; FTA; Spn Clb; Letter Chrldng; GAA; IM Sprt; PPFtbl; Ski Club; Bowling Green St Univ; Law Correctn.

KRAFCHECK, ANTOINETTE; La Brae HS; Warren, OH; 1/178 Cls Rep Soph Cls; Cl Rep Jr Cls; Am Leg Aux Girls St; Cmnty Wkr; Hon Rl; Hosp Ade; Sec JA; Pres NHS; PAVAS; Red Cr Ade; Coll; Psych.

KRAFFT, JIM; Hackett HS; Kalamazoo, MI; Pres Frsh Cls; Stu Cncl; Bsbl; Hockey; Socr; Loyola Univ; Poli Sci.

KRAFFT, WILLIAM; Richwood HS; Richwood, WV; 4/180 Sec Frsh Cls; Cls Rep Soph Cls; Cl Rep Jr Cls; Cls Rep Sr Cls; Am Leg Boys St; NHS; Natl Merit Schl; Mic State Univ; Social Sci.

KRAFT, ELLEN; Roy C Start HS; Toledo, OH; Chrs; Chrh Wkr; Cmnty Wkr; Sec Girl Scts; Hon Rl; Jr NHS; NHS; Sct Actv; Stg Crw; Spn Clb; Univ; Jrnlsm.

KRAFT, JENNIFER; London HS; London, OH; 5/141 Cls Rep Sr Cls; Hon Rl; NHS; Quill & Scroll; Stg Crw; Stu Cncl; Rptr Yrbk; 4-H; Fr Clb; 4-H Awd; Wittenberg Univ; Acctg.

KRAFT, JUNE; Greenville Sr HS; Greenville, MI; Band; Hon Rl; 4-H; Letter Bsktbl; IM Sprt; PPFtbl; Univ.

KRAFT, KIMBERLY; Stow HS; Stow, OH; 22/550 Band; Chrs; Hon Rl; JA; Treas NHS; Stu Cncl; Lat Clb; JA Awd; Coll; Busns.

KRAFT, KIMBERLY; Edwardsburg HS; Niles, MI; Band;.

KRAFT, TIMOTHY; Bishop Duenger HS; Ft Wayne, IN; Hon Rl; NHS; Sch Pl; Stg Crw; Key Clb; Purdue Univ; Aero Engr.

KRAFTY, SANDY; St Marys Cntrl Cath HS; Sandusky, OH; Cl Rep Jr Cls; Girl Scts; Hon Rl; NHS; 4-H; Spn Clb; GAA; Mat Maids; College.

KRAGERUD, TAMMY; Brownsburg HS; Brownsburg, IN; Hon Rl; Stu Cncl; Pep Clb; Gym; Letter Swmmng; Letter Trk; GAA; Mat Maids; PPFtbl; Most Improved Track Runner Going To Regnls As Hurdler 79; Univ; Enviro Design.

KRAGT, DANIEL; Kent City HS; Casnovia, MI; Trs Sr Cls; Band; Hon Rl; Yth Flsp; Bsbl; Bsktbl; Ftbl; Trk; Natl Merit Schl; Hope Coll; Med.

KRAHE, DIANA; Onekama Consolidated HS; Onekama, MI; 2/72 Cls Rep Frsh Cls; Cls Rep Soph Cls; Cl Rep Jr Cls; Cls Rep Sr Cls; Sal; Band; Chrs; Chrh Wkr; Hope College; Psych.

KRAJNAK, KATHRYN; Bishop Watterson HS; Worthington, OH; 5/250 Cls Rep Soph Cls; Chrs; Chrh Wkr; Girl Scts; Hon Rl; Jr NHS; NHS; Sch Mus; Sch Pl; Sct Actv; Univ; Psych.

KRAJNIK, MIKE; Traverse City St Francis HS; Traverse City, MI; Cls Rep Sr Cls; Hon Rl; Rptr Yrbk; Ftbl; Opertn Bentley 79 Partcpnt Olivet Coll 79; Right Ot Life March Wa DC 79; Photog Schl; Photog.

KRAJNYAK, KIM; Martins Ferry HS; Martins Ferry, OH; Sec Frsh Cls; Cl Rep Jr Cls; Hon Rl; Off Ade; Stu Cncl; Y-Teens; Yrbk; Sci Clb; Spn Clb; GAA; Technical Coll; Sec.

KRAKER, DAVID; Allendale HS; Allendale, MI; 2/72 Sal; Band; Hon Rl; Pres NHS; Grand Rapids Jr Coll Foundtn Schlrshp 79; St Of Mi Comp Schlrshp Prog Cert Of Recogntn 79; 4 1st Plc Photo; Grand Rapids Jr Coll; Bus Admin.

KRAL, LYDIA; James Ford Rhodes HS; Cleveland, OH; 9/309 Cls Rep Soph Cls; Chrh Wkr; Hon Rl; NHS; Mas Awd; Casewestern Reserve Univ; Phys Ther.

KRALL, JUDY; Defiance Sr HS; Defiance, OH; Girl Scts; Hon Rl; Off Ade; Rptr Yrbk; Scr Kpr; Bus Schl; Cosmetology.

KRALL, KAREN; Parkway HS; Willshire, OH; Am Leg Aux Girls St; Band; Yth Flsp; Pep Clb; Crs Cntry; PPFtbl; Scr Kpr; Cross Cntry Team Co Capt 79; Mbr Of Pepe Band; Univ; Engr.

KRALL, LISA; Onsted HS; Onsted, MI; 20/125 Band; FCA; Girl Scts; Hon Rl; Sch Pl; Stg Crw; Yth Flsp; Yrbk; 4-H; Bsktbl; Interlochen Fine Arts Camp; 1/2 Money Value Bnd 76; Jr High Hon Bnd; Players 75; Adrian Coll; Hstry.

KRALL, MARTHA; Linden HS; Fenton, MI; Band; Hon Rl; Hosp Ade; JA; NHS; Off Ade; Orch; Sch Mus; Stg Crw; Pres Spn Clb; Mim Comptn Schlrshp Awd 79; Michigan St Univ; Bus.

KRALLMAN, PAT; Edwardsburg HS; Edwardsburg, MI; Cls Rep Sr Cls; Stu Cncl; Letter Chrldng; College; Stenography.

KRAMAN, ANN; Carroll HS; Kettering, OH; 15/285 Cmnty Wkr; Drl Tm; FCA; Hon Rl; NHS; Stu Cncl; Pres Rus Clb; GAA; College; Bus.

KRAMER, ANTHONY; Wapakoneta Sr HS; Wapakoneta, OH; Chrs; Hon Rl; Sch Pl; Pres Fr Clb; Bsbl; Ftbl; Trk; Coach Actv; Cit Awd; Pres Awd; Ohio St Univ; Bio Sci.

KRAMER, CAROLYN; Mc Auley HS; Cleves, OH; 22/254 Chrh Wkr; Hon Rl; Rptr Sch Nwsp; Pres Lat Clb; Socr; College; Journalism.

KRAMER, DEBORAH; Springboro HS; Springboro, OH; Chrs; Girl Scts; Hon Rl; Hosp Ade; Sct Actv; Stg Crw; Spn Clb; PPFtbl; Miami Univ; Nursing.

KRAMER, DONNA; Reeths Puffer HS; Muskegon, MI; Chrs; Girl Scts; Hon Rl; Yth Flsp; Muskegon Comm College; Sec.

KRAMER, JEANNE; St Johns HS; St Johns, MI; Band; Hon Rl; NHS; 4-H; Bsktbl; IM Sprt; Ctrl Michigan Univ; Comp Sci.

KRAMER, JEFF; Franklin HS; Westland, MI; 7/600 Boy Scts; Hon Rl; Stu Cncl; Letter Socr; Letter Ten; College.

KRAMER, J MCLAIN; Linsly Military Inst; Wheeling, WV; 14/63 FCA; ROTC; Sch Mus; Stg Crw; Rptr Sch Nwsp; FSA; Key Clb; Geo Tech; Aerospace Eng.

KRAMER, KARA; Fairmont West HS; Kettering, OH; Sec Frsh Cls; Cls Rep Soph Cls; Cl Rep Jr Cls; Hon Rl; Stu Cncl; Rptr Yrbk; Sch Nwsp; Pep Clb; Chrldng; Coach Actv; High Hon Roll 74 79; Univ; Cmnctns.

KRAMER, KATHLEEN; Archbishop Alter HS; Centerville, OH; 86/290 Drl Tm; Hosp Ade; Sch Pl; Yrbk; Rptr Sch Nwsp; Drama Clb; Rdo Clb; Letter Trk; GAA; 1st Hnrs 90% Or Abv Avg Every Qtr 76 78; Miami Bowling Green Univ; Cmnctns.

KRAMER, KELLEY; Thomas Carr Howe HS; Indianapolis, IN; 29/579 Hon Rl; NHS; Air Force; Vet.

KRAMER, KELLY; Western Michigan Chrstn HS; Grand Haven, MI; Pres Frsh Cls; VP Frsh Cls; Chrh Wkr; Hon Rl; NHS; Sch Pl; Ed Yrbk; Rptr Sch Nwsp; Capt Glf; Ferris State College; Optmtry.

KRAMER, LINDA; Holy Name Nazareth HS; Strongsville, OH; Chrs; Hon Rl; Exc In Chem Awd; NCTE Writing Awd; Math Tutor; Univ.

KRAMER, PAMELA; Marion Local HS; Osgood, OH; 10/88 Chrs; Hon Rl; NHS; 4-H; FTA; Pep Clb; Sci Clb; Trk; Bus Schl; Sec.

KRAMER, PAULA; Huntington North HS; Huntington, IN; 199/572 Band; Chrh Wkr; Orch; Sch Mus; Marion Univ; Med.

KRAMER, SHARON; Ayersville HS; Defiance, OH; Band; Chrs; Sch Mus; 4-H; Fr Clb; FBLA; FHA; Tmr; 4-H Awd; Northwest Tech Sch; Draftsmen.

KRAMER, STEPHEN A; Ft Wayne R Nelson Snider HS; Ft Wayne, IN; 500/749 Chrh Wkr; Hon Rl; Quill & Scroll; Yth Flsp; Sprt Ed Yrbk; Sprt Ed Sch Nwsp; Rptr Sch Nwsp; Ger Clb; Sci Clb; Bsbl; Ltrmns Club; All City Bsbl 79; Sci Fair Hnrbl Mntn 76; AACBC Coll Bsbl Recrutng Hnr 79; 2 Yr Perfct Attend; Des Moines Area Cmnty Coll; Chem.

KRAMER, WILLIAM; Moeller HS; Cincinnati, OH; 6/260 Pres Jr Cls; Trs Sr Cls; Cls Rep Sr Cls; Hon Rl; NHS; Sch Pl; Stu Cncl; IM Sprt; Miami Univ; Com Sci.

KRAMERICH, GEORGE; Gilmour Academy; Lyndhurst, OH; Boy Scts; Cmnty Wkr; Debate Tm; Hon Rl; NHS; Sct Actv; Sch Nwsp; Boys Clb Am; Letter Ftbl; IM Sprt; Univ; Bus Mgmt.

KRAML, DEBORAH; Bay HS; Bay Vill, OH; Chrh Wkr; Drl Tm; Orch; Sch Pl; Stu Cncl; Rptr Sch Nwsp; Pep Clb; PPFtbl; Univ; Occup Ther.

KRAMP, KENNETH; Lokata HS; Cincinnati, OH; Boy Scts; Chrh Wkr; Hon Rl; JA; IM Sprt; Univ Of Cincinnati; Bus.

KRANTZ, CINDY; Licking Hghts HS; Reynoldsburg, OH; 8/104 VP Jr Cls; Band; Hon Rl; Ed Sch Nwsp; OEA; Sec.

KRANTZ, JODI; Dover HS; Dover, OH; Hst Frsh Cls; Trs Jr Cls; Cls Rep Sr Cls; Chrs; Hon Rl; Jr NHS; Off Ade; Stu Cncl; Sch Nwsp; Pep Clb; Ohio Univ; Jrnlsm.

KRAPFF, JENNIFER; North Farmington HS; Farmington Hill, MI; Chrs; Hon Rl; College.

KRAPOHL, GRAYDON; Napoleon HS; Jackson, MI; 14/166 Pres Jr Cls; Natl Forn Lg; NHS; Stu Cncl; Drama Clb; Bsktbl; Crs Cntry; Univ Of Mic.

KRASKA, THOMAS; Chaminade Julienne HS; Dayton, OH; Chrh Wkr; Y-Teens; Bsbl; Ftbl; Coach Actv; Apprentcshp; Machinery Repairman.

KRASNEWICH, MICHELE; Our Lady Of Mercy HS; Farm Hls, MI; Chrs; Hon Rl; NHS; Sch Mus; Sch Pl; Yrbk; Chrldng; Coach Actv; Univ; Bus.

KRATOFIL, ELLEN; North Ridgeville HS; N Ridgeville, OH; 21/376 Band; Chrh Wkr; Hon Rl; NHS; Yth Flsp; Fr Clb; Letter Trk; Mount Union Coll; Music.

KRATT, LORA; Sidney HS; Sidney, OH; Trs Sr Cls; Hon Rl; Lbry Ade; NHS; Off Ade; Drama Clb; Spn Clb; Scr Kpr; College.

KRATZ, JAMES; Caro Cmnty HS; Caro, MI; Chrh Wkr; Hon Rl; NHS; Letter Ftbl; Letter Trk; JC Awd; Univ; Metallurgical Engr.

KRAUS, AMY; Fairless HS; Wilmot, OH; Am Leg Aux Girls St; Band; Hon Rl; Y-Teens; Sch Nwsp; 4-H; Letter Bsktbl; Trk; GAA; 4-H Awd; College.

KRAUS, ANN; Edwardsburg HS; Edwardsburg, MI; Girl Scts; Hon Rl; NHS; Yrbk; Ger Clb; IM Sprt; Univ; Psych.

KRAUS, BARBARA; St Joseph Academy; Fairview Pk, OH; Hosp Ade; Y-Teens; Rptr Sch Nwsp; Fr Clb; Univ; Acctg.

KRAUS, DAVID; St Marys HS; Sandusky, OH; Hon Rl; NHS; Ger Clb; Sci Clb; Letter Bsbl; Mgrs; Univ; Sci.

KRAUS, MARY; Monroe HS; Monroe, MI; 15/553 Cmp Fr Grls; Chrs; Hon Rl; Mdrgl; NHS; Orch; PAVAS; Sch Mus; Sch Pl; Stg Crw; Michigan St Univ; Vet.

KRAUS, SUZANNE; Whitehall HS; Whitehall, MI; 17/154 Trs Sr Cls; Hon Rl; NHS; Sch Mus; Sch Pl; Drama Clb; Trk; Chrldng; PPFtbl; Pres Awd; Aquinas College; Psychology.

KRAUSE, KATHRYN; Normandy HS; Parma, OH; 6/697 VP Frsh Cls; Cls Rep Frsh Cls; Sec Soph Cls; Cls Rep Soph Cls; Sec Jr Cls; Cl Rep Jr Cls; Sec Sr Cls; Cls Rep Sr Cls; Chrs; Girl Scts; Kent St Univ; Nursing.

KRAUSS, CARLA; Michigan Lutheran Seminary; Freeland, MI; Chrs; Chrh Wkr; Hon Rl; Sch Nwsp; 4-H; Key Clb; IM Sprt; Pom Pon; PPFtbl; Dr Martin Luther College; Elem Educ.

KRAUSS, GEORGE W; West Genuga HS; Novelty, OH; Band; Boy Scts; Hon Rl; Ten; IM Sprt; College.

KRAUSS, MARGARET A; Creston HS; Grand Rapids, MI; 2/400 Band; Chrh Wkr; Hon Rl; Hosp Ade; Jr NHS; NHS; Pol Wkr; Ger Clb; Scr Kpr; Elk Awd; Michigan St Univ; Chem Engr.

KRAUSS, MIKE; Ben Davis HS; Indianapolis, IN; 1/750 FCA; Mod UN; NHS; Fr Clb; Letter Bsktbl; Chrldng; Coach Actv; IM Sprt; Univ; Med.

KRAUTTER, KEITH; Meigs HS; Pomeroy, OH; Pres Soph Cls; Am Leg Boys St; Band; Boy Scts; Chrs; Chrh Wkr; Cmnty Wkr; Drm Bgl; Hon Rl; PAVAS; Ohio Univ; Comp Sci.

KRAWCZYK, KENNETH; St Alphonsus HS; Dearborn, MI; Band; Hon Rl; Detrioit Bus College; Bookeeping.

KRAWCZYK, KEVIN; North Union HS; Richwood, OH; FFA; Ftbl; Vocational School.

KRAWCZYK, SUSAN; Pinconning Area HS; Pinconning, MI; Pres Soph Cls; Pres Jr Cls; Hon Rl; Natl Forn Lg; NHS; Stu Cncl; Ed Yrbk; Bsbl; Bsktbl; Scr Kpr; College; Health.

KRAY, KRISTIN; Andrean HS; Hobart, IN; Hon Rl; NHS; Sch Nwsp; GAA; Columbus Coll; Bfa.

KRAYNAK, ELIZABETH; Ursuline & Chaffin Ctr; Youngstown, OH; 147/286 Chrh Wkr; Yth Flsp; VICA; Univ; Comm Art.

KREBER, THOMAS; Bishop Watterson HS; Columbus, OH; Hon Rl; Yrbk; Rptr Sch Nwsp; Spn Clb; College.

KREBS, BERND; Coloma HS; Coloma, MI; Hon Rl; Ger Clb; Univ; Sci.

KREBS, DAVID; Hanover Central HS; Cedar Lake, IN; 16/121 Chrh Wkr; Cmnty Wkr; Hon Rl; Jr NHS; NHS; Rptr Sch Nwsp; Letter Crs Cntry; Valparaiso Univ; Accgt.

KREBS JR, RAY; Tippecanoe HS; Tipp City, OH; 9/196 Pres Soph Cls; Cl Rep Jr Cls; Boy Scts; Hon Rl; NHS; Sct Actv; Stu Cncl; Ftbl; Trk; Wittenberg; Premed.

KRECEK, JACINTA; Central Cath HS; Lafayette, IN; Chrs; Cmnty Wkr; Hon Rl; NHS; Stg Crw; Yth Flsp; Fr Clb; Pep Clb; Trk; PPFtbl; Purdue Univ; Environmental Design.

KRECIOCH, JOHN; East Detroit HS; East Detroit, MI; 200/700 Boy Scts; NHS; Red Cr Ade; Sct Actv; Letter Bsktbl; Letter Crs Cntry; Letter Trk; Mic Tech College; Chem Engr.

KREDO, CARL; Center Line HS; Warren, MI; Band; Hon Rl; JA; Jr NHS; NHS; Sci Clb; Ten; Opt Clb Awd; Univ Of Mich; Computer Science.

KREEGER, LISA; Theodore Roosevelt HS; Kent, OH; 4/350 Chrs; Drl Tm; Hon Rl; Sch Mus; Sch Pl; Pep Clb; Bsktbl; Chrldng; Pom Pon; High Booster Pt Awd For Jr Cls 78; Sqd Leader 78; 1st Pl Drill Team Comp 78; Univ; Law.

KREFT, MARIA; La Porte HS; Laporte, IN; Hon Rl; Sch Mus; Pres Fr Clb; Pep Clb; Letter Trk; Treas GAA; IM Sprt; Vlybl Varsity Ltr 76; Indiana Univ; Radiology.

KREGAR, DORI; Ursuline HS; Girard, OH; Chrs; Hon Rl; NHS; FTA; Ger Clb; VP Lat Clb; Youngstown St Univ.

KREGEL, KEN; East Kentwood HS; Kentwood, MI; 1/600 Hon Rl; IM Sprt; Univ Of Mich; Acctg.

KREGER, JOYCE; Ferndale HS; Oak Park, MI; 88/493 Cl Rep Jr Cls; Cls Rep Sr Cls; Sch Mus; Sch Pl; Stg Crw; Stu Cncl; Drama Clb; Mich State Univ; Communications.

KREGER, MICHELLE; Henry Ford Ii HS; Stelring Hts, MI; 27/435 Cls Rep Frsh Cls; Pres Soph Cls; Cls Rep Sr Cls; Band; Girl Scts; Hon Rl; Hosp Ade; NHS; PPFtbl; College.

KREH, GLORIA; Peru HS; Peru, IN; 21/290 Sec Chrh Wkr; Hon Rl; NHS; Off Ade; Yth Flsp; Rptr Yrbk; Fr Clb; Letter Bsktbl; Trk; GAA; Bethel Coll; Bus Admin.

KREHER, COLLEEN; Douglas Mac Arthur HS; Saginaw, MI; 48/306 Sec Frsh Cls; Sec Soph Cls; Pres Jr Cls; Cls Rep Sr Cls; Chrh Wkr; Debate Tm; Hon Rl; Sch Pl; Stu Cncl; Pep Clb; 4yr Varsity Skiing Team Captain; Can Amera Games Forensics Team 2nd Plc; Miss J Board Rep Jacobsons; College; Communications.

KREHER, TASHA; Douglas Mac Arthur HS; Saginaw, MI; Chrh Wkr; Cmnty Wkr; Girl Scts; Hosp Ade; Yth Flsp; Fr Clb; Swmmng; Tmr; St Of Mi Schlstc Achvmnt Awd 79; V P & Pres Of Church Youth Grp 77 78 & 79; Treas Of Girls Clb 78; Northwood Inst; CPS.

KREICKER, CLAUDIA; Warsaw Cmnty HS; Warsaw, IN; 25/394 Treas FCA; Hon Rl; Sch Pl; Spn Clb; Bsktbl; Glf; Trk; GAA; Opt Clb Awd; Pres Awd; Univ; Bus.

KREIDER, LADONNA; Whitko HS; Pierceton, IN; 32/143 Chrs; Hon Rl; Natl Forn Lg; NHS; Sch Mus; Yrbk; Drama Clb; Pres OEA; Donald E Love Memrl Awd For Excellnc In Bus 1979; Indiana Univ; Acctg.

KREIDER, SUE; Central Christian HS; Wadsworth, OH; 1/69 Sec Soph Cls; Sec Jr Cls; Sec Sr Cls; Val; Chrs; Chrh Wkr; Hon Rl; Pres Yth Flsp; Scr Kpr; Cit Awd; Bob Jones Univ; Biologyu.

KREIDLER, MARIANNE C; Austintown Fitch HS; Youngstown, OH; 1/662 Cl Rep Jr Cls; Val; NHS; Sec Yth Flsp; Sec Fr Clb; Elk Awd; NCTE; Ohio St Univ; Natrl Rsrcs Mgmt.

KREIDLER, SUSAN; Heritage Christian HS; Indianapolis, IN; 27/62 Chrs; Hon Rl; Lbry Ade; Sch Mus; Univ.

KREIENBRINK, ELISE; Northrop HS; Ft Wayne, IN; FCA; Ten; Chrldng; Cit Awd; Univ; Acctg.

KREIGBAUM, JULIE; Midpark HS; Middleburg Hts, OH; 3/600 AFS; NHS; Ed Yrbk; Martin W Essex Schl For Gifted; College; Elem Ed.

KREIGHBAUM, DEBRA; Farwell Area HS; Lake, MI; 3/121 Pres Frsh Cls; Trs Soph Cls; Trs Jr Cls; Trs Sr Cls; Cls Rep Sr Cls; Band; Hon Rl; NHS; Sch Mus; Central Mic Univ; Acctg.

KREINBRING, KEVIN; Imlay City HS; Imlay City, MI; Am Leg Boys St; Hon Rl; Jr NHS; Sci Clb; Univ; Eng Tchr.

KREINBRINK, ANNETTE; Buckeye Central HS; Tiro, OH; 1/88 Sec Soph Cls; Pres Jr Cls; Am Leg Aux Girls St; Chrs; Hon Rl; VP Spn Clb; IM Sprt; Scr Kpr; Am Leg Awd; Cit Awd; Ohio St Univ; Nursing.

KREINBRINK, DON; Van Buren Local HS; Findlay, OH; 17/87 Boy Scts; Chrh Wkr; Hon Rl; Jr NHS; NHS; Sct Actv; IM Sprt; Natl Merit Ltr; Ohio St Univ; Elec Engr.

KREINBRINK, JOHN; Ottawa Glandorf HS; Ottawa, OH; Boy Scts; Hon Rl; Sch Mus; Sch Pl; Sct Actv; Stg Crw; Fr Clb; Ger Clb; Ftbl; Wrstlng; Northwest Business College.

KREINBRINK, T; Miller City HS; Leipsic, OH; Trs Jr Cls; Trs Sr Cls; Hon Rl; Treas NHS; Yrbk; Sec 4-H; Bsktbl; Chrldng; Dnfth Awd; Univ; Disc Jockey.

KREIS, JEFFREY; Dublin HS; Dublin, OH; 25/287 Chrh Wkr; Cmnty Wkr; Hon Rl; VP JA; Pres Yth Flsp; Ftbl; Ten; IM Sprt; JA Awd; European Hist Cntst 79; Univ; Engr.

KREISS, DIRK; Westerville HS; Columbus, OH; 51/280 Aud/Vis; Boy Scts; Hon Rl; Lbry Ade; Quill & Scroll; Ed Sch Nwsp; Pres Key Clb; Freedoms Foundation Vly Forge Yth Ldrshp Awd; Ohio Univ; Journalism.

KREITMAN, KEVAN; Detroit Cntry Day HS; Southfield, MI; VP Jr Cls; Pres Sr Cls; Sal; Hon Rl; NHS; Treas Sch Pl; Sec Key Clb; Mth Clb; Socr; Ten; Univ Of Michigan; Med.

KREJCI, LISA; Lutheran HS; N Olmsted, OH; Am Leg Aux Girls St; Hon Rl; Mod UN; NHS; Stu Cncl; Boys Clb Am; Mth Clb; Sci Clb; Natl Merit Ltr; Natl Merit SF; College; Sci.

KREJSA, JULIE; Lumen Cordium HS; Northfield, OH; Sec Frsh Cls; Trs Soph Cls; Chrh Wkr; Hon Rl; Stu Cncl; Mgrs; Cuyahoga Cmnty Coll; Intr Dsgn.

KREMER, DEBRA; Versailles HS; Rossburg, OH; 19/133 Pres Chrh Wkr; Hon Rl; Hst Frsh Cls; VP 4-H; FHA; Spn Clb; 4-H Awd; Miami Valley Schl Of Nursing; Rn.

KREMER, GAIL; Coldwater Exempted HS; Coldwater, OH; 15/140 Cls Rep Frsh Cls; Cls Rep Soph Cls; Sec Jr Cls; Hon Rl; Jr NHS; Stu Cncl; Yrbk; Pep Clb; Spn Clb; Gym; Bowling Green State Univ; Acctg.

KREMER, KATHERINE; Chaminade Julienne HS; Dayton, OH; 5/249 Band; Chrs; Chrh Wkr; Cmnty Wkr; Girl Scts; Hon Rl; Jr NHS; Orch; Sch Mus; Sch Pl; College.

KREMER, LISA; St Henry HS; St Henry, OH; Chrs; Chrh Wkr; FCA; Hon Rl; Sec Yth Flsp; Treas FHA; FTA; OEA; JA Awd; JETS Awd; Voc Schl; Sec.

KREMER, TAMARA A; Versailles HS; Rossburg, OH; 38/135 Sec Jr Cls; Cl Rep Jr Cls; Sec Sr Cls;

Am Leg Aux Girls St; Chrs; Chrh Wkr; JA; Wright State; Bus.

KREMPASKY, FRANCES; Holy Redeemer HS; Detroit, MI; Hon Rl; Lit Mag; NHS; Rptr Sch Nwsp; Trk; Michigan St Univ; Jrnlsm.

KREMPEL, JOHN T; Washington HS; Dalton, OH; AFS; Band; Hon Rl; NHS; Rptr Yrbk; Ger Clb; Akron Univ; Psych.

KREMPEL, MARCIE; Sault Area HS; Sault Ste Marie, MI; 15/350 Sec Frsh Cls; Band; Debate Tm; Hon Rl; Yth Flsp; Yrbk; Rptr Sch Nwsp; Gym; Chrldng; Ski Clb; Speech Clb; Special Olympics Gymnastics Reg Judge; Work With Mentally Retarded; Lake Superior St Coll; Med.

KREMS, MARY JO; Seton HS; Cincinnati, OH; 2/255 Chmn Jr NHS; Chmn NHS; Fr Clb; Univ.

KRENRICK, MARY; Loudonville HS; Loudonville, OH; Val; Am Leg Aux Girls St; Band; Chrs; Chrh Wkr; Hon Rl; VP NHS; Sch Pl; Treas Yth Flsp; Rptr Yrbk; Grace Coll Mert Schslp 1216 79; John Phillip Sousa Band Awd 79; Wayne Smith Acad Schlshp 79; Grace Coll; Elem Educ.

KRENTZ, J; Laporte HS; Laporte, IN; AFS; NHS; Sch Mus; Sch Pl; Fr Clb; Ind Univ.

KRENTZ, JANICE; Fraser HS; Fraser, MI; Chrh Wkr; Hon Rl; NHS; Capt Bsbl; Letter Ten; PPFtbl; Ferris St Coll; Med Tech.

KRESS, JANE M; Perry HS; Massillon, OH; Cls Rep Frsh Cls; Sec Soph Cls; Sec Jr Cls; NHS; Quill & Scroll; Stu Cncl; Yrbk; FHA; Crs Cntry; Trk; Outstanding Fres Girl Candidate; Coed Magazine Correspondent; College.

KRESS, KAREN; Chamberlin HS; Twinsburg, OH; Band; Bsktbl; Letter Gym; Outstndng Band Mbr; Merit Roll Awd; Coll.

KRESTIK, JEFFREY; Port Huron HS; Port Huron, MI; 2/327 Sal; Chrs; Treas Chrh Wkr; Hon Rl; Sch Pl; Drama Clb; Mth Clb; Natl Merit SF; Concordia Ann Arbor; Music Ther.

KRETCHMAN, SUE; Lakeshore Sr HS; St Joseph, MI; 21/299 Band; Drl Tm; Hon Rl; Orch; Sch Pl; 4-H; Sec FFA; Michigan State Univ; Animal Sci.

KRETOWICZ, KAREN; Grand Rapids Creston HS; Grand Rapids, MI; 10/395 Trs Jr Cls; VP Sr Cls; Am Leg Aux Girls St; NHS; Sch Pl; Rptr Sch Nwsp; Natl Merit Ltr; Mic State Univ; Bus Admin.

KREUTZER, ANNE; Peru HS; Peru, IN; 50/294 Band; Chrs; Debate Tm; Hon Rl; MMM; Sch Mus; Sch Pl; Drama Clb; Fr Clb; Butler Univ; Interior Design.

KREUTZER, MARY E; Mother Of Mercy HS; Cincinnati, OH; Girl Scts; Hon Rl; Hosp Ade; NHS; Red Cr Ade; Lat Clb; VP Sci Clb; Univ Of Cincinnati; Nursing.

KREUZ, ROGER J; St Johns HS; Swanton, OH; Hon Rl; Ed Sch Nwsp; Rptr Sch Nwsp; Sch Nwsp; Univ Of Toledo.

KREUZMANN, CINDY L; Northwest HS; Cincinnati, OH; 3/438 Cl Rep Jr Cls; Cls Rep Sr Cls; Hon Rl; Jr NHS; VP NHS; Yrbk; Rptr Sch Nwsp; Pres Spn Clb; Letter Trk; U S Military Academy; Natl Sec.

KREWSON, SCOTT; Maumee HS; Maumee, OH; 36/316 Hon Rl; Spn Clb; Letter Bsbl; Bsktbl; Letter Crs Cntry;.

KRICHBAUM, JANET; Watkins Memorial HS; Pataskala, OH; Band; Chrs; Chrh Wkr; Hon Rl; Fr Clb; Sec FNA; Univ; Nursing.

KRICK, TODD; Bishop Flaget HS; Chillicothe, OH; Chrh Wkr; Cmnty Wkr; Hosp Ade; Stg Crw; Spn Clb; Bsbl; Bsktbl; Crs Cntry; Oh St Sci Fair Excellnt Rating 78; Military Acad; Comp Sci.

KRIDER, TAMMERA; Northrop HS; Ft Wayne, IN; Band; Lbry Ade; Gym; Letter Mgrs; Pom Pon; Cit Awd; Indiana Univ; Comp Prog.

KRIDER, WANDA; Columbia City Joint HS; Columbia City, IN; 69/307 Band; Pres Chrh Wkr; Spn Clb; Fort Wayne Bible Coll; Missions.

KRIDLER, ELIZABETH; Hubbard HS; Hubbard, OH; Off Ade; Spn Clb; Gym; IM Sprt; Mat Maids; Scr Kpr; Tmr; College; Soc Work.

KRIEG, CONNIE; Lakeview HS; Cortland, OH; Chrs; Chrh Wkr; Off Ade; Yth Flsp; Y-Teens; Pres 4-H; Lat Clb; Mth Clb; Pep Clb; Letter Bsbl; Year End Awd 4 H 76; Year End Awd 4 H 77; Church Choir Awd 75; Univ; Pharm.

KRIEG, KENDALL; Harrison HS; Lafayette, IN; 25/300 Band; Boy Scts; Drm Bgl; Hon Rl; Jr NHS; NHS; Sct Actv; 4-H; Pep Clb; Mgrs; Purdue Univ; Engr.

KRIEGER, JEFFREY; Troy HS; Troy, MI; 10/350 Cls Rep Frsh Cls; Cls Rep Soph Cls; Cl Rep Jr Cls; Cls Rep Sr Cls; Hon Rl; Stu Cncl; Sprt Ed Yrbk; Bsbl; Ftbl; Wrstlng; Tech Schl; Mech Engr.

KRIEGER, KEVIN; Wauseon HS; Wauseon, OH; Hon Rl; Bsbl; Bsktbl; Ftbl; Trk; IM Sprt; Toledo Univ; Comp Sci.

KRIEGER, LAURA; Nordonia HS; Northfield, OH; Chrh Wkr; Girl Scts; Sch Pl; Stg Crw; Pep Clb; Bsktbl; Letter Trk; IM Sprt; Scr Kpr; Voice Dem Awd; College; Forestry.

KRIELOW, LAUREL; West Geauga HS; Chagrin Falls, OH; 63/352 Chrs; Hon Rl; Off Ade; Pep Clb; Bsktbl; IM Sprt; PPFtbl; Scr Kpr; Ohio State Univ; Vet.

KRIGLINE, KATHY; N Canton Hoover HS; North Canton, OH; 9/425 Am Leg Aux Girls St; Capt Band; Chrh Wkr; Cmnty Wkr; Pres Girl Scts; Hon Rl; NHS; Rptr Yrbk; Mth Clb; Sci Clb; Honorable Mention Ohio Tests Of Scholastic Achievmnt 1st Yr Algebra; College; Home Ec.

KRINOS, ELEANOR; Memorial HS; Campbell, OH; Cls Rep Frsh Cls; Cls Rep Soph Cls; Cl Rep Jr Cls; Sec Sr Cls; Chrs; Chrh Wkr; Lbry Ade; Off Ade; VP Stu Cncl; Pep Clb; X Ray Tech.

KRINSKY, ALISA; Northville HS; Northville, MI; VP Frsh Cls; Pres Jr Cls; Cmnty Wkr; Hon Rl; Stu Cncl; Ger Clb; Pep Clb; Chrldng; College; Bio Sci.

KRISER, LYNN A; Coldwater HS; Coldwater, MI; 1/295 Band; Cmp Fr Grls; Chrs; Chrh Wkr; Cmnty Wkr; Hon Rl; Lbry Ade; NHS; Pol Wkr; Sch Mus; Judson Coll; Music.

KRISHER, ANN; Berea HS; Berea, OH; 13/551 Cls Rep Frsh Cls; Cls Rep Soph Cls; Cl Rep Jr Cls; Chrs; Chrh Wkr; Hon Rl; Hosp Ade; NHS; Sch Mus; Sch Pl; Univ; Med.

KRISHER, JAMES W; Lordstown HS; Warren, OH; 26/54 VP Band; Chrs; Sch Mus; Sch Pl; Stg Crw; Pep Clb; Bsktbl; Crs Cntry; Trk; Am Leg Awd; College; Comp Tech.

KRISPIN, LORETTE; Algonac HS; Harsens Island, MI; Chrh Wkr; Girl Scts; Hon Rl; Lbry Ade; NHS; Boys Clb Am; St Clair Community College; Data Pro.

KRISTANC, ELEANOR; Girard HS; Girard, OH; 32/200 AFS; Chrs; Cmnty Wkr; Girl Scts; Lbry Ade; Y-Teens; Rptr Yrbk; Rptr Sch Nwsp; Pep Clb; Bsbl; Youngstown St Univ; Law Enforcement.

KRISTAPOVICH, LARRY; Calumet HS; Ahmeek, MI; VP Frsh Cls; Pres Sr Cls; Am Leg Boys St; Chrh Wkr; Hon Rl; Sch Pl; Fr Clb; Letter Ftbl; Am Leg Awd; Lion Awd; Mic Tech; Comp Sci.

KRISTEN, POLLY; Ernest W Seaholm HS; Birmingham, MI; 18/636 Cls Rep Frsh Cls; Cls Rep Soph Cls; Cl Rep Jr Cls; Cls Rep Sr Cls; Chrs; Debate Tm; Hon Rl; VP Jr NHS; Mod UN; Natl Forn Lg; Cornell Univ; Bio Engr.

KRISTIN, MATTHEW L; Ithaca HS; Ithaca, MI; Band; Boy Scts; Chrh Wkr; Hon Rl; Sct Actv; Bsbl; Bsktbl; Crs Cntry; Ftbl; IM Sprt; Bsbk 1st Team All Regnl Cls C 79; Bsbl Hon Mntn All Lg 79; Data Proc Wrkshp Schlshp Ferris St 79; Ferris St Coll; Data Proc.

KRISTOFF, KATHRYN; Lumen Christi HS; Pleasant Lake, MI; 1/242 Trs Jr Cls; Cls Rep Sr Cls; Val; Hon Rl; Sec NHS; Sch Mus; Stu Cncl; Univ Of Mic; Sci.

KRITZELL, THOMAS; Manchester HS; Akron, OH; 44/210 Boy Scts; Chrh Wkr; Cmnty Wkr; Sct Actv; Letter Trk; Ohio Univ; Comp Sci.

KRITZER, BONNIE E; Sidney HS; Sidney, OH; Chrs; Hon Rl; NHS; Orch; Sch Mus; Stu Cncl; Fr Clb; Coll; Engr.

KRIUTHOFF, THERESA; Zeeland HS; Zeeland, MI; Chrs; FCA; Hon Rl; Univ; Asst Ofc Mgmt.

KRIVE, JULIE; Interlochen Arts Academy; Big Rapids, MI; VP Soph Cls; Band; Hon Rl; Orch; Stu Cncl; Rptr Yrbk; Rptr Sch Nwsp; Fr Clb; Am Leg Awd; Cit Awd; Carleton Coll; Medicine.

KROCHMAL, ELAINE; Regina HS; Euclid, OH; Chrs; Hon Rl; Jr NHS; Pres Orch; Sch Mus; Yrbk; Rptr Sch Nwsp; Drama Clb; Coll; Bio Chem.

KROCHMALNY, MICHAEL; Divine Child HS; Dearborn Hts, MI; Cmnty Wkr; Hockey; IM Sprt; St Of MI Schlrshp Merit Awd 79; Michigan St Univ; Engr.

KROCKER, JAMES; Tuscarawas Central Cath HS; New Phila, OH; Cls Rep Frsh Cls; Hon Rl; NHS; Stu Cncl; Bsbl; Letter Ftbl; Awds In Local & Dist Sci Fairs 77 78 & 79; Kent St Univ; Engr.

KROEGER, CRAIG; Rossford HS; Rossford, OH; Cls Rep Frsh Cls; Cls Rep Soph Cls; Cl Rep Jr Cls; Band; Hon Rl; JA; PAVAS; Sch Mus; Sch Pl; Stu Cncl; First Pres & Organizer Of Thespian Club At Rossford High 79; Univ; Law.

KROEGER, JAYNE; Wood Memorial HS; Elberfield, IN; Chrh Wkr; Cmnty Wkr; Lbry Ade; PAVAS; Yth Flsp; Pep Clb; Spn Clb; College.

KROENING, LAURIE; Lakeshore HS; Stevensville, MI; Cmnty Wkr; Hon Rl; NHS; Off Ade; Sch Nwsp; Trk; Am Leg Awd; Cit Awd; Working At Win Schulers.

KROES, WILLIAM; Mc Bain Rural Agrl HS; Mc Bain, MI; 10/61 Band; Hon Rl; NHS; Stu Cncl; Letter Bsbl; Letter Bsktbl; Capt Ftbl; Ferris State; Plastics Tech.

KROETSCH, JUDY; Novi Sr HS; Novi, MI; Sec Soph Cls; Sec Jr Cls; Cmnty Wkr; Capt Drl Tm; Sch Mus; Stg Crw; Rptr Yrbk; Spn Clb; Trk; Busns Schl; Exec Sec.

KROFFT, LISHS S; Sheridan HS; Mt Perry, OH; 46/180 Chrs; Debate Tm; Hon Rl; Lbry Ade; Sec Sch Nwsp; Pres 4-H; Pres OEA; Pep Clb; Mgrs; Mat Maids; Ambassador Awd 78; Stateswoman Awd 78; Fresh Homecoming Attendant 75; Exec Sec.

KROGER, RICHARD J; La Salle HS; Cincinnati, OH; Cmnty Wkr; Hon Rl; Hosp Ade; Mod UN; Socr; Coach Actv; IM Sprt; Cincinnati Notre Dame Univ; Bus Mktg.

KROGULECKI, MATHEW; Redford Bishop Borgess HS; Dearborn Heigh, MI; Hon Rl; NHS; Capt Trk; IM Sprt; Natl Merit SF; Michigan St Univ.

KROHTA, JULIE; Trenton HS; Trenton, MI; 46/554 Chrs; Chrh Wkr; Hon Rl; NHS; Stu Cncl; Univ Of Mich; Political Science.

KROL, JIM; Bishop Noll Inst; Hammond, IN; 32/364 Am Leg Boys St; Hon Rl; Mth Clb; Letter Trk; College; Med.

KROL, MARCIA J; St Agatha HS; Detroit, MI; Chrh Wkr; Debate Tm; Hon Rl; NHS; Off Ade; Sct Actv; Fr Clb; Schoolcraft Coll; Med Rec.

KROL, SUSAN; Harry S Truman HS; Taylor, MI; Hon Rl; NHS; Sch Nwsp; Letter Trk; Scr Kpr; Univ; Med.

KROLICKI, COLETTE; St Clement HS; Detroit, MI; Girl Scts; Hon Rl; Jr NHS; NHS; Sct Actv; Pep Clb; Letter Bsbl; Letter Bsktbl; Chrldng; GAA; MVP Bsltbl Awd; All League Bsktbl; All Catholic All Cnty Bsktbl; Univ Of Michigan; Phys Ed.

KROLIKOWSKI, ANITA; Our Lady Of Mt Carmel HS; Wyandotte, MI; 10/63 Sec Sr Cls; Hon Rl; Pep Clb; Cit Awd; Bus School; Bus.

KROMAR, JACK; St Joseph HS; Cleveland, OH; 38/300 Chrs; Chrh Wkr; Cmnty Wkr; Hon Rl; NHS; Bsbl; Bsktbl; Bowling Green St Univ; Phys Ther.

KROMAR, JOHN; St Joseph HS; Cleveland, OH; 38/300 Chrs; Hon Rl; NHS; Key Clb; Capt Bsbl; Capt Bsktbl; Univ; Phys Ther.

KROMER, DONNA; Chalker HS; Southington, OH; 9/65 Cls Rep Soph Cls; Band; Boy Scts; Hon Rl; NHS; Stu Cncl; Y-Teens; Rptr Yrbk; Ed Sch Nwsp; Beta Clb; AJBC Schlrshp 79; West Virginia Univ; Phys Ther.

KROMER, WENDY; Sandusky St Marys Ctrl HS; Sandusky, OH; 38/122 Cls Rep Sr Cls; Band; Cmp Fr Grls; Hon Rl; 4-H; Spn Clb; GAA; Notre Dame Coll; Design Merch.

KROMKOWSKI, JOHN D; Saint Josephs HS; Baltimore, MD; 4/273 Hon Rl; Orch; Pol Wkr; Sch Pl; Sch Nwsp; Crs Cntry; Letter Trk; College; Poli Sci.

KRON, ELIZABETH S; Lansing Everett HS; Lansing, MI; Chrs; Cmnty Wkr; Debate Tm; Lbry Ade; Pol Wkr; Natl Merit Ltr; Kalamazoo Coll.

KRONDON, BEVERLEY; Bramwell HS; Rock, WV; 2/35 Sec Soph Cls; Sal; VP Chrs; NHS; Yrbk; Pres Drama Clb; Bluefield St Coll; Busns.

KRONE, DIANNE; Beallsville HS; Jerusalem, OH; Chrs; Chrh Wkr; FCA; Rptr Yrbk; 4-H; Fr Clb; FHA; Letter Bsktbl; Ohio Univ; Bus Mgmt.

KROPKA, JUDI; Buckeye South HS; Smithfield, OH; 19/120 FCA; Hon Rl; Y-Teens; Drama Clb; Pep Clb; Spn Clb; Ohio Univ; Medicine.

KROSKY, KAREN; Admiral King HS; Lorain, OH; Band; Chrs; Hon Rl; JA; Gym; JA Awd; Cuyahoga Cnty Cmnty Coll; Dent Hygns.

KROTZER, KATHLEEN; Herbert Henry Dow HS; Midland, MI; JA; 4-H; JA Awd; Delta Coll; Acctg.

KROUPA, MICHAEL; Mancelona HS; Mancelona, MI; Cls Rep Frsh Cls; Band; Hon Rl; Wrstlng; College.

KROWNAPPLE, E; East Knox HS; Howard, OH; 13/66 Pres Jr Cls; Pres Sr Cls; Band; Chrs; Yrbk; Drama Clb; Chrldng; GAA; North Ctrl Tech Coll; Nursing.

KROZAL, ROBERT; Adlai E Stevenson HS; Livonia, MI; 240/776 Cmnty Wkr; Off Ade; Letter Wrstlng; St Of MI Comp Schlshp Awd 79; Livonia Citizens Schlrshp Fndtn Awd 79; Livonia Pblc Schls Voc Dent Asst Prg; Northern Michigan Univ; Pre Dent.

KRPICAK, JANET; Chaney HS; Youngstown, OH; Hon Rl; Y-Teens; Youngstown St Univ; Soc Worker.

KRUCZ, JOAN; St Francis Desales Cntrl HS; Morgantown, WV; Spn Clb; Letter Bsktbl; Letter Trk; College; Pharmacy.

KRUDER, PAM; Plymouth HS; Plymouth, IN; Chrs; Chrh Wkr; Girl Scts; Pol Wkr; Yth Flsp; 4-H; 4-H Awd; Ivy Tech; Nursing.

KRUECK, MARGIE; South Amherst HS; So Amherst, OH; 6/69 Pres Frsh Cls; Pres Band; Chrs; Drm Mjrt; Hon Rl; NHS; Sch Pl; Yth Flsp; Yrbk; Drama Clb; U S Marine Awd Distngshd Musician 79; Ella Weiss Educ Fund Schlshp 79; Ohio St Univ; Bus Admin.

KRUEGER, CHERI; Fruitport HS; Fruitport, MI; 14/281 Band; Chrh Wkr; Debate Tm; Drl Tm; Drm Bgl; Hon Rl; Hosp Ade; NHS; Orch; Sch Mus; Lions Ofmi All St Badn 78 & 79; Fruitport HS Quiz Bwl Team 79; St Ofmi Schslp Comp 79; Muskegon Cmnty Coll; Dent Hygnst.

KRUEGER, DIANE; Williamston HS; Williamston, MI; Trs Frsh Cls; Pres AFS; Debate Tm; VP JA; Jr NHS; Yth Flsp; Drama Clb; VP JA Awd; Natl Merit Ltr; Lansing Cmnty Coll; Limnology.

KRUEGER, KIM; Highland HS; Medina, OH; Band; Chrs; Chrh Wkr; Hon Rl; VP 4-H; Key Clb; Lat Clb; 4-H Awd; College; Animal Studies.

KRUEGER, MARJORIE; Mt Pleasant HS; Mt Pleasant, MI; 27/372 Band; Hon Rl; 4-H; Lat Clb; Bsbl; IM Sprt; Natl Merit Ltr; Mic State Univ; Chem Engr.

KRUEGER, MARK; Chippewa Hills HS; Weidman, MI; 1/212 VP Jr Cls; Val; Band; VP NHS; Orch; Pres Stu Cncl; Trk; Elk Awd; Natl Merit Ltr; Michigan Tech Univ; Civil Engr.

KRUEGER, MARLENE; Mississinewa HS; Gas City, IN; 20/189 Chrs; Hon Rl; NHS; Sch Mus; Drama Clb; Fr Clb; Pres Pep Clb; PPFtbl; Elk Awd; JC Awd; Ball St Univ; Soc Work.

KRUEGER, MICHAEL; Chippewa Hills HS; Weidman, MI; 1/212 Val; Band; Hon Rl; NHS; Elk Awd; Natl Merit SF; Michigan Tech Univ; Chem Engr.

KRUEGER, P; Highland HS; Medina, OH; 80/208 Chrs; Hon Rl; NHS; Stu Cncl; Pres 4-H; IM Sprt; Ohi State Univ; Agri.

KRUEGER, RICHARD; Lutheran East HS; Warren, MI; Band; Chrs; Hon Rl; NHS; Rptr Yrbk; Rptr Sch Nwsp; Drama Clb; Natl Merit Ltr; Alma College; Music.

KRUG, JONI; Reeths Puffer HS; Muskegon, MI; 76/396 Boy Scts; Hon Rl; Off Ade; Yrbk; Trk; PPFtbl; Ferris State Coll; Bus Field.

KRUG, KAREN; Tuslaw HS; N Lawrence, OH; 42/160 Cls Rep Frsh Cls; Cls Rep Soph Cls; Y-Teens; Pres 4-H; Pep Clb; Chrldng; 4-H Awd; Bus Schl; Bus.

KRUG, KAREN E; Belleville HS; Belleville, MI; 14/514 Band; Hon Rl; NHS; Sch Mus; Stg Crw; Univ; Acctg.

KRUGER, BECKY; Whitmer Sr HS; Toledo, OH; 123/910 Band; Chrh Wkr; Girl Scts; Hon Rl; Hosp Ade; Spn Clb; Voc Schl; Nursing.

KRUGER, KATHY; West Central Jr Sr HS; Francesville, IN; 4/98 Band; Cmnty Wkr; Capt Drl Tm; Pol Wkr; Yth Flsp; Ed Yrbk; Drama Clb; Pres 4-H; FHA; OEA; West Central Schrlshp 1979; St Jr Leader Conf 1979; Ball St Univ; Exec Sec.

KRUGER, KIMBERLY; Tecumseh HS; Tecumseh, MI; 33/212 Cl Rep Jr Cls; Cls Rep Sr Cls; Hon Rl; NHS; Stu Cncl; Pep Clb; Chrldng; Scr Kpr; Natl Merit Schl; Cntrl Michigan Univ.

KRUGER, RANDELL; Oscoda Area HS; Oscoda, MI; 26/233 Band; Boy Scts; Drm Bgl; Hon Rl; Jr NHS; NHS; Orch; Sct Actv; Trk; God Cntry Awd; Univ Of Michigan.

KRUGER, ROBERT; Vinton Cnty Consolidated HS; Mc Arthur, OH; 8/160 Band; Boy Scts; Chrs; FCA; Hon Rl; Jr NHS; NHS; Sch Mus; 4-H; Fr Clb; District Algbra 1 20th Plc 76; District Plane Geomtry 10th Plc 77; District Algbra 2 17th Plc 78; Univ Of Kentucky; Bus Admin.

KRUGER, SUE; Clay HS; S Bend, IN; Hon Rl; Ger Clb; Lat Clb; Trk; Butler Univ; Pharm.

KRUGLER, CHARLES; Reed City HS; Reed City, MI; 9/165 Cl Rep Jr Cls; Cls Rep Sr Cls; Band; Chrh Wkr; Hon Rl; NHS; VP Yth Flsp; Pep Clb; Capt Twrlr; Valparaiso Univ.

KRUGLIAK, AMANDA; Timken Sr HS; Canton, OH; Cls Rep Soph Cls; Chrs; Hon Rl; Jr NHS; Natl Forn Lg; Off Ade; Sch Mus; Sch Pl; Sch Nwsp; Drama Clb; Univ.

KRUITHOF, DANIEL; Holland HS; Holland, MI; 5/280 Band; Hon Rl; NHS; IM Sprt; Hope College; Biology.

KRUITHOF JR, GLENN; Benton Harbor HS; Benton Hbr, MI; Band; Hon Rl; NHS; Yth Flsp; Mth Clb; Engr.

KRUK, DIANE; Marian HS; S Bend, IN; Band; Chrh Wkr; Drl Tm; Orch; Stg Crw; Yth Flsp; Pep Clb; Pom Pon; Bowling Club; Indiana Univ; Dent Tech.

KRUKEMYER, TERRY; Eastwood HS; Pemberville, OH; 11/185 Hon Rl; NHS; Treas Stu Cncl; Treas 4-H; Key Clb; Bsbl; Capt IM Sprt; Scr Kpr; Ohio State Univ.

KRUKOWSKI, SHARON; Shelby Sr HS; Shelby, OH; 25/290 Cls Rep Frsh Cls; Cls Rep Soph Cls; Pres Sr Cls; Am Leg Aux Girls St; Chrs; Hon Rl; Stu Cncl; Lat Clb; Letter Bsktbl; Am Leg Awd; Ohio Univ; Bio.

KRULIKOSKI, SANDRA; Traverse City HS; Traverse City, MI; 89/693 Band; Hon Rl; Lbry Ade; Sch Mus; Sch Pl; Stg Crw; Drama Clb; Mth Clb; Mich State Univ; Med.

KRUMBACK, LINDA; Alcona Comm HS; Harrisville, MI; 2/115 Sec Soph Cls; Band; Hon Rl; Jr NHS; Pep Clb; Spn Clb; Chrldng; PPFtbl; Alpena Hlywd Schl Of Bty; Beautcn.

KRUMLAW, MOLLIE; Ashland HS; Ashland, OH; Cls Rep Soph Cls; Cl Rep Jr Cls; Chrs; Hon Rl; Off Ade; Sch Pl; Stu Cncl; Yth Flsp; Yrbk; Letter Trk;.

KRUMME, MELISSA; St Ursula Academy; Cincinnati, OH; Hon Rl; Jr NHS; Ed Yrbk; Bsktbl; Ten; Natl Merit Ltr; Univ; Bus.

KRUPA, SANDY; Terre Haute South Vigo HS; Terre Haute, IN; FCA; Hon Rl; NHS; Off Ade; Y-Teens; Bsktbl; Swmmng; Indiana St Univ.

KRUPER, MARTIN; Avon HS; Avon, OH; Band; Boy Scts; Hon Rl; NHS; College.

KRUPINSKI, ALICE; St Florian HS; Detroit, MI; 15/103 Sec Frsh Cls; Sec Soph Cls; Trs Jr Cls; Hon Rl; Sct Actv; Rptr Sch Nwsp; Fr Clb; Spn Clb; Sci & Engr Fair Of Metro Detroit Hon Mention 1975 & Exhibitor In 1976; Univ.

KRUPINSKI, VICTORIA; Griffith Sr HS; Griffith, IN; 32/310 Trs Jr Cls; Cmnty Wkr; Hon Rl; Jr NHS; Off Ade; Stu Cncl; Sch Nwsp; Pep Clb; Bsbl; GAA; Indiana Univ; Elem Educ.

KRUPP, DOUGLAS; Gibsonburg HS; Helena, OH; 5/101 Hon Rl; Rptr Yrbk; Yrbk; 4-H; Sci Clb; Cit Awd; 4-H Awd; Bowling Green State Univ; Bus Admin.

KRUPP, KEVIN; Lorain Catholic HS; Lorain, OH; Band; Boy Scts; Chrs; Chrh Wkr; Hon Rl; NHS; Sch Pl; Sct Actv; Drama Clb; College.

KRUPP, ROB; Carey HS; Carey, OH; Cls Rep Soph Cls; Cl Rep Jr Cls; Cls Rep Sr Cls; Am Leg Boys St; Chrs; Hon Rl; Jr NHS; Stu Cncl; 4-H; Mth Clb; Univ; Comp Sci.

KRUSE, ALIX; Grosse Pointe North HS; Grosse Pointe, MI; Cls Rep Frsh Cls; Cls Rep Soph Cls; Cl Rep Jr Cls; Cls Rep Sr Cls; Chrs; Chrh Wkr; FCA; Hosp Ade; DECA; Letter Ten; Mich State Univ; Advertising.

KRUSE, CHRISTINE; Bishop Ready HS; Columbus, OH; Hon Rl; Hosp Ade; Sch Mus; OEA; Letter Trk; Letter Chrldng; Franklin Univ; Med.

KRUSE, JOHN S; Shaker Heights HS; Shaker Hts, OH; Hon Rl; Letter Swmmng; Tmr; NCTE; Natl Merit Schl; Univ Of Rochester.

KRUSHINSKI, MATTHEW; St Johns HS; Toledo, OH; Band; Hon Rl; Sch Pl; Ed Sch Nwsp; Sch Nwsp; Letter Socr; Letter Trk; IM Sprt; Pres Awd; Hnbrl Mntn In Feature Wrtng In HS Jrnlsm Comptn 79; Ensmbl Awd For Band Both From Bowling Grn 79; Univ; Musical Art.

KRUSIC, JACQUELYN A; Manistique HS; Manistique, MI; 2/150 Sal; Band; Hon Rl; Natl Forn Lg; Pep Clb; Capt Bsktbl; Trk; Chrldng; Coach Actv; IM Sprt; Central Michigan Univ; Phys Ed.

KRUSNIAK, MARY; Frankenmuth HS; Frankenmuth, MI; Band; Chrs; Hon Rl; Natl Forn Lg; NHS; PAVAS; Sch Mus; Sch Pl; Delta Coll; Fine Arts.

KRUSS, ROBERT; Riverside HS; Dearborn Hts, MI; Chrs; Hon Rl; Jr NHS; NHS; Sch Mus; Sch Pl; Sec Drama Clb; Pres Fr Clb; Univ Of Michigan; Bus.

KRUSZKA, RICHARD; Elyria Catholic HS; Elyria, OH; Am Leg Boys St; Band; Hon Rl; Hosp Ade; Sch Mus; Sch Pl; Yrbk; Rptr Sch Nwsp; Spn Clb; Univ.

KRUSZYNSKI, BARBARA; Andrean HS; Merrillville, IN; 22/284 Chrs; Cmnty Wkr; Hon Rl; Lat Clb; College; Pre Med.

KRUTEL, ELIZABETH; Baldwin HS; Bitely, MI; Hon Rl; Bsbl; Wrstlng; IM Sprt; Ferris State Univ; Data Processing.

KRUTEL, ELIZABETH M; Baldwin Comm HS; Bitely, MI; Hon Rl; Off Ade; IM Sprt; Muskegon Bsns Coll; Acctg.

KRUTHAUP, MERNA; Clermont Northeastern HS; Batavia, OH; 7/215 Pres Soph Cls; Sec Jr Cls; Chrh Wkr; FCA; Hon Rl; NHS; Yrbk; Pep Clb; Spn Clb; Chrldng; Southern St Cmnty Coll; Acctg.

KRUTTLIN, PHILLIP; Alcona Comm HS; Harrisville, MI; Hon Rl; Jr NHS; NHS; Capt Ftbl; Trk; Coll; Sci.

KRUZAN, JOSEPH; Bishop Noll Institute; E Chicago, IN; Chrs; Chrh Wkr; Hon Rl; Sch Mus; Sch Pl; Sct Actv; Stg Crw; Drama Clb; Chrl Minor & Major Ltr 78; Eagle Scout With Brnz Palm 75; Univ; Acctg.

KRYCH, LYNETTE; Lumen Cordium HS; Bedford, OH; Cmp Fr Grls; Debate Tm; Drl Tm; Hon Rl; Hosp Ade; Off Ade; Sch Pl; Stg Crw; Sch Nwsp; Fr Clb; College; Child Psych.

KRYLING, JOHN; Mc Comb Local HS; Mc Comb, OH; Bsbl; Bsktbl; Ftbl; Scr Kpr; Lima Tech Voc Schl; Elec.

KRYNICKI, CYNTHIA; Waldron HS; Flat Rock, IN; Hon Rl; 4-H; Fr Clb; FFA; Letter Bsktbl; Letter Trk; Northwood Inst.

KRYSTEK, CHRISTOPHER; Warren Sr HS; Warren, MI; Band; Sct Actv; Socr; Commendation In S E Michigan Scholastic Writing Awd; Michigan St Univ; Engr.

KRZISNIK, WILLIAM; Allen Park HS; Allen Park, MI; 1/365 Val; Treas Band; Ten; Am Leg Awd; Kiwan Awd; Wayne State Univ; Mech Engrn.

KRZYZANOWSKI, DAN; Upper Arlington HS; Columbus, OH; 74/610 Hon Rl; Sch Nwsp; Ger Clb; IM Sprt; Ohio St Univ; Graphic Arts.

KSIONZEK, DONNA; St Andrew HS; Detroit, MI; 1/99 Chrh Wkr; Hon Rl; NHS; Rptr Yrbk; Pep Clb; Eastern Michigan Univ; Medicine.

KUBACKI, KAREN; Ubly Cmnty HS; Ubly, MI; 8/120 Cls Rep Sr Cls; Chrh Wkr; Hon Rl; NHS; Stu Cncl; Pep Clb; Letter Trk; PPFtbl; Univ.

KUBALSKI, SHARON; Lumen Cordium HS; Garfield Hgts, OH; 10/92 Cl Rep Jr Cls; Drl Tm; Hon Rl; Hosp Ade; Stu Cncl; Spn Clb; GAA; Univ Of Akron; Comm Art.

KUBAN, BARRY; Port Clinton HS; Pt Clinton, OH; 10/280 Aud/Vis; Band; Boy Scts; Chrh Wkr; Hon Rl; NHS; Yrbk; Fr Clb; Mth Clb; Ftbl; Univ; Sci.

KUBIAK, C; Comstock Park Secondary HS; Comstock Pk, MI; Pres Soph Cls; VP Jr Cls; NHS; Rptr Yrbk; Pep Clb; Chmn Chrldng; College.

KUBIAK, KEVIN; West Geauga HS; Chesterland, OH; Hon Rl; Letter Bsbl; IM Sprt; Univ; Acctg.

KUBIT, NANCY; Lamphere HS; Mt Clemens, MI; Fr Clb; Spn Clb; Swmmng; Albion; Interpretor.

KUCEK, JOHN; William A Wirt HS; Gary, IN; 5/240 Chrh Wkr; Debate Tm; Hon Rl; NHS; Mth Clb; Am Leg Awd; US Naval Sea Cadet Corps Officers Awd; Post Tribune Bsns Achvmnt Awd; Purdue Univ; Elec Engr.

KUCENSKY, DAVID; Normandy HS; Parma, OH; 17/600 Aud/Vis; Band; Hon Rl; Lit Mag; Quill & Scroll; Stu Cncl; Ger Clb; Univ; Chem.

KUCHAREK, MARY; Central Lake Public HS; Central Lake, MI; Trs Sr Cls; Band; Girl Scts; Hon Rl; Lbry Ade; Bsktbl; Univ; Nursery Schl Tchr.

KUCHERA, APRIL; Marian HS; Cincinnati, OH; JA; Lbry Ade; Spn Clb; Univ.

KUCHERAVY, MARY; New Albany HS; New Albany, OH; Am Leg Aux Girls St; Chrs; Girl Scts; Hon Rl; Lbry Ade; NHS; Sch Pl; Stg Crw; Drama Clb; Pep Clb; Univ; Sci.

KUCHINIC, KARA; Herbert Henry Dow HS; Midland, MI; Hon Rl; Quill & Scroll; Stu Cncl; Sprt Ed Yrbk; Ed Sch Nwsp; Rptr Sch Nwsp; Sch Nwsp; Ger Clb; Glf; Awd Of Excllnc Ball St Jrnlsm Workshop 78; Exllnc In Writing Update Staff 78 79; St Of Mi Comp Schlrshp 79; Michigan St Univ; Bus Admin.

KUCHTA, STEVE; Benedictine HS; Highland Hts, OH; Hon Rl; Stg Crw; Drama Clb; Ger Clb; IM Sprt; Mgrs; Scr Kpr; College.

KUCK, KAROL; Waterford Mott HS; Drayton Plains, MI; VP Band; Chrs; Hon Rl; Sch Mus; Ed Yrbk; Drama Clb; PPFtbl; Albion College; Music Educa.

KUCKUCK, RONALD; Bryan HS; Bryan, OH; Aud/Vis; Chrs; JA; JA Awd; Huntington Coll; Wildlife Mgmt.

KUCMANIC, CHRISTINE; Euclid HS; Euclid, OH; Cls Rep Soph Cls; Cl Rep Jr Cls; Hon Rl; Cleveland State; Art.

KUCZINSKI, DONNA; St Joseph Acad; Fairview Pk, OH; 15/254 Cmnty Wkr; Girl Scts; Hosp Ade; Red Cr Ade; Chrldng; GAA; College; Nurse.

KUCZYNSKI, MICHELLE; Kenston HS; Chagrin Fl, OH; Cls Rep Frsh Cls; Cls Rep Soph Cls; Band; Drm Mjrt; Hon Rl; Sch Nwsp; Spn Clb; Letter Trk; PPFtbl; Twrlr; Nursing.

KUDEJ, GARY; Normandy HS; Seven Hls, OH; 26/640 Hon Rl; Ger Clb; IM Sprt; Cit Awd; College; Busns.

KUDER, JANICE M; Columbian HS; Tiffin, OH; 1/330 AFS; Band; Chrs; Chrh Wkr; Hon Rl; JA; Sch Mus; Sch Pl; Stg Crw; Yth Flsp; Univ; Elem Educ.

KUDRAK, DONALD; Theodore Roosevelt HS; Wyandotte, MI; Band; Hon Rl; Ten; Michigan Tech Univ; Mech Engr.

KUDSIN, KATHLEEN; Roseville HS; Roseville, MI; 6/400 Cls Rep Soph Cls; VP Jr Cls; Band; Chrh Wkr; Drm Mjrt; Hon Rl; NHS; Univ Of Det; Dental.

KUEBEL, SUSAN; Lawrenceburg HS; Lawrenceburg, IN; Treas FCA; Hon Rl; Hosp Ade; Rptr Yrbk; Treas Fr Clb; Pep Clb; Bsktbl; Glf; Trk; Mgrs; Thomas More Coll; Nursing.

KUEHN, DALE; Trenton HS; Trenton, MI; 64/549 Chrh Wkr; Hon Rl; Jr NHS; NHS; Yth Flsp; Letter Swmmng; Michigan Tech Univ; Fisheries Bio.

KUEHN, KELLY; South Spencer HS; Rockport, IN; Band; Chrs; Drl Tm; Hon Rl; Sch Mus; Stg Crw; 4-H; Chrldng; Capt Pom Pon; Intl Thespian Soc; Tri State Beauty Schl; Cosmetology.

KUEHR, LISA; Scecina Memorial HS; Indianapolis, IN; Chrh Wkr; Hon Rl; NHS; Off Ade; Pol Wkr; Stg Crw; Yrbk; Marian College; Elementary Ed.

KUENTZ, SCOTT; Copley Sr HS; Akron, OH; Band; Chrs; Hon Rl; Sch Pl; Drama Clb; Spn Clb; Univ Of Akron.

KUENZEL, KEELY; Western Reserve HS; Wakeman, OH; 4/120 Band; Sec Chrs; Hon Rl; Hosp Ade; NHS; Yth Flsp; 4-H; Letter Bsktbl; PPFtbl; Univ.

KUENZER, JOANNE; Hudson Area HS; Hudson, MI; Cls Rep Frsh Cls; Am Leg Aux Girls St; Band; Hon Rl; NHS; Spn Clb; Pom Pon; Scr Kpr; Univ; Engr.

KUENZI, JOLENE; St Johns HS; St Johns, MI; Band; Hon Rl; Yth Flsp; 4-H; IM Sprt; Tmr; 4-H Awd; Michigan St Univ; Bus Law.

KUENZLI, JOLENE; St Johns HS; St Johns, MI; Hon Rl; 4-H; 4-H Awd; Mic St Univ; Bus Law.

KUESS, BARBARA K; Celina Sr HS; Celina, OH; 8/241 Chrh Wkr; Cmnty Wkr; Hon Rl; NHS; Pres 4-H; Pres FBLA; Pep Clb; Letter Ten; GAA; PPFtbl; Univ; Mktg.

KUESS, DEB; Celina Sr HS; Celina, OH; Drm Bgl; Girl Scts; Hon Rl; Lbry Ade; NHS; Off Ade; FBLA; FHA; Voc Schl; Stewardess.

KUESTER, JENNY; Acad Of Immaculate Cncptn; Cincinnati, OH; 20/68 Aud/Vis; Chrs; Chrh Wkr; Hon Rl; JA; NHS; Sch Pl; Stg Crw; Sch Nwsp; Drama Clb; Univ; Music.

KUEY, PERRY; Warren Sr HS; Sterling Hts, MI; VP Sr Cls; Hon Rl; Jr NHS; NHS; Stu Cncl; Ten; Trk; Mgrs; Wayne St Univ; Fine Arts.

KUGLER, THOMAS; Coloma HS; Coloma, MI; Band; NHS; VP Fr Clb; Capt Glf; Letter Ten; Am Leg Awd; Univ; Phys Sci.

KUHAR, MARIANNE; Ursuline HS; Youngstown, OH; 1/340 VP Jr Cls; Hon Rl; NHS; Off Ade; Stu Cncl; FTA; Spn Clb; Crs Cntry; Trk; Chrldng; Univ; Speech Pathology.

KUHARIC, KATHARINE; John Adams HS; So Bend, IN; 67/400 Hon Rl; JA; Yrbk; 4-H; Lat Clb; College; Art.

KUHL, DEANN; Unionville Sebewaing HS; Sebewaing, MI; 13/119 Sec Frsh Cls; Trs Frsh Cls; Trs Soph Cls; Chrh Wkr; Cmnty Wkr; Hon Rl; Hosp Ade; FHA; Chrldng; Lake Superior State College; Nursing.

KUHL, JULIE; Lumen Christi HS; Jackson, MI; 105/242 Hon Rl; PAVAS; Sch Pl; Stg Crw; Yth Flsp; Sch Nwsp; Drama Clb; Jackson Community Coll; Medical Asst.

KUHL, KIM; Edison HS; Milan, OH; Band; Stg Crw; Yrbk; Sprt Ed Sch Nwsp; Drama Clb; 4-H; Sci Clb; Bsktbl; Mgrs; Mat Maids; Toledo Univ; Retail Marketing.

KUHL, LOU ANN; Niles Mc Kinley HS; Niles, OH; 17/379 AFS; Hon Rl; NHS; Pres Red Cr Ade; Sch Mus; Yrbk; Drama Clb; Key Clb; Treas Pep Clb; Kiwan Awd; Trumbull Mem Scholl; Nursing.

KUHL, TERI; Maumee HS; Maumee, OH; Drm Mjrt; Girl Scts; Stg Crw; Y-Teens; Sch Nwsp; 4-H; Bsktbl; Coach Actv; IM Sprt; Mgrs; Awd Honorable Mention 79; Photog Awd 79; Bowling Green Univ; Jrnlsm.

KUHLMAN, DIANE; New Riegel HS; New Riegel, OH; 11/51 Sec Soph Cls; Pres Jr Cls; Band; Hon Rl; Lbry Ade; NHS; Sch Mus; Yrbk; FHA; Pep Clb; Work.

KUHN, ANDY; Triton HS; Etna Green, IN; 8/98 Chrh Wkr; FCA; Hon Rl; Hosp Ade; Lit Mag; NHS; Off Ade; College; Pre Med.

KUHN, ANNETTE; Columbian HS; Tiffin, OH; Chrs; Chrh Wkr; Cmnty Wkr; Girl Scts; 4-H; Spn Clb; Trk; IM Sprt; Scr Kpr; 4-H Awd; CYO Staff Bd 78; Bowling Green Univ; Soc Work.

KUHN, BARBARA; Cameron HS; Glen Easton, WV; 8/105 Chrs; Chrh Wkr; Hon Rl; Sch Nwsp; NHS; Y-Teens; FHA; Lat Clb; Pep Clb;.

KUHN, DAVE; Rocky River HS; Rocky River, OH; Boy Scts; Hon Rl; Ftbl; Cit Awd; Law Schl.

KUHN, HOLLY; Northrop HS; Ft Wayne, IN; Chrs; Hon Rl; Hosp Ade; Sec JA; JA Awd; 2nd Rnnr Up Miss In Job Daughter Pgnt 78; J A Achvrs & Jr Exec Awd 78; High Hon Cls At Northrop HS 79; Indiana Univ; Comp Progr.

KUHN, JOHN; Culver Military Academy; El Centro, CA; ROTC; Yrbk; Ed Sch Nwsp; Sprt Ed Sch Nwsp; Rptr Sch Nwsp; Sch Nwsp; Swmmng; IM Sprt; Am Leg Awd; Regimental Aide To Chaplin Lt 79; Op Serg 78; Four Gun Drill Artillery Op Hnr Org Of The Artillery 77 79; Univ; Poli.

KUHN, JOHN; Willoughby South HS; Willoughby, OH; 3/470 Hon Rl; NHS; Yrbk; Sch Nwsp; Sci Clb; Bausch & Lomb Awd; Univ Of Michigan Freshman Schlr 79; Frank Weiss Memrl Schlrshp 79; HS Hnr Awds 76; Univ Of Michiga; Naval Archt.

KUHN, JON; Theodore Roosevelt HS; Kent, OH; Hon Rl; Bsbl; Ftbl; Art Awd 75 76; Jaycees 50th Awd For Logo Cntst 79; Ski Club & Skiing Each Yr; Univ; Indstrl Arts.

KUHN, RANDY; Bridgeport HS; Bridgeport, MI; Boy Scts; Chrs; JA; Sch Pl; Sct Actv; Yth Flsp; 4-H; Rdo Clb; IM Sprt; Saginwa Valley State; Elec Tech.

KUHN, RICHARD; Hazel Park HS; Hazel Park, MI; 16/306 Boy Scts; Hon Rl; NHS; Sch Pl; Sct Actv; Crs Cntry; Ftbl; Trk; Natl Merit SF; Wayne St Univ; Comp Sci.

KUHN, RITA; Scott HS; Foster, WV; Hon Rl; Jr NHS; 4-H; Pep Clb; 4-H Awd;.

KUHN, SHELLY J; Parkway Local HS; Rockford, OH; 12/83 Cmp Fr Grls; Hon Rl; Lbry Ade; Bsbl; Bsktbl; PPFtbl; Wright St Univ; Legal Sec.

KUHN, STEVEN; Parkway Local HS; Rockford, OH; 18/95 Pres Frsh Cls; Pres Soph Cls; Chrh Wkr; Hon Rl; Stu Cncl; Bsbl; Bsktbl; College; History.

KUHN, WILLIAM; Cadiz HS; Hopedale, OH; 20/104 Hon Rl; Jr NHS; Lbry Ade; NHS; Pep Clb; Spn Clb; Letter Bsbl; Letter Ftbl; Acad Ach Spanish 2; College; Broadcasting.

KUHN JR, JOHN E; Calvert HS; Tiffin, OH; 40/98 Boy Scts; FCA; Hon Rl; Sct Actv; Stg Crw; Ger Clb; Bsktbl; Ftbl; Ten; Cit Awd; Clemsen Univ; Med.

KUHNS, SUSAN; New Philadelphia HS; New Phila, OH; 63/289 Chrh Wkr; Hon Rl; DECA; Kent State; Rn.

KUHNY, JAYNE; Clay HS; S Bend, IN; Chrh Wkr; Off Ade; Yth Flsp; Rptr Sch Nwsp; Pep Clb; Ball St Univ; Tchr.

KUHR, DAVID; Brooklyn HS; Brooklyn, OH; 17/174 AFS; Chrs; Hon Rl; Lbry Ade; NHS; Yth Flsp; Sprt Ed Sch Nwsp; Mth Clb; VICA; Trk; Kent State Univ; Acctg.

KUHR, MELANIE; Walnut Hills HS; Cincinnati, OH; Cls Rep Frsh Cls; Cls Rep Soph Cls; Cl Rep Jr Cls; Hon Rl; Sch Mus; Rptr Yrbk; Ger Clb; Swmmng; Marrieta College; Law.

KUHR, W; Moeller HS; Cincinnati, OH; 15/275 Hon Rl; NHS; Eng Clb; Letter Crs Cntry; Letter Trk; IM Sprt; Univ Of Cincinnati; Archt.

KUJAWA, ANDREA; Hammond HS; Hammond, IN; Cls Rep Sr Cls; Chrs; Hon Rl; Mdrgl; NHS; Sch Pl; Stg Crw; Drama Clb; Fr Clb; Scr Kpr; Lake Forest Coll; Bio.

KUJAWSKI, JAMES; Rogers HS; Toledo, OH; 2/400 Chrh Wkr; Hon Rl; Jr NHS; NHS; Pres Yth Flsp; Ger Clb; Sci Clb; Letter Bsbl; NCTE; Univ; Chem.

KUJAWSKI, JAMES W; Rogers HS; Toledo, OH; Chrh Wkr; Hon Rl; NHS; Pres Yth Flsp; Sci Clb; Bsbl; College; Chemistry.

KUKIS, SUSAN; Holy Redeemer HS; Detroit, MI; 3/130 Cl Rep Jr Cls; Cls Rep Sr Cls; Debate Tm; Hon Rl; Lit Mag; NHS; Pol Wkr; Ed Sch Nwsp; Mic Tech Univ; Engineering.

KUKLO, JANE; Perry HS; Canton, OH; Band; FCA; Girl Scts; Hon Rl; NHS; Off Ade; Stu Cncl; Yth Flsp; Fr Clb; Pep Clb; Akron Univ; Acctg.

KUKULA, CATHERINE; Central Catholic HS; Wheeling, WV; 6/132 Chrh Wkr; Drl Tm; Hon Rl; NHS; Sch Mus; Sch Pl; Stg Crw; Drama Clb; 4-H; Fr Clb; Univ; Nursing.

KUKURA, LINDA; Woodrow Wilson HS; Youngstown, OH; NHS; Off Ade; Red Cr Ade; Y-Teens; Rptr Sch Nwsp; Sec Ger Clb; Key Clb; Pep Clb; Tri Hi Y Pres; Woodrow Wilson Exclinc In Jrnlsm Awd; Univ; Med Tech.

KULBA, ALEEN L; Harrison HS; Farmington Hls, MI; 1/400 Hon Rl; Jr NHS; Sec NHS; Orch; Sch Mus; Sci Clb; Spn Clb; Letter Trk; IM Sprt; Univ.

KULBACK, TRACY; Scottsburg HS; Scottsburg, IN; Cls Rep Frsh Cls; Cls Rep Soph Cls; Cl Rep Jr Cls; Band; Chrh Wkr; 4-H; Pep Clb; Chrldng; GAA; College; History.

KULCZAK, BARBARA; Scecina Mem HS; Indianapolis, IN; 10/197 Cls Rep Frsh Cls; Cls Rep Soph Cls; Cl Rep Jr Cls; Pres Sr Cls; Hosp Ade; NHS; Sch Mus; Fr Clb; Letter Ten; IM Sprt; Hnrs Prog; Univ.

KULEK, KAREN; Arenac Eastern HS; Omer, MI; 5/30 Sec Soph Cls; Band; Hon Rl; NHS; Yrbk; 4-H; Letter Bsbl; Letter Bsktbl; 4-H Awd; Basc Educ Opport Grant 79; Mi Financl Aid 79; Top 10 Hon Stndt & Art Awd 78; Baker Jr Coll; Exec Sec.

KULESIA, MICHAEL; Ross Beatty HS; Vandalia, MI; Cls Rep Frsh Cls; Boy Scts; Hon Rl; Sprt Ed Yrbk; Rptr Yrbk; Yrbk; Ten; College; Architect.

KULESIA, STEVEN; Ferndale HS; Ferndale, MI; Cl Rep Jr Cls; Boy Scts; Hon Rl; Sct Actv; Ger Clb; Wrstlng; Cit Awd; Northern Michigan Univ; Forestry.

KULHANEK, ELAINE; Battle Creek Central HS; Battle Crk, MI; 1/467 Val; Cmnty Wkr; Hon Rl; Hosp Ade; Lit Mag; NHS; Yrbk; Ed Sch Nwsp; Fr Clb; DAR Awd; Michigan St Univ; Jrnlsm.

KULHANEK, ELAINE; Battle Creek Central HS; Battle Creek, MI; 1/467 Val; Cmnty Wkr; Hon Rl; Hosp Ade; Lit Mag; NHS; Yrbk; Ed Sch Nwsp; DAR Awd; Mic State Univ; Journalism.

KULIK, PAMELA P; Schafer HS; Southgate, MI; Cl Rep Jr Cls; Chrs; Cmnty Wkr; Hon Rl; JA; Off Ade; Sch Pl; OEA; Ten; Trk; Univ Of Michigan; Nursing.

KUMAR, SANJAY; Park Hills HS; Fairborn, OH; Sal; Hon Rl; NHS; IM Sprt; Natl Merit Schl; Wright; Medical.

KUME, RENAE; Pymatuning Vly HS; Andover, OH; Am Leg Aux Girls St; Chrs; Drl Tm; Hon Rl; NHS; Sch Pl; Scr Kpr; Thiel Coll; Bus Admin.

KUMFER, VICKI; Columbia City Joint HS; Columbia City, IN; Band;.

KUMHALL, LISA; Holy Name Nazareth HS; Brunswick, OH; Chrh Wkr; Cmnty Wkr; Hon Rl; NHS; Red Cr Ade; Sch Mus; Stg Crw; Drama Clb; Cuyanoga Comm College; Law Enfrcment.

KUMLER, FELICIA; Wadsworth HS; Wadsworth, OH; 126/356 Cls Rep Frsh Cls; Cls Rep Soph Cls; Pres Jr Cls; Girl Scts; Natl Forn Lg; NHS; Sct Actv; Pres Stu Cncl; Bowling Green State Univ; Pblc Rltns.

KUMM, MICHELLE; Walled Lake Western HS; Milford, MI; 10/450 Cls Rep Frsh Cls; Cls Rep Soph Cls; Hon Rl; NHS; Stu Cncl; Rptr Yrbk; Letter Gym; Letter Swmmng; Letter Trk; Ferris St Merit Schlrshp 500.

KUMMER, DAWN; Calvert HS; Tiffin, OH; Aud/Vis; Stg Crw; Coach Actv; Mat Maids; Coll; Sci.

KUMMER, TERESA; Huntington North HS; Roanoke, IN; 57/652 Am Leg Aux Girls St; Chrh Wkr; Cmnty Wkr; Girl Scts; Jr NHS; Lbry Ade; Yth Flsp; Ten; Ball State Univ; Archt.

KUMMERER, MICHELLE; Tiffin Columbian HS; Tiffin, OH; 16/347 Trs Jr Cls; Band; Chrs; Girl Scts; Hon Rl; 4-H; Spn Clb; Univ; Bilingual Elem Educ.

KUMOR, MICHAEL; St Alphonsus HS; Dearborn, MI; Cls Rep Frsh Cls; Cls Rep Soph Cls; Cl Rep Jr Cls; Chrs; Hon Rl; NHS; Sch Mus; Pres Stu Cncl; Letter Bsbl; Opt Clb Awd; College; Business Admin.

KUMPF, CHARLOTTE; Cloverdale HS; Cloverdale, IN; 5/89 Sec Frsh Cls; Cls Rep Soph Cls; Trs Sr Cls; FCA; Hon Rl; NHS; Sch Mus; Stg Crw; Stu Cncl; 4-H; Phys Ed.

KUNARD, DOUGLAS; Perry Central HS; Tell City, IN; Am Leg Boys St; Hon Rl; NHS; Fr Clb; Pep Clb; Schlrshp Awd Alg Civics & Attdc Certf 77; Schlrshp Alg French Eng Attdnc 78; French Awd; Schlrshp 79; Univ.

KUNARD, STEVE; Hopkins HS; Dorr, MI; Hon Rl; Michigan Tech Univ; Forestry.

KUNATH, LINDA; Anchor Bay HS; New Baltimore, MI; 17/250 VP Chrs; Chrh Wkr; Hon Rl; Jr NHS; NHS; Sch Mus; Sch Pl; Stg Crw; Drama Clb; OEA; Macomb Cnty Cmnty Coll; Acctg.

KUNDINGER, BRUCE; Unionvill Sebewaing Area HS; Sebewaing, MI; Chrh Wkr; Yth Flsp; Pres FFA; Bsbl; Farming.

KUNDINGER, ERIC; Unionville Sebewaing HS; Sebewaing, MI; Hon Rl; Engr.

KUNDRAT, LAURE; Newbury HS; Newbury, OH; Hon Rl; Jr NHS; NHS; Sch Mus; Sch Pl; Drama Clb; Capt Chrldng; Ursuline Coll; Nursing.

KUNGL, DAVID B; Akron East HS; Akron, OH; 2/348 Am Leg Boys St; Hon Rl; NHS; Letter Bsbl; Letter Glf; Coll; Math.

KUNIEWICZ, THERESA; Sebring Mc Kinley HS; Sebring, OH; 9/76 Sec Frsh Cls; Trs Soph Cls; Band; Chrs; Hon Rl; NHS; Sch Mus; Rptr Sch Nwsp; Lat Clb; Chrldng; Nursing.

KUNISCH, PAULA; Unionville Sebewaing HS; Sebewaing, MI; Chrh Wkr; Hon Rl; Ed Yrbk; Rptr Yrbk; 4-H; Chrldng; Michigan St Univ; Animal Tech.

KUNK, JOSEPH; Coldwater HS; Coldwater, MI; 11/294 JA; NHS; Pol Wkr; JA Awd; Rotary Awd; Michigan St Univ; Comp Sci.

KUNK, MIKE; Coldwater HS; Coldwater, OH; Chrs; Hon Rl; Sch Mus; Sch Pl; Stg Crw; Drama Clb; Spn Clb; Letter Ftbl; Letter Trk; IM Sprt; Eastern Michigan Coll; Acctg.

KUNKEL, CHRISTINE; Mc Donald HS; Mc Donald, OH; 23/95 VP Jr Cls; Lbry Ade; Stu Cncl; Bsbl; Swmmng; Chrldng; Kent State Univ; Speech Therapist.

KUNKEL, KARLA; Madison Comprehensive HS; Mansfield, OH; Band; Drl Tm; Girl Scts; JA; Yth Flsp; Y-Teens; Fr Clb; FHA; Pom Pon; JA Awd; North Central Tech Coll; Comp Prog.

KUNKEL, MELISSA; Cadillac HS; Cadillac, MI; Chrs; Sch Mus; Stg Crw; Letter Chrldng; Coach Actv; PPFtbl; PPFtbl; Northern Michigan Univ; Speech.

KUNKLE, THOMAS; Montpelier HS; Montpelier, OH; VP Frsh Cls; Pres Soph Cls; Pres Jr Cls; Band; Chrs; NHS; Sch Mus; Ed Yrbk; Fr Clb; College; Art.

KUNKLE, THOMAS J; Montpelier HS; Montpelier, OH; Pres Soph Cls; Pres Jr Cls; Band; Chrs; Hon Rl; NHS; Sch Mus; Ed Yrbk; Univ; Art.

KUNKLE, TIMOTHY; Gorham Fayette HS; Fayette, OH; Am Leg Boys St; Chrh Wkr; Hon Rl; NHS; Sch Pl; Yth Flsp; Spn Clb; Wrstlng; Am Leg Awd; College; Medicine.

KUNOL, MARTIN; East HS; Akron, OH; 31/367 Am Leg Boys St; Band; Cmnty Wkr; FHA; Letter Ten; Univ Of Cincinnati; Chem.

KUNTER, DREW; Bellefontaine Sr HS; Bellefontaine, OH; 89/245 Am Leg Boys St; Boy Scts; Chrh Wkr; Cmnty Wkr; Debate Tm; Sch Pl; Sct Actv; Stg Crw; Drama Clb; Ger Clb; De Molay; Exch Stu To W Germany 79; Univ; Cmnctns.

KUNTZ, ANN; Brookville HS; Brookville, IN; 16/169 Hon Rl; Rptr Yrbk; 4-H; FHA; Ten; GAA; Mgrs; Univ.

KUNTZ, GREGORY; Jasper HS; Jasper, IN; 18/289 Am Leg Boys St; Boy Scts; Hon Rl; Jr NHS; NHS; Sct Actv; Key Clb; Bsktbl; Letter Ftbl; Wrstlng; Univ.

KUNTZ, KAREN; Washington HS; Massillon, OH; 27/463 Band; Boy Scts; Hon Rl; Jr NHS; NHS; Off Ade; Pep Clb; Hannah Mullins Schl; Nursing.

KUNTZ, PATTY; Brookville HS; Brookville, IN; 46/197 Band; Chrh Wkr; Drama Clb; 4-H; Pep Clb; 4-H Awd; God Cntry Awd; Connersville Area Voc Tech; Sec.

KUNZ, GEORGIA; Madison Comprehensive HS; Mansfield, OH; Chrs; Cmnty Wkr; Girl Scts; Lbry Ade; Sct Actv; Mansfield Genrl Hosp; Reg Nurse.

KUNZ, TAMMY; Madison Comprehensive HS; Mansfield, OH; Chrs; Hon Rl; Lbry Ade; Fr Clb; Spn Clb; Bowling Green St Univ; Psych.

KUO, CHEN F; Southgate HS; Southgate, MI; Sec Frsh Cls; Cls Rep Soph Cls; VP Jr Cls; VP Sr Cls; Jr NHS; NHS; Stu Cncl; Mth Clb; Trk; Pres Awd; Univ Of Michigan; Chem Engr.

KUPEC, JANET; Cleveland Central Cath HS; Cleveland, OH; Cmp Fr Grls; Chrh Wkr; Hon Rl; Hosp Ade; JA; Yrbk; JA Awd; Cleveland St Univ; Acctg.

KUPELIAN, MARK; Austintown Fitch HS; Youngstown, OH; 1/700 Aud/Vis; Chrh Wkr; Hon Rl; Jr NHS; Lbry Ade; NHS; Fr Clb; Youngstown State; Chem.

KUPETS, KELLY; Berea HS; Berea, OH; 79/533 Cls Rep Frsh Cls; Cls Rep Soph Cls; Cl Rep Jr Cls; Cls Rep Sr Cls; Hon Rl; NHS; Bsktbl; Trk; Chrldng; IM Sprt; Ohio Univ; Busns Mgmt.

KUPFER, MICHAEL D; Euclid Senior HS; Euclid, OH; 2/703 Aud/Vis; Boy Scts; Hon Rl; NHS; Orch ; Sch Mus; Rptr Yrbk; Ger Clb; Key Clb; Sci Clb; Univ; Comp Sci.

KURDUNOWICZ, MARY J; Aquinas HS; Lincoln Park, MI; Cls Rep Sr Cls; Treas Band; Chrs; Cmnty Wkr; Hon Rl; Orch; Sch Mus; Sch Pl; Stu Cncl; Rptr Yrbk; Wayne St Univ; Busns Admin.

KURILCHIK, LAUREN; Divine Child HS; Dearborn Hts, MI; Hon Rl; NHS; Ten; Univ Of Mic; Engr.

KURJIAN, CHRISTINE; Cloverleaf Sr HS; Medina, OH; Band; Chrh Wkr; Hon Rl; Univ; Med.

KURKA, SUSAN; Ovid Elsie HS; Ovid, MI; 4/170 Girl Scts; Hon Rl; Sch Pl; FHA; PPFtbl; Scr Kpr; College.

KURKER, CHRIS; Cardinal Ritter HS; Indianapolis, IN; 1/150 Val; Am Leg Boys St; Hon Rl; NHS; Pres Stu Cncl; Spn Clb; Capt Crs Cntry; Letter Trk; Natl Merit Ltr; MIT; Engr.

KURKO, GEORGIA; Martins Ferry HS; Martins Ferry, OH; Chrs; Chrh Wkr; Hon Rl; JA; Lbry Ade; Sch Mus; Ohio State Univ; Home Ec.

KURLEY, JACQUELINE; William A Wirt HS; Gary, IN; 20/230 Hon Rl; Pres Jr NHS; VP NHS; Stu Cncl; Rptr Yrbk; Spn Clb; Bsktbl; Letter Trk; GAA; IM Sprt; Indiana N W Univ; Labor Mgmt.

KURNOT, VICTORIA A; Highland HS; Medina, OH; 17/262 Cl Rep Jr Cls; Am Leg Aux Girls St; Band; Chrs; Chrh Wkr; Cmnty Wkr; Drl Tm; Girl Scts; Hon Rl; Lbry Ade; Coll; Med.

KURSEY, MICHAEL; Martinsburg HS; Martinsburg, WV; 32/220 Cls Rep Soph Cls; Cl Rep Jr Cls; Chrh Wkr; Hon Rl; Pres Stu Cncl; Boys Clb Am; Treas Key Clb; Ftbl; Dnfth Awd; Military Acad; Computer Science.

KURT, CLIFFORD; St Johns HS; Toledo, OH; Band; Yth Flsp; Sec Sch Nwsp; Bowling Green St Univ; Communication.

KURT, GINNY; Margaretta HS; Castalia, OH; Band; Chrs; Chrh Wkr; Sch Nwsp; Pres 4-H; Sec FHA; Bsktbl; IM Sprt; Scr Kpr; Cit Awd; Youth Amer Gvrnmtn; Ohio State Univ; Home Ec.

KURTH, CONSTANCE; Whitmer HS; Toledo, OH; 34/810 Chrs; Hon Rl; NHS; Sch Mus; Spn Clb; PPFtbl; Univ Of Toledo; Music.

KURTH, LORI; Escanaba Area Public HS; Escanaba, MI; 5/437 Treas Chrh Wkr; Debate Tm; Hon Rl; Lbry Ade; NHS; Yth Flsp; 4-H; 4-H Awd; Western Michigan Univ; Med Asst.

KURTI, JUDY A; N Ridgeville Sr HS; N Ridgeville, OH; Cls Rep Sr Cls; Hon Rl; Sec NHS; Stg Crw; Drama Clb; Pep Clb; Spn Clb; Cleveland St Univ; Med Tech.

KURTS, KATHERINE; Evart Public HS; Evart, MI; Chrs; Hon Rl; Lbry Ade; Sch Pl; Stg Crw; Rptr Yrbk; Spn Clb; Bsbl; Mgrs; Tmr; Voc Schl.

KURTZ, DEBRA; Bellefontaine HS; Bellefontaine, OH; Am Leg Aux Girls St; Band; Chrs; Drm Bgl; Hon Rl; Off Ade; Sch Mus; Y-Teens; Yrbk; 4-H; Clark Tech College; Executive Sec.

KURTZ, GERALD L; Roy C Start HS; Toledo, OH; Off Ade; Sch Pl; Stu Cncl; Trk; Toledo Univ; Entertainer.

KURTZ, LISA; East Canton HS; E Canton, OH; 3/110 Band; Hon Rl; Jr NHS; NHS; Drama Clb; Sci Clb; Spn Clb; Trk; Letterman In Track; VP Of Jr Natl Hnr Soc; Pres Of Spanish Clb; College; Drama.

KURTZ, MELANIE; North Royalton HS; N Royalton, OH; 108/286 Rptr Sch Nwsp; Spn Clb;.

KURTZ, STEVEN; Mc Nicholas HS; Cincinnati, OH; 49/227 Cl Rep Jr Cls; Hon Rl; JA; NHS; Spn Clb; Ftbl; Coach Actv; IM Sprt; Scr Kpr; Univ Of Cincinnati; Bus.

KURYLO, VALERIE; East Kentwood HS; Grand Rapids, MI; Band; Chrs; Drl Tm; Drm Bgl; Hon Rl; NHS; Sch Mus; Sch Pl; Stg Crw; Rptr Sch Nwsp; Stdnt Ocuncl Spec Serv 75; Musicale Mst Outstndng Dnacer 76; Contrbtn In Tutoring Middle Schl Stdnt 78; Michigan St Univ; T V Jrnlsm.

KURZER, ANN; Meadowdale HS; Dayton, OH; 14/275 Band; Chrs; Hon Rl; NHS; Sch Pl; Bsbl; IM Sprt; Ohio St Univ; Science.

KURZHALS, KAREN; John Adams HS; S Bend, IN; 100/395 Pres Chrh Wkr; Hon Rl; Lbry Ade; Yth Flsp; 4-H; Mgrs; 4-H Awd; Started On Girls St Vllybl Champ Tm 78; Pres Of Church Youth Grp 78; South Western Michigan Coll; Med Sec.

KUSCH, DAVID; Kalkaska HS; Williamsbrg, MI; 5/132 VP Frsh Cls; Chrh Wkr; Lbry Ade; NHS; Pol Wkr; Quill & Scroll; Sch Pl; Ed Sch Nwsp; NEDT Test Awd 78; Photogr Ed For HS Yrbk 78; Qualifr In St Of Mi Schlrshp Progr 79; Concordia Coll; History.

KUSHNAK, KAREN; Munster HS; Munster, IN; Chrh Wkr; Drm Bgl; Girl Scts; NHS; Orch; Drama Clb; Ger Clb; Bsktbl; Tmr; Purdue Univ; Civil Engr.

KUSIAN, AMY; Clay Sr HS; Oregon, OH; Pres Frsh Cls; Chrs; Hon Rl; Off Ade; Pep Clb; Chrldng; Kiwan Awd; Univ Of Toledo; Psych.

KUSINA, PAMELA; Calvin M Woodward HS; Toledo, OH; Sec Jr Cls; Drl Tm; Hon Rl; Jr NHS; NHS; Stu Cncl; Rptr Yrbk; OEA; Busns Schl; Sec.

KUSS, MICHAEL; Griffith HS; Griffith, IN; Chrh Wkr; Hon Rl; Letter Bsbl; Ftbl; Letter Wrstlng; Purdue Univ; Engr.

KUSSMAUL, ANDREW; Grand Ledge HS; Lansing, MI; Am Leg Boys St; Hon Rl; NHS; Letter Bsbl; Letter Bsktbl; Capt Crs Cntry; Michigan State Univ; Math.

KUSSY, LEISA; Washington Catholic HS; Washington, IN; Band; Chrs; Hon Rl; Quill & Scroll; Sch Pl; Drama Clb; Fr Clb; Keyettes; Pep Clb; GAA; Indiana Univ; Pharm.

KUSTER, MITCHELL; Cambridge HS; Blytheville, AR; 82/280 Univ Of Arkansas; Bus Admin.

KUSTRON, EDWARD; Lake Catholic HS; Mentor, OH; Boy Scts; Hon Rl; IM Sprt; Top 10% On Natl Educ Devlpmt Test 78; Schlstc Awd In German 78; Univ; Archt.

KUTAY, MIKE; Bishop Donahue HS; Moundsville, WV; Chrs; Hon Rl; NHS; VP Stu Cncl; Pres Key Clb; Spn Clb; Ftbl; Lettermens Clb Sec 78 79 & 80; Ftbl 3 Yr Letterman; Hon Mention For All OVAC & All Valley; West Virginia Univ; Elec Engr.

KUTCHIN, JULIE; Hammond HS; Hammond, IN; 1/333 Am Leg Aux Girls St; Debate Tm; Natl Forn Lg; NHS; Sch Pl; Mth Clb; Ten; VFW Awd; Voice Dem Awd; Collegef Engineering.

KUTIE, JANET; Lake Catholic HS; Painesville, OH; Hon Rl; Letter Ftbl; Mgrs; Univ; Sec.

KUTSCHBACH, LAINE; Unioto HS; Chillicothe, OH; Hon Rl; NHS; Quill & Scroll; FTA; Lat Clb; Mgrs; 4-H Awd; Ohio Univ; Sec Tech.

KUTSICK, DEBORAH; Carl Brablec HS; Roseville, MI; Girl Scts; Hon Rl; NHS; Off Ade; Red Cr Ade; Sch Mus; Rptr Sch Nwsp; Socr; Cit Awd; Saginaw Vly St Coll; Acctg.

KUTTER, CHRISTINE; Centerville HS; Centerville, IN; Chrs; Chrh Wkr; Debate Tm; Hon Rl; Y-Teens; FBLA; Trk; Scr Kpr;.

KUTTER, LISA; Ubly Community HS; Ubly, MI; Pres Sr Cls; Hon Rl; NHS; Sch Pl; Ed Sch Nwsp; FHA; Letter Trk; Letter Chrldng; Mgrs; Delta; Secretarial.

KUVER, RAHUL; Carman HS; Flint, MI; 5/400 VP Boy Scts; NHS; Socr; Kalamazoo Coll; Med.

KUWAMOTO, KATHY; Waldron HS; Waldron, IN; 3/69 Chrs; Girl Scts; Hon Rl; Lbry Ade; NHS; Sch Pl; Ed Yrbk; Drama Clb; FHA; Sec Pep Clb; Purdue Univ; Actuary Sci.

KUWAMOTO, KATHY J; Waldron HS; Waldron, IN; 2/68 Sal; Chrs; Girl Scts; Hon Rl; Lbry Ade; Sch Pl; Ed Yrbk; Drama Clb; FHA; Sec Pep Clb; Purdue Univ; Math.

KUYERS, KATHLEEN; West Ottawa HS; Holland, MI; 6/325 Band; Chrh Wkr; Cmnty Wkr; Hon Rl; NHS; Orch; Pol Wkr; Sch Mus; Ferris St Coll; Med Tech.

KUYKEADALL, DEBRA; Bishop Noll Inst; Lansing, IL; 14/321 Hon Rl; NHS; Yrbk; Mth Clb; Pom Pon; College; Communications Major.

KUYKENDALL, BETH; Franklin HS; Livonia, MI; Hon Rl; Cit Awd; College; Architect.

KUZAK, DEBORAH; Marion L Steele HS; Amherst, OH; 32/355 Hon Rl; NHS; Red Cr Ade; Pep Clb; Spn Clb; Swmmng; PPFtbl; Ski Club 79; Sr Ftbl Scrapbook Comm 78; Red Cross Volunteer; Providence Hosp Schl; RN.

KUZALA, ELIZABETH A; Hartland HS; Hartland, MI; 14/250 Sec Frsh Cls; Sec Soph Cls; Sec Jr Cls; Hon Rl; NHS; Off Ade; Sch Pl; Stu Cncl; Rptr Yrbk; Sprt Ed Sch Nwsp; Michigan St Univ; Phys Therapy.

KUZDA, KIMBERLEY; Strongsville HS; Strongsville, OH; Cls Rep Soph Cls; Cl Rep Jr Cls; Hon Rl; Jr NHS; NHS; Stu Cncl; Fr Clb; Lat Clb; Coll; Nursing.

KUZIMSKI, NANCY; Houghton Lake HS; Hoghton Lk, MI; Band; Hon Rl; Univ; Comp Prog.

KUZMA, SHARON; Clio HS; Clio, MI; 8/390 Hon Rl; NHS; 4-H; Capt Bsktbl; Swmmng; GAA; IM Sprt; Mgrs; 4-H Awd; Michigan Tech Univ; Engr.

KUZMYN, JOHN; Memorial HS; St Marys, OH; 35/223 Am Leg Boys St; Hon Rl; Sprt Ed Yrbk; Rptr Yrbk; Sprt Ed Sch Nwsp; Ohio State Univ; Bus.

KUZNAR, CARLA; Valley Forge HS; Parma, OH; 111/777 Drm Bgl; Girl Scts; Hon Rl; Opt Clb Awd; Drum & Bugle Corp 76; Honor Roll 77; Bowling Green Univ; Intr Dsgn.

KVARNBERG, STEVE; Chelsea HS; Chelsea, MI; Boy Scts; Debate Tm; Hon Rl; JA; NHS; Sch Pl; Stg Crw; Crs Cntry; Trk; Univ Of Michigan; Architect.

KVASNICKA, CINDY; N Royalton HS; N Royalton, OH; Chrh Wkr; Hon Rl; NHS; Sch Mus; Sch Pl; Stg Crw; Sch Nwsp; Drama Clb; Pep Clb; Chrldng; J V Sftbl Awd 78; Bowling Green S Univ; Forestry.

KVITKO, MIKE; R B Chamberlin HS; Twinsburg, OH; 3/180 AFS; Aud/Vis; Chrs; Hon Rl; NHS; Sch Pl; Stg Crw; Boys Clb Am; Rensselaer Polytechnic Inst; Engr.

KWAISER, MICHAEL; Bridgept Spaulding Cmnty HS; Birch Run, MI; 85/350 Band; Boy Scts; Sch Mus; Pep Clb;.

KWAPIS, LANETTE; Crestwood HS; Dearborn Hts, MI; Chrh Wkr; Hon Rl; Drama Clb; Central Mich Univ; Teaching.

KWASNESKI, DANIEL; St Peter & Paul HS; Swartz Creek, MI; Chrs; Chrh Wkr; Yrbk; 4-H; Rdo Clb; Letter Bsktbl; Letter Socr; IM Sprt; Univ; Math.

KWIATKOWSKI, ANN; Maumee HS; Maumee, OH; 2/300 Hon Rl; Lbry Ade; NHS; Y-Teens; Rptr Yrbk; Fr Clb; IM Sprt; PPFtbl; University.

KWIATKOWSKI, GREGORY C; Sts Peter & Paul Area HS; Saginaw, MI; 1/140 Trs Frsh Cls; Cls Rep Soph Cls; Cl Rep Jr Cls; Chrs; Chrh Wkr; Hon Rl; Mdrgl; NHS; Sch Mus; Sch Pl; Kalamazoo Coll; Engr.

KYLE, ELLEN; East Palestine HS; Negley, OH; 21/140 Cmp Fr Grls; Cmnty Wkr; Pol Wkr; Sct Actv; FTA; God Cntry Awd; Voice Dem Awd; Geneva College; Bus Admin.

KYLE, KAROLE; Newcomerstown HS; Newcomerstown, OH; Band; Girl Scts; Hon Rl; FBLA;.

KYLE, LISA; Jennings County HS; N Vernon, IN; 62/358 Band; NHS; Stg Crw; Yth Flsp; 4-H; Fr Clb; Pep Clb; Univ Of In; Social Work.

KYLE, TIM; Port Clinton HS; Port Clinton, OH; Hst Sr Cls; Chrs; Hon Rl; Sct Actv; Sch Nwsp; DECA; Wartburg Coll; Bus Admin.

KYLER, LINDA; Columbia City Joint HS; Columbia City, IN; 27/273 Band; Girl Scts; Hon Rl; Natl Forn Lg; Pres 4-H; Pres FHA; Pep Clb; 4-H Awd; College; Home Ec.

L

LAANSMA, RICHARD; Walled Lake Central HS; Union Lake, MI; 30/300 Boy Scts; Letter Swmmng; Mic Tech Univ; Elec Engr.

LA BADIE, DENISE; East Detroit HS; Warren, MI; Hon Rl; Off Ade; Macomb Co Comm Coll; Busns.

LA BADIE, MARK; Harrison HS; Harrison, MI; Band; NHS; Pres Awd; Adio Coll Of Chiropractic; Doctor.

LA BARBARA, FRANCIS E; George Washington HS; Charleston, WV; Boy Scts; JA; Sct Actv; JA Awd; Natl Merit SF; Univ; Bio Med Engr.

LABASAN, JANET; Greenon HS; Fairborn, OH; 9/260 VP Frsh Cls; Band; Hon Rl; NHS; Spn Clb; GAA; Twrlr; Perfect Attnd 78; Univ; Sci.

LABBE, THERESA; Badin HS; Fairfield, OH; 3/226 Hon Rl; JA; NHS; Drama Clb; Fr Clb; Swmmng; Trk; IM Sprt; Univ; Comp Sci.

LA BEAU, ANNETTE D; St Mary Academy; Monroe, MI; 27/104 Cls Rep Frsh Cls; Cls Rep Soph Cls; Hon Rl; Hosp Ade; NHS; Treas Stu Cncl; Rptr Sch Nwsp; Lat Clb; Sci Clb; Swmmng; College; Medicine.

LA BEAU, KATHRINE; Manton HS; Manton, MI; Cls Rep Frsh Cls; Cl Rep Jr Cls; Debate Tm; Drm Mjrt; Hon Rl; JA; Off Ade; Quill & Scroll; Sch Pl; Wexford; Air Force.

LA BEAU, MICHAEL; Central Lake Pub HS; Central Lake, MI; Band; Chrs; Natl Forn Lg; Sch Mus; Rptr Yrbk; Rptr Sch Nwsp; Voice Dem Awd;.

LA BELLE, LINDA; Kenowa Hills HS; Grand Rapids, MI; NHS; 4-H; Gym; Pom Pon; PPFtbl; Cit Awd; 4-H Awd; College.

LA BELLE, MARGARET; Ishpeming HS; Ishpeming, MI; 1/124 VP Frsh Cls; Val; Band; Chrs; Debate Tm; Girl Scts; Hon Rl; Mdrgl; Natl Forn Lg; NHS; Michigan Tech Univ; Comp Sci.

LABEOTS, LAURA; Munster HS; Munster, IN; 36/444 Chrs; Chrh Wkr; Hon Rl; Hosp Ade; NHS; Swmmng; Letter Trk; GAA; IM Sprt; Mat Maids; Northwestern Ill Univ; Medicine.

LABER, MARK; Lake Fenton HS; Fenton, MI; 7/170 Band; Chrh Wkr; Hon Rl; Pres NHS; Sch Pl; Yth Flsp; Univ Of Mich Flint; Comp Progr.

LABER, ROBIN; Lake Fenton HS; Fenton, MI; 5/204 Hon Rl; NHS; Sch Mus; Sch Pl; Yrbk; Cit Awd;.

LA BERGE, MARY; L Anse HS; Lanse, MI; Cl Rep Jr Cls; Cls Rep Sr Cls; Chrh Wkr; Hon Rl; Off Ade; Sch Pl; Pres Stu Cncl; Capt Bsktbl; Capt Hockey; Letter Trk; Northern Michigan Univ; Special Educ.

LABIS, FRANK; Lorain Catholic HS; Lorain, OH; Hon Rl; Ohio St Univ; Comp Sci.

LABO, LORINNE; Wadsworth HS; Wadsworth, OH; Am Leg Aux Girls St; Chrh Wkr; Lat Clb; Natl Merit Ltr; Univ; Bio Chem.

LA BONTE, M; Parkside HS; Jackson, MI; Band; Hon Rl; Ger Clb; Pep Clb; Trk; Michigan State.

LABORIE, JOAN; Elmwood HS; Fostoria, OH; 5/105 Cls Rep Sr Cls; Sec Chrs; Chrh Wkr; Hon Rl; JA; NHS; Sch Mus; Sch Pl; Stg Crw; Stu Cncl; BGSU; Educ.

LABOY, ANGELA; Glen Oak HS; Cleveland, OH; Chrh Wkr; Cmnty Wkr; Debate Tm; Hon Rl; JA; Jr NHS; Off Ade; Stu Cncl; Sci Clb; Spn Clb; A Better Chance Schlrshp; 5 Yr Spanish Awd; Univ; Med.

LA BRASH, JOHN; Bremen HS; Bremen, IN; Trs Frsh Cls; VP Sr Cls; Band; Hon Rl; Pol Wkr; Stu Cncl; Yth Flsp; Drama Clb; Fr Clb; Letter Crs Cntry; College; Pharmacy.

LABUDA, MONICA; Strongsville HS; Strongsville, OH; Cmp Fr Grls; Chrh Wkr; Girl Scts; Hon Rl; Jr NHS; Sct Actv; Y-Teens; FHA; IM Sprt; Opt Clb Awd; Mt Union; Accounting.

LABUDA, PAMELA; Trinity HS; Seven Hills, OH; Cls Rep Frsh Cls; Cls Rep Soph Cls; Chrs; Hon Rl; Stu Cncl; Rptr Sch Nwsp; Fr Clb; Pep Clb; Std Trainer; 17 Mag Natl Yth Cncl; Higbee Teen Bd; Univ.

LA BUMBARD, KEVIN J; Tri Township Schools; Rapid River, MI; 4/53 VP Frsh Cls; Cls Rep Soph Cls; Cl Rep Jr Cls; Cls Rep Sr Cls; Hon Rl; Stu Cncl; Letter Trk; Natl Merit Schl; Phys Fitness 78; Michigan Tech Univ; Forestry.

LACARIA, CHRISTOPHER; Washington Irving HS; Clarksburg, WV; 23/150 Hon Rl; NHS; Yth Flsp; Key Clb; Lat Clb; Crs Cntry; Ftbl; Socr; Mat Maids; C of C Awd; West Virginia Univ; Engr.

LACER, HOWARD; Linton Stockton Jr Sr HS; Linton, IN; Boy Scts; Hon Rl; NHS; Sct Actv; Mth Clb; Sci Clb; Ftbl; Purdue Univ; Comp Progr.

LACEY, CHERYL; Farmington Sr HS; Farmington Hls, MI; Hon Rl; Jr NHS; Off Ade; Rptr Sch Nwsp; Fr Clb; Bsktbl; Trk; Michigan St Univ; Bus.

LACEY, JAMES; Moeller HS; Cincinnati, OH; 20/238 Cl Rep Jr Cls; Boy Scts; Chrs; Hon Rl; Natl Forn Lg; NHS; Stu Cncl; Rptr Sch Nwsp; Scr Kpr; Xavier Univ; Radio Tv.

LACEY, LINDA; Frankfort Senior HS; Frankfort, IN; Band; Chrh Wkr; Cmnty Wkr; Drm Bgl; Girl Scts; NHS; Orch; Sch Mus; Sct Actv; Pep Clb; Z Club 1976; Spanish Excellence 1976; F # Club 1977; Indiana Univ; Law.

LACEY, MARTIN; Moeller HS; Cincinnati, OH; 20/260 Sec Soph Cls; Sec Jr Cls; Sec Sr Cls; Boy Scts; Hon Rl; NHS; Sch Pl; Stu Cncl; Rptr Sch Nwsp; Univ Of Dayton; Chem Engr.

LACEY, MERRILL; North HS; Youngstown, OH; 2/103 VP Jr Cls; Girl Scts; Hon Rl; Sch Pl; Stu Cncl; Pep Clb; Univ; Med.

LACH, PATRICIA; Grandview HS; Columbus, OH; 46/128 Sec Jr Cls; Sec Sr Cls; Treas Band; Chrs; FCA; Girl Scts; Hon Rl; Mdrgl; Sch Pl; Stu Cncl; Otstndng Sr; Homecoming Ct; John Carroll Univ.

LACHAJEWSKI, SUE; Mason Cnty Central HS; Ludington, MI; 4/150 Girl Scts; Hon Rl; Cit Awd; JA Awd; Natl Merit Ltr; Central Michigan Univ; Math.

LACHEY, JODI; Minster Local HS; Minster, OH; 10/80 Chrs; Girl Scts; Hon Rl; FTA; Pep Clb; Spn Clb; College; Social Services.

LACK, JULIE; Norton HS; Norton, OH; Cls Rep Frsh Cls; Cls Rep Soph Cls; Cl Rep Jr Cls; Band; Hon Rl; Off Ade; Sch Mus; Stg Crw; Bsktbl; Trk; Arkon Univ; Psycology.

LACKEY, ANNE E; Anderson HS; Anderson, IN; 161/443 Sec Frsh Cls; Cls Rep Soph Cls; Cl Rep Jr Cls; Chrs; Girl Scts; Hon Rl; Mdrgl; Sch Mus; Y-Teens; Eng Clb; Indiana Univ; Child Psych.

LACKEY, CONSTANCE C; Vinson HS; Huntington, WV; 26/112 Band; Chrs; Chrh Wkr; Girl Scts; Hon Rl; NHS; Off Ade; Rptr Sch Nwsp; Fr Clb; Keyettes; W Va All St Chorus; Majorette; Marshall Univ; Journalism.

LACKEY, LYNDA; Copley Sr HS; Copley, OH; Girl Scts; Hon Rl; Hosp Ade; Yth Flsp; FHA; Pep Clb; Spn Clb; Trk; Scr Kpr; Tmr; Univ; Med.

LACKEY, SCOTT W; Walnut Hills HS; Cincinnati, OH; Band; Hon Rl; Orch; Sch Mus; Ger Clb; US Collegiate Wind Bnd Eurp Tour 78; Pres Of Strategy & Tactics Club 78; Ohio Wesleyan Univ; Hstry.

LACKMAN, MARGERY A; Reading HS; Reading, OH; 2/230 Band; Drl Tm; NHS; Sch Mus; Sch Pl; Sec Stu Cncl; Drama Clb; Pres Fr Clb; Trk; Natl Merit SF; College.

LACKNEY, JEFFREY; St Francis De Sales HS; Toledo, OH; 23/187 Boy Scts; Hon Rl; Sct Actv; Stg Crw; Sch Nwsp; Bsktbl; Coach Actv; IM Sprt; Michigan St Univ; Archt.

LACONIS, JANINE; Berkley HS; Hunt Woods, MI; Band; Off Ade; Swmmng; Trk; IM Sprt; Univ; Cmnctns.

LACOSTE, HELENE; Brishton HS; Howell, MI; Hon Rl; Sch Pl; Kiwan Awd; Natl Merit In Bio 79; Studied Only 1 Yr In The US; Prior Std In French Schl In Montreal Ca; Univ Of Michigan; Bio.

LA COX, LEBANON L; Doddridge County HS; Salem, WV; Cmp Fr Grls; Chrh Wkr; Hon Rl; Lbry Ade; Quill & Scroll; Yth Flsp; Fr Clb; FBLA; Pep Clb; Wv Univ.

LA CROSS, DIANE; Buckeye South HS; Rayland, OH; 25/120 Band; Drm Mjrt; Hon Rl; NHS; Y-Teens; Pep Clb; Twrlr; Tech Schl; Dent Asst.

LACUMSKY, TAMARA; Port Clinton HS; Port Clinton, OH; 4/275 Chrs; Chrh Wkr; Hon Rl; Treas NHS; Natl Merit Ltr; Bowling Green St Univ; Spec Educ.

LACY, ANNE; Zionsville Comm HS; Zionsville, IN; VP Jr Cls; Chrs; Chrh Wkr; Cmnty Wkr; FCA; Hon Rl; Rptr Yrbk; Pep Clb; Spn Clb; Letter Bsktbl; Deanery Representative For CYO; Diocese VP For CYO; Rep To Natl Board Of Dir Meeting In Wash D C CYO; Univ; Poli Sci.

LACY, KIMBERLY; Belmont HS; Dayton, OH; Sec Frsh Cls; Cl Rep Jr Cls; Hon Rl; NHS; FHA; Univ; Nursing.

LACY, ROBERT; Stivers Patterson Coop HS; Dayton, OH; Chrh Wkr; Cmnty Wkr; Hon Rl; NHS; VICA; Sinclear Comm College; Elec.

LADD, BRUCE; Summerfield HS; Petersburg, MI; Cls Rep Frsh Cls; Hon Rl; Sch Mus; Boys Clb Am; 4-H; Letter Ftbl; Letter Glf; Scr Kpr; Univ; Cmnctns.

LADD, GERALYN; Muskegon Catholic Cntrl HS; Muskegon, MI; Band; NHS; Sch Mus; Sct Actv; Stg Crw; Ed Yrbk; Pep Clb; Natl Merit Ltr; Muskegon Cnty Cmnty Fdn Sclshp 79; Mi Comp Schslp Awd 79; Wayne St Univ; Phys Ther.

LADD, GREG; Bridgeport Sr HS; Bridgeport, WV; Band; Hon Rl; NHS; Glf; DAR Awd; West Virginia Univ; Chem Engr.

LADD, KAREN; Wooster HS; Wooster, OH; Cls Rep Frsh Cls; Cls Rep Soph Cls; Cl Rep Jr Cls; Chrs; Sch

Mus; Sch Pl; Treas Stu Cncl; 4-H; Fr Clb; Spn Clb; Bowling Green St Univ; Busns Admin.

LADD, KELLI; Mohawk HS; Sycamore, OH; Trs Frsh Cls; Am Leg Aux Girls St; Chrs; Chrh Wkr; Hon Rl; Jr NHS; NHS; Sec Yth Flsp; Drama Clb; FTA; Bowling Green State Univ; Spec Educ.

LADD, STEPHENIE; Whitehall HS; Whitehall, MI; Cls Rep Soph Cls; Trs Sr Cls; Girl Scts; Hon Rl; NHS; Off Ade; Sch Pl; Stu Cncl; Drama Clb; VP Ger Clb; Coll.

LADEGAARD, KEVIN; Avon HS; Avon, OH; 4/155 AFS; Am Leg Boys St; Hon Rl; NHS; Yrbk; Kent St Univ; Med.

LADEN, PHILLIP; S Pemiscot HS; Steele, MO; Chrh Wkr; Bsktbl; Ftbl; Coach Actv; Kiwan Awd; Coll.

LADERMANN, JOANN; Greenville Sr HS; Greenville, MI; 13/238 Hon Rl; Hosp Ade; VFW Awd; Mercy Cntrl Schl Of Nursing; RN.

LADSON, STEVEN; Lutheran HS East; Detroit, MI; Band; Crs Cntry; Wrstlng; Univ; Psych.

LA DUE, JOHN D; Manistee Catholic Ctrl HS; Manistee, MI; Hon Rl; Rptr Sch Nwsp; Bsbl; Bsktbl; Ftbl; Univ; Pre Med.

LA DUKE, MICHAEL; South Central HS; Elizabeth, IN; Band; Hon Rl; Sch Pl; Stg Crw; Drama Clb; Pres 4-H; Fr Clb; Treas FFA; Mth Clb; Letter Mgrs; FFA Area Judgng Contst 2nd 79; Indiana St Univ; Athltc Training.

LA DUKE, RICHARD; Hartland HS; Hartland, MI; Aud/Vis; Chrs; Hon Rl; Sch Nwsp; Spn Clb; Ferris St Coll; Graphic Arts.

LADYGO, LINDA; Jefferson Area HS; Rock Creek, OH; 1/160 AFS; Chrh Wkr; NHS; VP Yth Flsp; FTA; VP Spn Clb; Am Leg Awd; Cedarville Coll; Math.

LAEUFER, KATIE; Upper Arlington HS; Columbus, OH; Chrs; Hon Rl; Sch Mus; Sch Pl; Drama Clb; Ger Clb; Pep Clb; GAA; Torch; Honors Awd Banquet; Allegheny Coll; Law.

LAFATA, MARYJO; Dominican HS; Detroit, MI; Cls Rep Frsh Cls; Cl Rep Jr Cls; Sal; Chrh Wkr; Cmnty Wkr; Hon Rl; Hosp Ade; Red Cr Ade; Sch Pl; IM Sprt; Univ Of Michigan; Nursing.

LAFFERTY, LINDA; Hoover HS; No Canton, OH; Cmp Fr Grls; Lbry Ade; Off Ade; Spn Clb; Kent State Univ; Med Tech.

LAFFOON, JAY; Petoskey HS; Petoskey, MI; Band; Chrh Wkr; Cmnty Wkr; Sct Actv; Yth Flsp; Sch Nwsp; Pep Clb; Letter Bsbl; Ftbl; IM Sprt; Michigan Tech Univ; Youth Ministry.

LAFFOON, LAURA; Northridge HS; Bristol, IN; Chrs; Drl Tm; Hon Rl; NHS; Sch Mus; Yth Flsp; Ger Clb; Pep Clb; Ten; College; Math.

LA FLEUR, DAVID; Flushing Sr HS; Flushing, MI; Cls Rep Soph Cls; Hon Rl; PAVAS; Pol Wkr; Pres Stu Cncl; Letter Ftbl; Trk; Opt Clb Awd; Pres Awd; Univ; Math.

LA FONTAINE, LINDA; New Riegel HS; New Riegel, OH; 5/51 VP Jr Cls; Band; Chrs; Hon Rl; NHS; Sch Mus; FTA; Pep Clb; Chrldng; Cit Awd; Providence Hosp Schl; Nursing.

LA FORCE, KATHY; Brazil HS; Brazil, IN; Cl Rep Jr Cls; Chrh Wkr; Hon Rl; NHS; Stu Cncl; Fr Clb; FBLA; FHA; Pep Clb; Letter Trk; Business Schl; Sec.

LA FORGE, LORI; Saline HS; Saline, MI; Trs Soph Cls; Band; Chrh Wkr; Hon Rl; NHS; Orch; Yth Flsp; E Michigan Univ; Bus.

LA FORGE, ROSEMARIE; Our Lady Of The Lakes HS; Waterford, MI; Cl Rep Jr Cls; Cls Rep Sr Cls; Boy Scts; Chrh Wkr; Cmnty Wkr; Hon Rl; Sch Pl; Stg Crw; Stu Cncl; Rptr Yrbk; Univ Of Michigan.

LA FOUNTAIN, KIM; Miller City HS; Continental, OH; VP Soph Cls; VP Jr Cls; VP Sr Cls; Chrs; Hon Rl; Yrbk; 4-H; FHA; Bsktbl; Trk; Home Ec III Awd; Univ; Home Ec.

LA FRAMBOISE, JEFFREY; Romulus Sr HS; Romulus, MI; Chrh Wkr; Cmnty Wkr; Hon Rl; Treas NHS; Sci Clb; Letter Ftbl; Letter Trk; Bausch & Lomb Awd; Kiwan Awd; Natl Merit Ltr; Math Awd 78; Michigan St Univ; Engr.

LA FRENIERE, PATRICK; Manistee Catholic Cntrl HS; Manistee, MI; Hon Rl; Capt Ten; Wrstlng; Cert Of Recgntn St O Mi Compttv Schlshp Progr 79; House Of Rep St Of Mi Cert Of Schlstc Acvhmnt 79; Great Lakes Maritime Acad; Deck Offc.

LAGAE, MIKE; Grosse Pointe N HS; Grosse Pt Wds, MI; Aud/Vis; Boy Scts; Hon Rl; Lbry Ade; Ger Clb; Sci Clb; Lawrence Inst Of Tech; Engr.

LAGEMAN, ANNETTE; New Knoxville HS; New Knoxville, OH; 4/43 Cls Rep Sr Cls; Am Leg Aux Girls St; Chrs; Hon Rl; Pres NHS; Sch Pl; Stu Cncl; Yth Flsp; Sec 4-H; FHA; Univ Of Cincinnati; Reg Nurse.

LAGER, MARIA; Colerain HS; Cincinnati, OH; Hon Rl; Jr NHS; Sec NHS; Sdlty; FHA; Sec Ger Clb; Sci Clb; JETS Awd; Ohio State Univ; Veterinary Medicine.

LAGEVEEN, KATHY; Kankakee Valley HS; De Motte, IN; Band; Girl Scts; Off Ade; Sct Actv; Stg Crw; Yth Flsp; Drama Clb; Pep Clb; Spn Clb; Trk; College.

LAGINESS, JAMES; River Rouge HS; River Rouge, MI; 10/227 Hon Rl; NHS; Bsbl; Bsktbl; Ten; Mgrs; Tmr; JC Awd; Central Mic Univ; Physical Therapist.

LAGINESS, MARIANNE; St Mary Academy; South Rockwood, MI; 3/132 Trs Frsh Cls; VP Soph Cls; Sal; Chrh Wkr; Hon Rl; VP NHS; Monroe County Comm Coll; Comp Sci.

LAGINESS, MARIANNE H; St Mary Academy; South Rockwood, MI; 3/130 Trs Frsh Cls; VP Soph Cls; Sal; Cmnty Wkr; Hon Rl; Pres NHS; Stu Cncl; Monroe County Cmnty Coll; Comp Sci.

LA GORIN, MARK W; Bedford North Lawrence HS; Saginaw, MI; Cls Rep Frsh Cls; Yth Flsp; Beta Clb; Key Clb; Swmmng; Trk; I H Crim Awd 79; Rockford Coll.

LA GROU, JAMES; Fremont Ross HS; Fremont, OH; Univ Of Toledo; Archaeology.

LA GROW, REBECCA S; Swan Valley HS; Saginaw, MI; 9/190 Jr NHS; Pres NHS; Sch Pl; Sec Stu Cncl; Drama Clb; Pres Pep Clb; Trk; Michigan St Univ; Law.

LAGUNZAD, ANASTACIA; Lincoln West HS; Cleveland, OH; Chrs; Chrh Wkr; Hon Rl; NHS; Off Ade; Cit Awd; Cleveland St Univ; Chem Engr.

LAHAB, REGINA; Cooley HS; Detroit, MI; Cmp Fr Grls; Chrs; Hon Rl; Lbry Ade; PAVAS; Sch Mus; Sch Pl; Drama Clb; Pep Clb; Chrldng; Michigan St Univ; Psych.

LAHAIE, LINDA; Caro HS; Caro, MI; Hon Rl; Off Ade; Rptr Sch Nwsp; Bsbl; Capt Bsktbl; Univ; Med Lab Tech.

LA HAISE, CATHERINE; Servite HS; Detroit, MI; Chrs; Chrh Wkr; Hon Rl; NHS; Sch Pl; VP Library Club; Pres Library Club; Vocal Music Awd; Wayne St Univ; Respiratory Therapy.

LAHETA, MICHAEL; Padua Franciscan HS; Parma, OH; 2/225 Hon Rl; JA; NHS; Pres Stu Cncl; IM Sprt; Scr Kpr; College; Elec Tech.

LAHIFF, BRIGID; Magnificat HS; Cleveland, OH; Chrs; Girl Scts; NHS; Sch Mus; Sct Actv; Stg Crw; Drama Clb; Bsbl; IM Sprt; Univ; Engr.

LAHM, MICHELE; Garaway HS; Sugarcreek, OH; Pres Jr Cls; Sec Band; Chrs; Drm Mjrt; Hon Rl; NHS; Sch Pl; Stu Cncl; Yth Flsp; Rptr Yrbk; College; Business.

LAHNA, REGINA; Newcomerstown HS; Newcomerstown, OH; 14/103 Chrs; Hon Rl; NHS; Sec FBLA; Treas FHA; FTA;.

LAHTI, ANITA; Harding HS; Fairport, OH; Chrs; Hon Rl; JA; Lbry Ade; Fr Clb; Pep Clb; Bsbl; Letter Bsktbl; Chrldng; Univ.

LAHTI, MYA; White Pine HS; White Pine, MI; Aud/Vis; Band; Hon Rl; Lbry Ade; NHS; Rptr Yrbk; Yrbk; Ed Sch Nwsp; Pep Clb; Sec.

LAHTINEN, JAMES S; Negaunee HS; Negaunee, MI; 38/150 Band; Chrs; Hon Rl; Bsbl; Letter Trk; Northern Mich Univ; Bus.

LA HUE, KARIN; Salem HS; Salem, OH; Am Leg Aux Girls St; Band; Chrs; Hon Rl; Sch Mus; 4-H; Fr Clb; Sci Clb; 4-H Awd; College; Engr.

LAIDLER, ROXANE; Lapeer W HS; Lapeer, MI; Am Leg Aux Girls St; Band; Chrh Wkr; Hon Rl; NHS; Sch Mus; Natl Merit SF; Lake Superior St Univ; Med Tech.

LAIL, CINDY; Hammond Baptist HS; Cedar Lake, IN; 1/73 Cls Rep Frsh Cls; Cls Rep Soph Cls; Cl Rep Jr Cls; Cls Rep Sr Cls; Band; Chrh Wkr; Hon Rl; NHS; Pol Wkr; Sch Mus; Cert Of Awds Bible Spanish Eng Geom & Typing; Valparaiso Univ; Law.

LAIN, TERESA; Bay HS; Bay Vill, OH; 28/373 Chrh Wkr; Girl Scts; Hon Rl; Sct Actv; Yth Flsp; Drama Clb; Rdo Clb; Sci Clb; PPFtbl; Kiwan Awd; Girls Var Vlybl Ltr 77 79; Baycrfters Art Schlrshp 78; Proj Earth Study 77 79; Univ; Geol.

LAING, LORI; Harper Creek HS; Battle Creek, MI; Cls Rep Frsh Cls; Cls Rep Soph Cls; Trs Jr Cls; Trs Sr Cls; Pres Stu Cncl; 4-H; Spn Clb; 4-H Awd; College.

LAINHART, SANDRA; Fairfield HS; Hamitlon, OH; 50/594 Cls Rep Frsh Cls; Hon Rl; JA; Sec Stu Cncl; OEA; Spn Clb; Wrstlng; Chrldng; Stenography.

LAIRD, THOMAS; Grand Ledge HS; Grand Ledge, MI; Band; Chrh Wkr; Sch Mus; Spn Clb; Letter Swmmng; Natl Merit Ltr; Mich State Univ; Vet Medicine.

LAITY, KATHRYN A; Waverly HS; Lansing, MI; 3/365 Hon Rl; NHS; Sch Nwsp; Spn Clb; Natl Merit SF; College.

LA JEUNESSE, TERRI; Negaunee HS; Flint, MI; VP Frsh Cls; Chrs; Hon Rl; Lbry Ade; Stu Cncl; Capt Chrldng; Voice Dem Awd; Michigan St Univ; Textiles.

LAJINESS, DANINE; Mason Consolidated HS; Erie, MI; Band; Hon Rl; Hosp Ade; Lbry Ade; NHS; Sch Pl; Drama Clb; Letter Chrldng; PPFtbl; Mercy College; Sci.

LAKANEN, EDWARD; Westwood HS; Ishpeming, MI; Cmnty Wkr; Bsktbl; Crs Cntry; Trk; Mgrs; Voc Schl; Carpentry.

LAKATOS, BRIAN; Chesterton HS; Chesterton, IN; Boy Scts; Chrh Wkr; Ftbl; Swmmng; Purdue Univ West Univ; Elec Engr.

LAKE, BRIAN; Canton South HS; Canton, OH; Cls Rep Frsh Cls; Aud/Vis; FCA; Hon Rl; Spn Clb; Bsbl; Bsktbl; Ftbl; Trk; Univ; Bus Admin.

LAKE, CHRIS; Summerfield HS; Petersburg, MI; 8/85 Cls Rep Frsh Cls; Cl Rep Jr Cls; Cls Rep Sr Cls; Band; Chrh Wkr; Hon Rl; Jr NHS; NHS; Sch Mus; Sch Pl; Awd For Bsktbl; Phys Fitness Awd; Univ Of Michigan; Engr.

LAKE, JERRY; Lebanon HS; Lebanon, OH; Lbry Ade; ROTC; Spn Clb; IM Sprt; Mgrs; Scr Kpr; Mas Awd; Bio.

LAKE, KIMBERLY; Mona Shores HS; Muskegon, MI; Band; Girl Scts; Hon Rl; JA; Rptr Sch Nwsp; 4-H; March Of Dimes Battered Boot; DECA Bronze Merit Awd; Grand Valley St Coll; Nursing.

LAKE, KIMBERY; Webster County HS; Hacker Valley, WV; Band; Chrh Wkr; Hon Rl; NHS; 4-H; Sci Clb; IM Sprt; 4-H Awd; Univ; Bio.

LAKE, RANDALL E; Marshall HS; Ceresco, MI; 10/256 Chrs; Debate Tm; Natl Forn Lg; NHS; Sch Mus; Sch Pl; Drama Clb; Central Mic Univ;.

LAKE, REGINA; Redford HS; Detroit, MI; Hon Rl; Off Ade; OEA; Cit Awd; Univ; Phys Ther.

LAKER, LIZABETH; South Dearborn HS; Aurora, IN; 29/218 Band; Drl Tm; Hon Rl; NHS; Sch Pl; Treas Stu Cncl; Pep Clb; Letter Glf; Ind Univ.

LAKER, ROSALIND; Scecina Memorial HS; Indianapolis, IN; Chrh Wkr; Hon Rl; CAP; Y-Teens; Bsktbl; IM Sprt; Scr Kpr; Indiana Bus Schl; Data Processing.

LAKIN, ROBIN; Brookville HS; Brookville, IN; Chrs; Chrh Wkr; Lbry Ade; FHA; Pom Pon; Potoagraphy School.

LAKINS, SHELLY; West Carrollton HS; Dayton, OH; Band; Girl Scts; Jr NHS; Rptr Yrbk; Pep Clb; Mgrs; PPFtbl; College.

LAKOS, WINONA; Cuyahoga Falls HS; Cuyahoga Falls, OH; 62/807 Chrh Wkr; Hon Rl; JA; Off Ade; OEA;.

LALAIN, MARCIA; Taylor Center HS; Taylor, MI; Cls Rep Soph Cls; Cl Rep Jr Cls; Band; Hon Rl; Lbry Ade; Pres Stu Cncl; PPFtbl; I Dare You Awd 79; Univ; Jrnlsm.

LALAMA, PAT A; Liberty HS; Youngstown, OH; Cl Rep Jr Cls; Chrs; Cmnty Wkr; Hon Rl; Stu Cncl; Ftbl; Capt Trk; IM Sprt; Youngstown State; Biology.

LALICH, JIM; Lebanon HS; Lebanon, OH; Chrs; Hon Rl; Sch Mus; Sch Pl; Ed Yrbk; Rptr Yrbk; Yrbk; Drama Clb; Eng Clb; College; Acctg.

LALLEMENT, GEORGE; East Palestine HS; E Palestine, OH; Chrs; Fr Clb; Natl Merit Ltr; Univ.

LA LONDE, ANNA; S Amherst HS; So Amherst, OH; 5/70 Pres Soph Cls; Pres Jr Cls; Pres Sr Cls; Band; Girl Scts; Hon Rl; NHS; Sch Pl; Ed Yrbk; Drama Clb; Sr Girl Athlete 79; Ohio St Univ; Poli Sci.

LA LONDE, LAURINA; Adelphian Acad; Saginaw, MI; Pres Frsh Cls; Chrh Wkr; Hon Rl; Hinsdale Hosp; Nursing.

LA LONDE, ROSEMARIE; Midland HS; Midland, MI; 103/498 Band; Chrh Wkr; Hon Rl; Off Ade; Orch; Fr Clb; Cit Awd; JA Awd; Natl Merit Schl; Midland Chem Awd 77; Saginaw Valley St Univ; Chem Engr.

LA LONDE, THOMAS; Croswell Lexington HS; Applegate, MI; 2/160 Sal; Am Leg Boys St; Band; Boy Scts; Hon Rl; NHS; Sch Mus; FFA; Letter Bsktbl; Saginaw Valley St College; Phys Ed.

LAM, WOON H; Clawson HS; Clawson, MI; 7/282 Hon Rl; Pol Wkr; Univ Of Michigan; Chem Engr.

LAMA, RAUL; Wayne HS; Dayton, OH; College; Air Force.

LAMAG, SANDRA; Wayne HS; Dayton, OH; College; Psych.

LA MANTIA, JOE; Lake Catholic HS; Euclid, OH; Hon Rl; NHS; Ed Sch Nwsp; Rptr Sch Nwsp; Cert Of Honor 1976; 2nd Pl Northeastern Oh Sci And Eng 1976; Cert Of Merit World Hist 1977; Univ; Sci.

LA MAR, DEE; Worthington Jefferson HS; Worthington, IN; 6/36 Trs Jr Cls; Letter Band; Hon Rl; NHS; Yrbk; Beta Clb; Pres Pep Clb; Letter Bsbl; Letter Wrstlng; Chrldng; B T Awrd 77; World Hist Awrd 77; Bus Schl; Acctg.

LA MAY, DELBERT; Yale HS; Goodells, MI; Boy Scts; Hon Rl; Yth Flsp; Letter Bsbl; Letter Bsktbl; Letter Ftbl; Univ.

LAMB, DAVID; Grosse Pointe North HS; Grosse Pte Woo, MI; Cl Rep Jr Cls; Cls Rep Sr Cls; Hon Rl; NHS; Ftbl; Natl Merit Schl; Mich State Univf Business.

LAMB, DEBBIE; Washington HS; Washington, IN; 11/216 Chrh Wkr; FCA; Hon Rl; Fr Clb; Pep Clb; Bsktbl; Letter Ten; Mgrs;.

LAMB, ELAINE; Washington HS; Washington, IN; 22/195 Band; Hon Rl; NHS; Ger Clb; Pep Clb; Indiana St Univ; Life Sci.

LAMB, ELEANOR; R B Chamberlin HS; Twinsburg, OH; 23/173 Cls Rep Frsh Cls; FCA; Hon Rl; JA; NHS; Rptr Yrbk; Pep Clb; Bsbl; Letter Bsktbl; Ftbl; Bowling Green St Univ; Acctg.

LAMB, GREG; South Dearborn HS; Aurora, IN; Band; Chrh Wkr; Hon Rl; Yth Flsp; Purdue Univ; Elec.

LAMB, GREG; Orleans HS; Orleans, IN; 2/45 Trs Jr Cls; Cls Rep Sr Cls; Sal; Chrh Wkr; Hon Rl; NHS; Stu Cncl; Yth Flsp; Rptr Yrbk; Letter Bsbl; Indiana Univ; Acctg.

LAMB, GREGG; Oceana HS; Oceana, WV; Hon Rl; Tech Traning Schl; Elec Tech.

LAMB, LAURI; St Peters HS; Mansfield, OH; Cls Rep Soph Cls; Chrh Wkr; Cmnty Wkr; Stu Cncl; Rptr Yrbk; Civ Clb; Ten; Chrldng; IM Sprt; JA Awd; College; Sci.

LAMB, NANCY; South Amherst HS; S Amherst, OH; Band; Drl Tm; Girl Scts; Hon Rl; Treas Off Ade; 4-H; JA Awd; Coll; Art.

LAMB, PAMELA N; Huntington HS; Huntington, WV; 18/287 Am Leg Aux Girls St; Chrh Wkr; Girl Scts; Hon Rl; Jr NHS; NHS; Stu Cncl; Pres Yth Flsp; Y-Teens; VP Lat Clb; Mbr Of Teen Missions Intl Grand Canyon Evangelistic Team; Awd For 4 Yr Of Latin; Peer Leadership Comm; Marshall Univ; Christian Ed.

LAMB, SHEILA; Marian HS; Blmfld Hls, MI; Trs Frsh Cls; Hon Rl; NHS; Fr Clb; Trk; Coll; Nursing.

LAMB, WILLIAM; South Amherst HS; S Amherst, OH; Am Leg Boys St; Boy Scts; Hon Rl; Sch Pl; Sct Actv; Drama Clb; Ftbl; Trk; Univ; Comm Art.

LAMBERG, RHONDA; Tri Twp HS; Rapid River, MI; 2/55 Sec Sr Cls; Sal; Am Leg Aux Girls St; Band; Chrh Wkr; Hon Rl; Sch Mus; Yrbk; Fr Clb; Scr Kpr; Northern Michigan Univ; Other.

LAMBERT, BILLIE; James A Garfield HS; Windham, OH; Girl Scts; Hon Rl; Pep Clb; Trk; Capt Chrldng; Coach Actv; Drama Schl; Drama.

LAMBERT, CHRIS; Bloomington North HS; Bloomington, IN; Boys Clb Am; Spn Clb; Ten; Univ; Aviation.

LAMBERT, DEBRA; Monroe HS; Monroe, MI; Chrh Wkr; Hon Rl; Cit Awd; Monroe County Comm College; Acctng.

LAMBERT, DOUG; Hampshire HS; Slanesville, WV; Band; Hon Rl; Jr NHS; Stu Cncl; Yth Flsp; Yrbk; Letter Bsktbl; Letter Ftbl; Letter Trk; Rotary Awd; Univ; Archt.

LAMBERT, GREGORY; Crown Point HS; Crown Point, IN; 27/557 Cls Rep Frsh Cls; Pres Soph Cls; VP Jr Cls; Debate Tm; Hon Rl; NHS; Sch Pl; Stu Cncl; Drama Clb; Fr Clb; All St Cross Cntry All Amer Cross Cntry Track; Whos Who In Foreign Lang; Univ; Poli Sci.

LAMBERT, JERRY; Grafton HS; Grafton, WV; Boy Scts; Chrh Wkr; Debate Tm; FCA; Hon Rl; Sdlty; Yth Flsp; Letter Ten; IM Sprt; Fairmont St Univ; Engr Tech.

LAMBERT, JOHN; Salem Cmnty Schools; Daleville, IN; Chrh Wkr; Cmnty Wkr; Lbry Ade; Yth Flsp; 4-H; Fr Clb; Post Master Counc Order Of De Molay Daleville Chptr 79; Voc Schl; Home Const.

LAMBERT, JONATHAN; Princeton HS; Princeton, WV; Cls Rep Soph Cls; FCA; Hon Rl; Stu Cncl; Fr Clb; Key Clb; Bsbl; Bsktbl; Tmr; Awd For Straight A In French 1 76; Univ; Elec Engr.

LAMBERT, MICHAEL; Harman HS; Wymer, WV; Pres Frsh Cls; Pres Soph Cls; VP Sr Cls; FFA;.

LAMBERT, RICKY; Pineville HS; Pineville, WV; VP Soph Cls; VP Jr Cls; Aud/Vis; Hon Rl; Jr NHS; Univ; Bus Admin.

LAMBERT, VICKI; L C Mohr HS; South Haven, MI; Sec Jr Cls; Hon Rl; NHS; Yth Flsp; Rptr Sch Nwsp; 4-H; Swmmng; Trk; Cit Awd; 4-H Awd; Mic State; Veterinary Science.

LAMBERT JR, KENNETH; London HS; S Vienna, OH; 30/141 Hon Rl; Sch Pl; 4-H; Pep Clb; Spn Clb; Ohio Inst Of Technology.

LAMBKE, MARY P; Marian HS; Blmfld Hls, MI; 35/169 Cl Rep Jr Cls; Chrh Wkr; Cmnty Wkr; Hon Rl; Mod UN; NHS; Sch Mus; Stu Cncl; Fr Clb; Qualified For Michigan Schlrshp; French Honor Soc; Univ; Social Work.

LAMBRIGHT, TERESA; Gorham Fayette HS; Alvordton, OH; Chrs; Drl Tm; Hon Rl; Lbry Ade; Rptr Sch Nwsp; Sch Nwsp; Rptr Sch Nwsp; Bsbl; Swmmng;.

LAMBROS, MARY J; Hamilton Taft Sr HS; Hamilton, OH; 60/400 Trs Soph Cls; Trs Jr Cls; Trs Sr Cls; Am Leg Aux Girls St; Band; Drl Tm; Hon Rl; Jr NHS; Lit Mag; Off Ade; Mbr Natl Super Str Drill Tm 78; Ltr Of Partcptn For Fresh Yr Only 1 Awd To Class 76; Univ; Med Tech.

LAMER, DEB; Zeeland HS; Zeeland, MI; Sec Soph Cls; Band; Chrs; Drl Tm; Girl Scts; Hon Rl; 4-H; Glf; Chrldng; PPFtbl; 4 H Clothing Appearance & Construction Awds; Lou Rog Vocational Schl; Cosmetology.

LAMERATO, DINA; Troy Athens HS; Troy, MI; Hon Rl; Hosp Ade; NHS; Off Ade; Red Cr Ade; FNA; Pep Clb; Letter Bsktbl; Coach Actv; IM Sprt; Univ Of Michigan; Nursing.

LAMERE, MARGARET; Bishop Noll Institute; Hammond, IN; 69/321 Trs Frsh Cls; Sec Soph Cls; Hon Rl; Sch Mus; Stu Cncl; Mth Clb; Indiana Univ; Bus.

LAMM, KIM; Liberty HS; Clarksburg, WV; Cls Rep Frsh Cls; Cls Rep Soph Cls; Trs Jr Cls; Band; Hon Rl; Stu Cncl; Drama Clb; Pep Clb; Gym; Capt Chrldng; Union Protestant Hosp; Radiology.

LAMME, MAJEL; Sheridan HS; Glenford, OH; 18/171 Letter Band; Treas Girl Scts; VP NHS; Sch Mus; Sec Yth Flsp; Rptr Sch Nwsp; FHA; Sec VICA; Yth Coordinating Committee; All Ohio Yth Cnfrnce; College; Cosmetology.

LAMMERS, WILLIAM; Minster HS; Minster, OH; 3/80 Am Leg Boys St; Chrh Wkr; Hon Rl; Jr NHS; NHS; Yth Flsp; Pep Clb; Spn Clb; Letter Bsbl; JC Awd; Univ; Elec Engr.

LAMMERT, ANNE; Mcauley HS; Cinti, OH; 5/260 Hon Rl; Mod UN; Sch Mus; Rptr Yrbk; Lat Clb; Ten; Coach Actv; Sec GAA; Miami Univ; Marketing.

LAMMIE, JAMES; St Francis De Sales HS; Toledo, OH; VP Frsh Cls; Pres Soph Cls; Cl Rep Jr Cls; Pres Sr Cls; Hon Rl; NHS; Stu Cncl; Univ Of Alabama; Mech Engr.

LAMMON, DEBORAH; Defiance Sr HS; Defiance, OH; Chrs; Chrh Wkr; Hon Rl; NHS; Yth Flsp; Letter Bsktbl;.

LAMMON, JILL; Defiance Sr HS; Defiance, OH; 35/263 Chrs; Chrh Wkr; Hon Rl; Sch Mus; Sch Pl; Sec Yth Flsp; Drama Clb; Select Chrl Grp; Univ; Fshn Mdse.

LAMMOTT, TRUDY; Twin Valley North HS; Fairfax, VT; Chrs; Hon Rl; Hosp Ade; Stu Cncl; Rptr Sch Nwsp; FHA; Pep Clb; Univ Of Vermont; Nursing.

LA MONT, LAURIE; Deckerville HS; Deckerville, MI; VP Frsh Cls; Drl Tm; Girl Scts; Hon Rl; Off Ade; Bsktbl; Chrldng; Ferris St College; Nursing.

LAMOREAUX, WAYNE; Elk Rapids Sr HS; Elk Rapids, MI; 12/90 Sec Frsh Cls; Sec Soph Cls; Sec Jr Cls; Sec Sr Cls; Band; Boy Scts; Chrh Wkr; Hon Rl; NHS; Sct Actv; Eagle Scout; Amos Alonzo Stag Awd Athleta Of Yr; All Conf Football Honorable Mention Both Offense & Defense; Michigan Tech Inst; Civil Engr.

LA MOTTE, STEVEN; Houghton HS; Houghton, MI; Band; Boy Scts; Chrs; Chrh Wkr; Hon Rl; Sch

Mus; Letter Ftbl; Letter Trk; Northern Michigan Univ; Math.

LAMOURIE, MATTHEW; Cabrini HS; Allen Park, MI; Cls Rep Frsh Cls; Cls Rep Soph Cls; Debate Tm; Hon Rl; Natl Forn Lg; NHS; Fr Clb; Crs Cntry; Trk; IM Sprt; Michigan St Univ; Engr.

LAMPE, PHIL; La Salle HS; Cincinnati, OH; 24/249 VP Jr Cls; Cl Rep Jr Cls; VP Sr Cls; Hon Rl; NHS; Stu Cncl; Bsktbl; Ftbl; Univ; Priv Bus.

LAMPEN, LOWELL; Portland HS; Lyons, MI; 2/146 Sal; Band; NHS; Stg Crw; Stu Cncl; Letter Ftbl; Univ Of Mic; Pre Med.

LAMPERT, JEFFREY; Minster Local HS; Minster, OH; Chrh Wkr; Hon Rl; Pep Clb; Spn Clb; Bsbl; Ftbl; Miami Univ; Busns Acctg.

LAMPERT, STEVEN; Lawrenceburg HS; Lawrenceburg, IN; 41/144 VICA; IM Sprt; Purdue Univ; Forestry.

LAMPHIEAR, LINDA; Comstock HS; Galesburg, MI; Hon Rl; JA; NHS; Bsktbl; Trk; Cit Awd; JA Awd; Pres Awd; W Mich Univ; Phys Educ.

LAMPKIN, RAMONA; Monongah HS; Carolina, WV; 12/53 Chrs; Chrh Wkr; Hon Rl; Y-Teens; FHA; Pep Clb; Capt Bsktbl; Trk; Elk Awd; Mas Awd; Univ Of Charleston; Nursing Instr.

LAMPKIN, THALIA; Buckhannon Upshur HS; French Creek, WV; Band; College; Nursing.

LANCASTER, BRENDA E; Eau Claire HS; Eau Claire, MI; 7/97 Band; Hon Rl; Sch Mus; 4-H; Pep Clb; Chrldng; Mat Maids; 4-H Awd; Western Michigan Univ; Busns Mgmt.

LANCASTER, CINDY; Springs Valley HS; Paoli, IN; 14/80 Chrh Wkr; Hon Rl; Treas 4-H; FFA; FHA; Letter Trk; Scr Kpr; 4-H Awd; Purdue Univ; Vet.

LANCASTER, JULIA; Kalamazoo Central HS; Kalamazoo, MI; 19/405 Band; Chrh Wkr; Girl Scts; Hon Rl; JA; NHS; Orch; Sch Mus; Mich St Univ; Cpa.

LANCASTER, ROBERT N; Greenon HS; Enon, OH ; Boy Scts; Hon Rl; Ed Yrbk; Spn Clb; Ftbl; Wrstlng; IM Sprt; Perfct Attndnc Record 12 Yr Of Schl; Onlu Stdnt In Clark Cnty Oh To Grad With Hons 79; Wittenberg Univ; Pre Law.

LANCASTER, SANDY; The Leelanau HS; Alpena, MI; 4/23 Cls Rep Soph Cls; Cl Rep Jr Cls; Chrh Wkr; Cmnty Wkr; Hon Rl; Off Ade; Stg Crw; College; Med.

LANCASTER, SUSAN; Wintersville HS; Wintersville, OH; Band; Chrs; Chrh Wkr; Hosp Ade; Sch Pl; Stg Crw; Drama Clb; FNA; Pep Clb; Chrldng; Mansfield Schl Nursing; Rn.

LANCE, D; Albion HS; Albion, MI; Cls Rep Frsh Cls; Boy Scts; Quill & Scroll; Sch Mus; Sch Pl; Stg Crw; Rptr Sch Nwsp; Sch Nwsp; Drama Clb; College; Actor.

LANCE, GAIL; Waynedale HS; Wooster, OH; 2/132 Cls Rep Frsh Cls; Cls Rep Soph Cls; Chrs; Hon Rl; NHS; Sch Pl; Stu Cncl; Rptr Yrbk; FTA; Spn Clb; Case Western Reserve Univ; Engr.

LANCE, KIM; Wadsworth HS; Wadsworth, OH; VP Sr Cls; FHA; OEA; Spn Clb; IM Sprt; Scr Kpr; Twrlr; Wayne Genrl & Tech Univ; Acctg.

LANCE, LORI; Southeast HS; Rootstown, OH; Chrs; Girl Scts; Hon Rl;.

LANCE, SHERI; Hillsdale HS; Jeromesville, OH; Trs Sr Cls; Sec Chrh Wkr; Girl Scts; Ed Yrbk; FHA;.

LANCELOT, ROBERT; St Joseph HS; St Joseph, MI; Cl Rep Jr Cls; Am Leg Boys St; NHS; Sch Mus; Sch Pl; Stg Crw; Lat Clb; Letter Bsbl; Coach Actv; College; Comp Engr.

LANCENDORFER, PATRICIA A; Southwestern HS; Detroit, MI; 1/225 Val; Girl Scts; NHS; Swmmng; Kiwan Awd; Delia P Hussey Schlr Athlete Awrd 79; Mn Outward Bound Schlrshp 77; Mi Tech Bd Of Control Schlrshp 79; Michigan Tech Univ; Forestry.

LANCHMAN, GREGORY; Cathedral Latin Schl; Highand Hts, OH; 2/80 Hon Rl; Treas NHS; Sci Clb; Bausch & Lomb Awd; Ohio St Univ; Natural Resources.

LANCY, SHERRI A; Struthers HS; Poland, OH; Hon Rl; Lbry Ade; Sprt Ed Sch Nwsp; Lat Clb; Pep Clb; Gym; Chrldng; Youngstown Vindicator Journalism One Week Ed Schlrshp; Kent St Univ.

LAND, ANGELA; Wyoming Park HS; Wyoming, MI; 8/236 Chrh Wkr; Sec NHS; Ed Yrbk; Davenport College Of Bus; Fshn Merch.

LAND, DEBORAH; Alba HS; Elmira, MI; Girl Scts; Hon Rl; Lbry Ade; Off Ade; Sch Mus; Rptr Yrbk; Rptr Sch Nwsp; 4-H; Pep Clb; Bsktbl; Coll.

LAND, REBECCA; Lincoln HS; Vincennes, IN; 21/279 Chrh Wkr; Hon Rl; Yth Flsp; FHA; FTA; Pep Clb; Indiana Univ; Pre Law.

LAND, WILLIAM; Centerville HS; Centerville, IN; Band; Pol Wkr; IM Sprt; Purdue Univ; Mech.

LANDAKER, BEVERLY; Tri Valley HS; Adams Mills, OH; 16/215 Girl Scts; Hon Rl; Spn Clb;.

LANDAU, LISA; Delta HS; Muncie, IN; 82/320 Chrh Wkr; Girl Scts; Pres JA; Lbry Ade; Red Cr Ade; Stu Cncl; Fr Clb; JA Awd; College; Spec Ed.

LANDELLS, JILL; Otsego HS; Otsego, MI; 1/215 Trs Soph Cls; Val; Am Leg Aux Girls St; Chrs; Hon Rl; NHS; Sch Mus; Treas Stu Cncl; Rptr Yrbk; Rptr Sch Nwsp; Mich State Univ; Vet.

LANDER, JEFFREY M; Avon Jr Sr HS; Plainfield, IN; FCA; Hon Rl; Eng Clb; Spn Clb; Letter Crs Cntry; Letter Trk; Indiana St Univ; Aviation.

LANDER, LISA; Stephen T Badin HS; Hamilton, OH; Hosp Ade; JA; Stg Crw; Lat Clb; Mt St Joseph Univ; Nursing.

LANDERFELT, CATHI; Licking County HS; Newark, OH; Cl Rep Jr Cls; Girl Scts; Hon Rl; Lbry Ade; Sch Mus; 4-H; OEA; Spn Clb; Trk; 4-H Awd; College; Exec Sec.

LANDERS, LINDA; Taft HS; Hamilton, OH; Hon Rl; Off Ade; Stu Cncl; Yth Flsp; Indiana Univ; Comp Sci.

LANDERS, MARY; Cardinal Mooney HS; Youngstown, OH; 50/300 Hon Rl; Off Ade; Treas Stu Cncl; Ed Yrbk; Rptr Sch Nwsp; Mth Clb; Trk; Mgrs; Tmr; Univ Of Cinn; Architectural Design.

LANDFRIED, BARBARA; Harbor HS; Ashtabula, OH; 3/97 Am Leg Aux Girls St; Band; Girl Scts; NHS; Yth Flsp; Fr Clb; Lion Awd; French II & III Awds; Worthy Advisor Of Order Of Rainbow Girls; Superior Rating At Solo Contest; College.

LANDHEER, SHERI; Unity Christian HS; Byron Center, MI; Chrs; Chrh Wkr; Hosp Ade; Lbry Ade; 4-H; 4-H Awd; Grand Rapids Jr College; Prac Nurse.

LANDIN, KEVIN; O Hoville Local HS; Ft Jennings, OH; Trs Soph Cls; Cl Rep Jr Cls; Am Leg Boys St; Band; Hon Rl; NHS; Sch Mus; Treas Stu Cncl; Pres 4-H; IM Sprt; Univ; Physics.

LANDIS, ANN; Columbia City Joint HS; Columbia City, IN; 9/273 Hon Rl; Sec JA; NHS; Pres Yth Flsp; Rptr Yrbk; Spn Clb; College.

LANDIS, GINA; Shakamak HS; Jasonville, IN; 43/86 Sec Frsh Cls; Sec Soph Cls; Sec Jr Cls; Sec Sr Cls; Chrs; Drl Tm; Quill & Scroll; Sch Nwsp; FHA; Sec Pep Clb; Indiana State; Business.

LANDIS, J; Linton Stockton HS; Linton, IN; Pres Frsh Cls; Hon Rl; NHS; Stu Cncl; FFA; Col Schl Of Mines; Mine Supervision.

LANDIS, J; River Vly HS; Caledonia, OH; Yrbk; Sci Clb; Spn Clb; Trk; Southeastern Acad; Travel.

LANDIS, REBECCA; Schoolcraft HS; Schoolcraft, MI; Band; Hon Rl; NHS; Yth Flsp; Trk; Western Mich Univ; Bus.

LANDIS, RUTH; Napoleon HS; Mc Clure, OH; Am Leg Aux Girls St; Band; Cmnty Wkr; Lit Mag; Natl Forn Lg; NHS; Sch Mus; Sch Pl; Yth Flsp; Voice Dem Awd; Ohi Northern Univ; Pharmacy.

LANDRETH, CHERYL; Cloverdale HS; Cloverdale, IN; 20/80 Chrs; Chrh Wkr; Cmnty Wkr; Drl Tm; Girl Scts; Sch Mus; Stg Crw; 4-H; Fr Clb; Pep Clb; Miss Cloverdale 76; Univ.

LANDRETH, DOUG; Harper Creek HS; Battle Creek, MI; Letter Ftbl; Letter Trk; Univ; Archt.

LANDRITH, LINDA; Carsonville Port Sanilac HS; Carsonville, MI; Pres Soph Cls; Pres Jr Cls; Pres Sr Cls; Chrs; Girl Scts; Hon Rl; Off Ade; Sch Pl; Stg Crw; Rptr Yrbk; St Clair Comm Coll; Busns.

LANDRU, MICHAEL; Warren Woods HS; Warren, MI; VP Frsh Cls; Cls Rep Frsh Cls; Cls Rep Soph Cls; VP Jr Cls; Pres Sr Cls; Off Ade; Sch Pl; Stu Cncl; Bsbl; Bsktbl; Northwood Inst; Bus Admin.

LANDRUM, JENNIFER R; Heath HS; Heath, OH; Chrs; Drl Tm; Girl Scts; Hon Rl; Mdrgl; Natl Forn Lg; Sch Mus; Sch Pl; Drama Clb; Scr Kpr; Ohio St Univ; Comp Prog.

LANDRY, DIANE; Bishop Borgess HS; Redford, MI; Hon Rl; NHS; Stg Crw; Stu Cncl; Bsktbl; IM Sprt; Am Leg Awd; Univ; Bio.

LANDRY, MARTHA; Highland HS; Wadsworth, OH; 10/202 Band; Chrs; Girl Scts; Hon Rl; NHS; Off Ade; Sch Mus; FTA; Key Clb; Spn Clb; Natl Hnr Soc & Highland Hnr Soc; All Ohio St Fair Band; Cincinnati Conservatory Of Music Schlrshp; Univ Of Cincinnati; Music.

LANDRY, MARY; St Ursula Acad; Toledo, OH; Girl Scts; Hon Rl; Orch; Red Cr Ade; Sch Mus; Sct Actv; Lat Clb; Univ Of Mia.

LANDY, MAUREEN; Boardman Sr HS; Youngstown, OH; 11/550 Chrs; Hon Rl; Jr NHS; NHS; Sch Mus; Univ; Spanish.

LANE, ANGIE; Benton Central HS; Fowler, IN; Jr NHS; Rptr Sch Nwsp; Pres OEA; Chrldng; IM Sprt; PPFtbl; Vincennes Univ; Legal Sec.

LANE, BARBARA; New Haven Sr HS; New Haven, IN; Band; FCA; Hon Rl; JA; Sch Pl; Drama Clb; Letter Bsktbl; Letter Trk; Univ; Paramedic.

LANE, C; Bridgeport HS; Saginaw, MI; Girl Scts; Hon Rl; Sct Actv; Bsktbl; Letter Ten; Letter Trk; Univ Of Mic; Pre Dentistry.

LANE, DAWN; Greenfield Central HS; Greenfield, IN; 110/325 Off Ade; Pol Wkr; Quill & Scroll; Ed Sch Nwsp; 4-H; FFA; Pep Clb; 4-H Awd; Amer Inst Of Cooperatives At Montana; Ball St Journalism Workshop; Hoosier Farmer Degree FFA;.

LANE, JAMES; Adlai Stevenson HS; Sterling Hts, MI; NHS; Univ; Elec Engr.

LANE, JEFFREY; Springs Valley HS; French Lick, IN; Am Leg Boys St; Band; Boy Scts; Chrh Wkr; Pres Yth Flsp; IM Sprt; Lion Awd; Ind Univ Se; Elem Educ.

LANE, JEFFREY S; Sharples HS; Sharples, WV; 1/25 Band; Chrh Wkr; Cmnty Wkr; Hon Rl; Jr NHS; NHS; Off Ade; Red Cr Ade; Rptr Sch Nwsp; Pres 4-H; 4 H Charting Pin; Conservation Camp Col Allen Woodburn Awd; 1st Pl Talent Show Piano; Marshall Univ; Math.

LANE, JILL; Mississinewa HS; Gas City, IN; 1/189 Val; Am Leg Aux Girls St; Hon Rl; NHS; Rptr Yrbk; Spn Clb; Ball St Univ; Acctg.

LANE, JUDY; West Branch HS; Beloit, OH; Cls Rep Frsh Cls; Cls Rep Soph Cls; Cl Rep Jr Cls; VP Sr Cls; Cls Rep Sr Cls; VP Chrs; Lbry Ade; NHS; VP Stu Cncl; FTA; College.

LANE, K; Kalkaska HS; Rapid City, MI; 23/160 Cl Rep Jr Cls; Off Ade; Sch Pl; Chrldng; College; Business.

LANE, KIMBERLY; George Washington HS; East Chicago, IN; Cls Rep Soph Cls; Cl Rep Jr Cls; Cls Rep Sr Cls; Hon Rl; NHS; Off Ade; FHA; Cit Awd; Purdue Univ; Crt Reporter.

LANE, KIMBERLY; Marion HS; Marion, IN; Hon Rl; Jr NHS; Lbry Ade; Off Ade; Stu Cncl; Sci Clb; VICA; 4-H Awd; Ind Univ; Psych.

LANE, LINDA; Dayton Christian HS; Dayton, OH; 19/92 Pres Soph Cls; Pres Jr Cls; Chrs; Hon Rl; NHS; Sprt Ed Yrbk; Capt Bsbl; Capt Bsktbl; Cit Awd; College; Health.

LANE, LOUIS; Mount View HS; Elbert, WV; Am Leg Boys St; Hon Rl; NHS; Key Clb; Bsktbl; Letter Ftbl; Wv Univ; Tchr.

LANE, LOUIS S; Mount View HS; Elbert, WV; Am Leg Boys St; Hon Rl; NHS; Key Clb; Bsktbl; Ftbl; West Virginia Univ; Tchr.

LANE, MICHAEL; Archbishop Alter HS; Kettering, OH; Chrh Wkr; Sch Mus; Key Clb; Bsktbl; Ftbl; Letter Glf; IM Sprt; Scr Kpr; College; Busns.

LANE, MYRON; Western Boone HS; Lebanon, IN; 8/142 Am Leg Boys St; Band; Hon Rl; NHS; Yth Flsp; Key Clb; Lat Clb; Rdo Clb; Ten; Trk; Whos Who In Foreign Language In Latin; Purdue Univ; Elec Engr.

LANE, NADINE; Mount View HS; Welch, WV; 12/240 Chrs; Hon Rl; Jr NHS; NHS; Yth Flsp; Y-Teens; FBLA; Keyettes; Pep Clb;.

LANE, NICOLETTE; Greenville Sr HS; Greenville, OH; 102/380 Chrh Wkr; Girl Scts; Sct Actv; Stg Crw; Sec Yth Flsp; Drama Clb; Theater Soc Best Comm Worker Awrd 79; The Defiance Coll; Psych.

LANE, OLIVIA; Fayetteville HS; Fayetteville, WV; 30/75 Am Leg Aux Girls St; Chrs; Chrh Wkr; Drl Tm; Girl Scts; Hon Rl; Stu Cncl; Pep Clb; Bsktbl; West Virginia St Coll; Soc Work.

LANE, PATHEA; Athens HS; Athens, WV; Trs Soph Cls; Trs Jr Cls; Hon Rl; Hosp Ade; NHS; Stu Cncl; Pres Fr Clb; FTA; Treas Keyettes; Pep Clb; Univ.

LANE, PHILLIP J; Marlington HS; Alliance, OH; 52/326 Hon Rl; Sec VICA; Ftbl; Trk; IM Sprt; Univ Of Akron; Elec Engr.

LANE, RANDY; Southern Wells HS; Poneto, IN; 3/90 Hon Rl; NHS; Spn Clb; Health Awd; World History Awd; Huntington Coll; Math.

LANE, SCOTT; West Carrollton Sr HS; W Carrollton, OH; 2/385 Chrh Wkr; Jr NHS; NHS; Ten; IM Sprt; Case Western Reserve Univ; Dent.

LANE, STEPHEN; Middletown HS; Middletown, OH; 70/550 Band; Hon Rl; Natl Forn Lg; NHS; Orch; Sch Mus; Sch Pl; Stg Crw; Drama Clb; Wittenburg Univ; Poli Sci.

LANE, SUSAN; South Knox HS; Vincennes, IN; 40/130 Sec Jr Cls; Chrh Wkr; Hon Rl; Stu Cncl; 4-H; FHA; FNA; FSA; Mth Clb; OEA; Indiana St Univ; Comp Sci.

LANE, SUSAN; Bloomington North HS; Bloomington, IN; Cmp Fr Grls; Chrh Wkr; NHS; Sci Clb; Univ; Bio.

LANE, TERESA K; Adena HS; Frankfort, OH; 26/94 Trs Soph Cls; Trs Jr Cls; Band; Chrh Wkr; Hon Rl; Off Ade; Yth Flsp; Yrbk; Chrldng; Tech Coll; Financial Mgmt.

LA NEVE, LISA; Olmsted Falls HS; Olmsted Falls, OH; Chrs; Drl Tm; Hon Rl; Stg Crw; Pom Pon; College; Busns.

LANEW, LINDA; Mackinaw City HS; Mackinaw City, MI; Girl Scts; Hon Rl; NHS; Bsktbl; Pom Pon; Natl Merit SF; Davenport Bus Coll; Fashion Mdse.

LANFEAR, COLLEEN; Bishop Foley HS; Royal Oak, MI; Chrs; Hon Rl; JA; Yrbk; Fr Clb; Chrldng;.

LANFORD, DAVE; Ben Davis HS; Clermont, IN; 57/834 Band; Chrs; Chrh Wkr; Natl Forn Lg; NHS; Sch Mus; Fr Clb; Drum Major; Mbr Indiana All State Marching Band; College; Art.

LANG, ANETTE M; Concord HS; Concord, MI; FHA; Trk; Univ; Spec Educ.

LANG, ANGELA; Waterford HS; Waterford, OH; 9/63 Chrs; Hon Rl; 4-H; Sci Clb; Spn Clb; Bsktbl; Chrldng; Am Leg Awd; 4-H Awd; Coll; Social Work.

LANG, BRIAN E; Maplewood Jr Sr HS; Cortland, OH; Band; Beta Clb; Technical Schl.

LANG, BROOKE; Canfield HS; Canfield, OH; Chrs; Debate Tm; Hon Rl; Sch Mus; Sch Pl; Stu Cncl; Rptr Yrbk; Rptr Sch Nwsp; Fr Clb; PPFtbl; Univ; Psychology.

LANG, CINDY; Champion HS; Warren, OH; 16/230 Hon Rl; NHS; Off Ade; Stg Crw; 4-H; Fr Clb; FNA; FTA; 4-H Awd; Kent St Univ; Speech Path.

LANG, DANIEL; Padua Franciscan HS; Parma, OH; Chrh Wkr; Hon Rl; Yth Flsp; Natl Merit Schl; Wheeling Coll; Pre Law.

LANG, ERIC; Wooster HS; Wooster, OH; Band; Chrh Wkr; Yrbk; Sch Nwsp; Fr Clb; IM Sprt; Univ Of Mic; Bio.

LANG, JACQUELINE; Geneva Secondary Complex HS; Rock Creek, OH; Rptr Yrbk; Fr Clb; Lakeland Comm College; Med Lab.

LANG, JAMES; Centreville HS; Centreville, MI; 4/70 Trs Sr Cls; Am Leg Boys St; Band; Chrh Wkr; Hon Rl; NHS; 4-H; FFA; Spn Clb; Wrstlng; Michigan St Univ; Tele Cmnctns.

LANG, JAMES C; Piketon HS; Piketon, OH; 5/100 Pres Soph Cls; Pres Jr Cls; Band; Boy Scts; Chrs; Chrh Wkr; Cmnty Wkr; Hon Rl; Lbry Ade; MMM; Annapolis Naval Academy; Engr.

LANG, JEANNE; Fordson HS; Dearborn, MI; Chrh Wkr; NHS; Ger Clb; Red Cr Ade; Mic State Univ; Sci.

LANG, JOYCE; North Farmington HS; Farm Hills, MI; Cls Rep Frsh Cls; Cls Rep Soph Cls; Chrs; Hon Rl; Natl Forn Lg; NHS; Stu Cncl; Rptr Sch Nwsp; Fr Clb; The Detroit News Scholastic Writing Awds; Schl Bowling League; College; Acctg.

LANG, L; Medina Highland HS; Medina, OH; Band; Drl Tm; Hon Rl; Yth Flsp; Drama Clb; Capt Key Clb; Hndbl; Mat Maids; Scr Kpr; College; Business;.

LANG, MARILYN; Fort Frye HS; Marietta, OH; 15/129 Hon Rl; NHS; Off Ade; Quill & Scroll; Sch Mus; Sch Pl; Sdlty; Stg Crw; Rptr Yrbk; Sch Nwsp;.

LANG, MARK; Benjamin Bosse HS; Evansville, IN; Hst Frsh Cls; Cl Rep Jr Cls; Band; Hon Rl; Stu Cncl; Pep Clb; Rdo Clb; Capt Ftbl; Cit Awd; Univ Of Evansville; Journalism.

LANG, MARY; Bishop Foley HS; Royal Oak, MI; 43/250 Hon Rl; Chrldng; Natl Merit SF; College; Accounting.

LANG, T; Fort Frye HS; Lowell, OH; Am Leg Boys St; Band; Boy Scts; Hon Rl; Sch Mus; Spn Clb; Coll; Engr.

LANG, TAMRA; Pittsford Area HS; Pittsford, MI; NHS; Stu Cncl; Rptr Yrbk; Spn Clb; Ferris St Coll; Optometric Tech.

LANGAN, ANNE M; Dominican HS; Detroit, MI; Pres Soph Cls; Band; Chrs; Hon Rl; Hosp Ade; NHS; Sch Mus; Marygrove College; English.

LANGDON, ANDREW; Vicksburg Community HS; Fulton, MI; NHS; Yth Flsp; Letter Ftbl; Trk; Army.

LANGDON, ANNETTA; Taft Sr HS; Hamilton, OH; 1/420 Cls Rep Sr Cls; Val; Am Leg Aux Girls St; Capt Drl Tm; Hon Rl; VP NHS; Stu Cncl; Pres Y-Teens; Sec OEA; Opt Clb Awd; Univ Of Tennessee; Law.

LANGDON, THERESE; St Augustine Academy; Lakewood, OH; Cl Rep Jr Cls; Chrs; Hon Rl; Hosp Ade; Stu Cncl; Y-Teens; Rptr Yrbk; Sci Clb; Bsbl; Scr Kpr; Marquette Univ; Physical Therapy.

LANGE, ANNETTE; Napoleon HS; Napoleon, OH; Band; Chrs; Hon Rl; NHS; Orch; Sch Mus; Yth Flsp; Drama Clb; Fr Clb; College.

LANGE, CARLA; Whittemore Prescott HS; Whittemore, MI; Band; Hon Rl; NHS; Sch Pl; Rptr Yrbk; Letter Bsbl; Letter Bsktbl; IM Sprt; PPFtbl; Typing I Achievement Awd 78 79; Outstanding Plys Ed Stdnt Awd; Univ; Crim Justice.

LANGE, CAROL; St Henry HS; St Henry, OH; Hon Rl; NHS; Stg Crw; Yth Flsp; Rptr Sch Nwsp; Drama Clb; Sec FHA; Drama Clb; OEA; Clerk.

LANGE, CAROLINE; Traverse City Sr HS; Traverse City, MI; Band; NHS; Orch; Michigan St Univ; Agri Engr.

LANGE, ERIC; Eau Claire HS; Sodus, MI; Band; Hon Rl; Ftbl; Wrstlng; College; Bus Admin.

LANGE, LARRY; Arthur Hill HS; Saginaw, MI; Band; Boy Scts; Chrh Wkr; Hon Rl; Sct Actv; Ftbl; Univ; Engr.

LANGE, PAUL; St Joseph HS; St Joseph, MI; Pres Frsh Cls; Pres Soph Cls; Cl Rep Jr Cls; FCA; Jr NHS; NHS; Stu Cncl; Lat Clb; Bsbl; Ftbl; College; Doctor.

LANGE, STEVEN D; Rogers HS; Toledo, OH; Ger Clb; Heidelberg Coll; Chemistry.

LANGE, WILLIAM; Minerva HS; Minerva, OH; 40/250 Cls Rep Sr Cls; Am Leg Boys St; Pres Band; Pres Chrs; Hon Rl; Pres NHS; Lat Clb; Kiwan Awd; Natl Choral Awd 79; Mbr Of Canton Civic Opera 79; Kent St Univ; Vocal Music.

LANGEN, DANNY; Washington HS; Wash Court Hse, OH; Pres Sr Cls; Am Leg Boys St; Yrbk; Letter Glf; Am Leg Awd; DAR Awd; Pres Awd; College; History.

LANGENBRUNNER, ELAINE; Colerain Sr HS; Cincinnati, OH; 3/696 Hon Rl; Jr NHS; NHS; Ger Clb; Mth Clb; Pep Clb; Treas Sci Clb; Univ Of Cincinnati; Art.

LANGENDERFER, BETH; Evergreen HS; Swanton, OH; Cls Rep Soph Cls; Cl Rep Jr Cls; Sec Band; Chrs; Hon Rl; Lit Mag; NHS; Sch Pl; Stu Cncl; Drama Clb; Coll Club Pres; Bowling Green Schlstc Tests; History Day 1st District 3rd State; Univ Of Toledo; Early Childhood Ed.

LANGENDERFER, JOHN; St Francis De Sales HS; Toledo, OH; Chrh Wkr; Hon Rl; JA; Sch Mus; Stg Crw; Rptr Yrbk; Rptr Sch Nwsp; Sch Nwsp; IM Sprt; JA Awd; College; Engr.

LANGENDERFER, LYNN; Notre Dame Academy; Toledo, OH; Cls Rep Soph Cls; Girl Scts; Off Ade; Sprt Ed Yrbk; Yrbk; Rptr Sch Nwsp; Sch Nwsp; Bowling Green Univ; Transportation.

LANGENFELD, PAUL; Rosedale HS; Rosedale, IN; Hon Rl; 4-H; Sci Clb; Indiana Univ.

LANGENKAMP, MICHAEL J; Versailles HS; Yorkshire, OH; 27/135 Cmnty Wkr; FCA; Off Ade; Yth Flsp; Sprt Ed Sch Nwsp; FSA; FTA; Mth Clb; Sci Clb; Capt Bsbl; Bowling Green Univ; Med Tech.

LANGER, TIM; Liberty HS; Salem, WV; 23/228 Hon Rl; Jr NHS; Orch; Ftbl; Wrstlng; West Virginia Univ; Eng.

LANGERAK, CYNTHIA; Calvin Christian HS; Grandville, MI; Chrs; Hon Rl; Off Ade; Yth Flsp; Bsktbl; Letter Trk; Davenport Bus Schl; Acctg.

LANGEVIN, SHARI; Delta HS; Delta, OH; Am Leg Aux Girls St; NHS; Sch Pl; Stg Crw; Rptr Sch Nwsp; Treas Fr Clb; FHA; Sci Clb; Ohi State; Interior Design.

LANGFELDT, C; Garrett HS; Garrett, IN; Sec Band; Hon Rl; NHS; Sec FHA; Ger Clb; OEA; Letter Bsktbl; Letter Trk; Ind.

LANGLEY, CRAIG; Elwood Community HS; Elwood, IN; 24/179 Band; Chrs; Stu Cncl; Rptr Yrbk; Yrbk; 4-H; IM Sprt; 4-H Awd; Opt Clb Awd; Purdue Univ; Agri.

LANGLOIS, NANCY; Muskegon Catholic Ctrl HS; Muskegon, MI; 3/200 Cls Rep Frsh Cls; Sec Soph Cls; Cl Rep Jr Cls; Hon Rl; NHS; Sch Mus; Pres Stu Cncl; 4-H; Pep Clb; Pres Spn Clb; Michigan St Univ; Vet Med.

LANGOON, MARK; Carman HS; Flint, MI; Chrh Wkr; Hon Rl; Univ; Acctg.

LANGSETH, KARL; Calumet HS; Calumet, MI; 32/142 Band; Hon Rl; Sch Mus; Sch Pl; Stg Crw; Crs Cntry; Trk; IM Sprt; Natl Merit Ltr; NDSU; Ag.

LANGSTON, SHELLEY M; Lorain County Joint Voc Ctr; Amherst, OH; VP Jr Cls; Cl Rep Jr Cls; Chrs; Chrh Wkr; Cmnty Wkr; Girl Scts; Hosp Ade; Off Ade; Pol Wkr; Stu Cncl; Voc Schl; Med Sec.

LANGWORTHY, ELDON; Big Rapids HS; Big Rpds, MI; Sch Nwsp; 4-H; Letter Wrstlng; 4-H Awd; Ferris State College.

LANHAM, DEBORAH; Mooresville HS; Camby, IN; AFS; Hon Rl; Treas JA; Off Ade; Fr Clb; Sci Clb; Purdue Univ; Mech Engr.

LANHAM, DEREK; Lincoln HS; Lumberport, WV; NHS; Rptr Yrbk; Fr Clb; Bsbl; Bsktbl; Ftbl; West Virginia Univ.

LANHAM, JAMES; Morgantown HS; Morgntwn, WV; Chrs; Chrh Wkr; Hon Rl; Lbry Ade; Sch Pl; Stg Crw; Stu Cncl; Rptr Yrbk; Rptr Sch Nwsp; Treas 4-H; West Virginia Univ; Bio Sci.

LANHAM, RHONDA; Lincoln HS; Lumberport, WV; Hon Rl; NHS; Stu Cncl; Yrbk; Chrldng; Fairmont St Coll; Sec.

LA NIER, KIMBERLY; Charles S Mott HS; Warren, MI; Chrs; Jr NHS; Mdrgl; NHS; Ger Clb; Crs Cntry; Capt Trk; Letter Mgrs; Letter Tmr; Western Mic Univ; Bus Admin.

LA NIER, LORI; Washington HS; Massillon, OH; Chrs; Debate Tm; Girl Scts; Hon Rl; Lbry Ade; Sch Pl; DECA; FFA; FHA; Distr Educ.

LA NIER, VICTORIA; Forest Park HS; Forest Park, OH; 120/372 Trs Frsh Cls; Cl Rep Jr Cls; Cls Rep Sr Cls; Chrs; Girl Scts; Lbry Ade; Off Ade; Sch Pl; Stu Cncl; Y-Teens; Univ; Nursing.

LANIGAN, ROBERT A; Madison Plains HS; London, OH; 4-H; Sec FFA; Bsbl; Ftbl; Wrstlng; 4-H Awd; Bus Schl; Voc Agri.

LANK, DENNIS E; Pioneer Jr Sr HS; Lucerne, IN; Am Leg Boys St; FCA; NHS; Fr Clb; Sec Key Clb; VP Pep Clb; Bsktbl; Capt Crs Cntry; Capt Trk; Indiana St Univ; Busns Mgmt.

LANK, JOHN; Benjamin Franklin HS; Livonia, MI; 14/535 Cls Rep Frsh Cls; Hon Rl; Letter Crs Cntry; Trk; Cit Awd; Univ Of Virginia; Chemistry.

LANKENAU, TIM E; Elmhurst HS; Ft Wayne, IN; 15/346 Hon Rl; Bsbl; Bsktbl; Letter Ten; C of C Awd; JETS Awd; Purdue Univ; Electrical Engr.

LANKHEET, BRENDA; Holland Christian HS; Holland, MI; Chrh Wkr; Yth Flsp; Rptr Yrbk; 4-H; Ger Clb; 4-H Awd; Calvin Coll.

LANNAN, CAROL; Bishop Hartley HS; Columbus, OH; 10/200 Hon Rl; NHS; Stg Crw; Drama Clb; Trk; Ohio St Univ; Comp Prog.

LANNAN, CATHY S; Mooresville HS; Mooresville, IN; Cl Rep Jr Cls; Chrs; FCA; Girl Scts; Hon Rl; Natl Forn Lg; NHS; Sch Mus; Stg Crw; Drama Clb; Univ; Nursing.

LANNAN, MICHAEL B; Linton Stocton HS; Linton, IN; Am Leg Boys St; Boy Scts; Hon Rl; NHS; Pres Stu Cncl; Treas 4-H; Sec FFA; Pep Clb; Letter Bsbl; Letter Bsktbl; Bsktbl Hustlr Awd 78; Purdue Univ; Econ.

LANNIGAN, LOIS; Belmont HS; Dayton, OH; 5/350 Cl Rep Jr Cls; Cls Rep Sr Cls; Hon Rl; NHS; Stu Cncl; Bsktbl; Letter Ten; Trk; Sci Awd For Sr Class; Schlrshp For Women In Engr Seminar; Ohio Bd Of Regents Cert For Acad Ach; Univ Of Dayton; Chem Engr.

LANNING, PENNY; Brookville HS; Brookville, IN; Chrh Wkr; Cmnty Wkr; Hon Rl; Yrbk; Sch Nwsp; FFA; Ger Clb; Am Leg Awd; Univ; Soc Work.

LANNING, SUSAN; Divine Child HS; Dearborn Hts, MI; Band; Debate Tm; Hon Rl; NHS; Orch; Sch Mus; Fr Clb; FTA; Mic State Univ; Bus.

LANNOM, JEFFERY T; Loveland Hurst HS; Loveland, OH; 36/256 VP Frsh Cls; VP Soph Cls; VP Jr Cls; VP Sr Cls; Am Leg Boys St; Chrh Wkr; FCA; Yth Flsp; Key Clb; Pres Spn Clb; Miami Univ; Architecture.

LANNON, BETH; St Joseph HS; St Joe, MI; Hon Rl; Lat Clb; IM Sprt; North Carolina St Univ; Vet Med.

LANPHIER, BRIAN; Badin HS; Hamilton, OH; Boy Scts; Sch Mus; Sct Actv; Yrbk; Fr Clb; Letter Crs Cntry; Letter Trk; Univ; Gen Educ.

LANSDALE, SANDRA; Turpin HS; Cincinnati, OH; 9/357 Band; Chrs; Chrh Wkr; NHS; Orch; Sch Mus; Yth Flsp; Univ; Reg Nurse.

LANTAGNE, LISA; Gladstone HS; Gladstone, MI; 16/211 Am Leg Aux Girls St; Lit Mag; NHS; Sec Quill & Scroll; Stu Cncl; Rptr Yrbk; Rptr Sch Nwsp; Pres Spn Clb; Letter Chrldng; Cit Awd; Univ Of Mich; Nurse.

LANTHORN, DANA; West Union HS; Winchester, OH; Band; Hosp Ade; 4-H; Pep Clb; Mgrs; 4-H Awd; Univ; Occupational Ther.

LANTRY, JOHN R; Ontonagon Area HS; Ontonagon, MI; Trs Soph Cls; Boy Scts; Hon Rl; NHS; Sch Pl; DECA; Drama Clb; Fr Clb; Rdo Clb; Ftbl; Michigan Tech Univ; Bus Admin.

LANTZ, DENISE; Goshen HS; Goshen, IN; 19/269 Chrs; Chrh Wkr; Hon Rl; Orch; Sch Mus; Pep Clb; Bob Jones Univ; Music.

LANTZ, JIM; Upper Arlington HS; Columbus, OH; Hon Rl; Quill & Scroll; Red Cr Ade; Sch Nwsp; IM Sprt; Quill & Scroll Ntl Goldkey Advrts 1978; Ohio St Univ; Aviation.

LANTZ, JONI; R Nelson Snider HS; Ft Wayne, IN; 60/600 Hon Rl; Indiana Univ; Fine Arts.

LANTZ, LORETTA; New Haven HS; New Haven, IN; Band; Girl Scts; Hon Rl; Sct Actv; Ger Clb; Letter Trk; Top Child Care Awd 1979; Honoralble Mention 1976; Earlham Bus Schl; Bus.

LANTZ, LUELLEN; Crestview HS; Mansfield, OH; Cls Rep Sr Cls; Hon Rl; NHS; Sch Pl; Rptr Sch Nwsp; Drama Clb; 4-H; FHA; Spn Clb; Letter Trk; Ohio St Univ; Home Ec.

LANTZ, RAMONA G; Coalton Twelve Yr HS; Ellamore, WV; 2/33 Sec Soph Cls; Sec Sr Cls; Sal; Chrs; Hon Rl; Lbry Ade; Stu Cncl; Yrbk; Sch Nwsp; Pep Clb;.

LANTZY, KIM; Bishop Foley HS; Warren, MI; 6/194 Hon Rl; Hosp Ade; NHS; Stu Cncl; Rptr Yrbk; Rptr Sch Nwsp; Letter Bsbl; Letter Bsktbl; Mgrs; PPFtbl; Univ; Nursing.

LANUM, KENT; Jeffersonville HS; Jeffersonville, IN; VP Soph Cls; Pres Sr Cls; Cls Rep Sr Cls; Letter Ftbl; Letter Swmmng; Letter Wrstlng; Opt Clb Awd; Boys State; Hoosier Schlr; Depauw Univ.

LANZ, KELLY; Fredericktown HS; Fredericktown, OH; 24/113 Am Leg Aux Girls St; VP Chrs; Hon Rl; NHS; Sch Mus; Pres Stu Cncl; Scr Kpr; Bowling Green State Univ; Inst Deaf.

LANZY, FABIAN; Redford Union HS; Redford, MI; Band; Chrh Wkr; Yth Flsp; Ed Sch Nwsp; Ger Clb; Lion Awd; First Chair Awd First Chair Of Amer; Michigan Competitive Schlrshp Prog; Mi St Chapt Order Of De Molay; Wayne St Univ; Instrumental Music.

LAO, NORMAN; Upper Arlington HS; Columbus, OH; 1/610 Hon Rl; NHS; Fr Clb; Natl Merit Ltr; Partcipated In John Von Neumann Math Seminar At SMU; Honor Roll With Dist; Mbr French Natl Honor Society; College; Math.

LAPADAT, MARY; Cardinal Ritter HS; Indianapolis, IN; 8/160 Cl Rep Jr Cls; Cls Rep Sr Cls; Hon Rl; NHS; Stu Cncl; Spn Clb; Chrldng; IM Sprt; Mat Maids; PPFtbl; De Pauw Univ; Pre Med.

LAPAIN, CHERYL; Dondero HS; Royal Oak, MI; Cls Rep Frsh Cls; Cls Rep Soph Cls; Band; Pres Chrh Wkr; Cmnty Wkr; Girl Scts; Lit Mag; Sct Actv; FNA; PPFtbl; Univ; Nursing.

LA PAN, ROSLEE; Paulding HS; Cecil, OH; 18/168 Cmnty Wkr; Hon Rl; Rptr Yrbk; Drama Clb; OEA; St Bd Of Educ Awd Of Dstnctn 79; Offc Educ Assoc Ambssdr Awd 79; Gregg Typing Awd For Achvmnt 78; Univ Of California; Marine Bio.

LA PEER, BECKY; Bridgeport Sr HS; Bridgeport, WV; 11/200 Band; Chrs; Chrh Wkr; Cmnty Wkr; Hon Rl; Jr NHS; NHS; Orch; PAVAS; Pol Wkr; Florida Inst Of Tech.

LA PEER, MELANIE; Inland Lakes HS; Afton, MI; Cls Rep Frsh Cls; Hon Rl; 4-H; Bsktbl; Trk; GAA; Mgrs; Northern Coll; RN.

LA PENSEE, LISA; Wilie E Groves HS; Birmingham, MI; Girl Scts; Hon Rl; JA; Lbry Ade; Stg Crw; Rptr Sch Nwsp; 4-H; Fr Clb; Socr; Coach Actv; Michigan St Univ; Bus Admin.

LAPHAM, DAVID; Wayland Union HS; Shelbyville, MI; Band; Chrs; Hon Rl; Off Ade; Sch Mus; Rus Clb; Sci Clb; Mim & Adrian Coll Schlrshp 79; Finalist Twice At Intl Sci & Engr Fair 77 & 79; 3rd Pl Zoology At ISEF; Adrian Coll; Pre Med.

LAPHAM, KATHLEEN; Wayland Union HS; Wayland, MI; Cl Rep Jr Cls; Sch Pl; Stu Cncl; Pres Yth Flsp; Yrbk; Swmmng; Trk; Pom Pon; PPFtbl; Tmr; Dept Of Mi Educ Tuition Grant 79; SEOG 79; BEOG 79; Davenport Coll Of Bus; Hotel Mgmt.

LAPHAM, NANCY; Kearsley HS; Flint, MI; 69/385 Cls Rep Frsh Cls; Cls Rep Soph Cls; VP Jr Cls; Band; Hon Rl; Off Ade; Sch Mus; Sct Actv; Stu Cncl; Rptr Yrbk; Canddt For Amer Lgn Girls St 78; Univ Of Michigan; Med Tech.

LA PINE, JILL; East Clinton HS; Lees Creek, OH; 28/102 Chrs; Drl Tm; Hon Rl; Off Ade; FHA; FTA; Pep Clb; Chrldng; FHA Queen 76; Most Otstndng Flag Corp Mbr 77 78 & 79; Awds For Drill Tm & Flag Corps 78;.

LAPINSKY, MARC T; Swartz Creek HS; Swartz Creek, MI; Hon Rl; NHS; Crs Cntry; Trk; Mgrs; Aviation.

LA POINT, MARCIA; Whitmer HS; Toledo, OH; 56/860 Cl Rep Jr Cls; VP Sr Cls; NHS; Off Ade; Quill & Scroll; Stu Cncl; Rptr Yrbk; Pres Pep Clb; Mgrs; Scr Kpr; Univ Of Toledo; Spec Ed.

LA POINTE, BETH; Ionia HS; Ionia, MI; 5/272 Cls Rep Frsh Cls; Cls Rep Soph Cls; Band; Pres Chrs; Debate Tm; Girl Scts; Hon Rl; NHS; Sch Mus; Stu Cncl; Edmond & Mary Chapin Schlrshp 79; MI St Univ Acdmc Excllnc Ared 79; MHEAA Awrd 79; Western Michigan Univ; Acctg.

LA POINTE, JANET; Whiteford HS; Ottawa, MI; 1/100 Pres Soph Cls; Pres Sr Cls; Chrs; Hon Rl; Sec NHS; Sch Mus; Drama Clb; 4-H; Pres Spn Clb; Letter Bsktbl; Univ Of Toledo; Reg Nurse.

LA PONSIE, DANIEL; Cass City HS; Cass City, MI; Chrh Wkr; Hon Rl; Jr NHS; Natl Forn Lg; PAVAS; Yth Flsp; Spn Clb; Wrstlng; Coll; Engr.

LA PORTE, DAVID; Washington HS; Massillon, OH; Ger Clb; Computer Programmer.

LA PORTE, LYNN; Manistee Catholic Ctrl HS; Manistee, MI; Sec Jr Cls; Cl Rep Jr Cls; Band; Hon Rl; NHS; Yrbk; Pep Clb; Chrldng; VFW Awd; Business School; Accounting.

LA PORTE, MARK; Hemlock HS; Hemlock, MI; 35/165 Hon Rl; NHS; Stg Crw; Bsbl; Ftbl; Ferris State College; Pharmacy.

LAPP, LINDA; Riverview HS; Coshocton, OH; 15/225 Pres Sr Cls; Am Leg Aux Girls St; Band; NHS; Red Cr Ade; Rptr Yrbk; 4-H; Bsktbl; Ohi State Univ; Pharmacy.

LAPP, THOMAS L; Morgantown HS; Mortantown, WV; Aud/Vis; Stg Crw; Drama Clb; Mth Clb; College; Elec Engr.

LA PRAIRIE, FAITH; Au Gres Sims HS; Au Gres, MI; 3/52 Sal; Hon Rl; NHS; Sdlty; Sch Nwsp; Capt Bsktbl; Chrldng; Mgrs; Voice Dem Awd; Central Mich Univ; Accounting.

LAPRES, SUSAN; Muskegon Cath Ctrl HS; Muskegon, MI; 11/186 Cls Rep Soph Cls; Cl Rep Jr Cls; Cls Rep Sr Cls; Chrh Wkr; CAP; Drl Tm; Hon Rl; Stu Cncl; Drama Clb; 4-H; Aquinas Coll; Nursing.

LA PRESTA, JULIE; Hubbard HS; Hubbard, OH; 8/330 Hon Rl; Rptr Sch Nwsp; Lat Clb; Youngstown St Univ; Sci.

LAPSLEY, TRACY; Lutheran East HS; E Cleveland, OH; 12/50 Trs Frsh Cls; Cls Rep Sr Cls; Chrs; Chrh Wkr; Drl Tm; Lbry Ade; Sch Mus; Drama Clb; Mth Clb; Pep Clb; Sawyer Bus Schl; Accountant.

LARCH, MELANIE; Herbert Hoover HS; Charleston, WV; Band; Chrs; Hon Rl; Jr NHS; Lbry Ade; Mod UN; Off Ade; Sch Pl; Rptr Yrbk; Rptr Sch Nwsp; All County & St Chorus; All County Band; College; Music.

LARCK, CYNTHIA; Bethel HS; Tipp City, OH; Band; Chrs; Capt Drl Tm; Hon Rl; Orch; Sch Mus; FHA; Letter Trk; Edison St Coll; Data Proc.

LARCOMB, PEGGY; Westerville N HS; Westerville, OH; Band; Chrs; Drl Tm; Hon Rl; Sch Mus; Sch Pl; Stg Crw; 4-H; College; Music.

LARES, JOHN S; Lewis County HS; Weston, WV; Am Leg Boys St; Boy Scts; Chrs; Chrh Wkr; Hon Rl; Jr NHS; NHS; Sct Actv; Natl Merit Ltr; Natl Merit SF; Alderson Broaddus Coll; Bio.

LAREW, ROBERTA; Union HS; Greenville, WV; Band; Drm Mjrt; Hon Rl; Sch Pl; Rptr Yrbk; Sch Nwsp; 4-H; FHA; Pep Clb; Chrldng; Berea Coll; Phys Ed.

LARGE, DUANE; Rochester HS; Rochester, IN; 1/159 Val; Hon Rl; NHS; Ger Clb; Crs Cntry; Tri Kappa Schlrshp 79; German Clb Schlrshp 79; Most Valuable Runner Cross Cntry 78; Purdue Univ; Law.

LARGE, FORREST; West Ottawa HS; Holland, MI; Cls Rep Sr Cls; Chrs; Chrh Wkr; Hon Rl; Mdrgl; Stu Cncl; Yth Flsp; Muskegon Bus College.

LARGER, MARY C; Ft Loramie HS; Ft Loramie, OH; Chrs; Girl Scts; Hon Rl; Jr NHS; NHS; Off Ade; Stg Crw; Yrbk; 4-H; FHA; 4th Regionals OOEA Genl Clerical II 1979; Letter A O Grade Average Sr Yr 1979;.

LARGUEZA, MARIA; Buckhannon Upshur HS; Buckhannon, WV; Pres Frsh Cls; Cl Rep Jr Cls; Chrs; Chrh Wkr; Drl Tm; Girl Scts; Hon Rl; Sct Actv; Stu Cncl; Sci Clb; W Va Wesleyan College; Nursing.

LARIME, MARK; Grand Blanc HS; Grand Blanc, MI; 61/650 Boy Scts; Cmnty Wkr; Hon Rl; Y-Teens; Letter Bsktbl; Coach Actv; IM Sprt; Scr Kpr; Tmr; Michigan St Univ; Law.

LARIMER, MYRON; Hammond Tech Voc HS; Hammond, IN; 3/160 Cls Rep Sr Cls; Chrh Wkr; Hon Rl; NHS; Pres VICA; Bsbl; Ten; Rotary Awd; Highst Schshtc Achvmnt Fo Ran Athlt 79; Bst Mental Atttd Bsbl 79; Ball St Univ; Archt.

LARIMORE, PAMELA; Roy C Start HS; Toledo, OH; Chrs; Chrh Wkr; FCA; Girl Scts; Hon Rl; Off Ade; Coach Actv; Univ Of Toledo; Comp Tech.

LARISON, REBECCA; Danville Community HS; Danville, IN; 12/155 Am Leg Aux Girls St; Chrs; Chrh Wkr; Debate Tm; Hon Rl; Natl Forn Lg; NHS; Off Ade; Indiana Central Univ; Eng.

LARKE, DANIEL; Carman HS; Flint, MI; Boy Scts; Hon Rl; Sct Actv; Letter Bsbl; Bsktbl; College.

LARKIN, ANNE; Marquette HS; Grand Beach, MI; 9/81 Trs Soph Cls; Hon Rl; Sch Mus; Sch Pl; Treas Stu Cncl; Sch Nwsp; Drama Clb; Fr Clb; Pep Clb; Glf; NEDT Cert 76 & 77; Univ; Med.

LARKIN, KAREN; Bentley HS; Livonia, MI; 40/727 Hon Rl; NHS; Sch Mus; Sch Pl; Stg Crw; Drama Clb; Natl Merit Ltr; Univ Of Mic; Fashion Merch.

LARKIN, REX; Hammond HS; Hammond, IN; Bsbl; Bsktbl; Univ; Engr.

LARKIN, RICHARD G; Mariemont HS; Terrace Park, OH; 5/150 AFS; Chrs; Sch Mus; Yrbk; Sch Nwsp; FFA; Ger Clb; Bsbl; Letter Socr; PPFtbl; Massachusetts Inst Of Tech; Bio Med.

LARKIN, RODNEY; Cass Technical HS; Detroit, MI; Chrh Wkr; Hon Rl; Off Ade; OEA; Capt IM Sprt; Wayne State Univ; Bus Admin.

LARKINS, MARIROSE; Bishop Foley HS; Troy, MI; Chrh Wkr; Cmnty Wkr; Jr NHS; IM Sprt; College.

LA ROCHE, CATHY L; Celina Sr HS; Celina, OH; 13/241 Band; Drl Tm; Hon Rl; Orch; Sch Mus; Pep Clb; Indiana Univ; Elem Educ.

LA ROCHE, PATTY; Mt Gilead HS; Cardington, OH; 4/114 Chrs; Hon Rl; Lbry Ade; NHS; Rptr Yrbk; 4-H; FHA; OEA; Pep Clb; Trk; Ach Awd For A's During Schl Yr; Perfect Attendance Awd; FHA Awd For 15 Pts Earned; College; Acctg.

LA ROSA, GERALD; Boardman HS; Youngstown, OH; Chrh Wkr; NHS; Youngstown State; Mathematics.

LA ROSA, JEFF; Notre Dame HS; Bridgeport, WV; Chrh Wkr; Hon Rl; FDA; Bsbl; Bsktbl; Ftbl; IM Sprt; Univ; Agri Mgmt.

LA ROSE, JOSEPH; Southeast HS; Ravenna, OH; VP Sr Cls; Hon Rl; NHS; Red Cr Ade; Sch Mus; Sch Pl; Stg Crw; Drama Clb; Wrstlng; College; Bio Physics.

LA ROUE, DENISE; Whitmore Lake HS; Whitmore Lk, MI; Hst Jr Cls; Band; Chrh Wkr; Hon Rl; Hosp Ade; Sch Mus; Sch Pl; Yrbk; Fr Clb; Chrldng; Univ Of Michigan; Nursing.

LA ROY, LAURA; Whiteford HS; Riga, MI; 2/94 Sec Soph Cls; Cls Rep Soph Cls; Sec Jr Cls; Sal; Hon Rl; VP NHS; Red Cr Ade; Stg Crw; Stu Cncl; Rptr Yrbk; Monroe Cnty Cmnty Coll; Acctg.

LARRICK, LORI; Western Hills HS; Cincinnati, OH; Cl Rep Jr Cls; Chrs; Chrh Wkr; Hon Rl; Pres Jr NHS; Sch Mus; Sch Pl; Stu Cncl; Yth Flsp; Sec Drama Clb; Intl Thespian Soc Sec; Yth In Cty Govt; College.

LARRICK, SCOTT; West Grauga HS; Chesterland, OH; Chrs; Chrh Wkr; Cmnty Wkr; Hon Rl; Letter Bsbl; Letter Ftbl; PPFtbl; Univ; Sci.

LARSEN, DOUGLAS D; Swan Valley HS; Saginaw, MI; Hon Rl; Jr NHS; VP NHS; Bsbl; MVP Skiing; Outstanding Jr Boy Awd; Albion Coll; Medicine.

LARSEN, FREDRICK A; Decatur Central HS; Indianapolis, IN; Chrh Wkr; Hon Rl; Hosp Ade; Quill & Scroll; Yrbk; Letter Glf; Purdue Univ; Criminal Justc.

LARSEN, JANET; Copley Sr HS; Copley, OH; Girl Scts; Hon Rl; Hosp Ade; Lbry Ade; Sig Crw; Spn Clb; Scr Kpr; Tmr; North East Univ; Med.

LARSEN, JEANETTE; Grosse Ile HS; Grosse Ile, MI; Band; Girl Scts; Hon Rl; 4-H; Bsktbl; 4-H Awd; Mic State Univ; Bus Mgmt.

LARSEN, JILL; Grand Haven Sr HS; Grand Haven, MI; 74/385 Band; Cmnty Wkr; Drm Bgl; Girl Scts; Hon Rl; Hosp Ade; NHS; Ed Yrbk; DECA; VFW Awd; Stendel Schslhp 79; Goff Memrl Schslhp 79; Valparaiso Univ; Acctg.

LARSEN, KIRK; Ann Arbor Pioneer HS; Ann Arbor, MI; Band; Boy Scts; Hon Rl; Orch; Sch Mus; Natl Merit SF; Music.

LARSEN, LORI; Menominee HS; Menominee, MI; Drm Bgl; Hon Rl; Letter Ten; Voc Schl; Lab Animal Care Tech.

LARSEN, LYNN; Hamilton Southeastern HS; Noblesville, IN; 45/180 Cmp Fr Grls; Hon Rl; Drama Clb; 4-H; Fr Clb; Ger Clb; Pep Clb; College; History Tchr.

LARSEN, RANDY; Detroit Catholic Central HS; Southfield, MI; VP Frsh Cls; Boy Scts; Hon Rl; Stg Crw; Rptr Yrbk; Bsktbl; Ftbl; Trk; IM Sprt; Natl Merit Ltr; Ftbl Mich St Western Mi Eastern Mi & Illinois Univ; Univ Of Illinois; Fine Arts.

LARSON, BETSY J; Alba Public HS; Alba, MI; Trs Frsh Cls; Chrs; Chrh Wkr; Hon Rl; Jr NHS; NHS; Off Ade; Sch Mus; Stu Cncl; Rptr Yrbk; Soc Dstngshd Amer HS Stu; Candidate For Christmas Queen; Northwestern Michigan Coll; English.

LARSON, ELEANOR; Big Rapids HS; Big Rapids, MI; Trs Jr Cls; Trs Sr Cls; Band; Natl Forn Lg; NHS; Sch Pl; Stu Cncl; Drama Clb; Cit Awd; Univ; Admin Asst.

LARSON, GLADYS; Stephenson HS; Stephenson, MI; 2/94 Sal; Band; Chrs; Chrh Wkr; Hon Rl; NHS; Yth Flsp; Ed Yrbk; Pres OEA; OEA Comptn Events Awd On Regional St & Natl 79; Chosen Number 2 Outstndg Stu At SHS For Schlrshp 79; Exec Sec.

LARSON, HOLLY; Upper Arlington HS; Columbus, OH; Girl Scts; Hon Rl; Sct Actv; Spn Clb; College; Equestrian Sci.

LARSON, INGRID; Romulus HS; Romulus, MI; 39/305 Sec Frsh Cls; Cls Rep Soph Cls; Cl Rep Jr Cls; Cls Rep Sr Cls; Band; Chrs; Chrh Wkr; Cmnty Wkr; Debate Tm; Drl Tm; Kiwanis For Hnr Stu Awd; Class Cncl; EMU Campus Leader Awd; E Michigan Univ; Busns Admin.

LARSON, KAREN; Inland Lakes HS; Indian River, MI; Cls Rep Soph Cls; Trs Sr Cls; Hon Rl; Chrldng; Univ; Bus Admin.

LARSON, KAREN S; Chagrin Falls HS; Chagrin Falls, OH; Band; Chrs; Chrh Wkr; Hon Rl; Sch Mus; Cmp Fr Grls; Yth Flsp; Ger Clb; Bowling Green St Univ; Music.

LARSON, KENT R; Gladstone Area HS; Gladstone, MI; 1/220 Hon Rl; Lbry Ade; NHS; Quill & Scroll; Yth Flsp; Rptr Sch Nwsp; Natl Merit SF; Michigan Tech Univ; Chem.

LARSON, KIMBERLY; Muskegon Sr HS; Muskegon, MI; 43/511 Cls Rep Frsh Cls; Cls Rep Soph Cls; Cls Rep Sr Cls; Drm Mjrt; Hon Rl; NHS; Off Ade; Stu Cncl; Fr Clb; Spn Clb; Hope Coll Schlrshp 79; Muskegon Womens Clb Schlrshp 79; Hope Coll; Med Dr.

LARSON, KRISTIN; Orange HS; Pepper Pike, OH; 5/250 Cls Rep Frsh Cls; VP Jr Cls; Chrs; Girl Scts; Hon Rl; Mod UN; NHS; Stu Cncl; Yrbk; Fr Clb; Yale Coll; French.

LARSON, LOWELL; Negaunee HS; Negaunee, MI; Band; Boy Scts; Hon Rl; Orch; Bsbl; Crs Cntry; Ftbl; Ten; Northern Michigan Univ; Comp.

LARSON, TODD; North Putnam Jr Sr HS; Bainbridge, IN; Band; Boy Scts; Chrh Wkr; Yrbk; Sch Nwsp; 4-H; Glf; IM Sprt; Cit Awd; 4-H Awd; Indiana St Univ; Brdcstng Radio.

LA RUE, MATTHEW; Midland HS; Midland, MI; Hon Rl; NHS; Letter Bsbl; Univ; Math.

LARZELERE, SHANNON; North Newton HS; Fair Oaks, IN; Hon Rl; Ed Yrbk; Sci Clb; PPFtbl; Univ; Pre Law.

LASENYIK, SUSAN; Holy Name HS; Parma, OH; 37/350 Band; Hon Rl; Hosp Ade; Jr NHS; NHS; Sch Pl; Pep Clb; IM Sprt; Cit Awd; Cleveland State Univ; Phys Ther.

LASER, JULIE; Waldron HS; Waldron, MI; 8/54 Drm Mjrt; Hon Rl; NHS; Sch Pl; Pres Spn Clb; Letter Bsktbl; Letter Trk; Chrldng; College; Acctg.

LASH, TONY; Reeths Puffer HS; Muskegon, MI; Cls Rep Frsh Cls; Cls Rep Soph Cls; Cl Rep Jr Cls; Cls Rep Sr Cls; Chrs; Chrh Wkr; Sch Pl; Rptr Sch Nwsp; Drama Clb; 4-H; Grand Rapids Bapt Coll; Brdcstng.

LASH, WILLIAM E; Terre Haute South Vigo HS; Terre Haute, IN; 6/420 Am Leg Boys St; Chrh Wkr; Hon Rl; Yth Flsp; 4-H; Lat Clb; Mth Clb; Sci Clb; JETS Awd; Natl Merit Ltr; College; Engr.

LASHBROOK, TINA; Clinton Prairie HS; Colfax, IN; 29/90 Chrs; Chrh Wkr; Hon Rl; Yth Flsp; Bsktbl; Trk;.

LASHER, JENNIFER; Shortridge HS; Indianapolis, IN; Chrh Wkr; Hon Rl; Lbry Ade; NHS; Quill & Scroll; Sch Pl; Stu Cncl; Ind State Univ.

LASHER, MICHELLE; Chaminade Julienne HS; Dayton, OH; 21/249 Chrs; Chrh Wkr; Girl Scts; Hon Rl; Lbry Ade; Stg Crw; Fr Clb; FHA; Coll; Early Childhood Ed.

LASHER, TERESA; Reitz Memorial HS; Evansville, IN; Hon Rl; Sci Clb; College.

LASK, DENISE; Benedictine HS; Detroit, MI; 19/169 Cls Rep Soph Cls; Cl Rep Jr Cls; Cls Rep Sr Cls; Hon Rl; NHS; Stu Cncl; Rptr Sch Nwsp; Letter Trk; Letter Chrldng; Natl Merit SF; Univ Of Michigan.

LASKEY, KIMBERLY; Eaton Rapids HS; Eaton Rapids, MI; Band; Cmp Fr Grls; Hon Rl; NHS; Letter Trk; Mgrs; PPFtbl; Tmr; Michigan Tech Univ; Comp Sci.

LASKO, MAUREEN; Beaumont Girls HS; Shaker Hts, OH; Hon Rl; Lbry Ade; Lit Mag; Rptr Yrbk; Fr Clb; Pep Clb; Natl Merit Ltr; Univ; History.

LASKOWSKI, JANE; Greensburg Community HS; Greensburg, IN; Chrs; Chrh Wkr; Hon Rl; Mdrgl; Yth Flsp; Ed Sch Nwsp; Fr Clb; Lat Clb; Sci Clb; Ind Univ; Journalism.

LASKOWSKI, JUDI; Washington HS; South Bend, IN; 8/355 Band; Chrh Wkr; Drm Mjrt; Hon Rl; Jr NHS; NHS; Sch Mus; Rptr Sch Nwsp; Sch Nwsp; Spn Clb; South Bend Tribune Schlrshp 79; Purdue Univ; Forestry.

LASKY, M; Parkside HS; Jackson, MI; Chrh Wkr; Hon Rl; Sch Pl; Bsbl; Ftbl; Hockey; Wrstlng; Coach Actv; IM Sprt; Scr Kpr; Michigan Univ; Engr.

LASOTA, FRANK; Plymouth Canton HS; Plymouth, MI; 30/445 Chrh Wkr; FCA; NHS; Bsbl; Bsktbl; Ftbl; Hndbl; Mgrs; Univ Of Mich Ann Arbor; Engr.

LASSER, DANIEL; Utica HS; Utica, MI; 80/390 Hon Rl; Letter Ftbl; Letter Swmmng; Trk;.

LASSETER, PAUL; Kyger Creer HS; Gallipolis, OH; 16/85 VP Jr Cls; Band; Key Clb; Lat Clb; Letter Bsbl; Letter Ftbl; Letter Trk; David Lipscomb.

LASSILA, HEIDI; Chassell HS; Chassell, MI; 1/26 VP Frsh Cls; Sec Soph Cls; Band; Girl Scts; Hon Rl; Hosp Ade; Lbry Ade; Mic State Univ; Vet.

LASTER, ALPHONSO; Pontiac Northern HS; Pontiac, MI; Chrh Wkr; Hon Rl; Rptr Sch Nwsp; Boys Clb Am; FBLA; USC; Law.

LASZLO, GAIL; Cass City HS; Deford, MI; 28/149 Girl Scts; Hon Rl; Lbry Ade; Off Ade; 4-H; Spn Clb; Trk; Letter Chrldng; PPFtbl; Scr Kpr; Delta Coll; Comp Prog.

LATA, SUSAN; Bishop Foley HS; Madison Hts, MI; Girl Scts; Hon Rl; NHS; Pol Wkr; Sch Mus; Yrbk; Trk; Chrldng; Coach Actv; Natl Merit Schl; Catholic Schl Lg Schlr Ath Awd Cheerldng 79; Marygrove Coll; Art.

LATESKY, HAZEL; Birch Run HS; Birch Run, MI; 13/147 Hon Rl; NHS; FHA; Pep Clb; Sci Clb; Saginaw Valley St Coll; Chem.

LATHAM, ANGELA; Clay City HS; Cory, IN; 3/54 Chrh Wkr; Hon Rl; NHS; Off Ade; Stu Cncl; Yth Flsp; 4-H; Lat Clb; Mth Clb; Pep Clb; Olivet Nazarene Coll; Communications.

LATHAM, LISA; Staunton HS; Staunton, IN; 3/46 VP Soph Cls; Cls Rep Soph Cls; Cl Rep Jr Cls; Drl Tm; NHS; Stu Cncl; Fr Clb; Bsktbl; GAA; ISU; Spec Ed.

LATHAM, TAMMY; Kenton Sr HS; Kenton, OH; 18/210 Chrs; Hon Rl; NHS; Sch Mus; Yth Flsp; 4-H; Scr Kpr; Am Leg Awd; Cit Awd; 4-H Awd; Univ Of Kentucky; Acctg.

LATHAM JR, WILLIAM; St Xavier HS; Batavia, OH; 133/264 Mod UN; Crs Cntry; Trk; Natl Merit Ltr; College; Bus Admin.

LATHER, J B; Traverse City HS; Traverse City, MI; 58/698 Cls Rep Frsh Cls; Hon Rl; NHS; Stu Cncl; Yth Flsp; Key Clb; Mic Tech Univ; Engr.

LATHERY, MICHAEL; Connersville Sr HS; Connersville, IN; 7/350 Boy Scts; Hon Rl; JA; Boys Clb Am; Sci Clb; Univ; Engr.

LATHWELL, JULIE; Benzie County Central HS; Frankfort, MI; Chrs; Chrh Wkr; Hon Rl; NHS; Off Ade; Yth Flsp; 4-H; Capt Bsktbl; Letter Trk; Coach Actv; College.

LATIMER, JEFF; Riverside HS; Quincy, OH; 4/81 Hon Rl; Lbry Ade; NHS; Sch Pl; Stg Crw; Glf; IM Sprt; 2nd Place Chemistry Awrd; MIP Golf; Edison State Univ; Ind Engr.

LATIMER, KEVIN; Lutheran HS West; Inkster, MI; 27/157 Band; Hon Rl; Jr NHS; NHS; Bsbl; Letter Bsktbl; Ftbl; Coach Actv; IM Sprt; Cit Awd; Stu Natl Achvmnt Schlrshp 78; Prog For Outstndg Negro Stu; Most Valuable Bsktbl Plyr 76 79; Henry Ford Coll; Bus.

LATOCHA, DEBORAH L; Mackinaw City HS; Mackinaw City, MI; Cls Rep Soph Cls; Band; Chrs; Girl Scts; Letter Hon Rl; Sec Frsh Cls; Drama Clb; Pep Clb; Chrldng; Mgrs; College; Soc Work.

LA TORRE, DONALD; Grosse Ile HS; Grosse Ile, MI; 6/209 Boy Scts; Chrh Wkr; Hon Rl; Sct Actv; Sch Nwsp; Spn Clb; VICA; Bsbl; Swmmng; Pres Awd; Case Western Reserve Univ; Dentistry.

LATOS, ANITA; Bishop Foley HS; Warren, MI; 1/193 Val; Hon Rl; Stg Crw; Rptr Yrbk; Rptr Sch Nwsp; Sec Sci Clb; Bausch & Lomb Awd; Wayne State Univ; Science.

LATREILLE, CAROLYN; Howell HS; Howell, MI; 5/500 Band; Hon Rl; VP NHS; Fr Clb; Univ; Psych.

LATSHAW, MICHAEL K; Nordonia HS; Macedonia, OH; 48/412 Band; Chrs; Chrh Wkr; Cmnty Wkr; Hon Rl; PAVAS; Sch Mus; Sch Pl; Drama Clb; Dist Bnd Contest Awd 79; UCLA; Theatre.

LATSHAW, SABRINA L; Decatur Central HS; Indianapolis, IN; 21/306 Girl Scts; Hon Rl; Lbry Ade; NHS; Rptr Yrbk; Pep Clb; Sci Clb; Spn Clb; 1st Yr Algebra Awd 77; Yrbk Staff Awd; Nursing Schl; Nursing.

LATTANNER, LYNN; Dublin HS; Columbus, OH; 47/163 Cls Rep Frsh Cls; Pres Soph Cls; Cl Rep Jr Cls; Cls Rep Sr Cls; Cmp Fr Grls; Chrs; Hon Rl; NHS; Sch Mus; Sch Pl; Mt Union Coll; Communications.

LATTANZI, LINDSAY; Fayetteville HS; Fayetteville, WV; Chrs; Cmnty Wkr; Hon Rl; 4-H; VP 4-H; Spn Clb; Ftbl; Trk; 4-H Awd; Wv Inst Of Tech; Elec Engr.

LATTIMORE, GWENDOLYN; Jame Addam Voc HS; Clevealnd, OH; Cmp Fr Grls; Chrs; Cmnty Wkr; Hon Rl; Lbry Ade; Off Ade; Orch; Red Cr Ade; Stu Cncl; Rptr Yrbk; Univ; Brdcstng.

LATTIMORE, SCOTT; Danbury Local HS; Lakeside, OH; Hon Rl; NHS; Off Ade; Sec Sci Clb; Spn Clb; Bsbl; Capt Ftbl; Physics Awd 78; Oh Youth & Sci Conference For High Ability Sci Stud 78; Tutor For Learning Disabilities 78; Univ; Aero Engr.

LATTNER, DAN; Reitz Memorial HS; Evansville, IN; 28/250 Hon Rl; NHS; Ten; IM Sprt; Indiana Univ; Phys Ther.

LATZ, KEN; Ovid Elsie HS; Elsie, MI; Cls Rep Frsh Cls; Cls Rep Soph Cls; Cl Rep Jr Cls; Band; Chrh Wkr; Hon Rl; Stu Cncl; Rptr Yrbk; Rptr Sch Nwsp; 4-H; Coll; Art.

LATZ, KENNETH; Ovid Elsie HS; Elsie, MI; Cls Rep Frsh Cls; Cls Rep Soph Cls; Cl Rep Jr Cls; Cls Rep Sr Cls; Band; Chrh Wkr; Hon Rl; Stu Cncl; Ed Yrbk; Rptr Yrbk; Univ; Art.

LATZ, MICHAEL; Brebeuf Prep Schl; Carmel, IN; Boy Scts; FCA; Hon Rl; Stg Crw; Pep Clb; Letter Crs Cntry; Letter Trk; Purdue Univ; Math.

LAU, AMY; Ann Arbor Pioneer HS; Ann Arbor, MI; Band; Chrh Wkr; Girl Scts; Hon Rl; Yth Flsp; Ger Clb; Chrldng; Coach Actv; PPFtbl; Michigan St Univ; Elem Educ.

LAUB, CYNTHIA; Reading Cmnty HS; Cincinnati, OH; 1/217 Val; Hon Rl; NHS; Spn Clb; Coach Actv; Scr Kpr; Kiwan Awd; Ohio St Univ; Dentistry.

LAUCHNER, DANNY; Richmond Sr HS; Richmond, IN; Voc Schl; Mech Engr.

LAUDEMAN, TERESA; Marion HS; Marion, IN; Hon Rl; NHS; Quill & Scroll; Sch Nwsp; Letter Gym; Chrldng; Coll; Math.

LAUDENSHLAGER, DAVID L; North Miami HS; Peru, IN; 13/122 Band; Boy Scts; Chrs; Chrh Wkr; Hon Rl; Sct Actv; Pres Yth Flsp; 1st & 2nd In Dist Bnd Solo Contst 76 78 & 79; Lincoln Tech Inst; Diesel Mech.

LAUDERBACK, JEFFREY; Princeton Community HS; Princeton, IN; Aud/Vis; Band; Stg Crw; Yth Flsp; Spn Clb; Indiana St Univ; Tele Cmnctns.

LAUDERDALE, AMY; North Posey HS; Wadesville, IN; Band; Hon Rl; NHS; IM Sprt; Cit Awd;.

LAUER, ELIZABETH; Loy Norrix HS; Kalamazoo, MI; Band; Girl Scts; Hon Rl; NHS; Sch Mus; Cit Awd; Univ; Med Tech.

LAUER, LYNN; Delphos St Johns HS; Delphos, OH; 10/139 Cls Rep Soph Cls; Cls Rep Sr Cls; Sec Band; Hon Rl; NHS; Sch Mus; Treas Stu Cncl; Rptr Yrbk; Rptr Sch Nwsp; IM Sprt; Bus Schl.

LAUER, TERESA; Bishop Dwenger HS; Ft Wayne, IN; Chrs; Hon Rl; Hosp Ade; Univ; Phys Ther.

LAUF, MARGARET; Bath HS; Lima, OH; Band; Chrs; Girl Scts; Hon Rl; Sch Mus; Y-Teens; 4-H; Fr Clb; Pep Clb; Bsktbl; Bowling Green St Univ; Bus Educ.

LAUF, TERI; Ayersville HS; Defiance, OH; Letter Band; Chrs; Hon Rl; Stg Crw; Stu Cncl; Rptr Yrbk; Fr Clb; FHA; College; Acct.

LAUFFER, BETH; Richmond HS; Richmond, IN; Girl Scts; Hosp Ade; Jr NHS; IM Sprt; Mat Maids; PPFtbl; 4-H Awd; Purdue Univ; Vet Medicine.

LAUGHLIN, RICHARD; Brooke HS; Wellsburg, WV; 59/403 FCA; Hon Rl; Jr NHS; Lit Mag; NHS; Lat Clb; Letter Bsbl; Letter Bsktbl; Letter Ftbl; Lion Awd; Baseball All Mountaineer League 79; Univ; Dent.

LAUGHLIN, VICKIE; Calhoun HS; Arnoldsburg, WV; Hon Rl; Mth Clb; Glenville Wv; Teacher.

LAUGHMAN, SUSAN; Bethel HS; Dayton, OH; 1/100 Hon Rl; Hosp Ade; Jr NHS; NHS; Off Ade; Fr Clb; College; Acctg.

LAUGHRY, BETSY; Prairie Heights HS; Orland, IN; 5/136 Chrs; Chrh Wkr; Girl Scts; Hon Rl; 4-H; Glen Oaks Bus.

LAUKKA, MARK; Negaunee HS; Negaunee, MI; Band; Debate Tm; Hon Rl; Natl Forn Lg; NHS; Natl Merit SF; Univ; Pre Med.

LAURELL, DENNIS; Northwood HS; Northwood, OH; VP Frsh Cls; Pres Soph Cls; VP Jr Cls; Chrs; JA; Sch Mus; Stu Cncl; Key Clb; Letter Wrstlng; Toledo Univ; Aviation.

LAURENT, BETH; Monsignor Hackett HS; Kalamazoo, MI; Pres Frsh Cls; Sec Soph Cls; Trs Soph Cls; Cl Rep Jr Cls; Hon Rl; Pres NHS; Stu Cncl; Pres Spn Clb; Swmmng; Trk; Univ.

LAURENZ, LINDA; Ithaca HS; Ithaca, MI; Boy Scts; Chrs; Chrh Wkr; Hon Rl; Yth Flsp; 4-H; Univ.

LAURIANTI, DONNA; Nordonia HS; Northfield, OH; Cl Rep Jr Cls; Treas Chrh Wkr; CAP; Girl Scts; Lbry Ade; Off Ade; Pep Clb; College; Phy Ther.

LAURIE, ROBYN; Calumet HS; Ahmeek, MI; Hon Rl; Hosp Ade; FNA; Bsktbl; Trk; Nursing.

LAURILA, LINNEA; Negaunee HS; Negaunee, MI; 1/153 Hon Rl; NHS; Treas Sci Clb; Bsktbl; Capt Trk; Michigan Tech Univ; Chem Engr.

LAURION, JACQUELYN; Vassar HS; Vassar, MI; 12/153 Band; Hon Rl; NHS; Fr Clb; Bsktbl; Trk; Top 3rd Yr French Awd 79; Schlstc Achvmnt Awd 79; U Of M Flint Merit Schlrshp 79; Univ Of Michigan; Elem Educ.

LAUTENBACH, KERRI; South Christian HS; Grand Rapids, MI; Cls Rep Soph Cls; Cl Rep Jr Cls; Band; Hon Rl; Stu Cncl; Yth Flsp; Yrbk; Trk; Calvin Coll; Nursing.

LAUTENSCHLAGER, LORI; Upper Scioto Valley HS; Belle Ctr, OH; 3/89 Cls Rep Frsh Cls; Cls Rep Soph Cls; Sec Jr Cls; Cl Rep Jr Cls; Am Leg Aux Girls St; Hon Rl; NHS; Pres Stu Cncl; Yth Flsp; Beta Clb; Ohio St Univ; Vet.

LAUTENSCHLAGER, PHILLIP E; Upper Scioto Valley HS; Belle Ctr, OH; Pres Frsh Cls; Pres Soph Cls; NHS; Stu Cncl; Beta Clb; 4-H; Pres FFA; Dairy Farmer.

LAUTENSCHLEGAR, BRENT; Loveland Hurst HS; Loveland, OH; 1/300 VP Soph Cls; Am Leg Boys St; Hon Rl; Lit Mag; NHS; Yrbk; VP Key Clb; Letter Socr; Am Leg Awd; Natl Merit SF; Congressional Scholarship Winner; Academic Ach; Member Cincinnati Council On Wolrd Affairs; Miami Univ; Physics.

LAUTERBACH, DAVID; Lutheran HS; N Olmsted, OH; Yrbk; Cleveland State Univ; Bus.

LAUTERMITCH, TIM; Upper Sandusky HS; Upper Sandusky, OH; Cls Rep Frsh Cls; VP Jr Cls; Am Leg Boys St; Band; FCA; Hon Rl; NHS; Bsbl; Letter Ftbl; IM Sprt; College; Science.

LAUTZENHEISER, JAEL; Fairless HS; Navarre, OH; Chrs; Chrh Wkr; Hon Rl; NHS; Sch Mus; Sch Pl; Yth Flsp; Drama Clb; College; Music.

LAUTZENHEISER, RANDAL; Van Wert HS; Van Wert, OH; Band; Hon Rl; NHS; Sch Pl; Lat Clb; Adrian College; Law.

LAUTZENHISER, FAYE; Tuslaw HS; N Lawrence, OH; Sec Sr Cls; VP Band; Chrs; Chrh Wkr; NHS; Sch Mus; Stu Cncl; Massillon Comm Hosp; Registered Nurs.

LAUX, CONNIE; Big Bay De Noc HS; Fayette, MI; Band; Chrs; Rptr Sch Nwsp; Sch Nwsp; 4-H; Bsbl; 4-H Awd;.

LAUX, ROBERT; Clawson HS; Royal Oak, MI; Boy Scts; Hon Rl; Pol Wkr; Mth Clb; Mic State Univ; Chem Engr.

LAUX, RUTH; Kiser HS; Dayton, OH; Hst Soph Cls; Hst Jr Cls; Hst Sr Cls; Val; Band; Chrs; Hon Rl; NHS; Sch Mus; Stu Cncl; U Of Dayton.

LAUZUN, DAVID; Holt HS; Holt, MI; 6/267 Pres NHS; Wrstlng; Cit Awd; Rotary Awd; Lansing Comm Coll.

LAVANIER, SUZANNE; St Ursula Acad; Cincinnati, OH; Chrs; Chrh Wkr; Hon Rl; Stg Crw; Swmmng; Tmr; College; Bus.

LA VANTURE, DENNIS; Glen Lake Cmnty HS; Cedar, MI; Trs Frsh Cls; Cls Rep Frsh Cls; VP Soph Cls; Cl Rep Jr Cls; Cls Rep Sr Cls; NHS; Bsbl; Ftbl; Glen Oaks Cmnty Coll; Bus Mgmt.

LAVELLE, LYNNE; Magnificat HS; N Olmstead, OH; Chrh Wkr; Sch Mus; Sch Pl; Coach Actv; Ohio St Univ; Engr.

LAVELLE, MEGAN; Lapel HS; Anderson, IN; Chrs; Hon Rl; Off Ade; Sch Mus; Yrbk; Rptr Sch Nwsp; Lat Clb; Pep Clb; IM Sprt; Ball State Univ; Spec Educ.

LAVENAU, DEBORA; Cloverdale HS; Quincy, IN; Girl Scts; Hon Rl; 4-H; 4-H Awd; Business School; Secretarial.

LAVERY, ALICE J; Lakota HS; Cincinnati, OH; Chrs; Orch; Stu Cncl; Spn Clb; Letter Ten; Bowling Green State Univ; Med Tech.

LAVERY, DAVID; Parkersburg Catholic HS; Vienna, WV; 1/41 Trs Sr Cls; Val; Hon Rl; Hosp Ade; NHS; Sch Mus; Sch Pl; Stg Crw; Bausch & Lomb Awd; Elk Awd; Va Polytechnic Inst; Chem Engr.

LAVEY, DAVID; Normandy Sr HS; Seven Hills, OH; 3/700 Cmnty Wkr; Debate Tm; Hon Rl; NHS; Orch; Sct Actv; Pres Lat Clb; Bsbl; Coach Actv; Natl Merit Ltr; Coll; Math.

LA VIGNE, DAVID A; Nitro HS; Nitro, WV; VP AFS; Band; Boy Scts; Chrh Wkr; Hon Rl; Sct Actv; Natl Merit Ltr; Natl Merit SF; Univ Of Charleston; Music.

LAVIGNETTE, AIMEE; West Lafayette HS; W Lafayette, IN; 60/185 Sec Frsh Cls; Sec Soph Cls; Sec Jr Cls; Chrs; FCA; Hon Rl; Sch Mus; Sch Pl; Stu Cncl; Sec Keyettes; Univ Of Kentucky; Nursing.

LA VINE, SHARON; Penn HS; Wyatt, IN; Chrs; Hon Rl; 4-H; Fr Clb; 4-H Awd;.

LAVIOLETTE, MICHELLE; Hemlock HS; Saginaw, MI; 45/210 Hon Rl; JA; Off Ade; Sch Pl; Rptr Yrbk; Trk; Chrldng; Mgrs; Pom Pon; Scr Kpr;.

LAVOLETTE, SCOTT; Eaton Rapids HS; Eaton Rapids, MI; 24/229 Hon Rl; Yth Flsp; Univ Of Mic.

LAVOY, RENEE; Carroll HS; Xenia, OH; 103/285 Cmnty Wkr; Off Ade; Scr Kpr; Tmr; Univ; Art.

LAVRENCHIK, DAVID J; Benedictine HS; Brunswick Hills, OH; 5/100 Hon Rl; NHS; Stu Cncl; Rptr Yrbk; Ger Clb; Key Clb; Case Inst Tech; Elec Engr.

LAW, BRUCE A; Mooresville HS; Mooresville, IN; 3/270 Pres Frsh Cls; Pres Soph Cls; Hon Rl; NHS; Sci Clb; Crs Cntry; Coach Actv; Univ; Engr.

LAW, JACQUELINE; Parkersburg South HS; Washington, WV; 4 Girl Scts; Hosp Ade; Civ Clb; Drama Clb; Marshall Univ; Accntg.

LAW, JEFFREY A; Dayton Christian HS; Dayton, OH; 5/125 Band; Hon Rl; Yth Flsp; Bsbl; Cit Awd; Univ; Bus Admin.

LAW, JOHN C; Bluefield HS; Bluefield, WV; 8/264 Am Leg Boys St; Hon Rl; Jr NHS; NHS; Pres Lat Clb; Pep Clb; Letter Bsbl; Natl Merit Ltr; Golden Horseshoe 76; Latin Clb Pres 77; Univ; Physics.

LAW, JULIE; Shelbyville Sr HS; Shelbyville, IN; 5/279 Chrh Wkr; Hon Rl; JA; NHS; Off Ade; Pep Clb; Spn Clb; PPFtbl; JA Awd; Univ.

LAW, KENT D; Crestline HS; Crestline, OH; Boy Scts; Hon Rl; Sct Actv; Stg Crw; Bsbl; Ohio State; Horticulture.

LAW, LORI; Carlisle Sr HS; Carlisle, OH; 2/185 Sal; Hon Rl; Jr NHS; VP NHS; Spn Clb; Dnfth Awd; Lion Awd; CERA; Vrsty Vllybll Mst Srvs Awrd; Vrsty Sftbll Lttr; Miami Univ; Bus Admin.

LAW, RAETA A; Cambridge HS; Cambridge, OH; Band; Chrh Wkr; Hon Rl; Hosp Ade; Lbry Ade; Red Cr Ade; Stu Cncl; Pres Yth Flsp; Mat Maids; Pensacola Christian Coll; RN.

LAW, SCOTT; Greenon HS; Enon, OH; 198/270 Boy Scts; Chrs; CAP; Sch Mus; Sch Pl; Sct Actv; Stg Crw; Drama Clb; Wright St Univ; Theater Dsgn.

LAWES, CAROL; St Peters HS; Mansfield, OH; Chrh Wkr; Girl Scts; JA; Red Cr Ade; Yrbk; Rptr Sch Nwsp; IM Sprt; Mat Maids; JA Awd; Jr Grad Of Dale Carnegie 78; Acad Awd Of Hon In Jrnlsm 79; Univ; Jrnlsm.

LAWHORN, JEFFREY A; Eastern HS; Lucasville, OH; Hon Rl; Letter Bsktbl; Trk; College.

LAWLER, SCOTT; Tri Valley HS; Frazeysburg, OH; 23/225 Band; VP Yth Flsp; VP 4-H; Letter Ftbl; Letter Trk; College; Archeology.

LAWLER, SCOTT A; Tri Valley HS; Frazeysburg, OH; Band; Hon Rl; VP Yth Flsp; VP 4-H; Lat Clb; Letter Ftbl; Letter Trk; College.

LAWLESS, MARK; Princeton HS; Princeton, WV; 64/374 FCA; Hon Rl; FHA; Key Clb; Sci Clb; Glf;.

LAWLIS, MARGARET; Grosse Pointe North HS; Grosse Pte Wds, MI; Hon Rl; Jr NHS; NHS; Rptr Yrbk; Spn Clb; Trk; Natl Merit Schl; Michigan St Univ; Engr.

LAWLOR, TERESA; Clear Fork HS; Beckley, WV; Hon Rl; Hosp Ade; NHS; Beckley Univ; Nursing.

LAWRENCE, ALYCE; Grand Ledge Academy; Eaton Rapids, MI; Cls Rep Frsh Cls; Cls Rep Soph Cls; VP Jr Cls; VP Sr Cls; Chrs; Hon Rl; Lbry Ade; Battle Creek Coll; Phys Ther.

LAWRENCE, DEBORAH; Sherman HS; Seth, WV; Band; Sch Pl; Yrbk; 4-H; Trk; Chrldng; Univ.

LAWRENCE, DOUG; Hastings HS; Hastings, MI; Boy Scts; Hon Rl; Bus Schl; Architecture.

LAWRENCE, ELIZABETH; Marion HS; Marion, IN; Am Leg Aux Girls St; Chrs; Chrh Wkr; Hon Rl; Jr NHS; NHS; Pol Wkr; Stu Cncl; Rptr Sch Nwsp; Ger Clb; Purdue Univ; Nursing.

LAWRENCE, ELIZABETH; W Geauga HS; Novelty, OH; 1/358 Val; Band; Hon Rl; NHS; Off Ade; Yth Flsp; Ed Yrbk; Letter Swmmng; IM Sprt; Dartmouth Coll; Math.

LAWRENCE, LISA; Jefferson Union HS; Toronto, OH; Band; Capt Drl Tm; Hon Rl; Off Ade; Orch; 4-H; FBLA; Letter Bsktbl; IM Sprt; 4-H Awd; Jefferson Cnty Grange Princess 77 & 78; Knoxville Bi Centnnl Queen 2nd Rnnr Up 76; Bus.

LAWRENCE, MARY; Carroll HS; Kettering, OH; 11/305 Hon Rl; Hosp Ade; NHS; Pep Clb; Spn Clb; Natl Merit Schl; Univ Of Cincinnati; Nursing.

LAWRENCE, MELISSA; Indianapolis Baptist HS; Greenwood, IN; 2/36 Girl Scts; Hon Rl; Jr NHS; Lbry Ade; Letter Trk; Indiana Univ; Nurse.

LAWRENCE, MELISSA; Pleasant HS; Marion, OH; VP Soph Cls; VP Jr Cls; Band; Hon Rl; Hosp Ade; Quill & Scroll; Rptr Yrbk; Rptr Sch Nwsp; Treas Drama Clb; Ohio St Univ.

LAWRENCE, MOLLY; Upper Arlington HS; Columbus, OH; 199/643 Aud/Vis; Cmp Fr Grls; Hon Rl; Lbry Ade; Orch; Quill & Scroll; Sch Mus; Sch Pl; Hon Rl; Yth Flsp; Ohio Univ; Journalism.

LAWRENCE, PAMELA; Perry HS; Laingsburg, MI; 3/150 Band; Hon Rl; NHS; Pep Clb; Spn Clb; Perfect Attendance Awd; Acad Letter; Band Letter; Michigan St Univ; Engr.

LAWRENCE, RANDY; Lapeer East HS; Lapeer, MI; Chrh Wkr; NHS; Red Cr Ade; Boys Clb Am; Bsbl; Bsktbl; Ftbl; Am Leg Awd; VFW Awd; Central Michigan Univ; Comp Sci.

LAWRENCE, STACY; Arlington HS; Indianapolis, IN; 3/436 Pres Jr Cls; VP Sr Cls; Am Leg Aux Girls St; Chrs; Chrh Wkr; Girl Scts; Hon Rl; JA; NHS; Pol Wkr; Outstndg Ctzn Of Hoosier Girls St 79; Pres Of Top Teens Of Amer Inc 79; 4th Runnr Up In 1st Annul Cotn Ball; Purdue Univ; Engr.

LAWRENCE, TAMARA; Northfield HS; Wabash, IN; 3/110 Cls Rep Sr Cls; Band; Chrh Wkr; Drl Tm; Hon Rl; NHS; Stu Cncl; Yrbk; Drama Clb; Pep Clb; Taylor Univ; Med Tech.

LAWS, TIMOTHY; Cowan HS; Muncie, IN; 20/79 Hon Rl; NHS; Indiana Voc Tech Coll.

LAWSON, BRENDA; Marlette HS; Snover, MI; Hon Rl; OEA; Busns Schl; Busns Sec.

LAWSON, CHERI; Blanchester HS; Blanchester, OH; 18/169 Band; Hon Rl; JA; Stu Cncl; Ed Yrbk; Pep Clb; Bsktbl; Trk; Chrldng; GAA; Sr Homecoming Attnd 1978; Pres Student Cncl 1978; Sr Flower Girl 1976; Gaa Treas 1979; Bus Schl.

LAWSON, DAN; Floyd Central HS; Floyd Knobs, IN; Hon Rl; Sch Pl; Lat Clb; Swmmng; Univ Of Ten; Engr.

LAWSON, DEBBIE; Sidney HS; Sidney, OH; Hon Rl; Off Ade; Orch; Stu Cncl; Yth Flsp; Picked To

Spend 3 Wks In Paris 79; Bowling Green St Univ; Foreign Lang.

LAWSON, DIANE; Cascade HS; Clayton, IN; Chrh Wkr; Hon Rl; Lbry Ade; Off Ade; VP 4-H; FBLA; Treas FHA; 4-H Awd; Univ; Tchr.

LAWSON, GARY L; Yellow Springs HS; Yellow Springs, OH; Aud/Vis; Chrh Wkr; Boys Clb Am; Letter Bsktbl; Letter Ftbl; Letter Trk; Natl Merit Schl; Univ; Bus Admin.

LAWSON, GLENDA; Jane Addams Vocational HS; Cleveland, OH; Chrs; Trk; Cit Awd; Univ; Legal Sec.

LAWSON, JEFFERSON; Pathfinder HS; Northport, MI; Pres Jr Cls; Pres NHS; Pres Quill & Scroll; Ed Sch Nwsp; Letter Socr; Letter Ten; Natl Merit Schl; Brown Univ.

LAWSON, JOHN; Strongsville HS; Strongsville, OH; Band; Boy Scts; Chrs; Chrh Wkr; Sct Actv; Bsbl; Univ; Elec Engr.

LAWSON, JOHN; St Francis De Sales HS; Columbus, OH; 115/189 Letter Ftbl; Trk; Wrstlng; Ohio St Univ; Landscaping.

LAWSON, KIMBERLY; Logan Sr HS; Logan, WV; Drl Tm; Girl Scts; Hon Rl; Hosp Ade; Jr NHS; NHS; Off Ade; Sct Actv; Ed Yrbk; Rptr Sch Nwsp; USAF; Admin.

LAWSON, LISA; Withrow HS; Cincinnati, OH; 10/561 Hon Rl; NHS; Fr Clb; Trk; Defiance Coll; Acctg.

LAWSON, RAY; Southeast Fountain HS; Attica, IN; 21/135 Boy Scts; Chrh Wkr; Hon Rl; 4-H; Mth Clb; Sci Clb; Letter Ftbl; Trk; Purdue Univ; Comp Prog.

LAWSON, RICKI; Wayne HS; Dayton, OH; Hon Rl; Jr NHS; Ger Clb; Bsbl; IM Sprt; Wright State Univ; Engr.

LAWSON, ROBIN; St Johns HS; De Witt, MI; Sec Sr Cls; Chrs; Girl Scts; Hon Rl; Hosp Ade; Lbry Ade; Sch Mus; Sch Pl; Stg Crw; Drama Clb; Ushers Club Sec & Treas 79; Univ Of Michigan; RN.

LAWSON, SANDRA; South Spencer HS; Rockport, IN; 78/160 Cmp Fr Grls; Chrs; Girl Scts; Lbry Ade; Off Ade; Sch Mus; Stg Crw; Yth Flsp; Rptr Sch Nwsp; FHA; Indiana St Univ; Mgmt Ind.

LAWSON, TERI; Granville HS; Granville, OH; 46/132 Hon Rl; Jr NHS; Y-Teens; Yrbk; Sch Nwsp; Capt Chrldng; GAA; Mat Maids; Ohio State Coll; Elem Ed.

LAWVER, LAURIE; Newcomerstown HS; Newcomerstown, OH; 5/136 Chrs; Hon Rl; NHS; Off Ade; Stg Crw; OEA; Spn Clb;.

LAXTON, GLEN; Pineville HS; Pineville, WV; Cls Rep Soph Cls; Cl Rep Jr Cls; Cls Rep Sr Cls; Hon Rl; Jr NHS; Stu Cncl; Pep Clb; Bsbl; Bsktbl; West Vir Univ.

LAY, CHUCK; Decatur Central HS; Camby, IN; 21/302 Am Leg Boys St; Boy Scts; Treas Chrh Wkr; Hon Rl; Treas JA; 4-H; Crs Cntry; Trk; Tmr; 4-H Awd; Indiana Univ; Chemistry.

LAY, DANICE; Lincoln HS; Vincennes, IN; Girl Scts; Hon Rl; Pep Clb; Spn Clb; GAA; Mgrs; PPFtbl; Indiana Univ; Med.

LAY, LAURA; Parkway HS; Celina, OH; 12/82 VP Frsh Cls; VP Soph Cls; VP Jr Cls; VP Sr Cls; Band; Hon Rl; NHS; FTA; Rdo Clb; PPFtbl; Bowling Green St Univ; Speech Ther.

LAY, LAURA; Parkway Local HS; Celina, OH; 11/82 VP Frsh Cls; VP Soph Cls; VP Jr Cls; VP Sr Cls; VP Band; Hon Rl; NHS; Sch Pl; FTA; VP Pep Clb; Bowling Green St Univ; Spec Educ.

LAY, RONALD; Holt HS; Lansing, MI; Band; Boy Scts; Sct Actv; Stg Crw; Sci Clb; Letter Ftbl; Trk; Wrstlng; Great Lakes Maritime Acad; Us Cst Gd.

LAYCOCK, CHARLENE; Clio HS; Clio, MI; Chrh Wkr; Rptr Yrbk; Pep Clb; Letter Bsktbl; Letter Trk; PPFtbl; Univ.

LAYCOCK, M; R Nelson Snider HS; Ft Wayne, IN; 4/565 Band; Hon Rl; Hosp Ade; Orch; Sch Mus; College; Bio Sci.

LAYFIELD, JEFFREY; Wirt County HS; Elizabeth, WV; Band; Boy Scts; Chrh Wkr; Cmnty Wkr; FFA; Farm Comm Chrmn; Earning & Svngs Comm Chrmn; Univ; Forest Ranger.

LAYMAN, CATHY; Clear Fork HS; Colcord, WV; 1/27 Pres Frsh Cls; Val; Am Leg Aux Girls St; Hon Rl; NHS; Sct Actv; Yrbk; Dnfth Awd; Wv Univ; Phys Ther.

LAYMAN, CATHY; Clear Fork HS; Culcord, WV; 1/27 Pres Frsh Cls; Val; Am Leg Aux Girls St; Girl Scts; Hon Rl; NHS; Yrbk; Kiwan Awd; West Virginia Univ; Forestry.

LAYNE, JANINE; Shadyside HS; Shadyside, OH; 29/102 Hst Sr Cls; Band; Hon Rl; Hosp Ade; Off Ade; Y-Teens; Drama Clb; Sec OEA; Ohio Valley General Hosp; Nursing.

LAYNE, KIMBERLY A; Tecumseh HS; New Carlisle, OH; VP Jr Cls; Pres Sr Cls; Hon Rl; Yrbk; Sch Nwsp; Pep Clb; Pres VICA; Bsktbl; Hockey; Capt Chrldng; Vocational Schl; Art.

LAYNE, MICHAEL; Danville HS; Danville, IN; Aud/Vis; Band; Drm Mjrt; Hon Rl; Sch Pl; Drama Clb; Pep Clb; Swmmng; General Motors Inst; Mech Engr.

LAYNE, TERENCE; Marquette HS; Marquette, MI; 29/427 Stg Crw; Drama Clb; Mic Tech Univ; Comp Sci.

LAYTON, DAVID; Kentwood HS; Kentwood, MI; Band; Boy Scts; Hon Rl; Sch Mus; Sch Pl; Sct Actv; God Cntry Awd; Awd Of Recgntn In J V Band 77; Univ; Diesel Mech.

LAYTON, DEANNA; Whitehall Yearling HS; Whitehall, OH; Cls Rep Frsh Cls; Cls Rep Soph Cls; Sec Jr Cls; Stu Cncl; Drama Clb; Pep Clb; Chrldng; GAA; Pom Pon; Ohio State Univ; Psych.

LAYTON, DON; Point Pleasant HS; Pt Pleasant, WV; 45/250 Boy Scts; Hon Rl; FFA; Wv Univ Of Outstndg Schlrshp & Ldrshp 79; Westerville Cmp Schlrshp 78; Marshall Univ; Agri.

LAYTON, REGINALD; Collinwood HS; Cleveland, OH; 4/338 Pres Jr Cls; Cl Rep Jr Cls; Pres Sr Cls; Cls Rep Sr Cls; Chrh Wkr; Hon Rl; Jr NHS; Stu Cncl; Letter Ten; Coach Actv; Case Wstrn Reserve Univ; Mgmt.

LAYTON, RICHARD; Washington HS; Massillon, OH; 17/450 Cls Rep Sr Cls; Hon Rl; Jr NHS; NHS; Stu Cncl; Mth Clb; Spn Clb; Letter Crs Cntry; Cit Awd; Cincinnati Univ; Engr.

LAYTON, ROBERT J; Walsh Jesuit HS; Stow, OH; Cmnty Wkr; Hon Rl; Pol Wkr; Bsbl; Bsktbl; IM Sprt; College; Medicine.

LAZAR, EDWARD; Woodhaven HS; Woodhaven, MI; Aud/Vis; Hon Rl; Lbry Ade; Univ Of Michigan; Film Making.

LAZAR, GEORGE; Valley Forge HS; Parma, OH; 100/800 Boy Scts; Chrh Wkr; Cmnty Wkr; Hon Rl; NHS; Pol Wkr; Sct Actv; Lat Clb; Bsbl; IM Sprt; OSU; Optometry.

LAZAREK, DAVID; Marquette HS; Michigan City, IN; Aud/Vis; Chrh Wkr; Hon Rl; Sci Clb; DAR Awd; Lion Awd; Opt Clb Awd; Univ; Med Resrch.

LAZAREK, R; La Porte HS; Laporte, IN; Chrh Wkr; Hon Rl; Orch; So Bend Univ; Radiology.

LAZARO, LEIGH; Notre Dame HS; Bridgeport, WV; VP Jr Cls; NHS; Stu Cncl; Yth Flsp; Mth Clb; Pep Clb; Sci Clb; Bsktbl; Ten; IM Sprt; West Virginia Univ; Med.

LAZARUS, BETH; Wheeling Park HS; Wheeling, WV; Cls Rep Soph Cls; Hon Rl; Lit Mag; Quill & Scroll; Stu Cncl; Pres Y-Teens; Ed Yrbk; Rptr Yrbk; Rptr Sch Nwsp; FBLA; Stone & Thomas Teen Bd 79; 1st Womn WV Wheeling Distance Race 79; 1st 17 & Under Oglebay Distance Race 79; Univ; Cmnctns.

LAZARUS, JEWEL; Carson City Crystal HS; Crystal, MI; 33/115 Cl Rep Jr Cls; Girl Scts; Hon Rl; PAVAS; Sch Pl; Stg Crw; Rptr Yrbk; Drama Clb; MCC Central Mic; Math.

LAZARUS, JILL; Homer HS; Homer, MI; Trs Sr Cls; Sal; Band; NHS; Sch Pl; Stu Cncl; Capt Chrldng; Argubrights Bus College; Exec Sec.

LAZEAR, DAVID; Medina Sr HS; Medina, OH; 98/341 Key Clb; Capt Bsktbl; Letter Ftbl; Univ.

LAZOR, DAVID A; Lakeview HS; Cortland, OH; Am Leg Boys St; Hon Rl; NHS; Rptr Sch Nwsp; Bsktbl; Lion Awd; College; Computer Programming.

LAZUR, ANDY; Harry S Truman HS; Taylor, MI; Hon Rl; Hockey; Letter Ten; Univ.

LAZZARO, LAURA; Westview Jr Sr HS; Shipshewana, IN; 3/84 Chrs; Chrh Wkr; Hon Rl; NHS; Yth Flsp; FHA; FTA; Pep Clb; Mgrs; Mat Maids; University; Med Tech.

LE, TIN T; Pontiac Northern HS; Pontiac, MI; 28/429 Hon Rl; NHS; Letter Ten; Kalamazoo Coll; Bio Chem.

LEABU, DANA; Belleville HS; Ypsilanti, MI; Hst Sr Cls; Hon Rl; NHS; Stu Cncl; Letter Gym; PPFtbl; Eastern Michigan Univ; Acctg.

LEABU, LINDA; Wayne Memorial HS; Westland, MI; FCA; Hon Rl; NHS; Rptr Yrbk; Ger Clb; Mth Clb; Letter Bsktbl; Underclass Hon Awd In Frgn Lang German 79; Univ; Med.

LEACH, DONNA; R B Chamberlin HS; Twinsburg, OH; 6/172 Band; NHS; Letter Ten; Letter Trk; GAA; Univ Of Akron; Bus Mgmt.

LEACH, GENEVA; Norwood HS; Norwood, OH; 187/375 Hon Rl; DECA; Pep Clb; Spn Clb; Ramond Walters Coll; Merchandising.

LEACH, JAMES; Les Cheneaux Comm HS; Cedarville, MI; Hon Rl; Letter Bsbl; Letter Bsktbl; Letter Crs Cntry; Letter Ftbl; Letter Trk; Ferris State College; Heavy Equip Tc.

LEACH, LORI; Madison Plains Sr HS; Mt Sterling, OH; Cmp Fr Grls; Chrs; Chrh Wkr; Girl Scts; Hon Rl; Hosp Ade; Off Ade; Yth Flsp; Sch Nwsp; Drama Clb; Math Club; Busns Schl; Comp Prog.

LEACH, MARK R; Midpark HS; Middleburg Hts, OH; 1/630 Am Leg Boys St; Band; Chrh Wkr; Hon Rl; NHS; Orch; Yth Flsp; Key Clb; Natl Merit SF; Case Western Reserve Univ.

LEACH, MICHELENE; Olmsted Falls HS; Olmsted Falls, OH; 52/240 Trs Sr Cls; AFS; Chrs; Hon Rl; Sch Mus; Stu Cncl; Ed Sch Nwsp; Rptr Sch Nwsp; Capt PPFtbl; Ohio St Univ.

LEACH, MIKE; Lynchburg Clay HS; Lynchburg, OH; Univ; Engr.

LEACH, ROBIN; Jackson HS; Jackson, OH; 64/230 Chrs; Drl Tm; Hon Rl; Sch Mus; Lat Clb; Pep Clb; PPFtbl; Flag Corps Cptn 79; Rio Grande Coll; Phys Ther.

LEADBETTER, DIANE; Tuslaw HS; Dalton, OH; 10/168 Band; Sec Chrs; Hon Rl; NHS; Orch; Sch Mus; Sch Pl; Am Leg Awd; Univ; Vocal Music.

LEADER, DIANA; Napoleon HS; Napoleon, OH; Hon Rl; Stg Crw; Sprt Ed Yrbk; Spn Clb; Gym; Trk; PPFtbl; Twrlr; Business School; Sec.

LEADHOLM, MARGARET; Monroe Jefferson HS; Monroe, MI; 5/170 Hon Rl; Jr NHS; Lbry Ade; NHS; 4-H; Capt Bsktbl; Letter Trk; Michigan St Univ; Geology.

LEAH, HOLYCROSS; Whitko HS; Columbia City, IN; Chrs; Sch Mus; Sch Pl; Yth Flsp; Rptr Yrbk; Drama Clb; 4-H; OEA; Ravenscroft Beauty Coll; Cosmotology.

LEAHY, BETSY; Our Lady Of Mercy HS; Farm Hls, MI; Cls Rep Frsh Cls; Cls Rep Soph Cls; Cl Rep Jr Cls; Hon Rl; Sch Mus; Sch Nwsp; Ger Clb; Letter Swmmng; Coach Actv; NCTE; 3.75 GPA; Swimming World Magazine Publication Feature On Girls Named To All Amer Tm; Coll; Med.

LEAHY, KELLY; Columbian HS; Tiffin, OH; Trs Frsh Cls; Cls Rep Frsh Cls; Cl Rep Jr Cls; AFS; Hon Rl; Stu Cncl; Drama Clb; Gym; IM Sprt; Miami Univ; Geneticist.

LEAHY, PATRICK; La Salle HS; Cincinnati, OH; 105/270 Hon Rl; Sch Mus; Sch Pl; Stg Crw; Drama Clb; Ftbl; Swmmng; Coach Actv; IM Sprt; Mgrs; Univ Of Cincinnati; Theatre Prod.

LEAHY, PEGEEN; Mc Auley HS; Cincinnati, OH; Hosp Ade; Pep Clb; Bsbl; Swmmng; Coach Actv; Pres GAA; IM Sprt; Christ Hosp School Of Nursing.

LEAK, RANDY; Oakridge HS; Muskegon, MI; 10/120 Band; Boy Scts; Hon Rl; Jr NHS; NHS; Sct Actv; Voice Dem Awd; Univ; Archt Drafting.

LEAMER, JERRY L; Westfield Washington HS; Westfield, IN; Chrh Wkr; Lbry Ade; Yth Flsp; Bsktbl; Ftbl; Trk; IM Sprt; PPFtbl; 2 All Range Lin Conf Medals In Track; Highest Point Man Awd In Track; 2nd In Cnty In Low Hurdles; Coll; Comp Sci.

LEAMON, LAURA; Penn HS; Granger, IN; 53/503 Lit Mag; NHS; Sch Pl; Yth Flsp; Ed Yrbk; Ind Univ; Journalism.

LEANO, ANN; Elyria Cath HS; N Ridgeville, OH; Cmnty Wkr; Hon Rl; Off Ade; Drama Clb; Spn Clb; Letter Bsktbl; Trk; Univ; Comm Art.

LEAR, BRIAN; Logan Elm HS; Laurelville, OH; 41/180 Band; Chrh Wkr; Hon Rl; Sch Pl; Stg Crw; Drama Clb; Fr Clb; Ohio Univ; History.

LEAR, FRANCIS; Moeller HS; Cincinnati, OH; Hon Rl; IM Sprt; College.

LEAR, GENIA; Point Pleasant HS; Gallipolis Ferr, Y ; Hon Rl; Hosp Ade; NHS; Red Cr Ade; Lat Clb; Spn Clb; VICA; Conservation Test 1st Pl; Latin I Avg Mdl Spanish I & II Avg; Nurse Aid 6 Week High Avg Pin; Marshall Univf Med Tech.

LEARMONT, DONALD; Calumet HS; Calumet, MI; 41/147 Hon Rl; Sch Pl; Scr Kpr; Crs Cntry; Ftbl; Trk; Coach Actv; GAA; Scr Kpr; Tmr; Northern Mich Univ; Sec Ed.

LEARNED, CLAUDIA; Lake Michigan Catholic HS; Benton Harbor, MI; Trs Frsh Cls; Chrs; Hon Rl; Sch Pl; Rptr Sch Nwsp; Fr Clb; Bsktbl; Trk; Chrldng; IM Sprt; Univ; Med.

LEARNER, SANDRA; Stow Sr HS; Munroe Falls, OH; 76/500 Cl Rep Jr Cls; AFS; Band; Chrs; Hon Rl; Lbry Ade; Off Ade; Sch Mus; Stu Cncl; Ger Clb; Univ; Phys Ther Asst.

LEASE, GENE; Riverdale HS; Mt Blanchard, OH; 1/105 Am Leg Boys St; Band; Boy Scts; Chrs; Hon Rl; Mdrgl; NHS; Sch Mus; Sct Actv; Stu Cncl; Soc Dstngshd Amer HS Stu; All Ohio Yth Choir & Band; Talented Able Gifted Organization; College; Vocal Music.

LEASER, KAREN; Sandusky HS; Sandusky, OH; Chrs; Hon Rl; Rptr Yrbk; Pep Clb; Letter Bsktbl; Trk; IM Sprt; PPFtbl; BGSU; Phys Educ.

LEASURE, LORA; Skyvue HS; Woodsfield, OH; Pres Jr Cls; Chrs; Hon Rl; Pres NHS; Sch Pl; Yrbk; Sch Nwsp; Fr Clb; Chrldng; DAR Awd;.

LEATH, ANDRE M; Northfork HS; Northfork, WV; 25/113 Chrh Wkr; Hon Rl; Jr NHS; NHS; Rptr Yrbk; Fr Clb; Key Clb; Bsktbl; Ftbl; Trk; Nc State Univ; Law.

LEATHERBURY, JANA; Union City HS; Sherwood, MI; Trs Jr Cls; Pres Sr Cls; Band; VP NHS; Sch Mus; Mat Maids; W Michigan Univ; Elem Ed.

LEATHERMAN, GAYLE; Norwayne HS; Wooster, OH; Trs Sr Cls; Band; Hon Rl; IM Sprt; Scr Kpr; Tmr; Univ; Actvst Ther.

LEATHERS, MARILEE; Climax Scotts Jr Sr HS; Climax, MI; 20/58 Hon Rl; PAVAS; Sch Pl; 4-H; Letter Mgrs; PPFtbl; Scr Kpr; Mi Comp Schlrshp 78; Schlrshp From Adrian Coll 79; Exchange Stu To Japan 77; Adrian Coll; Law.

LEATHERS, NEAL; Whiteford HS; Ottawa Lk, MI; Hon Rl; NHS; Sch Pl; Stg Crw; Yrbk; Sprt Ed Sch Nwsp; Drama Clb; Sci Clb; Spn Clb; Natl Merit Ltr; Univ Of Toledo; Aerospace Engr.

LEAVENS, PAMELA K; Pinconning Area HS; Linwood, MI; 1/250 Val; Band; Chrs; Debate Tm; NHS; Sch Pl; Pres Drama Clb; NCTE; Natl Merit SF; Voice Dem Awd; MTU Brd Schlrshp; Michigan Tech Univ; Tech Cmnctns.

LEAVER, ROBERT; Copley HS; Fairalwn, OH; Chrh Wkr; Spn Clb; Crs Cntry; Trk; Stanford; Med.

LEAVITT, JENNIFER; Fostoria HS; Fostoria, OH; Chrs; Hon Rl; 4-H; Trk; Pres Awd; Med.

LEAVY, KAREN; Northville HS; Northville, MI; JA; Alma College; Engr.

LE BAY, JULIE; Arcadia HS; Fostoria, OH; 3/57 Chrs; Hon Rl; NHS; Stg Crw; Yrbk; 4-H; VP FHA; College; Art.

LEBEAN, DANIAL; Davison HS; Davison, MI; Chrs; Hon Rl; Mdrgl; Sch Mus; Sch Pl; Stg Crw; Stu Cncl; Drama Clb; Michigan State Univ; Law.

LEBEDNICK, MARK; Grand Rapids Cath Cntrl HS; Wyoming, MI; Cl Rep Jr Cls; Cls Rep Sr Cls; Am Leg Boys St; NHS; Chmn Stu Cncl; Capt Crs Cntry; Letter Trk; St Of Mi Schshp 79; Michigan Tech Univ; Mech Engr.

LEBER, CHERYL; Monroeville HS; Monroeville, OH; 7/86 Trs Jr Cls; Pres Sr Cls; Am Leg Aux Girls St; Chrh Wkr; Girl Scts; Hon Rl; Jr NHS; NHS; PAVAS; Red Cr Ade; Firelands Bus Schl.

LEBER, DAVID; Taylor HS; Cincinnati, OH; Hon Rl; Univ Of Cincinnati; Chem Engr.

LEBICH, BILL; Menominee HS; Menominee, MI; Bsbl; Ftbl; Ten; Michigan St Univ; Archt.

LE BLANC, JAMES; Tuscarawas Vly HS; Bolivar, OH; 68/138 Band; Hon Rl; Stu Cncl; Fr Clb; Pep Clb; Bsbl; Bsktbl; Ftbl; Glf; Coach Actv; Malone Univ; Comm Art.

LE BLANC, JEANETTE; Regina HS; Shaker Hts, OH; Chrs; Hon Rl; Orch; Stg Crw; Rptr Sch Nwsp; IM Sprt; Pres Awd; Miami Univ; Bus Admin.

LE BLANC, JOHN; Lake Cath HS; Wickliffe, OH; Boy Scts; NHS; Glf; IM Sprt; Case Western Reserve Coll; Engr.

LE BLANC, REGINA; Romulus Sr HS; Romulus, MI; 31/315 Cls Rep Frsh Cls; Cls Rep Soph Cls; Trs Jr Cls; Hon Rl; NHS; Rptr Yrbk; Fr Clb; VICA; IM Sprt; Mat Maids; VICA Participation Awd 78; Certf Of Awd 79; Michigan Tech Univ; Bio.

LEBO, GARY; Rochester HS; Rochester, IN; Hon Rl; Off Ade; FFA; Pep Clb; Bsbl; Capt Ftbl; Wrstlng; PPFtbl; Coll.

LEBRECHT, LAURA; Prairie Hts HS; Angola, IN; 2/140 Chrh Wkr; Hon Rl; NHS; Sch Pl; Stg Crw; Rptr Yrbk; Ed Sch Nwsp; Sprt Ed Sch Nwsp; Rptr Sch Nwsp; Sec Drama Clb; College.

LECH, LEO; Bishop Noll Inst; Hammond, IN; 82/337 Hon Rl; Top Score In Schl On Natl Math Exam; Business Honor Soc; Loyola Univ; Medicine.

LECHNAR, ANNE; St Frances Cabrini HS; Allen Pk, MI; Girl Scts; Hon Rl; Jr NHS; NHS; Fr Clb; Ger Clb; Letter Ten; Univ Of Mic; Psych.

LE CLAIRE, DENA; North Vermillion HS; Cayuga, IN; Am Leg Aux Girls St; Band; Chrs; Hon Rl; Treas NHS; Sec FHA; Pep Clb; Spn Clb; US Hist Excel Awd 79; Clothing Excel Awd 79; Danville Jr Coll; Nurse.

LE CLAIRE, MARY; Dominican HS; Detroit, MI; Chrh Wkr; Jr NHS; NHS; Sch Pl; Sct Actv; Mic State; Acct.

LE CLEAR, LAURA; Tri County Area HS; Howard City, MI; 4/87 Band; Hon Rl; Fr Clb; Bsktbl; GAA; Western Michigan Univ; Bio.

LE COCQ, SHERRI; Shakamak HS; Jasonville, IN; Hon Rl; Off Ade; DECA; 4-H; FHA; Voc Schl; Bus.

LECOURS, DAVID; Pontiac Catholic HS; Waterford, MI; Hon Rl; Sch Mus; Sch Pl; Drama Clb; Capt Ftbl; Hockey; Michigan Tech Univ; Engr.

LECTURE, RAY; La Salle HS; Cincinnati, OH; 17/249 Hon Rl; Jr NHS; Ftbl; Letter Wrstlng; IM Sprt; College.

LE CUREUX, DONNA; Southwestern HS; Flint, MI; Band; Girl Scts; Hon Rl; NHS; Sch Pl; Mich Competitive Schrshp; Cert Of Hnr; Secondary Gifted Stu; Michigan St Univ; Vet.

LE CUREUX, SUSAN; North Branch HS; Columbiaville, MI; 4/180 VP Band; Chrs; Chrh Wkr; Hon Rl; NHS; Red Cr Ade; Sch Mus; Pres Fr Clb; Spn Clb; Lion Awd; #1 Math Stu Of High 78; Hugh O Brien Ldrshp Sem Rep 78; Chem Awd 78; Michigan St Univ; Law.

LEDA, MICHAEL; Washington HS; South Bend, IN; Band; Boy Scts; Wrstlng; Coach Actv; Coll; Computer Tech.

LEDBETTER JR, DAN; Little Miami HS; Maineville, OH; Chrs; Chrh Wkr; Hon Rl; Sec JA; Lbry Ade; NHS; Sch Mus; Sch Pl; Yth Flsp; College; Comp Sci.

LEDDICK, JULIE; Clio HS; Montrose, MI; Band; Girl Scts; Jr NHS; Stg Crw; Drama Clb; Spn Clb; Lake Superior State College; R N.

LEDERLE, J R; S Range HS; Salem, OH; Chrs; Hon Rl; Lbry Ade; NHS; Sch Mus; Stg Crw; Letter Crs Cntry; Coll.

LEDERLE, TIMOTHY; Traverse City St Francis HS; Traverse City, MI; JA; Ftbl; IM Sprt; Univ; Forestry.

LEDERLEITNER, MARGARET A; Interlochen Arts Academy; Mt Prospect, IL; Band; Chrh Wkr; Debate Tm; Hon Rl; Sch Mus; 4 Yr Half Schlrshp To De Pauw Univ; Ill Music Assn Contests & Concerto With Dist Orchestra; De Pauw Univ; Music.

LE DESMA, JOSE; Western HS; Detroit, MI; Chrh Wkr; Cmnty Wkr; Hon Rl; Off Ade; Coll; Elec Engr.

LEDESMA JR, BRUNO; Spencer Sharples HS; Holland, OH; 1/24 Pres Sr Cls; Aud/Vis; Hon Rl; Stu Cncl; Trk; Mgrs; Cit Awd; 1st To Win An Awd In Mech Drawing For Schl Of Spencer Ahrples 78; Univ; Drafting.

LEDFORD, CHRIS; West Central HS; Winamac, IN; 14/105 Hon Rl; NHS; Sch Pl; Drama Clb; FFA; Letter Bsktbl; Capt Ftbl; Letter Trk; Natl Merit Ltr; Indiana St Schlrshp; West Central HS Schlarship; Purdue Univ; Busns Mgmt.

LEDFORS, ROBERT; Cadiz HS; Cadiz, OH; Hon Rl; NHS; Ftbl; JA Awd;.

LEDINGTON, TAMMY; Fayetteville Perry HS; Fayetteville, OH; Chrs; Debate Tm; Girl Scts; Hon Rl; Lbry Ade; Fr Clb; IM Sprt; Univ; Jrnlsm.

LE DOUX, HEIDI; Western HS; Kokomo, IN; Chrs; Chrh Wkr; FCA; Yth Flsp; Yrbk; Ten; Trk; PPFtbl; Anderson College; Psy Soc.

LE DOUX, MICHELLE; Central Catholic HS; Canal Fulton, OH; Hon Rl; Sch Mus; Sch Pl; Stg Crw; Rptr Sch Nwsp; Drama Clb; 4-H; Fr Clb; FBLA; Opt Clb Awd; Univ Of Akron; Acctg.

LE DUC, DONNA; St Alphonsus HS; Dearborn, MI; 20/181 Sec Frsh Cls; Sec Soph Cls; Sec Jr Cls; Hon Rl; NHS; Sch Pl; Stu Cncl; Fr Clb; Bsbl; Swmmng; Univ; Med.

LEDY, JANA; Arthur Hill HS; Saginaw, MI; 650/700 Chrh Wkr; Hon Rl; Ambassador College; Comm Art.

LEE, ALAN J; Oakwood HS; Dayton, OH; 3/150 Chrh Wkr; Hon Rl; IM Sprt; Univ; Aero Engr.

LEE, B; Regina HS; St Clair, MI; Cls Rep Soph Cls; VP Jr Cls; Cls Rep Sr Cls; Hon Rl; NHS; Stu Cncl;

Rptr Yrbk; Coach Actv; PPFtbl; Scr Kpr; College; Law Enforcement.

LEE, BAILEY; Franklin HS; Livonia, MI; Hon Rl; Natl Merit Ltr; Univ Of Mic; Med.

LEE, BRENDA; Hauser HS; Hope, IN; 10/100 Band; Hon Rl; NHS; Sch Pl; Stg Crw; Fr Clb; FHA; Pep Clb; IUPUI; Accounting.

LEE, BRENDA; Roosevelt HS; Gary, IN; Chrh Wkr; Girl Scts; Hon Rl; Orch; ROTC; Y-Teens; FHA; Cit Awd; Purdue Univ; Bus.

LEE, BRYAN; Fairborn Baker HS; Fairborn, OH; 246/300 Aud/Vis; Lbry Ade; ROTC; Sch Pl; Rptr Yrbk; Drama Clb; Wright State Univf Chem.

LEE, BYRON; Westview Jr Sr HS; Middlebury, IN; Pres Soph Cls; VP Jr Cls; Hon Rl; NHS; Yth Flsp; 4-H; FFA; Letter Crs Cntry; IM Sprt; 4-H Awd; Purdue Univ; Vet Med.

LEE, CHRISTIAN H; Bridgeport Sr HS; Bridgeport, WV; 25/200 Band; Boy Scts; Hon Rl; NHS; Sch Pl; Stu Cncl; Yth Flsp; Mth Clb; Letter Wrstlng; William & Mary Coll; Bio Sci.

LEE, CRYSTAL; Mount View HS; Welch, WV; Chrs; Girl Scts; Hon Rl; Lbry Ade; Voc Schl; Nursing.

LEE, CYNTHIA F; Southern Local HS; Racine, OH; Chrs; Chrh Wkr; Hon Rl; Jr NHS; Coll.

LEE, DANIEL; Timken HS; Canton, OH; Hon Rl; Ohio State.

LEE, DAVE; Solon HS; Solon, OH; 39/288 Hon Rl; NHS; Key Clb; Capt Socr; Letter Wrstlng; IM Sprt; Miami Univ; Poli Sci.

LEE, GERALD; Adrian HS; Adrian, MI; 17/386 Am Leg Boys St; Boy Scts; Hon Rl; NHS; Sct Actv; Stu Cncl; Lat Clb; Mth Clb; Mgrs; God Cntry Awd; Adriam Coll 79; Mi Compt Schlshp 79; Natl Math Test 3rd Pl At Adrian HS 79; Adrian Coll; Pharm.

LEE, GERRY O; North Vermillion HS; Cayuga, IN; 33/98 VP Frsh Cls; VP Soph Cls; VP Sr Cls; FCA; Hon Rl; Off Ade; Sch Mus; Sch Pl; Drama Clb; Letter Bsbl; Inter Natl Thespian Soc 78; S Illinois Univ.

LEE, GREGORY; H H Dow HS; Midland, MI; Band; Boy Scts; Hon Rl; Pol Wkr; Sct Actv; Mth Clb; Rdo Clb; Sci Clb; Natl Merit SF; 1st Plc Delta Coll Advncd Elec 77; 1st Plc Delta Coll Digital Elec Comp 78; Michigan Tech Univ; Elec Engr.

LEE, JACKIE; Sandy Valley HS; Waynesburg, OH; 1/150 Chrh Wkr; Hon Rl; JA; Lbry Ade; Natl Forn Lg; NHS; Quill & Scroll; Sch Nwsp; Fr Clb; Spn Clb; Oral Roberts Univ; Math.

LEE, JAN; Bedford North Lawrence HS; Bedford, IN; 12/385 Chrh Wkr; Hon Rl; NHS; Beta Clb; Univ; Mech Engr.

LEE, KAM KIN; Rogers HS; Toledo, OH; 28/417 Boy Scts; Hon Rl; Off Ade; Mth Clb; Sci Clb; Univ Of Toledo; Medicine.

LEE, KATHY; Charles F Brush HS; Lyndhurst, OH; Cls Rep Frsh Cls; Cl Rep Jr Cls; Chrh Wkr; Letter Bsbl; Letter Bsktbl; Letter Ten; Univ; Bus.

LEE, KENNY; Sebring Mc Kinley HS; Sebring, OH; Am Leg Boys St; Hon Rl; NHS; Letter Bsbl; Letter Bsktbl; Univ; Acctg.

LEE, LAURA; Elmwood HS; Wayne, OH; Sec Band; Chrs; Hon Rl; Mdrgl; MMM; Sch Mus; Treas Yth Flsp; Bowling Green; Acctg.

LEE, LINDA; La Crosse HS; La Crosse, IN; 1/38 Val; Hon Rl; NHS; Sch Pl; Ed Yrbk; Drama Clb; 4-H; Pep Clb; 4-H Awd; Purdue Univ; Occup Ther.

LEE, LINDA K; Seton HS; Cincinnati, OH; 14/387 Chrh Wkr; Girl Scts; Hon Rl; NHS; Pol Wkr; FBLA; Spn Clb; Bsbl; Gym; St Dominic Fr Stockelman Schlrshp To Seton HS; Univ; Spec Ed.

LEE, LISA; Wayland Union HS; Wayland, MI; 20/193 Sec Sr Cls; Chrs; Sch Mus; Sch Pl; Stu Cncl; Yth Flsp; Sch Nwsp; FTA; Chrldng; IM Sprt; Nazareth Coll; Nurse.

LEE, LISA; Coshocton HS; Coshocton, OH; 5/178 Band; Hon Rl; Hosp Ade; NHS; Yrbk; FTA; Sci Clb; Treas Spn Clb; PPFtbl; Univ; Acctg.

LEE, MARCHELLE; Edgerton HS; Montpelier, OH; 5/87 Band; Chrh Wkr; Hon Rl; NHS; Sch Mus; Sec Yth Flsp; Pep Clb; Spn Clb; Spanish Club Schlrshp; Grange Yth Princess; Busns Schl; Bilingual Exec Sec.

LEE, MARIANNE; Southern Local HS; Lisbon, OH; Off Ade; Pres FHA; FNA; OEA; Kent St Ext Univ; Public Relations.

LEE, MARTY; Sandusky HS; Sandusky, MI; Cmnty Wkr; Hon Rl; Pol Wkr; Bsbl; Coach Actv; College; Bookkeeping.

LEE, MARY; Douglas Mac Arthur HS; Saginaw, MI; Cmnty Wkr; Hon Rl; NHS; Pol Wkr; Sch Mus; Sct Actv; Treas Spn Clb; Letter Pom Pon; Nominated For People To People Stu Ambassdr 78; Spnsh Awd 79; Captn Var Pom Pon 79; Univ Of Michigan; Pre Med.

LEE, MIKE; R Nelson Sr HS; Ft Wayne, IN; 17/575 Hon Rl; Fr Clb; Letter Bsbl; Hockey; Letter Ten; IM Sprt; Univ; Med.

LEE, NANCY; Elmwood HS; Bloomdale, OH; Hon Rl; Chrldng; Mat Maids; Bus Schl; Sec.

LEE, REBECCA; Admiral King HS; Lorain, OH; Aud/Vis; Chrh Wkr; FCA; Hon Rl; Quill & Scroll; Yth Flsp; Rptr Sch Nwsp; Drama Clb; Letter Bsktbl; Swmmng; Lorain Cmnty Coll; Jrnlsm.

LEE, ROBERT; Detroit Catholic Ctrl HS; Dearborn Heigh, MI; 10/189 NHS; Pres Stu Cncl; Sch Nwsp; Fr Clb; Trk; IM Sprt; Am Leg Awd; Gabriel Richard GPA; Univ Of Notre Dame; Elec Engr.

LEE, ROBERT; Mt Pleasant HS; Mt Pleasant, MI; Hon Rl; NHS; Letter Bsbl; Letter Bsktbl; Letter Ftbl; Univ; Bus.

LEE, ROBERT; Parkside HS; Jackson, MI; Hon Rl; NHS; Univ Of Mic; Journalism.

LEE, ROGER; Canton South HS; Canton, OH; Hon Rl; OEA; St Brd Of Ed Awd 1979; Schlstc Awd 1979; OEA 3rd Pl In Region 1979; Stark Tech Coll; Acctg.

LEE, RORY G; Kalkaska Public HS; Rapid City, MI; Band; Chrh Wkr; Cmnty Wkr; Hon Rl; NHS; Sct Actv; Letter Bsbl; Letter Bsktbl; Letter Ftbl; IM Sprt;.

LEE, RUTH; Loudonville HS; Loudonville, OH; Band; Chrs; Girl Scts; Hon Rl; NHS; Off Ade; Sch Pl; Stg Crw; Yth Flsp; 4-H; Capital Univ; Nurse.

LEE, SALLY; Finneytown HS; Cincinnati, OH; Band; Hon Rl; Hosp Ade; NHS; Sch Nwsp; Scr Kpr; Tmr; Natl Merit SF; Stern Coll; Sci.

LEE, SANDRA; Hughes HS; Cincinnati, OH; Cls Rep Frsh Cls; Cmnty Wkr; Hon Rl; NHS; Fr Clb; Cit Awd; Purdue Univ; Computer Engr.

LEE, SANDRA; Rutherford B Hayes HS; Delaware, OH; 7/305 AFS; Band; Girl Scts; Hon Rl; NHS; Y-Teens; Pres FTA; Key Clb; Tmr; Dnfth Awd; Ohio Wesleyan Univ; Psych.

LEE, SHARON; Vanlue HS; Mt Blanchard, OH; Hon Rl; NHS; Sec Work.

LEE, SONJIA; Northern HS; Detroit, MI; Trs Soph Cls; VP Sr Cls; Band; Girl Scts; Hon Rl; NHS; Off Ade; FHA; Cit Awd; Marygrove Coll; Bus Admin.

LEE, STEVE; Swan Valley HS; Saginaw, MI; Band; Boy Scts; Chrh Wkr; Hon Rl; JA; Lbry Ade; Pol Wkr; Boys Clb Am; Hockey; Mic State Univ; Electric Engr.

LEE, SUSIE; Lawrence Central HS; Indianapolis, IN; Chrs; Treas Chrh Wkr; Drl Tm; NHS; Sch Mus; Cmnty Awd 77; Music Awd Piano 79; Purdue Univ; Comp Analist.

LEE, TANDA; Jefferson HS; Kearneysville, WV; Cls Rep Frsh Cls; Band; Chrh Wkr; Hon Rl; NHS; Stu Cncl; Spn Clb; Trk; Pom Pon; Natl Merit Ltr; West Virg Univ.

LEE, TIM; Fostoria HS; Fostoria, OH; Hon Rl; Ftbl; Letter Wrstlng; Bowling Green.

LEE, TODD; Inland Lakes HS; Indian Rvr, MI; 15/89 Band; Hon Rl; Sprt Ed Yrbk; Rptr Yrbk; Yrbk; College; Psych.

LEE, YONG PYO; John F Kennedy HS; Warren, OH; 1/180 Val; Chrs; Hon Rl; Natl Forn Lg; NHS; Rptr Yrbk; FSA; Mth Clb; Sci Clb; Natl Merit SF; Univ.

LEEBER, ANGELA; Woodrow Wilson HS; Mabscott, WV; 62/508 Cls Rep Sr Cls; Hon Rl; Lbry Ade; Off Ade; Ed Sch Nwsp; Fr Clb; IM Sprt; Univ Of Kentucky; Psych.

LEECH, JOHN W; Malabar HS; Mansfield, OH; 12/300 Boy Scts; Hon Rl; NHS; Orch; Sct Actv; Stu Cncl; Key Clb; Mth Clb; Ohio St Univ; Sci.

LEEDOM, CAROLE; Central Baptist HS; Cincinnati, OH; VP Soph Cls; Cls Rep Soph Cls; Trs Jr Cls; Chrs; Sch Pl; Stu Cncl; Rptr Yrbk; Capt Chrldng; Work.

LEEDOM, SUE; Wadsworth Sr HS; Wadsworth, OH; 16/367 Chrs; Off Ade; Ed Sch Nwsp; Drama Clb; Fr Clb; Pep Clb; Scr Kpr; Univ Of Akron; Recreation.

LEEDS, BOBBY; Western Hills HS; Cincinnati, OH; Pres Frsh Cls; Pres Soph Cls; Cl Rep Jr Cls; Chrs; Girl Scts; Sch Pl; Stu Cncl; Yth Flsp; Drama Clb; Swmmng; Univ Of Cincinnati; Ct Clerk.

LEEDS, CATHY; Weir Sr HS; Weirton, WV; 48/343 Hon Rl; JA; NHS; Off Ade; Pep Clb; GAA; JA Awd; Fairmont St Coll; Acctg.

LEEDY, PAUL; Madison Comprehensive HS; Athens, OH; 100/480 Chrs; Hon Rl; VP JA; Lbry Ade; Pol Wkr; Sch Mus; Yth Flsp; Pres Spn Clb; JA Awd; Ohio Univ; Music Educ.

LEEPER, A; Fort Frye HS; Beverly, OH; Cls Rep Frsh Cls; Cls Rep Soph Cls; Cl Rep Jr Cls; Band; Chrh Wkr; Cmnty Wkr; Sch Mus; Stu Cncl; 4-H; Pep Clb; College; Teaching.

LEEPER, BECKY; Morgan HS; Mc Connelsville, OH; 3/232 Cls Rep Frsh Cls; Cls Rep Soph Cls; Cl Rep Jr Cls; Hon Rl; NHS; Off Ade; Stu Cncl; Spn Clb; Chrldng; IM Sprt; Univ.

LEEPER, JILL; Bremen HS; Plymouth, IN; 6/121 Chrs; Chrh Wkr; Hon Rl; NHS; Sch Pl; Stg Crw; Yth Flsp; Yrbk; Sch Nwsp; Drama Clb; Ball St Univ; Radio & T V.

LEESBURG, JAYNE; Portsmouth East HS; Wheelersburg, OH; 16/82 Sec Band; Chrh Wkr; Hon Rl; Lbry Ade; NHS; Stg Crw; Lat Clb; Letter Ten; Shawnee St Coll.

LEESBURG, SHERI; Portsmouth East HS; Wheelesburg, OH; Trs Frsh Cls; Trs Soph Cls; Trs Jr Cls; Chrs; Chrh Wkr; Hon Rl; Mdrgl; Sch Mus; Shawnee State; Med Asst.

LEESON, CAROLINE; Bridgeport Sr HS; Bridgeport, WV; Band; Chrs; Hon Rl; Jr NHS; NHS; Fairmont St Univ; Music.

LEETH, JOHN E; Western HS; Bainbridge, OH; 2/79 Pres Frsh Cls; Pres Soph Cls; Pres Jr Cls; Hon Rl; NHS; Yrbk; Fr Clb; Pres Sci Clb; Bsktbl; Univ.

LEE VAN, MICHELLE; Washington HS; South Bend, IN; 5/300 Hon Rl; JA; NHS; Fr Clb; JA Awd; Purdue Univ; Engineering.

LE FEBRE, RENA; Meigs HS; Pomeroy, OH; Trs Jr Cls; Band; Chrs; Chrh Wkr; Girl Scts; Hon Rl; NHS; 4-H; Fr Clb; OEA; Vocational Schl.

LE FEVRE, BRUCE; Herbert Henry Dow HS; Midland, MI; 73/460 Boy Scts; Hon Rl; NHS; Sct Actv; Stu Cncl; Yth Flsp; Sci Clb; Letter Swmmng; Tmr; Natl Merit Ltr; Michigan Tech Univ; Elec Engr.

LE FEVRE, LYNNE; Edwin Denby HS; Detroit, MI; 23/341 Girl Scts; Hon Rl; Hosp Ade; JA; Off Ade; Bsbl; Bsktbl; Swmmng; Trk; Scr Kpr; Mi Schlstc Grant 79; Basic Ed Opportunity Grant Progr Pndg 79; ADF Contest Dvlpmnt Appeal 75; Detroit Coll Of Bus; Acctg.

LE FEVRE, ROBYN; Fairmont West HS; Kettering, OH; 10/489 Cmnty Wkr; Girl Scts; Hon Rl; NHS; Orch; Sch Mus; Sch Pl; Fr Clb; Pep Clb; IM Sprt; Ohio St Univ; Engr.

LEFF, GAIL; Meadowdale HS; Dayton, OH; Am Leg Aux Girls St; Hon Rl; Hosp Ade; NHS; Rptr Yrbk; Pep Clb; College; Medicine.

LEFFLER, KEN; Cedar Lake Academy HS; Woodridge, IL; Cls Rep Soph Cls; VP Jr Cls; Band; Chrs; Hon Rl; Mdrgl; IM Sprt; Scr Kpr; Tmr; Andrews Univ; Bus Admin.

LEFKOWITZ, MICHAEL; Bexley HS; Columbus, OH; Trs Sr Cls; Hon Rl; Sch Pl; Stu Cncl; Yth Flsp; Rptr Sch Nwsp; Drama Clb; Fr Clb; IM Sprt; Natl Merit Ltr; College; Business.

LEFLER, BRIAN; Wylie E Groves HS; Southfield, MI; 46/532 Cls Rep Frsh Cls; Chrh Wkr; Hon Rl; NHS; Sch Pl; Stg Crw; Stu Cncl; Drama Clb; Fr Clb; Swmmng; Mich State Univ; Fashion.

LE FORT, MICHAEL; Taylor Center HS; Taylor, MI; Hon Rl; Sch Nwsp; Glf; Letter Ten; Highst SAT Scr In Cls 78; Asst Ed Featr Ed Staff Art Schl Newsppr 79; Univ; Jrnlsm.

LEFTRICT, FRED T; Nettie Lee Roth HS; Dayton, OH; 7/225 Boy Scts; Chrh Wkr; Hon Rl; JA; Natl Forn Lg; Pres NHS; Sct Actv; Sch Nwsp; Letter Bsbl; Natl Merit Ltr; 1st Pl Riverdale Optimist Club; 1st Pl Downtown Optimist Club; Natl Sci Fndtn Schlrshp; College; Computer Engr.

LEFURGE, TODD; Waverly HS; Wyoming, MI; Michigan St Univ; Pre Law.

LE GALLEE, JULIE; Philip Barbour HS; Philippi, WV; Chrh Wkr; Cmnty Wkr; Girl Scts; Hon Rl; NHS; Sch Pl; Yrbk; Drama Clb; Keyettes; IM Sprt; Univ Of Colo; Journalism.

LEGG, BECKY; High School; Charleston, WV; Pres Jr Cls; Cl Rep Jr Cls; Cmp Fr Grls; Chrh Wkr; Girl Scts; Hon Rl; Jr NHS; Lbry Ade; NHS; PAVAS; West Virginia St Coll; Art Ther.

LEGG, PATRICIA; Fairland HS; Proctorville, OH; 4/153 Band; Hon Rl; NHS; Sch Mus; Ed Yrbk; Sch Nwsp; 4-H; Mth Clb; Pep Clb; 4-H Awd; Fairland HS Correspondent/huntington Adv; Ohio Univ HS Scholar Cert; All County Concert Band; College.

LEGG, WILLIAM L; Poca HS; Poca, WV; Cls Rep Frsh Cls; Cls Rep Soph Cls; Cl Rep Jr Cls; Am Leg Boys St; Band; Boy Scts; Chrh Wkr; FCA; Hon Rl; Sch Pl; 2nd Pl Regnl Sci Fair 79; Best Algebra 2 Stud 78; Best Chem Stud 79; Univ; Med.

LEGHART, C; Lorain Catholic HS; Amherst, OH; Drl Tm; Hon Rl; NHS; Trk; Chrldng; Pom Pon; College; Vet.

LEGHART, CATHERINE; Lorain Catholic HS; Amherst, OH; Chrs; Girl Scts; Hon Rl; NHS; Pep Clb; Trk; Chrldng; Pom Pon; Univ; Vet.

LEGLER, MARK; Tri County HS; Remington, IN; 8/75 Hon Rl; Mth Clb; Spn Clb; Letter Glf; IM Sprt; Work.

LE GROS, SANDRA L; Southeast HS; Deerfield, OH; 3/150 Band; Girl Scts; Hon Rl; MMM; Stu Cncl; Yth Flsp; Rptr Sch Nwsp; Pep Clb; Bsktbl; Trk; Portage Chapter De Molay Sweetheart; Ohio Univ Summer Scholar Prog; College.

LEHENBAUER, PHILIP; Patrick Henry HS; Deshler, OH; 3/121 Cls Rep Frsh Cls; Cls Rep Soph Cls; Am Leg Boys St; Band; Chrs; Chrh Wkr; Hon Rl; Treas NHS; Sch Mus; Stu Cncl; Univ; Music.

LEHIGH, ELIZABETH A; Tuscarawas Central Cath HS; Zoar, OH; Cls Rep Frsh Cls; Chrs; Sec Girl Scts; Hon Rl; NHS; Sch Pl; Sct Actv; Stu Cncl; Y-Teens; Drama Clb; Awd Of Special Recog Miss Teenage Amer; Cert Of Ed Dev Natl For Superior Perf; College; Archt.

LEHMAN, BRENT; Lima Perry HS; Lima, OH; VP Jr Cls; Band; Chrs; Hon Rl; Yrbk; Bsbl; Ftbl; College; Math.

LEHMAN, CARLTON; Lexington HS; Mansfield, OH; 98/271 Boy Scts; Yth Flsp; Sci Clb; God Cntry Awd; College; Physics.

LEHMAN, DANIEL; Archbishop Alter HS; Dayton, OH; 1/277 Aud/Vis; Hon Rl; NHS; Sec Stg Crw; Rptr Yrbk; Key Clb; IM Sprt; College; Sci.

LEHMAN, DEIRDRE; Adams Central HS; Monroe, IN; Sec Soph Cls; Sec Jr Cls; Band; Drm Mjrt; FCA; Mdrgl; NHS; Pres Spn Clb; Ten; Chrldng; Ind Univ; Spanish.

LEHMAN, GREG; Bloomfield HS; Bloomfield, IN; 18/107 Am Leg Boys St; Boy Scts; Chrh Wkr; FCA; Hon Rl; Jr NHS; NHS; Sct Actv; Stu Cncl; Yth Flsp; Indiana Univ; Finance.

LEHMAN, JILL; Evart Public Schools; Evart, MI; Cls Rep Frsh Cls; Cls Rep Soph Cls; Cl Rep Jr Cls; Cls Rep Sr Cls; Chrs; Chrh Wkr; Cmnty Wkr; Girl Scts; Hon Rl; Sch Mus; Univ; Bus.

LEHMAN, RAMONA; Mt Gilead HS; Mt Gilead, OH; Chrh Wkr; Hon Rl; 4-H; Fr Clb; FHA; Trk; GAA; 4-H Awd; JC Awd; Ohio St Univ; Home Ec.

LEHMAN, TERRI; Hilltop HS; W Unity, OH; Am Leg Aux Girls St; Band; Chrs; Hon Rl; Sch Pl; Rptr Yrbk; 4-H; Swmmng; Coach Actv; Findlay Coll; Elem Educ.

LEHMAN, TONY; Garrett HS; Garrett, IN; Hon Rl; NHS; Letter Bsktbl; Letter Trk; Univ; Acctg.

LEHMAN, TONYA; Northwest HS; Jackson, MI; Cls Rep Sr Cls; Band; Chrh Wkr; Drm Bgl; Hon Rl; Mdrgl; NHS; Davenport College Of Bus; Med Sec.

LEHMANN, GABRIELE; Warren HS; Troy, MI; Chrh Wkr; Girl Scts; Hon Rl; NHS; Orch; Sch Mus; Sch Pl; Drama Clb; Natl Merit Ltr; Natl Merit SF; General Motors Inst; Engr.

LEHMANN, GLORIA; Brooklyn HS; Brooklyn, OH; 1/170 Cls Rep Frsh Cls; Cls Rep Sr Cls; Val; Band; Chrs; Chrh Wkr; NHS; Orch; Sch Mus; Sch Pl; Evangel Coll; Mental Health.

LEHMANN, JOANNE; Geneva Secondary HS; Geneva, OH; 3/240 AFS; Chrh Wkr; NHS; Off Ade; Sch Pl; Rptr Yrbk; Drama Clb; FBLA; Lat Clb; Bill Wasulko Memrl Schlrshp 79; Oh Bd Of Regents Distinction Awrd 79; Kent St Univ; Elem Educ.

LEHMANN, PAMELA; Berrien Springs HS; Berrien Spgs, MI; Band; Chrs; Chrh Wkr; Cmnty Wkr; Hon Rl; Hosp Ade; Off Ade; Pol Wkr; Stg Crw; Yth Flsp; Bronson Univ; RN.

LEHMKUHL, CATHERINE A; Versailles HS; Versailles, OH; Chrs; Girl Scts; Lbry Ade; Sch Mus; Drama Clb; Pres FHA; Tiger Bell Track St 78; Relgn Tchr 1st Grd 76; Coll Club 78; Thespian Adv Drama 78; Ohio St Univ; Home Ec.

LEHMKUHL, VANCE; Cincinnati Cntry Day HS; Middletown, OH; Chrs; Hon Rl; Sch Mus; Sch Pl; Ed Sch Nwsp; Sch Nwsp; Mth Clb; Rus Clb; Letter Socr; IM Sprt; Oberlin Coll; Music.

LEHNEN, DIANE; St Johns HS; St Johns, MI; Band; Girl Scts; Hon Rl; Orch; Sct Actv; Yth Flsp; College; Music.

LEHNER, BECKY; Harding HS; Marion, OH; Band; Hon Rl; Capt Chrldng;.

LEHNER, DANIEL; Pleasant HS; Marion, OH; 37/145 Boy Scts; Hon Rl; JA; 4-H; Fr Clb; Key Clb; Bsktbl; Glf; Miami Of Ohio; Archetecture.

LEHNER, SANDRA; Liberty HS; Yngstn, OH; Cls Rep Soph Cls; Cl Rep Jr Cls; Chrs; Cmnty Wkr; Hon Rl; Sch Pl; Sch Mus; Stu Cncl; Yth Flsp; Drama Clb; Coll; Busns Admin.

LEHNHART, KEVIN; Lucas HS; Lucas, OH; Band; Chrh Wkr; Cmnty Wkr; 4-H; Treas FFA; IM Sprt; 4-H Awd; Mas Awd; Farm Bureau P 1979; Hocking Tech Schl; Timber Hrvstng.

LEIBY, NED; Marquette HS; Michigan City, IN; Cls Rep Frsh Cls; Chrh Wkr; Pol Wkr; Stu Cncl; Spn Clb; College; History.

LEICHER, ANN; Midpark HS; Brook Park, OH; 39/636 Sec Soph Cls; Band; Stu Cncl; OEA; Chrldng; Mat Maids; Cuyahoga Community Coll; Bsns Mgmt.

LEICHT, YOLANDA; Mt Vernon Acad; Galion, OH; Band; Chrs; Hon Rl; Sch Pl; Rptr Sch Nwsp; Sthern Missionary Coll; Young People.

LEIDEN, DIANNE; Beaumont Girls HS; Cleveland, OH; 8/129 Hon Rl; Hosp Ade; NHS; Rptr Yrbk; Fr Clb; Univ Of Miami.

LEIDY, JEANNE; Lima Sr HS; Lima, OH; 8/443 Cls Rep Frsh Cls; Band; Hon Rl; Tmr; Case Western Reserve Univ; Math.

LEIDY, RAE; North Central HS; Pioneer, OH; Chrs; Hon Rl; Lbry Ade; FTA; Trk; Mgrs; Siena Heights; Psychology.

LEIGH, TERESA; Cuyahoga Falls HS; Silver Lake, OH; Chrs; FCA; Hon Rl; NHS; College; Medicine.

LEIGHNER, PENNY; Parkway Local HS; Rockford, OH; 13/83 Bsktbl; Crs Cntry; Coach Actv; GAA; Scr Kpr; Bowling Green State U; Phys Educ.

LEIGHTON, KAYE; Northport Public Schl; Northport, MI; 2/28 Cls Rep Frsh Cls; Trs Soph Cls; Sec Sr Cls; Band; Hon Rl; NHS; Stu Cncl; 4-H; Spn Clb; Letter Bsktbl; Univ.

LEIJA, ABIGAIL; Salem HS; Salem, OH; 84/295 Cls Rep Frsh Cls; Band; Chrh Wkr; Hon Rl; Quill & Scroll; Sch Mus; Stu Cncl; Sch Nwsp; Spn Clb; Trk; Univ Of Alabama; Law.

LEIN, JOHNATHAN; Brethren HS; Kaleva, MI; Cls Rep Frsh Cls; Cls Rep Soph Cls; Band; Boy Scts; Chrh Wkr; Debate Tm; FCA; Hon Rl; Lbry Ade; Stu Cncl; St Of Mi Competitive Schlrshp; Hope Coll Social Studies & Acad Schlrshps; Awd For Most Religious Boy Sr Cls; Hope Coll; History.

LEINBACH, EARL T; Oregon Davis HS; Hamlet, IN; Hon Rl; FFA; Letter Glf; Trk; IM Sprt; Mgrs; Univ; Med.

LEINENGER, TANYA; Clarkston Sr HS; Lake Orion, MI; Hon Rl; Fr Clb; Spn Clb; Chrldng; Pom Pon; PPFtbl; Ferris St Coll; Intl Bus.

LEININGER, NANCY; Lynchburg Clay HS; Lynchburg, OH; 26/92 Band; Chrh Wkr; Girl Scts; Hon Rl; Off Ade; Stu Cncl; Yrbk; Sch Nwsp; 4-H; Chrldng;.

LEINONEN, NANCY; Cheboygan Area HS; Cheboygan, MI; Band; Chrs; Chrh Wkr; Hon Rl; Fr Clb; College; Vocal Music.

LEIRSTEIN, KEVIN; Livonia Franklin HS; Westland, MI; Hon Rl; Coach Actv; IM Sprt; Central Michigan Univ; Bus.

LEIS, STEVEN; Ansonia HS; Ansonia, OH; 13/68 Band; Boy Scts; Chrs; Hon Rl; Sct Actv; VP Yth Flsp; FFA; IM Sprt; Ohio State Univ; Agri Economics.

LEISHMANN, VANESSA; Sandy Valley HS; Waynesburg, OH; Cl Rep Jr Cls; Hon Rl; Off Ade; Sch Nwsp; Fr Clb; OEA; Kent St Univ.

LEISING, CHARLENE; Connersville Sr HS; Connersville, IN; 100/400 Chrs; Chrh Wkr; Sch Mus; Sch Pl; Drama Clb; 4-H; FHA; Ger Clb; Mat Maids; 4-H Awd; Marian Coll; Nursing.

LEITCH, CARMEN; Churubusco HS; La Otto, IN; 8/125 Sec Sr Cls; Chrs; Chrh Wkr; Hon Rl; NHS; Sch Mus; Sch Pl; Yth Flsp; Drama Clb; 4-H; Coll; Music.

LEITCH, DAVID; Jackson Milton HS; N Jackson, OH; Trs Frsh Cls; Am Leg Boys St; Chrh Wkr; Hon Rl; Lbry Ade; NHS; Ftbl; Oh Talents For Christ Winner In Boys Publc Speaking 79; Coll; Minister.

LEITCH, MARY A; Central Noble HS; Albion, IN; 45/122 Chrs; Chrh Wkr; Mdrgl; Sch Mus; Sch Pl; Yth Flsp; Rptr Yrbk; Sec Drama Clb; Pep Clb; Gym; Reciefed A 2nd Rating At NISBOVA Contest; Intnl Order Of Rainbow For Girls Worth Assoc Advisor; International Busns Schl; Legal Sec.

LEITE, JOSEPH; Fremont Ross HS; Fremont, OH; Am Leg Boys St; Hon Rl; Rptr Sch Nwsp; Ftbl; Swmmng; Trk; Schlsp From The Vet Admin 79 80; 3 Yr Ltr Winner Track & Swimmng 77 79; Mount Union Coll; Acctg.

LEITENBERGER, JUDY; Hilliard HS; Hilliard, OH; 8/350 AFS; Am Leg Aux Girls St; Band; Hon Rl; Jr NHS; NHS; Off Ade; Orch; Yth Flsp; Spn Clb; Univ Of Cincinnati; Nursing.

LEITMAN, MINDY; Southfield HS; Southfield, MI; Chrs; Cmnty Wkr; Hon Rl; Quill & Scroll; Sch Mus; Sch Pl; Stg Crw; Rptr Yrbk; Drama Clb; MI All St Hnrs Chr 78; Schlrshp Bus & Pro Wmns Club 79; Schlrshp MI St Dept Of Ed 79; Univ; Music.

LEITOW, BRENDA; Kalkacka HS; Kalkaska, MI; 2/120 VP Sr Cls; Sal; NHS; Sch Pl; Stu Cncl; Sch Nwsp; 4-H; GAA; Scr Kpr; 4-H Awd; Michigan Tech Univ; Forestry.

LEKAN, CAROL; Cleveland Central Cath HS; Cleveland, OH; Chrh Wkr; Hon Rl; Mod UN; NHS; Quill & Scroll; Sch Mus; Sch Pl; Ed Yrbk; Sprt Ed Yrbk; Rptr Sch Nwsp; Case Western Reserve Univ; Sci.

LEKAS, CONSTANTINE; Pontiac Central HS; Pontiac, MI; Lit Mag; 3rd Pl Regnl Hon In Mi Indsut Educ Awd 79; Acad Hon Roll 77 &78 & 79; Genrl Motors Inst; Engr.

LEKAS, NICHOLAS; Clarkston HS; Clarkston, MI; Hon Rl; Bsbl; Bsktbl; Ftbl; Trk; Central Michigan; Business Admin.

LEKSAN, MARK; St Ignatius HS; Richmond Hgts, OH; 14/280 Chrh Wkr; Hon Rl; Yrbk; Sch Nwsp; Wrstlng; Univ Of Toledo; Pharmaccy.

LEKSON, JEFF; Eastlake North HS; Willowick, OH; 16/708 Band; Boy Scts; Hon Rl; Jr NHS; NHS; Letter Trk; Air Force ROTC; Comp Sci.

LELAND, AL; Lustre Christian HS; Chicago, IL; 2/12 VP Soph Cls; Pres Jr Cls; Sal; Band; Chrs; Hon Rl; Stu Cncl; Ed Sch Nwsp; Capt Bsktbl; Capt Crs Cntry; Univ; Math.

LELAND, JOHN; Loudonville HS; Loudonville, OH; Cl Rep Jr Cls; Hon Rl; Sch Pl; Stu Cncl; Rptr Sch Nwsp; Lat Clb; Spn Clb; Univ; Dr.

LEMA, MARLENE F; Garfield Sr HS; Hamilton, OH; 11/376 AFS; Hon Rl; Jr NHS; Lbry Ade; NHS; Off Ade; PAVAS; Sch Pl; Drama Clb; VP Fr Clb; College; Foreign Language.

LEMAL, MARY; Toronto HS; Toronto, OH; Sec Frsh Cls; Band; Drl Tm; Hon Rl; Sch Mus; Sch Pl; Pep Clb; Spn Clb; Trk; Pom Pon; Ohio State Univ; Doctor.

LEMAN, SUELEEN; West Central Jr Sr HS; Francesville, IN; 6/105 Cls Rep Frsh Cls; Band; Chrs; Chrh Wkr; Hon Rl; Jr NHS; NHS; Stu Cncl; FHA; Ger Clb; Coll; Radiologist.

LE MASTER, LAUREL; Wheelersburg HS; Wheelersburg, OH; Band; Chrh Wkr; Girl Scts; Hon Rl; H osp Ade; Off Ade; Sch Pl; Y-Teens; Twrlr; Miss River Days Candidate From Wheelersbury HS 79; Univ; Phys Ther.

LE MASTER, MIKE; Crestline HS; Crestline, OH; Boy Scts; Hon Rl; Yth Flsp; Glf;.

LE MASTER, PAUL; Ayersville HS; Defiance, OH; 5/85 Am Leg Boys St; Band; Hon Rl; NHS; Spn Clb; Ftbl; Ten; Natl Merit SF; Gnrl Mtrs Mark Of Excel Awd 78; 1st Pl Dist 18th Pl St In Oh Tests Of Schlstc Achvmnt & Chem 78; General Mtrs Inst; Inds Engr.

LE MASTER, TODD; Cedarville HS; Cedarvl, OH; Pres Frsh Cls; Pres Soph Cls; Pres Jr Cls; FCA; Ftbl; Trk; Communications.

LE MASTERS, DIANA; Wellsville HS; Wellsville, OH; Am Leg Aux Girls St; Hosp Ade; NHS; Y-Teens; Rptr Yrbk; FNA; Pep Clb; Ohio Vly Hosp Schl Of Nursing; Nurse.

LE MASTERS, MARTHA; Cameron HS; Cameron, WV; Chrs; College.

LE MASTERS, NOREEN J; Tyler County HS; Middlebourne, WV; 37/105 Band; Chrs; Hon Rl; Off Ade; Drama Clb; FTA; Pep Clb; Who Who In Music Awd; College; Nursing.

LE MAY, DIANE; William V Fisher Cath HS; Lancaster, OH; Am Leg Aux Girls St; Girl Scts; Hon Rl; NHS; Red Cr Ade; Sct Actv; Rptr Yrbk; Civ Clb; VP Fr Clb; VP FDA; Hugh O Brian Yth Leadrshp Canddt 78; Var F Mbr 76 79; Amer Lgn Jr Aux 75 79; Univ; Pediatrician.

LE MAY, MARLENE A; Grove City HS; Grove City, OH; Cmnty Wkr; Hon Rl; Jr NHS; Off Ade; OEA; IM Sprt; Perfect Attendance Awds; Clark Tech Coll; Stenographer.

LE MAY, RENEE; Westfall HS; Circleville, OH; 18/138 Am Leg Aux Girls St; Band; Sdlty; Yth Flsp; 4-H; Fr Clb; FFA; FTA; Sci Clb; Scr Kpr; French II Awrd 76; Grand Cross Of Color Rainbow Girls 76; Chptr Queen For Future Farmers Of Amer 78; Ohio St Univ; Spec Educ.

LEMCKE, BELINDA J; N Royalton HS; Cleveland, OH; 79/300 Cmnty Wkr; Girl Scts; Off Ade; Pol Wkr; Sch Pl; Stu Cncl; Sch Nwsp; Drama Clb; Lat Clb; Socr; Stewardess.

LE MIEUX, CATHERINE; Taylor HS; Cleves, OH; Trs Soph Cls; Pres Jr Cls; Pres Sr Cls; Chrh Wkr; Drl Tm; Hon Rl; Off Ade; Stu Cncl; Key Clb; Pep Clb; Boc Schl; Med Asst.

LE MIEUX, THERESA; Reeths Puffer HS; Muskegon, MI; 1/300 Val; Hon Rl; NHS; Pol Wkr; Yrbk; Spn Clb; PPFtbl; Natl Merit Ltr; Awd Of Hon In Foreign Lang 79; Muskegon Cmnty Coll.

LE MIRE, EDMUND; St Francis Cabrini HS; Allen Pk, MI; Hon Rl; NHS; Glf; IM Sprt; Univ; Math.

LE MIRE, GERARD; West Catholic HS; Grand Rapids, MI; Chrs; Hon Rl; Mdrgl; Bsbl; Socr; IM Sprt; College; Pharmacy.

LEMISH, MARY; St Philip Catholic Ctrl HS; Battle Crk, MI; Cl Rep Jr Cls; Hon Rl; Chrldng; Bus Schl; Med Sec.

LEMKE, LEE; Ridgedale Local HS; Marion, OH; 7/108 VP Frsh Cls; Pres Soph Cls; FCA; Hon Rl; Stg Crw; Yth Flsp; Bsktbl; Ohio Northern Univ; Acctg.

LEMKE, LYLA; Marion Adams HS; Sheridan, IN; 3/100 Band; Hon Rl; Jr NHS; Lbry Ade; NHS; Trk; Pres Pom Pon; Univ Of Oregon; Oceanography.

LEMKE, LYLA J; Marion Adams HS; Sheridan, IN; 3/99 Band; Hon Rl; Lbry Ade; NHS; Pom Pon; Oregon St Univ; Oceanography.

LEMKE, MICHAEL; Bishop Borgess HS; Redford, MI; Aud/Vis; Boy Scts; Chrh Wkr; Rdo Clb; Sci Clb; IM Sprt; Natl Merit Schl; MSU; Vet.

LEMLEY, PATRICIA; Benzie Central HS; Copemish, MI; Am Leg Aux Girls St; Chrs; Debate Tm; Sch Mus; Stg Crw; Rptr Yrbk; Yrbk; Rptr Sch Nwsp; Sch Nwsp; Michigan St Univ; Landscape Archt.

LEMLEY, ROBERT; Clay Battelle HS; Core, WV; FFA;.

LEMMEN, B; Holland Christian HS; Holland, MI; Chrh Wkr; Hon Rl; Ger Clb; Bsktbl; Letter Socr; Letter Trk; Calvin Coll.

LEMMER, JOHN; Father Gabriel Richard HS; Ann Arbor, MI; Pres Soph Cls; Trs Jr Cls; Am Leg Boys St; Hon Rl; NHS; Ftbl; Trk;.

LEMMERMANN, LOIS A; Charles F Brush HS; Lyndhurst, OH; 14/600 NHS; Stu Cncl; Pep Clb; PPFtbl; Natl Merit SF; College.

LEMMINK, JENNY; Mother Of Mercy HS; Cincinnati, OH; 6/237 Band; Girl Scts; Hon Rl; Hosp Ade; Treas NHS; Red Cr Ade; Lat Clb; Sci Clb; Univ Of Cincinnati; Nursing.

LEMMON, S; Heritage HS; Hoagland, IN; Band; Chrh Wkr; Cmnty Wkr; Hon Rl; JA; Sch Pl; Yth Flsp; Fr Clb; IM Sprt; Coll; Ministry.

LEMMON, STEPHANIE; Columbia City Joint HS; Columbia City, IN; 21/273 Cls Rep Frsh Cls; Cls Rep Soph Cls; Cl Rep Jr Cls; Cls Rep Sr Cls; FCA; NHS; Ed Yrbk; Pep Clb; Letter Ten; Cit Awd; Univ; Phys Ther.

LEMNA, BRIAN; South Newton Jr Sr HS; Kentland, IN; 1/110 Am Leg Boys St; Band; Chrh Wkr; Hon Rl; NHS; Sch Mus; Sch Pl; FTA; Lat Clb; Sci Clb; Hi Y Clb; Health Careers Clb; Edward Rector Schlrshp Nom; Notre Dame Univ; Writing.

LEMNA, JILL; Northrop HS; Ft Wayne, IN; Cl Rep Jr Cls; Drl Tm; Hon Rl; Off Ade; Stu Cncl; Rptr Yrbk; Rptr Sch Nwsp; Gym; Chrldng; Pom Pon; Univ; Dent Hygnst.

LE MON, ANITA; Spencer HS; Spencer, WV; Band; Girl Scts; Sch Pl; Yth Flsp; Drama Clb; Pep Clb; Letter Chrldng; IM Sprt; Order Of Rainbow For Girls 1976; Frsh Homecomg Princess 1976; Mt Vernon Nazarene Coll; Sec Sci.

LE MON, BRYANT; Washington HS; Massillon, OH; Chrs; Chrh Wkr; Cmnty Wkr; Hon Rl; Off Ade; Sch Mus; Stg Crw; Boys Clb Am; Spn Clb; Ftbl; Univ; Psych.

LE MON, DAVID; Taylor Center HS; Taylor, MI; VP Soph Cls; Band; Hon Rl; Jr NHS; NHS; Orch; Yth Flsp; Mgrs; Oral Roberts Univ; Psych.

LE MON, JOANN; Eastern HS; Beaver, OH; 1/65 Pres Frsh Cls; Pres Soph Cls; VP Jr Cls; Pres Sr Cls; Band; Chrs; Chrh Wkr; Drl Tm; Hon Rl; MMM; Goshen Coll; Nursing.

LE MON, LEIGH; Maysville HS; S Zanesville, OH; Hon Rl; NHS; Stu Cncl; Rptr Yrbk; Chrldng; Univ; Elem Educ.

LE MON, SUSAN; Ravenna HS; Ravenna, OH; 37/313 Cls Rep Sr Cls; Pres AFS; Am Leg Aux Girls St; Band; Chrh Wkr; Drm Mjrt; Girl Scts; NHS; Quill & Scroll; Sec Stu Cncl; Kent St Univ; Spec Educ.

LE MON, TARA; Cass Technical HS; Detroit, MI; Chrs; Univ; Interior Decor.

LE MON, THOMAS R; St Johns HS; Toledo, OH; 3/270 Chrh Wkr; Cmnty Wkr; Hon Rl; PAVAS; Pol Wkr; Sch Pl; Drama Clb; Ger Clb; Crs Cntry; Trk; Univ; Acctg.

LEMORIE, STEVEN; Cheboygan Area HS; Cheboygan, MI; Hon Rl; Ftbl; Trk; Divine Instit Of Tech; Commer Diving.

LEMUT, MARIE; Holyname Nazareth HS; Seven Hills, OH; Cl Rep Jr Cls; Chrs; Cmnty Wkr; Hon Rl; Hosp Ade; NHS; Sch Pl; Drama Clb; IM Sprt; College; Nursing.

LEN, DAVID; St Andrew HS; Detroit, MI; 12/99 Hon Rl; NHS; Stg Crw; Rptr Yrbk; Yrbk; Letter Trk; College; Archt.

LEN, DOUGLAS; Ovid Elsie HS; Ovid, MI; 55/170 Chrh Wkr; Hon Rl; NHS; Pep Clb; Bsktbl; Ftbl; Natl Merit SF; St Schlshp Awd 79; Lansing Cmnty Coll; Law.

LENARD, JOSEPH; Cabrini HS; Allen Pk, MI; Hon Rl; IM Sprt; Scr Kpr; Tmr; Natl Merit Ltr; Mic State Univ; Bus.

LENART, MARK; Solon HS; Solon, OH; 84/288 Pres Frsh Cls; Pres Soph Cls; Pres Jr Cls; Pres Sr Cls; FCA; NHS; Key Clb; Bsbl; Ftbl; IM Sprt; Univ; Communicatons.

LENDER, JOYCE; North HS; Willowick, OH; 33/669 Chrh Wkr; Hon Rl; JA; Jr NHS; NHS; Off Ade; Yth Flsp; Rptr Yrbk; Rptr Sch Nwsp; Sch Nwsp; Bowling Green St Univ; Med Tech.

LENDRUM, J ERIC; Norwalk HS; Norwalk, OH; Band; Hon Rl; Letter Bsbl; Letter Ftbl; College; Oceanography.

LENDVAY, JOHN; West Geauga HS; Novelty, OH; Cls Rep Soph Cls; Band; Hon Rl; Lbry Ade; NHS; Orch; Red Cr Ade; Stu Cncl; IM Sprt; Cit Awd; Sci Lab Asst 77 & 78; Voter Infrmtn Dir For W Geauga Sd 78; Hiram Coll; Chem.

LENEGAR, CHRIS; Vinton Cnty Consolidated HS; Mc Arthur, OH; Aud/Vis; FCA; Hon Rl; Jr NHS; Lbry Ade; NHS; Spn Clb; Letter Ten; Univ.

LENGERLIOGLU, G; Bluefield HS; Bluefield, WV; Chrs; Hon Rl; Fr Clb; College; Commercial Designer.

LENGERLIOGLU, GULFERI; Bluefield HS; Bluefield, WV; Hon Rl; Fr Clb; W Virginia Univ; Music.

LENHART, BEVERLY; Spencerville HS; Spencerville, OH; 3/99 Hon Rl; NHS; Stg Crw; Bsktbl; Coach Actv; GAA; IM Sprt; Bowling Green; Phys Educ.

LENHART, GARY; Winfield HS; Scott Depot, WV; Aud/Vis; JA; Fr Clb; JA Awd; West Virginia Univ; Poli Sci.

LENHART, JENNIFER; Defiance Sr HS; Defiance, OH; 12/281 Sec Chrs; Debate Tm; Capt Drl Tm; Jr NHS; Mdrgl; NHS; Off Ade; Sch Mus; Sch Pl; Stg Crw; Vassar Coll; Econ.

LENHART, SHELIA; Arcadia Local HS; Fostoria, OH; 8/64 Band; Hon Rl; NHS; Yrbk; 4-H; Letter Trk; 4-H Awd; College; Busns.

LENHART, VIRGINIA N; Detiance Sr HS; Defiance, OH; Band; Chrs; Chrh Wkr; Jr NHS; NHS; Sch Mus; Stu Cncl; Yth Flsp; Rptr Yrbk; Mth Clb; Defiance Coll; Mkrtg.

LENIO, JAMES; Heath HS; Heath, OH; 4/150 VP Jr Cls; FCA; NHS; Pres Fr Clb; Key Clb; JA Awd; Rotary Awd; Ohio State Univ; Aeronautical Engr.

LENK, ANITA; Deer Park HS; Cincinnati, OH; Chrs; Hon Rl; NHS; Sch Mus; Sch Pl; Stg Crw; Rptr Sch Nwsp; Drama Clb; College; Math.

LENK, DANIEL; Edgewood Sr HS; Ashtabula, OH; Chrs; NHS; PAVAS; Sch Mus; Sch Pl; Stg Crw; Drama Clb; Cit Awd; Porthse Actng Apprent Progr Schlrshp Kent St U 79; Kent St Univ; Theatre Arts.

LENNARTZ, SANDY; Memorial HS; St Marys, OH; Band; Chrh Wkr; Drm Mjrt; Hon Rl; Y-Teens; 4-H; Bsktbl; Letter Gym; Letter Trk; Letter GAA; Lima Tech Schl; Sec.

LENNON, LISA; Msgr Hackett HS; Kalamazoo, MI; 2/133 Sec Sr Cls; Trs Sr Cls; Hon Rl; Sec NHS; Stu Cncl; IM Sprt; PPFtbl; Univ; Med.

LENNON, SEAN; Newark Sr HS; Newark, OH; 2/700 Am Leg Boys St; Hon Rl; NHS; Sci Clb; Coll; History.

LENSING, PAMELA; Harrison HS; Evansville, IN; Cls Rep Soph Cls; Cl Rep Jr Cls; Am Leg Aux Girls St; Chrh Wkr; Hon Rl; Stu Cncl; Cit Awd; Univ; Dr Of Pathology.

LENSS, VIESTURS; Henry Ford HS; Detroit, MI; Boy Scts; Chrh Wkr; Hon Rl; Mod UN; Sct Actv; Natl Merit Schl; Univ Of Michigan; Aero Engr.

LENTS, BRETT; Grtr Jasper Consolidated HS; Jasper, IN; 59/289 Am Leg Boys St; FCA; Hon Rl; Capt Bsktbl; Letter Crs Cntry; Ftbl; Letter Trk; Coach Actv; Univ; Acctg.

LENTS, DANA; Loogootee HS; Loogootee, IN; 7/117 Cl Rep Jr Cls; Band; Hon Rl; Stu Cncl; Ed Yrbk; Drama Clb; Pep Clb; Spn Clb; DAR Awd; 4-H Awd; Indiana Univ; Counseling.

LENTS, DEBBIE; Marysville HS; Marysville, MI; 3/190 Cls Rep Soph Cls; Sec Jr Cls; Am Leg Aux Girls St; Hon Rl; NHS; Quill & Scroll; Stu Cncl; Ed Yrbk; Letter Ten; Cit Awd; St Clair County Cmnty Coll; Med.

LENTZ, ANGELA; Danville Comm HS; Danville, IN; Sec Band; Drl Tm; FCA; Hosp Ade; NHS; Sch Mus; Pep Clb; Spn Clb; IUPUI; Phys Ther.

LENTZ, CHERYL; Lake Catholic HS; Euclid, OH; Chrs; Chrh Wkr; Hon Rl; Treas JA; Yth Flsp; Pep Clb; JA Awd; Outsdng Achvmnt In French I Awd 76; Univ; Acctg.

LENTZ, CHERYL; Sandusky HS; Sandusky, OH; Band; Girl Scts; Hon Rl; Orch; Sch Mus; Sch Pl; Ger Clb; IM Sprt;.

LENTZ, MARJORIE; Avon HS; Indianapolis, IN; Chrh Wkr; Hon Rl; Spn Clb; Letter Gym; Letter Trk; Indiana St Univ; Phys Ed.

LENTZ, SANDRA; Sheridan HS; Somerset, OH; 12/179 Am Leg Aux Girls St; Chrs; FCA; Hon Rl; NHS; Sch Mus; Bsktbl; IM Sprt; Mgrs; Cntrl Ohio Tech Coll; Radio Tech.

LENTZ, SANDRA J; Sheridan HS; Somerset, OH; Am Leg Aux Girls St; Chrs; FCA; Hon Rl; NHS; Sch Pl; Bsktbl; IM Sprt; Mgrs; Central Ohio Tech Coll; X Ray Tech.

LENY, MARK; Escanaba Area HS; Wells, MI; 86/450 Am Leg Boys St; Band; NHS; Central Mich; Infor Systems.

LENZER, HERBERT; Moeller HS; Blue Ash, OH; Hon Rl; MMM; Univ Of Cincinnati; Home Desgn.

LEO, CHERYL; Chaminade Julienne HS; Dayton, OH; 54/250 Band; Chrs; Drl Tm; Hon Rl; Trk; Wright St Univ; Acctg.

LEO, JAMES; St Clement HS; Warren, MI; Boy Scts; Stg Crw; Letter Bsbl; Letter Bsktbl; IM Sprt; Grand Valley; Physical Educ.

LEO, JANIE; Highland HS; Marengo, OH; 1/120 Trs Jr Cls; Trs Sr Cls; Am Leg Aux Girls St; Chrs; FCA; NHS; Sch Mus; Yth Flsp; Letter Bsktbl; Letter Trk; Ohio Univ; Phys Therapy.

LEO, LAURIE; Chippewa Valley HS; Mt Clemens, MI; Chrs; Girl Scts; Hon Rl; Hosp Ade; Sch Mus; Stg Crw; FHA; IM Sprt; Okland Univ; Nursing.

LEON, KELLY A; Seton HS; Cincinnati, OH; 87/271 Cls Rep Frsh Cls; Pres Soph Cls; Cl Rep Jr Cls; Sec Sr Cls; Chrs; Hon Rl; Lbry Ade; Orch; Pol Wkr; Stu Cncl; Univ; Communctns.

LEONARD, CHRISTINE; Lorain Catholic HS; Amherst, OH; Chrs; Chrh Wkr; Hon Rl; NHS; Spn Clb; Bsktbl; GAA; Achiev Awd 3rd Yr Span 78; Univ; Elem Educ.

LEONARD, CYNTHIA; R B Chamberlin HS; Twinsburg, OH; 9/180 Trs Soph Cls; Hon Rl; NHS; Stg Crw; Drama Clb; Pep Clb; GAA; Kent State Univ; Bus.

LEONARD, DARLA; St Louis HS; St Louis, MI; 2/127 Sal; Chrs; NHS; Off Ade; Treas Pom Pon; Natl Merit SF; Univ Of Michigan; Psych.

LEONARD, DIANE; Newton HS; Laura, OH; 7/55 Trs Sr Cls; Band; Hon Rl; NHS; Off Ade; Drama Clb; Univ; Bus.

LEONARD, JAMES; Norton HS; Norton, OH; 57/312 Band; Hon Rl; Orch; Rptr Yrbk; IM Sprt; Akron Univ; Bus Admin.

LEONARD, JAMES A; Trotwood Madison HS; Laura, OH; 2/493 Band; Boy Scts; Hon Rl; Jr NHS; NHS; Orch; Sct Actv; Natl Merit Ltr; Natl Merit SF; Opt Clb Awd; Ohio St Univ; Engr.

LEONARD, KAREN; Bishop Gallagher HS; Detroit, MI; 116/333 Cls Rep Soph Cls; Cl Rep Jr Cls; Treas Girl Scts; Hon Rl; Sct Actv; Stu Cncl; Rptr Yrbk; PPFtbl; Univ Of Michigan; Engr.

LEONARD, KAREN T; Union Sr HS; Grand Rapids, MI; 14/365 Cmp Fr Grls; Chrs; Capt Cmnty Wkr; Hon Rl; VP JA; Lit Mag; NHS; Pol Wkr; Pres Quill & Scroll; Stg Crw; Central Mich Univ; Broadcasting.

LEONARD, KATHRYN; Niles Mc Kinley Sr HS; Niles, OH; Chrs; Debate Tm; Hon Rl; NHS; Off Ade; Rptr Yrbk; Drama Clb; Letter Chrldng; PPFtbl; College.

LEONARD, KATHY; Worthington HS; Worthington, OH; Chrh Wkr; Stg Crw; Stu Cncl; DECA; IM Sprt; Intl Thespai Soc Troupe 1851 1978; Worthington PTA Schlshp 1979; DECA Dist Parliamntarn 4th Rnnr Up 1978; Bowling Green St Univ; Fashion Mdse.

LEONARD, LORI; R Nelson Snider HS; Ft Wayne, IN; 27/564 Cls Rep Frsh Cls; Band; Chrs; Chrh Wkr; Girl Scts; Hon Rl; Orch; Sch Mus; Sct Actv; Stu Cncl; Univ.

LEONARD, PATRICIA; Port Huron Northern HS; Port Huron, MI; 15/408 Chrh Wkr; Drl Tm; Girl Scts; Hon Rl; NHS; Letter Pom Pon; Mi Comp Schlrshp 79; Mbr Of Mardi Gras Queens Crt Jr & Sr Jr 77 79; Michigan St Univ; Animal Phys.

LEONARD, STEPHEN; Morgantown HS; Morgntwn, WV; Aud/Vis; Boy Scts; Chrs; Debate Tm; Lbry Ade; Sch Mus; Sct Actv; Sec Ger Clb; Sci Clb; IM Sprt; 3 In 1 Awd Boy Scouts 75; Order Of Arrow 76; West Virginia Univ; Mining Engr.

LEONARD, STEPHEN M; Wyoming HS; Wyoming, OH; 28/212 Pres Sr Cls; Am Leg Boys St; Band; Hon Rl; NHS; Sprt Ed Sch Nwsp; Rptr Sch Nwsp; Sch Nwsp; Letter Bsktbl; Letter Ftbl; College.

LEONARD, TIMOTHY; Greenfield Cntrl HS; Greenfield, IN; Chrs; Debate Tm; Mdrgl; Natl Forn Lg; PAVAS; Pol Wkr; Drama Clb; Leo Clb; Spn Clb; Opt Clb Awd; Coll; Drama.

LEONARD, TODD; Shelbyville Sr HS; Shelbyville, IN; Boy Scts; Chrh Wkr; Hon Rl; JA; Yrbk; Sch Nwsp; Sci Clb; Spn Clb; Ten; Mas Awd; Youth For Understanding/lilly Foundation Schlr; Master Councilor Intl Order Of De Molay; Hnr Carrier Of Yr; Purdue Univ; Foreign Languages.

LEONBERGER, M; E A Johnson Memorial HS; Clio, MI; Cls Rep Frsh Cls; Hon Rl; Hosp Ade; Quill & Scroll; Sch Mus; Sch Pl; Stg Crw; College; Drama.

LEONE, MICHAEL; Madison HS; N Madison, OH; 19/325 Hon Rl; NHS; Key Clb; Letter Trk; Natl Hnr Soc 79; Univ; Systems Analyst.

LEONHARD, LAURA; Indian Valley South HS; Port Washington, OH; 5/95 Sec Frsh Cls; Cls Rep Soph Cls; Band; Hon Rl; Jr NHS; NHS; Ed Yrbk; OEA;.

LEONHARDT, CHARLES W; Sault Area Public HS; Sault Ste Mari, MI; 1/280 VP Jr Cls; Pres Sr Cls; NHS; IM Sprt; Rotary Awd; Lake Superior State Coll; Acctg.

LEONHARDT, MARY; Shelby Sr HS; Shelby, OH; 1/280 Cl Rep Jr Cls; Val; Hon Rl; Stg Crw; Drama Clb; Lat Clb; Letter Ten; Attended Operation Yth In Cincinnati Summer Of 79; Ohio St Coll; Acctg.

LE PAGE, MICHELE; Bishop Foley HS; Rochester, MI; Girl Scts; Hon Rl; PPFtbl; Univ; Bus Mgmt.

LE PAGE, REBECCA; John Glenn HS; New Concord, OH; 4/193 Chrs; FCA; Hon Rl; NHS; VP Yth Flsp; Lat Clb; Letter Crs Cntry; Letter Trk; Univ.

LE PAGE, TODD; Hoover HS; North Canton, OH; 8/422 Pres Jr Cls; Cl Rep Jr Cls; Cls Rep Sr Cls; Treas FCA; Hon Rl; VP NHS; VP Stu Cncl; Treas Yth Flsp; College; Med.

LE PARD, CATHERINE; Grand Blanc HS; Grand Blanc, MI; 83/690 Hon Rl; NHS; Letter Bsktbl; Natl Merit Schl; Captain 2 Letters Varsity Sftbl Tm; Varsity Vlybl Letter Earned; Induction Into Whos Who In Poetry; Kalamazoo Coll; Lib Arts.

LEPINE, CECILIA; Marysville HS; Smiths Creek, MI; 82/179 Chrs; Hon Rl; Lbry Ade; Macomb Cnty Cmnty Coll; Dent Asst.

LEPP, MARGARET; Andrean HS; Hobart, IN; Chrh Wkr; Hon Rl; NHS; Rptr Yrbk; Pres Mth Clb; Sci Clb; Natl Merit Ltr; Purdue Univ; Law.

LEPPER, DAVID; Fremont Ross HS; Fremont, OH; Hon Rl; Sci Clb; Ohio State Univ; Engineering.

LERCH, MELODY A; Oregon Davis HS; Grovertown, IN; 1/60 Band; Chrh Wkr; Drl Tm; Hon Rl; Lbry Ade; Yrbk; Sch Nwsp; 4-H; Pep Clb; Mgrs; Michiana Coll Of Commerce; Sec.

LE ROUX, EVETTE; Maumee HS; Maumee, OH; Cls Rep Frsh Cls; Cls Rep Soph Cls; Pres Jr Cls; Debate Tm; Hon Rl; Natl Forn Lg; NHS; Stu Cncl; Y-Teens; Fr Clb; Cornell Univ; Hotel Admin.

LE ROY, DENNIS; Roosevelt Wilson HS; Stonewood, WV; Chrh Wkr; Hon Rl; Leo Clb; VICA; Letter Ftbl; Glf; Mgrs; 4-H Awd; Fairmont St Coll; Busns.

LE ROY, JAMES; Rocky River HS; Rocky River, OH; Boy Scts; Chrh Wkr; Hon Rl; Sct Actv; Yth Flsp; Letter Trk; Mgrs; Tmr; College; Art.

LERUTH, MICHAEL; St Francis De Sales HS; Toledo, OH; 7/200 Capt Debate Tm; Hon Rl; VP Natl Forn Lg; NHS; Pol Wkr; Stu Cncl; IM Sprt; Voice Dem Awd; College; Poli Sci.

LESAUSKI, CARMEN; Concordia Lutheran HS; Ft Wayne, IN; Hon Rl; FBLA; Ger Clb; Letter Trk; Univ.

LESCHUK, TINA; High School; Brown City, MI; Band; Chrs; Hon Rl; NHS; Sch Mus; FHA; FTA; Pep Clb; Michigan Tech; Engineering.

LESHOCK, VICI; Wadsworth HS; Wadsworth, OH; 45/368 Hosp Ade; NHS; Off Ade; Fr Clb; Pep Clb; Chrldng; IM Sprt; Univ Of N Alabama; Nursing.

LESHOK, DAVID; St Alphonsus HS; Detroit, MI; 63/177 Cls Rep Soph Cls; Hon Rl; Off Ade; Sprt Ed Yrbk; Bsbl; Capt Bsktbl; Trk; Scr Kpr; Natl Merit Ltr; Henry Ford Cmnty Coll.

LESIUK, MARK; Washington HS; South Bend, IN; 124/355 Hon Rl; Letter Bsbl; Letter Ftbl; Coll; Engr.

LESKELA, JENNIE; Ewen Trout Creek HS; Bruce Crossing, MI; 2/50 Pres Frsh Cls; Cls Rep Soph Cls; Cl Rep Jr Cls; Sal; Band; Hon Rl; Off Ade; Stu Cncl; Rptr Yrbk; Northern Mic Univ; Soc Work.

LESKO, JOHN; Seecina Memorial HS; Indianapolis, IN; 67/194 Hon Rl; Mgrs; Indiana Univ; Soc Work.

LESKO, MARIA; South Dearborn HS; Aurora, IN; Chrs; Stu Cncl; Sch Nwsp; Pres Drama Clb; Pep Clb; Ftbl; Trk; IM Sprt; PPFtbl; Franklin Univ; Phys Ther.

LESKUSKI, DONA; Buckhannon Upshur HS; Buckhannon, WV; 25/300 Trs Frsh Cls; Cls Rep Sr Cls; Band; Chrh Wkr; Cmnty Wkr; Hon Rl; NHS; Orch; Sch Mus; Sch Pl; 450 In Shclsp For The Univ Of Mimai Band 79; Univ Of Miami; Marine Sci.

LESLEY, LISA; Manistee HS; Manistee, MI; Hon Rl; Off Ade; Letter Bsktbl; Letter Trk; Chrldng; GAA; IM Sprt; Michigan St Univ; Soc Work.

LESLIE, ANDREW; Rutherford B Hayes HS; Delaware, OH; AFS; Chrs; Debate Tm; Hon Rl; Jr NHS; Natl Forn Lg; NHS; Orch; Sch Mus; Sch Pl; Univ; Pre Med.

LESLIE, CARMEN; Saranac HS; Saranac, MI; Band; Hon Rl; NHS; Sch Mus; Pres FBLA; Bsktbl; PPFtbl; Dnfth Awd; Lansing Business Inst; Data Processi.

LESLIE, CAROL; Charles F Brush HS; Lyndhurst, OH; Cls Rep Frsh Cls; Cls Rep Soph Cls; Cl Rep Jr Cls; Chrs; Girl Scts; Hon Rl; Stu Cncl; Letter Bsbl; Letter Swmmng; Letter Ten; Completed 2nd Yr Of Cnslr Training & Recd Highest Hon In Swimming Sailing & Canoeing At Private Girls Camp; Coll; Bus.

LESLIE, DOROTHY; Solon HS; Solon, OH; Cl Rep Jr Cls; Cls Rep Sr Cls; AFS; Chrs; Hon Rl; MMM; NHS; PAVAS; Pol Wkr; Sch Mus; Thespian 1976; Univ; Music.

LESLIE, LISA; Kenton Ridge HS; Springfield, OH; Chrs; Chrh Wkr; Cmnty Wkr; Girl Scts; Hon Rl; Hosp Ade; Sch Pl; Sct Actv; Yrbk; Drama Clb; Spanish Honor Soc 77 78; Varsity K 78; Miami Univ; Eng.

LESLIE, PAUL; Brighton HS; Brighton, MI; Boy Scts; Chrs; Hon Rl; Sch Mus; Sch Pl; Sct Actv; Stu Cncl; Rptr Sch Nwsp; FBLA; Pep Clb; Univ; Bus Admin.

LESLIE, TERRY; Edwardsburg HS; Niles, MI; Boy Scts; Hon Rl; Sct Actv; 4-H; Crs Cntry; Trk; Wrstlng; Eagle Scout; College; Medicine.

LESNESKI, TIMOTHY; Hale HS; Hale, MI; Band; Hon Rl; NHS; Sch Pl; Letter Bsbl; Capt Bsktbl; Capt Ftbl; Capt Trk; Mgrs; Ferris St Coll; Pharm.

LESNIAK, ANDREA; North Newton HS; De Motte, IN; 6/142 VP Frsh Cls; VP Soph Cls; Trs Sr Cls; Hon Rl; NHS; Off Ade; Yrbk; FBLA; Lat Clb; Ball State Univ.

LESNIAK, MICHELLE; All Saints Central HS; Bay City, MI; Trs Frsh Cls; Hon Rl; Lbry Ade; Lit Mag; Rptr Sch Nwsp; Sch Nwsp; IM Sprt; Adrian College; Interior Design.

LESNOSKI, TOM; Warren Western Reserve HS; Warren, OH; 41/462 Hon Rl; NHS; Swmmng; Ohi Univ; Bus Admin.

LESSER, ROBIN; Wadsworth HS; Wadsworth, OH; 48/367 Chrh Wkr; NHS; Stu Cncl; Pep Clb; Spn Clb; Ten; Chrldng; IM Sprt; Brigham Young Univ; Bus Mgmt.

LESTER, CHARLA; Lewis County HS; Weston, WV; Am Leg Aux Girls St; Hon Rl; Jr NHS; Lbry Ade; NHS; Delegate To IOOF UN Pilgrimage For Yth; Rainbow Girls; Theta Rho Girls; Fairmont St Coll; Respiratory Ther.

LESTER, CYNTHIA; North HS; Columbus, OH; 17/325 Hon Rl; NHS; Off Ade; OEA; Mat Maids; Office Work.

LESTER, DAVID; Chesapeake HS; Chesapeake, OH; Cl Rep Jr Cls; Cls Rep Sr Cls; Am Leg Boys St; Hon Rl; NHS; Stu Cncl; College.

LESTER, JAYNE; Marquette Sr HS; Marquette, MI; Am Leg Aux Girls St; Hon Rl; Sch Pl; Drama Clb; Ger Clb; Spn Clb; Am Leg Awd; 4-H Awd; FHA; Special Ed Aid; Northern Michigan Univ; Special Ed.

LESTER, MICHAEL P; Hurricane HS; Hurricane, WV; 26/182 Hon Rl; NHS; Quill & Scroll; Rptr Yrbk; Rptr Sch Nwsp; Glf; IM Sprt; West Virginia Tech Univ; Civil Engr.

LESTER, REBECCA; Sullivan HS; Sullivan, IN; 7/150 Band; Chrs; Chrh Wkr; Drl Tm; Hon Rl; Lbry Ade; NHS; Sch Mus; Yth Flsp; Beta Clb; Indiana St Univ Schlrhsp 79; Indiana St Univ.

LESTER, VANESSA; Shenandoah HS; Pleasant City, OH; 3/87 Sec Frsh Cls; Sec Jr Cls; Chrh Wkr; Hon Rl; Off Ade; Sch Pl; Y-Teens; Rptr Yrbk; Rptr Sch Nwsp; Beta Clb; Eng I & II Awd 77 & 78; Earth Sci Awd 77; Bowling Green St Univ; Pre Law.

LESTI, CHRISTINE; Stow HS; Stow, OH; 15/535 Band; Chrs; Hon Rl; Sec NHS; Off Ade; Stu Cncl; Rptr Sch Nwsp; Ger Clb; Sec Lat Clb; Mth Clb; Outstanding Squad Ldr Marching Band; Rec Superior Rating At Ohio Music Ed Assn; 1st Pl Costume Contest; Coll; Busns.

LETCAVITS, JOI; Washington HS; Massillon, OH; Cls Rep Frsh Cls; Cls Rep Soph Cls; Cl Rep Jr Cls; Cls Rep Sr Cls; Chrs; Girl Scts; Hon Rl; Jr NHS; NHS; Sch Mus; Timken Mercy Hosp; X Ray Tech.

LETCHER, LAURA; Fowlerville HS; Fowlerville, MI; Sec Jr Cls; Sec Sr Cls; Cmnty Wkr; Hon Rl; Lbry Ade; Off Ade; Sch Pl; Stu Cncl; Letter Chrldng; IM Sprt; Lib Essay Awd 75; Univ; R N.

LETIZIA, DONALD; Bishop Dwenger HS; Ft Wayne, IN; Cls Rep Frsh Cls; Boy Scts; Chrs; Hon Rl; JA; Off Ade; Stu Cncl; FDA; Key Clb; Pep Clb; Notre Dame Univ; Medicine.

LETIZIA, LORI A; Garrett HS; Garrett, IN; 20/144 Am Leg Aux Girls St; Cmp Fr Grls; Chrs; Girl Scts; Hon Rl; Sch Mus; Sch Pl; Sct Actv; Y-Teens; 4-H; College; Elem Ed.

LETTAU, MOLLY; Wylie E Groves HS; Birmingham, MI; Michigan St Univ; Fshn Mdse.

LETTENEY, NEAL; Martinsville HS; Martinsville, IN; 110/400 Band; Chrs; Mdrgl; Sch Mus; Yth Flsp; IM Sprt; Kiwan Awd; Butler Univ; Music Performance.

LETWIN, SHAWN; Lake Orion HS; Lake Orion, MI; 31/336 Cls Rep Soph Cls; Cl Rep Jr Cls; Am Leg Boys St; Hon Rl; NHS; Opt Clb Awd; Outstndng Chem Awd 79; Sci Stdnt Awd 79; Eastern Michigan Univ; Chem.

LEUNG, ANNIE; Whitehall Yearling HS; Whitehall, OH; Hon Rl; NHS; Ohi State Univ; Acctg.

LEUTERITZ, ROBERT; Arlington HS; Indianapolis, IN; 18/435 Cls Rep Sr Cls; Hon Rl; NHS; Stu Cncl; Letter Ftbl; Letter Trk;.

LEUTY, STEVE; Benton Harbor HS; Benton Hbr, MI; Cls Rep Soph Cls; Band; Chrs; Hon Rl; Jr NHS; NHS; Sch Mus; Fr Clb; Key Clb; IM Sprt; Univ; Psych.

LEVACY, BETH; William V Fisher Cath HS; Lancaster, OH; Chrs; Chrh Wkr; Hon Rl; Pol Wkr; Ohio Univ; Art Tchr.

LE VALLY, BRIAN; Ridgemont HS; Ridgeway, OH; Boy Scts; Chrh Wkr; VICA; Letter Bsbl; Bsktbl; Ftbl; Ten; Trk; Scr Kpr; Tmr; Northwestern Bus Schl.

LEVEILLE, RENE; Engadine HS; Gould City, MI; Sec Soph Cls; Sec Sr Cls; Hon Rl; Sch Pl; Sch Nwsp; Muskegon Bus School; Sec Work.

LEVELLE, RANDY; Clay Battelle HS; Core, WV; NHS; Sch Pl; Drama Clb; 4-H; Letter Bsbl; Letter Ftbl; 4-H Awd; I Was Awd A 5 Day Trip To Our Capital In Charleston 79; West Virginia Univ; Bus Admin.

LEVELY, MELISSA E; Beaverton HS; Beaverton, MI; ł/130 Chrh Wkr; Hon Rl; Jr NHS; VP NHS; Ed Yrbk; Rptr Yrbk; Pres Spn Clb; Mich St Univ Awd Academ Excllnc 1979; Stu Foundtn Cntrl Mich Univ 1978; Michigan St Univ.

LEVENDIS, CALIOPE; Campbell Mem HS; Campbell, OH; Cl Rep Jr Cls; Am Leg Boys St; Hon Rl; Hosp Ade; NHS; VP Drama Clb; Mth Clb; Sec Spn Clb; Trk; Pres Awd; Youngstown St Univ; Med.

LEVERANZ, LINDA; James Ford Rhodes HS; Cleveland, OH; 3/359 Cls Rep Frsh Cls; Am Leg Aux Girls St; Boy Scts; Hon Rl; Jr NHS; NHS; Off Ade; Orch; Fr Clb; FDA; Christian Schmidt Carl E Von Czoernig 600.

LEVERETT, REGINA; East HS; Cleveland, OH; 5/227 Drl Tm; Girl Scts; Hon Rl; JA; Jr NHS; NHS; Cit Awd; 2 Martha Holden Jennings Schlship 77; Cleveland Schlrshp 79; East High Alumni Schlrshp 79; Ohio Univ; Comp Engr.

LEVERONI, CHARLES; Western Reserve Academy; Hudson, OH; 6/90 Hon Rl; Stu Cncl; Ed Yrbk; Rptr Yrbk; Rptr Sch Nwsp; Lat Clb; Capt Bsbl; Glf; Hndbl; Letter Socr; Brown Univ; Bus.

LEVI, ANTHONY; Anderson HS; Anderson, IN; 69/391 Pres Frsh Cls; Cls Rep Frsh Cls; Pres Soph Cls; Cls Rep Soph Cls; Cl Rep Jr Cls; Cls Rep Sr Cls; Hon Rl; Lbry Ade; Off Ade; Stu Cncl; Univ; Engr.

LEVIHN, DIANE; Yorktown HS; Muncie, IN; 6/180 Am Leg Aux Girls St; Chrh Wkr; Cmnty Wkr; Hon Rl; Hosp Ade; NHS; FBLA; Ger Clb; Pep Clb; Indiana Univ; Occup Ther.

LEVIN, MICHELLE P; Donald E Gavit Jr Sr HS; Hammond, IN; VP Soph Cls; Hon Rl; Stu Cncl; Pep Clb; Chrldng; GAA; Mat Maids; PPFtbl; Scr Kpr; Tmr; Football Homecoming Court; Basketball Homecoming Court; Purdue Univ; Stewardess.

LE VINE, ELLIOT; Eastmoor HS; Columbus, OH; 5/290 Cls Rep Sr Cls; Hon Rl; Jr NHS; NHS; Stu Cncl; Sprt Ed Sch Nwsp; Coach Actv; Ohio St Univ; Chem Engr.

LE VINE, ROBERT; Jackson HS; Jackson, MI; 35/322 Sch Pl; Rptr Yrbk; Lat Clb; Capt Glf; Ferris State Coll; Optometry.

LEVINER, DONNA; Calumet HS; Gary, IN; JA; Quill & Scroll; Yrbk; FSA; Lat Clb; Sci Clb; PPFtbl; Coll; Vet.

LEVINGS, AMY; Cardington Lincoln HS; Cardington, OH; Drl Tm; Fr Clb; Sci Clb; Cumberland Coll; Nursing.

LEVINSOHN, JANE; Pike HS; Indpls, IN; Band; Cmnty Wkr; Girl Scts; Hon Rl; Jr NHS; Orch; Sch Pl; Sct Actv; Stu Cncl; College; Educ.

LEVINSON, RALPH; Linsly Inst; Steubenville, OH; Chrs; Hon Rl; ROTC; Sch Mus; Sch Pl; Eng Clb; Fr Clb; Pres Key Clb; Sci Clb; Bsktbl; 2nd Pl In Wv St Key Clb Oratory Contest 79; Ohio St Univ; Pre Med.

LEVO, DIANE M; Ursuline Academy; Cincinnati, OH; 1/140 Hon Rl; NHS; Sch Pl; Drama Clb; Natl Merit Ltr; Natl Merit SF; Univ; Phys Sci.

LEVY, ALEXANDRA; Shaker Hts HS; Shaker Hts, OH; Hon Rl; Off Ade; Pol Wkr; Ed Yrbk; Swmmng; College; Psych.

LEVY, CHERYL; Northrop HS; Ft Wayne, IN; 23/600 Chrs; Hon Rl; JA; Coll; Elem Ed.

LEVY, THADDEUS L; Elmhurst HS; Ft Wayne, IN; 62/400 Cls Rep Frsh Cls; Boy Scts; Hon Rl; Stu Cncl; Letter Trk; IM Sprt; Univ; Bus.

LEWALLEN, KYLE; Niles Sr HS; Niles, MI; 1/450 Cls Rep Frsh Cls; Cls Rep Soph Cls; Cl Rep Jr Cls; Am Leg Boys St; Chrs; Hon Rl; NHS; Sch Mus; Chmn Stu Cncl; Drama Clb; Univ; Pre Med.

LEWANDOWSKI, DOLORES; Ladywood HS; Dearborn, MI; Cl Rep Jr Cls; Cls Rep Sr Cls; Chrs; Cmnty Wkr; Hon Rl; Pres NHS; Off Ade; Quill & Scroll; Sch Mus; Stg Crw; Eastern Michigan Univ; Med Tech.

LEWANDOWSKI, GREGORY; St Francis De Sales HS; Toledo, OH; Sec Sr Cls; Boy Scts; Hon Rl; Sct Actv; Ger Clb; Letter Swmmng; IM Sprt; College; Marine Biology.

LEWANDOWSKI, K MARTIN; Springfield HS; Springfield, MI; Bsbl; Bsktbl; Glf; Natl Merit Ltr; Coll.

LEWANDOWSKI, LISA; Bishop Donahue HS; Wheeling, WV; Chrs; Hon Rl; Rptr Yrbk; Vocational Schl; Travel Agent.

LEWANDOWSKI, MICHELLE; Norwell HS; Roanoke, IN; 77/193 VP Soph Cls; Chrs; Hon Rl; Eng Clb; 4-H; Key Clb; Pep Clb; Sci Clb; Spn Clb; Cit Awd; Business Schl; Accounting.

LEWANDOWSKI, RICHARD; Fraser HS; Roseville, MI; Swmmng; Trk; College; Electrician.

LEWANDOWSKI, STEVE J; Swan Valley HS; Saginaw, MI; NHS; Pol Wkr; Yth Flsp; Michigan St Univ; Chem Engr.

LEWANDOWSKI, STEVEN; Swan Vly HS; Saginaw, MI; 4/182 NHS; Pol Wkr; Michigan St Univ; Chem Engr.

LEWANDOWSKI, STEVEN; St Alphonsus HS; Detroit, MI; Chrs; Letter Bsktbl; Letter Trk; Univ; Math.

LEWANDOWSKI, TOM; Lake Catholic HS; Mentor, OH; Aud/Vis; Boy Scts; Hon Rl; Ger Clb; Cleveland Univ; Engr.

LEWARCHIK, GREG; Nordonia HS; Northfield, OH ; VICA; Glf; Socr; Trk; Univ; Foreign Lang.

LEWE, ROBERT; Fostoria HS; Fostoria, OH; 2/200 VP Sr Cls; Am Leg Boys St; Pres NHS; Chmn Glf; Chmn Ten; Bausch & Lomb Awd; Elk Awd; Case Western Reserve Univ; Med.

LEWELLYN, DEBRA; Western HS; Russiaville, IN; 9/210 Am Leg Aux Girls St; Band; Drl Tm; FCA; NHS; Pol Wkr; Stu Cncl; Bsktbl; GAA; Pom Pon; College; Bus Mgmt.

LEWINSKI, LISA J; Luther L Wright HS; Ironwood, MI; 2/179 Debate Tm; NHS; Pres Stu Cncl; Rptr Yrbk; Rptr Sch Nwsp; Fr Clb; Key Clb; Pep Clb; Letter Crs Cntry; Natl Merit SF; Northern Michigan Univ; Soc Work.

LEWIS, ANNIE; Chadsey HS; Detroit, MI; Chrs; Hon Rl; Lbry Ade; Off Ade; Sch Pl; Stu Cncl; Mth Clb; Pep Clb; Bsbl; Cit Awd; Univ Of Detroit; Law.

LEWIS, ANTOINETTE; Northeastern HS; Detroit, MI; Sec Sr Cls; Hon Rl; NHS; PAVAS; Sch Mus; Fr Clb; Pep Clb; Chrldng; Lewis Coll Of Business; Exec Sec.

LEWIS, BELL; Clay Battelle HS; Fairview, WV; Cls Rep Soph Cls; Chrs; Cmnty Wkr; Hon Rl; Lbry Ade; Sch Pl; Stg Crw; Stu Cncl; Drama Clb; FHA; Tutor For Jr High Stu; Working Program; College; Sociology.

LEWIS, BOBBIE J; Bruceton HS; Bruceton Mills, WV; Trs Jr Cls; Chrs; Hon Rl; Sch Pl; Stu Cncl; 4-H; FHA; FTA; Keyettes; Bsktbl; William & Mary Coll; Marine Bio.

LEWIS, BOBBY D; Highland Park HS; Highland Park, MI; Aud/Vis; Hon Rl; Sch Pl; Stg Crw; Boys Clb Am; Drama Clb; Spn Clb; Crs Cntry; Letter Trk; Coach Actv; Wayne St Univ.

LEWIS, BRENDA; Perrysburg HS; Perrysburg, OH; Chrs; Girl Scts; Hon Rl; 4-H; Ger Clb; Pep Clb; Mat Maids; 4-H Awd; Outstndng Stdnt Of Yr; Univ; Vet Med.

LEWIS, BRENDA; Centerville HS; Dayton, OH; 50/670 Aud/Vis; Cmp Fr Grls; Chrh Wkr; Cmnty Wkr; FCA; Hon Rl; NHS; Stu Cncl; Yth Flsp; DECA; E Kentucky Univ; Interior Design.

LEWIS, BRENDA; Eaton HS; Camden, OH; Hon Rl; Jr NHS; Spn Clb; Bsktbl; Trk; Busns Schl; Acctg.

LEWIS, BRENDA; South HS; Akron, OH; 1/104 VP Jr Cls; VP Sr Cls; Val; Cmnty Wkr; Hon Rl; NHS; Off Ade; Fr Clb; FHA; Key Clb; Akron Univ.

LEWIS, BRENDA; Parkersburg HS; Parkersburg, WV; 209/720 Band; Hon Rl; JA; Off Ade; PAVAS; Y-Teens; Drama Clb; FNA; Parkersburg Comm College; Nursing.

LEWIS, CHRISTOPHER; Kearsley Community HS; Flint, MI; Band; Debate Tm; Hon Rl; Orch; Pol Wkr; Sch Pl; Stg Crw; Stu Cncl; Rptr Yrbk; Drama Clb; Eastern Michigan Univ; Cmmrcl Art.

LEWIS, CHUCK; Barberton HS; Barberton, OH; JA; Off Ade; Sch Mus; Sch Pl; Drama Clb; Lat Clb; IM Sprt; Proj Prep Depauw Univ 79; Univ; Theatre.

LEWIS, CYNTHIA; John Hay HS; Cleveland, OH; Band; Chrh Wkr; Hon Rl; NHS; Orch; Sch Mus; Cit Awd; Univ; Chem Engr.

LEWIS, DARLENE; Nettie Lee Roth HS; Dayton, OH; Cls Rep Frsh Cls; Sec Soph Cls; Sec Jr Cls; Drl Tm; Hon Rl; JA; Pres NHS; Stu Cncl; Pom Pon; Bowling Green St Univ; Comp Sci.

LEWIS, DARRYL; Garfield HS; Akron, OH; Aud/Vis; Hon Rl; Off Ade; OEA; Sci Clb; Cit Awd; U S Air Force; Computer Tech.

LEWIS, DAVID A; Vicksburg HS; Vicksbrg, MI; Chrh Wkr; Hon Rl; Jr NHS; NHS; Spn Clb; Glf; Ten; Univ Of Mich; Science Or Med Fld.

LEWIS, DEBORAH; Farmington HS; W Farmington, OH; Hon Rl; Rptr Yrbk; Beta Clb;.

LEWIS, DEBORAH; North Ridgeville Sr HS; N Ridgeville, OH; Cmnty Wkr; Hon Rl; VP JA; Sch Pl; Honorable Mention Dist & St In English Test Of Scholastic Ach; Bowling Green St Univ; Psych.

LEWIS, DELINDA; Whiteland Cmnty HS; Greenwood, IN; Band; Hon Rl; VP FBLA; OEA; PPFtbl; Voc Schl; Sec.

LEWIS, DONNA; Meadow Bridge HS; Danese, WV; 8/62 Chrs; Hon Rl; NHS; Sch Pl; Yrbk; Rptr Sch Nwsp; Sch Nwsp; Eng Clb; Wv Univ; Bus.

LEWIS, DUANE S; Bellefontaine Sr HS; Bellefontaine, OH; 23/250 Cl Rep Jr Cls; Cls Rep Sr Cls; Chrs; Cmnty Wkr; Hon Rl; Sch Mus; Sch Pl; Stu Cncl; 4-H; Ftbl; Ohio St Univ; Oceanographer.

LEWIS, EUGENE; Detroit Central HS; Detroit, MI; Cmnty Wkr; Hon Rl; Sci Clb; Letter Ten; Cit Awd; Wayne State Univ; Bus Mgmt.

LEWIS, GERALD F; Boardman HS; Youngstown, OH; Boy Scts; Cmnty Wkr; Hon Rl; Sct Actv; Yth Flsp; Bsktbl; Ftbl; Trk; Youngstown State Univ; Bio.

LEWIS, HORACE; Southwestern HS; Hanover, IN; Cls Rep Sr Cls; Boy Scts; Hon Rl; Lbry Ade; Rptr Sch Nwsp; Boys Clb Am; Letter Bsktbl; Letter Trk; Kiwan Awd; Coll.

LEWIS, J; Bellaire HS; Neffs, OH; Hon Rl; Ohio Valley Coll; Art.

LEWIS, JACQUELINE; Chesapeake HS; Chesapeake, OH; Cls Rep Frsh Cls; Trs Soph Cls; Cls Rep Soph Cls; Trs Jr Cls; Cl Rep Jr Cls; Cls Rep Sr Cls; Am Leg Aux Girls St; Hon Rl; Stu Cncl; Scr Kpr; Marshall Univ; Recreation.

LEWIS, JAMES; L C Mohr HS; South Haven, MI; Cls Rep Frsh Cls; Cls Rep Soph Cls; Cl Rep Jr Cls; Hon Rl; Stg Crw; Stu Cncl; Eng Clb; Letter Bsktbl; Letter Ftbl; College.

LEWIS, JEFFREY; United Local HS; Hanoverton, OH; Hon Rl; Sch Pl; Stg Crw; Rptr Sch Nwsp; Fr Clb; Coach Actv; Leaders In Training Nomination LIT; College; History.

LEWIS, JEFFREY; South Haven HS; So Haven, MI; 16/230 Chrs; Chrh Wkr; Hon Rl; NHS; Letter Ftbl; Lake Michigan Coll; Automotive Tech.

LEWIS, JENNY; Point Pleasant HS; Pt Pleasant, WV; Am Leg Aux Girls St; Band; Sec NHS; VP Yth Flsp; Rptr Sch Nwsp; 4-H; DAR Awd; College.

LEWIS, JENNY; Licking Cnty Jt Voc HS; Granville, OH; 3/386 OEA; GAA; Ambassador Awd; Statesmen/stateswomen Awd; Diplomat Awd; Busns Schl; Sec.

LEWIS, JERILYN; Fr Thomas Scecina Memrl HS; Indianapolis, IN; 19/194 Girl Scts; Hon Rl; JA; NHS; Letter Trk; IM Sprt; Letter Mgrs; Tmr; IU-PUI; Bus Admin.

LEWIS, JIM; L C Mohr HS; S Haven, MI; Cls Rep Frsh Cls; Cls Rep Soph Cls; Cl Rep Jr Cls; Hon Rl; Stg Crw; Stu Cncl; Letter Bsktbl; Letter Ftbl; College.

LEWIS, JITA; Barnesville HS; Barnesville, OH; 13/115 Trs Jr Cls; Trs Sr Cls; Band; Hon Rl; Hosp Ade; Lbry Ade; NHS; Sch Mus; Yrbk; Fr Clb; Ohio Univ; Elem Educ.

LEWIS, JO; Shakamak HS; Jasonville, IN; Chrs; Sch Nwsp; DECA; FHA; Pep Clb; Bsktbl; GAA; Indiana St Univ; Phys Educ.

LEWIS, JOHN; Coleman Community HS; Coleman, MI; 4/96 Cls Rep Frsh Cls; Sec Jr Cls; Trs Jr Cls; Pres Sr Cls; NHS; Letter Bsktbl; Letter Ftbl; Letter Trk; Central Mic Univ; Chem.

LEWIS, KATHY; Thomas Carr Howe HS; Cumberland, IN; 50/562 Chrs; Girl Scts; Hon Rl; Hosp Ade; NHS; Orch; Sch Mus; Drama Clb; 4-H; Fr Clb; 1 Yr Music Schlrshp For Violin Lessons 76; Univ; Pharm.

LEWIS, KATHY; Mitchell HS; Mitchell, IN; 10/263 Chrs; Chrh Wkr; Hon Rl; Jr NHS; NHS; Sch Pl; Yth Flsp; Bob Jones Univ; Christian Educ.

LEWIS, KELLY; Lakeland HS; La Grange, IN; 10/146 Trs Frsh Cls; Cls Rep Frsh Cls; Cls Rep Soph Cls; CAP; Hon Rl; NHS; Sch Mus; Stu Cncl; Pep Clb; Spn Clb; Purdue Univ; Social Sci.

LEWIS, KEVIN; Oxford HS; Leonard, MI; Cls Rep Frsh Cls; Cls Rep Soph Cls; Am Leg Boys St; Capt Bsbl; Capt Bsktbl; Letter Ftbl; Florida Central Univ; Elec.

LEWIS, KIM; Our Lady Of Mercy HS; Inkster, MI; Cls Rep Frsh Cls; Cls Rep Soph Cls; Cl Rep Jr Cls; Chrh Wkr; Cmnty Wkr; Hosp Ade; Stu Cncl; Sci Clb; Spn Clb; College; Med.

LEWIS, LAURA; Elmhurst HS; Ft Wayne, IN; 6/413 VP Frsh Cls; VP Soph Cls; VP Jr Cls; Am Leg Aux Girls St; Band; Chrs; Hon Rl; Mdrgl; Sct Actv; Stu Cncl; Natl H S Athletic Coaches Assn; NHS ACA All American Athlete ; Most Valuable All Area Gymnast; College; Medicine.

LEWIS, LEE ANN; Escanaba Public HS; Escanaba, MI; 16/450 Hon Rl; NHS; IM Sprt; St Of Mi Educ Sclshp 78; Ferris St Coll; Office Admin.

LEWIS, LEE R; Pocahontas County HS; Marlinton, WV; Boy Scts; Rptr Yrbk; Rptr Sch Nwsp; FTA; Fairmont St Coll; Soc Work.

LEWIS, LELANA; William Henry Harrison HS; Laf, IN; Stg Crw; Rptr Sch Nwsp; Sch Nwsp; Fr Clb; Pep Clb; Sci Clb; PPFtbl; Purdue; Zoology.

LEWIS, LISA; Regina HS; Cleveland Hts, OH; Chrs; Drl Tm; Hon Rl; JA; Jr NHS; Sch Mus; Drama Clb; FTA; Natl Hon Soc 79; Case Western Reserve Univ; Civ Engr.

LEWIS, LISA; Trenton HS; Trenton, MI; Cls Rep Soph Cls; Hon Rl; Stu Cncl; Letter Gym; GAA; Univ; Med.

LEWIS, LISA; Magnolia HS; New Martinsvile, WV; 25/195 Am Leg Aux Girls St; Band; Girl Scts; Hon Rl; Hosp Ade; Sct Actv; Fr Clb; FTA; Marshall Univ; Soc Work.

LEWIS, LYDIA; Anderson HS; Anderson, IN; Band; Chrs; Drm Bgl; JA; Lbry Ade; Quill & Scroll; Yth Flsp; Rptr Sch Nwsp; Mgrs; College; Journalism.

LEWIS, MARK; Fraser HS; Mt Clemens, MI; Band; Ftbl;.

LEWIS, MARSHA A; J W Sexton HS; Lansing Mich, MI; Cls Rep Soph Cls; Pres JA; Stu Cncl; Rptr Yrbk; Ed Sch Nwsp; Mgrs; JA Awd; St Of Mi Schlrshp 79; Delta Sigma Theta Schlrshp 79; Western Michigan Univ; Forestry.

LEWIS, MECHELI; East HS; Columbus, OH; Girl Scts; Hon Rl; Arizona St Univ; Mktg.

LEWIS, MICHAEL; Bishop Foley HS; Royal Oak, MI; 30/200 Boy Scts; Hon Rl; Sct Actv; Capt Wrstlng; Coach Actv; IM Sprt; College; Aero.

LEWIS, MILTON; Newton Falls HS; Newton Falls, OH; Hon Rl; NHS; Sci Clb; Spn Clb; Letter Bsktbl; Ftbl; IM Sprt; Am Leg Awd; Natl Merit Ltr; College; Engineering.

LEWIS, MONICA; William A Wirt HS; Gary, IN; 24/235 Hon Rl; NHS; Y-Teens; Pom Pon; Purdue Univ.

LEWIS, NITA L; Emmerigh Manual HS; Indianapolis, IN; 12/400 Hon Rl; JA; NHS; OEA; Scr Kpr; Tmr; NCTE; Soc Stds Awd For All As 1978; Mmbr For 4yrs In Lge Of Hon; Depauw Univ; Bus Jrnlsm.

LEWIS, PAMELA; Crothersville HS; Crothersville, IN; 10/69 Trs Frsh Cls; Band; Chrs; Drl Tm; Girl Scts; Hon Rl; Yth Flsp; FHA; Pep Clb; GAA; Home Economics; Purdue Univ; Nursing.

LEWIS, P EMILY; Fairfield Union HS; Rushville, OH; 14/147 Chrs; Hon Rl; Hosp Ade; NHS; Sch Pl; Stu Cncl; Yth Flsp; Sec 4-H; Pres Fr Clb; Treas FBLA; Ohio St Univ; Reg Nurse.

LEWIS, REGINA; Immaculata HS; Detroit, MI; Band; Cmp Fr Grls; Chrs; Chrh Wkr; Cmnty Wkr; Girl Scts; Hon Rl; Pol Wkr; Sch Mus; Sch Pl; Honor Roll; Serv Awd; Religion Awd; Wayne Cnty Comm Coll; Nursing.

LEWIS, REGINA; Dayton Christian HS; Trotwood, OH; Chrh Wkr; Drl Tm; Girl Scts; Hon Rl; Hosp Ade; Letter Trk; Scr Kpr; 3 Bowling Trophies; Excellnct Ribbon & Cert In Sci Fair 79; Univ; Pre Med.

LEWIS, RENEE; Creston HS; Grand Rapids, MI; 1/395 Sec Frsh Cls; Cls Rep Sr Cls; Val; Chrs; Chrh Wkr; Hon Rl; Jr NHS; Mdrgl; Treas NHS; Sch Mus; Pres Schlrshp At Hope Coll 79; Hope Coll; Sci.

LEWIS, ROBIN; Corunna HS; Perry, MI; 6/235 Band; Chrh Wkr; Hon Rl; Mod UN; NHS; Orch; Yrbk; 4-H Awd; Univ Of Colorado; Med.

LEWIS, ROBIN R; Springfield HS; Holland, OH; 9/245 Sec Soph Cls; NHS; Stu Cncl; Ed Yrbk; Spn Clb; Capt Trk; GAA; Mat Maids; Pres Awd; Spring Arbor Coll; Medicine.

LEWIS, ROGER; Baker HS; Fairborn, OH; Band; Drm Bgl; Hon Rl; Natl Forn Lg; Quill & Scroll; Sch Pl; Stg Crw; Rptr Yrbk; Yrbk; Drama Clb; Wright State; Veterinarian.

LEWIS, ROSE; Firelands HS; Oberlin, OH; Trs Sr Cls; Chrs; Lbry Ade; Off Ade; Yth Flsp; 4-H; FHA; Bsbl; Bsktbl; IM Sprt; Lorain Cnty Cmnty Coll; Acctg.

LEWIS, ROSELA A; Ripley HS; Ripley, WV; 34/265 Band; Hon Rl; Jr NHS; Off Ade; FNA; Capt Pom Pon; College.

LEWIS, SANDY; Huntington HS; Huntington, WV; 13/287 Hon Rl; Jr NHS; NHS; Lat Clb; Treas Mth Clb; Pep Clb; Sigma Sr Publicity Ofc; Final In West Virginia Natl Teenager Contest; Ohio St Univ; Vet.

LEWIS, SCOTT; Linsly Institute; Wheeling, WV; 7/60 VP Soph Cls; Cls Rep Sr Cls; Cmnty Wkr; FCA; Hon Rl; ROTC; Stu Cncl; Key Clb; Spn Clb; Ftbl; Stud Athlete Schlrshp Awd 77 80; Univ; Engr.

LEWIS, SHERRY K; Jane Addams Voc HS; Cleveland, OH; Sec Jr Cls; Cl Rep Jr Cls; Chrs; Drl Tm; Lbry Ade; Pep Clb; VICA; Pom Pon; Cit Awd; Natl Merit Ltr; College; Drama.

LEWIS, SUSAN; Fairland HS; Proctorvll, OH; Hon Rl; NHS; 4-H; Mth Clb; 4-H Awd; 10th Pl In 1st Yr French Div II In O U Dist Ohio Test Of Schlstc Achvmtn 79; Oh Univ HS Schlr 79; Marshall Univ; Bus Admin.

LEWIS, SUSAN; Elmwood HS; Wayne, OH; Cls Rep Soph Cls; Cls Rep Sr Cls; Band; Chrs; Stu Cncl; Yrbk; Rptr Sch Nwsp; FTA; Tiffin Univ; Acctg.

LEWIS, TAMARA J; Flushing HS; Flushing, MI; 37/495 Rptr Sch Nwsp; 4-H; Fr Clb; 4-H Awd; Med Explrs Clb 78; Univ; Bio Sci.

LEWIS, TAMMY; Ogemaw Heights HS; Gaylord, MI; 1/23 Band; Girl Scts; Hon Rl; Sct Actv; Bsktbl; Letter Trk; Chrldng; Mgrs; Davenport Coll Of Bus; Acctg.

LEWIS, TERRI; East HS; Columbus, OH; 20/272 Cls Rep Frsh Cls; Cls Rep Soph Cls; Cl Rep Jr Cls; Cls Rep Sr Cls; Band; Chrh Wkr; Cmnty Wkr; Drl Tm; Drm Mjrt; Hon Rl; Ohio St Univ; Bus Admin.

LEWIS, TERRI B; Linton Stockton HS; Linton, IN; Sec Jr Cls; Am Leg Aux Girls St; Band; Chrh Wkr; Girl Scts; Hon Rl; NHS; Ger Clb; Pep Clb; Chrldng; Sftbl 2 Ltrs MVP 77 79; Vllbl 77 79; Univ.

LEWIS, TIM; West Washington HS; Campbellsburg, IN; 24/99 Trs Frsh Cls; Trs Soph Cls; Trs Jr Cls; Trs Sr Cls; Band; Boy Scts; Yth Flsp; FFA; Ind Univ.

LEWIS, TIMOTHY; Park Hills HS; Fairborn, OH; Chrs; Hon Rl; Stg Crw; Yth Flsp; Lat Clb; Cit Awd; Coll; Math.

LEWIS, TRACEY; Kettering Sr HS; Detroit, MI; Hon Rl; NHS; FHA; Cit Awd; Ferris St Univ; Cosmetologist.

LEWIS, WILLIAM G; East Catholic HS; Detroit, MI; Pres Jr Cls; Stu Cncl; Rptr Yrbk; Yrbk; Rptr Sch Nwsp; Sch Nwsp; Voice Dem Awd; Univ; Communication.

LEWTER, ABBE; Speedway HS; Speedway, IN; Cls Rep Frsh Cls; Cls Rep Soph Cls; Cl Rep Jr Cls; Am Leg Aux Girls St; Girl Scts; Hon Rl; Jr NHS; NHS; Stu Cncl; Yth Flsp; Scholarship Awds; AAA Awd; Schol Traffic Safety Poster Contest; Indiana Univ; Archt.

LEWTON, DWIGHT; Marion HS; Marion, IN; Cls Rep Frsh Cls; Yth Flsp; La Tourneau Univ; Aviation.

LEY, JOYCE; East Noble HS; Avilla, IN; 33/273 Chrh Wkr; Hon Rl; 4-H; Pep Clb; IBC.

LEYPOLDT, ROSEMARIE S; Grandview Hts HS; Columbus, OH; Band; Chrs; Hon Rl; Orch; Yrbk; FTA; Capital Univ; Music Comp & Theory.

LEYPOLDT, ROSEMARIE; Grandview Hts HS; Columbus, OH; Band; Chrs; Hon Rl; Jr NHS; NHS; Orch; PAVAS; Rptr Yrbk; Yrbk; FTA; Univ; Theory.

LEYRER, KELLEY; Gladwin HS; Gladwin, MI; Hon Rl; Sch Pl; Stg Crw; Drama Clb; Bsbl; IM Sprt; Hon Roll Pin Frsh Yr 76; Michigan St Univ; Bus Tchr.

LEZAN, MICHELE; Parma Sr 'S; Parma, OH; Cls Rep Frsh Cls; Cls Rep Soph Cls; Cl Rep Jr Cls; Stu Cncl; Chrldng; GAA; Ohio St Univ.

LI, JENNIFER; North Central HS; Indianapolis, IN; 5/1194 Cmnty Wkr; Debate Tm; Hon Rl; Lit Mag; NHS; Rptr Yrbk; Rptr Sch Nwsp; Fr Clb; NCTE; Natl Merit SF; Univ; Bio Chem.

LIABENOW, DANIAL; Manton Consolidated HS; Manton, MI; Band; Hon Rl; Yrbk; FTA; Spn Clb; College; History.

LIACCO, MARIANO; Gilmour Acad; Highland Hts, OH; 15/80 Band; Hon Rl; NHS; Orch; Fr Clb; Scr Kpr; Univ; Bus.

LIADIS, DIANE; Adlai E Stevenson HS; Livonia, MI; Chrs; Chrh Wkr; Cmnty Wkr; Hon Rl; Hosp Ade; Orch; Red Cr Ade; VP Yth Flsp; Bsktbl; Swmmng; Wayne St Univ; Pharm.

LIASKOS, VIOLET; Hammond HS; Hammond, IN; 68/334 Drl Tm; Hon Rl; Sch Pl; Drama Clb; Capt Pom Pon; Scr Kpr; Tmr; Univ.

LIAUW, ANDREW V; Lorain Catholic HS; Lorain, OH; VP Frsh Cls; Cmnty Wkr; FCA; Rptr Sch Nwsp; Trk; Univ; Pathologist.

LIBAUSKAS, MARY; Andrean HS; Gary, IN; Chrh Wkr; Cmnty Wkr; Hon Rl; Sch Mus; Drama Clb; Univ; Bus Admin.

LIBB, CINDY; Rising Sun HS; Rising Sun, IN; VP Soph Cls; Cl Rep Jr Cls; Band; Chrs; Chrh Wkr; Girl Scts; Hon Rl; Stu Cncl; Yth Flsp; Y-Teens; Volleyball Letter; Track Statistician; College; Special Ed.

LIBBERT, MELISSA; South Dearborn HS; Dillsboro, IN; Am Leg Aux Girls St; Band; Chrh Wkr; NHS; Rptr Sch Nwsp; FTA; Bsktbl; College; Accgt.

LIBBERT, TAMMY; Southridge HS; Huntngbrg, IN; Chrh Wkr; Cmnty Wkr; Hon Rl; VP 4-H; Pres FHA; Pep Clb; PPFtbl; 4-H Awd; Univ; Bus.

LIBBY, DAVID; Cros Lex HS; Lexingtn Hts, MI; Boy Scts; Chrs; Spn Clb;.

LIBBY, MICHAEL; Rogers City HS; Hawks, MI; 18/145 Boy Scts; Hon Rl; Sch Pl; Stg Crw; Letter Ftbl; Letter Trk; Ferris St Coll; Bus Mgmt.

LIBER, SALLY; Our Lady Of Angels HS; Cincinnati, OH; 19/169 Girl Scts; Hon Rl; Spn Clb; Bsktbl; Ten; Trk; GAA; IM Sprt; Indiana Univ; Phys Therapy.

LIBERTIN, MARK; Campbell Memorial HS; Campbell, OH; 1/225 Val; Chrh Wkr; Hon Rl; Hosp Ade; Jr NHS; NHS; Sch Pl; Stg Crw; Stu Cncl; Y-Teens; Ohio St Univ; Med.

LIBERTOWSKI, JOHN; Washington HS; South Bend, IN; 52/455 Chrs; Hon Rl; Jr NHS; Sprt Ed Sch Nwsp; Bsbl; Univ; Jrnlsm.

LIBES, STEPHANIE; Delta HS; Muncie, IN; 3/380 Hon Rl; JA; NHS; Ed Yrbk; Fr Clb; FHA; Sci Clb; JA Awd; Purdue Univ; Comp Sci.

LIBEVATI, DOUGLAS P; Bellaire HS; Bellaire, OH; 38/223 Aud/Vis; Hon Rl; Stg Crw; Sch Nwsp; Pres Fr Clb; Trk; Univ; Bio Sci.

LICATA, ANTONIO; Weirton Madonna HS; Weirton, WV; 4/99 Lit Mag; VP NHS; Rptr Yrbk; Key Clb; IM Sprt; NEDT Cert 77; West Virginia Univ; Physician.

LICAUSE, GAIL; Wadsworth Sr HS; Wadsworth, OH; VP Frsh Cls; Cls Rep Frsh Cls; Cls Rep Soph Cls; Pres Jr Cls; Cl Rep Jr Cls; Chrs; Cmnty Wkr; Girl Scts; Hosp Ade; Pol Wkr; Akron General Schl; Nursing.

LICHNEY, JEAN; Boardman HS; Youngstown, OH; Cls Rep Frsh Cls; Cls Rep Soph Cls; Cls Rep Sr Cls; Hon Rl; Sch Mus; Stu Cncl; Fr Clb; Sci Clb; Chrldng; Youngstown State Univ; Retail Mark.

LICHT, DONALD; Escanaba HS; Escanaba, MI; Aud/Vis; Yrbk; Hockey; Scr Kpr; Amer Vets Dodge Dist 1 Driver Excellnc 2nd Pl 79; Michigan Tech Univ; Drafting.

LICHTE, KIM; North Knox HS; Bicknell, IN; 14/173 Hosp Ade; NHS; 4-H; FHA; Lat Clb; Mth Clb; Pep Clb; Bsbl; DAR Awd; Vincennces Univ; Phys Ther.

LICHTE, LORI; Brownsburg HS; Pittsboro, IN; Cmp Fr Grls; Chrs; Chrh Wkr; Hon Rl; Mdrgl; Sch Mus; Stg Crw; Yth Flsp; 4-H; Pep Clb; Supr Rating Cert IN Schl Music Assc 78 & 79; 1st Pl IN St Choral Solo & Qrt 79; Ball St Univ; Med.

LICHTENBERG, GARY; Westlake HS; Westlake, OH; 120/290 Ftbl; Ten; IM Sprt; Univ; Math.

LICHTLE, CAROLYN; Adams Central HS; Decatur, IN; 6/107 Pres Frsh Cls; Pres Soph Cls; Sec Sr Cls; Hon Rl; VP NHS; Ed Yrbk; Rptr Sch Nwsp; Pep Clb; Lion Awd; Parkview Schl Of Nrsng; Nursing.

LICHTLE, CAROLYN M; Adams Central HS; Decatur, IN; 6/113 Pres Frsh Cls; Pres Soph Cls; Sec Sr Cls; FCA; Hon Rl; VP NHS; Stu Cncl; Ed Yrbk; Yrbk; Rptr Sch Nwsp; Parkview Methodist Schl; Nursing.

LICK, HARVEY; Vanderbilt Area HS; Vanderbilt, MI; Sch Nwsp; Bsbl; Ftbl;.

LICK, WILLIAM; Vanderbilt Area HS; Vanderbilt, MI; 4/27 Boy Scts; Hon Rl; Letter Bsktbl; Letter F tbl; Trk; Ohio Inst Of Tech; Elec.

LICKEY, BETH; Huntington North HS; Huntington, IN; 27/600 Stg Crw; IUPU At Ft Wayne; Acctg.

LICKING, JEFFREY; Michigan Center HS; Michigan Center, MI; Pres Sr Cls; Bsktbl; Ftbl; Glf; College.

LICKLY, JOYCE; Pittsford Area HS; Pittsford, MI; Band; Chrs; Chrh Wkr; Cmnty Wkr; Girl Scts; Hon Rl; Hosp Ade; NHS; Off Ade; Yrbk; Coll; Busns.

LICO, ISABELLA; Our Lady Star Of The Sea HS; Grse Pt Shr, MI; 1/52 Val; Hon Rl; Natl Forn Lg; NHS; Quill & Scroll; Sch Mus; Sch Pl; Mic Univ; Pre Med.

LIDDLE, SHELLEY; Delaware Hayes HS; Delaware, OH; Cls Rep Frsh Cls; AFS; Girl Scts; JA; Stu Cncl; Y-Teens; Fr Clb; Pep Clb; Letter Bsktbl; GAA; Bowling Green Univ; Phys Ed.

LIEBAU, JOSEPH; St Philip Catholic Ctrl HS; Battle Creek, MI; 27/70 Pres Jr Cls; Pres Sr Cls; Cmnty Wkr; Hon Rl; Jr NHS; NHS; Stu Cncl; Yth Flsp; Rptr Sch Nwsp; Letter Bsktbl; Kalamazoo Coll; Med.

LIEBAU, SHERRI; Novi HS; Novi, MI; 24/240 Pres Frsh Cls; Hon Rl; Lbry Ade; NHS; Pol Wkr; Rptr Yrbk; Rptr Sch Nwsp; Mgrs; Capt Twrlr; Michigan St Univ; Pre Law.

LIEBELT, ERICA; Kent Roosevelt HS; Kent, OH; 5/378 Cls Rep Frsh Cls; Pres Sr Cls; Sec AFS; Band; Chrs; Cmnty Wkr; Girl Scts; Hon Rl; NHS; Sch Mus; Awd Of Distnctn For Basic Std 79; Schlshp Hon Awd For Top Ten Sr 79; Duke Univ; Psych.

LIEBER, KATHLEEN; Mayville HS; Millington, MI; 1/82 Trs Jr Cls; Trs Sr Cls; Val; Band; Hon Rl; NHS; FTA; Pep Clb; Letter Bsktbl; Letter Trk; Alma Pres Schlrshp; St Of Michigan Awd; Natl HS Exc Awd; Alma Coll; Med.

LIEBER, KRISTA; Lanesville HS; Lanesville, IN; Chrs; FCA; Hon Rl; 4-H; FHA; Pep Clb; Bsktbl; Mgrs; Pom Pon;.

LIEBERMAN, KATHY; Stonewall Jackson HS; Charleston, WV; Cls Rep Frsh Cls; Am Leg Aux Girls St; Band; Stu Cncl; Fr Clb; Letter Bsktbl; Crs Cntry; Letter Ten; Univ.

LIEBETRAU, KURT; Cadillac Sr HS; Cadillac, MI; Cls Rep Frsh Cls; Cls Rep Soph Cls; Hon Rl; Sch Mus; Sch Pl; Stu Cncl; Letter Ftbl; Hockey; Ten; IM Sprt; Homecoming Court Fresh Yr; Most Valuable Player Last Yr; Picked For The North Central All Star; Michigan St Univ; Hotel Mgr.

LIEBNAU, GREG; Libbey HS; Toledo, OH; Boy Scts; Hon Rl; Jr NHS; NHS; Sct Actv; Wrstlng; Tmr; Cit Awd; College; Tech Fields.

LIEBRECHT, KATHLEEN; Miller City HS; Continental, OH; 8/68 Trs Sr Cls; Am Leg Aux Girls St; Chrs; Hon Rl; NHS; Yrbk; Treas FHA; Am Leg Awd; St Vincent Schl; Reg Nurse.

LIEBSCH, DAWN; Athens HS; Athens, WV; Chrh Wkr; Girl Scts; Hosp Ade; Sch Pl; Stg Crw; Bsbl; Bsktbl; Mgrs; Scr Kpr; College; Design Art.

LIECHTI, SANDRA; Parkside HS; Jackson, MI; Cls Rep Frsh Cls; Cls Rep Soph Cls; Cl Rep Jr Cls; Cls Rep Sr Cls; Band; Hon Rl; Letter Trk; Univ; Med Tech.

LIELL, KATHARINE; Bloomington South HS; Bloomington, IN; 24/318 Band; Debate Tm; FCA; NHS; Pol Wkr; Stu Cncl; 4-H; Trk; Chrldng; PPFtbl; De Pauw Univ; Law.

LIEN, BRIAN; Hill Mc Cloy HS; Montrose, MI; Am Leg Boys St; Hon Rl; NHS; Sprt Ed Yrbk; Rptr Sch Nwsp; Letter Ftbl; Letter Trk; Letter Wrstlng; IM Sprt; Am Leg Awd; Univ; Elec.

LIENAU, ALAN; Lakeview HS; St Clair Shore, MI; 105/532 Cntr For Creative Stds; Advert Dsgn.

LIEPACK, KAREN; Whitehall Yearling HS; Whitehall, OH; Am Leg Aux Girls St; Aud/Vis; Boy Scts; Cmnty Wkr; Drl Tm; Lbry Ade; Off Ade; PAVAS; Red Cr Ade; Sch Pl; 2nd Runner Up In Miss Whitehall Pageant 79; Ohio St Univ; Brdcst Jrnlsm.

LIESER, CARL; Buckeye Central HS; Tiro, OH; Band; Boy Scts; Chrs; Chrh Wkr; Hon Rl; NHS; Sch Mus; Yth Flsp; Lat Clb; Mgrs; Blue Ribbon For #1 Ratng In Cls C Soph Ensmbl Singing 77; Red Ribbon For #2 Rating In Cls B Jr Ensbml 78; Coll.

LIETO, JOSEPH; Monroe Catholic Central HS; Monroe, MI; 9/95 Trs Frsh Cls; Cl Rep Jr Cls; Trs Sr Cls; Boy Scts; Hon Rl; NHS; 4-H; Pep Clb; Bsbl; Bsktbl; Michigan St Univ; Criminal Just.

LIEVERDINK, DEREK; N Michigan Christian HS; Falmouth, MI; Band; Boy Scts; Hon Rl; Sch Mus; Sch Pl; Yth Flsp; Boys Clb Am; Spn Clb; PPFtbl; Central Michigan Univ; Radio Brdcstn.

LIFER, J DAVID; Clearfork HS; Butler, OH; 22/186 Band; Chrh Wkr; Hon Rl; NHS; Yth Flsp; Pres 4-H; Pres FFA; 4-H Awd; St Farmers Degree 1979; Agri Tech Inst; Agri Educ.

LIFER, STEVEN T; Clear Fork HS; Butler, OH; 6/182 Band; Chrh Wkr; Hon Rl; NHS; Stu Cncl; Yth Flsp; Pres 4-H; Pres FFA; Mth Clb; Sci Clb; Ohio St Univ; Engr.

LIGGETT, DEBRA; Jackson Milton HS; North Jackson, OH; 7/111 VP Jr Cls; Hon Rl; Treas NHS; Capt Bsktbl; Letter Trk; College; Accounting.

LIGGETT, JAMES; Padua Franciscan HS; Parma, OH; Cls Rep Frsh Cls; Cls Rep Soph Cls; Cl Rep Jr Cls; Boy Scts; Hon Rl; JA; NHS; Letter Ftbl; Letter Wrstlng; Air Force Academy; Aeronautics.

LIGGETT, JO DEE; Brooke HS; Wellsburg, WV; 14/403 Sec Frsh Cls; Chrs; Chrh Wkr; Hon Rl; Yth Flsp; Fr Clb; Letter Trk; Letter Chrldng; IM Sprt; Univ; Med.

LIGGINS, TONI; East HS; Columbus, OH; 12/276 Band; Debate Tm; Hon Rl; Hosp Ade; Natl Forn Lg; NHS; Fr Clb; VICA; Scr Kpr; Twrlr; Wright St Univ; Med Tech.

LIGGITT, MELINDA; Jackson Milton HS; North Jackson, OH; 17/116 VP Frsh Cls; Am Leg Aux Girls St; Band; Chrs; Chrh Wkr; Cmnty Wkr; Girl Scts; College; Advertising.

LIGHT, BRIAN; Liberty Benton HS; Finlay, OH; Trs Frsh Cls; Pres Sr Cls; Am Leg Boys St; Chrh Wkr; Pres JA; Jr NHS; Sct Actv; Pres Yth Flsp; Sec FFA; Letter Bsktbl; U Of Arizona; Busns.

LIGHT, LISA; Saint Joseph Cntrl Catholic; Fremont, OH; 17/87 VP Jr Cls; Cls Rep Sr Cls; Cmp Fr Grls; Chrh Wkr; Hon Rl; Sch Pl; Stu Cncl; Ed Yrbk; Pep Clb; Siena Heights College; Child Develop.

LIGHT, MARK; Woodward HS; Batavia, OH; Am Leg Boys St; Band; Drm Bgl; Hon Rl; NHS; Rdo Clb; Spn Clb; Crs Cntry; Trk; Capt Wrstlng; College; Mechanical Engr.

LIGHT, MARK R; Woodward HS; Batavia, OH; Am Leg Boys St; Band; Drm Bgl; Hon Rl; NHS; Rdo Clb; Spn Clb; Crs Cntry; Trk; Capt Wrstlng; College; Mechanical Eng.

LIGHTALL, KAREN; Southfield Sr HS; Southfield, MI; Cmp Fr Grls; Chrs; Hon Rl; Off Ade; Sch Pl; Stu Cncl; Ten; Mgrs; Univ; Paramedic.

LIGHTCAP, DANIEL; Pontiac Northern HS; Pontiac, MI; Chrh Wkr; Cmnty Wkr; Hon Rl; Jr NHS; Lit Mag; NHS; Sch Mus; Sch Pl; Yth Flsp; Drama Clb; Will O Way Repertory Theatre; Wayne St Univ; Communications.

LIGHTFOOT, BELINDA; Hilliard HS; Galloway, OH; Chrs; Chrh Wkr; Hon Rl; Yth Flsp; College.

LIGHTFOOT, CHANDREA D; Broad Ripple HS; Indianapolis, IN; 17/355 Cls Rep Sr Cls; Cmnty Wkr; Debate Tm; Hon Rl; NHS; Off Ade; Pres Yth Flsp; Letter Glf; Natl Merit Ltr; Univ Of California; Journalism.

LIGHTFOOT, LORI; Massillon Washington HS; Massillon, OH; Pres Soph Cls; Pres Jr Cls; Pres Sr Cls; Am Leg Aux Girls St; Band; Chrs; Chrh Wkr; NHS; Yrbk; Lat Clb; Coll; Busns Admin.

LIGHTFOOT, MARK A; Bluefield HS; Bluefield, WV; 125/290 Cls Rep Frsh Cls; Boy Scts; Hon Rl; Stu Cncl; 4-H; Key Clb; Pep Clb; Spn Clb; Letter Bsbl; Letter Ftbl; Athlete Of The Yr For Track 76; Honorable Mention All Area Bsbll Team 79; Univ; Bus Mgmt.

LIGHTFOOT, TINA; Harbor Springs HS; Harbor Spgs, MI; 4-H; Sec FFA; Treas Spn Clb; 4-H Awd; Meredith Manor Voc Schl; Equestrian.

LIGHTHALL, KIMBERLY; Adrian HS; Brandon, FL; 8/386 Hon Rl; NHS; Pep Clb; Bsktbl; Trk; Eastern Mich Univ.

LIGHTLE, TIMOTHY R; Highland HS; Fredericktown, OH; Yth Flsp; Rptr Yrbk; Rptr Sch Nwsp; Spn Clb; Crs Cntry; Wrstlng; IM Sprt; Miami Univ; Sci.

LIGHTNER, MICHELE; Huntington North HS; Huntington, IN; 32/605 Cls Rep Soph Cls; Cl Rep Jr Cls; Chrs; Chrh Wkr; Sch Mus; Stg Crw; Stu Cncl; Letter Trk; Letter Chrldng; Tmr; Ball St Univ; Acctg.

LIGOTTI, JOSEPHINE; Yale HS; Yale, MI; Sec Frsh Cls; VP Sr Cls; Cmnty Wkr; Hon Rl; 4-H; Sci Clb; Crs Cntry; Letter Trk; 4-H Awd; College; Phys Ther.

LIHANI, TERESA; Parma Sr HS; Parma, OH; Band; Hon Rl; Lit Mag; Sch Mus; Spn Clb; NCTE; Highest Hon All Poin Avrgs 76; Hon In Modern European History 78; Spanish Hon Soc 79; Cleveland St Univ; Eng.

LIIMAKKA, MIA; Luther L Wright HS; Ironwood, MI; Band; Chrh Wkr; Girl Scts; Hon Rl; NHS; Sch Pl; 4-H; Letter Ten; 4-H Awd; Gogebic Cmnty Coll; Comp Sci.

LIINANGI, LISA; Clawson Sr HS; Clawson, MI; 320299 AFS; Band; Cmp Fr Grls; Girl Scts; Hon Rl; NHS; Quill & Scroll; Mi St Schslp 79; Michigan St Univ; Eng.

LIJEWSKI, MARYANN; New Buffalo Jr Sr HS; Union Pier, MI; Hon Rl; Off Ade; Sch Nwsp; Bsktbl; Trk; Coach Actv; GAA; Mgrs; Scr Kpr; Tmr; Michigan St Univ; Bus.

LIKE, JULIE; Lincoln HS; Vincennes, IN; 47/281 Chrh Wkr; Sec Debate Tm; Drm Mjrt; Hon Rl; Sch Mus; Sct Actv; Rptr Sch Nwsp; Sch Nwsp; Drama Clb; Pep Clb; Miss Indiana Natl Teenager & 4th Runner In Natl Pageant Schlrshp To Coll Of Choice; Marchng Cncrt Jazz Bnd; Indiana State Univ; Medicine.

LIKES, SHERRY; St Joe Sr HS; St Joseph, MI; 13/350 Girl Scts; JA; Sct Actv; 4-H; JV Softball 79; Univ; Bus.

LILLER, DAWN; Frankfort HS; Ridgeley, WV; Cl Rep Jr Cls; Chrh Wkr; Drl Tm; Hon Rl; Hosp Ade; NHS; Stu Cncl; Yrbk; Mth Clb; Voice Dem Awd; West Virginia Univ; Nursing.

LILLEY, BRIAN; Stevenson HS; Livonia, MI; JA; God Cntry Awd; JA Awd; Lawrence Tech; Mech Tech.

LILLEY, DANIEL; Lapeer East HS; Lapeer, MI; Band; Chrh Wkr; NHS; Yth Flsp; Fr Clb; Ten; College.

LILLIBRIDGE, LINDA; Coshocton HS; Coshocton, OH; 38/170 Chrh Wkr; Hon Rl; Off Ade; Stu Cncl; Yth Flsp; Rptr Yrbk; Yrbk; VP 4-H; FTA; Spn Clb; Bowling Green St Univ; Bus Admin.

LILLICH, LORI; Cedarville HS; Cedarville, OH; Band; Chrs; Chrh Wkr; FCA; Yth Flsp; 4-H; Fr Clb; IM Sprt; Scr Kpr; 4-H Awd; Clark Tech.

LILLICH, WILLIAM; Glen Este Sr HS; Cincinnati, OH; Cls Rep Sr Cls; Am Leg Boys St; Pres Band; Drm Mjrt; Hon Rl; NHS; Sch Mus; Spn Clb; Cit Awd; U S Air Force Acad; Chem.

LILLIE, DAVID; Roosevelt HS; Marenisco, MI; Cls Rep Frsh Cls; Cls Rep Soph Cls; Cl Rep Jr Cls; Cls Rep Sr Cls; Band; Chrs; Hon Rl; 4-H; Bsbl; Bsktbl; Voc Schl.

LILLY, CARL; Chesapeake HS; Chesapeake, OH; Cls Rep Frsh Cls; Boy Scts; Hon Rl; Sch Pl; Stg Crw; Stu Cncl; Rptr Yrbk; Sch Nwsp; Glf; Wrstlng; Marshall Univ; Jrnlsm.

LILLY, JAMIE; Chesapeake HS; Chesapeake, OH; Am Leg Aux Girls St; Girl Scts; Hon Rl; NHS; Off Ade; Yrbk; Beta Clb; Spn Clb;.

LILLY, KEVIN; Talcott HS; Hinton, WV; Cl Rep Jr Cls; VP Sr Cls; Cls Rep Sr Cls; Chrh Wkr; Cmnty Wkr; Hon Rl; Sch Mus; Stg Crw; Stu Cncl; Yth Flsp; West Virginia Tech Univ; Elec.

LILLY, KIMBERLY D; Shady Spring HS; Cool Ridge, WV; 8/150 Band; FCA; Hon Rl; Jr NHS; NHS; Sch Pl; Drama Clb; Pep Clb; Twrlr; Beckley Coll; Banking.

LILLY, LINDA K; Independence HS; Slab Fork, WV; Chrh Wkr; Hon Rl; NHS; Beta Clb; FBLA; FHA;.

LILLY, RICHARD D; Shady Spring HS; Daniels, WV; Cls Rep Frsh Cls; VP Jr Cls; Cl Rep Jr Cls; Boy Scts; Chrs; Chrh Wkr; Hon Rl; Jr NHS; NHS; Sch Mus; Univ Of Tennessee; Archt.

LILLY, ROBERT; Whitehall Yearling HS; Whitehall, OH; Band; Chrs; Chrh Wkr; Hon Rl; Lbry Ade; Ten;.

LILLY, ROBIN; Shady Spring HS; Shady Spring, WV; Band; Chrs; Chrh Wkr; Cmnty Wkr; Girl Scts; Hon Rl; NHS; Yth Flsp; Rptr Yrbk; Pep Clb; Beckley Coll; Steno.

LILLY, SANDRA; Princeton HS; Princeton, WV; 33/350 Jr NHS; NHS; FHA; Pep Clb; Spn Clb; Bluefield State; Bus Mgmt.

LILLY, STEPHEN; Walnut Hills HS; Cincinnati, OH; Cls Rep Frsh Cls; Boy Scts; Chrs; Chrh Wkr; Hon Rl; VP Yth Flsp; Rptr Sch Nwsp; IM Sprt; Cit Awd; Kiwan Awd; College; Journalism.

LIM, DAVID J; W Lafayette HS; W Lafayette, IN; 82/190 Hon Rl; Orch; Sch Mus; Sch Pl; Ten; Trk; IM Sprt; Cit Awd; Most Val Orch Mbr Awd 77; Lafayette Symphony Gld Msc Schlrshp 77; 1st Ind St Music Cntst 77; Purdue Univ; Engr.

LIMBACH, JEANNE; Greenon HS; Enon, OH; 16/267 Band; Chrs; Hon Rl; NHS; Sch Mus; Fr Clb; FTA; Mth Clb; Chrldng; GAA; Univ; Comp Prog.

LIMBACHER, TAMMY; Garaway HS; Baltic, OH; 4/85 Hon Rl; NHS; Stu Cncl; Yth Flsp; 4-H; Pep Clb; Spn Clb; Gym; Trk; Capt Chrldng; Acctg.

LIMER, CHERYL; Royal Oak Kimball HS; Troy, MI; 73/597 Hon Rl; Hosp Ade; NHS; FDA; Mgrs; Natl Merit Ltr; Natl Merit SF; Kalamazoo Coll; Pre Med.

LIMONGI, LISA; Niles Mckinley HS; Niles, OH; Girl Scts; Hon Rl; PAVAS; Pep Clb; Chrldng; PPFtbl; College; Art.

LIMONOFF, LAWRENCE; Fowlerville HS; Webberville, MI; Cls Rep Soph Cls; Cl Rep Jr Cls; Boy Scts; Hon Rl; Stu Cncl; 4-H; Spn Clb; Letter Bsbl; Bsktbl; Letter Crs Cntry; College; Medicine.

LINABURY, LISA; Southfield Christian HS; Birmingham, MI; Band; Chrh Wkr; Hon Rl; Yth Flsp; Drama Clb; Fr Clb; Chrldng; Pres Awd; Daughters Of The Amer Revolutn Citizenshp Awrd; Michigan State Univ; Fash Merch.

LINCH, ARNETTA; Roosevelt Wilson HS; Stonewood, WV; 11/122 Hon Rl; Hosp Ade; NHS; FNA; FTA; Ten; Letter Trk; Fairmont State Univ; Med Tech.

LINCOLN, STEPHEN; Okemos HS; Okemos, MI; 79/326 Band; Boy Scts; Chrs; Chrh Wkr; Sch Mus; Yth Flsp; Trk; IM Sprt; Mgrs; 4-H Awd; Western Michigan Univ; Bus.

LINCZER, RON; St Joseph HS; Mishawaka, IN; Hon Rl; Sch Mus; Sch Pl; Letter Crs Cntry; Trk; Univ.

LIND, DAVID; Colerain HS; Cincinnati, OH; Aud/Vis; Band; Hon Rl; Jr NHS; NHS; Sch Mus; Sch Pl; Letter Socr; Univ Of Cincinnati; Engr.

LIND, JENNY; Goshen HS; Goshen, IN; 79/256 Band; Cmp Fr Grls; Chrh Wkr; FCA; Orch; Yth Flsp; 4-H; Fr Clb; Pep Clb; Letter Glf; College.

LIND, SCOTT; Madison Heights HS; Anderson, IN; 58/500 Cls Rep Frsh Cls; Boy Scts; Chrs; Chrh Wkr; Cmnty Wkr; FCA; Hon Rl; Mdrgl; Sch Mus; Sch Pl; Ball State Univ; Bus.

LINDAMOOD, SCOTT; Marietta HS; Marietta, OH; Hon Rl; Marietta College; Bus Admin.

LINDAUER, KELVIN; Perry Central HS; St Meinrad, IN; 54/95 Band; 4-H; Pep Clb; Cit Awd; 4-H Awd;.

LINDAUER, SHARON M; Forest Park HS; Ferdinand, IN; 10/134 Hon Rl; NHS; Stu Cncl; Beta Clb; 4-H; Pep Clb; Letter Ten; Chrldng; GAA; College; Med Tech.

LINDBERG, MARK C; Worthington HS; Worthington, OH; 20/563 Hon Rl; JA; Orch; Natl Merit SF; Ohio St Univ; Aero Engr.

LINDEMAN, DAVID; Holland Sr HS; Holland, MI; Band; Chrh Wkr; Hon Rl; Pol Wkr; Yth Flsp; IM Sprt; Michigan Tech Univ; Engr.

LINDEMAN, DAVID; Upper Arlington HS; Columbus, OH; Pol Wkr; Sch Mus; Sch Pl; Treas Drama Clb; VP Ger Clb; Natl Merit Schl; Ohio St Univ; Physn.

LINDEMAN, JAMES; Henry Ford II HS; Sterling Hts, MI; 43/455 VICA; Crs Cntry; Trk; VICA St Skill Olympics Archt Comp; Mich Comp Schlrshp Awd; Lawrence Inst Of Tech; Archt.

LINDEMAN, LISA; Ottoville Local HS; Ft Jennings, OH; Chrs; Hon Rl; Off Ade; Sch Mus; Rptr Yrbk; Drama Clb; FHA; Trk; Tech Schl; Dent Asst.

LINDEMANN, ALLAN; Ann Arbor Pioneer HS; Ann Arbor, MI; Chrh Wkr; JA; Yth Flsp; Sch Nwsp; 4-H; Bsktbl; Ftbl; IM Sprt; Mgrs; Scr Kpr; Michigan St Univ; Wildlife Mgmt.

LINDEMANN, DANA; Lansing Everett HS; Lansing, MI; Jr NHS; NHS; Exerett HS Math Dept Awrd 78; MSEA Schlrshp Based On Act Score; Michigan St Univ; Vet Med.

LINDER, CINDY; Woodridge HS; Hudson, OH; Chrs; Chrh Wkr; Girl Scts; Hon Rl; Off Ade; Sct Actv; Stg Crw; Yth Flsp; Pep Clb; C of C Awd; Ohio St Univ; Educ Tchr.

LINDER, MAUREEN; Bishop Dwenger HS; Ft Wayne, IN; Cls Rep Soph Cls; Cl Rep Jr Cls; Chrs; Hon Rl; Stu Cncl; 4-H; Pep Clb; Letter Pom Pon; 4-H Awd; Univ; Spanish.

LINDERMAN, KAREN; Huron HS; Ann Arbor, MI; 12/588 Hon Rl; Fr Clb; Natl Merit Ltr; Oberlin College.

LINDERMAN, MICHAEL; Medina Sr HS; Medina, OH; 8/341 Am Leg Boys St; Hon Rl; NHS; Pres Key Clb; Letter Crs Cntry; Letter Trk; Coll; Engr.

LINDERMAN, MICHAEL D; Medina Sr HS; Medina, OH; 8/341 Am Leg Boys St; Hon Rl; NHS; Pres Key Clb; Capt Crs Cntry; Trk; Univ; Engr.

LINDGREN, ANNE; Kearsley HS; Flint, MI; Trs Frsh Cls; VP Jr Cls; Pres Sr Cls; NHS; Stu Cncl; Univ Of Mic Flint; Bus.

LINDH, CINDY A; Clinton HS; Clinton, MI; Band; Pep Clb; Treas Spn Clb; Letter Trk; Chrldng; GAA; Scr Kpr; 3 Yr Cheerleading Awd 79; Ski Club Mbr; Western Michigan Univ; Med.

LINDHOLM, CARRIE; North Dickinson Cnty Schl; Iron Mtn, MI; Band; Chrh Wkr; Hon Rl; 4-H; Bsktbl; Trk; Chrldng; IM Sprt; Scr Kpr; 4-H Awd; Ferris St Coll; Med Sec.

LINDKE, GARY; Gaylord HS; Gaylord, MI; 36/200 Cls Rep Sr Cls; Band; Hon Rl; NHS; Stu Cncl; Capt Trk; Letter Wrstlng; Vrsty Lttr Earned All 4 Yrs & Capt 78; Wrstlng 75; Part In The Univ Of Mi Med Outreach 77; Attnd St Police; Michigan St Univ; Bus Law.

LINDLEY, LORI; Talawanda HS; Oxford, OH; 40/272 Am Leg Aux Girls St; Chrh Wkr; Hon Rl; NHS; Off Ade; Sch Pl; Stu Cncl; Yth Flsp; Drama Clb; Dnfth Awd; Miami Univ; Educ.

LINDLEY, PATRICK; Tipton HS; Tipton, IN; 7/189 Sec Jr Cls; Pres Sr Cls; Cls Rep Sr Cls; Am Leg Boys St; Hon Rl; Treas NHS; Stu Cncl; Beta Clb; Pres 4-H; FFA; Most Improved Bsktbl Player; All Sec Bsktbl; Grade Point Awd; Univ; Bus.

LINDNER, DONALD A; Ontonagon Area HS; Ontonagon, MI; Aud/Vis; Boy Scts; Cmnty Wkr; Hon Rl; Lbry Ade; NHS; Stg Crw; Rdo Clb; Natl Merit Ltr; Univ; Elec Rsrch & Dsgn.

LINDOWER, KAREN; Clay HS; South Bend, IN; 52/382 Band; Chrs; Chrh Wkr; Girl Scts; Hon Rl; NHS; Orch; Quill & Scroll; Sch Mus; Stu Cncl; Manchester Coll; Medicine.

LINDOWER, PAUL; Fairmont West HS; Kettering, OH; 35/496 Hon Rl; NHS; Mth Clb; Letter Trk; Earlham College; Med.

LINDOWER, S; Clay HS; S Bend, IN; 49/449 Chrs; Chrh Wkr; Hon Rl; NHS; Orch; Sch Mus; Stu Cncl; Sch Nwsp; Eng Clb; 4-H; Coll; Acctg.

LINDQUIST, SCOTT; William G Mather HS; Munising, MI; 13/98 Aud/Vis; Band; Boy Scts; Chrh Wkr; Hon Rl; Sch Pl; Sct Actv; Stg Crw; Letter Glf; VFW Awd; Michigan Tech Univ; Mech Engr.

LINDQUIST, VALERIE S; Pine River Jr Sr HS; Le Roy, MI; Sec Frsh Cls; Sec Jr Cls; Band; Hon Rl; NHS; Stu Cncl; Fr Clb; Pep Clb; Chrldng; Ferris St Coll; Med Record Tech.

LINDSAY, BEVERLY; Union HS; Losantville, IN; Sec Frsh Cls; Trs Soph Cls; Aud/Vis; Band; NHS; Rptr Yrbk; FHA; Bsktbl; Trk; Coll.

LINDSAY, BRENDA; Tygarts Valley HS; Valley Bend, WV; 4/54 Trs Jr Cls; Band; Hon Rl; NHS; Stu Cncl; 4-H; Sec Leo Clb; Letter Bsktbl; Potomac St Coll; Med Sec.

LINDSAY, NANCY; Maumee HS; Maumee, OH; 13/320 Pres Soph Cls; Hon Rl; NHS; Off Ade; Y-Teens; Fr Clb; Ten; Chrldng; IM Sprt; PPFtbl; Ohio State; Elem Ed.

LINDSAY, PAUL; Parkside HS; Jackson, MI; 85/350 Pres Frsh Cls; Band; Debate Tm; Hon Rl; Stg Crw; Yth Flsp; Capt Socr; Natl Merit SF; Pres Awd; Albion Coll; Busns.

LINDSEY, ANNE; Bremen HS; Bremen, IN; 11/102 Hon Rl; NHS; Drama Clb; 4-H; Fr Clb; 4-H Awd; Tri Kappa Hnrs 77; Univ; Vet.

LINDSEY, ERIC; Baldwin HS; Idlewild, MI; 10/70 Pres Frsh Cls; Cls Rep Frsh Cls; VP Soph Cls; Cls Rep Soph Cls; VP Jr Cls; Pres Sr Cls; Band; Chrs; Chrh Wkr; Cmnty Wkr; Bus.

LINDSEY, JAMES J; Cuyahoga Falls HS; Cuyahoga Falls, OH; 10/800 Debate Tm; Hon Rl; Lbry Ade; Mod UN; Pres Natl Forn Lg; NHS; Natl Merit SF; Opt Clb Awd; Rotary Awd; Voice Dem Awd; College; Law.

LINDSLY, TERRI; Lakota HS; W Chester, OH; 8/496 Chrs; Girl Scts; Hon Rl; NHS; Sch Mus; Y-Teens; Drama Clb; Sec Fr Clb; IM Sprt; Natl Merit Ltr; Outstndng Spanish Stdnt 78; Awd For Except Acad Achvmtn 77; Univ Of Cincinnati; Med.

LINDSTEAD, MARK; Parkersburg HS; Parkersburg, WV; Band; Hon Rl; Letter Trk; Wrstlng; Sci Fair 1st Pl Physics; Rice Univ; Archt.

LINDSTEDT, KEVIN; Chesterton HS; Chesterton, IN; 14/474 Band; Hon Rl; NHS; Off Ade; Orch; 4-H; Pep Clb; 4-H Awd; Oustndg Pep Band Mbr 78; Indiana Voc Tech Coll; Drftng.

LINE, ERIC; Sidney HS; Sidney, OH; Band; Chrs; Hon Rl; Orch; Key Clb; Univ; Law.

LINE, JENNI; Heritage Christian HS; Anderson, IN; Band; Hon Rl; Quill & Scroll; Ed Yrbk; Mgrs;.

LINE, KENDRA; Elida HS; Lima, OH; 14/255 Sec Soph Cls; Trs Soph Cls; Pres Sr Cls; Sec Band; Chrh Wkr; Hon Rl; NHS; Rptr Yrbk; DECA; Lat Clb; Ohio St Univ; Elem Educ.

LINEBAUGH, MICHELLE; Belding Area HS; Belding, MI; Am Leg Aux Girls St; Band; Chrh Wkr; NHS; Orch; Sch Pl; Stu Cncl; Pep Clb; Lion Awd; Natl Merit Schl; St Of Mi Schlrshp 79; Grand Rapids Univ; Psych.

LINEDECKER, ANGIE; Mc Cutcheon HS; Clarks Hill, IN; Sec Jr Cls; Band; Hon Rl; Jr NHS; Natl Forn Lg; Off Ade; Sch Mus; Fr Clb; FHA; Pep Clb; Univ; Med.

LINENKUGEL, WESLEY; Robert S Rogers HS; Toledo, OH; Band; JA; Orch; Sch Mus; Sch Pl; Stg Crw; Ger Clb; JA Awd; Univ; Archt.

LINERODE, LYLE; Marlington HS; Alliance, OH; 56/264 Am Leg Boys St; Chrs; Chrh Wkr; Hon Rl; NHS; Off Ade; Sch Mus; Yth Flsp; Key Clb; Am Leg Awd; Malone Coll; Public Rel.

LINES, SCOTT; Ashtabula HS; Ashtabula, OH; 4/208 VP Jr Cls; Pres Sr Cls; Cls Rep Sr Cls; Hon Rl; NHS; Stu Cncl; Sprt Ed Yrbk; Sprt Ed Sch Nwsp; Letter Bsktbl; Letter Ftbl; ICM Schl Of Bus; Comp Analyst.

LINFORD, LISA A; Regina HS; Detroit, MI; Hon Rl; Natl Forn Lg; VP NHS; Pol Wkr; Sci Clb; PPFtbl; Tmr; Mercy Coll; R N.

LING, VICKI A; Madison Comprehensive HS; Mansfield, OH; Chrs; Chrh Wkr; Girl Scts; Hon Rl; Jr NHS; Lbry Ade; Orch; Sch Mus; Sch Pl; Yrbk; Busns Schl; Vocation.

LINGAUR, KEN; St Marys HS; Lake Leelanau, MI; Chrh Wkr; Hon Rl; Sch Pl; Stg Crw; Yrbk; Univ; History.

LINGENFELTER, BARBARA; Liberty HS; Youngstown, OH; Girl Scts; Hon Rl; Lbry Ade; Treas Yth Flsp; FTA; Trumbull Mem Schl; Nursing.

LINGER, CYNTHIA J; Oak Glen HS; Chester, WV; Band; Chrh Wkr; Girl Scts; Hon Rl; NHS; Fr Clb; Pep Clb; Chrldng; IM Sprt; Clark & Gilbert Voc Schl; Cosmetolog.

LINGER, DARLENE; Lewis County HS; Buckhannon, WV; Band; Hon Rl; VP Jr NHS; NHS; Stu Cncl; Y-Teens; VP 4-H; West Virginia Weslyan Univ.

LINGER, DARRELL; Buckhannon Upshur HS; Buckhannon, WV; Aud/Vis; NHS; Bsbl; West Virginia Univ.

LINGER, DWAYNE; Stow HS; Munroe Fall, OH; Aud/Vis; Chrh Wkr; Hon Rl; Rptr Sch Nwsp; Hndbl; IM Sprt; Akron Univ; Acctg.

LINGER, JANE; Beaver Local HS; Negley, OH; Hon Rl; NHS; Eng Clb; Fr Clb; Sci Clb; Trk; Mgrs; Scr Kpr; Natl Merit SF; Univ; Elem Ed.

LINGER, LINDA; Bridgeport Sr HS; Bridgeport, WV; Hon Rl; Jr NHS; Red Cr Ade; Stu Cncl; Pres Y-Teens; Pep Clb; Merit Awd Glenville St Coll Annual Art Exhibit; Honorable Mention Clarksburg Harrison Public Library; Vocational Schl; Interior Design.

LINGER, MARILYN; Buckhannon Upshur HS; Buckhannon, WV; Trs Frsh Cls; Girl Scts; 4-H; Pep Clb; Letter Bsktbl; Swmmng; Capt Trk; IM Sprt; 4-H Awd; Youth Fitness Achvmnt Awd 76; Vlybl Capt & Ltr 77; AAU Jr Olympics Medals 79; Marshall Univ; Pre Law.

LINGER, RUSSELL T; Washington Irving HS; Clarksburg, WV; Am Leg Boys St; Hon Rl; Treas NHS; Rptr Yrbk; Yrbk; Rptr Sch Nwsp; Sch Nwsp; Fr Clb; Treas Sci Clb; West Virginia Univ; Pharm.

LINGNAU, BERNIE; Bishop Ready HS; Galloway, OH; Chrh Wkr; Cmnty Wkr; Hon Rl; NHS; Crs Cntry; Wrstlng; IM Sprt; Univ; Engr.

LINK, CAROL; Our Lady Of Mercy HS; W Bloomfield, MI; Swmmng; Pom Pon; Michigan St Univ; Bus.

LINK, CHRISTINE; Marion Local HS; Maria Stein, OH; Chrs; Hon Rl; Hosp Ade; Rptr Sch Nwsp; Pep Clb; Sci Clb; Scr Kpr; Miami Valley Univ; Nursing.

LINK, DAVID; Bowsher HS; Toledo, OH; 128/519 Band; Rptr Sch Nwsp; Sch Nwsp; College; Computer Tech.

LINK, JEANNE; Wyoming HS; Wyoming, OH; AFS; Chrs; Girl Scts; Hon Rl; Hosp Ade; Sch Mus; FDA; Trk; Chrldng; GAA; Miami Univ; Med.

LINK, JEFF S; Celina Sr HS; Celina, OH; 29/241 Hon Rl; Jr NHS; NHS; Lat Clb; IM Sprt; Ohio St Univ; Engr.

LINK, KAREN; Lehman HS; Sidney, OH; 5/98 VP Band; Girl Scts; Hon Rl; NHS; Sch Mus; Pres 4-H; Bsktbl; Trk; Am Leg Awd; 4-H Awd; Mt Saint Joseph; Math.

LINK, PENNY; Decatur Central HS; Canby, IN; Chrh Wkr; Drl Tm; Pol Wkr; 4-H; Pep Clb; IM Sprt; Pom Pon; 4-H Awd; College; Acctg.

LINK, TED; North HS; E Lake, OH; 107/655 Boy Scts; Chrh Wkr; Cmnty Wkr; Hon Rl; Sct Actv; Bsktbl; Trk; Cit Awd; Voc Schl; Elec.

LINK, VIRGINIA; Lehman HS; Sidney, OH; 3/98 Am Leg Aux Girls St; Hon Rl; Jr NHS; NHS; Red Cr Ade; Sch Pl; Ed Yrbk; Pres 4-H; Pres Fr Clb; Pep Clb; Edison State; Nursing.

LINKE, SONJA; Bay HS; Bay Vill, OH; 15/270 Band; Hon Rl; NHS; Yrbk; Pres Ger Clb; PPFtbl; Cleveland State Univ; Accountant.

LINKOUS, NELSON; Bluefield HS; Bluefield, WV; Band; Chrs; Chrh Wkr; Hon Rl; Rdo Clb; VICA; Bluefield St Univ; Elec Tech.

LINN, BRADLEY; Whitko HS; South Whitley, IN; Chrs; Rptr Sch Nwsp; North Amer Schl Of Firearms; Gunsmth.

LINN, BRENDA; Wakefield HS; Wakefield, MI; Sec Jr Cls; Band; FCA; Hon Rl; Off Ade; Sch Pl; Yth Flsp; Yrbk; Univ.

LINN, LORI; Laurel HS; Rushville, IN; Band; Chrh Wkr; Hon Rl; NHS; Yrbk; Sch Nwsp; College; Nursing.

LINN, PAUL; Wynford HS; Bucyrus, OH; Chrs; Chrh Wkr; Hon Rl; NHS; Sch Pl; Pres Yth Flsp; 4-H; Sec FFA; Trk; Wrstlng; Ohio St Univ; Agri.

LINN, PAULA; Catholic Central HS; Steubenville, OH; Hon Rl; Hosp Ade; NHS; Stu Cncl; FHA; Spn Clb; Bsktbl; Letter Ten; Wrstlng; IM Sprt; Univ; Med Tech.

LINN, SANDRA; Willow Run HS; Ypsilanti, MI; Hon Rl; NHS; Rptr Yrbk; Trk; Mat Maids; College.

LINN, SHERRY; Union City Cmnty HS; Union City, IN; 14/105 Band; Hon Rl; Lbry Ade; NHS; Stu Cncl; Yrbk; Eng Clb; 4-H; Fr Clb; OEA; Univ; Eng.

LINNEE, DIANE; Gwinn HS; Gwinn, MI; Drl Tm; Hon Rl; Gym; Chrldng; College; Special Education Teacher.

LINS, REBECCA; Penn HS; Mishawaka, IN; Chrs; Chrh Wkr; Cmnty Wkr; Hon Rl; Mdrgl; Sch Mus; Coll; Music.

LINSON, RICHARD E; W Lafayette HS; W Lafayette, IN; 52/185 Band; Boy Scts; Chrh Wkr; Hon Rl; Yth Flsp; Rptr Yrbk; Cit Awd; J Philip Sousa Awd 78; Univ; Comp Sci.

LINT, DON; Cadillac HS; Cadillac, MI; Cls Rep Frsh Cls; Hon Rl; Stu Cncl; Wrstlng; Univ; Bus Admin.

LINTON, MICHAEL D; Circleville HS; Circleville, OH; 1/225 Pres Soph Cls; Pres Jr Cls; Am Leg Boys St; Hon Rl; Jr NHS; NHS; Stu Cncl; Yth Flsp; Ed Yrbk; Lat Clb; Whos Who In Frgn Lang 77; Eng Merit Soc 77 79; Latin Hnr Soc 77 79; Law.

LINTON, RICHARD; Hedgesville HS; Martinsburg, WV; Pres Frsh Cls; Pres Jr Cls; Chrh Wkr; Hon Rl; Stu Cncl; Pres 4-H; Pres FFA; Crs Cntry; St Farmer Degree 79; Star St Farmer Awd 79; Dairy Farm Oper.

LINVILLE, SUSAN D; Lincoln HS; Lumberport, WV; Hon Rl; NHS; Sch Mus; Sch Pl; Stu Cncl; Treas Y-Teens; Drama Clb; Chrldng; Fairmont St Coll; Exec Sec.

LIO, SUZANNE; L C Mohr HS; South Haven, MI; Cmp Fr Grls; Chrh Wkr; Cmnty Wkr; Hon Rl; C of C Awd; Outstndng Stdnt Awd 76; Hon Stdnt At Grad 78; Muskegon Bus Schl; Legal Aid.

LIOSSIS, KATHY; Tuslaw HS; Massillon, OH; 9/175 Band; Hon Rl; NHS; Y-Teens; FNA; Lat Clb; Univ Of Akron; Med Tech.

LIOTTI, JENNIFER A; Carmel HS; Carmel, IN; 9/664 Cls Rep Soph Cls; Cl Rep Jr Cls; Cls Rep Sr Cls; Hon Rl; Lit Mag; NHS; Chmn Stu Cncl; Pep Clb; Scr Kpr; JETS Awd; Zoology Awd; Purdue Univ Cert Of Recog; Purdue Univ; Chemical Engr.

LIPINSKI, RICHARD; Cardinal Mooney HS; Youngstown, OH; Hon Rl; IM Sprt; Youngstown St Univ; Comp.

LIPINSKI, SUSAN; Calvin M Woodward HS; Toledo, OH; 12/350 Band; Hon Rl; Jr NHS; NHS; Fr Clb; OEA; Am Leg Awd; Univ Of Toledo; Bus Admin.

LIPINSKI, THEODORE; Brooke HS; Weirton, WV; 63/405 Hon Rl; Ger Clb; Sci Clb; Bsbl; Ftbl; College; Sci.

LIPKA, JOHN M; Morton Sr HS; Hammond, IN; 10/450 Cls Rep Soph Cls; JA; NHS; Sch Pl; Stg Crw; Rptr Sch Nwsp; Sci Clb; Letter Crs Cntry; Letter Trk; IM Sprt; Univ Of Chicago.

LIPKA, JUDY; Warren Woods HS; Warren, MI; Band; Chrh Wkr; Hon Rl; NHS; Stu Cncl; Coach Actv; Life Chiropractic College; Med.

LIPPENCOTT, JON; Graham HS; Urbana, OH; Band; Boy Scts; Chrs; Chrh Wkr; Cmnty Wkr; Debate Tm; 4-H; Ohi State.

LIPPERT, CINDY; Cedar Lake Academy; Alma, MI; 45/83 Chrs; Hon Rl; FHA; VFW Awd; Voice Dem Awd; Andrews Univ; Sec.

LIPPIATT, LORIE; West Branch HS; Salem, OH; AFS; Chrs; Hon Rl; Lbry Ade; Natl Forn Lg; NHS; Rptr Yrbk; 4-H; Rdo Clb; Scr Kpr; Youngstown St Univ.

LIPPINCOTT, ROGER; Connersville Sr HS; Connersville, IN; 2/400 Aud/Vis; Hon Rl; NHS; Sch Pl; Stg Crw; Drama Clb; Ger Clb; Sci Clb; Kiwan Awd; 1st Pl In Altrusa Clb Young Artist Contest 73 & 75 & 77; Oberlin Coll; Music.

LIPPOLD, SHARON; North Miami HS; Peru, IN; 3/114 VP Sr Cls; Pres Chrs; Chrh Wkr; Hon Rl; Mdrgl; Pres MMM; Pres NHS; Sec Stu Cncl; Pres 4-H; Key Clb; Purdue Univ; Engr.

LIPPS, ANN; Providence HS; New Albany, IN; Hst Frsh Cls; Cls Rep Soph Cls; Cl Rep Jr Cls; Cls Rep Sr Cls; Chrs; Chrh Wkr; Girl Scts; Hon Rl; Sch Pl; Sct Actv; Indiana Univ; Phys Educ.

LIPPS, JACKIE J; Union City Community HS; Union City, IN; DECA; FHA; Indiana Univ East.

LIPPS, LINDA; Tri Village HS; New Madison, OH; Trs Jr Cls; Chrs; Sch Mus; Yrbk; Rptr Sch Nwsp; FHA; OEA; Miami Jacobs Jr Coll Bus; Legal Sec.

LIPS, JANET; St Josephs HS; S Bend, IN; 9/229 Hon Rl; Jr NHS; NHS; Sdlty; Ball State Univ; Bus.

LIPSCHUTZ, JOSH; West Lafayette HS; W Lafayette, IN; Boy Scts; Chrh Wkr; Debate Tm; Hon Rl; JA; Sch Mus; Sch Pl; Yth Flsp; Drama Clb; Glf; Univ; Law.

LIPSCOMB, BETHANY; Ripley HS; Cottageville, WV; 10/260 Sec Chrh Wkr; Hon Rl; Treas Hosp Ade; Pres JA; NHS; Off Ade; Sch Pl; Stg Crw; Pres Yth Flsp; Pres FHA; W V Wesleyan Coll; Nursing.

LIPSCOMB, LARRY; Bruceton HS; Bruceton Mills, WV; Band; West Virginia Univ; Engr.

LIPSCOMB, SUSAN; Federal Hocking HS; Coolville, OH; 2/115 VP Jr Cls; Am Leg Aux Girls St; Hon Rl; Jr NHS; Yth Flsp; Rptr Yrbk; 4-H; Mth Clb; Spn Clb; 4-H Awd; Ohio Univ; Social Work.

LIPSEY, NANETTE; Union HS; Grand Rapids, MI; Band; Cmp Fr Grls; Chrs; Chrh Wkr; Girl Scts; Hon Rl; Jr NHS; Off Ade; Yth Flsp; Cit Awd; Michigan St Univ; Comp Sci.

LIPTAK, LISA; Pocahontas County HS; Arbovale, WV; 37/125 Girl Scts; Sch Pl; Sct Actv; 4-H; Sec 4-H Awd; Potomac State; Phys Ther.

LIQUORI, DIANE; Niles Mc Kinley HS; Niles, OH; Cl Rep Jr Cls; Hon Rl; Jr NHS; NHS; Sch Mus; Stu Cncl; Rptr Yrbk; Sch Nwsp; Drama Clb; OEA; Youngstown St Univ; Bus Admin.

LIQUORI, DONNA; Niles Mckinley HS; Niles, OH; Hon Rl; Youngstown State; Teacher.

LISHNESS, TODD; Wapakoneta Sr HS; Wapakoneta, OH; Boy Scts; Chrh Wkr; Hon Rl; Pres Yth Flsp; 4-H; Fr Clb; Letter Wrstlng; Univ.

LISI, ANNETTE; Midpark HS; Brook Park, OH; Sec Frsh Cls; Cls Rep Soph Cls; Cl Rep Jr Cls; NHS; Pep Clb; Trk; Chrldng; Tmr; Cuyahaga Comm Coll; Dental Hygiene.

LISKIEWICZ, JULIA; Saint Alphonsus HS; Detroit, MI; Hon Rl; Hosp Ade; College; Veterinarian.

LISS, MICHAEL; Cincinnati Cntry Day HS; Cincinnati, OH; Boy Scts; JA; Pres Jr NHS; Lit Mag; Mod UN; NHS; Yrbk; Mth Clb; Socr; Elk Awd; Univ Of Penn; Bus.

LISSAKERS, LARS; Loudonville HS; Perrysville, OH; Band; Boy Scts; Sch Pl; Sct Actv; Stg Crw; Natl Merit Ltr; Univ; Elec Engr.

LIST, DIANE; North Farmington HS; Farm Hills, MI; Hon Rl; NHS; Fr Clb; College.

LISTER, TONI; Bellmont HS; Decatur, IN; 42/244 Hon Rl; Ger Clb; Pep Clb; Bsbl; Bsktbl; Ftbl; Gym; Mgrs; Scr Kpr; Ind Univ; Law.

LISTO, DAN; Purcell HS; Cincinnati, OH; Pres Frsh Cls; Pres Soph Cls; Pres Jr Cls; Stu Cncl; Yth Flsp; Yrbk; Bsbl; Bsktbl; Chrldng; Univ; Draftng.

LISTON, HEATHER C; Burris Lab HS; Muncie, IN; 1/50 Sec Sr Cls; Band; Chrs; Mdrgl; Sch Pl; Rptr Sch Nwsp; Univ; Theatre.

LISTON, PAUL; Bloomington South HS; Bloomington, IN; Band; Letter Crs Cntry; Trk; Voc Schl; Elec.

LITKA, LISA; Hoover HS; North Canton, OH; Am Leg Aux Girls St; Band; Hon Rl; Stu Cncl; Y-Teens; Yrbk; Rptr Sch Nwsp; Lat Clb; Pep Clb; Swmmng; Miami Univ; Poli Sci.

LITT, RORI; Meadowdale HS; Dayton, OH; VP Frsh Cls; VP Soph Cls; VP Jr Cls; VP Sr Cls; Chrs; Chrh Wkr; Cmnty Wkr; Hon Rl; NHS; Off Ade; Denison Univ.

LITTERAL, BRIAN; Emmerich Manual HS; Indianapolis, IN; JA Awd; JETS Awd; California Tech Univ; Math.

LITTERAL, DAVID; Loveland Hurst HS; Loveland, OH; Boy Scts; Chrs; Chrh Wkr; Stg Crw; Key Clb; Spn Clb; Wrstlng; IM Sprt; Schl Serv Group 77 78 & 79; Brigham Young Univ; Bus Mgmt.

LITTLE, ANTHONY A; Cahdsey HS; Detroit, MI; Cls Rep Frsh Cls; Cls Rep Soph Cls; Cl Rep Jr Cls; Band; Drl Tm; Orch; Sch Mus; Bsbl; Bsktbl; Ftbl; Univ; TV Brdtstng.

LITTLE, CAMILLE; Bishop Hartley HS; Columbus, OH; Cls Rep Soph Cls; Girl Scts; Sct Actv; Stu Cncl; Drama Clb; Trk; Intrudctn To Findmntls Of Engr OSU 79; Exclinc Dist Sci Day Oh Acad Of Sci 76; Univ; Comp Engr.

LITTLE, CAROL; Cass City HS; Cass City, MI; 5/149 Trs Soph Cls; Cl Rep Jr Cls; Pres Sr Cls; Band; FCA; Girl Scts; Hon Rl; Jr NHS; NHS; Orch; Julia Murray Schlrshp; St Of Michigan Schlrshp; Michigan St Univ; Med Tech.

LITTLE, CAROLYN; Bay City Central HS; Bay City, MI; 5/535 Cl Rep Jr Cls; Sec Sr Cls; Chrh Wkr; Cmnty Wkr; Hon Rl; Lbry Ade; NHS; Off Ade; Pol Wkr; Quill & Scroll; Alma Coll Pres Schlrshp 79; Alma Coll Frsh Talent Awd Leadership 79; Alma Coll; Nuclear Physics.

LITTLE, CINDY; Teays Valley HS; Grove Port, OH; 18/198 Hon Rl; Hosp Ade; NHS; 4-H; Lat Clb; Mas Awd; Lab Asst 76 79; Whos Who Among Amer HS Stu 77; Ohio St Univ; Nurse.

LITTLE, DARCY; Bad Axe HS; Bad Axe, MI; 8/138 Band; Hon Rl; Natl Forn Lg; NHS; Orch; Sch Mus; 4-H; Pep Clb; Bsktbl; Trk; Alma College; Art.

LITTLE, DAVID B; Swan Valley HS; Saginaw, MI; 15/188 Cls Rep Soph Cls; NHS; VP Stu Cncl; Bsktbl; Ftbl; Ten; Natl Merit SF; Opt Clb Awd; Outstanding Stu Class; College; Busns Admin.

LITTLE, DEBORAH; Elgin HS; La Rue, OH; Hon Rl; Letter Bsktbl; Gym; Letter Trk; Chrldng; PPFtbl; Mst Valuable Track Plyr 79; Nursing.

LITTLE, DIANE; Turpin HS; Cincinnati, OH; 1/371 Chrs; Hon Rl; Sch Pl; Drama Clb; Mth Clb; Swmmng; Letter Trk; PPFtbl; DAR Awd; Outstanding Performance Math 1977; Pro Song & Dance Grp; Univ; Math.

LITTLE, JEAN; Elgin HS; Larue, OH; Cls Rep Soph Cls; Cl Rep Jr Cls; Cls Rep Sr Cls; Hon Rl; Stu Cncl; FFA; Gym; Trk; Homecoming Ct 76 77 & 78; Homecoming Queen 79; State Beauty Acad; Cosmetology.

LITTLE, JEANETTE; Youngstown South HS; Youngstown, OH; 1/372 Trs Frsh Cls; Cls Rep Soph Cls; Chrh Wkr; Hon Rl; Stu Cncl; Rptr Sch Nwsp; FHA; Cit Awd; Youngstown St Univ; Prof Sec.

LITTLE, JENNIFER; Okemos HS; East Lansing, MI; 57/350 Chrs; Hon Rl; Mdrgl; Sch Pl; 4-H Awd; Western Michigan Univ; Music Theatre.

LITTLE, KATHLEEN; Ontario HS; Mansfield, OH; 15/145 Chrh Wkr; Drl Tm; Hon Rl; Off Ade; Red Cr Ade; 4-H; Pep Clb; Tmr; 4-H Awd; NCTC; Bus.

LITTLE, KENT; Greeneview HS; Jamestown, OH; 45/110 Band; Hon Rl; FTA; Wrstlng; Mgrs;.

LITTLE, KIM; North Putnam Jr Sr HS; Greencastle, IN; FCA; Girl Scts; 4-H; Pep Clb; Spn Clb; Letter Bsktbl; Letter Swmmng; Letter Trk; GAA; Mat Maids; Univ; Med.

LITTLE, LORI; Woodhaven HS; Woodhaven, MI; Chrs; Hon Rl; Pep Clb; Bsktbl; Chrldng; Coach Actv; Scr Kpr; Detroit College Of Bus; Acctg.

LITTLE, MARK; Malabar HS; Mansfield, OH; 9/216 Cl Rep Jr Cls; Boy Scts; Hon Rl; NHS; Orch; Sch Pl; Sct Actv; Stg Crw; Yth Flsp; Rptr Yrbk; Univ Of Cincinnati; Engr.

LITTLE, SHELLY; St Johns HS; St Johns, MI; Girl Scts; Hosp Ade; 4-H; 4-H Awd; Natl Merit Ltr; Ferris State College; Med Asst.

LITTLE, SUZANNE; Cass City HS; Cass City, MI; Band; Chrs; Chrh Wkr; Hon Rl; NHS; Sch Mus; Yth Flsp; Yrbk; Western Michigan Univ; Art.

LITTLEFIELD, DAVID; North Olmsted HS; N Olmsted, OH; AFS; Band; Boy Scts; Hon Rl; NHS; Orch; Sch Mus; Trk; God Cntry Awd; Les Exclnt 1st 2nd 4th Qtrs 78; Full Tiution & Extra Schlrshp 79; Ohio Bd Of Regents 2nd Pl 79; Univ Of Cincinnati; Archt.

LITTLEJOHN, DAVE; Sidney HS; Sidney, OH; Am Leg Boys St; Chrs; Hon Rl; NHS; Am Leg Awd; Miami Univ; History.

LITTNER, JAY; La Salle HS; Cincinnati, OH; 100/300 Chrs; Hon Rl; Sch Mus; Sch Pl; Drama Clb; Univ Of Cincinnati; Broadcasting.

LITTON, LISA; Olentangy HS; Delaware, OH; 8/149 Hon Rl; NHS; Pep Clb; Sci Clb; Spn Clb; Am Leg Awd; Schlrshp Awd Frsh Yr 77; Cert Of Hnr Soph Yr 78; Cert Of Hnr H Jr Yr 79; Univ; Educ.

LITWILLER, JAN; Fulton HS; Ithaca, MI; Chrh Wkr; Hon Rl; Lbry Ade; Off Ade; Yth Flsp; Rptr Yrbk; Rptr Sch Nwsp; 4-H; FHA; 4-H Awd; Ctrl Michigan Univ; Exec Sec.

LITWIN, TERRI; Chaney HS; Youngstown, OH; Hon Rl; NHS; Off Ade; Y-Teens; Ger Clb; Pep Clb; Letter Ten; Cert Of Achvmnt 78; C Pin 79; Univ; Med.

LITZ, LEANDRA; Madison Heights HS; Anderson, IN; 40/267 Chrs; Chrh Wkr; Cmnty Wkr; Hon Rl; Off Ade; FHA; Pep Clb; Letter Gym; Letter Trk; Letter Chrldng; Univ; Psych.

LITZ, SARA; Madison Hts HS; Anderson, IN; 41/371 Chrs; Chrh Wkr; Cmnty Wkr; Hon Rl; NHS; Off Ade; Pep Clb; Letter Gym; Trk; Letter Chrldng; Univ; Math.

LIUTAUD, GREG; Culver Military Acad; Cary, IL; VP Frsh Cls; Pres Soph Cls; Pres Jr Cls; Pres Sr Cls; Debate Tm; Drl Tm; Hon Rl; Jr NHS; NHS; Pol Wkr; Univ; Engr.

LIUTKUS, INDRE; Shaker Hts HS; Shaker Hts, OH; Chrs; Hon Rl; Fr Clb; Swmmng; Cit Awd; Univ; Interior Design.

LIVELY, KYLE; Tipton HS; Atlanta, IN; Chrh Wkr; Hon Rl; NHS; FFA; Letter Bsbl; IM Sprt; Purdue Univ.

LIVELY, MICHELLE; Upper Arlington HS; Columbus, OH; 208/645 Chrs; Chrh Wkr; Hon Rl; Sch Pl; Ed Yrbk; Drama Clb; Pep Clb; Ohi State Univ; Dental Hygiene.

LIVELY, SUSAN; Roosevelt Wilson HS; Clarksburg, WV; 30/122 Chrh Wkr; Cmnty Wkr; Hon Rl; Sch Pl; Yth Flsp; Y-Teens; 4-H; Am Leg Awd; 4-H Awd; Fairmont College; Early Chldhd Educ.

LIVENGOOD, KATHY; Perry HS; Massillon, OH; Chrs; Chrh Wkr; Girl Scts; Hon Rl; NHS; Sct Actv; Yth Flsp; Sec OEA; Pep Clb; Stark Tech Coll; Data Processing.

LIVERETT, MICHAEL A; Charles Stewart Mott Sr HS; Warren, MI; Boy Scts; 4-H; Sci & Engr Fair Of Metropolitan Detroit Special Awd; Univ Of Michigan; Engr.

LIVERMORE, BRAD; Pioneer HS; Ann Arbor, MI; Cls Rep Frsh Cls; Stu Cncl; Lat Clb; Ftbl; Wrstlng; IM Sprt; College.

LIVERNOIS, JAMES L; Vandercook Lake HS; Jackson, MI; 14/90 VP Sr Cls; Band; Hon Rl; NHS; Sch Pl; Rptr Sch Nwsp; Sch Nwsp; Letter Glf; Letter Trk; Mgrs; Michigan Competitive Schlrshp; Michigan St Univ; Criminal Justice.

LIVERS, RITA; North HS; Akron, OH; Drm Mjrt; Hon Rl; NHS; Red Cr Ade; FNA; Twrlr; Howard; Nursing.

LIVEZEY, KELLY; Walter P Chrysler Mem HS; New Castle, IN; 44/418 Band; Drl Tm; Hon Rl; Sch Mus; Sch Pl; Stg Crw; Ed Sch Nwsp; Drama Clb; DAR Awd; Indiana Univ; Jrnlsm.

LIVINGSTON, CYNTHIA; Harry S Truman HS; Taylor, MI; Hon Rl; NHS; Letter Gym; Univ Of Mic; Med.

LIVINGSTON, ELLEN; Clay City HS; Centerpoint, IN; 7/59 VP Soph Cls; Band; Drm Mjrt; Hon Rl; NHS; Pep Clb; Sci Clb; Letter Bsbl; Letter Socr; Letter Chrldng; Ind State Univ; Commercial Art.

LIVINGSTON, JEFF; Pt Pleasant HS; Leon, WV; Yth Flsp; 4-H; FFA; Home Imprvmnt Awd 1977; De Kalb Awd 1978; Converstn Trip Awd 1976;.

LIVINGSTON, LINDA; R Nelson Snider HS; Ft Wayne, IN; Hon Rl; Letter Bsktbl; Letter Trk; Ball St Univ.

LIVINGSTON, LISA; Lawrence Central HS; Lawrence, IN; 9/295 Chrs; Girl Scts; JA; NHS; Pres Orch; Sch Mus; Yth Flsp; Beta Clb; Key Clb; Chrldng; Purdue Univ; Soc Wrk.

LIVINGSTON, MARCIA; Heath HS; Heath, OH; Sec Frsh Cls; Sec Soph Cls; Sec Jr Cls; NHS; Treas Key Clb; Letter Gym; Letter Chrldng; Dnfth Awd; Lion Awd;.

LIVINGSTON, MARY; Clay City HS; Center Point, IN; 6/60 Chrs; NHS; Sci Clb; Trk; GAA; Univ; Phys Ther.

LIVINGSTON, PAMELA; Wadsworth Sr HS; Wadsworth, OH; 9/349 Chrh Wkr; Girl Scts; Hon Rl; NHS; Yth Flsp; Spn Clb; Letter Trk; Scr Kpr; Univ; Sci.

LIVON, LISA; North Farmington HS; W Blmfield, MI; Band; Pres Chrh Wkr; Drm Mjrt; Girl Scts; Hon Rl; Lbry Ade; Orch; Fr Clb; GAA; Twrlr; College.

LIXEY, CHERYL; Lamphere HS; Madison Height, MI; 20/347 Hon Rl; NHS; Pol Wkr; Stu Cncl; Trk; Chrldng; Pom Pon; Natl Merit SF; Oakland Univ; Optometrist.

LLOYD, ANTHONY; Watkins Memorial HS; Pataskala, OH; Debate Tm; Hon Rl; NHS; Spn Clb; IM Sprt; Opt Clb Awd; Univ; Physics.

LLOYD, BRIAN; Hamilton Southeastern HS; Noblesville, IN; Fr Clb; Bsktbl; Trk;.

LLOYD, C; Fairmont West HS; Kettering, OH; 1/471 Hon Rl; Fr Clb; Natl Merit SF; West Point Military Acad; U S Army.

LLOYD, CAROL; Lapel HS; Lapel, IN; 6/83 Hon Rl; Sec NHS; Off Ade; Sec Stu Cncl; Rptr Yrbk; VP 4-H; Lat Clb; Bsktbl; Trk; Ball State; Secretarial.

LLOYD, CATHY; Lee M Thurston HS; Redford, MI; Hon Rl; Hosp Ade; NHS; Natl Merit Ltr; Univ Of Michigan; Bus Admin.

LLOYD, CONNIE; Lincolnview HS; Van Wert, OH; Sec Band; Chrs; Chrh Wkr; Sec Yth Flsp; Pres 4-H; Pres FHA; 4-H Awd; Sec.

LLOYD, K; Delphos Jefferson HS; Delphos, OH; 19/110 Band; Chrh Wkr; Hon Rl; NHS; Yth Flsp; Sci Clb; Bsktbl; College; Accounting.

LLOYD, NANCY; West HS; Columbus, OH; 1/330 Val; Am Leg Aux Girls St; Band; Hon Rl; NHS; Orch; Yrbk; Ed Sch Nwsp; Sch Nwsp; Mth Clb; Ohio St Univ; Journalism.

LLOYD, TAMMIE; East Canton HS; E Canton, OH; VP Soph Cls; Am Leg Aux Girls St; Chrs; Chrh Wkr; Hon Rl; Jr NHS; NHS; Fr Clb; FTA; Sci Clb; Tech Coll; Dent Hygnst.

LOAR, DEBBIE; Hampshire HS; Kirby, WV; 40/218 AFS; Am Leg Aux Girls St; Band; Girl Scts; Hon Rl; Sct Actv; VP Yth Flsp; Sprt Ed Yrbk; 4-H; FBLA; Coll; Bus Admin.

LOBBAN, JOHN; Greenbrier East HS; Alderson, WV; 1/380 4-H; FFA; Ftbl; West Virginia Univ; Biology.

LOBBEZOO, TIMOTHY; Creston HS; Grand Rpds, MI; Cls Rep Soph Cls; Cls Rep Sr Cls; Hon Rl; Jr NHS; Stg Crw; Yth Flsp; IM Sprt; Calvin Coll; Pre Med.

LOBERGER, SCOTT R; North Farmington HS; Farmington Hlls, MI; VP Frsh Cls; Cls Rep Soph Cls; Debate Tm; Hon Rl; Natl Forn Lg; Sch Mus; Sch Pl; Stu Cncl; Ger Clb; Michigan; Chiropractor.

LOBO, JAMES; St Joseph HS; Huntington, WV; Ho n Rl; Sch Pl; Yrbk; Socr; Engr.

LOCEY, ELLEN; Monsignor HS; Kalamazoo, MI; Cls Rep Frsh Cls; Cls Rep Soph Cls; Stu Cncl; Lat Clb; Spn Clb; Bsktbl; Swmmng; Trk; GAA; IM Sprt; Western Michigan Univ; Cmnctns.

LOCH, AMY; Galion HS; Galion, OH; Hon Rl; VP JA; IM Sprt; Natl Merit Ltr; College; Biochemistry.

LOCHER, MARY; John F Kennedy HS; Taylor, MI; 4/400 Cls Rep Soph Cls; Cl Rep Jr Cls; Cls Rep Sr Cls; Cmp Fr Grls; Hon Rl; Jr NHS; VP NHS; Sch Mus; Alma College; Bio.

LOCHNER, PAUL D; Riverside HS; Dearborn Hts, MI; Boy Scts; Hon Rl; Sch Pl; Fr Clb; Hockey; Univ Of Mic; Law.

LOCHNERT, TODD; Bexley HS; Bexley, OH; Cls Rep Soph Cls; Cl Rep Jr Cls; Chrh Wkr; FCA; Hon Rl; Stu Cncl; Fr Clb; Mth Clb; Letter Bsbl; Letter Bsktbl; Duke Univ; Pre Law.

LOCHOTZKI, MARCIA; Sandusky St Marys Cntrl HS; Sandusky, OH; VP Jr Cls; Sec Sr Cls; Trs Sr Cls; Band; Hon Rl; NHS; Stu Cncl; Ger Clb; Sci Clb; Bsktbl; College; Nursing.

LOCHTOFELD, CAROLYN; Ft Recovery HS; Ft Recovery, OH; 4/90 Chrs; Chrh Wkr; Hon Rl; Jr NHS; NHS; Off Ade; Sch Mus; 4-H; OEA; Pep Clb; Mt St Joseph Univ; Intr Design.

LOCKE, CYNTHIA A; Charlotte HS; Charlotte, MI; 82/322 Cl Rep Jr Cls; Band; Chrs; Chrh Wkr; Sch Pl; Stu Cncl; Pres 4-H; Sec FFA; Am Leg Awd; 4-H Awd; Outstndng Jr FFA Agri Awrd 1979; Outstndng Cnty Holstein Jr 1978; Michigan St Univ; Animal Tech.

LOCKE, JEANNE; St Charles HS; Brant, MI; Band; Hon Rl; NHS; Orch; Stu Cncl; Univ; Acctg.

LOCKE, KRISTI; Allen East HS; Lima, OH; 10/120 Band; Girl Scts; Orch; Rptr Sch Nwsp; Treas 4-H; VP Lat Clb; Scr Kpr; 4-H Awd; College; Educa.

LOCKE, LYNN; Celina Sr HS; Celina, OH; 55/273 Chrs; Hon Rl; NHS; Yth Flsp; Ger Clb; Wright St Univ; Banking.

LOCKER, HOLLY; Sandy Valley HS; Magnolia, OH; Chrs; Girl Scts; Hon Rl; Lbry Ade; NHS; Pep Clb; Sci Clb; Spn Clb; Univ; Educ.

LOCKER, LORETTA J; Eastlake N HS; Willowick, OH; 69/669 Girl Scts; Hon Rl; Hosp Ade; JA; Jr NHS; Lakeland Univ; X Ray Tech.

LOCKER, MIKE A; Houston HS; Sidney, OH; Am Leg Boys St; Band; Boy Scts; Chrs; Hon Rl; Sci Clb; Letter Crs Cntry; Letter Trk; Am Leg Awd; Edison St Univ; Acctg.

LOCKETT, PATRICIA; Osborn HS; Detroit, MI; Cl Rep Jr Cls; Chrs; Chrh Wkr; Hon Rl; NHS; Orch; Stu Cncl; Spn Clb; Cit Awd; Cnslr Aide 79; AFRO Amer Club 78; Michigan St Univ; Spec Educ.

LOCKHART, DIANE; Buckeye Valley HS; Ashley, OH; Band; Chrh Wkr; Drl Tm; Hon Rl; Sct Actv; Yth Flsp; Rptr Yrbk; Spn Clb; Ohio St Univ; Soc Work.

LOCKHART, DYKE; Chesapeake HS; Chesapeake, OH; Hon Rl; Letter Wrstlng; Marshall Univ; Sci.

LOCKHART, GERALD; Parkersburg South HS; Mineral Wells, WV; 3/480 Cls Rep Soph Cls; Band; Chrs; Chrh Wkr; Hon Rl; Mdrgl; Natl Forn Lg; Sch Mus; 4-H; Fr Clb; John Philip Sousa Awd 75; All State Band; Graduated With Gold Hon Cord; West Virginia Univ; Applied Music.

LOCKHART, KEVIN; Belpre HS; Belpre, OH; Band; Boy Scts; Chrh Wkr; Drl Tm; Hon Rl; Orch; Sct Actv; Fr Clb; Cit Awd; Lion Awd; Bandmn Of Yr Awd 79; Jazz Bnd Mbr 76 79; Pre So Yth Grp At Church 79; Ohio St Univ; Music.

LOCKHART, LISA; Avon HS; Plainfield, IN; 1/158 Cls Rep Frsh Cls; Cls Rep Soph Cls; Cmp Fr Grls; Hon Rl; NHS; Stu Cncl; Yrbk; Spn Clb; Whos Who In In & Ky Foreign Lang 78; Pin For Best Stud In Algebra 3 & 4 79; Spanish Awds 77 78; Math Awd 77; Purdue Univ; Math.

LOCKMAN, RICHARD; Aquinas HS; Lincoln Pk, MI; FCA; Hon Rl; Sch Nwsp; Mth Clb; Rdo Clb; Ftbl; Wrstlng; Coach Actv; IM Sprt; Western Michigan Univ; Bus.

LOCKWOOD, CHARLA; Carroll HS; Ft Wayne, IN; 31/225 Chrs; Chrh Wkr; CAP; Capt Drl Tm; NHS; Sch Mus; Sec Stu Cncl; Sch Nwsp; VP 4-H; Spn Clb; Honors With Distinction Honor Ball 1979; Indiana Univ; Intr Desgn.

LOCKWOOD, DEBBIE; Morgan HS; Mc Connelsville, OH; 42/232 Hon Rl; 4-H; Sec FHA;.

LOCKWOOD, JOAN; Skeels Northern Chrstn HS; Harrison, MI; Chrh Wkr; Hon Rl; Off Ade; Yrbk; Var Vllybll Ltr Trophy 79; Var Sftbl Ltr Trophy 79; Var Sftbl Ltr Hon Mntn 77; Grand Rapids Baptist Coll; Tchr.

LOCKWOOD, LAURA; Lima Perry HS; Lima, OH; 3/74 Band; Chrs; Girl Scts; Hon Rl; Lbry Ade; NHS; Off Ade; Yth Flsp; 4-H; Spn Clb; Whos Who In Music 79; Century Three Ldr 78; Amer Bus Wmns Assoc Schlrshp Finalist 79; OSU; Music.

LOCKWOOD, LISA; Sandusky HS; Sandusky, MI; 28/140 Band; Chrs; Chrh Wkr; Debate Tm; Girl Scts; Hon Rl; Natl Forn Lg; Orch; Sch Pl; Sct Actv; Central Mic Univ; Criminal Justice.

LOCKWOOD, M; Fairmont West HS; Kettering, OH; 20/500 Band; FCA; Hon Rl; Capt Yth Flsp; VP Fr Clb; Mth Clb; Rdo Clb; Letter Crs Cntry; Letter Trk; Yale Univ; Liberal Arts.

LOCKWOOD, MARY JO; Cass City HS; Cass City, MI; 1/148 Val; Band; Chrs; Chrh Wkr; Debate Tm; Hon Rl; Jr NHS; NHS; Yth Flsp; FTA; Spring Arbor Coll; Scndry Educ.

LOCKWOOD, TERESA; Hamilton Comm HS; Hamilton, IN; 2/55 Sal; Chrs; Drl Tm; Hon Rl; NHS; Off Ade; Sch Mus; Drama Clb; Pep Clb; Pom Pon; Secretary.

LOCOCO, LEAH; Grandview Hts HS; Columbus, OH; Hon Rl; Jr NHS; NHS; Quill & Scroll; Yrbk; Fr Clb; Letter Hockey; Mat Maids; Cit Awd; De Pauw Univ; Art.

LOE, CHRISTINA; Whitko HS; Larwill, IN; Hon Rl; OEA; Bsktbl; Glf; Univ.

LOEHR, SHERI J; Oxford HS W; Oxford, MI; Cls Rep Sr Cls; Band; Chrs; Chrh Wkr; Hon Rl; Mdrgl; Sch Mus; Sch Pl; Letter Trk; Eastern Michigan Univ; Music Ther.

LOEHRLEIN, JANE; Reitz Memorial HS; Evansville, IN; 19/226 Girl Scts; Hon Rl; Red Cr Ade; Sct Actv; Cert Of Merit In An Essay Contest; College; Spec Ed.

LOEHRLEIN, THERESA; Central HS; Evansville, IN; 38/500 Cls Rep Frsh Cls; Cls Rep Soph Cls; Cl Rep Jr Cls; Hon Rl; Jr NHS; Stu Cncl; Gym; PPFtbl; Opt Clb Awd; Purdue Univ; Sci.

LOEL, BRENDA; Chillicothe HS; Chillicothe, OH; 4/375 Aud/Vis; Chrs; Hon Rl; JA; Jr NHS; NHS; O ff Ade; Ten; Chrldng; JA Awd; Univ.

LOEMBER, MARY; Oakwood HS; Dayton, OH; 12/120 Chrh Wkr; Debate Tm; Hon Rl; JA; Natl Forn Lg; NHS; Sch Pl; Stg Crw; Univ.

LOESER, MARY; St Joseph Central HS; Huntington, WV; 1/39 VP Soph Cls; Sec Jr Cls; Val; Hon Rl; Jr NHS; NHS; Sch Pl; Y-Teens; Pres FSA; Sec Keyettes; College; Medicine.

LOESER, THOMAS J; St Joseph Central Cthlc HS; Huntington, WV; 3/54 Sec Soph Cls; VP Jr Cls; Boy Scts; Chrh Wkr; Hon Rl; Jr NHS; NHS; Key Clb; Glf; Wrstlng; W Point Military Acad; Military Sci.

LOESING, DIANA M; Seton HS; Cincinnati, OH; 3/271 Hon Rl; Jr NHS; Mod UN; NHS; Off Ade; Fr Clb; Natl Merit SF; Univ Of Cincinnati; Chem.

LOEWER, MICHELE; Guernsey Catholic Ctrl HS; Cambridge, OH; 17/27 Chrs; Chrh Wkr; Cmnty Wkr; Girl Scts; Sch Mus; Sch Pl; Sct Actv; Stg Crw; Pep Clb; College; Education.

LOFTIS, NANCY; Nitro HS; Sumerco, WV; AFS; Hon Rl; Mth Clb; Univ.

LOFTUS, ANDREW; Hastings HS; Hastings, MI; Hon Rl; Sch Pl; Stg Crw; Drama Clb; College; Forest Tech.

LOFTUS, HOWARD; Ashtabula HS; Ashtabula, OH; Chrh Wkr; Hon Rl; Rptr Sch Nwsp; Voice Dem Awd; Liberty Bapt Coll.

LOGA, KEVIN; Ida Public HS; Ida, MI; 28/185 Band; Chrh Wkr; Hon Rl; NHS; Rptr Yrbk; Sprt Ed Sch Nwsp; Rptr Sch Nwsp; 4-H; Bsktbl; Ftbl; Univ Of Toledo; Educ.

LOGAN, CAROL J; Marion Harding HS; Marion, OH; AFS; Chrs; Sec Chrh Wkr; Hon Rl; Lit Mag; Off Ade; Rptr Sch Nwsp; Sch Nwsp; Drama Clb; Pres Spn Clb; Won The Title Of Miss Oh Teen Queen 78; Placed 4th In A E & S Spanish Contest 79; Rcvd The Lcl Sci Awd 77; Univ; Lang.

LOGAN, CHRISTINA; Archbishop Alter HS; Kettering, OH; Chrs; Hon Rl; Jr NHS; Lbry Ade; NHS; Drama Clb; Pres Fr Clb; GAA; IM Sprt; Pres Awd; Univ Of Dayton; Engr.

LOGAN, CYNTHIA; Lima Sr HS; Lima, OH; Chrs; Cmnty Wkr; Hon Rl; Off Ade; Orch; Sch Mus; Pep Clb; Spn Clb; Chrldng; Pom Pon; Arthur Mitchell Schl; Pro Dance.

LOGAN, DAVID; Deerfield HS; Deerfield, MI; 5/38 Cls Rep Frsh Cls; Cls Rep Soph Cls; VP Jr Cls; Cl Rep Jr Cls; Am Leg Boys St; VP NHS; Pres Stu Cncl; Letter Bsbl; Letter Bsktbl; Letter Trk; College; Engr.

LOGAN, JOANNA; Lamphere HS; Madison Hts, MI; Spn Clb; PPFtbl; Bus Schl.

LOGAN, KAREN; Fromberg HS; Fromberg, MT; Chrh Wkr; Hon Rl; Lbry Ade; Sch Pl; FHA; Mas Awd; Bus Schl.

LOGAN, KENDRA K; North Putnam Jr Sr HS; Russellville, IN; Sec Frsh Cls; Sec Soph Cls; Sec Jr Cls; Sec Sr Cls; Am Leg Aux Girls St; Treas Band; Chrh Wkr; Pres FCA; NHS; Pres OEA; Sr Of Month Optimist Clb; Mental Attitude Swimming; Outstndng Bus Stu; Indiana St Univ; Sec.

LOGAN, LINDA; Roosevelt HS; Gary, IN; 44/525 Chrh Wkr; Hon Rl; FSA; FTA; Lat Clb; Schslts Achvmnt Trophy 78; Hoosier Schr 78; Hon Stdnt Cert 78; Earlham Coll; Vet Med.

LOGAN, MICHELE; Archbishop Alter HS; Kettering, OH; 10/276 Chrs; Girl Scts; Hon Rl; Lbry Ade; NHS; Off Ade; Sch Pl; Drama Clb; VP Fr Clb; GAA; English & History Dept Awds; Natl Ed Devel Test Awd; Univ Of Dayton; Psych.

LOGAN, PATRICK J; Carmel HS; Indianapolis, IN; 23/785 Hon Rl; Off Ade; Mth Clb; Letter Trk; IM Sprt; Natl Merit SF; Purdue Univ.

LOGAN, RAE; West Carrollton HS; W Carrollton, OH; Band; Girl Scts; Jr NHS; Lit Mag; Natl Forn Lg; Sct Actv; Ger Clb; Pep Clb; Ohi Wesleyan Univ; Speech.

LOGAN, THERESA; Notre Dame Acad; Toledo, OH; Chrs; Chrh Wkr; Cmnty Wkr; 4-H; Fr Clb; IM Sprt; Cit Awd; College; Nurse.

LOGERTWELL, JENNY; Berea HS; Berea, OH; Band; Girl Scts; Hon Rl; Hosp Ade; Jr NHS; Lbry Ade; NHS; Spn Clb; Swmmng; Ten; Univ.

LOGSDON, BRENDA; Penn HS; Granger, IN; Chrh Wkr; VP JA; Sec Natl Forn Lg; Sch Pl; Rptr Yrbk; Rptr Sch Nwsp; Sch Nwsp; Spn Clb; Capt Mat Maids; Induction Into Thespians 79 80; Univ; Jrnlsm.

LOGSDON, BRIAN; Teays Valley HS; Ashville, OH; 58/208 Am Leg Boys St; Aud/Vis; Band; FCA; Sch Mus; Stg Crw; Gold Music Awd For Outstndng Band Mbr 79; Soung System Tech 77; Jazz & Marching Band 76; Ohio St Univ; Music.

LOGSDON, CYNTHIA A; Upper Sandusky HS; Upper Sandusky, OH; Chrs; Chrh Wkr; Hon Rl; JA; Jr NHS; Stu Cncl; Yrbk; Ohio St Univ; Cosmetology.

LOGSDON, JEFFREY; Bosse HS; Evansville, IN; Chrh Wkr; Hon Rl; Rptr Yrbk; Sprt Ed Sch Nwsp; Rptr Sch Nwsp; Pep Clb; Cit Awd; Univ; Cmnctns.

LOGSDON, KEITH; Plymouth Canton HS; Plymouth, MI; Hon Rl; Letter Ten; Coach Actv; Opt Clb Awd; Voice Dem Awd; Lawrence Inst Of Tech; Archt.

LOGSDON, LYNN; Bedford North Lawrence HS; Bedford, IN; 16/417 Hon Rl; NHS; Red Cr Ade; Beta Clb; Mth Clb; Spn Clb; GAA; IM Sprt; PPFtbl; N Lawrence Cmnty Schls Bd Of Trustee Schlrshp Awd 79; The St Of In A Hoosier Schlr Awd 79; Indiana Univ; Allied Health.

LOGUE, KEVIN M; Belpre HS; Belpre, OH; Am Leg Boys St; Chrh Wkr; Hon Rl; VP Yth Flsp; Pres Spn Clb; Letter Bsbl; Bsktbl; Letter Ftbl; Swmmng; Coach Actv; Univ; Engr.

LOGUE, LORRAINE; Ursuline HS; Youngstown, OH; 61/305 Hon Rl; Off Ade; FTA; College.

LOH, JUDY; Andrean HS; Gary, IN; 4/272 Hon Rl; Hosp Ade; Stu Cncl; Rptr Yrbk; Fr Clb; Mth Clb; Pep Clb; Pom Pon; Sci Awd 79; Hoosier Schlr 79; Univ Of Michigan Fresh Schlr 79; Purdue Univ; Med.

LOHER, SUELLEN; Warsaw Comm HS; Warsaw, IN; Band; Chrh Wkr; FCA; Yth Flsp; Rptr Sch Nwsp; Sch Nwsp; 4-H; Bsktbl; Trk; DAR Awd; Bsktbl Most Improved Player Varsity Letter; Track Letter; Coll; Phys Ed.

LOHMAN, LYNN; Montague HS; Rothbury, MI; Hon Rl; Bsktbl; Muskegon Comm College; Beekeeper.

LOHMAN, SUSAN; Charlestown HS; Charlestown, IN; 4/187 FCA; Hon Rl; Treas JA; Lbry Ade; NHS; Ed Sch Nwsp; Rptr Sch Nwsp; Drama Clb; Pres 4-H; FHA; Ele Conf Cncl & Chrmn; Purdue Univ; Pharmacy.

LOHMANN, GINI; Newark Catholic HS; Newark, OH; 3/82 Band; Chrs; Chrh Wkr; Cmnty Wkr; Girl Scts; Hon Rl; NHS; Sch Mus; Stu Cncl; GAA; College; Pre Med.

LOHMEYER, CINDY; Wadsworth HS; Wadsworth, OH; 50/460 Cls Rep Soph Cls; Cl Rep Jr Cls; Cls Rep Sr Cls; Chrs; Chrh Wkr; Girl Scts; Hon Rl; Jr NHS; Yth Flsp; Spn Clb; Ohio St Univ; Mktg.

LOHN, JOE; Berea HS; Berea, OH; 39/552 Hon Rl; NHS; Letter Ftbl; Letter Wrstlng; IM Sprt; Ohio State Univ; Wild Life Mgmt.

LOHR, MELANIE; Vandalia Butler HS; Dayton, OH; Cls Rep Frsh Cls; Sec Soph Cls; Cls Rep Soph Cls; Sec Jr Cls; Cl Rep Jr Cls; Band; Cmp Fr Grls; Hon Rl; Hosp Ade; Jr NHS; College; Broadcasting.

LOHR, ROBERT; Hoover HS; North Canton, OH; Chrs; Hon Rl; Stg Crw; Fr Clb; Natl Merit Ltr; College.

LOHRER, JOANN; Michigan Lutheran Seminary; Owosso, MI; Chrs; Sch Nwsp; PPFtbl; Dr Martin Luther King Coll; Tchr.

LOHRSTORFER, JEFF; South Central HS; Elizabeth, IN; Band; Chrs; Hon Rl; Lit Mag; Mth Clb; Spn Clb; Trk;.

LOJO, ANTHONY; Washington HS; Massillon, OH; Boy Scts; FCA; Hon Rl; Boys Clb Am; Spn Clb; Swmmng; Univ; Civil Engr.

LOKAR, KEVIN; Lake Linden Hubbell HS; Lake Linden, MI; 1/63 Band; Hon Rl; Yrbk; Ferris State College; Pharmacy.

LOKAR, PETER; Stevenson HS; Plainwell, MI; Letter Ftbl; Mic State Univ; Bus Admin.

LOKMER, ADREIENE; Canfield HS; Canfield, OH; 3/258 Trs Jr Cls; Girl Scts; Hon Rl; Lit Mag; NHS; Stg Crw; Ger Clb; Spn Clb; Letter Trk; GAA; Univ; Engr.

LOKUTA, RUSSELL G; Our Lady Of Mt Carmel HS; Wyandotte, MI; 6/71 Trs Soph Cls; Trs Sr Cls; Chrs; Chrh Wkr; Hon Rl; NHS; Sch Mus; Sch Pl; Stu Cncl; Rptr Yrbk; Univ Of Michigan; Med.

LOMAS, KRISTI; St Alphonsus HS; Detroit, MI; Band; Hon Rl; Off Ade; Orch; Fr Clb; PPFtbl; Outstndng Musicnship Awd 78; Western Univ; Math.

LOMBARDI, JONI; Central Catholic HS; Canton, OH; Band; Boy Scts; Chrs; Drm Mjrt; Hon Rl; Sct Actv; Twrlr; Ohi Northern; Pharmacy.

LOMBARDI, WENDY; Bishop Foley HS; Clawson, MI; Hon Rl; Rptr Sch Nwsp; Capt Crs Cntry; Capt Trk; Univ; Acctg.

LOMBARDO, PINA; Warren Sr HS; Sterling Hts, MI; Chrs; Hon Rl; Sch Mus; Best Coll Awd 79; Awd For Outsdng Achvmnt In French 77; Univ; Med.

LOMNANN, LARS; High School; Grosse Pt Shrs, MI; Band; Hon Rl; Jr NHS; NHS; Sch Pl; Ger Clb; Spn Clb; Socr; IM Sprt; Univ.

LOMONT, KATHY; Heritage HS; New Haven, IN; 11/176 Quill & Scroll; Ed Sch Nwsp; Rptr Sch Nwsp; Letter Gym; Coach Actv; Univ.

LONCHAR, MICHELLE; Euclid Sr HS; Euclid, OH; Chrh Wkr; Letter Gym; Letter Swmmng; Cit Awd; Mbr Of Natl Atheltic Schlrshp Soc Of Scndry Schls 78; Schlstc Excllnc Awd 78; Distinguished Hon Awd 76; Art Inst Of Pittsburg; Cmmrcl Art.

LONCHAR, ROBBIN M; Bergland HS; Center Line, MI; Hon Rl; NHS; Graphic Arts Hnr 79; Madonna Coll; Cmmrcl Art.

LONDON, BETH; Shaker Hts HS; Shaker Hts, OH; Hon Rl; Hosp Ade; Univ; Soc Work.

LONG, ANGELA; Archbishop Alter HS; Dayton, OH; Chrs; Chrh Wkr; Cmnty Wkr; Hon Rl; Lbry Ade; Off Ade; Spn Clb; Natl Merit Ltr; Miami Univ; Medicine.

LONG, BRIAN; Tecumseh HS; Tecumseh, MI; Hon Rl; NHS; Yth Flsp; 4-H; FFA; Letter Bsbl; IM Sprt; 4-H Awd; 4 H Leadership & Ach Awd; Michigan St Univ; Engr.

LONG, BRIAN; Ashland HS; Ashland, OH; Cls Rep Frsh Cls; Cls Rep Soph Cls; Cl Rep Jr Cls; Cls Rep Sr Cls; Hon Rl; Off Ade; Stu Cncl; Bsbl; Ftbl; Taylor Univ; Ministry.

LONG, CARLTON; William A Wirt HS; Gary, IN; Boy Scts; Chrs; Hon Rl; Lbry Ade; Lit Mag; NHS; Ed Sch Nwsp; Treas Lat Clb; Pep Clb; Pres Spn Clb; De Pauw Univ; Psych.

LONG, CHERYL; Southmont HS; Ladoga, IN; 12/187 Hon Rl; Jr NHS; NHS; FHA; Spn Clb; College.

LONG, CHRIS; Rensselaer Central HS; Rensselaer, IN; 14/154 Chrh Wkr; Hon Rl; Coll.

LONG, DANA; Goshen HS; Goshen, IN; 83/201 Chrh Wkr; Debate Tm; Girl Scts; Hon Rl; Off Ade; Rptr Sch Nwsp; 4-H; Pep Clb; 4-H Awd; Miles Sci Lab; Math.

LONG, DEBBIE; Fairview HS; Dayton, OH; Hon Rl; Pom Pon; Alpha Kappa Alpha Sor Achvmtn Awd 76; Roberta Lynns Acad Of Dance Cert Of Achvmtn 76; Wright St Univ; Educ.

LONG, DEIDRE; John F Kennedy HS; Cleveland, OH; Chrs; JA; Twrlr; Cit Awd; JA Awd; Wright St Univ; Nursing.

LONG, DENA; North HS; Akron, OH; 8/365 Chrh Wkr; Girl Scts; Hon Rl; JA; NHS; Off Ade; Sch Nwsp; Univ Of Akron; Medical Tech.

LONG, DENNIS; Port Clinton HS; Pt Clinton, OH; Voc Schl; Comp Tech.

LONG, DOUG; Reitz Memorial HS; Boonville, IN; 5/200 Sec Frsh Cls; Hon Rl; Jr NHS; Sch Mus; Sch Pl; Stu Cncl; Rptr Yrbk; Letter Ftbl; Letter Glf; IM Sprt; Letter For Above 3.5 Grade Aver 3yrs; Stu Life Edit Of Yrbk; Vanderbilt Univ; Law.

LONG, DWIGHT E; Dwight HS; Chillicothe, OH; 7/385 Chrs; Debate Tm; Hon Rl; Natl Forn Lg; NHS; Sch Mus; Pres Sci Clb; Ten; Univ Of Cincinnati; Archt.

LONG, G; Northeastern HS; Williamsburg, IN; 6/109 Pres Band; Boy Scts; Hon Rl; NHS; Sch Mus; Stg Crw; Ftbl; Wrstlng; Coll; Marine Bio.

LONG, GRAHAM; Andover HS; Bloomfield Hls, MI; 60/440 Boy Scts; Hon Rl; NHS; Sct Actv; Fr Clb; Sci Clb; Kalamazoo Coll; Pre Med.

LONG, J; Fort Frye HS; Lowell, OH; Am Leg Aux Girls St; Chrh Wkr; Hon Rl; Stg Crw; Eng Clb; 4-H; FTA; GAA; 4-H Awd; Ohio St Univ; Bus Admin.

LONG, JAMIE; Rivet HS; Vincennes, IN; 20/46 Sec Sr Cls; Chrs; Chrh Wkr; Hosp Ade; Sch Mus; Rptr Yrbk; FHA; Pep Clb; Bsktbl; Trk; Vincennes Univ; Music.

LONG, JANE; Willard HS; Willard, OH; Chrs; Sch Mus; Chrldng; IM Sprt; Mgrs; Ohio State Univ; Dental Hygienist.

LONG, JANICE; Fort Frye HS; Lowell, OH; Am Leg Aux Girls St; Hon Rl; Eng Clb; FTA; GAA; 4-H Awd; Ohio St Univ; Bus Admin.

LONG, JANIE; North Knox HS; Bruceville, IN; Cls Rep Sr Cls; Band; Cmp Fr Grls; Chrh Wkr; Girl Scts; Lbry Ade; Off Ade; Rptr Sch Nwsp; Oakland City College; Art.

LONG, JAY; Connersville HS; Glenwood, IN; 68/400 Band; Boy Scts; Hon Rl; Stg Crw; Ger Clb; IM Sprt; Vincennes Univ; TV Brdcstng.

LONG, JEFF; Princeton HS; Cincinnati, OH; Chrs; Hon Rl; Ger Clb; Mth Clb; Crs Cntry; JETS Awd; Univ Of Cincinnati; Archt Engr.

LONG, JEFFREY; Jefferson Area HS; Jefferson, OH; Chrh Wkr; Sch Mus; Sch Pl; Stg Crw; Yth Flsp; Fr Clb; Spn Clb; Ftbl; Trk; College; Aviation.

LONG, JILL; Elgin HS; Marion, OH; 8/139 Band; Chrs; Chrh Wkr; Hon Rl; Jr NHS; Mod UN; NHS; Off Ade; Yth Flsp; 4-H; Ohio St Univ; Soc Work.

LONG, JOAN; Washington HS; Massillon, OH; Off Ade; Quill & Scroll; Y-Teens; Yrbk; Drama Clb; Pep Clb; Spn Clb; Scr Kpr; Kent State Univ; Phot Journalism.

LONG, JOSEPH; Bishop Fenwick HS; Middletown, OH; 1/90 Cl Rep Jr Cls; Chrh Wkr; Hon Rl; NHS; Stu Cncl; Bsktbl; Ftbl; Medicine.

LONG, KAREN; Cleveland Cntrl Catholic HS; Cleveland, OH; Cls Rep Frsh Cls; Pres Soph Cls; Cls Rep Soph Cls; Drl Tm; Hon Rl; Stg Crw; Stu Cncl; OEA; IOE.

LONG, KATHY; Coleman HS; Coleman, MI; 2/123 VP Frsh Cls; Band; Girl Scts; Hon Rl; NHS; FTA; Pep Clb; Letter Bsktbl; Chrldng; Univ; Psych.

LONG, KIM; Lincolnview HS; Middle Pt, OH; Cmp Fr Grls; Chrs; NHS; Sch Mus; Stu Cncl; Yth Flsp; Rptr Sch Nwsp; GAA; Scr Kpr; Sec.

LONG, KRISTEN; Lynchburg Clay HS; Lynchburg, OH; Pres Frsh Cls; VP Soph Cls; VP Jr Cls; Sec Band; NHS; Pres 4-H; Letter Trk; Voice Dem Awd; Ohio Northern Univ; Pharmacy.

LONG, LAURA; Tecumseh HS; New Carlisle, OH; 34/364 AFS; Hon Rl; Jr NHS; Sch Mus; Sch Pl; Rptr Yrbk; Ed Sch Nwsp; Drama Clb; Fr Clb;.

LONG, LINDA; Ben Davis HS; Indianapolis, IN; Chrs; Hon Rl; Off Ade; Fr Clb; OEA; Mas Awd;.

LONG, LISA; Paint Valley HS; Chillicothe, OH; 14/90 Sec Fr Cls; Hon Rl; Yth Flsp; FHA; Pep Clb; Mgrs; Scr Kpr; Bus Schl.

LONG, LORRAINE; North Side HS; Ft Wayne, IN; 21/499 Band; Debate Tm; Drl Tm; Letter Natl Forn Lg; Sch Mus; Sch Pl; Capt Pom Pon; Cit Awd; Ball St Univ; Commercial Art.

LONG, MARGARET; Lakeshore HS; St Joseph, MI; 44/292 Cls Rep Frsh Cls; Cls Rep Soph Cls; VP Jr Cls; Cl Rep Jr Cls; Band; Chrh Wkr; Hon Rl; Sch Mus; Stu Cncl; Yth Flsp; Berrien Cnty Fed Of Wmns Clubs Nursing Schlrshp 79; Lake MI Coll Nursing Div Schlrshp 79; Lake Michigan Coll; Nursing.

LONG, MARK; Brown County HS; Nineveh, IN; Hon Rl; Mth Clb; Sci Clb; Spn Clb; Crs Cntry; Varsity Lettermens Club 78 79; Indiana St Univ; Comp Sci.

LONG, MELINDA; Clay Battelle HS; Hundred, WV; Yrbk; Bsktbl; Wv Univ; Art.

LONG, PAUL; Rogers HS; Toledo, OH; Band; Boy Scts; Hon Rl; JA; Jr NHS; Sct Actv; Ten; JA Awd; Univ Of Toledo.

LONG, PAUL; Washington HS; Massillon, OH; FCA; Hon Rl; Yth Flsp; Boys Clb Am; Civ Clb; Letter Glf; Ten; Stark Tech.

LONG, PHILLIP; Hoover HS; North Canton, OH; Band; Boy Scts; Chrh Wkr; Hon Rl; Hosp Ade; Sci Clb; Spn Clb; Cit Awd; Natl Merit Ltr; Univ Of Akron; Bio.

LONG, RANAE; Breckenridge Jr Sr HS; Breckenridge, MI; 7/96 Pres Frsh Cls; Band; Chrh Wkr; NHS; Stu Cncl; Yth Flsp; Rptr Yrbk; Letter Bsktbl; Letter Trk; Chrldng; Coll; Bus.

LONG, REBECCA A; Kankakee Valley HS; Wheatfield, IN; 16/195 Chrs; Hon Rl; NHS; Ger Clb; Sci Clb; Pom Pon; Valparaiso Univ; Med.

LONG, RICHARD S; Wilbur Wright HS; Dayton, OH; Pres Jr Cls; Val; Am Leg Boys St; Hon Rl; NHS; Sch Pl; Rptr Yrbk; Ed Sch Nwsp; Fr Clb; Ten; Univ Of Dayton; English.

LONG, SHELLEY; Bloomfield HS; Bloomfield, IN; Sec Frsh Cls; Sec Soph Cls; Sec Jr Cls; Chrs; Chrh Wkr; Drl Tm; FCA; Hon Rl; Stu Cncl; Yth Flsp; Indiana Central Bus Coll; Sec.

LONG, SHERYL; Marysville HS; Marysville, OH; Cls Rep Frsh Cls; Cls Rep Soph Cls; Am Leg Aux Girls St; Chrs; Hon Rl; Hosp Ade; NHS; Stu Cncl; Yth Flsp; 4-H; Coll.

LONG, SUSAN; Marietta Sr HS; Marietta, OH; 11/428 Chrs; Hon Rl; NHS; Fr Clb; Pres OEA; Otstndng Bus & Office Educ Stud Awd By BPW Clb 79; Coop Office Educ Awd Of Distinctn 79; 1st Pl Acctg 79;.

LONG, TAFFY; St Bernard Elmwood Place HS; St Bernard, OH; Aud/Vis; Band; Chrh Wkr; Drl Tm; Lbry Ade; Sch Mus; Sch Pl; Stg Crw; Yrbk; Drama Clb; College; Drama.

LONG, THOMAS; Buckeye Central HS; New Washington, OH; Band; Chrs; Drm Mjrt; Hon Rl; NHS; Sch Mus; Pep Clb; Letter Bsbl; Am Leg Awd; Univ; Music.

LONG, WANDA; Atherton HS; Burton, MI; Band; Chrs; Chrh Wkr; Hon Rl; NHS; Orch; Bob Jones Univ; Church Sec.

LONG, WILLIAM; St Marys HS; Belmont, WV; 3/126 Pres Frsh Cls; Cls Rep Soph Cls; Am Leg Boys St; Hon Rl; NHS; Sch Pl; Treas Stu Cncl; Rptr Sch Nwsp; Key Clb; Spn Clb; Spnch Hnrry Scty 78; WV Key Clb Dstrct Otstndng Brd Mmbr 78; SMHS Schlrshp Lttr 78; Univ; Opthamology.

LONGABERGER, TAMALA; Tri Valley HS; Dresden, OH; 36/216 Sec Frsh Cls; Cls Rep Soph Cls; Sec Sr Cls; Am Leg Aux Girls St; Aud/Vis; Drl Tm; Hon Rl; NHS; Sch Pl; Stg Crw; Ohio St Univ; Bus Admin.

LONGANACRE, TIMOTHY; Mullens HS; Mullens, WV; 17/87 Cls Rep Soph Cls; Am Leg Boys St; Band; Chrh Wkr; Hon Rl; Jr NHS; NHS; Treas Stu Cncl; Yth Flsp; Yrbk; Hnr Guard 79; Band Awd 77; West Point Military Acad; Engr.

LONGBOTTOM, GARY; Field HS; Suffield, OH; 19/238 Band; Boy Scts; Hon Rl; NHS; Sch Pl; Sct Actv; Stg Crw; Drama Clb; Sci Clb; Spn Clb; Univ Of Akron; Poli Sci.

LONGBRAKE, KAREN; Tecumseh HS; Medway, OH; 2/402 FCA; Hon Rl; Jr NHS; Scr Kpr; Schlrshp Test Team Mathmatics; College; Comp Sci.

LONGENBERGER, SHERYL; Bluffton HS; Bluffton, IN; Cls Rep Frsh Cls; Cls Rep Soph Cls; Cl Rep Jr Cls; Drl Tm; Hon Rl; Stu Cncl; Y-Teens; Rptr Yrbk; Rptr Sch Nwsp; 4-H; OEA Dist Cntst Inf Cmnctns II 1st Pl 79; OEA Dist Cntst Job Interview I 4th Pl 79; Bus Schl; Sec.

LONGERBONE, ANGELA; North Central HS; Indianapolis, IN; 218/999 Chrs; Hon Rl; Sch Mus; Yth Flsp; Fr Clb; Butler Univ; Elem Tchr.

LONGHI, PAT; Madonna HS; Weirton, WV; 15/105 Cls Rep Soph Cls; Pres Jr Cls; VP Sr Cls; Hon Rl; NHS; Sch Mus; Stu Cncl; Yrbk; Letter Bsbl; Letter Ftbl; Duquesne Univ; Pharm.

LONGLEY, BRENDA; Penn HS; Granger, IN; Cls Rep Frsh Cls; Band; Cmp Fr Grls; Chrh Wkr; Drl Tm; FCA; Hon Rl; JA; Jr NHS; Lbry Ade; Manchester Coll; Acctg.

LONGLEY, PATTY; Hubbard HS; Hubbard, OH; 23/330 Chrh Wkr; Girl Scts; Hon Rl; Off Ade; Pres Yth Flsp; IM Sprt; Mbr Of Tri Hi Y Club & Business Club; Youngstown State Univ; Med Sec.

LONGMIRE JR, WILBERT; Hughes HS; Cincinati, OH; Boy Scts; Cmnty Wkr; FCA; Hon Rl; Sprt Ed Yrbk; Sprt Ed Sch Nwsp; Boys Clb Am; Letter Bsbl; Bsktbl; Ftbl; Var Bslb Ltr 78; Reserve Bsktbl Citznshp Awd 78; Cmnty Worker 79; Intrmrl Sports 79; Var Ftbl 79; Univ; Eng.

LONGNECKER, KIM; Frontier HS; Newport, OH; Sch Pl; Stg Crw; FFA; College.

LONGPRE, CAROLE; Atlanta Community School; Atlanta, MI; 5/68 Sec Frsh Cls; Pres Soph Cls; Band; Hon Rl; NHS; Sch Pl; Stu Cncl; Rptr Yrbk; Pep Clb; Letter Bsbl; World Hist Awd 77; Leadership Awd 78; Univ; Art.

LONGPRE, THERESA; Coloma HS; Coloma, MI; Girl Scts; Hon Rl; NHS; Yrbk; Fr Clb; Pep Clb; Ten; Trk; College.

LONGSHAW, DENISE; Collinwood HS; Cleveland, OH; Hon Rl; JA; NHS; Sch Mus; Stu Cncl; Rptr Sch Nwsp; Drama Clb; JA Awd; Univ.

LONGSHORE, KATHI; Columbiana HS; Columbiana, OH; 22/110 Trs Jr Cls; Trs Sr Cls; Hon Rl; Stu Cncl; Fr Clb; Univ.

LONGSTRETH, JOAN; Zanesville HS; Zanesville, OH; Cmnty Wkr; Girl Scts; Hon Rl; NHS; Y-Teens; Chrldng; Tmr; Coll.

LONGUSKI, REBECCA; Immaculata HS; Detroit, MI; Cls Rep Soph Cls; Sec Jr Cls; Cls Rep Sr Cls; Girl Scts; Hon Rl; Lbry Ade; Sct Actv; Stu Cncl; Fr Clb; Central Michigan Univ; Elem Schl Tch.

LONGWELL, RONA; Hundred HS; Littleton, WV; Sec Soph Cls; Sec Jr Cls; Hon Rl; Yrbk; Letter Chrldng; Art Club; College; Art.

LONIEWSKI, EDWARD; Detroit Catholic Cntrl HS; Detroit, MI; Chrh Wkr; Hon Rl; JA; Pol Wkr; Spn Clb; Ftbl; Swmmng; Trk; Wrstlng; Coach Actv; St Of Michigan Schlrshp Fund; Most Dedicated Swimmer; 2 Time Catholic League Champ In Swimming; Michigan St Univ; Hotel Mgmt.

LONIK, BARRY; Berkley HS; Oak Park, MI; Cls Rep Frsh Cls; Cls Rep Soph Cls; Cl Rep Jr Cls; Cls Rep Sr Cls; Hon Rl; Stu Cncl; Capt Bsktbl; Trk; Albion Coll; Busns.

LONSWAY, BOB; Cardinal Stritch HS; Oregon, OH; 50/212 Band; Boy Scts; Hon Rl; NHS; Orch; Sch Mus; Sct Actv; College; Aero Engr.

LONSWAY, MARJORIE; St Joseph Ctrl Cath HS; Fremont, OH; 9/100 Band; Cmp Fr Grls; Chrs; Chrh Wkr; Hon Rl; Hosp Ade; FTA; Pep Clb; Scr Kpr; Univ; Sci.

LONSWAY, ROBERT; Cardinal Stritch HS; Oregon, OH; Band; Boy Scts; Hon Rl; NHS; Orch; Sch Mus; Sct Actv; Toledo Univ; Aeronautical Engr.

LOO, GREGORY; West Branch HS; Beloit, OH; Band; Hon Rl; Univ; Comp Sci.

LOOK, BONNIE; Tawas Area HS; E Tawas, MI; Sec Frsh Cls; Cls Rep Frsh Cls; Cls Rep Soph Cls; Cl Rep Jr Cls; Off Ade; Sch Pl; VP Stu Cncl; Bsktbl; Glf; Trk; Northwood Inst; Busns Mgmt.

LOOLEN, SANDRA; Norwalk HS; Norwalk, OH; Cmp Fr Grls; Girl Scts; Hon Rl; Hosp Ade; Off Ade; Red Cr Ade; Sct Actv; Fr Clb; Pep Clb; Bsktbl; Ohio Northern Univ; Phys Educ.

LOOMAN, CHARLES; Steubenville Cath Cntr HS; Mingo, OH; 15/205 Am Leg Boys St; FCA; Hon Rl; Jr NHS; NHS; Sch Pl; 4-H; Letter Ftbl; College; Engr.

LOOMAN, LORI; Mt Pleasant HS; Mt Pleasant, MI; Band; Chrs; Chrh Wkr; Girl Scts; Hon Rl; Hosp Ade; Red Cr Ade; Yth Flsp; Rptr Yrbk; Lat Clb; Mid Michigan Cmnty Coll; Nursing.

LOOMIS, BETHANN; Highland HS; Medina, OH; Cls Rep Frsh Cls; Cls Rep Soph Cls; Cl Rep Jr Cls; Cls Rep Sr Cls; Chrs; Drl Tm; Hon Rl; Ohio Univ; Journalism.

LOOMIS, KIM; Waterloo HS; Atwater, OH; Girl Scts; Hon Rl; Beta Clb; 4-H; FHA; OEA; Sci Clb; Trk; Cit Awd; 4-H Awd; Genrl Clercl Contst 1st 1979; Home Ec Awd 1977; Univ; Sec.

LOOMIS, MARK; Old Trail School; Medina, OH; VP Sr Cls; Sec Sr Cls; Trs Sr Cls; Band; Boy Scts; Cmnty Wkr; Debate Tm; Lbry Ade; Sct Actv; Stu Cncl; Baldwin Wallace Univ; Med.

LOOMIS, M FERN; Sidney HS; Sidney, OH; 1/245 Val; Chrh Wkr; NHS; VP FTA; NCTE; Natl Merit Ltr; Natl Merit SF; Miami Univ; Educ.

LOOMIS, TINA; Heath HS; Heath, OH; FCA; Hosp Ade; Off Ade; Sch Pl; FHA; Key Clb; Letter Gym; Trk; Ohio St Univ; Elem Ed.

LOONEY, JOYCE; Yellow Springs HS; Yellow Springs, OH; 26/74 Band; Letter Bsktbl; Letter Socr; Letter Trk; Chrldng; Clark Tech College; Commercial Art.

LOOS, CYNTHIA; West Washington HS; Hardingsburg, IN; Chrh Wkr; Girl Scts; Sch Pl; Yrbk; Drama Clb; Pep Clb; Spn Clb; Chrldng; 4-H Awd; College; Education.

LOOSBROCK, MICHAEL J; Father Joseph Wehrle Mem HS; Columbus, OH; 11/115 Chrh Wkr; Debate Tm; Hon Rl; Sch Nwsp; Spn Clb; U S Air Force Acad; Astronomy.

LOOSER, LISA; Lincolnview HS; Middle Pt, OH; Chrs; JA; 4-H; Bsktbl; GAA; Tmr; 4-H Awd; JA Awd; VFW Awd; Coll; Art.

LOPER, CHERYL; Chesaning HS; Chesaning, MI; Chrs; Chrh Wkr; Hon Rl; NHS; Off Ade; Ed Yrbk; Yrbk; Drama Clb; FHA; Pep Clb; Grand Rapids Baptist Coll.

LOPEZ, ELDA; Hammond Tecnical Voc HS; Hammond, IN; Cls Rep Frsh Cls; VP Soph Cls; Chrs; Hon Rl; Sch Mus; Sch Pl; Stg Crw; Pres Stu Cncl; Letter Ten; Chmn Pom Pon; Ind Univ; Spec Ed.

LOPEZ, FELICIA; Fremont Ross HS; Fremont, OH; Hon Rl; Hosp Ade; Stg Crw; Yrbk; Drama Clb; 4-H; FHA; 4-H Awd; Terro Tech Coll; Graphics.

LOPEZ, FERMIN; Holland HS; Holland, MI; Hope Coll; Drama.

LOPEZ, MARY C; Liberty HS; Clarksburg, WV; Band; NHS; Sch Mus; Stu Cncl; Drama Clb; Pep Clb; Gym; Chrldng; Marshall Univ.

LOPEZ, MICHAEL M; Washington HS; E Chicago, IN; 15/289 Hon Rl; Key Clb; Mth Clb; Capt Crs Cntry; Capt Trk; Univ Of Notre Dame; Archt.

LOPEZ, PALO; Holy Redeemer HS; Detroit, MI; Cls Rep Soph Cls; Cl Rep Jr Cls; Boy Scts; Chrh Wkr; Hon Rl; NHS; Stu Cncl; FDA; Socr; College; Pre M ed.

LOPEZ, RICARDO; High School; Filbert, WV; Cls Rep Frsh Cls; Pres Sr Cls; Am Leg Boys St; Hon Rl; Jr NHS; NHS; Yth Flsp; Y-Teens; Key Clb; Bsbl; Univ; Engr.

LOPEZ, RICARDO; Mount View HS; Filbert, WV; 7/250 Cls Rep Frsh Cls; Pres Sr Cls; Am Leg Boys St; Hon Rl; Jr NHS; NHS; Yth Flsp; Key Clb; Bsbl; Am Leg Awd; Univ; Engr.

LOPEZ, SUZANNE; Lincoln HS; Vincennes, IN; Hon Rl; Lbry Ade; Rptr Yrbk; Sci Clb; Pres Spn Clb; Ten; Ball St Univ Jrnlsm Wrkshp; Volleyball Captain; Indiana Univ; Med.

LOPEZ, THEODORE; Notre Dame HS; Bridgeport, WV; Chrh Wkr; Cmnty Wkr; Yth Flsp; Key Clb; Letter Bsktbl; Letter Ftbl; Fairmont St Univ; Acctg.

LORAFF, RICHARD; Eau Claire HS; Eau Claire, MI; FCA; Hon Rl; Jr NHS; Bsbl; Ftbl; Gym; Capt Wrstlng; Boys Phys Ed Awrd 78; St Qualified Wrestling 77 78; Univ.

LORD, LOREN; Kelloggsville HS; Wyoming, MI; 1/150 Hon Rl; NHS; Univ; Comp Prog.

LORE, DIANE; Willow Run HS; Ypsilanti, MI; Cls Rep Frsh Cls; Sec Soph Cls; Trs Soph Cls; Cl Rep Jr Cls; Girl Scts; Hon Rl; Stu Cncl; Rptr Yrbk; Yrbk; College; Law.

LORELLE, ROGER; Archbishop Alter HS; Centerville, OH; Chrh Wkr; Crs Cntry; Trk; IM Sprt; Coll; Sci.

LOREN, BRIAN; Yale HS; Goodells, MI; Hon Rl; NHS; Sch Pl; Rptr Sch Nwsp; Pres Spn Clb; Michigan State Univ; Vet.

LOREN, MATT; Hillsdale HS; Hillsdale, MI; NHS; Rptr Yrbk; Rptr Sch Nwsp; Key Clb; Univ.

LORENGER, PETER; University Of Detroit HS; Detroit, MI; 21/130 Chrs; Chrh Wkr; Hon Rl; NHS; Sch Mus; Sch Pl; Sch Nwsp; Fr Clb; IM Sprt; Natl Merit SF; Univ Of Detroit; Elec Engr.

LORENGER, PETER M; Univ Of Detroit HS; Detroit, MI; 16/138 Pres Chrs; Chrh Wkr; Hon Rl; NHS; Sch Mus; Sch Pl; Stg Crw; Drama Clb; Fr Clb; Natl Merit SF; College; Elec Engr.

LORENSEN, PATRICIA; Port Clinton HS; Port Clinton, OH; 5/266 Band; Treas Chrh Wkr; Cmnty Wkr; Hon Rl; NHS; Sch Nwsp; 4-H; Ger Clb; Mth Clb; Capt Chrldng; College; Biosci.

LORENT, RHONDA; Niles Mckinley HS; Niles, OH; 35/346 Chrs; Girl Scts; Hon Rl; JA; Rptr Yrbk; JA Awd; Youngstown State Univ.

LORENZ, ANN; Centerville HS; Dayton, OH; NHS; Stu Cncl; Yth Flsp; Spn Clb; Socr; Coach Actv; Scr Kpr; Miami Univ; Bus.

LORENZ, JOHN T; Pike HS; Indpls, IN; 45/350 VP Soph Cls; Cls Rep Soph Cls; Cl Rep Jr Cls; VP Sr Cls; Cls Rep Sr Cls; Hon Rl; Stu Cncl; Ger Clb; Bsktbl; Letter Ftbl; Two Yrs Serv Awd Indpls Star 78; Sup Serv Awd Indpls Star 78; Hon Cert Indpls Star 76; Purdue Univ; Engr.

LORENZ, TIMOTHY; Garaway HS; Baltic, OH; 4/100 Am Leg Boys St; Band; Hon Rl; NHS; Ger Clb; Scr Kpr; College; Comp Sci.

LORENZETTI, DAVID; Fairborn Baker HS; Fairborn, OH; 1/275 Am Leg Boys St; Boy Scts; Chrh Wkr; Hon Rl; Lit Mag; Mod UN; NHS; Quill & Scroll; Sct Actv; Sch Nwsp; 1st Pl Jr Div Engr NM St Sci & Engr Fair 77; Honors Sem Of Metro Dayton 78 80; C J Brown Cong Yth Council; Univ.

LORI, JAMES; Norway HS; Norway, MI; 19/96 Chrh Wkr; Hon Rl; Stg Crw; Letter Bsktbl; Capt Ftbl; Trk; Ferris St Univ; Bus Mgmt.

LORICK, JERARD; Arsenal Technical HS; Indianapolis, IN; Cls Rep Frsh Cls; Cls Rep Soph Cls; Cl Rep Jr Cls; Cmnty Wkr; FCA; Hon Rl; Stu Cncl; Letter Bsktbl; Capt Ftbl; Letter Trk; Ind St Univ; Social Work.

LORING, ANGELA; Taylor HS; Cincinnati, OH; Pres Frsh Cls; Cls Rep Soph Cls; Trs Jr Cls; Cls Rep Sr Cls; Chrh Wkr; Cmnty Wkr; Capt Drl Tm; FCA; Girl Scts; Hon Rl; All Amer Drill Tm 78 80; I Set A Hgh Kickng Record In Drill Tm Of 1150 Kicks 79; Stu Aid 4 Yrs 77 80; Christ Hospital Nursing Schl; RN.

LORITZ, LINDA; Escanaba Area Public HS; Escanaba, MI; 45/250 Band; Cmp Fr Grls; Chrs; Girl Scts; Hon Rl; DECA; 4-H; Trk; Mgrs; 4-H Awd; St Of Mi Schlshp Awd 79; Northern Michigan Univ; Sociology.

LORMS, MAUREEN; Bishop Ready HS; Columbus, OH; Chrs; JA; Bsbl; Crs Cntry; Trk; Coach Actv; JA Awd; Univ; Tchr.

LORTON, SHERRI; Ursuline Academy; Cincinnati, OH; Chrs; Cmnty Wkr; JA; Sch Pl; Math Awd From Oh Council Of Tchrs Of Math 79; Eng Awd 6th Pl In Mi Univ Dist 77; Eng Awd 15th Pl In Oh 77; Univ; Med Tech.

LORTZ, MARK; Carey HS; Carey, OH; Band; Chrs; Hon Rl; Sch Pl; Treas Yth Flsp; Rptr Yrbk; 4-H; Trk; Natl Merit Schl;.

LOSCALZO, BETH; Kalamazoo Central HS; Kalamazoo, MI; 107/460 Band; Chrs; Chrh Wkr; Cmnty Wkr; Debate Tm; Drm Mjrt; Hon Rl; Mdrgl; Natl Forn Lg; Orch; N Amera Pageant Systms Miss Teenage Snowflake Miss Metro West Miss Teen Oakland Cnty 2 Med 1978; Twrlng 197; Western Michigan Univ; Psych.

LOSEE, KIMBERLY; North Muskegon HS; N Muskegon, MI; Band; Girl Scts; Hon Rl; Off Ade; Y-Teens; Fr Clb; Chrldng; Coach Actv; PPFtbl; Muskegon Jr Coll; Bus Admin.

LOSTOSKI, DAN; Field HS; Kent, OH; Hon Rl; Jr NHS; NHS; Univ Of Akron; Engr.

LOTHES, CAROLYN; Caldwell HS; Beverly, OH; 3/100 Sec Frsh Cls; Cls Rep Soph Cls; Band; Hosp Ade; NHS; Stu Cncl; 4-H; Trk; Scr Kpr; Lion Awd; College.

LOTHRIDGE, KEVIN; South Dearborn HS; Aurora, IN; 39/263 Pres Jr Cls; Am Leg Boys St; Boy Scts; Hon Rl; Lbry Ade; Sch Pl; Sct Actv; Stg Crw; Pep Clb; Letter Ftbl; Boy Scouts Of Amer Eagle Scout 76; Coacher Outstndg Sportsmanshp Awd 77; Eastern Kentucky Univ; Forensic Sci.

LOTRIDGE, CHRIS; Botkins HS; Botkins, OH; Hon Rl; Sci Clb; Letter Bsbl; Bsktbl; Letter Glf; Mt Vernon Nazarene Coll; Bus Admin.

LOTT, NAJA; Whitehall Yearling HS; Whitehall, OH; Girl Scts; Hon Rl; Red Cr Ade; Y-Teens; Pres OEA; Spn Clb; Busns Schl; Legal Sec.

LOTTES, MARSHA; Barr Reeve HS; Loogootee, IN; Sec Jr Cls; Sec Sr Cls; Chrh Wkr; Cmnty Wkr; Hon Rl; Off Ade; Beta Clb; FHA; Pep Clb; Chrldng; Univ; Nursing.

LOUCAS, CATHY; Weir Sr HS; Weirton, WV; Cls Rep Frsh Cls; VP Soph Cls; Cl Rep Jr Cls; Cmp Fr Grls; Hon Rl; NHS; Stu Cncl; Pep Clb; Spn Clb; Chrldng; West Virginia Univ; Bsns Marketing.

LOUCHART, DONALD; Freeland HS; Freeland, MI; 2/115 Sal; Hon Rl; NHS; Sch Pl; Drama Clb; Saginaw Valley State College; Engr.

LOUCHART, LISA; Clio HS; Mt Morris, MI; 9/320 Cls Rep Frsh Cls; Hon Rl; Jr NHS; NHS; Stu Cncl; OEA; Chrldng; Gold Carpet Awd 79; MBSA Schslhp 79; Var Ltre 78; Detroit Coll Of Bus; Acctg.

LOUCKS, CHRISTOPHER; Eaton Rapids Sr HS; Eaton Rapids, MI; Boy Scts; Pres Stu Cncl; Sch Nwsp; Letter Swmmng; Tmr; Amer Coll Test Schlsp 79; Cntrl Michigan Univ; Pre Law.

LOUDEN, JEFFREY; New Haven HS; New Haven, IN; Bsbl; IM Sprt; Univ.

LOUDEN, JULIE; Whitmer HS; Toledo, OH; 42/910 Cls Rep Frsh Cls; Hon Rl; Stu Cncl; Pep Clb; Spn Clb; Letter Bsktbl; Letter Gym; Letter Trk; Letter Chrldng; PPFtbl; Univ.

LOUDEN, LAWRENCE; Edgewood HS; Kingsville, OH; Aud/Vis; Sch Mus; Sch Pl; Stg Crw; Drama Clb; Sci Clb; Kent State Univ; Comp Sci.

LOUDENSLAGER, BONNIE; Colon HS; Burr Oak, MI; Band; Chrs; Off Ade; 4-H; Key Clb; Cit Awd; 4-H Awd; Leadership; College; Interior Design.

LOUDENSLAGER, LYNN; Ridgedale HS; Marion, OH; 13/113 VP Jr Cls; Chrs; Chrh Wkr; Cmnty Wkr; FCA; Hon Rl; Hosp Ade; Jr NHS; NHS; Sch Mus; Flying Farmer St Teen Offc 79; Ohio St Univ; Phys Ther.

LOUDERBACK, DARLA; Western Brown Sr HS; Bethel, OH; Sec Frsh Cls; Cls Rep Soph Cls; Band; Cmnty Wkr; Hon Rl; Sch Mus; Stg Crw; Schlrshp Tm Eng 79; Bnd Serv Awd 77; Poetry Awd High Point Aver In This Class 79; Coll; Cmnctns.

LOUDERBACK, RONALD; Felicity Franklin HS; Felicity, OH; 4/90 Trs Soph Cls; Band; Chrs; Chrh Wkr; Cmnty Wkr; Hon Rl; NHS; Sch Pl; Yth Flsp; Sprt Ed Yrbk; Pl 2nd In Dist Chem; Its Acad Team; Univ; Physics.

LOUDERMILK, CAROL S; Licking County Joint Voc HS; Hebron, OH; Cls Rep Frsh Cls; Pres Jr Cls; Cl Rep Jr Cls; Chrs; Chrh Wkr; Girl Scts; Fr Clb; Ohi State Univ; Legal Sec.

LOUDIN, ANNE; Medina HS; Medina, OH; 111/359 Aud/Vis; Chrs; Capt Drl Tm; Red Cr Ade; Sch Mus; Sch Nwsp; Pep Clb; PPFtbl; Wv Univ; Bus.

LOUDIN, DAVID A; Braxton County HS; Sutton, WV; Cls Rep Sr Cls; Band; Chrs; Chrh Wkr; Hon Rl; NHS; Stu Cncl; Key Clb; Mth Clb; Natl Merit SF; West Virginia Univ; Elec Engr.

LOUDIN, MELINDA; Buckhannon Upshur HS; Buckhannon, WV; Cl Rep Jr Cls; Chrs; Hon Rl; NHS; Sch Mus; Stu Cncl; VP 4-H; Pep Clb; IM Sprt; West Virginia Univ; Busns Mgmt.

LOUDON, MARCIA; Salem Sr HS; Salem, OH; 31/243 Pres Band; Hon Rl; Hosp Ade; Sch Mus; Stu Cncl; Y-Teens; Yrbk; Pres Fr Clb; FSA; Pep Clb; Kent St Univ; Nursing.

LOUGH, NANCY; Bridgeport HS; Bridgeport, WV; Hst Jr Cls; Am Leg Aux Girls St; Band; Girl Scts; Hon Rl; Jr NHS; NHS; 4-H; Twrlr; 4-H Awd; College.

LOUGH, PHILIP H; Lewis County HS; Jane Lew, WV; Am Leg Boys St; Aud/Vis; Band; Hon Rl; NHS; Yth Flsp; Am Leg Awd; DAR Awd; NSF/SSTP Coal Sci Proj 79; West Virginia Univ; Chem.

LOUGH, SANDY; Spencer HS; Spencer, WV; Chrh Wkr; Jr NHS; VP Drama Clb; Center City Coll; Keypunch Operator.

LOUGHMILLER, DONNA; Our Lady Of Providence HS; New Albany, IN; 1/168 Val; Am Leg Aux Girls St; Hon Rl; Stu Cncl; Mth Clb; Crs Cntry; IM Sprt; Ind Univ Southeast; Law.

LOUGHMILLER, SUSAN; Decatur Central HS; Indpls, IN; Sec Sr Cls; Am Leg Aux Girls St; Chrh Wkr; Hon Rl; Mod UN; Pres NHS; Quill & Scroll; Stu Cncl; Sprt Ed Yrbk; Sprt Ed Sch Nwsp; Ball State Univ; Journalism.

LOUGHRIDGE, BILL; Celina HS; Celina, OH; Hon Rl; Fr Clb; Letter Bsktbl; Letter Ftbl; Business School.

LOUGHRIGE, CLAIRE; Celina Sr HS; Celina, OH; 20/241 Band; Chrs; Girl Scts; Hon Rl; NHS; Off Ade; Sch Mus; Sch Pl; Stu Cncl; Rptr Yrbk; Miami Univ; Acctg.

LOUGHRIN, ELLEN; Hastings HS; Hastings, MI; 21/271 Cls Rep Soph Cls; Cl Rep Jr Cls; Chrh Wkr; Hon Rl; NHS; Sch Pl; Stu Cncl; Rptr Yrbk; Ed Sch Nwsp; Drama Clb; Mic Tech Univ; Tech Communications.

LOUIS, CAROL; Nordonia HS; Sagamore Hl, OH; 111/450 Chrs; Chrh Wkr; Hon Rl; Sch Mus; Pres Yth Flsp; Rptr Yrbk; VFW Awd; College; Spec Educ.

LOUIS, DEBORAH; Osborn HS; Detroit, MI; Cl Rep Jr Cls; Hon Rl; Pep Clb; Cit Awd; Bus.

LOUIS, LORI; Madeira HS; Madeira, OH; 30/200 Pres Sr Cls; Chrh Wkr; Pol Wkr; Sch Pl; Drama Clb; Ger Clb; Cit Awd; Indiana Univ; Spec Educ.

LOUIS, MARK; Brecksville Sr HS; Broadview Hts, OH; 54/376 Chrh Wkr; Hon Rl; Jr NHS; NHS; Ger Clb; Ftbl; Letter Trk; IM Sprt; Cit Awd; John Carroll Univ; Acctg.

LOUK, LALA LEANNE; Wintersville HS; Wintersville, OH; Cls Rep Frsh Cls; Cls Rep Sr Cls; Hon Rl; Stu Cncl; Fr Clb; Capt Chrldng; GAA; PPFtbl; Ohio Univ; Airline Hostess.

LOUKS, GERALD R; Marion Adams HS; Sheridan, IN; 1/99 Pres Sr Cls; Hon Rl; Jr NHS; NHS; Stu Cncl; FFA; Bsbl; Bsktbl; Crs Cntry; Ftbl; Purdue Univ; Math.

LOUKS, SCOTT; Arthur Hill HS; Saginaw, MI; Boy Scts; Chrh Wkr; Cmnty Wkr; Sct Actv; Stu Cncl; Bsktbl; Ftbl; Letter Trk; Michigan Ctrl Univ; Med.

LOUNSBURY, THOMAS; Pinckney HS; Pinckney, MI; Tri St Univ; Aero Engr.

LOUTHAN, MICHAEL; Hamilton Southeastern Sr HS; Noblesvle, IN; Sec Jr Cls; Cls Rep Sr Cls; FCA; Hon Rl; Sch Pl; Spn Clb; Letter Bsbl; Letter Ftbl; Letter Wrstlng; Florida St Univ; Brdcstng.

LOUZON, RANDALL; Harry S Truman HS; Taylor, MI; Chrh Wkr; Hon Rl; Letter Bsbl; Hockey; Wayne St Univ; Denistry.

LOVE, CHRISTOPHER; Kettering HS; Kenney, MI; Hon Rl; Jr NHS; Lbry Ade; NHS; Sch Pl; Wayne St Univ; Jrnlsm.

LOVE, J; Central Baptist HS; Cincinnati, OH; Trs Frsh Cls; Cls Rep Soph Cls; Pres Jr Cls; Boy Scts; Chrs; Chrh Wkr; Letter Socr; Univ.

LOVE, JOYCE M; Cheboygan HS; Cheboygan, MI; VP Frsh Cls; Band; Chrs; Girl Scts; Stu Cncl; IM Sprt; Central Michigan Univ; Acctg.

LOVE, KIMBERLY; Cambridge HS; Cambridge, OH; 6/280 Band; Hon Rl; NHS; Off Ade; Orch; Rptr Yrbk; 4-H; Bsktbl; GAA; Ohi Valley College.

LOVE, LAMARA; Eastmoor HS; Columbus, OH; 34/290 Chrs; Off Ade; Pep Clb; Ohio St Univ; Nursing.

LOVE, RICKIE R; Emerson HS; Gary, IN; Pres Soph Cls; Am Leg Boys St; Hon Rl; JA; Stu Cncl; Drama Clb; Letter Ten; Pres Awd; College.

LOVE, TAMMY L; Stow HS; Stow, OH; Hon Rl; Lbry Ade; Off Ade; Yrbk; Drama Clb; Sec Pep Clb; Kent St Univ; Zoology.

LOVE, TIMOTHY; Missinewa HS; Marion, IN; Boy Scts; Hon Rl; Sch Pl; Sct Actv; Stg Crw; DECA; Drama Clb; Spn Clb; I V Tech; Auto Mechanics.

LOVE, VICKIE; St Ladislaus HS; Hamtramck, MI; Cls Rep Frsh Cls; Cls Rep Soph Cls; Sec Jr Cls; Sec Sr Cls; Chrh Wkr; Cmnty Wkr; Hon Rl; Off Ade; Sec Stu Cncl; Sprt Ed Yrbk; Mi Schlhsp Grant 79; Serv Awd 79; Wayne St Univ; Bus Admin.

LOVEDAY, JOHN A; Walter P Chrysler Memrl HS; New Castle, IN; 91/419 Chrs; FCA; JA; Letter Glf; JA Awd; 1st Pl In St Music Contst Piano 75; 3rd Pl In St Music Contst Piano 76; 1st Pl St Music Contst Piano 78; Indiana Tech Univ; Engr.

LOVEGROVE, NORMAN; Frankfort HS; Elberta, MI; Pres Frsh Cls; Hon Rl; NHS; Sci Clb; Spn Clb; Univ; Physicist.

LOVEJOY, PAULA; Jonathan Alder HS; Plain City, OH; 29/108 Trs Frsh Cls; Cls Rep Frsh Cls; Sec Soph Cls; Sec Jr Cls; Cl Rep Jr Cls; Sec Sr Cls; Hon Rl; Hosp Ade; Lbry Ade; NHS; Fresh Attendent 1975; Homecoming Queen 1978; Univ; Dent Hygn.

LOVEJOY, TAMMY; Edon HS; Montpelier, OH; Pres Jr Cls; Chrs; Sch Mus; Sch Pl; Rptr Yrbk; Rptr Sch Nwsp; 4-H; Spn Clb; John Hurd Memorial Schlrshp 79; Poetry Awrd 79; Pro Life Speech Cntst 2nd 79; Univ; Law.

LOVELACE, JOHN; Stivers Patterson Co Op HS; Dayton, OH; Cmnty Wkr; Hon Rl; JA; Yth Flsp; VICA; JA Awd; Natl Tool Die Prcsn Assn; Tool Mkr.

LOVELADY, STEPHEN; Warsaw Community HS; Warsaw, IN; 13/356 Am Leg Boys St; Band; Chrh Wkr; Hon Rl; Sch Mus; Grace College.

LOVELESS, ANDREA; Robert A Taft HS; Cincinnati, OH; 1/150 Cls Rep Frsh Cls; Cls Rep Soph Cls; Cl Rep Jr Cls; Trs Sr Cls; Hon Rl; Jr NHS; Stu Cncl; Rptr Yrbk; OEA; Cit Awd; Mercantile Lib Membshp 1978; Certf For Century 21 Shorthand 1978; Citizenship Awd 1977; Univ Of Cincinnati; Bus Admin.

LOVELESS, MICHAEL; Olivet HS; Olivert, MI; Band; Boy Scts; Hon Rl; Sch Pl; Stg Crw; Drama Clb; Letter Bsbl; Letter Bsktbl; Letter Ftbl; Letter Ten; Us Air Force.

LOVELL, PAMELA; Dexter HS; Dexter, MI; VP Frsh Cls; Trs Sr Cls; Band; Girl Scts; Hon Rl; Jr NHS; NHS; Sct Actv; Yth Flsp; 4-H; Eastern Michigan Univ; Nursing.

LOVELL, RICHARD; Garfield HS; Akron, OH; 32/464 Hon Rl; Yrbk; Letter Ftbl; College; Business.

LOVELL, ROB R; N Ridgeville Sr HS; N Ridgeville, OH; Band; Hon Rl; NHS; Sch Pl; Stg Crw; Stu Cncl; Y-Teens; Drama Clb; Fr Clb; Glf; Univ Of Michigan; Dentistry.

LOVELL, RUSSELL; East Palestine HS; Negley, OH; Boy Scts; Chrs; Red Cr Ade; Ftbl; Ohio St Univ; Law.

LOVELL, VICKIE; Winchester Community HS; Winchester, IN; 24/162 Chrs; Hon Rl; Lbry Ade; Sch Mus; Yrbk; FBLA; FHA; Ft Wayne Intl Bus Coll; Bus.

LOVERN, JON M; Princeton HS; Princeton, WV; 24/330 Band; Jr NHS; NHS; Rptr Sch Nwsp; Key Clb; Capt Ten; Dnfth Awd; Kiwan Awd; Pres Awd; WVU; Med.

LOVERN, VICKIE; Yorktown HS; Yorktown, IN; 48/200 Cl Rep Jr Cls; Sec Sr Cls; Band; Chrh Wkr; Girl Scts; Sch Mus; Rptr Yrbk; Drama Clb; FHA; Indiana St Univ; Psych.

LOVETT, LAURA; Hampshire HS; Capon Bridge, WV; 24/225 Am Leg Aux Girls St; Cmnty Wkr; Hon Rl; Yth Flsp; Yrbk; Drama Clb; 4-H; Letter Bsktbl; GAA; 4-H Awd; College; Journalism.

LOVEY, KEVIN; Marsh Fork HS; Arnett, WV; Trs Soph Cls; Hon Rl; Jr NHS; NHS; Stu Cncl; Pep Clb; Concord Coll; Bus Mgmt.

LOVILL, STEVEN; Southfield Sr HS; Southfield, MI; Chrs; Hon Rl; Sch Pl; Stg Crw; Rptr Sch Nwsp; Rdo Clb; Bsbl; Socr; IM Sprt; Scr Kpr; Univ Of Michigan; Radio Brdcstng.

LOVINSKI, JONI; Steubenville Catholic HS; Wintersville, OH; 67/204 Hon Rl; Fr Clb; Pep Clb; College; Communications.

LOVRIC, MIRO; St Ignatius HS; Euclid, OH; 30/254 Cls Rep Sr Cls; Boy Scts; Hon Rl; NHS; Stu Cncl; Yrbk; Letter Ftbl; Letter Socr; Trk; IM Sprt; Columbia Univ; Pre Med.

LOVSE, VALERIE; Waterford Twp HS; Union Lake, MI; 38/380 Treas Band; Debate Tm; Hon Rl; NHS; Sch Mus; Rptr Yrbk; Rptr Sch Nwsp; Letter Trk; Chrldng; Natl Merit Ltr; Ferris Merit Schlrshp; Ferris St Coll; Med Tech.

LOW, NANCY; Newark HS; Newark, OH; Chrs; Drl Tm; Lbry Ade; Rptr Yrbk; FHA; Pep Clb; Art Awd; College; Art.

LOWDEN, MICHAEL; Northeastern Wayne HS; Richmond, IN; Boy Scts; Hon Rl; Yrbk; Drama Clb; Navy; Nuclear Field.

LOWDERMILK, REBECCA; Clay City HS; Clay City, IN; 7/59 Cls Rep Frsh Cls; Cls Rep Soph Cls; VP Jr Cls; Cl Rep Jr Cls; VP Sr Cls; Cls Rep Sr Cls; Am Leg Aux Girls St; Band; Hon Rl; NHS; Indiana St Univ; RN.

LOWE, ALICE; Huron HS; Huron, OH; Chrs Hon Rl; JA; NHS; Sch Mus; Spn Clb; Great Bks Forum 77 78 & 79; Vocal Awds 75 79; Bowling Green Univ; Music.

LOWE, BRUCE; Robert S Rogers HS; Toledo, OH; Boy Scts; Sct Actv; Ger Clb; Ftbl; Univ.

LOWE, BRUCE A; Robert S Rogers HS; Toledo, OH; Boy Scts; Hon Rl; Sct Actv; Ger Clb; Bowling Green Univ.

LOWE, DEIRDRE; West Side HS; Gary, IN; 2/650 Sal; Chrh Wkr; Cmnty Wkr; Hon Rl; NHS; Civ Clb; Pres Lat Clb; Pres Sci Clb; Schlrshp To Spend 10 Days Traveling In Italy 79; Salutatorian Of Class 79; Purdue Univ; Pre Med.

LOWE, DELENA; Buffalo HS; Huntington, WV; Chrs; Chrh Wkr; Hon Rl; Y-Teens; FBLA; Bus Schl; Sec.

LOWE, JEFFRE; Clerance M Kimball HS; Royal Oak, MI; Letter Swmmng; Coach Actv; Natl Merit SF; Cal State Univ; Pol Sci.

LOWE, JOHN B; Timken HS; Canton, OH; 3/800 Cls Rep Sr Cls; Boy Scts; Hon Rl; Jr NHS; NHS; Sct Actv; Sprt Ed Yrbk; Rptr Yrbk; Letter Ten; Ohio State Univ; Engr.

LOWE, JOSEPH; Milford HS; Milford, MI; 30/365 Am Leg Boys St; Boy Scts; Chrh Wkr; VP NHS; Stu Cncl; Pep Clb; Spn Clb; Letter Bsktbl; Letter Ftbl; Mich Tech Univ; Engr.

LOWE, KATHERINE; Loudonville HS; Loudonville, OH; Hosp Ade; Pres Stu Cncl; DECA; FNA; Letter Chrldng; Mansfield Grnl Nursing Schl; RN.

LOWE, KIMBERLY; Liberty HS; Bristol, WV; Hon Rl; Jr NHS; NHS; Stu Cncl; Pres FFA; Awrd Chaptr Farmer Degree 79; Whos Who Among Amer HS Stdnts 79; Army Reserve.

LOWE, LINDA; H H Dow HS; Midland, MI; Girl Scts; Hon Rl; Yth Flsp; Pep Clb; Trk; IM Sprt; PPFtbl; Valparaiso Univ; Soc Work.

LOWE, LISA; Wirt County HS; Elizabeth, WV; Chrh Wkr; Hon Rl; Yth Flsp; 4-H; FHA; Pep Clb; PPFtbl;.

LOWE, PATRICIA; Garber HS; Essexville, MI; Hon Rl; Off Ade; Rptr Sch Nwsp; Bsktbl; Pres Awd; Bay City Bus Coll; Sec.

LOWE, RENEE; Dominican HS; Detroit, MI; Cl Rep Jr Cls; Cls Rep Sr Cls; Chrs; Chrh Wkr; Drl Tm; Girl Scts; Sch Pl; Stu Cncl; Pep Clb; Spn Clb; Miss Mi Venus Runner Up Finalist Contestant 79; Perfect Attendance Awd 77; Wayne County Cmnty Coll; Psych.

LOWE, SCOTT; Seeger Memorial HS; Williamsport, IN; 1/150 Cls Rep Soph Cls; Cl Rep Jr Cls; Am Leg Boys St; Hon Rl; NHS; Stu Cncl; Letter Bsbl; Letter Bsktbl; Ftbl; IM Sprt; Phys Sci Phys Ed Health Bio Awds; Purdue Univ; Engr.

LOWE, THOMAS; Pinconning Area HS; Linwood, MI; Chrh Wkr; Bsbl; Capt Glf; Michigan St Univ; Law Enforce.

LOWER, DIANE; Beaver Local HS; Negler, OH; 5/221 Band; Chrs; Trs Frsh Cls; Orch; Rptr Yrbk; Eng Clb; Fr Clb; Summi Decem 75 79; Univ; Acctg.

LOWER, ELAINE; Ridgewood HS; Fresno, OH; Debate Tm; Hon Rl; NHS; Sch Pl; Yrbk; VP 4-H; Fr Clb; Aultman Hosp Schl Of Nrsng; Reg Nrse.

LOWERY, ANNETTE; Arcadia Local HS; Fostoria, OH; 15/64 Band; Chrs; Hon Rl; NHS; Sch Mus; Rptr Yrbk; FHA; Gym; Trk; Ohio St Univ; Phys Therapy.

LOWERY, LISA; Shady Spring HS; Daniels, WV; 3/155 Sal; Am Leg Aux Girls St; Band; Chrh Wkr; FCA; Hon Rl; NHS; Ed Yrbk; 4-H; Cit Awd; Concord Coll; Med Tech.

LOWERY, MICHAEL; Hopewell Loudon HS; Fostoria, OH; 35/108 Band; Sch Mus; Spn Clb;.

LOWERY, MITCHELL; Clarkston HS; Davisburg, MI; Cl Rep Jr Cls; Hon Rl; Jr NHS; Ed Sch Nwsp; Trk; Scr Kpr; Univ; Bus Admin.

LOWERY, PAMELA; Arcadia Local HS; Fostoria, OH; 6/65 Am Leg Aux Girls St; Band; Chrs; Hon Rl; NHS; Sch Mus; Sch Pl; Stg Crw; Rptr Yrbk; Drama Clb; Bowling Green St Univ; Law Enfor.

LOWREY, SHANE; East HS; Akron, OH; Aud/Vis; Hon Rl; Lbry Ade; Fr Clb; JA Awd; Otstndng Math Stud 78; Rank 165 Out Of 25190 On Natl HS Math Exam 79; Univ Of Akron; Chem.

LOWRY, BARBARA J; Kalamazoo Central HS; Kalamazoo, MI; 1/430 Band; Chrs; Girl Scts; Hon Rl; Lit Mag; Mdrgl; Sec NHS; Orch; Quill & Scroll; Sch Mus; Northwestern Univ; Jrnlsm.

LOWRY, DIANA; Gull Lake HS; Richland, MI; Chrh Wkr; Hon Rl; JA; NHS; DECA; Western Michigan Univ.

LOWRY, ERIC; Scottsburg HS; Scottsburg, IN; 10/165 Boy Scts; Chrs; Hon Rl; Drama Clb; Fr Clb; Sci Clb; Woodmen Of The World Amer History Awd; 10th Dist Ach Test In Biology; Hanover Univ; Comp Sci.

LOWRY, ERIC; Lima Sr HS; Lima, OH; Hon Rl; JA; Sch Nwsp; DECA; Wrstlng; Bus Schl; Bus.

LOWRY, LINDA S; Eastwood HS; Perrysburg, OH; 14/180 Trs Soph Cls; Am Leg Aux Girls St; Band; Chrs; Chrh Wkr; Cmnty Wkr; Girl Scts; Hon Rl; NHS; Orch; OSU; Med Bio.

LOWRY, MARIE; Redford Union HS; Redford, MI; Chrh Wkr; Girl Scts; Hon Rl; Fr Clb; Trk; Natl Merit SF; Univ Of Michigan.

LOWTHER, JEFF; William A Wirt HS; Gary, IN; Hon Rl; College; Busns.

LOY, DEBORAH G; Edgewood HS; Ellettsville, IN; 7/194 Band; Drl Tm; Girl Scts; Hon Rl; Hosp Ade; NHS; Sch Mus; Stg Crw; Rptr Yrbk; Ger Clb; Indiana Univ; Phys Ther.

LOY, DEBRA; Bloom Carroll HS; Lancaster, OH; 5/155 Am Leg Aux Girls St; Band; NHS; Rptr Yrbk; 4-H; FFA; C of C Awd; Cit Awd; 4-H Awd; Iowa St Univ; Ag.

LOY, JONATHAN T; Fairless HS; Brewster, OH; Boy Scts; Sct Actv; Letter Ftbl; Letter Trk; IM Sprt; Art Awds 79; Univ Of Akron; Cmmrcl Art.

LOY, TRACY; Roosevelt Wilson HS; Clarksburg, WV; Chrs; Hon Rl; Off Ade; Sch Pl; Stu Cncl; Y-Teens; Rptr Sch Nwsp; Drama Clb; 4-H; Leo Clb; All St Chorus; Charting Pin 4 H; Alderson Broaddus Univ; Music.

LOYA, ANDREA; Parma Sr HS; Parma, OH; 45/800 Band; Girl Scts; Hon Rl; Off Ade; Sec Fr Clb; Pep Clb; Cleveland St Univ; Phys Ther.

LOYCHIK, MARK; Mc Kinley HS; Niles, OH; Boy Scts; Hon Rl; Fr Clb; Ftbl;.

LOYD, JANITH; Black River HS; Wellington, OH; 19/120 Band; Hon Rl; Sch Pl; Ed Yrbk; Yrbk; Beta Clb; VP 4-H; FTA; Sci Clb; Sec Spn Clb; Bowling Green; Special Ed.

LOZANO, NORMA A; St Francis De Sales HS; Westerville, OH; 49/186 Cls Rep Soph Cls; Cl Rep Jr Cls; Am Leg Aux Girls St; Drl Tm; Stg Crw; Stu Cncl; Drama Clb; Spn Clb;.

LOZANO, PAUL; Upper Sandusky HS; Upper Sandusky, OH; 6/213 Cl Rep Jr Cls; Cls Rep Sr Cls; Am Leg Boys St; Hon Rl; NHS; Sch Pl; Stu Cncl; Rptr Yrbk; Letter Crs Cntry; Letter Trk; Martin W Essex Schl For The Gifted 79; Purdue Univ Minority Engr Prog 79; Amer Legn Jr Cadet Ohio Hwy Ptrl; Univ; Med.

LOZEAU, RENEE; Bridgman HS; Bridgman, MI; Trs Frsh Cls; VP Jr Cls; Am Leg Aux Girls St; Band; Drm Mjrt; Hon Rl; NHS; Sch Pl; FHA; Trk; Univ; Interior Decorating.

LOZIER, IDA; Marlington HS; Paris, OH; 54/265 Chrh Wkr; Hon Rl; Yth Flsp; FFA; Horticultural Cert Of Completion; Ohio St Univ; Greenhouse Mgmt.

LOZON, RAYMOND J; Lakeview HS; St Clair Shore, MI; Hon Rl; Natl Merit Schl; USJC Awd; Univ Of Detroit; Engr.

LUBAHN, DEBORAH; Fulton HS; Ashley, MI; VP Sr Cls; Aud/Vis; Band; Chrs; Drl Tm; Hon Rl; Lbry Ade; Sprt Ed Yrbk; Rptr Yrbk; Ed Sch Nwsp; Univ; Eng.

LUBBE, THERESA; Divine Child HS; Dearborn, MI; Treas Spn Clb; Letter Trk; Tmr;.

LUBBERT, LINDA; Dayton Christian HS; Dayton, OH; 1/125 Band; Chrs; Chrh Wkr; Hon Rl; Fr Clb; Chrldng; IM Sprt; Scr Kpr; Cit Awd; College; Business.

LUBBINGE, LISA; Rogers HS; Wyoming, MI; Hon Rl; Lbry Ade; NHS; Spn Clb; Chrldng; Junior College; Exec Sec.

LUBECK, JEFFREY; East Detroit HS; East Detroit, MI; Band; Boy Scts; Hon Rl; Pres Mth Clb; Rdo Clb; Attendnc Cert 79; Cert Of Recogntn For Otstndng Acad Achvmnt In St Of Mi Schlrshp Comp 79; Macomb Cnty Cmnty Coll; Sci.

LUBECKY, DAVID; West Geauga HS; Novelty, OH; Band; Chrs; Hon Rl; Pol Wkr; IM Sprt; Univ; Pre Law.

LUBIENSKI, MARIA; Our Lady Of Mercy HS; Dearborn Hts, MI; Cl Rep Jr Cls; NHS; Off Ade; Pol Wkr; Rptr Yrbk; Sec Spn Clb; Letter Ten; Univ Of Mic; Law.

LUBINSKI, ANNETTE; Springfield HS; Holland, OH; 3/200 Cls Rep Frsh Cls; VP Soph Cls; VP Jr Cls; VP Sr Cls; Am Leg Aux Girls St; Band; Jr NHS; Pres FTA; Spn Clb; Mat Maids; Acdmc Achvmnt Awd Sci 1979; Pres Honor Roll 1977 1978; Toledo Hosp Nursing Schl; R N.

LUBKOWSKI, LEONA; Carl Brablec HS; Roseville, MI; 36/407 Hon Rl; Jr NHS; NHS; Off Ade; Fr Clb; Sci Clb; Chrldng; Sci & Engr Fair Of Metropolitan Detroit 2nd Awd; 4th Pl Schl Sci Project; Outstanding Fresh; Wayne St Univ.

LUC, CHRISTINE; Erieview Catholic HS; Cleveland, OH; 9/115 Chrs; Hon Rl; Lit Mag; Sch Mus; Sch Pl;.

LUCAS, BARBARA; Medina Sr HS; Medina, OH; 120/370 Band; Girl Scts; Orch; PPFtbl; Univ Of Cincinnati; Soc Wkr.

LUCAS, BEVERLY; Brown County HS; Nashville, IN; 64/208 Hon Rl; FHA; Perfect Attend Awd 74; Univ; Pre Law.

LUCAS, CONNIE; Martins Ferry HS; Martins Ferry, OH; Trs Frsh Cls; Cls Rep Soph Cls; Band; Chrs; Hon Rl; Orch; Twrlr; Ohio Valley Nursing Schl; Nurse.

LUCAS, DARLENE; Thomas W Harvey HS; Painesville, OH; 9/176 Hon Rl; Stu Cncl; Rptr Sch Nwsp; Key Clb; OEA; Spn Clb; Ten; Chrldng; Lakeland Univ; Banking.

LUCAS, ELIZABETH; Grand Rapids Christian HS; Grand Rapids, MI; Letter Trk; Davenport Coll Of Bus; Retail Mgmt.

LUCAS, ERIC; Terre Haute North Vigo HS; Terre Haute, IN; 26/600 Aud/Vis; Hon Rl; Boys Clb Am; Crs Cntry; Letter Glf; Ten; IM Sprt; College.

LUCAS, GENEVA; Upper Sandusky HS; Upper Sandusky, OH; Band; Chrs; Chrh Wkr; Hon Rl; NHS; Sch Mus; Sch Pl; Yrbk; Sch Nwsp; Drama Clb; Capital Univ; Bus.

LUCAS, J BRADLEY; Bloomfield HS; Bloomfield, IN; 5/85 Trs Frsh Cls; Cls Rep Soph Cls; Band; Hon Rl; NHS; Sch Mus; Sch Pl; Stg Crw; Stu Cncl; Drama Clb; Rotary Top Ten Students Dinner; Indiana St Univ; Law.

LUCAS, JIM D; Port Clinton HS; Port Clinton, OH; 48/230 Bsktbl; Ftbl; Wrstlng; Toledo Univ; Busns Admin.

LUCAS, JUNE; Our Lady Of Mercy HS; Detroit, MI; Aud/Vis; Chrh Wkr; Cmnty Wkr; Girl Scts; Hosp Ade; Lbry Ade; Pol Wkr; Univ Of Mic; Economics.

LUCAS, KAREN; United Local HS; Kensington, OH; VP Jr Cls; Hon Rl; Off Ade; Rptr Yrbk; 4-H; OEA; 4-H Awd; Med Sec.

LUCAS, KEVIN; Union Local HS; Belmont, OH; 8/143 Cls Rep Sr Cls; Hon Rl; NHS; Stu Cncl; Yrbk; 4-H; Fr Clb; FTA; Sci Clb; Foreign Exchange Program 78;.

LUCAS, LOIS; Marion Harding HS; Marion, OH; 3/449 Band; Sec Chrs; NHS; Sch Mus; Sch Pl; Drama Clb; Fr Clb; IM Sprt; Rotary Awd; Ohio St Univ; Bus Admin.

LUCAS, MARGARET; Bishop Borgess HS; Detroit, MI; 51/475 Cmnty Wkr; Hon Rl; Lbry Ade; Natl Forn Lg; NHS; Sch Mus; Fr Clb; Sci Clb; Mercy Coll Of Detroit; Law Enfrcmnt.

LUCAS, MARILYN D; Arsenal Technical HS; Indianapolis, IN; 32/597 Cls Rep Frsh Cls; Trs Soph Cls; Trs Jr Cls; Pres Sr Cls; Am Leg Aux Girls St; Hon Rl; Stu Cncl; Ball State Univ.

LUCAS, MARK J; Girard HS; Girard, OH; 19/216 Trs Soph Cls; Band; Debate Tm; Mdrgl; Sch Pl; Drama Clb; Fr Clb; Sci Clb; Univ; Marine Bio.

LUCAS, MARY; Edsel Ford HS; Dearborn, MI; Hon Rl; NHS; GAA; IM Sprt; Univ Of Mic; Bus Mgmt.

LUCAS, PAMELA; Willard HS; Willard, OH; Band; Chrs; Girl Scts; Sch Mus; Sch Pl; Stg Crw; Pres 4-H; Letter Bsktbl; Letter Trk; Letter Scr Kpr; Phys Ther.

LUCAS, RHONDA; Colerain Sr HS; Cincinnati, OH; Cmnty Wkr; Hon Rl; Lit Mag; Off Ade; Pol Wkr; Pres Eng Clb; Ger Clb; Mth Clb; Pep Clb; Sci Clb; Coll; Foreign Lang.

LUCAS, SUZI; Norton HS; Norton, OH; Hon Rl; Natl Forn Lg; OEA; Vocational Schl; Sec.

LUCCHESI, LISA; Washington HS; Massillon, OH; 200/484 Band; Boy Scts; Hosp Ade; Orch; Spn Clb; College; Nursing.

LUCE, DAVID R LUCE; Upper Arlington HS; Columbus, OH; Aud/Vis; Quill & Scroll; Stg Crw; Ohio St Univ; Comp Sci.

LUCE, MARRIE; Columbian HS; Tiffin, OH; 3/400 Band; Chrs; Chrh Wkr; Hon Rl; PAVAS; Sch Mus; Stu Cncl; Gym; Trk; Letter Chrldng; Miami Univ; Ingerior Designer.

LUCENTE, MARIA; Notre Dame HS; Clarksburg, WV; 5/55 Am Leg Aux Girls St; Chrh Wkr; Cmnty Wkr; Hon Rl; Hosp Ade; Jr NHS; NHS; Pol Wkr; Sch Pl; Stg Crw; Fairmont St Univ; Elem Ed.

LUCHETTI, ADELAIDE; Wheeling Park HS; Triadelphia, WV; 3/600 Am Leg Aux Girls St; Hon Rl; NHS; Sec Fr Clb; Chrldng; Mat Maids; Natl Merit Ltr; Brown Univ Bk Awd For Acad Excellnc In Eng 79; Stifel Prz Compttv Test Taken Within Each Grd Level 78; Univ; Eng.

LUCHS, BRENDA; Whitmore Lake HS; Whitmore Lk, MI; 2/82 Girl Scts; Hon Rl; Jr NHS; NHS; Rptr Yrbk; Univ.

LUCIER, CYNTHIA; Southgate HS; Southgate, MI; Band; Hon Rl; College; Art Tchr.

LUCIUS, BILLY; Kearsley HS; Flint, MI; 20/400 Hon Rl; Off Ade; Sch Mus; Sch Pl; Mott Commm College; Radio Annoncing.

LUCK, ROBERT; Roscommon HS; Roscommon, MI; Chrs; Bsktbl; Trk; Univ; Bus Mgmt.

LUCK, TINA; New Richmond HS; Bethel, OH; Chrs; Hon Rl; PAVAS; Quill & Scroll; Sch Mus; Sch Pl; Rptr Sch Nwsp; Sch Nwsp; Drama Clb; 4-H; Chorus St & Dist Comp Superior Ratng 79; Troubadours Letter & Ltr Guard Awrd 78; Drama Pin Comp Awrd 79; Cincinnati Univ; Singer.

LUCKE, JANICE; Delphos St Johns HS; Delphos, OH; 2/164 Am Leg Aux Girls St; Band; Hon Rl; Sec NHS; Letter Bsktbl; Letter Trk; Coach Actv; Letter Mgrs; Mission Soc Rep; Honor Stu; Fresh & Soph Scholarship Teams; College.

LUCKEL, MARK; Hammond Baptist HS; Lowell, IN; Chrh Wkr; Hon Rl; NHS; Sch Mus; Yth Flsp; Bsktbl; Crs Cntry; Letter Socr; Senior Class Off Chaplain 1978; Hyles Anderson Coll; Theology.

LUCKEN, BEVERLY; Taft HS; Hamilton, OH; Chrs; Drl Tm; Hon Rl; Jr NHS; PAVAS; Sch Mus; Sch Pl; Drama Clb; Ger Clb; Chrldng; Univ Of Cincinnati; Music.

LUCKETT, PATRICK; William A Wirt HS; Gary, IN; Am Leg Boys St; Jr NHS; Lit Mag; NHS; Rptr Sch Nwsp; Sch Nwsp; Mth Clb; Spn Clb; Letter Crs Cntry; Letter Trk; Univ.

LUCKIEWICZ, JAMES; Andrean HS; Merrillville, IN; 27/230 Hon Rl; Spn Clb; Bsbl; Bsktbl; Crs Cntry; Ftbl; Trk; Am Leg Awd; Cit Awd; Opt Clb A wd; Univ.

LUCKY, BRADLEY; Wilbur Wright HS; Dayton, OH; Aud/Vis; Rptr Sch Nwsp; Letter Ftbl; Letter Gym; Coach Actv; College; Law.

LUCKY, NATHANIEL; Central HS; Detroit, MI; Cls Rep Frsh Cls; Cls Rep Soph Cls; Cl Rep Jr Cls; Cls Rep Sr Cls; Cit Awd; Marygrove.

LUCZKOWSKI, MARGARET; La Salle HS; South Bend, IN; 24/488 Hon Rl; NHS; Quill & Scroll; Sch Nwsp; Letter Ten; Chrldng; Univ; Bus Admin.

LUCZKOWSKI, MARY; Washington HS; South Bend, IN; 38/355 Cmp Fr Grls; Chrs; Hon Rl; Sch Mus; Sch Pl; Drama Clb; Fr Clb; Pom Pon; Maureice Matthys Sftbl Sportmnshp Awd 77; Univ; Phys Ther.

LUDEMAN, RANDALL; Whitmer HS; Toledo, OH; Cls Rep Soph Cls; Band; Cmnty Wkr; Hon Rl; NHS; Stu Cncl; Ger Clb; Bsbl; Bsktbl; Ftbl; Toledo Univ; Law.

LUDLAM, SHERI L; Benton Harbor HS; Benton Harbor, MI; 1/451 Val; Band; Hon Rl; NHS; Mth Clb; Spn Clb; Letter Trk; Natl Merit SF; Michigan St Univ; Vet.

LUDLOW, LORI; Dominican HS; Detroit, MI; Chrs; Hon Rl; Hosp Ade; JA; Lbry Ade; NHS; Off Ade; Stg Crw; Michigan St Univ; Bus Admin.

LUDLOW, PATRICIA; Waverly HS; Lansing, MI; Cls Rep Frsh Cls; Cl Rep Jr Cls; Chrs; Girl Scts; Hon Rl; Pol Wkr; Sch Mus; Spn Clb; IM Sprt; Natl Merit Ltr; Michigan St Univ; Soc Sci.

LUDLUM, MARK; Sylvania Southview HS; Sylvania, OH; 63/363 Quill & Scroll; Yrbk; Sch Nwsp; JA Awd; Michigan St Univ; Photojournalism.

LUDOLPH, BARBARA J; West Branch HS; Salem, OH; 35/260 AFS; Chrs; Hon Rl; NHS; Off Ade; Stg Crw; Stu Cncl; Yth Flsp; Pep Clb; Spn Clb; Youngstown State Univ; Psych.

LUDOWESE, KATHY; Wooster HS; Wooster, OH; Band; Orch; Sch Mus; Ger Clb; Ohi Univ; Bus Admin.

LUDWICK, DIANE; Jenison Public HS; Jenison, MI; Cls Rep Soph Cls; Cl Rep Jr Cls; Cls Rep Sr Cls; Hon Rl; Sch Pl; Stu Cncl; Chrldng; Letter Pom Pon; PPFtbl; Carthage Coll; Spec Educ Tchr.

LUDWICK, KATHY; Hampshire HS; Augusta, WV; Chrh Wkr; Cmnty Wkr; Girl Scts; Hon Rl; Lbry Ade; FBLA; FHA; Hndbl; GAA; Work Training; Lirarian.

LUDWIG, ANNE; Meridian HS; Sanford, MI; Pres Frsh Cls; Cls Rep Soph Cls; Am Leg Aux Girls St; Chrh Wkr; Hon Rl; NHS; Sch Pl; Stu Cncl; Yth Flsp; Michigan State Univ; Elem Educ.

LUDWIG, KEITH; La Salle HS; Cincinnati, OH; 98/290 Cmnty Wkr; Hon Rl; Bsktbl; Coach Actv; IM Sprt; Univ Of Cincinnati; Indus Mgmt.

LUDWIG, LONN; Shelby HS; Shelby, MI; 27/129 Band; Hon Rl; NHS; Bsbl; Letter Ftbl; Elk Awd; Mich St Univ; Elec Engr.

LUDWIG, PAULA K; Plymouth HS; Plymouth, IN; Band; Cmp Fr Grls; Chrh Wkr; Hon Rl; NHS; Pol Wkr; Sch Mus; Drama Clb; Eng Clb; 4-H; Purdue Univ; Acctg.

LUEBKE, KURT; Concordia Lutheran HS; Ft Wayne, IN; 67/180 Chrh Wkr; Boys Clb Am; Letter Glf; IM Sprt; Scr Kpr; Purdue Univ; Forestry.

LUECK, BARBARA; Herbert Henry Dow HS; Midland, MI; 47/466 Hon Rl; NHS; Orch; Yth Flsp; Ger Clb; Natl Merit Ltr; Pres Scghslhp 79; Lutheran Pers Schslhp 79; Valparaiso Univ; Med.

LUECKE, WILLIAM E; Valparaiso HS; Valparaiso, IN; Chrh Wkr; Hon Rl; Sch Pl; Stu Cncl; IM Sprt; JETS Awd; Univ; Engr.

LUECKEN, BOB; Copley HS; Akron, OH; Boy Scts; Chrs; VP JA; Sct Actv; Yth Flsp; Socr; JA Awd; Natl Merit Ltr; Coll; Psychology.

LUEDER, MIKE; Hanover Central HS; Cedar Lake, IN; 10/137 Cls Rep Frsh Cls; Cl Rep Jr Cls; Hon Rl; Jr NHS; NHS; Sch Mus; Sch Pl; Stu Cncl; Rptr Yrbk; Rptr Sch Nwsp; U S Air Force Academy; Law.

LUEDTKE, MARK; Taft HS; Hamilton, OH; 1/400 Hon Rl; Jr NHS; NHS; Off Ade; Ger Clb; 1 Of 5 Top Sci Stud 78; Awrd For 91st % On German 2 Achvmnt Test 78; Chosen For Achvmnt Test Chem 1 78; Rice Univ; Research Physicist.

LUEDTKE, ROBIN; Lee M Thurston HS; Redford, MI; 32/478 Band; NHS; Sch Mus; Ger Clb; Bsbl; Bsktbl; Earned Letters In Sftbl Bsktbl & Band; Acquired 1st & 2nd Ratings In Music Festivals; Received Sftbl Awds; Ferris St Coll; Pre Sci.

LUEHMANN, CHRIS; Delta HS; Delta, OH; Band; Chrs; Girl Scts; Hon Rl; Lbry Ade; NHS; 4-H; Columbus Tech Inst; Vet.

LUEHRMANN, PAUL; Moeller HS; Cincinnati, OH; Boy Scts; Hon Rl; NHS; Sch Pl; Stg Crw; Lat Clb; Mgrs; Natl Merit Ltr; Blue Ash Womans Club Schlrshp; Univ Of Pittsburg Schlrshp; 2nd Pl Univ Of Cincinnati Sci Exibits; Purdue Univ; Physics.

LUEKE, STEVEN; Big Rapids HS; Big Rpds, MI; Hon Rl; Natl Forn Lg; NHS; Sch Pl; Drama Clb; Michigan St Univ; Bus.

LUELLMAN, PATTY; Edison Sr HS; Lake Sta, IN; Chrs; Hon Rl; Tchr.

LUERSMAN, TERESA; Delphos St Johns HS; Delphos, OH; 22/150 Cls Rep Frsh Cls; Cls Rep Soph Cls; Cl Rep Jr Cls; Pres Sr Cls; Am Leg Aux Girls St; Band; Hon Rl; Fr Clb; Letter Trk; Chrldng; Univ.

LUERSSEN, ANN; Munster HS; Munster, IN; 11/441 NHS; Capt Glf; Capt Ten; Miami Univ; Econ.

LUETH, CATHY; Memphis HS; Memphis, MI; Girl Scts; Hon Rl; Hosp Ade; Sct Actv; Rptr Yrbk; 4-H; Letter Trk; IM Sprt; PPFtbl; 4-H Awd; Navy; Elec.

LUFT, DI ANN; Owosso HS; Owosso, MI; Chrs; Chrh Wkr; Cmnty Wkr; Yth Flsp;.

LUFT, JOAN; North Central Area HS; Carney, MI; 16/73 Sec Band; Chrh Wkr; Treas Stu Cncl; Rptr Yrbk; Pres 4-H; Trk; IM Sprt; Mgrs; Pom Pon; 4-H Awd; Mich Tech Univ; Business Admin.

LUFT, KATHRINE; North Central Area HS; Powers, MI; Chrh Wkr; Hon Rl; NHS; Sch Pl; Spn Clb; Mgrs; Pom Pon; Tmr; College; Law.

LUFT, PAUL; North Central HS; Carney, MI; 3/63 Cls Rep Frsh Cls; Cls Rep Soph Cls; Cl Rep Jr Cls; Pres Sr Cls; Cls Rep Sr Cls; Am Leg Boys St; Band; Hon Rl; Sch Pl; Stu Cncl; Mich Tech Univ; Engr.

LUGABIHL, STEVEN E; Parkway Local School; Rockford, OH; 6/82 Am Leg Boys St; Band; Chrs; Chrh Wkr; Hon Rl; NHS; Lat Clb; Sci Clb; Letter Ftbl; Trk; Adrian Coll; Sci.

LUGABIHL, STEVEN E; Parkway Local HS; Rockford, OH; 6/84 Am Leg Boys St; Chrs; FCA; Hon Rl; NHS; Lat Clb; Sci Clb; Ftbl; Chrldng; Chem.

LUGAR, ELIZABETH; Oceana HS; Oceana, WV; 1/135 Am Leg Aux Girls St; Girl Scts; NHS; Quill & Scroll; Ed Sch Nwsp; Pres Beta Clb; Pep Clb; Sec Spn Clb; Capt Chrldng; DAR Awd; Univ; Theatre.

LUGAR, JIM; Westfield Washington HS; Westfield, IN; Hon Rl; Fr Clb; Outstndg Achvmnt Ind Arts 78; Outstndg Achmvnt Martial Arts Karate 76; Achmvnt Of Blk Belt 78; Univ.

LUGAR, LISA; Oceana HS; Oceana, WV; 1/130 Am Leg Aux Girls St; NHS; Quill & Scroll; Ed Sch Nwsp; Beta Clb; Sec Spn Clb; Capt Chrldng; DAR Awd; College; Theatre.

LUGINBILL, DEANNA F; Parkway HS; Rockford, OH; 24/83 Cls Rep Frsh Cls; Cls Rep Soph Cls; Cl Rep Jr Cls; Cls Rep Sr Cls; Band; Chrs; Chrh Wkr; Hon Rl; Stu Cncl; Yth Flsp; Wright St Branch Coll; Data Process.

LUIBRAND, MARLENE; Lakeview HS; St Clair Shores, MI; 5/350 Hon Rl; NHS; PPFtbl; Natl Merit Schl; Wayne St Univ; Engr.

LUKAC, LOUIS; North Judson San Pierre HS; N Judson, IN; 3/200 Pres Jr Cls; Am Leg Boys St; Chrh Wkr; Sec NHS; Pres FFA; Mth Clb; Sci Clb; IM Sprt; Purdue Univ; Landscape Archt.

LUKACHKO, MARK; Admiral King HS; Lorain, OH; Am Leg Boys St; Hon Rl; Pol Wkr; Rptr Yrbk; Yrbk; Am Leg Awd; Ski Clb; Miami Univ; Comp Sci.

LUKAS, LYNNE; Old Trail HS; Brecksville, OH; Cls Rep Soph Cls; Cl Rep Jr Cls; Cls Rep Sr Cls; Chrh Wkr; Hon Rl; Sch Mus; Rptr Yrbk; Fr Clb; Letter Bsbl; Bsktbl; College.

LUKAS, SUZANNE; Cardinal HS; Middlefield, OH; Pres Jr Cls; AFS; Band; Cmp Fr Grls; Chrs; Chrh Wkr; Cmnty Wkr; Girl Scts; College.

LUKASCHEWSKI, MELANIE; S Lyon HS; New Hudson, MI; 6/279 Cl Rep Jr Cls; Cls Rep Sr Cls; Hon Rl; NHS; Letter Bsbl; Scr Kpr; Natl Merit Ltr; Oakland Cnty Comm Trust Schlrshp; Acad Exc Awd; Eng & Bio Medals; Michigan St Univ; Vet.

LUKASZEWICZ, NICHOLAS; Fairview HS; Fairview Pk, OH; Band; Hon Rl; Ftbl; IM Sprt; Univ; Fisheries Bio.

LUKE, CARLESSA; Buena Vista HS; Saginaw, MI; Cls Rep Sr Cls; Chrs; Chrh Wkr; Cmnty Wkr; Girl Scts; Hon Rl; Pep Clb; Mgrs; Pom Pon; Scr Kpr; Patricia Stevens College; Fashion.

LUKE, JAMES; South Dearborn HS; Dillsboro, IN; Band; 4-H; Letter Bsbl; Letter Bsktbl; Letter Ftbl; Letter Wrstlng; IM Sprt; Vincennes; Drafting.

LUKE, KAREN; South Dearborn HS; Dillsboro, IN; 5/263 Am Leg Aux Girls St; Chrs; Chrh Wkr; Hon Rl; NHS; 4-H; NEDT Awd High Standards Local 78; Purdue Univ; Acctg.

LUKE, MARY; Milan Jr Sr HS; Dillsboro, IN; 2/80 Trs Jr Cls; Trs Sr Cls; Am Leg Aux Girls St; Chrs; Chrh Wkr; Hon Rl; NHS; Stg Crw; Yrbk; Drama Clb; Univ.

LUKE, PAULA; George A Dondero HS; Royal Oak, MI; Chrs; Girl Scts; Drama Clb; FBLA; Ger Clb; PPFtbl; Scr Kpr; Univ; Bus Mgmt.

LUKE, SHELLY; Geneva Secondary Complex HS; Geneva, OH; Cl Rep Jr Cls; Cls Rep Sr Cls; AFS; Chrs; Off Ade; Sch Mus; Bsktbl; Kent St Ashtabula Branch Coll; Bio.

LUKE, SUSAN; Yorktown HS; Muncie, IN; Hon Rl; NHS; Yth Flsp; Spn Clb; Letter Swmmng; Univ; Acctg.

LUKEN, KIM; Mother Of Mercy HS; Cincinnati, OH; Aud/Vis; Chrs; Girl Scts; JA; GAA;.

LUKEN, PATTY; Richmond Sr HS; Richmond, IN; 39/650 Girl Scts; Hon Rl; Hosp Ade; Treas JA; NHS; 4-H; Fr Clb; JA Awd; Rotary Awd; St Marys Coll; Eng.

LUKIN, JONATHAN; Austintown Fitch HS; Austintown, OH; 23/660 NHS; Fr Clb; College; Physics.

LUKING, ROBERT B; Rivet HS; Vincennes, IN; Cl Rep Jr Cls; Aud/Vis; Chrs; Hon Rl; Mdrgl; Sch Mus; Stu Cncl; Fr Clb; IM Sprt; Grnd Concours Of Indiana; Indiana State Schl Music Assoc; College; Medicine.

LUKONEN, DARA; Atherton HS; Flint, MI; 1/160 Val; Band; Chrh Wkr; Hon Rl; Sch Pl; Letter Bsktbl; DAR Awd; Michigan St Univ; Vet.

LUKONEN, DARA; Atherton HS; Burton, MI; Val; Orch; Sch Pl; Letter Bsbl; Letter Bsktbl; DAR Awd; Mic State College; Vet.

LUKOTCH, DEBORAH; Lorain Catholic HS; Lorain, OH; 11/156 Cls Rep Frsh Cls; Trs Soph Cls; Trs Jr Cls; Trs Sr Cls; Band; Chrs; Hon Rl; NHS; Sch Pl; Stu Cncl; Oh St Cert Of Mert 79; Miami Univ; Bus Admin.

LUKSA, ROSANNA; Normandy HS; Parma, OH; 49/649 Drl Tm; Hon Rl; Jr NHS; VICA; Vocational Schl; Nursing.

LULKO, DEBORA; Adlai E Stevenson HS; Livonia, MI; Chrh Wkr; Cmnty Wkr; Drm Mjrt; Lit Mag; Natl Forn Lg; Stu Cncl; Spn Clb; Twrlr; Natl Merit SF; Voice Dem Awd; Marygrove Coll Scholar Award 79; Marygrove Coll; Foreign Lang.

LUM, ROBERT P; Fairborn Park Hills HS; Fairborn, OH; AFS; Am Leg Boys St; Band; Chrs; Debate Tm; Hon Rl; VP Jr NHS; Natl Forn Lg; Treas NHS; Sch Pl; Stanford Univ; Med.

LUMB, MARY; Ursuline Academy; Cincinnati, OH; Hon Rl; Rptr Sch Nwsp; Lat Clb; IM Sprt; Natl Merit Ltr; Univ; Bio.

LUMBATIS, PAIGE; Woodsfield HS; Lewisville, OH; Sec Soph Cls; Sec Jr Cls; Sec Sr Cls; Am Leg Aux Girls St; Band; Chrs; Chrh Wkr; Hon Rl; Lbry Ade; Off Ade; Univ; Music.

LUMLEY, DAVID; Gladwin HS; Gladwin, MI; 49/150 DECA; Adrian College; Bio.

LUMMER, CHERYL; Bellbrook HS; Bellbrook, OH; Band; Chrh Wkr; Drm Bgl; Girl Scts; Off Ade; Yth Flsp; GAA; Twrlr; Sinclair Comm Collegef Exec Sec.

LUMPCIK, MELINDA; New Philadelphia HS; New Phila, OH; Chrs; Chrh Wkr; Hon Rl; Off Ade; Fr Clb; Univ; Jrnlsm.

LUMPKIN, CAROLYN; Southwestern HS; Detroit, MI; Band; Chrh Wkr; Hon Rl; NHS; Off Ade; Sch Mus; Stu Cncl; Rptr Sch Nwsp; Sch Nwsp; Gold Medal Record Keeping; Silver Medal Typing; Michigan St Univ; Mass Comm.

LUND, JULIE; Cedar Springs HS; Cedar Spgs, MI; Girl Scts; Hon Rl; Jr NHS; NHS; Fr Clb; FFA; FHA; Kent Skills Cntr Voc Schl; Art.

LUND, LAURIE; Climax Scotts HS; Fulton, MI; 13/58 Chrh Wkr; Cmnty Wkr; Hon Rl; Lbry Ade; Sch Pl; Stg Crw; Yth Flsp; 4-H; Trk; Mgrs; Adrian Coll; Eng.

LUNDBERG, DONALD; Rapid River HS; Rapid River, MI; Aud/Vis; Boy Scts; Chrs; Chrh Wkr; Hon Rl; Sct Actv; 4-H; Letter Bsktbl; Letter Crs Cntry; Letter Ftbl; PE Fitness Awd Scoring In Top 70% Of Yth 78; Northern Michigan Univ; Bookeepng.

LUNDBERG, DONALD; Lumen Christi HS; Jackson, MI; Hon Rl; Letter Bsktbl; Letter Crs Cntry; Letter Ftbl; Letter Trk; IM Sprt; Jackson Community College; Arch Engr.

LUNDBERG, KELLY; Keaisley HS; Davison, MI; Sec Frsh Cls; Sec Soph Cls; Sec Jr Cls; Sec Sr Cls; Hon Rl; Sch Pl; Stu Cncl; Coach Actv; Mgrs; Univ Of Colorado; Psych.

LUNDBERG, THOMAS; St Francis De Sales HS; Toledo, OH; Boy Scts; Hon Rl; NHS; Bsbl; St Pius X Shugrue Scholarshp 76; Bio Award 78; Eng Award 78; Sci Award 77; Highest Averages; Univ; Orthodontist.

LUNDBLAD, BETH; Columbia City Joint HS; Columbia City, IN; FCA; Girl Scts; Spn Clb; Letter Bsktbl; Letter Ten;.

LUNDGREN, ALLYSON; Taft Sr HS; Hamilton, OH; 12/412 AFS; Hon Rl; Jr NHS; Sec NHS; Off Ade; Yrbk; Ger Clb; Univ Of Cincinnati; Fshn Dsgn.

LUNDQUIST, KIM; Highland HS; Medina, OH; Trs Frsh Cls; Band; Capt Drl Tm; Hon Rl; Hosp Ade; NHS; Stu Cncl; Treas 4-H; FHA; Key Clb; Univ.

LUNDSTROM, KAREN; Chagrin Falls HS; Chagrin Falls, OH; Chrh Wkr; Girl Scts; Hon Rl; Lit Mag; Rptr Yrbk; Sch Nwsp; Ger Clb; IM Sprt; PPFtbl; College; Psych.

LUNEKE, PATRICIA; Tecumseh HS; New Carlisle, OH; Hon Rl; Jr NHS; Letter Trk; Ohio St Univ; Vet.

LUNG, MATILDA; Benzie County Central HS; Beulah, MI; 10/128 Band; Chrs; Chrh Wkr; Off Ade; Rptr Yrbk; Rptr Sch Nwsp; Drama Clb; 4-H; NMC; Sec.

LUNGARO, JOAN; Cody HS; Detroit, MI; 6/450 Band; Chrh Wkr; Hon Rl; Lbry Ade; NHS; Beta Clb; Mth Clb; OEA; Sci Clb; Am Leg Awd; Wayne St Univ Merit Schlrshp; Summa Cum Laude; Cody HS Chapt Ofc Co Op Of Yr; Wayne St Univ; Busns Admin.

LUNGERHAUSEN, EMILIE; North Central Area HS; Hermansville, MI; 1/80 Band; Chrh Wkr; Hon Rl; NHS; Orch; Yth Flsp; Rptr Yrbk; Yrbk; 4-H; FHA; Univ Of Michigan; Sci.

LUNSFORD, ELLEN C; Shawe Memorial HS; Madison, IN; 12/36 Cls Rep Soph Cls; Sec Jr Cls; Girl Scts; Hon Rl; Sch Pl; Stu Cncl; Yrbk; Rptr Sch Nwsp; 4-H; Pep Clb; Ivy Tech Schl; Med Tech.

LUNSFORD, GINA; Brookville HS; Laurel, IN; Chrs; Cmnty Wkr; Girl Scts; Hon Rl; Sch Mus; Sct Actv; Drama Clb; 4-H; Trk; GAA; Beautician Schl.

LUNSFORD, LARRY; Brookville HS; Brookville, IN; 13/215 Hon Rl; Rptr Sch Nwsp; FFA; Letter Bsktbl; Letter Ftbl; Letter Trk; Univ.

LUNSFORD, TED; Chillicothe HS; Chilicother, OH; Hon Rl; Jr NHS; College.

LUNT, GREGORY; Carrollton HS; Saginaw, MI; 11/120 Band; Boy Scts; Chrh Wkr; Hon Rl; MMM; NHS; Off Ade; Orch; Sch Mus; Sct Actv; Aquinas; Psych.

LUOMA, KRISTINE; Logan HS; Logan, OH; Band; Chrh Wkr; Hon Rl; NHS; Orch; Stu Cncl; Rptr Yrbk; Treas Fr Clb; Lat Clb; Scr Kpr; St Olaf Coll; Poli Sci.

LUPFER, BRUCE; Timken HS; Canton, OH; Band; Boy Scts; Sct Actv; Colo State; Wildlife Bio.

LUPICA, MARY ANN; Normandy HS; Parma, OH; 50/650 Chrs; Lbry Ade; Lit Mag; Off Ade; Sch Mus; Lat Clb; Cuyahoga Cmnty Coll; Litry Writer.

LUPKE, MARK; Concordia Lutheran HS; Ft Wayne, IN; Hon Rl; Orch; Sch Pl; Lat Clb; Crs Cntry; Trk; Dir Awd Purdue Acadmc Ldrshp Seminar 78; Mbr MENSA 79; Brd Of Dir Ft Wayne Astro Soc 79; Univ; History.

LUPPINO, TOM; Medina HS; Medina, OH; 32/360 Hon Rl; NHS; Letter Socr; Univ Of Akron; Elec Engr.

LUSBY, DOUG; Mt Healthy HS; Cincinnati, OH; 71/572 Hon Rl; Letter Bsbl; Bsktbl; Letter Ftbl; Univ; Bus Admin.

LUSCOMB, SUSAN; Northwest HS; Jackson, MI; Chrs; Chrh Wkr; Hosp Ade; Jackson Community College; Elem Educ.

LUSE, VERL; Whiteford HS; Riga, MI; Am Leg Boys St; Lbry Ade; NHS; Orch; Sch Mus; Yth Flsp; Ed Sch Nwsp; Rptr Sch Nwsp; Drama Clb; Ftbl; Eastern Mich Univ; Law.

LUSH, ELIZABETH; Lake Central HS; Dyer, IN; 35/468 Cls Rep Soph Cls; Cl Rep Jr Cls; Cls Rep Sr Cls; NHS; Quill & Scroll; Sch Mus; Stu Cncl; Rptr Yrbk; PPFtbl; Indiana Univ; Medical.

LUSK, CLAUDIA J; Bridgeport HS; Bridgeport, WV; Chrh Wkr; Cmnty Wkr; Girl Scts; Hon Rl; Lbry Ade; NHS; Sch Pl; Sct Actv; Stg Crw; Yth Flsp; Fairmont State Coll; Elem Ed.

LUSK, SHELIA; Montcalm HS; Duhring, WV; Chrs; Chrh Wkr; Hon Rl; Sch Mus; Sch Pl; 4-H; FBLA; FHA; Pep Clb; Sci Clb; Concord Coll; Voice.

LUSK, TAMMY J; Princeton HS; Bluefield, WV; 3/300 Am Leg Aux Girls St; VP Band; NHS; Rptr Sch Nwsp; Keyettes; Capt Twrlr; Natl Merit SF; Salem Coll; Music Educ.

LUSK, TRACY; Princeton HS; Princeton, WV; Jr NHS; Ftbl; Concord Coll; Law.

LUST, JEFFERY L; Jackson Baptist HS; Concord, MI; Band; Chrs; Chrh Wkr; Yth Flsp; 4-H; Jordan Coll; Indust Elec.

LUST, JENNY; Wynford HS; Bucyrus, OH; 5/120 Band; Hon Rl; Hosp Ade; Lbry Ade; NHS; Off Ade; VP Yth Flsp; 4-H; FHA; Busns Schl; Sec.

LUSTIG, RICHARD; West Geauga HS; Novelty, OH; Cls Rep Frsh Cls; Band; Chrs; Hon Rl; Stu Cncl; Spn Clb; Wrstlng; IM Sprt; College.

LUTA, JACQUELYN J; Bridgeport Cmnty HS; Bridgeport, MI; 37/365 Band; Drl Tm; Hon Rl; NHS; Twrlr; Line Commander In Marching Bnd; Recog Schlrshp Awd; Cum Laude; Delta Coll; Psych.

LUTE, DANIEL; South Central HS; Hanna, IN; Pres Frsh Cls; Pres Sr Cls; Boy Scts; Chrs; Chrh Wkr; Debate Tm; Sch Mus; Sch Pl; Yth Flsp; Bsbl; Univ; Public Relations.

LUTES, CYNTHIA J; Lawrence Central HS; Lawrence, IN; JA; Stg Crw; Pres DECA; Pep Clb; Lawrence Kiawnis Clb Voc Schlshp 1979; 1st In Apparel & Accissrs In St Contst 1979; Vincennes Univ; Marketing.

LUTES, JULIE; Brown County HS; Nashville, IN; Chrs; Rptr Yrbk; DECA; 4-H; Pep Clb; 4-H Awd; Bus Schl; Fashion Mdse.

LUTES, PAMELA G; Brownstown Central HS; Brownstown, IN; 32/145 Band; Quill & Scroll; Sch Mus; Ed Sch Nwsp; 4-H; FTA; Lat Clb; Pep Clb; Sci Clb; Twrlr; Ball St Univ; Elem Ed.

LUTHER, JAYNE; Springboro HS; Springboro, OH; Drm Bgl; Hon Rl; Jr NHS; NHS; Univ; Soc Wrk.

LUTHER, LINDA; Bishop Foley HS; Madison Hts, MI; Am Leg Aux Girls St; Capt Debate Tm; Hon Rl; Lit Mag; NHS; Sch Mus; Eng Clb; Letter Crs Cntry; Letter Trk; Univ; Fine Arts.

LUTJEN, MARY B; Beaumont School For Girls; Shaker Hts, OH; Hosp Ade; Ten; College; Bus.

LUTON, DEBBIE; Kalkaska HS; Kalkaska, MI; 21/138 Sec Soph Cls; Sec Jr Cls; Girl Scts; Hon Rl; Sch Pl; Rptr Yrbk; Rptr Sch Nwsp; Letter Bsbl; Letter Bsktbl; Pres Awd; Bus School; Manager.

LUTTERBACH, LISA; Memorial HS; Evansville, IN; Chrs; Cmnty Wkr; Hon Rl; Hosp Ade; Sch Mus; Sch Pl; Rptr Sch Nwsp; 4-H; Fr Clb; Pep Clb; Whos Who In Indiana For French & Ky HS 78; Univ.

LUTTIG, LINDA; High School; St Johns, MI; Band; FCA; Girl Scts; Hon Rl; Stg Crw; Drama Clb; Spn Clb; Swmmng; Tmr; Univ; Sci.

LUTZ, BRIAN; Tawas Area HS; National City, MI; Ftbl; Ferris St Univ; Real Estate.

LUTZ, CAROLINE; Chaminade Julienne HS; Dayton, OH; 4/249 Chrh Wkr; Cmnty Wkr; Sec Girl Scts; Hon Rl; NHS; Pol Wkr; Sch Pl; Sct Actv; Ed Yrbk; Rptr Yrbk; Univ; Jrnlsm.

LUTZ, H; Roy C Start HS; Toledo, OH; Band; Chrs; Sch Mus; Sch Pl; Drama Clb; Eng Clb; Fr Clb; Rus Clb; Univ; Lang.

LUTZ, JERRY; Grand Haven HS; Grand Haven, MI; Chrh Wkr; Hon Rl; NHS; Trk; Mic Tech Univ; Applied Physics.

LUTZ, JOANNE; The Andrews School; Phillipsburg, NJ; Chrs; Drm Bgl; Girl Scts; Yrbk; IM Sprt; Nursing Schl; Nursing.

LUTZ, LAURA; Southeast HS; Ravenna, OH; Chrs; Drl Tm; Hon Rl; MMM; Off Ade; Rptr Sch Nwsp; Sch Nwsp; Pep Clb; Bsktbl; Scr Kpr; Univ; Forest Ranger.

LUTZ, LAWRENCE; Central HS; Evansville, IN; Cls Rep Frsh Cls; Cl Rep Jr Cls; Aud/Vis; Chrh Wkr; NHS; Stg Crw; Stu Cncl; VP Rdo Clb; Letter Bsbl; Crs Cntry; Acad Schsp To ISUE 79; Hoosier St Hon Schslp 79; Indiana St Univ; Elec Engr.

LUTZ, LORI; Memorial HS; St Marys, OH; 8/222 Am Leg Aux Girls St; Chrh Wkr; Hon Rl; Lbry Ade; NHS; Pol Wkr; Treas Yth Flsp; Y-Teens; Sprt Ed Sch Nwsp; FDA; Schl Winner Of Century III Leaders; Ohio St Univ; Vet Med.

LUTZ, MARK; Fairfield Sr HS; Fairfield, OH; Ger Clb; Miami Univ.

LUTZ, MICHAEL; Orchard View HS; Muskegon, MI; Cl Rep Jr Cls; Aud/Vis; Hon Rl; Lbry Ade; Navy; Elec.

LUTZ, RAE A; South Vigo HS; Terre Haute, IN; 55/630 Chrs; Chrh Wkr; Hon Rl; NHS; Off Ade; Sch Mus; Sch Pl; Y-Teens; Sch Nwsp; Drama Clb;.

LUTZ, ROBERT; St Joseph HS; Euclid, OH; 15/285 Cls Rep Soph Cls; Cl Rep Jr Cls; Cls Rep Sr Cls; FCA; Hon Rl; NHS; Stu Cncl; Capt Bsbl; Wrstlng; IM Sprt; Bowling Green State Univ; Commnctn.

LUTZ, SEABRIGHT; West Geavga HS; Chesterland, OH; 109/352 Chrs; Cmnty Wkr; Hon Rl; Lbry Ade; NHS; Sch Mus; Sch Pl; Stg Crw; Rptr Sch Nwsp; Pres Drama Clb; Univ Of Miami; Theater.

LUU, DANIEL; Carmel HS; Indianapolis, IN; Hon Rl; NHS; Yth Flsp; DECA; Fr Clb; Mth Clb; IM Sprt; Outstanding Stu Of Distr Ed; Boy Stu Of Yr DECA; DECA St Treas & Chapt Pres; Purdue Univ; Busns Mgmt.

LUZOADER, ANN; Northside HS; Muncie, IN; 28/231 Cls Rep Soph Cls; Sec Jr Cls; VP Sr Cls; Sec NHS; Stu Cncl; Rptr Sch Nwsp; Pep Clb; Spn Clb; Chrldng; Indiana Univ; Tele Cmnctns.

LY, MARGARET A; Jay County HS; Portland, IN; 51/474 Band; Hon Rl; Jr NHS; NHS; Mth Clb; Sci Clb; Ten; Wnnr Of The Portland Jr HS Spelling Champ 75; Wnnr Of The Judge Haynes Elem Schl Spelling Champ 74; Univ Of Michigan; Pre Med.

LYBARGER, JERRI; Shelby HS; Shelby, OH; Cls Rep Frsh Cls; Sec Sr Cls; Girl Scts; Pol Wkr; Sch Pl; Ed Yrbk; Ed Sch Nwsp; 4-H; Sci Clb; Letter Trk; Ohio Univ; Communications.

LYDDON, JULIA A; Chillicothe HS; Chillicothe, OH; Chrs; Debate Tm; Hon Rl; Natl Forn Lg; NHS; Off Ade; Ohi State Univ.

LYDEN, THOMAS; Turpin HS; Cincinnati, OH; 36/371 Band; Stg Crw; Letter Swmmng; Mgrs; Drum Major 1978; Univ; Engr.

LYKINS, BETH; Norwood HS; Norwood, OH; VP Soph Cls; Cl Rep Jr Cls; Drl Tm; Hon Rl; Jr NHS; Stu Cncl; Y-Teens; Mth Clb; Pep Clb; Capt Bsktbl; Univ Of Cincinnati; Interior Design.

LYKINS, CHRIS; Our Lady Of Angels HS; Cincinnati, OH; 25/140 Hon Rl; NHS; Stg Crw; Drama Clb; Pep Clb; Trk; GAA; Capt IM Sprt; Univ; X Ray Tech.

LYKINS, SANDRA; Utica HS; Utica, MI; Debate Tm; Drl Tm; Hon Rl; Jr NHS; NHS; Rptr Yrbk; Pep Clb; Spn Clb; Pom Pon; Michigan St Univ; Spanish.

LYKINS, ZEBORAH; Bishop Fenwick HS; Middletown, OH; DAR Awd; Miami Univ.

LYLE, JODIE; Union Local HS; Flushing, OH; 51/150 Band; Hon Rl; Stu Cncl; Yrbk; Rptr Sch Nwsp; Fr Clb; Pep Clb; Sci Clb; Letter Chrldng; Tmr; Belmont Tech Coll; Exec Sec.

LYLES, CALVIN; Highland Park Community HS; Highland Park, MI; Band; Hon Rl; NHS; Letter Wrstlng; Univ Of Mich; Math.

LYLES, MARY; Salem HS; Salem, IN; Letter Bsktbl; GAA; PPFtbl; JA Awd; Prosser Univ; Med.

LYMAN, ADRIAN; St Agatha HS; Redford Twsp, MI; 11/145 Cls Rep Sr Cls; Hon Rl; Letter Ftbl; Letter Trk; College; Business Admin.

LYMAN, ADRIAN; St Agatha HS; Detroit, MI; 8/135 Cls Rep Sr Cls; Boy Scts; Hon Rl; Stu Cncl; Letter Ftbl; Letter Trk; Central Michigan Univ; Bus.

LYMAN, M; Flushing HS; Flushing, MI; Trs Jr Cls; Mgrs; Univ; Engr.

LYNAM, EDWARD P; Brookfield Sr HS; Hubbard, OH; Hon Rl; Treas NHS; Sct Actv; Beta Clb; Lat Clb; Univ; Engr.

LYNCH, ANTHONY; Kenowa Hills HS; Grand Rapids, MI; Pres Frsh Cls; Am Leg Boys St; Band; Drm Mjrt; Pres NHS; Stu Cncl; Glf; Univ Of Mic; Law.

LYNCH, CHRIS; Ravenna HS; Ravenna, OH; Hst Jr Cls; Cmp Fr Grls; Hon Rl; Off Ade; 4-H; IM Sprt; 4-H Awd; Business School; Legal Secretary.

LYNCH, DANIEL J; Lapeer East HS; Lapeer, MI; Hon Rl; NHS; Bsbl; Bsktbl; Ftbl; Rotary Awd; College.

LYNCH, DONNA; Springs Valley HS; W Baden, IN; 3/87 Am Leg Aux Girls St; Band; Girl Scts; Hon Rl; NHS; OEA; Pep Clb; Sullivan Jr Coll; Acctg.

LYNCH, DONNA; Springs Valley HS; West Baden, IN; 1/100 Band; Girl Scts; Hon Rl; OEA; Pep Clb; Sullivan Jr Bus Schl; Acctg.

LYNCH, JAMES; Pineville HS; Pineville, WV; Trs Frsh Cls; Boy Scts; Chrh Wkr; Hon Rl; Jr NHS; NHS; Stu Cncl; Drama Clb; Pep Clb; Sci Clb; Univ; Pharm.

LYNCH, KENT; Wabash HS; Wabash, IN; 34/191 Pres Frsh Cls; Chrs; Chrh Wkr; FCA; Hon Rl; Sch Pl; Boys Clb Am; Letter Bsbl; Letter Bsktbl; Letter Ten; Ball St Univ; Acctg.

LYNCH, LARRY; Southwestern HS; Lexington, IN; 8/100 Cls Rep Frsh Cls; Cls Rep Soph Cls; Cl Rep Jr Cls; Cls Rep Sr Cls; Letter Band; Boy Scts; Hon Rl; NHS; Sch Pl; Stg Crw; Purdue Univ; Elec Engr.

LYNCH, LAURA; Floyd Central HS; Floyd Knobs, IN; Girl Scts; Pep Clb; Indiana Univ; Nursing.

LYNCH, LOLA; North HS; Columbus, OH; 8/325 Hon Rl; Jr NHS; NHS; Off Ade; Capt Trk; IM Sprt; Ohio St Univ; Acctg.

LYNCH, MARGARET; Father Wehrle Memorial HS; Columbus, OH; 15/119 Cls Rep Soph Cls; VP Jr Cls; Cl Rep Jr Cls; Am Leg Aux Girls St; Chrh Wkr; Hon Rl; Lbry Ade; Sch Mus; Stu Cncl; 4-H; Ohio Dominican Coll; Secondary Ed.

LYNCH, MARTHA; Our Lady Star Of The Sea HS; Grse Pt Shr, MI; Cls Rep Frsh Cls; Sch Pl; Stu Cncl; Letter Bsktbl; Letter Swmmng; Letter Ten; Coach Actv; GAA; IM Sprt; Purdue Univ.

LYNCH, MARY; Grafton Sr HS; Grafton, WV; Cls Rep Frsh Cls; Chrs; Hon Rl; Sch Mus; Sch Pl; Stg Crw; Pres Drama Clb; Bsktbl; Chrldng; Capt PPFtbl; Fairmont St Coll; Elem Ed.

LYNCH, MARY ANN; Wirt County HS; Palestine, WV; GAA;.

LYNCH, P; Triton HS; Bourbon, IN; Band; Boy Scts; Chrs; Chrh Wkr; Pres FCA; Hon Rl; Sct Actv; VP Stu Cncl; Pres Yth Flsp; 4-H; Indiana Central Univ; Elem Educ.

LYNCH, PATRICIA; Mother Of Mercy HS; Cincinnati, OH; Chrh Wkr; Cmnty Wkr; Hon Rl; Mod UN; NHS; Off Ade; Pol Wkr; Sch Pl; Fr Clb; Dnfth Awd; Univ; Bus Law.

LYNCH, PATRICIA A; Mother Of Mercy HS; Cincinnati, OH; 1/240 Chrh Wkr; Cmnty Wkr; Hon Rl; Mod UN; NHS; Off Ade; Pol Wkr; College; Bus.

LYNCH, RICHARD H; St Xavier HS; Maineville, OH; 75/270 Cls Rep Frsh Cls; Cls Rep Soph Cls; Cl Rep Jr Cls; Cls Rep Sr Cls; Chrs; Cmnty Wkr; Hon Rl; Hosp Ade; Sch Nwsp; Pep Clb; 1st Plc In Sci Fair 76; Rank Of 12th In Cincinnati For Tennis In Age Grp 75; Hon Every Sem At St Xavier 79; Georgia Tech Univ; Law.

LYNCH, ROBERT; Wilbur Wright HS; Dayton, OH; Pres Jr Cls; Sch Pl; Rptr Yrbk; Sch Nwsp; Letter Ftbl; Letter Gym; Letter Trk; Univ Of Dayton; Education.

LYNCH, STEVEN; Cedar Springs HS; Sand Lakes, MI; Jr NHS; Univ; Chem.

LYNCH, SUSAN M; Notre Dame Academy; Toledo, OH; 13/134 Pres Sr Cls; Chrs; Hon Rl; JA; Mod UN; NHS; Quill & Scroll; Sch Pl; Stg Crw; Stu Cncl; Miami Univ; Bus.

LYNCH, T; Euclid Sr HS; Euclid, OH; Hon Rl; Trk; Pres Awd; Univ; Med.

LYNEMA, SCOTT; Zeeland HS; Zeeland, MI; Band; Boy Scts; Cmnty Wkr; Hon Rl; Natl Forn Lg; Sct Actv; Yth Flsp; Pep Clb; Letter Bsbl; Letter Bsktbl; Univ; Law.

LYNN, BRYON G; Arlington HS; Indianapolis, IN; 6/326 Hon Rl; NHS; Orch; Sch Mus; Sch Pl; Drama Clb; Letter Swmmng; Letter Ten; JETS Awd; Pres Awd; Purdue Univ; Elec Engr.

LYNN, DAWN; Bloomington HS N; Bloomington, IN; 41/425 Cl Rep Jr Cls; Cmnty Wkr; Hon Rl; Jr NHS; Off Ade; Bsktbl; PPFtbl; Scr Kpr; Natl Merit Ltr; Varsity Vlybl Tm Ltrs 77 79; Univ Of Northern Colorado; Phys Ed.

LYNN, JEAN; Nettie Lee Roth HS; Dayton, OH; Chrh Wkr; Cmnty Wkr; Hon Rl; NHS; FHA; Univ Of Cincinnati; Intr Dsgn.

LYNN, LORRAINE; Reeths Puffer HS; Muskegon, MI; 3/271 Chrh Wkr; Hon Rl; Jr NHS; NHS; 4-H; Spn Clb; Muskegon Comm Coll; Busns.

LYNN, SHERI; Indianapolis Baptist HS; Indianapolis, IN; Trs Frsh Cls; Chrh Wkr; Hon Rl; Off Ade; Stg Crw; Chrldng; Mat Maids; Business School; Real Estate.

LYNN, THERESA; Negaunee HS; Negaunee, MI; Cls Rep Frsh Cls; Cls Rep Soph Cls; Pres Jr Cls; Chrs; Hon Rl; Stu Cncl; Pep Clb; Sci Clb; Trk; Chrldng; Univ; Psych.

LYON, ANNE; Van Wert HS; Van Wert, OH; 12/205 Chrh Wkr; Hon Rl; NHS; Lat Clb; Sci Clb; Bluffton College; Med Tech.

LYON, FRANK; Elmhurst HS; Ft Wayne, IN; 123/400 Boy Scts; Chrh Wkr; Hon Rl; Sct Actv; Ftbl; IM Sprt; Univ; Archt.

LYON, JAN; Van Wert HS; Van Wert, OH; 6/221 Am Leg Aux Girls St; Chrh Wkr; Hon Rl; NHS; Yth Flsp; Treas 4-H; FHA; Lat Clb; Univ; Nursing.

LYON, JANICE; Van Wert HS; Van Wert, OH; Am Leg Aux Girls St; Chrh Wkr; Hon Rl; NHS; 4-H; FHA; Lat Clb; Univ; Nursing.

LYON, JOHN; Brownsburg HS; Pittsboro, IN; Rptr Sch Nwsp; Ger Clb; Crs Cntry; Letter Glf; Swmmng; Letter Ten; Ind Univ; Sports Reporter.

LYON, KELLY; East Kentwood HS; Kentw Ood, MI; Girl Scts; Hon Rl; NHS; Bsktbl; PPFtbl; Cit Awd;.

LYON, KELLY; Marietta Sr HS; Marietta, OH; Chrs; Hon Rl; JA; Off Ade; Sch Pl; Ger Clb; Chrldng; Mat Maids; JA Awd; Pres Awd; Univ.

LYON, SHARON C; John Glenn HS; Cambridge, OH; 7/193 Chrs; Chrh Wkr; Hon Rl; NHS; Yth Flsp; Fr Clb; College; Art.

LYONETTE, JOHN; Boardman HS; Youngstown, OH; 55/594 Band; Hon Rl; NHS; Orch; Sch Mus; Sch Pl; Fr Clb; Outstndg Jazz Musicians Awd 79; Summer Jazz Clinic Schlrshp 77; Schlrshp To YSU 79; Youngstown State Univ; Acctg.

LYONS, BRIAN; Northfield HS; Roann, IN; Band; Boy Scts; JA; 4-H; 4-H Awd; JA Awd; Lincoln Inst Of Tech; Auto Mech.

LYONS, BRIDGID; Fenwick HS; Middletown, OH; VP Frsh Cls; Pres Jr Cls; Band; Chrh Wkr; Sch Mus; Sch Pl; Stu Cncl; Drama Clb; Spn Clb; Bsbl; Coll; Eng.

LYONS, DANIEL; Central HS; Grand Rapids, MI; Band; Boy Scts; Debate Tm; Sch Mus; Bsbl; Capt Bsktbl; Ftbl; Socr; Coach Actv; Mgrs; Phys Fittness Awd; Grand Valley Coll; Comp Sci.

LYONS, GARY; Miami Vly HS; Dayton, OH; Bsktbl; Letter Socr; Letter Trk; Natl Merit Ltr; Univ; Engr.

LYONS, GAYLE; Pershing HS; Detroit, MI; Chrs; Hon Rl; Cit Awd; Natl Merit Schl; Music Award; Scholastic Ach Awrd; Outstndng Performance In Ensemble; Eastern Michigan Univ; Phys Therapy.

LYONS, JORY; William A Wirt HS; Gary, IN; Hon Rl; Jr NHS; NHS; Univ.

LYONS, LORI; Jackson Memorial HS; Canton, OH; Cl Rep Jr Cls; VP Sr Cls; Band; Orch; Sch Mus; Yth Flsp; Akron Univ; Music.

LYONS, MEL; Edon HS; Edon, OH; 8/76 Pres Frsh Cls; Trs Soph Cls; Trs Jr Cls; Band; Chrs; Chrh Wkr; Drl Tm; Drm Mjrt; Hon Rl; NHS; Bowling Green State Univ; Music Ed.

LYONS, MELMOTH; Edon HS; Edon, OH; 8/68 Pres Frsh Cls; Trs Soph Cls; Trs Jr Cls; Band; Chrs; Chrh Wkr; Drl Tm; Univ Of Toledo; Music Educ.

LYONS, REGINA; Elk Garden HS; Elk Garden, WV; Trs Frsh Cls; Sec Soph Cls; Band; Drm Mjrt; Hon Rl; Hosp Ade; Lbry Ade; Sch Pl; Stu Cncl; 4-H; West Virginia Univ; Nurse.

LYONS, RISA; Madison HS; N Madison, OH; Cls Rep Frsh Cls; Cls Rep Sr Cls; Hon Rl; Stu Cncl; Y-Teens; Pep Clb; Spn Clb; Scr Kpr; Univ; Stewardess.

LYONS, SHELLI A; Northside HS; Muncie, IN; Pres Soph Cls; VP Soph Cls; Hon Rl; Hosp Ade; Stu Cncl; Ger Clb; Gym; Chrldng; Coach Actv; Indiana Univ; Phys Ther.

LYONS, SHERRY; Henryville HS; Memphis, IN; 2/71 Trs Frsh Cls; Sec Band; Hon Rl; 4-H; FTA; Sec Pep Clb; Letter Bsbl; Modeling Schl; Modeling.

LYONS, WILBUR M; Bluefield HS; Bluefield, WV; Cls Rep Frsh Cls; Chrs; Chrh Wkr; Sch Mus; Stu Cncl; Letter Ftbl; Fresh Yr Mdl Outstndg Male Chr Mbr; Fresh Yr Mdl Superior Ensemble Male Chr Mbr Song Ldr; Concord Coll; Music.

LYSHER, VICKI; Davison HS; Davison, MI; 8/450 Am Leg Aux Girls St; Band; Chrs; Chrh Wkr; Girl Scts; Hon Rl; NHS; Alma College; Bus Admin.

LYSIK, KIMBERLY; Fitzgerald HS; Warren, MI; Cl Rep Jr Cls; Cls Rep Sr Cls; Chrs; Hon Rl; NHS; Sch Mus; Sch Pl; Stg Crw; Stu Cncl; Drama Clb; Michigan St Univ; Theatre.

LYSLE, BRIAN; Bay HS; Bay Vill, OH; Cls Rep Frsh Cls; Cls Rep Soph Cls; Lbry Ade; Lit Mag; Rptr Sch Nwsp; Sch Nwsp; Ger Clb; Cleveland St Univ; Jrnlsm.

LYSYJ, MARTHA; North Royalton HS; N Royalton, OH; Hon Rl; Off Ade; Pres Spn Clb; Tri C Cmnty Coll; Criminal Law.

LYTKOWSKI, GREG; Solon HS; Solon, OH; Boy Scts; FCA; Sch Nwsp; Univ; Acctg.

LYTLE, DANA; Penn HS; Mishawaka, IN; Band; VP Cmp Fr Grls; FCA; Girl Scts; Hon Rl; NHS; Sch Pl; Stg Crw; Drama Clb; Mgrs; Univ.

LYTLE, LINCOLN L; Paint Valley HS; Bourneville, OH; 7/90 Chrs; Hon Rl;.

LYTTON, MARSHALL; Princton HS; Princeton, WV; Chrh Wkr; Debate Tm; VP FCA; Hon Rl; Yth Flsp; Spn Clb; Letter Ftbl; Letter Trk; Tmr; Pres Awd; Flag Carrier At Grad 78; Univ; Amer Std.

LYZENGA, DIANE; South Christian HS; Grand Rapids, MI; 41/180 Sec Frsh Cls; VP Jr Cls; VP Sr Cls; Band; Chrs; Chrh Wkr; Hon Rl; Hosp Ade; Jr NHS; NHS; Calvin College.

M

MA, MARCO; Jared Finney HS; Detroit, MI; 1/260 Val; Hon Rl; Jr NHS; VP NHS; Off Ade; Cit Awd; Natl Merit SF; College; Computer Engr.

MAAG, MICHELE; Orrville HS; Orrville, OH; 1/180 Cls Rep Frsh Cls; Cls Rep Soph Cls; Cl Rep Jr Cls; Cls Rep Sr Cls; Am Leg Aux Girls St; FCA; Hon Rl; NHS; Pres Stu Cncl; FTA; Ashland Coll; Scndry Educ.

MAAG, TIM; Ft Jennings HS; Ft Jennings, OH; Trs Frsh Cls; Hon Rl; Fr Clb; Crs Cntry; College; Comp Prog.

MAANIKA, DAVID; Calumet HS; Laurium, MI; Hon Rl; Ftbl; Based On ACT Score Qulfd For St Schlsp Consdrtn 80; Mb Ro Fst Runner Up Midgeta Jr Hockey Team 78; Michigan Tech Univ; Engr.

MAASEIDVAAG, LISE; Pioneer HS; Ann Arbor, MI; Band; Chrs; Girl Scts; Hon Rl; Off Ade; Orch; Sch Mus; Drama Clb; Lat Clb; Pep Clb; Univ; Engr.

MABE, B; Bluefield HS; Bluefld, WV; Hon Rl; NHS; Yrbk; Spn Clb; Virg Polytech Inst; Engineering.

MABIE, DENISE; Cedar Springs HS; Cedar Spgs, MI; 4/147 Hon Rl; NHS; PPFtbl; Ferris St Univ; Med Tech.

MABIN, PATRICIA; High School; Gary, IN; Sec Soph Cls; Cmnty Wkr; Drl Tm; Hon Rl; ROTC; Sch Pl; Stu Cncl; Y-Teens; Civ Clb; 4-H; Coll; Comp Tech.

MABRY, GARY L; Greenbrier East HS; Caldwell, WV; Cls Rep Frsh Cls; Hon Rl; Univ; Envrnmnt Study.

MABRY JR, WILLIAM; Pontiac HS; Pontiac, MI; 20/650 Cmnty Wkr; Hon Rl; Red Cr Ade; Fr Clb; Swmmng; Trk; College; Wildlife Bio.

MAC, MICHELLE; Wayne Memorial HS; Wayne, MI; Cls Rep Sr Cls; Am Leg Aux Girls St; Hon Rl; VP NHS; Quill & Scroll; Ed Sch Nwsp; Sprt Ed Sch Nwsp; Mth Clb; Spn Clb; Underclass Honor Awd In Math & Social Studies; College; Biochemical Engr.

MACASKILL, BRIAN D; Menominee HS; Menominee, MI; Band; Chrh Wkr; Jr NHS; Y-Teens; Spn Clb; Crs Cntry; Michigan Tech Univ; Civil Engr.

MACCAULEY, MICHAEL; Reitz Memorial HS; Evansville, IN; Cls Rep Frsh Cls; Cls Rep Soph Cls; Chrs; Debate Tm; Hon Rl; Sch Mus; Sch Pl; Drama Clb; IM Sprt; VFW Awd; 1st Rating St Competition For Ind St Music Assn; Leading Roles In Civic Theatres Last 2 Shows; College; Drama.

MACCHIA, ANNETTE; Archbishop Alter HS; Kettering, OH; Am Leg Aux Girls St; Chrh Wkr; Girl Scts; Sch Nwsp; Fr Clb; Rdo Clb; Univ Of Dayton; Comm Arts.

MACDONALD, A; Walled Lake Western HS; Walled Lk, MI; 1/450 Band; CAP; Hon Rl; Voice Dem Awd; Natl Science Fdn SSTP Kalamazoo Coll 79; Massachusetts Inst Of Tech; Physics.

MACDONALD, DAVID W; Bay City All Saints Cntl HS; Bay City, MI; Sec Sr Cls; Chrh Wkr; Hon Rl; Stu Cncl; Yrbk; Sch Nwsp; Letter Ten; Capt Trk; Coach Actv; Natl Merit SF; College; Pharmacy.

MACDONALD, FAITH; Hudsonville HS; Hudsonville, MI; Chrs; Chrh Wkr; Hon Rl; Lbry Ade; Rptr Sch Nwsp; Mich Busns Schls Assn Competetive Schlrshp; Amer Legion Schlrshp; Davenport Coll Of Busns; Exec Sec.

MACDONALD, HEATHER; Algonac HS; Algonac, MI; Band; Chrh Wkr; Hon Rl; Lbry Ade; Off Ade; Rptr Sch Nwsp; Sch Nwsp; St Scholar 79; Michigan St Univ; Vet.

MACDONALD, SCOTT; Allendale HS; Allendale, MI; Band; Boy Scts; Debate Tm; FCA; Hon Rl; Mod UN; NHS; Stu Cncl; 4-H; Rdo Clb; Bsktbl Varsity Letters Team All Conf; 4 H Ctznshp Shortcourse Jr Leader; Nazareth Coll; Phys Therapy.

MACE, DOUG; Miami Trace HS; Washington Ch, OH; Pres Soph Cls; Cls Rep Soph Cls; Cl Rep Jr Cls; Hon Rl; Stu Cncl; 4-H; VP FFA; Letter Bsktbl; Coach Actv; College.

MACE, JOYCE; Jackson Mem HS; Massillon, OH; Am Leg Aux Girls St; Chrs; Hon Rl; Pres NHS; Fr Clb; JC Awd; Univ; Bus.

MACE, SHERRY; Vinton County HS; Mc Arthur, OH; 8/165 Sec Jr Cls; Sec Sr Cls; Band; FCA; NHS; Yrbk; Drama Clb; Shawnee State Comm College; Denthygn.

MACE, TAMA; Central Preston HS; Kingwood, WV; 6/150 Cls Rep Frsh Cls; Cls Rep Soph Cls; Sec Jr Cls; Cmnty Wkr; Hon Rl; Stu Cncl; Yth Flsp; Rptr Yrbk; 4-H; FHA; West Virginia; Medicine.

MACE JR, GERALD; Southington Chalker HS; W Farmington, OH; 2/70 Chrs; Chrh Wkr; Hon Rl; Yth Flsp; Sch Nwsp; Beta Clb; Bsbl; Ftbl; Tacoa Falls Coll.

MACEK, RICHARD; Roy C Start HS; Toledo, OH; 15/450 Sec Sr Cls; Am Leg Boys St; Chrh Wkr; Hon Rl; NHS; Stu Cncl; Yth Flsp; Ger Clb; Ten; Univ Of Toledo; Chem Engr.

MACESICH, AMANDA; Normandy HS; Parma, OH; 50/649 Cls Rep Frsh Cls; Chrs; Sch Mus; Stu Cncl; Spn Clb; Capt Chrldng; Scr Kpr; Coll; Geology.

MACEYKO, RONALD; Campbell Memorial HS; Campbell, OH; Boy Scts; Chrh Wkr; Hon Rl; NHS; Fr Clb; Mth Clb; Sci Clb; Capt Glf; Ten; Ohi State Univ; Dentistry.

MACGREGOR, JANA; Southfield Lathrup Sr HS; Southfield, MI; VP Frsh Cls; Cls Rep Soph Cls; Sec Jr Cls; Chrs; Hon Rl; Off Ade; Sch Pl; Stu Cncl; Sprt Ed Sch Nwsp; Pep Clb; Phys Ed Awd; Michigan St Univ; Psych.

MACH, BARBARA J; Elkhart Memorial HS; Elkhart, IN; Chrs; Hon Rl; Bsktbl; Ind Univ Sb; Bus Mgmt.

MACHESKE, FELICIA M; Harrison HS; Harrison, MI; Hon Rl; Central Michigan Univ; Commcl Art.

MACHI, JOSEPH; Solon HS; Solon, OH; Am Leg Boys St; Chrs; Hon Rl; MMM; NHS; Orch; Mth Clb; Comp.

MACHIELA, JEFF; Zeeland Public HS; Zeeland, MI; Am Leg Boys St; Boy Scts; Hon Rl; Sch Pl; Yth Flsp; 4-H; Lat Clb; Letter Ftbl; Letter Wrstlng; IM Sprt; Calvin Univ.

MACHIELE, P; Holland Christian HS; Holland, MI; 9/224 Mdrgl; Univ; Sci.

MACHLEIT, KELLEY; Alcona Comm HS; Spruce, MI; 4/125 Hon Rl; Pep Clb; Spn Clb; Chrldng; PPFtbl; Michigan Tech Univ; Engr.

MACHNACKI, DAVE; Our Lady Of Mt Carmel HS; Wyandote, MI; 2/65 VP Frsh Cls; Hon Rl; NHS; Pep Clb; Bsbl; Ftbl; IM Sprt; Univ; Med.

MACHUCA, ANGELO; Bishop Noll Institute; E Chicago, IN; 143/321 Hon Rl; Ftbl; Trk; Wrstlng; IM Sprt; Kiwanis Sponsorship To Ball St Seminar 79; Ball St Univ; Law.

MACICAK, SUSAN; Holland HS; Holland, MI; Hon Rl; Mod UN; NHS; Orch; PAVAS; Sch Mus; Sch Pl; Hope College;; Theatre.

MACICAK, WILLIAM; Holland HS; Holland, MI; 8/300 Hon Rl; Natl Forn Lg; Orch; Univ; Archt Engr.

MACIEJEWSKI, BARBARA; Holy Name Nazareth HS; Middlebg Hts, OH; Chrh Wkr; Hon Rl; Fr Clb; Ohio St Univ; Med.

MACIEJEWSKI, JUDITH; Central HS; Grand Rapids, MI; Hon Rl; Trk; Scr Kpr; Tmr; Grand Rapids Univ; Foods.

MACINA, OREST; Padua Franciscan HS; Cleveland, OH; 30/276 Boy Scts; Hon Rl; Sci Clb; Case Western Reserve Univ; Bio Med.

MACIOCI, JODIE; William V Fisher Cath HS; Lancaster, OH; Chrh Wkr; Cmnty Wkr; Hon Rl; Jr NHS; NHS; Sch Pl; Yrbk; Rptr Sch Nwsp; Capt Chrldng; Univ; Fshn Mdse.

MACK, BARBARA; Covington HS; Bradford, OH; Am Leg Aux Girls St; Band; Chrh Wkr; NHS; Sch Mus; Yth Flsp; Pres 4-H; Treas FHA; College.

MACK, CAROL; Mason HS; Mason, MI; Lbry Ade; Off Ade; College; Interior Decorating.

MACK, DANIEL; Bedford HS; Toledo, OH; Adrian College.

MACK, DENNIS; Union City HS; Union City, MI; 2/93 Cls Rep Frsh Cls; Pres Soph Cls; Sal; Hon Rl; Off Ade; Stu Cncl; Bsbl; Bsktbl; Ftbl; Trk; Central Michigan Univ; Indus Ed.

MACK, KEVIN; Malabar HS; Mansfield, OH; Cls Rep Frsh Cls; Cls Rep Soph Cls; Cl Rep Jr Cls; Cls Rep Sr Cls; Am Leg Boys St; Boy Scts; Chrs; Stu Cncl; Memphis State Univ; Bus.

MACK, MICHELE L; Cadillac Sr HS; Cadillac, MI; 7/300 Cls Rep Frsh Cls; Cls Rep Soph Cls; Pres Jr Cls; Pres Sr Cls; Am Leg Aux Girls St; Band; Cmnty Wkr; Debate Tm; Girl Scts; Hon Rl; Princeton Univ; Intl Relations.

MACKALL, LYNN; West Muskingum HS; Zanesville, OH; Pres Band; Chrs; Girl Scts; Orch; Stg Crw; Sch Nwsp; FTA; VP Mth Clb; Sci Clb; Trk; Englsh 10 Scholastic Ach Test; Nom For Mc Donalds All Amer HS Bnd; 1st Pl Sr HS Solo & Ensemble Contest; Miami Univ; Bio Sci.

MACKAY, DAVID S; Colerain Sr HS; Cincinnati, OH; Aud/Vis; Chrs; Hon Rl; Jr NHS; Mdrgl; NHS; Off Ade; Pres Stu Cncl; Crs Cntry; Swmmng; College; Math.

MACKAY, RODRIC A; North Farmington HS; Farmington Hill, MI; Cls Rep Frsh Cls; Hon Rl; NHS; Letter Swmmng; Univ Of Michigan; Bus Admin.

MACKE, JEFF; Mater Dei HS; Evansville, IN; 1/184 Pres Frsh Cls; Am Leg Boys St; Hon Rl; Jr NHS; Stu Cncl; Letter Bsbl; Letter Crs Cntry; Socr; IM Sprt; Univ.

MACKELLAR, ERIC; Reed City HS; Reed City, MI; Boy Scts; Hon Rl; 4-H; Michigan Tech Univ; Energy.

MACKENZIE, DAVID; Plymouth Salem HS; Plymouth, MI; VP Sr Cls; FCA; Hon Rl; Jr NHS; NHS; Stu Cncl; Rptr Sch Nwsp; Ftbl; Socr; Letter Trk; Central Michigan Univ.

MACKENZIE, TRACEY; St Agatha HS; Detroit, MI; 25/150 Hon Rl; NHS; Rptr Yrbk; Yrbk; Drama Clb; Fr Clb; Trk; Ferris St Coll; Reg Rcd Admin.

MACKERT, DENISE; Holy Name Nazareth HS; Parma, OH; Cmnty Wkr; Girl Scts; Red Cr Ade; Stg Crw; Drama Clb; Bsbl; Chrldng; Coach Actv; IM Sprt; Scr Kpr; College; Psych.

MACKEY, HELEN; Cadillac Sr HS; Cadillac, MI; 52/302 VP Sr Cls; Band; Natl Forn Lg; Sch Mus; Yrbk; Rptr Sch Nwsp; Sch Nwsp; 4-H; Cit Awd; 4-H Awd; 4h Cnty Delegate To Ctznshp 77 In WA D C 77; Selected As A Jr Rotarian Rep 78; Aquinas Coll; Cmnctns.

MACKEY, JOHN; Yale HS; Avoca, MI; 48/180 Hon Rl; 4-H; Bsbl; Bsktbl; Capt Ftbl; College; X Ray Tech.

MACKEY, JOSEPH; Yale HS; Avoca, MI; Bsbl; Bsktbl; Ftbl; Coll; Machinist.

MACKEY, SCOTT; Solone HS; Solon, OH; Chrs; Hon Rl; Mdrgl; VP NHS; Sch Mus; Drama Clb; Mth Clb; Pres Of Hon Music Soc 79; Mbr Of Mu Alpha Theta Math Frat; Top Rating In Music Contst Solo & Ensmbl 78; Univ; Sci.

MACKEY, TAMMY; Okemos HS; East Lansing, MI; 38/309 Hon Rl; Letter Bsbl; Bsktbl; IM Sprt; Mgrs; Western Mic Univ; Med Tech.

MACKIE, DAVID; Waterford Township HS; Pontiac, MI; Boy Scts; Hon Rl; Mic State Univ; Mech Engr.

MACKIE, HUGH; Sault Area HS; Sault Ste Marie, MI; Band; NHS; Ftbl; Mgrs; Michigan Tech Univ; Mech Engr.

MACKIN, ANN; Alpena Sr HS; Alpena, MI; Aud/Vis; Cmnty Wkr; Hon Rl; Lbry Ade; NHS; Off Ade; Pol Wkr; Am Leg Awd; Elk Awd; Natl Merit Ltr; Stu Of The Mnth 79; Stu Of The Yr 79; Western Mi Univ Academic Schl 79; Western Michigan Univ; Psych.

MACKLAY, HOLLY; George Washington HS; Charleston, WV; Band; Hon Rl; Hosp Ade; Sch Mus; Sch Pl; Keyettes; Pep Clb; Spn Clb; Gym; Swmmng; Univ; RN.

MACKLEY, DEBRA; Pinconning HS; Linwood, MI; Band; Hon Rl; Socr; Stewardess.

MACKLEY, TIM W; Big Walnut HS; Sunbury, OH; Chrs; Chrh Wkr; FCA; Hon Rl; VP Yth Flsp; VP 4-H; FFA; Bsktbl; Ftbl; Trk; Elec Engr.

MACKLING, TOD R; Hicksville HS; Hicksville, OH; Aud/Vis; Boy Scts; Hon Rl; Ohio Univ; Elec Engr.

MACKNIGHT, DEBBIE; Wahama HS; New Haven, WV; Am Leg Aux Girls St; Band; Chrs; Cmnty Wkr; Girl Scts; Hon Rl; Yth Flsp; FHA; Chrldng; GAA; W Virginia Univ; Elem Tchr.

MACKNIGHT, DENISE; Licking Valley HS; Newark, OH; Cl Rep Jr Cls; Chrs; Chrh Wkr; Girl Scts; Hon Rl; Sch Mus; Stu Cncl; Yth Flsp; Y-Teens; 4-H; Newark Coll; Math.

MACKO, JIM; Padua Fransiscan HS; Parma, OH; 24/270 Hon Rl; NHS; Red Cr Ade; Letter Wrstlng; Busns Schl; Acctg.

MACKO, PHIL; Mineral Ridge HS; Mineral Ridge, OH; 12/70 Pres Jr Cls; Pres Sr Cls; Chrs; Hon Rl; JA; Yrbk; Letter Ftbl; Letter Trk; IM Sprt; PPFtbl; Kent St Univ; Govt.

MACKOOL, SAM; Harper Woods Secondary HS; Harper Woods, MI; Hon Rl; Stu Cncl; Letter Bsbl; Letter Bsktbl; Letter Ftbl; College; Mech Engr.

MACLACHLAN, CINDY; Swan Valley HS; Saginaw, MI; Off Ade; Sch Pl; Drama Clb; Spn Clb; Trk; Chrldng;.

MACLEAN, DOUGLAS; Mason Cnty Eastern HS; Custer, MI; 5/58 Band; Chrs; Chrh Wkr; Hon Rl; Sch Mus; Sch Pl; Ed Yrbk; Yrbk; Pep Clb; Cit Awd; W Michigan Univ; Music.

MACLELLAN, JOHN J; Harry S Truman HS; Taylor, MI; Univ; Sci.

MACLELLAN, VINCENT; Harry S Truman HS; Taylor, MI; Boy Scts; Hon Rl; College; Airline.

MACLEOD, CHARI; Spring Lake Sr HS; Spring Lake, MI; 35/185 Hon Rl; Hosp Ade; Yth Flsp; IM Sprt; Muskegon Bus Coll; Data Proc.

MACLEOD, MARY ANN; Cass Technical HS; Detroit, MI; 106/889 Hon Rl; Off Ade; Michigan St Univ; Bus.

MACMAIN, R; Flushing HS; Flushing, MI; Band; Hon Rl; NHS; Coach Actv; Pres Awd; General Motors Inst; Engr.

MACMANN, SCOTT; Sycamore HS; Blue Ash, OH; 54/425 Boy Scts; Chrs; Debate Tm; Pres Mod UN; Sct Actv; Rptr Sch Nwsp; IM Sprt; Mgrs; College; Poli Sci.

MACNALL, KATHLEEN; Alpena HS; Alpena, MI; Hon Rl; NHS; 4-H; Ger Clb; Pep Clb; Swmmng; Michigan St Univ; Chem.

MACNAUGHTON, ELIZABETH; R B Chamberlin HS; Twinsburg, OH; Trs Frsh Cls; Cls Rep Soph Cls; Band; Chrs; Chrh Wkr; Drl Tm; FCA; Girl Scts; Hon Rl; Hosp Ade; Florida Inst Of Tech; Oceanography.

MACNEILL, DAVID G; Clay HS; Niles, MI; 46/460 Chrh Wkr; Cmnty Wkr; Hon Rl; Ger Clb; Swmmng; College; Medicine.

MACNICOL, DEAN; Hillman Community HS; Hillman, MI; Cls Rep Frsh Cls; Band; Chrs; Chrh Wkr; Cmnty Wkr; Hon Rl; Lbry Ade; Sct Actv; Stg Crw; Stu Cncl; Baker Junior College; Data Proc.

MACOWAN, VANESSA; Twin Lakes HS; Monticello, IN; 33/217 Hon Rl; Jr NHS; Sch Pl; 4-H; 4-H Awd; Purdue Univ; Vet Med.

MACPHERSON, KIM; Highland HS; Highland, IN; 7/496 Hon Rl; Jr NHS; NHS; Quill & Scroll; Sprt Ed Yrbk; Capt Bsbl; Capt Crs Cntry; PPFtbl; Scr Kpr; Indiana Univ; Bus Admin.

MACPHERSON, MARGO; Bloomfield Hills Andover HS; Birmingham, MI; 55/435 Sec Frsh Cls; VP Jr Cls; Hon Rl; NHS; Sprt Ed Yrbk; Sci Clb; Socr; Wrstlng; IM Sprt; Mic State Univ; Ved Med.

MACPHERSON, MICHAEL; Comstock HS; Kalamazoo, MI; Ftbl; Glf; Ten; Lake Superior St Coll; Amer History.

MACQUEEN, LYNETTE M; Springfield Local HS; Holland, OH; 25/243 Sec Jr Cls; Chrs; FCA; Hon Rl; NHS; Off Ade; Stg Crw; Stu Cncl; Drama Clb; 4-H; Bowling Green St Univ; Sec Bus.

MACRAE, KELLEY; Clinton HS; Clinton, MI; 1/106 VP Soph Cls; Band; Chrs; Chrh Wkr; Girl Scts; Hon Rl; NHS; Sch Mus; Sch Pl; Sct Actv; Michigan St Univ; Vet.

MACUGA, RICH; Chadsey HS; Detroit, MI; Cls Rep Frsh Cls; Boy Scts; Hon Rl; Letter Ftbl; Cit Awd; Natl Merit Ltr; Ferris St Coll; Phys Educ.

MACWOOD, PEG; Upper Arlington HS; Columbus, OH; 181/610 Hon Rl; Fr Clb; FTA; Ger Clb; Bsbl; Bsktbl; Letter Hockey; GAA; Explorer Post Archt 77; Univ; Bus.

MACZUGA, ANTHONY; St Alphonsus HS; Detroit, MI; Aud/Vis; Boy Scts; Chrh Wkr; Cmnty Wkr; Hon Rl; Sct Actv; Yth Flsp; Y-Teens; Crs Cntry; Tmr; Univ; Elec.

MADAY, MARGARET; Sts Peters & Paul Area HS; Sainaw, MI; Trs Soph Cls; Cls Rep Soph Cls; Pres Jr Cls; Cl Rep Jr Cls; VP Sr Cls; Cls Rep Sr Cls; Chrs; Hon Rl; NHS; Off Ade; Rcvd Achvmnt Awd In Acctg Ath Psych 78; Rcvd Serv Awd To My Class 78; Perfrm As Master Of Cer At Schl Rally; Univ; Bus.

MADDAMMA, GIOVANNA; Lincoln West Sr HS; Parma, OH; 13/300 Cls Rep Sr Cls; Hon Rl; Jr NHS; Off Ade; Rptr Yrbk; Yrbk; Citizenship Awrd 76; History Day Achvmnt Awrd 79; Baldwin Wallace Coll; Psych.

MADDEN, BONNIE; Carlisle HS; Miamisburg, OH; Chrh Wkr; Hon Rl; NHS; Off Ade; Rptr Yrbk; Rptr Sch Nwsp; Spn Clb; General Writing.

MADDEN, JERRY; Deer Park HS; Cincinnati, OH; Trs Sr Cls; Off Ade; Sch Mus; Stg Crw; Bsbl; Bsktbl; Ftbl; Coach Actv; Univ; Marketing.

MADDEN, JOELLA; Warren Central HS; Indianapolis, IN; 20/850 Aud/Vis; Chrs; Hon Rl; JA; OEA; Indiana Univ; Computer Sci.

MADDEN, LYNN; Port Clinton HS; Pt Clinton, OH; Chrs; Hon Rl; Fr Clb; Swmmng; College; Dental Hygenist.

MADDOCK, KIM; St Joseph HS; St Joseph, MI; Girl Scts; Drama Clb; Fr Clb; Swmmng; Trk; Tmr; Michigan St Univ; Marine Bio.

MADDOX, DENISE; Baldwin HS; Idlewild, MI; 6/67 Sec Soph Cls; Sec Jr Cls; Hon Rl; NHS; Mgrs; Scr Kpr; Tmr; Girls Varsity Softball Tm; Girls Varsity Volleyball Tm; Varsity Club Sec & Member; Muskegon Busns Coll; Secretary.

MADDOX, J; Hurricane HS; Hurrican, WV; Girl Scts; NHS; Rptr Sch Nwsp; 4-H; Pep Clb; Trk; C hrldng; 4-H Awd; Marshall Univ; Acctg.

MADDOX, J THOMAS; Benjamin Bosse HS; Evansville, IN; 24/280 Band; Chrh Wkr; Hon Rl; Orch; Sch Mus; Stg Crw; Yth Flsp; Pres Spn Clb; IM Sprt; Cit Awd; Music Ltr Awd 76; Indiana St Univ; Pre Dent.

MADDOX, LISA; Shenandoah HS; Middletown, IN; 7/150 Chrs; Cmnty Wkr; Hon Rl; NHS; Yth Flsp; Pep Clb; Spn Clb; Loma Linda Univ; Phys Ther.

MADDOX, MARK; Richmond Sr HS; Richmond, IN; Pres Jr Cls; Pres Sr Cls; Am Leg Boys St; Chrh Wkr; Hon Rl; NHS; Pol Wkr; Stu Cncl; Capt Swmmng; Wabash Coll; Law.

MADDOX, MIKE; Southern Wells HS; Keystone, IN; 7/96 Hon Rl; NHS; Sch Mus; 4-H; FFA; Letter Crs Cntry; Trk; Ball St Univ; CPA.

MADDOX, SHARON; Cassopolis Ross Beatty HS; Cassopolis, MI; Pres Jr Cls; Cls Rep Sr Cls; Band; Chrh Wkr; Girl Scts; Hon Rl; Sch Pl; Sct Actv; Stu Cncl; Rptr Yrbk; Univ.

MADDRILL, JANE; Thomas Carr Howe HS; Indianapolis, IN; 52/637 Hon Rl; NHS; Sch Mus; Stu Cncl; Trk; Letter Chrldng; Mgrs; Scr Kpr; Olivet Nazarene Coll.

MADDY, NELLIE; Shady Springs HS; Daniels, WV; Cmp Fr Grls; Chrs; Chrh Wkr; Hon Rl; Off Ade; Yrbk; Bsbl; Gym; Trk; Raleigh County Voc Schl; Nursing.

MADEKA, JOHN P; Hammond Tech Vocational HS; Hammond, IN; 3/200 Cls Rep Frsh Cls; Cls Rep Soph Cls; Cl Rep Jr Cls; Cls Rep Sr Cls; Am Leg Boys St; Boy Scts; Hon Rl; NHS; Purdue Univ; Engr.

MADHANI, PARAG; Sault Area HS; Sault St Marie, MI; Trs Jr Cls; NHS; Quill & Scroll; Sch Pl; Stg Crw; Rptr Sch Nwsp; Lat Clb; Ten; Univ Of Michigan; Med.

MADIA, LISA; Washington Irving HS; Clarksburg, WV; Hon Rl; Jr NHS; NHS; Lat Clb; Trk; West Virginia Univ; Nursing.

MADIA, MARIAN; Notre Dame HS; Clarksburg, WV; Chrs; Chrh Wkr; Cmnty Wkr; Drm Mjrt; Pol Wkr; Lat Clb; Pep Clb; Swmmng; Twrlr; Voc Schl; Sec.

MADIGAN, DEBRA; St Frances Cabrini HS; Allen Pk, MI; 6/154 Pres Frsh Cls; Pres Jr Cls; Chrs; Drl Tm; Hon Rl; Jr NHS; Mdrgl; NHS; Sch Mus; Pres Stu Cncl; Univ Of Michigan; Soc Work.

MADIGAN, NELL; Wadsworth Sr HS; Wadsworth, OH; Band; Hon Rl; Mth Clb; Spn Clb;.

MADISON, CLARENCE; Strongsville HS; Strongsville, OH; Hon Rl; Jr NHS; Rptr Yrbk; Univ; Art.

MADISON, KAREN; Ogemaw Heights HS; West Branch, MI; Sec Frsh Cls; Sec Soph Cls; Sec Jr Cls; Sec Sr Cls; Band; Girl Scts; NHS; Stu Cncl; Letter Trk; Capt Chrldng; Alma Coll; Bsns Admin.

MABITZ, TOM; Roosevelt Wilson HS; Clarksburg, WV; 1/120 Trs Soph Cls; Val; Hon Rl; VP NHS; Sch Pl; Stu Cncl; Leo Clb; Scr Kpr; Tmr; God Cntry Awd; Fairmont St Coll; Math.

MADITZ JR, THOMAS; Roosevelt Wilson HS; Clarksburg, WV; 7/122 Sec Soph Cls; Trs Soph Cls; Cls Rep Sr Cls; Val; Hon Rl; VP Hon Rl; VP NHS; Sch Pl; Stu Cncl; Leo Clb; Fairmont St Coll; Math.

MADORE, KAREN; Davison Sr HS; Davison, MI; Girl Scts; Sct Actv; Ferris St Coll; Acctg.

MADSEN, LISA; Cascade HS; Coatesville, IN; Am Leg Aux Girls St; Drl Tm; Girl Scts; Pres Stu Cncl; Yrbk; VP FBLA; Pep Clb; Mat Maids; Pom Pon; Art Schl.

MADSEN, MELISSA; Mt Vernon Acad; St Anne, IL; Hon Rl; Univ; Sci.

MADSEN, TIM; St Johns HS; St Johns, MI; Boy Scts; Hon Rl; 4-H; Bsbl; Ftbl; IM Sprt; College; Archt.

MADSEN, WENDY; Liberty HS; Bristol, WV; Chrs; Chrh Wkr; Girl Scts; Pep Clb; Spn Clb; Chrldng; Salem Coll; Nursing.

MADURA, MICHELE; Hammond HS; Hammond, IN; 9/334 Cls Rep Frsh Cls; Hon Rl; Jr NHS; NHS; Stg Crw; Pom Pon; Tmr; Univ; Fshn Mdse.

MADVEK, VALERIE; Andrean HS; Merrillville, IN; 91/254 Bus Schl; Bus.

MADZIA, KAREN L; Tuslaw HS; Massillon, OH; 21/185 Band; Hon Rl; Hosp Ade; Off Ade; Pres 4-H; Treas OEA; Bsktbl; Trk; GAA; 4-H Awd; Admin Mgmt Soc Busns Stu Of Yr; College; Sec.

MAECKER, HOLDEN; R Nelson Snider HS; Ft Wayne, IN; Boy Scts; Hon Rl; Orch; Stu Cncl; Fr Clb; Ten; Natl Merit Ltr; Univ; Bio.

MAERKER, GRETCHEN; Coshocton HS; Coshocton, OH; NHS; Stu Cncl; Rptr Yrbk; Spn Clb; PPFtbl; College.

MAESCH, JACKIE; Staunton HS; Staunton, IN; 9/48 Drl Tm; Hon Rl; Ed Sch Nwsp; Sec FBLA; Key Clb; Pep Clb; Bsktbl; Chrldng; Ivy Tech Voc Inst; Sec.

MAFIELD, CHARLES; Mannington HS; Metz, WV; Band; Boy Scts; Hon Rl; Sct Actv; Voc School; Welding.

MAGADA, PAUL; Austintown Fitch HS; Youngstown, OH; Chrs; Debate Tm; Natl Forn Lg; Key Clb; Youngstown St Univ; Math.

MAGALSKI, BRIAN; South HS; Cleveland, OH; 3/350 Aud/Vis; Hon Rl; NHS; Ed Sch Nwsp; Cit Awd; Amherst Coll; Psychiatry.

MAGAZINE, VICTOR; Barberton HS; Barberton, OH; Boy Scts; Hon Rl; Jr NHS; Sec Spn Clb; Ftbl; Wrstlng; Univ; Aviation.

MAGDA, PATRICIA; Ursuline HS; Youngstwn, OH; 53/292 Cl Rep Jr Cls; Hon Rl; NHS; Off Ade; Sch Pl; Sch Nwsp; FNA; Key Clb; Sec Spn Clb; Youngstown State Univ; Advertising.

MAGDICH, LESLIE; Northville HS; Northville, MI; 9/340 Girl Scts; Hon Rl; NHS; Sch Mus; Rptr Yrbk; Pep Clb; Letter Trk; GAA; Natl Merit Ltr; W Mich Univ Acad Schlrshp; Michigan St Univ; Psych.

MAGDYCH, NANCY; Maplewood HS; Farmdale, OH; 14/89 Chrh Wkr; NHS; Beta Clb; Fr Clb; FTA; OEA; Pep Clb;.

MAGEE, ANNETTE; Gary Roosevelt HS; Gary, IN; Band; Chrh Wkr; Hon Rl; JA; Orch; Sch Mus; Scr Kpr; Cit Awd; Ind Univ; Medical Techology.

MAGEE, KELVIN B; Martin Luther King Sr HS; Detroit, MI; 8/150 Cls Rep Frsh Cls; Cls Rep Sr Cls; Aud/Vis; Band; ROTC; Stu Cncl; Ed Yrbk; Sprt Ed Sch Nwsp; Rptr Sch Nwsp; Crs Cntry; Arizona St Univ; Poli Sci.

MAGEE, ROBIN; Cass Technical HS; Detroit, MI; Chrs; Chrh Wkr; Cmnty Wkr; JA; Pol Wkr; Sch Pl; Stu Cncl; Univ Of Mich; Poli Sci.

MAGER, ANN; Delphos St Johns HS; Delphos, OH; 20/140 Girl Scts; Hon Rl; Orch; Sch Mus; Sch Pl; Rptr Yrbk; Rptr Sch Nwsp; Fr Clb; FTA; Mth Clb; Bowling Green St Univ; Spec Educ.

MAGER, CAROL; Franklin HS; Livonia, MI; Chrs; Hon Rl; Sch Mus; Sch Pl; Stu Cncl; Rptr Yrbk; Drama Clb; Cit Awd; Univ; Med Tech.

MAGERA, CRAIG; St Josephs HS; S Bend, IN; Hon Rl; Treas Fr Clb; VP Mth Clb; VP Sci Clb; Letter Glf; Tri State Univ; Mech Engr.

MAGGARD, JON; Willow Run HS; Ypsilanti, MI; Cls Rep Soph Cls; Crs Cntry; Coll; Eng.

MAGGARD, LAURA; Buckeye Valley HS; Sunbury, OH; Band; Hon Rl; Lit Mag; Rptr Sch Nwsp; Pep Clb; Ohi State Univ.

MAGGIANO, ANNETTE; Warren Western Reserve HS; Warren, OH; Cls Rep Frsh Cls; Cls Rep Soph Cls; Cmnty Wkr; Hosp Ade; JA; Off Ade; Stu Cncl; Y-Teens; Drama Clb; Fr Clb; Kent St Univ; Comp Sci.

MAGGIANO, HOLLY; Howland HS; Warren, OH; Band; Hon Rl; Orch; Yth Flsp; Pep Clb; Best 77 Marcher 1977; Trophy 4 Point Avarage 1976; Youngstown Univ; Med.

MAGGINIS, KELLY; Springfield HS; Monclova, OH; 5/219 Am Leg Aux Girls St; Chrs; Debate Tm; Hon Rl; NHS; Off Ade; Am Leg Awd; Elk Awd; JC Awd; Capital Univ; Government.

MAGIERA, LAURA; Highland HS; Highland, IN; 5/509 Sec Sr Cls; Sal; Hon Rl; Jr NHS; NHS; Pep Clb; Bsktbl; Pom Pon; Indiana Univ; Bus.

MAGIERA, LYNN; Highland HS; Highland, IN; 10/509 Hon Rl; Jr NHS; NHS; Pep Clb; GAA; Mgrs; Scr Kpr; Purdue Calumet; Comp Progr.

MAGILL, MONTE; Park Hills HS; Fairborn, OH; 17/336 Cls Rep Frsh Cls; Boy Scts; Chrs; Hon Rl; NHS; Sch Mus; Sch Pl; Stg Crw; Stu Cncl; Yth Flsp; Lions Clb Schlrshp 79; Ohio Wesleyan Univ; Bio Chem.

MAGILL, RONDA; Crawford County HS; English, IN; 1/135 Band; Chrs; Hon Rl; NHS; Sch Mus; 4-H; Fr Clb; Ind Univ Souhtern; Comp Sci.

MAGINN, BRUCE; Scecina Memorial HS; Indianapolis, IN; 65/196 Bsktbl; Crs Cntry; Trk; College.

MAGNACCA, DAVID; St Francis De Sales HS; Columbus, OH; 25/200 Am Leg Boys St; Letter Band; Hon Rl; Sch Mus; Ohio St Univ; Pre Law.

MAGNER, ANNE; St Joseph HS; South Bend, IN; 19/263 Hon Rl; Jr NHS; NHS; Pol Wkr; Quill & Scroll; Stg Crw; Ed Yrbk; Sprt Ed Yrbk; Rptr Yrbk; Drama Clb; Univ Of Notre Dame; Poli Sci.

MAGNER, TOM; Carroll HS; Dayton, OH; Stg Crw; Stu Cncl; Fr Clb; Ger Clb; Wrstlng; Law.

MAGNUS, JOAN; Archbishop Alter HS; Dayton, OH; 50/300 Chrs; Girl Scts; Hon Rl; Lbry Ade; Sct Actv; Fr Clb; FDA; Swmmng; Coach Actv; Ohi State Univ; Pre Med.

MAGNUSON, LESLIE; Reeths Puffer HS; Muskegon, MI; Band; Chrh Wkr; Hon Rl; Stg Crw; Trk; Presidential Phys Fitness Awd; Kalamazoo Coll; Translator.

MAGNUSON, RONALD; La Ville Jr Sr HS; Plymouth, IN; Am Leg Boys St; Chrh Wkr; Yth Flsp; 4-H; Pres Mth Clb; Sci Clb; Pres Spn Clb; Letter Glf; IM Sprt; Ball St Univ; Comp Sci.

MAGOLAN, MONICA; Fitzgerald HS; Warren, MI; Sec Girl Scts; Hon Rl; Lbry Ade; VP NHS; Treas Fr Clb; Coach Actv; PPFtbl; Tmr; Wayne State Univ; Occupational Ther.

MAGOTO, KAREN; Russia Local HS; Russia, OH; 2/44 VP Jr Cls; Chrs; Hon Rl; NHS; Sch Pl; Stu Cncl; Rptr Yrbk; Drama Clb; Univ; Acctg.

MAGOULAKIS, STACEY; Boardman HS; Boardman, OH; Girl Scts; Hon Rl; Jr NHS; Orch; Y-Teens; Mth Clb; Sci Clb; Spn Clb; IM Sprt; 4-H Awd; Univ; Pharm.

MAGUIRE, GARY; St Alphonsus HS; Dearborn, MI; 1/171 Cls Rep Frsh Cls; Cls Rep Soph Cls; Cl Rep Jr Cls; Hon Rl; Stu Cncl; Crs Cntry; Trk; College.

MAGUIRE, TERI; Brownsburg HS; Brownsburg, IN; Cls Rep Frsh Cls; Cls Rep Soph Cls; Cl Rep Jr Cls; Band; Cmnty Wkr; Girl Scts; Hon Rl; Hosp Ade; Off Ade; Stu Cncl; IUPUI; Nursing.

MAGUSIN, LISA; Southgate HS; Southgate, MI; 1/350 VP Frsh Cls; VP Soph Cls; Pres Jr Cls; Band; Hon Rl; Jr NHS; NHS; Sch Mus; Sch Pl; Stu Cncl; Univ; Med Tech.

MAGYARI, JOHN; Nordonia Hills HS; Sagamore Hls, OH; 35/440 Letter Bsbl; Letter Bsktbl; Letter Socr;.

MAGYAROS, BARRY R; Salem Sr HS; Salem, OH; 7/260 Pres Jr Cls; Cl Rep Jr Cls; Pres Sr Cls; Am Leg Boys St; Chrh Wkr; FCA; Hon Rl; Sch Pl; Stu Cncl; Mth Clb; Univ; Petroleum Engr.

MAHADEVIAH, STUART; Cardinal Mooney HS; Youngstown, OH; Band; Boy Scts; Hon Rl; Orch; Sct Actv; Sch Nwsp; Fr Clb; Lat Clb; Mth Clb; Sci Clb; Univ; Archt.

MAHAFFEY, ROBERT; Elmwood HS; Wayne, OH; 32/120 Boy Scts; Hon Rl; Stg Crw; Rptr Yrbk; VP OEA; Sci Clb; Letter Bsbl; Letter Ftbl; Swmmng; Tmr; Bowling Green St Univ; Busns.

MAHAFFY, DEBIE; Marlette HS; Snover, MI; 30/130 Sec Jr Cls; Trs Sr Cls; Band; NHS; Stu Cncl; 4-H; OEA; Pep Clb; Dnfth Awd; Central Michigan Univ; Bus.

MAHANEY, CATHY; Bishop Rosecrans HS; Zanesville, OH; 6/80 Am Leg Aux Girls St; Hon Rl; JA; NHS; Sch Pl; Sec Stu Cncl; Rptr Sch Nwsp; Drama Clb; Pep Clb; Letter Bsktbl; Sec Ohio Yth For Life; Xavier Univ; Criminal Justice.

MAHANEY, WILLIAM; Green HS; Akron, OH; Chrs; Bsktbl; Ftbl; Coach Actv; Bowling Green St Univ; Brdcstng.

MAHAR, LORRAINE; Fordson HS; Dearborn, MI; Hon Rl; Fr Clb; Hockey; Trk; GAA; IM Sprt; St Of Mi Schslhp; Silver F Pin; French; Michigan Tech Univ; Bus Admin.

MAHER, CHARLEY; Mendon HS; Mendon, MI; Boy Scts; Chrh Wkr; Hon Rl; Sct Actv; Yth Flsp; 4-H; Letter Wrstlng; Scr Kpr; 4-H Awd; Us Navy; Math.

MAHER, JAMES; Holy Redeemer HS; Detroit, MI; 5/180 Cls Rep Soph Cls; Chrh Wkr; Cmnty Wkr; Hon Rl; NHS; IM Sprt; College; Psych.

MAHER, RUTH; Immaculate Conception Acad; Milan, IN; 7/70 Cmnty Wkr; Hon Rl; Off Ade; Y-Teens; 4-H; Ger Clb; Key Clb; Mth Clb; Sci Clb; Spn Clb; Univ Of Notre Dame; Nutrition.

MAHER JR, JOHN F; St Joseph Prep Seminary; St Marys, WV; 3/9 Trs Frsh Cls; Trs Soph Cls; Trs Jr Cls; Boy Scts; Chrs; Sch Pl; Ed Sch Nwsp; Bsktbl; Ten; IM Sprt; Xavier Univ; Bus.

MAHIN, CLARISSA; Morgantown HS; Morgantown, WV; Band; Hon Rl; Orch; 4-H; Fr Clb; IM Sprt; Mat Maids; Bus Educ Honorary Club & Awd 78; West Virginia Univ; Acctg.

MAHLE, CINDY; Bellbrook HS; Xenia, OH; 32/166 Cls Rep Sr Cls; Hon Rl; Stu Cncl; Pres 4-H; Coach Actv; GAA; 4-H Awd; Sinclair Cmnty Coll; Exec Sec.

MAHLE, PAMELA; Jefferson Area HS; Jefferson, OH; 4/200 NHS; Quill & Scroll; Rptr Sch Nwsp; Sch Nwsp; Fr Clb; FTA; Spn Clb; IM Sprt; DAR Awd; Rotary Awd; Hiram College; Journalism.

MAHLE, PEGGY; Harding HS; Marion, OH; Chrs; Hon Rl; Lit Mag; Rptr Sch Nwsp; Sch Nwsp; Sec 4-H; Spn Clb; Marion Tech College; Lab Tech.

MAHLER, CHERYL; Penn HS; Osceola, IN; Chrh Wkr; Girl Scts; NHS; Yth Flsp; 4-H; 4-H Awd;.

MAHLERWEIN, TERRY; Blanchester HS; Blanchester, OH; 3/153 Treas Band; Chrs; Hon Rl; NHS; Sch Mus; Stu Cncl; Rptr Yrbk; Fr Clb; Pres FTA; GAA; Wilmington Coll; General Arts.

MAHON, BARBARA; Hilliard HS; Columbus, OH; Cls Rep Frsh Cls; Sec FCA; Jr NHS; Rptr Yrbk; Yrbk; Trk; Chrldng; GAA; College.

MAHON, DAVID; St Ignatius HS; Middleburg Hts, OH; 13/272 Chrh Wkr; Hon Rl; Hosp Ade; NHS; Stu Cncl; Rptr Yrbk; Sprt Ed Sch Nwsp; Boys Clb Am; Trk; IM Sprt; St Louis Univ; Physn.

MAHON, MARGARET; St Augustine Academy; Lakewood, OH; Cls Rep Frsh Cls; Pres Soph Cls; VP Jr Cls; Cls Rep Sr Cls; Hon Rl; NHS; Stu Cncl; Capt Bsbl; Capt Bsktbl; IM Sprt; John Carroll Univ; Educ.

MAHON, ROBERT; Crestview HS; Shiloh, OH; Band; Boy Scts; Chrh Wkr; Drl Tm; Hon Rl; JA; Sct Actv; Sdlty; Am Leg Awd; Voice Dem Awd; College; Communication.

MAHONEY, ANNE; La Porte HS; La Porte, IN; 55/492 MMM; NHS; Orch; Sch Mus; Fr Clb; Indiana Univ; Busns.

MAHONEY, DARLENE; Gods Bible School HS; Milton, KY; 6/38 Chrs; Chrh Wkr; Hon Rl; FHA; Spn Clb; Hnr Awd 94 Grd Average 78; Perf Attend 76; Ivy Tech Voc Schl; Bus.

MAHONEY, DORIS; Anderson Sr HS; Anderson, IN; Hon Rl; FHA; Anderson Coll; Cmmrcl Art.

MAHONEY, JEFFREY; T L Handy HS; Bay City, MI; Aud/Vis; Hon Rl; NHS; Fr Clb; Bsktbl; Letter Ftbl; Coach Actv; DAR Awd; Delta Cmnty Coll; Pre Law.

MAHONEY, JOLEEN; Washington HS; Massillon, OH; Hon Rl; Hosp Ade; Lbry Ade; Off Ade; Sch Pl; Ed Yrbk; Drama Clb; Fr Clb; Voc Schl; Recording Engr.

MAHONEY, LINDA; Mt Notre Dame HS; Sharonville, OH; Trs Frsh Cls; Trs Soph Cls; Trs Jr Cls; Cls Rep Sr Cls; Cmnty Wkr; Hon Rl; Lit Mag; NHS; Stu Cncl; Rptr Sch Nwsp; Xavier Univ; Comp Sci.

MAHONEY, MAUREEN; Herbert Henery Dow HS; Midland, MI; Ger Clb; Letter Trk; PPFtbl; Michigan St Univ; Bus Admin.

MAHONEY, PATRICK; Niles Mc Kinley HS; Niles, OH; Hon Rl; Civ Clb; Bsktbl; Ftbl; IM Sprt; Univ; Civil Engr.

MAHONEY, SHERRI; Montague HS; Montague, MI; Hon Rl; Muskegon Business Coll; Retail & Mrk.

MAHURIN, MELISSA A; New Albany HS; New Albany, IN; 1/600 Hon Rl; Rdo Clb; Gym; IM Sprt; Capt Pom Pon; PPFtbl; Twrlr; Univ; Cmnctns.

MAI, TAI X; Lasalle HS; S Bend, IN; 58/488 Hon Rl; Mth Clb; Sci Clb; Purdue Univ; Elec.

MAIDA, CHERLYN; Bay City All Sts Cntrl HS; Bay City, MI; Girl Scts; Sch Pl; Univ.

MAIDEN, SAMUEL; Jackson Cnty Parma W HS; Jackson, MI; Band; Boy Scts; Debate Tm; JA; Lbry Ade; Pol Wkr; Boys Clb Am; Fr Clb; Bsktbl; Natl Merit Ltr; Michigan St Univ; Bus.

MAIDEN, SAMUEL; Western HS; Jackson, MI; Band; Boy Scts; Debate Tm; JA; Lbry Ade; Pol Wkr; Yth Flsp; Boys Clb Am; Fr Clb; Natl Merit Ltr; Michigan St Univ; Busns Admin.

MAIER, CAROL L; St Josephs Central Cath HS; Fremont, OH; 5/100 Band; Cmp Fr Grls; Hon Rl; NHS; Letter Bsktbl; Coach Actv; Univ; Biology.

MAIER, JOSEPH; Lansing Catholic Central HS; Lansing, MI; Chrh Wkr; Hon Rl; JA; NHS; Cl Rep Jr Cls; JA Awd; Mic State Univ; Acctg.

MAIER, LINDA C; North Posey Sr HS; Wadesville, IN; 32/189 Am Leg Aux Girls St; Band; Natl Forn Lg; Sch Pl; Stu Cncl; Drama Clb; 4-H; Pep Clb; 4-H Awd; Purude Univ; Agri.

MAIER, THERESE; Oscar A Carlson HS; Trenton, MI; 3/250 Hon Rl; Lbry Ade; NHS; Ger Clb; IM Sprt; Natl Merit Schl; Michigan St Univ; Intr Design.

MAIERS, PATRICIA; Cousino Sr HS; Warren, MI; Band; Chrh Wkr; Cmnty Wkr; Girl Scts; Hon Rl; Jr NHS; Lbry Ade; Orch; Red Cr Ade; Y-Teens; Mercy Coll Of Detroit; Nursing.

MAIKE, DIANE; Chesaning HS; Chesaning, MI; 2/280 Trs Frsh Cls; Sec Soph Cls; Cl Rep Jr Cls; Band; Chrh Wkr; Drl Tm; Hon Rl; NHS; Off Ade; 4-H; Central Michigan Univ; Bus Admin.

MAILLEY, K; Brandon HS; Clarkston, MI; 12/186 Chrs; Debate Tm; Hon Rl; Lbry Ade; Natl Forn Lg; Sch Mus; Rptr Sch Nwsp; College; Dietetics.

MAIN, JANET; Eastwood HS; Bowling Green, OH; Band; Girl Scts; Hon Rl; Spn Clb; Bus.

MAIN, J TODD; Bowling Green HS; Bowling Green, OH; Band; Chrs; Mdrgl; Sch Mus; Sch Pl; Stg Crw; Wrstlng; Bowling Green St Univ; Music.

MAINO, DEBRA; Luman Christi HS; Mich Ctr, MI; Band; Chrs; Girl Scts; Hon Rl; Hosp Ade; NHS; Sch Mus; Spn Clb; Chrldng; Cit Awd; Ferris State Coll; Med.

MAINO, MARY; Lumen Christi HS; Michigan Center, MI; Hon Rl; Spn Clb; Theology Awd 76; Michigan St Univ; Acctg.

MAINS, ROBIN; Willoughby South HS; Will Hills, OH; Cls Rep Frsh Cls; Cls Rep Soph Cls; Cl Rep Jr Cls; Cls Rep Sr Cls; Am Leg Aux Girls St; Band; Chrs; Hon Rl; NHS; Off Ade; Drama Awd 78 & 79; Homcmng Ct 79; Ohio Univ; Poli Sci.

MAIORANA, BARBARA; Ursuline HS; Youngstown, OH; 59/350 Drl Tm; Drm Mjrt; Hon Rl; Mth Clb; Pep Clb; Spn Clb; Pom Pon; Twrlr; 1st Pl Jr Cls In Natl Math Achvmnt Test 79; Co Capt & Ltr On Danceliner 79; Youngstown St Univ; Brdcstng.

MAIORANA, GAIL E; John F Kennedy HS; Taylor, MI; 4/450 Cls Rep Soph Cls; Cmnty Wkr; Hon Rl; Treas NHS; Ed Sch Nwsp; Rptr Sch Nwsp; Sch Nwsp; Ger Clb; Natl Merit SF; Scholastic Writing Honorable Memtion; State Fin Michigan Natl Teen Ager Pageant; Arizona St Univ; Jrnlsm.

MAIORANO, JAMIE; Cousino HS; Warren, MI; Hon Rl; Jr NHS; NHS; Bsktbl; IM Sprt; PPFtbl; Natl Merit Ltr; Oakland Univ; Comp Sci.

MAISH, WILLIAM A; R Nelson Snider HS; Ft Wayne, IN; 83/564 Aud/Vis; Boy Scts; Chrs; Chrh Wkr; Hon Rl; Mdrgl; Sch Mus; Sch Pl; Sct Actv; Yth Flsp; Univ; Pre Med.

MAISNER, KIMBERLY A; Marshall HS; Ceresco, MI; Band; Hon Rl; 4-H; Twrlr; College.

MAIURI, MARLA G; Dominican HS; Detroit, MI; Cls Rep Frsh Cls; Cl Rep Jr Cls; Hon Rl; Lbry Ade; NHS; Pol Wkr; Stg Crw; Stu Cncl; Yrbk; U S Air Force; Law Enforcmnt.

MAIVILLE, KATERI; Leslie HS; Onondaga, MI; 1/150 Hon Rl; Treas NHS; Michigan St Univ; Engr.

MAJERCZAK, DORIS R; Wooster HS; Wooster, OH; 22/365 Band; Orch; Spn Clb; Bsktbl; Sec GAA; PPFtbl; Softbl Letter Winner 1978; Volleybal Letter Winner 1977; Art Show 1st Pl; Ohio Wesleyan Univ; Bio.

MAJESKE, VICKIE; Charles Stewart Mott HS; Warren, MI; 36/765 Girl Scts; Hon Rl; Jr NHS; NHS; Stg Crw; Chrldng; GAA; Lawrence Inst Of Tech; Math.

MAJESKI, PETER V; Penn HS; Mishawaka, IN; Hon Rl; NHS; Spn Clb; Ten; Trk; NHS; College; Aviation.

MAJEWSKI, KAREN; Clay HS; S Bend, IN; 80/425 Band; Girl Scts; Hon Rl; Orch; Sch Mus; Ger Clb; Letter Bsktbl; Trk; Scr Kpr; Ball St Univ; Phys Ed.

MAJEWSKI, SUSAN; Reitz Memorial HS; Evansville, IN; 33/265 Cl Rep Jr Cls; Drl Tm; Hon Rl; Stu Cncl; Letter Gym; Purdue.

MAJIDZADEH, STASIA; Worthington HS; Worthington, OH; 25/565 Debate Tm; Hon Rl; Jr NHS; Natl Forn Lg; NHS; Pol Wkr; Sch Pl; Yrbk; Am Leg Awd; DAR Awd; Case Western Reserve Univ; Poli Sci.

MAJKA, DEBRA; Brecksville HS; Broadview Hts, OH; 20/374 NHS; Capt Bsbl; Capt Bsktbl; Capt Chrldng; Coach Actv; Baldwin Wallace Univ; Elem Educ.

MAJKA, KAREN; Berkshire HS; Huntsburg, OH; AFS; Chrs; Girl Scts; Hon Rl; NHS; Yrbk; GAA; Gov Hon Prg Awd; Natl Merit Ltr; 12th Dist Hon Mention St Eng 2 Oh Tests Of Schlstc Achvmnt 78; Hon Mention Amer Hist Oh Test Of Achvmnt 79; Univ; Acctg.

MAJNARIC, LIDIJA; Mt Vernon Academy; Akron, OH; VP Jr Cls; Chrs; Hon Rl; Yrbk; IM Sprt; Soc Sec Of SA 79; Bus Schl; Legl Sec.

MAJOROS, ROBERT; Lake Catholic HS; Lyndhurst, OH; Chrh Wkr; Hon Rl; NHS; College; Communications.

MAKAR, ELAINE; Lumen Cordium HS; Cleveland, OH; Am Leg Aux Girls St; Hon Rl; NHS; GAA; IM Sprt; Natl Merit Ltr; George Washington Univ; Engr.

MAKARA, YVONNE; St Johns HS; St Johns, MI; Hon Rl; Ed Yrbk; Letter Bsktbl; IM Sprt; Central Mich Univ.

MAKAREWICZ, DONNA; Gaylord HS; Elmira, MI; 16/190 Band; Chrh Wkr; Girl Scts; Hon Rl; Lbry Ade; NHS; Off Ade; Ferris St Coll; Med Asst.

MAKELA, RANDAL; White Pine HS; Ontonagon, MI; Trs Soph Cls; Pres Jr Cls; Am Leg Boys St; Band; Hon Rl; NHS; Bsktbl; Ftbl; Trk; Natl Merit SF; Michigan Tech Univ; Med.

MAKER, RONALD; Clawson HS; Clawson, MI; Band; Boy Scts; Hon Rl; NHS; Spn Clb; Letter Ftbl; Letter Trk; Letter Wrstlng; St Of Mi Schlste Schslhp 79; Hon Police Chf Stdnt Govt Day 79; Youth Asst Cmnty Serv Awd 79; Western Michigan Univ; Bus Admin.

MAKI, DIANE; Marquette Sr HS; Marquette, MI; 11/425 Band; Chrh Wkr; Sch Mus; Stg Crw; Sci Clb; Trk; Mgrs; Natl Merit Schl; Northern Michigan Univ; Soc Work.

MAKI, GAYLE; Baraga HS; Baraga, MI; 14/59 Hon Rl; Fr Clb; Northern Mic Univ; Criminal Justice.

MAKI, KIM; Chassell HS; Chassel, MI; 6/26 Band; Hon Rl; Stg Crw; Stu Cncl; Yrbk; Hockey; Mich Tech Univ; Mech Engr.

MAKI, PATRICE D; Marquette Sr HS; Marquette, MI; Band; Drm Bgl; Girl Scts; Yth Flsp; 4-H; IM Sprt; 4-H Awd; Northern Michigan Univ; Med.

MAKI, PATRICIA; West Iron County HS; Caspian, MI; Sec Frsh Cls; Chrh Wkr; Hon Rl; NHS; Off Ade; Stu Cncl; Yrbk; Pres OEA; Chrldng; Mat Maids; Davenport Coll Of Bus; Sec Sci.

MAKLEY, THERON; Bath HS; Lima, OH; Pres Band; Boy Scts; Hon Rl; Sch Mus; Sch Pl; Sct Actv; Stg Crw; Ger Clb; Scr Kpr; Tmr; Cincinnati Univ; Elec Engr.

MAKOWSKI, JOEL; Bluffton HS; Bluffton, IN; 27/136 Cls Rep Soph Cls; Cl Rep Jr Cls; Am Leg Boys St; Chrh Wkr; Hon Rl; Spn Clb; Letter Bsbl; Ten; Sr Rotarion 79; Vc Pres Of Debblers Club 79; Asst Admin Of Teen Ag Rep Club 78; Ball St Univ; Archt.

MAKOWSKI, MARY; Berkshire HS; Burton, OH; Cmp Fr Grls; Chrh Wkr; Hon Rl; Lbry Ade; NHS; Red Cr Ade; Pres Stu Cncl; Treas 4-H; 4-H Awd; Var Vllybl Lg Hon Mntn 77; Mt Union Coll; Bio Sci.

MAKRA, MELISSA; Green HS; Uniontown, OH; Hon Rl; Lbry Ade; Off Ade; Yrbk; Rptr Sch Nwsp; Academic Tm 76 78; Hnrbr Mentn Oh Sclstc Achvmnt Test Spnsh 1 76; Hnrbl Mentn Oh Schlstc Achvmnt Test Spnsh; Univ Of Michigan; Med.

MAKROGLOU, GEORGE; Normandy HS; Parma, OH; 54/665 Case Western Reserve Univ; Med.

MAKSUT, ANDA LYNN; Princeton HS; Princeton, WV; 78/367 Cmnty Wkr; Girl Scts; Hon Rl; Fr Clb; Bluefield St Coll; Radiology.

MAKSYM, JOHN; Univ Of Detroit HS; Grosse Point, MI; 28/130 Cls Rep Sr Cls; Hon Rl; Mod UN; Natl Forn Lg; NHS; Pol Wkr; Rptr Yrbk; Yrbk; Sch Nwsp; Michigan St Univ; Poli Sci.

MALARKEY, DAWN S; Lemon Monroe HS; Monroe, OH; Cl Rep Jr Cls; Band; Drl Tm; Hon Rl; VP NHS; Sch Mus; Stg Crw; Ed Yrbk; Rptr Yrbk; Bsktbl; Scholarshp Awd; JV Basketball; M M L Championshp; Grls Tennis; Pennsylvania State Univ; Law.

MALAYER, BRAD; North Putnam HS; Bainbridge, IN; VP Frsh Cls; NHS; Sch Mus; Sch Pl; Stg Crw; Drama Clb; 4-H; Sci Clb; Socr; Trk; Purdue Univ; Pre Vet.

MALBURG, ANTHONY; Pentwater Public HS; Hart, MI; 4/32 Pres Jr Cls; Cl Rep Jr Cls; Pres Sr Cls; Hon Rl; Stu Cncl; Yrbk; Letter Bsbl; Mic Tech Univ; Metallurgical Engr.

MALBURG, KRISTINE; Capac Jr Sr HS; Capac, MI; Band; Chrh Wkr; Hon Rl; NHS; Stu Cncl; Yrbk; Rptr Sch Nwsp; 4-H; GAA; Univ; Sec.

MALBURG, MARTHA; Hart HS; Hart, MI; 16/140 Chrh Wkr; Hon Rl; NHS; Rptr Yrbk; Rptr Sch Nwsp; Drama Clb; OEA; PPFtbl; Cit Awd; DAR Awd; W Shore Cmnty Coll Acad Schlrshp 79; West Shore Cmnty Coll; Bus.

MALCOLM, JOYCELYN; Pershing HS; Detroit, MI; Chrh Wkr; Trk; Univ; Jrnlsm.

MALCOMB, CHARLES R; Pickens HS; Helvetia, WV; 4/10 Pres Frsh Cls; Pres Jr Cls; Chrh Wkr; Hon Rl; NHS; 4-H; Bsktbl; 4-H Awd; Wv St Sen Page 78; Aldersn Bradodus Coll Sci Workshop 78; West Virginia Univ; Engr.

MALCOMNSON, DEBBIE; Harrison Cmnty HS; Harrison, MI; Lbry Ade; Sprt Ed Yrbk; Letter Bsktbl; Letter Trk; M J Murphy Bty Schl.

MALDONADO, ROSARIO; Hammond HS; Hammond, IN; 18/343 Hon Rl; Jr NHS; NHS; Sch Pl; Stg Crw; Bsktbl; Letter Trk; Vrsty Vllybll Team Lttr 78; Ctzn Apprntcshp Prgrm 78; Art Clb 77; Univ; Art.

MALE, BECKY; Lakeland Christian Academy; Warsaw, IN; 5/20 Cls Rep Frsh Cls; Cls Rep Soph Cls; Chrs; Chrh Wkr; Hon Rl; Sch Pl; Stu Cncl; Drama Clb; Fr Clb; Pep Clb; Grace Coll; Elem Educ.

MALE, ROBERT; Cuyahoga Falls HS; Cuyahoga Falls, OH; 10/826 Band; Hon Rl; NHS; IM Sprt; Rotary Awd; Univ.

MALEC, GEORGE P; Lake Catholic HS; Willoughby, OH; Band; Boy Scts; Chrh Wkr; Cmnty Wkr; Hon Rl; Red Cr Ade; Sct Actv; Ed Sch Nwsp; FBLA; Coach Actv; Univ; Acctg.

MALEC, VALERIE; Fitzgerald HS; Warren, MI; Cls Rep Soph Cls; Cl Rep Jr Cls; Hon Rl; NHS; Chrldng; PPFtbl; College; Fashion Mdse.

MALEK, LAURIE; Yale HS; Yale, MI; 16/162 Chrs; Girl Scts; Hon Rl; Stg Crw; Rptr Sch Nwsp; Mgrs; Ferris St College; A A S Retail Fshn.

MALEY, ADRIENNE; Peck HS; Peck, MI; Hon Rl; Lbry Ade; Yrbk; Sch Nwsp; 4-H; Letter Trk; Mgrs; 4-H Awd; Univ; Advrtsng Art.

MALEY, GARY; Clawson HS; Clawson, MI; Band; Orch; Sch Mus; Sprt Ed Yrbk; Yrbk; Sch Nwsp; PPFtbl; Cit Awd; Mich State Univ.

MALEY, KIMBERLY; Elwood Community HS; Elwood, IN; Hon Rl; FBLA; OEA; Spn Clb; Mat Maids; International Bus Coll; Legal Sec.

MALILA, SHAUN E; Huron HS; Ann Arbor, MI; 20/604 Sec Band; Chrh Wkr; Hon Rl; Hosp Ade; Gym; NCTE; Univ Of Michigan; Pre Med.

MALINAR, DRINA; Elyria Catholic HS; N Ridgeville, OH; 25/200 Chrh Wkr; Cmnty Wkr; Girl Scts; Hon Rl; Jr NHS; Stg Crw; Drama Clb; 4-H; Ger Clb; 4-H Awd; Akron Univ; Int Design.

MALINOWSKI, ANNE M; Bishop Foley HS; Royal Oak, MI; 29/198 Hon Rl; JA; Letter Bsbl; Letter Bsktbl; PPFtbl; Business Schl; Accounting.

MALINOWSKI, ROBERT; Divine Child HS; Dearborn Hts, MI; FCA; Hon Rl; Ger Clb; Letter Bsbl; Letter Ftbl; IM Sprt; St Of MI Competitve Schlrshp 78; Who Who Among Amer HS Stu 77; Met Detroit Sci Fair First Awd 76; Univ Of Detroit; Dent.

MALINZAK, MIKE; Ravenna HS; Ravenna, OH; 91/350 AFS; Aud/Vis; FCA; Hon Rl; JA; Lbry Ade; Pol Wkr; Yth Flsp; Eng Clb; FDA; Kent St Univ; Elec Engr.

MALJARIK, DEBORAH A; Eastlake North HS; Willowick, OH; 71/695 Hon Rl; Off Ade; Pep Clb; Capt Chrldng; Univ; Bus.

MALKOWSKI, APRIL; St Andrew HS; Detroit, MI; Cmnty Wkr; Hon Rl; NHS; Bsbl; Bsktbl; Mgrs; Univ; Med Tech.

MALLARD, CHRITINA; Clay HS; So Bend, IN; Chrs; Chrh Wkr; Girl Scts; JA; Yrbk; Drama Clb; Lat Clb; Ten; College; Psychiatrist.

MALLARD, JAMES; Kearsley HS; Flint, MI; Aud/Vis; Chrs; Cmnty Wkr; Lbry Ade; Sch Mus; Stg Crw; Coll; Educ.

MALLCHOK, WILLIAM; Haslett HS; Haslett, MI; Band; Hon Rl; NHS; 4-H; Capt Swmmng; 4-H Awd; Natl Merit SF; Mic State Univ.

MALLERNEE, KIMBERLY; Cadiz HS; Cadiz, OH; 1/134 Sec Frsh Cls; Am Leg Aux Girls St; Band; Chrs; Drm Mjrt; Hon Rl; Hosp Ade; NHS; Off Ade; Sch Mus; Univ Of Akron; Nursing.

MALLEY, MICHAEL; Struthers HS; Struthers, OH; Hon Rl; Spn Clb; Letter Ftbl; IM Sprt; Univ.

MALLICOAT, JERRY L; Springboro HS; Franklin, OH; Chrh Wkr; Hon Rl; NHS; Stu Cncl; Rptr Sch Nwsp; Pres OEA; Voice Dem Awd; Ohio St Univ; Acctg.

MALLIS, MARCIA; Bedford HS; Bedford, OH; Chrs; Girl Scts; Hon Rl; NHS; Off Ade; Pres Spn Clb; Capt Bsbl; College; X Ray Tech.

MALLORY, CARRIE; Harrison Community HS; Harrison, MI; Sec Sr Cls; Girl Scts; Hon Rl; NHS; Sch Pl; 4-H; Pep Clb; Chrldng; PPFtbl; Cit Awd; Coll; RN.

MALLORY, CRYSTAL B; Huntington East HS; Huntington, WV; Cls Rep Soph Cls; Cl Rep Jr Cls; Band; Chrs; Chrh Wkr; Cmnty Wkr; Drl Tm; Hon Rl; Jr NHS; Mdrgl; Natl Honor Soc; Huntington Busns Coll; Music.

MALLORY, STEVE; South Ripley HS; Versailles, IN; 49/120 Cls Rep Soph Cls; Aud/Vis; Hon Rl; Stu Cncl; Yth Flsp; Rptr Sch Nwsp; DECA; FFA; IM Sprt; Southeastern Indiana Voc Schl; Bus.

MALLOY, COLLEEN; Kelloggsville HS; Kentwood, MI; Hon Rl; NHS; Sch Pl; Stg Crw; Ten; Trk; PPFtbl; Central Mich Univ.

MALLOY, DAVID; Moeller HS; Cincinnati, OH; 52/260 Cincinnati Univ; Aerospace Engr.

MALLOY, JIM; Washington Irving HS; Clarksburg, WV; Chrh Wkr; Cmnty Wkr; Hon Rl; Stg Crw; Yth Flsp; Sci Clb; Cert Of Merit Awd Soccer; Old Dominion Univ; Oceanography.

MALLOY, SUSAN; Wintersville HS; Steubenville, OH; 112/283 Cls Rep Soph Cls; Cl Rep Jr Cls; Chrs; Hosp Ade; Mdrgl; Sch Pl; Stg Crw; Stu Cncl; Drama Clb; VP Spn Clb; Jr Womens Club Of Wintersville 500 Schlshp 79; Jr Womens Lg Of Wintersville 100 Schlshp 79; Ohio St Univ; Med.

MALNOFSKI, MICAHEL; Saint Xavier HS; Cincinnati, OH; 25/268 Hon Rl; Fr Clb; Sci Clb; IM Sprt; College.

MALOLEPSZY, CHRISTINE; Bishop Foley HS; Madison Hts, MI; 11/205 Cls Rep Soph Cls; Cl Rep Jr Cls; Chrs; Chrh Wkr; Girl Scts; Hon Rl; Mdrgl; NHS; Stu Cncl; Bsbl; Comm Coll; Music.

MALONE, DAPHNE; South Point HS; South Point, OH; Sec Frsh Cls; Hon Rl; JA; Yth Flsp; Pep Clb; Chrldng; Morehead Univ; Fash Merch.

MALONE, JOHN; New Albany HS; New Albany, IN; Cls Rep Soph Cls; Cl Rep Jr Cls; Pres Band; Chrh Wkr; Jr NHS; NHS; Orch; Stu Cncl; Sprt Ed Yrbk; Pres FTA; Serv On Stud Advisory Bd At In Univ S E; Top 5 Engr Dept; Univ; Engr.

MALONE, KATHLEEN; George Washington HS; Charleston, WV; 13/250 Hon Rl; Bsktbl; Trk; Amer Soc Of Mech Engrs Schlrshp; Presidential Phys Fitness Awd; West Virginia Univ; Mech Engr.

MALONE, KATHY; Lake HS; Walbridge, OH; Band; Chrs; Drm Mjrt; Hon Rl; FBLA; FTA; Spn Clb; Twrlr; Owens Tech; Sec.

MALONE, NANCY; Fairview HS; Fairview Pk, OH; 11/281 Hon Rl; NHS; Fr Clb; Letter Trk; Scr Kpr; Tmr; Bowling Green St Univ; Phys Ther.

MALONE, ROBERT; East HS; Cleveland, OH; Bsbl; Bsktbl; Ftbl; MVP Jur Var Ftbl Tm 76 79; Mst Imprvd Plyr On Bsktbl Tm 75; Akron Univ; Bus Admin.

MALONE, STEVEN; Rock Hill HS; Pedro, OH; Hst Sr Cls; Cmnty Wkr; Hon Rl; Stu Cncl; Sprt Ed Yrbk; Ed Sch Nwsp; Sprt Ed Sch Nwsp; Rptr Sch Nwsp; Sch Nwsp; Pres Civ Clb; Ohio Univ; Bus Mgmt.

MALONE, TAMARA; E Kentwood HS; Grand Rapids, MI; Cls Rep Frsh Cls; Cls Rep Soph Cls; Cl Rep Jr Cls; Debate Tm; Drl Tm; Hon Rl; Off Ade; Sch Pl; Stu Cncl; Y-Teens; Univ.

MALONEY, BRIAN P; Calvert HS; Tiffin, OH; 2/95 Am Leg Boys St; Boy Scts; Chrs; Debate Tm; Hon Rl; JA; Pres NHS; Sct Actv; Stu Cncl; Glf; College; Med.

MALONEY, JANET; Wheeling Ctrl Catholic HS; Wheeling, WV; 18/132 Cls Rep Frsh Cls; Cls Rep Soph Cls; Cl Rep Jr Cls; Sec Band; Capt Drl Tm; Hon Rl; Pres JA; Orch; Stu Cncl; Drama Clb; Whos Who 1976; Nasa Awd 1977; Rep Of Internatl Sci Fair 1977; Univ.

MALONEY, JOHN; Lakeview HS; Cortland, OH; Boy Scts; Cmnty Wkr; Hon Rl; Sch Pl; Sct Actv; Lat Clb; Letter Ftbl; Letter Trk; IM Sprt; Natl Merit Schl; Kent St Univ; Comp Sci.

MALONEY, KATHLEEN; Tiffin Calvert HS; Tiffin, OH; 1/99 Cls Rep Soph Cls; Val; Chrs; Hon Rl; VP JA; Sec NHS; Sch Mus; Heidelberg College; Bus Admin.

MALONEY, LAWRENCE; Admiral King HS; Lorain, OH; Band; Chrs; Hon Rl; Off Ade; Pol Wkr; Sch Mus; Yrbk; Letter Bsbl; Letter Bsktbl; Natl Sci Foundation Summer Training In Engr 79; Team Mbr Acad Challenge T V Prog 78; Univ; Engr.

MALONEY, MARTHA; Mount Notre Dame HS; Cincinnati, OH; 21/173 Cls Rep Soph Cls; Chrh Wkr; Hon Rl; NHS; Stu Cncl; Rptr Sch Nwsp; Spn Clb; Raymond Walters Voc Schl; Bsns Mgmt.

MALONEY, MEGAN; Grosse Pointe North HS; Grosse Pt Wds, MI; Chrs; Hon Rl; NHS; Sch Pl; Drama Clb; Swmmng; IM Sprt; Tmr; Natl Merit Ltr; College.

MALONEY, VINCENT; Brownsburg HS; Brownsburg, IN; 2/292 Sal; Am Leg Boys St; Band; Hon Rl; Lit Mag; NHS; 4-H; Fr Clb; Crs Cntry; Trk; Purdue Univ; Horticulture.

MALOTT, DEBORAH E; Peru HS; Peru, IN; Chrs; Cmnty Wkr; Hon Rl; Hosp Ade; Sch Pl; Yth Flsp; Yrbk; OEA; Pep Clb; Upper Wabash Voc Schl; Legal Sec.

MALOTTE, MICHELLE; Pike Central HS; Petersburg, IN; Cl Rep Jr Cls; Band; Chrh Wkr; Hon Rl; Lbry Ade; NHS; Sch Pl; Stu Cncl; Drama Clb; FHA; Indiana St Univ; Exec Sec.

MALTBIE, BETSY; South Range HS; Canfield, OH; Am Leg Aux Girls St; Hon Rl; Spn Clb; Univ; Med.

MALTBY, HOLLIS; Elmwood HS; Wayne, OH; Am Leg Aux Girls St; Chrs; Hon Rl; Mdrgl; MMM; NHS; Sch Mus; Ed Sch Nwsp; Rptr Sch Nwsp; Drama Clb; Musical Theatre.

MALTBY, STEVE; Lumen Christi HS; Jackson, MI; 67/248 Hon Rl; Crs Cntry; Trk; IM Sprt; Natl Merit Ltr; Univ; Aeronautical Engr.

MALUGIA, TIMOTHY; Bishop Noll Inst; Hammond, IN; Chrh Wkr; Letter Ten; Trk; College; Optometry.

MALWITZ, MICHAEL; Kenowa Hills HS; Marne, MI; Boy Scts; Hon Rl; Sct Actv; Bsbl; Univ; Archt.

MALYN, SHARI; Eastmoor Sr HS; Columbus, OH; 17/307 Pres Sr Cls; Am Leg Aux Girls St; Chrs; Drl Tm; Hon Rl; Jr NHS; NHS; Stg Crw; Yrbk; Ten; Parsons Schl Of Art; Illustrtr.

MAMAKOS, JOANNE; Wheeling Park HS; Wheeling, WV; Cls Rep Frsh Cls; AFS; Am Leg Aux Girls St; Hon Rl; NHS; Stu Cncl; VP Fr Clb; Capt Chrldng; Wv Univ; Pre Law.

MAMUZIC, BOJANA; West Lafayette Sr HS; W Lafayette, IN; 35/185 Chrs; Hon Rl; Quill & Scroll; Sch Mus; Yrbk; Drama Clb; Keyettes; Purdue Univ; Engr.

MANCE, CHARITY K; Park Tudor HS; Indianapolis, IN; VP Frsh Cls; Chrs; Hon Rl; Mod UN; VP Sct Actv; Rptr Yrbk; Pres Sch Pl; VP Spn Clb; Natl Merit Ltr; Part In Ind Univ Hon Prog In Foreign Lang For H S Stu 1978; Univ; Med.

MANCINA, MARY; Notre Dame HS; Clarksburg, WV; Cls Rep Frsh Cls; Chrs; NHS; Stu Cncl; Rptr Yrbk; FBLA; FTA; Sci Clb; Chrldng; W Vir Univ; Hosp Admin.

MANCINELLI, CORRIE; St Francis Desales HS; Morgantown, WV; 1/70 VP Frsh Cls; VP Soph Cls; VP Jr Cls; Chrh Wkr; Hon Rl; NHS; Off Ade; Sch Pl; Yrbk; Drama Clb; Univ; Nutrition.

MANCINI, ANNA M; Valley Forge HS; Parma Hgts, OH; 35/777 Cmnty Wkr; Hon Rl; Hosp Ade; Sch Pl; Pep Clb; Spn Clb; College; Pre Med.

MANCINI, LEO; Schafer HS; Southgate, MI; Band; Hon Rl; Jr NHS; NHS; Capt Wrstlng; Natl Merit Ltr; 2nd Tm All Area Wrestling Squad 78 79; 4 Varsity Letters Wrestling; Henry Ford Cmnty Coll; Civil Engr.

MANCINI, MICHAEL; Marian HS; South Bend, IN; Hon Rl; Rptr Sch Nwsp; IM Sprt; Scr Kpr; Univ.

MANCUSO, D; Nordinia HS; Northfield, OH; Cls Rep Frsh Cls; Cls Rep Soph Cls; Cmp Fr Grls; Orch; Sch Pl; Drama Clb; Pep Clb; Ten; PPFtbl; Ursiline; Nurse.

MANCUSO JR, PAUL R; Washington Irving HS; Clarksburg, WV; 10/139 Am Leg Boys St; Hon Rl; Fr Clb; VP Key Clb; Lat Clb; Letter Ftbl; Letter Wrstlng; West Virginia Univ; Acctg.

MANCZ, MARY; Waterloo HS; Atwater, OH; 16/169 Band; Hon Rl; Hosp Ade; Jr NHS; NHS; Orch; Stu Cncl; Rptr Yrbk; Rptr Sch Nwsp; Beta Clb; Ohio St Univ; Psych.

MANDALFINO, LEE A; Trinity HS; Seven Hills, OH; 67/150 Chrs; Chrh Wkr; Girl Scts; Hon Rl; Off Ade; Sch Mus; Sct Actv; Cuyahoga Cmnty Coll; Comp Tech.

MANDERS, LINDA; Calvin M Woodward HS; Toledo, OH; Hst Sr Cls; Chrh Wkr; Hon Rl; Pep Clb; College; Art Educ.

MANDERSCHEID, JANE M; East Lansing HS; East Lansing, MI; 5/380 Sec Hosp Ade; NHS; Stg Crw; Y-Teens; Natl Merit SF; College.

MANDOLI, T; Calumet HS; Calumet, MI; Sec Frsh Cls; Trs Frsh Cls; Band; Cmp Fr Grls; Cmnty Wkr; Hon Rl; Hosp Ade; ROTC; FNA; Pep Clb; Northern Mich Univ; Nurse.

MANDULA, JOSEPH; Padua Franciscan HS; Seven Hills, OH; 54/265 Boy Scts; Hon Rl; JA; Lbry Ade; NHS; Stu Cncl; Rptr Sch Nwsp; FSA; Letter Swmmng; Ohio St Univ; Pre Med.

MANDZIA, LESIA; Holy Name Nazareth HS; Cleveland, OH; Chrh Wkr; Hon Rl; Sdlty; Bsktbl; Socr; Ten; Trk; IM Sprt; Cert Of Apprctn Cert Of Mert 76; Pres Phys Ftnss Awd I & II 75 & 76; Univ; Nursing.

MANEELY, STEVEN; Maysville HS; Zanesville, OH; 50/194 Band; Hon Rl; Ohi Univ.

MANENTE, MELISSA; Liberty HS; Girard, OH; Cl Rep Jr Cls; Cmnty Wkr; Hon Rl; Hosp Ade; Rptr Yrbk; Sch Nwsp; Pep Clb; Gym; Youngstown Univ; Jrnlsm.

MANENTI, JOHN; Girard HS; Girard, OH; 22/215 Am Leg Boys St; Band; Jr NHS; VP NHS; Orch; Yrbk; Fr Clb; Ger Clb; Sci Clb; Hiram Coll; Bio.

MANFREDI, JOHN; Troy Athens HS; Troy, MI; Chrs; Hon Rl; Mdrgl; Natl Forn Lg; NHS; Sch Mus; Sch Pl; Stg Crw; Pres Drama Clb; Ftbl; Bst Supprng Actr 77; Thespian Soc 78; Mst Courageous Plyr Ftbl 78; Kenyon Coll; Theatre.

MANG, STEVEN; Frankfort HS; Lebanon, IN; 89/256 Boy Scts; Off Ade; Boys Clb Am; Lat Clb; Bsktbl; Crs Cntry; Wrstlng; College; Elec.

MANGAN, JOHN; Moeller HS; Loveland, OH; Chrh Wkr; Hon Rl; Sch Mus; Sch Pl; Sct Actv; Stg Crw; Lat Clb; Glf; Wrstlng; IM Sprt; Raymond Walters; Pre Medicine.

MANGANO, MARK; Oak Glen HS; Newell, WV; 30/300 Am Leg Boys St; Band; Boy Scts; Hon Rl; NHS; Sct Actv; Sprt Ed Yrbk; Key Clb; Glf; Wrstlng; West Virginia Univ; Bus.

MANGAS, JONI; Union City Comm HS; Union City, IN; 7/107 Sec Frsh Cls; Sec Soph Cls; Sec Jr Cls; Band; Hon Rl; NHS; Off Ade; VP Fr Clb; FHA; Chrldng; College; Elem Ed.

MANGEN, DEBBIE; Versailles HS; Versailles, OH; JA; FHA; FNA; Pres FTA; Spn Clb; Lion Awd; Coll; Nursing.

MANGEN, STEVEN D; Celina HS; Celina, OH; Chrs; Chrh Wkr; Hon Rl; Sch Mus; Stg Crw; Co llege; Acctg.

MANGIN, MARILYN; Washington Catholic HS; Washington, IN; Chrs; Hon Rl; Ed Yrbk; Rptr Sch Nwsp; Drama Clb; Pep Clb; Chrldng; Univ; Soc Work.

MANGOLD, JULIE; Wayne HS; Dayton, OH; 60/600 Chrh Wkr; Hon Rl; Jr NHS; Lbry Ade; NHS; Sch Mus; Yth Flsp; Fr Clb; OEA; Shrthnd Theory 1st Pl 79; Natl Achvmnt Campt Piano Solo 1st Pl 78; Music With Purpose 1st Pl Schslp 77; Grace Coll; Music.

MANGOLD, NORMA; Mother Of Mercy HS; Cincinnati, OH; 35/215 Chrs; Chrh Wkr; Cmnty Wkr; Girl Scts; Hon Rl; JA; Pol Wkr; Sch Pl; Sct Actv; Spn Clb; College; Comp Sci.

MANGOLD, NORMA J; Mother Of Mercy HS; Cincinnati, OH; 36/213 Chrs; Girl Scts; Hon Rl; JA; Pol Wkr; Sch Pl; Spn Clb; Socr; Coach Actv; GAA; Univ; Comp Sci.

MANGOLD, TERESA; Whiteland Community HS; New Whiteland, IN; AFS; Treas FCA; Off Ade; Key Clb; Kiwan Awd; IUPUI; Nursing.

MANGRAF, JENNY; Arcadia Local HS; Findlay, OH; 8/62 Band; Cmp Fr Grls; Chrs; Hon Rl; Jr NHS; Sch Mus; Stg Crw; 4-H; FFA; FHA; Ohio St Univ; Vet Med.

MANGUS, MARLO; La Ville Jr Sr HS; Lakeville, IN; Cls Rep Sr Cls; Aud/Vis; Chrs; Chrh Wkr; Cmnty Wkr; Hon Rl; NHS; Sch Pl; Stu Cncl; Yth Flsp; Mc Pherson Coll; Agri Tchr.

MANGUS, WILLIAM; Dunbar HS; Dunbar, WV; 1/180 Pres Soph Cls; Hon Rl; JA; NHS; Stu Cncl; Letter Bsbl; Bsktbl; Letter Ftbl; Glf; Letter Trk; Univ; Dent.

MANI, BETH; Garaway HS; Sugarcreek, OH; Band; Drm Mjrt; Hon Rl; Pep Clb; Spn Clb; Bsktbl; Gym; Trk; Chrldng; IM Sprt; Voc Schl; Acctg.

MANIAK, STEVEN T; Robt S Rogers HS; Toledo, OH; 19/420 Boy Scts; Orch; Sch Pl; Stg Crw; Lat Clb; Mth Clb; Pres Sci Clb; Univ Of Toledo; Chemistry.

MANION, ANNETTE; Brookfield HS; Masury, OH; VP Frsh Cls; VP Soph Cls; Pres Jr Cls; Boy Scts; Hon Rl; Jr NHS; NHS; Stu Cncl; Yrbk; Beta Clb; Kent State.

MANKO, DENNIS; Waterford Township HS; Pontiac, MI; 1/406 Cls Rep Sr Cls; Boy Scts; Hon Rl; NHS; Stu Cncl; Rptr Sch Nwsp; Sch Nwsp; Natl Merit Ltr; Mi St Univ Awd For Acad Excllnc 79; Mi St Univ Clb Schlrshp 79; St Of Mi Schlrshp Prog Cert Of Rec 79; Michigan St Univ; Comp Sci.

MANKOWSKI, SHARON; Sacred Heart Academy; Mt Pleasant, MI; 20/50 Chrs; Chrh Wkr; Cmnty Wkr; Girl Scts; Hon Rl; Pep Clb; Letter Chrldng; Univ; Eng.

MANKOWSKI, TERI; St Marys Cathedral HS; Gaylord, MI; 10/59 Sec Soph Cls; Cls Rep Soph Cls; Pres Jr Cls; Band; NHS; Yrbk; Pep Clb; Letter Bsbl; Letter Chrldng; 4-H Awd; Jr Coll; Engr.

MANLEY, DEBORAH L; Springfield Local HS; Holland, OH; 4/228 Band; Chrs; Hon Rl; Off Ade; 4-H; Letter Bsktbl; Letter Crs Cntry; Gym; Trk; Chrldng; College; English.

MANLEY, KATHY; Cardinal Ritter HS; Indianapolis, IN; Hon Rl; 4-H; Chrldng; Pom Pon; Vocational Schl.

MANLEY, KAY; Northville HS; Northville, MI; Debate Tm; Hon Rl; Natl Forn Lg; NHS; Yrbk; Ger Clb; Kalamazoo Coll; Vet.

MANLEY, THOMAS J; John Adams HS; South Bend, IN; 120/468 Cl Rep Jr Cls; Band; Boy Scts; Drm Bgl; Hon Rl; Orch; Red Cr Ade; Sct Actv; Letter Swmmng; Indiana Univ; Busns.

MANLEY, TROY; Olentangy HS; Powell, OH; 13/136 FCA; Hon Rl; JA; NHS; Sprt Ed Sch Nwsp; 4-H; Pep Clb; Sci Clb; Spn Clb; Letter Bsbl; Ohio State; Engineer.

MANLEY, WILLIAM; La Salle HS; South Bend, IN; Band; Boy Scts; Hon Rl; Orch; Sct Actv; Sci Clb; Purdue Univ; Elec Engr.

MANLY, SHERMAN; Roosevelt HS; E Chicago, IN; 49/219 Band; Univ; Printing.

MANN, ARTHUR; Marshall HS; Marshall, MI; 2/258 Pres Jr Cls; Cls Rep Sr Cls; Sal; Am Leg Boys St; Jr NHS; NHS; Sch Pl; Stg Crw; Pres Spn Clb; Rotary Awd; Stephen F Austin St Univ; Eng.

MANN, D; Decatur Central HS; Indnpls, IN; Cmp Fr Grls; Lbry Ade; Rptr Sch Nwsp; 4-H; OEA; GAA; PPFtbl; Cit Awd; 4-H Awd; College; Photo.

MANN, DANIEL W; Napoleon HS; Napoleon, OH; Band; Chrs; Chrh Wkr; Hon Rl; Orch; Yth Flsp; 4-H; Trk; 4-H Awd; Univ; Sci.

MANN, JEFF; Portsmouth East HS; Portsmouth, OH; 6/78 Chrs; Chrh Wkr; Hon Rl; Mdrgl; Spn Clb; Ten Temple Univ; Christian Worker.

MANN, KEVIN; Lawrence HS; Lawrence, MI; VP Frsh Cls; Cls Rep Sr Cls; Boy Scts; Hon Rl; Stg Crw; 4-H; FTA; Bsbl; Bsktbl; Capt Ftbl; Schlrshp Olivet Coll; David Small Awd; Ftbl 1st Tm All Conf; Olivet Coll; Busns Admin.

MANN, KIMBERLY; Warren Central HS; Indpls, IN; 187/768 Cls Rep Soph Cls; Cl Rep Jr Cls; Cmnty Wkr; FCA; Girl Scts; PAVAS; Sch Mus; Ball State Univ; Cmmrcl Art.

MANN, MARTIN; Mooresville HS; Mooresville, IN; 136/255 Hon Rl; Ger Clb; Mth Clb; Sci Clb; Bsktbl; Ftbl; Trk; Mgrs; ITT.

MANN, MARY; Chatard HS; Indianapolis, IN; 60/200 Hon Rl; Indiana Univ; Spec Ed.

MANN, MICHAEL; Washington HS; Massillon, OH; VP Sr Cls; Hon Rl; Off Ade; Sch Pl; Stg Crw; Sci Clb; Spn Clb; Ftbl; Swmmng; Trk; Stark Tech; X Ray Tech.

MANN, MIRIAM; River Valley HS; Waldo, OH; 6/208 Sec Band; Chrh Wkr; Cmnty Wkr; Hon Rl; NHS; Orch; Sch Mus; Stu Cncl; Sec Yth Flsp; Lat Clb; Oral Roberts Univ; Elem Educ.

MANN, RANDY; Fredericktown HS; Fredericktown, OH; Trs Soph Cls; Trs Jr Cls; Chrs; FCA; Hon Rl; DECA; 4-H; Bsktbl; Ftbl; IM Sprt; Coll; Law.

MANN, TIM; Peterstown HS; Lindside, WV; Sci Clb; Univ.

MANNER, JAN; Marshall HS; Marshall, MI; Band; Chrs; Chrh Wkr; Debate Tm; FCA; Hon Rl; Yth Flsp; Y-Teens; FHA; Pep Clb; Michigan St Univ; Pre Vet.

MANNERS, WENDY; Columbiana HS; Columbiana, OH; Cmp Fr Grls; Hon Rl; 4-H; OEA; Spn Clb; Exec Diplomat St Women & Ambassador Awds 78; Voc Schl; Comp Tech.

MANNING, ANN B; Northwestern HS; West Salem, OH; Chrs; Chrh Wkr; Cmnty Wkr; Hon Rl; Jr NHS; Sec Yth Flsp; Sprt Ed Yrbk; Sprt Ed Sch Nwsp; Rptr Sch Nwsp; Voc Schl; Stewardess.

MANNING, LETITIA; St Peters HS; Danville, OH; 1/90 Pres Soph Cls; NHS; Red Cr Ade; Sch Mus; Pres Stu Cncl; Ed Yrbk; Rptr Sch Nwsp; Sch Nwsp; 4-H; Am Leg Awd; Georgetown Univ; Med.

MANNING, LYNNE; Bishop Hartley HS; Columbus, OH; Hon Rl; Letter Chrldng; Univ; Bus.

MANNING, N; Atherton HS; Burton, MI; Band; Boy Scts; NHS; Sct Actv; Mgrs; Michigan St Univ; Vet.

MANNING, STUART; Bruceton HS; Bruceton Mills, WV; Boy Scts; Hon Rl; Stg Crw; Wv Univ.

MANNING, TAMMY; Fairbanks HS; Plain City, OH; 20/96 Band; Chrs; Sch Mus; Sch Pl; Rptr Yrbk; Drama Clb; 4-H; FHA; Spn Clb; Coach Actv; Columbus Symphony Youth Orch 79; All Oh St Fair Band 79; Oh MAA Schl Awd 78; Univ; Music Educ.

MANNING, THOMAS; East Lansing HS; East Lansing, MI; 6/352 Band; VP Mod UN; NHS; Orch; Sch Nwsp; NCTE; Opt Clb Awd; Mic State Univ; Animal Physiology.

MANNION, JUNE; Bishop Noll Inst; Hammond, IN; 1/385 Cls Rep Sr Cls; Cmnty Wkr; VP Girl Scts; Pres NHS; Sct Actv; Mth Clb; IM Sprt; Natl Merit SF; College; Medicine.

MANNION, RANDOLPH; Bishop Noll Institute; Hammond, IN; 2/321 Hon Rl; Stu Cncl; VP Mth Clb; Superior Cert Of Achvmnt In History Day 79; Purdue Univ; Elec Engr.

MANNISTO, LISA M; William G Mather HS; Munising, MI; 13/115 Sec Frsh Cls; Sec Soph Cls; Sec Sr Cls; Band; Hon Rl; NHS; Sch Pl; Yrbk; Ed Sch Nwsp; Chrldng; Stephens; Acting.

MANNIX, TRACY; Brookville HS; Orlando, FL; 7/190 Band; Chrs; Chrh Wkr; Drl Tm; Girl Scts; Hon Rl; Jr NHS; NHS; Sch Pl; Stg Crw; Hanover Coll; Law.

MANNO, CHARLES; St Edward HS; Cleveland, OH; 25/400 Chrh Wkr; Hon Rl; Pol Wkr; Y-Teens; Yrbk; Spn Clb; IM Sprt; Univ; Intl Bus.

MANNON, CYNTHIA; Hamlin HS; W Hamlin, WV; 5/62 Pres Sr Cls; Chrh Wkr; Cmnty Wkr; Hon Rl; Sec Jr NHS; NHS; Pol Wkr; 4-H; FHA; VP Ger Clb; All Tournmt Cheerldr; Pres Baptist Yth Fndtn; Marshall Univ; Soc Workr.

MANNOR, CATHERINE; Clio HS; Clio, MI; Chrs; Girl Scts; Hon Rl; NHS; Sch Pl; Sct Actv; Stg Crw; Drama Clb; 4-H; Spn Clb; Bus Schl; Acctg.

MANNOR, DENISE M; Genesee HS; Genesee, MI; 3/36 VP Frsh Cls; VP Soph Cls; VP Jr Cls; VP Sr Cls; Cmp Fr Grls; Chrs; Girl Scts; Hon Rl; Lbry Ade; NHS; Baker Jr Coll Of Busns; Exec Sec.

MANNOR, LINDA; Kearsley HS; Flint, MI; 106/375 Cl Rep Jr Cls; Cls Rep Sr Cls; Band; Boy Scts; Girl Scts; Hon Rl; Sct Actv; Stu Cncl; Yrbk; Chrldng; Eastern Michigan Univ; Psych.

MANOLOVICH, GEORGE; Crown Point HS; Crown Point, IN; Chrh Wkr; NHS; Arizona St Univ; Philosophy.

MANOLUKAS, JOHN; Boardman HS; Youngstown, OH; Band; Chrh Wkr; Hon Rl; Orch; Sch Mus; Sch Pl; Ger Clb; Mth Clb; Sci Clb; Univ Of Solonika; Med.

MANON, JEFF; De Kalb HS; Auburn, IN; NHS; Ger Clb; Sci Clb; Letter Bsbl; Letter Crs Cntry; IM Sprt; Gov Hon Prg Awd; Indiana Univ.

MANON, LORA; Bryan HS; Bryan, OH; 11/185 Band; Hon Rl; NHS; Orch; Sch Mus; Rptr Sch Nwsp; Sch Nwsp; Pres 4-H; Spn Clb; Am Leg Awd; Bowling Green St Univ; Music Educ.

MANON, MARY; Defiance Sr HS; Defiance, OH; 30/290 Girl Scts; Hon Rl; Hosp Ade; Treas JA; Jr NHS; Lbry Ade; Off Ade; DECA; Fr Clb; JA Awd; Northwest Tech Coll; Comp Prog.

MANOR, NANCY J; Martinsburg HS; Martinsburg, WV; Cls Rep Frsh Cls; Cls Rep Soph Cls; Cl Rep Jr Cls; Hon Rl; Stu Cncl; Sec Keyettes; Letter Bsbl; Letter Bsktbl; Chrldng; College; Busns Mgmt.

MANOS, DEBORAH; Cloverleaf Sr HS; Seville, OH; 16/290 Chrs; Girl Scts; Hon Rl; 4-H; Spn Clb; Ten; Pony Club Achvmnt Of D Rating 74; Schlshp Eng 78; Akron Univ; Legal Stenog.

MANOUS, LAURA; Highland HS; Highland, IN; 14/494 Hon Rl; Sec NHS; Pep Clb; Pom Pon; Natl Merit Ltr; Indiana Univ.

MANRING, BEN; St Johns HS; De Witt, MI; Trs Sr Cls; Boy Scts; Jr NHS; Sch Pl; Pres Yth Flsp; Yrbk; Sci Clb; Swmmng; Mic State Univ; Theoretical Physics.

MANSEL, OLIVER; Inkster HS; Inkster, MI; Cls Rep Frsh Cls; VP Soph Cls; Cls Rep Soph Cls; Cl Rep Jr Cls; Boy Scts; Debate Tm; Hon Rl; Stg Crw; Stu Cncl; Yth Flsp; Los Angeles City Coll; Bus Admin.

MANSEL, WYMAN; Inkster HS; Inkster, MI; Trs Frsh Cls; Hon Rl; Bsktbl; Letter Ftbl; Coach Actv; Purdue Univ; Engr.

MANSFIELD, CHERYL; Harper Creek HS; Battle Creek, MI; 50/244 Cls Rep Frsh Cls; Cls Rep Soph Cls; Cl Rep Jr Cls; Cmnty Wkr; Girl Scts; Hon Rl; Sch Mus; Yth Flsp; Fr Clb; Mgrs; Intl Fine Arts Coll; Fash Merch.

MANSFIELD, G; Sault Area HS; Slt Ste Marie, MI; Band; Chrh Wkr; Hon Rl; Lat Clb; Crs Cntry; Letter Swmmng; Trk; College; Bio Sci.

MANSFIELD, JERRY; Continental Local HS; Continental, OH; 2/60 Pres Frsh Cls; Pres Jr Cls; Pres Sr Cls; Am Leg Boys St; Band; Chrs; Chrh Wkr; Hon Rl; Pres NHS; Off Ade; Bowling Green St Univ; RN.

MANSKE, ROGER; Knox Sr HS; Knox, IN; PAVAS; Sch Pl; Sct Actv; Sch Nwsp; 1st Plc Sci Fair 76; Blue Ribbon Sci Fair 78; Locksmithing Inst; Theatre.

MANSOUR, AMAL; Berkley HS; Oak Park, MI; Off Ade; Orch; Sch Mus; Spn Clb; Capt Crs Cntry; Trk; Scr Kpr; SEOVEC; Cosmetology.

MANSOUR, ELIZABETH; Ursuline HS; Youngstown, OH; 72/314 Sec Soph Cls; Cl Rep Jr Cls; Hon Rl; Off Ade; Stu Cncl; Ohio State Univ; Advertising.

MANSOUR, JENNIFER; Carman Sr HS; Flint, MI; Trs Jr Cls; Band; Debate Tm; Hon Rl; NHS; Letter Chrldng; Debate 8th Spkr Awd 78; Girls Varsity Tennis Awd Mst Imprvd Plyr 78; Mi Schl Band Orch Ass Solo Ensemble 78; Univ; Sci.

MANTYCH, BEVERLY; Manistee Catholic Central H; Manistee, MI; Hon Rl; NHS; VP Stu Cncl; Sch Nwsp; Pep Clb; Fash Inst Of Tech; Fashion Designer.

MANTYCH, CANDACE; Manistee Catholic Ctrl HS; Manistee, MI; Cmnty Wkr; Hon Rl; Yth Flsp; Letter Ten; West Shore Cmnty Coll; Sec.

MANTYCH, CYNTHIA; Manistee Catholic Cntrl HS; Manistee, MI; Chrh Wkr; Cmnty Wkr; Hon Rl; Sprt Ed Sch Nwsp; Sch Nwsp; Letter Ten; Univ.

MANUDHANE, PRADEEP; Turpin HS; Cincinnati, OH; 6/357 Treas JA; NHS; Pres Of Chss Club Earned Lttr Turpin High Champ; Mbr Of The Its Academic Tm; Univ; Med.

MANUEL, CARLA; North Vigo HS; Terre Haute, IN; Chrs; Hon Rl; Stu Cncl; Y-Teens; Pep Clb; PPFtbl; Indiana St Univ.

MANUEL, CARMEN J; Southern Local HS; Racine, OH; Fr Clb; Rio Grande College; Teacher.

MANUEL, MARCIA; Cass Technical HS; Detroit, MI; Cls Rep Frsh Cls; Cls Rep Soph Cls; Cl Rep Jr Cls; Band; Chrs; Drl Tm; Orch; Stu Cncl; GAA; IM Sprt; Pepperdine Univ; Comp Sci.

MANUEL, RICK; Bethesda Christian HS; Lebanon, IN; Pres Frsh Cls; Chrs; Chrh Wkr; Hon Rl; Sch Pl; Stg Crw; Sci Clb; Letter Bsbl; Letter Bsktbl; Letter Socr; Univ.

MANUSAKIS JR, NICHOLAS; Western Reserve HS; Warren, OH; Cls Rep Sr Cls; Aud/Vis; Boy Scts; Cmnty Wkr; Ftbl; IM Sprt; Ohi Univ; Pro Football.

MANUSZAK, KAREN; St Marys Cathedral HS; Gaylord, MI; 11/63 Sec Sr Cls; Chrs; Hon Rl; Sec NHS; Off Ade; Sch Mus; Stu Cncl; Rptr Yrbk; Sec Drama Clb; Pep Clb; Davenport Coll Of Bus; Legal Sec.

MANWELL, LORI; Midland HS; Midland, MI; 81/489 Girl Scts; Hon Rl; Sch Pl; Drama Clb; Fr Clb; Pep Clb; Schlrshp Act Test Natl Merit 79; Awd For Dancing & Acting 76; Central Michigan Univ; Interior Dec.

MANYPENNY, JAMES; Oak Glen HS; Newell, WV; 51/285 Pres Frsh Cls; Am Leg Boys St; Stg Crw; Stu Cncl; Letter Bsbl; Bsktbl; Letter Ftbl; Coach Actv; College; Acctng.

MANYPENNY, RANDY; Marlington HS; Alliance, OH; 48/311 Chrs; Chrh Wkr; Mdrgl; Sch Mus; Sch Pl; Stg Crw; Rptr Sch Nwsp; Univ; Music.

MANZANO, MELODY; Eastern HS; Lansing, MI; 8/458 Chrs; Hon Rl; NHS; Pol Wkr; Rptr Sch Nwsp; FDA; Capt Swmmng; Tmr; Elk Awd; Runner Up 1st For Interlochen Piano Scslhp 76 & 77; HS Engr Inst 78; Quetico Wildrns Progr 2 Sci Crdts 79; Lyman Briggs Coll; Pre Med.

MANZO, CATHY; Brookside HS; Sheffield Lake, OH; 16/240 Hon Rl; Jr NHS; NHS; Bsktbl; Trk; Univ; Med Tech.

MANZO, LUCIO; Fairmont West HS; Kettering, OH; Hon Rl; Socr; IM Sprt; Wright St Univ; Vet.

MANZO, TOM; Hammond Tech HS; Hammond, IN; Pres Jr Cls; Am Leg Boys St; Hon Rl; JA; NHS; Rptr Yrbk; Sch Nwsp; VICA; Bsbl; Socr; Purdue Univ; Chem Engr.

MAO, CONNIE; Northville HS; Northville, MI; Hon Rl; NHS; Sch Mus; Ed Sch Nwsp; Rptr Sch Nwsp; Sch Nwsp; Trk; IM Sprt; Natl Merit Ltr; Univ.

MAPES, CHRISTINA; Wellston HS; Wellston, OH; 2/90 Sal; Band; Hon Rl; Lbry Ade; Mth Clb; Pep Clb; Ohio Univ; Zoology.

MAPES, CRAIG; Lake Catholic HS; Willowick, OH; Boy Scts; Hon Rl; Letter Socr; IM Sprt; College.

MAPLE, KATHRYN; Lebanon HS; Lebanon, OH; Am Leg Aux Girls St; Cmnty Wkr; Hon Rl; NHS; Sch Mus; VP Stu Cncl; Spn Clb; Chrldng; Marietta Coll; Cmnctns.

MARAGOS, CONSTANCE; Jefferson Union HS; Toronto, OH; Pres Frsh Cls; Pres Soph Cls; Pres Jr Cls; Pres Sr Cls; VP Sr Cls; Sec Sr Cls; Chrs; Chrh Wkr; Girl Scts; Stu Cncl; Nursing.

MARANEY, DONALD; St Francis HS; Star City, WV; Chrh Wkr; Spn Clb; Capt Bsbl; Bsktbl; Letter Ftbl; All Star City Bsbl Tm; 1st Pl Miniature Golf Tournament; 1st Pl Derby Race Car; West Virginia Univ; Engr.

MARANG, KEITH; Washington HS; Massillon, OH; Band; Chrs; Sch Mus; Stg Crw; Fr Clb; Rdo Clb; Sci Clb; College; Music.

MARANO, JOHN; Taylor Center HS; Taylor, MI; 2/388 Sal; Am Leg Boys St; Aud/Vis; Debate Tm; Hon Rl; JA; Natl Forn Lg; NHS; Ed Yrbk; Letter Glf; Gen Motors Inst; Mech Engr.

MARANSKY, JEFF; Heath HS; Heath, OH; 29/165 NHS; Spn Clb; Bsktbl; Ftbl; Trk; Ohio St Univ; Agricultural Engineeri.

MARAZITA, ELIZABETH; Waverly HS; Lansing, MI; 3/370 Cls Rep Frsh Cls; Pres Soph Cls; Cls Rep Soph Cls; Cl Rep Jr Cls; Cls Rep Sr Cls; Sal; Am Leg Aux Girls St; Band; Debate Tm; Hon Rl; Top 10 In Class; Top Sr Ldrshp Awd; Pres Of French Clb; Varsity Debater; Quarter St Finals; Coll; Intl Culture.

MARBURGER, SCOTT; Northrop HS; Ft Wayne, IN; 168/590 JA; Rptr Yrbk; Yrbk; Rptr Sch Nwsp; Sch Nwsp; Socr; IM Sprt; College; Advertising Art.

MARBURY, BEVERLY; M L King Jr Sr HS; Detroit, MI; Hon Rl; Hosp Ade; Off Ade; Stu Cncl; Y-Teens; DECA; OEA; Pep Clb; Trk; Busns Schl; Exec Sec.

MARCELAIN, ANDREW; Newark Cath HS; Newark, OH; Cls Rep Frsh Cls; Cls Rep Soph Cls; Trs Jr Cls; Chrh Wkr; Sch Pl; Rptr Yrbk; Ftbl; Univ; Bus.

MARCH, KELLY; Reese HS; Reese, MI; 24/120 Band; Debate Tm; Hon Rl; Univ; Med.

MARCH, LINDA; Green HS; Uniontown, OH; Band; Girl Scts; Hon Rl; Off Ade; Stu Cncl; Y-Teens; Pep Clb; Bsbl; Wrstlng; Mat Maids; Perf Attendance 76; Honor Awd 76; Ohio St Univ; Med.

MARCH, RICHARD; Buchanan HS; Buchanan, MI; Cls Rep Frsh Cls; Band; Boy Scts; Chrh Wkr; Hon Rl; NHS; Orch; Sch Mus; Sch Pl; Sct Actv; Cert Of Awd In Lang Arts Math Sci Speling Amer Hist Band & Geog 75 & 78; Solo Ensmbl Fest 1st Div 75 & 76; Univ; Bus.

MARCHAL, ELIZABETH; Greenville HS; Greenville, OH; Cls Rep Soph Cls; Chrh Wkr; Hon Rl; Quill & Scroll; Yth Flsp; Ed Sch Nwsp; Rptr Sch Nwsp; 4-H; Spn Clb; College.

MARCHANT, ROBERT N; Central HS; Evansville, IN; Cls Rep Frsh Cls; Cls Rep Sr Cls; Boy Scts;

NHS; Yth Flsp; 4-H; IM Sprt; Mgrs; 4-H Awd; Natl Merit SF; Rose Hulman Inst Of Tech; Sci.

MARCHANT, ROY; Central HS; Evansville, IN; Cls Rep Soph Cls; Boy Scts; NHS; Sch Mus; Yth Flsp; 4-H; IM Sprt; Mgrs; 4-H Awd; Natl Merit Ltr; Rose Hulman Inst Of Tech; Engr.

MARCHESE, CHRISTINE; Monroe HS; Monroe, MI; 24/586 Band; Chrs; Hon Rl; Jr NHS; NHS; Orch; Sch Mus; Stu Cncl; Ger Clb; Ferris State Univ; Pharmacy.

MARCHESI, JANET; St Anne HS; Warren, MI; Chrh Wkr; Girl Scts; Hon Rl; Jr NHS; NHS; Ed Yrbk; Rptr Yrbk; Univ; Jrnlsm.

MARCHINO, ANGELA; Danville Community HS; Danville, IN; Band; Hon Rl; Lbry Ade; Ten; General Motors Inst; Engineering.

MARCHIONE, NATALIE; Berkley HS; Huntington Wds, MI; Chrh Wkr; Cmnty Wkr; Girl Scts; Hon Rl; NHS; Sci Clb; Bsbl; Mich State Univ; Vet Med.

MARCHLENSKI, MARIE; Bishop Donahue HS; M c Mechen, WV; VP Cmnty Wkr; Hon Rl; Stu Cncl; Univ; Psych.

MARCHMAN, YVONNE; John Adams HS; Cleveland, OH; Cl Rep Jr Cls; Chrs; Chrh Wkr; Treas Drm Mjrt; Hon Rl; Jr NHS; NHS; Stu Cncl; OEA; Cit Awd; Youngstown St Univ; Sec Stds.

MARCIAL, MICHAEL R; Windham HS; Windham, OH; Hon Rl; Red Cr Ade; Spn Clb; Letter Ftbl; Scr Kpr; Tmr; Tech Schl; Elec.

MARCINIAK, GREGORY; St Francis De Sales HS; Toledo, OH; Band; Boy Scts; Orch; Sch Mus; Natl Merit Ltr; Ohio St Univ; Vet.

MARCINIAK, PENNY; Elston Sr HS; Mich City, IN; 71/350 Cls Rep Frsh Cls; Cls Rep Soph Cls; Cl Rep Jr Cls; Cls Rep Sr Cls; Jr NHS; Sch Mus; Yrbk; Drama Clb; Spn Clb; Ten; Indian Univ; Dent Hygnst.

MARCIS, SHARON; Lutheran East HS; Cleveland, OH; 3/50 Trs Frsh Cls; Sec Soph Cls; Trs Soph Cls; Chrs; Chrh Wkr; Hon Rl; Off Ade; Sch Mus; Sch Pl; Sec Stu Cncl; Univ; Educ.

MARCKEL, KAREN; Whiteford HS; Ottawa Lk, MI; Hon Rl; Pep Clb; Spn Clb; Capt Trk; Plcd 8th In St For Track Recieved Medal For 220 Yd 77; Plcd 10th In St For 440 Yd Dash 79; Univ Of Toledo; Paralegal.

MARCOTTE, ANN; Ben Davis HS; Indianapolis, IN; FCA; Girl Scts; Stu Cncl; Ger Clb; Pep Clb; Gym; Letter Trk; Letter Chrldng; Mgrs; Mat Maids; Univ; Soc Work.

MARCOTTE, GREG; Negaunee HS; Negaunee, MI; Hon Rl; Northern Michigan Univ.

MARCOTTE, RON; Bishop Fenwick HS; West Chester, OH; Chrs; Sprt Ed Sch Nwsp; Rptr Sch Nwsp; Sch Nwsp; Crs Cntry; Hockey; Write Short Stories 78; 3rd In Schl On PSAT; Johns Hopkins Univ; Thero Physics.

MARCOUX, JEAN; River Rouge HS; River Rouge, MI; Boy Scts; Chrh Wkr; Hon Rl; NHS; Sct Actv; Ten; Univ Of Michigan; Poli Sci.

MARCOZZI, MARY; Catholic Central HS; Steubenville, OH; Chrs; Hon Rl; Sch Mus; Sch Pl; Stg Crw; Stu Cncl; Drama Clb; College Of Steubenville; Acctg.

MARCUM, ALLEN M; Barboursville HS; Huntington, WV; Am Leg Boys St; Hon Rl; Jr NHS; NHS; Rptr Sch Nwsp; Boys Clb Am; Mth Clb; Letter Ten; Tag History Awd 77; Algebra 2 Awd 78; 1st Pl Econ Div Wv St Soc Studies Fair 79; Univ; Aero.

MARCUM, CINDIE; Oceana HS; Kopperston, WV; Band; Hon Rl; MMM; NHS; Yth Flsp; Pep Clb; Letter Bsktbl; GAA; Softball Letter 78; All Regl Band 77; Wyoming Voc Tech Ctr; Mach Acctg.

MARCUM, PAMELA S; Little Miami HS; Maineville, OH; Chrs; Chrh Wkr; Hon Rl; Hosp Ade; Lbry Ade; Lit Mag; NHS; Yrbk; Fr Clb; Most Otstndng French 3 Stud 78; Schlrshp Tm French 2 77; Univ.

MARCY, BRYAN; Edgewood Sr HS; Kingsville, OH; 2/300 AFS; Hon Rl; Ger Clb; Sci Clb; Wrstlng; Am Leg Awd; Awd Of Hon Cert Straight A 78; HS Ltr Shcsltc 79; Univ Of Akron; Acctg.

MARDAVICH, DEBORAH; Medina Sr HS; Medina, OH; AFS; Band; Chrs; Chrh Wkr; Girl Scts; Yth Flsp; Pep Clb; Swmmng; Trk; GAA; Partcpt In All Oh St Fair Band 79; Univ.

MARDER, JENNY; Amelia HS; Amelia, OH; Sec Sr Cls; NHS; Letter Trk; College; Med.

MARDONES, DANIEL; Liberty HS; Clarksburg, WV; 5/188 Boy Scts; Chrh Wkr; Hon Rl; NHS; Treas Mth Clb; Treas Sci Clb; Oral Roberts Univ; Bio.

MARDOSA, DEBBIE; Port Clinton HS; Pt Clinton, OH; 36/265 Chrs; Hon Rl; Fr Clb; GAA; Ohio State.

MARECKI, MARY; St Florian HS; Detroit, MI; 2/75 Trs Sr Cls; Chrs; Girl Scts; Hon Rl; NHS; Sch Mus; Sct Actv; Sdlty; Yrbk; Sci Clb; Univ; Med.

MAREK, ANTOINETTE; Reed City HS; Reed City, MI; Am Leg Aux Girls St; Chrh Wkr; Debate Tm; Hon Rl; Pres NHS; Coll.

MAREK, JOHN; Port Clinton HS; Gypsum, OH; Orch; Cert Of Merit; Univ; Cmnctns.

MAREK, JOHN; Shaker Hts HS; Shker Hts, OH; Boy Scts; Hon Rl; Stg Crw; IM Sprt; College; Engr Prog.

MAREK, MICHAEL; Reed City HS; Reed City, MI; 1/172 Val; Am Leg Boys St; Debate Tm; Hon Rl; Lbry Ade; Natl Forn Lg; Pres NHS; Mth Clb; Sci Clb; Trk; Michigan Tech Univ; Chem Engr.

MAREN, JOHN; Hamilton Southeastern HS; Noblesville, IN; Hon Rl; JA; Quill & Scroll; Yrbk; Sch Nwsp; Ger Clb; Pep Clb; ISU; Pre Med.

MARENTETTE, STEPHEN; Whittemore Prescott HS; Prescott, MI; Boy Scts; Debate Tm; Hon Rl; Drama Clb; Ger Clb; Western Michigan Univ; Comp Sci.

MARGESON, GARY; Brookhaven HS; Columbus, OH; Band; Hon Rl; NHS; Orch; Sprt Ed Sch Nwsp; Letter Bsktbl; Mgrs; Kiwan Awd; Rotary Awd; Michigan St Univ.

MARGO, KIM; Edgewood HS; Conneaut, OH; 31/290 AFS; Hon Rl; Sci Clb; Spn Clb; College; Accounting.

MARGOLIS, J; Springfield North HS; Springfield, OH; Cls Rep Frsh Cls; Cls Rep Soph Cls; Cl Rep Jr Cls; Band; Chrs; Orch; Pol Wkr; Sch Mus; Stu Cncl; Natl Merit Ltr; Schlshp Awd 77; Univ; Radio Cmnctns.

MARGOLIS, K; Revere Sr HS; Akron, OH; Cls Rep Soph Cls; Band; Hon Rl; Natl Forn Lg; Univ.

MARGUARDT, TOM; Bay HS; Bay Vill, OH; Ftbl;.

MARGUGLIO, B TROY; Parkside HS; Jackson, MI; NHS; Ten; Univ.

MARHEINEKE, MARK; R S Tower HS; Warren, MI; VP Frsh Cls; Cls Rep Soph Cls; Cl Rep Jr Cls; Cls Rep Sr Cls; Aud/Vis; Band; Chrs; Cmnty Wkr; Hon Rl; Off Ade; Eastern Michigan Univ; Psych.

MARIA, JEANETTE; Medina Sr HS; Medina, OH; 32/334 NHS; Letter Gym; Univ; Jrnlsm.

MARIANI, ANNA MARIE; Cousino HS; Warren, MI; Band; Chrh Wkr; Hon Rl; Jr NHS; NHS; Sch Mus; Mth Clb; IM Sprt; General Motors Inst; Industrial Admi.

MARIANI, BARBARA; Seaholm HS; Birmingham, MI; 67/700 Aud/Vis; Hon Rl; JA; Jr NHS; NHS; Stg Crw; Michigan St Univ; Cmnctns.

MARIANI, CARL; Benedictine HS; Cleveland, OH; 1/100 Hon Rl; NHS; Rptr Sch Nwsp; Ger Clb; Case Western Reserve; Medicine.

MARIETTI, JAMES; Wintersville HS; Steubenville, OH; 26/267 Boy Scts; Hon Rl; Rptr Sch Nwsp; Spn Clb; Aviation.

MARIN, CARLA; Honland HS; Warren, OH; 77/430 AFS; Band; Hon Rl; Y-Teens; Yrbk; Fr Clb; Miami Univ; Psych.

MARINACCI, LISA; Fairfield Union HS; Lancaster, OH; 5/147 Hst Soph Cls; Band; Chrs; Drm Mjrt; Hon Rl; Jr NHS; NHS; Drama Clb; Eng Clb; 4-H; Hillsdale Coll; Mgmt.

MARINCH, MICHAEL; Eastlake North HS; Willowick, OH; 133/639 Boy Scts; Hon Rl; Sct Actv; Capt Crs Cntry; Letter Trk; Tmr; Bowling Green Univ; Bus Admin.

MARINER, SHARI; Hoover HS; North Canton, OH; Hon Rl; Yth Flsp; Pep Clb; Spn Clb; Tmr; St Thomas Schl; Nursing.

MARINI, JILL; Warren Western Reserve HS; Warren, OH; 17/430 Chrs; Hon Rl; NHS; Y-Teens; Rptr Sch Nwsp; Letter Bsbl; Letter Bsktbl; Letter Glf; Treas GAA; IM Sprt; Univ; Acctg.

MARINO, MICHELLE; Howland HS; Niles, OH; 11/430 Chrs; Hon Rl; NHS; Rptr Yrbk; Fr Clb; Letter Trk; Kent State Univ; French.

MARINO, TODD; Sts Peter & Paul Area HS; Saginaw, MI; Cls Rep Sr Cls; Boy Scts; Chrs; Hon Rl; Jr NHS; NHS; Fr Clb; FDA; Bsbl; Bsktbl; Coll; Dentistry.

MARINO JR, FRANK; Salem Sr HS; Salem, OH; Hon Rl; FSA; Univ; Med.

MARIOL, SALLY R; Canton South HS; Canton, OH; Chrs; Hon Rl; Lbry Ade; Off Ade; Drama Clb; Ten; Scr Kpr; Stark Tech Voc Schl; Legal Sec.

MARION, MICHELLE; Our Lady Of Mercy HS; Plymouth Twp, MI; Chrs; Girl Scts; NHS; Swmmng; Univ Of Detroit; Engr.

MARION, SHEILA; Walnut Hills HS; Cincinnati, OH; AFS; Hon Rl; Hosp Ade; Off Ade; Sch Nwsp; Ger Clb; Univ Of Pennsylvania; Chem Engr.

MARIZETTE, REGINALD; John Hay HS; Cleveland, OH; 11/310 Hon Rl; Jr NHS; Letter Ftbl; Letter Trk; Cit Awd; Wilmington Coll; Mech Engr.

MARJOMAKI, DANA L; Gwinn HS; Gwinn, MI; Pres Jr Cls; Cl Rep Jr Cls; Am Leg Aux Girls St; Cmnty Wkr; Hon Rl; Crs Cntry; Gym; Trk; Chrldng; Am Leg Awd; Mic State Univ; Phy Ed.

MARK, DAVID P; E A Johnson HS; Clio, MI; Boy Scts; Hon Rl; Sct Actv; Univ; Elec Engr.

MARK, MICHELE R; Paint Valley HS; Chillicothe, OH; VP Soph Cls; Cmp Fr Grls; Hon Rl; NHS; OEA; Pep Clb; Sci Clb; Bsktbl; Trk; Chrldng;.

MARKEE, THERESA; Valley Local HS; Lucasville, OH; Cls Rep Frsh Cls; Hon Rl; Hosp Ade; Bsbl; Bsktbl; IM Sprt; Natl Merit Ltr; College; Computer Science.

MARKEL, JAMEY; Croswell Lexington HS; Croswell, MI; 4-H; Capt Crs Cntry; Letter Trk; College; Vet.

MARKEL, MARY; Rock Hill Sr HS; Pedro, OH; 39/161 Girl Scts; Hon Rl; Lbry Ade; Yrbk; GAA; Scr Kpr; Ashland Cmnty Coll.

MARKEL, SALLY; Rock Hill HS; Pedro, OH; 48/142 Aud/Vis; Chrs; Chrh Wkr; Hon Rl; Trk; Chrldng; GAA; 4-H Awd; Ohio Univ; Busns.

MARKER, JAMIE; Greenville HS; Gettysburg, OH; 49/360 Trs Frsh Cls; Trs Soph Cls; Trs Jr Cls; Trs Sr Cls; Drl Tm; NHS; OEA; Trk;.

MARKER, LISA; Tri Village HS; New Madison, OH; Hon Rl; Lbry Ade; NHS; 4-H; FHA; OEA; Pep Clb; Letter Trk; 4-H Awd; Richmond Bus Coll; Sec.

MARKER, RHONDA; South Dearborn HS; Aurora, IN; Chrs; Chrh Wkr; Lbry Ade; Sch Mus; Pep Clb; Good Samaritan Schl Of Nrsng; Nurse.

MARKERT, CHRISTOPHER; Medina HS; Medina, OH; 22/356 Band; Boy Scts; Hon Rl; NHS; 4-H; Letter Socr; Letter Ten; Univ Of Notre Dame; Mech Engr.

MARKERT, DAVID; Medina HS; Medina, OH; 17/353 Band; Boy Scts; Hon Rl; NHS; Sct Actv; 4-H; Key Clb; Socr; 4-H Awd; College.

MARKEY, CHARLES; Glade Valley School; Fenton, MI; Occupational Therapist.

MARKGRAF, PHIL; Moeller HS; Cincinnati, OH; 10/300 Aud/Vis; Hon Rl; Sch Mus; Sch Pl; Stg Crw; Eng Clb; Crs Cntry; Trk; Univ Of Cincinnati; Engr.

MARKHAM, DELYNN; Madison HS; Madison, OH; 12/252 Band; Drl Tm; Hon Rl; NHS; Lat Clb; Pep Clb; Scr Kpr; College; Nursing.

MARKHAM, SUZANNE K; Harper Creek HS; Cersesco, MI; 39/260 Girl Scts; Hon Rl; Jr NHS; NHS; Sprt Ed Yrbk; Yrbk; 4-H; Fr Clb; Pep Clb; Letter Bsktbl; Kellogg Community College; Business.

MARKIEWICZ, ANN; Kokomo HS; Kokomo, IN; 120/356 Cls Rep Frsh Cls; Cls Rep Soph Cls; Cl Rep Jr Cls; Cls Rep Sr Cls; Band; Chrh Wkr; FCA; Girl Scts; Off Ade; Sch Mus; St Joseph Coll; Sci.

MARKINS, EDDIE; Ironton HS; Ironton, OH; 9/190 Cls Rep Frsh Cls; Cls Rep Soph Cls; Cl Rep Jr Cls; Hon Rl; NHS; Stu Cncl; Pres Ger Clb; Letter Ten; Capt IM Sprt; Ohio State Univ; Medicine.

MARKLAND, GL; Floyd Central HS; Lanesville, IN; 28/375 Band; Hon Rl; Univ; Engr.

MARKLAND, MALCOLM; Switzerland County HS; Vevay, IN; 4/120 Am Leg Boys St; Band; Hon Rl; MMM; NHS; Sch Mus; Stg Crw; Drama Clb; Glf; Purdue Univ; Ag.

MARKLE, GARRY; Woodmore HS; Woodville, OH; Am Leg Boys St; Band; Boy Scts; Hon Rl; Sch Mus; Ftbl; Trk; Mgrs; Am Leg Awd; Natl Merit Schl; Univ; Engr.

MARKLEY, CYNTHIA; Philip Barbour HS; Junior, WV; 11/300 Hon Rl; Jr NHS; NHS; Off Ade; Am Leg Awd; West Virginia Univ; Fine Arts.

MARKLEY, DIANE; Lincolnview HS; Middle Pt, OH; Am Leg Aux Girls St; NHS; Sch Nwsp; 4-H; FHA; Mgrs; 4-H Awd; Univ; Math.

MARKLEY, JULIE; Kewanna HS; Kewanna, IN; Trs Frsh Cls; VP Soph Cls; Trs Jr Cls; Hon Rl; Off Ade; 4-H; Pep Clb; Spn Clb; Chrldng; Pom Pon; Honor Awds; Home Ec Awd; Typing Awd; Bsns Schl; Bsns.

MARKLEY, JULIE A; Richmond Sr HS; Richmond, IN; 69/650 Cls Rep Sr Cls; Band; Hon Rl; Natl Forn Lg; Orch; Quill & Scroll; Rptr Yrbk; Gym; Chrldng; PPFtbl; Lutheran Hosp Nursing Schl; RN.

MARKLEY, MICHAEL; Bishop Luers HS; Ft Wayne, IN; Chrh Wkr; JA; Lbry Ade; Sch Pl; Sct Actv; Pep Clb; Bsktbl; Scr Kpr; Indiana Univ; Ratio/TV Cmnctns.

MARKO, MICHELLE; Harrison HS; Harrison, MI; Hon Rl; NHS; Letter Bsbl; Letter Chrldng; 4-H Awd; Pres Awd; Vocational Schl; Cosmetology.

MARKO, RANDY; River Valley HS; Three Oaks, MI; 16/148 Hon Rl; NHS; Wrstlng; Cit Awd; Lake Mic College.

MARKOPOULOS, CHRISTY; Niles Mc Kinley HS; Niles, OH; 24/420 Hon Rl; Jr NHS; NHS; Lat Clb; Trk; Mgrs; PPFtbl; Ohio St Univ; Vet Med.

MARKOVICH, C; Albion Sr HS; Albion, MI; Cls Rep Frsh Cls; Cl Rep Jr Cls; Hon Rl; Off Ade; Stu Cncl; Swmmng; Chrldng; Pom Pon; W Michigan Univ.

MARKOVICH, DEBRA; Munster HS; Munster, IN; 17/402 Cls Rep Soph Cls; Cl Rep Jr Cls; Pres Sr Cl s; Hon Rl; NHS; Quill & Scroll; Yrbk; Pep Clb; IM Sprt; College; Math.

MARKOVICH, WILLIAM; Hammond HS; Hammond, IN; 25/350 Cls Rep Frsh Cls; Cls Rep Soph Cls; Cl Rep Jr Cls; NHS; Rptr Sch Nwsp; Crs Cntry; Ftbl; Glf; Trk; Wrstlng; College.

MARKOWSKI, TERESA; Muskegon Catholic Cntrl HS; Muskegon, MI; Hon Rl; Off Ade; Yrbk; Rptr Sch Nwsp; Pep Clb; Spn Clb; Muskegon Community College; Soc Work.

MARKS, DEBBIE; Gilmer County HS; Orlando, WV; Band; Drm Mjrt; Girl Scts; Hon Rl; Yth Flsp; Rptr Yrbk; Rptr Sch Nwsp; 4-H; VICA; Letter Trk; 2nd Rnr Up Black Walnut Majorette 1977; Fairmont Cmnty Coll; RN.

MARKS, DORIS G; Walnut Hills HS; Cincinnati, OH; Hon Rl; Sch Mus; Sch Pl; Lat Clb; Spn Clb; College; English.

MARKS, JAMES C; Brazil Sr HS; Brazil, IN; Band; Chrh Wkr; Hon Rl; Mod UN; NHS; Orch; Quill & Scroll; Sch Pl; Yth Flsp; Yrbk; Indiana Univ; Comp Sci.

MARKS, JERRI; Parkersburg South HS; Washington, WV; Cls Rep Frsh Cls; Cls Rep Soph Cls; Cl Rep Jr Cls; Chrs; Chrh Wkr; Cmnty Wkr; Hon Rl; Off Ade; Quill & Scroll; Yrbk; Sci Fair 76; Washington County Tech Univ; CPA.

MARKS, JIM; Manchester HS; N Manchester, IN; 49/138 VP Aud/Vis; Red Cr Ade; Stg Crw; FBLA; Sec Key Clb; Pep Clb; Letter Bsbl; Capt Ftbl; Capt Wrstlng; Am Leg Awd; Awd Schlrshp From 1st Natl Band Of Wabash; Was Choosen Counties Most Valuable Wrestler; Purdue Univ; Forestry.

MARKS, KARLA; Hamilton Southeastern HS; Fishers, IN; Band; Girl Scts; Hon Rl; Yth Flsp; 4-H; Pep Clb; Letter Bsktbl; Bus Schl; Bus.

MARKS, KATHY; Mt Notre Dame HS; Cincinnati, OH; 1/180 Chrh Wkr; Hon Rl; NHS; Ed Sch Nwsp; Sprt Ed Sch Nwsp; Rptr Sch Nwsp; Spn Clb; Letter Socr; Capt Trk; IM Sprt; Univ.

MARKS, MARY; Our Lady Of Mercy HS; Birmingham, MI; Cls Rep Frsh Cls; Cls Rep Soph Cls; Cl Rep Jr Cls; Chrs; Chrh Wkr; Girl Scts; NHS; Stu Cncl; Mth Clb; Spn Clb; Univ.

MARKS, SARAH; Plymouth Salem HS; Plymouth, MI; 86/540 Hon Rl; NHS; Letter Bsktbl; Letter Trk; Miami Univ; Bus Admin.

MARKS, STEVEN; Charles F Brush HS; Lyndhurst, OH; Pres Frsh Cls; Cls Rep Soph Cls; Cl Rep Jr Cls; Cls Rep Sr Cls; Band; Pres Stu Cncl; Univ Of Michigan; Poli Sci.

MARKSTROM, DARRYL; Les Cheneaux HS; Cedarville, MI; 2/53 VP Frsh Cls; VP Soph Cls; Trs Jr Cls; Pres Sr Cls; Hon Rl; NHS; Off Ade; Bsktbl; Crs Cntry; Ftbl; Mic Tech Univ; Civil Engr.

MARKSTROM, STEVEN; Sault Area HS; Sault Ste Marie, MI; Chrh Wkr; Hon Rl; DECA; Glf; IM Sprt; Ferris State Coll; Pro Golf Mgmt.

MARKUS, RONALD; Colon Jr HS; Colon, MI; Am Leg Boys St; Chrs; Hon Rl; NHS; PAVAS; Yrbk; FFA; FSA; JA Awd; NCTE; Drafting II.

MARLATT, JILL; North Newton HS; Demotte, IN; 4/140 Hon Rl; NHS; Off Ade; Rptr Yrbk; VP FBLA; Spn Clb; GAA; PPFtbl; Univ.

MARLATT, MARGOT S; Interlochen Arts Acad; Klamath Falls, OR; Cls Rep Frsh Cls; Band; Hon Rl; Mdrgl; Orch; Drama Clb; Fr Clb; Gym; Chrldng; Kiwan Awd; College; Concert Cellist.

MARLETT, CHRISTINE; Grand Rapids HS; Grand Rapids, MI; 7/293 Band; Hon Rl; JA; NHS; Sch Mus; Ed Sch Nwsp; Sch Nwsp; Glf; Twrlr; JA Awd; Treas Sec Of Agona Club 78; Jr Coll HS Bus Day 1st Pl Acctg Div I 3rd Pl Accrf Div 2 79; Davenport Coll Of Bus; Acctg.

MARLETT, SALLY; Bishop Borgess HS; Dearborn Hts, MI; Chrh Wkr; Girl Scts; NHS; Fr Clb; Trk; Mgrs; Tmr; College; Educ.

MARLEWSKI, LISA; Stephen T Badin HS; Fairfield, OH; 18/230 Girl Scts; Hon Rl; Sch Mus; FHA; Gym; Trk; Opt Clb Awd; Bus Schl; Sec.

MARLEY, JON; Western HS; Russiaville, IN; 30/220 VP Frsh Cls; VP Soph Cls; FCA; Hon Rl; Stu Cncl; 4-H; Capt Ftbl; Capt Wrstlng; Purdue.

MARLIN, CYNTHIA L; Clay HS; South Bend, IN; Pres Frsh Cls; Cls Rep Frsh Cls; VP Soph Cls; Cls Rep Soph Cls; VP Jr Cls; Cl Rep Jr Cls; Pres Sr Cls; Chrs; Chrh Wkr; Cmnty Wkr; Ball State Univ; Bus.

MARLOW, BARRY; Otsego HS; Grand Rpds, OH; 30/133 Trs Sr Cls; Am Leg Boys St; Band; Boy Scts; Chrs; Chrh Wkr; Cmnty Wkr; Hon Rl; Pol Wkr; Sch Mus; Ohio St Univ; Agri Bus.

MARLOW, PAMELA D; Morton Sr HS; Hammond, IN; Chrh Wkr; Hon Rl; Rptr Sch Nwsp; Fr Clb; Pep Clb; Sec Sci Clb; Capt Trk; PPFtbl; Capt Twrlr; Pur due Calumet Coll; Computer Sci.

MARLOW, SHIRLEY; East HS; Cleveland, OH; 21/227 Hon Rl; Off Ade; Red Cr Ade; Sch Nwsp; Fr Clb; IM Sprt; Cit Awd; Bowling Green St Univ; Spec Ed.

MARLOW, TIMOTHY R; Warren Local HS; Little Hocking, OH; Hon Rl; Sch Pl; Pres Stu Cncl; Rptr Yrbk; Drama Clb; Fr Clb; Natl Merit SF; Top Ten Of Class; Essay Published In Natl Essay Press; Awd For Outstndng Ach In Chemistry; West Virginia Univ; Radiology.

MARLOW, TRACY; William Mason HS; Mason, OH; Trs Frsh Cls; Trs Soph Cls; Chrs; Drl Tm; Hon Rl; Off Ade; Sch Mus; Sch Pl; Stg Crw; DECA; Southern Ohio Coll.

MARLOWE, WANDA M; Holly HS; Holly, MI; 20/298 Hst Jr Cls; Band; Cmp Fr Grls; Chrs; Chrh Wkr; Hon Rl; NHS; Sch Mus; Yth Flsp; 4-H; Whos Who Music 1979; 4 H All Stars 1979; Michigan St Univ.

MARMADUKE, ANITA; Greenwood Community HS; Greenwood, IN; 15/289 Cmp Fr Grls; Hon Rl; Hosp Ade; JA; Yrbk; 4-H; Treas OEA; Pep Clb; Mat Maids; 4-H Awd; Dipolmat Awd In OEA; Indiana Univ; Systems Analyst.

MARMADUKE, ELIZABETH; St Vincent St Mary HS; Akron, OH; 2/265 Sal; Hon Rl; Lit Mag; NHS; Mth Clb; Natl Merit Schl; Firestone Schlrshp 79; 17th Pl Oh Schlstc Achvmnt Test 79; Excel In Math & Outstndg Soc Studies Stu 79; Univ Of Akron; Math.

MARMIE, CRAIG; Newark Catholic HS; Newark, OH; Cl Rep Jr Cls; Hon Rl; Stu Cncl; Fr Clb; Letter Bsbl; Coach Actv; IM Sprt; College; Architecture.

MARMILICK, DIANE; Gladstone Area HS; Gladstone, MI; Hon Rl; Quill & Scroll; Ed Sch Nwsp; Rptr Sch Nwsp; Sch Nwsp; Chrldng; PPFtbl; Northern Michigan Univ; Journalism.

MARMON, ELLEN; Anderson HS; Anderson, IN; 1/560 Band; Chrh Wkr; Hon Rl; Yth Flsp; Lat Clb; Am Leg Awd; Cit Awd; Univ; Educ.

MARNON, LEIGH; Redford Union HS; Redford, MI; Pres Sr Cls; Hon Rl; PAVAS; Sch Mus; Yrbk; Pep Clb; Spn Clb; Letter Bsbl; Chrldng; Am Leg Awd; Univ; Dance.

MARO, CINDY; Ursuline HS; Youngstown, OH; 31/340 Hon Rl; NHS; Off Ade; Pres 4-H; FNA; Ger Clb; Key Clb; Trk; 4-H Awd; Ohio State; Vet.

MAROON, MICHAEL; Linsly Military Inst; Wheeling, WV; 3/60 Band; Chrs; Drm Bgl; Hon Rl; NHS; ROTC; Beta Clb; Fr Clb; Treas Key Clb; IM Sprt; West Virginia Univ; Pre Med.

MAROSI, SHARON; Solon HS; Solon, OH; Chrs; FCA; Hon Rl; NHS; College; Bus.

MARPLE, CHERYL; Buckhannon Upshur HS; Buckhannon, WV; Chrs; Girl Scts; Hon Rl; Lbry Ade; Sct Actv; Yth Flsp; 4-H; Pep Clb; Art Instruction Schls 79; Regional Sci Fair; Air Force Awd 75; Hon Mention 76; Cmrcl Art.

MARQUARDT, ONALEE; T L Handy HS; Bay City, MI; 17/321 Girl Scts; Hon Rl; Lit Mag; NHS; Stu Cncl; Ger Clb; Delta Cmnty Coll; RN.

MARQUART, GREGORY; Wheeling Cntrl Catholic HS; West Alexander, PA; 9/131 Hon Rl; Sch Mus;

Sch Pl; Stg Crw; Drama Clb; Key Clb; NEDT Certificate; West Virginia Univ; Engr.

MARQUART, TODD; Maumee HS; Toledo, OH; Cls Rep Frsh Cls; Boy Scts; Hon Rl; JA; Jr NHS; Orch; Sct Actv; Ftbl; Trk; JA Awd; Bowling Awd Patches & Trophies 77; Sftbll Trophy 78; Univ; Archt.

MARQUEDANT, JOE; Leslie HS; Leslie, MI; Letter Ftbl; Letter Trk; Univ.

MARQUEZ, RODOLFO; Plymouth HS; Plymouth, IN; 10/225 AFS; Hon Rl; NHS; Rptr Sch Nwsp; Eng Clb; Mth Clb; Trk; Natl Merit Ltr; Indiana Univ; Communications.

MARQUIS, MOLLY; Fremont Ross HS; Fremont, OH; Trs Frsh Cls; Cl Rep Jr Cls; Cls Rep Sr Cls; Chrs; Chrh Wkr; Hon Rl; Hosp Ade; Jr NHS; Mod UN; Natl Forn Lg; Purdue Univ; Communications.

MARQUISS, STEVE; Midland HS; Midland, MI; Hon Rl; Ferris State.

MARRA, ROBERT A; Bridgeport HS; Bridgeport, WV; Cls Rep Frsh Cls; Cls Rep Soph Cls; Cl Rep Jr Cls; Chrh Wkr; Hon Rl; Jr NHS; NHS; Stu Cncl; Key Clb; Spn Clb; Baseball Basketball & Football Awds; College; Dentistry.

MARRA, STEVE; Oakwood HS; Dayton, OH; Trs Soph Cls; Band; Chrs; FCA; Hon Rl; Sct Actv; Bsbl; Bsktbl; Ftbl; Trk; College; Pre Med.

MARRIAGE, ELDINA; Ovid Elsie HS; Ovid, MI; 2/179 Trs Soph Cls; Sal; Band; Chrh Wkr; Drl Tm; Hon Rl; NHS; Rptr Yrbk; Pep Clb; Letter Bsktbl; 3 Ltrs In Volleybl; Cntrl Michigan Univ; Law.

MARRINAN, PATRICK; Carroll HS; Dayton, OH; Trs Frsh Cls; Trs Soph Cls; Stu Cncl; Yth Flsp; Ed Sch Nwsp; Spn Clb; Letter Socr; Kiwan Awd; Univ Of Dayton; Education.

MARSEE, SHARON; Monrovia HS; Martinsville, IN; 31/140 Chrs; Drl Tm; Hon Rl; Lbry Ade; Off Ade; Y-Teens; Drama Clb; Spn Clb; PPFtbl; Ben Davis Voc Schl.

MARSH, CARL; Grosse Pointe North HS; Grosse Pt Wds, MI; Hon Rl; Trk; Univ.

MARSH, DANIEL; New Richmond HS; New Richmond, OH; 26/195 Hon Rl; Lit Mag; NHS; Quill & Scroll; Rptr Yrbk; Yrbk; Fr Clb; VP FSA; Univ Ov Cincinnati; Pharmacy.

MARSH, DEBBIE; Wilbur Wright HS; Dayton, OH; Drl Tm; Girl Scts; Hon Rl; Lbry Ade; Stu Cncl; Yrbk; Sch Nwsp; Boys Clb Am; Fr Clb; FHA; Miami Coll; Chemistry.

MARSH, DOUGLAS E; Edison HS; Milan, OH; AFS; Am Leg Boys St; Boy Scts; Jr NHS; NHS; Sch Pl; Stg Crw; Drama Clb; Mth Clb; Spn Clb; Ohio State Univ; Sci.

MARSH, DOUGLAS J; Oregon Davis HS; Hamlet, IN; Hon Rl; Jr NHS; FFA; IM Sprt;.

MARSH, ELIZABETH; Maumee HS; Maumee, OH; 10/336 Hon Rl; NHS; Sch Pl; Chmn Y-Teens; Yrbk; Drama Clb; Chrldng; Kiwan Awd; Skidmore Coll.

MARSH, GAIL; Medina Senior HS; Medina, OH; Chrs; Sch Mus; 4-H; Pep Clb; College; Bus.

MARSH, GINA E; Graham HS; St Paris, OH; 29/185 Hon Rl; FHA; JA Awd; Natl Merit Ltr; Bus Schl.

MARSH, GREGORY B; Strongsville Sr HS; Strongsville, OH; Hon Rl; Bsbl; Glf; Letter Ten; IM Sprt; Natl Merit SF; Coll; Chem Engr.

MARSH, IWANDA K; Oregon Davis HS; Hamlet, IN; 1/68 Am Leg Aux Girls St; Band; Hon Rl; NHS; Pres Yth Flsp; Rptr Yrbk; Drama Clb; 4-H; Pres FHA; Treas Pep Clb; Ball St Univ; Spec Ed.

MARSH, JAMIE; Eaton Rapids HS; Eaton Rapids, MI; 37/229 Trs Frsh Cls; Trs Soph Cls; Cmp Fr Grls ; Hon Rl; Off Ade; Stu Cncl; Rptr Yrbk; Rptr Sch Nwsp; 4-H; Spn Clb; Univ.

MARSH, JULIE; Ben Davis HS; Indianapolis, IN; Band; FCA; Hon Rl; Pep Clb; IM Sprt; PPFtbl; College; Lab Tech.

MARSH, KAREN; Mt Vernon Academy; Toledo, OH; Chrs; FCA; Hon Rl; Gym; Coach Actv; Scr Kpr; Cit Awd; Univ; Sec.

MARSH, LISA; Northside HS; Muncie, IN; Trs Frsh Cls; Sec Soph Cls; Cl Rep Jr Cls; Cls Rep Sr Cls; Sec FCA; Hon Rl; Jr NHS; NHS; Pep Clb; Letter Gym; Ball St Univ; Spec Educ.

MARSH, MARLA; Akron East Sr HS; Akron, OH; Cl Rep Jr Cls; Cls Rep Sr Cls; Chrh Wkr; Cmnty Wkr; JA; Off Ade; Stu Cncl; Pres Fr Clb; Pep Clb; Pres Spn Clb; Ltrmns Club Sec 79; Ushers Club Treas 78; Spirit Comm Co Chrpsn 79; Univ; Phys Ther.

MARSH, MELANIE; Monongah HS; Worthington, WV; 17/96 Cl Rep Jr Cls; Hon Rl; Stu Cncl; Yth Flsp; Y-Teens; Fr Clb; Pep Clb; Chrldng; Fairmont State; Med Asst.

MARSH, MICHAEL; Normandy HS; Seven Hls, OH; 19/650 Hon Rl; Lat Clb; Crs Cntry; Trk; IM Sprt; Univ; Engr.

MARSH, MONICA; Akron East Sr HS; Akron, OH; Cls Rep Sr Cls; Chrh Wkr; Cmnty Wkr; JA; Off Ade; Stu Cncl; Sec Fr Clb; Pep Clb; Sec Spn Clb; Letter Socr; Mbr Of Akron Pblc Schl Superintendent Stdnt Seminar; Ushers Club Pres; Mbr East High Lettermens Club; College; Phys Therapy.

MARSH, PAM; Peru Sr HS; Peru, IN; Band; Chrs; Chrh Wkr;.

MARSH, SHELLEY R; Owosso HS; Owosso, MI; 137/450 Band; Chrs; Drm Mjrt; Hon Rl; Orch; 4-H; 4-H Awd; Eastern Michigan Univ; Occptnl Ther.

MARSH, STEVEN; Bexley HS; Bexley, OH; Band; Hon Rl; Sch Pl; Stg Crw; Drama Clb; Fr Clb; Mth Clb; Univ.

MARSH, TERRI; Ross Sr HS; Hamilton, OH; Band; Hon Rl; Orch; FFA; College; Horticulture.

MARSH, WANDA; Oregon Davis HS; Hamlet, IN; 1/66 Val; Am Leg Aux Girls St; Band; Hon Rl; NHS; Pres Yth Flsp; Rptr Yrbk; Treas 4-H; Pres FHA; Treas Pep Clb; Ball St Univ; Spec Ed.

MARSHAL, BRENDA; Versailles HS; Versailles, OH; 42/125 Band; Chrs; Sch Mus; Sch Pl; 4-H; Chrldng; 4-H Awd; Coll; Stewardess.

MARSHALL, B; Richmond Sr HS; Richmond, IN; 26/550 CAP; Hon Rl; VP JA; Jr NHS; NHS; Y-Teens; Rptr Sch Nwsp; Spn Clb; Letter Mgrs; Univ; Dentist.

MARSHALL, BARBARA; Northview HS; Grand Rapids, MI; 42/289 Sec Sr Cls; Band; Boy Scts; Drm Mjrt; Hon Rl; Stu Cncl; Swmmng; Mgrs; Tmr; Rotary Awd; Stdnt Govt Schslhp 79; Prom Ct 79; Michigan St Univ; Pre Nursing.

MARSHALL, BRUCE; North Vermillion Schl Corp; Covington, IN; 7/101 Band; Chrh Wkr; FCA; Hon Rl; NHS; Y-Teens; Sci Clb; Letter Ftbl; Socr; Trk; Schlr In Athletics Awd 76 77 & 78; Seltd To Amer HS Athlete 78; Best Defensive Player Soccer 76; Danville Area Cmnty Coll.

MARSHALL, BRYAN; Richmond Sr Shs; Richmond, IN; 26/550 CAP; Hon Rl; VP JA; NHS; Y-Teens; Rptr Sch Nwsp; Spn Clb; IM Sprt; Letter Mgrs; I U Hon Progr For HS Stndt For Std Progr 79; Altrnt For Hoosier Boys St 79; Univ; Pre Dent.

MARSHALL, CAROL; Eastern HS; Salem, IN; 5/91 Sec Soph Cls; VP Jr Cls; Hon Rl; NHS; Off Ade; Pep Clb; Sec Spn Clb; Letter Trk; Letter Chrldng; GAA; Business Schl; Legal Sec.

MARSHALL, DAVID; Thomas W Harvey HS; Painesville, OH; Band; Hon Rl; NHS; Orch; Sch Pl; Stg Crw; Drama Clb; Pep Clb; Ohio St Univ; Dentistry.

MARSHALL, DENISE; Graham HS; St Paris, OH; 22/165 Band; Chrs; Hon Rl; Lit Mag; Rptr Sch Nwsp; 4-H; FHA; GAA; Ohio St Board Of Ed Awd Of Distinction For Completion Of St Ed Course Of Basic Studies; Barbizon Schl Of Fashion; Fash Merch.

MARSHALL, DIANE; Trinity HS; Garfield Hts, OH; 15/175 Cls Rep Frsh Cls; Pres Soph Cls; Cl Rep Jr Cls; Pres Sr Cls; Chrs; Drm Mjrt; Hon Rl; NHS; Letter Bsbl; Bsktbl;.

MARSHALL, DORINDA; North Vermillion HS; Perrysville, IN; 5/59 Band; Chrs; Chrh Wkr; Hon Rl; Lbry Ade; NHS; Drama Clb; Scr Kpr; Butler Univ; Cmnctns.

MARSHALL, DOROTHY K; Centennial HS; Columbus, OH; 108/216 Drl Tm; Hon Rl; Rptr Sch Nwsp; Sch Nwsp; VP DECA; VICA; Coach Actv; IM Sprt; PPFtbl; Scr Kpr; Amer Jr Bowling Congress Jr Leader; Ohio St Univ; Busns Admin.

MARSHALL, H; Saint Joseph Central HS; Huntington, WV; Cl Rep Jr Cls; Boy Scts; Hon Rl; Sch Pl; Sct Actv; Stu Cncl; Sch Nwsp; FBLA; FSA; Mth Clb; West Virginia Inst; Mechanical Engin.

MARSHALL, JANNICE; Charles F Kettering HS; Detroit, MI; Hst Jr Cls; Hst Sr Cls; Hon Rl; NHS; Univ Of North Carolina; Bus Admin.

MARSHALL, JEAN; Athen HS; Troy, MI; Band; Cmp Fr Grls; Chrs; Hon Rl; NHS; Sct Actv; Oakland Univ; Soc Work.

MARSHALL, JODIE; Bedford Sr HS; Bedford Hts, OH; 48/533 Hon Rl; NHS; Fr Clb; Ger Clb; Spn Clb; IM Sprt; Westminster Coll; Foreign Lang.

MARSHALL, J RENA; Buffalo HS; Kenova, WV; 4/141 Am Leg Aux Girls St; Band; Girl Scts; Hon Rl; Mod UN; Sec NHS; Sch Pl; Stg Crw; Drama Clb; VP 4-H; Marshall Univ.

MARSHALL, KAREN; Coshocton HS; Coshocton, OH; 1/231 Val; Band; VP Band; Cmnty Wkr; Hon Rl; Sec NHS; Sch Pl; Yth Flsp; Rptr Sch Nwsp; PPFtbl; Ohio St Univ; Music Educ.

MARSHALL, KAREN A; East Technical HS; Cleveland, OH; Cls Rep Frsh Cls; Cls Rep Soph Cls; Cl Rep Jr Cls; Cls Rep Sr Cls; Band; Drl Tm; Lbry Ade; Off Ade; Pol Wkr; Stu Cncl; Schslp Finslt With Clevelnd Sclshp 79; Allied Health & Offc Aide 79; Akron Univ; Resp Ther.

MARSHALL, KELLY; Marlington HS; Alliance, OH; Hon Rl; Lbry Ade; Rptr Sch Nwsp; Sci Clb; Spn Clb; Scr Kpr; Ohio Univ; Pharmacy.

MARSHALL, KRISTINE K; Rochester Sr HS; Utica, MI; 67/400 Hon Rl; NHS; Federal Grant; Oakland Univ; History.

MARSHALL, LANA; Monrovia HS; Monrovia, IN; 15/105 VP Soph Cls; VP Jr Cls; VP Sr Cls; Sec NHS; Off Ade; Rptr Yrbk; 4-H; Bsktbl; 4-H Awd;.

MARSHALL, LISA; Lakeview HS; Cortland, OH; Am Leg Aux Girls St; Band; Hon Rl; Yrbk; Beta Clb; Spn Clb; Letter Trk; Youngstown St Univ; Criminology.

MARSHALL, MARY; Chesaning Union HS; Burt, MI; Cmp Fr Grls; Chrh Wkr; Hon Rl; Letter Swmmng; Chrldng; Cosmetologists School.

MARSHALL, MIKE; John F Kennedy HS; Warren, OH; Band; Youngstown St Univ.

MARSHALL, RENA; Buffalo HS; Kenova, WV; 4/141 Am Leg Aux Girls St; Band; Girl Scts; Hon Rl; Mod UN; NHS; Sch Pl; 4-H; FHA; Mth Clb; Marshall Univ.

MARSHALL, RHONDA; Forest Park HS; Birdseye, IN; 70/136 Pres Sr Cls; VP Sr Cls; Chrs; Quill & Scroll; Sch Mus; Yrbk; Rptr Sch Nwsp; Sch Nwsp; 4-H; FHA; Voc Schl; Photog.

MARSHALL, ROBERT; Waverly HS; Waverly, OH; Boy Scts; Sct Actv; Spn Clb; College; Comp Sci.

MARSHALL, ROBERT; George Washington HS; Charleston, WV; 37/350 Cls Rep Soph Cls; Cl Rep Jr Cls; VP Sr Cls; Cls Rep Sr Cls; Aud/Vis; Cmnty Wkr; Hon Rl; Jr NHS; Red Cr Ade; Trk; Washington & Lee Univ; Engr.

MARSHALL, SANDRA; Wilmington Sr HS; Wilmington, OH; Chrh Wkr; Drl Tm; Girl Scts; Hon Rl; Off Ade; Pres Y-Teens; Trk; Coach Actv; Univ.

MARSHALL, SHERRI L; Union HS; Grand Rapids, MI; Chrh Wkr; Girl Scts; Pres Jr NHS; Lbry Ade; Off Ade; Gym; Chrldng; Pom Pon; Cit Awd; Western Univ; Busns Admin.

MARSHALL, STEPHANIE; Sandusky HS; Sandusky, OH; Cl Rep Jr Cls; Band; Hon Rl; Jr NHS; NHS; Orch; Ger Clb; Ohio St Univ.

MARSHALL, SUSAN; Waldron HS; Shelbyville, IN; 4/72 Cls Rep Frsh Cls; Cl Rep Jr Cls; Hosp Ade; Stu Cncl; Rptr Sch Nwsp; Lat Clb; Pep Clb; Letter Trk; Chrldng; Miami Univ; Political Sci.

MARSISCHKY, JOHN; Bloomington HS; Bloomington, IN; 95/393 Pres Orch; Sch Mus; IM Sprt; Ind Univ; Archeology.

MARSOLF, CHRIS; Rosedale HS; Rockville, IN; 1/69 Val; Band; NHS; 4-H; Sci Clb; Rose Hulman Inst Of Tech; Comp Sci.

MARSON, EDWIN C; Rocky River HS; Rocky River, OH; Boy Scts; Hon Rl; Orch; Sch Mus; Sch Pl; Sct Actv; Yrbk; Sch Nwsp; Univ; Lib Arts.

MARSON, MARY; Saint Clement HS; Centerine, MI; 1/125 Girl Scts; Hon Rl; JA; NHS; Sch Pl; Stu Cncl; Rptr Sch Nwsp; Coll; Nursing.

MARSTELLER, LYNNE D; Lakota HS; W Chester, OH; 57/459 Band; Chrh Wkr; Cmnty Wkr; Hon Rl; Off Ade; Yth Flsp; Ger Clb; Letter Bsbl; Ohio St Univ; Engr.

MARTEN, LINDA; Bowling Green HS; Bowling Green, OH; 61/325 Cls Rep Frsh Cls; Band; Chrs; Chrh Wkr; Hon Rl; Jr NHS; NHS; Off Ade; Yth Flsp; 4-H; Ohio State Univ; Medical.

MARTENEY, ALAN; Bridgeport Sr HS; Bridgeport, WV; Am Leg Boys St; Jr NHS; NHS; Sch Pl; Ten; West Virginia Univ; Civil Engr.

MARTENS, BRENDA; Magnificat HS; Fairview Pk, OH; Boy Scts; Chrh Wkr; JA; Off Ade; Sct Actv; IM Sprt; Bowling Green State Univ; Bus.

MARTENS, CHARITA; Woodward HS; Toledo, OH; Chrh Wkr; Cmnty Wkr; Hosp Ade; JA; Red Cr Ade; FNA; FSA; VICA; Cit Awd; JA Awd; Coll; Nursing.

MARTENSEN, LISA; George Rogers Clark HS; Whiting, IN; 14/218 Cls Rep Soph Cls; Band; Girl Scts; Jr NHS; NHS; Orch; Quill & Scroll; Sch Pl; Stu Cncl; Yrbk; Catholic Youth Organ Sec 78; Indiana Univ; Graphic Art.

MARTENY, NELSON; South Harrison HS; Mt Clare, WV; 10/86 Hon Rl; Jr NHS; NHS; Sch Pl; Yth Flsp; Boys Clb Am; Am Leg Awd; Dnfth Awd; Fairmont State Coll; Acctg.

MARTILOTTA, ROBERT; Bishop Gallagher HS; Detroit, MI; Cl Rep Jr Cls; Val; Hon Rl; NHS; Quill & Scroll; Sch Mus; Sch Pl; Rptr Sch Nwsp; Sch Nwsp; Letter Trk; Univ Of Detroit; Psych.

MARTILOTTA, ROBERT J; Bishop Gallagher HS; Detroit, MI; 1/350 Hon Rl; NHS; Quill & Scroll; Sch Pl; Stu Cncl; Sch Nwsp; Letter Trk; Natl Merit SF; Psych.

MARTIN, ALLEN; South Central HS; Elizabeth, IN; 1/65 Trs Frsh Cls; Hon Rl; NHS; Sch Pl; Stg Crw; Yth Flsp; Drama Clb; Fr Clb; Letter Crs Cntry; College; Engr.

MARTIN, ALLEN; South Central Jr Sr HS; Elizabeth, IN; 1/60 Trs Frsh Cls; Hon Rl; NHS; Sch Pl; Ed Yrbk; Fr Clb; Letter Crs Cntry; Univ; Physics.

MARTIN, ANITA; Bloomfield HS; N Bloomfield, OH; 2/43 Cl Rep Jr Cls; Band; Chrs; Chrh Wkr; Hon Rl; Hosp Ade; Lbry Ade; NHS; Off Ade; Sch Mus; Kent St Univ; Nursing.

MARTIN, ANN; Martinsville HS; Martinsville, IN; 43/391 Chrh Wkr; NHS; Rptr Yrbk; Rptr Sch Nwsp; Spn Clb; Univ.

MARTIN, ANNE; Culver Girls Academy; Laredo, TX; 18/200 Cls Rep Frsh Cls; Chrs; Girl Scts; Hon Rl; Sct Actv; Stu Cncl; Rptr Yrbk; 4-H; Sci Clb; Letter Ten; Univ; Bus.

MARTIN, ANNETTE; Morgantown HS; Morgantown, WV; Band; Chrs; Chrh Wkr; Cmnty Wkr; Hon Rl; Jr NHS; Pol Wkr; Quill & Scroll; Yth Flsp; Yrbk; West Virginia Univ; Comp Sci.

MARTIN, BARBARA J; Grove City HS; Grove City, OH; 38/449 Cls Rep Frsh Cls; Aud/Vis; Band; Chrs; Chrh Wkr; Cmnty Wkr; Hon Rl; JA; Orch; Stg Crw; Cincinnati Consrv Of Music; Entertnr.

MARTIN, BILL; Griffith HS; Griffith, IN; Hon Rl; Sci Clb; Bsbl; Letter Ftbl; IM Sprt; College.

MARTIN, BILL; Moorefield HS; Moorefield, WV; 11/80 Cls Rep Frsh Cls; Am Leg Boys St; Hon Rl; Jr NHS; NHS; Sch Pl; Stu Cncl; 4-H; FFA; 4-H Awd; West Virginia Univ; Agri.

MARTIN, BLAINE; Rockville HS; Rockville, IN; Hon Rl; Yrbk; Lat Clb; Bsbl; Ten; Ind State Univ; Commercial Design.

MARTIN, BRENDA; Watkins Memorial HS; Pataskala, OH; 53/226 Band; Hon Rl; Yth Flsp; 4-H; FFA; FFA Schlrshp Awd; FFA Queen; FFA Horse Proficiency Awd; Central Ohio Tech Coll; Nursing.

MARTIN, BRENDA; Chadsey HS; Detroit, MI; Hon Rl; Mth Clb; Wayne Univ; Comp Engr.

MARTIN, BRIAN; Taylor Center HS; Taylor, MI; 16/400 Cls Rep Frsh Cls; Am Leg Boys St; Hon Rl; NHS; Sch Nwsp; Letter Bsbl; Letter Ftbl; PPFtbl; Am Leg Awd; Ferris St Coll; Optometry.

MARTIN, CAROL; Brookville HS; Oxford, OH; Cls Rep Soph Cls; Band; Hosp Ade; Lbry Ade; Stu Cncl; Rptr Yrbk; Rptr Sch Nwsp; 4-H; Pep Clb; Bsktbl; Christ Hospital Of Nursing; RN.

MARTIN, CATHY; Northrop HS; Ft Wayne, IN; 41/554 Chrh Wkr; FCA; Girl Scts; Hon Rl; Hosp Ade; Letter Ten; Chrldng; Vllybl Ltr Highst Serv % Awd 78 &79; Ball St Univ; Acctg.

MARTIN, CHRISTINA; London HS; London, OH; 4/155 Jr NHS; Lit Mag; NHS; PAVAS; Sch Mus; Sch Pl; Fr Clb; Chrldng; Cit Awd; Kiwan Awd; Ent Into The M Exxex Schl For The Giftd 79; Field Study To Anddros Island Bahamas Through 78 The Intl Field; Univ; Oceanography.

MARTIN, CLIFFORD; South HS; Youngstown, OH; 1/330 Trs Frsh Cls; Val; Hon Rl; Jr NHS; NHS; JETS Awd; Natl Merit Ltr; Carneige Mellon Univ; Engr.

MARTIN, CLIFTON; Valley View HS; Frmrsvl, OH; Hon Rl; NHS; Yth Flsp; Letter Bsbl; Bsktbl; Cit Awd; College.

MARTIN, CONNIE; Woodrow Wilson HS; Beckley, WV; Hon Rl; NHS; Stu Cncl; Sprt Ed Yrbk; Yrbk; Pep Clb; Trk; Chrldng; West Virginia Univ; Phys Ther.

MARTIN, CURTIS; Grandville HS; Grand Rapids, MI; Band; Debate Tm; Letter Trk; Grand Rapids Bapt Coll.

MARTIN, CYNTHIA; John Hay HS; Cleveland, OH; Cls Rep Sr Cls; Hon Rl; Jr NHS; NHS; Rptr Sch Nwsp; Univ Of Bridgeport; Marine Bio.

MARTIN, DANIEL; David Anderson HS; Leetonia, OH; 50/116 Aud/Vis; Chrs; Sch Mus; Sch Pl; Stg Crw; Yth Flsp; Sprt Ed Yrbk; Boys Clb Am; 4-H; Sci Clb; Hiram Coll; Bio.

MARTIN, DARICK; Toledo Scott HS; Toledo, OH; Cls Rep Frsh Cls; Cls Rep Soph Cls; Hon Rl; NHS; Boys Clb Am; Mth Clb; Spn Clb; Letter Bsbl; Letter Bsktbl; Univ; Law.

MARTIN, DARLENE; Toronto HS; Toronto, OH; Band; Chrs; Chrh Wkr; Hosp Ade; Sch Mus; Stg Crw; Sec Yth Flsp; Spn Clb; Coll; Chldhd Educ.

MARTIN, DAVE; East HS; Akron, OH; 103/350 Boy Scts; Chrh Wkr; Sch Pl; Sct Actv; Stu Cncl; Fr Clb; Letter Bsbl; Crs Cntry; IM Sprt; Ariz State Univ; Math.

MARTIN, DAVID; Wayland HS; Wayland, MI; 1/200 Cls Rep Sr Cls; Val; Boy Scts; Debate Tm; Natl Forn Lg; NHS; Sch Pl; Sci Clb; Wrstlng; Natl Merit Ltr; Overall 1s Tpl Blossom Land Regnl Sci Fair 79; 3rd Pl Intl Sci Fair 79; St Finlst Extempore Spkng 79; Univ Of Michigan; Engr.

MARTIN, DAVID; Bluefield HS; Freeman, WV; 24/285 Am Leg Boys St; Hon Rl; NHS; Quill & Scroll; Yrbk; Fr Clb; Key Clb; Bsktbl; Crs Cntry; Trk; All Cntry Bnd; Stu Cncl Exec Comm; Eng Typing & Frnch Awd; Virginia Tech Univ; Bus Admin.

MARTIN, DAVID; Theodore Roosevelt HS; Wyandotte, MI; Band; Chrh Wkr; Cmnty Wkr; Debate Tm; Hon Rl; Jr NHS; NHS; Sch Mus; Sch Pl; Pres Stu Cncl; Michigan Tech Univ; Chem Engr.

MARTIN, DEAN; La Ville Jr Sr HS; Plymouth, IN; Am Leg Boys St; Hon Rl; Am Leg Awd; Brick Layer.

MARTIN, DEANNA; Southwood HS; Somerset, IN; 23/118 Band; Chrs; Chrh Wkr; FCA; Hon Rl; Sch Pl; Yth Flsp; Drama Clb; 4-H; Pep Clb; Purdue Univ; Science.

MARTIN, DEBORAH; Northeastern HS; Fountain Cy, IN; 5/139 Drl Tm; Hon Rl; Hosp Ade; NHS; Sec 4-H; FFA; Lat Clb; Trk; Pom Pon; 4 H Grand Champion Plant Sci; Coll; Med.

MARTIN, DEBORAH; Adrian HS; Blissfield, MI; 19/384 Chrs; Hon Rl; Sch Mus; Yrbk; Michigan Dept Of Educ 79; Michigan St Univ; Music Ther.

MARTIN, DEBORAH; Dunbar Sr HS; Dunbar, WV; Hon Rl; Lbry Ade; NHS; 4-H; Pres Fr Clb; IM Sprt; 4-H Awd; West Virginia Wesleyan Univ; Comp Pr.

MARTIN, DENISE; M L King HS; Detroit, MI; 4/200 Cls Rep Sr Cls; Chrs; Cmnty Wkr; Hon Rl; JA; NHS; Stu Cncl; OEA; Sci Clb; Trk; Michigan St Univ; Elec Engr.

MARTIN, DENNIS; Salem HS; Salem, IN; 2/170 Chrs; Hon Rl; NHS; Sci Clb; Letter Crs Cntry; Letter Trk; Purdue Univ; Engr.

MARTIN, E; Lumen Christi HS; Jackson, MI; 11/231 Cls Rep Frsh Cls; Cls Rep Soph Cls; Cl Rep Jr Cls; Hon Rl; NHS; Stu Cncl; Fr Clb; Capt Gym; Michigan State Univ; French.

MARTIN, EDDIE; Marsh Fork HS; Dry Creek, WV; Pres Frsh Cls; Hon Rl; NHS; Ed Yrbk; Yrbk; Rptr Sch Nwsp; Drama Clb; Pep Clb; Concord Coll; Bus Admin.

MARTIN, ELIZABETH; Sullivan HS; Shelburn, IN; Chrs; Girl Scts; Hon Rl; Lbry Ade; Sch Mus; FHA; Lat Clb; Pep Clb; PPFtbl; Indiana St Univ; Comp Tech.

MARTIN, ELIZABETH; Meadowbrook HS; Cumberland, OH; 6/179 Hon Rl; NHS; Rptr Yrbk; Pres 4-H; FTA; Key Clb; Sec Mth Clb; Pep Clb; Sci Clb; Spn Clb; Ohio State Univ; Agri Communications.

MARTIN, FELICIA; Notre Dame HS; Stonewood, WV; Yrbk; Drama Clb; FBLA; FTA; Chrldng; Fairmont State; Erly Chldhd Educ.

MARTIN, FREDRICK; River Valley HS; Three Oaks, MI; Hon Rl; NHS; Yth Flsp; 4-H; 4-H Awd; Univ; Comp Progr.

MARTIN, GERARDINE; Pewamo Westphalia HS; Fowler, MI; Band; Drm Bgl; Hon Rl; 4-H; 4-H Awd; Lansing Cmnty Coll; Data Proc.

MARTIN, GINGER; St Philip Catholic Ctrl HS; Battle Creek, MI; Cl Rep Jr Cls; Am Leg Aux Girls St; Hon Rl; NHS; Stu Cncl; Lat Clb; Pep Clb; Capt Chrldng; Coach Actv; Univ; Med Lab Tech.

MARTIN, GREGORY; St Albans HS; St Albans, WV; Cls Rep Sr Cls; Hon Rl; Stg Crw; Stu Cncl; Spn Clb; Letter Bsbl; Babe Ruth Bsbl Athlete Of Yr 76; Interact Clb Pres 78; Univ; Bio Chem.

MARTIN, GREGORY; Whiteford HS; Ottawa Lk, MI; Sch Mus; Sch Pl; Stg Crw; Drama Clb; Bsbl; Letter Ftbl; College; Forestry.

MARTIN, J; Richmond HS; Richmond, IN; Hon Rl; Sch Pl; Y-Teens; Drama Clb; Spn Clb; College; Pharmacy.

MARTIN, J; Trenton HS; Trenton, MI; Band; Boy Scts; Chrs; Chrh Wkr; Hon Rl; Jr NHS; Ger Clb; College; Med.

MARTIN, JACKIE; Lincoln HS; Shinnston, WV; Girl Scts; Hon Rl; Yrbk; Swmmng; Voc Schl; Comp Prog.

MARTIN, JACQUELINE; East Catholic HS; Detroit, MI; 3/67 Cls Rep Frsh Cls; Sec Soph Cls; Trs Jr Cls; Trs Sr Cls; Chrs; Sec Chrh Wkr; Hon Rl; Off Ade; Pol Wkr; Bsktbl; Univ Of Detroit; Poli Sci.

MARTIN, JAMES; Culver Military Acad; Culver, IN; 15/198 Hon Rl; ROTC; Yth Flsp; Ed Yrbk; Rptr Yrbk; Yrbk; Rptr Sch Nwsp; Sch Nwsp; Letter Glf; Letter Socr; Coll Of William & Mary; Pre Med.

MARTIN, JAMES; Monongah HS; Worthington, WV; 14/51 Band; Hon Rl; 4-H; Fr Clb; Elk Awd; 4-H Awd; Lion Awd; Voice Dem Awd; Fairmont State College; Elec Engr.

MARTIN, JAMES A; George Washington HS; Charleston, WV; Cls Rep Frsh Cls; Boy Scts; Sch Pl; Ed Yrbk; Rptr Yrbk; Yrbk; Drama Clb; Univ Of Cincinnati; Archt.

MARTIN, JAMES K; Princeton HS; Princeton, WV; Hon Rl; Jr NHS; Pres NHS; Quill & Scroll; Sch Nwsp; Key Clb; Spn Clb; Letter Bsktbl; Crs Cntry; DAR Awd; Davidson Coll; Bio.

MARTIN, JEFF; Kings HS; Loveland, OH; 2/157 Hon Rl; NHS; Sprt Ed Yrbk; Yrbk; Fr Clb; Ftbl; Letter Glf; Pres Of Natl Hon Soc 79; Comp Tech Prog.

MARTIN, JEFFREY; St Francis De Sales HS; Temperance, MI; 11/203 Cmnty Wkr; Debate Tm; Hon Rl; Pres Natl Forn Lg; NHS; Stu Cncl; Rptr Sch Nwsp; IM Sprt; Univ; Bus.

MARTIN, JIM; Warsaw Community HS; Warsaw, IN; Trs Jr Cls; Hon Rl; Stg Crw; Stu Cncl; DECA; IM Sprt; Gov Hon Prg Awd; Vincennes Univ; Law.

MARTIN, JIM; Father Joseph Wehrle Mem HS; Columbus, OH; 1/115 Aud/Vis; Hon Rl; Lbry Ade; NHS; Sch Pl; Stg Crw; Drama Clb; Fr Clb; Ten; Office Helper; French Awd For 2 Yrs; Typing Awd 75 Words A Minute; Ohio St Univ; Law.

MARTIN, JIM; Bishop Fenwick HS; Middletown, OH; Hon Rl; Bsbl; Ftbl; IM Sprt; Ohi Univ; Sales Mrktg.

MARTIN, JODI; Bishop Watterson HS; Columbus, OH; 20/244 Cl Rep Jr Cls; Hon Rl; Jr NHS; NHS; Letter Bsktbl; PPFtbl; Wright St Univ; Phys Educ.

MARTIN, JOHN; Cheboygan Area HS; Cheboygan, MI; Boy Scts; Hon Rl; Fr Clb; IM Sprt; Western Col Univ; Accounting.

MARTIN, JOHN S; Dexter HS; Ann Arbor, MI; 1/175 Val; Am Leg Boys St; Band; Hon Rl; Lit Mag; NHS; Sch Pl; Sct Actv; Stg Crw; Yrbk; Univ; Law.

MARTIN, JULE; Coloma HS; Coloma, MI; Cls Rep Frsh Cls; Hon Rl; Lbry Ade; Stu Cncl; 4-H; Trk; Mat Maids; Scr Kpr; 4-H Awd; Ferris State; Law.

MARTIN, JULIE; Washington HS; Massillon, OH; Band; Hon Rl; Jr NHS; NHS; Y-Teens; Pep Clb; Tmr; Stark Tech Voc Schl; Resp Ther.

MARTIN, KARIN; Grand Ledge HS; Dewitt, MI; NHS; Lansing Community College; Sci.

MARTIN, KATHLEEN; Green HS; Uniontown, OH; Sch Mus; Sch Pl; Y-Teens; Trk; IM Sprt; Pom Pon; Scr Kpr; Univ Of Georgia; Mgmt Acctg.

MARTIN, KELLY; Philo HS; Philo, OH; 78/205 Band; Girl Scts; Hon Rl; Lit Mag; Stg Crw; Yrbk; Rptr Sch Nwsp; Sch Nwsp; Spn Clb; Trk;.

MARTIN, KENNETH; Jefferson Area Local HS; Jefferson, OH; 9/192 Chrh Wkr; Hon Rl; Stg Crw; Yth Flsp; Fr Clb; Ten; Top Male Score In Amer Lgns Amer Test; Varsity Ltr In Ftbl; Usher For Grad; Prom Decrtn Comm; Bowling Green St Univ; Bus Mgmt.

MARTIN, KEVIN; Northmont HS; Englewood, OH; 61/517 Trs Soph Cls; Trs Jr Cls; VP Sr Cls; Boy Scts; Hon Rl; 4-H; Ftbl; Univ Of Ohi; Bus Acct.

MARTIN, KIM; Girard HS; Girard, OH; 6/200 Trs Jr Cls; Hon Rl; Stu Cncl; Y-Teens; Spn Clb; Gym; Scr Kpr; College; Elem Ed.

MARTIN, LAURI; Indian Hill HS; Cincinnati, OH; 16/280 Chrh Wkr; Hon Rl; Stu Cncl; Yth Flsp; Yrbk; Hndbl; Swmmng; Coach Actv; IM Sprt; PPFtbl; College; Med Career.

MARTIN, LAWRENCE; Castle Sr HS; Newburgh, IN; Chrh Wkr; Hon Rl; 4-H; Bsbl; Coach Actv; IM Sprt; 4-H Awd; Univ Of Indiana; Visual Arts Tchr.

MARTIN, LINDA; Little Miami HS; Loveland, OH; Chrs; Chrh Wkr; Girl Scts; Hon Rl; Lit Mag; NHS; Sct Actv; Yth Flsp; Ger Clb; Spn Clb; Otstndng Spanish 4 Stud 79; Studied Piano 74; Univ; Lang.

MARTIN, LINDA; Marsh Fork HS; Dry Creek, WV; Am Leg Aux Girls St; Band; Chrs; Chrh Wkr; Cmnty Wkr; Debate Tm; Hon Rl; VP NHS; Sch Mus; Sch Pl; Concord Univ; Psych.

MARTIN, LORA; West Carrollton HS; W Carrollton, OH; 37/418 Letter Band; Chrs; Chrh Wkr; Cmnty Wkr; Hon Rl; Jr NHS; Natl Forn Lg; NHS; College.

MARTIN, LUTHER W; St Xavier HS; Springdale, OH; 107/270 Band; Mth Clb; Sci Clb; JETS Awd; Natl Merit SF; Purdue Univ; Chem Engr.

MARTIN, LYNN; Cedar Springs HS; Cedar Spgs, MI; Band; Hon Rl; Jr NHS; Rptr Yrbk; Ten; Trk; Natl Merit Ltr; Univ Of Michigan; Spch Ther.

MARTIN, MARGARET; Southgate HS; Southgate, MI; 10/365 NHS; Scr Kpr; College; Health.

MARTIN, MARJORIE M; Warren Sr HS; Warren, MI; Cls Rep Frsh Cls; Cmp Fr Grls; Chrh Wkr; Hon Rl; NHS; Ed Sch Nwsp; Letter Bsktbl; Letter Trk; Pres Awd; MVP Bsktbl; Univ Of Michigan; Psych.

MARTIN, MARY; St Marys Ctrl Catholic HS; Castalia, OH; 24/119 Chrs; Hon Rl; Treas JA; GAA; Univ Of Redlands; Acctg.

MARTIN, MARY; Inland Lakes HS; Topinaee, MI; 30/90 Girl Scts; Hon Rl; Off Ade; Pep Clb; Bsktbl; GAA; Univ; Phys Ther.

MARTIN, MICHAEL; Mason HS; Holt, MI; Trs Soph Cls; Cl Rep Jr Cls; Cls Rep Sr Cls; Boy Scts; NHS; Stu Cncl; Sci Clb; Bsbl; Capt Bsktbl; Mic Tech Univ; Geol Engr.

MARTIN, MICHAEL; Boardman HS; Youngstown, OH; Boys Clb Am; IM Sprt; Youngstown St Univ; Acctg.

MARTIN, MICHELLE; Clay HS; S Bend, IN; 16/430 Cmp Fr Grls; Hon Rl; Sec JA; NHS; Rptr Yrbk; Ger Clb; Lat Clb; Pep Clb; Ten; Capt Pom Pon; City Spelling Champion South Bend; Date Carnegie Awd; College; Photography.

MARTIN, MICHELLE; River Valley HS; Caledonia, OH; 27/207 Pres Band; Chrs; Hon Rl; JA; Orch; Sch Mus; Fr Clb; Rdo Clb; Sci Clb; Busns Schl.

MARTIN, MITCHELL; Lincoln HS; Shinnston, WV ; Boy Scts; Hon Rl; Pol Wkr; FTA; Pres Spn Clb; Bsktbl; Letter Crs Cntry; Letter Trk; West Virginia Univ; Aero Engr.

MARTIN, NANCY; Gabriel Richard HS; Ann Arbor, MI; Cls Rep Frsh Cls; Band; Sec Girl Scts; Sch Pl; Sct Actv; Ed Yrbk; Drama Clb; Eng Clb; Pep Clb; Sec Spn Clb; Outstndngn Serv Awd 78 & 79; Marywood Univ; Tchr.

MARTIN, NANCY; Immaculata HS; Detroit, MI; Chrs; Chrh Wkr; Hon Rl; JA; Yth Flsp; Sch Nwsp; Pep Clb; Cit Awd; Henry Ford Nursing Schl; Rn.

MARTIN, PATRICIA; Salem HS; Salem, IN; Chrh Wkr; Girl Scts; JA; Sct Actv; Yth Flsp; Rptr Yrbk; Ed Sch Nwsp; Drama Clb; Pep Clb; VP Spn Clb; Indiana Univ; Scndry Educ.

MARTIN, RENEE; Summerfield HS; Petersburg, MI; Trs Jr Cls; Trs Sr Cls; Band; Hon Rl; NHS; Sch Pl; Rptr Yrbk; 4-H; Pep Clb; Sci Clb; Michigan St Univ; Bio.

MARTIN, ROBERT; Lincoln HS; Shinnston, WV; Spn Clb; VICA; Vocational Schl; Elec Tech.

MARTIN, ROBERT; Delaware Hayes HS; Delaware, OH; 20/300 Am Leg Boys St; Chrs; Debate Tm; Hon Rl; Jr NHS; Natl Forn Lg; Pol Wkr; Yth Flsp; Letter Socr; Trk; Ohio Wesleyan; Law.

MARTIN, ROBIN; Marion Adams HS; Sheridan, IN; 3/86 Band; Chrs; Chrh Wkr; FCA; Hon Rl; Hosp Ade; Jr NHS; Anderson College; Nursing.

MARTIN, RON; Rogers HS; Toledo, OH; 5/394 Am Leg Boys St; Boy Scts; Hon Rl; Jr NHS; NHS; Sci Clb; Letter Trk; Letter Wrstlng; Ohio St Univ; Civil Engr.

MARTIN, SCOTT; Troy HS; Troy, MI; 97/282 Chrh Wkr; Sec FCA; Hon Rl; Letter Bsktbl; Cit Awd; Mis State; Mech Engr.

MARTIN, SCOTT; Fountain Ctrl HS; Newtown, IN; Pres Frsh Cls; Cls Rep Soph Cls; VP Jr Cls; Cls Rep Sr Cls; Am Leg Boys St; Hon Rl; NHS; Stu Cncl; Sch Nwsp; Letter Trk; Indiana St Univ; Archt.

MARTIN, SHEILA; Wirt County HS; Elizebeth, WV; 1/106 Cls Rep Frsh Cls; Sec Soph Cls; Cl Rep Jr Cls; Cls Rep Sr Cls; Val; Band; Chrh Wkr; Cmnty Wkr; Drl Tm; Hon Rl; Voted Most Dependable Sr 78; PCC Schlrshp 79; Robert C Byrd Schlstc Awd 79; Parkersburg Cmnty Coll; Bus Admin.

MARTIN, SHELIA; Chadsey HS; Detroit, MI; FCA; Hon Rl; Off Ade; Pep Clb; Letter Ten; Capt Trk; GAA; Capt Mic State; Draftsman.

MARTIN, SHERRI; West Washington HS; Campbellsbg, IN; Sec Jr Cls; Sec Sr Cls; Band; Drl Tm; NHS; Treas Stu Cncl; Drama Clb; 4-H; Voc Schl.

MARTIN, SONIA; Redford HS; Detroit, MI; Trs Frsh Cls; Chrh Wkr; Hon Rl; JA; NHS; Off Ade; Sch Pl; Yrbk; Drama Clb; 4-H; Wayne St Univ; Nursing.

MARTIN, STEPHEN; Salem HS; Salem, IN; Cmnty Wkr; Hon Rl; JA; Sch Nwsp; Pres Spn Clb; Trk; Prosser Voc Schl; Data Processing.

MARTIN, STEVEN; Thomas A Edison Jr Sr HS; Lake Station, IN; 4/171 Band; Letter Ftbl; Letter Trk; Univ; Comp Sci.

MARTIN, SUE; Medora HS; Medora, IN; 4/22 VP Jr Cls; Am Leg Aux Girls St; Hon Rl; Yrbk; Beta Clb; 4-H; FHA; Trk; Chrldng; GAA; Univ.

MARTIN, SUSY; Meadowdale HS; Dayton, OH; Ed Yrbk; Wright St Univ; Mrktng.

MARTIN, TAMMY; Lincoln HS; Shinnston, WV; Sec Soph Cls; Sec Jr Cls; Cl Rep Jr Cls; Band; Hon Rl; Jr NHS; NHS; Stu Cncl;.

MARTIN, TOM; Lincoln HS; Vincennes, IN; 61/283 Cls Rep Frsh Cls; Cls Rep Soph Cls; Cl Rep Jr Cls; Cls Rep Sr Cls; Chrs; FCA; Sch Mus; Stu Cncl; Letter Ftbl; Harding Coll; Education.

MARTIN, TYRELL; Thomas Cooley HS; Detroit, MI; Hon Rl; NHS; Letter Bsktbl; Suomi College; Acctg.

MARTIN, WENDY; Western HS; Auburn, MI; 10/438 Chrs; Chrh Wkr; Hon Rl; NHS; Chrldng; Concordia College; Soc Work.

MARTINDALE, CHRISTINE; Greenville Sr HS; Gettysburg, OH; 23/380 Am Leg Aux Girls St; Band; Chrh Wkr; Hon Rl; NHS; Orch; Sch Mus; Yth Flsp; 4-H; Lat Clb; Univ; Engr.

MARTINDALE, STEVEN; New Albany HS; New Albany, OH; VP Soph Cls; Chrh Wkr; Hon Rl; Yth Flsp; Letter Bsktbl; Letter Ftbl; Letter Trk; Cit Awd;.

MARTINDALE, THOMAS; Grosse Pointe South HS; Grosse Pt Farms, MI; Cls Rep Sr Cls; Hon Rl; Pres Yth Flsp; Ten; Trk; IM Sprt; Michigan St Univ; Bus.

MARTINEAU, MARY; St Ursula Academy; Toledo, OH; Hon Rl; Ger Clb; IM Sprt; Mgrs; Univ; Psych.

MARTINES, THERESA; Kearsley HS; Flint, MI; Lbry Ade; Off Ade;.

MARTINEZ, ABELINA; River Rouge HS; River Rouge, MI; Cls Rep Frsh Cls; Cls Rep Soph Cls; Cl Rep Jr Cls; Chrs; Hon Rl; NHS; Drama Clb; Rdo Clb; Spn Clb; Ten; Univ; Pre Law.

MARTINEZ, ALICIA; Hammond Voc Tech HS; Hammond, IN; 46/207 Band; Chrs; Hon Rl; Sch Mus; Sch Pl; FBLA; Lat Clb; Spn Clb; Ten; Pom Pon; Purdue Univ; Bus.

MARTINEZ, DAVID; Elmhurst HS; Ft Wayne, IN; Aud/Vis; Red Cr Ade; Voc Sch; Elec.

MARTINEZ, E; Washington HS; E Chicago, IN; Band; Boy Scts; Orch; Boys Clb Am; Purdue Univ; Mech.

MARTINEZ, EDD; Anthony Wayne HS; Swanton, OH; Cls Rep Frsh Cls; Cls Rep Soph Cls; Cl Rep Jr Cls; Aud/Vis; Hon Rl; NHS; Stu Cncl; Letter Crs Cntry; Letter Trk; IM Sprt; 2nd Team All Lg Cross Cntry 78; Coll; Archaeology.

MARTINEZ, FRANCES; Fr Gabriel Richard HS; Ypsilanti, MI; Sec Sr Cls; Girl Scts; Hon Rl; NHS; Red Cr Ade; Sch Pl; Stg Crw; Drama Clb; Pep Clb; Univ Of Mic; Chem.

MARTINEZ, MARIA; South Dearborn HS; Aurora, IN; Cmp Fr Grls; Chrs; Girl Scts; Hon Rl; Sch Pl; Drama Clb; Pep Clb; Natl Merit Ltr; Beta Sigma Phi 77; Univ Of Chicago.

MARTINEZ, MARY F; George Washington HS; East Chicago, IN; 5/286 Cls Rep Soph Cls; Cl Rep Jr Cls; Cls Rep Sr Cls; Hon Rl; NHS; Stu Cncl; Fr Clb; FHA; Treas FTA; Key Clb; Purdue Univ; Indust Engr.

MARTING, PEGGY; Cuyahoga Falls HS; Cuyahoga Fls, OH; Sec Frsh Cls; Hon Rl; JA; NHS; Off Ade; Stg Crw; Sec Stu Cncl; Sch Nwsp; Ger Clb; Pres JA Awd; Otstndng Achvmnt Awrd Eng 77; Univ; Med.

MARTINI, BETTY A; Seton HS; Cincinnati, OH; Cls Rep Frsh Cls; Cl Rep Jr Cls; Cls Rep Sr Cls; Band; Drl Tm; Girl Scts; Hon Rl; JA; Lbry Ade; Off Ade; Mount St Joseph Univ; Med Tech.

MARTINI, DANIEL C; La Salle HS; Cincinnati, OH; 5/250 Cls Rep Soph Cls; Boy Scts; Hon Rl; Jr NHS; Sct Actv; Stu Cncl; Rptr Sch Nwsp; Capt IM Sprt; Univ; Bus.

MARTINI, ROBERT; Grass Lake HS; Grass Lk, MI; Chrh Wkr; Ftbl; Mic Tech Univ; Engr.

MARTINI, THERESA; Mc Auley HS; Cincinnati, OH; 12/252 Hon Rl; Fr Clb; Letter Ten; GAA; IM Sprt; Miami Univ; Bus Admin.

MARTINI, VICTORIA; Holy Redeemer HS; Detroit, MI; Hon Rl; Fr Clb; GAA; Henry Ford Comm Coll; Nursing.

MARTINO, JOSEPH J; Brooke HS; Follansbee, WV; 75/466 VP Soph Cls; VP Jr Cls; VP Sr Cls; Am Leg Boys St; FCA; Hon Rl; Jr NHS; NHS; DECA; Bsbl; DECA Occupational Manual WV 2nd Pl 78; DECA Human Relations WV 3rd Pl 78; DECA Fin & Cred WV 4th Pl; West Virginia Univ; Bus Admin.

MARTINO, LYNN; Washington Irving HS; Clarksburg, WV; Am Leg Aux Girls St; Hon Rl; Lbry Ade; NHS; FBLA; Lat Clb; Bus Schl; Sec.

MARTINO, VICKY; Archbishop Alter HS; Dayton, OH; 50/332 Band; Drl Tm; Hon Rl; NHS; Off Ade; Miami Univ; Lib Arts.

MARTON, MATTHEW; Parma Sr HS; Parma, OH; 3/782 Chrs; Chrh Wkr; Hon Rl; NHS; Sch Mus; Scr Kpr; NCTE; Coll; Bio Sci.

MARTT, GINGER; Georgetown HS; Georgetown, OH; VP Soph Cls; Sec Sr Cls; Am Leg Aux Girls St; Band; Hosp Ade; NHS; Treas Stu Cncl; Yrbk; Pres 4-H; Bsbl; Miami Univ; Bus Mgmt.

MARTY, DOUG; West Branch HS; Salem, OH; 2/260 Band; Chrs; Hon Rl; Pres NHS; Sch Mus; Bsbl; Letter Ftbl; College; Comp Sci.

MARTYNIAK, BRENT; Trenton HS; Trenton, MI; Hon Rl; IM Sprt; Natl Merit Ltr; Univ.

MARTYNIUK, KATHERINE; Woodridge HS; Cuyahoga Fls, OH; Trs Sr Cls; Band; Hosp Ade; Lbry Ade; Stu Cncl; Pep Clb; Spn Clb; Bsktbl; Letter Trk; Scr Kpr; Ohio St Univ; Phys Ther.

MARTZ, BARNEY; Revere HS; Richfield, OH; 90/290 FCA; Lbry Ade; Yth Flsp; Rptr Sch Nwsp; Wrstlng; Coach Actv; Ripon; Economics.

MARTZ, MICHAEL; Edison HS; Milan, OH; Chrs; Chrh Wkr; Hon Rl; College; Engr.

MARVEL, STEPHEN; William Henry Harrison HS; Evansville, IN; 19/466 Cls Rep Frsh Cls; Cls Rep Soph Cls; Treas Chrs; Hon Rl; Sch Mus; Sch Pl; Stu Cncl; Sch Nwsp; Pep Clb; God Cntry Awd; Univ; Acting.

MARVIG, JEFF; Cheboygan HS; Cheboygan, MI; Band; Hon Rl; Orch; Double Reed Camp Schlrshp For Bassoon 78 79; Michigan St Univ; Vet Med.

MARVIN, BRENDA; Evergreen HS; Swanton, OH; Band; Chrs; Chrh Wkr; Hon Rl; Off Ade; Spn Clb; GAA; Vocational Schl; Sec.

MARVIN, KELLEY A; Hartland Consolidated Schls; Howell, MI; Hon Rl; Rptr Sch Nwsp; Sch Nwsp; Fr Clb; Cntrl Michigan Univ; Lang.

MARVIN, SHIRLEY; Fredericktown Sr HS; Fredericktown, OH; 5/117 Band; Chrs; Chrh Wkr; Hon Rl; Lbry Ade; Off Ade; Yrbk; OEA; Outstanding IOE II Award 1979; Honor Student 1979; Typesetter.

MARX, LORI; Father Wehrle HS; Columbus, OH; 25/115 Aud/Vis; Chrh Wkr; Drl Tm; Hon Rl; Sec Jr NHS; Lbry Ade;.

MARX, SHEILA E; Bexley HS; Columbus, OH; Chrs; Cmnty Wkr; Sch Mus; Mth Clb; Spn Clb; Bsktbl; GAA; Ohi State Univ; Comp Sci.

MARZ, MICHAEL; St Josephs HS; South Bend, IN; 16/240 Boy Scts; Hon Rl; NHS; Yrbk; Rptr Sch Nwsp; Capt Crs Cntry; Trk; IM Sprt; Scr Kpr; Natl Merit SF; Notre Dame Univ; Mech Engr.

MARZEC, BOB J; Woodward HS; Toledo, OH; Cls Rep Frsh Cls; Quill & Scroll; Letter Bsbl; Letter Ftbl; Letter Wrstlng; Univ; Telephone Installer.

MARZINSKI, BARBARA; Manistee Cath Central HS; Manistee, MI; Cls Rep Frsh Cls; Trs Soph Cls; VP Sr Cls; Chrh Wkr; Hon Rl; Hosp Ade; Drama Clb; Pep Clb; Trk; 4-H Awd; Western Michigan Univ; Occup Ther.

MARZKA, KURTIS J; Capac HS; Capac, MI; Hon Rl; Yrbk; Letter Bsktbl; Letter Glf; Letter Trk; Beloit Coll; Chem.

MARZOLF, TERESA; St Joseph HS; South Bend, IN; 34/200 Band; Hon Rl; Pres JA; Sch Pl; Pep Clb; Letter Crs Cntry; Letter Trk; Scr Kpr; Natl Merit Ltr; Pres Awd; Univ; Comp Sci.

MARZOLINO, GREGORY; Aquinas HS; Southgate, MI; Hon Rl; NHS; Letter Socr; Letter Ten; IM Sprt; Michigan St Univ; Med.

MASCARO, ANGELA; Washington Irving HS; Clarksburg, WV; Cl Rep Jr Cls; Sec Sr Cls; Am Leg Aux Girls St; VP Band; Hon Rl; NHS; Lat Clb; Pep Clb; West Virginia Univ; Med.

MASCHARKA, JEFFREY; Franklin HS; Livonia, MI; Crs Cntry; Trk; Natl Merit Ltr;.

MASCHERINO, TINA M; Bishop Watterson HS; Columbus, OH; NHS; Sch Mus; Sch Pl; Franklin Univ; Legal Sec.

MASCHMEIER, JENNIE; East HS; Akron, OH; Off Ade; Sch Pl; Rptr Sch Nwsp; Drama Clb; Spn Clb; Gym; Univ.

MASCK, BRIAN; West Catholic HS; Grand Rapids, MI; Cls Rep Frsh Cls; Cls Rep Soph Cls; Cl Rep Jr Cls; Am Leg Boys St; Band; Hon Rl; JA; Pol Wkr; Sch Mus; Rptr Yrbk; College.

MASCK, MARYBETH A; West Catholic HS; Grand Rapids, MI; 2/300 Cls Rep Frsh Cls; VP Soph Cls; Sal; Band; Hon Rl; VP NHS; Stu Cncl; Letter Swmmng; Aquinas Coll; Eng.

MASHNI, BETTY; Lake Ville Mem HS; Otter Lake, MI; 15/190 Sec Sr Cls; Chrh Wkr; Lbry Ade; NHS; Rptr Yrbk; GAA; Mgrs; Univ Of Michigan; Pre Med.

MASICA, GREGORY; Coshocton HS; Coshocton, OH; 9/253 Hon Rl; Pres NHS; Sch Pl; Swmmng; Ohio State; Engineering.

MASICH, JOSEPH; Barberton HS; Barberton, OH; 42/498 Am Leg Boys St; Hon Rl; Jr NHS; NHS; Off Ade; Stu Cncl; Ger Clb; Key Clb; Sci Clb; Letter Ftbl; N Michigan Univ; Criminology.

MASLOWSKI, SUSAN; Milton Union HS; W Milton, OH; 1/216 Hon Rl; NHS; Off Ade; Pres FBLA; FTA; Letter Ten; Mgrs; Ohio Northern Univ; Phys Ed.

MASNYK, MICHAEL; Rossford HS; Rossford, OH; 7/150 Am Leg Boys St; Hon Rl; NHS; Letter Bsbl; Bsktbl; Miami Univ; Law.

MASON, ANDREW; Heath HS; Heath, OH; 14/152 VP Sr Cls; Chrh Wkr; FCA; Hon Rl; NHS; Yth Flsp; Key Clb; Spn Clb; Bsktbl; Cincinnati Bible Coll; Ministry.

MASON, BETH; Westerville South HS; Westerville, OH; Hon Rl; Sprt Ed Yrbk; Rptr Yrbk; Rptr Sch Nwsp; Letter Bsbl; Letter Bsktbl; GAA; IM Sprt; PPFtbl; Franklin Univ; Busns.

MASON, DANIEL; Zanesville HS; Zanesville, OH; 35/383 Hon Rl; NHS; Letter Wrstlng; Mgrs; Ohio Univ; History.

MASON, DEBORAH S; Philo HS; Newport News, VA; 36/205 VP Jr Cls; Chrs; Capt Drl Tm; NHS; Sec Stu Cncl; Yrbk; 4-H; GAA; Tech College.

MASON, DIANA; Ortonville Brandon HS; Goodrich, MI; Cmnty Wkr; Hon Rl; Letter Bsktbl; Letter Trk; Coach Actv; Coll; Busns Admin.

MASON, DOROTHY; Richmond Sr HS; Richmond, IN; 70/521 Cls Rep Frsh Cls; Sal; Chrh Wkr; Hon Rl; Jr NHS; Lbry Ade; NHS; Stu Cncl; Yth Flsp; Lat Clb; Earlham Coll; Chem Librn.

MASON, INGRID; Lakeland HS; Milford, MI; 25/375 NHS; Fr Clb; Pep Clb; Trk; IM Sprt; Mich Tech Univ; Eng.

MASON, JIM; St Edward HS; Parama, OH; FCA; Hon Rl; Pol Wkr; Stu Cncl; Trk; Wrstlng; Coach Actv; C of C Awd; Math.

MASON, JODY; Port Clinton HS; Port Clinton, OH; 10/280 Band; Girl Scts; Hon Rl; GAA; Mat Maids; Scr Kpr; Tmr; Delgt To Buckeye Girls State; Flute Player.

MASON, JOHN A; St Ignatius HS; N Olmsted, OH; 7/304 Cls Rep Soph Cls; Stu Cncl; Rptr Sch Nwsp; Lat Clb; Mth Clb; Letter Bsbl; Letter Ftbl; IM Sprt; JETS Awd;.

MASON, JOHNNY; Berkeley Springs HS; Berkeley Spg, WV; 13/133 Cls Rep Frsh Cls; Cls Rep Sr Cls; Hon Rl; NHS; Stu Cncl; Capt Bsbl; Letter Ftbl; Capt Wrstlng; IM Sprt; Shepherd Coll; Bus.

MASON, JON; Parkersburg HS; Parkersburg, WV; 127/725 Chrh Wkr; Cmnty Wkr; Pres Yth Flsp; College; Busns.

MASON, JULIE; Hillard HS; Columbus, OH; FCA; Girl Scts; Hon Rl; Lbry Ade; Rptr Sch Nwsp; Drama Clb; FHA; GAA; Scr Kpr; Univ; Soc Work.

MASON, KAREN L; North Newton HS; De Motte, IN; NHS; Am Leg Awd;.

MASON, LARRY; Tyler County HS; Middlebourne, WV; Cls Rep Soph Cls; Pres Jr Cls; Trs Sr Cls; Hon

Rl; JA; NHS; Sch Pl; Stu Cncl; Ed Yrbk; Yrbk; Marshall Univ; Occupt Health.

MASON, LYNN; Bad Axe HS; Bad Axe, MI; Trs Jr Cls; Band; Chrs; Drl Tm; Hon Rl; Jr NHS; NHS; Off Ade; Sch Mus; Pep Clb; Michigan St Univ; Med.

MASON, MARGIE; Washington HS; Massillon, OH; Chrs; Chrh Wkr; Girl Scts; Hon Rl; Off Ade; Sch Mus; Sct Actv; Yth Flsp; Drama Clb; Jr Womens Club; Ski Club; Jobs Daughters; College; Animal Behavior.

MASON, MARK; Sparta Highland HS; Marengo, OH; 13/135 VP Frsh Cls; VP Soph Cls; VP Jr Cls; VP Sr Cls; Hon Rl; Jr NHS; NHS; Stu Cncl; 4-H; FFA; Varsity Club Pres; St Farmer Degree; Paliamentry Procedure Tm; College; Busns.

MASON, MARSHA; Zanesville HS; Zanesville, OH; Cls Rep Frsh Cls; Drl Tm; Hon Rl; NHS; Off Ade; Stu Cncl; Yth Flsp; Sci Clb; Chrldng; IM Sprt; College; Dental Hygienist.

MASON, MICHELLE; Yellow Springs HS; Yellow Sprg, OH; 29/75 VP Jr Cls; VP Sr Cls; Band; Girl Scts; Bsktbl; Univ; Mech Engr.

MASON, RHONDA A; Walnut Ridge HS; Columbus, OH; 14/429 Cmp Fr Grls; Hon Rl; Lit Mag; NHS; Ger Clb; Crs Cntry; Trk; Natl Merit SF; Member Stratford Shakespeare Fest Workshop; College; Math.

MASON, RICHARD L; Dover HS; Dover, OH; Band; Boy Scts; Hon Rl; Sct Actv; Stu Cncl; FBLA; Cit Awd; Pres Awd; Stud Tutor Awd 78; Kent St Univ; Advert Photog.

MASON, TAMARA; Field HS; Mogadore, OH; Chrs; Chrh Wkr; Hon Rl; Jr NHS; NHS; Orch; Yth Flsp; Rptr Sch Nwsp; Fr Clb; College; Cmmrcl Art.

MASON, TIMOTHY; Grosse Pointe South HS; Grss Pte Pk, MI; Debate Tm; Hon Rl; Ger Clb; Michigan St Univ; Envir Law.

MASONI, ANITA; Buckeye Vly HS; Delaware, OH; Chrs; Hon Rl; Stg Crw; Pres DECA; Drama Clb; Mgrs; Univ; Bus.

MASS, TIMOTHY; Clay HS; S Bend, IN; Chrs; Chrh Wkr; Sch Mus; Yth Flsp; 4-H; Letter Ftbl; Trk; 4-H Awd; College; Architect.

MASSA, TAMERA; Rockville Jr Sr HS; Rockville, IN; 4/83 Am Leg Aux Girls St; Band; Chrs; Hon Rl; NHS; Pep Clb; Spn Clb; Letter Trk; Twrlr; Indiana St Univ; Educ.

MASSAY, SHERYL; Jackson HS; Jackson, OH; 29/230 Girl Scts; Hon Rl; NHS; 4-H; Letter Bsktbl; Trk; GAA; IM Sprt; PPFtbl; Ohio State; Physical Therapy.

MASSELA, NTUMBA M; Bloomington North HS; Bloomington, IN; Band; Girl Scts; Univ; Med.

MASSEY, ALAN; Loveland HS; Loveland, OH; 50/221 Chrh Wkr; Hon Rl; Ftbl; Socr; Trk; Wrstlng; Mgrs; Miami Univ; Civil Engr.

MASSEY, DEBRA A; Shady Spring HS; Shady Spring, WV; Band; Chrh Wkr; Hon Rl; Sch Pl; Yth Flsp; Civ Clb; FHA; Concord Coll; Music.

MASSEY, DOUGLAS; Ithaca Pub HS; Ithaca, MI; 2/138 Sal; Hon Rl; Jr NHS; Lbry Ade; NHS; Rptr Yrbk; Pres Fr Clb; Treas FTA; Pres Spn Clb; Ferris St Univ; Acctg.

MASSEY, JEFFERY; Elwood Community HS; Elwood, IN; 16/260 Boy Scts; Hon Rl; Jr NHS; NHS; Industrl Tech Awd 76 78; Anderson Coll; Acctg.

MASSEY, KAREN; Indian Creek HS; Martinsvll, IN; 3/161 Sec Frsh Cls; Sec Soph Cls; Am Leg Aux Girls St; Hon Rl; Pres NHS; Pres 4-H; FHA; FTA; Lat Clb; Pep Clb; Public Rltns.

MASSEY, MELANIE; Manton Cons HS; Manton, MI; Cls Rep Soph Cls; Cl Rep Jr Cls; Hon Rl; Sec Stu Cncl; Letter Chrldng; Letter GAA; Voc Schl; Med.

MASSEY, REBECCA; Clear Fork HS; Colcord, WV; 2/40 Am Leg Aux Girls St; Boy Scts; Chrh Wkr; Cm nty Wkr; Girl Scts; Hon Rl; NHS; Yth Flsp; FBLA; Pep Clb; College.

MASSEY, TRACI; Midland Trail HS; Ansted, WV; Band; Chrs; Hon Rl; NHS; Rptr Yrbk; Fr Clb; FHA; Pep Clb; PPFtbl; West Virginia Univ; Phys Ther.

MASSEY, W; Midland Trail HS; Ansted, WV; Hon Rl; 4-H; 4-H Awd; Wv Hstry Bowl 1st Pl Team 79; Chess Team Ltr 76 80; Southern Coll Of Optometry; Optmtry.

MASSIE, B; Buffalo HS; Prichard, WV; Hon Rl; Ftbl; College.

MASSIE, BRENDA; Mifflin HS; Columbus, OH; Hon Rl; Off Ade; Yth Flsp; Pres Fr Clb; Scr Kpr; Engr For A Day 79; PTSA Acad Awd 77; Muskingum Univ; Cmnctns.

MASSIE, BRENT; Buffalo HS; Prichard, WV; Hon Rl; Letter Ftbl; College.

MASSIE, BRIAN; Buffalo HS; Prichard, WV; Hon Rl; Letter Ftbl; College; Bio Sci.

MASSIE, IRMA; Kearsley HS; Burton, MI; 40/400 Am Leg Aux Girls St; Chrs; Hon Rl; Sch Mus; Sch Pl; Pep Clb; Chrldng; Univ Of Mich; Child Psych.

MASSIE, KIMBERLY; Libbey HS; Toledo, OH; Hon Rl; Jr NHS; Rptr Yrbk; Rptr Sch Nwsp; FHA; Lat Clb; Toledo Univ; Pediatrician.

MASSIE, SHARON; Mackenzie HS; Detroit, MI; 45/420 Hon Rl; Stu Cncl; Yrbk; Pep Clb; Letter Hockey; Chrldng; Mich Competitive Schlrshp; Michigan St Univ; Busns Admin.

MASSIE, WILLIAM; Port Clinton HS; Pt Clinton, OH; 34/260 Am Leg Boys St; Boy Scts; Hon Rl; Orch; Stu Cncl; Ger Clb; Letter Ftbl; Wrstlng; All Conf 2nd Team Middle Guard Football; All Conf 2nd Team Wrestling; College; Medicine.

MASSING, ANGIE; Greenfield Central HS; Pendleton, IN; Chrs; Hon Rl; Yth Flsp; Sch Nwsp; Ger Clb; Gym; Mgrs; PPFtbl; College; Med Tech.

MASSOGLIA, DAVID; Calumet HS; Laurium, MI; Hon Rl; NHS; Letter Bsktbl; Capt Crs Cntry; Coach Actv; IM Sprt; Elk Awd; Natl Merit Schl; Michigan Tech Univ.

MASSON, JO ANN; St Ursula HS; Cincinnati, OH; Chrs; Hon Rl; Capt Chrldng; Coach Actv; Xavier Univ; Montessori Educ.

MAST, DAVID; Avon Jr Sr HS; Indianapolis, IN; Am Leg Boys St; Band; Boy Scts; Chrs; Hon Rl; NHS; Sch Mus; Geom Awd 78; Univ; Engr.

MAST, KURT; Holland Christian HS; Holland, MI; Am Leg Boys St; FCA; Ger Clb; Crs Cntry; Trk; Calvin Coll; Chem.

MAST, LISA; Bay City Cntrl HS; Bay City, MI; 16/464 Cl Rep Jr Cls; Chrs; Hon Rl; Hosp Ade; NHS; Sch Mus; Stu Cncl; Eng Clb; PPFtbl; Stdnt Cncl V P 79; Queens Crt 77; Frndshp Ambsdr Poland 78; Univ; Nursing.

MAST, RENEE; Jimtow HS; Elkhart, IN; Lbry Ade; Yth Flsp; VICA; Ten; JC Awd; Kiwan Awd; Univ; Engr Drafting.

MASTALERZ, KATHLEEN; Wheeling Park HS; Wheeling, WV; Chrh Wkr; Hon Rl; Natl Forn Lg; Sch Pl; Stg Crw; College; Med.

MASTEL, JON P; Walnut Township HS; Millersport, OH; Cls Rep Frsh Cls; Cl Rep Jr Cls; Trs Sr Cls; Am Leg Boys St; Cmnty Wkr; Treas FCA; Hon Rl; Stu Cncl; Spn Clb; Bsbl; Amer HS Athlete Publicatn Ftbl 27 Trophies & Cert Of Mert In All Sports 79; Univ; Acctg.

MASTEN, KATHRYN; Cloverdale HS; Cloverdale, IN; 1/88 Chrs; Chrh Wkr; Girl Scts; Hon Rl; NHS; Sch Mus; Sch Pl; Sec Yth Flsp; Drama Clb; Fr Clb; De Pauw Coll; Nursing.

MASTEN, PATRICIA; St Alphonsus HS; Dearborn, MI; Hon Rl; Rptr Sch Nwsp; Sch Nwsp; Mic State; Communication.

MASTERS, JENNIFER; Waterford Twp HS; Waterford, MI; 14/405 Girl Scts; NHS; Stu Cncl; Fr Clb; Pep Clb; Pom Pon; Grand Vly St Coll Hnr Schrlshp; E Mich Univ Reg HS Awd; E Michigan Univ; Lang.

MASTERS, JOSEPH E; Bishop Donahue HS; Moundsvl, WV; 14/54 Boy Scts; Chrh Wkr; Hon Rl; NHS; Sct Actv; 4-H; Capt Ftbl; Cit Awd; DAR Awd; 4-H Awd; WVIT; Mech Engr.

MASTERS, KARA; Oakwood HS; Dayton, OH; 25/150 AFS; Hon Rl; MMM; NHS; PAVAS; Sch Pl; Y-Teens; Socr; IM Sprt; College; Bio.

MASTERS, KAREN; Rushville Consolidated HS; Carthage, IN; 1/290 Val; Chrs; VP NHS; Treas Stu Cncl; 4-H; FHA; Lat Clb; Mth Clb; Letter Bsktbl; Trk; Hanover Coll; Math.

MASTERS, MAUREEN; W G Mather HS; Munising, MI; Hon Rl; College; Sci.

MASTERS, PAULA; Mannington HS; Mannington, WV; 8/113 Cls Rep Soph Cls; Hon Rl; Stu Cncl; Rptr Yrbk; Fr Clb; Chrldng; Pres GAA; IM Sprt; Pom Pon; Twrlr; Fairmont State College.

MASTERS, ROGER; Coventry HS; Akron, OH; Band; Hon Rl; Sch Mus; Pep Clb; Spn Clb; Vocational School.

MASTERSON, ANGELA; Chesapeake HS; Chesapeake, OH; Am Leg Aux Girls St; Band; Cmp Fr Grls; Hon Rl; Sch Pl; Stu Cncl; Ed Yrbk; Sprt Ed Yrbk; Sprt Ed Sch Nwsp; Beta Clb; Marshall Univ; Jrnlsm.

MASTERSON, ANGELA M; Chesapeake HS; Chesapeake, OH; 20/140 Cls Rep Frsh Cls; Cls Rep Soph Cls; Hon Rl; Stu Cncl; Ed Yrbk; Sprt Ed Yrbk; Sprt Ed Sch Nwsp; Beta Clb; Scr Kpr; Marshall Univ; Journalism.

MASTERSON, ANGIE; Elmhurst HS; Fort Wayne, IN; 8/357 Hon Rl; NHS; Letter Ten; Trk; Dnfth Awd; IUPU; Sec.

MASTERSON, LYNN; Normandy HS; Parma, OH; 41/649 Band; Hon Rl; Cmmrcl Art.

MASTERSON, MICHAEL; Okemos HS; Okemos, MI; Cls Rep Frsh Cls; Orch; Stu Cncl; Rptr Sch Nwsp; Kalamazoo Coll.

MASTERSON, WAYNE; Eau Claire HS; Eau Cliare, MI; Band; Boy Scts; Hon Rl; Sch Mus; Sct Actv; Sprt Ed Yrbk; Bsbl; Bsktbl; Glf; College; Prof Baseball.

MASTEY, JOE; Lake Central HS; Schererville, IN; 15/460 NHS; Ger Clb; Pep Clb; Sci Clb; Letter Bsbl; Purdue Univ.

MASTRANGELO, SANDRA A; North HS; Eastlake, OH; 36/669 Hon Rl; NHS; Spn Clb; Bsktbl;.

MASTROIANNI, ENZO; St Alphonsus HS; Dearborn, MI; 18/181 Pres Jr Cls; VP Sr Cls; Aud/Vis; Hon Rl; Stg Crw; Stu Cncl; Ftbl; Trk; Michigan Tech Univ; Civil Engr.

MASTRONADE, JOHN; Campbell Memorial HS; Campbell, OH; 98/210 Hon Rl; NHS; VP Key Clb; Mth Clb; Sci Clb; Spn Clb; Letter Bsktbl; Letter Ftbl; IM Sprt; College; Pharmacy.

MASTROVASELIS, CHRISTINE; Campbell Memorial HS; Cmapbell, OH; Band; Hosp Ade; JA; Orch; Yrbk; VP Spn Clb; Bsktbl; Trk; Tmr; JA Awd; Youngstown St Univ; Psych.

MASTURZO, LORIE; East HS; Akron, OH; 1/292 Val; Hon Rl; Natl Forn Lg; NHS; Quill & Scroll; Sch Pl; Rptr Sch Nwsp; Drama Clb; Pres Fr Clb; Letter Crs Cntry; Washington & Jefferson Coll.

MASUGA, PAULA; W Iron Cnty HS; Caspian, MI; Sec Soph Cls; Sec Jr Cls; Band; Hon Rl; Off Ade; Stu Cncl; 4-H; Fr Clb; Key Clb; Gym; Univ.

MATA, MARY; Jefferson HS; La Salle, MI; 95/172 Cmp Fr Grls; Chrh Wkr; Hosp Ade; Off Ade; FHA; Pep Clb; Monroe Cntry Comm Coll; Lib Arts.

MATA, MIGUEL; Decatur HS; Decatur, MI; Univ; Fine Arts.

MATANGUIHAN, GREGORIO; Moeller HS; Cincinnati, OH; 40/260 Cls Rep Frsh Cls; Cls Rep Soph Cls; Cls Rep Sr Cls; Hon Rl; JA; Stg Crw; Stu Cncl; Ten; JA Awd; Hrt Of Gold Awd 78; Altrn Of Homcmng Ct; Univ Of Cincinnati; Pre Med.

MATARRESE, MICHAEL; Upper Arlington HS; Columbus, OH; 103/610 Hon Rl; Orch; Ger Clb; Crs Cntry; Trk; Ohio St Univ; Aeronautical Engr.

MATASH, TERESA; Campbell Memorial HS; Campbell, OH; 20 218 Chrh Wkr; Hon Rl; NHS; Red Cr Ade; Sch Pl; Rptr Yrbk; Rptr Sch Nwsp; Drama Clb; Mth Clb; Spn Clb; Youngstown State; Respiratory Ther.

MATE, LOIS; Stow HS; Stow, OH; 1/508 Val; Debate Tm; Natl Forn Lg; NHS; Sch Pl; Stu Cncl; Y-Teens; Pres Drama Clb; Mth Clb; Natl Merit Ltr; Univ Of Vir; Architecture.

MATERN, TERRANCE; Connersville HS; Connersville, IN; 20/400 Hon Rl; NHS; Sci Clb; Spn Clb; Ftbl; Trk; Purdue Univ; Bio.

MATERNOWSKI, AMY; Manistee Catholic Cent HS; Manistee, MI; Cl Rep Jr Cls; Band; Cmnty Wkr; Hon Rl; Stu Cncl; Pep Clb; Bsktbl; Trk; GAA; Mich State Univ; Lawyer.

MATERNOWSKI, AMY; Manistee Catholic Ctrl HS; Manistee, MI; Cls Rep Frsh Cls; Cls Rep Soph Cls; Cl Rep Jr Cls; Band; Cmnty Wkr; Hon Rl; Stu Cncl; Pep Clb; Bsktbl; Trk; Michigan St Univ; Law.

MATESICH, MARK; Newark Catholic HS; Newark, OH; Letter Bsktbl; Ten; Univ; Phys Ther.

MATESZ, DONALD; Whitmer Sr HS; Toledo, OH; 13/810 Hon Rl; Univ Of Toledo Honor Schlrshp; Ohio Acad Schlrshp; Among Top Ten Grad Sr In Ohio; Univ Of Toledo; Medicine.

MATHENEY, STEVEN; Lake HS; Walbridge, OH; Aud/Vis; Pres JA; Lbry Ade; Sch Pl; Stg Crw; Drama Clb; Spn Clb; JA Awd; Miami Univ; Mass Comm.

MATHENY, SCOTT; Wauseon HS; Wauseon, OH; Pres Jr Cls; Cl Rep Jr Cls; Pres Sr Cls; Cls Rep Sr Cls; Boy Scts; Chrs; Chrh Wkr; Hon Rl; Sch Mus; Sct Actv; Actvty W Awd 79; Univ; Phys Ther.

MATHER, CYNTHIA; Salem Sr HS; Salem, OH; Hst Jr Cls; Trs Sr Cls; Cmp Fr Grls; Hon Rl; Yth Flsp; Kent St Univ; Acctg.

MATHERLY, ANITA; Independence HS; Sophia, WV; Chrh Wkr; Hon Rl; NHS; Ed Yrbk; Yrbk; FBLA; FHA; Salutatorian 1979; Beckley Coll; Acctg.

MATHERS, DAVID; Springs Valley HS; French Lick, IN; 7/97 Hon Rl; Treas FFA; VP VICA; VP Trk; Mgrs; Scr Kpr; Tmr; Ball St Univ; Archt.

MATHERS, PAUL; Springs Valley HS; French Lick, IN; Pres FFA; Trk; American Schl Of Heavy Equipment.

MATHESON, PAUL; Central HS; Evansville, IN; 20/650 Stu Cncl; Air Force Academy.

MATHEWS, ANN M; Bishop Gallagher HS; Detroit, MI; VP Soph Cls; Cl Rep Jr Cls; Hon Rl; Stu Cncl; Bsbl; Bsktbl; Coach Actv; JC Awd; College; Medicine.

MATHEWS, BARB; Pine River Jr Sr HS; Le Roy, MI; Chrs; Hon Rl; Letter Bsbl; Letter Bsktbl; College.

MATHEWS, BRENDA; Kent City HS; Casnovia, MI; 1/95 Val; Band; Hon Rl; Jr NHS; Lbry Ade; NHS; Sch Mus; Yth Flsp; Bausch & Lomb Awd; Western Michigan Univ; Acctg.

MATHEWS, BRENDA; North HS; Columbus, OH; VP Frsh Cls; Cls Rep Frsh Cls; Chrs; Chrh Wkr; Hon Rl; JA; Lbry Ade; Off Ade; Fr Clb; Bsktbl; Florida Univ; Psychologist.

MATHEWS, COLLEEN; St Joseph HS; S Bend, IN; Chrs; Hon Rl; Sch Mus; Sch Pl; Stg Crw; Drama Clb; JA Awd; Univ Of Dayton; Theatre.

MATHEWS, DANNA; Columbiana HS; Columbiana, OH; 14/100 Band; Chrh Wkr; Hon Rl; Orch; Sch Mus; Sch Pl; Yrbk; 4-H; Fr Clb; 4-H Awd; Yngstown Yth Symphny; Superior Rating Class A Solo & Ensemble Cont; Exc Rating Class Solo & Ensemble Cont; Baldwin Wallace Coll; Music.

MATHEWS, GWENDOLYN; Parchment HS; Kalamazoo, MI; Chrh Wkr; Hon Rl; Off Ade; Ed Yrbk; Bsbl; Bsktbl; Natl Merit SF; Michigan St Univ; Nursing.

MATHEWS, JERRY L; Centerville HS; Centerville, IN; Cmnty Wkr; Hon Rl; Yrbk; 4-H; Ftbl; Wrstlng; Mgrs; 4-H Awd; College.

MATHEWS, JULIE A; Richwood HS; Nettie, WV; Hon Rl; Yrbk; Sch Nwsp; Pep Clb; Marshall Univ; Special Ed.

MATHEWS, LISA; Harbor Springs HS; Hrbr Spgs, MI; Chrs; Cmnty Wkr; Girl Scts; Hon Rl; Hosp Ade; Off Ade; Sct Actv; Stu Cncl; Yrbk; 4-H; 7th Stu Cncl Treas; Sold Most Girl Scout Cookies All HS Yrs; Sold Avon & Included In Pres Celebration; W Michigan Univ; Occup Therapy.

MATHEWS, MARY; Yale HS; Goodells, MI; Band; Hon Rl; 4-H; 4-H Awd; St Clair Cmnty Coll; Gen Studies.

MATHEWS, STANLEY; Mingo HS; Mingo Jct, OH; Am Leg Boys St; Band; Debate Tm; Hon Rl; NHS; Lat Clb; Am Leg Awd; Steubenville College; Engineering Sc.

MATHEWS, STEPHANIE C; Hinton HS; Hinton, WV; 4/145 Cls Rep Frsh Cls; Am Leg Aux Girls St; Band; Chrh Wkr; Cmnty Wkr; Hon Rl; Pres Jr NHS; VP NHS; Treas Stu Cncl; Yrbk; Acctg.

MATHEWS, TERRI; Whetstone HS; Columbus, OH; Chrs; Chrh Wkr; Hon Rl; Jr NHS; NHS; Off Ade; Yth Flsp; Swmmng; Ohi State Univ; Educa.

MATHEWS, TIMOTHY; Whitmer HS; Toledo, OH; 220/950 Hon Rl; Spn Clb; Bsbl; Trk; Wrstlng; IM Sprt; Toledo Univ; Bus.

MATHEWS, TRICIA; Cardinal Mooney HS; Youngstown, OH; 25/288 Cls Rep Soph Cls; Cls Rep Sr Cls; NHS; Rptr Yrbk; Mth Clb; VP Spn Clb; Univ; Pre Med.

MATHEWSON, MICHELLE; Lawrence Ctrl HS; Indianapolis, IN; Sch Pl; Yth Flsp; Yrbk; Drama Clb; Capt Bsktbl; Socr; Indiana Univ; Cmnctns.

MATHEY, LAURIE; Perry HS; Massillon, OH; Chrs; Chrh Wkr; Cmnty Wkr; Girl Scts; Hon Rl; Natl Forn Lg; Off Ade; Quill & Scroll; Stg Crw; Yrbk; Ohio Northern Univ; Pharmacy.

MATHEY, SUE; Salem HS; Salem, OH; 43/296 AFS; Chrs; Chrh Wkr; Cmnty Wkr; Lbry Ade; Pol Wkr; Eng Clb; Fr Clb; FSA; Voice Dem Awd; College; Med.

MATHIAS, ANGELA; William A Wirt HS; Gary, IN; 10/260 Girl Scts; Hon Rl; Jr NHS; NHS; Rptr Yrbk; Pep Clb; Letter Swmmng; Letter Trk; GAA; PPFtbl; Indiana Univ; Commercial Art.

MATHIAS, DOUG; Southridge HS; Huntngbrg, IN; Band; FCA; Hon Rl; 4-H; Ger Clb; Pep Clb; Bsktbl; Glf; Wrstlng; Univ; Merch.

MATHIAS, NANCY; Carroll HS; Kettering, OH; 31/290 Band; Drl Tm; Hon Rl; NHS; Yth Flsp; Pep Clb; Trk; College.

MATHIAS, VINCENT; Lancaster Sr HS; Lancaster, OH; 321/700 AFS; Am Leg Boys St; Girl Scts; Sch Mus; Sch Pl; Stg Crw; Stu Cncl; Yth Flsp; Drama Clb; FBLA; Prfct Attndnc Lancaster HS 78; Ohio Univ; Poli Sci.

MATHIAS, VIRGINIA; North Miami HS; Roann, IN; 53/196 Chrs; FCA; Hon Rl; MMM; Off Ade; Stg Crw; 4-H; FFA; FHA; Bsktbl; Dist Horticulture & Nursery Oper 1st Pl 1978; Volleyball 1978; St Choral Award 1st 1978;.

MATHIEU, KAREN; Our Lady Of Mercy HS; Livonia, MI; Cls Rep Frsh Cls; Chrs; Univ Of Michigan; Lang.

MATHIS, ERNIE; Brown County HS; Columbus, IN; 12/205 Hon Rl; Bsbl; Bsktbl; Crs Cntry; Vincennes Univ; Conserv Law Enfrcmnt.

MATHIS, LISA; Brazil Sr HS; Brazil, IN; 3/200 Am Leg Aux Girls St; Band; Hon Rl; Mod UN; Pres NHS; Quill & Scroll; Stu Cncl; Ed Sch Nwsp; Sci Clb; Spn Clb; Purdue Academic Ldrshp Seminar; Stu Legislative Assembly; College; Phys Therapy.

MATHIS, SALLY; Hamilton Southeastern HS; Noblesville, IN; Am Leg Aux Girls St; Capt Drl Tm; Hon Rl; Sec NHS; Fr Clb; Pep Clb; Capt Pom Pon; Top Ten Percent Of Class; College.

MATHIS, WILLIAM; Goodrich HS; Goodrich, MI; Letter Bsbl; Letter Ftbl; Letter Hockey;.

MATIASH, JEAN; Whitehall HS; Whitehall, MI; 18/150 Am Leg Aux Girls St; Band; Girl Scts; Sch Pl; Drama Clb; Ten; Trk; Chrldng; PPFtbl; Central Mich Univ; Comp Progr.

MATKO, ALEXIS; Notre Dame HS; Clarksburg, WV; Sch Pl; Ten; IM Sprt; College.

MATKOVICH, MARYANNE; Wylie E Groves HS; Birmingham, MI; Girl Scts; Hon Rl; Lbry Ade; Off Ade; Orch; W Michigan St Univ; Busns Admin.

MATLICK, SHELLY; Indian Valley North HS; New Phila, OH; VP Frsh Cls; VP Soph Cls; VP Jr Cls; VP Sr Cls; Debate Tm; Girl Scts; Hon Rl; NHS; Off Ade; Ed Yrbk; Kent St Univ; Elem Educ.

MATLICK, SHELLY D; Indian Valley North HS; New Phila, OH; VP Frsh Cls; VP Soph Cls; VP Jr Cls; Sec Sr Cls; Cmnty Wkr; Hon Rl; NHS; Off Ade; Ed Yrbk; Rptr Yrbk; Kent State Univ; Accounting.

MATNEY, PAMELA S; Bluefield HS; Bluefld, WV; 27/286 Chrs; Girl Scts; Hon Rl; Jr NHS; Quill & Scroll; Yrbk; Fr Clb; Univ.

MATOUSEK, PAUL; Benedictine HS; Newburgh Hts, OH; 3/113 VP Soph Cls; VP Jr Cls; Hon Rl; NHS; Stu Cncl; Rptr Sch Nwsp; Fr Clb; Letter Crs Cntry; Letter Trk; Coach Actv; Partial Academic Schlrshp; Varsity Lettermans Clb; College.

MATRAS, ERIC E; St Alphonsus HS; Dearborn, MI; 17/180 Boy Scts; Hon Rl; Rptr Sch Nwsp; Fr Clb; Letter Crs Cntry; Letter Trk; Coach Actv; Scr Kpr; Univ Of Michigan; Medicine.

MATRISCIANO, KATHLEEN; Lumen Cordium HS; Twinsburg, OH; Chrs; Hon Rl; Hosp Ade; Off Ade; Fr Clb; FNA; Pep Clb; Crs Cntry; GAA; GAA; Marymount School Of Nursing.

MATRONIA, TAMMY; Canton South HS; Canton, OH; 69/309 Band; Girl Scts; Hon Rl; JA; Lbry Ade; 4-H; OEA; Pep Clb; Scr Kpr; 4-H Awd; Stark Technical School; Legal Sec.

MATSAKIS, EMMANUEL; Shadyside HS; Shadyside, OH; 20/120 Am Leg Boys St; NHS; Stu Cncl; Letter Ftbl; Letter Trk; Letter Wrstlng; Univ Of Ken; Dentistry.

MATSON, BETH; James A Garfield HS; Garrettsville, OH; Sch Mus; Stu Cncl; Drama Clb; Sci Clb; Letter Bsktbl; Letter Trk; Kent St Univ.

MATSON, KIM; Forest Park HS; Crystal Falls, MI; 8/95 Band; Hon Rl; IM Sprt; No Mich Univ; Registered Nurse.

MATSON, LAURIE; Ottoville Local School; Cloverdale, OH; Girl Scts; Hon Rl; Sch Mus; Stg Crw; Ed Yrbk; FHA; OEA; Ohio St Univ; Art.

MATSON, THOMAS H; South Side HS; Fort Wayne, IN; 3/429 Band; Hon Rl; Orch; Natl Merit SF; Purdue Univ; Engr.

MATTACHIONE, MIKE; Timken HS; Canton, OH; Hon Rl; Gym; Trk; Wrstlng; Akron Univ; Electrical Engineer.

MATTALIANO, VIRGINIA; Philip Barbour HS; Philippi, WV; Hon Rl; Off Ade; Y-Teens; Treas Civ Clb; Treas FDA; West Virginia Univ.

MATTEO, MELISSA; Chaney HS; Youngstown, OH; 39/323 Cl Rep Jr Cls; Hon Rl; Hosp Ade; Jr NHS; NHS; Off Ade; Stu Cncl; Capt Pom Pon; PPFtbl; Youngstown St Univ.

MATTER, JULEEN; Bluffton HS; Bluffton, OH; VP Jr Cls; Pres Sr Cls; Am Leg Aux Girls St; Band; Chrs; Hon Rl; Jr NHS; NHS; Rptr Sch Nwsp; Fr Clb; Bowling Green State Univ.

MATTER, M; Western Reserve Acad; Canton, OH; Aud/Vis; Hon Rl; Stg Crw; Mth Clb; Rdo Clb; Natl Merit SF; Univ; Elec Engr.

MATTERN, DIANE; Wabash Jr Sr HS; Wabash, IN; 19/200 Cls Rep Frsh Cls; Cls Rep Soph Cls; VP Jr Cls; Chrs; Hon Rl; NHS; Off Ade; Sch Mus; Stu Cncl; Ger Clb; Indiana Univ.

MATTERN, DOROTHY; East Liverpool HS; E Liverpool, OH; 10/337 Trs Sr Cls; Chrs; Pep Clb; Spn Clb; E Liverpool Hosp Lab Sch; Lab Asst.

MATTERN, NORMAN; Beaver Local HS; Wellsville, OH; 134/242 Cls Rep Frsh Cls; VP Jr Cls; FCA; Sch Pl; Stu Cncl; Eng Clb; Fr Clb; Mth Clb; Mgrs; Most Outstndg Sr Awrd 79;.

MATTES, BONNIE; North Royalton HS; N Royalton, OH; 1/275 Band; Hon Rl; NHS; Drama Clb; Fr Clb; OEA; Sec.

MATTESON, BURTON; Penn HS; Mishawaka, IN; Chrh Wkr; Hon Rl; Treas Yth Flsp; Bethel College; Bio.

MATTESON, JACK; Parkersburg HS; Parkersburg, WV; Chrs; Sch Mus; San Diego Univ; Zoology.

MATTHAI, CATHERINE; Mt Notre Dame HS; Loveland, OH; 1/180 Band; Cmnty Wkr; Hon Rl; NHS; Fr Clb; Gym; Capt Chrldng; Coach Actv; GAA; IM Sprt; Univ Of Dayton; Chem Engr.

MATTHEIS, MARK; Hagerstown HS; Hagerstown, IN; Am Leg Boys St; Band; Sch Mus; Sch Pl; Yrbk; Sch Nwsp; Letter Swmmng; Letter Trk; Letter Mgrs;.

MATTHEW, TANICE; North White HS; Reynolds, IN; 17/75 Hon Rl; 4-H; Ger Clb; Mth Clb; Sci Clb; Ivy Tech Schl; Med Asst.

MATTHEWS, CINDY; South Spencer HS; Rockport, IN; 1/160 Trs Frsh Cls; Cl Rep Jr Cls; Cls Rep Sr Cls; Val; Am Leg Aux Girls St; Band; Chrs; Chrs; Cmnty Wkr; Girl Scts; Univ Of Evansville.

MATTHEWS, CLARISSA; Sandusky HS; Sandusky, OH; Chrs; Chrh Wkr; Girl Scts; Hon Rl; JA; NHS; Off Ade; Orch; Ohio Northern Univ; Child Psych.

MATTHEWS, JOHN; Montpelier HS; Montpelier, OH; 5/109 Aud/Vis; Chrs; Debate Tm; Hon Rl; Jr NHS; NHS; Sch Pl; Rptr Yrbk; Mth Clb; JETS Awd; Ohio Awd Of Distinction; Martin Sprocket & Grear Inc Math & Sci Schlrshp; Rensselaer Poly Tech Inst; Physics.

MATTHEWS, KATHLEEN L; Walter E Stebbins HS; Kettering, OH; Cmnty Wkr; Letter Ten; Mat Maids; Wright State Univ; Comp Sci.

MATTHEWS, KEVIN; Escanaba Area HS; Escanaba, MI; 46/438 Univ.

MATTHEWS, KIMBERLY; Onsted HS; Onsted, MI; Trs Frsh Cls; Trs Soph Cls; Trs Jr Cls; Hon Rl; Hosp Ade; Off Ade; Sch Pl; Yrbk; FHA; FTA; R N.

MATTHEWS, MARK; Loogootee Community HS; Loogootee, IN; 7/150 Pres Jr Cls; Cl Rep Jr Cls; Pres Sr Cls; Cls Rep Sr Cls; Am Leg Boys St; Chrh Wkr; Stu Cncl; Spn Clb; IM Sprt; Mgrs; College; Social Sci.

MATTHEWS, MELANIE; Hale Area HS; Hale, MI; 10/60 Band; Chrh Wkr; Cmnty Wkr; Hon Rl; Red Cr Ade; Yth Flsp; 4-H; 4-H Awd; Coll; Pharmacy.

MATTHEWS, NANCY; Bishop Foley HS; Madison Hts, MI; Cls Rep Sr Cls; Girl Scts; Hon Rl; NHS; Sch Pl; Stu Cncl; Yrbk; Letter Crs Cntry; Letter Trk; IM Sprt; Univ; Cmnctns.

MATTHEWS, PAMELA; William Henry Harrison HS; Evansville, IN; Cls Rep Soph Cls; Cl Rep Jr Cls; Cls Rep Sr Cls; Chrs; Chrh Wkr; Cmnty Wkr; Girl Scts; Hon Rl; JA; Orch; Grtr Evanbsville Yth Symp Orch 77; Pres Gld Teens Clb 78; Evansville Coll; Music.

MATTHEWS, RANDY; Bath HS; Laingsburg, MI; Sec Frsh Cls; Debate Tm; Hon Rl; Sch Pl; Rptr Sch Nwsp; Sch Nwsp; Wrstlng; Scr Kpr; Alma Coll; Acting.

MATTHEWS, STEVEN G; Winfield HS; Scott Depot, WV; VP Frsh Cls; Am Leg Boys St; Band; FCA; Hon Rl; Jr NHS; Stu Cncl; Beta Clb; Bsktbl; Crs Cntry; Marshall Univ; Criminal Justice.

MATTHEWS, TAMI; Martinsburg HS; Martinsburg, WV; 8/250 Cls Rep Frsh Cls; Cls Rep Soph Cls; Cls Rep Sr Cls; Hon Rl; Stu Cncl; Rptr Yrbk; Rptr Sch Nwsp; Pep Clb; Letter Chrldng; Scr Kpr; Morris Harvey Coll; Computer Sci.

MATTHEWS, VICKIE; Miller HS; Corning, OH; Band; Chrs; Hon Rl; NHS; Sch Pl; Yrbk; Sch Nwsp; FBLA; IM Sprt; Scr Kpr;.

MATTHEWS, VICKY; Onekama Consolidated School; Kaleva, MI; Band; Girl Scts; Hon Rl; Lbry Ade; Sch Pl; Stg Crw; Yrbk; Drama Clb; 4-H; FHA; Michigan Tech Univ; Marine Bio.

MATTHIS, DOREEN E; Williamsburg HS; Batavia, OH; 1/94 Val; Chrs; Capt Drl Tm; Hon Rl; NHS; Sec Yth Flsp; Drama Clb; Pres 4-H; 4-H Awd; Univ; Acctg.

MATTHIS, F D; Williamsburg HS; Batavia, OH; Cls Rep Frsh Cls; Am Leg Boys St; Hon Rl; NHS; Stu Cncl; Yth Flsp; Mas Awd; Computer Science.

MATTHIS, F DALE; Williamsburg HS; Batavia, OH; 3/99 Cls Rep Frsh Cls; Chrh Wkr; Hon Rl; NHS; Stu Cncl; Yth Flsp; 4-H; Sci Clb; Spn Clb; Letter Ftbl; College; Accounting.

MATTICE, MICHAEL S; Trenton HS; Trenton, MI; Band; Boy Scts; Yth Flsp; Letter Wrstlng; Syracuse Univ; Comp Engr.

MATTIELLO, JOSEPH; Ferndale HS; Oak Park, MI; 7/370 Band; Hon Rl; NHS; Ger Clb; Mth Clb; Univ Of Michigan; Comp Engr.

MATTIN, MATT; Delta Sr HS; Delta, OH; Letter Wrstlng; Voc Schl; Elec.

MATTINAT, BETSY; Hubbard HS; Hubbard, OH; 17/330 Girl Scts; Hon Rl; Off Ade; Bsktbl; Am Leg Awd; Univ; Acctg.

MATTINGLY, WANDA; George Rogers Clark HS; Whiting, IN; 57/253 Cmp Fr Grls; Chrs; Chrh Wkr; Cmnty Wkr; Drl Tm; Drm Mjrt; Hon Rl; JA; Off Ade; Orch; Mst Valbl Chr Mbr 77; 3 1st & 6 2nd In Twrlng 75 78; Patol Awd Sci Fari 1st Pl 6,; Purdue Univ; Phys Ther.

MATTIS, JULIA; Millersport HS; Thornville, OH; 1/65 Am Leg Aux Girls St; Treas Band; Chrs; Chrh Wkr; FCA; Girl Scts; Hon Rl; Hosp Ade; Jr NHS; Lbry Ade; Attend Michigan Tech Univ Because Of Sci & Math Grades; Schlrshp Team Gen Sci; Sci Fair Winner Cnty & State; Muskingum Univ; Biological Research.

MATTIS, JULIE; Frankenmuth HS; Birch Run, MI; 1/183 VP Frsh Cls; Cls Rep Soph Cls; Val; Band; NHS; Rptr Yrbk; Capt Chrldng; Bausch & Lomb Awd; Natl Merit Ltr; SAR Awd; Michigan Tech Univ; Envir Engr.

MATTISON, STANLEY; Cass Technical HS; Detroit, MI; Aud/Vis; Debate Tm; Hon Rl; Pol Wkr; Stu Cncl; IM Sprt; Cit Awd; Marines Corps.

MATTOX, RANDY; Indian Creek HS; Trafalgar, IN; Boy Scts; Hon Rl; Sct Actv; Yth Flsp; Sci Clb; Natl Merit Ltr; Purdue Univ; Sci.

MATTSON, JODI; Allen Park HS; Allen Park, MI; 35/436 Band; Chrs; Girl Scts; Hon Rl; Jr NHS; Sct Actv; Ed Sch Nwsp; Sch Nwsp; Fr Clb; Michigan St Univ; Jrnlsm.

MATTSON, MARGO; Adelphian Academy; Livonia, MI; Pres Sr Cls; Band; Mdrgl; NHS; Off Ade; Red Cr Ade; Rptr Sch Nwsp; Bsbl; Hockey; IM Sprt; Andrews Univ; Theology.

MATTSON, MARLENE; Adelphian Academy; Livonia, MI; 3/54 Band; Chrs; Hon Rl; NHS; Quill & Scroll; Ed Sch Nwsp; Bsbl; Bsktbl; Capt Hockey; Stu Assn Pres; Andrews Univ; Medicine.

MATUJA, LESLIE; Bishop Gallagher HS; Roseville, MI; Cls Rep Soph Cls; Band; Chrh Wkr; Cmnty Wkr; Hon Rl; Jr NHS; PAVAS; Pol Wkr; Stu Cncl; Rptr Sch Nwsp; University; Law.

MATUREN, RENEE; Reed City Public HS; Reed City, MI; 18/170 Cls Rep Sr Cls; Chrs; Chrh Wkr; Girl Scts; Hon Rl; Hosp Ade; Lbry Ade; Off Ade; Sch Mus; Sch Pl; Central Michigan Univ; Cmnctns.

MATUSEK, JANE; Polaris Joint Voc Schl; Middleburg Hts, OH; Cls Rep Frsh Cls; Debate Tm; Girl Scts; Sch Pl; Pres DECA; Bsbl; IM Sprt; Twrlr; Cit Awd; JC Awd; Cuyahoga Cmnty Coll; Sales Rep.

MATUSIC, KAREN; Buckeye West HS; Adena, OH; Band; Hon Rl; NHS; Sch Pl; Yth Flsp; Rptr Sch Nwsp; Drama Clb; 4-H; FTA; Sci Clb; Ohio St Univ; Agri Educ.

MATUSKA, DEANNA; Seton HS; Cincinnati, OH; Chrs; Girl Scts; Hon Rl; NHS; Stg Crw; Mth Clb; Pres Spn Clb; Kiwan Awd; Univ Of Notre Dame; Engr.

MATUSZAK, JANE; Lorain Catholic HS; Lorain, OH; Cls Rep Soph Cls; Chrs; Hon Rl; Stu Cncl; Yrbk; Sch Nwsp; Trk; Univ.

MATUSZAK, MICHELLE; St Marys Cathedral HS; Elmira, MI; Cls Rep Soph Cls; Band; Hon Rl; NHS; Stu Cncl; Ed Yrbk; Yrbk; Rptr Sch Nwsp; Pep Clb; PPFtbl; Lake Superior State Coll; Child Dev.

MATUSZEWSKI, LISA; John Glenn HS; Bay City, MI; 4/360 VP Jr Cls; Band; Hon Rl; Natl Forn Lg; NHS; Orch; Sch Pl; Letter Swmmng; Pom Pon; Natl Merit Schl; Marquette Univ; Med Tech.

MATUSZEWSKI, MARK; Bay City All Sts Ctrl HS; Bay City, MI; Pres Frsh Cls; Band; Hon Rl; Mdrgl; Sch Pl; Bsbl; Glf; Cit Awd; Univ; Med.

MATZ, MICHAEL; Lebanon HS; Lebanon, OH; 1/275 Hon Rl; NHS; Sch Pl; Yth Flsp; Bsbl; Letter Ftbl; Trk; Wrstlng; Univ; Engr.

MATZAS, JOANNE; Aquinas HS; Southgate, MI; Chrh Wkr; Hon Rl; NHS; Sch Pl; Drama Clb; Siena Heights College; Poli Sci.

MAU, CAROL; Owosso HS; Owosso, MI; Am Leg Aux Girls St; Band; Chrh Wkr; Hon Rl; NHS; Lat Clb; Pep Clb; Swmmng; Pom Pon; Twrlr; Univ Of Mich; Engring.

MAUCH, CYNTHIA; Glen Este HS; Cincinatti, OH; Cls Rep Frsh Cls; Drm Mjrt; Hon Rl; NHS; Stu Cncl; Pep Clb; Spn Clb; Letter Chrldng; Twrlr; Am Leg Awd; Coll; Elem Educ.

MAUCK, LINDA; Heath HS; Heath, OH; Cls Rep Soph Cls; Band; Chrs; Hon Rl; Yrbk; Spn Clb; Univ.

MAUDER, KIM; Worthington Jefferson HS; Worthington, IN; 10/40 Pres Frsh Cls; VP Soph Cls; Chrs; Hon Rl; Lbry Ade; Off Ade; Sprt Ed Yrbk; Yrbk; Beta Clb; FHA; Univ; Phys Ed.

MAUDLIN, JULIE R; Corunna HS; Bancroft, MI; Band; Hon Rl; 4-H; 4-H Awd; LCC; Jrnlsm.

MAUDLIN, TIM; E Washington Schl Corp HS; Pekin, IN; 10/84 Chrh Wkr; Cmnty Wkr; Hon Rl; NHS; Sch Nwsp; 4-H; Bsktbl; 4-H Awd; Purdue Univ; Cmmrcl Artist.

MAUE, ROBIN; Whitehall HS; Whitehall, MI; Hon Rl; 4-H; Trk; GAA; College; Photography.

MAUEL, KATHERINE; Clay HS; South Bend, IN; Cls Rep Frsh Cls; Aud/Vis; Hon Rl; NHS; Rptr Sch Nwsp; Lat Clb; Letter Swmmng; Letter Trk; Natl Merit SF; College; Chem Engr.

MAUGHAN, MARY; Rochester Community HS; Rochester, IN; 15/169 Band; Chrs; Chrh Wkr; FCA; Hon Rl; NHS; Sch Mus; Yth Flsp; Fr Clb; Pep Clb; Univ.

MAUHAR, PETER; Gladstone HS; Gladstone, MI; 2/203 Sal; Am Leg Boys St; Band; Pres NHS; Pres Stu Cncl; Rptr Sch Nwsp; Letter Bsktbl; Letter Ftbl; Mic Tech Univ; Mech Engr.

MAUK, DEBBIE; Ehove Vocational School; Sandusky, OH; 25/240 Cls Rep Frsh Cls; Hst Sr Cls; Cls Rep Sr Cls; Band; Chrs; Drl Tm; Hon Rl; Sch Mus; Stu Cncl; DECA;.

MAUK, JANE; Bath HS; Lima, OH; VP Jr Cls; Band; Hon Rl; NHS; Sch Mus; Sch Pl; Sprt Ed Yrbk; Rptr Yrbk; Fr Clb; Ohio St Univ; Nursing.

MAULER, ANITA; Belpre HS; Belpre, OH; Band; Chrh Wkr; Hon Rl; Hosp Ade; NHS; Yth Flsp; JETS Awd; Otterbein Coll; Acctg.

MAUPIN, KIRK; Eaton HS; Eaton, OH; 7/150 Band; Chrs; Chrh Wkr; Cmnty Wkr; FCA; Hon Rl; Sch Mus; Sch Nwsp; Air Force Academy; Pilot.

MAURE, MARTHA; Washington HS; South Bend, IN; 17/300 Chrh Wkr; Girl Scts; Hon Rl; NHS; Sct Actv; Pep Clb; Spn Clb; Am Leg Awd; Purdue Univ; Speech Ther.

MAUREN, MARK; St Joseph Prep Seminary; Portland, MI; Boy Scts; Cmnty Wkr; Hon Rl; Sch Pl; Sct Actv; Rptr Yrbk; Rptr Sch Nwsp; Lat Clb; Spn Clb; Letter Bsbl; Lansing Cmnty Coll; Media Tech.

MAURER, CAROLYN; Elmhurst HS; Ft Wayne, IN; Sec Soph Cls; Trs Soph Cls; Cls Rep Soph Cls; Cl Rep Jr Cls; Cls Rep Sr Cls; Drl Tm; Hon Rl; Stu Cncl; Yth Flsp; Flag Captain; Social Chairman Of Jr Class; Indiana St Univ; Nursing.

MAURER, CHERYL; Terre Haute South Vigo HS; Terre Haute, IN; 139/630 Trs Frsh Cls; Chrh Wkr; Cmnty Wkr; Drl Tm; Hon Rl; Sch Mus; Stu Cncl; Y-Teens; Rptr Sch Nwsp; Gym; Indiana St Univ; Occupt Ther.

MAURER, DENISE; Chaminade Julienne HS; Dayton, OH; JA; Rptr Sch Nwsp; Univ; Phys Ther.

MAURER, DIANE; St Johns HS; Dewitt, MI; Trs Frsh Cls; Trs Soph Cls; Cls Rep Sr Cls; Girl Scts; Hon Rl; NHS; Stu Cncl; Pep Clb; Gym; Ten; Central Michigan Univ; Bus Admin.

MAURER, DOUGLAS; Ridgewood HS; W Lafayette, OH; 17/150 Am Leg Boys St; Cmnty Wkr; Hon Rl; NHS; Letter Bsbl; Letter Bsktbl; Ohio Univ; Comp Sci.

MAURER, HEIDI; Mendon Union HS; Mendon, OH; 2/35 Trs Frsh Cls; Cls Rep Sr Cls; Band; Chrs; Chrh Wkr; Hon Rl; NHS; Off Ade; Sch Pl; Stu Cncl; Univ; Phys Ed.

MAURER, KAREN; Harbor Beach HS; Bad Axe, MI; Chrs; Hon Rl; NHS; Off Ade; Sch Mus; Stg Crw; Eng Clb; 4-H; FHA; Pep Clb; Baker Jr Coll; Sec.

MAURER, KAREN L; Grove City HS; Grove City, OH; 1/548 Chrs; Chrh Wkr; Cmnty Wkr; Hon Rl; NHS; Off Ade; OEA; Opt Clb Awd; Stdnt Of The Yr 78; Exec & Dipl Awd 78; 2nd In Nation In Extemperaneous Verbal Cmnctn 79; Franklin Univ; Bus Admin.

MAURER, MICHELE; Bishop Ready HS; Columbus, OH; Girl Scts; Hon Rl; Hosp Ade; Sch Mus; Sch Pl; Sct Actv; College; Nursing.

MAURER, SHARON; Hubbard HS; Hubbard, OH; 20/330 Hon Rl; JA; Sec Lat Clb; Youngstown Univ; B F A.

MAURICE, KEITH; Melvindale HS; Allen Park, MI; 3/281 Cls Rep Frsh Cls; Cls Rep Soph Cls; Cl Rep Jr Cls; Cls Rep Sr Cls; NHS; Stu Cncl; VP Key Clb; Pres Sci Clb; VP Spn Clb; Capt Wrstlng; Detroit Assoc Of Phi Beta Kappa Awd 79; Chosen As Treas City Allen Pk Stud Govt Day 79; Adrian Coll; Bus Admin.

MAUSER, JEAN; Denby HS; Detroit, MI; VP Band; Jr NHS; NHS; Hockey; Univ; Psych.

MAUSSER, MARGE; Valley Forge HS; Parma, OH; 54/704 Cls Rep Sr Cls; Chrs; Hon Rl; NHS; Stu Cncl; Chrldng; Univ Of Akron; Acct.

MAUST, MARIETTA; North Daviess Jr Sr HS; Montgomery, IN; 1/92 Cls Rep Sr Cls; Val; Hon Rl; Beta Clb; 4-H; FHA; Spn Clb; DAR Awd; Vincennes Univ; Nursing.

MAUTER, TAMMY; Newark Catholic HS; Newark, OH; Chrs; Hon Rl; NHS; Fr Clb; Sci Clb; Swmmng; Trk; Chrldng; GAA; IM Sprt; College; Elementary Education.

MAUTZ, SHARON; Heath HS; Newark, OH; Hon Rl; Spn Clb; Letter Gym; Trk; Art.

MAUZY, CAMILLA A; Laurel HS; Laurel, IN; Band; Chrh Wkr; Hon Rl; NHS; Rptr Yrbk; Sch Nwsp; 4-H; Purdue Univ; Vet.

MAUZY, TIMOTHY J; Circleville HS; Riverton, WV; Cl Rep Jr Cls; Band; Cmnty Wkr; Hon Rl; Sch Mus; Yrbk; Rptr Sch Nwsp; Sch Nwsp; Spn Clb; 4-H Awd; West Virginia Univ; Bus Mgmt.

MAVIS, CHARLES; Deckerville Community School; Sandusky, MI; Aud/Vis; Band; Hon Rl; Treas NHS; Sch Pl; Pres Stu Cncl; Drama Clb; Trk; Letter Coach Actv; Letter Mgrs; Northwood Inst Univ; Retail Mdse.

MAWBY, CHARLIE; Rockford HS; Rockford, MI; 44/364 Band; Hon Rl; Sch Mus; Lat Clb; Sci Clb; Grand Rapids Jr College; Chem Engr.

MAWBY, MICHAEL; St Ignatius HS; S Euclid, OH; 54/309 Trs Frsh Cls; Cls Rep Soph Cls; Cl Rep Jr Cls; Hon Rl; NHS; Bsktbl; Crs Cntry; IM Sprt; Coll; Acctg.

MAXCY, JEFFREY; Marion HS; Marion, IN; 5/645 Band; Boy Scts; Hon Rl; Pres Mdrgl; NHS; Orch; Sch Mus; Kiwan Awd; Rotary Awd; Outstndn Gpercussnst Med W Swing Chr Contst 79; NISBOUA 3 Ust Pl St Medl 78; Purdue Univ; Vet Med.

MAXEY, MICHAEL; Willow Run HS; Ypsilanti, MI; Boy Scts; Hon Rl; Sch Pl; Sct Actv; Boys Clb Am; Sci Clb; Bsktbl; Letter Ftbl; JETS Awd; Auburn Univ; Engr Tech.

MAXEY, STEPHANIE; Arlington HS; Indianapolis, IN; 19/479 Am Leg Aux Girls St; Hon Rl; NHS; Stu Cncl; Rptr Yrbk; 4-H; Sci Clb; Spn Clb; PPFtbl; JA Awd; Purdue Univ; Engr.

MAXFIELD, CHERYL; Deckerville Cmnty HS; Sandusky, MI; Trs Frsh Cls; Sec Soph Cls; Trs Jr Cls; Trs Sr Cls; OEA; Chrldng; St Clair Cnty Cmnty Coll; CPA.

MAXFIELD, SUE; Madison Comprehensive HS; Mansfield, OH; Lit Mag; Girl Scts; Orch; Stu Cncl; 4-H; FHA; Spn Clb; Ten; Mat Maids; Scr Kpr; Univ; Poli Sci.

MAXIE, SHEILA; Crothersville HS; Crothersville, IN; Sec Frsh Cls; Trs Soph Cls; Sec Jr Cls; FCA; Hon Rl; NHS; Ed Yrbk; Pep Clb; Chrldng; Dnfth Awd;.

MAXSON, CRYSTAL; Bridgeport HS; Bridgeport, WV; 36/189 Hon Rl; NHS; Stg Crw; Stu Cncl; Rptr Yrbk; Rptr Sch Nwsp; Sec Keyettes; VP Pep Clb; Wesleyan Coll.

MAXSON, KIMBERLY; Fairlawn HS; Conover, OH; Sec Jr Cls; Chrs; Hon Rl; Jr NHS; Sch Mus; Yth Flsp; Yrbk; Pres 4-H; FHA; Ger Clb; Ohio Northern Univ; Eng Tchr.

MAXSON, LOIS; Elkins HS; Elkins, WV; 70/227 Chrs; Chrh Wkr; Cmnty Wkr; Hon Rl; Hosp Ade; Rptr Sch Nwsp; VICA; Grad From Nursing Schl With 540 Hrs Nurse Asst 79; Activ Mbr Tri Hi Y 76 79; Partcptd Youth Govt Progr 78; Alderson Broaddus Coll; Voc Rehab.

MAXSON, TAMMY; Fremont HS; Fremont, MI; Chrs; FCA; Hon Rl; Yrbk; Pres FBLA; Treas Spn Clb; Gym; Chrldng; Grand Rapids Baptist Coll; Sec.

MAXTON, SHELIA; Hamilton HS; Angola, IN; 6/55 Band; Chrs; Chrh Wkr; Cmnty Wkr; Hon Rl; NHS; Stg Crw; 4-H; 4-H Awd; Kiwan Awd; Ball St Univ; Elem Educ.

MAXWELL, ARDITH; Cedar Springs HS; Cedar Springs, MI; Band; Cmnty Wkr; Hon Rl; Jr NHS; College.

MAXWELL, CARL; Nitro HS; Charleston, WV; Boy Scts; Hon Rl; Sch Pl; Stu Cncl; Drama Clb; 4-H; Mth Clb; Univ; Archt.

MAXWELL, DONALD; Avon Jr Sr HS; Indianpls, IN; 1/188 Val; Band; Treas NHS; Sch Mus; Rptr Sch Nwsp; Pres Lat Clb; Trk; Butler Univ; Music Educ.

MAXWELL, ELANDA; Ridgewood HS; W Lafayette, OH; 18/156 Band; Hon Rl; NHS; Off Ade; Red Cr Ade; 4-H; Bsktbl; Trk; GAA; Muskingum Area Tech; Data Proc.

MAXWELL, HENRY; Grafton HS; Thornton, WV; Sec Frsh Cls; Cls Rep Sr Cls; Chrs; Chrh Wkr; Cmnty Wkr; Hon Rl; Stu Cncl; 4-H; FFA; Pep Clb; Wv Univ; Vet.

MAXWELL, LARY; Warren Woods HS; Warren, MI; 39/364 NHS; Letter Ftbl; Capt Trk; Coach Actv; Adrian Coll; Bus Admin.

MAXWELL, MARY; West Carrollton HS; W Carrollton, OH; Band; Chrh Wkr; Debate Tm; Girl Scts; JA; Jr NHS; Natl Forn Lg; NHS; Ger Clb; Mgrs; Univ Of Cincinnati.

MAXWELL, SANDRA; Columbus Central HS; Columbus, OH; Trs Jr Cls; Chrs; Drl Tm; Hon Rl; Treas JA; NHS; Sch Mus; Stg Crw; Stu Cncl; Yth Flsp; Univ.

MAXWELL, SHELIA; University HS; Morgantown, WV; Cls Rep Frsh Cls; Cls Rep Soph Cls; Am Leg Aux Girls St; Stu Cncl; Crs Cntry; Gym; Trk; Chrldng; IM Sprt; College; Phys Educ.

MAXWELL, TRISHA; Claymont HS; Uhrichsville, OH; 9/200 Band; Drl Tm; Hon Rl; Sec NHS; FTA; Treas Pep Clb; VP Spn Clb; Letter Bsktbl; Letter Trk; PPFtbl; Univ Of Akron Assoc Schlrshp 79; Akron Univ; Elem Educ.

MAXWELL JR, GLENN E; Bellaire HS; Bellaire, OH; 6/225 Boy Scts; FCA; Hon Rl; NHS; Yth Flsp; Fr Clb; Bsbl; Ftbl; God Cntry Awd; Eagle Scout 76; Ohio St Univ.

MAY, ANTHONY; Blue Rover Valley HS; New Castle, IN; 1/95 Cls Rep Frsh Cls; Cls Rep Sr Cls; Am Leg Boys St; Chrs; Chrh Wkr; Hon Rl; Lbry Ade; Pres NHS; Sch Pl; Stu Cncl; Indiana Univ; Poli Sci.

MAY, ARDITH; Albion HS; Homer, MI; Cmp Fr Grls; Cmnty Wkr; Hon Rl; Hosp Ade; Off Ade; Stg Crw; Drama Clb; 4-H; Central Mic Univ; Secondary Educ.

MAY, BARBARA; Midland Trail HS; Clifftop, WV; Band; Chrh Wkr; Hon Rl; Sch Pl; Yrbk; Rptr Sch Nwsp; Drama Clb; 4-H; FHA; Pep Clb; Univ; Theatre Arts.

MAY, BONNIE; Maple Vly HS; Nashville, MI; 54/119 Chrs; Chrh Wkr; Hon Rl; Voc Schl; Sec.

MAY, BRUCE A; Pontiac Central HS; Clarkston, MI; Am Leg Boys St; Band; Debate Tm; Hon Rl; Natl Forn Lg; Orch; Sch Mus; Partial Schlrshp To Interlochen Music Comp 78; 80 Class Band Mbr Of The Yr 77 79; Univ; Bus.

MAY, CHARLES J; Dayton Christian HS; Arcanum, OH; Band; Chrs; Chrh Wkr; Cmnty Wkr; FCA; Yth Flsp; Letter Crs Cntry; Letter Trk; Assoc Dayton Museum Of Natural History; American HS Athlete; Air Force Academy; Science.

MAY, DAVID P; Sandy Valley HS; Magnolia, OH; 4/160 Band; Chrh Wkr; Hon Rl; NHS; Sch Mus; Yth Flsp; Bsbl; Bsktbl; Ochosen For Buckeye Boys St Delegate; College; Math.

MAY, DEANNA; South HS; Columbus, OH; Drl Tm; Hon Rl; Jr NHS; NHS; Off Ade; Stu Cncl; Sch Nwsp; Eng Clb; Treas FHA; Treas OEA; Awd From The Ohio Hse Of Rep; College; Sec.

MAY, DEBRA; Perrysburg HS; Perrysburg, OH; Sec Sr Cls; Chrs; Hon Rl; Hosp Ade; NHS; Stu Cncl; Drama Clb; Fr Clb; Ten; Mat Maids; Miami Univ; Jrnlsm.

MAY, EMMA L; Jane Addams Voc HS; Cleveland, OH; Cmp Fr Grls; Chrh Wkr; Cmnty Wkr; Girl Scts; Sch Pl; Bsbl; Hndbl; Swmmng; Ten; Trk; Jane Addams Voc Schl; Food Serv.

MAY, GREG; E Canton HS; E Canton, OH; Sprt Ed Sch Nwsp; Spn Clb; Bsbl; Bsktbl; College; Business.

MAY, JACQUELINE; Mississinawa Vly HS; New Weston, OH; 8/88 Sec Soph Cls; Cl Rep Jr Cls; Cls Rep Sr Cls; Pres Band; Drm Mjrt; Pres NHS; Sec Stu Cncl; Pres 4-H; Sci Clb; Chrldng; Mt Carmel Schl Of Nursing; Nurse.

MAY, JOHN; St Marys Ctrl Catholic HS; Sandusky, OH; 11/125 Pres Frsh Cls; Pres Soph Cls; Am Leg Boys St; Boy Scts; Chrs; Chrh Wkr; Hon Rl; College.

MAY, JORG; East Preston Sr HS; Terra Alta, WV; VP Frsh Cls; Aud/Vis; Hon Rl; Yth Flsp; Sprt Ed Yrbk; Drama Clb; VICA; Letter Bsktbl; Letter Glf; Coach Actv; Univ; Pharm.

MAY, KAREN; Martinsvilla HS; Martinsville, IN; 41/450 Band; Chrh Wkr; Girl Scts; Off Ade; Stu Cncl; Pep Clb; Scr Kpr; College; Law.

MAY, KAROL; Jay Cnty HS; Portland, IN; 22/474 AFS; Band; Chrh Wkr; FCA; Hon Rl; Jr NHS; NHS; Yth Flsp; Y-Teens; Fr Clb; Milligan Coll; Soc Work.

MAY, KATHLEEN; Edgewood HS; Bloomington, IN; VP Frsh Cls; Band; Chrh Wkr; Sch Pl; Stg Crw; Drama Clb; Spn Clb; 4-H Awd; Indiana Univ; Med.

MAY, KENNETH; North Miami HS; Peru, IN; Hon Rl; NHS; Ed Sch Nwsp; Trk; College; Forest.

MAY, LAURA A; Lemon Monroe HS; Monroe, OH; Band; Chrs; Chrh Wkr; Drl Tm; Girl Scts; Off Ade; Sch Mus; Sch Pl; Sct Actv; Yrbk; Dee Russell Lee; Sec.

MAY, MICHAEL P; Northwest HS; Cincinnati, OH; VP Sr Cls; FCA; Jr NHS; NHS; Lat Clb; Mth Clb; Letter Wrstlng; Cit Awd; Straight A Stu Reds Awd; Hnr Stu Awd; Univ Of Cincinnati; Chem Engr.

MAY, MILLIE; Windham HS; Windham, OH; 1/109 Cls Rep Frsh Cls; Trs Soph Cls; Hon Rl; NHS; Sch Pl; Stu Cncl; Rptr Sch Nwsp; Bsbl; Letter Trk; Capt Chrldng; Two Yr All Star Summer Softbl League 1977; Volleyball 1976; Buckeye Girls St Candidate 1979; Kent St Univ; Labor & Bus Mgmt.

MAY, RENETTA; Point Pleasant HS; Pt Pleasant, WV; Girl Scts; Hon Rl; Hosp Ade; Off Ade; Yrbk; FHA; Marshall Univ; Comp Prog.

MAY, RICHARD; Madison Hts HS; Anderson, IN; Hosp Ade; VICA; TUPVI; Nursing.

MAY, RONALD K; Edgewood HS; Bloomington, IN; 12/223 Boy Scts; Chrh Wkr; FCA; Hon Rl; Sct Actv; Key Clb; Letter Ftbl; Letter Wrstlng; Naval Academy; Aero Engr.

MAY, SCOTT; Shakamak HS; Jasonville, IN; Band; Hon Rl; NHS; Quill & Scroll; Sch Pl; Yth Flsp; Sch Nwsp; Drama Clb; Indiana State; Spanish.

MAY, TAMMY; Central Baptist HS; Cincinnati, OH; 3/20 Trs Frsh Cls; Chrh Wkr; Hon Rl; Off Ade; Sch Pl; Drama Clb; Scr Kpr; Pensacola Christian Coll; Scndry Edc.

MAY, YELANDRA; Marian HS; Cincinnati, OH; Pres Jr Cls; Band; Treas NHS; Stu Cncl; Coach Actv; IM Sprt; Dnfth Awd; Spelman Coll; Bio Chem.

MAYBERRY, DALE; Norwayne HS; Sterling, OH; VICA; Letter Glf; Letter Swmmng; Machinist.

MAYBERRY, JANE E; Highland Sr HS; Highland, IN; 56/494 Debate Tm; Girl Scts; NHS; Stg Crw; Yth Flsp; Drama Clb; Pres Sci Clb; Natl Merit SF; Natl Merit Schl; Pres Awd; Purdue Univ; Engr.

MAYBURY, CATHERINE; Shortridge HS; Indianapolis, IN; 8/500 Cls Rep Frsh Cls; Cls Rep Soph Cls; Hon Rl; NHS; Quill & Scroll; Sch Mus; Stu Cncl; Rptr Yrbk; Rptr Sch Nwsp; Sch Nwsp; I U Hon Progr Sime Finlst 78; Whos Who Among In & Ky For Lang Stdnt 77; Mu Alpha Theat Mbr 78; Univ; Cnslr.

MAYE, BRENDA; Withrow HS; Cincinnati, OH; 4/563 Pres Jr Cls; Cl Rep Jr Cls; Pres Sr Cls; Hon Rl; NHS; Top 10% 79; Voc Achvmnt 79; Univ Of Cincinnati; Legal Sec Tech.

MAYEDA, MARY LYNN; Loy Norrix HS; Kalamazoo, MI; Pres Soph Cls; Chrs; Chrh Wkr; Hon Rl; NHS; Sch Mus; Yth Flsp; Mic State Univ; Comm.

MAYER, DAN; Princeton HS; Cincinnati, OH; 125/669 FCA; Hon Rl; Quill & Scroll; Rptr Sch Nwsp; Beta Clb; Key Clb; Bsktbl; Scr Kpr; Miamo Of Ohi; Mass Communications.

MAYER, DENISE; Rudyard HS; Fibre, MI; VP Frsh Cls; VP Soph Cls; Trs Jr Cls; Pres Sr Cls; Hon Rl; Jr NHS; NHS; FHA; OEA; Capt Chrldng; Muskegon; Sec.

MAYER, ED; St Xavier HS; Cincinnati, OH; 97/314 Cmnty Wkr; Hon Rl; Rptr Yrbk; Boys Clb Am; Pep Clb; Spn Clb; Trk; IM Sprt; Essay Contest Winner; 4th Pl Natl Ftbl Contest;.

MAYER, JOHN; Padua HS; Parma, OH; Boy Scts; Letter Hockey; Socr; Coach Actv; IM Sprt; Tmr; College.

MAYER, JOHN S; St Francis De Sales HS; Toledo, OH; Hon Rl; Stg Crw; Trk; IM Sprt; Univ Of Toledo; Theatre Arts.

MAYER, MARK; Stephenson HS; Stephenson, MI; 15/98 Aud/Vis; Band; Chrs; Chrh Wkr; Cmnty Wkr; Hon Rl; Lbry Ade; Lit Mag; Sch Pl; Stg Crw; Mic Tech; Engr.

MAYER, MARK W; Wheeling Park HS; Wheeling, WV; 96/579 Am Leg Boys St; Band; Drama Clb; Letter Ftbl; Trk; Letter Wrstlng; Univ; Med.

MAYERNIK, SHAWN; Lake Catholic HS; Eastlake, OH; Cls Rep Frsh Cls; Cls Rep Soph Cls; Cl Rep Jr Cls; Am Leg Boys St; Letter Bsktbl; Letter Ftbl; IM Sprt; All Crown Athtc Conf Ftbl 78; News Herald Plyr Of Wk; Univ.

MAYERS, STEPHANIE; Delta Sr HS; Delta, OH; Am Leg Aux Girls St; Chrs; Girl Scts; NHS; Off Ade; Red Cr Ade; Sch Pl; Yth Flsp; Rptr Yrbk; 4-H; College.

MAYERSON, MARC S; The Miami Valley HS; Dayton, OH; Pres Jr Cls; Pol Wkr; Stu Cncl; Rptr Yrbk; Ed Sch Nwsp; Mth Clb; Natl Merit SF; College; Busns.

MAYES, JANE; Mt Pleasant HS; Mt Pleasant, MI; Hon Rl; NHS; Pep Clb; Chrldng; IM Sprt; Acad Hon 77 79; Outstndng Achvmtn Natl Hon Soc 79; Outstndngl Achmvnt Interior Decoration 79; Univ; Interior Designer.

MAYES, JANE C; Heritage Christian HS; Indianapolis, IN; Trs Sr Cls; Hon Rl; Sch Pl; Yrbk; Trk; Am Leg Awd; Univ; Elem Educ.

MAYES, LEAH; Chesterton HS; Chesterton, IN; 16/454 Band; Debate Tm; Jr NHS; Lit Mag; Natl Forn Lg; Sch Pl; Ger Clb; Mat Maids; College; Archaeology.

MAYFIELD, ELIZABETH M; Huntington East HS; Huntington, WV; Band; Chrs; Girl Scts; Hon Rl; Hosp Ade; Mdrgl; Sch Mus; DECA; FBLA; Keyettes; Marshall Univ; Marketing.

MAYFIELD, LARRY W; Tucker County HS; Parsons, WV; 3/120 Am Leg Boys St; Band; Chrh Wkr; Hon Rl; NHS; Yth Flsp; Yrbk; Rptr Sch Nwsp; 4-H; Key Clb; West Virginia Univ; Mining Engr.

MAYFIELD, SONYA; Roosevelt HS; Gary, IN; Band; Hon Rl; Jr NHS; Lbry Ade; NHS; Orch; Fr Clb; FSA; Gary All City Band 78; Purdue Univ; Engr.

MAYHAK, SHELLY; Coloma HS; Rockford, MI; Hon Rl; NHS; Off Ade; Sch Mus; Sch Pl; Stg Crw; Drama Clb; Ger Clb; Chrldng; College.

MAYHEW, ELIZABETH; Parkersburg HS; Parkersburgh, WV; Chrs; Drl Tm; Sch Mus; Pep Clb; GAA; Fairmont St Coll; Speech Ther.

MAYHEW, JULIE; S Newton Jr/sr HS; Kentland, IN; 23/120 Band; Sch Mus; Sch Pl; Stu Cncl; Rptr Yrbk; FBLA; FHA; Lat Clb; Pep Clb; GAA; College; Acctg.

MAYHOMES, GWENDOLYN; Emerson HS; Gary, IN; Band; Hon Rl; Orch; Sch Pl; Stu Cncl; Boys Clb Am; Letter Bsktbl; Letter Trk; Cit Awd; Bus Schl.

MAYHUGH, REXINE; Ida Public HS; Petersbrg, MI; 15/157 Cls Rep Soph Cls; Cl Rep Jr Cls; Am Leg Aux Girls St; NHS; Stu Cncl; Ed Yrbk; Rptr Yrbk; Yrbk; Sprt Ed Sch Nwsp; Rptr Sch Nwsp; Vrsty Lttr In Sftbl Two Yrs 78; Made All Conf 1st Tm Sftbl Two Yrs 78; Oakland Univ; Jrnlsm.

MAYLATH, GLEN; Paw Paw HS; Paw Paw, MI; 15/187 Band; Boy Scts; Hon Rl; NHS; Sct Actv; Yth Flsp; Crs Cntry; Trk; Kalamazoo College; Pre Med.

MAYLE, CARLA; East Canton HS; E Canton, OH; Chrs; Girl Scts; Hon Rl; Jr NHS; NHS; Drama Clb; Fr Clb; FHA; FTA; Pep Clb; Univ; Med.

MAYLE, DALE; Littlefield HS; Alanson, MI; 2/32 Sal; Hon Rl; NHS; Rptr Yrbk; Rptr Sch Nwsp; Dnfth Awd; Ferris St Coll; Refrigeration.

MAYLE, JOY; Canton South HS; Canton, OH; Band; Chrs; Hon Rl; Hosp Ade; Lat Clb; Pep Clb; College; Sci.

MAYLE, KEN; Perry HS; Canton, OH; College.

MAYLE, ROGER L; Warren Local HS; Belpre, OH; Cl Rep Jr Cls; Cls Rep Sr Cls; Am Leg Boys St; Band; Chrh Wkr; Cmnty Wkr; Hon Rl; Orch; Sch Pl; Stu Cncl; Tracy Found Awd; Placed In Dist In Spanish II Test; Pres Of Spanish Hnr Soc; Coll; Engr.

MAYNARD, CINDY; Zane Trace HS; Laurelville, OH; 16/100 Cl Rep Jr Cls; Cls Rep Sr Cls; Hon Rl; Lbry Ade; NHS; Y-Teens; Sch Nwsp; 4-H; Fr Clb; Pep Clb; Ohio Univ; Social Work.

MAYNARD, DEWEY; Salem Sr HS; Salem, OH; 40/265 FCA; Hon Rl; Off Ade; Fr Clb; Key Clb; Ftbl; Trk; Univ; Pre Law.

MAYNARD, GREGORY; Muncie Southside HS; Muncie, IN; 38/322 Chrh Wkr; Hon Rl; JA; Stu Cncl; Pres Yth Flsp; Rptr Yrbk; Rptr Sch Nwsp; Glf; Scr Kpr; Ball St Univ; Law.

MAYNARD, J D; Buffalo HS; Kenova, WV; 1/141 Trs Jr Cls; Am Leg Boys St; Hon Rl; Lbry Ade; Mod UN; NHS; Stg Crw; Stu Cncl; Sch Nwsp; Drama Clb; Know Your St Gov Day; Golden Horseshoe; College; Psych.

MAYNARD, JEFF; Fairland HS; Proctorville, OH; 25/153 VP Jr Cls; Hon Rl; NHS; Sct Actv; Stu Cncl; Rptr Yrbk; Mth Clb; Pep Clb; Ftbl; Trk; Georgetown Univ; Phys Ed.

MAYNARD, JOHNNY D; Lenore HS; Lenore, WV; Boy Scts; Chrh Wkr; Hon Rl; FHA; Bsktbl; Ftbl; Mgrs; College.

MAYNARD, KEVIN; Lenore HS; Lenore, WV; Cls Rep Frsh Cls; Band; Chrs; Hon Rl; Stu Cncl; Beta Clb; Bsbl; Bsktbl; Ftbl; West Virginia Univ; Engr.

MAYNARD, LORI; Eastmoor Sr HS; Columbus, OH; 21/290 Cls Rep Frsh Cls; Band; Chrs; Girl Scts; Hon Rl; Hosp Ade; NHS; Orch; Sch Mus; Stu Cncl; Ohio St Univ; Bus Admin.

MAYNARD, MINETTA L; Wayne HS; Wayne, WV; Cl Rep Jr Cls; Hon Rl; NHS; Yrbk; Ten; College; Art.

MAYNARD, PATRICIA; Cleveland Central Cthlc HS; Cleveland, OH; 2/130 Chrh Wkr; Drl Tm; Hon Rl; Sec NHS; Quill & Scroll; Ed Yrbk; Sprt Ed Yrbk; Yrbk; Rptr Sch Nwsp;.

MAYNARD, ROBERT; Gilmour Academy; Shaker Hts, OH; 3/82 Band; NHS; Yrbk; Bsbl; Letter Bsktbl; Univ; B A.

MAYNARD, SCOTT; Anderson HS; Anderson, IN; Hon Rl; Jr NHS; Lit Mag; Quill & Scroll; Yth Flsp; Ed Sch Nwsp; Sprt Ed Sch Nwsp; Capt Ftbl; College.

MAYNARD, VERA; Indiana Academy; Columbus, IN; Sch Mus; 4-H; Southern Missionary Univ; Phys Ther.

MAYNE, TERESA D; Garfield Sr HS; Hamilton, OH; 3/376 Hon Rl; Jr NHS; NHS; Off Ade; Rptr Yrbk; Spn Clb; Gym; Letter Ten; Letter Trk; College; Busns Admin.

MAYNOR, KIMBERLY; West Side HS; Gary, IN; Cl Rep Jr Cls; Chrs; Hon Rl; NHS; Lat Clb; Ind Univ; Comp Sci.

MAYNOR, MICHAEL; Southmont HS; Crawfordsville, IN; 43/196 Band; Drm Bgl; Orch; Sch Mus; Ind State Univ; Geol.

MAYO, ALLEN; Zanesville HS; Zanesville, OH; 34/500 Cl Rep Jr Cls; Cls Rep Sr Cls; Aud/Vis; Chrs; PAVAS; Sch Mus; Sch Pl; Stg Crw; Stu Cncl; Sch Nwsp; Ohio Univ; Radio.

MAYO, ANTHONY; Bexley HS; Bexley, OH; 39/184 Hon Rl; NHS; Off Ade; Socr; IM Sprt; Andrews Univ; Med Tech.

MAYO, CAROLYN; Bridgeport Sr HS; Bridgeport, WV; Cls Rep Sr Cls; Band; Chrh Wkr; Cmnty Wkr; Hon Rl; Sch Pl; Stu Cncl; Y-Teens; Pep Clb; Letter Bsktbl; Fairmont St Coll; Bus.

MAYO, LAURA; Anderson HS; Cincinnati, OH; 61/350 Am Leg Aux Girls St; Chrs; Girl Scts; Hon Rl; NHS; Sprt Ed Sch Nwsp; Trk; Chrldng; PPFtbl; Am Leg Awd; Univ Of Cincinnati; Elem Educ.

MAYO, LAURA; Turpin HS; Cincinnati, OH; 11/371 Band; VP Yth Flsp; Univ; Psych.

MAYO, MATTHEW; Elmwood HS; Cygnet, OH; Chrs; Mdrgl; MMM; Sch Nwsp; IM Sprt;.

MAYO, STEVEN; Central HS; Grand Rapids, MI; 9/300 Am Leg Boys St; Band; Boy Scts; Chrs; Chrh Wkr; Debate Tm; Hon Rl; Jr NHS; NHS; ROTC; Grand Rapids Bapt Coll; Religion.

MAYOCK, PETER; Bluffton HS; Bluffton, IN; 6/134 Band; Treas Chrh Wkr; Hon Rl; Pol Wkr; Rptr Yrbk; Spn Clb; Letter Swmmng; College.

MAYRBERGER, TORSTEN; Warren HS; Troy, MI; Band; Hon Rl; Crs Cntry; Univ; Sports Med.

MAYROSE, RAEANN; Staunton HS; Brazil, IN; 3/47 Band; Hon Rl; Treas NHS; Off Ade; Stu Cncl; Fr Clb; VP Pep Clb; Bsktbl; Chrldng; Scr Kpr; Indiana St Univ; Elem Ed.

MAYS, CELESTIA L; Immaculata HS; Detroit, MI; 10/93 Cls Rep Soph Cls; Cl Rep Jr Cls; Cls Rep Sr Cls; Chrs; Chrh Wkr; Debate Tm; Hon Rl; Hosp Ade; JA; NHS; Serv To French Club; Cert Of Merit YMCA Youth In Legis; Cert Of Merit Hse Of Representatives; Univ Of Michigan; Medicine.

MAYS, ERIC; Montgomery Cnty Jnt Voc Schl; Trotwood, OH; Jr NHS; NHS; Fr Clb; Treas OEA; Oh Academic Schlrshp Progr 79; Office Ed Assoc Ambassador Awd 79; Office Ed Assoc Statesmn Awd 79; Wright St Univ; Comp Sci.

MAYS, JEFF; Toronto HS; Toronto, OH; Chrh Wkr; Stg Crw; Kent State Univ; Accountant.

MAYS, KEVIN; Northwest Sr HS; Cincinnati, OH; Cls Rep Sr Cls; FCA; Hon Rl; Jr NHS; Lat Clb; Bsktbl; Ftbl; Letter Trk; Cit Awd; SAR Awd; Univ; Math.

MAYS, MELEDY; E Liverpool HS; E Liverpool, OH; 12/324 Cl Rep Jr Cls; Cls Rep Sr Cls; Am Leg Aux Girls St; Chrh Wkr; Girl Scts; Hon Rl; Pres NHS; Off Ade; Sch Pl; Treas Yth Flsp; Metz Harper Schlrshp; Fellowship Awd Beth Shalom Congregati on; Hi Tri Pres; Ohio St Univ; Medicine.

MAYS, SANDRA L; North Ridgeville HS; N Ridgeville, OH; Chrs; Drl Tm; Hon Rl; Mdrgl; Sch Pl; Pom Pon; Homecomg Queen 1978; Sextet 1977; Piano Scholrshp 1975; Baldwin Wallace Univ; Bus.

MAYS, WANETA; Ainsworth Sr HS; Flint, MI; 2/253 Sal; Band; Chrh Wkr; Hon Rl; NHS; Sch Mus; Natl Merit SF; John Phillip Sousa Band Music Awd 79; Al Serra Chevrolet Schlrshp Awd 300.

MAZANEC, MARILYN; Midland HS; Midland, MI; 9/486 Chrs; Girl Scts; Hon Rl; Mdrgl; Treas NHS; Yrbk; Ger Clb; Natl Merit SF; Mich Tech Univ; Mech Engr.

MAZANEC, MARILYN A; Midland HS; Midland, MI; Chrs; Girl Scts; Hon Rl; Mdrgl; Treas NHS; Yrbk; Ger Clb; Natl Merit SF; Michigan Tech Univ; Mech Engr.

MAZAREK, JACQUELINE; Farmington Local HS; W Farmington, OH; VP Soph Cls; Pres Jr Cls; Sec Sr Cls; Sal; Hon Rl; Pres NHS; Pres Beta Clb; FTA; Letter Bsktbl; Letter Trk; Trumbull Business Sch; Med Secretary.

MAZE, KIMBERLY; Godwin Hts HS; Wyoming, MI; Cls Rep Sr Cls; Band; Cmp Fr Grls; Hon Rl; Orch; Stu Cncl; Ger Clb; Gym; Trk; Chrldng; Univ; Bus Mgmt.

MAZEROSKI, ROBERT; Cadiz HS; Cadiz, OH; 9/105 Cls Rep Frsh Cls; Cls Rep Soph Cls; Am Leg Boys St; Chrs; Hon Rl; NHS; Sch Mus; Sch Pl; Stu Cncl; Yth Flsp; Univ; CPA.

MAZEZKA, GEORGE; Brooke HS; Follansbee, WV; 5/450 Pres Sr Cls; Band; Chrh Wkr; NHS; Ger Clb; Elk Awd; God Cntry Awd; Eagle Scout 78; Univ Of Rochester; Acoustical Engr.

MAZIK, PAT; Solon HS; Solon, OH; 9/288 Chrh Wkr; Hon Rl; NHS; Sec Yth Flsp; Mth Clb; Pep Clb; Bsbl; Gym; Bowling Green St Univ; Marine Bio.

MAZUK, STEPHAN M; Sturgis HS; Sturgis, MI; 3/234 Band; NHS; Orch; Stg Crw; Natl Merit SF; Univ Of Michigan; Physics.

MAZUR, JAMES; Hammond HS; Hammond, IN; 20/267 Am Leg Boys St; Hon Rl; Natl Forn Lg; NHS; Quill & Scroll; Ed Yrbk; Ed Sch Nwsp; Rotary Awd; Indiana Univ; Bus.

MAZURE, GREG; Bad Axe HS; Bad Axe, MI; 2/200 Cls Rep Soph Cls; Chrh Wkr; Debate Tm; FCA; Hon Rl; Natl Forn Lg; NHS; Sch Pl; Drama Clb; Fr Clb; West Point Acad; Bus Admin.

MAZURE, WADE R; Harbor Beach Community HS; Harbor Beach, MI; 7/120 Hon Rl; NHS; FFA; Mic State Univ; Dairy Sci.

MAZZA, LARRY; Notre Dame HS; Clarksburg, WV; Cls Rep Frsh Cls; Cls Rep Soph Cls; Cl Rep Jr Cls; Chrh Wkr; Off Ade; Sch Pl; Pres Stu Cncl; Rptr Yrbk; Drama Clb; FBLA; Commodor Of The Ship Of State; 2nd Pl In Century III Leadershp Contest; University; Law.

MAZZAFERRI, MARK; Maple Hts HS; Maple Heights, OH; 1/460 Pres Band; Treas NHS; Beta Clb; Crs Cntry; Trk; Scr Kpr; Tmr; JC Awd; Rotary Awd; Walsh Coll; Engr Physist.

MAZZARA, CHRISTOPHER; Rochester Adams HS; Rochester, MI; 1/537 Chrh Wkr; Cmnty Wkr; Hon Rl; NHS; Stg Crw; Stu Cncl; Ger Clb; Sci Clb; Crs Cntry; Trk; Univ; Chem.

MAZZEI, MARY; Mcauley HS; Cincinnati, OH; Girl Scts; Sct Actv; Rptr Sch Nwsp; Spn Clb; Trk; College; Eng.

MAZZELLA, HENRY; Lasalle HS; Cincinnati, OH; 25/250 Hon Rl; VP NHS; Yrbk; Letter Crs Cntry; Letter Trk; Univ Of Cincinnati; Engr.

MAZZOLA, LINDA; St Francis De Sales HS; Columbus, OH; Chrs; Drm Mjrt; Hon Rl; Rptr Yrbk; Drama Clb; 4-H; Key Clb; Pep Clb; Spn Clb; Gym; Meritorious Awd; Ohio St Barber Coll Schlrshp; Schlstc Ach; Ohio St Barber Schl.

MAZZONE, JOHN; Weirton Madonna HS; Weirton, WV; 44/112 Chrs; Chrh Wkr; Cmnty Wkr; Hon Rl; Stg Crw; Yrbk; Sch Nwsp; FDA; Pep Clb; Sci Clb; Ftbl Hon Mntn Linmn Of Wk 79; 1st Pl Relgs Art Contst 76; West Virginia Univ; Mech Engr.

MCABEE, JACKIE; Norwood Sr HS; Norwood, OH; Chrs; Hon Rl; Jr NHS; Off Ade; DECA; Lat Clb; Pep Clb; Univ Of Cincinnati; Medicine.

MCAFEE, BONITA; Eau Claire HS; Eau Claire, MI; 26/100 Pres Frsh Cls; Chrh Wkr; Hon Rl; NHS; Trk; Chrldng; Davenport; Legal Sec.

MCAFEE, LISA; Floyd Central HS; Floyd Knobs, IN; 44/300 Band; Chrh Wkr; Cmnty Wkr; Girl Scts; Rdo Clb; Swmmng; Pom Pon; PPFtbl; Tmr; College; Nursing.

MCALEAR, THOMAS; Cardinal Stritch HS; Rossford, OH; Pres Sr Cls; Am Leg Boys St; Boy Scts; Chrh Wkr; Hon Rl; NHS; Off Ade; College; Pre Med.

MCALEAR, THOMAS G; Cardinal Stritch HS; Rossford, OH; 12/230 Pres Sr Cls; Am Leg Boys St; Aud/Vis; Boy Scts; Hon Rl; Jr NHS; NHS; Stu Cncl; Fr Clb; Bsbl; Univ; Med.

MCALLISTER, CATHERINE; Carroll HS; Dayton, OH; 3/285 Band; Hon Rl; Hosp Ade; NHS; Stu Cncl; Key Clb; Natl Merit Ltr; Univ Of Dayton; Pre Dentistry.

MCALLISTER, CLARKE; Rogers HS; Toledo, OH; Band; Boy Scts; Chrh Wkr; Hon Rl; Orch; Sch Mus; Yth Flsp; Toledo Univ; Music.

MCALLISTER, KAREN; Anderson Sr HS; Cincinnati, OH; Chrs; Hon Rl; JA; Sch Mus; DECA; JA Awd;.

MCALLISTER, LORI; Ithaca HS; Ithaca, MI; 1/125 Pres Jr Cls; Val; Am Leg Aux Girls St; Debate Tm; Hon Rl; Mdrgl; NHS; Sch Mus; Pres Stu Cncl; Chrldng; Central Michigan Univ; Law.

MCALLISTER, LYNN; Plymouth Canton HS; Plymouth, MI; 140/550 Cls Rep Frsh Cls; Trs Soph Cls; Trs Jr Cls; Cls Rep Sr Cls; Band; Chrh Wkr; Cmnty Wkr; Girl Scts; Hon Rl; Stu Cncl; Eastern Michigan Univ; Spec Educ.

MCALPIN, CHUCK; Vandalia Butler HS; Dayton, OH; 74/325 Chrh Wkr; Letter Bsbl; Letter Crs Cntry; Dave Sabek Athltc Memrl Awd 79; Mst Vlbl Runner Cross Country 78 & 79; All Confrnc Bsbl 79; Michigan Christian Coll; Indust Arts.

MCALVEY, DAVID; Holt HS; Holt, MI; 10/274 NHS; Sprt Ed Sch Nwsp; Rptr Sch Nwsp; Letter Bsbl; Letter Crs Cntry; Letter Ftbl; Michigan Tech Univ; Engr.

MCAMMON, V; Washington HS; So Bend, IN; Chrs; Hon Rl; Hosp Ade; PAVAS; Sch Mus; Sch Pl; Drama Clb; Letter Bsbl; Coach Actv; Pom Pon; IU; Med.

MCANDREW, RANDY; Benton Harbor HS; Benton Hbr, MI; Ten; College; Construction.

MCANDREWS, SANDRA; Whiteland Cmnty HS; Greenwood, IN; 17/194 Hon Rl; Lbry Ade; Sch Pl; Fr Clb; FHA; OEA; Indiana Ctrl Univ; Acctg.

MCANLIS, KAREN A; Wadsworth HS; Wadsworth, OH; Sec Soph Cls; Trs Soph Cls; Cls Rep Soph Cls; Chrh Wkr; Hon Rl; Hosp Ade; Stu Cncl; Yth Flsp; Drama Clb; Fr Clb; Univ; Communications.

MCARDLE, KATHLEEN; Bridgman HS; North Canton, OH; Am Leg Aux Girls St; Hon Rl; Jr NHS; NHS; Sch Nwsp; Pres Fr Clb; Letter Bsbl; College; Math.

MCAREE, LAURA; Park Tudor HS; Indianapolis, IN; Hon Rl; Yrbk; Fr Clb; Sci Clb; Capt Hockey; Swmmng; Pom Pon; College; Medicine.

MCARN, CRAIG H; Western Reserve Academy; Hudson, OH; 30/86 Hon Rl; Off Ade; Ftbl; Letter Lcrss; IM Sprt; Red Cross Jr Lifesaving 77; Bus & Pro Womens Clb Otstndng Driver Of Yr 79; Univ.

MCATEE, BEVERLY; Loogootee HS; Loogootee, IN; Band; Drl Tm; Yrbk; 4-H; Pep Clb; Trk; IM Sprt; Pom Pon; 4-H Awd; Univ; Ag.

MCATEE, SHARON; Loogootee HS; Loogootee, IN; Trs Frsh Cls; VP Soph Cls; VP Jr Cls; VP Sr Cls; Am Leg Aux Girls St; Pres Chrh Wkr; Cmnty Wkr; Hon Rl; Sch Mus; Sch Pl; Indiana State Univ; Nursing.

MCAVOY, MARY; Groveport Madison HS; Columbus, OH; Cmnty Wkr; Hon Rl; Hosp Ade; Lbry Ade; Off Ade; Yrbk; Pres FHA; Spn Clb; PPFtbl; Scr Kpr; Columbus Tech Inst; Bus Mgmt.

MCAVOY, RUTH; Kenmore HS; Akron, OH; Chrh Wkr; Off Ade; Sch Pl; Pres Yth Flsp; Univ Of Akron; Bus.

MCAVOY, WILLIAM; Watkins Memorial HS; Pataskala, OH; Boy Scts; Chrh Wkr; Hon Rl; Lbry Ade; NHS; Sct Actv; Yrbk; Spn Clb; Letter Crs Cntry; Letter Trk; Bowling Green State Univ; Med Tech.

MCBRIDE, BARRY; West Geauga HS; Novelty, OH; Band; Debate Tm; Hon Rl; Natl Forn Lg; Mbr Of 1st Pl In Oh Plane Geom Tm 75; St Debate Champnshp Semi Fnlst 78; Natl Forensic Lg Rgnl Champnshp 78; Ohio St Univ; Politics.

MCBRIDE, BRIAN; Cardinal Mooney HS; Youngstown, OH; Comp Analyst.

MCBRIDE, CHRIS; Malabar HS; Mansfield, OH; 30/280 Band; Off Ade; Red Cr Ade; Stu Cncl; Mth Clb; Chrldng; Scr Kpr; Mas Awd; College; Psych.

MCBRIDE, CYNTHIA; Lexington Sr HS; Mansfield, OH; 35/270 NHS; Y-Teens; Fr Clb; Tchr Aide; Ohio St Univ; Bus.

MCBRIDE, JANET; Owen Valley HS; Spencer, IN; 18/193 Cls Rep Frsh Cls; Cls Rep Soph Cls; Cl Rep Jr Cls; Cls Rep Sr Cls; Band; Hon Rl; Hosp Ade; Mod UN; Stu Cncl; Yth Flsp; Indiana Univ; Med.

MCBRIDE, KIMBERLY A; North Putnam Jr Sr HS; Greencastle, IN; VP Frsh Cls; VP Soph Cls; VP Jr Cls; FCA; Hon Rl; 4-H; OEA; Pep Clb; Spn Clb; Bsktbl; Indiana Busns Coll; Busns.

MCBRIDE, LORRAINE; New Haven HS; New Haven, IN; 53/283 Chrh Wkr; Cmnty Wkr; Lbry A de; Sct Actv; Ger Clb; Pep Clb; Mgrs; College; Business.

MCBRIDE, MELODY; Spanishburg HS; Flat Top, WV; Bsbl; Mercer Co Vo Tech Center; Nursing.

MCBRIDE, RICHARD; Boardman HS; Youngstown, OH; 128/600 Cmnty Wkr; Hon Rl; Off Ade; Letter Wrstlng; Bowling Green State Univ; Gen Bus.

MCBRIDE, SCOTT; John Glenn HS; New Concord, OH; Band; Boy Scts; Chrs; Hon Rl; Mdrgl; Orch; Sch Mus; Sch Pl; Sct Actv; Yrbk; Cornell Univ; Elec Engr.

MCBRIDE, SUSAN; Bellbrook HS; Xenia, OH; 40/170 Band; Drm Mjrt; Off Ade; Yrbk; Key Clb; Pep Clb; GAA; Twrlr; Sinclair Univ; Bus Acctg.

MCBRIDE, TERRY; Tri HS; Lewisville, IN; Treas NHS; Capt Bsktbl; Crs Cntry; Indiana Univ; Bus.

MCBROOM, CHARLES; Watkins Mem HS; Granville, OH; 1/212 Hon Rl; NHS; Letter Bsbl; Letter Ftbl; IM Sprt; Air Force Academy; Aviation.

MCCABE, JAMES; Huntington North HS; Markle, IN; Band; Boy Scts; Sch Mus; Ten; Purdue Univ; Vet.

MCCABE, JAMES; Stonewall Jackson HS; Charleston, WV; Cls Rep Soph Cls; Am Leg Boys St; Hon Rl; JA; Jr NHS; Pres NHS; Red Cr Ade; Yth Flsp; FBLA; Pres Mth Clb; Washington & Lee Univ; Med.

MCCABE, MARGARET; Servite HS; Detroit, MI; 10/90 VP Jr Cls; Hon Rl; Jr NHS; NHS; Fr Clb; Letter Bsbl; Letter Bsktbl; Coach Actv; Mic State; Social Srvcs.

MCCABE, MICHAEL; South Point HS; South Point, OH; Hon Rl; Jr NHS; NHS; Rptr Sch Nwsp; Fr Clb; College; Architect.

MCCABE, MICHAEL; Dublin HS; Dublin, OH; Band; Boy Scts; Hon Rl; Rptr Sch Nwsp; Eng Clb; Fr Clb; Mth Clb; Ftbl; Ten; IM Sprt; OSU.

MCCABE, SUSAN; Cameron HS; Cameron, WV; Band; Chrs; Hon Rl; Jr NHS; NHS; Sch Nwsp; FHA; IM Sprt; West Liberty St Coll; Psych.

MCCABE, TAMI; South Point HS; South Point, OH; Jr NHS; Pep Clb; Trk; Univ; Med Tech.

MCCAFFERTY, MARY; St Joseph Academy; N Olmsted, OH; Cls Rep Sr Cls; Sal; Cmnty Wkr; Hon Rl; NHS; Quill & Scroll; Fr Clb; Sci Clb; Natl Merit SF; John Carroll Univ; Chem.

MCCAFFERY, KELLY; Westfall HS; Williamsport, OH; Band; Cmnty Wkr; Hon Rl; Stu Cncl; Yrbk; Fr Clb; Letter Trk; Letter Chrldng; Bus Schl; Key Punch.

MCCAFFERY, KEVIN; Rock Hill Sr HS; Ironton, OH; Band; Chrh Wkr; Cmnty Wkr; Drm Bgl; Hon Rl; JA; PAVAS; Ed Yrbk; Rptr Yrbk; Sprt Ed Sch Nwsp;.

MCCAIGE, DANIEL; Holt HS; Holt, MI; Letter Bsbl; Letter Bsktbl; Letter Ftbl; Letter Socr; IM Sprt; College.

MCCAIN, ANNETTE; Clarkston Sr HS; Drayton Plns, MI; Girl Scts; Hon Rl; Lbry Ade; Sch Nwsp; Bakers Coll; Acctg.

MCCAIN, MICHELLE; Woodward HS; Cincinnati, OH; Hon Rl; Letter Ten; Ohi State; Rn.

MCCAIN, VERONICA; Shaw HS; East Cleveland, OH; 8/490 Sec Soph Cls; Sec Jr Cls; Band; Chrh Wkr; Hon Rl; JA; Sch Pl; Stu Cncl; Sch Nwsp; Fr Clb; College; Law.

MCCALISTER, KEITH; Bosse HS; Evansville, IN; Hon Rl; NHS; Letter Wrstlng; Coll; Mech Engr.

MCCALL, JO ANN; John Hay HS; Cleveland, OH; Cls Rep Sr Cls; Band; Chrs; Chrh Wkr; Hon Rl; Jr NHS; Lbry Ade; NHS; Cit Awd; Participate In The J Carroll Univ GYSP Goes To Coll Progr 79; I Am Asstnt MU Ldr Yng Peoples Soc 79; Univ; Physician.

MCCALL, KATHLEEN; Mariemont HS; Cincinnati, OH; 41/149 AFS; Chrs; Sch Mus; Rptr Yrbk; Pep Clb; Letter Gym; Altrnt For Girls St 78; Head Of Sr Sect Of Yrbk 79; Univ.

MCCALL, LISA; Warsaw Comm HS; Warsaw, IN; 69/405 Chrs; Debate Tm; Hon Rl; Treas JA; Natl Forn Lg; Sch Pl; Stg Crw; Drama Clb; Pep Clb; JA Awd; Coll; Telecomm.

MCCALL, PAM; Seton HS; Cincinnati, OH; 154/276 Cls Rep Frsh Cls; Chrs; Chrh Wkr; Drl Tm; FCA; Hon Rl; Stu Cncl; Letter Bsktbl; Trk; GAA; Ohio State Univ; Medicine.

MCCALL, SAROLL; Warrensville Hts HS; Warrensvl Hts, OH; Band; Orch; Sch Mus; Pep Clb; Rdo Clb; Letter Bsbl; Letter Bsktbl; Airco Inst; Bus.

MCCALL, SCOTT; Trenton HS; Trenton, MI; Hon Rl; Rptr Sch Nwsp; Univ Of Detroit; Pre Dentistry.

MCCALL, TERRI; John Adams HS; Cleveland, OH; Cl Rep Jr Cls; Cls Rep Sr Cls; Hon Rl; Off Ade; Sch Pl; Rptr Yrbk; Trk; Coach Actv; Twrlr; Duke Coll; Acctg.

MCCALLA, JULIE; Williams HS; Williamston, MI; Trs Frsh Cls; Trs Soph Cls; Trs Jr Cls; Band; Cmp Fr Grls; Hon Rl; Jr NHS; College.

MCCALLISTER, JULIE; St Francis De Sales HS; Columbus, OH; Pres Band; Hst Frsh Cls; Hon Rl; Lbry Ade; NHS; Orch; Sch Mus; Sch Pl; Yth Flsp; Spn Clb; Univ; Elem Educ.

MCCALLISTER, MARY; New Albany HS; New Albany, IN; 95/565 Band; Jr NHS; Orch; DECA; Mgrs; Voc Schl; Lab Tech.

MCCALLUM, AMY D; Breckenridge Jr Sr HS; Breckenridge, MI; 2/109 Stu Cncl; 4-H; Sec FFA; Capt Pom Pon; Natl Merit SF; Michigan St Univ.

MCCALLUM, LORI; Waterford Kettering HS; Drayton Plains, MI; 24/374 Band; Hon Rl; NHS; Letter Bsbl; Mic State Univ; Med Tech.

MCCAN, DONALD; Laville Jr Sr HS; Plymouth, IN; Band; Lbry Ade; Mth Clb; Sci Clb; Letter Bsbl; Letter Ten; IM Sprt; Am Leg Awd; Indiana Voc Schl; Elec.

MCCAN, SCOTT; Laville Jr Sr HS; Plymouth, IN; 2/160 Am Leg Boys St; NHS; Fr Clb; Mth Clb; Sci Clb; Sec Bsbl; Bsktbl; Am Leg Awd; Cit Awd; Pres Awd; Purdue Univ; Engr.

MCCANDLESS, JOHN; Midland HS; Midland, MI; Hon Rl; Letter Bsbl; Coach Actv; Michigan St Univ; Law Enforcement.

MCCANDLESS, TAMARA; Brown Cnty HS; Nashville, IN; 20/208 Cls Rep Frsh Cls; Cls Rep Soph Cls; Cl Rep Jr Cls; FCA; Hon Rl; NHS; Off Ade; Stu Cncl; Yrbk; Bsktbl; Univ; Natural Sci.

MCCANN, EDNA; Hebron HS; Hebron, IN; 14/63 Aud/Vis; Chrs; Chrh Wkr; Cmnty Wkr; Girl Scts; Mdrgl; Sch Pl; Stg Crw; Yth Flsp; Ed Sch Nwsp; Navy.

MCCANN, FREDERICK W; Huntington HS; Chillicothe, OH; Chrh Wkr; Hon Rl; Jr NHS; Lbry Ade; NHS; FFA; Employment.

MCCANN, GREGORY; Bishop Foley HS; Sterling Hts, MI; 30/190 Cls Rep Frsh Cls; VP Sr Cls; Am Leg Boys St; NHS; Stu Cncl; Rptr Yrbk; Ftbl; Trk; Dnfth Awd; Univ; Sci.

MCCANN, KATHY; Regina HS; Cleveland Hts, OH; Cls Rep Sr Cls; Girl Scts; Hon Rl; Stg Crw; Stu Cncl; Yrbk; Rptr Sch Nwsp; Sch Nwsp; GAA; Awd For Work As Page Ed For Schl Newspaper 78; Awd For Grp Leadr On Conservtn & Water Analysis 77; Univ; Law.

MCCARRON, LYNN; Field HS; Kent, OH; 29/275 Cls Rep Soph Cls; Cl Rep Jr Cls; Am Leg Aux Girls St; Hon Rl; NHS; Stu Cncl; Rptr Yrbk; Ten; Trk; Chrldng; Kent St Univ; Vet.

MCCARTAN, LORRAINE; Calvert HS; Tiffin, OH; Sch Nwsp; Bus Schl; Cmnctns.

MCCARTER, LOU; Tipton HS; Tipton, IN; Cls Rep Frsh Cls; Am Leg Aux Girls St; Chrs; NHS; Sch Pl; Stu Cncl; Sch Nwsp; Drama Clb; 4-H; Pep Clb; Most Improved Acress Thespian Soc 78; Univ Of Colorado; Comp.

MCCARTHY, CHARLENE; Hubbard HS; Hubbard, OH; Chrs; Girl Scts; Ten; School For Cooking; Cheg.

MCCARTHY, CHRISTINE; Lakota HS; Hamilton, OH; Chrs; Off Ade; DECA; Swmmng; Chrldng; IM Sprt; Tmr;.

MCCARTHY, CHRISTOPHER; Bishop Chatard Catholic HS; Indianapolis, IN; Cmnty Wkr; Hon Rl; Yth Flsp; IM Sprt;.

MCCARTHY, CORRINE; Bishop Foley HS; Madison Heights, MI; Band; Cmnty Wkr; Girl Scts; Hon Rl; Y-Teens; Swmmng; Coach Actv; GAA; IM Sprt; PPFtbl; Swimming Letter 77; Recvd Most Improved Swimmer Trophy 77; Eastern Michigan Univ; Phys Educ.

MCCARTHY, EDWARD; Norwood HS; Norwood, OH; Hon Rl; Jr NHS; Mth Clb; Ftbl; Wrstlng; Massachusetts Institute Of Tech;vet.

MCCARTHY, GENEVIEVE; Marian HS; Birmingham, MI; Cls Rep Frsh Cls; Cls Rep Soph Cls; Cl Rep Jr Cls; Cls Rep Sr Cls; Hon Rl; NHS; IM Sprt; College.

MCCARTHY, GWEN; Lake Michigan Catholic HS; Benton Hrbr, MI; Band; Chrh Wkr; Hon Rl; 4-H; Capt Crs Cntry; Letter Trk; 4-H Awd;.

MCCARTHY, JOAN; De Kalb Central HS; Auburn, IN; Band; Hon Rl; NHS; Yrbk; Drama Clb; Spn Clb; Ten; Letter Trk; PPFtbl; College; Biology.

MCCARTHY, KEVIN; Ann Arbor Huron HS; Ypsilanti, MI; 154/620 Band; Chrh Wkr; JA; Sch Pl; Drama Clb; Fr Clb; Ftbl; Capt Wrstlng; Natl Merit Ltr; I Compt Schlshp 79; 3 Yrs Of Var Ltr Awd 79; Michigan Tech Univ; Forestry.

MCCARTHY, MARIA; Dunbar HS; Dunbar, WV; Pres Frsh Cls; Pres Jr Cls; VP Sr Cls; Hon Rl; NHS; Off Ade; Stg Crw; Stu Cncl; Bsktbl; IM Sprt; College; Business Admin & Mgmt.

MCCARTHY, MARYANN; Eau Claire HS; Eau Claire, MI; Hon Rl; 4-H; Univ; Forestry.

MCCARTHY, MAUREEN; Magnificat HS; Rocky River, OH; Band; Cmp Fr Grls; Chrs; Chrh Wkr; Girl Scts; Hosp Ade; Sch Pl; Sct Actv; Stg Crw; Rptr Sch Nwsp; Univ; Eng.

MCCARTHY, MICHAEL; Bloomington South HS; Bloomington, IN; Stu Cncl; Boys Clb Am; IM Sprt; Indiana Univ; Mktg.

MCCARTHY, RUSSELL; Cameron HS; Cameron, WV; 11/345 Am Leg Boys St; Hon Rl; NHS; FFA; Letter Ftbl; IM Sprt; College; Law.

MCCARTHY, STEVEN; La Salle HS; Cincinnati, OH; 7/275 Cls Rep Frsh Cls; Boy Scts; Hon Rl; Mod UN; Sec Stu Cncl; Mth Clb; Its Academic Team Capt; Jr Council On World Affairs Sec; Ohio Test Of Schlstc Achvmnt Algebra I & Ii; College; Law.

MCCARTHY, TAMMY; Lakewood HS; Newark, OH; Cl Rep Jr Cls; Band; Hon Rl; Jr NHS; Stu Cncl; 4-H; Fr Clb; Letter Chrldng; GAA; 4-H Awd; Miami Univ Of Ohio; French.

MCCARTNEY, BRENDA; Lewis County HS; Weston, WV; Chrs; Hon Rl; Hosp Ade; Lbry Ade; NHS; Stg Crw; Stu Cncl; Y-Teens; Ed Sch Nwsp; Dnfth Awd; West Virginia Univ; RN.

MCCARTNEY, JILL; Calhoun HS; Grantsville, WV; Chrs; Hon Rl; Hosp Ade; Sch Mus; Yrbk; Sch Nwsp; Mth Clb; Sci Clb; Hugh O Brian Leadshp Semnr 78; Goldn Horseh Winner 76; Top 10 Mag Sales Mn 2nd Highst 78; Glenville St Coll; Dr.

MCCARTNEY, KEVIN; Watkins Mem HS; Granville, OH; FCA; Hon Rl; Sch Pl; Spn Clb; Letter Trk; IM Sprt; Ohio St Univ; Elec Engr.

MCCARTNEY, LINDA; Saints Peter & Paul Area HS; Saginaw, MI; Cls Rep Frsh Cls; Cls Rep Soph Cls; Cl Rep Jr Cls; Hon Rl; Jr NHS; NHS; PAVAS; Stu Cncl; Ten; GAA; College; Visual Communications.

MCCARTT, PAULA; Bloomington South HS; Bloomington, IN; Band; Chrs; Chrh Wkr; Off Ade; Yth Flsp; 4-H; Scr Kpr; Tmr; 4-H Awd; Natl Merit Ltr; Ind Univ.

MCCARTY, DONALD L; Lincoln HS; Lumberport, WV; 2/158 Trs Soph Cls; Hosp Ade; NHS; Rptr Yrbk;.

MCCARTY, KAREN; Bradford HS; Versailles, OH; Am Leg Aux Girls St; Band; Chrh Wkr; Hon Rl; NHS; Sch Pl; Yth Flsp; Ed Yrbk; Am Leg Awd; Lion Awd; College; Nutrition.

MCCARTY, TIM; Flushing HS; Flushing, MI; Boy Scts; Statewide Ind Art Aair Winner 76 79; Univ; Naval Archt.

MCCAULEY, DANIEL; Elk Rapids Sr HS; Traverse City, MI; 78/90 Pres Soph Cls; Cl Rep Jr Cls; Cls Rep Sr Cls; Hon Rl; Sch Pl; Pres Stu Cncl; Letter Bsktbl; Capt Crs Cntry; Trk; Natl Merit SF; Michigan St Univ; Engr.

MCCAULEY, DAVID; Liberty HS; Clarksburg, WV; 32/232 Cl Rep Jr Cls; Am Leg Boys St; Hon Rl; Jr NHS; NHS; Stu Cncl; Mth Clb; Letter Bsktbl; Letter Crs Cntry; Wv Univ; Chem.

MCCAULEY, JODY; Zanesville HS; Zanesville, OH; Drl Tm; Hon Rl; Sch Pl; Stg Crw; Rptr Sch Nwsp; Pres Lat Clb; Bsbl; Letter Bsktbl; GAA; Scr Kpr; Head Trainer For Yr; Ohio St Univ; Nursing.

MCCAULEY, LORIE; Park Hills HS; Fairborn, OH; Hon Rl; Hosp Ade; Off Ade; Spn Clb; Var Sftbl 79; Voluntr At Elem Schl 78; Ohio St Univ; Phys Ther.

MCCAULEY, MICHELE; Malabar HS; Mansfield, OH; 30/251 Cl Rep Jr Cls; VP Band; Treas NHS; Orch; Mth Clb; Trk; Chrldng; Mat Maids; Tmr; Bowling Green Univ; Music.

MCCAULEY, RHONDA; Ravenswood HS; Ravenswood, WV; 4/192 Cls Rep Soph Cls; Cl Rep Jr Cls; Cls Rep Sr Cls; Chrh Wkr; Hon Rl; Hosp Ade; JA; NHS; Quill & Scroll; Stu Cncl; West Virginia Univ; Phys Therapy.

MCCAW, LISA; Gahanna Lincoln HS; Gahanna, OH; 50/440 Band; Lit Mag; NHS; Fr Clb; Twrlr; Univ Of Akron; Dance.

MCCHANCY, CLAUDIA; Euclid Sr HS; Euclid, OH; 3/714 Hon Rl; VP NHS; Quill & Scroll; Red Cr Ade; Ed Sch Nwsp; Letter Ten; Natl Merit Ltr; Kent State Univ Honors Schlrshp Awd; Kent State Univ; Nursing.

MCCHRISTY, SUZANNE; Fowlerville HS; Fowlerville, MI; 4/150 Band; Hon Rl; NHS; Off Ade; Rptr Sch Nwsp; Fr Clb; Whos Who In Music 79; All Star Band 79; County Honors Bands 79; Univ; Music.

MCCLAIN, CONNIE; Miller HS; Shawnee, OH; Sec Jr Cls; Band; Chrs; Hon Rl; Sec NHS; Sch Pl; Rptr Yrbk; Rptr Sch Nwsp; VP FBLA; Pep Clb; Hocking Tech; Computer Mgmt.

MCCLAIN, HEATHER; Talawanda HS; Oxford, OH; 1/321 Pres Jr Cls; VP Sr Cls; Am Leg Aux Girls St; Girl Scts; Hon Rl; NHS; Orch; Stu Cncl; Pep Clb; Letter Hockey; Univ.

MCCLAIN, JAMES; Franklin Sr HS; Franklin, OH; Band; Drm Bgl; Hon Rl; NHS; Sch Mus; Sch Pl; Stu Cncl; Rptr Sch Nwsp; Fr Clb; Letter Mgrs; Joe Mc Cabe Memrl Schlrshp Oratory 75 76 & 77; Optomist St Speech Cntst 2nd 76; Ohio St Univ; Radio.

MCCLAIN, PENNY; Fairview HS; Farmington, WV; Cls Rep Soph Cls; Cl Rep Jr Cls; Chrh Wkr; Debate Tm; Hon Rl; Off Ade; Stu Cncl; Pres Yth Flsp; VP Fr Clb; Fairmont St Coll; Nursing.

MCCLAIN, ROBERT; Wintersville HS; Wintrvl, OH; 18/290 Am Leg Boys St; Boy Scts; Chrh Wkr; Hon Rl; NHS; Yrbk; Sch Nwsp; Spn Clb; Bsktbl; Letter Ftbl; Service Acad; Comp Engr.

MCCLAIN, SYLVESTER; Libbey HS; Toledo, OH; Cls Rep Frsh Cls; Val; Sal; Hon Rl; Jr NHS; NHS; Cit Awd; God Cntry Awd; Natl Merit SF; Natl Merit Schl; Ohi State; Med.

MCCLAIN, TIM; East Kentwood HS; Kentwood, MI; Mich State Univ; Lawyer.

MCCLARDY, MARK; Pontiac Northern HS; Pontiac, MI; Hon Rl; Lbry Ade; Letter Wrstlng; Cit Awd; College; Acct.

MCCLARY, ANDREW S; Heritage Christian HS; Indianapolis, IN; Cl Rep Jr Cls; Band; Hon Rl; Stu Cncl; Yth Flsp; College; Busns.

MCCLARY, BRUCE; Big Walnut HS; Westerville, OH; 12/225 Pres Sr Cls; Am Leg Boys St; Hon Rl; Sec NHS; Stu Cncl; FFA; FHA; Letter Ftbl; Letter Trk; IM Sprt; Bowling Green St Univ; Busns Admin.

MCCLARY, JUANITA; Ironton HS; Ironton, OH; 20/200 Band; Chrh Wkr; Hon Rl; JA; Mod UN; Orch; Quill & Scroll; Sch Mus; Sch Pl; Yth Flsp; Sci Fair Superior Fating; Top Biology Sci Fair Project; Purdue Univ; Med Tech.

MCCLASKEY, KATHERINE S; Huntington East HS; Huntington, WV; 1/340 Sec Jr Cls; Sec Sr Cls; Band; Hon Rl; Jr NHS; NHS; Stu Cncl; Yth Flsp; FHA; Lat Clb; Majorette; Marshall Univ.

MCCLAUGHLIN, DAVID; Bridgeport HS; Saginaw, MI; 97/365 Band; Boy Scts; Chrh Wkr; Sct Actv; Stg Crw; Yth Flsp; Letter Ten; Saginaw Valley State College; Chem.

MCCLEARY, KEN; West Vigo HS; W Terre Haute, IN; 1/191 Pres Frsh Cls; Pres Soph Cls; Val; Am Leg Boys St; Chrs; FCA; Hon Rl; Jr NHS; Mod UN; NHS; Rose Hulman Inst Of Tech; Chem Engr.

MCCLEERY, BONNIE; Struthers HS; Struthers, OH; 76/289 Chrs; Chrh Wkr; Girl Scts; Hon Rl; Sct Actv; Yth Flsp; Y-Teens; OEA; Pep Clb; Rdo Clb; OEA Diplomat Awd; Pres For Churchs Youth Group; College; Sec.

MCCLEERY, MICHAEL; Flat Rock Sr HS; Flat Rock, MI; Hon Rl; NHS; Sci Clb; Letter Bsbl; Letter Ftbl; College.

MCCLEERY, ROBBIN P; Summerfield HS; Petersburg, MI; 3/100 Hon Rl; NHS; Rptr Yrbk; Rptr Sch Nwsp; Sch Nwsp; Sci Clb; Letter Bsbl; Voc Schl; Electronics.

MCCLELLAN, APRIL; John F Kennedy HS; Cleveland, OH; Pres Frsh Cls; Cls Rep Soph Cls; Chrs; Drl Tm; Stu Cncl; Rptr Sch Nwsp; Pep Clb; Bsktbl; Univ; Tele Cmnctns.

MCCLELLAN, MIKE; Field HS; Mogadore, OH; 21/290 Cls Rep Frsh Cls; Band; Chrh Wkr; Cmnty Wkr; Hon Rl; NHS; Sch Mus; Sch Pl; Ed Sch Nwsp; VP Drama Clb; Kent State Univ; Archt.

MCCLELLAND, KELLY; Mt Gilead HS; Mt Gilead, OH; 33/115 Sec Jr Cls; Cmnty Wkr; Hon Rl; Lbry Ade; Off Ade; Sch Pl; Stg Crw; Rptr Yrbk; Rptr Sch Nwsp; Drama Clb; Grange Member St Officer; Farm Bureau Member As Regional Cabinet Representative; Morrow Co Jr Miss St Kodak; Bowling Green St Univ; Communication.

MCCLELLAND, LESLIE; Clay HS; S Bend, IN; 78/430 Hon Rl; Ftbl; College; Engr.

MCCLENIC, BRIAN K; Wylie E Groves HS; Birmingham, MI; Band; Boy Scts; Natl Merit Ltr; Univ; Pre Med.

MCCLENNING, MARK; Bethesda Christian HS; Brownsburg, IN; 3/25 Band; Chrs; Chrh Wkr; Hon Rl; Sch Mus; Sch Pl; Ed Sch Nwsp; Fr Clb; Pep Clb; Grace College; Music.

MCCLINCUCK, KELLY; Perry HS; Navarre, OH; Band; Cmnty Wkr; Drm Bgl; Orch; FHA; Pep Clb; Mat Maids; Twrlr; 3 Music Awd For Bnd Participation 78; Akron Univ; RN.

MCCLINTOCK, CATHY; The Andrews School; Madison, OH; Girl Scts; Hosp Ade; Lbry Ade; Off Ade; Stg Crw; Fr Clb; Ger Clb; Miami Univ; Psych.

MCCLISH, BRENT; Miami Trace HS; Washington, OH; Pres Jr Cls; AFS; Am Leg Boys St; Hon Rl; NHS; Stu Cncl; 4-H; FFA; Scr Kpr; 4-H Awd; Univ; Dairy Farmer.

MCCLISH, PENNY; Colon HS; Colon, MI; Hon Rl; Stg Crw; 4-H; Letter Bsktbl; Letter Trk; PPFtbl; Tmr; 4-H Awd; Central Michigan Univ; Phys Ed.

MCCLOREY, ANNE M; Our Lady Of Mercy HS; Novi, MI; 18/331 Girl Scts; Hon Rl; Off Ade; Pol Wkr; Rptr Sch Nwsp; Bsktbl; Chrldng; Coach Actv; Notre Dame Univ; Pre Law.

MCCLOSKEY, DARLENE; Bishop Borgess HS; Detroit, MI; 35/530 Cmnty Wkr; Hon Rl; Lbry Ade; NHS; Sch Pl; Fr Clb; Sci Clb; St Comp Schlrshp Prog Cert 79; Outstdg French 79; Henry Ford Cmnty Coll; Nursing.

MCCLOSKEY, JACALYN A; Bishop Gallagher HS; Roseville, MI; 1/350 Hon Rl; Yrbk; Ed Sch Nwsp; Rptr Sch Nwsp; Univ; Med Tech.

MCCLOSKEY, TIMOTHY; Franklin HS; Livonia, MI; Am Leg Boys St; Band; Boy Scts; Chrs; Chrh Wkr; Hon Rl; Sch Mus; Sct Actv; Alma College; Medicine.

MCCLOUD, DEBRA; North Putnam HS; Roachdale, IN; 30/103 Chrs; Chrh Wkr; Cmnty Wkr; Hon Rl; Lbry Ade; NHS; Pol Wkr; FHA; OEA;.

MCCLOUD, PAMELA E; Monroe Gregg HS; Mooresville, IN; 8/105 Hon Rl; JA; Lbry Ade; NHS; Off Ade; JA Awd; Natl Merit Ltr;.

MCCLOUGHAN, KIM; Tippecanoe Valley HS; Akron, IN; Chrs; Girl Scts; Hon Rl; NHS; 4-H; Indiana Univ; Science.

MCCLOY, CHRIS; Pennsboro HS; Pennsboro, WV; Sec Frsh Cls; Trs Frsh Cls; VP Soph Cls; VP Jr Cls;

Band; Natl Forn Lg; NHS; Drama Clb; West Virginia Univ; Radiology.

MCCLUE, DENISE; Houghton Lake HS; Houghton Lk, MI; 68/152 Cmp Fr Grls; Girl Scts; Hon Rl; Lbry Ade; 4-H; Fr Clb; Spn Clb; Siena Heights Coll; Interior Dec.

MCCLUNG, JANET K; Tri West Hendricks HS; Pittsboro, IN; 12/121 Hon Rl; NHS; 4-H; 4-H Awd; Voc Schl.

MCCLUNG, JEFFREY; South Charleston HS; S Charleston, WV; Hon Rl; NHS; Sprt Ed Sch Nwsp; Bsbl; Bsktbl; Glf; IM Sprt; JA Awd; Marshall Univ; Bus Mgmt.

MCCLUNG, KAREN; Parkersburg South HS; Parkersburg, WV; 86/640 Chrs; Chrh Wkr; Cmnty Wkr; Girl Scts; Hon Rl; Pol Wkr; Y-Teens; Pep Clb; Sci Clb; Pres Mat Maids; Parkersburg Cmnty Coll; Radiology.

MCCLUNG, TINA R; Richwood HS; Leivasy, WV; Hon Rl; Hosp Ade; Lbry Ade; Lit Mag; Sch Pl; Sec Yth Flsp; Yrbk; Rptr Sch Nwsp; Drama Clb; 4-H; Candystriper Hat & Pin; Vocational Schl; Busns.

MCCLUNG, TONYA; Lewis County HS; Weston, WV; FCA; Hon Rl; NHS; PAVAS; Sec Stu Cncl; Gym; Chrldng; Friends Of The Weston Lewis Cnty Creative Cntst I 79; Recd 2nd Pl & A Plaque; Miss LCHS Sweetheart 78; Fairmont St Coll; Nurse.

MCCLURE, CATHERINE A; Plymouth HS; Plymouth, IN; 8/240 Trs Soph Cls; Trs Jr Cls; Trs Sr Cls; AFS; Am Leg Aux Girls St; Band; Hon Rl; NHS; Pres Stu Cncl; Ed Yrbk; St Marys Coll; Acctg.

MCCLURE, CINDY; Lake Orion HS; Lake Orion, MI; Band; Cmp Fr Grls; Hon Rl; NHS; Drama Clb; Spn Clb; Twrlr; Northern Michigan Univ; Aviatn Tech.

MCCLURE, DENNIS D; Bishop Dwenger HS; New Haven, IN; 11/268 Chrh Wkr; Hon Rl; NHS; Bsktbl; Ftbl; Mgrs; Scr Kpr; Tmr; JETS Awd; Natl Merit Schl; Indiana St Schlshp 1979; Hoosier Schlr 1979; Purdue Univ Hons 1979; Hon In Chem 1979; Notre Dame Univ; Chem Engr.

MCCLURE, ELIZABETH; Rivet HS; Vincennes, IN; 11/46 Trs Frsh Cls; VP Jr Cls; Pres Sr Cls; FHA; Pep Clb; Cit Awd; Vincennes Univ; Forestry.

MCCLURE, JENNIFER; Thomas Carr Howe HS; Indianapolis, IN; 32/600 Chrs; Chrh Wkr; Hon Rl; NHS; Sch Mus; Stg Crw; Sch Nwsp; Mat Maids; Scr Kpr; Cit Awd; Univ; Public Relations.

MCCLURE, JENNY L; Whiteland Comm HS; Whiteland, IN; 39/229 FCA; FBLA; Key Clb; Letter Bsktbl; Trk; IM Sprt; Mgrs; PPFtbl; Pres Phys Fitness Awrd; College; Law.

MCCLURE, KAREN L; Hurricane HS; Hurricane, WV; Hon Rl; Off Ade; Pep Clb; Trk;.

MCCLURE, MARY; Northrop HS; Ft Wayne, IN; 69/600 Sec Frsh Cls; Trs Frsh Cls; Chrs; Hon Rl; Stu Cncl; Rptr Sch Nwsp; Letter Ten; Cit Awd; Jrnlsm 76 78; Latin 78; Ball St Univ; Law.

MCCLURE, SUSAN; South Spencer HS; Eockport, IN; Band; Girl Scts; Hon Rl; Lbry Ade; Sch Mus; Sch Pl; Ed Yrbk; Rptr Yrbk; Rptr Sch Nwsp; Drama Clb; Welborn Bpts Hosp Sch Radiolgy; Xray.

MCCLURE, TERESA; Salem HS; Salem, IN; Band; Girl Scts; Hon Rl; Lbry Ade; Drama Clb; FHA; Pep Clb; Watterson Coll; Med Lab Tech.

MCCLURE, TERESA; Jonesville HS; Horton, MI; Band; Girl Scts; Hon Rl; 4-H; 4-H Awd; College; Comp Prog.

MCCLURG, PAULA; Jefferson Union HS; Irondale, OH; Letter Band; Cmp Fr Grls; Chrs; Chrh Wkr; Cmnty Wkr; Hon Rl; Jr NHS; Yth Flsp; Rptr Sch Nwsp; Beta Clb; Univ; Nursing.

MCCLURKIN, HEIDI L; Avon Lake HS; Avon Lake, OH; 28/280 AFS; Band; Chrh Wkr; Drl Tm; Hon Rl; NHS; Sch Mus; Ger Clb; Mth Clb; Pep Clb; Georgia Inst Of Tech; Archt.

MCCLUSKEY, R; Grand Ledge HS; Grnd Ldg, MI; Band; Debate Tm; NHS; Letter Glf; Univ.

MCCOLLISTER, KELLY; Zanesville HS; Zanesville, OH; Drl Tm; Hon Rl; Chrldng; Muskingum Area Tech Coll; X Ray Tech.

MCCOLLUM, CHERYL; Tri County HS; Wolcott, IN; 4/73 Cls Rep Frsh Cls; Trs Soph Cls; Trs Jr Cls; Band; Chrh Wkr; Hon Rl; NHS; Off Ade; Sch Mus; 4-H; Purdue Univ; Elem Educ.

MCCOLLUM, SCOTT; Beavercreek HS; Dayton, OH; 315/750 Boy Scts; Chrh Wkr; Sct Actv; Boys Clb Am; Ftbl; Gym; Trk; Wrstlng; Air Force; Comp Tech.

MCCOLLUM, SUSAN; Monrovia HS; Clayton, IN; 2/104 Sec Frsh Cls; Sec Soph Cls; Sec Jr Cls; Sec Sr Cls; Sal; Am Leg Aux Girls St; Band; Chrh Wkr; Hon Rl; VP NHS; Purdue Univ; Family Studies.

MCCOLLUM, SUSAN C; Monrovia HS; Clayton, IN; 2/109 Sec Frsh Cls; Sec Soph Cls; Sec Jr Cls; Sec Sr Cls; Sal; Am Leg Aux Girls St; Band; Chrh Wkr; Hon Rl; VP NHS; Purdue Univ; Home Ec.

MCCOMAS, ANGELA L; Hannan HS; Pliny, WV; 1/30 Hon Rl; VP Stu Cncl; Pres Yth Flsp; Yrbk; FHA; Cit Awd; DAR Awd; Busns Schl; Legal Sec.

MCCOMAS, SANDRA K; Barboursville HS; Barboursville, WV; 100/426 VP Soph Cls; Cl Rep Jr Cls; FCA; Hon Rl; Jr NHS; Yth Flsp; Pep Clb; Letter Crs Cntry; Letter Ten; Letter Chrldng; West Virginia Univ; Law.

MCCOMBS, JIM; New Albany HS; New Albany, OH; 7/110 Band; Chrs; Chrh Wkr; FCA; Hon Rl; Sch Mus; Sch Pl; IM Sprt; College; Electronics.

MCCOMBS, KAREN; Sycamore HS; Cincinnati, OH; 84/445 Hon Rl; Hosp Ade; Rptr Sch Nwsp; Fr Clb; Hockey; Ohio Univ; Psych.

MCCONAHAY, SUSAN; Thomas Carr Howe HS; Indianapolis, IN; Chrs; Hon Rl; Lit Mag; Off Ade; Sci Clb; IM Sprt; Scr Kpr; Tmr; Awd For Chorus 79; Indiana Univ; Med.

MCCONIGA, DAVID; Northrop HS; Ft Wayne, IN; Sec Soph Cls; Trs Soph Cls; Notre Dame Club Jr Of Yy Awd 79; Mc Donalds All Amer HS Mrch Band 79; 2 Yrs Part In All City Hon Orch 78; Univ; Law.

MCCONKEY, CRYSTAL A; Tippecanoe Valley HS; Rochester, IN; 3/168 Sec Frsh Cls; Chrs; Hon Rl; Lbry Ade; NHS; 4-H; Pep Clb; Gym; Swmmng; Ten; Univ.

MCCONNELL, DIANE; Magnificat HS; Rocky River, OH; Girl Scts; JA; Mod UN; Sch Pl; Rptr Sch Nwsp; Trk; College; Bus.

MCCONNELL, GREG; Yale HS; Yale, MI; 18/160 Am Leg Boys St; Aud/Vis; Boy Scts; Chrh Wkr; Hon Rl; Stu Cncl; Bsktbl; Ten; Ferris St Coll.

MCCONNELL, KAREN; Fremont HS; Fremont, IN; VP Band; Chrh Wkr; Sec NHS; Drama Clb; Pres Fr Clb; Pep Clb;.

MCCONNELL, KATHY; Parchment HS; Lakeside, CA; Chrs; Chrh Wkr; Girl Scts; Hon Rl; NHS; Sch Mus; Stu Cncl; Ten; Chrldng; PPFtbl; San Diego State Univ; Nurse.

MCCONNELL, KATHY; Washington HS; Massillon, OH; 92/482 AFS; Hon Rl; NHS; Quill & Scroll; Stg Crw; Y-Teens; Yrbk; Drama Clb; Pep Clb; IM Sprt; Ohi Univ; Recreation.

MCCONNELL, KATHY; La Salle HS; South Bend, IN; 47/488 Chrs; Hon Rl; Off Ade; Sch Mus; Stu Cncl; Drama Clb; Letter Swmmng; Tmr; Cit Awd; DAR Awd; Purdue Univ; Pre Med.

MCCONNELL, MARJORIE; Quincy HS; Quincy, MI; Band; Chrh Wkr; Hon Rl; NHS; Yth Flsp; Fr Clb; College; Teacher.

MCCONNELL, MARK; Warsaw Cmnty HS; Warsaw, IN; Band; Boy Scts; Sch Mus; Sct Actv; Rptr Sch Nwsp; Ball St Univ; Archt.

MCCONNELL, MELISSA; Lakewood HS; Newark, OH; 13/194 Cl Rep Jr Cls; Hon Rl; NHS; Pres OEA; Ohio St Univ; Bus Admin.

MCCONNELL, THOMAS; South Vigo Terre Haute HS; Terre Haute, IN; Band; Chrh Wkr; Hon Rl; Yth Flsp; Indiana St Univ; Bldg Engr.

MCCOOL, LONNIE; Daleville HS; Daleville, IN; 12/70 Band; Boy Scts; Jr NHS; VP NHS; Fr Clb; Pep Clb; De Molay Sr Decon Scribe; Perfect Attndnc 77 78 & 79; Purdue Univ; Forestry Wildlife Mgmt.

MCCORD, DIANE L; Bishop Flaget HS; Chillicothe, OH; 2/33 Cls Rep Frsh Cls; Cmnty Wkr; Hon Rl; NHS; Sch Mus; Sch Pl; Ed Yrbk; Sprt Ed Sch Nwsp; VP Fr Clb; Sec Pep Clb; Ohio Univ; Jrnlsm.

MCCORD, KATHY; River Valley HS; Marion, OH; 17/207 Chrh Wkr; Cmnty Wkr; Treas Girl Scts; Treas JA; Sch Mus; Drama Clb; Lat Clb; Sci Clb; JA Awd; Bowling Green Univ; Busns Admin.

MCCORD, SANDRA K; Barr Reeve HS; Loogootee, IN; 21/48 Hon Rl; FFA; FHA; Pep Clb; VICA; Chrldng; IM Sprt; Pom Pon; Vincennes Univ; Comp Prog.

MCCORD, TONY; Bryan HS; Bryan, OH; 12/192 Hon Rl; NHS; Key Clb; Letter Bsbl; Ftbl; Capt IM Sprt; Letter Mgrs; Scr Kpr; Tmr; Bowling Green St Univ; Soc Sci.

MCCORKLE, KIM; Walter P Chrysler Mem HS; New Castle, IN; 46/414 Girl Scts; Hon Rl; Lbry Ade; Stu Cncl; Ed Yrbk; 4-H; Pep Clb; Spn Clb; Mat Maids; Purdue Univ; Pharmacy.

MCCORKLE, RUTH; Jackson Milton HS; N Jackson, OH; Sec Jr Cls; Trs Sr Cls; Hon Rl; NHS; Off Ade; 4-H; OEA; Letter Chrldng; Scr Kpr; College; Word Processing.

MCCORKLE, STEVE; Port Huron N HS; North Street, MI; 17/385 Hon Rl; NHS; Lawrence Inst Of Tech Acad Schlrshp; Detroit News Mich Indus Ed Awd; Lawrence Inst Of Tech; Archt.

MCCORMACK, SUSAN; Union Cnty HS; College Corner, OH; 4/130 Band; Girl Scts; Hon Rl; NHS; Yth Flsp; 4-H; Fr Clb; Pep Clb; Letter Bsktbl; Letter Trk; Univ; Phys Ed.

MCCORMICK, ALICE; Airport HS; Carleton, MI; Treas Band; Drm Mjrt; NHS; 4-H; Fr Clb; Pep Clb; Twrlr; 4-H Awd; Mic State Univ; Educ.

MCCORMICK, DANNY; Green HS; No Canton, OH; 46/317 NHS; Letter Dnfth Awd; IM Sprt; Cit Awd; Univ Of Dayton; Pre Med.

MCCORMICK, DAVID; Green HS; North Canton, OH; 44/319 Cls Rep Frsh Cls; Band; Hon Rl; Orch; Stg Crw; Stu Cncl; Drama Clb; IM Sprt; Univ; HS Tchr.

MCCORMICK, JANET; Wadsworth Sr HS; Wadsworth, OH; 87/367 FCA; Girl Scts; Hosp Ade; Jr NHS; NHS; Lat Clb; Treas VICA; Letter Bsktbl; Capt Trk; JC Awd; Univ Of Michigan; Nursing.

MCCORMICK, JENNIFER; Princeton HS; Princeton, WV; Pep Clb; Pom Pon; Dancing Awd; Concord Coll; Education.

MCCORMICK, JOHN; Stivers Patterson Coop HS; Dayton, OH; 64/414 Debate Tm; Hon Rl; NHS; Sch Pl; Sch Nwsp; Boys Clb Am; Wright St Univ; Acting.

MCCORMICK, LESHIA; Anderson HS; Cincinnati, OH; 100/383 Chrs; Girl Scts; Hosp Ade; Off Ade; Orch; Fr Clb; FBLA; PPFtbl; Past Honored Queen Jobs Daughters 77; Eastern Kentucky Univ; Pediatric Ast.

MCCORMICK, LINDA; Norton HS; Norton, OH; 30/287 Cl Rep Jr Cls; Cmnty Wkr; Girl Scts; Hon Rl; Jr NHS; Orch; Sct Actv; Sec Fr Clb; Pep Clb; Cit Awd; Univ Of Akron; Child Psych.

MCCORMICK, MARK; Pontiac Cntrl HS; Pontiac, MI; Mgrs; Scr Kpr; College; Acctg Cpa.

MCCORMICK, MICHAEL; Michigan Lutheran Seminary; Toledo, OH; Aud/Vis; Chrs; Hon Rl; Ger Clb; Lat Clb; Mth Clb; IM Sprt; Scr Kpr; Tmr; Northwestern Univ; Ministry.

MCCORMICK, NANCY; Cloverdale HS; Cloverdale, IN; 7/85 Chrs; FCA; Hon Rl; Sch Mus; Pep Clb; Chrldng; GAA; Mgrs;.

MCCORMICK, PAM; Boardman HS; Boardman, OH; 76/538 Girl Scts; Hon Rl; Orch; Sch Mus; VP Sct Actv; Fr Clb; Sci Clb; College; Music.

MCCORMICK, THOMAS; Monroe Catholic Central HS; Carleton, MI; Yrbk; Letter Ten; IM Sprt; Monroe Cnty Cmnty Coll; Comp Sci.

MCCORMICK, TIM; Groveport Madison HS; Groveport, OH; 11/373 Hon Rl; 4-H; FFA; Ftbl; Cert Of Academic Ach; French Cert Of Merit; FFA Schlrshp Awd; FFA Beef Production Awd; Ohio St Univ; Ag Lab Tech.

MCCORMICK, TOM; Groveport Madison HS; Groveport, OH; 11/373 Hon Rl; 4-H; FFA; Ftbl; Cert Of Academic Ach; FFA Schlrshp Awd; FFA Beef Production Awd; FFA Greenhand Degree; FFA Treasurer; Ohio St Univ; Voc Ag Instructor.

MCCORRY, ERICA; Warrensville Heights HS; Warrensville, OH; Cmnty Wkr; Drl Tm; Hon Rl; JA; Off Ade; Stu Cncl; Rptr Yrbk; Yrbk; Pep Clb; Spn Clb; College; Intl Bus.

MCCORRY, TRACEY L; Warrensville Heights HS; Warrensvlle Hts, OH; Pres Soph Cls; Cl Rep Jr Cls; Cls Rep Sr Cls; Chrs; Sch Mus; Stu Cncl; Yrbk; Rptr Sch Nwsp; VP DECA; Pep Clb; Miami Univ; Tele Communications.

MCCOURT, ANITA; Webster County HS; Camden Gauley, WV; Hon Rl; Rptr Sch Nwsp; Pep Clb; Bsktbl; Trk; Chrldng; GAA; Bus Schl; Stewardess.

MCCOWAN, BARBARA; Jay Cnty HS; Redkey, IN; Chrh Wkr; Hon Rl; NHS; Yth Flsp; Y-Teens; OEA; College; Secretarial Progr.

MCCOWAN, MELODY; Jay County HS; Redkey, IN; 24/474 Am Leg Aux Girls St; Band; Hon Rl; Jr NHS; NHS; Sch Mus; Stg Crw; Y-Teens; Drama Clb; Fr Clb; Univ; Interior Dsgn.

MCCOWAN, SUSAN; Brookside HS; Sheffield Lake, OH; Cls Rep Soph Cls; Sec Jr Cls; Sec Sr Cls; Hon Rl; Jr NHS; Lbry Ade; NHS; Off Ade; Stu Cncl; Pres FTA; Lorain Cnty Cmnty Coll; Bus.

MCCOWIN, JODI; East Palestine HS; E Palestine, OH; Sec Jr Cls; Hon Rl; Ten; Chrldng; Scr Kpr; Ohio State Univ; Nursing.

MCCOY, BARBARA; Hundred HS; Burton, WV; 5/47 Hon Rl; FFA; FHA; Pep Clb; Bus School; Sec.

MCCOY, BRENDA; W Ottawa HS; Holland, MI; Cmp Fr Grls; Chrs; Chrh Wkr; Hon Rl; JA; IM Sprt; JA Awd; Muskegon Busns Coll; Acctg.

MCCOY, CYNTHIA; Union Scioto HS; Chillicothe, OH; 1/123 Pres Jr Cls; Hosp Ade; NHS; Off Ade; Quill & Scroll; Ed Sch Nwsp; Ten; Ohi State Univ.

MCCOY, DAVID R; Washington HS; Washington, IN; 14/216 Boy Scts; FCA; Hon Rl; Beta Clb; Lat Clb; Letter Ftbl; Letter Swmmng; IM Sprt; Math.

MCCOY, DOUGLAS; Bridgman HS; Bridgman, MI; Pres Frsh Cls; Chrs; Hon Rl; Sch Mus; Stg Crw; Sci Clb; Bsktbl; Trk; Mgrs; Western Michigan Univ; Bus Mgmt.

MCCOY, ERIN; Lima Sr HS; Lima, OH; Chrs; Cmnty Wkr; Girl Scts; Hon Rl; Lbry Ade; Off Ade; Rptr Sch Nwsp; Letter Bsktbl; IM Sprt; Ohio St Univ; Pre Med.

MCCOY, ERIN; Sts Peter & Paul HS; Saginaw, MI; Sec Frsh Cls; Sec Sr Cls; Hon Rl; NHS; Sch Mus; Stu Cncl; Rptr Yrbk; Trk; Pom Pon; PPFtbl; College; Natural Science.

MCCOY, GARY; Beaver Local HS; Calcutta, OH; Chrh Wkr; Cmnty Wkr; Sch Pl; Stg Crw; Yth Flsp; Sci Clb; Ftbl; Trk; Wrstlng; Coach Actv; Jefferson Tech Voc Schl; Carpenter.

MCCOY, IRENE; Waterloo Sr HS; Atwater, OH; 5/135 Band; Girl Scts; Hon Rl; Jr NHS; NHS; Beta Clb; Mth Clb; Sci Clb; Letter Crs Cntry; Letter Trk;.

MCCOY, J; Redford HS; Detroit, MI; Pres Sr Cls; Chrh Wkr; Hon Rl; JA; Stu Cncl; FSA; VICA; Ftbl; Cal State; Elec Engr.

MCCOY, KAREN L; Valley Forge HS; Parma Heights, OH; Cls Rep Frsh Cls; Cls Rep Soph Cls; Chrs; Cmnty Wkr; Girl Scts; Hon Rl; Lbry Ade; Lit Mag; Off Ade; PAVAS; Kent State Univ; Graphic Design.

MCCOY, KATHY; Perry HS; Canton, OH; Band; Chrs; Chrh Wkr; Hon Rl; Natl Forn Lg; NHS; Sch Mus; Stg Crw; Drama Clb; Spn Clb; College; Music.

MCCOY, KATY; Piketon HS; Waverly, OH; 4/115 Cls Rep Soph Cls; Cl Rep Jr Cls; Band; Chrs; Hon Rl; Sch Mus; Treas Stu Cncl; Sprt Ed Yrbk; Sec 4-H; FTA; Varsity Volleyball Lettered Co Capt Co MVP; Algebra I Schlrshp Team; Ohio St Univ; Nuclear Engr.

MCCOY, LEONARD; Buffalo HS; Lavalette, WV; 4/141 Hon Rl; NHS; Sch Pl; VP FFA; Mth Clb; Letter Bsbl; Letter Bsktbl; Letter Ftbl; Trk; College; Engineering.

MCCOY, LORI; Pike HS; Indianapolis, IN; 25/303 Band; Girl Scts; Hon Rl; Jr NHS; NHS; Yth Flsp; FBLA; Bsktbl; PPFtbl;.

MCCOY, PATTY; Elkins HS; Elkins, WV; Clarksburg; Sec.

MCCOY, SARAH; Frontier HS; Nw Mtmrs, OH; Hon Rl; Off Ade; Stg Crw; OEA; GAA;.

MCCOY, SHAWNA E; Upper Valley Jnt Voc Schl; Piqua, OH; 47/321 Chrs; Chrh Wkr; Cmnty Wkr; Drl Tm; Hon Rl; Yth Flsp; Y-Teens; DECA; Spn Clb; Bsbl; Top 100 1978; Univ Of Houston; Radio & Tv.

MCCOY, TAMMY; St Clement HS; Warren, MI; 2/115 Sal; Chrs; Girl Scts; Hon Rl; NHS; Sch Pl; Stg Crw; Drama Clb; Pep Clb; Natl Merit SF; Macomb Cnty Cmnty Coll; Engr.

MCCOY, THOMAS; Ridgewood HS; Fresno, OH; Am Leg Boys St; Chrh Wkr; Hon Rl; Sct Actv; Yth Flsp; Bsbl; Bsktbl; Crs Cntry; Am Leg Awd; Dnfth Awd; Dollars For Scholars 79; Judson Coll; Comp Sci.

MCCOY, TIMOTHY; Williamson HS; Sprigg, WV; 6/100 Hon Rl; Jr NHS; NHS; Pep Clb; Sci Clb; Trk; Bausch & Lomb Awd; DAR Awd; West Virginia Tech Inst; Elec Engr.

MCCOY, TONI; Henry Ford HS; Detroit, MI; Chrs; Univ; Psych.

MCCOY, TROY; Pocahontas County HS; Hillsboro, WV; FFA; Marshall Univ; Law Enforcement.

MCCOY, VALERIE J; Cass Tech HS; Detroit, MI; Cmp Fr Grls; Chrh Wkr; Hon Rl; Jr NHS; Yrbk; FTA; Schlrshp Detroit Heritage Hse; Honrbl Mention AAA Safety Poster Contest; Michigan St Univ; Commercial Art.

MCCRACKEN, BONITA; North Decatur Jr Sr HS; Greensburg, IN; 20/90 VP Jr Cls; Chrs; Chrh Wkr; Hon Rl; Off Ade; Yth Flsp; Rptr Sch Nwsp; Drama Clb; 4-H; Pres Fr Clb; Bus Schl.

MCCRACKEN, BONITA S; North Decatur HS; Greensburg, IN; 20/88 VP Jr Cls; Off Ade; Yth Flsp; Rptr Sch Nwsp; Drama Clb; 4-H; Fr Clb; FTA; Letter Bsktbl; Letter Trk;.

MCCRACKEN, CHERYL; Washington HS; Washington, IN; 5/194 Chrs; Hon Rl; Mdrgl; NHS; Pol Wkr; Sch Mus; Sch Pl; Beta Clb; Drama Clb; 4-H; Purdue Univ; Pharm.

MCCRACKEN, JOYLENE; Bad Axe HS; Bad Axe, MI; 3/141 Band; Hon Rl; Jr NHS; NHS; Off Ade; Rptr Yrbk; Rptr Sch Nwsp; FHA; Saginaw Vly St Coll; Nursing.

MCCRACKEN, KELLY S; Hubbard HS; Hubbard, OH; 3/330 Band; Chrh Wkr; Hon Rl; Orch; Sch Mus; Yth Flsp; Lat Clb; Youngstown St Univ; Psych.

MCCRACKEN, LISA; Centerburg HS; Centerburg, OH; 5/71 Sec Sr Cls; Am Leg Aux Girls St; Chrs; Debate Tm; Hon Rl; NHS; Stg Crw; Stu Cncl; Yrbk; Drama Clb; Colorado Bus Univ; Acctg.

MCCRACKEN, MARTIN; Sullivan HS; Sullivan, IN; Am Leg Boys St; Band; Chrs; Hon Rl; Orch; Sch Mus; Y-Teens; Rptr Yrbk; Sch Nwsp; Pres Spn Clb; Ind Univ; Journalism.

MCCRACKEN, SHERRI; Lincolnview HS; Middle Point, OH; 35/78 Chrs; Hon Rl; Lbry Ade; Rptr Sch Nwsp; Sec DECA; 3rd In DECA Food Sercie Contest;.

MCCRAKEN, MARY; North Royalton HS; N Royalton, OH; Cmnty Wkr; Girl Scts; Off Ade; Sch Pl; Drama Clb; OEA; Univ; Psych.

MCCRARY, LESIA; South Knox HS; Wheatland, IN; 7/106 Chrh Wkr; Girl Scts; Hon Rl; NHS; Sch Pl; Drama Clb; Pep Clb; Bsktbl; Trk;.

MCCREA, TIM; Northrop HS; Ft Wayne, IN; 35/600 Band; Chrs; Hon Rl; Mdrgl; Orch; Coll; Music.

MCCREA, TIMOTHY; Northrop HS; Ft Wayne, IN; 35/600 Band; Chrs; Hon Rl; Mdrgl; Orch; College; Elec Engr.

MCCREADY, KEITH; Tawas Area HS; Tawas City, MI; 3/200 Band; Boy Scts; Chrh Wkr; Debate Tm; VP NHS; Sch Pl; Wrstlng; Voice Dem Awd; Univ; Sci.

MCCREARY, DAVID; Brooke HS; Wellsburg, WV; 108/405 Cls Rep Soph Cls; Am Leg Boys St; Boy Scts; FCA; Hon Rl; Sct Actv; Stu Cncl; Sprt Ed Sch Nwsp; Key Clb; Spn Clb; Univ; Engr.

MCCREARY, DAVID F; Brooke HS; Wellsburg, WV; 108/403 Trs Frsh Cls; Cls Rep Soph Cls; Pres Jr Cls; Am Leg Boys St; Boy Scts; Chrh Wkr; FCA; Hon Rl; NHS; Sct Actv; College; Engr.

MCCREARY, JOSEPH; Owen Vly HS; Spencer, IN; 25/147 Band; FCA; Red Cr Ade; Sch Mus; Stg Crw; Drama Clb; Rus Clb; Ftbl; Trk; Pres Awd; Purdue Univ.

MCCREARY, MARK; James Ford Rhodes HS; Cleveland, OH; Ohi State; Eng.

MCCREE, CEDRIC; Cass Tech HS; Detroit, MI; Chrs; Chrh Wkr; Drl Tm; Hon Rl; Orch; ROTC; Natl Merit Ltr; Mi St Schlrshp 79; Fine Arts Camp Schlrshp 75; Natl Music Camp Schlrshp 78; Eastern Michigan Univ; Jrnlsm.

MCCREERY, BETH; Fort Frye HS; Lowell, OH; 9/129 Am Leg Aux Girls St; Hon Rl; Jr NHS; NHS; Sec Pep Clb; Spn Clb; Letter Bsktbl; Letter Chrldng; Am Leg Awd; Bausch & Lomb Awd; Glenville St Coll; Elem Ed.

MCCREERY, JIM; Grand River Academy; Poland, OH; Boy Scts; Chrh Wkr; Off Ade; Sch Pl; Drama Clb; Bsbl; Socr; IM Sprt; Serv Awd 78; Univ; Law Enforcement.

MCCREIGHT, KATHLEEN; Hillsboro HS; Hillsboro, OH; Band; Sch Pl; Yth Flsp; Fr Clb; Lat Clb; Order Of Rainbow For Girls Schlrshp Awd; Most Outstanding Rainbow Girl Of 7 Masonic Dist; Bliss Coll; Court Reporting.

MCCREIGHT, KATHY; Mt Pleasant HS; Mt Pleasant, MI; 13/365 Band; Chrs; Hon Rl; Treas NHS; Sch Mus; Sch Pl; Stg Crw; Central Mic Univ; Reatle Estate.

MCCRONE, TAMI; Andrew School; Painesvll, OH; Hon Rl; NHS; Off Ade; Quill & Scroll; Hndbl; Ten; Chrldng; Mgrs; Scr Kpr; Tmr; Hon Coll In Sr Yr 79; Lakeland Coll; Comp Sci.

MCCRUTER, VERA; St Peters HS; Mansfield, OH; Cls Rep Sr Cls; Chrs; Chrh Wkr; Cmnty Wkr; Lbry Ade; Off Ade; PAVAS; Sch Mus; Sch Pl; Stg Crw; Bowling Green; Retailing.

MCCUBBIN, LAWRENCE W; Covington HS; Covington, IN; 1/110 Cls Rep Frsh Cls; Pres Soph Cls; Pres Jr Cls; Chrh Wkr; Hon Rl; Sch Pl; Stu Cncl; Sprt Ed Sch Nwsp; Rptr Sch Nwsp; Letter Bsbl; Harding Univ; Acctg.

MCCULLARS, VALERIE; John R Buchtel HS; Akron, OH; Chrs; Lbry Ade; Off Ade; Sch Pl; FDA; Bsktbl; Trk; GAA; Univ Of Akron; Sec.

MCCULLOCH, L; Bluefield HS; Bluefield, WV; 23/286 Jr NHS; NHS; Rptr Sch Nwsp; Spn Clb; Letter Ten;.

MCCULLOGH, LEIGH; Bluefield HS; Bluefield, WV; 23/286 NHS; Rptr Sch Nwsp; Spn Clb; Letter Ten; Montreat Anderson Coll.

MCCULLOUGH, E; Shakamak HS; Lewis, IN; 12/84 Chrh Wkr; Hon Rl; NHS; Sct Actv; VP 4-H; FFA; Mgrs; 4-H Awd; Coll.

MCCULLOUGH, EVELYN; River Rouge HS; River Rouge, MI; Cls Rep Soph Cls; Pres Jr Cls; Band; Chrh Wkr; Cmnty Wkr; Hon Rl; Lbry Ade; NHS; Sch Pl; Stu Cncl; Univ Of Michigan; Law.

MCCULLOUGH, KAREN; Springport HS; Fort Wayne, IN; Band; Chrs; 4-H; Chrldng; 4-H Awd;.

MCCULLOUGH, LARRY; Reitz Memorial HS; Evansville, IN; 82/250 Am Leg Boys St; Chrs; Hon Rl; Chmn Bsbl; IM Sprt; Purdue; Mech Engr.

MCCULLOUGH, LINDA; Morton Sr HS; Hammond, IN; 13/419 Cl Rep Jr Cls; Debate Tm; Hon Rl; Pres JA; Natl Forn Lg; Quill & Scroll; Rptr Sch Nwsp; Fr Clb; Pep Clb; Spn Clb; Univ; Bus Mgmt.

MCCULLOUGH, PAM; Parkway HS; Rockford, OH; 8/84 Band; Chrs; Hon Rl; NHS; Ger Clb; Sci Clb; Spn Clb; Defiance College; Psychology.

MCCULLOUGH, PAMELA; Parkway HS; Rockford, OH; 8/85 Band; Chrs; Chrh Wkr; Hon Rl; NHS; Ger Clb; Sci Clb; Spn Clb; Dist III Band 1977; Clarinet Quartet 1976; Symphonic Choir 1977; Manchester Coll; Psych.

MCCULLUM, CYNTHIA; Westfield Washington HS; Westfield, IN; Cmnty Wkr; Hon Rl; NHS; VP Yth Flsp; 4-H; Spn Clb; Am Leg Awd; College.

MCCULLUM, ROBERT; Westland HS; Columbus, OH; Hon Rl; ROTC; FBLA; OEA; Univ; Travel Agent.

MCCUMBER, ERIC; Cadillac HS; Cadillac, MI; Chrs; Chrh Wkr; FCA; Hon Rl; NHS; Letter Crs Cntry; Letter Trk; College.

MCCUMMINS, RONALD; Mathews HS; Fowler, OH; 42/152 Aud/Vis; Hon Rl; Sch Pl; DECA; Pres 4-H; Fr Clb; FTA; Pep Clb; Capt Ftbl; Capt Trk; All Amer In Track 79; Ohio St Univ; Agri Educ.

MCCUNE, DEBBIE; Du Pont HS; Charleston, WV;

MCCUNE, PAMELA; Kokomo HS; Kokomo, IN; 34/319 Sec Chrh Wkr; Hon Rl; Off Ade; Outstndng Stdnt Awd In Acctg I & II 79; Univ; Acctg.

MCCURDY, CHARLOTTE; Austintown Fitch HS; Austintown, OH; Drm Bgl; Hosp Ade; Y-Teens; Spn Clb; Mat Maids; PPFtbl; Univ; Comm Art.

MCCURDY, DAWN K; Pleasant HS; Marion, OH; Chrh Wkr; Hon Rl; Jr NHS; Pres Lbry Ade; Lit Mag; NHS; 4-H; Sci Clb; IM Sprt; Natl Merit SF; Bowling Green St Univ; Microbio.

MCCURDY, JOAN; Otsego HS; Grand Rapids, OH; 2/150 Am Leg Aux Girls St; Band; Hon Rl; Jr NHS; NHS; Sch Pl; Yrbk; Pres Drama Clb; Fr Clb; Tmr; College; Elem Ed.

MCCURDY, LARRY; Centerville HS; Richmond, IN; 5/170 Trs Frsh Cls; Boy Scts; Chrh Wkr; Hon Rl; JA; NHS; Sct Actv; FFA; Crs Cntry; Trk; Eagle Scout Awd & 3 Palms; College; Science.

MCCUTCHEN, CINDY; Lawrence Central HS; Lawrence, IN; 55/365 Cl Rep Jr Cls; Chrh Wkr; Debate Tm; Hon Rl; Natl Forn Lg; NHS; Yth Flsp; Fr Clb; Pep Clb; Letter Bsktbl; 2 Ribbons For Impromto Spkng On Spch Team 78; Semi Finlst Fo RIU Hon Progr 78; Miami Univ; French.

MCCUTCHEON, ELLEN; Bellbrook HS; Bellbrook, OH; Band; GAA; College.

MCCUTCHEON, MARY J; Woodrow Wilson HS; Beckley, WV; 12/508 Sec Sr Cls; JA; NHS; Stg Crw; 4-H; Keyettes; Pep Clb; Spn Clb; JA Awd; West Virginia Univ; Engr.

MCDANIEL, AMY; Wehrle HS; Columbus, OH; 1/118 Hon Rl; Stu Cncl; Rptr Sch Nwsp; Voice Dem Awd; Ohio Dominican Univ; Social Work.

MCDANIEL, CHRIS; Indian Hill HS; Cincinnati, OH; Boy Scts; Hon Rl; Mod UN; Sct Actv; Lat Clb; Letter Ftbl; Trk; Letter Wrstlng; IM Sprt; Univ Of Cincinnati; Engr.

MCDANIEL, CHRISTIAN; Aquinas HS; Allen Park, MI; Hon Rl; NHS; Stg Crw; Ed Sch Nwsp; Rptr Sch Nwsp; Drama Clb; Natl Merit SF; Michigan St Univ; Soc Sci.

MCDANIEL, DARLENE; Macomber Whitney HS; Toledo, OH; Cls Rep Soph Cls; Girl Scts; JA; VICA; Bowling Green; Pharmacist.

MCDANIEL, ERNEST; Lapeer East Sr HS; Lapeer, MI; Debate Tm; Hon Rl; ROTC; Stg Crw; Crs Cntry; Coll; History.

MCDANIEL, GARY; Berkeley Springs HS; Unger, WV; 23/145 Boy Scts; PAVAS; Sch Mus; Sch Pl; Sct Actv; Stg Crw; Ed Sch Nwsp; Drama Clb; Fr Clb; Pep Clb; West Virginia Univ; Drama.

MCDANIEL, GINNY A; Hedgesville HS; Martinsburg, WV; 11/219 Hon Rl; Sch Mus; 4-H; Fr Clb; Pep Clb; Chrldng; DAR Awd; Pres Awd; Shepherd Coll; Math.

MCDANIEL, JANICE; Columbian HS; Tiffin, OH; Band; Chrh Wkr; Yth Flsp; Pep Clb; 4-H Awd; College.

MCDANIEL, JILL; Manton HS; Manton, MI; 6/50 Cls Rep Soph Cls; VP Sr Cls; Band; Hon Rl; Mod UN; Stu Cncl; Rptr Yrbk; Rptr Sch Nwsp; Pep Clb; Letter Bsktbl; Cadillac Womens Clb Schlrshp For Nursing 79; Mi Interschlstc Press Assoc Awd Of Excllnc 79; Northwestern Michigan Coll; RN.

MCDANIEL, KEVIN C; Davison HS; Davison, MI; Band; Hon Rl; NHS; Cit Awd; Gov Hon Prg Awd; JETS Awd; Natl Merit Ltr; Natl Merit SF; Natl Merit Schl; Pres Awd; College; Draftsman.

MCDANIEL, LENA E; Mount Hope HS; Beckley, WV; 26/87 Hst Frsh Cls; Chrh Wkr; Cmnty Wkr; Girl Scts; Hon Rl; Lbry Ade; Yth Flsp; FBLA; FHA; Pep Clb; Bookkeeping Awd; Typing Awd; Filing Awd;.

MCDANIEL, PAMELA; Princeton Community HS; Francisco, IN; 10/203 Cl Rep Jr Cls; Jr NHS; NHS; Yth Flsp; Pep Clb; Purdue Univ; Vet Tech.

MCDANIEL, RHONDA; Patterson Co Op HS; Dayton, OH; Sec Jr Cls; Band; Cmp Fr Grls; Chrh Wkr; Cmnty Wkr; Drl Tm; OEA; Pep Clb; Glf; Clark Coll; Comp Sci.

MCDANIEL, RHONDA P; Patterson Co Op HS; Dayton, OH; Sec Jr Cls; Band; Chrh Wkr; Cmnty Wkr; OEA; Pep Clb; Glf; Ten; Clark College; Computer Specialist.

MCDANIEL, SCOTT; Northeastern Jr Sr HS; Richmond, IN; Hon Rl; NHS; 4-H; Fr Clb; 4-H Awd; Ball St Univ; Archt.

MCDANIEL, TERESA; W Carrollton HS; W Carrollton, OH; 20/450 Band; Girl Scts; Hon Rl; Jr NHS; Natl Forn Lg; NHS; Yth Flsp; Pep Clb; Trk; Ohio State Univ; Fashion Mdse.

MCDANIELS, JACQUELINE A; Buckhannon Upshur HS; Buckhannon, WV; Girl Scts; Hon Rl; NHS; Sct Actv; Stu Cncl; FBLA; Univ.

MCDANIELS, RODNEY; Buckhannon Upshur HS; Buckhannon, WV; Sec Sr Cls; Hon Rl; Jr NHS; NHS; Sct Actv; Stu Cncl; Key Clb; Bsktbl; IM Sprt; Mgrs; Univ.

MCDANIELS, ROXANNE; Athens HS; East Leroy, MI; Chrh Wkr; Pol Wkr; 4-H; 4-H Awd; Grand Valley Coll; Nursing.

MCDANNEL, TRACY; Canton South HS; Canton, OH; Band; Hon Rl; NHS; Spn Clb; College; Comp Sci.

MCDAVID, BRAD; Centerburg HS; Centerburg, OH; 2/78 Cls Rep Frsh Cls; Cls Rep Soph Cls; Pres Band; Chrs; Hon Rl; NHS; Sch Mus; Sch Pl; Pres Stu Cncl; Rptr Yrbk; Ohio St Univ; Music Educ.

MCDERMITT, ERIC; Memorial HS; St Marys, OH; Band; Orch;.

MCDERMOTT, BRIAN; Crown Point HS; Crown Point, IN; Band; Chrh Wkr; Cls Rep Frsh Cls; Sch Mus; Yth Flsp; Purdue Univ; Chem Engr.

MCDERMOTT, KELLY; Ursuline HS; Youngstown, OH; 60/350 Girl Scts; Hon Rl; Sec Ger Clb; Hnrbl Mntn In Geometry Div 1 Kent St Univ Dist Ohio Test Of 78; Schlstc Achvmnt; Merit Awd Tutoring 77 & 78; Univ; Med.

MCDERMOTT, MIKE; Plymouth HS; Plymouth, IN; Treas Aud/Vis; Chrh Wkr; Stg Crw; Swmmng; Tmr; College; Elec Engr.

MCDERMOTT, PAT; Kirtland HS; Kirtland, OH; 21/100 Hon Rl; JA; Yth Flsp; Key Clb; Trk; Wrstlng; Graduate Schl; Bus Admin.

MCDERMOTT, TAMALETTE; Chaminade Julienne HS; Dayton, OH; 27/270 Chrh Wkr; Hon Rl; Lbry Ade; Fr Clb; Ohio Univ; Med Tech.

MCDEVITT, AMY; Boardman HS; Youngstown, OH; 99/600 Chrh Wkr; Hon Rl; Fr Clb; Univ; Educ.

MCDEVITT, JOHN; Oak Glen HS; Chester, WV; 15/263 Am Leg Boys St; Band; Chrh Wkr; Hon Rl; Pres NHS; Yrbk; Sch Nwsp; Ten; IM Sprt; Bethany College; Vet Medicine.

MCDEVITT, LAURE; Madison Comprehensive HS; Mansfield, OH; Cl Rep Jr Cls; Drl Tm; Stu Cncl; FHA; Spn Clb; Mat Maids; Scr Kpr; Univ; Home Ec.

MCDIFFETT, AMY; Talawanda HS; Oxford, OH; 1/321 Chrh Wkr; Hon Rl; NHS; Scr Kpr; Kiwan Awd; Natl Merit Ltr; 4th Pl Reg Cmptn By Amer Chem Soc 79; Sigma Xi Miami Univ Rec As Outsdng Loc HS Sci Stu 79; Awd In Math; Univ; Math.

MCDIVITT, GREGORY T; Eaton HS; Eaton, OH; 36/175 Hon Rl; Fr Clb; Natl Merit Ltr; Pres Awd; Fairhaven Baptist Coll; Theol.

MCDONALD, ALLEN; Perry HS; Canton, OH; Boy Scts; Chrs; Sch Pl; Boys Clb Am; Bsbl; Ftbl; Mgrs; Armed Services.

MCDONALD, BONNIE; Mc Nicholas HS; Cincinnati, OH; Hon Rl; Univ; Bus.

MCDONALD, BRENDA; Yale HS; Goodells, MI; 3/162 Sec Jr Cls; Band; Chrs; Drm Mjrt; Hon Rl; NHS; Sch Pl; Rptr Yrbk; Rptr Sch Nwsp; 4-H; SCCCC; Med.

MCDONALD, BRUCE; Ida HS; Monroe, MI; Boy Scts; Chrs; Hon Rl; Sct Actv; Drama Clb; 4-H; Ftbl; Coach Actv; Cit Awd; 4-H Awd; Univ Of Mich; Bus.

MCDONALD, CAROLYN; Ctrl Preston Sr HS; Kingwood, WV; Band; Chrh Wkr; Girl Scts; Hon Rl; Sch Mus; Sch Pl; Yth Flsp; Drama Clb; FTA; Twrlr; Pittsburgh Schl; Dance.

MCDONALD, CHERYL; Washington HS; Washington, IN; 2/194 Sal; Band; Hon Rl; NHS; Pol Wkr; Yth Flsp; Beta Clb; Sec 4-H; Ger Clb; Pep Clb; Homemakers Schlrshp 1979; 4 H Speech & Demonstration Area Winner 1978; Purdue Univ; Pharm.

MCDONALD, CYNTHIA; Adelphian Academy; Holly, MI; 7/49 Chrs; Chrh Wkr; Hon Rl; Lbry Ade; Graduated With High Honor Award; Andrews Univ; Elem Ed.

MCDONALD, DAVID N; John Glenn HS; Westland, MI; 1/762 Debate Tm; Hon Rl; NHS; Sch Mus; Sch Pl; Stg Crw; Ger Clb; VP Lat Clb; Natl Merit SF; MSU; Chem Engr.

MCDONALD, DONA; Loy Norrix HS; Kalamazoo, MI; Girl Scts; Hon Rl; JA; Letter Crs Cntry; Letter Trk; JA Awd; Univ; Home Ec.

MCDONALD, DOUGLAS A; Beal City HS; Mt Pleasant, MI; Band; Chrh Wkr; Hon Rl; 4-H; FFA; Sci Clb; Letter Bsbl; 4-H Awd; Central Mich Univ.

MCDONALD, JERRY E; Sacred Heart Academy; Mt Pleasant, MI; Chrh Wkr; Cmnty Wkr; Hon Rl; NHS; Sch Pl; Yrbk; Lat Clb; Bsktbl; Letter Ftbl; IM Sprt; Altrnt Delgt To 43rd Walverian Boys St 79; Michigan St Univ; Vet.

MCDONALD, JILL; Michigan Lutheran Seminary; Bridgeport, MI; Cls Rep Frsh Cls; Cls Rep Soph Cls; Cl Rep Jr Cls; Cls Rep Sr Cls; Band; Chrs; Drm Bgl; Hon Rl; Stu Cncl; Pep Clb; Univ; Med.

MCDONALD, JODIE; Paw Paw HS; Paw Paw, WV; Pres Jr Cls; Band; Hon Rl; NHS; Sch Pl; Stu Cncl; Rptr Yrbk; Rptr Sch Nwsp; FHA; Scr Kpr; West Virginia Univ; Psych.

MCDONALD, JUDI; East HS; Akron, OH; 33/334 Chrs; Hosp Ade; JA; Off Ade; Sch Mus; Sch Pl; Fr Clb; JA Awd; Akron City Hospital; Rn.

MCDONALD, KAREN; Cass Technical HS; Detroit, MI; Cmnty Wkr; Drl Tm; Hon Rl; ROTC; FTA; Am Leg Awd; JETS Awd; Wayne St Univ; Engr.

MCDONALD, KAREN; West Catholic HS; Grand Rapids, MI; 23/280 Cls Rep Frsh Cls; Cl Rep Jr Cls; Hon Rl; NHS; FDA; Lat Clb; Sci Clb; Socr; Mic State Univ; Med.

MCDONALD, KATHLEEN; Marquette HS; Michigan City, IN; 2/66 Cls Rep Frsh Cls; Sec Sr Cls; Chrh Wkr; Hon Rl; NHS; Stu Cncl; Rptr Yrbk; Yrbk; Sch Nwsp; Fr Clb; Purdue Univ; Comp Sci.

MCDONALD, KELLY; Farmington HS; Farmington, MI; Chrh Wkr; Hon Rl; Yth Flsp; Bsktbl; GAA; Scr Kpr; Pres Awd; Univ Of Michigan.

MCDONALD, KIM; Calumet HS; Laurium, MI; Cmp Fr Grls; Hon Rl; NHS; FTA; VP Pep Clb; Michigan St Univ; Law.

MCDONALD, KRIS; Tecumseh HS; Tecumseh, MI; Trs Jr Cls; Girl Scts; Hon Rl; Orch; 4-H; Pep Clb; Letter Bsktbl; Letter Trk; 4-H Awd; Michigan St Univ; Bio Sci.

MCDONALD, LEA; New Castle HS; New Castle, IN; Cl Rep Jr Cls; FCA; Lbry Ade; Yth Flsp; Gym; Swmmng; Trk; Coach Actv; IM Sprt; Pom Pon; Coll; History.

MCDONALD, LISA; Knightstown HS; Knightstown, IN; 22/160 Sec Soph Cls; VP Jr Cls; Hon Rl; Stg Crw; Yrbk; Sch Nwsp; Drama Clb; Spn Clb; IM Sprt; Mat Maids; Thespian Most Dedicated In Non Performance Area; Indiana Univ; Dental Hygiene.

MCDONALD, MARIA; Lake Michigan Cath HS; Benton Hrbr, MI; Hon Rl; Rptr Yrbk; Yrbk; Vocational Schl; Radiology Tech.

MCDONALD, MARK; River Valley HS; Marion, OH; Boy Scts; Bsns Awd; Civics & Bsns Math Awd; Bookkeeping II Awd; Business Schl; Acctg.

MCDONALD, MONICA; Dupont HS; Belle, WV; Chrs; Chrh Wkr; Girl Scts; Off Ade; Sch Mus; Sct Actv; Ohi Valley College; Sec Educ.

MCDONALD, NADINE; Warren HS; Warren, MI; Hon Rl; NHS; PAVAS; Stg Crw; Ed Sch Nwsp; Letter Ten; Mgrs; Dennis Mc Lean Awd For Leadrshp & Serv On Stage Crew 79; 1st All Confrnc Tm Hon For Girls Tennis 79; Univ; Eng.

MCDONALD, PETER; West Lafayette Sr HS; W Lafayette, IN; 31/185 Chrs; Hon Rl; Sch Mus; Ten; Wrstlng; IM Sprt; Duke Univ; Pre Med.

MCDONALD, RENEE; Milford HS; Milford, MI; Stu Cncl; Rptr Yrbk; Rptr Sch Nwsp; Spn Clb; Letter Ten; Letter Trk; PPFtbl; Northwood Inst; Advertising.

MCDONALD, RICK; Pine River HS; Luther, MI; Sec Soph Cls; Boy Scts; Hon Rl; Off Ade; Sct Actv; Rptr Yrbk; Yrbk; Boys Clb Am; Letter Bsbl; Letter Wrstlng;.

MCDONALD JR, ALBERT; Mifflin HS; Columbus, OH; Hon Rl; JETS Awd; Ohi State; Comp Engr.

MCDONNELL, AMY; Bad Axe HS; Bad Axe, MI; Cl Rep Jr Cls; Band; Hon Rl; NHS; Sch Mus; Yrbk; Sch Nwsp; Sci Clb; Michigan State Univ; Jrnlsm.

MCDONNELL, MARY ANN; Erieview Catholic HS; Cleveland, OH; 4/98 Trs Jr Cls; Chrs; Cmnty Wkr; Hon Rl; Pres Stu Cncl; Rptr Yrbk; Rptr Sch Nwsp; Univ; Elem Educ.

MCDONNELL, PHILLIP; Marquette HS; Michigan City, IN; Pres Jr Cls; Chrh Wkr; Hon Rl; Pol Wkr; Sch Mus; Stu Cncl; Letter Socr; Letter Ten; Letter Trk; Lion Awd; Univ Of Notre Dame; Dentistry.

MCDONOUGH, ALAN; St Joseph HS; Richmond Hts, OH; 58/286 Aud/Vis; Chrh Wkr; Hon Rl; Lbry Ade; NHS; Sch Mus; Stg Crw; Ed Sch Nwsp; Rptr Sch Nwsp; IM Sprt; Exploring BSA Subsidary; E Side Chariman; Varsity Bowling Tm; John Carroll Univ; Acctg.

MCDONOUGH, CAROL; Harrison HS; Farmington Hlls, MI; 1/368 Val; Hosp Ade; Treas Jr NHS; NHS; Orch; Red Cr Ade; Ger Clb; Chrldng; Mich State Univ; Bus.

MCDONOUGH, WILLIAM; Beaver Island HS; St James, MI; 2/6 Pres Sr Cls; Sal; Boy Scts; Cmnty Wkr; Hon Rl; Sch Pl; Stu Cncl; Sch Nwsp; Bsbl; Ftbl; Davenport Coll Of Bus; Bus Mgmt.

MCDOUGAL, BARBARA; Nitro HS; St Albans, WV; AFS; Band; Hon Rl; NHS; Stu Cncl; West Virginia Univ; Sci.

MCDOUGAL, FREDA C; Berrien Springs HS; Niles, MI; Hon Rl; JA; Yth Flsp; Trk; Lake Michigan Coll; Drafting.

MCDOUGAL, TERRI; Jackson Milton HS; North Jackson, OH; 2/108 Am Leg Aux Girls St; Chrh Wkr; Hon Rl; Off Ade; Treas Yth Flsp; Rptr Sch Nwsp; VP 4-H; Treas FHA; Pres Ger Clb; Am Leg Awd; Youngstown St Univ; English.

MCDOUGLE, MARK; Carey HS; Carey, OH; 2/100 Am Leg Boys St; Hon Rl; NHS; Sch Pl; Yth Flsp; Ed Sch Nwsp; Rptr Sch Nwsp; Spn Clb; Crs Cntry; Trk; Ohio St Univ; Engr.

MCDOUGLE, SHAWN M; Clay HS; Oregon, OH; Chrs; Hon Rl; Hosp Ade; Jr NHS; Sch Mus; Stg Crw; 4-H; FTA; Pep Clb; College; Med Sec.

MCDOWELL, BARBARA; Boyne City HS; Boyne City, MI; Chrh Wkr; Girl Scts; Hosp Ade; Orch; Sch Mus; Stg Crw; IM Sprt; Valparaiso Univ.

MCDOWELL, CLIFFORD; Buena Vista HS; Saginaw, MI; Hon Rl; JA; Sch Pl; Drama Clb; 4-H; Bsktbl; Ftbl; Trk; IM Sprt; JA Awd; Delta Cc; Bus Admin.

MCDOWELL, DAVID; Whitehall Yearling HS; Whitehall, OH; Hon Rl; Sch Pl; Rptr Sch Nwsp; Ten; College.

MCDOWELL, DORTHEA; Southwestern HS; Detroit, MI; Chrs; Cmnty Wkr; Hon Rl; Off Ade; Sch Mus; Bsbl; Socr; Cit Awd;.

MCDOWELL, JAMES K; Brookhaven HS; Columbus, OH; 1/350 Hon Rl; VP NHS; Stu Cncl; Spn Clb; Socr; Capt Ten; Ohio St Univ; Engr.

MCDOWELL, KENNETH N; Chillicothe HS; Chillicothe, OH; Am Leg Boys St; Band; Boy Scts; Chrh Wkr; Orch; Sct Actv; Spn Clb; Wrstlng; Ohi State; Pilot.

MCDOWELL, KIM; Muncie Central HS; Muncie, IN; 40/340 Chrh Wkr; Girl Scts; Hon Rl; Off Ade; Yth Flsp; Rptr Sch Nwsp; Twrlr; 4-H Awd; Ball St Univ; Busns.

MCDUFFIE, DARRYL; Collinwood HS; Cleveland, OH; Cls Rep Frsh Cls; Cls Rep Soph Cls; Cl Rep Jr Cls; Hon Rl; Fr Clb; Lat Clb; Cit Awd; Case Western Reserve Univ.

MCELHANEY, EVELYN; Ridgewood HS; Coshocton, OH; 5/150 Am Leg Aux Girls St; Chrs; Chrh Wkr; Hon Rl; NHS; Off Ade; Sch Pl; Stu Cncl; Yth Flsp; Ohi State Univ; Comp Sci.

MCELHENY, ROBERT; Plymouth HS; Plymouth, IN; Coach Actv; IM Sprt; Bus Sch; Bus.

MCELHONE, WILLIAM K; Benedictine HS; Detroit, MI; 12/121 Hon Rl; NHS; Rptr Yrbk; Pres Sci Clb; Crs Cntry; Trk;.

MCELRAVY, CINDY; Brookfield HS; Brookfield, OH; Sec Sr Cls; Hon Rl; Off Ade; Quill & Scroll; Sprt Ed Yrbk; Pres Spn Clb; Kent State Univ; Bus Admin.

MCELROY, AMBER; Univ HS; Westover, WV; 53/142 Band; Chrs; Chrh Wkr; Drm Mjrt; Yth Flsp; Ger Clb; Modern Bus Awd; West Virginia Univ; Eng.

MCELROY, DEBBIE; Elgin HS; Green Camp, OH; 10/185 VP Jr Cls; Band; Chrh Wkr; Girl Scts; Hon Rl; Jr NHS; NHS; Yth Flsp; 4-H; FTA; Letter Chrldng; Band Dir Awd 76; 2nd Yr Awd For Vlybl 79; 3rd Yr Awd For Cheerldng 79; Lima Tech Univ; Dent Hygnst.

MCELROY, STEPHEN G; Harbor HS; Ashtabula, OH; 25/172 VP Jr Cls; VP Sr Cls; JA; NHS; Stu Cncl; Bsbl; Glf; Bowling Green Univ; Bus Admin.

MCELROY, WEONTAH; Fairview HS; Dayton, OH; Cmp Fr Grls; Chrh Wkr; Hon Rl; Lbry Ade; Sch Nwsp; Bsktbl; Bus Schl; Sec.

MCELROY JR, ROBERT; Leslie HS; Onondasa, MI; 5/111 Hon Rl; NHS; Letter Ten; Univ Of Michigan; Comp Sci.

MCELWAIN, RAMONA; New Buffalo HS; New Buffalo, MI; 5/68 Cls Rep Sr Cls; Chrh Wkr; Cmnty Wkr; Hon Rl; NHS; Sch Pl; Stg Crw; Stu Cncl; Drama Clb; Spn Clb; Olivet Nazarene Coll; Elem Ed.

MCELWAIN, RITA; Madonna HS; Weirton, WV; 25/102 Hon Rl; Treas NHS; Pep Clb; Wv Univ; Pharmacy.

MCELWAIN, VINCE E; North Marion HS; Worthington, WV; 10/110 Hon Rl; Yth Flsp; Mth Clb; Letter Ftbl; Letter Trk; Univ; Forestry.

MCELWEE, MICHELE; Marquette HS; Michigan City, IN; 21/73 Hon Rl; Quill & Scroll; Stg Crw; Sprt Ed Yrbk; Drama Clb; Fr Clb; Ball St Univ; Jrnlsm.

MCENDREE, JILL; Buckeye North HS; , ; Pres Frsh Cls; Trs Soph Cls; Trs Jr Cls; Band; Hon Rl; NHS; Sch Pl; Drama Clb; Fr Clb; Pep Clb; Jeff Tech Busns Schl; Sec.

MCENDREE, LORI; Buckeye North HS; Brilliant, OH; 4/119 Trs Frsh Cls; Sec Jr Cls; Chrs; Chrh Wkr; Hon Rl; Jr NHS; NHS; Off Ade; Stu Cncl; Pep Clb; College.

MCEUEN, SCOTT; Hobart Sr HS; Hobart, IN; 13/395 Am Leg Boys St; Treas FCA; Hon Rl; Jr NHS; NHS; Pres Stu Cncl; VP Ger Clb; Mth Clb; Sci Clb; Letter Crs Cntry; Outstndng 9th Grd Boy 1976; His Awd D F P 1978; Wabash Univ.

MCEVERS, BECKY; Rochester HS; Rochester, MI; Band; Hon Rl; NHS; Yth Flsp; Univ.

MCEVOY, DANIELLE; Franklin HS; Livonia, MI; Chrs; Girl Scts; Hon Rl; Orch; Sch Mus; Sch Pl; Sct Actv; Stg Crw; Drama Clb; Univ.

MCEVOY, LAURA; St Joseph Academy; Lakewood, OH; Chrh Wkr; Hon Rl; NHS; Orch; Sch Mus; Rptr Yrbk; Drama Clb; FSA; Mth Clb; NCTE; Magna Cum Laude Latin 78; Chem Awd 79; Natl Math Exam Awd 79; Univ; Pre Med.

MCEWEN, SUSAN; David Anderson HS; Lisbon, OH; 7/115 FCA; Hon Rl; Crs Cntry; Trk; Coll; Bio.

MCFADDEN, CATHY; New Albany HS; Westerville, OH; 2/110 Sec Jr Cls; Girl Scts; Hon Rl; 4-H; Pep Clb; Sci Clb; College; Fashion.

MCFADDEN, DAWN; Lawrence HS; Lawrence, MI; 4/57 Pres Soph Cls; Cls Rep Soph Cls; Pres Jr Cls; NHS; Off Ade; Sch Pl; Stu Cncl; Pep Clb; Capt Chrldng; Dnfth Awd; Western Michigan Univ; Pre Law.

MCFADDIN, DONALD; Rockville HS; Rockville, IN; 23/98 Aud/Vis; Boy Scts; Lbry Ade; Ftbl; Letter Mgrs; Mas Awd; Purdue; Aero Engr.

MCFADDIN, MELANIE; Culver Girls Academy; Bellaire, TX; 47/191 Hon Rl; Lbry Ade; Sch Pl; Drama Clb; IM Sprt; Univ.

MCFARLAND, BRUCE E; Northwest Sr HS; Cincinnati, OH; 13/438 Band; Hon Rl; Jr NHS; Mth Clb; Letter Glf; Trk; Natl Merit SF; Univ; Math.

MCFARLAND, CHARLA; New Richmond HS; New Richmond, OH; 23/194 Sec Band; Chrh Wkr; Hon Rl; NHS; Orch; FSA; 1st Pl 2nd Pl Clermont Cnty Soil & Water Consrvtn Art Conts T79; 1 Ratng In Cls Music In Oh Music Educ 79; Cedarville Coll; Elem Art Tchr.

MCFARLAND, DANIEL D; Martins Ferry HS; Martins Ferry, OH; Cls Rep Frsh Cls; VP Jr Cls; Hon Rl; Stu Cncl; Fr Clb; Letter Bsbl; Letter Ftbl; Cit Awd; Univ; Engr.

MCFARLAND, DAVID W; Bucyrus HS; Bucyrus, OH; 1/200 Cls Rep Frsh Cls; Hon Rl; JA; NHS; Sch Mus; Sch Pl; Natl Merit SF; Honor Med St Of Oh Schlshp In Bio & Chem; Univ; Physics.

MCFARLAND, JANNA; Bryan HS; Bryan, OH; Band; Chrs; Hon Rl; JA; Rptr Yrbk; GAA; JA Awd; Univ Of Toledo; Respiratory Ther.

MCFARLAND, MICHAEL B; Bedford Sr HS; Lambertville, MI; 61/550 Boy Scts; FCA; JA; Lbry Ade; NHS; Pol Wkr; Crs Cntry; Tmr; JA Awd; Natl Merit SF; Reed Coll; Philosophy.

MCFARLAND, SUSAN M; Northwest Sr HS; Cincinnati, OH; 1/425 Band; Hon Rl; Jr NHS; NHS; Yrbk; Cit Awd; JETS Awd; Natl Merit Ltr; College.

MCFARLAND, TERRI; West Ottawa HS; Holland, MI; 23/322 Trs Jr Cls; Cls Rep Sr Cls; Band; FCA; Hon Rl; Treas NHS; Bsktbl; Central Mich Univ; Secondary Educ.

MCFARLAND, YOLANDA J; East HS; Columbus, OH; Treas Chrh Wkr; Hon Rl; Treas Jr NHS; VP Stu Cncl; Sec FHA; Pres Spn Clb; Columbus Bus Univ.

MCFARLANE, JOY; Augus Sims HS; Augres, MI; 15/48 Cls Rep Soph Cls; Trs Jr Cls; Trs Sr Cls; Band; Girl Scts; Hon Rl; Sch Mus; Yrbk; 4-H; GAA; Ferris State; Med.

MCFARLANE, ROXANNE; Henry Ford II HS; Sterling Hts, MI; 58/469 Hosp Ade; Pep Clb; Bsbl; PPFtbl; Macomb Cnty Cmnty Coll; Dent Hygnst.

MCFARLIN, DEBRA; Elkhart Mem HS; Elkhart, IN; Chrs; Pres JA; Yth Flsp; Y-Teens; JA Awd; Purdue Univ; Sci.

MCFARLING, BRUCE R; Watkins Mem HS; Pataskala, OH; Boy Scts; Orch; 4-H; Miami Univ.

MCFEELEY, ELIZABETH; Meadowdale HS; Dayton, OH; 31/274 Hon Rl; NHS; Off Ade; OEA; Pep Clb; Chrldng; Sinclair Cmnty Coll; Exec Sec.

MCGAFFICK, BRENDA; Otsego HS; Kalamazoo, MI; Cls Rep Soph Cls; Val; Band; Chrh Wkr; Hon Rl; Hosp Ade; NHS; Off Ade; Sch Nwsp; 4-H; Bronson Meth Hsp Schl Of Nrsg; Nrsg.

MCGANN, BETH; Mishawaka Shs; Mishawaka, IN; 4/439 Am Leg Aux Girls St; Cmp Fr Grls; Chrs; Hon Rl; Mdrgl; NHS; Sch Mus; Sch Pl; Stg Crw; Stu Cncl; Indiana Univ; Theatre.

MCGANNON, JUDITH; Clermont Northeastern HS; Williamsburg, OH; VP Frsh Cls; Cls Rep Frsh Cls; Cls Rep Soph Cls; Drl Tm; Hon Rl; Spn Clb; Letter Trk; Pres Awd; Adrian; Business.

MCGARVEY, S; Mason HS; Mason, MI; Band; Chrs; Chrh Wkr; Lbry Ade; Mdrgl; Sch Mus; Sch Pl; Yth Flsp; College.

MCGAUGHEY, ANNE; North Putnam Jr Sr HS; Bainbridge, IN; 7/170 NHS; 4-H; Lat Clb; Mth Clb; Scr Kpr; Tmr; Purdue Univ; Vet.

MCGAUGHEY, RITA; North Putnam HS; Russellville, IN; 22/175 Am Leg Aux Girls St; Band; Cmnty Wkr; FCA; NHS; Yth Flsp; Yrbk; Sch Nwsp; 4-H; College; Educ.

MCGEE, BRIAN; Austintown Fitch HS; Austintown, OH; Boy Scts; Chrh Wkr; Hon Rl; Sct Actv; Yth Flsp; Crs Cntry; Trk; Military Acad; Acctg.

MCGEE, DIANE E; South Charleston HS; So Charleston, WV; Cls Rep Frsh Cls; Hon Rl; Jr NHS; Lbry Ade; NHS; Stu Cncl; FBLA; Pep Clb; Spn Clb; Trk; Marshall Univ.

MCGEE, FRED B; Buckeye North HS; Smithfield, OH; 26/100 Am Leg Boys St; Hon Rl; Pep Clb; Letter Ftbl; Letter Trk; Coach Actv; IM Sprt; Natl Merit Ltr; College; Elec Engr.

MCGEE, L; Barnesville HS; Barnesville, OH; Cl Rep Jr Cls; Band; Chrs; Drl Tm; Hon Rl; Orch; Sch Mus; Stg Crw; Stu Cncl; Drama Clb; Nursing.

MCGEE, LISA; Gaylord Community HS; Gaylord, MI; 9/200 Sec Frsh Cls; Hon Rl; Jr NHS; Lbry Ade; NHS; Off Ade; Red Cr Ade; Stu Cncl; Muskegon Business College; Med Sec.

MCGEE, MARLANA; Brookhaven HS; Columbus, OH; Sch Pl; Stg Crw; Rptr Yrbk; Drama Clb; Eng Clb; Spn Clb; Trk; Coach Actv; Scr Kpr; Cit Awd; Ohio St Univ; Psych.

MCGEE, SHAUN; William Mason HS; Mason, OH; 26/195 AFS; Band; Boy Scts; Cmnty Wkr; Drm Bgl; Hon Rl; Jr NHS; NHS; Orch; PAVAS; Air Force Academy; Aviation.

MCGEE, SPANISH W; Wintersville HS; Bloomingdale, OH; 5/289 Cls Rep Frsh Cls; Cls Rep Soph Cls; Cl Rep Jr Cls; Hon Rl; NHS; Sch Pl; Yrbk; Sch Nwsp; FSA; Mth Clb; Yale Univ; Engr.

MCGEE JR, FRED; Buckeye North HS; Smithfield, OH; Am Leg Boys St; FCA; Hon Rl; NHS; Sct Actv; Letter Ftbl; Letter Trk; Coach Actv; John Carroll Univ; Electrical Engr.

MCGEORGE, SUSAN; Traverse City Sr HS; Traverse City, MI; Aud/Vis; Chrh Wkr; Hon Rl; Bsktbl; Letter Trk; Bronze Gold Keys; Mi Schlrshp Awd; Spring Arbor Coll; Tchr Educ.

MCGERVEY, MARGARET; Magnificat HS; Avon, OH; Chrh Wkr; Cmnty Wkr; Mod UN; Pol Wkr; Sch Mus; Sch Pl; Drama Clb; Fr Clb; Univ; Phys Ther.

MCGHAN, MARK; Muskegon HS; Muskegon, MI; Band; Chrs; Hon Rl; Lbry Ade; Sch Mus; Sch Pl; Stg Crw; Yrbk; Drama Clb; Pep Clb; Mich State; Physical Therapist.

MCGHEE, GARY; Eaton Rapids HS; Dimondale, MI; 2/231 Band; Hon Rl; Jr NHS; NHS; Orch; Sch Mus; Pres Stu Cncl; Mich State Univ; Med Dr.

MCGHEHEY, ELIZABETH; Westfield Washington HS; Westfield, IN; Cmp Fr Grls; Chrs; Hon Rl; Sch Mus; Sch Pl; Yth Flsp; FHA; Pep Clb; Purdue Univ; Veterinarian.

MCGILL, CRAIG; Yellow Springs HS; Yellow Sprg, OH; Band; Boy Scts; Chrh Wkr; Yth Flsp; IM Sprt; Morehouse Coll.

MCGILL, JOHN; Carroll HS; Flora, IN; Am Leg Boys St; Chrh Wkr; FCA; Hon Rl; NHS; Fr Clb; Bsbl; Bsktbl; Am Leg Awd; Cit Awd; Purdue Univ; Engr.

MCGILL, MARY C; Doddridge County HS; West Union, WV; Trs Frsh Cls; Band; Hon Rl; Stu Cncl; FBLA; FHA; Pep Clb; Parkersburg Cmnty Coll; Nursing.

MCGINNIS, MARY T; Liberty HS; Clarksburg, WV; 1/228 VP Jr Cls; Cls Rep Sr Cls; Am Leg Aux Girls St; Band; Hon Rl; Jr NHS; NHS; Sch Mus; Sch Pl; Stg Crw; West Virginia Univ; Med.

MCGINNIS, SALLY; Servite HS; Detroit, MI; Hon Rl; NHS; Letter Bsktbl; Natl Merit Schl; Wayne State College.

MCGINNIS, TAMARA; W Bloomfield HS; Keego Harbor, MI; Band; Girl Scts; Hon Rl; NHS; Sch Mus; Sct Actv; VICA; Swmmng; Trk; Tmr; Oakland Univ; Health Sci.

MCGINNIS, TERRY M; Tippecanoe HS; Tipp City, OH; Cl Rep Jr Cls; Am Leg Boys St; Hon Rl; NHS; Stu Cncl; Letter Bsbl; Bsktbl; Letter Ftbl; IM Sprt; Top Schlr Awd; Lamp Of Learning Awd; Coll.

MCGINTY, ANTHONY; Valley Forge HS; Parma Hgts, OH; 210/777 Chrs; Cmnty Wkr; Hon Rl; Lit Mag; Rptr Yrbk; Spn Clb; Trk; IM Sprt; Mgrs; Scr Kpr; Ohio St Univ; Psych.

MCGINTY, CORLYN; Malabar HS; Mansfield, OH; 7/280 Cls Rep Soph Cls; Cl Rep Jr Cls; Band; Chrh Wkr; Hon Rl; Jr NHS; Orch; Trk; Ohio State Univ; Dent Hygiene.

MCGINTY, SHERRI L; Lutheran East HS; Detroit, MI; Cls Rep Frsh Cls; Girl Scts; Hon Rl; Lbry Ade; NHS; Off Ade; Rptr Yrbk; Rptr Sch Nwsp; Ger Clb; Cit Awd; College; Comp Sci.

MCGIVENS, DENISE; Mumford HS; Detroit, MI; Hon Rl; NHS; Off Ade; VP Stu Cncl; Pep Clb; Rdo Clb; Spn Clb; Wayne State Univ; Phys Ther.

MCGIVERN, CAROLE; Washington Irving HS; Clarksburg, WV; Hon Rl; Yth Flsp; Y-Teens; Fr Clb; Pep Clb; Sci Clb; College; Accounting.

MCGLINSEY, VICKI; Marcellus Cmnty HS; Marcellus, MI; Chrs; Hon Rl; NHS; Spn Clb; Univ; Sec.

MCGLONE, LISA; Sheridan HS; Thornville, OH; Band; Hon Rl; NHS; Off Ade; Rptr Sch Nwsp; Drama Clb; 4-H; FTA; Lat Clb; Ohio State Univ; Bus Admin.

MCGLOTHEN, YVETTE; Ursuline HS; Youngstown, OH; 32/369 Cls Rep Frsh Cls; Cls Rep Soph Cls; Cl Rep Jr Cls; Chrh Wkr; Cmnty Wkr; Drl Tm; Hon Rl; Hosp Ade; Off Ade; Orch; Attend N E Coll Of Medicine For Minority Stu Seminars; Youth Coordinator Christian Study Center; Youngstown St Univ; Chemistry.

MCGLOTHLIN, TERAH; Scottsburg Sr HS; Scottsburg, IN; 1/232 Chrh Wkr; Hon Rl; NHS; Fr Clb; Pep Clb; Kiwan Awd; Hanover Coll; Math.

MCGLYNCHEY, LISA; Waterford Township HS; Union Lake, MI; 5/411 Cls Rep Frsh Cls; Cls Rep Sr Cls; Chrh Wkr; Girl Scts; Hon Rl; Jr NHS; NHS; Red Cr Ade; Stu Cncl; Sprt Ed Sch Nwsp; St Marys Coll.

MCGONAGLE, KATHERINE; Kenston HS; Chagrinfl, OH; Band; Chrs; Girl Scts; Hon Rl; Orch; Sch Mus; Spn Clb; PPFtbl; Outstndng Schlstc Ach Awd Middle East; Miami Univ.

MCGONAGLE, MOLLY ANN; W V Fisher Catholic HS; Lancaster, OH; Cls Rep Frsh Cls; Trs Soph Cls; Trs Jr Cls; VP Sr Cls; Am Leg Aux Girls St; Cmnty Wkr; Hon Rl; NHS; VP Stu Cncl; Fr Clb; Xavier.

MCGOUGH, CERVANTE; Aquinas HS; Westland, MI; Band; Drm Mjrt; Hon Rl; Yth Flsp; Spn Clb; USC; Journalism.

MCGOVERN, BRIAN; Canton South HS; Canton, OH; Cls Rep Frsh Cls; Boy Scts; Chrh Wkr; Hon Rl; JA; Lbry Ade; Yrbk; Bsktbl; Ftbl; Letter Trk; Art Inst; Interior Dsgn.

MCGOVERN, LINDA; Pike HS; Indpls, IN; 47/286 Band; Hon Rl; Jr NHS; NHS; Letter Swmmng; Univ.

MCGOVERN, MICHAEL; St Francis De Sales HS; Columbus, OH; Hon Rl; Sch Nwsp; Ftbl; Ohio Dominican College; Statistics.

MCGOVERN, MICHELLE; Dublin HS; Dublin, OH; 17/153 Trs Jr Cls; Trs Sr Cls; Band; Chrs; Hon Rl; NHS; Lat Clb; Letter Chrldng; Univ; Law.

MCGOVNEY, CAROL; Ohio Valley Vocational HS; Stout, OH; VP Soph Cls; Pres Jr Cls; Pres Sr Cls; Chrs; Drl Tm; NHS; Stu Cncl; 4-H; FFA; FHA;.

MCGOWAN, D; New Philadelphia HS; New Phila, OH; Chrh Wkr; Hon Rl; JA; Lbry Ade; Sch Pl; FNA; Pep Clb; Spn Clb; Trk; IM Sprt; Massillon City Hosp Schl; Nursing.

MCGOWAN, D SCOTT; Columbian HS; Tiffin, OH; 28/378 Cls Rep Frsh Cls; Cls Rep Soph Cls; Hon Rl; JA; Stu Cncl; Lat Clb; Ten; IM Sprt; Scr Kpr; Univ; Bus Admin.

MCGOWAN, KATHLEEN; Salem Sr HS; Salem, OH; Cmp Fr Grls; Yth Flsp; Y-Teens; Pres FHA; Pep Clb; Spn Clb; Scr Kpr; Coll; Home Ec.

MCGOWAN, MARVIN; Benedictine HS; Cleveland, OH; 24/90 VP Band; Hon Rl; NHS; Orch; Sch Mus; Drama Clb; IM Sprt; Case Western Reserve Univ; Chem Engr.

MCGOWAN, PATRICK J; East Liverpool HS; E Liverpool, OH; Cls Rep Soph Cls; Cl Rep Jr Cls; Sprt Ed Sch Nwsp; Bsbl; Letter Bsktbl; University; Journalism.

MCGOWAN, RHONDA; Warrensville Heights HS; Warrensville, OH; Off Ade; Pep Clb; Univ Of Akron; Bus Admin.

MCGOWAN, SUE; Champion HS; Warren, OH; Chrs; Mdrgl; NHS; Off Ade; Sch Mus; Sch Pl; VP Drama Clb; Spn Clb; Kent St Univ; Med Tech.

MCGRAE, LESLIE; Carman HS; Flint, MI; Chrs; NHS; Letter Swmmng; Univ Of Michigan; Pre Med.

MCGRANE, MARY; Bishop Gallagher HS; Detroit, MI; 135/333 Cls Rep Soph Cls; Cl Rep Jr Cls; Chrs; Hon Rl; Sch Mus; Sch Pl; Am Leg Awd; Cit Awd; Wayne St Univ; Legal Sec.

MCGRATH, CHRIS; Northwest HS; Canal Fulton, OH; Aud/Vis; Band; Drm Bgl; Hon Rl; Lbry Ade; Pol Wkr; Stg Crw; Yth Flsp; Y-Teens; Yrbk; Canton College; Med Lab Assistant.

MCGRATH, RHONDA; Meadowbrook HS; Zanesville, OH; Sch Pl; Rptr Sch Nwsp; Sch Nwsp; Fr Clb; FHA; Pep Clb; Chrldng; PPFtbl; Univ; Child Care.

MCGRATH, ROBERT; Romulus HS; Romulus, MI; Chrh Wkr; FCA; Off Ade; Sch Pl; Sct Actv; Stg Crw; Yth Flsp; Rptr Sch Nwsp; Ftbl; Bill And Howell; Comupter Elec.

MCGRAW, CARMELA; Eastern HS; Beaver, OH; 28/66 Cls Rep Frsh Cls; Cls Rep Soph Cls; Sec Jr Cls; Sec Sr Cls; Band; Chrs; Chrh Wkr; Hon Rl; Sch Mus; Sch Pl; Shawnee St Comnty Coll; Nurse.

MCGRAW, DEBORAH; Athens HS; Athens, WV; 19/68 Chrs; Girl Scts; Off Ade; Yrbk; Keyettes; Pep Clb; Chrldng; Mgrs; Dnfth Awd; Kiwan Awd; Concord Coll; Phys Ed.

MCGRAW, JAMES; Midland Trail HS; Ansted, WV; Hon Rl; VICA; Bsktbl; Military Serv; Civil Engr.

MCGRAW, SANDRA; Trinity HS; Garfield Hts, OH; Cmp Fr Grls; Chrs; Drm Mjrt; Hosp Ade; JA;.

MCGRAW, TAMMY; Portsmouth East HS; Portsmouth, OH; 7/81 Sec Sr Cls; Chrs; Chrh Wkr; Cmnty Wkr; Hon Rl; NHS; Off Ade; Rptr Yrbk; Ed Sch Nwsp; Lat Clb; Shawnee St Cmnty Coll; Sec.

MCGREEVY, JEANETTE; Versailles HS; Versailles, OH; 20/133 Band; Chrs; Girl Scts; Sch Mus; Stg Crw; Drama Clb; Fr Clb; Miami Univ; Home Ec.

MCGREGOR, DANE S; Midland HS; Midland, MI; Sec Chrh Wkr; Hon Rl; Sch Mus; Sch Pl; Stg Crw; Yth Flsp; Yrbk; Sch Nwsp; Drama Clb; 4-H; Univ.

MCGREGOR, TROY; Grand Ledge HS; Lansing, MI; 200/416 Boy Scts; IM Sprt; Scr Kpr; Lansing Cmnty Coll; Bus Mgmt.

MCGREW, CHERI M; Rockville HS; Rockville, IN; Band; Chrs; Cmnty Wkr; Hon Rl; Sch Nwsp; 4-H; Spn Clb; Bsktbl; Letter Trk; Univ; Cmnctns.

MCGREW, RICHARD; East Liverpool HS; E Liverpool, OH; Chrs; Sch Mus; Ftbl; Coach Actv; Univ.

MCGREW, ROBERT; High School; Marietta, OH; 21/405 Hon Rl; NHS; Yth Flsp; Letter Trk; Letter Wrstlng; Univ; Vet.

MCGREW, STEVE; Moeller HS; W Chester, OH; 64/262 Boy Scts; Hon Rl; Pres Yth Flsp; Bsbl; Bsktbl; Ftbl; Coach Actv; Full Ftbl Schlrshp 79; GCL All Star Tm Ftbl 79; E W All Star Tm Ftbl 79; North Carolina Univ; Pre Med.

MCGREW, TAMRA; Dunbar HS; Charleston, WV; 9/165 VP Jr Cls; Chrh Wkr; Hon Rl; NHS; Off Ade; Stu Cncl; Mth Clb; Pep Clb; Mgrs; Dnfth Awd; Univ Of Charleston; Radiologic Tech.

MCGRIFF, MELISSA; Newton HS; Laura, OH; 3/59 Hon Rl; Pres NHS; Off Ade; Pol Wkr; Stu Cncl; Rptr Yrbk; Drama Clb; OEA; Scr Kpr; Am Leg Awd; Univ Od Cincinnati; Psych.

MCGUGIN, DAN J; Lucas HS; Lucas, OH; 6/67 Pres Soph Cls; Am Leg Boys St; NHS; Yrbk; 4-H; FHA; Bsbl; Bsktbl; Trk; 4-H Awd; Bowling Green; Architecture.

MCGUIGGAN, ANNE; East Noble HS; Kendallville, IN; Chrh Wkr; Hon Rl; Fr Clb; Ten; Cit Awd; Voc Schl; Bus Sec.

MCGUINNESS, COLLEEN; Park Hills HS; Fairborn, OH; 24/350 Drl Tm; Hon Rl; NHS; ROTC; Fr Clb; Wright St Univ; Med Tech.

MCGUINNESS, EILEEN; Port Clinton HS; Pt Clinton, OH; Cls Rep Sr Cls; Drm Bgl; Hon Rl; Hosp Ade; Sch Pl; Stg Crw; Rptr Yrbk; Yrbk; Drama Clb; Chrldng; Bowling Green State; Special Ed.

MCGUINNESS, MARY; Our Lady Of Mercy HS; Detroit, MI; 1/350 Cls Rep Frsh Cls; Cls Rep Soph Cls; Cmnty Wkr; Hon Rl; NHS; Stg Crw; Fr Clb; Crs Cntry; Trk; Univ; Life Sci.

MCGUIRE, BARBARA; Catholic Central HS; Grand Rapids, MI; Chrs; Cmnty Wkr; Girl Scts; Hon Rl; Off Ade; Grand Rapids Acad; Data Processing.

MCGUIRE, KAREN; Wadsworth Sr HS; Wadsworth, OH; 5/367 Band; Hon Rl; NHS; Orch; Yth Flsp; 4-H; Fr Clb; Mth Clb; 4-H Awd; JC Awd; Akron Univ; Chem Engr.

MCGUIRE, MELANIE; Southeastern HS; Chillicothe, OH; Sal; Hon Rl; Jr NHS; NHS; Yrbk; FTA; Chrldng; DAR Awd;.

MCGUIRE, MICHELE; Lincoln HS; Milton, IN; 18/138 Capt Band; Chrs; Chrh Wkr; Hon Rl; Mdrgl; Orch; Rptr Yrbk; Letter Ten; Earlham Univ; Eng.

MCGUIRE, STEPHEN; Jefferson HS; Lafayette, IN; Cls Rep Soph Cls; Cl Rep Jr Cls; Cls Rep Sr Cls; Am Leg Boys St; Band; Boy Scts; Hon Rl; Natl Forn Lg; NHS; Stu Cncl; Univ; Pre Med.

MCGURK, JANE; Covington HS; Covington, IN; 4/100 Chrs; Girl Scts; Hon Rl; Hosp Ade; Off Ade; Sch Pl; Stu Cncl; Pep Clb; Chrldng; GAA; Purdue Univ.

MCHAFFIE, SCOTT E; Elmwood HS; Bloomdale, OH; CAP; Hon Rl; Sct Actv; Yth Flsp; Sch Nwsp; OEA; Bsbl; Ftbl; Wrstlng; IM Sprt; USC; Bus.

MCHALE, ROSEMARY; Oak Park HS; Oak Park, MI; 24/342 Cls Rep Frsh Cls; Cls Rep Soph Cls; Cl Rep Jr Cls; Cls Rep Sr Cls; VP Stu Cncl; Wayne St Univ; Med.

MCHARGUE, LARRY; Monroe HS; Monroe, MI; Chrh Wkr; Hon Rl; NHS; Stu Cncl; Yth Flsp; Sprt Ed Sch Nwsp; Rptr Sch Nwsp; Bsbl; Bsktbl; Letter Ten; Marion Coll.

MCHENRY, DANIEL S; Tyler Co HS; Middlebourne, WV; Am Leg Boys St; NHS; Ed Sch Nwsp; Spn Clb; Letter Bsktbl; Letter Ftbl; Letter Trk; Coach Actv; All Amer HS Athlete Basketball; Soc Of Dist Amer HS Stu; West Virginia Univ; Law.

MCHENRY, DARLA; Tyler County HS; Middlebourne, WV; Am Leg Aux Girls St; Hon Rl; JA; Stu Cncl; Yth Flsp; Treas FTA; Pep Clb; Spn Clb; West Liberty Coll; Acctg.

MCHENRY, DARLA; Tyler Cnty HS; Middlebourne, WV; 2/96 Am Leg Aux Girls St; Hon Rl; JA; NHS; Stu Cncl; Yth Flsp; Treas FTA; Pep Clb; Spn Clb; West Liberty Univ.

MCHENRY, DENZIL; University HS; Morgantown, WV; Cls Rep Frsh Cls; Cls Rep Soph Cls; Cl Rep Jr Cls; Cls Rep Sr Cls; Aud/Vis; Band; Orch; Sch Mus; Sch Pl; Univ; Elec.

MCHENRY, JAMES; Timken HS; Canton, OH; Chrh Wkr; Hon Rl; DAR Awd; College; Sci.

MCHUGH, KATHLEEN; St Augustine Acad; Cleveland, OH; Cls Rep Soph Cls; Sec Jr Cls; VP Sr Cls; Chrs; Hon Rl; Stu Cncl; Yth Flsp; College; Educ.

MCHUGH, KELLY; Maysville Sr HS; Zanesville, OH; Chrs; Hon Rl; Rptr Sch Nwsp; Sch Nwsp; 4-H; Pep Clb; Mgrs; Scr Kpr; 4-H Awd; Oh St Horse Judging Tm 78; Muskingum Cnty Horsebowl Tm Tri Cnty Rep 76 77; Oh Clb Congress 79; Univ; Equestrian Studies.

MCHUTCHON, PAMELA; Revere HS; Akron, OH; AFS; Letter Band; Hon Rl; Stu Cncl; Yth Flsp; Letter Trk; Lancaster Univ; Human Geog.

MCILDUFF, EDWARD; Columbiana HS; Columbiana, OH; Boy Scts; Hon Rl; Sct Actv; Spn Clb; Bsbl; Bsktbl; God Cntry Awd; JA Awd; Rotary Theodore Detwiler Memrl Awrd For Otstndng Achvmnt In Scouting 78; Univ; Engr.

MCILRATH, MITCHELL; Western HS; Russiaville, IN; Aud/Vis; Lbry Ade; Stg Crw;.

MCINERNEY, LORI; Mt Clemens HS; Mt Clemens, MI; Hon Rl; Letter Ten; Mgrs; Michigan St Univ; Comp.

MCINERNEY, PATRICIA; Bishop Noll Inst; Highland, IN; 31/321 Hon Rl; PAVAS; Stg Crw; Drama Clb; Pep Clb; Sci Clb; Chrldng; Coach Actv; GAA; Mat Maids; Univ; Bus.

MCINERNEY, THOMAS; Notre Dame HS; Mt Clemens, MI; 80/205 Cls Rep Frsh Cls; Hon Rl; Trk; Mich State Univ; Engr Comp.

MCINERNY, DAVE; St Josephs HS; S Bend, IN; Hon Rl; Bsktbl; Trk; IM Sprt; Univ Of Notre Dame; Arts.

MCINNES, SUSAN; Washington HS; Massillon, OH; Cls Rep Soph Cls; Cl Rep Jr Cls; Cls Rep Sr Cls; Chrs; Chrh Wkr; Hon Rl; Lbry Ade; Lit Mag; Mdrgl; Akron Univ; Elem Teach.

MCINTIRE, CHERYL; Hillsdale HS; Jeromesville, OH; 10/103 Band; Chrs; Hon Rl; NHS; Rptr Yrbk; 4-H; 4-H Awd; Ohio 4 H Fash Board; Alternat Make It Yourself With Wool Cntst; Delegate To Ohio Club Congress; College; Fash Merch.

MCINTIRE, KATHRYN; Lincoln HS; Worthington, WV; Hon Rl; FBLA; Pep Clb; Spn Clb; Lion Awd; Fairmont St Coll; Sec.

MCINTIRE, LILAH L; Monongah HS; Monongah, WV; 18/51 Hon Rl; Yth Flsp; Y-Teens; Fr Clb; FHA; Pep Clb; Fairmont State College; Home Ec.

MCINTOSH, ANTOINETTE; Jane Addams Voc HS; Cleveland, OH; Hon Rl; Jr NHS; Rptr Yrbk; Beta Clb; Mth Clb; Cit Awd; ECI Cmnctns Awrd Charles W Elliot Jr HS; Univ.

MCINTOSH, BRYAND; Benedictine HS; Detroit, MI; Boy Scts; Cmnty Wkr; FCA; Hon Rl; Sct Actv; Stg Crw; Bsktbl; Coach Actv; IM Sprt; Scr Kpr; Univ Of Louisiana; Bus.

MCINTOSH, CAROLYN; Walled Lake Western HS; Jackson, KY; Hon Rl; Off Ade;.

MCINTOSH, DEBBIE; Carlisle HS; Carlisle, OH; Band; Hon Rl; Jr NHS; NHS; College.

MCINTOSH, ROBIN; David Anerson HS; Lisbon, OH; Cls Rep Soph Cls; Cl Rep Jr Cls; Band; Hon Rl;

Sch Mus; Stu Cncl; Yth Flsp; Y-Teens; Ed Yrbk; Fr Clb; Radiologic Schl Of Tech; Radiologic.

MCINTOSH, SANDRA; Seeger Memorial HS; Williamsport, IN; 3/132 Chrh Wkr; FCA; Girl Scts; Hon Rl; NHS; Off Ade; Sch Pl; Stg Crw; Yth Flsp; DECA; Purdue Univ; Pre Vet.

MCINTOSH, SHELLEY; Bloom Local HS; Wheelersburg, OH; VP Jr Cls; FHA; OEA; Chrldng; Bus Schl.

MCINTYRE, BETTY; Rock Hill Sr HS; Kitts Hill, OH; 1/142 Val; Band; Chrh Wkr; Hon Rl; NHS; Stu Cncl; Rptr Yrbk; Rptr Sch Nwsp; Beta Clb; 4-H; St Marys Nursing Schl; RN.

MCINTYRE, K; Triton HS; Tippecanoe, IN; Chrh Wkr; FCA; Yth Flsp; 4-H; FBLA; Letter Bsbl; Crs Cntry; Ftbl; DAR Awd; 4-H Awd; Liberty Baptist College.

MCINTYRE, KATHLEEN; Kalamazoo Central HS; Kalamazoo, MI; Chrs; Hon Rl; Natl Forn Lg; Sch Mus; Sch Pl; Stg Crw; Yrbk; Drama Clb; W Michigan Univ; Cmnctns.

MCINTYRE, KEVIN; Dublin HS; Columbus, OH; Boy Scts; Cmnty Wkr; Hon Rl; JA; 4-H; FFA; Ftbl; Letter Glf; IM Sprt; Univ; Horticulture.

MCINTYRE, LORI; Arthur Hill HS; Saginaw, MI; 16/522 Hon Rl; JA; NHS; Drama Clb; Pep Clb; Coach Actv; PPFtbl; Alma Coll Trustee Hon Schlshp; Mi Compttv Schlshp; Alma Coll; Chem.

MCINTYRE, MARK; Columbiana HS; Columbiana, OH; 7/105 Am Leg Boys St; Band; Boy Scts; Chrh Wkr; Hon Rl; NHS; Sct Actv; Stu Cncl; Yth Flsp; Rptr Sch Nwsp; Univ; Cmnctns.

MCINTYRE, MARY; Lakota HS; W Chester, OH; 3/464 Pres Soph Cls; Cl Rep Jr Cls; Cls Rep Sr Cls; Am Leg Aux Girls St; Univ Of Cincinnati; Engr.

MCINTYRE, REBECCA; South Decatur HS; Westport, IN; Trs Frsh Cls; Chrs; Hon Rl; Off Ade; 4-H; Pep Clb; Letter Bsktbl; Trk; Chrldng; Scr Kpr; Huffer Beauty Coll; Cosmetology.

MCINTYRE, TIM; Belleville HS; Belleville, MI; 28/519 Hon Rl; NHS; Capt Crs Cntry; Letter Trk; Univ; Educ.

MCKAIN, TERESA; Sullivan HS; Merom, IN; Cls Rep Frsh Cls; Cls Rep Soph Cls; Band; Chrs; Hon Rl; Stu Cncl; Beta Clb; Gym; Trk; Chrldng; Butler Univ; Pharm.

MCKAMEY, LISA A; Cloverdale HS; Cloverdale, IN; Am Leg Aux Girls St; Band; Hon Rl; Sch Mus; Drama Clb; 4-H; FTA; Pep Clb; VP Spn Clb; Letter Bsktbl; Ball St Univ; Music Educ.

MCKANNA, JEFF; Columbus Grove HS; Colombus Grove, OH; Pres Frsh Cls; Pres Sr Cls; Am Leg Boys St; Band; Chrs; NHS; Sch Mus; Stu Cncl; VP FFA; Wrstlng; Wooster Agric Inst; Crop Prod.

MCKARNS, SUSAN; Southern Local HS; Kensington, OH; VP Sr Cls; Chrh Wkr; Hon Rl; JA; Jr NHS; NHS; 4-H; FNA; Lat Clb; Bsktbl; College; Medcial.

MCKAY, JANE; Mount Vernon Acad; Hillsboro, OH; Chrs; Hon Rl; Chmn Bsbl; Letter Bsktbl; Chmn Ftbl; Scr Kpr; Columbia Union College; History Tchr.

MCKAY, LILLIAN; Our Lady Of Mercy HS; Birmingham, MI; Stg Crw; Pep Clb; Wayne St Univ; Bus.

MCKAY, LISA; Alcona HS; Black River, MI; 6/124 Sec Sr Cls; Jr NHS; Spn Clb; College; Business.

MCKAY, MICHAEL; Madison Hts HS; Anderson, IN; 12/450 FCA; Hon Rl; NHS; Ten; Coll; Engr.

MCKAY, MOLLY; Hamilton Southeastern HS; Fortville, IN; 6/160 Am Leg Aux Girls St; Band; Hon Rl; MMM; NHS; Fr Clb; Crs Cntry; Trk; Natl Merit Ltr; Univ; Foreign Language.

MCKAY, TIMOTHY; L C Mohr HS; S Haven, MI; Band; Chrs; Hon Rl; Jr NHS; NHS; Letter Bsktbl; Trk; Michigan Tech Coll; Civil Engr.

MCKEE, ANN; Imlay City HS; Imlay City, MI; Band; Chrh Wkr; Hon Rl; NHS; Yth Flsp; 4-H; Sci Clb; 4-H Awd; Michigan St Univ; Chem Engr.

MCKEE, BRUCE; North Vigo HS; Terre Haute, IN; Band; Hon Rl; Orch; Sci Clb; Ball State; Architecture.

MCKEE, BRUCE; Avon Jr Sr HS; Plainfield, IN; Hon Rl; Letter Ten; Trk; Purdue Univ; Vet Med.

MCKEE, BRYAN; Groveport Madison Sr HS; Columbus, OH; 8/350 Chrs; Chrh Wkr; Hon Rl; NHS; Off Ade; Orch; Sch Mus; Fr Clb; Hon Mention Col Symph Orch Contest 75; Mbr Of Oclumbus Youth Symphony Orch 78; 1 Of 5 Schl For Gifted 75; Ohio St Univ; Vet Med.

MCKEE, GARY; Tippecanoe Vly HS; Akron, IN; Chrh Wkr; Hon Rl; NHS; Yth Flsp; Bsbl; Ftbl; Univ.

MCKEE, JEFFREY A; Mt Clemens HS; Mt Clemens, MI; 18/400 Cls Rep Frsh Cls; Pres Soph Cls; Pres Jr Cls; Cls Rep Sr Cls; Am Leg Boys St; Hon Rl; Jr NHS; Stu Cncl; Ed Sch Nwsp; Sprt Ed Sch Nwsp; Univ Of Mich.

MCKEE, JOAN; Vassar HS; Vassar, MI; 7/150 Sec Soph Cls; Band; Hon Rl; NHS; Off Ade; Sch Mus; Yth Flsp; Rptr Sch Nwsp; VP Fr Clb; GAA; United Fund Queen; Central Michigan Univ; Elem Educ.

MCKEE, LORI; Timken Sr HS; Canton, OH; Stu Cncl; Pep Clb; Chrldng;.

MCKEE, PAM; Bowling Green HS; Lima, OH; Band; Chrh Wkr; Lbry Ade; Owebs Tech Schl; Comp Sci.

MCKEE, SUE; Delphos Jefferson Sr HS; Delphos, OH; Am Leg Aux Girls St; Pres Band; Chrs; Hon Rl; NHS; Sch Mus; Sch Pl; Stu Cncl; Fr Clb; IM Sprt; College; Photography.

MCKEE, TANYA; Huntington HS; Chillicothe, OH; 1/97 Sec Soph Cls; Pres Jr Cls; Val; Hon Rl; NHS; Chrldng; Nursing Schl; Nursing.

MCKEE, TERRY; North HS; Springfield, OH; Bsktbl; Wuttenburg Univ; American History.

MCKEEN, DEBRA; Brooke HS; Bethany, WV; 13/466 Cls Rep Soph Cls; Hon Rl; Lit Mag; Sec NHS; Quill & Scroll; Stu Cncl; Treas Y-Teens; West Liberty College; Bio.

MCKEEN, LE ANNE; Chatard HS; Indianapolis, IN; 2/200 Sec Frsh Cls; Hon Rl; Hosp Ade; NHS; Stu Cncl; Sprt Ed Yrbk; Rptr Yrbk; Fr Clb; Chrldng; IM Sprt; College; Journalism.

MCKEETHEN, CONSTANCE; George Washington HS; E Chicago, IN; 16/264 Cls Rep Soph Cls; Pres Sr Cls; Chrs; Hon Rl; JA; NHS; Boys Clb Am; FHA; Key Clb; Pep Clb; Howard Univ; Nursing.

MCKEEVER, BELINDA; Cody HS; Detroit, MI; VP Soph Cls; Pres Jr Cls; Cl Rep Jr Cls; Band; Cmnty Wkr; Hon Rl; JA; Sch Mus; Wayne Michigan; Business Admin.

MCKEEVER, CARLA; Wardensville 12 Yr School; Wardensville, WV; Pres Soph Cls; Girl Scts; Hon Rl; Sch Pl; Stu Cncl; 4-H; FBLA; Pep Clb; Chrldng; 4-H Awd;.

MCKEEVER, MICHAEL; Stanton HS; Empire, OH; 2/75 Boy Scts; Chrs; Chrh Wkr; Hon Rl; NHS; Sct Actv; Bsktbl; NROTC; Comp Engr.

MCKEIVER, PATRICK; West Catholic HS; Grand Rapids, MI; Hon Rl; Spn Clb; IM Sprt; Mgrs; College; Acctg.

MCKELVEY, CINDY; Saint Francis Desales HS; Westerville, OH; Cmp Fr Grls; Drl Tm; Sch Mus; Sch Pl; Stg Crw; Yth Flsp; Drama Clb; Pep Clb; Bowling Green State Univ; Drama.

MCKEMEY, SUZANNE; Clay City HS; Bowling Green, IN; 3/62 Am Leg Aux Girls St; NHS; Sec 4-H; FHA; VP Sci Clb; 4-H Awd; Voice Dem Awd; Franklin Coll; Pre Med.

MCKENNA, JENNIFER; St Marys Central Cath HS; Sandusky, OH; Chrs; Chrh Wkr; Girl Scts; Off Ade; Sdlty; Y-Teens; Sch Nwsp; Spn Clb; Chrldng; GAA; Univ Of Dayton.

MCKENNA, KAREN; Fenton HS; Fenton, MI; 15/302 Letter Band; Chrs; Cmnty Wkr; Girl Scts; Hon Rl; NHS; Pol Wkr; PPFtbl; Schlstc Honor Roll; W Michigan Univ; Comp Sci.

MCKENNEY, MELISSA; Andover HS; Bloomfield Hls, MI; Hon Rl; Natl Merit Ltr; Univ Of Mic.

MCKENNEY, TIMOTHY; Holly HS; Holly, MI; Band; IM Sprt; Bravender Math Awd 1979; Univ Of Notre Dame; Bus Admin.

MCKENZIE, B; Parkside HS; Jackson, MI; Cls Rep Frsh Cls; Cls Rep Soph Cls; Band; Hon Rl; IM Sprt; Univ Of Michigan; Engineering.

MCKENZIE, CRAIG; Shelby Senior HS; Shelby, OH; Band; Boy Scts; Chrs; Chrh Wkr; Hon Rl; Sch Mus; Stg Crw; Pres Yth Flsp; Sch Nwsp; Lat Clb; Wittenburg; Music Education.

MCKENZIE, DARLENE; Ravenna HS; Ravenna, OH; 14/327 AFS; Hon Rl; Hosp Ade; Lbry Ade; NHS; Fr Clb; Cit Awd; Cert Of Awd Enrched Amer Hist 76; Cert Of Achvmnt Sci Fair 76; Univ; Educ.

MCKENZIE, DEBORAH; Jackson HS; Jackson, MI; 16/326 Band; Drm Mjrt; Hon Rl; NHS; Coach Actv; Pom Pon; Twrlr; Spring Arbor College; Bus Admst.

MCKENZIE, JULIE; Fowlerville HS; Fowlerville, MI; Band; Drm Bgl; Girl Scts; Hon Rl; Off Ade; 4-H; IM Sprt; PPFtbl; Ferris State College; Pharmaceutical.

MCKENZIE, LEANN; Romeo Sr HS; Romeo, MI; Debate Tm; Hon Rl; NHS; Drama Clb; Fr Clb; Gym; Letter Swmmng; GAA; IM Sprt; PPFtbl; Michigan St Univ.

MCKENZIE, RENE; Southern Local HS; Wellsville, OH; 4/110 Pres Sr Cls; Sec Chrs; Hon Rl; NHS; Sch Pl; 4-H; FNA; Pres OEA; Chrldng; 4-H Awd; Kent State Univ; Accounting.

MCKENZIE, THOMAS L; Mason HS; Mason, MI; AFS; Band; Boy Scts; Chrs; Chrh Wkr; Cmnty Wkr; Hon Rl; Jr NHS; NHS; Sch Mus; Hope Coll; Chem Engr.

MCKEVURY, ANN; Cheboygan Area HS; Cheboygan, MI; Band; Hon Rl; NHS; Sch Pl; College; Soc Work.

MCKIERNAN, JUDY; High School; Memphis, MI; Chrs; Hon Rl; Stu Cncl; Yth Flsp; 4-H; Bsbl; Chrldng; Mgrs; PPFtbl; 4-H Awd; Univ; Interior Dsgn.

MCKIM, PAMELA; North Huron HS; Kinde, MI; 6/52 Sec Frsh Cls; VP Soph Cls; Cls Rep Soph Cls; Cl Rep Jr Cls; Hon Rl; NHS; Stu Cncl; Yth Flsp; Yrbk; 4-H; Achvmnt Awd Art 2 78; Achvmnt Awd Yrbk 79; Achvmnt Awd Academic Excel 79; Coll; Cmmrcl Art.

MCKINLEY, JAY; Plymouth Canton HS; Plymouth, MI; 100/446 Cls Rep Frsh Cls; Cls Rep Soph Cls; Pres Jr Cls; VP Sr Cls; Sch Mus; Stu Cncl; Letter Bsktbl; Letter Ftbl; Mic St.

MCKINLEY, JEFFREY; West Carrollton HS; Dayton, OH; 1/420 Band; Drm Mjrt; Hon Rl; Jr NHS; Pres NHS; Orch; Pep Clb; Opt Clb Awd; Mastr Hnr Carrier For The Dayton Daily Nws 76 78; Schlrshp To Smith Walbridge Drm Majr Camp 78; Univ; Bus.

MCKINLEY, LISA A; Winamac Cmnty HS; Winamac, IN; Cl Rep Jr Cls; Chrh Wkr; Drl Tm; Hon Rl; Hosp Ade; Jr NHS; Sch Mus; Sec Stu Cncl; Drama Clb; Sec Lat Clb; Butler Univ; Med Tech.

MCKINLEY, MARK S; New Haven HS; Fort Wayne, IN; Band; Stg Crw; Letter Ftbl; Trk; Wrstlng; Bst Mntl Attd Ftbl 76; Bst Def Back Ftbl 77; Air Force; Engr.

MCKINLEY, MICHAEL D; New Richmond HS; New Richmond, OH; Rptr Sch Nwsp; IM Sprt; Mgrs; Scr Kpr; Tmr; College; Educ.

MCKINLEY, MICHELLE; Jenison HS; Jenison, MI; 79/358 Cls Rep Frsh Cls; Cls Rep Soph Cls; Cl Rep Jr Cls; Cls Rep Sr Cls; Band; Girl Scts; Hon Rl; Natl Forn Lg; Sch Mus; Sch Pl; Univ Of Toledo; Med Asst.

MCKINLEY, ROBERT; Ridgemont HS; Kenton, OH; 4-H; FFA; Spn Clb; Ftbl; 4-H Awd;.

MCKINLEY, TAMARA SUE; Indiana Academy; Carmel, IN; Sec Soph Cls; Chrs; Hon Rl; Lbry Ade; Sec Off Ade; Sch Pl; Sct Actv; Pres Stu Cncl; Rptr Sch Nwsp; College.

MCKINNEY, CHARLES; Carlisle HS; Franklin, OH; Band; Boy Scts; Spn Clb; Crs Cntry; Ftbl; Trk; Xavier; Pre Law.

MCKINNEY, DERRICK; John F Kennedy HS; Cleveland, OH; Hon Rl; Cit Awd; Univ; Elec Engr.

MCKINNEY, DOUGLAS; Franklin Community HS; Franklin, IN; 80/350 Cls Rep Frsh Cls; Cls Rep Soph Cls; Cl Rep Jr Cls; FCA; Hon Rl; Stu Cncl; VP Y-Teens; Boys Clb Am; VP Pep Clb; Sci Clb; Indiana Univ; Telecmnctns.

MCKINNEY, EVELYN; Tecumseh Sr HS; Tecumseh, MI; 33/265 Chrs; Chrh Wkr; Girl Scts; Hon Rl; Treas NHS; Yrbk; 4-H; Pres Spn Clb; 4-H Awd; Spanish Club Schlrshp To Mexico; Eastern Michigan Univ; Publications.

MCKINNEY, GERRI; Madison HS; Adrian, MI; Band; Hon Rl; Hosp Ade; VP NHS; Pres Quill & Scroll; Sec Stu Cncl; Ed Yrbk; Yrbk; Rptr Sch Nwsp; Key Clb; Outstndng Bio Awrd 1978; Profncy In Eng 1978; All Cnty Band 1979;.

MCKINNEY, JACQUELINE V; Glen Oak School; Cleveland, OH; Chrs; Chrh Wkr; Cmnty Wkr; Off Ade; PAVAS; Sch Mus; Yrbk; Drama Clb; Fr Clb; Pep Clb; Better Chance Schlshp 76; Performing Arts Awd 79; Outstndng Eng Achvmnt Awd 79; Univ; Child Psych.

MCKINNEY, JAMES; Medora HS; Norman, IN; 3/21 VP Frsh Cls; Pres Soph Cls; Cl Rep Jr Cls; Am Leg Boys St; Hon Rl; Sch Pl; Stg Crw; Stu Cncl; Beta Clb; Sci Clb; Prfct Attndnc 76 79; IUPUI; Agri Bus.

MCKINNEY, KAREN; Mt Gilead HS; Mt Gilead, OH; Cls Rep Sr Cls; Chrs; Hon Rl; Jr NHS; NHS; Stg Crw; Stu Cncl; Rptr Sch Nwsp; Sch Nwsp; Pep Clb; Ohio St Univ; Cmnctns.

MCKINNEY, KIM; Franklin Comm HS; Greenwood, IN; VP Frsh Cls; VP Soph Cls; VP Jr Cls; VP Sr Cls; Chrh Wkr; Cmnty Wkr; Hon Rl; Hosp Ade; Jr NHS; NHS; Salutatorian Of Class; Delegate To 1st Annual Lugars Symposium For Tomorrows Leader; Awd For Exc In French; Taylor Univ; Psych.

MCKINNEY, KIM; Northwest HS; Indianapolis, IN; Girl Scts; Hon Rl; Letter Gym; Chrldng; IM Sprt; Scr Kpr; Pres Awd; Indiana St Univ; Phys Ed.

MCKINNEY, MELANIE; Jackson HS; Jackson, OH; Chrs; Hon Rl; Lbry Ade; Off Ade; Red Cr Ade; OEA; Letter Trk; PPFtbl; Delgt At Regnl Meetng In Pickaway Ross 78; Head Of Actvts Comm In OEA 78; Jr Sr Pbom Comm 78; Truck Driver.

MCKINNEY, NANCY; Washington HS; Washington, IN; 20/203 Hon Rl; Jr NHS; NHS; Sch Pl; Stg Crw; Sec Beta Clb; Drama Clb; Fr Clb; Pres Awd; Univ Of Evansville; Social Work.

MCKINNEY, PAMELA; Herndon HS; Herndon, WV; 3/35 Sec Soph Cls; Pres Jr Cls; Hon Rl; Lbry Ade; VP NHS; Pres Stu Cncl; Fr Clb; FBLA; FHA; W V Univ; Pre Med.

MCKINNEY, PATRICK S; Pineville HS; New Richmond, WV; Aud/Vis; Band; Chrs; Debate Tm; Drl Tm; Drm Bgl; Hon Rl; Jr NHS; Off Ade; Orch; Dir Spec Awd For Band 78; Dir Asst Band 77; Pres Of Percussion Corps 78; S W Virginia Cmnty Coll; Law.

MCKINNEY, PATTI; Woodward HS; Toledo, OH; Chrs; Drl Tm; Hosp Ade; Stu Cncl; Drama Clb; Pep Clb; Owens Tech; Nursing.

MCKINNEY, PAULA; Gleneste HS; Cincinnati, OH; 26/250 Am Leg Aux Girls St; Chrs; Chrh Wkr; Hon Rl; NHS; FHA; OEA; Spn Clb; Am Leg Awd; Pres Clsrm Delgte 1979; Bus Schl; Bus Admin.

MCKINNEY, TOM; Brownstown Central HS; Freetown, IN; Chrh Wkr; Hon Rl; Yth Flsp; IM Sprt; Voc Schl; Mech.

MCKINNEY, YVONNE; Herndon HS; Bud, WV; 3/35 VP Frsh Cls; Sec Jr Cls; Chrh Wkr; Hon Rl; Stu Cncl; Yth Flsp; 4-H; FBLA; FHA; Pep Clb; Bus Schl; Bus Admin.

MCKINNON, JANET; Denby HS; Detroit, MI; 8/350 Hon Rl; Off Ade; Univ Of Mic.

MCKINSEY, KATHLEEN S; Delta HS; Muncie, IN; 29/320 Trs Frsh Cls; Trs Sr Cls; Band; Cmp Fr Grls; Chrs; Drl Tm; Girl Scts; Hon Rl; Sch Mus; Sch Pl; Purdue Univ; Dietics.

MCKITRICK, JENIFER; Greenville Sr HS; Greenville, OH; 12/360 Hon Rl; Lit Mag; NHS; Quill & Scroll; Fr Clb; Spn Clb; Trk; Kent St Univ.

MCKITRICK, MINDY; Dublin HS; Columbus, OH; 19/155 Trs Frsh Cls; Cls Rep Soph Cls; Sec Jr Cls; Cls Rep Sr Cls; Chrs; Chrh Wkr; Drm Mjrt; Hon Rl; NHS; Sch Mus; Miami Univ; Interior Dsgn.

MCKNIGHT, C; Groveport Madison HS; Columbus, OH; Am Leg Boys St; Band; Hon Rl; NHS; Trk; Ohio State; Bio Chem.

MCKNIGHT, DEBRA; Peebles HS; Peebles, OH; VP Frsh Cls; Chrs; Hon Rl; Sch Pl; Drama Clb; FHA; Twrlr; College.

MCKNIGHT, IVAN; Dunbar HS; Dunbar, WV; Boy Scts; Chrh Wkr; CAP; Hon Rl; Red Cr Ade; Yth Flsp; Spn Clb; Letter Crs Cntry; Letter Trk; Voice Dem Awd; Air Force Academy; Aero.

MCKOWN, LYNNE; Willard HS; Plymouth, OH; Band; Chrs; Chrh Wkr; Hon Rl; NHS; Orch; Sch Mus; Sch Pl; Yrbk; IM Sprt; College.

MCKUNE, AMY; Shortridge HS; Indianapolis, IN; 5/326 Hon Rl; NHS; Quill & Scroll; Yrbk; Sch Nwsp; Fr Clb; Univ.

MCKUNE, DAWN; Clawson HS; Clawson, MI; Girl Scts; Hon Rl; Trk; PPFtbl; Oakland Univ; Nursing.

MCLACHLAN, DANIEL; Norton HS; Magnolia, OH; 2/287 Sal; Band; Chrs; NHS; Sch Mus; Sch Pl; Drama Clb; Fr Clb; Mth Clb; Am Leg Awd; Ohio Northern Univ; Mech Engr.

MCLAIN, ELAINE S; Memorial HS; St Marys, OH; 18/233 Band; Chrs; Hon Rl; Red Cr Ade; Sch Mus; Yrbk; 4-H; FTA; GAA; IM Sprt; Ag Tech Inst; Equestrian.

MCLAIN, JOHN R; Niles HS; Niles, MI; 13/703 Band; Hon Rl; Sch Mus; Natl Merit SF; Univ Of Michigan; Bus Admin.

MCLAIN, TIM; New Lexington HS; New Lexington, OH; 2/165 Boy Scts; Jr NHS; NHS; Yth Flsp; Lat Clb; Letter Sci Clb; Letter Bsktbl; Letter Ftbl; Marietta Univ; Acctg.

MCLANE, JOLINE; William G Mather HS; Munising, MI; Sal; Band; Chrh Wkr; Girl Scts; Hon Rl; MMM; NHS; Sch Nwsp; 4-H; 4-H Awd; Univ; Spec Ed.

MCLAREN, BRADLEY; Hillman Comm HS; Hillman, MI; Cls Rep Frsh Cls; Cls Rep Soph Cls; Cls Rep Sr Cls; Band; Chrh Wkr; Hon Rl; Stu Cncl; Sprt Ed Yrbk; Rptr Sch Nwsp; Letter Bsbl; C S Mott Comm Coll; Journalism.

MCLAREN, THOMAS; Kimball HS; Royal Oak, MI; Hon Rl; NHS; Rptr Yrbk; Rptr Sch Nwsp; Fr Clb; I Was Subjct Of A Staffing For Except Stdnts 78; Univ; Jrnlsm.

MCLAUGHLIN, AMY; Northridge HS; Middlebury, IN; Chrs; Chrh Wkr; Girl Scts; Hon Rl; 4-H; Univ; Law.

MCLAUGHLIN, DAWN; Meridian Sr HS; Sanford, MI; 107/121 Chrs; Girl Scts; Hon Rl; NHS; Sct Actv; Saginaw Valley St Coll; Nursing.

MCLAUGHLIN, DAWN; Jimtown HS; Elkhart, IN; 7/93 Trs Soph Cls; Cls Rep Soph Cls; Band; Girl Scts; Hon Rl; JA; NHS; Drama Clb; 4-H; Fr Clb; Valparaiso Univ; Bus Law.

MCLAUGHLIN, ELIZABETH; Williamston HS; Williamston, MI; Treas AFS; Band; Debate Tm; Hon Rl; Pres Jr NHS; Off Ade; Sch Pl; Yth Flsp; Treas Drama Clb; Blue Lake Fine Arts Camp Internatl Band 79; Michigan St Univ; Bus Admin.

MCLAUGHLIN, JAMES; St Joseph Prep Seminary HS; Barnesville, OH; 1/19 Pres Frsh Cls; Pres Soph Cls; Pres Jr Cls; Val; Pres Jr NHS; Pres NHS; Pres Stu Cncl; Bsbl; Bsktbl; IM Sprt; Univ; History.

MCLAUGHLIN, JEFFREY; Brooke HS; Wellsburg, WV; 20/466 Am Leg Boys St; NHS; Quill & Scroll; Sprt Ed Yrbk; DECA; Letter Bsktbl; West Virginia Univ; Acctg.

MCLAUGHLIN, KELLY; Mogadore HS; Mogadore, OH; 2/78 Am Leg Aux Girls St; Band; Chrs; Hon Rl; NHS; Fr Clb; Hockey; PPFtbl; Am Leg Awd; Natl Merit Schl; Univ; Law.

MCLAUGHLIN, KEVIN; West Lafayette HS; W Lafayette, IN; 8/185 Trs Sr Cls; Band; Hon Rl; Stu Cncl; Ed Yrbk; Yrbk; Cit Awd; DAR Awd; Kiwan Awd; Natl Merit Ltr; Purdue Univ; Engr.

MCLAUGHLIN, LISA; Highland HS; Anderson, IN; Sec Jr Cls; Cls Rep Sr Cls; Band; Stu Cncl; Spn Clb; IM Sprt; PPFtbl; Ind Univ.

MCLAUGHLIN, MARY; Norwalk HS; Norwalk, OH; Chrh Wkr; Sch Mus; Pep Clb; Letter Bsbl; Mat Maids; PPFtbl; Scr Kpr; Tmr; M B Johnson Schl Of Nursing; RN.

MCLAUGHLIN, MARY B; Beaumont School For Girls; Clevlnd, OH; Cls Rep Sr Cls; Cmnty Wkr; Hon Rl; Lit Mag; NHS; Pol Wkr; Stu Cncl; Spn Clb; World Hist Awd 78; Andrews Schlshp Stdnt For Acvmnt Leadshp Loylty & Serv To Schl & Cmnty 79; Univ; Jrnlsm.

MCLAUGHLIN, MAUREEN; St Joseph Acad; Cleveland, OH; Cls Rep Frsh Cls; Cls Rep Soph Cls; Cl Rep Jr Cls; Chrs; Chrh Wkr; Cmnty Wkr; Drl Tm; Girl Scts; Hon Rl; Hosp Ade; Univ Of Dayton; Dietetics.

MCLAUGHLIN, ROBIN; Jimtown HS; Elkhart, IN; 8/95 VP Frsh Cls; Trs Jr Cls; Cl Rep Jr Cls; Cls Rep Sr Cls; Hon Rl; NHS; Sch Pl; Stu Cncl; DECA; Drama Clb; Indiana Univ; Bus.

MCLAUGHLIN, TAMARA; Morgantown HS; Morgantwn, WV; Chrs; Sch Mus; Sch Pl; Stg Crw; Rptr Sch Nwsp; Drama Clb; WVU.

MCLAUGHLIN, THOMAS; North Branch HS; North Branch, MI; Cls Rep Soph Cls; Pres Jr Cls; Hon Rl; Letter Bsktbl; Ferris State & Wayne State; Sci.

MCLAUGHLIN, TRACY; South Vigo HS; Terre Haute, IN; Hon Rl; PAVAS; Sch Mus; Y-Teens; Pep Clb; Spn Clb; Glf; Trk; GAA; Mgrs; Univ; Bus.

MCLAUGHLIN, VICKI; Fort Frye HS; Beverly, OH; Band; Chrs; Chrh Wkr; Cmnty Wkr; Drl Tm; Hon Rl; NHS; Sch Mus; Sch Pl; Stu Cncl; Univ; Psych.

MCLAURIN, BRENDA; Brookhaven; Columbus, OH; 86/434 Chrh Wkr; Drl Tm; Girl Scts; Hon Rl; Jr NHS; NHS; Lbry Ade; Lit Mag; Off Ade; Sct Actv; Yth Flsp; Ohio Dominican Coll; Bus.

MCLAVY, MARK; Elizabeth Ann Johnson Sr HS; Mt Morris, MI; Band; Boy Scts; Chrh Wkr; Hon Rl; Orch; Yth Flsp; Cert Of Otstndng Performnc In World History; Bethel Coll; Chem.

MCLAY, TRACEY; Sault Area HS; Ss Mclay, MI; Cmnty Wkr; Stg Crw; Pep Clb; Chrldng; Northern Michigan; Elem Teacher.

MCLEAN, DOUGLAS; Mansfield Madison Comp HS; Mansfield, OH; Band; Lbry Ade; Yrbk; Sch

Nwsp; Spn Clb; Capt Glf; Capt IM Sprt; Univ; Pre Dent.

MCLEAN, SUSAN; North Farmington HS; W Bloomfield, MI; Chrs; Chrh Wkr; Hon Rl; NHS; Stg Crw; Pep Clb; Chrldng; Mgrs; Scr Kpr; Michigan St Univ; Nursing.

MCLELLON, DOUGLAS P; Pontiac Central HS; Ann Arbor, MI; 39/469 Band; Boy Scts; Hon Rl; NHS; Orch; Stg Crw; Yth Flsp; Voice Dem Awd; Michigan Tech Univ; Forestry.

MCLEMORE, CHARLENE; Cass Technical HS; Detroit, MI; Hon Rl; Jr NHS; Off Ade; Sct Actv; OEA; Sci Clb; Cit Awd; Univ Of Michigan; Comp Sci.

MCLEMORE, KIMBERLY J; Logan HS; Logan, WV; 68/296 Trs Frsh Cls; Chrh Wkr; Girl Scts; Hon Rl; Off Ade; Quill & Scroll; Sprt Ed Sch Nwsp; Beta Clb; Spn Clb; Gym; All County Cheerleader; 1st Attendent To Miss Pacesetter; Kiwanis Bowl Qn For Logan HS; West Virginia Univ; Pharmacy.

MCLEMORE, LISA; Frankton HS; Anderson, IN; 35/136 Band; Chrh Wkr; Hosp Ade; Rptr Yrbk; Rptr Sch Nwsp; Hoosier Schlr 79; Houghton Coll; Psych.

MCLENAGHAN, COLLEEN; Roscommon HS; St Helen, MI; Sec Soph Cls; Trs Jr Cls; Sec Sr Cls; Am Leg Aux Girls St; Band; Girl Scts; Letter Chrldng; GAA; Letter Mgrs; Letter Mat Maids; Mich State; Architecture.

MCLENITHAN, JOHN; Tri Township Tribune HS; Rapid Rvr, MI; Cls Rep Frsh Cls; Cls Rep Soph Cls; Boy Scts; Hon Rl; Stu Cncl; Capt Bsbl; Bsktbl; Ftbl; Trk; Scr Kpr; Bsktl Capt All CUP Confrnc & All Skyline Confrnc MVP & MIP & Outstndng Plyr Awd; Univ.

MCLEOD, BRENDA; Green HS; Akron, OH; 41/322 Chrs; Chrh Wkr; Hon Rl; Off Ade; Sch Mus; Sch Pl; Stg Crw; Yth Flsp; Rptr Sch Nwsp; Drama Clb; Cedarville College; Government.

MCLEOD, CHRISTOPHER; East Kentwood HS; Kentwood, MI; NHS; Michigan Tech Univ; Civil Engr.

MCLEOD, DEAN; Houghton Lake HS; Houghton Lkae, MI; Cmnty Wkr; Hon Rl; Univ; Math.

MCLEOD, KATHLEEN; Our Lady Mercy HS; Detroit, MI; Treas Girl Scts; Off Ade; Univ Of St Thomas; Rn.

MCLEOD, MARK; Sault Area HS; Sault Ste Marie, MI; Hon Rl; Jr NHS; NHS; Sch Pl; Stg Crw; Lat Clb; Bsktbl; Crs Cntry; Glf; Lake Superior State College; Pre Med.

MCLIMORE, JOHN R; Heritage Christian School; Indianapolis, IN; 1/6 Chrh Wkr; Hon Rl; NHS; Sch Pl; Drama Clb; Key Clb; Letter Bsktbl; Letter Socr; Letter Trk; Wabash Univ; Med.

MCLIN, DENISE L; Washington HS; Massillon, OH; Chrs; Fr Clb; Mount St Joseph Univ; Nursing.

MCLINDEN, MEIGHAN; Central Cath HS; Canton, OH; 14/249 VP Chrs; Cmnty Wkr; Hon Rl; NHS; Yrbk; Washington Univ.

MCLOED, LAWRENCE; Brownsburg HS; Brownsburg, IN; Cls Rep Soph Cls; Hon Rl; NHS; IM Sprt; Purdue Univ; Engr.

MCLOED, MARTIN; Brownsburg HS; Brownsbrg, IN; 13/314 Hon Rl; Letter Bsbl; Letter Ftbl; Letter Wrstlng; Univ.

MCLONIS, KRISTINE; St Hedwig HS; Detroit, MI; Chrs; Hon Rl; Off Ade; Orch; Sch Pl; FTA; College; Religion.

MCMAHAN, CONNIE; North Newton HS; Lk Village, IN; Hon Rl; FBLA; Spn Clb; Bus Schl; Bus.

MCMAHON, COLLEEN; Marian HS; Mishawaka, IN; Hon Rl; NHS; Pep Clb; Capt Trk; Chrldng; IM Sprt; Marquette Univ; Phys Ther.

MCMAHON, THERESA A; Carroll HS; Dayton, OH; 80300 Band; Hon Rl; NHS; Stu Cncl; Key Clb; Rus Clb; JETS Awd; Natl Merit Ltr; Univ; Elec Engr.

MCMAINS, DONNA; St Bernard Elmwood HS; St Bernard, OH; Chrs; Drl Tm; Red Cr Ade; Sch Mus; VICA; Swmmng; Coach Actv; Pom Pon; Scr Kpr; Scarlet Oaks Voc Schl; Cosmetology.

MCMAKEN, JULIE; Covington HS; Covington, OH; Cl Rep Jr Cls; Cls Rep Sr Cls; Chrs; Hon Rl; Off Ade; Sch Mus; Sch Pl; Sec Stu Cncl; Yrbk; Pep Clb; Night Schl; Bus.

MCMANIGELL, SHAWN; St Charles Prep; Columbus, OH; Sch Nwsp; Fr Clb; Letter Trk; Wrstlng; IM Sprt; College; Pilot.

MCMANUS, ANNETTE; Charlestown HS; Charlestown, IN; 15/155 Cmnty Wkr; NHS; Lat Clb; Letter Bsktbl; Letter Crs Cntry; Letter Trk; Bryan Coll; Bio.

MCMANUS, KATHLEEN; Harrison HS; Farmington Hil, MI; 73/376 Band; Hon Rl; Letter Bsbl; Letter Bsktbl; PPFtbl; Univ Of Michigan; Bio.

MCMANUS, M; Lumen Christi HS; Jackson, MI; 83/238 Band; Hon Rl; JA; NHS; Orch; PAVAS; Sch Mus; Sch Pl; Stg Crw; Drama Clb; Mic St Univ; Elec Engr.

MCMANUS, M; Maplewood HS; N Bloomfield, OH; Pres Frsh Cls; Sec Soph Cls; Cl Rep Jr Cls; Girl Scts; Hosp Ade; Stu Cncl; Rptr Sch Nwsp; 4-H; 4-H Awd; Vocational School; Nursing.

MCMANUS, MARGARET; Eastlake North HS; Willowick, OH; 86/669 VP Band; Hon Rl; Off Ade; Rptr Sch Nwsp; Spn Clb; Bowling Green Univ; Bus.

MCMANUS, MARK; Bishop Flaget HS; Chillicothe, OH; 6/36 Pres Sr Cls; Chrh Wkr; Hon Rl; Hosp Ade; NHS; Sch Mus; Sch Pl; Sct Actv; VP Stu Cncl; Fr Clb; Xavier Univ; Agric Chem.

MCMANUS, MARK W; Bishop Flaget HS; Chillicothe, OH; Pres Sr Cls; Aud/Vis; Boy Scts; Chrh Wkr; Cmnty Wkr; Hon Rl; NHS; Sch Mus; Sch Pl; Stu Cncl; Xavier Univ; Ag.

MCMANUS, PAM; Anderson HS; Anderson, IN; 50/400 Chrs; Chrh Wkr; Hon Rl; Mdrgl; NHS; Yth Flsp; Fr Clb; FHA; Pep Clb; Trk; Anderson College.

MCMANUS, WILLIAM L; Colon Comm HS; Colon, MI; Trs Jr Cls; Am Leg Boys St; Hon Rl; Letter Bsktbl; Scr Kpr; Tmr; College; Math.

MCMASTER, TIMOTHY; Traverse City HS; Traverse City, MI; 27/700 NHS; Letter Crs Cntry; Letter Trk; Mic Tech Univ; Elec Engr.

MCMASTERS, MARK; Bellaire HS; Bellaire, OH; 6/223 Am Leg Boys St; Aud/Vis; Boy Scts; Hon Rl; VP NHS; Spn Clb; Letter Crs Cntry; IM Sprt; Ohi State Univ; Rsrch Chem.

MCMASTERS, TIM; Martinsburg HS; Martinsburg, WV; 13/230 Am Leg Boys St; NHS; Crs Cntry; Trk; Univ; Poli Sci.

MCMATH, MARK; Indian Valley South HS; Gnadenhutten, OH; 8/95 Band; Chrs; Chrh Wkr; Hon Rl; NHS; Sch Pl; Stu Cncl; Fr Clb; Mth Clb; Pep Clb; Kent St Univ; Mech Engr.

MCMEEKING, JOHN; Lake Shore HS; St Clair Shore, MI; 9/700 Band; Boy Scts; Hon Rl; Orch; Sch Mus; Sct Actv; Natl Merit Schl; Michigan Tech Univ; Elec Engr.

MCMENEMY, CATHERINE; Cabrini HS; Allen Pk, MI; 1/163 Chrh Wkr; Cmnty Wkr; Hon Rl; Jr NHS; Natl Forn Lg; NHS; Sch Pl; Stg Crw; VP Drama Clb; Spn Clb; Trophy Forensics; Cert & Medals District & Reg/public Forensics; Honorable Mention Cert; Detroit News; Univ Of Michigan; Phys Therapy.

MCMICHAEL, JOANNE; Onsted HS; Adrian, MI; 45/122 Sec Band; Cmp Fr Grls; Chrh Wkr; Hon Rl; Sch Pl; FHA; Crs Cntry; Capt Trk; IM Sprt; Mat Maids; Jackson Cmnty Coll.

MCMICHAEL, LE; Southwestern HS; Edinburgh, IN; 3/65 Cls Rep Soph Cls; Band; Hon Rl; Hosp Ade; NHS; Sch Pl; Stg Crw; Stu Cncl; Sprt Ed Yrbk; Drama Clb; Evansville Univ; Nursing.

MCMICHAEL, LISA; Paulding Exempted Vlg HS; Paulding, OH; Cls Rep Frsh Cls; Cls Rep Soph Cls; Cl Rep Jr Cls; Band; Chrs; Chrh Wkr; Girl Scts; Hon Rl; Sch Mus; Sch Pl; Mt Vernon Nazarene Coll; Psych.

MCMICHAEL, MARTHA J; Lakewood HS; Newark, OH; Hon Rl; Treas Jr NHS; Lit Mag; VP NHS; Treas Fr Clb; Natl Merit Ltr; Natl Merit SF; Ohio Univ; Graphic Design.

MCMILLAN, BOBBIE; Rochester HS; Rochester, MI; Girl Scts; Sct Actv; Adrian College; Teacher.

MCMILLAN, DEBBIE; Walled Lake Sr HS; Wixom, MI; Cls Rep Frsh Cls; Chrs; Chrh Wkr; Cmnty Wkr; Girl Scts; Hon Rl; Univ; Soc Sci.

MCMILLAN, JODI; Garrett HS; Garrett, IN; Cls Rep Sr Cls; Girl Scts; Sch Pl; Stu Cncl; Yth Flsp; Y-Teens; Pep Clb; Spn Clb; Glf; Pom Pon; Coll; Accntg.

MCMILLAN, LAURENA; North Newton HS; Morocco, IN; 24/139 Hon Rl; NHS; Off Ade; Ed Yrbk; FHA; Spn Clb; Talent Grant Schl Of Bus In St Univ 79; Disabled Ver Awd 79; IRIS 78; Indiana St Univ; Bus.

MCMILLAN, MIKE; Springfield HS; Springfield, MI; Boy Scts; Hon Rl; Sct Actv; Bsbl; Bsktbl; Ftbl; Am Leg Awd; Voc Schl; Printing.

MCMILLAN, TONYA; Walnut Hills HS; Cincinnati, OH; Cls Rep Sr Cls; AFS; Chrh Wkr; Cmnty Wkr; Hon Rl; JA; Sch Mus; Spn Clb; Natl Merit Ltr; Spelman Univ; Comp Sci.

MCMILLAN, WENDELL B; Fredericktown HS; Fredericktown, OH; 12/125 Band; Chrh Wkr; Hon Rl; NHS; Off Ade; Yth Flsp; Univ; Pre Law.

MCMILLEN, BILL; Malvern HS; Malvern, OH; Ftbl; Wrstlng; Voc Schl.

MCMILLEN, BRAD; Tecumseh HS; Medway, OH; 60/360 Cls Rep Frsh Cls; Band; Boy Scts; Hon Rl; NHS; Sct Actv; FBLA; Pep Clb; Spn Clb; VICA; Ohio Industrial Arts Awd Of Merit Elec; First Place Industrial Arts Awd Tecumseh Elec; Clark Tech Coll; Elec Engr.

MCMILLEN, CHERYL; Canton South HS; Canton, OH; 38/300 Cls Rep Soph Cls; Chrh Wkr; Girl Scts; Hon Rl; JA; NHS; Sct Actv; Stg Crw; Yth Flsp; Rptr Sch Nwsp; Coll; Wildlife Conservation.

MCMILLIN, MARK; Revere HS; Akron, OH; 9/300 Cl Rep Jr Cls; Cls Rep Sr Cls; AFS; Aud/Vis; Band; Boy Scts; Hon Rl; NHS; Stg Crw; Key Clb; Univ Of Cincinnati; Engr.

MCMILLIN, SHARON; Reading Community HS; Reading, OH; 6/240 Band; Chrh Wkr; Hon Rl; NHS; Orch; Fr Clb; Ky Christian Coll; Educ.

MCMILLION, DONNA J; Woodrow Wilson HS; Beckley, WV; Cmnty Wkr; Hon Rl; JA; Sch Pl; Drama Clb; Keyettes; Spn Clb; 4-H Awd; JA Awd; Miss Teenage So WV 79; Conservation Club 77 79; West Virginia Univ; Psych.

MCMILLION, RAELEEN; Fort Frye HS; Summersville, WV; 30/125 Sec Frsh Cls; Pres Soph Cls; VP Soph Cls; Cls Rep Soph Cls; Cls Rep Sr Cls; Chrs; Chrh Wkr; Cmnty Wkr; Hon Rl; NHS; West Liberty Coll; Communications.

MCMILLION, SHEILA; Liberty HS; Fairdale, WV; 8/73 Cls Rep Sr Cls; Hon Rl; Jr NHS; Lbry Ade; NHS; Stu Cncl; FHA; Pep Clb; Gov Hon Prg Awd; Miss All Amer Tngr & Sthrn W V Teen Semi Finalist 1978; Jr Miss Miss Sprt Awd & 1st Runner Up 1978; Fshn Model.

MCMINN, BETH; Marlington HS; Alliance, OH; Sec Jr Cls; Sec Sr Cls; Chrs; Girl Scts; Hon Rl; Lbry Ade; Off Ade; Sch Mus; Sch Pl; Stg Crw; Tech Schl; Fshn Modeling.

MCMINN, RODNEY; Elwood Community HS; Elwood, IN; Trs Jr Cls; Trs Sr Cls; Aud/Vis; Lbry Ade; Spn Clb; Ball St Univ; Bus Mgmt.

MCMONIGLE, SHIRLEY; Lanesville HS; Lanesville, IN; Band; Chrs; FCA; Hon Rl; NHS; Sch Mus; Stu Cncl; Yrbk; Pres FHA; Bsktbl; Univ; Med.

MCMULLEN, JOSEPH; Jefferson Union HS; Toronto, OH; Band; Hon Rl; Stg Crw; Beta Clb; Ohi State; Eng.

MCMULLEN, JULIE; Rocky River HS; Rocky River, OH; 15/285 Cls Rep Soph Cls; Cl Rep Jr Cls; Band; Capt Drl Tm; Hon Rl; Hosp Ade; NHS; Stu Cncl; Drama Clb; Ten; Univ; Phys Ther.

MCMULLEN, MAURINE; Pinconning Area HS; Pinconning, MI; Chrs; Hon Rl; Lbry Ade; Sch Mus; Northwood Inst; Fashion Mdse.

MCMULLEN, SANDY; Peru HS; Peru, IN; Am Leg Aux Girls St; Hon Rl; NHS; Fr Clb; Dnfth Awd; Whos Who In For Lang 77; Univ; Bus.

MCMULLEN, TAMALYN; Rockville Jr Sr HS; Rockville, IN; 12/94 Cls Rep Frsh Cls; Cls Rep Soph Cls; Chrh Wkr; Cmnty Wkr; FCA; Girl Scts; Hon Rl; NHS; Stu Cncl; Yth Flsp; Runner Up To FFFA Sweetheart Queen; St Jr Leadr Confrnc Cnslr; Vllybl 2 Ltrs; Purdue Univ; Agri Bus.

MCMULLIN, PATRICIA A; Norwood Sr HS; Norwood, OH; 1/367 Pres Soph Cls; Aud/Vis; Chrh Wkr; Girl Scts; Hon Rl; JA; Jr NHS; Lit Mag; NHS; Pol Wkr; Univ; Psych.

MCMURRAY, EDWARD; Greenbrier East HS; Lewisbrg, WV; 9/434 Am Leg Boys St; Chrs; Hon Rl; Pres MMM; NHS; Pres Yth Flsp; Letter Ftbl; Letter Glf; Ten; IM Sprt; Univ; Engr.

MCMURRAY, KIMBERLY; Boardman HS; Youngstown, OH; 134/558 Treas Band; Red Cr Ade; Y-Teens; Pres FNA; Youngstown State Univ; Rn.

MCMURTRY, LUANN; Warren Central HS; Indianapolis, IN; FCA; VP JA; Fr Clb; FHA; Lat Clb; Iv Tech; Bus.

MCMURTRY, TROY; Rockville HS; Rockville, IN; 15/100 Aud/Vis; Band; Chrh Wkr; FCA; Hon Rl; NHS; Yth Flsp; Lat Clb; Letter Glf; Letter Wrstlng; Purdue Univ; Elec Engr.

MCNABB, LYNNADA; Ithaca Public Schls; Ithaca, MI; Band; Chrs; Debate Tm; Hon Rl; Orch; Sch Mus; Yrbk; 4-H; 4-H Awd; Central Michigan Univ; Music.

MCNABB, MICHAEL; Grosse Ile HS; Grosse Ile, MI; Trk; Pres Awd; Univ; Mech Engr.

MCNABB, NANCY L; Marlington HS; Alliance, OH; Hon Rl; Lbry Ade; NHS; Red Cr Ade; Sch Mus; Rptr Yrbk; Spn Clb; Trk; Bus Schl; Acctg.

MCNAIR, BRUCE G; Western Hills HS; Cincinnati, OH; 9/780 Am Leg Boys St; Boy Scts; Chrh Wkr; Hon Rl; Jr NHS; Lat Clb; Letter Crs Cntry; Letter Glf; Letter Trk; Cit Awd; Univ; Math.

MCNAIR, LA TONIA; Roosevelt HS; Gary, IN; 6 7/534 Band; Chrh Wkr; Cmnty Wkr; Hon Rl; Jr NHS; Off Ade; ROTC; Sch Mus; Sch Pl; Trk; Indiana Univ; Law.

MCNALLY, STEVE; Lakeview HS; Battle Creek, MI; Boy Scts; Hon Rl; Capt Bsbl; IM Sprt; Finalist In Mi Math Prz Comptn 78; Central Michigan Univ; Engr.

MCNAMARA, DIANNE; Midland HS; Midland, MI; Hon Rl; NHS; Yth Flsp; DECA; Swmmng; Pom Pon; Tmr; Wayne St Univ; Law.

MCNAMARA, JAY; Ross Sr HS; Hamilton, OH; 8/240 Cls Rep Frsh Cls; Cls Rep Soph Cls; VP Jr Cls; Am Leg Boys St; Hon Rl; Pres NHS; Bsbl; Bsktbl; Univ.

MCNAMARA, MAUREEN; Owosso HS; Owosso, MI; Girl Scts; Y-Teens; Lat Clb; Swmmng; GAA;.

MCNAMARA, NANCY; St Mary Academy; Indianapolis, IN; 42/148 Sec Frsh Cls; Pres Soph Cls; Chrs; Chrh Wkr; Hon Rl; JA; Red Cr Ade; Stu Cncl; Fr Clb; Hoosier Schlr 79; Purdue Univ; Agri.

MCNAMARA, ROSEMARY; Willoughby S HS; Willoughby, OH; 42/416 Hon Rl; NHS; Stu Cncl; Capt Bsktbl; Cleveland St Univ; Acctg.

MCNAMARA, THOMAS; Fairview HS; Fairview Pk, OH; 20/230 Hon Rl; NHS; Fr Clb; Bsbl; Glf; IM Sprt; Ohio Univ; Bus Exec.

MCNARY, ANNA; Mechanicsburg HS; Mechanicsburg, OH; Band; Hon Rl; NHS; Stu Cncl; Rptr Yrbk; 4-H; Ger Clb; Pep Clb; Spn Clb; Letter Trk; Ohio St Univ; Micro Bio.

MCNASH, ROBBIN; Morton Sr HS; Hammond, IN; 7/419 Hon Rl; Sprt Ed Sch Nwsp; Bsbl; Letter Bsktbl; Am Leg Awd; Baseball Girls Sr League Softball State For Indiana ANA Champs; Volleyball; Univ.

MCNEAL, DAVID; Martins Ferry HS; Martins Ferry, OH; 3/215 Treas NHS; Spn Clb; Natl Merit Ltr; Rotary Awd; Univ Of Cincinnati; Chem Eng.

MCNEAL, ELLEN; Ridgemont HS; Ridgeway, OH; 1/65 Sec Frsh Cls; Pres Soph Cls; Sec Jr Cls; Pres Band; Sec Chrs; Hon Rl; NHS; Pres Yth Flsp; Ed Sch Nwsp; Sec 4-H; Univ; Music.

MCNEAL, ROSE; Southwestern HS; Oak Hill, OH; Hst Frsh Cls; Pres Soph Cls; Cl Rep Jr Cls; Pres Sr Cls; Band; Chrs; Chrh Wkr; Cmnty Wkr; Drm Mjrt; Hon Rl; Rio Grande Coll; Busns Mgmt.

MCNEAL, ROSE L; Southwestern HS; Oak Hill, OH; 2/42 Pres Soph Cls; Cl Rep Jr Cls; Pres Sr Cls; Band; Chrs; Chrh Wkr; Drm Mjrt; Hon Rl; Lbry Ade; NHS; Dist Miss Ohio FHA Hero; Gallia County Miss Congeniality; Rio Grande Coll; Busns Admin.

MCNEEL, SAMUEL; Pocahontas County HS; Hillsboro, WV; Boy Scts; VP Yth Flsp; 4-H; FFA; College.

MCNEEL, TODD; Battle Creek Central HS; Battle Crk, MI; 5/467 Cls Rep Frsh Cls; Cls Rep Soph Cls; Cl Rep Jr Cls; Aud/Vis; Debate Tm; FCA; Hon Rl; Jr NHS; Natl Forn Lg; NHS; Michigan St Univ; Geol.

MCNEELY, EILEEN; Logan Sr HS; Peach Creek, WV; Hon Rl; NHS; Off Ade; Pres 4-H; 4-H Awd;.

MCNEELY, KAREN K; Park Hills HS; Fairborn, OH; 6/336 Band; Hon Rl; NHS; Stu Cncl; Fr Clb; Lat Clb; Trk; Letter Chrldng; Mgrs; Appionmnt To Hon Semnr Of Metrpltn Dayton 77; Chosen As Top Sci Stdnt By Wilmington Coll 79; Wright St Univ; Nursing.

MCNEICE, BARBARA; Inland Lakes HS; Indian River, MI; Band; Hon Rl; Rptr Yrbk; 4-H; Bsktbl; GAA; IM Sprt; Mgrs; Michigan St Univ; Bus Admin.

MCNEICE, CINDY; Frank Cody HS; Detroit, MI; 35/550 Girl Scts; Hon Rl; Sct Actv; Coach Actv; GAA; Univ Of Detroit; Dental Hygienist.

MCNEIL, JEANNE; Grand Ledge HS; Lansing, MI; 1/400 Val; Hon Rl; Jr NHS; VP NHS; Stu Cncl; Yrbk; Lat Clb; IM Sprt; Natl Merit Ltr; Michigan St Univ; Acctg.

MCNEIL, THOMAS; Edward Lee Mc Clain HS; Greenfield, OH; Am Leg Boys St; Boy Scts; Quill & Scroll; Ed Sch Nwsp; Glf; Swmmng; Am Leg Awd; Univ Of Cincinnati; Art.

MCNEILL, CAROL A; Pocahontas County HS; Buckeye, WV; Band; Chrs; Chrh Wkr; Cmnty Wkr; Sch Pl; Drama Clb; 4-H; Pep Clb; Chrldng; 4-H Awd; Honors Prog; College.

MCNEVIN, ANNE M; Carmel HS; Indianapolis, IN; 347/657 Hon Rl; DECA; Lat Clb; Arizona Univ; Law Enforcement.

MCNICHOLS, CHRISTY; Southeastern HS; Londonderry, OH; 19/100 VP Jr Cls; Band; Jr NHS; NHS; Stu Cncl; Yrbk; FTA; Spn Clb; Letter Trk; Chrldng; Coll.

MCNICHOLS, KIM; Zane Trace HS; Laurelville, OH; Band; Chrs; Debate Tm; Girl Scts; Hon Rl; Pol Wkr; Rptr Sch Nwsp; 4-H; OEA; Rcvd All Four Torch Awrds In Offc Educ Assoc Exec & Diplomat 78 & Stateswmn & Ambassador 79; Circleville Bible Coll; Sec.

MCNISH, ALAN J; Arthur Hill HS; Saginaw, MI; Hon Rl; Letter Glf; Hockey; Univ; Civil Engr.

MCNULTY, JAMES M; Oakwood HS; Dayton, OH; Boy Scts; Hon Rl; Y-Teens; Capt Ftbl; Trk; College; Law Bus.

MCNULTY, JENNIFER; Livonia Franklin HS; Westland, MI; Cls Rep Frsh Cls; Chrh Wkr; Hon Rl; Letter Bsbl; Letter Bsktbl; Trk; GAA; Summa Cum Laude 77 78 & 78 79; Univ; Drama.

MCNULTY, REGAN; Northmont HS; Dayton, OH; Boy Scts; Hon Rl; Notre Dame Univ; Mech Engr.

MCPEAK, BARBARA; Sandusky HS; Sandusky, OH; Chrh Wkr; Hon Rl; Univ; Educ.

MCPEEK, DAVID; Watkins Memorial HS; Pataskala, OH; Boy Scts; Chrs; Chrh Wkr; Sct Actv; Yth Flsp; Ohio St Univ; Photo Jrnlsm.

MCPHAIL, DIANNE; Adlai Stevenson HS; Sterling Hts, MI; 137/570 Band; Hon Rl; Sch Mus; Macomb County Comm Coll; Med.

MCPHEE, KATHLEEN M; Adlai Stevenson HS; Livonia, MI; 1/700 Cls Rep Sr Cls; Val; Am Leg Aux Girls St; Cmp Fr Grls; Chrs; Chrh Wkr; Cmnty Wkr; Debate Tm; Hosp Ade; Lit Mag; Univ Of Michigan; Pre Med.

MCPHERSON, DALE; Pontiac Central HS; Pontiac, MI; Hon Rl; Rptr Sch Nwsp; Michigan St Univ; Engr.

MCPHERSON, LORI; Napoleon HS; Napoleon, OH; 1/250 Cls Rep Frsh Cls; Cls Rep Soph Cls; Cl Rep Jr Cls; Cls Rep Sr Cls; Band; Chrh Wkr; Girl Scts; Hon Rl; NHS; Orch; Miami Univ; Elem Ed.

MCPHERSON, ROBERT; Grosse Point North HS; Grosse Pt Wds, MI; 20/500 Hon Rl; College; Optometry.

MCPHILLIPS, MICHAEL; Lake Catholic HS; Chesterland, OH; Am Leg Boys St; Hon Rl; Sch Mus; Sch Pl; Stg Crw; Treas Stu Cncl; Drama Clb; Am Leg Awd; John Carroll Univ.

MCPIKE, JEFFREY D; Medora HS; Medora, IN; VP Frsh Cls; VP Soph Cls; Pres Sr Cls; Am Leg Boys St; Chrh Wkr; Hon Rl; Jr NHS; NHS; Stu Cncl; Yrbk; Perfect Attendance Awd; Lettermens Club; Pres Stu Council; Indianapolis Univ; Ind Engr.

MCPIKE, JONATHAN D; Bedford N Lawrence HS; Bedford, IN; 36/400 Band; Chrh Wkr; Cmnty Wkr; Hon Rl; Mdrgl; NHS; Orch; Pol Wkr; Sch Mus; Beta Clb; GMI; Engr.

MCPIKE, SARAH J; Bedford N Lawrence HS; Springville, IN; 4/380 Band; Chrs; Chrh Wkr; Cmnty Wkr; Hon Rl; Hosp Ade; NHS; Beta Clb; Fr Clb; Mth Clb; Harding Coll; Spec Educ.

MCQUADE, PATRICIA; Willow Run HS; Ypsilanti, MI; Cls Rep Frsh Cls; Cls Rep Soph Cls; Cl Rep Jr Cls; Hon Rl; Jr NHS; NHS; Rptr Yrbk; Yrbk; Bsbl; Swmmng; Mic State; Med.

MCQUAID, JEANIE; Chesapeake HS; Chesapeake, OH; Pres Chrs; Chrh Wkr; Hon Rl; Sch Mus;.

MCQUAID, PAM; Lincoln HS; Lumberport S, WV; Cls Rep Frsh Cls; Cl Rep Jr Cls; Cmp Fr Grls; Chrs; Chrh Wkr; Cmnty Wkr; Hon Rl; Jr NHS; Lbry Ade; NHS; West Liberty St Coll; Dent Hygnst.

MCQUAIN, CRYSTAL; Grafton HS; Grafton, WV; Band; Chrs; Hon Rl; Lbry Ade; Pol Wkr; Sch Pl; Drama Clb; 4-H; Pep Clb; Letter Chrldng; Coach Of Pop Warner Ree Weed Pom Pom Cheerldrs 78; Church Girls Vllybll Tm Won St Champ 77; Alderson Broaddus Univ; Phys Asst.

MCQUARTERS, REGINA; Cass Tech HS; Detroit, MI; Chrh Wkr; NHS; Y-Teens; Metropolitan Detroit Yth Found Awd; Univ Of Michigan; Elem Ed.

MCQUAY, GINA M; Waverly HS; Waverly, OH; 33/167 Sec Jr Cls; Band; Drl Tm; Off Ade; Fr Clb; Pep Clb; Trk; Pom Pon; Pres Awd; Track 1st Pl Mile

Relay 77 & 78; Schslhp Team Altrn French M76 & 77; Shcslh Team Altrnt Algbr 2i 78; Univ; Acctg.

MCQUEEN, BECKY; Laurel HS; Laurel, IN; 2/29 Cls Rep Frsh Cls; Cls Rep Soph Cls; Pres Jr Cls; Cl Rep Jr Cls; Cls Rep Sr Cls; Chrs; Hon Rl; Sec NHS; Pres Stu Cncl; Ed Yrbk; Indiana Ctrl Univ.

MCQUEEN, EUGENE; Princeton Community HS; Princeton, IN; Chrh Wkr; FCA; Boys Clb Am; Bsktbl; Ftbl; Trk; Wrstlng; IM Sprt; Rose Hulman; Engineering.

MCQUEEN, JULIE; Morrice Area School; Owosso, MI; 1/80 Trs Soph Cls; Cl Rep Jr Cls; Pres Sr Cls; Hon Rl; NHS; Sch Pl; Fr Clb; Letter Bsbl; Letter Bsktbl; Chrldng; Math & Sci Awd; Eng Awd; Michigan St Univ; Bio.

MCQUEEN, LISA; Laurel HS; Laurel, IN; 3/31 VP Sr Cls; Band; Chrs; Drl Tm; Hon Rl; Sec NHS; Yrbk; Sch Nwsp; Indiana Cntrl Univ; Reg Nurse.

MCQUEEN, LORI M; Southwestern HS; Flat Rock, IN; 7/72 Sec Frsh Cls; Cls Rep Soph Cls; Sec Jr Cls; Band; Hon Rl; NHS; Rptr Sch Nwsp; Drama Clb; 4-H; Pep Clb; Purdue Univ; Bio Sci.

MCQUEEN, SUSAN; Marian HS; Bloomfield Hl, MI; Girl Scts; Stg Crw; Rdo Clb; Bsktbl; Gym; Socr; IM Sprt; Northern Mich; Tchr.

MCQUIGG, MOLLY; Rutheford B Hayes HS; Delaware, OH; AFS; Band; Chrs; Hon Rl; Jr NHS; Orch; Quill & Scroll; College; Pre Med.

MCQUILKIN, BRIAN; Salem Sr HS; Salem, OH; 35/300 Band; FCA; Hon Rl; Off Ade; Letter Ftbl; Letter Ten; Ohio St Univ; Coach.

MCQUILLAN, DAN; Lake Michigan Catholic HS; St Joseph, MI; Pres Soph Cls; Cl Rep Jr Cls; Hon Rl; Stu Cncl; Letter Bsbl; Letter Bsktbl; Letter Ftbl; Bausch & Lomb Awd; Holy Cross Coll; Medicine.

MCQUILLAN, DANIEL; Lake Michigan Cath HS; St Joseph, MI; 5/100 Pres Soph Cls; Cl Rep Jr Cls; Chrh Wkr; Hon Rl; NHS; Pol Wkr; FDA; Spn Clb; Letter Bsbl; Letter Bsktbl; Univ; Pre Med.

MCQUISTON, GREGORY; Richmond HS; Richmond, IN; 12/550 Cls Rep Soph Cls; VP Jr Cls; Cls Rep Sr Cls; NHS; Yth Flsp; Lion Awd; Natl Merit Ltr; General Motors Inst; Mech Engr.

MCQUISTON, MARILOU; Ashley Community HS; Brant, MI; 7/28 Sec Frsh Cls; Sec Soph Cls; Sec Jr Cls; Trs Sr Cls; Hon Rl; NHS; Off Ade; Lansing Bus Inst; Exec Secretary.

MCRAE, JOSEPH; Quincy HS; Quincy, MI; Band; JA; Off Ade; Orch; PAVAS; Sch Pl; Drama Clb; 4-H; Fr Clb; Univ; Pre Law.

MCRAE, MARY; Thomas M Cooley HS; Detroit, MI; 10/495 Chrh Wkr; Hon Rl; NHS; Off Ade; Yth Flsp; Mic St Univ; Chem Engr.

MCRAE, STEVEN A; West Side HS; Gary, IN; Band; Chrs; Chrh Wkr; Cmnty Wkr; JA; Natl Forn Lg; Orch; Sch Mus; Sch Pl; Stg Crw; Ivy Tech; Radio & Tv.

MCREYNOLDS, MICHELE M; Adlai Stevenson HS; Livonia, MI; 13/810 Am Leg Aux Girls St; Sec Chrs; Cmnty Wkr; Debate Tm; Natl Forn Lg; Stu Cncl; Natl Merit SF; Voice Dem Awd; Univ Of Michigan; Bus.

MCRILL, BRIAN; Riverdale HS; Arlington, OH; Am Leg Boys St; Chrs; Chrh Wkr; Hon Rl; Voc Schl; Elec.

MCRILL, JANE; Riverdale HS; Mt Blanchard, OH; Chrs; Chrh Wkr; Hon Rl;.

MCROBERTS, BILL; Mathews HS; Cortland, OH; 19/160 Band; Boy Scts; Hon Rl; Off Ade; Orch; Fr Clb; FTA; Cit Awd; Kiwan Awd; Youngstown St Univ; Comp Sci.

MCROBERTS, LORI; Danville Comm HS; Danville, IN; 3/150 Band; Chrh Wkr; Hon Rl; NHS; Sch Mus; Spn Clb; Trk; Cit Awd; Outstanding Soph Awd; Olivet Nazarene Coll; Medicine.

MCROBERTS, THOMAS E; Piketon HS; Piketon, OH; 7/105 Pres Frsh Cls; Chrs; Chrh Wkr; Cmnty Wkr; Hon Rl; Pres NHS; Sch Mus; Stg Crw; Yrbk; 4-H; Ohio St Univ; Agri.

MCSORLEY, JOHN A; St Florian HS; Detroit, MI; Boy Scts; Chrs; Chrh Wkr; Hon Rl; NHS; Yrbk; Mth Clb; Sci Clb; Lawrence Inst Of Tech; Elec Engr.

MCSWINEY, GARY; Centerville HS; Cnterville, OH; 286/685 Cls Rep Frsh Cls; Band; Hon Rl; Natl Forn Lg; NHS; Off Ade; Orch; Boys Clb Am; Univ Of Cin; Law.

MCTAGGART, MELINDA; Bad Axe HS; Bad Axe, MI; 4/137 Trs Frsh Cls; Cls Rep Soph Cls; Pres Jr Cls; Pres Sr Cls; Hon Rl; NHS; Sch Mus; Sch Pl; Stu Cncl; 4-H; Michigan St Univ; Bus.

MCTYRE, JAMES W; Huntington HS; Huntington, WV; 5/300 Am Leg Boys St; Chrs; Debate Tm; NHS; Stu Cncl; Drama Clb; Eng Clb; Key Clb; Lat Clb; Mth Clb; Univ.

MCVAN, MAUREEN; Woodridge HS; Cuyahoga Fls, OH; 10/132 Trs Jr Cls; Chrs; Debate Tm; Drl Tm; Hon Rl; MMM; Sec NHS; College.

MCVAY, RANDALL R; Ripley HS; Ripley, WV; 15/250 Am Leg Boys St; Hon Rl; Jr NHS; Off Ade; Pol Wkr; Stg Crw; IM Sprt; West Virginia St Univ; Bus Admin.

MCVETY, STEVEN; Minster Local HS; Minster, OH; Cmnty Wkr; Hon Rl; Pol Wkr; Stg Crw; Drama Clb; Coach Actv; Mgrs; Scr Kpr; Tmr; Univ Of Cincinnati; Education.

MCVEY, BARBARA; Marion HS; Marion, IN; 28/745 Chrh Wkr; Hon Rl; Jr NHS; NHS; Pep Clb; Purdue Univ; Speech And Hearing Ther.

MCVEY, KRISTY; Vinton Cnty Consolid HS; New Plymouth, OH; 7/150 Band; Chrs; FCA; Hon Rl; Jr NHS; NHS; Sch Pl; Ed Yrbk; Rptr Sch Nwsp; Drama Clb; Ohi Univ; Bus Admin.

MCVEY, MARK; Midland Trial HS; Ansted, WV; Band; Hon Rl; Jr NHS; NHS; Stg Crw; Drama Clb; 4-H; Pep Clb; VICA; Scr Kpr; Glenville Univ; Forestry.

MCVEY, SHERYL; Marion Adams HS; Sheridan, IN; 20/100 Band; FCA; Letter Trk; Voc Schl; Body Shop.

MCVICKER, CURT; Madison Comprehensive HS; Mansfield, OH; Am Leg Boys St; Band; Lbry Ade; NHS; VP Fr Clb; Key Clb; Letter Bsktbl; Letter Ftbl; Letter Trk; Most Imprvd Plyr Bsktbl 78; Lg Leading Punter Ftbl 78; Comp Sci.

MCVICKER, PATRICK; St Francis De Sales HS; Toledo, OH; Chrs; Hon Rl; Sch Mus; Crs Cntry; Trk; IM Sprt; Ohi State Univ; Bus Admin.

MCVICKER, TERRI; R B Chamberlin HS; Twinsburg, OH; VP Jr Cls; Yth Flsp; Coll; Radiologic Tech.

MCVITTY, KELLY; South Harrison HS; Lost Creek, WV; 15/85 Sec Frsh Cls; Pres Soph Cls; Sec Jr Cls; Band; Girl Scts; Hon Rl; Jr NHS; NHS; Stg Crw; Stu Cncl; Vllybl Team Explorers; Fairmont St Coll; X Ray Tech.

MCWATERS, SUSAN; Inland Lakes HS; Afton, MI; VP Soph Cls; VP Jr Cls; VP Sr Cls; Band; Hon Rl; Stu Cncl; 4-H; Cit Awd; 4-H Awd; Northern Central Mi College; Nursing.

MCWILLIAMS, CINDY; Clay HS; South Bend, IN; 63/496 Cls Rep Frsh Cls; Cl Rep Jr Cls; Band; Chrs; Chrh Wkr; Cmnty Wkr; Drl Tm; Girl Scts; Hon Rl; Jr NHS; Ball St Univ; Social Science.

MEACHAM, ROGER; Penn HS; Mishawaka, IN; 51/498 Cls Rep Frsh Cls; Cl Rep Jr Cls; Boy Scts; Cmnty Wkr; FCA; Hon Rl; Jr NHS; Mod UN; Natl Forn Lg; NHS; Univ Of Alabama; Golf Course Mgmt.

MEAD, C; Beal City Public HS; Weidman, MI; Cls Rep Frsh Cls; VP Soph Cls; Band; Chrh Wkr; Hon Rl; Lbry Ade; Sch Mus; Sch Pl; Stg Crw; Stu Cncl; Central Michigan Univ; Med Tech.

MEAD, LONNIE; Pymatuning HS; Andover, OH; Aud/Vis; Sch Pl; Stg Crw; 4-H; FFA; FTA; Bsktbl; Crs Cntry; Talen Prog Ntl FFA Convention 1978; Washington Conf Prog 1977; St Farmer Degree FFA 1979; Kent St Univ; Agri Educ.

MEAD, MICHELE; Alcona HS; Lincoln, MI; Band; Hon Rl; Jr NHS; NHS; Pep Clb; Letter Trk; PPFtbl; Lake Superior St Coll; Reg Nurse.

MEAD, PATRICIA; Adrian HS; Adrian, MI; 91/386 Chrh Wkr; Hon Rl; Spn Clb; Central Mic Univ.

MEADE, BRYAN; Chillicothe HS; Chillicothe, OH; Boy Scts; Chrs; Hon Rl; NHS; Off Ade; 4-H; Ftbl; Trk; Mgrs; 4-H Awd; Ohio State Univ; Commrcl Pilot.

MEADE, DREXEL; Chapmanville HS; Chapmanville, WV; Pres Frsh Cls; Cls Rep Soph Cls; Pres Jr Cls; Am Leg Boys St; Hon Rl; Jr NHS; Stu Cncl; VP Beta Clb; Letter Bsktbl; Letter Ftbl; Pres Physical Fitness Awd; All Logan Cnty Ftbl & Bsktbl & Phys Ed; Mechanical Drawing Awd; College; Busns Mgmt.

MEADE, MICHAEL; Tecumseh HS; Medway, OH; 57/344 AFS; Chrs; Hon Rl; Jr NHS; NHS; Fr Clb; Perfect Attndnce Awrd 1977; Wright St Univ; Bio.

MEADER, ALISON; Bay HS; Bay Village, OH; Drl Tm; Gym; Chrldng; Pom Pon; Ohio St Univ; Dance.

MEADOR, CHERYL; Charlestown HS; Otisco, IN; 30/179 Band; Girl Scts; Hon Rl; JA; Drama Clb; Fr Clb; FTA; Crs Cntry; Trk; Mgrs; Bus Schl; Med Sec.

MEADOR, CONNIE; Willow Run HS; Ypsilanti, MI; Hon Rl; Off Ade; Cit Awd; Awrd Of Honor 76; Awrd Of Honor 77; Univ Of Michigan; Bus Admin.

MEADOR, DAPHNE; Ursuline Academy; Cincinnati, OH; Schl Of Nursing; Nurse.

MEADOWS, ARCHIE; Hannan Trace HS; Crown City, OH; Pres Frsh Cls; Pres Soph Cls; Trs Jr Cls; Hon Rl; Stu Cncl; Beta Clb; 4-H; Pep Clb; Letter Bsktbl; Capt Ftbl; 4 H 5 Trophies In Entomology & 2 Pins; 1 Trphy In Beef Cattle 70; Eng II III Hstry Alg Geom Sci Dr Ed Awd; Univ.

MEADOWS, DEBORAH; Pt Pleasant HS; Henderson, WV; 4/270 NHS; Stu Cncl; FHA; Spn Clb; DAR Awd; Hi Y Clb Historian 79; Harold Harding Memrl Essay Contest Winner 79; Univ; Med Lab Tech.

MEADOWS, JACQUELINE; South Charleston HS; S Charleston, WV; Pres Jr Cls; VP Jr Cls; Band; Chrs; Girl Scts; Hon Rl; Sch Mus; Sct Actv; Stu Cncl; Yth Flsp; Vc Pres Of Kanawha Cnty Assn Of Stdtn Councl 79; Mbr Of Spansih Honsoc 78 80; S Charelstn Chrl 79; Fshns.

MEADOWS, KAREN; Lemon Monroe HS; Middletown, OH; 29/278 Chrs; Cmnty Wkr; Hon Rl; Hosp Ade; NHS; Off Ade; Sch Mus; Sch Pl; Stu Cncl; Trk; Eastern Kentucky Univ.

MEADOWS, KAREN; Princeton HS; Princeton, WV; 53/378 Trs Frsh Cls; Band; Chrs; Hon Rl; Mdrgl; Stu Cncl; Drama Clb; Keyettes; Ten; Concord College; Music.

MEADOWS, KRISTINA JO; Independence HS; Crab Orchard, WV; VP Jr Cls; Band; Chrh Wkr; Girl Scts; Hon Rl; JA; Beta Clb; 4-H; Treas Fr Clb; Pres FHA; Bio Awd 1978; Phys Ed Awd 1978; Glenville St Coll; Elem Educ.

MEADOWS, LINETTE; Ovid Elsie HS; Ovid, MI; Band; Girl Scts; Hon Rl; Hosp Ade; Sch Pl; Yth Flsp; 4-H; Trk; PPFtbl; 4-H Awd; Univ Of Mic; Phys Ther.

MEADOWS, LORI; Taylor HS; Kokomo, IN; 6/200 Am Leg Aux Girls St; Band; Hon Rl; Sec NHS; Sec Stu Cncl; 4-H; Pep Clb; Bsktbl; Ball State Univ; Accgt.

MEADOWS, MARY; Groveport Madison HS; Columbus, OH; 7/400 Drl Tm; Hon Rl; NHS; Rptr Sch Nwsp; Mat Maids; Franklin Univ; Acctg.

MEADOWS, MICHAEL; Lawrence North HS; Indianapolis, IN; 1/390 Pres Frsh Cls; Cls Rep Soph Cls; Cl Rep Jr Cls; Val; Chrs; FCA; NHS; Bsbl; Bsktbl; Ftbl; Hanover.

MEADOWS, NELSON; Spanishburg HS; Princeton, WV; 15/33 Princeton Voca Tech Center; Welding.

MEADOWS, PAMELA J; Athens HS; Athens, WV; 12/60 Sec Frsh Cls; Girl Scts; Hon Rl; Rptr Yrbk; FHA; FTA; Keyettes; Pep Clb; Sci Clb; Bsbl; Educ.

MEADOWS, PAMEY R; Edgewood HS; Ellettsville, IN; 19/194 VP Soph Cls; Cls Rep Soph Cls; Cl Rep Jr Cls; Cls Rep Sr Cls; Band; Drl Tm; FCA; Hon Rl; NHS; Off Ade; Bus Schl; Sec.

MEADOWS, TOMMY; Whitko HS; N Manchester, IN; 20/150 FFA; Sci Clb; Nashville Auto Diesel Coll; Mechanic.

MEAL, CYNTHIA; Kelloggsville HS; Kentwood, MI; Trs Soph Cls; Pres Jr Cls; Hon Rl; Lbry Ade; NHS; Rptr Sch Nwsp; Letter Ten; Pom Pon; DAR Awd; Natl Merit Schl; Michigan St Univ; Art.

MEALEY, SHAWN; Midland HS; Midland, MI; Chrh Wkr; FCA; Hon Rl; Yth Flsp; Letter Ftbl; Mgrs; Univ; Theology.

MEANEY, LEO; Ashtabula County Jt Voc HS; Jefferson, OH; 27/208 Cls Rep Sr Cls; Hon Rl; OEA; Lakeland Comm Coll; Data Processing.

MEANS, KAREN; Marysville HS; Marysville, OH; Am Leg Aux Girls St; Band; Girl Scts; Hon Rl; Lit Mag; NHS; Sch Mus; Stu Cncl; Yth Flsp; 4-H; Attnded Hon Banquet My Frsh Soph & Jr Yrs; Columbus Tech Inst; Bus.

MEANS, KELLI; Doddridge County HS; West Union, WV; Hon Rl; NHS; Sch Pl; Stu Cncl; Yth Flsp; Rptr Yrbk; Ed Sch Nwsp; Fr Clb; Pep Clb; Twrlr; Coll; Jrnlsm.

MEANS, LAWRETTA; Warrensville Heights HS; Warrensvl Hts, OH; Cls Rep Frsh Cls; Cmp Fr Grls; Drl Tm; Hon Rl; JA; Jr NHS; Sch Mus; Sch Pl; Stu Cncl; Rptr Yrbk; Cincinnati State; Psychology.

MEANS, TAMI; Stivers Patterson Co Op HS; Dayton, OH; Chrs; Girl Scts; JA; Sct Actv; Yth Flsp; VICA; Dayton Bible Coll.

MEARA, JOSEPH; St Charles Prep; Worthington, OH; Boy Scts; Hon Rl; Yrbk; Sch Nwsp; Crs Cntry; Letter Trk; Univ; Chem.

MEARS, ROGER; Avon HS; Indianapolis, IN; 5/200 Chrh Wkr; Hon Rl; Ger Clb; Sci Clb; Ten; IM Sprt; Indiana Univ; Pre Med.

MEARS, SHARON; Seymour HS; Seymour, IN; 10/340 Band; Chrs; Hon Rl; Sch Mus; Sch Pl; Stg Crw; Yth Flsp; Y-Teens; Drama Clb; FTA; Swing Choir Pres; FTA Sec Elect; Majorette Feature Twirler Asst Head Majorette; Head Majorette; Butler Univ; Music.

MEARS, WILLIAM; Bill Mears HS; Munster, IN; Hon Rl; Ger Clb; Bsktbl; Crs Cntry; Glf; Trk; Indiana St Univ; Real Estate.

MECKFESSEL, SUSAN; George Washington HS; Charleston, WV; Cls Rep Sr Cls; Hon Rl; Jr NHS; Stu Cncl; Yth Flsp; Keyettes; Bsktbl; Trk; Natl Merit SF; Coll; Languages.

MECYSSINE, JOSEPH; Munster HS; Munster, IN; Aud/Vis; Boy Scts; Hon Rl; Lbry Ade; Off Ade; Univ Of Colorado.

MEDAK, KATHY; Hubbord HS; Hubbard, OH; Chrh Wkr; Hon Rl; Off Ade; Sch Mus; Sdlty; IM Sprt; Natl Merit Ltr; Lewis Weinberger; Cosmetology.

MEDAR, MELISSA; Berea HS; Berea, OH; 48/551 Cls Rep Frsh Cls; Cls Rep Soph Cls; Hst Jr Cls; Cls Rep Sr Cls; Band; Chrh Wkr; Cmnty Wkr; Girl Scts; Hon Rl; Hosp Ade; Sr Girl Scout Ach Awd; Outstndng Jr Data Processing; Grand Escort For Grand Assemble For Rainbow For Girls; Ohio St Univ; Law.

MEDARIS, GINA; Brownsburg HS; Brownsburg, IN; 3/314 Band; Chrh Wkr; Drm Mjrt; Hon Rl; Jr NHS; Lit Mag; NHS; Baylor Univ; Journalism.

MEDELLIN, MARY; Roosevelt HS; E Chicago, IN; Rptr Sch Nwsp; Sec Civ Clb; FHA; FTA; Lat Clb; Spn Clb; Chrldng; Mat Maids; Pom Pon; Bus Schl; Bus.

MEDEN, BRENDA; Gwinn HS; Gwinn, MI; VP Soph Cls; VP Jr Cls; Cl Rep Jr Cls; Band; Drl Tm; Hon Rl; Rptr Yrbk; 4-H; Letter Gym; Letter Ten; Univ; Stewardess.

MEDINA, ENRICO; Bishop Noll Institute; Munster, IN; 80/321 Hon Rl; Mth Clb; Bsktbl; Letter Socr; Univ; Pre Dent.

MEDINA, TINA M; Ursuline HS; Campbell, OH; 82/286 Chrs; Hon Rl; Off Ade; FNA; VP Sci Clb; St Elizabeth Schl Of Nrsg; Nrs.

MEDIODIA, LISA; Grosse Pointe North HS; Grosse Pt Shrs, MI; Girl Scts; Hon Rl; Hosp Ade; NHS; Letter Swmmng; Letter Trk; College; Nursing.

MEDLER, GREG; Berkley HS; Berkley, MI; Boy Scts; Chrh Wkr; Off Ade; Yth Flsp; Letter Crs Cntry; Swmmng; Trk; Wrstlng; Michigan St Univ; Engr.

MEDLEY, CAROL; Fort Frye HS; Lower Salem, OH; Hon Rl; Stu Cncl; Rptr Sch Nwsp; Sec FTA; Letter Bsktbl; English Honorary & Awd; College; Journalism.

MEDLEY, JAMES; Cadiz HS; Cadiz, OH; 1/102 Cls Rep Sr Cls; Val; Am Leg Boys St; Aud/Vis; FCA; Hon Rl; NHS; Yth Flsp; Lat Clb; Ftbl; Awds For Outstndng In Class 1975; Bio Health Algebra II 1977; American Lit Latin III Acctg I 1979; Univ; Math.

MEDLEY, TODD; Shelby Sr HS; Shelby, OH; Chrs; Chrh Wkr; Sch Mus; Sch Pl; Stg Crw; Rptr Yrbk; Drama Clb; Fr Clb; Bsktbl; Trk; Univ; Tchr.

MEDLICOTT, BECKY; Madeira HS; Cincinnati, OH; 1/170 Val; Hon Rl; NHS; Sch Mus; Sch Pl; Sec Drama Clb; OEA; Wittenberg Univ; Psychology.

MEDLICOTT, CAROL; Franklin Community HS; Franklin, IN; 1/300 Val; AFS; Band; Chrs; Chrh Wkr; Cmnty Wkr; Hon Rl; Lbry Ade; Mdrgl; NHS; Latin Club Sec & Pres; Drum Major In Training; Butler Univ; Poli Sci.

MEDORS, SCOTT; Westerville S HS; Westerville, OH; Pres Jr Cls; Cl Rep Jr Cls; Pres Sr Cls; Cls Rep Sr Cls; FCA; Hon Rl; Stu Cncl; Yth Flsp; Spn Clb; Letter Bsbl; Ohio Capital Cnfrnce Scholar Athlete Of The Yr; All League Running Back; Kenyon Coll; History.

MEDOWS, CYNTHIA; Marion HS; Marion, IN; 13/648 Chrh Wkr; Hon Rl; Mdrgl; NHS; Orch; Sch Mus; Sch Pl; Stu Cncl; 4-H; Spn Clb; Marion College; Spec Educ.

MEDUNA, LORRIE; Manistee Cath Cntrl HS; Manistee, MI; Hon Rl; Stg Crw; Pep Clb; Bsktbl; Chrldng; Mat Maids; Muskegon Busns Coll; Sec.

MEDVED, ANNETTE; Sandy Valley HS; Waynesburg, OH; 5/100 Chrs; Hon Rl; Lbry Ade; NHS; Quill & Scroll; Ed Yrbk; Rptr Yrbk; Rptr Sch Nwsp; Fr Clb; Univ; Bus.

MEDVES, LEE; Kirtland HS; Kirtland, OH; 13/120 Chrh Wkr; Cmnty Wkr; Hon Rl; Jr NHS; NHS; Spn Clb; Chrldng; PPFtbl; Scr Kpr; College; Public Relations.

MEDVEZ, MARY; Ursuline HS; Campbell, OH; 1/330 Chrh Wkr; Cmnty Wkr; Hon Rl; NHS; FTA; Spn Clb; Religious Ed For The Deaf Awd; College; Health.

MEDWICK, LORI; Champion Sr HS; Warren, OH; Band; Drm Bgl; Drm Mjrt; Girl Scts; Off Ade; Sch Mus; Sch Pl; Yrbk; Twrlr; College; Modeling.

MEE, ROBERT; St Johns HS; De Witt, MI; Am Leg Boys St; Hon Rl; 4-H; FFA; Swmmng; Pres Awd; Michigan St Univ; Jrnlsm.

MEECE, ANNA; Valparaiso HS; Valparaiso, IN; 101/465 Chrs; Girl Scts; Hon Rl; NHS; Sch Mus; Sct Actv; Stg Crw; Y-Teens; Drama Clb; Pres 4-H; 4 H Jr Leader Pres; Mbr Children Of The Amer Revolution; Girls St Fair Schl Awd; Valparaiso Univ; Music.

MEEDS, BOB; Greenville HS; Greenville, OH; Hon Rl; NHS; Quill & Scroll; Ed Yrbk; Rptr Yrbk; Ball St Univ; Jrnlsm.

MEEHAN, BARBARA; Rudyard HS; Rudyard, MI; Band; Chrs; Drm Mjrt; Hon Rl; Jr NHS; NHS; Rptr Yrbk; 4-H; Letter Bsktbl; Capt Swmmng; St Of Mich Competitive Schlrshp; Rudyard Ed Assn Schlrshp; Michigan St Univ; Phys Ed.

MEEHAN, PATRICIA; Notre Dame Acad; Toledo, OH; Hon Rl; Mod UN; NHS; Spn Clb; Bsktbl; IM Sprt; College; Architecture.

MEEK, AMANDA; Wilmington Sr HS; Wilmington, OH; Chrs; Drl Tm; Girl Scts; Stg Crw; Drama Clb; Pep Clb; Mgrs; Univ; Math.

MEEK, CHRISTINE; Galion Sr HS; Kingsport, TN; Band; Chrh Wkr; Girl Scts; Hon Rl; Hosp Ade; NHS; Sch Mus; Pres 4-H; Sec Fr Clb; French Frgn Lang Awd 79; Univ; Librarian.

MEEK, DEBRA; Fairless HS; Brewster, OH; Chrs; Hosp Ade; Off Ade; Stg Crw; Voc Schl; Child Care.

MEEK, TERESA; Coshocton HS; Coshocton, OH; VP Jr Cls; Hst Sr Cls; Hon Rl; Off Ade; Stu Cncl; Sch Nwsp; 4-H; Key Clb; Gym; PPFtbl;.

MEEKER, BRIAN; Fraklin HS; Franklin, OH; Hon Rl; Stg Crw; Fr Clb; IM Sprt; Miami Of Middleton; Dent.

MEEKS, BILLIE; Franklin HS; Franklin, OH; Band; Chrs; Chrh Wkr; Hon Rl; Sch Mus; Sch Pl; Sec Stu Cncl; Pep Clb; VICA; Capt Chrldng; Cosmetologist.

MEEKS, FRANK; Kettering Sr HS; Detroit, MI; College; Nursing.

MEEKS, JERYL A; Orrville Sr HS; Marshallville, OH; 8/177 Band; Chrh Wkr; Hon Rl; NHS; Orch; Treas Y-Teens; Sec FTA; Natl Merit Ltr; Scholastic Honors Awd; Luther Awd; Ohio St Univ; Engr.

MEEKS, LAURIE; Knightstown HS; Knightstown, IN; Chrs; Chrh Wkr; Hon Rl; Sch Mus; Yth Flsp; Rptr Yrbk; FFA; Trk; GAA; IM Sprt;.

MEEKS, LINDA; Kokomo HS; St Mary Of Wds, IN; Stu Cncl; VP Fr Clb; Pep Clb; St Mary Of Woods Univ; French.

MEEKS, LINDA; L C Mohr HS; S Haven, MI; Band; Cmp Fr Grls; Chrs; Chrh Wkr; Girl Scts; Hon Rl; NHS; Central Michigan Univ; Pre Med.

MEEKS, LINDA; L C Mohr HS; South Haven, MI; Band; Cmp Fr Grls; Chrs; Chrh Wkr; Girl Scts; Hon Rl; NHS; Univ Of Mic; Med Doctor.

MEEKS, MARYE; National Trail HS; W Manchester, OH; Band; Chrh Wkr; Hon Rl; NHS; Indiana Voc Tech Schl; Med Tech.

MEEKS, PHYLLIS; Fremont HS; Fremont, IN; 5/50 Am Leg Aux Girls St; Band; Girl Scts; Hon Rl; Treas NHS; Sch Mus; Am Leg Awd; Indiana Univ; X Ray Tech.

MEERSCHAERT, CAROL; Troy HS; Troy, MI; Cls Rep Frsh Cls; Sch Pl; Stu Cncl; Drama Clb; Natl Merit Schl; Univ Of Michigan; Med Tech.

MEES, PAM; Meigs HS; Pomeroy, OH; Band; Off Ade; Fr Clb; Ohio Univ.

MEESE, ANDREW; Cabrini HS; Allen Pk, MI; Hon Rl; NHS; Sch Pl; Drama Clb; Spn Clb; Kiwan Awd; Natl Merit Ltr; Univ Of Mich; Engr.

MEESE, DEWAYNE; Williamsburg HS; Batavia, OH; Boy Scts; Hon Rl; NHS; Sci Clb; Spn Clb; Bsbl; Glf; Mgrs; College; Design Engr.

MEETH, JANINE; Kalamazoo Central HS; Kalamazoo, MI; Cmnty Wkr; Girl Scts; Hon Rl; Mdrgl; Orch; Sch Mus; Swmmng; Opt Clb Awd; W Michigan Univ; Theatre.

MEEUWSEN, LORI; Zeeland HS; Zeeland, MI; Band; Chrh Wkr; Debate Tm; Girl Scts; Hon Rl; Rptr Yrbk; Rptr Sch Nwsp; Lat Clb; PPFtbl; College; Bus.

MEEVES, TERRI; Traverse City HS; Traverse City, MI; Cls Rep Frsh Cls; Band; Hon Rl; Rptr Yrbk; Pep Clb; Letter Trk; Chrldng; Western Mic Univ; Criminal Justice.

MEFFERD, DEBORAH; Dayton Christian HS; Dayton, OH; 1/117 Chrs; Hon Rl; NHS; Sch Pl; Sec Yth Flsp; Rptr Sch Nwsp; 4-H; Huntington Coll.

MEGENITY, NIKKI; Jeffersonville HS; Jeffersonville, IN; FCA; Hon Rl; Hosp Ade; Bsktbl; Trk; PPFtbl; Univ Of Evansville; Spec Educ.

MEGERIAN, MAUREEN; North Farmington HS; Farmington, MI; Cl Rep Jr Cls; Cls Rep Sr Cls; Natl Forn Lg; NHS; Off Ade; Sch Pl; Stg Crw; Drama Clb; College; Journalism.

MEGGITT, JOHN; Milan HS; Milan, MI; 10/180 Hon Rl; NHS; Sch Pl; Stg Crw; Drama Clb; VICA; Western Mich Univ; Pringting Mgmt.

MEGISON, LESLIE; Indian Hill HS; Cincinnati, OH; 12/265 Hon Rl; NHS; Fr Clb; IM Sprt; College; Law.

MEGLAN, DWIGHT; Olentangy HS; Galena, OH; 4/139 Pres Jr Cls; Am Leg Boys St; NHS; Sch Mus; Sch Pl; Drama Clb; 4-H; Fr Clb; Am Leg Awd; DAR Awd; Ohio State Univ; Mech Engr.

MEHL, CATHERINE; Bellaire HS; Neffs, OH; 3/240 Am Leg Aux Girls St; Band; Hon Rl; NHS; Y-Teens; Fr Clb; Rdo Clb; Scr Kpr; Voice Dem Awd; Ohio St Univ; Phys Ther.

MEHLE, ANTHONY; Girard HS; Girard, OH; 1/225 AFS; Band; Capt Debate Tm; Key Clb; Pres Sci Clb; Pres Spn Clb; Am Leg Awd; Univ.

MEHNERT, AMY; Michigan Lutheran Seminary; Bay City, MI; Chrh Wkr; Hon Rl; Yth Flsp; IM Sprt; PPFtbl; Dr Martin Luther Coll; BSE.

MEHNERT, DANA; Alliance HS; Alliance, OH; 7/380 Pres Sr Cls; Am Leg Boys St; CAP; Drl Tm; Hon Rl; VP NHS; Pol Wkr; Stu Cncl; Sci Clb; Spn Clb; Harvard Univ; Law.

MEHOLICK, CAROL; Regina HS; Mayfield Hts, OH; Band; Chrs; Cmnty Wkr; Girl Scts; Hon Rl; Off Ade; Orch; Sch Mus; Sch Pl; Sct Actv; N E Ohio Sci Fair 76; Catholic Educ Endowment Trust 78 79; Miami Univ; Sci.

MEHRINGER, TERRI; Jasper HS; Jasper, IN; VP Soph Cls; Hon Rl; Stu Cncl; Indiana St Univ; Nursing.

MEIBERS, DANIEL; Purcell HS; Cincinnati, OH; Band; Chrh Wkr; Hon Rl; Pol Wkr; Sch Mus; Sch Pl; Drama Clb; Lat Clb; IM Sprt; Univ; Vet.

MEIER, BARBARA; St Francis Desales HS; Columbus, OH; Hon Rl; Red Cr Ade; Trk; Mgrs; Columbus Tech Inst; Engr.

MEIER, JOHN; St Charles Prep; Columbus, OH; Am Leg Boys St; Hon Rl; Jr NHS; NHS; Rptr Yrbk; Notre Dame Univ; Cmnctns.

MEIER, STEVEN; R B Chamberlin HS; Twinsburg, OH; 17/200 Hon Rl; NHS; Bsktbl; Crs Cntry; Trk; IM Sprt; Mgrs; Natl Hnr Soc; 3rd Yr Awd In Track; Tm Capt Awd In Cross Cntry; Ohio St Univ; Civil Engr.

MEIER, STEVEN F; Wickliffe Sr HS; Wickliffe, OH; 1/300 Am Leg Boys St; Band; Boy Scts; Hon Rl; Jr NHS; NHS; Sch Mus; Bsbl; Schlshp Awd Top 9th Grd Stdtn 77; Outstndng Soph Band Mbr 78; Outstndng Jr Band Mbr 79; Univ; Bio.

MEIERS, JULIE J; Lakeland HS; Highland, MI; Band; Chrs; Hon Rl; Jr NHS; Sch Mus; Sch Pl; Stu Cncl; Ten; Pres Awd; Michigan Tech Univ; Engr.

MEIERS, SUSAN; Cabrini HS; Allen Pk, MI; 1/162 Cls Rep Frsh Cls; Chrh Wkr; Cmnty Wkr; Hon Rl; Natl Forn Lg; NHS; Sch Pl; Stg Crw; Stu Cncl; Rptr Sch Nwsp; Univ; Bus Admin.

MEIGH, MARTHA J; Bridgeport HS; Brideport, OH; Girl Scts; Hon Rl; Hosp Ade; 4-H; FHA; Lat Clb; Pep Clb; Mat Maids; RN.

MEIGHEN, MARTIN; Norwood HS; Norwood, OH; Treas Chrh Wkr; Hon Rl; JA; Jr NHS; Lbry Ade; Lit Mag; Stu Cncl; Fr Clb; Key Clb; Mth Clb; Univ.

MEILINK, KIM; Sylvania Southview HS; Toledo, OH; 14/275 Chrh Wkr; Cmnty Wkr; Girl Scts; Hon Rl; NHS; Pres PAVAS; Quill & Scroll; Ed Yrbk; Rptr Yrbk; Scr Kpr; Columbus Coll; Commercial Art.

MEIMARIDIS, JOHN; Lake Ridge Academy; Lorain, OH; Aud/Vis; Band; CAP; Debate Tm; Hon Rl; JA; Pol Wkr; Sch Mus; Rptr Yrbk; Sch Nwsp; NEDT Cert For Super Perfrmnc In Natn Wide Admin 77; Univ; Med.

MEINERT, MICHELE; Flushing Sr HS; Flushing, MI; Chrh Wkr; Girl Scts; Pep Clb; Letter Pom Pon; Opt Clb Awd; Ferris Univ; Pharm.

MEINHARDI, LAURA; Whitehall HS; Whitehall, MI; Band; Chrs; Chrh Wkr; Girl Scts; Hon Rl; Hosp Ade; Off Ade; Harding Univ; Home Ec.

MEINHARDT, MAUREEN; Adlai E Stevenson HS; Sterling Hts, MI; 22/570 Am Leg Aux Girls St; Band; Cmp Fr Grls; Drl Tm; Hon Rl; NHS; Off Ade; Pol Wkr; Fr Clb; OEA; Alma Coll; Busns Admin.

MEININGER, MICHELE; Fairmont West HS; Kettering, OH; 45/468 Girl Scts; Hon Rl; NHS; Orch; Sch Mus; Pres Stu Cncl; Yth Flsp; 4 Yr Mbr Dayton Philharmonic Youth Orch; Orch String Quarter; Stu Body Pres; Kettering Summer Field Studies; Coll; Music.

MEINTZ, BRENDA; North Central Area HS; Powers, MI; VP Jr Cls; Am Leg Aux Girls St; Band; Hon Rl; NHS; Sec Beta Clb; 4-H; Pres FHA; Spn Clb; 4-H Awd; College; Fashion Mdse.

MEIRING, GRACE; Pike Delta York Sr HS; Delta, OH; Chrs; Off Ade; 4-H; Fr Clb; FTA; Mth Clb; 4-H Awd; 4 H Sec Of Delta Experts 77; 4 H Pres Of Delta Experts 79; Toledo Univ; Elem Tchr.

MEIRING, JOHN; Southwest Local HS; Ft Recovery, OH; 4/97 Cls Rep Frsh Cls; Chrs; Hon Rl; Jr NHS; NHS; Stg Crw; Ger Clb; Rdo Clb; Sci Clb; Am Leg Awd; Indiana Inst Of Tech; Aerospace.

MEISEL, CINDY; Vermilion HS; Vermilion, OH; 10/250 Am Leg Aux Girls St; Hon Rl; Sec NHS; Quill & Scroll; Sch Pl; Rptr Yrbk; Drama Clb; Fr Clb; Spn Clb; Heidelberg College; Foreign Language.

MEISEL, JANET; Douglas Macarthur HS; Saginaw, MI; Hon Rl; Hosp Ade; VP Fr Clb; Mic State Univ; Pre Law.

MEISENHEIMER, RHONDA; Fruitport HS; Fruitport, MI; 39/280 Band; Chrh Wkr; Hon Rl; NHS; Letter Trk; Muskegon Cmnty Coll; Elem Educ.

MEISER, PATTY; Ross Beatty HS; Dowagiac, MI; Cls Rep Soph Cls; Hon Rl; NHS; 4-H; Grand Champion Market Pig 4 H 78; Southwestern Coll; Sec.

MEISER, VICKIE; Lockland HS; Cincinnati, OH; 9/59 Chrs; Girl Scts; Hon Rl; NHS; OEA; GAA; Legl Sec.

MEISTER, DAVE; La Salle HS; Cincinnati, OH; 4/249 Hon Rl; NHS; Letter Swmmng; Univ Of Cincinnati; Fashion Design.

MEISTER, JEFF; Plymouth HS; Plymouth, IN; Boy Scts; Hon Rl; Jr NHS; Mth Clb; Glf; Swmmng; Ten; Ind Univ; Orthodontics.

MEISTER, LORI; Liberty Center HS; Napoleon, OH; 1 Pres Jr Cls; Cls Rep Sr Cls; Band; Chrs; Chrh Wkr; Hon Rl; MMM; Bowling Green St Unvi; Spec Sci.

MEISTER, PATRICIA; R B Chamberlin HS; Twinsburg, OH; Trs Frsh Cls; Sec Soph Cls; VP Jr Cls; Band; Chrs; FCA; Girl Scts; Hosp Ade; Sch Pl; Stg Crw; Univ Of Toledo; Pre Med.

MEISTER, SHAUNE; Onekama HS; Manistee, MI; 4/70 Band; Hon Rl; NHS; Sch Mus; Sch Pl; Drama Clb; FHA; Bsktbl; 4-H Awd; Natl Merit SF; Grand Valley State College; Spec Ed.

MEITZ, PHILLIP; Cedar Springs HS; Cedar Spgs, MI; Am Leg Boys St; Band; Boy Scts; Cmnty Wkr; Hon Rl; Jr NHS; NHS; Sch Pl; Yrbk; Sci Clb; Blue Lk Music Camp 76; Ferris Univ; Pharm.

MEJIA, SYLVIA; Emerson HS; Gary, IN; Hon Rl; Lat Clb; Cit Awd;.

MEKIS, CAROL; Walled Lake Central HS; W Bloomfield, MI; Hon Rl; Off Ade; Trk; Tmr; Univ Of Michigan; Acctg.

MELANSON, RICHARD; Hubbard HS; Hubbard, OH; Hon Rl; Letter Ftbl; IM Sprt; Pres Awd; Coll; Civil Engr.

MELBARDIS, VICTOR; Brownsburg HS; Brownsbg, IN; Cls Rep Frsh Cls; Hon Rl; Stu Cncl; Ger Clb; Ftbl; Letter Wrstlng; IM Sprt; IUPUI; Math.

MELCHER, JANE; Northridge HS; Mc Allen, TX; 4/144 Drl Tm; Hon Rl; Hosp Ade; NHS; Pep Clb; Bsktbl; Hockey; Trk; Mat Maids; Pom Pon; Coll; Nursing.

MELCHIORI, MARK; Jackson County Western HS; Spring Arbor, MI; Boy Scts; Off Ade; Bsbl; Ftbl; Hockey; Coach Actv; IM Sprt; Mich Tech; Engineering.

MELCHIORRE, RENEE; Magnificat HS; Brook Pk, OH; Trs Soph Cls; Sec Jr Cls; Cls Rep Sr Cls; Chrs; Chrh Wkr; NHS; Sch Pl; Stu Cncl; Yrbk; Cuyahoga Cmnty Coll; Office Admin.

MELDRUM, CHRIS; Centerline HS; Warren, MI; 160/450 Band; Boy Scts; Chrh Wkr; CAP; Hon Rl; Sch Mus; Sct Actv; Sci Clb; Letter Crs Cntry; Letter Trk; Univ; Elec.

MELENDY, JOANNA; Olivet HS; Olivet, MI; Am Leg Aux Girls St; Hon Rl; Bsbl; Trk; PPFtbl; Oceanography.

MELESKI, KEVIN; Swan Valley HS; Saginaw, MI; Boy Scts; Chrh Wkr; Cmnty Wkr; Jr NHS; Red Cr Ade; Sct Actv; Letter Bsbl; Letter Ftbl; Letter Hockey; Patrick C Coffey Memrl Schslp 79; Cmnty Educ Awd 78; Michigan St Univ.

MELFI, JOSEPH; Millersport HS; Thornville, OH; Am Leg Boys St; Boy Scts; FCA; Hon Rl; Bsbl; Bsktbl; Ftbl; Letter Trk; DAR Awd; Columbus Tech; Comp.

MELICK, DIANN; Southern Wells Jr Sr HS; Petroleum, IN; 3/95 Am Leg Aux Girls St; Hon Rl; Pres NHS; Letter Bsktbl; Letter Trk; Chrldng; DAR Awd; St Josephs Coll; Law.

MELICK, MARK; Southern Wells Jr Sr HS; Petroleum, IN; 4/90 Cls Rep Soph Cls; Chrh Wkr; Hon Rl; NHS; Pres Yth Flsp; Bsktbl; Ftbl; Letter Glf; Mgrs; Univ; Cmmrcl Art.

MELINIS, CATHY; Brecksville Sr HS; Broadview Hts, OH; Cls Rep Soph Cls; Cl Rep Jr Cls; Band; Chrh Wkr; Off Ade; Red Cr Ade; Sch Mus; Sch Pl; Stg Crw; Treas Stu Cncl; 1st Pl Skit Youngstown Univ Foreign Lang Day 1977; Active In Singing Angels 5 Yrs 1972; Univ; Theater.

MELJAC, MARK; Maple Heights HS; Maple Heights, OH; Hon Rl; NHS; Stg Crw; Cleveland State Univ; Landscape Arch.

MELKA, JANICE; Marquette HS; Marquette, MI; 44/427 Band; Hon Rl; Mgrs; Scr Kpr; Tmr; Mic Tech Univ; Forestry.

MELKERSON, MARK; Anchor Bay HS; New Baltimore, MI; 1/270 Hon Rl; Jr NHS; NHS; VFW Awd; Michigan St Univ; Micro Bio.

MELLEN, CATHY; Olentangy HS; Delaware, OH; 10/133 Hon Rl; NHS; Yth Flsp; 4-H; Fr Clb; Spn Clb; Mgrs; Scr Kpr; Bowling Green St Univ; Child Fam Ser.

MELLEN, DWAINE; Carney Na Deau HS; Carney, MI; 4/26 Pres Jr Cls; Am Leg Boys St; Band; Hon Rl; Sch Pl; Drama Clb; 4-H; Capt Bsktbl; Trk; Cit Awd; Northern Michigan Univ.

MELLERT, BETH; Buckeye HS; Medina, OH; 12/173 Band; Chrs; Girl Scts; Hon Rl; Pep Clb; Spn Clb; GAA; PPFtbl; Race Harness Horses.

MELLOTT, LYNN; Lakeview HS; Cortland, OH; Band; Trs Frsh Cls; VP NHS; VP Stu Cncl; Y-Teens; Yrbk; Beta Clb; Pres Fr Clb; Mth Clb; Univ.

MELLOTT, MARK; Old Fort HS; Old Fort, OH; 4/54 Am Leg Boys St; Band; Boy Scts; Hon Rl; NHS; Sct Actv; Stg Crw; Yrbk; Lat Clb; Bsbl; Air Force Acad; Sci.

MELLOTT, TIMOTHY; Madison Hts HS; Anderson, IN; Ger Clb; VICA; Trk; Voc Schl; Elec.

MELLSTEAD, TIM; Charlotte HS; Charlotte, MI; Boy Scts; Chrh Wkr; FCA; Sch Pl; Sct Actv; 4-H; Pep Clb; IM Sprt; Cit Awd; 4-H Awd;.

MELNICK, BOBBY; Shaker Heights HS; Shaker Hts, OH; Cls Rep Frsh Cls; Hst Soph Cls; Cl Rep Jr Cls; Cls Rep Sr Cls; Cmnty Wkr; Hon Rl; Lit Mag; Rptr Sch Nwsp; FDA; Letter Bsbl; Washington Univ.

MELNICK, KATHLEEN; Milan HS; Milan, MI; Band; Hon Rl; NHS; Sch Mus; Stg Crw; Sec Yth Flsp; Yrbk; Drama Clb; Letter Chrldng; Tmr; Michigan St Univ.

MELOTT, KAREN L; Magnolia HS; New Martinsvile, WV; 9/187 Hon Rl; FBLA; West Virginia Univ; Chem Engr.

MELOY, CAROL; Theodore Roosevelt HS; Kent, OH; 48/350 VP Soph Cls; Cmp Fr Grls; Chrh Wkr; Cmnty Wkr; Girl Scts; Hon Rl; NHS; Letter Hockey; Letter Trk; Coach Actv; College; Law.

MELSA, SUSAN; Clay HS; S Bend, IN; Am Leg Aux Girls St; Boy Scts; Girl Scts; Hon Rl; JA; NHS; Quill & Scroll; Sct Actv; Ed Yrbk; JA Awd; College; Pre Med.

MELSON, DEE; Fairfield HS; Leesburg, OH; Sec Soph Cls; Hst Jr Cls; Band; Cmp Fr Grls; Capt Drl Tm; Hon Rl; Stg Crw; Rptr Yrbk; Drama Clb; FTA;.

MELTON, DON; Lakeland Christian Academy; Warsaw, IN; 1/18 VP Frsh Cls; Pres Soph Cls; Hon Rl; Stu Cncl; Letter Bsktbl; Grace Coll; Bus.

MELTON, ELIZABETH; Magnolia HS; New Martinsvle, WV; Chrh Wkr; Hon Rl; Yth Flsp; Drama Clb; Pep Clb; Mod Dance & Exercise Club; Homecoming Comm; Projct Talented & Gifted; Marshall Univ; Psych.

MELTON, LISA; Poca HS; Poca, WV; Band; Hon Rl; NHS; Off Ade; FBLA; Trk; Chrldng; Marshall Univ; Education.

MELVIN, MARIAN; Elwood Cmnty HS; Elwood, IN; 15/350 Cls Rep Frsh Cls; Cls Rep Soph Cls; Cl Rep Jr Cls; VP Sr Cls; Am Leg Aux Girls St; Hon Rl; Jr NHS; Stu Cncl; Pep Clb; Spn Clb; Univ; Med.

MELZAK, JEFF; Charles F Brush HS; Lyndhurst, OH; Band; Chrs; Hon Rl; Sch Mus; Yrbk; Letter Ten; IM Sprt; Case Western Reserve Univ; Engr.

MEMMER, KATERI; Chesaning Union HS; Chesaning, MI; Aud/Vis; Chrh Wkr; Girl Scts; Hon Rl; Rptr Yrbk; Yrbk; 4-H; FHA; Pep Clb; 4-H Awd; Michigan St Univ.

MENACHER, JULIE; Menominee HS; Menominee, MI; 9/250 Hon Rl; NHS; Northern Michigan Univ.

MENAFEE, LORI A; East HS; Columbus, OH; Hon Rl; OEA; Spn Clb; Univ; Archt Engr.

MENARD, ANNETTE; St Peter & Paul Area HS; Saginaw, MI; 16/116 Sec Am Leg Aux Girls St; Chrs; Girl Scts; Hon Rl; NHS; Off Ade; Yrbk; Ger Clb; Achvmnt Awd In Art 78; John W & Rose E Watson Schlrshp 78; Delta Coll.

MENARD, RENE; Carney Nadeau Pub HS; Nadeau, MI; Cmp Fr Grls; Chrs; Girl Scts; Hon Rl; Sch Pl; Drama Clb; FHA; Pep Clb; Letter Bsktbl; Letter Trk; Coll; Real Estate.

MENAS, GEORGANNE; Fairview HS; Farmington, WV; 11/50 Band; Chrs; Chrh Wkr; Girl Scts; Hon Rl; Lbry Ade; NHS; Off Ade; Stu Cncl; Yth Flsp; West Virginia Univ; Biology.

MENCK, DOUGLAS; Otsego HS; Otsego, MI; 46/216 Boy Scts; Hon Rl; Sct Actv; 4-H; Mgrs; Michigan Tech Univ; Comp Sci.

MENDEL, C; Clinton HS; Manchester, MI; Hon Rl; Sch Mus; Spn Clb; Trk; Univ; Chem Engr.

MENDELSON, STEWART; Wheeling Park HS; Wheeling, WV; Boy Scts; Debate Tm; Fr Clb; Hockey; Miami Univ; Bus Law.

MENDENHALL, ANN; Marion Adams HS; Sheridan, IN; 18/84 Sec Band; Hon Rl; NHS; Off Ade; Capt Bsktbl; Manchester College; Acctg.

MENDENHALL, MARK A; Frontier HS; Newport, OH; 22/120 Cls Rep Frsh Cls; Cls Rep Soph Cls; Cl Rep Jr Cls; NHS; Stu Cncl.

MENDENHALL, SHERRY; Wadsworth Sr HS; Wadsworth, OH; Univ.

MENDEZ, DIANE; Hudson HS; Lyons, OH; Cmp Fr Grls; Chrs; Chrh Wkr; Sch Mus; Sch Nwsp; 4-H; Ten; 4-H Awd; Cert Of Attndnc 72; March Of Dimes Walk Recgntn 76; Recgntn Of Serv Achvmnt Camp Fire 73; Bus Schl; Legal Sec.

MENDEZ, MICHELLE; South Harrison HS; Mt Clare, WV; 9/115 Cls Rep Frsh Cls; Cls Rep Soph Cls; Cl Rep Jr Cls; Band; Chrh Wkr; Hon Rl; Jr NHS; NHS; Sch Pl; Pres Stu Cncl; Public Speaking Pin 77; Citizenship Awd 78; St Wnr Of Poultry Visual Presentations 4 H 77; West Virginia Univ; Law.

MENDEZ, THOMAS; Ontario HS; Mansfield, OH; 4/200 Aud/Vis; Band; Cmnty Wkr; Hon Rl; Jr NHS; NHS; Stg Crw; Stu Cncl; C of C Awd; Univ; Music Educ.

MENDICK, MAUREEN; Floyd Central HS; Lanesville, IN; 51/359 Cls Rep Soph Cls; Chrs; Hon Rl; Pres JA; Stu Cncl; 4-H; Trk; Mgrs; PPFtbl; JA Awd; Mas Inst Of Tech; Engr.

MENDOZA, LAURA; Notre Dame HS; Clarksburg, WV; 7/54 Hosp Ade; Natl Forn Lg; Rptr Yrbk; Mth Clb; Sci Clb; IM Sprt; Twrlr; Pittsburgh Univ; Med.

MENGE, AMY; Ann Arbor Pioneer HS; Ann Arbor, MI; Chrh Wkr; Ger Clb; Letter Bsktbl; Letter Trk; Univ; Oceanogrphy.

MENGEL, PATRICIA; John Adams HS; S Bend, IN; 55/395 Hon Rl; Off Ade; Gym; Trk; PPFtbl; Scr Kpr; College; Recreation.

MENGER, MARCY; Brandon HS; Ortonville, MI; 19/250 Chrs; Girl Scts; Hon Rl; NHS; Sct Actv; Bsbl; Oakland Univ; Med.

MENGERINK, TERESA; Napoleon HS; Napoleon, OH; Chrs; Girl Scts; Hon Rl; Lat Clb; Univ.

MENKEDICK, KEVIN; Greensburg Community HS; Greensburg, IN; 33/203 Band; Hon Rl; JA; NHS; Orch; Ftbl; Purdue Univ; Mech Engr.

MENNINGEN, LINDA; Carey HS; Carey, OH; VP Soph Cls; Sec Jr Cls; Hon Rl; NHS; Sch Pl; Y-Teens; Pres 4-H; Lat Clb; Mth Clb; GAA; Excllnc In Schlrshp Awd 78; Whos Who In Foreign Lang 78; 1st In Cnty For Bread Proj 4 H 76; Nursing Schl; RN.

MENOUGH, ELIZABETH; James A Garfield HS; Garrettsville, OH; Cls Rep Frsh Cls; Pres Soph Cls; Trs Jr Cls; Am Leg Aux Girls St; Band; Chrs; Chrh Wkr; Cmnty Wkr; Hon Rl; NHS; Univ; Psychtrst.

MENTE, MICHAEL; Midland HS; Midland, MI; 17/490 Boy Scts; Hon Rl; Sct Actv; Natl Merit Ltr; Univ Of Mich; Engineer.

MENTEL, MICHAEL; Bishop Ready HS; Columbus, OH; Chrh Wkr; Cmnty Wkr; Pol Wkr; Boys Clb Am; Civ Clb; Letter Ftbl; Trk; Wrstlng; Coach Actv; IM Sprt; Attended Wa Workshop Congressional Seminar 79; Attended Univ Of Notre Dam Summer Sports Camp 78; Univ Of Notre Dame; Pre Law.

MENTER, ANNMARIE; Lumen Christi HS; Jackson, MI; 14/247 Band; Chrs; Hon Rl; JA; NHS; Sch Mus; Sch Pl; Stg Crw; Yth Flsp; Sch Nwsp; Jackson Cmnty Coll; Bus Admin.

MENTER, DAVID; Imlay City HS; Imlay City, MI; 7/162 Am Leg Boys St; Band; NHS; Fr Clb; Crs Cntry; Letter Glf; Trk; Cit Awd; Northwestern Univ.

MENTING, TERESA; La Villa Jr Sr HS; South Bend, IN; NHS; 4-H; Pres Ger Clb; Am Leg Awd; St Josephs Coll; Bus Admin.

MENZEL, TOM; Owendale Gagetown HS; Sebewaing, MI; 15/57 Chrh Wkr; Hon Rl; Sch Pl; Stg Crw; Yth Flsp; Rptr Yrbk; Pres 4-H; Bsktbl; Trk; IM Sprt;.

MERANDA, DONA; Avon Jr Sr HS; Danville, IN; Band; Drl Tm; Girl Scts; Lbry Ade; Yth Flsp; 4-H; Pep Clb; Trk; Mgrs; Twrlr; Bst Rifle Sqd Awds 78; Coll; Retail.

MERCER, DARCIE; Covington HS; Covington, OH; 10/86 Band; Chrs; Hon Rl; Lbry Ade; NHS; Orch; 4-H; Fr Clb; FHA; Pep Clb; Miami Univ.

MERCER, JEFFREY; Padua Franciscan HS; Parma, OH; Band; Chrh Wkr; Hon Rl; Orch; Spn Clb; Univ; Bus Admin.

MERCER, JIM; Jackson HS; Jackson, OH; 29/200 Hon Rl; PAVAS; Lat Clb; Sci Clb; Rio Grande College; Elect Tech.

MERCER, KENNETH L; Jefferson HS; Shenandoah Jct, WV; Cls Rep Soph Cls; Cl Rep Jr Cls; Cls Rep Sr Cls; Band; Hon Rl; NHS; Ten; Wrstlng; Mgrs; Tmr; Golden Horseshoe Wnr 76; Shepherd Coll; Sci.

MERCER, MIKE; Kings HS; South Lebanon, OH; 23/153 Boy Scts; Hon Rl; ROTC; Sch Pl; Sch Nwsp; Spn Clb; Bsbl; Ftbl; IM Sprt; Wagner Univ; Bus Admin.

MERCER, PAUL; Crest View HS; Columbiana, OH; Chrh Wkr; Hon Rl; Yth Flsp; 4-H; Key Clb; Lion Awd; Goshon Coll; Agri Engr.

MERCER, SHARRENE; Montpelier HS; Montpelier, OH; 32/100 Band; Drm Mjrt; Girl Scts; Sch Mus; Fr Clb; GAA; Mat Maids; Twrlr; College; Business Admin.

MERCER, TERESA; Clay Sr HS; Curtice, OH; 33/323 Chrh Wkr; FCA; Girl Scts; Hon Rl; NHS; 4-H; OEA; Bsktbl; GAA;.

MERCHANT, JANE; Marysville HS; Marysville, MI; Cmnty Wkr; NHS; Rptr Sch Nwsp; Fr Clb; Pep Clb; Chrldng; Univ.

MERCHANT, LISA; Greenfield Central HS; Greenfield, IN; PAVAS; Y-Teens; 4-H; OEA; PPFtbl; College; Tech Illistration.

MERCIER, CAROL; Edison Sr HS; Lake Sta, IN; 7/190 Am Leg Aux Girls St; Chrh Wkr; Hon Rl; Jr NHS; Sch Mus; Sec Stu Cncl; Fr Clb; GAA; Outstndngn Stndt 76; Outstndng GAA Mbr 76; Cumberland Coll; Christian Educ.

MERCIER, JULIE; Marquette Sr HS; Marquette, MI; Sec Frsh Cls; Trs Frsh Cls; VP Soph Cls; Cl Rep Jr Cls; Debate Tm; Drl Tm; Drm Mjrt; Hosp Ade; Orch; Stu Cncl; Univ; Med.

MERCIER, KEITH A; Kearsley HS; Flint, MI; Boy Scts; Hon Rl; Sct Actv; Boys Clb Am; Spn Clb; Swmmng; Johnson & Wales Coll; Culinary Arts.

MERCIER, TERESA; Flushing HS; Flushing, MI; 115/522 Cl Rep Jr Cls; Chrs; Cmnty Wkr; Girl Scts;

Hon Rl; Lbry Ade; Mdrgl; Mic State Univ; Pre Med.

MERCK, MARY; Westerville North HS; Westerville, OH; Band; Drl Tm; Hon Rl; NHS; Yth Flsp; Drama Clb; Fr Clb; Pom Pon; PPFtbl; Flag Corp; Alpha Omega; Outstndng Sr Drill Team Mbr; College.

MERCKEL, ROBERT; Turpin HS; Cincinnati, OH; 3/371 Hon Rl; Quill & Scroll; Sch Pl; Yrbk; Ed Sch Nwsp; Drama Clb; Univ; Jrnlsm.

MERCKLE, MARJORIE; Buckeye North HS; Mingo Junction, OH; Chrh Wkr; Hon Rl; Yth Flsp; Bsktbl; Mgrs; Scr Kpr;.

MERCS, LINDA; Marysville HS; Marysville, OH; Hosp Ade;.

MERDIAN, SHARON; Lake Michigan Cath HS; Benton Harbor, MI; 7/102 Hon Rl; Jr NHS; NHS; Cit Awd; Ferris St Univ; Pharm.

MEREDITH, BRIDGET; Miami Trace HS; Wash C H, OH; 1/300 Sec Soph Cls; Am Leg Aux Girls St; Chrh Wkr; Hon Rl; Off Ade; Pres Stu Cncl; Ed Sch Nwsp; 4-H; FTA; GAA; Miami State.

MEREDITH, CHARLES; Fairmont Sr HS; Fairmont, WV; Band; Chrs; Hon Rl; Sch Mus; Sch Pl; Key Clb; Coll; Engr.

MEREDITH, MICHAEL R; Interlochen Arts Acad; Dearborn, MI; Hon Rl; Yrbk; Rptr Sch Nwsp; Mgrs; Pres Awd; Wanye State Univ; Pre Med.

MEREDITH, WILLIAM V; Brookhaven HS; Columbus, OH; 29/434 Cls Rep Frsh Cls; Cls Rep Soph Cls; Cl Rep Jr Cls; Cls Rep Sr Cls; Band; Boy Scts; Chrs; Debate Tm; Hon Rl; NHS; Acad Schlrshp 79; Pres 79 VP 78 Ski Clb; Diploma Of Distinction 79; In The Know Tm 78; Ohio Dominican Univ; Bus.

MERGEL, CAROL A; Shrine HS; Royal Oak, MI; 7/176 Hon Rl; NHS; Rptr Yrbk; Rptr Sch Nwsp; Natl Merit SF; Univ Of Michigan; Engr.

MERICAL, STEVE; Beaver Local HS; East Liverpool, OH; 35/242 Band; Boy Scts; Hon Rl; NHS; OEA; Letter Glf; IM Sprt; Ohio Inst Of Tech; Elec Engr.

MERILLAT, BARBARA; Waldron HS; Waldron, MI; Band; Chrs; Hon Rl; NHS; Sch Nwsp; Treas FHA; Pep Clb; Spn Clb; Letter Trk; GAA; Amer & Me Essay Contest 2nd Pl At Waldron 75; Univ; Nursing.

MERILLAT, KATHLEEN; Liberty Center HS; Liberty Cntr, OH; Band; MMM; Orch; Fr Clb; Bsbl; Capt Chrldng; Univ Of Bowling Green; Airline Atten.

MERK, DAVID; William V Fisher Cath HS; Lancaster, OH; Chrh Wkr; Hon Rl; NHS; FDA; Key Clb; Bsbl; Bsktbl; Ftbl; Glf; Xavier Univ; Pre Med.

MERK, HEIDI; Kirtland HS; Kirtland, OH; 3/130 Am Leg Aux Girls St; Band; Hon Rl; Jr NHS; NHS; Letter Bsktbl; Ten; PPFtbl; Case W Reserve Univ; Bio Med Engr.

MERKEL, DAVID; Floyd Central HS; New Albany, IN; Band; Debate Tm; Hon Rl; Mod UN; Orch; Sch Pl; Ger Clb; Letter Swmmng; Univ; Pre Med.

MERKEL, ELIZABETH; Chelsea HS; Chelsea, MI; 2/250 Debate Tm; Hon Rl; NHS; Fr Clb;.

MERKLE, BARB; Bishop Dwenger HS; Ft Wayne, IN; Cl Rep Jr Cls; Cmnty Wkr; Hon Rl; NHS; Fr Clb; Letter Gym; De Pauw Univ; Engr.

MERKLE, TERRY; Loy Norrix HS; Kalamazoo, MI; 22/400 Hon Rl; NHS; IM Sprt; Natl Merit SF; WMU Acad Schlrshp 79; Western Michigan Univ; Comp Sci.

MERKLIN, KIM; Ben Davis HS; Indianapolis, IN; Cls Rep Soph Cls; Cl Rep Jr Cls; Hon Rl; NHS; Stu Cncl; Spn Clb; Letter Swmmng; Letter Trk; GAA; Particip Awd For Outsdng Achvmnt In Swim 76 77 & 78; All Conf Swim Tm 77; Scarborough Peace Games Swim 79; Univ; Dent Hygnst.

MERLINO, DONNA; Benjamin Franklin HS; Westland, MI; Cls Rep Frsh Cls; Hon Rl; Letter Ten; Univ; CPA.

MERRELL, TONY; Olentangy HS; Galena, OH; Boy Scts; Chrh Wkr; Yrbk; Rptr Sch Nwsp; 4-H; Bsbl; Wrstlng; PPFtbl; 4-H Awd; Univ; Creative Arts.

MERRELLS, NATHAN; Warren HS; Little Hocking, OH; Sec Jr Cls; Chrs; Hon Rl; Sch Mus; Sch Pl; Stu Cncl; Rptr Yrbk; Drama Clb; Tenn Temple Univ; Bus Admin.

MERRIAM, DANIEL; Tri Valley HS; Adamsville, OH; 12/220 Hon Rl; Jr NHS; NHS; Letter Bsbl; Bsktbl; Crs Cntry; College; Busns.

MERRIAM, WINTHROP J; Bruceton HS; Bruceton Mills, WV; 4/55 Am Leg Boys St; Band; Chrh Wkr; Hon Rl; 4-H; Fr Clb; Mth Clb; Letter Bsktbl; Am Leg Awd; 4-H Awd; West Virginia Univ; Law.

MERRICK, KRISTIN; Northridge HS; Goshen, IN; 2/130 Band; Hosp Ade; Pres NHS; Sch Mus; Bsktbl; Trk; Bausch & Lomb Awd; Purdue Univ; Biology.

MERRICK, LEE; Marine City HS; Marine City, MI; Cls Rep Soph Cls; Cl Rep Jr Cls; Cls Rep Sr Cls; Hon Rl; Hosp Ade; Sch Pl; 4-H; Trk; Chrldng; Saint Clair County Community College.

MERRILL, BRAD; Bentley HS; Burton, MI; Cls Rep Frsh Cls; Cls Rep Soph Cls; Cl Rep Jr Cls; Cls Rep Sr Cls; Boy Scts; Hon Rl; NHS; Off Ade; Stg Crw; Sci Clb; Regents Alumni Schlrshp; Univ Of Michigan; Pre Med.

MERRILL, BRIAN; Wirt County HS; Elizabeth, WV; Band; Hon Rl; Boys Clb Am; Treas FBLA; W Vir Univ; Bus Admin.

MERRILL, GLENN; Montabella Community HS; Blanchard, MI; Hon Rl; Spn Clb; Ferris State College; Conservation.

MERRILL, JOHN; Penn HS; Granger, IN; Boy Scts; Hon Rl; Bsktbl; Trk; IM Sprt; Indiana Univ; CPA.

MERRILLI, MARIANNE; Bishop Gallagher HS; Roseville, MI; 16/322 Cls Rep Sr Cls; Hon Rl; Natl Forn Lg; PAVAS; Pol Wkr; Sch Mus; Sch Pl; Stu Cncl; Y-Teens; Rptr Yrbk; Michigan St Univ; Psych.

MERRIMAN, MARIAN; Deckerville Cmnty HS; Deckervll, MI; Am Leg Aux Girls St; Band; Chrs; Hon Rl; Sch Mus; OEA; Letter Bsktbl; Letter Trk; Letter Chrldng; Univ; Acctg.

MERRIMAN, MAUREEN; Monsignor John R Hackett HS; Kalamazoo, MI; Cls Rep Soph Cls; Hon Rl; NHS; Stu Cncl; Swmmng; Letter Trk; College.

MERRIMAN, PEGGY; Tuslaw HS; Massillon, OH; 11/180 Sec Frsh Cls; Trs Soph Cls; Trs Jr Cls; Cls Rep Sr Cls; Hon Rl; Jr NHS; NHS; Stu Cncl; Y-Teens; Pep Clb; Wayne Tech College; Med Tech.

MERRIMAN, RANDAL; Maysville HS; So Zanesville, OH; Hon Rl; Cit Awd; DAR Awd; Capital Univ; Speech.

MERRITT, BARBARA; Linden Mc Kinley HS; Columbus, OH; Capt Drl Tm; Hon Rl; Sch Nwsp; OEA; CBU.

MERRITT, CHERIE; East Technical HS; Cleveland, OH; Cls Rep Frsh Cls; Cls Rep Soph Cls; Trs Jr Cls; AFS; Chrs; Hon Rl; Lbry Ade; VICA; Pom Pon; Cit Awd; Ashland Coll; Engr.

MERRITT, DONALD G; Barboursville HS; Ona, WV; Am Leg Boys St; Hon Rl; NHS; Sch Mus; Rptr Yrbk; Key Clb; Spn Clb; Letter Bsbl; Letter Bsktbl; Letter Ftbl; Marshall Univ; Engr.

MERRITT, MATTHEW; Clio HS; Clio, MI; 34/350 Jr NHS; NHS; Letter Glf; Grand Vly St Coll; Bus Admin.

MERRIWEATHER, DOROTHY; Lima Sr HS; Lima, OH; Chrs; Hon Rl; Jr NHS; Off Ade; Sch Mus; 4-H; Bsktbl; 4-H Awd; California St Univ; Psych.

MERRY, CONNIE; Mitchell HS; Mitchell, IN; VP Jr Cls; Chrs; Off Ade; VP Stu Cncl; Pep Clb; Chrldng; GAA; Natl Merit Ltr; Pres Awd; Sullivan Jr College; Business.

MERRY, MICHAEL; North Vermilion HS; Cayuga, IN; Boy Scts; Hon Rl; NHS; Fr Clb; Bsktbl; Letter Swmmng; Purdue Univ; Engr.

MERRYMAN, CHRISTE; Tri Valley HS; Adamsville, OH; 55/226 Sec Jr Cls; Sec Sr Cls; Hon Rl; Lbry Ade; Off Ade; Yrbk; 4-H; Lat Clb; GAA; Mat Maids; Ohio Univ; R N.

MERS, MARY; St Ursula Acad; Cincinnati, OH; Chrs; Hon Rl; Mod UN; Sch Mus; Sch Pl; Socr; College; Engineering.

MERSCH, CRISTINA; Blanchester HS; Pleasant Plain, OH; 15/165 Trs Jr Cls; Band; Chrs; Hon Rl; NHS; Sch Mus; Rptr Yrbk; 4-H; GAA; Univ; Music.

MERSCH, ROGER; Moeller HS; Cincinnati, OH; 21/260 Chrh Wkr; Hon Rl; VP JA; Trk; Univ Of Cincinnati; Architecture.

MERTA, LORI; River Rouge HS; River Rouge, MI; Cmnty Wkr; Hon Rl; NHS; Drama Clb; Swmmng; Scr Kpr; Tmr; College; Medicine.

MERTZ, BARBARA; Lewis Cnty HS; Jan Lew, WV; Sec Frsh Cls; Band; Cmnty Wkr; Hon Rl; 4-H; FHA; Glenville St Coll; Education.

MERTZ, CAROL; Lutheran East HS; Detroit, MI; Chrh Wkr; Hon Rl; Drama Clb; Pep Clb; Letter Bsbl; Bsktbl; Trk; Chrldng; PPFtbl; Natl Merit Ltr; St John Hosp; Radiology.

MERTZ, EDWARD; Marysville HS; Marysville, MI; Cls Rep Frsh Cls; Cls Rep Soph Cls; Cl Rep Jr Cls; Am Leg Boys St; Hon Rl; Sch Pl; VP Stu Cncl; Yth Flsp; Letter Ftbl; Letter Hockey; Marysville Library Summer Reading Club Winner; Sci Fair 2nd Plc; Michigan St Univ; Poli Sci.

MERTZ, JANICE; Botkins HS; Botkins, OH; 2/49 Sal; Band; Chrs; Chrh Wkr; Hon Rl; VP NHS; Pres 4-H; FHA; Sec FTA; Pres Sci Clb; Ohio St Univ; Food Sci.

MERULLO, KAREN A; Whetstone HS; Columbus, OH; Chrs; Hon Rl; Off Ade; Sch Mus; OEA; Spn Clb; Trk; Mat Maids; Cit Awd; Ohio St Univ; Busns Admin.

MERVENNE, MARY; Marian HS; Birmingham, MI; Cls Rep Frsh Cls; Cl Rep Jr Cls; Cls Rep Sr Cls; Hon Rl; Mod UN; NHS; Fr Clb; Univ; Bio.

MERZ, MERCEDES; Portage Lakes Joint Voc HS; Nw Canton, OH; Pres Jr Cls; Hon Rl; Sch Pl; Stg Crw; Drama Clb; Pep Clb; VICA; Ohio State; R N.

MESCHEN, RONALD E; Rockville Jr Sr HS; Montezuma, IN; Pres Frsh Cls; Cls Rep Soph Cls; Cl Rep Jr Cls; Cls Rep Sr Cls; FCA; Hon Rl; VP Stu Cncl; Yrbk; Letter Ten; Univ; Sci.

MESCHER, DALE; Chaminade Julienne HS; Dayton, OH; Boy Scts; JA; Wrstlng; Univ; Oceanography.

MESI, DOUGLAS; Gilmour Acad; Shaker Hts, OH; 26/82 Band; Hon Rl; Letter Ftbl; College.

MESIK, CORINNA; Allegan HS; Hopkins, MI; Band; Chrh Wkr; Debate Tm; Natl Forn Lg; Sch Pl; Pep Clb; Pres Spn Clb; Trk; Brigham Young Univ.

MESKO, CONNIE; Crestwood HS; Mantua, OH; 13/241 VP Jr Cls; AFS; Bowling Green St Univ; Home Ec.

MESKUNAS, BRENDA; Eastlake North HS; Willowick, OH; 55/730 Hon Rl; Jr NHS; Lbry Ade; PAVAS; Sch Mus; Sch Pl; Stg Crw; Rptr Sch Nwsp; Sch Nwsp; Drama Clb; Best English Stu Fresh Yr; Outstanding English Acv Jr Yr; Best Actress; San Francisco St Univ; English.

MESNARD, RICHARD W; Tiffin Columbian HS; Tiffin, OH; Cls Rep Sr Cls; Hon Rl; JA; Pol Wkr; Ger Clb; Am Leg Awd; JA Awd; Natl Merit SF; Univ.

MESSENGER, CHARLES; George Rogers Clark HS; Whiting, IN; 13/250 Band; Trk; Natl Merit Ltr; Purdue; Scientific Research.

MESSENGER, TIMOTHY; Bristolville Local HS; New Waterford, OH; Chrh Wkr; Hon Rl; Stg Crw; Voc Schl; Bus Mgmt.

MESSER, BRENDA K; Penn HS; Mishawaka, IN; Chrs; Off Ade; Sch Mus; Stg Crw; 4-H; Pep Clb; Sci Clb; NISBOVA Contst Piano Perfrmnc 1st Div Ratng 76 & 78; NISBOVA Contst Concert Chr 1st Div Ratng 79; IUSB; Music Educ.

MESSER, MELODY; Montabella HS; Holland, MI; Off Ade; Yrbk; FTA; Pep Clb; Mat Maids; Pom Pon; Montcalm Cmnty Coll; Legal Sec.

MESSER, ROCHELLE; Cass City HS; Gagetown, MI; Hon Rl; NHS; Letter Bsbl; Letter Bsktbl; Central Michigan Univ.

MESSERLY, ROBERT; William V Fisher Cath HS; Lancaster, OH; Am Leg Boys St; Boy Scts; NHS; Sch Pl; Sct Actv; Sprt Ed Sch Nwsp; Ten; IM Sprt; Univ; Pre Law.

MESSICK, KEVIN; Allen East HS; Lafayette, OH; 2/105 Hon Rl; NHS; Sch Nwsp; Letter Crs Cntry; Letter Trk; Mgrs; Ohio Northern Univ; Elec Engr.

MESSICK, REBECCA; Southwestern Community HS; Flint, MI; Band; Drm Bgl; Hon Rl; NHS; Orch; Red Cr Ade; Natl Merit SF; Mich State Univ; Pre Medical.

MESSING, KAREN; Ubly HS; Ruth, MI; Cl Rep Jr Cls; Band; Hon Rl; Lbry Ade; Stu Cncl; 4-H; Coll; Elem Ed.

MESSING, PAULINE; Ubly Comm HS; Ruth, MI; 30/111 Cls Rep Sr Cls; Hon Rl; Sch Pl; Rptr Yrbk; 4-H; FFA; Chrldng; PPFtbl; Coll; Nursing.

MESSING, SUE; Harbor Beach Cmnty HS; Ruth, MI; 38/122 Cl Rep Jr Cls; Aud/Vis; Chrh Wkr; Cmnty Wkr; Hon Rl; Hosp Ade; Lbry Ade; NHS; Sch Mus; Stg Crw; Ferris St Coll.

MESSING, TIMOTHY; Ubly Cmnty HS; Ruth, MI; Letter Bsbl; Letter Bsktbl; Letter Ftbl; IM Sprt; Scr Kpr; Tmr; Univ; Phys Ed.

MESSINGER, DAVID; Clay HS; Granger, IN; Boy Scts; Cmnty Wkr; Hon Rl; Jr NHS; NHS; Lat Clb; Spn Clb; Bsktbl; Letter Crs Cntry; Trk; Univ Of Tennessee; Law.

MESSMER, KEITH; Jasper HS; Jasper, IN; 45/326 Hon Rl; Ftbl; Trk; Ind State; Bus.

MESSNER, BETH; Goshen HS; Goshen, IN; 29/268 Hon Rl; Lbry Ade; Sch Pl; Drama Clb; Spn Clb; Goshen College; Art.

MESSNER, DANIEL R; Southfield Christian HS; Pontiac, MI; Band; Chrh Wkr; Hon Rl; Sch Mus; Yth Flsp; Drama Clb; Bsbl; Bsktbl; Most Improved Baseball & Basketball Player; College; Business.

MESSNER, DIANA; Western HS; Spring Arbor, MI; Band; Sch Mus; Fr Clb; Letter Gym; Univ; Micro Bio.

MESTELLE, DAVID J; Eastern HS; Lansing, MI; Band; Chrh Wkr; Hon Rl; NHS; Sch Mus; Natl Merit SF; Mic State Univ; Engineering.

MESZAROS, JOLENE; Washington HS; South Bend, IN; 45/355 Hon Rl; Indiana Univ; Acctg.

METCALF, ELIZABETH; Kirtland HS; Waite Hil Vlg, OH; Sec Jr Cls; Sec Sr Cls; AFS; Band; Cmnty Wkr; Girl Scts; Hon Rl; Jr NHS; NHS; Spn Clb; College; Engr.

METCALF, RICHARD; Tawas Area HS; E Tawas, MI; 12/155 Cls Rep Sr Cls; Hon Rl; NHS; Letter Ftbl; Mic Tech Univ; Bio Engr.

METCALF, SCOTT; Sidney HS; Sidney, OH; Band; Chrh Wkr; FCA; Letter Ftbl; Letter Trk; Univ; Psych.

METCALFE, DARIAN; Horace Mann HS; Gary, IN; Cls Rep Frsh Cls; Cls Rep Soph Cls; Cl Rep Jr Cls; Hon Rl; JA; Jr NHS; NHS; Stu Cncl; Yrbk; Purdue Univ; Indus Engr.

METHENY, SANDRA; Morgantown HS; Morgantwn, WV; Chrs; Chrh Wkr; Hon Rl; Sprt Ed Yrbk; Pres FBLA; Pep Clb; Coach Actv; IM Sprt; Scr Kpr; Tmr; West Vir Univ; Acctg.

METIVA, RANDY C; Bridgeport HS; Bridgeport, MI; Letter Band; Boy Scts; Sct Actv; DECA; Letter Trk; Saginaw News Top 40 Carrier Awd 75; Saginaw News Mert Awd 74; Saginaw Vly St Coll; Music.

METROVICH, NINA; Beaver Local HS; E Liverpool, OH; 17/221 Band; Cmp Fr Grls; Chrh Wkr; Hon Rl; NHS; Off Ade; Sch Pl; Drama Clb; Eng Clb; Chrldng; Kent St Univ; Med Sci.

METTERT, JON; Brandywine HS; Niles, MI; NHS; Letter Bsbl; Letter Ftbl; IM Sprt; PPFtbl; Scr Kpr; BEOG 1226 79; Mi Compttv Schlshp 1200 79; Adrian Schlshp 1010 79; Adrian Coll; Med Tech.

METTERT, KERRY; R Nelson Snider HS; Ft Wayne, IN; 131/526 Band; Boy Scts; Chrh Wkr; FCA; Hon Rl; Yth Flsp; Fr Clb; Letter Ftbl; Trk; IM Sprt; Anderson Coll; Religion.

METTERT, R; Garrett HS; Auburn, IN; Chrh Wkr; Hon Rl; Jr NHS; FFA; Glf; IM Sprt; Purdue Univ; Electronic Draftsman.

METTEY, ELLEN; Mount Notre Dame HS; Cincinnati, OH; 23/179 Band; Chrh Wkr; Hon Rl; NHS; Off Ade; Sch Mus; Sch Pl; Stg Crw; Rptr Sch Nwsp; Sch Nwsp; Univ Of Cincinnati; English Lit.

METTEY, ELLEN; Mt Notre Dame HS; Cincinnati, OH; 23/179 Cls Rep Frsh Cls; Cls Rep Sr Cls; Sec Band; Hon Rl; NHS; Sch Mus; Sch Pl; Stg Crw; Rptr Sch Nwsp; Sch Nwsp; Univ Of Cincinnati; Jrnlsm.

METTILLE, MICHAEL J; Newark HS; Newark, OH; 31/550 Debate Tm; Sec Frsh Cls; NHS; Eng Clb; Fr Clb; Key Clb; Lat Clb; Mth Clb; Sci Clb; Natl Merit SF; Cal Inst Of Tech; Chemical Engr.

METTLER, JAMES; Paw Paw HS; Paw Paw, MI; 43/193 Boy Scts; Hon Rl; NHS; Stg Crw; Rptr Sch Nwsp; W Mich Univ; Elec Engr.

METTS, LORI; Marietta HS; Marietta, OH; 19/419 Band; Chrh Wkr; Drm Mjrt; Girl Scts; Hon Rl; NHS; Sch Pl; Spn Clb; Mgrs; Twrlr; Marietta Coll; Business.

METZ, ELIZABETH; Calhoun Co HS; Mtzion, WV; Sec Frsh Cls; Cl Rep Jr Cls; Am Leg Aux Girls St; Chrs; Chrh Wkr; Girl Scts; Hon Rl; Stu Cncl; 4-H; Sci Clb; West Virginia Univ; Nursing.

METZ, LILLIE; Maysville HS; Zanesville, OH; Sec Band; Hon Rl; JA; NHS; Sch Mus; Treas 4-H; FHA; College.

METZGER, CAROL; New Riegel HS; Carey, OH; 4/48 Band; Hon Rl; NHS; Stg Crw; 4-H; Pres FHA; Pep Clb; Cit Awd;.

METZGER, DELORES; Perry HS; Canton, OH; 160/470 Chrs; Chrh Wkr; Cmnty Wkr; FHA; Saftey Town 78; Stark Tech Coll; Med Asst.

METZGER, DENNIS; St Johns HS; Delphos, OH; Boy Scts; Chrh Wkr; Cmnty Wkr; Hon Rl; Crs Cntry; Coach Actv; IM Sprt; Univ Of Toledo.

METZGER, KAREN; Bryan HS; Bryan, OH; 19/191 AFS; Chrs; Chrh Wkr; Cmnty Wkr; Hon Rl; NHS; Beta Clb; Bowling Green State; Poli Sci.

METZGER, SHARON; New Riegel HS; New Riegel, OH; 4/51 Band; Chrs; Hon Rl; Off Ade; Sch Mus; Sch Pl; 4-H; VP FHA; Cit Awd; Bowling Green Voc Schl; Nursing.

METZGER, SUSAN; Ft Jennings HS; Delphos, OH; Sec Jr Cls; Band; Girl Scts; Hon Rl; Sch Mus; Stu Cncl; 4-H; Fr Clb; Ten; Chrldng; Lima Tech Coll; Dent Hygnst.

METZNER, CHERYL; Jefferson Area HS; Rock Crk, OH; 3/176 Cls Rep Frsh Cls; AFS; Chrs; NHS; Sch Nwsp; Pres Spn Clb; Gym; Math Awd 75; Sftbl Var Ltr All GRC Team 78 & 79; Univ; Transptrn.

MEURER, DAVE; North Daviess Cougars HS; Plainville, IN; Cls Rep Frsh Cls; VP Soph Cls; Chrs; Chrh Wkr; Hon Rl; Sch Mus; Sch Pl; Bsbl; Bsktbl; Crs Cntry; Dist Contest Winner In Piano & State Contest; Ind Teachers Music Assn; Vincennes Univ; Medicine.

MEWHORTER, JAMES; Perrysburg HS; Perrysburg, OH; Hon Rl; Bsbl; IM Sprt; Colorado St Univ; Psych.

MEYER, ANGIE; Brookville HS; Brookville, IN; Band; Chrh Wkr; Hon Rl; Lbry Ade; Sch Mus; 4-H; Pep Clb; GAA;.

MEYER, BARRY; R Nelson Snider HS; Ft Wayne, IN; 2/526 Band; FCA; Hon Rl; Stu Cncl; Letter Trk; C of C Awd; Indiana Univ; Public Acctg.

MEYER, CAROLYN; Bremen HS; Bremen, IN; 7/101 FCA; Hon Rl; NHS; Sch Pl; Treas Stu Cncl; Yth Flsp; Sec Drama Clb; Fr Clb; Sec OEA; Pep Clb; Messiah Coll; French.

MEYER, CHRISTOPHER; Toronto HS; Toronto, OH; Cls Rep Frsh Cls; Cl Rep Jr Cls; Cls Rep Sr Cls; Boy Scts; Chrh Wkr; Sct Actv; Stu Cncl; Letter Glf; Wrstlng; Ohio St Univ.

MEYER, CRISTOPHER A; Indian Hill HS; Cincinnati, OH; 4/285 Band; Chrs; Hon Rl; Lit Mag; NHS; Orch; Sch Mus; Rptr Sch Nwsp; Sch Nwsp; Ger Clb; Univ Of Virginia; Med.

MEYER, DALE; Calvin Christian HS; Wyoming, MI; Chrs; Lbry Ade;.

MEYER, DAN; Napoleon HS; Napoleon, OH; Chrh Wkr; Yth Flsp; Spn Clb; Bsbl; Ftbl; Wrstlng; IM Sprt; Owens Tech; Agri Engr.

MEYER, DAVE; Deer Park HS; Cincinnati, OH; Aud/Vis; Boy Scts; Chrh Wkr; Cmnty Wkr; FCA; Hon Rl; Sct Actv; Letter Ftbl; Letter Trk; Letter Wrstlng; Univ Of Cinti; Accounting.

MEYER, DAVID; Romulus HS; Romulus, MI; 46/330 Band; Boy Scts; Chrh Wkr; Hon Rl; Sch Pl; Sct Actv; Rptr Sch Nwsp; Drama Clb; Letter Trk; College.

MEYER, DEBORAH; William Henry Harrison HS; Harrison, OH; 10/243 Pres Soph Cls; Hon Rl; NHS; Stu Cncl; Drama Clb; Pres 4-H; Mat Maids; 4-H Awd; Ohio St Univ; Pre Vet Med.

MEYER, DEBRA; Mother Of Mercy HS; Cincinnati, OH; Aud/Vis; Chrs; Hon Rl; Hosp Ade; Sch Mus; Sch Pl; Stg Crw; Drama Clb; Fr Clb; GAA; Univ; Nursing.

MEYER, DORTHY; Tinora HS; Defiance, OH; 3/108 Hst Sr Cls; Chrs; Chrh Wkr; Hon Rl; Treas Hosp Ade; Treas NHS; Sch Mus; 4-H; FHA; OEA; Coll; Data Proc.

MEYER, DOUGLAS; La Salle HS; South Bend, IN; Hon Rl; NHS; Bsbl; Letter Bsktbl; Coach Actv; Cit Awd; Univ; Law.

MEYER, ELIZABETH; Eastwood HS; Pemberville, OH; 1/179 Hon Rl; Lbry Ade; NHS; Off Ade; Stu Cncl; 4-H; Lat Clb; 4-H Awd; College; Medicine.

MEYER, GAYLE; Mapleton HS; New London, OH; 10/125 Am Leg Aux Girls St; Sec Band; Drl Tm; Hon Rl; Sec NHS; Yrbk; 4-H; Lat Clb; GAA; IM Sprt; Ohi Northern Univ; Pharmacy.

MEYER, GINA; Fairview HS; Bryan, OH; 2/120 VP Jr Cls; Sal; Chrs; Capt Drl Tm; Hon Rl; Sec NHS; Off Ade; Sch Mus; Sch Pl; Stg Crw; Wittenberg Univ; Eng.

MEYER, GORDON; Brookville HS; Brookville, IN; Boy Scts; Chrh Wkr; Sct Actv; Key Clb; Letter Bsbl; Mgrs; Projector Club Pres; College; Conservation.

MEYER, GREGORY; Sandusky HS; Sandusky, OH; Band; Hon Rl; Red Cr Ade; IM Sprt; Hocking Tech Coll; Forestry Mgmt.

MEYER, JACQUELINE; All Saints HS; Bay City, MI; Chrs; Chrh Wkr; Cmnty Wkr; Girl Scts; Hon Rl; Hosp Ade; Red Cr Ade; Saginaw Valley State College; Rn.

MEYER, JENNETTE; Stryker HS; Stryker, OH; 14/50 Trs Frsh Cls; Sec Soph Cls; Am Leg Aux Girls St; Band; Chrs; Chrh Wkr; Hon Rl; NHS; Off Ade; Pol Wkr; Bowling Green St Univ; Home Ec.

MEYER, JENNY; Bridgeport HS; Bridgeport, WV; 4/199 Cls Rep Sr Cls; Am Leg Aux Girls St; Band;

Chrs; Chrh Wkr; Cmnty Wkr; Girl Scts; Hon Rl; Hosp Ade; Jr NHS; WV Delegate To Washington Wrkshp 1978; Outstndng Yng Amer 1978; Publication Of Poetry In 3 Natl Antholog; Purdue Univ; Pharm.

MEYER, JUDITH; Lakeshore HS; Saint Joseph, MI; Chrh Wkr; NHS; 4-H; Spn Clb; 4-H Awd; Michigan St Univ; Indust Rel.

MEYER, JUDY; Minster HS; Minster, OH; 27/80 Hon Rl; Pres 4-H; FHA; OEA;.

MEYER, JULIE; Whetstone HS; Columbus, OH; Chrs; Hon Rl; Jr NHS; Fr Clb; IM Sprt; Prtcptn In The Oh Tests Of Schlstc Achvmnt 77; Knight Chancellor Accumltv High Grd Avr For Grds 7 To 9 77; Univ.

MEYER, KAREN; Madison Comprehensive HS; Lucas, OH; Band; Chrh Wkr; Girl Scts; Orch; FHA; Ger Clb; Spn Clb; Univ; Med.

MEYER, KATHERINE; Woodmore HS; Elmore, OH; 1/140 AFS; Band; Chrs; Chrh Wkr; Girl Scts; Sch Mus; Yth Flsp; 4-H; Cit Awd; Natl Merit Schl; Bowling Green St Univ; Music.

MEYER, KATHLEEN L; Seton HS; Cincinnati, OH; 23/255 Girl Scts; Hon Rl; JA; NHS; Stg Crw; Univ Of Cincinnati; Acctg.

MEYER, KIMBERLY; Whitmer HS; Toledo, OH; 48/810 Band; Hon Rl; NHS; Fr Clb; PPFtbl; Toledo Univ; Engineering.

MEYER, KRISTAN; Traverse City HS; Traverse City, MI; VP Frsh Cls; Sec Soph Cls; Sec Jr Cls; VP Sr Cls; Hon Rl; NHS; Orch; Stu Cncl; Ed Yrbk; Rptr Sch Nwsp; Univ Of Mic; Eng.

MEYER, KURT; Kiser HS; Dayton, OH; 10/210 Band; Trs Frsh Cls; NHS; OEA; 1st Pl Acctg & Related I Region 3 Of Ohio; Rating Of Superior At Wright St Univ Invitational Acctg; Sinclair Comm Coll; Acctg.

MEYER, LINDA; Mcauley HS; Cinti, OH; Aud/Vis; Chrh Wkr; Cmnty Wkr; Hon Rl; Coach Actv; GAA; IM Sprt; Univ Of Cincinnati; Special Ed.

MEYER, LYNN; Heritage Hills HS; Chrisney, IN; Sec Frsh Cls; Band; FCA; Hon Rl; NHS; Stu Cncl; Pep Clb; Letter Trk; Chrldng; Twrlr; W Kentucky Univ; Bus Tchr.

MEYER, MARK E; Prairie Hts Sr HS; Howe, IN; 2/150 Trs Frsh Cls; Trs Soph Cls; Hon Rl; NHS; College; Math.

MEYER, MARTIN; Clyde HS; Clyde, OH; Am Leg Boys St; Chrh Wkr; FCA; Hon Rl; Jr NHS; Spn Clb; Crs Cntry; Trk; Coll; Phys Ed.

MEYER, MARY; Liberty Benton HS; Findlay, OH; Sec Jr Cls; Sec Sr Cls; NHS; Off Ade; Sch Mus; Sch Pl; Rptr Yrbk; VP FHA; N W Busns Coll; Med Ofc Asst.

MEYER, MIKE; Oscoda HS; Oscoda, MI; 3/240 Trs Sr Cls; Am Leg Boys St; Band; Boy Scts; Chrh Wkr; Chmn Ftbl; Letter Trk; Central Mic Univ.

MEYER, MONDA; S Ripley Jr Sr HS; Cross Plains, IN; Band; Chrh Wkr; Hon Rl; Lbry Ade; 4-H; FNA; Lat Clb; Pep Clb; Sci Clb; Coll; Med.

MEYER, NANCY; Immaculate Conception Acad; Cincinnati, OH; 3/68 Pres Frsh Cls; Chrs; Hon Rl; NHS; Quill & Scroll; Sch Mus; Sch Pl; Rptr Yrbk; Sch Nwsp; Fr Clb; College; Graphic Arts.

MEYER, PEGGY; Robert S Rogers HS; Toledo, OH; Band; Hon Rl; Jr NHS; NHS; Off Ade; Orch; Yth Flsp; Ger Clb; Sci Clb; German Amer Festival Society Awd; Greater Toledo Council Of Tchrs Of Math Awd; Ohio State Univ; Sci.

MEYER, RANDY; Crestwood HS; Mantua, OH; Band; Bsktbl; Glf; Ohio Inst Of Tech; Elec.

MEYER, RITA; Attica Jr Sr HS; Covington, IN; 6/75 Sec Soph Cls; Trs Soph Cls; Trs Sr Cls; Hon Rl; NHS; Off Ade; Letter Trk; VP GAA; Purdue Univ; Home Ec.

MEYER, S; Kenston HS; Chagrin Fl, OH; Boy Scts; Hon Rl; Stg Crw; Stu Cncl; Fr Clb; Rdo Clb; Crs Cntry; College; Engr.

MEYER, S; Miller City HS; Leipsic, OH; VP Band; Chrs; Chrh Wkr; Hon Rl; Pres NHS; Sch Mus; Yrbk; Pep Clb; Bsktbl; College; Music Ther.

MEYER, SANDRA; Decatur Central HS; Indianapolis, IN; 55/305 Sec Band; Chrh Wkr; Girl Scts; Hon Rl; Off Ade; Sch Mus; 4-H; In Univ Bloomington; Dental Hygiene.

MEYER, SANDY; Washington Township HS; Valparaiso, IN; 1/36 Trs Frsh Cls; Cl Rep Jr Cls; Aud/Vis; Hon Rl; Lit Mag; Sch Pl; Rptr Sch Nwsp; Treas 4-H; Spn Clb; Letter Bsktbl; Hoosier Girls St Delgt 1979;.

MEYER, STEPHEN J; Fairfield Local HS; Ocala, FL; Band; FFA; Spn Clb; Cit Awd; Univ Of Florida; Politics.

MEYER, THOMAS; Carroll HS; Dayton, OH; 31/285 Hon Rl; Treas Yth Flsp; Sec Ger Clb; Coll.

MEYER, THOS; Highland HS; Highland, IN; Hon Rl; Marquette Univ; Bus.

MEYER, WILLIAM; Wylie E Groves HS; Birmingham, MI; Natl Merit SF; Mic State Univ; Poli Sci.

MEYERS, CLAYTON; Calvert HS; Republic, OH; Chrh Wkr; Toledo Univ; Mech Engr.

MEYERS, COLLEEN; Salem Sr HS; Salem, OH; 24/248 Trs Jr Cls; Pres Sr Cls; Cmp Fr Grls; Hon Rl; Lbry Ade; Off Ade; Yrbk; 4-H; DAR Awd; 2nd Pl In Reg 7th In St IOE Com 77; 6th In Reg 1st In St & 2nd In Natl IOE Comp 78; St Awd Of Distnctn 78; Kent St Univ; Bus Admin.

MEYERS, DAVID; John Adams HS; South Bend, IN; 132/450 Boy Scts; FCA; Hon Rl; Y-Teens; Bsbl; Ftbl; IM Sprt; Purdue Univ; Sci.

MEYERS, DEBRA; Mississinewa HS; Jonesboro, IN; Cl Rep Jr Cls; Cls Rep Sr Cls; Band; Hon Rl; Jr NHS; Spn Clb; Taylor Univ; Comp Sci.

MEYERS, JAMES; Ravenna HS; Coopersville, MI; 6/100 Cls Rep Sr Cls; Chrh Wkr; Cmnty Wkr; Hon Rl; VP NHS; Sch Pl; Stu Cncl; Yrbk; Rptr Sch Nwsp; Sch Nwsp; Muskegon Cmnty Coll; Graphic Arts.

MEYERS, JANE; Chaminade Julienne HS; Dayton, OH; FCA; Hon Rl; NHS; Bsktbl; PPFtbl; Univ Of Dayton; Comp Sci.

MEYERS, JANET; North Farmington HS; Farm Hills, MI; 32/389 Cls Rep Frsh Cls; Cls Rep Soph Cls; Cl Rep Jr Cls; Cls Rep Sr Cls; Hon Rl; NHS; Sch Mus; VP Stu Cncl; Rptr Yrbk; Opt Clb Awd; Mich State Univ; Speech Pathology.

MEYERS, MARY; Clare HS; Clare, MI; Cls Rep Frsh Cls; Cls Rep Soph Cls; Trs Jr Cls; Cl Rep Jr Cls; Cls Rep Sr Cls; Band; FCA; Hon Rl; Off Ade;.

MEYERS, PAMELA; Carroll HS; Dayton, OH; 11/285 Chrh Wkr; Cmnty Wkr; Hon Rl; NHS; Spn Clb; Bsktbl; College.

MEYERS, PATTI; Circle HS; Circle, MT; Cls Rep Soph Cls; Drl Tm; Hon Rl; Off Ade; Sch Pl; Stu Cncl; Drama Clb; Pep Clb; Chrldng; PPFtbl; 1st Pl Sci Fair Wnr; Eastern Montana Coll; Bus Mgmt.

MEYERSON, BENJAMIN; Wylie E Groves HS; Birmingham, MI; Hon Rl; NHS; Swmmng; Wrstlng; Natl Merit Ltr; College; History.

MIARS, JULIE; Anna HS; Anna, OH; 1/96 Trs Jr Cls; Trs Sr Cls; Am Leg Aux Girls St; Band; Chrs; Chrh Wkr; Hon Rl; Jr NHS; Lbry Ade; NHS; Bowling Green Univ; Music.

MIATECH, SCOTT; Ann Arbor Pioneer HS; Ann Arbor, MI; Hon Rl; Rptr Yrbk; Rptr Sch Nwsp; Letter Socr; Univ; Natrl Bio Sci.

MICHAEL, ANN; Mc Auley HS; Cinti, OH; 15/252 Hon Rl; Sdlty; Univ Of Cincinnati; Med Tech.

MICHAEL, BEV; Whitko HS; S Whitley, IN; Cls Rep Frsh Cls; Cl Rep Jr Cls; Hon Rl; Stu Cncl; Sch Nwsp; 4-H; Fr Clb; OEA; Pep Clb; Chrldng; Purdue Univ; Bus Mgmt.

MICHAEL, CARLA; Central Noble HS; Albion, IN; Band; Cmnty Wkr; Drl Tm; Drm Mjrt; Hon Rl; Pep Clb; Chrldng; Capt Pom Pon; PPFtbl; Ball St Univ; Phys Educ.

MICHAEL, CRAIG; Taft Sr HS; Hamilton, OH; Aud/Vis; Hon Rl; VP Jr NHS; Stg Crw; Fr Clb; Ger Clb; Letter Bsbl; Letter Bsktbl; IM Sprt; Univ; Med.

MICHAEL, DAVID; Wyoming HS; Wyoming, OH; 1/163 Cls Rep Soph Cls; Band; Debate Tm; Hon Rl; Orch; Sch Pl; Stu Cncl; Sci Clb; JETS Awd; MIT; Engr.

MICHAEL, DIANNE; Hicksville HS; Hicksville, OH; Cls Rep Frsh Cls; Chrs; Chrh Wkr; Hon Rl; NHS; Rptr Sch Nwsp; Spn Clb; Bsktbl; Trk; PPFtbl; Bowling Green State Univ; Chemistry.

MICHAEL, DONNA; Hampshire HS; Romney, WV; 18/235 Sec Frsh Cls; Sec Soph Cls; Sec Jr Cls; AFS; Am Leg Aux Girls St; Band; Chrh Wkr; Cmnty Wkr; Hon Rl; Stg Crw; Shepherd College; Med Tech.

MICHAEL, ELIZABETH; Northside HS; Muncie, IN; 5/260 NHS; Orch; Lat Clb; Mth Clb; Kiwan Awd; Univ Of Cincinnati; Actuarial Sci.

MICHAEL, GREG; Little Miami HS; Loveland, OH; Hon Rl; Lit Mag; IM Sprt; Natl Merit Ltr; Miami Univ; Bio.

MICHAEL, JOHN; John Patrick Michael HS; Indianapolis, IN; VP Jr Cls; Chrs; Hon Rl; Mdrgl; Sch Mus; Sci Clb; Spn Clb; Letter Glf; Letter Socr; Univ; Bus.

MICHAEL, KAREN; Gibsonburg HS; Gibsonburg, OH; 1/101 Hon Rl; Hosp Ade; Lit Mag; Sch Pl; Drama Clb; 4-H; Am Leg Awd; 4-H Awd; Univ Of Toledo; Arts.

MICHAEL, KATHERINE; Marysville HS; West Mansfield, OH; Band; Chrs; Chrh Wkr; Drl Tm; Yth Flsp; 4-H; IM Sprt; Scr Kpr; 4-H Awd; Hocking Tech; Paramedics.

MICHAEL, LANA; West Lafayette HS; W Lafayette, IN; 83/187 Chrs; FCA; Girl Scts; Hon Rl; Hosp Ade; JA; Sch Nwsp; Pep Clb; Letter Bsktbl; Letter Ten; Purdue Univ; Acctg.

MICHAEL, LESLIE; Eau Claire HS; Eau Claire, MI; Hosp Ade; 4-H Clb; Lake Mich Coll;.

MICHAEL, M; Our Lady Star Of The Sea HS; Grosse Pre Shr, MI; Yrbk; Rptr Sch Nwsp; IM Sprt; Albion Coll; Bus.

MICHAEL, MAUREEN; Admiral King HS; Lorain, OH; Band; Chrs; Girl Scts; Hon Rl; JA; Sch Mus; Sch Pl; Stg Crw; Drama Clb; Gym; Univ; Dent Hygn.

MICHAEL, NANCY; Tri Valley HS; Frazeysburg, OH; 7/215 Hon Rl; Jr NHS; Sec NHS; Off Ade; 4-H; Bsktbl; GAA;.

MICHAEL, NANCY; Redford Union HS; Redford, MI; Am Leg Aux Girls St; Chrs; Chrh Wkr; Hon Rl; Orch; Yth Flsp; Treas Spn Clb; GAA; Tmr; Twrlr; Univ; Music.

MICHAEL, RANDY; Huntington North HS; Huntington, IN; Bsktbl; Letter Ftbl; Socr; Letter Trk; IM Sprt; Indiana Univ; Pre Law.

MICHAEL, RICHMOND; The Leelanau School; Cadillac, MI; VP Jr Cls; Boy Scts; Letter Socr; Letter Trk; Univ.

MICHAELIS, KIM; Otsego HS; Bowling Grn, OH; Pres Frsh Cls; Cls Rep Frsh Cls; VP Soph Cls; Cls Rep Soph Cls; Trs Jr Cls; Cl Rep Jr Cls; Am Leg Aux Girls St; Band; Jr NHS; Treas Stu Cncl; Wood Cnty Jr Fair Queen 78; Oh Cnty & Indpndnt Fair Queen 78; 4th Runner Up In Miss Oh St Fair Pgnt 78; Bowling Green St Univ; Bus.

MICHAELIS, MARIA A; Patrick Henry HS; Hamler, OH; 4/100 Chrs; Hon Rl; FHA; OEA; Sec.

MICHAELS, KELLY; Allen Park HS; Allen Pk, MI; Chrs; Cmnty Wkr; Hon Rl; Jr NHS; NHS; Pol Wkr; Yrbk; Ed Sch Nwsp; Spn Clb; Coach Actv; St Of Mi Comp Shclsp 79; Michigan St Univ; Spec Educ.

MICHAELSON, MARGARET; Huntington North HS; Huntington, IN; Girl Scts; Rptr Sch Nwsp; Sch Nwsp; DECA; Ger Clb; Gov Hon Prg Awd; 3rd Pl Advtsng Layots In DECA 79; The Cmpus Bst Writer Trphy 79; Jrnlsm 79; Coll; Advtsng Layout.

MICHAILENKO, ANN; Holy Name Nazareth HS; Parma, OH; Chrh Wkr; Hon Rl; Jr NHS; NHS; Orch; Stg Crw; Rptr Yrbk; Rptr Sch Nwsp; Fr Clb; Pep Clb; Sci Awd In The Field Of Chem 78; Case Western Reserve Univ; Poli Sci.

MICHALAK, MARTIN; St Alphonsus HS; Detroit, MI; 1/180 Cls Rep Frsh Cls; Debate Tm; Hon Rl; Natl Forn Lg; NHS; Stu Cncl; Trk; Opt Clb Awd; Voice Dem Awd; Univ Of Detroit; Engr.

MICHALAK, MICHAEL; Bishop Borgess HS; Dearborn, MI; Hon Rl; Bsbl; IM Sprt; Business School; Bus.

MICHALSKI, EDWARD; Admiral King HS; Lorain, OH; Chrs; Hon Rl; Rptr Yrbk; Yrbk; Rptr Sch Nwsp; Sch Nwsp; Trk; College.

MICHALSKI, ELIZABETH A; Lexington HS; Lexington, OH; 8/271 Hon Rl; NHS; Orch; Pres Y-Teens; Univ; Psych.

MICHALSKI, JEFFREY; Bay City Central HS; Bay City, MI; Band; ROTC; Fr Clb; Missouri St Univ.

MICHAUD, LISA; Parkway HS; Willshire, OH; 6/96 Band; Chrh Wkr; Hon Rl; Pres Yth Flsp; Treas FHA; Pep Clb; Trk; PPFtbl; Univ.

MICHAUD, MARK; R Nelson Snider HS; Ft Wayne, IN; Hon Rl; Fr Clb; Gov Hon Prg Awd; Indiana Univ; Med.

MICHAUD, MICHAEL; Roscommon HS; Roscommon, MI; 1/120 Pres Sr Cls; Chrh Wkr; Hon Rl; Sch Mus; Letter Bsbl; Capt Bsktbl; Capt Ftbl; Aguinas College; Comp Prog.

MICHAUX, SHARON; Galion Sr HS; Galion, OH; Am Leg Aux Girls St; Chrh Wkr; Cmnty Wkr; Hon Rl; Yth Flsp; Y-Teens; Letter Swmmng; Trk; Tmr; Bowling Green Coll; Psych.

MICHEL, ANN; Sandusky HS; Sandusky, OH; Cls Rep Frsh Cls; Band; Cmp Fr Grls; Chrs; Drm Bgl; Girl Scts; Hon Rl; Mdrgl; Mod UN; Stu Cncl; Phillips Petro Co Free Enterp 3rd Pl; Kiwanis Club Cert Of Appreciation; Bauder Fashion Coll; Fash Merch.

MICHEL, DIANE; Southridge HS; Huntingbrg, IN; Chrs; FCA; Girl Scts; Sch Mus; Sch Pl; Rptr Yrbk; FHA; Ger Clb; Pep Clb; Swmmng; Univ Of Evansville.

MICHEL, MATTHEW; Sandusky HS; Sandusky, OH; Band; Hon Rl; JA; IM Sprt; Wright St Univ; Comp Engr.

MICHEL, MICHAEL; St Thomas Aquinas HS; Louisville, OH; Wrstlng; Univ; Engr.

MICHEL, NANCI S; Seton HS; Cincinnati, OH; Chrs; Jr NHS; Mod UN; Red Cr Ade; Sci Clb; Kiwan Awd; College; Medicine.

MICHEL, RITA; Benedictine HS; Detroit, MI; Cls Rep Frsh Cls; Girl Scts; Hon Rl; Sprt Ed Yrbk; Rptr Yrbk; Fr Clb; Capt Trk; Chrldng; Cit Awd; Grand Valley College; Phy Theapist.

MICHEL, SUSAN; Sandy Valley HS; Waynesburg, OH; 4/172 VP Soph Cls; Am Leg Aux Girls St; Chrs; Hon Rl; Jr NHS; Pres Natl Forn Lg; NHS; VP Quill & Scroll; Sch Mus; Sch Pl; Kent St Univ; Elem Ed.

MICHELI, LAUREN; Marian HS; Cincinnati, OH; Trs Jr Cls; Girl Scts; NHS; Coll; Art.

MICHELI, MARIO; Fordson HS; Dearborn, MI; 30/553 Hon Rl; Quill & Scroll; IM Sprt; Bus Awd; Social Studies Awd; Slvr Pin 79; St Of Mic Cert 79; MHEAA 79; Univ Of Michigan; Bus Admin.

MICHELINI, THERESA; Ladywood HS; Plymouth, MI; Chrh Wkr; Hon Rl; Treas JA; NHS; Off Ade; Sch Pl; Rptr Yrbk; Treas Drama Clb; Spn Clb; Voice Dem Awd; Michigan St Univ; Sci.

MICHELS, CAROL; Maumee HS; Maumee, OH; 17/331 Girl Scts; NHS; Sct Actv; Trk; IM Sprt; Bowling Green State Univ; Med Tech.

MICHELS, OLIVER; Morgantown HS; Morgantwn, WV; Aud/Vis; Band; Boy Scts; Chrh Wkr; Lbry Ade; Orch; Red Cr Ade; Sct Actv; Yth Flsp; 4-H; Univ; Comp Sci.

MICHELSEN, BARBARA; Liberty Benton HS; Findlay, OH; Band; Cmp Fr Grls; Chrs; Hon Rl; NHS; Off Ade; Letter Bsktbl; Letter Trk; Coach Actv; IM Sprt; Bowling Green Univ; Art.

MICHELSON, KATHY; Roy C Start HS; Toledo, OH; Chrs; Sch Mus; Fr Clb; College; Bus Admin.

MICHIELUTTI, ANNE; Lakeview HS; St Clair Shores, MI; 18/450 Band; Hon Rl; NHS; Off Ade; Orch; Sch Mus; Stu Cncl; Yth Flsp; Fr Clb; Letter Swmmng; St Marys Coll; Law.

MICINSKI, ANNE; Marian HS; Mishawaka, IN; 50/170 Cls Rep Frsh Cls; Cls Rep Soph Cls; Cl Rep Jr Cls; Cls Rep Sr Cls; Stg Crw; Rptr Yrbk; Sprt Ed Sch Nwsp; Pep Clb; Chrldng; IM Sprt; Valparasio Univ; Nursing.

MICK, ELIZABETH; Jefferson Area HS; Jefferson, OH; Band; Girl Scts; NHS; Sct Actv; Yth Flsp; Spn Clb; Med Explorers; Bowling Green St Univ; Med Tech.

MICK, JUDY; Fairless HS; Navarre, OH; Chrs; Hon Rl; NHS; Sch Mus; Sch Pl; Stg Crw; Stu Cncl; Drama Clb; FTA; Pep Clb; Akron Univ.

MICK, REBECCA; Beaver Local HS; Lisbon, OH; Chrh Wkr; Stg Crw; Y-Teens; Eng Clb; 4-H; FNA; Pep Clb; Sci Clb; Letter Trk; Univ; RN.

MICK, WALTER; Sheridan HS; Thornville, OH; 8/180 Cls Rep Sr Cls; Chrs; FCA; Hon Rl; Pres NHS; Sch Mus; Stu Cncl; Capt Ftbl; Capt Wrstlng; Miami Univ; Med Tech.

MICK, WILLIAM; Defiance Sr HS; Defiance, OH; 29/300 Hon Rl; JA; DECA; JA Awd; Ohio St Univ; Math.

MICKA, DIANN; Maumee HS; Maumee, OH; 26/319 Chrs; Girl Scts; Hon Rl; Yth Flsp; Y-Teens; Fr Clb; IM Sprt; PPFtbl; Bowling Green Univ; Special Ed.

MICKELINC, NANCY; Martinsburg HS; Martinsburg, WV; Hon Rl; Stu Cncl; Pep Clb; College; Communications.

MICKELSON, KIM; Taylor HS; Kokomo, IN; 3/180 Band; Hon Rl; NHS; Sch Pl; Rptr Yrbk; Sch Nwsp; Drama Clb; 4-H; Fr Clb; Johnson Bible Coll; Education.

MICKELSON, ROB; A D Johnston HS; Bessemer, MI; Hon Rl; Rptr Sch Nwsp; Bsktbl; Letter Ftbl; Trk; IM Sprt; Nothern Mich Univ; Forestry.

MICKENS, E; Warrensville Heights HS; Warrensville, OH; Band; Chrh Wkr; Drl Tm; Sch Pl; Yth Flsp; Drama Clb; Wrstlng; Scr Kpr; Capt Twrlr; JA Awd; New York Univ; Pschology.

MICKEY, FELECIA; Woodrow Wilson HS; Raleigh, WV; 121/512 Cl Rep Jr Cls; Cls Rep Sr Cls; Hon Rl; Lbry Ade; Rptr Sch Nwsp; Sec Sci Clb; IM Sprt; Natl Merit SF; West Virginia Univ; Animal Sci.

MICKLE, KIMBERLY; Miami Trace HS; Washington Ch, OH; 80/249 Band; Lbry Ade; Sec 4-H; FNA; Sec 4-H Awd; College; Bus.

MICKLEY, KEITH; Danville HS; Danville, OH; 7/62 Chrh Wkr; Hon Rl; Stg Crw; FFA; Ftbl; Trk; COTC Voc Schl; Elect Engr.

MICKLOS, MARY; Fairmont West HS; Kettering, OH; 215/500 Cls Rep Frsh Cls; Cls Rep Sr Cls; Stu Cncl; GAA; Kiwan Awd; Ball St Univ; Business Admin.

MICKOW, MARY; Oregon Davis HS; Hamlet, IN; Cls Rep Frsh Cls; Chrs; Chrh Wkr; FCA; Hon Rl; Lbry Ade; Off Ade; Sch Pl; Stg Crw; Rptr Yrbk; Bus School; Bus.

MICULKA, LAWRENCE; Dublin HS; Dublin, OH; 11/153 Sec Frsh Cls; Pres Sr Cls; Band; NHS; Letter Bsbl; Letter Ftbl; Cit Awd; Ohi State Univ; Chem Engr.

MIDCAP, DOUGLAS W; Wheeling Park HS; Wheeling, WV; Trs Frsh Cls; Am Leg Boys St; Hon Rl; NHS; Letter Wrstlng; IM Sprt; College; Med.

MIDDAUGH, KENNETH; East Canton HS; E Canton, OH; 10/107 Sec Jr Cls; Band; Boy Scts; Hon Rl; Jr NHS; NHS; Stu Cncl; Yrbk; Fr Clb; Sci Clb; Univ Of Cincinnati; Indus Engr.

MIDDAUGH, WENDY; Fairhaven Christian Academy; Chesterton, IN; 1/13 Pres Frsh Cls; Cls Rep Frsh Cls; Band; Chrs; Chrh Wkr; Hon Rl; Lbry Ade; Orch; Pol Wkr; Sch Mus; Fairhaven Coll; Missionary.

MIDDENDORF, KAREN; Franklin Heights HS; Columbus, OH; 10/180 Band; Hon Rl; Treas NHS; Stg Crw; Key Clb; Otterbein College; Educ.

MIDDENDORF, LISA; Mother Of Mercy HS; Cincinnati, OH; 95/247 Girl Scts; Hosp Ade; PAVAS; Pol Wkr; Red Cr Ade; Sch Pl; Stg Crw; Rptr Sch Nwsp; Pres Drama Clb; Pep Clb; Univ Of Cincinnati; Psych.

MIDDENDORF, NANCY; Greensburg Community HS; Greensburg, IN; 36/206 Chrs; Hon Rl; NHS; Sch Mus; Sch Nwsp; Lat Clb; Sci Clb; Indiana St Univ; Bk P Mag Illustratr.

MIDDLEKAUFF, WILLIAM B; Walnut Hills HS; Cincinnati, OH; Band; Chrh Wkr; Hon Rl; Quill & Scroll; Stu Cncl; Yth Flsp; Yrbk; Rptr Sch Nwsp; Mth Clb; Natl Merit SF; Univ; Psych.

MIDDLETON, BETH; Crown Point HS; Crown Point, IN; NHS; Letter Ten; GAA; Mat Maids; Pom Pon; PPFtbl; Purdue Univ; Comp Sci.

MIDDLETON, DORANN; North Central HS; Indianapolis, IN; Chrh Wkr; Cmnty Wkr; Girl Scts; Hon Rl; JA; Lbry Ade; Trk; GAA; JA Awd; Natl Achvmnt Schlrshp For Outstndng Blck Students; Indiana St Univ; Biology.

MIDDLETON, JULIE; Crown Point HS; Crown Point, IN; 1/550 Pres Frsh Cls; Trs Jr Cls; Sec Sr Cls; Val; NHS; Stu Cncl; Letter Ten; Am Leg Awd; DAR Awd; Kiwan Awd; Univ Of Notre Dame; Chem.

MIDDLETON, LEWIS; Grayling HS; Frederic, MI; Band; Hon Rl; NHS; Letter Bsbl; Letter Bsktbl; Ftbl; Ten; Central Michigan Univ; Acctg.

MIDDLETON, MIKE; Zanesville HS; Zanesville, OH; Bsktbl; Ftbl; Trk; Ohi State.

MIDDLETON, SCOTT; Lebanon HS; Lebanon, OH; 63/309 Band; Pres Chrs; Hosp Ade; Sch Mus; Pres Yth Flsp; Sch Nwsp; Spn Clb; Outstndng Musicl Accomplshmnt Awd 78; 4 Superior Ratng At Oh Educ Music Assoc 76 79; Nyack Univ; Ministry.

MIDDLETON, TODD L; Benedictine HS; Cleveland, OH; 13/99 Band; Hon Rl; NHS; Orch; Letter Ftbl; Cit Awd; 3 Yr ABC Scholarship; Member Tots & Teens Inc; Natl Youth Organization; College; Acctg.

MIDEA, ANTHONY C; North Royalton HS; North Royalton, OH; 1/286 Am Leg Boys St; Band; Hon Rl; Jr NHS; Bsktbl; Ftbl; Wrstlng; IM Sprt; Am Leg Awd; JA Awd; College; Aviation.

MIDKIFF, ANDREA; Watkins Memorial HS; Pataskala, OH; 78/202 Cmp Fr Grls; Chrh Wkr; Yth Flsp; Sch Nwsp; 4-H; Pep Clb; Ohio St Univ; Home Econ.

MIDLA, TODD; Mishawaka Marian HS; S Bend, IN; 24/154 Chrh Wkr; Hon Rl; Rptr Yrbk; Rptr Sch Nwsp; 4-H; Spn Clb; Bsbl; Ind Univ; Biology.

MIEHLKE, TODD J; Manistee Cath Central HS; Manistee, MI; 10/65 Pres Frsh Cls; Pres Jr Cls; Pres Sr Cls; Am Leg Boys St; Hon Rl; 4-H; Am Leg Awd; 4-H Awd; Northwestern Univ.

MIELE, MICHELE; Farmington HS; Farmington, MI; Girl Scts; Hon Rl; Letter Ten; Univ; Bus Admin.

MIELE, SHERI; Kearsley HS; Davison, MI; Girl Scts; Off Ade; Fr Clb; Letter Bsktbl; Trk; Coach Actv; IM Sprt; Bus Schl; Sec.

MIELENZ, JOY; Morton Sr HS; Hammond, IN; Chrh Wkr; Girl Scts; Hon Rl; Hosp Ade; Jr NHS; Sec FHA; Purdue Univ; RN.

MIELKE, DEBBIE; Gladwin HS; Gladwin, MI; Chrs; Hon Rl; Lbry Ade; Stg Crw; 4-H; FFA; 4-H Awd; Bus Schl; Legal Sec.

MIENTKIEWICZ, KAREN; Niles Mc Kinley HS; Niles, OH; 7/421 AFS; Chrs; Girl Scts; Hon Rl; Natl Forn Lg; VP NHS; VP PAVAS; Drama Clb; Chrldng; GAA; Youngstown St Univ.

MIENTKIEWICZ, TIMOTHY J; Mckinley HS; Niles, OH; 13/378 AFS; Am Leg Boys St; Boy Scts; Hon Rl; NHS; Red Cr Ade; Sch Mus; Sch Pl; Sct Actv; College; Engr.

MIERAS, LYNN; Newaygo HS; Newaygo, MI; Drl Tm; Hon Rl; NHS; Yth Flsp; Rptr Yrbk; FTA; OEA; Spn Clb; Swmmng; Grand Rapids Jr Coll; Med Asst.

MIERZWIAK, SUSAN; Notre Dame Academy; Toledo, OH; Chrh Wkr; Girl Scts; Hosp Ade; Stg Crw;.

MIES, MICHAEL; Bishop Borgess HS; Livonia, MI; Hon Rl; NHS; Ed Sch Nwsp; IM Sprt; 3rd And 4th In Principals Writing Awd Cntst; Certificate Of Merit S E Mich Scholastic Writing Awd Cntst; College; Journalism.

MIESIAK, STEPHEN; Troy HS; Troy, MI; Jr NHS; NHS; Mert Scclhsp Awd 79; Wayne St Univ; Comp Engr.

MIESNER, JOHN; Washington Irving HS; Clarksburg, WV; 35/172 Cls Rep Frsh Cls; Cl Rep Jr Cls; Cls Rep Sr Cls; Am Leg Boys St; Band; Boy Scts; Chrh Wkr; Hon Rl; College; Soc Sci.

MIESZKOWSKI, JULIA; Utica HS; Utica, MI; Chrs; Hon Rl; Jr NHS; NHS; Orch; Sch Mus; Piano Schlrshp; Piano Performance Awds; I Rating Every Dist Solo Ensemble; Univ Of Michigan; Music.

MIETLA, HELEN M; Swan Valley HS; Saginaw, MI; 17/189 Chrh Wkr; Hon Rl; NHS; Off Ade; Yrbk; Drama Clb; Pep Clb; Trk; Principals Award; Saginaw Valley State Coll; Sec Ed.

MIFFLIN, JAMES; Park Hills HS; Fairborn, OH; Band; Chrs; Drm Bgl; Drm Mjrt; Hon Rl; Off Ade; Orch; Lat Clb; Gym; Wri State Univ; Bio.

MIFFLIN, KARL A; Nordonia Sr HS; Macedonia, OH; 33/486 Band; Hon Rl; Orch; Sch Mus; Sch Pl; Sct Actv; Stg Crw; Drama Clb; Bsbl; Bsktbl; Nordonia HS Hon Awd 78; Music Amer Select Band European Concert Tour 78; Univ; Chem Engr.

MIGALA, JEFFREY A; St Joseph HS; St Joseph, MI; Cls Rep Frsh Cls; Boy Scts; Chrs; FCA; Hon Rl; Stg Crw; Stu Cncl; Lat Clb; Sci Clb; Letter Ftbl; Eagle Rank Of Boy Scout; Notre Dame Univ; Psych.

MIGNANO, ANTONINA M; St Mary Academy; Monroe, MI; 14/133 Pres Debate Tm; Hon Rl; Mod UN; Sci Clb; Swmmng; Trk; GAA; Opt Clb Awd; Michigan St Univ; Pre Law.

MIGNELLA, MICHELE; Cardinal Mooney HS; Poland, OH; 26/294 Hon Rl; Jr NHS; NHS; Lcrss; Wrstlng; Coach Actv; Mat Maids; Bausch & Lomb Awd; Dnfth Awd; DAR Awd; Youngstown St Univ ; Med Tech.

MIGOCKI, BETTY; Warren HS; Sterling Hts, MI; Chrh Wkr; Hon Rl; NHS; Sch Nwsp; Letter Pom Pon; Letter Scr Kpr; Letter Tmr; College; Nurse.

MIHAJLOV, ANDREA; Barberton HS; Barberton, OH; 1/460 Am Leg Aux Girls St; Hosp Ade; NHS; Off Ade; Sct Actv; Yth Flsp; FDA; Ger Clb; Univ; Vet.

MIHALKO, TERRIE; Northwest HS; Canal Fulton, OH; 11/165 Band; Chrs; Chrh Wkr; Girl Scts; Hon Rl; NHS; Off Ade; Yth Flsp; Y-Teens; Rptr Yrbk; Bowling Green State Univ; Nurse.

MIHALYO, MICHAEL P; Mingo HS; Mingo Jct, OH; 5/129 Cl Rep Jr Cls; Am Leg Boys St; Sec Band; Chrs; Chrh Wkr; NHS; Pres Stu Cncl; VP Key Clb; Ohio Music Ed Assn Awd Superior Piano; Thursday Music Clb Wheeling Chapt Musically Advanced Superior; Cincinnati Conservatory; Music.

MIHOJEVICH, NANCY; Brethren Christian Schl; Elkhart, IN; 1/31 Band; Chrs; Chrh Wkr; Hon Rl; Ed Yrbk; Yrbk; Sch Nwsp; Opt Clb Awd; Univ; Graphic Arts.

MIILLER, JEFFREY; South Newton HS; Goodland, IN; 27/105 Chrh Wkr; Yth Flsp; FBLA; FFA; Ger Clb; Ftbl; Univ; Engr.

MIILU, MARY; Ontonagon Area HS; Mass City, MI; 2/85 Trs Sr Cls; Am Leg Aux Girls St; Cmnty Wkr; Hon Rl; Hosp Ade; NHS; Sch Pl; Stg Crw; Yth Flsp; Ed Yrbk; Coll Of St Scholastica; Nursing.

MIJARES, PATSY; Springfield HS; Holland, OH; 20/150 Trs Jr Cls; Band; Chrs; Hon Rl; Off Ade; Orch; Stu Cncl; Pep Clb; Spn Clb; Michigan St Univ; Interpreter.

MIKA, RICHARD; Bay City All Saints HS; Bay City, MI; Chrs; Cmnty Wkr; Hon Rl; Boys Clb Am; FBLA; Pep Clb; Bsbl; Bsktbl; Ten; Olttrs On Varsity Tem For 3 Yrs; Rcvd 2 Golden Glove Awdds As Catcher For Team; Tennis 2 Ltrs On Varsty Tm; Northwood Inst; Mrktng.

MIKE, KAREN; Heath HS; Heath, OH; Trs Jr Cls; Chrh Wkr; Cmnty Wkr; Hon Rl; Key Clb; Chrldng; College; Bus.

MIKELONIS, MICHELLE; Madeira HS; Madeira, OH; 9/207 Trs Soph Cls; Trs Jr Cls; Trs Sr Cls; Drl Tm; Hon Rl; Lit Mag; NHS; Fr Clb; Bsktbl; GAA; Arizona St Univ; Bio.

MIKESELL, YUKARI; Centerville HS; Dayton, OH; 77/687 NHS; Orch; Lat Clb; Mth Clb; Rus Clb; Sci Clb; Miami Univ; Micro Bio.

MIKKILA, JANET A; Fairview HS; Fairview Pk, OH; 30/280 Sec Frsh Cls; Pres Soph Cls; Pres Jr Cls; VP Sr Cls; Girl Scts; Hon Rl; Sch Pl; Chrldng; Scr Kpr; Ohio St Univ; Nursing.

MIKLE, LORRAINE; Mount Clemens HS; Mt Clemens, MI; Cls Rep Frsh Cls; Chrh Wkr; Girl Scts; Hon Rl; Hosp Ade; NHS; Lat Clb; Letter Swmmng; Albion College; Premed.

MIKLIS, ELLEN; Charles F Brush HS; Lyndhurst, OH; AFS; Chrs; Girl Scts; Off Ade; Rptr Yrbk; Yrbk; Mth Clb; Cleveland Press Spelling Bee Finalist; Coll; Med.

MIKLOWSKI, MARY; North Royalton HS; N Royalton, OH; Band; Cmp Fr Grls; Girl Scts; Hon Rl; Jr NHS; VICA; IM Sprt; Ohio State; Veterinarian.

MIKOLAICZIK, DONNA; Arthur Hill HS; Saginaw, MI; Hon Rl; Y-Teens; Letter Bsktbl; GAA; Ferris St Univ; X Ray Tech.

MIKOLAJCZAK, LINDA; Rensselaer Cntrl HS; Rensselaer, IN; 17/162 Cls Rep Frsh Cls; Sec Soph Cls; Cls Rep Sr Cls; Chrs; Chrh Wkr; FCA; Hon Rl; Hosp Ade; NHS; Sch Mus; Univ Of Evansville; Nursing.

MIKOLAJCZAK, MARY; Bay City All Saints Ctrl HS; Bay City, MI; Trs Soph Cls; Cl Rep Jr Cls; Cls Rep Sr Cls; Chrh Wkr; Hon Rl; Hosp Ade; NHS; Red Cr Ade; Sch Mus; Stu Cncl; College; Vocational Rehabilitation.

MIKOVITS, C; Flushing HS; Mt Morris, MI; Girl Scts; Lbry Ade; Yth Flsp; Cit Awd; Univ Of Flint; Conservation.

MIKSIS, GEORGIANA; Oak Hill HS; Oak Hill, WV; Hon Rl; NHS; Sch Mus; Sch Pl; Yrbk; Drama Clb; Sci Clb; 3rd Pl In Cnty Sci Fair 77; 2nd Pl An Oral Interpartn Contst 78; Univ; Bio.

MIKULA, CYNTHIA; Old Trail School; Wadsworth, OH; Sec Frsh Cls; Sec Soph Cls; Pres Jr Cls; Pres Sr Cls; Val; Chrs; Girl Scts; Hon Rl; Sct Actv; Pres Stu Cncl; Wittenberg Univ; Bio.

MIKULSKI, MARIA; Holy Redeemer HS; Detroit, MI; Cls Rep Frsh Cls; Sec Soph Cls; Hon Rl; Univ.

MIKUTOWICZ, JOHN; Holy Rosary HS; Burton, MI; Hon Rl; Univ.

MILANO, MARK; Clarence M Kimball HS; Royal Oak, MI; 31/605 NHS; Sch Pl; Letter Ftbl; Hon Schlrshp For Cntrl Mi Univ 79; Central Michigan Univ; Dent.

MILANO, STEVE; Coventry HS; Barberton, OH; 3/18 Pres Jr Cls; Cl Rep Jr Cls; Pres Sr Cls; Hon Rl; Stu Cncl; Ed Yrbk; Key Clb; VICA; Dnfth Awd; Pres Awd; Ntnl Rfle Assctn Awrd Of Shrpshter 78; Diesel Mech.

MILANOVIC, ZORAN; Donald E Gavit HS; Hammond, IN; 1/250 Val; Hon Rl; Jr NHS; NHS; Off Ade; Stu Cncl; Sci Clb; Bausch & Lomb Awd; Natl Merit Ltr; Univ Of Chicago; Physical Science.

MILANOWSKI, CHRISTINE; West Catholic HS; Grand Rapids, MI; Cls Rep Soph Cls; Debate Tm; Hon Rl; VP JA; Mdrgl; Sch Mus; College; Chem.

MILAR, KARA; Norton HS; Norton, OH; 3/285 Chrh Wkr; Hon Rl; Pres Jr NHS; Treas NHS; Yth Flsp; Rptr Sch Nwsp; Lat Clb; Mth Clb; Scr Kpr; Bowling Green St Univ; Acctg.

MILARCH, JODI; Manistee Catholic Cntrl HS; Manistee, MI; Hon Rl; 4-H;.

MILASKY, CHRISTINE; Lorain Catholic HS; Lorain, OH; Chrs; Hon Rl; Coach Actv; PPFtbl; College.

MILBAUER, KRISTINA; Beaver Local HS; E Liverpool, OH; 40/245 Am Leg Aux Girls St; Hon Rl; Eng Clb; Pres Fr Clb; Pep Clb; Trk; IM Sprt; Mgrs; Kent St Univ; Acctg.

MILBERT, DEBBIE; Buckeye W HS; Mt Pleasnat, OH; Hst Soph Cls; Am Leg Aux Girls St; Hon Rl; NHS; Drama Clb; 4-H; FHA; OEA; Pep Clb; Sci Clb; Bradford Busns Schl; Steno Clerk.

MILBERT, DEBBIE S; Buckeye West HS; Mt Pleasant, OH; Hst Soph Cls; Hon Rl; Jr NHS; NHS; Drama Clb; FHA; OEA; Pep Clb; Sci Clb; Bsktbl; Business Schl; Secretary.

MILDER, SUSAN; Greenon HS; Enon, OH; 4/236 Hon Rl; NHS; Fr Clb; Coll; Vet.

MILENIUS, KEITH; Rocky River HS; Rocky Rvr, OH; Band; Boy Scts; Hon Rl; Sct Actv; Socr; Univ; Bus.

MILES, HENRY G; Lake HS; Hartville, OH; VP Sr Cls; Am Leg Boys St; Hon Rl; JA; Jr NHS; Pres NHS; Ed Yrbk; Sci Clb; Bsktbl; Letter Ten; Oh St Police Cadet Progr W Am Leg Auxilary 79; Univ; Pre Med.

MILES, JANET E; Northland HS; Columbus, OH; 1/425 Cls Rep Soph Cls; Cls Rep Sr Cls; Val; Aud/Vis; Boy Scts; Cmp Fr Grls; Chrs; Chrh Wkr; Cmnty Wkr; Hon Rl; Hugh O Brien Yth Awd; BSA Exploring Young Amer Awd; Reg Soroptimist Yth Citizenship Awd; Ohio St Univ; Medicine.

MILES, JOHN T; Beavercreek HS; Fairborn, OH; 9/702 Hon Rl; Natl Merit SF; 9th Pl In Geometry Test; 8 Pl Chem Div I; Case Western Reserve Univ; Physics.

MILES, LINDA; Clio HS; Clio, MI; Girl Scts; NHS; Sch Pl; Stg Crw; Yth Flsp; Drama Clb; Spn Clb; Trk; Chrldng; Hope Coll; Drama.

MILES, LOIS; Western Brown Sr HS; Georgetown, OH; 19/160 Treas Band; Hon Rl; MMM; NHS; Stg Crw; Pres Yth Flsp; Spn Clb; Purdue Mrch Band Awd 78; Southern St Coll; Real Estate.

MILES, LORI; North Muskegon HS; N Muskegon, MI; 38/108 Band; Chrs; Hon Rl; Off Ade; Orch; Sch Mus; Sch Pl; Fr Clb; Capt Chrldng; GAA; Central Michigan Univ.

MILES, NANCY; West Jefferson HS; W Jefferson, OH; 15/105 Am Leg Aux Girls St; Band; Cmp Fr Grls; Chrs; Chrh Wkr; Hon Rl; NHS; Quill & Scroll; Sch Mus; Sch Pl; Franklin Univ; Nursing.

MILES, STEVE; Richmond Sr HS; Richmond, IN; Cls Rep Frsh Cls; Cls Rep Soph Cls; Hon Rl; IM Sprt; Univ.

MILES, THERESA; Shortridge HS; Indianapolis, IN; 42/444 Cls Rep Sr Cls; Chrs; Chrh Wkr; Cmnty Wkr; Hon Rl; Off Ade; Orch; Stu Cncl; Civ Clb; 4-H; State Finalist Miss United Teenager Pageant; Upward Bound; Indiana Univ; Busns.

MILETI, DIANA; Rocky River HS; Rocky Rvr, OH; 56/300 Cl Rep Jr Cls; Hon Rl; Stu Cncl; Rptr Yrbk; Yrbk; IM Sprt; Mat Maids; Tmr; Cit Awd; Cleveland St Univ; Bus Admin.

MILETI, RAY; West Geauga HS; Chesterland, OH; 33/352 Hon Rl; NHS; Letter Glf; Univ Of Akron; Acctg.

MILEWSKI, GREG; East Detroit HS; E Detroit, MI; Band; Hon Rl; Jr Pin In Jazz Ensmbl 78; Univ; Music.

MILEY, ELIZABETH; Harrison HS; Evansville, IN; 10/475 Cl Rep Jr Cls; Hon Rl; Natl Forn Lg; NHS; Orch; Sch Mus; Sch Pl; Stg Crw; Stu Cncl; Yth Flsp; Univ Of Evansville; Cmnctns.

MILEY, KIMBERLY; Northmor HS; Galion, OH; 6/109 Chrh Wkr; FCA; Hon Rl; Hosp Ade; NHS; Chrldng; Mansfield Gen Schl; Nursing.

MILFORD, WILLIAM R; Green HS; North Canton, OH; 21/319 Band; Boy Scts; Chrs; Hon Rl; JA; Lbry Ade; Mdrgl; NHS; Sch Mus; Sct Actv; College; Elec Engr.

MILHOLLAND, KATRINA; South Western HS; Flat Rock, IN; 18/65 Band; Sch Mus; Sch Pl; Rptr Yrbk; Rptr Sch Nwsp; Drama Clb; Pep Clb; Bsktbl; Mgrs; Scr Kpr; Univ Of Evansville; Nursing.

MILING, DAN; Howell HS; Howell, MI; 49/395 Trs Sr Cls; Hon Rl; JA; NHS; JA Awd; Mich State Univ; Bus.

MILING, DANIEL; Howell HS; Howell, MI; 49/395 Trs Sr Cls; Boy Scts; Hon Rl; JA; NHS; JA Awd; Natl Merit Ltr; Michigan St Univ; Bus.

MILIONIS, W KELLY; Douglas Mac Arthur HS; Saginaw, MI; Pol Wkr; Rptr Sch Nwsp; Ger Clb; Pep Clb; People To People Stdnt Ambssdr Progr 78; Washington Workshp 79; Michigan St Univ; Intl Relations.

MILKS, MATTHEW; Loy Norrix HS; Kalamazoo, MI; Letter Bsbl; Letter Ftbl; Ferris State Coll; Bus.

MILKS, ROBERT; Benzie Central HS; Copemish, MI; Band; Boy Scts; Hon Rl; Crs Cntry; Univ; Cmmrcl Airline Pilot.

MILLAGE, KYLE; Shenandoah HS; Middletown, IN; 13/118 Hon Rl; Mth Clb; Sci Clb; Purdue Univ; Chem Engr.

MILLAGER, JODY; Bluffton HS; Bluffton, OH; Band; Trs Frsh Cls; VP Soph Cls; Gym; IM Sprt;.

MILLARD, BECKY; Ashtabula Harbor HS; Ashtabula, OH; 27/207 AFS; Hon Rl; JA; Rptr Yrbk; Pep Clb; Sec Spn Clb; Bsbl; JA Awd; Univ Of Akron Data Proc.

MILLBERG, CHRIS; Bishop Luers HS; Fort Wayne, IN; 33/222 Chrh Wkr; Hon Rl; OEA; Indiana Purdue Univ; Comp Tech.

MILLEN, JOHN; Northville HS; Northville, MI; Chrh Wkr; Cmnty Wkr; Hon Rl; JA; Red Cr Ade; Fr Clb; Pep Clb; Letter Bsbl; Letter Ftbl; Letter Swmmng; Oakland Univ; Engr.

MILLEN, SUSAN; Whitmore Lake HS; Whitmore Lake, MI; 16/89 Band; Girl Scts; Hon Rl; Jr NHS; NHS; Treas Stu Cncl; Pep Clb; Chrldng; Captian Jr Vrsty Cheerldrs 1976; Various Band Awrds; Eastern Univ; Acctg.

MILLER, ALAN; Jackson HS; Jackson, OH; Boy Scts; Chrs; Jr NHS; PAVAS; Sch Nwsp; Lat Clb; VP Of The Pep Club 78; 5th Pl In The Dist Eng Schlrshp Test 77; Rio Grande Univ; Advtsng.

MILLER, AMY; Crown Point HS; Crown Point, IN; Cls Rep Soph Cls; Cmnty Wkr; Off Ade; Awd For Straight A In Semester Class 78; IUN; Nurse.

MILLER, ANGELA; Monroeville HS; Monroevle, OH; Trs Sr Cls; Band; Chrh Wkr; Hon Rl; Bsktbl; GAA; Sandusky School Of Practical Nursing.

MILLER, ANGELA; Hilliard HS; Columbus, OH; Cls Rep Frsh Cls; Chrs; Chrh Wkr; Cmnty Wkr; Hon Rl; NHS; Sch Pl; Stu Cncl; Fr Clb; Pres FTA; OSU; Real Estate.

MILLER, ANGELA; Benjamin Logan HS; W Mansfield, OH; Hon Rl; Jr NHS; Sch Mus; Yrbk; Sch Nwsp; OEA; Letter Gym; Letter Trk; Chrldng; Bus.

MILLER, ANGELA R; Terre Haute South Vigo HS; Terre Haute, IN; 49/620 VP Jr Cls; VP Sr Cls; Chrh Wkr; Hon Rl; Off Ade; Pol Wkr; Yth Flsp; Y-Teens; DECA; OEA; Vincennes Univ; Phys Ther.

MILLER, ANNE; Grand Ledge HS; Grand Ledge, MI; Girl Scts; Hon Rl; NHS; Lat Clb; Natl Merit Ltr; Mic State Univ; Engr.

MILLER, ANNEMARIE; De Kalb HS; Waterloo, IN; Band; Chrh Wkr; Debate Tm; JA; Natl Forn Lg; NHS; Sch Mus; Stg Crw; VICA; Art Inst Of Pittsburgh; Inter Dsgn.

MILLER, BARBARA; Bexley HS; Columbus, OH; Pres AFS; Band; Hon Rl; ROTC; Sch Pl; Drama Clb; VP Spn Clb; Tmr; Cum Laude Soc 78; Part In Amer Assoc Of Gchr Of Spanish & Porugese 76 78; Univ; Bilingual Educ.

MILLER, BECKY; Meadowbrook HS; Byesville, OH; Cls Rep Soph Cls; Cl Rep Jr Cls; VP Sr Cls; Cls Rep Sr Cls; Chrh Wkr; Hon Rl; Jr NHS; NHS; Off Ade; Sch Pl; Bookkeeper.

MILLER, BETH; Hiland HS; Millersburg, OH; Cls Rep Frsh Cls; Am Leg Aux Girls St; Chrh Wkr; Hon Rl; NHS; Off Ade; Sch Pl; Yth Flsp; 4-H; FHA; E Mennonite Coll; Home Econ.

MILLER, BETH; Mitchell HS; Williams, IN; 1/143 Val; Hon Rl; Oakland City Coll; Acctg.

MILLER, BILL; Milton Union HS; W Milton, OH; 30/232 Chrh Wkr; Hon Rl; NHS; Pol Wkr; FTA; Ten; Wrstlng; Univ Of Dayton; Dentistry.

MILLER, BILLY; Huntington E HS; Huntington, WV; Band; Chrs; Chrh Wkr; Hon Rl; Lit Mag; Mdrgl; Sch Mus; Yth Flsp; Lat Clb; Music Awd; Citizenship Honor Roll; Recognition 3 Yrs In Literary Magazine; Marshall Univ; Music.

MILLER, BLAIR; Greenville Sr HS; Gettysburg, OH; 17/360 Chrh Wkr; Hon Rl; NHS; Quill & Scroll; Yth Flsp; Sprt Ed Yrbk; Letter Ten; Manchester Coll; Chem.

MILLER, BONNIE; Meadowbrook HS; Byesville, OH; Cls Rep Frsh Cls; Sec Soph Cls; Cl Rep Jr Cls; Band; Chrs; Chrh Wkr; Drm Mjrt; Hon Rl; Off Ade; Stu Cncl; Univ; Comp Sci.

MILLER, BONNIE L; Vanlue Local School; Carey, OH; Trs Sr Cls; Band; Chrs; Debate Tm; Hon Rl; Jr NHS; Lbry Ade; NHS; Sch Mus; Sch Pl; Bus Schl; Comp Sci.

MILLER, BRENT; John Glenn HS; New Concord, OH; FCA; Hon Rl; Off Ade; Capt Bsktbl; Letter Ftbl; College; Law.

MILLER, BRIAN; Mona Shores HS; Muskegon, MI; Hon Rl; Lbry Ade; Sprt Ed Yrbk; Sprt Ed Sch Nwsp; IM Sprt; Jr Var Ltr In Ftbl 77; Muskegon Cmnty Coll; Acctg.

MILLER, BRIAN; Anderson HS; Anderson, IN; Cls Rep Frsh Cls; Cls Rep Soph Cls; Cl Rep Jr Cls; Cls Rep Sr Cls; Boy Scts; FCA; Hon Rl; Quill & Scroll; Stu Cncl; Rptr Yrbk; Ball State.

MILLER, BRIAN; Jackson HS; Massillon, OH; 12/409 Hon Rl; Sci Clb; Wittenberg Univ; Pre Med.

MILLER, BRIAN; Philo HS; Roseville, OH; Sec Sr Cls; Chrh Wkr; Rptr Sch Nwsp; 4-H; Pres Fr Clb; FTA; Sci Clb; 4-H Awd; College; Astro Physics.

MILLER, BRUCE; Harbor Sr HS; Ashtabula, OH; 3/185 Cls Rep Frsh Cls; Cls Rep Soph Cls; Cl Rep Jr Cls; Cls Rep Sr Cls; AFS; Am Leg Boys St; Band; Chrh Wkr; Cmnty Wkr; Hon Rl; Mercy Hurst Coll; Govt.

MILLER, CANDY; Green HS; Greensburg, OH; Sec Soph Cls; Cls Rep Soph Cls; Sec Jr Cls; Cl Rep Jr Cls; Chrs; Hon Rl; NHS; Stu Cncl; Y-Teens; Treas Pep Clb; Sr Of Month 79; Bus Dept Awd 79; Homecoming Attendant 77; Univ Of Akron; Math.

MILLER, CAROL; Grove City HS; Grove City, OH; 1/500 Am Leg Aux Girls St; Treas NHS; Yth Flsp; Bsktbl; Opt Clb Awd; Univ; Phys Educ.

MILLER, CAROL; Edinburgh Cmnty HS; Franklin, IN; 10/92 Cl Rep Jr Cls; Hosp Ade; Off Ade; Stu Cncl; Pres 4-H; Fr Clb; VP Pep Clb; Trk; Am Leg Awd; 4-H Awd; Univ.

MILLER, CAROL; Warren HS; Warren, MI; Hon Rl; NHS; Red Cr Ade; Pres Swmmng; GAA; IM Sprt; Tmr; Natl Merit Schl; Michigan St Univ; Zoology.

MILLER, CAROLE; Southgate HS; Southgate, MI; 1/350 Cls Rep Frsh Cls; Cl Rep Jr Cls; Cls Rep Sr Cls; Girl Scts; Hon Rl; Pres Jr NHS; VP NHS; Sct Actv; Stu Cncl; Yth Flsp; Univ; Vet Med.

MILLER, CAROLYN; Marian HS; Cincinnati, OH; Cmp Fr Grls; Chrs; JA; Off Ade; Orch; Sch Mus; Stu Cncl; Spn Clb; Bsbl; Bsktbl; Univ; Cmnctns.

MILLER, CATHERINE; Lake Catholic HS; Newbury, OH; 16/340 Lit Mag; NHS; Rptr Sch Nwsp; Fr Clb; Kent State Univ; Education.

MILLER, CATHY; Msgr John R Hackett HS; Kalamazoo, MI; Girl Scts; Hon Rl; Yth Flsp; 4-H; Bsktbl; 4-H Awd; College.

MILLER, CHARISSA; North Putnam HS; Fillmore, IN; 24/150 Am Leg Aux Girls St; Capt Drl Tm; FCA; Sec NHS; Sch Mus; 4-H; Pres Lat Clb; Treas Mth Clb; Spn Clb; Capt Pom Pon; College; Nursing.

MILLER, CHARLES; Hamilton Taft HS; Hamilton, OH; 7/435 AFS; Band; Chrh Wkr; Hon Rl; Jr NHS; NHS; Yth Flsp; Rptr Sch Nwsp; Miami Univ; Pulp & Paper Tech.

MILLER, CHARLES; Delphos Jefferson HS; Delphos, OH; 13/110 Treas Band; Chrs; Drm Bgl; Hon Rl; NHS; Sch Mus; Fr Clb; Spn Clb; Letter Trk; Bowling Green State Univ.

MILLER, CHERYL; Eisenhower HS; Saginaw, MI; 15/344 Cls Rep Soph Cls; Pres Jr Cls; Cls Rep Sr Cls; Hon Rl; NHS; Stu Cncl; Sec Pep Clb; Letter Swmmng; Letter Ten; Natl Merit SF; Homecoming Ct 79; Michigan St Univ; Pre Med.

MILLER, CHERYL; Rutherford B Hayes HS; Delaware, OH; 23/294 Band; Hon Rl; Sch Mus; 4-H; FFA; Ohi State Univ; Agri Field.

MILLER, CHRISTIAN; Decatur Jr Sr HS; Decatur, MI; Pres Sr Cls; Pol Wkr; Crs Cntry; Trk; Am Leg Awd; Cit Awd; Alternate Camp Minewanka; College; Biology.

MILLER, CHRISTINA; Western Boone Jr Sr HS; Throntown, IN; Hon Rl; NHS; Spn Clb; Ind Purdue Univ; Nursing.

MILLER, CHRISTINE; Howell HS; Howell, MI; 34/365 Trs Jr Cls; Chrs; Chrh Wkr; Hon Rl; Sch Mus; Yth Flsp; Bsbl; Lansing Community College; Nursing.

MILLER, CINDY; Maplewood HS; Cortland, OH; Band; Chrh Wkr; Hon Rl; Hosp Ade; Yth Flsp; DECA; Fr Clb; Bsbl; Bsktbl; Trumbull Coll Joint Voc Schl; Nurse.

MILLER, CONNIE; Westview Jr Sr HS; Topeka, IN; 6/84 Chrs; Drl Tm; Hon Rl; Jr NHS; NHS; Yth Flsp; FHA; Pep Clb; Mat Maids; Pom Pon; Business.

MILLER, CORINNE J; Rogers HS; Toledo, OH; VP Soph Cls; Chrh Wkr; Debate Tm; Hon Rl; Off Ade; Sch Pl; Stg Crw; Stu Cncl; Yth Flsp; Rptr Yrbk; Univ Of Toledo; Social Sci.

MILLER, CORRINA; Saint Clement HS; Detroit, MI; 14/115 Sec Jr Cls; Girl Scts; Hon Rl; Treas NHS; Sch Pl; Stg Crw; Stu Cncl; GAA; Wayne State Univ; Acctg.

MILLER, CORRINA; St Clement HS; Detroit, MI; 14/115 Sec Jr Cls; Chrs; Girl Scts; Hon Rl; Treas NHS; Sch Pl; Stg Crw; GAA; Wayne St Univ; Acctg.

MILLER, C RENE; Terre Haute South Vigo HS; Terre Haute, IN; Cls Rep Frsh Cls; Cls Rep Soph Cls; Cl Rep Jr Cls; Cls Rep Sr Cls; Chrs; FCA; Girl Scts; Hon Rl; Hosp Ade; Sct Actv; Purdue Univ; Sci.

MILLER, CYNTHIA; Flint Central HS; Flint, MI; Cls Rep Frsh Cls; Cl Rep Jr Cls; Band; Hon Rl; Lbry Ade; NHS; Orch; Stu Cncl; Yth Flsp; Mich State Univ; Applied Music.

MILLER, CYNTHIA; Green HS; Uniontown, OH; 1/320 Drl Tm; Hon Rl; NHS; Y-Teens; Drama Clb; Fr Clb; Pep Clb; Letter Ten; Pom Pon; College.

MILLER, D; Timken HS; Canton, OH; Boy Scts; Chrh Wkr; JA; Sct Actv; Fr Clb; Ftbl; IM Sprt;.

MILLER, DALE; Indian Valley South HS; Port Washington, OH; Cls Rep Frsh Cls; Cls Rep Soph Cls; Cl Rep Jr Cls; Band; Chrs; Chrh Wkr; Hon Rl; NHS; Sch Pl; VP Stu Cncl; Ohio St Farmer Degree; 4 Yr Schlrshp Awd Plaque; All Ohio St FFA Band; Wittenberg Univ; Medicine.

MILLER, DALE R; Indian Valley South HS; Port Washington, OH; 10/95 Cls Rep Frsh Cls; Cls Rep Soph Cls; Cl Rep Jr Cls; Band; Chrs; Sec Chrh Wkr; Hon Rl; NHS; Sch Pl; VP Stu Cncl; Wittenberg Univ; Radiation Med.

MILLER, DAN; St Philip Catholic Cntrl HS; Battle Creek, MI; Hon Rl; NHS; Lat Clb; Letter Bsbl; Letter Bsktbl; College.

MILLER, DANIEL B; Maumee HS; Maumee, OH; Am Leg Boys St; Aud/Vis; Boy Scts; Chrh Wkr; Cmnty Wkr; Drl Tm; Drm Bgl; Hon Rl; Yth Flsp; Boys Clb Am; Superior Rating Dist & St Sci Fair 79; USMA; Chem.

MILLER, DARRELL; Norwood Sr HS; Norwood, OH; Chrs; Chrh Wkr; Cmnty Wkr; Hon Rl; DECA; Mas Awd; David Livingsto Awd; Bus Schl; Bus Mgmt.

MILLER, DARRYL; Woodhaven HS; Romulus, MI; Letter Band; Chrh Wkr; NHS; Sch Pl; Stg Crw; Drama Clb; VICA; Farris St Univ; Elec Tech.

MILLER, DARYL J; Marlington HS; Louisville, OH; 81/278 Chrh Wkr; Cmnty Wkr; Pol Wkr; Pres Yth Flsp; Bsbl; Bsktbl; IM Sprt; Univ Of Akron; Bus Admin.

MILLER, DAVE; Walsh Jesuit HS; Akron, OH; 3/170 Cls Rep Frsh Cls; Hon Rl; Red Cr Ade; Rptr Sch Nwsp; Capt Glf; Letter Trk; Univ Of Akron; Med.

MILLER, DAVID; Walsh Jesuit HS; Akron, OH; 3/170 Cls Rep Frsh Cls; Hon Rl; ROTC; Stu Cncl; Rptr Sch Nwsp; Capt Glf; Socr; Trk; Phi Beta Kappa Awd; St Louis Univ Schlrshp; Univ Of Akron.

MILLER, DAVID; Loudonville HS; Loudonville, OH; 2/130 Band; Boy Scts; Hon Rl; NHS; Sch Pl; Stg Crw; Rptr Sch Nwsp; Sch Nwsp; Lat Clb; Bowling Green Univ; CPA.

MILLER, DAVID; Brooklyn HS; Brooklyn, OH; Band; Chrh Wkr; Red Cr Ade; Yth Flsp; Spn Clb; Crs Cntry, Hockey, Trk, Coach Actv, IM Sprt; Univ; Bio.

MILLER, DAVID; Lake Catholic HS; Wickliffe, OH; Cls Rep Frsh Cls; Cls Rep Soph Cls; Hon Rl; IM Sprt; Univ.

MILLER, DAVID P; Orrville HS; Orrville, OH; 5/160 Am Leg Boys St; Band; Hon Rl; JA; Jr NHS; Sch Pl; Yth Flsp; Rptr Yrbk; IM Sprt; JA Awd; College; Engineering.

MILLER, DEAN; Jasper HS; Jasper, IN; 6/326 Am Leg Boys St; Chrs; Cmnty Wkr; Hon Rl; NHS; Stg Crw; 4-H; Letter Ftbl; Letter Trk; Letter Wrstlng; Purdue Univ; Comp Sci.

MILLER, DEBBIE; John F Kennedy HS; Taylor, MI; Band; Chrs; Debate Tm; Hon Rl; Lbry Ade; Natl Forn Lg; Sct Actv; Yth Flsp; PPFtbl; Cit Awd; Univ; Law.

MILLER, DEBBIE; Rensselaer Central HS; Rensselaer, IN; 20/162 Hon Rl; NHS; 4-H; FHA; Cit Awd; 4-H Awd;.

MILLER, DEBORAH; Henry Ford II HS; Sterling Hts, MI; 5/456 Band; NHS; Off Ade; Chrldng; Scr Kpr; Tmr; Mi St Univ Awd Of Acad Excllnc 79; French Medal 79; Mi Comp Schlrshp 79; Michigan St Univ; Pre Med.

MILLER, DEBORAH; Warren Central HS; Indpls, IN; VP Girl Scts; JA; Natl Forn Lg; Pres 4-H; Pep Clb; Spn Clb; 4-H Awd; Whos Who Medln For Home Ec 76; Home Ec Awd For Foods 76; Hrnbl Diploma Awd For Spnsh 76; Ball St Univ; Tchr.

MILLER, DEBORAH; Field HS; Kent, OH; 2/300 Am Leg Aux Girls St; Chrh Wkr; Hon Rl; NHS; Yth Flsp; Bsbl; Letter Bsktbl; GAA; Univ; Phys Ther.

MILLER, DEBRA; White Pigeon HS; White Pigeon, MI; 6/94 Band; Hon Rl; NHS; Fr Clb; Letter Trk; Mgrs; PPFtbl; Western Mic Univ; Pre Med.

MILLER, DEBRA A; Defiance Sr HS; Defiance, OH; 24/321 Chrh Wkr; Hon Rl; Jr NHS; NHS; FTA; Bsbl; Bsktbl; Concordia Coll; Home Ec.

MILLER, DENISE; Marietta HS; Marietta, OH; Band; NHS; Orch; Marietta Coll.

MILLER, DENISE; Atherton HS; Grand Blanc, MI; 3/150 Hon Rl; Sprt Ed Sch Nwsp; Rptr Sch Nwsp; Letter Bsktbl; Coach Actv; IM Sprt; Scr Kpr; Tmr; Univ Of Michigan; Jrnlsm.

MILLER, DENNIS; Tri Village HS; New Madison, OH; Cls Rep Soph Cls; Band; Chrs; Hon Rl; Stu Cncl; Bsktbl; Letter Trk; Am Leg Awd; Univ; Comp Sci.

MILLER, DIANA; Peebles HS; Peebles, OH; 15/101 Chrs; Chrh Wkr; Cmnty Wkr; Debate Tm; Hon Rl; Sch Mus; Sch Pl; Ed Yrbk; Rptr Yrbk; Rptr Sch Nwsp; Ohio St Univ; Agri.

MILLER, DIANE; Arthur Hill HS; Saginaw, MI; Band; Chrs; Chrh Wkr; Hon Rl; Lbry Ade; Mdrgl; NHS; Orch; Sch Mus; Sch Pl; Morley Music Schlrshp; Teens Involved Music Comp; College; Legal Se.

MILLER, DIANE; Tuslaw HS; Massillon, OH; 14/151 Chrs; Chrh Wkr; Pres Girl Scts; Hon Rl; JA; Pres Yth Flsp; FDA; Pep Clb; Spn Clb; Cleveland State Univ; Phys Therpst.

MILLER, DONALD; St Johns HS; Sylvania, OH; Hon Rl; Lit Mag; Yrbk; Trk; IM Sprt; Ind Univ; Pre Med.

MILLER, DONALD; Napolen HS; Mcclure, OH; Am Leg Boys St; Chrs; Chrh Wkr; Cmnty Wkr; Debate Tm; Hon Rl; Sch Mus; Sch Pl; Stg Crw; Yth Flsp; Univ; Elem Ed.

MILLER, DONALD; Eastern Pike HS; Beaver, OH; VP Frsh Cls; VP Soph Cls; Hon Rl; Stu Cncl; Sprt Ed Yrbk; Bsbl; Bsktbl; Univ.

MILLER, DONALD C; Springfield HS; Akron, OH; Am Leg Boys St; Chrs; Chrh Wkr; Hon Rl; NHS; Off Ade; VICA; Cit Awd; Bowling Green St Univ; Bus Admin.

MILLER, DON E; Napoleon HS; Mc Clure, OH; Am Leg Boys St; Chrs; Chrh Wkr; Cmnty Wkr; Debate Tm; Hon Rl; Sch Mus; Sch Pl; Stg Crw; Rptr Yrbk; Univ.

MILLER, DONNA; Avondale HS; Pontiac, MI; 7/270 Hon Rl; Jr NHS; NHS; Yrbk; Rptr Sch Nwsp; VICA; Trk; Chrldng; Mish State Univ;.

MILLER, DONNA L; West Technical HS; Lakewood, OH; Hon Rl; Jr NHS; Treas NHS; Ed Yrbk; Univ; Acctg.

MILLER, DONNA S; Defiance Sr HS; Defiance, OH; 25/295 Hon Rl; Jr NHS; Letter Bsbl; Bsktbl; Most Improved & Most Sets Volleyball Jv & Vrsty; Honorable Mention Western Buckeye League All Teams Vllybl; Purdue Univ; Engr.

MILLER, DOUGLAS; Central HS; Elkhart, IN; Boy Scts; Chrh Wkr; Cmnty Wkr; Debate Tm; Hon Rl; Jr NHS; Mth Clb; Sci Clb; Ten; Mgrs; College; Architecture.

MILLER, DOUGLAS; Vicksburg HS; Vicksbrg, MI; Cls Rep Sr Cls; Boy Scts; Stu Cncl; Sch Nwsp; Fr Clb; Bsbl; Bsktbl; Natl Merit Ltr; Coll.

MILLER, DOUGLAS S; Hastings HS; Bedford, MI; Band; Boy Scts; Chrh Wkr; Hon Rl; Sch Mus; Sch Pl; Drama Clb; Pres Fr Clb; Key Clb; Spn Clb; Southern Missouri St Univ; For Lang.

MILLER, EARL; Loy Norrix HS; Kalanazoo, MI; 15/454 Hon Rl; Lbry Ade; NHS; Rptr Sch Nwsp; Natl Merit SF; Natl Merit Schl; Univ Of Fla; Forestry.

MILLER, EARL; Kalamazoo Loy Norrix HS; Kalamazoo, MI; 15/454 Hon Rl; Lbry Ade; Pol Wkr; Sch Nwsp; Natl Merit SF; Univ Of Florida; Forestry.

MILLER, EDWARD F; Reitz Memorial HS; Evansville, IN; Cls Rep Soph Cls; Cl Rep Jr Cls; Chrh Wkr; Cmnty Wkr; Hon Rl; NHS; Stg Crw; Stu Cncl; VP Ger Clb; VP Sci Clb; Service Awd; Community Leader Of Tomorrow; Edward E Meyer Educational Trust Schlrshp; Purdue Univ; Mech Engr.

MILLER, ELIZABETH; St Josephs HS; South Bend, IN; Band; Hon Rl; Jr NHS; NHS; Orch; Stg Crw; Yrbk; Sch Nwsp; JETS Awd; NCTE; Univ Of Chicago; Phys Sci.

MILLER, EMILY M; University HS; Westover, WV; Cls Rep Frsh Cls; Hon Rl; VP Jr NHS; Lit Mag; Quill & Scroll; Ed Yrbk; Rptr Sch Nwsp; 4-H; Sci Clb; Scr Kpr; Alderson Broaddus Coll; Med.

MILLER, ERIC; Bullock Creek HS; Midland, MI; 20/152 Band; Chrh Wkr; Hon Rl; JA; NHS; Yth Flsp; St Of Mi Compttv Schslhp 79; Sr Soc Std Awd 79; Cntrl Michigan Univ; Acctg.

MILLER, GARY; New Haven HS; New Haven, IN; Aud/Vis; Purdue Univ; Comp Prog.

MILLER, GARY J; Centreville HS; Centreville, MI; 3/69 Band; Hon Rl; NHS; Yth Flsp; FFA; Bsbl; Ftbl; St Farmer Degree FFA; Glen Oaks Acad Schlrshp Tuition; Clara Abbott Found For Schl Yr; Glen Oaks Cmnty Coll; Comp Prog.

MILLER, GENE; Wadsworth Sr HS; Wadsworth, OH; Band; Chrh Wkr; Hon Rl; Orch; Sct Actv; Yth Flsp; Mth Clb; Spn Clb; Univ; Chem.

MILLER, GLENN; Howell HS; Howell, MI; 39/400 Aud/Vis; Band; Boy Scts; Chrh Wkr; Pres CAP; Hon Rl; NHS; Pres Sct Actv; Yth Flsp; Yrbk; Lansing Comm Coll; Aviation.

MILLER, GLYNN; Hartford HS; Hartford, MI; 2/100 Pres Jr Cls; Pres Sr Cls; VP Band; Drm Mjrt; NHS; Sch Pl; Stg Crw; Letter Crs Cntry; Letter Trk; Dnfth Awd; Univ Of Mic; Aviation Engr.

MILLER, GORDON; Field HS; Mogadore, OH; Band; Boy Scts; Chrh Wkr; Cmnty Wkr; Hon Rl; Red Cr Ade; Sct Actv; Yth Flsp; Wrstlng; Pres Awd; Letter For Concert Band 79; Mbr Of Post 2267 Exployers Soffield Fire Dept 77 78 & 79; Univ; Law.

MILLER, GREG; Port Clinton HS; Port Clinton, OH; 1/300 Band; Hon Rl; NHS; Lat Clb; Univ Of Toledo; Chem Engr.

MILLER, GREG; Sandy Valley HS; Magnolia, OH; Band; Boy Scts; Chrs; Chrh Wkr; Hon Rl; Jr NHS; Lbry Ade; Lbry Ade; NHS; Kent State Univ; Bus.

MILLER, GREGORY; St Philip Catholic Cntrl HS; Battle Creek, MI; 4/70 Hon Rl; Pres NHS; Lat Clb; Letter Bsbl; Letter Bsktbl; Coach Actv; Natl Merit SF; Univ Of Notre Dame; Bus Admin.

MILLER, GRETCHEN; Hanover Central HS; Cedar Lake, IN; 22/137 Girl Scts; Hon Rl; Jr NHS; NHS; Stu Cncl; Pep Clb; Spn Clb; Letter Trk; Letter Chrldng; PPFtbl; Indiana Univ; Medicine.

MILLER, IRENE; Clyde HS; Clyde, OH; 7/200 NHS; Letter Trk; College.

MILLER, JAMES; Rossford HS; Rossford, OH; 8/150 Band; Hon Rl; JA; NHS; IM Sprt; Ohio State Univ; Elec Engr.

MILLER, JAMES G; Grosse Pointe North HS; Grosse, MI; Band; Chrs; Chrh Wkr; Cmnty Wkr; Hon Rl; NHS; Orch; Ferris State College; Optometry.

MILLER, JAMES R; Linsly Institute; Wheeling, WV; Boy Scts; ROTC; Sch Mus; Sch Pl; Sct Actv; Sprt Ed Sch Nwsp; Lat Clb; Letter Socr; IM Sprt; Cit Awd; ROTC Achvmnt Awd For Marksmanship Exec 79; Eagle Scout Awd 77; West Virginia Inst Of Tech; Engr.

MILLER, JANA; Marietta HS; Marietta, OH; 22/405 Band; Chrh Wkr; Hosp Ade; NHS; Sec Yth Flsp; Sec FNA; Ger Clb; Ohi State Univ; Comp Sci.

MILLER, JANET; Hale HS; Hale, MI; Cls Rep Sr Cls; Girl Scts; Hon Rl; Lbry Ade; Off Ade; Stu Cncl; 4-H; Letter Bsktbl; Scr Kpr; 4-H Awd; Grand Vly St Coll; Public Relations.

MILLER, JANET S; Rushville Consolidated HS; Rushville, IN; 11/315 Am Leg Aux Girls St; Band; Chrh Wkr; Hon Rl; Lit Mag; NHS; Fr Clb; Lat Clb; Pep Clb; Elk Awd;.

MILLER, JANICE; Manistee Catholic HS; Manistee, MI; 1/64 Sec Frsh Cls; Cls Rep Frsh Cls; Sec Band; Hon Rl; NHS; Red Cr Ade; Pres Stu Cncl; Pep Clb; Swmmng; Chrldng; Muskegon Business Coll.

MILLER, JANIS; Grand Haven Sr HS; Grand Haven, MI; Hon Rl; Jr NHS; NHS; Yth Flsp; Trk; Grand Valley St Coll; Acctg.

MILLER, JEANNIE; Medina Sr HS; Medina, OH; 29/365 Chrs; Girl Scts; Hon Rl; NHS; Sch Mus; Drama Clb; 4-H; Keyettes; 4-H Awd; Dollars For Schlrs Schlrshp 79; RPM Nursing Schlrshp 79; Golden Tassel Recipnt 10% Of Grad Class 79; Univ Of Akron; Nursing.

MILLER, JEFF; Buckeye HS; Valley City, OH; VP Soph Cls; VP Jr Cls; Pres Sr Cls; Chrh Wkr; FCA; Pres Yth Flsp; Pres 4-H; FFA; Capt Bsktbl; Ftbl; Grain Farmer.

MILLER, JEFF; Tecumseh HS; New Carlisle, OH; 39/324 Band; Boy Scts; Chrh Wkr; Treas FCA; Hon Rl; VP Jr NHS; NHS; Orch; Sct Actv; Pep Clb; College; Oceanography.

MILLER, JEFF D; Greenville HS; Greenville, OH; 116/390 Chrs; Sch Mus; Sch Pl; Stg Crw; Treas Drama Clb; 4-H; Sci Clb; Ftbl; College; Broadcasting.

MILLER, JEFFREY; Greenville HS; Greenville, OH; Chrh Wkr; Spn Clb; Ftbl; Trk; Mgrs; Columbus Coll; Cartooning.

MILLER, JEFFREY S; Mc Comb HS; Mc Comb, OH; Hon Rl; NHS; Rptr Yrbk; Voc Schl; Interior Decorating.

MILLER, JENNY; Whiteland Comm HS; Whiteland, IN; 35/220 Pres Soph Cls; Hon Rl; NHS; Sch Mus; Sch Pl; Stu Cncl; Yrbk; Drama Clb; Key Clb; Pom Pon; Indiana Tech; Med Tech.

MILLER, JERI; Greenfield Central HS; Greenfield, IN; Am Leg Aux Girls St; Chrs; Chrh Wkr; Hon Rl; Mdrgl; NHS; Pol Wkr; Sch Mus; Rptr Sch Nwsp; Fr Clb; Hancock Band & Trust Awd 77 78 & 79; Whos Who In Foreign Lang In Midwestern HS 77; Indiana Univ.

MILLER, JERRY L; Breckenridge Jr Sr HS; Breckenridge, MI; 1/100 Boy Scts; Hon Rl; NHS; Yth Flsp; Spn Clb; Letter Bsbl; Letter Ftbl; PPFtbl; Math Awd 1977; Sci Awd 1976; Soc Of Distg Amer Hs Stu 1977; Univ.

MILLER, JILL; Meadowbrook HS; Cumberland, OH; Cls Rep Soph Cls; Hon Rl; Off Ade; Sch Pl; Stu Cncl; Yth Flsp; Mth Clb; Pep Clb; Sci Clb; Spn Clb; College; Phys Therapy.

MILLER, JILL; Newark HS; Newark, OH; Cls Rep Frsh Cls; Cls Rep Soph Cls; Cl Rep Jr Cls; Cls Rep Sr Cls; Band; Chrs; Drl Tm; Girl Scts; Hon Rl; Lit Mag; Ohio St Univ; Publications.

MILLER, JIM; Pine River HS; Tustin, MI; 1/90 Cls Rep Sr Cls; Val; Band; Hon Rl; NHS; Sch Pl; Stu Cncl; Yth Flsp; Bsbl; Bsktbl; Ferris State Coll; Acctg.

MILLER, JOANNE; Seneca East HS; Republic, OH; 1/90 Cl Rep Jr Cls; Cls Rep Sr Cls; Treas Chrs; Chrh Wkr; Hon Rl; Jr NHS; NHS; Sch Pl; Stg Crw; Stu Cncl; Bowling Green St Univ; Med Tech.

MILLER, JOE; Field HS; Tallmadge, OH; FHA; Bsktbl; Bus Schl; Bus Mgr.

MILLER, JOHN; Miami Trace HS; Washington Ch, OH; Fr Clb; Sci Clb; Spn Clb; 8th In Dist 92nd % In St Oh Schlstc Test Of Achvmnt Spanish 2 Test 78; 82nd % St In OSA Test French 1 79; Arizona St Univ; Meteorology.

MILLER, JOHN; Central Catholic HS; Wheeling, WV; 5/131 Cls Rep Frsh Cls; Hon Rl; Stu Cncl; Key Clb; Wrstlng; Soc Dstngshd Amer HS Stu; French Awds; Phys Sci Cert Of Awd; College; Medicine.

MILLER, JOLENE; Newton HS; Plsnt Hl, OH; Trs Frsh Cls; Band; Drl Tm; Hon Rl; NHS; Sch Pl; Pres Yth Flsp; Sec FHA; Sec VICA; Voice Dem Awd; Ohio Univ; Journalism.

MILLER, JONI; Waldron HS; Shelbyville, IN; Band; Chrs; Chrh Wkr; Drl Tm; Rptr Sch Nwsp; 4-H; Lat Clb; Pep Clb; Chrldng; 4-H Awd; Bus Schl.

MILLER, JOSEPH; Lakeview HS; Battle Creek, MI; Boy Scts; Chrh Wkr; FCA; Hon Rl; Yth Flsp; Letter Swmmng; IM Sprt; Tmr; 4-H Awd; Central Mich Univ; Engr.

MILLER, JOYCE A; Ottoville Local HS; Ft Jennings, OH; 11/68 Sec Sr Cls; Hon Rl; Sch Mus; Stu Cncl; Rptr Yrbk; FHA; OEA;.

MILLER, JOYCE ANN; Ottoville Local HS; Ft Jennings, OH; 11/68 Sec Sr Cls; Hon Rl; Sch Mus; Stu Cncl; Rptr Yrbk; Fr Clb; FHA; OEA; Exec Sec.

MILLER, JUDY; West Branch HS; Salem, OH; 4/250 Pres AFS; Band; Hon Rl; Boy Scts; Pep Clb; Part In Flute Trio At Solo & Ensmbl Rcvd A Sup Rtng 79; Ohio St Fnlst For Miss Untd Teenager Pageant 77; Univ; X Ray Tech.

MILLER, JUDY; Covington HS; Bradford, OH; 33/100 Hon Rl; Lbry Ade; Off Ade; Letter Bsktbl; PPFtbl; Coll; Phys Ed.

MILLER, JULIE; Perrysburg HS; Perrysburg, OH; 72/247 Hon Rl; Forgn Lang Cert Of Achvmnt 79; Awd For Spanish 79; Ohio St Univ; Phys Ther.

MILLER, JULIE; S Newton Jr/sr HS; Kentland, IN; Sch Mus; Sch Pl; Yth Flsp; Pres 4-H; FBLA; VP FHA; Pep Clb; Letter Mgrs; PPFtbl; 4-H Awd; 4 H Leadership Awd Citizenship Awd; Purdue Univ; Home Ec.

MILLER, JULIE; Ottoville Local HS; Ottoville, OH; 18/67 Band; Hon Rl; Pep Clb; Business School; Med Office Asst.

MILLER, JULIE; Northwood HS; Northwood, OH; 1/67 Band; Chrs; Hon Rl; NHS; Sch Mus; 4-H; Letter Bsbl; Letter Bsktbl; 4-H Awd; JETS Awd; Univ Of Toledo; Med Tech.

MILLER, JULIE; Cabrini HS; Lincoln Park, MI; Drl Tm; Hon Rl; Quill & Scroll; Ed Yrbk; Rptr Sch Nwsp; Sch Nwsp; Mgrs; Capt Pom Pon; PPFtbl; Pres Awd; Wayne Cnty Cmnty Coll; Stewardess.

MILLER, KAREN; N Canton Hoover HS; North Canton, OH; Hon Rl; Jr NHS; NHS; Stu Cncl; Boys Clb Am; Spn Clb; Chrldng; Jr College; Transportation.

MILLER, KAREN; Washington Catholic HS; Washington, IN; Hon Rl; Drama Clb; Rdo Clb; Bsktbl; IM Sprt; Vincennes.

MILLER, KAREN; Miami Trace HS; Washington Ch, OH; Cmp Fr Grls; Chrs; Chrh Wkr; Hosp Ade; Yth Flsp; Drama Clb; Pres 4-H; FHA; FNA; Morehead Univ; Fshn Mdse.

MILLER, KAREN; Broad Ripple HS; Indianapolis, IN; 6/445 Cls Rep Frsh Cls; Cl Rep Jr Cls; Am Leg Aux Girls St; Cmp Fr Grls; Hon Rl; Jr NHS; NHS; Off Ade; Quill & Scroll; Ind Univ; Advertising.

MILLER, KATE; Lake Catholic HS; Newbury, OH; 5/305 Drl Tm; Lit Mag; NHS; Sch Nwsp; Fr Clb; Kent State Univ.

MILLER, KATHERINE; Merrill HS; Merrill, MI; 10/120 Girl Scts; Hon Rl; Hosp Ade; Rptr Yrbk; Rptr Sch Nwsp; Pep Clb; Bsktbl; Trk; Saginaw Valley State College; Nursin.

MILLER, KATHLEEN; Everett HS; Lansing, MI; 11/700 Chrs; Hon Rl; Jr NHS; NHS; Sch Mus; Yth Flsp; Rptr Yrbk; Rptr Sch Nwsp; Trk; College; Journalism.

MILLER, KATHLEEN; Catholic Central HS; Ada, MI; Band; Cmnty Wkr; Drm Bgl; MMM; Stg Crw; Pep Clb; IM Sprt; PPFtbl; Am Leg Awd; Pres Awd; Western Univ; Music.

MILLER, KATHLEEN; Hamady HS; Flint, MI; Trs Sr Cls; Chrh Wkr; Hon Rl; Stu Cncl; Yth Flsp; Scr Kpr; Kiwan Awd; Univ Of Detroit; Archt.

MILLER, KATHRYN; Lorain Catholic HS; Lorain, OH; Cl Rep Jr Cls; Cls Rep Sr Cls; Band; Chrh Wkr; Hon Rl; Stu Cncl; Yrbk; Rptr Sch Nwsp; Coach Actv; IM Sprt; Coll; Med.

MILLER, KATHY; Logan HS; Logan, OH; Sec Frsh Cls; Trs Soph Cls; VP Jr Cls; Hon Rl; Off Ade; Sch Mus; Stu Cncl; 4-H; Pep Clb; Chrldng;.

MILLER, KEITH; Chesapeake HS; Chesapeake, OH; VP Frsh Cls; Hon Rl; Letter Bsbl; University.

MILLER, KEN; Indian Hill HS; Cincinnati, OH; 70/280 Band; Hon Rl; Orch; Sch Mus; DECA; Pep Clb; Bsbl; Bsktbl; Coach Actv; IM Sprt; College; Bus.

MILLER, KENNETH M; Warren G Harding HS; Warren, OH; 100/443 Chrs; Hon Rl; Yrbk; Ski Club 1979; Vocal Chamber Ensmbl 1979; Univ Of Cincinnati; Bus Admin.

MILLER, KEVIN; Albion Sr HS; Albion, MI; Aud/Vis; Boy Scts; CAP; Debate Tm; Hon Rl; Sct Actv; Yth Flsp; Sch Nwsp; Ten; IM Sprt; Northwood Inst Univ; Automotive Engr.

MILLER, KIMBERLIE L; Cowan HS; Muncie, IN; Cls Rep Soph Cls; FCA; Hon Rl; NHS; Sec Stu Cncl; FHA; Letter Bsktbl; Letter Trk; Chrldng; 4-H Awd; College; Lawyer.

MILLER, KURT; Northwood HS; Northwood, OH; Cls Rep Frsh Cls; Cl Rep Jr Cls; Band; Chrs; Sec Stu Cncl; Key Clb; Letter Bsbl; Letter Ftbl; VP JA Awd; Univ; Bus Admin.

MILLER, LAMONI R; East HS; Cleveland, OH; Off Ade; Quill & Scroll; Stu Cncl; Rptr Yrbk; Ed Sch Nwsp; Pep Clb; Rdo Clb; IM Sprt; Jane Addams & Huron Rd Schl; Nsng.

MILLER, LAURA; South Spencer HS; Richland, IN; 28/151 Chrs; Hon Rl; Sch Mus; Yrbk; 4-H; OEA; Trk; Chrldng; GAA; Indiana St Univ; Health.

MILLER, LAURA; Reeths Puffer HS; N Muskegon, MI; 14/281 Girl Scts; Hon Rl; JA; NHS; Muskegon Cmnty Coll.

MILLER, LAURA; Grosse Ile HS; Grosse Ile, MI; Band; Chrs; Hon Rl; Yrbk; Sch Nwsp; Pep Clb;

Letter Chrldng; GAA; IM Sprt; Michigan St Univ; Nursing.

MILLER, LAUREN; Galien Township HS; Galien, MI; Cls Rep Frsh Cls; Cls Rep Soph Cls; Cl Rep Jr Cls; Cls Rep Sr Cls; Band; Girl Scts; Hon Rl; Sch Pl; Sec Stu Cncl; 4-H; Homecoming Ct Rep; Jr Var Vllybl Team Capt; Sftbl Team Capt 1980; Grand Valley St Coll; Lab Tech.

MILLER, LAURETTA; St Joe Central Catholic HS; Fremont, OH; 7/100 Am Leg Aux Girls St; Band; Pres Cmp Fr Grls; Hon Rl; NHS; 4-H; Drama Clb; Pep Clb; Chrldng; 4-H Awd; College; Teaching.

MILLER, LAURETTA; St Joseph Cntrl Catholic HS; Fremont, OH; Band; Cmp Fr Grls; Hon Rl; NHS; 4-H; FTA; Pep Clb; Sec Chrldng; IM Sprt; 4-H Awd; Univ.

MILLER, LAURIE; Archbishop Alter HS; Springboro, OH; Hon Rl; Hosp Ade; Stu Cncl; 4-H; Spn Clb; GAA; College; Commercial Design.

MILLER, LEANN M; Ottoville Local HS; Cloverdale, OH; 14/70 Chrs; Chrh Wkr; Hon Rl; VP NHS; Sch Mus; Rptr Yrbk; Yrbk; Rptr Sch Nwsp; Drama Clb; Bowling Green State Univ; Univ Div.

MILLER, LEISHA; Bedford Sr HS; Lambertville, MI; 81/465 Pres Frsh Cls; VP Soph Cls; Pres Jr Cls; Pres Sr Cls; Cmp Fr Grls; Chrs; Chrh Wkr; Cmnty Wkr; FCA; Hon Rl; Glendale Cmnty Coll; Art.

MILLER, LINDA; Cass Tech HS; Detroit, MI; Trs Sr Cls; Cls Rep Sr Cls; Hon Rl; NHS; Y-Teens; Rptr Yrbk; OEA; Pep Clb; Twrlr; Cit Awd; Oakland Univ; Mgmt.

MILLER, LINDA; Four County Joint Voc HS; Swanton, OH; Sec Soph Cls; VP Jr Cls; Chrh Wkr; Hon Rl; NHS; FHA; OEA; Ohio Academic Shlrshp; Univ Of Toledo; Busns Mgmt.

MILLER, LINDA; Niles Mc Kinley HS; Niles, OH; Hon Rl; Jr NHS; NHS; Off Ade; Stu Cncl; Pep Clb; PPFtbl; Sec For Italian Club 2 Yrs 77 & 79; Recgntn Of Schlshp 79; Cert From Italian Contst 76 77 & 78; Trumbull Univ; Nurse.

MILLER, LINDA; Seneca East HS; Republic, OH; Pres Frsh Cls; Cls Rep Soph Cls; Cl Rep Jr Cls; Chrs; Hon Rl; Jr NHS; NHS; Sch Pl; Stu Cncl; Yth Flsp; Ohio St Univ; Psych.

MILLER, LINDA; Rockford HS; Rockford, MI; Band; Cmp Fr Grls; Drl Tm; Hon Rl; Fr Clb; Bsbl; Gym; Aquinas; Comm Art.

MILLER, LINDA; Bremen HS; Bremen, IN; Chrh Wkr; Lbry Ade; Seamstress.

MILLER, LINDA; Tri County HS; Remington, IN; Boy Scts; Chrs; Sct Actv; Chrldng; Bus Schl; Acctg.

MILLER, LISA; Waynesfield Goshen HS; Waynesfield, OH; Pres Jr Cls; Pres Sr Cls; Band; Hon Rl; Off Ade; Stu Cncl; Pres OEA; PPFtbl; Outstanding Serv Awd; All Ohio Voc Stu Conf; OEA Ambassador Awd; Business Schl; Sec.

MILLER, LISA; Lima Sr HS; Lima, OH; 52/553 Cl Rep Jr Cls; Chrs; Girl Scts; Hon Rl; Orch; Sch Mus; Sch Pl; Stg Crw; Stu Cncl; Gym; OSU; Minestry.

MILLER, LISA; Belpre HS; Belpre, OH; Sec Frsh Cls; Cl Rep Jr Cls; Cls Rep Sr Cls; Band; Hon Rl; Off Ade; FHA; Pep Clb; Spn Clb; Trk; Ohio State Univ; Home Ec.

MILLER, LISA; Toronto HS; Toronto, OH; Hosp Ade; Lbry Ade; Rptr Sch Nwsp; Fr Clb; Pep Clb; Trk; Univ; Nursing.

MILLER, LISA; Napoleon HS; Napoleon, OH; 60/265 Chrh Wkr; Hon Rl; FHA; Ger Clb; Northwest Tech Schl; Comp Prog.

MILLER, LISA; Minerva HS; Minerva, OH; Band; Cmp Fr Grls; Chrh Wkr; Cmnty Wkr; Drm Mjrt; Hon Rl; Off Ade; Red Cr Ade; Sct Actv; Pep Clb; Stark Tech Coll; Sec.

MILLER, LISA; Lincoln HS; Cambridge, IN; 28/129 Hon Rl; Hosp Ade; Y-Teens; OEA; Cert Of Awd For Participating In Free Interprise Cntst 78; IU East Bus Schl; Bus.

MILLER, LISA D; Edon HS; Edon, OH; 21/81 Trs Jr Cls; Band; Chrs; Off Ade; Sch Mus; 4-H; Pep Clb; Bsktbl; Letter Trk; Letter Chrldng; Northwest Tech Coll; Pblc Acctg.

MILLER, LOIS; Seneca East HS; Attica, OH; Band; Chrs; Hon Rl; Sch Mus; Sch Pl; Yth Flsp; Drama Clb; Pep Clb; Trk; Chrldng; Ohio St Univ; Speech Ther.

MILLER, LONITA; Faribanks HS; Marysville, OH; 5/100 Chrh Wkr; Hon Rl; NHS; Red Cr Ade; Yth Flsp; Yrbk; Drama Clb; FHA; Spn Clb; GAA; Univ.

MILLER, LOREN; High School; Columbus, OH; Chrs; JA; NHS; PAVAS; Yrbk; Sch Nwsp; Drama Clb; Spn Clb; Natl Merit Ltr; College; Engr.

MILLER, LORI; Oakridge HS; Muskegon, MI; 2/118 VP Frsh Cls; Pres Soph Cls; Pres Jr Cls; Sal; Band; Hon Rl; NHS; Off Ade; Stg Crw; Stu Cncl; I Dare You Awd 79; Grnd Valley Hrn Schlrshp 79; Cert Of Recogntn St Of Mi Comptn Schlrship Progr 79; Grand Valley St Univ; Frgn Lang.

MILLER, LORI; Ross HS; Hamilton, OH; 33/240 Band; Girl Scts; Hon Rl; Hosp Ade; Yth Flsp; 4-H; Fr Clb; Sci Clb; 4-H Awd; Good Samaritan; Nursing.

MILLER, LORI; Lincolnview Local HS; Van Wert, OH; VP Soph Cls; Chrh Wkr; JA; Lbry Ade; NHS; Stg Crw; Yth Flsp; Fr Clb; Bsktbl; Trk; College; Teacher.

MILLER, LORI; Prairie Hts HS; Mongo, IN; Drl Tm; Girl Scts; Hon Rl; Off Ade; FTA; Pep Clb; Bsktbl; Trk; GAA; Pom Pon; Intl Bus Coll; Sec.

MILLER, LORI; Cory Rawson HS; Mt Cory, OH; Band; Hon Rl; Sch Pl; Sch Nwsp; Pep Clb; Mat Maids; Scr Kpr; Twrlr;.

MILLER, LORI A; River Rouge HS; River Rouge, MI; Cls Rep Frsh Cls; Cls Rep Sr Cls; Drm Mjrt; Girl Scts; Hon Rl; Hosp Ade; JA; Jr NHS; NHS; FHA; Acad Excll Awd 77; Whos Who Amer H S Std 78; Shrthnd Prof Awd 79; Homemaking Awd 79; De Vry Inst Of Tech; Comp Sci.

MILLER, LYNN; Marysville HS; Raymond, OH; 15/240 Pres Frsh Cls; Am Leg Boys St; Band; Yth Flsp; 4-H; Pres FFA; Bsbl; Ftbl; Wrstlng; IM Sprt; Ohio State Univ; Ag Ec.

MILLER, M; Elmhurst HS; Ft Wayne, IN; Boy Scts; Hon Rl; Trk; Indiana Univ.

MILLER, MARCELLUS; Cleveland Cntrl Catholic HS; Cleveland, OH; Hon Rl; Fr Clb; Bsbl; Ftbl; Univ; Engr.

MILLER, MARCIA; Coldwater HS; Coldwater, OH; Chrs; Hon Rl; IM Sprt; Univ; Nursing.

MILLER, MARIAN; Lumen Christi HS; Jackson, MI; 40/242 Hon Rl; NHS; Sch Mus; Sprt Ed Sch Nwsp; Rptr Sch Nwsp; 4-H; Lat Clb; Gym; Trk; Natl Mert Commnded Stdnt 78; Whos Who In Amer HS Stndt 78; 4 H Awd In Achvmnt Learhp & Spkng 78; Ferris St Coll; Pesticide Tech.

MILLER, MARJORIE L; Bellevue Sr HS; Bellevue, OH; 2/240 Chrs; Chrh Wkr; Hon Rl; Hosp Ade; NHS; FHA; FNA; IM Sprt; Elk Awd; Natl Merit SF; Univ Of Toledo; Psych.

MILLER, MARK; Willard HS; Willard, OH; Am Leg Boys St; Hon Rl; Letter Bsbl; Letter Bsktbl; Letter Ftbl; Letter Trk; College; Engineering.

MILLER, MARK; New Albany HS; New Albany, OH; 1/95 Cls Rep Frsh Cls; Pres Sr Cls; Am Leg Boys St; Hon Rl; NHS; Rptr Yrbk; Sci Clb; Letter Bsbl; Letter Ftbl; Am Leg Awd; College; Accounting.

MILLER, MARK W; Grosse Pointe South HS; Grosse Pointe, MI; 30/550 Debate Tm; NHS; Treas Lat Clb; Natl Merit SF; Univ; Law.

MILLER, MARVIN; Fairview Area Schools; Fairview, MI; Trs Frsh Cls; Trs Soph Cls; VP Jr Cls; Chrs; Hon Rl; Yrbk; Rptr Sch Nwsp; Sch Nwsp; Drama Clb; FFA; Jrnlsm Awrd 79; Yearbook Awrd 79; Drama Clb Playr Of The Yr 79; Univ.

MILLER, MARVIN; Belmont HS; Dayton, OH; Boy Scts; Cmnty Wkr; Hon Rl; Boys Clb Am; Letter Ten; Ohio St Univ; Dent.

MILLER, MARVIN P; Lakeland Christian Academy; Warsaw, IN; 2/20 VP Jr Cls; Band; Chrs; Chrh Wkr; Hon Rl; Stu Cncl; Fr Clb; Bsktbl; Socr; Cit Awd; Grace Coll.

MILLER, MARY; North Union HS; Mt Victory, OH; 6/119 VP Jr Cls; Hon Rl; Lat Clb; Chrldng;.

MILLER, MARY; Watkins Mem HS; Pataskala, OH; 49/229 Hon Rl; FHA; Pep Clb; PPFtbl;.

MILLER, MARY A; St Joseph Central Cath HS; Fremont, OH; 39/100 Cmp Fr Grls; Hon Rl; Hosp Ade; JA; Stg Crw; Yrbk; Drama Clb; 4-H; Pep Clb; 4-H Awd; Tiffin Univ; Sec.

MILLER, MARY B; Washington Irving HS; Clarksburg, WV; Cl Rep Jr Cls; Cls Rep Sr Cls; Chrh Wkr; Hon Rl; NHS; Rptr Sch Nwsp; Treas Drama Clb; Fr Clb; Pres Lat Clb; Treas Pep Clb; 39th Annual Conservation Camp; VP Of Sci & Modical Club; Coll; Social Work.

MILLER, MARY C; Hanover Central HS; Cedar Lake, IN; 8/126 Hon Rl; Jr NHS; Sch Mus; Sch Pl; Drama Clb; Pep Clb; Spn Clb; Ten; Trk; Chrldng; Indiana Univ; Theatre Arts.

MILLER, MAURICE C; Cedar Lake Academy; Taylor, MI; Chrs; Chrh Wkr; Hon Rl; Stu Cncl; Rptr Sch Nwsp; Bsktbl; IM Sprt; College.

MILLER, M C; Anderson HS; Cinncinnati, OH; Cls Rep Frsh Cls; Sec Chrs; Girl Scts; Hon Rl; Sec NHS; Sec Orch; Stu Cncl; Socr; College.

MILLER, MELANIE; Shawnee HS; Springfield, OH; 18/209 Hon Rl; Hosp Ade; Orch; Pres 4-H; FDA; Mat Maids; 4-H Awd; Univ Of Flo; Occupational Ther.

MILLER, MELISSA; R Rogers HS; Toledo, OH; 18/412 Cls Rep Frsh Cls; Cls Rep Soph Cls; Cls Rep Sr Cls; Sec Band; Chrs; Hon Rl; NHS; Off Ade; VP Orch; IM Sprt; Ohio Univ; Music Educ.

MILLER, MICHAEL; Washington Irving HS; Clarksburg, WV; 35/139 Am Leg Boys St; Chrh Wkr; Cmnty Wkr; Hon Rl; Fr Clb; Key Clb; Letter Ftbl; Letter Trk; Letter Wrstlng; Am Leg Awd; Wa Irving Outstng Ftbl Ath Of The Yr 78; All Harrison Cnty Captain Big Ten Hnrbl Mntion Plyer Of Wk 78; West Virginia Univ; Pharm.

MILLER, MICHAEL; St Joseph HS; St Joseph, MI; Rptr Sch Nwsp; FNA; Ferris St Coll; Data Proc.

MILLER, MICHAEL; Rogers HS; Michigan City, IN; Boy Scts; Chrs; Hon Rl; Jr NHS; Sct Actv; Stu Cncl; Fr Clb; Mth Clb; Ftbl; IM Sprt; Purdue Univ; Comp Sci.

MILLER, MICHAEL; Watterson HS; Columbus, OH; Cls Rep Soph Cls; Cl Rep Jr Cls; Cls Rep Sr Cls; Hon Rl; Jr NHS; NHS; Stu Cncl; Letter Bsbl; Letter Ftbl; Univ.

MILLER, MICHELE; Allegan Sr HS; Allegan, MI; 10/197 Band; Hon Rl; Natl Forn Lg; NHS; Sch Pl; Valparaiso Univ Residential Schlrshp; Top Ten Of Sr Class; St Solo Proficiency III Exam 1st Division; Valparaiso Univ; Music.

MILLER, MICHELLE; Kingston HS; Clifford, MI; 2/59 Sec Sr Cls; Chrh Wkr; Hon Rl; Lbry Ade; NHS; Off Ade; Delta College; Acctg.

MILLER, MICHELLE; Sullivan HS; Sullivan, IN; 5/147 Hon Rl; Beta Clb; FHA; GAA; Indiana St Univ; Elem Ed.

MILLER, MICHELLE; James Ford Rhodes HS; Cleveland, OH; Trs Soph Cls; VP Jr Cls; VP Sr Cls; PAVAS; Sprt Ed Sch Nwsp; Rptr Sch Nwsp; Fr Clb; UCLA; Public Relations.

MILLER, MOLLY; Dover HS; Dover, OH; Hon Rl; Jr NHS; NHS; Yth Flsp; Ger Clb; Sci Clb; Letter Bsktbl; Letter Ten; College.

MILLER, MONICA; Midland Trail HS; Ansted, WV; Chrs; NHS; Sch Pl; Stu Cncl; Ed Yrbk; Rptr Yrbk; Rptr Yrbk; Drama Clb; Fr Clb; Treas FHA; All Cnty Chr 79; Univ.

MILLER, NANCY; Marion Adams HS; Sheridan, IN; 24/86 Am Leg Aux Girls St; Chrs; Chrh Wkr; FCA; Girl Scts; Sch Pl; Pres 4-H; VP FHA; Bsktbl; Anderson College; Minister.

MILLER, NORMA; Fountain Central HS; Veedersburg, IN; 2/147 Sec Band; Chrh Wkr; Hon Rl; NHS; Sch Pl; Rptr Yrbk; Rptr Sch Nwsp; Drama Clb; Sec FHA; DAR Awd; Univ; Bus.

MILLER, PAM; Withrow HS; Cincinnati, OH; Chrh Wkr; Cmnty Wkr; Hon Rl; JA; Stu Cncl; Univ Of Cincinnati; Chem Engr.

MILLER, PAM; Springfield HS; Akron, OH; Chrh Wkr; Akron Univ; Busns.

MILLER, PAMELA; Greenville Sr HS; Greenville, OH; Cls Rep Soph Cls; Chrh Wkr; Hon Rl; Orch; Sch Mus; Sch Pl; Stg Crw; Yth Flsp; Rptr Sch Nwsp; Drama Clb; Coll; Bus.

MILLER, PAMELA; Edgewood HS; Ashtabula, OH; Cls Rep Frsh Cls; Cls Rep Sr Cls; Chrs; Hon Rl; Stu Cncl; Y-Teens; Pep Clb; Chrldng; Pom Pon; Cit Awd; Kent State; Registered Nurse.

MILLER, PAMELA; Arcanum HS; Arcanum, OH; 11/99 Chrs; Chrh Wkr; Cmnty Wkr; Drm Bgl; Hon Rl; Sch Mus; Sch Pl; Yth Flsp; 4-H; 4-H Awd; Univ.

MILLER, PAMELA S; Rogers HS; Toledo, OH; Chrh Wkr; Girl Scts; Jr NHS; Yth Flsp; Spn Clb; Univ; Sci.

MILLER, PATRICIA; Riverview HS; Riverview, MI; 2/250 Hon Rl; Jr NHS; Pres NHS; Letter Ten; Univ Of Michigan; Med.

MILLER, PATRICK; New Castle Chrysler HS; New Castle, IN; Band; Boy Scts; Pol Wkr; Lat Clb; Bsktbl; Univ; Med.

MILLER, PAUL; Green HS; Uniontown, OH; Pres Soph Cls; Pres Jr Cls; Pres Sr Cls; Am Leg Boys St; Chrs; Chrh Wkr; Hon Rl; College.

MILLER, PAUL; Columbia HS; Columbia Sta, OH; Chrh Wkr; Cmnty Wkr; Hon Rl; Spn Clb; Cit Awd; Voice Dem Awd; Air Force; Auto Mech.

MILLER, PHIL; Lakewood HS; Hebron, OH; 3/210 Hon Rl; Spn Clb; Bsbl; Bsktbl; Univ; Criminal Justice.

MILLER, PHILIP; Gilmour Acad; Lakewood, OH; 20/85 Sec Frsh Cls; Sec Soph Cls; Sec Jr Cls; Sec Sr Cls; Hon Rl; NHS; Stu Cncl; Letter Ftbl; Univ Of Notre Dame; Acctg.

MILLER, PHILIP; Manistee Catholic Centl HS; Manistee, MI; Cls Rep Frsh Cls; Trs Soph Cls; Trs Jr Cls; Hon Rl; Stg Crw; Stu Cncl; Letter Ftbl; Letter Ten; Trk; Mic State Univ; Pre Law.

MILLER, RALYNN; Jackson HS; Jackson, OH; 1/210 Val; Am Leg Aux Girls St; Band; Chrh Wkr; Trs Frsh Cls; NHS; Yth Flsp; Y-Teens; Pres 4-H; Rio Grande Coll; Med Lab Tech.

MILLER, RANDAL; Rogers HS; Toledo, OH; Letter Band; Chrh Wkr; Jr NHS; NHS; Off Ade; Orch; Yth Flsp; Pep Clb; Sci Clb; Letter Bsbl; College.

MILLER, RANDAL S; Rogers HS; Toledo, OH; Band; Chrh Wkr; Hon Rl; Jr NHS; NHS; Orch; Stu Cncl; Yth Flsp; Sci Clb; Bsbl; Univ; Engr.

MILLER, REBECCA; Sidney HS; Sidney, OH; Band; Chrs; Chrh Wkr; Orch; Ohio Music Educ Assoc 1976; Piano Rating 1 Sidney HS Music Dept 1st Awd 1978; Univ.

MILLER, REBECCA; Kouts HS; Madison, MO; 1/68 Trs Frsh Cls; Cls Rep Frsh Cls; Pres Soph Cls; Cls Rep Soph Cls; Cl Rep Jr Cls; Band; Chrs; Hon Rl; Jr NHS; NHS; Brigham Young Univ; Music.

MILLER, REBECCA; Woodlan HS; Woodburn, IN; 6/150 Band; Chrs; Chrh Wkr; FCA; Hon Rl; Pres Yth Flsp; FHA; Letter Bsktbl; IM Sprt; PPFtbl; Goshen Coll; Soc Work.

MILLER, REBECCA; Chesaning HS; Burt, MI; Band; Cmp Fr Grls; Hon Rl; Sec NHS; Off Ade; Sch Mus; Sch Pl; Stg Crw; Drama Clb; Spn Clb; Central Mich Univ.

MILLER, RENEE; Bedford HS; Bedford Hts, OH; 32/625 Band; Chrs; Hon Rl; NHS; Treas Yth Flsp; Bsbl; Letter Bsktbl; GAA; Coll; Busns.

MILLER, RENEE; Sebring Mckinley HS; Sebring, OH; 2 Trs Frsh Cls; Am Leg Aux Girls St; NHS; Sch Mus; Rptr Yrbk; Ger Clb; Chrldng; College.

MILLER, RHONDA; Crooksville HS; Crooksville, OH; 10/96 Sec Frsh Cls; Trs Frsh Cls; VP Soph Cls; VP Sr Cls; Band; Hon Rl; NHS; Sch Pl; Yth Flsp; Chrldng; Univ; Educ.

MILLER, RICHARD; Brooke HS; Follansbee, WV; 78/466 Band; Boy Scts; Chrh Wkr; Hon Rl; Orch; Sch Mus; Sct Actv; Pres Ger Clb; God Cntry Awd; Pres Awd; Blue Belt In Karate 1978; Outstndng Sr Band Mbr 1979; Order Of The Arrow 1976; West Liberty Univ; Cmmrcl Art.

MILLER, RICHARD; Zanesville HS; Zanesville, OH; FCA; Hon Rl; Sch Pl; Stg Crw; Stu Cncl; Treas Lat Clb; Mth Clb; Sci Clb; Ftbl; Letter Swmmng; Ohio State Univ; Med.

MILLER, RICHARD; Catholic Central HS; Detroit, MI; 12/205 Aud/Vis; Hon Rl; Jr NHS; NHS; Red Cr Ade; Sdlty; Yrbk; Sci Clb; Scr Kpr; Gabriel Richard Soc; Michigan St Univ; Engr.

MILLER, RITA; Wauseon HS; Wauseon, OH; Chrs; Chrh Wkr; Cmnty Wkr; Hon Rl; Sch Mus; Stg Crw; Y-Teens; Ed Yrbk; Rptr Sch Nwsp; Fr Clb; Univ; Med.

MILLER, ROBERT; Tecumseh HS; Medway, OH; 71/350 Band; Chrh Wkr; Drm Bgl; FCA; Hon Rl; Sec NHS; Orch; Sch Mus; Treas Yth Flsp; Rptr Sch Nwsp; Music Schlrshp Morehead St Univ; HS Band Merit Awd; Morehead St Univ; Music.

MILLER, ROGER; Southridge HS; Huntingburg, IN; 26/172 Band; Boy Scts; Chrs; FCA; Hon Rl; Sch Mus; Sch Pl; Sct Actv; 4-H; Ger Clb; Indiana Univ; Dent.

MILLER, ROMA; Piketon HS; Piketon, OH; Chrs; Hon Rl; MMM; Sch Mus; Stu Cncl; Yrbk; Drama Clb; FTA; Pep Clb; Chrldng; Univ; Drama.

MILLER, ROSS A; Waynedale HS; Wooster, OH; 7/122 Boy Scts; Chrs; Hon Rl; Pres NHS; Yth Flsp; FTA; Capt Ftbl; Capt Socr; Capt Wrstlng; Kenyon Coll; Pre Med.

MILLER, ROXANE; Jackson County Western HS; Spring Arbor, MI; Cls Rep Frsh Cls; Cls Rep Soph Cls; Band; Chrs; Chrh Wkr; Cmnty Wkr; Girl Scts; Stu Cncl; Pep Clb; Trk; Jackson Cmnty Coll; Law Enfrmnt.

MILLER, RUSSELL B; Clay City HS; Clay City, IN; 4/70 Hon Rl; NHS; Stu Cncl; Yth Flsp; Lat Clb; Letter Bsbl; Letter Bsktbl; Coach Actv; Lion Awd; Voice Dem Awd; Indiana Univ; Pre Med.

MILLER, SANDRA L; Archbold HS; Archbold, OH; 9/120 Trs Soph Cls; Chrs; Hon Rl; Sch Mus; Sec FHA; Pep Clb; Ohio St Univ; Nursing.

MILLER, SARA; Barnesville HS; Barnesville, OH; Band; Hon Rl; Jr NHS; Sch Pl; Drama Clb; FHA; FTA; Letter Trk; GAA; Univ; Bus.

MILLER, SARAH; Ridgedale HS; Marion, OH; 8/96 Cls Rep Frsh Cls; Cls Rep Soph Cls; Am Leg Aux Girls St; Chrs; Hon Rl; Jr NHS; Sch Mus; Stu Cncl; Pres FHA; Letter Trk; College.

MILLER, SCOT; Henry Ford II HS; Sterling Hts, MI; 47/423 Chrh Wkr; NHS; Letter Bsbl; Letter Bsktbl; Letter Ftbl; Outstndng Sr Athlt Of Yr 1978; Univ.

MILLER, SCOTT; Caldwell HS; Dexter City, OH; 5/104 Aud/Vis; Hon Rl; NHS; Spn Clb; Crs Cntry; Trk; College.

MILLER, SCOTT; Garaway HS; Sugarcreek, OH; 2/103 VP Frsh Cls; Pres Soph Cls; VP Sr Cls; Am Leg Boys St; Band; Boy Scts; Hon Rl; NHS; Stu Cncl; Sprt Ed Sch Nwsp; Univ.

MILLER, SCOTT; Cambridge HS; Cambridge, OH; Am Leg Boys St; Pres Chrs; Chrh Wkr; Hon Rl; Pres NHS; Key Clb; Letter Bsktbl; Capt Ftbl; Letter Trk; Ohio Valley Coll; Bus Law.

MILLER, SHANNON; Shakamak HS; Jasonville, IN; Band; Girl Scts; Lbry Ade; Y-Teens; FBLA; FHA; Pep Clb; Letter Bsktbl; Trk; GAA; Indiana St Univ; Law.

MILLER, SHARI; Montpelier HS; Montpelier, OH; 21/101 Band; Chrs; Hon Rl; NHS; Off Ade; Sch Mus; Sch Pl; Stg Crw; 4-H; Treas Fr Clb; Ohio St Univ; Acctg.

MILLER, SHARI; Liberty HS; Clarksburg, WV; Hon Rl; DECA; Fr Clb; FBLA; West Va; Comp Sci.

MILLER, SHERI; Athens HS; Athens, MI; Sec Frsh Cls; Sec Soph Cls; Sec Jr Cls; Sec Sr Cls; Hon Rl; NHS; Off Ade; Quill & Scroll; Red Cr Ade; Sch Pl; College; Nursing.

MILLER, SIEANNA; Bishop Flaget HS; Chillicothe, OH; 4/38 Cls Rep Soph Cls; Pres Jr Cls; Hon Rl; Hosp Ade; 4-H; Fr Clb; Treas Pep Clb; Ten; Chrldng; Coach Actv; Univ Of Cincinnati; Bus Admin.

MILLER, STARR B; London HS; London, OH; 17/161 Band; Pres Stg Crw; Chrh Wkr; Hon Rl; NHS; Sch Pl; Stu Cncl; Pres Yth Flsp; Treas 4-H; Fr Clb; College; Engr.

MILLER, STEPHEN; Lima Sr HS; Lima, OH; Am Leg Boys St; Band; Chrs; Hon Rl; Orch; Sch Mus; Am Leg Awd; West Jr High Orchestra Awd; Outstanding Jazz Soloist At Ohio Northern Jazz Festival; Superior Ratings; Ohio St Univ; Poli Sci.

MILLER, STEPHEN; Sandy Valley HS; Magnolia, OH; Chrs; Letter Trk; Mount Union; Geol.

MILLER, STEVE; Western HS; Russiaville, IN; 10/224 Hon Rl; Natl Forn Lg; NHS; VP Sci Clb; Perfect Attendance Awd 76; Purdue Univ; Math.

MILLER, STEVEN; William Henry Harrison HS; Lafayette, IN; 75/340 Cls Rep Frsh Cls; Jr NHS; Letter Crs Cntry; Letter Trk; IM Sprt; College; Bus Mgmt.

MILLER, STEVEN; Van Buren HS; Finlay, OH; Sec Soph Cls; Hon Rl; Mth Clb; Letter Bsktbl; Letter Ftbl; Coach Actv; IM Sprt; Univ; Bio.

MILLER, STEVEN; Wadsworth Sr HS; Wadsworth, OH; 44/349 FCA; NHS; Pres Yth Flsp; VP Key Clb; Letter Ftbl; IM Sprt; Cit Awd; Univ.

MILLER, STEVEN; Sandy Valley HS; Sandyville, OH; 17/171 Hon Rl; Jr NHS; Natl Forn Lg; Sec Quill & Scroll; Stg Crw; Yrbk; Sprt Ed Sch Nwsp; Letter Crs Cntry; Trk; Cit Awd; Marietta College; Petro Engr.

MILLER, STEVEN S; Shakamak HS; Jasonville, IN; 26/84 Chrs; Hon Rl; NHS; 4-H; FFA; 4-H Awd; Ivy Tech Voc Schl; Inds Elect.

MILLER, SUE; Copley HS; Copley, OH; 65/315 Cl s Rep Frsh Cls; Band; Hon Rl; Sec DECA; Sec 4-H; FHA; 4-H Awd; DECA Dist & St Wnr Natl Participant 1979; Bowling Green Univ; Fash Mdse.

MILLER, SUSAN; Charlevoix HS; Charlevoix, MI; 12/160 Cls Rep Frsh Cls; Cls Rep Soph Cls; Trs Jr Cls; Sec Sr Cls; Band; Debate Tm; Drl Tm; Hon Rl; Natl Forn Lg; Sch Mus; Part In Opertn Bently; Hope Coll Hon Schlshp; St Of Mi Compt Schslhp; Hope Coll; Soc Work.

MILLER, SUSAN; North HS; Springfield, OH; Swmmng; Univ; Mgmt.

MILLER, SUSAN; Griffith Sr HS; Griffith, IN; 4/308 Band; Chrh Wkr; Hon Rl; Jr NHS; NHS; Sch Mus; Busns Schl; Busns Mgmt.

MILLER, SUSAN; Bowling Green HS; Bowling Green, OH; 1/300 Val; Band; Chrs; Chrh Wkr; Hon Rl; NHS; Orch; Sch Mus; Miami; Environmental Studies.

MILLER, SUZANNE; Lebanon HS; Lebanon, OH; Cls Rep Frsh Cls; Band; Chrs; Drl Tm; Hon Rl; NHS; Stu Cncl; Letter Ten; Letter Trk; Capt Chrldng; Virginia Poly Tech Univ; Pre Law.

MILLER, TAMARA; Columbia City Joint HS; Columbia City, IN; Band; Spn Clb; Cit Awd; College; Music Educ.

MILLER, TAMARA; Defiance HS; Defiance, OH; Band; Sch Mus; Sch Pl; Stg Crw;.

MILLER, TAMERRA L; St Clairsville HS; St Clairsville, OH; Chrs; Girl Scts; Hon Rl; Hosp Ade; Treas JA; Y-Teens; FHA; OEA; Pep Clb; JA Awd; West Virginia N Cmnty Coll; Acctg.

MILLER, TAMMY; Father Joseph Wehrle Mem HS; Columbus, OH; Chrh Wkr; Drl Tm; Hon Rl; Busns Schl; Busns.

MILLER, TAMMY; Blissfield HS; Blissfield, MI; 21/111 Chrh Wkr; Hon Rl; Off Ade; Pep Clb; GAA; IM Sprt; Mgrs; Scr Kpr; Adrian Coll; Pre Law.

MILLER, TARA; Frankfort HS; Ridgeley, WV; 20/129 Hon Rl; Hosp Ade; NHS; Fr Clb; Mth Clb; Pep Clb; Chrldng; GAA; Fairmont St Coll; Nursing.

MILLER, TERESA; Whiteland Comm HS; Whiteland, IN; 9/200 Hon Rl; Sec FBLA; OEA; Indiana Central Univ; Sec.

MILLER, TERESA; East Noble HS; Kendallville, IN; 4/279 Am Leg Aux Girls St; Chrs; Hon Rl; Hosp Ade; JA; Mod UN; NHS; Y-Teens; FHA; OEA; Notre Dame Univ; Law.

MILLER, TERESA; Elmhurst HS; Ft Wayne, IN; 21/346 Hon Rl; Sch Pl; DECA; Bus.

MILLER, TERI; Marian HS; S Bend, IN; Cls Rep Frsh Cls; Cls Rep Soph Cls; Cl Rep Jr Cls; Cls Rep Sr Cls; Hon Rl; Mdrgl; Pol Wkr; Stu Cncl; Rptr Yrbk; Rptr Sch Nwsp; Purdue Univ; Public Relations.

MILLER, THERESA; Rensselaer Central HS; Rensselaer, IN; 13/161 Pres Jr Cls; Cl Rep Jr Cls; Am Leg Aux Girls St; Band; Hon Rl; NHS; Orch; Pol Wkr; Stu Cncl; 4-H; Loren Karns Memrl Schlrshp 79; Hoosier Schlr 79; Attended Rotary Top 20 Dinner 79; Internatl Bus Coll; Acctg.

MILLER, THERESA; Pike Central HS; Petersburg, IN; 10/196 Cls Rep Sr Cls; Band; Chrh Wkr; Cmnty Wkr; FCA; Hon Rl; Lbry Ade; VP NHS; Treas Stu Cncl; Sch Nwsp; Univ Of Texas; Elem Ed.

MILLER, THERESA; Charlestown HS; Charlestown, IN; 32/155 Chrs; JA; Spn Clb; Univ Of Ken; Journalism.

MILLER, THOMAS; St Johns HS; Lambertville, MI; Hon Rl; Ger Clb; Rdo Clb; IM Sprt; St Of Mi Comp Schlrshp 79; Univ; Elec Engr.

MILLER, THOMAS; Pontiac Northern HS; Pontiac, MI; 12/500 Hon Rl; NHS; Sprt Ed Sch Nwsp; Ger Clb; Capt Glf; Natl Merit SF; PTA Schlrshp 4 Yrs; Oakland Univ; Cartooning.

MILLER, THOMAS J; Manistee Cath Ctrl HS; Onekama, MI; 8/64 Band; Boy Scts; Chrh Wkr; Hon Rl; Natl Forn Lg; Sct Actv; Stg Crw; Ftbl; Michigan Tech; Bio.

MILLER, TIM; Boardman HS; Youngstwn, OH; 94/597 FCA; Hon Rl; NHS; Boys Clb Am; Spn Clb; Letter Crs Cntry; Letter Trk; IM Sprt; Univ Of Cincinnati; Engineering.

MILLER, TIMOTHY; Calvin Christian HS; Grandville, MI; 7/160 Pres Band; Chrh Wkr; Hon Rl; NHS; Yth Flsp; Sch Nwsp; Sci Clb; Bsbl; IM Sprt; Univ Of Mi Regnst Almn Schslp 79; Aquinas Coll Acad Mert Awd 79; Calvin Coll Frshn Schslhp 79; Aquinas Coll; Acctg.

MILLER, TODD M; Twin Valley South HS; West Alexandria, OH; 3/93 Am Leg Boys St; Hon Rl; NHS; Rptr Sch Nwsp; Sci Clb; College; Pre Med.

MILLER, TONY; Spencer HS; Spencer, WV; Hon Rl; Jr NHS; Sch Pl; Stg Crw; Drama Clb; Bsktbl; Glf; Princeiples Honor List; College.

MILLER, TRACY; Pike Central HS; Stendal, IN; 44/192 Band; Hon Rl; Lbry Ade; Treas NHS; Stg Crw; 4-H; Treas FHA; Pep Clb; Letter Swmmng; Letter Chrldng; Univ; Bus.

MILLER, TRACY; Wheeling Park HS; Wheeling, WV; Cls Rep Frsh Cls; Cl Rep Jr Cls; Hon Rl; Hosp Ade; Off Ade; Sch Mus; Stu Cncl; Yth Flsp; IM Sprt; Mgrs; Stifel Awrd 76; WPHS Art Show Merit Awrd 78; Univ; Forestry.

MILLER, VALORIE; Sissonville HS; Sissonville, WV; Cl Rep Jr Cls; Cmnty Wkr; Girl Scts; Hon Rl; Jr NHS; Lbry Ade; NHS; Off Ade; Stu Cncl; Ed Yrbk; Comm Of The Shp Of St 78; Amb Of Goodwl Of Wv 78; Grd Corss Of Clr For The Ord Of Rainbow For Girls 78; Univ; Cmnctns.

MILLER, VICKI; Seton HS; Cincinnati, OH; Chrs; JA; Sch Mus; FBLA; Bsktbl; IM Sprt; Mgrs; Tmr; Cincinnati Tech College; Secretary.

MILLER, VICKY; Colon HS; Mendon, MI; Band; Chrs; Drl Tm; Lbry Ade; Pep Clb; Chrldng; Coll.

MILLER, VICKY; Woodhaven HS; Woodhaven, MI; VP Sr Cls; Girl Scts; Hon Rl; NHS; Stu Cncl; Rptr Yrbk; Spn Clb; Twrlr; Mic State Univ.

MILLER, VIRGINIA A; Lincoln HS; Vincennes, IN; 1/282 Hon Rl; Off Ade; Sch Nwsp; Pep Clb; Spn Clb; Ten; Trk; PPFtbl; Vincennes Univ; Medical Tech.

MILLER, VONNIE; Whitehall Yearling HS; Whitehall, OH; Chrs; Hon Rl; Lbry Ade; Off Ade; Orch; Yth Flsp; VFW Awd; Psych.

MILLER, WENDY; Columbiana HS; Columbiana, OH; Sec Sr Cls; Hon Rl; Pres OEA; Sec Spn Clb; Chrldng; Sec.

MILLER, WILLIAM E; Hubbard HS; Hubbard, OH; 15/350 Boy Scts; Hon Rl; Sct Actv; Fr Clb; Key Clb; IM Sprt; Ohio Test Of Schlstc Aptitude French I; Ohio Test Of Schlstc Aptitude French II; Ohio Schlstc Amer Hist; Youngstown St Univ; Comp Sci.

MILLER, WILLIAM R; Lake Catholic HS; Chesterland, OH; 2/315 Boy Scts; Hon Rl; NHS; Sct Actv; Natl Merit Ltr; Case Western Reserve Univ; Sci.

MILLER JR, MICHAEL A; Central Hower HS; Akron, OH; 42/400 Hon Rl; Red Cr Ade; Ne Oh Univ; Med.

MILLET, JOHN; Kenston HS; Chagrin Fl, OH; Aud/Vis; Boy Scts; Chrh Wkr; Cmnty Wkr; Hon Rl; Sct Actv; Boys Clb Am; Rdo Clb; Trk; Kent St Univ; Chem.

MILLETT, MICHAEL; Stivers Patterson Co Op HS; Dayton, OH; 14/426 Hon Rl; Jr NHS; NHS; Orch; Sch Mus; DECA; 1st Pl Dayton Philhrmnc Concerto Competn 1978; 1st Pl Radio Advrtsg 1977; Solo With Philharmnc Orchestra; Cincinnati Conservatory Of Music.

MILLHOF, RODERICK; High School; Chargrin Fl, OH; Chrh Wkr; Ger Clb; Capt Socr; Trk; IM Sprt; Scr Kpr; Univ; Bio.

MILLHOUSE, ANNE; Centerville HS; Dayton, OH; 72/687 Band; Chrh Wkr; Girl Scts; NHS; Orch; Sch Mus; Sct Actv; Stg Crw; Yth Flsp; Trk; Purdue Univ.

MILLICH, CAROL; Brooke HS; Weirton, WV; 116/450 Hon Rl; Hosp Ade; JA; Fr Clb; Sci Clb; JA Awd; Mercy Hosp Schl Of Nursing; Nurse.

MILLIGAN, MICHAEL; Upper Arlington HS; Columbus, OH; FCA; Hon Rl; Red Cr Ade; Bsktbl; Capt Crs Cntry; Glf; Trk; Spansih Natl Hon Soc 79; Prom Comm; Ohio St Univ; Pre Vet.

MILLIGAN, NANCY; Richmond Sr HS; Richmond, IN; 60/700 Cls Rep Frsh Cls; Cl Rep Jr Cls; Cls Rep Sr Cls; Am Leg Aux Girls St; Hon Rl; JA; Pol Wkr; Stu Cncl; Yth Flsp; 4-H; Denison Coll.

MILLIKAN, LORI; Madison Hts HS; Anderson, IN; 4/376 Cl Rep Jr Cls; Am Leg Aux Girls St; Treas JA; Treas NHS; Treas Stu Cncl; Pres FHA; Mgrs; Treas JA Awd; NCTE; Shlchp From In Assn Of CPA 79; Indiana Univ; Acctg.

MILLIKEN, DONALD; Farmington HS; W Farmington, OH; 2/26 Pres Jr Cls; Sec Sr Cls; Am Leg Boys St; Boy Scts; Pres NHS; Sec Stu Cncl; Beta Clb; Letter Crs Cntry; Letter Trk; College; Aerospace Engr.

MILLIKEN, JOHN; Adena HS; Frankfort, OH; 14/84 AFS; Am Leg Boys St; Hon Rl; Lbry Ade; NHS; Sch Pl; Stg Crw; Rptr Yrbk; Yrbk; 4-H; Ohio Univ; Forensic Chem.

MILLIRON, DAVID; Marion Harding HS; Marion, OH; Spn Clb; IM Sprt; OSU; Engr.

MILLIRON, KELLY; Benzie Central HS; Benzonia, MI; Band; Chrh Wkr; Drl Tm; Hon Rl; Lbry Ade; NHS; Orch; Yth Flsp; Yrbk; 4-H; Northwestern Michigan Univ; Nursing.

MILLISER, KAY; Grace Baptist Church HS; S Bend, IN; Chrs; Chrh Wkr; Hon Rl; NHS; Sch Mus; Sch Pl; Yth Flsp; 4-H; Hyles Anderson College; Sec Educ.

MILLISOR, ROD; Ridgedale HS; Marion, OH; Cls Rep Frsh Cls; Cls Rep Soph Cls; Cl Rep Jr Cls; VP Sr Cls; Band; Chrh Wkr; FCA; Hon Rl; Jr NHS; NHS; Ohio Northern Univ; Bus Admin.

MILLOTT, CORRINE; Blackriver HS; Spencer, OH; Band; Chrh Wkr; Hon Rl; Yth Flsp; 4-H; FFA; Pep Clb; Bsbl; Scr Kpr; Tmr; MB Johnson Univ; Nurse.

MILLS, BELINDA; Corydon Central HS; New Middletown, IN; 27/165 Girl Scts; Rptr Yrbk; Rptr Sch Nwsp; Drama Clb; Fr Clb; FBLA; Pep Clb; Business School; Data Proc.

MILLS, CHRISTOPHER; Whitehall Yearling HS; Whitehall, OH; Cls Rep Soph Cls; Cl Rep Jr Cls; Pres Sr Cls; Boy Scts; Orch; VP Stu Cncl; Pres Yth Flsp; Ed Sch Nwsp; Letter Bsbl; Letter Swmmng; Otterbein Coll; Math.

MILLS, GEORGE; Griffith HS; Griffith, IN; Cls Rep Frsh Cls; Hon Rl; Bsbl; Ftbl; Univ; Math.

MILLS, HOWARD; Mansfield HS; Mansfield, OH; 32/300 Hon Rl; Letter Wrstlng; Coll; Marine Engr.

MILLS, JANE; Upper Arlington HS; Upper Arlington, OH; 1/645 Val; Sec Chrh Wkr; VP NHS; Quill & Scroll; Rptr Yrbk; Ed Sch Nwsp; Crs Cntry; Trk; Sec Mat Maids; Tmr; Univ Of Virginia; Acctg.

MILLS, JANET; Warren Central HS; Indianapolis, IN; 236/857 Boy Scts; Chrh Wkr; Hosp Ade; Sct Actv; Yth Flsp; Swmmng; Scr Kpr; Purdue Univ; Animal Sci.

MILLS, JEFFERY; Lake Fenton HS; Lake Fenton, MI; 50/179 Hon Rl; Pol Wkr; Letter Bsbl; Letter Ftbl; Hockey; Albion College; Pol Sci.

MILLS, JENNY; Bedford North Lawrence HS; Oolitic, IN; Cls Rep Soph Cls; Cl Rep Jr Cls; Cls Rep Sr Cls; Drl Tm; Off Ade; Stu Cncl; Sch Nwsp; DECA; Keyettes; OEA; Indiana Univ; Psych.

MILLS, JIM; Marietta Sr HS; Marietta, OH; 53/405 Am Leg Boys St; NHS; Yth Flsp; Bsbl; Letter Ftbl; Crew Team; Certified Scuba Diver; Service Academies; Petroleum Engr.

MILLS, JOEL; Benzie Central HS; Beulah, MI; Boy Scts; Hon Rl; Letter Bsbl; Letter Swmmng; IM Sprt; College; Bus.

MILLS, KATHY; Washington Irving HS; Clarksburg, WV; Hon Rl; Jr NHS; NHS; Quill & Scroll; Rptr Yrbk; Yrbk; Rptr Sch Nwsp; Lat Clb; Cit Awd; Fairmont State College; Elem Ed.

MILLS, KENT; Penn HS; Mishawaka, IN; Chrs; Hon Rl; Natl Forn Lg; Yth Flsp; IM Sprt; Purdue; Physics.

MILLS, LINDA; Edison HS; Norwalk, OH; 43/155 Hon Rl; Jr NHS; NHS; Sch Nwsp; 4-H; FBLA; FHA; Trk; Mgrs; Scr Kpr; Bowling Green St Univ; Sec Admin.

MILLS, MARY; Valley Local HS; Lucasville, OH; 11/107 VP Sr Cls; Band; Chrs; Drm Mjrt; NHS; Sch Pl; Stu Cncl; FHA; FTA; Capt Bsktbl; Univ Of Cincinnati; Nurse Anesthetis.

MILLS, NELSON; Brooke HS; Colliers, WV; 47/449 Chrh Wkr; Cmnty Wkr; Hon Rl; Yth Flsp; Brooke Voc Ed Outstndg Achvmnt Awd 78; W Virginia Inst Of Tech; Mech Engr.

MILLS, RICHARD; Roosevelt Wilson HS; Nutter Fort, WV; 5/123 Am Leg Boys St; Band; Hon Rl; NHS; Orch; Sch Pl; Rptr Yrbk; Sec Fr Clb; Leo Clb; Mth Clb; West Virginia Univ; Comp Sci.

MILLS, ROBERT; Wintersville HS; Steubenville, OH; Boy Scts; Fr Clb; History Awd; Steubenville Coll; Acctg.

MILLS, ROY; Penn HS; Bremen, IN; 43/480 Cls Rep Frsh Cls; Band; Boy Scts; Chrh Wkr; Hon Rl; Sct Actv; Stu Cncl; Yth Flsp; 4-H; Fr Clb; Bible Quiz Trophy; Jazz Ensemble Top Five 79; History Day Proj 79; Purdue Univ; Agri.

MILLS, SANDRA; Chagrin Falls HS; Chagrin Falls, OH; Hon Rl; Sch Mus; Ten; PPFtbl; Ohio St Univ; Spanish.

MILLS, STUART L; Parkside Shs; Jackson, MI; Band; Chrs; Debate Tm; Hon Rl; Natl Forn Lg; Orch; Sch Mus; Lat Clb; Univ; Law.

MILLS, SUSAN; Carroll HS; Bringhurst, IN; 32/135 Girl Scts; 4-H; Fr Clb; Pep Clb; Trk; Mat Maids; PPFtbl; 4-H Awd; Bus Schl; Acctg.

MILLS, SUSAN; Port Clinton HS; Pt Clinton, OH; Band; Hon Rl; Orch; Sch Pl; Drama Clb; Ohio State Univ; Elem Ed.

MILLS, TERESA; Union HS; Losantville, IN; Band; Chrs; Chrh Wkr; Off Ade; Ed Yrbk; FHA; Ball St Univ; Elem Ed.

MILLS, TERI; Hamilton Southeastern HS; Noblesville, IN; 56/136 Girl Scts; Hon Rl; Sec JA; Sct Actv; Ger Clb; Pres OEA; JA Awd; Ball St Univ; Bus Mgmt.

MILLS JR, J; Central Hower HS; Akron, OH; 49/450 Boy Scts; Hon Rl; Jr NHS; Lbry Ade; Natl Forn Lg; Red Cr Ade; Sct Actv; Rptr Sch Nwsp; FDA; Mth Clb; Case Western Reserve Acad; Med.

MILNE, JEFFREY; North Branch HS; North Branch, MI; Boy Scts; Hon Rl; FFA; Letter Trk; Natl Merit Schl; Cum Laude Hon Schslhp From Cntrl Mi Univ 79; Hon Progr At Cntrl Mi Univ 79; Cntrl Michigan Univ; Comp Sci.

MILNER, JOHN; Northwestern HS; Kokomo, IN; 25/190 Trs Frsh Cls; Trs Soph Cls; Band; Boy Scts; Hon Rl; JA; Sci Clb; IM Sprt; Rotary Awd; Purdue Univ.

MILNER, LISA Y; Cincinnati Country Day Schl; Cincinnati, OH; Chrh Wkr; Cmnty Wkr; Hon Rl; Rptr Yrbk; Yrbk; Sch Nwsp; Letter Trk; Mgrs; Mat Maids; Scr Kpr; Univ; Dr.

MILNER, MARLA; Rossville HS; Frankfort, IN; 10/50 Trs Frsh Cls; Trs Soph Cls; Trs Jr Cls; Hon Rl; Natl Forn Lg; Stu Cncl; Yth Flsp; Drama Clb; 4-H; Pom Pon; Purdue Univ; Agri.

MILNES, BETH; Perry HS; Canton, OH; Girl Scts; Hosp Ade; NHS; Off Ade; FHA; Pep Clb; Publicity Crew Schl Play & Music; Teen Cncl Rep Sec Aultman Hosp; Univ Of Akron; Nursing.

MILNIKEL, LYNNE; Grandville HS; Grand Ville, MI; Band; Drm Bgl; Hon Rl; Bsbl; Bsktbl; Ten; GAA; PPFtbl; Central Mich Univ; Ct Reporting.

MILO, DIANNE; Jackson Milton HS; N Jackson, OH; 11/117 Sec Soph Cls; Hon Rl; NHS; Bsktbl; Trk; Chrldng; Vocational Schl; Art.

MILOSEVIC, JANE; James Ford Rhodes HS; Cleveland, OH; Hon Rl; Jr NHS; NHS; Red Cr Ade; DECA; Letter Bsktbl; Letter Trk; Coach Actv; IM Sprt; Scr Kpr; Univ.

MILOSTAN, MICHAEL; Lake Catholic HS; Mentor, OH; Chrs; Letter Bsbl; Letter Ftbl; IM Sprt; Arizona St Univ; Data Proc.

MILSTEIN, JEFF; Brush HS; Lyndhurst, OH; Hon Rl; Univ.

MILTENBERGER, S; Springfield HS; Springfield, MI; Girl Scts; Hon Rl; NHS; Pep Clb; Bsbl; Bsktbl; Chrldng; PPFtbl; Western Michigan Univ; Acctg.

MILTNER, DOUG; Bellbrook HS; Bellbrook, OH; 40/160 Letter Bsbl; Letter Ftbl; College; Law.

MILTON, ELBERT; St Hedwig HS; Detroit, MI; Band; NHS; Capt Bsktbl; Letter Ftbl; Univ; Elec Engr.

MILTON, JOE; Cleveland Ctrl Catholic HS; Cleveland, OH; 45/131 Boy Scts; Sct Actv; Boys Clb Am; Capt Bsktbl; Scr Kpr; 3 Var Bsktbl Lt 76 79; Leadng Rebounder 3rd Leadng Scorer 76; Len Janiak Awd Tri Capt 78; Univ Of Akron; Civil Engr.

MILTON, NANCY; Elkton Pigeon Bay Port Laker; Bad Axe, MI; Band; Hon Rl; NHS; 4-H; OEA; Spn Clb; 4-H Awd; Saginaw Valley St Coll; Bus Mgmt.

MILUM, BARBARA; Ontario HS; Mansfield, OH; 32/155 Cls Rep Sr Cls; Stu Cncl; Letter Trk; Ohi State Univ; Acctg.

MILUM, RAYMOND L; Malabar HS; Mansfield, OH; 26/216 Band; Boy Scts; Hon Rl; Sct Actv; Yth Flsp; Key Clb; Wrstlng; God Cntry Awd; Eagle Scout 75; Summer Scjlr At Ohio Univ 78; Miami Univ; Bus Admin.

MIN, JANET; Mt Clemens HS; Mt Clemens, MI; 9/291 Band; Hon Rl; NHS; Sec Key Clb; Natl Merit Ltr; Univ Of Michigan; Sci.

MINAMYER, TAMI; Canfield HS; Canfield, OH; Cmnty Wkr; Hon Rl; Hosp Ade; Sch Pl; Stg Crw; Drama Clb; Fr Clb; FSA; Pep Clb; Honorary Mention From DAR; Runner Up For Brooks Contest; Ohio St Univ; Nursing.

MINAR, JOHN; Central HS; Evansville, IN; Ftbl; Purdue; Elec Engr.

MINARD, MIKE; Notre Dame HS; Clarksburg, WV; 18/56 Pres Frsh Cls; Pres Soph Cls; VP Jr Cls; Cls Rep Sr Cls; Am Leg Boys St; NHS; Stu Cncl; Letter Bsbl; Letter Bsktbl; Capt Ftbl; Glenville State Coll; Bus Admin.

MINCEK, JOSEPH; Benedictine HS; Cleveland, OH; 12/98 Chrh Wkr; Treas NHS; Fr Clb; Bsktbl; Ftbl; Trk; IM Sprt; Ohio Northern Univ; Pharmacy.

MINCEY, KATHY; Benedictine HS; Detroit, MI; 7/270 Cls Rep Frsh Cls; Cls Rep Soph Cls; VP Jr Cls; Cls Rep Sr Cls; Cmnty Wkr; Girl Scts; Hon Rl; NHS; PAVAS; Pol Wkr; Awd In Bio & Geometry 77; Close Up Participants Cert Awd; 4 Yrs Working In Stud Govt; Wayne St Univ; Law.

MINCH, RICHARD; St Ignatius HS; Euclid, OH; 26/283 Chrh Wkr; Cmnty Wkr; FCA; Hon Rl; NHS; Rptr Sch Nwsp; Rdo Clb; Letter Bsbl; Coach Actv; Cit Awd; Bat Boy Cleveland Indians; College; Broadcasting.

MINCH, SARA; Catholic Central HS; Mingo Jct, OH; 29/226 Hon Rl; NHS; Drama Clb; Good Samaritan Hosp; Nursing.

MINCH, VALORIE; Pershing HS; Detroit, MI; Hon Rl; Jr NHS; NHS; Heritage Univ; Languages.

MINCHELLA, MICHAEL; Northwood HS; Northwood, OH; Hon Rl; Toledo Univ; Pharm.

MINDA, MICHELE; Admiral King HS; Lorain, OH; Band; Hon Rl; Orch; Rptr Yrbk; Ohio St Univ; Lib Arts.

MINDER, TAMMY; Frontier HS; New Matamoras, OH; 6/122 Cls Rep Sr Cls; Band; Girl Scts; Hon Rl; NHS; Off Ade; Sch Pl; Stu Cncl; Sec OEA; Spn Clb; Washington Tech Coll; Acctg Tech.

MINDER, VESTA; Frontier HS; New Matamoras, OH; Band; Chrs; Girl Scts; Hon Rl; Sch Pl; Pres Stu Cncl; OEA; Treas Spn Clb; GAA; Washington Tech Schl; Sec.

MINDERMAN, LORI; Lincoln HS; Vincennes, IN; 11/300 Trs Jr Cls; Trs Sr Cls; Band; Hon Rl; Yth Flsp; FTA; Pep Clb; Spn Clb; Ten; Coll; Med Tech.

MINEER, LYDIA A; Madeira HS; Cincinnati, OH; 35/165 AFS; Hon Rl; Fr Clb; Trk; Univ Of Florida; Dent Hygnst.

MINELLA, BARB; Mother Of Mercy HS; Cincinnati, OH; Hon Rl; Hosp Ade; Red Cr Ade; Fr Clb; Socr; GAA; Univ Of Cincinnati; Nursing.

MINER, GREG; Quincy HS; Fremont, IN; 2/110 VP Sr Cls; Am Leg Boys St; Band; Chrs; Chrh Wkr; NHS; PAVAS; Sch Pl; Stg Crw; Pres Yth Flsp; Univ Of Michigan; Med.

MINER, JACK G; Hastings HS; Hastings, MI; Cls Rep Soph Cls; Cl Rep Jr Cls; Am Leg Boys St; Band; Boy Scts; Chrh Wkr; Hon Rl; Stu Cncl; Fr Clb; Key Clb; Univ Of Mich; Marine Bio.

MINER, KIMBERLY; Hastings HS; Hastings, MI; Hon Rl; Beta Clb; Key Clb; PPFtbl; Western Univ; Art.

MINER, LINDA; Quincy HS; Fremont, IN; Band; Chrs; Chrh Wkr; Cmnty Wkr; Hon Rl; NHS; Yth Flsp; 4-H; 4-H Awd; Coll; Bus.

MINER, NANCY; Adena HS; Frankfort, OH; 25/85 Cls Rep Soph Cls; AFS; Band; Chrs; Hon Rl; Stu Cncl; Y-Teens; Rptr Sch Nwsp; 4-H; Ger Clb; Col Tech; Medl Sec.

MINERD, MARGARET; John F Kennedy HS; Niles, OH; 13/175 Band; Hon Rl; NHS; Sch Mus; FTA; Pep Clb;.

MING CHU, TAI; Stow HS; Stow, OH; Chrs; Chrh Wkr; Hon Rl; NHS; Sch Mus; Stg Crw; Mth Clb; Univ Of Akron;pre Med.

MINGE, DEBORAH; Springboro HS; Springboro, OH; Chrs; Hon Rl; Lbry Ade; Off Ade; Stu Cncl; 4-H; 4-H Awd; Miami Univ; Social Sci.

MINGERINK, DON; South Christian HS; Ada, MI; Hon Rl; College; Restaurant Mgmt.

MINGLE, MICHELLE; Fairborn Bakes HS; Fairborn, OH; Orch; Rptr Sch Nwsp; College; Med.

MINGLE, THOMAS; Highland HS; Middletown, IN; 21/439 Hon Rl; NHS; FFA; Trk; Am Leg Awd; Pres Awd; 1 In County Soil Judging Competition Awd; On Top Soil Judging Team Awd; College; Agri.

MINGO, DENISE; South HS; Akron, OH; Cls Rep Soph Cls; Pres Jr Cls; Pres Sr Cls; Am Leg Aux Girls St; Chrs; Hon Rl; Jr NHS; NHS; Off Ade; Sch Mus; College; Comp Sci.

MINGUS, DEAN; Edison HS; Berlin Heights, OH; Band; Chrs; Orch; Sch Mus; Sch Pl; Drama Clb; Glee Club; Ski Club;.

MINICHIELLO, MELISSA; Turpin HS; Cincinnati, OH; Band; Hon Rl; Stu Cncl; Hugh O Brian Youth Found Final 1977; Scholarship Awrd 1976; Schl Scholrshp Merit Awrd 1976; Univ; Doctor.

MINIX, TERRY; Oregon Davis HS; Walkerton, IN; 19/60 VP Frsh Cls; Cls Rep Soph Cls; Chrh Wkr; FCA; Hon Rl; Stu Cncl; Sprt Ed Sch Nwsp; Pep Clb; Letter Bsbl; Letter Bsktbl; College; Radio & Tv Broadcasting.

MINK, ANTHONY; Copley HS; Copley, OH; Aud/Vis; Boy Scts; Chrs; Chrh Wkr; Sch Mus; Rptr Sch Nwsp; Boys Clb Am; DECA; Mgrs; Univ; Med.

MINNECI, ELIZABETH; Seton HS; Cincinnati, OH; Chrs; Hon Rl; Pep Clb; Spn Clb; Western Hills Schl; Cosmetology.

MINNELLI, KAREN; Taft HS; Hamilton, OH; 9/444 NHS; Off Ade; Lion Awd; Rotary Awd; Miami Univ; Eng.

MINNEMEYER, HOLLY; Hilltop HS; W Unity, OH; 11/72 Band; Chrh Wkr; Cmnty Wkr; Girl Scts; Hon Rl; FHA; College.

MINNER, ELIZABETH; Delta HS; Eaton, IN; Cls Rep Frsh Cls; Cls Rep Soph Cls; Cl Rep Jr Cls; Pres Sr Cls; Chrs; FCA; Girl Scts; JA; Sch Mus; Stu Cncl; Ball St Univ; Phys Ther.

MINNEY, LISA; Windham HS; Windham, OH; Sec Jr Cls; VP Band; VP Chrs; Chrh Wkr; Girl Scts; Hon Rl; Sec NHS; Stu Cncl; Yth Flsp; Spn Clb; Ohio Vlly Christian Coll; Dent Tech.

MINNEY, ROGER; Jefferson HS; Monroe, MI; JA; Rptr Yrbk; Sch Nwsp; Sci Clb; Swmmng; Ten; Trk; Coach Actv; Monroe County Comm College; Med Tech.

MINNICH, EUGENE; Lorain Catholic HS; Lorain, OH; Cl Rep Jr Cls; Band; Chrs; Cmnty Wkr; Sch Pl; Stu Cncl; Rptr Sch Nwsp; DECA; Drama Clb; 4-H; Pres Lorain Cnty Yth Assoc 77; Outsdng Yth Grp Mbr 77; Citizen For Outsdng Work In Loraine Cnty; Bowling Green St Univ; Spec Educ.

MINNICH, KAREN; Our Lady Of Mercy HS; Lathrup, MI; 3/313 Cls Rep Frsh Cls; Chrh Wkr; Girl Scts; Hon Rl; Lbry Ade; Stg Crw; Mth Clb; Sci Clb; Glf; Tmr; Univ; Sci.

MINNICH, SCOTT; Arthur Hill HS; Saginaw, MI; Letter Bsbl; Letter Ftbl; IM Sprt; Michigan St Univ; Vet.

MINNIEAR, JULIE; Northfield HS; Wabash, IN; Band; Chrh Wkr; Drl Tm; Quill & Scroll; Rptr Yrbk; Rptr Sch Nwsp; 4-H; Pep Clb; Quill & Scroll Awd Of Mrt; Upper Wabash Voc Schl; Sec.

MINNIS, GAYLE V; Emerson HS; Gary, IN; Trs Frsh Cls; Hon Rl; Off Ade; FBLA; Bloomington; Registered Nurse.

MINOR, BRENDA; Clinton HS; Clinton, MI; Hon Rl; Sch Mus; Bsktbl; Cleary; Secretarial.

MINOR, PATRICIA; Buckeye HS; Medina, OH; 29/173 Cmp Fr Grls; Chrh Wkr; Off Ade; Lat Clb; Evangel College; Nursing.

MINOR, SANDRA; Clinton HS; Clinton, MI; 4/94 Sec Jr Cls; Trs Sr Cls; Hst Sr Cls; Cls Rep Sr Cls; Hon Rl; NHS; Off Ade; Siena Heights College; Bus Admin.

MINOR, STEVE; Tyler County HS; Middlebourne, WV; 3/97 Band; Boy Scts; Chrs; Hon Rl; JA; NHS; Off Ade; Sch Pl; Ed Sch Nwsp; Sch Nwsp; Marshall Univ.

MINORE, JEFFREY; Flint Central HS; Flint, MI; Hon Rl; Mod UN; NHS; Yrbk; Bsktbl; Chmn Ten; Mic State Univ.

MINOSKY, STEPHEN; Padua Franciscan HS; Broadview Hts, OH; Debate Tm; Hon Rl; IM Sprt; College; Bus Admin.

MINSTERMAN, DIANA; Greenville Sr HS; Greenville, OH; Band; Drl Tm; Hon Rl; NHS; Off Ade; Yth Flsp; Yrbk; Univ; Speech Ther.

MINTON, CLAY; Williamstown HS; Williamstown, WV; 35/117 Cmnty Wkr; JA; Bsbl; Bsktbl; Ftbl; IM Sprt; Letter Mgrs; JA Awd; Wv Conservation Camp 79; Marietta Coll; Petroleum Engr.

MINTON, ELLEN; Point Pleasant HS; Pt Pleasant, WV; Hosp Ade; Stu Cncl; Y-Teens; Yrbk; Keyettes; Pep Clb; Chrldng; W Vir Univ; Med Tech.

MINTON, KARIN; Medina Sr HS; Medina, OH; 24/341 Drl Tm; Hon Rl; NHS; Ger Clb; Pep Clb; Pom Pon; Scr Kpr; Natl Merit Ltr; Univ.

MINTON, LISA; David Anderson HS; Lisbon, OH; 34/95 Cl Rep Jr Cls; Aud/Vis; Cmp Fr Grls; Chrs; Chrh Wkr; Cmnty Wkr; FCA; Hon Rl; Red Cr Ade; Sch Mus; Ohio State Univ; Communications.

MINTON, PAMELA A; Lordstown HS; Warren, OH; Pres Band; Chrs; Chrh Wkr; Hon Rl; Sch Mus; Sch Pl; Stu Cncl; Beta Clb; Pres Drama Clb; Pep Clb; Hiram Coll; Art.

MINTON, SHERRY; Milan HS; Milan, MI; Sec Frsh Cls; Cls Rep Soph Cls; Band; Hon Rl; NHS; Stu Cncl; Yrbk; 4-H; Letter Trk; Track Team Mst Imprvd Awd 79; 4 H 5 Grand Champ Awd 76 78; Michigan St Univ; Cmnctns.

MINX, RUSSELL D; East HS; Akron, OH; Band; Boy Scts; Chrh Wkr; Cmnty Wkr; JA; Sct Actv; Yth Flsp; 4-H; Swmmng; Boy Scout Eagle Awd 79; Childrn Of Amer Revoltn So Pres 76; Childrn Of Amer Rev St Of Oh Soc Chaplain 79; Glenville St Coll; Forestry.

MIOTKE, KATHLEEN; Charles Stewart Mott HS; Warren, MI; 2/700 Sal; Chrs; Hon Rl; Jr NHS; Natl Forn Lg; NHS; Stu Cncl; Wayne State Univ; Psychology.

MIRACLE, ANITA; Western Brown Sr HS; Bethel, OH; 10/165 Chrh Wkr; Hon Rl; Hosp Ade; NHS; Yth Flsp; 4-H; Spn Clb; Berea Coll; Nursing.

MIRACLE, MARY; Lockland HS; Cincinnati, OH; Sec Jr Cls; Band; Chrs; Hon Rl; NHS; Pep Clb; Spn Clb; Twrlr; Cit Awd; SAR Awd; Univ Of Cincinnati; Bus.

MIRACLE, PAMELA; Lakewood HS; Newark, OH; Chrh Wkr; Hon Rl; Jr NHS; Lit Mag; NHS; Pres Yth Flsp; Rptr Sch Nwsp; Sch Nwsp; College; Psychiatry.

MIRAMONTI, STEVE; Mt Clemens HS; Mt Clemens, MI; Cls Rep Frsh Cls; Cls Rep Soph Cls; Cl Rep Jr Cls; Cls Rep Sr Cls; Chrh Wkr; Hon Rl; NHS; Stu Cncl; Letter Bsbl; Letter Glf; Lettered Varsity Vlybl As Mgr; Coll; Med.

MIRANDA, AIDA; Clearview HS; Lorain, OH; 21/125 Band; Chrs; Hon Rl; NHS; FTA; Pep Clb; Spn Clb; Lorain Cnty Cmnty Coll; Cosmetology.

MIRANDA, MICHELLE; Gods Bible School; Chandler, OK; Sec Sr Cls; Chrs; Chrh Wkr; Orch; Central St Univ; Nursing.

MIREE, PATRICIA; Cass Tech HS; Detroit, MI; Band; Chrh Wkr; Hon Rl; Sch Mus; Howard Univ; Med.

MIRICH, MICHELE; Andrean HS; Crown Pt, IN; 30/250 Cls Rep Frsh Cls; VP Sr Cls; Hon Rl; Hosp Ade; NHS; Stu Cncl; Treas Pep Clb; Chrldng; Coach Actv; Scr Kpr; Univ; Med.

MIRON, GARY; Port Huron Northern HS; Northstreet, MI; Hon Rl; NHS; Pres 4-H; Capt Crs Cntry; Letter Trk; Letter Wrstlng; Coach Actv; 4-H Awd; Natl Merit SF; Natl Merit Schl; N Mich Univ; Chem.

MIRON, RONALD; Atherton HS; Holly, MI; 40/141 Pres Sr Cls; Hon Rl; Stg Crw; Letter Bsbl; Letter Bsktbl; Letter Ftbl; Opt Clb Awd; Grant For MSU 79; MSU; Agri.

MIROS, NEIL; Portland HS; Eagle, MI; Band; Hon Rl; Sch Mus; Bsbl; Ftbl; Wrstlng; Mgrs; Scr Kpr; Lansing Community College; Comp Prog.

MIS, LISA; Caro HS; Caro, MI; Sec Soph Cls; Band; Hon Rl; NHS; Fr Clb; Capt Chrldng; Western Mich Univ; Psych.

MISAK, ERIC; Bluefield HS; Bluefield, WV; 52/285 Chrh Wkr; Hon Rl; Fr Clb; Pep Clb; Coach Actv; IM Sprt; Scr Kpr; Wv Univ; Chem Engr.

MISCH, L; Rensselaer Central HS; Rensselaer, IN; Cls Rep Sr Cls; Drm Bgl; Hon Rl; NHS; Stu Cncl; Rptr Yrbk; Fr Clb; Purdue Univ; Elem Educ.

MISCHLER, FRED; Oakwood HS; Dayton, OH; Boy Scts; Chrs; Hon Rl; JA; Natl Forn Lg; NHS; Sch Mus; Sch Pl; Sct Actv; Stg Crw; Cert Of Hon From Intl Thespian Soc M9; St Louis Univ; Engr.

MISCHLER, LISA; Mater Dei HS; Evansville, IN; 18/171 Sec Frsh Cls; Cls Rep Soph Cls; Sec Jr Cls; VP Sr Cls; Am Leg Aux Girls St; Hon Rl; VP Jr NHS; Sec NHS; Sct Actv; Univ.

MISCISKIA, ANNETTE; Liberty HS; Girard, OH; 46/242 Cl Rep Jr Cls; Cls Rep Sr Cls; Cmnty Wkr; Girl Scts; Hon Rl; NHS; Sch Mus; Sct Actv; Stu Cncl; OEA; 1st Plc Trophies In Modeling; Chairman Of Prom In Charge Of Decorations; Mount Union Coll; Acctg.

MISCONISH, JOHN; Stanton HS; Stratton, OH; Cls Rep Frsh Cls; Cls Rep Soph Cls; Aud/Vis; Boy Scts; Chrs; Hon Rl; Jr NHS; Sch Mus; Stu Cncl; Yrbk; Univ.

MISHLER, K; Parkside HS; Jackson, MI; Hon Rl; Sch Pl; Mic St Univ; Communications.

MISIAK, DAVID; De La Salle Collegiate HS; Detroit, MI; Boy Scts; Hon Rl; IM Sprt; Lawrence Inst Of Tech; Mech Engr.

MISIK, CURTIS; Howland HS; Warren, OH; Hon Rl; Letter Glf; Wrstlng; College.

MISITI, A J; Woodrow Wilson HS; Beakley, WV; 3/550 Cls Rep Frsh Cls; Cls Rep Soph Cls; Pres Jr Cls; Cl Rep Jr Cls; Am Leg Boys St; Chrh Wkr; Hon Rl; NHS; Stu Cncl; Sprt Ed Sch Nwsp; Virginia Tech Univ; Engr.

MISKIMEN, CATHY; Perry HS; Canton, OH; 24/480 Chrh Wkr; Hon Rl; NHS; Off Ade; Fr Clb; LPN Nursing Prog; Nursing.

MISKIN, JAMES; William Henry Harrison HS; W Lafayette, IN; Band; Pres Chrh Wkr; Sct Actv; Yth Flsp; Bsktbl; Letter Ftbl; Trk; God Cntry Awd; JC Awd; Pres Awd; Brigham Young Univ; Forestry.

MISKINIS, DONALD J; Lake Catholic HS; Chesterland, OH; Hon Rl; Pol Wkr; Sch Mus; Sch Pl; IM Sprt; College; Busns.

MISNER, DEBBIE; Wyoming Park HS; Wyoming, MI; Band; Pol Wkr; Ger Clb; Junior Coll; Social Worker.

MISSAD, MATTHEW; Ottawa Hills HS; Grand Rapids, MI; 1/379 Pres Sr Cls; Val; Hon Rl; NHS; Letter Bsbl; Letter Wrstlng; Am Leg Awd; Hope Coll; Bus.

MISSAD, N; Central HS; Grand Rapids, MI; Letter Ten; Grand Rapids Jr Coll; Pre Law.

MISSLER, SUSAN; Lima Ctrl Cath HS; Lima, OH; 5/183 Am Leg Aux Girls St; Hon Rl; NHS; Sch Pl; Stu Cncl; Ed Yrbk; Sprt Ed Yrbk; Lat Clb; Bsbl; Bsktbl; Cath Yth Org Hnr; G Andrews Schlrshp; Awd Of Distinction St Bd Of Educ; Schlrshp Recog Awd; Ohio Northern Univ; Psych.

MISTER, MELONEY A; West Side Sr HS; Gary, IN; Band; Girl Scts; Hon Rl; Lbry Ade; Y-Teens; Capt Twrlr; Cit Awd; Humn Reltns Club; Pen Pal Club; Modeling Schl; Purdue Univ; Civil Engr.

MISTERAVICH, MICHAEL; Lorain Catholic HS; Farmington Hlls, MI; Boy Scts; Rptr Sch Nwsp; Fr Clb; College; Bus Admin.

MITCH, MARK; Revere HS; Akron, OH; Boy Scts; Natl Forn Lg; Sch Mus; Sch Pl; Drama Clb; Hiram College; Biology.

MITCH, SHARI; Meigs HS; Pomeroy, OH; 16/200 Cls Rep Frsh Cls; Pres Jr Cls; Cl Rep Jr Cls; Cls Rep Sr Cls; VP NHS; Sch Pl; VP Stu Cncl; Yrbk; GAA; Dnfth Awd; Rio Grande Coll; Med Lab Tech.

MITCHEL, LEE A; Adams Central HS; Decatur, IN; Trs Frsh Cls; Cls Rep Sr Cls; Band; Chrs; Chrh Wkr; Cmnty Wkr; Hon Rl; Manchester College; Soc Work.

MITCHELL, ALITA; Inkster HS; Westland, MI; Hon Rl; NHS; Sch Pl; Eastern Mic Univ; Bus Admin.

MITCHELL, ANGELA; Grant HS; Grant, MI; Girl Scts; Hon Rl; 4-H; Letter Bsbl; GAA; W Michigan Univ; Comp Sci.

MITCHELL, ANTHONY; Central HS; Detroit, MI; Boy Scts; Chrs; Hon Rl; Cit Awd;.

MITCHELL, BELINDA; Madison Comprehensive HS; Mansfield, OH; Cl Rep Jr Cls; Chrh Wkr; Drl Tm; JA; Red Cr Ade; Fr Clb; FHA; Capt Chrldng; Pom Pon; JA Awd; Univ; Spec Educ.

MITCHELL, CAROL; Napoleon HS; Napoleon, OH; Chrs; Hon Rl; Off Ade; Orch; Sch Mus; Sch Pl; Stg Crw; Yth Flsp; Drama Clb; 4-H; Tech Coll; Bus.

MITCHELL, CHARLES; Magnolia HS; New Martinsvle, WV; 17/189 Cls Rep Soph Cls; Band; Chrs; Hon Rl; Treas NHS; Sch Mus; Letter Crs Cntry; College; Engr.

MITCHELL, CYNTHIA L; Springfield HS; Toledo, OH; Band; Chrs; Chrh Wkr; Drl Tm; Hon Rl; Lbry Ade; Sch Pl; Sprt Ed Sch Nwsp; Rptr Sch Nwsp; Drama Clb; College; Medicine.

MITCHELL, DANIEL; Mount View HS; Wilcoe, WV; Aud/Vis; Hon Rl; Jr NHS; Mod UN; NHS; Key Clb; Letter Trk; Letter Wrstlng; Am Leg Awd; Marshall Univ; Architectural Eng.

MITCHELL, DARLENA; South HS; Youngstwn, OH; 46/200 JA; Lat Clb; Bsktbl; Trk; Mgrs; Scr Kpr; College In Atlanta Geo.

MITCHELL, DARREN; Anderson HS; Cincinnati, OH; 150/425 Boy Scts; Chrs; Ger Clb; IM Sprt; PPFtbl; Cit Awd; College.

MITCHELL, DAVID D; Huntington HS; Waverly, OH; 10/89 Hon Rl; NHS; Yrbk; OEA; Exec Awd 78; Diplomat & Statesman Awd 79; Gold Cert For Victor Calculator Test 79; Coll; Data Proc.

MITCHELL, DEBBIE; Gilbert HS; Gilbert, WV; 3 Chrs; Hon Rl; NHS; Stu Cncl; Rptr Sch Nwsp; Ger Clb; Mth Clb; Pep Clb; Chrldng; Mas Awd; Marshall Univ; Bus Mgmt.

MITCHELL, DIANA; Franklin HS; Franklin, WV; 4/82 VP Sr Cls; Hon Rl; NHS; Sch Pl; Stu Cncl; FHA; West Virginia Univ; Med Tech.

MITCHELL, ELIZABETH; Covert HS; South Haven, MI; 3/34 Trs Frsh Cls; Trs Soph Cls; Band; Hon Rl; Mod UN; NHS; Stu Cncl; Yth Flsp; FHA; Pep Clb; Soc Of Dstngshd Amer HS Students; Ferris St Coll; Acctg.

MITCHELL, ELLIOT; Shaker Hts HS; Shaker Hts, OH; Chrs; Hon Rl; Sch Mus; Sch Pl; Stg Crw; Yrbk; Drama Clb; Fr Clb; Univ; Bio.

MITCHELL, GAIL; Rutherford B Hayes HS; Delaware, OH; Cl Rep Jr Cls; Cls Rep Sr Cls; Chrs; Hon Rl; NHS; Sch Mus; Stu Cncl; Pep Clb; Spn Clb; Chrldng; Univ Of Cincinnati; Phys Therapy.

MITCHELL, GREGORY; S Dearborn HS; Dillsboro, IN; Band; Chrs;.

MITCHELL, JANE M; Newton HS; Pleasant Hill, OH; 6/57 Cl Rep Jr Cls; Cls Rep Sr Cls; Girl Scts; Hon Rl; Lbry Ade; NHS; Off Ade; Stu Cncl; FHA; OEA; State Degree FHA; Ambassador Awd; Top Medical Terminology Stu Awd; College; Medical Steno.

MITCHELL, JEFF; Fayetteville HS; Fayetteville, OH; Band; Boy Scts; Chrs; Debate Tm; Lbry Ade; PAVAS; Stg Crw; Stu Cncl; 4-H; Bsbl;.

MITCHELL, JENNIFER; Rochester HS; Rochester, IN; 22/160 Cls Rep Sr Cls; VP Band; Chrs; FCA; Hon Rl; NHS; Sch Mus; Yth Flsp; Pep Clb; Capt Bsktbl; Ball St Univ; Educ.

MITCHELL, JILL T; Cheboygan Area HS; Cheboygan, MI; 15/197 Sec Jr Cls; Band; Hon Rl; Treas Stu Cncl; Rptr Sch Nwsp; Spn Clb; Michigan St Univ; Travel Mgmt.

MITCHELL, JIM; Delta HS; Eaton, IN; Cls Rep Sr Cls; Aud/Vis; Hon Rl; Stu Cncl; DECA; Letter Crs Cntry; Letter Glf; Mgrs; DECA Pres 79; Ball St Univ; Acctg.

MITCHELL, JOHN; Rapid River HS; Rapid Rvr, MI; 2/75 Pres Frsh Cls; Am Leg Boys St; Band; Hon Rl; Stu Cncl; Letter Bsktbl; Letter Ftbl; Letter Trk; Am Leg Awd; Upper Michigan Today T V Show 76; HS Bowl Show PBS 79; HS Jaxx Band Awrd 77; Marquette Univ; Sci.

MITCHELL, JUDITH; Rutheford B Hayes HS; Delaware, OH; 4-H; Spn Clb; Bsktbl; Socr; GAA; IM Sprt; 4-H Awd; Ohio St Univ; Bus.

MITCHELL, JULIA; Western Boone HS; Thorntown, IN; Am Leg Aux Girls St; Band; Hon Rl; NHS; Off Ade; Orch; Sch Mus; FHA; Pres OEA; Bus Schl; Bus.

MITCHELL, KELLY; Mendon HS; Three Rivers, MI; 5/61 Cls Rep Frsh Cls; Cls Rep Soph Cls; VP Jr Cls; Cls Rep Sr Cls; Band; Hon Rl; NHS; Stu Cncl; Rptr Yrbk; Rptr Sch Nwsp; Ferris St Coll; Dent Hygnst.

MITCHELL, KENNETH; Fountain Central HS; Veedersburg, IN; 12/150 Aud/Vis; Boy Scts; FCA; Hon Rl; NHS; Off Ade; Spn Clb; Letter Ftbl; Letter Trk; Purdue Univ; Aero Tech.

MITCHELL, KEVIN; Colonel Crawford HS; Bucyrus, OH; Band; Boy Scts; Drm Mjrt; Hon Rl; JA; Sch Pl; Sct Actv; Yrbk; Fr Clb; Swmmng; Stdnt Yth Progr At Mi Tech Univ Cert In Med Tech 78; Ohio St Univ; Med Tech.

MITCHELL, KEVIN; Eau Claire HS; Eau Claire, MI; 26/101 Band; Boy Scts; Chrh Wkr; FCA; Hon Rl; Letter Bsbl; Capt Bsktbl; Letter Ftbl; Letter Trk; Schlrshp From Clark Pro Women Organztn 79; Most Athletic Awd 79; Nominee For County Sports Writer Awd 79; Southwestern Michigan Coll; Archt.

MITCHELL, KIMBERLY; George Washington HS; S Charleston, WV; Chrh Wkr; Hon Rl; Jr NHS; Off Ade; Sct Actv; Stu Cncl; Pep Clb; Spn Clb; Trk; Chrldng; Univ; Psych.

MITCHELL, LAURA; Whiteland Community HS; Whiteland, IN; 10/205 FCA; NHS; VP FHA; Indiana St Univ; Elem Educ.

MITCHELL, LISA A; Churchill HS; Livonia, MI; 10/660 Band; Chrs; Cmnty Wkr; Drm Bgl; Hon Rl; Orch; Civ Clb; Sci Clb; Cit Awd; Univ Of Michigan; Civil Engr.

MITCHELL, LISA J; Anderson HS; Rensselaer, IN; 38/443 Sec Chrh Wkr; Hon Rl; Hosp Ade; NHS; Sch Pl; Stg Crw; Lat Clb; Pep Clb; Treas Spn Clb; Natl Latin Exam Medalist Maxima Cumlaude 77; Natl Latin Exam Awd Cum Laude 78; Outstndng Stdnt In Eng 76; Univ; Med.

MITCHELL, LORI; Winfield HS; Winfield, WV; 90/124 Cls Rep Soph Cls; Chrh Wkr; Hon Rl; Jr NHS; NHS; Stu Cncl; Yth Flsp; Yrbk; FHA; Mth Clb; West Virginia St Coll; Math.

MITCHELL, MARK; Madison HS; Madison, OH; Band; Hon Rl; Sch Mus; Sch Pl; Drama Clb; Ger Clb; High Ratings In Solo Ensemble Contest; All Ohio St Fair Bnd; Cincinnati Conservatory; Music.

MITCHELL, MARK; Hammond Baptist HS; Griffith, IN; VP Soph Cls; Hon Rl; Letter Bsktbl; Letter Socr; Letter Trk; College; Journalism.

MITCHELL, MARK; Rossville HS; Frankfort, IN; 7/50 Am Leg Boys St; Band; Chrh Wkr; Cmnty Wkr; Hon Rl; Natl Forn Lg; NHS; Yth Flsp; Sch Nwsp; Pres Key Clb; Purdue Univ; Engineering.

MITCHELL, MARSHA; Clinton Central HS; Frankfort, IN; 2/97 Band; Drl Tm; FCA; Hon Rl; Pres NHS; Off Ade; Sch Mus; Drama Clb; FFA; Pres Lat Clb; Purdue Univ; Engr.

MITCHELL, MARY; Hartland HS; Hartland, MI; Cl Rep Jr Cls; Hon Rl; Spn Clb; Coll; Busns.

MITCHELL, MARY J; St Joseph Acad; Cleveland, OH; Hon Rl; Lit Mag; Sch Nwsp; Mth Clb; GAA; IM Sprt; Heidelberg Coll; Vet.

MITCHELL, MELANIE; Buckeye West HS; Adena, OH; 2/92 Chrs; Hon Rl; NHS; Off Ade; Sch Mus; Sch Pl; Yth Flsp; Drama Clb; FTA; Sci Clb; Ohio Univ; Child Psych.

MITCHELL, MELVERN; St Johns HS; Toledo, OH; Chrh Wkr; Hon Rl; Yth Flsp; Bsktbl; IM Sprt; Evangel Coll; Bus Admin.

MITCHELL, MICHAEL; Kearsley HS; Burton, MI; Hon Rl; Sct Actv; Stu Cncl; Yth Flsp; Fr Clb; Bsbl; Ftbl; Glf; Hockey; Cit Awd; Hockey All Lge 2nd Tm 78; Univ; Bus Mgmt.

MITCHELL, MICHELLE; Kenmore HS; Akron, OH; NHS; Gym; Chrldng; Akron Univ.

MITCHELL, OVIE H; Withrow HS; Cincinnati, OH; Cls Rep Soph Cls; Cl Rep Jr Cls; Band; Hon Rl; JA; NHS; Drama Clb; Letter Trk; Ombudsman; Mass Inst Of Tech; Engr.

MITCHELL, PATRICIA L; Fredericktown HS; Fred, OH; Cls Rep Soph Cls; Band; Chrs; Drl Tm; Sch Mus; Stu Cncl; FHA; OSU; Vet.

MITCHELL, PEGGY; E Kentwood HS; Rockford, MI; Hon Rl; Rptr Sch Nwsp; Sch Nwsp; Fr Clb; Oakland Univ; Journalism.

MITCHELL, REBECCA; Fredericktown HS; Fredericktown, OH; 12/113 Cls Rep Soph Cls; Cl Rep Jr Cls; Cls Rep Sr Cls; Am Leg Aux Girls St; Band; Debate Tm; Hon Rl; NHS; Off Ade; Quill & Scroll; Kent St Univ; Chem.

MITCHELL, REITA A; Fairview HS; Fairview Pk, OH; 31/268 Band; Chrh Wkr; Hon Rl; Sch Mus; Stg Crw; Yth Flsp; Drama Clb; Spn Clb; College; Spec Educa.

MITCHELL, RICHARDA; Notre Dame Acad; Toledo, OH; Sec Frsh Cls; VP Soph Cls; VP Jr Cls; Mod UN; NHS; Ger Clb; Cert Of Ach Whos Who In Foreign Lang; Found For Lifes Essay Contest; Cert Of Commendation Of Perfect Attend; Univ Of Notre Dame; Busns Admin.

MITCHELL, ROBIN; Whiteland Community HS; Franklin, IN; 16/180 Cls Rep Frsh Cls; Cls Rep Soph Cls; Drl Tm; Hon Rl; JA; Jr NHS; NHS; Stu Cncl; FHA; Key Clb; Vllybl Letter 79; Typing Awd 78 79; Colorado St Univ; Archt.

MITCHELL, ROBIN; Creston HS; Grand Rpds, MI; 12/400 Treas Band; Hon Rl; JA; Jr NHS; NHS; Orch; HS Engr Inst Mich St Women Engrs 79; Michigan St Univ; Chem Engr.

MITCHELL, SANDRA M; Franklin Hts HS; Columbus, OH; Sch Pl; Yth Flsp; Key Clb; Chrldng; Scr Kpr; Ohio Dominican Coll; Med.

MITCHELL, SHANNON; Elmhurst HS; Ft Wayne, IN; 14/400 Band; Hon Rl; Letter Gym; Natl Merit Ltr; Hugh Kariger Citizenship Awd 77; Most Imprvd Gymnast 79; Univ.

MITCHELL, TAMARA; North Posey HS; Poseyville, IN; 11/162 Pres Frsh Cls; Pres Soph Cls; Am Leg Aux Girls St; Hon Rl; NHS; Off Ade; Sec Stu Cncl; Pep Clb; GAA; IM Sprt; College; Med.

MITCHELL, TERRI L; Hurricane HS; Hurricane, WV; Sec Jr Cls; Cl Rep Jr Cls; Drl Tm; Girl Scts; Hon Rl; JA; Jr NHS; Off Ade; Pol Wkr; Peer Cnslr 78; Murricane HS Chem Awd 78; Marshall Univ; Sci.

MITCHELL, THERESA; Dominican HS; Detroit, MI; Cls Rep Frsh Cls; VP Jr Cls; Pres Sr Cls; Hon Rl; Hosp Ade; NHS; Sch Mus; Capt Bsbl; Capt Bsktbl; College; Rn.

MITCHELL, TINA; Midland Trail HS; Ansted, WV; VP Soph Cls; Cl Rep Jr Cls; Chrs; Chrh Wkr; Cmnty Wkr; Hon Rl; Stu Cncl; Yth Flsp; Fr Clb; Pep Clb; Marshall Univ; Nursing.

MITCHELL, TOBIN; Lowell HS; Lowell, IN; Boy Scts; Hon Rl; 4-H; VICA; 1st Pl At In St Power & Auto Contest 79; Florida Inst Of Tech; Flight Tech.

MITCHELL, TRACY A; Owendale Gagetown Area HS; Gagetown, MI; Girl Scts; Off Ade; 4-H; FHA; Chrldng; Delta Bus Schl; Sec.

MITCHELL, WILLIAM; Washington HS; E Chicago, IN; 19/292 Pres Chrs; Hon Rl; NHS; Boys Clb Am; Am Leg Awd; Vincennes Univ; Printing Mgmt.

MITCHELL, YVONNE; Griffith HS; Griffith, IN; Band; Chrs; Hon Rl; Jr NHS; Sch Mus; Yth Flsp; Y-Teens; Pep Clb; College; Biology.

MITCHELSON, J; Atherton HS; Burton, MI; Cls Rep Frsh Cls; VP Soph Cls; Aud/Vis; Band; Hon Rl; NHS; Stu Cncl; Mic State Univ; Bus Admin.

MITCHEM, BERNICE L; Spanishburg HS; Kegley, WV; Civ Clb; FBLA; Bluefield State.

MITCHEM, SHARI; North Dickinson HS; Iron Mtn, MI; Sec Soph Cls; Sec Jr Cls; Band; Chrh Wkr; Hon Rl; Acad Achvmnts Awd 79; Math Awd 79; Bus Awd 79; Michigan Tech Univ; Engr.

MITEFF, GANIE; Lansing Eastern HS; Lansing, MI; Cls Rep Soph Cls; Cl Rep Jr Cls; Cls Rep Sr Cls; Chrh Wkr; Hon Rl; Off Ade; Stu Cncl; IM Sprt; Principals Awd For Otstndng Serv To Schl 79; Var Awd In Vllybl; Lansing Cmnty Coll.

MITRO, KATHIE M; Merrillville Sr HS; Merrillville, IN; Off Ade; Sch Nwsp; Pep Clb; Spn Clb; Letter Chrldng; Merriillville HS Cheerldng Awd 77; Harrison Jr Hgh Schl H Emblem 77; Harrison Jr HS H Emblem Lib Aid 77; Indiana Univ; Cmnctns.

MITROVICH, BRUCE; Hubbard HS; Hubbard, OH; Band; Boy Scts; Stg Crw; Diesel Mech.

MITTEN, BRIGHAM; Southeastern HS; Chillicothe, OH; Cl Rep Jr Cls; Band; Boy Scts; Jr NHS; 4-H; Fr Clb; Letter Ftbl; Trk; 4-H Awd; College; Dent.

MITTEN, MARY; Maumee HS; Toledo, OH; Sch Pl; Stg Crw; Y-Teens; Yrbk; Fr Clb; Pep Clb; PPFtbl; Twrlr; College; Mech Drawing.

MITTENTHAL, JAMES P; Cranbrook HS; Huntington Wds, MI; Aud/Vis; Band; Debate Tm; Hon Rl; Lit Mag; Yrbk; Rptr Sch Nwsp; Sch Nwsp; IM Sprt; Natl Merit Ltr; Univ Of Michigan; Law.

MITTERMAIER, MARSHA L; Upper Sandusky HS; Upper Sandusky, OH; Chrs; Girl Scts; Hosp Ade; Lbry Ade; Stg Crw; 4-H; FNA; OEA; Tri Rivers Voc Tech.

MITTOWER, MARVIN A; Taylor HS; Kokomo, IN; 29/230 Cls Rep Frsh Cls; Boy Scts; Chrs; Chrh Wkr; Cmnty Wkr; Hon Rl; JA; Mod UN; Sch Nwsp; Boys Clb Am; Outstndg Achvmnt Amer Hstry 76; Participant Eng Achvmnt Day BSU 78; Model UN Awd For Coun Accellence 78; Univ; Law.

MITZEL, CINDY; Washington HS; Massillon, OH; Hon Rl; Lbry Ade; Drama Clb; Ger Clb; Pep Clb; Kent State; Parole Officer.

MITZELFELD, JIM; Wylie E Groves HS; Birmingham, MI; 152/600 Cls Rep Soph Cls; Quill & Scroll; Ed Sch Nwsp; Sprt Ed Sch Nwsp; Rptr Sch Nwsp; Rdo Clb; Bsbl; Socr; IM Sprt; Michigan St Univ; Journalism.

MITZO, KAREN; Nordonia HS; Northfield, OH; Cls Rep Frsh Cls; Cls Rep Soph Cls; Cl Rep Jr Cls; Band; Chrs; Chrh Wkr; Drl Tm; FCA; Girl Scts; Lbry Ade; 1st Pl Talent Show Playcut Awd For Directing; Univ; Pre Med.

MIX, DAN; Baker HS; Dayton, OH; 52/300 Band; Boy Scts; Chrh Wkr; Drm Bgl; Hon Rl; Sch Mus; Sct Actv; Stg Crw; Yth Flsp; Y-Teens; Wright State Univ; Bio.

MIX, DOUG; Fairview HS; Sherwood, OH; 5/105 Hon Rl; NHS; Mth Clb; Bsktbl; Letter Ftbl; Letter Trk; St Rank Elem Alg Div II OH Schlstc 77; St Rank Geo Div II OH Schlstc Achiev 78; Maumee Vlly Math Cont; Univ; Engr.

MIX, SCOTT C; Jackson Milton HS; Berlin Center, OH; 7/108 Band; Hon Rl; NHS; Yth Flsp; Ger Clb; Mth Clb; Ftbl; Trk; Wrstlng; IM Sprt; Soc Adv HS Studnt 1977; Dist Amer HS Studnt 1977; Kent St Univ; Engr.

MIX, STEVE; New Albany HS; New Albany, IN; 39/565 Cls Rep Frsh Cls; Cls Rep Soph Cls; Cl Rep Jr Cls; Hon Rl; NHS; Stu Cncl; Letter Ftbl; Hanover Coll; Busns.

MIXELL, PHILIP; Yorktown HS; Muncie, IN; 29/180 Boy Scts; FCA; Hon Rl; Fr Clb; Rptr Sch Nwsp; Sci Clb; Ftbl; Capt Swmmng; Ball St Univ; Accts.

MIXON, STEPHANY; East HS; Akron, OH; Chrs; Chrh Wkr; JA; Lbry Ade; Pep Clb; Trk; Chrldng; Mat Maids; Natl Merit Ltr; Univ; Dentistry.

MIXTER, STEPHEN; Whetstone HS; Columbus, OH; Am Leg Boys St; Hon Rl; NHS; IM Sprt; Natl Merit Ltr; Ohi State Univ; Eng.

MIXTER, STEVE; Ubly HS; Ruth, MI; 11/110 Pres Jr Cls; Chrh Wkr; NHS; Sch Pl; Stu Cncl; FFA; Capt Ftbl; Letter Trk; Mgrs; Voice Dem Awd; Central Mich Univ; Auto Engr.

MIXTER, THOMAS K; Whetstone HS; Columbus, OH; 17/325 Hon Rl; Ger Clb; Natl Merit Ltr; Natl Merit SF; Ohio St Univ; Phys Sci.

MIZE, WILLIAM; Fairview HS; Fairview Pk, OH; Band; Treas NHS; Orch; Stg Crw; Spn Clb; Letter Swmmng; Natl Merit Ltr; Univ.

MIZELL, DAVID; Bloomington North HS; Bloomington, IN; 25/500 Band; Hon Rl; Jr NHS; NHS; Sch Mus; Sch Pl; Drama Clb; Spn Clb; Univ Of Illinois; Archt Engr.

MIZER, EILEEN; Berea HS; Berea, OH; Cls Rep Soph Cls; AFS; Chrs; Girl Scts; NHS; Yth Flsp; Sch Nwsp; Swmmng; IM Sprt; Tmr; 1st Clss Girl Scout 77; Univ; Acctg.

MIZER, LINDA; Guernsey Cath Ctrl HS; Cambridge, OH; 1/26 Val; Chrs; Hon Rl; NHS; Sch Pl; Yrbk; Pep Clb; Bsbl; Letter Chrldng; VFW Awd; Ohio St Univ; Med.

MIZER, TODD; Dover HS; Dover, OH; 30/240 Chrh Wkr; Hon Rl; Jr NHS; NHS; Yth Flsp; Bsbl; Bsktbl; Ftbl; Cincinnati Univ; Archt.

M JONES, TENO D M; Buena Vista HS; Saginaw, MI; 30/167 Cls Rep Frsh Cls; Cls Rep Soph Cls; Cl Rep Jr Cls; Cls Rep Sr Cls; Chrh Wkr; Hon Rl; Sch Pl; Sprt Ed Yrbk; Sprt Ed Sch Nwsp; Drama Clb; Grambling St Univ; Sports Brdcstng.

MLACHAK, NATALIE; Villa Angela Acad; Euclid, OH; Chrh Wkr; Hon Rl; Pol Wkr; Stg Crw; Lat Clb; Coll; Nursing.

MLAKER, MANUELA; Erieview Cath HS; Cleveland, OH; 14/96 Cls Rep Soph Cls; Trs Jr Cls; Chrs; Hon Rl; Mod UN; NHS; Sch Pl; Stu Cncl; Trk; Univ Of Boulder; Med Tech.

MLYNARIK, KAREN; William Henry Harrison HS; W Lafayette, IN; Sec Frsh Cls; Band; Girl Scts; Off Ade; Stu Cncl; Rptr Yrbk; Letter Gym; Letter Swmmng; Capt Chrldng; PPFtbl; Purdue Univ; Home Econ.

MOAK, DANIEL; Upper Arlington HS; Columbus, OH; 133/610 Chrh Wkr; FCA; Hon Rl; Stu Cncl; Ger Clb; Lcrss; Univ Of Cincinnati; Forestry.

MOBERG, NANCY; Kankakee Vly HS; Wheatfield, IN; 4/249 Hon Rl; Lbry Ade; NHS; Off Ade; Stg Crw; Treas Yth Flsp; Drama Clb; Spn Clb; Spanish Typing & Creative Writing Awds; Purdue Univ; Busns Admin.

MOBLEY, ANTHONY; George Washington HS; E Chicago, IN; Chrs; Chrh Wkr; Cmnty Wkr; Bsbl; Cit Awd; Elk Awd; Coll.

MOBLEY, JEFFREY; Strongsville HS; Strongsville, OH; Hon Rl; Jr NHS; Letter Wrstlng; Univ Of Akron; Science.

MOBLEY, KEITH; Carlisle HS; Carlisle, OH; Band; Chrs; Hon Rl; Off Ade; Bsktbl; Coach Actv; IM Sprt; College; History.

MOBLEY, LISA; Villa Angela Acad; Cleveland, OH; Chrh Wkr; Cmnty Wkr; Hon Rl; Hosp Ade; Lat Clb; Natl Merit SF; Case Institute Of Tech; Chemicalengr.

MOBLEY, MARK C; Big Walnut HS; Sour Lake, TX; Band; Chrs; 4-H; Letter Crs Cntry; Trk; Letter Wrstlng; College; Civil Engr.

MOBLEY, NORMA; Parkside HS; Jackson, MI; Pres Sr Cls; Chrh Wkr; Cmnty Wkr; Debate Tm; Girl Scts; Orch; Stu Cncl; Pep Clb; Chrldng; Michigan St Univ; Medicine.

MOBLEY, PAMELIA; Elgin HS; Marion, OH; 1/130 Am Leg Aux Girls St; Band; Chrs; Chrh Wkr; Hon Rl; NHS; Off Ade; Yth Flsp; FTA; DAR Awd; Marion Tech Coll; Data Proc.

MOBLEY, SUSAN; Harding HS; Marion, OH; Band; Chrh Wkr; Orch; Sch Mus; Trk; Columbus College Of Art & Design;art.

MOCHAN, LINDA; Lincoln HS; Warren, MI; 3/357 Cls Rep Frsh Cls; Cl Rep Jr Cls; Chrs; Hon Rl; Jr NHS; NHS; Stu Cncl; Sci Clb; Spn Clb; Capt Gym; Macomb Cnty Cmnty Coll; Chem.

MOCHERMAN, TODD E; Edon HS; Edon, OH; Band; Hon Rl; Sch Mus; 4-H; Spn Clb; Crs Cntry; 4-H Awd; Tri State Univ; Computer Engr.

MOCILNIKER, MARGARET; Erieview Catholic HS; Cleveland, OH; 4/117 Chrs; Chrh Wkr; Hon Rl; Lit Mag; Sch Pl; Sch Nwsp; Bsbl; Bsktbl; Univ; Acctg Tchr.

MOCIULEWSKI, LISA; Henry Foro Ii HS; Sterling Hts, MI; 7/455 Band; Chrs; Chrh Wkr; Debate Tm; Hon Rl; Natl Forn Lg; NHS; Central Mi Univ; Music.

MOCK, BRENDA; Tri Valley HS; Frazeysburg, OH; Girl Scts; Hon Rl; Lbry Ade; Yth Flsp; Rptr Yrbk; Yrbk; 4-H; Lat Clb; 4-H Awd; Univ; Vet Asst.

MOCK, DALE; Union City Community HS; Union City, IN; VP Soph Cls; Cls Rep Sr Cls; Band; Chrs; Pres Chrh Wkr; Cmnty Wkr; Stu Cncl; Pres DECA; Ten; Mgrs; Northwestern Bus Coll; Acctg.

MOCK, GREG; Winchester Community HS; Winchester, IN; Business; Business.

MOCK, KATHY; Madison Comprehensive HS; Mansfield, OH; Cmnty Wkr; Girl Scts; Lbry Ade; Spn Clb; Outstanding Stu Awd; U S Naval Academy.

MOCK, MARY; Huntington HS; Huntington, WV; 1/280 Cls Rep Soph Cls; Cls Rep Sr Cls; Val; Sec NHS; Stu Cncl; Yth Flsp; Fr Clb; Sec Mth Clb; Pep Clb; Trk; Centre College.

MOCK, PATRICIA J; Heritage HS; Monroeville, IN; 13/175 Band; Chrs; Hon Rl; Sch Pl; 4-H; Gym; 4-H Awd; Univ; Phys Ther.

MOCK, STANLEY; Jay County HS; Dunkirk, IN; 95/504 Band; Stu Cncl; Rptr Yrbk; Pep Clb; Swmmng; Ball State Univ; Cpa.

MOCKENSTURM, DAVID; St Francis De Sales HS; Toledo, OH; 22/170 FCA; Hon Rl; NHS; Fr Clb; Letter Ftbl; Wrstlng; IM Sprt; Univ Of Dayton; Comp Sci.

MOCZEK, BETH; Bishop Donahue HS; Moundsville, WV; 5/54 Pres Soph Cls; Trs Jr Cls; Pres Sr Cls; Hon Rl; NHS; Stu Cncl; Ed Yrbk; Spn Clb; GAA; Lion Awd; Wv Univ; Bus.

MOCZEK, BETH A; Bishop Donahue HS; Moundsville, WV; 5/55 Pres Soph Cls; Trs Jr Cls; Pres Sr Cls; Hon Rl; NHS; Stu Cncl; Ed Yrbk; Pep Clb; Spn Clb; Bsktbl; West Virginia Univ; Bus Admin.

MODLIN, RUSSELL; Greenbrier East HS; Lewisbrg, WV; 1/480 Hon Rl; NHS; Yth Flsp; Rptr Sch Nwsp; Fr Clb; Letter Crs Cntry; Letter Trk; Letter Wrstlng; Natl Merit SF; Univ; Comp Engr.

MODOS, MARYANN; Clay HS; South Bend, IN; Chrs; Hon Rl; Sch Mus; Pep Clb; Michiana Coll Of Commerce; Exec Sec.

MODRESKI, JO; Manistee Catholic Cntrl HS; Manistee, MI; 5/64 Chrs; Chrh Wkr; Girl Scts; Hon Rl; Hosp Ade; Off Ade; Red Cr Ade; Sch Pl; Stg Crw; Drama Clb; Aquinas Coll; Psych.

MOE, DUANE; Meridian HS; Midland, MI; Band; Boy Scts; Sct Actv; Yth Flsp; Rptr Sch Nwsp; Letter Ftbl; Letter Wrstlng; God Cntry Awd; Ferris; Law.

MOE, JEFFREY; Morgantown HS; Morgantown, WV; Aud/Vis; Band; Chrs; Hon Rl; Orch; Rptr Yrbk; Mth Clb; College; Engin Aerospace.

MOEDER, JIM; Coldwater HS; Celina, OH; 8/130 Hon Rl; Lat Clb; Spn Clb; Letter Bsbl; Bsktbl; IM Sprt; Bowling Green State Univ; Law.

MOEDER, SUSAN; Chaminade Julienne HS; Englewood, OH; Hon Rl; NHS; Sch Pl; Sct Actv; Stg Crw; Drama Clb; Univ; Nursing.

MOEGGENBORG, JEFF; Shepherd HS; Shepherd, MI; Hon Rl; Yrbk; Rptr Sch Nwsp; Pep Clb; Letter Ftbl; Letter Trk; College; Acctg.

MOEHLMAN, TIM; Elmwood HS; Bloomdale, OH; 6/120 Am Leg Boys St; Hon Rl; NHS; Sch Mus; Rptr Sch Nwsp; Sci Clb; Mgrs; Am Leg Awd; John Hopkins Univ; Pre Med.

MOEHLMAN, TIMOTHY; Elmwood HS; Bloomdale, OH; 6/120 Hon Rl; NHS; Sch Mus; Rptr Sch Nwsp; Sci Clb; Mgrs; Am Leg Awd; College; Pre Med.

MOELLER, CHERYL; St Charles HS; St Charles MI; Cls Rep Frsh Cls; Band; Hon Rl; NHS; Sch Mus; Sec Stu Cncl; 4-H; Pep Clb; Letter Trk; Ctrl Michigan Univ; Elem Ed.

MOELLER, DONNA; Bellbrook HS; Bellbrook, OH; 17/176 AFS; Band; Hon Rl; Stg Crw; Indiana Univ; Music.

MOELLER, JILL; Carman HS; Flint, MI; Cls Rep Frsh Cls; Pres Soph Cls; Pres Jr Cls; Chrs; Chrh Wkr; Hon Rl; NHS; College.

MOELLER, JOSEPH; Greensburg Cmnty HS; Greensburg, IN; 2/200 Cls Rep Frsh Cls; Cls Rep Soph Cls; Pres Jr Cls; Cl Rep Jr Cls; Sal; Am Leg Boys St; Hon Rl; NHS; Pres Stu Cncl; VP Lat Clb; Purdue Univ; Indus Mgmt.

MOELLER, LISA; Marion Local HS; Chickasaw, OH; Pep Clb; Sci Clb; Letter Bsktbl; IM Sprt; Bowling Green Univ; Phys Educ.

MOELLER, MARK; South Ripley HS; Versailles, IN; 3/100 Hon Rl; NHS; Sch Pl; Drama Clb; Pres Sci Clb; Crs Cntry; Trk; Cit Awd; DAR Awd; Lion Awd; Florida Inst Of Tech.

MOELLER, MARY M; Lansing Catholic Ctrl HS; Lansing, MI; 5/140 Cls Rep Frsh Cls; VP Soph Cls; VP Jr Cls; VP Sr Cls; Girl Scts; Hon Rl; NHS; Sch Pl; Sct Actv; Pep Clb; Univ Of Mi Hon Trphy Awd 79; Mi Competitive Schlrshp 79; John & Elizabeth Whitely Fnd Schlrshp 79; Michigan St Univ; Gen Bus Admin.

MOELLER, NINA; Deckerville Community HS; Palms, MI; Band; 4-H; OEA; Trk; 4-H Awd; Bus Schl; Legal Sec.

MOENART, STEPHEN; Pershing HS; Detroit, MI; Hon Rl; Macomb County Comm Coll; Engineering.

MOERDYK, KARLA; Lincoln HS; Vincennes, IN; 1/300 Band; Hon Rl; FTA; Mth Clb; Pep Clb; Spn Clb; Mgrs; College; Education.

MOFF, DIANE; Archbishop Alter HS; Centerville, OH; 16/290 Band; Hon Rl; Lbry Ade; NHS; Sch Mus; Fr Clb; College; Nursing.

MOFF, DIANE; Archbishop Alter HS; Centervll, OH; 17/290 Band; Hon Rl; Lbry Ade; NHS; Sch Mus; Fr Clb; Univ.

MOFF, DONNETTE; Columbiana HS; Columbiana, OH; 25/90 Band; Cmp Fr Grls; Chrs; Drm Mjrt; Hon Rl; Off Ade; OEA; Pep Clb; Spn Clb; Swmmng; Ambassador Awd In OEA; Intensive Ofc Educ Class Pres; 3sd Pl In Typing & Related II Region; Honor Roll;.

MOFF, GREGORY; Boardman HS; Canfield, OH; 93/600 Hon Rl; Jr NHS; NHS; Pres 4-H; Letter Trk; Dnfth Awd; 4-H Awd; Ohio State Univ; Agri.

MOFFATT, BETH; St Joseph Sr HS; St Joseph, MI; Band; Chrs; Chrh Wkr; Girl Scts; PAVAS; Sch Mus; Yth Flsp; Rptr Sch Nwsp; Sch Nwsp; Drama Clb; Jr Coll; Cmmrcl Dsgn.

MOFFETT, JERRY; Central HS; Evansville, IN; 27/580 Cmnty Wkr; Hon Rl; Jr NHS; NHS; Boys Clb Am; IM Sprt; Cit Awd; Natl Merit Ltr; College; Engr.

MOFFETT, KATHERINE; Big Rapids HS; Big Rapids, MI; Hon Rl; Ferris St Coll; Acctg.

MOFFETT, TANYA; Southwestern HS; Detroit, MI; Band; Chrs; Chrh Wkr; Hon Rl; Off Ade; Rptr Yrbk; Rptr Sch Nwsp; Harwick Awd For Spelling 79; Michigan St Univ; Jrnlsm.

MOFFITT, CAROL; Liberty Benton HS; Benton Ridge, OH; Band; Chrs; Hon Rl; NHS; Sch Mus; Sch Pl; Rptr Yrbk; Drama Clb; Trk; All Ohio State Fair Band 1977; Schlrshp Team 1976; All Ohio HS Reading Band 1978; Univ.

MOFFITT, VICTORIA S; Mc Comb HS; Mc Comb, OH; 1/66 Band; Chrs; Chrh Wkr; Girl Scts; Hon Rl; Jr NHS; NHS; Yth Flsp; Rptr Sch Nwsp; 4-H; Bowling Green State Univ; Comp Sci.

MOGUL II, ARTHUR; Winfield HS; Winfield, WV; Band; Hon Rl; Jr NHS; NHS; Fr Clb; Mth Clb; Ten; Natl Merit Ltr; Davis & Elkins College; Sci.

MOHAMMED, KAMI; Edison HS; Milan, OH; Cls Rep Frsh Cls; Band; Chrs; Hon Rl; Hosp Ade; NHS; Drama Clb; Mth Clb; Sci Clb; College; Lib Arts.

MOHAMMED, SARA; Edison HS; Milan, OH; 3/164 Trs Frsh Cls; VP Soph Cls; Cls Rep Soph Cls; Band; Hon Rl; NHS; Sch Mus; Sch Pl; Stg Crw; Drama Clb; Univ.

MOHAR, KATHY; White Pine HS; White Pine, MI; Band; Hon Rl; Sch Nwsp; PPFtbl; Coll; Pre Law.

MOHLER, EDWARD; St Francis De Sales HS; Toledo, OH; 72/192 Band; Chrh Wkr; Hon Rl; Hosp Ade; Sch Mus; Y-Teens; Trk; Coach Actv; IM Sprt; Univ; Pre Law.

MOHLER, H CRAIG; Union HS; Union, WV; 4/100 Boy Scts; NHS; Sch Pl; Yrbk; Sch Nwsp; Pres Beta Clb; Pres FBLA; Bsbl; Letter Ftbl; Dnfth Awd; College; Journalism.

MOHLER, JANICE; Marysville Sr HS; Marysville, OH; Chrh Wkr; Hon Rl; NHS; Stg Crw; Stu Cncl; Yrbk; 4-H; Pep Clb; Letter Trk; IM Sprt; Univ; Art.

MOHLER, JEAN; Briggs HS; Columbus, OH; Band; Girl Scts; Off Ade; Yrbk; DECA; Ger Clb; College; Psych.

MOHLER, TAMELA; Ft Recovery HS; Ft Recovery, OH; 9/90 Chrs; Chrh Wkr; Hon Rl; Jr NHS; NHS; Stu Cncl; OEA; Pep Clb; Gym; GAA; Cincinnati Bible Coll; Bus Educ.

MOHLMASTER, WENDY; Ellet HS; Akron, OH; 46/363 Band; NHS; Yth Flsp; Ger Clb; Wooster Coll; Acctg.

MOHNASKY, CAREY; Maple Hts HS; Maple Hgts, OH; Cls Rep Soph Cls; Cl Rep Jr Cls; Sec Sr Cls; Hon Rl; NHS; Stu Cncl; FHA; Pep Clb; Ohio State; Recreation.

MOHNEY, LESLIE; Springfield Local HS; New Springfield, OH; Boy Scts; 4-H; Spn Clb; IM Sprt; College; Forestry.

MOHR, BETTY; Sault Ste Marie Area HS; Saultstemarie, MI; Band; Cmp Fr Grls; Chrh Wkr; Hon Rl; NHS; Orch; Pol Wkr; Lat Clb; IM Sprt; Mic State Univ.

MOHR, BRENT; Van Wert HS; Van Wert, OH; Boy Scts; Hon Rl; Yrbk; Ger Clb; Ftbl; Ten; College; Bus.

MOHR, BRUCE; Carroll HS; Dayton, OH; 20/290 Band; Hon Rl; Orch; Sch Mus; Boys Clb Am; IM Sprt; Univ; Aeronautical Engr.

MOHR, DONNA; Waldron Jr Sr HS; Waldron, IN; 1/68 Drl Tm; FCA; Hon Rl; Lat Clb; Pep Clb; Letter Trk; Univ.

MOHR, KATHRYN; Onsted HS; Adrian, MI; Sec Soph Cls; Sec Jr Cls; Chrh Wkr; Hon Rl; Lit Mag; Off Ade; Pol Wkr; Sch Pl; Treas FTA; Keyettes; Univ; Pre Law.

MOHR, KIM A; Sebring Mc Kinley HS; Sebring, OH; 8/93 Trs Jr Cls; Chrh Wkr; Hon Rl; Sec NHS; Off Ade; Quill & Scroll; Ed Sch Nwsp; Lat Clb; Capt Chrldng; Am Leg Awd; Alternate To Buckeye Girls State; Career Schl; Airlines.

MOHR, SUE; Marlington HS; Paris, OH; Hon Rl; FFA; Trk; Kent St Univ; Acctg.

MOHR, TINA; Michigan Lutheran Seminary; Morenci, MI; Chrs; Hon Rl; Bsktbl; IM Sprt; PPFtbl; DMLC; Educ.

MOHR, WILLIAM; Benton Harbor HS; Benton Hbr, MI; Band; Girl Scts; NHS; Yth Flsp; Mth Clb; Natl Merit SF; Univ.

MOHRFIELD, GINNI; Goshen HS; Pleasant Plain, OH; Sec Frsh Cls; Sec Soph Cls; Sec Jr Cls; Band; Drm Mjrt; Sch Mus; Pres Yth Flsp; Sec 4-H; Pep Clb; Letter Trk;.

MOHSENZADEH, MOHAMMAD; Richmond Sr HS; Richmond, IN; Socr; Ten; Univ; Elec Engr.

MOILANEN, DAVID; Ewene Trout Creek HS; Trout Creek, MI; 20/54 Cls Rep Frsh Cls; Cl Rep Jr Cls; Sprt Ed Yrbk; Bsbl; Bsktbl; Ftbl; Trk; IM Sprt; Univ Of Wisconsin; Phys Ed.

MOILANEN, DAVID; Einen Trout Creek HS; Trout Creek, MI; 21/50 Cls Rep Frsh Cls; Cls Rep Soph Cls; Cl Rep Jr Cls; Sal; Sprt Ed Yrbk; Bsbl; Bsktbl; Ftbl; Trk; IM Sprt; Central Michigan Univ.

MOINE, JO DEE; Wadsworth Sr HS; Wadsworth, OH; Aud/Vis; Sch Nwsp; Sec DECA; Fr Clb; Spn Clb; Bsktbl; Letter Ten; Coach Actv; IM Sprt; Mgrs; Tennis Conf Comp Doubles 78; Wadsworthopen Tennis Ntourn 2nd Pl Singles & Doubles 78; Wads Art Exh 2 Hnrs; Wayne General & Tech Univ; Psych.

MOLCHAN, WILLIAM; Padua Franciscan HS; Parma, OH; 60/263 Boy Scts; Chrh Wkr; Cmnty Wkr; Debate Tm; Hon Rl; JA; NHS; Pol Wkr; Sct Actv; Stu Cncl; Jr Achvmnt Pres Of Yr 79; Jr Achvmnt Schlrshp 79; Univ Of Dayton; Acctg.

MOLES, BRUCE E; Calhoun County HS; Nicut, WV; Cls Rep Frsh Cls; Hon Rl; Stu Cncl; FHA; Capt Bsbl; Capt Ftbl; Wrstlng; Coach Actv; IM Sprt; Glenville St Coll; Spec Educ.

MOLES, LISA; Elida HS; Lima, OH; 7/250 Am Leg Aux Girls St; Band; Debate Tm; Drl Tm; Hon Rl; NHS; Pol Wkr; Bluffton College; Theater.

MOLESKI, KEN; Ovid Elsie HS; Ovid, MI; 20/130 Aud/Vis; Boy Scts; Chrh Wkr; Lbry Ade; Yth Flsp; Rptr Yrbk; Sprt Ed Sch Nwsp; Capt Bsktbl; Ftbl; Letter Trk; Airlines.

MOLIN, GREG; Kearsley HS; Burton, MI; 15/400 Chrs; Chrh Wkr; Yth Flsp; Fr Clb; IM Sprt; Cedarville College; Bus.

MOLINA, BRENDA; Theodore Roosevelt HS; E Chicago, IN; 10/215 Cls Rep Frsh Cls; Band; NHS; Orch; Yrbk; Sch Nwsp; Fr Clb; FHA; Mth Clb; Sci Clb; Honor & Service & Lenin Awd 79; Purdue Univ; Phys Ther.

MOLINA, MICHAEL D; Notre Dame HS; Anmoore, WV; 8/54 Cls Rep Soph Cls; Pres Jr Cls; Chrh Wkr; Cmnty Wkr; Natl Forn Lg; Red Cr Ade; Sch Pl; Stg Crw; Stu Cncl; Drama Clb; Marshall Univ; Speech Pathlgy.

MOLINARI, FRANCESCO; Henry Ford II HS; Strlng Hts, MI; Cmnty Wkr; Hon Rl; Off Ade; Drama Clb; Eng Clb; Fr Clb; Natl Merit Schl; Wayne St Univ; Eng.

MOLINARI, MICHAEL; Champion HS; Warren, OH; 31/226 Hon Rl; Lbry Ade; Sch Pl; Stg Crw; Rptr Sch Nwsp; Ten; Trk; IM Sprt; Kent State; Computer Technology.

MOLINE, DENISE K; Cheboygan Area HS; Cheboygan, MI; 1/193 Sec Sr Cls; Treas Band; VP Chrs; Chrh Wkr; Hon Rl; Mdrgl; Pol Wkr; Sch Mus; Sch Pl; Stu Cncl; Mercy Coll; Med Rcrd Admin.

MOLITORS, ELIZABETH; Our Lady Of The Elms HS; Akron, OH; 1/35 Pres Jr Cls; Pres Sr Cls; Hon Rl; Sprt Ed Sch Nwsp; Rptr Sch Nwsp; Letter Bsktbl; Dnfth Awd; College; Psych.

MOLL, JONATHAN; Arthur Hill HS; Saginaw, MI; Hon Rl; Pol Wkr; Sch Mus; Fr Clb; Sci Clb; Natl Merit Ltr; Univ Of Mic; Bio.

MOLLAUN, KELLY; Lawrenceburg HS; Lawrenceburg, IN; 14/150 Trs Jr Cls; VP Sr Cls; Am Leg Boys St; FCA; Hon Rl; NHS; Key Clb; Pep Clb; Letter Bsktbl; Glf; Tri Kappa Wd 75; Its Acad 78; Univ; Bus Mgmt.

MOLLE, CATHERINE; Bishop Noll Institute; Hammond, IN; Cl Rep Jr Cls; Am Leg Aux Girls St; Band; Hon Rl; Stu Cncl; Mth Clb; Mat Maids; Regnl Music Contest 1st Plc Solo Clarinet Trio & Quartet 77; Girls St Cnty Comminssioner 79; Univ; Nursing.

MOLLER, KATHY; Reeths Puffer HS; N Muskegon, MI; 151/281 Aud/Vis; Chrs; Girl Scts; Hon Rl; JA; Lbry Ade; 4-H; 4-H Awd; Muskegon Comm; Educ.

MOLLERAN, VIRGINIA M; Seton HS; Cincinnati, OH; 12/274 Girl Scts; Hon Rl; Sec JA; NHS; Fr Clb; Univ; Physician.

MOLLET, LONNIE; West Washington HS; Salem, IN; Band; Sch Mus; Sch Pl; Stg Crw; Rptr Sch Nwsp; Sch Nwsp; Drama Clb; Spn Clb; VICA; Voc Schl; Carpenter.

MOLLITOR, ELISABETH; Jackson County Western HS; Parma, MI; Band; Chrs; Chrh Wkr; Cmnty Wkr; Sch Pl; Y-Teens; Fr Clb; Gym; IM Sprt; College; Vet.

MOLLOHAN, SUE; Woodrow Wilson HS; Beckley, WV; Hon Rl; Pep Clb; Chrldng; PPFtbl; West Virginia Univ.

MOLNAR, BRENDA; Springfield Local HS; Poland, OH; 8/152 Band; Drm Mjrt; Hon Rl; Treas NHS; 4-H; Pres FTA; Pep Clb; Spn Clb; 4-H Awd; JC Awd; Youngstown State Univ; Computer.

MOLNAR, CATHY; Woodhaven HS; Woodhaven, MI; 4/200 Chrs; Hon Rl; Jr NHS; NHS; Ed Yrbk; Rptr Yrbk; Yrbk; Letter Ten; PPFtbl; Tmr; Univ Of Mic; Bus Admin.

MOLNAR, LORI; Boardman HS; Youngstown, OH; 5/550 Cmp Fr Grls; Hon Rl; NHS; Quill & Scroll; Ed Yrbk; Rptr Yrbk; Treas Fr Clb; Mth Clb; Sci Clb; College; Math.

MOLNAR, THERESA M; Bishop Flaget HS; Chillicothe, OH; Val; Am Leg Aux Girls St; Chrh Wkr; Cmnty Wkr; Debate Tm; Hon Rl; Hosp Ade; Natl Forn Lg; Pres NHS; Sch Mus; Coll Of Mt St Joseph; Dietetics.

MOLNER, PATTY; Madison HS; Madison Hts, MI; 1/250 Val; Hon Rl; Jr NHS; Pres NHS; Sci Clb; Pres Spn Clb; Chrldng; Wayne State Univ; Med Tech.

MOLONEY, JOHN W; Fairlawn HS; Sidney, OH; 3/45 Pres Frsh Cls; Cls Rep Soph Cls; Cl Rep Jr Cls; Am Leg Boys St; Hon Rl; NHS; Stg Crw; Stu Cncl; 4-H; VICA; Edison St Univ; Carpentry.

MOLTER, ROBERT; Coloma HS; Coloma, MI; 10/225 Cls Rep Soph Cls; Cl Rep Jr Cls; Pres Sr Cls; Band; Hon Rl; NHS; Stu Cncl; Capt Ftbl; Dnfth Awd; Ferris Mert Schlshp 79; St Ofmi Chmpttv Schlhp 79; Mb Rof Coloma High Quiz Bowl Team 78; Ferris St Coll; Optometrist.

MOLZAN, DAVIE; James Ford Rhodes HS; Cleveland, OH; Eng Clb; Ger Clb; Letter Bsktbl; Letter Trk; IM Sprt; Mgrs; Cit Awd; JA Awd; Pres Awd; Air Force; Tech.

MOMANY, SHARON; Davison HS; Davison, MI; Band; Drl Tm; Girl Scts; Coach Actv; Univ Of Michigan; Data Proc.

MOMYER, GENE; Gorham Fayette HS; Fayette, OH; VP Frsh Cls; Trs Soph Cls; Am Leg Boys St; Hon Rl; Sch Pl; Ed Sch Nwsp; 4-H; FFA; Letter Crs Cntry; Letter Trk; College; Pre Law.

MONACHINO, THOMAS; Thomas W Harvey HS; Painesville, OH; Aud/Vis; Hon Rl; JA; Yrbk; Rptr Sch Nwsp; Sch Nwsp; Ten; JA Awd; Ohio Univ; Radio Announcer.

MONAGHAN, MICHAEL; Ida HS; Ida, MI; Hon Rl; NHS; Letter Bsbl; Letter Glf; Western Mic; Flight Tech.

MONCK, TIMOTHY; Sault Area HS; Sault Stemarie, MI; Boy Scts; Drl Tm; Hon Rl; NHS; Pol Wkr; ROTC; Sct Actv; IM Sprt; Lion Awd; VFW Awd; Lake Superior St Coll; Law.

MONCZYNSKI, ANGELA; Lumen Cordium HS; Macedonia, OH; Pres Frsh Cls; Pres Jr Cls; Drl Tm; Hon Rl; Off Ade; Sch Mus; Sch Pl; Stu Cncl; Drama Clb; Spn Clb; Mother Mary Joseph Schlrshp 77; Serv Awd 77; Perfect Attnd 79; Univ.

MOND, JOSHUA; Beachwood HS; Beachwood, OH; Debate Tm; Mod UN; Natl Forn Lg; Capt Glf; Coll; Law.

MONDAK, JEFFERY; St Edward HS; Middleburg Hts, OH; Debate Tm; Hon Rl; Lit Mag; Natl Forn Lg; NHS; Sch Nwsp; Am Leg Awd; College.

MONDOC, ERIC; Brookfield Sr HS; Hubbard, OH; Cls Rep Soph Cls; Hon Rl; NHS; Beta Clb; Lat Clb; Univ; Marine Bio.

MONDORA, CHRISTINA; Struthers HS; Poland, OH; Cmp Fr Grls; Chrs; Chrh Wkr; Cmnty Wkr; JA; Sch Pl; Stg Crw; Y-Teens; Drama Clb; 4-H; Bowling Green Univ; Speech Ther.

MONDS, JOANNA; Cloverdale Community Schools; Poland, IN; Sec Band; Drl Tm; Drm Mjrt; FCA; Sch Mus; Yrbk; Drama Clb; FTA; Pep Clb; Spn Clb; Altemt To Girls St 78; Univ.

MONETTE, JANENE; Fremont Public HS; Brunswick, MI; 7/238 Hon Rl; Lbry Ade; NHS; 4-H; Letter Bsbl; Sec Pom Pon; Dnfth Awd; Natl Merit Schl; Central Mic Univ; Bus Admin.

MONETTE, RICHARD; Notre Dame HS; Grosse Pte Wds, MI; Hon Rl; NHS; Univ Of Mich Dearborn; Bus Admin.

MONEY, DEREK; Horace Mann 'S; Gary, IN; Hon Rl; Jr NHS; Natl Forn Lg; NHS; Sch Mus; Sch Pl; Mth Clb; Trk; Cit Awd; Outstanding Speech Stu Of Horace Mann HS 77; 2nd Pl Awd Citywide Forensic Tourn 78; Indiana Univ; Theatre Arts.

MONEY, JANIS; Milford Christian Academy; Goshen, OH; Sec Sr Cls; Band; Chrs; Chrh Wkr; FCA; Hon Rl; Sch Mus; Rptr Sch Nwsp; Spn Clb; IM Sprt; Tennessee Temple Univ; Elem Educ.

MONEYPENNY, MOLLY; Nordonia Sr HS; Macedonia, OH; Sec Band; Drl Tm; Hon Rl; Sawyer Coll Of Bus; Legal Sec.

MONFILS, CHRISTINE; Roseville HS; Roseville, MI; 9/423 Treas Band; Hon Rl; Off Ade; Sch Mus; Bausch & Lomb Awd; Cit Awd; Kiwan Awd; Michigan St Univ; Music Ther.

MONFREDA, GREGG; Decatur Central HS; Camby, IN; Am Leg Boys St; Hon Rl; NHS; Letter Crs Cntry; IM Sprt; Univ; Comp Sci.

MONGINE, MARK; Niles Mckinley HS; Niles, OH; 32/365 AFS; Band; Hon Rl; NHS; Sch Mus; Sch Pl; Stg Crw; Drama Clb; Key Clb; Letter Glf; Ohi Northern Univ; Pharmacy.

MONICO, KAREN; Girard HS; Girard, OH; 28/200 AFS; Stu Cncl; Y-Teens; Rptr Yrbk; Rptr Sch Nwsp; Pep Clb; GAA;.

MONING, JOSEPH L; La Salle HS; Cheviot, OH; 2/270 Boy Scts; Chrh Wkr; Hon Rl; JA; NHS; Yrbk; Cit Awd; XUF; Comp Sci.

MONK, GREG; Marshall HS; Marshall, MI; Hon Rl; Lat Clb; Am Leg Awd; Univ Of Western Mic.

MONNIER, CHRIS; Russia Local HS; Russia, OH; 4/44 Band; Hon Rl; NHS; Stu Cncl; Spn Clb; Letter Bsktbl; Letter Chrldng; College; Health.

MONNIER, CHRIS; Russia Local School; Russia, OH; 4/44 Band; Chrs; Hon Rl; NHS; Stu Cncl; Drama Clb; Spn Clb; Letter Bsktbl; Chrldng; Univ; Health.

MONNIG, JULIA; Archbishop Alter HS; Centervl, OH; 36/320 Hon Rl; NHS; 4-H; Keyettes; Spn Clb; Trk; Univ Of Dayton; Bus Mgmt.

MONNIN, BARB; Russia Local HS; Russia, OH; 4/34 Pres Frsh Cls; Pres Jr Cls; Chrs; Hon Rl; NHS; Off Ade; Sch Pl; Ed Sch Nwsp; Chrldng; GAA; College.

MONNIN, L; Versailles HS; Versailles, OH; Band; Chrs; Chrh Wkr; Girl Scts; Hon Rl; Sch Mus; FNA; College; Nursing.

MONNIN, TAMMY; Russia Local HS; Russia, OH; Sec Soph Cls; Trs Jr Cls; Chrs; Hon Rl; Hosp Ade; VP NHS; Sch Pl; Rptr Yrbk; Drama Clb; Spn Clb; Miami Valley Schl; Nursing.

MONNIN, TAMMY; Russia Local School; Russia, OH; 1/35 Sec Soph Cls; Trs Jr Cls; Chrs; Hon Rl; Hosp Ade; VP NHS; Sch Pl; Rptr Yrbk; Drama Clb; VP Pep Clb; Miami Valley Schl Of Nursing; RN.

MONNOT, BETTE; Central Catholic HS; Canton, OH; 6/247 Band; Chrh Wkr; Cmnty Wkr; Girl Scts; Hon Rl; Hosp Ade; NHS; Bowling Green State Univ; Nurse.

MONROE, ALISON; Paint Valley HS; Bourneville, OH; 9/90 Hon Rl; FHA; Lat Clb; Spn Clb; Letter Bsktbl; 4th Pl SAT English Test; Holzer Medical Ctr; Nursing.

MONROE, CHERYL; Econse HS; Ecorse, MI; Cls Rep Frsh Cls; Cls Rep Soph Cls; Sec Jr Cls; Sec Sr Cls; Band; Hon Rl; Off Ade; Stu Cncl; Chrldng; Capt Pres Awd; Wayne State Univ; Medical Social Wkr.

MONROE, CHRISTINE; Father Gabriel Richard HS; Ann Arbor, MI; Hon Rl; Lit Mag; Pol Wkr; Stu Cncl; Rptr Yrbk; Spn Clb; Letter Bsktbl; Letter Trk; IM Sprt; Univ Of Michigan; Criminal Justice.

MONROE, CYNTHIA; Lakeville HS; Otisville, MI; 3/199 Cls Rep Sr Cls; Sal; Hon Rl; NHS; Sec Stu Cncl; Ed Sch Nwsp; Spn Clb; Cntrl Michigan Univ; Bus Admin.

MONROE, DEBRA; South Ripley Jr Sr HS; Versailles, IN; 23/102 Chrs; Chrh Wkr; Hon Rl; Lit Mag; Quill & Scroll; Sch Mus; Yth Flsp; Rptr Yrbk; Rptr Sch Nwsp; 4-H; Georgetown Coll; Cmnctn Arts.

MONROE, JOSEPH T; Martinsburg Sr HS; Martinsburg, WV; 3/227 Cls Rep Soph Cls; Pres Jr Cls; Cl Rep Jr Cls; Am Leg Boys St; Boy Scts; Hon Rl; NHS; Rptr Yrbk; Key Clb; Glf; Univ; Pre Med.

MONROE, LISA; Sandy Valley HS; Magnolia, OH; Cls Rep Sr Cls; Chrs; Cmnty Wkr; Hon Rl; NHS; Quill & Scroll; Stg Crw; Stu Cncl; Kent State; Health.

MONROE, SUSAN; Johnstown HS; Gahanna, OH; 10/140 Band; Pres Girl Scts; Hon Rl; NHS; Rptr Sch Nwsp; 4-H; Fr Clb; Ohio Univ; Vet.

MONROE, THOMAS; Marion L Steele HS; Amherst, OH; Cls Rep Frsh Cls; Cls Rep Soph Cls; Boy Scts; Stu Cncl; Boys Clb Am; Spn Clb; Hockey; Pres Awd; Ohio St Univ; Archt.

MONSON, LORI; Crestwood HS; Dearborn Hts, MI; Chrh Wkr; Hon Rl; NHS; Sch Pl; Stu Cncl; Key Clb; Bsbl; Chrldng; Henry Ford Comm College; Dancing.

MONTAG, MIKE; La Salle HS; Cincinnati, OH; 20/249 Hon Rl; Bsbl; Ftbl; IM Sprt; Univ.

MONTAGNESE, RENEE; Licking Valley HS; Newark, OH; VP Frsh Cls; Sec Jr Cls; Hon Rl; Stu Cncl; Yrbk; Key Clb; Pep Clb; Bsktbl; Chrldng; Scr Kpr; Bowling Green Univ; Tchr Biol.

MONTAGUE, MARY; Ursuline Academy; Cincinnati, OH; Chrs; Girl Scts; Sct Actv; Yrbk; Rptr Sch Nwsp; Sch Nwsp; Socr; Scr Kpr; Cit Awd; Natl Merit SF; College; Lawyer.

MONTAN, VASILE; Indian Valley North HS; Nw Philadelphia, OH; Band; Boy Scts; Hon Rl; Sct Actv; 4-H; Ger Clb; God Cntry Awd; Univ; Math.

MONTANARO, CRISTINE; Ashtabula HS; Ashtabula, OH; 22/266 VP Soph Cls; VP Jr Cls; Pres Sr Cls; AFS; Hon Rl; Jr NHS; Off Ade; Stu Cncl; FTA; College; Bus.

MONTANYA, DAVID; Mansfield Christian HS; Lexington, OH; Pres Band; Bsktbl; Crs Cntry; Trk; Ohio State Univ; Optometry.

MONTAVON, BOB; Chaminade Julienne HS; Dayton, OH; Cls Rep Soph Cls; Band; Boy Scts; Chrh Wkr; Hon Rl; Orch; Sct Actv; Stg Crw; Stu Cncl; Swmmng; Univ Of Dayton; Acctg.

MONTE, ANGIE; Green HS; Akron, OH; Cls Rep Sr Cls; Chrs; Hon Rl; Off Ade; Sch Mus; Sch Pl; Stu Cncl; Y-Teens; Drama Clb; Pep Clb; Univ; Soc Serv.

MONTE, GINA M; Wellsville HS; Wellsville, OH; Band; Chrs; Cmnty Wkr; Drm Mjrt; Lbry Ade; PAVAS; Sch Pl; Stg Crw; Y-Teens; Rptr Sch Nwsp; American Academy Of Drama; Theatre.

MONTE CALVO, ANTHONY J; Warren Western Reserve HS; Warren, OH; 1/431 Am Leg Boys St; Hon Rl; NHS; Yrbk; Fr Clb; Sci Clb; Trk; Am Leg Awd; Ohio St Univ; Aero Engr.

MONTELEONE, MARC; Notre Dame HS; Clarksburg, WV; 7/62 Cls Rep Frsh Cls; Cls Rep Soph Cls; VP Jr Cls; VP Sr Cls; Am Leg Boys St; Stu Cncl; Key Clb; Lat Clb; Mth Clb; Bsktbl; Notre Dame Univ; Acctg.

MONTELEONE, TERESA; Maple Heights Sr HS; Maple Hts, OH; 3/500 Cl Rep Jr Cls; AFS; Hon Rl; NHS; Off Ade; Drama Clb; Crs Cntry; Letter Trk; Letter IM Sprt; Kiwan Awd; Coll Of Wooster; Liberal Arts.

MONTEMURRO, MICHELLE; Robert S Rogers HS; Toledo, OH; Sec Soph Cls; Hon Rl; Sch Mus; Sch Pl; Stg Crw; FHA; Sci Clb; Socr; IM Sprt; Sci Honrr Soc 1978; Astronomy Club Sec 1978; Soccer Club 1979; Univ Of Toledo; Sci.

MONTERUSSO, MARY; Lake Shore HS; St Clair Shore, MI; 4/650 Hon Rl; Jr NHS; NHS; Pol Wkr; Natl Merit Ltr; Wayne St Univ; Acctg.

MONTES, CARLOS; Aquinas HS; Romulus, MI; 27/211 Boy Scts; Chrh Wkr; Hon Rl; NHS; Letter Bsbl; Letter Bsktbl; Letter Crs Cntry; IM Sprt; Mgrs; Scr Kpr; Michigan Tech Univ; Engr.

MONTES, MICHELLE L; Munster HS; Munster, IN; Lit Mag; Quill & Scroll; Stg Crw; Yrbk; Drama Clb; Fr Clb; IM Sprt; Mat Maids; Scr Kpr; Tmr; Purdue Univ; Bio.

MONTGOMERY, BOB; Perrysburg HS; Perrysburg, OH; 41/251 Rptr Yrbk; Pres 4-H; 4-H Awd; College; Pre Med.

MONTGOMERY, BONITA S; Perry HS; Massillon, OH; 146/453 4-H; Pep Clb; Sci Clb; VICA; 4-H Awd; St Bd Of Educ Awd Of Distinction 79; Shawnee St Cmnty Coll; Dent Hygnst.

MONTGOMERY, BRENDA; Eastern HS; Melbourne, FL; Band; Cmnty Wkr; Hon Rl; Sch Pl; Stg Crw; Sch Nwsp; Drama Clb; 4-H; FHA; Pep Clb; Shawnee St Coll; Retail Mktg.

MONTGOMERY, BRENDA; Henryville HS; Henryville, IN; 6/64 Band; Hon Rl; Mod UN; NHS; Sch Pl; 4-H; VP Spn Clb; Indiana Univ; Spanish.

MONTGOMERY, CAROLYN; Kalkaska HS; Rapid City, MI; Hon Rl; DECA; Spn Clb; Letter Bsktbl; Suomi Hancock; Gen Studies.

MONTGOMERY, CHRISTIE L; Waldron HS; St Paul, IN; VP Frsh Cls; Sec Soph Cls; Trs Soph Cls; Cl Rep Jr Cls; Sec Sr Cls; Hon Rl; Lbry Ade; Off Ade; Sch Pl; Stu Cncl;.

MONTGOMERY, DEBBIE; St Bernard Elmwood Place HS; St Bernard, OH; Drl Tm; Stg Crw; Stu Cncl; Rptr Yrbk; Rptr Sch Nwsp; DECA; Pep Clb; Spn Clb; Scr Kpr; Pres Awd; Vocational Schl; Cosmetology.

MONTGOMERY, DEBORAH; Greenbrier East HS; Renick, WV; 28/413 Band; Chrs; Chrh Wkr; Hon Rl; NHS; Treas Yth Flsp; Pres 4-H; College; Bus Admin.

MONTGOMERY, DIANA; Lake Central HS; Schererville, IN; Hon Rl; Lbry Ade; Ind State Univ; Nursing.

MONTGOMERY, DODIE; Brooke HS; Follansbee, WV; 53/403 VP Frsh Cls; VP Soph Cls; VP Jr Cls; VP Sr Cls; Am Leg Aux Girls St; FCA; Hon Rl; NHS; Quill & Scroll; Sprt Ed Yrbk; West Virginia Univ; Phys Ther.

MONTGOMERY, ELIZABETH; Centerburg HS; Centerburg, OH; 1/65 Val; Am Leg Aux Girls St; Chrs; Cmnty Wkr; Debate Tm; Hon Rl; Jr NHS; NHS; Off Ade; Stg Crw; Univ Of Akron; Respiratory Therapy.

MONTGOMERY, G; Immaculata HS; Detroit, MI; Girl Scts; Hon Rl; Off Ade; Sct Actv; Pep Clb; Spn Clb; IM Sprt; College; Prof Dance Instructor.

MONTGOMERY, GENA; Yellow Springs HS; Yellow Sprg, OH; 22/72 Chrs; Chrh Wkr; Cmnty Wkr; Rptr Yrbk; Drama Clb; Awd For Outstndng Achvmnt In Eng II 78; Awd For Profcncy In Typing III 78; Outstndng Achvmnt In Spnsh 78; Univ; Bus.

MONTGOMERY, JACK; North Central HS; Indianapolis, IN; JA; NHS; Sch Mus; Sch Pl; Stu Cncl; OEA; IM Sprt; Ind Univ; Acctg.

MONTGOMERY, JAMES; Hill Community HS; Lansing, MI; Trs Sr Cls; Band; Chrh Wkr; Hon Rl; Jr NHS; NHS; Natl Merit Ltr; Michigan St Univ; Comp Sci.

MONTGOMERY, JANET; University HS; Morgantown, WV; 20/125 Cls Rep Frsh Cls; Cls Rep Soph Cls; Band; Hon Rl; Stu Cncl; Ger Clb; Sci Clb; Letter Bsktbl; Letter Trk; Chrldng; North Texas St Univ; Acctg.

MONTGOMERY, JEFFREY; Wellston HS; Wellston, OH; Pres Jr Cls; NHS; Stu Cncl; Mth Clb; Letter Bsbl; Letter Bsktbl; Letter Ftbl; Marshall Univ; Civil Engr.

MONTGOMERY, JIL; Columbia Ctrl HS; Brooklyn, MI; Band; Cmp Fr Grls; Debate Tm; Girl Scts; Hon Rl; NHS; Sch Mus; Fr Clb; Pres FTA; Eastern Michigan Univ; Spec Ed.

MONTGOMERY, JILL; Green HS; N Canton, OH; Cls Rep Frsh Cls; Cls Rep Soph Cls; Cl Rep Jr Cls; Cls Rep Sr Cls; Chrs; Mdrgl; Sch Mus; Stu Cncl; Pres Pep Clb; Chrldng; College; Speech Therapy.

MONTGOMERY, KAREN; Jefferson Area HS; Jefferson, OH; Band; Chrh Wkr; Hon Rl; NHS; Off Ade; Yth Flsp; Fr Clb; Sci Clb; College; Nursing.

MONTGOMERY, KAREN; Marian HS; Birmingham, MI; Cls Rep Frsh Cls; Chrh Wkr; Cmnty Wkr; Hon Rl; Sch Nwsp; Spn Clb; Trk; Mercy College; Nursing.

MONTGOMERY, KATHY; Hamilton Hts HS; Cicero, IN; Sec Jr Cls; Girl Scts; Hon Rl; 4-H; Lat Clb; Pep Clb; Chrldng; PPFtbl; Indiana Univ; Nursing.

MONTGOMERY, KENNETH; Danville HS; Danville, IN; 15/170 Trs Frsh Cls; Trs Soph Cls; Trs Jr Cls; Trs Sr Cls; Am Leg Boys St; Hon Rl; Red Cr Ade; Glf; Ten; Am Leg Awd; Purdue Univ; Engr.

MONTGOMERY, KRISTI; Avon HS; Indianapolis, IN; Chrs; Hon Rl; Off Ade; Stu Cncl; Rptr Yrbk; Lat Clb; Pep Clb; Chrldng; Pres Awd; Whos Who Cheerldng 1977; Whos Who Amer High Schl Stdnts 1977; Miss Cresendo Cand 1977; Ball St Univ; Spec Educ.

MONTGOMERY, L; Triton HS; Bourbon, IN; Band; Cmp Fr Grls; Drl Tm; Drm Mjrt; Sprt Ed Yrbk; Rptr Yrbk; Fr Clb; Spn Clb; Ten; Pom Pon; Indiana Univ; Journalism.

MONTGOMERY, LORI; Marlington HS; Alliance, OH; 45/258 Band; Chrh Wkr; Hon Rl; NHS; Off Ade; Yrbk; Pres 4-H; Letter Trk;.

MONTGOMERY, LORIE; Henryville HS; Henryville, IN; Red Cr Ade; Rptr Yrbk; FHA; Spn Clb; Indiana Univ; Mktg.

MONTGOMERY, LORI L; Marlington HS; Alliance, OH; 41/289 Band; Chrh Wkr; Off Ade; Yrbk; Pres 4-H; Letter Trk; Coach Actv; Mgrs; 4-H Awd; JA Awd; Stark Tech Schl; Med Sec.

MONTGOMERY, MICHAEL; Toronto HS; Toronto, OH; Band; Boy Scts; Hon Rl; College; Biol.

MONTGOMERY, MICHELLE; Concord HS; Jackson, MI; Cmp Fr Grls; Hon Rl; 4-H; Bsktbl; Trk; Cit Awd; Bus Schl.

MONTGOMERY, SHERRY; James Ford Rhodes HS; Cleveland, OH; Band; Jr NHS; Orch; Sch Mus; Yth Flsp; Fr Clb; IM Sprt; Solo Ensemble Contest Solo 2 Duet 1 Trio 1; Baldwin Wallace Coll; Math.

MONTGOMERY, STEPHANIE; Mc Comb HS; Mc Comb, OH; Band; Girl Scts; Lbry Ade; Off Ade; Yth Flsp; Rptr Sch Nwsp; 4-H; FTA; Spn Clb; GAA; Akron Univ; Bus.

MONTGOMERY, TIMOTHY; Argos HS; Argos, IN; 10/66 Band; Hon Rl; Bsktbl; Capt Crs Cntry; Capt Glf; Socr; Ball St Univ; Math.

MONTICELLO, JAMES; St Agatha HS; Redford, MI; VP Frsh Cls; Hon Rl; Drama Clb; Pres Fr Clb; Bsktbl; Trk; Univ Of Mich.

MONTISANO, JOE; Garfield HS; Akron, OH; Debate Tm; Pres JA; Sch Mus; Sch Pl; Stg Crw; Yrbk; Pres Fr Clb; Sci Clb; Glf; Trk; Akron Univ; Political Science.

MONTMORENCY, MICHELE; Grosse Pointe North HS; Grosse Pt Wds, MI; Chrh Wkr; Cmnty Wkr; FCA; DECA; Chrldng; Letter Mgrs; PPFtbl; Letter Tmr; Univ.

MONTNEY, CHARLES; New Haven HS; New Haven, MI; Chrs; Hon Rl; NHS; Sch Pl; Yrbk; Drama Clb; Computer Science.

MONTONEY, CAROL; Stow HS; Stow, OH; Band; Chrs; Hon Rl; Off Ade; Quill & Scroll; Stu Cncl; Ed Sch Nwsp; Rptr Sch Nwsp; OEA; Pres Pep Clb; Coll; Sec.

MONTPETIT, ANNE; Grosse Pointe South HS; Grosse Pt Pk, MI; 34/580 Cls Rep Sr Cls; Girl Scts; Hon Rl; JA; Sct Actv; Stu Cncl; Letter Gym; PPFtbl; 4-H Awd; JA Awd; Wayne St Univ; Psych.

MONTRI, PATTY; Ida HS; Ida, MI; 31/160 Letter Bsktbl; Letter Trk; GAA; IM Sprt; Coll; Busns.

MOOD, PAULINE; Bloomington HS South; Bloomington, IN; 53/310 Band; Chrh Wkr; NHS; Off Ade; FHA; OEA; Indiana Univ; Exploratory.

MOOD, SHARYN; High School; Ypsilanti, MI; Band; Cmnty Wkr; Girl Scts; Hon Rl; Stu Cncl; Art.

MOODESPAUGH, PAMELA; Big Walnut HS; Sunbury, OH; 1/240 Chrs; Chrh Wkr; Hon Rl; NHS; Off Ade; Yth Flsp; FTA; Pep Clb; Chrldng; Scr Kpr; Univ; Comp Sci.

MOODY, MARLA K; South Ripley Jr Sr HS; Versailles, IN; 16/105 Band; Chrs; Hon Rl; NHS; Quill & Scroll; Sch Mus; Sch Pl; Yrbk; Ed Sch Nwsp; Drama Clb; Indiana Univ; Journalism.

MOODY, PATRICIA A; Trinity HS; Cleveland, OH; 68/139 Cmp Fr Grls; Chrs; Cmnty Wkr; Pol Wkr; Sch Nwsp; Cit Awd; Markette Univ; Micro Bio.

MOODY, ROBIN L; Springfield HS; Akron, OH; Chrs; Hon Rl; Lbry Ade; Natl Forn Lg; Stu Cncl; Cit Awd; Haromano Girls Honor Soc; Florida Coll; Spec Ed.

MOODY, SHARON; West Side HS; Gary, IN; Hon Rl; Jr NHS; NHS; Spn Clb; Ball St Univ; Sociology.

MOOK, JULIE; Floyd Central HS; Floyds Knobs, IN; Cls Rep Soph Cls; Band; Girl Scts; Hon Rl; Stu Cncl; 4-H; Letter Ten; PPFtbl; Bus Schl; Exec Sec.

MOOMAW, CRISTY; Edon Northwest HS; Montpelier, OH; 5/78 Band; Chrs; Drm Mjrt; Hon Rl; Sch Mus; Beta Clb; 4-H; Pep Clb; Chrldng; GAA; Univ.

MOOMAW, JANET; River Valley HS; Sawyer, MI; 3/150 Sec Soph Cls; Sec Jr Cls; Sec Sr Cls; Band; Hon Rl; NHS; Stg Crw; Ed Sch Nwsp; Drama Clb; Pres Spn Clb; Marquette Univ; Busns.

MOON, ANNA; Ithaca HS; Ithaca, MI; Chrs; Hon Rl; Hosp Ade; Univ.

MOON, BARBARA; Belding Sr HS; Belding, MI; Chrs; FFA; Spn Clb; Trk; Voice Dem Awd; College; Cosmetology.

MOON, CAROLYN; Rensselaer Central HS; Rensselaer, IN; 17/161 Sec Jr Cls; Hon Rl; 4-H; Fr Clb; Pres Mat Maids; Tmr; Ball State; Math.

MOON, DEBBIE; Charlotte HS; Charlotte, MI; 37/347 Girl Scts; Hon Rl; Stu Cncl; Pep Clb; Capt Chrldng; Coach Actv; Pom Pon; Michigan St Univ; Advert.

MOON, DOUGLAS E; Oscoda Area HS; East Tawas, MI; 16/230 Pres Frsh Cls; Pres Soph Cls; Boy Scts; Pres Chrh Wkr; Hon Rl; Jr NHS; NHS; Stu Cncl; Letter Ftbl; Univ; Bio.

MOON, ERNEST; High School; Cleveland, OH; Bsbl; Bsktbl; Cit Awd; Bowling Green Univ; Phys Educ.

MOON, JEFF; Fulton HS; Maple Rapids, MI; Pres Band; Boy Scts; Hon Rl; Orch; Sct Actv; Bsbl; Bsktbl; Crs Cntry; Glf; College.

MOON, JOHN; Bellefontaine HS; Bellefontaine, OH; 5/241 Boy Scts; FCA; Hon Rl; Kiwan Awd; Rotary Awd; Univ; Med.

MOON, JUDITH; Tucker Cnty HS; Davis, WV; 14/136 VP Sr Cls; Hon Rl; NHS; 4-H; FHA; VICA; Letter Bsktbl; Kiwan Awd; Alderson Broaddus Coll; Nursing.

MOON, ROBERTA; Fort Gay HS; Fort Gay, WV; Chrs; Hon Rl; FHA; Spn Clb; Trk; Chrldng; Mgrs; Pikeville Coll; Nurse.

MOON, SUSAN; Alma HS; Alma, MI; Hon Rl; NHS; Yrbk; Swmmng; Alma Prod Schlrshp; Adrian Coll Schlrshp; Voc Educ Cert; Adrian Coll; Art.

MOONE, JEFF; Whitehall Yearling HS; Whitehall, OH; 12/273 Chrh Wkr; Hon Rl; NHS; Business Administration.

MOONEY, JAMES F; Grosse Pointe South HS; Grosse Pte Frms, MI; Hon Rl; Lbry Ade; Pol Wkr; Yrbk; Treas Ger Clb; Ten; Natl Merit SF; Natl Merit Schl; Univ; Med.

MOONEY, KIMBERLY; Niles HS; Niles, MI; Pres 4-H; College; Fashion Designer.

MOONEY, LINDA; Benedictine HS; Detroit, MI; 5/172 Hon Rl; NHS; Rptr Sch Nwsp; Fr Clb; Wayne St Univ.

MOONEY, MARTA; Wyoming HS; Wyoming, OH; 13/196 Girl Scts; Hon Rl; NHS; Sch Mus; Rptr Yrbk; Pep Clb; Capt Chrldng; Fashion Dsgn.

MOONEY, MELISSA; New Lexington Sr HS; New Lexington, OH; Cls Rep Soph Cls; Chrs; Girl Scts; Hon Rl; NHS; Red Cr Ade; Sch Mus; Stu Cncl; Yrbk; 4-H; Univ Of Cincinnati; Exec Sec.

MOONEY, STEPHEN; St Clairsville HS; St Clairsville, OH; 2/240 Sal; Chrh Wkr; VP NHS; Yth Flsp; Yrbk; Fr Clb; Pres FTA; Natl Merit SF; Coll Of Wooster.

MOORE, ADRIENNE; Broad Ripple HS; Indianapolis, IN; Cls Rep Frsh Cls; Cls Rep Soph Cls; Cl Rep Jr Cls; Chrs; Hon Rl; Stu Cncl; Pep Clb; Spn Clb; Honor Awd Ribbon; Merit Awd Ribbon; Art & Ribbons; Ball St Univ; Psych.

MOORE, ALISON; Madison Heights HS; Anderson, IN; 4/436 Chrh Wkr; Hon Rl; Lbry Ade; NHS; Off Ade; Yth Flsp; Lat Clb; Taylor Univ; Christian Educ.

MOORE, AMY; Medina HS; Medina, OH; 13/341 Hon Rl; Off Ade; Rptr Sch Nwsp; Sch Nwsp; Pep Clb; Spn Clb; Scr Kpr; College; Psych.

MOORE, ANGELA; Centerville HS; Centerville, OH; 167/689 Chrs; Chrh Wkr; Drl Tm; Off Ade; Yth Flsp; OEA; Pep Clb; PPFtbl; Mississippi St Univ; Bus Admin.

MOORE, BREDINA; Mannington HS; Mannington, WV; Hon Rl; Lbry Ade; Y-Teens; Fairmont State College; Secretary.

MOORE, BRIAN; Redford Union HS; Redford, MI; Band; Chrs; Hon Rl; Orch; Rptr Sch Nwsp; Boys Clb Am; Trk; Am Leg Awd; Cit Awd; Coll; Chiropractor.

MOORE, BRIAN; Watkins Memorial HS; Pataskala, OH; Hon Rl; Lbry Ade; Rptr Yrbk; Fr Clb; College; Bus.

MOORE, CAROL E; Westfield Washington HS; Westfield, IN; Sec Frsh Cls; VP Soph Cls; Am Leg Aux Girls St; Hon Rl; Pres NHS; Sch Mus; Yth Flsp; Sec Fr Clb; Pep Clb; Bsktbl; Taylor Univ; Elem Ed.

MOORE, CHERYL; Rogers HS; Toledo, OH; Band; Hon Rl; Lit Mag; JA Awd; Toledo Univ Tech Coll; Bus Mgmt.

MOORE, CHRISTINE M; Gallia Academy; Gallipolis, OH; Cmp Fr Grls; Girl Scts; Hosp Ade; Sch Nwsp; Fr Clb; Gym; Twrlr; Marshall Univ; Bio.

MOORE, CYNTHIA; Collinwood HS; Cleveland, OH; Hon Rl; Sec Jr NHS; Rptr Sch Nwsp; Cit Awd; Martha Holden Jennings Award; College; Journalism.

MOORE, DANA; West Branch HS; Damascus, OH; Aud/Vis; Chrs; Lbry Ade; Yth Flsp; Job Custmr Rltns At R J Moore Int; Toured OH & MI W Cho Grp; Restr Antique Trks As A Hobby Own 34 Ford; Ohio St Univ; Law.

MOORE, DANIEL; Merrillville HS; Merrillville, IN; 28/596 Cls Rep Sr Cls; Hon Rl; NHS; Stu Cncl; Ftbl; Schlrshp Harvard Univ 79 83; Harvard Univ; Chem.

MOORE, DANIEL; Monroe HS; Monroe, MI; Boy Scts; Hon Rl; Natl Merit Ltr; Adrian Coll; Acctg.

MOORE, DAVID; Hartford HS; Hartford, MI; Band; Hon Rl; Voc Schl.

MOORE, DEANNE; Fenton HS; Fenton, MI; 8/315 Band; Hon Rl; NHS; Letter Bsktbl; Michigan St Univ.

MOORE, DEBBIE; Elyria Catholic HS; Elyria, OH; Cls Rep Frsh Cls; Cmnty Wkr; Hon Rl; Hosp Ade; Off Ade; Red Cr Ade; Stu Cncl; Fr Clb; Capt Swmmng; Coach Actv; 4th Pl The Real Goodness Of Amer 76; Acad Letter Cntest 79; Tutor 78; Univ; Tchr.

MOORE, DEBBIE; Rock Hill Sr HS; Ironton, OH; 32/142 Hon Rl; Yrbk;.

MOORE, DEBORA L; Waldron Jr Sr HS; Waldron, IN; 3/64 VP Jr Cls; Band; Chrh Wkr; Y-Teens; Hon Rl; NHS; Sch Pl; Stu Cncl; Rptr Yrbk; 4-H; Purdue Univ; Home Econ.

MOORE, DEDRIA; Big Creek HS; Bartley, WV; Cls Rep Frsh Cls; Cls Rep Soph Cls; VP Jr Cls; Band; Chrh Wkr; Drm Mjrt; Girl Scts; Hon Rl; Hosp Ade; Red Cr Ade; Univ; Bus.

MOORE, DELORES; Scott HS; Toledo, OH; Chrs; Chrh Wkr; Girl Scts; Hon Rl; Hosp Ade; Lbry Ade; 4-H; Fr Clb; Pep Clb; Trk; College; Business.

MOORE, DELVEDA J; Shortridge HS; Indianapolis, IN; 36/444 AFS; Cmp Fr Grls; Chrs; Chrh Wkr; Hon Rl; JA; NHS; PAVAS; Sch Pl; Stu Cncl; Butler; Ped.

MOORE, DENA; Parkersburg HS; Vienna, WV; Cls Rep Frsh Cls; AFS; Cmnty Wkr; Girl Scts; Hosp Ade; Sct Actv; Rptr Sch Nwsp; Lat Clb; Pep Clb; Marshall Univ; Med.

MOORE, DEVON; Bloomington South HS; Bloomington, IN; 56/375 Band; Chrh Wkr; Yth Flsp; College; Acctg.

MOORE, DIEDRA; Linden Mc Kinley HS; Columbus, OH; 16/300 Cls Rep Soph Cls; Cl Rep Jr Cls; Chrh Wkr; Drl Tm; Hon Rl; NHS; Off Ade; Stu Cncl; OEA; Bsbl;.

MOORE, D MICHAEL; Southeastern HS; Chillicothe, OH; Band; Boy Scts; Hon Rl; Jr NHS; NHS; Lat Clb; Letter Crs Cntry; Letter Ftbl; Letter Trk; 4-H Awd; Univ; Engr.

MOORE, DON; Grove City HS; London, OH; Pres Soph Cls; NHS; Rptr Yrbk; Letter Ftbl; Letter Trk; Cit Awd; Young Life 79; Otterbein Coll; Bus Admin.

MOORE, DUANE A; Woodhaven HS; Woodhaven, MI; Band; NHS; Orch; Crs Cntry; College; Marine Bio.

MOORE, ELISABETH J; Minerva HS; Minerva, OH; 5/268 Band; Chrh Wkr; Girl Scts; Hon Rl; Hosp Ade; Orch; Eng Clb; FHA; Spn Clb; County Sci Fair Part; Univ Of Akron; Psych.

MOORE, ELIZABETH M; Bluefield HS; Bluefield, WV; 10/250 Cls Rep Soph Cls; Cl Rep Jr Cls; Sec Sr Cls; Jr NHS; NHS; PAVAS; Quill & Scroll; Stu Cncl; Yth Flsp; Ed Yrbk; Woodmen Of The Wrld Hstry Awd 77; Laurel Leaf Short Stry Awd 79; Captan T V Current Events Guiz Tm 78 80; Concord Coll; Commercial Art.

MOORE, ELIZABETH; East Liverpool HS; E Liverpool, OH; 18/365 Cl Rep Jr Cls; Am Leg Aux Girls St; Chrh Wkr; Hon Rl; Pep Clb; Am Leg Awd; Perfct Attndnc 77; Hi Tri 78; Nike 78; E Liverpool City Hosp; Lab Tech.

MOORE, ELLEN; Kenowa Hills HS; Grand Rapids, MI; Cls Rep Soph Cls; Chrs; Chrh Wkr; Hon Rl; Jr NHS; Treas NHS; Stu Cncl; 4-H; Capt Gym; Capt Trk; Univ.

MOORE, FRANCES; Bay HS; Bay Village, OH; 70/350 Cls Rep Soph Cls; Cl Rep Jr Cls; Stu Cncl; Rptr Yrbk; Pep Clb; Swmmng; Chrldng; PPFtbl; Scr Kpr; Tmr; Poem Publshd In Lit Mag 78; Schl Record Holder Diving; Univ Of Arizona.

MOORE, GARY; New Richmond HS; New Richmond, OH; Aud/Vis; Chrh Wkr; Cmnty Wkr; FCA; Lbry Ade; Yth Flsp; Crs Cntry; Swmmng; Trk; Grad Of Culver Militry Acad 76; Champ Indian Dancer For 3 Yr 72 76; Univ; Med.

MOORE, GINA G; Charleston HS; Charleston, WV; Chrs; Hon Rl; JA; Sch Pl; Pep Clb; Spn Clb; Ten; Chrldng; GAA; JA Awd; Fresh Yr Sewing Awd; College; Fash Design.

MOORE, GLENN; Northrop HS; Ft Wayne, IN; Chrh Wkr; FCA; Hon Rl; Yrbk; Letter Crs Cntry; Letter Trk; College; Coach.

MOORE, GREGORY; Madison Plains HS; So Solon, OH; Debate Tm; Mod UN; Civ Clb; Eng Clb; Fr Clb; Pep Clb; Spn Clb; Bsbl; Ftbl; Wright State; Bus.

MOORE, HAROLD E; Liberty HS; Clarksburg, WV; 36/238 Boy Scts; Chrs; Hon Rl; Jr NHS; Lbry Ade; NHS; Sch Nwsp; Fr Clb; Mth Clb; Sci Clb; Fairmont St Univ; Elem Educ.

MOORE, HERMIE G; Buckhannon Upshur HS; Rock Cave, WV; Hosp Ade; Off Ade; Pep Clb; IM Sprt; W Vir Univ; Psych.

MOORE, IVY T; Glen Oak HS; Cleveland, OH; Chrh Wkr; Hon Rl; Jr NHS; Lbry Ade; Off Ade; Sci Clb; Cit Awd; Natl Merit Schl; College; Med Tech.

MOORE, JAMES; Clarkston Sr HS; Clarkston, MI; Boy Scts; Hon Rl; Spn Clb; Genrl Motors Inst Of Tech; Acctg.

MOORE, JANE; North Canton Hoover HS; North Canton, OH; Hon Rl; Jr NHS; Off Ade; Stu Cncl; Yth Flsp; 4-H; Pep Clb; Scr Kpr; 4-H Awd; Univ; Bus Admin.

MOORE, JEFF; Charles F Brush HS; S Euclid, OH; Business School; Business.

MOORE, JENNIFER; Tri Valley HS; Dresden, OH; 3/215 Hon Rl; NHS; Off Ade; Yth Flsp; Yrbk; FHA; Spn Clb; Art Inst Of Pittsburgh; Photography.

MOORE, JILL; Imlay City Comm HS; Imlay City, MI; Hon Rl; Lbry Ade; Univ Of Mich; Psych.

MOORE, JOEL; Tri Valley HS; Dresden, OH; 8/220 Hon Rl; VP FFA; Lat Clb; Letter Ftbl; Letter Trk; Letter Wrstlng; Univ; Law.

MOORE, JOSEPH; Central HS; Detroit, MI; Am Leg Boys St; Band; Drm Bgl; Hon Rl; Orch; Yth Flsp; Am Leg Awd; Cit Awd; JETS Awd; Wayne Coll; Music.

MOORE, JUDITH A; Arthur Hill HS; Saginaw, MI; Cls Rep Sr Cls; Boy Scts; Chrs; Pres Chrh Wkr; Cmnty Wkr; Debate Tm; Girl Scts; Hon Rl; Hosp Ade; JA; Ms Saginaw Cnty Schlrshp Pgnt 1000 Dollars 150 Dollars Talent Awd 79; Mbr Blue Lk Fine Arts Camp Intl Chr; Western Michigan Univ; Music Ther.

MOORE, JULIE; Arsenal Technical HS; Indianapolis, IN; 213/560 Cl Rep Jr Cls; Cls Rep Sr Cls; Hon Rl; Stu Cncl; IUPUI; Occptnl Ther.

MOORE, KANDI; Huntington East HS; Huntington, WV; Cls Rep Soph Cls; Trs Jr Cls; Hon Rl; Jr NHS; NHS; Off Ade; Stu Cncl; Mth Clb; Spn Clb; Chrldng; Univ; Med Tech.

MOORE, KATHY; Triton Central HS; Indianapolis, IN; Am Leg Aux Girls St; Cmp Fr Grls; Girl Scts; Hon Rl; Lbry Ade; Off Ade; FBLA; Cit Awd; Vocational School; Bus.

MOORE, KELLY; Big Rapids HS; Big Rapids, MI; 25/200 Hon Rl; Rptr Sch Nwsp; Mth Clb; Pep Clb; Rdo Clb; Chrldng; GAA; St Annes Schl Nursing; Nursing.

MOORE, KEVIN; Coalton HS; Mabie, WV; Hon Rl; Sch Pl; Stg Crw; Yth Flsp; Sec Frsh Cls; 4-H; Sci Clb; VICA; 4-H Awd; W Va Inst Of Tech; Drafting.

MOORE, KIMBERLEY; Clermont Northeastern HS; Batavia, OH; Hon Rl; Mod UN; NHS; DECA; Spn Clb; 250.

MOORE, KIMBERLY; Northrop HS; Ft Wayne, IN; Hon Rl; Orch; Sch Mus; Lat Clb; College.

MOORE, KIMBERLY; Hartland HS; Holly, MI; Hon Rl; Letter Ten; Mgrs; Twrlr; Perf Attndnc Awd 79; Varsity Clb 79; Sci Aid 79; Oakland Cmnty Univ; Acctg.

MOORE, LANCE; University School; Cleveland, OH; Boy Scts; Chrh Wkr; Sch Pl; Rptr Yrbk; Rptr Sch Nwsp; Key Clb; Stanford Univ; Economics.

MOORE, LANCE; University Schl; Cleveland, OH; 8/90 Chrh Wkr; Hon Rl; Off Ade; Rptr Yrbk; Rptr Sch Nwsp; Sch Nwsp; Eng Clb; IM Sprt; Stanford Univ; Econ.

MOORE, LARRY; Shenandoah HS; Quaker City, OH; 26/87 Hon Rl; FFA; Letter Bsbl; Letter Ftbl; Tech Schl; Ag.

MOORE, LAURIE; Findlay HS; Findlay, OH; 85/650 Am Leg Aux Girls St; Band; Chrs; Girl Scts; Hon Rl; NHS; Off Ade; Sch Mus; Sch Pl; Trk; Bluffton College; Elem Ed.

MOORE, LERDINE D; West Side HS; Gary, IN; Hon Rl; Jr NHS; NHS; Univ; Bus.

MOORE, LINDA; Clay Battelle HS; Burton, WV; Trs Jr Cls; Lbry Ade; Off Ade; Sch Pl; Stu Cncl; 4-H; FHA; Pep Clb; Bsktbl; Trk; Voc Schl.

MOORE, LISA; East Clinton HS; Sabina, OH; 21/112 VP Frsh Cls; Cl Rep Jr Cls; Cls Rep Sr Cls; Band; Drm Mjrt; NHS; Sch Pl; Stu Cncl; Yrbk; Chrldng;.

MOORE, LISA; West Side HS; Gary, IN; Cls Rep Frsh Cls; Band; Chrh Wkr; Hon Rl; Lbry Ade; Off Ade; Sch Pl; Stu Cncl; FHA; Cit Awd; Ala State; Court Reporting.

MOORE, LORI; Cannelton Jr Sr HS; Cannelton, IN; 3/31 VP Jr Cls; Band; Hon Rl; Pres NHS; Ed Yrbk; Ed Sch Nwsp; OEA; Pep Clb; Future Sec Of Amer Sec; Office Ed Assn 5th Pl Winner; Business Schl; Med Sec.

MOORE, LORI; Brown Cnty HS; Nashville, IN; Girl Scts; Hon Rl; FHA; Pep Clb;.

MOORE, LOU; Shawe Mem HS; Madison, IN; 5/32 Hon Rl; Jr NHS; NHS; Rptr Sch Nwsp; Sch Nwsp; Pep Clb; Coll; Theatre.

MOORE, LYNN A; North Farmington HS; Frmngtn Hls, MI; Chrs; Hon Rl; Lbry Ade; Sch Mus; Pep Clb; Letter Swmmng; Mgrs; Mat Maids; Culinary Inst Of Amer; Food Serv.

MOORE, MARY; Gwinn HS; Little Lake, MI; 23/110 Am Leg Aux Girls St; Girl Scts; Hon Rl; Lbry Ade; Red Cr Ade; Bsktbl; Crs Cntry; Trk; Coach Actv; Natl Merit Ltr; Mich State; Crim Just.

MOORE, MARY; Mt Gilead HS; Mt Gilead, OH; 12/114 Sec Sr Cls; Am Leg Aux Girls St; Chrs; NHS; Off Ade; Sch Pl; Sec Stu Cncl; Sch Nwsp; Treas Drama Clb; Otterbein College; B A In Speech.

MOORE, MARY; Salem HS; Salem, OH; 40/245 Cmnty Wkr; Hon Rl; Hosp Ade; Lbry Ade; Off Ade; Y-Teens; 4-H; Pep Clb; 4-H Awd; Ohi State Univ; Dietetics.

MOORE, MARY L; Reeths Puffer HS; Muskegon, MI; 249/600 Cls Rep Frsh Cls; Cls Rep Soph Cls; Trs Jr Cls; Cmp Fr Grls; Chrs; Chrh Wkr; Cmnty Wkr; Girl Scts; Hon Rl; Hosp Ade; Michigan St Univ; Nursing.

MOORE, MELISSA; Western HS; Kokomo, IN; 22/222 Band; Drl Tm; Hon Rl; Sec NHS; Off Ade; Pres 4-H; Pep Clb; Ten; PPFtbl; Tmr; Univ; Phys Ther.

MOORE, MELVIN; Philip Barbour HS; Kasson, WV; Hon Rl; 4-H; FFA; Am Leg Awd;.

MOORE, MICHAEL; Horace Mann HS; Gary, IN; Treas Band; Hon Rl; Jr NHS; Sch Mus; Sch Pl; Cit Awd; Berklee College Of Music; Music Educ.

MOORE, MICHAEL; St Johns HS; St Johns, MI; Sec Frsh Cls; Hst Soph Cls; Aud/Vis; Band; Chrh Wkr; Hon Rl; Off Ade; Sch Mus; Sch Pl; Sct Actv; Internatl Thespian Soc; 1st Pl St Drama Championship; Individual Excellents Awd Drama; Alma Coll; Medicine.

MOORE, MICHAEL; Parma Sr HS; Parma, OH; Hon Rl; VICA; Letter Wrstlng; Univ; Engr.

MOORE, MICHELE; Ishpeming HS; Ishpeming, MI; 9/123 Hon Rl; NHS; Northern Mich Univ; Nursing.

MOORE, MICHELLE; Jay Cnty HS; Portland, IN; 10/506 Am Leg Aux Girls St; Band; FCA; Hon Rl; NHS; Y-Teens; 4-H; Sci Clb; Letter Ten; Purdue; Chem.

MOORE, MIKE; Johnstown Monroe HS; Johnstown, OH; Aud/Vis; Sch Pl; Stg Crw; Yth Flsp; 4-H; FFA; Spn Clb; Letter Bsbl; Bsktbl; Ftbl; Star Green Hand Local FFA Chapter; Recv State Farmer Degree; Ohio State Univ; Commercial Ag.

MOORE, NANCY; Parkersburg South HS; Parkersburg, WV; 37/525 AFS; Band; Boy Scts; Chrh Wkr; Girl Scts; Hon Rl; Sct Actv; Sec Yth Flsp; Ohio State Univ; Vet.

MOORE, NANCY; Elwood Cmnty HS; Elwood, IN; 1/260 Cmnty Wkr; Hon Rl; NHS; Off Ade; Red Cr Ade; Mth Clb; Sci Clb; Ivy Tech Coll; EMT.

MOORE, N KENT; Wintersville HS; Steubenvl, OH; 61/282 Boy Scts; Sct Actv; Rptr Sch Nwsp; Spn Clb; Letter Ftbl; Univ; Psych.

MOORE, PAM; Jimtown HS; Elkhart, IN; 4/95 Hon Rl; NHS; Off Ade; Yrbk; Pep Clb; Spn Clb; Chrldng; PPFtbl; Univ; Bus.

MOORE, PAMELA; Perry HS; Cridersville, OH; Hon Rl; Sch Nwsp; Letter Bsktbl; Letter Trk; Chrldng; Scr Kpr; Rotary Awd; O Northern; Business.

MOORE, PATRICIA; Millersport HS; Millersport, OH; Am Leg Aux Girls St; Band; Chrs; Chrh Wkr; Cmnty Wkr; Hon Rl; Sch Mus; Sch Pl; Drama Clb; FHA; Ohio State Univ; Pre Law.

MOORE, PATRICIA; Kenston HS; Chagrin Falls, OH; 25/192 Hon Rl; Rptr Yrbk; Ed Sch Nwsp; Bsktbl; Crs Cntry; GAA; PPFtbl; Wittenberg Univ; Bus Admin.

MOORE, PAUL; Gabriel Richard HS; Brigton, MI; Band; Boy Scts; Hon Rl; Sct Actv; Ger Clb; Bsbl; Ftbl; Univ Of Mich; Engr.

MOORE, PAUL; Walnut Hills HS; Cincinnati, OH; Boy Scts; Hon Rl; Sct Actv; FBLA; VP Mas Awd; Univ; Engr.

MOORE, PENNY; Ithaca HS; Ithaca, MI; Cl Rep Jr Cls; Band; Hon Rl; Stu Cncl; Bsktbl; Tmr; College; Nursing.

MOORE, PHILLIP; Emerson HS; Gary, IN; 1/146 Cls Rep Frsh Cls; Cls Rep Soph Cls; Cls Rep Sr Cls; Val; AFS; Am Leg Boys St; Cmnty Wkr; Hon Rl; Jr NHS; Lbry Ade; Pres Clssrm For Yng Amercns 1979; Top 5 Soph Prog At Purdue Univ 1977; Howard Univ; Bus Admin.

MOORE, REDA; E Liverpool HS; E Liverpool, OH; 38/351 Band; Chrh Wkr; Hon Rl; Hosp Ade; Lbry Ade; Off Ade; Red Cr Ade; Pres 4-H; Sec Lat Clb; 4-H Awd; Cedarville Coll; Music.

MOORE, ROBIN; Garfield HS; Akron, OH; 1/433 Cls Rep Frsh Cls; Chrs; Drl Tm; Hon Rl; Jr NHS; NHS; ROTC; Fr Clb; Sci Clb; Spn Clb; US Naval Academy; Nuclear Physicist.

MOORE, ROBYN; John Adams HS; So Bend, IN; 33/395 Band; Hon Rl; Jr NHS; NHS; Off Ade; Sch Mus; Drama Clb; Lat Clb; TBE Bandswoman Of Yr/purdue Summer Band; Natl Band Assn Awd; TBE Schlrshp Purdue Summer Camp; College; Music.

MOORE, SALLY E; Fairfield Sr HS; Fairfield, OH; 208/598 Ohio St Univ; Tech Bio Sci.

MOORE, SHARON E; Benedictine HS; Detroit, MI; Chrs; Chrh Wkr; Cmnty Wkr; Hon Rl; Hosp Ade; Pol Wkr; Sch Mus; Sch Pl; Yth Flsp; Rptr Yrbk; 5th Pl Medl Track & Field Natl Agr Grp Champ 79; 2nd Pl Natl AAU Champ 79; Univ; Med.

MOORE, SHEILA; Bishop Watterson HS; Columbus, OH; Cmnty Wkr; Hon Rl; Hosp Ade; Jr NHS; NHS; Fr Clb; Lat Clb; Capt Ten; College; Special Ed.

MOORE, SHELBY; Jonesville HS; Jonesville, MI; Band; Chrs; Hon Rl; Hosp Ade; Orch; Rptr Sch Nwsp; South Central Michigan Univ; Nursing.

MOORE, SUSAN; Boardman HS; Poland, OH; Hon Rl; JA; JA Awd; College; Acctg.

MOORE, SUSAN; Mannington HS; Wallace, WV; Hon Rl; 4-H; Sci Clb; IM Sprt; 4-H Awd; Florida Inst Of Tech Univ; Bio.

MOORE, TAMI; Eaton HS; Eaton, OH; Band; Chrs; Hon Rl; 4-H; Pep Clb; Spn Clb; Bsktbl; GAA; PPFtbl; Univ; Jrnlsm.

MOORE, TERRY; Fairmont West HS; Kettering, OH; Band; Chrh Wkr; Hon Rl; Orch; Pol Wkr; Yth Flsp; Natl Merit Ltr; Participnt In Kettering Youth Govt Day 79; Univ Of Cincinnati; Bus Admin.

MOORE, TERRY; Parkersburg South HS; New England, WV; Chrh Wkr; Cmnty Wkr; Hon Rl; Glenville St Coll; Soc Work.

MOORE, TERRY; Parkside HS; Jackson, MI; Boy Scts; FFA; Michigan St Univ; Criminology.

MOORE, THOMAS W; St Johns HS; Perrysburg, OH; 102/264 Aud/Vis; Cmnty Wkr; Lit Mag; Sch Pl; Stg Crw; Rptr Sch Nwsp; Sch Nwsp; Letter Crs Cntry; Trk; IM Sprt; Bucknell; Chem Engr.

MOORE, TODD; Terre Haute North Vigo HS; Terre Haute, IN; 20/600 Cl Rep Jr Cls; Band; Boy Scts; Hon Rl; JA; Sct Actv; Stu Cncl; Rptr Sch Nwsp; Boys Clb Am; Letter Glf; Univ; Engr.

MOORE, TOM; Terre Haute So Vigo HS; Terre Haute, IN; 40/630 Chrs; Hon Rl; NHS; Sct Actv; Key Clb; IM Sprt; Rose Hulman.

MOORE, VALERIE; West Lafayette HS; W Lafayette, IN; 16/185 Hon Rl; Keyettes; Pep Clb; Letter Trk; Indiana Univ; Law.

MOORE, VERONICA; Jane Addams Vocational HS; Cleveland, OH; Chrh Wkr; Hon Rl; Lbry Ade; Y-

Teens; DECA; Eng Clb; Gym; Ten; Cit Awd; Ohi State Univ; Med Lab Tech.

MOORE, VICTORIA; Carroll HS; Fairborn, OH; 6/287 Drl Tm; Hon Rl; NHS; VP Fr Clb; Rus Clb; Letter Trk; College; Translator.

MOORE, VICTOR S; West Side HS; Gary, IN; Cls Rep Frsh Cls; Band; Boy Scts; Chrh Wkr; Hon Rl; Jr NHS; Lbry Ade; Letter Ftbl; Trk; Ohio State; Eletrical Engineering.

MOORE, WALTER; Creston HS; Grand Rpds, MI; FCA; Letter Bsktbl; Letter Ftbl; Univ; Engr.

MOORE, WILLIAM T; Mona Shores HS; Muskegon, MI; VP NHS; Trk; Bausch & Lomb Awd; Mich Tech Univ; Comp Engr.

MOORHEAD, JANE; South Ripley Jr Sr HS; Versailles, IN; Am Leg Aux Girls St; Band; Chrs; Chrh Wkr; Drl Tm; Hon Rl; NHS; Quill & Scroll; Sch Pl; Yrbk; Varsity Letter Awd In Volleyball; Church State Guild Grls Highest Awd; College; Phys Ed.

MOORMAN, BRENDA; Minster HS; Minster, OH; 27/81 Trs Frsh Cls; Chrs; Chrh Wkr; Bsbl; Scts; Hon Rl; Off Ade; Sct Actv; FTA; OEA; Pep Clb; Ohio Class A Girls St Track Champions 77; Offc Work.

MOORMAN, CHARISSE; Chaminade Julienne HS; Dayton, OH; Band; Chrs; Drl Tm; Girl Scts; Hon Rl; Jr NHS; Pep Clb; Bsbl; 4 Yr Schlshp To Chaminade Julienne 76; Miss Sftbl Amer All Star 78; Univ Of Cincinnati; Acctg.

MOORMAN, DAVID L; Chaminade Julienne HS; Dayton, OH; 88/264 Ger Clb; JETS Awd; Case Inst Of Tech; Engr.

MOORMAN, JOSEPH C; Valley Forge HS; Parma, OH; 11/777 Pres Jr Cls; Am Leg Boys St; Chrs; Cmnty Wkr; Jr NHS; Lit Mag; Mdrgl; Sch Mus; Sch Pl; Drama Clb; College; Communications.

MOORMAN, KAREN; Russia Local HS; Russia, OH; Band; Chrs; Chrh Wkr; Cmnty Wkr; Girl Scts; Hosp Ade; Off Ade; Sch Pl; Stg Crw; Rptr Yrbk; Nurse.

MOORMAN, MICHELLE; Minster HS; Minster, OH; 42/80 FCA; Girl Scts; Hon Rl; Off Ade; FTA; OEA; Pep Clb; Letter Trk; Scr Kpr; Bus Schl; Legal Sec.

MOORTHY, RAMANA; Pike HS; Indianapolis, IN; 8/265 Band; Hon Rl; Treas NHS; Mth Clb; Letter Ten; Mr Technology Awd Fron Indianapolis Sci & Engr Fdn 79; Univ; Engr.

MOOSBRUGGER, LAURENE; Fairview HS; Dayton, OH; 2/124 Trs Sr Cls; Drl Tm; Hon Rl; Jr NHS; NHS; Sch Mus; Sch Pl; Letter Bsbl; Pom Pon; College; Comp Sci.

MOOSE, DOUG; Sebring Mc Kinley HS; Sebring, OH; Boy Scts; Hon Rl; NHS; Sct Actv; Am Leg Awd; Natl Merit Schl; Mt Union Univ; Bio.

MOOSE, GRACE; Boyne City HS; Casa Grande, AZ; 3/109 Chrh Wkr; Hon Rl; Rptr Yrbk; Yrbk; Rptr Sch Nwsp; Fr Clb; Arizona St Univ; Archt.

MOOTZ, SANDY; Lynchburg Clay HS; Hillsboro, OH; Band; Chrs; Yrbk; Vocational Schl; Comp Training.

MORABITO, JACQUELINE; Euclid Sr HS; Euclid, OH; 77/746 Cl Rep Jr Cls; Am Leg Aux Girls St; Aud/Vis; Chrs; Hon Rl; NHS; Sch Mus; Sch Pl; Capt Tmr; Cit Awd; Miami Univ.

MORABITO, NICK; St Joseph Central Cath HS; Huntington, WV; Cl Rep Jr Cls; Univ; Med.

MORAD, HELEN; Ripley HS; Ripley, WV; Cls Rep Frsh Cls; Cls Rep Soph Cls; Cl Rep Jr Cls; Cls Rep Sr Cls; Band; Hon Rl; Jr NHS; Natl Forn Lg; Pres Stu Cncl; Sprt Ed Yrbk; Most Outstndg Jr Stu Cncl Mbr 78 79; Electd Pres Stu Govmnt 79 80; Univ; Poli Sci.

MORAHAN, SUSAN; Magnificat HS; Avon, OH; Chrh Wkr; NHS; Quill & Scroll; Sch Nwsp; Pres 4-H; Pres Fr Clb; Gym; 4-H Awd; Lion Awd; Ohio St Univ; Vet.

MORAJA, LAURA; Eaton HS; Eaton, OH; Am Leg Aux Girls St; Band; Girl Scts; Sct Actv; Stg Crw; Drama Clb; 4-H; Spn Clb; Trk; GAA; Ohio Univ; Soc Wrk.

MORALES, AIDA; Wilson HS; Youngstwn, OH; Chrh Wkr; Lbry Ade; Treas DECA; Youngstown; Bus.

MORALES, EGDILIO; St Ignatius HS; Cleveland, OH; Cls Rep Frsh Cls; Cls Rep Soph Cls; Chrh Wkr; Capt Debate Tm; Hosp Ade; Mod UN; Natl Forn Lg; Stu Cncl; Univ; Pre Med.

MORALES, EMMA; Saginaw HS; Saginaw, MI; Girl Scts; Jr NHS; Spn Clb; Letter Ten; Michigan Tech Univ; Math.

MORALES, JOSEPH; Washington HS; E Chicago, IN; Band; Hon Rl; NHS; Bsbl; Ftbl; Am Leg Awd; College; Law.

MORALES, MONICA; Kankakee Valley HS; De Motte, IN; Chrh Wkr; Girl Scts; NHS; Sct Actv; Sci Clb; Spn Clb; PPFtbl; Gov Hon Prg Awd; Purdue Univ; Meterorology.

MORAN, DANIEL; Mason County Central HS; Scottville, MI; 5/180 Boy Scts; Hon Rl; Sch Mus; Sch Pl; Sct Actv; Ed Yrbk; Spn Clb; Bsktbl; Crs Cntry; Trk; Univ Of Mich; Eng.

MORAN, DAVID; Houghton Lake HS; Prudenville, MI; 30/149 Chrh Wkr; Hon Rl; Kirtland Comm College; Police Admin.

MORAN, JUDITH; Lewis County HS; Weston, WV; 6/266 FCA; Hon Rl; Jr NHS; Pres NHS; Stu Cncl; Pep Clb; Letter Bsktbl; Coach Actv; Fairmont St Coll; Acctg.

MORAN, JULIE; St Stephens HS; Saginaw, MI; VP Sr Cls; Hon Rl; Treas Pep Clb; Swmmng; Pom Pon; Central Univ; Comp Sci.

MORAN, KAY; Jefferson Union HS; Toronto, OH; Sec Frsh Cls; Band; Chrs; Chrh Wkr; Off Ade; Sch Mus; Yth Flsp; Y-Teens; Rptr Sch Nwsp; Drama Clb; Fred J Miller Clinic Awd Indiana Univ PA 78; Shrthnd Achvmnt Awd 79; Univ; Public Rltns.

MORAN, LESLIE; Liberty HS; Reynoldsville, WV; 41/228 Band; Hon Rl; Rptr Yrbk; Rptr Sch Nwsp; FDA; Lat Clb; Univ Of South Carolina; Jrnlsm.

MORAN, MELONY; Redford HS; Detroit, MI; Drl Tm; Girl Scts; Hon Rl; NHS; Orch; ROTC; Cit Awd; Voc Schl; Med Sec.

MORAN, MICHAEL E; East Preston HS; Terra Alta, WV; Trs Frsh Cls; Am Leg Boys St; Stu Cncl; Yth Flsp; Ger Clb; Letter Bsbl; Letter Bsktbl; Letter Ftbl; College.

MORAN, NANCY; Roosevelt Wilson HS; Clarksburg, WV; Hon Rl; FTA; Salem College; Elem Ed.

MORAN, P; Lewis County HS; Weston, WV; Am Leg Aux Girls St; FCA; Hon Rl; NHS; Pep Clb; Letter Bsktbl;.

MORAN, PATRICIA A; Huntington Local School; Chillicothe, OH; 7/92 Pres Frsh Cls; Chrh Wkr; Cmnty Wkr; Hon Rl; Hosp Ade; Lbry Ade; NHS; Sch Pl; Yth Flsp; Rptr Yrbk; Shawnee St Coll; Med Lab Tech.

MORAN, PATRICK; Lamphere HS; Madison Hts, MI; 43/330 NHS; Rptr Yrbk; Spn Clb; Letter Swmmng; Outsdndng Ach In Spanish; Yrbk Staff; Serv Awd As A Sr; Michigan St Univ.

MORAN, SALLY J; Alcona Community HS; Lincoln, MI; 14/127 VP Frsh Cls; Pres Soph Cls; Pres Jr Cls; Band; Hon Rl; Sch Mus; Sch Pl; Sec Stu Cncl; Yrbk; Ed Sch Nwsp; N Ctrl Mich Coll; Resp Therapy.

MORAN, TIM; Jefferson Union HS; Toronto, OH; 20/150 Cls Rep Frsh Cls; Cls Rep Soph Cls; Chrs; Hon Rl; Jr NHS; NHS; Stu Cncl; Beta Clb; Sci Clb; Spn Clb; Hiram College.

MORAND, MARY C; St Ursula Acad; Cincinnati, OH; Chrs; Chrh Wkr; Cmnty Wkr; Hon Rl; Mod UN; NHS; Sch Pl; Yrbk; Sch Nwsp; Drama Clb; Ohi State Univ; Ther.

MORANDY, DEBORAH L; Novi Sr HS; Novi, MI; Band; Capt Drl Tm; Hon Rl; Off Ade; Sch Mus; Chrldng; Pom Pon; Letter Band & Drill Team 1977; 1st Pl & 2nd Pl & 3rd Pl Ribbons At NCA Drill Team Camps 1977; Central Michigan Univ; Tchr.

MORAN JR, FRANK R; Andrean HS; Portage, IN; 20/251 Hon Rl; Jr NHS; Ger Clb; Mth Clb; Letter Ten; Univ; Engr.

MORANTY, MARTHA; Annapolis HS; Dearbornhts, MI; Hon Rl; Stu Cncl; Northern Mic Univ; Forestry.

MORASKA, SUSAN; Norway HS; Norway, MI; Band; Chrh Wkr; Hon Rl; Sch Pl; Yth Flsp; Ed Yrbk; Drama Clb; 4-H; Dnfth Awd; 4-H Awd; Ferris State College; Court Reportin.

MORAT, CAROLEE; Whitehall HS; Whitehall, MI; Sec Jr Cls; Chrs; Chrh Wkr; Hon Rl; Hosp Ade; Mdrgl; Sch Mus; Sch Pl; Stg Crw; Yth Flsp; Western Michigan Univ; Music.

MORAVETZ, CLIFFORD; Cedar Lake Academy; Dowagiac, MI; Univ; Forestry.

MORAWA, BRENDA; Troy HS; Troy, MI; 3/80 Pres Frsh Cls; Band; Hon Rl; NHS; Bsbl; Bsktbl; IM Sprt; Natl Merit SF; Univ Of Miami; Biomedical Engineer.

MORAWA, ROSEANN; St Hedwig HS; Detroit, MI; Trs Frsh Cls; Hon Rl; Yrbk; Wayne State Univ; Occu Therapy.

MORBITZER, MARY T; Seton HS; Cincinnati, OH; 1/274 Hon Rl; Pres Jr NHS; Treas NHS; Pres Fr Clb; C of C Awd; DAR Awd; JC Awd; Its Academic; Catholic Knghts Of Ohio; Engr Soc Of Cincinnati; College; Law.

MORDARSKI, BARBARA; Madison HS; Madison Hts, MI; 1/250 Val; Chrh Wkr; Hon Rl; Pres NHS; Sci Clb; Spn Clb; Capt Swmmng; Trk; Tmr; Univ; Acctg.

MORDIS, LISA; Rochester HS; Rochester, MI; Band; Drl Tm; Hon Rl; NHS; Stg Crw; Drama Clb; Pep Clb; Cit Awd; Univ; Engineering.

MOREE, STEPHEN; Troy HS; Troy, MI; Chrh Wkr; Ger Clb; Univ.

MOREHEAD, CATHERINE E; Parkside HS; Jackson, MI; Chrs; Chrh Wkr; Cmnty Wkr; Hon Rl; Hosp Ade; Crs Cntry; Univ; Nursing.

MOREHEAD, CATHERINE; Parkside HS; Jackson, MI; Chrh Wkr; Cmnty Wkr; Hon Rl; Jackson Community College; Med.

MOREHOUSE, DENISE; Delta HS; Muncie, IN; 35/298 Sec Chrs; Chrh Wkr; Sec FCA; Hon Rl; Sch Mus; 4-H; FHA; Sci Clb; Spn Clb; 4-H Awd; Tournmt & Lg Champnshp 78; Rgnl Sci Fair Participate 76 78; My Singing Grp Won Dist Rgnl & St 78; Ball St Univ; Spec Educ.

MOREHOUSE, KIM; Stockbridge HS; Stockbridge, MI; 1/128 Val; Band; Pres NHS; Yth Flsp; Letter Wrstlng; Brds Of Control Schlrshp At MTU 79; St Of Mi Comptn Schlrshp 79; Gauss Math Schlrshp; F Nash Math Awd 79; Michigan Tech Univ; Chem Engr.

MORELAND, ALLEN; Paw Paw HS; Paw Paw, WV; Band; Chrh Wkr; Hon Rl; Sch Pl; Yth Flsp; Sprt Ed Sch Nwsp; Pep Clb; Sci Clb; Letter Bsbl; Letter Bsktbl;.

MORELAND, BECKY; Licking Valley HS; Newark, OH; Band; Chrs; Hon Rl; Stu Cncl; Yrbk; 4-H; Key Clb; Pep Clb; Bsktbl; Trk; Ohio Univ; Bio.

MORELAND, ROB; De Kalb HS; Auburn, IN; 5/290 Cls Rep Soph Cls; Cl Rep Jr Cls; FCA; Natl Forn Lg; NHS; Sch Pl; Pres Stu Cncl; Letter Ftbl; Natl Merit SF; College; Law.

MORELAND, RUTH; Big Walnut HS; Westerville, OH; 24/233 VP Frsh Cls; Cls Rep Soph Cls; Pres Jr Cls; Cl Rep Jr Cls; Cls Rep Sr Cls; Band; Hon Rl; NHS; Off Ade; Pres Stu Cncl; Runner Up On Century III Local Competition; Scholarship To Camp Miniwanea; Bowling Green Univ; Soc Services.

MORELL, THOMAS; Vassar HS; Vassar, MI; 41/158 Sch Mus; Sch Pl; Fr Clb; Alma Coll; Fine Arts.

MORELLA, DIANE; Springfield Local HS; Poland, OH; Cls Rep Frsh Cls; Cls Rep Soph Cls; Chrs; Girl Scts; Stu Cncl; 4-H; Fr Clb; FTA; Pep Clb; Chrldng; Univ.

MORELLI, EVA; Madison HS; Madison Hts, MI; Chrh Wkr; Cmnty Wkr; Girl Scts; Hon Rl; Hosp Ade; NHS; Drama Clb; Sci Clb; Spn Clb; Wayne State; Med Asst.

MORELLI, L; Steubenville Cath Ctrl HS; Steubenvll, OH; Hon Rl; NHS; Fr Clb; Pep Clb; Letter Ten; Ohio Univ; Bus.

MORELLI, THERESA; Garfield Sr HS; Akron, OH; 11/443 Hon Rl; NHS; Off Ade; Lat Clb; Spn Clb; Univ Of Akron.

MOREMAN, TINA; Forest Park HS; Cincinnati, OH; 4/400 Hon Rl; Gym; Chrldng; Natl Merit SF; College; Busns.

MORENO, JORGE; Andrean HS; Schererville, IN; 29/251 Hon Rl; Spn Clb; Trk; Purdue Univ; Engr.

MORENO, KATHLEEN; Bishop Luers HS; Ft Wayne, IN; Cl Rep Jr Cls; Girl Scts; Stu Cncl; Key Clb; Coll; Acctg.

MORETTI, DEBRA; Riverview Comm HS; Riverview, MI; 28/250 Cls Rep Sr Cls; Chrh Wkr; Cmnty Wkr; Hon Rl; Hosp Ade; Jr NHS; Natl Forn Lg; NHS; Sch Mus; Sch Pl; W Michigan Univ; Liberal Arts.

MORETTI, MARY; Struthers HS; Struthers, OH; 22/252 VP Frsh Cls; VP Soph Cls; VP Jr Cls; NHS; Pres Stu Cncl; Y-Teens; Ed Yrbk; FTA; Spn Clb; VFW Awd; College.

MOREY, JOHN; South Range Local HS; Canfield, OH; Cl Rep Jr Cls; Cls Rep Sr Cls; Am Leg Boys St; Sch Mus; Sch Pl; Sct Actv; Stu Cncl; Drama Clb; Letter Crs Cntry; Letter Trk; Mount Union College; Accounting.

MOREY, LORI; Olivet HS; Olivet, MI; 21/101 Girl Scts; Hon Rl; Off Ade; Sch Mus; Sch Pl; Drama Clb; Pep Clb; Bsktbl; Trk; Coach Actv; Capt Of Bsktbl 79; All Confrnc 78; MVP Bsktbl & 2(d Team 79; Mst Pts For Track 77 78 &79; Trade Schl.

MOREY, SUE; Geneva HS; Geneva, OH; Hst Jr Cls; Stu Cncl; Sec Yth Flsp; OEA; Voc Schl; Police Cmnctns.

MORFAS, PETE; Hammond HS; Hammond, IN; 18/324 Cls Rep Frsh Cls; VP Jr Cls; Hon Rl; Jr NHS; Rptr Sch Nwsp; Mth Clb; Letter Glf; Letter Ten; Univ; Math.

MORFORD, DEAN; Grayling HS; Grayling, MI; 9/143 Am Leg Boys St; Boy Scts; Chrh Wkr; Hon Rl; Lbry Ade; NHS; Sct Actv; Yth Flsp; Bausch & Lomb Awd; Natl Merit Ltr; Mich Tech.

MORFORD, JUDY; Warren Central HS; Indianapolis, IN; 106/807 Hon Rl; Jr NHS; Off Ade; Stu Cncl; Yth Flsp; Mgrs; Mat Maids; College; Acctg.

MORFORD, SUSAN; Mt Vernon Academy; Canton, OH; Cls Rep Frsh Cls; Cls Rep Soph Cls; Chrs; Chrh Wkr; Hon Rl; Off Ade; Sch Pl; Bsbl; Bsktbl; Ftbl; Univ; RN.

MORGAN, ALISON; Tecumseh HS; Medway, OH; 8/364 Aud/Vis; Hon Rl; Jr NHS; Lbry Ade; NHS; Off Ade; Drama Clb; Pep Clb; Scr Kpr; Sinclair Cmnty Coll; Acctg.

MORGAN, ANDREA; Madison Comprehensive HS; Mansfield, OH; Band; Chrs; Girl Scts; Off Ade; Yth Flsp; Yrbk; Pres 4-H; IM Sprt; Mgrs; 4-H Awd; North Central Tech Coll; Radiology.

MORGAN, BECKY; Fairbanks HS; Ostrander, OH; Pres Jr Cls; Hosp Ade; Off Ade; Stu Cncl; Yth Flsp; Rptr Yrbk; Rptr Sch Nwsp; 4-H; FHA; GAA; 4 H Ohio Club Congress 78; F F A Queen Candidate 78; Ftbll Homecoming Attednt 77; Univ.

MORGAN, BEVERLY; Mount View HS; Wilcoe, WV; Concord College; Lawyer.

MORGAN, BOB; Hubbard HS; Hubbard, OH; 24/33 0 Hon Rl; Yth Flsp; Bsktbl; College; Engr.

MORGAN, BRIDGETT; William Henry Harrison HS; Harrison, OH; VP Soph Cls; Hst Jr Cls; VP Sr Cls; Am Leg Aux Girls St; Hon Rl; Stu Cncl; Pep Clb; GAA; IM Sprt; PPFtbl; Univ Of Cincinnati; Educ.

MORGAN, BROOKE; North Muskegon HS; North Muskegon, MI; 12/105 Cls Rep Frsh Cls; Cls Rep Soph Cls; Cl Rep Jr Cls; Chrs; Lit Mag; NHS; Sch Mus; Sch Pl; VP Stu Cncl; Rptr Yrbk; Western Michigan Univ; Engl.

MORGAN, CATHY; Jackson HS; North Canton, OH; Pres Band; Chrh Wkr; FCA; Sch Mus; Yth Flsp; Y-Teens; Pep Clb; Spn Clb; Mas Awd; Aultman Hosp Schl Of Nursing.

MORGAN, CHRIS; Attica Jr Sr HS; Attica, IN; Aud/Vis; Lbry Ade; Off Ade; Pres 4-H; Pres FFA; Glf; IM Sprt; Pres 4-H Awd; Univ; Agri.

MORGAN, COLLEEN; Memphis HS; Emmett, MI; 4/100 Pres Frsh Cls; VP Soph Cls; Cl Rep Jr Cls; VP Sr Cls; Hon Rl; Off Ade; Stu Cncl; Rptr Sch Nwsp; Trk; Chrldng; St Clair Cnty Cmnty Coll; Bus.

MORGAN, COLVIN; Hinton HS; Sandstone, WV; Cls Rep Frsh Cls; Cls Rep Soph Cls; Pres Jr Cls; Pres Sr Cls; Band; Hon Rl; Jr NHS; Stu Cncl; Yrbk; 4-H Awd; Wv Inst Of Tech; Surveying.

MORGAN, DARREN; Warren G Harding HS; Warren, OH; Ftbl; Trk; All Amer Conference Honorable Mention; Trumbull Cnty Hnr Mention; College.

MORGAN, DEBORAH; Oak Glen HS; Chester, WV; 3/242 NHS; Rptr Yrbk; Pres Fr Clb; West Virginia Univ; Chem Engr.

MORGAN, DOUGLAS J; Pineville HS; Pineville, WV; VP Frsh Cls; Hon Rl; Sch Pl; Stu Cncl; Pep Clb; Bsbl; Ftbl; IM Sprt; Scr Kpr; Tmr; College; Welding.

MORGAN, DREAMA K; Mount View HS; Hemphill, WV; Hon Rl; Hosp Ade; Jr NHS; Off Ade; Quill & Scroll; Stu Cncl; Yrbk; Keyettes; Pep Clb; Chrldng; Bluefield State College; Elem Ed.

MORGAN, ELEANOR; Stanton HS; Hammondsville, OH; 12/62 Band; Chrs; Hon Rl; Sch Pl; Stg Crw; Yrbk; Fr Clb; Pep Clb; Letter Bsktbl; Letter Trk; Kent St Univ.

MORGAN, G; Greenbrier East HS; Caldwell, WV; Chrh Wkr; Hon Rl; NHS; Off Ade; Potomic St Univ; Sci.

MORGAN, JEFFREY; Parkersburg HS; Parkersburg, WV; Band; Sch Mus; Lat Clb; West Virginia Univ; Comm Art.

MORGAN, JO; Williamsburg HS; Williamsburg, OH; Cls Rep Soph Cls; Cl Rep Jr Cls; Band; Treas Chrs; Drl Tm; Lbry Ade; Sch Mus; Sch Pl; Stu Cncl; Ed Yrbk; Univ.

MORGAN, JOHN; Rivet HS; Vincennes, IN; 15/45 Cls Rep Frsh Cls; Cls Rep Soph Cls; Cl Rep Jr Cls; Cmnty Wkr; Hon Rl; Stu Cncl; Ed Yrbk; Fr Clb; Pep Clb; Indiana Univ.

MORGAN, KAREN; Norton HS; Norton, OH; 81/354 Chrh Wkr; Girl Scts; Hon Rl; Off Ade; Y-Teens; Pep Clb; Spn Clb; IM Sprt; Mgrs; Scr Kpr; Akron Univ; Sci.

MORGAN, KARIN; Chelsea HS; Chelsea, MI; Chrs; Hon Rl; Sch Mus; FFA; IM Sprt; Michigan State; Animal Technologist.

MORGAN, KELLY; Brandon HS; Ortonville, MI; Debate Tm; Girl Scts; Hon Rl; Lbry Ade; Off Ade; Sch Mus; Sch Pl; Sct Actv; Sch Nwsp; 4-H; Univ; Sci.

MORGAN, LEE; Saginaw Sts Peter & Paul HS; Reese, MI; Band; Hon Rl; NHS; Sprt Ed Sch Nwsp; Rptr Sch Nwsp; Fr Clb; Letter Glf; IM Sprt; College; Medicine.

MORGAN, LESA; Pineville HS; Pineville, WV; Hon Rl; Jr NHS; Off Ade; FHA; Pep Clb; Letter Chrldng; Coach Actv; YMCA Camp Horseshoe Ldrshp Camp 79; Psych Clb & Photog Clb; Minutemen Clb 3 Yrs; W Virginia S Cmnty Coll; Phys Ther.

MORGAN, LINDA; Sandusky HS; Sandusky, MI; VP Frsh Cls; VP Soph Cls; VP Jr Cls; Chrh Wkr; Girl Scts; Hon Rl; NHS; Trk; Chrldng; Pres Awd; College; Phys Therapy.

MORGAN, LINDA; Harry Hill HS; Lansing, MI; Cl Rep Jr Cls; Cls Rep Sr Cls; Chrh Wkr; Hon Rl; NHS; Swmmng; Natl Merit SF; Var Club Schsp 79; Greater Lansing Panhellenic Awd 79; Lansing Jr Bd Of Educ 77 79; Michigan St Univ; Police Admin.

MORGAN, LISA; Herbert Hoover HS; Clendenin, WV; Pres Frsh Cls; Cls Rep Soph Cls; Cl Rep Jr Cls; Sec Band; Chrh Wkr; Hon Rl; Jr NHS; Pres Stu Cncl; Pres Yth Flsp; 4-H; Alderson Broaddus; Spec Ed.

MORGAN, LISA; Archbold HS; Archbold, OH; Chrs; Chrh Wkr; Hon Rl; Sch Mus; Stg Crw; Rptr Yrbk; Coll; Interior Design.

MORGAN, LISA A; Austin HS; Austin, IN; 1/100 Trs Frsh Cls; Band; Chrs; FTA; Pep Clb; Sci Clb; VP Spn Clb; Purdue Univ; Phmcy.

MORGAN, LORI; Knightstown HS; Knightstown, IN; 17/145 Cl Rep Jr Cls; Am Leg Aux Girls St; Chrh Wkr; Hon Rl; NHS; Sch Pl; Stg Crw; Rptr Yrbk; Drama Clb; Fr Clb; Coll; Math.

MORGAN, LUCINDA; Toronto HS; Toronto, OH; Chrs; Chrh Wkr; Hon Rl; Sch Mus; Sch Pl; Rptr Sch Nwsp; Sch Nwsp; Fr Clb; Pep Clb; IM Sprt; Coll; Journalism.

MORGAN, M; Flushing Sr HS; Flushing, MI; Letter Ftbl; Letter Trk; IM Sprt;.

MORGAN, MICHELLE; Lancaster HS; Lancaster, OH; AFS; Band; Chrh Wkr; Hon Rl; Orch; Y-Teens; Fr Clb; FBLA; Chrldng; GAA; Coll.

MORGAN, MICHELLE; West Muskingum HS; Zanesville, OH; Girl Scts; Hon Rl; JA; NHS; Sch Pl; Drama Clb; 4-H; FHA; JA Awd; Brigham Young Univ; Food Sci.

MORGAN, NATALIE; Inland Lakes HS; Indian River, MI; Band; Girl Scts; Hon Rl; Univ.

MORGAN, PAMELA; Rochester HS; Rochester, IN; 8/165 Chrs; Hon Rl; NHS; Sch Mus; Sch Pl; Stg Crw; Beta Clb; Drama Clb; Ger Clb; Sci Clb; Purdue Univ; Wildlife Bio.

MORGAN, PAULA; Stanton HS; Hammondsville, OH; Band; Chrs; Pres Chrh Wkr; Hon Rl; Off Ade; Sch Mus; Yth Flsp; Rptr Yrbk; Pep Clb; Letter Bsktbl; Jefferson Cnty Tech Coll; Med Sec.

MORGAN, PHILLIP; Elwood Community HS; Elwood, IN; 25/295 Cls Rep Frsh Cls; Trs Soph Cls; Pres Sr Cls; Aud/Vis; FCA; Hon Rl; Jr NHS; Mod UN; Stu Cncl; Drama Clb; Lettermns Clb 77 78 & 79; In Senate Pg 78; Miami Univ; Psych.

MORGAN, PHILLIP; Pittsford HS; Osseo, MI; 12/59 Trs Frsh Cls; Pres Soph Cls; Hon Rl; Spn Clb; Bsbl; Bsktbl; Ftbl; Trk; Hillsdale Coll; Pre Law.

MORGAN, ROBERT; Whetstone Sr HS; Columbus, OH; Chrs; Hon Rl; PAVAS; Pres Stu Cncl; Rptr Sch Nwsp; Ger Clb; Letter Bsbl; Letter Wrstlng; Coach Actv; IM Sprt; Coll; Med.

MORGAN, ROBIN; Strongville Sr HS; Strongsville, OH; Drl Tm; Hon Rl; Stu Cncl; Mat Maids; PPFtbl; Ohio St Univ; Med.

MORGAN, SANDRA; Euclid HS; Euclid, OH; 30/742 Cl Rep Jr Cls; Am Leg Aux Girls St; Debate

Tm; Hon Rl; Natl Forn Lg; Pres NHS; Pol Wkr; Cit Awd; College; Bio.

MORGAN, SAUNDRA; Hubbard HS; Hubbard, OH; Chrs; Sch Mus; Pep Clb; Univ; Music.

MORGAN, SCOTT; Parkersburg HS; Parkersburg, WV; Boy Scts; FCA; Lit Mag; Sct Actv; Pres Yth Flsp; Letter Ftbl; IM Sprt; God Cntry Awd; 3rd Pl In Wood Cnty Sci Fair; Parkersburg Cmnty Coll.

MORGAN, SCOTT E; Jay County HS; Portland, IN; 6/406 Band; Debate Tm; Hon Rl; Stu Cncl; 4-H; Fr Clb; Mth Clb; Sci Clb; Natl Merit SF; Cornell Univ; Medicine.

MORGAN, SHELLY; Clay HS; Curtice, OH; Cls Rep Frsh Cls; Hon Rl; NHS; FTA; Pep Clb; Bauder Fashion College; Fash Merch.

MORGAN, STEPHAN; Henry Ford HS; Detroit, MI; Hon Rl; Letter Ftbl; Letter Trk; Univ.

MORGAN, STEPHAN W; Henry Ford HS; Detroit, MI; Hon Rl; Letter Ftbl; Letter Trk; College.

MORGAN, STEVEN R; Milton Union HS; W Milton, OH; 30/190 Am Leg Boys St; Boy Scts; Hon Rl; Off Ade; Stu Cncl; FTA; Letter Bsbl; Ftbl; Glf; Coach Actv; College; Bus Admin.

MORGAN, SUE; Olmsted Falls HS; Olmsted Falls, OH; Cls Rep Frsh Cls; Chrs; Chrh Wkr; Drl Tm; Hon Rl; Off Ade; Stu Cncl; Scr Kpr; Univ; Fashion.

MORGAN, SUE; Hicksville HS; Hicksville, OH; Chrh Wkr; Hon Rl; Sch Pl; Stg Crw; OEA; Coll; Data Proc.

MORGAN, SUSAN; Our Lady Of Mercy HS; W Bloomfield, MI; Cls Rep Frsh Cls; Cls Rep Soph Cls; Cl Rep Jr Cls; Chrs; Mdrgl; Pol Wkr; Stu Cncl; FSA; Sci Clb; Letter Swmmng; College; Law.

MORGAN, SUSAN; South Spencer HS; Richland, IN; 40/147 Trs Soph Cls; Chrs; Chrh Wkr; Hon Rl; Sch Mus; Sch Nwsp; DECA; Fr Clb; Trk; Brescia College; Photo.

MORGAN, TAMMI; Augres Sims HS; Au Gres, MI; Hon Rl; Lbry Ade; 4-H; Letter Bsktbl; Letter Trk;.

MORGAN, TAMMY JEAN; Goshen HS; Loveland, OH; 21/200 Sec Frsh Cls; Sec Soph Cls; VP Sr Cls; Chrs; Off Ade; Stu Cncl; Rptr Sch Nwsp; Pep Clb; Letter Chrldng; Letter Mgrs; Bowling Green St Univ; Bus Admin.

MORGAN, TARITA; Whiteland Comm HS; Whiteland, IN; 22/196 FCA; Girl Scts; Hon Rl; Jr NHS; FBLA; Letter Trk; IM Sprt; PPFtbl; Business School.

MORGAN, TODD A; Rivesville HS; Rivesville, WV; Am Leg Boys St; Hon Rl; Lbry Ade; NHS; Sch Mus; Yrbk; Sprt Ed Sch Nwsp; Sci Clb; Letter Bsktbl; IM Sprt; West Virginia Univ; Mining Engr.

MORGAN, VICKIE; John Glenn HS; Bay City, MI; 5/322 Cls Rep Soph Cls; Band; Chrh Wkr; Cmnty Wkr; Girl Scts; Hon Rl; Natl Forn Lg; NHS; Sch Mus; Sct Actv; Bd Of Trustees Schlrshp Delta Coll 79; Gertrude Hamme Mem Schlrshp 79; Delta Coll; RN.

MORGANO, CARMELO; Maple Heights HS; Maple Hgts, OH; Hon Rl; Cit Awd; Cleveland St Univ; Engr.

MORGENROTH, LORI; Calumet HS; Gary, IN; 10/305 Cls Rep Frsh Cls; Cl Rep Jr Cls; Hon Rl; Jr NHS; NHS; Treas Stu Cncl; Treas Pep Clb; Pom Pon; Red Cross Lifesaving Cert; College.

MORGENSTERN, M; North Eastern HS; Richmond, IN; Cls Rep Frsh Cls; Hon Rl; Spn Clb; Mgrs; PPFtbl; Ball State; Bus Admin.

MORGENSTERN, RUTH; Roscommon HS; Roscommon, MI; 1/120 VP Frsh Cls; Cls Rep Soph Cls; Cl Rep Jr Cls; Band; Chrs; Chrh Wkr; Cmnty Wkr; Girl Scts; Hon Rl; NHS; Michigan St Univ; Pharmacy.

MORIARITY, TOM; Napoleon HS; Napoleon, OH; Hon Rl; Jr NHS; NHS; Sch Pl; Stg Crw; Fr Clb; Bsbl; IM Sprt; BGSU; Bus.

MORIARTY, TODD; Fairless HS; Navarre, OH; 31 Am Leg Boys St; Key Clb; Ftbl; Trk; Us Air Force Acad; Engr.

MORIARTY, TODD A; Fairless HS; Navarre, OH; 31/218 Am Leg Boys St; Key Clb; Ftbl; Trk; United States Air Force Acad; Engr.

MORIKIS, PETE; Thomas A Edison Sr HS; Lake Station, IN; 40/170 Cls Rep Frsh Cls; Cls Rep Soph Cls; Am Leg Boys St; Boy Scts; Stu Cncl; Fr Clb; Sci Clb; Spn Clb; VICA; Letter Ftbl; College; Phys Ed.

MORIN, COLLEEN; Aquinas HS; Southgate, MI; Hon Rl; Letter Bsktbl; College; Bus.

MORIN, DOUGLAS; Marion HS; Marion, IN; 154/745 Am Leg Boys St; Band; Chrs; Debate Tm; NHS; Sch Mus; Drama Clb; Spn Clb; Indiana Univ; Law.

MORIN, MAUREEN; Marian HS; Mishawaka, IN; 2/150 Trs Soph Cls; Cl Rep Jr Cls; Hon Rl; NHS; Stu Cncl; Pep Clb; IM Sprt; Univ; Bus.

MORIN, MICHAEL J; Houghton HS; Dodgeville, MI; Letter Ftbl; Letter Trk; Mich Tech Univ; Bus.

MORK, JAMES; Northport Public HS; Northport, MI; 9/26 Pres Soph Cls; Cl Rep Jr Cls; Boy Scts; NHS; Yrbk; Letter Bsktbl; Socr; Letter Socr; Mgrs; Opt Clb Awd; Soccer Varsity Letter; College; Comp Sci.

MORLAN, TOM; Highland HS; Marengo, OH; Chrh Wkr; NHS; Sch Mus; Stu Cncl; Boys Clb Am; VP Spn Clb; Letter Ftbl; Letter Trk; Capt Wrstlng; College; Science.

MORLEY, MARK; Ursuline HS; Youngstown, OH; 98/450 Hon Rl; Youngstown State Univ; Bus.

MORLOCK, MARK; Elmwood HS; Wayne, OH; 2/105 Am Leg Boys St; Band; Hon Rl; Pres NHS; VP FFA; Sci Clb; Letter Ftbl; Ohio St Univ; Agri.

MORMAN, BRETT; Walnut Ridge HS; Columbus, OH; 80/429 Hon Rl; Y-Teens; Spn Clb; Ohio St Univ; Dentistry.

MORMOL, LESLIE; Bexley HS; Columbus, OH; Hon Rl; Stu Cncl; Yrbk; Spn Clb; Letter Gym; Letter Hockey; Socr; Wrstlng; IM Sprt; Mat Maids; College; CPA.

MOROKOFF, CAROL; Arlington HS; Indianapolis, IN; 10/300 Am Leg Aux Girls St; Hon Rl; NHS; Sch Mus; Sch Pl; Stg Crw; Rptr Sch Nwsp; Drama Clb; Eng Clb; PPFtbl; Indiana Univ; Jrnlsm.

MORON, MICHAEL; Chippewa Valley HS; Mt Clemens, MI; Cmnty Wkr; Hon Rl; NHS; Rptr Yrbk; Rptr Sch Nwsp; Letter Socr; Letter Swmmng; Letter Trk; Wayne St Univ; Pre Dent.

MORONY, CATHERINE; Eastlake North HS; Willowick, OH; 40/613 Band; Chrh Wkr; Drl Tm; Hon Rl; NHS; Pep Clb; Univ; Bus Admin.

MOROS, CHERYL; Benedictine HS; Detroit, MI; Cl Rep Jr Cls; Cls Rep Sr Cls; Cmnty Wkr; Girl Scts; Hon Rl; NHS; Stu Cncl; Mic State Univ; Vet.

MORPHIS, DAN; Bluefield HS; Bluefield, WV; 46/287 Hon Rl; Key Clb; Lat Clb; Pep Clb; Letter Bsbl; Bsktbl; Am Leg Awd; Appalachian State; Physical Ed.

MORR, GLEN; East Noble HS; Kendallvile, IN; Band; Boy Scts; Chrh Wkr; Hon Rl; VP JA; Bsktbl; Wrstlng; Purdue Univ; Engr.

MORRAN, ALISON; Revere HS; Arlington, TX; 27/270 Cls Rep Soph Cls; AFS; Band; Hon Rl; Pres Jr NHS; Lbry Ade; NHS; Off Ade; Sch Pl; Treas Yth Flsp; Univ.

MORRELL, GREG; East Detroit HS; E Detroit, MI; 15/752 Cls Rep Frsh Cls; NHS; Stu Cncl; Boys Clb Am; Mth Clb; Coach Actv; Mgrs; Scr Kpr; Tmr; Ctrl Mic Univ; Acctg.

MORREN, KAREN; Ottawa Hills HS; Grand Rapids, MI; Cl Rep Jr Cls; Cls Rep Sr Cls; Hon Rl; NHS; Off Ade; Stu Cncl; Treas OEA; Letter Chrldng; Natl Merit SF; Grand Rapids Jr Coll; Med Sec.

MORRETT, LISA; Connersville HS; Connersville, IN; 4/393 Chrh Wkr; Drl Tm; Hon Rl; NHS; Stu Cncl; Drama Clb; VP Ger Clb; Anderson College; Math.

MORRICAL, WAYNE; Waterford Kettering HS; Pontiac, MI; Ed Yrbk; Yrbk; Sch Nwsp; Center For Creative Studies; Phtgrhr.

MORRIS, ALICIA; Sebring Mckinley HS; Sebring, OH; 17/96 Chrs; Chrh Wkr; Girl Scts; Hon Rl; NHS; Off Ade; Quill & Scroll; Sch Mus; Malone College; Music Ed.

MORRIS, ANDRA; Clay County HS; Bickmore, WV; 44/170 Band; Chrs; Girl Scts; Hon Rl; Off Ade; Bsktbl; Clenville State College; History.

MORRIS, BEVERLY; Keyser HS; Keyser, WV; Band; Chrs; Chrh Wkr; Drl Tm; Yth Flsp; Rptr Sch Nwsp; 4-H; Keyettes; Potomac St Coll; Music Ther.

MORRIS, BRIAN; Hackett HS; Kalamazoo, MI; 1/140 Hon Rl; NHS; IM Sprt; Natl Merit SF; College; Physics.

MORRIS, CINDY; Louisville Sr HS; Louisville, OH; Cls Rep Soph Cls; Cl Rep Jr Cls; Cls Rep Sr Cls; Am Leg Aux Girls St; Chrs; Hon Rl; NHS; Stu Cncl; Y-Teens; Yrbk; Sec.

MORRIS, CINDY; Fairfield HS; Leesburg, OH; 11/60 Capt Drl Tm; Sch Pl; Sec Stu Cncl; Yrbk; Drama Clb; 4-H; Sec FHA; Pep Clb; Treas Spn Clb; Trk; Southern St Univ; Busns.

MORRIS, CONNIE; Grandview Hts HS; Columbus, OH; Cmp Fr Grls; Chrs; Cmnty Wkr; Drl Tm; FCA; Hon Rl; PAVAS; Sch Pl; Sct Actv; Yrbk; Ohio Univ; Fine Arts.

MORRIS, CURTIS; Saginaw HS; Saginaw, MI; JA; Coll; Elec.

MORRIS, DANIEL; Edwin Denby HS; Detroit, MI; Hon Rl; Jr NHS; Red Cr Ade; College.

MORRIS, DANIEL; North Central HS; Indianapolis, IN; 92/1068 Band; Chrs; Hon Rl; NHS; Sch Mus; Sch Pl; Stg Crw; IM Sprt; NCTE; Natl Merit SF; Univ; Soc Sci.

MORRIS, DAVID; Chelsea HS; Chelsea, MI; Boy Scts; Chrh Wkr; Hon Rl; Natl Forn Lg; Letter Bsbl; Letter Ftbl; College.

MORRIS, DAVID; Cuyahoga Vly Christn Academy; Tallmadge, OH; 1/70 Trs Jr Cls; Band; Hon Rl; Stu Cncl; Sprt Ed Sch Nwsp; Rptr Sch Nwsp; Trk; Univ; Med.

MORRIS, GREGORY; Parkersburg HS; Vienna, WV; Chrs; FCA; Hon Rl; Sch Mus; Boys Clb Am; Pep Clb; Bsktbl; Trk; Coach Actv; IM Sprt; West Virginia Univ.

MORRIS, HEIDI; Chaminade Julienne HS; Brookville, OH; 5/273 Band; Chrs; Chrh Wkr; Cmnty Wkr; Hon Rl; NHS; Orch; Red Cr Ade; Rptr Yrbk; VP Fr Clb; Ohio St Univ; Pre Med.

MORRIS, JACKIE; Springs Valley HS; French Lick, IN; Band; Chrs; Chrh Wkr; Drl Tm; Hon Rl; Stg Crw; Fr Clb; Pep Clb; Trk; GAA;.

MORRIS, JAMES P; Marian HS; Mishawaka, IN; Cmnty Wkr; Hon Rl; Ten; Mas Awd; Indiana Univ; Orthodontist.

MORRIS, JEANNIE; Eastern HS; Salem, IN; 19/94 Trs Sr Cls; Chrh Wkr; NHS; Stu Cncl; Pres FHA; Pep Clb; Spn Clb; Scr Kpr; Indiana St Univ.

MORRIS, JOE; Whiteland Comm HS; Franklin, IN; 52/222 FCA; Hon Rl; Pres DECA; FTA; Gym; Trk; Mgrs; College; Marketing.

MORRIS, JOHN; Claymont HS; Uhrichsville, OH; 54/198 VP Sr Cls; FCA; Hon Rl; Jr NHS; Sch Pl; Drama Clb; Lat Clb; Letter Ftbl; Letter Wrstlng; Mt Union; Chemical Engr.

MORRIS, JOHN D; John Hay HS; Cleveland, OH; Cls Rep Frsh Cls; Cls Rep Soph Cls; Cl Rep Jr Cls; Cls Rep Sr Cls; Hon Rl; Jr NHS; Stu Cncl; Ohi Inst Tech; Aerospace Engr.

MORRIS, JULIE; Redford Union HS; Redford, MI; Hon Rl; JA; Letter Crs Cntry; Letter Trk; Univ; Health.

MORRIS, KAREN; Berne Union HS; Sugar Grove, OH; 4/64 Treas Band; Chrh Wkr; Sec NHS; Pres Yth Flsp; Pres FHA; Letter Bsktbl; Scr Kpr; Valparaiso Univ; Journalism.

MORRIS, KATHY; Gahanna Lincoln HS; Gahanna, OH; 168/440 Cls Rep Frsh Cls; Cls Rep Soph Cls; Hon Rl; Lbry Ade; Off Ade; Stu Cncl; DECA; Fr Clb; Gym; PPFtbl; Ohio St Univ; Bus Educ.

MORRIS, KELLY; Jackson Center Local Schl; Jackson Cntr, OH; Band; Boy Scts; Yrbk; Glf; Voc Schl; Elec Engr.

MORRIS, LARRY; Ida HS; Ida, MI; 45/130 Boy Scts; Chrh Wkr; Capt Crs Cntry; Capt Trk; Coach Actv; IM Sprt; C of C Awd; Flo College; Preacher.

MORRIS, LAURA; Lee M Thurston HS; Redford, MI; 16/484 Band; Pres Chrs; Cmnty Wkr; Pres Girl Scts; Hon Rl; Hosp Ade; Jr NHS; Mdrgl; NHS; Sch Mus; Natl Schl Choral Awd; Natl Hnr Soc Schlrshp; Wayne St Univ Merit Schlrshp; Wayne St Univ; Theatre Arts.

MORRIS, LINDA; Marietta Sr HS; Marietta, OH; 126/450 Cmnty Wkr; 4-H; FHA; OEA; 4-H Awd; Cert Of Comltn For 1520 Hr In Coop Offc Educ 79; Ambssdr Awd 79; Exec Awd OEA 78; Marietta Coll; Bus.

MORRIS, M ELAINE; Woodrow Wilson HS; Youngstown, OH; 45/345 Cls Rep Frsh Cls; Stu Cncl; Y-Teens; Key Clb; Pep Clb; Victor George Bty Acad; Cosmetology.

MORRIS, MICHAEL; Coshocton HS; Coshocton, OH; 4-H; Sci Clb; Ftbl; Trk; Wrstlng; Marine Phys Fitness Test; Univ; Wildlife Mgmt.

MORRIS, MITCH; Springboro HS; Springboro, OH; Band; Boy Scts; Drm Bgl; Hon Rl; Sct Actv; Spn Clb; Trk; IM Sprt; Ohio St Univ; Dentistry.

MORRIS, PATRICIA; Lumen Christi HS; Jackson, MI; Cmnty Wkr; Hon Rl; PAVAS; Fr Clb; Pep Clb; Trk; IM Sprt; JCC.

MORRIS, PHILLIP; Churubusco HS; Churubusco, IN; 10/125 Hon Rl; NHS; Yth Flsp; Letter Ftbl; Letter Glf; Scr Kpr; Univ.

MORRIS, RALPH; W Lafayette HS; W Lafayette, IN; 35/185 Cls Rep Soph Cls; Cl Rep Jr Cls; Am Leg Boys St; Boy Scts; Hon Rl; Sch Mus; Sch Pl; Stu Cncl; Ind Univ; Bus.

MORRIS, ROBIN; John Glenn HS; Westland, MI; Chrs; Girl Scts; Hon Rl; Jr NHS; Off Ade; Drama Clb; Fr Clb; FHA; Cit Awd; VAW Essay Awd For Subject In God We Trust; Henry Ford Cmnty Coll; Bus Admin.

MORRIS, SHARON; Carlisle HS; Carlisle, OH; Band; Chrh Wkr; Hon Rl; Yth Flsp; FTA; Bsktbl; Trk; Nrthwst Bible College; Christian Ed.

MORRIS, SORONA; Franklin Cmnty HS; Franklin, IN; 5/266 Sec Chrs; Mdrgl; NHS; Sch Mus; 4-H; OEA; VP Mat Maids; Hoosier Schlr Awd 1979; David Lipscomb Chrstn Coll; Acctg.

MORRIS, STEVE; Utica HS; Utica, MI; Hon Rl; Rptr Sch Nwsp; Ger Clb; Univ; Mech Engr.

MORRIS, STEVEN; Canton South HS; Canton, OH; Aud/Vis; FCA; Hon Rl; JA; Spn Clb; Bsbl; Bsktbl; Ftbl; Notre Dame Univ.

MORRIS, SUSAN; St Marys Cathedral HS; Gaylord, MI; 2/59 Sec Jr Cls; Sal; Band; Cmnty Wkr; Hon Rl; NHS; Pep Clb; Bausch & Lomb Awd; JC Awd; N Cntrl Michigan Coll; RN.

MORRIS, TAMMY; Groveport Madison Sr HS; Columbus, OH; 7/377 Girl Scts; Hon Rl; NHS; Spn Clb; Letter Chrldng; GAA; PPFtbl; Student Of Year 1976; Ohio Test Of Scholst Achv Hnrbl Men In Dist 1976; Univ; Elem Educ.

MORRIS, THOMAS; Frontier HS; Newport, OH; Cls Rep Sr Cls; Hon Rl; Jr NHS; NHS; Sch Pl; Stu Cncl; Pres 4-H; Sci Clb; Pres Awd; Marietta Coll; Physics.

MORRIS, TONIA; Tippecanoe Valley HS; Claypool, IN; Chrs; Hon Rl; Rptr Sch Nwsp; Drama Clb; 4-H; FTA; Pep Clb; Trs Soph Cls; Chrldng; Ball St Univ; Eng.

MORRIS, TRACY; Oak Hill HS; Oak Hill, WV; Cls Rep Soph Cls; Cl Rep Jr Cls; Pep Clb; Letter Ftbl; Var Clb 78; Clean Up Comm 78; Hi Teen Comm 77; Stud Communication Council 78; Glenville Univ; Mining Engr.

MORRISH, DEBBIE; Atherton HS; Burton, MI; 32/150 Band; Chrs; Chrh Wkr; Girl Scts; Hon Rl; Mdrgl; Yth Flsp; Letter Trk; Mgrs; Twrlr;.

MORRISON, ANN; R Nelson Snider HS; Ft Wayne, IN; Hon Rl; Stu Cncl; Fr Clb; Letter Chrldng; Purdue Univ; Math.

MORRISON, BARBARA; Walnut Ridge Sr HS; Reynoldsburg, OH; Cls Rep Sr Cls; Band; Chrs; NHS; Off Ade; Orch; Stu Cncl; Pres Spn Clb; Trk; Ohio St Univ; Busns.

MORRISON, CHRISTINA; Cloverdale HS; Cloverdale, IN; Aud/Vis; Lbry Ade; Sch Mus; Sch Pl; Stg Crw; Drama Clb; VP 4-H; OEA; Pres Sci Clb; GAA; Purdue Univ; Agri.

MORRISON, CINDY; Milton Sr HS; Milton, WV; Cls Rep Frsh Cls; Cl Rep Jr Cls; Band; Chrs; Hon Rl; Jr NHS; NHS; Stu Cncl; FBLA; Pep Clb; Univ.

MORRISON, DEANA; South Harrison HS; W Milford, WV; 3/87 Trs Sr Cls; Band; Chrs; Chrh Wkr; Drm Mjrt; Hon Rl; Jr NHS; NHS; Sch Pl; NHS; Farimont St Coll; Physics.

MORRISON, JAMES; Harber Beach Cmnty HS; Harborbeach, MI; Boy Scts; Hon Rl; Lbry Ade; Off Ade; Rptr Yrbk; Yrbk; Rdo Clb; Letter Glf; Natl Merit SF; Michigan St Univ.

MORRISON, JEANETTE; Chelsea HS; Chelsea, MI; 9/210 Trs Frsh Cls; Cls Rep Soph Cls; Cl Rep Jr Cls; Treas Band; Hon Rl; NHS; Treas Stu Cncl; Ten; Chrldng; Michigan St Univ; Bus Admin.

MORRISON, JEFF; Winchester Community HS; Farmland, IN; Chrh Wkr; Hon Rl; Fr Clb;.

MORRISON, KATHY; Brookhaven HS; Columbus, OH; 1/434 Val; Band; Chrs; Hon Rl; Hosp Ade; Jr NHS; NHS; Off Ade; Acadmc Schlrshp From Spring Arbor Coll 79; Spring Arbor Coll; Math.

MORRISON, KEVIN; Algonac HS; Algonac, MI; 1/215 Val; Hon Rl; Jr NHS; NHS; OEA; Letter Crs Cntry; Letter Ten; Letter Trk; Letter Wrstlng; Bausch & Lomb Awd; Univ Of Michigan Dearborn Chancellors Schlrshp 79; Michigan St Univ Awd For Academic Exc 79; Comp Schlrshp; Univ Of Michigan; Sys Analysis.

MORRISON, MARILEE; New Buffalo HS; New Buffalo, MI; 1/63 Sec Sr Cls; Val; Chrs; Hon Rl; NHS; Ed Yrbk; Rptr Sch Nwsp; Fr Clb; DAR Awd; Oakland Univ; Psych.

MORRISON, NEIL; John F Kennedy HS; Romulus, MI; Chrs; Debate Tm; Hon Rl; Natl Forn Lg; Sch Mus; Sch Pl; Stg Crw; Sch Nwsp; Pres Drama Clb; Sci Clb; Univ Of Mich; Anatomy.

MORRISON, ROBERT; Manchester HS; Manchester, OH; FFA;.

MORRISON, THEODORE; Hughes HS; Cincinnati, OH; Cl Rep Jr Cls; Cmnty Wkr; C of C Awd; Cit Awd; Columbus Dsgn Of Art Coll; Artist.

MORRISON, TOM; North Adams HS; Osseo, MI; Boy Scts; Debate Tm; Hon Rl; Sct Actv; Yth Flsp; FFA; Bsktbl; Letter Trk; Scr Kpr; Tmr; College; History.

MORRISON, TREVA; John Glenn HS; New Concord, OH; 8/198 Band; Chrs; Hon Rl; Orch; 4-H; Pres FHA; College; Home Econ.

MORRISON, TROY; Philo HS; Philo, OH; FCA; Hon Rl; Pres Beta Clb; Pres FTA; Spn Clb; Letter Ftbl; Letter Glf; Capt Trk; Academic Ltr For Hon Roll 79; League & Sectional Track Champ 880 79; Pennsylvania St Univ; Radio Cmnctns.

MORRISSEY, VICKIE; Potterville HS; Dimondale, MI; 5/60 VP Sr Cls; Band; Girl Scts; Hon Rl; NHS; Sct Actv; Sci Clb; PPFtbl; Bausch & Lomb Awd; Var Ltr Sftbl 76; Var Ltr Vllybl 78; Schslp Regnl HS Awd From E Mi Univ 79; E Michigan Univ; Marine Bio.

MORRISSON, JOHN; George Rogers Clark HS; Hammond, IN; 46/217 College.

MORROW, ANITA F; Bedford N Lawrence HS; Springville, IN; 23/380 Chrh Wkr; Cmnty Wkr; Hon Rl; Hosp Ade; Mdrgl; NHS; Yrbk; Beta Clb; 4-H; Fr Clb; Indiana Univ; Bus Mgmt.

MORROW, BEVERLY; Woodrow Wilson HS; Youngstown, OH; Cmp Fr Grls; Chrs; Hon Rl; Hosp Ade; NHS; Red Cr Ade; Y-Teens; Lat Clb; Youngstown St Univ; Dental Hygiene.

MORROW, CHRISTINA; Greenville Sr HS; Greenville, OH; Band; Chrh Wkr; Cmnty Wkr; Orch; Sch Mus; 4-H; Univ; Music.

MORROW, CRAIG A; Castle HS; Newburg, IN; Stg Crw; Letter Ftbl; Indiana St Schlrshp Honorary; Western Kentucky Univ; Busns Mgmt.

MORROW, DAVE; East Clinton HS; Sabina, OH; Hon Rl; Bsbl; Bsktbl; Ftbl; Trk; Univ; Tchr.

MORROW, JACK; Brookside HS; Sheffield Lake, OH; Chrs; Chrh Wkr; Debate Tm; Hon Rl; Lbry Ade; Yth Flsp; DECA; Bsbl; Bsktbl; Ftbl; Bus Schl; Mgmt.

MORROW, MARIA; Hamilton Heights HS; Noblesville, IN; 12/131 VP Soph Cls; Pres Jr Cls; Band; Hon Rl; Jr NHS; 4-H; Fr Clb; Lat Clb; Pep Clb; Letter Bsktbl; Rangeline Conf Team 2 Basketball 1 Volleyball 1 Track; Noblesville Ledger All Cnty Team Bsktbll & Volleybl; College; Education.

MORROW, MARSHA; Collinwood HS; Cleveland, OH; Cls Rep Soph Cls; Cl Rep Jr Cls; Band; Hon Rl; NHS; Orch; Sec Yth Flsp; Yrbk; College; Nuclear Sci.

MORROW, PAUL; Ontario HS; Ontario, OH; 36/189 Hon Rl; Letter Bsktbl; Coach Actv; Bowling Green State Univ; Math.

MORROW, THOMAS; Catholic Central HS; Grand Rapids, MI; Band; Boy Scts; Chrs; Chrh Wkr; Drm Bgl; Hon Rl; Stg Crw; Letter Ftbl; Letter Ten; IM Sprt; Marquette Univ; Med.

MORROW, VIVIAN; Madison HS; Madison, OH; Band; Girl Scts; Hon Rl; JA; Twrlr; Lttr In HS Bnd & Corresponding Bars 77; US Army; Voice Interceptor.

MORSE, JAMES; Hill HS; Lansing, MI; 7/703 Hon Rl; Jr NHS; NHS; Trk; Natl Merit Ltr; Mich State Univ; Med.

MORSE, JENELLE; The Leelanau Schl; Glen Arbor, MI; 4/30 Sec Frsh Cls; Sec Soph Cls; Band; Hon Rl; Sch Pl; Yth Flsp; 4-H; Bsktbl; Trk; Chrldng; Michigan St Univ.

MORSE, JENELLE; Leelanau HS; Glen Arbor, MI; 5/30 Sec Frsh Cls; Pres Soph Cls; Band; Hon Rl; Sch Pl; 4-H; Letter Bsktbl; Letter Trk; Pom Pon; 4-H Awd; Colorado St Univ; Vet.

MORSE, MARY J; Fairbanks HS; Milford Center, OH; Band; Hon Rl; Sch Pl; Drama Clb; Spn Clb; GAA; Ohi State Univ; Psych.

MORSE, SHERI; Fennville HS; Fennville, MI; Chrs; Hon Rl; NHS; Yth Flsp; Yrbk; Bsktbl; Gym; Ten; Chrldng; Mi Bus Schl Assoc Shlrshp 79; Cert Of Recognition St Of Mi Competitive Schlrshp Progr 79; Bus Awd Tn HS 79; Davenport Coll; Acctg.

MORTENSEN, ANNE; H H Dow HS; Midland, MI; 18/490 Chrs; Chrh Wkr; Hon Rl; Orch; Pol Wkr; Pres Yth Flsp; 4-H; Natl Merit Schl; Wheaton Coll.

MORTON, CHERYL A; Allen Park HS; Allen Park, MI; Chrs; Chrh Wkr; Cmnty Wkr; Hon Rl; Jr NHS; Sch Mus; Yth Flsp; Treas Drama Clb; Alma Music Talent Awd; Alma Coll.

MORTON, CONNIE; Fredericktown HS; Fredericktown, OH; 4/125 Hon Rl; Off Ade; Sch Mus; FHA; Pep Clb; Business School; Sec.

MORTON, ELLEN; Andrean HS; Merrillville, IN; 56/251 Chrh Wkr; Girl Scts; Hon Rl; Hosp Ade; Sch Mus; Sch Pl; Bsktbl; GAA; Opt Clb Awd; Phys Ther.

MORTON, JEFFREY; Logan Elm HS; Stoutsville, OH; Band; FCA; Hon Rl; NHS; Sch Pl; Yth Flsp; Key Clb; Bsbl; Dnfth Awd; Ohio St Univ; Engr.

MORTON, MATT; Fountain Central HS; Veedersburg, IN; Hon Rl; Stg Crw; Rptr Yrbk; Rptr Sch Nwsp; FSA; Mth Clb; Sci Clb; College; Systems Analist.

MORTON, PAUL; Admiral King HS; Lorain, OH; Rptr Yrbk; Univ; Jrnlsm.

MORTON, RICHARD; Buckeye HS; Medina, OH; 21/176 Hon Rl; NHS; Letter Bsbl; Letter Ftbl; Letter Trk; Letter Wrstlng; Coach Actv; Dnfth Awd; JETS Awd; Marietta Coll; Petroleum Engr.

MORTON, ROBBIN; Belpre HS; Belpre, OH; VP Jr Cls; VP Sr Cls; Band; Hon Rl; NHS; Drama Clb; Fr Clb; Mth Clb; Pep Clb; Sci Clb; Parkersburg Cmnty Coll; RN.

MORTON, SHEILA; Bishop Dwenger HS; Ft Wayne, IN; Cl Rep Jr Cls; Chrs; Chrh Wkr; Cmnty Wkr; Girl Scts; Hon Rl; Hosp Ade; Lbry Ade; Off Ade; Sct Actv; Univ.

MORTON, TERESA; Mt De Chantal Visatatn Acad; Wheeling, WV; 8/31 Chrs; Cmnty Wkr; NHS; Orch; Pol Wkr; Sch Mus; Stg Crw; Ed Yrbk; Rptr Sch Nwsp; Pres Fr Clb; Butler Univ; Music.

MORTON, THOMAS; George Washington HS; Charleston, WV; Hon Rl; Spn Clb; Bsktbl; Co Captain Merit Valuble Bsktbl 79; 1st Tm All Kan Valley Conf 79; 2nd Team All St 79; Univ Of S Florida; Bus Admin.

MORTON, VALERIE D; Triway HS; Wooster, OH; 18/168 VP Soph Cls; Am Leg Aux Girls St; Band; Chrs; Chrh Wkr; Drl Tm; Drm Mjrt; FCA; Hon Rl; JA; Teenager Of The Month; Miss Triway HS; Choral Awd; Head Majorette; Sr Bsktbl Attendant; Mansfield Schl; Nursing.

MORTON, WALTER; Watkins Memorial HS; Reynoldsbg, OH; 4/250 Band; Boy Scts; Chrh Wkr; Hon Rl; Lit Mag; Sch Mus; Sch Pl; Sct Actv; Stg Crw; Yth Flsp; Miami Univ; Sci.

MORVAI, ANN; Barberton HS; Barberton, OH; Cl Rep Jr Cls; Cls Rep Sr Cls; Val; AFS; Am Leg Aux Girls St; Chrs; Cmnty Wkr; FCA; Hon Rl; Jr NHS; The U L Light Jr Hi Memrl For Highest Schlr 77; Mbr Of Homecoming Court 78; Univ; Bio.

MORVAY, LAURIE; Boardman HS; Youngstown, OH; 51/562 Hon Rl; NHS; Y-Teens; Pres Spn Clb; Gym; Univ; Frgn Lang.

MORWAY, WILLIAM M; St Hedwig HS; Detroit, MI; Pres Frsh Cls; VP Soph Cls; Hon Rl; NHS; Bsbl; Univ; Health.

MORYL, ANN MARIE; New Prairie HS; Rolling Prairie, IN; 11/167 Sec Frsh Cls; Trs Jr Cls; VP Sr Cls; Hon Rl; NHS; Quill & Scroll; Ed Yrbk; Rptr Yrbk; Yrbk; Rptr Sch Nwsp; Indiana Univ; Bio Sci.

MOSBAUGH, LAURA; Marion Adams HS; Sheridan, IN; 35/96 Chrs; Lbry Ade; Sch Mus; FHA; Pep Clb; Bsbl; Chrldng; Mat Maids; Pom Pon; Hon Queen Jobs Daughters; Bat Girl For Bsbl Tm 4 Yrs; Indiana St Univ; Inter Dsgn.

MOSBY, LORI; Cooley HS; Detroit, MI; Cls Rep Soph Cls; Sec Sr Cls; Chrh Wkr; Hon Rl; Rptr Yrbk; Eng Clb; Pep Clb; Wayne State Univ; Psych.

MOSCATO, LORI A; Buckeye South HS; Yorkville, OH; Band; Chrh Wkr; Hon Rl; Sch Pl; Y-Teens; Rptr Yrbk; Drama Clb; Pep Clb; Bsktbl; Am Leg Awd; Coll.

MOSCHEL, JAMES; Lutheran N HS; Warren, MI; Am Leg Boys St; Aud/Vis; Hon Rl; Lbry Ade; Yrbk; Crs Cntry; Trk; Mgrs; Valparaiso Univ; Criminal Justice.

MOSELEY, JULIE; Kent Roosevelt HS; Kent, OH; 50/360 Chrs; Chrh Wkr; Hon Rl; NHS; Spn Clb; IM Sprt; College; Soc Work.

MOSER, DON; Elgin HS; Prospect, OH; 31/155 Trs Soph Cls; Am Leg Boys St; Hon Rl; Lat Clb; Bsktbl; Letter Crs Cntry; Letter Trk;.

MOSER, MARY; South Harrison HS; Jane Lew, WV; Chrh Wkr; Hon Rl; Jr NHS; Lbry Ade; NHS; Bus Schl; Sec.

MOSER, RICHARD; Ottawa Hills HS; Grand Rapids, MI; Band; Hon Rl; Natl Forn Lg; NHS; Orch; ROTC; Univ Of Michigan; Acctg.

MOSES, ELIZABETH; Genoa Area HS; Curtice, OH; 40/180 Hon Rl; JA; NHS; FHA; College; Public Acct.

MOSES, REGINA; Chippewa Valley HS; Mt Clemens, MI; Chrs; Hon Rl; Lbry Ade; NHS; Off Ade; Sch Mus; IM Sprt; Oakland Univ; Bus Admin.

MOSES, ROBERT; Oak Hill HS; Thurman, OH; 1/110 Band; Chrs; Chrh Wkr; Pres NHS; Sch Mus; 4-H; Bsbl; Letter Bsktbl; Letter Crs Cntry; Letter Ftbl; Rio Grande Coll; General Engr.

MOSES, SCOTT; Copley Sr HS; Akron, OH; Chrs; Chrh Wkr; Hon Rl; NHS; Sch Nwsp; Mth Clb; Spn Clb; Bsbl; Glf; Arizona St Univ; Pre Med.

MOSES, TAMMY; Edison HS; Huron, OH; Band; Stg Crw; 4-H Awd; Kiwan Awd; Miami Univ.

MOSHER, JANET M; Lake Catholic HS; Mentor, OH; Band; Hon Rl; Off Ade; Sch Pl; Boys Clb Am; 4-H; Coach Actv; IM Sprt; Mgrs; 4-H Awd; College; Acctng.

MOSHER, KATHLEEN C; Theodore Roosevelt HS; Kent, OH; AFS; Chrs; Cmnty Wkr; Hon Rl; NHS; Sch Pl; Yth Flsp; Ed Sch Nwsp; VP 4-H; Fr Clb; Kent State Univ; Journalism.

MOSHER, LORI; Houghton Lake HS; Prudenville, MI; Girl Scts; Hon Rl; NHS; Yrbk; Rptr Sch Nwsp; Pep Clb; Spn Clb; Chrldng; Coach Actv; Central Michigan Univ; Jrnlsm.

MOSHER, RUSTY; West Branch HS; Salem, OH; 20/250 Am Leg Boys St; Chrs; Hon Rl; VP NHS; Bsktbl; Ftbl; Trk; Bowling Green Univ; Bus.

MOSHER, SCOTT C; Michigan Lutheran Seminary; Webberville, MI; Cls Rep Frsh Cls; Cls Rep Soph Cls; Cl Rep Jr Cls; Pres Sr Cls; Cls Rep Sr Cls; Chrs; Hon Rl; Pres Stu Cncl; 4-H; IM Sprt; Northwestern Coll; Ministry.

MOSHER, WENDY; Leelanau HS; Kentwood, MI; Cl Rep Jr Cls; Cls Rep Sr Cls; Chrh Wkr; Hon Rl; NHS; Off Ade; PAVAS; Stu Cncl; Ten; Trk; WMU; Social Work.

MOSHIER, AMY; Oxford Area Community HS; Oxford, MI; 129/240 Band; Cmnty Wkr; Girl Scts; Hon Rl; Lbry Ade; Schlrshp Oxford Music Boosters 76 77 & 78; Diploma Sherwood Music Schl From Course In Piano 79; Adrian Coll; Author.

MOSHIER, CHRIS; Scecina Memorial HS; Indianapolis, IN; Cls Rep Frsh Cls; Cls Rep Soph Cls; Chrs; Sch Mus; Sch Pl; Bus Schl; Eng.

MOSHIER, JACQUELINE; Ubly Community HS; Ubly, MI; 26/124 Band; Girl Scts; Hon Rl; NHS; Sch Pl; Mgrs; PPFtbl; Scr Kpr; College; Music.

MOSIER, DEBBIE; North Union HS; Raymond, OH; Band; Hon Rl; Pep Clb; Pres Spn Clb; IM Sprt; PPFtbl; Am Leg Awd; Schlstc Team Mbrshp Sci Spanish & Amer Hist; Schltc Achvmnt 15th Pl Amer Hist Div II Schls 78; Univ; Soc Std.

MOSKO, D; Steubenville Catholic HS; Mingo Jct, OH; 35/200 Cl Rep Jr Cls; Am Leg Boys St; Hon Rl; NHS; Stu Cncl; Fr Clb; Letter Ftbl; Letter Trk; IM Sprt; College.

MOSKOSKY, JAMES; Campbell Memorial HS; Campbell, OH; 1/205 Boy Scts; Hon Rl; NHS; Mth Clb; Sci Clb; Spn Clb; Letter Bsbl; Letter Ftbl; IM Sprt; Natl Merit Ltr; Babe Ruth Bsbll Hall Of Fame Ahtletes Of Yr 76; All Steel Valley Bsbll Tm Shortstop 79; Univ; Math.

MOSKOWITZ, TODD; West Geauga HS; Chesterland, OH; 27/352 Hon Rl; NHS; Yrbk; Letter Ten; IM Sprt; JETS Awd; Univ Of Mic; Cpa.

MOSKUS, LOUISE; Theodore Roosevelt HS; E Chicago, IN; 2/199 Band; NHS; Stu Cncl; Fr Clb; FHA; Mth Clb; Sci Clb; PPFtbl; Coll; Computer Science.

MOSKWA, LINDA; Ontonagon Area HS; Ontonagon, MI; 6/85 Pres Jr Cls; Am Leg Aux Girls St; Chrh Wkr; Hon Rl; NHS; Sch Nwsp; OEA; Bsktbl; Letter Trk; N Michigan Univ; Psych.

MOSLEY, CHERYL; Pickerington HS; Pickerington, OH; Band; Chrs; Drl Tm; Girl Scts; Hon Rl; Sec NHS; Spn Clb; Swmmng; Mat Maids; Pickerington Mdl Schl Spelling Champ 76; Stu Of The Mnth 78; Schlrshp Tm 77; Miami Univ; Hlth.

MOSLEY, DIANE; Adelphian Academy; Detroit, MI; 5/49 Cls Rep Soph Cls; VP Band; Chrs; Hon Rl; Pres Stu Cncl; Ed Sch Nwsp; Rptr Sch Nwsp; John Philip Sousa Awd; Girls Clb Chorister; High Honors Grad; Andrews Univ; Bio.

MOSLEY, EVA; High School; Columbiaville, MI; Cls Rep Frsh Cls; Cls Rep Soph Cls; Cl Rep Jr Cls; Girl Scts; JA; Orch; Sct Actv; Yth Flsp; IM Sprt; Indiana Univ.

MOSLEY, LYNNE; Archbishop Alter HS; Dayton, OH; Cmp Fr Grls; Drl Tm; Hon Rl; Yth Flsp; Sch Nwsp; Fr Clb; IM Sprt; Mbr Of The Explorers Clb 78; Marian Council Knights Of Columbus Awrd 76; Applicant In Miss Teenage Oh 76; Univ Of S California; Bus Admin.

MOSLEY, MATTHEW; Sycamore HS; Cincinnati, OH; Hon Rl; Univ; Engr.

MOSLEY, RONALD A; John R Buchtel HS; Akron, OH; 11/365 Band; Hon Rl; NHS; Lat Clb; Ftbl; Coach Actv; IM Sprt; Cit Awd; Natl Merit SF; College; Engr.

MOSORIAK, MARK; George Rogers Clark HS; Whiting, IN; Hon Rl; IM Sprt; Northland Coll; Forestry.

MOSPENS, CATHERINE; Tippecanoe HS; Tipp City, OH; Cls Rep Frsh Cls; Cl Rep Jr Cls; Cls Rep Sr Cls; AFS; Chrh Wkr; Hon Rl; Treas NHS; Stu Cncl; Trk; GAA; Top Schlr Awd 2 Yrs; Lamp Of Learning 1 Yr; Univ; Bus.

MOSS, CHARLES; William Henry Harrison HS; Evansville, IN; 1/466 Cls Rep Sr Cls; Boy Scts; Pres Debate Tm; Hon Rl; Pres Natl Forn Lg; Stu Cncl; Civ Clb; Sci Clb; Spn Clb; Natl Achvmtn Ltr; Rose Hulman Inst Of Tech; Chem Engr.

MOSS, DOUG; Teays Valley HS; Ashville, OH; 13/200 Treas Am Leg Boys St; FCA; Hon Rl; NHS; Stu Cncl; Yth Flsp; Pres Key Clb; Pres Lat Clb; Letter Bsktbl; Letter Trk; Ohio St Univ; Chem Engr.

MOSS, EDWARD; Michigan Ctr HS; Mich Center, MI; 4/136 Cls Rep Frsh Cls; Cls Rep Sr Cls; Hon Rl; NHS; Crs Cntry; Capt Trk; Jackson Cmnty Coll; Civil Engr.

MOSS, JEFF; Madison Plains HS; Mt Sterling, OH; 4/146 Am Leg Boys St; Hon Rl; Mod UN; VP NHS; Stu Cncl; Fr Clb; Letter Bsktbl; Letter Glf; Ohi State Univ; Engr.

MOSS, JERRI; West Branch HS; Salem, OH; Chrs; Girl Scts; Lbry Ade; Sch Mus; 4-H; FHA; Pep Clb; Capt Chrldng; Tmr; Perfect Attendance Awd Fresh; Univ Of Akron; Comp Sci.

MOSS, JOANNE; Wadsworth Sr HS; Wadsworth, OH; Band; Treas Girl Scts; Sct Actv; Sec 4-H; Forest Ranger.

MOSS, KELLIE; Atlanta HS; Atlanta, MI; Letter Band; Chrh Wkr; Hon Rl; Off Ade; Natl Forn Lg; Orch; Rptr Yrbk; Rptr Sch Nwsp; Pep Clb; Dist Solo Ensemble Festral Mdl 77; Assembly Of God Ath Achvmnt Awd 77; Univ; Med Asst.

MOSS, NANCY L; Bishop Noll Inst; E Chicago, IN; 78/321 Cl Rep Jr Cls; Hon Rl; NHS; Stu Cncl; Rptr Yrbk; Rptr Sch Nwsp; Pep Clb; Scr Kpr; College; Dental Hyg.

MOSS, RAYMOND O; Lordstown HS; Warren, OH; Am Leg Boys St; Boy Scts; Pres Chrs; Hon Rl; Sch Mus; Sch Pl; VP Yth Flsp; Rptr Yrbk; Rptr Sch Nwsp; Treas Drama Clb; Anderson Coll; Music.

MOSS, SCOTT; Woodhaven HS; Flat Rock, MI; Hon Rl; Sprt Ed Yrbk; Rptr Sch Nwsp; Crs Cntry; Ten; Natl Merit SF; Univ Of Michigan; Cmnctns.

MOSS, S MICHAEL; Heritage Christian HS; Indianapolis, IN; VP Frsh Cls; VP Soph Cls; VP Jr Cls; Chrh Wkr; Sch Pl; Sprt Ed Sch Nwsp; Drama Clb; Fr Clb; Letter Bsktbl; Letter Socr; College; Busns.

MOSS, THERON; Patterson Co Op HS; Dayton, OH; Chrs; Chrh Wkr; Cmnty Wkr; Hon Rl; Stu Cncl; Boys Clb Am; VICA; Letter Bsbl; Bsktbl; IM Sprt; Sinclair Coll; Archt.

MOSS, TIM; De Kalb HS; Auburn, IN; Chrs; Cmnty Wkr; Hon Rl; NHS; Sch Mus; Sch Pl; Drama Clb; Ger Clb; Indiana Univ; Music.

MOSS, TINA; St Francis De Sales HS; Westerville, OH; Chrh Wkr; Hon Rl; Sch Mus; Sch Pl; Stg Crw; Drama Clb; Socr; Otterbein Coll; Theatre.

MOSS, TINA K; Washington Irving HS; Clarksburg, WV; Pres Boy Scts; Hosp Ade; Quill & Scroll; Sch Mus; Yrbk; Sch Nwsp; Pres Fr Clb; Lat Clb; Sci Clb; College; Med.

MOSSBARGER, TERESA L; Chillicothe HS; Chillicothe, OH; Hon Rl; NHS; Yth Flsp; Lat Clb; Ten; St Dept Educ Ohio Test Schl Achvmnt Gen Sci 77; St Sci Fair Exhbt 77; Mead Paper Co Sci Essay Cont 78; Univ; Christian Educ.

MOSSBURG, ROBERT E; Summerfield HS; Petersburg, MI; 2/100 Pres Frsh Cls; Pres Soph Cls; Cl Rep Jr Cls; Cls Rep Sr Cls; Sal; Am Leg Boys St; Aud/Vis; Hon Rl; Jr NHS; Lbry Ade; Hugh O Brien Ldrshp Awd; Mich St Univ Acad Exc Awd; Summerfield Sprtmnshp Awd; Michigan Comp Schlrshp; Michigan St Univ; Hotel Mgmt.

MOSSER, LORI; Perry HS; Canton, OH; Hon Rl; Quill & Scroll; Yrbk; FHA; College.

MOSSING, MARIANNE; St Ursula Academy; Swanton, OH; Band; Chrs; Hon Rl; Off Ade; Sch Mus; Sch Nwsp; 4-H; Univ; Bus Admin.

MOSS JR, PONCE D; Warrensville Sr HS; Warrensville, OH; Boy Scts; Chrs; Chrh Wkr; Drl Tm; Sct Actv; Yth Flsp; Sprt Ed Sch Nwsp; Rptr Sch Nwsp; Pep Clb; Ftbl; Cleveland St Univ; Drafting.

MOSSOR, GARY; Buckeye North HS; Rayland, OH; VP Soph Cls; Boy Scts; FCA; Sch Pl; Pres OEA; Ftbl; Wrstlng; IM Sprt; Scr Kpr; Tmr; College; Law.

MOST, KIMBERLY; St Louis HS; St Louis, MI; 32/128 Chrh Wkr; Hon Rl; Lbry Ade; Rptr Yrbk; Pep Clb; Davenport Inst; Legal Sec.

MOST, ROGER; Ithaca HS; Ithaca, MI; Hon Rl; NHS; FFA; Wrstlng; Univ; Engr.

MOSTER, LEROY; Wilmington HS; Wilmington, OH; 28/298 Chrs; Hon Rl; Sch Mus; Sch Pl; Stg Crw; Drama Clb; Crs Cntry; Purdue Univ; Meterologist.

MOSTOLLER, JEFFREY; Niles Mc Kinley HS; Niles, OH; Band; Hon Rl; Red Cr Ade; Coach Actv; IM Sprt; North Side Hosp; Radiological Tech.

MOSTROM, CHERYL; Centreville HS; Sturgis, MI; Sec Soph Cls; Chrh Wkr; Hon Rl; NHS; Pep Clb; Spn Clb; Letter Trk; Letter Chrldng; Dnfth Awd; Whos Who Mdwstern H S Forgn Lang 79; Cheerldg 1st Regnl Comp 79; Univ; Med.

MOSTYN, PAUL; East HS; Akron, OH; Band; Sch Mus; Mgrs; Akron Univ; Hist.

MOTHERSBAUGH, AMY; Our Lady Of The Elms HS; Akron, OH; Chrh Wkr; Cmnty Wkr; Hon Rl; PAVAS; Sch Pl; Stg Crw; Rptr Sch Nwsp; Cit Awd; Arizona Coll; Lang Interperter.

MOTL, MARK; South Spencer HS; Grandview, IN; 19/150 Band; Chrh Wkr; Cmnty Wkr; Hon Rl; NHS; Sct Actv; Yrbk; Letter Bsktbl; Letter Ftbl; Trk; Achvmnt Awd For Schlrshp 79; Tri Kappa Schlrshp 79; Victor Moore Schlrshp 79; Univ Of Kentucky; Engr.

MOTLEY, DOROTHEA; Franklin Hts HS; Columbus, OH; Chrh Wkr; Cmnty Wkr; Off Ade; OEA; Bsktbl; Scr Kpr; Wilbur Force Coll; Bus Admin.

MOTLEY, NORMA B; Saint Thomas Aquinas HS; Canton, OH; 49/174 Chrh Wkr; Cmnty Wkr; Hon Rl; Natl Forn Lg; Yth Flsp; Natl Merit Ltr; Natl Forensic League Trophy; Univ Of Akron; Law.

MOTLEY, PHILLIPIE; Kenston HS; Chagrin Fl, OH; Band; Chrs; Cmnty Wkr; Drm Bgl; Hon Rl; Sch Pl; Stu Cncl; Rptr Sch Nwsp; 4-H; Bsktbl; Ohio St Univ; Bio Chem.

MOTLEY, TIMOTHY; East Technical HS; Cleveland, OH; Pres Soph Cls; Pres Jr Cls; Lbry Ade; PAVAS; Sch Pl; Stu Cncl; Rptr Sch Nwsp; Drama Clb; Trk; Kiwan Awd; Emerson Coll; Peforming Arts.

MOTSCO, CHERYL; Bedford Senior HS; Bedford, OH; 4/533 Hon Rl; NHS; Spn Clb; Scr Kpr; Wittenberg Univ; Veterinary Medicine.

MOTSINGER, NANCY; Eastern HS; Salem, IN; 13/91 Chrs; Chrh Wkr; Hon Rl; NHS; Stg Crw; Rptr Sch Nwsp; Drama Clb; Southeastern Acad.

MOTT, CHERI; Valley HS; Pine Grove, WV; 1/77 Pres Soph Cls; Val; NHS; Sch Pl; Stg Crw; Rptr Yrbk; Sec FFA; Letter Trk; West Liberty College; Med Tech.

MOTT, KEVIN; Andrean HS; Gary, IN; 65/260 Boy Scts; Cmnty Wkr; Hon Rl; JA; Jr NHS; DECA; Purdue Univ; Pre Law.

MOTT, LYNNE; West Carrollton Sr HS; Dayton, OH; Cls Rep Sr Cls; Jr NHS; Lit Mag; Stu Cncl; Rptr Yrbk; Trk; Chrldng; Univ.

MOTT, MARTHA; Richmond HS; Richmond, MI; Trs Sr Cls; Chrs; Chrh Wkr; Hon Rl; Mdrgl; NHS; Yrbk; Sprt Ed Sch Nwsp; Rptr Sch Nwsp; Capt Chrldng; Spanish Awd & Geom Awd 77; St Of Mi Schlshp 79; Stdtn Actvts Scshlhp 79; Saginaw Valley Coll; Acctg.

MOTT, NORBERT; Chaminade Julienne HS; Dayton, OH; Cl Rep Jr Cls; Chrh Wkr; Cmnty Wkr; Hon Rl; Pol Wkr; Stu Cncl; Rptr Sch Nwsp; Spn Clb; IM Sprt; Cit Awd; Explorers Law Clb; Univ; Law.

MOTT, SYLVIA; Olivet HS; Olivet, MI; Band; Chrh Wkr; Drl Tm; Girl Scts; Hon Rl; Sch Mus; Sch Pl; Sct Actv; Stg Crw; Stu Cncl; Cerm Proj Top Ten Awds 78; Cosmetology Schl; Cosmtlgst.

MOTTELER, CLINTON; Houghton HS; Houghton, MI; Band; Chrs; Drm Bgl; Hon Rl; Lbry Ade; Orch; Yrbk; Drama Clb; Grand Valley College; Music.

MOTTER, DEBBY; Piqua Central HS; Piqua, OH; Girl Scts; Off Ade; Sec 4-H; Sec Pep Clb; Spn Clb; Edison State.

MOTTES, DEBORAH; Gwinn HS; Gwinn, MI; Band; Cmnty Wkr; Hon Rl; Pep Clb; Gym; Chrldng; Coach Actv; Pres Awd; Univ; Bus.

MOTTONEN, TAMMY; Calumet HS; Laurium, MI; Band; Cmp Fr Grls; Chrh Wkr; Drm Mjrt; Hon Rl; Hosp Ade; 4-H; Fr Clb; FNA; FTA; Jr Honor Guard For 79 Graduating Class; Winter Olympics Speed Skating 1st & 2nd Pl Awds; College; Law.

MOTZ, CINDY; Northrop HS; Ft Wayne, IN; Cls Rep Frsh Cls; Cls Rep Soph Cls; Cl Rep Jr Cls; VP Sr Cls; Hon Rl; Stu Cncl; Lat Clb; Cit Awd; Purdue Univ; Home Ec.

MOTZ, DAVID; North Posey Sr HS; Wadesville, IN; Boy Scts; Hon Rl; NHS; FFA; Ger Clb; Letter Bsbl; Letter Ftbl; IM Sprt; Univ; Forestry.

MOTZ, TIMOTHY; St Johns HS; St Johns, MI; Chrh Wkr; Hon Rl; Eng Clb; VICA; 4-H Awd; Ohio Diesel Inst Tech; Diesel Mech.

MOTZA, AMY; West Union HS; Winchester, OH; 13/118 Chrs; Hon Rl; Rptr Sch Nwsp; Pres Fr Clb; Southern St Cmnty Coll; Acctg.

MOUHLAS, CYNTHIA; Trinity HS; Parma, OH; 12/150 Band; Chrs; Drm Bgl; Girl Scts; Hon Rl; NHS; Orch; Sch Mus; Sct Actv; Letter Bsktbl; Schlrshp Awd 78; Music Schlrshp 77; Vllybll MVP 2 Yr Letter Winner 78; Cleveland St Univ; Sci.

MOULD, GARY A; N Ridgeville HS; N Ridgeville, OH; Hon Rl; FFA; Wrstlng; Nursery & Lndscpng.

MOULD, MARCIA; St Francis De Sales HS; Columbus, OH; 10/190 Chrh Wkr; Hon Rl; NHS; Sch Mus; Sch Pl; Spn Clb; Crs Cntry; Swmmng; Letter Trk; IM Sprt; Univ; Med.

MOULDEN, REBECCA; N Daviess Jr Sr HS; Elnora, IN; 3/93 VP Jr Cls; Am Leg Aux Girls St; Band; Chrh Wkr; Hon Rl; Lbry Ade; Rptr Yrbk; Rptr Sch Nwsp; Beta Clb; Freshman Band Cncl Rep; Whos Who In Indiana & Ky HS Foreign Languages; Read A Book For Cerebral Palsied; Indiana St Univ; Busns Admin.

MOULDS, BRENDA; North Muskegon HS; North Muskegon, MI; Band; Chrs; Girl Scts; Hon Rl; NHS; Sch Mus; Yrbk; Trk; PPFtbl; Natl Merit SF; Kendall Schl Of Design; Advert Desgn.

MOULOS, TAMMY; Fairless HS; Navarre, OH; Sec Soph Cls; Sec Jr Cls; Sec Sr Cls; Am Leg Aux Girls St; Chrh Wkr; Hon Rl; JA; Jr NHS; Bowling Green College; Communication.

MOULTHROP, JEANNE; Charles F Brush HS; Lyndhurst, OH; AFS; Debate Tm; Hon Rl; Hosp Ade; Natl Forn Lg; PAVAS; Stg Crw; Yth Flsp; Drama Clb; Natl Merit SF; College; Psych.

MOUNCE, TAMARA; Central Baptist HS; Norwood, OH; VP Frsh Cls; Sec Soph Cls; Chrs; Chrh Wkr; Stu Cncl; Pep Clb; Bsktbl; Chrldng; Dnfth Awd; Bethesba Schl Of Nursing; Rn.

MOUNSEY, TORI A; Southern Wells HS; Montepllier, IN; 22/96 Band; Sec Chrh Wkr; Hosp Ade; NHS; Drama Clb; Fr Clb; FHA; Letter Trk; GAA; In St Schlrshp Honorary 79; Taylor Univ.

MOUNT, LAURA; Grant Public HS; Grant, MI; Hon Rl; Lbry Ade; 4-H; Muskegon Comm College; Data Procesin.

MOUNT, MASON; Wooster HS; Apple Creek, OH; Val; Boy Scts; FCA; Hon Rl; Sct Actv; Beta Clb; Pep Clb; Sci Clb; Spn Clb; Bsktbl; OU; Physics.

MOUNTAIN, CATHY; Grove City HS; Grove City, OH; Cls Rep Frsh Cls; Cls Rep Soph Cls; Cl Rep Jr Cls; Cls Rep Sr Cls; Hon Rl; Sec Jr NHS; Lbry Ade; Sec NHS; Yth Flsp; Rptr Yrbk; Ohio St Univ; Public Relations.

MOUNTAIN, DONALD; Streetsboro HS; Streetsboro, OH; 53/349 Ftbl; Letter Wrstlng; Mgrs; Scr Kpr; Univ.

MOUNTS, BRENDA G; Guyan Valley HS; Ranger, WV; 12/100 Cl Rep Jr Cls; Cls Rep Sr Cls; Chrh Wkr; Cmnty Wkr; Hon Rl; NHS; Rptr Yrbk; Ed Sch Nwsp; Rptr Sch Nwsp; FBLA;.

MOUNTZ, DEBRA L; Marlington HS; Louisville, OH; 32/280 Band; Drl Tm; Girl Scts; Hon Rl; Hosp Ade; NHS; Pres FNA; CAP; Massillon Cty Schl Of Nursing; Nurse.

MOURAD, BRIAN; Grosse Pointe North HS; Grosse Pt Shor, MI; IM Sprt; Mich State Univ; Intl Relations.

MOURAND, CARRIE; Negaunee HS; Negaunee, MI; Cls Rep Frsh Cls; Cls Rep Soph Cls; Band; Hon Rl; Stu Cncl; Pep Clb; Letter Gym; Capt Chrldng; Univ; Med.

MOUSER, CINDY; Park Tudor School; Indianapolis, IN; Cl Rep Jr Cls; Chrs; Hon Rl; Mdrgl; Sch Mus; Sch Pl; Stg Crw; Yrbk; Civ Clb; Drama Clb; Univ; Bio Sci.

MOUSER, JANICE; Ithaca HS; Ithaca, MI; 1/140 Boy Scts; Chrs; Debate Tm; Hon Rl; Pres Natl Forn Lg; NHS; Sch Mus; Yth Flsp; Central Michigan Univ; Poli Sci.

MOUSER, MICHAEL S; Lakeview Sr HS; Stow, OH; AFS; Chrh Wkr; Hon Rl; Fr Clb; Top Ten Awd 77; Schlrshp Awd 77; Ohio Valley Coll; Poli Sci.

MOUSSEAU, BARBARA; Reese HS; Reese, MI; Hon Rl; Off Ade; 4-H; Letter Bsktbl; Trk; PPFtbl; Tmr; Delta Coll; Bookkeeping.

MOUSSEAU, SCOTT; Grandville HS; Grandville, MI; Chrs; Hon Rl; Natl Forn Lg; Sch Mus; Sch Pl; Rptr Yrbk; Rptr Sch Nwsp; Drama Clb; Scr Kpr; Aquinas College; Jrnlsm.

MOUZON, LESLIE; Little Miami HS; Oregonia, OH; Hon Rl; VICA; Bsktbl; Crs Cntry; Ftbl; Trk; Warren County Jvs.

MOVALSON, TRACY; La Salle HS; Moran, MI; Cls Rep Frsh Cls; Cmp Fr Grls; Hon Rl; JA; Stu Cncl; Chrldng; Central Michigan Univ; Health.

MOWATT LARSSEN, ERLING; Howland HS; Warren, OH; 28/400 Band; Hon Rl; NHS; Orch; Fr Clb; Bsbl; Swmmng; Purdue Univ; Engr.

MOWBRAY, LINDA; Wayne HS; Dayton, OH; Hon Rl; Sch Pl; Pep Clb; 2nd Pl In Bicent Coin Cntst For Cmnty 76; Whos Who Amon Amer HS Stu 77; Wright St Univ; Cmnctns.

MOWDER, LYNN; Rogers HS; Toledo, OH; Jr NHS; NHS; Sec Fr Clb; Sci Clb; Ten; College.

MOWERY, GAIL; Southwood HS; Wabash, IN; Cls Rep Frsh Cls; Cls Rep Soph Cls; VP Jr Cls; Band; FCA; Stu Cncl; 4-H; FHA; Pep Clb; Pom Pon; Upper Wabash Voc Schl; Sec.

MOWERY, JAY; Allen East HS; Lima, OH; Band; Boy Scts; Hon Rl; 4-H; Fr Clb; Indianapolis Tech; Heating.

MOWERY, JULIE; Waynesfield Goshen HS; Wapakoneta, OH; 2/57 Band; Chrs; Drl Tm; Hon Rl; Jr NHS; NHS; Sch Mus; Ed Yrbk; Rptr Yrbk; 4-H; College; Science.

MOWERY, REX; North Knox HS; Bruceville, IN; Hon Rl; NHS; 4-H; IM Sprt; Natl Merit Ltr; Vincennes Univ; Elec Tech.

MOWERY, REX P; North Knox HS; Bruceville, IN; 5/154 Hon Rl; NHS; 4-H; IM Sprt; Vincennes Univ.

MOWERY, RHONDA; Northfield HS; Wabash, IN; 27/114 Sec Sr Cls; Band; Drl Tm; Hon Rl; Stg Crw; Yrbk; Rptr Sch Nwsp; Drama Clb; OEA; IU; Dent Hygnst.

MOWERY, TERESA; Eastbrook HS; Marion, IN; FCA; Hon Rl; Stu Cncl; Rptr Sch Nwsp; Pep Clb; Bsktbl; Trk; Mgrs; Pom Pon; PPFtbl; Gold Medal In MIC For Track 77; Taylor Univ; Doctor.

MOWERY, THOMAS; Bedford Sr HS; Toledo, OH; 17/440 NHS; Mgrs; Univ Of Toledo; Engr.

MOWREY, PHILLIP; Central HS; Evansville, IN; 51/528 Cls Rep Frsh Cls; Cls Rep Soph Cls; Cl Rep Jr Cls; Cls Rep Sr Cls; Band; Boy Scts; Ed Sch Nwsp; Letter Ftbl; Letter Trk; C of C Awd; Wabash Coll; Law.

MOWRY, ANN; Sault Area HS & Skills Cntr; Sault Ste Marie, MI; Cl Rep Jr Cls; Band; Chrh Wkr; Hon Rl; Sch Pl; Stu Cncl; Yth Flsp; Drama Clb; Lat Clb; Letter Trk; Univ; Civil Engr.

MOWRY, DEANNE M; Spencer HS; Spencer, WV; Pres Chrs; Hon Rl; Jr NHS; Sec Stu Cncl; VP Yth Flsp; Sch Nwsp; VP FHA; IM Sprt; Coll; Home Ec.

MOXLEY, DENISE; Mio Au Sable HS; Mio, MI; 15/48 Band; Hon Rl; Orch; Sch Mus; Blue Lk Fine Arts Mus Cmp Schlrshp 77; Blue Lk Fine Arts Cmp Music Camp Schlrshp 78; John P Sousa Awd 79; Ferris St Coll; Acctg.

MOY, KATHY; Greenville Sr HS; Greenville, MI; Chrh Wkr; Hon Rl; Stu Cncl; GAA; Mgrs; PPFtbl; Scr Kpr; Opt Clb Awd; Univ; Educ.

MOYE, ANGELA; Michigan Lutheran Seminary; Detroit, MI; Sch Pl; Drama Clb; General Motors Inst; Comp Sci.

MOYE, MARK; Matoak HS; Rock, WV; 3/66 Pres Soph Cls; Am Leg Boys St; Band; Hon Rl; NHS; Pres Stu Cncl; Yrbk; Chmn Bsktbl; Dnfth Awd; Univ; Mining Engr.

MOYE, PAULA; Pontiac Central HS; Pontiac, MI; Band; Drm Mjrt; Hon Rl; Sch Mus; Sch Pl; Drama Clb; Twrlr;.

MOYE, STUART; Field HS; Kent, OH; Hon Rl; DECA; San Diego State; Sports Broadcasting.

MOYER, CHERYL; Portland HS; Eagle, MI; Band; Cmnty Wkr; Debate Tm; Girl Scts; Hon Rl; NHS; Sch Mus; Sch Pl; Stg Crw; Drama Clb; Univ; Soc Sci.

MOYER, CYNTHIA; Hamilton Southeastern HS; Noblesville, IN; 25/140 VP Jr Cls; Pres Sr Cls; Hon Rl; Stu Cncl; Fr Clb; OEA; Sci Clb; Trk; Chrldng; Mat Maids; College; Bus.

MOYER, DAWN; Clyde HS; Clyde, OH; Cl Rep Jr Cls; Drm Mjrt; Hon Rl; Stu Cncl; Spn Clb; Chrldng; Scr Kpr; Twrlr; College; Special Educ.

MOYER, DIANE; Cory Rawson HS; Mt Cory, OH; Band; Chrh Wkr; Cmnty Wkr; Hon Rl; Off Ade; Sch Pl; Yth Flsp; Fredricks Beauty Coll; Cosmetology.

MOYER, JULIE; Edison HS; Milan, OH; 30/168 Band; Hon Rl; Jr NHS; NHS; Quill & Scroll; Yrbk; Sprt Ed Sch Nwsp; Mth Clb; Capt Bsktbl; Trk; Univ Of Toledo; Spec Ed.

MOYER, KENT; Arcadia Local School; Findlay, OH; 2/60 Sec Frsh Cls; Trs Soph Cls; Band; Chrs; Hon Rl; NHS; Sch Mus; Stu Cncl; Yth Flsp; FFA; Univ.

MOYER, LINDA; Buckeye Valley HS; Ashley, OH; Chrs; Girl Scts; JA; Yth Flsp; DECA; FHA; Spn Clb; Bluffton Univ; Elem Ed.

MOYER, MARY; Catholic Central HS; Wyoming, MI; Chrs; Hon Rl; Lat Clb; Univ; RN.

MOYER, MARY; Bluffton HS; Bluffton, OH; Band; Chrs; Fr Clb; Lat Clb; Coll Of William & Mary; Spec Ed.

MOYER, MITZI; Cass Tech HS; Detroit, MI; 50/780 Band; Girl Scts; Hon Rl; Lbry Ade; NHS; Sct Actv; Natl Merit SF; Ferris St Coll; Educ.

MOYER, ROBERT; Plymouth Canton HS; Plymouth, MI; Band; Hon Rl; Orch; Trk; Natl Merit Ltr; Michigan Tech Univ; Mech Engr.

MOYER, ROBIN; Andrews HS; Ecorse, MI; Trs Soph Cls; Band; Chrs; Chrh Wkr; Hon Rl; JA; Sec Sr Cls; Off Ade; Stg Crw; Stu Cncl; Selected For Spec Recog 1980 Salute To The Good In Youth By St Rep M Mc Neely; College; Busns Admin.

MOYER, SHEELAH; Chaminade Julienne HS; Dayton, OH; Band; Drl Tm; NHS; Red Cr Ade; Sch Pl; Yrbk; Chrldng; Coach Actv; PPFtbl; Recreational Mgr.

MOYER, STEVEN; Bishop Rosecrans HS; Zanesville, OH; 10/80 Cls Rep Frsh Cls; Trs Soph Cls; Cl Rep Jr Cls; Hon Rl; Jr NHS; NHS; Yrbk; Bsktbl; Ftbl; Trk; Ohio St Univ; Metallurgical Engr.

MOYER, T; Roosevelt Wilson HS; Clarksbrg, WV; Trs Jr Cls; VP Chrs; Chrh Wkr; Cmnty Wkr; Hon Rl; Off Ade; Sch Mus; Stu Cncl; Yth Flsp; Y-Teens; College; Elem Educa.

MOYER, TERRY; Regina HS; S Euclid, OH; Cls Rep Soph Cls; Chrs; Hon Rl; Stg Crw; Stu Cncl; Univ; Dent Hygnst.

MOYER, VICTORIA L; Norwalk HS; Norwalk, OH; 2/182 Sal; Hon Rl; NHS; Off Ade; Sch Mus; 4-H; Pres OEA; Firelands Voc Schl; Acctg.

MOYERS, KATHY; Marietta HS; Marietta, OH; 143/419 Pres JA; Off Ade; Y-Teens; Drama Clb; OEA; Spn Clb; Swmmng; Exec Sec.

MOYERS, PAMELA; Bridgeport HS; Bridgeport, WV; 2/189 Hon Rl; Hosp Ade; Jr NHS; Lbry Ade; NHS; Stg Crw; Fr Clb; Alderson Brooaddus; Med Sci.

MOYLE, JUNE; Lake Linden Hubbell HS; Calumet, MI; 2/53 Pres Soph Cls; Sal; Band; Hon Rl; Sch Pl; Stu Cncl; Yrbk; Bsktbl; Cit Awd; Natl Merit Ltr; Michigan Tech Univ; Bus Admin.

MOYZIS, ELIZABETH J; Fairmont East HS; Kettering, OH; Girl Scts; Hon Rl; Sct Actv; Yth Flsp; Yrbk; Spn Clb; JETS Awd; Natl Merit Ltr; Univ Of Cincinnati; Chem Engr.

MOZDIAN, RAYANNE; Van Wert HS; Van Wert, OH; Chrs; Hon Rl; Y-Teens; FHA; Lat Clb; Pep Clb; Sci Clb; Kent St Univ; Law.

MOZENA, BARBARA; Tri Valley HS; Dresden, OH; 43/220 Band; Chrh Wkr; Hon Rl; Orch; Pres Yth Flsp; Sec 4-H; FTA; Spn Clb; 4-H Awd; Baldwin Wallace; Music.

MOZOLITS, DEBBIE; West Lutheran HS; North Olmsted, OH; Chrs; Girl Scts; Sch Mus; Mgrs; Purdue Univ; Nursing.

MOZUKE, TAMMY; Williamstown HS; Williamstown, WV; 10/129 Band; Hon Rl; Y-Teens; Sprt Ed Yrbk; Rptr Sch Nwsp; Sch Nwsp; Pep Clb; Letter Trk; GAA; Scr Kpr; Wva Univ; Law.

MRAS, PATRICIA; Monrovia HS; Mooresville, IN; 6/134 Hon Rl; NHS; Rptr Yrbk; Ed Sch Nwsp; Spn Clb; Mgrs; Scr Kpr; College; Busns Admin.

MROCKA, SANDRA; Hartland HS; Brighton, MI; Cmnty Wkr; Hon Rl; Univ; Comp Sci.

MROZ, RICHARD; Andrean HS; Gary, IN; 24/251 Hon Rl; Sci Clb; Spn Clb; Lew Wallace Natl Honor Soc Awd; College; Business.

MROZEK, ERIC; Hartland HS; Howell, MI; 18/250 Band; Pres Chrh Wkr; Hon Rl; Sec NHS; Sch Pl; Stg Crw; Drama Clb; Crs Cntry; Capt Trk; Univ; Elec Engr.

MROZOWSKI, EDWARD; Chadsey HS; Detroit, MI; Hon Rl; Sch Nwsp; Boys Clb Am; Michigan State.

MRUSEK, MARK; Carlisle HS; Miamisburg, OH; Off Ade; Sch Pl; Bsbl; Ftbl; Gym; Trk; Wrstlng; IM Sprt; PPFtbl; Tmr; College; Dentistry.

MTICHELL, RONDA; Jane Addams Vocational HS; Cleveland, OH; Chrh Wkr; Hosp Ade; NHS; Off Ade; DECA; Bsbl; Trk; Chrldng; Coach Actv; Cit Awd; College; Bus Admin.

MUCCIANTE, MICHELE; Eisenhower HS; Utica, MI; Cmp Fr Grls; Hon Rl; Off Ade; Sch Mus; Sch Pl; Letter Bsktbl; Letter Trk; Oakland Univ; Vet.

MUCCIO, MARIA; Niles Mc Kinley HS; Niles, OH; Hon Rl; Jr NHS; NHS; Off Ade; Pep Clb; Ten; College.

MUCK, CHERYL; Ellet HS; Akron, OH; 34/361 Chrs; Hon Rl; Ger Clb; Univ Of Akron; Psych.

MUCK, PETE; Southern Local HS; Summitvll, OH; Aud/Vis; Chrh Wkr; Hon Rl; 4-H; Lat Clb; IM Sprt; 4-H Awd; Univ.

MUDD, EILEEN M; Big Walnut HS; Westerville, OH; Hst Soph Cls; Chrs; Girl Scts; Hon Rl; Red Cr Ade; Sct Actv; Fr Clb; FHA; Letter Chrldng; Am Leg Awd; College.

MUDD, LOUISE; Anderson HS; Anderson, IN; 5/400 Sec Sr Cls; Am Leg Aux Girls St; VP NHS; Ed Sch Nwsp; Sec Lat Clb; Am Leg Awd; C of C Awd; Opt Clb Awd; Rotary Awd; Notre Dame; Elec Engr.

MUDRACK, BRENDA; Northside HS; Ft Wayne, IN; AFS; Girl Scts; PAVAS; Sch Mus; Sch Pl; Stg Crw; Drama Clb; Fr Clb; Rdo Clb; Spn Clb; Univ; Drama.

MUELLAUER, SUE; Brooklyn HS; Brooklyn, OH; 6/172 Chrs; Hon Rl; NHS; Sch Pl; Yrbk; Eng Clb; OEA; VICA; Coll; Busns.

MUELLE, MARY; Marquette Sr HS; Marquette, MI; Cls Rep Sr Cls; Chrs; Off Ade; Sch Mus; Rptr Yrbk; Yrbk; FNA; Ger Clb; Pep Clb; Tmr; Northern Michigan Univ; X Ray Tech.

MUELLER, ALFRED; Riverside HS; Dearborn Hgts, MI; Chrs; Hon Rl; Wayne State Univ; Liberal Arts.

MUELLER, DAWN; Little Miami HS; Maineville, OH; Hon Rl; Jr NHS; Lit Mag; Off Ade; Sct Actv; Stg Crw; Yrbk; 4-H; Fr Clb; Ten; I Have Had Art Wrk & Poems Publshed 77 79; Cincinnati Univ; Juv Justice.

MUELLER, GARY; Warren Woods HS; Warren, MI; 6/350 Band; Chrs; Mdrgl; Pres NHS; Sch Mus; Stg Crw; Treas Drama Clb; Natl Merit Ltr; Univ Of Michigan; Chem.

MUELLER, GEORGE; Reading HS; Reading, MI; FFA; Bsktbl; Ftbl; Univ.

MUELLER, K; Hastings HS; Hastings, MI; 11/325 Chrh Wkr; Hon Rl; FBLA; Univ; Educ.

MUELLER, KEVIN; Greenville Sr HS; Greenville, OH; Hon Rl; Spn Clb; Crs Cntry; Trk; Univ.

MUELLER, MICHAEL; Reese HS; Reese, MI; 11/131 Pres Frsh Cls; Trs Jr Cls; Am Leg Boys St; Chrh Wkr; NHS; Ger Clb; Trk; Ferris State College; Optometry.

MUELLER, MONICA; Madonna HS; Weirton, VA; Hon Rl; Lit Mag; Pep Clb; Trk; Letter Wrstlng; Capt Chrldng; Wheeling Barber Coll; Barber.

MUELLER, RITA; Garfield HS; Akron, OH; 1/460 Band; Chrs; Chrh Wkr; Hon Rl; Orch; ROTC; JC Awd; May Festival 1973; Stage Band 1975; Composers Contst Awrd 1973; Conservatory Of Music; Music.

MUELLER, ROBERT J; Pine River HS; Le Roy, MI; Michigan St Univ; Archt.

MUELLER, SHELLEY; East Kentwood HS; Kentwood, MI; Chrh Wkr; Letter Trk; Letter Pom Pon; Western Michigan Univ; Bus.

MUELLER, THERESA; Villa Angela HS; Cleveland, OH; Chrh Wkr; Girl Scts; Hon Rl; Orch; Sch Mus; Sch Pl; Sct Actv; Mth Clb; Sci Clb; Dayton Univ; Engr.

MUELLER, TIMOTHY; Western HS; Bay City, MI; 1/470 Val; Band; Chrh Wkr; Hon Rl; NHS; DAR Awd; Natl Merit Ltr; Concordia College; Eng.

MUELLER, WES; Lexington HS; Mansfield, OH; 4/270 Hon Rl; NHS; Letter Bsbl; Letter Bsktbl; Natl Merit SF; College; Chemical Engr.

MUESING, NATALIE; East Noble HS; Kendallville, IN; 11/249 Trs Frsh Cls; Cl Rep Jr Cls; Cls Rep Sr Cls; Band; Chrh Wkr; Hon Rl; Natl Forn Lg; NHS; Stu Cncl; 4-H; Open Div Judging Team Natl Jr Horticulture Convention; St Jr Leader Cncl; Mbr Of Team In Mid St 4 H Team; Purdue Univ; Ag.

MUGAN, THERESE C; Dominican HS; Detroit, MI; Band; Trk; Wayne State Univ; Liberal Arts.

MUGFORD, REBECCA L; Zanesville HS; Zanesville, OH; Chrs; Girl Scts; Hon Rl; Hosp Ade; Sch Mus; Stu Cncl; Schlstc Outstndng Achvmnt 76; Schlrshp Awrd 77; Natl Youth Phys Fitness 77; Univ.

MUGRIDGE, LORI; Atherton HS; Flint, MI; 12/126 Band; Chrs; Mdrgl; Val; Red Cr Ade; ROTC; Sch Mus; Mich State Univ; History.

MUHAL, COLLEEN; Hartland HS; Brighton, MI; Chrh Wkr; Hon Rl; Hosp Ade; NHS; Spn Clb; Ten; IM Sprt; Scr Kpr; Grand Valley State College; Rn.

MUHLEMAN, GEORGIA; Salem HS; Salem, OH; 61/273 Trs Frsh Cls; Cls Rep Frsh Cls; Trs Soph Cls; Cls Rep Soph Cls; Trs Jr Cls; Cl Rep Jr Cls; Trs Sr Cls; Cls Rep Sr Cls; VP Cmp Fr Grls; Hon Rl; Ohi State Univ; Sci.

MUHLENKAMP, RICK; Parkway HS; Celina, OH; Chrh Wkr; Cmnty Wkr; Hon Rl; IM Sprt; Univ; Agri Engr.

MUIDERMAN, JEFFREY; Creston HS; Holland, MI; 25/433 NHS; Ed Sch Nwsp; Hope Coll; Jrnlsm.

MUIRHEAD, GREG; North Central HS; Indianapolis, IN; NHS; Sec Key Clb; IM Sprt; Ball St Univ; Archt.

MUKANS, ELIZABETE; Kenowa Hills HS; Grand Rapids, MI; Band; Girl Scts; Hon Rl; NHS; 4-H; Capt PPFtbl; 4-H Awd; Grand Rapids Jr Coll; Nursing.

MULCAHY, MARTHA; St Francis HS; Traverse City, MI; Pres Soph Cls; Pres Jr Cls; Chrs; JA; Sch Mus; Stu Cncl; Yrbk; Bsktbl; Letter Crs Cntry; Ten; St Catherines Coll; Lib Arts.

MULDER, DAVID; Jenison HS; Jenison, MI; Boy Scts; Hon Rl; VP JA; Lit Mag; Yrbk; Rptr Sch Nwsp; JA Awd; Natl Merit Ltr; Grand Valley State Coll.

MULDER, MELVIN; Tell City HS; Tell City, IN; Band; Boy Scts; 4-H; Letter Crs Cntry; Letter Ftbl; Letter Trk; Tmr; Dnfth Awd; 4-H Awd; Purdue Univ; Bio.

MULDOON, MARLENE; Southwestern HS; Edinburgh, IN; 1/56 Sec Soph Cls; Val; Am Leg Aux Girls St; Chrs; Chrh Wkr; Hon Rl; NHS; Off Ade; Sch Mus; Yth Flsp; Vlybl Capt; Sunshine Soc; Coll; Sec.

MULHALL, PAM; Fenwick HS; Middletown, OH; Sec Frsh Cls; Hon Rl; Sch Mus; Stu Cncl; Fr Clb; Letter Swmmng; Letter Chrldng; Miami Univ; Spec Educ.

MULHEIM, PATTY; Perry HS; Navarre, OH; 51/480 Cmnty Wkr; Girl Scts; Hon Rl; Hosp Ade; Lbry Ade; NHS; Off Ade; Quill & Scroll; Stg Crw; Ed Yrbk;.

MULHERN, ELLEN; Regina HS; Detroit, MI; 2/137 Sal; Debate Tm; Hon Rl; Hosp Ade; JA; Natl Forn Lg; Sec Sci Clb; PPFtbl; Univ Of Detroit; Bus.

MULHERN, LISA; Vinton County Consol HS; Mc Arthur, OH; 32/160 Band; Hon Rl; Off Ade; Rptr Yrbk; 4-H; Sec FHA; Pep Clb;.

MULHOLLAN, JULIE; Highland HS; Wadsworth, OH; Cls Rep Sr Cls; Girl Scts; Hon Rl; Hosp Ade; Sct Actv; Stu Cncl; Sec Lat Clb; Miami Univ; Cmnctns.

MULHOLLAND, CHERYL; Lima Perry HS; Lima, OH; 1/74 Band; Chrs; Hon Rl; Sch Mus; Rptr Yrbk; 4-H; Pep Clb; Spn Clb; Trk; Chrldng; Spanish I Awd; Optimist Oratoricl Cntst Winner; Outstndng Pianist Hnr; Ohio State Univ; CPA.

MULHOLLAND, JOSEPH; Bishop Noll Inst; Hammond, IN; 9/337 Pres Band; Hon Rl; NHS; Orch; Sch Mus; Capt Trk; Ind Univ.

MULHOLLAND, MARTIN; Bishop Noll Institute; Hammond, IN; 16/321 Band; Hon Rl; Orch; Mth Clb; Letter Trk; Univ.

MULKA, STEVE; Utica HS; Utica, MI; Hon Rl; JA; IM Sprt; Mocomb County Community College;arch.

MULL, JOHN; Wauseon HS; Wauseon, OH; 9/151 Am Leg Boys St; Chrh Wkr; FCA; Hon Rl; NHS; Pres Yth Flsp; Pres 4-H; Pres FFA; Letter Ftbl; College; Agriculture.

MULL, KAREN; Stow HS; Stow, OH; Am Leg Aux Girls St; Band; Girl Scts; Hon Rl; NHS; Sch Pl; Sct Actv; Stu Cncl; Drama Clb; Am Leg Awd; Univ Of Akron; Nursing.

MULL, MICHELLE; Henryville HS; Henryville, IN; Sec Band; Chrh Wkr; Drm Mjrt; Hon Rl; Mod UN; Treas NHS; Sec Spn Clb; Letter Trk; Letter Chrldng; Coach Actv; Ball St Univ; Spanish.

MULL, STEVE; Marquette HS; Michigan City, IN; 9/73 Pres Frsh Cls; Pres Jr Cls; Pres Sr Cls; Am Leg Boys St; Quill & Scroll; Rptr Sch Nwsp; Capt Crs Cntry; Letter Socr; Letter Trk; Univ; Pre Law.

MULLALLY, MARY; Holy Rosary HS; Mt Morris, MI; 4/60 Girl Scts; Hon Rl; NHS; Capt Crs Cntry; Letter Trk; Chrldng; Flint Exchng Club Awd; Univ Of Michigan; Nursing.

MULLALLY, TOM; Holy Rosary HS; Mt Morris, MI; 1/45 Pres Frsh Cls; Trs Jr Cls; Cls Rep Sr Cls; Val; Boy Scts; Hon Rl; NHS; Sch Pl; Stu Cncl; Crs Cntry; Captain All League In Cross Cntry; 4 Yr State Finalist In Cross Cntry; A Avg In HS; Univ Of Michigan; Medicine.

MULLALY, COLLEEN M; Berkley HS; Berkley, MI; 12/487 Trs Jr Cls; Trs Sr Cls; Cls Rep Sr Cls; Chrh Wkr; Cmnty Wkr; Girl Scts; Lbry Ade; NHS; Off Ade; Pol Wkr; Kalamazoo College.

MULLANEY, ANNE; Marion HS; Blmfld Hls, MI; Cls Rep Soph Cls; Hon Rl; JA; Lbry Ade; Off Ade; Sch Nwsp; Eng Clb; Oakland Univ; Bus Admin.

MULLANEY, JACK; Marysville HS; W Mansfield, OH; Chrh Wkr; Hon Rl; NHS; Yth Flsp; 4-H; Lat Clb; Bsbl; Bsktbl; Ftbl; Ohi State Univ; Eng.

MULLARKEY, PATRICK; Wadsworth HS; Wadsworth, OH; 54/360 Chrs; Chrh Wkr; Hon Rl; NHS; Bsktbl; Crs Cntry; Trk; IM Sprt; Miami Univ; Pulp & Paper Tech.

MULLEN, CATHERINE; St Augustine Acad; Bay Vlg, OH; 19/133 Hon Rl; Rptr Yrbk; Drama Clb; Key Clb; Inst Of Comp Mgmt; Comp Sci.

MULLEN, CATHERINE; Sault Area HS; Slt Ste Marie, MI; Fr Clb; Pep Clb; Lake Superior St Coll; Nurse.

MULLEN, JAMIE; Bloom Local S Webster HS; Beaufort, SC; Cl Rep Jr Cls; Cls Rep Sr Cls; Chrs; Chrh Wkr; FCA; Pol Wkr; FHA; OEA; Shawnee St Univ; Bus Admin.

MULLEN, JENNIFER; Floyd Central HS; Georgetown, IN; 78/350 Cls Rep Soph Cls; Cl Rep Jr Cls; Cls Rep Sr Cls; Am Leg Aux Girls St; Hon Rl; Stu Cncl; Pep Clb; DAR Awd; Opt Clb Awd; College; Medicine.

MULLEN, JUDITH M; Washington Catholic HS; Washington, IN; Sec Frsh Cls; VP Soph Cls; VP Jr Cls; Chrs; Chrh Wkr; Cmnty Wkr; Girl Scts; Hon Rl; Jr NHS; Sch Mus; Ind Univ; Soc Work.

MULLEN, JULIA; Ben Davis HS; Indianapolis, IN; Band; FCA; Girl Scts; Hon Rl; Off Ade; Stu Cncl; 4-H; Fr Clb; Pep Clb; Chrldng; All Cnty Tm Vllybl 78; 2nd Tm All Star Select US Jr Olymp Natl Vllybl Champ 79; Univ.

MULLEN, LISA; Jefferson HS; Lafayette, IN; Chrh Wkr; JA; Stu Cncl; Rptr Sch Nwsp; Pres DECA; Pep Clb; Spn Clb; Purdue Univ; Bus Mgmt.

MULLEN, MICHAEL; Cadillac Sr HS; Cadillac, MI; Am Leg Boys St; Boy Scts; FCA; Hon Rl; Capt Bsbl; Letter Bsktbl; Letter Crs Cntry; Rotary Awd; Western Michigan Univ; Bus.

MULLEN, ROGER; Floyd Central HS; Georgetown, IN; 72/340 Aud/Vis; Cmnty Wkr; Hon Rl; Mod UN; NHS; Sch Mus; Stg Crw; IM Sprt; Rotary Awd; YCC 78; Radio WNAS FM 77; Rose Hulman Univ; Elec Engr.

MULLEN, SHEILA; Alter HS; Dayton, OH; 90/270 Chrh Wkr; Hon Rl; Yth Flsp; Spn Clb; Univ; Acctg.

MULLENIX, DEBORAH; Goshen HS; Goshen, OH; Cls Rep Frsh Cls; Chrs; Chrh Wkr; Girl Scts; Off Ade; Red Cr Ade; Sch Mus; Stu Cncl; Yth Flsp; Pep Clb; Finalist In State Final Of The 79 Miss U S Teenage Pagnt 79; Law.

MULLENNEX, TERESA; Harman HS; Job, WV; 4/18 Sec Sr Cls; Band; Chrs; Hon Rl; NHS; Sch Pl; Rptr Yrbk; FFA; Salem Coll; Aviation.

MULLENS, PAM; Shakamak HS; Jasonville, IN; 3/80 VP Frsh Cls; VP Soph Cls; VP Jr Cls; VP Sr Cls; Am Leg Aux Girls St; Treas Chrs; Chrh Wkr; Drl Tm; Hon Rl; Treas NHS; Prom Queen 79; Mbr Of Friendly Grove Gospel Singers 77 79; Voted Mst Depndble By Entire Stu Body 77; ISU; Elem Educ.

MULLER, ANDREA; Paw Paw HS; Pawpaw, MI; Chrs; Girl Scts; Hon Rl; Jr NHS; NHS; Treas 4-H; Treas Spn Clb; Pom Pon; 4-H Awd; Kellogg Comm Coll; Phys Therapy.

MULLET, DAVID; Groveport Madison Sr HS; Columbus, OH; Hon Rl; NHS; Letter Trk; Univ; Archt.

MULLETT, AMY; Magnolia HS; New Martinsvle, WV; Cls Rep Soph Cls; Cmnty Wkr; Girl Scts; Hon Rl; Off Ade; Sct Actv; Stu Cncl; Ten; College; Art.

MULLETT, BRENDA; Magnolia HS; New Martinsvle, WV; Sec Frsh Cls; Cl Rep Jr Cls; Band; Hon Rl; Stu Cncl; FTA; Busns Schl; Sec.

MULLETT, CRAIG; Chippewa HS; Rittman, OH; Am Leg Boys St; Hon Rl; Spn Clb; Letter Ten; Wrstlng; IM Sprt; Univ; Civil Engr.

MULLIGAN, JOSEPH; Theodore Roosevelt HS; Wyandotte, MI; Chrs; Lbry Ade; Red Cr Ade; Sch Mus; Stu Cncl; Drama Clb; Fr Clb; Amer Cancer Soc Stu Against Smoking 78; St Of Mi Cmptn Schlrship 79; Michigan St Univ; Chem.

MULLIGAN, MONICA; St Agatha HS; Detroit, MI; 3/98 Girl Scts; Hon Rl; NHS; Bsbl; Bsktbl; PPFtbl; College; Computer Tech.

MULLIKIN, JOHN; Jennings County HS; No Vernon, IN; Chrs; Sch Mus; Sch Pl; Spn Clb; Ftbl; Wrstlng; Hanover Univ.

MULLIN, JOAN; Carrollton HS; Saginaw, MI; Girl Scts; Hon Rl; DECA; Fr Clb; Bsbl; Crs Cntry; Gym; Mgrs; Delta Mic State Univ; Data Proc.

MULLIN, MARIE; Wayne Memorial HS; Westland, MI; 30/650 Cls Rep Soph Cls; Cl Rep Jr Cls; Trs Sr Cls; Hon Rl; NHS; Sch Nwsp; Letter Ten; Michigan St Univ; Radio Brdcstng.

MULLING, CRAIG; Berea HS; Berea, OH; NHS; Letter Bsbl; Letter Glf; IM Sprt; College; Bus.

MULLINIX, MATT; Princeton HS; Sharonville, OH; 110/651 Chrh Wkr; Hon Rl; Quill & Scroll; Rptr Yrbk; Rptr Sch Nwsp; Sch Nwsp; College; Finance.

MULLINS, ALICIA; Watkins Mem HS; Pataskla, OH; 26/228 Sec Jr Cls; Hon Rl; Stu Cncl; Yrbk; Bsktbl; Gym; Trk; Chrldng; IM Sprt; PPFtbl; COTC; Bus.

MULLINS, CHRISTINA M; Eastern Local HS; Lucasville, OH; Chrs; Chrh Wkr; Cmnty Wkr; Hon Rl; Off Ade; Sch Mus; Sch Pl; Stg Crw; Yrbk; Sch Nwsp; Shawnee St Univ; Respiratory Ther.

MULLINS, CINDY; Bucyrus HS; Bucyrus, OH; Am Leg Aux Girls St; Chrs; Hon Rl; NHS; Stu Cncl; Y-Teens; Fr Clb; Pep Clb;.

MULLINS, CLINTON L; Iaeger HS; Paynesville, WV; Cls Rep Frsh Cls; Am Leg Boys St; Band; Chrs; Hon Rl; Pres Jr NHS; Pres NHS; Off Ade; Pol Wkr; Red Cr Ade; 1st Pl Sci Fairs 77 & 78; French I & French II Awds 78 & 79; Outstndnng Leadrshp & Serv Awd 79; West Virginia Univ; French.

MULLINS, DEBBIE; Iaeger HS; Iaeger, WV; Band; Hon Rl; Sch Mus; Pep Clb; Bsktbl; Letter Trk; IM Sprt; Concord College; Physical Ed.

MULLINS, FRANK; Green HS; N Canton, OH; 17/328 Chrs; Hon Rl; Ed Sch Nwsp; IM Sprt; Univ Of Akron; Law.

MULLINS, JAMES A; Gahanna Lincoln HS; Gahanna, OH; 1/475 Am Leg Boys St; Hon Rl; VP Yth Flsp; Ed Yrbk; Pres Beta Clb; Letter Ftbl; Natl Merit Ltr; Univ Of Ken; Chem.

MULLINS, KATHY; Rock Hill Sr HS; Ironton, OH; Cls Rep Frsh Cls; Cls Rep Soph Cls; Cmp Fr Grls; Girl Scts; Hon Rl; Hosp Ade; Sct Actv; Stu Cncl; Yrbk; FHA; Ashland Cmnty Bus Coll; CPA.

MULLINS, KRISTINA; Willow Run HS; Ypsilanti, MI; 5/200 Cls Rep Frsh Cls; Cls Rep Soph Cls; VP Jr Cls; Hon Rl; NHS; Stu Cncl; Yrbk; Letter Swmmng; Tmr; Rotary Awd; E Michigan St Univ; Med Tech.

MULLINS, MELONEY; Philip Barbour HS; Galloway, WV; Chrh Wkr; Cmnty Wkr; Hon Rl; NHS; Yth Flsp; Drama Clb; Mth Clb; Sunday Schl Tchr; Univ.

MULLINS, REBECCA; Clarenceville HS; Farmington, MI; Band; Girl Scts; Hon Rl; NHS; Sch Mus; Stg Crw; Drama Clb; Leo Clb; Madonna College; Nursing.

MULLINS, STEPHEN; Gallia Academy; Gallipolis, OH; Cls Rep Frsh Cls; VP Soph Cls; Band; Chrs; Sch Mus; Stu Cncl; Key Clb; Pep Clb; Spn Clb; Letter Ten; 1st Team All SEOAL Tennis 77 & 78; 1st Trombn All Oh Readingclinic 78; Univ Of Cincinnati; Music Perfrmnc.

MULLINS, TAMMY; Attica HS; Attica, IN; Girl Scts; Hosp Ade; Sch Pl; Drama Clb; Pep Clb; Letter Bsktbl; Swmmng; Letter Trk; GAA; PPFtbl; Bsktbl Mst Impvd Trophy 77; Bsktbl Mental Attitute; Girls Bsktbl Clinic 78; Summer Swim Tm Mntl Attitude 76; Indiana Voc Tech Schl; Rn.

MULLINS, TAMMY; Baker HS; Fariborn, OH; Chrs; Chrh Wkr; Hon Rl; Quill & Scroll; Rptr Sch Nwsp; PPFtbl; Wright St Univ; Bio.

MULLINS, TERESA; Richmond HS; Richmond, IN; 30/690 Chrs; Chrh Wkr; Hon Rl; JA; NHS; Sch Pl; Y-Teens; Spn Clb; College; Physics.

MULLOOLY, CATHERINE; Lewis Cnty HS; Weston, WV; Pres FCA; Hon Rl; NHS; Bsktbl; PPFtbl; Kiwan Awd; West Virginia Univ; Psych.

MULLOOLY, JOHN; Lewis County HS; Weston, WV; Chrs; FCA; Key Clb; Letter Bsbl; Letter Bsktbl; Coach Actv; Glenville State College; Bus.

MULROONEY, KIM; Wintersville HS; Wintersville, OH; Cls Rep Frsh Cls; Cls Rep Soph Cls; Band; Hosp Ade; Pep Clb; Bsktbl; Trk; Letter Chrldng; GAA; Mat Maids; Softball 1978; Univ; Elem Educ.

MULVAINE, ROBERT; Marion Harding HS; Marion, OH; 1/449 Val; Band; Pres Chrs; NHS; Sch Mus; Sch Pl; Pres Yth Flsp; Pres Drama Clb; Wheaton Coll.

MULVEY, LORI; Wheeling Park HS; Wheeling, WV; Off Ade; Stu Cncl; Y-Teens; Rptr Sch Nwsp; Fr Clb; Chrldng; College; Sec.

MULVEY, MARY E; Magnificat HS; Middleburg Hts, OH; Girl Scts; Hosp Ade; Yrbk; Gym; Chrldng; Coach Actv; Bowling Green; Marketing Research.

MUMAW, CLARK; Northridge HS; Middlebury, IN; 7/160 Chrs; Hon Rl; Yth Flsp; 4-H; Pep Clb; Letter Wrstlng; Goshen Coll.

MUMAW, JOHN; Whetstone HS; Columbus, OH; 34/336 Chrs; Hon Rl; Lbry Ade; Orch; Rptr Sch Nwsp; Spn Clb; Natl Merit SF; Natl Merit Semifinalist; Top 10% Statewide Sci Test; Captain Of Chess Team; Ohio State Univ; Pharmacy.

MUMAW, L ALAN; Orrville HS; Orrville, OH; FCA; Hon Rl; Lat Clb; Swmmng; IM Sprt; Univ Of South Carolina.

MUMPER, LORNA; Loudonville HS; Loudonville, OH; Band; Hon Rl; NHS; Letter Bsktbl; Letter Trk; Trade School; Cosmetology.

MUNAW, LISA V; Grafton HS; Grafton, WV; Hon Rl; NHS; Quill & Scroll; Rptr Yrbk; Yrbk; Ed Sch Nwsp; Sprt Ed Sch Nwsp; Rptr Sch Nwsp; Sch Nwsp; Fr Clb; College; Journalism.

MUNCIE, PEGGY; Staunton HS; Cory, IN; 1/52 Trs Frsh Cls; Val; Chrh Wkr; Hon Rl; NHS; Off Ade; Rptr Sch Nwsp; Olivet Nazarene Coll; Elem Educ.

MUNCY, PAULA; Shelbyville HS; Shelbyville, IN; 49/288 Band; Drl Tm; Drm Bgl; Hon Rl; Sec JA; Lat Clb; Pom Pon; PPFtbl; Univ.

MUNDAY, DONALD; Wood Memorial HS; Oakland City, IN; Boy Scts; Letter Ftbl; Letter Wrstlng; ISU; Auto Engr.

MUNDAY, MICHELLE; Troy HS; Troy, MI; Cls Rep Sr Cls; Chrh Wkr; Hon Rl; NHS; Off Ade; Stu Cncl; Rptr Sch Nwsp; Bsbl; GAA; PPFtbl; Mich; Pre Med.

MUNDAY, SUZANNE; Hilltop HS; W Unity, OH; 3/67 Band; Hon Rl; NHS; Sch Pl; 4-H; Letter Crs Cntry; Letter Trk; 4-H Awd; Pres Awd; Ohio St Univ; Vet.

MUNDORFF, ANDREA; Hoover HS; North Canton, OH; Chrs; Hon Rl; Sch Mus; Pep Clb; Spn Clb; Trk; Scr Kpr; Tmr; Pres Awd; Univ; Acctg.

MUNDSTOCK, MICHELLE; Huntington East HS; Huntington, WV; Lbry Ade; Yth Flsp; DECA; 4-H; FHA; Marshall Univ; Phys Ed.

MUNDY, RHONDA; Meadowdale HS; Dayton, OH; Chrs; NHS; IM Sprt; Most Improved Player Softball; Debutante; Perfect Attendance; Howard Univ; Civil Engr.

MUNGER, JULIE; Penn HS; Mishawaka, IN; Band; Drl Tm; Hon Rl; NHS; Pep Clb; Bsktbl; Letter Trk; Pom Pon; Indiana Univ; Bus Admin.

MUNGER, PAMELA; Fruitport HS; Muskegon, MI; 93/300 Chrs; Hon Rl; PAVAS; Sch Pl; Stg Crw; Drama Clb; Olivet Coll; Music.

MUNGUIA, RANDY; Brother Rice HS; Birmingham, MI; 93/250 Aud/Vis; CAP; Hon Rl; Lbry Ade; Rptr Sch Nwsp; Sch Nwsp; IM Sprt; Congrssnl Nomntn U Smilitary Acad 79; Michigan Compttn Schlshp 79; Cert Of Recgntn Alliance Francaise 79; Michigan St Univ; Cmnctns.

MUNK, MARTHA; Wintersville HS; Stuebnvl, OH; Letter Band; Chrh Wkr; Hosp Ade; Sch Pl; Stg Crw; Yrbk; Drama Clb; Lat Clb; Letter Trk; GAA; Univ; Speech Path.

MUNN, DAVID; Maple Valley HS; Vermontville, MI; 45/121 Cls Rep Soph Cls; Cls Rep Sr Cls; Hon Rl; Sch Pl; Rptr Sch Nwsp; Bsbl; Bsktbl; Capt Crs Cntry; Trk; All Conf Cross Country & Track; Western Michigan Univ; Education.

MUNNING, JOSEPH H; Washington Catholic HS; Washington, IN; 8/65 Am Leg Boys St; Hon Rl; NHS; Stg Crw; Key Clb; Glf; IUPUI; Med.

MUNOZ, ANDREA; Our Lady Of Mercy HS; Southfield, MI; Chrs; Chrh Wkr; Stg Crw; Swmmng; Tmr; Wayne St Univ; Jrnlsm.

MUNOZ, ANNE; Hammond HS; Hammond, IN; Jr NHS; NHS; Sch Pl; Stg Crw; Stu Cncl; Drama Clb; Letter Trk; Am Leg Awd; College; Cmmrcl Art.

MUNRO, DONNA M; East Grand Rapids HS; Grand Rapids, MI; Hon Rl; Lit Mag; Mod UN; Natl Merit Ltr; William James Coll; Writing.

MUNRO, JAMES; James A Garfield HS; Akron, OH; Trs Sr Cls; Cmnty Wkr; FCA; Hon Rl; Lbry Ade; NHS; Lat Clb; Spn Clb; Coach Actv; Scr Kpr; Young Ctzns Awd 77 78 & 79; Univ.

MUNSON, ANDREA; Arthur Hill HS; Saginaw, MI; 3/499 Chrh Wkr; Hon Rl; NHS; Yth Flsp; Pep Clb; Delta College; Dent Hygiene.

MUNSON, MARY; Portland HS; Portland, MI; 1/143 Cls Rep Sr Cls; Val; Hon Rl; NHS; Trk; Bausch & Lomb Awd; Voice Dem Awd; Albion Coll Presidents Schlrshp 79; Rochester Natl Schlrshp 79; State Of Mich Schlrshp 79; Albion Coll; Pre Med.

MUNSON, ROBERT; Strongsville HS; Strongsville, OH; Chrh Wkr; Cmnty Wkr; Hon Rl; Jr NHS; Yth Flsp; IM Sprt; Ohio St Univ; Aeronautics.

MUNSON, SANDRA; Lake Central HS; St John, IN; 35/468 Cls Rep Frsh Cls; NHS; Sch Mus; Y-Teens; OEA; Pep Clb; Chrldng; PPFtbl; Columbia Coll.

MUNZER, DEBBIE; East Clinton HS; Sabina, OH; 23/110 Chrh Wkr; Capt Drl Tm; Hon Rl; Off Ade; Sprt Ed Yrbk; Sec FTA; Mth Clb; Pep Clb; Sci Clb; Eastern Kentucky Univ; Bus Educ.

MURACO, PATRICIA; Kirtland HS; Kirtland, OH; 2/117 Sal; AFS; Cmp Fr Grls; Chrs; Hon Rl; Jr NHS; NHS; Scr Kpr; Am Leg Awd; Bowling Green Univ; Bus Admin.

MURAD, MARK R; Charles F Brush HS; So Euclid, OH; Univ; Elec Engr.

MURATORI, MICHAEL; Reeths Puffer HS; Muskegon, MI; Band; Chrs; Hon Rl; NHS; Ten; Ferris State College; Acctg.

MURAWA, MICHELLE; Benedictine HS; Detroit, MI; 2/173 Sal; Hon Rl; VP NHS; Stu Cncl; Ed Yrbk; Letter Trk; DAR Awd; Lawrence Inst Of Tech; Mech Engr.

MURAWSKI, CHRISTINE C; John R Buchtel HS; Akron, OH; 164/460 Chrs; Hon Rl; Red Cr Ade; Sch Mus; Fr Clb; Pep Clb; PPFtbl; Ricks College; Actrs.

MURAWSKI, DEBORAH; Lamphere HS; Madison Hts, MI; 17/316 Band; Chrs; Hon Rl; NHS; Sch Mus; 4-H; Oakland Univ; Acctg.

MURCHAKE, JENNIFER; Upper Arlington HS; COlumbus, OH; 33/610 VP AFS; Girl Scts; Hon Rl; NHS; Stg Crw; Pep Clb; Spn Clb; Scr Kpr; College; Vet Medicine.

MURCHEK, PAULETTE; Morton Sr HS; Hammond, IN; Chrs; Girl Scts; Hon Rl; Swmmng; Mgrs; Univ.

MURCHLAND, SHARI; Weir Sr HS; Weirton, WV; Cls Rep Soph Cls; Hst Jr Cls; Cl Rep Jr Cls; Hon Rl; Hosp Ade; Stu Cncl; Y-Teens; Pep Clb; Spn Clb; Capt Chrldng; May Ct Attendant; Cheerleader All Four Yrs; Fairmont Coll; Respiratory Therapy.

MURDOCH, CYNTHIA; Cadillac Sr HS; Cadillac, MI; 43/350 Chrh Wkr; Hon Rl; Natl Forn Lg; NHS; Sch Pl; Yrbk; Ed Sch Nwsp; Bsktbl; Letter Trk; GAA; N W Michigan Coll; Marketing.

MURDOCK, KIRA; Forest Park HS; Forest Park, OH; Cls Rep Sr Cls; Chrs; Off Ade; Sch Mus; Stu Cncl; Drama Clb; Ger Clb; Letter Gym; Letter Chrldng; Pres Awd; Nominated For Miss Crescends Cheerleading Camp; Ohio State Univ; Fash Merch.

MURDOCK, RANDY; Anderson HS; Anderson, IN; Quill & Scroll; Rptr Sch Nwsp; Sch Nwsp; Fr Clb; Hoosier Scholar; Youth Reporter Anderson Newspapers; Best News Story & Most Inches Printed; Indiana Univ; Journalism.

MURDOCK, VICKI; Ubly Cmnty Schls; Ubly, MI; 7/403 Hon Rl; Lbry Ade; NHS; Sch Pl; Stg Crw; Stu Cncl; 4-H; Letter Bsktbl; Letter Glf; Letter Wrstlng; Baker Jr Coll; Data Proc.

MURFF, LORRAINE; Martin Luther King HS; Detroit, MI; Cls Rep Frsh Cls; Chrs; Chrh Wkr; FCA; Hon Rl; Stu Cncl; OEA; Ten; Central State Univ; Bsns Admin.

MURFIELD, BRAD; Hayes HS; Delaware, OH; Boy Scts; Chrh Wkr; Hon Rl; Sct Actv; Yth Flsp; Letter Bsbl; Bsktbl; IM Sprt; God Cntry Awd; Cincinnati Bus Schl; Archt.

MURILLO, RUBEN; West Side HS; Gary, IN; Band; Boy Scts; Jr NHS; ROTC; Air Force; Aviation Maintenance.

MURIN, MELISSA; Munster HS; Munster, IN; 35/430 Band; Hon Rl; NHS; Sch Mus; Pep Clb; Letter Gym; Chrldng; Coach Actv; GAA; PPFtbl; Letterwomans Clb; Most Val Gymnast Awd; St Gymnastic Medal Winner; All Conf Gymnast; Indiana Univ; Elem Ed.

MURLEY, S; Our Lady Of Mercy HS; Detroit, MI; Cmnty Wkr; Hon Rl; U Of M Dearborn; Cpa.

MURNEN, BRIAN; Central Catholic HS; Toledo, OH; Boy Scts; Hon Rl; Letter Socr; Univ Of Toledo; Med.

MURNEN, PETER T; St Johns HS; Toledo, OH; PAVAS; Sch Pl; Stu Cncl; Drama Clb; Socr; Wrstlng; Bowling Green St Univ; Communication.

MURNEY, KATHLEEN; Dublin HS; Dublin, OH; 30/157 Cmp Fr Grls; Chrs; Hon Rl; NHS; Sch Mus; Stg Crw; Spn Clb; OSU; Comp Sci.

MURPHY, ANTHONY S; Barr Reeve HS; Montgomery, IN; 1/65 Pres Frsh Cls; Pres Jr Cls; Pres Sr Cls; Val; Am Leg Boys St; Hon Rl; Sch Pl; Stu Cncl; Yrbk; Sprt Ed Sch Nwsp; Univ Of Notre Dame; Engr.

MURPHY, BERNADETTE; Servite HS; Detroit, MI; 45/90 Cmnty Wkr; Hon Rl; NHS; Sch Pl; Drama Clb; Spn Clb; Letter Bsktbl; Mic State Univ; Nursing.

MURPHY, BEULAH; Parkersburg South HS; Parkersburg, WV; Chrs; Chrh Wkr; Hon Rl; Sch Pl; Yth Flsp; DECA; Tech Schl; Nursing.

MURPHY, CAROL; Jane Addams Voc HS; Cleveland, OH; Chrh Wkr; Lbry Ade; FHA; Cit Awd; John Carroll Univ; Comp Sci.

MURPHY, CATHY; Bay City All Saints Ctrl HS; Bay City, MI; Pres Soph Cls; Hon Rl; Red Cr Ade; Stg Crw; Pep Clb; Vc Pres Stdnt Councl 79; Univ; Med.

MURPHY, CATHY; Hurricane HS; Hurricane, WV; Cls Rep Frsh Cls; Pres Soph Cls; Cls Rep Soph Cls; Cl Rep Jr Cls; Cls Rep Sr Cls; Chrh Wkr; Drl Tm; Hon Rl; Treas NHS; Stu Cncl; Marshall Univ; Business.

MURPHY, CHRISTY; Shawe Mem HS; Madison, IN; 2/32 VP Soph Cls; FCA; Hon Rl; Jr NHS; NHS; Rptr Sch Nwsp; Pep Clb; Bsktbl; Coll; Busns.

MURPHY, CINDA; Maple Valley HS; Nashville, MI; 13/138 Hon Rl; NHS; Sch Pl; VP Stu Cncl; Yth Flsp; GAA; 4-H Awd; Natl Merit SF; Lansing Community College;architect.

MURPHY, DEBRA; Pennsboro HS; Pennsboro, WV; Cls Rep Frsh Cls; Am Leg Aux Girls St; Band; Hon Rl; Pres 4-H; FHA; FTA; Bsktbl; GAA; PPFtbl; 2nd Pl St 4 H Competition 78; 4 H Exchange Camper To Va 77; Parkersburg Cmnty Coll; RN.

MURPHY, DENNIS; Moeller HS; Cincinnati, OH; 28/250 Pres Sr Cls; Chrh Wkr; NHS; Off Ade; Sch Mus; Sch Pl; Yrbk; Sch Nwsp; Pep Clb; DAR Awd; Thomas More Coll; Theatre Director.

MURPHY, GERRY; Scecina Memorial HS; Indianapolis, IN; Hon Rl; Ger Clb; Letter Bsbl; Mgrs; Univ; Brdcstng.

MURPHY, JANET; Harry S Truman HS; Taylor, MI; Hon Rl; Sci Clb; Bus Schl; Acctg.

MURPHY, JEAN; Southeast HS; Deerfield, OH; Band; Chrh Wkr; Hon Rl; Jr NHS; NHS; Off Ade; 4-H; Bsktbl; Trk; IM Sprt; Univ; Vet Med.

MURPHY, JEFF; East Clinton HS; Wilmington, OH; 13/103 VP Jr Cls; Pres Band; Hon Rl; NHS; Pres 4-H; Sec FFA; Pep Clb; Sci Clb; Spn Clb; Whos Who In Music; St Farmer Degree; Music Dir Awd; Ohio St Univ; Agri.

MURPHY, JEFF; Tippecanoe Valley HS; Akron, IN; 68/190 Boy Scts; Spn Clb; Bsbl; Bsktbl; Capt Crs Cntry; Ten; Purdue; Banking & Finance.

MURPHY, JOHN; Centerville Sr HS; Centerville, IN; 18/160 Chrs; Jr NHS; Stu Cncl; IM Sprt; Bus Schl; Math.

MURPHY, JULIE; Muskegon HS; Muskegon, MI; Hon Rl; Hosp Ade; NHS; Yrbk; Drama Clb; Fr Clb; Tmr; Am Leg Awd; College; Aviation.

MURPHY, KAREN; Streetsboro HS; Streetsboro, OH; 6/179 AFS; Am Leg Aux Girls St; Hon Rl; NHS; Bsktbl; The Univ Of Akron; Vet Med.

MURPHY, KATHERINE; Bentley HS; Livonia, MI; Cmp Fr Grls; Sec Chrs; Chrh Wkr; Hon Rl; NHS; Sch Mus; Yth Flsp; Alma Coll; Vocal Music.

MURPHY, KATHLEEN; Port Clinton HS; Pt Clinton, OH; Cls Rep Soph Cls; Band; Girl Scts; Stu Cncl; Yth Flsp; Yrbk; 4-H; Ten; Tmr; Univ; Med.

MURPHY, KATHLEEN K; Huron HS; Huron, OH; 15/175 Cls Rep Frsh Cls; Cls Rep Soph Cls; Pres Jr Cls; Pres Sr Cls; Band; Chrs; Hon Rl; Mdrgl; NHS; Sch Mus; Jacksonville Univ; Acctg.

MURPHY, KATHY; Streetsboro HS; Streetsboro, OH; 12/179 AFS; Am Leg Aux Girls St; Hon Rl; NHS; Univ Of Akron; Acctg.

MURPHY, KELLY; Vinton Cnty HS; Mc Arthur, OH; 16/150 Cl Rep Jr Cls; Am Leg Aux Girls St; Band; Chrs; Girl Scts; Hon Rl; Jr NHS; NHS; Yrbk; Rptr Sch Nwsp; Hocking Tech Coll; Exec Sec.

MURPHY, KEVIN; Lake Catholic HS; Painesvl, OH; 54/310 Hon Rl; Letter Bsbl; Letter Ftbl; Letter Wrstlng; Baldwin Wallace Univ; Math.

MURPHY, LEE; Revere HS; Akron, OH; Hon Rl; Ftbl; Akron Univ; Art.

MURPHY, LINN; Claymont HS; Dennison, OH; 34/198 Band; Chrh Wkr; Hon Rl; Jr NHS; NHS; Sch Mus; Sch Pl; Drama Clb; VP FTA; Mas Awd; Kent St Univ; Elem Educ.

MURPHY, LUCINDA; Lincoln HS; Lumberport, WV; 5/150 Cls Rep Frsh Cls; Sec Soph Cls; Cls Rep Soph Cls; Am Leg Aux Girls St; Band; Chrh Wkr; Hon Rl; NHS; Sch Pl; Stu Cncl; Fairmont St Coll; Acctg.

MURPHY, MARY; Gladwin HS; Gladwin, MI; Cls Rep Soph Cls; Trs Jr Cls; Cl Rep Jr Cls; Hon Rl; NHS; Stu Cncl; Bsktbl; Trk; College; Med.

MURPHY, MARY ANNE; Cadillac Sr HS; Cadillac, MI; Hon Rl; Jr NHS; Spn Clb; Trk; Chrldng; Varsity Letter For Cheerleading; Track No & Track Cert 78; Coll; Nursing.

MURPHY, MAUREEN; Clarence M Kimball HS; Royal Oak, MI; Band; Hon Rl; NHS; Off Ade; Stu Cncl; Letter Bsktbl; Letter Trk; IM Sprt; College; Airplane Pilot.

MURPHY, MICHAEL; Kalamazoo Central HS; Kalamazoo, MI; Univ Of Mic; Philology.

MURPHY, MICHAEL; Lasalle HS; Cincinnati, OH; 41/293 Chrh Wkr; Hon Rl; Civ Clb; Letter Socr; Letter Wrstlng; Univ Of Cincinnati; Comp Engr.

MURPHY, MICHELLE; Ottawa Hills HS; Grand Rapids, MI; Cls Rep Frsh Cls; Hon Rl; NHS; Sch Pl; Stg Crw; Drama Clb; Natl Merit Ltr; Univ; Theatre Arts.

MURPHY, MONIQUE; Greenville Sr HS; Greenville, OH; Cls Rep Soph Cls; Hon Rl; NHS; Off Ade; Stu Cncl; Yth Flsp; 4-H; OEA; Spn Clb; Trk; Vocational Schl; Stewardess.

MURPHY, NANCY; Our Lady Of The Elms HS; Medina, OH; Chrh Wkr; Cmnty Wkr; Off Ade; Yth Flsp; Rptr Yrbk; 4-H; 4-H Awd; Univ; Sociology.

MURPHY, PAMELA; Shawe Memorial HS; Madison, IN; 1/34 Am Leg Aux Girls St; FCA; Girl Scts; Hon Rl; Jr NHS; NHS; Rptr Sch Nwsp; 4-H; Pep Clb; Chrldng; Univ; Bus.

MURPHY, PATRICIA; Akron Central Hower HS; Akron, OH; Band; Chrs; Hon Rl; Jr NHS; Orch; PAVAS; Sch Mus; Sch Pl; Stg Crw; Pep Clb; Akron Univ; Theater.

MURPHY, PATRICIA; Wheeling Central Cath HS; Wheeling, WV; Hon Rl; Business Schl; Court Reporter.

MURPHY, PATRICIA A; Franklin HS; Franklin, WV; Cls Rep Soph Cls; Chrh Wkr; Hon Rl; NHS; Stu Cncl; FHA; Pep Clb; Swmmng; Letter Chrldng; IM Sprt; College; Journalism.

MURPHY, PATRICK; East Kentwood HS; Kentwood, MI; 21/416 Hon Rl; NHS; Hockey; Coach Actv; Mgrs; Cit Awd; Ferris State Coll; Acctg.

MURPHY, PATRICK; Defiance HS; Defiance, OH; Hon Rl; Jr NHS; Bsbl; Ftbl; Wrstlng; College; Sec Educ.

MURPHY, PATTY; Eastern HS; Stanford, IN; Cls Rep Frsh Cls; Band; Chrs; Chrh Wkr; Stu Cncl; Yth

Flsp; Pep Clb; Bsktbl; GAA; Pom Pon; Vincense Univ; Bus.

MURPHY, RICHARD L; Moeller HS; Cincinnati, OH; 20/300 Hon Rl; Letter Glf; Letter Swmmng; St Of Oh Distinction 79; Louisiana St Univ; Sci.

MURPHY, SANDRA; Groveport Madison Sr HS; Obetz, OH; Band; Cmp Fr Grls; Hon Rl; Fr Clb; Scr Kpr; Tmr; Ohio St Univ; Poli Sci.

MURPHY, SHAROLYN; Woodrow Wilson HS; Youngstwn, OH; 1/350 Am Leg Aux Girls St; Chrs; Chrh Wkr; Hon Rl; JA; Jr NHS; Stg Crw; Yth Flsp; Capt Chrldng; College; Psych.

MURPHY, THOMAS; Oakwood HS; Dayton, OH; Band; Boy Scts; Chrh Wkr; Sct Actv; Yth Flsp; Pres 4-H; Rdo Clb; Crs Cntry; Letter Trk; College; Engr Mgmt.

MURPHY, W; Albion HS; Albion, MI; Chrh Wkr; Hon Rl; Natl Forn Lg; Red Cr Ade; Yth Flsp; Letter Ten; Letter Wrstlng; JA Awd; Coll; Elec Engr.

MURR, DAVE; Springboro HS; Springboro, OH; Hon Rl; Letter Ftbl; Letter Trk; IM Sprt; Cumberland Coll.

MURR, KENDRA; Memorial HS; St Marys, OH; 63/220 Cmnty Wkr; Hon Rl; Y-Teens; Pep Clb; Treas Spn Clb; GAA; IM Sprt; Rainbow Past Worthy Advisor; Rainbow Grand Prompter In Ohio Grand Assembly; College; Sec.

MURRAY, AMY; Plainwell HS; Plainwell, MI; Sec Frsh Cls; Sec Jr Cls; Sec Sr Cls; Band; Hon Rl; NHS; Ed Yrbk; Rptr Yrbk; Yrbk; Spn Clb; Notre Dame; Chem.

MURRAY, ANDY; Tuscarawas Valley HS; Bolivar, O H; 1/138 Hon Rl; NHS; Capt Bsktbl; Bausch & Lomb Awd; Cls Valedictrn 79; Schlst Awd 4th Yr 79; Akron Univ; Engr.

MURRAY, BRIAN; South Dearborn HS; Dillsboro, IN; 16/260 Band; Chrs; Chrh Wkr; Hon Rl; NHS; Sch Mus; Sch Pl; Stu Cncl; Drama Clb; Sci Clb; Univ; Law.

MURRAY, B S; Reitz Memorial HS; Evansville, IN; 14/253 Pep Clb; Trk; Pom Pon; Cit Awd; College.

MURRAY, CAROLYN; Pershing HS; Detroit, MI; Hon Rl; JA; NHS; Eng Clb; Cit Awd; ; Stenographer.

MURRAY, CHRISTINA; La Ville Jr Sr HS; Bremen, IN; 12/130 Chrs; Chrh Wkr; Mdrgl; NHS; Sch Mus; Stg Crw; Rptr Yrbk; Yrbk; Rptr Sch Nwsp; Sch Nwsp; Indiana Univ; Music.

MURRAY, DAVID; Central Preston Sr HS; Tunnelton, WV; Band; Hon Rl; Mth Clb; Sci Clb; Univ; Elec Engr.

MURRAY, JACQUELINE; Warren Central HS; Indpls, IN; 34/768 Cl Rep Jr Cls; Band; Girl Scts; Hon Rl; Jr NHS; NHS; Off Ade; Stg Crw; Stu Cncl; Drama Clb; Part In Natl Leadrshp Conf 79; 4 Tim St Jr Judo Champ 75 78; Indiana Univ; Pre Med.

MURRAY, JACQUELINE; Western Reserve HS; Norwalk, OH; 5/108 VP Soph Cls; Trs Jr Cls; Band; Chrh Wkr; Hon Rl; NHS; Spn Clb; N Central Tech Coll; Radiology.

MURRAY, JAMES; Creston HS; Grand Rapads, MI; FCA; Hon Rl; Jr NHS; NHS; Ger Clb; Letter Ftbl; Letter Hockey; Natl Merit SF; Michigan St Univ; Busns.

MURRAY, JO DEE; South Knox HS; Vincennes, IN; Drl Tm; Girl Scts; Hon Rl; Off Ade; Red Cr Ade; Yth Flsp; Treas 4-H; Pres FHA; FNA; OEA; Vincennes Univ; Fashion Mdse.

MURRAY, JULIE; New Lexington Sr HS; New Lexington, OH; 41/140 Chrs; Hon Rl; Lbry Ade; NHS; Off Ade; Sch Mus; Yrbk; FHA; Pep Clb; Ohio Uni; Acctg.

MURRAY, KATHRYN; Elyria Catholic HS; Elyria, OH; 3/188 Cls Rep Soph Cls; Trs Jr Cls; Am Leg Aux Girls St; VP Chrs; Hon Rl; Jr NHS; Sch Mus; Sch Pl; Stu Cncl; Rptr Yrbk; Univ Of Dayton.

MURRAY, KELVIN; John Marshall HS; Indianapolis, IN; Hon Rl; Beta Clb; DECA; Univ; Aero Engr.

MURRAY, KENNETH; Penn HS; Osceola, IN; 133/467 Aud/Vis; Cmnty Wkr; Hon Rl; Ger Clb; Letter Glf; IM Sprt; Tmr; Indiana Univ; Engr.

MURRAY, LISA; Gallia Academy; Gallipolis, OH; Cmnty Wkr; Hon Rl; Stu Cncl; 4-H; Fr Clb; OEA; 4-H Awd; Busns Schl; Sec.

MURRAY, LISA; Marian HS; Birmingham, MI; Cls Rep Frsh Cls; Sec Soph Cls; Cl Rep Jr Cls; Hon Rl; JA; Lit Mag; Stu Cncl; Fr Clb; IM Sprt; Mgrs; Univ Of Michigan; Bus.

MURRAY, M ARLA; De Kalb HS; Auburn, IN; 3/279 Band; Chrs; Chrh Wkr; Cmnty Wkr; Hon Rl; Lbry Ade; NHS; Yth Flsp; Treas Ger Clb; Designate From De Kalb In Congressional Stu Prog; Tri Kappa Scholastic Awd; College; Elem Ed.

MURRAY, MARYANN; Howell HS; Howell, MI; Hon Rl; Lit Mag; NHS; Yrbk; 4-H; Letter Ten; 4-H Awd; Univ; Art.

MURRAY, MICHAEL D; Morton Sr HS; Schererville, IN; 23/436 Cls Rep Soph Cls; VP Sr Cls; Am Leg Boys St; Hon Rl; Jr NHS; Quill & Scroll; Sch Nwsp; Bsktbl; Dnfth Awd; Ball State Univ; Journalism.

MURRAY, MICHELLE; River Rouge HS; River Rouge, MI; 28/200 Chrh Wkr; Drl Tm; Hon Rl; Lbry Ade; Off Ade; ROTC; FBLA; FHA; OEA; Spn Clb; Henry Ford Cmnty Coll; Bus Admin.

MURRAY, PHILLIP; Madison Plains HS; Mt Sterling, OH; Am Leg Boys St; Band; Debate Tm; Hon Rl; Mod UN; NHS; Sch Nwsp; Sci Clb; Letter Bsbl; Letter Ftbl; College; Elec.

MURRAY, RENEE; Tippecanoe Valley HS; Rochester, IN; 8/158 Chrs; Chrh Wkr; Drl Tm; Hon Rl; NHS; Yrbk; 4-H; Pom Pon; 4-H Awd; Manchester Coll; Acctg.

MURRAY, SCOTT; Bentley HS; Burton, MI; Am Leg Boys St; Hon Rl; NHS; Letter Bsbl; Letter Ftbl; Univ; Dentistry.

MURRAY, SHARON; Field HS; Kent, OH; Band; Girl Scts; Hon Rl; Hosp Ade; NHS; Sch Mus; Spn Clb; Letter Bsktbl; Letter Crs Cntry; Kent State Univ; Vet.

MURRAY, SUSAN; Buckeye West HS; Mt Pleasant, OH; 13/85 Chrh Wkr; Cmnty Wkr; Girl Scts; Hon Rl; Off Ade; FHA; OEA; Bus Schl.

MURRAY, T; Delphi Community HS; Delphi, IN; Boy Scts; Chrh Wkr; 4-H; Pep Clb; Spn Clb; Letter Bsbl; Letter Crs Cntry; IM Sprt; 4-H Awd; College; Engr.

MURRAY, TERRI; Piketon HS; Piketon, OH; Band; Chrs; Cmnty Wkr; Hon Rl; Lbry Ade; Sch Mus; Stg Crw; 4-H; FTA; Pep Clb; Ohio St Univ; Jrnlsm.

MURRAY, TIMOTHY; Bark River Harris HS; Bark River, MI; VP Frsh Cls; Band; Boy Scts; Chrh Wkr; Hon Rl; JA; NHS; Baydenoc Comm College; Elec Engr.

MURRELL, MARY ANN; Whitehall HS; Whitehall, MI; Band; Girl Scts; Hon Rl; Off Ade; Mat Maids; Mic State.

MURTHA, MICHAEL; Sault Area HS & Skill Ctr; Sault Ste Marie, MI; Hon Rl; Ftbl; Trk; Univ; Law.

MURTHA, THOMAS; Ursuline HS; Youngstown, OH; 23/360 Debate Tm; Hon Rl; Lbry Ade; Lit Mag; Natl Forn Lg; NHS; Sch Nwsp; Ger Clb; Trk; Urban Planning.

MURTHY, KALPANA; Worthington HS; Worthington, OH; 14/575 Cl Rep Jr Cls; Am Leg Aux Girls St; Hon Rl; Hosp Ade; NHS; Sch Pl; Drama Clb; Spn Clb; Vanderbilt Univ; Bus.

MURTIFF, TRACEE; Delta Sr HS; Delta, OH; Sec Soph Cls; Band; Stu Cncl; Rptr Yrbk; Yrbk; 4-H; Spn Clb; 4-H Awd; Toledo Univ; CPA.

MUSACCHIA, BETH; Fairless HS; Brewster, OH; 17/215 Cls Rep Frsh Cls; Cls Rep Soph Cls; Cl Rep Jr Cls; Cls Rep Sr Cls; Am Leg Aux Girls St; Chrs; Hon Rl; Jr NHS; Sec NHS; Stu Cncl; Historian Varsity F Club 78; Univ; Bus Admin.

MUSCAT, TERESE; Our Lady Of The Lakes HS; Clarkston, MI; Sec Frsh Cls; Pres Jr Cls; Hon Rl; Sch Clb; Bsbl; Bsktbl; Michigan St Univ; Psys Therapy.

MUSCOTT, DEBORAH; Vestaburg Cmnty HS; Riverdale, MI; Chrs; Hon Rl; Jr NHS; Off Ade; Sch Mus; Sch Pl; Yrbk; Drama Clb; FHA; Bus Schl; Sec.

MUSE, YVONNE S; Tri Valley HS; Trinway, OH; 23/280 Sec Band; Girl Scts; Hon Rl; Sch Pl; Stg Crw; Yth Flsp; Yrbk; Drama Clb; VP 4-H; Pres FHA; High Scorer/marine Crps Phys Fittness Test; Univ Of Hawaii; Interior Decorator.

MUSGRAVE, JEFFERY; Carey HS; Carey, OH; VP Jr Cls; Am Leg Boys St; Hon Rl; NHS; Sch Pl; Y-Teens; VP Spn Clb; College; Coaching Sports.

MUSGRAVE, MARK; Hayes HS; Delaware, OH; Am Leg Boys St; Band; Hon Rl; Orch; Sch Mus; Letter Socr; Trk; Mgrs; PTSA Instum Music Awd 77; Selctd To All St Concert Band Of Ny 77; Awd For Otstndng Part In Phys Educ 77; Univ; Bio.

MUSGRAVE, TAMMY; Jasper HS; Jasper, IN; Girl Scts; Hon Rl; Hosp Ade; Lbry Ade; 4-H; Pep Clb; IM Sprt; Bus Schl; Bus.

MUSGROVE, GINA; Williamsburg HS; Williamsburg, OH; 25/95 Chrs; Chrh Wkr; Drl Tm; Girl Scts; Hon Rl; Sch Mus; Stg Crw; Yth Flsp; Drama Clb; VP Sci Clb; Univ Of Cincinnati; Med.

MUSIC, LOLA; Crestline HS; Crestline, OH; 38/118 VP Soph Cls; Pres Jr Cls; Pres Sr Cls; Hon Rl; 4-H; VICA; Bsktbl; Trk; Chrldng; Cit Awd; Mansfield Branch Univ; Phys Educ.

MUSICK, DOUGLAS; Watkins Memorial HS; Pataskala, OH; 16/209 Pres Sr Cls; Hon Rl; Pres NHS; Sch Pl; Drama Clb; Fr Clb; Nancys Flower Shop 300 Dollar Schlrshp 79; St Board Of Educ Awd Of Distinction; Ohio St Univ; Broadcast Jrnlsm.

MUSICK, JEFF; Fairborn Baker HS; Dayton, OH; Hon Rl; Letter Bsbl; Coach Actv; Miami Univ.

MUSROCK, WILLIAM; Valley HS; Hastings, WV; Hst Jr Cls; Boy Scts; Chrh Wkr; Hon Rl; NHS; Sch Pl; Yrbk; Letter Bsktbl; Letter Ftbl; Letter Trk; RESA VI Math & Sci Summr Cmp 78; Stu Of The Mnth 76; Mech Drawing Awd 77; West Virginia Tech Univ; Elec Engr.

MUSSELMAN, BEVERLY; Westfall HS; Orient, OH; Band; Cmnty Wkr; Hon Rl; Jr NHS; NHS; Orch; 4-H; FNA; Spn Clb; Letter Trk;.

MUSSELMAN, KRISS A; Charlotte HS; Charlotte, MI; 69/304 Band; Boy Scts; Off Ade; Sprt Ed Yrbk; Rptr Yrbk; 4-H; Ftbl; Glf; 4-H Awd; Golf Acad; Arnold Palmer Golf Acad; Schl Photog; Ferris St Coll; Busns Mgmt.

MUSSER, DARLENE; Wapakoneta Sr HS; Wapakoneta, OH; Chrs; Chrh Wkr; Girl Scts; Pres Quill & Scroll; Sch Mus; Yth Flsp; Y-Teens; Yrbk; Sch Nwsp; Lat Clb; Coll; Child Psych.

MUSSER, DENISE; Norton HS; Norton, OH; 85/325 Cl Rep Jr Cls; Band; Cmp Fr Grls; Chrh Wkr; Cmnty Wkr; Girl Scts; Hon Rl; Hosp Ade; JA; Quill & Scroll; Ohio St Univ.

MUSSER, NANCY; Pine River HS; Luther, MI; VP Jr Cls; Hon Rl; NHS; Fr Clb; Letter Bsktbl; Trk; College.

MUSSER, RENE; Bishop Foley HS; Troy, MI; 25/195 Chrs; Hon Rl; NHS; Pep Clb; Gym; Letter Trk; Letter Chrldng; Tmr; Wayne St Univ; Phys Ther.

MUSSER, STEPHEN; Padua Franciscan HS; Cleveland, OH; Chrh Wkr; Hon Rl; Ger Clb; Sci Clb; Ftbl; PPFtbl; Heidelberg Coll; Pre Dent.

MUSSER, SUSAN; Utica HS; Sterling Hts, MI; 96/395 Hon Rl; Off Ade; Pep Clb; Gym; Letter Swmmng; Tmr; Univ; Psych.

MUSSO, PAUL; Padua Franciscan HS; Brook Pk, OH; Hon Rl; Bsbl; Letter Wrstlng; High Hons 78; Univ; Bus Admin.

MUSTER, KELLIE; Thomas W Harvey HS; Canton, OH; 14/167 Chrs; Hon Rl; NHS; Bsktbl; Ten; Mgrs; Tmr; Am Leg Awd; Cit Awd; Harriet B Stove Schlrshp 79; PTA Schlrshp 79; Bowling Green St Univ; Bus.

MUSZYNSKI, THOMAS; Manister Cath Ctrl HS; Manistee, MI; Band; Hon Rl; NHS; Mgrs;.

MUTERSPAW, LISA; Springboro HS; Springboro, OH; Lbry Ade; NHS; Sch Pl; Rptr Yrbk; Drama Clb; 4-H; Letter Bsktbl; 4-H Awd; Univ.

MUTH, SHARI; Grandview Heights HS; Columbus, OH; 2/125 Girl Scts; Hon Rl; Jr NHS; NHS; Sci Clb; Letter Ten; Letter Chrldng; College; Med.

MUTH, TERESA; St Joseph HS; St Joseph, MI; Cls Rep Sr Cls; Chrs; Lit Mag; NHS; Quill & Scroll; Yrbk; Sch Nwsp; S W Michigan Coll; Bus Admin.

MUTSCHLER, JACQUELINE; Tecumseh HS; New Carlisle, OH; 1/400 Cls Rep Frsh Cls; AFS; Am Leg Aux Girls St; Chrs; Drl Tm; Hon Rl; Jr NHS; NHS; Sch Pl; Stu Cncl; Clark Cnty Sci Fair Supr Rating 76; Ohio Test Of Schlrshp Achvmnt Team 77 & 78; Schl & Cnty Sci Fair Judge; Wright St Univ; Archaeology.

MUTSKO, DEBORAH; St Ursula Acad; Toledo, OH; Cl Rep Jr Cls; Chrs; Hon Rl; Stu Cncl; Ed Sch Nwsp; Rptr Sch Nwsp; IM Sprt; Univ Of Toledo; Bus Mgmt.

MUZIO, NANCY; Cuyahoga Vlly Christian Acad; Akron, OH; Sec Jr Cls; Band; Drl Tm; Hon Rl; VP NHS; Orch; Stu Cncl; Yth Flsp; Scr Kpr; Natl Merit Ltr; Univ; Engr.

MUZZIN, MICHAEL; Northville HS; Northville, MI; Socr; Coach Actv; Stud Life Schlrshp 79; Oakland Univ; Mech Engr.

MYAARD, BRUCE; Grand Haven Sr HS; Spring Lake, MI; Chrh Wkr; Hon Rl; Ftbl; Capt Wrstlng; IM Sprt; St Of Mi Compttv Awd 79; Western Michigan Univ; Elec Engr.

MYATT, FRANKLIN J; Northrop HS; Ft Wayne, IN; VP Frsh Cls; Cls Rep Soph Cls; Cl Rep Jr Cls; Cls Rep Sr Cls; Band; Boy Scts; Chrs; Chrh Wkr; Cmnty Wkr; Stu Cncl; Ind Univ; Fine Arts.

MYATT, GREGORY; Brandon HS; Ortonville, MI; Univ Of Mi Rgnts Alumni Schlr 79; Brandon Achvmnt Awd For Soc Studies 79; Nominated For The Natl Hnr Soc 78; Univ Of Michigan; Acctg.

MYCHALCZAK, ROMA; Immaculate Conception HS; Warren, MI; Sec Jr Cls; Cls Rep Sr Cls; Chrs; Girl Scts; Hon Rl; NHS; Stu Cncl; Rptr Yrbk; Rptr Sch Nwsp; Chrldng; Wayne St Univ; Med.

MYER, ERIC; Notre Dame HS; Bridgeport, WV; 9/54 Boy Scts; Sct Actv; Univ.

MYER, TAMMA; Dansville Agricultural HS; Mason, MI; Hon Rl; Off Ade; Sch Pl; Yrbk; 4-H; FHA; Spn Clb; Bsktbl; Letter Trk; 4-H Awd; Michigan St Univ; Psych.

MYERS, ALICE; Clarksville HS; Clarksville, TN; Cl Rep Jr Cls; Cls Rep Sr Cls; Chrs; VP FCA; Stu Cncl; Fr Clb; Mth Clb; Letter Trk; Chrldng; Univ Of Ten; Med.

MYERS, AMY; Ravenna HS; Ravenna, OH; 38/313 Cls Rep Soph Cls; Cl Rep Jr Cls; Band; Hon Rl; Hosp Ade; Jr NHS; NHS; Off Ade; Quill & Scroll; Stu Cncl; Mary Mason Schlrshp Eng Excllnc 79; Principals Awd Serv 79; Oh Bd Of Regents Acad Schlrshp Prog 79; Bowling Green St Univ; Spec Educ.

MYERS, ANNE; Willard HS; Willard, OH; Drl Tm; Hon Rl; Hosp Ade; VP Stu Cncl; Ed Yrbk; Sprt Ed Yrbk; Letter Bsktbl; Letter Ten; Letter Trk; IM Sprt;.

MYERS, ANTHONY; Forest Park HS; Crystal Falls, MI; 2/79 Sal; Chrh Wkr; Hon Rl; Boys Clb Am; Pres 4-H; Letter Ftbl; IM Sprt; Dnfth Awd; 4-H Awd; Michigan Tech Coll; Bio Sci.

MYERS, BARBARA; Canton South HS; Canton, OH; 1/300 Cls Rep Soph Cls; Am Leg Aux Girls St; Hon Rl; Jr NHS; NHS; Lat Clb; Mth Clb; Univ; Architecture.

MYERS, BETH; Roscommon HS; Roscommon, MI; 7/120 Band; Chrs; Chrh Wkr; Girl Scts; Lbry Ade; NHS; Orch; Sch Mus; Sch Pl; Sct Actv; Cntrl Michigan Univ.

MYERS, BRAD; West Washington HS; Campbellsbg, IN; 5/96 NHS; FFA; Bsktbl; Trk; DAR Awd;.

MYERS, BRAD A; Miami Valley HS; Dayton, OH; VP Chrh Wkr; Cmnty Wkr; Hockey; Socr; Ten; Natl Merit SF; College.

MYERS, BRET S; Washington HS; Washington, IN; Chrs; Chrh Wkr; Hon Rl; Treas Yth Flsp; Letter Crs Cntry; Letter Trk; Capt IM Sprt; College; Ministry.

MYERS, BRIAN; North Newton HS; Morocco, IN; 2/240 Hon Rl; NHS; 4-H; Lat Clb; Purdue Univ; Animal Sci.

MYERS, BRIAN; Hopkins HS; Dorr, MI; 1/90 Pres Soph Cls; Cls Rep Soph Cls; Pres Sr Cls; Hon Rl; Jr NHS; Pres NHS; Treas FFA; Letter Bsbl; Letter Ftbl; IM Sprt; Michigan St Univ; Engr.

MYERS, CAROLYN; Fairfield Union HS; Pleasantville, OH; 25/158 Band; Hon Rl; Jr NHS; Yth Flsp; FDA; FTA; Sec Spn Clb; Ohio State Univ; Elem Ed.

MYERS, CARRIE S; Madison Comprehensive HS; Mansfield, OH; Cl Rep Jr Cls; Band; Chrh Wkr; Girl Scts; Sch Pl; 4-H; Spn Clb; Trk; 4-H Awd; Coll; Agri.

MYERS, CHRISTIE; Zanesville HS; Znaesville, OH; Chrs; Girl Scts; Hon Rl; Sch Mus; Lat Clb; Bsktbl; Chrldng; Central State; Math.

MYERS, CHRISTINA; Greensburg Comm HS; Greensburg, IN; 27/200 Cl Rep Jr Cls; Cls Rep Sr Cls; Band; Cmp Fr Grls; Chrh Wkr; FCA; Hon Rl; NHS; PAVAS; Sec Stu Cncl; College.

MYERS, CHRISTOPHER; Dunbar HS; Dunbar, WV; Cls Rep Soph Cls; Band; Hon Rl; Rptr Sch Nwsp; Crs Cntry; Trk; IM Sprt; Univ; Restaurant Mgmt.

MYERS, C JEFF; Attica Jr Sr HS; Attica, IN; 4/87 Cls Rep Soph Cls; Cl Rep Jr Cls; Cls Rep Sr Cls; Hon Rl; NHS; Pres Stu Cncl; Yth Flsp; Rptr Sch Nwsp; Letter Bsbl; Letter Bsktbl; Ball St Univ.

MYERS, DALE; Vandercook Lake HS; Jackson, MI; 4/94 Hon Rl; Lbry Ade; NHS; Sch Pl; Pres Stu Cncl; Treas Yth Flsp; Letter Bsktbl; Letter Ftbl; Trk; Univ; Pre Med.

MYERS, DAVID; Winfield HS; Scott Depot, WV; Boy Scts; Chrs; Pres JA; Sct Actv; Letter Ftbl; Letter Trk; Mas Awd; Coll.

MYERS, DEANA; Shelbyville HS; Indianapolis, IN; Girl Scts; Hon Rl; Off Ade; DECA; Pep Clb; PPFtbl; Fashion Mdse.

MYERS, DEBBIE; Highland HS; Hinckley, OH; 40/207 Band; Chrs; Hosp Ade; Akron Univ; Nurse.

MYERS, DEBORAH; Tuslaw HS; N Lawrence, OH; 3/181 Band; Chrs; Hon Rl; NHS; Sch Mus; Ed Yrbk; FNA; FTA; Twrlr; Lion Awd; Stark Tech Coll; Med Asst.

MYERS, DEREK; Tri Valley HS; Frazeysburg, OH; 14/220 Sec Frsh Cls; Trs Soph Cls; Trs Jr Cls; Trs Sr Cls; NHS; Pres 4-H; Pres Lat Clb; Letter Ftbl; Letter Wrstlng; College.

MYERS, DEREK D; Tri Valley HS; Frazeysburg, OH; Sec Frsh Cls; Trs Soph Cls; Trs Jr Cls; Hon Rl; Yth Flsp; 4-H; Lat Clb; Letter Ftbl; Letter Wrstlng; 4-H Awd; Univ; Math.

MYERS, DIANE; Sand Creek HS; Adrian, MI; Sec Sr Cls; Hon Rl; NHS; Sch Pl; Rptr Yrbk; 4-H; 4-H Awd; Natl Merit Ltr; Siena Hts Coll.

MYERS, DOUGLAS; Sycamore HS; Cincinnati, OH; Boy Scts; Hon Rl; Off Ade; Sct Actv; Yth Flsp; Sch Nwsp; Key Clb; Lat Clb; Mth Clb; College; Engr.

MYERS, DOUGLAS G; Rose D Warwick HS; Tekonsha, MI; Band; Hon Rl; Stg Crw; 4-H; Pep Clb; Ftbl; Mgrs; 4-H Awd; Mic State Univ; Agri.

MYERS, FRANK; Attica HS; Attica, IN; 5/80 Cls Rep Soph Cls; Cl Rep Jr Cls; Cls Rep Sr Cls; Am Leg Boys St; Hon Rl; NHS; Glf; Ten; IM Sprt; Mgrs; Rose Hulman Inst Of Tech; Civil Engr.

MYERS, GENA; North Marion HS; Farmington, WV; Band; Hon Rl; Hosp Ade; NHS; Y-Teens; Ed Yrbk; 4-H; Fr Clb; Trk; West Virginia Univ; Phys Ther.

MYERS, GRANT; Prairie Hts HS; Angola, IN; Band; Sch Mus; Sch Pl; Stg Crw; Stu Cncl; Drama Clb; Tri St Univ; Acctg.

MYERS, GREGORY; Cambridge HS; Cambridge, OH; Hon Rl; VICA; Wrstlng; Univ.

MYERS, HOWARD; Euclid HS; Euclid, OH; Cls Rep Frsh Cls; Cmnty Wkr; Hon Rl; Off Ade; Y-Teens; Letter Bsbl; Letter Wrstlng; Letter Mgrs; Pres Awd; Ohio State Univ; Law.

MYERS, JACQUELINE; Marshall HS; Marshall, MI; Hon Rl; Off Ade; Yth Flsp; 4-H; Spn Clb; 4-H Awd; Western Michigan Univ; Bus.

MYERS, JAMES; Bethel Local HS; Tipp Cty, OH; 12/100 Chrs; Hon Rl; Sch Mus; Fr Clb; Letter Ftbl; Univ.

MYERS, JAMES R; Archbishop Hoban HS; Akron, OH; 2/165 Chrh Wkr; Hon Rl; NHS; Sch Pl; Stg Crw; Ed Sch Nwsp; Crs Cntry; IM Sprt; Am Leg Awd; Natl Merit SF; Univ Of Akron; Chem Engr.

MYERS, JANICE; Seton HS; Cincinnati, OH; 37/271 Cl Rep Jr Cls; Cls Rep Sr Cls; Girl Scts; Hon Rl; JA; NHS; Stu Cncl; Pres Lat Clb; Pep Clb; GAA; Univ Of Cin; Pre Pharmacy.

MYERS, JEFF; Columbus E Sr HS; Columbus, IN; Chrs; Hon Rl; Lbry Ade; Off Ade; DECA; DECA Comp 1st Pl Dist & St 1978; Outstnd Jr D E Student Chapter 1978; DECA Natl Career Devpmnt Expost Pa; Northwood Inst; Resteraunt Mgr.

MYERS, JEFF; Attica Jr Sr HS; Attica, IN; 4/74 Hon Rl; NHS; Stu Cncl; Rptr Sch Nwsp; FTA; Bsbl; Bsktbl; Ftbl; Am Leg Awd; Hanover Coll; Law.

MYERS, JEFFREY W; North Knox HS; Freelandville, IN; 15/154 Chrh Wkr; Cmnty Wkr; FCA; Hon Rl; NHS; Treas Yth Flsp; 4-H; Letter Bsbl; Letter Bsktbl; Letter Crs Cntry; Vincennes Univ; Bldg Tech.

MYERS, JEFFRY A; St Joseph HS; Mayfield Vlg, OH; 26/290 Aud/Vis; Band; Boy Scts; Chrh Wkr; Hon Rl; Lbry Ade; Lit Mag; NHS; Rptr Sch Nwsp; IM Sprt; John Carroll Univ; Bus.

MYERS, JOHN; Gallia Academy HS; Gallipolis, OH; Muskingum Univ; Radiologist Tech.

MYERS, JOHN; St Peters HS; Mansfield, OH; Spn Clb; IM Sprt; Bus Schl; Bus.

MYERS, JONATHAN; Whitko HS; S Whitley, IN; 5/146 Cls Rep Sr Cls; Am Leg Boys St; Chrs; VP Natl Forn Lg; Treas NHS; Stu Cncl; Pres Ger Clb; Pres Sci Clb; Letter Bsktbl; Mgrs; Univ Of Notre Dame; Internatl Law.

MYERS, JOY; Bowling Green HS; Bowling Green, OH; 74/325 Cls Rep Sr Cls; Jr NHS; Stg Crw; Rptr Sch Nwsp; Drama Clb; Sci Clb; Bsktbl; Ohio State Univ; Aeronautical.

MYERS, KELLEY; Meridian HS; Sanford, MI; 21/149 Chrs; Girl Scts; Hon Rl; Hosp Ade; Sch Mus; Sct Actv; Fr Clb; FHA; Pep Clb; College.

MYERS, KELLY; Madison Heights HS; Anderson, IN; Cl Rep Jr Cls; Chrs; FCA; Hon Rl; Spn Clb; Letter Ten; Ball State Univ; Secretary.

MYERS, KIM; North Miami HS; Denver, IN; Pres Frsh Cls; Pres Soph Cls; Chrs; Hon Rl; MMM; Drama Clb; Pep Clb; Spn Clb; Letter Chrldng; Mat Maids; Prudue Univ.

MYERS, LORENA; Pleasant HS; Marion, OH; Band; Drl Tm; Hon Rl; Yth Flsp; Rptr Sch Nwsp; Drama Clb; 4-H; Sci Clb; IM Sprt; Pom Pon; Ohio St Univ.

MYERS, LYNN; Liberty Center HS; Liberty Ctr, OH; 18/70 Band; Chrh Wkr; Hon Rl; Off Ade; Red Cr Ade; Stu Cncl; Yth Flsp; Rptr Sch Nwsp; Sch Nwsp; FTA; Northwest Tech Coll; Exec Sec.

MYERS, LYNNE; Anderson HS; Anderson, IN; 18/430 Drm Bgl; Drm Mjrt; Hon Rl; Hosp Ade; NHS; Off Ade; FHA; Spn Clb; Purdue Univ; Speech Ther.

MYERS, MARTIN; Lakeland Christian Acad; Pierceton, IN; Band; Chrs; Chrh Wkr; Drm Bgl; Pol Wkr; Rptr Sch Nwsp; Fr Clb; Purdue; Accounting.

MYERS, MARTIN H; Beachwood HS; Beachwood, OH; Cls Rep Frsh Cls; Pres Soph Cls; Pres Jr Cls; Pres Sr Cls; Debate Tm; Natl Forn Lg; NHS; Sch Mus; Sch Pl; Stg Crw; Acad Challenge 78; 3rd Pl Inoh 2n 4 Man Debt 79; 1 Star Thepian 79; Case Western Reserve Univ; Law.

MYERS, MARY; Willard HS; Willard, OH; Band; Bsktbl; Crs Cntry; Trk; GAA; Elk Awd; Jayne Reynolds Educ Schlrshp 79; Verna Williams Outstndng Sr Female Athlete Honor 78; Ashland Coll; Home Ec.

MYERS, MARY; Shakamak HS; Jasonville, IN; Chrh Wkr; DECA; ISU; Elem Ed.

MYERS, MATT; South Point HS; South Point, OH; Cl Rep Jr Cls; Boy Scts; Sec Chrh Wkr; Hon Rl; JA; NHS; Treas Stu Cncl; Boys Clb Am; Treas 4-H; Pep Clb; Ohio Univ HS Schlr; Coll; Engr.

MYERS, MICHAEL; Ellet HS; Akron, OH; 20/360 Boy Scts; Hon Rl; JA; NHS; Red Cr Ade; Stu Cncl; Spn Clb; Letter Ten; IM Sprt; College; Medicine.

MYERS, MICHAEL; Paden City HS; Paden City, WV; 7/85 VP Sr Cls; Am Leg Boys St; Band; Boy Scts; Hon Rl; JA; Sch Pl; Sct Actv; Rptr Yrbk; Rptr Sch Nwsp; Tyler County Schlstc Awd 79; West Virginia Univ; Law.

MYERS, MIKE; Sturgis HS; Sturgis, MI; Am Leg Boys St; Hon Rl; NHS; VICA; Bsktbl; Letter Ten; Univ Of Western Mic; Industrial Arts.

MYERS, PATRICIA; Scecina Memorial HS; Indianapolis, IN; 33/200 Cl Rep Jr Cls; Chrs; FCA; Hon Rl; Bsktbl; GAA; IM Sprt; College; Optometry.

MYERS, PHILIP; Evergreen HS; Berkey, OH; Chrh Wkr; Hon Rl; Rptr Sch Nwsp; Sch Nwsp; Fr Clb; Univ Of Toledo; Busns.

MYERS, RANDALL J; Park Hills HS; Fairborn, OH; 14/344 Am Leg Boys St; Chrs; Chrh Wkr; Cmnty Wkr; Hon Rl; NHS; Off Ade; Sch Mus; Sch Pl; Stu Cncl; College; Computer Sci.

MYERS, REBECCA; Elmwood HS; Bloomdale, OH; Cls Rep Frsh Cls; Cls Rep Soph Cls; Cl Rep Jr Cls; Band; Drl Tm; Girl Scts; Hon Rl; NHS; Treas Stu Cncl; Sprt Ed Yrbk; Univ; Envrnmntl Chem.

MYERS, RENE; Newton Falls HS; Newton Falls, OH; 1/169 Cls Rep Soph Cls; Val; Band; Cmp Fr Grls; Hon Rl; Hosp Ade; NHS; Off Ade; Sch Pl; Stu Cncl; College; Biology.

MYERS, RICHARD; Rossville Consolidated Schl; Rossville, IN; 16/50 Boy Scts; Hon Rl; Purdue Univ; Aero Engr.

MYERS, RICHARD; Central HS; Evansville, IN; 62/570 Cls Rep Frsh Cls; Cls Rep Soph Cls; Cl Rep Jr Cls; Boy Scts; Chrs; Chrh Wkr; Cmnty Wkr; Debate Tm; Hon Rl; Natl Forn Lg; Indiana Univ; Bus Admin.

MYERS, ROBERT; Keystone HS; La Grange, OH; Band; Boy Scts; Off Ade; Sct Actv; 4-H; FFA; FTA; Agri Tech Inst; Hog Mgmt.

MYERS, ROGER; Morgantown HS; Morgantwn, WV; Boy Scts; Chrs; Lbry Ade; Sch Pl; Sct Actv; Stg Crw; Yth Flsp; Rptr Yrbk; Tmr; Natl Merit Ltr; West Virginia Univ; Comp Sci.

MYERS, SHARON; Andrews Acad; Berrien Center, MI; Band; Chrs; Hon Rl; Sch Mus; Sch Nwsp; Fr Clb; Spn Clb; Band Cert Awd; Creative Writing Awd; Andrews Univ; Clinical Child Psych.

MYERS, STACEY; River Valley HS; Marion, OH; Hon Rl; Lbry Ade; Rptr Yrbk; Rptr Sch Nwsp; PPFtbl; Bowling Green; Spec Ed.

MYERS, STEPHANIE; John Marshall HS; Indianapolis, IN; 90/611 Girl Scts; Hon Rl; JA; Sct Actv; Stu Cncl; Indiana Univ Bloomington; Med.

MYERS, STEVE; Adams Central HS; Monroe, IN; 21/100 Band; Hon Rl; NHS; Pres Yth Flsp; Rptr Yrbk; Rptr Sch Nwsp; VP 4-H; Fr Clb; College; Architectural.

MYERS, STEVEN; Evart HS; Evart, MI; VP Frsh Cls; Pres Soph Cls; Hon Rl; NHS; Sch Pl; Bsbl; Bsktbl; Ftbl; Bsbl Hnrble Mention; Ferris St Coll; Bus Mgmt.

MYERS, SUE; Hamtramck Sr HS; Hamtramck, MI; 22/113 Hon Rl; Off Ade;.

MYERS, TAMMY; Prairie Heights HS; Mongo, IN; 49/150 Cls Rep Frsh Cls; Cls Rep Soph Cls; Sec Jr Cls; Cl Rep Jr Cls; Boy Scts; Girl Scts; Hon Rl; Stu Cncl; 4-H; FTA; Outsdng Stu Cncl Mbr 76; Stu Ldrshp Conf 77; Natl Stu Cncl Conv 78; 4 H Princess 79; Bus Schl; Acctg.

MYERS, TEENA; Sandusky HS; Sandusky, OH; Chrs; Hon Rl; Off Ade; Lat Clb; Mth Clb; Ten; IM Sprt; Mgrs; Scr Kpr; Ticket Selling 79; Univ; Med Tech.

MYERS, TODD; Wauseon HS; Wauseon, OH; 41/116 Pres Frsh Cls; Pres Soph Cls; Pres Jr Cls; Pres Sr Cls; Stu Cncl; Pres FFA; Sci Clb; Ohio Univ.

MYERS, TRACY; Monongah HS; Monongah, WV; Trs Frsh Cls; Cls Rep Frsh Cls; Sec Stu Cncl; Fr Clb; Bsktbl; Coach Actv; Fairmont State College; Phys Educ.

MYERS, TYRONE; Wauseon HS; Wauseon, OH; 36/151 Cls Rep Sr Cls; Am Leg Boys St; Chrh Wkr; FCA; Yth Flsp; FFA; Capt Ftbl; Letter Trk; FFA Sec Book 1st In Dist & State; Amer Inst Of Coop; Attended FFA Washington Cnfrnce; Coll.

MYLENEK, COLLEEN; St Andrew HS; Detroit, MI; 4/115 Cmnty Wkr; Hon Rl; Sec NHS; Pol Wkr; Rptr Yrbk; Rptr Sch Nwsp; Pep Clb; Natl Merit SF; Wayne St Univ; Engr.

MYLES, VIANNA; Fowlerville HS; Webberville, MI; Capt Trk; Mgrs; PPFtbl; Univ; Forestry.

MYLIUS, JENNIFER; Hoover HS; North Canton, OH; 15/342 Hst Jr Cls; Pres Sr Cls; Hon Rl; NHS; Quill & Scroll; Yth Flsp; Ed Yrbk; Cit Awd; 4-H Awd; Opt Clb Awd; Akron Univ; Optometry.

MYLLYLA, MARY; Escanaba Area Public HS; Escanaba, MI; Band; Chrh Wkr; Hon Rl; Jr NHS; NHS; 4-H; Gym; Mgrs; 4-H Awd; Bay Community Coll; Educ.

MYNER, KIM; Plainwell HS; Kalamazoo, MI; Band; Girl Scts; Hon Rl; NHS; Stu Cncl; Pres 4-H; Fr Clb; Spn Clb; Gym; 4-H Awd; Univ; Med.

MYNY, KEVIN; Algonac HS; Algonac, MI; Band; Hon Rl; NHS; Coll; Engr.

MYSLIWIEC, MARK; Lake Central HS; Dyer, IN; 69/518 Aud/Vis; Band; Chrs; Chrh Wkr; Cmnty Wkr; Hon Rl; Mdrgl; MMM; NHS; Orch; Indiana State Univ.

MYSONA, JENNIFER; Holy Name HS; Garfield Ht, OH; Cmnty Wkr; Hon Rl; NHS; Sch Mus; Yrbk; Ed Sch Nwsp; Fr Clb; IM Sprt; Cit Awd; College; Journalism.

MYSZENSKI, PATRICIA; Robert S Tower HS; Warren, MI; 20/384 Cls Rep Sr Cls; Cmnty Wkr; Hon Rl; Sec NHS; Sch Mus; Sch Pl; Stg Crw; Stu Cncl; Drama Clb; Letter Swmmng; St Of Mi Comp Schlrshp 79; Oakland Univ; Pre Med.

N

NAAS, CHERYL; Carroll HS; Dayton, OH; 48/285 Sec Soph Cls; Band; Chrh Wkr; Cmnty Wkr; Drl Tm; Hon Rl; NHS; Orch; Stu Cncl; Trk; College; Psychology.

NABERHAUS, JANE; Mount Notre Dame HS; Cincinnati, OH; 7/178 Hon Rl; Sec NHS; Stu Cncl; Spn Clb; Pres Schlrshp To Edgcliff Coll 79; Whos Who Among Amer HS Stud 78; Edgecliff Univ; Elem Educ.

NABOZNY, MICHAEL; High School; Lincoln Pk, MI; Bsbl; Ftbl; IM Sprt; College; Acctg.

NACARATO, NATALIE; Ursuline HS; Youngstown, OH; 36/300 Hon Rl; Off Ade; Youngstown Univ; Marketing.

NACHBAR, SHARON; Upper Sandusky HS; Upper Sandusky, OH; Band; Hon Rl; NHS; Off Ade; Stg Crw; Sec Yth Flsp; Algebra II Schlrshp Team; College; Education.

NACHMAN, JOE; Stanton HS; , ; Band; Chrs; Chrh Wkr; Hon Rl; NHS; Orch; Sch Mus; Sch Pl; Ed Yrbk; Univ; Engr.

NACHMAN, JOSEPH; Stanton HS; Stratton, OH; 3/64 Band; Chrs; Chrh Wkr; Hon Rl; NHS; Orch; Sch Mus; Sch Pl; Stg Crw; Ed Yrbk; Cincinnati Univ; Civil Engr.

NADEAU, KAY; Monroe HS; Monroe, MI; Hon Rl; JA; Off Ade; JA Awd; Henry Ford Comm Coll; Sec

NADER, ANNETTE; Normandy HS; Seven Hls, OH; 25/650 Hon Rl; Lit Mag; NHS; Quill & Scroll; VP Fr Clb; Crs Cntry; Trk; IM Sprt; Cit Awd; Natl Merit Ltr; University; Doctor.

NADER, MARIA; Timken Sr HS; Canton, OH; Chrs; Chrh Wkr; Girl Scts; Hosp Ade; Lbry Ade; Off Ade; Sch Mus; Sch Pl; Stu Cncl; Y-Teens; Brigham Yng Univ; Med.

NADOUD, JEFFREY; St Francis De Sales HS; Toledo, OH; Cls Rep Frsh Cls; Cls Rep Soph Cls; Cl Rep Jr Cls; Band; Hon Rl; Sch Pl; Lat Clb; Hockey; Swmmng; IM Sprt; Miami; Pre Law.

NAEYAERT, GARY; Carl Brablec HS; Roseville, MI; 36/391 Pres Frsh Cls; Pres Soph Cls; Pres Jr Cls; Pres Sr Cls; Chrh Wkr; Cmnty Wkr; Hon Rl; Natl Forn Lg; NHS; Pol Wkr; Proclomation From City Council 79; Front Pg Articl About Me In Local Newspr 78; Michigan St Univ; Soc Sci.

NAGEL, CARLA; St Marys Cntrl Catholic HS; Sandusky, OH; Band; Chrs; 4-H; Ger Clb; Bsktbl; GAA; IM Sprt; Scr Kpr; Bowling Green Univ; Music Educ.

NAGEL, KAREN; Deer Park HS; Cincinnati, OH; 18/217 Cl Rep Jr Cls; Hon Rl; VP Hosp Ade; JA; NHS; Rptr Yrbk; Univ Of Cincinnati; Nurse.

NAGEL, LISA; Hilltop HS; W Unity, OH; 4/72 Band; Girl Scts; Hon Rl; Sct Actv; 4-H; FHA; Trk; Coach Actv; Univ Of Toledo; Health.

NAGEL, WILLIAM; Howell HS; Howell, MI; Ferris Auto; Disel Mech.

NAGELE, FRAN; Allegan HS; Allegan, MI; 2/193 Sal; Hon Rl; NHS; Yrbk; Michigan St Univ.

NAGENGAST, MARTHA; Madeira HS; Cincinnati, OH; 40/165 Cmp Fr Grls; JA; Off Ade; Coll; Bus Admin.

NAGI, JANET; Eisenhower HS; Utica, MI; 6/602 Chrs; Chrh Wkr; Cmnty Wkr; Hon Rl; NHS; Sch Mus; Stg Crw; Sec Fr Clb; Saint Marys College; Natural Sci.

NAGLE, CATHLEEN; Meridian Sr HS; Sanford, MI; 27/114 Drm Mjrt; Girl Scts; Hon Rl; JA; Off Ade; Sch Mus; Yrbk; 4-H; Pep Clb; Delta Cmnty Coll; Bus.

NAGLE, LINDA; Cleveland Cntrl Catholic HS; Cleveland, OH; Hon Rl; FFA; Bus Schl; Acctg.

NAGLE III, EDWIN; St Francis HS; Toledo, OH; Cl Rep Jr Cls; VP Sr Cls; Aud/Vis; Hon Rl; Sch Mus; Stg Crw; Letter Ftbl; IM Sprt; Indiana Inst Of Tech; Bus.

NAGLICH, JULIANNE; Andrews Schl; Geneva, OH; 11/72 Cls Rep Frsh Cls; Pres Soph Cls; Cl Rep Jr Cls; Pres Sr Cls; Aud/Vis; Chrs; Cmnty Wkr; Girl Scts; Hon Rl; Lbry Ade; Akron Univ; Bus Admin.

NAGORSKI, AMY; St Annes Warren HS; Warren, MI; Cl Rep Jr Cls; Cmp Fr Grls; Orch; Trk; Chrldng; Michigan St Univ.

NAGRANT, BARB; Our Lady Of Mercy HS; Farm Hls, MI; Cls Rep Frsh Cls; Cl Rep Jr Cls; Chrh Wkr; Cmnty Wkr; Lat Clb; Rus Clb; College; Medicine.

NAGY, DAVID; Bedford HS; Bedford, OH; 250/600 Spn Clb; Letter Bsbl; Letter Bsktbl; Letter Ftbl; IM Sprt; Baldwin Wallace; Bus Admin.

NAGY, DEBRA J; Manistique HS; Manistique, MI; 18/150 Hon Rl; 4-H; Chrldng; Pom Pon; 4-H Awd; Bsns Schl; Legal Sec.

NAGY, JAN; Hubbard HS; Hubbard, OH; 40/350 Band; Chrs; Debate Tm; Girl Scts; Hon Rl; Quill & Scroll; Sch Mus; Rptr Sch Nwsp; Sch Nwsp; FTA; College; X Ray Tech.

NAGY, LYNNE; Valley Forge HS; Parma Hts, OH; Cls Rep Frsh Cls; Cls Rep Soph Cls; Cl Rep Jr Cls; Band; Hon Rl; VP Stu Cncl; Drama Clb; Fr Clb; Capt Bsktbl; College.

NAGY, P; Highland HS; Hinckley, OH; 4/208 Hon Rl; NHS; Lat Clb; Voice Dem Awd; Miami Univ; Pre Med.

NAGY, SHELLY; Clearview HS; Lorain, OH; 4/109 Sec Band; Drm Mjrt; Hon Rl; NHS; Off Ade; Ed Yrbk; Rptr Yrbk; Rptr Sch Nwsp; FTA; Trk; Ohio Univ; TV/RADIO Cmnctns.

NAGY, STEVEN M; Flat Rock Sr HS; Flat Rock, MI; Chrs; FCA; Hon Rl; Jr NHS; NHS; Y-Teens; Sci Clb; Ftbl; Letter Trk; Pres Awd; Univ Of Michigan; Chem Engr.

NAGY, TAMMY; Geneva Secondary Complex HS; Geneva, OH; 47/298 Trs Frsh Cls; Pres Soph Cls; Band; Chrs; Chrh Wkr; Sch Pl; Drama Clb; Chrldng; Kent State Univ; Bus Tech.

NAGYVATHY, SANDI; Firelands HS; Wakeman, OH; Cls Rep Frsh Cls; Cls Rep Soph Cls; Cl Rep Jr Cls; Sch Pl; Stu Cncl; Drama Clb; Spn Clb; Bsbl; Bsktbl; Chrldng; Univ.

NAHHAT, EDWARD; Clarence M Kimball HS; Royal Oak, MI; Chrs; JA; Mdrgl; Natl Forn Lg; Sch Mus; Sch Pl; Stg Crw; Rptr Sch Nwsp; Drama Clb; Rdo Clb; Wayne St Univ; Acting.

NAHRA, JANE; Our Lady Of The Elms HS; Akron, OH; 14/36 Cl Rep Jr Cls; Hon Rl; Sch Pl; Sch Nwsp; Univ; Law.

NAKAGAWA, JAMES; Wickliffe Sr HS; Wickliffe, OH; 13/320 Cls Rep Sr Cls; Band; Chrh Wkr; Hon Rl; Jr NHS; Mod UN; NHS; Stu Cncl; Ten; IM Sprt; Bowling Green St Univ; Geol.

NAKASHIGE, SUZANNE; Lutheran West HS; Parma, OH; Sec Frsh Cls; Sec Soph Cls; Sec Jr Cls; VP Sr Cls; Hon Rl; NHS; Rptr Yrbk; Pep Clb; Spn Clb; Chrldng; Homecoming Queen 79; Spanish Awd 78 79; Hon Roll; Bowling Green Univ; Bus Admin.

NAKFOOR, GUS; Okemos HS; Okemos, MI; Cls Rep Frsh Cls; Cl Rep Jr Cls; Sch Nwsp; Socr; Scr Kpr; Michigan St Univ.

NAKONECZNY, LAWRENCE; Henry Ford HS; Detroit, MI; Boy Scts; Hon Rl; Fr Clb; Letter Glf; College; Law.

NALLENWEG, RICHARD M; Morton Sr HS; Hammond, IN; 26/419 Boy Scts; Hon Rl; Letter Ftbl; Coach Actv; DAR Awd; M Club 1977; Army Awd; Sci Fair Proj 1974; Univ.

NALLEY, KEITH; Grand Haven Sr HS; Grand Haven, MI; Boy Scts; Hon Rl; NHS; Capt Ftbl; Letter Trk; Letter Wrstlng; Ferris St Univ; Pharm.

NALLEY, PATRICK T; Miami Valley School; Farnklin, OH; Band; Stg Crw; Rptr Yrbk; Yrbk; Drama Clb; Fr Clb; Letter Crs Cntry; Letter Trk; IM Sprt; Univ Of Colorado; Bus.

NALLEY, TAMELA; Wood Memorial HS; Oakland City, IN; Am Leg Aux Girls St; Band; Chrs; Chrh Wkr; Debate Tm; Drm Bgl; Hon Rl; Lbry Ade; NHS; Orch; 1st Pl Ratng At In St Music Contst 79; Univ; Law.

NALTNER, L SCOTT; Bishop Luers HS; Ft Wayne, IN; Cmnty Wkr; Hon Rl; Red Cr Ade; Key Clb; Letter Trk; IM Sprt; Amer Red Cross; Mbr Brd Of Dir VP Teen Club; Disaster Tm Mbr; Instruct Aid Swimmngs & First Aid; Univ; Comp Sci.

NAMEN, KIMBERLEE; Solon HS; Solon, OH; Chrs; Drl Tm; Hon Rl; NHS; Capt Pom Pon; College; Stewardess.

NAMEROFF, NATALIE B; Indian Hill HS; Cincinnati, OH; Chrs; Cmnty Wkr; Drl Tm; Hon Rl; Rptr Yrbk; Rptr Sch Nwsp; Drama Clb; PPFtbl; Intl Thespian Soc 79; Bna Brth Yth Org 78; Univ; Telecmnctns.

NANCE, APRIL; Wapakoneta Sr HS; Cridersville, OH; 13/323 Band; Hon Rl; NHS; Stu Cncl; FTA; Lat Clb; Letter Ten; Trk; Chrldng; Bowling Green St Univ; Elem Ed.

NANCE, CHERYL; Eastern Local HS; Lucasville, OH; 7/65 Cls Rep Frsh Cls; Trs Soph Cls; Trs Jr Cls; Trs Sr Cls; Pres Stu Cncl; Sch Nwsp; Capt Bsktbl; Chrldng;.

NANCE, PAM; Piketon HS; Piketon, OH; 15/93 Band; Chrs; Chrh Wkr; Cmnty Wkr; Girl Scts; Hon Rl; Lbry Ade; NHS; Orch; Sch Mus; Pittsburg Art Inst; Art.

NANDRASY, KATHRYN; Highland HS; Wadsworth, OH; 37/203 Hon Rl; NHS; Off Ade; Quill & Scroll; Ed Yrbk; 4-H; Mgrs; Scr Kpr; 4-H Awd; Oh Univ; Journalism.

NANDRASY, LAURA; Highland HS; Wadsworth, OH; 53/202 VP Sr Cls; Cls Rep Sr Cls; Chrs; Chrh Wkr; Hon Rl; NHS; Off Ade; Quill & Scroll; Stg Crw; Stu Cncl; Wittenberg Univ; Poli Sci.

NANI, ROBERT; Adams HS; Rochester, MI; Boy Scts; Hon Rl; Jr NHS; NHS; Red Cr Ade; Spn Clb; Swmmng; Trk; Coach Actv; Tmr;.

NANNI, SUSAN; Carl Brablec HS; Roseville, MI; Girl Scts; Hon Rl; Jr NHS; NHS; Quill & Scroll; Ed Yrbk; Yrbk; Spn Clb; Bsktbl; Trk; Community Coll; Dentistry.

NANNINI, GREGG; St Agatha HS; Redford, MI; Hon Rl; Lbry Ade; Letter Crs Cntry; Letter Trk; Northern Michigan Univ; Jrnlsm.

NAPIER, CATHY; Grosse Ile HS; Grosse Ile, MI; Cls Rep Frsh Cls; Band; Cmp Fr Grls; Chrs; Hon Rl; Mdrgl; Sch Mus; Mic State Univ; Sociology.

NAPIER, GEORGE H; Univ Of Detroit HS; Detroit, MI; 63/133 Cmnty Wkr; ROTC; Stg Crw; JETS Awd; AFROTC Schlrshp 1979; Michi Schlrshp Fnlst 1978; Natl Achvmnt Semi Fnlst 1978; Univ Of Michigan; Aero Engr.

NAPIER, NICKI; Twin Valley South HS; W Alexandria, OH; Chrs; Chrh Wkr; Cmnty Wkr; Hon Rl; JA; Jr NHS; Lbry Ade; Pres 4-H; Sec FFA; Gym; FFA St Chrs Dist 3 3rd Pl Sec 79; Prod Horticultaure Acctg Awd 79; Pt System 3rd In Fruit Sales 79; Mont Co JVS; Equestrian Std.

NAPIER, REGINA; New Lexington Sr HS; New Lexington, OH; 9/176 VP Frsh Cls; Chrs; Hon Rl; PAVAS; Sch Mus; Sch Pl; Stg Crw; Stu Cncl; Yrbk; Rptr Sch Nwsp; Wilmington Coll Schlrshp; Best Stu Director Of Yr; Wilmington Coll; Pre Med.

NAPIER, VALORIA; Central Baptist HS; Reading, OH; Trs Frsh Cls; Sec Soph Cls; VP Jr Cls; Chrs; Chrh Wkr; FCA; Hon Rl; Off Ade; Sch Mus; Stg Crw; Volleyball Co Capt & All Conf Team; Cert Of Schlrshp All Subj; Acctg Schlrshp Of Recognition; Deaconess Nursing Schl; RN.

NAPIERALA, LAURIE; Evergreen HS; Swanton, OH; Band; Capt Drl Tm; Hon Rl; NHS; Off Ade; 4-H; Fr Clb; GAA; Capt Pom Pon; Univ Of Toledo; Nursing.

NAPOLI, GINA; Brookfield HS; Brookfield, OH; 1/157 Cls Rep Frsh Cls; VP Jr Cls; Cl Rep Jr Cls; Trs Sr Cls; Cls Rep Sr Cls; Val; Hon Rl; Pres NHS; Quill & Scroll; VP Stu Cncl; Ohio St Univ; Comp Sci.

NAPON, GINA; Kennedy Christian HS; Hiram, OH; 50/53 Hst Jr Cls; Sal; Am Leg Boys St; Aud/Vis; Cmp Fr Grls; CAP; Natl Forn Lg; Sct Actv; Boys Clb Am; 4-H; Harvard Univ; Law.

NARDECCHIA, DEAN; Norwalk HS; Norwalk, OH; Ed Yrbk; Sprt Ed Yrbk; Ftbl; Wrstlng; Coach Actv; Univ.

NARDI, MARION; Berkley HS; Berkley, MI; Band; Hon Rl; Bsktbl; GAA; Suomi Coll; Recreation Leadership.

NARHI, PAMELA; Hartland HS; Linden, MI; Pres Chrh Wkr; Hon Rl; NHS; Pres Fr Clb; Ten; Univ Of Mich; Foreign Language.

NARO, KEVIN; Clearview HS; Lorain, OH; 8/96 Band; Pres Chrs; Hon Rl; NHS; Stu Cncl; FTA; Lat Clb; Ashland College; Bus.

NAROWITZ, DANIEL; Muskegon Sr HS; Muskegon, MI; Boy Scts; JA; NHS; Rptr Sch Nwsp; Boys Clb Am; JA Awd; Eagle Sct 77; Art Serv Awd 77; Michigan St Univ; Vet.

NARR, JULIE; Lutheran HS; Fraser, MI; 4/110 Band; Chrh Wkr; Girl Scts; Hon Rl; NHS; Rptr Yrbk; Wayne St Univ; Chem.

NARTKER, DEBRA J; Bullock Creek HS; Midland, MI; Band; FSA; Pep Clb; Sci Clb; Spn Clb; Trk; Brigham Young Univ; Pre Med.

NARTKER, JOSEPH; Stephen T Badin HS; Hamilton, OH; 27/225 Cmnty Wkr; Hon Rl; NHS; Fr Clb; Letter Bsbl; Letter Crs Cntry; Trk; IM Sprt; Cit Awd; Ohio State Univ; Optometry.

NASEMAN, REGINA; Anna HS; Anna, OH; VP Frsh Cls; Trs Soph Cls; Trs Jr Cls; Band; Chrs; Drl Tm; Girl Scts; Hon Rl; Sch Mus; Sch Pl; Volleyball; Best Actress For The Night Of The One Acts; Mbr Of The Tam Ettes; College; Elem Ed.

NASH, ALICIA; Warren Western Reserve HS; Warren, OH; 10/437 Band; Hon Rl; Jr NHS; NHS; Sch Pl; Stg Crw; Yrbk; Drama Clb; Fr Clb; Sci Clb; Coll; Med.

NASH, BECKY; Gladwin HS; Gladwin, MI; Girl Scts; Hon Rl; NHS; Sct Actv; Rptr Sch Nwsp; Civ Clb; 4-H; Bsktbl; Trk; 4-H Awd; Bus Schl.

NASH, CONNIE S; Cardinal Ritter HS; Indianapolis, IN; 68/147 Band; Chrs; Girl Scts; Hon Rl; Hosp Ade; JA; Mdrgl; Off Ade; Scr Kpr; PPFtbl; Dale Carnegie Grad Asst 1978; Girls Ensmble St Winner 1978; Sci Fair Proj 1st Pl 1975; Indiana Central Univ; Nursing.

NASH, DEBBIE; Bethesda Christian HS; Brownsburg, IN; Chrs; Chrh Wkr; Girl Scts; Hon Rl; College.

NASH, DIANE; Bethany Christian HS; Sterling Hts, MI; 2/32 Cls Rep Soph Cls; VP Jr Cls; Pres Sr Cls; Chrs; Chrh Wkr; Hon Rl; Off Ade; Sch Mus; Sch Pl; Stu Cncl; Mi Competitive Schlrshp 79; Wayne St Univ; MD.

NASH, LILLIE; John F Kennedy HS; Cleveland, OH; Cls Rep Frsh Cls; Aud/Vis; Chrs; Cmnty Wkr; Lbry Ade; Stu Cncl; DECA; FTA; Univ; Counseling.

NASH, LISA; St Clement HS; Centerline, MI; Chrh Wkr; Hon Rl; Rptr Yrbk; Yrbk; Rptr Sch Nwsp; Sch Nwsp; Gym; Trk; Tmr; Voice Dem Awd; Macomb County Community Coll; Art.

NASH, LOUISA; Shaker Hts Sr HS; Shaker Hts, OH; 55/554 AFS; Hon Rl; Red Cr Ade; Ed Yrbk; Spn Clb; Letter Hockey; Indiana Univ; Spanish.

NASH, TONYA; Allegan Sr HS; Allegan, MI; Hon Rl; Stu Cncl; Bsbl; Bsktbl; Coach Actv; PPFtbl; Alma Coll; Phys Ed.

NASON, MARY; Brecksville HS; Brecksville, OH; 92/376 Band; Girl Scts; Sch Mus; Sct Actv; Stg Crw; GAA; Cuyahoga Comm Coll; Respiratory Ther.

NASS, DEANNA; Lapeer East HS; Lapeer, MI; Trs Jr Cls; Band; Hon Rl; NHS; Red Cr Ade; Pep Clb; College; Med.

NASSAR, FREDERICK; Hampshire HS; Romney, WV; 67/210 Hon Rl; FFA; Pres Rdo Clb; Letter Bsbl; Ftbl; IM Sprt; Voice Dem Awd; Univ Of South Fla; Elec Engin.

NASSAR JR, FREDERICK; Hampshire HS; Romney, WV; Hon Rl; FFA; Pres Rdo Clb; Letter Bsbl; Ftbl; Bowling Team Captain; Univ Of South Florida; Elec Engr.

NASSER, ANNETTE; Houghton Lake HS; St Helen, MI; VP Frsh Cls; Pres Soph Cls; Cl Rep Jr Cls; Hon Rl; NHS; Off Ade; Stu Cncl; Rptr Yrbk; Rptr Sch Nwsp; Pep Clb; Coll; Med.

NASTALLY, MIKE; Garrett HS; Garrett, IN; Band; Hon Rl; Orch; Ger Clb; Crs Cntry; Glf; Wrstlng; Coll.

NASTAS, GLORIA; Bishop Foley HS; Detroit, MI; 3/193 Hon Rl; JA; Treas Sci Clb; JA Awd; Schlshp To Bishop Foley HS 1978; 1st In Schl Sci Fair 1978; Amer Soc Of Distgshd Students; Univ; Pre Med.

NASTWOLD, SCOTT; Harry S Truman HS; Taylor, MI; 5/550 Cls Rep Frsh Cls; Am Leg Boys St; Band; Hon Rl; NHS; Gym; Univ; Pharm.

NATHANSON, KEITH M; North Farmington HS; Frmngtn Hls, MI; Hon Rl; Stu Cncl; Sch Nwsp; Univ Of Michigan.

NATOLI JR, FRANK; Niles Mc Kinley HS; Niles, OH; 10/421 AFS; Hon Rl; Jr NHS; Pres NHS; Stg Crw; Drama Clb; Sec Key Clb; IM Sprt; Kiwan Awd; Youngstown St Univ.

NAU, KEVIN; Arcadia Local HS; Fostoria, OH; 4/63 Cls Rep Frsh Cls; Cls Rep Soph Cls; Band; Boy Scts; Hon Rl; NHS; Sch Mus; Stu Cncl; Yth Flsp; Yrbk; Ohio St Univ; Agri Tech Engr.

NAUGLE, AMY; Mariemont HS; Cincinnati, OH; 20/149 Sec Frsh Cls; Cls Rep Soph Cls; Chrs; NHS; Sch Mus; Sch Pl; Stu Cncl; Rptr Sch Nwsp; Drama Clb; Pep Clb; Univ; Speech.

NAUMAN, BRIAN; North Union HS; Richwood, OH; Am Leg Boys St; Hon Rl; NHS; FFA; Lat Clb; Letter Bsbl; Letter Bsktbl; Coach Actv; PPFtbl; 4-H Awd; All CBL Boys Bsktbll Teamm All Union Cnty Union Cnty Ldng Scorer Mst Dedctd HS All Amer 78; Univ; Educ.

NAUMANN, SARA; Bay HS; Bay Vill, OH; Pep Clb; Letter Bsktbl; Crs Cntry; GAA; IM Sprt; PPFtbl; Scr Kpr; Univ; Math Tchr.

NAUS, CHRISTINE; Liberty Benton HS; Findlay, OH; Band; Cmp Fr Grls; Chrs; Drm Bgl; Hon Rl; NHS; Orch; Sch Pl; Drama Clb; 4-H; FFA Awd For Public Speaking 77 & 78; 4 H 1st Pl Hancock Cnty Awd For Mgmt 78; Bowling Green Univ; Psych.

NAUTA, BETH; West Ottawa HS; Holland, MI; Cls Rep Frsh Cls; Cls Rep Soph Cls; Cl Rep Jr Cls; Cls Rep Sr Cls; Hon Rl; Lbry Ade; Natl Forn Lg; Yth Flsp; Letter Trk; Pres Awd; Hope Coll; Communications.

NAVARINI, BARBARA; Notre Dame HS; Clarksburg, WV; Cl Rep Jr Cls; VP Sr Cls; Band; Chrs; Chrh Wkr; Cmnty Wkr; Hon Rl; Stu Cncl; Mth Clb; Pep Clb; West Virginia Univ; Pre Law.

NAVARRA, JOSE; Finney HS; Detroit, MI; Hon Rl; Ftbl; Wayne St Univ; Dent.

NAVARRE, WILLIAM F; Lumen Christi HS; Clark Lk, MI; Hon Rl; Fr Clb; Hockey; IM Sprt; Ctrl Michigan Univ; Law.

NAVE, PAM; South Ripley HS; Versailles, IN; 13/110 Cls Rep Frsh Cls; Chrh Wkr; Cmnty Wkr; Hon Rl; 4-H; FHA; 4-H Awd; Tenn 4 H Hnr Clb 1974; Dist VP Of Distrbtv Educ Clbs Of Amrca 1977; Asstnt Mgr Of Sprmrkt.

NAVE, SCOTT; Parkway Local HS; Rockford, OH; 15/96 Band; Chrs; Chrh Wkr; Hon Rl; VP Yth Flsp; Lat Clb; Sci Clb; College; Music.

NAVEAU, MARY J; Russia Local HS; Russia, OH; 2/35 Sec Band; Chrs; Hon Rl; Treas NHS; Sct Actv; Sec Stu Cncl; Rptr Yrbk; Rptr Sch Nwsp; Drama Clb; Am Leg Awd; Bowling Green St Univ.

NAVILLE, ROBERT J; Floyd Central HS; Floyds Knobs, IN; 1/352 Cls Rep Soph Cls; Cls Rep Sr Cls; Val; Am Leg Boys St; Band; Chrh Wkr; Cmnty Wkr; Hon Rl; Jr NHS; NHS; Hoosier Boys St Frank M Mc Hale Schlrshp 78; AFROTC 4 Yr Schlrshp 79; Purdue Univ; Engr.

NAVY, PATTY; Struthers HS; Struthers, OH; 157/272 Chrh Wkr; Treas JA; Lbry Ade; Off Ade; Yth Flsp; Y-Teens; Drama Clb; Treas OEA; Pep Cl b; IM Sprt; Diplomat Ward; Honor Role; Jr Ach Awd; Youngstown St Univ.

NAWROCKI, JANICE; West Catholic HS; Grand Rapids, MI; Chrs; Hon Rl; NHS; Lat Clb; Am Leg Awd; Mercy Central School; Nursing.

NAWROCKI, LAURA; Andrean HS; Merrillville, IN; 78/251 Hon Rl; Hosp Ade; Pep Clb; Trk; Chrldng; GAA; Pom Pon; PPFtbl; Univ; Busns.

NAWROCKI, MARY; West Catholic HS; Grand Rapids, MI; Band; Orch; Sch Mus; VP Lat Clb; Letter Ten; Jr Coll; Dentistry.

NAWROCKI, SANDRA; Caledonia HS; Alto, MI; 25/185 Trs Sr Cls; Chrs; Hon Rl; JA; Sch Mus; Yrbk; Ed Sch Nwsp; Letter Bsbl; Letter Ten; Cit Awd; Beloit College; Pre Law.

NAY, LESA; Lincoln HS; Shinnston, WV; Band; Chrh Wkr; Hon Rl; Jr NHS; Pep Clb; Spn Clb; Letter Trk; Univ; Tchr.

NAY, TRUDY; Lincoln HS; Shinnston, WV; 21/148 Sec Soph Cls; Pres Jr Cls; Sec Sr Cls; Am Leg Aux Girls St; Band; Hon Rl; NHS; Stu Cncl; FTA; Am Leg Awd; West Virginia Univ; Music Ed.

NAZARETH, LEE; Holy Name Nazareth HS; Seven Hills, OH; 2/200 Chrs; Girl Scts; Hon Rl; Hosp Ade; Univ; Nursing.

NEAL, BRIAN; Barberton HS; Barberton, OH; 33/520 Chrs; Hon Rl; Jr NHS; NHS; Off Ade; Letter Ftbl; Letter Glf; Letter Wrstlng; Univ Of Akron; Law.

NEAL, BRUCE; Jackson HS; Jackson, OH; Cl Rep Jr Cls; Stu Cncl; Pres Pep Clb; Letter Bsktbl; Letter Trk; Univ.

NEAL, BRUCE; Mogadore HS; Mogadore, OH; Cls Rep Frsh Cls; Hon Rl; Sch Pl; Yth Flsp; Letter Bsbl; Letter Bsktbl; Glf; Akron Univ.

NEAL, CATHY; Western Brown Sr HS; Mt Orab, OH; 6/200 Trs Soph Cls; Cl Rep Jr Cls; Cls Rep Sr Cls; Chrs; Hon Rl; NHS; Off Ade; Sch Pl; Stg Crw; Drama Clb; Morehead St Univ; Pre Phys Ther.

NEAL, CHERYL; Herbert Hoover Sr HS; Elkview, WV; 1/278 Cl Rep Jr Cls; Cls Rep Sr Cls; Val; Chrh Wkr; Girl Scts; Hon Rl; Jr NHS; Stu Cncl; Yth Flsp; Rptr Sch Nwsp; Texas A & M Univ; Geophysics.

NEAL, JULIE; North Knox HS; Bicknell, IN; 6/153 Sec Jr Cls; FCA; Hon Rl; NHS; FHA; Bsbl; Bsktbl; Vincennes Univ; Nursing.

NEAL, KENDRA; Yorktown HS; Muncie, IN; Band; Chrh Wkr; Girl Scts; Yth Flsp; 4-H; Pep Clb; Bsktbl; Swmmng; Trk; Chrldng; Univ; Phys Ed.

NEAL, KIMBERLY; Blue River Valley Jr Sr HS; Mooreland, IN; 5/93 Cls Rep Frsh Cls; Sec Soph Cls; Trs Soph Cls; Sec Jr Cls; Trs Jr Cls; Am Leg Aux Girls St; Hon Rl; NHS; OEA; Oakland City Coll Schlrshp; Typing I Awd 78; Typing II Awd 79; Shorthand I Awd 79; Outstanding Soph & Jr; Ball St Univ; Bus.

NEAL, MARK; Shenandoah HS; Middletown, IN; 14/139 Band; Hon Rl; NHS; Sprt Ed Yrbk; 4-H; Mth Clb; Bsbl; Ball St Univ; Math.

NEAL, MARSHA; Yorktown HS; Yorktown, IN; Am Leg Aux Girls St; Chrs; Chrh Wkr; Hon Rl; VP NHS; Ger Clb; Pep Clb; IM Sprt; Coll; Educ.

NEAL, REBECCA; Lawrence Central HS; Indianapolis, IN; 2/300 Am Leg Aux Girls St; Band; NHS; Yth Flsp; PPFtbl; Depauw Univ; Pre Med.

NEAL, RONALD; Indian Creek HS; Columbus, IN; Sec Band; Chrs; Quill & Scroll; Sch Mus; Stg Crw; Ed Sch Nwsp; Rptr Sch Nwsp; Sch Nwsp; Swmmng; Mgrs; Purdue Univ; Pharm.

NEAL, SUE; Pike Central HS; Petersburg, IN; Pres Frsh Cls; Sec Soph Cls; VP Jr Cls; Band; Girl Scts; Hon Rl; NHS; FHA; Pep Clb; Letter Ten; Univ; Elem Educ Tchr.

NEAL, SUSAN; Arlington HS; Williamstown, OH; 6/43 Band; Chrh Wkr; Hon Rl; Lbry Ade; NHS; Off Ade; Yrbk; Pep Clb; GAA; Scr Kpr; Lima Tech College; Nurse.

NEAL, WALLACE; Upper Scioto Valley HS; Alger, OH; 16/78 VP Sr Cls; Hon Rl; Beta Clb; FFA; Bsktbl; 1st Pl In Hardin Co In Algebra I Test 78; 1st Pl In Hardin Co In Geom Test 79; Stu Adv In Our FFA Club 79; Coll; Math.

NEARHOOD, CHERI; Clyde Sr HS; Clyde, OH; 99/210 Cmp Fr Grls; Chrs; Chrh Wkr; Hon Rl; Hosp Ade; Off Ade; Yth Flsp; Sandusky Schl; Nursing.

NEARY, CHRISTOPHER; Marietta HS; Marietta, OH; Ohio St Univ; Acctg.

NEARY, MAUREEN; St Agatha HS; Redford, MI; 19/93 Bsktbl; Gym; Trk; Chrldng; PPFtbl; Bus Schl.

NEASE, PHILLIP; Austin HS; Austin, IN; Hon Rl; Yth Flsp; Rptr Yrbk; Rptr Sch Nwsp; Lat Clb; Pep Clb; Letter Bsbl; Bsktbl; Letter Ten; IM Sprt; Indiana Univ S E; Marketing.

NEBBERGALL, TOM; Millersport HS; Millersport, OH; Am Leg Boys St; Aud/Vis; Hon Rl; Stg Crw; Drama Clb; Spn Clb; Bsktbl; Trk; IM Sprt; College; Engr.

NEBEL, CHARLES; Mather HS; Munising, MI; 7/110 VP Frsh Cls; VP Jr Cls; Pres Sr Cls; Hon Rl; NHS; Sch Pl; Bsktbl; Ftbl; Trk; Coach Actv; Mbrshp In Hi Y An All Boys Organization; Albion Coll; Law.

NEBLETT, JAMES; Crispus Attucks HS; Indianapolis, IN; Cls Rep Soph Cls; Hon Rl; VP JA; Off Ade; Sec Stu Cncl; DECA; FBLA; JA Awd; Bowling Awds ISNB Bowling Lg 76 & 77; Purdue Univ; Acctg.

NECAMP, MICHAEL; Copley HS; Akron, OH; Hon Rl; Letter Ftbl; College; Engr.

NECKER, ROBIN; Franklin HS; Livonia, MI; Band; Chrs; Chrh Wkr; Hon Rl; NHS; Off Ade; FTA; Cit Awd; Eastern Mich.

NEE, VICTORIA; John Adams HS; South Bend, IN; Hon Rl; NHS; Orch; Sch Mus; Drama Clb; Natl Merit SF; Univ; Music.

NEEB, DOUGLAS A; Midland HS; Hope, MI; 155/476 Hon Rl; Letter Wrstlng; Stu Financial Aid Schlrshp; Coll; Busns Mgmt.

NEEB, JOHN MICHAEL; New Palestine HS; Fountntwn, IN; 15/204 Band; Boy Scts; Hon Rl; Sdlty; Fr Clb; College; Sci Indust Hyg.

NEEB, ROBIN; Freeland HS; Freeland, MI; Chrs; Girl Scts; Hon Rl; 4-H; Pep Clb; PPFtbl; Univ Of Mich; Geology.

NEEDHAM, JAMIE; New Albany HS; New Albany, IN; 16/500 Cl Rep Jr Cls; Am Leg Aux Girls St; Hon Rl; Jr NHS; NHS; Off Ade; Quill & Scroll; Stu Cncl; Yth Flsp; Ed Yrbk; Hanover Coll; Elem Ed.

NEEDLER, GLORIA; Newton Falls HS; Newton Falls, OH; Band; Hon Rl; NHS; Off Ade; Sch Pl; Y-Teens; Rptr Yrbk; Yrbk; Rptr Sch Nwsp; FNA; Youngstown St Univ; Nurse.

NEEL, RICHARD R; Linsly Military Inst; Dillonvale, OH; 2/48 Band; Boy Scts; Chrs; FCA; Hon Rl; Capt ROTC; Sch Mus; Trk; Letter Wrstlng; Tmr; US Air Force Acad; Engr.

NEEL, WAYNE; Fairborn Park Hills HS; Fairborn, OH; Hon Rl; Bsbl; Ftbl; Letter Wrstlng; College.

NEELEY, STEVEN; Lebanon HS; Lebanon, OH; Boy Scts; Hon Rl; NHS; ROTC; Sct Actv; Ohio State Univ; Elec Engr.

NEELIS, LAURIE; Cheboygan Catholic HS; Chbeoygan, MI; Cls Rep Soph Cls; Cl Rep Jr Cls; Chrs; Hon Rl; Sch Mus; Stu Cncl; Rptr Yrbk; Univ Of Wyo; Phys Educ.

NEELY, ANTHONY; New Albany HS; New Albany, IN; 34/576 Boy Scts; Chrs; Hon Rl; NHS; Sch Mus; Yth Flsp; 4-H; Lat Clb; College; Medicine.

NEELY, JILL; Jimtown HS; Elkhart, IN; Hon Rl; NHS; Yrbk; 4-H; Fr Clb; Pep Clb; Chrldng; Ball St Univ; Sec.

NEELY, LENELL; Horace Mann HS; Gary, IN; Cls Rep Sr Cls; Boy Scts; Hon Rl; Jr NHS; Sch Pl; Sch Nwsp; Drama Clb; Purdue Univ; Comp Sci.

NEELY, LISA D; Worthington HS; Worthington, OH; 167/538 Cls Rep Sr Cls; Chrs; Chrh Wkr; Drl Tm; Hon Rl; Pep Clb; Trk; Chrldng; Pom Pon; Scr Kpr; Boston Univ; Systm Engr.

NEELY, YVONNE; Jefferson Area HS; Dorset, OH; Sch Pl; Stg Crw; Fr Clb; Gym; Trk; IM Sprt; Tmr; College.

NEENAN, R TIMOTHY; Central Catholic HS; Toledo, OH; DECA; Letter Glf; Letter Hockey; Coach Actv; Toledo Univ; Bus Admin.

NEER, JOAN; Morgan County HS; Mc Connelsville, OH; Band; Hon Rl; Jr NHS; NHS; Orch; Sch Mus; Stg Crw; 4-H; Spn Clb; IM Sprt; Univ.

NEES, GARY; Clay City HS; Cory, IN; 5/60 Chrh Wkr; Cmnty Wkr; Hon Rl; NHS; FBLA; Lat Clb; OEA; Voice Dem Awd; Dist Honor Stu Of Amer; Indiana St Univ; Busns.

NEES, JAMES; Moeller HS; Cincinnati, OH; Band; Boy Scts; Hon Rl; Orch; Sch Mus; Pep Clb; Swmmng; Natl Merit Ltr; Washington Univ; Mech Engr.

NEES, SHARON; Franklin Central HS; Indianapolis, IN; 38/260 Hon Rl; Sch Pl; FTA; Pep Clb; Swmmng; Univ; Home Econ.

NEES, SUSAN; Cloverdale HS; Poland, IN; 3/89 Am Leg Aux Girls St; Chrs; Hon Rl; NHS; Off Ade; Sch Mus; Sch Pl; Stg Crw; Yth Flsp; Ed Sch Nwsp; Vincennes Univ; Exec Sec.

NEESE, QUINTANNA; Brownsburg HS; Brownsburg, IN; 42/314 Cls Rep Frsh Cls; Cls Rep Soph Cls; Cl Rep Jr Cls; Pres Chrs; Chrh Wkr; Debate Tm; Girl Scts; Hon Rl; Mdrgl; Sch Mus; 1st Pl Piano Solo Div 2 78; Dir Awd 78; Schlrshp Music Clinic 78; Butler Univ; Musical Ther.

NEESON, JOSEPH; Oxford Area Community HS; Oxford, MI; 26/226 Am Leg Boys St; Chrh Wkr; Hon Rl; NHS; Letter Bsbl; Letter Bsktbl; Letter Ftbl; Rotary Awd; Monetray Schslp From St Of Mi 79; Bsbl All Lg Hon Mntn 78; Ftbl All Area 78; Cntrl Michigan Univ; Bus.

NEFF, ANNEKE; Buckhannon Upshur HS; Buckhannon, WV; Sec Frsh Cls; Hon Rl; Mgrs; College.

NEFF, BARB; Zane Trace HS; Adelphi, OH; 8/105 Hon Rl; NHS; Rptr Sch Nwsp; 4-H;.

NEFF, GARY; Mio Au Sable HS; Mio, MI; Hon Rl; Rptr Sch Nwsp; Sch Nwsp; 4-H; Letter Trk; Univ.

NEFF, GORDON L; Terre Haute South Vigo HS; Terre Haute, IN; 1/710 Band; Hon Rl; Orch; Sch Mus; Treas Key Clb; Rdo Clb; Sci Clb; Letter Bsktbl; JETS Awd; College; Elec Engr.

NEFF, JENNIFER; Southfield HS; Southfield, MI; Band; Yth Flsp; Trk; Mich State Univ; Math.

NEFF, JOSEPH; North Miami HS; Macy, IN; Band; Chrs; Hon Rl; Mdrgl; Stg Crw; Yth Flsp; Indiana Univ; Pro Musician.

NEFF, KATHARINE; North Canton Hoover HS; North Canton, OH; 65/430 Band; Hon Rl; Lbry Ade; Leo Clb; Swmmng; Mat Maids; Tmr; Miami Univ; Systems Analyst.

NEFF, KATHRYN; Richmond HS; Richmond, IN; 1/625 Hon Rl; Jr NHS; NHS; Orch; Stu Cncl; 4-H; Letter Swmmng; Letter Trk; DAR Awd; Natl Merit Ltr; College; Science.

NEFF, KATHY; Richmond HS; Richmond, IN; 1/625 Cls Rep Frsh Cls; Cl Rep Jr Cls; Hon Rl; Jr NHS; NHS; Orch; 4-H; Letter Swmmng; Letter Trk; DAR Awd; Oberlin College; Sci.

NEFF, LAUREN; St Joseph Academy; Cleveland, OH; Chrh Wkr; JA; Drama Clb; GAA; Bowling Green Univ; Intr Dsgn.

NEFF, MARK; Bluffton HS; Bluffton, IN; 33/136 Ger Clb; Bsbl; Capt Ftbl; Wrstlng; IM Sprt; Air Force Acad.

NEFF, ROBERT; Richmond Sr HS; Richmond, IN; 1/650 Band; FCA; Hon Rl; NHS; Orch; Sch Mus; Letter Crs Cntry; Letter Trk; IM Sprt; Natl Merit Ltr; Univ; Elec Engr.

NEFF, SALLY; Indian Lake HS; Bellefontaine, OH; Hon Rl; OEA; Indiana St Univ; Computer Prog.

NEFF, SANDRA; Washington HS; Washington, IN; 13/200 Pres Chrs; Hon Rl; Jr NHS; Mdrgl; NHS; Sch Mus; Sch Nwsp; Beta Clb; Drama Clb; Eng Clb; Indiana Univ; Jrnlsm.

NEFF, THERESA; Parma Sr HS; Parma, OH; 71/782 NHS; Univ; Spanish.

NEFTZER, CONNIE; Amelia HS; Amelia, OH; Band; Girl Scts; Sct Actv; Yth Flsp; Trk; IM Sprt; Pres Awd; Univ; Educ.

NEGRI, MARY; Adrian Sr HS; Adrian, MI; Band; Hon Rl; NHS; Off Ade; Lat Clb; Mth Clb; Bsktbl; Mgrs; I Rcvd Recogntn At Hnrs Night For My Participation In Physic 78; I Rcvd A Superior Rating At A Band Fest 77; Univ; Pre Med.

NEHRIG, KAY P; Clinton Prairie HS; Mulberry, IN; Trs Jr Cls; Band; Drm Mjrt; Hon Rl; Off Ade; Sch Mus; Sch Nwsp; Treas FBLA; FHA; FTA; Outstndng Soph Mrchr; Busns Schl.

NEHRING, LORI; Gladwin HS; Gladwin, MI; 54/200 Chrs; Chrh Wkr; Hon Rl; 4-H; Crs Cntry; Gif; PPFtbl; Lansing Bus Inst; Comp Sci.

NEIBERT, TRUDY; Indian Valley North HS; New Phila, OH; Band; Chrs; Hon Rl; Spn Clb; Am Leg Awd; Technical Schl; X Ray Tech.

NEIDERT, JEFF; Garfield HS; Akron, OH; 11/400 Cl Rep Jr Cls; Cls Rep Sr Cls; Pres Chrs; Hon Rl; Natl Forn Lg; NHS; Sch Mus; Pres Drama Clb; Fr Clb; Opt Clb Awd; Participated In Advnced Placement English Course; Received A Rating Of I At The Omea Solo & Ensemble Cntst; Kent State Univ; Tele Communications.

NEIDLINGER, ANNE; Jenison HS; Jenison, MI; 34/334 Sec Frsh Cls; Cls Rep Soph Cls; Sec Jr Cls; Band; Hon Rl; Sch Pl; Stu Cncl; Rptr Sch Nwsp; Bsktbl; Trk; Univ.

NEIGER, CHRIS; St Edward HS; Westlake, OH; Boy Scts; NHS; Sch Mus; Sch Pl; Stg Crw; Boys Clb Am; Univ; Engr.

NEIHARDT, DEBRA; Sturgis HS; Sturgis, MI; Hosp Ade; Yth Flsp; Letter Swmmng; Chrldng; PPFtbl; Nazareth Coll; Nursing.

NEIHEISEL, M; Mother Of Mercy HS; Cincinnati, OH; 19/215 Girl Scts; Hon Rl; NHS; IM Sprt; Univ Of Cincinnati; Civil Engr.

NEIL, KATHRYN; Williamston HS; Williamston, MI; Band; Chrh Wkr; Girl Scts; 4-H; 4-H Awd; Brigham Young Univ; Nursing.

NEIL, TAMMY; Rock Hill Sr HS; Kitts Hill, OH; Trs Soph Cls; Band; Chrs; Chrh Wkr; Hon Rl; NHS; Stu Cncl; Treas Beta Clb; Civ Clb; 4-H; Coll.

NEILING, TIM; Eastwood HS; Dunbridge, OH; VP Frsh Cls; Band; Hon Rl; Stu Cncl; OEA; Glf; IM Sprt; Tenta Cnty Voc Schl; Data Processing.

NEILL, HOLLY; Chesterton HS; Porter, IN; 35/450 Cls Rep Sr Cls; Band; Girl Scts; Hon Rl; NHS; Stg Crw; Yth Flsp; 4-H; Spn Clb; 4-H Awd; Purdue; Med Tec.

NEILS, THOMAS L; Allegan HS; Allegan, MI; 1/280 Pres Frsh Cls; Cls Rep Frsh Cls; Am Leg Boys St; Chrh Wkr; Hon Rl; Jr NHS; VP NHS; Sch Nwsp; Letter Bsktbl; Letter Ftbl; Michigan Tech Univ; Chem Engr.

NEILSON, JEANNA L; Bluefield HS; Bluefld, WV; Chrh Wkr; Hon Rl; NHS; Spn Clb; Hnr Eng; West Virginia Univ.

NEILSON, WILLIAM S; Charles F Brush HS; South Euclid, OH; 3/635 Boy Scts; Chrs; Chrh Wkr; Hon Rl; NHS; Sct Actv; Rptr Yrbk; Mth Clb; Letter Mgrs; Natl Merit SF; Eagle Scout 1975; Natl Sci Fdn Stu Sci Traing Prog 1978; 113th Among H S Math Stu In Ohio 1978; Univ; Math.

NEIMAYER, ALLAN; Jewett Scio HS; Scio, OH; 3/78 Band; Chrh Wkr; Hon Rl; NHS; Spn Clb; JC Awd; Ohio St Univ; Architecture.

NEISWINGER, MICHAEL; Morton Sr HS; Hammond, IN; Pres Aud/Vis; Chrs; Chrh Wkr; FCA; Hon Rl; VP NHS; Sch Mus; Sch Pl; Stu Cncl; Sci Clb; Purdue Univ; Mech Engr.

NEITZEL, JULIE; Vestaburg Cmnty HS; Edmore, MI; 6/75 VP Jr Cls; Hst Sr Cls; Hon Rl; NHS; Off Ade; FHA; PPFtbl; Bausch & Lomb Awd; Natl Merit Ltr; Natl Merit Schl; Michigan Tech Univ; Pre Med.

NEITZEL, PATSY; Hanover Central HS; Cedar Lake, IN; 3/137 Trs Soph Cls; Hon Rl; Sec Jr NHS; VP NHS; Stu Cncl; VP Yth Flsp; Pep Clb; Letter Trk; Chrldng; PPFtbl;.

NEITZKE, LISA; Breckenridge Jr Sr HS; Wheeler, MI; Debate Tm; Girl Scts; Hon Rl; Sct Actv; Yth Flsp; 4-H; FFA; Twrlr; 4-H Awd; Michigan State Univ; Bsns.

NELLIS, BRETT; Stow HS; Stow, OH; Letter Ftbl; Letter Trk; Univ Of Akron; Busns.

NELMS, AMIE; Shadyside HS; Shadyside, OH; Sal; Am Leg Aux Girls St; Band; VP Chrs; Girl Scts; Hon Rl; NHS; Ohi Univ; Math.

NELMS, TOM; Shadyside HS; Shadyside, OH; 4/120 Am Leg Boys St; Boy Scts; Hon Rl; NHS; Sch Mus; Yth Flsp; Spn Clb; Letter Bsbl; Letter Bsktbl; Letter Ftbl; Ohio St Univ; Engr.

NELSON, ARDENA; Muskegon HS; Muskegon, MI; Sec Frsh Cls; Am Leg Aux Girls St; Band; Chrh Wkr; Hon Rl; Stg Crw; Am Leg Awd; Muskegon Cmnty Coll; Nursing.

NELSON, BOBBIE; Monroe HS; Monroe, MI; Cl Rep Jr Cls; Cls Rep Sr Cls; Hon Rl; Off Ade; Stu Cncl; Sch Nwsp; Ger Clb; Monroe Co Community Coll; Bus.

NELSON, BRIAN; Pike Central HS; Petersburg, IN; Hon Rl; NHS; Engr.

NELSON, CARRI; Ripley HS; Essex Jct, VT; Chrs; Chrh Wkr; Hon Rl; Sch Pl; VP Yth Flsp; VP 4-H; Rep For Nazarene World Youth Confrnc 79; Univ; Radio.

NELSON, CASSANDRA; Willard HS; Willard, OH; Band; Chrs; Chrh Wkr; Hosp Ade; Orch; Sch Mus; Sch Pl; 4-H; IM Sprt; Univ Of Dayton; Criminal Justice.

NELSON, CATHERINE; South Newton HS; Brook, IN; 7/103 Chrs; Capt Drl Tm; Hon Rl; NHS; Pres 4-H; FBLA; Letter Bsktbl; Manchester College; Acctg.

NELSON, CHARLES; Lumen Christi HS; Jackson, MI; Band; Hon Rl; JA; Orch; Michigan St Univ.

NELSON, COLLEEN; Grosse Pointe North HS; Gs Pte Wds, MI; Cls Rep Soph Cls; Cl Rep Jr Cls; Cls Rep Sr Cls; Cmnty Wkr; Hon Rl; Off Ade; Sch Nwsp; Fr Clb; Michigan St Univ; Jrnlsm.

NELSON, CONNIE; Mississinewa HS; Gas City, IN; 5/170 Hon Rl; NHS; Off Ade; Pres DECA; Outsdng Bus Awd 79; 1st Pl At DECA Dist Cntst In The Fd Serv Ind 79; Bus.

NELSON, CYNTHIA; Strongsville HS; Strongsville, OH; Trs Soph Cls; Sec Jr Cls; Trs Sr Cls; Stu Cncl; Capt Gym; Trk; Chrldng; GAA; Mat Maids; PPFtbl; Bowling Green Univ; Social Psych.

NELSON, DANA W; Our Lady Of Angels HS; Cincinnati, OH; 20/100 Cls Rep Frsh Cls; Cmp Fr Grls; Chrh Wkr; Girl Scts; Stg Crw; Stu Cncl; Beta Clb; Univ Of Cincinnati; Scientist.

NELSON, DAVID; South Range HS; Salem, OH; Chrh Wkr; Sprt Ed Sch Nwsp; Drama Clb; Crs Cntry; Trk; Scr Kpr; College; Communications.

NELSON, DAWN; Brandon HS; Ortonville, MI; Cl Rep Jr Cls; Girl Scts; Hon Rl; Jr NHS; Sct Actv; Stu Cncl; Ten; Scr Kpr; College; Med Pro.

NELSON, DONNA; South Range HS; Salem, OH; Chrh Wkr; Hon Rl; Sch Pl; Sch Nwsp; Bsktbl; PPFtbl; Bus Schl; Math.

NELSON, DOTTIE; Circleville HS; Seneca Rocks, WV; 16/30 Chrs; Chrh Wkr; Cmnty Wkr; Hon Rl; Sch Pl; Yth Flsp; Yrbk; Rptr Sch Nwsp; FBLA; FHA; South Branch Voc; Bus Sec.

NELSON, GRANT; Howland HS; Warren, OH; 13/418 Band; Boy Scts; Chrh Wkr; Hon Rl; Jr NHS; Orch; Sct Actv; Ger Clb; IM Sprt; Ohio State Univ; Sci.

NELSON, GREG; Walnut Ridge HS; Edmond, OK; 59/435 Hon Rl; NHS; Spn Clb; Capt Bsbl; All City Bsbl 79; Murray St Univ; Comp Sci.

NELSON, GRETCHEN; North Dickinson HS; Foster City, MI; Trs Jr Cls; Band; Hon Rl; Lbry Ade; Natl Forn Lg; Drama Clb; North Park Coll; Lit.

NELSON, HEIDI; Grant Public HS; Grant, MI; Hon Rl; Sch Pl; 4-H; FFA; Sci Clb; Spn Clb; Letter Ten; Letter Trk; GAA; Cit Awd; Michigan St Univ; Vet Med.

NELSON, JAMES; Rock Hill HS; Ironton, OH; Hon Rl; Beta Clb; Mth Clb; Sci Clb; Trk; Coll; Engr.

NELSON, JAMES F; Athens HS; Sherwood, MI; Hon Rl; Jr NHS; Trk; Vocational Schl; Auto Mech.

NELSON, JEFFREY; Decatur HS; Decatur, MI; Am Leg Boys St; Hon Rl; Letter Wrstlng; Attndnc Awd 78 & 79; S W Michigan Univ; Aviation.

NELSON, JOHN; Valley HS; Beards Fork, WV; Am Leg Boys St; Hon Rl; NHS; WVIT; Comp Sci.

NELSON, JOYCE; Fruitport HS; Nunica, MI; 45/281 Girl Scts; Hon Rl; 4-H; Spn Clb; Cert Of Achvmnt In Coop Wrk 79; Mi Comptn Schlrshp 79; Basic Ed Opportnty Awd 79; Comptd 3 Yrs Of Hnrs Eng; Ferris St Coll; Data Proc.

NELSON, JULIANNA; North Royalton HS; N Royalton, OH; Drl Tm; Off Ade; Sch Mus; Sch Pl; Stg Crw; Stu Cncl; Drama Clb; Lat Clb; Sci Clb; Akron Univ; Bus Admin.

NELSON, JULIE; Crestwood HS; Dearborn Hts, MI; 6/400 Sec Frsh Cls; Cls Rep Frsh Cls; Sec Soph Cls; Cls Rep Soph Cls; Sec Jr Cls; Cl Rep Jr Cls; Sec Sr Cls; Am Leg Aux Girls St; Cmnty Wkr; Hon Rl; Michigan St Univ; Psych.

NELSON, JULIE; Alexandria Monroe HS; Alexandria, IN; Band; Girl Scts; Hon Rl; Sch Mus; Spn Clb; GAA; Ball State; Elem Teacher.

NELSON, JULIE G; Central Catholic HS; Massillon, OH; 6/249 Cmnty Wkr; Girl Scts; Hon Rl; Hosp Ade; OEA; Spn Clb; Frsh Schlrshp Awd 1976; Stark Tech Coll; Comp Sci.

NELSON, KAREN; Greencastle HS; Greencastle, IN; Cls Rep Frsh Cls; Cls Rep Soph Cls; Trs Jr Cls; Chrh Wkr; Cmnty Wkr; FCA; Girl Scts; Stu Cncl; Yth Flsp; 4-H; Univ; Bus.

NELSON, KEITH; Howell HS; Howell, MI; Band; Chrs; Hon Rl; NHS; Sch Mus; Stu Cncl; 4-H; Letter Bsbl; Bsktbl; Letter Ftbl; Top County Schlr; Hon Band; Blue Lk Music Camp Schlrshp; Univ; Med.

NELSON, KENNETH; Elk Garden HS; Keyser, WV; Cls Rep Frsh Cls; Pres Soph Cls; Chrs; Sch Pl; Stg Crw; Stu Cncl; Yth Flsp; Bsbl; Bsktbl; Crs Cntry; Potomac St Coll; Phys Ed.

NELSON, KIM; Burr Oak HS; Burr Oak, MI; 3/30 Sec Frsh Cls; VP Jr Cls; Pres Sr Cls; Hon Rl; Hosp Ade; NHS; Off Ade; Yrbk; Letter Chrldng; PPFtbl; Typng & Shorthand Spped Awd 77; Glen Oaks Cmnty Coll; Exec Sec.

NELSON, KIM; Southridge HS; Huntingburg, IN; 18/175 Hon Rl; Treas JA; NHS; FHA; JA Awd;.

NELSON, KIMBERLY; Au Gres Sims HS; Au Gres, MI; Band; Hon Rl; Natl Forn Lg; NHS; Off Ade; Sch Pl; Rptr Yrbk; Drama Clb; 4-H; Bsktbl; Univ; Eng.

NELSON, KRISTINE; Andrean HS; Merrillville, IN; Girl Scts; Hon Rl; Sct Actv; Rptr Sch Nwsp; Fr Clb; Coach Actv; Valparaiso; Bus Admin; Acctg.

NELSON, LISA; Luther L Wright HS; Ironwood, MI; 25/178 Band; Hon Rl; Yrbk; Pres DECA; Pres Pep Clb; Bsbl; Letter Bsktbl; Letter Gym; Letter Trk; Chrldng; Wis Indianhead Tech Inst; Fshn Mdse.

NELSON, LISA; South Newton HS; Brook, IN; 20/100 Chrs; Drl Tm; Sec 4-H; FBLA; FFA; Letter Bsktbl; Trk; Pom Pon; Purdue Univ; Vet Asst.

NELSON, LORI; Lakeview HS; Cortland, OH; Girl Scts; Hon Rl; Y-Teens; Fr Clb; Chrldng; Ct Reporting Academy; Ct Reporter.

NELSON, MARJIANNE; Upper Arlington Sr HS; Columbus, OH; Hon Rl; Rptr Yrbk; Ed Sch Nwsp; Lat Clb; IM Sprt; Northwestern Univ.

NELSON, MARJORIE C; Crooksville HS; Crooksville, OH; VP Frsh Cls; Trs Soph Cls; Cl Rep Jr Cls; Cmnty Wkr; Hon Rl; Sch Pl; Stu Cncl; 4-H; FTA; Pep Clb; Hnrbl Mentn Vlybl L& Bsktbl 78; Rio Grand Univ; Phys Educ.

NELSON, MARK R; Madison Heights HS; Anderson, IN; Band; Boy Scts; JA; Sct Actv; Crs Cntry; Gym; JA Awd; Univ; Engr.

NELSON, MARTHA; Our Lady Of Mercy HS; Detroit, MI; Cl Rep Jr Cls; Hon Rl; NHS; FSA; Sci Clb; Coach Actv; Univ; Phys Sci.

NELSON, MARTINDALE; Valley HS; Lucasville, OH; 7/107 Band; NHS; Orch; Sch Pl; Sprt Ed Yrbk; 4-H; FHA; FTA; Crs Cntry; Ftbl; Ohio St Univ; Engr.

NELSON, MARY; Waverly HS; Lansing, MI; 9/359 Treas NHS; Capt Bsktbl; Michigan St Univ.

NELSON, MICHAEL; Mt Healthy HS; Cincinnati, OH; 35/450 Hon Rl; Natl Forn Lg; Ed Yrbk; Fr Clb; FBLA; Sci Clb; Univ Of Texas; Psych.

NELSON, PATTY; George Rogers Clark HS; Whiting, IN; 108/219 Chrs; Drl Tm; Fr Clb; Pom Pon; Scr Kpr; Coll; Math.

NELSON, R; Interlochen Arts Acad; Charlotte, MI; Girl Scts; Hon Rl; Glf; College; Fine Arts.

NELSON, ROXANNE; Bedford HS; Lamb, MI; Band; Hon Rl; Lbry Ade; Stu Cncl; Ed Sch Nwsp; Swmmng; Trk; Michigan St Univ; Advrtsng.

NELSON, SHARA; Franklin HS; Westland, MI; Chrs; Chrh Wkr; Girl Scts; Hon Rl; Ricks College; Bus Admin.

NELSON, SHARON; Martin Luther King HS; Detroit, MI; 2/200 Hon Rl; Hosp Ade; NHS; Yth Flsp; Fr Clb; FDA; Pep Clb; Cit Awd; Michigan St Univ; Medicine.

NELSON, STELLA D; Hannan HS; Glenwood, WV; 5/30 Hon Rl; Jr NHS; Lbry Ade; NHS; Yrbk; FHA; Pep Clb; Univ.

NELSON, STUART; Rapid River HS; Rapid Rvr, MI; 4-H; Trk; 4-H Awd; Univ.

NELSON, TANYA; Toronto HS; Toronto, OH; 25/135 Chrs; Chrh Wkr; Cmnty Wkr; Hon Rl; Jr NHS; Sch Mus; Sch Pl; Yth Flsp; Fr Clb; Pep Clb; Mt Vernon Nezerene Coll; Med Tech.

NELSON, TERESA; Marshall HS; Marshall, MI; Am Leg Aux Girls St; Hon Rl; Lbry Ade; NHS; 4-H; Pep Clb; Mgrs; College; Comp Sci.

NELSON, TERRY A; Galesburg Augusta Cmnty HS; Galesburg, MI; 16/115 Hon Rl; Lbry Ade; Spn Clb; Letter Bsbl; Purdue Univ; Vet Med.

NELSON, TRACEY L; Redford HS; Detroit, MI; Chrh Wkr; Hon Rl; JA; Stu Cncl; College; Marketing Mgmt.

NELSON, VICKI; Mississinewa HS; Marion, IN; Band; Chrh Wkr; Hon Rl; Jr NHS; Yth Flsp; Y-Teens; Drama Clb; 4-H; Fr Clb; PPFtbl;.

NELTNER, ANNETTE; Mc Nicholas HS; Cincinnati, OH; Chrs; Girl Scts; Sch Mus; Sch Pl; Univ Of Cincinnati; Comp Engr.

NEMANIC, SHELLEY; Douglas Mac Arthur HS; Saginaw, MI; Cl Rep Jr Cls; Band; Hon Rl; NHS; Stu Cncl; Lat Clb; Pep Clb; Pom Pon; College.

NEMENZ, JUDY; Springfield Local HS; Poland, OH; Chrh Wkr; Cmnty Wkr; Drl Tm; Girl Scts; Hon Rl; Off Ade; Sct Actv; Yth Flsp; 4-H; Pep Clb; Univ.

NEMETH, CHRIS; Clay HS; S Bend, IN; 90/450 Cl Rep Jr Cls; Hon Rl; VP Stu Cncl; Ger Clb; Ten; IM Sprt; Awd Of Merit In Drafting; Ball St Univ; Archt.

NEMETH, F; John Adams HS; So Bend, IN; 63/395 Hon Rl; Lit Mag; Univ; Elec Engr.

NEMETH, HEIDI; Fairmont West HS; Kettering, OH; Hon Rl; NHS; Off Ade; DECA; Pep Clb; Wright St Univ; Busns.

NEMETH, JEANINE; Admiral King HS; Lorain, OH; Mb Johnson Schl Of Nursing.

NEMETH, JEFF; Clay HS; S Bend, IN; 83/360 Hon Rl; NHS; Stu Cncl; Capt Ftbl; Kiwan Awd; Hanover Coll; Bus.

NEMETH, JULIE; Bowling Green HS; Bowling Green, OH; 1/322 Cls Rep Soph Cls; Cl Rep Jr Cls; Band; Chrs; Hon Rl; Jr NHS; NHS; Bowling Green State Univ; Pre Med Pr.

NEMETH, NANCY; Marian HS; S Bend, IN; 8/162 Hon Rl; Ind Univ; Med.

NEMETI, JEAN; Buckeye South HS; Tiltonsville, OH; 14/110 Am Leg Aux Girls St; Band; Girl Scts; Hon Rl; NHS; Stu Cncl; Rptr Yrbk; Drama Clb; Pep Clb; Spn Clb; Kent State; Business.

NENNINGER, KATHY; Warren Woods HS; Warren, MI; 65/350 Hon Rl; Lbry Ade; NHS; Off Ade; OEA; Macomb Cnty Cmnty Coll; Bus Mgmt.

NEPHEW, KURT; Midland HS; Midland, MI; Band; Boy Scts; Hon Rl; Letter Swmmng; Natl Merit Ltr; Stu Grant From Michigan St Univ; Schlrshp From St Of Michigan; Mbr Of Eagle Scout Class Of 76; Michigan St Univ; Med.

NERI, PATTI; Hubbard HS; Hubbard, OH; 37/335 Girl Scts; Hon Rl; FBLA; Spn Clb; Letter Trk; PPFtbl; College; Business Major.

NERO, JUDITH; Solon HS; Solon, OH; Cl Rep Jr Cls; Pres AFS; Chrs; Hon Rl; Hosp Ade; NHS; Sch Mus; Sch Pl; College; Nursing.

NERSESIAN, NANCY; Divine Child HS; Dearborn Hts, MI; 14/200 Band; Hon Rl; NHS; Orch; Red Cr Ade; Rptr Sch Nwsp; Swmmng; Univ Of Mich; Architecture.

NERVIG, APRIL; Berea HS; Berea, OH; Hon Rl; NHS; Yrbk; Letter Swmmng; College; Aerospace.

NESBIT, LARRY; Bellbrook HS; Bellbrook, OH; 3/178 Cls Rep Frsh Cls; Sch Mus; Fr Clb; Pep Clb; Spn Clb; Ftbl; IM Sprt; Coll; Law.

NESBITT, DANIEL; Parkersburg South HS; Parkersburg, WV; Boy Scts; Chrs; FCA; Pol Wkr; Yth Flsp; Key Clb; Letter Ftbl; Wrstlng; IM Sprt; Mgrs; Navy.

NESE, JON; Steubenville Cath Ctrl HS; Steubenville, OH; 2/220 Am Leg Boys St; Hon Rl; NHS; Stu Cncl; Letter Bsktbl; Capt Glf; Trk; Bausch & Lomb Awd; Natl Merit SF; Penn State Univ; Meteorology.

NESS, GREGORY; Columbia City HS; Columbia City, IN; Cls Rep Frsh Cls; Cls Rep Soph Cls; Cl Rep Jr Cls; Bsbl; Bsktbl; Ftbl; College.

NESS, SUZANNE; Huntington Catholic HS; Huntington, IN; Cls Rep Soph Cls; Girl Scts; Hon Rl; Stu Cncl; Trk; Capt Chrldng; GAA; IM Sprt; Indiana Univ; Engl.

NESTELL, DEAN; Benzie Central HS; Interlochen, MI; Boy Scts; Chrh Wkr; Hon Rl; Sct Actv; Sch Nwsp; Bsktbl; Crs Cntry; Trk; Cit Awd; God Cntry Awd; Wester Mich Univ; Comm Art.

NESTER, BRENDA; Hicksville HS; Hicksville, OH; VP Frsh Cls; Pres Soph Cls; Pres Jr Cls; Hon Rl; NHS; 4-H; Bsktbl; GAA; 4-H Awd; Pres Awd; Farriers College.

NESTER, BRYAN; Salem HS; Salem, IN; Hon Rl; JA; NHS; Lat Clb; Capt Ftbl; Letter Trk; DAR Good Citizenship Awd; Outstanding History Stu; College; Engr.

NESTER, KELLY A; Lake Catholic HS; Painesville, OH; Cls Rep Sr Cls; Chrs; Hon Rl; Sch Mus; Sch Pl; Stu Cncl; Pep Clb; IM Sprt; PPFtbl; Merit Ach Awd; Hmcmng Chrmn; Coll; Busns.

NESTER, SUSAN; Archbishop Alter HS; Kettering, OH; Chrs; Chrh Wkr; Cmnty Wkr; Girl Scts; Lbry Ade; Red Cr Ade; Stu Cncl; Sch Nwsp; Drama Clb; Pep Clb; Univ; Engr.

NESTER, VICKY; Calhoun County HS; Millstone, WV; Hon Rl; Hosp Ade; NHS; Rptr Sch Nwsp; Pres 4-H; Treas VICA; GAA; 4-H Awd; Parkersburg Comm Coll; X Ray Tech.

NESTOR, BRENDA; Nicholas County HS; Summersville, WV; 57/214 Chrs; Hon Rl; Sch Mus; Fr Clb; FHA; FTA; Univ; Nursing.

NESTOR, SHARON; Philip Barbour HS; Philippi, WV; Aud/Vis; Hon Rl; Lbry Ade; DECA; Mat Maids; Bus Schl.

NESTOR, TERRY; Pickens HS; Pickens, WV; Sec Frsh Cls; VP Soph Cls; Cl Rep Jr Cls; Rptr Yrbk; Rptr Sch Nwsp; Scr Kpr; W Virginia Wesleyan Coll; Elem Ed.

NETH, BRENDA; Columbia HS; Columbia Sta, OH; Band; Chrs; Sch Pl; Yrbk; Sch Nwsp; Drama Clb; Kent State Univ; Journalism.

NETHERLAIN, DOUGLAS; Shakamak HS; Jasonville, IN; 46/86 FFA; Terra Haute Iv Tech; Welding.

NETHERS, MARY L; Licking County Jt Voc HS; Nashport, OH; 14/142 Hon Rl; Stu Cncl; Y-Teens; Rptr Yrbk; Pres 4-H; OEA; Mat Maids; Scr Kpr; 4-H Awd; Received Ambassador Awd; Education Assoc 1st Pl Regional Level; Vocational Schl; Admin Sec.

NETHERS, MIKE; Newark Sr HS; Newark, OH; 34/600 Trs Sr Cls; Boy Scts; Natl Forn Lg; NHS; Orch; Sct Actv; Treas Stu Cncl; Bsktbl; Ftbl; YMCA Youth In Gov Prog Ele Clerk Of House; Ohio St Univ; Medicine.

NETHERTON, STEVE; Tipton HS; Tipton, IN; Hon Rl; Ftbl; IM Sprt; Purdue Univ; Mechanicis.

NETHERY, KATI; Mansfield Christian HS; Mansfield, OH; Cls Rep Soph Cls; Band; Chrh Wkr; Hon Rl; Stu Cncl; Drama Clb; Bsktbl; Gym; Swmmng; Trk; Univ; Theatre.

NETTLE, GREGORY; Northwest HS; Clinton, OH; Cls Rep Frsh Cls; Cls Rep Sr Cls; Chrs; Chrh Wkr; FCA; Hon Rl; Jr NHS; Natl Forn Lg; NHS; Sch Mus; Cincinnati Bible Coll; Music.

NETTLE, LISA; Northwest HS; Clinton, OH; Pres Frsh Cls; Pres Soph Cls; Pres Jr Cls; Pres Sr Cls; Chrs; Hon Rl; Lbry Ade; NHS; Sch Mus; Yth Flsp; Univ; Home Ec.

NETTLETON, ELAINE; Hillsdale HS; Jeromesville, OH; 2/90 Pres Band; Chrh Wkr; Hon Rl; NHS; Pres Yth Flsp; 4-H; Lat Clb; 4-H Awd; Pres Awd; Sel Rep Stud Mgmt Day Ohio Dept Of Trasn 1978; Grace Coll; Poli Sci.

NETZLEY, LORI L; Swan Valley HS; Saginaw, MI; 18/188 Band; Chrh Wkr; Drm Mjrt; Girl Scts; Hon Rl; Jr NHS; NHS; Yth Flsp; Pep Clb; Letter Swmmng; Solo Esmble Band Comp; Pep Band; Central Michigan Univ; Commnctns.

NETZLY, PAULETTE; Northeastern HS; S Charleston, OH; Band; Hon Rl; Yth Flsp; 4-H; Fr Clb; Heidelberg; Elem Educ.

NEU, DALE; Allen East HS; Lima, OH; 29/120 Boy Scts; Hon Rl; Stg Crw; Sprt Ed Yrbk; Bsbl; Ftbl; Trk; IM Sprt; Hon Mention Ftbl 77; Univ Of Arizona; Conservation.

NEU, DEANNE; Unionville Sebewaing HS; Unionville, MI; 14/113 Band; Hon Rl; Yth Flsp; Concordia Coll; Tchr.

NEUBAUER, AGNES; Eastmoor Sr HS; Columbus, OH; 11/290 Hon Rl; NHS; Stern Coll For Women; Archt.

NEUBAUER, KIMBERLY; St Joseph HS; St Joseph, MI; Band; Hosp Ade; Treas JA; Yth Flsp; Fr Clb; Trk; Central Michigan; Sociology.

NEUENDORF, NANCY; Niles HS; Niles, MI; 38/380 Cl Rep Jr Cls; Cls Rep Sr Cls; Band; Hon Rl; Hosp Ade; NHS; Sch Mus; Sch Pl; Stu Cncl; 4-H; William Woods Coll.

NEUFELD, FRANCENE; Bluffton HS; Bluffton, OH; Band; Chrs; Chrh Wkr; Hon Rl; Sch Mus; Sch Pl; Pres Yth Flsp; Eng Clb; Fr Clb; Pep Clb; Bluffton Coll.

NEUFELD, LES; Bexley HS; Columbus, OH; VP Sr Cls; AFS; Chrs; Hon Rl; NHS; Sch Mus; Sch Pl; Stu Cncl; Yrbk; Sch Nwsp; College; Medicine.

NEUFELDT, SANDRA A; West Lafayette HS; W Lafayette, IN; 39/176 Band; Hon Rl; Sch Mus; Sch Nwsp; Drama Clb; Ger Clb; Pep Clb; Bsktbl; Letter Trk; Indiana Univ; Jrnlsm.

NEUGEBAUER, KATHLEEN; West Lafayette HS; W Lafaytt, IN; Band; FCA; Hon Rl; Sprt Ed Yrbk; IM Sprt; Pom Pon; Purdue Univ; Sci.

NEUHART, CHARLES; Shenandoah HS; Quaker City, OH; Sec Jr Cls; Cls Rep Sr Cls; Hon Rl; NHS; Sch Mus; Sch Pl; Stu Cncl; Rptr Yrbk; Rptr Sch Nwsp; Mth Clb; Ohio St Univ; Civil Engr.

NEUHART, ERIC; Meadowbrook HS; Senecaville, OH; VP Frsh Cls; Cls Rep Frsh Cls; Cl Rep Jr Cls; Hon Rl; Sch Pl; Pep Clb; Bsktbl; IM Sprt; Ohio St Univ; Educ.

NEUHART, ROBERT; Meadowbrook HS; Senecaville, OH; 7/190 VP Frsh Cls; Cls Rep Frsh Cls; Cls Rep Soph Cls; Cl Rep Jr Cls; Pres Sr Cls; Debate Tm; Hon Rl; ROTC; Mth Clb; Pep Clb; Ohio St Univ; Comp Engr.

NEUHART, TERRY; Morgan HS; Mc Connelsville, OH; 4/273 Hon Rl; Lbry Ade; NHS; Mth Clb; Sci Clb; Spn Clb; Ohio State; Engr.

NEUMAN, BETH; Ludington HS; Ludington, MI; 16/260 Hon Rl; NHS; Rptr Yrbk; Rptr Sch Nwsp; Letter Swmmng; Coach Actv; GAA; Tmr; West Shore Community College; Bio.

NEUMAN, MARY; Rocky River HS; Rocky Rvr, OH; Hon Rl; Letter Ten; Chrldng; GAA; IM Sprt; Univ.

NEUMANN, BARRY; Galion HS; Galion, OH; 18/275 Crs Cntry; Letter Swmmng; Univ Of Cincinnati; Civil Engr.

NEUMANN, CARRIE; Bellbrook HS; Bellbrook, OH; AFS; Chrs; Drl Tm; Girl Scts; Sch Mus; Stg Crw; Yth Flsp; Pep Clb; Spn Clb; GAA; College; Health.

NEUMANN, INGRID; Fairview HS; Fairview Pk, OH; Chrs; Hon Rl; Lit Mag; Mod UN; Sch Pl; Stg Crw; Drama Clb; Sci Clb; IM Sprt; Univ; Comm Art.

NEUMANN, NANCY; Kearsley HS; Flint, MI; 16/379 Girl Scts; Hon Rl; Jr NHS; NHS; Glf; Ten; Mic Tech Univ; Physics.

NEUMANN, RICHARD; Big Rapids HS; Big Rpds, MI; Band; Boy Scts; Hon Rl; Sct Actv; Bsktbl; Crs Cntry; Trk; God Cntry Awd; Central Mich Univ; Bio.

NEUMEYER, JEFFERY; Chesaning Union HS; Chesaning, MI; Chrh Wkr; Hon Rl; Spn Clb; Letter Crs Cntry; Letter Trk; IM Sprt; College; Spanish.

NEUMEYER, JUDY; Western HS; Saginaw, MI; 47/487 Hon Rl; Sec NHS; Rptr Yrbk; Letter Trk; Varsity Vllybl Letter 77; Delta Coll; Soc Work.

NEUTZLING, CONNIE; Madison Comp HS; Mansfield, OH; Sec Jr Cls; Sec Sr Cls; Band; Hon Rl; Stu Cncl; Fr Clb; Scr Kpr; Univ; HS Math Tchr.

NEVELS, LOIS; Bishop Luers HS; Ft Wayne, IN; Chem.

NEVEU, GIGI A; Soo Area HS; Sault Ste Marie, MI; Hst Jr Cls; Band; Chrh Wkr; Cmnty Wkr; Hon Rl; Orch; Eng Clb; Lat Clb; Bsbl; Lake Superior State; Forestry.

NEVILLE, KATHRYN; East Detroit HS; East Detroit, MI; Cmp Fr Grls; Hon Rl; Lbry Ade; NHS; Off Ade; Yrbk; Swmmng; Chrldng; Tmr; Siena Heights; Bus.

NEVILLE, MYRON; Broad Ripple HS; Indianapolis, IN; Chrh Wkr; FCA; Hon Rl; Sct Actv; Yth Flsp; Boys Clb Am; Ger Clb; Wrstlng; Legion Of Merit; Indiana Univ; Computer Sci.

NEVISKA, TIMOTHY; Brookhaven HS; Columbus, OH; Band; Hon Rl; Jr NHS; NHS; Sch Pl; Stg Crw; Drama Clb; Fr Clb; Pres Rdo Clb; Bsktbl; Knight Chancellor Esquire & Page 76; Acad Of Scholars 78; Diploma Of Distnctn 79; Ohio St Univ; Mech Engr.

NEVITT, JERI; Hamilton Southeastern HS; Noblesville, IN; VP JA; 4-H; OEA; Mgrs; Scr Kpr; JA Awd; 4th Pl Acctg Cntst For Offc Educ Assn 79; Voting Delegate At St OEA Cntst 79; Indiana Univ; Acctg.

NEVITT, MELINDA; South Newton Jr Sr HS; Goodland, IN; Band; Chrs; Off Ade; Sch Mus; Sch Pl; FBLA; Lat Clb; Tmr;.

NEVIUS, MARY; Chaminade Julienne HS; Dayton, OH; 12/249 Chrh Wkr; Cmnty Wkr; FCA; Hon Rl; NHS; Boys Clb Am; Chrldng; Coach Actv; GAA; PPFtbl; Univ; Mech Engr.

NEVSETA, TRISA; Kelloggsville HS; Kentwood, MI; Cls Rep Frsh Cls; Cls Rep Soph Cls; Trs Jr Cls; Cl Rep Jr Cls; Cmp Fr Grls; Hon Rl; Sch Pl; Sec Stu Cncl; Ed Yrbk; Sprt Ed Yrbk; Univ; Dramatic Arts.

NEW, NANCY; Henryville HS; Henryville, IN; 13/62 Capt Drl Tm; Girl Scts; Hon Rl; Lbry Ade; NHS; Sch Pl; Rptr Yrbk; Yrbk; FTA; Pep Clb; Indiana St Univ; Linguistics.

NEWBERG, LENITA; Taylor HS; Kokomo, IN; Band; Drm Mjrt; Hon Rl; Orch; Pres Yth Flsp; Fr Cl b; Bsktbl; Whos Who In Music 78; Univ; Music Educ.

NEWBERRY, CYNTHIA; London City HS; London, OH; Band; Hon Rl; Fr Clb; Univ Of Portland; Psych.

NEWBERRY, JUDY; New Richmond HS; Moscow, OH; Band; Hon Rl; NHS; Orch; Sch Mus; Sch Pl; Stg Crw;

Drama Clb; Fr Clb; Sci Clb; Spn Clb; Spanish Natl Hnr Soc 76; Univ; Work With Mentally Retarded.

NEWBERRY, ROBERT; Struthers HS; Struthers, OH; Hon Rl; Lat Clb; Bsbl; Ftbl; IM Sprt; Univ; Vet.

NEWBERRY, STEVEN; Anderson HS; Cincinnati, OH; 11/380 Chrs; Hon Rl; NHS; Orch; Sch Mus; Stu Cncl; Pres Awd; SAR Awd; Univ Of Cinti; Music.

NEWBERRY, TINA; Meridian HS; Sanford, MI; 29/123 Hon Rl; Hosp Ade; JA; Off Ade; Sch Mus; Sch Pl; Stg Crw; Mid Mic Community College; Paramedic.

NEWBORN, MARY; Lawrence Central HS; Indianapolis, IN; 43/370 Band; Chrh Wkr; Girl Scts; Hon Rl; NHS; Sct Actv; Sec Yth Flsp; Pep Clb; IM Sprt; PPFtbl; Center For Leadership Dev Participant; 1st Class Girl Scouts Of Amer Awd; College; Poli Sci.

NEWBROUGH, AVIS; Lakeview HS; Cortland, OH; 12/180 Chrs; Girl Scts; Hon Rl; Lbry Ade; NHS; Y-Teens; Rptr Yrbk; Beta Clb; 4-H; Mth Clb; St Cert; Cert Of Perfct Attndnc 5 Yrs; Alderson Univ; Vet.

NEWBURG, JULIA L; Cathedral HS; Indianapolis, IN; 10/148 Chrs; Girl Scts; Hon Rl; NHS; Red Cr Ade; Stu Cncl; Rptr Sch Nwsp; Spn Clb; Hoosier Schlr 79; Internatl Stud Leadrshp Inst 78; Acad Letter & Gold Bar For Achvmnt; Spirit Awd; Professional Careers Inst; Dent.

NEWBURN, DELANO; Lasalle HS; South Bend, IN; 56/488 Band; Chrs; Chrh Wkr; Girl Scts; Hon Rl; JA; Sch Mus; Sch Pl; Drama Clb; Pep Clb; Top 5 Black Soph Program Mbr; Black Cultural Soc V Pres; Purdue Univ; Civil Engr.

NEWBURN, SANDRA; Jefferson Union HS; Bloomingdale, OH; Band; Sch Mus; Stg Crw; Pres Yth Flsp; Beta Clb; Pres 4-H; Bsbl; Bsktbl; GAA; PPFtbl; Muskingum Univ; Educ.

NEWBY, KRISTIN; Marion Adams HS; Sheridan, IN; 1/85 Val; Girl Scts; Hon Rl; Jr NHS; NHS; Capt Bsktbl; Rotary Awd; Purdue Univ; Sci.

NEWCOM, DWAYNE; Coldwater HS; Coldwater, OH; 23/146 Chrh Wkr; Cmnty Wkr; Hon Rl; NHS; Rptr Yrbk; Sprt Ed Sch Nwsp; Letter Bsbl; Letter Bsktbl; Coach Actv; Bowling Green St Univ; Mgmt.

NEWCOMB, PATRICIA; Morgantown HS; Morgantwn, WV; 15/500 Jr NHS; Lbry Ade; Orch; Spn Clb; Natl Merit Ltr; Creative Writing 76 77; Spanich 76 77; Hnrbl Merit Magna Cum Laude Natl Latin Exam 77 78; Oberlin Univ; Med.

NEWCOMB, VICKIE L; James A Garfield HS; Garrettsville, OH; Cl Rep Jr Cls; Off Ade; Stu Cncl; Rptr Sch Nwsp; Drama Clb; 4-H; Fr Clb; Pep Clb; Scr Kpr; 4-H Awd; Fashion Merchantdising.

NEWELL, RYAN; Frontier HS; Newport, OH; Chrh Wkr; Hon Rl; NHS; Sch Pl; Spn Clb; Letter Bsbl; Letter Bsktbl; Ftbl; All PVC Bsbl 79; All OVAC Bsktbl Hon Ment 79; Sel To Attend Boys St 79; Univ; Educ.

NEWHART, JULIE; Western Boone HS; Jamestown, IN; Sec Sr Cls; Am Leg Aux Girls St; Sec Chrh Wkr; Cmnty Wkr; FCA; NHS; Sch Mus; Valparaiso; Nursing.

NEWHART, NEAL; Clinton Prairie HS; Frankfort, IN; 10/90 Cl Rep Jr Cls; VP Sr Cls; Hon Rl; NHS; Sch Mus; Stg Crw; Stu Cncl; Rptr Sch Nwsp; FFA; Lat Clb; Purdue Univ; Vet.

NEWHOUSE, ANDREA B; Webster Cnty HS; Webster Springs, WV; Chrs; Chrh Wkr; Cmnty Wkr; Hon Rl; Pol Wkr; Yth Flsp; Yrbk; Sch Nwsp; Drama Clb; 4-H; Career Coll; Acctg.

NEWING, LAURA; Robert S Rogers HS; Toledo, OH; Band; Girl Scts; Hon Rl; Jr NHS; NHS; Sch Mus; Sec Ger Clb; Sci Clb; College; Science.

NEWKIRK, DAVID; Mumford HS; Detroit, MI; Cls Rep Frsh Cls; Cls Rep Sr Cls; Boy Scts; Chrh Wkr; Cmnty Wkr; Hon Rl; Jr NHS; NHS; Sch Pl; Sct Actv; Mumford Hnr Soc 76 77 78; Natl Hnr Soc 76 77 78; Univ Of Michigan; Bus Admin.

NEWKIRK, SANDY; Wilmington Sr HS; Wilmington, OH; Band; Off Ade; Pep Clb; Eastern Kentucky Univ; Bus Admin.

NEWLON, PHILIP; St Francis Desales HS; Westerville, OH; Band; Hon Rl; Letter Wrstlng; Columbus Tech Inst; Mechanics.

NEWLOVE, DANE; North Baltimore HS; Cygnet, OH; 3/57 Trs Sr Cls; Band; Chrs; NHS; Orch; Sch Mus; Ed Sch Nwsp; Bowling Green State; Music Ed.

NEWMAN, CHARLES L; North Adams HS; Seaman, OH; 15/100 Am Leg Boys St; Band; Chrh Wkr; Cmnty Wkr; Drm Bgl; Hon Rl; Sch Pl; Stu Cncl; 4-H; IM Sprt; Ohio St Univ; Engr.

NEWMAN, CINDY; Shaker Hts HS; Shaker Hts, OH; Hon Rl; Lit Mag; Yrbk; Fr Clb; Univ; Cmnctns.

NEWMAN, DEBORAH; Liberty HS; Youngstown, OH; 5/214 Chrs; Hon Rl; Lit Mag; NHS; Spn Clb; Univ; Med.

NEWMAN, FREDERICK; Clare HS; Clare, MI; Hon Rl; Mi Comp Schlshp 79; Clare HS Stdnt Councl 79; Michigan Tech Univ; Engr.

NEWMAN, GREG; Ontario HS; Mnsfld, OH; Hon Rl; Letter Ftbl; Trk; College; Engr.

NEWMAN, GREG; Eaton HS; Eaton, OH; 27/175 Band; Chrs; OSU.

NEWMAN, JANET; Logan Elm HS; Laurelville, OH; 8/182 Sec Frsh Cls; Trs Sr Cls; Cls Rep Sr Cls; Hon Rl; NHS; Stu Cncl; Yth Flsp; OEA; Bsktbl; Letter Trk;.

NEWMAN, JON; R Nelson Snider HS; Ft Wayne, IN; Fr Clb; Whos Who Among Amer HS Stud 77; Mbr Of Distinguished Schlrs 76 79; De Pauw Univ; Exploratory.

NEWMAN, JULIE; St Stephen Area HS; Saginaw, MI; 2/85 Pres Frsh Cls; VP Jr Cls; Sal; Hon Rl; NHS; Sch Pl; Stu Cncl; Mic Tech; Engr.

NEWMAN, KEVIN; Elder HS; Cinn, OH; 140/384 Ohi College Of Appl Sci; Elec Tech.

NEWMAN, KRISTA; Sacred Heart Academy; Clare, MI; Cls Rep Sr Cls; Chrs; Chrh Wkr; Hon Rl; PAVAS; Stu Cncl; Yrbk; 4-H; Trk; Chrldng; 10 Yr Hon Awd For Dancing 79; Jr Class Homecoming Attendant 79; Grand Champ 4 H Foods Demo & T V Appearnce; Cntrl Michigan Univ; Exec Sec.

NEWMAN, LAURA; Big Creek HS; Caretta, WV; 17/154 Cl Rep Jr Cls; Band; Girl Scts; Hon Rl; Rptr Yrbk; Pep Clb; Spn Clb; Letter Bsktbl; Letter Ten; Letter Mgrs; Rec 2nd Pl 3rd Pl Hnr Mention On Photog Work; Marshall Univ; Acctg.

NEWMAN, LORI; Washington Irving HS; Clarksburg, WV; 14/140 VP Sr Cls; Band; Hon Rl; Hosp Ade; Stg Crw; Stu Cncl; Yth Flsp; Y-Teens; Fr Clb; Lat Clb; West Virginia Univ; Vet Sci.

NEWMAN, MICHAEL; Yellow Springs HS; Yellow Sprg, OH; 13/87 Boy Scts; Chrs; Off Ade; Orch; Sch Mus; Stg Crw; Drama Clb; Letter Crs Cntry; Natl Merit SF; UNK; Bio.

NEWMAN, RICHARD; West Lafayette HS; W Lafayette, IN; 61/185 Band; Hon Rl; Yth Flsp; Letter Trk; IM Sprt; Purdue Univ.

NEWMAN, SHERRI; L Anse Creuse HS; Mt Clemens, MI; 1/260 Val; Chrs; Chrh Wkr; Hon Rl; Jr NHS; Sec NHS; Treas Yth Flsp; Capt Trk; Capt PPFtbl; Tmr; Michigan St Univ; Soc Work.

NEWMAN, TAMMY; Old Fort HS; Old Fort, OH; 16/53 Band; Hon Rl; Sch Pl; Stg Crw; Rptr Yrbk; Rptr Sch Nwsp; FHA; Spn Clb; Letter Trk; IM Sprt; MVP Vllybl 78; Vllybl Ltr 4 Yrs;.

NEWMAN, TERRI; Washington HS; Washington, IN; 5/216 Cmp Fr Grls; Chrs; Chrh Wkr; Hon Rl; Lbry Ade; Orch; Red Cr Ade; Sch Mus; Sch Pl; Stg Crw; Univ; Conslr.

NEWMARCH, BARBARA; Kingsley Area HS; Kingsley, MI; 1/49 Val; Band; Hon Rl; NHS; Cit Awd; Mich State Univ; Vet Med.

NEWMASTER, BRUCE; Central HS; Evansville, IN; 171/511 Chrs; Hon Rl; Sch Mus; Stg Crw; Stu Cncl; Yth Flsp; 4-H; Finlst For Navy ROTC Schskp 79; Illinois Inst Of Tech; Civil Engr.

NEWMYER, EDWARD; Fruitport HS; Muskegon, MI; 3/281 Hon Rl; NHS; Trk; Natl Merit Ltr; Natl Merit SF; Suomi Coll; Law.

NEWPORT, ALAN; William Henry Harrison HS; Harrison, OH; Band; Hon Rl; Sch Mus; All Ohio St Fair Band; All Ohio HS Bnd; Hnr H Awd; Univ Of Cincinnati; Music.

NEWPORT, PENNY; Wapakoneta HS; Wapakoneta, OH; Chrs; Hon Rl; Jr NHS; Lat Clb; Lima Branch Univ; Radiologic Tech.

NEWPOWER, SHERRI; Bay City All Saints HS; Bay City, MI; Cmnty Wkr; Hon Rl; Univ Of Mic; Phy Ther.

NEWSAD, DAVID; Northmont HS; Dayton, OH; Am Leg Boys St; Boy Scts; Chrh Wkr; Hon Rl; Sct Actv; Yth Flsp; Sch Nwsp; IM Sprt; God Cntry Awd; Eagle Scout 77; 3 Yr Masters Hon Carrier Dayton Daily News 78; Sci Projct Awd 76; Wright St Univ; Pre Med.

NEWSOM, DEAN; Morgan HS; Malta, OH; 3/232 Pres Jr Cls; Am Leg Boys St; Hon Rl; Treas NHS; Rptr Yrbk; Mth Clb; Spn Clb; Letter Bsbl; Letter Bsktbl; Letter Crs Cntry; WTAP Quiz Shw Tm; Pre Med Clb; Univ; Petro Engr.

NEWSOME, KIMBERLY; Rogers HS; Toledo, OH; Chrh Wkr; Girl Scts; Hon Rl; JA; Sch Mus; Spn Clb; Trk; Chrldng; 4-H Awd; JA Awd; Univ Of Michigan; Spanish.

NEWTON, BILL R; Turpin HS; Cincinnati, OH; 35/357 Off Ade; Letter Bsbl; Letter Bsktbl; Letter Ftbl; Oklahoma St Univ; Educ.

NEWTON, BRENDA; Clinton Central HS; Michigantwn, IN; 6/100 Am Leg Aux Girls St; FCA; NHS; 4-H; Pep Clb; Sci Clb; Letter Bsktbl; Sci.

NEWTON, JEFFREY; Goods Bible Schl; Mocksville, NC; 3/42 Pres Jr Cls; VP Sr Cls; Chrs; Chrh Wkr; Hon Rl; Sch Pl;.

NEWTON, LORI; West Lafayette HS; W Lafayette, IN; 19/185 Pres Band; Drm Mjrt; JA; Lit Mag; NHS; Quill & Scroll; Sch Mus; Stu Cncl; Sch Nwsp; Pep Clb; Ind Univ; Marketing.

NEWTON, LUCINDA; Waldron Area HS; Waldron, MI; 11/39 Sec Sr Cls; Hon Rl; Lbry Ade; NHS; Off Ade; Stg Crw; Rptr Sch Nwsp; Pep Clb; Trk; Busns Schl; Busns Admin.

NEWTON, MARY; Valley Local HS; Lucasville, OH; 4/110 Chrh Wkr; Hon Rl; Yrbk; FHA; FTA; Pep Clb; Berea Coll; Bus Admin.

NEWTON, PAUL; Croswell Lexington HS; Croswll, MI; NHS; Letter Ten; St Clair Cnty Cmnty Coll; Archt.

NEWTON III, JOSEPH A; Brooke HS; Wellsburg, WV; 6/400 Aud/Vis; Hon Rl; Lit Mag; NHS; Pres Yth Flsp; Ger Clb; Sci Clb; Coll; Freelance Writer.

NEWYEAR, DAVID; Interlochen Arts Academy; Willoughby, OH; Band; Hon Rl; Orch; Stg Crw; Gradutd With Hons 1979; Awded Schlshp From Baldwin Wallace Coll 1979; Northwestern Univ; Music.

NEYLON, BRENDA; James Ford Rhodes HS; Cleveland, OH; Chrs; Chrh Wkr; Stu Cncl; Ger Clb; Chrldng; Coll; Elem Ed.

NGUYEN, ANH N; Mt Hope HS; Mt Hope, WV; Sch Nwsp; Univ Of Wv.

NGUYEN, HOA; St Johns HS; St Johns, MI; 66/300 Chrh Wkr; Hon Rl; NHS; Letter Gym; Bausch & Lomb Awd; Hope Coll; Pre Med.

NGUYEN, HUNG; Lasalle HS; Mont Clair, CA; 17/500 Chrh Wkr; Cmnty Wkr; Hon Rl; Civ Clb; JA Awd; Hnr Awd For Meritorius Serv For Chgo Mtr Club 77; Awd Of Merit In Schlrshp 79; Awd Of Merit In Perfct Atten; California Inst Of Tech; Elec Engr.

NGUYEN, MAI; Thomas W Harvey HS; Painesville, OH; Hst Frsh Cls; Hon Rl; JA; Jr NHS; PAVAS; FSA; Bausch & Lomb Awd; Case Western Reserve Univ; Chem Engr.

NGUYEN, SON; Thomas W Harvey HS; Painesville, OH; Boy Scts; Hon Rl; Sci Clb; Ftbl; Socr; Trk; DAR Awd; Univ; Elec Engr.

NIBERT, PAMELA; Hannan HS; Apple Grove, WV; Hon Rl; NHS; Off Ade; Stu Cncl; Rptr Yrbk; 4-H; FHA; Pep Clb; DAR Awd; Glenville Coll.

NICELY, RANDY; Lockland HS; Lockland, OH; Cl Rep Jr Cls; Cls Rep Sr Cls; Band; Boy Scts; Chrh Wkr; Drm Bgl; Hon Rl; Lbry Ade; Sch Mus; Sch Pl; Univ; Eng.

NICEWANDER, KRISTEN A; Washington HS; Massillon, OH; Cl Rep Jr Cls; Cls Rep Sr Cls; AFS; Band; Pres Chrs; Hon Rl; NHS; Sch Mus; Stu Cncl; Yth Flsp; Univ; Music.

NICHOLAS, CAROLINE; Beaumont HS For Girls; Lyndhurst, OH; Cls Rep Soph Cls; Pres Sr Cls; Chrh Wkr; Hon Rl; Hosp Ade; Lit Mag; Off Ade; Stu Cncl; Chrldng; Dance A Thon Chrmn For Mentally Retarded 79; Volntr Awd 78; John Carroll Univ; Hosptl Admin.

NICHOLAS, GREGG; Cedar Lake Academy; Bessemer, MI; Band; Chrh Wkr; Debate Tm; Hon Rl; Off Ade; Fr Clb; Andrews Univ; Chem.

NICHOLAS, JAMIE; Mendon HS; Mendon, MI; Band; Hon Rl; Hosp Ade; Red Cr Ade; 4-H; Fr Clb; Pep Clb; Bsktbl; PPFtbl; Tmr; Kalamazoo Vly Cmnty Coll; Sci.

NICHOLAS, JENNIFER; Warren Sr HS; Warren, MI; Sec Frsh Cls; Trs Soph Cls; Trs Jr Cls; Trs Sr Cls; Band; Hon Rl; Jr NHS; Stu Cncl; Rptr Sch Nwsp; Wayne St Univ; Phys Ther.

NICHOLAS, JONATHAN; George Washington Sr HS; Charleston, WV; Trs Jr Cls; Cls Rep Sr Cls; Am Leg Boys St; Hon Rl; Off Ade; Stu Cncl; FBLA; Treas Key Clb; Natl Merit Ltr; Univ; Law.

NICHOLAS, LORI; Laporte HS; Mill Creek, IN; Hon Rl; Fr Clb;.

NICHOLAS, TAMMY; Hagerstown Jr Sr HS; Hagerstown, IN; 6/142 Chrs; Chrh Wkr; Girl Scts; Hon Rl; VP FHA; Bus Schl; Bus.

NICHOLES, CAROL; Creston HS; Grand Rapids, MI; Band; NHS; Mgrs; Jr Coll; Child Dev.

NICHOLL, JOHN; Annapolis HS; Dearborn Hgts, MI; Trs Jr Cls; Am Leg Boys St; Chrs; Sch Pl; Stu Cncl; Sprt Ed Sch Nwsp; Drama Clb; Ftbl; Wrstlng; Kiwan Awd; College; Engr.

NICHOLLS, SCOTT; Warsaw Cmnty HS; Warsaw, IN; 110/350 Boy Scts; Chrh Wkr; JA; Pol Wkr; Sct Actv; Rptr Yrbk; Rptr Sch Nwsp; DECA; Glf; Ball St Univ; Bus.

NICHOLS, BARBARA; Bennett HS; Marion, IN; Hon Rl; NHS; Off Ade; Fr Clb; Pep Clb; Bsktbl; Ft Wayne Univ; Sec.

NICHOLS, BRENDA; Pike HS; Indianapolis, IN; 78/312 Chrs; Chrh Wkr; Girl Scts; Hon Rl; Jr NHS; Off Ade; 4-H; FBLA; Ten; C of C Awd; Manchester Coll; Bus.

NICHOLS, BRYAN; Northrop HS; Ft Wayne, IN; Sct Actv; Mgrs;.

NICHOLS, CINDY S; Waterford HS; Waterford, OH; Trs Sr Cls; Chrh Wkr; Hon Rl; NHS; Yth Flsp; Sch Nwsp; OEA; Dnfth Awd; Natl Merit Ltr; Tech Coll; Sec.

NICHOLS, DEBBIE; Spencer HS; Reedy, WV; Band; Chrh Wkr; Cmnty Wkr; Hon Rl; Sch Pl; Stg Crw; Yth Flsp; Rptr Sch Nwsp; 4-H; FBLA; Parkersburg Voc Schl; Cosmetology.

NICHOLS, DENISE; Redford Union HS; Detroit, MI; 8/525 Cls Rep Frsh Cls; Cls Rep Soph Cls; Cl Rep Jr Cls; Band; Chrs; Hon Rl; NHS; VP Stu Cncl; Mic State Univ; Music Educ.

NICHOLS, E; Concordia Lutheran HS; Ft Wayne, IN; 41/181 Chrh Wkr; JA; 4-H; Pep Clb; PPFtbl; Elk Awd; JA Awd; Purdue Univ; Vet Med.

NICHOLS, GINA; North Daviess HS; Plainville, IN; 7/92 Band; Chrs; Hon Rl; Sch Pl; Beta Clb; 4-H; FHA; Pep Clb; Bsktbl; Trk; College; Acctg.

NICHOLS, GREGORY R; Buckeye HS; Valley City, OH; 91/208 Am Leg Boys St; Band; Chrh Wkr; Sch Mus; Rptr Yrbk; Drama Clb; Lat Clb; Tri C Univ; Phys Asst.

NICHOLS, HARRY E; Walled Lake Central HS; Union Lake, MI; Chrh Wkr; Hon Rl; Jr NHS; NHS; Orch; Sch Mus; Letter Bsktbl; IM Sprt; Won 3 First Prizes & 2nd Prize In Mi Ind Ed Fair; Univ Of Michigan; Mech Engr.

NICHOLS, JACQUELINE; Plymouth Canton HS; Livonia, MI; 42/450 Chrs; Girl Scts; Hon Rl; Lbry Ade; Sch Mus; Sct Actv; Rptr Sch Nwsp; Sch Nwsp; Pep Clb; Ten; Mi Schlrshp Dept Of Educ 79; Mi Competitive Schlrshp Awd 79; Gen Bus Excell 9th Gd 75; Eastern Michigan Univ.

NICHOLS, JANE; Williamston HS; Williasmton, MI; 5/160 Cls Rep Soph Cls; Cl Rep Jr Cls; Chrh Wkr; Hon Rl; Jr NHS; Treas Stu Cncl; Treas Yth Flsp; Chrldng; Grand Rapids Baptist.

NICHOLS, JENNIFER; Cloverdale HS; Poland, IN; Am Leg Aux Girls St; Chrs; Sch Mus; Sch Pl; Stg Crw; Drama Clb; VP 4-H; VP FFA; Pep Clb; Sci Clb; Purdue Univ; Ag.

NICHOLS, KEITH; Southeastern HS; Chillicothe, OH; 3/100 Pres Jr Cls; Chrh Wkr; FCA; Hon Rl; Jr NHS; NHS; Lat Clb; Crs Cntry; Trk; Scr Kpr; Coll; Comp Sci.

NICHOLS, LINDA; Madison HS; Madison, OH; Cmp Fr Grls; Chrs; Chrh Wkr; Girl Scts; Hon Rl; Hosp Ade; Drama Clb; Ger Clb; Pep Clb; College; Nursing.

NICHOLS, LUELLA; Braxton County HS; Ireland, WV; 44/180 Band; Chrh Wkr; Girl Scts; Hon Rl; NHS; 4-H; FBLA; Pep Clb; Trk; PPFtbl; Glenville State Coll; Acctg.

NICHOLS, LUELLA J; Braxton Co HS; Ireland, WV; Band; Chrh Wkr; Cmnty Wkr; Hon Rl; Sch Mus; 4-H; FBLA; Pep Clb; IM Sprt; Mat Maids; Math Bowl Team; FBLA Leadership Conference; Glenville St Coll; Acctg.

NICHOLS, MARGARET A; Shrine HS; Royal Oak, MI; Sec Frsh Cls; Sec Soph Cls; Cl Rep Jr Cls; Cls Rep Sr Cls; Chrs; Chrh Wkr; Cmnty Wkr; Girl Scts; Hon Rl; Lbry Ade; Michigan St Univ; Journalism.

NICHOLS, ROBERT; Griffith HS; Griffith, IN; Band; Hon Rl; Jr NHS; Letter Ten; College.

NICHOLS, SANDRA Y; Mendon HS; Three Rivers, MI; Band; Chrh Wkr; Hon Rl; NHS; Off Ade; Cit Awd; Schlstc Achv; Excellence In Schlrshp; College; Communications.

NICHOLS, STEPHANIE; Harper Creek HS; Battle Creek, MI; Band; Sec Chrh Wkr; Hon Rl; 4-H; Capt Trk; PPFtbl; LCC; Math.

NICHOLS, SUSAN; St Josephs HS; South Bend, IN; 14/240 Hon Rl; Lit Mag; NHS; NCTE; Natl Merit SF; Univ Of Chicago.

NICHOLS, TOBEY; St Marys HS; St Marys, WV; Rptr Sch Nwsp; DECA; Ohio Valley Coll; Pharm.

NICHOLSEN, LAURA; Niles HS; Niles, MI; Band; Chrh Wkr; Girl Scts; Hon Rl; Sch Mus; 4-H; Fr Clb; Pep Clb; Twrlr; 4-H Awd; College; Psych.

NICHOLSON, CARL; Hastings HS; Hastings, MI; Band; Chrh Wkr; Hon Rl; Yth Flsp;.

NICHOLSON, DOUGLAS; Greensburg Community HS; Greensburg, IN; 38/200 Band; Boy Scts; Hon Rl; Sprt Ed Yrbk; Bsktbl; Ftbl; Mgrs; Mas Awd; 1st Pl Sci Fair Chem 1977; Masonic Natl Order De Molay For Boys 1977; Univ; Engr.

NICHOLSON, JAMES; Fairfield Union HS; Lancaster, OH; 7/158 Hon Rl; Stu Cncl; 4-H; Letter Bsbl; Bsktbl; Letter Glf; Ohio Univ.

NICHOLSON, KAREN; Columbiana HS; Columbiana, OH; 5/98 Cls Rep Frsh Cls; Cls Rep Soph Cls; Cl Rep Jr Cls; Cls Rep Sr Cls; Treas Band; Chrs; Chrh Wkr; Cmnty Wkr; Hon Rl; Treas Jr NHS; Youngstown St Univ; Pre Med.

NICHOLSON, KELLIE; East Liverpool HS; E Liverpool, OH; Cls Rep Frsh Cls; Cls Rep Soph Cls; Cl Rep Jr Cls; Cls Rep Sr Cls; Am Leg Aux Girls St; Sec NHS; Quill & Scroll; Sch Mus; Sch Pl; Stu Cncl; Ohio St Univ; Law.

NICHOLSON, LORI; Eastern HS; Pekin, IN; Cls Rep Frsh Cls; Sec Soph Cls; Cls Rep Soph Cls; Cl Rep Jr Cls; Drl Tm; Hon Rl; NHS; Stu Cncl; 4-H; Pep Clb; Indiana St Univ.

NICHOLSON, MYRA; South Spencer HS; Rockport, IN; 4/150 Am Leg Aux Girls St; Band; Girl Scts; Hon Rl; Jr NHS; NHS; Off Ade; Pol Wkr; Sch Mus; Sch Pl; Western Kentucky Univ; Bus Admin.

NICHOLSON, NANCY; Loy Norrix HS; Kalamazoo, MI; Chrs; Chrh Wkr; Hon Rl; Sch Mus; Yth Flsp; Fr Clb; College.

NICHOLSON, RENNE; Chillicothe HS; Chillicothe, OH; Hon Rl; NHS; Sch Nwsp; OEA; Mat Maids; Stenographer.

NICHOLSON, RONALD; Boardman HS; Youngstn, OH; 39/594 Cls Rep Frsh Cls; Cls Rep Soph Cls; Hon Rl; JA; NHS; Stu Cncl; DECA; Ger Clb; JA Awd; College; Bus.

NICHOLSON, TERRY; University HS; Jere, WV; VP Frsh Cls; Hon Rl; FBLA; Pep Clb, Chrldng; Mat Maids; Bus Schl.

NICKEL, ANNETTE; St Joseph Sr HS; St Joseph, MI; Cls Rep Soph Cls; Cl Rep Jr Cls; Cls Rep Sr Cls; Chrh Wkr; NHS; Sch Mus; Sch Pl; Drama Clb; Treas 4-H; Treas Fr Clb; S W MI Delegate To The 4 H Ctznshp Short Course Wash DC 79; Univ; Pre Law.

NICKEL, MICHELE; Romulus HS; Romulus, MI; Cls Rep Frsh Cls; Cls Rep Soph Cls; Band; Girl Scts; Hon Rl; JA; Jr NHS; NHS; Orch; Stu Cncl;.

NICKEL, RETANA; Bellbrook HS; Xenia, OH; Sec AFS; Hon Rl; Sch Pl; VP Fr Clb; Letter Scr Kpr; Letter Tmr; Univ; Psych.

NICKEL, WALTER; Brooklyn HS; Brooklyn, OH; 29/174 NHS; Letter Trk; IM Sprt; Cleveland St Univ; Commercial Art.

NICKELL, RENEE C; Midland Trail HS; Hico, WV; 3/111 Sec Frsh Cls; Sec Jr Cls; Hon Rl; NHS; Stu Cncl; Yrbk; Bsktbl; PPFtbl;.

NICKELL, WESLEY H; Buckhannon Upshur HS; Buckhannon, WV; Trs Soph Cls; Trs Sr Cls; Am Leg Boys St; Band; Chrh Wkr; Hon Rl; NHS; Yth Flsp; Letter Bsktbl; 4-H Awd; Wv Wesleyan Coll; Comp Sci.

NICKELS, DAPHNE; Manchester Community HS; Manchester, MI; 20/106 Hon Rl; Sch Nwsp; Eastern Mich Univ; Arch.

NICKELS, THERESA J; High School; Ft Wayne, IN; 61/400 AFS; Treas Girl Scts; Pres JA; Red Cr Ade; Sct Actv; Mgrs; PPFtbl; JA Awd; Purdue Univ; Nursing.

NICKELSON, CRAIG; Kelloggsville HS; Kentwood, MI; Hon Rl; Jr NHS; NHS; Letter Ten; Letter Mgrs; Meteorology.

NICKERSON, JENNY; Hamilton Township HS; Columbus, OH; 4/175 Chrh Wkr; Hon Rl; Pres NHS; Sch Mus; Sch Pl; VP Stu Cncl; Ed Sch Nwsp; Sch Nwsp; College; Med.

NICKERSON, LYNDA; Cloverdale HS; Boca Raton, FL; 15/89 Am Leg Aux Girls St; Band; Hon Rl; Sch

Mus; Yrbk; Ed Sch Nwsp; Rptr Sch Nwsp; Sch Nwsp; Pep Clb; Sci Clb; Jrnlsm Hon Awd 78; Pres Of Band 78; Whos Who Of Sr Class Most Musical 78; Coll Of Boca Raton; Jrnlsm.

NICKERSON, SUSAN; Grosse Pointe North HS; Harper Woods, MI; Hon Rl; JA; DECA; Fr Clb; Univ Of Detroit; Tax Attorney.

NICKODEMUS, DANIEL; Reese HS; Richville, MI; 7/139 Am Leg Boys St; Chrs; Hon Rl; NHS; Sch Pl; Yth Flsp; Natl Merit SF; Central Mich Univ; Pre Law.

NICKS, MONIQUE; Heath HS; Heath, OH; 1/155 Am Leg Aux Girls St; Chrh Wkr; Cmnty Wkr; Hon Rl; Jr NHS; Natl Forn Lg; NHS; Stu Cncl; Chrldng; Cit Awd; College; Chemical Engineering.

NICODEMUS, CAROL; Churubusco HS; Churubusco, IN; 10/105 Hon Rl; Off Ade; 4-H; Pres OEA; 4-H Awd;.

NICODEMUS, MERRIE; Churubusco HS; Churubusco, IN; Chrs; Drl Tm; FCA; Hon Rl; Jr NHS; NHS; Sch Mus; Rptr Sch Nwsp; College; Inter Design.

NICOL, MARK; Dublin HS; Dublin, OH; 25/155 Band; Chrh Wkr; Yth Flsp; Lat Clb; Engr.

NICOL, MARY; Marlington HS; Homeworth, OH; 85/312 Chrs; Chrh Wkr; Lbry Ade; Sch Mus; Stg Crw; 4-H; Lat Clb; Spn Clb; Kent State Univ; Busns Admin.

NICOL, SUSAN; North Farmington HS; Farmington Hil, MI; Cls Rep Soph Cls; Chrs; Chrh Wkr; Hon Rl; Off Ade; Western Mic Univ; Psych.

NICOLAOU, HELEN; Lockland HS; Cincinnati, OH; 18/59 Hon Rl; Stg Crw; Rptr Yrbk; Spn Clb; Bsktbl; Chrldng; GAA; IM Sprt; College; Fash Merch.

NICOLLS, KRISTI; Huntington East HS; Huntington, WV; Cls Rep Soph Cls; Chrs; Stg Crw; Stu Cncl; DECA; Bsktbl; 1st Female Pres Of St DECA; Treas Of Stu Body; Mem Of Pres Council; Marshall Univ; DECA Advisor.

NIDAY, DAVID S; Wayne HS; Lavalette, WV; VP Soph Cls; Pres Jr Cls; Am Leg Boys St; Chrh Wkr; Hon Rl; Jr NHS; NHS; Pres Yth Flsp; Rptr Sch Nwsp; Lat Clb; Univ; Med.

NIDAY, KIM; Lewis County HS; Weston, WV; Cls Rep Frsh Cls; Cl Rep Jr Cls; Hon Rl; Stu Cncl; Sch Nwsp; Pep Clb; Mat Maids; Natl Merit Ltr; W Virginia Univ; Law.

NIDINI, KELLY; St Charles HS; St Charles, MI; Debate Tm; Hon Rl; Pres NHS; Ftbl; JC Awd; Lion Awd; Schlr Athlete Of Yr 78; All Area All Saginaw Cnty All Conf Hnrbl Mtn All St 78; Cptn Ltr Ernd 78 79; Iowa St Univ; Comp Engr.

NIEBAUER, LINDA; Clarkston HS; Clarkston, MI; Aud/Vis; Band; Chrs; Girl Scts; Hon Rl; Spn Clb; IM Sprt; PPFtbl; Scr Kpr; Univ; Bio.

NIEC, CYNTHIA; Marquette HS; Michigan City, IN; Hon Rl; Spn Clb; Purdue Univ; Sec.

NIEDBALA, PETER; Monroe Catholic Central HS; Monroe, MI; 3/94 Cl Rep Jr Cls; Pres Sr Cls; Band; Cmnty Wkr; Hon Rl; Lit Mag; NHS; Pol Wkr; Sch Mus; Sch Pl; Schlstc Medals & Crtfct 1976; Vrsty Band Monagram & Med 1977; Band Drum Maj; Univ.

NIEDBALSKI, WILLIAM; Clay Sr HS; S Bend, IN; 69/382 Boy Scts; Chrs; Hon Rl; NHS; Rptr Sch Nwsp; VICA;.

NIEDERBAUMER, DARRYL; South Dearborn HS; Dillsboro, IN; 15/260 Chrs; Chrh Wkr; Hon Rl; Lbr y Ade; NHS; Bsbl; Bsktbl; Cincinnati Tech Schl; Elec.

NIEDERER, WILLIAM G; Rochester Cmnty HS; Rochester, IN; 1/166 Band; Chrs; Hon Rl; Mdrgl; NHS; Sch Mus; Sch Pl; Stg Crw; Drama Clb; FTA; Ball St Univ; Music.

NIEDERHAUSER, BRIAN; Hillsdale HS; Hillsdale, MI; 18/190 Hon Rl; Jr NHS; NHS; Key Clb; Letter Ftbl; Rotary Awd; Mic State Univ; Acctg.

NIEDERMEIER, CYNTHIA; Willard HS; Willard, OH; Hon Rl; Jr NHS; 4-H; Sec.

NIEDERMEYER, CHERYL; St Alphonsus HS; Detroit, MI; Band; Chrh Wkr; Drm Mjrt; Hon Rl; Sch Mus; Sch Pl; Stu Cncl; Twrlr; Pres Of Missions Club 78; All A's In Hstry Instructional Aid & Typing 78; 1st Rnnr Up For Miss Ukraine 78; Univ Of Michigan; Phys Ther.

NIEDERMIER, KAREN; Buckeye Central HS; New Washington, OH; 25/94 Band; Girl Scts; Sch Pl; Sec Stu Cncl; Sec 4-H; FHA; Spn Clb; IM Sprt; Ohio State Univ; Nursing.

NIEDERMIER, STEVEN; Seneca East HS; Attica, OH; Chrh Wkr; Cmnty Wkr; Hon Rl; Jr NHS; Bsbl; Bsktbl; Glf;.

NIEDNER, CARL D; Granville HS; Granville, OH; 8/144 NHS; Letter Crs Cntry; Natl Merit SF; Univ.

NIEDZIELSKI, ANDREW; Central Catholic HS; Toledo, OH; 6/350 Band; Hon Rl; NHS; Orch; Sch Mus; Bowling Green St Univ; Chem.

NIEHAUS, MARK; La Salle HS; Cincinnati, OH; 1/249 Hon Rl; NHS; VP Civ Clb; Letter Wrstlng; IM Sprt; Kiwan Awd; Univ; Mech Engr.

NIEHAUS, TWYALA; Castle HS; Elberfeld, IN; 12/400 Chrh Wkr; Girl Scts; Hon Rl; Natl Forn Lg; NHS; Sch Mus; Stu Cncl; Yth Flsp; College; Doctor.

NIEHUS, BRIAN; Avon HS; Danville, IN; 16/196 Am Leg Boys St; Hon Rl; NHS; Pres Ger Clb; Sci Clb; Letter Ftbl; Capt Wrstlng; Dnfth Awd; Purdue Univ; Engr.

NIELSEN, BRIAN; Cedar Springs HS; Cedar Spgs, MI; FCA; Bsbl; PPFtbl; College; Sci.

NIELSEN, DEBORAH; Central Lake HS; Eastport, MI; Cl Rep Jr Cls; Hon Rl; Treas Stu Cncl; Rptr Yrbk; Rptr Sch Nwsp; Fr Clb; Chrldng; Pom Pon; Davenport College Of Business; Fash.

NIELSEN, JOANNE; Highland HS; Wadsworth, OH; 76/202 Off Ade; Quill & Scroll; Y-Teens; Yrbk; Spn Clb; Scr Kpr; Ken St; Arts And Sciences.

NIELSEN, KAREN; Cass Technical HS; Detroit, MI; Hon Rl; NHS; Fr Clb; Lat Clb; Kalamazoo Coll.

NIELSEN, LISA; Houghton Lake HS; Houghton Lake, MI; Band; Hon Rl; Jr NHS; Business School; Account.

NIELSEN, PAUL; Lamphere HS; Madison Hts, MI; Band; Chrh Wkr; NHS; Spn Clb; Letter Ftbl; IM Sprt; Wayne St Univ; Law.

NIEMAN, DAVID; Lawrenceburg HS; Lawrenceburg, IN; 32/150 Cls Rep Soph Cls; Chrh Wkr; Cmnty Wkr; Hon Rl; Stu Cncl; Sci Clb; College; Bus Accnt.

NIEMAN, KEVIN; Whiteford HS; Ottawa Lk, MI; Trs Frsh Cls; VP Soph Cls; Chrh Wkr; Hon Rl; Jr NHS; NHS; Pep Clb; Bsbl; Letter Bsktbl; College; Engr.

NIEMAN, RICHARD; Flint Carman HS; Flint, MI; Hon Rl; Ed Yrbk; Socr; Univ; Energy Engr.

NIEMAN, ROBERT; John Glenn HS; New Concord, OH; AFS; Chrs; Hon Rl; NHS; Sch Mus; Drama Clb; Pres Mth Clb; Spn Clb; Univ; Sci.

NIEMANN, ALICE; Franklin Hts HS; Columbus, OH; Cmp Fr Grls; Girl Scts; Orch; Yth Flsp; Cit Awd; Franklin Univ; Acctg.

NIEMANN, SUZANNE; Central Baptist HS; Loveland, OH; Sec Jr Cls; Chrs; Chrh Wkr; Cmnty Wkr; Sch Mus; Stg Crw; Yrbk; Pep Clb; Letter Bsktbl; IM Sprt; Selected In Miss Teen USA As A St Finalst 79; Univ.

NIEMELA, LORI; White Pine HS; White Pine, MI; 7/35 Band; Chrh Wkr; Hon Rl; Rptr Yrbk; Swmmng; Lion Awd; Northern Mic Univ; Med Sec.

NIEMENSKI, LAURIE; St Alphonsus HS; Livonia, MI; 60/177 Hon Rl; NHS; Ed Yrbk; Letter Bsbl; Swmmng; Scr Kpr; Mi St Schslhp 79; Madonna Coll; Bus.

NIEMEYER, LISA; St Johns HS; Delphos, OH; Hon Rl; Sec JA; 4-H; Fr Clb; FTA; Voc Schl; Nursing.

NIEMEYER, NANCY; East Lansing HS; East Lansing, MI; 68/380 Chrs; Pres Chrh Wkr; Cmnty Wkr; Lbry Ade; NHS; Sch Mus; Coach Actv; IM Sprt; Mgrs; 4-H Awd; Central Michigan Univ; Rec Admin.

NIEMEYER, PAUL; Norwood HS; Cincinnati, OH; 2/347 Cls Rep Frsh Cls; Band; Hon Rl; JA; Jr NHS; Treas NHS; Orch; Mth Clb; Math Awd; College.

NIEMEYER, STEPHANIE; Thomas A De Vilbiss HS; Toledo, OH; Chrs; Hon Rl; Hosp Ade; NHS; Quill & Scroll; Sch Mus; Stu Cncl; Rptr Yrbk; Fr Clb ; Univ; Psych.

NIEMI, LORAINE; Calumet HS; Copper City, MI; 12/163 Band; Chrh Wkr; Hon Rl; Hosp Ade; NHS; Yrbk; 4-H; FNA; Pep Clb; IM Sprt; N Michigan Univ; Nursing.

NIEMI, SANDRA; Sault Area HS; Slt Ste Marie, MI; 21/287 Debate Tm; Hon Rl; NHS; IM Sprt; Michigan St Univ; Bio Sci.

NIEMI, TINA; Lakeview HS; Cortland, OH; 1/180 Trs Frsh Cls; Girl Scts; Hon Rl; NHS; Y-Teens; Yrbk; Beta Clb; Mth Clb; Spn Clb; Univ; Bio.

NIEMIEC, BRIAN; Livonia A Stevenson HS; Livonia, MI; 90/749 Cls Rep Sr Cls; Chrh Wkr; Stu Cncl; Ftbl; IM Sprt; Michigan St Univ.

NIEMIEC, FRANK; Bishop Noll Institute; Griffith, IN; 37/321 Am Leg Boys St; Band; Boy Scts; Chrh Wkr; Hon Rl; Jr NHS; NHS; Sch Mus; Sct Actv; Mth Clb; De Paul Univ; Music.

NIEMIEC, PHILLIP; High School; Redford, MI; Marygrove College; Social Work.

NIEMIEC, RICHARD; Morton Sr HS; Hammond, IN; 27/436 Aud/Vis; Hon Rl; Jr NHS; NHS; Sch Pl; Stg Crw; Rptr Sch Nwsp; Drama Clb; FSA; Letter Bsbl; Purdue Univ; Engr.

NIEMINEN, LAURA; William Henry Harrison HS; W Laf, IN; Chrs; Sch Mus; Yth Flsp; Ger Clb; Mth Clb; Letter Swmmng; Arion Awd For Outstndg Achvmnt Vocal Music 78; Culver Lmilitary Acad Summer Schl Gld Slvr & Brz Tuxis 76 78; Univ; Music.

NIENDORF, VICKI; La Porte HS; La Porte, IN; 17/550 Hon Rl; Jr NHS; Fr Clb; Mat Maids; Univ; Elem Ed.

NIENHAUS, LYNNE; Divine Child HS; Dearborn, MI; Pres Jr Cls; VP Sr Cls; Pres Chrs; Cmnty Wkr; Hon Rl; NHS; Stu Cncl; Letter Bsbl; GAA; College.

NIERGARTH, JERRI L; Pellston HS; Levering, MI; Cls Rep Frsh Cls; Chrh Wkr; Girl Scts; Hon Rl; Sec NHS; Sct Actv; Stu Cncl; FTA; Bsbl; Pom Pon; N Ctrl Michigan Coll; Med.

NIERMAN, KIMBERLY; Garrett HS; Auburn, IN; Sec Soph Cls; Chrh Wkr; Girl Scts; Hon Rl; Hosp Ade; NHS; Sch Mus; Y-Teens; Ger Clb; Pep Clb; Univ Of Indiana; Sci.

NIES, VICTORIA; St Ursula & Summit HS; Cincinnati, OH; Sch Mus; Sdlty; Stg Crw; Sch Nwsp; Drama Clb; Gym; Coach Actv; Univ; Primary Educ.

NIESE, ANNE; Medina Sr HS; Medina, OH; 80/380 Cl Rep Jr Cls; Am Leg Aux Girls St; Chrh Wkr; Cmnty Wkr; Girl Scts; Hon Rl; Hosp Ade; Off Ade; Red Cr Ade; Y-Teens; Bowling Green Univ; Spch & Hrng.

NIESE, LESLIE; Wapakoneta Sr HS; Wapakoneta, OH; Am Leg Aux Girls St; FBLA; VP OEA; Spn Clb; Gym; Voc Schl; Sec.

NIESSNER, ROBERT; Mathews HS; Cortland, OH; Am Leg Boys St; Aud/Vis; NHS; Pol Wkr; Letter Ftbl; Letter Trk; Air Force; Pilot.

NIESZALA, GREG; St Francis De Sales HS; Toledo, OH; Boy Scts; Stg Crw; 4-H; Letter Bsbl; Ftbl; Coach Actv; IM Sprt; Scr Kpr; 4-H Awd; Univ; Bus Admin.

NIETO, MICHAEL; Andrean HS; Gary, IN; 80/275 Hon Rl; Sprt Ed Sch Nwsp; Sch Nwsp; Spn Clb; Letter Ftbl; Letter Trk; H J Grant Foundation Schlrshp Journalism Form Marquette; Marquette Univ; Journalism.

NIETZKE, KEVIN; Waterford Mott HS; Pontiac, MI; Band; Boy Scts; CAP; Debate Tm; Orch; Fr Clb; Mic Tech; Elec Engr.

NIEUWENKAMP, HEIDI A; Rapid River HS; Rapid River, MI; Sec Frsh Cls; VP Frsh Cls; Pres Sr Cls; Band; Girl Scts; Hon Rl; Off Ade; Stu Cncl; Capt Chrldng; Bay De Noe Cmnty Coll; Sec.

NIEWENHUIS, DEBRA; Wm Henry Harrison HS; Okeana, OH; Band; Chrh Wkr; Hosp Ade; JA; Sch Mus; Sch Pl; Stg Crw; Drama Clb; Trk; Calvin College; Phys Ther.

NIEWIADOMSKI, JEFF; La Porte HS; Laporte, IN; Fr Clb; Wrstlng; Purdue N Ctrl Univ; French.

NIEWIROWICZ, LISA; Redford Union HS; Redford, MI; Band; Chrs; Hon Rl; Treas JA; Pom Pon; College; Wildlife Conservation.

NIEZER, TED; Bishop Dwenger HS; Ft Wayne, IN; 25/256 Cls Rep Frsh Cls; Pres Soph Cls; Cl Rep Jr Cls; Aud/Vis; Hon Rl; Key Clb; Ftbl; Trk; Coach Actv; Notre Dame Univ; Bus.

NIGBOR, DEB; St Alphonsus HS; Detroit, MI; Cmp Fr Grls; Cmnty Wkr; Drm Mjrt; Hon Rl; Lbry Ade; College.

NIGG, DENNIS; Springs Valley HS; French Lick, IN; Hon Rl; Glf; IM Sprt; Purdue Univ; Meteorology.

NIGGEMEYER, GINGER; Heath HS; Heath, OH; 14/160 Cls Rep Frsh Cls; Chrs; FCA; Hon Rl; Stu Cncl; Key Clb; Spn Clb; Letter Trk; Chrldng; COTC; Nursing.

NIGGEMYER, MARY; Central Catholic HS; Wheeling, WV; Hosp Ade; Bsktbl; GAA; Mat Maids; Wheeling College.

NIGH, MINDY; Galion Sr HS; Galion, OH; Sec Soph Cls; Cmnty Wkr; Red Cr Ade; 4-H; Gym; Swmmng; Chrldng; GAA; 4-H Awd; Bowling Green St Univ; Therapy.

NIGH, PHILLIP; Cory Rawson HS; Findlay, OH; Trs Jr Cls; Chrs; Hon Rl; Jr NHS; NHS; Rptr Yrbk; Mth Clb; Bsktbl; Ftbl; Trk; Case Western Reserve Univ; Comp Engr.

NIGHTENHELSER, STUART; Hamilton Heights HS; Atlanta, IN; 5/96 Hon Rl; Jr NHS; NHS; Pres Stu Cncl; Drama Clb; Treas Mth Clb; Pres Sci Clb; Spn Clb; Letter Bsbl; Letter Trk; Academic Ach Awd In English Literature; Academic Ach Awd In Industrial Art; Whos Who In Indiana & Ky HS; Butler Univ; Physics.

NILES, MATTHEW; Brighton HS; Brighton, MI; Hon Rl; Ger Clb; Letter Ftbl; Letter Trk; Coach Actv; Mst Valbl Running Back In Ftbl 78; All Cnty Al Llg All Are Track 77; Boys St; Univ Of Detroit; Archt.

NILLES, JAIME; Northwest HS; Canal Fulton, OH; 2/174 VP Soph Cls; Cl Rep Jr Cls; Cls Rep Sr Cls; Sal; Hon Rl; NHS; Chmn Bsktbl; C of C Awd; Cit Awd; Ohio Northern Univ; Math.

NINE, DIANE; Kingswood School; Bloomfld Hls, MI; VP Sr Cls; Hon Rl; Mod UN; Pol Wkr; Sch Nwsp; Bsbl; Bsktbl; Letter Glf; Var Ltr In Vllybl Capt 77 80; Var Club Pres 79; Stdnt Intern On White Hs Staff For Summer 79; Univ; Law.

NINOTTI, JOHN; Pontiac Catholic HS; Pontiac, MI; Cls Rep Frsh Cls; Trs Soph Cls; Cl Rep Jr Cls; Band; Debate Tm; Hon Rl; JA; Stu Cncl; Univ Of Mic; Chem Engr.

NIPPES, CINDY; Wayne Memorial HS; Westland, MI; Hon Rl; NHS; Stg Crw; Ed Yrbk; Rptr Yrbk; Home Ec Awd 1977; Yearbook Outstndg Awd 1978; Cum Laude Dipl 1979; Univ; Med Asst.

NIQUETTE, CYNTHIA; Bennett HS; Marion, IN; 1/32 Hon Rl; NHS; Off Ade; Beta Clb; Drama Clb; Fr Clb; Crs Cntry; Trk; Univ Of Dayton; Comp Sci.

NISEVICH, LISA; Munster HS; Munster, IN; 151/402 Cls Rep Soph Cls; Cls Rep Sr Cls; AFS; Chrs; Girl Scts; Lbry Ade; Off Ade; Sch Pl; Stu Cncl; Rptr Yrbk; Natl Offc Educ Assoc Ambssdr Awd 79; Drama Club & Thespians Vtd Biggst Contrbtn To Spring Play 79; Univ; Bus Admin.

NISKALA, KATHY; Edwardsburg HS; Edwardsburg, MI; 6/148 Band; Hon Rl; NHS; Chrldng; Pom Pon; Western Mich Univ; Muscic Therapy.

NITSCHKE, MATT; Sparta HS; Sparta, MI; Band; Chrs; Hon Rl; Mdrgl; Sch Pl; Drama Clb; Sci Clb; Michigan Tech Univ; Elec Engr.

NITZ, JOSEPH I; Tygarts Valley HS; Beverly, WV; Pres Band; Orch; 4-H; Bsbl; Bsktbl; 4-H Awd; West Virginia Univ.

NIX, DEBBIE; Robert S Tower HS; Warren, MI; Hon Rl; OEA; Macomb Cnty Cmnty Coll; Legal Sec.

NIX, PATRICK; Bishop Dwenger HS; Ft Wayne, IN; Boy Scts; Chrh Wkr; Hon Rl; Wrstlng; College; Medicine.

NIX, THERESA; Huntington Catholic HS; Huntington, IN; Cls Rep Sr Cls; Hon Rl; Sch Pl; Stg Crw; Rptr Yrbk; Trk; Capt Chrldng; Mgrs; Indiana Univ; Jrnlsm.

NIXON, CHARLES; Cadillac HS; Cadillac, MI; 36/300 Chrh Wkr; Cmnty Wkr; FCA; Hon Rl; NHS; Yth Flsp; Capt Crs Cntry; Letter Trk; Ohi Inst Of Tech; Elec Engr.

NIXON, LYNELL; Fountain Central HS; Hillsboro, IN; 7/135 Chrh Wkr; Drl Tm; Girl Scts; Hon Rl; Lbry Ade; NHS; Sct Actv; Yth Flsp; Sch Nwsp; Drama Clb; Indiana Univ; Commctns.

NOACK, BRENDA; Flushing Sr HS; Flushing, MI; Hon Rl; Hosp Ade; Spn Clb; Cert Of Achvmnt For Compltn Of 900 Hrs Of Pratcl Nursing Instrctn 79; Nazareth Coll; Nursing.

NOACK, MARY B; Coloma Sr HS; Coloma, MI; 19/227 Hon Rl; NHS; Recvd Varsity Letter In Girls Sftbl 76 79; Recvd Varsity Letter In Girls Vllybl 78 79; Ferris St Coll; Acctg.

NOAH, MARY LYNN; Chelsea HS; Gregory, MI; 7/213 Trs Sr Cls; Band; Chrh Wkr; Girl Scts; Hon Rl; NHS; Pol Wkr; Stu Cncl; 4-H; 4-H Awd; Michigan St Univ; Business.

NOAH, PAUL; Thornapple Kellogg HS; Middleville, MI; 1/160 Pres Frsh Cls; Cls Rep Sr Cls; Val; NHS; Stu Cncl; Letter Crs Cntry; Letter Swmmng; Letter Ten; IM Sprt; Bausch & Lomb Awd; Mich State Univ; Pre Med.

NOBILIO, DEBBIE; Mayfield HS; Mayfield Hts, OH; 74/530 AFS; Band; Chrs; Drl Tm; Hon Rl; Hosp Ade; Drama Clb; Fr Clb; Pom Pon; College; Law Enforcement.

NOBIS, GRETCHEN; Colerain Sr HS; Cincinnati, OH; Band; Chrs; Girl Scts; Hosp Ade; Lbry Ade; Off Ade; Orch; Quill & Scroll; Sch Mus; Sch Pl; Miami Univ; Nursing.

NOBLE, ANDREW; Broad Ripple HS; Indianapolis, IN; 4/375 Cl Rep Jr Cls; Chrs; Hon Rl; Mdrgl; Pres NHS; Sch Mus; Sch Pl; VP Drama Clb; Ind Univ; Bus Law.

NOBLE, CHERRI L; Chesapeake HS; Chesapeake, OH; 15/145 Band; Cmp Fr Grls; Chrs; Hon Rl; Beta Clb; Marshall Univ; Medicine.

NOBLE, LOWELL; Deckerville Cmnty HS; Deckerville, MI; Band; Boy Scts; Chrs; Debate Tm; Hon Rl; NHS; Orch; Sch Mus; Sch Pl; Sct Actv; Adrian Univ; Physics.

NOBLE, MIKE; Chippewa HS; Marshallville, OH; Boy Scts; Chrh Wkr; Hon Rl; Sct Actv; Crs Cntry; IM Sprt; College; Wildlife Mgmt.

NOBLE, SHELLY; Garfield HS; Akron, OH; Sec Band; Sec Chrs; Hon Rl; Pres JA; Orch; Red Cr Ade; Drama Clb; Fr Clb; JA Awd; College; Medicine.

NOBLE, SHERRY; West Branch HS; Alliance, OH; Treas Band; Chrh Wkr; Cmnty Wkr; Girl Scts; Hon Rl; Jr NHS; NHS; Akron Univ; Med.

NOBLE, TERESA; Shepherd HS; Shepherd, MI; Hon Rl; 4-H; FHA; Letter Bsktbl; Letter Trk; Tmr; 4-H Awd; College; Data Proc.

NOBLE, TERRI; Sandy Valley HS; Sandyville, OH; Chrs; Stu Cncl; OEA; Letter Bsktbl; Scr Kpr; Ashland Coll; Sec Sci.

NOCUS, JONI; Rockville HS; Rockville, IN; 13/84 Band; Chrs; Chrh Wkr; Girl Scts; NHS; Sct Actv; Sec FHA; Lat Clb; Twrlr; Univ Of Evansville; Music.

NOE, DONALD A; Wadsworth Sr HS; Wadsworth, OH; 48/360 FCA; Hon Rl; 4-H; Lat Clb; Letter Ftbl; Letter Trk; IM Sprt; Natl Merit Ltr; Tulane Univ; Biomed Engr.

NOECHEL, JEANETTE; Servite HS; Detroit, MI; Hon Rl; Sch Pl; Stg Crw; Servite Schlrshp; College; Sci.

NOEL, ALICE; Maysville Sr HS; Zanesville, OH; 34/252 Chrh Wkr; Hon Rl; Hosp Ade; JA; Lbry Ade; Off Ade; Sch Pl; Rptr Sch Nwsp; Drama Clb; FHA; Honor Chord For Grad; Most Improved Girl At MJHS; Muskingum Area Tech Coll; Med Asst.

NOEL, DEBBIE; Hubbard HS; Hubbard, OH; 31/350 Cls Rep Frsh Cls; Cls Rep Sr Cls; AFS; Am Leg Aux Girls St; Hon Rl; Hosp Ade; JA; Lit Mag; Off Ade; Quill & Scroll; Youngstown St Univ; Medicine.

NOEL, ERIC; Worthington Jefferson HS; Worthington, IN; Cls Rep Frsh Cls; Sec Soph Cls; VP Jr Cls; Band; Chrh Wkr; Hon Rl; NHS; 4-H; Ten; Mgrs; Voc Schl.

NOEL, JILL; West Side HS; Gary, IN; Band; Chrs; Hon Rl; Orch; Ball State Univ; Foreign Language.

NOEL, LISSA; Arcadia Local HS; Fostoria, OH; 11/65 Band; Chrs; Chrh Wkr; NHS; Sch Mus; Sch Pl; Yth Flsp; Yrbk; 4-H; 4-H Awd; Ohio St Schl; Cosmetology.

NOEL, THOMAS; Waverly HS; Waverly, OH; 8/167 Boy Scts; Hon Rl; NHS; Stg Crw; 4-H; Fr Clb; Ftbl; Miami Univ.

NOFFSINGER, STEVE; Wadsworth Sr HS; Wadsworth, OH; 20/380 Pres Soph Cls; Cl Rep Jr Cls; Band; Boy Scts; Hon Rl; Treas Stu Cncl; Yth Flsp; Fr Clb; Pres Key Clb; Letter Ftbl; Hugh O Brian Yth Found Awd; Wadsworth Sr HS Stu Of Mnth; College; Engr.

NOFS, DENISE; Harper Creek HS; Battle Creek, MI; Pres Frsh Cls; Sec Chrs; Chrh Wkr; Cmnty Wkr; Hon Rl; Mdrgl; Mod UN; NHS; Sch Mus; Yth Flsp; Albion Coll; Pre Med.

NOFTZ, DAWN; Columbian HS; Tiffin, OH; Chrs; Hon Rl; Lbry Ade; Stu Cncl; Ed Sch Nwsp; Sch Nwsp; Drama Clb; Fr Clb; Pep Clb; IM Sprt; Bowling Green Univ; Public Relations.

NOFZIGER, BRENDA; Pettisville HS; Wauseon, OH; Trs Soph Cls; Cl Rep Jr Cls; Chrs; Hon Rl; Sch Pl; Stu Cncl; Yth Flsp; Rptr Sch Nwsp; GAA; IM Sprt; Goshen Univ; Elem Ed.

NOFZIGER, SARA; Stryker HS; Stryker, OH; Cls Rep Frsh Cls; Cls Rep Soph Cls; Band; Chrs; NHS; Stu Cncl; VP 4-H; Scr Kpr; Tmr; Goshen Coll; Nursing.

NOFZINGER, JOLENE; Morenci Area HS; Morenci, MI; Cls Rep Soph Cls; Cl Rep Jr Cls; Cls Rep Sr Cls; Am Leg Aux Girls St; Band; Chrs; Chrh Wkr; Lbry Ade; NHS; VP Stu Cncl; Huntington Coll; Comp Sci.

NOFZINGER, SARA; Stryker HS; Stryker, OH; Cls Rep Frsh Cls; Cls Rep Soph Cls; Band; Chrs; Hon Rl; Stu Cncl; Yth Flsp; Pres Fr Clb; Scr Kpr; Tmr; Univ; Nursing.

NOGA, MARY; St Augustine Acad; Cleveland, OH; Chrs; Sch Mus; Sch Pl; Drama Clb; Sci Clb; Trk; Ohi State Univ; Dent Hygen.

NOGGLE, MICHAEL; Mohawk Local HS; Melmore, OH; 5/127 Am Leg Boys St; Band; Treas Boy Scts; Chrs; Chrh Wkr; Cmnty Wkr; Hon Rl; Lit Mag; NHS; Orch; Bowling Green St Univ; Pre Law.

NOKES, LINDA; Vinton County Cons HS; Ray, OH; Hon Rl; NHS; Yrbk; Rptr Sch Nwsp; FHA; OEA;.

NOLAN, BERT; Valley HS; Pine Grove, WV; VP Jr Cls; Band; Hon Rl; NHS; Sch Pl; 4-H; Bsktbl; Ftbl; West Virginia Univ; Bio.

NOLAN, BRIGID; Our Lady Of Mercy HS; Farm Hls, MI; Cls Rep Soph Cls; Chrh Wkr; Cmnty Wkr; Girl Scts; NHS; FSA; Mth Clb; Sci Clb; Spn Clb; Univ Of Mi; Phys Ther.

NOLAN, CHARLOTTE; Bridgman HS; Bridgman, MI; Am Leg Aux Girls St; Band; Hon Rl; FHA; Letter Bsktbl; Letter Trk; Coll; Bus Mgmt.

NOLAN, LAURA; Hanover Central Jr Sr HS; Cedar Lake, IN; 12/137 Trs Jr Cls; Chrh Wkr; Girl Scts; Hon Rl; Jr NHS; NHS; Fr Clb; Pep Clb; Trk; Pom Pon; College; Psych.

NOLAN, LE; Mitchell HS; Mitchell, IN; Band; Chrs; Hon Rl; Pep Clb; 4-H Awd; Univ; Sec.

NOLAN, PAUL; William Henry Harrison HS; Harrison, OH; 39/223 Hon Rl; Jr NHS; Bsktbl; Crs Cntry; Trk; Univ.

NOLAN, PEGGY; Seton HS; Cincinnati, OH; 45/285 Cls Rep Soph Cls; Cmnty Wkr; Hon Rl; NHS; Stu Cncl; Bsktbl; GAA; Univ; Art.

NOLAN, SCOTT; Lincolnview HS; Van Wert, OH; Chrs; Chrh Wkr; Yth Flsp; 4-H; FFA; Bsbl; Bsktbl; Glf; College; Animal Sci.

NOLAN, TERESE; James Ford Rhodes HS; Cleveland, OH; Girl Scts; Hon Rl; NHS; Orch; Sct Actv; Stu Cncl; Letter Crs Cntry; Letter Trk; GAA; IM Sprt; Univ Of Mich; Law.

NOLAN, TIMOTHY; Maysville HS; Zanesville, OH; Hon Rl; NHS; Mgrs; Muskingum Area Joint Voc.

NOLAND, MARK; Pleasant HS; Prospect, OH; Band; Hon Rl; JA; College.

NOLCOX, DION; North HS; Springfield, OH; Pres Frsh Cls; Chrh Wkr; Cmnty Wkr; Hon Rl; Jr NHS; NHS; Spn Clb; Letter Ftbl; Cit Awd; SAR Awd; O V Brown Athletic Schlrshp Awd 76; Dorothy M Digel Schlrshp Awd 76; Univ; Engr.

NOLF, KARLA; Wintersville HS; Steubenvl, OH; Am Leg Aux Girls St; Band; Drl Tm; Sec Fr Clb; Chrldng; College.

NOLF, KELLY; Cadillac Sr HS; Cadillac, MI; 275/314 Sec Frsh Cls; VP Sr Cls; Band; Chrs; Chrh Wkr; Hon Rl; MMM; PAVAS; Sch Mus; Stg Crw; Olivet Coll; Vocal Perfrmnc.

NOLFI, JULIE; Stow HS; Stow, OH; Hon Rl; Mth Clb; Univ; Cmnctns.

NOLL, GARY; Carson City Crystal HS; Carson City, MI; 14/130 Am Leg Boys St; Boy Scts; Hon Rl; Treas NHS; Stu Cncl; Treas Sci Clb; Pres Spn Clb; Central Mich Univ; Retail Mgmt.

NOLL, P; Woodmore HS; Woodville, OH; 5/129 Cls Rep Sr Cls; Am Leg Boys St; Hon Rl; Jr NHS; NHS; Am Leg Awd; Kiwan Awd; Bowling Green St Univ; Comp Sci.

NOLL, SUSAN; Amanda Clearcreek HS; Lancaster, OH; Band; Drl Tm; Hon Rl; Sec Stu Cncl; Pres 4-H; FHA; FTA; Sci Clb; IM Sprt; 4-H Awd; Univ; Music.

NOLLENBERGER, SCOTT; Elkins HS; Montrose, WV; 48/275 Debate Tm; Hon Rl; JA; Sch Pl; Stg Crw; Yrbk; Sch Nwsp; VICA; IM Sprt; JA Awd; Voc Schl; Engr.

NOLOT, BECKY; Floyd Central HS; Floyds Knobs, IN; 21/359 Chrs; Chrh Wkr; Drl Tm; Hon Rl; Pep Clb; Pom Pon; PPFtbl; College; Public Relations.

NOLTE, TAMERA; Scecina Mem HS; Indianapolis, IN; 5/194 Am Leg Aux Girls St; Band; Hon Rl; VP NHS; Sch Mus; Stu Cncl; Ed Yrbk; Fr Clb; Marian Coll; Acctg.

NOLTE, TERRI; Reading Comm HS; Reading, OH; Cls Rep Soph Cls; Cl Rep Jr Cls; Cls Rep Sr Cls; Band; Chrh Wkr; Hon Rl; NHS; Fr Clb; Univ Of Cincinnati; Nursing.

NOLTY, PEGGY; Brookville HS; Brookville, IN; Trs Jr Cls; Cl Rep Jr Cls; Drl Tm; Hon Rl; Stu Cncl; Trk; GAA; Mgrs;.

NOMMAY, NANCY; North Central HS; Indianapolis, IN; 219/999 Chrs; Girl Scts; Hon Rl; NHS; OEA; Office Educ Assoc Serv Mbr Of Yr 79;.

NONNENMACHER, ANITA; Father J Wehrle Mem HS; Columbus, OH; 11/115 Hon Rl; Yrbk; Pep Clb; Busns Schl; Busns.

NONTE, CATHY; Jasper HS; Jasper, IN; 42/289 Hon Rl; Ten; Purdue Univ; Vet.

NOONAN, JOHN; Groves HS; Birmingham, MI; Hon Rl; Bsbl; Ftbl; Miami Of Ohi Univ; Bus.

NOONAN, KEN; Bellmont HS; Decatur, IN; Am Leg Boys St; Band; Boy Scts; Hon Rl; NHS; Sct Actv; Lat Clb; Sci Clb; Univ; Geol.

NOONAN, PATRICIA; Delphos St Johns HS; Delphos, OH; 13/139 Band; Hon Rl; NHS; Sch Mus; Yrbk; Rptr Sch Nwsp; Ohio St Univ; Optometry.

NOONAN, THOMAS; Mount Healthy HS; Mt Healthy, OH; 54/580 Band; Cmnty Wkr; Hon Rl; Y-Teens; Glf; Ten; Univ; Comp Engr.

NOORDYKE, BRIAN; Grand Rapids Christian HS; Grand Rapids, MI; 10/345 Hon Rl; Yth Flsp; Sch Nwsp; Letter Bsbl; Letter Ftbl; Letter Wrstlng; IM Sprt; Calvin Coll; Architecture.

NOPOLA, DEBORAH; L Anse HS; Covington, MI; 8/96 Hst Jr Cls; Hst Sr Cls; Chrh Wkr; Hon Rl; NHS; Off Ade; Chrldng; IM Sprt; Mgrs; VFW Awd; Northern Mich Univ.

NORANDER, JOHN; Aquinas HS; Detroit, MI; Chrh Wkr; Cmnty Wkr; Hon Rl; Bsbl; Bsktbl; Ftbl; Coach Actv; Mgrs; Basic Educ Opportunity Grant 79; Coll Work Study 79; Natl Direct Stdnt Loan 79; Univ Of Miami; Bus Admin.

NORDEN, CINDY; Bishop Watterson HS; Hilliard, OH; Cls Rep Frsh Cls; Cls Rep Soph Cls; Chrs; Hon Rl; Orch; Sch Mus; Stu Cncl; 4-H; 4-H Awd; College.

NORDGREN, LORI L; Edwardsburg HS; Niles, MI; Trs Frsh Cls; Band; Chrh Wkr; Girl Scts; Hon Rl; NHS; Sch Mus; Yth Flsp; 4-H; VICA; Bethel Coll; Med.

NORDMAN, JERRY; La Salle HS; Cincinnati, OH; Band; Boy Scts; Hon Rl; Orch; Sch Mus; Univ Of Cincinnati; Busns.

NORGAARD, KURT; Manchester HS; Manchester, MI; 7/120 Chrh Wkr; Hon Rl; NHS; Crs Cntry; Trk; Natl Merit Ltr; Spring Arbor Univ; Engr.

NORLANDER, CATHERINE; John Glenn HS; Westland, MI; Hon Rl; Jr NHS; Ger Clb; Chrldng; Pom Pon; Univ Of Michigan; Med Tech.

NORLUND, KRISTINE; Redford HS; Detroit, MI; Chrh Wkr; Hon Rl; OEA; Henry Ford Community College; Educa.

NORMAN, ANDREA; Anthony Wayne HS; Whitehouse, OH; 43/312 Cl Rep Jr Cls; Sec Sr Cls; Hon Rl; Sch Mus; Sch Pl; Stu Cncl; Rptr Yrbk; PPFtbl; Owens Tech Coll; Art.

NORMAN, DEENA; Leroy Pine River HS; Tustin, MI; 19/98 Cls Rep Sr Cls; Hon Rl; NHS; Stu Cncl; Sec Yrbk; Capt Crs Cntry; Grand Rapids Jr Coll; Occup Ther.

NORMAN, GREG; Holy Rosary HS; Flint, MI; 5/65 Hon Rl; Bsbl; Ftbl; Michigan St Univ; Data Processing.

NORMAN, KIM; Tippicanoe Valley HS; Akron, IN; Chrs; Chrh Wkr; Sch Mus; Sch Pl; Stg Crw; Yth Flsp; Drama Clb; Gulf Coast Bible Coll; Psych.

NORMAN, MARK; Garaway HS; Sugarcreek, OH; Aud/Vis; Spn Clb; Crs Cntry; Starb Tech Coll; Elec Tech.

NORMAN, MARY; Theodore Roosevelt HS; Gary, IN; Mod UN; Pres Girl Scts; Hon Rl; Jr NHS; NHS; Pres Yth Flsp; Pres Y-Teens; Sec FSA; Spn Clb; Scr Kpr; Univ; Math.

NORMAN, SHERI; Point Pleasant HS; Pt Pleasant, WV; Band; Hosp Ade; Lbry Ade; Sch Mus; Y-Teens; Yrbk; FHA; West Virginia Univ; Home Ec.

NORMANDIN, CASSANDRA; Quincy HS; Quincy, MI; 5/116 Cls Rep Frsh Cls; Hst Soph Cls; Cls Rep Soph Cls; Hst Jr Cls; Hst Sr Cls; Cls Rep Sr Cls; NHS; Pres Stu Cncl; Rptr Yrbk; Sec 4-H; Western Mich Univ; Bus Admin.

NORRED, JEFF; Taylor Center HS; Taylor, MI; Band; Boy Scts; Debate Tm; Hon Rl; Glf; Ten; Univ Of Michigan; Archt Engr.

NORRIS, ANDREW; Sycamore HS; Cincinnati, OH; 9/470 Mod UN; Pres NHS; Stg Crw; Sch Nwsp; Drama Clb; VP Ger Clb; Natl Merit SF; Capt Its Academic 1976; Top Math Stdnt 1976; Top Sci Stdnt 1976; Awrd Winner Natl AATG 1977; Ohio St Univ; Comp Sci.

NORRIS, CARLA; Conotton Valley HS; Uhrichsville, OH; 6/59 Chrs; Chrh Wkr; Lbry Ade; Mdrgl; Beta Clb; FHA; 4-H Awd; Univ Of Ten; Secretarial Sci.

NORRIS, CAROLE; Upper Arlington HS; Columbus, OH; 1/648 Val; FCA; Hon Rl; NHS; Sch Mus; Stu Cncl; Yrbk; Pep Clb; Chrldng; Natl Merit Ltr; French Natl Hnr Soc; Duke Univ; English.

NORRIS, CHERYL; Sandusky HS; Sandusky, OH; Band; Chrh Wkr; Hon Rl; NHS; Orch; Sch Mus; Yth Flsp; Lat Clb; Coll.

NORRIS, DEBORAH L; Ironton HS; Ironton, OH; Band; Hon Rl; Sch Nwsp; Boys Clb Am; Fr Clb; Sci Clb; Trk; GAA; DAR Awd; Univ; Med.

NORRIS, DENNIS; Woodsfield HS; Woodsfield, OH; 12 Chrh Wkr; Hon Rl; 4-H; Bsbl; Bsktbl; Am Leg Awd; 4-H Awd; Kiwan Awd; Ohio Univ; Civil Engr.

NORRIS, DENNIS; Pontiac Central HS; Pontiac, MI; Band; Boy Scts; Chrh Wkr; Hon Rl; Orch; Sct Actv; Yth Flsp; Pep Clb; Wrstlng; Univ; Med.

NORRIS, GEORGE; High School; Huntngbrg, IN; Band; Chrh Wkr; Pres Soroptimist; Ind Univ; Music.

NORRIS, GLORIA J; Parkside HS; Jackson, MI; Cl Rep Jr Cls; Cls Rep Sr Cls; Band; Debate Tm; Hon Rl; Natl Forn Lg; Stu Cncl; Sch Nwsp; College; Medicine.

NORRIS, JAMES; New Palestine HS; New Palestine, IN; 66/238 FCA; Hon Rl; Yrbk; Sch Nwsp; FHA; Spn Clb; VICA; Wrstlng; IM Sprt;.

NORRIS, JOEY; Northfork HS; Northfork, WV; 1/150 Pres Soph Cls; Pres Jr Cls; Pres Sr Cls; Jr NHS; Ed Yrbk; Fr Clb; Key Clb; Letter Ftbl; Am Leg Awd; DAR Awd; Univ Of W V; Political Science.

NORRIS, KATHY; Buchtel University HS; Akron, OH; Cls Rep Frsh Cls; Cls Rep Soph Cls; Hon Rl; Off Ade; Fr Clb; Ger Clb; Pep Clb; Spn Clb; Collge; Foreign Language.

NORRIS, KENT; Tecumseh HS; Tecumseh, MI; Pres Frsh Cls; Am Leg Boys St; Stu Cncl; Pres Yth Flsp; Letter Crs Cntry; Trk; Michigan St Univ; Law.

NORRIS, KEVIN; Vinson HS; Huntington, WV; Boy Scts; Chrs; Hon Rl; Sct Actv; Boys Clb Am; DECA; FHA; Key Clb; Bsbl; Letter Ten; Richland J Kirkland Citznshp Awd 78; Letter In Tennis 79; Glenville St Univ; Forestry.

NORRIS, KIMBERLY; Cass Tech HS; Detroit, MI; Girl Scts; Off Ade; ROTC; FDA; Pep Clb; Chrldng; Mic State Univ; Pre Med.

NORRIS, LINDA; South Point HS; Charleston, WV; 16/160 Cl Rep Jr Cls; Band; Chrh Wkr; Girl Scts; Hon Rl; Hosp Ade; Lbry Ade; NHS; Yth Flsp; FHA; Ohio Univ; Fshn Mdse.

NORRIS, PAMELA; Westfield Washington HS; Zionsville, IN; Band; Hon Rl; 4-H; Fr Clb; Trk; 4-H Awd; Univ.

NORRIS, ROXSANNA; Northeastern Jr Sr HS; Fountaincty, IN; Hon Rl; Pres JA; Sch Nwsp; Pres JA Awd; Bus Schl; Bus Mgmt.

NORRIS, RUTH; Ontario Sr HS; Mansfield, OH; AFS; Band; Chrs; Lbry Ade; Sch Mus; Sch Pl; Stg Crw; Drama Clb; Ten; Mgrs; Heidelberg Coll; Theatre.

NORRIS, SARA; N Muskegon HS; N Muskegon, MI; 30/108 Band; Hon Rl; Jr NHS; NHS; Off Ade; Orch; Sch Mus; Sct Actv; Fr Clb; Letter Bsktbl; Coll; Phys Therapy.

NORRIS, SUSAN; St Joseph HS; Bethel Park, PA; Cls Rep Frsh Cls; Cls Rep Soph Cls; Cl Rep Jr Cls; Chrs; FCA; Stu Cncl; Rptr Yrbk; IM Sprt; Natl Merit SF; Univ; Bus.

NORRIS, TAMMY; Springfield HS; Springfield, MI; 18/104 Cls Rep Frsh Cls; Cls Rep Soph Cls; Hon Rl; NHS; Stu Cncl; FHA; Pep Clb; Bsktbl; Twrlr; Bus Schl; Office Mgmt.

NORRIS, TERRY L; Reeths Puffer HS; Muskegon, MI; 20/350 Letter Ftbl; Western Michigan Univ; Law.

NORRIS, TIMOTHY; Colon HS; Leonidas, MI; 3/80 Band; Hon Rl; NHS; FFA; Univ Of Michigan; Comp Sci.

NORRIS, TONI; Southern Wells HS; Poneto, IN; 17/90 Band; Chrs; Chrh Wkr; Cmnty Wkr; Hon Rl; NHS; Off Ade; Yth Flsp; FHA; Pep Clb; Olivet Nazarene Coll; Home Ec.

NORTH, ISHMEAL; Saginaw HS; Saginaw, MI; Pres Frsh Cls; Pres Soph Cls; JA; Jr NHS; Stg Crw; Stu Cncl; Yth Flsp; Pep Clb; Bsbl; JETS Awd; Michigan St Univ.

NORTH, JUDI A; Southside HS; Muncie, IN; Hon Rl; NHS; Quill & Scroll; Ed Yrbk; Sch Nwsp; College; Busns.

NORTH, JULI A; Southside HS; Muncie, IN; 20/300 Hon Rl; JA; NHS; Quill & Scroll; Yth Flsp; Yrbk; Am Leg Awd; JC Awd; Kiwan Awd; Rotary Awd; Ball St Univ; Elem Ed.

NORTH, KAREN; Roeper City & Country HS; Union Lake, MI; Sch Mus; Sch Pl; Rptr Yrbk; Sch Nwsp; Univ; Drama.

NORTH, LORI D; East Noble HS; Wolcottville, IN; 49/269 Pres Soph Cls; Band; FCA; Hon Rl; Sch Pl; Stg Crw; Drama Clb; 4-H; Crs Cntry; Gym; Natl Honor Soc; Marothons; College; Archt.

NORTH, SUZANNE; Grosse Ile HS; Grosse Ile, MI; 12/220 Sec Soph Cls; Cl Rep Jr Cls; Chrs; Chrh Wkr; Hon Rl; Pres NHS; Sec Stu Cncl; Fr Clb; Glf; Letter Ten; Univ; Intl Bus.

NORTHROP, PATRICK; Hillman Cmnty HS; Hillman, MI; 5/55 Band; Chrh Wkr; NHS; Sch Pl; Ftbl; Univ; Physics.

NORTHROP, SHERRI; Marcellus HS; Marcellus, MI; Cls Rep Soph Cls; Cls Rep Sr Cls; Hon Rl; Pep Clb; Spn Clb; Trk; Chrldng; GAA; W Mic Univ; Psych.

NORTHROP, TINA; Ida HS; Temperance, MI; Hon Rl; Yrbk; Sch Nwsp; Pep Clb; Mat Maids; Monroe Comm Coll; Flight Attendent.

NORTHRUP, LORI; Montpelier HS; Montpelier, OH; 7/110 VP Soph Cls; Am Leg Aux Girls St; Band; Chrs; Chrh Wkr; Cmnty Wkr; Girl Scts; Hon Rl; NHS; Orch; 78 79 Sr Queen; St English Awd; St Music Awd; Bowling Green St Univ; Medicine.

NORTHRUP, RICHARD C; Okemos HS; Okemos, MI; 60/300 Pres Sr Cls; Band; NHS; Pol Wkr; Yth Flsp; Coach Actv; Awd Mst Imprvd Skier 77; Cvtn Youth Leadrshp Seminar Adrian Coll 79; Comptd In CUSSA Ctrl U S Ski Assoc 77; Univ; Bus Admin.

NORTON, B; Madison HS; Madison, OH; 24/295 Band; Cmnty Wkr; Hon Rl; Stg Crw; Sch Nwsp; Drama Clb; 4-H; Fr Clb; College; Bus Management.

NORTON, DIANE; Licking Cnty Joint Voc HS; Newark, OH; Cl Rep Jr Cls; Cls Rep Sr Cls; Girl Scts; Hosp Ade; Rptr Yrbk; OEA; Ambassador Awd Jr & Sr Yr Ofc Ed Assn; 1st Pl Parliamentary Tm Regional Competition; OEA Person Of Week; Busns Schl; Busns Admin.

NORTON, JEROME; Fremont St Joseph HS; Fremont, OH; Hon Rl; Y-Teens; Wrstlng; Univ; Forestry.

NORTON, MARCI; Keystone HS; Elyria, OH; Chrs; Lbry Ade; NHS; Pep Clb; Lorain County Cmnty Coll; Mdse.

NORTON, STEPHANIE; Deer Park HS; Cincinnati, OH; Hon Rl; JA; Pres Pep Clb; Univ; Vet.

NORTON, TAMMY; United Local HS; East Rochester, OH; Hon Rl; Jr NHS; Yth Flsp; FHA; OEA; Columbiana Cnty Joint Voc Schl.

NORTON, TODD; Coldwater HS; Coldwater, MI; Cl Rep Jr Cls; Boy Scts; Hon Rl; Sch Pl; Sci Clb; Letter Ftbl; Letter Trk; IM Sprt; Natl Merit SF; Mich St Univ; Comp Sci.

NORVELL, LUCY; Gallia Acad HS; Gallipolis, OH; Band; Chrh Wkr; Drl Tm; Girl Scts; Rptr Yrbk; Rptr Sch Nwsp; Drama Clb; FNA; Lat Clb; Sci Clb; College.

NORWOOD, REBECCA; Huntington N HS; Huntington, IN; 78/560 Cls Rep Frsh Cls; Chrs; Chrh Wkr; Hon Rl; NHS; Sch Mus; Yth Flsp; 4-H; Pep Clb; 4-H Awd; Internatl Busns Coll; Sec.

NOSS, JULIE; Pike Delta York Sr HS; Delta, OH; Sec Jr Cls; Sec Sr Cls; Cls Rep Sr Cls; Am Leg Aux Girls St; Band; Girl Scts; Hon Rl; Hosp Ade; Sec NHS; Sch Pl; Voc Schl; Bus.

NOSS, YVONNE; Edgewood Sr HS; Conneaut, OH; AFS; Band; Hon Rl; Lbry Ade; Sch Mus; Sch Pl; Y-Teens; Pep Clb; Sci Clb; Spn Clb; Defiance Univ; Marine Bio.

NOSSETT, DARIN; Wood Memorial HS; Oakland City, IN; 3/88 Pres Soph Cls; Am Leg Boys St; Band; Chrh Wkr; Hon Rl; Orch; Sct Actv; Stu Cncl; Yth Flsp; Bsktbl; Biology Chemistry History & Band Awds; Nazarene Church Teen CARE Corps To Virgin Islands; Olivet Nazarene Coll.

NOSSETT, JAMES R; Bethesda Christian HS; Lebanon, IN; Pres Soph Cls; Pres Jr Cls; Chrs; Chrh Wkr; Cmnty Wkr; Hon Rl; Quill & Scroll; Sch Mus; Stg Crw; Yth Flsp; Whos Who In Forgn Languages 1977; 1st Pl Dist & St Ensemble 1977; Yth Of Wk Brownsburg Pol Dept Cadts 1977; Wabash Coll; Med.

NOTA, ELIZABETH M; Belleville HS; Belleville, MI; 43/507 Cls Rep Soph Cls; VP Jr Cls; VP Sr Cls; Chrs; Hon Rl; NHS; Stu Cncl; Ed Yrbk; Bsbl; Chrldng; College; Spec Ed.

NOTARBERARDINO, TERI; Brookside HS; Sheffield Lke, OH; Hon Rl; Lbry Ade; NHS; Stg Crw; Stu Cncl; Bsbl; Lorain Cnty Cmnty Coll; Sec Sci.

NOTESTINE, TONYA A; Mohawk HS; Sycamore, OH; Am Leg Aux Girls St; Chrs; Chrh Wkr; Cmnty Wkr; Girl Scts; Hon Rl; Jr NHS; NHS; Sch Mus; Y-Teens; Navy; Dent Tech.

NOTTEBOOM, CHRISTINE; Marian HS; Mishawaka, IN; 8/156 Hon Rl; NHS; IM Sprt; Mgrs; SAR Awd;.

NOURSE, JAMI; Kenton Ridge HS; Springfield, OH; 34/140 Hon Rl; JA; FHA; Letter Ten; Chrldng; Clark Tech Schl; Med Sec.

NOUSS, LINDA; Hamilton Twp HS; Papillion, NE; Cmp Fr Grls; Girl Scts; Sdlty; Pres 4-H; Fr Clb; FHA; Pep Clb; Chrldng; Pom Pon; Humane Soc Cert Of Apprctn 1976; Pres Physical Fitness Award 1976; Award Of Excell 1976; Ohio St Univ; Elem Educ.

NOVAK, ANN; Polaris Joint Voc HS; Olmsted Townshp, OH; Pres Jr Cls; Pres Sr Cls; Girl Scts; Stg Crw; Rptr Yrbk; Yrbk; Pres FFA; Trk; Scr Kpr; Tmr; Schlrshp Honor Awd; Recognition Of Service In Art; Customer Service Awd; College; Plant Biology.

NOVAK, CAROLINE; Marquette HS; Michigan City, MN; Chrs; Hon Rl; JA; Sch Mus; Drama Clb; Pres Awd; College.

NOVAK, CHARLES; Donald E Gavit Jr Sr HS; Hammond, IN; Boy Scts; Hon Rl; Letter Swmmng; B Hnr Roll Awd 77; B Hnr Roll Awd 76; Univ; Comp Sci.

NOVAK, ERIC; Willow Run HS; Ypsilanti, MI; Boy Scts; Cmnty Wkr; Hon Rl; Bsbl; Ftbl; Wrstlng; Coach Actv; Scr Kpr; Eastern Mic Univ; Comp Tech.

NOVAK, GENEVIEVE A; La Porte HS; Laporte, IN; Cmp Fr Grls; Hon Rl; Fr Clb; Jr Hnr Roll 78; Carnegie Mellon Univ; Archt.

NOVAK, LAUREEN; West Muskingum HS; Newark, OH; Cls Rep Soph Cls; Cl Rep Jr Cls; Chrs; Hon Rl; NHS; Sch Mus; Y-Teens; Sprt Ed Yrbk; 4-H; Trk; Univ Of S Carolina; Busns Admin.

NOVAK, MARGARET; Munster HS; Munster, IN; 1/406 Band; Chrh Wkr; Hon Rl; NHS; Orch; Ger Clb; Mth Clb; Natl Merit Ltr; Purdue Univ; Chem Engr.

NOVAK, MICHELLE; Meridian Sr HS; Auburn, MI; 2/120 Sec Soph Cls; Pres Jr Cls; Sal; Band; Chrs; Hon Rl; NHS; Sch Mus; Sch Pl; Stg Crw; Acdmc Schlrshp From Cntrl Mi Univ 79; Central Michigan Univ; Educ.

NOVAK, NATALIE; Our Lady Of Mt Carmel HS; Wyandotte, MI; Aud/Vis; Chrs; Chrh Wkr; Sch Mus; Spn Clb; Completed Intro Course For Basic Catechetics 1977; Univ; Music.

NOVAK, NATALIE J; Flint Central HS; Flint, MI; Band; Hon Rl; Sec NHS; Chrldng; Schlrshp For Mi St HS Engr Inst; St Of Mich Schlrshp; Grad With High Distinction; Michigan St Univ; Econ.

NOVAK, SUSAN; Rocky River HS; Rocky Rvr, OH; Sec Jr Cls; Sec Sr Cls; Band; Hon Rl; JA; Ger Clb; Pep Clb; Ten; IM Sprt; Univ Of Mic; Communication.

NOVELLI, ROBIN; Warren G Harding HS; Warren, OH; 35/385 Cls Rep Sr Cls; Am Leg Boys St; Chrs; Chrh Wkr; Hon Rl; Jr NHS; NHS; Yth Flsp; Pep Clb; Letter Ten; College; Math.

NOVICK, TONI; St Francis Cabrini HS; Dearborn Hts, MI; Girl Scts; Hon Rl; Spn Clb; Bsbl; Bsktbl; Scr Kpr; ALL Area Hon Mention For All Leag 79; Vet.

NOVIN, MARGRETE; Memorial HS; St Marys, OH; 5/239 VP Frsh Cls; Band; Hon Rl; JA; Lbry Ade; NHS; Rptr Yrbk; Ger Clb; Sci Clb; Kiwan Awd; Univ; Psych.

NOVOSEL, LINDA; Hubbard HS; Hubbard, OH; 20/350 Band; Hon Rl; NHS; Youngstown St Univ; Soc Work.

NOVOTNY, JEFF; Clay HS; S Bend, IN; 21/450 Cls Rep Frsh Cls; Boy Scts; Chrh Wkr; Hon Rl; NHS; Sct Actv; Yrbk; Fr Clb; Letter Ftbl; Hockey; Dana Corp Doctor Of Motors Engine Overhaul Crtfctn 79; Notre Dame Univ; Mech Engr.

NOVOTNY, THOMAS; Cabrini HS; Allen Pk, MI; Cl Rep Jr Cls; Sprt Ed Yrbk; Mi Comp Schlrshp 79; Morality In Media Writing Contest Winner 78; Henry Ford Cmnty Coll; Aero Engr.

NOVY, ROSE; Cuyahoga Heights HS; Brooklyn Hts, OH; Cls Rep Frsh Cls; Trs Soph Cls; Trs Jr Cls; Trs Sr Cls; Band; Chrs; Drm Mjrt; Hon Rl; Sch Pl; Stg Crw; Univ; Phys Ther.

NOW, LAURIE; Celina Sr HS; Celina, OH; Chrh Wkr; Hon Rl; Sch Mus; Sch Pl; Stg Crw; Yth Flsp; Ed Yrbk; Trk; Voc Schl; Ticket Agent.

NOWAK, ANNE; Posen Consolidated Schl; Posen, MI; Band; Hon Rl; NHS; Stu Cncl; Rptr Sch Nwsp; Fr Clb; FHA; Pep Clb; Btty Crckr Awd; Alpena C mnty Coll; Acctg.

NOWAK, COLLEEN; Ubly Cmnty HS; Ubly, MI; 5/110 VP Frsh Cls; Cls Rep Sr Cls; Band; Hon Rl; NHS; Sch Pl; Stu Cncl; Trk; Univ; Soc Work.

NOWAK, LYNDA; Whitmore Lake HS; Whitmore Lake, MI; 22/85 Sal; Band; Cmnty Wkr; Drm Mjrt; Girl Scts; Hon Rl; Jr NHS; Off Ade; PAVAS; Fr Clb; Siena Heights Coll; Acctg.

NOWAK, LYNNE; Ubly Community HS; Ubly, MI; 2/110 Sec Soph Cls; Sal; Chrh Wkr; Hon Rl; NHS; Chrldng; Pres Awd; Saginaw Vly St College; Computer.

NOWAK, MARILYN; Ravenna HS; Ravenna, OH; Chrh Wkr; Cmnty Wkr; FCA; Hon Rl; Lbry Ade; NHS; Yth Flsp; Pep Clb; Taylor Univ; Psych.

NOWAK, RENEA; Perrysburg HS; Perrysburg, OH; AFS; Hon Rl; Hosp Ade; JA; Ger Clb; Pep Clb; Letter Ten; JA Awd; Ohio St Univ; Psych.

NOWAK, ROBERT; St Francis HS; Traverse City, MI; Boy Scts; Ftbl; Wrstlng; Mgrs; Pres Awd; Fordham.

NOWAK, SUE; Bishop Noll Inst; Chicago, IL; 89/321 Hon Rl; Pep Clb; Nurses Training.

NOWAKOWSKI, JANET; St Ursula Acad; Sylvania, OH; Cmnty Wkr; JA; Drama Clb; Lat Clb; Spn Clb; Univ Of S Florida; Vet.

NOWC, NANCY; Carl Brablec HS; Roseville, MI; Chrs; Hon Rl; JA; NHS; Spn Clb; Adrian Coll; Math.

NOWELL, KEITH T; Dunbar HS; Dunbar, WV; Hon Rl; JA; PAVAS; Bsktbl; Letter Crs Cntry; Letter Ftbl; Letter Trk; College; Bus.

NOWELL, TERLYN; Cass Technical HS; Detroit, MI; Chrh Wkr; Cmnty Wkr; Girl Scts; Hon Rl; Lbry Ade; NHS; FTA; Sci Clb; Gym; Trk; Univ Of Mich; Comp Sci.

NOWELS, DEBRA K; East Noble HS; Kendallville, IN; 54/236 Pres Soph Cls; Band; Debate Tm; Hon Rl; Natl Forn Lg; Sch Pl; Drama Clb; OEA; Pep Clb; VICA; Olive B Cole Foundtn Schlshp 1979; St Stdnt Asst Commssn Of In A Hoosier Scholr 1979; Valparaiso Univ; Psych.

NOWICKI, MICHELE; Mott HS; Warren, MI; Cls Rep Frsh Cls; Cls Rep Soph Cls; Cl Rep Jr Cls; Girl Scts; Hon Rl; Jr NHS; Off Ade; Sch Pl; Sct Actv; DECA; Macomb; Conselor.

NOWICKI, PATTI; Wapakoneta Sr HS; Wapakoneta, OH; Hon Rl; NHS; Pres 4-H; Spn Clb; 4-H Awd; Tech Schl; Nurse.

NOWING, REBECCA; Crothersville HS; Crothersville, IN; 12/66 VP Jr Cls; Capt Drl Tm; Hon Rl; Yth Flsp; Pep Clb; Pom Pon; Purdue Univ; Pre Law.

NOWINSKI, DOUGLAS; Western Reserve Academy; Columbia Sta, OH; Hon Rl; Off Ade; Letter Bsbl; Letter Lcrss; Letter Socr; Schl Caucus 79; Coll.

NOWINSKI, GREGORY; Riverside HS; Dearborn Hts, MI; Pres Soph Cls; Cl Rep Jr Cls; Hon Rl; NHS; VP Stu Cncl; Fr Clb; Letter Bsktbl; Letter Ftbl; Univ Of Mich; Medicine.

NOWLIN, VICKI J; Eastwood HS; Luckey, OH; 7/180 Cls Rep Soph Cls; Am Leg Aux Girls St; Band; Cmnty Wkr; FCA; Hon Rl; NHS; Sch Mus; Drama Clb; Pep Clb; Univ Of Toledo.

NOYES, SCOTT; Memorial HS; Elkhart, IN; Chrs; Hon Rl; Stu Cncl; Rptr Sch Nwsp; Serv Clbs Hon Roll Awd 76; Serv Awd Newspaper Staff 77; Perfect Attndnc Awd 75 76 & 77; IUSB; Music.

NUBER, TIMOTHY; Columbus N HS; Columbus, OH; 28/350 Cls Rep Frsh Cls; FCA; Hon Rl; Jr NHS; NHS; Stu Cncl; VICA; Ftbl; Letter Wrstlng; IM Sprt;.

NUCKOLLS, CAROL; Shakamak HS; Lewis, IN; 2/100 Sec Soph Cls; Trs Soph Cls; Sec Jr Cls; Sal; Band; VP NHS; Quill & Scroll; Ind State Univ; Math.

NUGENT, DAVID; Kouts HS; Kouts, IN; 1/64 Am Leg Boys St; Band; Drm Mjrt; Hon Rl; Pres NHS; Sch Pl; Sct Actv; Stg Crw; Stu Cncl; Sci Clb; Wa Wrkshp Congressnl Seminar 79; Pres Porter Cnty Vt Assoc 79; Slctd For Amer Outstndg Names & Faces 78; Purdue Univ; Vet Med.

NUHRING, CAROL; Southridge HS; Huntngbrg, IN; 8/175 Hon Rl; Treas JA; Pres 4-H; VP FHA; Letter Trk; 4-H Awd; Vincennes Univ Jasper Center; Sec.

NULL, DAVID; Edgewood HS; Ellettsville, IN; 14/194 VP Frsh Cls; Am Leg Boys St; FCA; NHS; Key Clb; Bsktbl; Ftbl; Am Leg Awd; Dnfth Awd; DAR Awd; Hanover Coll; Tchr.

NULL, JOHN W; Wooster HS; Wooster, OH; 1/330 Am Leg Boys St; Band; Boy Scts; NHS; Spn Clb; Letter Crs Cntry; Letter Trk; College; Med.

NULL, LESA; Winfield HS; Scott Depot, WV; 1/125 Band; Hon Rl; Jr NHS; NHS; Stu Cncl; Beta Clb; Fr Clb; Pep Clb; Bsktbl; Scr Kpr; College; Law.

NULLS, CHERI; Bay Davis HS; Indianapolis, IN; Chrs;.

NUMMIKOSKI, DAVE; Holland HS; Holland, MI; 44/290 Hon Rl; NHS; Letter Bsbl; Letter Bsktbl; Letter Ftbl; Natl Merit Ltr; College; Bus Admin.

NUNEZ, CYNTHIA M; Aquinas HS; Taylor, MI; Pres Frsh Cls; Pres Soph Cls; Pres Jr Cls; Hon Rl; NHS; Bsbl; Capt Chrldng;.

NUNEZ, JOANN; Fordson HS; Dearborn, MI; Cls Rep Sr Cls; Hon Rl; NHS; Stu Cncl; Pres Spn Clb; IM Sprt; Univ Of Mic; Educa.

NUNEZ, SYLVIA; Union City Cmnty HS; Union City, IN; 9/100 Drl Tm; Hon Rl; Lbry Ade; NHS; Stu Cncl; Eng Clb; Fr Clb; FHA; Bsktbl; Trk; Univ; Math.

NUNN, J; Perrysburg HS; Perrysburg, OH; Boy Scts; Hon Rl; Jr NHS; Ger Clb; Bsbl; Ten; Univ; Law Enforcement.

NUNN, KRISTIE; Center Line HS; Center Line, MI; 10/425 Band; Hon Rl; Jr NHS; NHS; Fr Clb; Sci Clb; Mbr Of HS Top 10 79; Michigan Tech Univ; Forestry.

NUNN, LAURA; La Porte HS; La Porte, IN; 45/492 Band; Chrs; MMM; NHS; Orch; Sch Mus; Yth Flsp; Fr Clb; IM Sprt; Twrlr; Purdue Univ; Vet Med.

NURENBERG, SUE; Pewamo Westphalia HS; Pewamo, MI; Hon Rl; 4-H; 4-H Awd; Active Mbr Of The Cath Order Of Foresters 2 Trophies For Bowling; Gifts For Spelling Bee; Prize For Min Glf; Lansing Comm Coll.

NURRE, ELLEN; Our Lady Of Angels HS; Cincinnati, OH; 42/125 Cls Rep Frsh Cls; Trs Soph Cls; Girl Scts; Hon Rl; Hosp Ade; Sch Mus; Sch Pl; Rptr Yrbk; Drama Clb; Letter Bsktbl; Xavier Univ; Cmnctns.

NUSBAUM, BETTY; Bluffton HS; Bluffton, OH; Hon Rl; FHA;.

NUSBAUM, TINA; Jimtown HS; Elkhart, IN; 17/96 Hon Rl; Pep Clb; Spn Clb; International Bus; Med Sec.

NUSKEN, ELIZABETH; Bexley HS; Columbus, OH; 42/186 AFS; Band; Hon Rl; Lit Mag; Orch; Y-Teens; Rptr Sch Nwsp; Swmmng; Rotary Awd; Miami Univ.

NUSS, CHRISTINE; Our Lady Of The Lakes HS; Pontiac, MI; 10/45 Pres Frsh Cls; Pres Jr Cls; Pres Sr Cls; Hon Rl; Jr NHS; NHS; Off Ade; Sch Nwsp; Pep Clb; Spn Clb; Oakland Univ; Early Child Dvlpmnt.

NUSS, KATHY; New Knoxville HS; New Knoxville, OH; 3/40 Band; Chrs; Drm Mjrt; Hon Rl; NHS; Yth Flsp; Rptr Sch Nwsp; FHA; Ger Clb; Sci Clb; Coll; Sci.

NUSSBAUM, JOHN M; Central Christian HS; Orrville, OH; 15/69 Chrh Wkr; Cmnty Wkr; Hon Rl; Yth Flsp; Ger Clb; Dnfth Awd; Eastern Mennonite College; Math.

NUSSBAUM, STEVEN; Central Christian HS; Smithville, OH; 6/72 Pres Sr Cls; Chrs; Hon Rl; Pres Yth Flsp; Y-Teens; Ger Clb; Letter Bsktbl; Letter Socr; Natl Merit Ltr; Teenager Of Mnth For Entire Schl; Selected To Travel In Europe People To People Yng Ambassador Prog; Oral Roberts Univ; Med.

NUSSBAUM, TIM; Central Christian HS; Kidron, OH; Hon Rl; Sch Pl; Yth Flsp; Yrbk; Sch Nwsp; Socr; Goshen Coll; Physics.

NUSSDORFER, MICHAEL; Shelby HS; Shelby, MI; Hon Rl; Letter Glf; Natl Merit Ltr; Univ; Health.

NUSSEL, CAROLE; Mayfield HS; Mayfield Hts, OH; AFS; Band; Drl Tm; Girl Scts; Hon Rl; Red Cr Ade; Stg Crw; Drama Clb; Pep Clb; Letter Gym; Special Ach Awd In Phys Ed; College.

NUSSMAN, RON; Northmont HS; Dayton, OH; 26/517 Hon Rl; Letter Bsbl; Letter Bsktbl; Bowling Green St Univ; Acctg.

NUTKIN, AMY; Beachwood HS; Beachwood, OH; AFS; Cmnty Wkr; Hosp Ade; Lit Mag; NHS; Off Ade; Sprt Ed Yrbk; Rptr Yrbk; Rptr Sch Nwsp; VP Fr Clb; Boston Univ; Nurse.

NUTT, KAREN; Bosse HS; Evansville, IN; 7/329 Cls Rep Soph Cls; Sec Jr Cls; Cl Rep Jr Cls; Pres Sr Cls; Cls Rep Sr Cls; Hon Rl; NHS; Pres Quill & Scroll; Stu Cncl; Ed Sch Nwsp; Mc Donalds Youth Salute Progr Rep; Univ Of Evansville; Spec Educ.

NUTT, LINDA; Washington Twp HS; Valparaiso, IN; 10/22 Pres Soph Cls; Pres Jr Cls; Hon Rl; Pres NHS; Yrbk; Sch Nwsp; Chrldng;.

NUTT, TAMMY; Mayfield HS; Mayfield Hts, OH; 62/500 AFS; Band; Drl Tm; Hon Rl; Hosp Ade; Pol Wkr; Sct Actv; Stg Crw; Letter Pom Pon; College; Criminal Justice.

NUTTALL, DENNIS; Faith Christian HS; Fruitport, MI; Band; Chrs; Chrh Wkr; FCA; Bsbl; Letter Bsktbl; Ftbl; Socr; Wrstlng; IM Sprt;.

NUTTER, JAN; Bridgeport Sr HS; Bridgeport, WV; Am Leg Aux Girls St; Band; Chrs; Chrh Wkr; Cmnty Wkr; Hon Rl; Jr NHS; Red Cr Ade; Y-Teens; Pres 4-H; 1st Pl St Youth Essay & 1st Pl West Fork Soil Conservation Dist Speech Contest; Amer Outstnding Name & Face; Fairmont St Coll; Elem Ed.

NUTTER, KIM; South Harrison HS; Jane Lew, WV; Pres Frsh Cls; Band; Hon Rl; NHS; Sch Pl; Stu Cncl; 4-H; FTA; Letter Bsktbl; 4-H Awd; College; Med Tech.

NUTTER, LISA; Fayetteville HS; Fayetteville, WV; Am Leg Aux Girls St; Off Ade; Treas Stu Cncl; Yth Flsp; VP Fr Clb; Centry III Ldr Schlrshp Wnnr In Wv 79; Sec Wv Assoc Of Stu Coun 77; Schls Hnr Coun 78& 79; Head Jr Cnslr; W Virginia Inst Of Tech; Comp Sci.

NUTTER, MARGUERITE; Marysville HS; Marysville, OH; 10/225 Band; Chrs; Debate Tm; Hon Rl; Natl Forn Lg; NHS; Sch Mus; Sch Pl; IM Sprt; DAR Awd; Purdue; Advertising.

NUTTER, NANCY; Calvert HS; Tiffin, OH; Chrs; Girl Scts; Cit Awd; Ashland Coll; Soc Work.

NUTTER, PATTY; Marysville HS; Marysville, OH; Chrs; Mdrgl; Sch Mus; Sci Clb; IM Sprt; Univ; Hist.

NUTTER, STEPHEN A; Plainwell HS; Allegan, MI; 32/215 NHS; Stu Cncl; Letter Crs Cntry; Trk; St Of Mi Comp Schlshp 79; Cntrl Michigan Univ; Bus.

NUTTLE, SANDY; Garrett HS; Garrett, IN; 13/130 Band; Hon Rl; Sch Mus; Y-Teens; Yrbk; Ger Clb; Trk; GAA; Mgrs; Ball St Univ; Math.

NUZUM, BRIAN; Hundred HS; Hundred, WV; Boy Scts; Cmnty Wkr; Hon Rl; Sch Pl; Sct Actv; FFA; Bsbl; Ftbl; Natl Merit Ltr; FFA Fdn Awd Chatp Star Agri Busmn 79; FFA Fdn Awd Agri Proc 79; Waitman Barr Bsktbl Champ 74; Wetzel Cnty Voc Tech Schl.

NUZUM, RONDA J; Fairview HS; Farmington, WV; Hon Rl; Lbry Ade; Off Ade; 4-H; Fr Clb; Fairmont St Coll; Acctg.

NYBERG, E; Frankfort HS; Arcadia, MI; Sec Jr Cls; Sec Sr Cls; Band; Hon Rl; NHS; Sch Mus; Stu Cncl; Ed Yrbk; W Michigan Univ; Busns Admin.

NYDEREK, JEANETTE; Springs Vly HS; W Baden, IN; 11/86 Chrs; Chrh Wkr; Girl Scts; Hon Rl; JA; Sct Actv; Yth Flsp; 4-H; Trk; JA Awd;.

NYDEREK, JULIE; Springs Valley HS; W Baden, IN; 20/71 Chrs; Chrh Wkr; Girl Scts; Hon Rl; Sct Actv; Stg Crw; Yth Flsp; 4-H; FHA; Trk; Sullivan College; Comp Progr.

NYE, BARBARA; Hopewell Loudon HS; Fostoria, OH; 3/94 Band; Hon Rl; Treas NHS; Treas Pep Clb; Spn Clb; Letter Bsktbl; Capt Chrldng; Bowling Green St Univ; Foreign Lng.

NYE, GARY; River Valley HS; Three Oaks, MI; Hon Rl; Yrbk; Bsktbl; Crs Cntry; Glf; College; Archt.

NYE, LORI; Otsego HS; Grand Rapids, OH; 14/133 Band; Hon Rl; Jr NHS; NHS; Fr Clb; Trk; Scr Kpr; Tmr; Bowling Green St Univ; Busns Admin.

NYE, NICKI; West Carrollton Sr HS; Dayton, OH; 6/450 Chrs; Cmnty Wkr; Hon Rl; Jr NHS; NHS; Stu Cncl; Pep Clb; Letter Bsktbl; Trk; IM Sprt; Vllybl Ltr Capt All MCC Hon Mntn; Sftbl Ltr All MCC Hon Mntn; Vc Pres Of Var Club; Miami Univ; Comp Sci.

NYE, PATTI; Napoleon HS; Napoleon, OH; Hon Rl; Lbry Ade; NHS; Off Ade; Ed Yrbk; Lat Clb; Letter Swmmng; Letter Ten; Coach Actv; Mgrs; Univ; Acctg.

NYGAARD, DAVID A; Wylie E Groves HS; W Bloomfield, MI; 5/559 Cl Rep Jr Cls; Boy Scts; Chrs; NHS; Sch Mus; Sch Pl; IM Sprt; Natl Merit SF; Opt Clb Awd; Syracuse Univ; Architect.

NYHUIS, BETH; Edwardsburg HS; Edwardsburg, MI; Band; Hon Rl; Lbry Ade; Rptr Sch Nwsp; Sch Nwsp; Bsktbl; GAA; Grand Rapids Bapt Coll; Psych.

NYKIEL, STEVE; La Ville Jr Sr HS; Bremen, IN; FFA; Sci Clb; Lion Awd; Purdue Univ; Aviation.

NYLAAN, COLLEEN; East Kentwood HS; Kentwood, MI; Hon Rl; Bsbl; Letter Ten; Chrldng; GAA; IM Sprt; PPFtbl; Michigan St Univ; Vet Med.

NYLAND, BRIAN; Cadillac Sr HS; Cadillac, MI; Hon Rl; NHS; Letter Glf; Letter Ten; Natl Merit Ltr; Ferris St Coll; Acctg.

NYO, Y!N Y; Middletown HS; Middletown, OH; Hon Rl; JA; NHS; Orch; Y-Teens; Yrbk; Fr Clb; Ohi State Univ; Pre Med.

NYPAVER, BERNARD; Parma Sr HS; Parma, OH; 50/782 Hon Rl; Jr NHS; NHS; Sci Clb; Bsbl; Bsktbl; Ftbl; Trk; Wrstlng; IM Sprt; John Carroll Univ; Med.

NYSTROM, MARGARET; Marquette Sr HS; Marquette, MI; Hon Rl; Hosp Ade; Bsktbl; Swmmng; Trk; IM Sprt; Univ; Spec Educ.

O

O, JACQUELINE J; Philip Barbour HS; Flemington, WV; Band; Chrh Wkr; Girl Scts; Hon Rl; Off Ade; Sch Mus; Sct Actv; Stg Crw; Yth Flsp; 4-H; Univ; Photog.

OAKERSON, MARNETTA; Union HS; Losantville, IN; Band; Hon Rl; NHS; FHA; Spn Clb; Letter Bsktbl; College; Phys Therapy.

OAKES, ANGELA K; South Charleston HS; S Charleston, WV; 5/282 Cls Rep Sr Cls; Hon Rl; Jr NHS; Lit Mag; NHS; Sec Yth Flsp; FBLA; FHA; Spn Clb; Lion Awd; Amer Outstndng Names & Faces; Sherriffs Yth Cmp; Dstngshd Amer HS Stu; Fairmont State Coll; Accounting.

OAKES, DAVID V; Glen Oak HS; Canton, OH; Fr Clb; Natl Merit SF; College.

OAKLAND, KAREN; Bishop Donahue HS; Moundsville, WV; Band; Chrs; Hon Rl; Yth Flsp; Rptr Yrbk; Sec Spn Clb; Twrlr; Univ; Lab Tech.

OAKLEY, BRENDA; Muncie Central HS; Muncie, IN; 10350 Am Leg Aux Girls St; Hon Rl; NHS; Quill & Scroll; Ed Sch Nwsp; Ger Clb; Keyettes; Pep Clb; Sci Clb; Kiwan Awd; Cert Of Awd From Exchng Club Of Muncie 78; Jrnlsm Hon Cert 78 & 79; Indiana Univ; Pre Med.

OAKLEY, CAROL; South Dearborn HS; Dillsboro, IN; VP Soph Cls; Cl Rep Jr Cls; Hon Rl; Sec NHS; Quill & Scroll; Sch Pl; Sec Stu Cncl; Ed Yrbk; Rptr Yrbk; Rptr Sch Nwsp; Whos Who Among Amer HS Stdnt 77; Spanish Awd 77; Jrnlsm Ed In Chief & Copywritng Medl 78; Banking Schl; Jrnlsm.

OAKLEY, DORIS C; Meadowbrook HS; Kipling, OH; Hon Rl; Off Ade; Stu Cncl; Yrbk; 4-H; Treas FHA; Pep Clb; Ohio Univ; Nursing.

OAKLEY, RICHARD; Marysville HS; Marysville, OH; 5/230 Cls Rep Frsh Cls; Boy Scts; Hon Rl; NHS; Stu Cncl; Yrbk; Lat Clb; Letter Ftbl; Letter Trk; Wrstlng; Univ; Chem.

OAKS, JOHN; Calumet HS; Gary, IN; 6/250 Pres Jr Cls; Pres Sr Cls; NHS; PAVAS; Sch Pl; Stu Cncl; Drama Clb; Fr Clb; FSA; Indiana Univ; Nursing.

OANCEA, DAVID M; Louisville Sr HS; Louisville, OH; 1/371 Pres Jr Cls; Am Leg Boys St; Band; Chrh Wkr; Debate Tm; Hon Rl; Pres Natl Forn Lg; VP NHS; Pres Stu Cncl; Rdo Clb; St Spch Tourn 79; Exl Int Ratng St Sci Fair 78; Teen Talk Part 78; Univ; Med.

OARD, JULIE; Beaverton HS; Gladwin, MI; 20/141 Band; Chrs; Chrh Wkr; Drm Mjrt; Hon Rl; Lbry Ade; NHS; Central Mic Univ; Bus.

OATES, BETH; Waldron Area HS; Waldron, MI; 4/52 Band; Chrh Wkr; Hon Rl; Hosp Ade; Sec NHS; Sch Pl; Stu Cncl; Bsktbl; Trk; Capt Chrldng; College; Rn.

OATES, BETH A; Waldron Area HS; Waldron, MI; 4/52 Cl Rep Jr Cls; Band; Hon Rl; Hosp Ade; NHS; Sch Pl; Stu Cncl; FHA; Pep Clb; Spn Clb; College; Nursing.

OATES, STEVEN; Riverdale Local HS; Forest, OH; 26/105 Band; Chrs; Chrh Wkr; Hon Rl; NHS; Sch Pl; 4-H; FTA; IM Sprt; 4-H Awd; College; Bus Admin.

O BAKER, RONALD O; Gaylord HS; Gaylord, MI; Hon Rl; NHS; College; Engr.

OBAL, LORIE; Wickliffe HS; Wickliffe, OH; Band; Hon Rl; Cleveland State; Bio.

O BANION, BRIAN S; East Lutheran HS; Warren, MI; 1/140 Am Leg Boys St; Chrh Wkr; Hon Rl; NHS; Key Clb; Letter Bsbl; Letter Bsktbl; Letter Ftbl; Cit Awd; Natl Merit SF; Univ; Chem Engr.

O BANION, MELBA A; Garfield HS; Akron, OH; Cls Rep Soph Cls; Cl Rep Jr Cls; Chrs; Hon Rl; Off Ade; Yrbk; Fr Clb; Sci Clb; Swmmng; Chrldng; College.

O BANNON, JENNIE; Collinwood HS; Cleveland, OH; Chrs; Cmnty Wkr; Lbry Ade; Off Ade; Civ Clb; Bsbl; Cit Awd; Dyke Bus School; Sec.

O BARA, NORMA; Kankakee Valley HS; Fair Oaks, IN; Band; Chrh Wkr; FCA; Hon Rl; Yth Flsp; Rptr Sch Nwsp; 4-H; Mth Clb; Pep Clb; Sci Clb; Coll; Music.

O BARRIOS, JUANA; Culver Girls Academy; Los Angeles, CA; 10/200 Pres Frsh Cls; Cls Rep Soph Cls; Cl Rep Jr Cls; Pres Sr Cls; Cls Rep Sr Cls; Chrs; Debate Tm; Hon Rl; JA; Jr NHS; Raymund Huningt on Gardner Amer Airlines Schlrshp 76 80; Yale Univ.

OBEE, PAMELA; Notre Dame Academy; Toledo, OH; Cls Rep Frsh Cls; Cls Rep Soph Cls; VP Jr Cls; Chrh Wkr; Girl Scts; Hon Rl; JA; NHS; Sct Actv; Stu Cncl; Whos Who In Frgn Lang 79; Sponsored As Participant In Oper Yth 79; Univ; Pre Med.

OBENDORF, SUNDA; Eastside Jr Sr HS; Butler, IN; Pres Frsh Cls; Cls Rep Soph Cls; Chrh Wkr; Hon Rl; Lbry Ade; NHS; Stg Crw; Pres Yth Flsp; Rptr Yrbk; Letter Bsktbl; Indiana Univ; Educ.

OBENDORFER, MARGARET; Stow HS; Stow, OH; FCA; Hon Rl; Hosp Ade; JA; NHS; Letter Ten; Cincinnati Univ; Pharm.

OBERFIELD, MEME; Newark Sr HS; Newark, OH; Drl Tm; Hon Rl; NHS; Stu Cncl; Univ; Psych.

OBERGEFELL, LOUISE A; Lake Catholic HS; Mentor, OH; 8/318 Band; Hon Rl; Jr NHS; Lit Mag; Letter Bsbl; Letter Bsktbl; Natl Merit SF; Univ; Mech Engr.

OBERHAUS, JERRY; Holgate HS; Holgate, OH; 4/59 Hst Soph Cls; Trs Jr Cls; Chrs; Chrh Wkr; Hon Rl; NHS; Sch Mus; Sch Pl; Stg Crw; Treas Stu Cncl; Bowling Green St Univ; Elem Ed.

OBERHAUS, KEVIN; Liberty Center HS; Napoleon, OH; 13/70 Cl Rep Jr Cls; Am Leg Boys St; Hon Rl; NHS; Sch Mus; Sch Pl; Stg Crw; Yrbk; Fr Clb; Am Leg Awd; College; Sci.

OBERHEU, ANNE; Oakwood HS; Dayton, OH; AFS; Chrs; FCA; Girl Scts; Hon Rl; Hosp Ade; JA; Sch Mus; Sch Pl; Ten; College; Med.

OBERHOLTZ, PATRICIA L; Ellet HS; Akron, OH; Cls Rep Sr Cls; Cmnty Wkr; Hon Rl; NHS; Red Cr Ade; Sec Stu Cncl; Ed Yrbk; Pres OEA; Voice Dem Awd; Akron Univ; Acctg.

OBERHOLTZER, TRACY; Western HS; Russiaville, IN; 35/195 Band; Boy Scts; Chrs; Chrh Wkr; FCA; Sct Actv; Yth Flsp; Yrbk; Wrstlng; Mgrs; Purdue Univ; Elec Engr.

OBERHOUSE, JAN; Eastwood HS; Pemberville, OH; VP Soph Cls; Band; Chrs; Chrh Wkr; FCA; Girl Scts; Hon Rl; NHS; Off Ade; Sch Mus; College; Law.

OBERLANDER, DEBORAH; Mt Pleasant HS; Mt Pleasant, MI; 1/319 Val; Band; Chrh Wkr; Girl Scts; Hon Rl; NHS; Sch Mus; Yth Flsp; Lat Clb; OEA; Bd Of Trustees Schlrshp 79; Mi Comp Schlrshp 79; Basic Educ Opportnty Grant 79; Cntrl Michigan Univ; Math.

OBERLEAS, TERI; Bremen Public HS; Bremen, IN; 6/95 Band; Cmp Fr Grls; Chrs; Sec Chrh Wkr; Hon Rl; NHS; Sch Mus; Drama Clb; Sec 4-H; Spn Clb; Tri Kappa 77 78 & 79; Misbova Vocal Solo 2nd At St 79; Vocal & Instumntl Awds 77 78 & 79; Univ; Math.

OBERLIN, CATHY; Shelby HS; Shelby, MI; 9/120 Band; Chrh Wkr; Cmnty Wkr; Hon Rl; NHS; Off Ade; Stg Crw; Cit Awd; Opt Clb Awd; Davenport College; Comp Progr.

OBERMESIK, PATRICIA; Hartford HS; Hartford, MI; Hon Rl; Sch Nwsp; Sec FFA; Spn Clb; Bsktbl; IM Sprt; Univ; Jrnlsm.

OBERMEYER, KATHLEEN; Taylor HS; N Bend, OH; 1/160 Am Leg Aux Girls St; Band; Chrh Wkr; FCA; Hon Rl; JA; Jr NHS; NHS; Pol Wkr; Sch Pl; Northwestern Univ.

OBERMILLER, REED; Crestline HS; Crestline, OH; Pres Sr Cls; Boy Scts; Chrh Wkr; Hon Rl; Sct Actv; Stu Cncl; Ger Clb; Bsktbl; Ftbl; Letter Glf; Tennis Mst Valuble Plyer Mst Wins 1979; Oh Ind Arts Assoc Bl Rbn 2 Yrs 1978; K Of C Ath Of Mnth 1978; Voc Schl.

OBERMYER, BETH; Woodmore HS; Woodville, OH; 6/130 Band; Treas Girl Scts; Hon Rl; NHS;

Orch; Sch Pl; VP Yth Flsp; Pres Lat Clb; Am Leg Awd; Ohio St Univ; Med Tech.

O BERNARD, RONALD; Seneca East HS; Attica, OH; 2/100 Pres Soph Cls; Am Leg Boys St; Hon Rl; Hosp Ade; NHS; Sch Pl; Stu Cncl; Rptr Sch Nwsp; Mth Clb; Sci Clb; Univ; Pre Med.

OBERSKI, DOUGLAS; Ida HS; Ida, MI; 8/152 Pres Jr Cls; Am Leg Boys St; Hon Rl; NHS; Stu Cncl; Letter Bsbl; Letter Bsktbl; Letter Ftbl; W Michigan Univ; Comp Sys Engr.

OBERT, JAN; Cardinal Stritch HS; Oregon, OH; 1/172 Val; Am Leg Aux Girls St; Hon Rl; JA; Sch Mus; Stu Cncl; Swmmng; Univ Of Toledo; Co Sci.

OBEY, MARY A; Hazel Park HS; Hazel Park, MI; Band; Chrh Wkr; Girl Scts; Hon Rl; NHS; Off Ade; Yth Flsp; Sch Nwsp; Swmmng; Cit Awd; Oakland Cmnty Coll; Eng.

O BOYLE, PAM; Breckenridge Jr Sr HS; Merrill, MI; 32/118 Band; Chrh Wkr; Hon Rl; NHS; Stg Crw; Drama Clb; 4-H; Pep Clb; Spn Clb; Letter Bsktbl; Cedarville Coll; Elem Ed.

O BRIEN, ANN; Bishop Watterson HS; Worthington, OH; 12/250 Band; Cmp Fr Grls; Hon Rl; Jr NHS; 4-H; Lat Clb; Spn Clb; Mat Maids; Scr Kpr; Ohio St Univ; Vet.

O BRIEN, CHERYLL; Traverse City St Francis HS; Williamburg, MI; Band; Drl Tm; Hon Rl; PPFtbl; Univ; CPA.

O BRIEN, COLLEEN; Franklin Community HS; Morgantown, IN; 29/310 Hon Rl; JA; Off Ade; 4-H; FFA; Pep Clb; Swmmng; Trk; 4-H Awd; Univ; Real Estate.

O BRIEN, CONNIE; Union Local HS; Flushing, OH; 3/165 Band; Chrh Wkr; Pres NHS; Stu Cncl; Ed Sch Nwsp; Fr Clb; FTA; Bowling Green Su; Music.

O BRIEN, DANIEL; Monroe Catholic Central HS; Monroe, MI; 3/96 VP Jr Cls; Chrh Wkr; Hon Rl; Lit Mag; NHS; Sch Pl; Stg Crw; Rptr Yrbk; Capt Ten; IM Sprt; Particptd In Alumni Schlrshp Prog 79; Edward Rector Schlrshp Prog 79; Acad Awds 75 79; Michigan St Univ; Vet Med.

O BRIEN, DEBRA; Pontiac Central HS; Pontiac, MI; VP Sr Cls; Band; Chrh Wkr; Girl Scts; Hon Rl; Hosp Ade; NHS; Stg Crw; Ten; Mich Tech Univ; Mech Engr.

O BRIEN, DOUG; Bishop Watterson HS; Columbus, OH; FCA; Bsbl; Bsktbl; Ftbl; IM Sprt; Famous Names & Faces 79; Ftbl MVP Off All St All CCL & Ctzn Jrnl Plyr Of Wk 78; Bsblbst Hitter 78; Miami Univ; Spec Educ.

O BRIEN, J; Mason Sr HS; Mason, MI; Cmnty Wkr; Hon Rl; Jr NHS; Pol Wkr; Ten; Coll.

O BRIEN, JUDY; Interlochen Arts Acad; Lubbock, TX; Debate Tm; Hon Rl; Orch; Sch Mus; Yth Flsp; Fr Clb; Opt Clb Awd; Univ; Music.

OBRIEN, JULIE A; Bishop Foley HS; Troy, MI; 83/200 Cls Rep Frsh Cls; Cls Rep Soph Cls; Cl Rep Jr Cls; Hon Rl; NHS; Sec Stu Cncl; Yth Flsp; Trk; Chrldng; PPFtbl; Nazareth Coll; Nurse.

O BRIEN, K; The Andrews School; Timber Lk, OH; Chrh Wkr; Hon Rl; VP Stu Cncl; Rdo Clb; Ten; Chrldng; Treas GAA; Mgrs; College; Business.

O BRIEN, KATHLEEN; Hilliard HS; Columbus, OH; AFS; Chrs; Hon Rl; Off Ade; PAVAS; Sch Mus; Sch Pl; Drama Clb; Spn Clb; Capital Univ; Spec Educ.

O BRIEN, KELLY; Brookfield HS; Brookfield, OH; Chrh Wkr; Hon Rl; Jr NHS; NHS; Trk; Am Leg Awd; Univ; Health Educ.

O BRIEN, KELLY; Girard HS; Girard, OH; 18/200 AFS; Hon Rl; Y-Teens; Yrbk; Ed Sch Nwsp; Pep Clb; Spn Clb; Scr Kpr; Honor Mention Spanish I Ohio Schol Achv 1976; Youngstown St Univ; Eng.

O BRIEN, LAURIE; Scecina Memorial HS; Indianapolis, IN; 14/194 Cls Rep Soph Cls; Trs Jr Cls; Cmnty Wkr; Hon Rl; NHS; Treas Stu Cncl; Fr Clb; Bsktbl; Ten; GAA; Scecina Hnrs Prog 78; Univ.

O BRIEN, MARILYN; Mc Nicholas HS; Cincinnati, OH; Cls Rep Soph Cls; Cl Rep Jr Cls; Chrh Wkr; JA; Sch Mus; Stu Cncl; Pep Clb; GAA; Univ Of Cincinnati; Soc Work.

O BRIEN, MARK; Central HS; Elkhart, IN; Boy Scts; Hon Rl; Orch; Sch Mus; Sch Pl; Stg Crw; Drama Clb; Socr; Natl Merit Ltr; College.

O BRIEN, MARY; Archbisop Alter HS; Centerville, OH; Chrs; Drl Tm; Hon Rl; Sch Mus; Sch Pl; Stu Cncl; Drama Clb; Communications.

O BRIEN, MAUREEN; Marian HS; Birmingham, MI; Hon Rl; Mod UN; NHS; 4-H; Fr Clb; Sci Clb; College; Science.

O BRIEN, MICHAEL; De La Salle Collegiate HS; Harper Woods, MI; Band; Chrh Wkr; Hon Rl; Natl Forn Lg; Sch Mus; Sch Pl; Yrbk; Drama Clb; Detoit Catholic Forensics League 78 79; Natl HS Awd For Excellence 78; Natl Essay Press Awd 79; Wayne St Univ; Pre Law.

O BRIEN, MONICA; Grand Haven Sr HS; Grand Haven, MI; Band; Cmnty Wkr; Debate Tm; Girl Scts; Hon Rl; Orch; Sch Mus; Michigan St Univ; Animal Tech.

O BRIEN, ROSEMARY; St Joseph Acad; N Olmsted, OH; Girl Scts; Hosp Ade; Sch Pl; Drama Clb; College; Law.

O BRIEN, SANDY; Vandercook Lake HS; Jackson, MI; VP Sr Cls; Hon Rl; NHS; Sch Pl; Letter Bsktbl; Cit Awd; Sftbl 3 Yrs Var Ltr Co Capt & Coaches Awd 77 79; Vllbyl Var Ltr 79; Univ; Bus Mgmt.

O BRIEN, SHERRI; Mother Of Mercy HS; Cincinnati, OH; Hon Rl; JA; Sch Mus; Sct Actv; GAA; Modeling.

O BRIEN, TERENCE; West Catholic HS; Grand Rapids, MI; Band; Hon Rl; Jr NHS; Sch Mus; Bsktbl; Wrstlng; Univ; Dentistry.

O BRIEN, TIM; Walled Lake Western HS; Walled Lk, MI; Boy Scts; Hon Rl; Fr Clb; Mic State; Pre Law.

O BRIEN, TIMOTHY; St Joseph HS; Richmond Hts, OH; 8/243 Hon Rl; NHS; Sch Mus; Sch Pl; Rptr Sch Nwsp; Spn Clb; Ftbl; Wrstlng; Univ; Med.

OBRINGER, DAVE; Buckeye Central HS; New Washington, OH; 2/96 VP Jr Cls; Pres Sr Cls; Am Leg Boys St; Chrs; Hon Rl; Sch Mus; Rptr Yrbk; Rptr Sch Nwsp; Fr Clb; Bsbl; Bowling Green State; Psych.

OBRINGER, LINDA; Ansonia HS; Rossburg, OH; 16/65 Band; Chrs; Chrh Wkr; Cmnty Wkr; Hon Rl; Hosp Ade; Yrbk; Sec.

OBRINGER, NANCY; Spencerville HS; Spencerville, OH; 32/100 Hon Rl; Off Ade; FTA; Letter Bsktbl; Letter GAA; Scr Kpr; Tmr;.

O BRYAN, MICHAEL; Grosse Pointe South HS; Grosse Pointe, MI; 11/552 Debate Tm; NHS; Pol Wkr; Ger Clb; Letter Crs Cntry; Letter Trk; Gov Hon Prg Awd; Natl Merit SF; Univ Of Michigan; Law.

OBRZUT, SUSAN; Bishop Noll Inst; Munster, IN; 66/321 Chrs; Hon Rl; NHS; Sch Mus; Natl Busns Honor Soc; College.

OBSUSZT, MICHAEL; Lutheran HS; Avon, OH; Pres Jr Cls; Chrh Wkr; Mod UN; Stg Crw; Pep Clb; Spn Clb; Letter Bsktbl; Glf; Trk; IM Sprt; College; Advertising.

O BUNKER, JEFFREY; Wintersville HS; Wintersville, OH; Band; Spn Clb; Brigham Young Univ; Archt.

OCACIO, DEBRA; Collinwood HS; Cleveland, OH; Cls Rep Frsh Cls; Cls Rep Soph Cls; Cl Rep Jr Cls; Cls Rep Sr Cls; Red Cr Ade; Stu Cncl; FTA; Cit Awd; Institution Of Comp Mgmt; Comp Prog.

OCHS, MARY; St Joseph Central Cath HS; Fremont, OH; Sec Sr Cls; Cls Rep Sr Cls; Band; Cmp Fr Grls; Chrh Wkr; Cmnty Wkr; Hon Rl; Hosp Ade; Phys Ther.

OCHS, THERESA; St Joseph Cntrl Catholic HS; Fremnt, OH; Band; Cmp Fr Grls; Yrbk; Pres 4-H; Pep Clb; Chrldng; IM Sprt; 4-H Awd; Davis Jr Coll; Interior Dsgn.

OCKER, SABINE; Fraser HS; Fraser, MI; 35/615 Cmnty Wkr; Hon Rl; Lit Mag; NHS; Quill & Scroll; Sct Actv; Stu Cncl; Ed Yrbk; Sch Nwsp; Macomb Cmnty Coll; Acctg.

OCKO, SUSANNE; Engadine Consolidated HS; Engadine, MI; VP Sr Cls; Hon Rl; Lbry Ade; Off Ade; Stu Cncl; Rptr Sch Nwsp; Sci Clb; Cit Awd; Outstndng Stu In World History; Winner Of Bsktbl Free Throw Cont; Michigan Tech Univ; Engr.

O CONNELL, COLLEEN; Stow HS; Stow, OH; Girl Scts; Hon Rl; Off Ade; Sch Pl; Drama Clb; Bsktbl; Letter Trk; Pres Awd; Bus Schl; Stewardess.

O CONNELL, ERIN; Houghton Lake HS; Prudenville, MI; Rptr Yrbk; Rptr Sch Nwsp; FHA; Pep Clb; Bsbl; Central Mich Univ; Social Work.

O CONNELL, KAY; Madison Comprehensive HS; Mansfield, OH; Chrs; Sec Spn Clb; College.

O CONNELL, MICHAEL; Struthers HS; Struthers, OH; 38/268 Hon Rl; Lat Clb; Voice Dem Awd; Outstanding Ach In Speech; Youngstown Univ; Math.

O CONNELL, TIMOTHY; Hedgesville HS; Martinsburg, WV; 1/250 Cls Rep Soph Cls; VP Jr Cls; Cl Rep Jr Cls; NHS; Stu Cncl; Letter Bsbl; Letter Crs Cntry; Pres Of Natl Hon Soc 79; VP Of Hi Y Clb 78; West Virginia Tech Univ; Elec Engr.

O CONNOR, C; George Rogers Clark HS; Whiting, IN; 18/218 Chrs; Girl Scts; Hon Rl; Jr NHS; Sct Actv; Sch Nwsp; Spn Clb; Bsbl; Trk; IM Sprt; College; Nursong.

OCONNOR, CHRISTINE; Central Catholic HS; Lafayette, IN; 17/100 Chrs; Hon Rl; Sch Mus; Sch Pl; Stg Crw; Rptr Yrbk; Pep Clb; Ten; Trk; GAA; Purdue Univ.

O CONNOR, GARY; Rogers HS; Toledo, OH; Bsbl; Glf; Socr; Collge; Bus.

O CONNOR, JANET; Barr Reeve HS; Montgomery, IN; 6/49 Band; Beta Clb; FHA; Pep Clb; Spn Clb; Bsktbl; Ten; Trk; Chrldng; Twrlr; Indiana State; Phy Educ.

O CONNOR, JILL; St Clair HS; St Clair, MI; Hon Rl; NHS; Letter Bsbl; St Clair County Comnty Coll.

O CONNOR, KAREN; Scecina Mem HS; Indianapolis, IN; 21/194 Girl Scts; Sct Actv; Ball St Univ; Bus Mgmt.

O CONNOR, KELLY P; Iaeger HS; Iaeger, WV; VP Jr Cls; Band; NHS; Stu Cncl; Yth Flsp; Fr Clb; Keyettes; Pep Clb; Trk; Twrlr; Virginia Poly Tech Univ; Law.

O CONNOR, LARY E; Cros Lex HS; Jeddo, MI; 50/190 Band; FCA; Hon Rl; Sct Actv; Yth Flsp; 4-H; FFA; Letter Bsbl; Letter Ftbl; Letter Wrstlng; Schlshp Awd FFA 79; Leadrshp Awd FFA 79; Michigan St Univ; Agri.

O CONNOR, LYNNE; Yale HS; Emmett, MI; 74/170 Hon Rl;.

O CONNOR, MARY; St Mary Cathedral HS; Gaylord, MI; Sec Frsh Cls; Band; Chrh Wkr; Hon Rl; Natl Forn Lg; NHS; Stg Crw; Drama Clb; Pep Clb; GAA; Michigan St Univ; Vet Med.

O CONNOR, MARY B; Bishop Noll Inst; Burnham, IL; 135/321 Cmnty Wkr; Girl Scts; Hon Rl; Hosp Ade; Sch Pl; Swmmng; Chrldng; College; Nursing.

O CONNOR, MICHAEL; Athens HS; Troy, MI; Am Leg Boys St; Band; Debate Tm; Hon Rl; Pol Wkr; St Of Mich Competitive Schlrshp 79; Eastern Michigan Univ; Poli Sci.

O CONNOR, PATRICIA; Walled Lake Central HS; Union Lake, MI; 3/425 Cl Rep Jr Cls; Hon Rl; NHS; Sch Pl; Stu Cncl; Rptr Sch Nwsp; Drama Clb; Letter Gym; Chrldng; Univ Of Michigan; Eng.

O CONNOR, PATRICK; Norton HS; Doylestown, OH; 160/380 Chrh Wkr; FSA; Spn Clb; Trk; Mgrs; Aron Univ; Botany.

O CONNOR, RAYMOND; Chesterton Sr HS; Chesterton, IN; 40/454 Chrh Wkr; Hon Rl; Ten; Trk; IM Sprt; Natl Merit Ltr; Valparaiso Univ; Law.

O CONNOR, SCOTT; Fenton HS; Fenton, MI; Chrs; Hon Rl; Sch Mus; Ftbl; Ten; College; Engr.

O CONNOR II, JACK T; Grand Ledge HS; Grand Ledge, MI; Hon Rl; Red Cr Ade; Letter Ftbl; Letter Wrstlng; Scr Kpr; Tmr; College.

O DANIEL, CHRISTOPHER; Columbus Acad; Westerville, OH; 22/45 Bsbl; Letter Swmmng; Coll Of Wooster; Bio.

O DANIEL, DAVID; St Philip Catholic Cntrl HS; E Leroy, MI; Trs Soph Cls; Chrs; Chrh Wkr; Hon Rl; NHS; Stu Cncl; Pres 4-H; Fr Clb; Mic State Univ; Railroad Oper.

O DAY, BRIAN; Marquette Sr HS; Marquette, MI; 19/365 Band; CAP; Debate Tm; Capt Swmmng; Kiwan Awd; Natl Merit SF; St Of Michigan Competitv Schlrshp Prog; Univ; Comp Sci.

O DELL, CONNIE; Stonewall Jackson HS; Charleston, WV; Band; CAP; Lbry Ade; Hon Rl; Jr NHS; Lbry Ade; NHS; Red Cr Ade; Rptr Yrbk; Sec Fr Clb; Florida St Univ; Med.

O DELL, KATHI; Hamilton S E HS; Noblesville, IN; Band; Chrh Wkr; Hon Rl; Off Ade; Quill & Scroll; Yth Flsp; 4-H; Fr Clb; Ger Clb; Pep Clb; Coll; Religion.

O DELL, LORETTA E; Lake Fenton HS; Fenton, MI; 2/215 Band; Chrs; Hon Rl; NHS; Sch Mus; Sch Pl; Yth Flsp; Sec Drama Clb; PPFtbl; Voice Dem Awd; College; Law.

O DELL, TAMLYN; Columbia Cntrl HS; Brooklyn, MI; 3/176 Am Leg Aux Girls St; Band; Hon Rl; NHS; Sci Clb; Gym; Univ Of Michigan; Law.

ODEN, CAROLINE; North Central HS; Inpls, IN; 569/999 Girl Scts; Hon Rl; Lbry Ade; Pol Wkr; Sct Actv; Stu Cncl; Trk; Letter Chrldng; Purdue Univ; Phys Educ.

ODENDAHL, RICHARD A; Tower HS; Warren, MI; 4/356 Hon Rl; NHS; Glf; Natl Merit SF; GMI; Engr.

O DETWEILER, RANDALL; Fairview Area School; Fairview, MI; Trs Jr Cls; Chrh Wkr; Hon Rl; Yth Flsp; Sch Nwsp; 4-H; Bsbl; Bsktbl; Glf; Coach Actv; Univ; Bus Admin.

ODGERS, BRETT; Bellbrook HS; Bellbrook, OH; 7/169 Cls Rep Sr Cls; Band; Boy Scts; Hon Rl; Sct Actv; Stu Cncl; Fr Clb; Letter Ftbl; Texas A & M Univ; Engr.

ODLE, SHARI; Seeger Memorial HS; Williamsport, IN; 2/126 Sal; Chrh Wkr; Hon Rl; Lbry Ade; NHS; Yrbk; Pep Clb; Spn Clb; Am Leg Awd; Elk Awd; Tennessee Temple Univ.

ODLEVAK, JANINE; Lumen Christi HS; Jackson, MI; Hon Rl; NHS; Pep Clb; Spn Clb; Ten; Univ; Spec Ed.

ODLEY, CATHERINE; Seton HS; Cincinnati, OH; Chrs; Girl Scts; Hon Rl; JA; Off Ade; Rptr Sch Nwsp; Sch Nwsp; Spn Clb; DAR Awd; Univ; Eng.

ODOM, DANIEL L; Tri West Hendricks HS; Danville, IN; 11/118 Hon Rl; NHS; Sch Nwsp; Univ; Elec Engr.

ODOM, KEVIN; Waverly HS; Lansing, MI; Cls Rep Frsh Cls; Cls Rep Soph Cls; NHS; Quill & Scroll; Rptr Yrbk; Sprt Ed Sch Nwsp; Bsktbl; Socr; Coach Actv; IM Sprt; Jrnlsm Awd 79; Amer Yuoth Soccer Assoc Soccer 78 & 79; Coach At Mi St Univ Youth Soccer Schl 79; Michigan St Univ; Tele Cmnctns.

ODOM, MARLETTE; Southwestern HS; Detroit, MI; 60/220 Cls Rep Frsh Cls; VP Soph Cls; Cl Rep Jr Cls; Chrs; Chrh Wkr; Hon Rl; Hosp Ade; JA; Jr NHS; Off Ade; Central State Univ; Comp Progr.

ODOM, MICHAEL; East Catholic HS; Detroit, MI; Trs Sr Cls; Chrh Wkr; Hon Rl; NHS; Stu Cncl; Spn Clb; Ftbl; Trk; Cit Awd; Wayne St Univ; Comp Engr.

O DONNELL, COLLEEN; Bedford HS; Bedford, OH; Cls Rep Frsh Cls; Cls Rep Soph Cls; Sec Jr Cls; VP Sr Cls; Chrs; Hon Rl; Spn Clb; Kent State; Educ.

O DONNELL, JACKLYN; Claymont HS; Uhrichsville, OH; 26/200 Am Leg Aux Girls St; Band; Drl Tm; Hon Rl; Off Ade; Quill & Scroll; Ed Yrbk; Rptr Sch Nwsp; Beta Clb; FTA; Akron Univ; Elem Educ.

O DONNELL, JENNIFER; New Richmond HS; New Richmond, OH; 6/198 NHS; Quill & Scroll; Sch Mus; Sch Pl; Rptr Yrbk; Sch Nwsp; Drama Clb; Fr Clb; Pep Clb; Sci Clb; Miami Univ; Bio.

O DONNELL, JOHN; Lake Catholic HS; Wickliffe, OH; Pol Wkr; Rptr Sch Nwsp; Letter Bsktbl; Letter Ftbl; IM Sprt; Univ; Bus Admin.

O DONNELL, KATHLEEN; Holland HS; Holland, MI; Chrh Wkr; Hon Rl; Mod UN; Rptr Yrbk; Rptr Sch Nwsp; Sch Nwsp; Fr Clb; Natl Merit Schl; Hope Hon Schlrshp 79; Cert Of Recogntn St Of Mi Comp Schlrshp Prog 79; Hope Coll; Sociology.

O DONNELL, MARY; Grove City HS; Grove City, OH; Sec Jr Cls; Am Leg Aux Girls St; Chrs; Hon Rl; NHS; Stu Cncl; Capt Ten; Franklin Univ; Busns Admin.

O DONNELL, MARY S; Carroll HS; Dayton, OH; Band; Chrh Wkr; Cmnty Wkr; Hon Rl; Red Cr Ade; Sch Mus; Stu Cncl; Sec Key Clb; Univ; Busns Admin.

O DONNELL, MIKE; Tyler Cnty HS; Sistersville, WV; Am Leg Boys St; Band; Chrs; Chrh Wkr; Hon Rl; Jr NHS; NHS; Sch Mus; Sch Pl; Drama Clb; West Virginia Univ; Civil Engr.

O DONNELL, PATRICIA; Chaminade Julienne HS; Englewood, OH; Cls Rep Soph Cls; Band; Drl Tm; Girl Scts; Stu Cncl; Fr Clb; PPFtbl; College; Math.

O DONOVAN, PATRICK; Mt Healthy HS; Cincinnati, OH; 1/536 Am Leg Boys St; Hon Rl; NHS; Rptr Sch Nwsp; Beta Clb; Ger Clb; College; Architecture.

O DOWD, MARGARET; St Agatha HS; Redford, MI; 18/98 Hon Rl; Fr Clb; Bsbl; Letter Bsktbl; Mgrs; PPFtbl; Bus Schl; Hotel Mgmt.

OECHSLE, JODY; Onsted HS; Onsted, MI; Chrh Wkr; Hon Rl; Sch Pl; Chrldng; Pom Pon; College; Art.

OEDING, JACQUELINE; Northeast Dubois HS; Jasper, IN; 10/79 Hon Rl; Lbry Ade; Beta Clb; FHA; Pep Clb;.

OEN, CHARLOTTE; Wapakoneta HS; Wapakoneta, OH; 22/308 Hon Rl; NHS; 4-H; FBLA; OEA; Spn Clb; 4-H Awd; College; Accounting.

OEN, RICHARD J; Brunnerdale Seminary HS; Wapakoneta, OH; 1/5 Trs Frsh Cls; Val; Chrs; Chrh Wkr; Hon Rl; Hosp Ade; NHS; Sch Pl; Stg Crw; Pres Stu Cncl; Ohio Northern Univ; Medicine.

OEN, SUZANNE; Memorial HS; St Marys, OH; Chrs; Girl Scts; Hon Rl; JA; Sct Actv; Yth Flsp; Y-Teens; Pep Clb; Gym; GAA; Univ.

OEN JR, RICHARD; Brunnerdale HS Seminary; Wapakoneta, OH; 1/5 Trs Frsh Cls; Val; Chrh Wkr; Hon Rl; Hosp Ade; NHS; Sch Pl; Stg Crw; Pres Stu Cncl; Sprt Ed Sch Nwsp; Ohio Northern Univ; Med.

OERTLIN, BONNIE; Kelloggsville HS; Kentwood, MI; VP Jr Cls; VP Sr Cls; Trk; Grand Rapids Jr Coll.

OESCH, KRISTI; Shelby HS; Shelby, OH; Chrs; Chrh Wkr; Cmnty Wkr; Hon Rl; Stu Cncl; Yth Flsp; 4-H; Lat Clb; Ohi State Univ; Home Economics.

OESCH, MICHAEL; Mich Lutheran Seminary HS; Pigeon, MI; VP Soph Cls; Chrs; Hon Rl; JA; Ger Clb; Lat Clb; Bsktbl;.

OESTERLE, MARY; Laurel Oaks Career Devel HS; New Holland, OH; 96/234 Cls Rep Sr Cls; Pres Cmp Fr Grls; Hon Rl; FBLA; Pres OEA; College; Data Processing.

OESTERLE, TRACIE; Washington Sr HS; Wash C H, OH; Trs Frsh Cls; Trs Sr Cls; AFS; Band; Cmp Fr Grls; Chrs; Chrh Wkr; Drl Tm; Hon Rl; Hosp Ade; Columbus Tech Inst Voc Schl; Med Sec.

OETZEL, RANDY; New Richmond HS; New Richmond, OH; Am Leg Boys St; Hon Rl; NHS; Quill & Scroll; Stu Cncl; Rptr Sch Nwsp; Sch Nwsp; 4-H; IM Sprt; 4-H Awd; Purdue Univ; Mech Engr.

OEXMAN, NELSON; Floyd Central HS; Georgetown, IN; Aud/Vis; Hon Rl; Boys Clb Am; Ftbl; IM Sprt; Indiana St Univ; Hist Tchr.

OFFENBERGER, BRENDA; Belpre HS; Belpre, OH; 21/230 Band; Letter Chrs; Chrh Wkr; Cmnty Wkr; Girl Scts; Hon Rl; Hosp Ade; Mdrgl; NHS; Off Ade; 1st Pl OEA Reg Cont Job Interview; Sec Of Yr Awd; 5 Free Hour Credits Ohio Univ; Ohio Univ; Busns Admin.

OFFILL, WINNA; Alliance HS; Alliance, OH; Aud/Vis; Cmnty Wkr; Hon Rl; JA; Lbry Ade; Univ; Marine Bio.

OFFUTT, JEFFREY; Cambridge HS; Cambridge, OH; Chrs; Hon Rl; Yth Flsp; Spn Clb; Air Force Cmnty Coll; Comp Sci.

O FLAHERTY, JANET; Carey HS; Carey, OH; Am Leg Aux Girls St; Girl Scts; Hon Rl; NHS; Off Ade; Stg Crw; Y-Teens; Ed Yrbk; Rptr Yrbk; 4-H; Univ.

O FLAHERTY, JANNA; Tri Valley HS; Frazeysburg, OH; Cls Rep Sr Cls; Am Leg Aux Girls St; Band; Hon Rl; NHS; Sch Pl; Pres 4-H; VP Lat Clb; Letter Trk; Pres GAA; Univ; Sci.

O FLAHERTY, JENNIFER; Walnut Hills HS; Cincinnati, OH; AFS; Boy Scts; Chrh Wkr; Hon Rl; Jr NHS; NHS; Pol Wkr; Stg Crw; Sch Nwsp; Fr Clb; Univ; Med.

OGAN, SCOTT F; Edgewood HS; Bloomington, IN; 8/201 Am Leg Boys St; Chrh Wkr; Hon Rl; Pres Jr NHS; Pres NHS; Treas Fr Clb; Key Clb; Bsbl; Dnfth Awd; Lion Awd; U S Army Jr Sci & Humanities Symposium Progr At ISU 79; U S Coast Guard Acad; Marine Sci.

OGDEN, SUZANNE; Ypsilanti HS; Ypsilanti, MI; Band; Chrs; Chrh Wkr; Girl Scts; Hon Rl; Sch Mus; Sch Pl; Sct Actv; Stg Crw; Yth Flsp; Thespian Soc; Chamber Singers; Campaign Comm For Board Of Ed; Colorado St Univ.

OGDEN, TAMMY; Buckeye South HS; Dillonvale, OH; Girl Scts; Hon Rl; 4-H; OEA; 4-H Awd; Jefferson Tech Coll; Photog.

OGLE, DANIEL; Rensselaer Central HS; Rensselaer, IN; Band; Hon Rl; Letter Bsktbl; Capt Crs Cntry; Capt Trk; Coach Actv; Indiana Univ.

OGLE, LISA; Yale HS; Yale, MI; 10/160 Pres Soph Cls; Pres Sr Cls; Am Leg Aux Girls St; Sec Chrs; Cmnty Wkr; Hon Rl; NHS; Sch Mus; Sch Pl; Treas Stu Cncl; Central Michigan Univ; Jrnlsm.

OGLE, MARK R; Perry Meridian HS; Greenwood, IN; 5/547 Cl Rep Jr Cls; Hon Rl; Jr NHS; NHS; Orch; Pol Wkr; Stu Cncl; Sci Clb; Spn Clb; Letter Ten; Natl Spelling Bee; Bicentennial Essay Cntst; Top 20 Marian Cnty Math Cntst; Wabash Coll; Medicine.

OGLE, MAUREEN; Crestline HS; Crestline, OH; Chrs; Hon Rl; Ed Yrbk; Ed Sch Nwsp; Bsktbl; Chrldng; Capt.

OGLESBEE, JOYCE; Lima Sr HS; Lima, OH; 128/486 Band; Chrs; Girl Scts; Hon Rl; JA; OEA; Mgrs; JA Awd; Bus Schl; Med Sec.

OGLESBY, TRACEY; Norwalk HS; Norwalk, OH; 16/216 Sec Frsh Cls; Drl Tm; Hon Rl; Jr NHS; NHS; Orch; Sch Mus; Sch Nwsp; 4-H; Pep Clb; Univ Of Miami; Poli Sci.

OGLETREE, GLENDAL; Independence HS; Columbus, OH; Sec Jr Cls; Cl Rep Jr Cls; Chrh Wkr; Hon Rl; Orch; Stu Cncl; Fr Clb; Pep Clb; Trk; Chrldng; All Star Cheerleader Award 1977; Univ; Jrnlsm.

OGONEK, EDWARD A; Walsh Jesuit HS; Barberton, OH; 9/170 Band; Boy Scts; Drm Bgl; Hon Rl; Lit Mag; Sct Actv; Pep Clb; IM Sprt; Am Leg Awd; College; History.

O GRADY, COLLEEN; Armada HS; Richmond, MI; 3/116 Chrh Wkr; Girl Scts; Hon Rl; NHS; Off Ade; Stg Crw; 4-H; Pep Clb; Capt Trk; Capt Chrldng; Okalnd Univ Stu Life Schlrshp; Armada Stu Cncl Schrlshp; Acad Ach In St Of Michigan Schlrshp Competition; Oakland Univ; Phys Therapy.

O GRADY, KATY; Regina HS; Beachwood, OH; Chrh Wkr; Cmnty Wkr; Hon Rl; Lbry Ade; Off Ade; Swmmng; College.

OGSTON, ELIZABETH; Eaton Rapids Sr HS; Eaton Rapids, MI; 32/230 Band; Girl Scts; Hon Rl; Sch Mus; Sct Actv; Spn Clb; Bsktbl; Letter Crs Cntry; Trk; Lake Superior St Coll; Archt.

O HAGAN, ANNIE; John Glenn HS; Farmington Hl, MI; Cls Rep Frsh Cls; Cls Rep Soph Cls; Band; Hon Rl; Jr NHS; Sch Pl; Fr Clb; Letter Chrldng; Cit Awd; Oakland Community College; French.

O HALLORAN, MARIANN; Boardman HS; Youngstown, OH; 1/550 Hon Rl; Jr NHS; NHS; Off Ade; Otterbein Coll Cert Of Achvmnt For Whos Who In For Lang 79; Awd For 3rd Pl Shrtnd Theory Yngstwn St Univ 79; Sec.

O HARA, BRIDGIT; Regina HS; Richmond Hts, OH; Chrs; Hon Rl; Carroll.

O HARA, JOSEPH; Ursuline HS; Youngstown, OH; 12/370 Pres Sr Cls; Hon Rl; Off Ade; Glf; Wrstlng; College; Math.

O HARA, KATHLEEN; Grosse Pointe N HS; Grosse Pte Shr, MI; Chrs; Hon Rl; Fr Clb; IM Sprt; Scr Kpr; Tmr; Cit Awd; Michigan Schlstc Awd; Michigan St Univ; Law.

O HARA, PATRICIA; Ursuline HS; Youngstown, OH; 90/365 Chrs; Hon Rl; Off Ade; Pep Clb; Youngstown State Univ; Bus.

O HARA, THOMAS; Gilmour Academy; Pepper Pk, OH; 30/80 Boy Scts; Hon Rl; Stg Crw; Drama Clb; Bsktbl; Capt Glf; Trk; IM Sprt; Univ; Archt.

O HARL, JAMES; Evansville Central HS; Evansville, IN; 1/610 NHS; Boys Clb Am; IM Sprt; Coll; Mining Engr.

O HATT, DOUGLAS; Allen Park HS; Allen Park, MI; Cls Rep Frsh Cls; Cls Rep Soph Cls; Cl Rep Jr Cls; Cls Rep Sr Cls; Chrs; Hon Rl; Stu Cncl; Capt Crs Cntry; Trk; Capt Wrstlng; Saginaw Vly St Coll; Jrnlsm.

O HEARN, COLLEEN; Chaminade Julienne HS; Dayton, OH; Hon Rl; JA; Stu Cncl; Letter Trk; PPFtbl; Ohi State; Occupational Ther.

O HEARN, COLLEEN; St Thomas Aquinas HS; Louisville, OH; 27/150 Sec Sr Cls; Chrs; Hon Rl; Natl Forn Lg; Sch Pl; Stg Crw; Yth Flsp; Rptr Sch Nwsp; Drama Clb; Pep Clb; Univ.

OHLENKAMP, CAROL; Lowell HS; Lowell, IN; Pres Frsh Cls; Cl Rep Jr Cls; Hon Rl; Sec Stu Cncl; Pep Clb; Chrldng; Mat Maids; Vocational School; Computer Program.

OHLINGER, TEDD; Pt Pleasant HS; Gallipolis Ferr, WV; 39/212 Boy Scts; FCA; Hon Rl; Stu Cncl; Bsktbl; Letter Ftbl; Ten; Letter Trk; IM Sprt; WVIT; Engr.

OHLMACHER, JULIE; Holly Sr HS; Holly, MI; 3/310 Hon Rl; Bsktbl; IM Sprt; Natl Merit Ltr; General Motors Inst; Engr.

OHM, MICHAEL D; Cuyahoga Falls HS; Cuyahoga Falls, OH; 51/807 Band; Boy Scts; Chrs; FCA; Hon Rl; Natl Forn Lg; NHS; Sch Mus; Sch Pl; Sct Actv; Univ Of Akron; Astronomer.

OHMANN, JAY; Edison Jr Sr HS; Lake Station, IN; Band; Sch Mus; Sch Pl; Fr Clb; Pep Clb; Bsbl; Ftbl; Trk; Wrstlng; Voc Schl; Mech.

OHMER, DEBORAH; Mother Of Mercy HS; Cincinnati, OH; 58/230 Drm Bgl; Hon Rl; Red Cr Ade; Fr Clb; Trk; Univ; Tech.

O HOLDEN, JOHN; Fayetteville HS; Fayetteville, OH; Pres Frsh Cls; Cls Rep Soph Cls; Cl Rep Jr Cls; Chrs; Chrh Wkr; Hon Rl; Lbry Ade; Sch Pl; Stg Crw; Pres Stu Cncl; Univ; Elec.

OJEDA, LISA; Seton HS; Cincinnati, OH; Chrs; Girl Scts; Hon Rl; Sch Mus; Pep Clb; Spn Clb; Letter Socr; Coach Actv; GAA; College; Bus Admin.

OKA, DAVID; Elder HS; Cincinnati, OH; 6/383 Cl Rep Jr Cls; Aud/Vis; Hon Rl; Pres NHS; Sch Mus; Stg Crw; Stu Cncl; Yrbk; Spn Clb; Capt Socr; Univ Of Cincinnati; Graphic Dsgn.

O KEEFE, KATHLEEN A; Parma Sr HS; Parma, OH; 29/782 Boy Scts; Chrs; Chrh Wkr; Cmnty Wkr; Hon Rl; Lbry Ade; VP NHS; Off Ade; Yth Flsp; Fr Clb; Univ; Bus Ed.

O KEEFE, KEVIN; Belleville HS; Ypsilanti, MI; Rptr Yrbk; Yrbk; Letter Wrstlng; Ctrl Michigan Univ; Bus Admin.

O KEEFE, KIM; Charles Mott Sr HS; Warren, MI; Hon Rl; Univ; Bus.

OKENFUSS, CHARLES; St Xavier HS; Cincinnati, OH; 156/264 Band; Orch; IM Sprt; Univ; Engr.

OKERSON, JAMES; Scecina Mem HS; Indianapolis, IN; 75/208 Cls Rep Frsh Cls; Spn Clb; Letter Bsktbl; Letter Ftbl; Coll.

OKERSTROM, DENISE; Cass City HS; Cass City, MI; 25/183 Hon Rl; NHS; Yth Flsp; Letter Bsbl; Ferris State Univ; Architecture.

OKO, KATHRYN; Maple Hts Sr HS; Maple Hgts, OH; Cls Rep Sr Cls; AFS; Letter Chrs; Chrh Wkr; Girl Scts; Jr NHS; NHS; Off Ade; Sch Mus; Sch Pl; Stu Govt Day; Hi Clb Pres; Intl Thespian Soc; College; Sociology.

OKRAGLY, RHONDA; Walled Lake Western Sr HS; Walled Lk, MI; Cl Rep Jr Cls; Hon Rl; Natl Forn Lg; NHS; PAVAS; Sch Mus; Stg Crw; Stu Cncl; Ten; Univ Of Michigan; Law.

O KRUTA, JOHN; Oak Glen HS; Newell, WV; 19/243 Am Leg Boys St; Chrs; NHS; Sch Mus; Sch Pl; Stg Crw; Rptr Yrbk; Drama Clb; West Virginia Univ; Vet.

OKULEY, JOHN; Ayersville HS; Defiance, OH; 4/88 Cls Rep Soph Cls; Band; Boy Scts; Chrs; Ohio State Univ; Agricultural.

OLASHUK, JOHN; Madonna HS; Weirton, WV; VP Sr Cls; Cls Rep Sr Cls; Boy Scts; Chrh Wkr; Cmnty Wkr; Hon Rl; Sct Actv; Stu Cncl; Yth Flsp; VICA; West Virginia Univ; Metallurgcl Engr.

OLASHUK, MARY; Madonna HS; Weirton, WV; 1/98 Cmp Fr Grls; Chrh Wkr; Cmnty Wkr; Hon Rl; Lit Mag; VP NHS; Letter Bsktbl; Ten; Letter Trk; Coach Actv; High Schl All Amer Honor Prog; NCTE Achievmnt Awd In Writing Candidate; Soc Of Distinguished Amer HS Stu; West Virginia Univ; Medicine.

OLBRICH, CARL; Milford HS; Milford, MI; Cls Rep Frsh Cls; Cls Rep Soph Cls; Aud/Vis; Sch Pl; Sct Actv; Stg Crw; Stu Cncl; Yth Flsp; Rptr Yrbk; Yrbk; Shclshp SAT Test 79; Awd Of Mert In Camp Cnsrl & Outdoor Rec 77; 10th Pl In Cls Of 395 78; Michigan St Univ; Engr.

OLBRYS, ROBIN; Parma Sr HS; Parma, OH; Chrs; Hon Rl; Stu Cncl; FFA; Gym; Vocational Schl; Dance.

OLDAKER, BRADLEY; Buckhannon Upshur HS; Buckhannon, WV; Band; Hon Rl; NHS; Ed Yrbk; Dnfth Awd; West Virginia Wesleyan Coll; Pre Law.

OLDAKER, MARY; Wahama HS; Hartford, WV; 20/96 Chrs; Hon Rl; Hosp Ade; Yth Flsp; 4-H; FFA; FHA; Pep Clb; VICA; Scr Kpr; Arch Moore Voc Tech Schl; Nursing.

OLDEN, SHIRLEY; North Ridgeville HS; N Ridgeville, OH; Hon Rl; Rptr Yrbk; Yrbk; Lorain County Comm Coll; Sec.

OLDENBROEK, DEBRA; Calvin Christian HS; Wyoming, MI; Band; Chrs; Chrh Wkr; Hon Rl; Hosp Ade; Red Cr Ade; Stg Crw; Pep Clb; Swmmng; IM Sprt; Calvin Coll; Sci.

OLDENBURG, SUSAN; John Glenn HS; Westland, MI; Hon Rl; NHS; PAVAS; Sch Mus; Sch Pl; Stg Crw; Drama Clb; Spn Clb; Glf; Natl Art Hnr Soc; Univ Of Michigan; Physics.

OLDER, PAMELA; Stonewall Jackson HS; Charleston, WV; Hon Rl; Jr NHS; Off Ade; Pep Clb; Spn Clb; Ten; Cit Awd; Bus Sch; Secretary.

OLDHAM, LESLIE A; Central HS; Evansville, IN; 22/528 Cls Rep Frsh Cls; Cls Rep Soph Cls; Cl Rep Jr Cls; Cls Rep Sr Cls; Chrh Wkr; Hon Rl; Jr NHS; NHS; Stu Cncl; Yth Flsp; Univ Of Tennessee; Bus.

OLDHAM, THOMAS; Centerville HS; Centerville, OH; Am Leg Boys St; Chrh Wkr; Letter Crs Cntry; Letter Trk; IM Sprt; Miami Univ; Pulp And Paper Tech.

OLDING, CARRI; N Muskegon HS; North Muskegon, MI; 32/105 Band; Hon Rl; Fr Clb; Bsktbl; PPFtbl; Muskegon Bus Coll; Marketing.

OLDS, DANIEL; Orchard View HS; Muskegon, MI; NHS; Bsktbl; Mich Tech Univ; Engr.

OLDS, JULIE; R B Chamberlin HS; Kent, OH; 10/150 AFS; Chrs; Drl Tm; Hon Rl; Mdrgl; NHS; Sch Pl; Stg Crw; Rptr Yrbk; Sec Drama Clb; Hiram Coll; Psych.

OLDS, JULIE; R B Chamberlin HS; Twinsburg, OH; 10/165 AFS; Hon Rl; Mdrgl; NHS; Sch Pl; Stg Crw; Drama Clb; Hiram College; Psych.

OLDS, ROBIN; Pike HS; Indianapolis, IN; 16/303 Sec Soph Cls; Pres Jr Cls; Cmnty Wkr; Hon Rl; NHS; Stu Cncl; Y-Teens; Rptr Yrbk; Rptr Sch Nwsp; FBLA; College; Economics.

OLDS, TENITIA; North Central HS; Indpls, IN; 113/999 Cls Rep Frsh Cls; Cls Rep Soph Cls; Cl Rep Jr Cls; Hon Rl; Trk; Chrldng; Univ.

O LEARY, PATRICIA; Eaton Rapids HS; Eaton Rapids, MI; 54/212 Cls Rep Frsh Cls; Hon Rl; Hosp Ade; Y-Teens; Yrbk; Mat Maids; PPFtbl; Western Michigan Univ; Occup Ther.

OLECH, BRIAN; St Alphonsus HS; Detroit, MI; 9/171 Hon Rl; Univ; Math.

OLECH, LAURA; Adlai Stevenson HS; Sterling Hts, MI; 1/535 VP Jr Cls; VP Sr Cls; Val; Band; Cmnty Wkr; Hon Rl; NHS; Sct Actv; Mic State Univ; Bus.

OLECHOWSKI, MARGARET; Cabrini HS; Lincoln Pk, MI; Hon Rl; Rptr Yrbk; Detroit Bus Schl.

OLEINICK, JEFFREY; Southfield Lathrup Sr HS; Southfield, MI; Chrs; Hon Rl; Off Ade; Red Cr Ade; Stu Cncl; Yth Flsp; FDA; IM Sprt; Univ Of Michigan; Med.

OLEN, THOMAS; West Catholic HS; Grand Rapids, MI; Band; Boy Scts; Chrh Wkr; Hon Rl; JA; IM Sprt; JA Awd; Michigan St Univ; Med.

OLENIK, JACQUELINE; St Augustine Academy; N Olmsted, OH; Cls Rep Frsh Cls; Cl Rep Jr Cls; Girl Scts; Hon Rl; Stu Cncl; IM Sprt; Cleveland St Univ; Bus Mgmt.

OLENIK, MICHELLE; Parma Sr HS; Parma, OH; Hon Rl; Lit Mag; PAVAS; Hockey; Art Cert For B And Better Avg 78; Spanish Crt 77; Hnr Roll Cert 76 & 79; Cleveland St Univ; Art.

OLENIK, ROBIN; Parma HS; Parma, OH; 166/710 Hon Rl; DECA; Univ Of Cin.

OLER, TIMOTHY; Northeastern Wayne HS; Willmsbrg, IN; 8/140 Cls Rep Frsh Cls; Cls Rep Soph Cls; Cl Rep Jr Cls; Cls Rep Sr Cls; Hon Rl; NHS; Stu Cncl; 4-H; Bsbl; Letter Ten; Purdue Univ; Wildlife Mgmt.

OLESEN, JAMES; Boardman HS; Boardman, OH; 105/597 Boy Scts; Chrs; Chrh Wkr; Hon Rl; Stg Crw; Yth Flsp; Spn Clb; IM Sprt; Bowling Green; Sci.

OLESEN, JIM; Boardman HS; Boardman, OH; 110/596 Boy Scts; Chrs; Chrh Wkr; Hon Rl; Stg Crw; Yth Flsp; Spn Clb; IM Sprt; Mgrs; Bowling Green; Sci.

OLESINSKI, RON; Nordonia HS; Macedonia, OH; 40/450 Cls Rep Sr Cls; Band; Chrs; Chrh Wkr; Cmnty Wkr; Hon Rl; Orch; Sch Mus; Sch Pl; Drama Clb; Univ; Archt.

OLESON, JAMES D; Elkins HS; Elkins, WV; 28/227 Am Leg Boys St; Boy Scts; Hon Rl; Rptr Sch Nwsp; Natl Merit Ltr; Univ; Sci.

OLESZKOWICZ, MICHAEL J; St Alphonsus HS; Dearborn Hts, MI; 23/181 Hon Rl; Voice Dem Awd; Univ; Bus Admin.

OLGY, WALTER C; William A Wirt HS; Gary, IN; 7/230 Band; Chrh Wkr; Hon Rl; Hosp Ade; NHS; Sci Clb; Spn Clb; N Indiana Schl Band Orchstr & Vocal Assoc 4 Gold Medals For Piano 1974; Regnl Sci Fair Hon Mention 1977; Wabash Coll; Pre Med.

O LINGER, LAURA JO; Southridge HS; Huntingburg, IN; Band; Drl Tm; FCA; Hon Rl; Sch Mus; Yth Flsp; Ed Yrbk; Rptr Yrbk; Ger Clb; Pep Clb; St Vlbl In Girsl Swimmng 77 & 78; Schlshp Awd From Lcl Std Club 76 77 & 78; Purdue Univ; Vet Med.

O LINGER, LYDIA; Forest Park HS; Ferdinand, IN; Band; Hon Rl; Beta Clb; Pep Clb; Ten; GAA; College; Bus.

OLIPHANT, CONNIE; Bloomfield HS; Bloomfield, IN; Girl Scts; Rptr Yrbk; FBLA; Lat Clb; Pom Pon; DAR Awd; Business.

OLIS, KATHLEEN; Kankakee Valley HS; De Motte, IN; 31/195 Hon Rl; NHS; Off Ade; Rptr Yrbk; College; Math Tchr.

OLIVER, AMY; Chillicothe HS; Ch Illicothe, OH; Cls Rep Sr Cls; Band; Drl Tm; Sch Mus; Sch Pl; Lat Clb; Ohio St Univ.

OLIVER, ANGELA; Norwayne HS; Bubbank, OH; Chrs; Hon Rl; Sec NHS; Sec Stu Cncl; Eng Clb; Pep Clb; Letter Trk; IM Sprt; Pom Pon; Twrlr; Univ Of Akron; Chem Engr.

OLIVER, BRAD; Norwayne HS; Burbank, OH; Band; Chrs; Hon Rl; Stu Cncl; 4-H; Letter Ftbl; Letter Trk; Letter Wrstlng; IM Sprt; Akron Univ; Comp Sci.

OLIVER, DAVID; Mount Clemens HS; Sang Base, MI; 16/258 Hon Rl; Jr NHS; NHS; Off Ade; Univ.

OLIVER, DAVID; Grand Haven HS; Grand Haven, MI; 121/374 Hon Rl; Letter Bsktbl; Letter Ftbl; Letter Trk; Western Mic Univ; Communications.

OLIVER, DEBBIE; Woodridge HS; Cuyahoga Fls, OH; 14/130 Band; Cmnty Wkr; Debate Tm; Hon Rl; Jr NHS; Natl Forn Lg; Off Ade; Fr Clb; Mgrs; Scr Kpr; Univ; Spec Educ.

OLIVER, GLENN; Muskegon Sr HS; Muskegon, MI; Cl Rep Jr Cls; Chrs; Chrh Wkr; Hon Rl; Sch Pl; Stg Crw; Stu Cncl; Boys Clb Am; 4-H; Ftbl; Coll; Law.

OLIVER, HEIDI; Buckeye West HS; Adena, OH; 1/87 Chrh Wkr; Debate Tm; Hon Rl; NHS; Off Ade; Pres OEA; Sci Clb; Am Leg Awd; DAR Awd; Cincinnati Bible Coll; Psych.

OLIVER, HEIDI JO; Buckeye West HS; Adena, OH; 1/87 Chrh Wkr; Debate Tm; Hon Rl; NHS; Off Ade; Yth Flsp; Pres OEA; Sci Clb; Am Leg Awd; DAR Awd; Cincinnati Bible Coll; Psych.

OLIVER, JILL; Genesee HS; Genesee, MI; Trs Frsh Cls; ROTC; Chrs; Hon Rl; Sch Mus; Yth Flsp; Bsktbl; Chrldng; College.

OLIVER, KARIN K; Jackson HS; Jackson, OH; 7/239 Band; Hon Rl; NHS; Rptr Sch Nwsp; 4-H; Treas Pep Clb; Trk; PPFtbl; 4-H Awd; Voc School; Comp Progr.

OLIVER, KELLEY; Benzie County Central HS; Beulah, MI; Hon Rl; 4-H; Mgrs; Mat Maids; 4-H Awd; College; Bus.

OLIVER, KEVIN; Brookville HS; Sioux City, IA; 16/210 Rptr Yrbk; FHA; GAA; Mgrs; 4-H Awd; Univ.

OLIVER, LAURA; Montpelier HS; Montpelier, OH; 1/100 Am Leg Aux Girls St; Drl Tm; Girl Scts; Hon Rl; NHS; Off Ade; Fr Clb; Trk; Chrldng; Scr Kpr; Univ; Bus Admin.

OLIVER, MARK; Carmel HS; Carmel, IN; 43/711 Band; Boy Scts; Chrs; Chrh Wkr; Jr NHS; Lit Mag; Mod UN; Sch Mus; Beta Clb; Eng Clb; Brigham Young Univ; Acctg.

OLIVER, MELAINE; Versailles HS; Versailles, OH; 10/134 Hon Rl; JA; NHS; Rptr Sch Nwsp; Sec Mth Clb; GAA; Scr Kpr; JA Awd; Ohio St Univ; Journalism.

OLIVER, MICHELLE; Coleman HS; Coleman, MI; NHS; Sch Pl; Ed Sch Nwsp; Drama Clb; Trk; St Of Mi Comp Schlrshp 79; Dow Corning Corp Youth For Understanding Schlrshp 78; Delta Coll; Jrnlsm.

OLIVER, MONICA; East HS; Akron, OH; Band; Chrs; Drl Tm; Hon Rl; Off Ade; Quill & Scroll; Ed Yrbk; Rptr Yrbk; Akron Univ; Transportn.

OLIVER, TAMI; Jackson HS; Jackson, OH; Trs Frsh Cls; Trs Soph Cls; Cl Rep Jr Cls; Band; Chrs; Drm Mjrt; Girl Scts; Hon Rl; Jr NHS; NHS; Ohio St Univ; Educ.

OLIVER, TERENCE; John Hay HS; Cleveland, OH; 26/260 Band; Boy Scts; Chrs; Chrh Wkr; Cmnty Wkr; Drm Bgl; Hon Rl; Hosp Ade; Yth Flsp; Sch Nwsp; Ferris St Coll; Tech Illustration.

OLIVER, TIMOTHY; Benjamin Logan HS; Bellefontaine, OH; Chrh Wkr; Hon Rl; Yth Flsp; 4-H; FFA; Columbus Tech Inst; Aviation.

OLIVERIO, JANE; West Geauga HS; Chesterland, OH; Chrs; Hon Rl; Jr NHS; Lbry Ade; NHS; Ed Yrbk; Rptr Yrbk; Letter Trk; Natl Merit Ltr; Univ.

OLIVERIO, JILL; Notre Dame HS; Clarksburg, WV; 1/59 VP Frsh Cls; Cls Rep Soph Cls; Chrh Wkr; Hon Rl; Stg Crw; Stu Cncl; Yrbk; Pep Clb; Sci Clb; Trk; College.

OLIVERIO, SAL; Notre Dame HS; Clarksburg, WV; Cls Rep Frsh Cls; Cls Rep Soph Cls; Sec Jr Cls; VP Sr Cls; Chrs; Chrh Wkr; Cmnty Wkr; Pol Wkr; Sch Mus; Sch Pl; Potomac St Jr Coll; Pre Pharm.

OLIVETO, CINDY; Lincoln HS; Lumberport, WV; 13/154 Sec Frsh Cls; Cls Rep Soph Cls; Hon Rl; NHS; Sch Mus; Sch Pl; Pres Stu Cncl; Y-Teens; Pres Drama Clb; Scr Kpr; Glenville St Univ; Horticulture.

OLIVIER, KATHLEEN; Marquette Sr HS; Marquette, MI; 17/428 Chrh Wkr; Drl Tm; Stg Crw; Northern Michigan Univ.

OLIVIER, LILA; Union HS; Grand Rapids, MI; Chrs; Chrh Wkr; Hon Rl; Hosp Ade; NHS; Orch; Sch Mus; Letter Gym; Olivet Nazarene Coll; Med.

OLLIS, RHONDA; Spanishburg HS; Kegley, WV; 7/36 Cl Rep Jr Cls; Chrs; Hon Rl; Sch Mus; Stu Cncl; Yrbk; FHA; Pep Clb; Sci Clb; Bsktbl; Bluefield St Coll; RN.

OLMSTEAD, VALERIE; Creston HS; Grand Rapids, MI; Hon Rl; NHS; Sch Pl; Spn Clb; Alma Coll; Lang.

OLNEY, CHERIE; Coloma HS; Benton Hrbr, MI; VP Sr Cls; Band; Chrh Wkr; Cmnty Wkr; Drl Tm; Girl Scts; Hon Rl; Jr NHS; NHS; Off Ade; Westen Michigan Univ; Dance.

OLNEY, DEANNA; Carman Sr HS; Flint, MI; Chrh Wkr; Cmnty Wkr; Yth Flsp; Univ; Phys Ther.

OLNEY, MARY; Clarkston HS; Clarkston, MI; Hon Rl; Eng Clb; Spn Clb; Gym; Trk; Chrldng; Coach Actv; PPFtbl; Univ Of Mich; Animal Trainer.

OLRICH, TRACY; Vestaburg HS; Edmore, MI; Cls Rep Frsh Cls; Band; Hon Rl; NHS; Yrbk; Ftbl; Trk; Wrstlng; Cntrl Michigan Univ; Phys Educ.

OLRY, KAY; North Side HS; Ft Wayne, IN; Cls Rep Frsh Cls; Cls Rep Soph Cls; Cl Rep Jr Cls; Am Leg Aux Girls St; JA; Stu Cncl; Sch Nwsp; DECA; Letter Bsktbl; College; Business Admin.

OLSEN, CARL; Fairmont West HS; Kettering, OH; 51/496 Aud/Vis; Boy Scts; Chrh Wkr; Hon Rl; Bsktbl; Glf; Socr; Trk; Miami Univ; Busns.

OLSEN, CAROL; Olivet HS; Charlotte, MI; 3/80 Hon Rl; NHS; Orch; PPFtbl; Univ Of Michigan.

OLSEN, DAVID; Ayersville HS; Defiance, OH; 1/82 Am Leg Boys St; Pres Band; VP Chrs; Hon Rl; NHS; Sch Pl; Yth Flsp; Sec Fr Clb; Letter Swmmng; Letter Ten; Univ.

OLSEN, JAMES; Ann Arbor Pioneer HS; Ann Arbor, MI; Band; Boy Scts; Hon Rl; Orch; Sct Actv; Trk;.

OLSEN, JOSEPH; Muskegon HS; Muskegon, MI; Hon Rl; NHS; Fr Clb; Ftbl; Letter Wrstlng; Univ Of Michigan; Elec Engr.

OLSEN, MARSHA; West Sr HS; Garden City, MI; 16/400 Am Leg Aux Girls St; Band; Chrh Wkr; Hon Rl; Jr NHS; Red Cr Ade; Sch Pl; Adrian Coll; Bus Admin.

OLSEN, SUSAN; Redford HS; Detroit, MI; Girl Scts; Hon Rl; Off Ade; Cit Awd; Detroit Coll Of Bus; Acctg.

OLSON, CATHERINE; Detour Area HS; Goetzville, MI; 2/37 Trs Sr Cls; Sal; Chrs; Debate Tm; Hon Rl; NHS; Yth Flsp; Mi Tech Univ; Computer Programming.

OLSON, JEAN; Talawanda HS; Oxford, OH; 1/270 AFS; Chrs; Chrh Wkr; Hon Rl; NHS; Yth Flsp; Drama Clb; Fr Clb; Letter Hockey; Univ.

OLSON, JILL; Brownsburg HS; Brownsburg, IN; 42/300 Band; Girl Scts; Hon Rl; NHS; Orch; Stg Crw; Drama Clb; 4-H; Fr Clb; Pep Clb; Univ Of Evansville; Nursing.

OLSON, JOSEPH; Traverse City HS; Traverse City, MI; Western Mic Univ; Elec Engr.

OLSON, KIRK; Ithaca HS; Ithaca, MI; VP Soph Cls; VP Jr Cls; Band; Chrs; Sch Pl; 4-H; Letter Ftbl; Letter Trk; Letter Wrstlng; 4-H Awd; Michigan St Univ; Vet.

OLSON, LISA; Pontiac Central HS; Pontiac, MI; Band; Debate Tm; PPFtbl; College.

OLSON, LORI; Forest Park HS; Crystal Falls, MI; 8/79 Cls Rep Frsh Cls; Cls Rep Soph Cls; Pres Jr Cls; Cl Rep Jr Cls; Cls Rep Sr Cls; Band; Debate Tm; Hon Rl; Stu Cncl; Yrbk; Michigan St Univ; Wildlife Bio.

OLSON, M; Charles F Brush HS; Lyndhurst, OH; Band; Drm Bgl; Orch; Sch Mus; College.

OLSON, MARK; Cedar Lake Acad; Munising, MI; Cls Rep Frsh Cls; Cls Rep Soph Cls; Band; Hon Rl; Andrews Univ; Pre Med.

OLSON, SALLY; South Vigo HS; Terre Haute, IN; Cl Rep Jr Cls; Drl Tm; JA; Off Ade; Y-Teens; Pep Clb; Letter Swmmng; Ten; Pom Pon; PPFtbl; ISU; Elem Education.

OLSON, SHARON; Muskegon Sr HS; Muskegon, MI; Girl Scts; Hon Rl; Hosp Ade; Am Leg Awd; Univ; RN.

OLSON, SIRI; Pioneer HS; Ann Arbor, MI; Band; Girl Scts; Hon Rl; Orch; 4-H; Ger Clb; IM Sprt; 4-H Awd; Natl Merit Ltr; Pres Awd; Univ.

OLSON, WARREN; Bay HS; Bay Village, OH; 70/373 Band; Boy Scts; Sct Actv; Letter Swmmng; Eagle Scout Rank; Jr Varsity Letter Lacrosse; Jr Varsity Letter Soccer; West Point Acad.

OLSON, WILLIAM; Lake Orion HS; Pontiac, MI; Cls Rep Frsh Cls; Cls Rep Soph Cls; Cl Rep Jr Cls; Cls Rep Sr Cls; Am Leg Boys St; Hon Rl; Jr NHS; Sci Clb; Capt Bsbl; Mgrs; All St Bsbl 78 & 79; All Regn 78 & 79; All League Bsbl 78; All Cnty Bsbl 79; Natl Merit Letter; Grand Valley Univ; Bus Admin.

OLSZEWSKI, CATHY; George Rogers Clark HS; Whiting, IN; 4/218 Cls Rep Frsh Cls; Cls Rep Soph Cls; Cl Rep Jr Cls; VP Sr Cls; Chrs; Drl Tm; Hon Rl; NHS; Sch Pl; Stu Cncl; Purdue.

OLSZEWSKI, GREGORY; Padua HS; Berea, OH; 10/267 Cl Rep Jr Cls; Pres Sr Cls; Hon Rl; NHS; Pres Stu Cncl; Lat Clb; Sci Clb; Wrstlng; Mgrs; Radar Wrstlng Awd 79; Univ Of Notre Dame; Bio.

OLSZEWSKI, LORI; Adlai Stevenson HS; Sterling Hgts, MI; Chrs; Chrh Wkr; Cmnty Wkr; Debate Tm; Hon Rl; NHS; Yth Flsp; Eastern Mic Univ; Spec Educ.

OLTHOUSE, VICTORIA; South Christian HS; Caledonia, MI; Band; Crs Cntry; Letter Trk; Pom Pon; PPFtbl; Grand Rapids Jr College; Language.

OLTMANNS, LISA; Mayfield HS; Cleveland, OH; 7/499 AFS; Band; Chrs; Girl Scts; Hon Rl; Jr NHS; NHS; Sch Mus; Rptr Yrbk; Drama Clb; Eastern Mich Univ; Language.

O MALLEY, ANNE; Brooklyn HS; Brooklyn, OH; Trs Frsh Cls; Cls Rep Soph Cls; Band; Debate Tm; JA; Orch; Sch Pl; Stu Cncl; Yrbk; Drama Clb; UCLA; Law.

O MALLEY, CHRISTOPHER; St Josephs HS; S Bend, IN; Hon Rl; Fr Clb; FDA; Ftbl; Trk; Mgrs; Indiana Univ; Pre Prof Med.

O MALLEY, COLLEEN; Beaumont HS; Cleveland Hts, OH; 8/160 Aud/Vis; Chrs; Hon Rl; VP NHS; Red Cr Ade; Sch Mus; Sch Pl; Stg Crw; Drama Clb; Swmmng; College; Music.

OMAN, JOHN D; North Union HS; Richwood, OH; Hon Rl; Pres FFA; Lat Clb; Letter Bsktbl; Letter Ftbl; Letter Trk; Am Leg Awd; Miami Univ Of Ohi; Bus Management.

OMAN, LESLIE; Highland HS; Highland, IN; 53/503 Chrh Wkr; NHS; Quill & Scroll; Stg Crw; Stu Cncl; Yrbk; Sch Nwsp; Drama Clb; Pres Spn Clb; Tmr; Univ Of Evansville.

OMAN, RACHEL; Cory Rawson HS; Findlay, OH; 1/66 Trs Soph Cls; Trs Sr Cls; Band; Chrs; Hon Rl; NHS; Pres Stu Cncl; 4-H; Letter Trk; Chrldng; Bowling Green St Univ; Comp Sci.

O MARA, JAMES; Deckerville Community HS; Deckervll, MI; Pres Soph Cls; Pres Sr Cls; Boy Scts; Hon Rl; Stu Cncl; Letter Bsbl; Letter Bsktbl; Letter Ftbl; Letter Trk; Pres Awd; College; Auto Sales.

O MARA, TOM; Jennings County HS; No Vernon, IN; Chrh Wkr; Hon Rl; Ger Clb; Pep Clb; Ftbl; Coach Actv; Indiana Univ; Cmnctns Tech.

O MEARA, CHERYL; Fairmont West HS; Kettering, OH; 11/471 VP Frsh Cls; Band; Chrs; Letter Drl Tm; Hon Rl; Natl Forn Lg; Orch; Sch Mus; Stu Cncl; Fr Clb; Kettering Youth Commsnn Mbr 76 Chrmn 77;.

OMIETANSKI, LYNN; Marietta HS; Marietta, OH; Aud/Vis; Band; Sch Pl; College.

OMLOR, JEAN; Calvert HS; Tiffin, OH; Band; Hon Rl; Stg Crw; Univ; Psych.

O MORTON, PHILIP; Admiral King HS; Lorain, OH; Hon Rl; Yrbk; Ohio State Univ; Cardiovascular Surg.

OMOTO, ROGER; Okemos HS; Okemos, MI; 30/309 Hon Rl; Letter Bsbl; Hockey; IM Sprt; Univ Of Oregon.

ONACKI, MARY; Dominican HS; Detroit, MI; Cmp Fr Grls; Cmnty Wkr; Hosp Ade; NHS; Off Ade; Univ Of Mic; Chemistry.

ONDERKO, KENNETH; Ursuline HS; Youngstown, OH; Chrh Wkr; Hon Rl; Spn Clb; Bsbl; Ftbl; Swmmng; Youngstown St Univ; Industrial Engr.

O NEAL, BARRY; Switzerland Cnty HS; Vevay, IN; Boy Scts; 4-H; Lat Clb; Bsktbl; Letter Crs Cntry;.

O NEAL, RHONDA; Madison Comprehensive HS; Mansfield, OH; 10/457 Treas Band; VP Boy Scts; Chrh Wkr; JA; NHS; Stg Crw; Fr Clb; Scr Kpr; College; Pre Med.

O NEAL, TESSA; Scottsburg Sr HS; Scottsburg, IN; Band; FCA; Girl Scts; Hon Rl; FHA; OEA; Gym; Chrldng; Indiana Bus Schl; Clerical Sec.

O NEIL, DOREEN; North Central Area HS; Spalding, MI; Band; Bsbl; Bsktbl; Chrldng; Bus Sch.

O NEIL, ERIN; Penn HS; Mishawaka, IN; VP Soph Cls; VP Jr Cls; Hon Rl; Stu Cncl; Spn Clb; PPFtbl; Indiana Univ.

O NEIL, TOM; Hubbard HS; Hubbard, OH; 25/350 VP Sr Cls; Treas FCA; Hon Rl; NHS; Stg Crw; Sec Key Clb; Bsbl; Ftbl; Trk; Wrstlng; Wooster Coll; Physics.

O NEIL KAHN, MAURA; Shawe Memorial HS; Madison, IN; 8/28 Cl Rep Jr Cls; FCA; Girl Scts; Hon Rl; Jr NHS; NHS; Sch Pl; Stu Cncl; Yth Flsp; Sprt Ed Yrbk; Var Vllybl 2 Ltr 77 79; Yunker Fdn 500 Schlsp 79; Hon Hoosier Schlhsp 79; St Marys Coll; Govt.

O NEILL, CATHERINE; Arcadia Local HS; Fostoria, OH; 8/64 Band; Chrs; Chrh Wkr; Girl Scts; Hon Rl; NHS; Orch; Sch Mus; Stg Crw; Yth Flsp; Univ Of Toledo; Archt Tech.

O NEILL, CATHERINE; Benedictine HS; Detroit, MI; Chrh Wkr; Hon Rl; Treas NHS; Pol Wkr; Stu Cncl; Cit Awd; College; Acct.

O NEILL, CATHERINE; Lumen Christi HS; Jackson, MI; Sec Soph Cls; VP Jr Cls; Trs Sr Cls; Hon Rl; NHS; Stu Cncl; Rptr Sch Nwsp; Fr Clb; Pep Clb; Trk; Mic St Univ.

O NEILL, EUGENE R; Valparaiso HS; Valparaiso, IN; 10/452 Cl Rep Jr Cls; Cls Rep Sr Cls; Hon Rl; Jr NHS; NHS; Stu Cncl; Boys Clb Am; 4-H; IM Sprt; Natl Merit SF; Univ; Pre Med.

O NEILL, GERALD; Benedictine HS; Detroit, MI; 15/173 Hon Rl; Pol Wkr; Wayne State Univ; Pre Law.

O NEILL, JAMES T; Charleston Catholic HS; Charleston, WV; Am Leg Boys St; JA; NHS; Bsktbl; Glf; IM Sprt; Univ Of Ten; Engr.

O NEILL, MARIA; Gabriel Richard HS; Ann Arbor, MI; 1/80 Cls Rep Frsh Cls; Am Leg Aux Girls St; Hon Rl; Hosp Ade; NHS; Stu Cncl; Drama Clb; Univ Of Mich; Attorney.

O NEILL, PENNY; Marietta Sr HS; Marietta, OH; 27/384 Am Leg Aux Girls St; Debate Tm; Drl Tm; Hon Rl; NHS; Pol Wkr; Sch Pl; Stu Cncl; VP Drama Clb; Fr Clb; Univ.

O NEILL, POLLY; Wadsworth Sr HS; Wadsworth, OH; 6/350 Chrh Wkr; Hon Rl; Off Ade; Pep Clb; Spn Clb; Chrldng; Scr Kpr; Miami Univ; Comp Sci.

O NEILL, THOMAS; Culver Military Acad; Campaign, IL; 41/202 Hon Rl; ROTC; Letter Swmmng; IM Sprt; C of C Awd; DAR Awd; Univ.

O NESTI, CHRISTINE; Campbell Mem HS; Campbell, OH; Trs Sr Cls; Chrs; Chrh Wkr; Hon Rl; Off Ade; Sch Mus; Rptr Yrbk; Rptr Sch Nwsp; Lat Clb; Sci Clb; Youngstown St Univ; Psych.

ONEY, MARK; Whitehall Yearling HS; Whitehall, OH; Hon Rl; Ed Sch Nwsp; Rptr Sch Nwsp; Police.

ONEY, MELINDA; Tecumseh Sr HS; New Carlisle, OH; 15/381 Cls Rep Soph Cls; Trs Jr Cls; AFS; Band; Hon Rl; Jr NHS; NHS; Fr Clb; Pep Clb; Letter Chrldng; Alternate A F ROTC 4 Yr Schlrshp; Letterd In Marching Band; Captain Of Flag Corps; Ohio St Univ; Dentistry.

ONSTOTT, JANET; Bay HS; Bay Village, OH; 42/379 AFS; Band; Chrs; Chrh Wkr; Cmnty Wkr; Hon Rl; VP JA; Lit Mag; Sch Mus; Stg Crw; Univ; Chem.

ONSTOTT, LISA D; Cuyahoga Vly Christian Acad; Cuyahoga Falls, OH; 10/68 Hon Rl; Sch Pl; Bsktbl; College.

ONTKO, KAREN; Woodrow Wilson HS; Younstwn, OH; 40/345 Off Ade; Stg Crw; Drama Clb; Pep Clb; Univ; Nursing.

ONTROP, PATRICK; Coldwater HS; Coldwater, OH; Chrs; Chrh Wkr; Cmnty Wkr; Hon Rl; Pol Wkr; IM Sprt;.

OOLEY, TINA; Mooresville HS; Mooresville, IN; Chrs; Chrh Wkr; Hon Rl; Yth Flsp; Y-Teens; Ger Clb; Sci Clb; Taylor Univ; Pre Med.

OOSTERWAL, WARONNE; Andrews Academy; Berrien Spring, MI; Chrh Wkr; Cmnty Wkr; Off Ade; Fr Clb; Ger Clb; IM Sprt; Andrews Univ; Psych.

OPAL, REBECCA; Manchester HS; Manchester, MI; 11/106 Hst Sr Cls; Chrs; Chrh Wkr; Hon Rl; NHS; Sch Mus; Stg Crw; Treas Yth Flsp; Drama Clb; Ger Clb; Spring Arbor Coll; Music.

OPALSKI, GLENN; Benton Harbor HS; Benton Harbor, MI; 6/400 Hon Rl; NHS; Letter Ftbl; Letter Ten; Letter Wrstlng; Lion Awd; Univ Of Notre Dame.

O PARKA, LYNN RAE; Harbor Beach Community HS; Harbor Beach, MI; Band; Hon Rl; NHS; Off Ade; Sch Mus; Pres 4-H; Mth Clb; Spn Clb; PPFtbl; 4-H Awd; College; Math.

OPEL, JEFFREY; John Marshall HS; Indianapolis, IN; 27/612 Hon Rl; Lbry Ade; Rptr Sch Nwsp; Swmmng; Ten; Mgrs; Purdue Univ; Chem Engr.

OPELL, PAULA J; Lincoln HS; Vincennes, IN; 14/284 Chrs; Chrh Wkr; Hon Rl; Hosp Ade; Mdrgl; Sch Mus; Sch Pl; Yth Flsp; Drama Clb; Anderson Coll; Christian Educ.

OPFERMANN, MARK; Monroe Jefferson HS; Monroe, MI; 5/180 Trs Soph Cls; Trs Jr Cls; Band; Hon Rl; Treas Jr NHS; Treas NHS; Rptr Yrbk; Rptr Sch Nwsp; Capt Ftbl; Central Michigan Univ; Jrnlsm.

OPPAT, WILLIAM; C S Mott HS; Warren, MI; 22/700 Hon Rl; Jr NHS; NHS; Stu Cncl; Mth Clb; Swmmng; Ten; IM Sprt; Cit Awd; Natl Merit Ltr; Univ Of Detroit; Orthodontist.

OPPENHEIM, ANNE M; Upper Arlington HS; Columbus, OH; 142/645 AFS; Hon Rl; Ger Clb; Ohio St Univ; Vet.

OPPER, SHARI; Norwalk HS; Norwalk, OH; Rptr Sch Nwsp; Pep Clb; Spn Clb; Chrldng; GAA; PPFtbl; Univ; Bus.

OPRIE, KATHY; St Joseph Central Cath HS; Fremont, OH; 3/100 Cls Rep Soph Cls; Band; Cmp Fr Grls; Hon Rl; Hosp Ade; Stu Cncl; 4-H; Pep Clb; Letter Chrldng; College; Math.

OPRISCH, BETH; Toronto HS; Toronto, OH; 2/119 Cls Rep Soph Cls; Cl Rep Jr Cls; Sal; Am Leg Aux Girls St; Band; Cmnty Wkr; FCA; Girl Scts; Hon Rl; Sch Mus; State Awd Of Distinction Perfect Attendance; Homecoming Volleyball Co Capt; Toronto Ed Assn Awd; Bowling Green St Univ.

OPRISCH, KARL; Toronto HS; Toronto, OH; Am Leg Boys St; Hon Rl; Bsktbl; Letter Ftbl; Letter Trk; Letter Wrstlng; IM Sprt; Cit Awd; College.

OPRSAL, SANDRA; Adrian HS; Adrian, MI; 7/386 Hon Rl; NHS; Letter Swmmng; Tmr; Michigan St Univ.

ORAC, VERA; Strongsville HS; Strongsville, OH; 2/451 Sal; Hon Rl; NHS; Quill & Scroll; Natl Merit SF; Oberlin Univ; Music.

ORAM, DAVID W; Adrian HS; Adrian, MI; 1/350 Am Leg Boys St; Pres Band; Hon Rl; VP NHS; Orch; Sch Mus; Mth Clb; Ten; Univ Of Mich; Premed.

ORANGE, LINDA; Douglas Mac Arthur HS; Saginaw, MI; Band; Hon Rl; Jr NHS; Ger Clb; Cit Awd; Sci Medal 76; Univ.

ORBAN, LISA; Calumet HS; Griffith, IN; 19/300 Hon Rl; Jr NHS; NHS; Quill & Scroll; Sch Nwsp; Fr Clb; Pep Clb; Pom Pon;.

ORCHARD, STEVE J; Clear Fork HS; Danville, OH; Band; Chrs; Chrh Wkr; Hon Rl; Sch Mus; Pres 4-H; FFA; Bsktbl; Crs Cntry; 4-H Awd; Univ Of Wyoming; Bus.

ORCUTT, BRIAN; Divine Heart Seminary; Chicago, IL; 1/10 VP Jr Cls; Boy Scts; Chrs; Chrh Wkr; Cmnty Wkr; Hon Rl; NHS; Quill & Scroll; Red Cr Ade; Sch Pl; American Newspapermens Assoc Most Valuable Staffer Awd 1979; Notre Dame Univ; Physician.

ORCUTT, SUZANNAH; North Central HS; Pioneer, OH; Pres Frsh Cls; Trs Jr Cls; Trs Sr Cls; Am Leg Aux Girls St; Chrs; Chrh Wkr; NHS; Yrbk; Sec 4-H; Letter Bsktbl; College; Med Tech.

ORDELL, DONNA; Center Line HS; Warren, MI; 4/425 Chrs; Chrh Wkr; Girl Scts; Hon Rl; Jr NHS; Natl Forn Lg; NHS; Sch Mus; Sch Pl; Sct Actv; Oakland Univ; Busns Admin.

O REAR, SHERRY; Westfield Washington HS; Westfield, IN; Hon Rl; Spn Clb; Letter Bsktbl; Letter Trk; Physical Educ.

O REILLY, CHRISTOPHER; Tecumseh HS; New Carlisle, OH; AFS; Band; Chrh Wkr; FCA; Hon Rl; Pres Jr NHS; NHS; Stu Cncl; Sch Nwsp; Pres FBLA; Dayton Univ; Radio Disc Jockey.

O REILLY, DONNA; Brighton HS; Brighon, MI; Hon Rl; Mich St College; Sci.

O REILLY, PATRICK; Orange HS; Pepper Pike, OH; 7/250 AFS; VP Debate Tm; Hon Rl; Lit Mag; Mod UN; Natl Forn Lg; NHS; Pol Wkr; VP Stu Cncl; Rptr Yrbk; Chairman Career Day Comm 1979; Close Up Fndtn 1979; Univ; Law.

O REILLY, PATTY; St Francis De Sales HS; New Albany, OH; 1/197 Cl Rep Jr Cls; Capt Drl Tm; Hon Rl; Sch Pl; Stg Crw; Drama Clb; PPFtbl; Rotary Awd; Miami Univ; Poli Sci.

OREM, GLENDA; Carroll HS; Bringhurst, IN; 1/130 Pres Soph Cls; Pres Jr Cls; Pres Sr Cls; Am Leg Aux Girls St; FCA; Hon Rl; NHS; Stg Crw; Stu Cncl; Pres Stu Cncl; Ind Univ; Law.

OREN, KERRY; Union HS; Losantville, IN; Trs Frsh Cls; Trs Soph Cls; VP Jr Cls; Chrh Wkr; Sci Clb; Spn Clb; Letter Wrstlng; Univ; Sci.

ORENDAS, STEPHANIE; Norton HS; Norton, OH; 18/350 Chrs; Chrh Wkr; Hon Rl; Jr NHS; NHS; Pol Wkr; Sch Mus; Mgrs; Mount Union Coll; Bus.

ORFE, RANDY; Avondale Sr HS; Bloomfield Hls, MI; Band; Quill & Scroll; Rptr Sch Nwsp; Rdo Clb; Univ; Profsnl Music.

ORIANS, LAURA; Carey HS; Carey, OH; Chrs; Off Ade; Y-Teens; 4-H; FHA; Spn Clb; Trk; GAA; 4-H Awd; Voc School; Beautician.

ORIANS, MARY; St Joseph Central Cath HS; Fremont, OH; Cmp Fr Grls; Chrs; Girl Scts; Hon Rl; Drama Clb; 4-H; Swmmng; Trk; GAA; Scr Kpr; Univ; Nursing.

ORIANS, NEIL; Carey HS; Carey, OH; 8/93 Am Leg Boys St; Hon Rl; VP NHS; Sprt Ed Yrbk; Lat Clb; Letter Ftbl; Trk; Wrstlng; Ohio State Univ; Engineering.

O RICE, SANDRA; Traverse City HS; Traverse City, MI; Band; Chrs; Debate Tm; Girl Scts; Hon Rl; Sch Mus; Sec 4-H; Great Lakes Acad; Deck Officer.

ORLANDI, ALLEN; Padua Franciscan HS; Seven Hills, OH; Hon Rl; NHS; Bsbl; IM Sprt; Mgrs; College.

ORLANDO, LAURA; Lake Michigan Catholic HS; Benton Hrbr, MI; 1/98 Cls Rep Frsh Cls; Cls Rep Soph Cls; Pres Jr Cls; NHS; Stu Cncl; Letter Bsktbl; Letter Trk; Am Leg Awd; Voice Dem Awd; University; Business.

ORLANDO, MICHAEL; St Thomas Aquinas HS; Homeworth, OH; 73/180 Chrh Wkr; Hon Rl; JA; Yrbk; Spn Clb; College; Busns Admin.

ORLANDO, ROSELLE; Edgewood Sr HS; N Kingsville, OH; VP Jr Cls; VP AFS; Am Leg Aux Girls St; Chrs; Chrh Wkr; Cmnty Wkr; Hon Rl; Lbry Ade; NHS; Sch Mus; Union Carbide Schlrshp Washington Workshop; American Yth Foundation Camp MFG Schlrshp Alternate; College.

ORLANDO, ROSE MARIE; St Ladislaus HS; Detroit, MI; Cmnty Wkr; JA; Sch Pl; Ed Yrbk; Yrbk; Ed Sch Nwsp; Sprt Ed Sch Nwsp; Fr Clb; Spn Clb; JA Awd; Whos Who In For Lang In Mid W 79; Whos Who Among Amer HS Stnd 77; N E Cong Of Tchr Of For Lang Awd 79; Mercy Coll; Drug Abuse Rehab.

ORLANDO, TIMOTHY; Charles Stewart Mott HS; Warren, MI; Boy Scts; Chrh Wkr; Cmnty Wkr; Hon Rl; Jr NHS; NHS; Sct Actv; Fr Clb; Univ Of Detroit; Busns Admin.

ORLIKOWSKI, CELESTE; St Florian HS; Hamtramck, MI; Sec Frsh Cls; Cls Rep Soph Cls; Cl Rep Jr Cls; Pep Clb; VICA; Macomb Cnty Comm; Marine Biology.

ORMAN, LOUIE; Shakamak HS; Jasonville, IN; 5/86 FCA; Hon Rl; NHS; Quill & Scroll; Yrbk; Pep Clb; Bsbl; Bsktbl; College; Math.

ORMOND, ALEXANDER; Cuyahoga Valley Academy; Akron, OH; Trs Soph Cls; Pres Jr Cls; Hon Rl; Letter Bsktbl; Letter Socr; Letter Trk; College; Biology.

ORN, JULIE; Ashtabula Harbor HS; Ashtabula, OH; 10/199 AFS; NHS; Rptr Yrbk; Fr Clb; College; Law.

ORNDOFF, ELIZABETH W; Wardensville HS; Wardensville, WV; Pres Frsh Cls; Pres Soph Cls; Cl Rep Jr Cls; Pres Sr Cls; Cls Rep Sr Cls; Chrh Wkr; Cmnty Wkr; Girl Scts; Hon Rl; Pol Wkr; Shenandoah Coll; Psych.

OROS, LYNDA; Madison HS; Madison, OH; 7/280 Chrs; Hon Rl; NHS; Pep Clb; Sci Clb; Spn Clb; Bowling Green State Univ; Med Tech.

O ROURKE, KIERAN; R B Chamberlin HS; Twinsburg, OH; 20/200 VP Frsh Cls; Cls Rep Sr Cls; FCA; Hon Rl; NHS; Yrbk; Letter Ftbl; Trk; Akron Univ; Physics.

OROURKE, MIKE; Rosecraws HS; Zanesville, OH; 10/90 Pres Sr Cls; Cls Rep Sr Cls; Am Leg Boys St; Aud/Vis; Hon Rl; NHS; Stu Cncl; Rptr Yrbk; Rptr Sch Nwsp; Key Clb; Univ Of Ohio; Engineering.

O ROURKE, TIERNEY A; Anderson HS; Cincinnati, OH; 142/424 VP Frsh Cls; Chrs; Chrh Wkr; Lbry Ade; Orch; Stu Cncl; Y-Teens; Pep Clb; Capt Crs Cntry; Letter Trk; Univ Of Tenn; Law.

ORR, CINDY; Medina Sr HS; Medina, OH; Chrs; Girl Scts; Stg Crw; 4-H; Pep Clb; Gym; Ten; Trk; Chrldng; GAA; Cuyahoga Cmnty Coll; Dent Hygnst.

ORR, DAVID; Zane Trace HS; Chillicothe, OH; 4/100 Trs Sr Cls; Mth Clb; Sci Clb; Crs Cntry; Trk; Bausch & Lomb Awd; Pres Awd; Univ Of Miami; Agri.

ORR, JOHN; Pinckney HS; Pinckney, MI; Band; Boy Scts; Chrs; Hon Rl; Mdrgl; Sct Actv; Pep Clb; Spn Clb; Chrldng; IM Sprt; Eagle Rank In Boy Scouts 79; Ltr In Band 79; Pep Band 76 79; Univ; Poli Sci.

ORR, JULIE; Ogemaw Heights HS; West Branch, MI; Trs Frsh Cls; Trs Soph Cls; Trs Jr Cls; Letter Trk; Capt Chrldng; 4-H Awd; Alma College.

ORR, MARY; Manistique HS; Manistique, MI; Band; Chrs; Drama Clb; Alma; Communications.

ORR, NANCY; Lehman HS; Piqua, OH; 1/90 Trs Frsh Cls; Cls Rep Soph Cls; Cl Rep Jr Cls; Band; Chrs; Chrh Wkr; Debate Tm; Hon Rl; NHS; Orch; St Marys Coll; Math.

ORR, RANDY; Gallia Academy HS; Gallipolis, OH; 10/221 Boy Scts; Chrs; Hon Rl; NHS; Sch Mus; Sct Actv; Stg Crw; Key Clb; Sci Clb; Spn Clb; Northwestern Univ; Bio Med Engr.

ORR, TAMARA; Bridgeport HS; Bridgeport, WV; Am Leg Aux Girls St; Hon Rl; Jr NHS; NHS; Yth Flsp; Y-Teens; Pep Clb; Spn Clb; Twrlr; Univ.

ORR, TIMOTHY; Milford HS; Milford, MI; Cmnty Wkr; NHS; Letter Bsbl; Capt Bsktbl; Letter Ftbl; Cmnty Coll.

ORSBURN, ELIZABETH J; Buckhannon Upshur HS; Tallmansville, WV; Girl Scts; NHS; Stu Cncl; 4-H; Treas FBLA; 1st Pl St FBLA Poster 79; Chosen & Attnd Rotary Clbs World Affairs Inst In Morganstown 79; Acctg.

ORSCHELL, SHERI; Brookville HS; Brookville, IN; Hon Rl; Yrbk; 4-H; FHA; 4-H Awd;.

ORSINI, PAUL; Catholic Cntrl HS; Toronto, OH; 12/227 Chrs; Hon Rl; NHS; Cit Awd; Coll Of Steubenville; Busns Admin.

ORSINI, SUSAN; St Francis Desales HS; Columbus, OH; Rptr Yrbk; Rptr Sch Nwsp; Key Clb; Mat Maids; PPFtbl; Scr Kpr; College; Acctg.

ORSINI, TONETTE; Steubenville Cath Cntrl HS; Mingo Jct, OH; 17/227 Hon Rl; NHS; Ed Yrbk; Spn Clb; Scr Kpr; Ohio St Univ.

ORSZYCKI, KARIN; Parma Sr HS; Parma, OH; 12/811 Band; Drl Tm; Drm Bgl; Hon Rl; Lit Mag; Orch; Yrbk; Rptr Sch Nwsp; Bsbl; IM Sprt; Baldwin Wallace Univ; Jrnlsm.

ORTEGA, DEBBIE; Port Clinton HS; Port Clinton, OH; 8/290 Am Leg Aux Girls St; Girl Scts; Hon Rl; Hosp Ade; Natl Forn Lg; NHS; Red Cr Ade; FDA; Mth Clb; Spn Clb; Wellesley Univ; Physician.

ORTEGON, CAROLINE; Hammond Tech Voc HS; Hammond, IN; 23/256 Chrs; Hon Rl; Mdrgl; Sch Mus; Sch Pl; Drama Clb; Ten; Chrldng; PPFtbl; Tmr; Indiana Univ; Psych.

ORTENBURG, ERYN; Gladwin HS; Gladwin, MI; Cls Rep Frsh Cls; VP Soph Cls; Cls Rep Soph Cls; Cl Rep Jr Cls; Hon Rl; Sec NHS; Stu Cncl; Treas Yth Flsp; Rptr Yrbk; Sch Nwsp; Mid Mich Community Coll; Bookkeeping.

ORTIZ, DEBRA; Morton HS; Hammond, IN; 32/384 Band; Chrh Wkr; Girl Scts; Hon Rl; Lat Clb; Spn Clb; Trk; Letter GAA; St Marys Of The Woods; Med.

ORTIZ, LYDIA; Ovid Elsie HS; Elsie, MI; Cl Rep Jr Cls; Band; Drl Tm; Pep Clb; Letter Trk; Chrldng; Pom Pon; PPFtbl; College; Foreign Language.

ORTIZ, NORMA; Emerson HS; Gary, IN; Lbry Ade; ROTC; Lat Clb; Cit Awd; Ivy Tech Schl; Horticulture.

ORTMAN, BOB; Edison HS; Milan, OH; Pres Jr Cls; Am Leg Boys St; Band; Boy Scts; Hon Rl; NHS; Sch Mus; Sct Actv; Mth Clb; Sci Clb; Purdue Univ; Engr.

ORTMAN, KAREN; Harrison HS; W Lafayette, IN; 16/302 Band; Chrh Wkr; Hon Rl; NHS; Orch; Sch Mus; Sch Pl; Rptr Yrbk; Rptr Sch Nwsp; Drama Clb; Univ.

ORTMAN, KIMBERLY; Calumet HS; Gary, IN; 1/293 Trs Frsh Cls; Cls Rep Frsh Cls; Trs Soph Cls; Cls Rep Soph Cls; Trs Jr Cls; Cl Rep Jr Cls; Cls Rep Sr Cls; Val; Am Leg Aux Girls St; Chrh Wkr; Most Otstndng Jr 78; Most Likely To Succeed 79; Most Contributing Newspaper Staff Mbr 77; Valparaiso Univ; Bio.

ORTON, KELLY K; Walnut Ridge HS; Columbus, OH; Chrs; Hon Rl; Off Ade; FTA; VICA; Columbus Tech Inst; Bus.

ORTOSKI, DEBRA; Brookside HS; Sheffield Lke, OH; 2/200 Hon Rl; NHS; Sprt Ed Yrbk; FTA; Kent State Univ; Comp Sci.

ORWICK, JAMES; Arlington HS; Forest, OH; 16/43 Band; Hon Rl; NHS; Orch; Pres Yth Flsp; VP FFA;

Letter Bsbl; Letter Ftbl; Scr Kpr; Lima Tech Schl; Data Process.

O RYAN, BARBARA; Arcanum Butler Sr HS; Arcanum, OH; 58/99 Girl Scts; Lbry Ade; Pep Clb; Air Force.

ORZO, BRIAN; Alliance HS; Alliance, OH; Boy Scts; Chrh Wkr; Hon Rl; NHS; Treas Sci Clb; IM Sprt; Ohi State Univ; Pharmacist.

OSBON, BARB; Colon HS; Colon, MI; 1/68 Val; Band; Hon Rl; NHS; Sch Mus; Sch Pl; Fr Clb; Trk; Bausch & Lomb Awd; Natl Merit Ltr; Oakland Univ; Comp Sci.

OSBORN, ABBY; Maumee HS; Maumee, OH; Chrs; Cmnty Wkr; Hon Rl; Sct Actv; Y-Teens; Yrbk; PPFtbl; College; Lib Arts.

OSBORN, DARRELL; Mathew HS; Vienna, OH; 30/155 Cls Rep Soph Cls; Cl Rep Jr Cls; Am Leg Boys St; Aud/Vis; Boy Scts; Hon Rl; Sch Pl; Sct Actv; Stg Crw; Stu Cncl; Youngstown St Univ; Comp Tech.

OSBORN, DAVID; United Local HS; Salem, OH; 1/140 Chrh Wkr; Hon Rl; NHS; Voice Dem Awd; Gold Medal Of Achvmnt In Royal Rangers 77; Asst Natl Scout Royal Rangers 76; Bell & Howell Tech Inst; Elec Engr.

OSBORN, DEANNA; Bear Lake HS; Bear Lake, MI; 3/37 Sec Frsh Cls; Pres Jr Cls; VP Sr Cls; Hon Rl; NHS; Rptr Yrbk; Letter Bsbl; Letter Bsktbl; West Shore Cmnty Coll; Educ.

OSBORN, DEE; Truman HS; Taylor, MI; Cls Rep Frsh Cls; Chrs; Hon Rl; Stu Cncl; GAA; Awd Of Merit Schlstc Hon 76; Awd Of Merit Swimming 77; Wayne Cmnty Coll; RN.

OSBORN, J; Lumen Christi HS; Jackson, MI; Chrs; Girl Scts; Off Ade; Sch Pl; Drama Clb; Lat Clb; Gym; IM Sprt; Scr Kpr; JA Awd; Jackson Cmnty Coll; Bus Admin.

OSBORN, JEAN; Maplewood HS; Farmdale, OH; Sec Jr Cls; Am Leg Aux Girls St; Chrh Wkr; Hon Rl; Hosp Ade; NHS; Off Ade; Yth Flsp; Beta Clb; Fr Clb; Nom For Warren Jr Womens League Teen Volunteer Awd; Univ; Phys Ther.

OSBORN, KARLA; Spring Lake HS; Spring Lake, MI; 19/190 Hon Rl; Hosp Ade; NHS; Gym; Letter Chrldng; IM Sprt; PPFtbl; Elk Awd; Davenport Coll; Fash Merch.

OSBORN, PHIL; Brownsburg HS; Brownsburg, IN; Hon Rl; Wrstlng; IM Sprt; Opt Clb Awd; Pres Awd; Motorcycle Racing 72; Univ; Archt.

OSBORN, TAMMY; Lima Perry HS; Lima, OH; 9/66 VP Frsh Cls; Cls Rep Frsh Cls; Sec Soph Cls; Cls Rep Soph Cls; Trs Jr Cls; Cl Rep Jr Cls; Pres Sr Cls; Sec Sr Cls; Cls Rep Sr Cls; Chrs; Ohio St Coll; Acctg.

OSBORNE, JAY; Jackson Milton HS; Diamond, OH; Pres Frsh Cls; Hon Rl; NHS; Stu Cncl; Yth Flsp; Yrbk; Rptr Sch Nwsp; Pres 4-H; Key Clb; Ohio St Univ; Med.

OSBORNE, JEAN; Parkersburg South HS; Parkersburg, WV; Chrs; Chrh Wkr; Girl Scts; Hon Rl; Lbry Ade; Off Ade; Sct Actv; Yth Flsp; Lib Awd Most Otstndng Asst 76; Letters For Being On Principals List 74; Voc Schl; Ornamental Horticulture.

OSBORNE, JOE; Licking Valley HS; Newark, OH; Chrh Wkr; Hon Rl; Pres Sci Clb; Bsktbl; Letter Trk; Wrstlng; Ohio St Univ; Bio Sci.

OSBORNE, KIM; Washington Irving HS; Clarksburg, WV; Am Leg Aux Girls St; Band; Chrh Wkr; Drm Mjrt; Hon Rl; Hosp Ade; NHS; Orch; Lat Clb; Sci Clb; West Virginia Univ; Nursing.

OSBORNE, MATTHEW; Vandercook Lake HS; Jackson, MI; 11/84 Cls Rep Soph Cls; Cl Rep Jr Cls; Cls Rep Sr Cls; Chrs; Chrh Wkr; Hon Rl; NHS; Sch Mus; Sch Pl; JCC.

OSBORNE, REX; Van Buren HS; Findlay, OH; Band; Bus Admin.; Boy Scts; Hon Rl; Bsktbl; Ftbl; Bowling Green Univ; Bus Admin.

OSBORNE, STEPHANIE; Bluefield HS; Bluefield, WV; 51/314 Hon Rl; Yth Flsp; Pep Clb; Bsktbl; Lcrss; Ten; Pres GAA; Phys Educ Awd 78; All Mercer Cnty Bsktbl Team 78; Superltv Mst Athtc; All Tourn Team Bsktbl 76 78; Univ; Phys Educ.

OSBORNE, STEPHANIE; Bluefield HS; Bluefld, WV; 51/314 Hon Rl; Pep Clb; Spn Clb; Letter Bsktbl; Letter Ten; Pres GAA; College; Phy Ed.

OSBORNE, TERESA; Piketon HS; Lucasville, OH; 3/103 VP Soph Cls; Band; Hon Rl; Sec NHS; Off Ade; VP OEA; Shawnee St Univ; Bus Tchr.

OSBORNE J, RONALD J; Western HS; Spring Arbor, MI; Trk; Wrstlng; Univ Of Mich; Chemistry.

OSBUN, LAURIE; Elmhurst HS; Ft Wayne, IN; Chrh Wkr; Hon Rl; DECA; Ravens Croft Coll; Cosmetology.

OSBURN, BECKY; North Central HS; Fairbanks, IN; 7/98 VP Soph Cls; VP Jr Cls; VP Sr Cls; Am Leg Aux Girls St; Aud/Vis; Band; Hon Rl; Sec NHS; Stu Cncl; Drama Clb; Purdue Univ; Fashion Mdse.

OSBURN, CYNTHIA; Lincolnview HS; Van Wert, OH; VP Jr Cls; Band; Chrs; Chrh Wkr; Cmnty Wkr; Lbry Ade; Stg Crw; Yth Flsp; Univ Of Dayton; Home Ec.

OSBURN, JAMES; Benton Harbor HS; Benton Hrbr, MI; Boy Scts; Treas FFA; U S Air Force.

OSBURN, LEISHA; Burris HS; Middletown, IN; 1/65 Trs Frsh Cls; Chrs; Hon Rl; Lbry Ade; Sch Mus; Stu Cncl; 4-H; Kiwan Awd; Purdue Univ; Vet.

OSBURN, SCOTT; Wintersville HS; Bloomingdale, OH; 33/267 Chrh Wkr; NHS; Sch Pl; Stg Crw; Pres Yth Flsp; Pres Drama Clb; Spn Clb; Letter Bsktbl; 1st Altrnt To Boys St 79; Bst Actr In Thspian 79; U S Air Force Acad.

O SCHROCK, RUSSELL; Pleasant HS; Marion, OH; Cls Rep Soph Cls; Cl Rep Jr Cls; Hon Rl; Quill & Scroll; VP Yth Flsp; Rptr Sch Nwsp; Pres Key Clb; Letter Bsktbl; Letter Ftbl; Letter Trk; Univ; Bus Admin.

OSENDOTT, BILL; Kermit HS; Kermit, WV; 1/37 Trs Frsh Cls; VP Soph Cls; Cl Rep Jr Cls; Hon Rl; Lbry Ade; Stu Cncl; Yrbk; Sch Nwsp; Beta Clb; Scr Kpr; Soc Of Dstngshed Amer HS Stu; Know Your State Gvrnmnt Day; College; Elec Engr.

OSENTOSKI, ANNA; Cass City HS; Cass City, MI; 10/169 Chrh Wkr; Hon Rl; NHS; NHS; Off Ade; Yth Flsp; Letter IM Sprt; Scr Kpr; Univ; Nursing.

OSGA, RONDA; St Johns HS; St Johns, MI; Hon Rl; 4-H; Letter Trk; 4-H Awd; College; Engr.

OSHINSKY, COLLEEN K; Streetsboro HS; Streetsboro, OH; 4/200 Cl Rep Jr Cls; Am Leg Aux Girls St; Hon Rl; NHS; Sec Stu Cncl; Rptr Yrbk; Rptr Sch Nwsp; VP FHA; FNA; FTA; Kent St Univ; Nurse.

OSIECKI, JULIE; Benedictine HS; Livonia, MI; 4/165 Cls Rep Frsh Cls; Cl Rep Jr Cls; Cls Rep Sr Cls; Chrh Wkr; Girl Scts; Hon Rl; JA; NHS; Stu Cncl; Rptr Yrbk; Wayne St Univ; Engr.

OSIER, LAURIE; Poca HS; Poca, WV; Chrs; Girl Scts; Hon Rl; Trk; Chrldng; GAA; Coll.

OSINSKI, KRYSTYNA; Erieview Catholic HS; Cleveland, OH; 3/105 Chrs; Chrh Wkr; Hon Rl; Lbry Ade; Mod UN; Off Ade; Pol Wkr; Ed Sch Nwsp; Univ; Med.

OSIVNIK, JAMES; Chippewa HS; Doylestown, OH; Band; Sch Mus; Sch Pl; Drama Clb; Sci Clb; Ten; Akron Univ.

OSKIN, ROBERT; Chesapeake HS; Chesapeake, OH; 11/98 Cls Rep Frsh Cls; Cls Rep Soph Cls; Cl Rep Jr Cls; Cls Rep Sr Cls; Hon Rl; Stu Cncl; Sprt Ed Yrbk; Sch Nwsp; Beta Clb; Bsktbl; Miami Univ.

OSLER, JAMES; Jackson HS; Clinton, OH; Boy Scts; Hon Rl; NHS; Pres Fr Clb; Key Clb; Ohio St Univ.

OSMON, CINDY; Yorktown HS; Muncie, IN; 3/250 Band; Cmp Fr Grls; Chrh Wkr; FCA; Girl Scts; Hon Rl; NHS; Off Ade; Sch Mus; Sct Actv; Pres Of Youth Fellowshp Grp 78; Sec Of Hon Soc 79; Whos Who In Foreign Lang 78; Univ.

OSSEGE, JULIANNE; Seton HS; Cincinnati, OH; Cls Rep Frsh Cls; Cls Rep Soph Cls; VP Jr Cls; Hon Rl; Hosp Ade; NHS; Pres Orch; Sch Mus; Am Leg Awd; DAR Awd; Bethesda Hosp Schl Of Nursing.

OSTBY, CATHY; Muskegon HS; Muskegon, MI; Hon Rl; Hosp Ade; JA; Jr NHS; NHS; Orch; PAVAS; Sch Mus; Sch Pl; Drama Clb; Muskegon Jr Coll; Archt.

OSTER, ROBERT; Ontario HS; Ontario, OH; 3/180 Cls Rep Frsh Cls; VP Soph Cls; Cl Rep Jr Cls; AFS; Band; Boy Scts; Hon Rl; Jr NHS; NHS; Sct Actv; Eagle Scout Silver Palm; Case Western Reserve Univ; Astrmny.

OSTER, TERI; R Nelson Snider HS; Ft Wayne, IN; Band; Hon Rl; Fr Clb; Univ; Eng.

OSTERHOUT, CARMEN; Bloomington HS North; Bloomington, IN; Am Leg Aux Girls St; Band; NHS; Ger Clb; Univ; Sci.

OSTERHOUT, J; Pike Delta York HS; Delta, OH; Boy Scts; Yth Flsp; Spn Clb; Bsbl; Bsktbl; Glf; Owens Tech; Acctg.

OSTERKAMP, JO ANN; Seton HS; Cincinnati, OH; 37/272 Chrs; Girl Scts; Hon Rl; Jr NHS; NHS; Red Cr Ade; Sch Pl; Sct Actv; Sprt Ed Sch Nwsp; Pep Clb; Xavier Univ; Elem Educ.

OSTERMAN, LORI; Arlington HS; Indianapolis, IN; 25/487 Girl Scts; Hon Rl; Lbry Ade; Sch Mus; Sct Actv; Stu Cncl; Rptr Sch Nwsp; 4-H; Ten; Letter Chrldng; Indiana St Univ; Jrnlsm.

OSTERMANN, JUDITH; St Philip Catholic Cntrl HS; Battle Creek, MI; 1/70 Trs Frsh Cls; VP Soph Cls; Pres Jr Cls; Cls Rep Sr Cls; Val; Am Leg Aux Girls St; Cmp Fr Grls; Hon Rl; NHS; Pol Wkr; Kellogg Co Schlrshp 79; Kellogg Cmnty Coll; Bus.

OSTERMEIER, BETH; Blanchester HS; Midland, OH; 13/150 Hon Rl; NHS; Stu Cncl; 4-H; FHA; Spn Clb; Univ; Psych.

OSTERWISCH, DALE; N Coll Hill HS; Cincinnati, OH; 30/200 Band; Chrh Wkr; Hon Rl; Orch; Sch Mus; Cit Awd; Kiwan Awd; Pres Awd; Univ Of Cincinnati; Mech Engr.

O STEWART, CHRISTOPHER; Princeton Cmnty HS; Princeton, IN; 39/204 Hon Rl; Mth Clb; Spn Clb; Letter Ten; Mgrs; Mc Donalds Yth Salute Progr 79; Design Princeton HS Flag 78; Univ; Archt.

OSTING, CINDY; Tri Jr Sr HS; Lewisville, IN; Sec Soph Cls; Cl Rep Jr Cls; Drama Clb; 4-H; FHA; Ten; Chrldng; Nurse.

OSTREK, SHERRIE; Chalker HS; Southington, OH; Sec Soph Cls; Trs Soph Cls; Off Ade; Y-Teens; Rptr Yrbk; Yrbk; Beta Clb; Sci Clb; Trk; Kent St Univ; Psych.

OSTRENGA, GREG; Menominee HS; Wallace, MI; 74/270 Chrh Wkr; Hon Rl; 4-H; Pep Clb; VICA; Letter Crs Cntry; Letter Trk; Letter Wrstlng; 4-H Awd; Farris St Coll; Gen Printing.

OSTRIC, ELIZABETH; Clay Sr HS; S Bend, IN; 17/430 Chrs; Hon Rl; NHS; Sch Mus; Stu Cncl; VP Fr Clb; PPFtbl; Univ Of Notre Dame; Archt.

OSTROSKI, ROBERT; Bishop Borgess HS; Detroit, MI; Chrh Wkr; Cmnty Wkr; Hon Rl; Y-Teens; Fr Clb; Coach Actv; IM Sprt; Cit Awd; College; Law.

OSWALD, FREDERICK; Bark River Harris HS; Bark River, MI; Band; Chrh Wkr; NHS; Sch Pl; Ed Yrbk; Rptr Yrbk; Drama Clb; Swmmng; Am Leg Awd; Bausch & Lomb Awd; Mi St Compttv Schlshp 79; 1st Natl Bank & Trust Of Escanaba Schslhp 79; Bay De Na Univ; Pre Engr.

OSWALD, GARY; Holy Name HS; Cleveland, OH; 11/359 Chrh Wkr; Hon Rl; Jr NHS; NHS; Pol Wkr; Sct Actv; Letter Glf; Letter Wrstlng; Coach Actv; IM Sprt; Univ; Vet.

OSWALD, HAROLD N; Waldron Area HS; Waldron, MI; 7/54 Sec Frsh Cls; Hon Rl; Lbry Ade; Sch Pl; Rptr Sch Nwsp; Spn Clb; Scr Kpr; Tmr; Cit Awd; College; Math.

OSWALD, JAMES R; Univ Of Detroit HS; Detroit, MI; 1/138 Cls Rep Frsh Cls; Cls Rep Soph Cls; Cl Rep Jr Cls; Sal; Chrs; Hon Rl; NHS; PAVAS; Sch Mus; Sch Pl; College; Theatre.

OSWALD, RICHARD E; South Lake HS; St Clair Shores, MI; 3/428 Boy Scts; Hon Rl; VP NHS; Pol Wkr; Sct Actv; Stg Crw; Yth Flsp; Boys Clb Am; Natl Merit SF; Pres Awd; Mayor Of The City For A Day; Univ Of Michigan; Medicine.

OSWALD, SUZANNE; Crestview HS; Mansfield, OH; Band; Chrs; Chrh Wkr; Hon Rl; Lbry Ade; Sch Mus; Sch Pl; Yth Flsp; Drama Clb; 4-H; Frosh Homecoming Attendent 76; Best Supporting Actress 2 Yrs In Row For Drama 77; Partial Schlrshp 79; Ashland Coll; Theater.

OSWALT, CONSTANCE; Mansfield Malabar HS; Mansfield, OH; 30/241 Cl Rep Jr Cls; Drl Tm; Jr NHS; Off Ade; Stu Cncl; Mth Clb; Letter Trk; Tmr; College; Flight Attnt.

OSZ, EDWARD; Wintersville HS; Wintrsvll, OH; Fr Clb; Univ.

OTCASEK, JULIET; Euclid Sr HS; Euclid, OH; Cl Rep Jr Cls; Cls Rep Sr Cls; Chrs; Hon Rl; Sch Mus; Stu Cncl; Drama Clb; Swmmng; Mgrs; Univ.

OTERO, JEFFREY B; Ernest W Seaholm HS; Birmingham, MI; 29/647 Sch Mus; Sch Pl; Stg Crw; Natl Merit SF; Univ Of Michigan; Architect.

O THAYER, CHARLES; Notre Dame HS; Clarksburg, WV; 3/59 Cls Rep Sr Cls; Am Leg Boys St; Band; Chrs; Chrh Wkr; Sch Mus; Sch Pl; Stu Cncl; Pres 4-H; FDA; Univ; Math.

OTHERSEN, CONNIE; Eaton HS; Eaton, OH; Band; Chrs; Drl Tm; Hon Rl; Off Ade; Fr Clb; Pep Clb; GAA; Mgrs; PPFtbl; Miami Bus Schl; Exec Sec.

OTMAN, MICHAEL; Southgate HS; Southgate, MI; 25/260 Band; Boy Scts; Hon Rl; Lbry Ade; Sct Actv; Stu Cncl; Bsbl; Bsktbl; Coach Actv; Mgrs; E Michigan Univ; Bus Admin.

O TOOLE, LORI; Rosecrans HS; Zanesville, OH; Hon Rl; Pep Clb; Tmr; Muskingum Area Tech Coll; Bus Mgmt.

OTT, ARLINE; Mc Nicholas HS; Cincinnati, OH; 6/240 Drl Tm; Hon Rl; NHS; St Dept Of Ed Hnbl Mntn Spanish 2 78; Cert Of Merit Outstndg Academic Achvmnt 77; First Hnr In Spnsh 3 78; Xavier Univ; Comp Sci.

OTT, JUDE; St Marys Central Cath HS; Sandusky, OH; FCA; Rptr Yrbk; Yrbk; Ten; IM Sprt; Vocation School.

OTT, KEVIN; La Porte HS; La Porte, IN; Band; Hon Rl; MMM; Orch; Rptr Yrbk; Ger Clb; IM Sprt; Mgrs; Vandercook Coll; Music Educ.

OTT, PAMELA; Valley Local HS; Lucasville, OH; 6/110 Band; Chrs; Hon Rl; Stu Cncl; Yth Flsp; Sch Nwsp; 4-H; FHA; Pep Clb; Chrldng; Louisiana St Univ; Med Tech.

OTT, SHELLEY; Belleville HS; Belleville, MI; 1/500 Cls Rep Sr Cls; Val; Hon Rl; NHS; Natl Merit SF; MHEAA Schlrshp 79; Univ Of Michigan Reagent Schlr 79; Univ Of Michigan; Pre Med.

OTT, SHERRY; Lanesville HS; Lanesville, IN; 5/57 Chrs; Drl Tm; Pres FCA; Hon Rl; NHS; Stu Cncl; Rptr Yrbk; Pres 4-H; FHA; Pep Clb; Ivy Tech Schl; Acctg.

OTT, TERRIE; Valley HS; Lucasville, OH; 21/107 Trs Jr Cls; Trs Sr Cls; Band; Chrs; Hon Rl; Hosp Ade; Off Ade; Sch Pl; Stu Cncl; Ed Yrbk; Marshall Univ; Legal Sec.

OTTEN, CHARLES; Holland Christian HS; Holland, MI; Chrh Wkr; Stg Crw; Ger Clb; Letter Bsktbl; Letter Glf; IM Sprt; Davenport College; Acctng.

OTTENWESS, NICK; Kenowa Hills HS; Grand Rapids, MI; Band; Chrh Wkr; Hon Rl; NHS; Letter Bsbl; Letter Ftbl; IM Sprt; College; Business.

OTTER, BARBARA; Switzerland Cnty Jr Sr HS; Vevay, IN; 12/120 Chrh Wkr; Drl Tm; Hon Rl; Off Ade; Sch Mus; Stg Crw; Drama Clb; Pep Clb; Mat Maids; S E Indiana Voc Schl; Cosmetology.

OTTNEY, CHERYL; Wheelersburg HS; Sciotoville, OH; Band; Hon Rl; Stg Crw; Fr Clb; Pep Clb; Bus Schl; Bus Admin.

OTTO, GINA; Whitehall Sr HS; Whitehall, MI; 35/150 Hon Rl; Yrbk; PPFtbl; Muskegon Cmnty Coll; Interior Dsgn.

OTTO, JAMES; Cathedral Latin School; Lyndhst Mayfld, OH; 1/80 Val; Band; Hon Rl; NHS; Orch; Stu Cncl; Sprt Ed Yrbk; Letter Bsbl; Letter Ftbl; IM Sprt; Dartmouth Univ; Hstry.

OTTO, JEFF; Midland HS; Midland, MI; Swmmng; Trk; College; Law.

OTTO, STEVE; Whitehall Yearling HS; Columbus, OH; Cls Rep Frsh Cls; Cls Rep Soph Cls; Cl Rep Jr Cls; Hon Rl; Stu Cncl; Bsbl; Bsktbl; Socr; Capt Of Bsktbl Team 77; Ltr In Bsktbl & Soccer 76 & 78; Ohio St Univ; Bus.

OTTOBRE, SAL; Solon HS; Solon, OH; 65/288 AFS; Hon Rl; Univ.

OTWELL, ROBERTA; Buchanan HS; Buchanan, MI; Chrs; Chrh Wkr; Hosp Ade; 4-H; S W Michigan Univ; Nursing.

OUELLETTE, ANDREW; Upper Arlington HS; Upper Arlington, OH; 59/610 Chrs; Hon Rl; Sch Pl; Spn Clb; Natl Merit Ltr; Natl Merit SF; College; Architecture.

OUELLETTE, BARRY; Northville HS; Northville, MI; Cls Rep Frsh Cls; Debate Tm; NHS; Fr Clb; Ten; College Prelaw And Law.

OUGHTON, JOHN; Brooke HS; Follansbee, WV; 17/403 Cl Rep Jr Cls; Am Leg Boys St; Hon Rl; IM Sprt; West Virginia Univ; Math.

OURANT, KAY; Upper Arlington HS; Columbus, OH; 190/610 Chrs; Hon Rl; Sec FHA; Ger Clb; Pep Clb; Spn Clb; GAA; Mgrs; Mat Maids; Coll; Fash Merch.

OUSLEY, ALICE; Marshall HS; Albion, MI; 89/258 Sec Chrh Wkr; Hon Rl; Pres 4-H; Lat Clb; GAA; IM Sprt; PPFtbl; Spring Arbor College; Bio.

OUSLEY, JILL; Clinton Massie HS; Wilmington, OH; Chrs; Drl Tm; Girl Scts; NHS; Stu Cncl; 4-H; Chrldng; Miami Univ; Bus Admin.

OUSLEY, KENT; Clinton Massie HS; Wilmington, OH; Cl Rep Jr Cls; NHS; Stu Cncl; 4-H; Letter Bsbl; Letter Bsktbl; Letter Ftbl; 4-H Awd; Miami Univ; Elec Tech.

OUSLEY, LADORA; Tuslaw HS; W, OH; 25/178 Band; Pres Chrh Wkr; Hon Rl; NHS; Sch Mus; Pres Yth Flsp; Sec FDA; FHA; Lat Clb; Twrlr; Ohio Univ; Psych.

OUSLEY, TERRY; Austin HS; Austin, IN; 5/90 Chrs; Chrh Wkr; Lbry Ade; Sch Mus; Sci Clb;.

OUTCALT, TODD; North Central HS; Shelburn, IN; 15/96 Am Leg Boys St; Hon Rl; Stu Cncl; Yth Flsp; FSA; Sci Clb; Spn Clb; Bsbl; Bsktbl; Indiana State Univ; Journalism.

OUTMAN, SANDRA; Northridge HS; Bristol, IN; Band; Chrs; Hon Rl; Mdrgl; NHS; Sch Mus; Yth Flsp; Ind Central Univ; Eng Educ.

OVEHOLT, CHRISTOPHER; Fredericktown HS; Fred, OH; Aud/Vis; Hon Rl; Lbry Ade; Ohio St Univ; Poli Sci.

OVERBEEK, CRAIG; Grand Rapids Christian HS; Grand Rapids, MI; Chrs; Ftbl; Wrstlng; Coach Actv; Calvin College; Bus Admin.

OVERDORF, LINDA; Tipton HS; Tipton, IN; 13/189 Cls Rep Frsh Cls; Cls Rep Soph Cls; Cl Rep Jr Cls; Sec Sr Cls; Cls Rep Sr Cls; Chrs; Chrh Wkr; Hon Rl; Sch Mus; Stu Cncl;.

OVERDORF, SCOT; Frankton HS; Frankton, IN; 1/134 Pres Sr Cls; Val; Am Leg Boys St; FCA; NHS; Stu Cncl; Drama Clb; Ball State Univ; Acctg.

OVERFIELD, GAYLE; William Henry Harrison HS; Evansville, IN; Trs Jr Cls; Trs Sr Cls; Am Leg Aux Girls St; Hon Rl; NHS; PAVAS; Sch Mus; Sch Pl; Stg Crw; Drama Clb; Univ; Comp Sci.

OVERHOLT, DAVID H; Ridgewood HS; West Lafayette, OH; Am Leg Boys St; Boy Scts; Hon Rl; Yth Flsp; 4-H; Letter Bsktbl; Letter Ftbl; Eastern Dist Hnrbl Mention Ftbl All Star Tm 77; Jewett Scio All Opponet Team Ftbl 78; Coll.

OVERLEY, BETH; Reeths Puffer HS; Twin Lake, MI; Hon Rl; NHS; Rptr Sch Nwsp; Univ; Creative Writing.

OVERLY, JANA; Miami Trace HS; Washington Ch, OH; AFS; Hosp Ade; DECA; 4-H; FDA; FNA; 4-H Awd; Vllybl 76 77 & 78; Pres Of Distrib Educ Clbs Of Amer 79; Ohio St Univ; Med.

OVERLY, STACIE; Pymatuning Valley HS; Andover, OH; 31/150 Band; Chrs; Drl Tm; Sch Pl; FHA; Pep Clb; Spn Clb; Bsbl; Bsktbl; Scr Kpr;.

OVERLY, STEVEN; Ridgemont HS; Ridgeway, OH; 6/66 Pres Frsh Cls; Cl Rep Jr Cls; Am Leg Boys St; Chrs; Hon Rl; NHS; VP Stu Cncl; FFA; Letter Bsbl; Letter Ftbl; Univ; Elec.

OVERMAN, MARY A; Brownsburg HS; Brownsburg, IN; 42/300 Sec Frsh Cls; Cls Rep Frsh Cls; Cls Rep Soph Cls; Cl Rep Jr Cls; Pres Sr Cls; Cls Rep Sr Cls; Hon Rl; Sec NHS; Quill & Scroll; Sch Mus; Purdue Univ; Comp Sci.

OVERMYER, LINDA; Niles HS; Niles, MI; Band; Girl Scts; Hon Rl; Sch Pl; Drama Clb; Fr Clb; Ten; Univ Of Michigan; Law.

OVERPECK, DOUGALS; Rockville Jr Sr HS; Rockville, IN; 18/96 Pres Sr Cls; Am Leg Boys St; Aud/Vis; Boy Scts; FCA; Hon Rl; NHS; Yth Flsp; Pep Clb; Bsbl; Purdue Univ; Mech Engr.

OVERPECK, DOUGLAS; Rockville HS; Rockville, IN; 18/96 Pres Sr Cls; Am Leg Boys St; Aud/Vis; FCA; Hon Rl; Letter Bsbl; Letter Bsktbl; Letter Ftbl; Purdue Univ; Mechanical Eng.

OVERTON, TINA; Washington Catholic HS; Washington, IN; Band; Cmp Fr Grls; Chrs; Chrh Wkr; Cmnty Wkr; Girl Scts; Hon Rl; Off Ade; Sch Mus; 4-H; College; Nursing.

OVERTON, TROY; Marion HS; Marion, IN; 7/700 VP Sr Cls; Boy Scts; Chrs; Hon Rl; NHS; Off Ade; Sch Mus; Yth Flsp; Letter Ftbl; Letter Trk; West Point Acad.

OVERTURF, MELODIE; Reynoldsburg HS; Reynoldsburg, OH; Chrs; Chrh Wkr; Cmnty Wkr; Girl Scts; Hon Rl; Lbry Ade; Off Ade; Sct Actv; Yth Flsp; FHA; Univ; Vet.

OVERWAY, CURT; Turpin HS; Cincinnati, OH; 24/357 Band; Hon Rl; Univ; Law.

OVOITT, DONALD; Bullock Creek HS; Midland, MI; Cls Rep Frsh Cls; Band; Debate Tm; Hon Rl; NHS; Stu Cncl; Sci Clb; Letter Bsbl; Letter Glf; Central Michigan Univ; Bio.

O WACHNER, HOWARD; Buena Vista HS; Saginaw, MI; Band; Boy Scts; Cmnty Wkr; Hon Rl; Orch; Sct Actv; Stg Crw; Sci Clb; Bsbl; Hohn Philip Sousa Awd Band 79; Saginaw Vly St Coll.

OWEN, ANITA; Greenfield Central HS; Greenfield, IN; 11/350 Band; Girl Scts; Hon Rl; NHS; 4-H; Spn Clb; Butler Univ; Zoology.

OWEN, APRIL; Springs Valley HS; West Baden, IN; 1/97 Band; Chrh Wkr; Treas Girl Scts; Hon Rl; Pep Clb; Letter Mgrs; Scr Kpr; Spanish Award; Top 10% Of Class; Indiana Univ; Spec Educ Tchr.

OWEN, CHRISTINE; Lakeville Memrl HS; Otisville, MI; 32/189 Sec Frsh Cls; Band; Hon Rl; NHS;

Chrldng; Sr Honro Stdt Silver Honor Cord 1979; Ceramics & Potters Whl Demstr 1979; Modeling Schl; Model.

OWEN, CRAIG; Cedar Lake Academy; Gobles, MI; Chrs; Gym; IM Sprt; Cert Of Recognition For Acad Ach In The St Of Michigan Schlrshp Competition; Coll; Health Care.

OWEN, J; Richmond Sr HS; Richmond, IN; 5/600 Sec Frsh Cls; Cls Rep Frsh Cls; Cls Rep Soph Cls; Cl Rep Jr Cls; AFS; Am Leg Aux Girls St; Band; Chrs; Hon Rl; Hosp Ade; Univ.

OWEN, JENNIFER; Loy Norrix HS; Kalamazoo, MI; Hon Rl; Hosp Ade; NHS; Orch; Sch Mus; Yth Flsp; Cit Awd; High Hnrs In Spanish; Citizenship Awd; Coll; Languages.

OWEN, JUDY; Davison Sr HS; Davison, MI; Band; Chrh Wkr; Girl Scts; Hon Rl; Orch; Sct Actv; 4-H; Sci Clb; Bsktbl; Trk; Word Of Life Schlrshps; Qualified For Regional Quizing 2 Yrs In A Row; Word Of Life Bible Inst; Paramedic.

OWEN, LISA; Whiteland Community HS; New Whiteland, IN; 1/197 Cls Rep Sr Cls; Am Leg Aux Girls St; Pres NHS; Stu Cncl; FHA; FTA; Mat Maids; DAR Awd; Indiana St Univ; Elem Educ.

OWEN, MICHELLE; Trenton HS; Trenton, MI; 130/560 Cls Rep Frsh Cls; Cls Rep Soph Cls; Sec Jr Cls; Cl Rep Jr Cls; Cls Rep Sr Cls; Hon Rl; NHS; Off Ade; Sch Pl; Stu Cncl; Eastern Michigan Univ; Math.

OWEN, PHILIP R; Heritage Christian HS; Indianapolis, IN; 2/64 VP Sr Cls; Band; Hon Rl; Pres Ger Clb; Letter Crs Cntry; Natl Merit SF; General Motors Inst; Mech Engr.

OWEN, REBECCA; New Albany HS; New Albany, IN; 32/565 Am Leg Aux Girls St; Hon Rl; NHS; Orch; FTA; Ger Clb; Rdo Clb; College; Math.

OWENS, BETH ANNE; Wintersville HS; Wintersville, OH; 4/267 Hon Rl; Rptr Yrbk; Lat Clb; Chrldng; GAA; College.

OWENS, CAROL; Redford Union HS; Redford, MI; Hon Rl; Lbry Ade; Pep Clb; Spn Clb; Bsbl; Bsktbl; Crs Cntry; Gym; Trk; Northern Ariz Univ; Med.

OWENS, CATHERINE; Okemos HS; Okemos, MI; Band; 4-H; Lansing Community College; Photog.

OWENS, CELESTE; West Side HS; Gary, IN; 49/650 VP Soph Cls; Cl Rep Jr Cls; Chrs; Chrh Wkr; Hon Rl; Jr NHS; Mdrgl; NHS; Yth Flsp; Y-Teens; Michigan St Univ; Pre Med.

OWENS, DANIEL; Clio HS; Clio, MI; 98/394 Band; Drm Mjrt; Drama Clb; Pep Clb; Capt Swmmng; Letter Ten; Mott Cmnty Coll; Auto Mech.

OWENS, DIANNA R; Tyler County HS; Jacksonburg, WV; 13/97 Chrs; Hon Rl; Off Ade; Drama Clb; FBLA; FTA; Whos Who In Music 78;.

OWENS, EDDIE; Marion Adams HS; Sheridan, IN; Hon Rl; Jr NHS; Rptr Yrbk; Sch Nwsp; Crs Cntry; Swmmng; Trk; Itt Tech Inst; Electronics.

OWENS, ELIZABETH C; West Lafayette HS; W Lafayette, IN; 43/184 Chrh Wkr; FCA; Girl Scts; Hon Rl; VP Orch; Pol Wkr; Sch Mus; Sch Pl; Yth Flsp; Yrbk; College; Marine Biology.

OWENS, JAMES; East HS; Cleveland, OH; Capt Bsktbl; Natl Honor Soc; College; Busns Admin.

OWENS, JENIE L; Father Joseph Wehrle Mem HS; Columbus, OH; 5/115 Drl Tm; Hon Rl; NHS; Spn Clb; Soph Awd For English; Soc Dstngshd Amer HS Stu; Natl HS Awd For Excellence; Cert Of Honor Composition; Ohio St Univ; Nursing.

OWENS, KELLI; Dayton Christian HS; Dayton, OH; 4/95 Hon Rl; Hosp Ade; NHS; Spn Clb; Bsktbl; Cit Awd; Spanish Natl Honor Soc 1976; Volybl & Softbl Varsity Letters 1977; Univ Of Cincinnati; Med.

OWENS, KIMBERLY; Norwood HS; Norwood, OH; Band; Cmp Fr Grls; Cmnty Wkr; Girl Scts; Hon Rl; Hosp Ade; Pol Wkr; Sct Actv; Stu Cncl; Fr Clb; Univ Of Cincinnati; Spec Educ.

OWENS, LORRAINE; Western Hills HS; Cincinnati, OH; 132/857 Cls Rep Soph Cls; Cl Rep Jr Cls; Cls Rep Sr Cls; Hon Rl; Off Ade; Lat Clb; Bsktbl; Trk; Scr Kpr; Ohio Univ; Pblc Affairs.

OWENS, RICHARD; Port Huron HS; Smiths Creek, MI; 13/357 Boy Scts; Chrh Wkr; Cmnty Wkr; Hon Rl; NHS; Stg Crw; Sch Nwsp; Bsbl; St Of Mi Comp Schlrshp Awd 79; Port Huron HS Art Dept Awd 79; Times Herald 3.5 Acad Achvmnt Awd 79; Ferris St Coll; Tech Illustration.

OWENS, RICK; Franklin Cmnty HS; Franklin, IN; 55/305 Cmnty Wkr; FCA; Hon Rl; Pol Wkr; Y-Teens; Boys Clb Am; Pep Clb; Sci Clb; Spn Clb; Bsbl; Univ; Bus Admin.

OWENS, SHEREE; De Vilbiss HS; Toledo, OH; VP Soph Cls; Cmnty Wkr; Girl Scts; Hon Rl; Jr NHS; DECA; OEA; Pep Clb; Spn Clb; Chrldng; Ohio St Univ; Secretary.

OWENS, SUSAN; Ridgewood HS; West Lafayette, OH; Am Leg Aux Girls St; Hon Rl; NHS; Sch Pl; Rptr Yrbk; Rptr Sch Nwsp; Pres Fr Clb; FTA;.

OWENS, TIMOTHY; Patterson Cooperative HS; Dayton, OH; 33/468 Boy Scts; VICA; Crs Cntry; Letter Trk; Hon Roll 77; Writing Merit Awd 77; Univ Of Cincinnati; Elec.

OWENS, TOM; Unioto HS; Chillicothe, OH; 3/140 Band; Chrs; Hon Rl; Sch Mus; Stu Cncl; Drama Clb; Spn Clb; Letter Glf; Letter Mgrs; Ohio State Univ; Elec Engr.

OWENS, WILLIAM A; Bluefield HS; Bluefld, WV; 4/280 Chrs; Hon Rl; Jr NHS; NHS; VP Lat Clb; Bausch & Lomb Awd; ACL & NJCL Natl Latn Exam Maxima Cum Laude Silvr Medl 78; Laurel Leaves Awd Short Story 78; Hampden Sydney Coll; Med.

OWENSBY, TAMMY; Norton HS; Norton, OH; Band; Chrs; Girl Scts; Sch Mus; Sch Pl; Stg Crw; Fr Clb; Trk; Juliard School Of Music; Vocalist.

OWINGS, LEE A; Chelsea HS; Hastings, MI; 5/250 Sec Soph Cls; Sec Jr Cls; Hon Rl; NHS; Yrbk; Bsktbl; College; Busns.

OWSLEY, ROBERT; Ernest W Seaholm HS; Troy, MI; Ftbl; IM Sprt; Michigan St Univ.

OXIER, SANDRA J; Toronto HS; Toronto, OH; 11/119 Hon Rl; Lbry Ade; Off Ade; Sch Mus; Sch Pl; DECA;.

OXLEY, AMY; Bishop Luers HS; Ft Wayne, IN; Band; Chrh Wkr; Girl Scts; Hon Rl; Lbry Ade; Orch; Sch Mus; Sch Pl; Sct Actv; Y-Teens; Soc Work.

OXLEY, LONNIE; Pike Central HS; Stendal, IN; Band; Chrh Wkr; Cmnty Wkr; Hon Rl; NHS; 4-H; FFA; Ftbl; IM Sprt; Purdue Univ.

OXLEY, SCOTT G; Ashland HS; Ashland, OH; Pres Jr Cls; Cl Rep Jr Cls; Pres Sr Cls; Cls Rep Sr Cls; Am Leg Boys St; Chrs; Stu Cncl; Letter Bsbl; Letter Ftbl; IM Sprt; Miami Univ; Pre Law.

OXLEY, TERESA; Union HS; Parker City, IN; 11/89 Band; Chrh Wkr; Hon Rl; NHS; Off Ade; 4-H; FHA; Spn Clb; 4-H Awd; Univ; Nursing.

OYER, DANNY; North Central HS; Pioneer, OH; Pres Soph Cls; Pres Jr Cls; Pres Sr Cls; Chrs; Stg Crw; Drama Clb; 4-H; FFA; 4-H Awd; 4 County Voc Schl; Auto Mech.

OYER, JEFFREY; Pettisville HS; Archold, OH; Am Leg Boys St; Chrs; Chrh Wkr; Hon Rl; Sch Pl; Stu Cncl; Spn Clb; Letter Bsbl; Glf; IM Sprt; Univ; Acctg.

OYER, SHARON; North Central HS; Pioneer, OH; 1/45 Band; Chrs; Chrh Wkr; Hon Rl; Lbry Ade; NHS; Yth Flsp; College.

OYLER, MARY; Hammond HS; Hammond, IN; Letter Band; Drm Mjrt; Girl Scts; Sct Actv; Tmr; College; Dentistry.

O YOUNG, BRETT A; Richmond Sr HS; Richmond, IN; Hon Rl; Hosp Ade; Y-Teens; 4-H; Spn Clb; 4-H Awd; Univ; Sci.

OZAK, ANNE; Les Cheneaux Comm HS; Cedarville, MI; 6/54 Cls Rep Soph Cls; Cl Rep Jr Cls; Cmp Fr Grls; Hon Rl; Hosp Ade; Off Ade; Stu Cncl; Rptr Yrbk; Letter Bsktbl; N W Michigan Coll; Nursing.

OZBURN, RODGER; South Harrison HS; Lost Creek, WV; Band; Hon Rl; Jr NHS; NHS; Sch Pl; Stu Cncl; Bsbl; Letter Wrstlng; West Virginia Univ; Wildlife Mgmt.

OZENBAUGH, TAMARA; Elwood Community HS; Elwood, IN; Band; Girl Scts; Hosp Ade; Jr NHS; Stu Cncl; Yth Flsp; 4-H; Chrldng; Twrlr; 4-H Awd; College; Nursing.

P

PAARLBERG, MARTHA; West Lafayette HS; W Lafayette, IN; 36/203 Cls Rep Soph Cls; Cl Rep Jr Cls; FCA; Hon Rl; Sch Pl; Stu Cncl; Rptr Yrbk; Yrbk; Keyettes; Pep Clb; Purdue Univ.

PAARNI, CINDY; Escanaba Area HS; Escanaba, MI; 30/442 Chrs; Chrh Wkr; Girl Scts; Hon Rl; NHS; Orch; Sch Mus; Michigan Tech Univ; Med Tech.

PAAUWE, LISA; Holland HS; Holland, MI; Cls Rep Frsh Cls; Band; Cmp Fr Grls; Hon Rl; NHS; Red Cr Ade; Rptr Yrbk; Rptr Sch Nwsp; Lat Clb; Pep Clb; Hope Coll Hon Schlrshp 79; Gold Cord 79; Sr Athletic Awd 79; Hope Coll; Bus.

PABLOW, FRANCES; Pinconning HS; Rhodes, MI; Trs Frsh Cls; PAVAS; Red Cr Ade; Sch Pl; Stu Cncl; Yth Flsp; Drama Clb; 4-H; Trk; Coach Actv; Vocational School; Peace Corp.

PACE, LYNN; Horace Mann HS; Gary, IN; Am Leg Aux Girls St; Band; Jr NHS; Pres NHS; Ten; College.

PACE, TERESA; William Mason HS; Mason, OH; 11/190 Sec Jr Cls; Sec Sr Cls; Am Leg Aux Girls St; Band; Drl Tm; NHS; Stu Cncl; Cit Awd; Natl Merit Ltr; Voice Dem Awd; Univ Of Kentucky; Bio.

PACH, RUSS; Centerline HS; Centerline, MI; Band; Hon Rl; Fr Clb; Pep Clb; Sci Clb; Macomb County Cmnty Coll; Musician.

PACHECO, SUSAN; North Framington HS; Farm Hills, MI; Cls Rep Soph Cls; Am Leg Aux Girls St; Band; Chrs; Hon Rl; NHS; Letter Socr; Letter Wrstlng; Coach Actv; Mgrs; College.

PACHOLEC, COLLETTE; St Florian HS; Hamtramck, MI; 13/75 Chrs; Hon Rl; Sch Mus; Sci Clb; Letter Bsbl; Mercy Coll; Med Tech.

PACHUTA, JOHN J; Guernsey Cath Cntrl HS; Cambridge, OH; 11/34 Pres Frsh Cls; Cls Rep Soph Cls; Cl Rep Jr Cls; Am Leg Boys St; Boy Scts; Chrs; Chrh Wkr; Hon Rl; NHS; Sch Pl; Coll; Phys Ed.

PACHUTA, MARY; St Marys Central Cthlc HS; Sandusky, OH; Cls Rep Frsh Cls; Hon Rl; Jr NHS; Lbry Ade; NHS; Sch Pl; Stu Cncl; GAA; Mat Maids; Univ; Elem Educ.

PACHUTA, SUSAN; Shady Spring HS; Daniels, WV; Band; Chrh Wkr; FCA; Girl Scts; Hon Rl; Stu Cncl; Yth Flsp; 4-H; Pep Clb; Trk; Marshall Univ; Architect.

PACK, DORA; Portsmouth E HS; Portsmouth, OH; 23/81 Hon Rl; Rptr Yrbk; Spn Clb; Ohio Cncl Of Teachers Of Math; Shawnee St Coll; Chem Engr.

PACK, GAIL; Bath HS; Lima, OH; Chrh Wkr; Hon Rl; Jr NHS; Letter Swmmng; IM Sprt; College; Elementary Ed.

PACK, JEANNE; Mullens HS; Mullens, WV; 13/100 Hon Rl; Beta Clb; Marshall Univ; Acctg.

PACK, PHIL; Waverly HS; Waverly, OH; Tech Schl.

PACKARD, DANIEL A; Interlochen Arts Academy; Grand Rapids, MI; Chrs; Pol Wkr; Stu Cncl; Bsbl; Natl Merit SF; Fndr & Frmr Pres Star Trek Club Of Grd Rpds 1976; Grd Rpds Chap Young Organists Assoc 1975; Organ Maj IAA; Univ.

PACKARD, STANLEY R; Athens HS; Athens, MI; Hon Rl; JA; Jr NHS; NHS; Trk; JA Awd; Mass Inst Of Tech; Elec Engr.

PACKARD, V; Brandon HS; Ortonvle, MI; Hon Rl; VP Spn Clb; Mic State Univ; Law.

PACKERT, RICHARD C; Port Clinton HS; Port Clinton, OH; FCA; Hon Rl; Lbry Ade; Stg Crw; Stu Cncl; Yth Flsp; Rptr Sch Nwsp; DECA; Ger Clb; Elk Awd; Bowling Green St Univ; Bus Admin.

PACOVSKY, MONICA; River Valley HS; Three Oaks, MI; Band; Girl Scts; Hon Rl; NHS; Ger Clb; Spn Clb; Spanish Club Vice Pres & Pres 78 & 79; Natl Hon Society Treas 79; Univ.

PACZEWITZ, DEAN; Woodhaven HS; Wyandotte, MI; Band; NHS; Pres VICA; Capt Crs Cntry; Capt Trk; All Lg Tm Cross Cntry & MVP St Comptn 78; Lgchamp Mile 2 Mile Track 79; St Comptn UECA Preprd Spch 78; Coll.

PADDOCK, GREG; Richmond Sr HS; Richmond, IN; 6/527 Cl Rep Jr Cls; Cls Rep Sr Cls; Band; Hon Rl; NHS; Stu Cncl; Treas Yth Flsp; VP Lat Clb; Coll Of William & Mary; Chem.

PADGETT, ANITA; North Daviess HS; Washington, IN; 42/100 Girl Scts; Hon Rl; 4-H; Spn Clb; 4-H Awd; Natl Merit Ltr; Coll; Law.

PADGETT, CHERYL; Big Creek HS; Yukon, WV; Hon Rl; Bsbl; Bsktbl; College; Comp Progr.

PADGETT, DEBORAH; Dayton Christian HS; Miamisburg, OH; Cls Rep Frsh Cls; Cls Rep Soph Cls; Cl Rep Jr Cls; Band; Sec Chrs; Girl Scts; Hon Rl; Sch Mus; Stu Cncl; Yth Flsp; Univ; Surgeon.

PADGETT, PAMELA; Clinton Prairie HS; Frankfort, IN; 7/90 Sec Soph Cls; Pres Jr Cls; Band; Chrs; Chrh Wkr; Cmnty Wkr; Girl Scts; Hon Rl; Lbry Ade; Mdrgl; Business Schl; Business.

PADGETT, TERRY; William Henry Harrison HS; W Lafayette, IN; 52/340 Hon Rl; NHS; Rdo Clb; Letter Ftbl; Univ; Engr.

PADLEY, CYNTHIA S; N Ridgeville HS; N Ridgeville, OH; Band; Chrh Wkr; OEA; Bus Schl; Sec.

PADO, LAURE; St Clement HS; Warren, MI; Off Ade; Sch Pl; Coach Actv; Mgrs; Scr Kpr; Mercy; Med Tech.

PADOLIK, PETER; Chagrin Falls HS; Chagrin Falls, OH; 8/165 Band; Boy Scts; Chrs; Hon Rl; NHS; Sch Mus; Letter Socr; Natl Merit SF; Wooster Coll; Med.

PADRO, RICHARD; Dover HS; Dover, OH; Ten; Pres Awd; College.

PADUAN, MARK; Houghton HS; Houghton, MI; Chrh Wkr; Hon Rl; Natl Merit Ltr; Coll; Religion.

PAESANO, DEBRA; Brooke HS; Follansbee, WV; 57/466 Sec Frsh Cls; Sec Soph Cls; Sec Jr Cls; Hon Rl; Jr NHS; NHS; Spn Clb; Chrldng; Selctd To Be In Miss USA Pageant 79; Homecoming Ct Top 10 78; Selctd For Miss Teen Wv Pageant 79; Modeling Schl; Teller.

PAFAHL, WALTER E; Huntington HS; Huntington, WV; 70/350 Band; Chrh Wkr; Hon Rl; Yth Flsp; Fr Clb; Key Clb; Wrstlng; IM Sprt; Med.

PAFF, DAVID A; Penn HS; South Bend, IN; Boy Scts; Sct Actv; Treas Yth Flsp; Ger Clb; JA Awd; Hon Cert Of Yr For S Bend Trib 77; Purdue Univ; Acctg.

PAFFORD, TAMARA S; Oceana HS; Oceana, WV; Cmp Fr Grls; NHS; Ed Yrbk; Beta Clb; FBLA; Pep Clb; Spn Clb; Pres Of Coed Hi Y 1979; Shorthnd I Awd 1978; Yrbk Awd 1978; Marshall Univ; Sec.

PAGAN, ANNETTE; Bishop Noll Inst; Hammond, IN; 67/321 Cls Rep Frsh Cls; Chrs; Chrh Wkr; Hon Rl; Stu Cncl; Spn Clb; Coll; Phys Therapy.

PAGAN, MIRIAM; East HS; Youngstown, OH; Band; Hon Rl; Lbry Ade; DECA; Nursing.

PAGE, ELIZABETH; Coldwater HS; Coldwater, MI; Girl Scts; Hon Rl; NHS; Sch Nwsp; Letter Bsktbl; Letter Trk; GAA; IM Sprt; Booster Club Schlrshp 79; Outsdng Young Woman 79; St Of Mi Competitive Schlrshp Acad 79; Adrian Coll.

PAGE, KATHRYN A; Fairfield Union HS; Rushville, OH; 8/147 Pres Band; Sec Chrs; Hon Rl; Jr NHS; NHS; Off Ade; Sch Pl; Yth Flsp; OEA; Bus Sec.

PAGE, RAY; Brookville HS; Brookville, IN; Cls Rep Frsh Cls; Cls Rep Soph Cls; Cls Rep Sr Cls; Boy Scts; Chrh Wkr; Stu Cncl; Spn Clb; Letter Bsktbl; Letter Ftbl; Letter Trk; Voc Schl.

PAGE, TERRI; Marietta HS; Marietta, OH; AFS; Band; Drm Bgl; Sch Pl; 4-H; OEA; Letter Trk; C ollege; Sec.

PAGGEOT, FRANCES; Pentwater Public HS; Pentwatr, MI; 3/25 Band; Hon Rl; Off Ade; Sch Mus; Pres Stu Cncl; Pep Clb; College; Med.

PAGLIALUNGA, JULIE; Union Local HS; Lafferty, OH; 22/157 Cls Rep Soph Cls; Cls Rep Sr Cls; Band; Hon Rl; Stu Cncl; Rptr Sch Nwsp; VP 4-H; Fr Clb; FTA; Sci Clb; 4 H Citznshp Shortcourse Delegate 79; 4 H Vet Sci Cnty Awd 77; 4 H Clb Congress Delegate 77; Univ Of Cincinnati; Nursing.

PAGLIALUNGO, DOMENIC; St Frances Cabrini HS; Allen Pk, MI; 20/162 Hon Rl; Spn Clb; Hockey; Ten; Natl Merit Ltr; 2 Crtfcts In Spanish 76 78; 1 Crtfct In Hockey 78; Univ Of Detroit; Dent.

PAGNUCCO, MARTY; West Branch HS; Alliance, OH; Hon Rl; Capt Glf; IM Sprt; USAF Acad.

PAHL, CHERYL; Gladwin HS; Gladwin, MI; Band; Drm Mjrt; Hon Rl; NHS; Yrbk; Sch Nwsp; Pep Clb; Capt Bsbl; Bsktbl; Lion Awd; Lions Club Awd Sftbl Most Improved; MVP Bsktbl; All Cnfrnce Bsktbl Sftbl; Spring Arbor Coll; Phys Ed.

PAHL, RICK; Traverse City HS; Traverse, MI; 218/864 Aud/Vis; Boy Scts; Sct Actv; Opt Clb Awd; Northwestern Mi Coll; Elem Educ.

PAIGE, VANESSA; East HS; Cleveland, OH; Cls Rep Frsh Cls; Band; Lbry Ade; Orch; Sch Mus; Fr Clb; Pep Clb; IM Sprt; Kiwan Awd; Northwood Inst; CPA.

PAINE, ERIC; Walled Lake Central HS; Union Lake, MI; 3/348 Mod UN; NHS; Yrbk; Ger Clb; Letter Crs Cntry; Letter Ten; Mgrs; Mic State Univ; Math.

PAINTER, CYNTHIA; St Peter & Paul Area HS; Saginaw, MI; Chrs; Girl Scts; Hon Rl; NHS; Red Cr Ade; Sct Actv; FBLA; Bsbl; Bsktbl; GAA; College; Bus Admin.

PAINTER, DENISE; Lincoln HS; Shinnston, WV; 8/175 Band; Drm Mjrt; Hon Rl; NHS; Sch Pl; Stu Cncl; Ed Sch Nwsp; Sch Nwsp; Drama Clb; Wv Univ; Pol Sci.

PAINTER, DONNA; Springs Valley HS; French Lick, IN; Band; Drl Tm; Girl Scts; Sct Actv; Yth Flsp; Pep Clb; College; Educ.

PAINTER, LAURI; Southeast HS; Ravenna, OH; Chrs; Girl Scts; Hon Rl; NHS; 4-H; Fr Clb; GAA; 4-H Awd; Univ; Military.

PAINTER, LINDA; Ypsilanti HS; Ypsilanti, MI; Band; Chrh Wkr; Drm Bgl; Girl Scts; Letter Bsbl; College; Bio.

PAINTER, PATRICIA; Shenandoah HS; Springport, IN; 15/150 Band; Hon Rl; NHS; Rptr Sch Nwsp; Pres 4-H; FHA; Mth Clb; Sec Sci Clb; Spn Clb; 4-H Awd; Purdue Univ; Agri.

PAINTER, PENNY; Waynesfield Goshen HS; New Hampshire, OH; Band; Hon Rl; Hosp Ade; Sec 4-H; FHA; Spn Clb; Letter Bsktbl; PPFtbl; 4-H Awd; Lima Tech College; Sec.

PAIRITZ, BARBARA; Central HS; Elkhart, IN; Cls Rep Frsh Cls; Cls Rep Soph Cls; Stg Crw; PPFtbl; Univ; Phys Ther.

PAIRITZ, DAVID; Elkhart Central HS; Elkhart, IN; NHS; Ftbl; Hockey; Chrldng; IM Sprt; Kiwan Awd; Notre Dame; Acctg.

PAISLEY, DAVID; Mona Shores HS; Muskegon, MI; Mic State Univ; Vet Med.

PAISLEY, DEBI; Cambridge HS; Cambridge, OH; Pres Frsh Cls; Cls Rep Soph Cls; Pres Jr Cls; Pres Sr Cls; Chrh Wkr; Hon Rl; Jr NHS; NHS; Stu Cncl; IM Sprt; Akron Univ; Radiologic Tech.

PAISLEY, JANET; Dominican HS; Detroit, MI; Hosp Ade; Mercy College Of Detroit; Nursing.

PAISLEY, KATINA; Philo HS; Chandlersville, OH; Pres Jr Cls; Band; Chrs; Hon Rl; NHS; Stg Crw; Stu Cncl; 4-H; Pep Clb; Letter Bsktbl; Varsity Clb; Bus Schl; Acctg.

PAISLEY, KIRK; Indian Valley North HS; Tuscarawas, OH; Am Leg Boys St; Boy Scts; Cmnty Wkr; Sct Actv; Ger Clb; Letter Bsktbl; Letter Ftbl; Letter Trk; Coach Actv; College; Bus.

PAITER, DENISE; Marenisco HS; Marenisco, MI; Cls Rep Frsh Cls; Cls Rep Soph Cls; Trs Jr Cls; Chrs; Hon Rl; Natl Forn Lg; Sch Mus; Stu Cncl; Rptr Yrbk; Bsktbl; Gogebic Community College; Ct Report.

PAITL, GEORGE J; Tawas Area HS; Tawas City, MI; Letter Ftbl; Capt Wrstlng; Coll.

PAK, BILL; Harrison HS; W Lafayette, IN; Band; Chrs; Letter Crs Cntry; Letter Trk; Purdue Univ; Intomology.

PAK, DOROTHY; William Henry Harrison HS; W Lafayette, IN; Band; NHS; Sch Mus; Sch Pl; Drama Clb; Sec Fr Clb; Keyettes; Pep Clb; Trk; Univ; Lib Arts.

PAK, GRACE; Plainfield HS; Plainfield, IN; 10/283 Band; Drm Mjrt; Hon Rl; Jr NHS; NHS; OEA; Pep Clb; JC Awd; Professional Typing & Shorthand Awds; Music Contest Awd; Accompanist To 1st Pl Solos At State Level; College; Music.

PAKARCIK, DOREEN A; Fitch HS; Youngstown, OH; Hosp Ade; Sch Pl; Y-Teens; Pep Clb; Spn Clb; Trk; PPFtbl; Youngstown St Univ; Chem Engr.

PAKE, SUZANNE; St Anne HS; Warren, MI; 13/52 Sec Sr Cls; Chrh Wkr; Hon Rl; Lbry Ade; Rptr Yrbk; Univ Of Mich Regents Alumni Schlr Bnd; Univ Of Michigan; Clinic Psych.

PAKKO, MICHAEL; Portage Central HS; Portage, MI; 11/379 Band; Chrh Wkr; Drm Bgl; Hon Rl; Orch; Pol Wkr; Chmn Swmmng; Mic State Univ; Law.

PAKSI, KIMBERLY; St Johns HS; Saint Johns, MI; Band; Hon Rl; NHS; Sec 4-H; Pep Clb; Voice Dem Awd; Michigan St Univ; Med.

PAKULSKI, STEVEN; Calvin M Woodward HS; Toledo, OH; Aud/Vis; Band; Hon Rl; JA; Jr NHS; NHS; Sct Actv; Wrstlng; Univ Of Toledo; Engr.

PALAIOLOGOS, ELAINE; Munster HS; Munster, IN; AFS; Chrh Wkr; NHS; Orch; Sch Mus; Purdue Univ; Micro Bio.

PALANCA, ROEL; Warrensville Hts HS; Warrensville, OH; 3/200 Hon Rl; Jr NHS; NHS; IM Sprt; Akron Univ; Hechanical Engr.

PALAZZO, PATRICIA; Ursuline HS; Youngstown, OH; 28/300 Cl Rep Jr Cls; Chrs; Hon Rl; Off Ade; Stu Cncl; Pep Clb; Youngstown State Univ; Social Work.

PALAZZO, SUSAN M; Ellet HS; Akron, OH; 40/362 Cls Rep Sr Cls; Hon Rl;.

PALCIC, PHIL; West Carrollton HS; W Carrollton, OH; 11/418 Am Leg Boys St; Boy Scts; NHS; Boys Clb Am; Chmn Ftbl; Trk; IM Sprt; College; Engr.

PALDANIUS, LOWRY; Marysville HS; Pt Huron, MI; Boy Scts; Sct Actv;.

PALENCHAR, ROBERT M; Lumen Christi HS; Parma, MI; 5/259 Trs Sr Cls; Cls Rep Sr Cls; NHS;

Spn Clb; IM Sprt; Natl Merit SF; Michigan Inst Of Tech; Nuclear Engr.

PALERMO, BECKY; Admiral King HS; Lorain, OH; Hon Rl; Yrbk; Bowling Green St Univ; Math.

PALFREY, DEBORAH A; Strongsville Sr HS; Strongsville, OH; VP Frsh Cls; VP Soph Cls; Chrs; Girl Scts; Red Cr Ade; Sec Yrbk; OEA; Crs Cntry; Swmmng; JA Awd; Greg Shorthand & Typing Awds; Regional Sec; Career Wmn Of Yr Awd;.

PALIGA, BRIAN; Cardinal Mooney HS; Struthers, OH; 16/288 Hon Rl; NHS; General Motors Inst; Elec Engr.

PALIN, SUE; Gaylord HS; Gaylord, MI; Chrs; Hon Rl; NHS; Off Ade; Drama Clb; Trk; Michigan St Univ; Vet.

PALING, WILLIAM; Memphis HS; Memphis, MI; Band;.

PALIWODA, JEFFREY W; Valley Forge HS; Parma Heights, OH; 15/704 Boy Scts; Chrh Wkr; NHS; VP Fr Clb; Mgrs; Scr Kpr; Natl Merit SF; Highest Honors 1975; Univ; Math.

PALLA, KATHLEEN; Bishop Noll Inst; E Chicago, IN; 12/347 Cls Rep Frsh Cls; Trs Soph Cls; Hon Rl; Jr NHS; NHS; Yth Flsp; Rptr Sch Nwsp; Mth Clb; Pep Clb; Scr Kpr; Purdue Univ; Pharmacy.

PALLANT, SUSAN; Jefferson Area HS; Rock Creek, OH; AFS; Band; Girl Scts; Sch Mus; Sct Actv; Fr Clb; College; Ther.

PALLAY, LOUIS; Saint Charles Prep; Bexley, OH; NHS; Rptr Yrbk; Bsktbl; Coach Actv; Ohio State Notre Dame; Architecture.

PALM, TIMOTHY; Ashtabula Harbor HS; Ashtabula, OH; Pres Frsh Cls; Pres Jr Cls; Am Leg Boys St; Aud/Vis; Boy Scts; FCA; Stu Cncl; Lat Clb; Ftbl; IM Sprt; Pres Of Stu Coun 79; 2 Yr Lttrmn; Bryant & Stratton Bus Schl; Bus Mgmt.

PALMBY, KEVIN; Hazel Park HS; Hazel Park, MI; 50/312 Hon Rl; NHS; Capt Crs Cntry; Letter Trk; IM Sprt; Mic State Univ; Med.

PALMER, ANNA K; Martins Ferry HS; Bridgeport, OH; 33/211 Sec Frsh Cls; Sec Sr Cls; Trs Sr Cls; Hon Rl; Hosp Ade; Off Ade; Y-Teens; Pep Clb; Sci Clb; VP Spn Clb; West Virginia Univ; Phys Ther.

PALMER, BRENDA; Jane Addams Voc HS; Cleveland, OH; VICA; Bsbl; Perfect Attendence Awd; College; Psych.

PALMER, BRENDA; Leslie HS; Leslie, MI; Band; Chrh Wkr; Girl Scts; Hon Rl; Sct Actv; Y-Teens; 4-H; Trk; College; Lpn.

PALMER, BRIAN; Marquette HS; La Porte, IN; 11/81 Hon Rl; Letter Bsktbl; Letter Crs Cntry; Letter Glf; Purdue Univ; Bus.

PALMER, DANIELLE; Cleveland Cntrl Catholic HS; Cleveland, OH; Cls Rep Sr Cls; Chrs; Chrh Wkr; Cmnty Wkr; Drl Tm; Hon Rl; Red Cr Ade; Yth Flsp; Mth Clb; Letter Pom Pon; Morehouse Univ; Math.

PALMER, DEAN; Milan HS; Milan, IN; 13/100 Hon Rl; Lat Clb; Univ.

PALMER, DENEE; Heath HS; Heath, OH; Letter Band; Debate Tm; Hon Rl; Letter Natl Forn Lg; Sch Pl; Yrbk; Drama Clb; Univ; Sci.

PALMER, DENISE; East HS; Akron, OH; Chrs; Girl Scts; Hon Rl; JA; Lbry Ade; Off Ade; Sch Nwsp; Pep Clb; Letter Gym; GAA; Akron Univ; Sec.

PALMER, DENNIS; Milan Jr Sr HS; Milan, IN; Hon Rl; Lat Clb; College; Electronics.

PALMER, JENNIFER E; Mater Dei HS; Evansville, IN; 24/184 Cl Rep Jr Cls; Hon Rl; Sch Pl; Stu Cncl; Rptr Sch Nwsp; Pep Clb; Chrldng; College; Science.

PALMER, JULIE; Lake Fenton HS; Fenton, MI; 2/178 VP Frsh Cls; Sal; Band; Girl Scts; Hon Rl; Stu Cncl; Sprt Ed Sch Nwsp; Rptr Sch Nwsp; Bsktbl; Trk; Michigan St Univ; Bsns Admin.

PALMER, KAREN; Benedictine HS; Detroit, MI; Cls Rep Sr Cls; Hon Rl; NHS; Stu Cncl; Rptr Yrbk; Fr Clb; Ski Clb 77; French Awrd 77; Univ Of Michigan; Med.

PALMER, KELLY G; Pioneer HS; Ann Arbor, MI; Cls Rep Frsh Cls; Cls Rep Soph Cls; Cl Rep Jr Cls; Cls Rep Sr Cls; Chrs; Chrh Wkr; Girl Scts; Hon Rl; Lbry Ade; Orch; Rnnr Up Century III Ldrshp Awrd 1978; Membrshp Natl Piano Plyng Gld 1971; Womens Schlrshp Natl Music Camp; Wellesley Coll; Econ.

PALMER, KIM; Sebring Mc Kinley HS; Sebring, OH; 36/91 Band; Chrs; Chrh Wkr; Girl Scts; Hon Rl; Hosp Ade; Orch; Sch Mus; Sch Pl; Sct Actv; College; Med Tech.

PALMER, KIMBERLY; Center Line HS; Warren, MI; Chrs; Hon Rl; Jr NHS; NHS; Stu Cncl; Fr Clb; Sci Clb; Scr Kpr; College; Law.

PALMER, KIRK; Fraser HS; Fraser, MI; Hon Rl; Letter Bsbl; Letter Bsktbl; Univ.

PALMER, LEWIS; Greenville HS; Greenville, MI; Pres Frsh Cls; Hon Rl; Fr Clb; Bsktbl; Letter Ftbl; Letter Trk; Letter Wrstlng; Coach Actv; Cit Awd; Voc Schl; Conservation.

PALMER, MARY; Green HS; Clinton, OH; 102/317 Cls Rep Frsh Cls; Chrs; Hon Rl; Yth Flsp; Yrbk; Letter Bsktbl;.

PALMER, MICHAEL; Pontiac Central HS; Pontiac, MI; 147/477 Cls Rep Soph Cls; Cl Rep Jr Cls; Cls Rep Sr Cls; Band; Boy Scts; Chrs; Chrh Wkr; Cmnty Wkr; Drm Mjrt; Hon Rl; Western Michigan Univ; Comp Sci.

PALMER, NANCY; Shadyside HS; Shadyside, OH; VP Frsh Cls; Cls Rep Frsh Cls; Cls Rep Soph Cls; Am Leg Aux Girls St; Chrs; Hon Rl; Off Ade; Sch Mus; Stu Cncl; Y-Teens;.

PALMER, PAUL D; Wilmington HS; Wilmington, OH; 1/270 Am Leg Boys St; NHS; Lat Clb; Letter Crs Cntry; Letter Trk; Bausch & Lomb Awd; Natl Merit Ltr; Coll; Aeronautical Engr.

PALMER, REAMA; Burr Oak HS; Burr Oak, MI; 10/33 Sec Soph Cls; Sec Jr Cls; Sec Sr Cls; Band; Hon Rl; Off Ade; Sch Pl; Ed Yrbk; Rptr Sch Nwsp; Letter Bsktbl; Kellogg Cmnty Coll; Legal Sec.

PALMER, ROBERT J; Champion HS; Warren, OH; 49/223 Aud/Vis; Chrh Wkr; Hon Rl; Lbry Ade; NHS; Letter Bsbl; Letter Bsktbl; Letter Ftbl; Letter Trk; Letter Mgrs; West Virginia Univ; Phys Educ.

PALMER, RODNEY; Haslett HS; Haslett, MI; 54/157 Cls Rep Frsh Cls; Chrs; Sch Pl; Lat Clb; Letter Bsbl; Letter Bsktbl; Trk; Coach Actv; OSU; Agri.

PALMER, THOMAS; Everett Vikings HS; Lansing, MI; NHS; Crs Cntry; Ftbl; Letter Swmmng; Letter Trk; Coach Actv; IM Sprt; Tmr; Diving 5th In Cty 25th In Rgn Ltr Mdl Cert 77; Div 5th In City 14th In Rgn Ltr 4th Pl Mdl In LCC Inv 78; Construction.

PALMIERI, TERESA; Henry Ford HS; Detroit, MI; Chrh Wkr; Cmnty Wkr; Hon Rl; Hosp Ade; Off Ade; Stg Crw; Yth Flsp; Rptr Sch Nwsp; Leo Clb; Spn Clb; Wayne Univ; Nurse.

PALMISANO, JAMES; Willoughby South HS; Willoughby, OH; 33/415 Am Leg Boys St; Hon Rl; NHS; Rptr Yrbk; Letter Ftbl; Letter Wrstlng; Ohio State Univ; Physics.

PALMITIER, SUE; Grandville HS; Grandville, MI; Band; Cmp Fr Grls; Hon Rl; Bsktbl; Trk; Central Michigan Univ; Acctg.

PALNAU, CARL P; Belleville HS; Belleville, MI; 15/535 Debate Tm; Hon Rl; Natl Forn Lg; NHS; Sch Mus; Sch Pl; Stg Crw; College; Communications.

PALO, DEBORAH; Engadine HS; Engadine, MI; 9/35 Hon Rl; Lbry Ade; Sch Pl; Chrldng; PPFtbl; Voice Dem Awd; Mst Outstndng Stndt Typing II 78; Honor Grad 79; MI Comp Schlrhsp 79; Univ; Acctg.

PALOSSARI, DAN; Chassell HS; Chassell, MI; Hon Rl; Stu Cncl; Yrbk; 4-H; Bsktbl; Crs Cntry; Trk; 4-H Awd; Michigan St Univ; Agri.

PALOVICH, BECKY; Hubbard HS; Hubbard, OH; 38/350 Treas Chrs; Girl Scts; Hon Rl; VP JA; Lit Mag; PAVAS; Sch Mus; Sch Pl; Stg Crw; Rptr Sch Nwsp; Guidepost Magzn Schlrshp Awrd 1979; Westminster Univ; Art.

PALUCH, STEVEN; Trenton HS; Trenton, MI; Hon Rl; Cit Awd; Air Force Acad; Aviation.

PALUMBO, MARYANNE; Sault Area HS; Sault Ste Marie, MI; 38/302 Drl Tm; Girl Scts; Hon Rl; Jr NHS; NHS; Swmmng; Lake Superior St Coll; Pharm.

PALUSAK, DEREK; Columbiana HS; Columbiana, OH; Hon Rl; College; Microbiology.

PANCAKE, LAURA; Archbishop Alter HS; Kettering, OH; Cl Rep Jr Cls; Chrs; Chrh Wkr; Stu Cncl; Drama Clb; Pep Clb; Univ; Psych.

PANCHER, JIM; Tuscarawas Central Cath HS; Uhrichsville, OH; VP Soph Cls; Hon Rl; Jr NHS; NHS; Rptr Yrbk; Sprt Ed Sch Nwsp; Letter Bsbl; Letter Bsktbl; Marietta Coll; Busns Admin.

PANCHOS, M; Perry HS; Massillon, OH; Chrs; Natl Forn Lg; Off Ade; Sch Mus; Sch Pl; Drama Clb; Sec Fr Clb; Pep Clb; GAA; Stark Tech College; Stenography.

PANDO, JEROME; West Iron HS; Stambaugh, MI; 20/135 Stu Cncl; Fr Clb; Letter Bsktbl; Letter Trk; Univ Of Michigan; Chem.

PANEK, JOSEPH; St Mary HS; Cedar, MI; 1/19 Chrh Wkr; Hon Rl; Yrbk; 4-H; Letter Bsbl; Letter Bsktbl; Dnfth Awd; 4-H Awd; Michigan St Univ; Elec Engr.

PANEPUCCI, ESTHER L; Buckeye South HS; Dillonvale, OH; Am Leg Aux Girls St; Band; Cmnty Wkr; Drl Tm; Girl Scts; Hon Rl; Hosp Ade; Y-Teens; Drama Clb; Pep Clb; West Liberty St Coll; Med Tech.

PANGBORN, CATHLEEN; Northmor HS; Edison, OH; 9/120 Sec Frsh Cls; Cl Rep Jr Cls; Am Leg Aux Girls St; Chrh Wkr; FCA; Hon Rl; NHS; Stu Cncl; Fr Clb; Spn Clb; North Central Tech Univ; Nursing.

PANGLE, JENNIFER; Caldwell HS; Caldwell, OH; 10/104 Trs Soph Cls; Band; Drl Tm; Girl Scts; Hon Rl; NHS; Sct Actv; Stu Cncl; Lat Clb; Pep Clb; Freshman Basktbl Homecoming Attent 76; Univ; Math Tchr.

PANICH, PEGGY; Traverse City Sr HS; Traverse City, MI; 64/650 Hon Rl; Jr NHS; Rptr Yrbk; Michigan Tech Univ.

PANICO, MINDY; Bridgman HS; Bridgman, MI; Band; Chrs; Chrh Wkr; Girl Scts; Hon Rl; Jr NHS; NHS; PAVAS; Sch Mus; Sch Pl; Blue Lake Fine Arts Intl Band; U S Collegate Wind Band; All Star Band; College; Music.

PANIWOZIK, NANCY; West Catholic HS; Grand Rapids, MI; Hon Rl; Treas JA; Lat Clb; Letter Swmmng; Letter Trk; Scr Kpr; JA Awd; Michigan St Univ; Vet.

PANKEY, MICHAEL; East HS; Akron, OH; Cls Rep Frsh Cls; Hon Rl; Jr NHS; NHS; Red Cr Ade; Yth Flsp; Sch Nwsp; Lat Clb; Spn Clb; Bsbl; Akron Univ;.

PANKOW, KATHY; Jefferson HS; Charles Town, WV; Chrs; Cmnty Wkr; Hon Rl; Mod UN; Rptr Yrbk; 4-H; Lat Clb; Letter Trk; Letter Chrldng; Modlng Schslhp 78; Track Ltr 78; Ice Sktng Medl 78; Dog World Awd Abednc & Dog Show Trophy 73 78; John Hopkins Univ; Pro Ice Skater.

PANNELL, LISA; Chesapeake HS; Chesapeake, OH; 7/140 Band; Hon Rl; NHS; Sch Pl; Beta Clb; Pep Clb; Bsbl; Marshall Univ.

PANNWNZIO, JOHN; Ursuline HS; Youngstown, OH; Cls Rep Frsh Cls; Cls Rep Soph Cls; Boy Scts; Hon Rl; IM Sprt; Youngstown St Univ; Bus Admin.

PANTAGES, MARTIN; Ellet HS; Akron, OH; 15/363 Pres Chrh Wkr; Hon Rl; NHS; Rptr Sch Nwsp; Sch Nwsp; Ger Clb; Letter Crs Cntry; Opt Clb Awd; Kent State; Journalism.

PANTALONE, COLEEN; Ravenna HS; Ravenna, OH; 122/313 Girl Scts; Hosp Ade; Treas OEA;.

PANTANO, LISA; Lamphere HS; Madison Hts, MI; 4/385 Cls Rep Frsh Cls; Cmnty Wkr; Hon Rl; Jr NHS; NHS; Sch Nwsp; PPFtbl; Albion College; Health.

PANTONE, MICHAEL; Magnolia HS; New Martinsvle, WV; 4/200 Cls Rep Frsh Cls; Cls Rep Soph Cls; Am Leg Boys St; Hon Rl; Pres NHS; Sch Pl; Yrbk; Capt Crs Cntry; Letter Trk; Wrstlng; Univ; Archt.

PANTZER, GREGORY; Marian HS; South Bend, IN; Boy Scts; Hon Rl; DAR Awd; Notre Dame Univ; Bus Admin.

PANZA, JOHN; Brooke HS; Follansbee, WV; 36/466 Cls Rep Frsh Cls; Cls Rep Soph Cls; Cl Rep Jr Cls; VP Sr Cls; Chrh Wkr; FCA; Hon Rl; NHS; Stu Cncl; DECA; Wv Univ; Acctg.

PANZECA, JENNIFER L; Seton HS; Cincinnati, OH; Cls Rep Frsh Cls; Cls Rep Soph Cls; Cl Rep Jr Cls; Hon Rl; Stu Cncl; Mth Clb; Spn Clb; Univ; Spec Educ.

PANZICA, CAROLYN; John Adams HS; S Bend, IN; 85/415 Cls Rep Frsh Cls; Cls Rep Soph Cls; Cl Rep Jr Cls; Cls Rep Sr Cls; Band; Hon Rl; Quill & Scroll; Sch Mus; Sch Pl; Yrbk; Ball St Univ; Elem Educ.

PANZL, BARBARA; North Muskegon HS; N Muskegon, MI; Chrh Wkr; Hon Rl; Yth Flsp; Capt Gym; Letter Trk; PPFtbl; College; Phys Ther.

PAOLELLO, MARY; Seton HS; Cincinnati, OH; 7/280 Cmp Fr Grls; Hon Rl; Jr NHS; NHS; Trk; GAA; Mgrs; Tmr; Rotary Awd; Xavier Univ; Mktg.

PAOLETTA, M; Solon HS; Solon, OH; Trs Frsh Cls; Cls Rep Soph Cls; Cl Rep Jr Cls; Trs Sr Cls; Hon Rl; Stu Cncl; Key Clb; Bsbl; Ftbl; College; Vet.

PAPACELLA, MICHAEL; Norton HS; Norton, OH; Chrh Wkr; Yth Flsp; Trk; Akron Univ; Surveying.

PAPACH, LAURA; Clay HS; S Bend, IN; 9/431 Cmp Fr Grls; Hon Rl; JA; NHS; Orch; Sch Mus; Ind Univ; Science.

PAPARIZOS, NIKEA; Eastlake N HS; Willowick, OH; 25/669 Hon Rl; NHS; Chrldng; Mgrs; Carnegie Mellon Univ; Bsns Admin.

PAPAS, COSTA; Wadsworth Sr HS; Wadsworth, OH; 35/370 Cls Rep Sr Cls; Band; Sec NHS; Stu Cncl; Key Clb; Mth Clb; Spn Clb; IM Sprt; Chosen As A Mbr Of The All Ohio St Fair Band; Carnegie Mellon Univ; Computer Sci.

PAPAY, KEITH; Lorain Catholic HS; Amherst, OH; Hon Rl; Sct Actv; Trk; Cle Tech Inst; Drafting.

PAPKE, LARRY; Mt Clemens HS; Mt Clemens, MI; Hon Rl; NHS; Sch Pl; Capt Ftbl; Wrstlng; Univ; Engr.

PAPOURAS, KATHERINE S; Regina HS; Cleve Hts, OH; 28/198 Cls Rep Frsh Cls; Chrs; Chrh Wkr; Girl Scts; Hon Rl; Fr Clb; Pep Clb; Glf; Chrldng; GAA; Ohio Wesleyan Univ; Pre Law.

PAPP, KARL; Barberton HS; Barberton, OH; Aud/Vis; Boy Scts; Chrs; Chrh Wkr; Hon Rl; Jr NHS; NHS; Sch Mus; Sch Pl; Sct Actv; Univ; Bio Sci.

PAPP, LAURIE; Orange HS; Chagrin Falls, OH; 10/250 AFS; Hon Rl; NHS; Yrbk; Fr Clb; Letter Hockey; St French Test Cert Of Of Merit; French Tutor; College; Busns Admin.

PAPPA, MIKE; Wheeling Central Cath HS; Wheeling, WV; 7/133 Cls Rep Soph Cls; Pres Jr Cls; Pres Sr Cls; Am Leg Boys St; Hon Rl; Natl Forn Lg; NHS; Sch Mus; Stu Cncl; Rptr Yrbk; Wheeling Coll; Fine Arts.

PAPPAS, MALA; Dexter HS; Whitemore Lk, MI; Chrh Wkr; Girl Scts; Lbry Ade; Sct Actv; Chrldng; Chrldr Spirit Awd 77; EMU; Bus.

PAPPAS, PAMELA; Mott HS; Warren, MI; Hon Rl; Jr NHS; NHS; Spn Clb; Cit Awd; Univ Of Michigan; Phys Ther.

PAPPAS, VICKI; Upper Arlington HS; Upper Arlington, OH; AFS; Chrs; Hon Rl; Hosp Ade; Treas JA; Pol Wkr; Rptr Sch Nwsp; Ger Clb; GAA; IM Sprt; Semi Finalist In Miss Teenage Columbus Pageant 77; Yth Cons Corps 77; Marshell Univ; Jrnlsm.

PAQUETTE, SCOTT; Boyne City HS; Boyne City, MI; Band; Bsktbl; Ftbl; Glf; Ten; Trk; North Central Mic College.

PAQUETTE, THOMAS; Hazel Park HS; Hazel Park, MI; 17/306 Cl Rep Jr Cls; Hon Rl; NHS; Red Cr Ade; Stu Cncl; Rptr Yrbk; Crs Cntry; Trk; Central Mic Univ; Chem.

PAQUIN, MARY A; Madison HS; Madison, OH; Cl Rep Jr Cls; Cls Rep Sr Cls; Band; Hon Rl; NHS; Twrlr; Univ.

PAQUIN JR, JOSEPH; Madison HS; Madison, OH; 1/288 Val; Band; Chrh Wkr; Cmnty Wkr; Hon Rl; Treas NHS; Rdo Clb; Letter Bsbl; Letter Glf; Am Leg Awd; Ohio St Univ; Engr Physics.

PARADINE, JULIA; Schoolcraft HS; Schoolcraft, MI; Am Leg Aux Girls St; Band; Hon Rl; NHS; Sch Pl; Yth Flsp; 4-H; Coll; Banking.

PARADISE, ROBERT; Hammond Tech Voc HS; Hammond, IN; 10/208 VP Jr Cls; VP Sr Cls; Am Leg Boys St; Hon Rl; Jr NHS; NHS; Drama Clb; Spn Clb; Ind State Univ; Law.

PARADISO, LINDA; Calvert HS; Tiffin, OH; Band; Chrs; Hon Rl; Orch; Sch Mus; Pep Clb; Chrldng; Scr Kpr; College.

PARADY, ELIZABETH A; Walnut Hills HS; Cincinnati, OH; Band; Chrh Wkr; Girl Scts; Hon Rl; Off Ade; Pol Wkr; Sch Pl; Sct Actv; Stg Crw; Yth Flsp; Cert For Work On March Of Dimes Walkathon 77; Brigham Young Univ; Acctg.

PARAGAS, DAVID; Normandy Sr HS; Parma, OH; 170/600 Debate Tm; Hon Rl; Natl Forn Lg; Pres Spn Clb; PPFtbl; Mas Awd; Spanish Hon Soc 77 78 & 79; Cert Of Merit 79; St Officer & 2nd Dist Chrmn Of Order Of De Molay 77 78 & 79; Ohio Wesleyan Univ; Pre Law.

PARAGINA, NADA; Munster HS; Munster, IN; 65/450 Chrh Wkr; Hon Rl; Hosp Ade; Jr NHS; Drama Clb; Ger Clb; OEA; Pep Clb; Purdue Univ; Pharm.

PARANIUK, MICHELLE; High School; Cincinnati, OH; Hon Rl; Stu Cncl; Sch Nwsp; Pep Clb; Spn Clb; Bsbl; Trk; Miami Univ; Med.

PARAVENTI, TINA; St Alphonsus HS; Detroit, MI; Cl Rep Jr Cls; Chrs; Chrh Wkr; Debate Tm; Hon Rl; Mdrgl; Natl Forn Lg; Sch Mus; Sch Pl; Stu Cncl; Univ; Drama.

PARCELL JR, ROBERT; Marine City HS; Marine City, MI; Cls Rep Frsh Cls; Cls Rep Soph Cls; Cl Rep Jr Cls; Cls Rep Sr Cls; Hon Rl; VP NHS; Sch Pl; Sprt Ed Sch Nwsp; Drama Clb; Capt Bsbl; General Motors Inst; Industrial Engi.

PARCELLS, BARBARA; Portage Northern HS; Portage, MI; Debate Tm; Hon Rl; Natl Merit SF; Natl Merit Schl; Mic State Univ; Gen Sci.

PARDIKE, PAUL; Rogers City HS; Rogers City, MI; 15/142 AFS; Band; Hon Rl; Ferris State College; Pharmacy.

PARDOE, BLAINE; Harper Creek HS; Battle Creek, MI; Cls Rep Soph Cls; Debate Tm; Hon Rl; NHS; Stu Cncl; Sch Nwsp; Central Mich Univ; Law.

PAREJA, JAIME G; Dublin HS; Columbus, OH; Boy Scts; Hon Rl; Socr; Harvard Univ; Neurologist.

PARELLO, RAYMOND; Catholic Central HS; Mingo Junction, OH; 5/236 Band; Chrs; Chrh Wkr; Cmnty Wkr; Hon Rl; NHS; Orch; FDA; Sci Clb; Spn Clb; Allegheny Coll; Pre Med.

PARENT, CELINE; West Lafayette HS; W Lafayette, IN; Chrs; Chrh Wkr; Purdue Univ; Pharm.

PARGOFF, ROBERT; Crentwood HS; Dearborn Hts, MI; Cls Rep Frsh Cls; Cls Rep Soph Cls; Cl Rep Jr Cls; Cls Rep Sr Cls; Hon Rl; Pol Wkr; Bsbl; Lawrence Inst; Business.

PARHAM, ERIC J; Reynoldsburg HS; Columbus, OH; 50/408 VP Jr Cls; Boy Scts; Chrs; Hon Rl; Lbry Ade; NHS; Sct Actv; Stu Cncl; Yth Flsp; Trk; Duke Univ; Law.

PARIKH, ABHAY; Northmont HS; Englewood, OH; 57/517 Boy Scts; Hon Rl; Sct Actv; Stu Cncl; FDA; IM Sprt; Ohio State Univ; Med.

PARILLO, TINA; Liberty HS; Girard, OH; Band; Chrh Wkr; Cmnty Wkr; Girl Scts; Hon Rl; Orch; Sch Mus; Sct Actv; Fr Clb; OEA; Youngstown St Univ; Bus Mgmt.

PARIS, GINA; Swartz Creek HS; Flint, MI; Hon Rl; Jr NHS; NHS; Ed Yrbk; Rptr Yrbk; Yrbk; Rptr Sch Nwsp; Pres Awd; Alma Coll; Bus Admin.

PARIS, LINDA; Lawrence Central HS; Indianapolis, IN; 36/365 Band; Chrh Wkr; Girl Scts; Hon Rl; JA; Beta Clb; Drama Clb; Mat Maids; PPFtbl; Band Awards; Ball State Univ; Nursing.

PARIS, MARY; Catholic Central HS; Mingo Jctn, OH; 50/200 Girl Scts; Hon Rl; Yrbk; Lat Clb; Bsktbl; Univ; Engr.

PARIS, PATTI; Franklin Cmnty HS; Franklin, IN; Hon Rl; Off Ade; Stu Cncl; 4-H; FHA; Pep Clb; Letter Trk; Chrldng; GAA; 4-H Awd; Vincennes Univ; Fashion Mdse.

PARIS, PETER; William Henry Harrison HS; Evansville, IN; Aud/Vis; Hon Rl; Pol Wkr; Pres Quill & Scroll; Stu Cncl; Yrbk; Ed Sch Nwsp; VP Fr Clb; Indiana Univ; Jrnlsm.

PARISE, JERRY; Niles Mc Kinley HS; Niles, OH; Cls Rep Frsh Cls; Cls Rep Soph Cls; Cl Rep Jr Cls; Am Leg Boys St; Boy Scts; Jr NHS; VP NHS; Pres Stu Cncl; Ftbl;.

PARISH, CHARLOTTE; Benedictine HS; Detroit, MI; 43/173 Cls Rep Sr Cls; Chrs; Hon Rl; Lbry Ade; NHS; Stu Cncl; Rptr Sch Nwsp; Detroit Coll Of Bus; Data Proc.

PARISH, DARRYL; Churubusco HS; Churubusco, IN; Chrs; FCA; Sch Mus; Sch Pl; Yth Flsp; Drama Clb; Bsktbl; Letter Ftbl; Letter Trk; Ball State Univ; Architect.

PARISH, JOE; Teays Valley HS; Stoutsville, OH; Aud/Vis; Chrs; FCA; Hon Rl; Lbry Ade; NHS; Stg Crw; VP 4-H; Lat Clb; 4-H Awd; College; Communication.

PARISH, RANDY; Mc Comb HS; Mccomb, OH; Hon Rl; Stg Crw; Ftbl; Trk; Wrstlng; Univ.

PARISH, SUE; Riverdale HS; Findlay, OH; 3/100 Pres Jr Cls; Pres Sr Cls; Chrs; Hon Rl; NHS; Off Ade; Quill & Scroll; Stg Crw; Ed Sch Nwsp; FTA; Lima Tech; Data Processing.

PARISH, TERRI; North Knox HS; Emison, IN; 38/150 Cls Rep Frsh Cls; Cls Rep Soph Cls; Cl Rep Jr Cls; FCA; Girl Scts; Hon Rl; Off Ade; Pol Wkr; FHA; Pep Clb; Vincennes Univ; Bookkpg.

PARISI, LISA; Arthur Hill HS; Saginaw, MI; 42/522 Pres Frsh Cls; Cls Rep Sr Cls; Hon Rl; NHS; Off Ade; Stu Cncl; Yrbk; Pep Clb; Letter Bsbl; Swmmng; Western Michigan Univ; Secondary Ed.

PARK, CAROLYN M; Richmond Sr HS; Richmond, IN; 57/665 Cls Rep Sr Cls; Band; Chrh Wkr; Hon Rl; Jr NHS; Stu Cncl; Yth Flsp; Pep Clb; Chrldng; PPFtbl; De Pauw Univ; English.

PARK, CHERYL; South Spencer HS; Rockport, IN; Cls Rep Sr Cls; Band; Chrs; Chrh Wkr; Girl Scts; Hon Rl; NHS; Sch Mus; Sch Pl; Stg Crw; Music Schlrshp 79; Western Kentucky Univ; Voice.

PARK, ELIZABETH A; Bexley HS; Bexley, OH; 3/185 Band; Boy Scts; Chrh Wkr; Girl Scts; Hon Rl;

Orch; Sch Mus; Sch Pl; Sct Actv; Stg Crw; Ohio St Univ; Physics.

PARK, JANE; Riverdale HS; Wharton, OH; Am Leg Aux Girls St; Chrs; Chrh Wkr; Hon Rl;.

PARK, TERI; Mt Vernon Academy; Chula Vista, CA; Cls Rep Frsh Cls; Chrs; Hon Rl; Yth Flsp; Coach Actv; Scr Kpr; Tmr; Univ; Phys Educ.

PARKE, EVAN; Shaker Hts HS; Shaker Hts, OH; 77/551 Cmnty Wkr; Hon Rl; Rptr Yrbk; Ohi Univ; Photojournalist.

PARKER, AMY; Jasper HS; Jasper, IN; 20/289 Cls Rep Frsh Cls; Cls Rep Soph Cls; Am Leg Aux Girls St; Chrh Wkr; Hon Rl; NHS; Stu Cncl; Pep Clb; Bsktbl; Vanderbilt Univ; Prospective Engr.

PARKER, ANN; Capac Community HS; Capac, MI; Band; Hon Rl; Yth Flsp; Pres 4-H; Mgrs; Mat Maids; Scr Kpr; Mic State; Creative Writing.

PARKER, ANNE E; John F Kennedy HS; Taylor, MI; Trk; Pres Awd; Wayne Cnty Cmnty Coll; Psych.

PARKER, BARRY; Warsaw Comm HS; Warsaw, IN; 67/400 Hon Rl; Off Ade; DECA; 4-H; Ftbl; Trk; IM Sprt; 4-H Awd; College; Bus.

PARKER, BRYAN; Allen East HS; Harrod, OH; 19/116 Chrh Wkr; Cmnty Wkr; Hon Rl; Pres Yth Flsp; 4-H; VP FFA; Bsbl; 4-H Awd;.

PARKER, CAROL; Owendale Gagetown HS; Gagetown, MI; 5/60 Sec Frsh Cls; Sec Jr Cls; Girl Scts; Hon Rl; NHS; Off Ade; Sch Pl; Stg Crw; Rptr Yrbk; Delta Coll; Data Proc.

PARKER, CINDY; Montcalm HS; Rock, WV; Pres Frsh Cls; VP Soph Cls; Cl Rep Jr Cls; Cls Rep Sr Cls; Chrs; Chrh Wkr; Cmnty Wkr; Hon Rl; NHS; Red Cr Ade; Concord Coll.

PARKER, CRAIG; Martinsburg HS; Martinsburg, WV; 40/206 Cmnty Wkr; Hon Rl; Stu Cncl; Boys Clb Am; Capt Bsktbl; Letter Ftbl; Letter Trk; Pres Of Martinsburg Boys Club; Glenville St Coll; Social Work.

PARKER, DAWN; Robert S Rogers HS; Toledo, OH; Pres Sr Cls; Chrh Wkr; Cmnty Wkr; Hon Rl; JA; NHS; Off Ade; College; Bus Admin.

PARKER, DEBRA A; Harrison HS; Harrison, MI; 1/150 Chrs; Chrh Wkr; Hon Rl; 4-H; Pres Spn Clb; French Awd; Composition Awd; Typing Awd; Michigan State Univ; Vet.

PARKER, DOLORES; Mannington HS; Mannington, WV; 2/113 Sal; Hon Rl; NHS; Off Ade; Mth Clb; Cit Awd; DAR Awd; W V Univ; Sec Educ.

PARKER, DOUG; Farmington HS; Farmington Hls, MI; Cmnty Wkr; Letter Bsktbl; Letter Ftbl; Letter Trk; Allison Univ; Math.

PARKER, GARY; Springfield North HS; Springfield, OH; Aud/Vis; Pres JA; Yrbk; Ger Clb; Lat Clb; JA Awd; Officer Of Yr Awd Jr Ach; Exc Awd Jr Ach; Jr Ach Travelship Awd To Ja Natl Convention; College; Business Admin.

PARKER, GARY; New Haven HS; New Haven, IN; Cls Rep Frsh Cls; Debate Tm; Fr Clb; College; Pre Med.

PARKER, GARY; Heritage Christian HS; Noblesville, IN; VP Jr Cls; VP Band; Sch Pl; Stg Crw; Yrbk; Socr; Trk; Christian Coll; Bus Engr.

PARKER, JACQUELYN; Big Rapids HS; Big Rapids, MI; Band; Hon Rl; Bsktbl; IM Sprt; Michigan St Univ; Vet.

PARKER, JAMES; Indianapolis Baptist HS; Indianapolis, IN; Hon Rl; 4-H; Letter Socr; Letter Wrstlng; 4-H Awd;.

PARKER, JAMES R; Marion Harding HS; Marion, OH; 5/494 Hon Rl; Sci Clb; Socr; Univ; Aerospace Engr.

PARKER, JANE; Centerville HS; Centerville, OH; Band; Chrh Wkr; Girl Scts; Eastern Ken Univ; Med Tech.

PARKER, JANE; St Francis De Sales HS; Columbus, OH; Sch Mus; Sch Pl; Stg Crw; Sec Drama Clb; Univ; Drama.

PARKER, JOHN P; Belpre HS; Belpre, OH; Am Leg Boys St; Hon Rl; JA; NHS; Stu Cncl; Boys Clb Am; Fr Clb; Pres Sci Clb; Bsbl; Civitan Youth Leadrshp Confrnc 78; Forensics 78; Ohio St Univ; Poli Sci.

PARKER, JULIE; Indianapolis Baptist HS; Indianapolis, IN; 3/41 Sec Jr Cls; Chrs; Chrh Wkr; Hon Rl; Pol Wkr; Ed Yrbk; Chrldng; Pensacola Christian Coll; Elem Ed.

PARKER, KIMBERLY; Immaculata HS; Detroit, MI; Chrh Wkr; Girl Scts; Hon Rl; NHS; Sct Actv; Yth Flsp; Lat Clb; Bsktbl; Mgrs; Cit Awd; Mich State; Bus.

PARKER, KIRK; Central HS; Grand Rapids, MI; Chrh Wkr; Cmnty Wkr; Hon Rl; Rptr Yrbk; Key Clb; Lat Clb; Ftbl; St Stephens Principals Awd 76; Univ Of Michigan; Med.

PARKER, LAURA; Rensselaer Central HS; Rensselaer, IN; Chrh Wkr; Hon Rl; Treas Yth Flsp; Spn Clb; Univ; Comp Engr.

PARKER, LAURA; Rutherford B Hayes HS; Delawre, OH; AFS; 4-H; Spn Clb; Bsktbl; Trk; 4-H Awd; Univ; Fshn Mdse.

PARKER, LAUREN; Anderson HS; Cincinnati, OH; 36/383 Chrs; Chrh Wkr; Cmnty Wkr; Hon Rl; NHS; Off Ade; Sch Mus; Sch Pl; Stu Cncl; Yth Flsp; Whos Who 77; Cross Cnbtry Meritorious Awd 77; Hon Prog 4th Yr 75 79; Univ Of Cincinnati; Cmrcl Art.

PARKER, LISA; Jesup W Scott HS; Toledo, OH; 13/272 Cls Rep Frsh Cls; Sec Soph Cls; Sec Jr Cls; Sec Sr Cls; Band; VP Chrs; FCA; Hon Rl; VP Yth Flsp; Treas Fr Clb;.

PARKER, LISA; John Adams HS; So Bend, IN; 3/395 Am Leg Aux Girls St; Band; Lit Mag; NHS; Quill & Scroll; Ed Sch Nwsp; Rptr Sch Nwsp; Sch Nwsp; College; English Tchr.

PARKER, LISA; Fruitport HS; Muskegon, MI; 54/281 Chrh Wkr; Hon Rl; NHS; Muskegon Bus Coll; Clerical Data Rec.

PARKER, LORI; Warsaw Community HS; Claypool, IN; 16/394 Band; Hon Rl; Hosp Ade; Jr NHS; Trk; Parkview Schl Of Nursing; Nursing.

PARKER, LUTRICIA; Linden HS; Linden, MI; 13/165 Cls Rep Frsh Cls; Cls Rep Soph Cls; Pres Jr Cls; Pres Sr Cls; Am Leg Aux Girls St; Hosp Ade; Off Ade; Sch Pl; Stu Cncl; Rptr Yrbk; Univ Of Mich; Chem Engr.

PARKER, MARSHALL; Bishop Gallagher HS; St Clr Shrs, MI; Cls Rep Frsh Cls; Cls Rep Soph Cls; Am Leg Boys St; Cmnty Wkr; FCA; Hon Rl; Letter Ftbl; Letter Swmmng; IM Sprt; Univ Pacific; Mech Engr.

PARKER, MELISSA; Herbert Hoover HS; Elkview, WV; Band; Hon Rl; Hosp Ade; Pep Clb; Chrldng; GAA; West Virginia Univ; Phys Therapy.

PARKER, MIKE; Hammond Baptist HS; Hammond, IN; Cls Rep Soph Cls; Cl Rep Jr Cls; Hon Rl; Sprt Ed Yrbk; Yrbk; Bsbl; Bsktbl; Ftbl; Wrstlng; College.

PARKER, NANCY; Shadyside HS; Shadyside, OH; 4/100 Band; Debate Tm; Hon Rl; NHS; Orch; Sch Mus; Sch Pl; Y-Teens; Rptr Yrbk; Sec Drama Clb; Univ Of Akron; Medical Technology.

PARKER, PAULA; Stanton HS; Toronto, OH; 1/70 Band; Chrs; Drm Mjrt; Hon Rl; NHS; Sch Mus; Stu Cncl; Fr Clb; Pep Clb; Letter Bsktbl; Choir & Girls Glee Clb; Cert Of Outstndng Ach In Academics; College; Pharmacy.

PARKER, PEG; Tippecanoe Valley HS; Claypool, IN; 6/158 Sec Soph Cls; Hon Rl; NHS; Off Ade; 4-H; FTA; Pom Pon; Natl Hnr Soc Treasurer; Future Educators In Action Pres;.

PARKER, PEGGY; Waterford Kettering HS; Drayton Plains, MI; Band; Chrh Wkr; Girl Scts; Hon Rl; Hosp Ade; NHS; Off Ade; Drama Clb; Pep Clb; PPFtbl; Wayne St Univ; RN.

PARKER, ROBERT; Prairie Hts HS; Hudson, IN; 16/145 Cls Rep Frsh Cls; Pres Soph Cls; Pres Jr Cls; Pres Sr Cls; FCA; Hon Rl; Jr NHS; NHS; Stu Cncl; Letter Ftbl; Univ; Math.

PARKER, ROSELEE; West Union HS; W Union, OH; Chrs; Chrh Wkr; Cmnty Wkr; Hon Rl; Pol Wkr; Yth Flsp; Eng Clb; 4-H; Fr Clb; 4-H Awd; Piano Awd 76; Sheep Awds In Open Class 77; French Club Awd; Ohio St Univ; Tchr.

PARKER, SANDRA K; Washington HS; Washington, IN; Band; Boy Scts; Chrs; Chrh Wkr; Cmnty Wkr; Drm Mjrt; Girl Scts; Hon Rl; Jr NHS; PAVAS; NEDT Schlstc Achv 1977; Pres Washgtn Catholics Red Cross Progr 1977; VP Explorers Pres Assn Area 4 1978; Indiana Univ; Engr.

PARKER, SUSAN G; Talawanda HS; Oxford, OH; 5/313 AFS; Hon Rl; NHS; Sec Fr Clb; Letter Mgrs; Natl Merit SF; College; Poli Sci.

PARKER, SUZY; Margaretta HS; Castalla, OH; 6/174 Am Leg Aux Girls St; Hon Rl; NHS; Off Ade; Quill & Scroll; Sch Nwsp; Letter Bsktbl; Scr Kpr; Volleyball Letter; Outstndng Jr Of MHS 79; Univ; Bus.

PARKER, TERRANCE L; Valley HS; Montgomery, WV; 15/127 Am Leg Boys St; Boy Scts; Chrh Wkr; Hon Rl; NHS; Sprt Ed Yrbk; Letter Bsbl; Letter Ftbl; IM Sprt; Am Leg Awd; West Virginia Tech Univ; Law.

PARKER, TERRI; Elwood Cmnty HS; Elwood, IN; 1/186 Cls Rep Soph Cls; Cl Rep Jr Cls; Cls Rep Sr Cls; Val; Am Leg Aux Girls St; Hon Rl; Jr NHS; Treas NHS; Sch Pl; Stu Cncl; Purdue Univ; Spanish.

PARKER, TIMOTHY T; Kalamazoo Cntrl HS; Kalamazoo, MI; 1/464 Dr Loy Norris Mem Awd; F W & Elsie L Heyle Sci Schlrshp; Kalamazoo Coll; Chem.

PARKINS, STEVE; Stonewall Jackson HS; Charleston, WV; 3/300 Am Leg Boys St; Boy Scts; Chrh Wkr; Cmnty Wkr; Hon Rl; Jr NHS; NHS; Sct Actv; Mth Clb; Spn Clb; Math Field Day Prtcptn 76; ACS Chem Test 79; Gifted Prog Prtcpnt 79; Univ Of Cincinnati; Acctg.

PARKINSON, ANNE E; Buckeye West HS; Adena, OH; 4/80 Pres Soph Cls; Pres Jr Cls; Band; Hon Rl; NHS; Sch Pl; Drama Clb; 4-H; FHA; FTA; Ohio State Univ; Vet Sci.

PARKINSON, SHEILA; Gaylord HS; Gaylord, MI; Chrs; NHS; Stu Cncl; Letter Bsbl; Letter Bsktbl; Coll; Educ.

PARKS, ALICE; Horace Mann HS; Gary, IN; Chrs; Chrh Wkr; Hon Rl; JA; Jr NHS; MMM; Sch Mus; Sch Pl; Drama Clb; Chrldng; Bloomington Univ; Actress.

PARKS, ANNETTE; West Side Sr HS; Gary, IN; Sec Sr Cls; Cmnty Wkr; Debate Tm; Hon Rl; Natl Forn Lg; NHS; Drama Clb; Univ Of Toledo; Criminal Law.

PARKS, DEANNA; Zionsville Community HS; Zionsville, IN; 16/149 VP Frsh Cls; Sec Jr Cls; Trs Sr Cls; Band; Chmn Drl Tm; Hon Rl; NHS; Ind Univ; Opto Tech.

PARKS, DERRICK; East Technical HS; Cleveland, OH; 3/302 Hon Rl; Jr NHS; NHS; Stu Cncl; Rptr Sch Nwsp; FDA; Key Clb; Mth Clb; Oberlin College; Pre Med.

PARKS, ELIZABETH D; Ironton HS; Ironton, OH; 12/250 Chrh Wkr; Girl Scts; Hon Rl; Hosp Ade; JA; Off Ade; Sct Actv; Yth Flsp; VP Spn Clb; Univ Of Cincinnati; Nursing.

PARKS, GAIL; Norwood HS; Norwood, OH; Chrs; Hon Rl; Jr NHS; Stu Cncl; Pep Clb; Trk; Spanish Natl Honor Soc; Awd For Best Stu Council Rep; College; Vet.

PARKS, GARY; Groveport Madison Sr HS; Columbus, OH; Cls Rep Frsh Cls; Band; FCA; Hon Rl; JA; Mod UN; Orch; Sch Mus; Sch Pl; Stg Crw; Engr.

PARKS, GLENN; Calumet HS; Laurium, MI; 29/143 Hon Rl; NHS; Letter Crs Cntry; Hockey; Trk; Michigan Tech Univ; Elec Engr.

PARKS, LYNNETTE; Ontario HS; Mansfield, OH; 15/205 Hon Rl; NHS; Off Ade; Chrldng; Sec Sr Cls; Homecoming Attendant; Honors Banquet Participant; Bowling Green St Univ.

PARKS, MARY; Edwardsburg HS; Edwardsburg, MI; Band; Cmnty Wkr; Drl Tm; Girl Scts; Hon Rl; Off Ade; Sch Pl; Yth Flsp; Y-Teens; Ed Sch Nwsp; S W Michigan Coll; Nursing.

PARKS, MELANIE; John Glenn Sr HS; New Concord, OH; 3/193 Sec Frsh Cls; VP Soph Cls; VP Jr Cls; Band; Hon Rl; NHS; Stu Cncl; Yth Flsp; Drama Clb; 4-H; Ohio St Univ; Agri.

PARKS, PAM; Huntington East HS; Huntington, WV; Cls Rep Frsh Cls; Cls Rep Soph Cls; Cl Rep Jr Cls; Cls Rep Sr Cls; Band; Cmp Fr Grls; Chrs; Drm Mjrt; Hon Rl; Hosp Ade; Music Awd 1976; Science Awd 1977; Marshall Univ; Med Sec.

PARKS, PATRICIA; Centennial HS; Columbus, OH; 1/217 Val; Am Leg Aux Girls St; Sec Chrs; Chrh Wkr; Pres NHS; VP Stu Cncl; Yth Flsp; Spn Clb; Miami Univ; Med.

PARKS, PRINCESS; Martin Luther King Jr Sr HS; Detroit, MI; Sec Sr Cls; Hon Rl; JA; Lbry Ade; DECA; Univ Of Detroit; Doctor.

PARKS, RHONDA; West Jefferson HS; W Jefferson, OH; Sec Frsh Cls; Sec Soph Cls; Chrs; Chrh Wkr; Hon Rl; Hosp Ade; Stu Cncl; Yth Flsp; Gym; Letter Chrldng; All Ohio Yth Chr 79; Cincinnati Univ; Nursing.

PARKS, SHERI; Mayfield HS; Highland Hts, OH; Chrs; Girl Scts; Hon Rl; Mod UN; Sct Actv; Drama Clb; Pep Clb; Swmmng; Tmr; Univ.

PARLETTE, TALLI; Divine Child HS; Dearborn Ht, MI; Chrs; Hosp Ade; Red Cr Ade; Sch Mus; Sch Pl; FNA; Pep Clb; Capt Chrldng; Pom Pon; College; Nurse.

PARLIN, ANITA; Athens HS; Athens, MI; Cls Rep Frsh Cls; Trs Jr Cls; Band; Cmp Fr Grls; Debate Tm; Hon Rl; Hosp Ade; Jr NHS; NHS; Off Ade; College; Flight Attendent.

PARLIN, CAROL; Athens HS; Athens, MI; 1/89 Band; Hon Rl; NHS; Quill & Scroll; Sch Pl; Stu Cncl; Ed Yrbk; VP Pep Clb; DAR Awd; College; Law.

PARLIN, DEBORAH; Colon HS; Leonidas, MI; 10/68 Trs Sr Cls; Band; Chrh Wkr; Hon Rl; NHS; Sch Mus; Sch Pl; Stg Crw; Fr Clb; Finlst In ACT Test 78; Awd By Schl For 4 Yr Of Coll Prep Math 76 79; Awd 5 Yrs Coll Prepn Sci 75 79; Michigan St Univ; Bus Mgmt.

PARMALEE, SANDRA; Henry Ford Ii HS; Stelring Hts, MI; Capt Swmmng; Mgrs; Scr Kpr; Tmr; College; Acctg.

PARMELEE, JULIE; Pine River Jr Sr HS; Le Roy, MI; Trs Frsh Cls; VP Soph Cls; Band; Hon Rl; NHS; Off Ade; Stu Cncl; Bsbl; Bsktbl; Trk; Central Mich Univ; Acctg.

PARMENTER, KYLE; Bloomington South HS; Bloomington, IN; Aud/Vis; Chrs; JA; Scr Kpr; Univ Of Col; Radio & Tv.

PARMENTER, RICK; Shawnee HS; Lima, OH; Band; Hon Rl; Univ Of Cincinnati; Bus Admin.

PARMENTER, SUSAN L; Cadillac Sr HS; Cadillac, MI; Cls Rep Soph Cls; Cl Rep Jr Cls; Chrs; Girl Scts; Hon Rl; NHS; Sch Mus; Stu Cncl; Chrldng; PPFtbl; Coll.

PARNELL, JOE; Cambridge HS; Cambridge, OH; 1/250 VP Frsh Cls; Pres Soph Cls; Cl Rep Jr Cls; Chrh Wkr; Hon Rl; NHS; Stu Cncl; Yth Flsp; Key Clb; Pep Clb; Vanderbuilt Univ; Engr.

PARNELL, MARY; Berkley HS; Berkley, MI; Chrh Wkr; Cmnty Wkr; Girl Scts; Hon Rl; NHS; Univ; Sci.

PARO, ELAINE; Barberton HS; Barberton, OH; 20/480 Cls Rep Sr Cls; Pres AFS; Chrs; Chrh Wkr; Hon Rl; JA; Jr NHS; NHS; Sch Mus; Stu Cncl; Buckey Girls St Altrnt 79; Champs In Vllybl 79; Oh Univ Jrnlsm Workshop 79; Univ; Med.

PAROLINE, PAMELA S; Martins Ferry HS; Martins Ferry, OH; Cls Rep Frsh Cls; Band; Chrs; Chrh Wkr; Hon Rl; Yth Flsp; Y-Teens; Ten; GAA; Bus Schl; Fashion Mdse.

PARR, JAMIE; Chaminade Julienne HS; Dayton, OH; Band; Hon Rl; PPFtbl; Ohio St Univ; Bus.

PARR, JULIE; Leslie HS; Leslie, MI; Cls Rep Sr Cls; Am Leg Aux Girls St; Girl Scts; Stu Cncl; Pep Clb; Letter Trk; Letter Chrldng; Lansing Comm College; Commericalart.

PARR, MARGO; Northrop HS; Ft Wayne, IN; 237/589 Chrs; Girl Scts; Hon Rl; Hosp Ade; Red Cr Ade; Rptr Yrbk; Sch Nwsp; FSA; Cit Awd; IUPU; X Ray Tech.

PARR, MICHAEL; Benton Harbor HS; Benton Hbr, MI; Chrh Wkr; Hon Rl; JA; JA Awd; Univ; Env Engr.

PARR, PATRICIA; Fenton HS; Fenton, MI; Fr Clb; Ferris State; Zoology.

PARR, REBECCA; Marysville HS; Marysville, OH; Band; Chrh Wkr; Hon Rl; Hosp Ade; Sch Mus; Stu Cncl; Sec 4-H; Lat Clb; 4-H Awd; Outdoor Club 78 79; Univ; Bio.

PARRETT, JULIA; Miami Trace HS; Washington Ch, OH; AFS; Hon Rl; Sch Pl; Yth Flsp; Rptr Yrbk; Sch Nwsp; Drama Clb; 4-H; FTA; Pep Clb; College; Social Work.

PARRETT, KARI; Milan HS; Milan, MI; Band; Chrh Wkr; Hon Rl; Hosp Ade; Sch Pl; Stg Crw; Stu Cncl; Yth Flsp; Drama Clb; VICA; Mi Compttv Schlshp Awd 78; Whos Who In Amer HS 77; Eastern Michigan Univ; Comp Systems.

PARRILL, SCOTT; Heath HS; Heath, OH; Cls Rep Frsh Cls; Hon Rl; Sch Pl; Stu Cncl; Drama Clb; Glf; Letter Trk; Ohio St Univ.

PARRIS, MELAINE; Frankfort HS; Frankfort, IN; Am Leg Aux Girls St; Chrs; Chrh Wkr; Drl Tm; NHS; Sch Mus; Sch Pl; Yth Flsp; Chmn Pom Pon; College; Airline Stewardess.

PARRIS, TERRY; Frankfort Sr HS; Frankfort, IN; 130/265 Sch Mus; Sch Pl; Drama Clb; Swmmng; College.

PARRISH, CHERYL K; Fairmont W HS; Kettering, OH; 44/471 Cl Rep Jr Cls; Drl Tm; Hon Rl; Sch Pl; Yth Flsp; Fr Clb; Capt Chrldng; Ohio Test Of Schlstc Achvmnt Hnrble Mention In State; Schlrshp To Camp Miniwanca From Pilots Club; College; Med Tech.

PARRISH, CYNTHIA; Mannington HS; Mannington, WV; 1/100 Trs Frsh Cls; Cls Rep Frsh Cls; Cls Rep Soph Cls; Sec Jr Cls; Am Leg Aux Girls St; Treas Stu Cncl; Treas Fr Clb; Chrldng; GAA; Mat Maids; Natl French Hnr Soc 79; Cystic Fibrosis Serv Awd 79; Stu Council Summer Workshp & St Convention 78; West Virginia Univ; Dent Hygnst.

PARRISH, DINA; Bryan HS; Bryan, OH; 16/188 Hon Rl; NHS; Ed Yrbk; Lat Clb; Pep Clb; Sci Clb; Letter Trk; Bowling Green State Univ; Bus Admin.

PARRISH, J C; Bryan HS; Bryan, OH; 5/195 Am Leg Boys St; Chrh Wkr; Hon Rl; NHS; Rptr Sch Nwsp; Lat Clb; Bsbl; Glf; Wrstlng; IM Sprt; Bowling Green Univ; Eng.

PARRISH, KATHLEEN; Hemlock HS; Saginaw, MI; Chrs; Hon Rl; Pep Clb; St Of Mi Comp Schlrshp 79; Basic Ed Opportunity Grant 79; Central Michigan Univ; Acctg.

PARRISH, KATHRINE; Loudonville HS; Loudonville, OH; 6/131 Band; Chrs; Hon Rl; NHS; Stg Crw; Sch Nwsp; 4-H; FTA; 4-H Awd; Univ Of Dayton; Scndry Educ.

PARRISH, MARGARET; Tippecanoe HS; Tipp City, OH; 10/190 Cls Rep Soph Cls; VP Jr Cls; Hon Rl; Hosp Ade; NHS; Stu Cncl; FHA; Letter Trk; Letter Chrldng; GAA; College.

PARRISH, MARK; Utica HS; Utica, MI; Hon Rl; Michigan St Univ; Mech Engr.

PARRISH, RORY; Archbishop Alter HS; Dayton, OH; 128/277 Boy Scts; Chrh Wkr; Cmnty Wkr; Pol Wkr; Yth Flsp; Beta Clb; Key Clb; IM Sprt; Cit Awd; Religion Achievmnt Awd; Stu Sci Program Univ Of Dayton; Ohio St Univ; Astronautical Engr.

PARRISH, THOMAS; Elk Garden HS; Elk Garden, WV; 4/34 Boy Scts; Chrh Wkr; Hon Rl; Stg Crw; Bsktbl; Cit Awd; Potomac State College.

PARRISH, VIDA; Lee HS; Wyoming, MI; 8/70 Pres Jr Cls; Trs Sr Cls; Treas Band; Hon Rl; Sec NHS; Pres Spn Clb; Chrldng; PPFtbl; Pres Leadrshp Schlrshp 79; St Comp Schlrshp 79; Differential Grant 79; Basic Educ Opportnty Grant 79; Aquinas Coll; Psych.

PARROTT, ALLEN; Hauser HS; Hartsville, IN; 17/85 Hon Rl; Letter Crs Cntry; Letter Trk; College; Bus Admin.

PARROTT, EDWARD; John Marshall HS; Indianapolis, IN; 97/632 Cls Rep Frsh Cls; Cls Rep Soph Cls; Cl Rep Jr Cls; Hon Rl; Off Ade; Stu Cncl; Sci Clb; College; Acctg.

PARROTT, ELIZABETH; Olivet HS; Olivet, MI; 1/80 Band; Girl Scts; Hon Rl; NHS; Ed Sch Nwsp; Rptr Sch Nwsp; 4-H; Letter Bsktbl; Letter Trk; Chrldng; Mbr Of The Natl Hon Soc 79; Olivet Coll; Bio.

PARROTT, JOETTE; Graham HS; St Paris, OH; Chrs; Chrh Wkr; Sch Mus; Sch Pl; Yth Flsp; Yrbk; Drama Clb; FHA; Chrldng; Miami Univ; Marketing.

PARROTT, KIMBERLY; Benton Harbor HS; Benton Hbr, MI; Girl Scts; Hosp Ade; Red Cr Ade; Sct Actv; Yth Flsp; Natl Merit Ltr; Coll; Bio.

PARROTT, TERRY; Inland Lakes HS; Indian River, MI; 12/73 Cls Rep Frsh Cls; VP Soph Cls; Band; Hon Rl; Stu Cncl; Rptr Yrbk; Pres Pep Clb; Trk; Chrldng; Natl Merit Schl; Schslp From Lake Superior St Coll 79; Lake Superior St Coll; Poli Sci.

PARRY, JAN; Vassar HS; Vassar, MI; Chrs; Debate Tm; Girl Scts; Hon Rl; Sch Pl; Yth Flsp; Sch Nwsp;.

PARSCH, MARY J; Imlay City HS; Imlay City, MI; Chrs; Chrh Wkr; Hon Rl; Sch Mus; Sct Actv; 4-H; 4-H Awd; College; Fashion Industry.

PARSDOSKI, ROSEANNE; Bishop Foley HS; Sterling Hts, MI; Hon Rl; Mod UN; Rptr Yrbk; Yrbk; Ed Yrbk; Spn Clb; PPFtbl; Univ; Soc Work.

PARSELL, PATRICIA; Peck Community HS; Peck, MI; 3/62 Trs Jr Cls; Am Leg Aux Girls St; Band; Girl Scts; Hon Rl; Pres NHS; Pep Clb; Letter Bsktbl; Letter Trk; Coach Actv; English Awd; Math Awd; Lake Superior State Univ; Nursing.

PARSHALL, DIANA; Niles Mc Kinley HS; Niles, OH; 72/370 Sec Band; Chrs; Drl Tm; Hon Rl; Treas NHS; Sch Mus; Sch Pl; VP Drama Clb; Pom Pon; Twrlr; Hon Thespian Soc; Youngstown St Univ; Bus Mrktng.

PARSLEY, ANDREA; Clay City HS; Clay City, IN; Band; NHS; 4-H; Fr Clb; FHA; GAA;.

PARSLEY, LAURA; South Spencer HS; Rockport, IN; 18/152 Band; Hon Rl; Hosp Ade; Sch Mus; Sch Pl; Capt Swmmng; Kiwan Awd; Deaconess Nursing Schl; RN.

PARSLEY, ROBIN E; Brown County HS; Nashville, IN; 4/200 Am Leg Aux Girls St; Hon Rl; Lbry Ade; NHS; Stg Crw; Sch Nwsp; Drama Clb; 4-H; Fr Clb; Pep Clb; Univ; Nuclear Engr.

PARSON, BRENDA; Hundred HS; Hundred, WV; Hon Rl; FHA; Pep Clb; Bus Schl; Bus.

PARSON, REGINA; East Sr HS; Akron, OH; Chrs; Sch Pl; Yrbk; Pep Clb; Letter Gym; Letter Trk; Chrldng; Akron Univ; Sec.

PARSONS, BRENDA; Logan Sr HS; Holden, WV; 8/278 Sec Frsh Cls; Hon Rl; JA; Jr NHS; NHS; FBLA; Cit Awd;.

PARSONS, GARY; Loogootee HS; Loogootee, IN; 40/160 Aud/Vis; Boy Scts; FCA; Hon Rl; JA; Lbry Ade; Pol Wkr; Sch Pl; Sct Actv; Rptr Sch Nwsp; Purdue Univ; Engr.

PARSONS, JANET; Hedgesville HS; Hedgesville, WV; 2/225 Band; Chrh Wkr; Hon Rl; VP NHS; Sec Stu Cncl; VP Y-Teens; VP FTA; DAR Awd; Univ.

PARSONS, JIM; Whitehall HS; Columbus, OH; Boy Scts; Chrs; Hon Rl; Sch Mus; Sch Pl; Stg Crw; Spn Clb; Socr; IM Sprt; Scr Kpr; Ohio St Univ; Music.

PARSONS, JULIE; Cambridge HS; Cambridge, OH; Cls Rep Frsh Cls; Cls Rep Soph Cls; Cl Rep Jr Cls; Hon Rl; Stu Cncl; Yth Flsp; Pep Clb; Mat Maids; Muskingum Coll; Child Psych.

PARSONS, KATHRYN M; Bishop Chatard HS; Indianapolis, IN; 2/200 Band; Girl Scts; Hon Rl; Sch Pl; Sct Actv; Stu Cncl; 4-H; IM Sprt; Purdue Univ; Math.

PARSONS, KATHY; Roosevelt Wilson HS; Nutter Fort, WV; 2/122 Pres Frsh Cls; Pres Soph Cls; Cl Rep Jr Cls; Sal; Am Leg Aux Girls St; Hon Rl; Jr NHS; Pres NHS; Sch Pl; Treas Stu Cncl; Fairmont St Coll.

PARSONS, LEANNA; Independence HS; Macar thur, WV; Hon Rl; Spn Clb; College; Math.

PARSONS, LINDA; Danville Community HS; Danville, IN; Band; Pres Girl Scts; Sec Lbry Ade; Sct Actv; Fr Clb; Sec FHA; Pep Clb; Stu Lib Awd 79; IUPUI; Phys Ther.

PARSONS, MELISSA; Federal Hocking HS; Guysville, OH; Band; Drm Mjrt; Girl Scts; Off Ade; Spn Clb; Hocking Tech; Bus Admin.

PARSONS, MELODY; North Daviess HS; Odon, IN; Band; Chrs; Hon Rl; Sch Mus; Pep Clb; Spn Clb; GAA; Vlybl Varsity Letter; Voc Schl; Photog.

PARSONS, MISTY; Zanesville HS; Zanesville, OH; 57/383 Hon Rl; NHS; Rptr Yrbk; Sci Clb; Gym; Ohi Univ.

PARSONS, NEVA; Waverly HS; Lansing, MI; Lbry Ade; Lit Mag; Sch Nwsp; Natl Merit SF; Northern Mic Univ; Psych.

PARSONS, RAY; Penn HS; Mishawaka, IN; Band; Chrs; Chrh Wkr; Hon Rl; Mdrgl; Letter Bsbl; IM Sprt; Bethel College; Baseball.

PARSONS, ROBERTA; Hubbard HS; Hubbard, OH; Band; Chrs; Chrh Wkr; Sch Mus; Stg Crw; Yth Flsp; Pres Pep Clb; IM Sprt; Youngstown St Univ; Nursing.

PARSONS, ROBERT L; University HS; Morgantown, WV; 25/146 Band; Boy Scts; Hon Rl; Lbry Ade; Sch Mus; Sct Actv; Drama Clb; Ger Clb; Sci Clb; IM Sprt; Outstanding Soph Band Mbr; College; Computer Sci.

PARSONS, SANDY; Fremont Ross HS; Fremont, OH; Chrs; Hon Rl; NHS; Yrbk; Spn Clb; Natl Org Of Wmns Schlrshp 79; Whos Who Amng Amer HS Stu 77; Ohio Tests Of Schlstc Achvmnt 76; Bowling Green St Univ; Frgn Lang.

PARSONS, SHERRY; Parkersburg South HS; Parkersburg, WV; Sec Sr Cls; Hon Rl; DECA;.

PARSONS, SUSAN; Magnolia HS; New Martinsvle, WV; 1/200 Hon Rl; VP NHS; Stu Cncl; Ed Yrbk; Sprt Ed Yrbk; Letter Bsktbl; Letter Trk; IM Sprt; Am Leg Awd; Rep To Know Your St Gov Day; Listed Among Amer HS Ath; History Clb; Vlybl Lettered Co Capt; Coll.

PARSONS, TERI; Greenon HS; Enon, OH; 28/280 Chrh Wkr; Hon Rl; NHS; Off Ade; Yth Flsp; 4-H; FHA; Treas FTA; Spn Clb; Trk; Ohio St Univ; Landscape Horticulture.

PARTAIN, DIANA; Bloomfield HS; Bloomfield, IN; Chrs; Chrh Wkr; Lbry Ade; Red Cr Ade; Sch Mus; Sch Pl; Yth Flsp; Drama Clb; Sci Clb; PPFtbl; Univ Of Evansville; Music Therapy.

PARTAIN, RENE; Hanover Central HS; Cedar Lake, IN; 29/137 Hon Rl; Jr NHS; Quill & Scroll; Sch Pl; Ed Yrbk; Pep Clb; Pom Pon; PPFtbl; College.

PARTELENO, PATRICIA; Struthers HS; Struthers, OH; 126 Pres Sr Cls; Stu Cncl; Sprt Ed Sch Nwsp; Rptr Sch Nwsp; Spn Clb; Letter Bsktbl; Letter Glf; Youngstowns St Univ; Sports Admin.

PARTICKA, MELANIE; Cass City HS; Ubly, MI; 1/170 Band; Chrh Wkr; Hon Rl; Jr NHS; NHS; Sch Mus; Sec 4-H; Spn Clb; 4-H Awd; Michigan St Univ; Med.

PARTIN, GARY; Romulus HS; Romulus, MI; Chrh Wkr; Cmnty Wkr; Spn Clb; VICA; IM Sprt; Cit Awd; Voc Ind Clubs Of Amer Awd 79; Eastern Michigan Univ; Med.

PARTOZOTI, ELIZABETH; North Judson San Pierre HS; Knox, IN; 27/144 Girl Scts; 4-H; Mth Clb; Spn Clb; PPFtbl; Knox Beauty Coll; Cosmtlgy Tchr.

PARTRIDGE, DALE; Clio HS; Clio, MI; 12/394 Chrh Wkr; Hon Rl; NHS; Yth Flsp; Spn Clb; VFW Awd; Univ Of Michigan; Archt Design.

PARTYKA, JEFF; Lake Central HS; Schererville, IN; Chrs; Hon Rl; Sch Mus; Stg Crw; Northern Mich Univ; Wild Life Mang.

PASANEN, WENDY; Harbor HS; Ashtabula, OH; 34/173 AFS; Capt Drl Tm; JA; Off Ade; Stu Cncl; Rptr Yrbk; Pep Clb; Kent St Univ; Educ.

PASCHE, THOMAS; Kearsley HS; Burton, MI; 13/378 Am Leg Boys St; Band; Hon Rl; Natl Forn Lg; Pres NHS; Pres Sct Actv; Letter Bsbl; Capt Ftbl; DAR Awd; Lion Awd; St Of Mi Compttv Schlshp Outstndng Achvmnt 79; Whos Who Among Amer HS Stdnts 77; All Confrcn Ftbl Team 79; Genrl Motors Inst; Engr.

PASCO, BEVERLY; Buckeye North HS; Smithfield, OH; 20/106 Band; Hon Rl; NHS; VP OEA; Pep Clb; PPFtbl;.

PASCOE, DAVID; John F Kennedy HS; Taylor, MI; VP Soph Cls; VP Jr Cls; Am Leg Boys St; Hon Rl; Y-Teens; Rptr Sch Nwsp;.

PASCUAL, FELINO A; Clarenceville HS; Farmington, MI; Cls Rep Soph Cls; Band; Hon Rl; Sci Clb; Cit Awd; Natl Merit Schl; Focus Hope Leadrshp Progr 77; Wayne St Univ; Physcn.

PASCUAL, HOLLY; Mt Vernon Acad; Elyria, OH; Cls Rep Frsh Cls; Band; Chrs; Hon Rl; Off Ade; Sch Mus; Stu Cncl; Yth Flsp; Letter Bsktbl; Andrews Univ; Optomistrist.

PASHKE JR, K; Catholic Central HS; Mingo Jct, OH; 51/204 Cls Rep Soph Cls; Cl Rep Jr Cls; Hon Rl; Stu Cncl; Spn Clb; College; Med Lab Tech.

PASK, JOHN; John Adams HS; So Bend, IN; Boy Scts; Hon Rl; Sct Actv; College; Math.

PASKELL, ANDREW; Bishop Watterson HS; Columbus, OH; Stg Crw; Stu Cncl; Letter Bsbl; Ohi St Univ; Engr.

PASLEY, CHARLOTTE; Hartford HS; Watervliet, MI; Lbry Ade; Univ; Airline Hostess.

PASLEY, KIM; Cody HS; Detroit, MI; Chrs; Chrh Wkr; Girl Scts; Hon Rl; Off Ade; Sch Mus; Pom Pon; Cit Awd; Wayne Community College; Pedia-Trici.

PASMAN, JERRY W; Harper Creek HS; Battle Creek, MI; Band; Orch; Sch Mus; Sch Nwsp; Natl Merit Ltr; Mi Youth Sym 1st Chari Bass 1978; Schlr Interlochen All State Orch 1974; Schlr Blue Laek Fine Arts 1976 Int; Univ; Music.

PASPEK, ANDREA; St Augustine Academy; Cleveland, OH; Girl Scts; NHS; Orch; Sch Mus; Fr Clb; Key Clb; VP JA Awd; Opt Clb Awd; Dale Carnegie Human Reltns Awd & Prepared Spch Champ 78; N E Ohio Sci Fair 1st Pl Chem Div 78; John Carroll Univ; Acctg.

PASQUALE, ALICIA; North HS; Willoughby, OH; 24/706 Am Leg Aux Girls St; Chrs; Chrh Wkr; Hon Rl; Mod UN; NHS; Spn Clb; Christian Church Of Ohio United Nations Seminar For Yth 79; Jr Fortnightly Musical Club; Univ; Med Tech.

PASQUALE, TERRY; Eastwood HS; Luckey, OH; Pres Soph Cls; Band; FCA; Hon Rl; Orch; Key Clb; Crs Cntry; Trk; IM Sprt; Owens Tech Coll; Hotel Mgmt.

PASQUALONE, RENEE; Geneva HS; Geneva, OH; 63/250 Cls Rep Frsh Cls; Cls Rep Soph Cls: Cl Rep Jr Cls; VP Sr Cls; AFS; Chrs; Off Ade; Sch Mus; Sch Pl; Yth Flsp; Chrldng Awds 75 79; Bst Actress 79; Ohio St Univ; Phys Ther.

PASSANTE, EDWARD; Padua Franciscian HS; Seven Hills, OH; 48/297 Cls Rep Frsh Cls; Cls Rep Soph Cls; Cl Rep Jr Cls; Chrh Wkr; Hon Rl; Glf; IM Sprt;.

PASSKIEWICZ, BRIAN; St Marys Prep; Kihei Maui, HI; 1/25 Hon Rl; NHS; Rptr Sch Nwsp; Socr; Mgrs; Tmr; Maui Cmnty Coll; Pre Med.

PASSKIEWICZ, BRIAN; St Marys Preparatory HS; Kihei Maui, HI; 1/25 Hon Rl; NHS; Rptr Sch Nwsp; Socr; Mgrs; Maui Cmnty Coll; Pre Med.

PASSKIEWICZ, JOE; Our Lady Of Lakes HS; Pontiac, MI; VP Soph Cls; Hon Rl; Fr Clb; Ftbl; IM Sprt; Central Michigan Univ; Busns Admin.

PASTERNAK, JACQUELINE; Mother Of Mercy HS; Cincinnati, OH; 3/230 Cmp Fr Grls; Hon Rl; NHS; Stg Crw; Fr Clb; Univ; Comp Sci.

PASTOR, CHRISTINA; Newbury HS; Newbury, OH; Pres Frsh Cls; Cls Rep Frsh Cls; Cl Rep Jr Cls; Cls Rep Sr Cls; Band; Chrs; Hon Rl; Sch Pl; Stu Cncl; 4-H; Univ Of Boston; Medicine.

PASTOR, JEFFREY; Malabar HS; Mansfield, OH; Stu Cncl; Bsbl; Univ; Aviation.

PASTOR, JIM; Bishop Noll Inst; Whiting, IN; 57/381 Hon Rl; Mth Clb; Socr; College; Engr.

PASTRE, RENEE; Buckeye North HS; Smithfield, OH; Band; Chrs; Drm Mjrt; Hon Rl; Off Ade; Rptr Yrbk; Pres Pep Clb; Spn Clb; Chrldng; Model Of The Yr 74; Candidate For Miss Teen Ohio 78; Aurora Princess 77; Univ; Spch & Hrng Ther.

PATAKY, GINGER K; Houghton Lake HS; Houghton Lk, MI; Letter Band; Rptr Yrbk; Rptr Sch Nwsp; Twrlr; Coll; Social Work.

PATCH, DAVID; Hilliard HS; Amlin, OH; 80/400 Cls Rep Frsh Cls; Aud/Vis; Chrs; Chrh Wkr; Hon Rl; Jr NHS; Mdrgl; Stg Crw; Stu Cncl; Yrbk; Perfect Attndnc 68 79; Pres Leadrshp Clb 76; Univ; Law.

PATCHEN, EDUARDO; West Geauga HS; Chesterland, OH; Cls Rep Sr Cls; Chrs; Hon Rl; PAVAS; Sch Mus; Sch Pl; IM Sprt; Schlstc Art Awd 76; Sr Achvmnt Awd For Scoring 5 On AP Tests 78; Pratt Inst Of Art; Fshn Dsgn.

PATCHETT, BECKY; Clinton Central HS; Frankfort, IN; 9/106 Sec Sr Cls; Cls Rep Sr Cls; Pres NHS; Lat Clb; Pep Clb; Sci Clb; Letter Chrldng; Purdue Univ; Gen Mgmt.

PATCHIMRAT, SITTIRAT; Mount Clemens HS; Mount Clemens, MI; Hon Rl; Sch Pl; Wayne St Univ; Physician.

PATE, CHRIS; Madison Plains HS; So Solon, OH; Boy Scts; Cmnty Wkr; Hon Rl; Mod UN; 4-H; Fr Clb; Spn Clb; 4-H Awd; Kiwan Awd; Beloit Univ; Anthropology.

PATE, JAMES; Kent City HS; Kent City, MI; Band; Chrs; Chrh Wkr; Hon Rl; Orch; Sch Mus; Sch Pl; 4-H; Crs Cntry; Letter Trk; 1st Div Medal Trumpet Solo Twice 77; United Electronics Inst; Elec.

PATE, KATHARINE; Monroe Gregg HS; Mooresville, IN; 12/150 Hon Rl; Lbry Ade; Lit Mag; Rptr Sch Nwsp; Spn Clb; Bsktbl; Trk; Univ; Spanish.

PATEL, AMIT; Portage Northern HS; Portage, MI; Ten; Univ Of Southern Cal; Bus.

PATEL, ROHANE; Athens HS; Troy, MI; 10/520 Band; Boy Scts; Hon Rl; NHS; Socr; College; Med.

PATERNI, PAMELA; St Agatha HS; Redford, MI; Cmnty Wkr; Hon Rl; Hosp Ade; College; Engr.

PATERRA, RHONDA; Greenville Sr HS; Greenville, OH; 10/360 Chrs; Hon Rl; NHS; Pres Fr Clb; Sci Clb; Spn Clb; Univ Of Michigan; Aerospace Engr.

PATERSON, SUSANNE; Anchor Bay HS; Dixon, IL; Debate Tm; Hon Rl; Spn Clb; Gym; Natl Merit Schl; Sauk Vly Comm Coll; Spec Ed.

PATHAK, SWATI; Normandy HS; Seven Hls, OH; 30/649 Band; Chrs; Hon Rl; NHS; Sch Pl; Stg Crw; Drama Clb; Lat Clb; Pep Clb; Twrlr;.

PATHIC, LOUANN; Peck HS; Peck, MI; Hon Rl; FHA; Letter Trk;.

PATRICK, ALLISON; New Philadelphia HS; New Phila, OH; Cls Rep Soph Cls; Cl Rep Jr Cls; Am Leg Aux Girls St; Hon Rl; Jr NHS; NHS; Pres Y-Teens; Ed Sch Nwsp; Pep Clb; Letter Ten; Hgh Scorer Awd For Girls Tennis 78; Univ.

PATRICK, CARLA; South Point HS; South Point, OH; 32/160 Band; Hon Rl; Lbry Ade; Off Ade; Yth Flsp; Beta Clb; Pep Clb; Sci Clb; Twrlr; Mas Awd; Huntington Bus College; Key Punch.

PATRICK, DAVE; Jackson Milton HS; Lake Milton, OH; Band; Off Ade; Stu Cncl; Trk; Kent State; Zoologist.

PATRICK, GREGG; Calumet HS; Mohawk, MI; Hon Rl; Bsbl; Hockey; College; Engr.

PATRICK, JOAN; Wheelersburg HS; Sciotsville, OH; Pres Frsh Cls; VP Soph Cls; Chrs; Hon Rl; Stu Cncl; Pep Clb; Spn Clb; Scr Kpr; Coll; Eng.

PATRICK, MICHAELENE; Howland HS; Warren, OH; Cmnty Wkr; Hon Rl; Hosp Ade; Off Ade; Pol Wkr; Y-Teens; Rptr Yrbk; Fr Clb; FNA; Pep Clb; Ohio St Univ; Nursing.

PATRICK, PAMELA J; Immaculata HS; Detroit, MI; Cl Rep Jr Cls; Hon Rl; Jr NHS; NHS; Stu Cncl; Rptr Yrbk; Spn Clb; Natl Merit SF; College; Communications.

PATRICK, RAYMOND; Milton HS; Milton, WV; Boy Scts; Chrs; Chrh Wkr; Hon Rl; NHS; Sch Pl; Boys Clb Am; Bsktbl; Letter Crs Cntry; Ftbl; Marshall Univ.

PATRICK, RICHARD; Vinton County Cnsldtd HS; New Plymouth, OH; 50/160 Rptr Yrbk; Yrbk; Lat Clb; Pep Clb; Trk; Wright State Univ; Fine Arts.

PATRICK, SHEILA; Immaculata HS; Detroit, MI; Cls Rep Soph Cls; Cl Rep Jr Cls; Hon Rl; Jr NHS; NHS; Stu Cncl; Trk; Univ; Fine Arts.

PATRICK, TIMOTHY; Saranac Comm HS; Saranac, MI; Boy Scts; Sprt Ed Sch Nwsp; 4-H; Bsbl; Ftbl; Wrstlng; Grand Valley Coll; Educ.

PATRICK, VIRGINIA; Brighton HS; Brighton, MI; Hon Rl; Sci Clb; Bsktbl; Crs Cntry; Trk; IM Sprt; College; Chem Engr.

PATRONE, TERESA; Mineral Ridge HS; Mineral Ridge, OH; 6/68 Trs Jr Cls; VP Sr Cls; Band; Hon Rl; NHS; Stg Crw; Stu Cncl; Beta Clb; Pep Clb; IM Sprt; Youngstown St Univ.

PATRY, MATT; Cardinal HS; Parkman, OH; Chrh Wkr; Hon Rl; Sch Pl; Capt Bsktbl; College; Comp Engr.

PATTERSON, CASSAUNDRA; Anderson HS; Anderson, IN; 145/415 Band; Sec Chrh Wkr; Debate Tm; Drl Tm; Drm Mjrt; JA; Pep Clb; Cit Awd; Opt Clb Awd; Top Pl Awd In Comp As Prt Of Spch Team 76 79; 500 Shclhp For 1st Pl In In Confrnc Youth Laymer Spch 78; Indiana Univ; Jrnlsm.

PATTERSON, CHRIS; Washington Catholic HS; Washington, IN; 42/64 Hon Rl; Drama Clb; Pep Clb; Chrldng; Pom Pon;.

PATTERSON, CYNTHIA J; Farmington Sr HS; Tustin, CA; Band; Chrs; Hon Rl; NHS; Stu Cncl; Ger Clb; Letter Socr; California St Univ; Forestry.

PATTERSON, DAWNELLE; Jasper HS; Jasper, IN; 70/320 Chrs; Cmnty Wkr; Hon Rl; JA; Sch Mus; Civ Clb; Drama Clb; 4-H; Pep Clb; JA Awd; Voc Schl; Bus Admin.

PATTERSON, DENISE; Cleveland Ctrl Catholic HS; Cleveland, OH; Cmp Fr Grls; Chrs; Chrh Wkr; Hon Rl; JA; Sch Mus; Yth Flsp; Cit Awd; Med Schl; Med.

PATTERSON, GREGORY; St Francis De Sales HS; Toledo, OH; 94/203 Cls Rep Frsh Cls; Sec Soph Cls; Trs Jr Cls; Hon Rl; Sch Mus; Swmmng; IM Sprt; Dist Champ In Divning 78 & 79; Hon Mnt From All Amer Bd In Diving 79; Univ; Psych.

PATTERSON, HEATHER; Parkersburg HS; Parkersburg, WV; Chrs; Girl Scts; Hon Rl; Yth Flsp; Y-Teens; Bwlng Wv BPA St Champ Family Twosome 76 Mixed Doubles 79; Bwlng Wv BPA Runner Up Team Champ 79; Univ; Law.

PATTERSON, JEFF; Penn HS; Mishawaka, IN; 57/480 Boy Scts; Chrh Wkr; FCA; Hon Rl; Sct Actv; Yth Flsp; 4-H; Purdue.

PATTERSON, JONI; West Holmes HS; Millersburg, OH; 4/190 Am Leg Aux Girls St; Hon Rl; NHS; Sec Stu Cncl; Rptr Yrbk; Rptr Sch Nwsp; VP Spn Clb; IM Sprt; Dnfth Awd; DAR Awd; Holmes Wayne Elec Coop Schlshp 79; Whos Who Among Amer HS Stdnt 77 & 78; HS Spanish I Awd 76; Sci Awd 77; North Cntrl Tech Coll; Rec Supervsr.

PATTERSON, JOSEPH; Dayton Christian HS; Brookville, OH; Boy Scts; Hon Rl; Sct Actv; Yth Flsp; Boys Clb Am; Bsbl; Sinclair Cmnty Coll; Bus Mgmt.

PATTERSON, KELLY S; Southern Wells Jr Sr HS; Keystone, IN; 8/96 Hon Rl; NHS; 4-H; Pep Clb; Letter Bsktbl; Letter Trk; 4-H Awd; Purdue Univ; Vet Med.

PATTERSON, KELVIN; Norwood HS; Norwood, OH; Boy Scts; Hon Rl; Off Ade; Stu Cncl; DECA; Ftbl; Trk; Wrstlng; 1st & 4th Pl DECA St & Dist Comp; 3rd Pl Norwood HS Art Show; Busns Schl; Sales Mgmt.

PATTERSON, LISA; Norwayne HS; Creston, OH; 6/118 Cls Rep Sr Cls; Treas Chrs; Girl Scts; Hon Rl; NHS; Pres Yth Flsp; Pom Pon; Lion Awd; Opt Clb Awd; Malone College; Elem Educ.

PATTERSON, LORI; Marlington HS; Louisville, OH; 47/289 Chrs; Hon Rl; Sprt Ed Sch Nwsp; VICA; Chrldng; IM Sprt; Radio Engr Inc Voc Schl; Radio & T V.

PATTERSON, MARK; North Canton Hoover HS; North Canton, OH; 200/426 FCA; Hon Rl; Stu Cncl; Letter Bsktbl; JC Awd; Univ; Comp Prog.

PATTERSON, MARK; Parchment HS; Kalamazoo, MI; Boy Scts; Chrh Wkr; Hon Rl; Sct Actv; Glf; Western Mic Univ; Elec Engr.

PATTERSON, MARK T; Colonel White HS; Dayton, OH; Cls Rep Frsh Cls; Cl Rep Jr Cls; VP Sr Cls; Am Leg Boys St; Band; Chrh Wkr; Hon Rl; NHS; Sch Pl; Stg Crw; Univ; Urban Studies.

PATTERSON, SCOTT; Wilbur Wright HS; Dayton, OH; 41/213 Band; Hon Rl; Orch; Sch Mus; Wrstlng; Drafting I Awd; Locker Squad; Coll; Elec Engr.

PATTERSON, SUSAN; Heritage Christian HS; Carmel, IN; Band; Socr; Letter Trk; College; Comp Sci.

PATTERSON, SUSAN J; Bluefield HS; Bluefield, WV; 52/385 Band; Hon Rl; Stu Cncl; 4-H; Spn Clb; 4-H Awd; Mercer County Foreign Language Week 2nd Plc Reproduction Drawing; Laurel Leaves 2nd Plc One Act Play; College; Psych.

PATTERSON, SUZANNE; Marquette Sr HS; Marquette, MI; 51/423 Trk; IM Sprt; N Michigan Univ; Phys Ed.

PATTERSON, TERI; St Johns HS; St Johns, MI; Band; Stg Crw; Drama Clb; 4-H; 4-H Awd; Lansing Bus Inst; Acctg.

PATTERSON, TRACY J; Instituto Carlos Gracida HS; Warsaw, IN; AFS; Chrs; Girl Scts; Hon Rl; Sch Pl; Stg Crw; FHA; Pep Clb; Pom Pon; Grace Coll.

PATTISON, TRACY; Wayne Mem HS; Wayne, MI; Cls Rep Frsh Cls; Hon Rl; Stu Cncl; Fr Clb; Swmmng; Trk; Tmr; College.

PATTON, ALISON; Delaware Hayes HS; Delaware, OH; AFS; Hon Rl; Jr NHS; Yth Flsp; 4-H; Fr Clb; Key Clb; Univ; Bio Sci.

PATTON, APRIL; Parkway Local HS; Willshire, OH; Cmp Fr Grls; JA; Pol Wkr; Quill & Scroll; Sprt Ed Sch Nwsp; Pep Clb; Sci Clb; Univ; Clergy.

PATTON, CHRISTINE; Bishop Ready HS; Columbus, OH; 2/147 Sal; Chrh Wkr; Cmnty Wkr; Hon Rl; NHS; Sch Pl; Stu Cncl; Sch Nwsp; Mat Maids; Gov Hon Prg Awd; Xavier Univ; Pre Med.

PATTON, DEBBIE; East Palestine HS; East Palestine, OH; Hst Frsh Cls; Hst Soph Cls; Band; Orch; Sch Nwsp; Bsktbl; Glf; Capt Ten; Outstndng Perfrmnc In Tennis 78; Univ; Phys Educ Tchr.

PATTON, JEFF; Miami Trace HS; Washington, OH; 26/250 Am Leg Boys St; Hon Rl; NHS; Sch Mus; Sch Pl; Stg Crw; Yrbk; Drama Clb; Pres Sci Clb; Univ Of Cincinnati; Aero Engr.

PATTON, LA DONNA; William Henry Harrison HS; Evansville, IN; Chrs; Hosp Ade; JA; Pep Clb; Spn Clb; Cit Awd; SIU; Spanish.

PATTON, LINDA K; Arcadia Local Schl; Arcadia, OH; 6/61 Sec Band; Chrs; Girl Scts; Hon Rl; NHS; Orch; Yth Flsp; Rptr Yrbk; FHA; Bsktbl;.

PATTON, LON; Sidney HS; Sidney, OH; Band; Chrs; Chrh Wkr; Hon Rl; NHS; Stg Crw; Key Clb; Bsktbl; Univ Of Cincinnati; Elec Audio Engr.

PATTON, MIKE; West Washington HS; Campbellsbg, IN; Univ.

PATTON, RODNEY; Shady Spring HS; Shady Spring, WV; 1/228 Chrh Wkr; Letter Debate Tm; FCA; Hon Rl; NHS; Stu Cncl; Pep Clb; Letter Crs Cntry; Letter Glf; Letter Trk; Ambassador To W Va Hugh O Brien Youth Leadership Seminar 1978; Nominee To Wv State Conservation Camp 1977; Univ; Med.

PATTON, RONNIE; Mt Vernon HS; Mt Vernon, IN; Pres FFA; Bsktbl; ISUE; Agri.

PATTON, SALLY; Garfield HS; Akron, OH; 20/400 Cls Rep Soph Cls; Cl Rep Jr Cls; Cls Rep Sr Cls; Chrs; Chrh Wkr; Cmnty Wkr; Debate Tm; Hon Rl; JA; Lit Mag; Bob Jones Univ; Speech.

PATTON, WAYNE; Parkside HS; Jackson, MI; Hon Rl; Swmmng; Mgrs; College; Engr.

PATTULLO, MIKE; Caro HS; Caro, MI; Hon Rl; NHS; Capt Crs Cntry; Trk; Voc Schl.

PATUTO, JEFFREY; Tiffin Columbian HS; Tiffin, OH; Cls Rep Frsh Cls; Hon Rl; Sch Mus; Sprt Ed Yrbk; Spn Clb; Glf; Natl Merit SF; Univ; Chem.

PAUGH, BECKY; Chatard HS; Indianapolis, IN; 5/200 Girl Scts; Hon Rl; Fr Clb; Mat Maids; Univ; Med Tech.

PAUGH, PATRICIA; Hampshire HS; Romney, WV; 36/213 AFS; Chrh Wkr; Cmnty Wkr; Hon Rl; Yth Flsp; Rptr Yrbk; Drama Clb; FBLA; Sheperd Coll; Elem Educ.

PAUGH, SCOTT; Grafton HS; Grafton, WV; 16/164 Am Leg Boys St; Hon Rl; NHS; Sprt Ed Yrbk; Sprt Ed Sch Nwsp; Fr Clb; Pres Sci Clb; Bsktbl; Golden Horeshoe Awd; Shrine Clb Stu Of Month; Fairmont St Coll; Electronics.

PAUL, ANNETTE; Philo HS; Zanesville, OH; 32/206 Band; Chrh Wkr; FCA; Hon Rl; NHS; Sch Mus; 4-H; FTA; Letter Trk; GAA; Muskingum Area Tech Univ; Enviro.

PAUL, CHERYL J; Shady Spring HS; Shady Spring, WV; Band; Hon Rl; NHS; Outstanding Musician

Award; All County Band Award; West Virginia Univ; Music Ed.

PAUL, DIANE; North Miami HS; Macy, IN; 39/122 Chrs; Chrh Wkr; Cmnty Wkr; Hon Rl; Pres MMM; Sch Mus; 4-H; Fr Clb; Pep Clb; 4-H Awd; Univ.

PAUL, JERRY; Beaverton HS; Beaverton, MI; 15/200 Boy Scts; Chrh Wkr; Hon Rl; Letter Ftbl; Letter Trk; Central Mic Univ; Forestry.

PAUL, JOSEPH; Jefferson Area HS; Rome, OH; 17/180 Rptr Sch Nwsp; 4-H; Ten; Letter Wrstlng; Coll; History.

PAUL, KAREN; Cass Technical HS; Detroit, MI; Hon Rl; NHS; Off Ade; Red Cr Ade; Y-Teens; Univ Of Michigan; Comp Sci.

PAUL, KEVIN C; Churchill HS; Livonia, MI; 2/680 Trs Jr Cls; Lit Mag; Stu Cncl; Capt Crs Cntry; Capt Trk; NCTE; Natl Merit Ltr; Univ; Illustration.

PAUL, LINDA; Utica Sr HS; Newark, OH; Cls Rep Frsh Cls; Band; Hon Rl; Y-Teens; Rptr Sch Nwsp; Drama Clb; 4-H; FHA; Treas Pep Clb; Treas Mat Maids; Bowling Green St Univ; Art.

PAUL, LYNN; Howland HS; Warren, OH; 7/439 AFS; Band; Hon Rl; Hosp Ade; Y-Teens; Rptr Yrbk; Fr Clb; FNA; Pep Clb; Univ; Nursing.

PAUL, MORGAN; James A Garfield HS; Garrettsville, OH; Band; Chrh Wkr; Cmnty Wkr; Girl Scts; Hon Rl; NHS; Off Ade; Pres Yth Flsp; Rptr Sch Nwsp; Treas 4-H; Thiel Coll; Engr.

PAUL, NELS; Hancock Central HS; Hancock, MI; Sch Pl; Bsktbl; Ftbl; Trk; Mic Tech; Bus Admin.

PAUL, TERRY; Beaverton HS; Beaverton, MI; Boy Scts; Hon Rl; Spn Clb; Letter Ftbl; Central Michigan Univ; Dentistry.

PAULAK, MARJORIE; Memorial HS; Elkhart, IN; Cls Rep Soph Cls; Chrs; Hon Rl; Sch Mus; Sch Pl; Stu Cncl; Yth Flsp; Drama Clb; IUSB; Dent Hygenistry.

PAULEY, FAITH; Pine River Jr Sr HS; Tustin, MI; Chrs; Chrh Wkr; Hon Rl; Lbry Ade; Natl Forn Lg; NHS; Sch Mus; Drama Clb; Central Michigan Univ; Education.

PAULEY, FAITH; Pine River HS; Tustin, MI; Chrs; Chrh Wkr; Hon Rl; Lbry Ade; Natl Forn Lg; NHS; Sch Mus; Cmu; Speech.

PAULEY, JO; Columbiana HS; Columbiana, OH; 15/103 Treas Band; Hon Rl; Yrbk; Sch Nwsp; Youngstown St Univ; Comp Prog.

PAULEY, RHODA; Pickerington HS; Pickerington, OH; 19/210 Trs Frsh Cls; Hon Rl; Jr NHS; Stu Cncl; Yth Flsp; Y-Teens; Ger Clb; Chrldng; Eng Schlrshp Tests 76 78; 2nd Pl In Plays German Day At Ohio St 76 & 78; Univ.

PAULEY, RITA M; Ripley HS; Liverpool, WV; 35/250 Hon Rl; Lbry Ade; Off Ade; Sch Pl; Stg Crw; Drama Clb; 4-H; Fr Clb; Mth Clb; Pep Clb; Berea Coll; Eng.

PAULIK, KAREN; Rochester Community HS; Rochester, IN; 6/165 FCA; Hon Rl; Jr NHS; Fr Clb; Letter Bsktbl; Letter Trk; PPFtbl; Univ; Frgn Lang.

PAULIK, PAUL; Manistee Catholic Cntrl HS; Manistee, MI; Sal; Boy Scts; Chrh Wkr; Hon Rl; Mod UN; NHS; Sch Pl; Sct Actv; Dnfth Awd; Kiwan Awd; Univ Of Detroit; Elec Engr.

PAULIK, THOMAS; Manistee Cath Central HS; Manistee, MI; Chrh Wkr; Cmnty Wkr; Hon Rl; Yrbk; College.

PAULL, SYLVIA; Lakeshore HS; St Clair Shores, MI; AFS; Debate Tm; Hosp Ade; Pol Wkr; Sch Mus; Sch Pl; Stg Crw; Wayne St Univ.

PAULSEN, CARLA; Buena Vista HS; Saginaw, MI; Hon Rl; Lbry Ade; NHS; Stu Cncl; 4-H; Sci Clb; Trk; Pom Pon; Univ; Bio.

PAULSIN, MICHAEL; Andrean HS; Merrillville, IN; 45/251 Chrh Wkr; Hon Rl; Jr NHS; Stu Cncl; Bsbl; Bsktbl; IM Sprt; Scr Kpr; Tmr; Cit Awd; MVP Bsbl 78; Univ; Psych.

PAULSON, MARY; Adelphian Academy; Mt Vernon, OH; Chrs; Hon Rl; Letter Gym; IM Sprt; Andrews Univ; Psych.

PAULUS, CAROL; Littlefield Public Schools; Oden, MI; 1/32 VP Frsh Cls; VP Soph Cls; Sec Jr Cls; Trs Sr Cls; Val; Am Leg Aux Girls St; Band; Hon Rl; Lbry Ade; NHS; Lambert Memorial Schlrshp 79; N Central Michigan Coll; Comp Progr.

PAULUS, CATHERINE; Our Lady Of Mercy HS; Detroit, MI; Univ; Comp Prog.

PAULUS, TIMOTHY; Washington HS; Massillon, OH; 56/459 Trs Frsh Cls; Trs Soph Cls; Trs Sr Cls; Band; Chrs; Chrh Wkr; Cmnty Wkr; Hon Rl; Orch; Rptr Yrbk; Univ; Engr.

PAULY, KATHLEEN; Rogers City HS; Rogers City, MI; 5/150 Band; Chrh Wkr; Hon Rl; NHS; Treas Yth Flsp; Rptr Yrbk; 4-H; Key Clb; Pep Clb; Pom Pon; Northwestern Michigan Coll; Dent Ast.

PAULY, MICHAEL; Tahota HS; W Chester, OH; Hon Rl; Sch Pl; Ger Clb; Sci Clb; Letter Socr; Congressional Nom To U S Air Force Acad 79; AFROTC Schlshp 79; Hon Mention For All Cincinnati Soccer Tm; Indiana Univ; Pre Med.

PAURAZAS, RUTH; Bloomington HS South; Bloomington, IN; Boy Scts; Hon Rl; Treas Sct Actv; Letter Swmmng; Letter Ten; Scr Kpr; Tmr; Kiwan Awd; Univ Of Evansville; Criminal Justice.

PAUSZEK, DAVID J; John Adams HS; South Bend, IN; Cl Rep Jr Cls; Hon Rl; NHS; Letter Swmmng; Monogram Club Tres; Elected To Stu Government; Southern Most Univ; Busns Admin.

PAVALKO, DIANE; Canfield HS; Canfield, OH; 69/278 Chrs; Debate Tm; Girl Scts; Hon Rl; Mdrgl; Natl Forn Lg; Sch Mus; Y-Teens; Sch Nwsp; PPFtbl; Ohio St Univ; Home Ec.

PAVELKA, DIANE L; Belleville HS; Belleville, MI; Hst Jr Cls; Debate Tm; Hon Rl; Stu Cncl; Ger Clb; Letter Chrldng; Natl Merit Ltr; Elected Honorary Judge For Van Buren Township 79; Univ Of Michigan; Phys Ther.

PAVELLA, CHERYL; Brighton HS; Brighton, MI; Hon Rl; PAVAS; Quill & Scroll; Rptr Yrbk; Yrbk; Rptr Sch Nwsp; Sch Nwsp; Pom Pon; Univ; Jrnlsm.

PAVER, JOHN; Cambridge HS; Cambridge, OH; Mgrs; Tmr; Ohi St.

PAVKOV, LYNORA; Manchester HS; Akron, OH; Cls Rep Soph Cls; VP Jr Cls; Sec Sr Cls; Chrh Wkr; Off Ade; Stu Cncl; OEA; Scr Kpr; Tmr; Portage Lakes Joint Voc Schl; Sec.

PAVLESCAK, RICHARD A; Cloverleaf HS; Medina, OH; Am Leg Boys St; Boy Scts; Jr NHS; Natl Forn Lg; Sch Mus; Yth Flsp; Ed Yrbk; Drama Clb; FTA; Voice Dem Awd; College; Psychology.

PAVLEY, SUSAN; Westerville South HS; Westerville, OH; 51/283 Girl Scts; Hon Rl; Sch Pl; OEA; Pep Clb; Spn Clb; IM Sprt;.

PAVLIK, TAMMIE; W V Fisher Catholic HS; Logan, OH; Cmnty Wkr; Hon Rl; Sch Pl; Y-Teens; Yrbk; 4-H; Fr Clb; Pep Clb; Gym; Chrldng; Univ.

PAVLOV, DON; Springfield Local HS; New Springfield, OH; Hon Rl; NHS; Spn Clb; Bsbl; Bsktbl; Capt Ftbl; Trk; Ftbl Homecoming Escort; 3 Yr Var Ltr Ftbl & Track; Univ; Jrnlsm.

PAVLYSHYN, MARY; James F Rhodes HS; Cleveland, OH; 87/309 Band; Chrh Wkr; Girl Scts; Hon Rl; Sch Mus; Sct Actv; Y-Teens; Letter Bsktbl; IM Sprt; Findlay Coll; Nature Interp.

PAVNICA, JOSEPH; Bishop Noll Inst; Highland, IN; 99/321 Hon Rl; Hockey; Ten; Univ; Acctg.

PAWELSKI, DANIEL; Dayton Christian HS; Dayton, OH; 16/112 Chrs; Hon Rl; Lbry Ade; Spn Clb; Bsbl; 1st Pl Medal Natl Spanish Exam 76 77 & 78; Perf Attend 75 78; Plaque In Bible Memorization 78; Asbury Univ; Math.

PAWINSKI, MONICA; George Rogers Clark HS; Hammond, IN; 2/218 Am Leg Aux Girls St; Chrs; NHS; Quill & Scroll; Sch Mus; Sch Pl; Stu Cncl; Ed Sch Nwsp; Dnfth Awd; Natl Merit Ltr; Wa Wrkshp Cngrssnl Sem Part 79; Univ; Poli Sci.

PAWLAK, EUGENE; Andrean HS; Merrillville, IN; 5/251 Chrh Wkr; Cmnty Wkr; Hon Rl; VP NHS; Sprt Ed Sch Nwsp; Letter Ftbl; Letter Trk; Letter Wrstlng; Gov Hon Prg Awd; Opt Clb Awd; Univ; Pre Med.

PAWLAK, JESS; Winston Churchill HS; Westland, MI; Hon Rl; Cit Awd; Natl Merit SF; Univ Of Michigan; Med.

PAWLEY, RHONDA; Wilmington HS; Wilmington, OH; Band; Chrs; Lit Mag; Sch Mus; Pres Yth Flsp; Drama Clb; Pres 4-H; 4-H Awd; Natl Merit Ltr; Ohio Yth Honors Chorale; Phi Delta Sigma; College; Music.

PAWLICKI, DIANE; Brunswick HS; Brunswick, OH; 14/481 Am Leg Aux Girls St; Chrh Wkr; Hon Rl; Pres Sr Cls; NHS; Quill & Scroll; Sch Mus; Sch Pl; Stg Crw; FTA; Univ Of Akron; Dietetics.

PAWLIK, GERALDINE; Bishop Gallagher HS; Detroit, MI; Hon Rl; Univ Of Michigan; Law.

PAWLIZAK, KRISTEN; Admiral King HS; Lorain, OH; Band; Chrs; Sch Mus; Key Clb; Gym; Mgrs; College.

PAWLOSKI, SHEILA; Schoolcraft HS; Kalamazoo, MI; Cls Rep Soph Cls; Hon Rl; Stu Cncl; Letter Trk; Letter Chrldng;.

PAWLOWSKI, JOAN; St Johns HS; De Witt, MI; Band; Hon Rl; Off Ade; Sch Pl; 4-H; Pep Clb; Spn Clb; Letter Bsbl; Letter Bsktbl; IM Sprt; Univ; Phys Ther.

PAWLOWSKI, STEVE; Howell HS; Howell, MI; Hon Rl; IM Sprt; Univ; Archt.

PAWLOWSKI, TINA; Bishop Borgess HS; Detroit, MI; 21/480 Hon Rl; Hosp Ade; NHS; Sch Mus; Sch Pl; Sci Clb; Ten; Mercy Coll; Nursing.

PAWLYSZYN, NADIA; Holy Name Nazareth HS; Severn Hills, OH; Chrs; Treas Girl Scts; Hon Rl; NHS; Sct Actv; Sdlty; Finlst From Oh In Msis Untd Teengr Pgnt 79; Univ; Nursing.

PAX, ARLENE; Celina HS; Celina, OH; Chrs; Girl Scts; Lbry Ade; Sct Actv; Ed Sch Nwsp; Rptr Sch Nwsp; FHA; GAA; WOBC; Child Care Mgmt.

PAX, KAREN; Coldwater Exempted Village; Coldwater, OH; Chrs; Drl Tm; Hon Rl; Hosp Ade; JA; Lbry Ade; Sch Mus; Rptr Sch Nwsp; Ger Clb; Mgrs; Univ; Secondary Educ.

PAX, RENEE; Memorial HS; St Marys, OH; Chrs; Girl Scts; Hon Rl; Hosp Ade; Y-Teens; Drama Clb; Pep Clb; Spn Clb; Gym; Letter GAA; College; Nursing.

PAXSON, CELESTE; Eaton HS; Eaton, OH; 45/177 Band; Chrs; Chrh Wkr; Girl Scts; Hosp Ade; Lbry Ade; Spn Clb; College; Spanish.

PAXTON, BRENDA; Walton Jr Sr HS; Walton, WV; Sec Sr Cls; Trs Sr Cls; Band; Drm Mjrt; Hon Rl; Sec Jr NHS; Pres NHS; Sch Pl; Treas Stu Cncl; Yth Flsp; All Area Band 78; Arch Moore Jr Voc Tech Schl; Sec.

PAXTON, MARGARET; Greenfield Central HS; Greenfield, IN; 2/300 Chrh Wkr; Hon Rl; Jr NHS; Lbry Ade; NHS; Yth Flsp; 4-H; Mth Clb; Spn Clb; 4-H Awd; Hancock Cnty Bank & Trust Awd 77; Purdue Univ.

PAYDEN, DAN; Stow HS; Stow, OH; Boy Scts; Sct Actv; Ftbl; IM Sprt; Scr Kpr; Tmr; Akron Univ; Drafting.

PAYETTE, PHYLLIS; Southfield Lathrup HS; Southfield, MI; Band; Hon Rl; Treas JA; Pep Clb; Letter Swmmng; Mich State Univ; Financial Admin.

PAYIAVLAS, ANTHONY; Warren G Harding HS; Warren, OH; Pres Soph Cls; VP Jr Cls; Pres Sr Cls; Am Leg Boys St; Chrs; Chrh Wkr; Cmnty Wkr; Hon Rl; Jr NHS; Mdrgl; Oh Assoc Of Stdnt Council St Rep 79; Trumbull Cnty Summer Stock Theatre 78; Univ; Fine Arts.

PAYICH, TODD; Liberty HS; Yngstn, OH; 12/238 VP AFS; Chrs; Debate Tm; Hon Rl; Sch Mus; Sch Pl; Drama Clb; Fr Clb; Ger Clb; Yngstwn St Univ Foreign Lang Day 1st Pl 78; Ohio Test Of Schlstc Achiev French 14th Dist HM St 79; Univ Of Dayton; Comp Sci.

PAYMENT, MICHELE M; De Tour Area HS; Drummond Is, MI; 1/37 Sec Jr Cls; Sec Sr Cls; Val; Hon Rl; NHS; Off Ade; Rptr Yrbk; Drama Clb; 4-H; Letter Bsktbl; Brd Of Contrl Schlrshp 4 Yrs Mi Tech Univ79; Stu Rep To Brd Of Ed 76 78; Mi Comptn Schlrshp 79 83; Michigan Tech Univ; Bus Admin.

PAYN, DEBORAH A; Northwestern HS; West Salem, OH; Band; Chrs; Chrh Wkr; Yth Flsp; 4-H; Fr Clb; FTA; Bsktbl; College.

PAYNE, ALLISON; Jackson HS; Jackson, OH; 1/235 Cl Rep Jr Cls; Band; Cmnty Wkr; NHS; Orch; 4-H; Pep Clb; Sci Clb; Scr Kpr; Tmr; College; Elem Educ.

PAYNE, DEBORAH L; Sissonville HS; Elkview, WV; Chrh Wkr; Hon Rl; Fr Clb; Mth Clb; Spn Clb; West Virginia Univ.

PAYNE, EUGENIA; Inkster HS; Westland, MI; 2/173 Sec Jr Cls; Chrh Wkr; Debate Tm; Hon Rl; VP NHS; Off Ade; Sec Stu Cncl; Sec Yth Flsp; Rptr Yrbk; Ohio St Univ; Busns Admin.

PAYNE, GARY; Herbert Hoover HS; Clendenin, WV; Pres Frsh Cls; Chrs; Hon Rl; Jr NHS; Pol Wkr; Stu Cncl; Ed Yrbk; Rptr Sch Nwsp; 4-H; Cit Awd; Musclear Dystrophe Grtst Aide 77; West Virginia Univ; Law.

PAYNE, IRIS; West Side Sr HS; Gary, IN; Chrs; Hon Rl; NHS; Drama Clb; Scr Kpr; Tmr; Natl Hon Soc 78; Hon Roll 76 79; Chrs 78; Michigan St Univ; Vet.

PAYNE, JEFFERY; East HS; Columbus, OH; Boy Scts; Hon Rl; Boys Clb Am; College.

PAYNE, JUDITH A; Philip Barbour HS; Volga, WV; Chrh Wkr; Cmnty Wkr; Hon Rl; NHS; Off Ade; Stu Cncl; 4-H; Pep Clb; 4-H Awd; Fairmont St Univ; Tchr.

PAYNE, KIM; Waldron HS; Waldron, IN; Band; FCA; Hon Rl; Rptr Yrbk; Sprt Ed Sch Nwsp; 4-H; Lat Clb; Pep Clb; Bsktbl; Trk; Univ.

PAYNE, LINDA; Garfield HS; Akron, OH; 80/400 Cls Rep Sr Cls; Chrs; Chrh Wkr; Hon Rl; JA; Lbry Ade; Pol Wkr; ROTC; Sch Mus; Sch Pl; Bicentenial Art Competition 2nd Pl; Best Gym Stu Awd; VEP Prgrm; Akron Univ; Computer Prog.

PAYNE, MARK; Warren Central HS; Indianapolis, IN; FCA; Hon Rl; Jr NHS; Pol Wkr; Bsbl; IM Sprt; College; Law.

PAYNE, PATRICIA J; Traverse City HS; Traverse City, MI; Cmnty Wkr; Hon Rl; Sec NHS; Red Cr Ade; Sprt Ed Yrbk; 4-H; Letter Crs Cntry; Ftbl; Gym; Letter Trk; 4th Yr Gold Schlrshp Key For A Or Better Avg; Central Migh Univ Board Of Trustees Schlrshp; Central Michigan Univ; Medicine.

PAYNE, RICHARD A; Rutherford B Hayes HS; Delaware, OH; AFS; Am Leg Boys St; Chrs; Chrh Wkr; Hon Rl; Sch Pl; Sct Actv; Yth Flsp; Sprt Ed Sch Nwsp; Rptr Sch Nwsp; Hnr Carrier Columbus Ctzn Jrnl 79; Sup Ratng St Mary Schl Sci Fair 75; Univ Of Notre Dame; Law.

PAYNE, SHIRLEY; Marion Harding HS; Marion, OH; 84/450 Chrs; Yrbk; Sch Nwsp; Spn Clb; Trk; IM Sprt; Armed Serv Navy.

PAYNE, SUETTA; Lawrence North HS; Indianapolis, IN; 50/366 Chrs; Girl Scts; JA; Lbry Ade; NHS; Off Ade; Pres Key Clb; OEA; JA Awd; Univ; Bus Mgmt.

PAYNE, TAMERA L; South Spencer HS; Grandview, IN; Cls Rep Frsh Cls; Cls Rep Soph Cls; Band; Chrh Wkr; Hon Rl; Sch Mus; Stu Cncl; Sch Nwsp; GAA; Pom Pon; Voc Schl; Elec.

PAYNE, TERI; Rosedale HS; Rosedale, IN; Band; Mod UN; Quill & Scroll; Rptr Yrbk; Rptr Sch Nwsp; Pep Clb; Am Leg Awd; Best Delegate Model U N 1978; Pres Of Soc Studies Clb 1978; Indiana St Univ; Law.

PAYNE, TRACY; Rogers HS; Rockford, MI; Band; Cmp Fr Grls; Hon Rl; JA; Orch; Sch Mus; Sch Pl; Close Up Clb Local St & Natl; Aquinas Coll; Busns Admin.

PAYTON, BEVERLY; Bloom HS; Wheelersburg, OH; 27/81 Chrs; Hon Rl; Off Ade; 4-H; FHA; OEA; IM Sprt; 4-H Awd; Portsmouth Bus College; Clerk Typist.

PAYTON, JANICE; St Peter & Paul Area HS; Sagnaw, MI; Sec Frsh Cls; Cl Rep Jr Cls; Chrh Wkr; Cmnty Wkr; Hon Rl; JA; Lbry Ade; MMM; Off Ade; Red Cr Ade; Michigan St Univ; Legal Sec.

PAZDZIOR, JOHN; Ida HS; Ida, MI; 10/160 Am Leg Boys St; Hon Rl; NHS; Bsktbl; Glf; Scr Kpr; Amer Hist Awrd 79; Univ; Comp Progr.

PAZILLO, PAM; Girard HS; Girard, OH; 28/202 AFS; Cmnty Wkr; Drl Tm; Hon Rl; Hosp Ade; Off Ade; Y-Teens; Rptr Sch Nwsp; OEA; Class Top Shorthand Stu; OOEA Shorthand I Competition; YSU Skill O Rama Shorthand Competition; College; Nursing.

PCOLINSKI, JOHN; Schlarman HS; Ft Wayne, IN; Hon Rl; JA; Sprt Ed Sch Nwsp; Bsktbl; Trk; IM Sprt; JA Awd; Natl Merit Ltr; Natl Merit SF; North Central Coll; Bus Admin.

PEA, JOHN; Northrop HS; Ft Wayne, IN; DECA; Letter Crs Cntry; Bus Schl; Bus Mgmt.

PEACE, PAMELA; Glen Este HS; Cincinnati, OH; Hon Rl; NHS; FHA; Spn Clb;.

PEACOCK, KENNETH; Shortridge HS; Indianapolis, IN; 42/340 Pres Frsh Cls; Cl Rep Jr Cls; VP Sr Cls; Hon Rl; JA; Key Clb; Mth Clb; Letter Ftbl; Letter Trk; C of C Awd; MVP Offensive In Varsity Ftbl; Completion Of Cntr For Ldrshp Dev Prog; Completion Of Minority Engr Adv Pgm; College; Medicine.

PEACOCK, KIM; Norwayne HS; Creston, OH; 9/131 Sec Jr Cls; Pres Sr Cls; Sec Sr Cls; Band; Chrh Wkr; Drl Tm; Hon Rl; 4-H; FHA; OEA; Outstndg Class Stu 78; Mabel Bibler Awd Outstndg Bus Stu 78; Regnl St & Natl Steno Wnnr 78; Wayne Business Coll; Sec.

PEACOCK, REBECCA E; Brandon HS; Ortonville, MI; 1/197 Cl Rep Jr Cls; Hon Rl; Hosp Ade; NHS; Rptr Sch Nwsp; 4-H; OEA; Letter Trk; 4-H Awd; Natl Merit SF; General Motors Inst; Mech Engr.

PEACOCK, VENA; North Newton HS; Morocco, IN; 4/150 Trs Jr Cls; Drl Tm; Hon Rl; NHS; FBLA; Sci Clb; Math Hon 76 & 77; Eng Hon 76 & 77; Typing Hon 77; Bus Schl; Acctg.

PEAK, CHRISTINE; Clinton Central HS; Frankfort, IN; Cls Rep Frsh Cls; Cls Rep Soph Cls; Cl Rep Jr Cls; Cls Rep Sr Cls; Hon Rl; Off Ade; Quill & Scroll; Pres Stu Cncl; Rptr Yrbk; Ed Sch Nwsp; IUPUI; Bus Mgmt.

PEAK, CYNTHIA; Pleasant HS; Marion, OH; Chrh Wkr; JA; Stg Crw; Yth Flsp; Drama Clb; Capital Univ; Languages.

PEAK, ELLEN; Mount View HS; Welch, WV; 69/250 Hon Rl; Jr NHS; Lbry Ade; FBLA; VP FHA; Pep Clb; Coll; Law.

PEAK, LORENE; Mount View HS; Welch, WV; 69/250 Hon Rl; Jr NHS; Lbry Ade; FBLA; VP FHA; Pep Clb; Coll; Law.

PEAKE, VANESSA; Redford HS; Detroit, MI; Chrh Wkr; Hon Rl; Off Ade; DECA; OEA; Trk; Univ Of Mch; Medical Field.

PEAKS, VON; Central HS; Columbus, OH; 19/173 Band; Chrh Wkr; Drm Bgl; Drm Mjrt; Hon Rl; NHS; Orch; Letter Glf; Letter Ten; Mgrs; Ohio St Univ; Archt.

PEARCE, LINDA; Elmwood HS; Portage, OH; Chrs; Hon Rl; OEA;.

PEARCE, RUTH; Sault Area HS & Skill Ctr; Sault Ste Marie, MI; Chrs; Chrh Wkr; Hon Rl; NHS; Yth Flsp; Lat Clb; Univ; Nurse.

PEARCY, JILL; Ravenna HS; Ravenna, MI; 2/98 Sal; Band; Hon Rl; NHS; Rptr Yrbk; FHA; Davenport Coll; Legal Sec.

PEARL, ALLYSON; New Albany HS; New Albany, IN; Chrh Wkr; Hon Rl; NHS; Orch; Yth Flsp; Ger Clb; Ten; Mgrs; Ind State Univ; Spch Hrng.

PEARL, LARRY; Bordan HS; Sellersburg, IN; 2/16 Cl Rep Jr Cls; Chrs; Hon Rl; Jr NHS; Sct Actv; Stu Cncl; Letter Bsbl; Letter Bsktbl; Letter Crs Cntry; VFW Awd;.

PEARL, TIMOTHY; East Lansing HS; East Lansing, MI; Cl Rep Jr Cls; Boy Scts; Stu Cncl; Michigan Tech Univ; Comp Sci.

PEARLMAN, LISA; East Grand Rapids HS; E Grand Rapids, MI; Hon Rl; Yrbk; Drama Clb; Pep Clb; Univ; Law.

PEARSALL, C ROBERT; Patrick Henry HS; Deshler, OH; 1/100 Aud/Vis; Chrh Wkr; Hon Rl; Pol Wkr; Pres Yth Flsp; Sci Clb; JETS Awd; St Sci Fair Supr Rating 1977; Intrnl Sci Engr 1977; Spkr Toledo Reg St Jr Sci Fari 1978; Mbr Ohio Academy; Univ; Elec Engr.

PEARSON, BARBARA; Barb Pearson HS; Hansens Island, MI; Girl Scts; Hon Rl; Jr NHS; NHS; Stu Cncl; FDA; Spn Clb; Bsbl; Gym; Michigan St Univ; Med.

PEARSON, BRIAN; Truman HS; Taylor, MI; Chrh Wkr; Hon Rl; Sch Pl; Stg Crw; Univ.

PEARSON, CINDY; Plainfield Jr Sr HS; Plainfield, IN; 3/283 Cls Rep Frsh Cls; Cls Rep Soph Cls; Cl Rep Jr Cls; Am Leg Aux Girls St; Chrs; Mdrgl; NHS; Sch Mus; Stu Cncl; Fr Clb; Butler Univ; French.

PEARSON, DAVID; Green HS; Akron, OH; 60/300 Ohio State Univ; Acctg.

PEARSON, JEFF; St Johns HS; De Witt, MI; Band; Chrh Wkr; Hon Rl; VP Yth Flsp; IM Sprt; Am Leg Awd; 4-H Awd; Voice Dem Awd; MSU.

PEARSON, KATHLEEN; Zanesville HS; Zanesville, OH; Hon Rl; NHS; Stu Cncl; Sci Clb; Letter Swmmng; Univ Of Mic.

PEARSON, MARIE; Sidney HS; Sidney, OH; VP Jr Cls; Chrs; Chrh Wkr; Drl Tm; Girl Scts; Hon Rl; Off Ade; OEA; Exec & Diplomat Awds;.

PEARSON, MARK; Tri Township HS; Rapid Rvr, MI; Hon Rl; Letter Trk; Vocational School.

PEARSON, NANCY; Jay County HS; Portland, IN; 1/475 Hon Rl; Jr NHS; Pres NHS; Pres Yth Flsp; 4-H; VP Mth Clb; VP Sci Clb; Sec Spn Clb; Bsktbl; 4-H Awd; Indiana Univ; Lang.

PEARSON, NATALIE; Columbus Eastmoor Sr HS; Columbus, OH; 26/290 Cl Rep Jr Cls; Chrs; Cmnty Wkr; Girl Scts; Hon Rl; Off Ade; Sch Mus; Stg Crw; Stu Cncl; OEA; Ohio Office Ed Assoc; Communications I Test 2nd Pl; Ohio State Univ; Busns.

PEARSON, PAT; Port Huron Northern HS; Pt Huron, MI; Chrs; Sch Mus; Letter Bsbl; Letter Ftbl; Letter Hockey; Univ.

PEARSON, SARA; Flushing HS; Flushing, MI; College; Soc Work.

PEARSON, STEPHEN E; St Xavier HS; Cincinnati, OH; 5/264 Debate Tm; Hon Rl; Mod UN; NHS; Sct Actv; Rptr Sch Nwsp; Mth Clb; Sci Clb; Crs Cntry; Trk; Univ; Physics.

PEARSON, TERESA; Philo HS; Roseville, OH; Hon Rl; Lbry Ade; VP 4-H; Fr Clb; FHA; College; Nursing.

PEARSON, VICKIE; Massillon Christian HS; Waynesburg, OH; Cls Rep Sr Cls; Band; Chrs; Chrh Wkr; Hon Rl; Natl Forn Lg; NHS; Sch Mus; Sch Pl; Yth Flsp; Sup Rating In Ntl Piano Plyng Auditions 76 79; St Qualifier In Oratorical Declamatn 2 Yrs 77; 2nd Pl Vocal; Univ; Music.

PEART, JAMIE; Madison Plains HS; London, OH; Hon Rl; Sch Pl; Stu Cncl; 4-H; FFA; Spn Clb; Wrstlng; IM Sprt; 4-H Awd; Recieved Awds For FFA Beef Showmanship; Ohio St Univ; Agronomist.

PEASE, JACQUELINE; Bellevue HS; Bellevue, MI; 3/87 Band; Lbry Ade; VP NHS; 4-H; Spn Clb; 4-H Awd; Western Michigan Univ; Paper Engr.

PEASE, JODY; Kent Roosevelt HS; Kent, OH; Hon Rl; Sch Pl; Drama Clb; Letter Crs Cntry; Letter Trk; College; Photog.

PEAVLY, JON; Mt View HS; Welch, WV; Am Leg Boys St; Hon Rl; Jr NHS; Key Clb; Ftbl; Ten; Wrstlng; Distinguished Serv Awd For Welch Key Clb 77; V P Of Stud In Action For Educ 79; Univ; Bus Admin.

PECCHIA, RICHARD; Campbell Memorial HS; Campbell, OH; Hon Rl; NHS; Mth Clb; Spn Clb; Univ.

PECENICA, NICK; Washington HS; E Chicago, IN; Cls Rep Frsh Cls; Cls Rep Soph Cls; Cl Rep Jr Cls; Key Clb; Indiana Univ; Bus.

PECHETTE, SUSAN; North Huron HS; Kinde, MI; Cl Rep Jr Cls; Sec Sr Cls; Hon Rl; Hosp Ade; Lbry Ade; NHS; Off Ade; Stu Cncl; Yrbk; 4-H; Saginaw Valley State Coll; Nursing.

PECHTA, LAURIE; Lasalle HS; Moran, MI; 5/103 Cls Rep Frsh Cls; Cls Rep Soph Cls; Hon Rl; NHS; Stu Cncl; Ed Yrbk; Letter Trk; Kiwan Awd; Ferris State; Bus.

PECK, DAVID; Rochester HS; Rochester, MI; 37/371 Hon Rl; NHS; Bsbl; Capt Bsktbl; Crs Cntry; Ftbl; IM Sprt; Scr Kpr; JC Awd; Central Mich Football; Med.

PECK, DEBRA I; Villa Angela Academy; Cleveland, OH; Cl Rep Jr Cls; Cmp Fr Grls; Cmnty Wkr; Hon Rl; Sch Pl; Sec Mth Clb; IM Sprt; Prtcptn In March Of Dimes Superwalk 78; Teen Rep For March Of Dimes Supewalk 79; Cuyahoga Cmnty Coll Credit; Univ; Civil Engr.

PECK, DENISE; West Lafayette HS; W Lafyt, IN; 45/190 Hon Rl; NHS; Keyettes; Pep Clb; Letter Gym; Letter Trk; Opt Clb Awd; Natl Spanish Contst 2nd Pl; Keyette Schlsp 100; Panorama Sr Girl Awd; Purdue Univ; Vet Med.

PECK, JACQUELINE; Gaylord St Mary Cathdrl HS; Gaylord, MI; 4/65 VP Frsh Cls; Cls Rep Soph Cls; Cl Rep Jr Cls; Chrs; Chrh Wkr; Hon Rl; NHS; Off Ade; Sch Mus; Sch Pl; North Central Michigan Coll.

PECK, JOHN A; Mount Clemens HS; Mt Clemens, MI; Cls Rep Frsh Cls; Cls Rep Sr Cls; Cmnty Wkr; FCA; Hon Rl; Lit Mag; NHS; Pol Wkr; Stg Crw; Stu Cncl; Univ; Eng.

PECK, MICHAEL; Theodore Roosevelt HS; Wyandotte, MI; Hon Rl; Hockey; Vocational School; Data Processing.

PECK, R; Kalkaska HS; Rapid City, MI; 14/140 NHS; Bsbl; Ftbl; Wrstlng; College; Wildlife Mgmt.

PECK, REBECCA E; Fruitport HS; Muskegon, MI; 2/300 Chrs; Chrh Wkr; Yth Flsp; Natl Merit SF; Soc Women Accountants; Grtr Muskegon Music Tchrs Assn Schlrshp Competition Awd; Univ Of Michigan; Medicine.

PECK, TERESA; Benton Central HS; Montmorenci, IN; Girl Scts; Lbry Ade; FHA; OEA; 4-H Awd; Med Sec.

PECK, TERRI; Clarkston Sr HS; Clarkston, MI; Chrs; Chrh Wkr; Girl Scts; Hon Rl; Sct Actv; Sdlty; Yth Flsp; Drama Clb; PPFtbl; Chorus; English; Social Studies; College; Drama.

PECK, TODD; Muskegon HS; Muskegon, MI; Chrh Wkr; Hon Rl; NHS; Fr Clb; Ten; Univ Mich; Pharmacy.

PECNIK, GREGORY; Euclid HS; Euclid, OH; Hon Rl; VICA; Cooper School Of Art; Artist.

PECORARO, DEBORAH; East Detroit HS; Roseville, MI; Hon Rl; Hosp Ade; NHS; FNA; Oakland Univ; Nursing.

PEDDICORD, ROBERT; Central Preston HS; Kingwood, WV; FCA; Off Ade; Sct Actv; Stu Cncl; Bsktbl; Ftbl; Trk; Coach Actv; Univ; Educ.

PEDDIE, JULIE; Bridgman HS; Bridgman, MI; Chrs; Sch Mus; Sch Pl; Stg Crw; Yth Flsp; Taylor Univ; Busns.

PEDDIE, M; Wylie E Groves HS; Franklin, MI; Chrs; Chrh Wkr; Hon Rl; Jr NHS; Sch Mus; Yth Flsp; Letter Bsbl; Letter Socr; IM Sprt; Michigan St Univ.

PEDDIE, MARCIA; Wylie Groves HS; Franklin, MI; Jr NHS; Sch Mus; Bsktbl; Letter Swmmng; Trk; Trk; Mgrs; Scr Kpr; Tmr; Michigan St Univ; Spec Educ.

PEDERSON, CHARLES; Dayton Christian HS; Dayton, OH; Chrh Wkr; Hon Rl; Letter Socr; Univ; Bus.

PEDERSON, DAVID; Livonia Franklin HS; Westland, MI; Cl Rep Jr Cls; Am Leg Aux Girls St; Band; Chrs; Chrh Wkr; Debate Tm; Hon Rl; Natl Forn Lg; Pol Wkr; Sch Pl; Wheaton Coll.

PEDICINI, BRIDGET; Ursuline Academy; Cincinati, OH; 12/106 Key Clb; Univ Of Cincinnat; Bio Med Engr.

PEDIGO, SUSAN; Plainfield Jr Sr HS; Plainfield, IN; 15/268 Chrs; Hon Rl; Lbry Ade; NHS; Off Ade; Sch Mus; Sch Pl; Stg Crw; Yth Flsp; Y-Teens; Indiana Schlr; Ball St Univ; Bus Admin.

PEDLEY, HAROLD J; Gilmour Acad; Shaker Hts, OH; 14/86 Sec Frsh Cls; Hon Rl; NHS; Rptr Sch Nwsp; Letter Bsktbl; Letter Crs Cntry; Letter Trk; IM Sprt; Coll; Mech Engr.

PEDONE, CHARLENE; Maple Heights Sr HS; Maple Hts, OH; Cl Rep Jr Cls; Hon Rl; Jr NHS; NHS; Off Ade; Stu Cncl; OEA; Pep Clb; Trk; Chrldng; College; Acctg.

PEDROTTI, MARY; Techumseh HS; Medway, OH; VP Frsh Cls; Pres Jr Cls; Sec Jr Cls; FCA; Hon Rl; Jr NHS; NHS; Fr Clb; Wright St Univ; Computer Sci.

PEEK, LORA; Philip Barbour HS; Junior, WV; Band; NHS; 4-H; West Virginia Univ.

PEEK, MICHAEL; Cody HS; Detroit, MI; Drl Tm; Hon Rl; Sch Nwsp; Wayne State Univ; History.

PEEL, LAURIE; Stow HS; Stow, OH; 7/550 Band; Chrs; NHS; Stu Cncl; Lat Clb; Univ.

PEELMAN, CARRIE; Kearsley Community HS; Flint, MI; 1/380 Val; Band; Chrs; Chrh Wkr; Hon Rl; Mdrgl; NHS; Sch Pl; College; Spec Ed.

PEEPS, DANA; Notre Dame Acad; Toledo, OH; Cmp Fr Grls; Chrh Wkr; Drl Tm; Hon Rl; NHS; Bsktbl; IM Sprt; Univ Of Toledo; Correctional Tech.

PEER, PAM; Calvert HS; Tiffin, OH; Girl Scts; Sct Actv; Mat Maids; Scr Kpr; Tmr; College; Med.

PEERMAN, TRACY; Harrison HS; Evansvile, IN; Chrh Wkr; Girl Scts; Pep Clb; Letter Ten; College.

PEERY, TINA; Lumen Cordium HS; Cleveland, OH; Cls Rep Frsh Cls; Cls Rep Soph Cls; Band; Chrs; Chrh Wkr; Drl Tm; Hon Rl; Pep Clb; Letter Trk; Letter Pom Pon; The Lumen Cordium Awd For Schlstc Ach; Univ Of Cincinatti; Law.

PEETS, TRUDY; Cheboygan Area HS; Cheboygan, MI; Band; Chrs; Chrh Wkr; Hon Rl; Orch; Univ; Bus Mgmt.

PEETZ, NANCY; Carsonville Port Sanilac HS; Carsonville, MI; 7/70 Sec Sr Cls; Band; Hon Rl; NHS; Sch Mus; Sch Pl; Stg Crw; Drama Clb; Scr Kpr; Oakland Univ; Health.

PEIFER, DENISE; Lake Central HS; Schererville, IN; Girl Scts; Hon Rl; Quill & Scroll; Stg Crw; Rptr Sch Nwsp; Sch Nwsp; 4-H; Fr Clb; Purdue Univ; Journalism.

PEIFFER, BAMBERLEE; Litchfield HS; Janesville, MI; Band; Girl Scts; Hon Rl; 4-H; Letter Bsktbl; Letter Trk; 4-H Awd; Business School; Secretary.

PEIFFER, GERARD; Tiffin Calvert HS; Tiffin, OH; Hon Rl; Treas NHS; Ed Sch Nwsp; Capt Bsktbl; Scr Kpr; Cit Awd; Miami Univ; Acctg.

PEIRCE, HOLLY; Holland HS; Holland, MI; 21/327 Aud/Vis; Trs Frsh Cls; PAVAS; Sch Mus; Sch Pl; Stg Crw; Rptr Yrbk; Drama Clb; Hope Coll; Theatre Arts.

PEIRCE, LEONARD; Hartford HS; Hartford, MI; Trs Frsh Cls; Band; Hon Rl; Stg Crw; Rptr Sch Nwsp; Drama Clb; Bsktbl; Coach Actv; Lake Michigan Coll.

PEIRCE, MARC; Bishop Noll Institute; Whiting, IN; 21/350 Chrh Wkr; Cmnty Wkr; Hon Rl; Ger Clb; Mth Clb; Letter Bsbl; Coach Actv; IM Sprt; Natl Bus Hon Soc 78; Schl Nominee To Serve As A Page In Congrss 79; Univ; Pre Law.

PEIRSOL, DEBRA; Buckeye Valley HS; Ostrander, OH; 21/185 AFS; Hon Rl; NHS; Rptr Yrbk; Yrbk; Rptr Sch Nwsp; Pres 4-H; Rdo Clb; Sci Clb; Spn Clb; Ohio Wesleyan Univ; Jrnlsm.

PEISERT, LAURIE; Greenville HS; Greenville, MI; 2/238 Chrs; Hon Rl; NHS; Off Ade; Sch Mus; Sch Pl; Sec FHA; FNA; W Mi Univ Acad Schlshp 78; Western Michigan Univ; Psych.

PEITSCH, BILL; Grosselle HS; Grosse Ile, MI; Cls Rep Frsh Cls; Cls Rep Sr Cls; Aud/Vis; Chrh Wkr; Cmnty Wkr; Hon Rl; Pol Wkr; Red Cr Ade; Stu Cncl; VICA; Tex A & M College; Auto Engr.

PEJUAN, SONIA; Allen Park HS; Allen Park, MI; Band; Chrh Wkr; Hon Rl; Hosp Ade; Red Cr Ade; Yth Flsp; Pep Clb; Spn Clb; Trk; Capt Twrlr; Mercy Coll; Nurse.

PEK, JEFF; Ann Arbor Pioneer HS; Ann Arbor, MI; Band; Boy Scts; Hosp Ade; Fr Clb; Glf; Mdrgl; Univ; Pre Med.

PEKAREK, PATRICIA; James Ford Rhodes HS; Cleveland, OH; 13/257 Chrs; Drl Tm; Hon Rl; Hosp Ade; NHS; Sch Mus; Y-Teens; Trk; Capital Univ; Nurse.

PELFREY, KIMBERLY; Maumee HS; Maumee, OH; Girl Scts; Y-Teens; PPFtbl; Univ.

PELFREY, ROBBIN; Spencer HS; Spencer, WV; Band; Hon Rl; NHS; Sch Pl; Drama Clb; Pep Clb; Letter Trk; IM Sprt; Scr Kpr; Lincoln Memorial Univ; Nursing.

PELHAM, DEBRA; Norwalk HS; Norwalk, OH; 20/185 Sec Sr Cls; Drm Mjrt; Hon Rl; Pep Clb; GAA; Twrlr; Univ; Phys Ther.

PELINO, EUGENE; St Francis De Sales HS; Columbus, OH; 5/200 Hon Rl; Pres NHS; Drama Clb; Pres Lat Clb; Natl Merit Ltr; Notre Dame; Comp Sci.

PELKEY, GARY; Jennings County HS; No Vernon, IN; 26/351 Chrs; Chrh Wkr; Hon Rl; NHS; Sch Mus; Yth Flsp; Bsktbl; Ftbl; Lettered In Ftbl Soph Yr Earned Jacket Jr Yr; Received Archt Medal; VP United Methodist Fellowship; Ball St Univ; Archt.

PELKIE, MARK; Gwinn HS; Gwinn, MI; 2/206 Sal; Band; Hon Rl; NHS; Sec Stu Cncl; Yth Flsp; Pres Key Clb; OEA; Letter Ten; IM Sprt; B O E C Awd; Data Processing Comp Emphasis 1st Place Natl 1st Place St 1st Place Regional; Bsns Arithmetic; Mass Inst Of Tech; Computer Sci.

PELL, LORIE; Mc Bain HS; Cadillace, MI; Band; Chrh Wkr; Girl Scts; Hon Rl; Sct Actv; Sec 4-H; 4-H Awd; Band 79; Honor Roll 78; Mercy Nursing Schl; RN.

PELLAND, CHERYL; Dollar Bay HS; Dollar Bay, MI; 13/27 Cls Rep Sr Cls; Stu Cncl; Letter Bsktbl; IM Sprt; Scr Kpr; Suomi Coll; Bus.

PELLEGRINI, GUY; Calumet HS; Calumet, MI; Hosp Ade; Sch Pl; Bsbl; Letter Ftbl; Letter Hockey; Letter Trk; Pres Fitness Awd For Athltc Achvmnt 76; Univ Of Michigan; Pre Med.

PELLEGRINI, LISA; Lima Sr HS; Lima, OH; Hon Rl; VP Yth Flsp; Yrbk; DECA; Pep Clb; Spn Clb; Coll; Med.

PELLEGRINI, MARIE; Gwinn HS; Gwinn, MI; 4/198 Band; Hon Rl; Off Ade; 4-H; Glf; Tmr; Northern Mic Univ; Cosmetologist.

PELLERIN, PHILIPPE A; Reeths Puffer HS; Muskegon, MI; 13/400 Boy Scts; Chrh Wkr; Hon Rl; NHS; Letter Bsbl; Ftbl; Cit Awd; Ferris St Univ; Pharm.

PELLETIER, LISA; Big Bay De Noe HS; Garden, MI; 5/45 Hon Rl; Stu Cncl; Sprt Ed Sch Nwsp; Sch Nwsp; 4-H; Bsktbl; 4-H Awd; Coll; Dent Asst.

PELLOCK, BETHANN; Adlai E Stevenson HS; Rochester, MI; Cls Rep Frsh Cls; Cls Rep Soph Cls; Debate Tm; Hon Rl; Natl Forn Lg; Stu Cncl; Rptr Yrbk; Pom Pon; VFW Awd; Michigan St Univ; Internatl Relation.

PELLY, JONATHAN; Lutheran HS East; Cleveland, OH; 12/47 Band; Sch Mus; Sch Pl; Bsbl; Bsktbl; Ftbl; IM Sprt; Univ; Engr.

PELON, DANIELLE; Aquinas HS; Taylor, MI; Hon Rl; Hosp Ade; Pol Wkr; Girl Scts; Pep Clb; PPFtbl; Univ Of Michigan.

PELSOR, LU; South Dearborn HS; Dillsboro, IN; 5/265 Cls Rep Soph Cls; Cl Rep Jr Cls; Am Leg Aux Girls St; Band; Chrs; Chrh Wkr; Girl Scts; Hon Rl; Lbry Ade; NHS; Ball St Univ; Poli Sci.

PELTIER, JACQUE; Russia Local HS; Russia, OH; Cls Rep Frsh Cls; Cls Rep Soph Cls; Cl Rep Jr Cls; Chrh Wkr; Hon Rl; NHS; Stu Cncl; Letter Bsbl; Letter Bsktbl; Letter Glf; College.

PELTO, MICHAEL; Marquette Sr HS; Marquette, MI; Band; Letter Glf; Univ; Vet.

PELTOMAA, LYNNE; W Jefferson HS; W Jefferson, OH; 1/100 Am Leg Aux Girls St; Hon Rl; NHS; Off Ade; Quill & Scroll; Rptr Yrbk; Sch Nwsp; Ohi State Univ; Guidance Cnslr.

PELTY, ROBERT; Timken HS; Canton, OH; Am Leg Boys St; Band; Boy Scts; Chrs; Chrh Wkr; Yth Flsp; Letter Glf; IM Sprt; Natl Merit Ltr; Fla Institute Of Technology.

PELUSO, GINA; Ashtabula County Jt Voc HS; Geneva, OH; Trs Jr Cls; Cl Rep Jr Cls; VP Sr Cls; Cls Rep Sr Cls; Band; Girl Scts; Ed Sch Nwsp; Sch Nwsp; Fr Clb; Pres OEA; College; Data Processing.

PEMBERTON, BETH; Brownsburg HS; Brownsbrg, IN; 43/300 Girl Scts; Hon Rl; Lbry Ade; NHS; Quill & Scroll; Sct Actv; Rptr Sch Nwsp; Sch Nwsp; 4-H; Sec Spn Clb; Indiana Univ; Nursing.

PEMBERTON, MARK; Chesapeake HS; Chesapeake, OH; 30/140 Letter Bsbl; Bsktbl; Univ; Engr.

PEMBERTON, SUSIE; Orleans HS; Orleans, IN; 10/62 Letter Band; Hon Rl; 4-H; Gods Bible School; Missionary Train.

PEMBERTON, TRACI A; Wapakoneta HS; Wapakoneta, OH; Am Leg Aux Girls St; Hon Rl; Pres Stu Cncl; Rptr Yrbk; Fr Clb; Mth Clb; Letter Gym; Letter Trk; Chrldng; Ohio St Univ; Dentistry.

PENA, MIRIAM; Hammond Technical Voc HS; Hammond, IN; 11/172 Trs Sr Cls; Chrh Wkr; Girl Scts; Hon Rl; NHS; OEA; Spn Clb; Letter Trk; GAA; Hoosier Schlr 79; Schlrshp In Span 79; Awd In Span Coop Office Educ Soc Std 79; Purdue Univ; Bus Mgmt.

PENA JR, REYNALDO; Mona Shores HS; Muskegon, MI; Cls Rep Frsh Cls; Cmnty Wkr; Hon Rl; Y-Teens; Pres Awd; Laredo St Univ; Educ.

PENCE, CONNIE; Anderson Sr HS; Anderson, IN; 55/460 Chrs; Girl Scts; Hon Rl; NHS; Sch Pl; Sec Y-Teens; Rptr Sch Nwsp; Drama Clb; Eng Clb; Opt Clb Awd; Intl Order Of Jobs Daughters; Honored Qn IOJD; Coll; Elec Engr.

PENCE, JACKIE; Eaton HS; Eaton, OH; Pres Frsh Cls; Hon Rl; Sch Mus; Stu Cncl; Yth Flsp; 4-H; Pep Clb; Chrldng; 4-H Awd; Findlay Coll; Equestrian Studies.

PENCE, KAREN M; National Trail HS; Eaton, OH; VP Frsh Cls; Pres Soph Cls; Pres Sr Cls; Am Leg Aux Girls St; Hon Rl; Treas NHS; Letter Bsktbl; Ftbl; Trk; Mgrs; Bowling Green St Univ; Bus Admin.

PENCE, KATHY; Greenville HS; Greenville, OH; 21/360 Chrs; Hon Rl; Sch Mus; 4-H; Spn Clb; Business School; Accounting.

PENCE, MICHAEL; Marion Adams HS; Sheridan, IN; 7/100 Band; Hon Rl; Jr NHS; NHS; Sch Pl; Letter Ftbl; Letter Swmmng; Letter Trk; Dnfth Awd; College; Sec Ed.

PENCE, T; Garrett HS; Garrett, IN; Chrh Wkr; Hon Rl; Stg Crw; Letter Bsbl; Letter Bsktbl; Letter Trk; Business; Accgt.

PENCE, TODD; Jefferson Twp Sr HS; Germantown, OH; 9/170 Hon Rl; Yrbk; Capt Ftbl; Univ Of Dayton; Mech Engr.

PENCE, TRACY; Carlisle HS; Carlisle, OH; Band; Chrs; Hon Rl; Pep Clb; Spn Clb; Bsktbl; Trk; Miami Vly Nurses Schl; RN.

PENCHEFF, THOMAS; St Francis De Sales HS; Toledo, OH; Band; Boy Scts; Hon Rl; Jr NHS; Boys Clb Am; Natl Merit Ltr; College; Vet.

PENCZAK, MICHELLE J; Donald E Gavit Jr Sr HS; Hammond, IN; 29/270 Hon Rl; NHS; Stu Cncl; Sec Fr Clb; Pres OEA; Mat Maids; Tmr; Kiwan Awd; Oea Dist Steno 6th Pl 1978; Oea Genl Clerical 4th Pl 1979; Indiana St Schlrshp Honry 1979; Purdue Calumet Campus; Med.

PENDER, JAMES; Ontonagon Area HS; Ontonagon, MI; 13/97 Boy Scts; Hon Rl; NHS; Rptr Sch Nwsp; Letter Bsktbl; Capt Ftbl; Letter Trk; Mic Tech Univ; Mech Engr.

PENDER, JULIE; Southwestern HS; Detroit, MI; 5/222 Hon Rl; OEA; Letter Ten; Cit Awd; Univ Of Michigan; Envir Studies.

PENDERGAST, DAVID; Walter E Stebbins HS; Dayton, OH; Hon Rl; NHS; Letter Bsktbl; Letter Glf; Letter Trk; IM Sprt; Miami Univ; Law.

PENDERGAST, PATRICIA; Ben Davis HS; Indianapolis, IN; Girl Scts; Hon Rl; Off Ade; Sct Actv; Stu Cncl; Yth Flsp; 4-H; Spn Clb; Purdue College; Graphic Artist.

PENDERGRAST, DAVID; Weir HS; Weirton, WV; Cmnty Wkr; Hon Rl; IM Sprt; West Virginia Univ; Bus Admin.

PENDLETON, JANE; Spring Lake Sr HS; Spring Lake, MI; Chrh Wkr; Cmnty Wkr; Hon Rl; Grand Valley St Coll; Bio.

PENDLETON, JEFF; Franklin HS; Franklin, OH; Boy Scts; Lbry Ade; Pol Wkr; Sct Actv; IM Sprt; Ohio St Univ; Archt.

PENDLETON, JENNIFER; Urbana HS; Urbana, OH; Hon Rl; NHS; 4-H; Letter Bsktbl; Letter Crs Cntry; Letter Trk; College; Phys Ed.

PENDLETON, KIM; River Valley HS; Waldo, OH; 35/207 Band; Chrs; Chrh Wkr; FCA; Hon Rl; Yth Flsp; Sci Clb; Bsktbl; Letter Crs Cntry; Letter Trk; Univ; Phys Ed.

PENDOCK, TAMMY; Newaygo HS; Grant, MI; VP Soph Cls; Band; Hon Rl; NHS; Fr Clb; Letter Bsbl; Letter Chrldng; Pom Pon; Univ.

PENDRED, MIKE; Augres Sims HS; Au Gres, MI; VP Soph Cls; VP Jr Cls; Hon Rl; Bsbl; Bsktbl; Letter Ftbl; Dnfth Awd; College.

PENDRY, CAROLYN JEAN; Greeneview HS; Sabina, OH; Band; Chrs; Lbry Ade; Sch Pl; Stg Crw; Yrbk; Drama Clb; 4-H; Fr Clb; FTA; Univ Of Dayton; Elem Educ.

PENDRY, VANESSA; Oceana HS; Matheny, WV; 10/150 Cl Rep Jr Cls; Chrh Wkr; Hon Rl; Stu Cncl; Yth Flsp; Fr Clb; FBLA; FHA; Spn Clb; 4-H Awd;.

PENHALE, ELIZABETH; Onaway HS; Onaway, MI; 8/93 Cls Rep Sr Cls; Band; Girl Scts; NHS; Off Ade; Sch Pl; Stu Cncl; Yth Flsp; 4-H; DAR Awd; Butterworth Schl Of Nrsg; Reg Nurse.

PENHALEGON, JANET; Bluffton HS; Bluffton, OH; Chrs; Hon Rl; Off Ade; Sch Mus; Sch Pl; Stg Crw; Pres Yth Flsp; Drama Clb; Pres 4-H; Lat Clb; Ohio St Univ; Nursing.

PENHORWOOD, TROY; Liberty Union HS; Baltimore, OH; Boy Scts; 4-H; FFA; Ftbl; Trk; DCT Voc Schl; Mech.

PENICK, DONNA; Samuel Mumford HS; Detroit, MI; Girl Scts; Hon Rl; Jr NHS; NHS; Stu Cncl; Pep Clb; Swmmng; ISNYC Head Start Prgrm; Word O Bowl Competition; Automobile Club Of Mich Serv Squad; Michigan State Univ; Retailing.

PENIX, TERESA; London HS; London, OH; 18/132 Band; Hon Rl; NHS; Yrbk; Rptr Sch Nwsp; Sch Nwsp; 4-H; Letter Bsktbl; GAA; Var Sftt 3 Ltr 79; Coll; X Ray Tech.

PENKOWSKI, BLASINE; Lake Catholic HS; Mentor, OH; 13/360 Cls Rep Frsh Cls; Cl Rep Jr Cls; AFS; Hon Rl; NHS; Stu Cncl; Ed Yrbk; Letter Bsbl; GAA; JC Awd; Varsity Letter Vlybl; Academic Exc Awd; Natl Ed Develp Test; College; Engr.

PENKOWSKI, CHERYL; Lake Catholic HS; Mentor, OH; 5/305 Cls Rep Soph Cls; Cl Rep Jr Cls; Sal; Am Leg Aux Girls St; NHS; Stu Cncl; Chrldng; Purdue Univ; Chem Eng.

PENLAND, HOLLI; Mayville HS; Mayville, MI; 5/92 Sec Jr Cls; Band; Hon Rl; NHS; 4-H; Pep Clb; Letter Bsbl; Chrldng; Central Mic.

PENLAND, HOWARD; John Hay HS; Cleveland, OH; Cls Rep Soph Cls; VP Jr Cls; Capt Ftbl; Cit Awd; Class Achvmnt Geo Fr 2 Bio Phys Ed Amer H G 76; Wilmington Coll; Elec.

PENN, CRYSTAL; Saint Ursula Acad; Toledo, OH; 1/111 Val; Hon Rl; Orch; Sch Mus; Fr Clb; FSA; Pres Sci Clb; IM Sprt; DAR Awd; Kiwan Awd; Mass Inst Of Tech; Engr.

PENN, GARY; Fenton HS; Fenton, MI; Boy Scts; CAP; Sch Nwsp; Drama Clb; College; Mech.

PENN, NORENE; Highland HS; Sunbury, OH; 7/110 Sec Jr Cls; Sec Sr Cls; Am Leg Aux Girls St; Hosp Ade; Lbry Ade; Pres NHS; Sec Stu Cncl; Ed Yrbk; Pres FHA; Sci Clb; College; Nursing.

PENNEKAMP, RICHARD; Turpin HS; Cincinnati, OH; Univ; Elec.

PENNEY, JOYCE D H; Freeland Community HS; Freeland, MI; 15/115 Band; Hon Rl; NHS; Quill & Scroll; Ed Sch Nwsp; PPFtbl; Natl Merit Ltr; Vllybll Varsity Letter Voted Most Improved 78 79; Schl Spirit Awd 79; Varsity Sftbll Varsity Letter 79; Ctrl Michigan Univ; Jrnlsm.

PENNINGTON, ANGELA; Penn HS; Osceola, IN; Chrh Wkr; JA; Lbry Ade; Sch Mus; Stg Crw; Yth Flsp; Spn Clb; VICA; Trk; JA Awd; St Fnlst VICA 79; Univ; Sci.

PENNINGTON, GARY W; Bluefield HS; Bluefld, WV; 25/300 Boy Scts; Hon Rl; Sct Actv; Fr Clb; Pep Clb; Ftbl; Univ; Dent.

PENNINGTON, JAMES A; Taylor HS; Cleves, OH; Band; Chrh Wkr; Hon Rl; Orch; Sprt Ed Yrbk; Yrbk; Key Clb; Univ; Engr.

PENNINGTON, LAVADA; Cloverdale HS; Quincy, IN; Chrs; 4-H; 4-H Awd; Shorthand I & Home Ec Schlrshps & Awd; College; Secretary.

PENNINGTON, LORI; Athens HS; Princeton, WV; 6/60 Band; Hon Rl; NHS; Yth Flsp; Fr Clb; FTA; Keyettes; Pep Clb; Letter Bsbl; Typing Ii 79; Concord Coll; Psych.

PENNINGTON, PENNY; North Gallia HS; Bidwell, OH; Sec Soph Cls; Pres Jr Cls; Trs Sr Cls; Chrs; Chrh Wkr; Cmnty Wkr; Drl Tm; Hon Rl; Hosp Ade; NHS; Buckeye Hills Career Ctr; Nurse.

PENNINGTON, PHYLLIS A; Southfield Lathrup Sr HS; Southfield, MI; Cls Rep Frsh Cls; Cls Rep Soph Cls; Hon Rl; Sec Pep Clb; Chrldng; Ice Capades Awds For Ice Skating; Skating Club Of Texas Awd; U S Figure Skating Assoc; College; Interior Design.

PENNINGTON, RICKY; Fayetteville Perry HS; Fayetteville, OH; Aud/Vis; Boy Scts; Chrs; Chrh Wkr; Debate Tm; Hon Rl; Sch Pl; Sct Actv; Stg Crw; Yth Flsp; Awd Vllybl Ltr; Awd Video Tech; Univ Of Cincinnati; Dent.

PENNINGTON, RITA; East Clinton HS; Wilmington, OH; 22/109 Band; Drl Tm; Sch Mus; Sch Pl; Drama Clb; 4-H; FHA; FSA; FTA; Pep Clb; Whos Who In Music 77; Brevard Univ; Psych.

PENNINGTON, ROSALIE; Brookville HS; Metamora, IN; 36/20 Chrh Wkr; Hon Rl; Lbry Ade; NHS; 4-H; FFA; FHA; Spn Clb; GAA; 4-H Awd; College.

PENNINGTON, TED G; Philo HS; Duncan Falls, OH; Spn Clb;.

PENNISTEN, DONALD E; South Point HS; South Point, OH; 14/160 Hon Rl; NHS; Ed Yrbk; Sprt Ed Yrbk; Rptr Yrbk; IM Sprt; Drafting Awd 79; Yearbook Awd 79; Ashland St Voc Tech Schl; Drafting.

PENNY, KIM; Muskegon HS; Muskegon, MI; Hon Rl; NHS; Letter Swmmng; Ferris State Univ; Dental Hygiene.

PENNYCUFF, VICKIE; Wayne HS; Dayton, OH; Cl Rep Jr Cls; Band; Chrh Wkr; Drm Bgl; FCA; Lbry Ade; Sch Mus; Sch Pl; Stg Crw; Pep Clb; Univ Of Cincinnati; Nursing.

PENNZA, JILL; Eastlake N HS; Willowick, OH; 144/621 Cmnty Wkr; Hon Rl; Pol Wkr; OEA; Bsbl; Chrldng; Sr Hon Awd For Mfg 79; Better Aver For Four Yrs; Lakeland Cmnty Coll; Acctg.

PENROD, DAVID; North Union HS; Magnetic Spgs, OH; Boy Scts; Hon Rl; Lbry Ade; Sch Pl; Pres Fr Clb; Spn Clb; Trk; Natl Merit Schl; Univ; Math.

PENRY, JIMMY; Emerson HS; Gary, IN; 17/149 Cls Rep Frsh Cls; Hon Rl; ROTC; FFA; Letter Bsktbl; Ftbl; Trk; College; Diesel Mech.

PENTECOST, GREGORY; Holt HS; Holt, MI; 13/362 Chrs; Hon Rl; NHS; Sch Mus; Bsktbl; Ftbl; Letter Ten; Coach Actv; IM Sprt; Natl Merit Ltr; Michigan Tech Univ; Comp Sci.

PENTONI, MICHELE; Athens HS; Athens, MI; Band; Debate Tm; IM Sprt; Natl Merit SF;.

PENTZ, NICOLE; Clearfork HS; Bellville, OH; 3/159 Am Leg Aux Girls St; Chrs; Chrh Wkr; Cmnty Wkr; Hon Rl; Hosp Ade; Jr NHS; NHS; Sch Mus; Stu Cncl; College; Rn.

PENWELL, LORA L; Western HS; Peebles, OH; 8/76 Cls Rep Soph Cls; Chrs; Hon Rl; Drama Clb; 4-H; FHA; 4-H Awd;.

PENZIEN, KORF; Howell HS; Howell, MI; 9/395 Pres Frsh Cls; VP Jr Cls; VP Sr Cls; NHS; Ger Clb; Letter Crs Cntry; Letter Trk; Univ Of Mich; Aero Engr.

PEOHLMAN, BECKY; Niles HS; Cassopolis, MI; Cls Rep Soph Cls; Cl Rep Jr Cls; Hon Rl; NHS; Stu Cncl; 4-H Awd; Pres Awd; College; Vet.

PEOPLES, BRENT; Loudonville HS; Loudonville, OH; 25/133 VP Frsh Cls; VP Sr Cls; Am Leg Boys St; NHS; Stu Cncl; Yth Flsp; Lat Clb; Bsktbl; Capt Ftbl; Capt Trk; Miami Univ; Law.

PEOPLES, BRIAN; Ashtabula Habor HS; Ashtabula, OH; Cl Rep Jr Cls; Debate Tm; Stu Cncl; Yrbk; 4-H; FTA; Spn Clb; Univ; Fshn Mdse.

PEOT, MARK; Bethel HS; New Carlisle, OH; Am Leg Boys St; Band; Hon Rl; NHS; Sch Mus; JETS Awd; Natl Merit Ltr; MIT; Electrical Eng.

PEPA, JAMES; Port Clinton HS; Port Clinton, OH; 23/233 Hon Rl; NHS; Lat Clb; Capt Crs Cntry; Letter Trk; Univ Of Dayton; Bus Admin.

PEPIN, HAROLD; Sault Area HS; Escanaba, MI; 15/280 Hon Rl; NHS; Crs Cntry; IM Sprt; Natl Merit Schl; Lake Superior State College; Draftin.

PEPIN, MIKE; Mona Shores HS; Muskegon, MI; Aud/Vis; Boy Scts; Chrh Wkr; Cmnty Wkr; Hon Rl; Stg Crw; Ftbl; Wrstlng; Scr Kpr; Tmr; Univ Of Michigan; Math.

PEPLINSKI, DAREN; Sterling Heights HS; Sterling Hts, MI; Drm Bgl; Hon Rl; Pres Orch; Pep Clb; Rus Clb; IM Sprt; Macomb Cnty Comm College; Arch.

PEPMEIER, KAREN; North Knox HS; Sandborn, IN; 18/150 VP Band; Hon Rl; Lbry Ade; NHS; Stu Cncl; Sec Yth Flsp; 4-H; Pep Clb; Bsktbl; Trk; North Knox Stu Cncl Schlrshp; Band Awd Jacket; Athletic Letter Jacket; Vincennes Univ; Dent Hygiene.

PEPPIN, GARY; Muskegon Catholic Ctrl HS; Muskegon, MI; 5/182 Trs Soph Cls; VP Jr Cls; Hon Rl; NHS; Sch Mus; Letter Ftbl; Natl Merit Ltr; Muskegon Cmnty Coll; Elec Engr.

PEPPLE, KIMBERLY J; Western Boone Jr Sr HS; Jamestown, IN; 20/168 Sec Jr Cls; Trs Jr Cls; Am Leg Aux Girls St; Chrs; Chrh Wkr; Girl Scts; Hon Rl; NHS; Sch Mus; Sch Pl; College; Medicine.

PEPPLER, JOHN; Parkersburg HS; Davisville, WV; 53/785 Pres Awd; Marrietta College; Engr.

PEQUIGNOT, JILL; Heritage Jr Sr HS; Hoagland, IN; Trs Frsh Cls; Chrh Wkr; Girl Scts; Hon Rl; Off Ade; Sct Actv; Pep Clb; Trk; Chrldng; IM Sprt; College; Sci.

PERALTA, CLARISSA; Bridgeport HS; Bridgeprt, MI; Cls Rep Soph Cls; Trs Jr Cls; Chrh Wkr; Hon Rl; JA; NHS; Sch Pl; Stu Cncl; Pep Clb; Mgrs; Shorthand Awd 79; Michigan St Univ; Travel Indust Mgmt.

PERALTA, DEANNA; Hamlin HS; Hamlin, WV; 1 Val; Band; Yth Flsp; Ger Clb; West Virginia Univ; Attorney.

PERAZZA, ANNE; Lakeview HS; St Clair Shore, MI; 7/550 Hon Rl; NHS; Quill & Scroll; Sch Mus; Sch Pl; Stg Crw; Ed Yrbk; Rptr Yrbk; Ed Sch Nwsp; Rptr Sch Nwsp; Central Michigan Univ; Cmnctns.

PERCELL, DAVID; Robert S Tower HS; Warren, MI; 13/400 Hon Rl; NHS; Mic Tech Univ; Comp Tech.

PERCH, VAN; Garfield HS; Akron, OH; VP Sr Cls; Hon Rl; NHS; Stg Crw; Stu Cncl; Fr Clb; Sci Clb; Letter Socr; Trk; College.

PERCY, KATHLEEN; Napoleon HS; Jackson, MI; 1/156 Chrh Wkr; Girl Scts; Hon Rl; Natl Forn Lg; Pres NHS; Drama Clb; 4-H; Spring Arbor College;psych.

PERDEW, LORI; Ogemaw Heights HS; West Branch, MI; 12/18 Cls Rep Sr Cls; Band; Chrh Wkr; Cmnty Wkr; Girl Scts; Hosp Ade; Pres NHS; Sct Actv; Stu Cncl; Yth Flsp; DOT Otstndng Stud Trainee 78; Grad Magna Cum Laude 79; Cert Of Recogntn St Of Mi Comp Schlrshp Prog 79; Ferris St Coll; Med Asst.

PERDUE, ANGEL; M Luther King Jr Sr HS; Detroit, MI; Pres Jr Cls; VP Jr Cls; Chrh Wkr; Hon Rl; JA; Mth Clb; Pep Clb; JA Awd; E Michigan Univ; Spec Ed.

PERDUE, JANIE; Vinson HS; Huntington, WV; 42/112 Band; Chrs; Chrh Wkr; Hon Rl; Finalist Miss Teenage Huntington Pageant; St Marys School; Nursing.

PERDUE, LEDA; Matoaka HS; Matoaka, WV; VP Jr Cls; Hon Rl; Stg Crw; Yrbk; Rptr Sch Nwsp; FBLA; Bkkpng II Awd 79; 1st Pl In Cirriculum Fair Offc Practc 79; Bluefield St Univ; Acctg.

PERDUE, RAMA D; Bluefield HS; Bluefield, WV; 95/325 Cls Rep Frsh Cls; Cl Rep Jr Cls; Cls Rep Sr Cls; Band; Hon Rl; Yrbk; Fr Clb; FTA; Twrlr; Mas Awd; Bluefield St Coll; Elem Ed.

PEREIRA, GREGG; Sylvania Southview HS; Sylvania, OH; Cmnty Wkr; Red Cr Ade; Rptr Yrbk; Yrbk; Rptr Sch Nwsp; Lat Clb; Ftbl; Letter Trk; Coach Actv; IM Sprt; College; Medicine.

PEREZ, ANA; Carroll HS; Centerville, OH; Chrh Wkr; Hon Rl; NHS; Key Clb; Spn Clb; Univ Of Dayton; Psych.

PEREZ, CINDY; Northrop HS; Howe, IN; 84/554 JA; Lbry Ade; Letter Socr; Activity Awd; College; Vet.

PEREZ, DELORES; Holy Redeemer HS; Detroit, MI; Cmnty Wkr; Hon Rl; Off Ade; Sch Nwsp; Spn Clb; Schlrshp GI Forum Pageant 1st Runner Up 78; Merit Awrd Schl Serv 79; Civil Serv.

PEREZ, ERNIE; Gavit HS; Hammond, IN; 37/252 VP Jr Cls; Hon Rl; Jr NHS; VP Stu Cncl; Spn Clb; Bsktbl; Crs Cntry; Capt Socr; Indiana Univ; Zoology.

PEREZ, GLORIA; Theodore Roosevelt HS; Wyandotte, MI; 19/424 Hon Rl; Lit Mag; NHS; Rptr Sch Nwsp; Letter Ten; ACT St Of Mi Comp Schlrshp 79; General Motors Inst; Mech Engr.

PEREZ, JUAN I; Carroll HS; Centerville, OH; 1/300 Hon Rl; NHS; Fr Clb; Ftbl; Trk; Natl Merit SF; MIT; Physics.

PEREZ, LINDA; South HS; Youngstown, OH; Chrh Wkr; Hon Rl; Lbry Ade; Off Ade; Univ; Accounting.

PEREZ, LINDA; Solon HS; Solon, OH; 11/300 Hon Rl; Lit Mag; Sch Nwsp; Voice Dem Awd; Ohio St Univ; Psych.

PEREZ, MARIA L; Warsaw Community HS; Winona Lake, IN; 80/450 Chrs; Chrh Wkr; Hon Rl; Sch Pl; Drama Clb; Pres Awd;.

PEREZ, MICHAEL J; Briggs HS; Columbus, OH; Pres Frsh Cls; Am Leg Boys St; FCA; Hon Rl; NHS; Spn Clb; Letter Bsbl; Crs Cntry; Letter Ftbl; College; Business.

PEREZ, MIKE; Bishop Watterson HS; Columbus, OH; 6/260 Am Leg Boys St; Hon Rl; Jr NHS; Off Ade; Sch Pl; Sch Nwsp; Spn Clb; Letter Ten; Coach Actv; IM Sprt; Notre Dame Univ; Med.

PEREZ, RAYMOND; Tallmadge HS; Tallmadge, OH; 11/349 Am Leg Boys St; Band; Boy Scts; Debate Tm; Hon Rl; Pres Natl Forn Lg; NHS; Lat Clb; Glf; IM Sprt; Kent St Univ; Med.

PEREZ, ROXANA; St Mary Cathedral HS; Saginaw, MI; 3/56 Hon Rl; NHS; Ed Sch Nwsp; Spn Clb; Natl Merit SF; Opt Clb Awd; Delta Coll; X Ray Tech.

PERFECT, BEVERLY; Big Walnut HS; Sunbury, OH; Cl Rep Jr Cls; Chrs; Girl Scts; Hon Rl; Off Ade; Rptr Sch Nwsp; DECA; Spn Clb; Bus Schl; Stenography.

PERFILI, LINDA; Cabrini HS; Southgate, MI; NHS; Spn Clb; Natl Merit Ltr; Michigan St Univ; Med Tech.

PERHALA, CHRISTOPHER; James Ford Rhodes HS; Cleveland, OH; Lat Clb; Crs Cntry; Trk; Wrstlng; Univ.

PERIGO, VADA; Boonville HS; Boonville, IN; 13/244 Chrh Wkr; Hon Rl; Hosp Ade; Pep Clb; Vinconnes Univ; Phys Ther.

PERISUTTI, STEVE; Highland HS; Hinckley, OH; 10/223 Am Leg Boys St; Hon Rl; NHS; Letter Bsbl; Letter Bsktbl; Scr Kpr; College.

PERK, SCARLETT; Riverside HS; De Graff, OH; 14/72 Band; Chrs; Girl Scts; Hon Rl; Lbry Ade; NHS; Sch Pl; Rptr Sch Nwsp; Rdo Clb; Chrldng; Clark Tech Coll.

PERKEY, JULIE; Four Cnty Joint Voc School; Ridgeville Crns, OH; 11/115 Am Leg Aux Girls St; Chrs; Chrh Wkr; Hon Rl; Stu Cncl; Yrbk; 4-H; OEA; GAA; Mat Maids; OEA Stateswoman 1979; OEA Reg Stenog I 1979; Typing I 1977; Voc Schl; Sec.

PERKINS, ANN; Philo HS; Duncan Falls, OH; Letter Band; Cmp Fr Grls; Chrs; Girl Scts; Letter Hon Rl; Hosp Ade; Lbry Ade; Lit Mag; Sch Mus; Pres Stu Cncl; Bus Schl; Bus Mgmt.

PERKINS, BRUCE; Nitro HS; Charleston, WV; Trs Frsh Cls; Cls Rep Frsh Cls; Cls Rep Soph Cls; Cl Rep Jr Cls; Cls Rep Sr Cls; Boy Scts; Chrs; Chrh Wkr; Cmnty Wkr; Hon Rl; Marshall Univ; Chem Engr.

PERKINS, CHERYL; Western Boone HS; Lebanon, IN; 26/166 Chrh Wkr; Hon Rl; NHS; Sch Mus; Drama Clb; 4-H; Pep Clb; Bethel College; Music.

PERKINS, CHRISTOPHER; Lima HS; Lima, OH; Boy Scts; Chrs; Treas Chrh Wkr; Hon Rl; Sct Actv; Treas Yth Flsp; Pep Clb; Tri St Univ; Aero Engr.

PERKINS, JACQUELYN; Colonel Crawford HS; Bucyrus, OH; VP Soph Cls; Band; Chrs; FCA; Hon Rl; JA; Rptr Yrbk; Pres 4-H; Fr Clb; VP FTA; Vlybl Ltr 78; Univ; Fshn Mdse.

PERKINS, JOHN; Climax Scotts HS; Scotts, MI; 11/57 Hon Rl; NHS; 4-H; Letter Bsktbl; Letter Trk; Mich State.

PERKINS, JULIE; Plainfield HS; Plainfield, IN; 25/283 Band; Hon Rl; NHS; Ind Univ; Phys Therap.

PERKINS, LAURA; Buffalo HS; Huntington, WV; 3/103 Chrh Wkr; Hosp Ade; NHS; Sch Pl; Ed Sch Nwsp; Fr Clb; Mth Clb; Pres Sci Clb; Spn Clb; VFW Awd; Ohio State Univ; Pre Med.

PERKINS, LAURIE D; R Nelson Snider HS; Fort Wayne, IN; 2/550 Chrs; Chrh Wkr; Hon Rl; Fr Clb; Trk; Natl Merit SF; Greenville College; Engineering.

PERKINS, LORRAINE; Whitmer HS; Toledo, OH; Chrs; Girl Scts; Hosp Ade; FNA; Owens Tech Inst; Nursing.

PERKINS, MATTHEW; Archbishop Alter HS; Centrvll, OH; 77/300 Chrh Wkr; Pol Wkr; Key Clb; Ftbl; Trk; Miami Univ; History.

PERKINS, PAMELA J; East HS; Columbus, OH; 50/500 Cls Rep Soph Cls; Aud/Vis; Hon Rl; JA; IM Sprt; Ohio State; Agriculture.

PERKINS, RHONDA; Magnolia HS; Varney, WV; Sec Frsh Cls; Cls Rep Soph Cls; Sec Jr Cls; Chrh Wkr; Hon Rl; Jr NHS; Lbry Ade; NHS; Stu Cncl; FHA; Marshall Univ; Early Childhood Ed.

PERKINS, SCOTT; Maple Valley HS; Nashville, MI; 27/124 Pres Sr Cls; Hon Rl; NHS; Stu Cncl; Wrstlng; Ferris State College; Mech Engr.

PERKINS, SHELLEY; Onaway HS; Onaway, MI; 3/97 Band; Hon Rl; NHS; Sch Pl; Stg Crw; 4-H; St Of Mi Schlrshp 79; Alpena Cmnty Coll; Educ.

PERKINS, STERLING; Fenwick HS; Middletown, OH; Boy Scts; Hon Rl; Fr Clb; College.

PERKOWSKI, SUSAN; Kent Theodore Roosevelt HS; Kent, OH; 73/375 Cls Rep Frsh Cls; Cmp Fr Grls; Chrs; Chrh Wkr; Cmnty Wkr; Hon Rl; NHS; Sch Mus; Miami Univ Of Ohi; Foreign Bus.

PERLOVE, KATHI; Ladywood HS; Livonia, MI; Pres Chrs; Girl Scts; Hon Rl; Hosp Ade; NHS; Pres Orch; Quill & Scroll; Sch Mus; Stu Cncl; Rptr Yrbk; Eastern Michigan Univ; Math.

PERNE, KIMBERLY; Forest Hills Central HS; Grand Rapids, MI;.Lbry Ade; Letter Ten; Michigan St Univ; Bus Admin.

PERNELL, MARK A; Roosevelt Wilson HS; Clarksburg, WV; Pres Frsh Cls; Cls Rep Soph Cls; Cl Rep Jr Cls; VP Sr Cls; Chrh Wkr; Cmnty Wkr; FCA; Hon Rl; JA; Pol Wkr; Marshall Univ; Archt.

PERNELL JR, ROBERT; R S Caldwell HS; Columbus, MS; Cmnty Wkr; Rptr Sch Nwsp; Ftbl; Socr; Trk; Coach Actv; IM Sprt; Scr Kpr; Twrlr; Voice Dem Awd; Miss State College; Law.

PERNIK, SUSIE; Alter HS; Kettering, OH; Off Ade; Fr Clb; Pep Clb; Ten; Univ; Comp Sci.

PERO, PAUL; Bishop Fenwick HS; Middletown, OH; Hon Rl; NHS; College; Mech Engr.

PERPICH, LAURA; Plymouth Salem HS; Canton, MI; Girl Scts; Hon Rl; Mod UN; NHS; Red Cr Ade; Capt Swmmng; Coach Actv; DAR Awd; Mich State Univ; Dietician.

PERRAS, JAMES L; Carney Nadeau HS; Carney, MI; 1/24 Trs Frsh Cls; Trs Soph Cls; Trs Jr Cls; Band; Hon Rl; Sch Pl; Stu Cncl; Drama Clb; 4-H; Letter Bsktbl; Univ; Civil Engr.

PERRELL, BRIAN; Brecksville HS; Braodview Hts, OH; 50/370 Chrh Wkr; FCA; NHS; Yth Flsp; Letter Bsbl; Ftbl; IM Sprt; Cit Awd; Univ Of Cincinnati; Civil Engr.

PERRICO, BARBARA; Canfield HS; Canfield, OH; Chrh Wkr; Girl Scts; Hon Rl; Yth Flsp; Y-Teens; Spn Clb; Socr; IM Sprt; PPFtbl; Scr Kpr; Youngstown St Univ.

PERRIN, CINDA; Millington HS; Millington, MI; Band; Chrh Wkr; Girl Scts; Hon Rl; Yth Flsp; 4-H; Fr Clb; Pep Clb; 4-H Awd; HS Ltr In Band 77; 2 Serv Bars In Band 78; Spec Rabbit Breeding Awd Trophies 77 79; Saginaw Valley St Coll; Cmmrcl Art.

PERRIN, JAMES; Hanover Central HS; Cedar Lake, IN; 38/121 Band; Hon Rl; Sch Mus; Sch Nwsp; Pep Clb; Bsbl; Letter Trk; Coach Actv; IM Sprt; Scr Kpr;.

PERRINE, MARTIN; Dansville HS; Dansville, MI; 3/65 Cls Rep Frsh Cls; Cls Rep Sr Cls; Band; Boy Scts; Chrh Wkr; Hon Rl; NHS; Off Ade; Sch Pl; Sct Actv; Michigan Tech Univ; Elec Engr.

PERRINO, MARIA L; St Ursula Academy; Cincinnati, OH; Cls Rep Sr Cls; Chrs; Chrh Wkr; Cmnty Wkr; Girl Scts; Hon Rl; Stu Cncl; Spn Clb; Trk; Chrldng; Xavier Univ; X Ray Tech.

PERRONE, ANNETTE; Catholic Ctrl HS; Steubenville, OH; Hon Rl; Rptr Sch Nwsp; FHA; Pep Clb; Spn Clb; Univ; Elem Ed.

PERROT, DAVE; Plymouth Canton HS; Plymouth, MI; 18/440 Hon Rl; Letter Trk; Univ Of Tenn; Transportation.

PERRY, AMY; Mohawk HS; Tiffin, OH; Hon Rl; Lit Mag; Stu Cncl; Yth Flsp; Y-Teens; 4-H; FHA; FTA; Pep Clb; Trk; Tiffin Univ; Exec Sec.

PERRY, ANDREA; Saint Alphonsus HS; Detroit, MI; Band; Hon Rl; Orch; Sch Mus; Sch Pl; Letter Swmmng; Letter Trk; Univ; Psych.

PERRY, ANGELA; Pontiac Central HS; Pontiac, MI; Cls Rep Frsh Cls; Cls Rep Soph Cls; Cl Rep Jr Cls; Band; Cmp Fr Grls; Hon Rl; Stg Crw; Stu Cncl; OEA; PPFtbl; Univ Of Michigan; Engr.

PERRY, ANTHONY; Cardinal Mooney HS; Boardman, OH; 20/288 Hon Rl; JA; Jr NHS; Mth Clb; Natl Merit Ltr; Highest Avg Comp Sci Comp Bus & Elec 1 78; Univ; Med.

PERRY, BRIAN; Benjamin Bosse HS; Evansville, IN; 37/329 Cl Rep Jr Cls; Cls Rep Sr Cls; Boy Scts; Chrs; Hon Rl; Pol Wkr; Sct Actv; Stu Cncl; Pep Clb; Letter Socr; College; Pharmacy.

PERRY, CHARLES; Reynoldsburg HS; Reynoldsburg, OH; Hon Rl; Pres JA; Yrbk; Sec Mth Clb; Hon Mntn In Geom In St Comp 77; 1 Month Trip To Bogota Columbia For Spanish Std 79; Univ; Comp Sci.

PERRY, CYNTHIA A; Whitko HS; Pierceton, IN; 20/151 Band; Hon Rl; Yrbk; 4-H; Ger Clb; OEA; Letter Trk; Mgrs; 4-H Awd; Busns Manager Annual Yrbk; Kosciusko Co 4h Horse & Pony; Track Letter & Jacket; Ivy Tech Univ; Accounting.

PERRY, DARRELL; Madison Comprehensive HS; Mansfield, OH; Aud/Vis; Band; Cmnty Wkr; Treas Hosp Ade; Red Cr Ade; Univ; Med.

PERRY, DAVID; Trenton HS; Trenton, MI; Hon Rl; JA; Wrstlng; Wayne St Univ; Acctg.

PERRY, DAVID; Rogers HS; Toledo, OH; Cls Rep Frsh Cls; Cls Rep Soph Cls; Chrs; Letter Bsbl; Letter Ftbl;.

PERRY, DAVID; Chesaning Union HS; Oakley, MI; 28/259 Hon Rl; Spn Clb; Letter Ftbl; Letter Trk; IM Sprt; Tmr; Central Michigan Univ; Comp Sci.

PERRY, DOUGLAS; Belleville HS; Belleville, MI; Hon Rl; NHS; Yrbk; Letter Bsbl; Natl Merit Ltr; Mi Comptn Schlrshp Honorary; Eastern Michigan Univ; Pre Pharm.

PERRY, GERTIE; Highland Park Comm HS; Highland Pk, MI; Chrh Wkr; Hon Rl; DECA; Business School; Marketing.

PERRY, GRETA; Marion Harding HS; Marion, OH; 1/500 Chrs; Chrh Wkr; Hon Rl; Sch Mus; Yth Flsp; Rptr Sch Nwsp; Sch Nwsp; Spn Clb; Natl Merit Ltr; Oh Test Of Schlstc Achvmnt 1st In St 77 In Spnsh I 77; Part In The M W Essex Schl For Giftd At OSU 79; Univ; Spnsh Tchr.

PERRY, INGER A; Liberty HS; Salem, WV; Chrh Wkr; Hon Rl; Hosp Ade; Jr NHS; Sch Mus; Sch Pl; Drama Clb; 4-H; Spn Clb; 4-H Awd; Salem Coll; Nursing.

PERRY, JEFF; Calvert HS; Tiffin, OH; Band; Sch Mus; Yth Flsp; Ftbl; Wrstlng; Voc Schl.

PERRY, JILL; Grosse Ile HS; Grosse Ile, MI; Chrs; Chrh Wkr; Hon Rl; Mdrgl; NHS; Sch Mus; Sch Pl; Drama Clb; Spn Clb; Bsbl; Michigan St Univ; Auto Design.

PERRY, JOHN; Wayne HS; Wayne, WV; 15/152 Pres Frsh Cls; Cl Rep Jr Cls; Trs Sr Cls; Am Leg Boys St; Chrh Wkr; Cmnty Wkr; Hon Rl; Jr NHS; NHS; Beta Clb; Sr Superlatv 79; YMC Model St Leg Chrmn 79; Marshall Univ; Bus Mgmt.

PERRY, KATHY; Hurricane HS; Hurricane, WV; Cl Rep Jr Cls; Hon Rl; Stu Cncl; Pep Clb; Trk; Chmn Chrldng; IM Sprt; Marshall Univ.

PERRY, KIMBERLY; Bedford Sr HS; Temperance, MI; 12/500 Band; Chrs; Treas Chrh Wkr; Hon Rl; Hosp Ade; Jr NHS; NHS; Red Cr Ade; Sch Mus; Sch Pl; Univ Of Toledo; Arts.

PERRY, LISA D; Mifflin Sr HS; Columbus, OH; 25/220 Chrs; Chrh Wkr; Girl Scts; Hon Rl; Sch Pl; Yth Flsp; Drama Clb; Treas OEA; Trk; Anderson Coll; Law.

PERRY, MICHAEL; East Kentwood HS; Kentwood, MI; VP Frsh Cls; Pres Jr Cls; Pres Sr Cls; Boy Scts; Yth Flsp; Letter Bsbl; Letter Ftbl; Central Michigan Univ; Bus.

PERRY, MICHELE M; Vinson HS; Huntington, WV; Chrs; Chrh Wkr; Hon Rl; Treas Stu Cncl; Yth Flsp; Y-Teens; FHA; Keyettes; Chrldng; Elk Awd; Miss Teenage & Congeniality 1978; Homecoming Queen 1978; W V All State Chorus 1978; Marshall Univ; Early Educ.

PERRY, PAUL; Bramwell HS; Bramwell, WV; VP Chrs; Hon Rl; NHS; Key Clb; Bsktbl; Crs Cntry; Trk; Cit Awd; College; Forestry.

PERRY, REBECCA; Tippecanoe Valley HS; Warsaw, IN; Chrs; Chrh Wkr; Stg Crw; Drama Clb; DAR Awd; Grace College; Nursing.

PERRY, ROGER; Calvert HS; Tiffin, OH; Hon Rl; Spn Clb; Letter Ftbl; Vocational School; Auto Mech.

PERRY, RONALD; Perry HS; Perry, MI; Band; Boy Scts; Hon Rl; Sct Actv; Letter Bsktbl; Letter Glf; Letter Trk; College; Elec.

PERRY, SANDRA; Annapolis HS; Dearborn, MI; Cls Rep Soph Cls; Cl Rep Jr Cls; Cls Rep Sr Cls; Hon Rl; NHS; Sch Pl; Stu Cncl; Trk; Chrldng; Western Michigan Univ.

PERRY, SHERRI; Rogers HS; Toledo, OH; Cls Rep Frsh Cls; Cl Rep Jr Cls; Hon Rl; Jr NHS; Off Ade; Stu Cncl; Rptr Sch Nwsp; Letter Trk; Jrnlsm Awd 78; Univ; Cmnctns.

PERRY, STEVEN D; West Lafayette HS; West Lafayette, IN; 3/185 Band; Hon Rl; NHS; Yrbk; Bsbl; Ftbl; Bausch & Lomb Awd; Kiwan Awd; Natl Merit SF; Purdue Univ; Engr.

PERRY, TAMMY; Watkins Memorial HS; Pataskala, OH; Girl Scts; Hon Rl; Lbry Ade; NHS; Off Ade; Yth Flsp; Rptr Sch Nwsp; Chrldng; IM Sprt; Scr Kpr; Schlrshp Awrd 75; Franklin Univ; Acctg.

PERRY, TRACEY M; Wadsworth HS; Wadsworth, OH; 20/375 Chrs; Chrh Wkr; FCA; Hon Rl; Red Cr Ade; Fr Clb; Key Clb; Pep Clb; Bsktbl; Chrldng; Univ.

PERRY, VERLAND; Buffalo HS; Kenova, WV; Hon Rl; Yth Flsp; 4-H; Sci Clb; Bsktbl; Capt Ftbl; Letter Trk; Marshall Univ.

PERRY, WENDY; Dearborn HS; Dearborn, MI; Chrs; Chrh Wkr; Cmnty Wkr; Girl Scts; Hon Rl; Hosp Ade; Lbry Ade; NHS; Sct Actv; Stu Cncl; Univ Of Mich; Accountant.

PERRY, WILLIAM M; South Newton HS; Kentland, IN; 16/101 VP Frsh Cls; VP Soph Cls; Quill & Scroll; Sch Pl; Stg Crw; Stu Cncl; Yrbk; Drama Clb; FBLA; Lat Clb; College; Bus.

PERSHING, BETH; Breckenridge Jr Sr HS; Breckenridge, MI; 3/105 Band; Chrh Wkr; Girl Scts; Hon Rl; NHS; Sch Mus; Sch Pl; Stg Crw; Sec Stu Cncl; Yth Flsp; Michigan Tech Univ; Math.

PERSHING, JENNY; Eastern HS; Sardinia, OH; Sec Frsh Cls; VP Soph Cls; VP Jr Cls; Cl Rep Jr Cls; Band; Chrs; NHS; Stu Cncl; Rptr Yrbk; Fr Clb; Raymond Walters Coll; Court Reporter.

PERSING, TERI; Lapel HS; Anderson, IN; 2/84 VP Jr Cls; VP Sr Cls; Pres Band; Chrs; Chrh Wkr; Capt Drl Tm; Hon Rl; Hosp Ade; NHS; Sch Mus; General Motors Inst; Engr.

PERSONS, SHARON; St Charles HS; St Charles, MI; Pres Chrs; Hon Rl; NHS; Sch Mus; Sch Pl; Stg Crw; Stu Cncl; Yth Flsp; Natl Merit SF; Albion; Med.

PERTICONE, ANNE; Lumen Christi HS; Jackson, MI; 6/250 Hon Rl; Treas NHS; Sch Mus; Rptr Yrbk; Drama Clb; Pep Clb; Chrldng; IM Sprt; Am Leg Awd; Jackson Cmnty Coll; Med Asst.

PERTNER, SANDRA; Gibsonburg HS; Gibsonburg, OH; 7/105 Pres Frsh Cls; Pres Soph Cls; Pres Jr Cls; Chrh Wkr; Cmnty Wkr; Girl Scts; Hon Rl; Off Ade; Yrbk; Sch Nwsp; Univ; Fshn Mdse.

PERTTUNEN, DARRYL; Howell HS; Howell, MI; 39/395 Hon Rl; Letter Ftbl; Letter Wrstlng; Michigan Tech Univ; Mech Engr.

PERUCCA, MELISSA; Terre Haute N Vigo HS; Terre Haute, IN; 41/597 Cls Rep Soph Cls; Hon Rl; Pres JA; NHS; Off Ade; Stu Cncl; Pres 4-H; Lat Clb; VP Sci Clb; 4-H Awd; Ind State Univ; Science.

PERUCCA, STEVE; C S Mott HS; Warren, MI; Band; Boy Scts; Hon Rl; NHS; Sct Actv; IM Sprt; Natl Merit Ltr; College; Physics.

PERUNKO, MAUREEN; Canfield HS; Canfield, OH; Band; Chrh Wkr; Cmnty Wkr; Debate Tm; Drl Tm; Girl Scts; Hon Rl; Sch Pl; Sct Actv; Y-Teens; Univ; Psych.

PERUSKI, DAVID; Ubly Community HS; Ruth, MI; 9/110 Trs Jr Cls; Chrh Wkr; Hon Rl; Lbry Ade; NHS; Stg Crw; 4-H; 4-H Awd; College; Rn.

PERUSKI, WANDA; Waterford Mott HS; Pontiac, MI; 7/397 Girl Scts; Hon Rl; NHS; PPFtbl; Central Mic Univ.

PERVOLARAKIS, D; Brandon HS; Ortonville, MI; Chrs; Hon Rl; Off Ade; Stu Cncl; Spn Clb; Letter Bsbl; Ftbl; Letter Glf; IM Sprt; Mich State; Law.

PERVOLARAKIS, DIMITRI; Brandon HS; Ortonville, MI; Hon Rl; Off Ade; Sch Pl; Stu Cncl; Spn Clb; Letter Bsbl; Ftbl; Letter Glf; IM Sprt; Cit Awd; Univ; Law.

PERZANOWSKI, MOLLY; Bellaire HS; Bellaire, OH; 46/218 VP Soph Cls; Treas FCA; Girl Scts; Hon Rl; Stu Cncl; IM Sprt; Scr Kpr; Ohio Valley Medical Ctr; Ansthslgy.

PESARESI, ANNAMARIA; Winamac Community HS; Winamac, IN; 10/150 VP Soph Cls; Sec Jr Cls; Band; Hon Rl; Jr NHS; NHS; Drama Clb; Lat Clb; Pep Clb; Ball State; Elem Teacher.

PESCH, RONALD; Muskegon Sr HS; Muskegon, MI; Hon Rl; JA; NHS; Pol Wkr; Yrbk; Muskegon Cmnty Coll; Comp Sci.

PETCH, ADRIENNE; James Ford Rhodes HS; Cleveland, OH; Chrs; Hon Rl; NHS; Orch; Sch Mus; Stu Cncl; Rptr Yrbk; Ger Clb; IM Sprt; Cit Awd; Soc Club Pres 76; All City Mbr 76; All City Orch Mbr 77; Univ; Eng.

PETER, JULIE; Hicksville HS; Hicksville, OH; 1/101 Chrs; Chrh Wkr; Hon Rl; NHS; Sch Pl; Rptr Sch Nwsp; Spn Clb; Letter Trk; Bowling Green; Pre Law.

PETER, MAX; Tyler County HS; Wilbur, WV; Band; Red Cr Ade; ROTC; 4-H; Treas FFA;.

PETER, MAZUR; Hammond HS; Hammond, IN; 8/340 Aud/Vis; Hon Rl; Jr NHS; Quill & Scroll; Rptr Yrbk; Yrbk; Sch Nwsp; Bsbl; Swmmng; Univ; Engr.

PETER, PHILIP; Perry Central HS; Tell City, IN; Am Leg Boys St; Chrh Wkr; Cmnty Wkr; Hon Rl; NHS; Pres 4-H; Pep Clb; Letter Ftbl; Trk; IM Sprt; Purdue Univ; Agriculture.

PETERFISH, SUSAN; Brookhaven HS; Columbus, OH; Sec Frsh Cls; Cls Rep Soph Cls; Cl Rep Jr Cls; Drl Tm; Hon Rl; Jr NHS; Off Ade; Sch Pl; Gym; Mat Maids; 1st Cl Girl Sct Awd 77; Ohio St Univ; Acctg.

PETERLIN, SUSAN; Holy Name Nazareth HS; Parma, OH; Sec Jr Cls; Sec Sr Cls; Cmnty Wkr; Girl Scts; Hon Rl; Stu Cncl; Bsktbl; Ten; Chrldng; Scr Kpr; Miami Univ.

PETERMAN, DAVID; Northwest HS; Canal Fulton, OH; Cls Rep Soph Cls; Hon Rl; NHS; Sch Pl; Stu Cncl; Lat Clb; Ftbl; IM Sprt; Univ Of Toledo; Engr.

PETERMAN, SALLY J; Indian Valley North HS; New Phila, OH; Cl Rep Jr Cls; Chrs; Stu Cncl; Rptr Yrbk; Sch Nwsp; FTA; OEA; Pep Clb; Bus Schl.

PETERMAN, SUSAN; Alma HS; Alma, MI; Chrh Wkr; FCA; Spn Clb; Bsktbl; Trk; Capt Chrldng; 4-H Awd; Kendall Coll; Applied Arts Fine Arts.

PETERS, BRIAN; East Bank HS; Winifrede, WV; 1/248 Trs Sr Cls; Chrh Wkr; Hon Rl; Treas JA; Treas Lbry Ade; Mod UN; Natl Forn Lg; Pres NHS; Sch Pl; Eng Clb; Wv Inst Of Tech; Comp Sci.

PETERS, CATHERINE A; Bishop Gallagher HS; Harper Woods, MI; 4/333 Chrs; Girl Scts; Hon Rl; Letter Ten; Univ; Med Research.

PETERS, CHERYL; Magnificat HS; No Olmsted, OH; Cls Rep Frsh Cls; Cl Rep Jr Cls; Cls Rep Sr Cls; Boy Scts; Chrh Wkr; Off Ade; Stu Cncl; Capt Bsbl; College; Business.

PETERS, DAVID W; Bishop Foley HS; Troy, MI; Boy Scts; Hon Rl; Off Ade; Rdo Clb; Massachuesetts Inst Of Tech; Chemist.

PETERS, DEBORAH; Marian HS; Mishawaka, IN; Chrs; Hon Rl; Lbry Ade; NHS; Sch Mus; Sch Pl; Rptr Yrbk; Sch Nwsp; Univ; Theatre.

PETERS, DIANE; Bellbrook HS; Dayton, OH; Cl Rep Jr Cls; Band; Girl Scts; Hon Rl; Stg Crw; Stu Cncl; Rptr Yrbk; College.

PETERS, E; Mason HS; Mason, MI; Cl Rep Jr Cls; Am Leg Boys St; Hon Rl; NHS; 4-H; Letter Bsbl; Letter Bsktbl; Fenis Univ; Optometry.

PETERS, ELAINE; Franklin HS; Livonia, MI; Cls Rep Soph Cls; Cl Rep Jr Cls; Chrs; Girl Scts; Lbry Ade; Sch Mus; Sch Pl; Stg Crw; Stu Cncl; Rptr Yrbk; Univ; Spanish.

PETERS, ERIC; Stow HS; Stow, OH; Hon Rl; JA; Sch Pl; Stg Crw; JA Awd; Kent State Univ; Art.

PETERS, GREG; Marquette Sr HS; Marquette, MI; Debate Tm; Natl Forn Lg; Yrbk; 1 Of 5 Marquette Stdnt Part In HS Bowl T V Series 79; Univ; Poli Sci.

PETERS, JANE; Eaton Rapids HS; Eaton Rapids, MI; VP Jr Cls; Chrs; Hon Rl; Sch Mus; Yth Flsp; Y-Teens; Spn Clb; Swmmng; Ten; Registered Nursing.

PETERS, JULIA M; Mancelona HS; Mancelona, MI; Chrh Wkr; Cmnty Wkr; Hon Rl; Hosp Ade; Sch Mus; Sch Pl; Sct Actv; Ed Yrbk; Ferris State College; Science.

PETERS, KEVIN; East Liverpool HS; E Liverpool, OH; Boy Scts; Cmnty Wkr; Key Clb; Kent St Univ; Vet.

PETERS, KIMBERLY; Walnut Hills HS; Cincinnati, OH; Chrh Wkr; Girl Scts; Hon Rl; Orch; 4-H; Fr Clb; Crs Cntry; Trk; 4-H Awd; College; Med.

PETERS, MARK; Revere HS; Bath, OH; Boy Scts; Cmp Fr Grls; Hon Rl; Sch Pl; Sct Actv; Ohio St Univ; Admin Sci.

PETERS, NICHOLAS; Brookville HS; Brookville, IN; Cls Rep Frsh Cls; Cls Rep Soph Cls; Cl Rep Jr Cls; Chrh Wkr; Hon Rl; Stu Cncl; Sch Nwsp; Key Clb; Spn Clb; Bsbl; Optimists Speech Contest; St Legislative Asst In 1976 & 1977; Natl Yth Leaders Amer Symposiuh; Indiana Central Univ; Busns Mgmt.

PETERS, RAY; Brownstown Central HS; Vallonia, IN; 17/150 Chrs; Hon Rl; NHS; Sch Mus; Stu Cncl; FFA; Purdue Univ; Engr.

PETERS, RENDA; Blanchester HS; Blanchester, OH; 7/146 Chrh Wkr; Cmnty Wkr; Hon Rl; NHS; GAA; Univ; Tchr.

PETERS, RUTHIE; Tri County Joint Voc HS; Albany, OH; Chrs; Chrh Wkr; Hon Rl; NHS; Off Ade; Yrbk; Sprt Ed Sch Nwsp; Rptr Sch Nwsp; Sch Nwsp; FHA; Hocking Tech; CPA.

PETERS, SARA; Tecumseh HS; New Carlisle, OH; Cls Rep Frsh Cls; Cl Rep Jr Cls; AFS; Hon Rl; Jr NHS; NHS; Off Ade; Stu Cncl; Yrbk; Rptr Sch Nwsp; Honor Roll; Intramural Volleyball Tm 1st In School; Superior Rating In School Sci Fair; College; Engr.

PETERS, STEVEN; Port Huron Northern HS; Pt Huron, MI; Hon Rl; VICA; Hobart Schl Of Welding; Welding.

PETERS, STORMY; Elmwood HS; N Baltimore, OH; Chrh Wkr; Yrbk; FTA; Sci Clb; IM Sprt; Univ; Cmnctns.

PETERS, SUSAN; Marquette Sr HS; Marquette, MI; Chrs; Gym; Capt Chrldng; College; Medicine.

PETERS, THERESE; Lake Cath HS; Mentor, OH; 15/369 Hon Rl; NHS; Bsbl; Letter Bsktbl; Coach Actv; IM Sprt; PPFtbl; Scr Kpr; Tmr; Acad Excel; Natl Hnr Soc; John Carroll Univ; Psych.

PETERS, TIMOTHY; Bad Axe HS; Bad Axe, MI; Chrh Wkr; FCA; Hon Rl; NHS; Ed Sch Nwsp; Sci Clb; Letter Bsbl; Bsktbl; Ftbl; Natl Merit SF; Mich Tech Univ; Forestry.

PETERS, VALERIE; Groveport Madison HS; Groveport, OH; 2/377 Sal; Treas NHS; Ed Sch Nwsp; Sec 4-H; Ten; Am Leg Awd; 4-H Awd; Rotary Awd; Ohio Dominican Coll; Bus Admin.

PETERS, VICKI; Fairview Area HS; Fairview, MI; Sec Fr Clb; College; Data Processing.

PETERSEN, ANNETTE; Patrick Henry HS; Hamler, OH; 3/99 Band; Chrs; Chrh Wkr; Girl Scts; Hon Rl; Orch; Sch Mus; Stg Crw; Yth Flsp; 4-H; Honor Mentn 1st Yr Algebra 1977; 2nd Yr Alg Ohio Tests 1978; Ohio Soc Professional Engr; Univ; Acctg.

PETERSEN, HOLLY; Lakeland HS; La Grange, IN; 3/150 Band; Chrh Wkr; FCA; Hon Rl; Pres NHS; Sch Mus; Stu Cncl; Lat Clb; Mth Clb; Pep Clb; Univ; Medicine.

PETERSEN, JAMES; Mccomb HS; Deshler, OH; Chrh Wkr; Hon Rl; Yth Flsp; 4-H; FFA; Bsbl; Bsktbl; Ftbl; Scr Kpr; Tmr; College; Engr.

PETERSEN, KAREN; Greenville HS; Greenville, MI; 10/238 Hon Rl; NHS; Stu Cncl; Rptr Yrbk; Yrbk; Spn Clb; Trk; IM Sprt; PPFtbl; Central Mic Univ; Journalism.

PETERSEN, RUTH; Medina Senior HS; Medina, OH; Cls Rep Soph Cls; Cl Rep Jr Cls; Stu Cncl; Drama Clb; Fr Clb; Pep Clb; Gym; Ten; Capt Chrldng; GAA; College.

PETERSON, AMY; Elkhart Memorial HS; Elkhart, IN; 57/541 Band; Chrh Wkr; Hon Rl; NHS; Orch; Quill & Scroll; Sch Mus; Sch Pl; Rptr Yrbk; Yrbk; Otstndng Rookie Of Yrbk Staff 78; Miami Of Ohio Univ; Cmnctns.

PETERSON, BOBBY; Miami Trace HS; Washington Ch, OH; 6/325 Band; NHS; Sch Pl; Pres Yth Flsp; Rptr Sch Nwsp; Treas Drama Clb; Pres 4-H; Treas FFA; FSA; Natl Merit SF; College.

PETERSON, BONNI; Lawrenceburg HS; Lawrenceburg, IN; 4/154 Cls Rep Soph Cls; Band; Drm Mjrt; Hon Rl; NHS; Off Ade; Sch Mus; Fr Clb; Key Clb; Pep Clb; French I Awd; Straight A Awd; Honor Stu Awd; College; Legal Sec.

PETERSON, CHARMAINE; Bellevue HS; Bellevue, MI; 16/87 Sec Sr Cls; Sec Band; Cmp Fr Grls; Chrh Wkr; Drm Mjrt; Hon Rl; NHS; Off Ade; Sch Mus; Sch Pl; Spring Arbor Coll; Music.

PETERSON, CINDY; Malabar HS; Mansfield, OH; 46/287 Chrs; Red Cr Ade; Scr Kpr; College; Bio.

PETERSON, DALE; Webberville HS; Webberville, MI; Band; Hon Rl; 4-H; Letter Bsbl; Letter Bsktbl; Crs Cntry; Scr Kpr; MSU; Acctg.

PETERSON, DIANA; Watervliet HS; Benton Harbor, MI; 7/90 Band; Chrs; Hon Rl; NHS; Off Ade; Sch Mus; Yth Flsp; 4-H; Mic State Univ.

PETERSON, ELAINE; Bentley HS; Livonia, MI; Cls Rep Frsh Cls; Cls Rep Sr Cls; Chrs; Pol Wkr; Stu Cncl; Spn Clb; Pom Pon; Univ Of Michigan; Psych.

PETERSON, ERICH; Archbold HS; Archbold, OH; Band; Hon Rl; Jr NHS; NHS; Orch; Letter Ftbl; Letter Trk; Coach Actv; Air Force Acad; Pilot.

PETERSON, GAIL; West Iron County HS; Iron River, MI; 23/127 Chrs; Hon Rl; Off Ade; Fr Clb; Northwestern Mic College; Data.

PETERSON, GARY; Carrollton HS; Carrollton, OH; 15/265 VP Soph Cls; Cls Rep Soph Cls; Cls Rep Sr Cls; Pres FCA; NHS; Bsbl; Bsktbl; Capt Ftbl; Univ Of Akron; Bus.

PETERSON, GRANT; Cory Rawson HS; Mt Cory, OH; Band; Chrs; Hon Rl; Sch Mus; 4-H; Pres FFA; Bsktbl; Crs Cntry; Ftbl; Trk; Star Chapt Farmer; Soil Judging Awd; College; Ag.

PETERSON, HEIDI; Kingswood HS; Pontiac, MI; Band; Chrh Wkr; Hon Rl; Ed Yrbk; Yrbk; 4-H; Univ.

PETERSON, JAMES; Ashtabula Harbor HS; Ashtabula, OH; Hst Frsh Cls; Cls Rep Soph Cls; Cl Rep Jr Cls; Val; AFS; Am Leg Boys St; Band; Boy Scts; Cmnty Wkr; Hon Rl; Univ.

PETERSON, JENNIFER; Harvey S Firestone Sr HS; Akron, OH; 7/365 Band; Chrh Wkr; Drl Tm; Hon Rl; NHS; Sch Mus; Yth Flsp; Rptr Yrbk; Drama Clb; Pep Clb; Coll; Economics.

PETERSON, JONATHAN; Muskegon HS; Muskegon, MI; Band; Chrh Wkr; FCA; Hon Rl; NHS; Ger Clb; Muskegon High Quiz Bowl Tm 78; Perfct Attndnc 2 Yrs 77; Univ; Bus.

PETERSON, JULIE; Cuyahoga Falls HS; Cuyahoga Falls, OH; Band; Hon Rl; Orch; Sch Mus; Sch Nwsp; IM Sprt; College.

PETERSON, JULIE; Manistique HS; Manistique, MI; Cls Rep Frsh Cls; VP Jr Cls; Stu Cncl; Rptr Sch Nwsp; 4-H; Letter Glf; 4-H Awd; Natl Merit SF; Western Michigan Univ; Paper Sci.

PETERSON, KARI; Clarkston HS; Clarkston, MI; Cls Rep Frsh Cls; Pres Soph Cls; Pres Jr Cls; Pres Sr Cls; Girl Scts; Hon Rl; Stu Cncl; Bsktbl; Coll; Bus Admin.

PETERSON, KATHRYN; Charles F Brush HS; Lyndhurst, OH; Girl Scts; Off Ade; Sct Actv; Letter Swmmng; Ohio St Univ; Rec Serv.

PETERSON, LANCE; Haslett HS; Haslett, MI; 32/180 Chrs; Hon Rl; Pol Wkr; Sch Pl; Yrbk; Swmmng; Ten; Central Mich Univ; Marketing.

PETERSON, LARRY; East Kentwood HS; Kentwood, MI; Band; Band; Orch; Sct Actv; Ed Sch Nwsp; Kalamazoo College; Engr.

PETERSON, RAMONA; Webberville Comm HS; Webberville, MI; Sec Jr Cls; Sec Sr Cls; Letter Band; Hon Rl; Sec NHS; 4-H; FHA; Letter Chrldng; Twrlr; Bsns Schl; Legal Sec.

PETERSON, RANDALL; Northrop HS; Norman, OK; Hon Rl; Yth Flsp; JA Awd; Oklahoma Univ; Comp Sci.

PETERSON, RICK L; Marlington HS; Alliance, OH; 20/278 Hon Rl; VICA; Bsbl; Ftbl; IM Sprt; Stark Tech Coll; Project Engr.

PETERSON, RONALD; Airport Comm HS; S Rockwood, MI; 15/210 Band; Debate Tm; Hon Rl; Orch; Sch Mus; Sch Pl; Yth Flsp; Sci Clb; Outstndng Awds In Bnd; Stu Dir Awd & Ach Awd; Monroe Comm Coll Bnd; Michigan St Univ; Music.

PETERSON, ROY; Beaverton HS; Beaverton, MI; Hon Rl; Ferris State College; Acctg.

PETERSON, SHERI; Fenton Sr HS; Fenton, MI; Sprt Ed Sch Nwsp; Rptr Sch Nwsp; FHA; PPFtbl; Home Ec Rltd Occptns Awd77; Named To Whos Who Amng Amer HS Stu 77; Part In HS & Byond Survey 78; Western Michigan Univ; Art.

PETERSON, SUSAN; David Anderson HS; Lisbon, OH; 1/95 Sec Sr Cls; Val; Am Leg Aux Girls St; Chrh Wkr; FCA; Hon Rl; NHS; Pres Stu Cncl; Yth Flsp; Y-Teens; Varsity Volleyball 3letters MVP; Ohio Board Of Regents Schlrshp; Columbiana Cnty All Star Softball Team; Marietta Coll; Petroleum Engr.

PETERSON, TANA; Froid Public HS; Froid, MT; VP Soph Cls; Band; Chrs; Chrh Wkr; Drama Clb; Pep Clb; Chrldng; GAA; Mgrs; College; Sec.

PETERSON, TERRI; Medina Sr HS; Medina, OH; 1/350 Hon Rl; NHS; Spn Clb; Medina Sr HS Outstanding Spanish Stdnt & Freshman Eng Stdnt Awd 76 77; Outstnading 78 79 Spanigh Stdnt Awd; Univ; Spanish.

PETERSON, THOMAS; Novi HS; Novi, MI; Aud/Vis; Boy Scts; Cmnty Wkr; Hon Rl; Sch Nwsp; VICA; IM Sprt; Univ; Aviation.

PETERSON, THOMAS W; Union City Community HS; Union City, IN; 1/95 Pres Frsh Cls; Pres Soph Cls; Am Leg Boys St; Boy Scts; NHS; Pres Stu Cncl; Ed Yrbk; Ten; Dnfth Awd; Natl Merit Ltr; Univ; Poli Sci.

PETHTEL, DONALD R; Lewis County HS; Weston, WV; Cls Rep Soph Cls; Cl Rep Jr Cls; FCA; Hon Rl; Stu Cncl; 4-H; Key Clb; Letter Bsbl; Ftbl; Wrstlng; Soph Yr 2nd Team Big 10 Confrnc Bsbl 2nd Base 78; Life Guard Lewis Cnty Park 78; Prin List 79;.

PETIT, THERESA; Norton HS; Clinton, OH; 21/338 Band; Hon Rl; Off Ade; Orch; Swmmng; Trk; Am Leg Awd; Univ Of Akron; Math.

PETITTO, MICHAEL; South Harrison HS; Clarsburry, WV; Band; Stg Crw; FFA; Wrstlng; Turf & Scape Mgnt Awd FFA 79; Univ.

PETIYA, SHARON; John F Kennedy HS; Warren, OH; 8/176 Band; Hon Rl; Jr NHS; Lit Mag; NHS; Sch Mus; Rptr Sch Nwsp; Kiwan Awd; Natl HS Awd For Excellnc 1977; NOSPA 3rd Pl Radio News Brdcstng 1978; Univ Of Houston; Eng.

PETKOF, MICHAEL; Southwestern HS; Detroit, MI; 6/280 FCA; Hon Rl; Pres NHS; Pres DECA; Am Leg Awd; SUOMI; Acctg.

PETRAKOS, C; Boardman HS; Youngstown, OH; Chrh Wkr; Girl Scts; Hon Rl; Off Ade; Orch; Sch Mus; Yth Flsp; Fr Clb; Youngstown State Univ; Pharmacy.

PETRASKA, REGINA; Euclid HS; Euclid, OH; Hon Rl; UCLA; Government.

PETREK, BEVERLY; Hubbard HS; Hubbard, OH; VP Frsh Cls; VP Soph Cls; VP Jr Cls; VP Sr Cls; Band; Off Ade; Stu Cncl; 4-H; Bsktbl; Trk; Travel Agent.

PETRELLA, M; Catholic Central HS; Steubenville, OH; 30/207 Hon Rl; Univ; Elec Engr.

PETRELLA, PHILIP; Bishop Ready HS; Columbus, OH; Chrh Wkr; Hon Rl; Treas NHS; Sch Mus; Ftbl; Letter Ten; IM Sprt; Dnfth Awd; College; Engr.

PETRELLA, SALLY; Seaholm HS; Birmingham, MI; Band; Chrs; Chrh Wkr; Girl Scts; Hon Rl; Off Ade; Sch Pl; Sct Actv; Yth Flsp; Fr Clb; College.

PETRETICH, JUDITH; Chaney HS; Youngstown, OH; 1/3 Am Leg Aux Girls St; Cmnty Wkr; Hon Rl; Jr NHS; Lbry Ade; NHS; Off Ade; Alderson Broaddus; Phys Assnt.

PETRI, CHRISTINE; Brighton Area HS; Brighton, MI; 6/373 Cls Rep Soph Cls; Chrs; Hon Rl; NHS; Sch Pl; Stu Cncl; Drama Clb; Spn Clb; Letter Trk; Mgrs; Top 10 Stdnt In Grad Cls 79; Pres Phys Ftnss Awd 76; Michigan Tech Univ; Chem.

PETRICH, RICHARD; Hubbard HS; Hubbard, OH; 25/350 Hon Rl; Sch Pl; Stg Crw; Yth Flsp; Key Clb; Ten; Youngstown St Univ; Chem Engr.

PETRIELLA, ANTHONY; Flushing HS; Flushing, M I; Cl Rep Jr Cls; Pres Sr Cls; Chrs; Cmnty Wkr; Hon Rl; NHS; Stu Cncl; Yth Flsp; Coach Actv; Mgrs; ACT Schlrshp Nominee 79; Univ Of Michigan; Med.

PETRILLI, JEFFERY; Niles Mckinley HS; Niles, OH; Letter Ftbl; IM Sprt; College; Pharmacist.

PETRISIN, SUSAN A; Alpena Sr HS; Ossineke, MI; Cls Rep Soph Cls; Hon Rl; Jr NHS; Lbry Ade; Treas Key Clb; Spn Clb; Letter Bsktbl; Mgrs; Am Leg Awd;.

PETRO, CHRISTINE; Strongsville Sr HS; Strongsville, OH; Cls Rep Soph Cls; Hon Rl; Jr NHS; NHS; Off Ade; Stu Cncl; Yrbk; Pep Clb; Scr Kpr; Opt Clb Awd; Schlstc Natl Art Exhibition Merit Awd 77 79; College; Archt Engr.

PETRO, LINDA; Wm A Wirt HS; Gary, IN; Hon Rl; Jr NHS; Rptr Yrbk; FBLA; Mth Clb; Purdue Univ; Busns Mgmt.

PETROFF, TIM; Marion HS; Marion, IN; Chrs; Hon Rl; IM Sprt; Indiana St Univ.

PETROU, PETER; Ontario HS; Mnsfld, OH; Hon Rl; Lbry Ade; Ftbl; Univ; Acctg.

PETROVICH, LISA; Perry HS; Massillon, OH; 14/480 Chrs; Hon Rl; NHS; Off Ade; Stg Crw; Rptr Sch Nwsp; Pep Clb; Letter Ten; Scr Kpr; Outstanding French Stu; Ohio Acad Schlrshp Program; Bowling Green St Univ; CPA.

PETROVICH, VERONICA; Northview HS; Grand Rapids, MI; 52/300 Cmp Fr Grls; Cmnty Wkr; Hon Rl; JA; Pep Clb; IM Sprt; Grand Rapids Jr College; Architectur.

PETRUCELLI, CAROL; Akron North HS; Akron, OH; 11/360 Hon Rl; Hosp Ade; Jr NHS; NHS; Rptr Yrbk; Chrldng; Bausch & Lomb Awd; Ohio St Univ; Pre Med.

PETRUS, MARY; St Joseph Academy; Lakewood, OH; 7/220 Hon Rl; NHS; Sch Pl; Yth Flsp; Yrbk; Ed Sch Nwsp; Rptr Sch Nwsp; Drama Clb; Bsbl; Magna Cum Laude Natl Latin Exam 77; Univ; Astronomy.

PETRUS, MARY H; Magnificat HS; Rocky River, OH; Cls Rep Frsh Cls; Cl Rep Jr Cls; VP Sr Cls; Val;

Chrh Wkr; Cmnty Wkr; Lit Mag; Mod UN; NHS; Sch Mus; N W Univ; Jrnlsm.

PETRUZZI, WILLIAM; Hubbard HS; Hubbard, OH; Cls Rep Soph Cls; Stu Cncl; Bsbl; Ftbl; Coll; Elec Engr.

PETTERSCH, ANNE; West Catholic HS; Grand Rapids, MI; Cls Rep Frsh Cls; VP Soph Cls; Cl Rep Jr Cls; Rptr Yrbk; Fr Clb; Letter Trk; Chrldng; Univ.

PETTET, MARIANNE; Rensselaer Central HS; Rensselaer, IN; Band; Hon Rl; Pep Clb; Spn Clb; Pom Pon; Vocational Schl; Dent Hyg.

PETTEYS, KIMBERLY; Dexter HS; Pinckney, MI; Band; Cmp Fr Grls; Chrs; Hon Rl; Lit Mag; 4-H; Spn Clb; 4-H Awd; Michigan St Univ; Spec Ed.

PETTIBONE, WILLIAM; Teays Valley HS; Ashville, OH; Am Leg Boys St; FCA; Hon Rl; Ed Sch Nwsp; Letter Bsbl; Letter Bsktbl; Letter Crs Cntry; Letter Ftbl; Am Leg Awd; Cit Awd; Ohio St Univ; Construction.

PETTIT, JENNIE L; Medina Sr HS; Medina, OH; AFS; Am Leg Aux Girls St; Chrs; Cmnty Wkr; Drl Tm; Girl Scts; Hon Rl; Lbry Ade; NHS; Sch Mus; Internatl Thespian Soc; Univ; Theatre.

PETTIT, STEVE; Elwood Cmnty HS; Elwood, IN; 9/273 Hon Rl; Jr NHS; NHS; Sct Actv; Letter Crs Cntry; Letter Trk; Natl Merit Ltr; Purdue Univ; Civil Engr.

PETTREY, JONNI L; Athens HS; Athens, WV; Band; Girl Scts; 4-H; FHA; Keyettes; Pep Clb; Bsbl; 4-H Awd;.

PETTWAY, PATRICIA; Highland Park Community HS; Highland Pk, MI; 9/32 Cls Rep Frsh Cls; Cls Rep Soph Cls; Sec Jr Cls; Cl Rep Jr Cls; Pres Chrs; Cmnty Wkr; Debate Tm; Girl Scts; Lbry Ade; MMM; Trip To Australia With Choir 79; Studying Music At Interlocen 78; Advance Tour Of Fl 78; Olivette Univ; Fine Arts.

PETTY, JAMES; Howell HS; Howell, MI; Am Leg Boys St; Chrh Wkr; Hon Rl; Fr Clb; Bsktbl; Trk; Coll; Cpa.

PETTY, KEVIN; Stonewall Jackson HS; Chrlstn, WV; Pres Frsh Cls; Cls Rep Soph Cls; Cl Rep Jr Cls; Pres Sr Cls; Am Leg Boys St; FCA; Hon Rl; Jr NHS; NHS; Sch Mus; College.

PETTY, KIMBERLY; Woodsfield HS; Woodsfield, OH; Band; Hon Rl; 4-H; Fr Clb; OEA; Pep Clb; Chrldng; Am Leg Awd; 4-H Awd; Kiwan Awd;.

PETTY, TAMMY; Washington Senior HS; Washington, IN; 7/216 Band; Hon Rl; Y-Teens; 4-H; Fr Clb; Pep Clb; Spn Clb; Trk; Chrldng; GAA; Pta Academic Award; 1973 4 H 1977; Senate Page 1979; Indiana St Univ; Nuclear Engr.

PETZ, BARBARA; Our Lady Of Mercy HS; Livonia, MI; Chrh Wkr; Off Ade; Stg Crw; Pep Clb; Art.

PETZKE, ANN; Berrien Springs HS; Berrien Spring, MI; 15/111 Cl Rep Jr Cls; Pres Sr Cls; Girl Scts; Hon Rl; Stu Cncl; Yth Flsp; Chrldng; Natl Merit Ltr; Homecoming Court 79; Michigan St Univ; Bus Law.

PEVER, DAN; Findlay HS; Findlay, OH; 39/686 Hon Rl; Jr NHS; Lit Mag; NHS; Quill & Scroll; Ed Sch Nwsp; Rptr Sch Nwsp; Trk; Ohio Univ; Jrnlsm.

PEVER, DENISE; Riverdale HS; Arlington, OH; 19/90 Band; Chrs; Hon Rl; NHS; Off Ade; Sch Mus; Yth Flsp; 4-H; Sec FTA; IM Sprt; Ohi State Univ; Soc Work.

PEVERLY, DALE; Edgerton HS; Edgerton, OH; 4/86 Trs Frsh Cls; Am Leg Boys St; Chrs; Hon Rl; NHS; Mth Clb; Bsbl; Bsktbl; Crs Cntry; Coach Actv; College.

PEYATT, PAMELA; Mt View HS; Capels, WV; 42/250 Chrh Wkr; Hon Rl; NHS; Sch Pl; Stg Crw; FBLA; Rdo Clb; 3rd Pl Wnnr In FBLA Conf In Job Intervw 79; Sec.

PEYSER, CYNTHIA; Our Lady Star Of The Sea HS; Grse Pt Shr, MI; VP Frsh Cls; VP Soph Cls; Pres Jr Cls; Pres Sr Cls; Chrh Wkr; Hon Rl; NHS; Univ Of Mic; Law.

PEYTON, BRIAN; Blanchester HS; Blanchester, OH; 4/151 VP Frsh Cls; VP Sr Cls; FCA; Hon Rl; JA; Pres NHS; Sch Pl; Stg Crw; Treas Stu Cncl; VP Drama Clb; Miami Univ; Med.

PEYTON, DEBRA; Buena Vista HS; Saginaw, MI; Cls Rep Frsh Cls; Cl Rep Jr Cls; Cls Rep Sr Cls; Band; Hon Rl; NHS; Stu Cncl; Sci Clb; Ten; Michigan St Univ; Zoology.

PEYTON, KATHLEEN; Huron HS; Huron, OH; Chrh Wkr; Hon Rl; NHS; Rptr Yrbk; Chrldng; Univ; Literature.

PEZET, MARY; Waterford Mott HS; Pontiac, MI; 56/367 Hosp Ade; Trk; Lake Superior State College; Prenurs.

PEZO, AMY; Millington Community HS; Millington, MI; 1/144 Hon Rl; Pres NHS; Capt Bsktbl; Coach Actv; Univ Of Mic; Natrual Resources.

PEZZUTTI, MARK; Bishop Hartley HS; Pickerington, OH; Hon Rl; Univ; Engr.

PFABE, VALINDA; Jefferson Union HS; Steubenville, OH; 17/160 Chrs; Girl Scts; Hon Rl; Y-Teens; Beta Clb; Pep Clb; GAA; PPFtbl; Perfect Attendance Award; Jefferson Co Coll; CPA.

PFAFF, BECKY J; Springfield HS; Holland, OH; Hon Rl; VP NHS; Pep Clb; Pres Spn Clb; Pres GAA; Pres Mat Maids; Capt PPFtbl; Wrestling Queen 1979; Soph Attndt 1977; Varsity Volleyball; Voc Schl; Travel Agent.

PFAFF, LINDA; Tri Jr Sr HS; Lewisville, IN; 3/82 Am Leg Aux Girls St; Band; Hon Rl; NHS; Sch Pl; Yrbk; Fr Clb; Chrldng; Dnfth Awd; Purdue Univ; Chem Engr.

PFALZGRAF, ELLEN; Western Hills HS; Cincinnati, OH; Chrs; Chrh Wkr; Capt Drl Tm; Hosp Ade; Jr NHS; Sch Mus; Stu Cncl; Univ Of Cincinnati; Acct Tech.

PFARRER, BARBARA; Northwestern HS; Kokomo, IN; 13/185 Band; NHS; 4-H; FHA; VP Pep Clb; Bloomington Univ; Med.

PFARRER, JEANNE; Archbishop Alter HS; Kettering, OH; 3/335 Chrs; Hon Rl; NHS; Sch Mus; Sch Pl; Drama Clb; Ger Clb; GAA; IM Sprt; Ohio St Univ; Vet.

PFAU, CINDY; Bexley HS; Bexley, OH; 60/186 Chrs; Chrh Wkr; Girl Scts; Hon Rl; Sct Actv; Pep Clb; Spn Clb; Letter Bsbl; Coach Actv; GAA; Ohio Univ; Spec Ed.

PFAU, CONSTANCE; Bekley HS; Bexley, OH; 9/190 Chrs; Girl Scts; Hon Rl; Lit Mag; NHS; Fr Clb; Pep Clb; Letter Bsktbl; GAA; IM Sprt; Mbr Of USVBA CJCA Tm; All Lag Lplyr In 78; Vlybl Hgh Schl Tm; MVP In The Olympc Dvlpmnt Camp Of Vlybl; Univ Of Cincinnati; Educ.

PFAU, SANDRA K; Defiance Sr HS; Defiance, OH; 1/295 Band; Chrh Wkr; Hon Rl; Jr NHS; Pres Yth Flsp; Pres 4-H; Pres Fr Clb; DAR Awd; 4-H Awd; Bowling Green State Univ; Bus Admin.

PFEFFER, ADAM; Jonesville HS; Jonesville, MI; Am Leg Boys St; Band; Letter Bsktbl; Letter Crs Cntry; Letter Ftbl; Letter Trk; College.

PFEFFER, LYNN; Ripley Union Lewis HS; Ripley, OH; 3/34 Sec Frsh Cls; Hosp Ade; Off Ade; Sch Pl; Pres Stu Cncl; Ed Yrbk; 4-H; Pres FHA; Natl Merit SF; Voice Dem Awd; Ohio State Univ; Medicine.

PFEIFER, CANDY; Tri West Hendricks HS; Pittsboro, IN; 7/118 FCA; NHS; Sch Pl; Ed Yrbk; Rptr Sch Nwsp; 4-H; Pep Clb; Mat Maids; Cit Awd; 4-H Awd; Herron Art Schl; Art.

PFEIFER, ELIZABETH; Cardinal Ritter HS; Indianapolis, IN; 46/186 Cls Rep Frsh Cls; Cls Rep Soph Cls; Band; Hon Rl; Sch Mus; Sch Pl; Stg Crw; Spn Clb; Trk; PPFtbl; Coll; Nursing.

PFEIFFER, CAROL; Henry Ford II HS; Sterling Hgts, MI; Band; Chrh Wkr; Debate Tm; Hosp Ade; NHS; Natl Merit Ltr; Sci Hon 79; Soc Studies Hon 79; Top Speaker Awd 78; Oakland Univ; Nursing.

PFEIFFER, GEOFFREY; Fraser HS; Fraser, MI; 1/617 Band; Debate Tm; Hon Rl; NHS; Orch; Sch Mus; Natl Merit Ltr; 1st Pl Sci Fair; MMA 1st Pl Ensemble; Stanford Univ; Bsns Mgmt.

PFEIFFER, KATHY; Lexington HS; Lexington, OH; Chrs; Hosp Ade; Yth Flsp; Coll; RN.

PFEIFFER, LINDA; Ridgedale HS; Morral, OH; Band; Chrs; Pres JA; Sch Mus; Rptr Yrbk; Rptr Sch Nwsp; Pres FHA; Leo Clb; Spn Clb; JA Awd; Marion Tech Coll; Acctg.

PFEIFFER, LISA; Chagrin Falls HS; Chagrin Falls, OH; Chrs; FCA; Girl Scts; Gym; Trk; Chrldng; PPFtbl; Univ; Model.

PFEIFFER, LISA; Warsaw Cmnty HS; Warsaw, IN; 47/394 Girl Scts; Hon Rl; Sch Nwsp; Pep Clb; Spn Clb; Voc Schl; Brdcstng.

PFEIFFER, M; Davison HS; Davison, MI; 30/450 Cmnty Wkr; Girl Scts; Hon Rl; Sct Actv; Mth Clb; Sci Clb; Spn Clb; Letter Trk; Scr Kpr; Tmr; Mich State Univ; Vet Med.

PFEIFFER, MICHELLE; Davison Sr HS; Davison, MI; Cmnty Wkr; Girl Scts; Hon Rl; Mth Clb; Sci Clb; Spn Clb; Letter Trk; Tmr; Michigan St Univ; Vet Med.

PFEIL, PATTY; Holy Name Nazareth HS; Brook Pk, OH; Cls Rep Frsh Cls; Chrh Wkr; Cmnty Wkr; Girl Scts; Lbry Ade; Off Ade; Sct Actv; Yth Flsp; Pep Clb; Spn Clb; College; Nursing.

PFINGSTON, PATTI; Pike Central Middle HS; Winslow, IN; Hon Rl; Off Ade; Pep Clb; Letter Trk; Chrldng; Coach Actv; Ahtlc Trophy For All Around Track & Field Girl 78; Athltc Trophy For High Pt Runner & All Around 79; Vincennes Bus Coll; Bus.

PFIRMAN, DANIEL; Moeller HS; Cincinnati, OH; Boy Scts; JA; Crs Cntry; Trk; IM Sprt; JA Awd; Carson Newman Marrietta; Forestry.

PFISTER, ALICE; Mater Dei HS; Evansville, IN; Sec Band; Chrs; Hon Rl; Jr NHS; Treas Natl Forn Lg; Sch Mus; Sch Pl; Pep Clb; Purdue Univ; Speech Ther.

PFISTER, ANNA; Niles Sr HS; Niles, MI; Band; Chrh Wkr; Cmnty Wkr; Girl Scts; Hosp Ade; Off Ade; Orch; Pol Wkr; Sct Actv; Yth Flsp; S W Michigan St Univ; Psych.

PFISTER, RUSSELL; Central Catholic HS; Canton, OH; 1/249 Capt Band; Hon Rl; Natl Forn Lg; Capt NHS; Natl Merit SF; Capital Univ; Mathematics Major.

PFLUEGER, JONATHAN J; Loudonville HS; Loudonville, OH; 10/130 Pres Frsh Cls; Am Leg Boys St; Band; Chrs; Hon Rl; NHS; Sch Mus; Stu Cncl; Yth Flsp; Rptr Sch Nwsp; All Ohio St Fari Band 79; Univ; Tchr.

PFLUGER, CINDY; Gwinn HS; Gwinn, MI; Cmp Fr Grls; Chrs; Hon Rl; Sch Mus; OEA; Gym; Swmmng; Trk; Pres Awd; Northern Michigan Univ; Busns.

PFLUM, JANET S; Connersville HS; Connersville, IN; 44/400 Hon Rl; NHS; Pol Wkr; Sec 4-H; Treas FFA; 4-H Awd; Purdue Univ; Agri.

PFOSCH, HEIDI; Novi HS; Northville Twp, MI; 26/230 Hon Rl; NHS; Orch; 4-H; Sci Clb; Mgrs; Mic Tech Univ; Forestry.

PHAGAN, LISA; Madison Heights HS; Anderson, IN; 6/371 Girl Scts; Hon Rl; NHS; Spn Clb; Letter Ten; Univ.

PHAM, CHAN; Jefferson HS; Lafayette, IN; Cls Rep Soph Cls; Cl Rep Jr Cls; Cls Rep Sr Cls; Am Leg Boys St; Chrs; Chrh Wkr; Hon Rl; Jr NHS; Natl Forn Lg; NHS; Univ; Pre Med.

PHAM, LANPHUONG; Eastmoor HS; Columbus, OH; Cls Rep Frsh Cls; Chrs; Girl Scts; Hon Rl; Sch Mus; Mth Clb; Spn Clb; College; Engr.

PHARES, MYRA ELAINE; Hagerstown Jr Sr HS; Hagerstown, IN; 10/142 VP Frsh Cls; Hon Rl; Sec Yth Flsp; Rptr Sch Nwsp; OEA; Sci Clb; Mgrs; Univ; Jrnlsm.

PHEANIS, SUSAN; Eaton HS; Eaton, OH; Chrs; Cmnty Wkr; Off Ade; Yrbk; Sch Nwsp; Fr Clb; Pep Clb; GAA; Mgrs; Univ Of Miami.

PHEGLEY, LINDA; North Knox HS; Bruceville, IN; Hon Rl; NHS; Sch Pl; Lat Clb;.

PHELAN, KATHLEEN; Marian HS; Birmingham, MI; Cls Rep Frsh Cls; Cmnty Wkr; Girl Scts; Lit Mag; Mod UN; PAVAS; Pol Wkr; Red Cr Ade; Pep Clb; Trk; College; Social Work.

PHELPS, CHARLES; Fairless HS; Canton, OH; Hst Jr Cls; Am Leg Boys St; Boy Scts; Hon Rl; NHS; Sch Nwsp; OEA; Crs Cntry; Trk; Coach Actv; Cross Country 4 Yr Lettermen 4 Yr Cpt 1974; Track 4 Yr Lettermen Sr Co Cpt Dst Qualifier 1978; Miami Univ; Bus Admin.

PHELPS, GARY; Barberton HS; Barberton, OH; 68/450 Band; Chrh Wkr; Hon Rl; Jr NHS; NHS; Yth Flsp; Bsktbl; Ftbl; Swmmng; IM Sprt; Military Acad; Oceanography.

PHELPS, JULIE; Greenville HS; Greenville, MI; Am Leg Aux Girls St; Hon Rl; Fr Clb; Bsktbl; Glf; Coach Actv; PPFtbl; College; Phys Ther.

PHELPS, KATHRYN; Sycamore HS; Cincinnati, OH; 245/455 Trs Frsh Cls; Cls Rep Soph Cls; Cl Rep Jr Cls; Band; Drm Mjrt; Hon Rl; Stu Cncl; VP Pep Clb; Socr; Miami Univ; Retail Mdse.

PHELPS, LEE A; Cambridge HS; Cambridge, OH; 47/270 Band; Chrh Wkr; Girl Scts; Hon Rl; NHS; Yth Flsp; Rptr Yrbk; Fr Clb; Aultman Hosp Schl Of Nursing; RN.

PHELPS, MARK; Kalkaska HS; Kalkoska, MI; Bsbl; Bsktbl; College; Chem.

PHELPS, MARSHA; Seeger Memorial HS; Attica, IN; Band; Chrh Wkr; Lbry Ade; VP Yth Flsp; Rptr Yrbk; Spn Clb; Evangel Coll; Bus Mgmt.

PHELPS, SUSAN J; Dansville HS; Stockbridge, MI; 1/65 Cls Rep Sr Cls; Band; Chrs; Hon Rl; NHS; Off Ade; Sch Pl; Sec Stu Cncl; Yth Flsp; 4-H; Michigan State Univ; Biochem.

PHELPS, THOMAS; Walled Lake Central HS; Union Lake, MI; Chrh Wkr; Hon Rl; Bsktbl; Ten; Michigan St Univ; Acctg.

PHELPS, WILLIAM; Deckerville HS; Carsonville, MI; Hon Rl; Off Ade; Letter Bsbl; Letter Ftbl; Letter Trk; IM Sprt; Scr Kpr; JA Awd; Pres Awd; Macomb Cnty Cmnty Coll; Archt.

PHIFER, LE TANYA; North HS; Youngstown, OH; 3/120 Chrh Wkr; Hon Rl; Jr NHS; NHS; Stu Cncl; Rptr Yrbk; Fr Clb; Chrldng; Bowling Green Univ; Psych.

PHILIBIN, DANIEL; Cardinal Mooney HS; Youngstown, OH; 80/288 Cls Rep Sr Cls; Hon Rl; Stu Cncl; Bsktbl; Ftbl; Trk; Coach Actv; IM Sprt; Mgrs; Scr Kpr; Univ.

PHILIPPI, MICHELLE; Kearsly HS; Burton, MI; Chrs; Chrh Wkr; Hon Rl; Glf; Univ Of Michigan; Med.

PHILIPS, STEVEN; Traverse City HS; Karlin, MI; Aud/Vis; Hon Rl; Lbry Ade; Spn Clb; Natl Merit Ltr; N W Michigan Coll; Bus.

PHILLABAUM, JAN; Boardman HS; Boardman, OH; 121/568 Hon Rl; Y-Teens; Fr Clb; Mat Maids; Youngstown St Univ; Acctg.

PHILLABAUM, MITCHELL; Valley View HS; Germantown, OH; 15/175 Trs Frsh Cls; Trs Soph Cls; Trs Jr Cls; Trs Sr Cls; Cmnty Wkr; Hon Rl; NHS; 4-H; Treas FFA; Letter Ftbl; St Farmer Degree In FFA; Dist Schlrshp Team Algebra; Star Chapter Farmer; Coll; Engr.

PHILLABAUM, VEE; Port Clinton HS; Port Clinton, OH; Band; Girl Scts; Hon Rl; NHS; Fr Clb; Mth Clb; Pep Clb; Letter Chrldng; Am Leg Awd; College; Chemistry.

PHILLABAUM, VOLITTA; Port Clinton HS; Pt Clinton, OH; FCA; NHS; DECA; Fr Clb; Mth Clb; Chrldng; Am Leg Awd; Univ.

PHILLIPICH, MARY; Grand Ledge HS; Lansing, MI; 8/416 Hon Rl; NHS; Letter Ten; Lansing Comm Coll; Med Tech.

PHILLIPPE, JOHN; Franklin HS; Franklin, OH; Hon Rl; Letter Bsbl; Trk; Miami Univ.

PHILLIPS, ALBERT; Jesup W Scott HS; Toledo, OH; Hon Rl; NHS; Boys Clb Am; Fr Clb; Mth Clb; Ftbl; Tech Soc Of Toledo 79; Ohio St Univ; Engr.

PHILLIPS, ALISON; Tecumseh Sr HS; Tecumseh, MI; 1/236 Val; Band; Chrh Wkr; Hon Rl; NHS; Orch; Spn Clb; Blue Lake Fine Arts Camp Interntl Band; Whos Who In Music; Univ Of Michigan.

PHILLIPS, AMY; Greenfield Central HS; Greenfield, IN; Band; Chrh Wkr; Hon Rl; NHS; 4-H; Fr Clb; Mth Clb; 4-H Awd; Whos Who In Midwestern Hgh Schls Frgn Lang 79; Hancock Bnk & Trst Awd Hgh Pt Avg 77; Univ.

PHILLIPS, ANDREW; Kalamazoo Central HS; Kalamazoo, MI; Kalamazoo College.

PHILLIPS, ANN; Edon Northwest Schl; Blakeslee, OH; 7/78 VP Jr Cls; Chrs; Hon Rl; Lbry Ade; Off Ade; Stg Crw; Spn Clb; Letter Trk; IM Sprt; Mgrs; Univ; Nursing.

PHILLIPS, BARBARA; Willard HS; Willard, OH; Cl Rep Jr Cls; Cls Rep Sr Cls; Hon Rl; Hosp Ade; NHS; Sch Pl; Stu Cncl; FHA; Crs Cntry; Trk; Coll; Nursing.

PHILLIPS, BARBARA A; Dayton Christian HS; Dayton, OH; Drl Tm; Hon Rl; Rptr Sch Nwsp; Sch Nwsp; Sinclair Comm Coll; Sec.

PHILLIPS, BRADLEY; Buckhannon Upshur HS; Buckhannon, WV; Trs Soph Cls; Off Ade; Yrbk; Sch Nwsp; Ar Ftbl Photog 78; Wesleyan Coll; Photog.

PHILLIPS, BRADLEY; Liberty Center HS; Liberty Center, OH; 11/64 Fr Clb; OEA; Univ Of Toledo; Data Proc.

PHILLIPS, CHERYL; Boonville HS; Gentryville, IN; 16/210 Band; Chrh Wkr; Drl Tm; Hon Rl; NHS; Off Ade; Stu Cncl; 4-H; Pep Clb; 4-H Awd; Purdue Univ; Med Tech.

PHILLIPS, CHERYL; Sidney HS; Sidney, OH; Chrs; Chrh Wkr; Cmnty Wkr; Debate Tm; Hon Rl; Hosp Ade; NHS; College.

PHILLIPS, CHRIS J; Miamisburg Sr HS; Dayton, OH; 1/316 Val; Band; Hon Rl; Hosp Ade; VP NHS; VP Orch; Sch Mus; FDA; Ger Clb; Am Leg Awd; Univ Of Dayton; Pre Med.

PHILLIPS, CHRISTINE; Maple Heights Sr HS; Maple Hts, OH; 12/375 Cls Rep Sr Cls; Hon Rl; Stu Cncl; FHA; Pres OEA; Pep Clb; Letter Trk; Cit Awd; Pres Awd; Univ; Bus Educ.

PHILLIPS, CINDEE; Ben Davis HS; Indianapolis, IN; 204/835 Chrs; Chrh Wkr; Natl Forn Lg; Off Ade; Stg Crw; Drama Clb; Univ; Psych.

PHILLIPS, CONNIE A; Lewis County HS; Weston, WV; Am Leg Aux Girls St; Band; Chrh Wkr; Cmnty Wkr; Hon Rl; NHS; Sch Pl; Y-Teens; Rptr Yrbk; Drama Clb; Fairmont St Coll; Social Studies.

PHILLIPS, DAVID; Kenmore HS; Akron, OH; Chrs; FCA; Swmmng; IM Sprt; Akron Univ; Doctor.

PHILLIPS, DEANNA; Bluefield HS; Bluefield, WV; 2/326 Sal; Capt Drl Tm; NHS; Stu Cncl; Yrbk; Civ Clb; Fr Clb; Univ Of Maryland; Accounting.

PHILLIPS, DEBORAH; Nicholas County HS; Summersville, WV; Band; Cmnty Wkr; Hon Rl; Lbry Ade; Lit Mag; Sch Pl; Stg Crw; Fr Clb; GAA; West Virginia St Univ; Eng.

PHILLIPS, DEBRA; Hickory HS; Hickory, MS; Pres Frsh Cls; Pres Soph Cls; Pres Jr Cls; Band; Hon Rl; Rptr Yrbk; Beta Clb; FFA; Bsbl; Letter Bsktbl; Univ; Psych.

PHILLIPS, DENISE; Clarence Kimball HS; Royal Oak, MI; 22/602 Chrh Wkr; Hon Rl; JA; NHS; Orch; Sch Pl; Stg Crw; Drama Clb; Mi Comp Schlrshp 78; Univ Of Michigan; Elec Engr.

PHILLIPS, DONALD; Mccomb HS; Mccomb, OH; Cls Rep Frsh Cls; Pres Soph Cls; Pres Jr Cls; Pres Sr Cls; Am Leg Boys St; Stu Cncl; 4-H; Letter Ftbl; Letter Wrstlng; Letter Trk; College; Architecture.

PHILLIPS, DONNA; Heritage HS; Townsend, TN; 55/375 AFS; Natl Forn Lg; Sch Mus; Sch Pl; Stg Crw; Drama Clb; Natl Merit SF; Univ; Bus Admin.

PHILLIPS, ELIZABETH; Carey HS; Carey, OH; Cls Rep Frsh Cls; Cls Rep Soph Cls; Cl Rep Jr Cls; Cls Rep Sr Cls; Am Leg Aux Girls St; Band; Chrs; Girl Scts; Hon Rl; NHS; Univ; Nursing.

PHILLIPS, ELLEN; West Jefferson HS; W Jefferson, OH; Band; Girl Scts; Hon Rl; NHS; Sct Actv; Rptr Yrbk; Fr Clb; Bsktbl; Univ; Art.

PHILLIPS, ERIC R; Shady Spring HS; Beaver, WV; Trs Frsh Cls; Cls Rep Frsh Cls; Cl Rep Jr Cls; Cls Rep Sr Cls; Chrh Wkr; Cmnty Wkr; FCA; Hon Rl; Stu Cncl; 4-H; College; Law.

PHILLIPS, HOLLY; Brookside HS; Sheffield, OH; 14/212 Trs Jr Cls; VP Sr Cls; Chrs; Hon Rl; NHS; VP Stu Cncl; Yrbk; Scr Kpr; College; Special Education.

PHILLIPS, JAMES; Cameron HS; Cameron, WV; 5/102 Am Leg Boys St; Hon Rl; NHS; 4-H; FFA; Key Clb; Letter Ftbl; Letter Trk; College; Ag.

PHILLIPS, JANE; John Glenn HS; Bay City, MI; Chrh Wkr; Hon Rl; Natl Forn Lg; NHS; Sch Mus; Sch Pl; Stg Crw; Drama Clb; Natl Merit Schl; Delta Coll; Speech Path.

PHILLIPS, JANINE; Fenton HS; Fenton, MI; 44/280 Sec Jr Cls; Band; Girl Scts; Hon Rl; NHS; Stu Cncl; 4-H; Bsktbl; Trk; 4-H Awd; College; Fine Arts.

PHILLIPS, JENNIFER; Heath HS; Heath, OH; 9/151 Chrs; Hon Rl; Mdrgl; NHS; Sch Pl; Stu Cncl; Ed Yrbk; Rdo Clb; DAR Awd; Ohio Univ; Cmnctns.

PHILLIPS, JILL; Meadowdale HS; Dayton, OH; 38/274 Cmp Fr Grls; Hon Rl; Off Ade; Pol Wkr; Sch Pl; Y-Teens; OEA; Capt Chrldng; PPFtbl; Scr Kpr; Bowling Green Univ; Bus Admin.

PHILLIPS, JODI; Eastside HS; Butler, IN; 2/90 VP Soph Cls; Pres Jr Cls; Pres Sr Cls; Hon Rl; NHS; Stu Cncl; Yrbk; VP OEA; Capt Chrldng; Am Leg Awd; Acctg Honorable Mention; Hoosier Honerary Schlrshp; Purdue Univ; CPA.

PHILLIPS, JOVITA; Chaminade Julienne HS; Dayton, OH; Cls Rep Soph Cls; Cl Rep Jr Cls; Chrh Wkr; Off Ade; Sch Nwsp; Pep Clb; Bsktbl; Coach Actv; Scr Kpr; Tmr; Miami Jacobs Jr Coll; Bus Mgmt.

PHILLIPS, JOY; Shelby Sr HS; Shelby, OH; Band; Chrs; Drm Mjrt; Girl Scts; Hon Rl; Yth Flsp; Lat Clb; Sci Clb; Trk; Columbus Inst; Comm Advertising.

PHILLIPS, JULIO A; Delphos Jefferson Sr HS; Delphos, OH; Chrs; CAP; JA; Lbry Ade; Stu Cncl; JA Awd;.

PHILLIPS, KAREN; Michigan Center HS; Michigancenter, MI; Hst Sr Cls; Girl Scts; Hon Rl; JA; Lbry Ade; Off Ade; St Of Mi Schlrshp 79; Hon Roll 76 79; Bus Educ Awd 79; Jackson Cmnty Coll; Exec Sec.

PHILLIPS, KAREN; Philip Barbour HS; Philippi, WV; Cls Rep Soph Cls; Chrs; Chrh Wkr; Girl Scts; Hon Rl; NHS; Off Ade; Sct Actv; Stu Cncl; Yth Flsp;.

PHILLIPS, KATHY; Gorham Fayette HS; Fayette, OH; Pres Jr Cls; Chrs; Hon Rl; NHS; Quill & Scroll; Sch Pl; Stu Cncl; Ed Yrbk; Sprt Ed Yrbk; Yrbk;.

PHILLIPS, KELLY; Central Hower HS; Akron, OH; 3/370 Aud/Vis; Chrs; Cmnty Wkr; Debate Tm; Hon

Rl; Sec JA; Lit Mag; Natl Forn Lg; NHS; Quill & Scroll; Close Up Essay Contst Schlshp Awd 1979; Kent St Univ; Photog.

PHILLIPS, KENNETH; Forest Park HS; Crystal Falls, MI; 15/90 Band; Hon Rl; Yth Flsp; Pep Clb; Letter Bsktbl; Capt Ftbl; Letter Trk; Nrthwstrn Mic; Deck Off.

PHILLIPS, KENNETH G; Gabriel Richard HS; Lincoln Park, MI; 40/159 Chrh Wkr; Pol Wkr; Lat Clb; St Of Mi Cert Of Recgntn Comptn Schslhp Progr 79; Recngtn Of Long Tem & Extradrnry Mert Serv Medl 79; Univ Of Detroit; Hist.

PHILLIPS, KIMBERLY; Carlisle Sr HS; Carlisle, OH; Chrs; Chrh Wkr; Girl Scts; Sch Nwsp; 4-H; OEA; Univ; Envir Sci.

PHILLIPS, LAURA; Magnificat HS; Westlake, OH; AFS; Chrs; Girl Scts; Hosp Ade; Red Cr Ade; Trk; Polaris Voc Ctr; Child Care.

PHILLIPS, LAURIE; Champion HS; Warren, OH; 77/245 Band; Hon Rl; Off Ade; Sprt Ed Yrbk; Yrbk; Sch Nwsp; Bsbl; Bsbl; IM Sprt; Scr Kpr; Levin Awd Yrbk Staff Awd 79; Photog.

PHILLIPS, LISA; Port Austin Public HS; Hickam AFB, HI; 2/25 Chrs; Hon Rl; IM Sprt; JA Awd; Varsity Ltr Sftbl 76; Captain Girls Volleyvall Team 78; Univ Of Hawaii.

PHILLIPS, MARK; Cuyahoga Falls HS; Cuyahoga Fls, OH; Band; Chrh Wkr; Hon Rl; NHS; Orch; Bsktbl; Rotary Awd; Cptn Of Bible Quiz Tm St Champ 78; Coach Of A Pk & Recreation Bsbl Tm 78; Cert Of Merit Ahron Beacn Jrnl 77; Univ; Bus.

PHILLIPS, MARK; Columbian HS; Tiffin, OH; Band; Hon Rl; ROTC; Pep Clb; Bsbl; Socr; Trk; IM Sprt; Scr Kpr; Tmr; St Dist & Local Sci Day Awds 78; Oh Music Educ Assoc Awd Brass Quartet & Solo 79; Univ; Music.

PHILLIPS, MARY F; Greenfield Central HS; Greenfield, IN; Chrs; Hon Rl; Mdrgl; Sch Mus; Spn Clb; Trk; PPFtbl; Tmr; Am Leg Awd; Univ; Public Cmmnctns.

PHILLIPS, MISTI; Ripley Union Lewis HS; Ripley, OH; Cls Rep Soph Cls; Cl Rep Jr Cls; Chrs; Chrh Wkr; Hosp Ade; Off Ade; Yrbk; Eng Clb; FHA; Southern State Univ; Office Educ.

PHILLIPS, MITZI; Washington HS; Massillon, OH; Band; Hon Rl; Orch; Fr Clb; Letter Swmmng; IM Sprt; Art Inst; Visual Cmnctns.

PHILLIPS, MONICA; John J Pershing HS; Detroit, MI; Cmnty Wkr; Girl Scts; Hon Rl; NHS; Orch; Sch Pl; Socr; Natl Merit Ltr; College; Law.

PHILLIPS, NANCY; Upper Valley HS; Covington, OH; Hst Jr Cls; Hon Rl; Hosp Ade; NHS; 4-H; FHA; OEA; IM Sprt; Scr Kpr; College.

PHILLIPS, NICHOLAS; Canfield HS; Canfield, OH; 4/258 Aud/Vis; Hon Rl; Lat Clb; Spn Clb; Natl Hon Soc 78; Univ; Chem Engr.

PHILLIPS, PAMELA; River HS; Powhatan Point, OH; 61/174 Band; Drl Tm; Girl Scts; Hon Rl; Hosp Ade; Off Ade; Ed Yrbk; FTA; Pep Clb; Chrldng;.

PHILLIPS, PAULA; Green HS; Akron, OH; Drm Bgl; Girl Scts; Off Ade; Rptr Yrbk; Pep Clb; Letter Trk; Scr Kpr; Akron Univ; Nursing.

PHILLIPS, REGINA; Winfield HS; Scott Depot, WV; Chrh Wkr; Hon Rl; Yth Flsp; Fr Clb; FHA; Gym; Ten; Chrldng; Miami Univ; Bio.

PHILLIPS, RICHARD; Morgantown HS; Morgantwn, WV; 77/400 Aud/Vis; Rptr Yrbk; Ger Clb; Mth Clb; Natl Merit Ltr; Univ.

PHILLIPS, RICK; Niles Mckinley HS; Niles, OH; 22/421 VP Frsh Cls; Cls Rep Frsh Cls; Cls Rep Soph Cls; Cl Rep Jr Cls; Cls Rep Sr Cls; Debate Tm; Hon Rl; Natl Forn Lg; NHS; Sch Mus; Univ Of Akron; Bus.

PHILLIPS, ROBERT L; Hannan Trace HS; Gallipolis, OH; Band; Boy Scts; Chrs; Chrh Wkr; FCA; MMM; Orch; Sch Mus; Yth Flsp; Mth Clb; College; Music.

PHILLIPS, SALLY; Shelby Senior HS; Shelby, OH; 3/259 Band; Girl Scts; Hon Rl; Lat Clb; College; Art.

PHILLIPS, STEPHEN; St Charles Prep; Columbus, OH; 3/62 Cl Rep Jr Cls; Boy Scts; Chrs; Hon Rl; NHS; Sch Mus; Sch Pl; The Ohi St Univ; Chem.

PHILLIPS, SUE; Walnut Ridge HS; Columbus, OH; Cl Rep Jr Cls; Drl Tm; Hon Rl; Jr NHS; NHS; Quill & Scroll; Ed Yrbk; Spn Clb; Chrldng; PPFtbl; Miami Univ; Graphic Dsgn.

PHILLIPS, SUSAN; Concord HS; Concord, MI; 6/90 Band; Drl Tm; Hon Rl; NHS; Sch Mus; Stu Cncl; Rptr Yrbk; Rptr Sch Nwsp; Scr Kpr; Awd For Creative & Expository Writing 79; Top Student In Algebra II 79; Michigan St Univ; Jrnlsm.

PHILLIPS, TAMIRA; North Gallia HS; Bidwell, OH; Drl Tm; Hon Rl; Hosp Ade; NHS; Stu Cncl; Beta Clb; 4-H; FNA; Holzer Schl Of Nrsng; Rn.

PHILLIPS, TERRI; Pineville HS; Pineville, WV; 5/80 Cls Rep Soph Cls; Hst Jr Cls; Aud/Vis; Band; Girl Scts; Hon Rl; Lit Mag; Jr NHS; Lbry Ade; NHS; Math Awd; Schl Serv Awd Honor To Schl; Brian Trust Honor; West Virginia Univ; Busns.

PHILLIPS, TERRI L; Springfield HS; Holland, OH; Hon Rl; NHS; Yrbk; OEA; Vocational Schl; Exec Sec.

PHILLIPS, TRACY; Southeast HS; Diamond, OH; Hon Rl; NHS; Sec Stu Cncl; Pres FHA; Sec Pep Clb; Scr Kpr; Coll; Elem Ed.

PHILLIPS, VICKI; Grant HS; Newaygo, MI; Hon Rl; Off Ade; Stg Crw; Spn Clb; Ten; Voc Schl; Data Proc.

PHILLIPS, WILLIAM; Olivet HS; Marshall, MI; Hon Rl; Stg Crw; Sprt Ed Sch Nwsp; Rptr Sch Nwsp; Sch Nwsp; Fr Clb; Bsbl; Bsktbl; Ftbl; Coach Actv; Northwood Inst Bus Schl; CPA.

PHILLIPSON, JACQULINE; Jefferson Union HS; Toronto, OH; 5/170 Trs Soph Cls; Trs Jr Cls; Trs Sr Cls; Band; Hon Rl; Lbry Ade; Orch; Stu Cncl; Y-Teens; Ed Yrbk; 19th Plc In Dist 2 For Algebra 1 77; Hon Mention In Dist 2 For Eng 3 79; Univ; Nursing.

PHILLIS, MELANIE JO; Miami East HS; Troy, OH; Drl Tm; Off Ade; Yth Flsp; Rptr Sch Nwsp; 4-H; Pep Clb; Chrldng; Btty Crckr Awd; 4-H Awd;.

PHILLIS, TAMI; Franklin HS; Columbus, OH; 6/192 Cls Rep Soph Cls; Am Leg Aux Girls St; Band; Chrh Wkr; Hon Rl; NHS; Stu Cncl; Stu Cncl; Key Clb; Spn Clb; Michigan Christian Univ; Sociology.

PHILMORE, VENITA; Beaumont Girls HS; Shaker Hts, OH; Girl Scts; FNA; Spn Clb; Howard Univ; Dent Asst.

PHILSON, RICHARD; River Valley Sr HS; Three Oaks, MI; Band; Hon Rl; Ger Clb; Rdo Clb; Glf; Wrstlng; Lions All St Bnd 1st Toured Jap 2nd Toured Can 78; Yrbk Photog 78; River Valley Quiz Bowl Team 78; Univ Of Michigan; Music In Educ.

PHIPPS, DEBRA; Taylor HS; Kokomo, IN; 28/204 Pres Chrh Wkr; Hon Rl; NHS; Pep Clb; Spn Clb; PPFtbl; Brigham Young Univ; Elem Educ.

PHIPPS, FREDERICK; Indiana Academy; Cincinnati, OH; Hst Frsh Cls; Chrs; Chrh Wkr; Hon Rl; Bsbl; Bsktbl; Ftbl; Coach Actv; IM Sprt; Scr Kpr; Andrews Univ; Aviation Tech.

PIA, RICK; Mona Shores HS; Muskegon, MI; Above Average 3.0 78 79; Voc Schl; Elec.

PIADE, JEFFREY I; Charles F Brush HS; Canoga Park, CA; Band; NHS; Orch; Natl Merit SF; College; Medicine.

PIASECZNY, KEITH; St Ladislaus HS; Hamtramck, MI; 9/109 Hon Rl; Sch Pl; Stu Cncl; Sprt Ed Yrbk; Ed Sch Nwsp; Sch Nwsp; Drama Clb; Gym; Swmmng; Trk; Manhattanville Coll; Psych.

PIATT, LYNNE; Perrysburg HS; Perrysburg, OH; Chrh Wkr; Yth Flsp; Sch Nwsp; Pep Clb; Mat Maids; Scr Kpr; Univ; Soc Work.

PIAZZA, RENEE; Lake Catholic HS; Euclid, OH; Chrh Wkr; Hon Rl; NHS; Off Ade; Y-Teens; Pep Clb; Cit Awd; College; Home Ec.

PICCIUTO, NICK; St Joseph Central Cath HS; Fremont, OH; 10/95 Cl Rep Jr Cls; Cls Rep Sr Cls; Hon Rl; NHS; Sch Mus; Stu Cncl; Key Clb; Letter Wrstlng; Am Leg Awd; Bowling Green St Univ; Acctg.

PICK, SANDRA; Brunswick HS; Brunswick, OH; 81/496 Am Leg Aux Girls St; Chrs; Red Cr Ade; Rptr Yrbk; 4-H; Spn Clb; Gym; Trk; IM Sprt; Scr Kpr; Ohio St Univ; Agronomy.

PICKARD, KIMBERLY; Unioto HS; Sardinia, OH; 9/125 Cl Rep Jr Cls; Am Leg Aux Girls St; Band; Hon Rl; Pep Clb; Mgrs; PPFtbl; Natl Merit Ltr; Ohio St Univ; Phys Ther.

PICKARD, LYNN; Port Huron Northern HS; North St, MI; 20/500 Trs Sr Cls; Chrs; Hon Rl; Stu Cncl; Beta Clb; 4-H; Ger Clb; Taylor Univ; Physh.

PICKEL, SHARON K; Unioto HS; Chillicothe, OH; 11/124 Band; Girl Scts; Hon Rl; Hosp Ade; Jr NHS; NHS; Sch Mus; Drama Clb; Schslhp Awd 75 79; Spanish Hon Soc 77 78 & 79; Sr Girls Ensmbl 79; Capital Univ; Soc Work.

PICKELHEIMER, DOUGLAS; Northrop HS; Ft Wayne, IN; Boy Scts; Sct Actv; Sci Fair Visual Arts Fair; 2 Man Art Show; Art Teachers Aid; College; Art.

PICKELL, BRUCE; North Adams Public HS; Jerome, MI; Trs Frsh Cls; Band; Hon Rl; Sch Pl; Drama Clb; Michigan St Univ; Vet.

PICKELL, GREGORY; Leslie HS; Leslie, MI; 15/130 Band; Drm Bgl; Hon Rl; Lbry Ade; Sch Mus; Stu Cncl; Crs Cntry; Mgrs; West Point Military Acad; Engr.

PICKENPAUGH, JULIA; Shenandoah HS; Quaker City, OH; 27/87 Aud/Vis; Chrs; Chrh Wkr; Hon Rl; Hosp Ade; Lbry Ade; Off Ade; Sch Mus; Sch Pl; Ed Yrbk; Mst Schl Spirit 75; Mst Christian Serv 77; Hghst Schlrstc Achvmnt 77; Malone Coll; Nursing.

PICKENS, JENIENE; High School; Deshler, OH; 9/82 Chrs; Hon Rl; NHS; Off Ade; Sch Pl; Stu Cncl; Yrbk; Pres Spn Clb; Letter Trk; Letter Mat Maids; OSU; Med Tech.

PICKENS, MARIE; Southern HS; Racine, OH; 23/103 Sec Jr Cls; Band; Chrs; Chrh Wkr; MMM; Sch Pl; FHA; Hocking Tech Coll; Comp Sci.

PICKERILL, DEBRA; Henryville HS; Henryville, IN; 19/62 Band; Hon Rl; Lbry Ade; Rptr Sch Nwsp; 4-H; FTA; Spn Clb; Bsktbl; IM Sprt; Cit Awd;.

PICKERILL, THEODORE; Jackson HS; North Canton, OH; 37/434 Band; Boy Scts; Chrh Wkr; JA; Univ.

PICKERING, JOHN; Wellsville HS; Wellsville, OH; Cl Rep Jr Cls; Am Leg Boys St; Stu Cncl; Ed Yrbk; Rptr Yrbk; VP Key Clb; Letter Ftbl; Letter Trk; Univ; Coach.

PICKERING, KATHY; Houston HS; Houston, OH; 2/83 VP Jr Cls; Am Leg Aux Girls St; Pres NHS; Ed Yrbk; FHA; Trk; Capt Chrldng; Soph Class Schlr; All Ohio St Fair Band; College.

PICKERING, KENNI; Frankfort Sr HS; Frankfort, IN; Am Leg Aux Girls St; Chrh Wkr; Girl Scts; Hosp Ade; Lbry Ade; Off Ade; Sch Nwsp; 4-H; FTA; Pep Clb; Sunshine Sec 78; Sunshine FBLA Dance Queens Crt 78; Sunshine Prs 79; Univ; Spec Educ.

PICKERING, KIRK; Charlotte HS; Charlotte, MI; Band; Chrh Wkr; Stg Crw; Yth Flsp; Kiwan Awd; Md Inst Of Tech; Pilot.

PICKERING, REBECCA; Brandon HS; Ortonville, MI; Cmp Fr Grls; Hon Rl; Off Ade; Red Cr Ade; Sch Pl; Stu Cncl; Pres 4-H; Ger Clb; IM Sprt; 4-H Awd; Mic St Univ; Dairy Sci.

PICKERING, ROBERT; Akron Garfield HS; Akron, OH; Boy Scts; Hon Rl; Y-Teens; Bsbl; Letter Socr; Letter Wrstlng; Coach Actv; Univ.

PICKERSGILL, DONALD; Fairview HS; Fairview Pk, OH; Band; Boy Scts; Sct Actv; IM Sprt; Univ.

PICKETT, JERRY; Grandview Heights HS; Columbus, OH; 32/130 Cl Rep Jr Cls; Chrs; Hon Rl; Jr NHS; Sch Mus; Sch Pl; Stu Cncl; Drama Clb; Ftbl; Ten; Brotherhood Of Rooks Schlrshp 79; Ohio St Univ; Music.

PICKETT, TRACEY; Pinckney HS; Brighton, MI; 10/254 Am Leg Aux Girls St; Chrh Wkr; Hon Rl; Lit Mag; NHS; Rptr Sch Nwsp; Drama Clb; Spn Clb; Whos Who Frgn Lang In Midwestern Hs 79; Bus Mgr Of Spnsh Tour Grp 77; St Of Mi Comptn Schlrshp 79; Univ Of Michigan; Bio.

PICKETTS, JULIA K; Harper Creek HS; Marshall, MI; 29/244 Hon Rl; 4-H; Trk; 4-H Awd; College; Vet.

PICKLE JR, ROBERT; North Muskegon HS; N Muskegon, MI; 17/108 Hon Rl; Fr Clb; FDA; Letter Bsktbl; Letter Ftbl; Letter Trk; Pres Awd; Univ; Pre Med.

PICKRELL, MARY; Zanesville HS; Zanesville, OH; 1/383 Val; Hon Rl; Lbry Ade; Treas NHS; Off Ade; Orch; Fr Clb; Sec Sci Clb; Pensacola Christian Coll; Acctg.

PICKUS, MIRIAM; Shaker Hts HS; Shaker Hts, OH; Cls Rep Sr Cls; Hon Rl; Off Ade; Stu Cncl; Sprt Ed Sch Nwsp; Natl Merit SF; Williams Coll Book Awd Recipient; Girls Leaders Clb Pres; Letter Winner On Girls Field Hockey Team & Sftbl; College; Journalism.

PIDCOCK, SANDRA K; Athens HS; East Leroy, MI; Cls Rep Sr Cls; Band; Hosp Ade; Red Cr Ade; Sch Pl; Rptr Yrbk; 4-H; Pep Clb; Pom Pon; Coldwater Coll; Nursing.

PIECHOWICZ, CHERYL; Lumen Cordium HS; Twinsburg, OH; 10/96 Cl Rep Jr Cls; Chrs; Chrh Wkr; Drl Tm; Hon Rl; Stu Cncl; Yrbk; Rptr Sch Nwsp; Sch Nwsp; Spn Clb; Akron Univ; Photog.

PIECHUTA, MARK; Buckeye HS; Litchfield, OH; 4/210 Pres Frsh Cls; Pres Soph Cls; Pres Jr Cls; Chrh Wkr; Hon Rl; NHS; Stu Cncl; Pres 4-H; Pres FFA; Letter Ftbl; Ohio State Univ; Ag.

PIEHLER, STEVE; Independence HS; Columbus, OH; 1/200 Am Leg Boys St; Band; Boy Scts; Pres NHS; Yth Flsp; God Cntry Awd; Kiwan Awd; Natl Merit Ltr; College; Computer Sci.

PIEKARSKI, SCOTT; Nordonia Sr HS; Sagamore Hl, OH; Honro & Merit Roll 76 79; Univ; Engr.

PIEKARSKI, SUSAN; Nordonia Sr HS; Sagamore Hl, OH; Off Ade; Coach Actv; Mat Maids; Scr Kpr; Tmr; Acctg 1; Typing 2 Yrs; Math 3 Yrs; Bus Schl; Bus.

PIEKENBROCK, KAREN; Marion Local HS; Maria Stein, OH; Chrs; Chrh Wkr; Cmnty Wkr; Hon Rl; Hosp Ade; FHA; Pep Clb; Sci Clb; Bsktbl; Trk; CYO Member; College; Medicine.

PIELA, DEBORAH; Northview HS; Grand Rapids, MI; 8/283 Chrs; Chrh Wkr; Hon Rl; NHS; Kiwan Awd; Univ Of Mich; Medicine.

PIELECH, DWAYNE; Buckeye South HS; Yorkville, OH; Am Leg Boys St; Hon Rl; NHS; Pres Stu Cncl; Drama Clb; Spn Clb; Letter Bsktbl; Letter Glf; Scr Kpr; College; Tv Radio Broadcasting.

PIEPER, CAROL; Portage Northern HS; Portage, MI; Chrs; Chrh Wkr; Girl Scts; Hon Rl; Hosp Ade; Lbry Ade; Off Ade; Pol Wkr; Sch Mus; Sch Pl; Western Michigan Univ; Mrktng.

PIEPSNY, RONALD; Padua Franciscan HS; Mid dleburg Ht, OH; Crs Cntry; Trk; Pres Awd; Cleveland State Univ; Engr.

PIER, TERRY; Eaton Rapids HS; Dimondale, MI; 34/226 Chrh Wkr; Hon Rl; Yrbk; Rptr Sch Nwsp; Sch Nwsp;.

PIERACINI, ANGELA; Carey HS; Carey, OH; Cl Rep Jr Cls; Band; Chrs; Cmnty Wkr; Hon Rl; Stu Cncl; Yrbk; Lat Clb; Trk; Chrldng; College; Nurse.

PIERACINI, ANGIE PIERAC; Carey HS; Carey, OH; Cl Rep Jr Cls; Band; Chrs; Cmnty Wkr; Hon Rl; Sch Pl; Stu Cncl; Y-Teens; Lat Clb; Trk; College; Nursing.

PIERATT, ANNE; Cuyahoga Falls HS; Kent, OH; 253/775 Sec Soph Cls; Sec Jr Cls; Sec Sr Cls; Cls Rep Sr Cls; Band; Girl Scts; Hon Rl; Off Ade; Stu Cncl; Yth Flsp; Cuyahoga Cmnty Coll; Dent Hygn.

PIERCE, ANGELA; Pennsboro HS; W Union, WV; Band; 4-H; 4-H Awd;.

PIERCE, BILL; Alexandria Monroe HS; Alexandria, IN; 33/141 Am Leg Boys St; Chrs; Chrh Wkr; Hon Rl; Bsbl; Bsktbl; Ten; IM Sprt; Ball St Univ; Busns.

PIERCE, DEANNA; Wilmington Sr HS; Wilmington, OH; Chrs; Drl Tm; Yth Flsp; Rptr Yrbk; Pres 4-H; Sec Fr Clb; FHA; Pep Clb; Capt Chrldng; GAA; Univ; Drama.

PIERCE, JEANNE; Danville Community HS; Danville, IN; 10/150 Chrs; Girl Scts; Hon Rl; Hosp Ade; NHS; Sch Mus; Sct Actv; Rptr Sch Nwsp; 4-H; Sci Clb; Univ; Med.

PIERCE, KATHERINE; Washington Irving HS; Clarksburg, WV; Trs Jr Cls; Hon Rl; Hosp Ade; NHS; Stu Cncl; Drama Clb; Lat Clb; Pep Clb; Sci Clb; World Affaird Inst In Morgantown Wv 79; Served As A Page In St Sen 79; West Virginia Univ; Med.

PIERCE, MICHAEL; Elk Rapids HS; Williamsburg, MI; Aud/Vis; Cmnty Wkr; Hon Rl; Lbry Ade; Stg Crw; Rdo Clb; Davenport College; Bus.

PIERCE, MICHAEL; West Lafayette HS; W Lafayette, IN; 85/189 Boy Scts; FCA; Hon Rl; Letter Ftbl; Mgrs; Purdue Univ; Aviation Technology.

PIERCE, MICHAEL; Bishop Noll Inst; Chicago, IL; 69/321 Band; Drm Bgl; Hon Rl; Sch Mus; Univ Of Ill; Mech Engr.

PIERCE, ROBERT T; Portsmouth HS; Portsmouth, OH; 11/237 Cls Rep Frsh Cls; Cls Rep Soph Cls; Cl Rep Jr Cls; Cls Rep Sr Cls; Chrh Wkr; Hon Rl; NHS; Pres Stu Cncl; Lat Clb; Letter Ten; Ohio St Univ; Admin Sci.

PIERCE, RON; Hagerstown Jr Sr HS; Hagerstown, IN; 8/142 Band; Hon Rl; 4-H; Sci Clb; Spn Clb; 4-H Awd; Ball St Univ.

PIERCE, RUSSELL; Lake Central HS; Schereville, IN; 17/526 Hon Rl; Jr NHS; NHS; Spn Clb; Letter Ftbl; Ind Univ Nw; Premed.

PIERCE, SCOTT; New Albany HS; New Albany, OH; 1/98 Sec Frsh Cls; VP Jr Cls; Cl Rep Jr Cls; Band; Chrs; Chrh Wkr; FCA; Hon Rl; Orch; Sch Pl; Science Student Of The Year; Freshmen Schlrshp Awd; Sophomore Schlrshp Awd; College.

PIERCE, THOMAS D; Eastlake North HS; Willowick, OH; 58/669 Chrs; Yrbk; Fr Clb; Key Clb; Art Inst Of Pittsburgh; Photog.

PIERCE, TY; Celina Sr HS; Celina, OH; Boy Scts; Hon Rl; 4-H; Bsbl; Glf; Univ Of Dayton; Bus Mgr.

PIERCEY, C; Warren HS; Troy, MI; Sec Frsh Cls; Cls Rep Soph Cls; Cl Rep Jr Cls; Chrs; Hon Rl; Stu Cncl; Alma College; Bus.

PIERDE, KELLIE; Groveport Madison HS; Groveport, OH; Chrs; Chrh Wkr; CAP; Girl Scts; Spn Clb; Scr Kpr; College.

PIERPOINT, LORA; Capitol City Christian Schl; Ionia, MI; 3/17 Pres Soph Cls; Chrs; Chrh Wkr; Girl Scts; Hon Rl; NHS; Sch Mus; VP Stu Cncl; Yth Flsp; Rptr Yrbk; Grace College; Nursing.

PIERRO, JEAN; Norton HS; Norton, OH; Band; Hon Rl; Fr Clb; Bsktbl; Ohio St Univ; Comp Sci.

PIERRON, ALICE; Notre Dame HS; Portsmouth, OH; Pres Frsh Cls; VP Soph Cls; Cmnty Wkr; Hon Rl; Jr NHS; NHS; Quill & Scroll; Stu Cncl; Rptr Sch Nwsp; Sch Nwsp; Xavier Univ; Dent Hygnst.

PIERSOL, J; Barnesville HS; Barnesville, OH; Band; Boy Scts; Sch Pl; Sct Actv; Boys Clb Am; Fr Clb; Sci Clb; Ohio State; Optometrist.

PIERSON, BRIAN; Sullivan HS; Merom, IN; 23/156 Hon Rl; Lbry Ade; Stu Cncl; 4-H; Lat Clb; Letter Ftbl; Letter Wrstlng; Mgrs; 4-H Awd; Univ; Engr.

PIERSON, LORI; Stephen T Badin HS; Hamilton, OH; 39/219 Hon Rl; JA; Sch Pl; Drama Clb; 4-H; Trk; 4-H Awd; Miami Univ; Spec Educ.

PIERSON, LYNNETTE; Quincy HS; Quincy, MI; Sec Sr Cls; Hon Rl; Off Ade; Rptr Yrbk; Yrbk; Rptr Sch Nwsp; 4-H; Pep Clb; Chrldng; 4-H Awd; Ferriss State College; Acctg.

PIERSON, MARY; Mc Auley HS; Cincinnati, OH; Cl Rep Jr Cls; Chrh Wkr; Cmnty Wkr; Girl Scts; Sch Mus; Sch Pl; Stu Cncl; Y-Teens; Beta Clb; Drama Clb; Univ Of Cincinnati; Brdcstng.

PIERSON, PAMELA; Grand Blanc Comm HS; Grand Blanc, MI; 35/614 Chrh Wkr; Hon Rl; NHS; IM Sprt; Michigan Christian Coll.

PIERSON, PAMELA; Coldwater HS; Coldwater, MI; 60/297 Cmp Fr Grls; Chrs; Hon Rl; Mdrgl; Sch Mus; 4-H; Spn Clb; C of C Awd; 4-H Awd; Siena Heights College; Social Work.

PIERSON, TARA; Port Huron N HS; Port Huron, MI; 22/388 Chrh Wkr; Hon Rl; NHS; Ger Clb; St Clair Cnty Comm Coll.

PIETENPOL, NANCY; Trenton HS; Trenton, MI; Girl Scts; Hon Rl; NHS; 4-H; Pep Clb; Cit Awd; 4-H Awd; Natl Merit Ltr; College; Vet.

PIGNATIELLO, MIKE; Centerville HS; Centerville, OH; 2/687 Band; Chrh Wkr; NHS; Fr Clb; Letter Ft bl; Letter Ten; Univ Of Dayton; Bio.

PIIEST, VICKI; Inland Lakes HS; Indian River, MI; 5/75 Hon Rl; Lbry Ade; Stu Cncl; Ed Yrbk; Rptr Sch Nwsp; Pep Clb; GAA; Lion Awd; Central Michigan Univ; Art.

PIKE, BRENDA; Unionvl Sebewaing Area Schl; Sebewaing, MI; Hon Rl; NHS; Stu Cncl; 4-H; Letter Hockey; Letter Trk; IM Sprt; Univ; Natural Sci.

PIKE, DENA; Caro HS; Unionville, MI; Band; Hon Rl; NHS; Yth Flsp; 4-H; Pep Clb; 4-H Awd; Michigan State; Clothing Retailer.

PIKE, ERIC; Eastlake North HS; Eastlake, OH; 124/706 Hon Rl; Letter Ftbl; Letter Trk; Univ; Lib Arts.

PIKE, JEFFREY; Mount View HS; Welch, WV; Band; Sch Pl; Key Clb; Ftbl; Trk; Wrstlng; Mgrs; Concord Coll; Pre Med.

PIKOVNIK, AMY; Andrews HS; Painesville, OH; Sec Jr Cls; Cmnty Wkr; Hon Rl; NHS; Sch Nwsp; Univ; Bus.

PIKTURNA, AUDREY G; Eastlake North HS; Willowick, OH; Girl Scts; Hon Rl; JA; Mod UN; Key Clb; Mth Clb; Sci Clb; Dyke Coll; Acctg.

PILATI, JOHN; Minerva HS; Minerva, OH; 19/241 Cls Rep Soph Cls; Pres Jr Cls; Hon Rl; Lbry Ade; Stu Cncl; Spn Clb; Bsktbl; Ftbl; College.

PILCHER, LISLE; Kenton Ridge HS; Springfield, OH; 30/140 Sch Nwsp; Spn Clb; Ten; Bowling Green Univ; Med.

PILCHER, PAMELA; S Vigo HS; Terre Haute, IN; Hosp Ade; Mod UN; Stu Cncl; Y-Teens; Sprt Ed Sch Nwsp; 4-H; Letter Bsktbl; Letter Ten; Sec GAA; DAR Awd; Univ; PE.

PILKENTON, RANDALL; Sturgis HS; Sturgis, MI; Cls Rep Frsh Cls; VP Soph Cls; Boy Scts; Hon Rl; JA; NHS; Stu Cncl; Yth Flsp; Bsktbl; Letter Glf; Oakland Univ; Comp Sci.

PILKEY, CINDY; Lutheran HS; N Ridgeville, OH; Band; Chrh Wkr; Hon Rl; NHS; Rptr Yrbk; Pep Clb; Architect.

PILLA, TERESA; Regina HS; E Cleveland, OH; Hon Rl; NHS; Stu Cncl; Yrbk; Swmmng; IM Sprt; Cleveland State Univ; Phys Ther.

PILLER, JOSEPH; La Salle HS; Cincinnati, OH; Hon Rl; Letter Bsbl; Bsktbl; Univ.

PILLIOD, KAREN; Evergreen HS; Swanton, OH; Trs Soph Cls; Chrs; Chrh Wkr; Hon Rl; Stu Cncl; Yth Flsp; Ed Sch Nwsp; Rptr Sch Nwsp; Sch Nwsp; 4-H; Univ.

PILLOW, KELLY; Coloma HS; Coloma, MI; 35/210 Chrs; Girl Scts; Hon Rl; Hosp Ade; Off Ade; Pep Clb; Letter Trk; LMC; Nurse.

PILNEY, DIANE; Buckeye South HS; Yorkville, OH; 20/135 Sec Soph Cls; Letter Band; Hon Rl; Hosp Ade; Ed Yrbk; Rptr Sch Nwsp; Drama Clb; Pep Clb; Spn Clb; Chrldng; 100 Hr Pin For Voluntr Work At Martins Ferry Hosp 79; Chrldr For 6 Yrs; Ohio Univ; Elem Educ.

PILON, CATHERINE; Goodrich HS; Holly, MI; Chrs; Hon Rl; Hosp Ade; JA; Sch Mus; Sch Pl; Letter Trk; Mic State Univ; Rn.

PILUTTI, JANINE; Carroll HS; Dayton, OH; 60/290 Chrh Wkr; Hon Rl; NHS; Red Cr Ade; Spn Clb; Coach Actv; IM Sprt; Opt Clb Awd; College; Nurse.

PINDOLEY, DONALD; Rossford HS; Rossford, OH; 6/150 Toledo Univ.

PINE, DENISE; Whitmore Lake HS; Whitmore, MI; 55/80 Cls Rep Frsh Cls; Cls Rep Soph Cls; Cl Rep Jr Cls; Girl Scts; Hon Rl; Captn Most Valbl Plyr Vollybll 78; Washtenaw Cmnty Coll; Dent Asst.

PINE, KATHRYN; Williamstown HS; Williamstown, WV; 1/103 Val; Am Leg Aux Girls St; Hon Rl; Sec NHS; Ed Yrbk; Rptr Sch Nwsp; Drama Clb; Pep Clb; Wv Univ; Doctor.

PINEVICH, ANTHONY; Wintersville HS; Wintersville, OH; 2/300 Hst Sr Cls; Sal; Am Leg Boys St; Band; Debate Tm; Drm Bgl; Hon Rl; NHS; Orch; Stu Cncl; Akron Med Schl; Physn.

PINGITORE, TAMMY; Yale HS; Avoca, MI; Band; Chrs; Hon Rl; 4-H; IM Sprt; Pom Pon; Twrlr; Certf Of Merit Twirling 77; Certf Of Merit Twirling Champion; Univ; Psych.

PINGLEY, BILL; Coalton 12 Year School; Norton, WV; 3/33 Cls Rep Soph Cls; VP Jr Cls; Hon Rl; NHS; Stu Cncl; Sch Nwsp; Sci Clb; VICA; Draftsman.

PINHO, JACKIE; George A Dondero HS; Royal Oak, MI; 8/450 Hon Rl; Lit Mag; NHS; Sch Mus; Sch Pl; Stg Crw; Sch Nwsp; VP Drama Clb; Fr Clb; NCTE; Wayne St Univ.

PINHO, JACQUELINE R; Dondero HS; Royal Oak, MI; 9/430 Chrs; Hon Rl; NHS; PAVAS; Sch Mus; Sch Pl; Sct Actv; Stg Crw; Rptr Sch Nwsp; VP Drama Clb; College.

PINION, JOHN A; Valley HS; Smithers, WV; 1/150 Am Leg Boys St; Band; Chrh Wkr; Hon Rl; NHS; Univ; Elec Engr.

PINKELMAN, DAVID; Evergreen HS; Swanton, OH; Chrh Wkr; Hon Rl; Lit Mag; FFA; Bsbl; Bsktbl; Coach Actv;.

PINKERTON, PAM; Sebring Mc Kinley HS; Sebring, OH; 5/93 Pres Jr Cls; Band; Chrh Wkr; Hon Rl; Off Ade; Quill & Scroll; Rptr Yrbk; Sch Nwsp; FHA; Letter Bsktbl;.

PINKLETON, MARILEE; Mississinewa HS; Jonesboro, IN; 6/189 Chrs; Chrh Wkr; Hon Rl; Pres NHS; Sch Mus; Yth Flsp; Treas 4-H; Fr Clb; 4-H Awd; Charlotte Mem Hosp Tech; Nuclear Med.

PINKOWSKI, JOHN L; Walsh Jesuit HS; Northfield Ctr, OH; 8/173 Band; Hon Rl; Y-Teens; Pep Clb; Letter Bsbl; Letter Ftbl; Trk; Received Academic Schlshp To Walsh Jesuit H S 1975; Whos Who Among Amrcn H S; Selected To Attend Med Schl; N E Ohio Univ; Med.

PINKS, TOBIN E; Hardin Northern HS; Dunkirk, OH; 13/54 Boy Scts; Hon Rl; Stu Cncl; 4-H; Fr Clb; Key Clb; 4-H Awd; Ohio St Univ; Vet.

PINKSTON, ANTHONY; Inkster HS; Inkster, MI; Cl Rep Jr Cls; Hon Rl; JA; NHS; Rptr Yrbk; Sci Clb; Bsbl; Bsktbl; Ftbl; Univ Of Detroit; Elec Engr.

PINKSTON, DUANE; North Posey Sr HS; Poseyville, IN; 10/162 Boy Scts; Hon Rl; Ger Clb; Pep Clb; Letter Bsbl; IM Sprt; Voice Dem Awd; Univ; Comp Sci.

PINNELL, WADE; John F Kennedy HS; Taylor, MI; 4/450 Am Leg Boys St; Chrh Wkr; Debate Tm; Hon Rl; Jr NHS; Treas NHS; Sch Pl; Stg Crw; Rep To The US Army Jr Sci & Humanities Symposian 78; VP Of Schl Spch Club 78; Univ Of Michigan; Aero Engr.

PINNELL, WILLIAM; Garden City East Sr HS; Garden City, MI; 7/400 Cls Rep Frsh Cls; Am Leg Boys St; Hon Rl; NHS; Yth Flsp; Ger Clb; Spn Clb; Capt Crs Cntry; Capt Trk; Cit Awd; Outstndng Sr Boy 78; Steven G Mc Keever Memrl Schlshp 78; Adrian Coll Acad Schlshp 78; Adrian Coll; Bus Admin.

PINNER, DAVID; East Knox Local HS; Howard, OH; IM Sprt; Univ; Elec.

PINNER, KEVIN L; Turpin HS; Cincinnati, OH; Sct Actv; Yth Flsp; Letter Socr; PPFtbl; Univ Of Cincinnati; Busns.

PINNEY, MELISSA; Woodlan HS; New Haven, IN; Trs Frsh Cls; Trs Soph Cls; Cl Rep Jr Cls; Chrs; Hon Rl; Off Ade; Stu Cncl; Drama Clb; FHA; Gym; Cand In Miss Teen USA Pageant 79; Humans Rel Comm 79; Purdue Univ; Opthalmic Tech.

PINO, DONNA; Highland HS; Highland, IN; 15/494 Chrs; Chrh Wkr; Hon Rl; Hosp Ade; Mdrgl; NHS; Sch Mus; Sct Actv; VP Ger Clb; Kiwan Awd; Camper In Leadership Training; Pres Schlrshp; German Natl Honor Society; Taylor Univ; Busns.

PINSONEAULT, GAIL; Wadsworth Sr HS; Wadsworth, OH; 34/367 Chrs; Cmnty Wkr; Girl Scts; Hon Rl; Jr NHS; NHS; Rptr Yrbk; Drama Clb; 4-H; Fr Clb; Univ; Home Ec.

PINTO, ANNA; Hackett HS; Kalamazoo, MI; NHS; Yrbk; Western Michigan Univ; Art.

PIONK, JULIANNE; Henry Ford II HS; Sterling Hts, MI; 12/364 Chrh Wkr; Girl Scts; Hon Rl; Hosp Ade; NHS; Sch Pl; Stg Crw; Chrldng; Central Michigan Univ; Pre Med.

PIONTKOWSKI, TIMOTHY; Rochester Adams HS; Rochester, MI; 65/532 Band; Cmnty Wkr; Hon Rl; NHS; Stg Crw; Rptr Yrbk; Sci Clb; Oakland Univ; Chemistry.

PIORKOWSKI, GARY; R B Chamberlin HS; Twinsburg, OH; Hon Rl; NHS; Bsktbl; Ftbl; Univ.

PIOTRKOWSKI, REBECCA; Villa Angela Acad; Cleveland, OH; Cl Rep Jr Cls; Chrs; Univ; Geol.

PIPER, CATHY; Norton HS; Norton, OH; 13/287 NHS; Sprt Ed Sch Nwsp; Rptr Sch Nwsp; FHA; GAA; Akron Univ; Comp Progr.

PIPER, JILL; Dexter HS; Dexter, MI; Girl Scts; Hon Rl; Pol Wkr; Sch Pl; Yth Flsp; Rptr Yrbk; Rptr Sch Nwsp; Drama Clb; VFW Awd; Voice Dem Awd; Georgetown Univ; Intl Govt.

PIPER, LAWRENCE; Holt HS; Lansing, MI; 28/395 Jr NHS; NHS; Sch Pl; Rptr Sch Nwsp; Sch Nwsp; Fr Clb; Univ.

PIPER, RICK; North Olmsted HS; N Olmsted, OH; 40/680 AFS; NHS; Coach Actv; IM Sprt; Ohio Univ.

PIPER, THOMAS L; Haslett HS; Haslett, MI; 44/154 Adv EMT.

PIPINO, MARY; John F Kennedy HS; Niles, OH; Cls Rep Soph Cls; Hon Rl; Jr NHS; NHS; Sch Mus; Stu Cncl; Y-Teens; Rptr Yrbk; Pres Fr Clb; Natl Merit Ltr; Univ; Spec Ed.

PIPPIN, MARK; Dayton Christian HS; Dayton, OH; Band; Hon Rl; NHS; Sch Mus; Yrbk; Trk; Natl Merit Ltr; Univ; Physics.

PIQUANT, NADIA; Andrean HS; Gary, IN; Band; Chrs; Hon Rl; Fr Clb; GAA; Univ; Nursing.

PIQUNE, ROSE; Southern Wells Jr Sr HS; Warren, IN; 10/100 Girl Scts; Hon Rl; NHS; Sct Actv; Yth Flsp; 4-H; FHA; Pep Clb; 4-H Awd; College; Acctg.

PIRRALLO, RONALD; Fraser HS; Fraser, MI; 6/617 Am Leg Boys St; Hon Rl; NHS; Sch Pl; Capt Ftbl; Ferris St Coll; Optometry.

PIRRUNG, DENISE M; Chaminade Julienne HS; Dayton, OH; 23/264 Cmp Fr Grls; Hon Rl; Sinclair Coll; Acctg.

PIRRUNG, THOMAS; Chaminade Julienne HS; Dayton, OH; 115/271 Chrh Wkr; Hon Rl; Univ Of Dayton; Bus.

PISARSKY, PAULA; Swartz Creek HS; Swartz Creek, MI; Band; Hon Rl; Stg Crw; Capt Chrldng; Coach Actv; Mgrs; Mich Higher Educ Schlrshp 1200 Dollars 79; Adiran Coll Awd 622 Dollars 79; Adrian Coll; Psych.

PISKIN, KENT; Central HS; Grand Rapids, MI; Hon Rl; NHS; Lat Clb; Acad Letter 79; Univ.

PISKOL, LOUISE; Washington HS; E Chicago, IN; 19/264 Hon Rl; NHS; FTA; Key Clb; Ten; Treas Harbor Cath Youth Org 78; Indiana St Univ; Acctg

PISKOS, GEORGE; Allen Park HS; Allen Park, MI; 23/300 Ftbl; Letter Ten; Natl Merit Ltr; Univ Of Michigan.

PISTEN, CAROL; R B Chamberlin HS; Twinsburg, OH; 10/180 Hon Rl; NHS; Rptr Yrbk; Pep Clb; Chrldng; GAA; IM Sprt; PPFtbl; Univ Of Cincinnati; Civil Engr.

PITCHER, BERTIE; L & M HS; Lyons, IN; Hon Rl; Lbry Ade; Beta Clb; FHA; Pep Clb; College; Acctg.

PITCHER, BRIAN; Richmond Sr HS; Richmond, IN; Sci Clb; Spn Clb; Univ Of New Mexico; Sciences.

PITCHER, DONALD J; Rensselaer Central HS; Rensselaer, IN; Hon Rl; Sch Nwsp;.

PITCHFORD, BRIAN E; Poca HS; Red House, WV; 9/154 Am Leg Boys St; Band; Chrh Wkr; Hon Rl; NHS; Pol Wkr; Sch Pl; Drama Clb; 4-H Awd; Oh State Univ; Aero Engr.

PITCOX, SHARON; Unioto HS; Chillicothe, OH; 27/124 Cls Rep Sr Cls; Chrs; Chrh Wkr; Hon Rl; FTA; Bsktbl; GAA; Ou Branch; Computer.

PITMAN, BRENDA; Greenville Sr HS; Greenville, OH; 29/380 Hon Rl; Orch; Sch Mus; Stg Crw; Drama Clb; Lat Clb; Sci Clb; Worthy Adv Internatl Order Of Rainbow For Girls 78; Univ; Acctg.

PITMAN, DENNIS; Union HS; Modoc, IN; 32/76 Cls Rep Frsh Cls; Cls Rep Soph Cls; Spn Clb; Letter Trk; Letter Wrstlng; Coach Actv;.

PITRELLI, MARTHA; Lehman HS; Sidney, OH; 7/87 Sec Sr Cls; Am Leg Aux Girls St; Chrs; Hon Rl; NHS; Sch Pl; Rptr Yrbk; Drama Clb; Pep Clb; Univ; Pro Art.

PITSCH, JENNIFER; Rockford Sr HS; Rockford, MI; 1/360 Cl Rep Jr Cls; Cls Rep Sr Cls; Val; Hon Rl; NHS; Pol Wkr; Stu Cncl; Lat Clb; Chrldng; PPFtbl; W Michigan Univ; Busns.

PITSCH, LAUREEN; Sparta HS; Sparta, MI; 6/195 VP Frsh Cls; VP Soph Cls; Cls Rep Soph Cls; Hon Rl; Pres NHS; Stu Cncl; Ed Yrbk; Capt Chrldng; Pom Pon; Western Mic Univ; Soc Work.

PITT, JIM; Newark HS; Newark, OH; Am Leg Boys St; Band; Boy Scts; Hon Rl; Jr NHS; NHS; Letter Crs Cntry; Letter Trk; Wrstlng; Rotary Awd; U S Air Force Acad; Pilot.

PITT, KATHLEEN; Chesaning Union HS; Chesaning, MI; 5/240 Hon Rl; NHS; 4-H; Spn Clb; Letter Bsbl; Mic Tech Univ; Engr.

PITT, RANDALL; St Xavier HS; Cincinnati, OH; 190/270 Hosp Ade; Pep Clb; IM Sprt; Univ; Engr.

PITTENGER, KELLI L; Muncie Northside HS; Muncie, IN; Cmnty Wkr; Hon Rl; NHS; Off Ade; Red Cr Ade; Ed Yrbk; Swmmng; Natl Merit Schl; Opt Clb Awd; Jrnlsm Awd For Yrbk Ed In Chief 79; Media Fair Awd In Photog Photo Essay 77; Indiana Univ; Dent Asst.

PITTMAN, CAROLYN; Merrillville HS; Merrillville, IN; 51/595 Hon Rl; Sch Pl; Trk; Tmr; Ball St Univ; Acctg.

PITTMAN, DAVID; Western Boone HS; Jamestown, IN; 14/141 VP Frsh Cls; Pres Soph Cls; Aud/Vis; Band; FCA; Hon Rl; NHS; Sch Mus; Stg Crw; Yrbk; Outstndng Ach In Bio; Selected To Natl Hnr Soc; Indiana St Univ; Elem Ed.

PITTMAN, DIANA; Jewett Scio HS; Scio, OH; Hon Rl; Yrbk; 4-H; Spn Clb; VICA; Trk; Chrldng; 4-H Awd; 1st Rnnr Up Scio Fall Festival Queen Contst 1977; Ohio Vly Coll.

PITTMAN, DIANA; James A Garfield HS; Ravenna, OH; Chrh Wkr; Hon Rl; NHS; Yth Flsp; 4-H; Fr Clb; FHA; Business School.

PITTMAN, GREGOIRE; Muskegon Heights HS; Muskegon Hts, MI; 11/161 Trs Soph Cls; Band; Hon Rl; Pres NHS; Stu Cncl; Rptr Sch Nwsp; Ftbl; Natl Merit SF; Louis Armstrong Jazz Awd 79; Lumbermans Bnk Deserving Schlrshp Awd 79; PUSH For Excellence Awd 79; Michigan St Univ; Poli Sci.

PITTMAN, LAURA; Herbert Hoover HS; Elkvw, WV; Cls Rep Frsh Cls; Chrs; Cmnty Wkr; Girl Scts; Hon Rl; Sch Pl; Stu Cncl; Yth Flsp; Fr Clb; FBLA; Univ; Law.

PITTMAN, RENEE; La Ville Jr Sr HS; Bremen, IN; Sec Frsh Cls; Aud/Vis; NHS; Stu Cncl; Ger Clb; Pep Clb; Chrldng; Am Leg Awd; DAR Awd; Bob Jones Univ; Dental Asst.

PITTS, BRIAN; Wilbur Wright HS; Dayton, OH; 15/199 Sec Frsh Cls; Cl Rep Jr Cls; Pres Band; Chrs; Chrh Wkr; Hon Rl; NHS; Off Ade; Orch; Pol Wkr; Fine Arts Awd; Commencement Keynote Speaker & Pianist; Blue Medal In St Solo & Ensemble Contest; Wright St Univ; Music.

PITTS, DANETTE; Parma Sr HS; Parma, OH; 110/710 Hon Rl; NHS; FFA; FFA St Degree; FFA Proficiency In Floriculture; Chapter Leadership Awd; Ohio St Univ; Floriculture.

PITTS, KEVIN; Collinwood HS; Cleveland, OH; Band; Hon Rl; JA; NHS; Stu Cncl; USMA Invt Academ Wrkshp Cert Of Completion 79; Kappa Alpha Psi Frat Cert Of Recgntn 79; CCC Awd 78; Case Western Reserve Univ; Engr.

PITTS, M; Perry HS; Massillon, OH; Band; Boy Scts; Coach Actv; Flo Inst Tech; Marine Sci.

PITTS, REVA L; Wilbur Wright HS; Dayton, OH; VP Jr Cls; Band; Chrh Wkr; Drl Tm; Hon Rl; Orch; Stu Cncl; FHA; Pres Awd; Wright St Univ; Medicine.

PITUCH, MARK G; St Clement HS; Warren, MI; Trk; Voc Schl; Tool & Die Maker.

PITZEN, TERRI; Plymouth HS; Plymouth, OH; Boy Scts; Sct Actv; Yrbk; Rptr Sch Nwsp; 4-H; FHA; FTA; Sec Spn Clb; North Central Tech Coll; Spec Ed.

PITZER, CINDY; Eastern HS; Long Bottom, OH; 15/73 Sec Jr Cls; Sec Chrs; Chrh Wkr; Cmnty Wkr; Hon Rl; Sec Hosp Ade; NHS; Off Ade; Sch Mus; Sch Pl; Meigs Co Outstndng Fha 1978; Natl Hnr Soc 1978; Club Congrss 4 H Recpt 1977; Ohio Univ; Home Ec.

PITZER, DWAIN; Clinton Central HS; Kirklin, IN; 2/120 Am Leg Boys St; Cmnty Wkr; FCA; Hon Rl; NHS; Yth Flsp; 4-H; VP FFA; Pep Clb; Sci Clb; FFA St Production Demonstration; Mbr Of Natl Dairy Judging Team; 1st In Dist FFA Essay Cont; Purdue Univ; Vet.

PITZER, ROGER; Whiteland Cmnty HS; Whiteland, IN; 59/216 Band; Boy Scts; Hon Rl; Yrbk; IM Sprt; Univ; Elec Engr.

PIXLEY, DAVID J; Interlochen Arts Academy; Rochester, MI; Cl Rep Jr Cls; Chrs; Hon Rl; Mdrgl; Sch Mus; Sch Pl; Stu Cncl; Drama Clb; Trk; Coll; Theatre Arts.

PIZATELLA, CATHY; Walnut Ridge HS; Columbus, OH; 30/450 Hon Rl; NHS; Spn Clb; PPFtbl; Ohio St Univ; Vet.

PIZZA, ANDREW; St Francis Desales HS; Toledo, OH; 22/195 Hon Rl; NHS; Bsbl; Letter Swmmng; IM Sprt; Univ Of Cincinnati; Archt.

PIZZALA, MICHAEL J; Linden Community HS; Linden, MI; Band; Cmnty Wkr; Hon Rl; Lbry Ade; NHS; Red Cr Ade; Sch Pl; Yrbk; Drama Clb; Med Explorers; Soc Activities Public Rel Dr 78; Mi St Comp Schlrshp Awd 79; Univ Of Michigan; Pre Med.

PIZZINI, JOHN; Trenton HS; Trenton, MI; Sch Mus; Wrstlng; Michigan State Univ; Air Force Rotc.

PIZZINO, SHAWN; Shady Spring HS; Shady Spring, WV; 19/155 Chrs; Chrh Wkr; Cmnty Wkr; FCA; Hon Rl; NHS; Yth Flsp; FHA; Pep Clb; Chrldng; College; Busns Mgmt.

PIZZUTI, JOHN; Brooke HS; Follansbee, WV; Cls Rep Sr Cls; Am Leg Boys St; Hon Rl; NHS; Spn Clb; Bsbl; Bsktbl; Coach Actv; Mr Hustle Awd For Bsktbl 78; Notre Dame Univ; Engr.

PLACE, DONALD E; St Marys HS; St Marys, WV; Cls Rep Frsh Cls; Band; Boy Scts; Sct Actv; VICA;.

PLACKE, LINDA; Guernsey Catholic Cntrl HS; S enecaville, OH; 6/27 Pres Jr Cls; Chrh Wkr; Hon Rl; NHS; Sch Pl; Yrbk; Pep Clb; Capt Bsktbl; Scr Kpr; Voice Dem Awd; Bowling Green State Univ; Speech Pat.

PLACKE, LYN; Archbishop Alter HS; Kettering, OH; 3/296 Chrs; Drl Tm; Hon Rl; NHS; Off Ade; Stu Cncl; Drama Clb; VP Keyettes; GAA; IM Sprt; Algebra Biology & English Special Awds; College; Medicine.

PLADARS, ELIZABETH; Columbus North HS; Columbus, OH; 7/300 VP Frsh Cls; Cls Rep Soph Cls; Cl Rep Jr Cls; Sec Sr Cls; Trs Sr Cls; Am Leg Aux Girls St; Band; Cmp Fr Grls; Chrs; Chrh Wkr; Ohio St Univ; RN.

PLAGEMAN, CHRIS M; St Xavier HS; Forest Park, OH; Cls Rep Soph Cls; Band; Boy Scts; Chrh Wkr; Hon Rl; NHS; Rptr Yrbk; Rptr Sch Nwsp; Fr Clb; Letter Socr; Univ; Engr.

PLAGENS, SANDRA; Divine Child HS; Dearborn Ht, MI; Chrh Wkr; Debate Tm; Hon Rl; Pol Wkr; Stg Crw; Pep Clb; Bsktbl; Trk; Wayne St Univ; Med.

PLAGENS, SHARON; Pellston HS; Pellston, MI; 4/70 Sec Soph Cls; Girl Scts; Hon Rl; Jr NHS; Off Ade; Yth Flsp; 4-H; FTA; Military.

PLAK, KAREN; Cardinal Mooney HS; Youngstown, OH; 8/288 Band; Hon Rl; NHS; Lat Clb; Mth Clb; Trk; Certf Awd For 2nd Highest Average In Algebra II & Trigonometry & Latin II; Univ; Chem.

PLAMBECK, MISSY; Douglas Macarthur HS; Saginaw, MI; Girl Scts; Hon Rl; Lbry Ade; Off Ade; Orch; Sch Nwsp; Trk; Pom Pon; PPFtbl; Cit Awd; College; Eng.

PLAMONDON, JOAN; St Mary HS; Lake Leelanau, MI; Hon Rl; Pep Clb; Letter Bsbl; Child Care.

PLANK, CHERYL; Carroll HS; Bringhurst, IN; Chrs; Hon Rl; Sch Mus; Sch Pl; Yrbk; Drama Clb; 4-H; Fr Clb; Pep Clb; 4-H Awd; Vincenney Univ; Nursing.

PLANK, KARLA; Fairfield Union HS; Bremen, OH; Cmnty Wkr; Hon Rl; Jr NHS; Rptr Yrbk; Ed Sch Nwsp; FBLA; OEA; Ohio Univ; Comp Sci.

PLANK, LAURIE; Lehman HS; Piqua, OH; Cl Rep Jr Cls; Band; Chrs; Hon Rl; Orch; Stu Cncl; Bsbl; Bsktbl; Crs Cntry; College.

PLANT, JACQUELINE; North Royalton HS; N Royalton, OH; 60/286 VP Soph Cls; VP Jr Cls; Pres Sr Cls; Cmnty Wkr; Hosp Ade; VP Stu Cncl; Yrbk; Drama Clb; Sci Clb; College; CPA.

PLANT, PATRICIA; Northfield HS; Wabash, IN; Cl Rep Jr Cls; Sec FCA; Hon Rl; NHS; Stg Crw; Stu Cncl; Drama Clb; Fr Clb; Capt Chrldng; Pom Pon; Ind Univ; Bus.

PLANTAMURA, CHARLES; Greenville Sr HS; Greenville, MI; Am Leg Boys St; Boy Scts; Chrh Wkr; Hon Rl; Quill & Scroll; Sct Actv; Stg Crw; Stu Cncl; Rptr Sch Nwsp; Sch Nwsp; Eagle Sct 78; Stdnt Cnsl Senator 77 & 78; Western Michigan Univ; Car Sales.

PLANTE, JOHN; Iron Mountain HS; Iron Mountain, MI; Cmnty Wkr; Hon Rl; Key Clb; IM Sprt; St Of Mi Comp Schlrshp 79; Dickinson Cnty War Vet Schlrshp 79; Northern Michigan Univ; Pre Dent.

PLANTZ, KIMBERLY; Milton HS; Milton, WV; Cls Rep Soph Cls; Cl Rep Jr Cls; Cls Rep Sr Cls; Am Leg Aux Girls St; Band; Hon Rl; Stu Cncl; Yrbk; Rptr Sch Nwsp; Flag Corps Capt; West Virginia Univ; Law.

PLAS, DEBORAH; Midview HS; Grafton, OH; 35/266 Hon Rl; JA; Lbry Ade; Stu Cncl; Fr Clb; Lorain Cnty Cmnty Coll; Med.

PLASKET, PAMELA; Hoover HS; North Canton, OH; 20/424 Cls Rep Frsh Cls; Hst Soph Cls; Am Leg Aux Girls St; Chrs; Chrh Wkr; Hon Rl; Hosp Ade; Jr NHS; NHS; Sch Mus; Univ; Med.

PLASS, SUSAN; Princeton HS; Princeton, WV; Chrs; Chrh Wkr; Cmnty Wkr; Girl Scts; Hon Rl; Hosp Ade; Off Ade; 4-H; Pep Clb; 4-H Awd; Sci Fair Awd 76; Soc Std Awd 78; Univ.

PLASSMAN, JANET; Archbold HS; Archbold, OH; Hon Rl; Rptr Sch Nwsp; Letter Trk; College; Law.

PLASSMAN, JEFFREY; Hicksville HS; Hicksville, OH; Hon Rl; NHS; Letter Bsbl; Univ; Dentistry.

PLATE, RITA; Creston HS; Grand Rapids, MI; Band; Cmp Fr Grls; Hon Rl; Jr NHS; NHS; Orch; Schlstc Letter; Univ Of Michigan; Educ.

PLATH, FRED; Tri County HS; Coral, MI; 3/88 VP Sr Cls; Boy Scts; Cmnty Wkr; Hon Rl; Jr NHS; NHS; Sch Pl; Mth Clb; Bsbl; Bsktbl; Mi Comp Schlrshp 1200.

PLATT, JAY; Snider HS; Ft Wayne, IN; 35/578 Cls Rep Frsh Cls; Band; Hon Rl; Orch; Crs Cntry; Letter Wrstlng; Coach Actv; Rotary Awd; Indiana Univ; Bio.

PLATT, PAMELA; Copley Sr HS; Copley, OH; Chrs; Chrh Wkr; Cmnty Wkr; Drl Tm; Hon Rl; Hosp Ade; Off Ade; Yth Flsp; Rptr Sch Nwsp; Pep Clb; Honor Roll Awd; Cert Of Commendation In Math; Univ Of Cincinnati; Nursing.

PLATTE, KATHY; Pewamo Westphalia HS; Fowler, MI; Band; Hon Rl; Hosp Ade; 4-H; PPFtbl; Scr Kpr; 4-H Awd; Mic State Univ; Med.

PLATZ, DAVID; Henry Ford Ii HS; Sterling Hts, MI; Chrh Wkr; Cmnty Wkr; Debate Tm; Pol Wkr; Sch Pl; Stg Crw; IM Sprt; Olivet College; Political Sci.

PLATZ, KATHERINE; Oscoda HS; Oscoda, MI; 16/200 Hon Rl; PPFtbl; Michigan St Univ; Acctg.

PLAUGHER, RADONNA; Liberty HS; Salem, WV; 19/228 Cls Rep Sr Cls; Band; Sec Chrh Wkr; Girl Scts; Hon Rl; NHS; Orch; Sch Mus; Stu Cncl; DECA; Salem Coll; Bio.

PLAUT, TOM; Madeira HS; Cincinnati, OH; 6/170 Hon Rl; NHS; Letter Bsbl; Letter Glf; Rotary Awd; College.

PLAVAC, THERESE; Eastlake North HS; Eastlake, OH; 83/706 Cl Rep Jr Cls; Hon Rl; NHS; Stu Cncl;

Ed Sch Nwsp; Rptr Sch Nwsp; Letter Trk; Coach Actv; Twrlr; College; Social Services.

PLAVSITY, ANN; Barberton HS; Barberton, OH; 22/480 Band; Hon Rl; Off Ade; Rptr Sch Nwsp; Mth Clb; Akron Univ; Acctg.

PLAWSKY, CAROL; Thomas A Devilbiss HS; Toledo, OH; Chrs; Debate Tm; Girl Scts; Hon Rl; Hosp Ade; Quill & Scroll; Sch Mus; Yrbk; Fr Clb; College; Special Ed.

PLEAK, PENNY; Avon HS; Indpls, IN; 58/158 Chrh Wkr; Girl Scts; Yth Flsp; Sprt Ed Sch Nwsp; Rptr Sch Nwsp; Sch Nwsp; Pep Clb; Bus Schl; Acctg.

PLEAK, VICKI; Avon HS; Indianapolis, IN; Chrh Wkr; Girl Scts; Lbry Ade; Off Ade; Sch Pl; Stg Crw; Yth Flsp; Drama Clb; Pep Clb; Univ; Acctg.

PLEAR, MONICA; Aiken Sr HS; Cincinnati, OH; Cls Rep Frsh Cls; Cl Rep Jr Cls; Chrh Wkr; Drl Tm; Hosp Ade; Sch Pl; Yrbk; Drama Clb; Fr Clb; Cert Of Ach Voluntary Participation In Serv To Community; Norma Sharkey Agency; Stewardess.

PLEAU, SCOTT; Menominee Area HS; Menominee, MI; Hon Rl; Sch Pl; Stg Crw; Boys Clb Am; IM Sprt; Univ Of Wisconsin; Auto Mech.

PLEDGER, ROBIN; Gavit HS; Hammond, IN; Band; Girl Scts; Hon Rl; Jr NHS; Off Ade; Quill & Scroll; Rptr Sch Nwsp; Pep Clb; Univ; Phys Ther.

PLEMONS, PHYLLIS; Lebanon HS; Lebanon, OH; Band; Hon Rl; NHS; Sch Mus; Fr Clb; Univ; Bus.

PLENUS, KATHY; Lake Central HS; Crown Point, IN; Chrs; NHS; Quill & Scroll; Sch Nwsp; Purdue Univ; Comp Sci.

PLESSAS, DENISE; Hammond HS; Hammond, IN; Chrs; Hon Rl; Jr NHS; Sch Pl; Drama Clb; Purdue Univ; Mgmt.

PLETCHER, JOAN; River Valley HS; Caledonia, OH; 15/215 Chrh Wkr; Hon Rl; NHS; Yth Flsp; Spn Clb; Letter Bsktbl; PPFtbl; College; Acctg.

PLETCHER, KURT; Bluefield HS; Bluefield, WV; 1/360 Am Leg Boys St; Hon Rl; JA; NHS; Lat Clb; Sci Clb; Letter Glf; Natl Merit Ltr; College; Med Sci.

PLETCHER, LISA; Lake Catholic HS; Mentor, OH; Hon Rl; Varsty Letter In Sftbl 79; Varsty Letter In Vllybl 77 & 78; John Carrol Univ; Bus.

PLETCHER, PAMELA; Niles HS; Niles, MI; Chrh Wkr; Cmnty Wkr; Hon Rl; Off Ade; Fr Clb; S W Michigan Coll; Comp Progr.

PLETCHER, STEPHEN; Argos Community HS; Argos, IN; 15/61 Aud/Vis; Band; Chrs; Chrh Wkr; Sch Mus; Sct Actv; Yth Flsp; Yrbk; 4-H; 4-H Awd; College; Music.

PLETCHER, VALISA; Chelsea HS; Chelsea, MI; Trs Soph Cls; Trs Jr Cls; Girl Scts; Hon Rl; NHS; Yth Flsp; Rptr Yrbk; Letter Chrldng; PPFtbl; Am Leg Awd; College; Educ.

PLETS, DANIEL; Robert S Tower Sr HS; Warren, MI; 17/340 Hst Sr Cls; Band; Chrs; Drm Mjrt; NHS; Sch Mus; Sch Pl; Yth Flsp; Drama Clb; Mgrs; Oakland Univ; Music.

PLEVICH, DAVE; St Francis HS; Morgantown, WV; JA; Sch Nwsp; Sci Clb; Bsktbl; Glf; Ten; IM Sprt; Mgrs; Allegary Comm College; Bus.

PLEW, JO ELLEN; Whitko HS; Pierceton, IN; 9/136 Chrs; Hon Rl; Sec NHS; Pres 4-H; Fr Clb; Sec Ger Clb; 4-H Awd; Indiana Voc Tech Schl; Acctg.

PLEWA, DAVID; Notre Dame HS; Warren, MI; NHS; Pol Wkr; Rptr Sch Nwsp; Capt Swmmng; Univ Of Michigan; Busns.

PLICHTA, DEAN; Fruitport HS; Muskegon, MI; Hon Rl; Bsbl; BEOG; St Of Mich; Fruitport Educ Assn; Muskegon Comm Coll; Busns.

PLOCHER, TODD; Shelby Senior HS; Shelby, OH; Hon Rl; Stu Cncl; FFA; Lat Clb; Letter Bsktbl; Letter Ftbl; Am Leg Awd; Ohio St Univ; Vet Medicine.

PLOETNER, JOHN; Jasper HS; Jasper, IN; 23/400 Hon Rl; Glf; IM Sprt; PTO Schlstc Awds 77 78 & 79; Whos Who In Mid W HS Foreign Lang 79; Univ; Med.

PLOOF, MICHELLE ANN; Morrice HS; Morrice, MI; Girl Scts; Hon Rl; Lbry Ade; Off Ade; 4-H; Elk Awd; 4-H Awd; Pres Awd; College; Art.

PLOOG, FLAVIA M; Oberlin Senior HS; Oberlin, OH; Orch; Yth Flsp; Yrbk; Pep Clb; Bsktbl; Scr Kpr; College; English History.

PLOTKOWSKI, PATRICIA; Bishop Gallagher HS; Mt Clemens, MI; 20/335 Cls Rep Soph Cls; Cl Rep Jr Cls; Chrh Wkr; Hon Rl; NHS; Off Ade; Ed Yrbk; Rptr Yrbk; Spn Clb; Marygrove Univ; Bus Admin.

PLOUGHMAN, LYNN; Portage Central HS; Kalamazoo, MI; 1/379 VP AFS; Chrs; Chrh Wkr; Hon Rl; Sch Mus; Yth Flsp; Rptr Yrbk; Ger Clb; Sci Clb; Hope Coll; Pre Med.

PLOUHAR, DAWN; Muskegon HS; Muskegon, MI; Sec Sr Cls; Chrs; Hon Rl; Jr NHS; Mdrgl; NHS; PAVAS; Sch Mus; Sch Pl; Grand Valley State College; Fsh Dsn.

PLOUHAR, JUDIE; Muskegon HS; Muskegon, MI; Cls Rep Frsh Cls; Band; Hon Rl; NHS; Pol Wkr; W Michigan Univ; Systems Analysis.

PLOUSSARD, JEFFEREY; Okemos HS; Okemos, MI; Sch Pl; Bsbl; Capt Bsktbl; Capt Glf; Capt Ten; IM Sprt; Rotary Awd; Michigan St Univ; Cmnctns.

PLOWRIGHT, JOHN; Chagrin Falls HS; Chagrin Falls, OH; Chrs; Cmnty Wkr; Hon Rl; Sch Mus; Yth Flsp; Natl Merit Ltr; College; Medical.

PLUE, RONALD; Elwood Community HS; Elwood, IN; 4/275 Cls Rep Frsh Cls; Cls Rep Soph Cls; Cl Rep Jr Cls; Hon Rl; Stu Cncl; Spn Clb; Ftbl; Wrstlng; Mas Awd; Ind Univ; Comp Sci.

PLUIMER, KAREN; Benton Central Jr Sr HS; Oxford, IN; 49/232 Chrs; Chrh Wkr; NHS; Sch Mus; Sch Pl; Rptr Sch Nwsp; Sec Drama Clb; Sec 4-H; PPFtbl; 4-H Awd; Ball St Univ; Psych.

PLUMER, MARSHALL; Ogemaw Heights HS; West Branch, MI; 3/207 Band; Chrh Wkr; Cmnty Wkr; Sch Mus; Drama Clb; VP Key Clb; Letter Crs Cntry; Letter Swmmng; Letter Trk; Michigan Tech Univ; Metallurgy.

PLUMLEY, CARL; Tucker Cnty HS; Parsons, WV; 24/125 Am Leg Boys St; NHS; VICA; Letter Ftbl; Letter Trk; Capt Wrstlng; Kiwan Awd; Fairmont St Coll; Indus Engr.

PLUMLEY, S; Heritage HS; Monroeville, IN; 37/175 Aud/Vis; Band; Boy Scts; Sch Pl; Crs Cntry; Ftbl; Glf; Ivy Tech Schl.

PLUMMER, DARRELL; Medina HS; Medina, OH; Band; Boy Scts; Chrs; Hon Rl; NHS; Orch; Sch Mus; Yth Flsp; Key Clb; IM Sprt; College; Nuclear Engr.

PLUMMER, DIANA; New Albany HS; New Albany, IN; Band; Chrh Wkr; Debate Tm; Hon Rl; NHS; Stu Cncl; Yth Flsp; Ger Clb; Rdo Clb; Swmmng; Univ; Comp Sci.

PLUMMER, DIANE; New Palestine HS; New Palestine, IN; NHS; Rptr Yrbk; Yrbk; 4-H; Spn Clb; Bsktbl; 4-H Awd; Purdue Univ; Chem.

PLUMMER, ELIZABETH; Aquinas HS; Allen Park, MI; JA; NHS; Univ; Med Tech.

PLUMMER, ELIZABETH; Aquinas HS; Allen Pk, MI; Univ; Lang.

PLUMMER, KEVIN D; North Knox HS; Edwardsport, IN; Aud/Vis; FCA; Hon Rl; VP Fr Clb; Bsbl; Bsktbl; Math.

PLUMMER, LEA; Tri Jr Sr HS; Straughn, IN; 4/89 Band; Chrh Wkr; Drl Tm; Hon Rl; JA; Lbry Ade; Natl Forn Lg; NHS; Orch; Sch Mus; Indiana Univ; Jrnlsm.

PLUMMER, PATRICIA; Fort Gay HS; Ft Gay, WV; 2/80 Pres Jr Cls; Chrs; Chrh Wkr; Hon Rl; NHS; Yth Flsp; FHA; Pep Clb; Spn Clb; Marshall Univ.

PLUMMER, PATTI; Martinsville HS; Martinsville, IN; 53/448 Band; Hon Rl; Orch; Sch Mus; Spn Clb; Ten; Recvd 2nd Alternt In In Univ Foreign Lang Prog Won 7 Wks In Mexico 79; Mbr Of Jazz Symphonic & Marchng Band; Indiana Univ.

PLUMMER, ROBERT; Brownstown Central HS; Vallon A, IN; 30/145 Cls Rep Frsh Cls; Cmnty Wkr; Hon Rl; Pres Y-Teens; Spn Clb; Bsktbl; Letter Crs Cntry; Letter Trk; Coach Actv; Scr Kpr; Univ; Psych.

PLUMMER, ROBIN; Shenandoah HS; Middletown, IN; 4/118 Hon Rl; Lbry Ade; Sch Nwsp; Mth Clb; Sci Clb; 3rd Pl Ribbon In Sci Fair 79; Ball St Univ.

PLUMMER, ROBIN; Athens HS; Athens, WV; 10/65 Hon Rl; NHS; Treas Stu Cncl; Yrbk; Pres Fr Clb; Pres Sci Clb; Bsktbl; Concord College; Bio.

PLUMMER, SANDRA J; Clinton Massie HS; Wilmington, OH; 15/96 Chrs; Chrh Wkr; Capt Drl Tm; NHS; Yth Flsp; 4-H; Bsbl; Chrldng; Twrlr; 4-H Awd; Hon Mntn Miss Teenage Amer 1979; Mbr Ohio St 4 H Livestock Judging Tm 1978; All Amer Natl H S Drill Tm 1979; Ohio St Univ; Animal Sci.

PLUMMER, SANDY; Chesapeake HS; Chesapeake, OH; 12/180 Cls Rep Frsh Cls; VP Soph Cls; VP Jr Cls; Am Leg Aux Girls St; Hon Rl; Off Ade; Stu Cncl; Beta Clb; Letter Trk; Mat Maids; Univ; Dent Tech.

PLUNKETT, MARY; Eaton HS; Eaton, OH; 2/160 Sec Sr Cls; Am Leg Aux Girls St; VP Band; Chrs; Chrh Wkr; Hon Rl; Hosp Ade; Jr NHS; NHS; Sch Mus; Manchester Coll; Scndry Educ.

PLUNKETT, PAMELA; Floyd Central HS; Floyd Knobs, IN; 33/359 Band; Hon Rl; Pres JA; Ger Clb; Pep Clb; Mat Maids; Tmr; JA Awd; Coll; Med.

PLUTA, RICHARD; West Ottowa HS; Holland, MI; Boy Scts; Chrh Wkr; Debate Tm; Natl Forn Lg; Pol Wkr; Sch Pl; Stg Crw; Coll; Peace Corp.

PLYLER, GERALD; Gwinn HS; Sawyer Afb, MI; 80/197 Band; Hon Rl; Orch; Sch Mus; Sct Actv; Glf; Capt Swmmng; California St Univ; Psych.

PLYLER, JONATHAN; Faith Christian HS; Muskegon, MI; Chrh Wkr; Debate Tm; Hon Rl; Yth Flsp; Devry Inst Of Tech; Elec Tech.

PLYMALE, AMY; Grove City HS; Grove City, OH; Rptr Sch Nwsp; Letter Ten; Wrstlng; PPFtbl; Ohio State Univ.

PLYMALE, TINA; East Clinton HS; Sabina, OH; 33/119 Cls Rep Sr Cls; Band; Drl Tm; Hon Rl; Sch Pl; 4-H; FFA; FHA; FTA; Mth Clb; Ohio St Univ; Ag.

POAT, JAMES; Anderson HS; Anderson, IN; 63/415 Am Leg Boys St; Boy Scts; Hon Rl; Quill & Scroll; Ed Sch Nwsp; Sprt Ed Sch Nwsp; Lat Clb; Bsbl; Bsktbl; Purdue Univ; Pre Med.

POCHEDLY, LYDIA; The Andrews HS; Willowick, OH; Hon Rl; NHS; Sch Mus; Sch Pl; Stg Crw; Drama Clb; Natl Merit Ltr; Ohio Univ.

POCHINI, STEVEN; Southgate Aquinas HS; Lincoln Pk, MI; Boy Scts; Hon Rl; IM Sprt; Natl Merit SF; College; Bus Admin.

POCHOP, RICK; Merrillville HS; Merrillville, IN; Aud/Vis; Boy Scts; Chrs; Hon Rl; NHS; Coll.

POCISK, SHERI; Maumee HS; Maumee, OH; 31/335 Debate Tm; Hon Rl; Hosp Ade; Jr NHS; Natl Forn Lg; NHS; Y-Teens; Fr Clb; Bsktbl; Letter Crs Cntry; Outstndng Soph Hugh O Brian Yth Ldrshp; Spec Recognition Army Awd Intl Sci; St Qualifications Mile Relay; Ohio St Univ; Med.

POCKEL, CAROL; Buena Vista HS; Saginaw, MI; Girl Scts; Hon Rl; Rptr Sch Nwsp; Sch Nwsp; Ger Clb; Ten; Trk; Michigan State; Archt.

POCOCK, CHERYL; Chillicothe HS; Chillicothe, OH; 2/350 Band; Chrs; Chrh Wkr; Debate Tm; Hon Rl; Natl Forn Lg; NHS; Orch; Stu Cncl; Yth Flsp; Wheaton Univ; Spanish.

POCTA, ANNMARIE; Lumen Cordium HS; Bedford, OH; Hon Rl; Sch Pl; Drama Clb; Spn Clb; Chrldng; College; Mathematics.

POCZEKAY, ANNE; Marquette HS; Michigan City, IN; 14/66 Cl Rep Jr Cls; Hon Rl; NHS; Stu Cncl; Yrbk; Key Clb; Letter Ten; Purdue Univ; Elem Educa.

PODCZERVINSKI, DENISE; St Alphonsos HS; Detroit, MI; Chrs; Hon Rl; Sch Mus; College; Med.

PODLASIAK, STEVE; Woodsfield HS; Woodsfield, OH; 6/66 Cls Rep Soph Cls; Am Leg Boys St; Band; Chrs; Stg Crw; Stu Cncl; Fr Clb; Letter Bsbl; Letter Ftbl; West Liberty State College; History.

PODOBA, DAWN M; Beaverton HS; Beaverton, MI; Cls Rep Sr Cls; Girl Scts; Hon Rl; NHS; Rptr Sch Nwsp; 4-H; Pep Clb; Spn Clb; Letter Chrldng; Twrlr; Mid Michigan Cmnty Coll; Bus Sec.

PODSEDLY, JUDY; Geneva HS; Geneva, OH; 34/250 Cls Rep Frsh Cls; Cls Rep Soph Cls; Sec Jr Cls; Sec Sr Cls; AFS; Chrh Wkr; Off Ade; Sch Pl; Stu Cncl; Yth Flsp; Univ; Nursing.

PODSEDLY, MARK; Maple Hts HS; Maple Hgts, OH; Rptr Yrbk; Letter Ten; Univ; Engr.

PODULKA, KIMBERLY; Montrose Hill Mccloy HS; Montrose, MI; Pres Jr Cls; Hon Rl; NHS; Off Ade; Stu Cncl; Yrbk; Bsktbl; Trk; College; Psych.

PODWYS, LAURIE; Brandon HS; Ortonville, MI; Hosp Ade; Natl Forn Lg; Stu Cncl; Letter Trk; PPFtbl; Pres Awd; Univ; Med.

POE, BRENDA; Hamady HS; Flushing, MI; Trs Jr Cls; Pres Sr Cls; Hon Rl; Natl Forn Lg; Mgrs; Univ Of Michigan; Public Relations.

POE, DARYL; Hilliard HS; Columbus, OH; 3/400 Band; Boy Scts; Hon Rl; Jr NHS; NHS; Stg Crw; IM Sprt; Natl Merit SF; Univ; Engr.

POE, LISA; Concordia Lutheran HS; Ft Wayne, IN; Girl Scts; Sct Actv; Ger Clb; Pep Clb; Gym; IM Sprt; PPFtbl; College; Dent Asst.

POE, MICHAEL G; Mid America Christain HS; Huntington, WV; Am Leg Boys St; Chrs; Chrh Wkr; FCA; Letter Bsktbl; Letter Glf; College; Forestry.

POEHNER, DAVID; Shelbyville HS; Shelbyville, IN; 21/320 Hon Rl; NHS; Boys Clb Am; Spn Clb; Univ; Engr.

POEL, LORI; Grand Haven HS; Spring Lake, MI; 1/487 Cls Rep Frsh Cls; Cls Rep Soph Cls; Trs Jr Cls; Trs Sr Cls; Val; Am Leg Aux Girls St; Band; Chrh Wkr; Hon Rl; Jr NHS; Oakland Univ; Pre Med.

POELLET, CAROL; Frankenmuth HS; Bridgeport, MI; Chrs; Chrh Wkr; Hon Rl; PAVAS; Sch Mus; Sch Pl; Stg Crw; FBLA; Pres Awd; Delta Coll; Legal Sec.

POEPPELMAN, LISA; Versailles HS; Versailles, OH; 30/134 Band; Chrs; FCA; NHS; Sch Mus; Sch Pl; VP Stu Cncl; Yrbk; Drama Clb; Swmmng; Univ Of Cincinnati.

POERIO, D; Grand Ledge HS; Lansing, MI; Ftbl; Wrstlng; College; Freestyle Art.

POET, CATHY; Clare HS; Clare, MI; FCA; Hon Rl; Spn Clb; Trk; Chrldng; 4-H Awd; Michigan St Univ; Legal Sec.

POET, DARLENE; West Ottawa HS; Holland, MI; 13/317 Hon Rl; Mdrgl; NHS; Sch Mus; Sch Pl; Yth Flsp; Drama Clb; Mic State Univ; Educ.

POETTER, NANCY; Wadsworth Sr HS; Wadsworth, OH; 39/349 Chrs; Chrh Wkr; FCA; Girl Scts; JA; NHS; Sch Mus; Yth Flsp; Fr Clb; Pep Clb; Ohio St Univ; Dent.

POGANY, PERRY J; Austintown Fitch HS; Austintown, OH; 203/660 Cmnty Wkr; Hon Rl; Pol Wkr; Red Cr Ade; Stu Cncl; VP Key Clb; Letter Bsktbl; Coach Actv; IM Sprt; Co Captn 2nd Tm All Stl Vly Mbr Of Mahoning Vly All Star Tm 79; Youngstown St Univ; Acctg.

POGGEMEYER, LAURIE; Eastwood HS; Luckey, OH; 17/187 Pres Jr Cls; Band; Chrh Wkr; Cmnty Wkr; Girl Scts; Hon Rl; Lbry Ade; Off Ade; Pol Wkr; Sch Pl; Bowling Green St Univ; Acctg.

POGORELC, SUSAN; Admiral King HS; Lorain, OH; Band; Chrs; Chrh Wkr; Hon Rl; Orch; Sch Mus; College; Comp Sci.

POGUE, JEFF; Mississinewa HS; Marion, IN; 24/202 Boy Scts; Hon Rl; Jr NHS; NHS; Yth Flsp; Spn Clb; Am Leg Awd; Bausch & Lomb Awd; Purdue Univ.

POHL, BARBARA; Portland HS; Portland, MI; Hon Rl; Fr Clb; FHA; Lansing Comm College; Spch Ther.

POHL, GREGORY; Coldwater HS; Coldwater, OH; 9/150 Cls Rep Sr Cls; Am Leg Boys St; Boy Scts; Hon Rl; NHS; Ftbl; Trk; Wrstlng; Univ Of Cin; Pre Dentistry.

POHL, JEAN; Marion Local HS; Maria Stein, OH; 1/88 Cl Rep Jr Cls; Am Leg Aux Girls St; Chrh Wkr; Hon Rl; NHS; Off Ade; Stu Cncl; Rptr Yrbk; FTA; Pep Clb; Miami Univ.

POHL, JEFFREY T; Marion Local HS; Osgood, OH; 10/93 Cls Rep Soph Cls; Am Leg Boys St; Hon Rl; NHS; Stu Cncl; Rptr Sch Nwsp; Sci Clb; Crs Cntry; Trk; Am Leg Awd; College; Architecture.

POHL, KRIS; Adrian HS; Adrian, MI; 36/368 Chrs; NHS; Sch Mus; Sch Pl; Drama Clb; Crs Cntry; Trk; Chrldng; Rotary Awd; Kalamazoo Coll; Bus.

POHL, MARK; Marion Local HS; Mariastein, OH; 5/93 Cls Rep Frsh Cls; Am Leg Boys St; Boy Scts; Hon Rl; NHS; Pres Stu Cncl; Rptr Sch Nwsp; VP FFA; Sci Clb; Letter Trk; Purdue Univ; Dairy Farmer.

POHL, MARY; Centerville HS; Centerville, OH; Hst Jr Cls; Hst Sr Cls; Cmnty Wkr; NHS; Yrbk; Arizona St Univ; Jrnlsm.

POHL, MICHAEL; Dublin HS; Dublin, OH; 42/156 Hon Rl; Yth Flsp; Lat Clb; Socr; Trk; Univ; Med.

POHLMAN, KIMBERLY; Northwest HS; Canal Fulton, OH; Band; Hon Rl; Hosp Ade; Jr NHS; NHS; Sch Pl; Rptr Yrbk; Bowling Green Univ.

POHLMAN, MICHELLE; Delphos St Johns HS; Delphos, OH; Aud/Vis; Hon Rl; Sch Pl; 4-H; FTA; Spn Clb; Chrldng; IM Sprt; 4-H Awd; Lima Tech Coll; Legal Sec.

POI, SUSAN; Griffith HS; Griffith, IN; 1/360 Cls Rep Soph Cls; Val; Pres Boy Scts; Chrs; Chrh Wkr; Cmnty Wkr; Pres Girl Scts; Hon Rl; JA; Jr NHS; Mem Hosp Schl; Pediatric Nursing.

POINDEXTER, TIMOTHY; East HS; Columbus, OH; Cl Rep Jr Cls; Lbry Ade; PAVAS; College; Architect.

POINDEXTER, TRACY; London HS; London, OH; Cls Rep Frsh Cls; Cls Rep Soph Cls; Cl Rep Jr Cls; Hon Rl; Sch Pl; Stu Cncl; Rptr Sch Nwsp; College; Communications.

POIRY, SCOTT; Clay HS; Oregon, OH; Boy Scts; Hon Rl; Sprt Ed Yrbk; Wrstlng; Pres Awd; Toledo Univ; Med.

POIT, T KEVIN; Lapeer West Sr HS; Lapeer, MI; Cmnty Wkr; Lbry Ade; NHS; Pep Clb; Spn Clb; Univ Of Michigan; Foreign Lang.

POITRA, CARYL; Yale HS; Melvin, MI; Hon Rl; 4-H; Crs Cntry; Trk; 4-H Awd; Pt Huron Jr Coll.

POKAS, JUDY; Martins Ferry HS; Martins Ferry, OH; Chrs; Chrh Wkr; Girl Scts; Hon Rl; Hosp Ade; Red Cr Ade; Y-Teens; Rptr Yrbk; Sci Clb; Letter Ten; College; Accounting.

POKELSEK, SUSAN; Harbor HS; Ashtabula, OH; 17/172 AFS; Am Leg Aux Girls St; NHS; Fr Clb; Letter Bsbl; Capt Bsktbl; Pres GAA; Am Leg Awd; Bowling Green St Univ; Bus.

POKORSKI, CAROLYN; Trinity HS; Brecksville, OH; 9/150 Sec Sr Cls; Chrs; Drl Tm; Hon Rl; Jr NHS; NHS; Pep Clb; Pom Pon; PPFtbl; Univ; Fshn Mdse.

POKORSKI, NADINE; St Annes HS; Sterling Hts, MI; 19/62 Cls Rep Frsh Cls; Chrh Wkr; Sec JA; Rptr Yrbk; Rptr Sch Nwsp; Bsbl; Bsktbl; Swmmng; Letter Trk; Hnr Certs; Univ; Dentistry.

POLACZYK, PAMELA; Riverview Comm HS; Riverview, MI; Chrs; Sch Mus; Sch Pl; Drama Clb; Fr Clb; Chrldng; Michigan St Univ; Psych.

POLAK, TIM; Flat Rock HS; Flat Rock, MI; Hon Rl; Jr NHS; NHS; Univ.

POLAK, TIMOTHY; Flat Rock HS; Flat Rock, MI; Hon Rl; Jr NHS; NHS; Univ.

POLAKOWSKI, JOHN; Leland Public HS; Maple City, MI; 6/36 VP Frsh Cls; Am Leg Boys St; Hon Rl; Pres NHS; Pres Stu Cncl; Letter Bsbl; Letter Bsktbl; Letter Socr; Michigan St Univ.

POLAND, RODNEY; Ctrl Preston Sr HS; Tunnelton, WV; 20/200 Cls Rep Frsh Cls; Pres Soph Cls; Band; Boy Scts; Hon Rl; NHS; Mth Clb; Bsbl; Bsktbl; Ftbl; West Virginia Univ; Chem Engr.

POLAND, SUSAN; Ben Davis HS; Indianapolis, IN; 3/865 Cl Rep Jr Cls; Sec Sr Cls; FCA; Girl Scts; Hon Rl; NHS; Stu Cncl; Spn Clb; Swmmng; Mgrs; Univ; Dent Hygnst.

POLATAS, STEVE; Green HS; Akron, OH; 5/255 Aud/Vis; Boy Scts; Chrh Wkr; Hon Rl; Jr NHS; NHS; Sct Actv; Ed Yrbk; Akron Univ; Engr.

POLEGA, DEBORAH; North Huron HS; Kinde, MI; 7/50 Sec Jr Cls; Chrh Wkr; Hon Rl; Yrbk; Acad Excllnc For 3 Marking Per 78; Voc Tech Educ For Clerk Typist 78; Cert Of Proficiency Typing 2 78; Bus Schl; Sec.

POLEN, DAVID; Wickliffe HS; Wickliffe, OH; 26/325 AFS; Am Leg Boys St; Chrs; Hon Rl; Mdrgl; Pres NHS; Sch Mus; Stu Cncl; Letter Bsbl; Ari State Univ; Optometry.

POLEN, STEPHEN; Southern Local HS; Salineville, OH; VP Jr Cls; Am Leg Boys St; Band; Hon Rl; NHS; Sch Pl; Lat Clb; Letter Bsktbl; Ftbl; Letter Trk; College.

POLETE, KIMBERLY; Goodrich HS; Goodrich, MI; 12/140 Hosp Ade; Pep Clb; Trk; Letter Chrldng; Tmr; Univ Of Michigan; Pre Med.

POLEWACH, SUSAN; Sandusky HS; Sandusky, MI; Band; Hon Rl; NHS; Yrbk; Letter Bsktbl; College; Med Tech.

POLHE, JOSEPH W; Bedford HS; Temperance, MI; 162/439 Boy Scts; Chrh Wkr; Hon Rl; Sct Actv; Drama Clb; Mgrs; Univ Of Toledo; Bio.

POLICH, NANCY; John Glenn HS; Westland, MI; Chrs; Hon Rl; Jr NHS; Sch Mus; Sch Pl; Stg Crw; Drama Clb; Fr Clb; Trk; IM Sprt;.

POLIFRONE, MICHAEL; James A Garfield HS; Garrettsville, OH; Trs Frsh Cls; Cl Rep Jr Cls; Aud/Vis; Boy Scts; Cmnty Wkr; Debate Tm; Hon Rl; JA; Lbry Ade; Pol Wkr; Bowling Green St Univ; Med.

POLING, BEV; Jennings Cnty HS; Butlerville, IN; 58/358 Band; Chrh Wkr; Drm Mjrt; NHS; 4-H; Key Clb; Pep Clb; Dnfth Awd; 4-H Awd; Ball St Univ; Acctg.

POLING, DANIEL; Philip Barbour HS; Philippi, WV; 23/205 Hon Rl; NHS; Pol Wkr; West Virginia Univ; Poli Sci.

POLING, DARL W; Woodrow Wilson HS; Beckley, WV; Pres Sr Cls; Am Leg Boys St; Chrh Wkr; Cmnty Wkr; Hon Rl; JA; NHS; Stu Cncl; Key Clb; Bsbl; Univ.

POLING, DEBORAH; Pittsford HS; Pittsford, MI; Am Leg Aux Girls St; Chrs; Chrh Wkr; Hon Rl; Lit Mag; NHS; Sch Pl; 4-H; Spn Clb; 4-H Awd; Schl Awrd For High Score On Mi Math Test 79; Speech & Drama Awrd 79; Eng Awrd 79; Univ; Speech.

POLING, DEBORAH; West Preston HS; Newburg, WV; 3/115 Hst Soph Cls; Cls Rep Sr Cls; Am Leg Aux Girls St; Band; Chrs; Chrh Wkr; Hon Rl; Lit Mag; NHS; Sch Pl; Fairmont St Univ; Music.

POLING, DIANA; Houston HS; Piqua, OH; Sec Jr Cls; Band; Cmp Fr Grls; Hon Rl; NHS; Yrbk; Rptr Sch Nwsp; Pres 4-H; FHA; Sci Clb; K Of C Otstndng Religous Awrd 77; Univ.

POLING, DONALD; Shady Spring HS; Beaver, WV; FCA; Hon Rl; NHS; Pep Clb; Letter Bsbl; Letter Bsktbl; Capt Crs Cntry; Capt Glf; College; Engr.

POLING, GARY; Woodrow Wilson HS; Beckley, WV; 3/500 Cls Rep Soph Cls; Chrh Wkr; Cmnty Wkr; Hon Rl; Jr NHS; NHS; Yth Flsp; Y-Teens; Soroptimist; Letter Ftbl; Univ; Pre Dent.

POLING, KAMELA; Logan Elm HS; Circleville, OH; 1/185 Val; FCA; Hon Rl; VP NHS; Sch Pl; Sch Nwsp; 4-H; Letter Trk; Capt Chrldng; Ohio State Univ; Art.

POLING, KAREN; Perry HS; Perry, OH; Girl Scts; Hon Rl; Off Ade; Sct Actv; 4-H; Spn Clb; 4-H Awd; Univ; Art.

POLING, POLLY; Urbana HS; Urbana, OH; Sec Band; Girl Scts; Hon Rl; Lit Mag; Treas NHS; Pres 4-H; Spn Clb; 4-H Awd; Grand Officer Of The St Of Oh Order Of Rainbow For Girls 78; Bowling Green St Univ; Educ.

POLING, REBECCA A; Berrien Springs HS; Berrien Spring, MI; 8/115 Sec Frsh Cls; Band; VP Chrs; Chrh Wkr; Girl Scts; Hon Rl; Lbry Ade; Lake Mich College.

POLING, S; Delphos Jefferson HS; Delphos, OH; 5/115 Band; Chrs; Hon Rl; Hosp Ade; NHS; Sch Mus; Stu Cncl; Sci Clb; Spn Clb; Chrldng; Ohio State Univ; Occupatnl Ther.

POLING, SHERRY; Ridgemont HS; Mt Victory, OH; 8/78 Band; Chrs; Chrh Wkr; Drl Tm; Drm Mjrt; Girl Scts; Hon Rl; NHS; Sch Mus; Stu Cncl; Miss Ohio Teen Queen; Simon Kenton Chptr & 16th Dist Demolay Sweetheart; 1st Pl Acctg Schlrshp Awd; College; Acctg.

POLING, SUSAN; Buckhannon Upshur HS; Buckhannon, WV; Chrs; Girl Scts; Hon Rl; NHS; Sch Mus; Sch Pl; Sct Actv; Stg Crw; Yth Flsp; Rptr Yrbk; Math Medal; Univ; Brdcstng.

POLINORI, TONI; Heath HS; Heath, OH; Chrs; Hon Rl; NHS; Sch Mus; FHA; Key Clb; Trk; Scr Kpr; Barbizon Modeling Schl.

POLIS, LORAINE; Cabrini HS; Allen Pk, MI; VP Frsh Cls; VP Soph Cls; Cl Rep Jr Cls; Cls Rep Sr Cls; Chrh Wkr; Hon Rl; NHS; Stu Cncl; Rptr Yrbk; Letter Bsbl; Univ Of Michigan; Indstrl Engr.

POLISKI, LEE; Roseville HS; Roseville, MI; 5/420 Cls Rep Frsh Cls; Chrh Wkr; Hon Rl; NHS; Letter Swmmng; Trk; Tmr; Detroit Coll Of Bus; CPA.

POLITE, LEE; Culver Military Academy; Munster, IN; 7/200 Band; Hon Rl; Jr NHS; ROTC; Ger Clb; Mth Clb; Sci Clb; IM Sprt; Cit Awd; Vrsty Fencing 4 Yrs Capt 77; Blue Key Soc Hon Soc 79; Cadet Lieutenant 80; Univ; Med.

POLITZER, JULIE; Mentor HS; Concord, OH; Cls Rep Frsh Cls; Hon Rl; Pres DECA; Scr Kpr; Rotary Awd; Lakeland Cmnty Coll; Bus.

POLK, DOUG; Shady Spring HS; Daniels, WV; Cls Rep Frsh Cls; Hon Rl; NHS; Stu Cncl; Sprt Ed Sch Nwsp; Pep Clb; Letter Bsktbl; Letter Ftbl; Letter Trk; IM Sprt; W Virginia Univ; Law.

POLK, JEROME; Gilmour Academy; Gates Mills, OH; 16/82 Lit Mag; NHS; Sch Mus; Sch Pl; Stg Crw; Drama Clb; IM Sprt; Natl Merit Ltr; Geogetown Univ; Foreign Studies.

POLK, LORIE; Buffalo HS; Prichard, WV; Band; Chrs; Girl Scts; Hon Rl; Mdrgl; Sch Mus; Sct Actv; Yth Flsp; OEA; Busns Schl; Acctg.

POLK, MALLORY; Charles F Brush HS; S Euclid, OH; Band; Drm Bgl; Girl Scts; Hosp Ade; Bsktbl; Trk; GAA; IM Sprt; Scr Kpr; Pres Awd; College; Nursing.

POLK, MELBA; Shortridge HS; Indianapolis, IN; 45/500 Hon Rl; Hosp Ade; Mth Clb; Spn Clb; College; Med Rsrchr.

POLKABLA, KELLY; Madison Hts HS; Anderson, IN; Cl Rep Jr Cls; Band; Hon Rl; Orch; 4-H; Gym;.

POLLAK, MARTIN R; John Adams HS; South Bend, IN; 8/400 Hon Rl; NHS; Orch; JETS Awd; Natl Merit Schl; Princeton Univ; Physics.

POLLARD, RACHEL; Vinton Cty Consolid HS; Mc Arthur, OH; 3/200 Sec Chrh Wkr; Hon Rl; NHS; Fr Clb; Spn Clb; Letter Bsktbl; Letter Trk; 4-H Awd; College; Electrical Engineer.

POLLAY, NANCY; Ashtabula Harbor HS; Ashtabula, OH; 14/200 Sec AFS; Fr Clb; FTA; Univ; Elem Educ.

POLLEY, AUDREY; Washington HS; Massillon, OH; Band; Hon Rl; Off Ade; Ger Clb; College; Eng Ed.

POLLEY, TAMMY; Windham HS; Windham, OH; 3/110 VP Soph Cls; Trs Sr Cls; Hon Rl; NHS; Stg Crw; Ed Yrbk; Rptr Yrbk; Yrbk; Spn Clb; Kent St Univ; Acctg.

POLLOCK, ARON; Aquinas HS; Southgate, MI; Hon Rl; Sch Pl; Drama Clb; Letter Ten; Scr Kpr; Wyane St Univ; Sci.

POLLOCK, GLEN R; Decatur Jr Sr HS; Decatur, MI; Band; Chrs; Hon Rl; Orch; Yth Flsp; Pep Clb; Gov Hon Prg Awd; Voc Schl; Elec Engr.

POLLOCK, JANE; North Dickinson HS; Iron Mtn, MI; Trs Soph Cls; Trs Jr Cls; Trs Sr Cls; Band; Chrh Wkr; Hon Rl; Hosp Ade; Lbry Ade; Off Ade; Chrldng; College; Secretary.

POLLOCK, MIKE; Jackson HS; Massillon, OH; Boy Scts; Chrh Wkr; Cmnty Wkr; FCA; Hon Rl; Sct Actv; Fr Clb; Key Clb; Letter Bsbl; Letter Ftbl; Voc Schl.

POLLOCK, SUSAN M; Highland HS; Hinckley, OH; Hon Rl; Lbry Ade; NHS; Gym; Scr Kpr; Schlsp From John Carroll Univ 79; John Carroll Univ; Pre Med.

POLLOCK, WALTER; Brooke HS; Wellsburg, WV; 74/466 Am Leg Boys St; Chrh Wkr; Cmnty Wkr; Hon Rl; Yth Flsp; Outstanding Building Construction Stu; Outstanding Vocational Ed Stu; West Virginia Univ; Civil Engr.

POLOMCAK, ANNETTE; Decatur Jr Sr HS; Decatur, MI; Sec Frsh Cls; Hon Rl; Lbry Ade; Bsktbl; Western Michigan Univ; Sec.

POLSON, CHRISTINA; Delta HS; Muncie, IN; Cl Rep Jr Cls; Band; Drl Tm; FCA; Hon Rl; JA; Stu Cncl; DECA; Pep Clb; Gym; Ball St Univ; Fshn Mdse.

POLSON, CRAIG; West HS; Cincinnati, OH; Band; Boy Scts; Chrh Wkr; Hon Rl; Spn Clb; Ftbl; Cert Of Achvmnt Awrd 76; Fire Prevention Week Schl Poster Awrd 73; Harvest Fest King Church Awrd 77; Univ Of Cincinnati; Drafting.

POLSTER, PAMELA; Cardinal Stritch HS; Toledo, OH; 9/160 Sec Band; Sec Boy Scts; Drm Mjrt; Hon Rl; NHS; Sch Mus; Sct Actv; Fr Clb; Twrlr; Ohio St Univ; Agri.

POLSTER, T; Genoa Area HS; Curtice, OH; 1/190 Cl Rep Jr Cls; Am Leg Aux Girls St; Hon Rl; NHS; Stu Cncl; Rptr Yrbk; Spn Clb; College.

POLTER, SHERYL; Fairview HS; Mark Center, OH; Cl Rep Jr Cls; Band; Chrh Wkr; Hon Rl; Yth Flsp; Sec 4-H; FHA; OEA; Pep Clb; GAA; Bowling Green Univ; Busns.

POLTORAK, DEBORAH; Charlotte HS; Charlotte, MI; Band; Girl Scts; Hon Rl; NHS; VP 4-H; 4-H Awd; Lansing Community Coll; Nurse.

POLTURANUS, NANCY; Theodore Roosevelt HS; Wyandotte, MI; Hon Rl; Univ.

POLUDNIAK, DANA; Shadyside HS; Shadyside, OH; 6/125 Band; Hon Rl; NHS; Sch Mus; Yth Flsp; Y-Teens; Spn Clb; Bsktbl; Coach Actv; GAA; Univ; Med.

POLUS, LINDA; Bishop Foley HS; Warren, MI; 13/231 Chrs; Cmnty Wkr; Girl Scts; Hon Rl; Mdrgl; NHS; Pep Clb; Crs Cntry; Trk; Natl Merit Ltr; Coll; CPA.

POLUS, PAUL N; Anderson HS; Anderson, IN; Pres Soph Cls; Cls Rep Soph Cls; Pres Jr Cls; Cl Rep Jr Cls; Cls Rep Sr Cls; Hon Rl; Jr NHS; NHS; Ind Iniv.

POLYAK, MIKE; Munster HS; Munster, IN; 52/403 Hon Rl; DECA; Deca Awds In Gnrl Merch 1979; Coll; Bus.

POLZIEN, ELLEN; Gladwin HS; Gladwin, MI; 7/146 Cls Rep Soph Cls; Debate Tm; Hon Rl; Lit Mag; NHS; Stu Cncl; Yrbk; Ed Sch Nwsp; Natl Merit Ltr; Michigan St Univ; Advtsng.

POMALES, MIRIAM; Horace Mann HS; Gary, IN ; 14/306 Chrh Wkr; Jr NHS; NHS; Cit Awd; College; Accnt.

POMBIER, PHILIP R; Everett HS; Lansing, MI; Hon Rl; Jr NHS; NHS; Letter Ftbl; Letter Wrstlng; IM Sprt; Am Leg Awd; Cit Awd; Michigan St Univ.

POMERANTZ, SHARON; Seton HS; Cincinnati, OH; Chrs; Drl Tm; Hon Rl; Sch Mus; FBLA; Letter Swmmng; Tch Handicapped Childrn To Swim 76; Probationary Mbr Of Natl Bus Hon Soc 78; Univ; Sec.

POMEROY, DEBRA E; Greenbrier West HS; Asbury, WV; Chrh Wkr; Hon Rl; NHS; Yth Flsp; FHA; FTA; Pep Clb; Chrldng; Cit Awd; Treas Of Hopewell Assn Baptist Youth; 2nd Runner Up Victory Qn; Pianist Quinwood 1st Baptist; College; Elem Ed.

POMEROY, JULIE; Maumee HS; Maumee, OH; 26/316 Band; Hon Rl; Orch; Y-Teens; Mat Maids; Univ; Acctg.

POMEROY, KIMBERLY A; Woodward HS; Toledo, OH; JA; Sch Pl; DECA; Drama Clb; Spn Clb; Socr; Univ; Psych.

POMEROY, LORI; North Muskegon HS; N Muskegon, MI; Girl Scts; Hon Rl; Hosp Ade; JA; Off Ade; Sct Actv; Yrbk; 4-H; PPFtbl; Tmr; Mst Imprvd Plyr For Girls Vllybl 78; Muskegon Cmnty Coll; Sec.

POMEROY, RANDALL; Hartford HS; Hartford, MI; 13/95 Pres Frsh Cls; Band; Drm Mjrt; Hon Rl; Mod UN; NHS; Sch Pl; Stg Crw; Stu Cncl; Rptr Sch Nwsp; Western Michigan Univ; History.

POMEROY, TIMOTHY; Ludington HS; Ludington, MI; Cls Rep Sr Cls; Boy Scts; Chrh Wkr; Cmnty Wkr; FCA; Hon Rl; Sch Mus; Sct Actv; Pep Clb; Bsbl; Ferris St Coll; Insurance.

POMIETLO, RAY; Perry HS; Perry, OH; Aud/Vis; Hon Rl; Sch Mus; Sch Pl; Stg Crw; Rptr Sch Nwsp; Key Clb; Letter Glf; Letter Wrstlng;.

POMINVILLE, LEANNE; Brighton HS; Brighton, MI; Sec Jr Cls; Sec Sr Cls; Hon Rl; Quill & Scroll; Ed Yrbk; Rptr Yrbk; Rptr Sch Nwsp; Sci Clb; Swmmng; Twrlr; College; Personnel Mgmt.

POMMERENKE, KIMBERLY S; Unionville Sebewaing HS; Sebewaing, MI; 18/109 Hon Rl; Rptr Yrbk; FHA; Scr Kpr; College; Home Ec.

POMORSKI, JOHN; Kelloggsville HS; Wyoming, MI; Hon Rl; Letter Ftbl; Letter Wrstlng; Mgrs; Voc Schl.

POMPA, ALFRED; Madonna HS; Follansbee, WV; Chrs; Hon Rl; Lit Mag; Sch Mus; Sch Pl; Stg Crw; Rptr Yrbk; St Vincent College; Theatre.

POMPEANI, MARISA; St Augustine Academy; N Olmsted, OH; Trs Jr Cls; Cl Rep Jr Cls; Chrs; Drl Tm; Girl Scts; Off Ade; Sch Pl; Stu Cncl; Bsbl; Bsktbl; Univ.

POMPY, LASONYA; Northern Sr HS; Detroit, MI; Girl Scts; Hon Rl; JA; FHA; Spn Clb; Cit Awd; Purdue Univ; Pediatrician.

PONADER, JONATHAN; Lawrence Central HS; Indianapolis, IN; Band; Chrh Wkr; VP Natl Forn Lg; NHS; Pres Yth Flsp; Yrbk; Drama Clb; Letter Ten; Univ; Indust Mgmt.

POND, ARLENE; West Liberty Salem HS; Urbana, OH; Chrs; Chrh Wkr; Cmnty Wkr; Hon Rl; JA; Sch Mus; Sch Pl; Pres Yth Flsp; Sch Nwsp; 4-H; 4 H Ldrshp Awd; 4 H Trip To Washington D C; College; Med Sec.

POND, CARRIE; Northwest HS; Pleasant Lake, MI; Cls Rep Frsh Cls; Cl Rep Jr Cls; Sec Sr Cls; Band; Chrs; Chrh Wkr; Cmnty Wkr; Drm Bgl; Girl Scts; Hon Rl; Grand Rapids Bapt Coll; Dent Hygnst.

POND, ROBERT; Chippewa HS; Doylestown, OH; Cl Rep Jr Cls; Hon Rl; Stu Cncl; Letter Ftbl; Letter Trk; IM Sprt; Mgrs; College.

POND, TEENA; Graham HS; St Paris, OH; 2/167 Band; Hon Rl; Jr NHS; NHS; Yrbk; 4-H; GAA; 4-H Awd; Ohio State Univ.

PONDER, CLAUDIA; Fountain Cntrl HS; Veedersburg, IN; 19/129 Capt Drl Tm; Hon Rl; NHS; Yth Flsp; 4-H; 4-H Awd; Purdue Univ; Elem Ed.

PONDER, COLLA; Baldwin HS; Baldwin, MI; Cls Rep Frsh Cls; Hon Rl; Letter Bsktbl; Crs Cntry; Letter Ftbl; Trk; Coach Actv; IM Sprt; Mgrs; Scr Kpr;.

PONTIOUS, TRACEY; Grant HS; Grant, MI; Band; Girl Scts; Hon Rl; Yth Flsp; Pep Clb; Letter Chrldng; GAA; Cit Awd; Ferris St Coll; Envir Sci.

PONTIUS, BARBARA; Munster HS; Munster, IN; 7/440 Cl Rep Jr Cls; Cls Rep Sr Cls; Am Leg Aux Girls St; Chrh Wkr; Hon Rl; Lbry Ade; NHS; VP Pep Clb; IM Sprt; Mat Maids; De Pauw Univ.

PONTIUS, BRIAN W; Bay HS; Bay Village, OH; 18/377 Band; Chrs; Hon Rl; Sch Mus; Sch Pl; Letter Ftbl; Natl Merit SF; Bay Mens Club Awd 1978; Superior Ratg Solo & Ensemble 1978; Homecomg Court 1978; Univ; Med.

PONZANI, WILLIAM S; Eastlake North HS; Willowick, OH; 66/669 Chrs; Jr NHS; NHS; Sch Mus; Sch Pl; Rptr Yrbk; VP Drama Clb; Comp Sci.

POOL, CYNTHIA; Madison Heights HS; Anderson, IN; 13/387 Chrh Wkr; Hon Rl; NHS; Pep Clb; Sci Clb; Spn Clb; Academic Schlrshp 79; Stu Of The Month 74; Olivet Nazarene Coll; Nursing.

POOLE, ANTHONY; Cleveland Benedictine HS; Cleveland, OH; 11/100 Band; Hon Rl; NHS; Orch; Stu Cncl; Boys Clb Am; Fr Clb; Ftbl; Elec Engr.

POOLE, EVELYN; Fennville HS; Fennville, MI; Cls Rep Sr Cls; Hon Rl; Stu Cncl; Fr Clb; Natl Merit Ltr; Western Mic Univ; Occup Therapy.

POOLE, MARJORIE; Colerain HS; Cincinnati, OH; Sec Soph Cls; Pres Jr Cls; Pres Sr Cls; Chrs; Off Ade; Stu Cncl; Drama Clb; Univ; Nursing.

POOLE, NADINE; Osborn HS; Detroit, MI; Chrh Wkr; Hon Rl; NHS; Stu Cncl; Yth Flsp; Pep Clb; Trk; Chrldng; PPFtbl; Cit Awd; Univ Of Detroit; Psych.

POOLE, PATRICIA; Flat Rock HS; Flat Rock, MI; Chrs; Chrh Wkr; Girl Scts; Hon Rl; NHS; Sch Pl; Yth Flsp; Sci Clb; PPFtbl; Scr Kpr; Michigan St Univ; Zoology.

POOLE, PATTY; Flat Rock HS; Flat Rock, MI; Chrs; Chrh Wkr; Girl Scts; Hon Rl; NHS; Sch Mus; Yth Flsp; Sci Clb; Scr Kpr; Univ Of Michigan; Biology.

POOLE, TAMI; Franklin Central HS; Indianapolis, IN; 53/243 Drl Tm; Girl Scts; Hon Rl; Sch Pl; Pep Clb; Pom Pon; Went To In St Univ For Summ Hon Progr 79; Opportunity To Learn Bus At Wabash Coll 79; An Awd For Hstry Clss; Ball St Univ; Comp Sci.

POOLE, TAMMY; Jennings County HS; North Vernon, IN; 32/351 Sec Chrs; Capt Drl Tm; Girl Scts; Hon Rl; Mdrgl; Sch Mus; Sch Pl; 4-H; Fr Clb; Pep Clb; All Amer Natl Drill Team Officer 79; Cntry 21 Typing Awd 79; Drill Team Lt & Cptn 78 80; Indiana St Univ; Elem Educ.

POOLE, TOM; Huntington North HS; Huntington, IN; Stg Crw; Letter Mgrs; Purdue Univ; Engr.

POOR, KIM; Bloomington South HS; Bloomington, IN; Chrs; Girl Scts; Hosp Ade; OEA; Pep Clb; Spn Clb; Swmmng; Tmr; Indiana Univ; Bus.

POOR, STEPHEN; Elwood Cmnty HS; Elwood, IN; 1/285 Debate Tm; Hon Rl; Jr NHS; NHS; Spn Clb; Letter Glf; Letter Mgrs; Natl Hnr Soc Chptr Pres 79; Purdue Univ; Comp Tech.

POORE, TIM; R Nelson Snider HS; Ft Wayne, IN; Band; Drm Bgl; Hon Rl; Stu Cncl; Cit Awd; Univ; Bus Admin.

POORMAN, ANNE; St Joseph Cntl Catholic HS; Fremont, OH; Cmp Fr Grls; Hon Rl; NHS; FTA; Pep Clb; Univ; Math.

POORMAN, ANNE; St Joseph Central Cath HS; Fremont, OH; Cmnty Wkr; Hon Rl; NHS; FTA; Pep Clb; Univ; Math.

POORT, SHIRLEY; Culver Community HS; Monterey, IN; 36/123 VP 4-H; Sec FHA; Bsbl; Capt Bsktbl; Capt Trk; Pom Pon; Twrlr; 4-H Awd; Capt & MVP Of Volleyball; 4 H Share The Fun Twirling Winner; Basketball Awds; Purdue Univ; Computer Tech.

POPA, DIANNA; Waterloo HS; Atwater, OH; 2/162 Am Leg Aux Girls St; Band; Sec Chrh Wkr; Hon Rl; VP NHS; Pres Stu Cncl; Am Leg Awd; Bausch & Lomb Awd; Dnfth Awd; Cedarville College; Optometrist.

POPA, PAUL; R S Tower HS; Warren, MI; Hon Rl; Letter Swmmng; Scr Kpr; Tmr; Alma Coll; Chem.

POPADAK, NANCY; St Joseph Acad; Cleveland, OH; Hon Rl; Coach Actv; GAA; Cleveland State Univ; Radiologist.

POPCHOCK, DIANE; Fitzgerald HS; Warren, MI; 1/300 Cls Rep Sr Cls; Val; Hon Rl; NHS; Stg Crw; Pep Clb; PPFtbl; Lion Awd; Wayne St Univ; Nursing.

POPE, CHARLES; Shakamak HS; Jasonville, IN; 4/84 Am Leg Boys St; Boy Scts; Chrh Wkr; FCA; Hon Rl; NHS; Quill & Scroll; Sprt Ed Sch Nwsp; Bsktbl; Trk; Ind State; Computer Sci.

POPE, D; Bloomington North HS; Bloomington, IN; Orch; Fr Clb; Gym; Natl Merit Ltr; Univ; Med.

POPE, JAMES; Greenfield Central HS; Greenfield, IN; Band; Boy Scts; Chrh Wkr; NHS; 4-H; Ger Clb; Valparaiso Univ; Bus Admin.

POPE, JOHN; Fostoria HS; Fostoria, OH; Cls Rep Sr Cls; Am Leg Boys St; Chrs; Hon Rl; Stu Cncl; Lat Clb; Ftbl; Letter Trk; Coll; Psych.

POPE, MARY; Lewis County HS; Camden, WV; 7/266 Cls Rep Frsh Cls; Chrs; Chrh Wkr; Cmnty Wkr; Hon Rl; NHS; 4-H; Pep Clb; DAR Awd; 4-H Awd; W Virginia Univ; Horticulture.

POPE, REINER; Lutheran East HS; Highland, MI; Hon Rl; Wrstlng; Coll; Elec.

POPE, STUART; Cowan HS; Muncie, IN; 1/85 Am Leg Boys St; Boy Scts; Debate Tm; FCA; NHS; Ger Clb; Spn Clb; Bsktbl; Glf; God Cntry Awd; Purdue Univ; Engr.

POPE, TONYA; Washington HS; Massillon, OH; Cls Rep Frsh Cls; Band; Chrs; Chrh Wkr; Off Ade; Rptr Yrbk; DECA; Fr Clb; Trk; College; Fashion Merch.

POPER, SHARIS; Hicksville HS; Hicksville, OH; Band; Drm Mjrt; Sch Pl; Stg Crw; Pep Clb; Gym; GAA; IM Sprt; PPFtbl; Twrlr;.

POPIEL, SHARON; Harry S Truman HS; Taylor, MI; 13/560 Cls Rep Frsh Cls; Cls Rep Soph Cls; Cl Rep Jr Cls; Cls Rep Sr Cls; Am Leg Aux Girls St; Hon Rl; Jr NHS; Sec NHS; Rptr Yrbk; Pom Pon; College; Bus.

POPOFF, CHRIS; River Valley HS; Marion, OH; 12/207 Am Leg Aux Girls St; NHS; Orch; Sch Mus; Yth Flsp; Fr Clb; Sci Clb; Letter Crs Cntry; Letter Trk; Univ.

POPOFF, CHRISTINE; River Valley HS; Marion, OH; Trs Sr Cls; Am Leg Aux Girls St; Hon Rl; Jr NHS; Orch; Sch Mus; Yth Flsp; Fr Clb; Sci Clb; Crs Cntry; Univ; Bus Mgmt.

POPOPAT, FRANK; St Josephs HS; Euclid, OH; Band; Hon Rl; Orch; Bsbl; Cleveland St Univ; Art.

POPP, JAMES R; Glen Este HS; Cincinnati, OH; Band; Boy Scts; Drl Tm; Hon Rl; Orch; Sch Pl; Sct Actv; Spn Clb; Socr; Trk; National Guard.

POPPE, HOLLY; William Henry Harrison HS; Miamitown, OH; Hon Rl; Bsktbl; GAA; IM Sprt; PPFtbl; UC; Med Tech.

POPPLEWELL, JUDI; Walter P Chrysler Mem HS; New Castle, IN; 41/420 VP Aud/Vis; NHS; Red Cr Ade; Stg Crw; Pres 4-H; Capt Pom Pon; Pres South Indiana Conference Youth; Miss Indiana Natl Teenager Pageant; St Health Occupations; Indiana Univ; Nursing.

POPPLEWELL, SHEILA; Brown County HS; Morgantown, IN; 21/250 Chrs; Girl Scts; Hon Rl; NHS; Sch Mus; Sch Pl; Stg Crw; Ed Sch Nwsp; Rptr Sch Nwsp; Drama Clb; Purdue Univ; Theater.

POQUETTE, KELLY; North Central Area HS; Hermansville, MI; 4/65 Trs Soph Cls; Trs Jr Cls; Trs Sr Cls; Band; Hon Rl; Sch Pl; Bsktbl; Chrldng; Bay Denoc Comm Coll; Elem Educ.

PORILE, JIM; West Lafayette HS; W Lafayette, IN; 15/187 Boy Scts; Hon Rl; Quill & Scroll; Sprt Ed Yrbk; Yrbk; Letter Ten; IM Sprt; Natl Merit Ltr; Univ.

PORKKA, SARAH; Lakeland HS; Highland, MI; 5/379 Am Leg Aux Girls St; Chrs; Hon Rl; NHS; Sch Mus; Sch Pl; Stu Cncl; Drama Clb; Fr Clb; Univ Of Michigan; Med.

PORN JR, J; Flushing HS; Flushing, MI; Band; Boy Scts; Drm Bgl; Orch; Sct Actv; Pep Clb; IM Sprt; SAR Awd; Cmmrcl Pilot.

PORSOSKA, MARY; Marquette HS; Michigan City, IN; 12/81 Cl Rep Jr Cls; Chrs; Drm Bgl; Hon Rl; Sch Mus; Stu Cncl; Yrbk; Spn Clb; Scr Kpr; DAR Awd; Univ; Math.

PORTARO, ROSS; St Edward HS; Westlake, OH; 10/400 Cls Rep Frsh Cls; Cls Rep Soph Cls; Jr NHS; NHS; Capt Swmmng; Capt Ten; IM Sprt; N E Oh Raquetbl Champ 78; 1st Pl In Mens Doulbes A Div Raquetbl 78; Univ Of Virginia; Med.

PORTE, DONNA; Coleman HS; Coleman, MI; Cl Rep Jr Cls; Hon Rl; Stu Cncl; Bsbl; Bsktbl;.

PORTEN, RICK; Ben Davis HS; Indianapolis, IN; Cls Rep Frsh Cls; Pres Soph Cls; Trs Jr Cls; Pres Sr Cls; FCA; Hon Rl; Stu Cncl; Ger Clb; Ftbl; Trk; Univ; Eng.

PORTER, AMY; Quincy HS; Quincy, MI; 7/110 VP Frsh Cls; VP Soph Cls; Hon Rl; Treas NHS; Off Ade; Rptr Yrbk; Rptr Sch Nwsp; Kellogg Community College; Acctg.

PORTER, ANDREW; Heath HS; Newark, OH; Band; Boy Scts; Chrh Wkr; Ohi State; Bus Admin.

PORTER, ANTHONY; North Putnam HS; Greencastle, IN; FCA; Hon Rl; NHS; 4-H; FFA; Mth Clb; Sci Clb; Spn Clb; IM Sprt; 4-H Awd; College; Aero Engr.

PORTER, BETTY; Brown County HS; Nineveh, IN; 19/139 Band; Drl Tm; VP NHS; Off Ade; Quill & Scroll; Stu Cncl; Ed Yrbk; Fr Clb; Treas Pep Clb; Ten; Bauder Fashion Coll; Fshn Mdse.

PORTER, BRENDA; Niles Mc Kinley HS; Niles, OH; 4/420 AFS; Chrs; Chrh Wkr; Hon Rl; NHS; Red Cr Ade; Sch Mus; Sch Pl; Ed Sch Nwsp; Drama Clb; Gods Bible Schl; Nursing.

PORTER, BRENDA; James A Garfield HS; Garrettsville, OH; Chrh Wkr; Off Ade; Spn Clb; Villa Maria Coll; Spec Ed.

PORTER, BRIAN; Madison Hts HS; Anderson, IN; 45/400 Boy Scts; Hon Rl; Sct Actv; Lat Clb; Stu Of The Year; Indiana St Univ; Geology.

PORTER, CAROL; Boardman HS; Youngstown, OH; Band; Girl Scts; Hon Rl; Sct Actv; Fr Clb; Pep Clb; Univ; Recreation.

PORTER, CINDY; Greensburg Community HS; Greensburg, IN; Band; Chrs; Girl Scts; Hon Rl; JA; Mdrgl; Sch Mus; Pep Clb; Spn Clb; Pom Pon; Ball State Univ; Social Work.

PORTER, DAVID E; Northrop HS; Ft Wayne, IN; Band; Boy Scts; Ftbl; Lion Awd; Ball St Univ.

PORTER, DEBORAH; Royal Oak C M Kimball HS; Royal Oak, MI; 12/610 Cls Rep Frsh Cls; Cls Rep Soph Cls; Cl Rep Jr Cls; Cls Rep Sr Cls; Hon Rl; NHS; Stu Cncl; PPFtbl; Natl Merit SF; Synchronized Swim Clb; Bd Of Trustees Hnrs Schlrshp Cntrl Michigan Univ; Awd For Acad Exc Michigan St Univ; Central Michigan Univ; Acctg.

PORTER, DONNA J; Clear Fork HS; Mansfield, OH; 11/168 Cls Rep Frsh Cls; Cls Rep Soph Cls; Chrh Wkr; Cmnty Wkr; Hon Rl; Red Cr Ade; Stu Cncl; Yth Flsp; OEA; Pep Clb; Sec.

PORTER, ERIC; Hartland HS; Howell, MI; Trs Jr Cls; Hon Rl; Jr NHS; NHS; Spn Clb; Letter Bsbl; Bsktbl; Ftbl; Ferris Coll; Pharm.

PORTER, JEFF; Shelbyville Sr HS; Shelbyville, IN; FCA; Hon Rl; Boys Clb Am; Lat Clb; Ftbl; Coach Actv; IM Sprt; Univ; Law.

PORTER, JOY; Carroll HS; Flora, IN; Band; Chrh Wkr; Cmnty Wkr; Girl Scts; Hon Rl; Sch Nwsp; 4-H; FHA; Spn Clb; 4-H Awd; College.

PORTER, JULIA; Lumen Christi HS; Jackson, MI; 16/240 Band; Chrh Wkr; Hon Rl; Jr NHS; Lbry Ade; NHS; PAVAS; Sch Mus; Yth Flsp; Spn Clb; Ferris State; Allied Health.

PORTER, KELLY; Stow Sr HS; Stow, OH; Chrh Wkr; Cmnty Wkr; Girl Scts; Hon Rl; NHS; Yth Flsp; Mth Clb; VP Of Explorer Post #2043 78; Univ; Math.

PORTER, MELINDA; Chesapeake HS; Chesapeake, OH; Chrh Wkr; Hon Rl; Off Ade; Beta Clb; FHA; OEA; College.

PORTER, MONICA; Pontiac Central HS; Pontiac, MI; Cl Rep Jr Cls; Cmp Fr Grls; Chrs; Debate Tm; Hon Rl; NHS; Off Ade; Stu Cncl; 4-H; Pep Clb; UCLA; Elec Tech.

PORTER, PAMELA; Batavia HS; Batavia, OH; Hon Rl; Off Ade; 4-H; Fr Clb; Pep Clb; Trk; Capt Chrldng; Scr Kpr; Bus Schl; Exec Sec.

PORTER, PAMELA; Niles HS; Niles, MI; Chrs; Hon Rl; Bus Schl.

PORTER, PATRICIA A; Catholic Central HS; Wintersville, OH; 45/215 Cls Rep Frsh Cls; Cls Rep Soph Cls; Hon Rl; NHS; Yth Flsp; Rptr Yrbk; FNA; Pep Clb; Spn Clb; Univ; Pre Med.

PORTER, PATRICK; Mt Gilead HS; Mt Gilead, OH; 6/100 Boy Scts; Hon Rl; Sdlty; Fr Clb; Ohio St Univ; Engr.

PORTER, RACHAEL; Rutherford B Hayes HS; Dealware, OH; AFS; Chrs; Lit Mag; Sch Mus; Sch Pl; Stg Crw; Drama Clb; Am Leg Awd; Opt Clb Awd; Best Short Story Awd 78; Univ; Music.

PORTER, REGINA; Indian Creek HS; Trafalgar, IN; 25/155 Band; Chrs; Girl Scts; Sch Mus; Sct Actv; F HA; Lat Clb; Sci Clb; Spn Clb; Arion Awd Band 78; Med.

PORTER, RITA; West Washington HS; Pekin, IN; 7/104 Band; Hon Rl; NHS; Sci Clb; Trk; ITT; Elec.

PORTER, ROBIN A; Groveport Madison HS; Columbus, OH; 77/573 Chrs; Girl Scts; Hon Rl; FFA; Spn Clb; PPFtbl; Scr Kpr; Ohio St Univ; Vet Med.

PORTER, RON; Carey HS; Carey, OH; Chrs; Cmnty Wkr; Drama Clb; Spn Clb; Ftbl; Wrstlng; College.

PORTER, ROSALIE; Field HS; Kent, OH; Band; Cmp Fr Grls; Girl Scts; Hosp Ade; Yrbk; FHA; Pep Clb; Spn Clb; Tmr; Univ; Nursing.

PORTER, SUSAN; Mingo HS; Mingo Jct, OH; 10/118 Band; Pres Chrh Wkr; Cmnty Wkr; Hon Rl; Off Ade; Yth Flsp; Sch Nwsp; Lat Clb; OEA; College; Busns.

PORTER, TAMARA; Lansing Eastern HS; Lansing, MI; Cls Rep Soph Cls; Cl Rep Jr Cls; Hon Rl; NHS; Stu Cncl; Swmmng; PPFtbl; Am Leg Awd; Univ; Interior Dsgn.

PORTER, TAMMY; New Richmond HS; New Richmond, OH; Cls Rep Sr Cls; Hon Rl; JA; NHS; Quill & Scroll; Rptr Sch Nwsp; Fr Clb; FSA; Pep Clb; Trk; Univ Of Cincinnati; Dent.

PORTER, WANDA; Henry Ford HS; Detroit, MI; 74/575 Chrs; Chrh Wkr; Cmnty Wkr; Hon Rl; Off Ade; Sch Mus; Yth Flsp; Drama Clb; Pep Clb; Chrldng; Focus Hope Cmnty Work1978; Elected Cmncmnt Spkr Sr Class 1979; Tennessee St Univ.

PORTERFIELD, GREGORY; Peterstown HS; Lindside, WV; FFA; Sci Clb; Voc Schl.

PORTERFIELD, JOHN; Caro HS; Caro, MI; 13/161 Hst Sr Cls; Hon Rl; NHS; Bsktbl; Ftbl; Trk; Cit Awd; Natl Merit Ltr; Mich Tech Univ; Electrical Eng.

PORTERFIELD, LINDA; Union Local HS; Flushing, OH; 20/154 Sec Chrh Wkr; Hon Rl; Lbry Ade; Off Ade; Sch Pl; Stu Cncl; Pres Y-Teens; Wv Career College; Bus.

PORTICE, JANET; Owasso HS; Owosso, MI; 2/406 Sal; Chrh Wkr; Girl Scts; Hon Rl; JA; NHS; Sch Mus; Sch Pl; Yth Flsp; Y-Teens; Grand Rapids Bapt Coll; Psych.

PORTMANN, VICKIE; Central Hower HS; Akron, OH; 21/400 Hon Rl; NHS; Red Cr Ade; Pep Clb; Letter Gym; Cleveland St Univ; Phys Ther.

PORTNOY, DARIN; Morgantown HS; Morgantown, WV; Boy Scts; Sct Actv; Letter Ten; IM Sprt; College; Medical.

POSEY, GAIL; North Knox HS; Freelandville, IN; 13/154 Chrh Wkr; Drl Tm; FCA; Hon Rl; NHS; Stu Cncl; Ed Yrbk; 4-H; Pep Clb; Sci Clb; Indiana St Univ; Med Tech.

POSEY, HEATHER; Rensselaer Central HS; Rensselaer, IN; 24/172 Band; Chrs; Chrh Wkr; Hon Rl; NHS; Pol Wkr; Sch Mus; Depauw Univ; Music.

POSGE, MARY; St Ursula Acad; Cincinnati, OH; Cincinnati Tech Coll; Pre Med.

POSIN, TAMARA F; Mount De Chantal Visitation; Wheeling, WV; Chrh Wkr; Cmnty Wkr; Hon Rl; Sch Mus; Sch Pl; Stu Cncl; Rptr Yrbk; VP Drama Clb; Spn Clb; Ohio St Univ; Occup Ther.

POSKEY, BONNIE; Ida HS; Monroe, MI; 35/160 Sec Frsh Cls; Band; Off Ade; Rptr Yrbk; Rptr Sch Nwsp; Pep Clb; Chrldng; GAA; Western Mic Univ; Comm Arts.

POST, CAROL; Centreville HS; Three Rivers, MI; Hon Rl; Sec NHS; Yth Flsp; Rptr Yrbk; Rptr Sch Nwsp; 4-H; Pep Clb; Bsktbl; Trk; 4-H Awd; Coll; Poli Sci.

POST, CHERYL; Miller HS; Corning, OH; Band; Chrs; NHS; Sch Pl; Stu Cncl; Rptr Yrbk; Rptr Sch Nwsp; FBLA; Ohi Univ; Cmmcrl Art.

POST, DEBRA; Perrysburg HS; Perrysburg, OH; Cls Rep Frsh Cls; Cls Rep Soph Cls; Chrs; Girl Scts; Hon Rl; Stu Cncl; Sprt Ed Sch Nwsp; Rptr Sch Nwsp; Fr Clb; Pep Clb; Univ; Flight Attendant.

POST, DONA K; Buckeye North HS; Rayland, OH; Band; Chrs; FCA; Hon Rl; Off Ade; Fr Clb; Pep Clb; Spn Clb; Chrldng; Ohio St Univ; Clinical Psych.

POST, DONNA; St Henry HS; St Henry, OH; 3/122 Cls Rep Sr Cls; Am Leg Aux Girls St; Chrh Wkr; Hon Rl; NHS; Pol Wkr; Sdlty; Wright State Univ; Law.

POST, JACQUELINE; South Harrison HS; Lost Creek, WV; Cl Rep Jr Cls; Chrh Wkr; Hon Rl; Jr NHS; Lbry Ade; NHS; Sch Pl; Yth Flsp; IM Sprt; Bob Jones Univ; Picture Prod.

POST, NANCY E; Spencer HS; Spencer, WV; Cmnty Wkr; Girl Scts; Hon Rl; Drama Clb; IM Sprt; Cit Awd; Acctg Profcncy Awd 79; Usherette 79; Univ; Acctg.

POST, TAMARA; Cheboygan Area HS; Cheboygan, MI; Hon Rl; Hosp Ade; FNA; Bsktbl; Trk; Pres Awd; Michigan St Little & Sr League Champ Softball; Most Improved Player Awd In Vlybl; All Conf Hnrbl Men Vlybl; College; Law Enforcement.

POST, TERESA; Jackson HS; Roy, OH; Chrh Wkr; Hon Rl; Lbry Ade; OEA; Ohi State Univ; Secretary.

POSTEL, GREG; Hoover HS; Canton, OH; Am Leg Boys St; Chrs; Chrh Wkr; Hon Rl; NHS; Sch Mus; Stu Cncl; Ger Clb; Sci Clb; Mas Awd; St Officer For Oh St Coucil Order Fo De Molay 78; Accompnst For Select Vocal Grp 79; Stud Of Piano Music; Univ; Med.

POSTELS, DOUGLAS; North Central HS; Indianapolis, IN; 152/999 Boy Scts; Hon Rl; Sec JA; NHS; 4-H; Fr Clb; Key Clb; JA Awd; Indiana Univ; Med.

POSTIY, EVA; Sebring Mc Kinley HS; Sebring, OH; Aud/Vis; Off Ade; Rptr Yrbk; Rptr Sch Nwsp; Lat Clb; GAA; Vocational Schl.

POSTLER, BETTY; Berkley HS; Hunt Woods, MI; NHS; Swmmng; Coll.

POSTMUS, KENT; Orchard View HS; Muskegon, MI; Sch Pl; Stg Crw; Ed Yrbk; Ftbl; Univ Of Miami; Bus Admin.

POSZUST, DIANE; Woodrow Wilson HS; Youngstwn, OH; 23/343 Letter Band; Chrs; Girl Scts; Hon Rl; NHS; Sct Actv; Keyettes; Bsktbl; Letter Mgrs; College; Law Enforcement.

POTERACK, KARL A; West Catholic HS; Grand Rapids, MI; 2/280 Debate Tm; NHS; Sprt Ed Sch Nwsp; Lat Clb; Capt Crs Cntry; Letter Trk; Natl Merit SF; College; Medicine.

POTES, ADAM; Wauseon HS; Wauseon, OH; 1/156 Am Leg Boys St; Band; Boy Scts; Chrs; Chrh Wkr; Hon Rl; NHS; Sch Mus; Sch Pl; Sct Actv; Univ; Engr.

POTH, JULIE; Eastwood HS; Pemberville, OH; Band; FCA; Girl Scts; Hon Rl; NHS; Pres 4-H; Treas Ger Clb; Trk; Chrldng; 4-H Awd; Univ; Fashion Mdse.

POTH, LORI; Mogadore HS; Mogadore, OH; Band; Chrs; Chrh Wkr; Cmnty Wkr; Drl Tm; Orch; Sch Mus; Sch Pl; Y-Teens; Yrbk; Akron Univ; Music.

POTHAST, LINDA; Delphos Jefferson Sr HS; Delphos, OH; Chrs; Girl Scts; Hon Rl; NHS; Rptr Yrbk; 4-H; Trk; Scr Kpr; Bus Schl.

POTHAST, LINDA; Delphos Jefferson Sr HS; Delphos, OH; Chrs; Girl Scts; Hon Rl; NHS; Rptr Yrbk; 4-H; Trk; Scr Kpr; Business Schl; Accounting.

POTOCZKY, MARGARET; La Ville Jr Sr HS; Lakeville, IN; 6/100 Cls Rep Frsh Cls; Cls Rep Soph Cls; Cl Rep Jr Cls; Chrs; NHS; Pol Wkr; Stu Cncl; 4-H; Fr Clb; Sci Clb; Stanford Univ; Engr.

POTRAFKE, DIANA; Batavia HS; Batavia, OH; Sec Jr Cls; Band; Drm Mjrt; Hon Rl; Hosp Ade; Lbry Ade; NHS; Yrbk; Fr Clb; Dnfth Awd; Univ Of Cincinnati; Bus Mgmt.

POTTEIGER, DANA; Eastmoor HS; Columbus, OH; 38/290 Chrs; Hon Rl; Off Ade; PAVAS; Sch Mus; Sch Pl; Stg Crw; Sch Nwsp; Spn Clb; Amer Ballet Schlrshp Ford Found; Schlrshp Medal Awd; Butler Univ; Dance.

POTTENGER, CONNIE; Cardinal Ritter HS; Indianapolis, IN; Band; Cmp Fr Grls; Chrs; Chrh Wkr; Drm Mjrt; Hon Rl; Mdrgl; MMM; NHS; Sch Mus; Indiana St Univ.

POTTER, BECKY; Chesapeake HS; Chesapeake, OH; 9/136 Cls Rep Frsh Cls; Pres Jr Cls; Cl Rep Jr Cls; VP Sr Cls; Cls Rep Sr Cls; Am Leg Aux Girls St; Band; Drm Mjrt; Hon Rl; NHS; Marshall Univ; Nursing.

POTTER, BETH; Lapeer East Sr HS; Lapeer, MI; Sec Frsh Cls; Cls Rep Soph Cls; Cl Rep Jr Cls; Chrs; Chrh Wkr; Stu Cncl; Yth Flsp; 4-H; Fr Clb; PPFtbl; Lapeer Cnty 4 H Queen 79; Univ; Elem Educ.

POTTER, BRADLEY; Lawrence Central HS; Indianapolis, IN; Band; Orch; Sch Mus; Yth Flsp; Letter Trk; PPFtbl; Outstanding Jr Bandsman Awd; Purdue Univ; Engr.

POTTER, BRIAN; Ayersville Local HS; Defiance, OH; Boy Scts; Hon Rl; Ten; Bus Schl; Acctg.

POTTER, DENNIS; James Ford Rhodes HS; Cleveland, OH; Cls Rep Frsh Cls; Aud/Vis; Hon Rl; Orch; Rptr Sch Nwsp; Ger Clb; Wrstlng; Mgrs; Cit Awd; Bus Driver.

POTTER, GREGG; Alma HS; Alma, MI; Val; Band; Hon Rl; NHS; Sch Pl; Stg Crw; Drama Clb; Bausch & Lomb Awd; Natl Merit Ltr; Alma Coll; Pre Law.

POTTER, JOHN T; Lutheran HS West; Cleveland, OH; Band; Boy Scts; Chrs; Chrh Wkr; Hon Rl; NHS; Orch; Pep Clb; Socr; Letter Trk; Schlrshp For A Smmr Course At The Art Inst In Cleveland 77; Cert Of Exc For Sup Achvmnt In Art 77; Univ; Lndscp Archt.

POTTER, JULIA A; Westerville North HS; Westerville, OH; Am Leg Aux Girls St; Girl Scts; VP Orch; Sch Mus; Sch Pl; Drama Clb; Key Clb; Kiwan Awd; Otterbein Music Schlrshp 79; Otterbein Coll; Music.

POTTER, KIMBER L; Van Buren HS; Brazil, IN; Chrs; Chrh Wkr; Drl Tm; Hon Rl; Sch Mus; Sch Pl; Stg Crw; Yth Flsp; Drama Clb; 4-H; Indiana St Univ; Speech Path.

POTTER, KIMBERLY; Mcnicholas HS; Cincinnati, OH; Cls Rep Frsh Cls; Cls Rep Soph Cls; Cl Rep Jr Cls; Cmnty Wkr; Drm Mjrt; Sch Mus; Stu Cncl; Pep Clb; Gym; Chrldng; College; Public Relations.

POTTER, PAMELA; Orchard View HS; Muskegon, MI; Band; Girl Scts; Hon Rl; 4-H; Trk; PPFtbl; College; Biology.

POTTER, REBECCA; Chesapeake HS; Chesapeake, OH; 6/139 Cls Rep Frsh Cls; Pres Jr Cls; Cl Rep Jr Cls; VP Sr Cls; Cls Rep Sr Cls; Am Leg Aux Girls St; Band; Capt Drm Mjrt; Hon Rl; NHS; Marshall Univ; Nursing.

POTTER, REBECCA; Atlanta Community School; Atlanta, MI; Trs Jr Cls; Chrh Wkr; Hon Rl; NHS; Sch Pl; Yth Flsp; Letter Bsbl; Baker Jr Coll Of Bus; Exec Sec.

POTTS, BRIAN; Redford Union HS; Redford, MI; Hon Rl; Wayne State Univ; Banking & Finance.

POTTS, JEFFREY; Linsly Military Inst; Columbus, OH; Band; Chrs; Chrh Wkr; Cmnty Wkr; Drl Tm; Drm Bgl; FCA; Orch; ROTC; Sch Mus; Univ; Brdcstng.

POTTS, JENNY; West Union HS; West Union, OH; Band; Chrh Wkr; Hon Rl; NHS; Southern St Comm Coll.

POTTS, LARRY; Bishop Donahue HS; Moundsville, WV; 2/55 VP Sr Cls; Boy Scts; Lit Mag; Treas NHS; Stu Cncl; Pres Yth Flsp; Key Clb; Pres Spn Clb; Letter Ftbl; Lion Awd; St Meinrad Coll; Psych.

POTTS, LAURA; Lehman HS; Sidney, OH; 3/100 VP Frsh Cls; Pres Soph Cls; VP Jr Cls; VP Sr Cls; Am Leg Aux Girls St; Hon Rl; Jr NHS; NHS; Sch Pl; Rptr Yrbk; Miami Univ.

POTTS, LAWRENCE R; Bishop Donahue HS; Moundsville, WV; 1/55 VP Sr Cls; Hon Rl; Treas NHS; Stu Cncl; Pres Yth Flsp; Sch Nwsp; Key Clb; Pres Spn Clb; Letter Ftbl; Lion Awd; Wheeling Coll; Religion.

POTTS, LORI; Penn HS; S Bend, IN; Chrh Wkr; Hon Rl; Lit Mag; Yth Flsp; Coach Actv; Bethel College; Journalism.

POTTS, PAULISA; North Daviess Jr Sr HS; Odon, IN; 10/93 Cl Rep Jr Cls; Am Leg Aux Girls St; Band; Chrh Wkr; FCA; Hon Rl; NHS; Pol Wkr; Stu Cncl; Yth Flsp; Var Vllybl 78; 3 Gregg Shorthand Awds 78; Miss Dariess County Queen 79; Vincennes Bus Coll; Legal Sec.

POULOS, NICHOLAS; Orange HS; Pepper Pike, OH; 1/250 Val; Pres Debate Tm; Hon Rl; Lit Mag; Mod UN; Natl Forn Lg; Pres NHS; Sch Pl; Crs Cntry; Trk; Top 100 In Ohio Cncl Of Teachers Math Cont; Algebra Honor; 1st Pl Essay Booster Writing Cont; Johns Hopkins Univ; Bio Engr.

POULSON, LINDA; Anderson HS; Anderson, IN; Red Cr Ade; Fr Clb; Pep Clb; Purdue Univ; Archt.

POUND, NANCY L; Newark HS; Newark, OH; Trs Frsh Cls; Chrs; Hon Rl; OEA; Bsbl; Bsktbl; GAA; Ohio State Univ.

POUNDS, BONNIE; Lumen Cordium HS; Maple Hts, OH; Am Leg Aux Girls St; Chrs; Hon Rl; Univ; Med.

POUPARD, BARRY; East Detroit HS; Warren, MI; Band; Chrh Wkr; Hon Rl; NHS; Sch Pl; College; Engl.

POUPARD, CAROL; Harper Woods HS; Harper Woods, MI; Hon Rl; Mich State; Vet.

POUZAR, S; Mason Sr HS; Mason, MI; Chrs; Hon Rl; Lbry Ade; 4-H; FFA; Spn Clb; Gym; Coll; Child Psych.

POVEROMO, MISTY; St Joseph Central HS; Huntington, WV; Trs Jr Cls; Hon Rl; Red Cr Ade; Sch Pl; Yrbk; Pep Clb; Sci Clb; Bsktbl; Ten; Scr Kpr; San Diego St Univ; Tele Cmnctns.

POVILUNAS, ANTHONY; Carsonville Port Sanilac HS; Pt Sanilac, MI; Hon Rl; Jr NHS; College; Architecture.

POVINELLI, KATHLEEN; Magnificat HS; Westlake, OH; VP Frsh Cls; Pres Soph Cls; Trs Jr Cls; Trs Sr Cls; Band; Chrs; Chrh Wkr; Jr NHS; NHS; Stu Cncl; Holy Cross Univ; Bsktbl.

POVROZNIK, STEPHEN; Washington Irving HS; Clarksburg, WV; Cls Rep Frsh Cls; Cls Rep Sr Cls; Boy Scts; Chrh Wkr; Stu Cncl; Fr Clb; Sec Leo Clb; Sci Clb; Ftbl; Letter Trk; Chess Club Treas & VP; Fairmont St Univ; Comp Sci.

POWELL, ALVA B; Holly HS; Royal Oak, MI; Boy Scts; Hon Rl; JA; Sch Mus; Sct Actv; Yth Flsp; Spn Clb; Bsktbl; Chrldng; Mgrs; Michigan Tech Univ; Chem Engr.

POWELL, AMBER; Pleasant HS; Prospect, OH; 7/153 Chrh Wkr; Girl Scts; Hon Rl; Jr NHS; Off Ade; Sch Pl; Yth Flsp; Yrbk; Drama Clb; FHA; Toccoa Falls Bible Coll; Elem Ed.

POWELL, AMY; Douglas Mac Arthur HS; Saginaw, MI; 17/300 Chrh Wkr; Hon Rl; NHS; Yth Flsp; Ed Sch Nwsp; Coll; Jrnlsm.

POWELL, ARLENE; Cheboygan Area HS; Che boygan, MI; Band; Chrs; Chrh Wkr; Hon Rl; Orch; Sch Pl; Liberty Baptist College; Music.

POWELL, BARBARA; Minerva HS; Minerva, OH; 1/217 Cls Rep Frsh Cls; Trs Sr Cls; Val; Band; Drm Mjrt; NHS; Treas Stu Cncl; VP Fr Clb; Bausch & Lomb Awd; Kent State Univ; Acctg.

POWELL, BETH; St Francis Central HS; Morgantown, WV; Band; Chrs; Hon Rl; Drama Clb; Pep Clb; Spn Clb; Trk; Chrldng; Natl Busns Coll; Fash Merch.

POWELL, BEVERLY; North Canton Hoover HS; Greentown, OH; 44/544 Chrs; Hon Rl; Hosp Ade; Sct Actv; Stg Crw; Yth Flsp; Drama Clb; Pep Clb; Spn Clb; Univ; Stewardess.

POWELL, BRIAN L; Big Walnut HS; Galena, OH; 18/245 Band; Cmnty Wkr; Hon Rl; NHS; Fr Clb; Letter Bsktbl; Letter Trk; Univ Of Denver; Archt.

POWELL, CHERYL; Minerva HS; Minerva, OH; 4/241 Band; Girl Scts; Hon Rl; VP Fr Clb; Pep Clb; Trk; Akron St Univ; Acctg.

POWELL, CYNTHIA; Walled Lake Central HS; W Bloomfield, MI; Cl Rep Jr Cls; Hon Rl; NHS; OEA; Letter Trk; St Of Mi Comp Shclsp 79; Is Tpl In Typing I 79; 6th Pl Acctg I At Regnl Leve Bus Oofc Educ Club 79; Oakland Cmnty Coll; Sec.

POWELL, DAVID; Manton Consolidated School; Manton, MI; Trs Frsh Cls; Band; Hon Rl; NHS; Sprt Ed Sch Nwsp; Bsbl; Bsktbl; Ftbl; Univ.

POWELL, DAVID; Eastmoor HS; Columbus, OH; Hon Rl; Jr NHS; Capital Univ; Optometry.

POWELL, DENISE; Boardman HS; Youngstown, OH; 48/597 Chrs; Chrh Wkr; Hon Rl; Mdrgl; NHS; Yth Flsp; FHA; Pep Clb; Mt Vernon Nazarene Coll; Elem Ed.

POWELL, DESIREE; Lutheran HS East; Cleveland, OH; 7/30 Sec Frsh Cls; Cl Rep Jr Cls; Band; Chrs; Chrh Wkr; Girl Scts; Hosp Ade; Sch Mus; Stu Cncl; Yth Flsp; All Amer Band; Cortland Univ; Phys Educ.

POWELL, DONALD; West Iron Cnty HS; Iron River, MI; 4/132 Pres Sr Cls; Debate Tm; Hon Rl; Lbry Ade; NHS; Sch Pl; Stg Crw; Stu Cncl; Drama Clb; 4-H; Northern Michigan Univ; Poli Sci.

POWELL, GORDON; Streetsboro HS; Streetsboro, OH; Aud/Vis; Band; JA; JA Awd; Otterbine; Music.

POWELL, GWENDOLYN; Warrensville Hts Sr HS; Warrensville, OH; .

POWELL, JAN; Ridgewood HS; Fresno, OH; 3/150 Am Leg Aux Girls St; Band; Hon Rl; Hosp Ade; NHS; Yth Flsp; 4-H; Otterben.

POWELL, JEFF; Monrovia HS; Mooresville, IN; 4/148 Hon Rl; NHS; Rptr Yrbk; Yrbk; Spn Clb; Mgrs; College; Finance.

POWELL, JUDY; West Muskingum HS; Hopewell, OH; Chrs; Chrh Wkr; Cmnty Wkr; Hon Rl; NHS; Sec Yth Flsp; Sec 4-H; Am Leg Awd; Cit Awd; 4-H Awd; Coll; Elem Ed.

POWELL, KAP; Cedar Lake Academy; Pittsford, MI; Trs Frsh Cls; Cls Rep Soph Cls; Chrs; Chrh Wkr; Cmnty Wkr; Hon Rl; NHS; Off Ade; Sch Pl; Stu Cncl; Andrews Univ; Med.

POWELL, LIONEL; Flint Northwestern HS; Flint, MI; 1/510 Hon Rl; Mth Clb; Natl Merit Ltr; St Of Michigan Comp Schlrshp; Schl Math Dept Awd; General Motors Inst; Engr.

POWELL, MARK; La Salle HS; Cincinnati, OH; 9/272 Hon Rl; NHS; Letter Bsbl; Letter Ftbl; Letter Trk; IM Sprt; Thomas More Coll; Acctg.

POWELL, PEGGY; Midland HS; Midland, MI; 11/486 Chrh Wkr; Hon Rl; JA; NHS; Letter Gym; Tmr; JA Awd; Michigan St Univ; Acctg.

POWELL, PERIANN; Martins Ferry HS; Martins Ferry, OH; 103/215 Hon Rl; Off Ade; Y-Teens; Fr Clb; Capt Bsktbl; Capt Trk; Pres GAA; Coll Of Steubenville; Cmnctns.

POWELL, RICHARD; Owendale Gagetown Area HS; Owendale, MI; 13/56 Cls Rep Frsh Cls; Trs Jr Cls; Trs Sr Cls; Band; Chrs; Hon Rl; Sch Pl; Stu Cncl; Letter Bsktbl; Letter Ftbl; Coll.

POWELL, SCOTT; Trinity HS; Garfield Hts, OH; 1/150 Hon Rl; Rptr Sch Nwsp; IM Sprt; Natl Merit Ltr; Trinity High Schlrshp; Commendation In Natl Test Of Assn Of Spanish; Won Election For Stu Senate Treas; Coll; Elec Tech.

POWELL, SELWYN K; Benedictine HS; Cleveland, OH; Hon Rl; NHS; Letter Wrstlng; IM Sprt; College; Electronics.

POWELL, STEPHANIE; Buena Vista HS; Sagimaw, MI; 15/185 Chrs; Chrh Wkr; Cmnty Wkr; Hon Rl; NHS; Mgrs; Pom Pon; Cit Awd; JETS Awd; Explorers Sec; Outstndng Serv In Youth Activities Awd; Perfect Attendance Awd; Michigan St Univ; Engr.

POWELL, STEVEN; Douglas Mac Arthur HS; Saginaw, MI; 14/307 Am Leg Boys St; Hon Rl; Pres NHS; Pol Wkr; Sch Pl; Stu Cncl; Spn Clb; Bsktbl; Alma Coll; Pre Law.

POWELL, SUZZETTE I; Harrison HS; Harrison, MI; Chrs; Chrh Wkr; Hon Rl; NHS; Off Ade; Yth Flsp; Mid Michigan Comm Coll; Sec.

POWELL, TERESA; Our Lady Of Mercy HS; Red Twp, MI; 3/325 Chrs; Chrh Wkr; Girl Scts; NHS; Sct Actv; Fr Clb; Trk; Natl Merit Ltr; College; Art.

POWER, ANN; Beaumont School For Girls; Shaker Hts, OH; Cls Rep Soph Cls; Cl Rep Jr Cls; VP Sr Cls; Sec Sr Cls; Girl Scts; Hosp Ade; Stu Cncl; Fr Clb; IM Sprt; Univ.

POWER, JAMES; Deer Park HS; Cincinnati, OH; Cls Rep Frsh Cls; Hon Rl; JA; Stu Cncl; Bsktbl; Trk; JA Awd; Univ Of Cincinnati; Mech Engr.

POWER, ROLFE; St Philip Catholic Cntrl HS; Battle Crk, MI; Cls Rep Frsh Cls; Cls Rep Soph Cls; Cl Rep Jr Cls; Cls Rep Sr Cls; Sal; Am Leg Boys St; Chrs; Chrh Wkr; Cmnty Wkr; Hon Rl; Battle Creek Exchange Clb Yth Of Month Awd; Elected To HS All Amer For Ldrshp Schlrshp; Rev G Owens Awd; Univ Of Notre Dame; Finance.

POWER, VICKIE; Utica HS; Newark, OH; 1/185 Val; Band; Hon Rl; Pres NHS; Off Ade; Capt Bsktbl; Letter Trk; OSU; Acctg.

POWERS, BEVERLY; Anderson HS; Anderson, IN; 48/438 Cls Rep Frsh Cls; Cls Rep Soph Cls; Cl Rep Jr Cls; Hon Rl; Jr NHS; NHS; Stu Cncl; Yrbk; Spn Clb; Tmr; Purdue Univ; Engr.

POWERS, DARRELL; Bluefield HS; Bluefield, WV; Chrh Wkr; Hon Rl; Spn Clb;.

POWERS, DEBORAH; Bedford HS; Bedford, OH; Off Ade; OEA; Vocational; Court Reporter.

POWERS, DENISE; New Haven HS; New Haven, IN; 8/300 Band; Chrs; Chrh Wkr; Cmnty Wkr; Girl Scts; Hon Rl; JA; Lbry Ade; Off Ade; Orch; Varsity Vllybll Letter 76; Outstndng Stdnt In Draftng 76; Outstndng Stdnt In Eng 76; Marion Coll; Elem Educ.

POWERS, JERRI; Indianapolis Baptist HS; Indianapolis, IN; 1/52 Pres Jr Cls; Band; Chrs; Hon Rl; Sch Pl; Yrbk; Sch Nwsp; Pep Clb; Chrldng; Univ; Pre Med.

POWERS, JOHN; Montpelier HS; Montpelier, OH; Boy Scts; Hon Rl; Ftbl; Gym; College; Engr.

POWERS, LAURETTE; Cardinal Stritch HS; Toledo, OH; 30/220 Cls Rep Frsh Cls; Cls Rep Soph Cls; Cl Rep Jr Cls; Hon Rl; NHS; Sch Pl; Stg Crw; Stu Cncl; Pep Clb; Spn Clb; Univ; Math.

POWERS, MICHAEL; Chaminade Julienne HS; Dayton, OH; Boy Scts; Socr; Letter Wrstlng; IM Sprt; Univ; Jrnlsm.

POWERS, MONICA; Saint Mary Academy; Monroe, MI; Cls Rep Frsh Cls; Cl Rep Jr Cls; Cls Rep Sr Cls; Chrh Wkr; Cmnty Wkr; Hon Rl; NHS; Stu Cncl; Rptr Yrbk; Monroe County Comm Coll.

POWERS, MONICA; St Mary Academy; Monroe, MI; 14/117 Cl Rep Jr Cls; Cls Rep Sr Cls; Chrh Wkr; Cmnty Wkr; Hon Rl; NHS; Stu Cncl; Rptr Yrbk; Monroe Cnty Cmnty Coll.

POWERS, NANCY R; Hathaway Brown Schl; Mayfield Hts, OH; Sec Sr Cls; AFS; Chrs; Chrh Wkr; Hon Rl; Pol Wkr; Yth Flsp; Ed Sch Nwsp; Bsbl; GAA; Univ.

POWERS, PEGGY; Mcauley HS; Cincinnati, OH; Cls Rep Frsh Cls; Cls Rep Soph Cls; JA; Bsbl; Bsktbl; Coach Actv; GAA; IM Sprt; Cincinnati Tech Coll; Bus.

POWERS, SANDRA E; Richmond HS; Richmond, IN; Hon Rl; Hosp Ade; NHS; Y-Teens; 4-H; Spn Clb; IM Sprt; Coll.

POWERS, SHARON; Warren Woods HS; Warren, MI; Girl Scts; Hon Rl; JA; Yth Flsp; Fr Clb; College; Law.

POWERS, TRACEY; Walnut Ridge HS; Columbus, OH; Chrs; Girl Scts; Hon Rl; Rptr Yrbk; Spn Clb; PPFtbl; Scr Kpr; Ohi State; Photographer.

POWERS, WENDY; Lakeville Memorial HS; Mt Morris, MI; Band; Hon Rl; NHS; GAA;.

POYNTER, BRENT; William Henry Harrison HS; Harrison, OH; Chrs; Hon Rl; Jr NHS; Lbry Ade; Stg Crw; Drama Clb; Spn Clb; Bsktbl; NSF Stdnt Sci Training Prog 78; Engr Sci Sem & Workshop 79; Univ; Naval Archt.

POYNTER, LISA; Whiteland Cmnty HS; Whiteland, IN; 32/210 Band; Chrs; Chrh Wkr; FCA; NHS; Sch Mus; Key Clb; Pep Clb; Bsktbl; Letter Ten; Ball St Univ; Spec Ed.

POZDOL, PEGGY; Marian HS; Birmingham, MI; Cls Rep Frsh Cls; Cls Rep Soph Cls; Cmnty Wkr; Girl Scts; Hon Rl; Lit Mag; NHS; PAVAS; Stu Cncl; Spn Clb; Univ Of Michigan; Dance.

POZNIK, JAMES; St Joseph HS; Euclid, OH; 48/300 Hon Rl; Key Clb; Spn Clb; IM Sprt; Cleveland St Univ; Civil Engr.

POZZUTO, JOANN; Maplewood HS; Cortland, OH; Cl Rep Jr Cls; Cls Rep Sr Cls; Chrs; Cmnty Wkr; Stu Cncl; Sch Nwsp; 4-H; 4-H Awd; College.

PRAHST, LINDA; James Ford Rhodes HS; Cleveland, OH; Chrs; Chrh Wkr; Hon Rl; JA; Jr NHS; NHS; Yth Flsp; Ger Clb; Sci Clb; College; Social Work.

PRAKEL, ANDY; Versailles HS; Versailles, OH; 15/125 Cls Rep Soph Cls; Boy Scts; NHS; Stu Cncl; Letter Bsktbl; Letter Glf; Letter Trk; Univ; Acctg.

PRANGE, GREGORY; Seymour HS; Seymour, IN; 18/288 VP Soph Cls; Am Leg Boys St; Chrh Wkr; Hon Rl; Yth Flsp; Rptr Yrbk; Bsktbl; Ftbl; IM Sprt; Elk Awd; Indiana Univ; Bus Admin.

PRASEK, PAM; West Geauga HS; Chesterland, OH; Sec Frsh Cls; Band; Chrs; Drl Tm; Hon Rl; Off Ade; Stu Cncl; Yrbk; Pep Clb; Capt Chrldng;.

PRATER, ANITA; Vinton County Consoldtd HS; Hamden, OH; Trs Sr Cls; Am Leg Aux Girls St; Band; Cmnty Wkr; Hon Rl; NHS; Fr Clb; Shawnee St Voc Schl; Dent Hygiene.

PRATER, BETTY J; Corunna HS; Corunna, MI; Cls Rep Frsh Cls; Hon Rl; Lbry Ade; College; Sec.

PRATER, DAVID L; Williamson HS; Williamson, WV; Am Leg Boys St; Chrh Wkr; Hon Rl; NHS; Sci Clb; Runnr Up St Bible Quiz Team 78; West Virginia Tech; Indust Chem.

PRATER, JOSEPH; John Glenn HS; Westland, MI; 65/725 Boy Scts; Orch; Sct Actv; Crs Cntry; Trk; Wrstlng; Eastern Michigan Univ; Elec Engr.

PRATER, RONDA; Bluffton HS; Bluffton, IN; Band; Chrs; Chrh Wkr; Hosp Ade; Yth Flsp; Ger Clb; Bsktbl; Letter Ten; Univ; Art Educ.

PRATHER, DORIAN; Servite HS; Detroit, MI; Chrs; Chrh Wkr; Letter Bsktbl; Letter Crs Cntry; Letter Trk; Scr Kpr; JC Awd; Univ; Psych.

PRATHER, SUSAN; Mount Healthy HS; Cincinnati, OH; 73/572 Chrs; Chrh Wkr; FCA; Hon Rl; Sch Mus; Sch Pl; Rptr Sch Nwsp; Beta Clb; Letter Ten; Christ; Nursing.

PRATT, ALAN; L C Mohr HS; South Haven, MI; Hon Rl; NHS; Crs Cntry; Trk; IM Sprt; Univ.

PRATT, BARB; Tippecanoe Valley HS; Rochester, IN; 53/160 Chrs; Yth Flsp; Yrbk; Drama Clb; 4-H; Fr Clb; Pep Clb; Ten; Chrldng; Capt IM Sprt; Vocational Schl; Cosmetology.

PRATT, CYNTHIA; Northwest HS; Canal Fulton, OH; Cls Rep Frsh Cls; Cls Rep Soph Cls; Cl Rep Jr Cls; Cls Rep Sr Cls; Band; Hon Rl; NHS; Stu Cncl; Yrbk; Pres Fr Clb; High Pt Rnk Trck Rnr 79; Univ; Law.

PRATT, GREGORY; Everett HS; Lansing, MI; Hon Rl; Jr NHS; Sch Pl; Ed Sch Nwsp; Swmmng; St Of Mich Financial Aid Schlrshp 79; Lansing Cmnty Coll; Pharm.

PRATT, JEFF; Doddridge County HS; Salem, WV; Treas Band; Drm Mjrt; Hon Rl; NHS; Stu Cncl; VP Yth Flsp; 4-H; Univ; Engr.

PRATT, KEN; New Bremen Local HS; New Bremen, OH; 12/63 Pres Frsh Cls; Trs Sr Cls; Am Leg Boys St; Chrs; Hon Rl; Jr NHS; NHS; Sprt Ed Sch Nwsp; Drama Clb; Capt Ftbl; West Point Military Acad.

PRATT, KIM; Grand Ledge HS; Mulliken, MI; Girl Scts; Hon Rl; Lbry Ade; 4-H; Lat Clb; 4-H Awd; Univ; Bio Chem.

PRATT, KRISTEN; Clinton HS; Clinton, MI; Cls Rep Frsh Cls; Trs Soph Cls; Trs Jr Cls; Hon Rl; NHS; Stg Crw; Pep Clb; Letter Bsbl; Letter Bsktbl; Letter Trk; Michigan St Univ; Phys Ed.

PRATT, LINDA; West Carrollton HS; Dayton, OH; Debate Tm; Yth Flsp; College; Eng.

PRATT, MICHELLE; Harman HS; Harman, WV; Band; Chrs; Hon Rl; FBLA; FFA; Bsktbl; College; Nursing.

PRATT, ROBIN; Lake Michigan Catholic HS; Benton Harbor, MI; 1/104 Cmnty Wkr; Hon Rl; Sch Mus; Sch Pl; Stg Crw; Drama Clb; IM Sprt; DAR Awd; Univ; Soc Work.

PRATT, WILLIAM; Lewis County HS; Weston, WV; West Vir Univ; Animal.

PRATT, WILLIAM; Caro HS; Caro, MI; Band; Hon Rl; NHS; Sch Mus; Yth Flsp; Fr Clb; Letter Ftbl; Capt Wrstlng; Tri Cnty Hnrs Band Timpianist; Catholic Yth Ministry Comm; AAU/USWF Freestyle Wrestling; Coll; Engr.

PRATT, YVETTE; East HS; Akron, OH; Sec Chrh Wkr; DECA; Pep Clb; Spn Clb; Trk; Akron Univ; Law.

PRAUSE, DOUG; Central Lake HS; Central Lake, MI; Hon Rl; Voc Schl; Auto.

PRAY, BETH; Ovid Elsie HS; Ovid, MI; Girl Scts; Hon Rl; Lbry Ade; Off Ade; Rptr Sch Nwsp; Chrldng; PPFtbl; Lansing Bus Inst; Sec.

PRCHLIK, JOE; Strongsville Sr HS; Strongsville, OH; Letter Ftbl; Letter Wrstlng; Ftbl UGCL Radio Plyr Of Wk 78; Wrstlng Of Wk 79; Brunswock Invttnl Wrstlngn Tourn Chap 175 Lbs 79; Univ; Hist.

PREAST, J; Midland Trail HS; Gauley Bridge, WV; Chrh Wkr; Cmnty Wkr; FCA; Hon Rl; VICA; Bsbl; Bsktbl; Ten; IM Sprt; Mgrs; WVU; Electrical Engr.

PREBENDA, MICHAEL; Catholic Central HS; Livonia, MI; Cmnty Wkr; Hon Rl; NHS; Pol Wkr; Ten; Kalamazoo Univ; Bio.

PRECHTEL, JANE; Reitz Memorial HS; Evansville, IN; Cls Rep Soph Cls; Chrs; Hon Rl; NHS; Stu Cncl; Yth Flsp; Fr Clb; Cit Awd; Purdue Univ.

PREDRAGOVICH, SHERRY; Eastern HS; Beaver, OH; 4/65 Hon Rl; Jr NHS; Sch Pl; Yrbk; Drama Clb; 4-H; FTA; Pep Clb; Spn Clb; Letter Bsktbl; Shawnee St Coll; Radiologic Tech.

PREECE, BRENDA; Tuslaw HS; Massillon, OH; 6/183 Cls Rep Sr Cls; Am Leg Aux Girls St; Chrs; Hon Rl; NHS; Sch Mus; Stu Cncl; Sec Y-Teens; Pep Clb; DAR Awd; Stark Tech Coll; Comp Prog.

PREECE, DIANNA; Wayne HS; Wayne, WV; Band; Hon Rl; Treas Jr NHS; NHS; Yth Flsp; Sprt Ed Sch Nwsp; Letter Bsktbl; Glf; Trk; Scr Kpr; Bst Sprts Page UHSP 79; 3rd Pl On Natl Math Exam 76; Univ.

PRENDERGAST, MARY; Villa Angela Academy; Cleveland, OH; Cls Rep Frsh Cls; Cls Rep Soph Cls; Cl Rep Jr Cls; Chrs; Chrh Wkr; Cmnty Wkr; Hosp Ade; Red Cr Ade; Stu Cncl; Lat Clb; Christian Cmnty Awd 77; Service 77; Univ; Nurse.

PRENGER, NANCY; Coldwater HS; Coldwater, OH; 11/137 Am Leg Aux Girls St; Band; Chrs; Chrh Wkr; Hon Rl; Sch Mus; Drama Clb; Gym; Swmmng; Trk; Univ Of Cincinnati; Architectureengr.

PRENTICE, DOUGLAS; Stow HS; Stow, OH; Aud/Vis; Hon Rl; Yth Flsp; Nyack Univ; Missionary.

PRENTICE, TRACY; Liberty HS; Niles, OH; Hon Rl; Red Cr Ade; Yth Flsp; Sec Job.

PRENTISS, J; St Francis HS; Morgantown, WV; 16/67 Pres Frsh Cls; Cl Rep Jr Cls; Hon Rl; NHS; Stu Cncl; Mth Clb; Spn Clb; Ten; West Virginia Univ.

PRESAR, DAVID; Perrysburg HS; Perrysburg, OH; Hon Rl; NHS; Letter Crs Cntry; Letter Trk; Univ.

PRESAR, SUSAN; Perrysburg HS; Perrysburg, OH; 5/250 Hon Rl; NHS; Spn Clb; Crs Cntry; Trk; Scr Kpr; Tmr; Univ.

PRESNELL, JENNY; Olmsted Falls HS; Olmsted Falls, OH; Cls Rep Soph Cls; Cl Rep Jr Cls; VP Chrs; Letter Drl Tm; Sch Mus; Sch Pl; Stu Cncl; Pres Drama Clb; Pres Ger Clb; PPFtbl; Best Actress; Winter Court Attendant; College; Music.

PRESSLER, BARBARA; Mississinewa HS; Gas City, IN; 1/209 Am Leg Aux Girls St; Chrs; Hon Rl; NHS; Sch Mus; Sch Pl; Ed Yrbk; Drama Clb; FTA; Sec Spn Clb; Manchester Coll; Library Sci.

PRESSLER, EDNA; Bloomington HS South; Bloomington, IN; 18/385 Trs Jr Cls; Cl Rep Jr Cls; Hon Rl; Jr NHS; Stu Cncl; Letter Swmmng; Univ; Liberal Arts.

PREST, NANCY; Cedar Lake Acad; Onaway, MI; Band; Chrh Wkr; Hon Rl; Off Ade; Sch Pl; IM Sprt; Andrews Univ; Hme Ec Tchr.

PRESTON, CINDY; Eaton HS; Eaton, OH; Am Leg Aux Girls St; Band; Hon Rl; Yrbk; Sch Nwsp; Drama Clb; Fr Clb; Pep Clb; GAA; Pres Awd; Brigham Young Univ; Architecture.

PRESTON, CONSTANCE; Gull Lake HS; Augusta, MI; 18/248 Sec Drm Mjrt; Hon Rl; Sec JA; NHS; Sch Mus; Yth Flsp; DECA; Crs Cntry; Ten; Western Michigan Univ; Aircraft Engr.

PRESTON, LOREE; Greenwood Cmnty HS; Cincinnati, OH; Band; Chrh Wkr; Hon Rl; Yth Flsp; 4-H; Taylor Univ; Acctg.

PRESTON, ROBERT J; Houston HS; Piqua, OH; 14/75 Cls Rep Frsh Cls; Cls Rep Soph Cls; Cl Rep Jr Cls; Cls Rep Sr Cls; Band; Boy Scts; Chrs; Hon Rl; Lbry Ade; Off Ade; All Ohio St Fair Band; Outstanding Band Mbr & John Phillip Sousa Awd; Ohio St Univ Reading Session; Ohio St Univ; Law.

PRESTON, STEVEN; North Muskegon HS; N Muskegon, MI; Pres Jr Cls; Hon Rl; Sch Pl; Stg Crw; Fr Clb; Letter Bsbl; Letter Ftbl; Hockey; Coach Actv; IM Sprt; College; Engr.

PRESTON, THOMAS; Moeller HS; Cincinnati, OH; 11/260 Boy Scts; Hon Rl; NHS; Off Ade; Sch Pl; Sct Actv; Sch Nwsp; Fr Clb; Pep Clb; Letter Trk; 1 Eng Hist & Rel 1978; 2 In French III 1978; 2 In French II 1977; Whos Who In Foreign Lang 1977; George Town Univ; Med.

PRETTY, STEVEN; Walled Lake Cntrl HS; Union Lake, MI; 32/350 Hon Rl; Hosp Ade; NHS; Ger Clb; Sci Clb; Am Leg Awd; Natl Merit SF; Cornell Univ; Molecular Biochem.

PREUSS, DAVID; Westlake HS; Westlake, OH; 1/310 Chrh Wkr; NHS; Glf; Capt Ten; IM Sprt; Cornell Univ; Pre Med.

PREUSSE, RICHARD S; North Central HS; Indianapolis, IN; 108/999 Hon Rl; Pres JA; Mod UN; NHS; Chmn Stu Cncl; Key Clb; JA Awd; Opt Clb Awd; Vanderbilt Univ; Med.

PREWITT, CLAUDIA; Blanchester HS; Blanchester, OH; 62/154 Drl Tm; Girl Scts; Hon Rl; JA; Stg Crw; Yth Flsp; Letter Trk; GAA; Twrlr; Pres Awd; Coll.

PRIBOR, DONALD; St Francis De Sales HS; Toledo, OH; Band; Hon Rl; NHS; Natl Merit SF; Winner Of J S Bach Internatl Cmptrs For Jr Pianists; 1st Pl Winner Of Ohio Music Tchrs Assoc Competition; College; Music.

PRICE, ANDREA; Admiral King HS; Lorain, OH; Chrs; Girl Scts; Hon Rl; Lbry Ade; Off Ade; FHA; Cincinatti Univ; Nursing.

PRICE, ANDREA J; Heritage Christian HS; Carmel, IN; Sec Frsh Cls; Aud/Vis; Band; Chrs; Hon Rl; NHS; Sch Mus; Drama Clb; Socr; College; Computer Sci.

PRICE, ART; Hilliard HS; Columbus, OH; Cls Rep Frsh Cls; Cl Rep Jr Cls; Hon Rl; Lbry Ade; Stu Cncl; Yrbk; Crs Cntry; IM Sprt; Mgrs; Tmr; Ohio State Univ; Architecture.

PRICE, BAMBI L; Point Pleasant HS; Pt Pleasant, WV; Band; Chrs; Hosp Ade; 4-H; Fr Clb; Letter Trk; Whos Who In Amer Music 78; West Virginia Univ; Music.

PRICE, BARBARA; Plymouth Salem HS; Plymouth, MI; Hon Rl; Off Ade; Sch Mus; Sch Pl; Stg Crw; Mic State Univ; Bus.

PRICE, CAROL; Forest Hills Central HS; Ada, MI; 51/240 Hon Rl; Quill & Scroll; Rptr Sch Nwsp; Letter Bsktbl; PPFtbl; Varsity Sftbl All Confrnc Selection; N Michigan Univ; Criminal Justice.

PRICE, CHRISTINE; Fairless HS; Canton, OH; VP Band; Sec Chrs; NHS; Sch Mus; Stu Cncl; Rptr Yrbk; 4-H; Bob Jones Univ; TV/RADIO Brdcstng.

PRICE, CONNIE; Berea HS; Berea, OH; AFS; Band; Hon Rl; NHS; Pep Clb; Chrldng; Tmr; Twrlr; Home Economics.

PRICE, DAN; Ridgedale HS; Marion, OH; 22/78 Hon Rl; Lit Mag; Quill & Scroll; Sch Mus; Stg Crw; Ed Sch Nwsp; Sprt Ed Sch Nwsp; Rptr Sch Nwsp; Sch Nwsp; Rdo Clb; Ohio St Univ; Jrnlsm.

PRICE, DAVE; River Valley HS; Marion, OH; 17/193 4-H; Treas FFA; Bsktbl; Letter Wrstlng; IM Sprt; 4-H Awd; Ohio St Univ; Math.

PRICE, DAWN; Roscommon HS; Roscommon, MI; Trs Frsh Cls; Cls Rep Soph Cls; Cl Rep Jr Cls; Band; Chrs; NHS; Off Ade; Sch Mus; Stu Cncl; Letter Bsktbl; Univ Of Michigan; Biology.

PRICE, DENISE; Bremen HS; Bremen, IN; 21/121 Band; Cmp Fr Grls; Chrs; Chrh Wkr; Hon Rl; Sch Mus; Stg Crw; Yth Flsp; VP 4-H; FTA; Hoosier Schlr & Schlrshp 79; Chr Solo & Ensemble Cntst 77 79; Tri Kappa Hnr Roll Awd 76; Ball St Univ; Elem Educ.

PRICE, DENISE; Vermillon HS; Vermilion, OH; VP Sr Cls; Girl Scts; Hon Rl; Off Ade; Sch Mus; OEA; Gym; Trk; Chrldng; C of C Awd; Varsity Volleyball 1978; Exec Sec.

PRICE, DENISE; Brookville HS; Brookville, IN; 50/200 Cls Rep Sr Cls; Band; Chrs; Drm Mjrt; Hon Rl; NHS; Stu Cncl; Ger Clb; Voc Schl; Sec.

PRICE, DIXIE; Terre Haute N Vigo HS; Terre Haute, IN; Band; Chrs; Chrh Wkr; Hon Rl; Orch; Sch Mus; Yth Flsp; Pres Y-Teens; VP Lat Clb; Am Leg Awd; Music Schlrshp; Depauw Univ; Music.

PRICE, DOROTHY G; Pike Central HS; Stendal, IN; Band; Hosp Ade; Off Ade; Sch Pl; Trk; PPFtbl; Girl Scts; Sch Mus; Yth Flsp; Drama Clb; Nat Guard; Bus.

PRICE, FAITH A; Hardin Northern HS; Dunkirk, OH; 11/59 Band; Chrs; Chrh Wkr; Cmnty Wkr; Hon Rl; Sec Yth Flsp; Rptr Sch Nwsp; Sch Nwsp; 4-H; OEA; Outstndng Bndmn Awd 79; Hall Of Fame Music Awd From Purdue Univ Solo & Trio Awd For Instrmntl Music; Sec.

PRICE, G JOSEPH; Rietz Mem HS; Newburgh, IN; Aud/Vis; FCA; Hon Rl; Pol Wkr; Rptr Sch Nwsp; Sch Nwsp; Key Clb; Letter Ftbl; Harlaxton Coll; Busns.

PRICE, GREGORY; Edwardsburg HS; Edwardsburg, MI; Hon Rl; Jr NHS; Bsbl; Bsktbl; Ftbl; Univ; Acctg.

PRICE, HAROLD; South Haven HS; S Haven, MI; Letter Band; Chrs; Hon Rl; NHS; Stg Crw; Letter Ftbl; Bd Of Educ Schlrshp Cert 77 78 & 79; Construction.

PRICE, JAMES; Utica HS; Utica, MI; Hon Rl; NHS; Swmmng; Mgrs; Tmr; Mas Awd; College.

PRICE, JEFFREY; Hardin Northern HS; Dunkirk, OH; VP Frsh Cls; Pres Jr Cls; Band; Hon Rl; NHS; Stu Cncl; Fr Clb; Key Clb; Letter Bsbl; Letter Bsktbl; Punt Pass Kick; Summer Bsbl HS Athletics; College; Education.

PRICE, JEFFREY; Jackson County Western HS; Spring Arbor, MI; Cls Rep Frsh Cls; Debate Tm; Natl Forn Lg; Off Ade; Pol Wkr; Sch Mus; Sch Pl; Stu Cncl; Drama Clb; Coach Actv; Pres Of Student Council 80; Ath Trainer Of Schl Sports 80; Dir Of Intramural Sports 80; Wayne St Univ; Law.

PRICE, JOE; Bellefontaine Sr HS; Bellfontaine, OH; Univ; Geology.

PRICE, KATHY A; Big Walnut HS; Sunbury, OH; 1/235 Band; Chrs; Chrh Wkr; Girl Scts; Hon Rl; Fr Clb; Univ; Math.

PRICE, KEVIN; Hardin Northern HS; Dunkirk, OH; Cmnty Wkr; Yth Flsp; Rptr Yrbk; Fr Clb; Air Force; Song Writer.

PRICE, KEVIN; East HS; Sciotoville, OH; 4/80 Chrh Wkr; Hon Rl; Lbry Ade; NHS; Sct Actv; Yrbk; Letter Bsbl; Schlrshp Team; Sci Placed 3sd In Dist; Bio; Lee Coll; Chem Engr.

PRICE, KIM; Zanesville HS; Zanesville, OH; Hon Rl; Lbry Ade; Off Ade; Orch; PAVAS; Red Cr Ade; Sch Mus; Sch Pl; Stu Cncl; 4-H; Ohio St Univ; Sociology.

PRICE, KIMBERLEY; Warren Central HS; Indianapolis, IN; 49/807 Girl Scts; Hon Rl; Jr NHS; NHS; Yth Flsp; Rptr Yrbk; Ger Clb; College; Elem Educ.

PRICE, KIMBERLY L; N Union HS; Richwood, OH; Band; Chrh Wkr; Cmnty Wkr; Hon Rl; Lbry Ade; Orch; Yth Flsp;.

PRICE, LARRY; Carlisle Sr HS; Carlisle, OH; 20/184 Chrs; Hon Rl; NHS; Off Ade; Ed Yrbk; Rptr Yrbk; Rptr Sch Nwsp; Spn Clb; Wright St Univ; English.

PRICE, LAURA; Yorktown HS; Yorktown, IN; 14/198 Hon Rl; NHS; FBLA; Sci Clb; Purdue Univ; Vet.

PRICE, LAURIE; Durand HS; Bancroft, MI; 2/213 Sal; Chrs; Chrh Wkr; Hon Rl; NHS; Rptr Yrbk; Rptr Sch Nwsp; 4-H; FFA; PPFtbl; Michigan Competitive Schlrshp; CMU Awd Trustees Outstndng HS Grad Awd; Central Michigan Univ; Journalism.

PRICE, LEWIS R; East HS; Columbus, OH; Hon Rl ; 4-H; FTA; 4-H Awd; Univ; Nursing.

PRICE, MARI; Brookville HS; Brookville, IN; 33/204 Band; Hon Rl; Rptr Sch Nwsp; Bsktbl; Glf; Ten; Trk; GAA; I U East ; Cpa.

PRICE, MARK; Columbia City Joint HS; Columbia City, IN; 10/253 Hst Jr Cls; Am Leg Boys St; Band; Drm Mjrt; Hon Rl; Natl Forn Lg; NHS; Pol Wkr; Sch Mus; Rptr Sch Nwsp; St Semi Finalist Century III Leaders Schlrshp; ECI Schlrshp Semi Finalist; Awd Of Exc Univ Of Dallas; Univ Of Dallas; Psych.

PRICE, MARK; North HS; Evansville, IN; 19/362 Chrs; Hon Rl; Jr NHS; Sch Mus; OEA; Letter Bsbl; Bsktbl; Cit Awd; In St Univ Evansville Acad Schlrshp 79; Hoosier Schlr St Schlrshp 79; Ambassador Awd In Office Educ Assoc; Indiana St Univ; Bus.

PRICE, MICHAEL J; Morton Sr HS; Hammond, IN; 35/477 Hon Rl; Ger Clb; Mth Clb; Letter Ten; Trk; Scr Kpr; Univ.

PRICE, MINDY; Muskegon Sr HS; Muskegon, MI; Hon Rl; JA; 4-H; Swmmng; 4-H Awd; Jr Coll Of Grand Rapids; Data Proc.

PRICE, PAULA; Mannington HS; Mannington, WV; Chrh Wkr; FFA; FFA Pres 79; FFA Star Green

Hand 78; FFA Chapt Sweetheart 78; Univ; Phys Educ Tchr.

PRICE, ROBERT A; Cambridge HS; Cambridge, OH; Cls Rep Frsh Cls; Hon Rl; Bsktbl; Trk; Natl Merit Ltr; Ohi State Univ; X Ray Tech.

PRICE, ROBERT M; Girard HS; Girard, OH; 11/212 Hon Rl; NHS; Yrbk; Letter Bsktbl; Letter Glf; Natl Merit Ltr; Younstown St Univ; Math.

PRICE, RONNY; North Knox HS; Oaktown, IN; 93/140 FCA; Fr Clb; Bsktbl; Crs Cntry; Swmmng; Wrstlng; Cit Awd; Wabash Vly Jr Coll; Auto Mech.

PRICE, SANDRA; Fulton HS; Perrinton, MI; 11/99 Hon Rl; Off Ade; Sch Pl; Sch Nwsp; 4-H; Mth Clb; Bsktbl; Trk; Pres Awd; CMU.

PRICE, TAMELA G; Loveland Hurst HS; Ft Worth, TX; Hon Rl; Health Occup Stdn Tof Amer Partlmntrn 78; Southern Methodist Univ; Law.

PRICE, TARA; Oakwood HS; Dayton, OH; Band; Chrh Wkr; Hon Rl; Off Ade; Yth Flsp; Letter Ten; College; Pharmacy.

PRICE, TERESA; North Union HS; Richwood, OH; Cl Rep Jr Cls; Am Leg Aux Girls St; Band; Chrs; Hon Rl; Lit Mag; NHS; Sch Mus; Stu Cncl; 4-H; Brnz Awd Eng 76; Bio Schlshp Test 16th Dist 77; Chopin Awd Chrs Gold Awd Chrs 78; Univ; Music.

PRICE, YOLANDA; Martin Luther King HS; Detroit, MI; Drl Tm; Hon Rl; ROTC; Rptr Sch Nwsp; Pep Clb; Letter Glf; Most Improved Player In Golf 79; Michigan St Univ; Engr.

PRICHARD, AMY; Bath HS; Lima, OH; 14/200 Am Leg Aux Girls St; Band; Chrs; Hon Rl; Jr NHS; NHS; Stu Cncl; Sci Clb; Spn Clb; Bsktbl; Northwestern Univ.

PRICHARD, MARY E; Wayne HS; Wayne, WV; Trs Frsh Cls; Girl Scts; Hon Rl; Jr NHS; Lbry Ade; NHS; Pres Stu Cncl; Rptr Sch Nwsp; Pres 4-H; Lat Clb; Schlrshp To Citizen Short Course In Washington D C; Competed In St 4 H Roundup; Rep In W Va St Fair Pageant; West Virginia Univ; Law.

PRICING, LINDA; Frankenmuth HS; Frankenmuth, MI; 17/193 Cls Rep Frsh Cls; Cl Rep Jr Cls; Band; Chrs; Chrh Wkr; Hon Rl; Jr NHS; Natl Forn Lg; NHS; Orch; Saginaw Symphony Yng Peoples Concert Assoc Wnnr 79; Musicla Arts Inc Schlrshp Wnnr 79; Univ Of Michigan; Music.

PRIEBE, DOUGLAS; Benton Harbor HS; Benton Hbr, MI; Band; Hon Rl; Univ; Engr.

PRIEBE, JOSEPH; Saint Francis De Sales HS; Sylvania, OH; Hon Rl; Sch Mus; Sch Pl; Stg Crw; Rptr Sch Nwsp; Sch Nwsp; IM Sprt; Univ Of Toledo; Wildlife Mgmt.

PRIEBE, LAURA; St Clement HS; Detroit, MI; Chrh Wkr; Hon Rl; Off Ade; Orch; Sch Nwsp; BEOG 79; Recgntn For The St Of Mi Comp Schlshp Progr 79; Wayne St Univ; Pre Phys Ther.

PRIEBE, SALLY; Clarkston Sr HS; Clarkston, MI; 41/510 Band; Chrs; Chrh Wkr; PAVAS; Sch Mus; Sch Pl; Stg Crw; Yth Flsp; Drama Clb; Pep Clb; Coll; Arts.

PRIEHS, GRANT; Carsonville Port Sanilac HS; Carsonville, MI; 1/70 Pres Soph Cls; Val; NHS; PAVAS; Sch Mus; Sch Pl; Ed Yrbk; St Clair Cnty Comm College; Advertis.

PRIELIPP, HAROLD; Deerfield Public HS; Deerfield, MI; Cmnty Wkr; Hon Rl; Yrbk; Univ; Archt.

PRIEM, BETSY; Magnificat HS; Middleburg Ht, OH; Chrh Wkr; Cmnty Wkr; NHS; Sch Mus; Rptr Sch Nwsp; Natl Merit Ltr; Univ; Chem Engr.

PRIEM, DAVID; Padua Franciscan HS; Middleburg Hts, OH; Chrh Wkr; Cmnty Wkr; Hon Rl; Pol Wkr; Stg Crw; Sci Clb; Rose Hulman; Mech Engr.

PRIEM, MARY E; Magnificat HS; Middleburg Hts, OH; Chrh Wkr; NHS; Sch Mus; Rptr Sch Nwsp; Natl Merit Ltr; Univ; Chem Engr.

PRIESMEYER, BILL; Scecing Memorial HS; Greenfield, IN; Trs Frsh Cls; Trs Soph Cls; Hon Rl; Sch Nwsp; 4-H; FFA; Mth Clb; Bsbl; Wrstlng; IM Sprt; Ind Univ; Geographer.

PRIESS, CHERYL; Yale HS; Goodells, MI; Sec Soph Cls; Hon Rl; NHS; 4-H; St Clair Cnty Comm Coll; Phys Ther.

PRIEST, DEBBIE; Fairfield HS; Highland, OH; 17/62 Lbry Ade; Off Ade; Sch Pl; Stg Crw; Yrbk; Rptr Sch Nwsp; Sch Nwsp; Drama Clb; FHA; FTA; Bus Schl.

PRIEST, RUTH; Edward Lee Mc Clain HS; Greenfield, OH; 11/161 Chrs; NHS; Sch Pl; Rptr Sch Nwsp; Drama Clb; 4-H; Chrldng; IM Sprt; 4-H Awd; Ohio Univ; Interior Decorating.

PRIESTLEY, SANDRA; Flushing HS; Flushing, MI; Girl Scts; Sct Actv; Fr Clb; Natl Merit Ltr; Natl Merit SF; Northwood Inst; Interior Mrktng.

PRILLIMAN, BRYAN; Kewanna HS; Kewanna, IN; 4/18 Pres Frsh Cls; Cls Rep Soph Cls; Pres Sr Cls; Band; Boy Scts; Chrs; Chrh Wkr; Cmnty Wkr; Hon Rl; Mdrgl; Milligan Coll; Personnel Mgmt.

PRINCE, DEIRDRE; Parkersburg HS; Parkersburg, WV; Pres Frsh Cls; Hon Rl; Y-Teens; Univ; Law Enfrcmnt.

PRINCE, EVELYN; Park Hills HS; Wp Afb, OH; Chrs; Chrh Wkr; Drl Tm; Girl Scts; Hon Rl; JA; Jr NHS; Spn Clb; Trk; Outstndng Stu Awd; Awd For Academic Distinction; College; Spanish.

PRINCE, JANICE; John Hay HS; Cleveland, OH; 140250 Drl Tm; Hon Rl; JA; NHS; Off Ade; Ger Clb; OEA; Pom Pon; Bright Future Award WYCA 79; Carlow Coll; Bus Mgmt.

PRINCE, JEANETTE; Buena Vista HS; Saginaw, MI; Pres Frsh Cls; Cls Rep Soph Cls; Pres Jr Cls; Cmnty Wkr; Hon Rl; Hosp Ade; Red Cr Ade; Stu Cncl; Drama Clb; Bsbl; Wayne St Univ; Phys Ther.

PRINCE, JENE; Rochester HS; Rochester, MI; Chrs; NHS; Letter Bsbl; PPFtbl; Michigan Tech Univ; Elec Engr.

PRINCE, KAREN; Akron South HS; Akron, OH; 10/134 Chrh Wkr; Girl Scts; Hon Rl; NHS; Pol Wkr; Key Clb; OEA; Pep Clb; Gym; Trk; Ohio Univ Athens; Bus Admin.

PRINCE, LENAYA; East Kentwood HS; Grand Rapids, MI; Natl Forn Lg; Orch; Rptr Sch Nwsp; Ger Clb; Central Michigan Univ; Jrnlsm.

PRINCE, MARK; Western Boone HS; Thorntown, IN; Band; Boy Scts; Chrh Wkr; Hosp Ade; Lbry Ade; Sch Mus; Sct Actv; Stg Crw; 4-H; Lat Clb; Univ; Nursing.

PRINCE, PATRICIA; Canfield HS; Canfield, OH; 5/270 Cls Rep Frsh Cls; Cls Rep Soph Cls; Cl Rep Jr Cls; Cls Rep Sr Cls; Am Leg Aux Girls St; Chrs; Girl Scts; Hon Rl; NHS; Sch Mus; Youngstown St Univ; Acctg.

PRINCE, THOMAS A; North Harrison HS; Palmyra, IN; 18/160 VP Frsh Cls; Aud/Vis; Chrs; Hon Rl; NHS; Sch Mus; Stu Cncl; Pep Clb; Letter Trk; JETS Awd; Purdue Univ; Engr.

PRINDLE, E; The Andrews Sch For Grls HS; Creston, OH; Band; Chrs; Girl Scts; Hon Rl; Sch Mus; Sch Pl; Yth Flsp; Trk; IM Sprt; College; Recording Eng.

PRINE, PAUL C; Fairborn Baker HS; Dayton, OH; Band; Chrs; Hon Rl; Jr NHS; Lit Mag; Mdrgl; Rptr Yrbk; Ftbl; Univ Of South Ala; Musician.

PRINE, RACHEL; Graham HS; St Paris, OH; Chrs; Hon Rl; Off Ade; Sch Mus; Yth Flsp; Rptr Yrbk; Yrbk; Rptr Sch Nwsp; FTA; Ger Clb; Foreign Lang.

PRINGLE, FRED J; Mifflin HS; Columbus, OH; Am Leg Boys St; Boy Scts; Hon Rl; Jr NHS; Sct Actv; VP Yth Flsp; VP Fr Clb; Crs Cntry; Trk; God Cntry Awd; West Point Acad; Aero Engr.

PRINGLE, GARRY; Millington HS; Clio, MI; 9/143 Ftbl; Wrstlng; General Motors Institute; Mgmt.

PRINGLE, GARY; Edgerton HS; Edgerton, OH; 7/87 Pres Frsh Cls; Pres Jr Cls; Am Leg Boys St; Hon Rl; NHS; Sch Mus; Stu Cncl; Spn Clb; Letter Ftbl; Letter Trk; College; Busns.

PRINGLE, GARY W; Edgerton HS; Edginton, OH; 8/85 Pres Frsh Cls; Cls Rep Soph Cls; Pres Jr Cls; Hon Rl; NHS; Sch Mus; Stu Cncl; Spn Clb; Ftbl; Wrstlng, Univ.

PRINGLE, KAY; Peck HS; Peck, MI; 12/61 Off Ade; Pres 4-H; Letter Bsktbl; Letter Trk; College.

PRINTZ, MARCIA; Crooksville HS; Crooksville, OH; Chrh Wkr; Drl Tm; Hon Rl; Sch Pl; Yth Flsp; 4-H; GAA; Mgrs; Pom Pon; 4-H Awd; Univ.

PRINZBACH, MARY; Princeton HS; Princeton, WV; 84/354 Hon Rl; Sdlty; 4-H; Fr Clb; Keyettes; Pep Clb; Concord Coll.

PRIOR, CAROLYN; West Geauga HS; Chagrin Falls, OH; 33/352 Cls Rep Frsh Cls; Cls Rep Soph Cls; Cl Rep Jr Cls; AFS; Band; Chrs; Girl Scts; Jr NHS; NHS; Otterbein College.

PRIOR, JODIE; Heath HS; Heath, OH; Band; Chrs; Chrh Wkr; Drl Tm; Lbry Ade; Mdrgl; Off Ade; Sch Mus; Stg Crw; Rptr Yrbk; Ohio State Branch; Real Estate.

PRISK, GAYL; Grosse Pointe N HS; Grosse Pt Wds, MI; 26/465 Band; Chrh Wkr; FCA; Girl Scts; Hon Rl; Lbry Ade; NHS; Orch; Ger Clb; Scr Kpr; Univ Of Michigan; Finance.

PRITCHARD, HEATHER; Delaware Hayes HS; Delaware, OH; Cls Rep Soph Cls; Sec Jr Cls; Trs Jr Cls; AFS; Hon Rl; Sec Pol Wkr; Stu Cncl; Pep Clb; Gym; Chrldng; Scholastic Awd; Miami Univ; Medicine.

PRITCHARD, JOHN; R Nelson Snider HS; Ft Wayne, IN; 5/570 Am Leg Boys St; Boy Scts; Hon Rl; Red Cr Ade; Spn Clb; Letter Ftbl; Am Leg Awd; C of C Awd; Amer Chem Soc 79; Xavier Univ 79; Univ Of Notre Dame; Pre Med.

PRITCHARD, JONNA; Monongah HS; Worthington, WV; Chrh Wkr; Hon Rl; Y-Teens; Fr Clb; FHA; Pep Clb; Univ.

PRITCHARD, LINDA; R B Chamberlin HS; Twinsburg, OH; 14/180 Sec AFS; Sec Band; FCA; Hon Rl; Sec NHS; Sch Mus; Sch Pl; Stg Crw; Drama Clb; FTA; Chrysler Yth Awd 79; Scholastic Awd 76 79; Best Crew Mbr 79; Miami Univ Of Ohio.

PRITCHARD, MARCHELLE; Northwood HS; Northwood, OH; Band; Chrs; Hon Rl; JA; Ger Clb; Bowling Green St Univ; Advert.

PRITCHARD, MARY J; Morgan HS; Mc Connelsville, OH; Cl Rep Jr Cls; Hon Rl; Lbry Ade; NHS; Stu Cncl; Bsbl; Bsktbl; Coach Actv; IM Sprt; DAR Awd; Univ; Pharm.

PRITCHARD, STEVEN; Malabar HS; Mansfield, OH; 42/278 Chrh Wkr; Bsbl; Bsktbl; Crs Cntry; College.

PRITCHETT, ALESIA; Roosevelt HS; Gary, IN; Cls Rep Soph Cls; Chrh Wkr; Cmnty Wkr; Girl Scts; Hon Rl; JA; NHS; FTA; Pep Clb; Scr Kpr; Purdue Univ; Acctg.

PRITCHETT, EVELYN; Otsego HS; Plainwell, MI; Band; Chrs; Hon Rl; Lbry Ade; Lit Mag; Sch Mus; Yrbk; 4-H; Western Mic Univ; Communications.

PRITT, DEBBIE; East Preston HS; Terra Alta, WV; Chrs; Chrh Wkr; Girl Scts; Hon Rl; Jr NHS; Lbry Ade; NHS; Pres Yth Flsp; Bausch & Lomb Awd; Voice Dem Awd; Fairmont State College; Second Educ.

PRIVETTE, MELINDA; United Local HS; Lsibon, OH; 1/160 Am Leg Aux Girls St; Cmp Fr Grls; Chrs; Chrh Wkr; Girl Scts; Hon Rl; NHS; Stu Cncl; 4-H; FHA; Univ; Sociology.

PROBST, JAMES R; Plymouth HS; Plymouth, IN; Aud/Vis; Band; Hon Rl; Stg Crw; Yth Flsp; Mth Clb; Rdo Clb; Letter Crs Cntry; Letter Trk; Coach Actv; Purdue Univ; Engr.

PROBST, KIMBERLY; South Dearborn HS; Aurora, IN; 23/260 Chrs; Chrh Wkr; Cmnty Wkr; Hon Rl; NHS; Off Ade; Evansville Univ; Phys Ther.

PROBST, MICHELE; Martinsburg HS; Martinsburg, WV; 26/226 Chrh Wkr; Hon Rl; Hosp Ade; Brigham Young Univ; Pre Pharm.

PROCHKO, ROBERT M; Midpark HS; Middleburg Hts, OH; 90/604 Cls Rep Frsh Cls; Cls Rep Soph Cls; Cl Rep Jr Cls; Orch; Stu Cncl; Rdo Clb; Natl Merit SF; Case Western Reserve Univ; Elec Engr.

PROCTOR, JANIS; Chelsea HS; Chelsea, MI; 7/210 Trs Sr Cls; Cmnty Wkr; Hon Rl; Lbry Ade; NHS; Central Michigan Univ; Education.

PROCTOR, PATRICIA; Fayetteville HS; Fayetteville, WV; Pres Sr Cls; Am Leg Aux Girls St; Pres Band; Hon Rl; Stu Cncl; Ed Yrbk; Sprt Ed Sch Nwsp; IM Sprt; College; Journalism.

PROCTOR, RICK; Nicholas Cnty HS; Summersville, WV; Am Leg Boys St; Hon Rl; Lit Mag; Sprt Ed Sch Nwsp; Rptr Sch Nwsp; FFA; Leo Clb; Letter Bsbl; Coach Actv; Univ.

PROCTOR, ROBERT; Kearsley HS; Flint, MI; Univ Of Michigan; Comp Sci.

PROFFITT, LAURA; Our Lady Of Mt Carmel HS; River Rouge, MI; 20/65 Hon Rl; Red Cr Ade; Rptr Sch Nwsp; Pep Clb; Am Leg Awd; Bus Schl; Stenography.

PROGER, MARY; Buckeye South HS; Rayland, OH; 20/120 Girl Scts; Hon Rl; Lbry Ade; Off Ade; Sct Actv; Y-Teens; Drama Clb; Pep Clb; W Liberty State Coll; Psych.

PROIETTI, JOHN T; Keyser HS; Keyser, WV; 11/248 AFS; Am Leg Boys St; Boy Scts; Hon Rl; NHS; Sch Pl; Stu Cncl; Key Clb; Am Leg Awd; Natl Merit Ltr; Potomac St Coll; Chem Engr.

PROIETTY, JOHN; Bedford Sr HS; Temperance, MI; Letter Crs Cntry; Trk; Michigan St Univ; Astronomy.

PROKOP, MARIA; Reed City HS; Reed City, MI; Band; Girl Scts; Hon Rl; Sch Pl; 4-H; Letter Trk; Mat Maids; PPFtbl; Scr Kpr; 4-H Awd; Davenport Busns Schl; Legal Sec.

PROLETTI, VICTOR D; Keyser HS; Keyser, WV; 6/262 AFS; Am Leg Boys St; NHS; Stu Cncl; Mth Clb; Bsktbl; Ftbl; Am Leg Awd; Potomac State College; Engr.

PROPER, CAROLYN; Southeastern HS; Londonderry, OH; Sec Jr Cls; Trs Jr Cls; Band; Hon Rl; Jr NHS; NHS; Stu Cncl; 4-H; OEA; Pep Clb; Bus Schl; Sec.

PROPER, JEFFREY; Ontonagon Area HS; Ontonagon, MI; 30/87 Hon Rl; ROTC; Sec Bsktbl; Letter Ftbl; Capt Glf; Capt Trk; Coach Actv; Voice Dem Awd; Ferris St Coll; Marketing.

PROPST, GRETA; Philip Barbour HS; Philippi, WV; 13/200 Am Leg Aux Girls St; Band; Chrs; Chrh Wkr; Girl Scts; Hon Rl; NHS; Stu Cncl; DECA; College.

PROSE, SHARON; Oakwood HS; Dayton, OH; Chrs; Girl Scts; Hon Rl; Sct Actv; Stg Crw; Yth Flsp; Rptr Sch Nwsp; Ten; Univ; Law.

PROSHEK, LELAND; Edward Drummond Libbey HS; Toledo, OH; Rptr Yrbk; Boys Clb Am; Letter Ftbl; Wrstlng; Scr Kpr; Tmr; Toledo Univ; Med.

PROSNICK, KEVIN; Columbiana HS; Columbiana, OH; 1/100 Pres Soph Cls; Val; Band; NHS; Pres Stu Cncl; Pres Spn Clb; Letter Bsbl; Univ Of Cincinnati; Industrial Eng.

PROSSER, EDWARD; Bloomington HS; Bloomington, IN; 25/373 Band; Boy Scts; NHS; IM Sprt; Natl Merit Ltr; Indiana Univ;co Sci.

PROTO, JULIE; Windham HS; Windham, OH; Pres Jr Cls; Pres Sr Cls; Hon Rl; Lit Mag; Sch Pl; Rptr Yrbk; Drama Clb; Sec Spn Clb; Trk; Scr Kpr; Univ; Cmnctns.

PROTOPAPAS, DOROTHY; Elgin HS; Prospect, OH; Hon Rl; JA; NHS; Fr Clb; Lat Clb; Univ; Med.

PROTZEK, BILL; Edison HS; Milan, OH; 29/152 Band; Chrs; Hon Rl; Orch; Rdo Clb; Sci Clb; Bowling Green St Univ; Music.

PROUGH, JEAN A; Huntington North HS; Huntington, IN; Chrs; Chrh Wkr; Cmnty Wkr; Yth Flsp; 4-H; Ger Clb; Pep Clb; Letter Chrldng; IM Sprt; Pres Awd; Busns Schl; Busns.

PROUGH, JUDITH; Onaway Area HS; Onaway, MI; Sec Jr Cls; Band; Hon Rl; NHS; Sch Pl; Stu Cncl; Yth Flsp; FHA; Concordia Coll; Elem Ed.

PROULX, CYNTHIA; Au Gres Sims HS; Au Gres, MI; 12/48 Cl Rep Jr Cls; Band; Chrs; Hon Rl; Lbry Ade; Orch; Sch Pl; Stu Cncl; Bsbl; Ferris St Univ; Med Sec.

PROULX, JOYCE; Au Gres Sims HS; Augres, MI; Chrh Wkr; Girl Scts; Hon Rl; Hon Rl; Lbry Ade; Stg Crw; Rptr Sch Nwsp; Drama Clb; Coll; Elem Ed.

PROVENCAL, KAREN; Quincy Community HS; Quincy, MI; 15/118 Sec Band; Hon Rl; NHS; Sch Pl; Stu Cncl; Yrbk; Pres Drama Clb; Pres Fr Clb; Trk; DAR Awd; Central Univ; Art.

PROVENCAL, KATHY; Quincy HS; Quincy, MI; 4/118 Sec Jr Cls; Sec Sr Cls; Band; Chrh Wkr; Hon Rl; Jr NHS; NHS; Stg Crw; Fr Clb; Letter Trk; Univ; Music.

PROVENCHER, RENEE; Kingsford HS; Kingsford, MI; Chrs; Chrh Wkr; Cmnty Wkr; Hon Rl; Hosp Ade; NHS; Cit Awd; Mi St Schlrshp ACT Test 79; Northern Michigan Univ.

PROVINS, BYRON A; United Local HS; Hemet, CA; 11/128 Pres Frsh Cls; Pres Soph Cls; Am Leg Boys St; Chrh Wkr; NHS; Sch Pl; Stu Cncl; Spn Clb; Letter Ftbl; DAR Awd; Appointment & Full Schlrshp To US Military Acad 79; US Military Acad; Engr.

PROVITT, JENNIFFER; Warren G Harding HS; Warren, OH; 110/405 Am Leg Aux Girls St; Band; Cmp Fr Grls; Chrh Wkr; Hon Rl; Lit Mag; Y-Teens; Yrbk; Ed Sch Nwsp; Sch Nwsp; Optimist Clb Essay 1st Pl You & The Raw 73; Ohio St Univ; Jrnlsm.

PROWANT, JEANIE; Continental Local HS; Continental, OH; Hon Rl; Stu Cncl; Treas Yth Flsp; Rptr Yrbk; Spn Clb; Tech School; Acctg.

PROWANT, JULIE; Bishop Dwenger HS; Ft Wayn, IN; Boy Scts; Hon Rl; Hosp Ade; 4-H; Fr Clb; Univ; Bus Admin.

PRUCY, DEBBIE; Highland HS; Highland, IN; Girl Scts; Hon Rl; Hosp Ade; Off Ade; FHA; N W Indiana Univ; Med Tech.

PRUDEN, KAREN; High School; Geneva, OH; 40/250 Chrs; Sct Actv; Stu Cncl; Yth Flsp; 4-H; Bsbl; Bsktbl; Gym; Trk; Chrldng; Univ; Piano Performance.

PRUETER, SUSAN; New Knoxville HS; New Knoxvll, OH; Chrh Wkr; Hon Rl; NHS; Sch Pl; Yth Flsp; Ed Sch Nwsp; Rptr Sch Nwsp; 4-H; Chrldng; 4-H Awd; College; Legal Secretary.

PRUETER, TIMOTHY; Reese HS; Reese, MI; 4/135 Am Leg Boys St; Chrh Wkr; Hon Rl; NHS; Bsbl; Bsktbl; Ftbl; IM Sprt; Michigan Tech Univ; Engr.

PRUETT, BRIAN; Maumee HS; Maumee, OH; Hon Rl; Ftbl; Trk; Univ; Comp Sci.

PRUETT, DEBBIE; Madison Hts HS; Anderson, IN; Cls Rep Frsh Cls; VP Jr Cls; FCA; Stu Cncl; Pep Clb; Gym; Chrldng; Participated In Prvte Gymnastics Team; Initiated Into Tri Gamm Sorority; Recv Vrsty Letter In Cheerleading; Indiana Univ; Acctg.

PRUETT, KARA; Oceana HS; Oceana, WV; Trs Sr Cls; Cls Rep Sr Cls; Treas Stu Cncl; Pep Clb; Spn Clb; Treas Alderson Broaddus; Business Economic.

PRUETT, KEITH; Bluefield HS; Bluefield, WV; 40/300 Band; Hon Rl; Jr NHS; Sec Yth Flsp; Fr Clb; Lat Clb; Pep Clb; Woodmen Of World Awd For America History; College; Poli Sci.

PRUIM, DAVE; Mona Shores HS; Muskegon, MI; Boy Scts; Chrh Wkr; Off Ade; Sct Actv; Letter Bsbl; Letter Bsktbl; Trk; Coach Actv; IM Sprt; Pres Awd; Bus Schl.

PRUITT, ARLON; Bluefield HS; Bluefield, WV; 114/487 Cls Rep Soph Cls; Chrh Wkr; Hon Rl; Off Ade; Stu Cncl; Yth Flsp; Sch Nwsp; Pep Clb; Spn Clb; Trk; Univ Of Tenn; Industrial Management.

PRUITT, DREAMA; Big Creek HS; Yukon, WV; 2/147 Pres Frsh Cls; Hst Soph Cls; Cl Rep Jr Cls; Band; Hon Rl; Jr NHS; Lbry Ade; NHS; Pep Clb; Spn Clb; Art Awd 77; Bluefield St Coll; Acctg.

PRUITT, JEFFREY A; Bellbrook HS; Bellbrook, OH; 4/168 Chrh Wkr; NHS; Swmmng; Am Leg Awd; Wright St Univ; Chem.

PRUITT, MICHAEL; Calumet HS; Gary, IN; 166/374 Pep Clb; Bsktbl; Ftbl; Las Vegas Univ; Draftmens.

PRUITT, PERRY; Whiteland Comm HS; New Whiteland, IN; 12/197 Band; Hon Rl; Orch; Pep Clb; IM Sprt; Rose Hulman Inst Of Tech; Elec Engr.

PRUITT, RODNEY; Buena Vista HS; Saginaw, MI; 16/157 Band; Boy Scts; Hon Rl; Jr NHS; NHS; Sch Nwsp; Pep Clb; Letter Bsbl; Letter Ftbl; Natl Merit Ltr; Boys Acadmc Awd 75; Attend Awd; Michigan St Univ; Engr.

PRUITT, TRESSIA; Big Creek HS; Cucumber, WV; Band; Hon Rl; Yrbk; Sch Nwsp; Coll; Art.

PRUNER, LISA; Terre Haute North Vigo HS; Terre Haute, IN; Cls Rep Soph Cls; Band; Chrs; Girl Scts; Hon Rl; Lbry Ade; Stu Cncl; Y-Teens; Eng Clb; 4-H; Vllybl MVP 78; Bsktbl Mst Rebounds 79; Univ.

PRUNTY, BRIAN; Washington Irving HS; Nutter Fort, WV; Chrh Wkr; Cmnty Wkr; Fr Clb; Key Clb; Crs Cntry; Trk; West Virginia Univ; Pre Pharm.

PRUNTY, JOHN; Monongah HS; Fairmont, WV; Hon Rl; Letter Bsbl; Fairmont State Coll; Carpenter.

PRUS, BOB; Elwood Community HS; Elwood, IN; Cl Rep Jr Cls; Cls Rep Sr Cls; Band; Chrs; Chrh Wkr; Hon Rl; Stu Cncl; DECA; Pep Clb; 1st Dist In Food Marktng Mgmt 1978; 1st St In Food Marktng Mgmt 1979; Delegt Tcareer Develpmnt Confrnc 1979; Ball St Univ; Acctg.

PRUSAKIEWICZ, CHERYL; St Marys Cathedral HS; Gaylord, MI; Band; Hon Rl; Trk; Univ; Nursing.

PRUSI, STEVE; Negaunee HS; Negaunee, MI; Hon Rl; Univ; Carpentry.

PRYOR, CHARLENE; Columbus East HS; Columbus, OH; 23/272 Chrh Wkr; Drl Tm; Girl Scts; Hon Rl; Jr NHS; Lbry Ade; NHS; OEA; Spn Clb; Am Leg Awd; Spanish Natl Hnr Soc 78; Ohio St Univ; Spec Educ.

PRYOR, CHARLENE D; East HS; Columbus, OH; 23/272 Chrh Wkr; Drl Tm; Girl Scts; Hon Rl; Lbry Ade; NHS; Sch Nwsp; Spn Clb; Am Leg Awd; Ohio St Univ; Spec Educ.

PRYOR, CYNTHIA M; Grafton HS; Bridgeport, WV; 8/164 Chrh Wkr; Hon Rl; NHS; Stu Cncl; Pres Nike 79; Athletic Ticket Comm Letter 76 79; Med Office Asst Cert 77 78 & 79; Fairmont St Coll; Med Lab Tech.

PRYOR, DANIEL; Philo HS; Zanesville, OH; Chrh Wkr; Hon Rl; Fr Clb; Bsktbl; Coll.

PRYOR, DEBORAH; Chaminade Julienne HS; Dayton, OH; Band; Chrs; Chrh Wkr; Girl Scts; Hon Rl; JA; NHS; Red Cr Ade; Sch Mus; Pep Clb; E Michigan St Univ; Communications.

PRYOR, GARY; Deer Park HS; Cincinnati, OH; Boy Scts; Hon Rl; Sch Pl; Sct Actv; Stg Crw; Glf; Ohio St Univ; Aerospace Engr.

PRYOR, JANELLE; Morgan HS; Mc Connelsville, OH; 6/265 Band; Hon Rl; NHS; 4-H; Fr Clb; 4-H Awd; Ohio St Univ; Med Tech.

PRYOR, JEFFREY; Charlestown HS; Charlestown, IN; 24/167 Hon Rl; Jr NHS; Sch Nwsp; 4-H; Trk; Cit Awd; 4-H Awd; VFW Awd; Voice Dem Awd; College.

PRYOR, LEOLLA; De Vilbiss HS; Toledo, OH; Chrh Wkr; Hon Rl; NHS; Fr Clb; Pep Clb; Ohio St Univ; Acctg.

PRYOR, LOIS; Collinwood HS; Cleveland, OH; Cls Rep Soph Cls; Cl Rep Jr Cls; Chrs; Hon Rl; NHS; Off Ade; Red Cr Ade; Stu Cncl; FTA; Coll; Engr.

PRYOR, LYNETTE; Fostoria HS; Fostoria, OH; 13/180 Band; Hon Rl; NHS; Vllybl Var Letter 78; Most Improved Awd In Vllybl 76; Ohio St Univ; Pharm Research.

PRYOR, MONICA; Shortridge HS; Indianapolis, IN; 48/444 Cls Rep Frsh Cls; Cls Rep Soph Cls; Cl Rep Jr Cls; Trs Sr Cls; Cmp Fr Grls; Girl Scts; Hon Rl; JA; Stu Cncl; 4-H; Coll.

PRYOR, RODNEY E; Woodrow Wilson HS; Beckley, WV; Cls Rep Sr Cls; Am Leg Boys St; Pres Band; Boy Scts; Chrh Wkr; Cmnty Wkr; Hon Rl; JA; Pol Wkr; Sch Pl; Hon Roll Awd 77; West Virginia Tech Univ; Acctg.

PRYOR, TODD; Brandon HS; Ortonville, MI; Hon Rl; Univ Of Michigan.

PRYSOCK, CHRISTINE; Toronto HS; Toronto, OH; Sec Sr Cls; Band; Girl Scts; Hosp Ade; Off Ade; Sch Mus; Sch Pl; Pep Clb; Spn Clb; Pom Pon; Univ Of Akron; Nursing.

PRYSOCK, WANTHA A; Patterson Cooperative HS; Dayton, OH; VP Sr Cls; Hst Sr Cls; Band; JA; Orch; OEA; JA Awd; College; Communications.

PRZEBIENDA, THERESA; Divine Child HS; Dearborn Hts, MI; 4/183 Am Leg Aux Girls St; Girl Scts; Hosp Ade; NHS; Stu Cncl; Sch Nwsp; FTA; Sec Spn Clb; Trk; Pres Awd; Wayne St Univ; Phys Ther.

PRZESLICA, JANE F; Fordson HS; Dearborn Hts, MI; VP Frsh Cls; Hon Rl; Pol Wkr; Letter Bsktbl; Letter Trk; GAA; Cit Awd; Pres Awd; Mich State Univ.

PRZYAGOCKI, JOAN; All Saints HS; Bay City, MI; Cls Rep Frsh Cls; Hon Rl; Pep Clb; Chrldng; Coach Actv; Delta Univ; Data Proc.

PRZYBYLSKI, CHRISTINE; St Andrew HS; Detroit, MI; Chrs; Hon Rl; Rptr Sch Nwsp; Bsbl; IM Sprt; Jrnlsm.

PRZYBYLSKI, DENISE; St Andrew HS; Detroit, MI; Hon Rl; NHS; Capt Bsbl; Letter Bsktbl; Coach Actv; IM Sprt; Business; Acct.

PRZYBYLSKI, PAMELA; Dearborn HS; Dearborn, MI; AFS; Chrh Wkr; Cmnty Wkr; Girl Scts; Hon Rl; NHS; Sch Pl; Yrbk; Spn Clb; Univ Of Michigan; Nursing.

PRZYBYLSKI, STEVEN; St Alphonsus HS; Detroit, MI; Cl Rep Jr Cls; Trs Sr Cls; Hon Rl; NHS; Sch Mus; Stu Cncl; Bsbl; Ftbl; Swmmng; Mgrs; College; Journalism.

PRZYGOCKI, JOAN; All Saints HS; Bay City, MI; Cls Rep Frsh Cls; Cmnty Wkr; FCA; Girl Scts; Hon Rl; Off Ade; Pep Clb; Chrldng; Delta Univ; Bus.

PSINKA, TAMARA; Campbell Memorial HS; Campbell, OH; 13/210 Band; Chrh Wkr; Cmnty Wkr; Hon Rl; Jr NHS; NHS; Orch; Yth Flsp; Fr Clb; Mth Clb; Youngstown State Univ; Chem Engr.

PTAK, WALLY; Our Lady Of Mt Carmel HS; Wyandotte, MI; 36/65 Pres Jr Cls; Chrs; Chrh Wkr; Hon Rl; Lbry Ade; Sch Mus; Stg Crw; Stu Cncl; Pep Clb; Scr Kpr; Michigan State Univ.

PUARIEA, DANIEL; Clay Sr HS; Oregon, OH; Ftbl; Trk; Univ; Acctg.

PUCEL, ROBERT; Strongsville HS; Strongsville, OH; 54/450 Hon Rl; Jr NHS; Trk; Letourneau College; Camping Admin.

PUCHALA, MARYANN; John Adams HS; So Bend, IN; Chrs; Chrh Wkr; Hon Rl; Orch; Sch Mus; Stg Crw; Drama Clb; Coll; Elem Ed.

PUCHALLA, VICTOR; Grant HS; Grant, MI; Pres Sr Cls; Band; Hon Rl; Quill & Scroll; Sch Pl; Sprt Ed Yrbk; Bsbl; Central Michigan Univ; Music.

PUCHARICH, MARY; Bishop Donahue HS; Glendale, WV; Trs Jr Cls; Hon Rl; Jr NHS; Stu Cncl; Rptr Yrbk; Rptr Sch Nwsp; Pep Clb; Spn Clb; Community Coll; Comp Progr.

PUCHLEY, THERESA; Gauit HS; Hammond, IN; 40/270 Hon Rl; NHS; Letter Bsktbl; Letter Ten; VP GAA; Capt PPFtbl; Franklin Coll; Bus.

PUCIK, DONOVAN J; Park Hills HS; W P AFB, OH; 3/370 Am Leg Boys St; Aud/Vis; Band; Boy Scts; Chrs; Chrh Wkr; Cmnty Wkr; Hon Rl; Jr NHS; Lit Mag; Univ Of Texas; Engr.

PUCKETT, ALLAN; Fostoria HS; Fostoria, OH; Pres Sr Cls; Chrs; Hon Rl; Stu Cncl; Fr Clb; Gov Hon Prg Awd; College; Physics.

PUCKETT, BRUCE; Bluefield HS; Bluefield, WV; Band; Hon Rl; Lat Clb; Pep Clb; Mgrs; Scr Kpr; Natl Latin Test Awd; Bluefield St Coll; Engr.

PUCKETT, CARLA L; Bluefield HS; Bluefield, WV; 33/280 Chrs; Chrh Wkr; Hon Rl; Sch Mus; Bob Jones Univ; Secretary.

PUCKETT, CAROL; Berea HS; Brookpk, OH; 12/578 Chrs; Hon Rl; Hosp Ade; NHS; Off Ade; Univ; Nursing.

PUCKETT, DAVID M; Redford Union HS; Novi, MI; 66/588 Cmnty Wkr; Hon Rl; NHS; Yth Flsp; Spn Clb; Schlrshp Bethel Coll & Notre Dame Coll; Michigan Competitive Schlrshp; Acceptance With Hnrs Valparaiso Univ; Univ Of Michigan; Engr.

PUCKETT, EDWARD; Peebles HS; Sinking Spg, OH; Band; Hon Rl; Stu Cncl; Drama Clb; 4-H; FFA; Pep Clb; Bsktbl;.

PUCKETT, JEFFREY M; Marlington HS; Alliance, OH; Pres Jr Cls; Boy Scts; FCA; Yth Flsp; Bsbl; Crs Cntry; Ftbl; Trk; IM Sprt; Bowling Green St Univ; Law.

PUCKETT, JENNIFER; Richmond Sr HS; Richmond, IN; 14/550 Cls Rep Frsh Cls; Cls Rep Soph Cls; Cl Rep Jr Cls; Am Leg Aux Girls St; Band; Hon Rl; NHS; Stu Cncl; Purdue Univ; Nursing.

PUCKETT, MICHAEL; Grass Lake HS; Grass Lake, MI; Cmnty Wkr; Hon Rl;.

PUCKETT, RODDY M; Gods Bible School; Goshen, OH; 4/21 Pres Soph Cls; Pres Jr Cls; Band; Chrs; Chrh Wkr; Hon Rl; Orch; Yrbk; VP Mth Clb; Spn Clb; Univ Of Cincinnati; Music Tchr.

PUCKETT, THOMAS J; London HS; London, OH; Hon Rl; Yth Flsp; Bsbl; Ftbl; Perfect Attendance Awrd; College; Art.

PUDELKO, SHELLY; Sandusky HS; Sandusky, MI; 7/114 Am Leg Aux Girls St; Chrh Wkr; Hon Rl; NHS; Letter Bsbl; DAR Awd; Sci Dept Awd 79; Mi Comp Schlrshp 79; Michigan Tech Univ; Med Tech.

PUDLO, ERIC; Adlai Stevenson HS; Sterling Hts, MI; 94/538 Hon Rl; NHS; Bsbl; Glf; Mich State Univ; Engr.

PUGH, BILL; Mariemont HS; Cincinnati, OH; Letter Bsktbl; Letter Ftbl; Scr Kpr; Univ Of Maryland; Bus Mgmt.

PUGH, BRIAN; Kimball HS; Royal Oak, MI; 65/600 Band; Boy Scts; Chrh Wkr; NHS; Orch; Sch Mus; Sct Actv; Yth Flsp; Michigan Tech Univ; Engr.

PUGH, BRIAN; Greenfield Central HS; Greenfield, IN; Chrh Wkr; Cmnty Wkr; Quill & Scroll; Yth Flsp; Rptr Sch Nwsp; Pep Clb; Spn Clb; Ftbl; Mgrs; Scr Kpr; Ball St; Journalism.

PUGH, CINDY; Munster HS; Munster, IN; Girl Scts; Hon Rl; Sch Pl; Sct Actv; Drama Clb; PPFtbl; Purdue Univ; Science.

PUGH, GARY; Mineral Ridge HS; Mineral Ridge, OH; 30/75 VP Frsh Cls; VP Soph Cls; Hon Rl; Bsktbl; Coach Actv; IM Sprt; PPFtbl; Scr Kpr; 3hr Varsity Ltd Wnr MVP Of MRHS Team Best Foul Shtr; Best Field Goal Precentage All Inter County League J; Univ; Park & Rec Dir.

PUGH, KAREN; Clarence M Kimball HS; Royal Oak, MI; 95/602 Band; Chrh Wkr; Girl Scts; NHS; Orch; Pres Yth Flsp; Drama Clb; Capt Gym; Albion Coll; Soc Serv Work.

PUGH, LINDA; Hampshire HS; Bloomery, WV; 5/212 AFS; Band; Chrh Wkr; Drl Tm; Drm Mjrt; Hon Rl; Jr NHS; Shepherd College; Med Tech.

PUGH, MELISSA L; Bluefield HS; Bluefld, WV; 31/232 Chrs; Hon Rl; Sec Jr NHS; Y-Teens; Fr Clb; Pep Clb; Univ; Med.

PUGH, RANDALL; Lawrence Central HS; Indianapolis, IN; Hon Rl; Ger Clb; Sci Clb; IM Sprt; Coll; Meteorology.

PUGH, SANDRA D; Clay City HS; Center Point, IN; Sec Frsh Cls; Cls Rep Frsh Cls; Cls Rep Soph Cls; Sec Jr Cls; Sec Sr Cls; Band; Girl Scts; Hon Rl; Hosp Ade; Stu Cncl; College; Fashion Illustrator.

PUGSLEY, THOMAS J; Dondero HS; Royal Oak, MI; NHS; Natl Merit SF; College; Astronomy.

PULEO, SUZANNE; Solon HS; Solon, OH; Cls Rep Soph Cls; Cl Rep Jr Cls; Chrs; Cmnty Wkr; FCA; Girl Scts; Hon Rl; Sec MMM; Sec NHS; Sch Mus; Ohio Northern Univ; Pharm.

PULFER, TONY; Lehman HS; Pt Jefferson, OH; Am Leg Boys St; Boy Scts; Hon Rl; NHS; Spn Clb; Letter Bsbl; Letter Wrstlng; Am Leg Awd; Univ.

PULLEN, MARY A; Winfield HS; Scott Depot, WV; Chrs; Girl Scts; Hon Rl; Jr NHS; NHS; Yth Flsp; FHA; Mth Clb; Central Bible College; Sacred Music.

PULLEN, SHEILA; Franklin Heights HS; Grove City, OH; Sec Jr Cls; Am Leg Aux Girls St; Hon Rl; Quill & Scroll; Sprt Ed Sch Nwsp; Key Clb; Gym; Trk; Chrldng; Scr Kpr; College; Medicine.

PULLEN, WILLIAM E; Patrick Henry HS; Napoleon, OH; 6/115 Aud/Vis; Pres Chrh Wkr; Cmnty Wkr; Hon Rl; Lbry Ade; NHS; Rptr Sch Nwsp; Sci Clb; Defiance Coll.

PULLEY, CYNTHIA; Thomas W Harvey HS; Painesville, OH; B Am Leg Aux Girls St; JA; Off Ade; FBLA; Spn Clb; Bsktbl; Scr Kpr; JA Awd; Acctg.

PULLEY, LINDA J; Southfield Christian HS; Southfield, MI; Band; Cmnty Wkr; Girl Scts; Pol Wkr; Sch Mus; Sch Pl; Drama Clb; Principals Awd; 1st Chair Flute Intermediate Bnd; Music Cmp; College; Physics.

PULLINS, TERRI; Eastern HS; Long Bottom, OH; Band; Chrs; Hosp Ade; Off Ade; Stg Crw; Yth Flsp; Pres 4-H; FHA; OEA; Trk; Delegate To 4 H Club Congress Columbus OH 1977; Mbr 4 H Club Advisory Comm 1978; Voc Schl; Sec Sci.

PULSKAMP, LYNN; Mother Of Mercy HS; Cincinnati, OH; Hon Rl; Off Ade; Sec.

PULTS, JOHN D; Pike HS; Indianapolis, IN; 5/301 Band; Hon Rl; Jr NHS; VP NHS; Orch; Sch Mus; Ger Clb; Mth Clb; Crs Cntry; Letter Trk; Rose Hulman Inst Of Tech; Engr.

PULVER, ROBERT; Bentley HS; Livonia, MI; Hon Rl; Wayne State Univ; Engr.

PUMFORD, ANGELIQUE; Bullock Creek HS; Midland, MI; 24/150 Pres Frsh Cls; Pres Jr Cls; Cls Rep Sr Cls; Hon Rl; NHS; Stu Cncl; Pep Clb; Spn Clb; Chrldng; Natl Merit Ltr; Northwood Inst; Fshn Mdse.

PUMFORD, LYNETTE; Ovid Elsie HS; Bannister, MI; Cls Rep Frsh Cls; Cls Rep Soph Cls; Cl Rep Jr Cls; Band; Drl Tm; Hon Rl; Swmmng; Chrldng; Pom Pon; PPFtbl; College; Aviation.

PUND, JOLENE; Southridge HS; Huntingburg, IN; Band; Drl Tm; Hon Rl; Yrbk; FHA; Pep Clb; Spn Clb; IM Sprt; Mat Maids; Tmr; Indiana St Univ; Bus.

PUNG, DAVID; St Johns HS; St Johns, MI; FCA; Sch Mus; Sch Pl; Drama Clb; 4-H; Letter Ftbl; IM Sprt; 4-H Awd; College; Engr.

PUNKE, MONICA; Catholic Central HS; Steubenville, OH; 730218 Hon Rl; NHS; Drama Clb; FHA; Lat Clb; Am Leg Awd; Coll Of Steubenville; Eng.

PUPEL, MARGARET M; Catholic Central HS; Grand Rapids, MI; Chrs; Chrh Wkr; Girl Scts; Hon Rl; Hosp Ade; Pol Wkr; Sch Mus; Drama Clb; Lat Clb; Aquinas Coll.

PURDON, THOMAS; Stow HS; Stow, OH; 55/590 Band; Boy Scts; Chrh Wkr; Hon Rl; Orch; Sct Actv; Yth Flsp; Ger Clb; Cin College; Chem Engr.

PURDUE, THOMAS; North Putnam HS; Roachdale, IN; 13/167 FCA; NHS; Spn Clb; Bsktbl; Letter Ftbl; Letter Ftbl; Letter Wrstlng; Univ.

PURDY, BRUCE; Northwestern HS; West Salem, OH; Band; Boy Scts; Hon Rl; Yth Flsp; FFA; Crs Cntry; Trk; Wrstlng; IM Sprt; College; Farmer.

PURDY, CHARLES; The Valley Schl; Pontiac, MI; Aud/Vis; Boy Scts; Sch Pl; Stg Crw; Drama Clb; FSA; Bsktbl; IM Sprt; Adrain Univ; Art.

PURDY, JOSEPH; Eastern Brown Cnty HS; Sardinia, OH; 10/91 Cls Rep Sr Cls; Chrs; Hon Rl; NHS; Sch Pl; Stu Cncl; Yth Flsp; 4-H; FFA; FTA;.

PURDY, JUDITH; Bishop Foley HS; Madison Hts, MI; Cl Rep Jr Cls; Hon Rl; Stu Cncl; Univ Of Mich; Med.

PURDY, LINDA; Terre Haute North Vigo HS; Terre Haute, IN; Aud/Vis; Band; Chrs; Girl Scts; Hon Rl; Hosp Ade; Orch; Quill & Scroll; Stu Cncl; Y-Teens; Ind St Univ; Nursing.

PURDY, MARY; Bloom Carroll HS; Carroll, OH; 1/154 Band; Drm Mjrt; Hon Rl; NHS; Off Ade; 4-H; Capt Chrldng; GAA; Scr Kpr; Tmr; Bowling Green St Univ; Bus Admin.

PURDY, PATRICIA; Our Lady Of The Elms HS; Stow, OH; Sch Pl; Yrbk; Ten; Chrldng; Univ Of Cincinnati; Interior Design.

PURDY, RAYMOND; Oscoda Area HS; Oscoda, MI; Boy Scts; NHS; Letter Bsbl; Letter Ftbl; Letter Swmmng; Cit Awd; Natl Merit Schl; Michigan St Univ; Law.

PURDY, THOMAS; Parkside HS; Annandale, VA; Hon Rl; Sprt Ed Sch Nwsp; VP Ger Clb; Bsktbl; Natl Merit Ltr; American Univ Dc.

PURK, SHELLEY; Fairview HS; Bryan, OH; Hon Rl; Yth Flsp; Ed Yrbk; Rptr Yrbk; Sprt Ed Sch Nwsp; Rptr Sch Nwsp; 4-H; FHA; FTA; Letter Bsktbl; Bus Schl; Acctg.

PURKHISER, JULIE; West Washington HS; Salem, IN; 2/100 Am Leg Aux Girls St; Band; Hon Rl; NHS; Sch Pl; Ed Yrbk; Drama Clb; Pres 4-H; FHA; Pres Spn Clb; Univ; Med Tech.

PURNEY, CHERYL; Genoa Area HS; Genoa, OH; 30/178 Chrh Wkr; Hon Rl; Off Ade; FBLA; Mercy Schl Of Nursing; RN.

PURPLE, LISA; Covington Cmnty HS; Covington, IN; 2/106 Sal; Band; Chrh Wkr; Girl Scts; Hon Rl; Lbry Ade; NHS; Quill & Scroll; Stu Cncl; Rptr Sch Nwsp; Tennessee Temple Univ; Elem Ed.

PURRENHAGE, JULIE; Dominican HS; Detroit, MI; Chrs; Chrh Wkr; Cmnty Wkr; Girl Scts; Sch Mus; Stg Crw; Rptr Yrbk; Sch Nwsp; Barnard Univ; Eng Lit.

PURTEE, CHERYL; Richmond HS; Richmond, IN; 45/550 Am Leg Aux Girls St; Band; Hon Rl; NHS; Pol Wkr; Sch Mus; Treas 4-H; Fr Clb; College; Poli Sci.

PURTILL, MARK; St Johns HS; St Johns, MI; Aud/Vis; Band; Boy Scts; PAVAS; Sch Pl; Drama Clb; Pep Clb; Letter Bsktbl; Letter Ftbl; Letter Trk; Michigan St Univ; Comp Tech.

PURTILO, KAREN E; Ashtabula Harbor HS; Ashtabula, OH; 8/200 AFS; Band; Hon Rl; Lbry Ade; Off Ade; FTA; Pep Clb; Spn Clb; Natl Merit Ltr; Toledo Univ; Communications.

PURVIANCE, JAMES; Bishop Dwenger HS; Ft Wayne, IN; Glf; IM Sprt; Chrstn Learshp Awd 79; Purdue Univ; Engr.

PURVIS, BRIAN; Ross Sr HS; Hamilton, OH; 63/220 Hon Rl; Orch; Sch Mus; Sch Pl; Sct Actv; Pep Clb; Bsbl; Bsktbl; Ftbl; Ten; Miami Univ; Music.

PURVIS, PATRICIA; Euclid Sr HS; Euclid, OH; Cls Rep Soph Cls; Cl Rep Jr Cls; Chrs; Drm Mjrt; Hosp Ade; JA; NHS; Stu Cncl; Rptr Sch Nwsp; College; Journalism.

PURVIS, SUSAN; Marquette HS; Marquette, MI; Band; Hosp Ade; Ger Clb; Chrldng; College.

PURVLICIS, ELZA; North Central HS; Indianapolis, IN; 115/999 Hon Rl; NHS; Letter Bsktbl; Letter Trk; Schlstic Awd 77 79; Bsktbl; All Metro; All County; All State Honorable Mention 78; Univ; Bus Admin.

PUSECKER, BETH; Dublin HS; Dublin, OH; 11/152 Cl Rep Jr Cls; Band; Cmp Fr Grls; Sch Mus; Treas Stu Cncl; Rptr Yrbk; Rptr Sch Nwsp; Fr Clb; Pep Clb; OSU; Social Work.

PUSHWAL, TAMMY; Crestwood HS; Mantua, OH; Chrs; Chrh Wkr; Cmnty Wkr; Hon Rl; Lbry Ade; Off Ade; OEA; Bus.

PUSKAS, SUZANNE; Union Local HS; Piedmont, OH; 31/147 Cmp Fr Grls; Chrs; Hon Rl; NHS; Off Ade; Stu Cncl; Yrbk; Rptr Sch Nwsp; Fr Clb; Ohio Valley Schl Of Nursing; RN.

PUSPOS, ELEONOR; Coopersville Sr HS; Coopersville, MI; 8/180 Trs Frsh Cls; Trs Soph Cls; Cls Rep Sr Cls; Band; Chrs; Chrh Wkr; Hon Rl; NHS; Stu Cncl; Ger Clb; Grand Rapids Jr Coll; Phys Ther.

PUSTAY, TERESA; Wadsworth HS; Wadsworth, OH; Cls Rep Soph Cls; Cl Rep Jr Cls; Cls Rep Sr Cls; Chrh Wkr; Girl Scts; NHS; Pres Sdlty; Sec Stu Cncl; 4-H; VP OEA; Student Council Awrd; Univ Of Akron; Accounting.

PUTALA, CONNIE; Hancock Central HS; Hancock, MI; 2/96 Sal; Lbry Ade; NHS; Sch Mus; Sch Pl; Trk; Michigan Tech Univ; Pre Med.

PUTATURO, NICOLETTA; North HS; Akron, OH; 14/361 Chrh Wkr; Cmnty Wkr; Hon Rl; Lbry Ade; NHS; Off Ade; Univ Of Akron; Civil Eng.

PUTHOFF, DAVE; Lasalle HS; Cincinnati, OH; 6/247 Cls Rep Frsh Cls; Hon Rl; Jr NHS; Mod UN; NHS; IM Sprt; SAR Awd; College; Elect Engr.

PUTHOFF, DAVID F; La Salle HS; Cincinnati, OH; 6/249 Cls Rep Frsh Cls; Boy Scts; Hon Rl; Mod UN; IM Sprt; SAR Awd; Soc Distingd Amer HS Stu 1978; Ohio St Univ; Math.

PUTHOFF, DENISE; Celina Sr HS; Celina, OH; Hon Rl; Jr NHS; NHS; Fr Clb; FBLA; GAA; IM Sprt;.

PUTHOFF, DIANA; Celina Sr HS; Celina, OH; Hon Rl; Jr NHS; NHS; Fr Clb; FBLA; GAA; IM Sprt;.

PUTKOVICH, MICHAEL; Niles Mc Kinley HS; Niles, OH; Cls Rep Frsh Cls; Hst Soph Cls; Cls Rep Soph Cls; Cl Rep Jr Cls; Boy Scts; Hon Rl; Off Ade; Stu Cncl; DECA; Lat Clb; Pennsylvania St Univ; Frstry.

PUTMAN, BRENT D; Argos HS; Argos, IN; 1/54 Pres Frsh Cls; Pres Soph Cls; VP Jr Cls; Pres Sr Cls; Hon Rl; NHS; 4-H; IM Sprt; Am Leg Awd; 4-H Awd; Purdue Univ; Elec Engr.

PUTMAN, DENISE; Pike Delta York Sr HS; Delta, OH; 1/130 Band; Chrh Wkr; Girl Scts; NHS; Sch Mus; Yth Flsp; Yrbk; Drama Clb; Fr Clb; FNA; Univ; Nurse.

PUTMAN, JANET; Blanchester HS; Blanchster, OH; 13/150 Band; Chrh Wkr; Hon Rl; NHS; Yth Flsp; Univ Of Dayton; Acctg.

PUTNAM, MARY; Troy HS; Troy, MI; Cls Rep Frsh Cls; Boy Scts; Chrh Wkr; Debate Tm; Girl Scts; Hon Rl; Jr NHS; Ten Tech Univ; Physics.

PUTNAM, NANCY A; Cheboygan Area HS; Cheboygan, MI; Band; Hon Rl; Sch Pl; 4-H; Fr Clb; Univ Of Mic; Law.

PUTNAM, THOMAS; Tuscarawas Ctrl Cath HS; Uhrichsville, OH; 2/78 Pres Frsh Cls; VP Jr Cls; Chrs; Chrh Wkr; Hon Rl; NHS; Stu Cncl; Yth Flsp; Civ Clb; 4-H; Univ; Engr.

PUTNEY, ROBERT; Peck HS; Melvin, MI; 1/45 Pres Frsh Cls; Val; Band; Boy Scts; Hon Rl; NHS; Letter Bsktbl; Letter Ftbl; Letter Trk; Michigan St Univ; Chem Engr.

PUTNEY, ROBERT L; Peck HS; Melvin, MI; Pres Frsh Cls; Pres Band; Off Ade; Letter Bsktbl; Letter Ftbl; Letter Trk; Michigan St Univ; Chem Engr.

PUTT, MARIA; Bay City Western HS; Auburn, MI; 63/456 Cls Rep Soph Cls; Cl Rep Jr Cls; Band; FCA; Girl Scts; NHS; Off Ade; Sch Mus; 4-H; Capt Bsktbl; Recvd All City Recogntn From Sports Pg 77; Mi Dept Of Educ Schlrshp Tuition Grant Prog Winner 79; Delta Coll; Law Enforcmnt.

PUTZ, LORI F; Aquinas HS; Melvindale, MI; 29/215 Hon Rl; Hosp Ade; Honor Roll; Wayne St Univ; Dentistry.

PUZZUOLI, TINA; Center Line HS; Center Line, MI; Cl Rep Jr Cls; NHS; Stu Cncl; Rptr Yrbk; OEA; Sci Clb; VP Spn Clb; Letter Swmmng; Scr Kpr; Voice Dem Awd; Wayne State Univ; Journalism.

PYDYN, DEBORAH; Crestwood HS; Dearborn Hts, MI; Pres Band; Chrs; Chrh Wkr; Girl Scts; Orch; Sct Actv; PPFtbl; Univ; Envr Bio.

PYERS, DEAN; Perrysburg HS; Perrysburg, OH; 3/260 Hon Rl; VP NHS; Scr Kpr; Natl Merit Ltr; Coll.

PYJAR, JOHN; Harbor Springs HS; Cross Vill, MI; 2/80 Pres Frsh Cls; Pres Sr Cls; Hon Rl; Sch Mus; Yrbk; Letter Ftbl; Letter Ten; IM Sprt; Mgrs; Cit Awd; Univ Of Texas; Urban Planning.

PYLE, BEV; Wayne HS; Dayton, OH; 37/590 Cls Rep Frsh Cls; Cls Rep Soph Cls; Cl Rep Jr Cls; Pres Sr Cls; Hon Rl; Jr NHS; NHS; Off Ade; Stu Cncl; DECA; Bowling Green St Univ; Bus Admin.

PYLE, BEVERLY; Wayne HS; Dayton, OH; 37/525 Cls Rep Frsh Cls; Cls Rep Soph Cls; Cl Rep Jr Cls; Pres Sr Cls; Hon Rl; Jr NHS; NHS; Bowling Green State Univ; Bus Amdin.

PYLE, BONNIE; Lakeview HS; Cortland, OH; 16/176 Cl Rep Jr Cls; Hon Rl; Off Ade; Lat Clb; OEA; Opt Clb Awd; Youngstown Coll Of Bus; Sec.

PYLE, GREGORY; Euclid Sr HS; Euclid, OH; Cls Rep Frsh Cls; Aud/Vis; Chrs; Cmnty Wkr; Red Cr Ade; Y-Teens; Letter Swmmng; Trk; Letter Wrstlng; Water Polo 77 79; Univ.

PYLE, JENNIFER R; Talawanda HS; Oxford, OH; AFS; Band; Hon Rl; NHS; Sch Pl; Yrbk; Drama Clb; Fr Clb; Mgrs; Natl Merit SF; Trigonometry Award; Science Award; College; Zoology.

PYLE, KAREN; Washington Irving HS; Clarksburg, WV; 81/158 Pres Chrh Wkr; Hon Rl; Mdrgl; Sch Mus; Sch Pl; Stg Crw; Sec 4-H; Pep Clb; 4-H Awd; West Virginia Univ; Speech Pathology.

PYLE, RISA; The Andrews School; Canton, OH; Hon Rl; Mod UN; Quill & Scroll; Sch Pl; Stg Crw; Stu Cncl; Ed Yrbk; Sch Nwsp; Drama Clb; Emerson Coll; Mass Cmnctns.

PYLE, RISE; Huntington Catholic HS; Huntington, IN; 3/33 Sec Frsh Cls; Sec Soph Cls; Hon Rl; Pres NHS; Sch Pl; Stg Crw; Sec Stu Cncl; Yrbk; Bsktbl; Trk; College.

PYLES, DANIEL B; Point Pleasant HS; Gallipolis Frry, WV; Am Leg Boys St; Boy Scts; NHS; 4-H;

Bsbl; DAR Awd; 4-H Awd; Marshall Univ; Archaeology.

PYLES, DAVID; Pennsboro HS; Pennsboro, WV; Hon Rl; FFA; Sci Clb; Parkersburg Cmnty Coll; Mech Drafting.

PYLES, GLENDA; Arcanum Butler HS; Castine, OH; 18/99 NHS; Off Ade; Pres Yth Flsp; VP FHA; Tmr; Jr FHA Degree; Chapter FHA Degree; College; Secondary Ed.

PYLES, HELEN; Buffalo HS; Kenova, WV; Chrh Wkr; Hon Rl; Hosp Ade; Mod UN; Sct Actv; Stg Crw; Rptr Yrbk; FHA; Spn Clb; Marshall Univ; Home Economist.

PYLES, MICHELE D; Hampshire HS; Points, WV; 81/213 Cmnty Wkr; Chmn Yth Flsp; Pres 4-H; FBLA; Bsktbl; Trk; GAA; 4-H Awd; Shepherd Coll; Bus.

PYLES, ROBIN; Waynesfield Goshen HS; Waynesfield, OH; 2/37 VP Sr Cls; Am Leg Boys St; Hon Rl; Jr NHS; NHS; Crs Cntry; Trk; Ohio St Univ; Chemical Engr.

PYLMAN, AMY; Evart HS; Sears, MI; Pres Frsh Cls; VP Jr Cls; Band; Hon Rl; NHS; Sch Pl; Cit Awd;.

PYLYPCHUK, CINDY; Bishop Donahue HS; Mc Mechen, WV; Trs Soph Cls; Sec Jr Cls; Girl Scts; Hon Rl; Treas NHS; Rptr Yrbk; Rptr Sch Nwsp; Pep Clb; Capt Chrldng; GAA; Wheeling Beauty Coll; Beautician.

PYPE, ROBYN; Medina Sr HS; Medina, OH; 20/350 AFS; Band; Chrs; Hon Rl; Orch; Sch Mus; Stg Crw; Drama Clb; PPFtbl; Univ; Math.

PYRON, JANE; Parkside HS; Jackson, MI; 20/389 Debate Tm; Natl Forn Lg; Lat Clb; Emory Univ; Pre Law.

PYSH, DAVID; Lake Station Edison HS; Lake Station, IN; Cl Rep Jr Cls; Cls Rep Sr Cls; Band; Hon Rl; Jr NHS; Fr Clb; Ten; Purdue; Computer Science.

PYTEL, MARK; De La Salle Collegiate HS; Detroit, MI; Boy Scts; Hon Rl; Jr NHS; NHS; Sch Mus; Drama Clb; Letter Ftbl; Michigan St Univ; Vet.

Q

QUA, CONSTANCE; Shaker Hts HS; Shaker Hts, OH; Cls Rep Frsh Cls; Cls Rep Soph Cls; Cl Rep Jr Cls; Cls Rep Sr Cls; Y-Teens; Univ; Nursing.

QUACKENBUSH, SHERRY; Hammond Baptist HS; Highland, IN; Chrs; Chrh Wkr; Hon Rl; Yth Flsp; Hyles Anderson Coll; Elem Ed.

QUAINTANCE, CHERRI; De Kalb HS; Auburn, IN; 55/287 Cls Rep Frsh Cls; Chrs; Debate Tm; Natl Forn Lg; NHS; Sch Pl; Yth Flsp; Ger Clb; Schlrshp 3rd Rnnrup For Miss N E IN 78; Bus.

QUALKENBUSH, DONALD R; Springs Valley HS; West Baden, IN; Sec Frsh Cls; Trs Soph Cls; Hon Rl; Glf; Univ; Archt.

QUALLEN, JOE; Purcell HS; Cincinnati, OH; Hon Rl; Bsbl; Ftbl; IM Sprt; Univ; Bus.

QUALLEN, JOHN; Wilmington HS; Wilmington, OH; 21/285 Chrh Wkr; Hon Rl; NHS; 4-H; Fr Clb; FFA; Bsbl; Bsktbl; 4-H Awd; MPV Of Var Bsbl Team 79; Univ.

QUALLS, PAULA; East HS; Akron, OH; Cls Rep Soph Cls; Pres Jr Cls; Chrh Wkr; Cmnty Wkr; FCA; Hon Rl; Stu Cncl; Pres OEA; Pep Clb; Capt Chrldng; Univ.

QUALLS, SYLVIA; Immaculata HS; Detroit, MI; Cmnty Wkr; Hon Rl; NHS; Pol Wkr; Trk; Peer Cnslr For Detoit Transi Alternative 78; Mbr Of Youth Advsy Comm Vor Natl Runaway Serv 79; Northwestern Univ; Soc Work.

QUALTIRE, PATRICK; Steubenville Cthlc Cntrl HS; Mingo Jct, OH; 25/250 Hon Rl; NHS; Letter Glf; Letter Ten; Univ Of Cincinnati; Bus Admin.

QUANDT, LINDA; Lutheran HS East; Roseville, MI; 4/130 Cls Rep Frsh Cls; Cls Rep Soph Cls; Chrs; Chrh Wkr; Hon Rl; Jr NHS; NHS; Stu Cncl; Ed Yrbk; Rptr Yrbk; Stud Council Sec 77; Univ Of Detroit Trustees Grant 79; CMU Acad Hon Schlrshp 79; Central Michigan Univ; Acctg.

QUARLES, JACQUELINE E; Broad Ripple HS; Indianapolis, IN; Band; Chrh Wkr; Girl Scts; Hon Rl; JA; Sct Actv; Yth Flsp; Ger Clb; Mgrs; Indiana Univ; Med.

QUATRINI, LINDA; Lahser HS; Blmfld Hills, MI; 30/415 Band; Hon Rl; NHS; Spn Clb; Natl Merit Ltr; Mic State Univ; Elem Educa.

QUATTRO, ANTHONY; Williamson HS; Williamson, WV; 3/81 Trs Jr Cls; Trs Sr Cls; Am Leg Boys St; Chrh Wkr; Lit Mag; Sch Pl; Yth Flsp; VP Drama Clb; Wendall Walker Cup; YMCA Youth In Govt Speaker Of Hse; Univ Of Florida; Biology.

QUEALY, ANGELA; Holy Name Nazareth HS; Cleveland, OH; Chrh Wkr; Cmnty Wkr; Girl Scts; Hon Rl; Jr NHS; NHS; Sct Actv; College; Math.

QUEARY, DENNIS; Bellbrook HS; Bellbrook, OH; Trs Frsh Cls; Yth Flsp; Mgrs; Letter Scr Kpr; Univ; Elec.

QUEEN, DONNA; Roosevelt Wilson HS; Clarksburg, WV; 3/122 Am Leg Aux Girls St; Chrh Wkr; Hon Rl; Hosp Ade; Lbry Ade; NHS; FNA; Sec FTA; Mas Awd; Alderson Broaddus Coll; Nursing.

QUEEN, KIMBERLY; Bluefield HS; Bluefld, WV; 12/287 Band; Drm Mjrt; Hon Rl; Jr NHS; NHS; Stu Cncl; Rptr Yrbk; Fr Clb; Keyettes; Pep Clb; Outstndng Stu Awd; Sportsmnshp Awd; Softbl Awd; Hon Ment All St Baskbl ; All Tournmnt Team Basktbl; Univ; Phys Educ.

QUEEN, NORMA; Wayne HS; Wayne, WV; Hon Rl; Beta Clb; 4-H; Pep Clb; Bus Schl; Admin.

QUEEN, SUSAN; Upper Arlington HS; Columbus, OH; 1/610 AFS; Chrh Wkr; Girl Scts; Hon Rl; JA; Lbry Ade; NHS; Sct Actv; Fr Clb; Pep Clb; Proj Bus Awd 77; Sci Fair Awds 77; French Natl Hon Soc 78; Columbus Dent Soc Awd; Amer Inst Of Mining Awd; Univ; Sci Research.

QUEEN, VICKIE; Springfield HS; Lakemore, OH; Hst Jr Cls; Chrs; Chrh Wkr; Hon Rl; OEA; Akron Univ; Busns Admin.

QUEENER, JOHN; South High HS; Youngstwn, OH; NHS; Letter Ftbl; College; Psychologist.

QUEENER, JOHN; South HS; Youngstown, OH; 11/327 Letter Ftbl; Ohio State Univ; Psych.

QUEENER, PEGGY; Wayne HS; Dayton, OH; Chrs; Drl Tm; Sch Mus; Sch Pl; VP Drama Clb; Other; Theater.

QUELLETTE, SARAH; Carrollton HS; Saginaw, MI; Band; Chrs; Chrh Wkr; Cmnty Wkr; Girl Scts; MMM; Off Ade; Pol Wkr; Red Cr Ade; Sct Actv; Grad Barbizon Model Schl 1977; Ms Tri Cnty Rnnr Up 1978; Yth For Undrstndg Exchg Stud 1979; Univ; Music Tchr.

QUELLHORST, BEVERLY; Memorial HS; New Bremen, OH; 16/223 Band; Chrs; Chrh Wkr; Hon Rl; NHS; Y-Teens; 4-H; Pres FHA; Pep Clb; GAA; Miami Vly Schl; Nursing.

QUELLO, ANGELA; Warsaw Cmnty HS; Warsaw, IN; Hon Rl; Purdue Univ; Vet.

QUERNER, KATHLEEN; Springboro HS; Springboro, OH; NHS; Trk; Coach Actv; Scr Kpr; College; Natural Resources.

QUERY, DAN; Owen Valley HS; Coal City, IN; .

QUESNELLE, FRANCIS; Bishop Gallagher HS; Detroit, MI; 20/335 Hon Rl; IM Sprt; College; Accounting.

QUICK, TERRI; N Central HS; Shelburn, IN; 10/100 Sec Frsh Cls; Sec Soph Cls; Sec Jr Cls; Sec Sr Cls; Hon Rl; Off Ade; Sch Pl; Stg Crw; Stu Cncl; Drama Clb; Univ; Psych.

QUICKEL, TERISSA; Lynchburg Clay HS; Lynchburg, OH; 12/96 Chrs; Girl Scts; Hon Rl; Sch Pl; FHA;.

QUILLEN, KELLY; East Canton HS; Canton, OH; 10/104 Treas Am Leg Aux Girls St; Chrh Wkr; NHS; Yth Flsp; Drama Clb; OEA; Pep Clb; Sci Clb; Crs Cntry; Letter Trk; Timken Company.

QUINCE, TANYA; Pontiac Central HS; Pontiac, MI; Sec Sr Cls; Band; Chrh Wkr; Cmnty Wkr; Hon Rl; Hosp Ade; NHS; Off Ade; Yth Flsp; Civ Clb; Whos Who Among Amer HS Stdtn 77; Wayne St Univ; Pre Med.

QUINCEL, DAWN; New Albany HS; New Albany, OH; Sec Sr Cls; Am Leg Aux Girls St; Hon Rl; Off Ade; 4-H; Pres Pep Clb; Capt Chrldng; IM Sprt; Mat Maids; PPFtbl; Chosen As All Star Cheerleader At Frnkln Hts HS; Track Queen; Homecoming Queen; College; Bsns Mgmt.

QUINLAN, PATRICIA; Cardinal Stritch HS; Northwood, OH; 34/180 Band; Chrs; Girl Scts; Jr NHS; NHS; Sch Mus; Pep Clb; Pres Spn Clb; Toledo Univ; Theatre.

QUINLAN, RUSSELL; Cardinal Stritch HS; Toledo, OH; 46/205 Hon Rl; Spn Clb; Univ Of Toledo; Aero Engr.

QUINLAN, SUSAN; Otsego HS; Bowling Grn, OH; 15/120 Hon Rl; Jr NHS; Spn Clb; Letter Bsktbl; IM Sprt; Mgrs; PPFtbl; Ohio St Univ; Pre Med.

QUINLIVAN, JONI; Lake HS; Walbridge, OH; Trs Frsh Cls; Trs Soph Cls; Sec Jr Cls; Hon Rl; Off Ade; PAVAS; Sch Mus; Sch Pl; Stg Crw; Sprt Ed Sch Nwsp; Univ; Nursing.

QUINN, BELINDA; Attica HS; Attica, IN; 18/72 Aud/Vis; Lbry Ade; Sch Nwsp; Fr Clb; Pres.

QUINN, BRIDGET; Manistee HS; Manistee, MI; Univ Of Michigan; Med Tech.

QUINN, FRANK; Salem Sr HS; Salem, OH; 23/245 Am Leg Boys St; Hon Rl; VICA; Letter Ftbl; Trk; St Awd Of Distnent For Drafting 79; Top Scorer In St Test Or Drafting 78 & 79; Univ; Mech Engr.

QUINN, JENNIFER; Mother Of Mercy HS; Cincinnati, OH; Aud/Vis; Chrs; Hon Rl; JA; Sch Mus; Spn Clb;.

QUINN, KEVIN; Highland HS; Chesterfield, IN; 3/400 Chrh Wkr; Hon Rl; NHS; Am Leg Awd; Opt Clb Awd; Ball St St Schlrshp 79; Ball St Univ; Archt.

QUINN, SEAN; Struthers HS; Struthers, OH; Chrs; Chrh Wkr; PAVAS; Sch Nwsp; Fr Clb; Bsbl; Bsktbl; Ftbl; IM Sprt; Mgrs; Norte Dame; Engineering.

QUINN, TAMARA; Traverse City HS; Traverse City, MI; 4-H; Socr; 4-H Awd; Natl Merit Ltr; Natl Merit SF; Natl Merit Schl; Northern Mic Univ; Argi.

QUINN, TERESA; Gladstone Area HS; Gladstone, MI; Band; Girl Scts; Hon Rl; Stg Crw; Drama Clb; Twrlr; Bay De Noc Community Coll; Spch Thrp.

QUINN, VICTORIA; John Marshall HS; Indianapolis, IN; Debate Tm; Hon Rl; JA; NHS; Orch; Sch Mus; Sch Pl; Fr Clb; Univ; Poli Sci.

QUINONEZ, STEVEN; Holy Redeemer HS; Detroit, MI; 62/112 Band; Chrh Wkr; Ed Yrbk; Rptr Yrbk; Yrbk; IM Sprt; Scr Kpr; Cit Awd; College; Architect.

QUIRE, KIMBERLY; Marian HS; Cincinnati, OH; Girl Scts; JA; Off Ade; FHA; College; Accounting.

QUIREY, STACY; Bosse HS; Evansville, IN; 34/329 Chrs; Girl Scts; Hon Rl; Hosp Ade; Yth Flsp; Ger Clb; Pep Clb; Trk; Univ Of Evansville; Nurse.

QUISENBERRY, JEFFREY J; Austintown Fitch HS; Austintown, OH; Aud/Vis; Chrs; JA; Mdrgl; NHS; Stg Crw; Natl Merit Ltr; Natl Merit SF; Natl Merit Schl; Ohio Scholastic Team Mbr; Pres Austintown Fitch Soc; Case Western Reserve Univ; Math.

QUIST, CHAD; East Noble HS; Kendallvle, IN; 3/258 FCA; Hon Rl; NHS; Yth Flsp; Ger Clb; Letter Ftbl; Letter Trk; Letter Wrstlng; Mgrs; PPFtbl; De Pauw Univ; Chem Engr.

QUIVEY, KATHIE; Meigs HS; Shade, OH; Band; Chrs; Chrh Wkr; Hon Rl; Sch Mus; Sch Pl; Stg Crw; Spn Clb; Flag Corp Liuet 78 80; Hero Club 78; Tchr Aide 78; Univ; Elem Educ.

QUOCK, KIM Y; Cass Technical HS; Detroit, MI; Cmnty Wkr; Hon Rl; Off Ade; Sch Nwsp; Mth Clb; Sci Clb; Spn Clb; Gov Hon Prg Awd; Was State Univ; Sci.

QUOTSON, PATRICK; Field Sr HS; Kent, OH; 1/275 Boy Scts; Hon Rl; Stg Crw; Yrbk; Kent St Univ; Graphic Art.

QURAISHI, CATHERINE A; River Valley HS; Caledonia, OH; 30/216 Trs Soph Cls; Sec Jr Cls; Pres Sr Cls; Cmnty Wkr; Girl Scts; Hon Rl; NHS; Sct Actv; Stu Cncl; Y-Teens; Ohio Northern Univ; Comp Sci.

QUYE, DAVID L; Clarkston HS; Clarkston, MI; Boy Scts; Chrh Wkr; Hon Rl; Sct Actv; Yth Flsp; 4-H; Bsktbl; Ftbl; Trk; Wrstlng; Warner Pacific; Architect.

R

RAAK, CHRISTINE; Otsego HS; Kalamazoo, MI; 19/215 Cls Rep Frsh Cls; Cls Rep Soph Cls; Cl Rep Jr Cls; Cls Rep Sr Cls; Band; Hon Rl; NHS; Off Ade; Sch Pl; Stu Cncl; Hope Coll Hnr Schlrshp; Hope Coll; Psych.

RAASCH, LORRAINE; Jefferson HS; Monroe, MI; 1/158 Val; Chrs; Chrh Wkr; Hon Rl; Hosp Ade; NHS; Sch Pl; Treas Drama Clb; Sec 4-H; Fr Clb; Aid Assoc For Lutheran Cmptve Nrsng Schlrshp 79; Monroe Cnty Cmnty Coll Pres Schlrshp 79; HS Dept Awd Sci; Monroe County Cmnty Coll; Nurse.

RABATIN, SUSAN; Bishop Noll Inst HS; E Chicago, IN; Girl Scts; Hon Rl; Lbry Ade; Yrbk; Mth Clb; Pep Clb; Am Leg Awd; Cit Awd; Tri St Univ; Elem Ed.

RABE, JULIE; Swan Valley HS; Saginaw, MI; Off Ade; Sch Pl; Spn Clb; Ten; Chrldng; Michigan State Univ.

RABEL, KATHY L; Madison Comprehensive HS; Mansfield, OH; Stu Cncl; Fr Clb; Mansfield General Hosp; Nurse.

RABER, MARK; Garaway HS; Sugarcreek, OH; Pres Frsh Cls; VP Jr Cls; Hon Rl; NHS; Yth Flsp; Pres FFA; Letter Bsktbl; Ohi St Wilmington; Agri.

RABER, STEPHEN; Hastings HS; Hastings, MI; 42/271 Chrs; Hon Rl; Sch Mus; Stu Cncl; Fr Clb; Key Clb; Pep Clb; Bsktbl; Ten; Ferris St Coll; Pharm.

RABIAH, PETER; Carman HS; Flint, MI; Band; NHS; Socr; Letter Swmmng; Letter Ten; Univ; Pre Med.

RABLE, DAVID; Champion HS; Warren, OH; 42/226 Hon Rl; Letter Ftbl; Coach Actv; IM Sprt; Acdmc Schlrshp From Youngstown St.

RABOLD, RON; Dublin HS; Dublin, OH; 3/157 Am Leg Boys St; Boy Scts; Chrh Wkr; Hon Rl; Jr NHS; Letter Bsktbl; Letter Socr; Univ.

RABY, ANNE; Regina HS; Cleveland Hts, OH; Aud/Vis; Cmnty Wkr; Hon Rl; JA; Jr NHS; Stu Cncl; Ed Sch Nwsp; Natl Merit SF; Univ; Jrnlsm.

RACE, ANTHONY; Calvert HS; Tiffin, OH; 14/99 Hon Rl; Yrbk; Sch Nwsp; IM Sprt; Coll; Psych.

RACHEL, DAWN; Lexington HS; Mansfield, OH; Band; Drl Tm; Sch Pl; Y-Teens; Drama Clb; Swmmng; Univ; Bio.

RACHWAL, DONNA; St Hedwig HS; Detroit, MI; 7/54 Chrs; Mercy Coll; Clinical Psych.

RACK, MARTIN; La Salle HS; Cincinnati, OH; 12/249 Band; Chrh Wkr; Hon Rl; Sch Mus; Letter Socr; Capt IM Sprt; Univ; Politics.

RACK, MARTIN J; La Salle HS; Cincinnati, OH; 11/290 Band; Hon Rl; NHS; Sch Mus; Sch Pl; Socr; IM Sprt;.

RACKAR, ROBERTA; Euclid Sr HS; Euclid, OH; 16/740 Band; Debate Tm; Lbry Ade; NHS; Quill & Scroll; Sch Mus; Rptr Sch Nwsp; Key Clb; Keyettes; Mgrs; Univ; T V Prod.

RACKETA, MARTHA; Medina Sr HS; Medina, OH; 3/66 Chrs; Girl Scts; Hon Rl; Lbry Ade; Sch Mus; Pep Clb; Ten; Mbr Of Thespians 79; Superior Rating In Chorus 79; Coll; Eng.

RACKLIFFE, SUE; Brecksville HS; Brecksville, OH; Hon Rl; Sch Mus; Sch Pl; Pres Sdlty; Sch Nwsp; Drama Clb; Pep Clb; Spn Clb; Scr Kpr; Tmr; College; Biochem.

RACZAK, DANA; Roosevelt HS; E Chicago, IN; Hon Rl; NHS; Fr Clb; College; English Tchr.

RACZKOWSKI, JUDITH; Manistee Catholic Ctrl HS; Manistee, MI; Chrs; Girl Scts; Hon Rl; Sch Pl; Ed Yrbk; Pep Clb; W Shore Cmnty Coll; Psych.

RADA, CHRISTOPHER; Heath HS; Heath, OH; 34/153 Am Leg Boys St; VP Chrh Wkr; Hon Rl; Letter Bsbl; Bsktbl; Trk; ROE Camp Cnslr 78; Camp Enterprise Delegate Rotary Clb 78; Univ; Bus Admin.

RADAK, TIMOTHY; Hazel Park HS; Hazel Park, MI; 59/550 Cls Rep Frsh Cls; Cl Rep Jr Cls; VP Sr Cls; Cls Rep Sr Cls; Boy Scts; Cmnty Wkr; Hon Rl; Pol Wkr; Sct Actv; Stu Cncl; Adrian Coll; Chem.

RADALIA, DONNA; Louisville HS; Louisville, OH; 17/351 Hon Rl; NHS; Off Ade; Pres 4-H; Bsktbl; Letter Trk; GAA; 4-H Awd; Muskingum College; Elem Educ.

RADCLIFF, DON E; Roosevelt Wilson HS; Mt Clare, WV; 4/122 Cl Rep Jr Cls; Cls Rep Sr Cls; Am Leg Boys St; Hon Rl; NHS; Sch Pl; Yth Flsp; Ed Sch Nwsp; 4-H; Fr Clb; West Virginia Univ; Pharmacy.

RADCLIFF, JOYCE; Lewis Cnty HS; Weston, WV; Chrh Wkr; Off Ade; Yth Flsp; Sch Nwsp; 4-H; FHA; Pep Clb; 4-H Awd; West Virginia Career Coll; Acctg.

RADCLIFF, KENDREA; Pike Central HS; Petersburg, IN; Trs Soph Cls; Pres Jr Cls; Hon Rl; Lbry Ade; NHS; Drama Clb; Indiana St Univ; Soc Worker.

RADCLIFF, ROBIN; Wellston HS; Wellston, OH; Cls Rep Sr Cls; Am Leg Aux Girls St; NHS; Stg Crw; FFA; Mth Clb; Gym; Trk; Capt Chrldng; Rotary Awd; Ohio St Univ; Natural Resources.

RADCLIFF, TONYA; Liberty HS; Clarksburg, WV; 11/226 Cl Rep Jr Cls; Pres Band; Chrs; Girl Scts; Hon Rl; Jr NHS; NHS; Orch; Sch Mus; Sch Pl; Fairmont St Coll; Med Lab Tech.

RADCLIFFE, LYNNE; Terre Haute S Vigo HS; Terre Haute, IN; Girl Scts; Hon Rl; Off Ade; Sch Mus; Yth Flsp; Y-Teens; 4-H; OEA; Spn Clb; 4-H Awd; Merit Awds; Purchase Prize SSAG Student Art Exhibition; Cert Of Merit; Sci Fair Awd; Indiana St Univ; Interior Design.

RADDANT, MEGAN; Novi HS; Novi, MI; 19/250 Am Leg Aux Girls St; Band; Cmnty Wkr; Girl Scts; Hon Rl; NHS; Sch Mus; Sch Pl; Stg Crw; Ed Yrbk; Stephens Coll; Cmnctns.

RADDATZ, MARIE; Summerfield HS; Petersburg, MI; 10/90 Chrs; Chrh Wkr; Cmnty Wkr; Hon Rl; Stg Crw; Yth Flsp; Sch Nwsp; 4-H; Twrlr; Cit Awd; Teachers Aid; Spec Ed Tutor; Newspaper Typist; College; Nursing.

RADE, JEFFREY J; Cardinal Mooney HS; Youngstown, OH; 18/295 Cls Rep Frsh Cls; Cls Rep Soph Cls; Cl Rep Jr Cls; Am Leg Boys St; Debate Tm; Hon Rl; Mod UN; Natl Forn Lg; Rptr Yrbk; Yrbk; Selection For Boys Nation; NEDT Test Top 10 Percent; North East Ohio Industrial Art Contest 1st Plc; Notre Dame Univ; Law.

RADEL, MARY; Napoleon HS; Napoleon, OH; Band; Hon Rl; Lit Mag; NHS; Sch Mus; Sch Pl; Drama Clb; Fr Clb; Bsktbl; Bowling Green St Univ; Med Lab Tech.

RADEMACHER, J; Grand Ledge HS; Grand Ledge, MI; Cmnty Wkr; Hon Rl; Hosp Ade; Lbry Ade; Pres 4-H; Key Clb; Lat Clb; 4-H Awd; Natl Merit Ltr; College; Reg Nurse.

RADEMACHER, STRATTON; Chelsea HS; Chelsea, MI; 65/200 Boy Scts; Hon Rl; Natl Forn Lg; Sprt Ed Sch Nwsp; Rptr Sch Nwsp; Sch Nwsp; Key Clb; Rdo Clb; Spn Clb; Glf; Colorado St Univ; Cmnctns.

RADEN, JONATHAN; Culver Military Academy; Dallas, TX; 68/191 Hon Rl; ROTC; Cit Awd; SAR Awd; Univ; Emergency Doctor.

RADENBAUGH, M; Davison HS; Davison, MI; Hon Rl; Ftbl; IM Sprt; U Of M; Industrial Electonics.

RADER, CLARITA; Copley HS; Akron, OH; 80/319 Band; Chrh Wkr; Cmnty Wkr; Girl Scts; Hon Rl; Hosp Ade; Letter Swmmng; Cit Awd; Univ Of Ten; Nursing.

RADER, ELIZABETH A; Newark Sr HS; Newark, OH; 1/550 Cls Rep Frsh Cls; Cls Rep Soph Cls; Cl Rep Jr Cls; VP Sr Cls; VP Trs Frsh Cls; VP Debate Tm; Drm Mjrt; Hon Rl; Jr NHS; NHS; 3rd Ohio Debate 1978; Northwestern Univ; Poli Sci.

RADER, JONATHAN; Mansfield Malabar HS; Mansfield, OH; Orch; Lat Clb; Mth Clb; Letter Ftbl; Socr; Letter Ten; Ohio State; Forestry.

RADER, KATHY; Huntington North HS; Huntington, IN; 13/565 Cls Rep Frsh Cls; Cls Rep Soph Cls; VP Jr Cls; Cl Rep Jr Cls; VP Sr Cls; Cls Rep Sr Cls; Am Leg Aux Girls St; Chrs; Chrh Wkr; Cmnty Wkr; Univ Of Wisconsin; Fshn Mdse.

RADER, LEESA; Crestline HS; Galion, OH; 1/114 Trs Jr Cls; Cl Rep Jr Cls; Val; Am Leg Aux Girls St; Hon Rl; NHS; Stu Cncl; Yth Flsp; Ed Yrbk; 4-H; Ohio St Univ; Pre Vet.

RADER, LOREN; Brookille HS; Brookville, IN; Pres Frsh Cls; Chrs; Stu Cncl; Sci Clb; IM Sprt; Ball State Univ; Architecture.

RADER, REBECCA; Van Buren HS; Brazil, IN; 24/97 Lbry Ade; Off Ade; Rptr Yrbk; Drama Clb; FBLA; FHA; Pep Clb;.

RADER, SUELLEN; Mc Comb HS; Mccomb, OH; 6/67 Band; Boy Scts; Hon Rl; NHS; Sch Pl; Sct Actv; Stu Cncl; Bowling Green State Univ; Microbio.

RADERMACHER, TINA; Anchor Bay HS; New Baltimore, MI; Girl Scts; Hon Rl; DECA; Pep Clb; Cmnty Serv Awd; Detroit Coll; Mktg.

RADFORD, ANITA; George Washington HS; Indianapolis, IN; Chrs; Chrh Wkr; Cmnty Wkr; Hon Rl; Lbry Ade; NHS; Off Ade; Sch Mus; Sch Pl; Drama Clb; Central State; Math.

RADFORD, STEPHANIE; Meigs HS; Pomeroy, OH; Am Leg Aux Girls St; Band; Chrs; Drl Tm; Drm Bgl; Hon Rl; Mdrgl; Sch Pl; Yrbk; 4-H; Tennessee Tech Univ; Music.

RADKE, PAUL; Fraser HS; Fraser, MI; Boy Scts; Chrh Wkr; Hon Rl; Red Cr Ade; Sct Actv; FTA; Swmmng; Trk; God Cntry Awd; Univ Of Michigan; Mech Engr.

RADLICK, JANICE M; Bishop Gallagher HS; Detroit, MI; 1/336 Cls Rep Sr Cls; Chrh Wkr; Cmnty Wkr; Hon Rl; Off Ade; Stu Cncl; Rptr Yrbk; Rptr Sch Nwsp; Sci Clb; PPFtbl; Univ Of Michigan; Law.

RADSAN, AFSHEEN; Grosse Ile HS; Grosse Ile, MI; 3/200 Pres Frsh Cls; Cls Rep Frsh Cls; Pres Sr Cls; Hon Rl; Stu Cncl; Spn Clb; Bsktbl; Ten; Stanford Univ; Chem Engr.

RADTKE, MICHAEL; Iron Mtn Sr HS; Iron Mountain, MI; 10/150 Hon Rl; NHS; Letter Ftbl; IM Sprt; Mgrs; Michigan Tech Univ; Elec Engr.

RADWAN, MARGARET; Walled Lake Central HS; West Bloomfield, MI; VP Frsh Cls; Chrs; Chrh Wkr; Girl Scts; Hon Rl; NHS; Orch; Sch Pl; Ger Clb; Univ Of Mich; Chem Engr.

RADWANSKI, MICHELLE; Rossford HS; Rossford, OH; 16/147 Sec Jr Cls; Cls Rep Sr Cls; Hon Rl; NHS; Sch Mus; Stu Cncl; Rptr Yrbk; Yrbk; Drama Clb; Sec Fr Clb; Bowling Green St Univ; Social Work.

RAEHL, CRYSTAL; Merrillville Sr HS; Merrillville, IN; 62/611 Hon Rl; Lbry Ade; Academic Awd Whos Who Amng Amer HS Stu 77; Upper 10% Of 79 Sr Grad Class;.

RAFF, MIKE; Fairless HS; Beach City, OH; 60/219 VP Frsh Cls; Am Leg Boys St; Cmnty Wkr; Sec Key Clb; Letter Ftbl; Letter Trk; Elec.

RAFFERTY, BRENDA; Rensselaer Central HS; Rensselaer, IN; 7/170 Chrh Wkr; Hon Rl; NHS; Stu Cncl; 4-H; Fr Clb; Key Clb; Mth Clb; Cit Awd; 4-H Awd; Purdue Univ; Aeronautical Engineer.

RAFTERY, SHARON; Garden City East HS; Garden City, MI; Chrh Wkr; Letter Bsbl; Capt Bsktbl; Coach Actv; Natl Merit Schl; Univ Of Mic; Engr.

RAGAN, CHRISTINA; Salem HS; Salem, OH; 10/260 Band; Hon Rl; MMM; Ger Clb; DAR Awd; Kent State Univ; Pre Vet.

RAGAN, CINDY; South Range HS; Poland, OH; Pres Jr Cls; Hon Rl; Y-Teens; Fr Clb; OEA; Bsbl; Bsktbl; IM Sprt; Scr Kpr; Tmr; Youngstown St Univ; Acctg.

RAGAN, NIKOLA; Kearsley HS; Burton, MI; 41/375 Chrs; Chrh Wkr; Hon Rl; Jr NHS; Mdrgl; NHS; Sch Pl; Drama Clb; Fr Clb; FHA; Cert Of Mbrshp To Natl Hnr Soc 77; Univ Of Alabama; RN.

RAGER, JAN; Whitko HS; Pierceton, IN; Chrs; Chrh Wkr; Natl Forn Lg; Off Ade; Sch Mus; Stg Crw; Drama Clb; Pep Clb; Univ; Eng.

RAGLAND, MARY E; East HS; Columbus, OH; Cls Rep Soph Cls; Band; Chrs; Hon Rl; Lbry Ade; NHS; Off Ade; Orch; IM Sprt; Southeast Career Cntr.

RAGONESI, SUSAN; Western HS; Parma, MI; Band; Chrh Wkr; Girl Scts; Sch Mus; Yth Flsp; Fr Clb; Trk; Chrldng; Grand Rapids Baptist College; Music.

RAGSDALE, JAN; William Henry Harrison HS; Evansville, IN; 113/467 Chrs; Chrh Wkr; Hon Rl; Yth Flsp; Fr Clb; Pep Clb; Glf; Kty Christian Coll; Vocal Music.

RAHE, SHERYL; Yorktown HS; Muncie, IN; 54/172 VP Sr Cls; Hon Rl; Spn Clb; Swmmng; Trk; Voc Schl; Cruise Dir.

RAHE, WENDE; Madison Heights HS; Anderson, IN; Band; Boy Scts; Chrh Wkr; Sct Actv; Yth Flsp; Pep Clb; Fort Wayne International; Legal Sec.

RAHI, ADELE; Wheeling Park HS; Wheeling, WV; 8/599 Cl Rep Jr Cls; AFS; Hon Rl; NHS; Off Ade; Stu Cncl; 4-H; Fr Clb; IM Sprt; Cit Awd; 2nd Pl Stifel Prize; W Liberty St Coll; Bio.

RAHMEL, AMY; Ayersville HS; Defiance, OH; 1/85 Pres Soph Cls; Am Leg Aux Girls St; Chrs; Cmnty Wkr; Hon Rl; Mdrgl; NHS; Sch Mus; Ykbk; VP Fr Clb; Genrl Motors Awd 76; Otstndng Algbr 2 Stud Awd 77; Otstndng Amer History Stud Awd 78; Bowling Green St Univ; Bus Admin.

RAHN, DENNIS; Mason County Central HS; Scottville, MI; 7/120 Band; Hon Rl; Rptr Sch Nwsp; 4-H; Spn Clb; Voice Dem Awd; Central Mic Univ; Broadcasting.

RAHN, WILLIAM G; John Glenn HS; Bay City, MI; 50/322 Boy Scts; Bsbl; IM Sprt; Crtfc Of Recgntn St Of MI Comptv Schlrshp Prog 79; The MI St Brd Of Educ Crtfict Of Recgntn Acdmc Achvmnt; Delta Coll; Engr.

RAHRIG, ANN; Mc Auley HS; Cincinnati, OH; 1/260 Cls Rep Soph Cls; Pres Jr Cls; Pres Sr Cls; Val; Am Leg Aux Girls St; Chrh Wkr; Cmnty Wkr; Xavier Univ; Bus.

RAIBLE, KIM; Mother Of Mercy HS; Cincinnati, OH; 6/254 Aud/Vis; Cmp Fr Grls; Chrs; Cmnty Wkr; Hon Rl; NHS; Sec 4-H; Fr Clb; College; Occup Therapy.

RAID, DUANE; Bellefontaine HS; Bellefontaine, OH; 17/245 Hon Rl; Letter Bsbl; Letter Ftbl; Univ.

RAIDERS, JAMES; Weir HS; Weirton, WV; 55/353 Boy Scts; Hon Rl; NHS; Sch Pl; Stg Crw; Drama Clb; Key Clb; God Cntry Awd; W Vir Inst Of Tech; Electrical Engin.

RAIFF, JULIE; Dayton Chaminade Julienne; Dayton, OH; Cls Rep Frsh Cls; Cl Rep Jr Cls; Cls Rep Sr Cls; Chrh Wkr; Sec FCA; Socr; Wrstlng; IM Sprt; PPFtbl; Scr Kpr; Fast Pitch Softball Varsity 78 & 79; Prest Church Teen Club 77 78 79 & 80; Volleyball Soph Yr Varsity; Coll; Marine Bio.

RAIKES, TAMMY; Bridgeport HS; Shinnston, WV; 12/189 Band; Chrs; Chrh Wkr; Hon Rl; Jr NHS; Pres Lbry Ade; NHS; Yth Flsp; Y-Teens; Pres 4-H; Bob Jones Univ; Elem Ed.

RAINBOLT, SHERRY; Bremen Sr HS; Bremen, IN; 13/105 Cls Rep Sr Cls; Chrh Wkr; FCA; Hon Rl; Off Ade; Pol Wkr; Sch Mus; Sch Pl; Stg Crw; Stu Cncl; Ball St Univ; Bus.

RAINE, RON; Arsenal Technical HS; Indianapolis, IN; Band; Hon Rl; Boys Clb Am; Bsbl; Bsktbl; Scr Kpr; Cit Awd; UCLA; Elec Engr.

RAINERY, PAMELA; Riverside HS; Painesville, OH; Band; Chrs; Chrh Wkr; Hon Rl; Univ; Internatl Rel.

RAINES, DALE; North Adams HS; Seaman, OH; 9/91 Pres Jr Cls; Band; Chrs; Hon Rl; NHS; Sch Mus; Sch Pl; Stu Cncl; Rptr Yrbk; 4-H; Morehead St Univ; Music.

RAINES, JAMES; Lasalle HS; Cincinnati, OH; Hon Rl; Letter Socr; Letter Trk; IM Sprt; College; Comp Elec.

RAINES, LORI; Northview HS; Grand Rapids, MI; 59/300 Chrs; Girl Scts; Hon Rl; JA; NHS; Pep Clb; IM Sprt; PPFtbl; Davenport Coll; Comp Prog.

RAINES, TODD; Spencer HS; Spencer, WV; Am Leg Boys St; Hon Rl; Jr NHS; NHS; Yrbk; Letter Trk; Glenville College.

RAINES III, WALTER; Kermit HS; Kermit, WV; Cls Rep Sr Cls; Chrh Wkr; FCA; Lbry Ade; NHS; Sch Pl; Stu Cncl; Pres Beta Clb; VP Spn Clb; Bsbl; Marshall Univ; Poli Sci.

RAINEY, DON; Le Banon HS; Lebanon, OH; Am Leg Boys St; Chrs; Hon Rl; Univ.

RAINEY, PATRICIA; Greenfield Central HS; Greenfield, IN; Chrs; Chrh Wkr; Natl Forn Lg; Sch Pl; Stg Crw; Yth Flsp; Rptr Yrbk; Drama Clb; Spn Clb; Ball St Univ; Jrnlsm.

RAINS, RICHARD; Highland HS; Anderson, IN; Boy Scts; Hon Rl; Mgrs; ITT Tech Inst; Auto Mech.

RAINS, STEVE; Waynesville HS; Lebanon, OH; Hon Rl; Letter Ftbl; IM Sprt; Univ; Bio Sci.

RAISCH, MARK; Valley View HS; Germantown, OH; VP Frsh Cls; Treas Band; Chmn Chrh Wkr; Pres NHS; Stu Cncl; Letter Bsktbl; Letter Ten; Capt IM Sprt; Miami Univ; Pre Dent.

RAIVZEE, DOLORES; Timken Sr HS; Canton, OH; VP Frsh Cls; Cls Rep Soph Cls; Cl Rep Jr Cls; Band; Chrh Wkr; Drm Bgl; Girl Scts; Hon Rl; Hosp Ade; NHS; Western Reserve Univ; Med.

RAKCZYNSKI, JANE; Manistee Cath Central HS; Manistee, MI; Hon Rl;.

RAKE, CARRIE; Washington County Jt Voc HS; Marietta, OH; Sec Frsh Cls; Sec Soph Cls; Hon Rl; NHS; Y-Teens; 4-H; Treas FFA; Bsktbl; VP GAA; Mat Maids; FFA Queen; Southeastern Acad; Travel Agent.

RAKEL, JULIE M; Turpin HS; Cincinnati, OH; Sec Soph Cls; Chrs; Girl Scts; Socr; Swmmng; Ten; PPFtbl; Tmr; College.

RAKESTRAW, DAVID; Edgewood Sr HS; Ashtabula, OH; 9/260 VP Jr Cls; VP Sr Cls; AFS; Chrh Wkr; Hon Rl; Lbry Ade; NHS; Stu Cncl; Lat Clb; Sci Clb; Bucknell Univ; Engr.

RAKESTRAW, JOHN; Rochester HS; Rochester, IN; 12/170 Pres Chrs; Hon Rl; Mdrgl; NHS; Sch Mus; Sch Pl; VP Drama Clb; Elk Awd; Ind Univ At Bloomington; Vocal Mus.

RALICH, STEVE; South Range HS; Salem, OH; Hon Rl; Off Ade; Ger Clb; Ftbl; Youngstown St Univ; Busns Admin.

RALL, PAT; Col Crawford HS; Crestline, OH; Am Leg Boys St; Chrh Wkr; JA; 4-H; Bsbl; Bsktbl; Ftbl; Capt IM Sprt; 4-H Awd; JA Awd; Univ.

RALL, PATRICK A; Col Crawford HS; Crestline, OH; Am Leg Boys St; Hon Rl; VP JA; 4-H; Bsbl; Bsktbl; Ftbl; IM Sprt; Pres JA Awd; Voc Schl.

RALPH, TERESE; St Joseph Acad; N Olmsted, OH; Drl Tm; Girl Scts; Sci Clb; College; Physical Therapy.

RALSTON, DAVID; Boonville HS; Newburgh, IN; 11/225 Am Leg Boys St; Hon Rl; NHS; Bsbl; Bsktbl; Ftbl; Wrstlng; Western Kentucky Univ; Phys Ed.

RALSTON, KARLA; Bellbrook HS; Bellbrook, OH; Off Ade; Sprt Ed Yrbk; Lat Clb; Bsktbl; Capt Trk; VP GAA; IM Sprt; Univ Of Tenn; Communications.

RALSTON, KATHLEEN A; Barnesville HS; Barnesville, OH; 14/130 VP Chrs; Hon Rl; Sch Mus; Sec Yth Flsp; Drama Clb; Fr Clb; FTA; West Liberty St Coll; Music Ed.

RALSTON, PAMELA; Marine Cty Ward Cottrell HS; Marine City, MI; Band; Chrs; Chrh Wkr; Cmnty Wkr; Drl Tm; Drm Mjrt; Hon Rl; NHS; Sch Pl; Rptr Sch Nwsp; St Clair Co Comm Coll; Journalism.

RALSTON, TIM; Eastern HS; Georgetown, OH; Hon Rl; Pol Wkr; Ger Clb; Am Leg Awd; Cit Awd; 7th In Miami Univ Dist In Ohio Tests Of Schlstc Achvmnt 79; Univ; Civil Engr.

RAMAGE, JEFF; Yale HS; Avoca, MI; CAP; Drl Tm; Sci Clb; Crs Cntry; Univ; Air Force Officer Trng.

RAMAKRISHNA, SARVA; George Washington Sr HS; Charleston, WV; 28/335 Chrs; Chrh Wkr; Jr NHS; Lbry Ade; Rptr Yrbk; Rptr Sch Nwsp; Spn Clb; Wellesley Coll; Bio.

RAMBO, ANGELA; Bridgman HS; Bridgman, MI; Band; Hon Rl; Lbry Ade; Off Ade; FHA; Pom Pon; 4-H Awd; Tri State Univ; Computer Sci.

RAMBO, T MICHAEL; Purcell HS; Cincinnati, OH; 16/195 Cls Rep Frsh Cls; Cls Rep Soph Cls; Cls Rep Sr Cls; Aud/Vis; Chrh Wkr; Cmnty Wkr; Hon Rl; JA; Jr NHS; NHS; Univ Of Texas; TV Brdcstng.

RAMBO, TODD; Oakwood HS; Dayton, OH; Chrs; Hon Rl; Sch Mus; Sch Pl; Stu Cncl; Drama Clb; Eng Clb; Socr; Trk; Coll; Sci.

RAMEY, BRIAN; Decatur Central HS; Indpls, IN; 1/260 Hon Rl; NHS; Lat Clb; Ten; Trk; IM Sprt; College.

RAMEY, CURTIS; Harts HS; Harts, WV; 1/48 Pres Frsh Cls; Cls Rep Soph Cls; Cl Rep Jr Cls; Val; Band; Hon Rl; NHS; Sch Nwsp; 4-H; Sci Clb; Marshall Univ; Pre Med.

RAMEY, DAN; Teays Valley HS; Ashville, OH; 24/171 Am Leg Boys St; Band; Chrh Wkr; FCA; Hon Rl; NHS; Sch Pl; Stg Crw; VP Yth Flsp; Drama Clb; Ohio St Univ; Music.

RAMEY, DEBBIE; Williamson HS; Williamson, WV; 15/143 Chrs; Girl Scts; Hon Rl; Lit Mag; FBLA; FHA; Pep Clb; Spn Clb; John F Kennedy Essey Awd 73; Univ.

RAMEY, DEBBIE; Walnut Ridge HS; Columbus, OH; Hon Rl; Yth Flsp; VP OEA; Univ; Med.

RAMEY, JANICE; Centerburg HS; Centerburg, OH; 3/65 Sec Jr Cls; Trs Sr Cls; Hon Rl; Hosp Ade; NHS; Stu Cncl; Y-Teens; Drama Clb; 4-H; Spn Clb; Cntrl Ohio Tech Coll; Nursing.

RAMEY, JILL; Winfield HS; Scott Depot, WV; Trs Frsh Cls; VP Sr Cls; Am Leg Aux Girls St; Hon Rl; Jr NHS; NHS; Beta Clb; FHA; Pep Clb; Capt Chrldng; Marshall Univ; Home Ec.

RAMEY, MARGO; Corington Comnty HS; Veedersburg, IN; 25/109 Sec Frsh Cls; Trs Frsh Cls; Cls Rep Soph Cls; Cl Rep Jr Cls; Chrs; Stu Cncl; Yrbk; OEA; Pep Clb; Chrldng; Danville Jr Coll; Acctg.

RAMEY, SANDRA; Heath HS; Heath, OH; 19/160 Band; Hon Rl; Natl Forn Lg; NHS; Sch Pl; Spn Clb; Univ; Theatre.

RAMEY, SHARON; Beech Grove HS; Beech Grove, IN; 29/216 Hon Rl; NHS; Stg Crw; Rptr Yrbk; OEA; Ten; IM Sprt; Busns Schl; Data Processing.

RAMEY, STEVE; Crum HS; Crum, WV; VP Frsh Cls; Sec Soph Cls; Hon Rl; Jr NHS; NHS; Bsbl; Bsktbl; Ftbl; IM Sprt; Voc Schl.

RAMEY, TAMMY; Jackson HS; Jackson, OH; Am Leg Aux Girls St; Band; Hon Rl; NHS; Quill & Scroll; Pres Yth Flsp; Ed Yrbk; VP 4-H; Sci Clb; Mas Awd; Delegate To Youth In Govt 79; Univ; Nurse.

RAMIREZ, SHARON; Bishop Noll Inst; Chicago, IL; 111/331 Band; Hon Rl; Orch; Trk; Tmr; College; Bus.

RAMM, BRIAN; Boardman HS; Boardman, OH; Boy Scts; Chrs; Hon Rl; Pol Wkr; Sch Pl; Stu Cncl; VP Sci Clb; Spn Clb; Letter Ten; Trk; 1st Pl Spnsh Drama 79; Natl Span Awd 78; Univ; Orthodontist.

RAMMEL, GARY; Northmont HS; Brookville, OH; Ger Clb; Us Army.

RAMONA, DAVID N; Euclid Sr HS; Euclid, OH; 13/714 Band; Hon Rl; Lit Mag; NHS; Pol Wkr; Rptr Sch Nwsp; Key Clb; NCTE; Natl Merit Ltr; Mbr Harvard U Pre Coll Prg 1978;.

RAMOS, ANASTASIA; William A Wirt HS; Gary, IN; 27/230 Cls Rep Sr Cls; Chrs; Chrh Wkr; Cmnty Wkr; Girl Scts; Hon Rl; NHS; Stu Cncl; Pep Clb; Capt Chrldng; Ball St Univ; Bus.

RAMOS, CARLOS E; Lutheran HS West; Cleveland, OH; Chrs; Stu Cncl; Yrbk; Ed Sch Nwsp; Rptr Sch Nwsp; Spn Clb; Trk; Wrstlng; IM Sprt; Mgrs; Univ; Art.

RAMOS, CYNTHIA; Calumet HS; Gary, IN; 65/294 Trs Sr Cls; Hon Rl; Sch Pl; Trk; College; Journalism.

RAMP, MICHAEL; Rensselaer Central HS; Ft Wayne, IN; 46/165 Aud/Vis; Hon Rl; Quill & Scroll; Sch Mus; Sch Pl; Stg Crw; Yth Flsp; Rptr Sch Nwsp; Drama Clb; ITT Tech; Elec.

RAMSAY, DONALD; Southmont Jr Sr HS; Crawfordsville, IN; 10/175 Jr NHS; NHS; Spn Clb; Letter Swmmng; Ten; Univ; Engr.

RAMSAY, SCOTT; Eastern Quakers HS; Lansing, MI; 57/416 NHS; Sct Actv; Bsbl; Ftbl; Glf; Letter Swmmng; Tmr; Natl Merit Ltr; Central Mich Univ; Bus.

RAMSBEY, MARK T; Plymouth HS; Plymouth, IN; 3/250 Am Leg Boys St; Sec Aud/Vis; Band; Treas Chrh Wkr; Hon Rl; NHS; Stg Crw; Yrbk; Fr Clb; Mth Clb; Purdue Univ; Physics.

RAMSDELL, DEANN; Hammond Baptist HS; Hammond, IN; Sec Soph Cls; Chrs; Chrh Wkr; Girl Scts; Hon Rl; Lbry Ade; Sch Mus; Yth Flsp; 4-H; Pep Clb; Bob Jones Univ; Bus.

RAMSDELL, RANDOLPH J; Groveport Madison HS; Columbus, OH; Cls Rep Frsh Cls; Aud/Vis; Hon Rl; Lbry Ade; NHS; Stu Cncl; Trk; Univ; Law.

RAMSEY, ALANA M; North Posey Sr HS; Poseyville, IN; 9/186 Band; Natl Forn Lg; NHS; Sch Mus; Sch Pl; Pres Yth Flsp; Pres FHA; Sec Pep Clb; Capt Pom Pon; Bloomington Univ; Phys Therapy.

RAMSEY, B; Lewis Cnty HS; Weston, WV; Band; Chrs; Hon Rl; Hosp Ade; Y-Teens; Pep Clb; Coll; X Ray Tech.

RAMSEY, BONNIE; Defiance Sr HS; Defiance, OH; Band; Chrs; Hon Rl; Lbry Ade; Off Ade; Sch Pl; Treas Yth Flsp; Rptr Sch Nwsp; Sec 4-H; FHA;.

RAMSEY, BUREN; Matoaka HS; Matoaka, WV; 13/62 Band; Chrs; Hon Rl; Lbry Ade; Mgrs; Lee Coll; Theol.

RAMSEY, CURTIS; William Henry Harrison HS; W Laf, IN; 50/340 Hon Rl; Jr NHS; Pol Wkr; Sch Nwsp; Bsktbl; Trk; Coach Actv; IM Sprt; Univ; Acctg.

RAMSEY, JEFF; Pineville HS; Pineville, WV; 100/110 Aud/Vis; Hon Rl; Lbry Ade; Yth Flsp; VICA; Ftbl; Va Tech; Elec Engr.

RAMSEY, JOSEPH; Daleville HS; Daleville, IN; Band; Chrs; Hon Rl; NHS; 4-H; 4-H Awd; Ball St Univ; Elem Educ.

RAMSEY, KENNETH; Ridgemont HS; Ridgeway, OH; 2/65 Chrs; Chrh Wkr; Hon Rl; NHS; Sch Mus; Yth Flsp; 4-H; FFA; FFA Star Greenhnd Degree 77; FFA Chapt Farmer Degree 78; FFA St Farmer Degree 79; Lima Tech Voc Schl; Paramedic.

RAMSEY, LISA; Mogadore HS; Mogadore, OH; Band; Chrs; Chrh Wkr; Hon Rl; NHS; Sch Pl; Chrldng; Twrlr; Lion Awd; Voice Dem Awd; 5th Pl In Div III Frnch II Oh Tests Of Schlrstc Achvmnts 78; Rating Of Excel At Dist VI Solo & Ens Cntst; Mt Union Coll; Cmnctns.

RAMSEY, LONUEL D; Parkersburg HS; Parkersburg, WV; Chrs; Hon Rl; Lat Clb; Mth Clb; Sci Clb; Marietta Coll; Nuclear Engr.

RAMSEY, LUANNE; Portsmouth East HS; Portsmouth, OH; Chrh Wkr; Girl Scts; Hon Rl; Hosp Ade; Lbry Ade; Sch Pl; Stg Crw; 4-H; Lat Clb; Coll; Med.

RAMSEY, PAMELA; John F Kennedy HS; Cleveland, OH; Cls Rep Sr Cls; Hon Rl; Jr NHS; NHS; Rptr Sch Nwsp; Beta Clb; OEA; Trk; Cit Awd; Exec Sec.

RAMSEY, ROLLIE C; Waterford HS; Waterford, OH; 6/64 Band; Chrs; Chrh Wkr; Hon Rl; NHS; Sch Pl; Yth Flsp; Sci Clb; Spn Clb; Glf; Judo 78; Var Club 77 80; Oh Sclstc Achvmnt Test 77; Ohio Univ; Elec Engr.

RAMSEY, SHELLY; Lapel HS; Lapel, IN; 9/84 Cls Rep Soph Cls; Chrs; Hon Rl; Sch Mus; Sch Pl; Rptr Yrbk; Bsbl; Letter Trk; Capt Wrstlng; Opt Clb Awd; Ind Instit Of Tech; Recreation Mgmnt.

RAMSEY, SHELLY; Capel HS; Lapel, IN; 9/84 Cls Rep Soph Cls; Chrs; Hon Rl; Sch Mus; Rptr Yrbk; Pep Clb; Spn Clb; Bsktbl; Letter Trk; Opt Clb Awd; Indiana Inst Of Tech; Rec Mgmt.

RAMSEY, SUSAN; Warren Central HS; Indianapolis, IN; 4/768 Cmp Fr Grls; Hon Rl; Jr NHS; NHS; Yth Flsp; Pep Clb; Scr Kpr; Tmr; 4-H Awd; Kiwan Awd; Spanish Awd 77; Swim Maid Captain 79; DEBZ Treas 76; Univ; Acctg.

RAMSEY, SUSAN J; North Posey HS; Wodesville, IN; 40/170 Chrh Wkr; Lbry Ade; Quill & Scroll; Rptr Yrbk; Rptr Sch Nwsp; Pep Clb; GAA; IM Sprt; Pom Pon; PPFtbl; Mid Florida Tech Univ; Florist.

RAMSEYER, RICK; Bluffton HS; Bluffton, OH; Sch Pl; Yth Flsp; Ed Sch Nwsp; Rptr Sch Nwsp; Letter Bsktbl; IM Sprt; Scr Kpr; Goshen Coll; Brdcstng.

RAMUNDO, MARIA; Mother Of Mercy HS; Cincinnati, OH; 17/245 Chrs; Chrh Wkr; Cmnty Wkr; Hon Rl; NHS; Sch Pl; Spn Clb; Univ; Nursing.

RANCE, DON P; Leetonia HS; Leetonia, OH; 1/80 VP Frsh Cls; Pres Soph Cls; Val; Am Leg Boys St; Hon Rl; NHS; Pres Stu Cncl; Yrbk; Capt Bsktbl; Marietta Coll; Petroleum Engr.

RANCURELLO, SUE; Archbishop Alter HS; Kettering, OH; 10/332 Chrs; Hon Rl; NHS; Stg Crw; Pres Drama Clb; Fr Clb; Univ; Theatre Arts.

RANDA, DENISE; Fairport Harding HS; Fairport Hbr, OH; 2/45 Cls Rep Soph Cls; Pres Jr Cls; Cl Rep Jr Cls; Am Leg Aux Girls St; Band; Hon Rl; NHS; Stg Crw; Stu Cncl; Y-Teens; Univ; Marine Bio.

RANDALL, AMY; Walnut Ridge HS; Columbus, OH; Chrs; Hon Rl; Jr NHS; Lit Mag; NHS; Quill & Scroll; Ger Clb; Pep Clb; Trk; Airline Acad; Travel Agent.

RANDALL, DANA; Westfield Washington HS; Carmel, IN; 16/125 Cls Rep Frsh Cls; Cls Rep Sr Cls; Chrh Wkr; Hon Rl; Pres NHS; Quill & Scroll; Stu Cncl; Sch Nwsp; Pep Clb; Letter Bsktbl; Indiana Central Univ; Phys Ed.

RANDALL, DAVID J; Austintown Fitch HS; Youngstown, OH; 18/646 Cls Rep Frsh Cls; Cls Rep Soph Cls; Cl Rep Jr Cls; Am Leg Boys St; Cmnty Wkr; Debate Tm; Hon Rl; Natl Forn Lg; Sch Pl; Stu Cncl; Natl Sci Foundation MSU 79; Univ; Med.

RANDALL, ELIZABETH M; Walnut Hills HS; Cincinnati, OH; Band; Girl Scts; Hon Rl; Scr Kpr; Tmr; Natl Merit Ltr; Univ; Premed.

RANDALL, ETHEL; Erieview Catholic HS; Cleveland, OH; Band; Chrh Wkr; Orch; Rptr Sch Nwsp; Bsktbl; Gym; Swmmng; Voc Schl; Modeling.

RANDALL, JULIA; Reed City HS; Reed City, MI; 20/150 Band; Hon Rl; Lbry Ade; NHS; Sch Pl; Stu Cncl; DAR Awd; Central Michigan Univ; Eng.

RANDALL, WILLIAM; Oakwood HS; Dayton, OH; Band; Boy Scts; Chrh Wkr; Hon Rl; Sct Actv; IM Sprt; Scr Kpr; Med.

RANDALL, YVONNE; Milan HS; Milan, IN; 44/82 Chrs; Hon Rl; Jr NHS; Lbry Ade; Lat Clb; Spn Clb; Trk; IM Sprt; Pres Awd; Ball St Univ; Med Tech.

RANDAZZO, FILIPPO; John Adams HS; So Bend, IN; Hon Rl; Sci Clb; Univ Of Notre Dame; Med.

RANDAZZO, ROSS J; Bedford HS; Bedford, OH; 55/627 Cl Rep Jr Cls; Am Leg Boys St; Hon Rl; Jr NHS; Stu Cncl; Pres Spn Clb; Letter Crs Cntry; Letter Trk; Coach Actv; Tmr; Natl Hnr Soc; Jr Most Ath; BGSU; Sci.

RANDELL, DENISE; West Geauga HS; Chesterland, OH; 77/352 Cls Rep Frsh Cls; Cls Rep Soph Cls; Cl Rep Jr Cls; Cls Rep Sr Cls; Chrs; Hon Rl; Lbry Ade; NHS; Sch Mus; Stu Cncl; Kent St Univ; Health Care.

RANDHAN, RITA; Elston HS; Michigan City, IN; 6/308 Cmnty Wkr; Hon Rl; NHS; Purdue North Central; Pharmacy.

RANDLE, CAROL; Clare HS; Clare, MI; Chrh Wkr; Cmnty Wkr; Girl Scts; Hon Rl; NHS; Quill & Scroll; Sct Actv; Yrbk; Natl Merit SF; Jrnlsm Awd For Work On Yrbk 79; Perfct Attndnc Awds 78; 1st Cl Awd In Girl Scouts 75; Mid Michigan Cmnty Coll; Pharm Tech.

RANDLE, DAVID; Washington HS; South Bend, IN; Pres Frsh Cls; Pres Soph Cls; Chrh Wkr; Hon Rl; IM Sprt; College; Science.

RANDOLPH, DELORES; Thomas M Cooley HS; Detroit, MI; Hon Rl; NHS; Y-Teens; Lawrence Inst Of Tech; Mech Engr.

RANDOLPH, JOSEPH M; Greenville HS; Greenville, OH; 30/360 Hon Rl; PAVAS; Sch Pl; Stg Crw; Rptr Sch Nwsp; Drama Clb; Key Clb; Spn Clb; Crs Cntry; IM Sprt; College; Engr.

RANDOLPH, LINDA; Grove City HS; Grove City, OH; 1/449 Sec Chrs; NHS; Sch Pl; Drama Clb; Fr Clb; Pep Clb; Am Leg Awd; Rotary Awd; Ohio St Univ; Music.

RANDOLPH, MARGUERITE C; Liberty HS; Salem, WV; 1/228 Am Leg Aux Girls St; Band; Chrs; Hon Rl; Sec Jr NHS; Lbry Ade; NHS; Sch Mus; Yth Flsp; Mth Clb; Salem Coll; RN.

RANDOLPH, REX E; Medina Sr HS; Medina, OH; 28/370 Hon Rl; NHS; Pol Wkr; Bsbl; IM Sprt; Gold

Tassel Recipient; St Of The Month 79; Liberty Baptist Coll; Acctg.

RANDOLPH, ROBERT; Mississinewa HS; Jonesboro, IN; Am Leg Boys St; Boy Scts; Hon Rl; Jr NHS; NHS; Yth Flsp; Y-Teens; College.

RANDOLPH, SHIRLEY; Martin Luther King HS; Detroit, MI; Hon Rl; ROTC; Rptr Sch Nwsp; Sch Nwsp; Pep Clb; Glf; Wayne; Psych.

RANDOLPH, VICKIE; Rensselaer Ctrl HS; Rensselaer, IN; Pres Chrh Wkr; Hon Rl; Rptr Sch Nwsp; Tennessee Temple Univ; Elem Ed.

RANDOLPH, W; Fountain Central Jr Sr HS; Veedersburg, IN; 18/135 Am Leg Boys St; Band; Chrh Wkr; Lbry Ade; NHS; Sch Pl; FSA; Sci Clb; Univ; Bapt Minister.

RANESBOTTOM, BARB; Pine River Jr Sr HS; Luther, MI; Sec Jr Cls; Sec Sr Cls; Band; Chrs; Hon Rl; NHS; Rptr Yrbk; Pres Fr Clb; Treas Pep Clb; Capt Chrldng; Ferris St Coll; Court Rprtng.

RANEY, B; Decatur Central HS; Indnpls, IN; Chrh Wkr; Hon Rl; NHS; Bsktbl; Glf; Bus Schl; Comp Progr.

RANEY, ELIZABETH; Dexter HS; Dexter, MI; Chrs; Chrh Wkr; Cmnty Wkr; Girl Scts; Hon Rl; Lit Mag; NHS; Yth Flsp; Sch Nwsp; 4-H; Michigan St Univ; Soc Work.

RANEY, SCOTT; Decatur Central HS; Indpls, IN; 8/400 Chrh Wkr; Hon Rl; NHS; Bsktbl; Glf; Business Schl; Accounting.

RANIERI, A; Tiffin Calvert HS; Tiffin, OH; Cls Rep Soph Cls; Am Leg Boys St; Sch Pl; Stu Cncl; Sprt Ed Yrbk; Rptr Yrbk; Sprt Ed Sch Nwsp; Letter Bsbl; Bsktbl; Am Leg Awd; Univ Of Toledo; Law.

RANIERI, ANNETTE; Parma Sr HS; Parma, OH; 372/710 FFA; Oklahoma St Univ; Horticulture.

RANIERI, ANTHONY; Tiffin Calvert HS; Tiffin, OH; Cls Rep Soph Cls; Am Leg Boys St; Stu Cncl; Rptr Yrbk; Sprt Ed Sch Nwsp; Rptr Sch Nwsp; Letter Bsbl; Letter Bsktbl; Am Leg Awd; Cit Awd; Univ Of Toledo; Law.

RANK, JOSEPH; Defiance HS; Defiance, OH; Hon Rl; NHS; Sprt Ed Sch Nwsp; Letter Trk; Eagle Scout; Pres Phys Fitness Awd; Coll; Busns.

RANK, NATHAN; Kalamazoo Central HS; Kalamazoo, MI; Hon Rl; NHS; Sch Mus; Sch Nwsp; Kalamazoo College; Bio.

RANKIN, SCOTT; Edward Drummond Libbey HS; Toledo, OH; Pres Jr Cls; Boy Scts; Hon Rl; Jr NHS; NHS; Red Cr Ade; Stu Cncl; Sprt Ed Yrbk; Boys Clb Am; Bsbl; Univ; Phys Ed.

RANKIN, STEVE; Archbishop Alter HS; Kettering, OH; 38/335 Hon Rl; NHS; Capt Bsbl; Letter Ftbl; Wrstlng; Scr Kpr; Tmr; Wittenberg Univ; Bus Admin.

RANKINEN, TODD; Republic Michigamme HS; Republic, MI; 1/35 Sec Soph Cls; Pres Sr Cls; Val; Chrh Wkr; Cmnty Wkr; Hon Rl; Stu Cncl; Fr Clb; Mic Tech Univ; Engr.

RANNEY, CHARLES G; Heritage HS; New Haven, IN; Boy Scts; Cmnty Wkr; Hon Rl; Off Ade; Pol Wkr; Sct Actv; Spn Clb; Wrstlng; IM Sprt; Eagle Scout Bronze Palm 77; Coll; Dent.

RANSBURG, SHARON; Brown County HS; Morgantown, IN; Drl Tm; Hon Rl; Off Ade; Pol Wkr; Yrbk; 4-H; Spn Clb; Bsktbl; Trk; GAA; Univ; Sci.

RANSBURGH, TWILA; Grove City HS; Grove City, OH; 48/452 Cls Rep Frsh Cls; Cls Rep Soph Cls; Cl Rep Jr Cls; Hst Sr Cls; Cls Rep Sr Cls; Cmnty Wkr; Stu Cncl; Yrbk; Pep Clb; Trk; Ohio St Univ; Pro Dancer.

RANSOM, ALLISON; Upper Arlington HS; Columbus, OH; 30/610 Pres AFS; Cmnty Wkr; Hon Rl; Fr Clb; Coll; Computer.

RANSOM, RONALD; East Noble HS; Avilla, IN; Am Leg Boys St; Band; Chrs; Chrh Wkr; Drm Bgl; Hon Rl; Sch Mus; Sch Pl; FFA; Wrstlng; Agri.

RANSOM, SHERRI; St Albans HS; St Albans, WV; 60/409 Cls Rep Frsh Cls; Cls Rep Sr Cls; Band; Chrh Wkr; Hon Rl; JA; Jr NHS; NHS; Sch Pl; Stu Cncl; Univ Of Charleston.

RANTA, DAN; Nordonia HS; Northfield, OH; 40/490 NHS; Sch Mus; Sch Pl; Spn Clb; Letter Bsktbl; Letter Glf; Letter Ten; Univ; Public Brdcsting.

RANZ, THOMAS T; St Xavier HS; Cincinnati, OH; 14/296 Cls Rep Frsh Cls; Cl Rep Jr Cls; Cls Rep Sr Cls; Cmnty Wkr; Hon Rl; Jr NHS; NHS; Pol Wkr; Stu Cncl; Rptr Sch Nwsp; Univ.

RANZINGER, YVONNE; Adelphian Academy; Union Lake, MI; Trs Jr Cls; Chrh Wkr; Hon Rl; Bsktbl; Bus Schl; Bus.

RAO, SHALINI; Au Gres Sims HS; Au Gres, MI; Girl Scts; Hon Rl; Chrldng; Natl Merit Ltr; Univ Of Michigan; Comp Sci.

RAPAPORT, SONIA; Athens HS; Athens, OH; Cl Rep Jr Cls; Cls Rep Sr Cls; NHS; Sch Mus; Sch Pl; Stu Cncl; Pres Drama Clb; NCTE; Natl Merit Schl; Univ Of Virginia; Physics.

RAPIN, THERESE; Tecumseh HS; Tecumseh, MI; Cl Rep Jr Cls; Hon Rl; Jr NHS; NHS; Stu Cncl; Pep Clb; Bsktbl; IM Sprt; Univ; English.

RAPP, BETH; Miami Trace HS; Washington C H, OH; AFS; Chrs; Drl Tm; Hon Rl; Rptr Yrbk; 4-H; FTA; Pom Pon; 4-H Awd; Bsns Schl; Sec.

RAPP, DENISE; Mc Kinley HS; Niles, OH; 80/420 AFS; Band; Chrh Wkr; Drl Tm; Hon Rl; Lbry Ade; Red Cr Ade; Stg Crw; Drama Clb; Lat Clb; Univ; Bus.

RAPP, MICHAEL; Clay HS; Oregon, OH; Band; Chrh Wkr; Hon Rl; Orch; Sch Mus; Yth Flsp; Fr Clb; Oral Roberts Univ; Grafic Art.

RAPP, MIKE; Clay HS; Oregon, OH; Band; Chrh Wkr; Hon Rl; Orch; Sch Mus; Yth Flsp; Beta Clb; Drama Clb; Fr Clb; Sci Clb; Oral Roberts Univ; Cmmrcl Design.

RAPP, PENNIE; Marion Harding HS; Marion, OH; 1/460 Band; Chrs; Hon Rl; Hosp Ade; Orch; Sch Mus; Sch Nwsp; Spn Clb; Natl Merit Ltr; Univ; Bio.

RAPP, ROBERT; Reading Community HS; Reading, OH; 35/210 Boy Scts; Hon Rl; Sct Actv; Univ Of Cin; Elec Engr.

RAPPLEY, KIM; Michigan Lutheran Seminary; Saginaw, MI; Chrs; Chrh Wkr; Cmnty Wkr; Y-Teens; Pep Clb; IM Sprt; PPFtbl; Cit Awd; Yth Conservation Corps; State Finalist Miss Teen USA & Hawaii Trip; Basis & Advanced Modeling; Kirkland Coll; Conservationist.

RARICK, HOLLY; Haslett HS; Haslett, MI; 24/189 VP Frsh Cls; Cls Rep Soph Cls; Sec Jr Cls; Pres Sr Cls; Band; Chrs; Chrh Wkr; Kalamazoo College; Pre Law.

RARICK, JANIS; Heath HS; Heath, OH; Pres FBLA; FNA; Bsktbl; Trk; Sec.

RARICK, JON; Dayton Christian HS; Dayton, OH; Cls Rep Frsh Cls; Band; Yth Flsp; Bsktbl; Crs Cntry; Trk; Cit Awd; Univ; Archt Engr.

RARICK, JULIE; Heath HS; Heath, OH; Band; Chrs; Drl Tm; FHA; FNA; Bsktbl; Sec.

RASAK, KENNETH; Carman HS; Flint, MI; Chrh Wkr; Hon Rl; Glf; IM Sprt; Univ Of Michigan; Jrnlsm.

RASCH, DAVID; West Catholic HS; Sparta, MI; Cls Rep Frsh Cls; Chrh Wkr; Cmnty Wkr; Hon Rl; Pol Wkr; 4-H; Spn Clb; Letter Bsbl; Letter Ftbl; Letter Swmmng; Grand Rapids Jr Coll.

RASCH, DONALD; West Catholic HS; Grand Rapids, MI; Hon Rl; 4-H; Letter Swmmng; Trk; 4-H Awd; Grand Rajsids Jr Coll.

RASCHE, PAM; Springs Valley HS; French Lick, IN; 16/97 Hon Rl;.

RASEMAN, RUTH; Gull Lake HS; Augusta, MI; 9/228 Sec Frsh Cls; Sec Soph Cls; VP Jr Cls; VP Sr Cls; Chrs; Chrh Wkr; Hon Rl; NHS; Yrbk; DECA; Michigan St Univ; Bus Admin.

RASEY, LAURA; Chalker HS; Southington, OH; Cls Rep Frsh Cls; VP Soph Cls; Band; Chrh Wkr; Off Ade; Stu Cncl; Yth Flsp; Rptr Yrbk; Ed Sch Nwsp; Beta Clb; Ohio Univ.

RASHAD, AHMAD; Grosse Ile HS; Grosse Ile, MI; Hon Rl; Sprt Ed Sch Nwsp; Spn Clb; Trk; Law.

RASHID, KALEEM; Calvin M Woodward HS; Toledo, OH; Drl Tm; Drama Clb; Bsbl; Bsktbl; College; Radio Elec.

RASI, CARMELLA; Mount View HS; Kimball, WV; 14/250 Am Leg Aux Girls St; Band; Hon Rl; Jr NHS; NHS; Yrbk; Beta Clb; 4-H; FBLA; FHA; Concord Coll; Acctg.

RASMUSSEN, KYLE; Aloena HS; Ossineke, MI; Band; Chrh Wkr; Hon Rl; Alpena Comm College; Liberal Arts.

RASMUSSEN, TRACY; Portage Central HS; Portage, MI; Cls Rep Sr Cls; Hon Rl; Off Ade; Stu Cncl; Pep Clb; Letter Chrldng; Tmr; Natl Merit Ltr; W Michigan Univ; Fash Mdse.

RASNICK, ROBERTA; Jefferson Area HS; Jefferson, OH; 5/230 Pres AFS; Am Leg Aux Girls St; Band; Chrs; Chrh Wkr; Drm Mjrt; NHS; Rptr Yrbk; Sec 4-H; College; Music.

RASO, MARIAN; Manton Consolidated HS; Manton, MI; Hon Rl; VP NHS; Off Ade; Yrbk; Treas FHA; Letter Trk; College.

RASOOL, KIM; Withrow HS; Cincinnati, OH; Chrs; Chrh Wkr; Hon Rl; Sch Mus; Univ Of California; Law.

RASOR, MARK; Lima Bath HS; Cairo, OH; Hon Rl; Ftbl; Trk; College; Cmmrcl Pilot.

RASSETTE, BARBARA; Regina HS; Harper Woods, MI; 12/130 Pres Drl Tm; Hon Rl; JA; Rptr Yrbk; Drama Clb; Trk; PPFtbl; Central Mic Univ; Cpa.

RASSMAN JR, JOHN; Columbiana HS; Columbiana, OH; 7/100 Cl Rep Jr Cls; Am Leg Boys St; Band; Boy Scts; Chrh Wkr; Hon Rl; JA; NHS; Sct Actv; Yth Flsp; Univ; Graphic Art.

RASTL, NATHAN; Columbia City Joint HS; Columbia City, IN; 1/270 Am Leg Boys St; Hon Rl; NHS; Ger Clb; Ten; College.

RATAJCZAK, JACLYNN; All Saints Central HS; Munger, MI; Band; Chrs; Hon Rl; Mdrgl; Sch Mus; College.

RATAY, DAVID; Archbishop Alter HS; Miamisburg, OH; Band; Chrh Wkr; Hon Rl; Sct Actv; Drama Clb; Spn Clb; IM Sprt; Univ Of Notre Dame; Civil Engr.

RATCLIFF, CHARLES; Baker HS; Fairborn, OH; Band; Boy Scts; Chrs; Chrh Wkr; Cmnty Wkr; Sch Mus; Sch Pl; Drama Clb; Mth Clb; Bsktbl; Abilene Christian Univ; Bible.

RATCLIFF, ELIZABETH; Regina HS; Cleveland, OH; Chrh Wkr; Cmnty Wkr; Hon Rl; Sch Mus; Sch Pl; Yth Flsp; Cit Awd; Case Western Reserve Univ; Med.

RATCLIFF, JOE; Gods Bible HS; Cincinnati, OH; 1/20 VP Frsh Cls; Trs Soph Cls; Trs Jr Cls; Chrs; Chrh Wkr; Hon Rl; NHS; Treas Yth Flsp; Mth Clb; Spn Clb; Gods Bible Schl.

RATCLIFF, TRACY; Southeastern HS; Chillicothe, OH; 1/93 Trs Sr Cls; Hon Rl; Jr NHS; NHS; Off Ade; Rptr Yrbk; Fr Clb; Ohi Univ; Physics.

RATCLIFFE, LAURA; St Augustine Acad; Lkwd, OH; Trs Soph Cls; Pres Jr Cls; Pres Sr Cls; Hon Rl; Hosp Ade; Stu Cncl; IM Sprt; Dnfth Awd; Cleveland State; Phys Ther.

RATES, GLYNIS V; Marquette HS; Michigan City, IN; Girl Scts; Hon Rl; Spn Clb; Bsbl; Pres Awd; Typing Awd 79; US Air Force Sci & Engr Fair Microbio 76; Purdue N Cntrl Univ; Cert Lab Asst.

RATH, DEBRA; Monroe HS; Monroe, MI; 13/603 Hon Rl; NHS; Ten; Natl Merit Ltr; Concordia College.

RATH, JOHN; Montpelier HS; Montpelier, OH; 8/105 Chrh Wkr; Hon Rl; Yth Flsp; 4-H; Letter Crs Cntry; Letter Ftbl; Letter Trk; 4-H Awd; Univ; Agri.

RATH, KAREN; Ironton HS; Ironton, OH; 3/169 Am Leg Aux Girls St; Hon Rl; Jr NHS; Sch Pl; Stg Crw; Drama Clb; Fr Clb; Sci Clb; College.

RATHBUN, BETH; Hilliard HS; Columbus, OH; Cmp Fr Grls; Girl Scts; Hon Rl; Jr NHS; Off Ade; Spn Clb; Gym; Trk; IM Sprt; Opt Clb Awd; High League Scorer Bsktbll 75; MVP Sftbll 78; Ohio St Univ; Sociology.

RATHBUN, BETH; Portage Lakes Joint Voc Schl; Akron, OH; Girl Scts; Hosp Ade; JA; Lbry Ade; OEA; Pep Clb; Hammell Actual Coll; Crt Reptr.

RATHBUN, LAURA; Wintersville HS; Wintersville, OH; 33/267 Girl Scts; Hon Rl; Hosp Ade; 4-H; Spn Clb; GAA; Mgrs; Ohio St Univ; Nursing.

RATHGABER, SCOTT; New Haven HS; New Haven, IN; 2/297 VP FCA; Hon Rl; Sch Mus; Treas Lat Clb; Bsbl; Capt Ten; Wabash Coll; Chem.

RATHJE, KENNETH W; Arthur Hill HS; Saginaw, MI; 44/552 Cls Rep Soph Cls; Cl Rep Jr Cls; Pres Sr Cls; NHS; Pol Wkr; Sct Actv; Pep Clb; Letter Ftbl; Letter Trk; Cit Awd; West Point Academy; Engr.

RATHKE, LISA; North Central Local HS; Montpelier, OH; Hon Rl; Hosp Ade; Sch Nwsp; 4-H; FFA; Trk; 4-H Awd;.

RATHS, MARGARET; Sts Peter & Paul Area HS; Saginaw, MI; Chrs; Cmnty Wkr; Hon Rl; NHS; Natl Merit Ltr; Univ.

RATHS, MICHELE; St Joseph Central Cath HS; Clyde, OH; 14/87 Cmp Fr Grls; VP Chrh Wkr; Hon Rl; NHS; FBLA; IM Sprt; Terra Tech Coll.

RATLIFF, CHERYL; Martin Luther King HS; Detroit, MI; VP Jr Cls; VP Sr Cls; Hon Rl; Hosp Ade; MMM; Off Ade; Stu Cncl; FDA; FNA; Pep Clb; Univ; Pediatrics.

RATLIFF, ERIC; Valley Local HS; Lucasville, OH; 10/103 Band; Chrs; Cmnty Wkr; Hon Rl; NHS; Sch Pl; Yrbk; Bsktbl; Crs Cntry; Swmmng; Ohio St Univ; Vet.

RATLIFF, JERA; Twin Valley North HS; Lewisburg, OH; VP Frsh Cls; VP Soph Cls; Pres Jr Cls; VP Band; Chrs; NHS; Sec Stu Cncl; Ed Yrbk; Sci Clb; Voice Dem Awd; College; Sci.

RATLIFF, KARL; Indiana Academy; Bloomington, IN; Chrh Wkr; Hon Rl; Sct Actv; 4-H; Trk; Pres Awd; History Awd; Andrews Univ; Religion.

RATLIFF, KEITH; Valley Local HS; Lucasville, OH; 6/110 Pres Jr Cls; Band; Boy Scts; Cmnty Wkr; Hon Rl; FHA; Pep Clb; Ftbl; Swmmng; Trk; Soc Dist Amer HS Stu; Scholarship Tms French I & French II; All Ohio St Youth Sci Conference; Ohio St Univ; Chem Engr.

RATLIFF, RHONDA; Watkins Memorial HS; Pataskala, OH; 9/216 Hon Rl; Lbry Ade; NHS; Sch Pl; Pep Clb; Gym; Trk; Chrldng; IM Sprt; PPFtbl; Ohio State Univ; Educ.

RATTERMAN, DENISE M; Dwight D Eisenhower Sr HS; Utica, MI; Hon Rl; Lbry Ade; NHS; Fr Clb; Case Western Reserve Univ; Bio.

RATZLAFF, RUTH; Chelsea HS; Chelsea, MI; Cls Rep Frsh Cls; Cls Rep Soph Cls; Cl Rep Jr Cls; Cls Rep Sr Cls; Chrh Wkr; Girl Scts; Hon Rl; Off Ade; Yth Flsp; Rptr Yrbk; Ferris St Univ; X Ray Tech.

RAU, DAVID W; Worthington HS; Worthington, OH; 113/563 Aud/Vis; Debate Tm; Hon Rl; Lbry Ade; Natl Forn Lg; Treas NHS; Sch Pl; Rptr Sch Nwsp; Drama Clb; Am Leg Awd; Ohio Univ Amer Hist Contest Finalist; Syracuse Univ; Journalism.

RAU, JAY; Charles Stewart Mott HS; Warren, MI; Rptr Yrbk; Rptr Sch Nwsp; Spn Clb; College; Journalism.

RAU, LORIE; Northview HS; Grand Rapids, MI; 6/350 Hon Rl; JA; NHS; Red Cr Ade; VP Ger Clb; Socr; Tmr; JA Awd; Kiwan Awd; Mich State Univ; Vet Med.

RAUB, SALLY; Springfield Local HS; New Middletown, OH; Cl Rep Jr Cls; AFS; Band; Cmnty Wkr; Girl Scts; Hon Rl; Sct Actv; Youngstown State Univ; Optometry.

RAUB, SALLY E; Springfield Local HS; New Mid dletown, OH; Cl Rep Jr Cls; AFS; Band; Girl Scts; Hon Rl; Sct Actv; Stu Cncl; 4-H; Fr Clb; Pep Clb; Ohio St Univ; Sci.

RAUCH, ELAINE; Warren Local HS; Little Hocking, OH; Chrs; Pres NHS; Sch Mus; Yrbk; Pres 4-H; Fr Clb; Pres FHA; Am Leg Awd; 4-H Awd; Jr Fair Bd Sec 78; Natl FHA Hero Conventn 77; Tracy Awd 76 79; Ohio St Univ.

RAUDABAUGH, DANA; Cory Rawson HS; Findlay, OH; 14/65 Chrs; Sec NHS; Off Ade; Sch Mus; Sch Pl; Treas Stu Cncl; Yrbk; Treas FHA; Chrldng; Am Leg Awd;.

RAUDMAN, RENEE; Kalkaska HS; Williamsburg, MI; 20/200 Cl Rep Jr Cls; Band; Girl Scts; Hon Rl; 4-H; Gym; Chrldng; Michigan St Univ; Music.

RAUE, PEGGY; Merrillville HS; Merrillville, IN; Letter Band; Chrs; Chrh Wkr; Hon Rl; NHS; Olivet Nazarene Coll; Music.

RAUHUT, MARK; Concordia Lutheran HS; Ft Wayne, IN; Chrs; Drl Tm; ROTC; Ger Clb; Rdo Clb; Letter Crs Cntry; Letter Trk; Am Leg Awd; Coll; Law Enforcement.

RAUP, TIMOTHY A; Msgr John R Hackett HS; Kalamazoo, MI; Boy Scts; JA; Sct Actv; Michigan St Univ; Phys Anthropology.

RAUPP, PATRICIA; Our Lady Of Mount Carmel HS; Ecorse, MI; 18/67 Red Cr Ade; Sch Mus; Pep Clb; IM Sprt; Henry Ford Comm; Court Reporter.

RAUSCH, KELLY; Buckeye Valley HS; Ostrander, OH; Band; Letter Bsktbl; Letter Trk; Vllybll Letter 2 Yrs Baron Awrd MVP 76 79; Univ; Phys Educ.

RAUSCH, KENNETH; Buckeye Valley HS; Ostrander, OH; Band; FFA; Letter Bsbl; Capt Bsktbl; Letter Crs Cntry; Letter Ftbl; Scr Kpr; Cit Awd; Univ Of Toledo; Accounting.

RAUSER, DORIS; Fairview HS; Fairview Pk, OH; 24/264 Hon Rl; Orch; Sch Mus; Ger Clb; IM Sprt; Summer Music Lesson Schlrshp 77 & 78; Cleveland St Univ; Engr.

RAVAI, KELLY; Munster HS; Munster, IN; 68/402 AFS; Hon Rl; NHS; Letter Trk; IM Sprt; Pres Awd; Purdue Univ; Zoology.

RAVER, BERNARD; Highland HS; Anderson, IN; 71/478 Band; Chrh Wkr; Swmmng; Am Leg Awd; Opt Clb Awd; Rotary Awd; Purdue Univ; Mech Engr.

RAVER, SUSAN; Highland HS; Anderson, IN; 29/434 Chrh Wkr; Girl Scts; Hon Rl; Hosp Ade; NHS; Spn Clb; C of C Awd; Purdue; Nursing.

RAWLES, MICHAEL; Western HS; Russiaville, IN; 46/226 Boy Scts; Hon Rl; NHS; Sct Actv; 4-H; Fr Clb; Hndbl; Wrstlng; 4-H Awd; Purdue Univ; Agri Econ.

RAWLINGS, TERESA; Stephen T Badin HS; Hamilton, OH; 50/225 Chrh Wkr; Cmnty Wkr; Hon Rl; Hosp Ade; Sch Mus; Sct Actv; Stg Crw; Drama Clb; Spn Clb; Mgrs; Eastern Kentucky Univ; Nursing.

RAWLINS, MARIE; Trinity HS; Garfield Hts, OH; 23/150 Chrs; Hon Rl; Hosp Ade; Sec Stu Cncl; GAA; Scr Kpr; Cuyahoga Comm Coll; Public Relations.

RAWLINS, MARY; Valley View HS; Frmrsvl, OH; Chrs; Hon Rl; Stu Cncl; Pep Clb; Sci Clb; Mat Maids; Tmr;.

RAWSON, JULIE; Toronto HS; Toronto, OH; Cmp Fr Grls; Hon Rl; Sch Mus; Sdlty; Treas Stu Cncl; Yrbk; Sch Nwsp; Pres Pep Clb; Spn Clb; Chrldng; Univ.

RAWSON, KELLY; Farwell HS; Farwell, MI; 6/121 Band; Debate Tm; Hon Rl; NHS; Sch Pl; Stu Cncl; Sch Nwsp; Drama Clb; Fr Clb; Bsbl; J Phillips Sousa Band Awd 79; All City Bsbl Queen 77; Bst Chrctr Actress 78; Bst Supprtng Actress 79; Ferris St Coll.

RAWSON, SHIRLEY; Jefferson Union HS; Toronto, OH; Chrs; Chrh Wkr; Hon Rl; 4-H; Spn Clb; 4-H Awd; X Ray Tech.

RAY, ALISA; Belleville HS; Belleville, MI; 16/500 Band; Hon Rl; NHS; Stg Crw; Ger Clb; Capt Bsbl; Letter Bsktbl; Township Supervsr For City Govt Day 79; Ltr In Var Vllybl 78; Catp Of Var Sftbl 1 Yr Ltr 2 Yrs 78 79; Univ Of Michigan; Jrnlsm.

RAY, CAROL; Green HS; Uniontown, OH; 17/310 Cls Rep Frsh Cls; Chrs; Chrh Wkr; Hon Rl; Lbry Ade; Mdrgl; NHS; Off Ade; Ed Sch Nwsp; Sch Nwsp; Coll; Busns.

RAY, DANIEL; Gilmour Academy; Chardon, OH; 4/82 Band; Boy Scts; Chrs; Hon Rl; NHS; Orch; Sch Mus; Sch Pl; Sct Actv; Rptr Yrbk; Headmstr List 79; Eagle Scout Awd 78; Outstndg Actor Awd 78; Kent St Univ Regional Awd For Chem 78; Notre Dame Univ; Biolgl Sci.

RAY, EVELYN; Stanton HS; Irondale, OH; Band; Chrs; Chrh Wkr; Hon Rl; Lbry Ade; NHS; Rptr Yrbk; Rptr Sch Nwsp; FHA; Bradford School; Accountant.

RAY, GREG; Jackson HS; Ray, OH; Band; Boy Scts; Chrs; Chrh Wkr; Sct Actv; Yth Flsp; 4-H; FFA; 4-H Awd; God Cntry Awd; Eagle Scout Awd 77; Yth Delegate On Admin Brd & Coun Of Christ United Meth Church Jackson 78; Morehead St Univ; Agri.

RAY, JAMIE; Alexander HS; Albany, OH; Chrh Wkr; Cmnty Wkr; Hon Rl; NHS; Sch Pl; FHA; Spn Clb; Rio Grande Coll.

RAY, JONATHAN C; Northrop HS; Ft Wayne, IN; Aud/Vis; Chrs; Chrh Wkr; Cmnty Wkr; JA; PAVAS; Rptr Yrbk; Yrbk; Rptr Sch Nwsp; Sch Nwsp; Univ; Comm Art.

RAY, JULIE; Bloomington HS; Bloomington, IN; Band; Chrh Wkr; Indiana Univ; Bus.

RAY, KELLY; Milton HS; Ona, WV; Aud/Vis; Cmnty Wkr; Hon Rl; Red Cr Ade; Sct Actv; Yrbk; Marshall Univ; Brdcstng.

RAY, KEVIN; Liberty HS; Girard, OH; Band; Boy Scts; Letter Bsbl; Bsktbl; Letter Ftbl; Wrstlng; Coll; Phys Educ.

RAY, LISA; Union Local HS; Bethesda, OH; Cl Rep Jr Cls; Am Leg Aux Girls St; Band; Hon Rl; Lbry A de; Sch Pl; Stg Crw; Fr Clb; Spn Clb; Ohio Merit Schlrshp; 1st Pl Drawing Awd Industrial Arts; 4 Yr Mbrshp In Schlrshp Team 4th Pl In Dist; Ohio Univ.

RAY, MICHAEL E; Jeffersonville HS; Long Beach, CA; Hon Rl; Jr NHS; Stu Cncl; Key Clb; Coll; Acctg.

RAY, ROBIN; Hamtramck HS; Hamtramck, MI; 2/109 Sal; Band; Hon Rl; NHS; Rptr Yrbk; Sch Nwsp; Fr Clb; FSA; Mth Clb; Sci Clb; Wayne State Univ; Engr.

RAY, RONALD; Loy Norrix HS; Kalamazoo, MI; Hon Rl; Orch; Sch Mus; Sch Pl; Stg Crw; Drama Clb; College; Music Prfrmnce.

RAY, SHARON; Western HS; Jackson, MI; Cls Rep Frsh Cls; Cls Rep Soph Cls; Cl Rep Jr Cls; Cmnty Wkr; Debate Tm; Off Ade; Stu Cncl; Fr Clb; Key Clb; Univ; Bus.

RAY, TAMMY V; East Tech HS; Cleveland, OH; Hon Rl; NHS; Cit Awd; Univ; Sci.

RAY, TIM L; John Marshall HS; Moundsville, WV; Cls Rep Frsh Cls; Cls Rep Sr Cls; Am Leg Boys St;

Chrh Wkr; Hon Rl; Jr NHS; NHS; Stu Cncl; Bsktbl; Letter Ftbl; Univ; CPA.

RAY, VANESSA; Elkins HS; Elkins, WV; Band; Chrs; Girl Scts; 4-H; FFA; FHA; Pep Clb; VICA; Beautician Schl; Beautician.

RAY, VIRGINIA; East Noble HS; Kendallvile, IN; Band; Chrs; Chrh Wkr; Cmnty Wkr; Debate Tm; Girl Scts; Hon Rl; JA; Natl Forn Lg; Sch Mus; Natl Jr Horticltry Assoc Natl Finlst 77 & 78; In Jr Horticltr Soc St Champ Team 77; Univ; Fshn Mdse.

RAYBURN, ETHEL; Green HS; Uniontown, OH; Chrh Wkr; Hon Rl; Lbry Ade; Acad Tm 77; Univ; Nursing.

RAYE, TONYA; Redford HS; Detroit, MI; Cls Rep Frsh Cls; Sec Jr Cls; Debate Tm; Stu Cncl; FBLA; Pep Clb; Trk; A & T; Law.

RAYLE, KIM; Marion Adams HS; Sheridan, IN; 13/98 Sec Frsh Cls; Pres Jr Cls; FCA; Girl Scts; Hon Rl; Jr NHS; Stu Cncl; FHA; OEA; Pep Clb;.

RAYMOND, DAWN; Bullock Creek HS; Midland, MI; Band; Girl Scts; Hon Rl; Hosp Ade; Treas JA; NHS; Pep Clb; GAA; IM Sprt; JA Awd; Jr Math Awd & Chem Awd 78; Bio Awd 76; All Star Bnd 75; Univ; Chem.

RAYMOND, DEBORAH; Shepherd Public HS; Shepherd, MI; Girl Scts; VP FHA;.

RAYMOND, LILY; John Adams HS; So Bend, IN; Cls Rep Soph Cls; Trs Jr Cls; Trs Sr Cls; Hon Rl; NHS; Orch; Stu Cncl; PPFtbl; Notre Dame; Psychiatry.

RAZZANO, JANICE L; Port Clinton HS; Port Clinton, OH; 8/280 Chrs; Hon Rl; Fr Clb; Chrldng; GAA; Attnd Football Dance Fr & Soph; Univ.

RCH, RUSSELL D BU; Greenfield Central HS; Greenfield, IN; 69/300 Pres Band; Chrh Wkr; Orch; Sch Mus; Sch Pl; Drama Clb; Ger Clb; Mth Clb; Mgrs; Scr Kpr; 1st Pl Rating State Solo Auditions Tuba; TV Academic Quiz Show; Olivet Nazarene Univ; Music.

REA, JULIA; Firestone Sr HS; Akron, OH; Cls Rep Frsh Cls; Cls Rep Soph Cls; Chrs; Hon Rl; NHS; Stu Cncl; Ed Yrbk; Rptr Sch Nwsp; Pep Clb; Capt Chrldng; Athletic Activity Girls Synchronized Swimming; Miami Univ Of Ohio; Bus.

REA, PAMELA; Creston HS; Grand Rapids, MI; 9/395 Chrs; Chrh Wkr; Hosp Ade; JA; Mdrgl; NHS; Sch Mus; Northwestern Univ; Fine Arts.

READ, JEFFREY; Anderson Sr HS; Anderson, IN; Boy Scts; Hon Rl; Jr NHS; NHS; Sct Actv; Ger Clb; Letter Wrstlng; Eagle Scout 76; Ball St Univ; Law.

READ, LYNN; Lincoln HS; Vincennes, IN; 15/282 Hon Rl; Off Ade; PAVAS; DECA; 4-H; FTA; Pep Clb; Chrldng; 4-H Awd; Whos Who In Foreign Language; Homecoming Queen; Mozart Clb; Purdue Univ; Vet Med.

READD, SALLY; Hilliard HS; Hilliard, OH; Band; Chrh Wkr; Girl Scts; Lbry Ade; Sch Pl; 4-H; Bsbl; Coach Actv; 4-H Awd; Mas Awd; CTI; Computer Analyst.

READER, DANIEL; Gladwin HS; Gladwin, MI; Cl Rep Jr Cls; Boy Scts; Hon Rl; NHS; Sct Actv; Lat Clb; IM Sprt; Univ; Engr.

READEY, KEVIN; Dublin HS; Dublin, OH; 58/153 Pres Sr Cls; Boy Scts; Sch Mus; Sch Pl; Rptr Sch Nwsp; Letter Bsbl; Letter Bsktbl; Letter Ftbl; Letter Ten; Ohio St Univ; Archt Drafting.

READMAN, KAREN; Howland HS; Niles, OH; Chrs; Girl Scts; Lbry Ade; Off Ade; Red Cr Ade; Y-Teens; Sch Nwsp; Fr Clb; Chrldng; Pom Pon; Youngstown St Univ; Health.

REAGAN, DEBRA; L And M HS; Bloomfield, IN; 5/24 Sec Frsh Cls; Trs Soph Cls; Trs Jr Cls; Sec Sr Cls; Chrh Wkr; Drl Tm; Hon Rl; Stu Cncl; Yrbk; Pom Pon; Ind State Univ; Home Ec.

REAGAN, THERESA; Creston HS; Grand Rpds, MI; 1/380 Pres Sr Cls; Hon Rl; Jr NHS; NHS; Off Ade; Lat Clb; Letter Trk; Am Leg Awd; Grand Rapids Jr Coll; Elem Ed.

REAGIN, PAMELA; Clay City HS; Cory, IN; 5/65 Aud/Vis; Band; Hon Rl; NHS; Off Ade; Pres Yth Flsp; Sch Nwsp; Fr Clb; Sci Clb; Voice Dem Awd; Concordia Coll; Dr Of Christian Educ.

REAKER, J; Laville HS; Plymouth, IN; Fr Clb; Sci Clb; Letter Bsbl; Letter Ftbl; College.

REALE, DEBRA; Brooke HS; Colliers, WV; 9/403 Band; Chrh Wkr; Hon Rl; Lit Mag; NHS; 4-H; Spn Clb; 4-H Awd; Beta Tri Hi V Mbr 78; Library Club 76; Poli Action Club 78 Electd Sec For 79; Bethany Coll; Pre Law.

REAM, BARBARA; Grant HS; Grant, MI; Band; Hon Rl; Yth Flsp; FNA; Cit Awd; JA Awd; College; Nursing.

REAM, MARLA; Benzie Central HS; Beulah, MI; Drl Tm; Hon Rl; 4-H; GAA; Pom Pon; Twrlr; 4-H Awd; Northwestern Univ; Interior Dsgn.

REAM, SHERRY; Buckeye Central HS; Chatfield, OH; 24/90 Chrs; Chrh Wkr; Hon Rl; Lbry Ade; Sch Mus; Treas Yth Flsp; Sch Nwsp; 4-H; Pep Clb; Spn Clb; Univ; Bus.

REAMAN, DEBBIE; Arch Bishop Alter HS; Kettering, OH; Ten; GAA; Ohi State Univ; Nursing.

REAMAN, RENEE; Goshen HS; Rockford, IL; Band; Chrs; Drl Tm; Girl Scts; Hon Rl; Yth Flsp; 4-H; Glf; IM Sprt; Mgrs; Rockford Coll.

REAMER, D; Calvert HS; Tiffin, OH; 23/101 Aud/Vis; Chrs; Chrh Wkr; Hon Rl; Sch Mus; Letter Bsbl; Letter Bsktbl; Letter Ftbl;.

REAMS, JANET; Northside HS; Muncie, IN; Boy Scts; Hon Rl; NHS; Spn Clb; Kiwan Awd; Rotary Awd; Ball State; Dentistry.

REARDON, JAYNE; Fenwick HS; Middletown, OH; Hon Rl; NHS;.

REAS, JOHN; St Francis De Sales HS; Toledo, OH; 6/171 Cmnty Wkr; Hon Rl; Natl Forn Lg; NHS; Sch Mus; Stu Cncl; Rptr Yrbk; Rptr Sch Nwsp; Letter Crs Cntry; Trk; Univ; Intl Affairs.

REASONER, GAYLE; Wintersville HS; Wintersville, OH; 2/282 Band; Chrs; Girl Scts; Sch Pl; Sct Actv; Stg Crw; Yth Flsp; Yrbk; Drama Clb; Spn Clb; Michigan St Univ; Spec Educ.

REASONER, LAURA; Marian HS; Birmingham, MI; Cls Rep Sr Cls; Cmp Fr Grls; Chrs; Chrh Wkr; Cmnty Wkr; Girl Scts; Hon Rl; Mdrgl; Mod UN; Sch Mus; Part Ms Teenage Amer W Virginia 77; Univ; Music.

REASOR, LENITA J; Springs Valley HS; French Lick, IN; 26/97 Chrs; Chrh Wkr; Hon Rl; Sch Pl; Fr Clb; FHA; Pep Clb; Mgrs; Oakland; Chiropractic.

REASOR, LOLITA A; Springs Valley HS; French Lick, IN; 24/97 Chrs; Chrh Wkr; Hon Rl; Fr Clb; FHA; Pep Clb; Mgrs; Oakland; Chiropractor.

REAVER, BRIAN; Pontiac Northern HS; Pontiac, MI; Cls Rep Frsh Cls; Band; Hon Rl; Letter Ftbl; Michigan Competitive Schlrshp; Oakland Univ.

REAVES, REGINA; Martin Luther King HS; Detroit, MI; Cls Rep Frsh Cls; Cls Rep Soph Cls; Cls Rep Sr Cls; Chrh Wkr; Cmnty Wkr; Hon Rl; Off Ade; Stu Cncl; Y-Teens; Ed Yrbk; Michigan St Univ; Fash Merch.

REAY, JENNIFER; Northport HS; Northport, MI; Cls Rep Frsh Cls; Hon Rl; Ten; Trk; Natl Merit Schl; Northern Michigan Univ; Crim Jstc.

REBANDT, DOROTHY; Gladwin HS; Gladwin, MI; 10/180 Pres Soph Cls; Hon Rl; Stu Cncl; Bsktbl; Trk; Mgrs; PPFtbl; Jr Civitan Clb Pres 79; Vllybl Letter & Co Captn 79; Farm Bureau Citznshp Seminar Stud 79; Michigan Tech Univ; Engr.

REBER, ALLISON; Clay HS; Curtice, OH; Band; Girl Scts; Mas Awd; Davis Business College; Sect.

REBER, JON; Goshen HS; Goshen, IN; Band; Boy Scts; Chrs; Chrh Wkr; FCA; Mdrgl; Sch Mus; Sct Actv; Yth Flsp; Bsbl; Goshen Coll; Youth Counslng.

REBER, TODD; Admiral King HS; Lorain, OH; Band; Chrh Wkr; Hon Rl; Off Ade; Stg Crw; Yth Flsp; Bsbl; Tmr; College; Engineering.

REBICH, NICK J; Wintersville HS; Steubenville, OH; Cmnty Wkr; Hon Rl; Fr Clb; Ohio St Univ; Elec Engr.

REBICH, RICHARD; Marquette HS; Michigan City, IN; Hon Rl;.

REBLE, DOUG; Hubbard HS; Hubbard, OH; 23/340 Band; Hon Rl; Orch; Fr Clb; Letter Crs Cntry; Swmmng; Youngstown State; Biology.

REBMAN, CHRIS; Madison Comp HS; Mansfield, OH; Band; Boy Scts; Chrs; Chrh Wkr; Hon Rl; Lbry Ade; Orch; Yth Flsp; Drama Clb; Fr Clb; Outstanding Musical Achievement Award; Univ; Concert Pianist.

RECHSTEINER, SALLY; Western HS; Bay City, MI; 18/470 Chrh Wkr; Hon Rl; NHS; Yrbk; 4-H; Sci Clb; Bsbl; Bsktbl; Delta Mic State College; Pre Vet.

RECK, DARYL; Covington HS; Covington, OH; 15/86 Band; Boy Scts; Chrh Wkr; Hon Rl; NHS; Sch Mus; Sct Actv; Yth Flsp; Outsntnd Carrier Awd Sr Div 77; Sci Fair Best Of Show 75; Perfct Attndnc 77 & 79; Univ.

RECK, GRETCHEN; Covington HS; Bradford, OH; Band; Hon Rl; Sch Pl; Pres Stu Cncl; Rptr Yrbk; Sec Fr Clb; Letter Trk; Capt Chrldng; PPFtbl; Twrlr;.

RECKART, CARMEN; Bruceton HS; Bruceton, WV; Pres Jr Cls; Hon Rl; Sch Pl; Stu Cncl; Yrbk; Treas FHA; VICA; Letter Bsktbl; Sec GAA; College; Photography.

RECKER, EARL; Continental HS; Cloverdale, OH; Am Leg Boys St; Band; Hon Rl; VP FFA; Am Leg Awd; Univ; Hist.

RECKER, SUSAN; Delphos St Johns HS; Delphos, OH; 35/150 Cls Rep Frsh Cls; Band; Hon Rl; JA; Stu Cncl; 4-H; Chrldng; Mgrs; 4-H Awd; God Cntry Awd; Ohio Northern Univ; Pharm.

RECKER, VICTORIA S; Seton HS; Cincinnati, OH; 81/283 FCA; Girl Scts; Hon Rl; Lbry Ade; Rptr Sch Nwsp; Pres Lat Clb; Pep Clb; Bsktbl; Capt Socr; Mgrs; Univ.

RECKNAGEL, JEFFREY; Mona Shores HS; Muskegon, MI; Chrh Wkr; Cmnty Wkr; Hon Rl; NHS; Sci Clb; Spn Clb; The Dr H Dykhuizen Sci Schlrshp 79; Mi Competitive Schlrshp 79; Muskegon Cnty Cmnty Found Schlrshp 79; Hope Coll; Physn.

RECTOR, CATHARINE; Madison Hts HS; Anderson, IN; 11/371 Hon Rl; NHS; Pres 4-H; Spn Clb; 4-H Awd; Kiwan Awd; Univ; Indus Engr.

RECZNIK, DENISE; Kent Roosevelt HS; Kent, OH; Band; Cmp Fr Grls; Chrs; Hon Rl; Lbry Ade; Orch; Pep Clb; Twrlr; Band Awd 77 78 & 79; Hoir Awd 77 78 & 79; Kent St Univ; Sci.

REDD, BARRY; West Side HS; Gary, IN; 43/750 Aud/Vis; Band; Hon Rl; Sch Mus; Sch Pl; Fr Clb; Letter Ten; Vandercook College Of Music.

REDD, LAURA M; Gabriel Richard HS; South Rockwood, MI; Cmnty Wkr; NHS; Pol Wkr; Sch Pl; Stg Crw; Drama Clb; Lat Clb; Pep Clb; College; Bus Mgmt.

REDD, LISA; Columbia City Joint HS; Columbia City, IN; Cmnty Wkr; Sch Mus; Sch Pl; Drama Clb; FTA; IM Sprt; Univ; Nurse.

REDDEN, RONALD; Griffith HS; Griffith, IN; Letter Crs Cntry; Capt Trk; Univ.

REDDER, MARSHALL; Jenison HS; Jenison, MI; 16/365 Chrh Wkr; Hon Rl; Sch Pl; Stu Cncl; Letter Bsbl; Letter Bsktbl; Letter Ftbl; Coach Actv; IM Sprt; Central Michigan Univ; Bus Admin.

REDDICK, LAURIE A; Hobart Sr HS; Hobart, IN; Sal; Pres AFS; Hon Rl; Jr NHS; NHS; Sch Mus; Sch Pl; Stu Cncl; Drama Clb; Fr Clb; Indiana Univ; Spec Ed.

REDDIG, DIANA; Harbor HS; Ashtabula, OH; AFS; Girl Scts; Off Ade; Fr Clb; Spn Clb; Bsbl; GAA; IM Sprt; Ohi State Univ; Sociology.

REDDING, BRENDA; Madison Plains HS; Mt Sterling, OH; Band; Cmp Fr Grls; Hon Rl; Sch Nwsp; Mt Vernon Nazarene Coll; Law.

REDDING, CYNTHIA; Onsted HS; Onsted, MI; 12/123 Cls Rep Frsh Cls; Cls Rep Soph Cls; Trs Jr Cls; Trs Sr Cls; Cls Rep Sr Cls; Band; Debate Tm; Hon Rl; Sch Pl; Stu Cncl; Central Michigan Univ; Phys Educ.

REDDING, DONNA; Brown City HS; Brown City, MI; 14/89 Girl Scts; Hon Rl; Lbry Ade; NHS; FNA; Letter Trk; PPFtbl; Tmr; Baker Bus School; Comp Progr.

REDDING, ROBERTA; Galien Township HS; Galien, MI; Sec Frsh Cls; Trs Frsh Cls; Cls Rep Soph Cls; Cl Rep Jr Cls; Trs Sr Cls; Cls Rep Sr Cls; Chrh Wkr; Debate Tm; Hon Rl; Natl Merit SF; Cntrl Michigan Univ; Lib Sci.

REDDING, STEPHEN F; Grosse Pointe S HS; Grosse Pte Pk, MI; 24/560 Boy Scts; Chrh Wkr; Hon Rl; NHS; Orch; Sct Actv; Pres Yth Flsp; Lat Clb; Swmmng; Natl Merit SF; Eagle Scout 1978; Univ; Engr.

REDDY, CATHERINE T; Ernest W Seaholm HS; Bloomfield Hls, MI; 53/636 Chrh Wkr; Red Cr Ade; Sct Actv; Sch Nwsp; Coach Actv; Natl Merit SF; Univ; Law.

REDEKER, JAMIE; Manistique HS; Manistique, MI; Chrh Wkr; Girl Scts; Hosp Ade; Sct Actv; Stu Cncl; 4-H; Trk; Cit Awd; 4-H Awd; Univ; Med.

REDEKER, JOEL; Holland HS; Holland, MI; Band; Hon Rl; Sch Pl; Letter Swmmng; Ten; Hope Coll; Bus Admin.

REDELMAN, RUTH; Greensburg Community HS; Greensburg, IN; 6/209 Band; Hon Rl; NHS; Sch Mus; 4-H; Pep Clb; 4-H Awd; Kiwan Awd; House Of James; Bus Curriculum.

REDER, CLIFFORD; Bay City Western HS; Kawkawlin, MI; 40/486 Boy Scts; Hon Rl; NHS; FBLA; IM Sprt; Cit Awd; Northwood Inst Bus Schl; Bus Admin.

REDER, JUDY; Western HS; Bay City, MI; VP Frsh Cls; Trs Sr Cls; Band; Chrh Wkr; Hon Rl; NHS; Stu Cncl; Sch Nwsp; Delta College; Communications.

REDERSTORF, LAURIE; Mona Shores HS; Muskegon, MI; Glf; Gym; Elk Awd; Pres Awd; Coll; Bus Admin.

REDIGER, JEFFREY; Columbia City Joint HS; Columbia City, IN; 43/256 Band; Chrh Wkr; Yth Flsp; Spn Clb; IM Sprt; Taylor Univ; Law.

REDLIN, GAIL; Bishop Gallagher HS; St Clair Shrs, MI; 9/328 Hon Rl; Univ.

REDLING, MARY; St Joseph Ctrl HS; Huntington, WV; 2/37 Pres Sr Cls; Cls Rep Sr Cls; Hon Rl; NHS; Stu Cncl; Rptr Sch Nwsp; Drama Clb; Keyettes; Pep Clb; Letter Bsktbl; Univ; Eng.

REDLING, MONICA; St Joseph Central HS; Huntington, WV; Cls Rep Frsh Cls; Pres Jr Cls; Cmnty Wkr; Hon Rl; Hosp Ade; Sch Pl; Sch Nwsp; Drama Clb; Keyettes; Pep Clb; Marshall Univ; Eng.

REDMAN, CHRISTIE; Euclid HS; Euclid, OH; Off Ade; Stg Crw; Mgrs; Tmr; Cedarville Coll; Home Ec.

REDMAN, DARCY; South Vermillion HS; Dana, IN; 20/170 Cls Rep Frsh Cls; Cls Rep Soph Cls; Cl Rep Jr Cls; Cls Rep Sr Cls; Am Leg Aux Girls St; NHS; Quill & Scroll; Stg Crw; Stu Cncl; Rptr Yrbk; Hoosier Grls St 1978 Outstndng Grl 1978; Voice Of Dmcrcy 1978; Purdue Univ; Nursing.

REDMAN, KIMBERLY; Clinton Massie HS; Wilmington, OH; 9/100 Cls Rep Frsh Cls; Girl Scts; Hon Rl; NHS; Off Ade; Chrldng; GAA; IM Sprt; PPFtbl; Raymond Walters Univ; Dent Hygiene.

REDMAN, PAM; Frankfort Sr HS; Frankfort, IN; 1/260 Sec Sr Cls; Band; NHS; Sch Mus; Stu Cncl; Drama Clb; Lat Clb; Capt Bsktbl; Letter Glf; Letter Ten; Purdue Univ; Pharmacy.

REDMAN, PAMELA; Miami Trace HS; Goodhope, OH; AFS; VP DECA; FHA; 1st Pl Tm Mgmt Dist DECA Comp 1979; AFS Summer Exchange Stdnt 1979; Barbizon Modeling Schl Grad 1978;.

REDMON, JOHN; Greenfield Central HS; Greenfield, IN; Hon Rl; Spn Clb; Chess Club; Span Natl Hon Soc; Ball St Univ; Chem.

REDMOND, DANIELLE; Shrine HS; Detroit, MI; 101/164 Chrs; Hon Rl; Hope Coll; Psych.

REDMOND, JOHN; Lake Catholic HS; Pnsvl, OH; Cls Rep Sr Cls; Boy Scts; Chrh Wkr; Hon Rl; Sch Mus; Yrbk; Sch Nwsp; Boys Clb Am; Socr; IM Sprt; Univ; Pre Law.

REDMOND, MAUREEN; Athens HS; Athens, MI; Hon Rl; Lbry Ade; NHS; Red Cr Ade; Pep Clb; Kellogg Cmnty Coll; Phys Ther.

REDMOND, TERRI; Pontiac Northern Sr HS; Pontiac, MI; Cl Rep Jr Cls; Chrs; Chrh Wkr; Drl Tm; Drm Mjrt; Hon Rl; Ed Sch Nwsp; Rptr Sch Nwsp; 4-H; Pep Clb; Eastern Michigan Univ; Acctg.

REDNOUR, MONICA; Shenandoah HS; New Castle, IN; 8/150 Band; Hon Rl; Lbry Ade; NHS; Drama Clb; 4-H; FHA; Spn Clb; Letter Trk; DAR Awd; Indiana St Univ; Pre Med.

REECE, CATHERINE; Marion HS; Marion, IN; 12/745 Chrh Wkr; Jr NHS; Mdrgl; NHS; Orch; Sch Mus; Yth Flsp; 4-H; Elk Awd; Hnr Music Schlrhsp To De Pauw Univ; Music Schlrshp Ball St Univ; Exchange Clb Dist Yth Of Yr; De Pauw Univ; Music.

REECE, JOHN; Westland HS; Galloway, OH; Am Leg Boys St; Band; Chrh Wkr; Jr NHS; NHS; Sch Mus; Sch Pl; OEA; Bsbl; IM Sprt; 2nd Pl In Reg & St OEA Acctg Cont; 8th Pl In Natl OEA Acctg Cont; Ohio St Univ; Acctg.

REECE, MARIAN; Jefferson HS; Lafayette, IN; Cls Rep Frsh Cls; Cls Rep Soph Cls; Cl Rep Jr Cls; Cls Rep Sr Cls; Stu Cncl; Y-Teens; Pep Clb; Trk; Chrldng; Tmr; Ball St Univ; Advertising.

REECE, TINA; Spanishburg HS; Rock, WV; 1/38 Sec Frsh Cls; Cls Rep Soph Cls; Cl Rep Jr Cls; Band; Chrs; Cmnty Wkr; Drm Mjrt; Hon Rl; Jr NHS; NHS; Bluefield St Coll; Nursing.

REECE, VIRGINIA; Marion HS; Marion, IN; 91/750 Band; Chrs; Chrh Wkr; Hon Rl; NHS; Orch; Yth Flsp; Drama Clb; 4-H; 4-H Awd; Purdue Univ; Consumer Sci.

REED, ANITA L; Nettle Lee Roth HS; Dayton, OH; Hst Frsh Cls; VP Soph Cls; Pres Jr Cls; Am Leg Aux Girls St; Chrh Wkr; Debate Tm; Girl Scts; Hon Rl; Sch Pl; Stu Cncl; Ohio House Rep Outstnd Achvrs 1976; Ohio St Univ; Psych.

REED, BARBARA; Muncie Southside HS; Muncie, IN; 12/323 Hon Rl; NHS; Rptr Yrbk; Sec.

REED, BRENDA; Wyoming Park HS; Wyoming, MI; 7/265 Band; NHS; Natl Merit SF; Rotary Awd; Grand Rapids Jr Coll; Busns.

REED, CARMELA; Buckhannon Upshur HS; Tallmansville, WV; Band; Chrh Wkr; Hon Rl; Lbry Ade; Off Ade; Keyettes; West Virginia Wesleyan Univ; Sec Sci.

REED, CAROL; Solon HS; Solon, OH; 58/290 AFS; Chrs; Chrh Wkr; FCA; Hon Rl; MMM; NHS; Stg Crw; Ed Yrbk; College; Busns Admin.

REED, CHERYL; Tippecanoe Valley HS; Rochester, IN; 27/147 Trs Jr Cls; Chrs; Chrh Wkr; Indiana Univ; Music.

REED, CHRIS; Springport Public HS; Charlotte, MI; Hon Rl; Letter Bsktbl; Letter Crs Cntry; Letter Trk; Jackson Cmnty Coll.

REED, CINDY; Buckeye Valley HS; Ostrander, OH; Band; Chrs; Stg Crw; Drama Clb; 4-H; FHA; FTA; Bsktbl; Scr Kpr; 4-H Awd; Ohio State Univ; Phys Therapy.

REED, CINDY; Jonesville HS; Hillsdale, MI; Chrh Wkr; Girl Scts; Hon Rl; NHS; VP Stu Cncl; Bsktbl; IM Sprt; College.

REED, CYNTHIA; Eastern HS; Lucasville, OH; 30/60 Chrs; Spn Clb; College; Busns Mgmt.

REED, DARRYL; Spanishburg HS; Camp Creek, WV; 10/41 VP Soph Cls; VP Jr Cls; Boy Scts; Hon Rl; Stu Cncl; VICA; Gym; IM Sprt; Scr Kpr; Mercer Cnty Vo Tech Ctr; Drafting.

REED, DAVID M; Elkins HS; Elkins, WV; 19/250 Am Leg Boys St; Band; Hon Rl; NHS; Spn Clb; Glf; Univ; Physics.

REED, DEBBIE; Bethesda Christian Schl; Pittsboro, IN; Sec Jr Cls; Chrs; Chrh Wkr; Hon Rl; Yrbk; Pep Clb; Letter Bsktbl; Volleyball Lettered Varsity 78; Univ.

REED, DEBBIE; Emerson HS; Gary, IN; Cmnty Wkr; Hon Rl; Jr NHS; ROTC; Pep Clb; Spn Clb; Cit Awd; General Busns Awd; College.

REED, DEBORAH; Our Lady Of Mercy HS; Detroit, MI; Girl Scts; Univ; Zoology.

REED, EDWINA; Doddridge Cnty HS; West Union, WV; 12/107 Trs Sr Cls; Sec Band; Hon Rl; NHS; Sec Stg Crw; Treas Pep Clb;.

REED, ELAINE; William Henry Harrison HS; Evansville, IN; Hon Rl; Off Ade; Spn Clb; Horsemanship.

REED, GERALD; Washington Irving HS; Clarksburg, WV; 37/149 Boy Scts; Hon Rl; Sct Actv; West Virginia Univ; Chem Engr.

REED, JAMES; Centreville HS; Constantine, MI; Pres Frsh Cls; FFA; Letter Bsbl; Letter Bsktbl; Letter Ftbl; MVP & Captain Bsbl 78; Univ.

REED, JAMES; Benjamin Logan HS; Belle Cntr, OH; Hon Rl; NHS; Sch Mus; Sch Pl; Yrbk; Drama Clb; 4-H; FFA; Mth Clb; Spn Clb; Univ; Law.

REED, JANICE; Charlotte HS; Charlotte, MI; Trs Sr Cls; Band; Drm Mjrt; Girl Scts; Hon Rl; NHS; Ger Clb; Pep Clb; Swmmng; Twrlr; Cntrl Michigan Univ; Chem.

REED, JILL; Crestview HS; Convoy, OH; Band; Hon Rl; Stu Cncl; Yth Flsp; 4-H; FHA; Pep Clb; Bsktbl; Trk; PPFtbl; Parliamentary Procedure FHA; Awd Of Merit; 1st Runner Up County Office FHA; Business Schl; Sec.

REED, JONATHAN; Amelia HS; Amelia, OH; 12/285 Band; Hon Rl; NHS; Sch Mus; Univ Of Cincinnati; Nuclear Engr.

REED, KAREN; Peebles HS; Peebles, OH; Sec Frsh Cls; Cl Rep Jr Cls; Band; Cmp Fr Grls; Chrs; Chrh Wkr; Cmnty Wkr; Drl Tm; Girl Scts; Hon Rl; Ohio St Univ.

REED, KAREN; Northrop HS; Ft Wayne, IN; 37/587 Band; Drm Mjrt; Hon Rl; Gym; Trk; Chrldng; Coll; Psychology.

REED, KATHLEEN M; Oregon Davis HS; Walkerton, IN; 5/60 Cls Rep Frsh Cls; Pres Jr Cls; Chrs; Hon Rl; Rptr Yrbk; Rptr Sch Nwsp; Drama Clb; 4-H; FHA; Lat Clb; Purdue Univ; Vet.

REED, KELLEY; Concord HS; Goshen, IN; Cls Rep Frsh Cls; Band; Hon Rl; JA; Jr NHS; Stu Cncl; Pep Clb; PPFtbl; St Of In Hoosier Schlr 78; Goshen Coll; Tchrs Aide.

REED, KEVIN; Elkins HS; Elkins, WV; 59/227 Cmnty Wkr; Hon Rl; Pol Wkr; Rptr Sch Nwsp; Key Clb; Letter Bsbl; Letter Bsktbl; Coach Actv; Letter Mgrs; All Tourn Tm Frsh Bsktbl 77; Page WV Hse Of Delegates 78; Elec Lieut Gov; WV Dist Key Club Intl 79; Univ; Bus.

REED, KIMBERLY D; Princeton HS; Princeton, WV; 100/327 Sec Soph Cls; Pep Clb; Capt Chrldng;.

REED, LAURA; Boardman HS; Boardman, OH; 6/500 Girl Scts; NHS; Orch; Sch Mus; Fr Clb; Univ; Music Perfmnce.

REED, LISA; Ridgewood HS; West Lafayette, OH; 55/150 Band; Chrs; Chmn Stu Cncl; Ed Yrbk; Yrbk; Rptr Sch Nwsp; FTA; GAA; PPFtbl; Am Leg Awd; Univ; Jrnlsm.

REED, LORI J; Eastern HS; Pekin, IN; Sec Jr Cls; Trs Sr Cls; Band; Drm Bgl; Hon Rl; NHS; Pep Clb; Univ.

REED, LYRONN; Crooksville HS; Crooksville, OH; Drl Tm; Hon Rl; Hosp Ade; Sch Pl; 4-H; GAA; Pom Pon; Acting Schl; Actor.

REED, MARK; Union HS; Elk Garden, WV; Cls Rep Frsh Cls; Cls Rep Soph Cls; Cl Rep Jr Cls; Cls Rep Sr Cls; Chrs; Chrh Wkr; Cmnty Wkr; Hon Rl; NHS; Sch Pl; Potomac St Coll; Med.

REED, MARSHA; Jefferson County HS; Shepherdstown, WV; Sch Mus; Sch Pl; Stg Crw; Drama Clb; Spn Clb; IM Sprt; Mgrs; Scr Kpr; Tmr; Univ Of West Virginia; Spec Educ.

REED, MICHAEL; Philip Barbour HS; Junior, WV; Band; Chrh Wkr; Rptr Sch Nwsp; VICA;.

REED, MIKE; Wilbur Wright HS; Dayton, OH; 3/250 Am Leg Boys St; Hon Rl; NHS; Mth Clb; Letter Bsbl; Letter Glf; Wright St Univ.

REED, MIKE; Napoleon HS; Napoleon, MI; Hon Rl; Off Ade; Letter Bsktbl; Letter Ftbl; Letter Trk; Chsn Nfor Schl Quiz Bowl Tm 79; Univ.

REED, PAM; Notre Dame HS; Portsmouth, OH; Girl Scts; Hon Rl; Quill & Scroll; Sct Actv; Rptr Sch Nwsp; Spn Clb; Bsktbl; Comm College; Den Hygiene.

REED, PAMELA; Caldwell HS; Caldwell, OH; Band; Chrh Wkr; Cmnty Wkr; Hon Rl; 4-H; FHA; Pep Clb; Spn Clb; Ohi State Univ; Nursing.

REED, RAMONA; Northfield HS; Wabash, IN; Am Leg Aux Girls St; Hon Rl; Spn Clb; Elem Educ.

REED, RAMONA J; Northfield HS; Wabash, IN; Am Leg Aux Girls St; Hon Rl; Univ; Art.

REED, ROBERT; New Albany HS; New Albany, IN; 151/551 Boy Scts; Univ.

REED, ROBERT R; Buckhannon Upshur HS; French Creek, WV; Band; Boy Scts; Hon Rl; Sch Mus; Sct Actv; Stu Cncl; 4-H; IM Sprt; Schl Stage Band 78; Solo Ensmlb Exclnt Ratng 79; Ws Hall Of Fame Track & Field Regnl Winner 440 77; West Virginia Wesleyan Coll; Music.

REED, ROBIN L; Harman HS; Whitmer, WV; Band; Chrs; Sec Chrh Wkr; Drm Mjrt; Hon Rl; Off Ade; Sch Pl; Treas Y-Teens; 4-H; FBLA; Davis & Elkins Univ; Sec.

REED, SHARON; Liberty HS; Bristol, WV; VP Frsh Cls; Cls Rep Soph Cls; Hon Rl; Jr NHS; NHS; Stu Cncl; Ed Yrbk; Pep Clb; Letter Bsktbl; Letter Ten; Concord Coll; Phys Ed.

REED, STACE; Bellmont HS; Decatur, IN; 51/244 Am Leg Boys St; Hon Rl; JA; Mod UN; Treas Spn Clb; Glf; Swmmng; Perfect Attendance 76 79; Purdue Univ; Nuclear Power.

REED, STEPHANIE; Traverse City HS; Traverse City, MI; NHS; Pep Clb; Northwestern Mich Coll; Bus.

REED, STEVEN; West Lafayette HS; W Lafayette, IN; FCA; Bsktbl; Ftbl; College; Acctg.

REED, SUE; Shelby Sr HS; Shelby, OH; Sec Soph Cls; Trs Soph Cls; Sec Jr Cls; Trs Jr Cls; Cl Rep Jr Cls; Sec Sr Cls; Trs Sr Cls; Cls Rep Sr Cls; Chrs; Chrh Wkr; Who Who Among Amer HS Stndt 77; Attndt Of HS Homcmng Ct 78; Bowling Green St Univ; Elem Educ.

REED, SUSAN; Walton HS; Elkview, WV; Hon Rl; Jr NHS; Lbry Ade; NHS; Off Ade; Sch Pl; FHA; Spn Clb; Cali State; Physical Therapy.

REED, SUSAN; East Canton HS; E Canton, OH; Hon Rl; Jr NHS; NHS; Stg Crw; Rptr Sch Nwsp; Drama Clb; FHA; Spn Clb; College; Law Enforcement.

REED, THOMAS; Theodore Roosevelt HS; Kent, OH; 4/360 Band; VP Chrs; Hon Rl; NHS; Orch; Sch Mus; Drama Clb; Natl Merit Ltr; Univ Of Michigan; Music Educ.

REED, THOMAS; Mt Healthy HS; Cincinnati, OH; Chrh Wkr; Hon Rl; Red Cr Ade; Yth Flsp; Pres 4-H; Ger Clb; Dnfth Awd; 4-H Awd; College; Animal Sci.

REED, THOMAS; Terre Haute North View HS; Terre Haute, IN; 146/676 Cls Rep Sr Cls; Aud/Vis; Band; Hon Rl; NHS; Orch; Rdo Clb; Wrstlng; Mgrs; Rose Halman Inst Of Tech; Elec Eng.

REED, TIM; Centreville HS; Constantine, MI; FFA; Letter Bsbl; Letter Bsktbl; Letter Ftbl; Univ.

REED, WENDY; Lucas HS; Lucas, OH; Sec Jr Cls; Am Leg Aux Girls St; Girl Scts; Hon Rl; NHS; Off Ade; Sch Mus; Sch Pl; Stg Crw; Rptr Yrbk; Participtd In Bus Skills Oly 79; Farm Bur Yth Grp; Bowling Green St Univ; Fshn Mdse.

REEDER, BRIAN; Medina Sr HS; Medina, OH; Boy Scts; Chrh Wkr; Sct Actv; Rptr Yrbk; Eagle Souct M8; Univ; Construction Engr.

REEDER, DAVID; Grosse Pointe South HS; Grss Pte Pk, MI; Chrh Wkr; Hon Rl; Bsbl; Bsktbl; Letter Ftbl; Trk; Mich State; Architecture.

REEDER, ERMA; Clinton Massie HS; Wilmington, OH; Girl Scts; Sct Actv; 4-H; Trk; 4-H Awd; Manager Training; Restaurant Manager.

REEDER, JENNIFER; Allen East HS; Harrod, OH; Cl Rep Jr Cls; Band; Chrs; Chrh Wkr; Cmnty Wkr; Sch Pl; Stu Cncl; 4-H; FHA; Chrldng; Tech Schl; Bus.

REEDER, JULIE; Stow HS; Stow, OH; 85/574 Band; Chrs; Chrh Wkr; Hon Rl; Trk; Band Awd; Outstanding Algebra Stu Awd; Vocational Schl; X Ray Tech.

REEDER, PAUL; Washington HS; Massillon, OH; Hon Rl; Yth Flsp; DECA; Vocational Schl.

REEDER, RACHELLE; National Trail HS; W Manchester, OH; Am Leg Aux Girls St; Band; Hon Rl; NHS; Stu Cncl; Rptr Yrbk; Rptr Sch Nwsp; Sec FTA; VP Spn Clb; College; Art Therapy.

REEDUS, ANNETTE; Linden Mc Kinley HS; Columbus, OH; 1/268 Val; Cmnty Wkr; Hon Rl; Off Ade; Ohio St Univ; Psych.

REEDY, DIANNE; Leetonia HS; Washingtonville, OH; 5/84 Am Leg Aux Girls St; Hon Rl; JA; NHS; Ed Sch Nwsp; VP Pep Clb; Spn Clb; Scr Kpr; VP JA Awd; Jr Achievement Officer Of The Yr; Star Of East Achievement Awd Ranked 5th In Class; Youngstown St Univ; Court Reporting.

REEF, MARTIN; Carroll HS; Cutler, IN; FFA; Purdue Univ; Elec Eng.

REERDERS, GAIL; Grand Haven Sr HS; Grand Haven, MI; Cls Rep Frsh Cls; Cl Rep Jr Cls; Am Leg Aux Girls St; Band; Hon Rl; Pres Jr NHS; NHS; Sch Mus; Stu Cncl; Yth Flsp; Southeastern Acad; Travel.

REES, DAVID; Tecumseh HS; Medway, OH; 24/360 Cls Rep Soph Cls; Cl Rep Jr Cls; Cls Rep Sr Cls; AFS; Am Leg Boys St; Chrs; Chrh Wkr; NHS; PAVAS; Sch Mus; Univ Of Cincinnati; Graphic Design.

REES, DONALD T; Gallia Academy; Gallipolis, OH; Sec Frsh Cls; Sec Soph Cls; Chrh Wkr; Yth Flsp; 4-H; Trk; Coach Actv; Mgrs; Tmr; Pres Awd; Track MVP; Record Track 2 Mile; Coll; Geology.

REES, ROBIN; Bridgman HS; Three Oaks, MI; Cmp Fr Grls; Chrh Wkr; Girl Scts; Hon Rl; Sch Pl; FHA; Sci Clb; Pom Pon; Voc Schl; Food Serv.

REESE, ANGELA; Jeffersonville HS; Jeffersonville, IN; Bus.

REESE, CECYLIA; Mumford HS; Detroit, MI; Hon Rl; Hosp Ade; Jr NHS; NHS; Y-Teens; Spn Clb; Michigan St Univ; Soc Work.

REESE, CHRISTOPHER; Lorain HS; Lorain, OH; 2/373 Sal; Chrs; Chrh Wkr; Cmnty Wkr; Hon Rl; NHS; Chmn Pol Wkr; Pres Stu Cncl; Rptr Yrbk; Bsktbl; Elected To Mayors Youth Advisory Council; Ohio State Univ; Medicine.

REESE, CYNTHIA; Yale HS; Yale, MI; Sec Frsh Cls; Cls Rep Frsh Cls; Sec Sr Cls; Chrs; Cmnty Wkr; Hon Rl; Stu Cncl; College; Nursing.

REESE, DENNIS; Lowell Sr HS; Hebron, IN; Aud/Vis; Chrs; Hon Rl; Lbry Ade; Stg Crw; Yth Flsp; Boys Clb Am; 4-H; IM Sprt; 4-H Awd; Patrol Boy Awd Bowling Awd & Trophy; Voc Schl; Operating Engr.

REESE, PAULA; Westfall HS; Orient, OH; Am Leg Aux Girls St; NHS; 4-H; FHA; FTA; Spn Clb; Westfall Home Ec Awds; Columbus Tech Inst; Med Lab Tech.

REESE, RICHARD; Grandville HS; Grand Rapids, MI; 37/340 Aud/Vis; Chrs; Hon Rl; Grand Rapids Jr Coll; Engr.

REESE, ROBERT; Central Catholic HS; Toledo, OH; Boy Scts; Chrh Wkr; Lbry Ade; Sprt Ed Sch Nwsp; Sch Nwsp; Coach Actv; IM Sprt; Bowling Green St Univ; Cmnctns.

REESE, SONYA; Marysville HS; Marysville, OH; Band; Chrs; Drl Tm; 4-H; Key Clb; Pep Clb; Letter Trk; Tech Schl; Data Proc.

REEVE, JACQUELINE; Bloomfield Hills Lahser HS; Bloomfield Hls, MI; Treas Chrs; Chrh Wkr; Debate Tm; NHS; Sch Mus; Sch Pl; Yth Flsp; Achvmnt Awd Alliance Fraanciase 79; Mert Schlshp Albion Coll 79; Acad Schlshp Venyon Coll 79; Univ Of Michigan.

REEVES, DAVID; Brownsburg HS; Brownsburg, IN; 49/300 Aud/Vis; Boy Scts; Chrh Wkr; Hon Rl; Lbry Ade; Sct Actv; Rptr Sch Nwsp; 4-H; Letter Bsktbl; Socr; Indiana St Univ; Comp Sci.

REEVES, DIANE; Pinconning Area HS; Pinconning, MI; Cmnty Wkr; Hon Rl; NHS; Sct Actv; Letter Bsktbl; Letter Trk; Coach Actv; PPFtbl; Ferris St Coll; Pharm.

REEVES, JENNIFER; Marion HS; Marion, IN; 45/675 Band; Chrs; Cmnty Wkr; Hon Rl; Hosp Ade; NHS; Sch Mus; Sch Pl; Drama Clb; Pres 4-H; Purdue Univ; Pre Pharm.

REEVES, JONI M; Wayne HS; Dayton, OH; 19/575 Cls Rep Frsh Cls; Cls Rep Soph Cls; Cl Rep Jr Cls; Cls Rep Sr Cls; Band; Hon Rl; Jr NHS; NHS; Stu Cncl; Chrldng; Miami Univ Of Ohio; Acctg.

REEVES, KAREN; Walled Lake Western HS; Walled Lk, MI; 10/450 Cls Rep Frsh Cls; Cls Rep Soph Cls; Cl Rep Jr Cls; Chrs; Hon Rl; Orch; Sch Mus; Yth Flsp; Letter Ten; Letter Chrldng; Oakland Univ; Music.

REEVES, LISA D; Lake Michigan Cath HS; Benton Harbor, MI; 8/102 Band; Drm Mjrt; Hon Rl; NHS; Sch Mus; Sch Pl; Stg Crw; Yrbk; Sec Drama Clb; Trk; Michigan St Univ; Vet.

REEVES, MARK; Waterford Kettering HS; Drayton Plains, MI; 1/400 Val; VP Band; Hon Rl; Jr NHS; NHS; Sch Mus; IM Sprt; Rcvd Div I Ratings At St Solo & Ensemble; Trustee Hnrs Schlrshp From Alma Coll 79; Philip Sousa Bnd Awd 79; Alma Coll.

REEVES, PAMELA; Hammond Christian Academy; Schererville, IN; 1/17 Pres Sr Cls; Cls Rep Sr Cls; Val; Chrs; Chrh Wkr; Drl Tm; Hon Rl; Off Ade; Orch; Sch Pl; College; Education.

REEVES, PAULA; Chaminade Julienne HS; Dayton, OH; Drl Tm; Hon Rl; Trk; Coll; Nursing.

REEVES, PHILIP; Norton HS; Norton, OH; 28/338 Band; Hon Rl; Socr; Adv Placmnt Amer Hstry Cl 78; Adv Placmnt Amer Hstry Tst 79; Univ; Engr.

REGAN, KATHRYN; Marian HS; Birmingham, MI; Mod UN; Spn Clb; Natl Merit SF; Art Schlrshp 76; Univ; Marine Bio.

REGAN, ROBERT; Memphis HS; Emmett, MI; Boy Scts; Hon Rl; Sch Pl; 4-H; Trk; 4-H Awd; Univ Of Michigan; Bus Admin.

REGAN, ROBIN; West Catholic HS; Comstock Pk, MI; Hon Rl; Off Ade; Sch Mus; Sch Pl; Pep Clb; Gym; PPFtbl; College; Phys Ther.

REGENSBURGER, AMY; Switzerland County HS; Vevay, IN; Hon Rl; Off Ade; Sch Pl; Rptr Sch Nwsp; Drama Clb; Fr Clb; Pep Clb; Wrstlng; Univ.

REGENSBURGER, AMY; Switzerland Cnty HS; Vevay, IN; Hon Rl; Sch Pl; Sch Nwsp; Drama Clb; Fr Clb; Pep Clb; Trk; Coll.

REGER, JANET; Lincoln HS; Shinnston, WV; Lbry Ade; Pep Clb; Voc Schl; Comp Prog.

REGER, KIRK W; Vinson HS; Huntington, WV; 3/100 Am Leg Boys St; Band; Chrs; Hon Rl; NHS; Boys Clb Am; Key Clb; Spn Clb; Letter Ftbl; Letter Ten; Marshall Univ.

REGILLO, NICKY; Mannington HS; Mannington, WV; Trs Jr Cls; Am Leg Boys St; Chrh Wkr; Hon Rl; Yth Flsp; Fr Clb; Letter Bsktbl; Coach Actv; IM Sprt; Scr Kpr; Ltr For Excelling In Bsktbl 78; Mt Vernon Nazarene Coll; Jrnlsm.

REGIS, CHERYL; Martins Ferry HS; Martins Ferry, OH; 32/213 Band; Hon Rl; Sch Mus; Y-Teens; Yrbk; Fr Clb; Letter Trk; GAA; Scr Kpr; Belmont Tech Coll; Sec.

REGNIER, MARK; Tipton HS; Tipton, IN; 56/175 Letter Bsbl; Letter Bsktbl; Letter Ftbl; IM Sprt; College.

REGRUT, MARY; Dublin HS; Dublin, OH; 37/153 Cls Rep Sr Cls; Chrs; Hon Rl; Sch Mus; Stu Cncl; Yth Flsp; Rptr Sch Nwsp; Fr Clb; Pep Clb; Mia Univ; Engr.

REGRUT, TOM; Dublin HS; Dublin, OH; 5/157 Hon Rl; NHS; Letter Ftbl; Ohi St Univ; Pre Med.

REGUEIRO, JENNY; Wadsworth Sr HS; Medina, OH; Girl Scts; Hon Rl; Eng Clb; 4-H; Fr Clb;.

REHAK, LORRAINE A; Springfield Local HS; New Springfield, OH; Hon Rl; Hosp Ade; Jr NHS; NHS; OEA; Sec.

REHARD, NANCY; Newcomerstown HS; Newcomerstown, OH; 13/105 Cl Rep Jr Cls; Am Leg Aux Girls St; VP Hst Frsh Cls; Hon Rl; Orch; Sch Mus; Sch Pl; Stg Crw; Stu Cncl; Univ Of Akron; Med Tech.

REHBERG, ANNE; Concordia Lutheran HS; Ft Wayne, IN; Chrs; Chrh Wkr; Capt Drl Tm; JA; Stu Cncl; 4-H; FBLA; GAA; Pom Pon; PPFtbl; Ball State Univ; Business.

REHFELD, RUTH; D D Eisenhower HS; Saginaw, MI; Band; Chrh Wkr; Hosp Ade; NHS; Sch Mus; Yrbk; Trk; Math Awd 76; John Philip Sousa Band Awd 78; Eisenhower Music Boosters Sr Schlrshp Awd 78; Michigan St Univ; Jrnlsm.

REHLING, CAROLYN A; St Francis De Sales HS; Westerville, OH; Drl Tm; Red Cr Ade; Pom Pon; Spelling Bee Winner; Tap & Jazz Dancer; Ohio St Univ.

REHMANN, KIMBERLY; Chesaning Union HS; Chesaning, MI; Aud/Vis; Hon Rl; Stu Cncl; Pep Clb; Letter Trk; Chrldng; Scr Kpr; Univ; Int Design.

REHMEL, ROBIN; Shakamak HS; Jasinville, IN; Band; Chrs; Chrh Wkr; Lbry Ade; Sch Mus; Sch Pl; Yth Flsp; Drama Clb; 4-H; Trk; ISU; Legal Sec.

REHMER, MARY; Bowling Green HS; Bowling Green, OH; Hon Rl; Off Ade; Stu Cncl; Fr Clb; FBLA; Ger Clb; Letter Gym; Letter Trk; Letter Chrldng; GAA; Bowling Green St Univ; Sec.

REIBEL, LISA; Mater Dei HS; Evansville, IN; 37/173 Girl Scts; Hon Rl; Stg Crw; 4-H; Pep Clb; Chrldng; GAA; Capt Twrlr; 4-H Awd; State Fair Showing Horses 76 & 75; Univ; Pharm.

REICH, BECKY; Medina HS; Medina, OH; 34/355 Band; Girl Scts; Hon Rl; Hosp Ade; NHS; Red Cr Ade; Stg Crw; 4-H; PPFtbl; 4-H Awd; Univ Of Akron; Nursing.

REICH, MARY E; Charlestown HS; Charlestwn, IN; 16/174 Pres Soph Cls; Band; Chrh Wkr; FCA; Girl Scts; Hon Rl; Hosp Ade; Mdrgl; Treas NHS; Pres Yth Flsp; Bus Schl; Fshn Mdse.

REICHANADTER, PERRY; Washington HS; South Bend, IN; 54/327 Yrbk; Sch Nwsp; Crs Cntry; Trk; Purdue Univ; Phys Ed.

REICHARD, RONALD; Carrollton HS; Saginaw, MI; Chrh Wkr; Hon Rl; Off Ade; Saginaw Vly St Coll; Bio.

REICHENBACH, ANN; Bishop Foley HS; Utica, MI; 17/193 Hon Rl; Stg Crw; Yrbk; Mercy Coll; Nursing.

REICHENBACH, KAREN; Whitmore Lake HS; Whitmore Lk, MI; Cl Rep Jr Cls; Chrs; Chrh Wkr; Hon Rl; NHS; Yth Flsp; Yrbk; Mich St Univ; Doctor.

REICHENBACH, ROGER; Whitmore Lake HS; Whitmore Lake, MI; Trs Sr Cls; Chrs; Chrh Wkr; Hon Rl; NHS; Pol Wkr; Pres Yth Flsp; Concordia; Md.

REICHERT, ANNE; Northwestern HS; West Salem, OH; 1/130 Band; Chrs; Chrh Wkr; Hon Rl; NHS; Sch Mus; Yth Flsp; Sec 4-H; Treas FTA; Lat Clb; Univ; Math.

REICHERT, JACQUELINE; Whitmer HS; Toledo, OH; Cls Rep Frsh Cls; Hon Rl; Stu Cncl; Pep Clb; Spn Clb; Trk; Mgrs; PPFtbl; Tmr; Univ Of Toledo; Banking.

REICHERT, MICHAEL A; Celina Sr HS; Montezuma, OH; Univ.

REICHLEY, JOHN; New Lexington HS; New Lexington, OH; Cls Rep Soph Cls; Sec Sr Cls; Cls Rep Sr Cls; Boy Scts; Hon Rl; Pol Wkr; Stu Cncl; 4-H; Fr Clb; Pep Clb; St Track Meet 78; Muskingum Coll; Dent.

REICHOW, LINDA; Albion HS; Albion, MI; Cls Rep Soph Cls; Am Leg Aux Girls St; Hon Rl; Lbry Ade; Sec NHS; Stg Crw; Stu Cncl; Yrbk; VP 4-H; Chrldng; Cntrl Michigan Univ.

REICKEL, ERIC; Dearborn HS; Dearborn, MI; Chrs; Debate Tm; Hon Rl; Mod UN; Natl Forn Lg; Sch Pl; Ger Clb; Bsktbl; Socr; Letter Ten; Univ Of Michigan; Eng Lit.

REICKEL, SUSAN; Dearborn HS; Dearborn, MI; Hon Rl; Tmr; Western Michigan Univ; Bus.

REID, ANNE E; Wylie E Groves HS; Southfield, MI; 97/559 Cls Rep Frsh Cls; Cls Rep Soph Cls; Cl Rep Jr Cls; Cls Rep Sr Cls; Pres AFS; Cmnty Wkr; Girl Scts; Jr NHS; Lbry Ade; Off Ade; Univ Of Michigan; Foreign Serv.

REID, ANNETTE; Douglas Mac Arthur HS; Saginaw, MI; Chrs; Swmmng; Delta Coll; Bus.

REID, BRIAN; Cloverdale HS; Quincy, IN; 2/80 Band; Drm Mjrt; Hon Rl; NHS; Sch Mus; Sch Pl; Treas Drama Clb; Spn Clb; De Molay Rd Awd; College; Medicine.

REID, DARLA J; Owosso HS; Owosso, MI; Chrs; Chrh Wkr; FCA; Hon Rl; JA; Sch Pl; Yth Flsp; Drama Clb; 4-H; Lat Clb; 4h Rcvd Svrl Sup Rtngs Sewng 73 79; Rep For Baptst Yth Fellowshp St Cabnt 79; Yth Missionry Intl Guatemala; Lansing Cmnty Coll; Occ Ther.

REID, ELIZABETH; Hubbard HS; Hubbard, OH; Band; Cmp Fr Grls; Hon Rl; Yth Flsp; Fr Clb; College; Vet.

REID, JAYNE; Hinton HS; Hinton, WV; Cmnty Wkr; Sec Jr NHS; Stu Cncl; Fr Clb; Treas Lat Clb; 90 Club Awd 76; Trait Of Character; Ctznshp Pageant 79; Tri Hi Y Club Mbr 3 Yrs 77; Univ; Chem.

REID, JOHN; Manistique HS; Gulliver, MI; Band; Chrs; Hon Rl; Trk; Wrstlng; IM Sprt; Michigan Tech Univ; Chem Engr.

REID, JUDITH A; High School; Traverse City, MI; Jr NHS; Pep Clb; Pom Pon; Natl Merit Ltr; Michigan St Univ; Bus Admin.

REID, KELLY J; Franklin HS; Westland, MI; Band; Girl Scts; Hon Rl; Off Ade; Sch Mus; Sch Pl; Sct Actv; Sprt Ed Sch Nwsp; Drama Clb; Trk; Michigan St Univ; Music.

REID, KENNETH; Brebeuf Prep Schl; Indianapolis, IN; 60/140 Boy Scts; Hon Rl; Letter Ftbl; Natl Merit Ltr; Univ; Engr.

REID, LONDA; River Rouge HS; Rivr Rouge, MI; Chrh Wkr; Cmnty Wkr; Girl Scts; Hon Rl; NHS; Rdo Clb; Cit Awd; Univ Of Michigan; Nursing.

REID, MICHAEL; Notre Dame HS; Grosse Pointe, MI; Hon Rl; Swmmng; IM Sprt; Natl Merit Ltr; Mic State Univ; Bio Chem.

REID, ROBERT; Marlette HS; Marlette, MI; Cls Rep Frsh Cls; Pres Soph Cls; Debate Tm; Hon Rl; NHS; Sch Pl; Stu Cncl; Rptr Yrbk; Pep Clb; Letter Bsbl; Northwood Inst; Busns Admin.

REID, SCOTT M; Swan Valley HS; Saginaw, MI; 16/185 Band; Boy Scts; Hon Rl; NHS; Red Cr Ade; Letter Swmmng; Letter Trk; God Cntry Awd; Delta Coll; Paramedic.

REID, TODD; Hampshire HS; Augusta, WV; 29/213 Hon Rl; Jr NHS; FFA; Wildlife Mgmt.

REID, TRACY; Holt Sr HS; Lansing, MI; 9/291 VP Jr Cls; Pres Sr Cls; Girl Scts; Hon Rl; Jr NHS; NHS; Stu Cncl; Ger Clb; Key Clb; Pep Clb; Michigan St Univ; Bus.

REIDER, STEPHEN; Perrysburg HS; Perrysburg, OH; FCA; Letter Ftbl; Letter Trk; Letter Wrstlng; Univ; Engr.

REIDY, DEBRA; Fairless HS; Navarre, OH; Band; Hon Rl; FHA; Swmmng; Bus Schl.

REIFENBERG, PHIL; Bishop Dwenger HS; Ft Wayne, IN; 49/300 Cls Rep Sr Cls; Hon Rl; JA; NHS; Stg Crw; Stu Cncl; Pres Key Clb; Ftbl; Trk; Wrstlng; Miami Univ; Busns.

REIGER, JEANNINE; Brooklyn HS; Brooklyn, OH; 4/185 Chrs; Hon Rl; JA; Lbry Ade; NHS; Sch Pl; Yrbk; Rptr Sch Nwsp; Eng Clb; Fr Clb; Baldwin Wallace Coll; Bus.

REIGLE, C; Laville HS; Mishawaka, IN; 8/180 Girl Scts; Hon Rl; Natl Forn Lg; NHS; Rptr Yrbk; Yrbk; 4-H; Spn Clb; Middle Tenn St Univ ; Recording.

REIHING, JACQUELINE; Clay Sr HS; Oregon, OH; 17/355 Pres Soph Cls; Cls Rep Sr Cls; Chrh Wkr; Cmnty Wkr; Girl Scts; Hon Rl; Jr NHS; NHS; Fr Clb; Culinary Inst; Caterer Mgr.

REIL, AUDREY; Wadsworth HS; Wadsworth, OH; 17/357 Chrh Wkr; Lat Clb; Spn Clb; Swmmng; Univ Of Akron; Internal Marketing.

REILLY, DEIRDRE; Cambridge HS; Cambridge, OH; Hon Rl; Off Ade; Fr Clb; Scr Kpr; Tmr; Univ; Bio Sci.

REILLY, JAN; Clarksville HS; Clarksville, IN; Chrh Wkr; Hon Rl; JA; Off Ade; Quill & Scroll; Ed Yrbk; Sch Nwsp; OEA; Pep Clb; Tmr; Vincennces Univ; Jrnlsm.

REILLY, MARGO P; Marquette HS; Marquette, MI; Band; Girl Scts; Off Ade; Sch Pl; Rptr Yrbk; 4-H; Fr Clb; FHA; Ten; Trk; N Mich Univ.

REILLY, REBECCA; Chippewa HS; Doylestown, OH; Band; Chrh Wkr; Hon Rl; Ten; Mat Maids; Tex A & M; Vet Med.

REILLY, TIM; Brown City HS; Brown City, MI; 2/87 Pres Frsh Cls; VP Soph Cls; VP Jr Cls; Sal; Band; Chrh Wkr; Pres NHS; Pres Stu Cncl; 4-H; Ftbl; Western Michigan Univ; Comp Engr.

REILMAN, TERRY; Mc Auley HS; Cincinnati, OH; Chrh Wkr; CAP; Orch; Bsbl; Bsktbl; Swmmng; Coach Actv; GAA; IM Sprt; Twrlr; College; Vet.

REIMER, RANDALL; Central Montcalm HS; Sheridan, MI; Band; Sch Mus; Stg Crw; Rptr Sch Nwsp; Drama Clb; Ftbl; Wrstlng;.

REIMER, THERESE; Ursuline Academy; Cincinnati, OH; 1/106 Band; Chrh Wkr; Cmnty Wkr; Pol Wkr; Rptr Sch Nwsp; Eng Clb; Rus Clb; SAR Awd; Univ; Lib Arts.

REIMER, TODD; Southwestern HS; Flat Rock, IN; Cls Rep Frsh Cls; Cls Rep Soph Cls; Cl Rep Jr Cls; Cls Rep Sr Cls; Chrs; Hon Rl; NHS; Sch Pl; Stu Cncl; Yth Flsp; Univ; Oceanography.

REIN, DEBORAH; Pinckney Cmnty HS; Pinckney, MI; 6/247 Sec Frsh Cls; Trs Jr Cls; Band; Chrh Wkr; Cmnty Wkr; Girl Scts; Hon Rl; Lbry Ade; NHS; Sct Actv; E Mi Campus Ldr Schlrshp 79; Natl Hnr Soc Awd Chosen For St Comp 79; St Of Mi Achvmnt Awd 79; Eastern Michigan Univ; Spch Path.

REIN, JUDY; Clermont Northeastern HS; Milford, OH; Band; Hon Rl; NHS; Sch Pl; Rptr Yrbk; Rptr Sch Nwsp; 4-H; Fr Clb; FHA; Scr Kpr; Coll; Jrnlsm.

REIN, MONIKA; Normandy HS; Seven Hills, OH; Chrs; Chrh Wkr; Hon Rl; Lit Mag; Off Ade; Sch Mus; FFA; Ger Clb;.

REINARD, KATHRYN; Streetsboro HS; Streetsboro, OH; Band; Chrs; Chrh Wkr; Girl Scts; Hon Rl; Lbry Ade; Off Ade; Sct Actv; Yth Flsp; OEA; College; CPA.

REINBERGER, BILL; South Dearborn HS; Dillsboro, IN; 11/265 Pres Frsh Cls; Pres Soph Cls; Hon Rl; NHS; Ed Sch Nwsp; Sprt Ed Sch Nwsp; FFA; Letter Bsbl; Bsktbl; Trk; Ball St Univ; Journalism.

REINBOLD, DENNIS; Cascade HS; Clayton, IN; 30/156 Cls Rep Sr Cls; Chrh Wkr; Cmnty Wkr; Hon Rl; Off Ade; Sch Mus; Pres Stu Cncl; Rptr Sch Nwsp; Lat Clb; Bsbl; Indiana Central Univ; Bus Admin.

REINCKE, BLAKE; Forest Hills Central HS; Ada, MI; 10/350 Cls Rep Soph Cls; Hon Rl; JA; Jr NHS; Mod UN; NHS; Stu Cncl; Letter Crs Cntry; Letter Trk; JA Awd; Sperry & Hutchinson Foundation Schlrshp St Of Michigan Comp 78; Schlrshp Sr Leadership Awd 78; Michigan St Univ; Chem Engr.

REINECK, JOHN; Pontiac Central HS; Pontiac, MI; Boy Scts; Chrs; Hon Rl; NHS; Sprt Ed Yrbk; Yrbk; JA Awd; Stg Crw; Rptr Yrbk; Rptr Sch Nwsp; Michigan State Univ.

REINER, WILLIAM R; Bloom Carroll HS; Carroll, OH; 12/170 Chrh Wkr; Hon Rl; Treas NHS; VP Yth Flsp; 4-H; Natl Merit SF; Univ; Natural Resources.

REINERT, JILL; Lutheran HS West; Detroit, MI; 14/163 NHS; Off Ade; Sch Pl; Drama Clb; Ger Clb; Valparaiso Univ.

REINERT, JOHN; Frankenmuth HS; Birch Run, MI; 29/189 Hon Rl; 4-H; IM Sprt; Lion Awd; Mic Tech Univ; Engr.

REINHARD, CURTIS; Fostoria HS; Fostoria, OH; Rdo Clb; Bsbl; Wrstlng; Spartan Univ; Aircraft Tech.

REINHARD, HERBERT; Southern Wells HS; Bluffton, IN; 1/97 Am Leg Boys St; Hon Rl; NHS; Dnfth Awd; Rotary Awd; Purdue Univ; Veterinarian.

REINHARDT, RENEE; Central HS; Detroit, MI; Chrs; Girl Scts; Lbry Ade; Off Ade; Sch Mus; Pep Clb; Swmmng; Cit Awd; Eastern Univ; Accounting.

REINHART, CARLA; Hopewell Loudon School; Tiffin, OH; 14/106 Band; Chrs; Hon Rl; NHS; Sch Mus; 4-H; Pep Clb; Bsktbl; Trk; Chrldng; Univ; Zoology.

REINHART, GORDON; Wayne Memorial HS; Westland, MI; 1/660 Val; Chrs; Debate Tm; FCA; Hon Rl; Natl Forn Lg; VP NHS; Orch; Sch Mus; Sch Pl; De Pauw Univ; Music.

REINHART, REBECCA; Bedford HS; Temperance, MI; 1/500 Chrh Wkr; Girl Scts; Hon Rl; NHS; Sct Actv; Univ Of Toledo; Engr.

REINHART, ROSEMARY; Anderson HS; Cincinnati, OH; 142/412 Cls Rep Frsh Cls; Cls Rep Soph Cls; Drl Tm; Hosp Ade; Sprt Ed Sch Nwsp; Letter Socr; Letter Swmmng; Letter Chrldng; Coach Actv; PPFtbl; Diving For Schl & AAU Meets 4th Pl Dist 2nd Cnty; Univ Of Dayton; Phys Ed.

REINHART, WENDY; Hopewell Loudon HS; Tiffin, OH; 3/106 VP Jr Cls; Chrs; Hon Rl; NHS; Sch Mus; Letter Trk; Letter Chrldng; Cit Awd; Bus Schl; Bus.

REINHEIMER, TERRI; Fairmont West HS; Kettering, OH; 25/500 Chrs; Hon Rl; NHS; Off Ade; Ten; Mgrs; Univ Of Dayton; Med Tech.

REINHOLD, GLEN; Rensselaer Cntrl HS; Rensselaer, IN; 5/154 Hon Rl; NHS; Mth Clb; Sci Clb; Letter Crs Cntry; Letter Trk; Coll.

REINHOLD, MARCI; Mother Of Mercy HS; Cincinnati, OH; 19/280 Chrh Wkr; Cmnty Wkr; Hon Rl; Hosp Ade; Jr NHS; NHS; Mth Clb; Swmmng; Ten; Regis College; Math.

REINHOLD, MARTA; Munster HS; Munster, IN; 21/410 AFS; Am Leg Aux Girls St; Chrs; Chrh Wkr; Debate Tm; Hon Rl; Jr NHS; NHS; Pol Wkr; Sch Nwsp; Oklahoma Univ; Geological Engr.

REINO, CHRISTOPHER; Gibsonburg HS; Gibsonburg, OH; Hon Rl; Crs Cntry; Trk; Col State Univ; Forestry.

REINOEHL, EILEEN; Walnut Ridge HS; Columbus, OH; 1/429 Band; Chrs; Pres Capital Univ; Math.

REINOEHL, TERRI E; Van Buren HS; Brazil, IN; Band; Chrh Wkr; Girl Scts; Hon Rl; Yth Flsp; Pep Clb; Letter Bsktbl; Gym; Letter Trk; Chrldng; Ivy Tech Schl; Sec.

REINSTATLER, JOE; Elder HS; Cincinnati, OH; Aud/Vis; Boy Scts; Sct Actv; Letter Crs Cntry; Letter Trk; IM Sprt; Coll.

REIS, CHRISTINE; Bedford Sr HS; Temperance, MI; NHS; Fr Clb; VP Mat Maids; Natl Merit Ltr; Univ Of Toledo Hnr Schlrshp 79; Univ Of Toledo; Pharm.

REIS, DANNA; Lumen Cordium HS; Aurora, OH; Cl Rep Jr Cls; Am Leg Aux Girls St; Cmp Fr Grls; VP Stu Cncl; Chrldng; Coach Actv; GAA; IM Sprt; Univ; Oceanography.

REIS, KATHLEEN; St Francis De Sales HS; Columbus, OH; Cl Rep Jr Cls; Hon Rl; Hosp Ade; Letter Gym; Chrldng; PPFtbl; Univ; Phys Ther.

REISCH, JAMES T; Marlington HS; Alliance, OH; Chrh Wkr; Hon Rl; NHS; VP Yth Flsp; Pres VICA; Trk; Univ Of Akron; Elec Tech.

REISDORF, WILLIAM C; Baraga HS; Baraga, MI; 2/63 Pres Soph Cls; Am Leg Boys St; Band; Hon Rl; Lbry Ade; NHS; Mgrs; Natl Merit Ltr; MI Upper Penninsula Honors Band 79; School Jazz Band 76; Univ; Phys Sci.

REISER, JAMES; Cadillac HS; Cadillac, MI; Hon Rl; Michigan Tech Univ; Civil Engr.

REISER, TIM; Napoleon HS; Napoleon, OH; Hon Rl; Letter Bsktbl; Univ; Phys Educ.

REISERT, MICHAEL; Middletown HS; Middletown, OH; 21/557 Band; Chrs; Debate Tm; Hon Rl; VP Orch; Sch Mus; Sch Pl; Purdue Univ; Chemical Engr.

REISIG, JEANNINE; Douglas Mac Arthur HS; Saginaw, MI; 8/302 Band; Hon Rl; MMM; NHS; People To People HS Stud Ambassador 78; Schlrshp From Mi St Univ 79; Distinguishd Stud Sci Awd 79; Michigan St Univ; Vet Med.

REISING, PAUL; North HS; Elberfield, IN; Chrh Wkr; Hon Rl; 4-H; VICA; 4-H Awd; North High Voc Progr; Machinist.

REISSLAND, GAIBRELLE; Father Joseph Wehrle Mem HS; Columbus, OH; Girl Scts; Hon Rl; Stu Cncl; VP Spn Clb; Bsktbl; GAA; IM Sprt; Capital Univ; Nursing.

REISTER, JENNIFER; Sparta HS; Sparta, MI; Band; Girl Scts; Hon Rl; Sch Pl; 4-H; 4-H Awd; Grand Rapids Jr Coll; Archt.

REITENGA, BARRY; Douglas Mac Arthur HS; Saginaw, MI; Ger Clb; Crs Cntry; Univ; Rest Mgmt.

REITENOUR, RONDA; North Farmington HS; Farmington Hls, MI; Chrs; Girl Scts; Hon Rl; Yrbk; Pep Clb; Spn Clb; IM Sprt; Ferris St Univ; Bus Admin.

REITER, NANCY A; Trenton HS; Trenton, MI; Chrh Wkr; Hon Rl; Pol Wkr; Yth Flsp; Ger Clb; Pep Clb; Bsktbl; GAA; IM Sprt; Michigan St Univ; Acctg.

REITER, PATRICK A; New Riegel HS; New Riegel, OH; Am Leg Boys St; Band; Hon Rl; JA; NHS; Orch; Sch Mus; Sch Pl; 4-H; Spn Clb; Univ; Hist.

REITZ, GREGG; Battle Creek Central HS; Battle Creek, MI; Band; Hon Rl; NHS; Letter Ten; Letter Wrstlng; Natl Merit Ltr; Kellogg Comm Coll; Busns Admin.

REITZEL, KAREN; Eastwood HS; Pemberville, OH; Band; Chrs; Chrh Wkr; Hon Rl; NHS; Orch; Sch Mus; Yrbk; 4-H; Mgrs; University.

REITZEL, KAY; Eastwood HS; Pemberville, OH; Cls Rep Soph Cls; Cl Rep Jr Cls; Chrs; Chrh Wkr; NHS; Sch Mus; Sec Stu Cncl; Rptr Yrbk; 4-H; 4-H Awd; University; Home Ec.

REIVA, JUDI; Monrovia HS; Mooresville, IN; 2/134 Band; Hon Rl; NHS; Yrbk; Spn Clb; Trk; Mat Maids; PPFtbl; Cit Awd; Geometry Awd; Zoology Lab Assistant; College.

RELAFORD, EUGENE; John Hay HS; Cleveland, OH; 36/251 Hon Rl; Bsktbl; Trk; IM Sprt; Cit Awd; Bell & Howell; Comp Tech.

RELLINGER, ANTOINETTE; Ottoville Local HS; Ft Jennings, OH; Sec Frsh Cls; Chrs; Hon Rl; NHS; Sch Mus; Rptr Yrbk; 4-H; FFA; Chrldng; Bus Schl; Bus.

RELYEA, KATHY; Fairview HS; Ney, OH; Hon Rl; Sec 4-H; FHA; Trk; Mgrs; Top American Hist Awd 78; Univ; Intr Dsgn.

RELYEA, KIM; Fairview HS; Ney, OH; 11/123 Am Leg Aux Girls St; Chrh Wkr; Hon Rl; Lbry Ade; Off Ade; Capt Trk; GAA; Am Leg Awd;.

RELYEA, MARK; Grove City HS; Grove City, OH; 130/512 Cls Rep Frsh Cls; Cls Rep Soph Cls; Cl Rep Jr Cls; Cls Rep Sr Cls; Cmnty Wkr; Hon Rl; Stu Cncl; Yth Flsp; Sprt Ed Yrbk; Rptr Yrbk; Muskingum Coll; Educ.

REMBELSKI, PHILLIP; St Alphonsus HS; Dearobrn, MI; 63/249 Debate Tm; Hon Rl; Natl Forn Lg; Univ.

REMBISH, TERRIE; Buckeye North HS; Brillinnt, OH; Band; Hon Rl; NHS; Sch Pl; Drama Clb; Spn Clb; College.

REMDERGAST, T; Bishop Watterson HS; Worthington, OH; 10/253 Hon Rl; Hosp Ade; Jr NHS; NHS; PPFtbl; College; Phys Ther.

REMIAS, KATHY; Champion HS; Warren, OH; VP Soph Cls; Chrs; Girl Scts; Hon Rl; Hosp Ade; Lbry Ade; Off Ade; Sch Mus; Sch Pl; Sct Actv; Natl Roller Skating Champ; Youth Conservation Corps; College; X Ray Tech.

REMIAS, KATHY; Kenston HS; Chagrin Fls, OH; Drl Tm; Spn Clb; College; Elec Tech.

REMICK, JUDITH; Charles S Mott HS; Warren, MI; 138/650 Letter Scr Kpr; Letter Tmr; Mic State Univ.

REMICK, MARK; Monsignor Hackett HS; Kalamazoo, MI; 6/139 Cls Rep Frsh Cls; Pres Soph Cls; Pres Jr Cls; VP Sr Cls; Boy Scts; Hon Rl; NHS; Sch Mus; Sct Actv; Stu Cncl; Eagle Scout; Notre Dame Univ; Vet Med.

REMILLARD, ANDREW; Bad Axe HS; Bad Axe, MI; Band; Chrs; Chrh Wkr; Hon Rl; NHS; Sch Mus; Yth Flsp; Coll; Music.

REMILLARD, ANTHONY; Wm Henry Harrison HS; Harrison, OH; Band; Hon Rl; NHS; Bsbl; Bsktbl; Glf; IM Sprt; College; Zoology.

REMILLARD, MICHELLE; Notre Dame Acad; Toledo, OH; Cl Rep Jr Cls; Hon Rl; JA; NHS; Fr Clb; FBLA; JA Awd; Univ.

REMKUS, JENNIFER; Thomas W Harvey HS; Painesville, OH; 2/166 Sal; Band; Hon Rl; NHS; Rptr Yrbk; Drama Clb; Mth Clb; Am Leg Awd; Univ Of Akron.

REMLEY, JULIE; Harrison HS; W Lafayette, IN; Band; Chrs; Girl Scts; Pep Clb; PPFtbl; Twrlr; Purdue Univ.

REMLINGER, THOMAS R; Delphos Saint Johns HS; Delphos, OH; Band; Cmnty Wkr; Hon Rl; Orch; Sch Mus; Yrbk; Fr Clb; Ten; IM Sprt; Natl Merit Ltr; Ohio State Univ; Pharmacy.

REMMELL, EDWARD C; Indian Hill HS; Cincinnati, OH; 4/132 Boy Scts; Debate Tm; Hon Rl; Pres JA; Lbry Ade; Orch; Sch Mus; Sct Actv; Mth Clb; Sci Clb; Awd Eagle Scout Rank 77; Semi Finalist In AMSA Piano Comp 76; 3rd Highest Of 1200 Stud Math Tournmt 79; Univ; Chem Engr.

REMMERS, SUE; Grand Ledge Academy; Washington, WV; 1/17 Pres Jr Cls; Trs Sr Cls; Val; Band; Hon Rl; NHS; Ed Yrbk; Univ; Acctg.

REMMERS, SUE; Grand Ledge Academy; Grand Ledge, MI; 1/18 Pres Jr Cls; Cl Rep Jr Cls; Trs Sr Cls; Val; Band; Chrs; Chrh Wkr; Hon Rl; NHS; Stu Cncl; Andrews Univ; Acctg.

REMMERS, SUSAN; Grand Ledge Academy; Berriew Sprgs, MI; 1/18 Pres Jr Cls; Trs Sr Cls; Band; Chrs; Chrh Wkr; Hon Rl; NHS; Andrews Univ; Acctg.

REMMLER, TERRY; Laurel HS; Laurel, IN; VP Frsh Cls; Cls Rep Frsh Cls; VP Soph Cls; Cls Rep Soph Cls; VP Jr Cls; Cl Rep Jr Cls; Hon Rl; NHS; Stu Cncl; Rptr Yrbk; Bus Schl; Real Estate.

REMUS, KATHIE; Avondale Sr HS; Auburn Heights, MI; Chrs; Girl Scts; Hon Rl; Sch Mus; Boys Clb Am; Trk; Chrldng; Pom Pon; PPFtbl; Mi Compt Schlhp 79; USCA Natl Grand Champ Team Mbr 78; MBSA Semin Fnlst; Baker Jr Coll; Bus Admin.

REMY, KATHLEEN; Lexington HS; Lexington, OH; VP Band; NHS; Pres Y-Teens; Fr Clb; Univ.

RENAKER, PATRICIA; Salem HS; Salem, IN; Aud/Vis; Chrs; Hon Rl; NHS; Stu Cncl; Ed Yrbk; Pep Clb; Spn Clb; Letter Trk;.

RENARD, JANET; New Albany HS; New Albany, IN; 1/500 Band; Hon Rl; NHS; Orch; Quill & Scroll; Sch Mus; Ed Sch Nwsp; Sch Nwsp; Natl Merit SF; Butler Univ; Music.

RENBERG, RENEE; Godwin Heights HS; Wyoming, MI; Band; Hon Rl; NHS; Pom Pon; College; Archt Engr.

RENEDO, D; Linsly Inst HS; Wheeling, WV; Cls Rep Sr Cls; Hon Rl; NHS; ROTC; Sch Pl; Rptr Sch Nwsp; Drama Clb; Spn Clb; Letter Bsbl; Capt Socr; Univ; Pre Med.

RENEKER, BELINDA; Claymont HS; Uhrichsville, OH; 15/206 Band; NHS; Sch Pl; Pres Drama Clb; Fr Clb; FTA; Spn Clb; College; Elem Ed.

RENICK, DEANNA; Indian Lake HS; Lewistown, OH; Am Leg Aux Girls St; Hon Rl; Sec Yth Flsp; VP 4-H; FHA; FTA; Mth Clb; Sci Clb; Capt Chrldng; 4-H Awd; Capital Univ; Nursing.

RENICK, SHELLIE; Hurricane HS; Hurricane, WV; Cls Rep Frsh Cls; Cls Rep Soph Cls; Chrh Wkr; Hon Rl; Off Ade; Stu Cncl; Yth Flsp; Pep Clb; Letter Bsktbl; Letter Trk; Marshall Univ.

RENICK, TAMARA; Miami Trace HS; Jeffersonville, OH; 33/234 NHS; Stg Crw; Sch Nwsp; Drama Clb; Sci Clb; Voc Schl.

RENICKER, JOANN; Fredericktown HS; Fredericktown, OH; 14/118 Pres Jr Cls; Am Leg Aux Girls St; VP Band; Chrs; Drm Mjrt; FCA; Hon Rl; Jr NHS; NHS; Sch Mus; 1st Runner Up In Knox Cnty Jr Miss Pagnt 78; Ohio St Univ; Fshn.

RENIFF, BECKY; Mahoning Cnty Jt Voc HS; Boardman, OH; Trs Jr Cls; Chrs; Hon Rl; DECA; Swmmng;.

RENIHAN, DONALD; Hamilton Southeastern HS; Noblesville, IN; FCA; Quill & Scroll; Rptr Yrbk; Sprt Ed Sch Nwsp; Spn Clb; Bsktbl; Ftbl; Glf; Coach Actv; All Cnty Bsktbl Team 79; All Cnty Ftbl Team 77; All Confrnc Golf Team 78 & 79; Univ; Tchr.

RENIHAN, MICHELLE; Franklin Community HS; Morgantown, IN; 80/310 Am Leg Aux Girls St; FCA; Hon Rl; Jr NHS; Stu Cncl; Sch Nwsp; Pres 4-H; Pres Keyettes; Pres Pep Clb; Trk; Purdue Univ; Vet Tech.

RENINGER, FRED; Field HS; Mogadore, OH; 17/245 Hon Rl; NHS; Sec 4-H; 4-H Awd; Sci Fair Awd; Agri Tech Inst; Equestrian.

RENKEMA, WILLIAM; Hudsonville HS; Hudsonville, MI; 15/280 VP Sr Cls; Am Leg Boys St; Chrh Wkr; Debate Tm; NHS; Sch Mus; Yrbk; Sch Nwsp; Bsbl; Capt Ftbl; Hope College; Engr.

RENKENBERGER, JERRY; Churubusco HS; Albion, IN; 7/102 Band; Chrs; Chrh Wkr; Cmnty Wkr; Hon Rl; NHS; Sch Mus; Sch Pl; Stg Crw; Yth Flsp; Purdue Univ; Cmnctns.

RENKIEWICZ, ANN; Hamtramck HS; Hamtramck, MI; 6/108 Hst Sr Cls; Pres Band; Capt Drm Mjrt; NHS; Quill & Scroll; Ed Sch Nwsp; Letter Bsbl; DAR Awd; Voice Dem Awd; Wayne State Univ; Music Education.

RENN, NEAL T; Floyd Central HS; Floyds Knobs, IN; 1/342 Cls Rep Soph Cls; Cl Rep Jr Cls; Cls Rep Sr Cls; Val; NHS; Letter Trk; JETS Awd; Natl Merit Ltr; Pres Awd; Rotary Awd; Purdue Univ; Mech Engr.

RENNELLS, LORI; Plymouth HS; Plymouth, IN; 26/200 Hon Rl; NHS; Civ Clb; Pep Clb; Office Work.

RENNER, BRENDA; Newton HS; Pleasant Hl, OH; Band; Chrs; Girl Scts; Lbry Ade; Sch Mus; Sch Pl; Rptr Yrbk; Rptr Sch Nwsp; FHA; Univ.

RENNER, CINDY; Sheridan HS; Thornville, OH; Sec Sr Cls; Hon Rl; NHS; FHA; OEA; 1st Pl Ofc Reprographiscs Region & St Comp; Executive Awd; Sec Of Yr Awd; Clerical Ii Eligible To St; College; Busns Admin.

RENNER, ERIC; Norwalk HS; Norwalk, OH; Boy Scts; Chrs; Hon Rl; Sch Mus; Sct Actv; Yth Flsp; 4-H; Letter Ten; IM Sprt; 4-H Awd; Univ; Elec Engr.

RENNER, MARC; Oak Park HS; Oak Park, MI; 13/340 Lit Mag; Pol Wkr; Eng Clb; FDA; Univ Of Michigan; Inteflex Progr.

RENNER, MELINDA; Elyria HS; Elyria, OH; 21/565 Am Leg Aux Girls St; VP Band; Chrs; Hon Rl; Lbry Ade; Mdrgl; NHS; Orch; Sch Mus; Stg Crw; Amer Legion Auxiliary Unit #12 Schlrshp; Spanish Clb Of Elyria HS Schlrshp; Bna Brith Haddasah Schlrshp; Bowling Green St Univ; Cmnctns.

RENNER, SHERRI; Berkshire HS; Burton, OH; Hon Rl; Jr NHS; Lbry Ade; NHS; Off Ade; Red Cr Ade; Stu Cncl; Yrbk; GAA; Columbus Tech Inst; Vet Asst.

RENNER, VAL; Springfield Local HS; Petersburg, OH; 23/150 Sec Jr Cls; Chrs; Chrh Wkr; Drl Tm; Hon Rl; NHS; Sch Nwsp; 4-H; Fr Clb; FNA; Youngstown St Univ; Nursing.

RENNEY, JOE; Grant HS; Grant, MI; Cl Rep Jr Cls; Band; Chrs; Hon Rl; Orch; Pol Wkr; Stu Cncl; Sci Clb; Spn Clb; Bsbl; Aquainus Univ; Dentistry.

RENNHACK, KATHLEEN; Berrien Springs HS; Berrien Spgs, MI; 5/144 Cls Rep Soph Cls; Sec Jr Cls; Cl Rep Jr Cls; Pres Sr Cls; FCA; Hon Rl; NHS; Sch Mus; Sch Pl; Stu Cncl; Coll; Sci.

RENNIE, GEORGE; Lincoln Park HS; Lincoln Park, MI; 51/573 Cls Rep Soph Cls; NHS; Bsbl; Ftbl; Bentley Coll; Acctg.

RENNIE, LAURIE; Benjamin Franklin HS; Livonia, MI; Treas Band; Chrh Wkr; Girl Scts; Hon Rl; Mth Clb; Cit Awd; Michigan St Univ; Sci.

RENNIE, MARY; Franklin HS; Livonia, MI; Band; Girl Scts; Hon Rl; JA; Yth Flsp; Yrbk; Sec Ger Clb; Scr Kpr; JA Awd;.

RENNING, CHRISTA; Concordia Lutheran HS; Ft Wayne, IN; 9/177 Cls Rep Soph Cls; Cl Rep Jr Cls; Cls Rep Sr Cls; Chrh Wkr; Cmnty Wkr; Hon Rl; Jr NHS; NHS; Off Ade; Sch Mus; Univ; Liberal Arts.

RENO, DANIEL; Bellaire HS; Bellaire, MI; 1/45 Trs Jr Cls; Trs Sr Cls; Val; Chrh Wkr; Hon Rl; NHS; Ftbl; Michigan Tech Univ; Engr.

RENOVETZ, SANDRA; Nordonia HS; Northfield, OH; Trs Frsh Cls; Trs Sr Cls; Band; Girl Scts; Hosp Ade; NHS; Stg Crw; Yrbk; Drama Clb; Natl Merit Ltr; College.

RENSBERGER, C; Northfield HS; Roann, IN; Pres Frsh Cls; VP Soph Cls; VP Jr Cls; Pres Sr Cls; Band; Stu Cncl; Pom Pon; Upper Wabash Voc Sch; Accounting.

RENTSCH, WAYNE D; Dover HS; Dover, OH; 12/260 Hon Rl; NHS; Letter Crs Cntry; Letter Trk; Natl Merit SF; Univ; Law.

RENTZ, TERRI; Marion Local HS; Rd, OH; 3/88 Band; Hon Rl; Sec NHS; Yrbk; 4-H; VP FTA; OEA; Pep Clb; Sci Clb; 4-H Awd; Univ; Acctg.

RENTZ, TOM; Patrick Henry HS; Malinta, OH; 7/100 Band; Chrh Wkr; Hon Rl; Pep Clb; Spanish Schlrshp 10th Pl Hnrbl Mtn State 1977; Univ Of Toledo; Engr.

REPASKY, ROBERT; Springfield Local HS; New Middletown, OH; 20/160 AFS; Boy Scts; Hon Rl; Pres NHS; Fr Clb; FTA; Letter Ftbl; Spartan Schl; Aviation.

REPASKY, SHERYL; Green HS; Uniontown, OH; Pres Frsh Cls; Cls Rep Frsh Cls; Sec Soph Cls; Cls Rep Soph Cls; Cl Rep Jr Cls; Sec Sr Cls; Cls Rep Sr Cls; Hon Rl; Pres Stu Cncl; Chrldng; College; Chemistry.

REPETTI, NANCY; Maumee HS; Maumee, OH; 28/300 Sec Frsh Cls; Cls Rep Sr Cls; Hon Rl; College; Science.

REPIC, TERESA; North Branch HS; North Branch, MI; 17/160 Trs Jr Cls; Hon Rl; NHS; Stu Cncl; Ed Yrbk; Rptr Yrbk; Chrldng; DAR Awd; Natl Merit SF; Prin Awd 75; Aquinas Coll; Pre Med.

REPKA, ANTHONY M; Genoa Area HS; Genoa, OH; 12/179 Boy Scts; Hon Rl; NHS; Ohio Buckeye Boys St Univ; HS Quiz Bowl; Aviation Explorers; Bowling Green St Univ; Comp Sci.

REPLOGLE, JEFF; Upper Valley HS; Houston, OH; Chrh Wkr; Hon Rl; NHS; Yth Flsp; OEA; Bsbl; Letter Glf; Mgrs; College; Acctg.

REPLOGLE, LISA D; South Vermillion HS; Clinton, IN; 14/180 Band; Hon Rl; Jr NHS; NHS; Beta Clb; Pres 4-H; Lat Clb; Bsktbl; Ten; PPFtbl; Outstndng Art Stu; Pres 4 H Horse Pony Clb; Washington Univ; Med Illustration.

REPLOGLE, SANDRA; Bremen HS; Bremen, IN; 8/131 Sec Jr Cls; Hon Rl; NHS; 4-H; Kiwan Awd; Indiana Univ; Bus.

REPO, JAMES R; Kaleva Norman Dickson Schls; Brethren, MI; 3/53 Pres Frsh Cls; VP Soph Cls; Pres Jr Cls; Pres Sr Cls; Band; Boy Scts; Hon Rl; Rptr Yrbk; Letter Bsbl; Letter Bsktbl; All N W Conference Bsktbll Tm 77 78 & 79; Farm Bureau Youth Citiznshp Seminar 78; Most Valuable Boy 79; West Shore Cmnty Coll; Bus.

REQUA, ROBIN; Jefferson Area HS; Jefferson, OH; Cls Rep Frsh Cls; Cls Rep Soph Cls; Cl Rep Jr Cls; AFS; Chrh Wkr; Lbry Ade; Off Ade; Sch Mus; Sch Pl; Stu Cncl; Exchange Stud To Thailand 78; Birmingham Southern Coll.

RESCH, STEVEN; Pickerington HS; Pickerington, OH; 49/205 VP Frsh Cls; Sec Soph Cls; Sec Jr Cls; Hon Rl; NHS; Ger Clb; Lat Clb; Socr; Ohio Dominican College; Cpa.

RESMER, RANDALL M; Pinconning HS; Pinconning, MI; 25/255 Boy Scts; Hon Rl; Letter Bsbl; Coach Actv; NCTE; Michigan St Univ; Vet.

RESS, NANCY; Tell City HS; Tell City, IN; 105/212 Hon Rl; NHS; Morehead State Univ; Animal Sci.

RESSLER, DARLA; Chesterton HS; Chesterton, IN; 58/409 Chrs; Chrh Wkr; Hon Rl; Hosp Ade; Yth Flsp; Rdo Clb; Scr Kpr; Univ; X Ray Tech.

RESSLER, GALEN; Edwardsburg HS; Edwardsburg, MI; 1/160 Cls Rep Frsh Cls; Pres Jr Cls; Band; Debate Tm; Hon Rl; NHS; Yth Flsp; Natl Merit Ltr; VFW Awd; Voice Dem Awd; Academic Excellence Awd; Outstndng Stu Of Social Studies; 3rd Pl Speaker 3 Rivers Novice Debate Tourney; College; Medicine.

RESTIFO, NICHOLAS; Lorain Catholic HS; Amherst, OH; Pres Jr Cls; Pres Sr Cls; Hon Rl; NHS; Ed Yrbk; Kiwan Awd; Natl Merit Ltr; Johns Hopkins; Medicine.

RETHAS, BARBARA; North Royalton HS; Lakewood, OH; Cmp Fr Grls; Chrs; Hon Rl; Off Ade; 4-H; 4-H Awd; Cuyahaga Cmnty Coll; CPA.

RETTELLE, MELONEY; Pinconning HS; Pinconning, MI; Yrbk; Mgrs; PPFtbl; Scr Kpr; DEHA; Psych.

RETTIG, ERIC; Redford Union HS; Redford, MI; Cls Rep Frsh Cls; Boy Scts; Chrs; Chrh Wkr; Hon Rl; JA; Mdrgl; Sch Pl; Western Mic Univ; Med.

RETTIG, SUSAN; Charles Holt Sr HS; Warren, MI; Girl Scts; NHS; Sct Actv; Treas Fr Clb; Tmr; Cit Awd; Univ; Comm Dsgn.

RETTINGER, ROMEL; Triton HS; Bourbon, IN; 11/92 Chrs; Hon Rl; NHS; Sch Mus; Pres Stu Cncl; Drama Clb; FBLA; Sci Clb; Pom Pon; Pres Awd; Purdue; Retailing.

RETTKE, REUBEN; Okemos HS; Okemos, MI; Yrbk; Mi Indust Educ Awds Photog Div1st & Bst Of Cat Regnk 75 1st St Comp 75; St Of Mi Shclsh Comp 79; Rochester Inst Of Tech; Photogillust.

RETTY, PATRICIA; Lutheran HS East; Detroit, MI; Chrs; Drl Tm; Hon Rl; Trk; IM Sprt; Pom Pon; PPFtbl; North Central Michigan Univ; RN.

RETZEL, ELIZABETH; Benedictine HS; Detroit, MI; Cls Rep Frsh Cls; Cl Rep Jr Cls; Cls Rep Sr Cls; Hon Rl; Hosp Ade; NHS; Letter Trk; Chrldng; Univ; Phys Ther.

REUFF, CHRIS; Hubbard HS; Hubbard, OH; 1/325 Band; Hon Rl; Off Ade; Spn Clb; Speech Tm; World Fair In Cincinatti; Kent Test Tms; Clarion St Coll; Law.

REUILLE, ELIZABETH; Heritage Jr Sr HS; New Haven, IN; 24/176 Chrh Wkr; Hon Rl; Off Ade; Quill & Scroll; Rptr Sch Nwsp; Eng Clb; IM Sprt; Indiana Univ; Jrnlsm.

REUNING, CHRISTA M; Concordia Lutheran HS; Fort Wayne, IN; 10/173 Cl Rep Jr Cls; Cls Rep Sr Cls; Chrs; Chrh Wkr; Cmnty Wkr; Hon Rl; Jr NHS; Lbry Ade; NHS; Off Ade; College; Lib Arts.

REUSS, GEORGE; Union County HS; Liberty, IN; Pres Frsh Cls; Hon Rl; Pol Wkr; Stg Crw; Yth Flsp; Sch Nwsp; Drama Clb; Bsbl; Ind State; Sports.

REUSSER, BRIAN; Bluffton HS; Bluffton, IN; Cls Rep Frsh Cls; Cls Rep Soph Cls; Cl Rep Jr Cls; VP Sr Cls; Am Leg Boys St; Hon Rl; NHS; Stu Cncl; Ger Clb; Bsbl; General Motors Inst; Mech Engr.

REUTEBUCH, KARIN; Winamac Community HS; Winamac, IN; 10/150 VP Jr Cls; Band; FCA; Hon Rl; Sch Pl; Drama Clb; Trk; Chrldng; Coach Actv; GAA; Purdue Univ; Nursing.

REUTER, BRIAN T; Aquinas HS; Southgate, MI; Hon Rl; NHS; Trk; Natl Merit Ltr; Univ Of Michigan; Elec Engr.

REUTER, CYNTHIA; Bedford North Lawrence HS; Bedford, IN; 1/417 Chrs; NHS; Sch Mus; Keyettes; Glf; Letter Ten; Letter Chrldng; Indiana Univ; Med.

REUTER, DEBBIE; East Liverpool HS; E Liverpool, OH; Sec Soph Cls; Band; VICA; Univ; Music.

REUTMAN, ANNETTE; Heritage Hills HS; Ferdinand, IN; 8/160 Band; FCA; Hon Rl; NHS; FHA; Pep Clb; Spn Clb; Letter Bsktbl; Letter Trk; PPFtbl; Purdue Univ; Vet Tech.

REUTTER, CLAIRE; Our Lady Of Mercy HS; Detroit, MI; 8/300 Chrh Wkr; Hon Rl; Ed Sch Nwsp; Rptr Sch Nwsp; Lat Clb; Spn Clb; Crs Cntry; Miami Univ; Journalism.

REUTTER, LAURA; Mt Gilead HS; Mt Gilead, OH; 1/1144 Val; Hon Rl; NHS; 4-H; Letter Trk; 4-H Awd; Ohio St Univ; Art.

REVALEE, RICHARD; Centerville HS; Centerville, IN; 17/153 Hon Rl; Jr NHS; NHS; Spn Clb; Bsbl; Bsktbl; Ftbl; Trk; IM Sprt; Natl Merit Ltr; St Schlrshp; Indinana Vocational Rehabilitation Benefits; Indiana Voc Tech.

REVELLE, DAVE; Chagrin Falls HS; Chagrin Fl, OH; 36/187 Chrh Wkr; Hon Rl; Yth Flsp; Ger Clb; Socr; Trk; Univ; Archt.

REVERE, BRENDA; Maple Hts Sr HS; Maple Heights, OH; 203/406 Cls Rep Sr Cls; Sec AFS; Off Ade; Yrbk; FHA; Pep Clb; Letter Trk; Track Trophy Most Impvd 77; Ohio St Univ; Vet Med.

REVESZ JR, JOHN; Cabrini HS; Allen Park, MI; Hon Rl; NHS; Trk; IM Sprt; Natl Merit Ltr; Univ Of Mich; Bioengr.

REVILOCK, DONNA; Holy Name Nazareth HS; Middleburg Ht, OH; Hon Rl; College.

REVITA, MARIA; Aquinas HS; Allen Pk, MI; Hon Rl; Hosp Ade; Pep Clb; Spn Clb; IM Sprt; Fritz Music Schl Hnr Awd; Cert Of Appreciation 100 Hr Awd; Wayne St Univ; Health.

REVITA JR, DIONISIO; Aquinas HS; Allen Park, MI; Hon Rl; Letter Wrstlng; Wayne St Univ; Liberal Arts.

REVOCK, RUSS; Padua Franciscan HS; Cleveland, OH; Hon Rl; Yrbk; Drama Clb; Acting Schl; Drama.

REWITZER, SHEILA; North Muskegon HS; N Muskegon, MI; Cls Rep Frsh Cls; Band; Chrh Wkr; Hon Rl; Off Ade; Sch Pl; Stg Crw; Drama Clb; Letter Ten; PPFtbl; College; Psychology.

REX, LAURA; Perry HS; Massillon, OH; 2/480 Lit Mag; NHS; Off Ade; Pol Wkr; Quill & Scroll; Yrbk; Rptr Sch Nwsp; DAR Awd; Bowling Green St Univ.

REXING, JOHN; Mater Dei HS; Evansville, IN; Hon Rl; Letter Glf; Letter Socr; College; Engineering.

REXRODE, SUSAN; Bluefield HS; Bluefield, WV; Chrh Wkr; Leo Clb; Pep Clb; Spn Clb; Univ.

REYELTS, FREDRIC; St Clair HS; St Clair, MI; 1/206 Pres Soph Cls; Cl Rep Jr Cls; Val; Hon Rl; NHS; Sch Pl; Pres Stu Cncl; Letter Crs Cntry; Letter Ftbl; Capt Trk; Geometry & Bio Awds; Chem Awd; All Area Wrestling Team; Alma Coll; Pre Med.

REYERING, JAMES; St Xavier HS; Cincinnati, OH; 33/280 Cmnty Wkr; Hon Rl; Jr NHS; Mod UN; NHS; Stg Crw; Sprt Ed Yrbk; Rptr Sch Nwsp; Univ; Agri.

REYES, CARMAN; Walnut Hills HS; Cincinnati, OH; Band; Girl Scts; Hon Rl; Pres Jr NHS; Off Ade; Sch Mus; Socr; Univ; Bus.

REYES, ELIZABETH; Northwood HS; Wakarusa, IN; Cls Rep Frsh Cls; Cls Rep Soph Cls; Band; FCA; Hon Rl; Pep Clb; Spn Clb; GAA; IM Sprt; Bus Schl.

REYES, GEORGIA; Buena Vista HS; Saginaw, MI; Hon Rl; Hosp Ade; Jr NHS; Stu Cncl; Ten; Cit Awd; Saginaw Vly Coll; Bio.

REYES, RICARDO; Western HS; Detroit, MI; Cls Rep Frsh Cls; Cls Rep Soph Cls; Cl Rep Jr Cls; Cls Rep Sr Cls; Hon Rl; Sch Nwsp; College; Art.

REYES, VERMAN E; Walter E Stebbins HS; Dayton, OH; Band; Bsktbl; Ftbl; Sacramento St Coll; Bus Mgmt.

REYNA, ELSA J; Mason Sr HS; Mason, MI; Chrs; Lbry Ade; Letter Bsbl; IM Sprt;.

REYNOLDS, BRENDA; Brenda Reynolds HS; Athens, MI; Sch Pl; Stu Cncl; Rptr Yrbk; Rptr Sch Nwsp; Pep Clb; Trk; Chrldng; Univ; Elem Educ.

REYNOLDS, CARSEL; Warrensville Hts HS; Warrensville, OH; Chrs; Chrh Wkr; Sch Mus; Sch Pl; Wrstlng; Coll; Bus Admin.

REYNOLDS, CHRIS; Garber HS; Essexville, MI; 10/172 Boy Scts; Hon Rl; Natl Forn Lg; NHS; Sct Actv; Wrstlng; Comm State; Mech Engr.

REYNOLDS, CHRISTOPHER; Garber HS; Essexville, MI; 10/172 Boy Scts; Hon Rl; Natl Forn Lg; NHS; Sct Actv; Wrstlng; Michigan St Univ; Envirnmtl Energy.

REYNOLDS, DELYNN; Alpena HS; Alpena, MI; 10/744 Band; Chrs; Girl Scts; Hon Rl; NHS; Sch Mus; Sch Pl; Yth Flsp; Hope College; Pre Med.

REYNOLDS, GARY; Mott HS; Warren, MI; Ger Clb; Mich Tech Univ; Math.

REYNOLDS, GERARD J; Bishop Dwenger HS; Ft Wayne, IN; Hon Rl; Bsktbl; Letter Ftbl; Indiana Inst Of Tech; Aero Engr.

REYNOLDS, JANICE; Port Clinton HS; Port Clinton, OH; 16/285 Band; Hon Rl; Orch; Treas Fr Clb; Mth Clb; GAA; French Natl Hon Soc; Dolfins Swim Clb; Univ; Bus Admin.

REYNOLDS, JEFF; Rocky River HS; Rocky Rvr, OH; 73/298 Cls Rep Frsh Cls; Cls Rep Soph Cls; Cl Rep Jr Cls; Pres Sr Cls; Chrs; Hon Rl; Jr NHS; Pres Stu Cncl; Bsbl; Letter Ftbl; College; Engr.

REYNOLDS, JENNY; Southport HS; Indianapolis, IN; Sec Frsh Cls; Cls Rep Soph Cls; Cls Rep Sr Cls; Chrs; Stu Cncl; Pep Clb; Chrldng; Indiana Univ.

REYNOLDS, JILL; Wadsworth Sr HS; Wadsworth, OH; 58/349 Cls Rep Frsh Cls; Sec Jr Cls; Trs Jr Cls; Chrs; Chrh Wkr; FCA; NHS; Stu Cncl; Pep Clb; Letter Trk; Univ; Educ.

REYNOLDS, KAREN; Algonac HS; Algonac, MI; Cls Rep Frsh Cls; Cls Rep Soph Cls; Cls Rep Sr Cls; Letter Hockey;.

REYNOLDS, KATHLEEN; Oakwood Sr HS; Dayton, OH; AFS; Chrs; Chrh Wkr; Cmnty Wkr; Girl Scts; Hon Rl; Lbry Ade; NHS; Stg Crw; Letter Socr; Univ.

REYNOLDS, LINDA; Columbia City Joint HS; Columbia City, IN; 34/273 Band; Hon Rl; JA; NHS; FTA; Pep Clb; Spn Clb; Letter Trk; GAA; Selctd To Attend Sen Lugars Seminar 78; Altemt For Girls St 79; Prom Comm Chrmn 79; Univ; Spec Educ.

REYNOLDS, LYNN; Bethel HS; Tipp City, OH; Band; Hon Rl; Jr NHS; Lbry Ade; IM Sprt; Univ Of Dayton; Law.

REYNOLDS, MICHAEL; Williamstown HS; Williamstown, WV; 25/115 Cls Rep Frsh Cls; Cls Rep Soph Cls; Cls Rep Sr Cls; Red Cr Ade; Stu Cncl; Letter Bsbl; Letter Bsktbl; Letter Ftbl; West Virginia Univ.

REYNOLDS, MICHAEL; Robert Rogers HS; Toledo, OH; Band; Orch; Sch Mus; Lat Clb; Toledo Univ; Music.

REYNOLDS, MICHAEL; Harrison HS; Evansville, IN; Aud/Vis; Boy Scts; Chrs; Pol Wkr; Sch Mus; Sch Nwsp; Cit Awd;.

REYNOLDS, MICHAEL J; Robert Rogers HS; Toledo, OH; Band; Hon Rl; Orch; Lat Clb; Univ; History.

REYNOLDS, NANCY; Forest Park HS; Cincinnati, OH; Chrs; Girl Scts; Hon Rl; Off Ade; Letter Socr; Coach Actv; GAA; IM Sprt; Pres Awd; Univ; Phys Ed.

REYNOLDS, PATRICIA; Brownstown Central HS; Brownstown, IN; 23/156 Cls Rep Sr Cls; Chrh Wkr; Girl Scts; Hon Rl; Hosp Ade; Jr NHS; NHS; Lat Clb; Sci Clb; Trk; IU; Phys Ther.

REYNOLDS, RICHARD; Waterford Twp HS; Union Lake, MI; Band; Boy Scts; JA; Jr NHS; NHS; Sprt Ed Yrbk; Ftbl; Tmr; JA Awd; Natl Merit Ltr; Hillsdale Trustee Schlrshp; Whayne St Merit Schlrshp; Ferris St Schlrshp; Hillsdale Coll; Engr.

REYNOLDS, SAKINA; Central HS; Detroit, MI; Pres Sr Cls; Hon Rl; Jr NHS; NHS; Quill & Scroll; Rptr Yrbk; Sch Nwsp; Harvard Book Awrd 79; Univ ; Psych.

REYNOLDS, SALLY; Black River HS; Spencer, OH; Chrh Wkr; Girl Scts; Y-Teens; FHA; Pep Clb; Spn Clb; Bsktbl; Trk; GAA; Cmnty Coll; Sec.

REYNOLDS, SUSAN; Seeger Metropolitan HS; W Lebanon, IN; 7/141 Hon Rl; Sch Pl; Stg Crw; Drama Clb; 4-H; FTA; Pep Clb; Mgrs; Top Clothing Stdnt 78; Top Housing Stdnt 79; Top Eng Stdnt 79; Univ; Tchr Of Interior Design.

REYNOLDS, TERRI; Frontier HS; Newport, OH; Band; Chrh Wkr; Off Ade; FHA; OEA; Cit Awd; Washington Tech College; Sec.

REYNOLDS, TWILA; St Albans HS; St Albans, WV; AFS; Chrh Wkr; Cmnty Wkr; Hon Rl; NHS; Off Ade; Sch Mus; Sch Pl; Stg Crw; Rptr Yrbk; Whos-who Amg Amer HS Stu 78; West Virginia St Coll; Fshn Mdse.

REYNOLDS, TYLER S; Sandy Valley HS; E Sparta, OH; Am Leg Boys St; Chrs; Chrh Wkr; Hon Rl; Bsktbl;.

REYNOLDS, WANDA; Medora HS; Medora, IN; 1/21 Sec Frsh Cls; Pres Jr Cls; Band; Chrs; Hon Rl; Sch Pl; Stu Cncl; Yrbk; Sec Beta Clb; Treas Sci Clb; Bedford N Lawrence Voc Schl; Bus.

REYOME, PATTY; Anthony Wayne HS; Waterville, OH; 12/266 Chrh Wkr; Hon Rl; NHS; Diploma Of Merit In Spanish Hnr In Foreign Language; Genral Schlstc Hnr; Bowling Green St Univ; Elem Ed.

REZEK, MARY; Calumet HS; Laurium, MI; VP Band; Cmp Fr Grls; Chrs; Chrh Wkr; Hon Rl; Jr NHS; Lit Mag; NHS; Orch; Mich Tech Univ; Engr.

REZMER, JANET; Pinconning Area HS; Linwood, MI; 5/272 Hon Rl; NHS; Sprt Ed Yrbk; Pres 4-H; Key Clb; Letter Trk; 4-H Awd; Saginaw Valley St Coll; Nursing.

REZNIK, SUE; Polaris Voc Center; Middleburg Hts, OH; Cl Rep Jr Cls; Sec Sr Cls; Cmnty Wkr; Hon Rl; NHS; Off Ade; Rptr Sch Nwsp; Sch Nwsp; 4-H; OEA; Berea High Academic Ach Awd; Polaris Voc Cntr Stu Of The Month; 3rd Place Prepared Verbal Communicatns Ii; Cleveland St Univ; Mass Comm.

RHEA, ROBIN; East HS; Columbus, OH; 62/272 Sec Frsh Cls; Chrs; Chrh Wkr; Drl Tm; Hon Rl; Jr NHS; Off Ade; Pol Wkr; OSU; Chldhd Psych.

RHEAD, LAURA; Bishop Foley HS; Warren, MI; Hon Rl; NHS; PAVAS; Ed Yrbk; Beta Clb; Bsbl; IM Sprt; Scr Kpr; College; R N.

RHEW, SHERRY; Bridgman HS; Bridgman, MI; Hon Rl; NHS; Letter Trk; Ferrio State College; Drafting.

RHINE, VICTORIA; Charleroix HS; Charleroix, MI; Band; Hon Rl; Sch Pl; Yrbk; FFA; Air Force; Administrative Ill.

RHINE, YVONNE; Southfield Lathrup HS; Southfield, MI; Hon Rl; Orch; Wayne State Univ; Comp Sci.

RHINEHART, PAULA; Walter E Stebbins HS; Dayton, OH; Chrh Wkr; Girl Scts; Orch; Spn Clb; Gym; Business School.

RHINEHART, ROSS; Wintersville HS; Steubenville, OH; Hon Rl; NHS; PAVAS; Fr Clb; Ftbl; Trk; Wrstlng; IM Sprt; Ohio St Univ.

RHOAD, TIM; Fostoria HS; Fostoria, OH; Boy Scts; Chrs; Hon Rl; NHS; Yrbk; Coll; Aerospace Engr.

RHOADES, CHRISTINE; Tippecanoe Valley HS; Silver Lake, IN; 1/179 Trs Frsh Cls; Chrs; Chrh Wkr; Hon Rl; NHS; Sch Mus; Sch Pl; Drama Clb; OEA; Ten; Most Improved Player; Most Valuable Jr Vrsty Cheerldr; 3rd Pl Typing & Related I; College; Foreign Language.

RHOADES, FELICIA; Bridgeport HS; Bridgeport, WV; Cls Rep Frsh Cls; Am Leg Aux Girls St; Hon Rl; Lbry Ade; Off Ade; Stu Cncl; Y-Teens; Ed Yrbk; Sch Nwsp; Pep Clb; West Virginia Univ; Pharmacy.

RHOADES, JOYCE; Ansonia HS; Rossburg, OH; 7/60 Band; Chrs; Hon Rl; NHS; Yth Flsp; Yrbk; Drama Clb; 4-H; OEA; 4-H Awd; College; Bus.

RHOADES, NANCY; Tippecanoe HS; Tipp City, OH; 22/198 Cls Rep Sr Cls; Chrs; Cmnty Wkr; Hon Rl; Hosp Ade; NHS; Stu Cncl; Yth Flsp; Mt Vernon Nazarene College.

RHOADES, RONALD; Notre Dame HS; Clarksburg, WV; Chrs; FDA; Mth Clb; Sci Clb; Trk; IM Sprt; West Virginia Univ; Elec Engr.

RHOADES, ROSE; Philo HS; Roseville, OH; VP Jr Cls; VP Sr Cls; Am Leg Aux Girls St; Girl Scts; JA; Off Ade; Stu Cncl; Sch Nwsp; Pres 4-H; Gym; Roseville Cmnty Days Queen 77; Coll; Phys Fitness.

RHOADES, TINA; Tecumseh HS; Dale, IN; Sec Jr Cls; Cl Rep Jr Cls; Chrs; Girl Scts; Lbry Ade; Sch Mus; Sch Pl; Stg Crw; Stu Cncl; Sprt Ed Yrbk; Lockepar Bus Schl.

RHOADS, CHRISTINE; Ridgedale HS; Marion, OH; VP Jr Cls; Chrs; Hon Rl; NHS; Off Ade; Sch Mus; Yrbk; 4-H; Spn Clb; Bsbl; Univ.

RHOADS, DIANE; Logan Elm HS; Circleville, OH; Trs Soph Cls; Sec Jr Cls; VP Sr Cls; Am Leg Aux Girls St; Band; Chrs; Capt FCA; Hon Rl; NHS; Sch Pl; Mt Carmel Schl; Nursing.

RHOADS, EDWARD R; Huntington HS; Chillicothe, OH; Band; Hon Rl; Sch Pl; 4-H; VICA; Ftbl; Am Leg Awd; Bus Schl; Bus Mgmt.

RHOADS, GARY; Peebles HS; Hillsboro, OH; 20/104 VP Frsh Cls; Hon Rl; Quill & Scroll; Sch Pl; Sch Nwsp; Drama Clb; FFA; Chapt Creed On Test FFA 1st Plc; Chapt Extemporaneous Speech FFA 3rd Plc; Southern St Coll; Journalism.

RHODEBACK, KARLA A; St Bernard Elmwood Pl HS; St Bernard, OH; Sec Frsh Cls; Sec Soph Cls; Sec Jr Cls; Band; Chrh Wkr; Drl Tm; Girl Scts; Hon Rl; Pres Jr NHS; Lbry Ade; Semi Fnlst In Child Internal Smr Village Prog 1973; Univ Of Cincinnati; Dental Hygn.

RHODEBECK, SARAH; Galion HS; Galion, OH; 1/280 Val; Am Leg Aux Girls St; Band; Chrh Wkr; Hon Rl; NHS; Orch; Yth Flsp; Ed Yrbk; Yrbk; Miami Univ; Arts.

RHODERICK, DANA; Shakamak HS; Jasonville, IN; 11/86 Band; Chrs; Drl Tm; NHS; Quill & Scroll; Rptr Sch Nwsp; FHA; Pep Clb; Pom Pon; Scr Kpr; College; Bus.

RHODES, CHRISTOPHER; Norton HS; Norton, OH; Boy Scts; Hon Rl; Sct Actv; Rptr Sch Nwsp; Sch Nwsp; Lat Clb; Swmmng; Letter Trk; IM Sprt; Akron Univ.

RHODES, DAN; Brooke HS; Follansbee, WV; Chrh Wkr; Hon Rl; Quill & Scroll; Sec Yth Flsp; Yrbk; Sch Nwsp; Key Clb; St Impact Team 3 Consectv Yrs; Comp In Local Zone St & Regnl Beble Quiz; Acctg.

RHODES, DAVID W; Tippecanoe Valley HS; Akron, IN; Cls Rep Frsh Cls; Cls Rep Soph Cls; Pres Jr Cls; Pres Aud/Vis; NHS; Yrbk; Bsktbl; Letter Ftbl; Letter Glf; IM Sprt; 1978 1st Team All State Quarterback; Clemson Univ; Med.

RHODES, JOHN; Negaunee HS; Negaunee, MI; Aud/Vis; Boy Scts; Hon Rl; Sct Actv; Natl Merit Ltr; Univ; Elec Engr.

RHODES, JULIE; Belding HS; Belding, MI; Girl Scts; Hon Rl; NHS; Drama Clb; 4-H; Pep Clb; Bsktbl; Trk; 4-H Awd; Ferris Univ; Bus.

RHODES, LANCE; Ripley HS; Ripley, WV; Hst Frsh Cls; Pres Sr Cls; Hon Rl; Jr NHS; NHS; Beta Clb; Mth Clb; Bsbl; Letter Wrstlng; IM Sprt; W Virginia Univ; Pre Med.

RHODES, LORI; Champion HS; Orwell, OH; 4/250 Band; Chrh Wkr; Orch; Sch Pl; Y-Teens; Yrbk; Pres Drama Clb; Fr Clb; Opt Clb Awd; St Stu Officer Intl Thespian Soc; French Schlstc Ach Test Honorable Mention; NEDT Top 10; College; Poli Sci.

RHODES, MARY; Bridgeport HS; Bridgeport, OH; Band; Hon Rl; Drama Clb; Spn Clb;.

RHODES, MEGAN; Crestview HS; Columbiana, OH; Chrs; Chrh Wkr; Hon Rl; NHS; Sch Mus; Pep Clb; Spn Clb; Chrldng; Scr Kpr; Jr Attdndt For 78 Ftbl Homecoming; Vice Prest Of Natl Honor Soc 79; Stewardess.

RHODES, NANCY; Newark Sr HS; Newark, OH; Cl Rep Jr Cls; Chrs; Chrh Wkr; Drl Tm; Drama Clb; Fr Clb; Univ; Fshn.

RHODES, ORLAND; Cambridge HS; Cambridge, OH; 60/280 Hon Rl; Muskingum Area Tech College; Petrole.

RHODES, REBECCA; Perrysburg HS; Perrysburg, OH; Chrh Wkr; JA; FTA; Leo Clb; Spn Clb; Coll; Art.

RHODES, ROBYNN; Southwestern HS; Detroit, MI; 5/220 Band; Girl Scts; Hon Rl; NHS; Sct Actv; Fr Clb; Gym; Olivet College; Music.

RHODES, SAMUEL; Chippewa HS; Doylestown, OH; Band; Chrh Wkr; Cmnty Wkr; Hon Rl; Orch; Sch Mus; Yth Flsp; Ed Sch Nwsp; Fr Clb; Spn Clb; Univ; Music.

RHODES, SHELLY; Bishop Ready HS; Columbus, OH; Cls Rep Frsh Cls; Cls Rep Soph Cls; Am Leg Aux Girls St; Girl Scts; Hon Rl; NHS; Off Ade; Pol Wkr; Quill & Scroll; VP Stu Cncl; Slctd To Prtcpt In Engr For A Day Prgrm By Ohio St Pro Engrs 79; Rcvd Schlstc Awrds In French I II & III; Massachusetts Inst Of Tech; Math.

RHODES, STACEY; Whitko HS; South Whitley, IN; 18/151 Chrh Wkr; Girl Scts; Hon Rl; Pres Yth Flsp; Rptr Yrbk; VP Fr Clb; VP Pep Clb; Sci Clb; Trk;.

RHODES, SUSAN; Tell City HS; Tell City, IN; Am Leg Aux Girls St; Hon Rl; Stg Crw; Drama Clb; Fr Clb; Pep Clb; Trk; IM Sprt; Mat Maids; Am Leg Awd; Ind Univ; Cytotechnology.

RHODES, SUSAN; Corydon Central HS; Corydon, IN; 1/159 Band; Hon Rl; NHS; Stu Cncl; Fr Clb; Pep Clb; Chrldng; GAA; Mgrs; PPFtbl; Indiana Univ; Clinical Psych.

RHODES, TODD; Versailles HS; Versailles, OH; Chrh Wkr; Hon Rl; Yth Flsp; Letter Bsbl; Letter Ftbl; Scr Kpr; Tmr; Lion Awd; Football All 3 Rvrs Conf 78; Cnty Sci Test 1st Pl Physics 79; Delegate Free Entrprse Rndtble Rotary 79; Heidelburg Coll; Comp Sci.

RHODES, VIRGINIA; Solon HS; Solon, OH; 2/288 Chrs; Hon Rl; Jr NHS; MMM; NHS; Off Ade; Stg Crw; Yth Flsp; Rptr Sch Nwsp; Mth Clb; Mbr Of Solon HS Acadmc Challenge Team; Accepted To Martin W Essex Schl For Gifted; Mount Union Coll; Medicine.

RHONE, EVETTE; Mumford HS; Detroit, MI; Chrs; Girl Scts; Hon Rl; JA; Jr NHS; NHS; Off Ade; Sch Mus; Sch Pl; Trk; Blue & Burgandy Honor Roll Track Ribbons; Track Trophy; Wayne St Univ; Mgmt.

RHONEMUS, JEFF; Lynchburg Clay HS; Lynchburg, OH; Band; Boy Scts; Hon Rl; Sch Mus; 4-H; FFA; Pep Clb; Ohio State Univ; Vet Med.

RHUDE, RACHEL; Blanchester HS; Blanchester, OH; 12/140 Trs Jr Cls; Band; Chrh Wkr; Cmnty Wkr; Hon Rl; NHS; Sch Mus; Drama Clb; Spn Clb; GAA; Univ; Nursing.

RHUDY, DAVID; Morgantown HS; Morgantwn, WV; Pres Sr Cls; Lbry Ade; Stu Cncl; Letter Bsktbl; Letter Ftbl; Trk; IM Sprt; William & Mary; Bus Mgmt.

RHUDY, VAUGHN; Woodrow Wilson HS; Beckley, WV; 1/550 Val; Boy Scts; Chrh Wkr; Hon Rl; Jr NHS; NHS; Sct Actv; Yth Flsp; Ed Yrbk; Cit Awd; Marshall Univ; Eng Tchr.

RHYNE, CYNTHIA; Euclid HS; Euclid, OH; 39/704 AFS; Chrs; Hon Rl; NHS; Sch Mus; Stg Crw; Rptr Yrbk; Univ Of Akron; Bus Admin.

RIAL, RANDY; Harper Creek HS; Battle Creek, MI; Cls Rep Frsh Cls; Cls Rep Soph Cls; Hon Rl; NHS; Rptr Sch Nwsp; Bsktbl; Ftbl; Trk; Am Leg Awd; College; Archetecture.

RIAN, TIM; Newark Catholic HS; Newark, OH; Am Leg Boys St; Hon Rl; Lat Clb; Sci Clb; Ftbl; Am Leg Awd; Ohio State Univ; Elec Engr.

RIBBLE, ANGELA; Philo HS; Blue Rock, OH; 5/204 Treas Chrs; Debate Tm; Girl Scts; Hon Rl; Hosp Ade; Lbry Ade; Lit Mag; Mdrgl; NHS; Miami Univ; Spanish.

RIBBLE, KEVIN; Philo HS; Blue Rock, OH; 9/205 Hon Rl; NHS; Pres Sci Clb; Spn Clb; Letter Glf; Am Leg Awd; Bausch & Lomb Awd; Lion Awd; Ohio St Univ; Chem.

RIBEIRO, PHILIPPE; John Glenn HS; Bay City, MI; Cl Rep Jr Cls; Am Leg Boys St; Sch Mus; Fr Clb; Letter Ten; Wrstlng; PPFtbl; Am Leg Awd; Elk Awd; Michigan St Univ; Pre Med.

RICCI, CAROLYN; Warren Western Reserve HS; Warren, OH; 13/425 Hon Rl; Hosp Ade; Jr NHS; NHS; Y-Teens; Rptr Yrbk; Spn Clb; Letter Swmmng; GAA; Tmr; Yearbook Editor In Chief; Yearbook Best Section Awd; College; Biology.

RICCI, CYNTHIA; N Farmington HS; Farm Hills, MI; Chrs; Chrh Wkr; Hon Rl; Lbry Ade; Off Ade; Fr Clb; Natl Merit SF; French Stu Awd; Coll; Acctg.

RICCI, PAULA; Kokomo HS; Kokomo, IN; 130376 Chrh Wkr; Hon Rl; Jr NHS; Stu Cncl; Sch Nwsp; Pep Clb; Spn Clb; Letter Trk; Chrldng; PPFtbl; Univ; Psych.

RICCIONI, FILOMENA; Ursuline HS; Youngstown, OH; 150/342 FTA; IM Sprt; Youngstown St Univ; Law.

RICCITELLI, KEITH; St Francis De Sales HS; Toledo, OH; Chrh Wkr; Hon Rl; Stg Crw; Yth Flsp; IM Sprt; Univ; Engr.

RICE, AARON; Chesapeake HS; Chesapeake, OH; 17/127 Chrh Wkr; Hon Rl; Sct Actv; Yth Flsp; Beta Clb; Letter Bsbl; Bsktbl; Letter Ftbl; IM Sprt; Scr Kpr; College; Phys Therapy.

RICE, BECKY; Westview HS; Shipshewana, IN; 4/89 Chrh Wkr; Hon Rl; NHS; Yth Flsp; Ed Sch Nwsp; Rptr Sch Nwsp; Sch Nwsp; FTA; Ger Clb; GAA; Anderson College; Professional.

RICE, BRYAN; North Ridgeville HS; N Ridgeville, OH; Band; Hon Rl; NHS; Sch Pl; Drama Clb; 4-H; Wrstlng; Voice Dem Awd;.

RICE, CALVIN; St Johns HS; St Johns, MI; 25/325 Am Leg Boys St; Band; Hon Rl; Yth Flsp; 4-H; Sci Clb; Letter Ftbl; Letter Gym; IM Sprt; Gym Awds; Michigan St Univ; Elec Engr.

RICE, CAROL J; Big Walnut HS; Sunbury, OH; 14/218 Band; Girl Scts; Orch; Yrbk; VP 4-H; FHA; 4-H Awd; Vocational Schl.

RICE, DAWN; La Salle HS; S Bend, IN; Chrh Wkr; Hon Rl; NHS; Off Ade; Sch Mus; Sch Pl; Stg Crw; Sec Drama Clb; De Paul Goodman Mem Coll; Dramatics.

RICE, DAWN; Stephenson HS; Stephenson, MI; 7/95 Band; Hon Rl; Pres NHS; Sch Pl; Yth Flsp; Yrbk; PPFtbl; Central Mic Univ.

RICE, DONNA; Mother Of Mercy HS; Cincinnati, OH; 30/256 Cls Rep Frsh Cls; Hon Rl; Off Ade; Fr Clb; Bsktbl; Socr; Trk; GAA; Tmr; God Cntry Awd; College; Phys Therapy.

RICE, DUANE; Sycamore HS; Cincinnati, OH; 49/445 Boy Scts; Chrh Wkr; Hon Rl; VP JA; JETS Awd; SAR Awd; College; Architecture.

RICE, ELIZABETH; Edison HS; Milan, OH; Am Leg Aux Girls St; Band; Chrs; Hon Rl; PAVAS; Sch Mus; Sch Pl; Yth Flsp; Drama Clb; Mgrs; Ohio St Univ; Child Psych.

RICE, GINNA; Quincy HS; Quincy, MI; Am Leg Aux Girls St; Hon Rl; NHS; Sch Pl; Trk; Capt Chrldng; Western Michigan Univ; Spec Educ.

RICE, GRETA; Alexander HS; Albany, OH; Band; Chrh Wkr; Girl Scts; Hon Rl; Sch Mus; Stg Crw; Fr Clb; FHA; Lat Clb; Ohio Univ; Home Ec.

RICE, JERRY; Fayetteville HS; Fayetteville, WV; Pres Jr Cls; Chrs; Chrh Wkr; Hon Rl; Sch Pl; Stg Crw; Stu Cncl; Drama Clb; Pep Clb; Spn Clb; West Virginia Inst Of Tech; Acctg.

RICE, JO; Zanesville HS; Zanesville, OH; Cls Rep Frsh Cls; Chrs; Chrh Wkr; Drl Tm; Hon Rl; NHS; Red Cr Ade; Stu Cncl; Yth Flsp; Y-Teens; 3 5 Club 77 78 & 79; Kentucky Christian Coll; Spec Ed.

RICE, JOHN; Sherman HS; Prenter, WV; Band; Boy Scts; Chrh Wkr; Sch Pl; Sct Actv; Yth Flsp; 4-H; Univ; Nursing.

RICE, JOHN; Brownsburg HS; Carmel, IN; 3/314 Hon Rl; Jr NHS; Stu Cncl; Yth Flsp; 4-H; Lat Clb; Pres Sci Clb; College; Physics.

RICE, KELLY; Austintown Fitch HS; Youngstown, OH; Capt Drl Tm; Girl Scts; NHS; Off Ade; Y-Teens; Key Clb; Mgrs; PPFtbl; Natl Dance Champ; Best Dancer Of Sr Class; Ohio & Penn St Dance Champs; Youngstown St Univ; Public Admin.

RICE, LAURICE; Andrean HS; Hobart, IN; 121/251 Cl Rep Jr Cls; Fr Clb; Pep Clb; GAA; Pom Pon; Univ.

RICE, LISA; Meadow Bridge HS; Rainelle, WV; Sec Jr Cls; Band; Cmnty Wkr; Hon Rl; Stg Crw; Fr Clb; Keyettes; College; Psych.

RICE, LISA C; De Vilbiss HS; Toledo, OH; Chrs; Chrh Wkr; Debate Tm; Hon Rl; JA; Sch Mus; Trk; JA Awd; Upward Bound Academic Excellence Awd; Jr Ach Sales Club Awd; Bowling Green St Univ; Commercial Ar.

RICE, MARY; Maplewood HS; Cortland, OH; 32/89 Hon Rl; Sec JA; Lbry Ade; Sch Pl; Yrbk; Beta Clb; Drama Clb; 4-H; Pep Clb; Spn Clb; Malone Coll; Soc Worker.

RICE, NELLIE; Carl Brablec HS; Roseville, MI; Cls Rep Soph Cls; Cl Rep Jr Cls; Hon Rl; Stu Cncl; Sch Nwsp; Fr Clb; Univ Of Michigan; Jrnlsm.

RICE, PAULA; Ross Beatty HS; Cassoplis, MI; Cls Rep Soph Cls; Hon Rl; NHS; Stu Cncl; Southwestern Michigan Univ; Sec.

RICE, STEVEN; Covington HS; Covington, OH; 14/86 Boy Scts; Cmnty Wkr; Hon Rl; NHS; Sct Actv; Glf; Local Sci Fairs 1st Pl Trophy & Superior; Oh Jr Academy Of Sci; Univ; Phys Sci.

RICE, SUSAN; Northfield HS; Lagro, IN; Band; FCA; Hon Rl; Yth Flsp; Sch Nwsp; 4-H; Pep Clb; Spn Clb; Bsbl; Bsktbl; Indiana Univ; Elem Educ.

RICE, TIMOTHY; Dunbar HS; Dunbar, WV; Hon Rl; JA; Jr NHS; NHS; Stu Cncl; Yth Flsp; Letter Bsbl; Capt Crs Cntry; Letter Ten; JA Awd; Appalachian St Univ; Psychology.

RICE, TIMOTHY; Montpelier HS; Montpelier, OH; 2/109 Cls Rep Frsh Cls; Cls Rep Soph Cls; Cl Rep Jr Cls; Cls Rep Sr Cls; Sal; Am Leg Boys St; Pres Band; Chrs; Chrh Wkr; Hon Rl; Miami Univ; Interdisciplinary Study.

RICE, TOM; Spencer HS; Reedy, WV; Hon Rl; Jr NHS; NHS; Bsktbl; Letter Ftbl; Letter Trk; Univ; Bio.

RICE, VIRGINIA; Allen Park HS; Allen Pk, MI; Chrs; Chrh Wkr; Hon Rl; Jr NHS; Drama Clb; GAA; Nomntd For Mst Outstndg Jr Awd To EMU 79; Univ; Archeology.

RICH, AMY; Nitro HS; Nitro, WV; Band; Chrh Wkr; Pres Girl Scts; Jr NHS; NHS; Pres Yth Flsp; Civ Clb; Sci Clb; Univ; Eng.

RICH, KEVIN; Loudonville HS; Perrysville, OH; Am Leg Boys St; Band; Hon Rl; Sch Pl; Stu Cncl; Sch Nwsp; Cincinnati Univ; Elec Engr.

RICH, LINDA; George C Schafer HS; Southgate, MI; Pres Band; Cmnty Wkr; Debate Tm; Hon Rl; JA; NHS; Off Ade; Sct Actv; Eng Clb; Cit Awd; Univ Of Michigan; Eng.

RICH, SANDRA; Hoover HS; N Canton, OH; 3/430 Hon Rl; Jr NHS; NHS; VP Fr Clb; Pep Clb; Tmr; Natl Merit Ltr; Pres Awd; Univ Of Akron; Poli Sci.

RICHARD, DAVID; Bryan HS; Bryan, OH; 5/200 Boy Scts; Hon Rl; Jr NHS; NHS; Off Ade; Spn Clb; Capt Ftbl; Bowling Green St Univ; Acctg.

RICHARD, DONNA; Patrick Henry HS; Mcclure, OH; 15/120 Cls Rep Soph Cls; Cl Rep Jr Cls; Cls Rep Sr Cls; Chrs; Drm Bgl; Drm Mjrt; Orch; Stu Cncl; Yrbk; Sci Clb; Bowling Green State Univ; Bus.

RICHARD, JAMES; Northrop HS; Ft Wayne, IN; 76/586 Boy Scts; Chrs; Chrh Wkr; Stg Crw; Univ; Engr.

RICHARD, MARIAN; Patrik Henry HS; Mcclure, OH; 17/121 Treas Chrh Wkr; Hon Rl; Yrbk; Pres 4-H; FHA; OEA; 4-H Awd; Sec.

RICHARDS, BARB; Houston HS; Covington, OH; Hon Rl; Hosp Ade; Lbry Ade; Off Ade; Sch Nwsp; Nurses Aide.

RICHARDS, CATHERINE; Regina HS; Detroit, MI; 52/134 Sec Drl Tm; Hon Rl; Sch Mus; Stg Crw; Rptr Yrbk; Drama Clb; Sci Clb; Swmmng; GAA; Mi Compttv Schshp; Cntrl Michigan Univ; Vet Med.

RICHARDS, DANIEL L; Greenville Sr HS; Greenville, OH; 39/378 Chrh Wkr; FCA; Hon Rl; Bsbl; Ftbl; Perfect Attend Awd For 76 78; Hon Roll Banquet; Softball For Church Tm; Xmas Church Play; Miami Univ; Chem.

RICHARDS, DAVID; Albion Sr HS; Albion, MI; Hon Rl; Ftbl; Trk; Wrstlng; Coll; Acctg.

RICHARDS, DEBBIE; Bishop Foley HS; Madison Hts, MI; 25/197 Cls Rep Soph Cls; Cl Rep Jr Cls; Cls Rep Sr Cls; Hon Rl; NHS; Stu Cncl; Yrbk; Letter Bsbl; Letter Bsktbl; Oakland Univ; Nursing.

RICHARDS, DEBORAH A; Bishop Foley HS; Madison Hts, MI; Cls Rep Soph Cls; Cl Rep Jr Cls; Cls Rep Sr Cls; Chrs; Hon Rl; NHS; Stu Cncl; Yrbk; Letter Bsbl; Letter Bsktbl; Oakland Univ; Nursing.

RICHARDS, GEORGEANNE; Lakewood HS; Lakewood, OH; Am Leg Aux Girls St; Chrh Wkr; Hon Rl; NHS; Stu Cncl; Yth Flsp; Swmmng; GAA; Ohi Northern Univ; Pharm.

RICHARDS, JANET; Lamphere HS; Madison Hts, MI; Band; Chrs; Chrh Wkr; Hon Rl; Sch Pl; Stu Cncl; Yth Flsp; IM Sprt; PPFtbl; Michigan Christian Coll; Psych.

RICHARDS, JANINE; Perry Meridian HS; Indianapolis, IN; 108/548 Cls Rep Frsh Cls; Cl Rep Jr Cls; Hon Rl; Off Ade; Stu Cncl; Rptr Yrbk; FHA; Pep Clb; Spn Clb; Ten; Univ; Jrnlsm.

RICHARDS, KAREN; Bloomington HS South; Bloomington, IN; Band; Chrh Wkr; Cmnty Wkr; Drl Tm; FCA; Pep Clb; Pom Pon; Scr Kpr; Tmr; Indiana Univ; Psych.

RICHARDS, KENNETH; Champion HS; Warren, OH; CAP; Gen Billy Mitchell Awd Cadet Of Yr; Gen Billy Henderson Awd; Coll; Mech Engr.

RICHARDS, MICHAEL S; Eaton HS; Eaton, OH; 15/175 Am Leg Boys St; Hon Rl; Treas Spn Clb; Bsktbl; Capt Crs Cntry; Letter Trk; Case Western Reserve Univ; Engr.

RICHARDS, NANETTE; Calvin M Woodward HS; Toledo, OH; Pres Frsh Cls; Cls Rep Soph Cls; Trs Sr Cls; Hon Rl; Off Ade; Stu Cncl; Rptr Yrbk; Fr Clb; Pep Clb; GAA; College; Public Relations.

RICHARDS, PAUL; Lowell HS; Ada, MI; 16/215 Hon Rl; Letter Bsbl; Letter Ftbl; Grand Rapids Jr Coll; Bus.

RICHARDS, ROBIN; Lake City Area HS; Lake City, MI; Chrs; Chrh Wkr; Hon Rl; NHS; Sch Pl; Yth Flsp; 4-H; FHA; Twrlr; 4-H Awd; Calvin Coll; Tchr.

RICHARDS, SCOTT; Eaton HS; Eaton, OH; Hon Rl; Spn Clb; Letter Crs Cntry; Letter Trk; Univ Of Cincinnati; Engr.

RICHARDS, SHARON; St Francis De Sales HS; Columbus, OH; Chrh Wkr; Cmnty Wkr; Hosp Ade; Ten; Coach Actv; Scr Kpr; College; Secondary Education.

RICHARDS, SHELLEY; Our Lady Of Mt Carmel HS; Ecorse, MI; 5/65 Cls Rep Soph Cls; Pres Sr Cls; Hon Rl; NHS; Pep Clb; Pres Awd; Eastern Mic; Med.

RICHARDS, SUZANNE; Upper Sandusky HS; Upper Sandusky, OH; 34/198 Cls Rep Soph Cls; Cl Rep Jr Cls; Cls Rep Sr Cls; Band; FCA; NHS; 4-H; Bsktbl; Capt Trk; Capt Oh Northern Univ; Phy Ed.

RICHARDS, THOMAS; Boardman HS; Boardman, OH; 75/594 Hon Rl; Bsbl; Ftbl; Wrstlng; Pres Awd; Baldwin Wallace Coll; Acctg.

RICHARDS, TODD; Harrison Hills HS; Cadiz, OH; Chrs; College; Surveying.

RICHARDS, WANDA; Tri Village HS; Hollansburg, OH; Hst Jr Cls; Hon Rl; Lbry Ade; Y-Teens; Mth Clb;.

RICHARDS JR, ROBERT; Chatard HS; Indianapolis, IN; Cls Rep Frsh Cls; Cls Rep Soph Cls; Boy Scts; Hon Rl; Sch Pl; Stu Cncl; Boys Clb Am; FBLA; Letter Crs Cntry; Ball State; Busines Mamt.

RICHARDSON, DAN; Salem HS; Salem, IN; Band; Boy Scts; Debate Tm; NHS; Pol Wkr; Rptr Yrbk; Rptr Sch Nwsp; Lat Clb; Letter Glf; Indiana Univ; Poli Sci.

RICHARDSON, DONNA; Bucyrus HS; Buryrus, OH; Band; Drl Tm; VP Y-Teens; Rptr Yrbk; Drama Clb; Pep Clb; GAA; Univ; Med.

RICHARDSON, ELIZABETH A; Charleston HS; Charleston, WV; Cls Rep Soph Cls; Cl Rep Jr Cls; Band; Stu Cncl; Yth Flsp; Chrldng; Univ.

RICHARDSON, GARY L; Atherton HS; Burton, MI; Letter Bsktbl; Letter Trk; General Motors Inst; Indst Engr.

RICHARDSON, JACKIE; Owengage HS; Sebewaing, MI; 12/52 Band; Chrs; Chrh Wkr; Girl Scts; Hon Rl; Hosp Ade; Off Ade; Sch Mus; Y-Teens; 4-H; College; Music.

RICHARDSON, JENNIFER J; Richmond Sr HS; Richmond, IN; Sec Frsh Cls; Band; Hon Rl; Orch; Stu Cncl; Pep Clb; PPFtbl; Kiwan Awd; Pres Awd; Tri Kappa Music Schslhp In Univ Sumer Music Clinic 78; Hugh O Brian Youth Fdn Learsdhp Canddt 78; Indiana Univ; Psych.

RICHARDSON, LATANGIA; Memphis HS; Smth Crk, MI; Chrh Wkr; Girl Scts; Mod UN; FHA; Wayne St Univ; Pediatrician.

RICHARDSON, LESLIE; Stivers Patterson Coop HS; Dayton, OH; 77/400 OEA; 3rd Pl In Region 3 Steno I Contest; 7th Pl In The State Steno I Contest; 2nd Pl Steno Theory; College; Stenography.

RICHARDSON, MARVIN; Cedar Springs HS; Cedar Spgs, MI; Jr NHS; FFA; Bsbl; Glf; College; Elec Tech.

RICHARDSON, MELANIE A; Montabella Cmnty HS; Remus, MI; 49/106 Band; Hon Rl; Hosp Ade; Sch Pl; Stg Crw; Drama Clb; Saginaw Vly St Coll; Nursing.

RICHARDSON, MICHAEL; Oak Hill HS; Oak Hill, WV; Hon Rl; NHS; Glenville St Univ; Forestry.

RICHARDSON, MICHAEL J; Northwest HS; Clinton, OH; 1/170 Pres Frsh Cls; Pres Soph Cls; Chrs; Chrh Wkr; Hon Rl; Mdrgl; NHS; Sch Mus; Pres Stu Cncl; Fr Clb; Ohio Univ; Psych.

RICHARDSON, MITZI; Farmington Sr HS; Farmington, MI; Band; Chrh Wkr; Cmnty Wkr; Girl Scts; Hon Rl; NHS; Off Ade; Mth Clb; Letter Bsktbl; Letter Socr; Michigan St Univ; Acctg.

RICHARDSON, ROBERT; Greenbrier East HS; Lewisburg, WV; Boy Scts; NHS; Stu Cncl; Yth Flsp; Pres 4-H; Bsktbl; 4-H Awd; College; Political Sci.

RICHARDSON, SHARON; West Branch HS; Beloit, OH; 20/200 AFS; Band; Girl Scts; Hon Rl; Hosp Ade; Fr Clb; FTA; Twrlr; Univ Of Akron; Acctg.

RICHARDSON, SUSAN; Henryville HS; Henryville, IN; Band; Girl Scts; Hon Rl; Yth Flsp; 4-H; FHA; 4-H Awd;.

RICHARDSON, TAMMY; Hamilton Taft HS; Hamilton, OH; Cl Rep Jr Cls; Chrs; Chrh Wkr; Y-Teens; Ger Clb; Pep Clb; IM Sprt; Miami Univ; Anthropology.

RICHARDSON, TAMRA; Dunbar HS; Dunbar, WV; Chrs; Chrh Wkr; Girl Scts; Hon Rl; Jr NHS; NHS; Off Ade; Sch Pl; Stu Cncl; College; Bus Educ.

RICHARDSON, TODD A; Benjamin Bosse HS; Evansville, IN; 1/375 Val; Chrs; Hon Rl; Jr NHS; Natl Forn Lg; NHS; Sch Mus; Pres Sch Pl; Pres Ger Clb; Pres Lat Clb; Harvard Univ; Philosophy.

RICHARDVILLE, CRAIG; Monroe Catholic Central HS; Monroe, MI; 3/96 Pres Frsh Cls; Pres Soph Cls; Chrs; Hon Rl; NHS; Sch Pl; Rptr Yrbk; Letter Ftbl; Wrstlng; IM Sprt; Mi Comp Schslhp 79; Michigan St Univ; Bus Mgmt.

RICHEY, BRENDA; Crestview HS; Wren, OH; Cl Rep Jr Cls; Chrs; Sch Mus; Sch Pl; Yth Flsp; Y-Teens; 4-H; FHA; Pep Clb; Scr Kpr; Palimentary Procedure; Historian Rating Perfect Score; St Homemakers Degree; College; Extenison.

RICHEY, DEBORAH; River Vly HS; Prospect, OH; Hosp Ade; VP Orch; 4-H; FHA; Sec Lat Clb; Sci Clb; 4-H Awd; Band Letter; Superiors At Cnty Dist Sci Fairs; Coll; Nursing.

RICHEY, NANCY; Crestview HS; E Palestine, OH; Sec Frsh Cls; Pres Jr Cls; Chrh Wkr; Cmnty Wkr; Hon Rl; NHS; Off Ade; Sch Pl; Stg Crw; 4-H; Youngstown State College; Comp Tech.

RICHEY, WILLIAM K; Xenia HS; Xenia, OH; 5/530 Cl Rep Jr Cls; Band; Chrs; Hon Rl; Pres NHS; Sch Mus; VP Stu Cncl; Fr Clb; Ger Clb; Key Clb; Honored By Wilmington Coll For Outstndng Acadc Achvmnt 77; Delegato To Bukeye Boys St 79; Med Schl; Med.

RICHEZ, JAY L; Owendale Gagetown HS; Cass City, MI; 14/54 Hon Rl; Sch Pl; Stg Crw; Stu Cncl; Yrbk; Sprt Ed Yrbk; Letter Ftbl; Trk; NROTC; Elec.

RICHHART, DEBORAH; Decatur Central HS; Indpls, IN; 15/306 Cls Rep Frsh Cls; Cls Rep Soph Cls; Cl Rep Jr Cls; Cls Rep Sr Cls; Hon Rl; NHS; Off Ade; Stu Cncl; Pep Clb; Letter Gym; Indiana St Univ; Bus.

RICHMAN, REBECCA; Floyd Central HS; Floyd Knobs, IN; 1/325 Chrs; Chrh Wkr; Girl Scts; Hon Rl; Jr NHS; NHS; Orch; Sch Mus; Stg Crw; Stu Cncl; Algebra Awrd 77; Geometry Awrd 78; 1st In 4 H St Demnstrtn 78; Univ; Elem Educ.

RICHMOND, ANNE; Walnut Hills HS; Cincinnati, OH; Sal; Band; Chrh Wkr; Yth Flsp; Fr Clb; Wrstlng; Natl Merit Ltr; Oberlin Coll.

RICHMOND, BETH; Redford Union HS; Detroit, MI; Cls Rep Frsh Cls; Cmp Fr Grls; Drl Tm; Hon Rl; JA; Stu Cncl; Pep Clb; Chrldng; GAA; Scr Kpr; Lake Supeiror Coll; Law Enforcement.

RICHMOND, DONALD C; Manistee Catholic Ctrl HS; Bear Lk, MI; Cls Rep Frsh Cls; Trs Soph Cls; Cls Rep Soph Cls; Am Leg Boys St; Hon Rl; NHS; Sch Pl; Capt Bsbl; Letter Bsktbl; Capt Ftbl; Western Michigan Univ; Comp Systems.

RICHMOND, DRUCEAN L; South HS; Cleveland, OH; Chrs; Drl Tm; Off Ade; Stu Cncl; Bsktbl; GAA; IM Sprt; Cleveland State Univ; Elec Engr.

RICHMOND, LISA; London HS; London, OH; 49/144 Band; Cmp Fr Grls; Cmnty Wkr; Hon Rl; Hosp Ade; Sch Pl; Rptr Sch Nwsp; 4-H; Scr Kpr; 4-H Awd; Rotary Exchng Stdnt To Brazil 77; Quill & Scroll Awd Hon Mbrshp; Sallie Dooris Poetry Awd Hon Mntn; Wittenberg Univ; Interior Dsgn.

RICHMOND, LOUIS L; High School; Dowagiac, MI; 98/215 Aud/Vis; Boy Scts; Chrs; Lbry Ade; Sch Pl; Sct Actv; Drama Clb; Ferris St Coll; Radio/TV Brdcstng.

RICHMOND, LUKE; Grand Blanc HS; Burton, MI; Band; Chrs; Debate Tm; Sch Mus; Univ Of Mic; Music.

RICHMOND, NORMAN; East Jackson HS; Jackson, MI; 1/130 Band; NHS; Sch Mus; Jackson Comm Coll; Elec Engr.

RICHMOND, PAMELLA; Centreville HS; Sturgis, MI; 28/76 Trs Soph Cls; Band; Chrs; Hosp Ade; Lbry Ade; Yth Flsp; Rptr Yrbk; Hesston College; Home Econ.

RICHMOND, PAT; Sacred Heart Academy; Mt Pleasant, MI; Am Leg Boys St; Boy Scts; Cmnty Wkr; Hon Rl; Sch Pl; Drama Clb; Pep Clb; Crs Cntry; Ftbl; Trk; Central Mic Univ; Business.

RICHMOND, RONACHELLE; Little Miami HS; Morrow, OH; 10/200 Cls Rep Frsh Cls; Cls Rep Soph Cls; Cl Rep Jr Cls; Am Leg Aux Girls St; Treas NHS; Sch Mus; Sch Pl; Pres Stu Cncl; Pres Fr Clb; DAR Awd; Ohi State Univ.

RICHMOND, STEVEN T; Jackson Cnty Western HS; Parma, MI; 11/271 Cls Rep Frsh Cls; Cls Rep Soph Cls; Band; Debate Tm; Mod UN; Pol Wkr; Sch Pl; Stu Cncl; Sch Nwsp; Fr Clb; Ctrl Michigan Univ; Bus Admin.

RICHNER, JENNIFER; R B Chamberlin HS; Twinsburg, OH; Band; Hon Rl; NHS; Letter Bsktbl; Letter Ten; Scr Kpr;.

RICHTER, MARK; La Salle HS; Cincinnati, OH; Boy Scts; Letter Socr; IM Sprt; Univ Of Cincinnati; Bus Mgmt.

RICHTER, ROBERT; Elder HS; Cinn, OH; 4/380 Cl Rep Jr Cls; Hon Rl; NHS; Yrbk; IM Sprt; Bausch & Lomb Awd; Xavier Univ; Med.

RICICA, NANCY; Tinora HS; Defiance, OH; Trs Soph Cls; Am Leg Aux Girls St; Hon Rl; NHS; Off Ade; Stu Cncl; OEA; Letter Bsktbl; Letter Trk; Scr Kpr; Northwest Tech Coll; Data Proc.

RICKARD, LAYNE; Teays Valley HS; Circleville, OH; 7/200 Am Leg Aux Girls St; Chrs; Chrh Wkr; FCA; Girl Scts; Hon Rl; NHS; Sch Mus; Sch Pl; Yth Flsp; All Oh Youth Choir 78; Math Awd 78; Natl Schl Choral Awd 79; Drama Schlrshp Awd Of Distinction 79; Roanoke Coll; Med Tech.

RICKEL, CHERYL; Ashland HS; Ashland, OH; Cls Rep Frsh Cls; Band; Chrs; Drl Tm; Hon Rl; Sch Mus; Stu Cncl; GAA; IM Sprt; Scr Kpr; Oh Test Of Schlstc Achvmnt 1 Yr French Hon Mntn 7;9 Nomintd For HS Ambssdr For U S 79; Univ; Elem Educ.

RICKENBACHER, MARK; Mt Blanchard Riverdale HS; Forest, OH; Band; Cmnty Wkr; Hon Rl; Yth Flsp; Bsbl; Bsktbl; Glf; College.

RICKENBACHER, STEVEN L; Kenton Sr HS; Kenton, OH; Am Leg Boys St; Chrh Wkr; Hon Rl; NHS; Sec 4-H; FFA; Glf; Ten; IM Sprt; 4-H Awd; Ohio St Univ; Ag.

RICKER, MARY; Delphos St Johns HS; Delphos, OH; Cls Rep Frsh Cls; Cls Rep Soph Cls; Cl Rep Jr Cls; Pres Sr Cls; Band; Hon Rl; NHS; Sch Mus; Stu Cncl; Rptr Yrbk; Lima Tech Coll; Nurse.

RICKERT, CYNTHIA; Wapakoneta Sr HS; Wapakoneta, OH; 17/332 Am Leg Aux Girls St; Chrs; Hon Rl; NHS; Quill & Scroll; Ed Yrbk; Yrbk; VP OEA; Mgrs; Univ Of Cincinnati; Med Sec.

RICKETTS, BECKY; Fairfield Union HS; Thornville, OH; 9/150 Hst Frsh Cls; Pres Soph Cls; Band; Drl Tm; Hon Rl; NHS; Off Ade; FBLA; FTA; OEA; Ohio St Univ; Admin.

RICKETTS, REYNE; Greenwood Community HS; Greenwood, IN; 19/236 Band; Hon Rl; NHS; St Josephs Coll.

RICKEY, KAREN; Heath HS; Heath, OH; Chrh Wkr; Hosp Ade; Lbry Ade; Yth Flsp; FNA; Future Nurses Of Amer Awd; College; Nursing.

RICKLI, JOHN; Hackett HS; Kalamazoo, MI; Letter Bsktbl; GAA; Letter Mgrs; Univ Of Mic; Comp Engr.

RICKMAN, MARCEL; Mt Clemens HS; Mt Clemens, MI; Cls Rep Frsh Cls; Cls Rep Soph Cls; Sec Sr Cls; Chrs; Chrh Wkr; Girl Scts; Hon Rl; JA; Sch Mus; Sch Nwsp; Crowned As Miss Debutante; 1st Runner Up Miss Mich; Set St Rec Fresh Yr 440 Yd Relay; Outstanding Soph; College; Busns.

RICKNER, PEGGY; Van Wert HS; Van Wert, OH; Cls Rep Frsh Cls; Cls Rep Soph Cls; Cl Rep Jr Cls; Cls Rep Sr Cls; Chrs; NHS; Sec Stu Cncl; Rptr Yrbk; Capt Trk; IM Sprt; Schlrshp From Ohio St Schl Of Cosmetology 79; Mile Relay St Champ 76; Ohio St Schl Of Cosmetology; Cosmlgy.

RICKSGERS, MAUREEN; Kelloggsville HS; Wyoming, MI; Band; Debate Tm; Hon Rl; NHS; Stg Crw; Spn Clb; Mic State Univ; Pre Vet Med.

RICKWALT, MELISSA; Caro Community HS; Caro, MI; Band; Chrs; Chrh Wkr; Drm Bgl; Drm Mjrt; Girl Scts; Hon Rl; Jr NHS; NHS; Off Ade; Ferris State Univ; Bus.

RIDDELL, KIMBERLY; West Carrollton HS; Dayton, OH; 43/367 Chrs; Hon Rl; JA; NHS; Off Ade; Ten; Univ Of Dayton; Acctg.

RIDDER, SAM; Eaton HS; Eaton, OH; 2/190 Cls Rep Frsh Cls; Cls Rep Soph Cls; Cl Rep Jr Cls; Band; Hon Rl; Stu Cncl; Ftbl; Trk; Wrstlng; IM Sprt; Astro Aeronautical Engr.

RIDDERING, GEORGE; Kenowa Hills HS; Grand Rapids, MI; Chrh Wkr; Hon Rl; NHS; Bsbl; Ftbl; Letter Glf; IM Sprt; Mgrs; Univ; Law.

RIDDIOUGH, DEBBIE; Madeira HS; Madeira, OH; 54/165 Band; Chrs; Chrh Wkr; Girl Scts; Hon Rl; Orch; Sch Mus; Sch Pl; Stg Crw; Yth Flsp; Coll.

RIDDIOUGH, ELIZABETH; Loveland Hurst HS; Loveland, OH; 32/270 Hon Rl; Hosp Ade; JA; NHS; Sec Yth Flsp; Treas Fr Clb; FHA; Ger Clb; College; Pre Med.

RIDDLE, DENNIS; Flushing HS; Flushing, MI; 142/538 Hon Rl; Lit Mag; Natl Merit SF; Ferris State College; Tv Prod.

RIDDLE, DIANE; Jefferson Union HS; Toronto, OH; Chrs; Hon Rl; Jr NHS; NHS; Beta Clb; Trk; PPFtbl; Ohio State Univ; Physical Therapy.

RIDDLE, LAURIE; East Palestine HS; E Palestine, OH; 17/155 Cls Rep Sr Cls; Treas Band; Cmp Fr Grls; Chrs; Chrh Wkr; Cmnty Wkr; NHS; Sch Mus; Stu Cncl; Ed Sch Nwsp; Univ.

RIDDLE, MONICA; Our Lady Of The Angels HS; Cincinnati, OH; 2/120 Treas Cmp Fr Grls; Chrh Wkr; Hon Rl; Hosp Ade; Treas NHS; Boys Clb Am; Spn Clb; Letter Bsktbl; GAA; IM Sprt; Univ Of Cincinnati; Acctg.

RIDDLE, NADINE; Edwin Denby HS; Detroit, MI; Girl Scts; Hon Rl; JA; FDA; Mich State Univ; Pre Med.

RIDDLE, NATALIE; Colonel Crawford HS; Bucyrus, OH; Band; Hon Rl; NHS; Yrbk; 4-H; 4-H Awd; Military Service.

RIDDLE, PATRICIA L; Mount View HS; Elbert, WV; Aud/Vis; Chrs; Chrh Wkr; Cmnty Wkr; Hon Rl; Yth Flsp; FHA; Keyettes; Univ.

RIDDLE, REBECCA; Owosso HS; Owosso, MI; Cmnty Wkr; Hon Rl; NHS; Yth Flsp; Lat Clb; Natl Merit Ltr; Univ Of Michigan; Nursing.

RIDDLE, RENEE; Amanda Clearcreek HS; Stoutsville, OH; 33/100 Pres Jr Cls; Pres Sr Cls; Am Leg Aux Girls St; Aud/Vis; Band; Chrs; Hon Rl; NHS; Off Ade; Stu Cncl; Schsp From Tchr At Schl At Its Org Called ACCTA For 150 79; Pauline Huston Memrl Sclshp 79; Ohio Univ; Lrng Dsblts.

RIDEN, MARK; John F Kennedy HS; Taylor, MI; Wayne County Comm College; Attorney.

RIDENOUR, CAROL J; Black River HS; Homerville, OH; 7/105 Band; Chrs; Hon Rl; Beta Clb; Drama Clb; 4-H; FHA; 4-H Awd; Univ; C P A.

RIDENOUR, CAROLYN; Bridgeport HS; Bridgeport, WV; 3/200 Girl Scts; Hon Rl; Jr NHS; Y-Teens; 4-H; Pep Clb; Spn Clb; Trk; 4-H Awd; Eng Pleasure Pony 3rd Pl In WV Horseman Assn 1974 & 1975; Morgantown Univ; Engr.

RIDENOUR, DEBORA; Coshocton HS; Coshocton, OH; 6/232 NHS; Sch Pl; Pres Yth Flsp; Rptr Yrbk; VP Fr Clb; Ten; 4-H Awd; Univ Of Cin; Industrial Engr.

RIDENOUR, MARILYN; Bridgeport HS; Bridgeport, WV; Girl Scts; Hon Rl; Jr NHS; 4-H; Pep Clb; 4-H Awd; Univ; Nursing.

RIDER, DENISE; Champion HS; Bristolville, OH; Band; Chrs; Chrh Wkr; Girl Scts; Hosp Ade; Off Ade; Red Cr Ade; Fr Clb; Letter In Band For 3 Yrs; Pin Awd For Outstanding Performance In Chorus; Kent St Univ; Nursing.

RIDER, DWAYNE; Greenbrier East HS; Alderson, WV; Band; Pres Chrs; Chrh Wkr; Cmnty Wkr; Hon Rl; MMM; NHS; Orch; Pres Yth Flsp; Marshall Univ.

RIDER, KIMBERLY; Milton HS; Ona, WV; Hon Rl; NHS; FBLA; Mth Clb; Mgrs; Scr Kpr; DAR Awd; Marshall Univ; Legal Administrator.

RIDGE, SUSAN; Jackson HS; Jackson, OH; 9/210 Cls Rep Sr Cls; Band; Chrs; Drm Mjrt; Hon Rl; NHS; Quill & Scroll; Sch Pl; Y-Teens; Yrbk; Ohio Univ; Journalism.

RIDGWAY, SCOTT; Bedford Sr HS; Walton Hills, OH; 57/625 Boy Scts; Hon Rl; Jr NHS; NHS; Letter Bsbl; Letter Ftbl; Trk; Wrstlng; Ohio St Univ; Med.

RIDILLA, ELAINA; Brooklyn HS; Brooklyn, OH; Band; Chrs; Sch Mus; Spn Clb; Bowling Green; Music.

RIDINGER, LYNN; Theodore Roosevelt HS; Kent, OH; Band; Girl Scts; Hon Rl; NHS; Yth Flsp; 4-H; Pep Clb; Letter Bsbl; Letter Bsktbl; Letter Hockey; Central Michigan Univ; Phys Ed.

RIDINGS, PHIL; Greenon HS; Enon, OH; Letter Ftbl; IM Sprt; Univ; Engr.

RIDL, JANICE; Adlai E Stevenson HS; Livonia, MI; Orch; Rptr Sch Nwsp; Sch Nwsp; Natl Merit SF; Schoolcraft Coll; Jrnlsm.

RIDLEY, MICHAEL; Purcell HS; Cincinnati, OH; 2/100 Chrs; Hon Rl; Sch Mus; Sct Actv; IM Sprt; College; Law.

RIDLEY, STEPHEN; E A Johnson HS; Clio, MI; 66/255 Band; Chrh Wkr; Drm Bgl; Hon Rl; Sch Mus; Stg Crw; Western Michigan Univ; Ind Ed.

RIEBE, PAMELA; Douglas Mac Arthur HS; Saginaw, MI; Chrs; Girl Scts; Hon Rl; Jr NHS; NHS; Sct Actv; Pep Clb; Chrldng; PPFtbl; Grand Champions At Cheerleading Camp; Delta Coll; Dental Hygiene.

RIECKEN, DEBBIE; Benjamin Bosse HS; Evansville, IN; 35/320 Sec Frsh Cls; Band; Hon Rl; Pres Quill & Scroll; Ed Yrbk; Sprt Ed Sch Nwsp; Sec Fr Clb; VP Pep Clb; Letter Glf; Letter Gym; Univ Of Evansville; Nursing.

RIEDEL, DOUGLAS; Buckeye Central HS; New Washington, OH; 10/90 Trs Sr Cls; Am Leg Boys St; Band; Hon Rl; NHS; Sch Mus; Yth Flsp; 4-H; Bsktbl; Letter Ftbl; Ohio State Univ; Civil Eng.

RIEDEL, HERBERT; Walled Lake Central HS; Union Lake, MI; Hon Rl; Bsbl; Crs Cntry; Letter Socr; Natl Merit Schl; Mich State.

RIEDEL, KELLY R; Geneva Secondary School; Geneva, OH; 1/250 Cls Rep Frsh Cls; Pres Soph Cls; Cls Rep Soph Cls; Pres Jr Cls; Pres Sr Cls; Cls Rep Sr Cls; AFS; Am Leg Boys St; Aud/Vis; Boy Scts; Schlstc Art & Photog Merit Awd 75; Eagle Scout 75; Ranked 94% On PSAT Test 78; Ohio St Univ; Pre Law.

RIEGE, MARK; Twin Valley South HS; W Alex, OH; 1/90 Trs Sr Cls; Val; Chrh Wkr; Cmnty Wkr; Hon Rl; NHS; Pol Wkr; FTA; Letter Trk; Lion Awd; Anderson Coll; Pre Med.

RIEGEL, MARGARET; Philip Barbour HS; Philippi, WV; Chrh Wkr; Hon Rl; NHS; Yrbk; Keyettes; Letter Ten; College; Communications.

RIEGEL, MARY A; Brownsburg HS; Brownsburg, IN; 58/315 Cls Rep Soph Cls; Chrh Wkr; Hon Rl; Jr NHS; NHS; 4-H; Fr Clb; PPFtbl; 4-H Awd; Pres Awd; Univ; Bus.

RIEGEL, TAMI; Logan Elm HS; Circleville, OH; Hon Rl; NHS; Off Ade; Stu Cncl; Yth Flsp; 4-H; Pep Clb; Letter Bsbl; Bsktbl; GAA; Soph Homecoming Attndnt; Pres Phys Fitnes Awd; Paul C Hayes Tech Trainng; Dent Tech.

RIEGER, BRIDGET; Strongsville HS; Strongsville, OH; Hon Rl; Jr NHS; Stg Crw; Letter Ten; IM Sprt; Hon Mntn In Algbr In Oh Test Of Schlts Achmnt 77; Eng Tchr Aide For Schl Yr 79; Univ; RN.

RIEGER, JACK; La Salle HS; Cincinnati, OH; 3/249 Band; Hon Rl; Jr NHS; Sch Mus; Yrbk; Sch Nwsp; Coll; Photog.

RIEGER, JACK B; La Salle HS; Cincinnati, OH; 3/249 Band; Hon Rl; Yrbk; Sch Nwsp; College; Photography.

RIEGER, RICKY; Northwest HS; Cincinnati, OH; Cls Rep Soph Cls; Cl Rep Jr Cls; Chrs; Hon Rl; Jr NHS; NHS; Stu Cncl; Univ Of Cin; Poli Sci.

RIEGERT, JULIE; Stephen T Badin HS; Fairfield, OH; 39/223 Chrh Wkr; Cmnty Wkr; Girl Scts; Hon Rl; FBLA; Gym; Univ; Bus.

RIEGLER, FRANCIS; St Xavier HS; Cincinnati, OH; Sch Pl; Stu Cncl; Pep Clb; Ftbl; Chrldng; IM Sprt; Xavier Univ; Engr.

RIEGLER, JONATHAN; Mona Shores HS; Muskegon, MI; Cls Rep Sr Cls; Band; Debate Tm; Hon Rl; Natl Forn Lg; Wrstlng; Cit Awd; Schl Part Schlrshp 79; St Of Mi Comptn Schlrshp 79; Michigan St Univ; Bus Admin.

RIEGLER, WALTER; Oakridge HS; Muskegon, MI; 12/155 Boy Scts; Jr NHS; Sch Pl; Stg Crw; Pep Clb; Trk; Univ; Aviation.

RIEGSECKE, STEVEN S; Goshen HS; Goshen, IN; 22/268 Hon Rl; Stu Cncl; Pep Clb; Letter Ftbl; Letter Swmmng; Trk; College; Pharmacy.

RIEGSECKER, S; Pike Delta York HS; Delta, OH; Chrs; Chrh Wkr; Sch Mus; Stu Cncl; Yth Flsp; Sch Nwsp; FHA; Pep Clb; Northwest Tech College; Prn.

RIEHL, LORI; Nordonia HS; Northfield, OH; Hon Rl; Sch Pl; Y-Teens; IM Sprt; Fench Awd 17th Pl 77; Prin Awd 76 & 77; Univ; Comp Sci.

RIEHL, MARK; Clyde HS; Clyde, OH; 19/212 Am Leg Boys St; Pres Chrh Wkr; Cmnty Wkr; Debate Tm; Hon Rl; NHS; VP FFA; Coach Actv; Ohio St Univ.

RIEHL, SUZANNE; Rossford HS; Rossford, OH; 1/147 Band; Chrh Wkr; Hon Rl; NHS; Red Cr Ade; Spn Clb; College; Engr.

RIEKER, MINETTE M; Carroll HS; Dayton, OH; Mod UN; Spn Clb; Wright St Univ; Acctg.

RIEMAN, DIANA; Cory Rawson HS; Bluffton, OH; Sec Frsh Cls; Trs Jr Cls; Cls Rep Sr Cls; Band; Chrs; Hon Rl; 4-H; Pep Clb; Mat Maids; Voc Schl.

RIEMAN, JOEL; Mt Healthy HS; Cincinnati, OH; 67/520 Hon Rl; Fr Clb; Pres VICA; Letter Ftbl; Letter Trk; Letter Wrstlng; Univ; Indus Tech.

RIEMAN, KATHLEEN; Bluffton HS; Columbus Grove, OH; 12/94 Chrs; Chrh Wkr; Hon Rl; PPFtbl; Lima Tech Coll; Data Proc.

RIEMAN, LYNN; Ottawa Glandorf HS; Ottawa, OH; 40/172 Cls Rep Sr Cls; Am Leg Aux Girls St; Chrh Wkr; Hon Rl; Off Ade; Sch Mus; Stu Cncl; Sch Nwsp; 4-H; Chrldng; Bowling Green Schl; R N.

RIEMENSCHNEIDER, BETH; Clay HS; South Bend, IN; Hon Rl; NHS; Stu Cncl; Fr Clb; Pep Clb; IM Sprt; College; Poli Sci.

RIEMENSCHNEIDER, WENDY; Cambridge HS; Cambridge, OH; Cls Rep Frsh Cls; Cls Rep Soph Cls; Cl Rep Jr Cls; Hon Rl; Stu Cncl; Rptr Yrbk; Pep Clb; Mat Maids; Scr Kpr; Tmr; College.

RIEMER, ANDREW; Ludington HS; Ludington, MI; 27/255 Cls Rep Frsh Cls; Cls Rep Soph Cls; Cls Rep Sr Cls; Chrh Wkr; Hon Rl; Pol Wkr; Stu Cncl; Yth Flsp; Yrbk; FSA; Ferris State Coll; Pharmacy.

RIEMERSMA, PETER; Saint Xavier HS; Cincinnati, OH; 28/310 Boy Scts; Hon Rl; NHS; Sct Actv; Fr Clb; Trk; College; Geol.

RIEPENHOFF, L; Miller City HS; Ottawa, OH; 1/53 Band; Chrs; Hon Rl; Sch Mus; Stu Cncl; Rptr Yrbk; FHA; Am Leg Awd; Natl Merit Ltr; College.

RIEPMA, PATRICK; Columbia Central HS; Brooklyn, MI; Pres Frsh Cls; Cls Rep Soph Cls; Cls Rep Sr Cls; Band; Hon Rl; NHS; Stu Cncl; Bsbl; Bsktbl; Ftbl; Hillsdale Coll; Bus Educ.

RIES, ELIZABETH; Wadsworth Sr HS; Wadsworth, OH; Band; Chrs; Chrh Wkr; Cmnty Wkr; Girl Scts; Off Ade; Rptr Sch Nwsp; Fr Clb; Pep Clb; Swmmng; Ohio Univ; Law.

RIES, MICHAEL; Redford HS; Detroit, MI; Band; Boy Scts; Hon Rl; Sct Actv; Stanford Univ; Art Intell.

RIES, ROGER; Mt Vernon Sr HS; Mt Vernon, IN; AFS; Chrh Wkr; Yth Flsp; 4-H; FFA; Letter Ftbl; Wrstlng; Coach Actv; Scr Kpr; 4-H Awd; FFA Awd For Ag Proficiency; Purdue Univ; Agronomy.

RIESER, KIMBERLY; St Francis Desales HS; Columbus, OH; Hon Rl; Trk; Columbus Tech Inst; Acctg.

RIESER, SHEILA L; Liberty HS; Clarksburg, WV; 15/228 Cl Rep Jr Cls; Trs Sr Cls; Band; Hon Rl; NHS; Stg Crw; Stu Cncl; Y-Teens; DECA; Drama Clb; Fairmont St Univ; Spec Educ.

RIESER, SUZANNE; Bishop Hartley HS; Columbus, OH; Cls Rep Soph Cls; Cl Rep Jr Cls; Hon Rl; Stu Cncl; Mat Maids; PPFtbl; Scr Kpr; CTI; Comp Prog.

RIESKAMP, MARY; Mother Of Mercy HS; Cincinnati, OH; 23/245 Chrs; Girl Scts; Hon Rl; Hosp Ade; Jr NHS; Lbry Ade; NHS; Off Ade; Red Cr Ade; Sct Actv; College; Medicine.

RIESKE, MICHAEL D; Fairmont West HS; Kettering, OH; Cmnty Wkr; Hon Rl; Off Ade; Sct Actv; Civ Clb; Socr; IM Sprt; Coll; Marine Bio.

RIESTER, DEAN; North Knox HS; Bicknell, IN; 22/179 Band; Chrh Wkr; Hon Rl; NHS; Orch; Rptr Yrbk; Trk; All Amer Bnd Hnr; Vincennes Univ; Business.

RIETHMAN, DUANE; Minster HS; Minster, OH; 26/80 Pres Soph Cls; Chrh Wkr; Hon Rl; NHS; Stu Cncl; Pres FFA; Pep Clb; Letter Bsktbl; Ohio St Univ; Agri.

RIFE, BARBARA; St Albans HS; St Albans, WV; 6/450 Sec Frsh Cls; Band; Hon Rl; Trs Frsh Cls; Off Ade; Orch; Sch Pl; Stu Cncl; Ed Yrbk; Univ Of Charleston; R N.

RIFE, BARBARA; Paulding HS; Paulding, OH; 35/180 Band; Hon Rl; Stg Crw; Drama Clb; Sci Clb; Scr Kpr;.

RIFE, CHARLES; Jay County HS; Dunkirk, IN; 30/479 Hon Rl; VP JA; NHS; Sch Nwsp; JA Awd; Mbr Schl Physics Comp Tm 78; Ball St Univ; Comp Sci.

RIFE, PENNY; Kyger Creek HS; Cheshire, OH; Chrs; Hon Rl; Off Ade; Rptr Yrbk; Ed Sch Nwsp; Rptr Sch Nwsp; FHA; Sec Keyettes; Scr Kpr; Schlshp Tchr Aide 79; Rio Grande Coll; Elem Educ.

RIFE, SHELLEY; Alexander HS; Albany, OH; 5/132 Hon Rl; Treas NHS; Sch Pl; Stu Cncl; Sch Nwsp; Pep Clb; Pres Spn Clb; Capt Chrldng; Hocking Tech Voc Schl; Sec.

RIFFE, ANDREW; Pendleton Hts HS; Middletown, IN; Cls Rep Soph Cls; Cl Rep Jr Cls; Trs Sr Cls; Aud/Vis; Boy Scts; Chrh Wkr; Cmnty Wkr; FCA; Lbry Ade; Pol Wkr; Xavier Univ; Law.

RIFFE, LYNN; Bellmont HS; Decatur, IN; Band; Drl Tm; PPFtbl; IUPU; Mental Health Tech.

RIFFEE, JENNIFER; Bridgeport HS; Bridgeport, WV; Band; Chrs; Hon Rl; Jr NHS; Lbry Ade; NHS; Yth Flsp; Y-Teens; College; Busns.

RIFFEL, KAREN; Jasper HS; Jasper, IN; 39/289 Chrs; Chrh Wkr; VP Cmnty Wkr; Hon Rl; Lbry Ade; Off Ade; Sch Mus; Sch Pl; Stg Crw; Drama Clb; Univ; Cmnctns.

RIFFLE, CHARLES; Elida HS; Lima, OH; Hon Rl; NHS; Pres Yth Flsp; Ftbl; Ohio St Univ.

RIFFLE, DIANA L; West Union HS; W Union, OH; Hon Rl; NHS; Drama Clb; 4-H; Trk; 4-H Awd; S St Merdith Manor Coll; Equestrian.

RIFFLE, DONNA; Morgantown HS; Morgantwn, WV; Cls Rep Frsh Cls; Chrs; FCA; Hon Rl; Yrbk; Mth Clb; Letter Bsktbl; IM Sprt; St Champ Girls Bsktbl Team 77; Univ; Math.

RIFICI, KIMBERLY; James Ford Rhodes HS; Cleveland, OH; 73/309 Sec Soph Cls; Pres Jr Cls; Pres Sr Cls; Chrs; Chrh Wkr; Drl Tm; JA; Pol Wkr; Sch Mus; Stu Cncl; Baldwin Wallace Coll; Poli Sci.

RIFKIN, WENDY; Dublin HS; Dublin, OH; Chrs; Hon Rl; Lbry Ade; Lit Mag; Sch Mus; Sch Pl; Stg Crw; 4-H; Fr Clb; Pep Clb; St Dept Of Educ Schlshp Awd In Eng II 79; Ohio St Univ; Vet Med.

RIGDON, DEBRA; Rockville Jr Sr HS; Rockville, IN; 3/97 VP Frsh Cls; VP Soph Cls; FCA; Hon Rl; Sch Pl; Yth Flsp; Sch Nwsp; Pep Clb; PPFtbl; Tmr; ISU; Nursing.

RIGDON, LISA; Greensburg Community HS; Greensburg, IN; 34/200 Band; Chrs; Hon Rl; Mdrgl; Sch Mus; VP FTA; Pep Clb; St Piano Contest 1st Pl 78; Ball St Univ; Elem Educ.

RIGEL, JACKIE L; Perry HS; Lima, OH; Cls Rep Frsh Cls; VP Sr Cls; Chrs; Chrh Wkr; Drl Tm; Hon Rl; Off Ade; Stu Cncl; Ed Yrbk; Pep Clb; Marion Coll; Bus.

RIGEL, SHERRY J; Austin HS; Austin, IN; 1/111 Band; Girl Scts; Hon Rl; NHS; Sct Actv; Stg Crw; Rptr Yrbk; Rptr Sch Nwsp; FTA; Lat Clb; Univ; Psych.

RIGELMAN, GREG; Edon HS; Montpelier, OH; 2/78 Hon Rl; Am Leg Awd; Univ; Sci.

RIGELSKY, JOSEPH; Ursuline HS; Youngstown, OH; 151/320 Hon Rl; Spn Clb; Bsktbl; Ftbl; IM Sprt; Scr Kpr; College.

RIGG, MICHAEL; Richmond Sr HS; Richmond, IN; 16/550 Band; Boy Scts; Lbry Ade; NHS; Sch Mus; Crs Cntry; Swmmng; Spanish Exchange Stu 79; Natl Scout Jamboree 77; Wolrd Scout Jamboree Sweden 77; Univ; Physics.

RIGG, NATHAN; Shelby HS; Shelby, OH; Band; Hon Rl; Lat Clb; Mgrs; BGSU; Comp Progr.

RIGGINS, KATHLEEN; Amanda Clearcreek HS; Lancaster, OH; Girl Scts; Spn Clb; GAA; Voc Schl; Data Proc.

RIGGIO, JAMES; Chippewa Valley HS; Mt Clemens, MI; 27/365 Chrs; Cmnty Wkr; Hon Rl; Hosp Ade; Jr NHS; Mdrgl; NHS; Sch Mus; Univ Of Detroit; Dentistry.

RIGGLE, ELLEN; Rossville HS; Frankfort, IN; 1/50 Hon Rl; NHS; Yrbk; 4-H; Letter Bsktbl; Letter Trk; Purdue Univ.

RIGGLE, JOHN; Kankakee Vly HS; De Motte, IN; 29/181 Hon Rl; Ger Clb; Crs Cntry; Letter Glf; Trk; Wrstlng; USJC Awd; Purdue Univ; Engr.

RIGGLEMAN, DANITA; Roosevelt Wilson HS; Clarksburg, WV; Band; Hon Rl; NHS; Orch; Sch Pl; Y-Teens; FBLA; Leo Clb; Bsktbl; Mgrs; Secretary.

RIGGS, JAYNE; Ironton HS; Ironton, OH; Cls Rep Frsh Cls; Cls Rep Soph Cls; Hon Rl; Off Ade; Sprt Ed Yrbk; Ger Clb; Capt Bsktbl; GAA; IM Sprt; Pres Awd; Univ; Law.

RIGGS, JEFF; Bloomington HS North; Bloomington, IN; Hon Rl; Jr NHS; NHS; Capt Glf; Coach Actv; Purdue Univ; Engr.

RIGGS, LETETIA; Swartz Creek HS; Swartz Crk, MI; Cls Rep Soph Cls; Sec Jr Cls; VP Sr Cls; Chrs; Hon Rl; NHS; Sch Mus; Sch Pl; Stu Cncl; Drama Clb; U S Coast Guard Acad.

RIGGS, MARTIN; Tyler County HS; Middlebourne, WV; 8/92 Cls Rep Frsh Cls; Cls Rep Soph Cls; Cl Rep Jr Cls; VP Sr Cls; Hon Rl; Jr NHS; NHS; Stu Cncl; Spn Clb; Letter Bsbl; Amer Outstg Names 79; Univ.

RIGGS, MICHELLE; Lutheran West HS; Elyria, OH; 28/99 Sec Band; Chrh Wkr; Hon Rl; NHS; Sch Mus; VP Ger Clb; Concordia Tchrs Coll; Secondary Ed.

RIGGS, PAULA; South Spencer HS; Rockport, IN; 89/147 Band; Chrs; Chrh Wkr; Girl Scts; Hon Rl; Lbry Ade; Off Ade; Sch Mus; Sch Pl; Sct Actv; 1st Class Cadette 76; Internatl Thespian Soc 79; Owensboro Bus Coll; Data Proc.

RIGGS, RHONDA; Shenandoah HS; Middletown, IN; 6/151 Am Leg Aux Girls St; Chrs; Girl Scts; Hon Rl; Lbry Ade; NHS; Sec FBLA; Pres Mth Clb; Pep Clb; Univ; Chem.

RIGGS, SHARI; Hilltop HS; W Unity, OH; 6/75 Sec Frsh Cls; Band; Chrs; Hon Rl; NHS; Chrldng; Scr Kpr; Vrsty Vlybl; Deb U's; Bowling Team; Univ Of Toledo; Spec Educ.

RIGLING, ANN; Stephen T Badin HS; Hamilton, OH; 12/225 VP Frsh Cls; Pres Soph Cls; Sec Sr Cls; Hon Rl; Stg Crw; Stu Cncl; Rptr Yrbk; Rptr Sch Nwsp; Swmmng; IM Sprt; College.

RIIKONEN, GLORIA L; Ontonagon Area HS; Mass City, MI; 5/85 Am Leg Aux Girls St; Cmnty Wkr; Hon Rl; Hosp Ade; NHS; Off Ade; Sch Pl; Stg Crw; Pres Yth Flsp; Yrbk; Univ Of Michigan; Busns Mgmt.

RILEY, ANGELA R; Barboursville HS; Barboursville, WV; Chrs; Girl Scts; Hon Rl; Off Ade; Fr Clb; FBLA; Pep Clb; Marching Choir Cabell County; Handballs; Marshall Coll; X Ray Tech.

RILEY, BERT; University HS; Westover, WV; Aud/Vis; NHS; Yth Flsp; Rptr Yrbk; Rptr Sch Nwsp; Sci Clb; Letter Ten; College; Communications Engineer.

RILEY, BRIAN M; Caro HS; Caro, MI; Am Leg Boys St; Band; Hon Rl; NHS; Orch; Pol Wkr; Pep Clb; Letter Glf; Scr Kpr; Natl Merit Ltr; Selected Outstanding Soph Of Schl & Attended Hugh O

Brien Yth Foundation Michigan Ldrshp Seminar; College; Chemistry.

RILEY, CASSANDRA; Warrensville Hts Sr HS; Warrensvlle Hts, OH; Hon Rl; DECA; Cit Awd; Merit Roll; Ohio St Univ; Busns Admin.

RILEY, CHRISTINA; Gladwin HS; Gladwin, MI; Band; Hon Rl; Natl Forn Lg; Trk; Cit Awd; 4-H Awd; Ferris State College; Law.

RILEY, CINDY; Roosevelt Wilson HS; Nutterfort, WV; Chrh Wkr; Hosp Ade; Y-Teens; FNA; VICA; United Career Center; Nursing.

RILEY, DIANA; Southwestern HS; Flat Rock, IN; 22/68 Cls Rep Frsh Cls; Cls Rep Soph Cls; Cl Rep Jr Cls; Cls Rep Sr Cls; Band; Cmnty Wkr; Girl Scts; Sch Mus; DECA; 4-H; IUPUI; Sec.

RILEY, DWAIN; Ontario HS; Mansfield, OH; Cls Rep Frsh Cls; Cls Rep Soph Cls; Cl Rep Jr Cls; Pres Sr Cls; Band; Boy Scts; Orch; Sch Mus; Sct Actv; Pres Stu Cncl; Univ; Civil Engr.

RILEY, JAME; Urbana HS; Urbana, OH; Boy Scts; Lit Mag; 4-H; Mth Clb; Letter Trk; Fla Inst Of Tech; Mech Engr.

RILEY, JEAN; Monroeville HS; Norwalk, OH; Cmp Fr Grls; Girl Scts; Hon Rl; Hosp Ade; Off Ade; Quill & Scroll; Rptr Sch Nwsp; Sch Nwsp; 4-H; FFA; Wooster Univ; Horticulture.

RILEY, KATHLEEN; Felicity Franklin HS; Felicity, OH; 4/69 Pres Sr Cls; Am Leg Aux Girls St; Chrh Wkr; Cmnty Wkr; Hon Rl; Hosp Ade; Lbry Ade; NHS; Ed Sch Nwsp; FHA; College; Journalism.

RILEY, KATHY; Father J Wehrie Memrl HS; Columbus, OH; Letter Hon Rl; Sch Mus; Sch Pl; Ohio Dominican; Psych.

RILEY, KEVIN; Benedictine HS; Garfield Hts, OH; 9/113 Pres Soph Cls; Pres Jr Cls; Hon Rl; NHS; Rptr Sch Nwsp; Fr Clb; Bsbl; Ftbl; IM Sprt; Biology Awd 1977; Schl Fund Raising 1977; Lettermens Club 1978;.

RILEY, LAUREN; Clay HS; Granger, IN; 29/430 Band; Hon Rl; NHS; Orch; Sch Mus; Fr Clb; Capt Swmmng; Stephens College; Fshn Merch.

RILEY, LEVENNA; Lincoln HS; Shinnston, WV; Cl Rep Jr Cls; Chrs; Hon Rl; Sch Pl; Sct Actv; VICA; Salem Coll; Nursing.

RILEY, LISA; Cannelton HS; Cannelton, IN; 7/38 Pres Frsh Cls; Pres Soph Cls; Pres Jr Cls; Drl Tm; Girl Scts; Hon Rl; Jr NHS; NHS; Stu Cncl; Yth Flsp; College; Busns.

RILEY, LISA; Jackson Cnty Western HS; Spring Arbor, MI; Cmp Fr Grls; Chrs; Chrh Wkr; Cmnty Wkr; Debate Tm; Girl Scts; Natl Forn Lg; Pol Wkr; Sch Mus; Sch Pl; Univ; Soc Work.

RILEY, LORA; East HS; Akron, OH; Chrs; Hon Rl; NHS; Yth Flsp; Univ Of Akron; Data Proc.

RILEY, LORI; Washington HS; Massillon, OH; Chrs; Hon Rl; Sch Mus; FHA; Pep Clb; Gym; Aultman Nursing Schl; Rn.

RILEY, LORI; Brookville HS; Brookville, OH; Band; Hon Rl; NHS; Orch; Fr Clb; Sci Clb; Ohio St Univ; Genetics.

RILEY, MICHAEL; Mount Vernon Academy; Proctorville, OH; Sec Frsh Cls; Trs Frsh Cls; VP Soph Cls; Pres Jr Cls; Cls Rep Sr Cls; Chrs; Chrh Wkr; Hon Rl; Orch; PAVAS; Southern Missionary Univ; Bio.

RILEY, NORM; Whiteford HS; Ottawa Lk, MI; Band; Drm Bgl; Hon Rl; NHS; Orch; Yrbk; Rptr Sch Nwsp; College.

RILEY, PAMELA; Gladwin HS; Gladwin, MI; Hon Rl; Lbry Ade; Sch Pl; Drama Clb; Bus Schl.

RILEY, PETER W; John Marshall HS; Indianapolis, IN; 11/584 Chrs; Hon Rl; Lbry Ade; Lit Mag; NHS; Sch Mus; Treas Fr Clb; Treas Key Clb; Mth Clb; JETS Awd; Amer Chem Soc In Regnl 2nd Pl 78; Outstndng Soph In Eng 78; Outstndng Stdnt In 1st Yr Algbr Geom 77 &78; Univ; Math.

RILEY, RICHARD; Andrews Academy; Berrien Spring, MI; Sec Frsh Cls; Yrbk; Rptr Sch Nwsp; Bsktbl; IM Sprt; Andrews Univ; Phys Educ.

RILEY, R TODD; Clay Sr HS; Granger, IN; 12/385 Pres Band; Hon Rl; NHS; Orch; Sch Mus; Sch Nwsp; Lat Clb; Capt Swmmng; Letter Trk; Purdue Univ; Engr.

RILEY, SUSAN; Redford Union HS; Redford, MI; 47/548 Cmnty Wkr; Hon Rl; NHS; Ed Sch Nwsp; Crs Cntry; Trk; Wayne State Univ; Bus.

RILEY, TERESA; Houghton Lake HS; Houghton Lk, MI; 26/150 Trs Frsh Cls; Trs Soph Cls; Band; Hon Rl; NHS; Bsktbl; Trk; Ferris St Coll; Ct Rptr.

RILEY, TERI; Avon Jr Sr HS; Danville, IN; 28/198 Sec Jr Cls; Sec Sr Cls; Cmp Fr Grls; Hon Rl; NHS; Off Ade; Stu Cncl; 4-H; Pep Clb; Gym; MVP Of Girlsl Track Team 77; 8 Ltr 3 In Chrldng 3 In Track & 2 In Gymnastc; Jr Miss Pgnt; Indiana Univ.

RILEY, THERESA; Whiteland Community HS; Whiteland, IN; 5/200 Cl Rep Jr Cls; AFS; Girl Scts; Hon Rl; Hosp Ade; NHS; Quill & Scroll; Sct Actv; Stu Cncl; Ed Yrbk; Air Traffic Cntrl.

RILEY, TINA; Crothersville HS; Crothersville, IN; Chrh Wkr; Girl Scts; Hon Rl; Hosp Ade; Yth Flsp; Rptr Yrbk; Rptr Sch Nwsp; 4-H; FHA; Pep Clb; Univ; Nursing.

RILEY, TRACEY; Bellbrook HS; Bellbrook, OH; Band; Drm Bgl; Letter Bsktbl; GAA; Bus Schl; Bus.

RILLEMA, TAMMY; Reeths Puffer HS; Muskegon, MI; Band; Girl Scts; Hon Rl; Sct Actv; Pep Clb; C hrldng;.

RIMBACH, CHRISTIAN; Marion Catholic HS; Marion, OH; Boy Scts; Hon Rl; Jr NHS; NHS; Sct Actv; Ger Clb; 3rd Pl In Ut St Fair Organ Comp 78; Superio Pl Awd Marion Cnty Oh Sci Fair 79; Univ; Chem.

RINARD, JACQUELINE; Frontier HS; Rnrd Mls, OH; Band; Hon Rl; NHS; Stg Crw; Yrbk; Sci Clb; Coll; Lab Tech.

RINCK, TODD; Broad Ripple HS; Indianapolis, IN; 30/450 Cls Rep Frsh Cls; Chrs; Hon Rl; Jr NHS; NHS; Sch Mus; Sch Pl; Drama Clb; Ftbl; Trk; Hanover College.

RINCKEL, LORI; Mc Auley HS; Cinti, OH; Pres Aud/Vis; Pres Girl Scts; Hon Rl; NHS; Sch Mus; Sch Pl; Sct Actv; Stg Crw; Drama Clb; Lat Clb; Xavier Univ; Bio.

RINDLER, JOYCE; St Henry HS; St Henry, OH; Sec Soph Cls; Chrs; Hon Rl; Sec NHS; Stu Cncl; Yrbk; Rptr Sch Nwsp; FSA; Treas OEA; Coll; Banking.

RINDLER, JULIE; Archbishop Alter HS; Kettering, OH; 9/330 Cl Rep Jr Cls; Hon Rl; Treas NHS; Bsktbl; Letter Ten; Letter Trk; GAA; Univ Of Dayton; Medicine.

RINDY, JILL; Hubbard HS; Masury, OH; 40/333 Pres Frsh Cls; Cls Rep Soph Cls; Cl Rep Jr Cls; Chrs; Hon Rl; NHS; Off Ade; Sch Mus; Sch Pl; Stu Cncl; Univ; Law.

RINEFORT, ANNE; Terre Haute South Vigo HS; Terre Haute, IN; 105/630 Band; Girl Scts; Hon Rl; Y-Teens; Spn Clb; Trk; Ind Univ.

RINEHART, JANET; River Valley HS; Waldo, OH; 1/206 Cls Rep Frsh Cls; Sec Soph Cls; Sec Jr Cls; Val; Am Leg Aux Girls St; Hon Rl; Hosp Ade; Lbry Ade; Lit Mag; NHS; Ohio St Univ.

RINEHART, KATHY; Taylor Center HS; Taylor, MI; Chrs; Hon Rl; Sch Pl; Stg Crw; Drama Clb; Lat Clb; Trk; GAA; PPFtbl; Univ Of Michigan; Law Enforcement.

RINEHART, KOLLETTE; Chelsea HS; Chelsea, MI; Hon Rl; NHS; Off Ade; Stg Crw; Drama Clb; Letter Swmmng; Mgrs; Tmr; Univ; Theatre.

RINEHART, LISA; Fostoria HS; Fostoria, OH; Hon Rl; NHS; Bsktbl; Trk; AAUW Outstndg Ath Achvmnt 78; Fostoria Ath Boosters Hnr Awd 78; All Lg Vlybl Dist Bsktbl 78; Univ.

RINEHART, ROBERT; Lexington HS; Mansfield, OH; Chrh Wkr; Cmnty Wkr; Lbry Ade; Yth Flsp; 4-H; Ftbl; Trk; IM Sprt; 4-H Awd; God Cntry Awd; Univ; Comp Tech.

RINEHART, SUSAN; Shady Spring HS; Shady Spring, WV; Band; Chrh Wkr; Drm Mjrt; FCA; Hon Rl; NHS; Orch; Sch Pl; Drama Clb; Pep Clb; West Virginia Univ; Optometry.

RINER, EBBONIE; Martinsburg HS; Martinsburg, WV; 18/206 Band; Chrs; Chrh Wkr; Drl Tm; Hon Rl; JA; Lbry Ade; Orch; Sch Mus; Sch Pl; Univ; Comp Prog.

RINES, CATHERINE; Jay County HS; Portland, IN; Girl Scts; Hon Rl; Jr NHS; NHS; Yth Flsp; Y-Teens; Fr Clb; Mth Clb; Pep Clb; Sci Clb; Univ; Interior Decor.

RINEY, MARIANNE; Aquinas HS; Southgate, MI; Hon Rl; Stu Cncl; Pep Clb;.

RING, CHRISTOPHER; Woodsfield HS; Woodsfield, OH; 16/71 Stg Crw; Drama Clb; 4-H; Fr Clb; Mgrs;.

RING, KATHRYN; Lockland HS; Cincinnati, OH; 2/73 Pres Soph Cls; Pres Jr Cls; Band; Hon Rl; NHS; Off Ade; Stu Cncl; Drama Clb; Fr Clb; Letter Bsktbl; College; Aeronautical Engr.

RING, MARY T; Hawken HS; Shaker Hts, OH; 4/105 Chrs; Debate Tm; Girl Scts; Hon Rl; Natl Forn Lg; Pres PAVAS; Sch Mus; Sch Pl; Sct Actv; Stg Crw; College; Theater Arts.

RING, WILLIAM D; Arch Bishop Alter HS; Centerville, OH; 52/277 Aud/Vis; Chrh Wkr; Cmnty Wkr; Hon Rl; Sch Mus; Stg Crw; Rptr Yrbk; IM Sprt; Stage Crew Awd; Excalibur Awd; Univ Of Cincinnati; Engr.

RINGEISEN, KAROL; East Kentwood HS; Kentwood, MI; Debate Tm; JA; JA Awd; Grand Rapids Jr Coll; Mktg.

RINGER, TINA; Annapolis HS; Dearborn Hts, MI; Pres Frsh Cls; Girl Scts; Hon Rl; Stu Cncl; Yrbk; Letter Chrldng; Michigan State Univ; Elem Ed.

RINGLE, LORI; Lakeview HS; Battle Creek, MI; Cmp Fr Grls; Chrh Wkr; Hon Rl; Sci Clb; IM Sprt; College; Phys Ther.

RINGLEIN, JULIE C; Clio HS; Midland, MI; 7/450 Cls Rep Soph Cls; Band; Hon Rl; Jr NHS; Sch Pl; OEA; Letter Chrldng; Pres Awd; Voice Dem Awd; SUSC; Criminal Justice.

RINGS, KEVIN; Dublin HS; Dublin, OH; 3/156 Cls Rep Sr Cls; Band; Boy Scts; Hon Rl; Jr NHS; Stu Cncl; Lat Clb; Bsbl; IM Sprt; College; Pre Law.

RINGWALD, ANDY; Shawe Memorial HS; Madison, IN; 6/32 Am Leg Boys St; Hon Rl; NHS; Sch Nwsp; 4-H; Rose Hulman Inst Of Tech; Elec Engr.

RINGWALD, ROSE; Bishop Flaget HS; Chillicothe, OH; 4/40 Trs Soph Cls; Trs Jr Cls; Hon Rl; Sch Mus; Rptr Yrbk; Rptr Sch Nwsp; 4-H; Bsktbl; Letter Ten; College; Archt.

RINI, TONY; Clyde Sr HS; Clyde, OH; 15/200 Am Leg Boys St; Boy Scts; Hon Rl; Spn Clb; Bsktbl; Ftbl; Trk; Coll; Sci.

RININGER, SHARON; Green HS; N Canton, OH; Cls Rep Frsh Cls; Cls Rep Soph Cls; Chrs; Off Ade; Stu Cncl; Y-Teens; Pep Clb; Pom Pon; College.

RINK, MICHAEL; Clay HS; S Bend, IN; 49/430 Cls Rep Frsh Cls; Aud/Vis; Chrh Wkr; Cmnty Wkr; Hon Rl; Jr NHS; NHS; Sch Mus; Stg Crw; Stu Cncl; Slctcd Page Rep SB At Gnrl Assmbly 79; Mst Val Tennis Plyr Awd 78; Captn Hcky Tm; Univ; Bus Mgmt.

RINKE, DEAN; Capac HS; Capac, MI; Pres Jr Cls; Band; Boy Scts; Hon Rl; Stu Cncl; 4-H; FFA; Letter Bsbl; Letter Bsktbl; College; Architecture.

RINKE, GORDON; St Anne HS; Warren, MI; Boy Scts; Hon Rl; JA; Bsktbl; Letter Crs Cntry; Letter Trk; IM Sprt; Univ; Engr.

RINKE, JAMES; Inland Lakes HS; Indian River, MI; Hon Rl; Bsktbl; Ftbl; Mgrs; Northern Mic Univ.

RINKEL, TONY; Edgerton HS; Bryan, OH; 12/66 Am Leg Boys St; NHS; Spn Clb; Bsktbl; Letter Crs Cntry; Letter Ftbl; Letter Trk; Track MVP Jr 1978; Part Stae Track Meet 1977; Tri State Univ; Engr.

RINKER, CAROL; Perrysburg HS; Perrysburg, OH; Chrh Wkr; Girl Scts; Off Ade; Stg Crw; Yth Flsp; 4-H; Spn Clb; Capt Socr; 4-H Awd; Miami Univ; Advertising.

RINKER, GINA; Marion HS; Marion, IN; Girl Scts; Hosp Ade; Yth Flsp; 4-H; Ger Clb; Sci Clb; Parkvw Methodist Hosp Schl; Nursing.

RINKER, ROBIN; Perrysburg HS; Perrysburg, OH; Hon Rl; NHS; Pep Clb; Spn Clb; Mat Maids; Univ; Fshn Mdse.

RINKES, JEANNIE; Buckeye West HS; Cadiz, OH; Chrh Wkr; Drl Tm; Girl Scts; Hon Rl; NHS; Off Ade; Yth Flsp; Yrbk; Drama Clb; 4-H; Receptionist.

RINKEVICH, SHARON; Lapeer East Sr HS; Metamora, MI; Cls Rep Sr Cls; Chrh Wkr; NHS; 4-H; Spn Clb; Natl Merit SF; Michigan Competitive Schlrshp;.

RINNE, ANNE L; Tecumseh HS; Clinton, MI; Pres Jr Cls; Chrh Wkr; Girl Scts; Hon Rl; Sec Yth Flsp; Sch Nwsp; 4-H; Chrldng; Univ.

RINYO, ANITA; Madison HS; Madison, OH; 69/295 Band; Chrh Wkr; Drl Tm; Girl Scts; Hon Rl; Off Ade; Orch; Sch Pl; Pep Clb; Spn Clb; Univ; Dance.

RIORDAN, TIMOTHY; Grosse Ile HS; Grosse Ile, MI; 15/226 Debate Tm; Hon Rl; VP NHS; Sch Pl; Sch Nwsp; Drama Clb; Letter Bsktbl; Letter Ten; Coach Actv; Pres Awd; Hillsdale Coll; Pre Law.

RIPEPI, LINDA; Valley Forge HS; Parma, OH; 82/704 Cls Rep Frsh Cls; Cls Rep Soph Cls; Cl Rep Jr Cls; Trs Sr Cls; Chrs; Hon Rl; NHS; Stu Cncl; Rptr Sch Nwsp; Pep Clb; Baldwin Wallace Coll.

RIPLEY, MOLLY; Hackett HS; Kal, MI; VP Frsh Cls; Hon Rl; NHS; Off Ade; Spn Clb; Ten; IM Sprt; Mic State Univ; Data Proc.

RIPLEY, PAM; Gahanna Lincoln HS; Gahanna, OH; 206/440 Girl Scts; JA; Sch Pl; Sct Actv; Stg Crw; DECA; Drama Clb; Spn Clb; 1st Pl Fd Mrktng Cmttn DECM 1979; Columbus Tech Inst; Retail Mgmt.

RIPLEY, SCOTT; West Carrollton HS; W Carrollton, OH; 10/405 Pres Jr Cls; Hon Rl; Pres Jr NHS; NHS; Sch Mus; Stu Cncl; Sch Nwsp; Beta Clb; Ftbl; USAF; Astronautical Engr.

RIPPEL, LINDA; Rudyard HS; Rudyard, MI; 1/64 Pres Band; Chrs; Chrh Wkr; Hon Rl; NHS; Yrbk; Letter Bsktbl; Trk; Scr Kpr; Mi Comp Schlrshp 79; Rudyard Educ Assoc Schlrshp 79; Northern Michigan Univ.

RIPPETOE, BECKY; Dunbar HS; Dunbar, WV; Sec Jr Cls; Band; Chrs; Chrh Wkr; Hon Rl; NHS; Sch Mus; Yrbk; Civ Clb; Spn Clb; Univ; Jrnlsm.

RISCHAR, STEPHEN; Southrange HS; Columbiana, OH; Band; Boy Scts; Hon Rl; Sch Mus; Sct Actv; 4-H; Ger Clb; College; Elec Engr.

RISER, DIANE; Wheeling Central Cath HS; Wheeling, WV; Cls Rep Soph Cls; Chrh Wkr; Cmnty Wkr; Hon Rl; NHS; Sch Pl; FDA; Bsktbl; Ten; West Virginia Univ; Phys Therapy.

RISHEL, MICHELE; Vinton County HS; Mc Arthur, OH; Band; Drl Tm; Girl Scts; Hon Rl; Off Ade; Sct Actv; 4-H; Fr Clb; Shawnee State College; Dent.

RISHER, ANNE; Upper Wabash Voc Schl; Wabash, IN; 10/107 Band; Hon Rl; Treas NHS; Sch Pl; Yrbk; Drama Clb; Pres 4-H; Pres OEA; Pep Clb; Spn Clb; Manchester Coll; Acctg.

RISING, STEPHANIE; Waldron Area HS; Waldron, MI; Chrh Wkr; Hon Rl; NHS; Sch Pl; Yth Flsp; Rptr Yrbk; Ed Sch Nwsp; Pep Clb; Spn Clb; Hillsdale Coll.

RISK, KAREN; Mc Cutcheon HS; Wingate, IN; Band; Jr NHS; Sch Mus; Sec Stu Cncl; 4-H; Fr Clb; Pep Clb; Gym; Trk; Capt Chrldng; Univ.

RISMILLER, FAYE; Ansomia HS; New Weston, OH; 16/70 Band; Chrs; Chrh Wkr; Hon Rl; Stu Cncl; Yrbk; FHA; OEA; Spn Clb; Trk; Univ; Elem Ed.

RISNER, ALEX; Allen East HS; Lima, OH; Hon Rl; Sch Pl; Sprt Ed Sch Nwsp; Fr Clb; Bsktbl; Crs Cntry; Glf; Trk; Univ Of Cincinnati; Science Eng.

RISNER, HOLLY; Fostoria HS; Fostoria, OH; Aud/Vis; Hon Rl; Rptr Sch Nwsp; Sch Nwsp; Univ; World Hist.

RISNER, MELINDA; Carey HS; Carey, OH; 6/104 Val; Am Leg Aux Girls St; Band; Chrs; NHS; Y-Teens; Rptr Yrbk; Mth Clb; IM Sprt; Mas Awd; Wittenberg Univ; Chem.

RIST, BEVERLY; Alexander HS; Athens, OH; Hon Rl; NHS; Yrbk; Rptr Sch Nwsp; Pep Clb; Ohi Univ.

RISTEV, CHRISTINE; Washington HS; Massillon, OH; Am Leg Aux Girls St; Chrs; Hon Rl; Jr NHS; NHS; Off Ade; Fr Clb; Akron Univ; Engr.

RISTOWSKI, SUE; Centerline HS; Centerline, MI; Cls Rep Frsh Cls; Hon Rl; Lbry Ade; NHS; Spn Clb; Bsbl; Wayne St Univ; Law.

RITCHEY, J; Windham HS; Garrettsvll, OH; Sec Soph Cls; VP Jr Cls; VP Sr Cls; Chrh Wkr; Hon Rl; NHS; Pep Clb; Ohi State Univ; Dental Hygiene.

RITCHEY, JENNIFER; Norwayne HS; Creston, OH; Chrh Wkr; Yth Flsp; Pres FHA; Pep Clb; Univ; Dietician.

RITCHEY, JENNIFER; Windham HS; Garrettsville, OH; Sec Soph Cls; VP Jr Cls; VP Sr Cls; Chrh Wkr; Hon Rl; NHS; Drama Clb; Pep Clb; Spn Clb; Letter Chrldng; Ohio St Univ; Dental Hygnst.

RITCHEY, KAREN; Philo HS; Zanesville, OH; Band; Sec Chrs; Hon Rl; 4-H; Sec Ger Clb; Pep Clb; Spn Clb; Trk; GAA; Sec 4-H Awd; MAJVS; Floristry.

RITCHEY, KATHLEEN; West Branch HS; Salem, OH; FHA; Bsktbl; College; Teacher.

RITCHIE, EDWINA; James A Garfield HS; Garrettsville, OH; Chrh Wkr; Hon Rl; Sec Yth Flsp; Rptr Yrbk; VP Fr Clb; Univ Of Kentucky; Forestry.

RITCHIE, KIM; Franklin Central HS; Indianapolis, IN; 8/273 Band; Hon Rl; JA; Lbry Ade; NHS; Off Ade; Stg Crw; 4-H; Pres FTA; Crs Cntry; 79 In HS Rodeo Queen 79; 1st Pl Animal Evalutn Clinic 78; B Evans In Horse Awd Wnnr 79; Indiana Univ; Law.

RITCHIE, RANDALL; Harrison HS; Gladwin, MI; Pres Soph Cls; Cl Rep Jr Cls; Sch Pl; Stg Crw; Stu Cncl; Drama Clb; Bsbl; Chrldng; Cntrl Michigan Univ; St Trooper.

RITCHIE, SHANNON; Frontier HS; Brookston, IN; Sec Jr Cls; Girl Scts; Hon Rl; NHS; Pep Clb; Bsktbl; Chrldng; Ball State; Computer Programming.

RITCHIE, SHARON; Onsted HS; Onsted, MI; Band; Chrs; Chrh Wkr; Girl Scts; Hon Rl; Lbry Ade; Stg Crw; 4-H; Twrlr; Am Leg Awd; College; Elem Ed.

RITCHIE, THERESA G; Hedgesville HS; Hedgesville, WV; 12/121 Girl Scts; Hon Rl; Hosp Ade; Jr NHS; Lbry Ade; Sec NHS; Potomac St Coll; Comp Tech.

RITCHISON, TERRI J; Parkside HS; Jackson, MI; Cl Rep Jr Cls; Band; Girl Scts; Hon Rl; Orch; Sct Actv; Stu Cncl; Rptr Yrbk; Univ; Phys Ther.

RITENOUR, LIBBY; Whiteford HS; Ottawa Lake, MI; 3/93 Band; Pres NHS; Sch Mus; Sch Pl; Drama Clb; 4-H; Sci Clb; Alma College; Pre Med.

RITTBERGER, SHERRI; Philo HS; Zanesville, OH; Cls Rep Frsh Cls; Cls Rep Soph Cls; Cl Rep Jr Cls; Cls Rep Sr Cls; Chrs; Drl Tm; Hon Rl; Sch Mus; Stu Cncl; Ger Clb; Synchronized Swimming Awd; College.

RITTER, AMY; Kingswood School; Orchard Lk, MI; VP Jr Cls; Girl Scts; Hon Rl; Sch Mus; All Area Metro Team Hon Mntn For Sftbl 78 & 79; New Stdtn Wlcmng Comm 79; Univ.

RITTER, CAROL; Mc Comb HS; Mccomb, OH; Cls Rep Frsh Cls; VP Jr Cls; Pres Band; VP Chrs; Chrh Wkr; Hon Rl; Off Ade; Sch Mus; Sch Pl; Stu Cncl; Bluffton Coll; Health.

RITTER, DENNIS; Harrison HS; Lafayette, IN; Band; NHS; Sch Mus; Sch Pl; Letter Wrstlng; Mgrs; Pres Awd; Purdue Univ; Elect Engr.

RITTER, JENNIFER; Bishop Fenwick HS; Middletown, OH; Sec Sr Cls; Band; Hon Rl; JA; NHS; Sch Mus; Yrbk; Sch Nwsp; Christ Hosp Schl; Nursing.

RITTER, LAURA; New Haven HS; New Haven, IN; Cl Rep Jr Cls; Chrs; Hosp Ade; JA; Pol Wkr; Stu Cncl; Lat Clb; Sci Clb; JA Awd; Elec Pres Of Stu Council For Next Yr; College; Medicine.

RITTER, MARY J; Sandusky HS; Sandusky, OH; Band; Hon Rl; Univ; Health.

RITTER, RHONDA; Grandview Hts HS; Columbus, OH; Hon Rl; Drama Clb; Sci Clb; Spn Clb; Scr Kpr; Ctzn Of Month 79; Sec Athletc Offc 79; Genrl Schlshp Team 76 77 & 79; Capital Univ; Nursing.

RITTER, RICHARD; North Daviess HS; Washington, IN; 1/96 Hst Jr Cls; Hon Rl; Beta Clb; VP FFA; IM Sprt; Natl Merit Ltr; Purdue Univ; Agri Engr.

RITTERSPACH, BETH; Westerville South HS; Westerville, OH; 14/270 Am Leg Aux Girls St; Hon Rl; NHS; Sch Pl; Stg Crw; Pep Clb; PPFtbl; Bowling Green St Univ; Art.

RITTGERS, TIMOTHY; Fairborn Park Hills HS; Fairborn, OH; Band; Boy Scts; Chrh Wkr; Hon Rl; Sct Actv; Wright St Univ; Vet Med.

RITTINGER, MELYNN; Chillicothe HS; Chillic othe, OH; Band; Girl Scts; 4-H; 4-H Awd; Opt Clb Awd; Ohio Univ; Elem Educ.

RITZ, CARRIE; Bishop Donahue HS; Wheeling, WV; Sec Jr Cls; Chrh Wkr; Hon Rl; NHS; Stu Cncl; Yrbk; 4-H; Spn Clb; Art College; Advertising.

RITZ, EVELYN; Seneca E HS; Attica, OH; Chrs; Chrh Wkr; Hon Rl; Sch Pl; 4-H; Capt Bsktbl; Chrldng; Cit Awd; 4-H Awd; Voice Dem Awd; Factory Wkr.

RITZ, GEORGE; Trenton HS; Trenton, MI; 11/538 Hon Rl; Jr NHS; NHS; IM Sprt; Phi Beta Kappa 79; Awd For Acad Excllnc 79; Cert Of Recogntn 79; Michigan St Univ; Pre Vet.

RITZ, NANCY; Edison HS; Berlin Hts, OH; 42/190 Chrs; Girl Scts; Hon Rl; Jr NHS; NHS; Quill & Scroll; Sprt Ed Yrbk; Rptr Yrbk; Rptr Sch Nwsp; 4-H; Air Force.

RITZENTHALER, ERIC; Bishop Watterson HS; Columbus, OH; Ftbl; Letter Wrstlng; Scr Kpr; Ohio St Univ.

RITZER, JEAN; Harrison Comm HS; Harrison, MI; VP Jr Cls; Pres Sr Cls; Band; Drl Tm; Lbry Ade; Stu Cncl; Rptr Sch Nwsp; Chrldng; Pom Pon; Letter Sftbl; College; Social Work.

RITZI, CHERYL; Franklin Central HS; Indianapolis, IN; Off Ade; Y-Teens; 4-H; Pep Clb; Letter Bsktbl; Letter Trk; Ind State;journalism.

RIVARD, RANDAL; Negaunee HS; Negaunee, MI; Band;.

RIVARD, RAY; Mater Dei HS; Evansville, IN; Band; Boy Scts; Cmnty Wkr; Debate Tm; Hon Rl; Natl Forn Lg; Orch; Sch Mus; Sch Pl; Stg Crw; Ball St Univ; Bio.

RIVARD, RUSS; Mater Dei HS; Evansville, IN; Band; Debate Tm; Natl Forn Lg; Orch; Sch Mus; Sch Pl; Rptr Sch Nwsp; 4-H; Spn Clb; 4-H Awd; Indiana State Univ; Communications.

RIVAS, LAURA; Bishop Noll Inst; E Chicago, IN; 86/331 Cls Rep Frsh Cls; Cl Rep Jr Cls; Chrs; Drl Tm; Hon Rl; Sch Mus; Sch Pl; Stg Crw; Yrbk; Spn Clb; Hnr Roll 76 78; Whos Who 78; Univ; Chld Psych.

RIVELLO, DAVE; Struthers HS; Struthers, OH; 44/266 Band; Boy Scts; Hon Rl; Orch; Spn Clb; Cit Awd; College; Music.

RIVERA, MICHELLE; Catholic Central HS; Steubenville, OH; Hon Rl; NHS; Fr Clb; Pep Clb; Coll.

RIVERA, NANCY; Southview HS; Lorain, OH; 18/310 VP Soph Cls; Trs Jr Cls; Trs Sr Cls; Chrh Wkr; Hon Rl; NHS; Off Ade; Spn Clb; Inst Of Comp Mgmt; Data Processing.

RIVERA NIEVES, ANGIE R; Fr Joseph Wehrle Memrl HS; Columbus, OH; 5/111 VP Frsh Cls; VP Soph Cls; VP Jr Cls; Pres Sr Cls; Am Leg Aux Girls St; Hon Rl; NHS; Stu Cncl; Sch Nwsp; Rotary Awd; Ohio Dominican Univ; Spec Educ.

RIVERS, DOROTHY; Holly Sr HS; Davisburg, MI; Chrs; Chrh Wkr; Cmnty Wkr; Hon Rl; Lbry Ade; NHS; Sch Mus; Rptr Yrbk; Yrbk; Ed Sch Nwsp; Central Michigan Univ; Jrnlsm.

RIVERS, TERESA; Negaunee HS; Negaunee, MI; Band; Chrs; Chrh Wkr; Hon Rl; Orch; Bethel Coll; Bio.

RIVET, DENISE; John Glenn HS; Bay City, MI; 19/337 Cls Rep Soph Cls; Cl Rep Jr Cls; Cls Rep Sr Cls; Hon Rl; NHS; Stu Cncl; Fr Clb; Swmmng; Scr Kpr; Tmr; Delta College; Pre Phrmcy.

RIVET, SUSAN; All Saints Central HS; Bay City, MI; Cls Rep Soph Cls; Cl Rep Jr Cls; Sec Sr Cls; Hon Rl; Jr NHS; NHS; Sch Mus; Stg Crw; Stu Cncl; Univ; Phys Ther.

RIVETTE, CLARENCE; Arthur Hill HS; Saginaw, MI; Trs Sr Cls; Band; Chrh Wkr; Stu Cncl; Pep Clb; Western Michigan Univ; Poli Sci.

RIVETTI _III, LOUIE; Greenville HS; Greenville, OH; 1/332 Val; Val; Pres NHS; Rptr Sch Nwsp; Fr Clb; Pres Lat Clb; DAR Awd; Univ Of Notre Dame; Theology.

RIVIR, KELLY; Huntington North HS; Huntington, IN; Jr NHS; Stu Cncl; Yth Flsp; 4-H; Pep Clb; Chrldng; GAA; Pom Pon; 4-H Awd; College; Business.

RIX, JAMES; Park Hills HS; Fairborn, OH; 56/350 Cls Rep Frsh Cls; Boy Scts; Chrs; Hon Rl; Mdrgl; Stu Cncl; Spn Clb; Crs Cntry; Wrstlng; College; Med.

RIZER, MARY; Chesterton HS; Chesterton, IN; 7/454 Chrh Wkr; Hon Rl; NHS; Quill & Scroll; Ed Yrbk; Fr Clb; Bsktbl; Gym; Letter Ten; Letter GAA; Coll.

RIZK, BOB; Groves HS; Birmingham, MI; Boy Scts; Capt Bsbl; Letter Ftbl; IM Sprt; Scr Kpr; Univ.

RIZOR, TRACY; Northport HS; Northport, MI; Cls Rep Soph Cls; Pres Sr Cls; AFS; Am Leg Aux Girls St; Chrs; Chrh Wkr; Hosp Ade; Sch Mus; Sch Pl; Stg Crw; Girls St Michigan At Olivet Coll; Music Schlrshp All St HS Choir Interlochen; Coll; Music.

RIZZA, ANNA; Chippewa Valley HS; Mt Clemens, MI; Cmnty Wkr; Hon Rl; Off Ade; Sch Nwsp; Eng Clb; Fr Clb; Ger Clb; Mth Clb; Spn Clb; Hockey; Voc Schl; Lang.

RIZZO, CHRIS; Southeast HS; Diamond, OH; 1/150 Pres Sr Cls; Boy Scts; Chrh Wkr; Hon Rl; Lbry Ade; Pres NHS; Quill & Scroll; Sch Mus; Sch Pl; Sct Actv; Akron Univ; Med.

RIZZO, MICHAEL; Southeast Local HS; Diamond, OH; Boy Scts; Chrh Wkr; Hon Rl; NHS; Sct Actv; Ftbl; Trk; Wrstlng; Kent Univ; Wildlife Mgmt.

RIZZUTO, PAMELA; Brunswick HS; Brunswick, OH; Cls Rep Frsh Cls; Band; Hst Frsh Cls; Sec Girl Scts; Hon Rl; Lit Mag; NHS; Sct Actv; Yth Flsp; Univ.

ROACH, BETSY; Reitz Memorial HS; Evansville, IN; Band; Chrh Wkr; Cmnty Wkr; Drm Mjrt; Girl Scts; Hon Rl; Lbry Ade; Orch; Red Cr Ade; Sch Mus; Univ; Marketing.

ROACH, DENISE; Bloomfield HS; Bloomfield, IN; Band; Chrh Wkr; Girl Scts; Hon Rl; Sct Actv; Pep Clb;.

ROACH, DIANA; Glen Este HS; Cincinnati, OH; 23/505 Chrs; Chrh Wkr; Hon Rl; NHS; Sch Mus; Sch Pl; Drama Clb; Clermont Univ; Comp Prog.

ROACH, JULIE; East Lansing HS; East Lansing, MI; 64/352 Chrs; Hon Rl; NHS; Drama Clb; Spn Clb; Bsktbl; Trk; IM Sprt; Natl Merit Schl; Pres Awd; Mi Comp Schlrshp 79; Michigan St Univ; Vet Med.

ROACH, MARCIA; Ben Davis HS; Indianapolis, IN; 8/834 Pres Chrs; Hon Rl; Hosp Ade; NHS; Sch Mus; Sec Fr Clb; Indiana Univ; Sci.

ROACH, PAULA; Rock Hill HS; Ironton, OH; Band; Hon Rl; Beta Clb; Mth Clb; Sci Clb; Spn Clb; Bsktbl; Chrldng; GAA;.

ROACH, PHIL; Moeller HS; Loveland, OH; Hon Rl; NHS; Ftbl; Trk; College.

ROACH, RENEE; North Central HS; Indianapolis, IN; Hon Rl; Jr NHS; NHS; Pol Wkr; Rptr Sch Nwsp; 4-H; Fr Clb; Ger Clb; Univ; Foreign Lang.

ROACH, VERONICA; Linton Stockton Jr Sr HS; Linton, IN; Am Leg Aux Girls St; Chrh Wkr; Hon Rl; Off Ade; VP Ger Clb; Pep Clb; Cit Awd; Schlrshp 76; Purdue Univ; Meteorlgy.

ROACH JR, GERALD; Gallia Academy HS; Gallipolis, OH; Chrs; Chrh Wkr; Mdrgl; Sch Mus; Stu Cncl; Pres 4-H; Pres Sci Clb; Letter Ftbl; Letter Trk; 4-H Awd; Ctznshp Shortcourse 79; Nalt 4 H Congrss 79; Ohio St Univ; Pre Vet Med.

ROALEF, DAVID R; Chaminade Julienne HS; Dayton, OH; 27/272 Hon Rl; Letter Ten; Natl Merit SF; Univ Of Dayton; Elec.

ROAN, KELLY; Washington HS; Massillon, OH; Chrs; Hon Rl; Y-Teens; Drama Clb; Pep Clb; Spn Clb; Mgrs; Tmr; Univ; Art.

ROARK, DARLENE; Lowell HS; Lowell, IN; 66/258 Hon Rl; Rptr Sch Nwsp; Pres 4-H; FHA; Mat Maids; 4-H Awd; 4 H Animal Sci Wrkshp & St Jr Ldr Conference; State Finalist In Miss United Teenager Pageant; Purdue Univ.

ROARK, JANICE; Brookville HS; Brookville, IN; 6/200 Band; Chrh Wkr; Hon Rl; NHS; Sch Pl; Stg Crw; Sch Nwsp; Purdue Univ; Law.

ROAT, TERESA; Marian HS; Cincinnati, OH; Girl Scts; Hon Rl; JA; Jr NHS; NHS; Spn Clb; College; Early Childhood Educ.

ROBARE, CONNIE; William G Mather HS; Munising, MI; 14/109 Sec Sr Cls; Band; Chrh Wkr; NHS; Sch Pl; Stu Cncl; Ed Yrbk; Rptr Sch Nwsp; Cit Awd; Northern Mic Univ; Bus Admin.

ROBARGE, MICHAEL; North Muskegon HS; North Muskegon, MI; 16/116 Hon Rl; Trk; IM Sprt; Muskegon Community College; Compsci.

ROBB, KRISTEN; Walled Lake Central HS; Orchard Lake, MI; Cl Rep Jr Cls; Band; Hon Rl; Sch Mus; Stg Crw; Stu Cncl; Ger Clb; Swmmng; Twrlr; College; Social Work.

ROBBINS, ANN; Holt Sr HS; Lansing, MI; Band; Girl Scts; Hosp Ade; Jr NHS; 4-H; Hope Coll.

ROBBINS, BRENT; Ben Davis HS; Indianapolis, IN; Band; Ivy Tech; Auto Mech.

ROBBINS, CARLA; Elmwood HS; Cygnet, OH; Band; Chrs; Hon Rl; Sch Pl; 4-H; 4-H Awd; Kiwan Awd;.

ROBBINS, CYNTHIA; Huntington East HS; Huntington, WV; Chrs; Chrh Wkr; Hon Rl; Mdrgl; Y-Teens; Lat Clb; Pep Clb; College; Inter Dec.

ROBBINS, DARRYL R; Terre Haute South Vigo HS; Terre Haute, IN; Rptr Sch Nwsp; Sch Nwsp; Ger Clb; Rdo Clb; Swmmng; Indiana St Univ; Music.

ROBBINS, DEBBIE; Westfield Washington HS; Westfield, IN; Cls Rep Sr Cls; Hon Rl; NHS; Sch Mus; Stu Cncl; Drama Clb; 4-H; Spn Clb; College; Pre Med.

ROBBINS, LISA; Mancelona HS; Mancelona, MI; 9/82 Sec Frsh Cls; Sec Jr Cls; VP Sr Cls; Trs Sr Cls; Band; Drm Mjrt; NHS; Eastern Mic Univ; Law.

ROBBINS, MARILYN; St Marys Cathedral HS; Highland Park, MI; Chrh Wkr; Hon Rl; Lbry Ade; Yrbk; Rptr Sch Nwsp; Spn Clb; Pom Pon; Watson Schlrshp 79; Newspaper Awd 79; Foreign Lang Day Awd 1st Pl 79; Hall Monitor; Kitchen Aide; Coll; Elem Educ.

ROBBINS, MARK; Prairie Hts Cmnty HS; La Grange, IN; 8/130 Hon Rl; NHS; Yrbk; FFA; Letter Ftbl; Trk; Mgrs; Cit Awd; Ivy Tech Schl; Auto Mech.

ROBBINS, MARK; Greenville Sr HS; Greenville, OH; Hon Rl; Yth Flsp; DECA; Key Clb; Wrstlng; Univ; Bus Mgmt.

ROBBINS, MARK K; Morgantown HS; Morgantown, WV; 15/400 Chrs; Debate Tm; Hon Rl; Sct Actv; Yth Flsp; Fr Clb; Treas Mth Clb; Crs Cntry; Trk; Natl Merit SF; Wittenberg Univ; Med.

ROBBINS, RICK; Daleville HS; Muncie, IN; Band; Hon Rl; Sprt Ed Yrbk; Letter Glf; Ball St Univ; Archt Design.

ROBBINS, RUTH; Yale HS; Goodells, MI; 17/170 Sec Jr Cls; Chrh Wkr; Hon Rl; Stu Cncl; 4-H; Pep Clb; Trk; Chrldng; Dnfth Awd; Varsity Letter For Cheerleading; College; Busns Mgmt.

ROBBINS, SARAH; Brookville HS; Brookville, IN; 13/200 Cls Rep Soph Cls; Band; Hon Rl; NHS; Off Ade; Pep Clb; Letter Trk; GAA; Eastern Kentucky Univ; Nursing.

ROBBINS, TANYA; North Putnam HS; Roachdale, IN; Sec Jr Cls; FCA; Hon Rl; OEA; Spn Clb; Bsktbl; Trk; Vin Univ; Acctng.

ROBECK, BRIAN; Grant HS; Grant, MI; Band; Boy Scts; Chrh Wkr; FCA; Yth Flsp; Letter Ftbl; Capt Wrstlng; Coach Actv; Scr Kpr;.

ROBEL, CONNIE M; Swan Valley HS; Saginaw, MI; 30/188 Jr NHS; NHS; Chrldng; Pom Pon; Saginaw Valley Univ; Bus.

ROBERDS, ANGIE; Bishop Fenwick HS; Middletown, OH; Drl Tm; Girl Scts; Hon Rl; Sch Pl; FBLA; Miami Univ; Sec.

ROBERSON, JUDY; Saginaw HS; Saginaw, MI; Pres Frsh Cls; Hon Rl; Jr NHS; Ed Yrbk; Ed Sch Nwsp; Letter Bsktbl; Trk; IM Sprt; Natl Merit Ltr; Black Hons Convocaton Awd 77; Jackson St Univ; Comp Progr.

ROBERSON, SHARON; Perry Central HS; Leopold, IN; Chrh Wkr; Drl Tm; Girl Scts; Hon Rl; Lbry Ade; Sch Pl; Stg Crw; Drama Clb; 4-H; Fr Clb; Univ; CPA.

ROBERSON, TERESA; John Hay HS; Cleveland, OH; Sec Jr Cls; Cls Rep Sr Cls; Hon Rl; Jr NHS; NHS; Stu Cncl; Bsktbl; Swmmng; Trk; Cit Awd; Art Inst Of Atlanta; Pro Photog.

ROBERSON, VERNON R; Belleville HS; Belleville, MI; Hon Rl; Cit Awd; Schlstc Achvmnt 78; Perfect Attndnc 75 78; Cleary Coll; Acctg.

ROBERTO, CHERYL; Ravenna HS; Ravenna, OH; 11/317 Am Leg Aux Girls St; Band; Girl Scts; Hon Rl; Sec NHS; Pol Wkr; Stu Cncl; Yrbk; Fr Clb; Lat Clb; Kent St Univ; Law.

ROBERTS, AMBER; Newton HS; Pleasant Hl, OH; VP Frsh Cls; VP Soph Cls; Pres Jr Cls; Band; Drl Tm; FCA; Hon Rl; Stg Crw; Stu Cncl; Drama Clb; College.

ROBERTS, B; Rocky River HS; Rocky River, OH; Chrh Wkr; Girl Scts; Hon Rl; Jr NHS; NHS; Sch Mus; Swmmng; College; Nursing.

ROBERTS, BART; Bishop Lvers HS; Ft Wayne, IN; Hon Rl; Key Clb; Ten; Ind Univ.

ROBERTS, BETH; Norwood HS; Norwood, OH; 14/378 Chrs; Chrh Wkr; Cmnty Wkr; Hon Rl; Jr NHS; NHS; Sch Mus; Pep Clb; Swmmng; N Kentucky Univ; Acctg.

ROBERTS, BETH; Circleville HS; Riverton, WV; 6/30 Pres Sr Cls; Chrs; Chrh Wkr; Cmnty Wkr; Girl Scts; Hon Rl; Lbry Ade; Sch Mus; Ed Yrbk; Rptr Sch Nwsp; Univ Of West Virginia; Psych.

ROBERTS, BILL; Harper Creek HS; Battle Creek, MI; 24/244 Drl Tm; Hon Rl; NHS; Letter Crs Cntry; Letter Trk; Univ; Aeronautical Engr.

ROBERTS, CATHY; Stow Sr HS Lakeview Bldg; Stow, OH; Band; Drm Bgl; Hon Rl; Lit Mag; Off Ade; Pol Wkr; Pres Y-Teens; Fr Clb; VP OEA; VP Pep Clb; Needs Assessment Comm 76; 1st US Twirling Team Went To Europe For Exhbtrs 77; Akron Univ; Legal Sec Sci.

ROBERTS, CHERYL; Tri Jr Sr HS; Lewisville, IN; 8/95 Trs Soph Cls; Sec Jr Cls; Sec Sr Cls; Sec Band; Hon Rl; Treas JA; Lbry Ade; NHS; Sch Pl; Stu Cncl; Indiana Univ; Acctg.

ROBERTS, CHRISTOPHER; Jesup W Scott HS; Toledo, OH; Cls Rep Frsh Cls; Cls Rep Soph Cls; Cl Rep Jr Cls; Cls Rep Sr Cls; Hon Rl; JA; NHS; Mth Clb; JA Awd; Univ; Bus Econ.

ROBERTS, CLARK; Wilmington Sr HS; Wilmington, OH; 18/365 Pres Sr Cls; Am Leg Boys St; Band; NHS; Yth Flsp; 4-H; Capt Bsbl; IM Sprt; 4-H Awd; Lion Awd; Ohio St Univ; Agri Bus Admin.

ROBERTS, CONNIE S; East Clinton HS; Sabina, OH; 29/103 Band; Debate Tm; Hon Rl; Lbry Ade; Stg Crw; Stu Cncl; FTA; Pep Clb; Trk; IM Sprt; Southern Ohio Coll; Med Sec.

ROBERTS, CYNTHIA; Mount Vernon Academy; Hinsdale, IL; Chrs; Chrh Wkr; Hon Rl; Mdrgl; Sch Mus; Sdlty; Yth Flsp; Yrbk; IM Sprt; Southern Missionary Coll; Acctg.

ROBERTS, CYNTHIA; Charles Stewart Mott 'S; Warren, MI; 46/650 Hon Rl; Spn Clb; Opt Clb Awd; Kalamazoo College; Inter Relations.

ROBERTS, DAN; Ross HS; Hamilton, OH; 1/230 Pres Frsh Cls; Cls Rep Frsh Cls; Cls Rep Soph Cls; Pres Sr Cls; Cls Rep Sr Cls; Am Leg Boys St; Hon Rl; NHS; Pol Wkr; Stu Cncl; Mbr Of Council Of Pres 79; Univ; Newspaper Jrnlsm.

ROBERTS, DAVID; Meadowbrook HS; Cumberland, OH; Hon Rl; 4-H; FFA; 4-H Awd;.

ROBERTS, DEIDRA; Carson City Crystal HS; Carson City, MI; Sec Jr Cls; Band; Cmp Fr Grls; FCA; Hon Rl; NHS; Stu Cncl; Yth Flsp; FHA; Pep Clb; Spanish Honor Soc; Grand Rapids Bapt Coll; Elem Ed.

ROBERTS, DERINDA; Chadsey HS; Detroit, MI; Chrh Wkr; Hon Rl; Off Ade; Yth Flsp; Rptr Yrbk; Yrbk; Univ Of Mic; Med.

ROBERTS, DIANE; Madison Heights HS; Anderson, IN; Hon Rl; NHS; Quill & Scroll; Sec Stu Cncl; Rptr Yrbk; Letter Swmmng; Ball State Univ; Spec Educ.

ROBERTS, EDWARD; Lutheran East HS; Detroit, MI; Hon Rl; NHS; Rptr Sch Nwsp; Ger Clb; Mgrs; Pom Pon; Univ.

ROBERTS, JAMES; Heath HS; Heath, OH; Pres Frsh Cls; Cls Rep Frsh Cls; Pres Soph Cls; Cls Rep Soph Cls; Pres Jr Cls; Cl Rep Jr Cls; Pres Sr Cls; Treas FCA; Hon Rl; NHS; Ldrshp Awd; Selected For Camp Enterprise By Rotary Club; Coll; Engr.

ROBERTS, JANICE; Ubly Community HS; Minden City, MI; 4/101 Cls Rep Frsh Cls; Hon Rl; NHS; Red Cr Ade; Stg Crw; Rptr Yrbk; Rptr Sch Nwsp; Sec FHA; PPFtbl; Central Mic Univ.

ROBERTS, JEFF; Madison Comprehensive HS; Mansfield, OH; 27/452 Band; Chrs; Chrh Wkr; Hon Rl; Lbry Ade; NHS; Orch; Sch Pl; Ger Clb; Spn Clb; Univ Of Akron; Music Educ.

ROBERTS, JEFFREY; Grandview Heights HS; Columbus, OH; 2/116 Sal; Hon Rl; Pres Jr NHS; Treas NHS; Sch Pl; Stg Crw; Stu Cncl; Drama Clb; Lat Clb; Univ; Comp Sci.

ROBERTS, JUDY; Washington HS; Washington, IN; 19/216 Band; Hon Rl; Lat Clb; Pep Clb; College; Busns.

ROBERTS, KEITH; Hamilton Southeastern HS; Fortville, IN; Glf; Swmmng; Wrstlng;.

ROBERTS, KIMBERLE; Roosevelt HS; Gary, IN; 21/525 Chrs; NHS; Spn Clb; Schlrshp Awd Serv Awd & Madrigal Singers Awd 79; Hoosier Schlr Schlstc Excllnc & Hon Grad Cert 79; Indiana Univ; Corp Law.

ROBERTS, KIMBERLY; Webster Cnty HS; Webster Springs, WV; Band; Chrh Wkr; Hon Rl; Yrbk; 4-H; Sci Clb; Letter Trk; 4-H Awd; Fairmont St Coll; Nursing.

ROBERTS, LINDA; Rockford Sr HS; Belmont, MI; 19/365 Cls Rep Frsh Cls; Cls Rep Soph Cls; Cl Rep Jr Cls; Pres Sr Cls; Hon Rl; NHS; Pol Wkr; Stu Cncl; Fr Clb; Pep Clb; G F Rounds Schlrshp Fund Awd 79; Rkfd Bd Of Ed Krause Stu Schlrshp; Schlrshp From W Mi Dent Ed Soc 79; Grand Rapids Jr Coll; Dent Hygnst.

ROBERTS, LINDA; Madison Comp HS; Mansfield, OH; Chrh Wkr; Orch; Ger Clb; Am Leg Awd; Alternate For Schl Academic Challenge Team; College.

ROBERTS, LOIS ANN; North Ridgeville HS; N Ridgeville, OH; Hon Rl; Yrbk; Sec DECA; Univ; Bus Mgmt.

ROBERTS, MADOLYN; Teays Valley HS; Ashville, OH; 9/210 Trs Frsh Cls; Pres Soph Cls; Am Leg Aux Girls St; Band; Pres Chrs; Debate Tm; FCA; Girl Scts; Hon Rl; NHS; Ohio St Univ.

ROBERTS, MARK P; Clare HS; Clare, MI; 8/128 Band; Chrh Wkr; Cmnty Wkr; Hon Rl; NHS; Southeastern Coll; Bilingual Elem.

ROBERTS, MARY E; Jane Addams Vocational HS; Cleveland, OH; Cl Rep Jr Cls; Chrs; Chrh Wkr; Cmnty Wkr; Hon Rl; JA; Stu Cncl; OEA; Chrldng; Cit Awd; College; Law.

ROBERTS, MELANIE; Warren Central HS; Indpls, IN; Chrs; Chrh Wkr; Girl Scts; Hon Rl; Hosp Ade; Sch Mus; Sch Pl; Pep Clb; Spn Clb; JA Awd; Ind Cntrl; Nursing.

ROBERTS, PAM; Jonesville HS; Jonesville, MI; 1/80 Pres Jr Cls; Band; Hon Rl; NHS; Stu Cncl; Rptr Sch Nwsp; 4-H; Pep Clb; Trk; Chrldng; English & Health Ed Awds; College; Acctg.

ROBERTS, PATTY; Nitro HS; Nitro, WV; Band; Hon Rl; Jr NHS; Off Ade; Sch Pl; Sct Actv; Drama Clb; Spn Clb; College; Medicine.

ROBERTS, PENNY; Croswell Lexington HS; Croswell, MI; Hst Jr Cls; Chrs; Hon Rl; NHS; Yrbk; Rptr Sch Nwsp; DECA; Voc Schl.

ROBERTS, RADELL; Shelby HS; Shelby, OH; Band; Chrs; Chrh Wkr; Hon Rl; Sch Pl; Yth Flsp; Rptr Sch Nwsp; Sch Nwsp; Drama Clb; Lat Clb; College.

ROBERTS, RITA; Scott HS; Foster, WV; Band; Chrh Wkr; Hon Rl; Drama Clb; Pep Clb; Annual Hon Banquet; GENESIS Performing Arts Prog; ACT Play Prod; Univ; Music.

ROBERTS, THEODORE; Madison Comprehensive HS; Mansfield, OH; 24/452 Cl Rep Jr Cls; Chrh Wkr; NHS; Orch; Sch Pl; Stu Cncl; Ger Clb; Ashland College; Music.

ROBERTS, VICKIE; Fulton HS; Perrinton, MI; Band; Chrs; FFA; Univ; Agri.

ROBERTS, WADE; Breckenridge Jr Sr HS; Breckenridge, MI; Debate Tm; Hon Rl; Yth Flsp; Yrbk; Rptr Sch Nwsp; 4-H; VP FFA; Letter Wrstlng; 4-H Awd; Michigan St Univ; Ag.

ROBERTS, WILDA; Edgewood HS; Spencer, IN; Band; Chrs; Hosp Ade; Lbry Ade; Off Ade; 4-H; Bus Schl; Bus.

ROBERTSON, ABEL; Rocky River HS; Rocky River, OH; Chrh Wkr; Hon Rl; Yth Flsp; Capt Swmmng; Scr Kpr; Case Western Univ.

ROBERTSON, BARBARA; Badin HS; Hamilton, OH; 21/215 Cls Rep Soph Cls; Trs Jr Cls; Cls Rep Sr Cls; Hon Rl; Stu Cncl; Rptr Yrbk; Fr Clb; Trk; IM Sprt; Univ Of Cincinnati; Nursing.

ROBERTSON, BRENDA; South Panola HS; Batesville, MS; Cl Rep Jr Cls; Chrh Wkr; Hon Rl; Stu Cncl; Rptr Sch Nwsp; Fr Clb; FBLA; FHA; FSA; Univ Of Miss; Journalism.

ROBERTSON, DALE; George Washington HS; Charleston, WV; Am Leg Boys St; Hon Rl; Jr NHS; Mod UN; Stu Cncl; Rptr Sch Nwsp; Key Clb; Letter Bsktbl; IM Sprt; Scheduling Team; College; Archt.

ROBERTSON, DARRELL A; Garfield Sr HS; Hamilton, OH; 8/350 Chrs; Cmnty Wkr; Hon Rl; Jr NHS; NHS; Fr Clb; Sci Clb; Ftbl; Univ; Vet Med.

ROBERTSON, DONNA; Morrice HS; Morrice, MI; Band; Chrh Wkr; Hon Rl; Natl Forn Lg; NHS; Off Ade; Yth Flsp; Rptr Yrbk; Rptr Sch Nwsp; Bsktbl; Voc Schl.

ROBERTSON, JANET; Springfield North HS; Springfield, OH; Chrs; Hon Rl; Pol Wkr; Sch Mus; Sch Pl; Stu Cncl; Fr Clb; Pep Clb; Swmmng; College; Cmmrcl Art.

ROBERTSON, JUDITH D; Fairfield Sr HS; Hamilton, OH; Cls Rep Frsh Cls; Cls Rep Soph Cls; Cl Rep Jr Cls; Band; Drl Tm; Quill & Scroll; Stu Cncl; Rptr Sch Nwsp; Fr Clb; Cit Awd; Miss Fort Hamilton; Mc Alpins Fashion Board; Principals Cabinet; College; Journalism.

ROBERTSON, JULIE A; Belpre HS; Parkersburg, WV; Pres Jr Cls; VP Sr Cls; Hon Rl; Hosp Ade; Off Ade; Sprt Ed Sch Nwsp; Eng Clb; Trk; 4-H Awd; Pres Awd; Exec Awd Diplomat Awd Stateswoman Awd & Ambassador Awd;.

ROBERTSON, KIMBERLY; Fairmont HS; Fairmont, WV; 11/235 Chrh Wkr; Hon Rl; Hosp Ade; Off Ade; Yth Flsp; Rptr Sch Nwsp; Sch Nwsp; College; Nursing.

ROBERTSON, LINDON; De Kalb HS; Auburn, IN; 18/283 Am Leg Boys St; Treas JA; Natl Forn Lg; NHS; Treas Stu Cncl; Ger Clb; Letter Trk; Univ; Law.

ROBERTSON, LORI; Pike Central HS; Petersburg, IN; 13/192 Trs Frsh Cls; Hst Soph Cls; Trs Jr Cls; Band; Chrs; Chrh Wkr; Drl Tm; Girl Scts; Hon Rl; Jr NHS; Olivet Nazarene Coll; Bus.

ROBERTSON, MARK; Madeira HS; Cincinnati, OH; 10/169 Boy Scts; Hon Rl; NHS; Red Cr Ade; ROTC; Lat Clb; Spn Clb; Ftbl; Letter Ten; Rotary Awd; Xavier Univ; Bus.

ROBERTSON, NANETTE; Edgewood HS; Kingsville, OH; 24/260 AFS; Chrs; Hon Rl; NHS; Y-Teens; Chrldng; Am Leg Awd; Ohi State Univ; Phys Ther.

ROBERTSON, PAIGE; Whitefish Twp HS; Paradise, MI; Trs Sr Cls; Hon Rl; Sch Pl; Stu Cncl; Yrbk; Bsktbl; Capt Chrldng; Univ; Liberal Arts.

ROBERTSON, RANDALL; North HS; Evansville, IN; 9/340 Chrs; Chrh Wkr; Hon Rl; Natl Forn Lg; NHS; Opt Clb Awd; Univ Of Evansville.

ROBERTSON, ROBYN; Buffalo HS; Huntington, WV; 15/102 Band; Chrh Wkr; Girl Scts; Hon Rl; Off Ade; Treas Red Cr Ade; Sch Pl; Y-Teens; Mas Awd;.

ROBERTSON, ROLAND L; Wheeling Park HS; Wheeling, WV; Am Leg Boys St; Aud/Vis; Band; Hon Rl; NHS; Letter Ftbl; Letter Trk; IM Sprt; Am Leg Awd; Marshall Univ; Dent.

ROBERTSON, STACY; Henryville HS; Henryville, IN; 12/76 Sec Soph Cls; Hon Rl; NHS; Stu Cncl; Ed

Sch Nwsp; 4-H; FHA; FTA; Pep Clb; Spn Clb; Univ.

ROBERTSON, SUSAN J; Marlington HS; Alliance, OH; 17/280 Cmnty Wkr; Girl Scts; Hon Rl; Hosp Ade; Lbry Ade; NHS; Off Ade; Sch Mus; Sct Actv; Yrbk; Univ Of Akron; Bus Admin.

ROBERTSON, TAMRA; Wayne Memorial HS; Wayne, MI; Cls Rep Frsh Cls; Aud/Vis; Chrs; Chrh Wkr; Girl Scts; Hon Rl; Hosp Ade; NHS; Stu Cncl; Spn Clb; Henry Ford Comm Coll; Sci.

ROBESON, BRYAN; Ontonagon Area HS; Ontonagon, MI; 12/100 Boy Scts; Chrh Wkr; Hon Rl; Lbry Ade; NHS; Sch Pl; Sct Actv; Yth Flsp; Drama Clb; Letter Ftbl; Upr Mich Winter Olympics Silver Medal In Volleyball 78; Michigan Tech Univ; Elec Engr.

ROBEY, VERNA; Lincoln HS; Shinnston, WV; Am Leg Aux Girls St; Hon Rl; Hosp Ade; Jr NHS; NHS; Pol Wkr; Fr Clb; Sci Clb; Part In Harrison County Math Field Day 76; West Virginia Univ; Mech Engr.

ROBIE, VERONICA; Lake Catholic HS; Mentor, OH; Chrs; Hon Rl; Hosp Ade; Sch Mus; Chrldng; PPFtbl; Schlstc Art Awd 77; Annl Schl Awds Contst For United Way 1st Pl 79; Univ.

ROBINETTE, CYNTHIA; Ctrl Bapt HS; Cincinnati, OH; Trs Soph Cls; Trs Jr Cls; Sec Chrh Wkr; NHS; Off Ade; Sch Mus; Sch Pl; Letter Chrldng; Scr Kpr; Cedarville Coll; Nursing.

ROBINETTE, DEANN; Shelby HS; Shelby, OH; Chrs; Hon Rl; Lat Clb; Letter Bsbl; Bus.

ROBINETTE, DUANA K; Garfield Sr HS; Hamilton, OH; Sec Frsh Cls; NHS; Sch Pl; Yth Flsp; Y-Teens; Drama Clb; OEA; Bsbl; Bsktbl; Chrldng; Hustle Awd Sftbl; Best Actress Theatre; English Academic Medal; College; Legal Sec.

ROBINS, CAREY; Crestview HS; New Waterford, OH; 22/74 Sec Sr Cls; Band; Cmp Fr Grls; Chrh Wkr; Cmnty Wkr; Hon Rl; Sch Pl; Yth Flsp; Rptr Yrbk; 4-H; Youngstown St Univ; Music Educ.

ROBINS, CARY; Oak Park HS; Oak Park, MI; Aud/Vis; Hon Rl; Lbry Ade; Lit Mag; Pol Wkr; Sch Pl; Stg Crw; Drama Clb; FDA; Cit Awd; Univ Of Mich; Engr.

ROBINSON, AMY; Ashtabula HS; Ashtabula, OH; 9/208 AFS; Band; Chrh Wkr; Hon Rl; NHS; Sch Mus; Stg Crw; Pres Yth Flsp; Yrbk; Ohio Wesleyan Univ.

ROBINSON, ANDREW; Mona Shores HS; Muskegon, MI; Band; Treas Chrh Wkr; Hon Rl; Mod UN; NHS; Olivet Nazarene Coll.

ROBINSON, ANGELA; Ursuline HS; Youngstown, OH; 69/250 Chrs; Chrh Wkr; Girl Scts; Hon Rl; Hosp Ade; Off Ade; Quill & Scroll; Sch Mus; Yth Flsp; Walsh College; Med Tech.

ROBINSON, ANNE; East Grand Rapids HS; Grand Rapids, MI; Chrs; Chrh Wkr; Sec JA; Sch Pl; Pres Yth Flsp; PPFtbl; JA Awd; Univ; Elem Ed.

ROBINSON, ANTHONY; Barberton HS; Barberton, OH; Pres Frsh Cls; Hon Rl; Jr NHS; NHS; Stu Cncl; IM Sprt; Univ Of Rkron; Engr.

ROBINSON, ANTHONY; Crestwood HS; Dearborn Hts, MI; Cmnty Wkr; Hon Rl; NHS; Pol Wkr; Ftbl; Univ Of Michigan; Law.

ROBINSON, BECKY; Brownstown Central HS; Vallania, IN; 22/145 Am Leg Aux Girls St; Hon Rl; Lbry Ade; Bus Schl; Sec.

ROBINSON, BECKY; Brownstown Central HS; Vallonia, IN; Am Leg Aux Girls St; Hon Rl; Lbry Ade; Business School; Secretary.

ROBINSON, BRENDA L; South HS; Youngstown, OH; 7/327 Chrh Wkr; Hon Rl; Off Ade; Yth Flsp; Rptr Yrbk; Sprt Ed Sch Nwsp; Drama Clb; Univ Of Akron; Nursing.

ROBINSON, CHRISTINE J; Reynoldsburg HS; Reynoldsburg, OH; Drm Bgl; Hon Rl; Yth Flsp; Yrbk; DECA; Mat Maids; PPFtbl; Bus Schl; Acctg.

ROBINSON, DAVE; Lake Michigan Catholic HS; St Joe, MI; NHS; Off Ade; Capt Crs Cntry; IM Sprt; Chem Engr.

ROBINSON, DAVID; Upper Arlington HS; Columbus, OH; Boy Scts; Hon Rl; Sct Actv; Lcrss; Wrstlng; Ohio State Univ; Bus Admin.

ROBINSON, DEBRA; John R Buchtel HS; Akron, OH; 119/487 Off Ade; DECA; Twrlr; Wilberforce Univ; Bio.

ROBINSON, DENISE; Bellaire HS; Bellaire, OH; Hon Rl; Y-Teens; GAA; Belmont Tech Coll; Comp.

ROBINSON, DENNIS; East Canton HS; E Canton, OH; Aud/Vis; Hon Rl; Sci Clb; Letter Crs Cntry; Letter Trk; Vocational School; Computer.

ROBINSON, DIANE; St Vincent HS; Akron, OH; Hon Rl; Jr NHS; NHS; Sprt Ed Sch Nwsp; Rptr Sch Nwsp; Fr Clb; Mth Clb; Capt Bsktbl; GAA; Ath Schlrshp Bsktbl; Bowling Green St Univ; Comp Sci.

ROBINSON, ELIZABETH; Lockland HS; Cincinnati, OH; 8/70 Trs Frsh Cls; Trs Soph Cls; Band; Hon Rl; NHS; Sch Mus; Sch Pl; Stu Cncl; Rptr Yrbk; Drama Clb; Drama Awd; Softball; Volleyball; Bowling Green St Univ; Bus Acctg.

ROBINSON, FRANKIE J; Wilmington HS; Wilmington, OH; Boy Scts; 4-H; Letter Ftbl; Letter Trk; Univ; Law.

ROBINSON, GARY; Bellaire HS; Bellaire, OH; Hon Rl; Ftbl; Gym; IM Sprt; Military.

ROBINSON, GEORGE; Miami Trace HS; Washington Ch, OH; 33/281 Hon Rl; Ftbl; Wrstlng; Purdue Univ; Civil Engr.

ROBINSON, GINGER L; Laurel HS; Laurel, IN; Sec Jr Cls; Trs Jr Cls; Cl Rep Jr Cls; Band; Girl Scts; Hon Rl; NHS; Stu Cncl; Rptr Yrbk; Sprt Ed Sch Nwsp; Notre Dame Univ; Jrnlsm.

ROBINSON, HARLESCIA; Lutheran East HS; Cleveland, OH; 1/44 Pres Soph Cls; Pres Jr Cls; Band; Chrh Wkr; Girl Scts; Hon Rl; JA; Stu Cncl; Yrbk; Capt Chrldng; Biology Award; Harvard Univ; Medicine.

ROBINSON, HAROLD; Highland HS; Anderson, IN; 45/397 Hon Rl; NHS; Cumberland Coll; Forestry.

ROBINSON, ISAAC; Bluefield HS; Bluefld, WV; 7/264 Sec Jr Cls; Chrh Wkr; Hon Rl; Jr NHS; NHS; Fr Clb; Lat Clb; Pep Clb; Engr.

ROBINSON, JAMES; Laura F Osborn HS; Detroit, MI; Debate Tm; Hon Rl; NHS; Mth Clb; Spn Clb; Natl Merit Ltr; Michigan St Univ; Acctg.

ROBINSON, JAMES; Westfield Washington HS; Westfield, IN; Band; Hon Rl; Stg Crw; Fr Clb; Ftbl; Glf; Letter Swmmng; Indiana Univ; Pre Med.

ROBINSON, JAN; Ridgewood HS; W Lafayette, OH; 1/150 Trs Sr Cls; Treas Band; Chrh Wkr; Debate Tm; Capt Drl Tm; Hon Rl; Treas Hon Rl; Orch; Yrbk; 4-H; The Ohio St Univ; Vet.

ROBINSON, JANELLE; Southern Local HS; Wellsville, OH; Chrh Wkr; Hon Rl; Sch Pl; Rptr Yrbk; 4-H; FHA; FNA; Lat Clb; OEA; Bsktbl; Kent State; Nursing.

ROBINSON, JANICE M; Our Lady Of Mercy HS; Detroit, MI; Hosp Ade; Stg Crw; FDA; FSA; Sci Clb; Spn Clb; Trk; Spanish Hnr Soc; Numerous Awds In Spanish; Michigan St Univ; Medicine.

ROBINSON, JEANNE; Jane Addams Voc HS; Cleveland, OH; Cl Rep Jr Cls; Drl Tm; Trk; Cit Awd; Univ; Med Sec.

ROBINSON, JILL; Bentley Sr HS; Davison, MI; Trs Frsh Cls; Trs Soph Cls; Trs Jr Cls; Trs Sr Cls; NHS; Stu Cncl; Letter Bsktbl; Letter Trk; Kiwan Awd; Michigan Schlrshp Or Tuition Grant; Adrian Coll; Spec Ed.

ROBINSON, JODY; William G Mather HS; Munising, MI; 14/108 Band; Hon Rl; Stg Crw; Rptr Sch Nwsp; 4-H; FHA; 4-H Awd; Univ; Music.

ROBINSON, JULIA; Lincoln HS; Haywood, WV; Cl Rep Jr Cls; Band; Chrs; Hon Rl; NHS; Stg Crw; Stu Cncl; Y-Teens; 4-H; FHA; Vocational Schl.

ROBINSON, KATHY; North Liberty HS; North Liberty, IN; Chrs; Chrh Wkr; Hon Rl; Sch Mus; Yth Flsp; 4-H; Spn Clb; Bsktbl; PPFtbl; 4-H Awd; Piano Awrds From Chorus 1977; 1st Pl Piano St Contst Indianapls 1978; 1st Pl John Adams HS Piano 1978; Bechel Coll; Music.

ROBINSON, KEVIN; Cameron HS; Cameron, WV; Hon Rl; NHS; Sch Pl; VP Stu Cncl; Drama Clb; 4-H; Pres FFA; Pres Sci Clb; Belmont Tech; Cnstrctn.

ROBINSON, KIM; Kelloggsville HS; Kentwood, MI; Cmp Fr Grls; Hon Rl; Yrbk; Jaycee Univ; Photog.

ROBINSON, LANA; West Jefferson HS; W Jefferson, OH; 30/88 Band; Cmp Fr Grls; Chrs; Chrh Wkr; Girl Scts; Hon Rl; Sch Pl; 4-H; Fr Clb; 4-H Awd; Typing Awd; First Aid To Injured Cert; Cedarvill Coll; Elem Ed.

ROBINSON, LAURA; Marquette HS; Michigan City, IN; Hon Rl; Sch Mus; Spn Clb; College; Court Reporting.

ROBINSON, LAURIE; Murray Wright HS; Detroit, MI; Cmp Fr Grls; Hon Rl; Off Ade; OEA; Cit Awd; Detroit Coll Of Bus; Acctg.

ROBINSON, LESLEIGH; Copley HS; Akron, OH; Cl Rep Jr Cls; Cls Rep Sr Cls; Band; Chrs; Hon Rl; Hosp Ade; Stu Cncl; Yth Flsp; Spn Clb; Trk; Ohio St Univ; Nursing.

ROBINSON, LINDA; Celina HS; Celina, OH; NHS; 4-H; GAA; IM Sprt; PPFtbl; 4-H Awd; College; Interior Design.

ROBINSON, LINDSAY; Highland HS; Medina, OH; Hon Rl; Rptr Sch Nwsp; Ger Clb; Scr Kpr; Bowling Green St Univ; Advertising.

ROBINSON, LISA; Lemon Monroe HS; Middletown, OH; Girl Scts; Hosp Ade; Sch Pl; Boys Clb Am; IM Sprt; Univ Of Maine; Law Enforcement.

ROBINSON, MARY A; Anderson HS; Anderson, IN; 3/425 Pres NHS; Lat Clb; Letter Ten; Chrldng; Am Leg Awd; Cit Awd; Rotary Awd; Purdue Univ; Comp Sci.

ROBINSON, MICHAEL; Cardington Lincoln HS; Cardington, OH; VP Sr Cls; Hon Rl; NHS; Stu Cncl; Fr Clb; Letter Bsbl; Letter Ftbl; Muskingum Coll; Pre Med.

ROBINSON, MICHAEL; S Haven HS; S Haven, MI; Band; Orch; Letter Crs Cntry; Ftbl; Letter Trk; Wrstlng; S W Michigan Univ.

ROBINSON, PATRICIA N; Emerson HS; Gary, IN; 7/146 Girl Scts; Hon Rl; Lbry Ade; OEA; Comp Sci.

ROBINSON, PHILLIP; Linsly Institute; Wheeling, WV; Boy Scts; Chrs; Drm Bgl; Hon Rl; Sch Mus; Sch Pl; Drama Clb; VP Key Clb; Spn Clb; 2nd Pl Hnr Awd 75; Univ; Engr.

ROBINSON, RANDY; Reed City HS; Hersey, MI; Chrh Wkr; Hon Rl; Ftbl; Trk; Wrstlng; Chem Awd 79; Ferris St Coll; X Ray Tech.

ROBINSON, ROBERT; Washington HS; Massillon, OH; 1/500 Hon Rl; Jr NHS; NHS; Ger Clb; Letter Swmmng; Texas Soc Of Pro Engr Sci Achvmnt 77; Univ; Med.

ROBINSON, ROBIN; Washington HS; Massillon, OH; Hon Rl; Lbry Ade; Sch Pl; Stg Crw; Ed Sch Nwsp; DECA; Drama Clb; Letter Gym; Trk; GAA; Awd Outstanding Female Athlete; Marine Test Awd; Class Treas Of DECA Club;.

ROBINSON, RONCENT; Dupont HS; Oxon Hill, MD; Am Leg Boys St; Hon Rl; Mod UN; Stu Cncl; Treas Mth Clb; Letter Crs Cntry; Trk; Letter Wrstlng; IM Sprt; Cumberland College; Civil Eng.

ROBINSON, ROSE; Charleston HS; Charleston, WV; 15/279 Pres Frsh Cls; VP Soph Cls; Sec Jr Cls; Trs Jr Cls; VP Sr Cls; Am Leg Aux Girls St; Chrh Wkr; Sec NHS; Stu Cncl; Capt Trk; West Virginia Univ; Comp Sci.

ROBINSON, SANDRA; Warren Central HS; Indpls, IN; Jr NHS; 4-H; Letter Swmmng; 4-H Awd; Univ; Bus.

ROBINSON, SCOTT; Jackson HS; North Canton, OH; FCA; Key Clb; Bsbl; Crs Cntry; Trk; Kent State Univ; Natural Resources.

ROBINSON, SCOTT A; Big Walnut HS; Galena, OH; 3/218 Hon Rl; Sch Pl; Yrbk; Drama Clb; Spn Clb; IM Sprt; Univ; Ministry.

ROBINSON, SHARI; Maumee HS; Maumee, OH; Pres Frsh Cls; Cls Rep Frsh Cls; Cmnty Wkr; Hon Rl; Hosp Ade; Lbry Ade; Off Ade; Stu Cncl; Yth Flsp; Yrbk; Univ; Data Proc.

ROBINSON, SHARON; Brilliant Buckeye HS; Smithfield, OH; Sec Frsh Cls; Chrs; FCA; Hon Rl; Lbry Ade; Stu Cncl; Drama Clb; Fr Clb; VP FHA; Pep Clb; Oh Test Of Schlstc Achvmtn Team 79; Campus Life Sec 78; Univ; Deaf Tchr.

ROBINSON, SHEILA; Mackenzie HS; Detroit, MI; 63/389 Cl Rep Jr Cls; Hon Rl; Off Ade; Yrbk; Pep Clb; Detroit Coll Of Busns; Exec Sec.

ROBINSON, SHERI; North Farmington HS; Farm Hills, MI; Am Leg Aux Girls St; Chrs; Pres Girl Scts; Hon Rl; Jr NHS; Lbry Ade; Natl Forn Lg; College; Bus Admin.

ROBINSON, TERESA; North Posey HS; Wadesville, IN; Chrs; Chrh Wkr; Natl Forn Lg; Sch Mus; Sch Pl; Stg Crw; Fr Clb; FHA; IM Sprt;.

ROBINSON, TERRI; Rockhill Sr HS; Kitts Hill, OH; 1/140 VP Soph Cls; Trs Jr Cls; Val; Band; Chrh Wkr; Drm Mjrt; VP NHS; Stu Cncl; Yth Flsp; Beta Clb; Spanish I Awd; St Marys Coll; Nursing.

ROBINSON, TIMOTHY P; Elkhart Mem HS; Elkhart, IN; Aud/Vis; Band; Boy Scts; Drm Bgl; Hon Rl; JA; Orch; Sch Mus; Sch Pl; Sct Actv; Univ; Studio Cameraman.

ROBINSON, TODD A; Miamisburg Sr HS; Miamisburg, OH; Cls Rep Sr Cls; Am Leg Boys St; Hon Rl; Sch Mus; Stu Cncl; Yrbk; Civ Clb; VP Fr Clb; Free Enterprise Progr 78;.

ROBINSON, TRACY; Chagrin Falls HS; Chagrin Falls, OH; Band; Cmp Fr Grls; Chrs; Chrh Wkr; Debate Tm; Hosp Ade; Sch Pl; Sch Nwsp; Ger Clb; Pep Clb; Univ; Psych.

ROBINSON, VALORI B; Lakeview HS; Cortland, OH; Band; Chrs; Hon Rl; Lbry Ade; Ger Clb; Lat Clb; Crs Cntry; Letter Gym; Letter Trk; Youngstown Univ; Music.

ROBINSON, VEDA; South Bend La Salle HS; South Bend, IN; 2/488 Cls Rep Soph Cls; Cl Rep Jr Cls; Sec Girl Scts; Hon Rl; Sec JA; Crs Cntry; Letter Trk; Coach Actv; IM Sprt; Top 5 Soph Prog At Purdue; Miss Congeniality At Purdue Academic Leadership Seminar; Univ Of Notre Dame; Biology.

ROBINSON, VERONICA; Cass Technical HS; Detroit, MI; Hon Rl; Lbry Ade; FHA; College; Dentistry.

ROBINSON, VINCENT P; Bishop Luers HS; Fort Wayne, IN; Cls Rep Frsh Cls; Chrh Wkr; Hon Rl; Pol Wkr; Sch Mus; Sch Pl; Sch Nwsp; Drama Clb; Commended Stu In The Natl Ach Prog; College; Law.

ROBINSON JR, ROBERT; Western HS; Detroit, MI; NHS; Mth Clb; Letter Ftbl; Wayne State Univ; Comp Engr.

ROBISON, ELYSE; Our Lady Of Mercy HS; Southfield, MI; 11/350 Cls Rep Frsh Cls; Cls Rep Soph Cls; Cl Rep Jr Cls; Chrs; Chrh Wkr; Lbry Ade; NHS; Stu Cncl; Univ; Law.

ROBISON, JEFF; North Knox HS; Freelandville, IN; Cls Rep Soph Cls; Cl Rep Jr Cls; Band; Hon Rl; NHS; Stu Cncl; 4-H; Fr Clb; Wrstlng; Vincennes Univ; Math.

ROBISON, KIMBERLY; Champion HS; Warren, OH; Chrs; Chrh Wkr; Hon Rl; JA; OEA; Spn Clb; OOEA Regnl II 5th Pl Inter Off Cmnctns 1 79; Bus Schl; Acctg.

ROBISON, LISA; Rutherford B Hayes HS; Delaware, OH; Chrs; Y-Teens; Key Clb; Pep Clb; Chrldng; Ohio St Univ; Biology.

ROBLESKI, DENNIS; Hastings HS; Hastings, MI; Boy Scts; Hon Rl; Pol Wkr; Sch Mus; Yrbk; Boys Clb Am; 4-H; IM Sprt; 4-H Awd; WMU; Acctg.

ROBLING, GREGORY; Central HS; Evansville, IN; Cl Rep Jr Cls; Boy Scts; Hon Rl; Pol Wkr; 4-H; 4-H Awd; Univ Of Evansville; Engr.

ROBOTHAM, SHELLY; Baldwin Comm HS; Bitely, MI; Trs Frsh Cls; Trs Soph Cls; Trs Jr Cls; Off Ade; Yrbk; Rptr Sch Nwsp; Busns Schl; Acctg.

ROBY, EILEEN; West Side HS; Gary, IN; Lbry Ade; VP DECA; Trk; Florida A & M Univ; Marketing.

ROBY, JENNIFER; Zanesville HS; Zanesville, OH; 83/415 Trs Frsh Cls; Band; Chrs; Hon Rl; Off Ade; Stu Cncl; Rptr Yrbk; Rptr Sch Nwsp; Lat Clb; Sci Clb; Muskingum Coll; Psych.

ROCCHIO, VINCENT; Hackett HS; Kalamazoo, MI; Cls Rep Soph Cls; Sch Mus; Sch Pl; Ed Yrbk; Yrbk; Drama Clb; Coach Actv; Natl Merit Ltr; Dayton Univ; Theater.

ROCCI, ERIC A; Grandview Hts HS; Columbus, OH; 18/115 Hon Rl; Jr NHS; Spn Clb; Ftbl; Ten; Coach Actv; Univ; Phys Educ.

ROCCO, JERALD J; A D Johnston HS; Ramsay, MI; Sec Frsh Cls; Trs Frsh Cls; Cls Rep Frsh Cls; Trs Soph Cls; Sec Jr Cls; Trs Jr Cls; Cl Rep Jr Cls; University; Mortician.

ROCHARD, MARK J; Griffith Sr HS; Griffith, IN; 45/289 Hon Rl; Jr NHS; Yrbk; Sch Nwsp; Wrstlng; Purdue Univ; Mech Engr.

ROCHELEAU, KRISTINE; Owendale Gagetown HS; Gagetown, MI; Girl Scts; Hon Rl; Lbry Ade; Stg Crw; Sch Nwsp; Ger Clb; Univ; Child Care Worker.

ROCHELEAU, RUTH; Grant HS; Grant, MI; VP Soph Cls; Band; Hon Rl; 4-H; Letter Bsbl; GAA; IM Sprt; Central Mic Univ; Music.

ROCHELEAU, SUSAN; Ithaca HS; Ithaca, MI; Hon Rl; Lbry Ade; Yth Flsp; Rptr Yrbk; Spn Clb; Trk; Ctrl Michigan Univ.

ROCHESTER, CHRISTIE; Tiffin Columbian HS; Bloomville, OH; Am Leg Aux Girls St; Chrs; Chrh Wkr; Cmnty Wkr; FCA; Hosp Ade; Pres 4-H; FFA; Ger Clb; Pres Leo Clb; FFA Pub Spkng Awd; Sining Solo Cls A Rating Superior; Capital Univ; RN.

ROCHHOLZ, PAULA; Schoolcraft HS; Schoolcraft, MI; Band; Drm Mjrt; Hon Rl; Off Ade; Sch Pl; Sct Actv; Yrbk; Scr Kpr; Twrlr; Kalamazoo Vly Cmm College; Dent Asst.

ROCHOTTE, BRET; New Riegel HS; Alvada, OH; 5/52 Cls Rep Frsh Cls; Pres Soph Cls; Cls Rep Soph Cls; Cl Rep Jr Cls; Cls Rep Sr Cls; Am Leg Boys St; Band; NHS; Pres Stu Cncl; Cit Awd; Ohio St Univ; Vet.

ROCK, DEBBIE; Fredericktown HS; Fredricktown, OH; 19/113 Chrh Wkr; FCA; Hon Rl; NHS; Sch Pl; Stu Cncl; Yth Flsp; Rptr Sch Nwsp; Drama Clb; 4-H; Capital Univ; Registered Nurse.

ROCK, DEE; Philo HS; Zanesville, OH; Cls Rep Soph Cls; Cl Rep Jr Cls; Chrs; Drl Tm; Hon Rl; Stu Cncl; 4-H; Ger Clb; GAA; Technical Coll.

ROCK, PEGGY; Ferndale HS; Ferndale, MI; Boston Univ; Chem Engr.

ROCK, TAMMY; Washington HS; Washington, IN; 12/200 Pres Chrs; Girl Scts; Hon Rl; Jr NHS; NHS; Sec Yth Flsp; Treas Beta Clb; Ger Clb; Pep Clb; Mas Awd; Indiana St Univ; Nursing.

ROCK, WILLIAM; Grosse Ile HS; Grosse Ile, MI; Band; Boy Scts; Hon Rl; Sch Mus; Sct Actv; Yrbk; 4-H; Trk; IM Sprt; Mgrs; College; Math.

ROCKAFELLOW, TRICIA; Alma HS; Elwell, MI; Cls Rep Soph Cls; Cl Rep Jr Cls; Band; Off Ade; 4-H; Pep Clb; 4-H Awd; Natl Merit Schl; Ferris State Coll; Acctg.

ROCKELEIN, RONALD; Colon HS; Leoniday, MI; Hon Rl; 4-H; Fr Clb; FFA; Univ; Vet Surgeon.

ROCKENSUESS, DALE; Lutheran HS; St Clair Shores, MI; Cls Rep Frsh Cls; VP Soph Cls; VP Jr Cls; Am Leg Boys St; Band; Hon Rl; NHS; Letter Ftbl; Carpenter.

ROCKETT, DEWRAIL; Buena Vista HS; Saginaw, MI; Cls Rep Soph Cls; Cl Rep Jr Cls; Cls Rep Sr Cls; Chrh Wkr; Hon Rl; Stu Cncl; Boys Clb Am; Capt Bsktbl; Letter Ftbl; Letter Trk; Aquinas; Bus.

ROCKSTRAW, DAVE; Chesterton HS; Chesterton, IN; 3/454 Hon Rl; Fr Clb; Ger Clb; Letter Glf; IM Sprt; Indiana Univ; Astronomy.

ROCKWELL, BEVERLY; Gallia Acad; Gallipolis, OH; Band; Girl Scts; Orch; FTA; 4-H Awd; College; Dent Hyg.

ROCKWELL, R; Nordonia HS; Northfield, OH; 91/401 Trs Frsh Cls; Bsktbl; Letter Ftbl; Letter Trk; Letter Wrstlng; Coach Actv; Ohio State.

RODA, ANN; Holy Rosary HS; Burton, MI; Girl Scts; Mgrs; Univ Of Michigan; Acctg.

RODAK, TONY; Keystone HS; La Grange, OH; Aud/Vis; NHS; Letter Ftbl; Tech Schl; Electronics.

RODAMMER, DEBRA; Frankenmuth HS; Vassar, MI; 12/180 Chrs; Debate Tm; Hon Rl; JA; Natl Forn Lg; Yth Flsp; Yrbk; Natl Merit SF; Delta Coll; Nursing.

RODAMMER, JANE; Vassar HS; Vassar, MI; 1/150 Band; Hon Rl; NHS; 4-H; Fr Clb; Letter Bsktbl; Letter Trk; GAA; 4-H Awd; Natl Merit Ltr; Saginaw Valley St Coll; Med Tech.

RODAMMER, MARK; Frankenmuth HS; Frankenmuth, MI; Pres Frsh Cls; Band; FCA; Hon Rl; Natl Forn Lg; NHS; Sch Mus; Sch Pl; Letter Bsbl; MLYA Boys St Bsktbl Champs 77; Univ; Sci.

RODDA, BARBARA; Bridgman HS; Bridgman, MI; Hon Rl; NHS; Pres Yth Flsp; VP 4-H; Letter Bsbl; Letter Trk; 4-H Awd; Joan Jewett Career Schl; Stewardess.

RODDEN, MAUREEN; Warren Central HS; Indpls, IN; 40/770 Cls Rep Soph Cls; Hon Rl; NHS; Stu Cncl; Hillsdale Coll; Educ.

RODDY, KATHY A; Big Walnut HS; Galena, OH; Band; Girl Scts; Hon Rl; Off Ade; Orch; Sch Pl; Sct Actv; Drama Clb; Spn Clb; Busns Schl.

RODECK, DEBORAH; Negaunee HS; Negaunee, MI; Chrh Wkr; Cmnty Wkr; Hon Rl; Off Ade; Red Cr Ade; Yrbk; Rptr Sch Nwsp; Pep Clb; Sci Clb; PPFtbl; 6 Type Writing Awds 78; N Michigan Univ; Surgery.

RODEHEAVER, ZANE; Parkersburg HS; Parkersburg, WV; Boy Scts; Chrh Wkr; Hon Rl; Sct Actv; IM Sprt; Univ; Engr.

RODEMSKY, EDWARD; Lake Fenton HS; Fenton, MI; Alma Coll; Pre Law.

RODEN, BARBARA A; Eaton Rapids Sr HS; Eaton Rapids, MI; 7/200 Hon Rl; NHS; Sch Mus; Y-Teens; Ed Yrbk; Swmmng; Dnfth Awd; Western Michigan Univ; Flight Tech.

RODEN, HALLIE; Girard HS; Girard, OH; 9/220 Band; Cmp Fr Grls; Chrh Wkr; Cmnty Wkr; Hon Rl; Hosp Ade; NHS; Yrbk; Sci Clb; Kent State Univ; Nursing.

RODENBERGER, JACKIE; Brownstown Central HS; Norman, IN; 10/133 Band; Chrs; Hon Rl; NHS; Pep Clb; Letter GAA; 4-H Awd; Vincennes Univ; Floriculture.

RODENISER, KELLE; Newark Sr HS; Newark, OH; Chrs; Cmnty Wkr; Letter Drl Tm; Hosp Ade; Sch Pl; Pep Clb; Gym; Trk; Chrldng; Pom Pon;.

RODER, LEE J; West Lafayette HS; W Lafayette, IN; 13/185 Debate Tm; Hon Rl; Am Leg Awd; Purdue Univ; Comp Sci.

RODERICK, DAWN; Chelsea HS; Chelsea, MI; Hon Rl; NHS; Off Ade; Pres 4-H; FFA; Cit Awd; 4 H Awd; 4 H Key Club Awd 78; Delegate To Natl 4 H Conference 78; Northern Michigan Univ; Soc Work.

RODEWALD, BETH; Reeths Puffer HS; Muskegon, MI; 76/271 Cls Rep Sr Cls; Cmnty Wkr; Girl Scts; Hon Rl; Hosp Ade; Mdrgl; Sch Pl; Sec Stu Cncl; Ed Yrbk; PPFtbl; Art Schlrshp From Muskegon Comm Coll; Muskegon Comm Coll; Arts.

RODEWALD, BONNIE; Reeths Puffer HS; Muskegon, MI; 40/345 Chrs; Girl Scts; Hon Rl; Hosp Ade; Stu Cncl; Spn Clb; PPFtbl; Muskegon Comm College; Sci.

RODFONG, TAMI S; E Liverpool HS; E Liverpool, OH; VP Frsh Cls; Cl Rep Jr Cls; Cls Rep Sr Cls; Cmp Fr Grls; Chrs; Cmnty Wkr; Hon Rl; Off Ade; Sch Pl; Stg Crw; Kent St Univ; Public Relations.

RODGERS, JOHN; Lutheran HS; Detroit, MI; Hon Rl; Letter Trk; College; Arch.

RODGERS, KELLY; Davison Sr HS; Davison, MI; Band; Hon Rl; Rptr Sch Nwsp; Pres OEA; Pres Awd; Communications Occu I Trophy; Busns Spelling & Proofreading Trophy; College; Admin Sec.

RODGERS, KENNETH; Tecumseh HS; Tecumseh, MI; Cmnty Wkr; Hon Rl; IM Sprt; Scr Kpr; Outstanding Craftsmanship Awd In Drafting 77; Michigan St Univ; Mech Engr.

RODGERS, LINDA K; Regina HS; Warrensville Ht, OH; Cmnty Wkr; Drl Tm; Girl Scts; Hosp Ade; JA; Lbry Ade; Off Ade; Sci Clb; Ten; Cit Awd; College; Med.

RODGERS, MARY; St Clair HS; St Clair, MI; 20/208 Cl Rep Jr Cls; Cls Rep Sr Cls; Hon Rl; NHS; Sch Pl; Stg Crw; Rptr Yrbk; Cit Awd; Natl Merit Ltr; St Clair Cmnty Coll; Civil Archt.

RODGERS, ROBIN; Lebanon HS; Lebanon, OH; Cls Rep Frsh Cls; Chrs; NHS; Sch Mus; Sch Pl; Drama Clb; Fr Clb; Chrldng; Univ; Music.

RODGERS, TAMMY; Danbury HS; Lakeside, OH; 21/64 Hon Rl; Off Ade; Spn Clb; Letter Bsktbl; Capt Trk; Wright St Univ; Bus Admin.

RODICH, TRACY; South Vermillion HS; Clinton, IN; Sec Jr Cls; Band; Girl Scts; Hosp Ade; JA; Off Ade; Sct Actv; Fr Clb; Pep Clb; Trk; Ivy Tech Bus Schl; Med Sec.

RODINO, HOLLY; William A Wirt HS; Gary, IN; Hon Rl; Jr NHS; Off Ade; Spn Clb; PPFtbl; Coll; Diagnostic Tech.

RODINO, LANA; Elkhart Central HS; Elkhart, IN; Cl Rep Jr Cls; Hon Rl; Lbry Ade; NHS; Sch Mus; Stu Cncl; Letter Gym; Univ; Dance.

RODKEY, SUSAN; Kent Roosevelt HS; Kent, OH; Hon Rl; Stg Crw; 4-H; 4-H Awd; Mereidth Manor Univ; Master Rider.

RODKEY, VIRGINIA; Rossville HS; Rossville, IN; 11/50 Pres Soph Cls; VP Jr Cls; Am Leg Aux Girls St; Band; Hon Rl; Natl Forn Lg; Off Ade; Sch Pl; Rptr Yrbk; Sch Nwsp; Outstndng Jr Band Mbr; St Elizabeth Schl; Nursing.

RODMAN, MARY; North Central Area School; Hermansville, MI; Am Leg Aux Girls St; Cmp Fr Grls; Chrh Wkr; Lbry Ade; Rptr Yrbk; 4-H; FHA; Spn Clb; Trk; Mi Compttv Schslhp 80; Univ.

RODOCKER, CONNIE C; Hicksville HS; Hicksville, OH; 3/112 Cl Rep Jr Cls; Am Leg Aux Girls St; Hon Rl; NHS; Stu Cncl; Letter Bsbl; Capt Chrldng; Toledo Univ; Med.

RODRIGUEZ, DAVE; Nordonia HS; Northfield, OH; Cmnty Wkr; Bsbl; Bsktbl; Ftbl; IM Sprt; College; Busines Admin.

RODRIGUEZ, DEBBIE; Lapeer West HS; Lapeer, MI; Band; Chrh Wkr; FCA; Hon Rl; Sct Actv; Yth Flsp; 4-H; Mic State Univ; Vet.

RODRIGUEZ, DOREEN; Finney HS; Detroit, MI; Band; Cmnty Wkr; Hon Rl; Off Ade; Yth Flsp; Sch Nwsp; Spn Clb; Cit Awd; Hnr From Afbany Model Acad 78; ATA Flight Schl 79; Michigan St Univ; Pro Soc Work.

RODRIGUEZ, HOPE; Grand Rapids Central HS; Grand Rapids, MI; Hon Rl; Grand Rapids Jr Coll; Fshn Mdse.

RODRIGUEZ, MAGDALENA; Hamtramck HS; Hamtramck, MI; Pres Sr Cls; Chrs; JA; Sch Pl; Rptr Yrbk; Sci Clb; Pres Awd; Univ; Soc Work.

RODRIGUEZ, MICHAEL; John Adams HS; South Bend, IN; Stu Cncl; Spn Clb; Ftbl; Wrstlng; Natl Merit Ltr; Purdue Univ; Mfg Engr.

RODRIGUEZ, MIRIAM; Ypsilanti HS; Ypsilanti, MI; Hon Rl; Off Ade; Gym; Letter Chrldng; College; X Tech.

RODRIGUEZ, RACHEL; Grant HS; Bailey, MI; VP Frsh Cls; VP Soph Cls; Cl Rep Jr Cls; Chrh Wkr; Hon Rl; Stu Cncl; Sprt Ed Sch Nwsp; Pep Clb; GAA; Cit Awd; Davenport; Legal Sec.

RODRIGUEZ, VICTORIA; Clyde Sr HS; Clyde, OH; Cmp Fr Grls; Chrh Wkr; Hon Rl; Lbry Ade; Off Ade; Sct Actv; Terra Tech Coll; Exec Sec.

ROE, BRIAN; Sand Creek HS; Adrian, MI; Cls Rep Frsh Cls; Trs Soph Cls; Band; Hon Rl; NHS; Letter Bsbl; Letter Bsktbl; Letter Glf; Ferris St Coll; Acctg.

ROE, KRISTIN; Clare HS; Clare, MI; 25/131 Chmn Cmnty Wkr; VP FCA; Hon Rl; NHS; Quill & Scroll; Rptr Yrbk; Ed Sch Nwsp; Letter Trk; Mich Interscholastic Press Assn Honorable Mentions; Central Mich Univ; Public Relations.

ROE, SHELLY; Van Buren HS; Harmony, IN; 7/84 Sec Frsh Cls; Band; Hon Rl; NHS; PAVAS; Indiana St Univ; Pediatrics.

ROE, TERRY; Ithaca HS; Pompeii, MI; 31/129 Boy Scts; Hon Rl; NHS; Fr Clb; Letter Bsbl; Letter Ftbl; Rotary Awd; Mi Comp Sclshp 79; Ferris St Coll; Drafting.

ROEDEL, SANDRA; Castle HS; Newburgh, IN; 10/333 Cls Rep Soph Cls; Am Leg Aux Girls St; Band; Chrs; Chrh Wkr; Drm Mjrt; Hon Rl; NHS; Off Ade; Orch; Univ Of Evansville; Jrnlsm.

ROEDEMA, DONNA; Lexington HS; Mansfield, OH; Hon Rl; Sch Pl; Y-Teens; Drama Clb; Fr Clb; Trk; Univ.

ROEDER, CLAUDIA; Rochester HS; Rochester, MI; Girl Scts; Hon Rl; NHS; Cit Awd; Natl Merit Ltr; Natl Merit SF; College; Interpeter.

ROEDER, KEVIN; St Francis De Sales HS; Toledo, OH; Hon Rl; Sch Mus; Sch Pl; Stg Crw; Rptr Yrbk; Sprt Ed Sch Nwsp; Spn Clb; Ftbl; IM Sprt;.

ROEDER, SCOTT A; Penn HS; Mishawaka, IN; Hon Rl; NHS; 4-H; Wrstlng; 4-H Awd; JETS Awd; Rose Hulman Inst Of Tech; Mech Engr.

ROEHRLE, DIANE; Continental HS; Continental, OH; 7/58 Sec Frsh Cls; Trs Jr Cls; Chrh Wkr; Hon Rl; NHS; Red Cr Ade; Stu Cncl; Spn Clb; Pres Bsktbl; Trk; Ohio Northern Univ.

ROELL, DONNA; Brookville HS; Cedar Grove, IN; Hon Rl; Off Ade; Sch Pl; Stg Crw; Rptr Sch Nwsp; VP Drama Clb; 4-H; Sci Clb; 4-H Awd;.

ROELL, STEVEN R; Sault Area HS; Sault Ste Marie, MI; Boy Scts; Hon Rl; NHS; Sct Actv; Glf; IM Sprt; U S Air Force Acad; Aero Engr.

ROEMBKE, KATHY; Roncalli HS; Indpls, IN; 9/187 Pres Frsh Cls; Hon Rl; Lat Clb; Chrldng; Ball State Univ; Sec.

ROEMER, DANIEL; Bishop Luers HS; Ft Wayne, IN; Aud/Vis; Chrh Wkr; IM Sprt; Mgrs; Sports Lttr Bsktbl Mngng 77; IUPU; TV Producer.

ROESCH, DOUGLAS C; Galion Sr HS; Galion, OH; Am Leg Boys St; Band; Chrh Wkr; Hon Rl; NHS; Yth Flsp; Rptr Yrbk; Mth Clb; Univ.

ROESCH, MONICA; Stephen T Badin HS; Fairfield, OH; 70/240 Cmnty Wkr; Girl Scts; Sch Mus; Rptr Sch Nwsp; Sch Nwsp; Gym; Chrldng; Coach Actv; Opt Clb Awd; Univ Of Dayton; Comp Sci.

ROESLER, DOUGLAS; Montague HS; Montague, MI; Cls Rep Sr Cls; Chrh Wkr; Hon Rl; Muskegon Community College; Crimjust.

ROESTEL, TAMMY; Michigan Lutheran Seminary; Pigeon, MI; Chrs; Chrh Wkr; FCA; Yth Flsp; 4-H; Pep Clb; IM Sprt; PPFtbl; 4-H Awd; JA Awd; Delta Coll; Child Dvlpmnt.

ROETH, JEFFERY; Houston HS; Piqua, OH; 1/62 Trs Frsh Cls; Pres Jr Cls; Chrs; Hon Rl; Treas NHS; Sch Pl; 4-H; Ohi State Univ; Agri.

ROETH, SUSAN; Upper Valley HS; Piqua, OH; 3/76 Pres Frsh Cls; Chrs; Hon Rl; Sprt Ed Yrbk; FHA; OEA; College; Acctg.

ROETTGER, ROSE; Brownstown Central HS; Seymour, IN; Am Leg Aux Girls St; Hon Rl; NHS; Yth Flsp; FBLA; Lat Clb; Pep Clb; Ten; Chrldng; GAA; Business School; Acctg.

ROETTKER, LISA; St Francis De Sales HS; Westerville, OH; 36/180 Hon Rl; Hosp Ade; Ten; Scr Kpr; College.

ROGALSKI, BRENDA; Forest Park HS; Crystal Falls, MI; 6/93 VP Sr Cls; Band; Hon Rl; 4-H; Letter Bsktbl; Letter Trk; IM Sprt; Univ.

ROGALSKI, EDWARD; Western HS; Detroit, MI; Boy Scts; Hon Rl; ROTC; DECA; Letter Ftbl; Letter Trk; Coll.

ROGAN, NARVETTA; Mt Clemens HS; Mount Clemens, MI; 28/314 Girl Scts; Hon Rl; Off Ade; Orch; Stu Cncl; Rptr Sch Nwsp; 4-H; Spn Clb; 4-H Awd; Natl Merit Schl; Michigan St Univ; Comp Tech.

ROGERS, ANTHONY; Warrensville Hts Sr HS; Warrensville, OH; Yrbk; Rptr Sch Nwsp; Sci Clb; Letter Ten; Harvard Univ; Astronomy.

ROGERS, BECKY; Lincoln HS; Lumberport, WV; 4/178 VP Soph Cls; Am Leg Aux Girls St; Band; Chrh Wkr; Hon Rl; NHS; Stu Cncl; 4-H; Chrldng; 4-H Awd; Potomac St Coll; Phys Therapy.

ROGERS, BRIAN; H H Dow HS; Midland, MI; 45/420 Hon Rl; NHS; Letter Bsktbl; Ten; IM Sprt; Hope College; Bus Admin.

ROGERS, CATHY; Meridian Sr HS; Midland, MI; 12/110 Girl Scts; Hon Rl; JA; Sch Pl; Yth Flsp; Rptr Yrbk; Pep Clb; Spn Clb; JA Awd; VFW Awd; Univ; Med Tech.

ROGERS, CHARLES R; Pt Pleasant HS; Pt Pleasant, WV; Cls Rep Soph Cls; Cl Rep Jr Cls; Cls Rep Sr Cls; Am Leg Boys St; Band; NHS; Sch Mus; Key Clb; Golden Horseshoe Awd; Wv Yth In Govt Part 77 79; Wv Oh Hy Y Councl Pres 78; Univ; Hist.

ROGERS, CHERYL; Bad Axe HS; Bad Axe, MI; 27/160 Cls Rep Frsh Cls; Cls Rep Soph Cls; Cl Rep Jr Cls; Cls Rep Sr Cls; Trk; Chrldng; Cit Awd; Delta College; Nurse.

ROGERS, CHRIS; Warsaw Community HS; Warsaw, IN; 39/394 Boy Scts; Sct Actv; DECA; Kappa Kappa Kappa Hon Awd 79; DECA Pres 79; Univ; Bus Mgmt.

ROGERS, CHRISTINE; Shenandoah HS; Caldwell, OH; 1/91 Sec Sr Cls; Val; Band; Hon Rl; Sch Pl; Ed Yrbk; Drama Clb; Mth Clb; Pep Clb; Mat Maids; Ohio St Univ; Comp Sci.

ROGERS, DARRYL; Greenville HS; Greenville, MI; Am Leg Boys St; Hon Rl; Stu Cncl; Rptr Yrbk; Fr Clb; Letter Ftbl; Trk; Capt IM Sprt; Montcalm Comm College; Bus.

ROGERS, DAV; Pineville HS; Pineville, WV; Sct Actv; Pres Yth Flsp; Spn Clb; College.

ROGERS, DAVE; Hammond Baptist HS; Hammond, IN; Chrh Wkr; Drl Tm; Hon Rl; NHS; Ed Sch Nwsp; Letter Bsbl; Letter Ftbl; Letter Trk; Letter Wrstlng; Sci Awd; Outstanding Stu; Hyles Anderson Coll; Education.

ROGERS, DENNA; Pennsboro HS; Pennsboro, WV; Cls Rep Soph Cls; Band; Hon Rl; Stu Cncl; Drama Clb; Fr Clb; Pep Clb; Bsktbl; GAA; Parkersburg Cmnty Coll.

ROGERS, DIANA; Kenston HS; Chagrin Fl, OH; Band; Chrs; Girl Scts; Hon Rl; Stg Crw; Rdo Clb; Gym; Trk; GAA; PPFtbl; College; Bio.

ROGERS, DIANA; Southern Local HS; Kensington, OH; Band; Hon Rl; Stu Cncl; Sec Yth Flsp; Sec 4-H; Lat Clb; Univ.

ROGERS, DIANE; Brown County HS; Morgantown, IN; Chrh Wkr; Fr Clb; Most Courteous Awd; Volleyball; Alternate Girls St & Model UN; College; Mental Health Tech.

ROGERS, GRADY; Taylor HS; Kokomo, IN; Aud/Vis; Boy Scts; Chrh Wkr; Hon Rl; Lbry Ade; NHS; Yth Flsp; Spn Clb; Indiana Bus Coll; Acctg.

ROGERS, JACQUELINE; Ridgemont HS; Ridgeway, OH; Band; Drl Tm; Girl Scts; Hon Rl; Sch Mus; 4-H; FHA; Trk; Chrldng; Columbus Art Schl; Art.

ROGERS, JANEEN; Rock Hill HS; Pedro, OH; VP Soph Cls; Band; Chrh Wkr; Girl Scts; NHS; Stu Cncl; Rptr Yrbk; Bsktbl; Trk; Chrldng; Univ; Educ.

ROGERS, JANET; Cheboygan Area HS; Cheboygan, MI; Band; Hon Rl; NHS; 4-H; Fr Clb; Spn Clb; 4-H Awd; Univ.

ROGERS, JEANNETTE; Fairborn Baker HS; Fairborn, OH; Chrs; Chrh Wkr; Drm Bgl; Girl Scts; Sch Pl; Stg Crw; Drama Clb; Lat Clb; Wright State; English.

ROGERS, JULIA; Roscommon HS; Roscommon, MI; 3/114 VP Soph Cls; Cls Rep Sr Cls; Sec Chrs; Chrh Wkr; Girl Scts; Hon Rl; NHS; Sch Mus; Letter Swmmng; Letter Trk; Lake Superior St Coll; Nursing.

ROGERS, KEITH; Benedictine HS; Detroit, MI; 17/143 Cls Rep Frsh Cls; Cls Rep Sr Cls; Chrh Wkr; Hon Rl; NHS; Fr Clb; Michigan St Univ.

ROGERS, KELLEY; Anna Local HS; Sidney, OH; 25/84 Sec Frsh Cls; Band; Chrs; Hon Rl; FHA; Sci Clb; Letter Bsktbl; Trk; Capt Chrldng; GAA; Tiffin Univ; Cosmotology.

ROGERS, KELLY; East Bank Sr HS; Cabin Creek, WV; Cls Rep Soph Cls; Cl Rep Jr Cls; Cls Rep Sr Cls; Chrh Wkr; Girl Scts; Hon Rl; Hosp Ade; Stu Cncl; Yth Flsp; Fr Clb; Univ; Nurse.

ROGERS, LARRY; Maple Heights Sr HS; Maple Hgts, OH; Hon Rl; Coll; Busns Admin.

ROGERS, LAURIE; Clyde HS; Clyde, OH; 11/260 Am Leg Aux Girls St; Band; Cmp Fr Grls; VP Chrh Wkr; Hon Rl; NHS; Off Ade; College; Nursing.

ROGERS, LINDA; Turpin HS; Cincinnati, OH; 22/359 Cls Rep Soph Cls; Cl Rep Jr Cls; Cmp Fr Grls; Chrh Wkr; Cmnty Wkr; Girl Scts; Hon Rl; Hosp Ade; NHS; Off Ade; Best Of Show In Art Contest 1977; 1st & 2nd Pl In Spring Art Show; Pres Of Art Club 1978; Auburn Univ; Interior Dsgn.

ROGERS, LINDA; Sault Area HS; Sault Ste Marie, MI; Chrh Wkr; Hon Rl; Bsktbl; Gym; Coach Actv; GAA; IM Sprt; Scr Kpr; Tmr; Northern Michigan Univ; Phys Educ.

ROGERS, LISA; Lincolnview HS; Van Wert, OH; Sec Jr Cls; Am Leg Aux Girls St; Band; NHS; Yth Flsp; Yrbk; Rptr Sch Nwsp; Twrlr; Bus School.

ROGERS, LISA; Grand Haven HS; Grand Haven, MI; 43/385 Hon Rl; Jr NHS; NHS; Yrbk; Sch Nwsp; Univ Of Mic; Law.

ROGERS, MARK; Divine Child HS; Dearborn Ht, MI; Chrs; Chrh Wkr; FCA; Yth Flsp; Sprt Ed Sch Nwsp; Spn Clb; Capt Bsktbl; Voice Dem Awd; Journalist.

ROGERS, MARK A; St Joseph Public HS; St Joseph, MI; 33/353 Treas JA; NHS; Orch; Mth Clb; Letter Bsbl; Natl Merit SF; Massachusetts Inst Of Tech; Elec Eng.

ROGERS, MARLENE; Southern Wells HS; Montpelier, IN; 6/96 Band; Chrs; Chrh Wkr; Hon Rl; NHS; Sch Mus; Sch Pl; Stg Crw; Sprt Ed Sch Nwsp; 4-H; ISU; Music Educ.

ROGERS, MARY; Sandy Valley HS; Magnolia, OH; Band; Chrs; Hon Rl; Sec Natl Forn Lg; Sch Mus; Sch Pl; Ger Clb; Sec Pep Clb; Trk; Bowling Green St Univ; Speech Cmnctn.

ROGERS, MELANIE; Bloomington HS; Bloomington, IN; Cl Rep Jr Cls; Chrs; FCA; Hon Rl; Jr NHS; NHS; Off Ade; Pep Clb; Ten; Pres Awd; Ind Univ; Medicine.

ROGERS, MICHAEL; Huntington North HS; Huntington, IN; Cls Rep Frsh Cls; Cls Rep Soph Cls; Boy Scts; Ftbl; Trk; Wrstlng; Opt Clb Awd; Scuba Diver For Civil Defence; Eagle Scout; Florida Inst Of Tech; Marine Bio.

ROGERS, RANDY; Washington Irving HS; Clarksburg, WV; 24/139 Cls Rep Sr Cls; Hon Rl; Stu Cncl; Fr Clb; Key Clb; Mth Clb; Sci Clb; Bsktbl; Letter Crs Cntry; Trk; Schl Winner In Century III Ldrshp Prog; Conservation Camp; Sandy Nininger Awd Outstanding Key Clubber; Fairmont St Univ; Landscape Archt.

ROGERS, REBECCA; Lincoln HS; Lumberport, WV; 4/148 Sec Soph Cls; Am Leg Aux Girls St; Band; Chrh Wkr; Hon Rl; NHS; Stu Cncl; 4-H; FFA; Pep Clb; Potomac St Univ; Comp Progr.

ROGERS, REX; Onaway HS; Onaway, MI; Cls Rep Frsh Cls; Cls Rep Soph Cls; Cl Rep Jr Cls; Lbry Ade; Sch Pl; Stu Cncl; Bsktbl; IM Sprt; Northern Michigan Univ.

ROGERS, ROSE; Lowellville HS; Lowellville, OH; 1/41 Val; Hon Rl; Lbry Ade; NHS; Off Ade; Y-Teens; Yrbk; Fr Clb; Pep Clb; Letter Bsktbl; Oh Bd Of Regnst Scslhp 4 Yrs 79; Youngstown St Univ Schlshp 79; Lowellville Bank Schsp 79; Youngstown St Univ; Acctg.

ROGERS, S; Central Hower HS; Akron, OH; Cmp Fr Grls; Drm Mjrt; Girl Scts; Hon Rl; Hosp Ade; Lbry Ade; Red Cr Ade; Univ Of Akron; Med.

ROGERS, SAMUEL; Lowellville HS; Lowellville, OH; Hon Rl; Yrbk; Rptr Sch Nwsp; Rdo Clb; Scr Kpr; Am Leg Awd; Ohio Univ; Acctg.

ROGERS, SANDI; Terre Haute North Vigo HS; Terre Haute, IN; Chrh Wkr; Hon Rl; Lbry Ade; Yth Flsp; Y-Teens; Whos Who In For Lang 79; Swope Gallery Stdnt Art Awd 77 & 79; St Paul Bible Coll; Art.

ROGERS, SCOTT; Oakridge HS; Muskegon, MI; 7/165 Cl Rep Jr Cls; Hon Rl; Jr NHS; NHS; Off Ade; Yrbk; Rptr Sch Nwsp; Cit Awd; Drafting Awd; Journalism I Awd; College; Photography.

ROGERS, SHEILA; Chadsey HS; Detroit, MI; Pres Jr Cls; Hon Rl; NHS; Sch Nwsp; Cit Awd; Region 2 Art Fair Awd; Stenography Gold Medal; College; Legal Secretary.

ROGERS, STEPHEN A; Central Catholic HS; N Canton, OH; 12/249 Cls Rep Sr Cls; Hon Rl; VP NHS; Letter Crs Cntry; Trk; IM Sprt; Marquette Univ; Metallurgcl Engr.

ROGERS, SUE; Hilliard HS; Amlin, OH; Hon Rl; Lbry Ade; Off Ade; Stu Cncl; OEA; Spn Clb; Columbus Tech Inst; Court Reporter.

ROGERS, TED; Elizabeth A Johnson HS; Mt Morris, MI; Band; Boy Scts; Bsktbl; Letter Ftbl; Letter Trk;.

ROGERS, TERRI F; Bedford HS; Temperance, MI; 1/431 Val; Sec Band; Hon Rl; Sec NHS; Sch Nwsp; Letter Trk; Mat Maids; Yth Of The Mnth Bedford Exchange Club 79; Pres Schlrshp Alma Coll 79; Alma Coll; Math.

ROGERS, WILLIAM; Baker HS; Wrightpatterson, OH; 45/550 Boy Scts; Chrs; Chrh Wkr; Jr NHS; Sct Actv; Swmmng; USAFA; Aero Engr.

ROGERSON, SCOTT; Rossford HS; Perrysburg, OH; 5/147 Band; Hon Rl; Univ Of Toledo; Acctg.

ROGGATZ, TIMOTHY; Lutheran North HS; Mount Clemens, MI; Aud/Vis; Band; Lbry Ade; PAVAS; Sct Actv; Stg Crw; Drama Clb; Letter Bsktbl; Letter Ftbl; Letter Trk; Adrian Coll; Cmnctns.

ROGGE, JULIE D; Northridge HS; Alexandria, OH; VP Sr Cls; Band; Girl Scts; Hon Rl; Yrbk; 4-H; Pep Clb; Letter Trk; Capt Chrldng; Scr Kpr; Busns Schl; Art.

ROGGE, KIMBERLY; Walnut Ridge Sr HS; Columbus, OH; 51/429 Band; Chrs; Hon Rl; NHS; Off Ade; Orch; Fr Clb; IM Sprt; Ohio St Bd Of Educ Awd Of Dist 79; Ohio St Univ.

ROGGENBUCK, JOY; Harbor Beach Cmnty HS; Harbor Beach, MI; 1/120 Hon Rl; Lbry Ade; VP NHS; Off Ade; 4-H; FHA; 4-H Awd; Ferris St Coll; Med Tech.

ROGGENBUCK, JOY; Harbor Beach Community HS; Harbor Beach, MI; 1/120 Hon Rl; Lbry Ade; VP NHS; Off Ade; 4-H; FHA; Key Clb; 4-H Awd; Ferris St Coll; Med Tech.

ROGGOW, SANDRA M; Athens HS; Athens, MI; 13/84 Band; Chrh Wkr; Drm Mjrt; Hon Rl; NHS; Stu Cncl; Pep Clb; Bsktbl; Chrldng; Twrlr; Arqubright Bus Coll; Med Sec.

ROGULSKI, ADAM; Bishop Gallagher HS; Detroit, MI; Band; Boy Scts; Debate Tm; Hon Rl; NHS; Quill & Scroll; Sch Mus; Sch Pl; Rptr Sch Nwsp; Letter Ftbl; Mass Inst Of Tech; Astro/aero Engr.

ROHAC, TRACEY; Owosso HS; Owosso, MI; Trs Jr Cls; Trs Sr Cls; Chrs; Hon Rl; NHS; PAVAS; Stu Cncl; Yrbk; Bsktbl; Trk; Colorado Inst Of Art; Cmmrcl Art.

ROHAL, DAVID; Stow HS; Stow, OH; Cl Rep Jr Cls; NHS; Ed Yrbk; Sprt Ed Sch Nwsp; Pres 4-H; Pres Lat Clb; Letter Ftbl; IM Sprt; JA Awd; Lion Awd; Univ; Engr.

ROHART, CARMEN; Stow HS; Stow, OH; Pres Chrs; Sec Chrh Wkr; Hon Rl; NHS; Stu Cncl; Rptr Sch Nwsp; Letter Ten; Wheaton College; Music.

ROHDENBURG, DONNA; Deer Park HS; Deer Park, OH; Sec Frsh Cls; Sec Soph Cls; Sec Jr Cls; Cls Rep Sr Cls; Am Leg Aux Girls St; Chrs; Girl Scts; Hon Rl; NHS; College; Elem Educ.

ROHLY, ROBERTA S; La Brae HS; Southington, OH; Cls Rep Soph Cls; Cl Rep Jr Cls; Am Leg Aux Girls St; Band; Girl Scts; Hon Rl; Treas NHS; Rptr Yrbk; Ed Sch Nwsp; Rptr Sch Nwsp; Stage Band 79; Flagline 79; Stud Council Award In Art 77; Elec.

ROHN, BARBARA; Ayersville HS; Defiance, OH; 2/93 Band; Chrs; Chrh Wkr; Hon Rl; Mdrgl; NHS; NHS; Sch Mus; Yth Flsp; Fr Clb;.

ROHN, ELIZABETH; Fairless HS; Navarre, OH; 1/231 Chrs; Chrh Wkr; Hon Rl; NHS; Off Ade; Sch Mus; Sch Pl; Y-Teens; Rptr Yrbk; Drama Clb; Kent Univ; Nursing.

ROHOVSKY, PATRICIA; Austintown Fitch HS; Youngstown, OH; Hon Rl; Off Ade; Y-Teens; VP Fr Clb; Pep Clb; Ten; PPFtbl; Youngstown St Univ; Comp Tech.

ROHR, EDWARD; West Preston HS; Masontown, WV; Hon Rl; IM Sprt; Univ; Art.

ROHR, LAURA; Jackson Sr HS; North Canton, OH; Girl Scts; Hon Rl; Fr Clb; Trk; Tmr; Univ; Mech Engr.

ROHRBACH, TIM; Memorial HS; St Marys, OH; 63/235 Band; Sch Pl; Sct Actv; Stg Crw; Drama Clb; Sci Clb; Voc Schl; Elec Engr.

ROHRBACHER, CHARLES; Delphos St John HS; Delphos, OH; Cls Rep Soph Cls; Cl Rep Jr Cls; Cls Rep Sr Cls; Boy Scts; Chrs; Chrh Wkr; Hon Rl; Sch Pl; Sct Actv; Sch Nwsp; Bluffton Coll; Acctg.

ROHRBACHER, COLLEEN; Clyde HS; Clyde, OH; Band; Chrs; Chrh Wkr; Hon Rl; Stg Crw; Trk; GAA; Nursing Schl.

ROHRBAUGH, KIMBERLY; South Harrison HS; Lost Creek, WV; Hon Rl; Hosp Ade; Lbry Ade; NHS; FTA; Glenville St Coll; Tchr.

ROHRBAUGH, SHERALYN; Louisville HS; Louisville, OH; Chrs; Girl Scts; Hon Rl; Hosp Ade; Off Ade; Sch Mus; Yrbk; Pep Clb; Univ; Photog.

ROHRBOUGH, ALISA; Lewis Cnty HS; Weston, WV; Chrh Wkr; Hon Rl; NHS; Yth Flsp; W Virginia Univ; Radiologic Tech.

ROHRER, KATHY; John Glenn HS; Walkerton, IN; 20/108 Trs Frsh Cls; Band; Chrh Wkr; Cmnty Wkr; FCA; Hon Rl; Sch Mus; Sch Pl; Stg Crw; Yth Flsp; Homecomg Queen Candidate 1975; Hon Bank 1976; Speaker For Amer Heart & Lung Assn 1978; Varsity Cheerleader; Indiana Univ; Soc Work.

ROHRER, LORI; Leetonia HS; Leetonia, OH; Band; Drm Bgl; Lbry Ade; Sch Mus; OEA; Pep Clb; Spn Clb; Bsktbl; Gym; GAA; Columbiania Cnty Voc Schl; Med Sec.

ROHRER, REBEKAH; Olmsted Falls HS; Olmsted Falls, OH; 7/244 Cls Rep Sr Cls; Chrs; Sec Chrh Wkr; Capt Drl Tm; Hon Rl; Sch Mus; Stg Crw; Stu Cncl; Yth Flsp; Schlrshp For High Scores ACT Test; Spring Arbor Coll; Education.

ROHRIG, BRIAN; Ironton HS; Ironton, OH; Jr NHS; NHS; Univ.

ROHRIG, ELIZABETH; Canton South HS; Canton, OH; Chrs; Girl Scts; Hon Rl; Hosp Ade; Sec JA; Lbry Ade; Y-Teens; Pep Clb; Spn Clb; JA Awd; Summer Art Schlrshp 78 & 79; JA Exec Sr & 100% Attendance 78; Akron Univ; Cyto Tech.

ROHRS, GAYLA; Liberty Ctr HS; Napoleon, OH; 7/70 Pres Soph Cls; Cls Rep Soph Cls; Cl Rep Jr Cls; Cls Rep Sr Cls; Band; Hon Rl; Pres MMM; Pres NHS; Red Cr Ade; Sch Mus; Toledo Med Ed Ctr; Med Asst.

ROHRS, JOAN; Stryker HS; Stryker, OH; 10/50 Band; Chrs; Debate Tm; Hon Rl; Yrbk; 4-H; FHA; Letter Gym; Univ; Acctg.

ROHRS, JOHN; Grand Haven Sr HS; Grand Haven, MI; Band; Boy Scts; Hon Rl; Jr NHS; Letter Ftbl; Ten; Michigan St Univ; Engr.

ROHRS, SUSAN; Fairview HS; Sherwood, OH; 9/123 Treas Band; Chrs; Hon Rl; NHS; Pres Yth Flsp; Pres 4-H; FTA; Pep Clb; Spn Clb; Bsktbl; Bowling Green St Univ; Elem Educ.

ROHWEDER, ROBERT; Clay Sr HS; Granger, IN; 71/430 Band; Chrh Wkr; Hon Rl; NHS; Ger Clb; Crs Cntry; Capt Wrstlng; Coach Actv; Var Letter Wrestling 78; Selctd 2nd Tm N In Confrnc Wrestling 79; Letter Wrestling Cross Cntry 77; Univ; Bus Admin.

ROJC, CAROL A; Regina HS; Euclid, OH; Trs Frsh Cls; Chrs; Hon Rl; Stg Crw; Ohio State; Dental Hygienist.

ROKICKI, LESLIE S; St Joseph Academy; Cleveland, OH; Cls Rep Frsh Cls; Trs Soph Cls; Stu Cncl; Bsbl; Coach Actv; Univ; Psych.

ROKOSZ, DEBRA; Lowell Sr HS; Lowell, IN; Cls Rep Frsh Cls; Sec Sr Cls; Am Leg Aux Girls St; Hon Rl; NHS; Off Ade; Ed Yrbk; Yrbk; OEA; Vllybll Varsity Letter 78; Univ; Acctg.

ROLAND, INEZ; Withrow HS; Cincinnati, OH; Cls Rep Soph Cls; Cl Rep Jr Cls; NHS; Stu Cncl; Univ Of Cinn; Math.

ROLAND, MARK; Mt Healthy HS; Cincinnati, OH; Boy Scts; Mod UN; Sct Actv; Rptr Sch Nwsp; Sch Nwsp; Univ; Jrnlsm.

ROLANDO, ANNETTE; Warren Woods HS; Warren, MI; Hon Rl; NHS; Sch Mus; ALMA; Pharm.

ROLENZ, KATHY; Ellet HS; Akron, OH; 79/360 Chrs; Girl Scts; Hon Rl; Hosp Ade; Mdrgl; Natl Forn Lg; NHS; Orch; Sch Mus; Sch Pl; Kent St Univ; Theatre.

ROLF, CHERYL; Kenston HS; Chagrin Fls, OH; Band; Chrs; Drl Tm; Girl Scts; Hon Rl; Sch Mus; Pres Yth Flsp; Rdo Clb; Mat Maids; Twrlr; Coll; Busns Mgmt.

ROLFES, JOSEPH; Western Hills HS; Cincinnati, OH; 5/860 VP Soph Cls; Pres Jr Cls; Am Leg Boys St; Stu Cncl; Letter Crs Cntry; Letter Trk; Chrldng; IM Sprt; Univ Of Cin; Bus.

ROLFES, LISA M; Seton HS; Cincinnati, OH; 48/271 Chrs; Drl Tm; Hon Rl; NHS; Spn Clb; College; Real Estate.

ROLFES, STEPHEN; William Henry Harrison HS; Harrison, OH; 32/254 AFS; Chrh Wkr; Jr NHS; Stg Crw; Treas Drama Clb; Spn Clb; Univ Of Cincinnati; Archt.

ROLKA, YVONNE; Fitzgerald HS; Sterling Hts, MI; Band; Girl Scts; Hon Rl; Jr NHS; NHS; Letter Trk; IM Sprt; Twrlr; Wayne St Univ; Med.

ROLL, KIM; Eastern HS; Pekin, IN; 14/91 Treas Band; Hon Rl; NHS; Sch Pl; Drama Clb; Pres Pep Clb; Letter Bsktbl; Letter Trk; Treas Of Sunshine Soc 78; 4 Yrs Prfct Attndnc 75 79; Bst Servng Percntg In Vllybll 78; Indiana St Univ; Math.

ROLLAND, BARB; Bridgeport HS; Bridgeport, WV; Y-Teens; Letter Bsktbl; Letter Ten; College; Bus Mngt.

ROLLER, VALERIE; Eastmoor Sr HS; Columbus, OH; 38/295 Cls Rep Sr Cls; Band; Chrs; Chrh Wkr; Hon Rl; Orch; Sch Mus; Stu Cncl; Lat Clb; Letter Trk; Ohio State Univ Prgrm For Prgress Outstndng Ach; Wittenberg Coll; Music.

ROLLETT, PATRICIA; Mater Dei HS; Evansville, IN; Cls Rep Sr Cls; Hon Rl; Quill & Scroll; Stg Crw; Yrbk; Sch Nwsp; Pep Clb; Letter Bsktbl; Letter Gym; Letter Chrldng; Honor Certificate; Evansville Schl; Medicine.

ROLLIN, MERRY; Hale HS; Hale, MI; Aud/Vis; Chrh Wkr; Girl Scts; Lbry Ade; Yrbk; 4-H; Swmmng; 4-H Awd; College; Medical Doctor.

ROLLINS, DENNIS L; Perry HS; Massillon, OH; 24/480 Boy Scts; Chrs; FCA; Hon Rl; NHS; Sct Actv; Stg Crw; Spn Clb; Letter Ftbl; Letter Wrstlng; Coll; Elec Engr.

ROLLINS, MALANIA; Rutherford B Hayes HS; Delaware, OH; 1/265 Pres Frsh Cls; Chrh Wkr; Hon Rl; Natl Forn Lg; NHS; Pres 4-H; Pres Fr Clb; Pep Clb; Chrldng; Cit Awd; Ohio Wesleyan Univ; Home Ec.

ROLLINS, SHARON; East HS; Youngstown, OH; 14/187 Sec Jr Cls; Band; Pres Chrh Wkr; JA; Lbry Ade; VP NHS; Stu Cncl; Sec Y-Teens; Pres DECA; Sec Key Clb; Choffin Voc Schl; LPN.

ROLLISON, KRIS; Bloomfield HS; Bloomfield, IN; 2/97 Band; FCA; Hon Rl; NHS; Ed Yrbk; Fr Clb; Pep Clb; Chrldng; Outstanding Preformance At Jrnlsm Inst 1978; Indiana Univ; Psych.

ROLLMAN, TEENA; Jefferson Area HS; Jefferson, OH; Girl Scts; NHS; Off Ade; Sch Pl; Stg Crw; Yth Flsp; Pres 4-H; Univ; Exec Sec.

ROLLYSON, CONNIE; Lewis County HS; Weston, WV; Hon Rl; NHS; Trk; PPFtbl; Natl Merit Ltr; West Virginia Univ; Sec Studies.

ROLLYSON, MIKE; Parkersburg HS; Parkersburg, WV; Boy Scts; Debate Tm; Natl Forn Lg; Sct Actv; Sch Nwsp; Boys Clb Am; Key Clb; Letter Ftbl; Letter Wrstlng; College; Pre Law.

ROLOFF JR, CARL; Lutheran West HS; Lakewood, OH; 4/96 Debate Tm; Hon Rl; Mod UN; NHS; Sct Actv; Sci Clb; Ftbl; Trk; IM Sprt; Natl Merit Ltr; Merit Roll; Coll; Sci.

ROLPH, LYNNE; Seymour HS; Seymour, IN; 1/394 Val; Am Leg Aux Girls St; Chrs; Hon Rl; Sch Mus; Pres Stu Cncl; VP Yth Flsp; Ed Yrbk; Spn Clb; Letter Bsktbl; De Pauw Univ; Medicine.

ROLSTON, VICTORIA; Williamstown HS; Williamstown, WV; 15/102 Girl Scts; Hon Rl; Hosp Ade; Sct Actv; Stg Crw; Yth Flsp; Drama Clb; Fr Clb; Pep Clb; Certf Of Serv As Vlntr 78; 3rd Pl Hnrs In Art Show 79; West Virginia Univ; Med Tech.

ROMAIN, FRANCINE R; Liberty HS; Clarksburg, WV; 65/228 Band; Boy Scts; Hon Rl; Lbry Ade; Sch Mus; Sch Pl; Sct Actv; Stu Cncl; Yth Flsp; Y-Teens; Fairmont St Univ; Comp Sci.

ROMAKER, ANTHONY; Wapakoneta Sr HS; Cridersville, OH; Cmnty Wkr; Hon Rl; NHS; Mth Clb; Spn Clb; Bsbl; Ftbl; Mgrs; Natl Merit SF; Bowling Green St Univ; Acctg.

ROMAN, BRIDGETTE; Canfield HS; Canfield, OH; Treas AFS; Chrs; Debate Tm; Girl Scts; Hon Rl; Treas JA; Lit Mag; Mdrgl; Natl Forn Lg; Orch; Ohio St Univ; Law.

ROMAN, FELISA; George Washington HS; East Chicago, IN; 3/286 Cls Rep Sr Cls; Sec Chrh Wkr; Hon Rl; Pres NHS; Orch; Rptr Yrbk; Sch Nwsp; Sec FHA; FTA; Spn Clb; Valparaiso Univ; Sociology.

ROMAN, JEROME; Padua HS; Parma, OH; Hon Rl; Ftbl; Ten; IM Sprt; Voc Schl; Elec.

ROMAN, SANTITA; Horace Mann HS; Gary, IN; Hon Rl; Jr NHS; Mth Clb; Spn Clb; Cit Awd; Sec.

ROMAN, SHIRLEY R; Alma HS; Alma, MI; Aud/Vis; Lbry Ade; 4-H; FHA; Pep Clb; College; Dance.

ROMANCZUK, BEV; Whiteoak HS; Hillsboro, OH; VP Jr Cls; Yrbk; FHA; Chrldng; Miami Jacobs Jr Coll; Fash Merch.

ROMANELLO, ANTHONY; Norwood Sr HS; Norwood, OH; 24/388 Chrs; Hon Rl; Jr NHS; Sch Mus; Pres Key Clb; Xavier Univ; Comp Prog.

ROMANIK, ELIZABETH; Our Lady Of Mercy HS; Northville, MI; CAP; VP JA; Mod UN; Ger Clb; JA Awd; Univ Of Michigan; Med.

ROMANO, NANCY; Forest Hills Central HS; Grand Rapids, MI; 3/270 VP Soph Cls; Hon Rl; Hosp Ade; Lbry Ade; NHS; Sch Pl; Y-Teens; Drama Clb; Fr Clb; Sci Clb; College; Biomedical Engr.

ROMANO, PETER; Holland HS; Holland, MI; 1/300 Pres Frsh Cls; Trs Soph Cls; Pres Sr Cls; Val; JA; NHS; Letter Bsbl; Capt Swmmng; Kalamazoo College; Medicine.

ROMANO, RHONDA; Malvern HS; Malvern, OH; Sec Jr Cls; Chrs; Hon Rl; Lbry Ade; NHS; Sch Mus; Yrbk; Pep Clb; Chrldng; Ohio St Univ; Psychology.

ROMANO, SHELLY; Willoughby South HS; Willoughby, OH; Chrs; Chrh Wkr; Off Ade; Sch Pl; DECA; 4-H; Bsktbl; Gym; GAA; God Cntry Awd; Willoughby Tech Sch; Major Course.

ROMANOWSKI, DIANE; Posen Consolidated HS; Posen, MI; Hon Rl; Rptr Yrbk; Rptr Sch Nwsp; Bsbl; Univ.

ROMATOWSKI, M; Trenton HS; Trenton, MI; Chrh Wkr; Hon Rl; Lbry Ade; NHS; Ger Clb; Ten; Voice Dem Awd; College; Dentist.

ROME, JO ANN; Garfield Sr HS; Hamilton, OH; Pres Sr Cls; Chrs; Hon Rl; NHS; Sch Mus; Pres Stu Cncl; Rptr Sch Nwsp; Chrldng; JC Awd; Rotary Awd; Outstndng Yth By Evening Optimist; Yth Of The Year; Bowling Green St Univ; Hosp Admin.

ROME, RUTH; Okemos HS; E Lansing, MI; 19/286 Chrs; Mdrgl; NHS; Sch Mus; Drama Clb; Lat Clb; Trk; IM Sprt; MSVA St Wmns Hnrs Chr 78; Music Patrons Schlrshp 79; Univ; Theater Arts.

ROMELL, KATE; Rocky River HS; Rocky River, OH; Cmp Fr Grls; Natl Forn Lg; Orch; PAVAS; Sch Mus; Sch Pl; Stg Crw; Drama Clb; Natl Merit SF; Denison Coll; Theatre Design.

ROMEO, KEITH; North Farmington HS; Farm Hills, MI; Aud/Vis; Boy Scts; Chrs; Chrh Wkr; Cmnty Wkr; FCA; Hon Rl; Lbry Ade; Off Ade; Pol Wkr; College; Engr.

ROMEO, MELINDA; Wickliffe Sr HS; Wickliffe, OH; 1/325 Val; AFS; Hon Rl; NHS; Stg Crw; Drama Clb; Fr Clb; Bowling Green St Univ; Bus.

ROMER, LYDIA; Carlisle HS; Carlisle, OH; 1/185 Am Leg Aux Girls St; Band; Chrs; Hon Rl; Hosp Ade; Jr NHS; NHS; Pres Stu Cncl; Rptr Yrbk; Ed Sch Nwsp; Schlshp Team 77; Carlisle Educ Recgntn Assoc 75; Excellnc In Acctg 79; Univ Of Dayton; Pre Med.

ROMEU, KATHLEEN; St Joseph Sr HS; St Joseph, MI; Cmnty Wkr; Hon Rl; Lbry Ade; Sch Mus; Sct Actv; 4-H; Letter Chrldng; Coach Actv; 4-H Awd; Lake Michigan Coll; Law.

ROMIE, JOAN; Centerville HS; Centerville, OH; 221/627 Girl Scts; Lbry Ade; Ftbl; Hockey; Trk; PPFtbl; Bowling Green St Univ.

ROMIG, AMY S; Claymont HS; Dennison, OH; Aud/Vis; Hon Rl; Lbry Ade; Quill & Scroll; Sch Mus; Sch Pl; Fr Clb; Spn Clb; Vocational Schl; Model.

ROMIGH, ALICIA; West Branch HS; Beloit, OH; Band; Yth Flsp; Scr Kpr; Twrlr; Natl Merit Ltr; Aultman Schl; Nursing.

ROMINE, SHARON; South Harrison HS; Mt Claire, WV; Am Leg Aux Girls St; Band; Hon Rl; Hosp Ade; Stu Cncl; Rptr Yrbk; Rptr Sch Nwsp; Sec 4-H; Mgrs; 4-H Awd; Fairmont St Coll; Med Asst.

ROMINE, TRACY; Pinckney HS; Brighton, MI; Cls Rep Sr Cls; Hon Rl; Chrldng; Pom Pon; Natl Merit SF; Michigan St Univ.

ROMINGER, JERRY P; Springs Valley HS; French Lick, IN; 1/109 Band; Chrs; Chrh Wkr; FCA; Hon Rl; Yth Flsp; Sch Nwsp; Bsktbl; Mgrs; Indiana Univ; Chemistry.

ROMITO, CLOTILDE; Lumen Cordium HS; Maple Hts, OH; Cls Rep Soph Cls; Hon Rl; Stu Cncl; Yrbk; Spn Clb; GAA; IM Sprt; College; Advertising.

ROMITO, TERESA; Campbell Memorial HS; Campbell, OH; Cls Rep Soph Cls; Cl Rep Jr Cls; Capt Hosp Ade; Treas JA; NHS; Mth Clb; Sci Clb; Pres Spn Clb; Trk; College.

ROMLEIN, JENNY; Pontiac N Sr HS; Pontiac, MI; Cmp Fr Grls; Hon Rl; Hosp Ade; Off Ade; Merit Awd N E Oakland Voc Ed Ctr; Schlrshp Fed Of Womens Clb; Mich Competitive Schlrshp; Oakland Univ; Nursing.

ROMME, RUSS; Lexington HS; Lexington, OH; 11/243 Hon Rl; Jr NHS; NHS; Letter Trk; Letter Wrstlng; Coach Actv; IM Sprt; Scr Kpr; Tmr; Ohio State Univ; Zoology.

ROMOHR, AMY; William Henry Harrison HS; Harrison, OH; 15/208 VP Sr Cls; Am Leg Aux Girls St; Band; Chrh Wkr; Jr NHS; NHS; Sch Mus; Sch Pl; Yrbk; Drama Clb; Miami Univ; Bus Admin.

ROMOSER, DONALD; Euclid HS; Euclid, OH; 97/701 Cls Rep Frsh Cls; Cls Rep Soph Cls; Cl Rep Jr Cls; NHS; Sch Pl; Stu Cncl; Sch Nwsp; Drama Clb; Crs Cntry; Ten; Miami Univ; Accounting.

ROMZEK, GERALDINE; Harbor Beach Cmnty HS; Ruth, MI; 14/126 Chrs; Hon Rl; NHS; FHA; Pep Clb;.

RONAYNE, AMY; Clarence M Kimball HS; Royal Oak, MI; Band; Hon Rl; Natl Forn Lg; NHS; Sch Mus; Sch Pl; Stg Crw; College; Law.

RONCONE, KAREN; Boardman HS; Youngstown, OH; Hon Rl; NHS; Off Ade; Pol Wkr; Quill & Scroll; Y-Teens; Rptr Sch Nwsp; Pep Clb; College; Bus Mgmt.

RONDEAU, WILLARD; Luther L Wright HS; Ironwood, MI; Hon Rl; VICA; IM Sprt; Michigan St Univ; Journalism.

RONDOT, PAULA; Bishop Luers HS; Ft Wayne, IN; 4 Cl Rep Jr Cls; Chrs; Hon Rl; Sch Mus; Sch Pl; Stg Crw; Stu Cncl; Drama Clb; Pep Clb; Chrldng; Ball St Univ; Elem Ed.

RONEY, DEIRDRE; Grosse Pointe North HS; Grosse Pt Shore, MI; Sec Jr Cls; Sec Sr Cls; Hon Rl; Pol Wkr; Sch Pl; Stu Cncl; IM Sprt; PPFtbl; Scr Kpr; Natl Merit SF; Univ Of Denver; Psychology.

RONEY, JANET M; Our Lady Star Of The Sea HS; Grosse Pt Shors, MI; Hon Rl; Hosp Ade; Natl Forn Lg; NHS; Stu Cncl; Ed Yrbk; Sprt Ed Yrbk; Rptr Yrbk; Yrbk; Drama Clb; Michigan St Univ; Travel.

RONEY, SHARON; Jackson HS; Massillon, OH; Chrs; Girl Scts; NHS; Sch Mus; Y-Teens; Yrbk; Pep Clb; Natl Merit Ltr; Ohio Wesleyan Spec Recognition Awd; Fresh Schlr At Ohio Wesleyan In The Fall; Ohio Wesleyan Univ; Vet.

RONNEBAUM, LINDA; Academy Of Immaculate Cncptn; Batesville, IN; 18/68 Chrs; Chrh Wkr; Cmnty Wkr; Hon Rl; Sec NHS; Quill & Scroll; Sch Mus; Sch Pl; Stg Crw; Yrbk; Journalism.

RONQUIST, RONALD; Sault Area HS; Sault Ste Mari, MI; 5/300 Band; Lat Clb; Letter Bsbl; Letter Bsktbl; Capt Ftbl; Letter Ten; Natl Merit Schl; Rotary Awd; Lake Superior State Collegef Med.

ROOD, BRIAN; Muskegon Cath Central HS; Muskegon, MI; Band; Hon Rl; Pres MMM; Pol Wkr; Sch Mus; Natl Merit Schl; Univ Of Michigan; Music.

ROOD, JOHN R; Lumen Christi HS; Jackson, MI; 83/231 Am Leg Boys St; Band; Boy Scts; PAVAS; Lat Clb; Spn Clb; Letter Trk; Earned Eagle Scout Awd; College; Engr.

ROOD, LINDA; Birch Run HS; Burt, MI; Girl Scts; Hon Rl; Stg Crw; Rptr Sch Nwsp; Fr Clb; IM Sprt; St Of Mi Schlshp 79; Cntrl Michigan Univ; Educ.

ROOD, ROBERT; Wellston HS; Wellston, OH; Band; Chrs; Chrh Wkr; Cmnty Wkr; Hon Rl; Sch Mus; Sch Pl; Stg Crw; Drama Clb; Ten; OSU; Pre Law.

ROOD, THERESA; Huntington HS; Huntington, WV; 1/500 Cmp Fr Grls; Hon Rl; Jr NHS; NHS; Drama Clb; Pres Lat Clb; Mth Clb; College; Law.

ROODBERGEN, SCOTT; Vicksburg HS; Scotts, MI; Yrbk; Sch Nwsp; Univ Of Mich; Architecture.

ROOF, LUCY; Wapakoneta HS; Wapakoneta, OH; Hon Rl; NHS; Sch Nwsp; OEA; Sec.

ROOF, ROBERT; Turpin HS; Cincinnati, OH; Bsktbl; Letter Ftbl; Socr; Gym; Air Force Academy; Aero Engr.

ROOKSTOOL, DEDRA; Talcott HS; Talcott, WV; Pres Frsh Cls; Chrh Wkr; Cmnty Wkr; Hon Rl; Stu Cncl; 4-H; Bsktbl; Cit Awd; 4-H Awd;.

ROOKSTOOL, ROBERT J; Meadow Bridge HS; Meadow Bridge, WV; 1/53 Am Leg Boys St; Hon Rl; NHS; Fr Clb; Bsktbl; Ftbl; Know Your St Govt Day 79; Know Your County Govt Day 79; Univ; Math.

ROOMES, SCOTT; Sidney HS; Sidney, OH; Hon Rl; Stu Cncl; Coach Actv; IM Sprt; Us Army Tank Corps.

ROONEY, KELLY; Stonewall Jackson HS; Chrlstn, WV; Cls Rep Frsh Cls; Cl Rep Jr Cls; Cls Rep Sr Cls; Cmp Fr Grls; Chrs; Hon Rl; Stu Cncl; Fr Clb; Pep Clb; Gym; Softball Team Little League; Coll.

ROONEY, PATTI; Bay HS; Bay Village, OH; 12/380 Trs Jr Cls; Trs Sr Cls; Hon Rl; NHS; Off Ade; Capt Ten; Trk; PPFtbl; College; Nursing.

ROONEY, SCOTT; Brother Rice HS; Birmingham, MI; Hon Rl; Lit Mag; Off Ade; Fr Clb; Bsktbl; Socr; Trk; IM Sprt; Marquette Univ; Pre Law.

ROOP, DEBRA; Mendon HS; Mendon, MI; Am Leg Aux Girls St; FCA; Hon Rl; NHS; Off Ade; 4-H; Gym; Letter Chrldng; Coach Actv; Tmr; Univ; Law.

ROOSE, ANNE M; Center Line HS; Warren, MI; 39/430 Hon Rl; Jr NHS; Natl Forn Lg; NHS; Sch Pl; Stu Cncl; VP Drama Clb; Fr Clb; OEA; Pres Sci Clb; Arizona St Univ; Busns.

ROOSE, GRETCHEN L; Hubbard HS; Hubbard, OH; 29/330 Cls Rep Frsh Cls; Band; Hon Rl; Stu Cncl; Rptr Sch Nwsp; Sch Nwsp; Swmmng; College; Journalism.

ROOSEN, BRENDA; Center Line HS; Center Line, MI; Hon Rl; Hosp Ade; OEA; Univ Of Detroit; Dent Hygenist.

ROOST, HEATHER A; Mason Sr HS; Mason, MI; VP Soph Cls; Cl Rep Jr Cls; Chrh Wkr; Girl Scts; Hon Rl; Lbry Ade; Orch; Yth Flsp; Fr Clb; Pep Clb; Univ.

ROOT, CHRISTINE; Black River HS; Spencer, OH; 2/78 VP Sr Cls; Am Leg Aux Girls St; Pres Band; Chrs; Hon Rl; Pres Beta Clb; Drama Clb; VP 4-H; Spn Clb; Scr Kpr; Florida St Univ; Bio Tchr.

ROOT, DAWN; Portage Central HS; Kalamazoo, MI; 1/379 Pres AFS; Chrs; Hon Rl; VP JA; Sch Mus; Fr Clb; Sci Clb; Mgrs; Scr Kpr; Natl Merit Ltr; Kalamazoo Coll; Math.

ROOT, JODIE; Olivet Community HS; Charlotte, MI; Hon Rl; NHS;.

ROOT, KIMBERLY; Shawnee HS; Camden, OH; Pres Soph Cls; Pres Jr Cls; Pres Sr Cls; Am Leg Aux Girls St; Chrs; Chrh Wkr; Drl Tm; Hon Rl; Off Ade; Sch Mus; Miami Univ; Mrktng.

ROOT, KRISTA; Owen Valley HS; Spencer, IN; 7/195 Band; Chrh Wkr; FCA; Hon Rl; Treas Jr NHS; Treas NHS; Sch Mus; Pep Clb; Indiana; Music.

ROOT, LAURA J; Black River HS; Spencer, OH; 2/105 Hst Soph Cls; Hst Jr Cls; Band; Chrs; Hon Rl; VP Beta Clb; 4-H; Sec FFA; Sci Clb; Twrlr; Coll.

ROOT, LISA; Niles HS; Niles, MI; 29/388 Girl Scts; Hon Rl; Yth Flsp; Mi Comp Schlrshp; Hon Grad Niles HS; Davenport Coll Of Bus.

ROOT, ROBERT; Grandville HS; Grandville, MI; Hon Rl; Sch Pl; Stg Crw; Rdo Clb; Grand Valley St College.

ROPER, THERESA; Peru HS; Peru, IN; Hon Rl; Jr NHS; Lit Mag; Natl Forn Lg; Sch Mus; Sch Pl; Stg Crw; Drama Clb; Pep Clb; VFW Awd; Coll; Secondary Ed.

RORABACHER, SHEILA; Plymouth Canton HS; Plymouth, MI; 35/435 Band; Hon Rl; NHS; Prin Hon Roll 78; Plymouth Caton Math Team 77; Aquinas Coll Schslp 78; Stdnt Serv Ctr 76; Aquinas Coll; Bus Admin.

RORABACK, ROSANNE; East Lansing HS; East Lansing, MI; 13/354 NHS; Natl Merit Ltr; Michigan St Univ; Educ.

RORICK, NANCY; Bishop Dwenger HS; Ft Wayne, IN; Chrh Wkr; Hon Rl; JA; Stu Cncl; College.

RORRER, TINA; Marsh Fork HS; Arnett, WV; Aud/Vis; Band; Hon Rl; Jr NHS; Off Ade; Univ; Vet Med.

ROSADO, EDUARDO; Mt Vernon Academy; Brooklyn, OH; Chrs; CAP; Hon Rl; Sch Pl; Stg Crw; Bsbl; Bsktbl; Ftbl; Socr; Swmmng; Coll; Aviation.

ROSAK, JOAN; Mogadore HS; Mogadore, OH; Cls Rep Frsh Cls; Cls Rep Soph Cls; Cl Rep Jr Cls; Aud/Vis; Chrs; Girl Scts; Hon Rl; Univ Of Akron; Art.

ROSALES, DEAN; Bishop Moll HS; E Chicago, IN; Mth Clb; Spn Clb; Crs Cntry; Trk; Wrstlng; IM Sprt; College; Mech Engr.

ROSANDER, DAWN; Oregon Davis HS; Hamlet, IN; 10/70 Sec Sr Cls; VP FCA; Hon Rl; Yrbk; Pep Clb; Sci Clb; Gym; Trk; Chrldng; VP GAA; Ancilla Coll.

ROSATI, MELISSA; Ashtabula Cnty Joint HS; Chardon, OH; Pres Sr Cls; Cls Rep Sr Cls; Hon Rl; Lakeland Comm College; Retailing.

ROSATI, PAMELA; St Mary Academy; Monroe, MI; 14/117 Cmnty Wkr; Hon Rl; Hosp Ade; NHS; Rptr Yrbk; Sci Clb; Michigan St Univ; Bio.

ROSCOE, KIM; Maplewood HS; Cortland, OH; Yrbk; Beta Clb; Fr Clb; FTA; Twrlr; Trumbull Voc Schl; Distrb Ed.

ROSCULET, JOHN; Grosse Pointe N HS; Grosse Pt Wds, MI; Band; Chrh Wkr; Cmnty Wkr; Hon Rl; NHS; Crs Cntry; Trk; Cert Of Hnr Soc Studies; 1st Chair Clarinet Player Symphony Bnd; Varsity Clb; Coll; Med.

ROSE, BEVERLY; Sylvania Northview HS; Sylvania, OH; VP Jr Cls; VP Sr Cls; Am Leg Aux Girls St; Band; Chrh Wkr; Girl Scts; Hon Rl; Hosp Ade; Natl Forn Lg; Sch Pl; Univ Of Toledo.

ROSE, CINDY M; Springs Valley Community HS; Frenchlick, IN; 13/81 Chrh Wkr; Hon Rl; NHS; Sch Pl; 4-H; Fr Clb; FFA; Purdue Univ; Veterinarian.

ROSE, CRAIG; West Muskingum HS; Zanesville, OH; Chrs; Hon Rl; NHS; Sch Mus; Pres FFA; Key Clb; Socr; Trk; IM Sprt; Tech Coll; Forester.

ROSE, CRYSTAL; Centerville HS; Centerville, OH; 18/680 Chrs; Sec Chrh Wkr; NHS; Pres OEA; Opt Clb Awd; 2nd In Ohio Ofc Ed Assn Reg Steno Cont; Stu Of Day; Runner Up Wash Twp Fire Dept Queen Cont;.

ROSE, DAVID; Mt Vernon Academy; Clyde, OH; Chrs; Hon Rl; Bsbl; Letter Ftbl; Ten; IM Sprt; Volleyball Captain 3yrs Lettered 3times; Worker Of The Montn Awd; Andrews Univ; Archt.

ROSE, DAVID; Gwinn HS; Ki Sawyer Afb, MI; 8/206 Boy Scts; Hon Rl; Sct Actv; Beta Clb; VICA; Natl Merit Ltr; Natl Merit SF; Univ Of Michigan; Mech Drafting.

ROSE, DAWN; C S Mott HS; Warren, MI; Cls Rep Soph Cls; Chrs; Girl Scts; Hon Rl; NHS; Stu Cncl; Rptr Sch Nwsp; Fr Clb; FTA; Letter Trk; College; Engineering.

ROSE, DICK; Sandy Valley HS; Magnolia, OH; Cls Rep Sr Cls; Am Leg Boys St; Hon Rl; Natl Forn Lg; Sch Pl; Bsbl; Kiwan Awd; College; Acctng.

ROSE, DORINDA; Calhoun County HS; Grantsville, WV; Cls Rep Sr Cls; Am Leg Aux Girls St; Chrh Wkr; Hon Rl; Lbry Ade; NHS; Off Ade; Sch Mus; Stu Cncl; Yrbk; Glenville St Univ; Acctg.

ROSE, ELIZABETH; Spanishburg HS; Flat Top, WV; Band; Hon Rl; Sch Mus; 4-H; FBLA; 4-H Awd; Beckley Coll; Bus.

ROSE, HEIDI; Edgewood Sr HS; Ashtabula, OH; AFS; Band; Off Ade; Stg Crw; Y-Teens; Rptr Yrbk; Pep Clb; Spn Clb; Scr Kpr; Univ; Bus.

ROSE, HILARY; Rochester HS; Rochester, MI; Band; Chrs; Mdrgl; NHS; Sch Mus; Sch Pl; Yrbk; Pep Clb; Glf; Natl Merit Ltr; Mic State Univ; Advertising.

ROSE, JULIA; David Anderson HS; Lisbon, OH; 9/116 Band; Cmp Fr Grls; Hon Rl; NHS; Sch Mus; Y-Teens; Rptr Sch Nwsp; Sch Nwsp; Fr Clb; Sci Clb; Univ Of Akron; Corp Law.

ROSE, KARL; Archbishop Alter HS; Kettering, OH; 22/270 Chrs; Chrh Wkr; Hon Rl; NHS; Rptr Sch Nwsp; Spn Clb; Letter Socr; Coach Actv; IM Sprt; Univ Of Dayton; Pre Med.

ROSE, KATHRYN; Aiken Sr HS; Cincinnati, OH; Cmp Fr Grls; Chrs; Hon Rl; JA; Yth Flsp; Fr Clb; Swmmng; Univ; Work With Children.

ROSE, KURT; Oakridge Sr HS; Muskegon, MI; Band; Boy Scts; Chrh Wkr; Hon Rl; Jr NHS; Orch; Crs Cntry; Trk; VFW Awd; Study Grant From W Shore Yth Symphony 78; Musician Of The Yr HS Band Schlrshp 78; Academic Schlrshp 79; Univ; Music.

ROSE, LINDA; Union City Cmnty HS; Union City, IN; 12/95 Band; Lbry Ade; NHS; Sch Mus; Eng Clb; Ten; Mas Awd; Univ; Elem Ed.

ROSE, LISA; Eastern HS; Salem, IN; Sec Frsh Cls; VP Soph Cls; Sec Sr Cls; Band; Hon Rl; Sch Mus; 4-H; Pep Clb; 4-H Awd; Coll; Lab Tech.

ROSE, LORI; Wapakoneta Sr HS; Wapakoneta, OH; Chrh Wkr; Cmnty Wkr; Hon Rl; Hosp Ade; Sec Yth Flsp; Sec Y-Teens; OEA; Letter Mgrs; Attndnc Cert Of Awd; Cert Of Proficiency; Lima Tech Coll; Acctg.

ROSE, MARSHA; University HS; Morgantown, WV; 9/175 Trs Frsh Cls; Cls Rep Soph Cls; Trs Sr Cls; Am Leg Aux Girls St; Band; Chrs; Chrh Wkr; Hon Rl; Jr NHS; NHS; West Virginia Univ; Acctg.

ROSE, MIKE; Austin HS; Austin, IN; 8/110 Pres Frsh Cls; Pres Soph Cls; Pres Jr Cls; Pres Sr Cls; Hon Rl; NHS; Sch Pl; Stu Cncl; FTA; Lat Clb; College; Busns Admin.

ROSE, MIKE; Edgewood Sr HS; Ashtabula, OH; Ed Yrbk; Spn Clb; Letter Trk; IM Sprt; Ohio Northern Univ.

ROSE, MYRA; Franklin HS; Franklin, OH; 85/302 Cls Rep Frsh Cls; Cls Rep Soph Cls; Cl Rep Jr Cls; Cls Rep Sr Cls; Off Ade; Stu Cncl; Yrbk; Pep Clb; Ten; MVP Tennis 77; Miami Univ.

ROSE, PATRICIA; Milan HS; Milan, MI; Band; Chrh Wkr; Hon Rl; NHS; Letter Bsbl; Letter Swmmng; Univ; Med.

ROSE, RITA; Lanse Creuse HS; Mt Clemens, MI; 13/260 Sec Soph Cls; Sec Jr Cls; Cls Rep Sr Cls; Hosp Ade; Lit Mag; NHS; Sch Mus; Sec Stu Cncl; Letter Trk; Mic State Univ; English.

ROSE, ROANNE; Bridgeport HS; Saginaw, MI; Chrs; Hon Rl; NHS; Rptr Sch Nwsp; Ger Clb;.

ROSE, STEPHANIE; Cadiz HS; Cadiz, OH; Chrs; Chrh Wkr; Girl Scts; Hon Rl; NHS; Jackson Coll; Music.

ROSE, TIMOTHY L; Streetsboro HS; Streetsboro, OH; Cmnty Wkr; Hon Rl; Rdo Clb; Bsbl; Ftbl; Wrstlng;.

ROSEBECK, RICHARD; Marion L Steele HS; Amherst, OH; Univ; Math.

ROSEBERRY, VIRGINIA; Brookhaven HS; Columbus, OH; Chrs; VP Chrh Wkr; Debate Tm; Lbry Ade; Sch Mus; Spn Clb; Trk; Tmr; St Paul Bible Coll; Nurse.

ROSEBOOM, DANIEL; Tri West Hendricks HS; Pittsboro, IN; 14/127 Boy Scts; Chrh Wkr; Cmnty Wkr; FCA; Hon Rl; NHS; Sch Pl; Stg Crw; Rptr Sch Nwsp; 4-H; Indiana St Univ; Printing.

ROSEBOOM, PATRICK; Portage Central HS; Portage, MI; Hon Rl; Sci Clb; St Of Mi Comp Schlrshp Prog 79; Cert Of Recogntn; Alpha Beta Awd 77 78 & 79; Northern Michigan Univ; Bio Chem.

ROSEBROCK, ANNETTE M; Fairview HS; Mark Center, OH; 9/120 Chrh Wkr; Hon Rl; Off Ade; 4-H; FHA; Bsktbl; Trk; GAA; 4-H Awd; County 4 H Fshn Bd 77 78 & 79; Univ; Med Tech.

ROSEBROCK, CAROL; Patrick Henry HS; Hamler, OH; Trs Soph Cls; Trs Jr Cls; Band; Chrs; Hon Rl; Orch; 4-H; Trk; 4-H Awd; Univ; Acctg.

ROSEBROCK, MELISSA; Whiteland Community HS; Whiteland, IN; 22/225 Cl Rep Jr Cls; Cls Rep Sr Cls; Am Leg Aux Girls St; FCA; Jr NHS; NHS; Treas Stu Cncl; 4-H; Pres FHA; Letter Trk; Purdue Univ; Animal Sci.

ROSE III, WILLIAM; Rochester HS; Rochester, MI; 25/400 Sec Sr Cls; Band; Hon Rl; NHS; Ger Clb; Crs Cntry; Trk; Univ Of Mic; Med.

ROSEKELLY, GEORGE; Edison HS; Huron, OH; 6/159 Hon Rl; Stu Cncl; Mth Clb; VP Sci Clb; C of C Awd; Kiwan Awd; Rifle Clb & Tm Varsity Lttr 78; Assembly Comm Chrmn 78; Co Capt Of Hi Q Tm 1st Plc In Oh 78; Univ; Engr.

ROSEKRANS, HEIDI; Walnut Hills HS; Cincinnati, OH; Girl Scts; Yth Flsp; VP Fr Clb; Ger Clb; Ten; Coach Actv; Kenyon Coll; Modern Foreign Lang.

ROSELLI, PHIL; N Farmington HS; Farmington Hls, MI; Hon Rl; Lbry Ade; NHS; Mth Clb; Sci Clb; Glf; Natl Merit Ltr; Coll; Med.

ROSEMA, RANDAL; Ottawa Hills HS; Grand Rapids, MI; VP Jr Cls; Chrh Wkr; NHS; Ten; Univ Albion; Accgt.

ROSEN, A; Southfield Sr HS; Southfield, MI; Sch Mus; Sch Pl; Sct Actv; Stg Crw; Univ Of Montana; Bus Admin.

ROSEN, MARC; William Henry Harrison HS; Harrison, OH; Aud/Vis; JA; Lbry Ade; Sch Mus; Sch Pl; Stg Crw; Drama Clb; Wrstlng; IM Sprt; Scr Kpr; Univ Of Cincinnati; Radio Cmnctns.

ROSENAU, LYNNE; Lutheran HS; E Detroit, MI; 3/149 Chrh Wkr; Hon Rl; Hosp Ade; NHS; Drama Clb; Pep Clb; Chrldng; Coll; Pediatrician.

ROSENAU, MARTIN; Notre Dame HS; Detroit, MI; 65/200 Cls Rep Frsh Cls; Cls Rep Soph Cls; Cl Rep Jr Cls; Cls Rep Sr Cls; Cmnty Wkr; Hon Rl; Jr NHS; Pol Wkr; Stu Cncl; Rptr Sch Nwsp; Michigan St Univ; Pre Law.

ROSENBAUM, BETH ELLEN; Morgantown HS; Morgantown, WV; 1/500 Chrs; Hon Rl; NHS; Sct Actv; Sec Fr Clb; Sec Mth Clb; Ten; Natl Merit SF; Voice Dem Awd; Coll; Music.

ROSENBAUM, BRUCE; Shaker Heights HS; Shaker Hts, OH; 33/545 Cls Rep Frsh Cls; Cl Rep Jr Cls; Cls Rep Sr Cls; Chrh Wkr; Debate Tm; Mod UN; Natl Forn Lg; Stu Cncl; Sch Nwsp; Natl Merit SF; Univ Of Mich.

ROSENBAUM, DEBORAH; Haworth HS; Kokomo, IN; 52/522 Girl Scts; Hon Rl; JA; Off Ade; Rptr Sch Nwsp; 4-H; Sec OEA; Pom Pon; PPFtbl; Am Leg Awd; College; Busns.

ROSENBAUM, GLENN; La Crosse HS; Wanatah, IN; Band; Cmp Fr Grls; Chrh Wkr; Cmnty Wkr; FCA; Sct Actv; Ger Clb; Pep Clb; Purdue; Real Estate.

ROSENBAUM, HEIDI; Marian HS; South Bend, IN; 11/145 Hon Rl; NHS; Sch Mus; Sch Pl; Stu Cncl; Pep Clb; Swmmng; Trk; Eng Awd 77; Amer Hist Awd 79; Spanish Hon 79; Univ; Cmnctns.

ROSENBECK, ANN; Marion Local HS; Chickasaw, OH; Pres Jr Cls; Hon Rl; Rptr Sch Nwsp; Drama Clb; FTA; Pep Clb; Bsktbl; IM Sprt; Ohio Univ; Bus Mgmt.

ROSENBECK, JOHN S; Coldwater HS; Coldwater, OH; Trs Frsh Cls; Am Leg Boys St; Band; Hon Rl; Rptr Yrbk; 4-H; Ger Clb; Glf; Univ; Mech Engr.

ROSENBERG, CRAIG; Hartford HS; Hartford, MI; 8/94 VP Jr Cls; Cl Rep Jr Cls; VP Sr Cls; Cls Rep Sr Cls; Letter Band; Hon Rl; NHS; Stu Cncl; Letter Bsktbl; Letter Crs Cntry; Kalamazoo Coll Acad Schlrshp 79; St Of Mi Competitive Schlrshp Awd 79; Kalamazoo Coll; Archt.

ROSENBERG, RACHEL; Talawanda HS; Oxford, OH; AFS; Cmp Fr Grls; Chrs; Hon Rl; Fr Clb; Pep Clb; Miami Univ; Oceanography.

ROSENBERY, CURTIS; Timken Sr HS; Canton, OH; Hon Rl; IM Sprt; Ohio St Univ; Aero Engr.

ROSENBLAT, FRANK; Oak Park HS; Oak Pk, MI; Band; Chrs; Cmnty Wkr; Lit Mag; Orch; Fr Clb; Univ Of Michigan; Pre Med.

ROSENBURY, ROBIN; Southwestern HS; Hanover, IN; VP Sr Cls; Girl Scts; Hon Rl; Hosp Ade; Jr NHS; NHS; Sch Pl; VP Yth Flsp; VP Drama Clb; 4-H; Univ.

ROSENCRANCE, JAMES G; Charleston HS; Charleston, WV; Am Leg Boys St; Chrs; Chrh Wkr; Hon Rl; NHS; Sch Pl; Yth Flsp; Drama Clb; Lat Clb; Bsbl; Jefferson Awd Univ Of Va Alumni 79; Also Play Piano & Pipe Organ Part In AGO Sponsored Recital 79; Univ; Med.

ROSENCRANS, KATHLEEN; Chesaning HS; Chesaning, MI; 11/250 Hon Rl; Off Ade; Stg Crw; Spn Clb; Letter Bsktbl; Mgrs; Central Mic Univ; Comp Sci.

ROSENFIELD, ANN; Grandview Hts HS; Columbus, OH; 7/130 Band; Chrs; Hon Rl; Jr NHS; NHS; Off Ade; Pol Wkr; Lat Clb; Miami Univ.

ROSENGARTEN, ANNE; Cloverdale HS; Poland, IN; 15/82 Chrs; Hon Rl; Lbry Ade; Sch Mus; Sch Pl; Rptr Yrbk; Sprt Ed Sch Nwsp; Drama Clb; FHA; FTA; St Mary Of The Woods; Eng.

ROSENGARTEN, J; Baebeuf Prep; Indianapolis, IN; Sec Frsh Cls; Trs Frsh Cls; Chrh Wkr; Hon Rl; NHS; Sch Pl; Stg Crw; Stu Cncl; Rptr Yrbk; Ed Sch Nwsp; Univ; Lib Arts.

ROSENTHAL, MARTIN; Walnut Hills HS; Cincinnati, OH; Hon Rl; MMM; Yrbk; Sch Nwsp; Mth Clb; IM Sprt; Natl Merit SF; Univ Of Cincinnati; History.

ROSENTHAL, ROBERT; Beachwood HS; Beachwood, OH; Cls Rep Frsh Cls; Stu Cncl; Sprt Ed Sch Nwsp; Bsbl; Letter Bsktbl; Capt Crs Cntry; Coach Actv; Law.

ROSENTRATER, PHIL; Northwood HS; Nappanee, IN; 23/221 Cl Rep Jr Cls; Chrh Wkr; Hon Rl; NHS; Sch Mus; Sch Pl; Stu Cncl; Drama Clb; Crs Cntry; IM Sprt; Messiah Coll; Poli Sci.

ROSFELD, RUTH; Wayne HS; Dayton, OH; Cls Rep Frsh Cls; Cls Rep Soph Cls; Trs Sr Cls; Hon Rl; Jr NHS; Treas DECA; IM Sprt; Miami Jacobs Jr Coll; Business Admin.

ROSHON, MELINDA; Northridge HS; Johnstown, OH; 3/124 FCA; Hon Rl; NHS; Stu Cncl; 4-H; VP Spn Clb; Bsktbl; Cit Awd; Univ; Dent.

ROSHON, MELISSA; Northridge HS; Johnstown, OH; 17/124 FCA; Hon Rl; NHS; Stu Cncl; 4-H; Spn Clb; Bsktbl; Chrldng; Cit Awd; Univ.

ROSIER, DAVID; Charlotte HS; Charlotte, MI; 39/303 Band; Hon Rl; Off Ade; Sch Mus; Sch Pl; Yrbk; Bsbl; Glf; Natl Merit SF; Michigan St Univ; Mortuary Sci.

ROSIN, BERNARD M; Louisville HS; Louisville, OH; Am Leg Boys St; Band; Boy Scts; JA; NHS; Sct Actv; IM Sprt; Univ Of Akron; Chemical Engineering.

ROSINE, CHERYL; Ainsworth Sr HS; Flint, MI; 1/161 Cls Rep Sr Cls; Val; Girl Scts; Hon Rl; JA; NHS; Sch Pl; Stu Cncl; PPFtbl; Michigan St Univ.

ROSINSKI, KAREN C; Garden City East Sr HS; Garden City, MI; Band; Cmnty Wkr; Girl Scts; Hon Rl; Jr NHS; Lbry Ade; NHS; Orch; Red Cr Ade; Sch Pl; Univ Of Michigan; Pediatrician.

ROSINSKI, RICK; All Saints Central HS; Bay City, MI; 18/200 Boy Scts; Hon Rl; Lbry Ade; Sct Actv; Rptr Yrbk; Trk; Coll.

ROSLOVIC, JOHN; Bexley HS; Columbus, OH; Chrs; Hon Rl; Bsktbl; OSU; Agri Engr.

ROSNER, HEIDI; Pontiac Central HS; W Bloomfield, MI; 3/550 Sal; Debate Tm; Hon Rl; Lbry Ade; Lit Mag; Natl Forn Lg; NHS; Sch Mus; Stg Crw; Swmmng; Univ Of Michigan; Comp Engr.

ROSOWICZ, JUDITH; Austintown Fitch HS; Austintown, OH; 61/625 Hon Rl; NHS; Off Ade; Sch Pl; Stg Crw; Y-Teens; Drama Clb; Treas Fr Clb; Scr Kpr; Ohio St Univ; Math.

ROSS, ANGELA; Wood Memorial HS; Oakland City, IN; Sec Sr Cls; Trs Sr Cls; Band; Chrs; Hon Rl; Orch; Rptr Sch Nwsp; Pres FHA; Sec Pep Clb; PPFtbl; ISU; Cmmnctns.

ROSS, CINDY; West Geauga HS; Novelty, OH; Cls Rep Frsh Cls; AFS; Drl Tm; Hon Rl; NHS; Pep Clb; Spn Clb; Letter Gym; Trk; Letter Chrldng; Chem Schlrshp Awd; Coll.

ROSS, CURTIS; Niles HS; Niles, MI; Cls Rep Frsh Cls; Pres Soph Cls; Trs Jr Cls; Cl Rep Jr Cls; Hon Rl; NHS; Stu Cncl; Yth Flsp; Letter Bsbl; Letter Ftbl; Bus.

ROSS, DEBRA; Mt View HS; Anawalt, WV; Band; Hon Rl; NHS; 4-H; Pep Clb; Letter Bsktbl; Fairmont State; Soc Work.

ROSS, DOUGLAS; Centreville HS; Centreville, MI; Cls Rep Frsh Cls; Cls Rep Soph Cls; Chrs; Stu Cncl; Drama Clb; Letter Bsktbl; Letter Ftbl; Letter Trk; Coach Actv; Mgrs; Coll.

ROSS, ELIZABETH; Galion HS; Galion, OH; 58/275 Band; Chrh Wkr; Cmnty Wkr; Off Ade; Whos Who Among Amer HS Stud 77; Worthy Advisor Order Of Rainbow 77; Grand Lecturer Order Of Rainbow 77; Milligan Coll; Bus Admin.

ROSS, ELIZABETH; River Valley HS; Marion, OH; Chrs; Hon Rl; Off Ade; Sch Mus; Trk; Scr Kpr; Miami Univ; Psych.

ROSS, GAYLE; Ravenna HS; Ravenna, OH; Trs Frsh Cls; Cls Rep Soph Cls; Hst Jr Cls; Cl Rep Jr Cls; Pres Sr Cls; Cmp Fr Grls; Girl Scts; Hon Rl; Stu Cncl; Sch Nwsp; Bus Schl; Fashion Mdse.

ROSS, GUY; Mumford HS; Ferndale, MI; Cmnty Wkr; Hon Rl; JA; Sch Pl; Rptr Sch Nwsp; Spn Clb; Letter Wrstlng; Michigan St Univ; Bio.

ROSS, JENNIE; Greeneview HS; Jamestown, OH; Sec Jr Cls; Sec Sr Cls; Chrs; Drl Tm; FCA; Hon Rl; Sch Pl; Stg Crw; Yth Flsp; Drama Clb; Central St Univ; Mgmt.

ROSS, KARIN; Huntington East HS; Huntington, WV; Cl Rep Jr Cls; Cls Rep Sr Cls; Band; Chrs; Chrh Wkr; Hon Rl; Jr NHS; NHS; Sch Mus; Rptr Yrbk; Marshall Univ; Busns Mgmt.

ROSS, KAY; Terre Haute North Vigo HS; Terre Haute, IN; Band; Cmnty Wkr; Drl Tm; Girl Scts; Hon Rl; Y-Teens; Fr Clb; Pep Clb; Chrldng; Pom Pon; Univ Of Illinois; Comp Sci.

ROSS, KIMBERLY; Valley Forge HS; Parma Hgts, OH; 48/777 Hon Rl; Bsbl; Bsktbl; College; Architecture.

ROSS, KISTAN; Southwestern HS; Detroit, MI; Hon Rl; Off Ade; Letter Ten; Cit Awd; Univ Of Texas; Comm Art.

ROSS, KRISTINA A; Triton Central HS; Indianapolis, IN; VP Frsh Cls; Hon Rl; Pol Wkr; Sch Pl; Sprt Ed Sch Nwsp; Rptr Sch Nwsp; Drama Clb; 4-H; Fr Clb; Letter Trk; Essey Awd From Triton Cntrl Tchr Assoc 1977; Sci Fair Awd From D J Angus Sci Tech Fdn 1976; Var Awd Vllybl; Indiana Univ; Med Research.

ROSS, LAURA; Castle HS; Newburgh, IN; Chrh Wkr; Hon Rl; JA; Lbry Ade; Letter Glf; JA Awd; Kiwan Awd; Spanish Hon Soc 79; Purdue Univ; Vet Med.

ROSS, MARILYN; Elkins HS; Beverly, WV; Chrh Wkr; Hon Rl; Sch Pl; Stu Cncl; Rptr Sch Nwsp; Keyettes; Crs Cntry; Letter Trk; GAA; Brigham Young Univ; Bus.

ROSS, MELODY; Olentangy HS; Galena, OH; 14/144 Chrs; Hon Rl; NHS; Stu Cncl; Yth Flsp; FHA; Pep Clb; Spn Clb; PPFtbl; Ralph Lahman Awd 79; Voc Awd Of Distnctn 79; Cert Of Awd The De Chapt Of Nalt Sec Assoc 79; Malone Univ; Acctg.

ROSS, MICHAEL; Fairmont West HS; Kettering, OH; Boy Scts; Chrh Wkr; Hon Rl; Pol Wkr; Sct Actv; Stu Cncl; IM Sprt; Mgrs; Scr Kpr; Cert Of Awd 77 & 78; Awd Cert In Soccer 77 & 78; Awd Cert In Bsktbl 78; MIT; Engr.

ROSS, MICHELLE; East HS; Akron, OH; Drl Tm; Hon Rl; College; Phys Educ.

ROSS, PAMELA; Centreville HS; Centreville, MI; 2/69 Pres Frsh Cls; Sal; Am Leg Aux Girls St; Hon Rl; Pres NHS; Sch Mus; Yth Flsp; Ed Yrbk; Pep Clb; Spn Clb; 2nd Runner Up Miss Centreville 78; 2nd Runner Up Miss Mi Tngr 79; Western Michigan Univ.

ROSS, PAULA; Southwestern HS; Detroit, MI; 35 Band; Hon Rl; Hosp Ade; Orch; FHA; Mi State Univ; Vet Med.

ROSS, RALPH; Madison Plains HS; Mt Sterling, OH; 13/153 Pres Frsh Cls; Pres Soph Cls; Pres Jr Cls; Pres Sr Cls; Pres Band; Pres Chrs; Chrh Wkr; Hon Rl; NHS; Sch Mus; Mt Vernon Nazarene Coll; Busns Admin.

ROSS, ROSALYN; West Side HS; Gary, IN; 116/650 Band; Cmp Fr Grls; Girl Scts; Hon Rl; Quill & Scroll; Yrbk; Ed Sch Nwsp; Rptr Sch Nwsp; Sch Nwsp; Pom Pon; Appointd Editor & Chief Of Newspaper 1978; Staff Achvmnt Awd Outstndng Dedication In Jrnlsm; Indiana Univ; Psych.

ROSS, SHERYL; Elgin HS; Prospect, OH; 37/155 Hon Rl; Stg Crw; Chrldng; Pom Pon; Ohio St Univ; Soc Work.

ROSS, STARLA D; Lakewood HS; Newark, OH; Cls Rep Frsh Cls; Cls Rep Soph Cls; Cl Rep Jr Cls; Cls Rep Sr Cls; Hon Rl; NHS; Off Ade; Stu Cncl; OEA; GAA; Homecoming Court; Queen Of Valentines Dance; High Grad Avg Awd; Technical Schl; Busns.

ROSS, TIM; Heritage Jr Sr HS; Ft Wayne, IN; 38/172 Boy Scts; Hon Rl; Yrbk; Lat Clb; Hndbl; Trk; Wrstlng; IM Sprt; Univ; Photog.

ROSSATO, ANNE; Iron Mtn HS; Iron Mountain, MI; 8/150 Band; Chrs; Hon Rl; NHS; Stg Crw; Rptr Yrbk; Rptr Sch Nwsp; Drama Clb; 4-H; FTA; Marquette Univ; Acctg.

ROSSEN, KENNETH J; Roeper City & Country HS; Detroit, MI; VP Jr Cls; Mdrgl; Off Ade; Sch Mus; Sch Mus; Sch Pl; Stg Crw; Rptr Yrbk; Sch Nwsp; Natl Merit SF; Univ; Math.

ROSSER, SALLY; Colerain Sr HS; Cincinnati, OH; Hon Rl; NHS; Off Ade; FHA; Pep Clb; Spn Clb; Chrldng; Letter Mat Maids; Natl Merit Schl;.

ROSSETTI, MANUEL; Perry HS; Canton, OH; Am Leg Boys St; Hon Rl; NHS; Univ; Acctg.

ROSSI, ANNE; Union HS; Grand Rapids, MI; Debate Tm; Hon Rl; JA; NHS; OEA; Spn Clb; Trk; Coach Actv; Aquinas College; Acctg.

ROSSI, DINA; Niles Mc Kinley HS; Niles, OH; Hon Rl; Pres Jr NHS; NHS; Stu Cncl; Yrbk; Sec FTA; Rochester Inst Of Tech; Photog.

ROSSI, KAREN; Euclid Sr HS; Euclid, OH; Cls Rep Frsh Cls; Cls Rep Soph Cls; Cl Rep Jr Cls; Cls Rep Sr Cls; Chrs; Chrh Wkr; Cmnty Wkr; Girl Scts; Hon Rl; Lbry Ade; Cooper Schl Of Art; Comm Art.

ROSSKOPF, REBA; Norwood Sr HS; Cincinnati, OH; 34/375 Band; Chrs; Chrh Wkr; Hon Rl; Jr NHS; Red Cr Ade; Sch Mus; Yth Flsp; Spanish Natl Honor Soc 79; Univ Of Cincinnati; Elem Educ.

ROSSMAN, KEVIN; The Columbus Acad; Columbus, OH; 10/45 Debate Tm; Hon Rl; Lit Mag; Off Ade; Rptr Sch Nwsp; Mth Clb; Bsktbl; Ten; IM Sprt; Univ Of Pen; Econ.

ROSSMAN, TOM; Owosso HS; Owosso, MI; Band; Boy Scts; Chrh Wkr; Pol Wkr; Sct Actv; Yth Flsp; 4-H; FFA; Lat Clb; Tmr; Graceland Coll; Vet.

ROSSMANITH, TIMOTHY; Kankakee Valley HS; De Motte, IN; Am Leg Boys St; Band; Hon Rl; NHS; Yth Flsp; Mth Clb; Sec Sci Clb; Crs Cntry; Trk; Oral Roberts Univ; Med.

ROSSMANN, GREG; Moeller HS; Cincinnati, OH; Aud/Vis; Hon Rl; PAVAS; Stg Crw; Stu Cncl; Pres Rdo Clb; Univ Of Cinn; Electricl Engnr.

ROSSMANN, JILL; Glen Este HS; Cincinnati, OH; Trs Sr Cls; Cls Rep Sr Cls; Chrs; Drl Tm; Girl Scts; Hon Rl; NHS; Sch Mus; Stu Cncl; Capt Chrldng; College; Med Tech.

ROSSY, JOE; Oak Glen HS; Chester, WV; 21/243 Band; NHS; Yth Flsp; Letter Glf; Stage Band 78; Explorers 78; West Virginia Univ; Indust Engr.

ROSTAR, JAMES; Boyne City HS; Flint, MI; Chrs; Hon Rl; Sch Mus; Sch Pl; Rptr Yrbk; Yrbk; Rptr Sch Nwsp; Sch Nwsp; Drama Clb; C S Mott Cmnty Coll; Comp Sci.

ROSTEN, ANN; Ishpeming HS; Ishpeming, MI; 13/123 Band; Hon Rl; NHS; OEA; Letter Bsktbl; Letter Swmmng; Voice Dem Awd; Northern Mic; Office Admin.

ROSZA, BEVERLY; Buckeye North HS; Dillonvale, OH; 11/109 Trs Sr Cls; Band; Capt Drl Tm; Hon Rl; NHS; Off Ade; Ed Yrbk; Chrldng; 4-H Awd; Ohio St Univ; Acctg.

ROSZAK, PAUL; Normandy Sr HS; Parma, OH; 107/597 Hon Rl; FFA; Rotary Awd; Ohio St Univ; Landscape Design.

ROSZAMN, CAROL; Owosso HS; Owosso, MI; Band; Hon Rl; NHS; Drama Clb; Pres 4-H; Mat Maids; 4-H Awd; College; Bus.

ROTENBERG, TRACEY; Morton Sr HS; Hammond, IN; 25/455 Chrs; Hon Rl; NHS; Quill & Scroll; Sch Mus; Stu Cncl; Rptr Sch Nwsp; Sch Nwsp; Pep Clb; PPFtbl; Purdue Univ; Jrnlsm.

ROTH, ALISHA; Field HS; Kent, OH; 23/253 Chrs; Chrh Wkr; Cmnty Wkr; Hon Rl; NHS; 4-H; 4-H Awd; Sftbl Ltrd 78; Vlybl Ltrd 78; Findlay Coll; Phys Educ.

ROTH, BRYAN; Sandusky Sr Marys Cntrl HS; Sandusky, OH; Cl Rep Jr Cls; Bsktbl; Letter Trk; Coach Actv; Univ; Acctg.

ROTH, CLAIRE; Sylvania Southview HS; Toledo, OH; 8/280 Hon Rl; NHS; Quill & Scroll; Sch Nwsp; Northwestern Univ.

ROTH, CONNIE; Indian Valley North HS; , ; Am Leg Aux Girls St; Band; Chrs; Hon Rl; NHS; Sch Pl; Yrbk· Sch Nwsp; VP 4-H; FTA; Ohio Test Of Schlstc Ach; Ohio St Univ; Journalism.

ROTH, DEBORAH; Willard HS; Willard, OH; Band; Girl Scts; Hon Rl; 4-H; Pep Clb; Bsktbl; Trk; GAA;.

ROTH, DEBRA T; Western Reserve Acad; Youngstown, OH; 1/85 Hon Rl; Hosp Ade; Lit Mag; NHS; Off Ade; Treas Stu Cncl; Rptr Sch Nwsp; Drama Clb; Fr Clb; IM Sprt; Univ; Poli Sci.

ROTH, DUANE; Monroe HS; Monroe, MI; Hon Rl; Jr NHS; NHS; Yrbk; Sch Nwsp; VICA; Letter Crs Cntry; Letter Trk; IM Sprt; Univ Of Michigan; Engr.

ROTH, ERIC; Broad Ripple HS; Indianapolis, IN; Hon Rl; Jr NHS; Mod UN; NHS; Pol Wkr; Quill & Scroll; Sch Pl; Rptr Yrbk; Lat Clb; Am Leg Awd; Senator Lugars HS Forum; U S Congress Page From Winning Rep Jacobs Essay; 4ea Natl Editorial Cont Hon Men; College; Law.

ROTH, GREGORY; Douglas Mac Arthur HS; Saginaw, MI; 33/315 Hon Rl; NHS; Mth Clb; Mic Tech; Mech Engr.

ROTH, GRIFFITH A; Hauser Jr Sr HS; Hope, IN; Cl Rep Jr Cls; Trs Sr Cls; Stu Cncl; Sci Clb; Bsbl; Bsktbl; Crs Cntry; Trk; Coach Actv; Ivy Tech Voc Schl; Construction.

ROTH, JOHN; Frankenmuth HS; Frankenmuth, MI; 8/180 Chrs; Chrh Wkr; Debate Tm; Natl Forn Lg; NHS; Sch Mus; Sch Pl; Concordia Lutheran College Ann Arbor.

ROTH, LESLIE; West Preston Sr HS; Arthurdale, WV; Chrs; Chrh Wkr; Hon Rl; Lit Mag; Sch Nwsp; West Virginia St Univ.

ROTH, NANCY; Chardon HS; Chardon, OH; Pres Chrs; Chrh Wkr; Hon Rl; MMM; NHS; Sec PAVAS; Sch Mus; Sch Pl; Stg Crw; Yth Flsp; Malone Coll; Music.

ROTH, ROSALYN; Clyde HS; Clyde, OH; 17/210 Chrs; Hon Rl; NHS; Off Ade; Stg Crw; Sprt Ed Yrbk; IM Sprt; Terra Tech College; Med Sec.

ROTH, SALLY; Toronto HS; Toronto, OH; Am Leg Aux Girls St; Treas Band; Girl Scts; Hon Rl; Hosp Ade; Lbry Ade; Rptr Sch Nwsp; Fr Clb; Pep Clb; Mat Maids; Univ Of Akron; Nursing.

ROTH, SARAH; Columbus North HS; Columbus, OH; Cls Rep Frsh Cls; Hon Rl; Stu Cncl; Y-Teens; Sec OEA; VP Spn Clb; Mgrs; Scr Kpr; Cit Awd; Sftbl & Vllybl Letter 77; Pg & Knight Hon Roll Awd 76; Booster Dr 78; Univ; Law.

ROTH, SCOTT; Lorain Catholic HS; Lorain, OH; Cls Rep Soph Cls; Pres Jr Cls; Cl Rep Jr Cls; Pres Sr Cls; Aud/Vis; Boy Scts; Chrh Wkr; Cmnty Wkr; Hon Rl; Off Ade; 3 Seprt Awds For Photog Excellnc By Kodak 77 & 79; 2 Term Pres Of Lorains B Naie B Rith Youth Org 76 79; Univ; Bus Law.

ROTHBAUER, PATRICIA; Southridge HS; Huntngbrg, IN; Sec Sr Cls; Band; Chrs; Hon Rl; Rptr Yrbk; Yrbk; Ger Clb; Pep Clb; PPFtbl; Scr Kpr; Evansville Univ; Soc Work.

ROTHER, ANDREA; Grand Ledge HS; Grand Ledge, MI; Band; Girl Scts; Ger Clb; Bsktbl; Michigan St Univ; Bio.

ROTHERMEL, JUDITH L; Castor Educational Center; Lucerne, IN; 2/60 Am Leg Aux Girls St; Chrs; Lbry Ade; NHS; Sch Pl; Sch Mus; Sec 4-H; FTA; Ger Clb; Purdue Univ; Library Sci.

ROTHERMEL, LYNNE; Norton HS; Norton, OH; Cls Rep Frsh Cls; Cls Rep Soph Cls; Cl Rep Jr Cls; Hon Rl; Hosp Ade; Jr NHS; NHS; Off Ade; Stu Cncl; FDA; Akron Univ; Music.

ROTHHASS, JODE; Franklin Cmnty HS; Franklin, IN; Band; Orch; Sch Mus; Sch Pl; Stg Crw; Yth Flsp; Drama Clb; 4-H; Pep Clb; Sci Clb; Franklin Coll; Elem Ed.

ROTHMAN, LORETTA E; Monroe HS; Riverview, MI; Hon Rl; NHS; Ger Clb; Univ Of Mic; Engr.

ROTHWELL, MICHAEL; Parkersburg HS; Vienna, WV; 36/740 AFS; Hon Rl; Pep Clb; Crs Cntry; Letter Glf; IM Sprt; Univ Of Alabama; Bus.

ROTMAN, MICHAEL; MSD Of Shakamak; Jasonville, IN; 18/75 Pres Frsh Cls; Pres Soph Cls; Pres Jr Cls; Pres Sr Cls; Am Leg Boys St; Chrh Wkr; Pres FCA; Letter Bsbl; Letter Bsktbl; Univ.

ROTRUCK, MARGO; Elk Garden HS; Elk Garden, WV; Trs Jr Cls; Chrs; Hon Rl; Sch Pl; Yrbk; Pep Clb; Outdoor Camp Councelor For Sixth Gr 78 79; Homecoming Princess 78 79;.

ROTTERMAN, MARY A; Archbishop Alter HS; Kettering, OH; GAA; Wright State Univ; Bus.

ROTTINGHAUS, JANE; St Ursula Acad; Cincinnati, OH; Chrs; Girl Scts; Hon Rl; NHS; PAVAS; Sch Pl; Yrbk; Sch Nwsp; Drama Clb; College; Rn.

ROTTINGHAUS, MARY J; Marian HS; Cincinnati, OH; Chrs; Chrh Wkr; Girl Scts; Hon Rl; NHS; Sct Actv; Stu Cncl; Yth Flsp; Spn Clb; Akron Univ; Spec Educ.

ROTTMAN, KATHY; Fremont HS; Fremont, MI; 11/238 Band; Chrh Wkr; Hon Rl; NHS; Sch Pl; Yth Flsp; Drama Clb; Ger Clb; Mic State Univ; Soc Sci.

ROUCH, MARILYN; Plymouth HS; Plymouth, IN; 30/250 Cmp Fr Grls; Girl Scts; Hon Rl; Yth Flsp; Yrbk; Pep Clb; PPFtbl; College; Tchr.

ROUDEBUSH, DARYL; Eaton City HS; Eaton, OH; Boy Scts; Chrs; Chrh Wkr; Hon Rl; Yth Flsp; Manchester Coll; Chem.

ROUDEBUSH, JENNIFER; Anderson HS; Anderson, IN; Hon Rl; Stu Cncl; Fr Clb; Beauty Schl; Beautician.

ROUDEBUSH JR, ROGER; Anderson HS; Anderson, IN; 9/400 Am Leg Boys St; Hon Rl; NHS; Quill & Scroll; VP Fr Clb; C of C Awd; DAR Awd; Wabash Coll; Med.

ROUGEAU, GINETTE; Carroll HS; Dayton, OH; 32/285 Band; Hon Rl; Orch; GAA; Westfield St Coll; Cmmrcl Art.

ROUGEAU, ROBERT; Detroit Catholic Central HS; Southfield, MI; 16/203 Debate Tm; Hon Rl; Jr NHS; Natl Forn Lg; NHS; IM Sprt; Natl Merit SF; Univ Of Ken; Bus Adm.

ROUHSELANG, PATTY; St Joseph HS; S Bend, IN; Cmp Fr Grls; Ger Clb; Glf; Chrldng; IM Sprt; PPFtbl; Pres Awd; Girls City Golf Champ 78; Carroll Coll; Aviation.

ROUNDHOUSE, ROYCE; William V Fisher Catholc HS; Lancaster, OH; Chrs; Cmnty Wkr; Sch Pl; Vaca Schl; Tv Broadcasting.

ROURK, RONALD; Bishop Hartley HS; Columbus, OH; Cls Rep Soph Cls; Cl Rep Jr Cls; Chrh Wkr; Sch Mus; Rptr Sch Nwsp; Drama Clb; Ftbl; Wrstlng; Coach Actv; Kiwan Awd; Univ Of Florida; Pre Law.

ROURKE, AARON; Bishop Flaget HS; Chillicothe, OH; 5/41 Cl Rep Jr Cls; Cmnty Wkr; Hon Rl; Stu Cncl; Fr Clb; Letter Bsktbl; Capt Crs Cntry; Capt Trk; Voice Dem Awd; Notre Dame Univ; Life Sci.

ROUSELL, DOUG; Mona Shores HS; Muskegon, MI; Band; Boy Scts; Chrh Wkr; Drl Tm; ROTC; Sct Actv; Yth Flsp; Natl Merit Ltr; Pres Awd; Eagle Scout; College; Music.

ROUSH, JOYCE; Dawson Bryant HS; Coal Grove, OH; 2/122 Trs Frsh Cls; Trs Soph Cls; Trs Jr Cls; Trs Sr Cls; Am Leg Aux Girls St; NHS; Stu Cncl; Rptr Yrbk; DAR Awd; Ashland Comm Coll; Accounting.

ROUSH, MIKE; Wahama HS; New Haven, WV; 3/100 Am Leg Boys St; Hon Rl; Pres NHS; Pres Key Clb; Rdo Clb; Pres Awd; Hocking Tech Coll; Ceramic Tech.

ROUSHER, THOMAS; Boardman HS; Youngstown, OH; 35/650 Hon Rl; NHS; Stu Cncl; VP Fr Clb; Mth Clb; College.

ROUSHER, TODD; Boardman HS; Youngstown, OH; 43/560 Hon Rl; Capt NHS; Mth Clb; Spn Clb; College; Computer Programmer.

ROUTH, MICHAEL; West Washington HS; Campbellsbg, IN; 10/90 Hon Rl; NHS; FFA; Pep Clb; Spn Clb; Bsktbl; Coach Actv; Var Bkstbk Free Throww Awd 79; Var Bsktbl Def Awd 79; 10th In St Of In Soil Judging Team 78; Univ Of Louisville; Civil Engr.

ROVDER, DENISE; Jackson Milton HS; Lake Milton, OH; Chrh Wkr; Stu Cncl; Custom Painter(automobile).

ROVELSTAD, CONSTANCE; St Francis Central HS; Morgantown, WV; Chrs; Chrh Wkr; Hon Rl; Lbry Ade; Mth Clb; Sci Clb; Trk; Wv Univ; Chemical Engr.

ROW, LISA; Willard HS; Willard, OH; Band; Chrs; Girl Scts; Sch Mus; Stg Crw; Chrldng; IM Sprt; Scr Kpr; Twrlr; Perf Attendance; Coll; Animal Tech.

ROWAN, THERESA A; Niles HS; Niles, MI; Debate Tm; Lat Clb; Gym; Chrldng; IM Sprt; Miami Florida Univ; Sci.

ROWAND, TIMOTHY M; Grafton HS; Grafton, WV; Am Leg Boys St; Band; Hon Rl; NHS; Key Clb; IM Sprt; Coll.

ROWE, BRETT; Vinson HS; Huntington, WV; Band; Hon Rl; Hosp Ade; Sch Mus; Stu Cncl; Treas Fr Clb; Univ; X Ray Tech.

ROWE, CHERRI; Wayne Trace/vantage HS; Cloverdale, OH; VP Sr Cls; Cmnty Wkr; Debate Tm; Hon Rl; FHA; OEA; Chrldng; Scr Kpr; Coll; Legal Sec.

ROWE, CINDY; Delta Sr HS; Delta, OH; 7/130 Girl Scts; NHS; Sch Pl; FHA; Scr Kpr; N W Tech Coll; Sec.

ROWE, DIANA; North Judson San Pierre HS; N Judson, IN; 31/126 Cls Rep Sr Cls; Drl Tm; Hon Rl; Rptr Sch Nwsp; FTA; Spn Clb; Bsktbl; Pom Pon; Indiana St Univ; Elem Ed.

ROWE, GREGORY; Flushing HS; Flushing, MI; Cls Rep Frsh Cls; Cls Rep Soph Cls; Cl Rep Jr Cls; AFS; Chrh Wkr; Hon Rl; Sch Pl; Stu Cncl; Yth Flsp; Drama Clb; Western Michigan Univ; Psych.

ROWE, KENNETH E; Stevenson HS; Livonia, MI; 23/810 Hon Rl; Pol Wkr; Letter Bsbl; Ftbl; Wrstlng; Natl Merit SF; Michigan State Math Prize Finalist; Career Intern Prgrm; Univ Of Michigan; Aero Engr.

ROWE, KIMBERLY; Goshen HS; Milford, OH; Cl Rep Jr Cls; Band; Drl Tm; Hon Rl; Sch Mus; Drama Clb; Sec Pep Clb; Bsktbl; Trk; Capt Chrldng; Univ; Comp Tech.

ROWE, LISA; High School; Manistee, MI; Chrh Wkr; Stu Cncl; Y-Teens; Aquinas; Art.

ROWE, MARILYN; Capitol City Christian HS; Holt, MI; Trs Sr Cls; Band; Chrs; Chrh Wkr; Off Ade; Letter Bsktbl; Grand Rapids Baptist Coll; Music.

ROWE, TOM; La Ville Jr Sr HS; Lakeville, IN; Pres Frsh Cls; Am Leg Boys St; Aud/Vis; Band; Chrs; Mdrgl; Sch Mus; Sch Pl; Stg Crw; Yth Flsp; Bible Inst; Theol.

ROWELL, DARWIN; Patterson Co Op HS; Dayton, OH; Chrs; Chrh Wkr; FCA; Hon Rl; PAVAS; Boys Clb Am; 4-H; Pep Clb; VICA; 4-H Awd; Embry Riddle Univ; Aviation.

ROWEN, NATHAN C; Gull Lake HS; Plainwell, MI; 41/242 Cls Rep Soph Cls; Aud/Vis; Band; Boy Scts; Hon Rl; Lbry Ade; NHS; Sch Mus; Sct Actv; Stu Cncl; Western Michigan Univ; Printing Mgmt.

ROWLAND, CARMA J; Adena HS; Frankfort, OH; 11/88 Sec Chrs; Drl Tm; Jr NHS; NHS; Ed Yrbk; Scr Kpr; Voice Dem Awd; Co Ed Sec 78; Arion Awd For Chorus 79; R W Pickens Schlrshp 79; Ohio Weslyan Festival Chorus 78 & 79; Ohio St Univ; Law.

ROWLAND, DAVID; Culver Military Acad; Kokomo, IN; Boy Scts; Hon Rl; ROTC; Lat Clb; Spn Clb; Glf; Wrstlng; Depaweer; Pre Dental.

ROWLAND, LISA; Flat Rock HS; Flat Rock, MI; Sec Jr Cls; Chrs; FCA; Hon Rl; Lbry Ade; Off Ade; Yrbk; Sci Clb; Coach Actv; Scr Kpr; College; Elem Educ.

ROWLAND, MELISSA A; Seton HS; Cincinnati, OH; 2/274 Cls Rep Frsh Cls; Cls Rep Soph Cls; Cl Rep Jr Cls; Cmp Fr Grls; Chrh Wkr; Hon Rl; NHS; Orch; Stu Cncl; VP Yth Flsp; College; Architecture.

ROWLANDS, GAIL; Cuyahoga Falls HS; Cuyahoga Falls, OH; 11/806 Hon Rl; Hosp Ade; NHS; Y-Teens; Rptr Yrbk; Spn Clb; Bausch & Lomb Awd; Natl Merit SF; Rotary Awd; Univ; Med.

ROWLANS, FAWNYA; Mc Comb HS; Mc Comb, OH; Band; Chrs; Chrh Wkr; Hon Rl; NHS; Stg Crw; Pep Clb; Capt Mat Maids; Scr Kpr; Ohio St Univ; Med Tech.

ROWLES, JAN; Washington HS; Massillon, OH; 1/450 Chrs; Hon Rl; Jr NHS; NHS; Off Ade; Sch Mus; Stg Crw; Yrbk; Fr Clb; Pep Clb; Univ; Food & Nutrition.

ROWLETT, ANN; Cuyahoga Falls HS; Cuyahoga Fls, OH; Cls Rep Soph Cls; Cl Rep Jr Cls; Hon Rl; JA; JA Awd; Rotary Awd; Cleveland St Univ; Eng.

ROWLETT, BENITA; La Salle HS; South Bend, IN; 28/417 Cls Rep Soph Cls; Trs Jr Cls; Trs Sr Cls; Band; Chrs; Chrh Wkr; Hon Rl; NHS; Orch; Sch Mus; Univ; Bus Admin.

ROWLEY, DAVID; John Marshall HS; Indianapolis, IN; Cl Rep Jr Cls; Cls Rep Sr Cls; Hon Rl; NHS; Quill & Scroll; Stu Cncl; Sprt Ed Sch Nwsp; Letter Swmmng; Ball St U; Journalism.

ROWLEY, LESLIE; Jefferson Union HS; Steubenville, OH; 56/105 Cls Rep Frsh Cls; Cls Rep Soph Cls; Cl Rep Jr Cls; Cls Rep Sr Cls; Chrs; Chrh Wkr; Girl Scts; Lbry Ade; Sch Mus; Sch Pl; Serv Awd 79; Jefferson Tech Inst; RN.

ROWLEY, MICHAEL; Ironton HS; Ironton, OH; 18/194 Cls Rep Frsh Cls; Band; Hon Rl; NHS; VP Stu Cncl; Sch Nwsp; Spn Clb; Letter Bsbl; Univ Of Cincinnati; Nuclear Engr.

ROWSE, JULIE; Bellevue 'S; Bellevue, MI; 7/89 Cls Rep Frsh Cls; VP Jr Cls; Letter Band; Cmp Fr Grls; NHS; Stu Cncl; Bsktbl; Chrldng; PPFtbl; Natl Merit SF; Volleyball Letter; Homecoming Ct Ftbl; Western Michigan Univ; Medicine.

ROY, CYNTHIA; Henryville HS; Underwood, IN; 6/71 Am Leg Aux Girls St; Hon Rl; Lbry Ade; NHS; Stu Cncl; Rptr Sch Nwsp; FHA; FTA; Spn Clb; Bsbl; West Point Military Acad.

ROY, DARRYL; Harman HS; Job, WV; 4/18 Hon Rl; Sch Pl; Yrbk; FFA; Bsktbl;.

ROY, RICHARD; Garden City East HS; Garden City, MI; Cl Rep Jr Cls; Cls Rep Sr Cls; Boy Scts; Stu Cncl; Bsktbl; Ftbl; Trk; God Cntry Awd; Grand Valley St College; Advertising.

ROY, STEPHEN; Cheboygan Area HS; Cheboygan, MI; Pres Frsh Cls; Hon Rl; Fr Clb; Letter Bsktbl; Ftbl; Letter Ten; Coach Actv; IM Sprt; Univ.

ROY, TERI; Howell HS; Howell, MI; Band; Hon Rl; Sec Mod UN; Sec 4-H; PPFtbl; 4-H Awd; Univ; Acctg.

ROYAL, RICKY; Emerson HS; Gary, IN; Chrs; Hon Rl; Jr NHS; Boys Clb Am; Sci Clb; Spn Clb; Letter Wrstlng; College; Med.

ROYALS, MICHELLE; Lake Michigan Cath HS; Savannah, GA; Chrs; Girl Scts; Hon Rl; Lbry Ade; NHS; Off Ade; Sch Mus; Sch Pl; Drama Clb; Gym; Spelman Univ; Interior Dsgn.

ROYALTY, JOHN; Corydon Central HS; Elizabeth, IN; Chrs; Sch Mus; Sch Pl; Rptr Yrbk; Ed Sch Nwsp; Sch Nwsp; Pres Drama Clb; College; Theatre.

ROYCE, CHRISTINE; Lacrosse HS; La Crosse, IN; 4/48 Sec Jr Cls; VP Sr Cls; Am Leg Aux Girls St; Hon Rl; Jr NHS; NHS; Drama Clb; Purdue Univ; Vet Tech.

ROYCE, JANICE; La Salle HS; South Bend, IN; 2/488 Chrs; Hon Rl; NHS; Sch Mus; Drama Clb; 4-H; Letter Swmmng; Chrldng; 4-H Awd; Miss United Teenager Pageant Finalist 77; Joseph M Boland Athletic Awrd 76; Univ; Retailing.

ROYER, K; Delphi Community HS; Delphi, IN; Chrs; Girl Scts; Hon Rl; 4-H; Spn Clb; Bsktbl; Ten; College; Accounting.

ROYER, PAUL; Bishop Watterson HS; Columbus, OH; 3/283 VP Frsh Cls; Cls Rep Soph Cls; Hon Rl; Jr NHS; NHS; Stu Cncl; Lat Clb; Sci Clb; Capt Ftbl; Wrstlng; All Cntrl Cathlc League Ftbl 78; Dstrct Qulaifier Wrstlng 78; All Star Wrstlr 77; Univ; Marine Bio.

ROZEBOOM, BRENDA; Holland Christian HS; Hollad, MI; Chrs; Chrh Wkr; 4-H; Pep Clb; Spn Clb; IM Sprt; Davenport Busns Coll; Acctg.

ROZIC, ROSEANNE; Malabar HS; Mansfield, OH; VP Frsh Cls; Cls Rep Soph Cls; Chrs; Cmnty Wkr; Red Cr Ade; Sch Pl; Ohio State Univ; Psych.

ROZINSKY, KIMBERLY; Eastlake North HS; Willowick, OH; Cls Rep Soph Cls; Cl Rep Jr Cls; Band; Hon Rl; Lbry Ade; Stu Cncl; College.

ROZMAN, IVANA M; Euclid Sr HS; Euclid, OH; Chrs; Chrh Wkr; Hon Rl; Jr NHS; NHS; Off Ade; Red Cr Ade; Rptr Yrbk; OEA; Letter Swmmng; College; Sec.

ROZMAN, JOSEPH; Univ Of Detroit HS; Birmingham, MI; 34/147 Cls Rep Frsh Cls; Cls Rep Sr Cls; Hon Rl; NHS; Stg Crw; Stu Cncl; Sci Clb; Bsbl; Cit Awd; Univ Of Detroit Coll; Elec Engr.

ROZMAN, MARTIN L; Maple Hts Sr HS; Maple Hgts, OH; Hon Rl; Sch Pl; IM Sprt; Cit Awd; Hnr & Ctznshp Awds 79; Schlstc Art Awds Cert Of Mrt For Art 77; Mech.

ROZSA, BEVERLY; Buckeye North HS; Dillonvale, OH; 10/106 Trs Sr Cls; Band; Chrs; Chrh Wkr; Drl Tm; Hon Rl; NHS; Off Ade; Sch Mus; Sch Pl; Ohio St Univ; Bus Admin.

ROZUM, DOUG; Campbell Mem HS; Campbell, OH; Hon Rl; NHS; Mth Clb; Sci Clb; Spn Clb; Bsktbl; Ftbl; Ten; Univ; Engr.

ROZZO, DAN; Hubbard HS; Hubbard, OH; 2/350 Cls Rep Frsh Cls; Pres Soph Cls; Cls Rep Soph Cls; Cl Rep Jr Cls; Cls Rep Sr Cls; Am Leg Boys St; Sec FCA; Hon Rl; Stg Crw; VP Stu Cncl; Ohio St Univ Alumni Dinner 1978; Rotary Club Hubbard Stu Of Month 1978; Took DAR Good Citizenship Test; Ohio St Univ; Optometry.

RPSE, LAMBERT; Elkins HS; Elkins, WV; 32/241 Band; Hon Rl; NHS; VICA; Worthy Advisor International Rainbow For Girls 79; Chaplain 79; Pres Fro Woodford Mrl Methodist Youth Grp 78; West Virginia Univ; RN.

RUARK, BECKY; Eastern Local HS; Beaver, OH; 10/70 Chrs; Girl Scts; Hon Rl; MMM; Orch; Sch Mus; Sch Pl; Sct Actv; Stg Crw; 4-H;.

RUARK, DEBRA A; South Putnam HS; Fillmore, IN; 3/135 Chrs; Chrh Wkr; Drl Tm; Hon Rl; NHS; Sch Mus; Sch Pl; Drama Clb; 4-H; Fr Clb; Purdue Univ; Sci.

RUBALCAVA, DULCIE; Jefferson Union HS; Steubenville, OH; VP Soph Cls; Cls Rep Soph Cls; Am Leg Aux Girls St; Hon Rl; NHS; Stu Cncl; PPFtbl; Pres Awd; College; Health.

RUBARD, ROXANNE; Madison HS; Madison, OH; 2/298 Chrs; Chrh Wkr; Girl Scts; Hon Rl; NHS; Ger Clb; Hockey; Trk; Am Leg Awd; Bob Jones Univ; Missions.

RUBCICH, MARTA; Shadyside HS; Shadyside, OH; 2/120 Sec Jr Cls; Sec Band; NHS; Y-Teens; Spn Clb; Letter Bsbl; Letter Bsktbl; GAA; Dnfth Awd; Natl Merit SF;.

RUBEIS, RITA; Mahoning Cnty Jt Voc HS; Youngstown, OH; 2/22 Hon Rl; DECA; Youngstown St Univ; Marketing.

RUBEL, DOUGLAS; Pemberville Eastwood HS; Pemberville, OH; 61/160 Trs Frsh Cls; Am Leg Boys St; Aud/Vis; Boy Scts; Cmnty Wkr; Hon Rl; Yth Flsp; Spn Clb; Letter Bsbl; Bsktbl; St Golf Participnt 78; Ohio St Univ; Cmnctns.

RUBERTUS, PAMELA; Carroll HS; Dayton, OH; Hon Rl; VP Fr Clb; College; Nursing.

RUBIN, DAVID; North HS; Springfield, OH; Chrh Wkr; JA; Off Ade; Yrbk; Key Clb; Rdo Clb; Spn Clb; Univ; Bus Admin.

RUBIN, PATRICIA; Charles F Brush HS; S Euclid, OH; Band; Hon Rl; Off Ade; Orch; Stg Crw; Yrbk; Drama Clb; Letter Bsbl; Letter Bsktbl; Natl Merit SF; Univ; Med.

RUBINGH, MARV; Ellsworth Cmnty HS; Ellsworth, MI; 4/24 Trs Jr Cls; Trs Sr Cls; Hon Rl; NHS; Yrbk; 4-H; Key Clb; Bsktbl; Trk; 4-H Awd; Dordt Coll; Agri Bus.

RUBIO, JAMES; Washington HS; Massillon, OH; Boy Scts; Hon Rl; Boys Clb Am; Spn Clb; Ftbl; Trk; Coach Actv; Am Leg Awd; Univ Of Akron; Bus Admin.

RUBLAITUS, DALE; Sandusky St Marys Cath HS; Sandusky, OH; Hon Rl; NHS; Sci Clb; Spn Clb; Bsktbl; Coll; Engr.

RUBLE, JAMES E; Parkersburg South HS; Parkersburg, WV; Am Leg Boys St; Hon Rl; Boys Clb Am; Letter Crs Cntry; Letter Trk; IM Sprt; Indiana St Univ; Drafting Engr.

RUBLE, LYNDA; Merrillville HS; Merrillville, IN; 21/603 Band; Girl Scts; Hon Rl; NHS; Sct Actv; 4-H; Pres Drama Clb; Ger Clb; OEA; GAA; Voc Exclenc 79; OEA Prepd Verbal Cmnctns 78; First Class Girl Scout 77; Univ; Court Reptr.

RUBY, GLENN E; North HS; Willowick, OH; 1/600 Val; Band; Boy Scts; Hon Rl; Jr NHS; NHS; Key Clb; Mth Clb; Rdo Clb; Sci Clb; Case Western Reserve Univ; Elec Engr.

RUCH, PATRICK; Mooresville HS; Mooresville, IN; Hon Rl; Drama Clb; Ger Clb; Sci Clb; Bsbl; Ftbl; Socr; Trk; Wrstlng; Mgrs; IUPUI; Physical Therapy.

RUCKEL, DWAIN; Mansfield Christian HS; Mansfield, OH; Boy Scts; Chrh Wkr; Rdo Clb; Class Numbers Fresh Bsktbl; Le Tourneau Coll; Drafting.

RUCKER, DANITA; Collinwood HS; Cleveland, OH; Cls Rep Soph Cls; Cl Rep Jr Cls; Chrs; Drl Tm; Trs Frsh Cls; JA; Orch; Stu Cncl; Pep Clb; Northwestern Univ; Computer Engr.

RUCKER, TAMI L; Marysville HS; Marysville, OH; Cls Rep Frsh Cls; Cls Rep Soph Cls; Cl Rep Jr Cls; Chrh Wkr; Debate Tm; Lit Mag; Natl Forn Lg; Stu Cncl; Yth Flsp; IM Sprt; Columbus Tech Inst; Acctg.

RUCKMAN, BRENDA; Bellaire HS; Bellaire, OH; 24/238 NHS; Yth Flsp; Fr Clb; Bluffton Coll; Elem Ed.

RUCKMAN, WAYNE; Mingo HS; Mingo Jct, OH; 12/120 VP Sr Cls; Am Leg Boys St; Hon Rl; VP NHS; VP Key Clb; Letter Ftbl; Letter Trk; Coll; Engr.

RUDD, TAMMY; Lemon Monroe HS; Middletown, OH; 37/275 Band; Hon Rl; Letter Bsktbl; Miami Univ; Nursing.

RUDDY, TERESE; Hale HS; Hale, MI; 6/61 Cls Rep Soph Cls; Band; VP Chrs; Drm Mjrt; Hon Rl; Sch Pl; Stu Cncl; Rptr Yrbk; Sch Nwsp; Drama Clb; Davenport Coll Of Bus; Legal Sec.

RUDE, RICHARD; Battle Creek Central HS; Battle Crk, MI; Chrh Wkr; Crs Cntry; Ten; Letter Trk; IM Sprt; Evangel Coll; Archt.

RUDER, KAREN; North Adams Public HS; Osseo, MI; NHS; VP Yth Flsp; Pres 4-H; Sec FFA; FTA; Letter Bsktbl; Trk; College.

RUDIG, SHELLY; Huntington North HS; Andrews, IN; Cls Rep Frsh Cls; Cls Rep Soph Cls; Cl Rep Jr Cls; Sch Mus; Stu Cncl; Letter Trk; Letter Chrldng; Opt Clb Awd; Barbizon Voc Schl; Modeling.

RUDKO, LYDIA; Eastlake North Sr HS; Willowick, OH; Sec Frsh Cls; Cls Rep Soph Cls; Cl Rep Jr Cls; Stu Cncl; Sprt Ed Yrbk; Sprt Ed Sch Nwsp; Spn Clb; Letter Crs Cntry; Chrldng; Bowling Green Univ; Jrnlsm.

RUDKO, LYDIA; Eastlake North HS; Willowick, OH; 176/706 Sec Frsh Cls; Hon Rl; Stu Cncl; Rptr Yrbk; Sprt Ed Sch Nwsp; Spn Clb; Letter Crs Cntry; Socr; Trk; Chrldng; Bowling Green Univ; Journalism.

RUDLAFF, SHARON; Berrien Springs HS; Berrien Spgs, MI; 6/110 Hon Rl; NHS; 4-H; Sec Ger Clb; Pep Clb; Trk; Pres Awd; Treas Lake Mich College; Medical.

RUDLOFF, WILLIAM; Newbury HS; Newbury, OH; Sec Frsh Cls; Sec Soph Cls; Pres Jr Cls; Band; Chrs; Chrh Wkr; Cmnty Wkr; Hon Rl; Sch Mus; Sch Pl; Salutatorian & Valedictorian Of Food Serv Voc Course; Bowling Green St Univ; Intl Busns.

RUDNIK, JOANNE; Union HS; Grand Rapids, MI; Hon Rl; JA; NHS; Yrbk; Sch Nwsp; JA Awd; Michigan St Univ; Acctg.

RUDOLPH, KAYE; Michigan Center HS; Michigan Center, MI; VP Jr Cls; Girl Scts; Sct Actv; Stu Cncl; Bsktbl; Trk; GAA; College; Phys Therapy.

RUDOLPH, MAX; Dearborn HS; Dearborn, MI; 15/540 Boy Scts; Hon Rl; NHS; Quill & Scroll; Rptr Sch Nwsp; Sch Nwsp; Ger Clb; Mth Clb; Letter Swmmng; Letter Trk; Michigan Tech Univ; Math.

RUDOLPH, REX; Traverse Cty Snt Francis HS; Traverse City, MI; 2/130 Pres Frsh Cls; Hon Rl; JA; NHS; Stu Cncl; Letter Bsbl; Letter Bsktbl; Letter Ftbl; Letter Ten; JA Awd; Mic State Univ; Comp.

RUDOLPH, STEVEN; Princeton Community HS; Princeton, IN; 16/222 Aud/Vis; Band; Boy Scts; Mdrgl; NHS; Sch Mus; Fr Clb; Mth Clb; Pep Clb; Opt Clb Awd; Purdue Univ; Hotel Mgmt.

RUDRICK, CONNIE; Centerburg HS; Centerburg, OH; 4/63 Trs Jr Cls; Am Leg Aux Girls St; Hon Rl; VP NHS; Y-Teens; Ed Yrbk; PPFtbl; Capital Univ; Nursing.

RUDY, JEFF; Sidney HS; Sidney, OH; Pres Soph Cls; Cl Rep Jr Cls; Chrh Wkr; Hon Rl; Lbry Ade; NHS; Off Ade; Treas Stu Cncl; Yrbk; College; Med.

RUDY, SCOTT; Washington HS; Massillon, OH; Boy Scts; Chrs; Hon Rl; Jr NHS; NHS; Sch Mus; Sct Actv; Stg Crw; Yth Flsp; Fr Clb; Chess Club; College; Computer Engr.

RUDY, TRACY; Edwardsburg HS; Edwardsburg, MI; Hon Rl; Sprt Ed Sch Nwsp; Rptr Sch Nwsp; Sch Nwsp; Ger Clb; Crs Cntry; Capt Trk; Chrldng; Michigan St Univ; Cycology.

RUDYNSKI, CHRISTOPHER; Clay HS; S Bend, IN; Hon Rl; NHS; Quill & Scroll; Ed Sch Nwsp; Rptr Sch Nwsp; Fr Clb; Letter Crs Cntry; Letter Trk; IM Sprt; 10 10 Percent Of Class; Coll; Jrnlsm.

RUDZINSKI, CHERYL; Fraser HS; Fraser, MI; Hon Rl; Spn Clb; Chrldng; Univ.

RUE, MATT; Greenon HS; Springfield, OH; Chrh Wkr; 4-H; FFA; Letter Ftbl; Letter Trk; College; Agri.

RUEBELMAN, TRACY L; Lake Orion HS; Lake Orion, MI; 2/550 Hon Rl; Jr NHS; VP Stu Cncl; Ed Yrbk; Rptr Yrbk; Yrbk; Pep Clb; Chrldng; Cit Awd; Nw Michigan St Univ; Communications.

RUEFF, J RUSSELL; Jeffersonville HS; Jeffersonville, IN; 16/633 Pres Jr Cls; Pres Sr Cls; Am Leg Boys St; Pres Chrs; NHS; Sch Mus; Sch Pl; Stu Cncl; Drama Clb; Opt Clb Awd; Wabash Coll.

RUEHL, LINDA; Allen Park HS; Allen Park, MI; Cls Rep Sr Cls; Chrs; Hon Rl; NHS; Sch Mus; Sch Pl; Stu Cncl; Yth Flsp; Sprt Ed Sch Nwsp; Drama Clb; Alma Coll; Journalism.

RUEHLMANN, MARK; St Xavier HS; Cincinnati, OH; Hon Rl; Mod UN; NHS; Stu Cncl; Sprt Ed Yrbk; Boys Clb Am; Ftbl; College; Bus.

RUELKE, JENNIFER; Robert S Rogers HS; Toledo, OH; Chrh Wkr; Girl Scts; VP Ger Clb; College; Foreign Lang.

RUELLE, JULIA; Mt Pleasant HS; Mt Pleasant, MI; 19/347 Band; Chrs; Hon Rl; Mdrgl; NHS; Orch; Sch Mus; Sch Pl; Yth Flsp; Rptr Sch Nwsp; Univ Of Michigan; Geo Physics.

RUEN, ROXIE; Continental HS; Continental, OH; Am Leg Aux Girls St; Band; Off Ade; FFA; Lima Tech; Sec.

RUF, SUSAN; Williamstown HS; Williamstown, WV; Pres AFS; Chrs; Chrh Wkr; Pres Yth Flsp; Fr Clb; Pep Clb; Letter Crs Cntry; Letter Trk; Mas Awd; Univ; Spec Ed.

RUFENACHT, JOEL S; Waldron HS; Waldron, MI; 2/45 Cls Rep Frsh Cls; Hon Rl; NHS; Sch Pl; Yth Flsp; Rptr Yrbk; FFA; Letter Bsbl; Letter Ftbl; Natl Merit Ltr; Goshen Coll; Agri Busns.

RUFF, DAVID; Crooksville HS; Crooksville, OH; 11/105 Pres Soph Cls; Hon Rl; NHS; Sch Pl; Stu Cncl; Spn Clb; Letter Bsbl; Letter Bsktbl; Ohio State Univ; Engr.

RUFF, DAWN; Plymouth HS; Plymouth, IN; Sec Frsh Cls; Sec Soph Cls; Chrs; Mdrgl; Pol Wkr; Sch Mus; Stu Cncl; 4-H; Fr Clb; Pep Clb; College.

RUFF, DEBBIE L; Bridgman HS; Bridgman, MI; Aud/Vis; Chrs; Chrh Wkr; Girl Scts; Hon Rl; Trs Frsh Cls; Lbry Ade; Off Ade; Sch Mus; Mic State; Social Work.

RUFF, LINDA; Bloom Carroll HS; Canal Wincheste, OH; 1/145 Trs Soph Cls; Am Leg Aux Girls St; Band; Chrs; Chrh Wkr; Hosp Ade; Pres NHS; Treas Stu Cncl; Treas 4-H; FTA; Ohio Univ; Elementary Education.

RUFF, MICHAEL; Monroe HS; La Salle, MI; 58/582 Band; Hon Rl; NHS; Orch; Univ Of Mich; Naval Architect.

RUFFENER, LESLEY; Wynford HS; Bucyrus, OH; 6/140 Sec Soph Cls; Sec Jr Cls; Sec Sr Cls; Pres Band; Chrs; Chrh Wkr; Hon Rl; NHS; PAVAS; Sch Mus; Ohio St Univ.

RUFFER, CHERYL; Centerline HS; Warren, MI; Cls Rep Soph Cls; Hon Rl; Jr NHS; Lbry Ade; GAA; IM Sprt; Wayne State; Bio Ecol Engin.

RUFFER, CINDY; Stryker HS; Stryker, OH; 5/50 NHS; VP Stu Cncl; Rptr Yrbk; Rptr Sch Nwsp; Capt Bsktbl; Trk; The Defiance Coll; Phys Ed.

RUFFER JR, WILLIAM; Bryan HS; Bryan, OH; Lat Clb; Natl Merit Ltr; Ohi State Univ; Bio.

RUFFING, ANDREW; Monroeville HS; Monroeville, OH; VP Jr Cls; Am Leg Boys St; Band; Hon Rl; NHS; Sch Pl; Bsbl; Crs Cntry; Wrstlng; Univ; Pre Med.

RUFFING, CHRISTOPHER; Huron HS; Huron, OH; AFS; Hon Rl; NHS; Eng Clb; Mth Clb; Sci Clb; Scr Kpr; Kenneth B Long Mem Schlrshp; Miami Univ; Busns Mgmt.

RUFFING, JEFFREY; Bellevue HS; Bellevue, OH; 56/224 Hon Rl; Ftbl; Letter Glf; Trk; Wrstlng; Scr Kpr; Kiwan Awd; Ohi St Univ; Astronomy.

RUFFING, KATHRYN; Monroeville HS; Monroeville, OH; Girl Scts; Hon Rl; Off Ade; Sch Pl; 4-H; FFA; Pep Clb; Letter Bsktbl; Scr Kpr; 4-H Awd; Ag Tech Inst; Landscaping.

RUFFING, KEVIN; Monroeville HS; Norwalk, OH; Trs Jr Cls; Am Leg Boys St; Band; Boy Scts; Chrh Wkr; Hon Rl; Treas JA; Sch Pl; Sct Actv; Stg Crw; Prfct Attndnc 78; Bluffton Coll; Bio.

RUFFING, WILLIAM; St Paul HS; Norwalk, OH; 3/45 VP Sr Cls; Am Leg Boys St; Hon Rl; NHS; 4-H; Fr Clb; Mth Clb; Bsktbl; Letter Ftbl; Letter Trk; Bowling Green St Univ; Acctg.

RUFFOLO, MICHAEL; Archbishop Alter HS; Kettering, OH; 25/350 Cls Rep Soph Cls; Cl Rep Jr Cls; Cls Rep Sr Cls; Hon Rl; NHS; Key Clb; Pres Rdo Clb; Univ Of Dayton; Comm Arts.

RUFFOLO, MIKE; Archbishop Alter HS; Kettering, OH; 20/340 Cls Rep Frsh Cls; Cls Rep Soph Cls; Cl Rep Jr Cls; Cls Rep Sr Cls; Hon Rl; NHS; Key Clb; Pres Rdo Clb; Letter Socr; Cit Awd; Univ Of Dayto n; Public Relations.

RUFH, KATHY; Niles Mc Kinley HS; Niles, OH; Off Ade; Rptr Yrbk; Drama Clb; Pep Clb; Letter Bsktbl; Letter Ten; Letter Trk; Univ; X Ray Tech.

RUGGERI, CATHRYN E; North HS; Willowick, OH; 1/659 Hon Rl; Jr NHS; NHS; Yrbk; Key Clb; Univ; Poli Sci.

RUGGIE, PATRICIA; Shaker Hts HS; Shaker Hts, OH; Cls Rep Frsh Cls; Cls Rep Soph Cls; Cl Rep Jr Cls; Mod UN; Off Ade; Pol Wkr; Quill & Scroll; Stu Cncl; Yrbk; Rptr Sch Nwsp; Coll; Law.

RUGGIERO, MICHAEL; Kent Theodore Roosevelt HS; Kent, OH; 1/350 AFS; Boy Scts; Cmnty Wkr; Hon Rl; Spn Clb; Swmmng; DAR Awd; College; Soc Sci.

RUGGIRELLO, MARIA; Carl Brablec HS; Roseville, MI; Hon Rl; NHS; Off Ade; Lat Clb; Ftbl; PPFtbl; Letter Scr Kpr; Achvd St Of Mi Competative Schlrshp 79; Hon Grad; Michigan St Univ; Sci.

RUGGLES, DAVID; Central Preston Sr HS; Tunnelton, WV; Trs Frsh Cls; Band; Boy Scts; Chrh Wkr; Hon Rl; Sch Mus; Sct Actv; High Avg Sci 76; West Virginia Univ; Engr.

RUGGLES, SUZANNE; Walled Lake Central HS; Union Lake, MI; Cls Rep Frsh Cls; Cls Rep Soph Cls; Cl Rep Jr Cls; Cls Rep Sr Cls; Hon Rl; Mod UN; Sch Pl; Pres Stu Cncl; Rptr Yrbk; Coach Actv; Grand Valley State; Theatre.

RUHE, MARY J; Penn HS; Mishawaka, IN; Chrs; Girl Scts; Hon Rl; NHS; Off Ade; PPFtbl; Univ; Pre Dent.

RUHL, CAROLE; Fredericktown HS; Fredericktown, OH; 10/117 Chrs; NHS; Yrbk; Treas 4-H; Pres OEA; Pep Clb; Vllybll 4 Yr Lttrmn Co Capt MVP Cchs Awrd 78; Gnrl Clrcl 2 Cntst 78; Otstndng Jr IOE Mmbr 77; Sec.

RUIS, CAROLYN; Big Rapids HS; Big Rapids, MI; Pres Band; Sec NHS; Sch Mus; VP Fr Clb; Natl Merit Ltr; Univ Of Michigan; Poli Sci.

RUIZ, ARLENE; Ashtabula Cnty Joint Voc Sch; Pierpont, OH; 2/18 Sec Jr Cls; Drl Tm; Hon Rl; Yrbk; FTA; OEA; Bsktbl; Trk; Scr Kpr; Cit Awd; Awd For St Competition In Parliamentary Procedures 1979; Awd For Spanish Declaration Contest I & II 1978; Univ.

RUIZ, CYNTHIA; Hammond Technical Voc HS; Hammond, IN; 6/256 Trs Soph Cls; Trs Jr Cls; Hon Rl; NHS; Stu Cncl; Ed Yrbk; Rptr Sch Nwsp; PPFtbl; Scr Kpr; Indiana Univ; Nursing.

RUIZ, HERMAN; Theadore Roosevelt HS; E Chicago, IN; 27/200 Cls Rep Soph Cls; Cl Rep Jr Cls; Pres JA; Stu Cncl; Pres Lat Clb; Mth Clb; VP Pep Clb; Sci Clb; Spn Clb; Pres JA Awd; Hon Roll B Soph Yr 77; Schl Spirit Awrd 77; Serv Charctr Awrd 78; Univ; Sci.

RUIZ, PHYLLIS; E Hammond HS; Hammond, IN; Cls Rep Sr Cls; Chrs; Hon Rl; Jr NHS; NHS; Sch Mus; Sch Pl; Drama Clb; Chrldng; PPFtbl; Most Outstndng Chrldr; Best Actress & Edwin Grabil Schlrshp; Outstndng Music Stu; Bsktbl Homecoming Queen; Ball State Univ.

RUJEVCAN, ADRIANE; Hobart Sr HS; Hobart, IN; Chrs; Hon Rl; Jr NHS; Off Ade; Stu Cncl; Ger Clb; Pep Clb; Univ; Math.

RUJEVCAN, BILL; Hobart Sr HS; Hobart, IN; 21/395 Hon Rl; Jr NHS; NHS; Ger Clb; Sci Clb; Ftbl; Trk; IM Sprt; U S Air Force Academy; Sci.

RULE, ANDREW; Clinton Central HS; Michigantown, IN; Boy Scts; FCA; Off Ade; Rptr Yrbk; Pep Clb; Sci Clb; Bsbl; Letter Ftbl; Glf; Letter Wrstlng;.

RULE, LAURA; Columbia Central HS; Brooklyn, MI; Hon Rl; NHS; Jackson Comm Coll; Secretarial.

RULLMAN, LISA; South Dearborn HS; Aurora, IN; 13/250 Band; Chrs; Hon Rl; NHS; Sch Pl; Stu Cncl; Drama Clb; Pep Clb; Pom Pon; Univ.

RULON, KIRBY; Terre Haute South Vigo HS; Terre Haute, IN; Chrs; Hon Rl; Sch Mus; 4-H; 4-H Awd; Grand Champ Gelding In St Fair 4 H Horse & Pony 76; Meredith Manor Schl; Breed Horse.

RUMBAUGH, GREG; Wapakoneta Sr HS; Cridersville, OH; Hon Rl; Lbry Ade; DECA; 3rd In Dist Comp Of Free Enterprise 1978; Perfect Attend Awd 1978; Library Aide Awd 1978; Auto Work.

RUMBOLD, JOHN; West Geauga HS; Chesterland, OH; Band; Chrs; Chrh Wkr; Hon Rl; MMM; NHS; Sch Pl; Trk; IM Sprt; Kent St Univ; Law.

RUMBOLD, LAURA; Aurora HS; Aurora, OH; 43/176 Chrh Wkr; NHS; Yrbk; Trk; Chrldng; Mat Maids; PPFtbl; Wittenberg Univ; Spec Ed.

RUMINSKI, LAURA; Villa Angela Acad; Euclid, OH; Aud/Vis; Chrs; Chrh Wkr; Hon Rl; NHS; Ed Yrbk; Rptr Yrbk; Yrbk; Lakeland Cmnty Coll; Advertising.

RUMISEK, KAREN; Chesaning Union HS; New Lothrop, MI; Cl Rep Jr Cls; Cls Rep Sr Cls; Band; NHS; Sch Mus; Stu Cncl; Rptr Sch Nwsp; Drama Clb; Natl Merit Schl; Rotary Awd; Michigan St Univ.

RUMLER, CRAIG; Lumen Christi HS; Jackson, MI; Hon Rl; Fr Clb; Trk; IM Sprt; Michigan St Univ; Comp Tech.

RUMMEL, MARTHA; Frankenmuth HS; Frankenmuth, MI; Hon Rl; Univ Of Michigan; Pre Med.

RUMORA, LYNN; Madonna HS; Weirton, WV; Hon Rl; NHS; Yrbk; Pep Clb; Trk; IM Sprt; West Liberty Univ; Bus Mgmt.

RUMP, DORA; Anna Local School; Sidney, OH; 1/82 Sec Soph Cls; Band; Chrs; Drm Mjrt; Hon Rl; NHS; Sch Mus; Rptr Yrbk; Drama Clb; 4-H; Univ; Elem Educ.

RUMPH, CHARLENE; Buchtel Univeristy HS; Akron, OH; Cls Rep Soph Cls; Chrs; Hosp Ade; JA; Off Ade; Sct Actv; 4-H; Ger Clb; OEA; Cit Awd; Univ Of Cincinnati; Bus Admin.

RUMPLE, CYNTHIA; Mississinewa HS; Marion, IN; 1/200 Hst Jr Cls; Am Leg Aux Girls St; Chrh Wkr; Hon Rl; Hosp Ade; Jr NHS; NHS; Stu Cncl; Yth Flsp; 4-H; Senator Lugar Symposium For Outstanding Jrs 78 79; Vllybll; Whos Whos In Foreign Lang 77 78 & 78 79; Univ; Med.

RUMPTZ, GARY; Ubly HS; Ubly, MI; 10/125 Band; Hon Rl; Jr NHS; Sch Pl; Stu Cncl; 4-H; FFA; Bsktbl; Ftbl; IM Sprt; Michigan St Univ; Agri.

RUMSCHLAG, CHARLES; New Riegel HS; New Riegel, OH; 12/47 Pres Soph Cls; Cls Rep Sr Cls; Hon Rl; Jr NHS; NHS; Stu Cncl; Spn Clb; IM Sprt; Am Leg Awd; Voice Dem Awd; Ashland Coll; Radio & T V.

RUMSEY, JEFFREY; Greensburg Community HS; Greensburg, IN; 28/200 Band; Drm Bgl; FCA; Hon Rl; Yth Flsp; Bsbl; IM Sprt; Mas Awd; College; Math.

RUNCO, JACQUELINE; William V Fisher Cath HS; Lancaster, OH; Aud/Vis; Chrs; Chrh Wkr; Cmnty Wkr; Hon Rl; Fr Clb; IM Sprt; Scr Kpr; Tmr; Ohio Univ; Phys Ther.

RUNDO, KIMBERLY; Maple Heights Sr HS; Maple Hgts, OH; Cls Rep Sr Cls; Hon Rl; Jr NHS; Off Ade; Rptr Yrbk; Letter Swmmng; Ursline Coll; Nursing.

RUNEVITCH, TAMMY; Buckeye West HS; Cadiz, OH; Trs Frsh Cls; Band; Chrs; Hon Rl; Drama Clb; 4-H; FHA; OEA; Chrldng; GAA; Bradford Bus Schl; Lgl Sec.

RUNKEL, EDWARD; Warren Central HS; Indpls, IN; 94/768 Jr NHS; Purdue Univ; Aero Engr.

RUNKEL, PAM; Sheridan HS; Thonrville, OH; 21/177 Hon Rl; NHS; Sch Mus; Sch Pl; Yrbk; Rptr Sch Nwsp; Sec Drama Clb; Pres FHA; FTA; Pep Clb; Miami Univ; Interior Design.

RUNKLE, RENAE; Black River HS; Wellington, OH; Hst Frsh Cls; Hon Rl; Off Ade; Sch Pl; Beta Clb; Pep Clb; Spn Clb; Bsktbl; Letter Gym; Trk; Bus Schl; Court Reporter.

RUNNEBAHM, MIKE; Waldron HS; Shelbyville, IN; Sec Jr Cls; Trs Jr Cls; Am Leg Boys St; Boy Scts; Chrh Wkr; NHS; IM Sprt; Mgrs; Univ.

RUNNELLS, KATHLEEN; Tippecanoe Valley HS; Warsaw, IN; 26/179 VP Frsh Cls; VP Soph Cls; VP Jr Cls; Band; Chrs; Drl Tm; Hon Rl; NHS; Stu Cncl; Pep Clb; Volleyball Capt; Purdue Univ; Phys Ed.

RUNNELS, TONY; Highland Park Community HS; Highland Pk, MI; Cls Rep Frsh Cls; Hon Rl; Off Ade; Y-Teens; Boys Clb Am; Bsbl; Bsktbl; Ftbl; Coach Actv; Scr Kpr; NBA/PEPSI Hot Shot Comp Runner Up 77; Best Athlete Best Sportsmnshp & MVP 76 77 & 78; Michigan St Univ; Phys Educ.

RUNNER, ERIK; Notre Dame HS; Bridgeport, WV; 11/54 Cls Rep Sr Cls; NHS; Sch Pl; Stu Cncl; Ed Sch Nwsp; Drama Clb; Fr Clb; IM Sprt; Univ; Law.

RUNNING, LESA; Bad Axe HS; Bad Axe, MI; Chrs; Chrh Wkr; Hon Rl; Jr NHS; Lbry Ade; Natl Forn Lg; NHS; Off Ade; Sch Pl; Stg Crw; Univ; Soc Work.

RUNOWSKI, ALEXANDER; L C Mohr HS; South Haven, MI; Band; Chrh Wkr; FCA; Hon Rl; Jr NHS; NHS; Swmmng; IM Sprt; Scr Kpr; Tmr; Univ Of Mic; Pre Med.

RUNYAN, COLLEEN; Mason HS; Mason, MI; Cls Rep Frsh Cls; Chrs; Hon Rl; Mdrgl; Sch Mus; Sch Pl; 4-H; IM Sprt; Natl Federation Of Music Clubs; Michigan Schl Vocal Assn; Intl Music Assn; Pres Phys Fitness; Michigan St Univ; Voice.

RUNYAN, LEE ANN; Zionsville HS; Zionsville, IN; 7/149 Pres Jr Cls; Am Leg Aux Girls St; Chrs; Mdrgl; VP MMM; NHS; Sch Mus; VP Stu Cncl; 4-H; Pep Clb; Most Otstndng Sr Choir Mbr 79; Most Talented Sr 79; Dr Spec Awd 78; Moody Bible Inst; Vocal Music.

RUNYAN, SUZANNE M; Rutherford B Hayes HS; Delaware, OH; Cls Rep Soph Cls; Cl Rep Jr Cls; AFS; Chrs; Debate Tm; Sch Mus; Stu Cncl; Drama Clb; Ger Clb; Key Clb; College; Broadcasting.

RUNYON, TERRI; Williamston HS; Williamston, MI; Bsktbl; Ten; PPFtbl; College; Business Management.

RUNYON, TODD; Centerville HS; Centerville, IN; Boy Scts; FCA; Sct Actv; 4-H; Spn Clb; IM Sprt; College; Math.

RUNZA, FRAN; Hackett HS; Kalamazoo, MI; Cls Rep Frsh Cls; Chrs; Cmnty Wkr; Debate Tm; Hon Rl; Off Ade; Stg Crw; Stu Cncl; Yrbk; Pep Clb; MVP Var Vllybl 78; Var Vllybl Capt & Ltr 78; Univ; Med.

RUPERT, BRYAN; Ursuline HS; Youngstown, OH; College; Restaurant Manager.

RUPERT, DAVID; Ravenna HS; Ravenna, OH; Am Leg Boys St; Boy Scts; Hon Rl; Jr NHS; NHS; Off Ade; Capt Ftbl; Trk; IM Sprt; College; Engineering.

RUPERT, GREGORY; Medina HS; Medina, OH; 93/360 Boy Scts; Sct Actv; Trs Jr Cls; Cls Rep Sr Cls; College; Oceanography.

RUPERT, LAURA; South Range HS; Salem, OH; AFS; Chrs; Hon Rl; Sch Mus; Sch Pl; Rptr Yrbk; Drama Clb; Rus Clb; PPFtbl; College; Math.

RUPP, BRENDA; Hilltop HS; W Unity, OH; 4/75 Sec Jr Cls; Band; Girl Scts; Hon Rl; NHS; FHA; Chrldng; Bowling Green; Elem Tchr.

RUPP, CATHY; Archbold HS; Archbold, OH; Cls Rep Soph Cls; Band; Chrs; Chrh Wkr; Hon Rl; NHS; Sch Mus; Stu Cncl; Yth Flsp; Pep Clb; Univ; Forensic Stds.

RUPP, MARY; Gorham Fayette HS; Fayette, OH; Trs Jr Cls; Am Leg Aux Girls St; Chrs; Hon Rl; NHS; 4-H; FHA; Chrldng; Am Leg Awd; Coll; Teaching.

RUPP, SAUNDRA; Valley Forge HS; Parma, OH; Drm Bgl; Hon Rl; Opt Clb Awd; VFW Awd; Voice Dem Awd; Univ; Jrnlsm.

RUPP, STANLEY; Hilltop HS; West Unity, OH; 1/65 Trs Soph Cls; VP Jr Cls; VP Sr Cls; Am Leg Boys St; Band; Chrs; Chrh Wkr; Hon Rl; Pres NHS; DAR Awd; Mt Vernon Nazarene College; Chemistr.

RUPP, THOMAS H; Davison HS; Davison, MI; 1/500 Debate Tm; Hon Rl; Natl Forn Lg; Sch Pl; Stg Crw; Mth Clb; Spn Clb; Glf; Voice Dem Awd; Univ Of Mic; Med.

RUPP, TIMOTHY; Davison HS; Davison, MI; Debate Tm; Hon Rl; Natl Forn Lg; NHS; VP Mth Clb; Treas Spn Clb; Letter Glf; VFW Awd; Voice Dem Awd; College; Med.

RUPP, TIMOTHY H; Davison HS; Davison, MI; Debate Tm; Hon Rl; Natl Forn Lg; VP Mth Clb; Treas Spn Clb; Letter Glf; VFW Awd; Voice Dem Awd; Univ; Dent.

RUPPEL, LESLIE; Clyde HS; Green Springs, OH; Trs Soph Cls; Trs Jr Cls; Trs Sr Cls; Chrs; Hon Rl; NHS; Rptr Sch Nwsp; Pres Spn Clb; Letter Trk; Animal Sci Inst; Zoo Keeper.

RUPPEL, MARY; Clio HS; Clio, MI; 32/400 Hon Rl; NHS; OEA; GAA; PPFtbl; Bakers Bus Coll; Acctg.

RUPPEL, SUSAN; South Knox HS; Vincennes, IN; 5/106 Hon Rl; NHS; Quill & Scroll; Sprt Ed Yrbk; FNA; OEA; Pep Clb;.

RUPPERT, JOHN; Lewis Cnty HS; Weston, WV; 2/270 Cl Rep Jr Cls; Chrs; FCA; Hon Rl; Jr NHS; NHS; Stu Cncl; Letter Ten; West Virginia Univ; Chem.

RUPPERT, MARY L; Lewis County HS; Weston, WV; Chrs; Hon Rl; Jr NHS; NHS; Sch Nwsp; Pep Clb; Ten; Trk; W V Univ; Psychology.

RUS, PATTI; Colerain Sr HS; Cincinnati, OH; Band; Hon Rl; Hosp Ade; JA; Jr NHS; Lit Mag; NHS; Stu Cncl; Drama Clb; Ger Clb; Ohio St Univ; Nursing.

RUSCH, LAURIE; Freeland HS; Saginaw, MI; 4/115 Band; Chrh Wkr; Hon Rl; NHS; Yth Flsp; Bsbl; Chrldng; St Of Mi Schlrshp 79; Central Mi Univ Hnrs Schlrshp 79; HS Acctg Awd 79; Central Michigan Univ; Bus.

RUSCHE, ROSALIE; Castle HS; Newburgh, IN; Hon Rl; NHS; Off Ade; FBLA; OEA; IM Sprt; 2nd Plc In OEA Reg Competition Acctg & Related II; Indiana St Univ; Acctg.

RUSCHER, KATHRYN; Madeira HS; Cincinnati, OH; Hon Rl; JA Awd;.

RUSCHMAN, ELISA J; Little Miami HS; Maineville, OH; Hon Rl; Sch Mus; 4-H; Fr Clb; Pep Clb; 4-H Awd; Univ; Zoology.

RUSCITTI, RINALDO; Girard HS; Girard, OH; 6/200 Cls Rep Soph Cls; AFS; Hon Rl; Keyettes; Sci Clb; Spn Clb; Trk; Wrstlng; Ohio Univ; Sci.

RUSCONI, MICHAEL; St Xavier HS; Cincinnati, OH; 70/270 Cls Rep Frsh Cls; Cls Rep Soph Cls; Cl Rep Jr Cls; VP Sr Cls; Chrs; Chrh Wkr; Cmnty Wkr; Hon Rl; Jr NHS; NHS; Mod UN; Univ; Bus.

RUSH, BETTY; Warrensville Hghts Sr HS; Warrensville, OH; Univ; Acctg.

RUSH, BRIAN; Hobart HS; Hobart, IN; Hon Rl; Jr NHS; Pol Wkr; Ftbl; Hndbl; Trk; Wrstlng; Indiana Univ; Bus.

RUSH, CATHERINE; Woodsfield HS; Woodsfield, OH; Hon Rl; Lbry Ade; NHS; Sch Pl; Ed Yrbk; Drama Clb; Fr Clb; Pep Clb; Mgrs; Kiwan Awd; Business School; Acct.

RUSH, DENISE; Union HS; Grand Rapids, MI; Hon Rl; Jr NHS; NHS; Michigan Competitive Schlrshp; Cert Of Merits In Art & Eng; Grand Rapids Jr Coll; Archt.

RUSH, KAREN; John Fitzgerald Kennedy HS; Cleveland, OH; Hon Rl; NHS; Off Ade; Pol Wkr; Ed Sch Nwsp; Sprt Ed Sch Nwsp; Sch Nwsp; Cit Awd; Lincoln Univ; Acctg.

RUSH, KEVIN; Parma Sr HS; Parma, OH; 36/844 Boy Scts; Hon Rl; Stu Cncl; Sch Nwsp; Wrstlng; Case Western Reserve Univ; Med.

RUSH, PATRICIA; Magnolia HS; New Martinsvle, WV; 6/200 Band; Hon Rl; NHS; Stu Cncl; FTA; Natl Merit Ltr; West Liberty St Coll; Math.

RUSH, STEVE; River Valley HS; Waldo, OH; 26/196 Am Leg Boys St; Band; FCA; Sch Mus; Stu Cncl; 4-H; Sci Clb; Crs Cntry; Trk; IM Sprt; College; Comp Sci.

RUSH, SUSAN; Little Miami HS; Loveland, OH; 57/200 Band; Debate Tm; Hon Rl; Lit Mag; Sch Mus; Sch Pl; Mas Awd; Ohio St Univ; Archt.

RUSHING, TORIE; Miller HS; Maxahala, OH; 32/96 Hon Rl; Jr NHS; Lbry Ade; NHS; Off Ade; Yrbk; Sch Nwsp; Letter Chrldng;.

RUSHTON, JEANNETTE; Holy Rosary HS; Davison, MI; Hon Rl; Sch Pl; Rptr Yrbk; Chrldng; Univ; Phys Ther.

RUSHTON, WILLIAM; Onaway HS; Onaway, MI; Trs Soph Cls; Boy Scts; Chrh Wkr; NHS; Sch Pl; Sct Actv; Yth Flsp; Letter Bsbl; Letter Ftbl; Letter Wrstlng; Air Force Academy; Pre Law.

RUSIN, JANE; Bishop Borgess HS; Detroit, MI; Hon Rl; Lbry Ade; NHS; Wayne State Univ; Doctor.

RUSIN, THOMAS; L C Mohr HS; South Haven, MI; Band; Chrh Wkr; Hon Rl; Ftbl; IM Sprt; Comptty Schlshp 79; Music Shslhp From LMC; Lake Michigan Coll; Music.

RUSKY, JIM; Comstock Park HS; Comstock Pk, MI; Aud/Vis; Hon Rl; Ftbl; Trk; Michigan St Univ; Engr.

RUSNAK, RONALD; Ursuline HS; Youngstown, OH; 85/360 Hon Rl; Glf; Mgrs; College; Science.

RUSS, BRIAN; Carroll HS; Xenia, OH; 12/330 Hon Rl; NHS; Sch Pl; Stg Crw; Mth Clb; Letter Ftbl; Letter Ten; Letter Trk; Natl Merit SF; St Louis Univ; Pre Med.

RUSS, TAMMY; Mt View HS; Welch, WV; 57/250 Chrs; Hon Rl; Jr NHS; Off Ade; Keyettes; Pep Clb;.

RUSSEL, JEFFREY E; Rocky River Sr HS; Rocky River, OH; 27/314 VP Band; Hon Rl; MMM; NHS; Orch; Sch Mus; Natl Merit SF; Michigan St Univ; Chem Engr.

RUSSELL, ALBERT; Whitehall Yearling HS; Whitehall, OH; Lit Mag; Sch Pl; Stg Crw; Sprt Ed Sch Nwsp; Rptr Sch Nwsp; Fr Clb; Ftbl Socr; Coach Actv; Univ; Env.

RUSSELL, CAROLYN; Calumet HS; Gary, IN; 37/200 Band; Hon Rl; Lbry Ade; Sch Pl; Cit Awd; Bell & Howell Inst Of Tech; Comp Sci.

RUSSELL, CHRISTIE; Gahanna Lincoln HS; Gahanna, OH; 46/440 Am Leg Aux Girls St; Band; NHS; Chrldng; Stu Cncl; Yth Flsp; Lat Clb; PPFtbl; Scr Kpr; Univ Of Ohi; Optmtry.

RUSSELL, DANA L; Midland HS; Midland, MI; Pres Soph Cls; Cl Rep Jr Cls; Cmnty Wkr; Hon Rl; Stu Cncl; Letter Bsktbl; Natl Merit SF; Michigan St Univ; Veterinary Med.

RUSSELL, DAVID; Evansville North HS; Evansville, IN; 4/330 Cls Rep Frsh Cls; Cls Rep Soph Cls; Band; Chrs; Chrh Wkr; Debate Tm; Hon Rl; VP Natl Forn Lg; VP NHS; Ger Clb; Univ Of Evansville; Chem.

RUSSELL, DEAN E; Richwood HS; Cottle, WV; Am Leg Boys St; Hon Rl; Letter Trk; Letter Wrstlng; IM Sprt; Univ; Archt.

RUSSELL, DONN M; Yorktown HS; Muncie, IN; 48/180 Cls Rep Frsh Cls; Cls Rep Soph Cls; Cl Rep Jr Cls; Cls Rep Sr Cls; Hon Rl; Stu Cncl; Spn Clb; Letter Bsbl; Letter Bsktbl; Letter Crs Cntry; Pres Of Spanish Club 79; VP Of Spanish Club 78; Arizona St Univ; Air Sci.

RUSSELL, ERROL; Kyger Creek HS; Cheshire, OH; Boy Scts; Hon Rl; JA; Sct Actv; Stu Cncl; Fr Clb; Key Clb; VICA; Bsbl; I Was On Schlrshp Tm 78 & 79; Apreniship Schl; Elec.

RUSSELL, GINNY; Wellsville HS; Wellsville, OH; Sec Band; Chrh Wkr; Girl Scts; NHS; Stg Crw; Yth Flsp; Y-Teens; Rptr Yrbk; Drama Clb; 4-H; Outstndng Jr Band Mbr; College.

RUSSELL, JAMES; Harbor HS; Ashtabula, OH; Pres Sr Cls; Pres AFS; Band, Mdrgl; Sch Mus; Sch Pl; Stu Cncl; Pres Spn Clb; College; Med.

RUSSELL, JANET; Indian Valley North HS; New Philadelphi, OH; Pres Frsh Cls; Sec Soph Cls; Pres Jr Cls; Chrs; Chrh Wkr; NHS; Rptr Yrbk; Rptr Sch Nwsp; Capt Bsktbl; Ohio Northern Univ; Biology.

RUSSELL, JANET S; Indian Valley North HS; New Philadelpha, OH; Pres Frsh Cls; Sec Soph Cls; Pres Jr Cls; Band; Chrs; Chrh Wkr; Cmnty Wkr; Hon Rl; NHS; Off Ade; Ohio N Univ; Bio.

RUSSELL, JEFFREY; New Lexington HS; New Lexington, OH; Cls Rep Frsh Cls; Cls Rep Soph Cls; VP Jr Cls; Hon Rl; Sch Pl; Stu Cncl; Pres Spn Clb; Capt Bsktbl; Ftbl; Trk; Ftbll 1st Team SEO 3rd Team Ohio Leading Yds; Track Hurdles 3rd Team SEO 2nd In St In Jr Olympic; Univ Of Wisconsin.

RUSSELL, JILL; North Knox HS; Bicknell, IN; 4/156 Chrh Wkr; Sec FCA; Girl Scts; Hon Rl; Treas NHS; Pol Wkr; Yth Flsp; Pres 4-H; FHA; Chrldng; Univ.

RUSSELL, JILL ANN; North Knox HS; Bicknell, IN; 4/156 Chrh Wkr; Sec FCA; Girl Scts; Hon Rl; Treas NHS; Pol Wkr; Yth Flsp; Pres 4-H; FHA; Pep Clb; Indiana St Univ; Educ.

RUSSELL, JULIE; Valley View HS; Kettering, OH; Cls Rep Soph Cls; Cl Rep Jr Cls; Chrh Wkr; Drl Tm; Hon Rl; Lbry Ade; Off Ade; Miami Univ; Pre Law.

RUSSELL, KAREN; Buckhannon Upshur HS; Tallmanville, WV; Hon Rl; Bus Tchr.

RUSSELL, KATHRYN S; Noblesville HS; Noblesville, IN; 4/240 Band; Debate Tm; Natl Forn Lg; NHS; Yth Flsp; Drama Clb; Ger Clb; Sci Clb; Letter Ten; Natl Merit SF; Purdue Univ; Science.

RUSSELL, KELLY; Western HS; Latham, OH; Cls Rep Frsh Cls; Band; Hon Rl; Stu Cncl; Drama Clb; 4-H; FHA; Bsktbl; Trk; Chrldng; Eng Schlrshp Awd 7th Dist 1978; Shawnee St Coll.

RUSSELL, KIMBERLY; Crothersville HS; Crothersville, IN; 12/66 Trs Soph Cls; Chrs; Chrh Wkr; Hon Rl; Pep Clb; Art III Awd 78;.

RUSSELL, LINDA; Monroe HS; Monroe, MI; 2/554 Sal; Pres Chrs; Hon Rl; NHS; Sch Mus; Drama Clb; Monroe County Community Coll; Educ.

RUSSELL, LINDA; Coloma HS; Hagar Shores, MI; Trs Sr Cls; Hon Rl; VP NHS; Pres Fr Clb; FTA; PPFtbl; Western Michigan Univ; Elem Ed.

RUSSELL, LISA; Midland HS; Midland, MI; 4/476 Chrs; Girl Scts; Hon Rl; NHS; Orch; Pol Wkr; Yrbk; Drama Clb; Natl Merit Schl; Lawrence Univ; Vocal Performance.

RUSSELL, MARGARET; Western Boone HS; Thorntown, IN; Am Leg Aux Girls St; Band; Chrs; Drl Tm; Girl Scts; Hon Rl; Sch Mus; Fr Clb; FHA; OEA;.

RUSSELL, MICHAEL D; Madison Comprehensive HS; Mansfield, OH; Chrh Wkr; Pol Wkr; Yth Flsp; Ger Clb; Wrstlng; IM Sprt; C of C Awd; Civil Engr.

RUSSELL, PAMELA; Lima Sr HS; Lima, OH; Band; Chrs; Girl Scts; Hon Rl; Hosp Ade; Lbry Ade; Sch Mus; Sct Actv; Rptr Yrbk; Yrbk; Lima Tech Branch; RN.

RUSSELL, PATRICIA; St Joseph Academy; Cleveland, OH; Cmnty Wkr; Hon Rl; Fr Clb; Univ; Bus Admin.

RUSSELL, PATRICIA; Harbor HS; Ashtabula, OH; 62/200 AFS; Chrh Wkr; Girl Scts; Fr Clb; Univ; Speech Ther.

RUSSELL, ROBERT; Pittsford HS; Osseo, MI; 9/57 Hon Rl; Lbry Ade; NHS; Sch Pl; 4-H; Spn Clb; Mgrs; Jackson Cmnty Coll; Acctg.

RUSSELL, SIDNEY; Mt Vernon Academy; Cleveland, OH; Chrs; Pres JA; Sch Pl; Rptr Sch Nwsp; Spn Clb; Bsktbl; IM Sprt; Cit Awd; Pres JA Awd; Career Awareness Pres 76; Varsity Bsktbl 78; Univ; Cmnctns.

RUSSELL, URETTA; Bedford Sr HS; Oakwood Village, OH; Cls Rep Sr Cls; Chrs; Cmnty Wkr; Drl Tm; Pol Wkr; Stu Cncl; OEA; Letter Trk; Intern For Youthwrk In Washington 80; Sr Class Cmmncmnt Spkr 79; Cleveland St Univ; Stewardess.

RUSSELL, VICKI; Ursulime HS; Youngstwon, OH; 86/315 Chrh Wkr; Debate Tm; Hon Rl; Natl Forn Lg; NHS; Drama Clb; Ger Clb; Lat Clb; Pep Clb; Univ Of Cincinnati; Cardiovascular.

RUSSELL, VINCENT; St Ignatius HS; N Royalton, OH; Hon Rl; Letter Socr; Univ; Engr.

RUSSNAK, BRIAN; Mount View HS; Gary, WV; 28/240 Pres Frsh Cls; Pres Soph Cls; Pres Jr Cls; Am Leg Boys St; Aud/Vis; Hon Rl; NHS; Stu Cncl; Key Clb; Ftbl; Concord Coll; Bus.

RUSSO, RON; La Salle HS; Cincinnati, OH; 25/285 Natl Honor Soc; Whos Who 77 78; La Salle Hnr Pin; Rose Hulman Inst Of Tech; Engr.

RUSSO, VINCENT; Carroll HS; Dayton, OH; Aud/Vis; Band; Hon Rl; Sch Mus; Sct Actv; College; Pre Med.

RUSTIC, JAMES; Valley Forge HS; Parma, OH; 57/704 Boy Scts; Pres Chrs; Chrh Wkr; Hon Rl; Mdrgl; NHS; Sch Pl; Sct Actv; Stg Crw; Stu Cncl; Coll Of Wooster.

RUSZ, JENNIFER; St Charles HS; St Charles, MI; Sec Soph Cls; Sec Jr Cls; Cl Rep Jr Cls; Cls Rep Sr Cls; Hon Rl; NHS; Stu Cncl; Saginaw Valley State College; Bio.

RUTCHOW, MARY; De Vilbiss HS; Toledo, OH; Band; Chrh Wkr; Hon Rl; Orch; Sch Mus; Eng Clb; Ger Clb; College; Medicine.

RUTERBUSCH, VICTOR; Saginaw St Peter & Paul HS; Linwood, MI; 7/115 Pres Frsh Cls; Chrs; Hon Rl; NHS; Sch Mus; Sch Pl; FDA; Letter Bsbl; Letter Ftbl; Letter Trk; Princeton Univ; Med.

RUTHERFORD, ANITA; Shelbyville Sr HS; Shelbyville, IN; 19/300 Hon Rl; JA; NHS; Sci Clb; Spn Clb; Purdue Univ; Sci.

RUTHERFORD, C; St Philip Catholic Ctrl HS; Battle Crk, MI; Cls Rep Frsh Cls; Cmnty Wkr; Hon Rl; Sch Pl; Yrbk; FBLA; Pep Clb; Chrldng; GAA; PPFtbl; Bus Schl; Legal Sec.

RUTHERFORD, JANET; Onekama Consolidated Schools; Manistee, MI; Trs Frsh Cls; Sec Soph Cls; Am Leg Aux Girls St; Band; Chrh Wkr; Debate Tm; Hon Rl; NHS; Orch; Sch Mus; Central Michigan Univ; Bus.

RUTHERFORD, LORI; Point Pleasant HS; Pt Plesant, WV; Cls Rep Frsh Cls; Cls Rep Soph Cls; Girl Scts; Hosp Ade; Sch Pl; Y-Teens; Keyettes; Pep Clb; Chrldng; Mat Maids; Marshall Univ; Nursing.

RUTHERFORD, SHANNON; Eastern HS; Pekin, IN; Am Leg Aux Girls St; Sec NHS; Spn Clb; Hanover Coll; Elem Educ.

RUTHERFORD, SHANNON S; Eastern HS; Pekin, IN; 4/93 Am Leg Aux Girls St; Hon Rl; Sec NHS; Stu Cncl; Spn Clb; Ind Univ; Elem Ed.

RUTHERFORD, SUE; Cannelton HS; Cannelton, IN; 4/35 Trs Frsh Cls; Trs Soph Cls; Trs Jr Cls; Band; Chrh Wkr; Girl Scts; Hon Rl; Jr NHS; NHS; Off Ade; Outsntdg Jr High Bandsmen Awd 1976; Homecomg Attndt Frsh & Jr Yr 1977;.

RUTHRUFF, CHRIS; Greenville HS; Greenville, MI; Am Leg Boys St; Hon Rl; Hosp Ade; Yth Flsp; Mth Clb; Letter Ftbl; PPFtbl; Nazareth Coll; Pre Med.

RUTKOSKI, CELIA; Shawe HS; Madison, IN; 10/31 Cls Rep Frsh Cls; Trs Jr Cls; Chrh Wkr; Hon Rl; Jr NHS; NHS; Stu Cncl; Yrbk; Pep Clb; Chrldng; Univ; Law.

RUTKOWSKI, CATHERINE; St Frances Cabrini HS; Allen Pk, MI; Chrh Wkr; Cmnty Wkr; Girl Scts; Hon Rl; Sec Fr Clb; Ger Clb; Letter Ten; GAA; College; Special Education.

RUTKOWSKI, CATHERINE; Lincoln HS; Warren, MI; 22/325 Band; Chrh Wkr; Drm Bgl; Girl Scts; Hon Rl; Jr NHS; Lbry Ade; NHS; VP Yth Flsp; Macomb Community College; Dent Asst.

RUTKOWSKI, KATHY; St Florian HS; Hamtramck, MI; 7/76 Chrs; Hon Rl; NHS; Rptr Sch Nwsp; Sch Nwsp; Mth Clb; Spn Clb; VICA; Univ Of Michigan; Pharm.

RUTKOWSKI, THOMAS; Athens HS; Troy, MI; Chrs; Hon Rl; Mdrgl; NHS; PAVAS; Sch Mus; Sch Pl; Stg Crw; Drama Clb; Ftbl; Hillsdale College; Comp Tech.

RUTLEDGE, CHRISTINE; Interlochen Arts Academy; Taylor, MI; Val; Hon Rl; Jr NHS; Natl Forn Lg; NHS; Orch; Sch Mus; Sch Pl; Drama Clb; Peabody Conservatory; Music.

RUTLEDGE, JANET; Wilbur Wright HS; Dayton, OH; 1/213 Am Leg Aux Girls St; Band; Chrh Wkr; NHS; Orch; Sch Mus; Sch Pl; Stu Cncl; Ger Clb; Rdo Clb; College; Math.

RUTLEDGE, LOIS; Chaminade Julienne HS; Dayton, OH; Chrs; Cmnty Wkr; NHS; Sch Pl; Stg Crw; Rptr Yrbk; Drama Clb; Spn Clb; College; Psych.

RUTLEDGE, MARK; Chillicothe HS; Chillicothe, OH; 18/400 Cls Rep Frsh Cls; VP Sr Cls; AFS; Boy Scts; Chrh Wkr; Cmnty Wkr; Hon Rl; Natl Forn Lg; NHS; Sch Pl; Coll Of Wooster; Chem.

RUTLEDGE, SUSAN M; Swan Valley HS; Saginaw, MI; 19/189 Cls Rep Sr Cls; Chrh Wkr; Girl Scts; NHS; Sch Pl; Stu Cncl; Drama Clb; Pom Pon; Scr Kpr; Central Michigan Univ; Med Tech.

RUTLEDGE, THOMAS; Whetstone HS; Columbus, OH; 1/320 Chrs; Rptr Sch Nwsp; Ten; Am Leg Awd; DAR Awd; JETS Awd; Natl Merit SF; Natl Merit Schl; Amherst Coll; Lib Arts.

RUTT, DONNA; Lake Orion HS; Lake Orion, MI; 5/465 Cls Rep Frsh Cls; Cls Rep Sr Cls; Hon Rl; Jr NHS; NHS; Rptr Yrbk; Rdo Clb; Bsktbl; Trk; Mat Maids; Univ Of Mic; Comm Broadcasting.

RUTTAN, BEVERLEE; Michigan Lutheran Seminary; Kawkawlin, MI; Cmnty Wkr; Hon Rl; Hosp Ade; Yth Flsp; Ed Sch Nwsp; Rptr Sch Nwsp; 4-H; Letter Trk; IM Sprt; PPFtbl; 3 Newspaper Articles Publshd By Saginaw Times 79; Michigan St Univ; Bus Mgmt.

RUTTER, CARA; Weir HS; Weirton, WV; 74/355 Chrh Wkr; Cmnty Wkr; Hon Rl; Lbry Ade; Off Ade; Yth Flsp; FBLA; Pep Clb; GAA; Freed Hardmen Coll.

RUTTER, PAULA; Britton Macon Area HS; Dundee, MI; Pres Frsh Cls; Sec Jr Cls; Sec Sr Cls; Band; Hon Rl; Stu Cncl; Yrbk; 4-H; Sci Clb; Spn Clb; College.

RUTTLEDGE, JANET; Wilbur Wright HS; Dayton, OH; 1/213 Cls Rep Frsh Cls; Cls Rep Soph Cls; Cl Rep Jr Cls; Am Leg Aux Girls St; Band; Chrh Wkr; Girl Scts; Hon Rl; NHS; College; Math.

RUTZEN, GREGORY; Laville HS; Plymouth, IN; Am Leg Boys St; Aud/Vis; NHS; Fr Clb; Sci Clb; Letter Bsbl; Letter Ftbl; Am Leg Awd; College.

RUUD, JOSEPH; Muskegon HS; Muskegon, MI; Band; College; Elec.

RUYBALID, MARK; Mt Vernon Academy; Wooster, OH; Pres Frsh Cls; Cls Rep Soph Cls; Hon Rl; VP Stu Cncl; Bsktbl; Southern Missionary Coll; Bus.

RUZ, IVETTE; Dublin HS; Columbus, OH; 22/153 VP Sr Cls; Cls Rep Sr Cls; NHS; Yrbk; Fr Clb; Pep Clb; Spn Clb; Ohi State Univ; Lawyer.

RUZICKA, DORIS; Holy Rosary HS; Flint, MI; 2/45 VP Jr Cls; VP Sr Cls; Hon Rl; NHS; Pol Wkr; Sch Pl; Bsktbl; Coach Actv; Univ Of Michigan.

RUZICKA, FRANK; Holy Rosary HS; Flint, MI; Pres Frsh Cls; VP Jr Cls; Hon Rl; Sch Pl; Bsbl; Bsktbl; Ftbl; Trk; Univ; Building.

RUZICKA, SHERI; Mona Shores HS; Muskegon, MI; Band;.

RYAN, BECKY; Tri Rivers Joint Voc HS; Marion, OH; Hon Rl; JA; Jr NHS; NHS; Pres OEA; JA Awd; Participated In OEA Regional Com & Recvd 3rd Pl In Acctg; Harding Girls Vlybl Team; Marion Tech Coll; Acctg.

RYAN, CARLA; Athens HS; Athens, OH; Chrs; Lbry Ade; NHS; Key Clb; Ohio Univ; Acctg.

RYAN, CHERYL; Peebles HS; Hillsboro, OH; VP Soph Cls; Band; Hon Rl; Bsbl; Bsktbl; Crs Cntry; Trk; College.

RYAN, CINDY; Herbert Hoover HS; Charleston, WV; Cl Rep Jr Cls; Chrs; Girl Scts; Stu Cncl; Pres Soph Cls; 4-H; FHA; Pep Clb; Ten; Chrldng; Bus Schl; Sec.

RYAN, DAN; Fredericktown HS; Fred, OH; 1/145 Debate Tm; Pres NHS; Orch; Stu Cncl; VP 4-H; Am Leg Awd; Dnfth Awd; College; Chem Sci.

RYAN, DAVID A; Oak Glen HS; Chester, WV; 34/260 Am Leg Boys St; Boy Scts; NHS; Sch Mus; Sch Pl; Sct Actv; Stg Crw; Spn Clb; Letter Ftbl; Air Force Acad; Mech Engr.

RYAN, DEBORAH; Lincoln HS; Warren, MI; 17/325 Trs Soph Cls; Hon Rl; Jr NHS; NHS; Sec Stu Cncl; Treas OEA; Sci Clb; Police Citznshp Awd 1979; Mac Thompson Schlrshp 1979; 8th Pl Awd Acctg Comp 1979; Ctrl Michigan St Univ; Bus Admin.

RYAN, DEITRA; Bedford North Lawrence HS; Bedford, IN; Cls Rep Frsh Cls; Am Leg Aux Girls St; Band; Hon Rl; Beta Clb; Keyettes; Pep Clb; Spn Clb; Chrldng; PPFtbl; Indiana Univ; Education.

RYAN, EDWARD; Defiance Sr HS; Defiance, OH; Cls Rep Frsh Cls; Cls Rep Soph Cls; Cl Rep Jr Cls; Hon Rl; Stu Cncl; Spn Clb; Univ; Math.

RYAN, GLENDA; Brownstown Central HS; Norman, IN; 7/145 Hon Rl; NHS; Treas Yth Flsp; Sec 4-H; FTA; Sci Clb; Outstanding Spanish II Stu; Indiana Univ; Elem Ed.

RYAN, JAMES; Warren HS; Belpre, OH; Am Leg Boys St; Boy Scts; Sch Mus; Sch Pl; Ed Yrbk; Fr Clb; Pep Clb; Trk; Mgrs; Am Leg Awd; Ohio St Univ; Sci.

RYAN, JEANNE; Grosse Pointe South HS; Grosse Pte, MI; Chrs; Chrh Wkr; Girl Scts; Hon Rl; Red Cr Ade; Trk; College; Computer Sci.

RYAN, JEFFREY W; Mariemont HS; Terrace Park, OH; 40/169 AFS; Am Leg Boys St; Boy Scts; Sprt Ed Yrbk; Rptr Sch Nwsp; Letter Bsbl; Letter Ftbl; Wrstlng; Coach Actv; IM Sprt; Univ; Law.

RYAN, JONATHAN; St Charles Prep; Worthington, OH; Cls Rep Soph Cls; Hon Rl; Pres NHS; Stu Cncl; Yrbk; Spn Clb; Letter Bsbl; Capt Bsktbl; IM Sprt; Am Leg Awd;.

RYAN, KAREN; Hoover HS; N Canton, OH; 11/427 Hon Rl; JA; Jr NHS; NHS; Off Ade; Sch Pl; Fr Clb; Mth Clb; Sci Clb; JA Awd; Univ Of Akron; Reg Nurse.

RYAN, KATHLEEN; St Francis De Sales HS; Columbus, OH; Cmnty Wkr; Spn Clb; Coll; Radio Communication.

RYAN, KELLIE; Woodhaven HS; Flat Rock, MI; 14/218 Band; Chrh Wkr; Drm Mjrt; Jr NHS; NHS; Sch Pl; Stu Cncl; Letter Bsbl; Letter Bsktbl; JC Awd; College.

RYAN, LANA; Pendleton Hts HS; Pendleton, IN; 5/305 Am Leg Aux Girls St; NHS; Pres Quill & Scroll; Ed Sch Nwsp; Beta Clb; Pep Clb; Spn Clb; Ball St Univ; Jrnlsm.

RYAN, NANCY; Lawrenceburg HS; Lawrenceburg, IN; 30/165 Band; Hon Rl; Jr NHS; Orch; 4-H; Key Clb; Pep Clb; Sci Clb; Spn Clb; Miami Univ; Fshn Mdse.

RYAN, PATRICIA M; Seton HS; Cincinnati, OH; 20/271 Cl Rep Jr Cls; Cls Rep Sr Cls; Chrs; Chrh Wkr; Drl Tm; Hon Rl; Jr NHS; NHS; Stu Cncl; Sch Nwsp; Univ; Comm Arts.

RYAN, PEGGIE; Bork River Horris HS; Harris, MI; Cls Rep Soph Cls; Hon Rl; Off Ade; Drama Clb; Chrldng; IM Sprt; Marion R Schmidt Mem Fund; Bay De Roc Comm Coll; Photog.

RYAN, RICHARD F; Lexington HS; Lexington, OH; 13/260 Pres Soph Cls; NHS; Stu Cncl; Key Clb; Mth Clb; Ftbl; Letter Ten; IM Sprt; US Military Acad; Comp Sci.

RYAN, RORY; Whiteoak HS; Hillsboro, OH; 5/65 VP Soph Cls; Hon Rl; NHS; Sch Pl; Stu Cncl; Sprt Ed Yrbk; Sprt Ed Sch Nwsp; 4-H; Lat Clb; Letter Bsbl; Univ Of Cincinnati; Eng.

RYAN, TERRY; Central Catholic HS; Wheeling, WV; 4/131 Cls Rep Soph Cls; Hon Rl; Stu Cncl; IM Sprt;.

RYAN, WILLIAM G; Green HS; Akron, OH; 85/315 Band; Chrh Wkr; Debate Tm; Orch; Sch Pl; Drama Clb; Sci Clb; Duquesne Univ; Chem.

RYBA, CAROLYN; Cody HS; Detroit, MI; Chrh Wkr; Girl Scts; Hon Rl; Univ.

RYBICKI, CYNTHIA; Byron Center HS; Byron Center, MI; 17/138 Band; Debate Tm; Girl Scts; Hon Rl; NHS; Sch Pl; Drama Clb; FDA; Letter Chrldng; IM Sprt; Aquinas Coll; CPA.

RYBICKI, GRACE; Hazel Park HS; Hazel Park, MI; 15/342 Cls Rep Frsh Cls; Band; Chrs; Drl Tm; Drm Mjrt; Girl Scts; Hon Rl; NHS; Sch Mus; Sct Actv; Michigan Tech Univ; Forestry.

RYBICKI, MICAHEL; Bishop Luers HS; Ft Wayne, IN; Band; Boy Scts; Chrs; Hon Rl; Fr Clb; Swmmng; Hnrs Awd Entrance To Salesianum HS; Indiana Univ; Psych.

RYBSKL, MARY; Bishop Watterson HS; Columbus, OH; Chrs; Chrh Wkr; Cmnty Wkr; Hon Rl; Hosp Ade; Lbry Ade; Fr Clb; Lat Clb; Letter Bsktbl; Letter Hockey; Ohi State Univ; Nursing.

RYCHAK, CAROLINE; Northside HS; Muncie, IN; 12/242 Jr NHS; NHS; Stu Cncl; Pres Ger Clb; Letter Trk; Tmr; Opt Clb Awd; Ball State Univ; Interpreting.

RYCHLAK, STEPHANIE; Mc Cutcheon HS; Lafayette, IN; 1/264 Val; Am Leg Aux Girls St; Pres Natl Forn Lg; Pol Wkr; Ed Sch Nwsp; VP Fr Clb; Capt Chrldng; Elk Awd; Opt Clb Awd; Rotary Awd; De Pauw Univ; Communications.

RYCKMAN, JILL; Morton Sr HS; Hammond, IN; 19/436 Cls Rep Soph Cls; Cl Rep Jr Cls; Cls Rep Sr Cls; Girl Scts; Hon Rl; NHS; Off Ade; Rptr Yrbk; Pep Clb; Bsktbl; Univ Of Indiana; Bus.

RYDBOM, JULIE; Southeast HS; Lk Milton, OH; Cmp Fr Grls; Chrs; Hon Rl; Letter Bsktbl; Letter Trk; Akron Coll; Med.

RYDER, BETH; Milton HS; Ona, WV; 7/200 Hon Rl; NHS; Stu Cncl; Mth Clb; Pep Clb; Gym; Capt Chrldng; GAA; Spanish Awd; W V St Finalist Miss Teen USA Pageant; College.

RYDER, C ANTHONY; Fairland HS; Proctorvll, OH; 23/153 CAP; Hon Rl; NHS; Yth Flsp; Fr Clb; Mth Clb; Pep Clb; Letter Ftbl; Univ; Comp Prog.

RYDER, NANCY; Schoolcraft HS; Kalamazoo, MI; Cls Rep Frsh Cls; Sec Soph Cls; Cls Rep Soph Cls; Sec Jr Cls; Am Leg Aux Girls St; Hon Rl; NHS; Off Ade; Stu Cncl; Trk; Kalamazoo Valley Cmnty Coll; Bus.

RYDZEWSKI, JOHN; St Alphonsus HS; Detroit, MI; 3/190 Debate Tm; Hon Rl; Natl Forn Lg; Rptr Sch Nwsp; Sch Nwsp; Fr Clb; Mth Clb; Sci Clb; Bsbl; Trk; General Motors Inst; Elec Engr.

RYERSON, LINDA; Norwalk HS; Norwalk, OH; Boy Scts; Girl Scts; Hon Rl; Hosp Ade; Lbry Ade; Sct Actv; Yth Flsp; 4-H; 4-H Awd; Natl Merit Ltr; Univ; Med Tech.

RYGIEL, SUZETTE; Franklin HS; Westland, MI; Cls Rep Soph Cls; Cl Rep Jr Cls; Cls Rep Sr Cls; Chrs; Chrh Wkr; Girl Scts; Sch Mus; Sct Actv; Stu Cncl; Yth Flsp; 1st Cls Girl Scout 78; Magna Cum Laude; Whos Who Among Amer French Stdnt 79; Univ.

RYKWALDER, CARLA; Allen Park HS; Allen Park, MI; Band; VP Chrh Wkr; Hon Rl; Jr NHS; VP Swmmng; Mgrs; College; Respiration Therapy.

RYLANDER, MARY; Highland HS; Highland, IN; 53/493 Letter Band; Chrh Wkr; Hon Rl; NHS; Augustana Coll; Foreign Lang.

RYLL, LAURA; Pickerington HS; Pickerington, OH; 39/204 Sec Sr Cls; Hon Rl; NHS; Stu Cncl; Chrldng; PPFtbl; Univ; Psych.

RYMASZ, NANCY; Liberty HS; Clarksburg, WV; Pres Frsh Cls; Band; Chrs; Chrh Wkr; Hon Rl; Red Cr Ade; Y-Teens; Rptr Yrbk; Fr Clb; FBLA; Marshall Univ; Busns.

RYNBRAND, SCOTT; Holland HS; Holland, MI; Hon Rl; Sch Pl; IM Sprt; Univ; Bus Admin.

RYNDERS, JANNA; Waterford Township HS; Union Lake, MI; 1/410 Band; Chrs; Debate Tm; Hon Rl; Mdrgl; NHS; Sch Mus; Hope College; Pre Vet.

RYNEARSON, STEPHEN; Lutheran HS; Detroit, MI; Band; Boy Scts; Hon Rl; NHS; Concordia Ann Arbor; Law.

RYON, MICHELLE; Herbert Henry Dow HS; Midland, MI; 86/450 Cls Rep Soph Cls; Girl Scts; Hon Rl; NHS; Stu Cncl; Yrbk; 4-H; Pep Clb; Chrldng; Mgrs; Delta Coll; Scndry Soc Std Educ.

RYOO, DAVID; Carson City Crystal HS; Carson City, MI; Boy Scts; Chrs; Hon Rl; NHS; Off Ade; Yth Flsp; Yrbk; Fr Clb; Letter Bsktbl; Letter Crs Cntry; Univ; Engr.

RYSZAWA, PATRICIA; St Florian HS; Detroit, MI; Trs Frsh Cls; Sec Soph Cls; Trs Jr Cls; Sec Sr Cls; Chrs; Girl Scts; Hon Rl; Lbry Ade; Natl Forn Lg; NHS; Univ Of Detroit; Poli Sci.

RYTIEWSKI, KAREN; Bay City Western HS; Auburn, MI; Sec Chrh Wkr; Hon Rl; NHS; Off Ade; Sch Mus; Sct Actv; Y-Teens; Coach Actv; Southeastern Acad; Travel Agent.

RZEPECKI, THOMAS; Catholic Cntrl HS; Dearborn Hts, MI; VP Frsh Cls; Hon Rl; NHS; Sct Actv; Sprt Ed Yrbk; Rptr Sch Nwsp; Pres Sci Clb; Northwestern Univ; Dentistry.

S

SAAD, BRIAN; George Washington HS; Houston, TX; FCA; Stg Crw; FBLA; Glf; Letter Trk; IM Sprt; Tex A & M; Acctg.

SAADA, CHRISTIANE; Shaker Hts Sr HS; Shaker Hts, OH; 13/557 Chrs; Debate Tm; Girl Scts; Hon Rl; Natl Forn Lg; Sch Mus; Letter Crs Cntry; Letter Ten; Letter Trk; Princeton Univ; Bio.

SAALMAN, GARY; Coldwater Exempted Vlg HS; Coldwater, OH; 10/150 Am Leg Boys St; Cmnty Wkr; NHS; Ed Yrbk; Drama Clb; 4-H; Crs Cntry; Trk; Amer & Gvt Awd 79; Buckeye Boys St Spec Bnking Awd 79; Univ; Law.

SABATINA, KATHY; Shadyside HS; Shadyside, OH; Am Leg Aux Girls St; Treas Band; Chrs; Hon Rl; NHS; Sdlty; Y-Teens; Spn Clb; Scr Kpr; Steubenville; Public Relations.

SABATINO, LORI; Minerva HS; Minerva, OH; 13/241 Am Leg Aux Girls St; Band; Cmnty Wkr; Girl Scts; Hon Rl; Jr NHS; NHS; Yrbk; FTA; Lat Clb; College; Politics.

SABATINO, NATALIE; Bellaire HS; Bellaire, OH; 10/243 Hon Rl; Off Ade; Y-Teens; Fr Clb; Sec Spn Clb; Chrldng; IM Sprt; Ohio State Univ.

SABATULA, ANNETTE; Lumen Cordium HS; Shaker Hts, OH; Chrs; Hon Rl; Yrbk; Schlstc Awd Readings In Amer Literature; Merit Awd Schlstc Ach; Busns Schl; Sec.

SABAU, GEORGENE; Morton Sr HS; Hammond, IN; Chrs; Chrh Wkr; Girl Scts; Hon Rl; JA; Stg Crw; Am Leg Awd; Purdue Calumet Univ.

SABELHAUS, MELISSA; Tell City HS; Tell City, IN; 36/225 Girl Scts; Hon Rl; IM Sprt; Tmr; Univ Of Evansville; Comp Engr.

SABELLI, JO ANN; Cardinal Mooney HS; Youngstown, OH; 24/265 Hon Rl; Sprt Ed Yrbk; Spn Clb; Univ; Health.

SABEN, DOUGLAS; Pewamo Westpha HS; Hubbardston, MI; Michigan St Univ; Elec Engr.

SABER, DEBRA; Jewett Scio HS; Scio, OH; 5/76 Trs Sr Cls; Am Leg Aux Girls St; Band; Hon Rl; NHS; Sch Mus; Sch Nwsp; Trk; Chrldng; Homcmng Attnednat 77; Homcng Queen 78; Prom Attendt 78; Flag Carrier; Airline Stewardess.

SABIN, DOUGLAS; East Kentwood HS; Kentwood, MI; Band; Chrs; Hon Rl; Sch Mus; Stu Cncl; Letter Ten; IM Sprt; Michigan Tech Univ; Mech Engr.

SABO, CAROLYN; Monroeville HS; Monroeville, OH; Band; Hon Rl; Hosp Ade; NHS; Sch Pl; Rptr Yrbk; 4-H; Pep Clb; GAA; Am Leg Awd; College; Registered Nurse.

SABO, RICHARD; Melvindale HS; Melvindale, MI; Hon Rl; NHS; Yrbk; VP Sci Clb; Natl Hnr Soc Schlrshp 78; Univ Of Mi Schlr 78; Allied Chem Sci Sut Of Yr 78; Univ Of Michigan; Med.

SABO, TAMARA A; Washington HS; East Chicago, IN; 8/286 Cls Rep Soph Cls; Cl Rep Jr Cls; Cls Rep Sr Cls; Am Leg Aux Girls St; NHS; Fr Clb; Rotary Awd; Purdue Calumet Univ; Bus.

SABO, TIM; Madison HS; Madison, OH; 5/300 Band; Hon Rl; NHS; Pol Wkr; Sct Actv; Key Clb; Bsbl; Letter Ftbl; IM Sprt; Am Leg Awd; Ohio State Univ; Prelaw.

SABOL, BRIAN; Struthers HS; Struthers, OH; 60/270 Hon Rl; Sch Nwsp; Spn Clb; IM Sprt; Ohio State Univ.

SABOL, JOE; Lewis Cnty HS; Bucksport, ME; Cls Rep Soph Cls; Band; Hon Rl; Jr NHS; NHS; Sch Pl; Stu Cncl; Ed Sch Nwsp; Univ; Math.

SABOL, MARGARET; Bay HS; Bay Vill, OH; 220/384 Band; Chrs; Sch Mus; Sch Pl; Sec Drama Clb; Ger Clb; Univ; Eng.

SACHA, THERESA; St Andrew HS; Detroit, MI; 5/109 Sec Jr Cls; Hon Rl; NHS; Pep Clb; Ten; IM Sprt; Mgrs; Univ; Ther.

SACK, ROBERT; Flint Carman HS; Flint, MI; Cls Rep Frsh Cls; Chrh Wkr; Hon Rl; Natl Forn Lg; Yth Flsp; Sprt Ed Sch Nwsp; Rptr Sch Nwsp; Rdo Clb; Bsktbl; Coach Actv; Univ Of Michigan; Busns Admin.

SACKA, LORI; Cabrini HS; Dearborn Hts, MI; Chrs; Girl Scts; Hon Rl; Hosp Ade; Sch Pl; Stg Crw; Civ Clb; Drama Clb; FNA; Ger Clb; Henry Ford Comm Coll; Nurse.

SACKENHEIM, JOSEPH; Stephen T Badin HS; Fairfield, OH; 50/211 Chrs; Chrh Wkr; Cmnty Wkr; Hon Rl; Sch Mus; Sch Nwsp; Fr Clb; Key Clb; Letter Crs Cntry; Letter Trk; Univ; Elec.

SACKS, VALERIE; Lakeview HS; Cortland, OH; Cls Rep Soph Cls; Pres Jr Cls; Hon Rl; Red Cr Ade; Y-Teens; Rptr Sch Nwsp; Sch Nwsp; Beta Clb; Letter Trk; Univ; Law.

SACKSTEDER, MICHAEL; Princeton Cmnty HS; Princeton, IN; 17/232 NHS; Sch Pl; Ed Sch Nwsp; Drama Clb; Fr Clb; Bsktbl; Capt Crs Cntry; Capt Trk; Natl Merit Ltr; Univ; Jrnlsm.

SADEWASSER, KAREN; Centreville HS; Centreville, MI; Chrs; Cmnty Wkr; Hon Rl; Lbry Ade; Yth Flsp; 4-H; Fr Clb; FTA; Pep Clb; Bsbl; Glen Oaks Cmnty Coll; Wildlife Tech.

SADLER, BETTY; O Hoville HS; Ottoville, OH; 17/69 Chrs; Chrh Wkr; Y-Teens; Girl Scts; Hon Rl; Yth Flsp; Spn Clb; Am Leg Awd; Columbus Bus Univ; Acctg.

SADLER, CHUCK; C S Mott HS; Warren, MI; Letter Ftbl; IM Sprt; Wayne St Univ; Mech Engr.

SADLER, MIKE; Caston HS; Kewanna, IN; 32/59 Boy Scts; Lbry Ade; Stu Cncl; 4-H; FFA; 4-H Awd; Purdue Univ; Ag.

SADOWSKI, GARY; Maple Heights HS; Maple Hgts, OH; 78/409 Chrs; Jr NHS; Ftbl; Univ; Med.

SADOWSKI, JOAN; Menominee HS; Menominee, MI; 46/300 Chrs; Chrh Wkr; Girl Scts; Hon Rl; Sch Mus; Sct Actv; Ger Clb; Amer & Me; Sci Fair Awd; College; Sci.

SAEVIG, DANIEL; Clay Sr HS; Oregon, OH; Cls Rep Sr Cls; Band; Hon Rl; Stu Cncl; 4-H; IM Sprt; Cit Awd; 4-H Awd; Ohio St Univ; Brdcstng.

SAFAR, JULIE; Coventry HS; Akron, OH; Cl Rep Jr Cls; Band; Chrs; Chrh Wkr; Sch Pl; Stu Cncl; Rptr Sch Nwsp; Swmmng; Scr Kpr; Twrlr; Akron Univ; Acctg.

SAFFLE, KELLY; Whitehall Yearling HS; Whitehall, OH; Band; Off Ade; Orch; Pol Wkr; Bsbl; Bsktbl; Scr Kpr; Tmr; Ohio State.

SAFKO, PAUL; Zanesville HS; Holmes Beach, FL; FCA; Hon Rl; Swmmng; College.

SAFRAN, DIANE; Howland HS; Warren, OH; AFS; Band; Chrs; Hon Rl; Mdrgl; Orch; Sch Mus; Sch Pl; Yrbk; Sch Nwsp; Musical Theater.

SAFREED, CARL; John Glenn HS; New Concord, OH; 2/184 Pres Sr Cls; Am Leg Boys St; Boy Scts; Hon Rl; NHS; Sct Actv; Lat Clb; Bsktbl; Letter Ftbl; Letter Trk; College; Engineering.

SAFREED, CARL; John Glenn HS; North Canton, OH; 4/180 Pres Sr Cls; Am Leg Boys St; Band; Boy Scts; Hon Rl; Lbry Ade; NHS; Sct Actv; Lat Clb; Bsktbl; Georgia Inst Of Tech; Engr.

SAGAN, VINCENT; Strongsville HS; Strongsville, OH; Boy Scts; Hon Rl; Jr NHS; NHS; Letter Ftbl; College; Engineering.

SAGARSEE, MELISSA; Shakamak HS; Linton, IN; Cls Rep Soph Cls; Hst Jr Cls; Hst Sr Cls; Band; Chrh Wkr; Sch Mus; Sch Pl; Stg Crw; Drama Clb; Bsbl; Ind State Univ; Law.

SAGARSEE, SAM; Shakamak HS; Linton, IN; Sch Mus; Letter Crs Cntry; Letter Trk;.

SAGE, DOUG; Matheus HS; Vienna, OH; VP Jr Cls; Pres Sr Cls; VP Band; Chrs; Hon Rl; NHS; Orch; Stu Cncl; Yth Flsp; Pres Key Clb;.

SAGE, MIKE; Wintersville HS; Wintersville, OH; 37/185 Hon Rl; Rptr Yrbk; Yrbk; Sch Nwsp; Spn Clb; College; Freelance Photog.

SAGE, TERESA; Princeton HS; Bluefield, WV; Band; Chrs; Chrh Wkr; Hon Rl; Orch; Sch Mus; Sch Pl; Bsbl; GAA; College.

SAGER, CATHERINE; Clay Sr HS; Oregon, OH; 5/340 Hon Rl; NHS; Yrbk; Sch Nwsp; Fr Clb; Honors Banquet Top 10% Of Sr Class 79; Merit Schlrshp To Univ Of Toledo 79; Awds Breakfast Honor Roll 79; Univ Of Toledo; Soc Work.

SAGER, CHERYL; Hagerstown Jr Sr HS; Hagerstown, IN; 116/172 FCA; Girl Scts; Hon Rl; Off Ade; Y-Teens; OEA; Pep Clb; Spn Clb; Bsktbl; Swmmng; Office Ed Assoc Dist Contest; Letter Jacket For Winning Five Varsity; Office Ed State Excutive Awd; Ball St Univ; Busns Admin.

SAGER, KATHRYN; Big Walnut HS; Jhnstn, OH; 53/210 Cls Rep Frsh Cls; Cls Rep Soph Cls; Cl Rep Jr Cls; Chrh Wkr; Cmnty Wkr; Off Ade; 4-H; CTI; Secretary.

SAGER, LINDA E; Hampshire HS; Delray, WV; 2/205 Am Leg Aux Girls St; Band; Jr NHS; NHS; VP Yth Flsp; Treas 4-H; Natl Merit SF; West Virginia Univ; Med.

SAGER, REBECCA; Lapel HS; Anderson, IN; Chrs; Girl Scts; Ed Yrbk; 4-H; Lat Clb; Pep Clb; Letter Mgrs; College; Forestry.

SAGRAVES, DANIEL E; Portsmouth HS; Portsmouth, OH; Band; Chrh Wkr; Cmnty Wkr; Orch; Pol Wkr; Sch Mus; Stg Crw; Pres Yth Flsp; Yrbk; Lat Clb; Past Master Cnslr 76; Rep De Molay 74; Whos Who Among Amer HS Stud 77; Shawnee St Coll; Elec Mech Engr.

SAGRAVES, DOUG; Waverly HS; Waverly, OH; 49/135 Hon Rl; Yrbk; Sch Nwsp; 4-H; Spn Clb; Art Inst Of Pittsburgh; Cmmrcl Art.

SAGUN, THERESE; Catholic Central HS; Steubenville, OH; 6/224 Chrs; Hon Rl; NHS; Fr Clb; FTA; Kent State Univ; Bus Admin.

SAHA, ELIZABETH; Pinconning Area HS; Pinconning, MI; Girl Scts; Hon Rl; NHS; Letter Bsktbl; Letter Trk; Mgrs; Scr Kpr; Tmr; College.

SAHAUDACK, LISA; Walled Lake Central HS; West Bloomfield, MI; Band; Girl Scts; Orch; Sch Mus; Stg Crw; Stu Cncl; Ger Clb; Swmmng; GAA; Pom Pon; Univ; Pblc Rltns.

SAHAYDAK, RACHEL; Unionvle Sebewaing Area HS; Akron, MI; Band; Chrh Wkr; Hon Rl; NHS; Yth Flsp; Calvin Coll; Nursing.

SAHO, CHERYL; Mc Auley HS; Cincinnati, OH; Aud/Vis; JA; Sch Mus; Sch Pl; Stg Crw; Stu Cncl; Drama Clb; Fr Clb; Swmmng; IM Sprt; Univ Of Cincinnati; Radio Tech.

SAHR, BRIAN; Franklin Heights HS; Columbus, OH; Quill & Scroll; Rptr Sch Nwsp; Rotary Awd; College; Med.

SAHR, KRISTINE; Reese HS; Saginaw, MI; Band; Hon Rl; NHS; 4-H; Trk; Michigan St Univ; Vet.

SAIKO, EDWARD J; Morgantown HS; Westover, WV; Hon Rl; Mth Clb; Letter Bsbl; Letter Bsktbl; Letter Crs Cntry; IM Sprt; West Virginia Univ; Busns Mgmt.

SAINATO, KATHLEEN; Watkins Memorial HS; Reynoldsburg, OH; Cmp Fr Grls; FCA; Hon Rl; NHS; Letter Bsktbl; Letter Trk; College; Vet Med.

SAITER, DELWYN; Waterford Mott HS; Pontiac, MI; Wayne St Merit Schlrshp; Outstanding Ach In Phys; Mbr Of Waterford Mott Hnr Soc; Wayne St Univ; Chem Engr.

SAJA, ALLAN; North Farmington HS; Farmington Hill, S ; Hon Rl; Off Ade; Sch Mus; Stg Crw; Spn C lb; Michigan Tech Univ; Comp Sci.

SAJOVEL, CAROL; Brush HS; S Euclid, OH; Cls Rep Frsh Cls; Cls Rep Soph Cls; Cl Rep Jr Cls; Cls Rep Sr Cls; Am Leg Aux Girls St; Stu Cncl; Yth Flsp; Letter Ten; Pom Pon; Twrlr; College; Marine Biology.

SAK, STANLEY M; Bay HS; Bay Village, OH; 39/377 Boy Scts; Hon Rl; Lbry Ade; Lit Mag; Quill & Scroll; Stu Cncl; Yrbk; Ger Clb; Natl Merit SF; Mech Engr.

SAKALOSKY, PAUL; Lumen Christ HS; Jerome, MI; Band; Chrh Wkr; Cmnty Wkr; Hon Rl; Quill & Scroll; Yrbk; Sch Nwsp; Fr Clb; Sci Clb; Socr; Anthropology Awd; Russian History Awd; French Awd; Biology Awd; College; Business.

SAKARA, NORMAN; John Adams HS; S Bend, IN; 47/395 Band; Hon Rl; NHS; Orch; Yrbk; Sch Nwsp; Pep Clb; Sci Clb; College; Automotive Design Engr.

SAKULICH, TIMOTHY J; Lake Orion Sr HS; Lake Orion, MI; VP Drama Clb; Opt Clb Awd;.

SALACH, PAMELA; St Joseph Sr HS; Saint Joseph, MI; Cls Rep Sr Cls; Chrs; Fr Clb; Sci Clb; Treas Pom Pon; Mi Comptn Schlrshp 79; Aquinas Coll; Math.

SALAMI, S; Bloomington North HS; Bloomington, IN; Cls Rep Frsh Cls; Pres Soph Cls; Cmnty Wkr; Pol Wkr; Stu Cncl; Yth Flsp; Y-Teens; Rptr Sch Nwsp; Eng Clb; FTA; Purdue Univ; Elec.

SALAMIE, GABRIEL; South Charleston Sr HS; S Charleston, WV; Am Leg Boys St; Hon Rl; NHS; Stu Cncl; Univ.

SALAMONY, SANDRA; Tawas Area HS; Tawas City, MI; Band; Hon Rl; Hosp Ade; Sec NHS; PPFtbl; College.

SALASEK, KATHY; Fairview HS; Fairview Pk, OH; Girl Scts; JA; Sct Actv; IM Sprt; Cincinnati Univ; Draftsmn.

SALATA, DAVID; Washington HS; South Bend, IN; Sprt Ed Yrbk; Swmmng; College; Chemistry.

SALATA, KAREN; Ursuline HS; Youngstown, OH; 171/342 Cl Rep Jr Cls; Band; Hon Rl; Stu Cncl; Youngstown St Univ; Elem Educ.

SALATA, LARRY; Springfield Local HS; New Middletown, OH; Cls Rep Soph Cls; Hon Rl; Letter Ftbl; Letter Trk; Univ.

SALATA, LAWRENCE; Springfield Local HS; New Middletown, OH; Cls Rep Soph Cls; Hon Rl; NHS; Stu Cncl; Letter Ftbl; Letter Trk; IM Sprt; College.

SALAY, MARY A; Sycamore HS; Cincinnati, OH; 18/465 Chrh Wkr; Hon Rl; Off Ade; Key Clb; Letter Bsktbl; Socr; Ten; Chrldng; Univ; Nursing.

SALAZAR, ROSENDO; Plymouth HS; Plymouth, IN; Boy Scts; Cmnty Wkr; Rptr Sch Nwsp; Ftbl; Capt Wrstlng; Voc Schl; Auto Engr.

SALB, SARA; Jasper HS; Jasper, IN; JA; Pep Clb; Ten; IM Sprt; JA Awd; Coll; Genrl Bus.

SALDANA, RUBEN; Deckerville Cmnty HS; Deckervll, MI; Hon Rl; FFA; Ftbl; St Clair Cmnty Coll; Auto Mech.

SALEM, GEORGE; Copley HS; Akron, OH; Debate Tm; NHS; Sch Pl; Letter Bsbl; Letter Bsktbl; Letter Glf; Natl Merit Ltr; Ashland Coll; Acctg.

SALENS, JOHN; Edwin Denby HS; Detroit, MI; 6/400 Hon Rl; Am Leg Awd; Wayne State; Mech Engr.

SALENSKI, KATHIE A; Kalkaska HS; Kalkaska, MI; 14/170 Band; Hon Rl; NHS; Off Ade; Glf; Capt Chrldng; Mgrs; Lake Superior St Coll; Legal Sec.

SALERMO, PATZI; Lincoln HS; Shinnston, WV; VP Frsh Cls; Hon Rl; Jr NHS; NHS; Stg Crw; Y-Teens; Drama Clb; FTA; Pep Clb; Spn Clb; West Virginia Univ; Psych.

SALERNO, CATHY; Jackson Milton HS; Lake Milton, OH; 4/108 Pres Sr Cls; VP NHS; Sec Key Clb; Bsktbl; Kent State Univ.

SALERNO, MARY; Regina HS; Cleve Hts, OH; Cls Rep Frsh Cls; Sch Nwsp; Ursuline Univ; Journalism.

SALGAT, ANTHONY; Northwestern HS; Kokomo, IN; Boy Scts; Treas JA; Lbry Ade; Drama Clb; Ger Clb; JA Awd; Purdue Univ; Engr.

SALGE, WILLIAM; Kenmore HS; Akron, OH; Aud/Vis; Boy Scts; Chrs; Sch Mus; Letter Crs Cntry; Capt Socr; Letter Trk; Univ; Running.

SALGOT, JANICE; Flint Holy Rosary HS; Mt Morris, MI; 10/57 Hon Rl; Crs Cntry; Trk; Chrldng; Flint Univ Of Michigan; Tchr.

SALIGA, ANN; Bishop Foley HS; Warren, MI; Chrs; Girl Scts; Hon Rl; Jr NHS; Off Ade; Fr Clb; Capt Crs Cntry; Trk; GAA; IM Sprt; Oakland Univ; Busns.

SALING, DANIEL; Southern Local HS; Lisbon, OH; Chrs; Hon Rl; 4-H; Lat Clb; Bsbl; Ftbl; Trk; 4-H Awd; Oh Schlrshp Test Hnrbl Mentn 79; Latin NII Awd 79; Fairboard Col Cnty St 4 H Club Congress 79; Ohio St Univ; Vet.

SALINGER, MARGARETE; Belleville HS; Ypsilanti, MI; Sch Pl; Belleville Bus & Pro Womens Club 79; Eastern Michigan Univ; Bio.

SALISBURY, BRAD; Fostoria HS; Fostoria, OH; 20/200 Cls Rep Frsh Cls; Chrh Wkr; Hon Rl; NHS; Stu Cncl; Yth Flsp; IM Sprt; Univ; Chem.

SALISBURY, KENNETH; Summerfield HS; Petersburg, MI; 38/42 Hon Rl; 4-H; Ftbl; Valley City St Coll; Bus Educ.

SALISBURY, LARRY; Theodore Roosevelt HS; Wyandotte, MI; Boy Scts; Lbry Ade; Key Clb; Forestry.

SALISBURY, MARY; Rockville Sr & Jr HS; Rockville, IN; Cmp Fr Grls; Chrs; FCA; Girl Scts; JA; Off Ade; Red Cr Ade; Sch Pl; Drama Clb; 4-H; Police Academy; Police Woman.

SALISBURY, TERRI; Archbold HS; Stryker, OH; Am Leg Aux Girls St; Band; Chrs; Chrh Wkr; Hon Rl; NHS; Sch Mus; Yth Flsp; IM Sprt; College; Engr.

SALISBURY, VICTORIA; Charlotte HS; Charlotte, MI; 22/303 Chrs; Sec Girl Scts; Hon Rl; NHS; Sct Actv; Cit Awd; Associated Schls Inc; Airlines.

SALISZ, DEBORAH; Petoskey HS; Petoskey, MI; Lat Clb; Natl Merit Schl; N Central Michigan Coll; Bus.

SALLADE, RONALD K; Poland Seminary HS; Poland, OH; 65/280 FCA; Hon Rl; Rptr Sch Nwsp; Lat Clb; Crs Cntry; Ftbl; Trk; Mgrs; Natl Merit SF; Ntl Merit Semi Fnlst 1978; Univ Of Virginia; Med.

SALLAK, REX A; Grace Baptist Church HS; Niles, MI; Val; Chrh Wkr; NHS; Sch Pl; Letter Bsbl; Letter Bsktbl; Letter Crs Cntry; Letter Socr; Cit Awd; Natl Merit SF; Cert Of Recognition; Hyles Anderson Coll; Education.

SALLAM, GALAL; Southwestern HS; Detroit, MI; Cls Rep Sr Cls; Chrh Wkr; Cmnty Wkr; Hon Rl; JA; Jr NHS; NHS; Sci Clb; Crs Cntry; Wayne State Univ; Acctg.

SALLAUM, SANDRA; Our Lady Of Mercy HS; Bloomfield Hls, MI; Cls Rep Frsh Cls; Hosp Ade; Mod UN; Sch Pl; Stg Crw; Stu Cncl; Letter Trk; Cert Of Merit AAA Art Poster Contest; Michigan St Univ; Advertising.

SALLEE, DIANE; Warsaw HS; Warsaw, IN; 10/360 Chrh Wkr; Hon Rl; Sch Pl; Pep Clb; Rotary Awd; St Marys Coll; Med Research.

SALLEE, DORA; Bosse HS; Evansville, IN; Cl Rep Jr Cls; Cls Rep Sr Cls; Hon Rl; JA; Pep Clb; Spn Clb; Mgrs; Univ; Pre Med.

SALLEE, DRUCILLA; Kings HS; S Lebanon, OH; Cl Rep Jr Cls; Cls Rep Sr Cls; Chrs; Chrh Wkr; Hon Rl; Jr NHS; NHS; Off Ade; 4-H; OEA; Voc Schl; Data Processing.

SALLER, CONNIE; St Joe Ctrl Cath HS; Fremont, OH; Cls Rep Frsh Cls; Treas Cmp Fr Grls; Hon Rl; Hosp Ade; Yrbk; Sec 4-H; Sec Pep Clb; IM Sprt; Univ; Dent Hygnst.

SALMER, SUZANNE; Ypsilanti HS; Brighton, MI; 16/408 Cmnty Wkr; Drm Bgl; Hon Rl; Lbry Ade; NHS; Orch; Ger Clb; Michigan Tech Univ; Chem Engr.

SALMON, BRET; Central HS; Evansville, IN; 100/534 Band; Chrh Wkr; FCA; NHS; Stu Cncl; Bsbl; Letter Bsktbl; Letter Glf; Purdue Univ; Vet.

SALMONS, RONALD; Guyan Valley HS; W Hamlin, WV; 6/100 Hon Rl; PAVAS; Pol Wkr; Ed Sch Nwsp; Sprt Ed Sch Nwsp; Rptr Sch Nwsp; Sci Clb; Spn Clb; Marshall Univ; Law.

SALO, LAURA; Westwood HS; Ishpeming, MI; Hon Rl; Bsktbl; Bus.

SALO, LYNN; Clarence Kimball HS; Royal Oak, MI; Sec Chrs; Chrh Wkr; Girl Scts; Hon Rl; Sch Mus; Sch Pl; Sct Actv; Drama Clb; Gym; Univ Of Mic; Bus Admin.

SALO, TINA; Grand Ledge HS; Grand Ledge, MI; Cls Rep Frsh Cls; Cls Rep Soph Cls; Cl Rep Jr Cls; Girl Scts; Hon Rl; Sch Pl; Sct Actv; Stu Cncl; Sprt Ed Yrbk; Yrbk; Lansing Cmnty Coll; Dent Hygiene.

SALOIS JR, JOHN K; St Alphonsus HS; Detroit, MI; 96/196 Cls Rep Frsh Cls; Cls Rep Soph Cls; Cl Rep Jr Cls; Cls Rep Sr Cls; Chrs; Hon Rl; Sprt Ed Sch Nwsp; Acct.

SALON, ELY J; Woodrow Wilson HS; Daniels, WV; 5/500 Pres Jr Cls; Pres Sr Cls; VP Sr Cls; Am Leg Boys St; Hon Rl; Mod UN; NHS; Off Ade; Sch Nwsp; Spn Clb; Sci Relgn Art Sci Ards 77; Alg Amer Stds Awd 78; Schlrshp Awd 78; Mc Gill Univ; Med.

SALOPEK, KRISTINE; Euclid Sr HS; Euclid, OH; 68/749 Girl Scts; Hon Rl; Hosp Ade; Pres Orch; Red Cr Ade; Sch Mus; Rptr Sch Nwsp; Tmr; Univ; Math.

SALSBERY, KRISTIN; Tri Central HS; Sharpsville, IN; 5/79 VP Frsh Cls; VP Soph Cls; VP Jr Cls; VP Sr Cls; Band; Chrh Wkr; Hon Rl; Lbry Ade; VP NHS; Yth Flsp; Taylor Univ; Christian Educ.

SALSBURY, KEVIN; Bryan HS; Bryan, OH; 1/184 Cls Rep Frsh Cls; Cls Rep Soph Cls; Cl Rep Jr Cls; Cls Rep Sr Cls; Val; Am Leg Boys St; Pres Chrs; Chrh Wkr; Hon Rl; NHS; Liberty Baptist Coll; Mission Work.

SALSGIVER, CHARLES; Madison Comp HS; , ; Aud/Vis; Boy Scts; CAP; Sct Actv; Spn Clb; Trk; Wrstlng; IM Sprt; Ohio State Univ; Math.

SALTER, MICHELLE; Mississinewa HS; Marion, IN; 13/205 Hon Rl; NHS; Off Ade; OEA; Pep Clb; Letter Trk; Letter Chrldng; Coach Actv; Mgrs; Scr Kpr; Cert For A Avr In Spanish II 78; Shrthnd Cert 78; 2ndpl In Job Intvw In Offc Educ Assoc Contst 78; Ball St Univ; Spanish.

SALTERS, VICKY; St Johns HS; St Johns, MI; Chrh Wkr; Cmnty Wkr; Hon Rl; Hosp Ade; Yth Flsp; 4-H; Letter Trk; 4-H Awd; Pres Awd; Western Univ; Ther.

SALTSGAVER, MARK; North Vermillion HS; Perrysville, IN; Band; FCA; Hon Rl; NHS; Off Ade; Bsktbl; Letter Ftbl; Scr Kpr; Univ; Math.

SALTSMAN, TERRI; Salem HS; Salem, OH; 1/240 Val; Cmp Fr Grls; Drm Mjrt; Pres Yth Flsp; Pres Ger Clb; Mth Clb; Bausch & Lomb Awd; Ohio Academic Schlrshp Awd Wnr 78; Elec Furnace Schlrshp 79; Martha Mc Cready Math Excel Awd 79; Univ Of Cincinnati; Chem Engr.

SALTTERY, PATRICK; Gilmour Academy; Highland Hts, OH; Cmnty Wkr; Hon Rl; NHS; Stg Crw; Yrbk; Drama Clb; Lion Awd; Univ; Archt.

SALTZMAN, JOYCE; Vanlue Local HS; Alvada, OH; 2/36 Hon Rl; NHS; Sch Pl; 4-H; FFA; FHA; Pep Clb; FFA Schlrshp 79; Vet Asst.

SALTZMANN, KIMBERLY; Bristol HS; Bristolville, OH; Sec Soph Cls; Chrs; Girl Scts; Hon Rl; Sch Mus; Sch Pl; Rptr Yrbk; Natl Schl Choral Awd; Awd Of Dist; Letter Of Merit; Kent St Univ; Spec Ed.

SALTZMANN, RICHARD; Bridgeport HS; Saginaw, MI; Boy Scts; Chrs; Chrh Wkr; Bsktbl; Letter Glf; Mgrs; Delta Coll; Engr.

SALUS, JOSEPH J; Morton Sr HS; Hammond, IN; 25/419 Chrh Wkr; Hon Rl; Sci Clb; Purdue Univ; Bio.

SALVATI, ANNE; Crestline HS; Crestline, OH; Cls Rep Frsh Cls; Trs Soph Cls; Cls Rep Soph Cls; Pres Jr Cls; Cl Rep Jr Cls; Cls Rep Sr Cls; VP Stu Cncl; Scr Kpr; Ohio State; Pre Med.

SALVI, CHARLES J; Arthur Hill HS; Saginaw, MI; Hon Rl; Univ; History.

SALYER, RANDY; Pleasant HS; Prospect, OH; Chrh Wkr; Hon Rl; Yth Flsp; FFA; FTA; Lat Clb; Bsbl; Letter Ftbl; IM Sprt; Ohio State.

SALYER, ROBIN; Rensselaer Ctrl HS; Rensselaer, IN; 9/162 Hon Rl; NHS; Spn Clb; DAR Awd; Univ; Spanish.

SALYER, T; Heritage HS; New Haven, IN; Hon Rl; Lbry Ade; Sec Fr Clb; FHA; PPFtbl; Coll; Acctg.

SALYERS, PAUL; Sandusky Comm HS; Marlette, MI; Am Leg Boys St; Band; Chrs; Chrh Wkr; CAP; Hon Rl; Natl Forn Lg; Yth Flsp; Capt Wrstlng; Opt Clb Awd; Central Mic Univ; Pre Law.

SALYERS, REBECCA; Sandusky HS; Sandusky, OH; AFS; Aud/Vis; Chrh Wkr; JA; Sch Pl; Stg Crw; Yth Flsp; Rptr Sch Nwsp; Sch Nwsp; Drama Clb; Firelands; Pschiatry.

SAMMON, JOHN; Saint Edward HS; Bay Village, OH; 97/360 Debate Tm; Hon Rl; Ger Clb; Key Clb; Pep Clb; College; Law.

SAMMUT, CHERYL; Allen Park HS; Allen Park, MI; Cls Rep Frsh Cls; Cls Rep Soph Cls; Cl Rep Jr Cls; Cmp Fr Grls; Chrs; Girl Scts; Hon Rl; Jr NHS; NHS; Sec Stu Cncl; College; Spec Educ.

SAMONAS, MARIA; South HS; Youngstown, OH; 4/327 Hon Rl; Hosp Ade; Rptr Yrbk; Rptr Sch Nwsp; Bsktbl; Letter Ten; Youngstown St Univ; Medicine.

SAMPLES, J ROBERT; Liberty HS; Salem, WV; Band; Chrs; Hon Rl; Jr NHS; Sch Pl; Fr Clb; Mth Clb; Sci Clb; Elk Awd; Academic Schlrshp To Salem Coll 79; Salem Coll; Chem.

SAMPLES, SUSAN; Lee M Thurston HS; Redford, MI; 100/484 Hst Soph Cls; Hon Rl; Jr NHS; Stu Cncl; Rptr Sch Nwsp; Letter Bsbl; GAA; PPFtbl; Natl Merit Schl; Michigan St Univ; Criminal Justice.

SAMPLES, SUSAN; Parkway HS; Rockford, OH; 1/82 Sec Soph Cls; Hon Rl; NHS; 4-H; Pres Ger Clb; VP Lat Clb; Sec Sci Clb; Letter Bsktbl; Letter Crs Cntry; Trk; Ohio Univ; Earth Sci.

SAMPSELL, JODIE; Warren Woods HS; Warren, MI; Sec Soph Cls; Chrs; Sch Mus; Chrldng; Scr Kpr; Natl Merit Ltr; Macomb Cnty Cmnty Coll; Bus Admin.

SAMPSON, CONNIE; Southeast HS; Ravenna, OH; Cls Rep Frsh Cls; Cls Rep Soph Cls; Cl Rep Jr Cls; Cls Rep Sr Cls; Band; Chrs; MMM; Pres Stu Cncl; 4-H; Pep Clb; Ohio St Univ; Bio.

SAMPSON, DAVE; Kelloggsville HS; Wyoming, MI; Sec Frsh Cls; Hon Rl; Jr NHS; NHS; Spn Clb; Letter Bsbl; Letter Bsktbl; Coach Actv; Mgrs; Michigan St Univ; Engr.

SAMPSON, SCOTT; Hardin Northern HS; Dunkirk, OH; Hon Rl; Rptr Yrbk; Yrbk; FFA; Key Clb; Bsbl; Bsktbl; Ftbl; Trk;.

SAMPSON, TERRI; Cameron HS; Cameron, WV; 17/104 Chrs; Girl Scts; Hon Rl; NHS; Pres Y-Teens; Sch Nwsp; Treas FHA; Pep Clb; Scr Kpr; Voc Schl; Soc Work.

SAMS, ANNETTE; South Dearborn HS; Sunman, IN; 4/230 Am Leg Aux Girls St; Band; Chrs; Chrh Wkr; Hon Rl; NHS; 4-H; Pep Clb; Sci Clb; Bsktbl; Cincinnati Coll; Respiratory Ther.

SAMSON, CARRIE; Adrian HS; Adrian, MI; Chrs; Cmnty Wkr; Hon Rl; NHS; PAVAS; Sch Mus; Drama Clb; Sci Clb; Univ; Sci.

SAMSON, DENISE M; Aquinas HS; Allen Park, MI; Hon Rl; NHS; Univ Of Michigan; Advertising.

SAMUEL, CHERYL; Muskegon Hts HS; Muskegon Hts, MI; 25/260 Cls Rep Frsh Cls; Cls Rep Soph Cls; Trs Jr Cls; Cls Rep Sr Cls; Chrs; Sec Chrh Wkr; Debate Tm; Hon Rl; Off Ade; PAVAS; Davenport Coll; Fshn Mdse.

SAMUEL, SUZANNE C; Aquinas HS; Inkster, MI; Girl Scts; Hon Rl; NHS; Mercy Coll; Nursing.

SAMUELS, BRAD; Frankton HS; Frankton, IN; 17/137 VP Jr Cls; FCA; NHS; Fr Clb; Letter Bsktbl; Capt Crs Cntry; Letter Trk; Elk Awd; Anderson Coll; Elem Educ.

SAMUELS, STEVEN; Pike HS; Indpls, IN; 23/298 Band; Boy Scts; Drm Mjrt; Hon Rl; Jr NHS; NHS; Orch; Sch Mus; Ger Clb; Pep Clb; In All St Bnd 78; Indiana Univ; Pre Med.

SAMUELS, TRACY; Niles Mckinley HS; Niles, OH; AFS; Debate Tm; Natl Forn Lg; Off Ade; Sch Mus; Sch Pl; Drama Clb; Univ; Wildlife Conservation.

SAMUELSON, JAMES; East Grand Rapids HS; E Grand Rapids, MI; Boy Scts; Chrh Wkr; FCA; Hon Rl; Off Ade; Pol Wkr; Sct Actv; Yth Flsp; Letter Wrstlng; Scr Kpr; Univ Of Michigan; Med.

SANABRIA, TONYA; Shenandoah HS; Middletown, IN; 23/138 Cls Rep Sr Cls; Stu Cncl; Sprt Ed Yrbk; Sprt Ed Sch Nwsp; 4-H; Mth Clb; Pep Clb; Sci Clb; Spn Clb; Letter Bsbl; Univ; Acctg.

SANBORN, ANN; Whitehall Yearling HS; Whitehall, OH; Band; Chrh Wkr; Hon Rl; Lit Mag; NHS; Red Cr Ade; Yth Flsp; Rptr Sch Nwsp; S E Travel Acad; Travel Agent.

SANBORN, HELEN; Cabrini HS; Allen Pk, MI; Hon Rl; Rptr Yrbk; Yrbk; Bsbl; Ten; Univ Of Dearbon; Airline Stewardess.

SANBORN, REBECCA; Northmont HS; Dayton, OH; 103/518 Band; Cmp Fr Grls; Chrh Wkr; Drl Tm; Hon Rl; Yth Flsp; Ed Sch Nwsp; Ger Clb; Huntington College; History.

SANBORN, SHARON; White Cloud HS; White Cloud, MI; 2/78 Sal; Band; Chrh Wkr; Hon Rl; Pep Clb; VICA; Arah Beach Schlrshp 79; Mi Bus Schls Assoc Schlrshp 79; St Of Mi Comp Schlrshp 79; Muskegon Bus Coll; Exec Sec.

SANCHEZ, CAROLINE; Pontiac Central HS; Pontiac, MI; Chrs; Off Ade; Lat Clb; Chrldng; GAA; Tmr; Oakland Community Coll; Emt.

SANCHEZ, GLORIA; St Andrew HS; Dearborn Hgts, MI; 11/109 Chrs; Chrh Wkr; Cmnty Wkr; Hon Rl; NHS; Pol Wkr; Sch Mus; Sch Pl; Stu Cncl; Rptr Yrbk; Univ Of Michigan; Med.

SAND, STEVEN; Warsaw Community HS; Warsaw, IN; 40/360 Hon Rl; Yth Flsp; Bsbl; Tri State Univ; Drafting.

SANDAHL, EDWARD; Allegan Sr HS; Allegan, MI; Debate Tm; Hon Rl; NHS; Chmn Stu Cncl; 4-H; Lat Clb; Treas Spn Clb; Natl Merit Finalist 79; Jr Rotarians 78; Kalamazoo Coll; Eng.

SANDEE, ROBIN; Union HS; Grand Rapids, MI; Cls Rep Frsh Cls; Hon Rl; JA; Off Ade; Stu Cncl; Trk; JA Awd; Grand Rapids Jr Coll; Exec Sec.

SANDEFER, KELLY; Lansing Everett HS; Lansing, MI; Boy Scts; Chrh Wkr; Hon Rl; Yth Flsp; Pep Clb; Letter Swmmng; Letter Trk; IM Sprt; Tmr; Cit Awd; Schlrshp Acad Achvmnt 77; Acad Achvmnt Received Letter 79; Univ Of Michigan; Dent.

SANDER, LORRIE; Mt Healthy HS; Cincinnati, OH; 20/576 Cls Rep Frsh Cls; Cls Rep Soph Cls; Cl Rep Jr Cls; Hon Rl; NHS; Off Ade; Stu Cncl; Sch Nwsp; Ger Clb; Gym; 2nd Pl Dst Ind Arts Display 79; Univ; Aero Space Engr.

SANDER, TINA; Tippecanoe Valley HS; Akron, IN; Cls Rep Frsh Cls; Chrs; Sch Mus; Stu Cncl; Yth Flsp; Sprt Ed Sch Nwsp; Rptr Sch Nwsp; Drama Clb; 4-H; Pep Clb; Anderson Coll; Journalism.

SANDERS, ARDAH; Collinwood HS; Cleveland, OH; Hon Rl; Cleveland State Univ; Bus Admin.

SANDERS, BRAD; Defiance HS; Defiance, OH; Chrs; Hon Rl; 4-H; Ftbl; Toledo Univ; Engr.

SANDERS, CHARLOTTE; East Chicago Roosevelt HS; E Chicago, IN; 19/199 Chrs; Chrh Wkr; Hon Rl; Pres FTA; Pep Clb; Chrldng; PPFtbl; Univ; Pediatrics Nurse.

SANDERS, CHERYL; Southfield Christian HS; Union Lake, MI; 5/65 Chrs; Chrh Wkr; Cmnty Wkr; Hon Rl; Jr NHS; NHS; Off Ade; Sch Pl; VP Stu Cncl; Drama Clb; Univ Of Michigan; Nursing.

SANDERS, DOROTHY; Black River HS; Sullivan, OH; Band; Lbry Ade; Stg Crw; Yrbk; FHA; Spn Clb; Lorian Cmnty Coll; Photojrnlsm.

SANDERS, GORDON; John F Kennedy HS; Warren, OH; Chrh Wkr; Hon Rl; Sch Mus; Sch Pl; Stg Crw; Yrbk; Sch Nwsp; Drama Clb; Fr Clb; College; Med.

SANDERS, GREGORY; North Dickinson HS; Hardwood, MI; Cls Rep Frsh Cls; Band; Chrh Wkr; Hon Rl; Sch Mus; Stu Cncl; 4-H; Bsktbl; Swmmng; Trk; Andrews Univ; Airline Pilot.

SANDERS, JANINE; Calvert HS; Tiffin, OH; Band; Girl Scts; Hon Rl; JA; Sct Actv; Cit Awd; JA Awd; Jr Achvmnt Fnlst For VP Of Finance N W Ohio 79; Jr Achvmnt Co Top Salesmn 79; Univ; Comp Sci.

SANDERS, JEFF; De Kalb HS; Auburn, IN; NHS; Stg Crw; Ger Clb; IM Sprt; De Pauw Univ.

SANDERS, JONATHAN; Walled Lake Central HS; Union Lake, MI; Band; Chrh Wkr; Hon Rl; Letter Bsktbl; Letter Mgrs; Lawrence Inst Of Tech; Elec Engr.

SANDERS, JUANITA; Roosevelt HS; Gary, IN; 58/547 Trs Soph Cls; Sec Sr Cls; Drl Tm; Girl Scts; Hon Rl; JA; NHS; ROTC; Boys Clb Am; Lat Clb; Typing Awd; Calumet Coll; Computer Sci.

SANDERS, KATHERINE; Central Preston Sr HS; Kingwood, WV; VP Soph Cls; Cl Rep Jr Cls; Hon Rl; Treas NHS; Stu Cncl; Treas FHA; FTA; VP Pep Clb; IM Sprt; West Virginia Univ; Nursing.

SANDERS, KATHRYN; Mannington HS; Mannington, WV; 11/95 Am Leg Aux Girls St; Chrh Wkr; Hon Rl; NHS; Quill & Scroll; Y-Teens; Rptr Sch Nwsp; Sch Nwsp; FHA; Elk Awd; College; Operating Room Tech.

SANDERS, LESHA; Milton HS; Milton, WV; 10/182 Cls Rep Frsh Cls; Pres Soph Cls; Pres Jr Cls; Cls Rep Sr Cls; Chrs; Chrh Wkr; Cmnty Wkr; Girl Scts; Hon Rl; Hosp Ade; Marshall Univ; Chem Engr.

SANDERS, LINDA; Southwestern HS; Flat Rock, IN; Band; Drama Clb; 4-H; Pep Clb; Letter Bsktbl; Trk; College; Vet.

SANDERS, LORI; Berkley HS; Berkley, MI; Sec Band; NHS; Stu Cncl; Pep Clb; Detroit College Of Bus; Accgt.

SANDERS, LYNN; Warsaw Community HS; Warsaw, IN; 4/395 Sec Debate Tm; FCA; Hon Rl; Natl Forn Lg; Off Ade; Sct Actv; Swmmng; Letter Trk; GAA; Tmr; Tri Kappa Hon Awd Bnaqt 79; Univ; Med.

SANDERS, PAMELA; Green HS; Akron, OH; Hon Rl; Off Ade; Red Cr Ade; FHA; OEA; Pep Clb; Gym; Trk; Chrldng; Bus Schl; Sec Std.

SANDERS, PAUL C; Summit Country Day Schl; Cincinnati, OH; Rptr Sch Nwsp; Letter Glf; Natl Merit SF; Univ; Med.

SANDERS, RANDALL L; Huntington HS; Chillicothe, OH; Band; Lbry Ade; NHS; Fr Clb; FTA; Trk; Chrldng;.

SANDERS, SANDRA; Lansing Everett HS; Lansing, MI; 42/504 Chrh Wkr; Hon Rl; Jr NHS; Off Ade; Stu Cncl; PPFtbl; I Partcptd In Jv Vlybl & Was Captn 77; Partcptd In Var Vlybl Ernd Ltr 78; Was On Teen Coun At Chrch 78; Michigan St Univ; Acctg.

SANDERS, STEPHEN; Clarkston Sr HS; Clarkston, MI; 6/530 Hon Rl; Yth Flsp; Letter Bsbl; Glf; IM Sprt; Natl Merit Ltr; Mst Outstndng Eng Stdt 76; Bob Jones Univ; Bus Admin.

SANDERS, STEPHEN; Sandusky HS; Sandusky, OH; AFS; Boy Scts; Chrs; Sct Actv; Fr Clb; Trk; College; Law Enforcement.

SANDERS, STEVE; Eastwood HS; Pemberville, OH; 7/187 Am Leg Boys St; Chrs; Hon Rl; NHS; Rptr Yrbk; FFA; Key Clb; Ohio State Univ; Accounting.

SANDERS, TAMMY; Washington Irving HS; Clarksburg, WV; 6/135 Chrh Wkr; Cmnty Wkr; Girl Scts; Hon Rl; Off Ade; Sch Pl; Yth Flsp; FBLA; Lat Clb; Trk; Fairmont Career Coll; Sec.

SANDERS, TERRI; Kankakee Valley HS; Wheatfield, IN; Trs Jr Cls; Chrs; Chrh Wkr; Girl Scts; Hon Rl; NHS; Off Ade; 4-H; Pep Clb; Trk; Typing Awd;.

SANDERS, VALINDA; John R Buchtal Univ; Akron, OH; 16/452 Drm Mjrt; Girl Scts; Hon Rl; NHS; Orch; Sch Mus; Fr Clb; Wright St Univ; Comp Sci.

SANDERSON, ANNE; Benedictine HS; Detroit, MI; 1/145 Cls Rep Frsh Cls; Cls Rep Soph Cls; Sec Jr Cls; Pres Sr Cls; Chrs; Hon Rl; Hosp Ade; NHS; Sch Pl; Letter Bsbl; Univ; Engr.

SANDERSON, DEBORAH J; Tiffin Columbian HS; Bloomville, OH; Band; Chrh Wkr; Hon Rl; Yth Flsp; Rptr Sch Nwsp; 4-H; Pep Clb; Spn Clb; Ohi State; Special D.

SANDERSON, JEFF; Bellmont HS; Decatur, IN; 32/245 Hon Rl; NHS; Pol Wkr; Letter Bsbl; Letter Ftbl; Coach Actv; IM Sprt; Univ; Mgmt.

SANDERSON, JOYCE; Sault Area HS; Sault Ste Marie, MI; Hon Rl; NHS; Quill & Scroll; Rptr Yrbk; Sch Nwsp; OEA; Lake Superior State College; Bus Adm.

SANDERSON, SUSAN; Montabella HS; Millbrook, MI; 6/115 Am Leg Aux Girls St; Band; Chrs; Drl Tm; Girl Scts; NHS; Sec Yth Flsp; Pep Clb; PPFtbl; Blue Lake Fine Arts Camp Intl Chr 79; Univ; Music Tchr.

SANDLIN, KAREN; Clarence M Kimball HS; Royal Oak, MI; Hon Rl; Red Cr Ade; Yrbk; PPFtbl; College; Pre Med.

SANDLING, HEIDI; Ferndale HS; Plsnt Rdg, MI; 15/450 Band; Cmp Fr Grls; Hon Rl; Mdrgl; NHS; Orch; Sch Mus; Yth Flsp; Ger Clb; Gym; Band Schlrshp To Attend Interlochens 77; Natl Music Camp In 79; Band Schlrshp 77 79; Music Schl; Music.

SANDNER, PAMELA; Fraser HS; Fraser, MI; Chrh Wkr; Sch Mus; Ed Sch Nwsp; Rptr Sch Nwsp; College; Technical.

SANDOR, MARY; Jewett Scio HS; Jewett, OH; Girl Scts; Hon Rl; Spn Clb; Kent State Univ; Nursing.

SANDOVAL, VIVIAN; East HS; Youngstown, OH; 14/181 Debate Tm; Hon Rl; Off Ade; VICA; Youngstown State Univ; Nursing.

SANDRI, DAVID; Forest Park HS; Amasa, MI; 6/80 Pres Soph Cls; Am Leg Boys St; Hon Rl; Sch Pl; Stg Crw; Mgrs; Scr Kpr; Voice Dem Awd; Michigan Tech Univ; Chem Engr.

SANDSTROM, KARALYN; Lawrence Central HS; Indianapolis, IN; 52/365 Cmnty Wkr; Hon Rl; NHS; Off Ade; Pol Wkr; Quill & Scroll; Sprt Ed Sch Nwsp; Rptr Sch Nwsp; Drama Clb; Feature Writing For Newspaper Quill & Scroll; College; Medicine.

SANDWISCH, MICHELE; Port Clinton HS; Pt Clinton, OH; Girl Scts; Hon Rl; Spn Clb; 4-H Awd; Terra Tech Bus Schl; Acctg.

SANDY, ARTHUR T; Parkersburg Catholic HS; Parkersburg, WV; Pres Frsh Cls; Cls Rep Soph Cls; Am Leg Boys St; Boy Scts; Hon Rl; NHS; Sch Pl; Sct Actv; Yrbk; Ftbl; Univ; Med.

SANDY, DAVE; Woodrow Wilson HS; Youngstwn, OH; 25/344 Hon Rl; NHS; Sprt Ed Sch Nwsp; Letter Bsktbl; Univ; Bus Admin.

SANDY, VICKIE L; Roosevelt Wilson HS; Mt Clare, WV; Band; Chrh Wkr; Hon Rl; Sec Yth Flsp; Rptr Sch Nwsp; Drama Clb; Natl Latin Hnr Soc; Explorers Post III; West Virginia Univ; Comp Sci.

SANETRIK, CHRISTINA; Univ HS; Morgantown, WV; 16/123 Chrh Wkr; Hon Rl; Jr NHS; NHS; Pres Quill & Scroll; Yrbk; Ed Sch Nwsp; Sci Clb; Letter Ten; West Virginia Univ; Advertising.

SANETRIK, CHRISTINE; University HS; Morgantown, WV; 19/166 Chrh Wkr; Hon Rl; Sec Jr NHS; NHS; Pres Quill & Scroll; Yrbk; Sprt Ed Sch Nwsp; 4-H; Sci Clb; Spn Clb; West Virginia Univ; Advertising Mgmt.

SANETRIK, ROBERT; Morgantown HS; Morgantwn, WV; Aud/Vis; Chrs; Hon Rl; Mth Clb; Wv Univ; Comp Sci.

SANFORD, CAROLYN; Andrews Girls HS; Clevelnd Hts, OH; Cls Rep Frsh Cls; Cls Rep Soph Cls; Girl Scts; Hon Rl; Hosp Ade; Mod UN; Treas Stu Cncl; Fr Clb; Hosp Aide; Stu Cncl Treas; French Clb; Univ Of N Carolina; Nursing.

SANFORD, JOHN C; St Xavier HS; Lebanon, OH; 60/289 Band; Cmnty Wkr; Hon Rl; Mod UN; Pol Wkr; Stu Cncl; Civ Clb; Natl Merit SF; Univ; Engr.

SANFORD, JULIE A; Concord Community HS; Concord, MI; 14/81 Trs Frsh Cls; NHS; PAVAS; Sch Mus; Sch Pl; Stu Cncl; Drama Clb; Bsbl; Trk; GAA; Music.

SANFORD, LORI; Bethesda Christian HS; Brownsburg, IN; Sec Sr Cls; Chrs; Chrh Wkr; Hon Rl; Pol Wkr; Sch Mus; Sch Pl; Sprt Ed Yrbk; Rptr Sch Nwsp; Pep Clb; Tenn Temple Univ; Sec.

SANFORD, SUSAN; Medina Sr HS; Medina, OH; 72/360 Hon Rl; Orch; Sch Mus; Pep Clb; PPFtbl; Kent St Univ; Drafting.

SANFORD, TRACY; Henry Ford HS; Detroit, MI; Cl Rep Jr Cls; Cmp Fr Grls; Chrs; Chrh Wkr; Hon Rl; Lbry Ade; Off Ade; Sch Mus; Sch Pl; Yth Flsp; Mich State; Midwifery.

SANFORD, WARD E; Jimtown HS; Elkhart, IN; 1/98 Am Leg Boys St; Chrh Wkr; Treas NHS; Sch Mus; Sch Pl; Stg Crw; VP Yth Flsp; Pres Drama Clb; Fr Clb; Purdue Univ; Geology.

SANGALANG, SANDRA; Chatard HS; Indianapolis, IN; Girl Scts; Hon Rl; Hosp Ade; Off Ade; Sch Pl; Rptr Yrbk; Spn Clb; INPI; Dent.

SAN GIACOMO, TERRY; Angola HS; Angola, IN; Band; Cmp Fr Grls; Chrs; Drl Tm; Sch Pl; Fr Clb; Pep Clb; Pom Pon; College; Psych.

SANGL, J; Southwestern HS; Shelbyvll, IN; Chrh Wkr; FFA; FFA Schlrshp Awd; Coll.

SANKER, ROBERT; Purcell HS; Norwood, OH; Sec Soph Cls; Trs Jr Cls; Hon Rl; Stu Cncl; Bsktbl; Chrldng; God Cntry Awd; College; Law.

SANKOVICH, SHARRON; Canton South HS; E Sparta, OH; Cl Rep Jr Cls; Girl Scts; Hon Rl; NHS; Lat Clb; Ohio Schlrshp Algebra I Test 15th In Dist; American P Jr Classical League Trst Maximae Cum Laude; College; Medicine.

SANNER, KAREN; Erieview Catholic HS; Cleveland, OH; 9/130 Chrh Wkr; Hon Rl; Hosp Ade; Lit Mag; Red Cr Ade; Stg Crw; Sch Nwsp; Ten; Dyke College; Legal Sec.

SANOR, KAREN; West Branch HS; Salem, OH; Cl Rep Jr Cls; Trs Sr Cls; Sec Band; Chrs; Chrh Wkr;

Hon Rl; NHS; Stu Cncl; 4-H; Delegate To Buckeye Girls St 79; Columbian Cty Grange Princess 79; Univ.

SANSOM, DEBBIE; Wayne HS; E Lynn, WV; Band; Chrh Wkr; Drm Bgl; Hon Rl; Hosp Ade; Jr NHS; VP NHS; Sch Pl; Ger Clb; Lat Clb; Marshall Univ; Nurse.

SAN TANA, BENNETT; Emerson HS; Gary, IN; Band; Hon Rl; Orch; Spn Clb; Coll; Law.

SANTANGELO, DENISE; Bishop Ready HS; Columbus, OH; 40/167 Cmp Fr Grls; JA; Rptr Yrbk; Fr Clb; Letter Trk; Letter Mat Maids; Ohio St Univ; Elem Ed.

SANTIAGO, CARLOS; St Francis De Sales HS; Toledo, OH; 12/200 Cl Rep Jr Cls; Sal; Hon Rl; NHS; Stu Cncl; Sch Nwsp; Bsktbl; Letter Ftbl; IM Sprt; Am Leg Awd; Cornell Univ; Comp Sci.

SANTIN, GLORIA; Toronto HS; Toronto, OH; Band; Hon Rl; Fr Clb; Pep Clb; Bsktbl; Trk; Pom Pon; Univ Of Missouri; Vet.

SANTNER, JAMES; Purcell HS; Cincinnati, OH; Debate Tm; Hon Rl; Mod UN; Y-Teens; Rptr Yrbk; Rptr Sch Nwsp; Mth Clb; IM Sprt; Scr Kpr; Univ; Law.

SANTNER, JIM; Purcell HS; Norwood, OH; 4/180 Debate Tm; Hon Rl; Mod UN; Rptr Sch Nwsp; Mth Clb; IM Sprt; Scr Kpr; Univ.

SANTORO, RANDAJO; Campbell Memorial HS; Campbell, OH; Cls Rep Frsh Cls; Cls Rep Soph Cls; Cl Rep Jr Cls; Hon Rl; JA; Sci Clb; Spn Clb; Letter Ten; JA Awd; Opt Clb Awd; Youngstown St Univ; Nursing.

SANTOS, MICHELLE; Utica Sr HS; Newark, OH; 1/193 Val; Hon Rl; Jr NHS; NHS; Drama Clb; VP Spn Clb; Letter Bsbl; Letter Chrldng; Ohio St Univ; Comp Sci.

SANTUCCI, KATHLEEN; Howland HS; Warren, OH; 110/410 Band; Girl Scts; Hon Rl; Off Ade; Sct Actv; Y-Teens; Pep Clb; Letter Gym; Letter Trk; Letter Chrldng; Bowling Green Univ; Phys Ed.

SAOUD, JEAN; Notre Dame HS; Clarksburg, WV; Cl Rep Jr Cls; Cls Rep Sr Cls; Jr NHS; Sch Pl; Stu Cncl; Drama Clb; Mth Clb; Pep Clb; Sci Clb; Ten; University.

SAPE, JEANINE; Whitmer HS; Toledo, OH; 66/800 Sec Soph Cls; Trs Soph Cls; Pres Jr Cls; Hon Rl; Jr NHS; Lbry Ade; NHS; Off Ade; Yth Flsp; DECA; Local Deca Cmptn Apprl 1st Pl 1979; St Ohio Deca Cmptn Apprl & Accssrs 2nd Pl 1979; Adv To Natl Cmptn 1979; Goshen Coll; Bus Mgmt.

SAPIANO, JOHN; Grosse Ile HS; Grosse Ile, MI; Aud/Vis; Chrs; Chrh Wkr; Hon Rl; Rptr Sch Nwsp; Eligbl For St Of Mi Schslhp 79; Univ Of Michigan; Mech Engr.

SAPLETAL, LAURA; West Iron Cnty HS; Iron River, MI; 1/130 Trs Jr Cls; Val; Band; Chrs; Chrh Wkr; Girl Scts; Hon Rl; NHS; Sch Pl; Rptr Yrbk; Michigan Tech Univ; Comp Sci.

SAPORITO, FRANK A; Fairmont Sr HS; Fairmont, WV; 42/237 Cl Rep Jr Cls; Am Leg Boys St; Chrs; Chrh Wkr; Hon Rl; Sch Mus; Sch Pl; Drama Clb; Treas Key Clb; Ftbl; Wv All St HS Chorus 79; West Virginia Univ; Pharm.

SAPP, DORCUS; Greenbrier West HS; Rainelle, WV; 29/150 Band; Sch Pl; Drama Clb; Pep Clb; Letter Bsktbl; Trk; Chrldng; IM Sprt; Mat Maids; Bluefield State Univ; Law.

SAPP, JACKIE; Parkway HS; Rockford, OH; 14/96 Band; FCA; Hon Rl; Letter GAA; PPFtbl; Scr Kpr; Pres Awd; Acctg.

SAPP, JODI; Jefferson Union HS; Toronto, OH; Band; Chrh Wkr; Girl Scts; Hon Rl; Y-Teens; Beta Clb; Drama Clb; 4-H; Fr Clb; Pep Clb; Univ; Phys Ed.

SAPP, KIMBERLY D; Monongah HS; Fairmont, WV; Lbry Ade; Y-Teens; Yrbk; Fr Clb; FHA; Pep Clb; Univ; Mentally Disabled Children.

SAPP, LYNETTE A; Celina Sr HS; Mendon, OH; 28/240 Trs Soph Cls; Sec Jr Cls; Sec Sr Cls; NHS; Off Ade; Yth Flsp; FBLA; FTA; GAA; IM Sprt; Sec.

SAPP, MIKE; Fremont HS; Fremont, IN; Hon Rl; Spn Clb; Bsktbl; Ftbl; Glf; College; Forestry.

SAPP, PAMELA; Lutheran HS East; Detroit, MI; 14/146 Chrh Wkr; Hon Rl; NHS; Stu Cncl; Pres Lat Clb; Letter Bsktbl; Univ; Chem Engr.

SAPP, VERA E; Eastbrook HS; Jonesboro, IN; Chrh Wkr; Hon Rl; Fr Clb; Gym; Univ; Elem Ed.

SAPPENFIELD, LORI L; Greenwood Comm HS; Greenwood, IN; 11/263 Hon Rl; OEA; Pep Clb; Clark Coll; Data Processing.

SAPPER, DANIEL A; Perkins HS; Sandusky, OH; Am Leg Boys St; Band; Hon Rl; NHS; Sch Mus; Sch Pl; VP Stu Cncl; Drama Clb; Lat Clb; Univ.

SAPUTO, RICK; Wylie E Groves HS; Birmingham, MI; 125/547 Cls Rep Frsh Cls; Cls Rep Soph Cls; Cl Rep Jr Cls; Cls Rep Sr Cls; Chrh Wkr; Cmnty Wkr; Swmmng; Ten; Coach Actv; Tmr; Western Michigan Univ; Bus Admin.

SARA, SARAH; Bloomington HS; Bloomington, IN; 110/432 Am Leg Aux Girls St; Letter Band; Girl Scts; Orch; 4-H; Fr Clb; Sci Clb; Letter Gym; Chrldng; PPFtbl; Miss Vincennes Cheerleader Awd; All Amer Shout It Outer Nominee; Mis Lake Lemon; Indiana Univ.

SARAFIN, CATHY; Lexington HS; Mansfield, OH; 8/260 Am Leg Aux Girls St; Band; Hosp Ade; NHS; Y-Teens; Fr Clb; Trk; Ohio St Univ; Med.

SARASIEN, JAMES; Northrop HS; Ft Wayne, IN; Aud/Vis; Boy Scts; Lbry Ade; Pol Wkr; Sct Actv; Key Clb; Lat Clb; Glf; Mgrs; Pres Awd; Business Schl; Busns.

SARE, KELLY; North Vermillion HS; Perrysville, IN; Band; Chrs; Hon Rl; NHS; Red Cr Ade; Pep Clb; Spn Clb; Bsktbl; Swmmng; Chrldng; Indiana St Univ; Pre Schl Educ.

SAREN, SCOTT R; St Thomas Aquinas HS; Lincoln Park, MI; Ftbl; Trk; IM Sprt; Northern Michigan Univ; Forestry.

SARGENT, ANNE M; Bullock Creek HS; Midland, MI; Band; Chrs; Girl Scts; Hon Rl; JA; NHS; Yth Flsp; 4-H; Fr Clb; 4-H Awd; Central Mic Univ.

SARGENT, CHERYL; Vassar HS; Vassar, MI; 16/150 Band; Hon Rl; Yth Flsp; Fr Clb; Trk; PPFtbl; St Of Mi Comp Schlrshp 79; Saginaw Valley St Coll; Health.

SARGENT, CRYSTAL; Clinton Massie HS; Clarksville, OH; 23/100 Chrs; Drl Tm; Hon Rl; Hosp Ade; Stu Cncl; 4-H; Chrldng; PPFtbl; 4-H Awd; Overall Home Furnshings Arts & Crafts Winner Fair 78; Univ; Anesthesia.

SARGENT, LAURIE; Bay Village HS; Bay Vill, OH; Off Ade; Fr Clb; Pep Clb; College; Child Psych.

SARGENT, STEVEN; W Lafayette HS; W Lafayette, IN; Aud/Vis; Boy Scts; Hon Rl; Sct Actv; Ftbl; Wrstlng; Chrldng; IM Sprt; Media Fair 79 Certif Of Merit; Purdue Univ; Busns Mgmt.

SARGENT, SUSAN; North Knox HS; Bicknell, IN; 2/153 FCA; Hon Rl; NHS; Stu Cncl; Yth Flsp; Yrbk; 4-H; Lat Clb; Capt Chrldng; 4-H Awd; Purdue Univ; Doctor.

SARGENT, TRACEY; Bedford N Lawrence HS; Bedford, IN; 115/437 Sec Soph Cls; Sec Jr Cls; Sec Sr Cls; Girl Scts; Hon Rl; Beta Clb; Keyettes; Pep Clb; Spn Clb; Capt Bsktbl; Hoosier Hills All Conf Most Rebounds MVP; HHC All Conf Most Assists; College; Phys Ed.

SARGENT, TROY A; Hobart Sr HS; Hobart, IN; Chrh Wkr; Hon Rl; Letter Bsbl; Letter Ftbl; Nom For Most Outstndg Fresh Boy; 3rd Hghst Grd Avg In Spnsh; Outstndg Ach Awrd For Acdmc & Nonacdmc Wrk; Indiana Univ; Medicine.

SARI, TINA; Margaretta HS; Bellevue, OH; Band; Girl Scts; Hon Rl; Yrbk; 4-H; Spn Clb; Bsktbl; Letter Trk; GAA; IM Sprt; 880 Relay Tm Record Holder Girls Track; Bnd Letter; Coll; Busns.

SARICH, JOHN; Cabrini HS; Dearborn, MI; Hon Rl; Letter Ftbl; Trk; IM Sprt; Natl Merit SF; Univ Of Mich; Bus.

SARIGIANI, LISA; Frank Cady HS; Detroit, MI; Band; Hon Rl; Jr NHS; Orch; Univ.

SARIN, JENNIFER G; Winston Churchill HS; Livonia, MI; Chrs; Hon Rl; Lbry Ade; Lit Mag; Off Ade; NCTE; Kalamazoo College; History.

SARISKY, JOHN; Woodrow Wilson Sr HS; Youngstown, OH; 1/300 Am Leg Boys St; Debate Tm; Hon Rl; Jr NHS; Sch Pl; Stg Crw; Ger Clb; Sci Clb; Natl Merit Ltr; Voice Dem Awd; Best Acad Stu Awd Paul C Bunn Schl; Massachusetts Inst Of Tech; Chem.

SARISKY, LAURINE; Woodrow Wilson HS; Youngstown, OH; 36/345 Jr NHS; Off Ade; Pep Clb; Trk;.

SARNES, CONSTANCE; Gibsonburg HS; Gibsonburg, OH; 2/98 Am Leg Aux Girls St; Band; Hon Rl; Stg Crw; Rptr Yrbk; Rptr Sch Nwsp; Drama Clb; Fr Clb; Mst Outstndng Jr 79; U S Coll Wind Band European Tour 79; Univ; Nursing.

SARNES, JEFFREY; Gibsonburg HS; Gibsonburg, OH; 7/101 Am Leg Boys St; Pres Band; Rptr Yrbk; Ed Sch Nwsp; Drama Clb; Treas Sci Clb; Glf; Unif Of Toledo; Civil Engr.

SAROSY, DONNA; Lumen Cordium HS; Bedford, OH; Hon Rl; NHS; Sch Pl; Stg Crw; Bsktbl; Chrldng; Coach Actv; VP GAA; Bowling Green State Univ; Bus.

SARPOLIS, KAREN; Winston Churchill HS; Livonia, MI; Cl Rep Jr Cls; Band; Chrs; Chrh Wkr; Hon Rl; Off Ade; Yth Flsp; Sprt Ed Yrbk; Pep Clb; Letter Crs Cntry; Kalamazoo Coll; Psych.

SARRETT, JEFF; Du Pont HS; Charleston, WV; Trs Frsh Cls; Am Leg Boys St; Stu Cncl; Letter Bsktbl; Coll.

SARSANY, PAUL; Champion HS; Warren, OH; 31/218 Band; Hon Rl; NHS; Orch; Sch Pl; Stg Crw; Drama Clb; IM Sprt; Univ Of Akron; Elec Engr.

SARTORE, J; Princeton Cmnty HS; Patoka, IN; 3/210 Boy Scts; Hon Rl; Jr NHS; NHS; Sct Actv; 4-H; FFA; FSA; Mth Clb; Pres Sci Clb; Purdue Univ; Vet.

SARVER, JOHN; South Spencer HS; Hatfield, IN; 29/147 VP Sr Cls; Chrh Wkr; Bsbl; Letter Ftbl; IM Sprt; JC Awd; Purdue Univ; Civil Engr.

SARVIS, WILLIAM; Perry HS; Painesville, OH; Am Leg Boys St; Hon Rl; NHS; Bsktbl; Letter Crs Cntry; Ftbl; Letter Ten; Letter Trk; Am Leg Awd; GRC Champion 2 Mile Run Grand River Conf Track; All Grand River Conf Team In Cross Cntry;.

SASAKI, PATTY A; West Geauga HS; Chesterland, OH; 35/352 Band; Cmp Fr Grls; Hon Rl; Natl Merit SF; Honorable Mention In Ohio Tests Of Scholastic Ach In English Ii; Ohio State Univ; Medicine.

SASALA, CONNIE; R B Chamberlin HS; Twinsburg, OH; FCA; Hon Rl; NHS; Sch Mus; Sch Pl; Rptr Yrbk; Mth Clb; Letter Trk; Chrldng; Pom Pon; College; Biological Research.

SASALA, STEVE; Pymatuning Valley HS; Jefferson, OH; 4/133 Cls Rep Frsh Cls; Cls Rep Soph Cls; Cl Rep Jr Cls; Am Leg Boys St; Band; Chrs; NHS; Sch Pl; Stu Cncl; Rptr Sch Nwsp; College; Lawyer.

SASS, BRETT A; Three Rivers HS; Three Rivers, MI; 51/229 Aud/Vis; Band; Chrh Wkr; Hon Rl; NHS; Sch Pl; Stg Crw; Yth Flsp; Yrbk; Rptr Sch Nwsp; Glen Oaks; Chem.

SASS, KYLE; Maumee HS; Maumee, OH; 61/315 Sec Aud/Vis; Letter Bsktbl; Letter Ten; Scr Kpr; Tmr; Univ Of Toledo; Chem Engr.

SASS, SHELLEE M; Winamac Comm HS; Star City, IN; Aud/Vis; Band; Chrh Wkr; Drl Tm; Hon Rl; JA; Off Ade; 4-H; Pep Clb; Spn Clb; Indiana Univ; X Ray Tech.

SASSANO, JOHN; North Sr HS; Akron, OH; 12/385 VP Sr Cls; Cmnty Wkr; Hon Rl; NHS; Pres Stu Cncl; Bsbl; Bsktbl; Glf; IM Sprt; Natl Merit Ltr; Missouri St Univ; Dent.

SATAWA, TAMARA A; Bishop Foley HS; Warren, MI; 8/193 Cmnty Wkr; Hon Rl; Sch Mus; Sch Pl; Yth Flsp; Rptr Yrbk; Rptr Sch Nwsp; Spn Clb; Chrldng; PPFtbl; Mercy Coll Of Detroit; Nursing.

SATCHWELL, JEFF; William Mason HS; Mason, OH; 2/200 Band; Debate Tm; Drm Bgl; Hon Rl; Orch; Sch Mus; Sch Pl; Stu Cncl; College; Chem.

SATCHWILL, GERALD; South Dearborn HS; Aurora, IN; 53/230 Band; Boy Scts; Hon Rl; Off Ade; Bsbl; Letter Bsktbl; Hanover Coll; Math Tchr.

SATER, KAREN; Strongsville HS; Strongsville, OH; Band; Girl Scts; Hon Rl; Sct Actv; Stg Crw; Pep Clb; IM Sprt; PPFtbl; College; Psych.

SATHER, TAMIE; Clio HS; Clio, MI; 10/400 VP Frsh Cls; VP Soph Cls; Cls Rep Soph Cls; Hon Rl; Jr NHS; NHS; Sch Pl; Stg Crw; Stu Cncl; Spn Clb; Univ Of Michigan; Medicine.

SATINK, DAN; Polaris Vocational Center; Berea, OH; Cls Rep Frsh Cls; Cls Rep Soph Cls; VP Jr Cls; Off Ade; Sch Pl; Stu Cncl; Yth Flsp; DECA; Bsbl; Crs Cntry; Akron Univ; Food Mkt.

SATKOWIAK, SUZANNE; Clay Sr HS; Oregon, OH; Hon Rl; Ownes Tech Coll; Radiologist.

SATTELE, DAVID; Charles F Brush HS; S Euclid, OH; Letter Socr; Colorado Mtn Coll; Forestry.

SATTERFIELD, JACQUELINE; Fr Joseph Wehrle Mem HS; Columbus, OH; Cl Rep Jr Cls; Cls Rep Sr Cls; Chrh Wkr; Stu Cncl; Capt Chrldng; Columbus Tech Inst; Bus.

SATTERFIELD, JERRY; Monongalt HS; Fairmont, WV; Pres Frsh Cls; Hon Rl; Stu Cncl; Letter Bsbl; Letter Bsktbl; Letter Ftbl; IM Sprt; College.

SATTERLEE, BETSY; William Henry Harrison HS; Evansville, IN; Cls Rep Frsh Cls; Cl Rep Jr Cls; Band; Chrh Wkr; Natl Forn Lg; Orch; Pep Clb; Spn Clb; Coach Actv; Cit Awd; Mbr Of Health Occupt Club Vc Pres 78; Pres Of Youth At Chyrch 78; Pub Chrmn Of Band 79; Gardner Webb S Bapt Coll; Deaf Ecuc.

SATTERWHITE, KENNETH; Mt Healthy HS; Cincinnati, OH; 74/597 Cl Rep Jr Cls; Chrh Wkr; Cmnty Wkr; Stu Cncl; Beta Clb; Stu Govt Pres; Minority Scholars Schlrshp; Fisk Univ; Poli Sci.

SATTLER, CAROL E; Rogers HS; Toledo, OH; Band; Girl Scts; Hon Rl; JA; Lbry Ade; Sec FFA; College; Floral Design.

SATTLER, RICHARD; Quincy HS; Quincy, MI; Boy Scts; FCA; Hon Rl; Rptr Yrbk; Rptr Sch Nwsp; Rdo Clb; VICA; Ftbl; Voc Schl; Building Tech.

SAUCEDA, JAMES; Lansing Eastern HS; Lansing, MI; 135/483 Cls Rep Frsh Cls; Band; Hon Rl; Bsbl; Brdcstg.

SAUCEDO, ANNABEL; Roosevelt HS; E Chicago, IN; 13/199 Chrh Wkr; Hon Rl; JA; Fr Clb; Ten; PPFtbl; Comp Sci.

SAUDER, DEB; High School; Lucas, OH; Pres Jr Cls; Band; Capt Drl Tm; Sch Mus; Drama Clb; Bsktbl; Letter Trk; Bus Schl.

SAUDER, NATHAN; Archbold HS; Archbold, OH; Chrs; Chrh Wkr; Stg Crw; 4-H; Ftbl; Ten; Mgrs; 4-H Awd; Univ; Phys Ed.

SAUER, J; Triton HS; Bourbon, IN; Am Leg Aux Girls St; Band; Chrh Wkr; Cmnty Wkr; Drm Mjrt; Hon Rl; FTA; Spn Clb; Twrlr;.

SAUER, JACKIE; Archbishop Alter HS; Dayton, OH; 130/276 Drl Tm; Hon Rl; Off Ade; Nursing.

SAUER, MARK; Schoolcraft HS; Schoolcraft, MI; Pres Jr Cls; Am Leg Boys St; Hon Rl; NHS; Sch Pl; Letter Ftbl; Letter Trk; Am Leg Awd; Michigan St Univ; Geol.

SAUER, MARY; Schoolcraft HS; Schoolcraft, MI; 6/83 Am Leg Aux Girls St; Chrh Wkr; Hon Rl; Lbry Ade; NHS; Sct Actv; 4-H; Kalamazoo College; Economics.

SAUER, TERREE; Little Miami HS; Clarksville, OH; Girl Scts; Hon Rl; Lit Mag; Fr Clb; Pep Clb; Socr; PPFtbl; Scr Kpr; College; Fashion Design.

SAUERMAN, LINDA; Euclid HS; Euclid, OH; Boy Scts; Chrs; Chrh Wkr; Drl Tm; Girl Scts; NHS; Pol Wkr; Scr Kpr; College; Acctg.

SAUL, DAWN; Bishop Ready HS; Columbus, OH; 14/130 Hon Rl; NHS; Sch Pl; DECA; OEA; Chrldng; Franklin Univ; Bus Admin.

SAULINO, CYNTHIA M; Jackson Milton HS; Lake Milton, OH; Am Leg Aux Girls St; Band; Pres Chrs; Off Ade; Sch Mus; Sch Pl; Sec FHA; FTA; Scr Kpr; Voc Schl; Cosmtlgy.

SAULMAN, LORI M; Floyd Central HS; Georgetown, IN; Chrs; Letter Drl Tm; Hon Rl; MMM; NHS; Red Cr Ade; Sch Mus; Stu Cncl; Pep Clb; Letter Pom Pon; Univ Of Louisville; Music.

SAULMAN, MICK; Corydon Central HS; Corydon, IN; FCA; Bsbl; Bsktbl; Ftbl; Trk; College; Bus.

SAULS, MARK D; Tippecanoe HS; Tipp City, OH; Cls Rep Soph Cls; Pres Sr Cls; Cls Rep Sr Cls; Hon Rl; Off Ade; Stu Cncl; Sch Nwsp; Bsbl; Bsktbl; Glf; Univ Of Dayton; Law.

SAUM, DAVID; Father J Wehrle Mem HS; Groveport, OH; Boy Scts; Chrh Wkr; Hon Rl; Franklin; Business Admin.

SAUM, DAVID; Amanda Clearcreek HS; Lancaster, OH; 5/97 Yth Flsp; Rptr Yrbk; Yrbk; 4-H; FFA; Sci Clb; Letter Bsbl; Scr Kpr; Ohio State Univ; Ag Engr.

SAUM, ROBERT; Memorial HS; St Marys, OH; 1/223 Trs Jr Cls; Am Leg Boys St; Band; Chrh Wkr; Cmnty Wkr; Hon Rl; NHS; Sch Mus; Sch Pl; Stg Crw; Univ Of Dayton; Math.

SAUNDERS, BRIAN; Briggs HS; Columbus, OH; 3/213 Pres Jr Cls; Am Leg Boys St; CAP; NHS; Pres Stu Cncl; Mth Clb; Pres Spn Clb; Letter Bsktbl; Letter Trk; Natl Merit Schl; Purdue Univ; Elec Engr.

SAUNDERS, CHERYL; Kokomo HS; Kokomo, IN; 11/323 Band; Hon Rl; Jr NHS; NHS; Sch Pl; Stu Cncl; Ger Clb; Mic State Univ; Wildlife Cnsrvtn.

SAUNDERS, CLAIRE; North Farmington HS; Frmngtn Hls, MI; Bsktbl; Wayne St Univ; Nursing.

SAUNDERS, DENISE; Lumen Cordium HS; Bedford, OH; Hon Rl; Stg Crw; Rptr Sch Nwsp; Capt Bsbl; Letter Bsktbl; GAA; IM Sprt; College.

SAUNDERS, JILL; Clarkston HS; Clarkston, MI; 17/489 Cmp Fr Grls; Hon Rl; NHS; Off Ade; Sch Pl; Drama Clb; 4-H; Fr Clb; Mth Clb; PPFtbl; Oakland Univ; Comp Sci.

SAUNDERS, MICHAEL; Milton HS; Ona, WV; Cls Rep Frsh Cls; Boy Scts; Chrs; Cmnty Wkr; Hon Rl; JA; Red Cr Ade; Sch Pl; Stg Crw; Rptr Yrbk; Marshall Univ Charleston; Communicat.

SAUNDERS, MONICA M; East HS; Columbus, OH; Cls Rep Frsh Cls; Cl Rep Jr Cls; Drl Tm; Hon Rl; Off Ade; Stu Cncl; Sch Nwsp; Pep Clb; Trk; Coll; Designer.

SAUNDERS, PATRICIA; Union Local HS; Belmont, OH; 7/167 Chrh Wkr; Hon Rl; NHS; Off Ade; Stu Cncl; Rptr Yrbk; Ed Sch Nwsp; Sch Nwsp; Fr Clb; Sci Clb; Barber College; Beautician.

SAUNDERS, VALERIE; Du Pont HS; London, WV; Hon Rl; Jr NHS; Shorthand Speed Awd 78; Bus Schl; Sec.

SAUNDRI, KATHRYN; Marquette Sr HS; Marquette, MI; Northern Michigan Univ; Bus.

SAUNTRY, MARTHA; Glen Este HS; Batavia, OH; 18/250 Hon Rl; NHS; FHA; Pep Clb; Spn Clb; Bsktbl; Univ Of Cincinnati; Acctg.

SAUS, JOE; Lake Catholic HS; Mayfield, OH; 38/312 Boy Scts; Chrh Wkr; Treas Spn Clb; Letter Ftbl; IM Sprt; Miami Univ; Pre Medd.

SAUSEN, LINDA; St Francis De Sls Cntrl HS; Morgantown, WV; 3/65 Chrs; Girl Scts; Hon Rl; NHS; Stg Crw; Drama Clb; Sci Clb; Spn Clb; IM Sprt; Coll; Nursing.

SAUTER, MARY JO; Lymen Christi HS; Jackson, MI; Sec Jr Cls; Hon Rl; Sec Stu Cncl; Lat Clb; Pep Clb; Trk; Chrldng; IM Sprt; Coll; Med.

SAUTER, SARAH; Grand Rapids Ctrl HS; Grand Rapids, MI; Trs Soph Cls; Trs Jr Cls; Trs Sr Cls; Band; Chrh Wkr; Hon Rl; JA; Jr NHS; Mod UN; NHS; Univ.

SAUTINS, IVETA; Perrysburg HS; Perrysburg, OH; 25/251 Hon Rl; Hosp Ade; NHS; Sch Mus; Stg Crw; Fr Clb; Pep Clb; Crs Cntry; Trk; French Clb Pres 78 79; Cross Cntry Meritorious Awd In Participation 79; Univ; Microbio.

SAUTO, JAMES W; Eastlake North HS; Willowick, OH; 34/669 Am Leg Boys St; Hon Rl; Jr NHS; NHS; Letter Ftbl; Letter Trk; Letter Wrstlng; Univ; Bio.

SAUVE, DAVID; Essexville Hamptn Garber HS; Essexville, MI; 18/172 Hon Rl; DAR Awd; Michigan St Univ; Comp Sci.

SAVAGE, CATHERINE M; St Clement HS; Centerline, MI; Trs Jr Cls; Trs Sr Cls; Cmnty Wkr; Girl Scts; Hon Rl; NHS; Pep Clb; Bsbl; GAA; IM Sprt; Univ Of Michigan; Dr Of Med.

SAVAGE, CHARLENE K; Caro Cmnty 'S; Caro, MI; 13/170 Band; Chrh Wkr; Girl Scts; Hon Rl; Hosp Ade; NHS; Pres Yth Flsp; Rptr Yrbk; FNA; Spn Clb; Mercy Central Schl; Nursing.

SAVAGE, DENISE; Avon HS; Indianapolis, IN; Band; Chrs; Drl Tm; Hon Rl; Mdrgl; MMM; Pom Pon; Scr Kpr; Most Improved Rifle 76; Most Improved Marcher 78; Basic & Advncd Clothing Awd 76 77 & 78; Indiana Univ; Bus.

SAVAGE, ELIZABETH; Chippewa Valley HS; Mt Clemens, MI; Cmnty Wkr; Girl Scts; Hon Rl; NHS; Pol Wkr; FHA; Spn Clb; Coach Actv; Lion Awd; Natl Merit Ltr; Michigan State; Vet.

SAVAGE, KATHLEEN; Colerain Sr HS; Cincinnati, OH; Band; Drl Tm; Girl Scts; Hon Rl; Hosp Ade; NHS; Sch Mus; Rptr Sch Nwsp; Fr Clb; Chrldng; College; Medicine.

SAVAGE, LINDA; Big Bay De Noc HS; Cooks, MI; Hon Rl; Lbry Ade; 4-H; Child Care.

SAVAGE, MARIA; Blanchester HS; Blanchester, OH; 3/160 Pres Frsh Cls; Cls Rep Frsh Cls; Cls Rep Soph Cls; Sec Jr Cls; Cls Rep Sr Cls; Band; Hon Rl; Jr NHS; NHS; Stu Cncl; Ohio St Univ; Pre Med.

SAVAGE, PAMELA; Allen Park HS; Allen Pk, MI; Cls Rep Sr Cls; Chrh Wkr; Hon Rl; Jr NHS; NHS; Tmr; College; Bio.

SAVAGE, PEGGY; Dublin HS; Columbus, OH; 45/157 Chrs; Chrh Wkr; Cmnty Wkr; Hon Rl; NHS; Sch Mus; Sch Pl; Rptr Sch Nwsp; Lat Clb; Twrlr; Ohio State Univ; Music.

SAVAGLIO, CLARE; Kimball HS; Royal Oak, MI; Chrh Wkr; Hon Rl; Lbry Ade; Lit Mag; Orch; Sch Mus; Sch Pl; Pres College; Sci.

SAVELLI, BRENDA; Kirtland HS; Kirtland, OH; 27/123 VP Chrs; Hon Rl; Rptr Sch Nwsp; Pep Clb; Chrldng; Twrlr; Am Leg Awd; Schlrshp To Fred Waring Music Workshop; Univ.

SAVERNIK, GREGOR E; Euclid Sr HS; Euclid, OH; Cls Rep Frsh Cls; Cls Rep Soph Cls; Boy Scts; Chrs; Chrh Wkr; Sch Pl; Sct Actv; Stu Cncl; Rdo Clb; Univ; Auto Design.

SAVILLE, MARY; Hampshire HS; Romney, WV; 19/213 Hst Frsh Cls; Am Leg Aux Girls St; Chrs;

NHS; Yth Flsp; Rptr Yrbk; Ten; Chrldng; Cit Awd; Fairmont St Coll; Archt Engr.

SAVOIE, EILEEN; North Central Area HS; Powers, MI; Trs Jr Cls; Band; Hon Rl; Yrbk; VP 4-H; Treas Spn Clb; Letter Mgrs; Pom Pon; 4-H Awd; Univ; Math.

SAVOIE, REBECCA; Durand Area HS; Lennon, MI; Cls Rep Sr Cls; Band; Chrs; Hon Rl; Jr NHS; Treas NHS; Off Ade; Stu Cncl; Fr Clb; Davenport College; Hospitality.

SAVORY, SHELLY; Whitmer HS; Toledo, OH; 32/835 Hon Rl; Jr NHS; NHS; Off Ade; Spn Clb; Bowling Green State Univ; Business.

SAWALL, FRED D; Hayes HS; Delaware, OH; Chrh Wkr; Debate Tm; Hon Rl; Natl Forn Lg; NHS; Spn Clb; Bsbl; Socr; Trk; College.

SAWAYDA, CYNTHIA; Champion HS; Warren, OH; 9/235 Sec Soph Cls; Sec Jr Cls; Sec Sr Cls; Am Leg Aux Girls St; Band; Hosp Ade; NHS; VP Stu Cncl; Letter Trk; IM Sprt; Cleveland St Univ; Phys Therapy.

SAWICKI, LESLIE; Maumee HS; Maumee, OH; Cls Rep Frsh Cls; Hon Rl; Off Ade; Stg Crw; Stu Cncl; Y-Teens; Yrbk; Fr Clb; Chrldng; PPFtbl; 5 Yr Cheerleader Awd; Top 5 In Maumee HS PSAT Math; Ohio St Univ; Special Ed.

SAWITKE, JANET; Mentor Sr HS; Mentor, OH; Cl Rep Jr Cls; Band; Chrs; Hon Rl; Orch; Red Cr Ade; Stu Cncl; Spn Clb; Univ; Bio.

SAWMILLER, JED; Waynesfield Goshen HS; Waynesfield, OH; 3/60 Pres Soph Cls; Chrs; Hon Rl; NHS; Sch Mus; Sch Pl; Rptr Yrbk; Rptr Sch Nwsp; 4-H; Bsktbl; Hiram Univ; Engr.

SAWVEL, BRYAN; Eastside Jr Sr HS; Hamilton, IN; 2/91 Sal; Am Leg Boys St; Aud/Vis; Hon Rl; NHS; Sci Clb; Spn Clb; Scr Kpr; Am Leg Awd; Rotary Awd; Indiana Univ; Comp Sci.

SAWYER, CYNTHIA L; Richmond Sr HS; Richmond, IN; Cls Rep Frsh Cls; Cls Rep Soph Cls; Cl Rep Jr Cls; Cls Rep Sr Cls; Chrh Wkr; Hon Rl; Orch; Pol Wkr; Stg Crw; Yth Flsp; Univ; Speech & Hearg Ther.

SAWYER, ELSPETH; Upper Arlington HS; Columbus, OH; 43/621 AFS; Band; Chrh Wkr; Hon Rl; Hosp Ade; NHS; Quill & Scroll; Sch Pl; Sch Nwsp; Drama Clb; Capital Univ Consrv; Music.

SAWYER, LISA; Princeton HS; Sharonville, OH; Boy Scts; Chrs; Cmnty Wkr; Girl Scts; Hon Rl; Sct Actv; Pep Clb; Spn Clb; Mas Awd; Intl Order Of Jobs Daughters; Explorers Sec/tres; Sharonville Fire Dept; Miami Univ; Law.

SAWYER, ROBERT; Mt Clemens HS; Selfridge, MI; 1/300 Cls Rep Frsh Cls; Cl Rep Jr Cls; Val; Am Leg Boys St; NHS; Ed Yrbk; Sch Nwsp; Letter Glf; Letter Socr; Letter Ten; Univ Of Michigan; Med.

SAWYER, RONALD; Norwalk HS; Norwalk, OH; JA; Fr Clb; JA Awd; Bowling Green State Univ; Bus Admin.

SAWYER, STACY; Evansville North HS; Evansville, IN; Hon Rl; NHS; DECA; FBLA; Kiwan Awd; Murray St Univ; Jrnlsm.

SAXON, MELANIE; Clay Battelle HS; Fairview, WV; Hon Rl; Lbry Ade; Spn Clb; Bsktbl; Univ; Engr.

SAXTON, JAY; Gallia Academy; Gallipolis, OH; VP Jr Cls; VP Sr Cls; Chrh Wkr; Hon Rl; Lbry Ade; VP Stu Cncl; Yth Flsp; Pres 4-H; Key Clb; Spn Clb; Won The Oh State Boys Class AA Bowling Team Chmpnshp; Recv Advanced Schlr Cert Summer Coll Classes; Univ Of Cincinnati; Vet.

SAXTON, PATRICIA; Hamilton HS; Columbus, OH; 31/175 Chrh Wkr; Sci Clb; Soroptimist; Air Force.

SAXTON, SHARON; Petoskey HS; Petoskey, MI; Cmnty Wkr; Lbry Ade; Natl Forn Lg; Off Ade; Red Cr Ade; FNA; Lat Clb; Pep Clb; Tmr; Natl Merit Schl; Univ Of Northern Michigan; Nurse.

SAYER, JAMES; Bellbrook HS; Belbrook, OH; Band; Orch; Sch Mus; Sch Pl; Letter Bsbl; Ftbl; IM Sprt; Wright State Univ; Music.

SAYER, MARK A; Morgan HS; Malta, OH; Hon Rl; Lbry Ade; NHS; VICA; Machinist.

SAYERS, LEANNE; Keystone HS; La Grange, OH; Cls Rep Frsh Cls; Cl Rep Jr Cls; Chrs; Off Ade; 4-H; Bsbl; Gym; Letter Trk; Chrldng; Lorain Cnty Cmnty Coll.

SAYERS, SUSAN P; Federal Hocking HS; Millfield, OH; 1/127 Am Leg Aux Girls St; VP Band; Drm Bgl; Girl Scts; Hon Rl; NHS; Spn Clb; Bsktbl; Trk; GAA; Ohio State Fair Band; Vlybl Tri Valley All Cnfrnce; Sftbl Tri Vly All Cnfrnce; Ohio Univ; Forensic Chem.

SAYGERS, JENNIFER; Alter HS; Centerville, OH; Chrs; Rptr Yrbk; Fr Clb;.

SAYLES, MARTHA; Midview HS; Grafton, OH; Cls Rep Frsh Cls; Cls Rep Soph Cls; Band; Hon Rl; Rptr Sch Nwsp; Spn Clb; M B Johnson Schl Of Nursing; RN.

SAYLOR, JO; Forest Park HS; Cincinnati, OH; Chrs; Chrh Wkr; Cmnty Wkr; Drl Tm; Girl Scts; Hosp Ade; MMM; Chrldng; Ohi St; Spec Ed Tchr.

SAYLOR JR, JOHN B; Centerville HS; Centerville, IN; Crs Cntry; Trk; College.

SAYRE, ALAN; Buckhannon Upshur HS; Buckhannon, WV; 1/281 Hon Rl; Jr NHS; Stu Cncl; Univ; Chem Engr.

SAYRE, BETINA; Point Pleasant HS; Leon, WV; 31/215 Chrs; NHS; Sch Pl; Rptr Yrbk; Sch Nwsp; Pres 4-H; VP Spn Clb; Cit Awd; 4-H Awd; Andersn Collge.

SAYRE, C; Parkside HS; Jackson, MI; Cl Rep Jr Cls; Debate Tm; Hon Rl; Natl Forn Lg; Orch; Ger Clb; Ten; Natl Merit SF; College; Bus Admin.

SAYRE, CHARLES; Parkersburg HS; Parkersburg, WV; Boy Scts; Hon Rl; Bsktbl; Letter Ftbl;.

SAYRE, RITA; Point Pleasant HS; Pt Pleasant, WV; Cls Rep Soph Cls; Cl Rep Jr Cls; Yth Flsp; Y-Teens; Rptr Yrbk; 4-H; Lat Clb; 4-H Awd; Huntington Beauty Culture.

SAYRE, RON; Belleville HS; Belleville, MI; 6/550 Hon Rl; NHS; Sch Mus; Sch Pl; Kalamazoo Coll; Pre Med.

SAYRE, SHERRIE; Floyd Central HS; Georgetown, IN; 130/360 Aud/Vis; Chrh Wkr; Cmnty Wkr; Hon Rl; JA; Off Ade; Stu Cncl; Y-Teens; 4-H; FHA; Perfct Attndnc 77; Univ Of Louisville; Acctg.

SAYRE, STEVEN; High School; Alexandria, IN; Chrs; Hon Rl; 4-H; Bsbl; Letter Wrstlng; 4-H Awd; Purdue.

SAYRE, TIMOTHY; Purcell HS; Cincinnati, OH; 52/171 Boy Scts; JA; Letter Crs Cntry; Letter Ftbl; Letter Swmmng; Architect.

SAZIMA, KIM; Bedford Sr HS; Bedford, OH; Cl Rep Jr Cls; Cls Rep Sr Cls; Off Ade; Yrbk; Pep Clb; Spn Clb; Tmr; Cooper Inst; Art.

SCACCIANOCE, MICHELE; North Royalton HS; N Royalton, OH; Drama Clb; 4-H; OEA; Bsbl; Bsktbl; Glf; Socr; IM Sprt; Scr Kpr; 4-H Awd; Cleveland State Univ; Bus.

SCAFE, JUDITH; Southwestern HS; Detroit, MI; 30/230 Drm Mjrt; Hon Rl; Rptr Yrbk; Cit Awd; Harwicke Bus Awd For Shorthand 79; Art Draw Paint Awd 76; Michigan St Univ; Jrnslm.

SCAFE, KEN; Romulus Sr HS; Romulus, MI; Cls Rep Sr Cls; Hon Rl; NHS; Stu Cncl; Sch Nwsp; Acad Achvmnt Awd 77; No Absents; Top Of Drafting Club; Michigan Tech Univ; Mech Engr.

SCAGGS, TAMI; Madison Plains HS; London, OH; Hon Rl; Lbry Ade; Rptr Yrbk; Yrbk; Spn Clb; Chrldng;.

SCAGLIONE, SUZANNE M; Salon HS; Solon, OH; Cls Rep Frsh Cls; Trs Soph Cls; Trs Jr Cls; VP Sr Cls; Hon Rl; Jr NHS; NHS; Stu Cncl; Chrldng; IM Sprt; Univ; Bus.

SCALES, ANNE; Wabash HS; Wabash, IN; 3/191 Hst Sr Cls; Band; Chrs; Chrh Wkr; Capt Drl Tm; FCA; Hon Rl; JA; NHS; Sch Mus; Coll Of Wooster.

SCALES, PAMELA; Bishop Ready HS; Columbus, OH; VP Jr Cls; Cmp Fr Grls; Chrs; OEA; Letter Bsbl; College.

SCALES, SCOTT; Southridge HS; Huntingburg, IN; 30/190 Cls Rep Frsh Cls; Cls Rep Soph Cls; VP Jr Cls; Boy Scts; Chrs; Chrh Wkr; Cmnty Wkr; FCA; Hon Rl; Pol Wkr; Grad Of Culver Milt Acad Summer Schl 77; Priv Pilot License From Culver Mit Acad 79; Purdue Univ; Advertising.

SCALES, SHARON; Lake Michigan Catholic HS; Saint Joseph, MI; Hon Rl; Natl Forn Lg; Sch Pl; Stg Crw; Rptr Yrbk; Fr Clb; Mic St Univ; Mdse.

SCALI, GERALYN M; North HS; Eastlake, OH; 7/699 Hon Rl; NHS; Pres 4-H; Lake Erie Coll; Equestrian.

SCAMAHORN, AMY; South Spencer HS; Rockport, IN; 18/146 Cls Rep Frsh Cls; Am Leg Aux Girls St; Band; Cmnty Wkr; Hon Rl; JA; Natl Forn Lg; NHS; Sch Mus; Sch Pl; Purdue Univ; Food.

SCAMP, JOSEPH; Romulus HS; Romulus, MI; 3/300 Sal; Aud/Vis; Hon Rl; NHS; Kiwan Awd; General Mtrs Inst; Elec Engr.

SCANLAN, SONYA; Wadsworth HS; Wadsworth, OH; Band; Hosp Ade; 4-H; Fr Clb; College; Registered Nurse.

SCARBERRY, BLANE; Clermont Northeastern HS; Goshen, OH; Cls Rep Frsh Cls; Cls Rep Soph Cls; Cl Rep Jr Cls; Sec Sr Cls; Cls Rep Sr Cls; FCA; Hon Rl; Off Ade; Sci Clb; Spn Clb; Univ; Bus.

SCARBERRY, CHRISTINE; Comstock HS; Kalamazoo, MI; Chrs; Girl Scts; Hon Rl; JA; Sch Pl; Natl Merit Ltr; Western Michigan Univ; Acctg.

SCARBERRY, GARY; Mt View HS; Welch, WV; Am Leg Boys St; Hon Rl; Jr NHS; Stg Crw; Yth Flsp; Key Clb; Letter Ftbl; Letter Mgrs; Distinguished Serv Jr Hon Soc 77; Distinguished Serv Awd Key Clb 76; West Virginia Univ; Athltc Training.

SCARBROUGH, GARY; Olentangy HS; Delaware, OH; Chrs; Hon Rl; Mdrgl; Sch Mus; Sch Pl; Drama Clb; Spn Clb; Most Promsng Freshmn Actor 1975; All Ohio St Fair Youth Choir 1978; Ohio Wesllyan Honor Choir 1978; Univ; Theater.

SCARBROUGH, KAREN; Kenmore HS; Akron, OH; 1/300 VP Sr Cls; Chrh Wkr; FCA; Hon Rl; Pres Jr NHS; NHS; Stu Cncl; Chrldng; Am Leg Awd; Univ; Pre Med.

SCARBROUGH, ROXANNE E; John Adams HS; So Bend, IN; 28/395 Chrh Wkr; Hon Rl; NHS; Yth Flsp; Gym; PPFtbl; Ohio Valley Christian Univ; Math.

SCARCHILLI, FRANK; Bishop Foley HS; Madison Hts, MI; Cls Rep Frsh Cls; Cls Rep Soph Cls; Cl Rep Jr Cls; Cls Rep Sr Cls; Hon Rl; NHS; Stu Cncl; Bsbl; IM Sprt; JETS Awd; Coll; Engr.

SCAREM, CAROLYN; Portsmouth HS; Portsmouth, OH; 4/264 Chrs; Chrh Wkr; Hon Rl; NHS; Sch Mus; Sch Pl; Yrbk; Treas Spn Clb; Milligan Coll.

SCARPELLA, JAY; Parkway HS; Rockford, OH; 15/85 Pres Soph Cls; Pres Jr Cls; Pres Sr Cls; Am Leg Boys St; Chrh Wkr; Pres FCA; Hon Rl; Sch Pl; Stu Cncl; Yth Flsp; Otterbein Coll; Elem Educ.

SCARPITTI, JOHN; Sebring Mckinley HS; Sebring, OH; 18/91 Am Leg Boys St; Aud/Vis; Hon Rl; NHS; Letter Bsktbl; Letter Glf; Dnfth Awd; Mount Union; Tchr.

SCEIFERS, JOE; New Albany HS; New Albany, IN; 197/565 Cls Rep Frsh Cls; Cl Rep Jr Cls; Boy Scts; Stu Cncl; Ger Clb; College; Acctg.

SCHAAD, A; Belpre HS; Belpre, OH; 18/192 Cls Rep Frsh Cls; Cls Rep Soph Cls; VP Sr Cls; Am Leg Aux Girls St; Band; Chrs; Chrh Wkr; Business School.

SCHAAF, KAREN; Walnut Ridge HS; Columbus, OH; 1/425 Chrs; Pres Chrh Wkr; Hon Rl; NHS; Sch Mus; Rptr Yrbk; 4-H; Fr Clb; Pep Clb; Natl Merit Ltr; Capital Univ.

SCHAAF, KURT; Reeths Puffer HS; Muskegon, MI; Hon Rl; NHS; Spn Clb; Letter Crs Cntry; Letter Ten; Michigan State Univ; Engr.

SCHAAR, DENNIS; Onaway Area Cmnty Schools; Onaway, MI; Band; NHS; Sch Pl; Stu Cncl; 4-H; Letter Bsbl; Letter Bsktbl; Letter Trk; Lake Superior St Coll; Engr.

SCHAB, PAUL; West Catholic HS; Grand Rapids, MI; 10/256 Band; Chrh Wkr; FCA; Hon Rl; Jr NHS; Orch; Lat Clb; Letter Bsktbl; Letter Trk; Letter Wrstlng; Western Michigan Univ; Mech Engr.

SCHACHT, CINDY; Meadowbrook HS; Cambridge, OH; Hon Rl; Yrbk; Mth Clb; Pep Clb; Sci Clb; Sec Spn Clb; Bus Schl; Sec.

SCHACHT, ERICH; Vicksburg HS; Portage, MI; 42/240 Band; Cmnty Wkr; Hon Rl; Michigan St Univ; Mech Engr.

SCHACHT, PATRICIA; Rogers HS; Michigan City, IN; 5/482 Cls Rep Frsh Cls; Band; Chrs; Hon Rl; JA; VP NHS; Sch Mus; Stg Crw; Stu Cncl; Yth Flsp; Purdue Univ; Educ.

SCHAD, KAREN; St Joseph Acad; Cleveland, OH; Girl Scts; Sch Pl; Sct Actv; Stg Crw; Drama Clb; Kent State; Speech.

SCHADE, BILL; Boardman HS; Youngstown, OH; 46/690 Hon Rl; NHS; Ger Clb; Letter Bsbl; Letter Bsktbl; Ftbl; Trk; Kent State Univ; Pre Dentistry.

SCHAEFER, CATHY; Magnificat HS; Olmsted Falls, OH; Aud/Vis; Chrh Wkr; Cmnty Wkr; Hosp Ade; NHS; Rptr Yrbk; Yrbk; Rptr Sch Nwsp; Sch Nwsp; Key Clb; College; Pre Med.

SCHAEFER, CHRISTINE; Capac Jr & Sr HS; Capac, MI; Band; Hosp Ade; Off Ade; FNA; Mgrs; St Clair County Cmnty Coll; Dent Hyg.

SCHAEFER, CONSTANCE; E Kentwood HS; Kentwood, Mi; Hon Rl; NHS; Swmmng; Pom Pon; Hope Coll; Busns Admin.

SCHAEFER, CYNTHIA; Newaygo HS; Newaygo, MI; Trs Jr Cls; Am Leg Aux Girls St; Band; Hon Rl; NHS; Stu Cncl; Letter Bsbl; Letter Bsktbl; Letter Trk; Letter Chrldng; Univ.

SCHAEFER, DAVE; Benedictine HS; Cleveland, OH; 12/95 Sec NHS; Treas Stu Cncl; Sch Nwsp; Treas Ger Clb; Crs Cntry; Trk; College; Psych.

SCHAEFER, DAVID G; Benedictine HS; Cleveland, OH; 12/113 Hon Rl; NHS; Sch Nwsp; Treas Ger Clb; Crs Cntry; Ftbl; Trk; Received A.

SCHAEFER, JODI; Escanaba Area HS; Escanaba, MI; 28/438 Band; Hon Rl; Y-Teens; 4-H; Trk; 4-H Awd; College; Accntg.

SCHAEFER, JONATHAN T; Oakridge HS; Muskegon, MI; 36/155 Band; Drm Mjrt; Treas Pep Clb; Bsktbl; Letter Trk; Tmr; Ferris St Coll Summer Band Camp Schlrshp; Spanish I Awd; Grand Rapids Bapt Coll; Music.

SCHAEFER, JULIE; Sparta HS; Conklin, MI; 14/176 Pres Soph Cls; Trs Sr Cls; Band; Chrh Wkr; Girl Scts; Hon Rl; NHS; Stu Cncl; 4-H; Pep Clb; Michigan St Univ; Psych.

SCHAEFER, JULIE; Archbishop Alter HS; Kettering, OH; 30/290 Hon Rl; NHS; Spn Clb; Letter Bsktbl; Purdue Univ; Phys Ed.

SCHAEFER, KENNETH; Fowler HS; Fowler, MI; 6/54 Cls Rep Soph Cls; Pres Jr Cls; Band; Boy Scts; Hon Rl; NHS; Pres Stu Cncl; Pres 4-H; IM Sprt; 4-H Awd; Lions Of Mi All St Band 78 & 79; High Schl Quiz Bowl 78; Michigan St Univ; Chem Engr.

SCHAEFER, PAULA; Reitz Memorial HS; Evansville, IN; Hon Rl; Hosp Ade; Red Cr Ade; Sch Mus; Sch Pl; 4-H; Ten; Univ Of Evansville; Hlth Occup Nrs.

SCHAEFER, SCOTT; Saint Charles Prep; Reynoldsbg, OH; Sch Mus; Sch Pl; Rptr Yrbk; Yrbk; Rptr Sch Nwsp; Drama Clb; Ohi State Univ; Communications.

SCHAEFER, SUSAN; Magnificat HS; Olmsted Falls, OH; Chrs; Hosp Ade; Sch Mus; Sch Nwsp; Key Clb; Spn Clb; Gym; John Carroll Univ; Pre Med.

SCHAEFF, MARY J; Douglas Mac Arthur HS; Saginaw, MI; Hon Rl; JA; NHS; Pep Clb; Ten; Coach Actv; Univ.

SCHAEFFER, JAMES; Clare HS; Clare, MI; 17/128 Band; Hon Rl; Lbry Ade; Ftbl; Mgrs; Opt Clb Awd; Citizens Band & Trust Schlrshp 79; Davenport Coll Of Bus; Acctg.

SCHAEFFER, JON; De Kalb HS; Waterloo, IN; 37/287 Band; Chrh Wkr; NHS; Sec FFA; Ten; IM Sprt; Purdue Univ; Agri Busns.

SCHAEFFER, JONNA; Tecumseh HS; New Carlisle, OH; 20/331 Sec Soph Cls; AFS; Am Leg Aux Girls St; Band; Cmnty Wkr; Hon Rl; Hosp Ade; Sec Jr NHS; Lbry Ade; NHS; Hanover Coll; Poli Sci.

SCHAEFFER, STANLEY; Lincoln HS; Cambridge City, IN; 2/150 Sal; Pres Band; Boy Scts; NHS; Pres Yth Flsp; Sch Nwsp; VP Key Clb; Bsktbl; Ten; Capt Trk; Purdue Univ; Engr.

SCHAEPER, JAMES D; Mt Healthy HS; Cincinnati, OH; 9/572 Hon Rl; Ger Clb; SAR Awd; Delta Epsilon Phi German Hon Assoc 78; Univ.

SCHAFER, BETH; La Ville Jr Sr HS; Bremen, IN; Band; Drl Tm; Sec NHS; Stu Cncl; 4-H; Fr Clb; Pep Clb; Sci Clb; Ten; Chrldng; Univ; Nursing.

SCHAFER, BRENDA; Chippewa Hills HS; Weidman, MI; Hon Rl; Lbry Ade; Drama Clb; Fr Clb; Delta College; Phys Ther.

SCHAFER, CAROL; St Mary Academy; Carleton, MI; Chrs; Hon Rl; NHS; Ed Yrbk; Rptr Yrbk; Yrbk; 4-H; Letter Trk; NCTE; Central Michigan Univ; Journalism.

SCHAFER, CRAIG; Beal City HS; Weidman, MI; 2/6 Pres Jr Cls; Band; Hon Rl; NHS; Sch Pl; Sci Clb; Letter Bsbl; Letter Bsktbl; Central Mic Univ; Educ.

SCHAFER, D; W Jefferson Roughriders HS; W Jefferson, OH; Am Leg Boys St; Hon Rl; NHS; Letter Bsktbl; Letter Ftbl; Letter Ten; Slippery Rock State; Biology.

SCHAFER, DAVID; Our Lady Of Providence HS; Clarksville, IN; 25/170 Boy Scts; Chrh Wkr; Hon Rl; Sch Mus; Sch Pl; Stg Crw; 4-H; Pep Clb; IM Sprt; 4-H Awd; Indiana Univ; Bus.

SCHAFER, GREG; Continental Local HS; Continental, OH; Aud/Vis; Band; Chrh Wkr; Hon Rl; Yth Flsp; 4-H; Pep Clb; Spn Clb; Bsktbl; Ten; Univ; Indus Art.

SCHAFER, KELLY; Garber HS; Essexville, MI; Chrs; Girl Scts; Hon Rl; Off Ade; Sch Mus; PPFtbl; Cit Awd; College; Business.

SCHAFER, KENNETH; Whitehall Yearling HS; Whitehall, OH; Aud/Vis; Band; Boy Scts; Chrh Wkr; Hon Rl; JA; Lbry Ade; Lit Mag; Off Ade; Orch; Most Concientious Musician 78; Perf Attndc; Ohio St Univ; Comp Engr.

SCHAFER, KIMBERLY; Wayne Memorial HS; Wayne, MI; Hon Rl; Spn Clb; Vir Farrel Beauty School; Cosom.

SCHAFER, MARY; Marian Hts Acad; Hanover, IN; 4/20 VP Frsh Cls; Cls Rep Soph Cls; Pres Jr Cls; Am Leg Aux Girls St; Chrs; Hon Rl; NHS; Sch Mus; Stu Cncl; Rptr Yrbk; Brescia Coll; Poli Sci.

SCHAFER, MICHAEL; Allen East HS; Lafayette, OH; 5/115 Chrs; Hon Rl; NHS; Yth Flsp; 4-H; Fr Clb; Letter Ftbl; Letter Trk; 4-H Awd;.

SCHAFER, REBECCA L; Winchester Comm HS; Winchester, IN; 22/154 Cls Rep Soph Cls; Cls Rep Sr Cls; Am Leg Aux Girls St; Band; Treas NHS; Sch Mus; Sch Pl; Sec Stu Cncl; Rptr Yrbk; Rdo Clb; John D Wilson Schlrshp; Hoosier Scholar; Miami Univ.

SCHAFER, ROBERTA; Eaton HS; Eaton, OH; Cls Rep Frsh Cls; Chrh Wkr; Girl Scts; Hon Rl; Off Ade; Orch; Sch Mus; Stu Cncl; Pep Clb; Spn Clb; College; Accounting.

SCHAFER, SHERYL; Lake Catholic HS; Krtlnd Hls, OH; Band; Girl Scts; JA; Sct Actv; College; Psych.

SCHAFER, SUSAN; Carl Brablec HS; Roseville, MI; Cls Rep Soph Cls; Cl Rep Jr Cls; Girl Scts; Hon Rl; NHS; Off Ade; Stu Cncl; Sci Clb; Capt Bsktbl; Chrldng; Cntrl Michigan Univ.

SCHAFER, TODD; Lumen Christi HS; Jackson, MI; 33/231 Chrh Wkr; Hon Rl; NHS; Sct Actv; Lat Clb; Crs Cntry; Trk; Natl Merit Ltr; Typing Cert 77; Hstry Cert 78; Latin Cert 78; Michigan Univ; Med.

SCHAFER, YVONNE; Pewamo Westphalia HS; Pewamo, MI; Sec Frsh Cls; Pres Soph Cls; Cl Rep Jr Cls; Hon Rl; Jr NHS; NHS; Stu Cncl; Rptr Yrbk; Letter Chrldng; College; Nursing.

SCHAFFER, ANDREA; St Pauls HS; Norwalk, OH; Band; Hosp Ade; Sch Pl; FNA; Pep Clb; Chrldng; Tmr; Providence Hosp School Of Nursing.

SCHAFFER, CHRISTINA; Au Gres Sims HS; Au Gres, MI; Sec Jr Cls; Cmp Fr Grls; Chrh Wkr; Cmnty Wkr; Hon Rl; Natl Forn Lg; 4-H; Community College; Communications.

SCHAFFER, LISA; St Paul HS; Norwalk, OH; 5/55 Am Leg Aux Girls St; Band; Hon Rl; NHS; Fr Clb; Pep Clb; Scr Kpr; Univ; Engr.

SCHAFFER, MARY; Monroeville HS; Norwalk, OH; Trs Soph Cls; Sec Sr Cls; Band; Hon Rl; Orch; 4-H; Pep Clb; Univ; Lib Art.

SCHAFFSTEIN, MARIBETH; Reitz Memorial HS; Evansville, IN; Pres Frsh Cls; Pres Soph Cls; Pres Sr Cls; Hon Rl; Sec Frsh Cls; NHS; Stu Cncl; IM Sprt; C of C Awd; Xavier Univ; Dental Hygn.

SCHAFFTER, LISA; Edon HS; Edon, OH; 3/77 Sec Frsh Cls; Band; Chrs; Hon Rl; Sch Mus; Sch Pl; Stg Crw; Spn Clb; Am Leg Awd; Adrian Coll; Computer Sci.

SCHAFFTER, STEVEN; Edon HS; Edon, OH; Band; Chrs; Chrh Wkr; Cmnty Wkr; Hon Rl; Sch Mus; Stg Crw; IM Sprt; Vocational School.

SCHAIBLE, JOAN; Manchester Community HS; Manchester, MI; 17/109 Am Leg Aux Girls St; Chrs; Chrh Wkr; Hon Rl; Lbry Ade; Sec NHS; Sch Mus; Sch Pl; Yth Flsp; Opt Clb Awd; Mich State; Nursing.

SCHAIK, CAROLYN; Oakwood HS; Dayton, OH; Chrs; Drl Tm; Hon Rl; Stg Crw; VP Drama Clb; Letter Bsktbl; College; Journalism.

SCHALK, CATHERINE; Hopewell Loudon HS; New Riegel, OH; Sec Sr Cls; Band; Chrh Wkr; Hon Rl; JA; Off Ade; Red Cr Ade; Sch Mus; Yrbk; FHA; 1 Of The Top 5 Salesprsn In Tiffin J A 79; FHA Natl Conv Delegate WA Dc 79; Red Cross Ldrshp Center 78; Coll; Elem Ed.

SCHALK, GREGORY H; Euclid Sr HS; Euclid, OH; 125/800 Aud/Vis; Quill & Scroll; Sprt Ed Sch Nwsp; Rptr Sch Nwsp; Letter Bsktbl; Letter Crs Cntry; Letter Trk; Mgrs; Am Leg Awd; College; Aeronautics.

SCHALK, PATRICIA; Hopewell Loudon HS; New Riegel, OH; 4/94 Hon Rl; JA; Sec NHS; Red Cr Ade; Sch Pl; Ed Yrbk; Sec FHA; Capt Pom Pon; Cit Awd; JA Awd; Schls Century 3 Leadrshp Recipient 79; Sec Of Yr Tiffin Finalist Nw Oh J A 79; Loudon Farm Wives Clb Awd 79; Univ; Cmnctns.

SCHALL, JENIFER; Bay HS; Bay Vill, OH; 12/380 Band; Boy Scts; Girl Scts; Hon Rl; NHS; Orch; Stg Crw; Drama Clb; Univ; Languages.

SCHALM, MARTY; Farmington HS; Farmington Hls, MI; Band; Boy Scts; Hon Rl; Natl Forn Lg; Sch Pl; Rptr Yrbk; Drama Clb; Ger Clb; Univ; Layout Magazines.

SCHALTENBRAND, ELIZABETH; New Albany HS; New Albany, IN; 27/512 Chrs; Chrh Wkr; Hon

Rl; Hosp Ade; NHS; Off Ade; Treas Orch; Pol Wkr; Sch Mus; Sch Pl; Indiana Univ S E.

SCHAMADAN, AMY; Malabar Sr HS; Mansfield, OH; 5/230 Trs Soph Cls; Trs Jr Cls; Cls Rep Sr Cls; Am Leg Aux Girls St; Band; Chrh Wkr; Hon Rl; Treas NHS; Stu Cncl; Rptr Sch Nwsp; Michigan St Univ; Journalism.

SCHAN, STEVE; Whitehall Yearling HS; Columbus, OH; Ohio State; Zoology.

SCHANTZ, PETER; Orrville HS; Orrville, OH; Chrs; FCA; Hon Rl; JA; Sch Mus; Sch Pl; Yth Flsp; Rptr Yrbk; College; Bus Admin.

SCHANTZ, RANDY; Thornapple Kellogg HS; M iddleville, MI; 7/156 Hon Rl; Lbry Ade; Pol Wkr; Sch Mus; Rptr Sch Nwsp; 4-H; Mic State Univ.

SCHANTZ, ROBERT; Allen East HS; Lima, OH; 3/120 VP Frsh Cls; VP Soph Cls; Band; Chrh Wkr; Hon Rl; Sch Pl; Pres Yth Flsp; VP Fr Clb; Sec FFA; Letter Bsbl; FFA Schlrshp Awd; FFA Schlrshp Awd; College; Medicine.

SCHARF, KATHLEEN; Villa Angela Acad; Cleveland, OH; Hon Rl; Sch Mus; GAA; Ohi State; Architectural Engr.

SCHARFENBERGER, JODEE; Indiana Schl For The Deaf; Indianapolis, IN; 1/49 Pres Frsh Cls; Sec Soph Cls; VP Jr Cls; VP Sr Cls; Am Leg Aux Girls St; Hon Rl; JA; Stu Cncl; Ed Yrbk; Ed Sch Nwsp; Gallaudet Coll; English.

SCHARICH, BETH; Unionville Sebewaing HS; Unionville, MI; 12/113 Sec Jr Cls; Hon Rl; Jr NHS; Lbry Ade; NHS; Stu Cncl; Yth Flsp; FHA; Lat Clb; Letter Bsbl; Mc Connell Schl; Travel Bus.

SCHARICH, JOANNE; Midland HS; Midland, MI; Girl Scts; Hon Rl; Off Ade; Yth Flsp; College.

SCHARICH, NANCY; Arthur Hill HS; Saginaw, MI; Stu Cncl; Yrbk; Pep Clb; Trk; Chrldng; Pom Pon; Delta Coll; Sci.

SCHARIO, KRISTEN; Hoover HS; North Canton, OH; Girl Scts; Hon Rl; Hosp Ade; NHS; Off Ade; Sci Clb; Spn Clb; Univ; Horticulture.

SCHARNITZKE, LYDIA; Garden City Sr HS East; Garden City, MI; 168/476 Chrs; Chrh Wkr; Sch Mus; Sch Pl; Yth Flsp; Rptr Sch Nwsp; Drama Clb; 4-H; Ger Clb; Pep Clb; Mi Readng Assoc Youth Author Awd 78; For Lang Trans Achvmnt 79; Var Mgr Awd In Vllybl 77 79; Concordia Lutheran Coll; German.

SCHAU, PAMELA; Shadyside HS; Shadyside, OH; Band; Chrs; Hon Rl; Sch Pl; Y-Teens; Spn Clb; West Liberty St Coll; Educ.

SCHAUB, RICHARD; Stebbins HS; Dayton, OH; Band; Chrh Wkr; Cmnty Wkr; MMM; Orch; Sch Pl; Stg Crw; Drama Clb; Ohio St Univ; Comp Engr.

SCHAUB, SANDRA L; Springfield Sr HS; Holland, OH; Sec Frsh Cls; Trs Frsh Cls; Cls Rep Soph Cls; Cl Rep Jr Cls; Cls Rep Sr Cls; Band; Chrs; Chrh Wkr; Hon Rl; JA; Art Awd; MVP Softball; Perfect Attendance; Michael J Owens Tech Coll; Archt.

SCHAUB, SHEILA; Walter E Stebbins HS; Dayton, OH; 1/420 Cls Rep Frsh Cls; Sec Soph Cls; Sec Jr Cls; Sec Sr Cls; Band; Chrh Wkr; Hon Rl; Red Cr Ade; Letter Chrldng; Bus Schl; Banking.

SCHAUDER, CRAIG; Lee M Thurston HS; Plymouth, MI; Pres Frsh Cls; Pres Soph Cls; Pres Jr Cls; Am Leg Boys St; Hon Rl; NHS; Spn Clb; Letter Bsbl; Capt Ftbl; Capt Wrstlng; Regnl Wrstlng Champ 78; Outstndng Jr 78; Outstndng Athlt 79; Albion Coll; Med.

SCHAUS, PAM; Unionville Sebewaing HS; Sebewain g, MI; Chrh Wkr; Hon Rl; Yth Flsp; 4-H; Letter Bsktbl; Letter Trk; 4-H Awd; College; Lab Technician Or Pilot.

SCHAUS, PAMELA; Unionville Sebewaing HS; Sebewaing, MI; Chrh Wkr; Yth Flsp; 4-H; Letter Bsktbl; Letter Trk; 4-H Awd; Univ; Lab Tech.

SCHAUS, TAMA; Jasper HS; Jasper, IN; 12/300 Cls Rep Frsh Cls; Cl Rep Jr Cls; Chrh Wkr; Hon Rl; Off Ade; Sch Pl; Stu Cncl; Drama Clb; Lat Clb; Pep Clb; Univ; Acctg.

SCHEAFNOCKER, LINDA; Benjamin Bosse HS; Evansville, IN; 46/329 Trs Frsh Cls; Cl Rep Jr Cls; Cls Rep Sr Cls; Band; Quill & Scroll; Stu Cncl; Sch Nwsp; Pep Clb; Ind State Univ; Physical Therapist.

SCHEBLO, DIANE; Marysville HS; Marysville, OH; Chrs; Girl Scts; Off Ade; 4-H; Fr Clb; FHA; Trk; Clark Tech Coll.

SCHEBOR, KARIN; Clarkston Sr HS; Clarkston, MI; Hon Rl; Spn Clb; Trk; Chrldng; IM Sprt; PPFtbl; Michigan St Univ; Hotel Mgmt.

SCHECK, RICHARD W; Triway HS; Shreve, OH; 27/165 Band; Chrs; Hon Rl; Sch Mus; Sch Pl; Stg Crw; Stu Cncl; Yrbk; Ed Sch Nwsp; Drama Clb; Natl Schlstc Art Awd; Reg Schlstc Art & Photog Awds; Photog Published On Cover Of Natl Art Magazine; Univ; Art.

SCHECTER, MARTIN; Bexley HS; Bexley, OH; Cls Rep Soph Cls; Trs Jr Cls; Band; Boy Scts; Hon Rl; NHS; Orch; Quill & Scroll; Sch Mus; Sch Pl; Cum Laude Soc 78; Superior Rating Class A & B At Oh Music Educ Assoc St Solo & Ensemble Contest 77 78 & 79; Univ; Pre Med.

SCHEEL, CONNIE; Monroeville HS; Monroeville, OH; Cls Rep Frsh Cls; Cls Rep Soph Cls; Sec Jr Cls; Hon Rl; NHS; Sch Pl; Yrbk; Pep Clb; Bsbl; Chrldng;.

SCHEEL, LINDA; Stanton HS; Stratton, OH; 7/71 Band; Chrs; Hon Rl; NHS; Yrbk; Treas Fr Clb; IM Sprt; Ohio St Univ; Dent.

SCHEELE, MARLENE; East Detroit HS; E Detroit, MI; Hon Rl; Business School; Bus.

SCHEER, DENISE; River Valley HS; Three Oaks, MI; Sec Frsh Cls; Sec Soph Cls; Trs Jr Cls; Sec Sr Cls; Band; Hon Rl; Sch Pl; Drama Clb; Ger Clb; Chrldng; Girls Varsity Sftbl Varsity Letter; Coll; Nursing.

SCHEERHORN, JEFFREY; Grandville HS; Grandville, MI; Hon Rl; NHS; Rptr Sch Nwsp; Letter Ftbl; Capt Trk; IM Sprt; PPFtbl; Natl Merit Ltr; Grand Rapids Jr Coll; Optometry.

SCHEESSELE, MIKE; South Spencer HS; Rockport, IN; 5/147 Chrh Wkr; Hon Rl; NHS; Ger Clb; Letter Crs Cntry; Letter Trk; Coach Actv; IM Sprt; Kiwan Awd; Fortune Underhill Academic Schlrshp 78; Purdue Univ; Comp Sci.

SCHEETZ, DAVID; Washington HS; Massillon, OH; Aud/Vis; Chrs; Hon Rl; Off Ade; Sch Mus; Stg Crw; Bsktbl; Voc Schl; Tele Cmnctns.

SCHEETZ, MINDY; Revere HS; Akron, OH; 66/280 Cls Rep Frsh Cls; Cls Rep Soph Cls; Hon Rl; Off Ade; OEA; Scr Kpr;.

SCHEFFLER, SCOTT; Northview HS; Grand Rapids, MI; Cls Rep Sr Cls; Yrbk; Pep Clb; Letter Crs Cntry; Ftbl; Capt Socr; Letter Wrstlng; Coach Actv; IM Sprt; Scr Kpr; Grand Rapids Jr Coll; Bus.

SCHEFLOW, ELIZABETH; Avonlake HS; Avon Lake, OH; Cl Rep Jr Cls; Drm Mjrt; Hon Rl; Off Ade; Sch Pl; Sct Actv; Stu Cncl; Pep Clb; Letter Chrldng; Twrlr; College; Psych.

SCHEIBER, DONA M; Whitko HS; Columbia City, IN; Hon Rl; 4-H; Pep Clb; Mat Maids; Voc Schl; Elem Ed.

SCHEIBER, JODI A; Huntington Catholic HS; Huntington, IN; 10/40 VP Jr Cls; Girl Scts; Hosp Ade; Sch Pl; Stg Crw; Ed Yrbk; Rptr Yrbk; Rptr Sch Nwsp; Trk; Chrldng; College; Special Ed.

SCHEICH, JANET; Dominican HS; Roseville, MI; Chrs; Chrh Wkr; Cmnty Wkr; Girl Scts; Hon Rl; NHS; Sch Mus; Sch Pl; College.

SCHEID, KATHY; Frankfort HS; Frankfort, IN; 6/270 Pres Frsh Cls; VP Jr Cls; VP Sr Cls; Band; NHS; Sch Mus; Stu Cncl; Swmmng; Am Leg Awd; Pres Awd; Indiana Univ; Bus.

SCHEIDLER, BETH; Lumen Cordium HS; Sagamore Hills, OH; 30/106 Chrs; Hon Rl; Sch Mus; Sprt Ed Yrbk; Yrbk; Sch Nwsp; Spn Clb; Sec GAA; Mgrs; Univ; Film Proc.

SCHEIDLER, MARY A; Mc Nicholas HS; Cincinnati, OH; 31/232 Sec Frsh Cls; Trs Soph Cls; Cl Rep Jr Cls; VP Sr Cls; Am Leg Aux Girls St; Hon Rl; Lit Mag; NHS; Stu Cncl; Sch Nwsp; Univ Of Cincinnati; Nursing.

SCHEINBERG, JEFF; Beachwood HS; Beachwood, OH; Boy Scts; Chrs; Hon Rl; Sch Mus; Rptr Sch Nwsp; Ftbl; Ten; Trk; Wrstlng; Spanish Awd 78; Art Awd 77; Newspaper Awd 76; Archt Schl; Archt.

SCHEINER, JACQUELINE; Bishop Luers HS; Woodburn, IN; 45/186 Band; Hon Rl; Off Ade; Sec 4-H; Coach Actv; IM Sprt; 4-H Awd; Evansville Univ; Music Ther.

SCHEIRER _II, JACK; Tecumseh HS; Tecumseh, MI; 13/248 Cls Rep Sr Cls; Band; Boy Scts; Hon Rl; NHS; Michigan St Univ; Comp Sci.

SCHELL, FRANK; Sandusky HS; Sandusky, MI; Cls Rep Frsh Cls; Cls Rep Soph Cls; Cl Rep Jr Cls; Cls Rep Sr Cls; Chrh Wkr; Debate Tm; FCA; Hon Rl; NHS; Sch Mus; St Debate; St Forensic; Ctznshp Seminar Awd By Farm Bureau; Michigan St Univ.

SCHELL, GEORGE; Harrison HS; Harrison, MI; Boy Scts; Hon Rl; Sch Pl; Rptr Yrbk; Rptr Sch Nwsp; College; Law Enforcement.

SCHELL, KATHLEEN; Ursuline HS; Youngstown, OH; Fr Clb; Univ; Jrnlsm.

SCHELL, KYLE; Newark Catholic HS; Newark, OH; Sec Frsh Cls; Cl Rep Jr Cls; Am Leg Aux Girls St; Chrs; Chrh Wkr; Cmnty Wkr; Hon Rl; Fr Clb; Chrldng; GAA; Rep To Camp Enterprs Kenyon Coll 79; N Cntrl Assn Evaluating Team 78; Capitol Univ; Law.

SCHELL, MICHAEL; Pike HS; Indpls, IN; 27/280 Debate Tm; Hon Rl; Lit Mag; NHS; Lat Clb; Mth Clb; Crs Cntry; Letter Gym; Socr; Bradley Univ; Med Tech.

SCHELL, PATRICK; Bucyrus HS; Bucyrus, OH; Cls Rep Frsh Cls; VP Jr Cls; Am Leg Boys St; Band; Hon Rl; NHS; Orch; Sch Mus; Sch Pl; Drama Clb; Univ.

SCHELL, RANDY M; Cedar Lake Academy; Hope, MI; 3/85 Cls Rep Frsh Cls; Cls Rep Soph Cls; Pres Jr Cls; Band; Chrs; Chrh Wkr; Debate Tm; Hon Rl; NHS; Off Ade; Andrews Univ; Med.

SCHELL, SANDRA; New Albany Sr HS; New Albany, IN; 113/535 Hon Rl; Pres JA; Sch Pl; Sct Actv; Stg Crw; Drama Clb; Ger Clb; Pep Clb; German Club 76; Drama Club 76; Indiana Univ; RN.

SCHELLBACHER, EMIL; Cabrini HS; Allen Pk, MI; 30/165 Cl Rep Jr Cls; Boy Scts; Letter Hon Rl; Quill & Scroll; Sch Pl; Stg Crw; Stu Cncl; Yrbk; Ed Sch Nwsp; Rptr Sch Nwsp; Univ; Pre Med.

SCHELLHASE, JOAN; Troy HS; Troy, MI; 16/300 Band; Chrh Wkr; NHS; Off Ade; Orch; Sch Pl; Stg Crw; Drama Clb; Wayne State; Phys Ther.

SCHELLIE, AVA; Posen Consolidated HS; Posen, MI; Band; Hon Rl; Lbry Ade; Sch Mus; Rptr Yrbk; Rptr Sch Nwsp; FHA; Gym; Ten; Trk; Coll; Chem.

SCHELLIN, STEVEN J; Xenia HS; Xenia, OH; 48/548 VP Sr Cls; Am Leg Boys St; Chrs; Pres Chrh Wkr; Hon Rl; Sch Mus; Stg Crw; Bsktbl; Letter Crs Cntry; Letter Ten; Earlham Coll; Ministry.

SCHEMAN, SUZANNA; Parma HS; Parma, OH; 64/782 Cls Rep Frsh Cls; Cls Rep Soph Cls; Cl Rep Jr Cls; Band; Cmnty Wkr; Hon Rl; Lbry Ade; Rptr Sch Nwsp; Ger Clb; Pep Clb; Data Processing.

SCHEMBER, RENEE; Cass City HS; Cass City, MI; Band; Chrs; Chrh Wkr; Jr NHS; NHS; Sch Mus; Yth Flsp; Spring Arbor College; Psych.

SCHEMBER, STEPHANIE; Elkton Pigeon Bay Port HS; Pigeon, MI; 10/130 Chrh Wkr; Debate Tm; Hon Rl; NHS; Off Ade; Sch Nwsp; 4-H; Chrldng; Eng 1 Awd 75; Typing 1 Awd 77; Bio 2 Awd 78; Bus Schlrshp 78; Baker Jr Coll Of Bus; Exec Sec.

SCHEMINE, STEVEN; Rutherford B Hayes HS; Delaware, OH; Am Leg Boys St; Chrs; Chrh Wkr; ROTC; Ftbl; Jr ROTC Dep Cmmndr 80; Reserve Off Assoc Medal 79; Univ; Military Pilot.

SCHEMPF, KEVIN; Interlochen Arts Academy; Mt Pleasant, MI; Band; Chrs; Hon Rl; Orch; Sch Mus; Rptr Sch Nwsp; Lat Clb; Eastman Schl Of Music; Pro Musician.

SCHENCK, BARBARA; Canfield HS; Canfield, OH; Band; Debate Tm; Hon Rl; JA; Y-Teens; Fr Clb; Key Clb; Gym; Trk; PPFtbl; Ashland Coll; Bus Admin.

SCHENCK, DENISE; Deckerville HS; Deckerville, MI; Girl Scts; Hon Rl; Stg Crw; GAA;.

SCHENCK, JENNIFER; Deer Park HS; Cincinnati, OH; Trs Soph Cls; Band; Capt Drl Tm; Hon Rl; NHS; Sch Pl; Letter Bsbl; Letter Bsktbl; Letter Trk; Scr Kpr; Naval Acad.

SCHENDEL, MARTIN; Plymouth Canton HS; Plymouth, MI; 127/430 Pres Sr Cls; Am Leg Boys St; Band; Hon Rl; Sch Mus; Drama Clb; Tmr; Am Leg Awd; Cit Awd; Kiwan Awd; Michigan Tech Univ; Engr.

SCHENDEN, ANNE; Our Lady Of Mercy HS; Farmington Hls, MI; Chrs; Cmnty Wkr; NHS; Stg Crw; Sec Pep Clb; College; Health.

SCHENK, KAREN; Reitz Memorial HS; Evansville, IN; 20/225 Sec Soph Cls; Drl Tm; Hon Rl; Hosp Ade; NHS; Sch Mus; Sch Pl; Stu Cncl; Rptr Sch Nwsp; Ger Clb; Butler Univ; Pre Med.

SCHENK, MICHAEL; Fenton Sr HS; Fenton, MI; 2/285 Cl Rep Jr Cls; Am Leg Boys St; Hon Rl; NHS; Stu Cncl; Letter Ftbl; Ten; IM Sprt; Ferris St Coll; Pre Optometry.

SCHENK, TOM; Indian Hill HS; Cincinnati, OH; Letter Socr; Univ; Med.

SCHENKEL, CINDY; William Mason HS; Mason, OH; 16/193 Cls Rep Frsh Cls; Cls Rep Soph Cls; Cl Rep Jr Cls; Cls Rep Sr Cls; Am Leg Aux Girls St; NHS; Pres Stu Cncl; 4-H; Chrldng; IM Sprt; Univ Of Houston; Poli Sci.

SCHENKEL, SUSAN; Northfield HS; Andrews, IN; 1/107 Band; Chrh Wkr; Hon Rl; NHS; Treas Yth Flsp; Rptr Yrbk; Sec 4-H; Pep Clb; Spn Clb; 4-H Awd; College; Math.

SCHENKS, PAMELA; Wood Memorial HS; Oakland City, IN; VP Sr Cls; Band; Chrs; Chrh Wkr; Off Ade; Orch; Rptr Sch Nwsp; FHA; Pep Clb; PPFtbl; ISUE; Dent Asst.

SCHEPIS, A; Solon HS; Solon, OH; Drl Tm; Hon Rl; Rptr Sch Nwsp; Pep Clb; PPFtbl; College; Journalist.

SCHEPPS, DONNA; Beachwood HS; Beachwood, OH; Chrh Wkr; Cmnty Wkr; Lit Mag; Ohio State Univ; Scientific Research.

SCHER, CYNTHIA; Huntington Catholic HS; Huntington, IN; 9/33 Trs Soph Cls; Chrh Wkr; Hon Rl; NHS; Pres Stu Cncl; Yrbk; FNA; Letter Trk; Opt Clb Awd; College; Nursing.

SCHER, CYNTHIA; Huntington North HS; Huntington, IN; 98/614 Cmp Fr Grls; Chrs; Chrh Wkr; Pol Wkr; Red Cr Ade; Stg Crw; Fr Clb; Pep Clb; Swmmng; Tmr; Purdue Univ; Marketing.

SCHERACH, SUSAN; Lorain Catholic HS; Lorain, OH; Band; Girl Scts; Hon Rl; Sct Actv; Pep Clb; Trk; Chrldng; Pom Pon; Coll.

SCHERFNER, CARL; Whittemore Prescott HS; Whittemore, MI; 23/120 Band; Boy Scts; Drm Mjrt; Hon Rl; Rptr Yrbk; Boys Clb Am; 4-H; College; Optometry.

SCHERGER, M; Calvert HS; Tiffin, OH; Band; Girl Scts; Hon Rl; 4-H; Cit Awd; Barbizon Sch Of Modeling.

SCHERGER, MARTHA; Calvert HS; Tiffin, OH; Band; Girl Scts; Hon Rl; Cit Awd; Barbizon School Of Modeling.

SCHERLEY, EDWIN; Tiffin Calvert HS; Republic, OH; Sch Pl; Stg Crw; Wrstlng; Hocking Tech Coll; Recreation.

SCHERMERHORN, SUZI; East Noble HS; Wawaka, IN; 19/258 Drl Tm; Hon Rl; Pom Pon; Univ; Comp Analysis.

SCHERZINGER, MICHAEL; Garfield HS; Hamilton, OH; 19/369 Chrh Wkr; Cmnty Wkr; NHS; Letter Crs Cntry; Letter Trk; IM Sprt; Campbellsville Univ; Acctg.

SCHETTERER, MIKE; Turpin HS; Cincinnati, OH; Orch; Sch Mus; Univ Of Cincinnati.

SCHEU, JANET; John Adams HS; South Bend, IN; 3/400 Cls Rep Frsh Cls; Trs Soph Cls; Cl Rep Jr Cls; Sec Sr Cls; Cmp Fr Grls; Hon Rl; NHS; 4-H; DAR Awd; Ball St Univ; Bus Admin.

SCHEUBER, MICHELE A; Huntington Catholic HS; Modesto, CA; Pres Jr Cls; Val; Hon Rl; NHS; Sch Pl; Rptr Yrbk; Sec 4-H; Letter Trk; IM Sprt; Modesto Junior College; Spec Ed.

SCHEUER, DAVID; Coloma HS; Coloma, MI; Band; Hon Rl; NHS; Ger Clb; Letter Bsbl; Coll; Comp Tech.

SCHEUERMAN, DANIEL; Adrian HS; Adrian, MI; 30/386 Chrh Wkr; Hon Rl; NHS; Sci Clb; Bsbl; Glf; IM Sprt; Natl Merit Ltr; Cntrl Michigan Univ.

SCHEUMANN, D; Heritage HS; Hoagland, IN; 3/172 Band; Chrs; Chrh Wkr; Cmnty Wkr; FCA; Hon Rl; Sch Mus; Sch Pl; Sec Stu Cncl; Yth Flsp; Owa State Univ; Forestry.

SCHEURICH, DENISE; Rensselaer Central HS; Rensselaer, IN; 42/162 Hon Rl; IM Sprt; Indiana State Univ; Pre Med.

SCHICK, JOHN; Marcellus HS; Vandalia, MI; 5/70 Cls Rep Frsh Cls; VP Soph Cls; Cls Rep Soph Cls; VP Jr Cls; Cl Rep Jr Cls; Pres Sr Cls; Cls Rep Sr Cls; Band; NHS; Stu Cncl; Grand Vly St Univ.

SCHICK, TOM; Romulus HS; Romulus, MI; 61/300 Hon Rl; NHS; Sch Pl; Stg Crw; Drama Clb; Bsbl; Bsktbl; Crs Cntry; Henry Ford C C.

SCHIEFER, DOUGLAS; Olentangy HS; Powell, OH; Cmnty Wkr; Fr Clb; Bsktbl; Ohio St Univ; Acctg.

SCHIEFER, STEVEN; Ridgedale HS; Marion, OH; 14/80 Band; Chrs; Hon Rl; Yth Flsp; Leo Clb; IM Sprt; 4-H Awd;.

SCHIEMANN, LONNIE; Gladwin HS; Gladwin, MI; 6/147 Band; Chrh Wkr; NHS; Pres Yth Flsp; 4-H; FFA; Lat Clb; Letter Bsktbl; Lion Awd; Hnrble Mention All Conf Vlybl; Bd Of Control Schlrshp; Vlybl Letter Winner; Lake Superior St Coll; Nursing.

SCHIEVE, MARYANN; St Augustine Acad; Brooklyn, OH; Hon Rl; Rptr Yrbk; Yrbk; Rptr Sch Nwsp; Pres Of Camera Clb; VP Of Camera Clb; Kent St Univ; Comm Arts.

SCHIFER, TIM; Wynford HS; Bucyrus, OH; 12/140 Pres Soph Cls; VP Jr Cls; Pres Sr Cls; Chrs; NHS; Key Clb; Letter Bsktbl; Letter Ftbl; Letter Trk; Am Leg Awd; College; Law.

SCHIFF, BELINDA; Lexington HS; Mansfield, OH; Drl Tm; Girl Scts; Off Ade; Stu Cncl; Y-Teens; Rptr Yrbk; Fr Clb; Twrlr; Ohio State Branch; Elem Educ.

SCHIFF, LEORA; George Washington HS; Charleston, WV; Cmnty Wkr; Debate Tm; Girl Scts; Hon Rl; Jr NHS; Mod UN; Orch; PAVAS; Pol Wkr; Rptr Sch Nwsp; Harvard Univ; Economics.

SCHIKNER, JEFFREY; West Carrollton Sr HS; Dayton, OH; 6/367 Band; Boy Scts; Jr NHS; NHS; Sct Actv; Yth Flsp; Opt Clb Awd; Virginia Polytech Inst; Math.

SCHILD, LAURA; Jenison Public HS; Jenison, MI; 49/339 Chrs; Chrh Wkr; Hon Rl; Natl Merit Ltr; Grand Rapids Baptist College; Psych.

SCHILDER, E; Grandview HS; Columbus, OH; Chrs; Hon Rl; PAVAS; Sch Mus; Sch Pl; Stg Crw; Rptr Sch Nwsp; Cols College Of Art & Design; Graph.

SCHILDHOUSE, MELISSA; Eastmoor HS; Columbus, OH; 25/300 Cls Rep Sr Cls; Chrs; Hon Rl; NHS; PAVAS; Sch Mus; Sch Pl; Yrbk; Drama Clb; Spn Clb; Vassar Univ; Soc Sci.

SCHILDMEIER, MARK; Hamilton Heights HS; Arcadia, IN; 10/131 Am Leg Boys St; Hon Rl; Jr NHS; Fr Clb; Sci Clb; Bsktbl; Letter Crs Cntry; Letter Trk; Letter Mens Club; Ball St Univ; Archt.

SCHILE, THOMAS; Archbishop Moeller HS; Cincinnati, OH; Hon Rl; IM Sprt; Oh Instructnl Grant; Xavier Univ; Info Systems.

SCHILL, DAVID; Crothersville Cmnty HS; Crothersville, IN; 5/69 VP Sr Cls; Am Leg Boys St; Chrs; Chrh Wkr; Hon Rl; NHS; Sch Mus; Yth Flsp; 4-H; FFA; Purdue Univ; Elec Tech.

SCHILL, DAVID; Crothersville Comm HS; Crothersville, IN; 5/69 VP Sr Cls; Am Leg Boys St; Chrs; Chrh Wkr; Hon Rl; NHS; Sch Mus; Yth Flsp; 4-H; Pres FFA; Purdue; Elec Tech.

SCHILLEMAN, JANA; Whitehall HS; Whitehall, MI; Trs Soph Cls; Trs Jr Cls; Trs Sr Cls; Band; Girl Scts; Hon Rl; Off Ade; Stg Crw; Letter Bsktbl; Letter Trk;.

SCHILLEMAN, LEESA; Montague HS; Montague, MI; 4/124 Trs Sr Cls; Am Leg Aux Girls St; Hon Rl; NHS; Letter Bsktbl; Letter Trk; Capt Chrldng; PPFtbl; Cit Awd; Hope Coll; Math.

SCHILLER, SUSAN; Tecumseh HS; Tecumseh, MI; 10/235 Band; Girl Scts; Hon Rl; 4-H; Spn Clb; 4-H Awd; Univ Of Toledo; Eng.

SCHILLING, DEANNA; Du Pont HS; Cedar Grv, WV; Cls Rep Frsh Cls; Cl Rep Jr Cls; Band; Drm Mjrt; Girl Scts; Hon Rl; Jr NHS; Lbry Ade; Sch Pl; Stu Cncl; Univ Of Florida; Psych.

SCHILLING, GLORIA J; Greenbrier E HS; Frankford, WV; Cls Rep Sr Cls; Girl Scts; Hon Rl; Off Ade; Stu Cncl; FBLA; Letter Trk; GAA; IM Sprt; Schl Math Tm Reg Math Tm Mbr; Coll; Comp Sci.

SCHILLING, JACQUELINE; Northwest HS; Canal Fulton, OH; 24/176 Band; Hon Rl; Jr NHS; NHS; Off Ade; Pres FTA; Lat Clb; Schlrshp; Wayne College; Education Major.

SCHILLING, JANE; Fort Frye HS; Beverly, OH; Hon Rl; NHS; Yrbk; Sch Nwsp; 4-H; FBLA; FTA; Letter Chrldng; 4-H Awd; Bus Schl.

SCHILLING, LISA; Princeton HS; Cincinnati, OH; 82/630 Band; Chrh Wkr; Hon Rl; NHS; Orch; Sch Mus; Rus Clb; Letter Bsktbl; Thespian Soc; Cincinnati Yth Symphony Orchestra Bassoon; Ohio St Univ; Busns Admin.

SCHILLING, NANCY; Hartford Public HS; Hartford, MI; Hon Rl; Yrbk; Pres 4-H; Treas FFA; Bsktbl; Ohi Diesel Tech; Diesel Mech.

SCHILLING, ROBERT; Northwest HS; Clinton, OH; Bsbl; Ftbl; Wrstlng; IM Sprt; Univ; Agri.

SCHILLING, SHERYL L; Westfall HS; Orient, OH; Cls Rep Soph Cls; Band; Girl Scts; Stu Cncl; 4-H; Treas Key Clb; Spn Clb; Bsktbl; 4-H Awd; Univ; Comp Progr.

SCHILLMAN, LAUREY; Davison Sr HS; Davison, MI; 23/455 Cl Rep Jr Cls; Am Leg Aux Girls St; Chrs; Chrh Wkr; Hon Rl; NHS; Orch; Sch Mus; Yth Flsp; OEA; Schlrshp To Interlochen All St Music Camp; Westminster Choir Coll Vocal Camp Schlrshp; Adrian Coll Schlrshp; Adrian Coll; Med.

SCHILLNE, SHERI; St Joseph HS; South Bend, IN; Cmnty Wkr; Hon Rl; Hosp Ade; Red Cr Ade; 4-H; Pep Clb; DAR Awd; St Marys Coll; Secondary Ed.

SCHILLO, ANGEL; Pontiac Ctrl HS; Pontiac, MI; Chrs; Chrh Wkr; Hon Rl; Hosp Ade; Sch Pl; Swmmng; Tmr; Univ; Dentistry.

SCHILTGES, CATHERINE; Bishop Foley HS; Warren, MI; Cmnty Wkr; Girl Scts; Letter Hon Rl; Jr NHS; NHS; Pol Wkr; Stg Crw; Eng Clb; Mth Clb; Rdo Clb; 1st Pl Spelling Bee Champ Fro Vacariate 74; 3rd Pl In Detroit News Spelling Bee Contest 76; Univ; Mech Draftsman.

SCHILTGES, DONNA; Bishop Foley HS; Warren, MI; 19/193 Hon Rl; PPFtbl; Mercy College; Nursing.

SCHIMMEL, CINDRA; Elwood Community HS; Elwood, IN; 30/236 Hon Rl; Sch Pl; Drama Clb; Lat Clb; Cit Awd; Indiana Univ; Dentist.

SCHIMMEL, JEFF; Benjamin Bosse HS; Evansville, IN; 15/319 Hon Rl; NHS; Quill & Scroll; Sprt Ed Yrbk; Sprt Ed Sch Nwsp; Pep Clb; Letter Ftbl; Western Ken Univ; Comp Sci.

SCHIMMEL, KEITH A; Franklin Central HS; Indianapolis, IN; 1/246 NHS; Sch Pl; Rdo Clb; Sci Clb; Gov Hon Prg Awd; JETS Awd; Natl Merit SF; Pres Awd; Rotary Awd; Purdue Univ; Chem Engr.

SCHIMMOELLER, ANN; Jennings HS; Ft Jennings, OH; 5/30 Band; Chrs; Hon Rl; Orch; Sch Mus; Sch Pl; Fr Clb; Capt Chrldng; Capt Twrlr; Lima Tech Coll; Radiologic Tech.

SCHINDEL, DIANNE; Jackson Ctr HS; Maplewood, OH; Trs Frsh Cls; Trs Soph Cls; Sec Jr Cls; Band; Chrs; Chrh Wkr; Drm Mjrt; Hon Rl; Sch Pl; Stg Crw; Soc Dstngshd Amer HS Stu; St Dist Sci Fairs; Wright St Univ; Nursing.

SCHINDERLE, MARY JO; Kingsford HS; Kingsford, MI; Hon Rl; Jr NHS; Stu Cncl; Sec 4-H; Keyettes; Gym; Letter Trk; Capt Chrldng; Cit Awd; Univ; Med.

SCHINDLER, JAMES R; Dayton Christian HS; Dayton, OH; Cl Rep Jr Cls; Cls Rep Sr Cls; Am Leg Boys St; Hon Rl; Sch Mus; Pres Stu Cncl; Yth Flsp; Drama Clb; IM Sprt; Am Leg Awd; Taylor Univ; Law.

SCHINDLER, JANICE; Henry Ford II HS; Utica, MI; 7/481 Hon Rl; Hosp Ade; JA; NHS; Ger Clb; Michigan St Univ; RN.

SCHINDLER, LISA; Churchill HS; Livonia, MI; Hon Rl; JA; Sch Pl; Ed Sch Nwsp; College; Business.

SCHINDLER, SCOTT; Celina Sr HS; Celina, OH; Chrs; Chrh Wkr; Hon Rl; NHS; Sch Mus; Sch Pl; Yth Flsp; Rptr Yrbk; Ger Clb; Solo & Ensemble Comp Piano Solo 78 & 79; Univ; Music Educ.

SCHINDLER, TONI; Chaminade Julienne HS; Dayton, OH; Cls Rep Frsh Cls; Pres Soph Cls; Chrs; Cmnty Wkr; FCA; JA; Pol Wkr; Sch Mus; Pres Stu Cncl; Rptr Yrbk;.

SCHIPPER, BRIAN; Holland Christian HS; Holland, MI; Aud/Vis; Mod UN; Orch; Stg Crw; Yrbk; Ger Clb; Natl Merit Ltr; College; Computer Eng.

SCHIPPER, KAREN; Chesaning Union HS; Chesaning, MI; Hon Rl; NHS; Rptr Yrbk; Pep Clb; Univ Of Detroit; Archt.

SCHIPPER, PHIL; Hammond Baptist HS; Merrillville, IN; Chrh Wkr; Drl Tm; Hon Rl; ROTC; Hyles Anderson Coll; Pastoral Theo.

SCHIPPER, TERRY; Chesaning Union HS; Chesaning, MI; Cls Rep Sr Cls; Chrh Wkr; Hon Rl; NHS; Stu Cncl; Rptr Sch Nwsp; Pres Pep Clb; Sci Clb; Univ; Genetic Engr.

SCHIRA, DIANA; Divine Child HS; Dearborn, MI; Band; Chrh Wkr; Sch Mus; Fr Clb; College; Med Tech.

SCHIRMANN, ERNEST; Muskegon HS; Muskegon, MI; Cls Rep Soph Cls; Cl Rep Jr Cls; Hon Rl; NHS; Stu Cncl; Letter Swmmng; Letter Ten; Am Leg Awd; Natl Merit Ltr; Chosen To Attend Operatn Bentley Poli Sci Seminar 79; Stud Faculty Admin Council Rep 77 80; Univ; Elec Engr.

SCHIRMER, THERESA M; Mother Of Mercy HS; Cincinnati, OH; 18/235 Chrs; Chrh Wkr; Girl Scts; Hon Rl; NHS; Sch Pl; Sct Actv; Fr Clb; Univ; Operations Research.

SCHIRTZINGER, KAREN; Westerville N HS; Westerville, OH; Trs Jr Cls; AFS; Cmp Fr Grls; Drl Tm; Hon Rl; Lbry Ade; NHS; IM Sprt; 1st Runner Up Most Outstanding Soph; Poetry Awds; College; Psych.

SCHLAAK, ANN; Huron HS; Huron, OH; VP Jr Cls; Band; Chrs; Chrh Wkr; Cmnty Wkr; Drl Tm; Girl Scts; Hon Rl; Hosp Ade; NHS; Univ; Dance.

SCHLABACH, MARILYN; Jonathan Alder HS; Plain City, OH; 13/130 Chrs; Chrh Wkr; Hon Rl; Yth Flsp; Y-Teens; FTA; Pep Clb; Spn Clb; Trk; Chrldng;.

SCHLABACH, PHIL; Garaway HS; Fresno, OH; 3/90 Trs Jr Cls; Chrs; Hon Rl; NHS; Sch Pl; Stu Cncl; Rptr Yrbk; Rptr Sch Nwsp; Crs Cntry; Natl Merit SF; College; Mathematics.

SCHLAFF, JUDY; Franklin HS; Livonia, MI; Orch; Trk; Cit Awd; College; Vet.

SCHLAGBAUM, ANNETTE; Ottoville Local HS; Ottoville, OH; Cls Rep Frsh Cls; Girl Scts; Hon Rl; Lbry Ade; NHS; Sch Mus; Treas 4-H; Trk; Chrldng; College; Bus.

SCHLAGBAUM, LYNETTE; St Johns HS; Delphos, OH; 8/141 Band; Chrh Wkr; Hon Rl; Jr NHS; NHS; Sch Mus; Rptr Sch Nwsp; FTA; Bowling Green State; Spec Edu.

SCHLAGER JR, BARRY; Swartz Creek HS; Swartz Creek, MI; Chrs; Chrh Wkr; Lit Mag; Sch Mus; Sch Pl; Stg Crw; Rptr Sch Nwsp; Univ Of Mic; Eng.

SCHLAUD, ANNETTE; Lapeer West HS; Lapeer, MI; 34/259 Chrs; Chrh Wkr; NHS; Sec PAVAS; Sch Mus; Sch Pl; Stg Crw; Sec Drama Clb; Natl Merit SF; Michigan St Univ; Psych.

SCHLECHT, ROSEMARY; Hilliard HS; Columbus, OH; 11/356 Hon Rl; Jr NHS; NHS; Off Ade; Sch Mus; VP Stg Crw; Pres Fr Clb; FHA; GAA; Mgrs; Ohio State Univ; Finance.

SCHLEDER, CINDY; Ithaca HS; Ithaca, MI; Band; Chrs; Hon Rl; Sch Mus; Fr Clb; Lansing Community; Art.

SCHLEICHER, MARY; Lake Catholic HS; Mentor, OH; College; Vet.

SCHLENSKER, TAMMY; Our Lady Of Providence HS; New Albay, IN; Chrh Wkr; Hon Rl; IM Sprt; Indiana Univ; Med Tech.

SCHLENVOGT, JULIE; Stephenson HS; Stephenson, MI; 1/95 Val; AFS; Band; Chrh Wkr; Hon Rl; NHS; Stg Crw; Stu Cncl; Yth Flsp; 4-H; Northern Michigan Univ; Music.

SCHLETTY, DEE ANN; Reynoldsburg HS; Reynoldsburg, OH; Hosp Ade; Yrbk; DECA; Fr Clb; PPFtbl; Ohio Univ; Fashion Buyer.

SCHLEY, LISA; Theodore Roosevelt HS; Wyandotte, MI; Hon Rl; Central Mic Univ.

SCHLEY, SANDY; Northwestern HS; W Salem, OH; 37/128 Band; Chrs; Drm Mjrt; Girl Scts; Orch; Sch Mus; Sch Pl; Yth Flsp; Rptr Yrbk; Yrbk; Univ; Jrnlsm.

SCHLEYER, CAROLE; Goshen HS; Goshen, OH; Chrs; Chrh Wkr; Girl Scts; Hon Rl; Off Ade; Sch Mus; Sch Pl; Stu Cncl; Yth Flsp; Drama Clb; College; Travel Agent.

SCHLEYER, COLLEEN; Port Huron HS; Port Huron, MI; 7/356 Band; Hon Rl; NHS; Boys Clb Am; Mth Clb; Trk; GAA; Voice Dem Awd; Mi Compttv Schslhp 79; Ther Times Herald City Newsppr Awd 79; Robert J Moenawd Band Awd For Learshp 79; St Clair Cnty Cmnty Coll; Elec.

SCHLICKMAN, KIMBERLY; Parkway HS; Willshire, OH; Am Leg Aux Girls St; Chrh Wkr; Hon Rl; Pres FHA; Sec Ger Clb; Pep Clb; Sci Clb; PPFtbl; Twrlr; Wright St Univ; Primary Ed.

SCHLIE, SHARON; Deer Park HS; Cincinnati, OH; Chrs; Hon Rl; NHS; Stg Crw; Coach Actv; GAA; Scr Kpr; Cit Awd; SAR Awd; Univ Of Cincinnati; Elem Ed.

SCHLOSSER, CINDY; Memorial HS; St Marys, OH; 7/223 Girl Scts; Hon Rl; NHS; Pres Y-Teens; VP FHA; Spn Clb; Letter GAA; Chmn IM Sprt; 4-H Awd; Ohio St Univ; Home Ec.

SCHLOSSER, D ANDRA; Litchfield HS; Litchfield, MI; 12/52 Cl Rep Jr Cls; Girl Scts; Hon Rl; Natl Forn Lg; VP Stu Cncl; Yrbk; 4-H; Letter Gym; 4-H Awd; Kendall Schl Of Design; Arts.

SCHLOSSER, KRAIG; Dekalb HS; Auburn, IN; FCA; NHS; Bsbl; Letter Ftbl; Letter Wrstlng; Univ; Engr.

SCHLUETER, JOY; Highland HS; Highland, IN; 17/503 Hon Rl; NHS; Spn Clb; Bsktbl; GAA; C of C Awd; Ind Univ.

SCHLUND, SUE; Solon HS; Solon, OH; Cls Rep Frsh Cls; Cls Rep Soph Cls; Cl Rep Jr Cls; FCA; Hon Rl; Stu Cncl; Pep Clb; Letter Bsktbl; Letter Ten; Trk; Miami Univ Oxford.

SCHLUNDT, DIANE; Elkhart Central HS; Elkhart, IN; Cls Rep Frsh Cls; Cls Rep Soph Cls; Hon Rl; Stu Cncl; Swmmng; Arizona Univ; Phys Ther.

SCHMAL, KRISTINE; St Joseph HS; Saint Joseph, MI; 54/310 Chrs; Sch Mus; Sch Pl; Drama Clb; Valparaiso Univ; Home Econ.

SCHMALENBERGER, DAVID; Interlochen Arts Academy; Wapakoneta, OH; Band; Hon Rl; Orch; Swmmng; Ten; Natl Merit Ltr; Pres Awd; Downbeat Recording Awds Honorable Mention; Ohio Northern Univ Band Camp Schlrshp; Capitol Univ; Music.

SCHMALL, SUE; Bedford HS; Temperance, MI; Chrh Wkr; Hosp Ade; NHS; Sch Pl; Stg Crw; Rptr Sch Nwsp; Sch Nwsp; Drama Clb; IM Sprt; Univ.

SCHMALSTIEG, SUZANNE; Madonna HS; Weirton, WV; Cmnty Wkr; Hon Rl; Lbry Ade; Spn Clb; Voc Schl; Nursing.

SCHMALTZ, BETTY; Bentley Sr HS; Davison, MI; Hon Rl; NHS; Off Ade; Sct Actv; Ed Yrbk; OEA; IM Sprt; Mgrs; Scr Kpr; Tmr; Busns Office Ed Club Spelling Awd Parlimentary Procedures Awd & Keypunching Awd; Ferris St Coll; Data Processing.

SCHMALTZ, TAD; Huron HS; Ann Arbor, MI; Boy Scts; Chrh Wkr; Cmnty Wkr; Hon Rl; Lat Clb; IM Sprt; Natl Merit Ltr; Kalamazoo Coll; Law.

SCHMEDDING, KAREN; Anderson Sr HS; Anderson, IN; 17/435 Cls Rep Soph Cls; Sec Jr Cls; Cl Rep Jr Cls; VP Sr Cls; Am Leg Aux Girls St; Hon Rl; VP NHS; Sec Ger Clb; Lat Clb; Twrlr; Purdue Univ; Comp Sci.

SCHMEISSER, CRAIG; Ironton HS; Ironton, OH; Cls Rep Soph Cls; Spn Clb;.

SCHMELTZER, KATHRYN; Gwinn HS; Gwinn, MI; 34/195 Aud/Vis; Chrs; Drm Bgl; Girl Scts; Hon Rl; Lbry Ade; Sch Pl; Stg Crw; OEA; Sec VICA; VICA Gold Medal Arch Drawing; Silver Medal Job Interview; Michigan Indust Awds; Cert Of Ach In Shorthand; Northern Michigan Univ; Sec.

SCHMELZER, JANET; Michigan Lutheran Semnry HS; Remus, MI; 7/62 Chrs; Hon Rl; Orch; Capt Trk; PPFtbl; Dr Martin Luther Coll; Educ.

SCHMELZER, PATRICIA; William V Fisher Cath HS; Lancaster, OH; Band; Chrs; Hon Rl; Sch Pl; 4-H; 4-H Awd; Univ.

SCHMELZER, STACIE; William V Fisher Cathlc HS; Lancaster, OH; Chrh Wkr; Girl Scts; Hon Rl; JA; Rptr Yrbk; Yrbk; IM Sprt; JA Awd; Bliss Bus Schl; Bus.

SCHMELZER, TIM L; Fairfield Union HS; Lancaster, OH; 14/158 Hon Rl; Jr NHS; Key Clb; Ftbl; Trk; Univ; Comp Tech.

SCHMETT, BRAD; Southridge HS; Huntingburg, IN; 8/180 Boy Scts; Chrh Wkr; Hon Rl; Sct Actv; Yth Flsp; 4-H; Spn Clb; Bsktbl; Crs Cntry; Glf; Indiana Univ; Psych.

SCHMID, ANGELA; Avondale HS; Troy, MI; Chrh Wkr; Jr NHS; NHS; Sch Mus; Sch Pl; Stg Crw; Stu Cncl; Yth Flsp; PPFtbl; Eastern Michigan Univ; Bus Mgmt.

SCHMID, KIMBERLY; Anchor Bay HS; New Baltimore, MI; 26/260 Trs Sr Cls; Girl Scts; Hon Rl; NHS; Sch Pl; Spn Clb; Trk; Chrldng; Natl Merit Schl; Voice Dem Awd; Mic State Univ.

SCHMID, STEPHANIE; Struthers HS; Struthers, OH; Yth Flsp; Y-Teens; Ed Yrbk; Drama Clb; Pep Clb; Spn Clb; Univ.

SCHMIDIKE, CYNTHIA; Schoolcraft HS; Schoolcraft, MI; 15/65 Chrh Wkr; Hon Rl; NHS; Off Ade; Sch Pl; Stu Cncl; Ed Yrbk; Sprt Ed Yrbk; Yrbk; 4-H; Amer Leg Good Ctznshp Awd 79; Western Michigan Univ; Bus Educ.

SCHMIDL, TERESA; Taylor HS; Cleves, OH; Trs Frsh Cls; Cl Rep Jr Cls; FCA; Hon Rl; Hosp Ade; Key Clb; Pep Clb; Swmmng; Chrldng; Coll; Nursing.

SCHMIDLIN, C; Pike Delta York HS; Delta, OH; 14/110 Band; Chrs; Drl Tm; NHS; Stu Cncl; Rptr Sch Nwsp; Pres 4-H; Fr Clb; FTA; Scr Kpr; Ohio State Univ; Horticulture.

SCHMIDLIN, GREGORY; Saint Xavier HS; Cincinnati, OH; 174/284 Cmnty Wkr; Wrstlng; IM Sprt; Xavier Univ; Bus.

SCHMIDT, ANN; Twin Valley North HS; Lewisburg, OH; Trs Sr Cls; Band; Cmp Fr Grls; Chrs; Chrh Wkr; Hon Rl; NHS; Off Ade; Stu Cncl; Yth Flsp; Sinclair; X Ray Tech.

SCHMIDT, BECKY; Reitz Memorial HS; Evansville, IN; 12/217 Cls Rep Frsh Cls; Cl Rep Jr Cls; Capt Drl Tm; Hon Rl; NHS; Off Ade; Stu Cncl; Indiana St Univ; Speech Therapy.

SCHMIDT, BETTY J; Sidney HS; Sidney, OH; 3/250 Chrh Wkr; Hon Rl; Lbry Ade; NHS; Orch; 4-H; FHA; OEA; 4-H Awd; Jr Data Proc Otstndg Studnt 1977; Sr Data Proc OEA Club Pres 1978; Dist Cncl 7 IUE Schlrshp 1979; Lima Tech Coll; Data Proc.

SCHMIDT, BRADLEY; Bullock Creek HS; Midland, MI; Hon Rl; NHS; Sch Pl; Wrstlng; Mich Tech Univ; Mech Engr.

SCHMIDT, BRENDA; Laporte HS; Laporte, IN; Cmp Fr Grls; Chrs; FCA; Girl Scts; Sch Pl; Fr Clb; Pep Clb; Trk; Mgrs; Mat Maids; College; Psych.

SCHMIDT, CATHERINE M; Perry HS; Canton, OH; 25/480 Trs Jr Cls; VP Sr Cls; Hon Rl; NHS; Off Ade; Stu Cncl; Perry Physics & Astronomy Asso C78; Schlshp Awd 3.5 Or Abv Avrge For 8 Consctv Sems 75 79; Ohio St Univ; Med.

SCHMIDT, CATHY; Reading Cmnty HS; Reading, OH; 7/230 Am Leg Aux Girls St; Cmnty Wkr; Hon Rl; Jr NHS; NHS; Pep Clb; Spn Clb; Mat Maids; Tmr; Univ Of Dayton; Spec Ed.

SCHMIDT, CRAIG; Greenville Sr HS; Greenville, OH; 106/385 Cls Rep Frsh Cls; Cl Rep Jr Cls; Hon Rl; Ftbl; Trk; Coll; Busns Admin.

SCHMIDT, CYNTHIA; Beechwood HS; Beachwood, OH; 1/130 Debate Tm; Drl Tm; Natl Forn Lg; VP NHS; Quill & Scroll; Ed Sch Nwsp; Pres Fr Clb; Rdo Clb; Ufrench 77 78; French Clb 78; Univ; Law.

SCHMIDT, DEBORAH; Lansing Everett HS; Lansing, MI; Band; Drm Mjrt; Hosp Ade; JA; Letter Trk; Twrlr; LCC; Travel.

SCHMIDT, DEBRA; Marian HS; S Bend, IN; Cmp Fr Grls; Hon Rl; Hosp Ade; Lbry Ade; Mdrgl; Yrbk; 4-H; 4-H Awd; A State Finalist For Miss Teenager Amer 79; IUSB Univ; RN.

SCHMIDT, DEBRA; Union City Cmnty HS; Union City, IN; 13/95 Trs Jr Cls; Trs Sr Cls; Hon Rl; NHS; DECA; Eng Clb; Fr Clb; OEA; Gym; Chrldng; Ball St Univ; Marketing.

SCHMIDT, DEBRA L; Union City Comm HS; Union City, IN; 14/95 Trs Jr Cls; Trs Sr Cls; Hon Rl; NHS; DECA; Eng Clb; OEA; Letter Gym; Ten; Chrldng; Ball St Univ; Marketing.

SCHMIDT, ED; Lasalle HS; Cincinnati, OH; 46/249 Band; Boy Scts; Hon Rl; Sch Pl; Sct Actv; Letter Crs Cntry; Letter Trk; IM Sprt; Miami; Aviation.

SCHMIDT, ELIZABETH; Archbishop Alter HS; Lebanon, OH; 35/350 Hon Rl; 4-H; Fr Clb; IM Sprt; Ohio St Univ; Pre Vet.

SCHMIDT, ELLEN A; Celina Sr HS; Celina, OH; 24/240 Chrs; Hon Rl; NHS; Sch Mus; Pep Clb; Ten; IM Sprt; Miami Univ; Soc Work.

SCHMIDT, GLENN; Beal City Public HS; Mt Pleasant, MI; Pres Frsh Cls; Pres Soph Cls; Aud/Vis; Band; Chrs; Chrh Wkr; Cmnty Wkr; Hon Rl; JA; NHS; Lawrence Inst Of Tech; Elec Engr.

SCHMIDT, GRETCHEN; Berea HS; Berea, OH; AFS; Band; Hosp Ade; NHS; Orch; IM Sprt; Tmr; Wittenburg Univ; Early Child Educ.

SCHMIDT, HOWARD; Celina HS; Celina, OH; 45/300 Hon Rl; NHS; Yrbk; Pep Clb; Bsktbl; Letter Ten; College; Bus.

SCHMIDT, JAMES; Grosse Pointe North HS; Grosse Pt Wds, MI; Band; FCA; Hon Rl; Letter Crs Cntry; Letter Trk; College.

SCHMIDT, JANET; Fairview HS; Fairview Pk, OH; 59/280 Girl Scts; Hon Rl; Hosp Ade; Stg Crw; 4-H; 4-H Awd; Coll; Nursing.

SCHMIDT, JEAN ANN; Whiteford HS; Riga, MI; 2/100 Pres Soph Cls; VP Jr Cls; Sal; Hon Rl; Sch Pl; Stg Crw; Rptr Yrbk; Rptr Sch Nwsp; Fr Clb; Mth Clb; Univ Of Toledo; Legal Asst.

SCHMIDT, JEFFREY; Wheeling Park HS; Wheeling, WV; Boy Scts; Bsbl; Elk Awd; WVU; Med.

SCHMIDT, JOE; Covington HS; Covington, OH; Hosp Ade; Jr NHS; NHS; Letter Bsktbl; Letter Ftbl; Univ.

SCHMIDT, JOHN; Frankenmuth HS; Frankenmuth, MI; 30/150 Cls Rep Frsh Cls; Cls Rep Soph Cls; Cl Rep Jr Cls; Cls Rep Sr Cls; FCA; Hon Rl; Jr NHS; NHS; Sch Pl; Stu Cncl; Univ; Math.

SCHMIDT, JONNA LEIGH; Plymouth Salem HS; Plymouth, MI; 1/593 Val; Hosp Ade; NHS; Sprt Ed Yrbk; Treas Sch Nwsp; Pep Clb; Swmmng; IM Sprt; Mgrs; Natl Merit SF; Essay Contest 1976; 4th Piano Contst 1977; Dist Wnnr Natl Piano Plyng 1977; Univ; Nursing.

SCHMIDT, JULIE; Kouts HS; Kouts, IN; 3/62 Trs Jr Cls; Cls Rep Sr Cls; Chrs; Hon Rl; VP NHS; Sch Pl; Treas Stu Cncl; Pres Yth Flsp; College; Comp Sci.

SCHMIDT, KAREN L; Greensburg Community HS; Indianapolis, IN; Band; Jr NHS; NHS; Sch Mus; VP Stu Cncl; Pres Sci Clb; Univ Of Ind Bloomington; Nursing.

SCHMIDT, LAURA; Seymour HS; Seymour, IN; VP Soph Cls; Chrs; Cmnty Wkr; Sch Mus; Pres 4-H; Pep Clb; VP Spn Clb; Gym; Chrldng; 4-H Awd; Indiana Univ; Educ.

SCHMIDT, LAURI A; Perry HS; Canton, OH; Hon Rl; NHS; Off Ade; Ten; Coach Actv; Tmr; Most Improved Player Tennis 77; MVP Tennis 78; Hon Mention Fedrl League Tennis 78; Cincinnati Univ; Archt.

SCHMIDT, MARGO; Elizabeth Ann Johnson HS; Mt Morris, MI; Cls Rep Sr Cls; Cmnty Wkr; Girl Scts; NHS; Sct Actv; Sterring Comm 79; Speedball Ltr 76 80; Stdnt Leader Of Child Devlpmt Clothing Drive 78; Mid Michigan Cmnty Coll; Radio Tech.

SCHMIDT, MELISSA; Mt Healthy HS; Cincinnati, OH; 103/529 Sec Sr Cls; Chrs; Drl Tm; Drm Bgl; Girl Scts; Hon Rl; Yrbk; Beta Clb; Gym; Pom Pon; Univ; Fshn Mdse.

SCHMIDT, NANCY; De Kalb HS; Auburn, IN; Chrs; Chrh Wkr; Cmnty Wkr; Natl Forn Lg; Sec NHS; Sch Pl; Pres Y-Teens; FTA; Pres Ger Clb; Indiana Univ; Recreation.

SCHMIDT, NANETTE; Shawe Memorial HS; Madison, IN; Rptr Yrbk; Rptr Sch Nwsp; Pep Clb; Ivy Tech Schl; Cmnctns.

SCHMIDT, PAMELA S; Madison Consolidated HS; Madison, IN; 5/290 Cls Rep Frsh Cls; Hon Rl; NHS; Sec Quill & Scroll; Sprt Ed Yrbk; Rptr Yrbk; Sec FBLA; Pep Clb; GAA; DAR Awd; Mahisco Yrbk Desgn Awd 1978; Miss Teenage Amer Hon Ment 1979; Cert Of Achvmnt 1976; Custer Oritrcl Cntst; Tri St Univ; Bus Mgmt.

SCHMIDT, PETER D; St Francis De Sales HS; Toledo, OH; Hon Rl; Jr NHS; NHS; Hockey; Socr; Trk; Univ.

SCHMIDT, PHILIP; Douglas Mac Arthur HS; Saginaw, MI; Hon Rl; Hosp Ade; NHS; Yth Flsp; Y-Teens; Letter Swmmng; Univ Of Michigan; Archt.

SCHMIDT, SHARI; Hubbard HS; Hubbard, OH; Chrh Wkr; Off Ade; FBLA; Pep Clb; Trk; Mgrs; Scr Kpr; Youngstown St Univ; Elem Ed.

SCHMIDT, STEPHEN; North Canton Hoover HS; North Canton, OH; Boy Scts; Chrs; Cmnty Wkr; Hon Rl; Sec JA; Sch Mus; Sch Pl; Sct Actv; Y-Teens; 4-H; Univ.

SCHMIDT, STEVE; Moeller HS; Cincinnati, OH; Stu Cncl; Rptr Yrbk; Rptr Sch Nwsp; Ftbl; Trk; U S Naval Academy.

SCHMIDT, SUSAN; Hoover HS; N Canton, OH; Chrs; Hon Rl; NHS; Sch Pl; Cit Awd; Mas Awd; Kent St Univ; Nursing.

SCHMIDT, TERESE; Charles F Brush HS; S Euclid, OH; 100/625 Sec Frsh Cls; Cls Rep Soph Cls; AFS; Band; Hon Rl; Hosp Ade; Off Ade; Letter Bsktbl; IM Sprt; Pres Awd; Univ Of Cincinnati; Nurse.

SCHMIDT, TIM; Jackson Milton HS; N Jackson, OH; 1/117 Chrh Wkr; Hon Rl; NHS; Yth Flsp; Pres 4-H; Key Clb; 4-H Awd; College.

SCHMIDT, TOM; La Salle HS; Cincinnati, OH; 10/277 Hon Rl; Jr NHS; NHS; Stg Crw; Ed Sch Nwsp; Capt Bsktbl; IM Sprt; Univ Of Cincinnati; Chem Engr.

SCHMIDT, VICKI; Mount Healthy HS; Cincinnati, OH; 54/572 Cls Rep Frsh Cls; VP Jr Cls; VP Sr Cls; Cls Rep Sr Cls; Hon Rl; Stu Cncl; Pep Clb;.

SCHMIDT II, WILLIAM; Hoover HS; N Canton, OH; 20/427 Boy Scts; FCA; Hon Rl; NHS; Sch Pl; Stu Cncl; Pres Mth Clb; Pres Sci Clb; Letter Ftbl; The Ohio State Univ; Pre Med.

SCHMIEDEKNECHT, DEAN; Jenison Sr 'S; Jenison, MI; Boy Scts; Hon Rl; Sch Pl; Sct Actv; Fr Clb; Ten; IM Sprt; Voice Dem Awd; Michigan Tech Inst; Engr.

SCHMIELEY, DONALD; Berea HS; Brook Pk, OH; Cls Rep Soph Cls; Cl Rep Jr Cls; Hon Rl; NHS; Stu Cncl; Ger Clb; Key Clb; Socr; Wrstlng; Univ; Ocean Engr.

SCHMIT, LAURIE; North College Hill HS; Cincinnati, OH; Chrh Wkr; Capt Drl Tm; Hon Rl; Bsbl; Bsktbl; Ten; GAA; Schl Of Cosmetology.

SCHMIT, MONICA; George A Dondero HS; Royal Oak, MI; Trs Sr Cls; Sec Band; Chrh Wkr; Cmnty Wkr; NHS; Orch; Sch Mus; Bsktbl; Mic State Univ; Music.

SCHMIT, THOMAS; St Johns HS; Delphos, OH; Cls Rep Frsh Cls; Cls Rep Soph Cls; Cl Rep Jr Cls; Pres Sr Cls; Band; Chrs; Chrh Wkr; Cmnty Wkr; Debate Tm; Hon Rl; Univ; Educ.

SCHMITIGAL, PHILIP; Hartland HS; Howell, MI; Chrh Wkr; Hon Rl; Off Ade; Yth Flsp; Fr Clb; Bsbl; Ftbl; Mch Tech Univ; Electrical Engineer.

SCHMITMEYER, KAREN; Anna HS; Anna, OH; 2/69 Am Leg Aux Girls St; Chrs; Hon Rl; Sch Mus; Drama Clb; 4-H; FHA; FTA; Pep Clb; Spn Clb; Honorbl Mention In St For Spanish I Schlshp Test 79; Bowling Green St Univ; Elem Educ.

SCHMITS, GEOFFREY; Princeton Community HS; Princeton, IN; 32/203 Boy Scts; Chrh Wkr; Cmnty

Wkr; Boys Clb Am; Mth Clb; Pep Clb; Sci Clb; Ftbl; IM Sprt; Ind Univ; Historian.

SCHMITT, ALICE; Our Lady Of Mercy HS; Garden City, MI; Cl Rep Jr Cls; Chrh Wkr; Hosp Ade; Lbry Ade; NHS; Stu Cncl; Fr Clb; Sci Clb; Univ; Pre Med.

SCHMITT, CHRIS; Jasper HS; Jasper, IN; Hon Rl; College; Interpreter.

SCHMITT, ELAINE; Mater Dei HS; Haubstadt, IN; 70/177 Chrh Wkr; Cmnty Wkr; 4-H; Pep Clb; 4-H Awd; Purdue Univ; Animal Sci.

SCHMITT, JOHN; North Posey HS; Evansville, IN; Hon Rl; Pep Clb; Bsktbl; Letter Ftbl; Letter Trk; IM Sprt; Elk Awd; Voice Dem Awd;.

SCHMITT, KAREN; Mcnicholas HS; Cincinnati, OH; 18/250 Cls Rep Sr Cls; Hon Rl; NHS; GAA; College.

SCHMITT, MARC; Mariemont HS; Terr Pk, OH; Boy Scts; Cmnty Wkr; Hosp Ade; Sch Pl; Sct Actv; Stg Crw; Yrbk; Fr Clb; Ger Clb; Bsbl; Awd Of Distinction; Natl Riflemens Awd; Art Awd; Xavier Univ; Comp Programming.

SCHMITT, MARY; Valley Forge HS; Parma Hgts, OH; 117/777 Chrs; Girl Scts; Hon Rl; Hosp Ade; Mod UN; Off Ade; Sch Pl; Drama Clb; Pep Clb; Spn Clb; Univ; Acctg.

SCHMITT, MICHAEL; Charles F Brush HS; S Euclid, OH; Hon Rl; PAVAS; Key Clb; Letter Socr; Letter Wrstlng; Univ; Elec Engr.

SCHMITT, SALLY; Canal Winchester HS; Cnl Winchester, OH; Chrs; Hon Rl; Lbry Ade; Stu Cncl; Drama Clb; Pep Clb; Spn Clb; Letter Bsbl; Letter Bsktbl; Capt Chrldng; Columbus Bsns Univ; Fash Merch.

SCHMITT, SUZANNE; Port Clinton HS; Port Clinton, OH; 1/300 Chrs; Hon Rl; 4-H; FDA; Ger Clb; Ohio St Univ; Veterinary.

SCHMITT, WINFIELD; Vinson HS; Huntington, WV; Band; Chrs; CAP; Hon Rl; Orch; Mth Clb; Louis B Armstrong Jass Awd; 79; Schlrshp Plaque 79; All Amer Young Mus Hall Of Fame 78; Sup WV Solo 77; Marshall Univ; Music.

SCHMITZ, CAROLYN; Ft Recovery HS; New Weston, OH; 2/90 Cl Rep Jr Cls; Sal; Am Leg Aux Girls St; Pres NHS; Off Ade; Stu Cncl; Ger Clb; GAA; IM Sprt; Am Leg Awd; Univ Of Toledo; Nursing.

SCHMITZ, LORI; West Muskingum HS; Zanesville, OH; VP Jr Cls; Cl Rep Jr Cls; Hon Rl; Hosp Ade; Jr NHS; Stu Cncl; Y-Teens; GAA; Univ.

SCHMITZ, MATTHEW; Imlay City Cmnty HS; Imlay City, MI; Boy Scts; Hon Rl; 4-H; Fr Clb; FFA; Sci Clb; Ftbl; Trk; Univ; Chem.

SCHMITZ, PETER M; Clay HS; S Bend, IN; 29/497 Hon Rl; Socr; Ten; Univ; Pre Dentstry.

SCHMOEKEL, RENEE; Mason HS; Mason, MI; Band; Chrs; Girl Scts; Hon Rl; Sch Mus; Stu Cncl; Yth Flsp; Civ Clb; Lansing Community College; Architect.

SCHMOLLINGER, STEVE; Hamilton Southeastern HS; Noblesville, IN; 4-H; Bsbl; Crs Cntry; Wrstlng; 4-H Awd;.

SCHMUCKER, BETH; Waldron Area HS; Waldron, MI; 4/39 Hst Frsh Cls; Cls Rep Sr Cls; Band; Pres NHS; Sec Stu Cncl; Pres Spn Clb; Capt Bsktbl; Chrldng; Coach Actv; GAA; Calvin Coll; Biology.

SCHMUCKER, CHERI; Eastside HS; Spencerville, IN; 3/90 Hon Rl; NHS; Off Ade; Rptr Sch Nwsp; 4-H; Fr Clb; Capt Gym; Trk; Am Leg Awd; DAR Awd; Homecoming Queen 78; FFA Sweetheart 78; Commented Stdnt 78; Ball St Univ.

SCHMUCKER, TONY; Stryker HS; West Unity, OH; Chrs; Sec Chrh Wkr; Hon Rl; VP Yth Flsp; 4-H; VP FFA; Bsbl; Bsktbl; Univ; Agric.

SCHMUHL, KAREN S; Parma Sr HS; Parma, OH; Hon Rl; Jr NHS; NHS; Ger Clb; Coll; Engr.

SCHMUKI, HEIDI; Fairless HS; Navarre, OH; Chrh Wkr; Cmnty Wkr; Hon Rl; VP NHS; Off Ade; Stu Cncl; Pres 4-H; Mth Clb; Pep Clb; Sci Clb; Ohio State Univ.

SCHMULDT, JANET; Jenison HS; Jenison, MI; Band; Chrh Wkr; Hon Rl; NHS; Pom Pon; Davenport Coll Of Bus; Exec Off Asst.

SCHNAITER, BRADLEY; Martinsville HS; Martinsville, IN; Treas 4-H; Treas Spn Clb; Wrstlng; Indiana Univ; Busns.

SCHNAPP, KARLYN; Maumee HS; Maumee, OH; 20/316 Am Leg Aux Girls St; Band; Chrh Wkr; Drm Mjrt; Hon Rl; NHS; Off Ade; Rptr Yrbk; Twrlr; Cincinatti Univ; Med Tech.

SCHNARR, DIANA; Washington HS; Washington, IN; 8/194 FCA; Hon Rl; NHS; Yth Flsp; Beta Clb; 4-H; Fr Clb; Pep Clb; Bsktbl; Letter Ten; Indiana Univ; Speech Ther.

SCHNARR, SHERRY; Loogootee HS; Loogootee, IN; 40/147 Sec Soph Cls; Sec Jr Cls; Band; Off Ade; Yrbk; Sch Nwsp; Pep Clb; Spn Clb; Trk; IM Sprt; Univ.

SCHNARRE, KAREN; Celina Sr HS; Celina, OH; Chrh Wkr; Yth Flsp; 4-H;.

SCHNAUTZ, DOUGLAS; Central HS; Evansville, IN; Chrs; Chrh Wkr; NHS; Treas Sct Actv; Ger Clb; Sci Clb; Univ Of Evansville; Comp Engr.

SCHNEBLE, PAULA; Archbishop Alter HS; Kettering, OH; 48/332 Chrs; Hon Rl; NHS; Sch Mus; Keyettes; Ohio St Univ; Pharm.

SCHNECK, MELODY; Salem HS; Little York, IN; 39/167 Lat Clb; OEA; Indiana Univ; Acctg.

SCHNEEWEIS, DAVID; Charles F Brush HS; Lyndhurst, OH; 1/500 Val; Band; NHS; Orch; Stu Cncl; Yrbk; Univ; Sci.

SCHNEIDER, ANDY; Malabar Shs; Mansfield, OH; 27/280 Boy Scts; Chrh Wkr; Hon Rl; Sct Actv; Yth Flsp; Ger Clb; Mth Clb; Bsbl; Miami Univ; Math.

SCHNEIDER, BETH; Indian Hill HS; Cincinnati, OH; Drama Clb; Pres 4-H; Chrldng; Dnfth Awd; 4-H Awd; 4 H Awds & Honors; Pres 4 H Jr Ldrshp Clb; College; Math.

SCHNEIDER, BETH; William Henry Harrison HS; Evansville, IN; 51/393 Band; Jr NHS; Fr Clb; FTA; Letter Trk; Chrldng; PPFtbl; Univ; Speech Pathology.

SCHNEIDER, BETH; Strongsville Sr HS; Strongsville, OH; Aud/Vis; Cmnty Wkr; Hon Rl; Lbry Ade; Off Ade; VP 4-H; Sec FFA; Ohio St Univ; Floriculture.

SCHNEIDER, BRENDA; Traverse City Sr HS; Traverse City, MI; 137/683 VP 4-H; Pep Clb; 4-H Awd; Northwestern Michigan Coll; Vet.

SCHNEIDER, BRYAN; Stow HS; Stow, OH; Boy Scts; Chrh Wkr; Hon Rl; Sct Actv; Wrstlng; IM Sprt; Cit Awd; College; Forestry.

SCHNEIDER, CHERYL; Botkins HS; Botkins, OH; 3/49 Am Leg Aux Girls St; Band; Chrs; Hon Rl; NHS; Off Ade; Sch Mus; Stg Crw; Yrbk; 4-H; Wright St Univ; Sci.

SCHNEIDER, DALE; Lanesville HS; Lanesville, IN; Val; Am Leg Boys St; Hon Rl; NHS; Stu Cncl; Yrbk; Bsbl; Bsktbl; DAR Awd; Natl Merit SF; Ind Univ; Broadcast Journalism.

SCHNEIDER, DAVE; Colerain Sr HS; Cincinnati, OH; Chrh Wkr; Pres Yth Flsp; Pres 4-H; Crs Cntry; Trk; Cit Awd; 4-H Awd; Kiwan Awd; Ohio St Univ; Engr.

SCHNEIDER, DAVID; Bishop Foley HS; Troy, MI; Boy Scts; Hon Rl; Jr NHS; Sct Actv; Spn Clb; Letter Bsbl; Letter Ftbl; Notre Dame Univ; Law.

SCHNEIDER, DEBBIE; North Branch HS; Clifford, MI; 8/162 Band; Hon Rl; NHS; 4-H; FHA; 4-H Awd; Michigan St Univ.

SCHNEIDER, DEBORAH M; Rogers HS; Toledo, OH; Cmp Fr Grls; Chrs; Jr NHS; NHS; Off Ade; Red Cr Ade; Yth Flsp; Rptr Sch Nwsp; Sci Clb; Crs Cntry; College; Medicine.

SCHNEIDER, DEE; Clyde Sr HS; Clyde, OH; 90/210 Cmp Fr Grls; Chrs; Hon Rl; OEA; Spn Clb; Trk; GAA; IM Sprt; Scr Kpr; Terra Tech Schl; Interior Dsgn.

SCHNEIDER, JANE; Walnut Hills HS; Cincinnati, OH; Mod UN; Pres Stu Cncl; Sec Mth Clb; Ten; Cit Awd; Univ Of Mich; Honors Program.

SCHNEIDER, JULIE; Circleville HS; Circleville, OH; 31/261 AFS; Hon Rl; Lbry Ade; Fr Clb; Capt Bsktbl; Ohi Weslleyam Univ; Romance Lang.

SCHNEIDER, JULIE; F J Reitz HS; Evansville, IN; Hon Rl; Jr NHS; Sec FBLA; Treas OEA; Cit Awd; Rotary Awd; Univ Of Evansville; Data Processing.

SCHNEIDER, KIM; Western Brown Sr HS; Hamersvll, OH; 6/165 Cls Rep Soph Cls; Cl Rep Jr Cls; Hon Rl; NHS; Stu Cncl; Pres 4-H; Spn Clb; PPFtbl; 4-H Awd; Acad Letter In Sci 79; Top Stud In Ancient Civilization 78; Ohio St Univ; Archt Design.

SCHNEIDER, LAWRENCE; Lanesville HS; Georgetown, IN; Chrh Wkr; Hon Rl; Jr NHS; NHS; 4-H; Pep Clb; Spn Clb; IM Sprt; 4-H Awd; Natl Merit Ltr; S E Indiana Univ; Data Processing.

SCHNEIDER, LISA; Cheboygan Area HS; Cheboygan, MI; Chrs; Hosp Ade; 4-H; Lk Superior State Coll; Obstet Rics.

SCHNEIDER, LORI; Ladywood HS; Livonia, MI; Chrs; Hon Rl; NHS; Orch; Sch Mus; Sch Pl; Drama Clb; Madonna College; Bus Admin.

SCHNEIDER, LORI; Chesapeake HS; Chesapeake, OH; 1/140 Trs Frsh Cls; Cls Rep Soph Cls; Cl Rep Jr Cls; Am Leg Aux Girls St; Hon Rl; Pres NHS; Stu Cncl; Sec Beta Clb; Letter Trk; Chrldng; Marshall Univ.

SCHNEIDER, MARK; Tecumseh HS; Medway, OH; 11/400 Cls Rep Frsh Cls; AFS; Chrs; Chrh Wkr; FCA; Hon Rl; Jr NHS; MMM; NHS; Pol Wkr; University.

SCHNEIDER, MARK A; Chesapeake HS; Chesapeake, OH; 8/140 Cls Rep Frsh Cls; Hon Rl; NHS; Stu Cncl; Beta Clb; Ftbl; Ftbl; Wrstlng; Univ Of Kentucky; Med.

SCHNEIDER, NANCY; Meadowdale HS; Dayton, OH; Cl Rep Jr Cls; VP Band; Hon Rl; NHS; Miami Univ; Math.

SCHNEIDER, PHILLIP; Moeller HS; Cincinnati, OH; 90/282 Chrs; Chrh Wkr; Hon Rl; Rptr Yrbk; Rptr Sch Nwsp; Sch Nwsp; Ftbl; Capt Trk; IM Sprt; Franklin Coll; Acctg.

SCHNEIDER, SANDRA; John Marshall HS; Cleveland, OH; 38/646 Boy Scts; Chrs; Chrh Wkr; Cmnty Wkr; Girl Scts; Hon Rl; Lbry Ade; NHS; Off Ade; Sct Actv; Cleveland St Univ; Comp Sci.

SCHNEIDER, SANDRA; Meadowdale HS; Dayton, OH; 8/230 Hon Rl; NHS; Miami Univ; Corporate Law.

SCHNEIDER, SHELLY L; East Kentwood HS; Kentwood, MI; Sec Jr Cls; Hon Rl; JA; NHS; Yth Flsp; Spn Clb; Trk; PPFtbl; JA Awd; Grand Rapids Jr Coll; Horticulture.

SCHNEIDER, STEPHANIE; Colerain Sr HS; Cincinati, OH; Hon Rl; Lbry Ade; Rptr Sch Nwsp; Drama Clb; VP Fr Clb; GAA; Natl French Hnr Soc; College; Med Tech.

SCHNEIDER, SUSAN; Norwood HS; Norwood, OH; 52/350 Drl Tm; Hon Rl; Stg Crw; Sec Fr Clb; Bsktbl; Letter Swmmng; Twrlr; College; Marine Bio.

SCHNEIDER, TAMMY; Washington Sr HS; Washington, OH; Cls Rep Frsh Cls; VP Soph Cls; Sec Jr Cls; Sec Jr Cls; AFS; Band; Hon Rl; Stu Cncl; Y-Teens; Rptr Yrbk; Nursing Schl; Reg Nurse.

SCHNEIDER, THERESA; Goshen HS; Goshen, IN; 64/232 Cls Rep Sr Cls; Aud/Vis; Chrs; Chrh Wkr; FCA; Stg Crw; Stu Cncl; Pep Clb; Bsktbl; Capt Ten; Grace Coll; Phys Ed.

SCHNEIDER, THOMAS; South Range HS; N Lima, OH; FCA; Yth Flsp; Bsktbl; Crs Cntry; Coach Actv; College; Bus Adm.

SCHNELL, CYNTHIA; Madeira HS; Cincinnati, OH; 85/185 Hon Rl; Lit Mag; Sch Pl; PPFtbl; Bowling Green St Univ; Advert.

SCHNELL, LAURA; Douglas Macarthur HS; Saginaw, MI; Band; Hon Rl; Pres MMM; NHS; Orch; Pol Wkr; Pep Clb; Spn Clb; Central Mic Univ; Music.

SCHNELL, STEPHEN; Our Lady Of Providence HS; Jeffersonville, IN; 23/168 Am Leg Boys St; Chrs; Hon Rl; Sch Mus; Sch Pl; Stu Cncl; Drama Clb; Letter Crs Cntry; Letter Trk; Opt Clb Awd; Booster Clb Athletic Awrd Achvmnt Awrd 79; Schl Record For Marathon 26 Mi 385 Yrds 2 Hrs 50;44 79; Rose Hulman Inst Of Tech; Engr.

SCHNELLE, ROBERT; Walda J Wood Memorial HS; Lynnville, IN; Hon Rl; OEA; Cert Of Attend 76 79; OEA Schrlshp 78; Oakland City Coll; Acctg.

SCHNEPF, SARAH; Delta HS; Muncie, IN; 13/315 Band; Hon Rl; Pres NHS; Sch Mus; Stu Cncl; 4-H; Fr Clb; Depauw Univ; Pre Law.

SCHNEPP, ROBERT; Huntington Catholic HS; Huntington, IN; 5/33 Trs Sr Cls; Boy Scts; Hon Rl; NHS; Sch Pl; Y-Teens; 4-H; Bsbl; Crs Cntry; Chrldng; Maint Elec.

SCHNEPP, SUSAN; Eaton Rapids Sr HS; Eaton Rapids, MI; 90/280 Band; Cmp Fr Grls; Hon Rl; 4-H; 4-H Awd; Univ; Med.

SCHNICK, DIANNE; Chesaning Union HS; Owosso, MI; Band; Hon Rl; NHS; Sch Mus; Sch Pl; Ed Sch Nwsp; VP Drama Clb; 4-H; Letter Mgrs; Central Mic Univ; Broadcasting.

SCHNIEGENBERG, RICHARD; Holy Name HS; Garfield Hts, OH; Cls Rep Soph Cls; Trs Jr Cls; Hon Rl; Jr NHS; NHS; Letter Bsktbl; IM Sprt; Cit Awd; Cert Of Recog; Serv Awd; Cert Of Appreciation; Coll; Broadcasting.

SCHNIPKE, KENNETH R; Brunnerdale HS; Ottawa, OH; 1/11 Sec Frsh Cls; Sec Soph Cls; Trs Soph Cls; Cmnty Wkr; Hon Rl; Lit Mag; NHS; Off Ade; Quill & Scroll; Stg Crw; St Josephs Coll.

SCHNIPKE, SHIRLEY; Delphos St Johns HS; Delphos, OH; 19/141 Hon Rl; NHS; Sch Pl; Rptr Yrbk; Rptr Sch Nwsp; 4-H; FTA; Capt Gym; Chrldng; IM Sprt; 2nd Plc On Floor Exercise Routine At Dist; ITT; Drafting.

SCHNITZ, RUTH; Bexley HS; Columbus, OH; Hon Rl; Fr Clb; GAA; IM Sprt; College.

SCHNORBERGER, JOHN; Monroe Catholic HS; Monroe, MI; 2/95 Pres Jr Cls; Cls Rep Sr Cls; Am Leg Boys St; Hon Rl; NHS; Stu Cncl; Letter Bsktbl; Crs Cntry; Trk; DAR Awd; College; Engineering.

SCHNORR, MICHAEL; Kenston HS; San Diego, CA; Pres Jr Cls; Boy Scts; Pep Clb; Rus Clb; Letter Crs Cntry; Letter Trk; Coach Actv; Hnr Trip To USSR With Russian Club 79; MVP Cross Cntry 78; San Diego St Univ; Aero Engr.

SCHOBELOCH, MELISSA; Chillicothe HS; Chillicothe, OH; 10/350 Band; Chrh Wkr; Debate Tm; Hon Rl; Hosp Ade; Jr NHS; Natl Forn Lg; Off Ade; Fr Clb; Cincinnati Univ; Accounting.

SCHOCH, DENISE; Mogadore HS; Mogadore, OH; 6/92 Chrs; Hon Rl; Hosp Ade; NHS; Off Ade; FHA; Bsktbl; Am Leg Awd; Lion Awd; Kent State Univ; Rn.

SCHOCH, EMILY; Chaminade Julienne HS; Dayton, OH; Hon Rl; Rptr Yrbk; Coll; Acctg.

SCHODORF, MIKE; Jackson HS; Canton, OH; VP Frsh Cls; VP Sr Cls; Trs Sr Cls; Cls Rep Sr Cls; FCA; Stu Cncl; DECA; Bsktbl; Ftbl; Trk; Stark Tech Inst; Busns Mgmt.

SCHODOWSKI, DANIEL; Padua Franciscan HS; Parma, OH; 11/256 Cls Rep Frsh Cls; Cls Rep Soph Cls; Hon Rl; NHS; VP Stu Cncl; Ftbl; Trk; IM Sprt; College; Bus.

SCHOECK, DANIEL; Padua Franciscan HS; Parma, OH; Hon Rl; NHS; Sci Clb; IM Sprt; Beloit Coll; Math.

SCHOECK, SUSAN; Holy Name Nazareth HS; Parma, OH; 12/288 Hon Rl; Stg Crw; Rptr Sch Nwsp; Drama Clb; Lat Clb; Ten; Amer Univ; Intntnl Studies.

SCHOELLKOPF, BETSY; Walnut Hills HS; Cincinnati, OH; Hon Rl; Lit Mag; Rptr Sch Nwsp; Fr Clb; Cit Awd; Univ Of Cincinnati; Linguistics.

SCHOEN, SUSAN; Northview HS; Comstock Park, MI; 14/289 Hon Rl; Sec NHS; Sch Nwsp; Spn Clb; Michigan St Univ; Vet.

SCHOEN, WANDA; St Henry HS; Ft Recovery, OH; Cl Rep Jr Cls; Am Leg Aux Girls St; Chrs; FCA; Hon Rl; NHS; Stu Cncl; FHA; FTA; OEA; Wright St Branch; Acctg.

SCHOENBORN, ELIZABETH A; Coopersville HS; Conklin, MI; Hst Jr Cls; Pres Sr Cls; Band; Chrh Wkr; Mod UN; NHS; Stu Cncl; 4-H; FNA; Ger Clb; Grand Vly St Coll; Nursing.

SCHOENEGGE, COLLETTE; Nordonia HS; Macedonia, OH; Cls Rep Frsh Cls; Sec Soph Cls; VP Jr Cls; Pres Sr Cls; Sch Mus; Sch Pl; Letter Bsktbl; Chmn Trk; IM Sprt; College; Phys Educ.

SCHOENER, DAVID; Ironton HS; Ironton, OH; Cls Rep Frsh Cls; Band; Hon Rl; Ger Clb; Bsbl; Capt Crs Cntry; Letter Trk; Natl Merit Ltr; Freshy Awd 76; Oh Univ HS Schlr Awd 78; Univ.

SCHOENHERR, ANN; Sturgis HS; Sturgis, MI; Trs Frsh Cls; Sal; Band; Girl Scts; Hon Rl; Pres NHS; Orch; Sch Mus; Sch Pl; Natl Merit Schl; Northwestern Univ; Integrated Sci.

SCHOENHERR, JOSEPH; Meridian HS; Midland, MI; Hon Rl; Sch Pl; Stg Crw; Cert List; Perfct Attndnc; Delta Coll; Carptner.

SCHOENHERR, PAUL; Adlai Stevenson HS; Sterling Hts, MI; 12/525 Chrs; Chrh Wkr; Hon Rl; NHS; Ger Clb; Macomb County Community College;bio.

SCHOENLE, GERALD; Bishop Dwenger HS; Ft Wayne, IN; VP Frsh Cls; Cls Rep Soph Cls; Cl Rep Jr Cls; Chrh Wkr; Hon Rl; NHS; Sch Pl; Stu Cncl; Fr Clb; Key Clb; Univ; Chem Engr.

SCHOENLEIN, LINDA M; Marion Local HS; Maria Stein, OH; Hon Rl; Off Ade; Stu Cncl; 4-H; Pep Clb; Sec.

SCHOENTRUP, ANITA R; Waldron HS; Shelbyville, IN; 3/67 Cl Rep Jr Cls; Chrs; Drl Tm; FCA; Girl Scts; Hon Rl; Sct Actv; Stu Cncl; 4-H; Lat Clb; Indiana Univ; Phys Ther.

SCHOETTINGER, JULIE; St Ursula Acad; Cinti, OH; Cls Rep Soph Cls; Cl Rep Jr Cls; Cls Rep Sr Cls; Chrs; Hon Rl; NHS; Pol Wkr; Sch Mus; Stu Cncl; Sch Nwsp; Ball St Univ; Urban Studies.

SCHOETTMER, JOHN; Alter HS; Kettering, OH; 84/360 Letter Ftbl; Letter Trk; Univ Of Dayton; Pre Med.

SCHOFIELD, AMY; Carman HS; Flint, MI; Sec Jr Cls; Chrh Wkr; Girl Scts; Hon Rl; Pol Wkr; Yth Flsp; College; Pharmacy.

SCHOFIELD, SHARON; Parkersburg HS; Vienna, WV; 61/746 Chrs; Chrh Wkr; Hon Rl; Hosp Ade; Sch Mus; Yth Flsp; FTA; Pep Clb; Coll; Nursing.

SCHOFNER, KEITH; Morristown Jr Sr HS; Shelbyville, IN; 24/100 Cls Rep Frsh Cls; Cls Rep Soph Cls; Cl Rep Jr Cls; Cls Rep Sr Cls; Pres Stu Cncl; Pres 4-H; FFA; Lat Clb; 4-H Awd; Outstndng Jr Leader Boy; Picked To Go To Boys St; Coll; Law.

SCHOLL, DAVID; Henryville HS; Henryville, IN; VP Frsh Cls; Band; Hon Rl; NHS; Pep Clb; Bsbl; C A Prosser Voc Schl; Brick Layer.

SCHOLL, JEFFREY T; Mancelona Public HS; Mancelona, MI; Hon Rl; Letter Ftbl; Wrstlng; Voc Schl; Elec.

SCHOLLE, JEAN; Archbishop Alter HS; Centerville, OH; Hon Rl; Pres 4-H; IM Sprt; 4-H Awd; Hocking Tech Inst; Wildlife.

SCHOLLMEYER, JEFFREY; Frankenmuth HS; Frankenmuth, MI; 47/170 Band; Hon Rl; Sch Mus; Sch Pl; Stg Crw; IM Sprt; Michigan St Univ; Music.

SCHOLTEN, CATHERINE; Cadillac HS; Cadillac, MI; Chrs; Hon Rl; NHS; Sch Mus; Rptr Yrbk; Univ Of Mic; Psych.

SCHOLTEN, KAREN; Gull Lake HS; Galesburg, MI; Band; Chrh Wkr; Girl Scts; Hon Rl; Natl Forn Lg; Sch Mus; Sch Pl; DECA; 4-H; Chrldng; State Finalist Forensic 1978; Kalamazoo Valley Cmnty Coll; Bus Adm.

SCHOLTEN, SHARI; East Kentwood HS; Kentwood, MI; Band; Hon Rl; NHS; Off Ade; Davenport Coll Of Bus; Med Asst.

SCHOLTEN, VICTORIA; Zeeland Public HS; Zeeland, MI; Band; Letter Trk;.

SCHOLZ, KENT; Northrop HS; Ft Wayne, IN; 8/581 Yth Flsp; 4-H; IM Sprt; Purdue Univ; Math.

SCHOLZ, RHONDA; Wickliffe HS; Wickliffe, OH; 47/325 Cls Rep Frsh Cls; Cls Rep Sr Cls; Chrs; Hon Rl; Treas JA; Stu Cncl; Chrldng; GAA; Southeastern Acad; Ticket Agent.

SCHONHOFT, MARTHA; Madeira HS; Cincinnati, OH; Sal; Hon Rl; NHS; Sch Pl; Stg Crw; Drama Clb; Fr Clb; Rotary Awd; Univ Of Cincinnati; Nursing.

SCHONING, JEFF; Ravenna HS; Ravenna, OH; Pres Jr Cls; Pres Sr Cls; Boy Scts; Hon Rl; NHS; Bsbl; Ftbl; Trk; IM Sprt; Sftbl 77 78 & 79; Lab Aide 79; Cincinnati Univ; Dnet.

SCHONK, CHARMAINE; Philip Barbour HS; Montrose, WV; Girl Scts; Hon Rl; Rptr Yrbk; 4-H; Fr Clb; Mth Clb; Bsbl; Bsktbl; Gym; Vocational School; Art.

SCHONOVER JR, JAMES; Garfield HS; Akron, OH; 39/390 Hon Rl; Jr NHS; NHS; Pres Yth Flsp; Ed Sch Nwsp; Socr; Ten; Univ Of Akron; Chemical Engr.

SCHOOLCRAFT, GARY; West Branch HS; North Benton, OH; 7/259 Band; Hon Rl; NHS; Orch; Sch Mus; Natl Merit Ltr; Ohio St Univ; Computer Science.

SCHOOLCRAFT, MARY; Coopersville HS; Muskegon, MI; Hon Rl; Hosp Ade; NHS; Off Ade; Stg Crw; Stu Cncl; Rptr Yrbk; Muskegon Comm Coll; Acctg.

SCHOOLER, ERIC; Cedarville HS; Cedarvl, OH; Band; Boy Scts; Chrh Wkr; FCA; Sch Pl; Sct Actv; Fr Clb; Bsbl; Bsktbl; Ftbl; Univ Of Colorado; Bio Sci.

SCHOOLEY, DAN; Ypsilanti HS; Ypsilanti, MI; Cmnty Wkr; Hon Rl; JA; Eastern Michigan Univ; Law.

SCHOONARD, TIMOTHY; Battle Creek Central HS; Battle Creek, MI; Cl Rep Jr Cls; Cls Rep Sr Cls; Boy Scts; Chrs; Debate Tm; Hon Rl; JA; Natl Forn Lg; Sch Mus; Stg Crw; Nation Forensic Lang Bronze Seal 78; Mi Bd Of Educ Tuition Grant 79; Male Chorus St Champ Mbr 78; Western Michigan Univ; Bio Med Sci.

SCHOONOVER, DOUG; Holt HS; Holt, MI; 108/340 Univ; Engr.

SCHOONOVER, KATHY; Elkins HS; Elkins, WV; 4-H Awd; Coll; Police Acad.

SCHOONOVER, KENNETH; Elkins HS; Elkins, WV; Boy Scts; VICA; Diploma In Bldg Trades; Meat Cutter.

SCHOPIERAY, JACQUELYN; Cadillac Sr HS; Cadillac, MI; 35/302 Girl Scts; Hon Rl; NHS; Pol Wkr; Bsktbl; GAA; Grand Valley St Univ; RN.

SCHOPNEYER, LORI; Clay City HS; Center Point, IN; 45/71 Band; Hon Rl; Lbry Ade; Yth Flsp; FHA; Bsktbl; Chrldng; GAA; 4-H Awd; Kiwan Awd; Indiana Univ; Law Enforcement.

SCHOPPEL, MARY; Oregon Davis HS; Hamlet, IN; 13/68 Band; Chrh Wkr; Hon Rl; Sch Pl; Stu Cncl; Yth Flsp; Rptr Sch Nwsp; Ind State Univ; Public Relations.

SCHOPPENHURST, ANNA; Fthr Thomas Scecina Mem HS; Indianapolis, IN; 9/194 Cmnty Wkr; Hon Rl; Univ Of Chicago; Anthropology.

SCHORK, CAROLYN R; William Mason HS; Mason, OH; 24/180 Hon Rl; Jr NHS; NHS; Yth Flsp; Socr; Chrldng; Natl Merit Ltr; Mst Outstndng Bio Wad 77; Univ Of Cincinnati; Nursing.

SCHORLE, PAMELA; Rittman HS; Rittman, OH; 13/113 Trs Soph Cls; Am Leg Aux Girls St; Band; NHS; Stg Crw; Ed Yrbk; Ed Sch Nwsp; VP Pep Clb; Wayne Gen & Tech College; Sec Std.

SCHOSKER, JULIE; Spencerville HS; Spencerville, OH; 6/95 Trs Sr Cls; Am Leg Aux Girls St; Band; Chrs; Chrh Wkr; Girl Scts; NHS; Sch Mus; Sch Pl; Yth Flsp; Ohio St Univ.

SCHOSTAK, BRIAN; Nordonia HS; Macedonia, OH; Hon Rl; Sct Actv; College; Civil Engr.

SCHOTT, JOAN; Colonel Crawford HS; Bucyrus, OH; 7/126 Am Leg Aux Girls St; Band; Chrs; NHS; Sec Sct Actv; Rptr Sch Nwsp; Pres 4-H; Letter Gym; 4-H Awd; Whos Who Among Amer HS Stud 77; Ohio St Univ; Comp Engr.

SCHOTT, SUSAN; Eastwood HS; Pemberville, OH; 10/185 Band; Boy Scts; Hon Rl; Pres JA; Sec Yth Flsp; Rptr Yrbk; Pres 4-H; Lat Clb; 4-H Awd; Toledo Univ; Pre Med.

SCHOUMACHER, VALERIE; Greenbrier East HS; Lewisburg, WV; 16/413 Cls Rep Frsh Cls; Cl Rep Jr Cls; Band; Chrh Wkr; Cmnty Wkr; Hon Rl; Hosp Ade; NHS; Pol Wkr; Sch Mus; Concord College; Educ.

SCHOUP, BRUCE; Upper Sandusky Sr HS; Upper Sandusky, OH; Chrh Wkr; Cmnty Wkr; Hon Rl; NHS; Sec Yth Flsp; IM Sprt; Coll; Bus.

SCHOUT, VALARIA; High School; Macedonia, OH; 28/450 Fr Clb; Sci Clb; Cit Awd; DAR Awd; Natl Merit SF; Ohio Northern Univ; Pre Med.

SCHRACK, BARB; Madison Comprehensive HS; Mansfield, OH; Cls Rep Soph Cls; Trs Sr Cls; Chrs; Stu Cncl; Y-Teens; 4-H; Ger Clb; Ten; 4-H Awd; Agricultural Tech Inst; Horse Mgmt.

SCHRACK, M BETH; Newton Falls HS; Newton Falls, OH; 6/165 Trs Sr Cls; Am Leg Aux Girls St; Band; Treas NHS; Y-Teens; Rptr Yrbk; Ed Sch Nwsp; Treas Spn Clb; Capt Pom Pon; Am Leg Awd; Genrl Motors Inst; Engr.

SCHRACK, RONALD; Loudonville HS; Loudonville, OH; 35/135 Hon Rl; NHS; Sch Pl; Stu Cncl; Sprt Ed Sch Nwsp; Lat Clb; Spn Clb; Letter Bsbl; Letter Ftbl; Coach Actv; Ohio St Univ; Engr.

SCHRAD, LINDA; Marian HS; Elkhart, IN; 1/152 Cls Rep Soph Cls; Hst Jr Cls; Chrs; Girl Scts; Hon Rl; Jr NHS; Mdrgl; Rptr Yrbk; Pep Clb; Natl Merit SF; College; Math.

SCHRADER, BETH; De Kalb HS; Waterloo, IN; 42/287 Cl Rep Jr Cls; Girl Scts; NHS; Sch Pl; Treas Stu Cncl; Rptr Sch Nwsp; Ger Clb; Pep Clb; Trk; PPFtbl; Purdue Univ; Engr.

SCHRADER, LORI K; Southeastern HS; Chillicothe, OH; Hon Rl; Jr NHS; NHS; FTA; Ger Clb; Intensive Office Educ.

SCHRADER, MELINDA; Bloom Local HS; S Webster, OH; Band; Chrs; Chrh Wkr; Drl Tm; Girl Scts; Hon Rl; Hosp Ade; NHS; Sch Pl; Yth Flsp; Brigham Young Univ; Animal Sci.

SCHRADER, RICHARD; Green HS; Akron, OH; 25/319 Boy Scts; Chrs; Chrh Wkr; Hon Rl; Sct Actv; IM Sprt; College.

SCHRADER, ROBERT; Green HS; Akron, OH; 23/319 Hon Rl; Coach Actv; IM Sprt; Scr Kpr; College; Mech Engr.

SCHRAGE, FRANCES; Dowagiac Union HS; Dowagiac, MI; 2/208 Hon Rl; NHS; Fr Clb; Am Leg Awd; Aquinas Coll; Music.

SCHRAGER, DAVID; William Henry Harrison HS; Evansville, IN; 25/466 Hon Rl; NHS; Spn Clb; Crs Cntry; Swmmng; N W Univ; Med.

SCHRAMKE, MARY; John Glenn HS; Bay City, MI; Cls Rep Frsh Cls; Pres Soph Cls; VP Jr Cls; Chrh Wkr; Hon Rl; Jr NHS; NHS; Stu Cncl; Fr Clb; Gym; Cheerleader Of The Year Awd 1978; Western Michigan Univ; Soc Work.

SCHRAMM, ALISSA; Solon HS; Solon, OH; Chrs; Hosp Ade; MMM; Ed Sch Nwsp; Rptr Sch Nwsp; Letter Ten; Trk; Univ; Jrnlsm.

SCHRAMM, ANN; Bishop Fenwick HS; Middletown, OH; Band; Chrh Wkr; Cmnty Wkr; Hon Rl; JA; NHS; Sch Mus; Rptr Yrbk; Fr Clb; Bsbl; General Motors Inst; Engr.

SCHRAMSKI, DONNA; St Joseph HS; S Bend, IN; Band; Chrs; Drl Tm; Sch Mus; 4-H; Ind Univ; Elem Educ.

SCHRAND, REBECCA; St Ursula Acad; Cincinnati, OH; Cmnty Wkr; Hon Rl; Spn Clb; Univ.

SCHRAND, STEVE; Southside HS; Muncie, IN; Boy Scts; Hon Rl; JA; Sct Actv; Rptr Yrbk; DECA; Fr Clb; Letter Glf; IM Sprt; JA Awd; Spelling Bee Champ Twice 1974; Offcr In Jr Achvmnt Co 1977; Michigan St Univ; Hotel Mgmt.

SCHRANK, DAVID; Union County HS; Liberty, IN; 15/130 Pres Jr Cls; Pres Sr Cls; Am Leg Boys St; Pres Chrs; Pres FCA; Hon Rl; NHS; Letter Bsbl; Letter Bsktbl; Dnfth Awd; College; Acctg.

SCHRECONGOST, BETH; West Geauga HS; Novelty, OH; Band; Hon Rl; Yth Flsp; IM Sprt; Tmr; Univ; Spec Educ.

SCHREIBER, DEBBIE; Loveland Hurst HS; Loveland, OH; 13/269 Hon Rl; NHS; FHA; Ger Clb; GAA; Schlrshp Pin; Acctg Awd; Miami Univ; Acctg.

SCHREIBER, JOY; Hanover Central HS; Cedar Lake, IN; 1/137 Sec Frsh Cls; VP Soph Cls; VP Jr Cls; Chrh Wkr; Hon Rl; Pres Jr NHS; NHS; Sch Pl; Pep Clb; Spn Clb; College.

SCHREIBER, KENNETH; Kirtland HS; Kirtland, OH; Cmnty Wkr; Hon Rl; VP JA; Civ Clb; Spn Clb; Letter Trk; IM Sprt; College; Mech Engr.

SCHREIBER, MICHELLE J; West Lafayette Sr HS; W Lafayette, IN; 40/185 Hon Rl; Sch Mus; Sch Pl; Yrbk; Drama Clb; Pep Clb; Letter Glf; Ten; Univ; Math.

SCHREIBMAN, STEVEN R; Glen Oak HS; Canton, OH; 49/700 Am Leg Boys St; Band; Chrs; Natl Forn Lg; NHS; Sch Mus; Sch Pl; Pres Drama Clb; Indiana University; Advertising.

SCHREINER, JACKIE; Brookville HS; Brookville, IN; 15/200 Am Leg Aux Girls St; Band; Drl Tm; Hon Rl; Jr NHS; Letter Bsktbl; Letter Glf; GAA; Pom Pon; MVP In Golf Last Two Yrs Conf Medalist Last Two Yrs 77; Univ; RN.

SCHREINER, MARTHA; Tiffin Calvert HS; Tiffin, OH; Sec Sr Cls; Chrs; Hon Rl; Jr NHS; NHS; Sch Mus; Stg Crw; Pep Clb; Letter Ten; Mgrs; Univ; Nursing.

SCHREUDER, KENNETH; Kalamazoo Christian HS; Kalamazoo, MI; Band; Hon Rl; NHS; Sch Pl; Yrbk; 4-H; Letter Ftbl; Coach Actv; 4-H Awd; Hope Coll; Civil Engr.

SCHRIEBER, GARY; Memorial HS; Campbell, OH; Mth Clb; Sci Clb; Spn Clb; Letter Ftbl; Trk; Univ; Math.

SCHRIER, JULIE; Brownsburg HS; Brownsburg, IN; Sec Frsh Cls; Cls Rep Frsh Cls; Cls Rep Soph Cls; Cl Rep Jr Cls; Trs Sr Cls; Cls Rep Sr Cls; Chrh Wkr; Hon Rl; Lbry Ade; Stu Cncl; Model Stu Awd; Most Dedicated To Frshmn Class; Phys Fitness Awd; Soph Class Princess;.

SCHROCK, ANITA; Colon HS; Mendon, MI; Cls Rep Frsh Cls; Cls Rep Soph Cls; Cl Rep Jr Cls; Cls Rep Sr Cls; Hon Rl; Stu Cncl; Fr Clb; Pep Clb; PPFtbl; Bus Sch.

SCHROCK, CLAUD R; Morton Sr HS; Hammond, IN; 31/439 Chrh Wkr; Hon Rl; Sci Clb; Ftbl; Purdue Univ; Vet.

SCHROCK, DEBBIE; Northridge HS; Bristol, IN; 6/128 Chrs; Hon Rl; Lbry Ade; NHS; Pep Clb; Glen Oaks; Nursing.

SCHROCK, HOWARD; St Agatha HS; Redford, MI; Am Leg Boys St; Hon Rl; NHS; Stg Crw; Letter Bsktbl; Capt Ftbl; Letter Trk; College; Business.

SCHROCK, JOY; Pettisville HS; Pettisville, OH; Cls Rep Frsh Cls; Chrs; Hon Rl; NHS; Sch Pl; Stu Cncl; Yth Flsp; Yrbk; Coll; Bookkeeping.

SCHROCK, SCOTT A; Waynedale HS; Apple Creek, OH; 13/121 VP Soph Cls; Hon Rl; Stu Cncl; Rptr Sch Nwsp; FTA; Natl Merit SF; Georgia Inst Of Tech; Aero Engr.

SCHROCK, TERESA; Goshen HS; Goshen, IN; Chrs; Chrh Wkr; Hon Rl; Orch; Fr Clb; Ball St Univ; Hist.

SCHRODER, ROBERTA; New Haven HS; New Haven, MI; Trs Jr Cls; Cl Rep Jr Cls; Band; Girl Scts; Hon Rl; NHS; OEA; Bsbl; Bsktbl; Trk; Univ; Mech Engr.

SCHROECK, THOMAS; La Salle HS; Cincinnati, OH; Hon Rl; Coach Actv; IM Sprt; Scr Kpr; College.

SCHROEDER, ARLENE; Switzerland County Jr Sr HS; Vevay, IN; 5/120 NHS; Rptr Sch Nwsp; Pep Clb; Spn Clb; Letter Bsktbl; Trk; Coach Actv; Univ; Comp Progr.

SCHROEDER, BARBARA; Pioneer Joint Vocational HS; Shelby, OH; 12/270 Hst Sr Cls; Band; Chrs; Chrh Wkr; Debate Tm; Hon Rl; Ed Sch Nwsp; Rptr Sch Nwsp; OEA; Cit Awd; 2nd Pl Regional & St Typing; Masters Thesis For Pioneer JVS Instructor; College; Archaeology.

SCHROEDER, BARBARA; New Prairie HS; Rolling Prairie, IN; Cl Rep Jr Cls; Chrh Wkr; Hon Rl; Off Ade; Pep Clb; Gym; Chrldng; IM Sprt;.

SCHROEDER, BARBARA; Jefferson Union HS; Bloomingdale, OH; Hon Rl; Lbry Ade; Rptr Sch Nwsp; Beta Clb; Ger Clb; Ohio St Univ; Bus Admin.

SCHROEDER, CRAIG; Chagrin Falls HS; Chagrin Falls, OH; AFS; Boy Scts; Chrh Wkr; Hon Rl; Lat Clb; Letter Bsbl; Letter Ftbl; Hockey; Coach Actv; Texas A & M Univ; Vet Med.

SCHROEDER, DEBBIE; Clay Sr HS; Oregon, OH; 19/323 Girl Scts; Hon Rl; NHS; Sct Actv; Sec OEA; Pep Clb; Letter Bsktbl; GAA;.

SCHROEDER, DEBRA; Clay Sr HS; Oregon, OH; 19/323 Girl Scts; Hon Rl; NHS; Sct Actv; Sec OEA; Pep Clb; Letter Bsktbl; GAA; Sec.

SCHROEDER, GARY; Napoleon HS; Napoleon, OH; 31/257 Band; Chrs; Chrh Wkr; Hon Rl; NHS; Orch; Sch Mus; Sch Pl; Yth Flsp; Drama Clb; Univ Of Cincinnati; Archt.

SCHROEDER, JILL; Bloomington North HS; Bloomington, IN; Chrs; Pep Clb; GAA; PPFtbl; Scr Kpr; Ind Univ; Arts.

SCHROEDER, KAREN; Big Rapids HS; Big Rapids, MI; Chrs; Girl Scts; Mdrgl; Sch Mus; Yth Flsp; 4-H; Trk; 4-H Awd; Ferris St Univ; Forestry.

SCHROEDER, LORI K; Concordia Lutheran HS; Decatur, IN; Hon Rl; NHS; Off Ade; Pol Wkr; Yrbk; Sec FBLA; Ger Clb; Pep Clb; Bus.

SCHROEDER, MARGIE; Norwood HS; Norwood, OH; Chrs; Drl Tm; Hon Rl; Sch Mus; Sec Stu Cncl; Fr Clb; Attended Operation Youth At Xavier Univ; Xavier Univ; Math.

SCHROEDER, PAUL; Richmond Sr HS; Richmond, IN; Univ.

SCHROEDER, ROBERT G; New Buffalo HS; New Buffalo, MI; Band; Boy Scts; Chrh Wkr; Hon Rl; Yth Flsp; Attndnc Awds 76 79; Univ; Acctg.

SCHROEDER, RONALD; Mt Vernon Sr HS; Mt Vernon, IN; 1/250 Am Leg Boys St; Chrh Wkr; Hon Rl; NHS; Stu Cncl; Pres Yth Flsp; Rptr Sch Nwsp; Pres 4-H; VP FFA; Sci Clb; Purdue Univ; Ag Engr.

SCHROEDER, SHARON; Saint Joseph HS; St Joseph, MI; 17/313 Hon Rl; Drama Clb; Spn Clb; Western Michigan Univ; Comp Sci.

SCHROEDER, SHEILA MIE; Cathedral HS; Indianapolis, IN; Cls Rep Frsh Cls; Sec Soph Cls; Cls Rep Soph Cls; Cl Rep Jr Cls; Girl Scts; Hon Rl; Hosp Ade; Off Ade; Sch Mus; Stu Cncl; Indiana Univ; Poli Sci.

SCHROEDER, STEVEN; Zionsville Commnty HS; Zionsville, IN; 4/175 Band; Boy Scts; Hon Rl; Sct Actv; Stg Crw; 4-H; Spn Clb; Letter Crs Cntry; Trk; Mgrs; Valparaiso Univ; Elec.

SCHROEN, SHERRI; Pinckney HS; Pinckney, MI; Chrh Wkr; Hon Rl; Pep Clb; Spn Clb; IM Sprt; Ja ckson Community College; Med Asst.

SCHROER, KATHY I; Defiance Sr HS; Defiance, OH; 13/110 Band; Chrh Wkr; Cmnty Wkr; Girl Scts; Hon Rl; NHS; Orch; Sch Mus; Treas Yth Flsp; Eng Clb; Regnl Sci Fair Honorable Mention 76; Univ; Scndry Educ.

SCHROERING, BRENDA; Northeast Dubois HS; Jasper, IN; 2/77 Trs Jr Cls; Sec Sr Cls; Am Leg Aux Girls St; FCA; Hon Rl; Beta Clb; FHA; Ger Clb; OEA; Pep Clb; Butler Univ; Bus Admin.

SCHROERING, JOYCE; Jasper HS; Jasper, IN; 20/289 Cls Rep Soph Cls; VP Sr Cls; Sec Band; Chrh Wkr; Drm Bgl; Hon Rl; NHS; Stu Cncl; Letter Bsktbl; 4-H Awd; College; Accounting.

SCHROLL, KATHRYN; Bishop Borgess HS; Detroit, MI; 160/485 Chrh Wkr; Debate Tm; Hon Rl; Lbry Ade; Natl Forn Lg; NHS; Off Ade; Rptr Sch Nwsp; Ger Clb; Cert Of Recognition St Of Mi Competitive Awd 79; Schlrshp Progr Awd; St Of Mi Spec Trib Fr C P Ogonoski 79; Henry Ford Cmnty Coll; RN.

SCHROTE, KAREN; River Valley HS; Marion, OH; 8/208 Chrs; NHS; Sch Mus; Stg Crw; Yth Flsp; 4-H; FHA; Lat Clb; 4-H Awd; Ohio St Univ; Fshn Mdse.

SCHROUDER, DEBORAH; Central HS; Grand Rapids, MI; 13/293 Cls Rep Frsh Cls; Cls Rep Soph Cls; Cl Rep Jr Cls; Cls Rep Sr Cls; Chrs; Chrh Wkr; Debate Tm; Hon Rl; Bob Jones Univ; Voice Major.

SCHROYER, DIANA; Heath HS; Heath, OH; Aud/Vis; Band; Chrh Wkr; Debate Tm; Girl Scts; Hosp Ade; Lit Mag; Natl Forn Lg; PAVAS; Red Cr Ade; 1st Pl In Dist & St Spanish; High Ranking Girl In Amer Legion In Govt; Mem Of St Bd For Intl Thespian Soc; Georgetown Univ; Military Sci.

SCHRUPP, LYNNE; Benedictine HS; Detroit, MI; Hon Rl; Rptr Yrbk; College; Science.

SCHRUTT, JIM; Pittsford HS; Pittsford, MI; Cl Rep Jr Cls; Boy Scts; Sch Pl; Stu Cncl; FFA; Ftbl; Voc Sch; Buidling Trades.

SCHUARTZ, STEPHEN; Cincinnati Country Day HS; Cincinnati, OH; Hon Rl; Mod UN; Sec Stu Cncl; Rptr Sch Nwsp; Sch Nwsp; Letter Bsktbl; Letter Trk; College; Engr.

SCHUBACH, TIMOTHY; Olentangy HS; Powell, OH; 2/146 Aud/Vis; Hon Rl; Lbry Ade; NHS; Fr Clb; Case Western Reserve Univ; Mech Engr.

SCHUBEL, CHERYL; Harbor Beach HS; Minden City, MI; 4/131 Chrs; Chrh Wkr; Hon Rl; NHS; Pep Clb; Off Ade; 4-H; Mic State Univ; Med Tech.

SCHUBERT, JANICE; Elyria HS; Elyria, OH; 15/565 Cl Rep Jr Cls; VP Sr Cls; Am Leg Aux Girls St; Chrh Wkr; Hon Rl; NHS; Pol Wkr; Rptr Yrbk; Spn Clb; Elk Awd; Case Western Reserve Univ; Math.

SCHUBERT, NANCY; Walnut Hills HS; Cincinnati, OH; Chrs; Girl Scts; Hon Rl; Hosp Ade; Pol Wkr; Sch Mus; Sprt Ed Yrbk; Capt Swmmng; Chrldng; GAA; Univ; Pre Med.

SCHUDDINCK, LISA; Avon Jr Sr HS; Danville, IN; Girl Scts; Sch Pl; Drama Clb; VP OEA; Glf; Ambssdr Awd For OEA 79; 1st Cls Girl Scout 77; Coll; Bus.

SCHUE, DELANA; Warsaw Community HS; Warsaw, IN; 88/405 Band; Hon Rl; JA; Yth Flsp; Pom Pon; JA Awd; Ind State Univ; Educ.

SCHUELER, SUSAN; Holy Name Nazareth HS; Strongsville, OH; Chrs; Girl Scts; Hon Rl; Sct Actv; Natl Merit Ltr; Univ.

SCHUELLER, DEAN; Fraser HS; Fraser, MI; 4/617 Hon Rl; NHS; Letter Bsbl; Letter Ftbl; Mgrs; Natl Merit Ltr; All A Honor Roll All Years; Univ Of Michigan; Med.

SCHUETER, ROBERT; Troy HS; Troy, MI; 3/300 Chrh Wkr; Hon Rl; Letter Swmmng; Tmr; Univ Of Mic; Engr.

SCHUETTE, DAVID; Armada HS; Armada, MI; 4/140 Am Leg Boys St; Band; Hon Rl; NHS; Sch Mus; Stg Crw; Pep Clb; Bsktbl; Ftbl; Trk; Western Michigan Univ.

SCHUETTE, DONNA; Michigan Center HS; Michigancenter, MI; Orch; Sch Mus; Mi Dept Of Educ Schlshp 79; Mi Compttv Schlsp Porgr Cert Of Recgntn 79; Jackson Cmnty Coll; Radiology Tech.

SCHUETTE, LINDA; Elkton Pigeon Bay Port HS; Pigeon, MI; 11/128 Chrh Wkr; Hon Rl; Rptr Yrbk; 4-H; 4-H Awd; Brd Of Trustee Schlrshp Grant Hnrs 79; Mi Comptn Schlrshp 79; Mi Department Of Ed 79; Central Michigan Univ; RN.

SCHUH, BRENDA; William Mason HS; Mason, OH; 1/180 Cls Rep Soph Cls; AFS; Drl Tm; Hon Rl; NHS; 4-H; Bsktbl; IM Sprt; Mgrs; Am Leg Awd; College; Architecture.

SCHUH, GERALD; Greenville HS; Greenville, OH; Cls Rep Soph Cls; Cl Rep Jr Cls; Chrs; Quill & Scroll; Yrbk; DECA; Busns Schl; Acctg.

SCHUITEMA, KEN; Tri County HS; Sand Lake, MI; 12/88 Chrh Wkr; Hon Rl; Letter Ftbl; IM Sprt; St Of Mi Compt Sclhp 79; Basic Educ Opprt Grant 79; Davenport Coll Of Bus; Acctg.

SCHULDHEIS, SUSAN; South HS; Willoughby, OH; 50/416 Cls Rep Soph Cls; Cl Rep Jr Cls; Cls Rep Sr Cls; Chrs; Hon Rl; NHS; Off Ade; Stu Cncl; Ger Clb; Pep Clb; John Carroll Univ; Pre Med.

SCHULER, DARLENE; Whitmer Sr HS; Toledo, OH; 88/810 Cls Rep Frsh Cls; Chrh Wkr; Cmnty Wkr; Girl Scts; Hon Rl; Sec DECA; Owens Tech Coll; Retail Merch.

SCHULER, PAMELA; Centerville HS; Spring Valley, OH; 7/687 Am Leg Aux Girls St; Band; Chrs; Hon Rl; NHS; Orch; Sch Pl; Drama Clb; Lat Clb; Mth Clb; Ohio Bd Of Regnts Schlrhsp Hon Mentn 78; Ohio St Univ; Vet Med.

SCHULER, SANDRA; Reitz Memorial HS; Evansville, IN; Band; Chrs; Chrh Wkr; Drl Tm; Hon Rl; Sch Mus; Sch Pl; Stg Crw; Pom Pon; College; Nurse.

SCHULIGER, LYNNE; Bexley HS; Columbus, OH; Cl Rep Jr Cls; Chrs; Chrh Wkr; Drl Tm; Hon Rl; Stu Cncl; College.

SCHULJAK, KIMBERLY; Munster HS; Munster, IN; 22/431 AFS; Band; Drl Tm; Drm Mjrt; Hon Rl; NHS; Sch Mus; Purdue Univ; German Interpreter.

SCHULT, BRENDA; Eastwood HS; Pemberville, OH; Band; Chrs; FCA; Hon Rl; Stg Crw; Yth Flsp; 4-H; Pep Clb; Crs Cntry; Trk; Univ; Nurse.

SCHULT, SUSAN; Warren HS; Warren, MI; 1/425 Chrs; Chrh Wkr; Hon Rl; Lbry Ade; NHS; Off Ade; Sch Mus; Oakland Univ; Biochemistry.

SCHULTE, CATHERINE; Mt Notre Dame HS; W Chester, OH; 38/181 Chrs; Girl Scts; Sch Mus; Stg Crw; FNA; Spn Clb; Wright State Univ; Elem Educ.

SCHULTE, DAVE; Lake HS; Genoa, OH; Band; Hon Rl; NHS; 4-H; Ftbl; 4-H Awd; Voc Schl; Agri.

SCHULTE, DONALD; Grosse Pointe North HS; Grosse Pte Wds, MI; 30/534 Aud/Vis; Cmnty Wkr; Hon Rl; Lit Mag; Rptr Yrbk; Yrbk; Natl Merit SF; Schlrshp Art Awd 2 Cert Of Merit 4 Gld Key 78; Schlstic Wrtng Awd Gld Key Art 79; Achvmnt In Ec Awd 79; Cntr For Creative Studies; Adv Phtgr.

SCHULTE, J; Brandon HS; Holly, MI; Band; Hon Rl; Wayne State Univ; Pre Med.

SCHULTE, JOHN; Catholic Central HS; Detroit, MI; Cls Rep Sr Cls; Hon Rl; Pep Clb; Letter Swmmng; Letter Trk; Chrldng; Indiana Univ; Busns.

SCHULTE, KENNETH; Reese HS; Reese, MI; 15/131 VP Boy Scts; Hon Rl; NHS; Sch Pl; Sct Actv; Pres Mth Clb; Letter Crs Cntry; Mic Tech Univ; Mech Engr.

SCHULTE, KURT; St Marys Cathedral HS; Saginaw, MI; 1/56 VP Sr Cls; Val; Boy Scts; Hon Rl; NHS; Stu Cncl; Sprt Ed Yrbk; Sprt Ed Sch Nwsp; Sci Clb; Letter Bsbl; Charles F Shea Memrl Awd Otstndng Atlete 79; Mi Tech Bd Of Control Schlrshp 79; Mi Dept Of Educ Schlrshp 79; Michigan Tech Univ; Mech Engr.

SCHULTE, MICHAEL; Norwood HS; Norwood, OH; 82/341 Chrs; Chrh Wkr; Hon Rl; Sch Mus; Sch Pl; Lat Clb; Ftbl; Wrstlng; IM Sprt; Northern Kentucky Univ.

SCHULTE, PATRICIA; Delphos St Johns HS; Delphos, OH; 23/160 Band; Drm Mjrt; Hon Rl; Fr Clb; Gym; Trk; IM Sprt; Twrlr; Miami Univ; Bus.

SCHULTE, STEPHEN; Clawson HS; Clawson, MI; Hon Rl; Yth Flsp; College; Chem Engr.

SCHULTE, SUSANNE; Port Hope Community HS; Port Hope, MI; Val; Chrs; Hon Rl; Yrbk; Rptr Sch Nwsp; Chrldng; IM Sprt; Letter Saginaw Vly State Coll; Comp Math.

SCHULTE, SUSANNE; Port Hope Comm HS; Port Hope, MI; Chrs; Girl Scts; Hon Rl; Ed Yrbk; Rptr Sch Nwsp; Chrldng; IM Sprt; Natl Merit Ltr; College.

SCHULTHEIS, REGINA; Reitz Memorial HS; Evansville, IN; 1/223 Am Leg Aux Girls St; NHS; Stg Crw; Yth Flsp; Sec 4-H; Letter Bsktbl; Crs Cntry; College; Sci.

SCHULTHEISS, PATRICIA; Logan HS; S Bloomingville, OH; 10/310 Am Leg Aux Girls St; Treas Band; Orch; Sch Mus; 4-H; Pep Clb; PPFtbl; Ohio Univ; Special Education.

SCHULTZ, B; Solon HS; Solon, OH; Hon Rl; NHS; Letter Bsbl; College; Aero Engr Pilot.

SCHULTZ, BARBARA; John Glenn HS; New Condord, OH; Chrh Wkr; Girl Scts; Hon Rl; Sch Pl; Yth Flsp; Drama Clb; Univ.

SCHULTZ, BEVERLY; Portage Lakes Jt Voc HS; Akron, OH; Hst Jr Cls; Cmp Fr Grls; Chrs; Off Ade; Sch Mus; OEA; Pep Clb; Swmmng; Coach Actv; IM Sprt; Univ; Data Proc.

SCHULTZ, BONNIE; Hubbard HS; Hubbard, OH; Am Leg Aux Girls St; Hon Rl; Jr NHS; Lit Mag; NHS; Quill & Scroll; Rptr Sch Nwsp; Bowling Green State Univ; Hos Adm.

SCHULTZ, BRIAN; Oakridge Sr HS; Muskegon, MI; Boy Scts; Hon Rl; Jr NHS; Sch Pl; Sct Actv; Stg Crw; Drama Clb; Trk; Univ; Chem Engr.

SCHULTZ, BRIAN; L'anse HS; Lanse, MI; Hon Rl; Ftbl; Trk;.

SCHULTZ, BRYAN D; Evart HS; Sears, MI; 3/100 Trs Soph Cls; Boy Scts; Hon Rl; NHS; Sch Pl; Pres 4-H; C of C Awd; God Cntry Awd; Natl Merit Ltr; Natl Merit SF; Lake Superior St Coll; Bio.

SCHULTZ, CHRISTINA L; Versailles HS; Versailles, OH; Trs Jr Cls; Yth Flsp; Ed Yrbk; Voc Schl.

SCHULTZ, CINDY; Bishop Ready HS; Columbus, OH; Hon Rl; NHS; DECA; Capital Univ; Bus.

SCHULTZ, CONNIE; T L Handy HS; Bay City, MI; 14/250 Hon Rl; NHS; Fr Clb; Delta Coll; Dental Hygiene.

SCHULTZ, CONNIE; Greenville HS; Gowen, MI; Hon Rl; Hosp Ade; Rptr Yrbk; Pep Clb; Spn Clb; Montcalm Community College; Lpn.

SCHULTZ, DEBRA; Holton HS; Holton, MI; 1/54 Trs Jr Cls; Val; Hon Rl; NHS; PAVAS; Sch Pl; Stg Crw; Yrbk; Drama Clb; 4-H; Muskegon Bus Coll; Med Asst.

SCHULTZ, DENISE; Piqua Central HS; Piqua, OH; 5/270 Band; Chrs; Hon Rl; Jr NHS; Lbry Ade; NHS; Sch Mus; Sch Pl; Stg Crw; Yth Flsp; Univ; Optometry.

SCHULTZ, EDWARD; Whiteford HS; Ottawa Lk, MI; Bsbl; College; Wildlife Mgmt.

SCHULTZ, GARY K; Van Buren HS; Brazil, IN; 12/80 Am Leg Boys St; Band; Hon Rl; Sch Pl; Yth Flsp; Sprt Ed Sch Nwsp; Sch Nwsp; Drama Clb; Key Clb; Spn Clb; Indiana St Univ; Jrnlsm.

SCHULTZ, GRETCHEN; Olmsted Falls HS; Olmsted Falls, OH; 4/244 Chrs; Drl Tm; Hosp Ade; Off Ade; Stu Cncl; Chrldng; College; Med Tech.

SCHULTZ, HEIDI; Olentangy HS; Delaware, OH; Treas Band; Pres Chrs; Mdrgl; Sch Mus; Pres Stu Cncl; Treas 4-H; Treas Fr Clb; PPFtbl; 4-H Awd; Ohio Valley Coll; Piano Tuner.

SCHULTZ, JAMES; Lawrenceburg HS; Lawrenceburg, IN; 2/150 Pres Soph Cls; Pres Jr Cls; Pres Sr Cls; Am Leg Boys St; Hon Rl; Pres Jr NHS; VP NHS; PAVAS; Sch Pl; Pres Stu Cncl; Univ; Bus.

SCHULTZ, JOANNE; Chagrin Falls HS; Chagrin Fl, OH; Trs Jr Cls; VP Debate Tm; Lit Mag; Natl Forn Lg; NHS; Sch Mus; Sch Pl; Pres Fr Clb; College; Journalism.

SCHULTZ, JOSEPH; Padua Franciscan HS; Parma, OH; Hon Rl; Sch Pl; Ohi State; Drama.

SCHULTZ, LAURA; Midland Trail HS; Clifftop, WV; Cl Rep Jr Cls; Am Leg Aux Girls St; Band; Drm Mjrt; Hon Rl; NHS; Pol Wkr; Sch Pl; Stu Cncl; Ed Sch Nwsp; Eng Awd 79; Jrnlsm Awd 79; Eng Bowl Team 79; Univ; Art.

SCHULTZ, LISA; Libbey HS; Toledo, OH; Chrh Wkr; Hon Rl; Jr NHS; NHS; Rptr Sch Nwsp; Fr Clb; Natl Merit Ltr; Bowling Green Univ; Speech Ther.

SCHULTZ, LYNN; All Saints HS; Bay City, MI; Chrs; Chrh Wkr; Hon Rl; Sch Mus; College.

SCHULTZ, MARY; Bishop Chatard HS; Indianaplis, IN; 8/195 Girl Scts; Hon Rl; Bsktbl; IM Sprt; College.

SCHULTZ, MARY; Oakridge HS; Muskegon, MI; 6/150 Hon Rl; Jr NHS; Stg Crw; Pep Clb; Bsbl; Univ Of Michigan; Law.

SCHULTZ, MICHAEL; Purcell HS; Cincinnati, OH; 17/180 Cl Rep Jr Cls; Hon Rl; Bsktbl; Crs Cntry; Ftbl; Ten; IM Sprt; Univ; Acctg.

SCHULTZ, MICHELE; St Joseph HS; St Joseph, MI; Cls Rep Frsh Cls; Cls Rep Soph Cls; Chrh Wkr; Cmnty Wkr; Drl Tm; Pol Wkr; Stu Cncl; Yth Flsp; 4-H; Lat Clb; Michigan St Univ; Pre Vet.

SCHULTZ, NANCY; Davison HS; Davison, MI; Hon Rl; Off Ade; PPFtbl; Ferris St Coll; Legal Asst.

SCHULTZ, RANDALL; Holly HS; Holly, MI; NHS; Letter Ftbl; Letter Wrstlng; GMAC; Chem Engr.

SCHULTZ, REBECCA; Bishop Donahue HS; Wheeling, WV; Band; Chrh Wkr; Hon Rl; Yth Flsp; Yrbk; Sch Nwsp; Pep Clb; Spn Clb; West Virginia Univ; Biol.

SCHULTZ, ROBERT A; Maple Hts Sr HS; Maple Hgts, OH; 15/450 Band; Cmnty Wkr; Hon Rl; Jr NHS; Ger Clb; Letter Ftbl; Letter Trk; Ski Clb; Jaycees Sponser Stu Govt Day; Akron Univ; Chem Engr.

SCHULTZ, SALLY; Mathews HS; Cortland, OH; Hon Rl; Hosp Ade; Stg Crw; Y-Teens; 4-H; Pep Clb; Spn Clb; Trk; Kent St Univ; Nursing.

SCHULTZ, SANDRA; Arthur Hill HS; Saginaw, MI; Chrh Wkr; Hon Rl; NHS; Off Ade; Sci Clb; Central Michigan Univ; Biology.

SCHULTZ, SHARON; Riverside HS; Painesville, OH; Cls Rep Soph Cls; Chrs; Chrh Wkr; Hon Rl; Stu Cncl; Yth Flsp; Letter Bsbl; Letter Bsktbl; Chrldng; GAA; College; Comp Engr.

SCHULTZ, STEPHEN R; St Thomas Aquinas HS; Louisville, OH; 7/143 Cls Rep Sr Cls; Am Leg Boys St; VP Chrh Wkr; VP Natl Forn Lg; Pres NHS; Sch Pl; Yrbk; Ed Sch Nwsp; Letter Wrstlng; IM Sprt; Univ; Med.

SCHULTZ, SUSAN; Kenston HS; Chagrin Fls, OH; Hon Rl; Rus Clb; Capt Chrldng; PPFtbl; Univ; Bus.

SCHULTZ, SUSAN; Trotwood Madison HS; Dayton, OH; 7/390 Chrs; Chrh Wkr; Hon Rl; Jr NHS; NHS; Off Ade; Sch Mus; Yth Flsp; Natl Merit SF; Opt Clb Awd; College; Music.

SCHULTZ, SUZANNE; Rensselaer Central HS; Rensselaer, IN; Band; Chrh Wkr; Hon Rl; Quill & Scroll; Stg Crw; Yth Flsp; Rptr Sch Nwsp; Sch Nwsp; Swmmng; A Schlrshp To Attend HS Jrnlsm Inst IN Univ Bloomington IN 78; Christian Educ.

SCHULTZ, CAROLINE; Lakeview HS; St Clair Shores, MI; Hon Rl; Lit Mag; Ger Clb; Hndbl; Macomb Cmnty Coll; Graphic Art.

SCHULZ, DONATA; Euclid HS; Euclid, OH; AFS; Hon Rl; NHS; Off Ade; Rptr Yrbk; Rptr Sch Nwsp; Letter Swmmng; Mgrs; Tmr; Coll; Lang.

SCHULZ, JENNIFER; Reitz Memorial HS; Evansville, IN; 15/231 Hon Rl; NHS; Letter Bsktbl; Coach Actv; Indiana State; Physical Education.

SCHULZ, PATRICIA; Crestwood HS; Manuta, OH; 107/238 Chrh Wkr; Cmnty Wkr; Girl Scts; Hon Rl; Hosp Ade; Off Ade; Stu Cncl; Pep Clb; Spn Clb; Btty Crckr Awd; Kent State; Special Educ.

SCHULZE, DANETTE; Charlotte HS; Charlotte, MI; 76/304 Boy Scts; Girl Scts; Sec 4-H; 4-H Awd; Natl Merit SF; Mic State Univ; Animal Tech.

SCHULZE, TODD; Central HS; Usaf Acad, CO; 8/528 VP Frsh Cls; Cls Rep Sr Cls; Chrs; Hon Rl; Jr NHS; NHS; Letter Bsbl; Chrldng; IM Sprt; Natl Merit Ltr; Us Air Force Acad; Aero Engr.

SCHUMACHER, JANE; Colon HS; Colon, MI; Girl Scts; Hon Rl; NHS; Stg Crw; Yth Flsp; 4-H; Fr Clb; Pep Clb; Trk; 4-H Awd; Univ.

SCHUMACHER, LYNDA; Woodsfield HS; Woodsfield, OH; Sec Frsh Cls; Hon Rl; NHS; 4-H; Fr Clb; Letter Bsktbl; Pioneer Valley Conf Awd For Bsktbl 78; MVP Bsktbl 78; Univ; Phys Ther.

SCHUMACKER, KAREN; Ripley Union Lewis HS; Ripley, OH; Chrh Wkr; Cmnty Wkr; Girl Scts; 4-H; FHA; Bsktbl; 4-H Awd; Coll; Home Econ.

SCHUMAKER, BETH; St Johns HS; St Johns, MI; Cls Rep Soph Cls; Cls Rep Sr Cls; Band; Hon Rl; NHS; Stg Crw; Stu Cncl; Yth Flsp; 4-H; Bus Schl; Sec.

SCHUMAKER, LAURA; Gull Lake HS; Augusta, MI; 77/228 Trs Frsh Cls; VP Soph Cls; Pres Jr Cls; Pres Sr Cls; Hon Rl; Stu Cncl; Ed Yrbk; Fr Clb; Sci Clb; Univ; Bus Admin.

SCHUMAKER, LORRAINE; Servite HS; Detroit, MI; Chrs; Hon Rl; NHS; Sch Pl; IM Sprt; College; Law.

SCHUMAKER, TINA; Medina HS; Medina, OH; Cl Rep Jr Cls; Stu Cncl; Yth Flsp; FHA; Ger Clb; Pep Clb; Chrldng; Coach Actv; GAA;.

SCHUMAN, KEITH; Whitko HS; Columbia City, IN; 25/150 Am Leg Boys St; Band; Hon Rl; NHS; VP 4-H; FFA; Sci Clb; 4-H Awd; Purdue Univ; Agri.

SCHUMAN, KEITH E; Whitko HS; Columbia City, IN; 25/150 Am Leg Boys St; Band; Hon Rl; NHS; VP 4-H; FFA; Sci Clb; 4-H Awd; Purdue Univ; Agri Econ.

SCHUMAN, LARILEE; East Noble HS; Del Norte, CO; Chrh Wkr; Hon Rl; JA; NHS; Y-Teens; 4-H; Pep Clb; Spn Clb; Cit Awd; 4-H Awd; Univ.

SCHUMANN, JUDI; Huntington North HS; Roanoke, IN; Am Leg Aux Girls St; Band; Chrs; Chrh Wkr; Drl Tm; Girl Scts; Hon Rl; Jr NHS; Orch; Pres Yth Flsp; Ball St Univ; Nursing.

SCHUMM, KAY; Parkway HS; Rockford, OH; 11/96 Hon Rl; Treas FHA; Univ; Sec.

SCHUMM, MICHAEL; Parkway HS; Willshire, OH; 10/84 Cls Rep Frsh Cls; Cls Rep Soph Cls; Cl Rep Jr Cls; Cls Rep Sr Cls; Chrh Wkr; FCA; Hon Rl; NHS; Stu Cncl; 4-H;.

SCHUMM, MIKE; Parkway Local HS; Willshire, OH; 9/83 Cls Rep Frsh Cls; Cls Rep Soph Cls; Cl Rep Jr Cls; Cls Rep Sr Cls; Band; FCA; Hon Rl; NHS; Sch Pl; Stu Cncl; Farming.

SCHUMUCKER, JEFFREY F; North Adams HS; N Adams, MI; 15/49 Pres Frsh Cls; Pres Soph Cls; VP Jr Cls; Pres Sr Cls; Eng Clb; Letter Bsktbl; Letter Crs Cntry; IM Sprt; Ferris St Coll; Brdcst Elec.

SCHUNEMANN, CYNTHIA; Wayne HS; Dayton, OH; 114/535 Chrs; Chrh Wkr; Hon Rl; JA; Lbry Ade; Lit Mag; Off Ade; Rptr Sch Nwsp; Sch Nwsp; Scr Kpr;.

SCHUNN, DARLENE; Vassar HS; Vassar, MI; Band; Chrs; Chrh Wkr; Girl Scts; Hon Rl; JA; Off Ade; Orch; Sch Mus; Sch Pl; Univ.

SCHURKO, STEVE; Woodrow Wilson HS; Youngstown, OH; 33/335 Band; Boy Scts; Chrh Wkr; Hon Rl; Jr NHS; Bsktbl; Letter Glf; Letter Trk; Youngstown State; Mech Engineer.

SCHURR, DENISE; L C Mohr HS; South Haven, MI; Band; Hon Rl; NHS; Coach Actv; College; Math.

SCHURR, MICHAEL; Culver Military Acad; Tampa, FL; 9/191 Boy Scts; Hon Rl; ROTC; Swmmng; College; Med.

SCHUSTER, BARBARA; Fairmont West HS; Kettering, OH; 15/490 AFS; Cmnty Wkr; Girl Scts; Hon Rl; Lit Mag; Sct Actv; Stu Cncl; Rptr Yrbk; Rptr Sch Nwsp; IM Sprt; Marian Awd & 1st Class Awd Girl Scouts 76 & 78; Hon Seminar Of Metropolitan Dayton 78; Univ; Sci.

SCHUSTER, DEBORAH; Grosse Ile HS; Grosse Ile, MI; Chrs; Sch Mus; Sch Pl; Drama Clb; GAA; Spring Arbor Coll; Bus.

SCHUSTER, MARK W; Fremont Ross HS; Fremont, OH; Am Leg Boys St; Band; Boy Scts; Chrs; Chrh Wkr; Hon Rl; Jr NHS; NHS; Sec Orch; Pol Wkr; Various GTCTM Math Cont Awd; Miami Univ; Pre Law.

SCHUSTER, SUE S; Swan Valley HS; Saginaw, MI; 1/188 Val; Band; Hon Rl; Jr NHS; NHS; Ten; Trk; Opt Clb Awd; Cntrl Michigan Univ.

SCHUT, SUZY; Gull Lake HS; Richland, MI; 34/250 Cls Rep Frsh Cls; VP Soph Cls; Pres Jr Cls; Pres Sr Cls; Jr NHS; NHS; Stu Cncl; Ed Yrbk; Letter Ten; Bradley Univ; Busns Admin.

SCHUTTE, JEANNE; Hamilton HS; Hamilton, MI; Hon Rl; Mdrgl; Sch Mus; Sch Pl; Stg Crw; Rptr Sch Nwsp; Davenport Coll; Fash Merch.

SCHUTTE, KELLY; Ross Sr HS; Hamilton, OH; 36/205 NHS; Off Ade; Sprt Ed Sch Nwsp; Pep Clb; Chrldng; GAA; Scr Kpr; Morehead St Univ; Med Sec.

SCHUTTER, KEITH; Moeller HS; Cincinnati, OH; Pres Sr Cls; CAP; Hon Rl; NHS; Stu Cncl; Rptr Sch Nwsp; Letter Crs Cntry; Letter Trk; U S Military Academy.

SCHUTZ, JAMES; Rapid River HS; Rapid River, MI; 4/56 Band; Chrs; Debate Tm; Yrbk; Rptr Sch Nwsp; Fr Clb; Letter Trk; St Of Michigan Schlrshp 79; Mc Donalds All American H S Band Nom 79; Patrick & Mary E Memrl Schlrshp 79; Michigan Tech Univ; Chem Engr.

SCHUTZ, LORI; Mater Dei HS; Evansville, IN; 5/174 Cls Rep Soph Cls; Cl Rep Jr Cls; Cls Rep Sr Cls; Hon Rl; Hosp Ade; Jr NHS; Natl Forn Lg; NHS; Pol Wkr; Stu Cncl; Coll; Nursing.

SCHUTZ, SUSAN M; Harrison Comm HS; Harrison, MI; 2/145 Sec Jr Cls; Sec Sr Cls; Band; Hon Rl; Hosp Ade; NHS; DAR Awd; Mid Michigan Comm College; Nursing.

SCHUYLER, GREGORY; William Mason HS; Mason, OH; 24/204 Hon Rl; Sct Actv; Letter Glf; Mas Awd; Univ; Elect Engr.

SCHWAB, ANGELA; Ironton HS; Ironton, OH; Band; Chrs; Chrh Wkr; Drl Tm; Hon Rl; NHS; Orch; Lat Clb; Oh Univ HS Scholr 79; Frsh Awd 77; Univ; Med Tech.

SCHWAB, C; Bishop Foley HS; Madison Hts, MI; Hon Rl; Sch Mus; Sch Pl; Pom Pon; Oakland Univ; Business Admin.

SCHWAB, ERIC; Bishop Foley HS; Madison Hts, MI; 5/193 Hon Rl; Sci Clb; Wayne St Univ; Med.

SCHWAB, JAYNE; Michigan Lutheran Seminary; Kawkawlin, MI; 11/61 Chrs; Hon Rl; Pep Clb; PPFtbl; Doctor Martin Luther College; Tchr.

SCHWAB, JOANNE; Vandalia Butler HS; Dayton, OH; Jr NHS; NHS; Spn Clb; Cit Awd; Cls Rep Frsh Cls; Cls Rep Soph Cls; Chrh Wkr; Bowling Green Univ; Secondary Ed.

SCHWAB, KAREN; Liberty Center HS; Napoleon, OH; Sec Frsh Cls; Cl Rep Jr Cls; Cls Rep Sr Cls; Band; Hon Rl; Red Cr Ade; Sch Pl; Yrbk; Capt Chrldng; Northwest Tech Coll; Nurse.

SCHWAB, MARY; Heath HS; Heath, OH; Chrs; Hon Rl; JA; Gym; Trk; Chrldng; Coll; Phys Ed.

SCHWAB, RAYMOND; Linden Mc Kinley HS; Columbus, OH; 4/260 Chrs; Hon Rl; NHS; Boys Clb Am; DECA; 4-H; Letter Crs Cntry; Letter Ftbl; Letter Trk; Capt Wrstlng; Ohio State Coll; Journalism.

SCHWAB, THERESA; Lakota HS; Cincinnati, OH; 5/464 Hon Rl; Jr NHS; NHS; Ger Clb; Letter Bsktbl; IM Sprt; Scr Kpr; Alumni Schlrshp 79; Cert Of Acad Achvmnt From Oh Bd Of Regents 79; MIP Trophy Var & J V Letters In Vllybl; Wiltenberg Univ; Lab Med.

SCHWABE, RICHARD; Northwest HS; Jackson, MI; Hon Rl; JA; NHS; Mgrs; JA Awd; Central Michigan Univ; Comp Sci.

SCHWANDNER, JODI; Lake HS; Walbridge, OH; 41/174 Trs Sr Cls; Chrs; Girl Scts; Hon Rl; Off Ade; Rptr Yrbk; Rptr Sch Nwsp; Drama Clb; 4-H; Bowling Green State Univ; Math.

SCHWANER, MICHAEL F; Lexington HS; Mansfield, OH; 120/250 Cmnty Wkr; Socr; Ten; Bowling Green Univ; Admin.

SCHWANKHAUS, KAREN; Norwood HS; Norwood, OH; Pres Frsh Cls; Hon Rl; Hosp Ade; Jr NHS; Lbry Ade; Stu Cncl; Fr Clb; Pep Clb; Chrldng; Hospital; RN.

SCHWANZL, MARIE; Central Catholic HS; Toledo, OH; 3/317 Hon Rl; JA; NHS; Letter Gym; Trk; Toledo Univ; Chiropractic.

SCHWARTZ, ALAN J; Seven Hills Schl; Cincinnati, OH; 4/50 Hon Rl; Rptr Sch Nwsp; Spn Clb; Letter Socr; Letter Ten; Natl Merit SF; Univ; Sci.

SCHWARTZ, ANN; Douglas Mac Arthur HS; Saginaw, MI; Pres Frsh Cls; Cls Rep Frsh Cls; Band; Cmp Fr Grls; FCA; Girl Scts; Hon Rl; Jr NHS; NHS; Sch Mus; Ferris Univ; Bus.

SCHWARTZ, CATHI; Bexley Sr HS; Bexley, OH; Chrs; Chrh Wkr; Cmnty Wkr; Girl Scts; Hon Rl; Hosp Ade; Off Ade; Sch Mus; Sct Actv; Stg Crw; Univ; Marine Bio.

SCHWARTZ, ERIC; Houghton HS; Houghton, MI; Trs Jr Cls; Band; Boy Scts; Lit Mag; Orch; Sch Pl; Spn Clb; Mic State; Journalism.

SCHWARTZ, FRIEDA; Houghton HS; Houghton, MI; Band; Chrs; Girl Scts; Hon Rl; Orch; Sch Mus; Sch Pl; Sct Actv; Rptr Yrbk; Northern Mich Univ.

SCHWARTZ, HENRY; Centerville HS; Sturgis, MI; Chrs; Chrh Wkr; Debate Tm; FCA; Jr NHS; NHS; Sch Mus; Stu Cncl; Bsbl; EMC; Food Sci.

SCHWARTZ, JAIMIE; Grandview Hts HS; Columbus, OH; Hon Rl; Yrbk; College.

SCHWARTZ, JANET; Lutheran W HS; Detroit, MI; 2/160 Sec Jr Cls; Cl Rep Jr Cls; Trs Sr Cls; Cls Rep Sr Cls; Sal; Girl Scts; Hon Rl; NHS; Stu Cncl; Yth Flsp; E Michigan; Occupational Therapy.

SCHWARTZ, JOSEPH; Colon HS; Bronson, MI; Sch Nwsp; Bsbl; Letter Crs Cntry; Ftbl; Trk; Am Leg Awd; Glen Oaks; Drafting.

SCHWARTZ, LAURIE; Centreville HS; Centreville, MI; Sec Frsh Cls; VP Soph Cls; Band; Hon Rl; NHS; Stu Cncl; Yth Flsp; Rptr Yrbk; Drama Clb; 4-H; Vllybl 3 Var Letters 77 78 & 79; Bsktbl All Confrnc 79; 4 H 1st In Sr Showmnshp 78; Univ.

SCHWARTZ, PATRICIA; Lorain Catholic HS; Lorain, OH; Chrs; Girl Scts; Hon Rl; NHS; Letter Bsbl; Bsktbl; Glf; Trk; Univ; Optometry.

SCHWARTZ, RANDALL C; Rogers HS; Toledo, OH; Chrs; Hon Rl; Jr NHS; NHS; Lat Clb; Sci Clb; Ftbl; Letter Trk; Wrstlng; Michigan Univ; Math.

SCHWARTZWALDER, DIANE; Lake HS; Millbury, OH; Cmp Fr Grls; Chrs; Girl Scts; Off Ade; Sct Actv; Drama Clb; FBLA; OEA; Pep Clb; GAA; Bowling Green College; Bus.

SCHWARZ, DEBBIE; Columbiana HS; Columbiana, OH; 4/100 Cls Rep Frsh Cls; Band; Capt Drl Tm; Hon Rl; NHS; Sch Pl; Stu Cncl; Rptr Sch Nwsp; Drama Clb; Fr Clb; Univ; Archt.

SCHWARZBEK, STEPHEN M; Frankenmuth HS; Frankenmuth, MI; 3/185 Am Leg Boys St; Band; Chrs; Chrh Wkr; Debate Tm; Hon Rl; NHS; Sch Mus; Sch Pl; Natl Merit SF; Univ; Phys Sci.

SCHWARZE, AMANDA; Chelsea HS; Chelsea, MI; Hon Rl; Bsbl; Chrldng; PPFtbl; College.

SCHWARZIN, HELMUT; Shortridge HS; Indianapolis, IN; Bsbl; Univ; Archt.

SCHWED, KATHY; Ironton HS; Ironton, OH; Cls Rep Soph Cls; JA; Trk; GAA; IM Sprt; Scr Kpr;.

SCHWEIFLER, REBECCA; Muskegon Sr HS; Muskegon, MI; Cl Rep Jr Cls; Cls Rep Sr Cls; Mdrgl; NHS; Orch; Treas Stu Cncl; Pres Ger Clb; Outstndng Regular Bapt Teengr Of Mich; Muskegon Exchnge Clb Yth Of The Mth; Word Of Life Clb Schlrshp; Grand Rapids Baptist Coll; Eng.

SCHWEIKERT, JUDY; Anderson Sr HS; Cincinnati, OH; Letter Chrs; Lat Clb; Letter Socr; Letter Mgrs; Letter Scr Kpr; Univ Of Cincinnati; Police Work.

SCHWEITZER, BRUCE; Wapakoneta HS; Wapakoneta, OH; Hon Rl; NHS; Letter Crs Cntry; Letter Trk; Univ Of Cincinnati; Architecture.

SCHWEITZER, EVELYN; Eastern HS; Winchester, OH; 9/100 Sec Sr Cls; Hon Rl; NHS; Sch Pl; Ed Yrbk; Sprt Ed Sch Nwsp; VP 4-H; Fr Clb; FFA; FTA; Morehead St Univ; Secondary Ed.

SCHWEITZER, MARY; Crown Pt HS; Crown Point, IN; 40/475 Chrh Wkr; Girl Scts; Hon Rl; Lit Mag; NHS; Quill & Scroll; Yrbk; 4-H; Lat Clb; Trusree Schlrshp 79; St Josephs Coll; Math Tchr.

SCHWEITZER, MELINDA; David Anderson HS; Lisbon, OH; 7/118 Am Leg Aux Girls St; Chrh Wkr; FCA; Hon Rl; NHS; Sch Mus; Pres Yth Flsp; Rptr Sch Nwsp; Sci Clb; Trk; College; Christian Educ.

SCHWEITZER, SHAREL; Maumee HS; Maumee, OH; 86/316 Cls Rep Sr Cls; Band; Girl Scts; Hon Rl; Off Ade; Y-Teens; Yrbk; Mat Maids; PPFtbl; Twrlr; Owens Tech Coll; Dent Hygnst.

SCHWENDEMAN, MARILYN; Fort Frye HS; Lowell, OH; 44/129 VP Sr Cls; Band; Hon Rl; Quill & Scroll; Stu Cncl; Pep Clb; Letter Chrldng;.

SCHWENK, CYNTHIA; Whitehall Yearling HS; Columbus, OH; Band; Girl Scts; Hon Rl; Drama Clb; Pep Clb; GAA; Mat Maids; CTI; Data Processing.

SCHWENK, REBECCA; Landmark Christian HS; Three Oaks, MI; Band; Chrs; Hon Rl; NHS; Off Ade; Trk;.

SCHWERER, DEBBIE; St Marys Cntrl Catholic HS; Sandusky, OH; Girl Scts; Hon Rl; Sprt Ed Yrbk; Sci Clb; Spn Clb; Letter Bsktbl; Letter Ten; Letter Trk; GAA; OSU Schl Of Nursing; RN.

SCHWERIN, VICTORIA; Indiana Academy; Angola, IN; Chrs; Hon Rl; NHS; Off Ade; Capt IM Sprt; Andrews Univ; Music.

SCHWERING, REGINA; Greensburg Cmnty HS; Greensburg, IN; 9/203 Band; Chrs; Capt Drl Tm; FCA; Hon Rl; NHS; Sch Mus; Pep Clb; Letter Gym; Purdue Univ; Engr.

SCHWERZLER, ANDREW; Jackson HS; Massillon, OH; Pres FCA; Capt Bsktbl; Univ Of Akron; Mech Engr.

SCHWIEBERT, PATRICIA; Napoleon HS; Napoleon, OH; 1/248 Hon Rl; Lbry Ade; NHS; Lat Clb; Bsktbl; Letter Trk;.

SCHWIETERING, DAN; Purcell HS; Cincinnati, OH; Cl Rep Jr Cls; Hon Rl; Stu Cncl; Rptr Sch Nwsp; Ftbl; IM Sprt; College; Bus Admin.

SCHWIETERMAN, JAMES; Marion Local HS; Maria Stein, OH; 5/92 Pres Frsh Cls; Pres Soph Cls; Am Leg Boys St; Pres Band; Hon Rl; Pres NHS; Pep Clb; Pres Sci Clb; Bsktbl; Trk; Univ.

SCHWIND, JANET; Clay HS; South Bend, IN; Chrh Wkr; Hon Rl; JA; NHS; Rptr Sch Nwsp; Trk; IM Sprt; JA Awd; College; Cmmrcl Artist.

SCHWIND, TAMI; Chagrin Falls HS; Chagrin Falls, OH; AFS; Girl Scts; Hosp Ade; Lit Mag; Yrbk; Rptr Sch Nwsp; Fr Clb; Pres FTA; Pres Ger Clb; Spn Clb; College; Languages.

SCHWING, JUDITH; Bay HS; Bay Vill, OH; 30/373 AFS; Chrs; Chrh Wkr; Girl Scts; Hon Rl; Jr NHS; Lit Mag; Sch Mus; Sct Actv; Yth Flsp; Univ; Foreign Lang.

SCHWING, MICHAEL; Brownsburg HS; Brownsbrg, IN; Ger Clb; Brain Game Tm 78; Rep From HS To Cntrl In Math Contest 76; IUPUI; Chem.

SCHWINGLE, DAN; West Branch HS; Salem, OH; Ftbl; Trk; College.

SCIBETTA, ANTHONY S; Perry HS; Canton, OH; Chrs; FCA; Lit Mag; Sch Mus; Sch Pl; Stg Crw; Ftbl; Trk; Wrstlng; Pres Of Choir 79; Dir Awd 77; Thespian Club 78; Univ; Engr.

SCIRANKO, DEBORAH; Trinity HS; Maple Hts, OH; Chrs; Hon Rl; NHS; Pep Clb; Spn Clb; Mat Maids; Capt Twrlr; Art Schlrshp Schlrshp Of Trinity HS; Sr Art Awd; Cooper Schl Of Art; Art.

SCITES, ERIC; Meigs HS; Pomeroy, OH; Band; Boy Scts; Chrh Wkr; Drm Bgl; Mdrgl; Sch Mus; Pres Fr Clb; Mas Awd; College; Music.

SCITES, TERESA; Huntington East HS; Huntington, WV; Band; Chrh Wkr; Girl Scts; Hon Rl; Jr NHS; 4-H; Lat Clb; Mth Clb; DAR Awd; 4-H Awd; Marshall Univ; Comp Sci.

SCOBBO, JAMES; Stow Sr HS; Stow, OH; Band; Hon Rl; Spanish Awd; Schlrshp Awd; Ski Clb Mbr; College.

SCOBEY, ROBERT; Wayland HS; Wayland, MI; Hon Rl; Natl Merit Ltr; Mi St Comptty Schlshp 79; Michigan St Univ; Fish Wildlife Mgmt.

SCOFIELD, BRADFORD L; Warren G Harding HS; Warren, OH; Chrs; Hon Rl; Ed Yrbk; Sci Clb; Univ Of Florida; Archt.

SCOLES, TODD; Westerville South HS; Westerville, OH; 35/270 Chrh Wkr; Hon Rl; NHS; Rptr Sch Nwsp; IM Sprt; Ohio St Univ; Admin Sci.

SCOLLON, THERESA; Interlochen Arts Academy; Cass City, MI; Pres Soph Cls; Band; Chrs; Chrh Wkr; Jr NHS; NHS; Sch Pl; Stu Cncl; Letter Gym; Natl Merit Ltr; Univ.

SCOOPS, SCOTT; Crestline HS; Crestline, OH; Hon Rl; NHS; Sch Mus; Sch Pl; Stg Crw; Yth Flsp; Rptr Sch Nwsp; Drama Clb; Eng Clb; Ohio St Univ; Theatre.

SCOPEL, ANNETTE; Crestline HS; Crestline, OH; Trs Frsh Cls; Pres Soph Cls; VP Jr Cls; Am Leg Aux Girls St; Stu Cncl; Bsktbl; Trk; Chrldng; M Power Awd Track 1978; Best Def Basktbl 1979; Most Rnng Pts Track 1979;.

SCOPEL, BABETTE M; Crestline HS; Crestline, OH; Off Ade; Bsktbl; Chrldng;.

SCOTT, ANGELA; Menton HS; Concord, OH; Chrh Wkr; Drl Tm; Girl Scts; Hon Rl; Jr NHS; Lbry Ade; Yth Flsp; Keyettes; Spn Clb; Letter Ten; Univ; Dent Hygiene.

SCOTT, BARB; Escanaba Area HS; Escanaba, MI; 7/415 Hon Rl; NHS; Pep Clb; Bsktbl; Glf; Coach Actv; IM Sprt; Univ Of Michigan; Bus.

SCOTT, BARBARA; John Adams HS; So Bend, IN; Band; Chrh Wkr; Cmnty Wkr; Drm Bgl; Hon Rl; 4-H; Trk; 4-H Awd; Univ; Spec Educ.

SCOTT, BARBARA A; Cloverleaf HS; Seville, OH; Hon Rl; Sec Spn Clb; Letter Gym; Trk; PPFtbl; College; Med.

SCOTT, BARBARA A; Rogers HS; Toledo, OH; Cl Rep Jr Cls; Chrs; NHS; Stg Crw; Pres Stu Cncl; Mth Clb; Sci Clb; Letter Trk; Capt Chrldng; Bowling Green St Univ.

SCOTT, BARBARA A; Edgewood HS; Ellettsville, IN; 1/194 Trs Sr Cls; Band; Chrh Wkr; FCA; Girl Scts; Hon Rl; NHS; Yrbk; 4-H; FHA; Purdue Univ; Interior Design.

SCOTT, BARBARA F; Cloverdale HS; Quincy, IN; 8/87 Band; NHS; Stu Cncl; Pep Clb; Sci Clb; Treas Spn Clb; GAA;.

SCOTT, BRETT; Gorham Fayette HS; Fayette, OH; Bsbl; Crs Cntry; Letter Trk; Bus Schl; Real Estate.

SCOTT, BRUCE; Western Boone HS; Jamestown, IN; 17/171 Cls Rep Frsh Cls; VP Soph Cls; Pres Jr Cls; Am Leg Boys St; Band; FCA; Hon Rl; College.

SCOTT, CHERYL; Watkins Mem HS; Pataskala, OH; Ed Yrbk; Rptr Yrbk; 4-H; FHA; 4-H Awd; Findlay Coll; Eng.

SCOTT, CYNTHIA; Oak Hill HS; Fayetteville, WV; Chrh Wkr; Cmnty Wkr; Girl Scts; Hon Rl; Lbry Ade; Off Ade; Pol Wkr; Stg Crw; VP Stu Cncl; Drama Clb; Selctd For Hon Council At Wv Assoc Of Stud Council Workshop 79; Lib Awd For Otstndng Girl 79; West Virginia Univ; Law.

SCOTT, DAVID; Mansfield Christian HS; Mansfield, OH; 2/47 Sal; Hon Rl; NHS; VP Stu Cncl; Rdo Clb; Letter Bsktbl; Socr; Am Leg Awd; Rotary Awd; Ohio St Univ; Wildlife Mgmt.

SCOTT, DAVID; Mississinewa HS; Gas City, IN; Pres Frsh Cls; Treas DECA; Letter Ftbl; Letter Trk; IM Sprt; Bus Schl; Bus Mgmt.

SCOTT, DAVID; Bullock Creek HS; Midland, MI; 9/152 Hon Rl; NHS; Trk; Univ Of Michigan; Law.

SCOTT, DAVID L; Gilmer County HS; Linn, WV; VP Frsh Cls; Cls Rep Soph Cls; Am Leg Boys St; Chrh Wkr; Hon Rl; NHS; Pol Wkr; Pres Stu Cncl; Yth Flsp; Pep Clb; West Virginia Univ; Engr.

SCOTT, DEBBIE; Marion Adams HS; Sheridan, IN; 17/99 FCA; Hon Rl; Jr NHS; Off Ade; FHA; OEA; Letter Bsktbl; Letter Trk; Chrldng; GAA; Butler Univ; Dance.

SCOTT, DEIRDRE; Villa Angela Acad; Cleveland, OH; Cls Rep Soph Cls; Chrh Wkr; Cmnty Wkr; Hon Rl; Hosp Ade; Off Ade; Yth Flsp; Fr Clb; Univ; Public Relations.

SCOTT, DELORA; Southern Wells Jr Sr HS; Keystone, IN; 11/96 Cls Rep Sr Cls; Am Leg Aux Girls St; Hon Rl; Treas NHS; Stu Cncl; Pres 4-H; Pep Clb; Letter Bsktbl; Trk; 4-H Awd; Ball St Univ; Health.

SCOTT, DIANA; Highland HS; Marengo, OH; 16/125 NHS; Letter Bsktbl; Am Leg Awd;.

SCOTT, DIANE J; Southern Wells HS; Keystone, IN; 9/90 Hon Rl; NHS; Yth Flsp; Sec 4-H; FHA; Pep Clb; Mgrs; PPFtbl; Twrlr; 4-H Awd; College; Landscaping.

SCOTT, DONNA; Wood Memorial HS; Francisco, IN; 13/100 Chrs; Chrh Wkr; Girl Scts; Hon Rl; Lbry Ade; Pres Orch; Sch Mus; Yth Flsp; VP Y-Teens; Pep Clb; Schslhp Awd 76 74 & 76; Reading 76; Home Ec 76; Anderson Coll; Med.

SCOTT, EARL A; Cedarville HS; Cedarville, OH; Band; Boy Scts; Hon Rl; NHS; Sch Pl; Rptr Sch Nwsp; Drama Clb; 4-H; Dnfth Awd; God Cntry Awd; Army Band Acad; Army Bandsman.

SCOTT, GARY; Princeton HS; Princeton, WV; 102/390 Band; Boy Scts; Chrs; Chrh Wkr; Cmnty Wkr; Hon Rl; Orch; 4-H; All Cnty Bnd; All Area Bnd; Bnd Schl Letter; Concord Coll; Music.

SCOTT, HEATHER; Otsego HS; Bowling Green, OH; 4/150 Am Leg Aux Girls St; Band; Chrh Wkr; Hon Rl; NHS; Sch Pl; Yrbk; Drama Clb; Fr Clb; Scr Kpr; Ohio State Univ; Journalism.

SCOTT, JAMES; Watkins Memorial HS; Pataskala, OH; Boy Scts; Drl Tm; ROTC; Rptr Sch Nwsp; Sch Nwsp; US Air Force; Art.

SCOTT, JANET; Woodward HS; Cincinnati, OH; 26/406 Band; Chrh Wkr; Hon Rl; Jr NHS; Off Ade; Daisy Chain Hon 78;awd Top 10% In Cls 79; 540 Voc Block Awd 79; Army; X Ray Spec.

SCOTT, JEAN; Galion HS; Galion, OH; Chrs; Hon Rl; Off Ade; Sch Mus; Sch Pl; Drama Clb; Treas 4-H; Fr Clb; Pep Clb; 4-H Awd; College; Radio.

SCOTT, JEFF; Lincolnview HS; Van Wert, OH; 1/80 Am Leg Boys St; Band; VP NHS; Fr Clb; Sci Clb; Letter Glf; Univ; Pre Med.

SCOTT, JEFFERY; Maysville HS; Zaneslille, OH; College; Chem.

SCOTT, JEROME; La Salle HS; Cincinnati, OH; 25/230 Band; Boy Scts; Hon Rl; Lat Clb; IM Sprt; Univ Of Cincinnati; Graphic Design.

SCOTT, JON; Schoolcraft HS; Schoolcraft, MI; Band; Sch Pl; Bsktbl; Glf; Ten; Univ.

SCOTT, JON W; Watkins Memorial HS; Granville, OH; Cls Rep Soph Cls; Cl Rep Jr Cls; Cls Rep Sr Cls; Hon Rl; Lbry Ade; Stu Cncl; Rptr Sch Nwsp; Letter Bsbl; Ohio State.

SCOTT, JULIE; Peebles HS; Peebles, OH; VP Soph Cls; Cls Rep Sr Cls; Chrh Wkr; Cmnty Wkr; Hon Rl; Rptr Yrbk; Sch Nwsp;.

SCOTT, KAREN; Midland Trail HS; Rainelle, WV; Band; Chrs; Girl Scts; Hon Rl; NHS; Sch Pl; Rptr Yrbk; Drama Clb; Fr Clb; FHA; Flag Carrier; Band Council & Sec; Glenville St Coll; Childhood Educ.

SCOTT, KAREN; Springfield HS; Uniontown, OH; 16/368 Am Leg Aux Girls St; Debate Tm; Hon Rl; Lbry Ade; Natl Forn Lg; Scr Kpr; Tmr; Georgetown Univ; RN.

SCOTT, KAREN; Copley HS; Copley, OH; 23/315 Cls Rep Sr Cls; Band; Am Leg Boys St; Hon Rl; Natl Forn Lg; NHS; Sch Mus; Sch Pl; Stg Crw; Yrbk; Univ Of Cincinnati; Graphic Design.

SCOTT, KARLA; Shawnee HS; Lima, OH; 3/260 Hon Rl; Treas NHS; VP Ger Clb; Crs Cntry; Glf; Lion Awd; Natl Merit Ltr; Univ Of Cincinnati; Architecture.

SCOTT, KELLEE; Collinwood HS; Cleveland, OH; Chrs; Hon Rl; NHS; Stu Cncl; Ten; Chrldng; Cit Awd; Miami Univ; Psych.

SCOTT, KEVIN; Madeira HS; Cincinnati, OH; 22/168 Aud/Vis; Band; Hon Rl; JA; Sch Mus; Sch Pl; Stg Crw; Drama Clb; Ger Clb; Natl Merit SF; College; Elec Engr.

SCOTT, KEVIN D; Lakota HS; West Chester, OH; 130250 Pres Frsh Cls; Cls Rep Frsh Cls; Cl Rep Jr Cls; Boy Scts; Chrh Wkr; Hon Rl; NHS; Ohi State; Bus Mgmt.

SCOTT, LAURA; Waterloo HS; Atwater, OH; Sec Frsh Cls; Pres Soph Cls; Cmnty Wkr; Girl Scts; Hon Rl; Hosp Ade; Lbry Ade; Stu Cncl; Drama Clb; 4-H; Akron Univ; Tchr.

SCOTT, LINDA; Salem HS; Salem, OH; 1/275 Am Leg Aux Girls St; Cmp Fr Grls; Hon Rl; Fr Clb; FHA; Pep Clb; Kiwan Awd; Bowling Green State Univ.

SCOTT, LISA; Munster HS; Munster, IN; FCA; Hon Rl; Lbry Ade; NHS; Off Ade; Capt Trk; Sec GAA; IM Sprt; Mgrs; Vllybl Ltr 78 & 79 All Conf 78 & 79 Capt 79; Asst Coach In Vllybl Camp 79; Univ; Bus Admin.

SCOTT, LISA; Muskegon Sr HS; Muskegon, MI; Hon Rl; NHS; Orch; Stu Cncl; Fr Clb; College; Nursing.

SCOTT, MARCIA L; Flint Central HS; Flint, MI; 33/300 Hon Rl; NHS; Yrbk; Sch Nwsp; Mott Cmnty Coll; Fine Arts.

SCOTT, MARTHA; Springfield Cathlc Ctrl HS; San Antonio, TX; 37/150 JA; NHS; Stu Cncl; Ten; Econ 79; Acctg I 79; Univ Of Texas; Finance.

SCOTT, PATRINA; Rock Hill HS; Wheelersburg, OH; 39/162 Cl Rep Jr Cls; FCA; Sch Pl; Yrbk; FHA; Bsktbl; Trk; Scr Kpr; Voc Schl.

SCOTT, PEGGY; Morton Sr HS; Hammond, IN; Cls Rep Sr Cls; Girl Scts; Hon Rl; Quill & Scroll; Stu Cncl; Rptr Sch Nwsp; Sch Nwsp; Pep Clb; GAA; PPFtbl; Univ.

SCOTT, PENNY; Huntington HS; Chillicothe, OH; Hon Rl; 4-H; FHA; Pep Clb; VICA; Trk; Chrldng; Scr Kpr; 4-H Awd; Pickaway Ross Voc Schl; Graphic Arts.

SCOTT, RANDY; Colonel Crawford HS; Bucyrus, OH; 2/120 Pres Soph Cls; Sal; Hon Rl; NHS; Sch Pl; Sct Actv; Ohio Univ Amer Hist Contst Finlst; Ohio St Univ.

SCOTT, ROBERT; Pineville HS; Pineville, WV; Hon Rl; Jr NHS; NHS; Yth Flsp; Rptr Yrbk; Ten; Concord Coll; Bus.

SCOTT, ROBERT; North White School Corp; Buffalo, IN; .

SCOTT, ROBIN; Maplewood Jr Sr HS; Cortland, OH; Boy Scts; Chrs; CAP; Red Cr Ade; Sch Pl; Sct Actv; Sprt Ed Sch Nwsp; Drama Clb; Letter Trk; Tmr; Colorado St Tech Inst; Elec Engr.

SCOTT, ROGER; Montpelier HS; Montpelier, OH; Am Leg Boys St; Hon Rl; Letter Bsbl; Coach Actv; Univ; Math.

SCOTT, RONALD; Pleasant HS; Marion, OH; 2/140 Hon Rl; NHS; Quill & Scroll; Sprt Ed Sch Nwsp; Rptr Sch Nwsp; Drama Clb; Treas 4-H; Key Clb; Letter Crs Cntry; Letter Trk; College; Law.

SCOTT, SELENE; Otsego HS; Tontosany, OH; Sec Frsh Cls; VP Soph Cls; Cl Rep Jr Cls; Trs Sr Cls; Am Leg Aux Girls St; Hon Rl; Off Ade; Rptr Yrbk; Drama Clb; 4-H; Bowling Green St Univ; Ed.

SCOTT, SHERI; Ridgedale HS; Marion, OH; Sec Jr Cls; Band; Chrs; Chrh Wkr; Hon Rl; Sch Mus; Yth Flsp; Yrbk; Leo Clb; Letter Bsbl; Toccoa Falls Bible Coll; Psych.

SCOTT, SUE; Jefferson Union HS; Steubenville, OH; 3/175 Band; Chrh Wkr; Cmnty Wkr; Girl Scts; Hon Rl; Orch; Stu Cncl; Beta Clb; Letter Bsktbl; Coach Actv; Kent St Univ; Nursing.

SCOTT, SUSAN; Pocahontas County HS; Hillsboro, WV; FBLA; FHA; Bsbl; Socr; Sec.

SCOTT, TAMMI; Clinton Central HS; Frankfort, IN; 10/110 Chrs; Chrh Wkr; Cmnty Wkr; Girl Scts; Hon Rl; Pol Wkr; Sch Pl; Stg Crw; Yth Flsp; Drama Clb; Drama Awd 78; Shorthand Awd 79; Indiana Univ; Psych.

SCOTT, THERESA; Spring Lake HS; Spring Lake, MI; 6/186 Girl Scts; Hon Rl; NHS; Mgrs; Elk Awd; Western Michigan Univ; Elem Ed.

SCOTT, TODD; St Johns HS; De Witt, MI; Band; Boy Scts; Hon Rl; Orch; Drama Clb; 4-H; Pep Clb; Crs Cntry; Trk; Coach Actv; Schlrshp To Blue Lake Band Camp For Otstndng Band Awd 77; All Confrnc Cross Cntry Gold Medal 77; Michigan St Univ; Pre Med.

SCOTT, TODD A; South Dearborn HS; Dillsboro, IN; Cls Rep Frsh Cls; Cls Rep Soph Cls; Cl Rep Jr Cls; Band; Boy Scts; Chrs; Drl Tm; Sch Pl; Stg Crw; Rptr Sch Nwsp; Vincennes Univ; Hotel & Rest Mgmt.

SCOTT, TRACY; Miami Trace HS; Jeffersonville, OH; 11/234 AFS; Cmp Fr Grls; Drl Tm; Hon Rl; NHS; Sch Mus; Y-Teens; Yrbk; Drama Clb; 4-H; Clark Tech Coll; Stenographer.

SCOTT, VANESSA; Roosevelt Wilson HS; Nutter Fort, WV; Chrh Wkr; Hon Rl; Red Cr Ade; Sch Pl; Yth Flsp; Y-Teens; VP DECA; Lat Clb; Leo Clb; Mth Clb; West Virginia Univ; Nursing.

SCOTT, VERNON; Struthers HS; Struthers, OH; Boy Scts; JA; Sct Actv; Yrbk; Spn Clb; Univ; Game Warden.

SCOTT, VICKIE; Field HS; Kent, OH; 8/310 Band; Hon Rl; NHS; Orch; Sch Mus; Sch Pl; Stg Crw; Yth Flsp; Ed Yrbk; Yrbk; Best Thespian Awd Natl Thespians 1979; Tennessee Tech Univ; Cmnctns.

SCOTT, WILLIAM; Washington HS; Massillon, OH; VP Soph Cls; VP Jr Cls; Cls Rep Sr Cls; Chrs; Hon Rl; NHS; Stu Cncl; Boys Clb Am; Letter Bsktbl; Letter Ftbl; Medicine Or Physcology.

SCOTT, WILLIAM R; Woodrow Wilson HS; Beckley, WV; 73/520 Chrh Wkr; Hon Rl; Treas DECA; Natl Merit SF; West Virginia Univ; Bsns Admin.

SCOWDEN, CINDY; William Henry Harrison HS; Lafayette, IN; 4/304 Band; Debate Tm; Hon Rl; Jr NHS; Natl Forn Lg; VP NHS; Orch; Sch Mus; Keyettes; Mth Clb; Top Speaker Top Debater Most NFL Points; 1st Place For Clarinet Solo; Most Improved Jr Bandsman; Purdue Univ; Mech Engr.

SCRAMLIN, CURT E; Vestaburg HS; Riverdale, MI; Cls Rep Sr Cls; Band; Chrh Wkr; Hon Rl; NHS; Stu Cncl; Rptr Sch Nwsp; Ftbl; Trk; Central Mi Univ; Math.

SCREWS, GREGORY; Saginaw HS; Saginaw, MI; VP Sr Cls; Band; Boy Scts; Chrh Wkr; FCA; Hon Rl; Jr NHS; NHS; Sch Mus; Stu Cncl; Lawrence Tech Univ; Comp Tech.

SCRIBNER, BARBARA M; Elizabeth Ann Johnson HS; Mt Morris, MI; Hon Rl; Off Ade; Hon Roll 73 74 & 76; Voc Schl; Med Asst.

SCRIMGER, BETH; Lapeer East HS; Lapeer, MI; Cls Rep Soph Cls; Cl Rep Jr Cls; Chrs; Girl Scts; NHS; Red Cr Ade; Sch Mus; Yrbk; Letter Trk; Natl Merit SF; Univ.

SCRIMGER, KENNETH; North Branch HS; North Branch, MI; Band; Chrh Wkr; Girl Scts; Hon Rl; NHS; Rdo Clb; Albion Coll; Physician.

SCRIPTER, MICHAEL; North Newton HS; Lake Village, IN; 16/141 Hon Rl; NHS; Sch Pl; Yrbk; Lat Clb; St Schlrshp 78; St Josephs Coll; Acctg.

SCROGGIE, JANET; High School; Greenfield, OH; 9/160 Band; Chrh Wkr; Cmnty Wkr; Girl Scts; NHS; Drama Clb; 4-H; FTA; Rotary Awd; Voice Dem Awd; Springfield Cmnty Hosp Schl; Nursing.

SCROGGINS, AMY; North Muskegon HS; N Muskegon, MI; 8/108 Cls Rep Frsh Cls; Cls Rep Soph Cls; Cl Rep Jr Cls; Am Leg Aux Girls St; Band; Chrs; Chrh Wkr; Hon Rl; Jr NHS; Sch Pl; Amer Wilderness Ldrshp Schl Schlrshp To 10 Days Env Experience 79; Univ Of Michigan.

SCROGGS, ANDY; Warren Central HS; Indpls, IN; 5/779 Cls Rep Soph Cls; Cl Rep Jr Cls; Cls Rep Sr Cls; Hon Rl; Jr NHS; NHS; Stu Cncl; Purdue Univ; Pre Med.

SCROGGS, BRENDA; Grafton Sr HS; Grafton, WV; Chrs; Hon Rl; NHS; Yth Flsp; FTA; Pep Clb; IM Sprt; PPFtbl; Vc Pres Of Natl Hon Soc 79; Vc Pres Of Stdnt Actn Of Educ M9; West Virginia Univ; Vet Med.

SCROGHAM, LOVEDA; Blue River Valley HS; New Castle, IN; 7/95 Am Leg Aux Girls St; Chrs; Drl Tm; Girl Scts; Hon Rl; Natl Forn Lg; NHS; Sch Pl; Yth Flsp; Pres 4-H; Ball State.

SCRUGGS, SANDY; Taylor HS; Kokomo, IN; 5/186 VP Frsh Cls; Cls Rep Soph Cls; Cl Rep Jr Cls; NHS; Stu Cncl; Yrbk; Gym; Trk; Chrldng; PPFtbl; College.

SCUBART, MARTINA; Hamilton Southeastern HS; Noblesville, IN; Cls Rep Frsh Cls; Cls Rep Sr Cls; Hon Rl; Stu Cncl; Pres Fr Clb; Ger Clb; Pep Clb; Bsktbl; Trk; Letter Chrldng; Purdue Univ; Nursing.

SCULLY, DAWN I; Berkeley Springs HS; Berkeley Spgs, WV; 40/133 Band; Chrh Wkr; Hon Rl; Sch Mus; Sch Pl; Stg Crw; Yrbk; Drama Clb; Fr Clb; Sci Clb; Shepherd Coll; Pre Sch Handcpd Child.

SCULLY, PAM; Bay HS; Bay Vill, OH; Cl Rep Jr Cls; Cls Rep Sr Cls; Drl Tm; Sch Pl; Stu Cncl; 4-H; Pep Clb; Trk; Chrldng; PPFtbl; Ohi St College; Bus Mgmt.

SCZENK, ALICIA; Madonna HS; Weirton, WV; 42/100 Lit Mag; Rptr Yrbk; College; Fashion Retail.

SEABERG, JEANETTE; Benzie Cnty Central HS; Traverse City, MI; Chrs; Debate Tm; Hon Rl; Natl Forn Lg; NHS; Sch Mus; Sch Pl; 4-H; 4-H Awd; Univ; Med.

SEABERG, JEANETTE; Benzie County Central HS; Traverse City, MI; Chrs; Debate Tm; Hon Rl; Natl Forn Lg; NHS; Sch Mus; 4-H; 4-H Awd; College; General Practitioner.

SEABOLT, BARBARA; Spencer HS; Spencer, WV; Cls Rep Frsh Cls; VP Soph Cls; Cl Rep Jr Cls; Cls Rep Sr Cls; Chrh Wkr; Hon Rl; NHS; Lbry Ade; Sch Pl; Chrldng; Boheckers Busns Schl; Acctg.

SEALS, JUDITH; Morgantown HS; Morgantwn, WV; Cl Rep Jr Cls; Cls Rep Sr Cls; Band; Chrh Wkr; Stu Cncl; Y-Teens; Letter Bsktbl; Letter Trk; Capt IM Sprt; Mat Maids; Rotary Clb Touchdown Clb Awd; U S Air Force Acad; Sci.

SEALS, SARAH; Fraser HS; Fraser, MI; Chrs; Hon Rl; Natl Forn Lg; Orch; Letter Trk; Letter Pom Pon; PPFtbl; Mercy Coll; Med Tech.

SEAMAN, MARTY; Lutheran North HS; Oxford, MI; VP Frsh Cls; Cls Rep Soph Cls; Band; Chrs; FCA; Hon Rl; Jr NHS; Sch Mus; Sch Pl; Letter Bsktbl; Univ; Pre Law.

SEAMON, LISA; Middletown HS; Middletown, OH; 63/585 Band; Chrs; Chrh Wkr; Cmnty Wkr; Capt Drl Tm; Drm Bgl; Hon Rl; Off Ade; Yth Flsp; Youth In Govt 78; Miami Univ; Banking.

SEARCY, BECKY; Bluffton HS; Bluffton, OH; Hon Rl; NHS; Yth Flsp; Rptr Yrbk; Rptr Sch Nwsp; Bsktbl; IM Sprt; Opt Clb Awd; College.

SEARFOSS, DAVID; Upper Sandusky HS; Upper Sandusky, OH; Chrh Wkr; Hon Rl; Univ; Engr.

SEARFOSS, LOIS; Ben Davis HS; Indianapolis, IN; 41/835 Chrh Wkr; Girl Scts; Hon Rl; JA; Sct Actv; Stg Crw; Drama Clb; 4-H; Pep Clb; Spn Clb; College; Busns.

SEARFOSS, STEVEN; Washington HS; South Bend, IN; 20/450 Chrs; Hon Rl; NHS; Sprt Ed Sch Nwsp; Rptr Sch Nwsp; Letter Bsbl; College; Journalism.

SEARING, RHONDA; Rosedale HS; Rosedale, IN; 12/55 Sec Sr Cls; Sec Band; Lbry Ade; Sec NHS; 4-H; Pep Clb; Letter Trk; Letter Chrldng; GAA; 4-H Awd; Indiana State Univ; Math.

SEARLES, GLORIA L; E Catholic HS; Detroit, MI; Hon Rl; JA; VP JA Awd; Univ Of Michigan; Law.

SEARLES, NANCY; Newbury HS; Newbury, OH; Chrs; Girl Scts; Hon Rl; Sch Pl; Stg Crw; Spn Clb; Bsktbl; Mgrs; Scr Kpr; Tmr; Univ; Educ.

SEARS, DIANE; Trinity HS; N Randall, OH; 34/150 Chrs; Hon Rl; Cert Of Honor 77 & 78; Univ; Soc Psych.

SEARS, JEFF; Centerburg HS; Mt Liberty, OH; 1/79 Cl Rep Jr Cls; Band; Chrh Wkr; Debate Tm; Hon Rl; NHS; Sch Mus; Stu Cncl; Perfect Attnd; Univ; Music.

SEARSON, JILL; Crown Point HS; Crown Point, IN; Debate Tm; Pep Clb; Letter Trk; GAA; IM Sprt; Pom Pon; PPFtbl; Tmr; Indiana Univ; Bus Mgmt.

SEASOCK, PHILLIP; Allen Park HS; Allen Park, MI; Chrs; Hon Rl; Rptr Sch Nwsp; Natl Merit Ltr; Ski Club Sponsor & Instr 1976; Eastern Michigan Univ; Tchr.

SEAVER, JOHN; Howland HS; Warren, OH; 75 Hon Rl; NHS; Letter Bsktbl; Youngstown St; Bus Admin.

SEAVOY, ANDREW; Baraga Twp HS; Barago, MI; Boy Scts; Hon Rl; Sch Mus; Letter Bsktbl; Letter Ftbl; Letter Trk;.

SEAWOOD, BRUCE; Indiana Academy; Indianpls, IN; Cls Rep Frsh Cls; Pres Soph Cls; Band; Chrs; Chrh Wkr; Cmnty Wkr; Hon Rl; NHS; Sch Mus; Coach Actv; Andrews Univ; Bio Med.

SEAY, ANN M; Trenton HS; Trenton, MI; Band; Hon Rl; Pol Wkr; Stg Crw; Ger Clb; Letter Bsktbl; College; Vet.

SEAY, DAVID; Scecina Memorial HS; Indianapolis, IN; 21/212 Hon Rl; NHS; Bsbl; Ftbl; IM Sprt; Scr Kpr; Ind Univ; Bio.

SEBASTIAN, DANA; Davison Sr HS; Davison, MI; Boy Scts; Debate Tm; Hon Rl; Sct Actv; Stu Cncl; Spn Clb; Letter Crs Cntry; Letter Trk; Coach Actv; Scr Kpr; Michigan St Univ; Law.

SEBASTIAN, LESHIA; Iaeger HS; Bradshaw, WV; Sec Jr Cls; Band; Debate Tm; Drl Tm; Drm Bgl; Hon Rl; Ed Sch Nwsp; Fr Clb; Keyettes; Trk; Univ; Pedtrcs.

SEBOLT, LOU; Olivet HS; Olivet, MI; Chrh Wkr; Girl Scts; Lbry Ade; Bsktbl; Trk; Chrldng; PPFtbl; Central Bible Coll.

SEBUSCH, DOUG P; Euclid Sr HS; Euclid, OH; 68/746 Hon Rl; JA; Sec Key Clb; Univ; Pre Law.

SECHLER, D; Mathews HS; Cortland, OH; 32/141 Key Clb; Trk; College; Mech Engr.

SECHLER, PATSY; Southeast Southeast HS; Newton Falls, OH; 10/200 Am Leg Aux Girls St; NHS; Quill & Scroll; Stu Cncl; Ed Yrbk; Rptr Sch Nwsp; FHA; Pep Clb; Crs Cntry; Letter Trk; Univ; Market Research.

SECOR, KELLEY; Concord HS; Elkhart, IN; Hon Rl; Pep Clb; PPFtbl; Ind Univ Bloomington.

SECORD, DUANE; Hastings HS; Hastings, MI; 30/425 Chrs; Chrh Wkr; Hon Rl; Univ; Psych.

SECREST, BRAD; Owen Valley HS; Spencer, IN; 19/198 Band; Hon Rl; Pol Wkr; Pep Clb; Sci Clb; Rose Hulman Inst Of Tech; Elec Engr.

SECREST, PAULA; Meadowbrook HS; Senecaville, OH; 32/186 Hon Rl; NHS; Sch Pl; Stu Cncl; Yth Flsp; 4-H; FHA; Mat Maids; 4-H Awd;.

SECRIST, GEOFF; Wadsworth Sr HS; Wadsworth, OH; Hon Rl; DECA; Lat Clb; Bsktbl; Letter Ftbl; Swmmng; Trk; IM Sprt; Wilmington Coll.

SECRIST, JACKIE; Tippecanoe Vly HS; Mentone, IN; 11/179 Girl Scts; Hon Rl; NHS; Sprt Ed Yrbk; Yrbk; 4-H; Pep Clb; Letter Swmmng; Pom Pon; 4-H Awd; Univ.

SECRIST, JACKIE; Tippecanoe Valley HS; Mentone, IN; 12/179 Drl Tm; Girl Scts; Hon Rl; NHS; Sct Actv; Sprt Ed Yrbk; Rptr Yrbk; Yrbk; 4-H; Pep Clb; Univ; Comp Progr.

SECRIST, TIMOTHY; Lexington HS; Lexington, OH; Band; Chrh Wkr; JA; Yth Flsp; Sci Clb; Crs Cntry; Trk; JA Awd; College; Aviation.

SECULOFF, NANCY; Bishop Dwenger HS; Ft Wayne, IN; Trs Soph Cls; Cl Rep Jr Cls; Hon Rl; NHS; Stg Crw; Stu Cncl; Pep Clb; Mat Maids; Indiana Univ; Phys Therapy.

SEDAM, MARK; Snider HS; Ft Wayne, IN; 174/564 Boy Scts; Cmnty Wkr; Hon Rl; Sct Actv; De Paw Univ; Chem.

SEDDON, DAVID; Peck HS; Peck, MI; Hon Rl; Yth Flsp; 4-H; Letter Bsbl; Letter Trk; 4-H Awd; College.

SEDGWICK, JENNIFER; Lincoln HS; Cambridge, IN; 7/135 Hon Rl; Lbry Ade; Sec NHS; FHA; OEA; Spn Clb; Office.

SEDLAR, JEFFREY; Chesaning Union HS; Chesaning, MI; Am Leg Boys St; Hon Rl; Jr NHS; NHS; Letter Bsbl; Letter Ftbl; Letter Swmmng; St Of Mi Comp Schlshp 79; Sci Awd 79; Schlstc Achvmnt Awd 79; Genrl Motors Inst; Mech Engr.

SEDLARIK, TERESA; Mendon HS; Three Rivers, MI; Band; Hon Rl; Hosp Ade; NHS; Bsktbl; Trk; PPFtbl; Voc Schl; Cosmetology.

SEE, CONNIE; Rochester HS; Rochester, IN; Chrh Wkr; FCA; Girl Scts; Hon Rl; Lbry Ade; Ger Clb;.

SEE, DIXIE; North Miami HS; Denver, IN; 22/122 Band; Chrh Wkr; Hon Rl; Hosp Ade; Pol Wkr; Sch Pl; Rptr Sch Nwsp; Drama Clb; FHA; Pep Clb; Lead In Lily The Felons Daughters 78; Brigham Young Univ; Bus Admin.

SEEBOHM, MONICA; North College Hill Jr Sr HS; Cincinnati, OH; 21/206 Cls Rep Soph Cls; Cl Rep Jr Cls; Cls Rep Sr Cls; AFS; Band; Chrh Wkr; Drl Tm; Hon Rl; Sch Mus; Sch Pl; Univ Of Cincinnati; Law.

SEEDORF, LORA; Liberty Center HS; Liberty Cntr, OH; Band; Chrs; Chrh Wkr; MMM; NHS; Sch Mus; Rptr Yrbk; Pres 4-H; Outstndg Jr In Chorus 79; Univ; Bus.

SEEGERT, KIMBERLY; Edon HS; Edon, OH; Cl Rep Jr Cls; Chrs; Hon Rl; Off Ade; Sch Mus; Sch Pl; Stu Cncl; Rptr Sch Nwsp; FHA; Spn Clb; Voc Schl; Stewardess.

SEEGMUELLER, HELEN; Brookville HS; Cedar Grove, IN; Band; NHS; Ed Yrbk; 4-H; Ger Clb; Letter Ten; 4-H Awd; Purdue; Vet.

SEEKER, DONNA; Barberton HS; Barberton, OH; Cls Rep Frsh Cls; Sec Chrh Wkr; Hon Rl; Jr NHS; Off Ade; Red Cr Ade; Sch Nwsp; FTA; OEA; Pep Clb; Schlrshp Grade Pt Average Over 3.5 For Four Yrs 1979; Night Schl; Sec.

SEELEY, ELIZABETH; East HS; E Grnd Rpd, MI; Cmnty Wkr; Girl Scts; Hon Rl; Off Ade; Pol Wkr; Sch Pl; Sch Nwsp; Fr Clb; Trk; Michigan State Univ; Pre Law.

SEELEY, SCOTT; Whitehall Yearling HS; Whitehall, OH; 14/300 VP Frsh Cls; Cls Rep Soph Cls; Cl Rep Jr Cls; Cls Rep Sr Cls; Am Leg Boys St; Band; Hon Rl; NHS; Yrbk; Sch Nwsp; Ohio State Univ; Civil Engr.

SEELY, DAVE; Barberton HS; Barberton, OH; 27/330 Band; Chrs; Hon Rl; Jr NHS; Spn Clb; Letter Ftbl; Univ; Bus.

SEEN, HARRY; Gwinn HS; Gwinn, MI; 50/250 Band; Hon Rl; Pres Stu Cncl; Sprt Ed Yrbk; Ftbl; Swmmng; Trk; Michigan St Univ; Tele Cmnctns.

SEESE, CHERYL D; Olentangy HS; Powell, OH; Cl Rep Jr Cls; Band; Drm Mjrt; Hon Rl; Yth Flsp; 4-H; Sci Clb; Spn Clb; Letter Bsbl; Chmn Bsktbl;.

SEESE, KIMBERLY; Springfield Local HS; Poland, OH; Girl Scts; Hon Rl; Lbry Ade; NHS; Orch; Fr Clb; FTA; Pep Clb; Bsktbl; Youngstown State.

SEEVERS, BILL; Frontier HS; Marietta, OH; Band; Stu Cncl; Rptr Yrbk; Sci Clb; Band Camp Best Leader; World Georaphy; College.

SEEVERS, WILLIAM; Frontier HS; Marietta, OH; Cls Rep Frsh Cls; Cls Rep Soph Cls; Cl Rep Jr Cls; Band; Sch Pl; Stu Cncl; Rptr Yrbk; Sci Clb; Univ; Elec Engr.

SEFCIK, DAVID; Chaney HS; Youngstown, OH; 1/360 Pres Frsh Cls; Cls Rep Frsh Cls; Hon Rl; NHS; Stu Cncl; VP Spn Clb; Letter Bsbl; Bsktbl; Trk; Coach Actv; Univ; Math.

SEFFRIN, NANCY; Union HS; Modoc, IN; Hon Rl; Sch Pl; Rptr Sch Nwsp; 4-H; FHA; Scr Kpr; 4-H Awd; Purdue Univ; Vet.

SEFJORD, MONA; London HS; London, OH; 27/144 Hon Rl; Bsbl; Swmmng; Yth For Understanding; Tri L; Art Club; Univ Of Oslo; Languages.

SEFTON, DONALD; La Crosse HS; La Crosse, IN; Hon Rl; Stg Crw; 4-H; Univ; Comm Art.

SEFTON, KATHLEEN R; Catholic Central HS; E Grand Rapids, MI; Chrs; Chrh Wkr; Hon Rl; JA; NHS; Stg Crw; Drama Clb; Lat Clb; Michigan St Univ; Elec Engr.

SEFTON, SUSAN; Fowlerville HS; Fowlerville, MI; College; Nursing.

SEGAARD, ELIZABETH; Port Clinton HS; Port Clinton, OH; 31/252 Girl Scts; Hosp Ade; Lbry Ade; Pol Wkr; Rptr Sch Nwsp; DECA;.

SEGAR, KAREN; The Miami Valley School; Dayton, OH; AFS; Chrs; Sprt Ed Yrbk; Bennington Coll.

SEGATTA, THOMAS J; Walsh Jesuit HS; Akron, OH; 2/180 Sal; Chrh Wkr; Hon Rl; Off Ade; Rptr Yrbk; Trk; IM Sprt; Bausch & Lomb Awd; Natl Merit Ltr; Georgia Tech Univ; Chem Engr.

SEGEDI, RHONDA K; Riverview Community HS; Riverview, MI; Sec Soph Cls; Sec Jr Cls; Sec Sr Cls; Chrh Wkr; Hon Rl; Jr NHS; NHS; Rptr Yrbk; Detroit Coll Of Bus; Bus.

SEGER, GAYLORD; Danville Comm HS; Danville, IN; 15/166 Cls Rep Soph Cls; Cl Rep Jr Cls; Cls Rep Sr Cls; Aud/Vis; Chrs; Chrh Wkr; Hon Rl; Lbry Ade; Natl Forn Lg; PAVAS; Indiana All St Choir;3rd Plc Central Indiana Regional Speeling Bee; Purdue Univ; Physics.

SEGERT, KATHY; Crown Point HS; Crown Point, IN; 1/500 Chrs; Chrh Wkr; Cmnty Wkr; Hon Rl; Mdrgl; NHS; Sch Mus; Sch Pl; Yth Flsp; Drama Clb; Soc Dstngshd Amer HS Stu; Thespian Soc; Runner Up Crown Point Jr Miss; Academic Schlrshp Indiana St Univ; Indiana St Univ; Accounting.

SEGIN, TRACI; Stow HS; Stow, OH; 45/600 Drl Tm; Hon Rl; NHS; Off Ade; Rptr Sch Nwsp; Spn Clb; Spanish Achvmtn Awd 76 & 77; Bus Schl; Exec Sec.

SEGRETARIO, DIANA; Struthers HS; Struthers, OH; Chrh Wkr; Cmnty Wkr; Pol Wkr; Y-Teens; Rptr Yrbk; Rptr Sch Nwsp; Drama Clb; 4-H; Fr Clb; Pep Clb; Chrldr 77; Stu Prints Nwspr 79; Kent St Univ; Telecmnctns.

SEGRIST, SUSAN; Marian HS; Norwood, OH; Cmp Fr Grls; Chrh Wkr; Cmnty Wkr; FHA; Spn Clb; Univ Of Cincinnati; Bookkeeper.

SEGUILIN, BRIAN; Maple Hts HS; Maple Hgts, OH; 1/425 Chrh Wkr; Hon Rl; Jr NHS; Lbry Ade; NHS; VP Stu Cncl; Ger Clb; IM Sprt; College; Computer Sci.

SEGUIN, JOEL; Timken HS; Canton, OH; Boy Scts; CAP; Sct Actv; Stg Crw; Letter Crs Cntry; Letter Gym; Letter Trk; College; Aero Engr.

SEGUIN, TONY; West Technical HS; Cleveland, OH; Cls Rep Soph Cls; Aud/Vis; Hon Rl; Lbry Ade; Sch Pl; Stu Cncl; Bsktbl; Socr; Trk; Cit Awd; Cleveland St Univ; Acctg.

SEGUINE, GLORIA; Whiteford HS; Ottawa Lk, MI; Pres Frsh Cls; Cls Rep Frsh Cls; Cls Rep Soph Cls; Cl Rep Jr Cls; Cls Rep Sr Cls; Chrs; Hon Rl; NHS; Sch Mus; Stu Cncl; I'm A Finalist For MI Miss United Teenager 79; Rep My Cnty At The St 4 H Horse Show 78; Univ; Phys Ther.

SEGULA, EDWARD; Trinity HS; Maple Hts, OH; Chrs; Hon Rl; JA; Pol Wkr; Sch Mus; Sch Pl; Stg Crw; Bsktbl; Crs Cntry; IM Sprt; Cleveland St Univ; Bus Mgmt.

SEGUR, JACQUELYNN; Ovid Elsie HS; Ovid, MI; Girl Scts; Hon Rl; Sch Nwsp; 4-H; Pep Clb; Letter Trk; Pom Pon; Joan Jewett Schl; Modeling.

SEHAFER, RUSSELL; Sacred Heart Acad; Mt Pleasant, MI; Band; Chrs; Hon Rl; Yrbk; Bsktbl; Crs Cntry; Trk; College; Bus Admin.

SEHL, RANDY; Bedford Senior HS; Temperance, MI; Band; Pres Chrh Wkr; Cmnty Wkr; Sch Nwsp; Fr Clb; Coach Actv; Prepared & Brdcst H S Editorial For WSPD TV 1978; Univ Of Toledo; Brdcstng.

SEIBEL, JANINE; Edwardsburg HS; Niles, MI; Cls Rep Soph Cls; Hon Rl; Stu Cncl; Bsktbl; Trk; Chrldng; Univ.

SEIBERT, ANITA; Frankfort Sr HS; Frankfort, IN; Band; Chrh Wkr; Girl Scts; Yth Flsp; Treas OEA; Pom Pon; Tmr; Office Education Assn Acctg Awd; Indiana Voc Tech Schl; Banking.

SEIBERT, JAMIE; Philip Barbour HS; Philippi, WV; Cl Rep Jr Cls; Chrh Wkr; Cmnty Wkr; Stu Cncl; VP 4-H; Sci Clb; Letter Ten; West Virginia Univ; Equestrian.

SEIBERT, JANE; Mater Dei HS; Evansville, IN; Trs Soph Cls; Hon Rl; Sch Pl; Pep Clb; Gym; Chrldng; Purdue Univ; Nursing.

SEIBERT, PAULA; Hoover HS; North Canton, OH; 32/423 Band; Chrs; Girl Scts; Hon Rl; NHS; Orch; Sch Mus; Yth Flsp; Drama Clb; 4-H; Ohio St Univ; Psych.

SEIBOLD, DAIVD; Upper Arlington HS; Upper Arlington, OH; 240/610 Aud/Vis; Band; Lbry Ade; Off Ade; Sch Mus; Sch Pl; Pres Stg Crw; Rptr Yrbk; Univ; Elec Engr.

SEIBOLD, STEVEN; Fountain Central HS; Veedersburg, IN; 39/124 Treas Chrh Wkr; Hon Rl; Sec Yth Flsp; Fr Clb; Pres Spn Clb; Olivet Nazarene Coll; Languages.

SEIDEL, JONI; Douglas Mac Arthur HS; Saginaw, MI; Chrh Wkr; Hon Rl; NHS; PPFtbl; Michigan St Univ; Soc Work.

SEIDEL, KURT; Reeths Puffer Sr HS; N Muskegon, MI; 16/351 Aud/Vis; Boy Scts; Chrs; Debate Tm; Hon Rl; Natl Forn Lg; NHS; Sch Pl; Drama Clb; Ger Clb; Michigan St Univ; Vet.

SEIDEN, PHILLIP; Goodrich HS; Goodrich, MI; 18/130 Boy Scts; Rptr Sch Nwsp; Letter Trk; Univ Of Mic; Comp.

SEIDNER, ELIZABETH; Western HS; Russiaville, IN; 1/202 Am Leg Aux Girls St; Capt Drl Tm; FCA; Treas NHS; Pres Yth Flsp; Treas 4-H; Letter Ten; Letter Trk; College; Computer Science.

SEIFERT, PAUL; John Glenn HS; Westland, MI; Hon Rl; NHS; Sch Mus; Stg Crw; Drama Clb; Ger Clb; Univ Of Michigan; Engr.

SEIFRIED, BARBARA; Herbert Henry Dow HS; Rhodes, MI; 42/405 Hon Rl; VP JA; NHS; JA Awd; Michigan St Univ; Landscaping.

SEIGLEY, LYNETTE; Tiffin Columbian HS; Tiffin, OH; 13/342 Band; Chrs; Hon Rl; 4-H; Spn Clb; Bsktbl; Trk; Trk 1st Yr Awd Mst Imprvd 78; Bsktbl 1st Yr Awd 78; Trk 2nd Yr Awd Mst Dedicated Mst Val Fld Tri Cptn 79; Coll Of Wooster.

SEILER, FRED; Central HS; Evansville, IN; 40/500 Purdue Univ; Chem.

SEILHAMER, DORA; Pickerington HS; Pickerington, OH; Chrs; Hon Rl; Orch; Lat Clb; Wittenberg Univ; Chem.

SEIM, KIMBERLY; Robert S Rogers HS; Toledo, OH; 25/412 Cls Rep Sr Cls; Cmp Fr Grls; Chrh Wkr; Hon Rl; JA; Jr NHS; NHS; Orch; Rptr Sch Nwsp; OEA; Univ Of Toledo; Acctg.

SEIPEL, CHARLES K; Bishop Ready HS; Columbus, OH; Hon Rl; NHS; Sch Mus; Sch Pl; Spn Clb; Lcl Natl Honor Soc V P 79; Camp Enterprise Roatry Clb Part 79; Univ; Acctg.

SEIPEL, GEORGE; Wm V Fisher Catholic HS; Lancaster, OH; Hon Rl; NHS; Stu Cncl; Pres Fr Clb; Key Clb; Bsbl; Bsktbl; Columbus Tech Council Sci Stud Awd 79; Amer Assoc Of Physics Tchrs Awd 79; Ohio St Univ; Elec Engr.

SEIPKE, KRISTEN; Grosse Pte North HS; Grosse Pt Wds, MI; Chrs; Chrh Wkr; Hon Rl; Sch Mus; Sch Pl; Yth Flsp; Ger Clb; Pep Clb; Bsbl; Crs Cntry; Baylor Univ; Nursing.

SEIPKE, STEVEN; Lutheran HS; Grosse Pte Wds, MI; Chrs; Chrh Wkr; FCA; Hon Rl; Orch; Yth Flsp; Letter Crs Cntry; Letter Trk; Hayne State Univ; Pre Law.

SEITER, DONNA; Pleasant HS; Marion, OH; 67/150 Hon Rl; Lbry Ade; Stg Crw; Rptr Sch Nwsp; Drama Clb; Coach Actv; IM Sprt; Mat Maids; Univ; Theater.

SEITTER, JEFF; Elgin HS; Prospect, OH; 15/160 Hon Rl; NHS; Pres 4-H; Ftbl; Trk; 4-H Awd; All Cnty Ftbl Tm 78; Hon Ment NCC 78; Best Off Lnmn & 500 Clb Of Elgin 78; Univ; Engr.

SEITZ, BARBARA; Erieview Catholic HS; Cleveland, OH; 7/92 Trs Sr Cls; Chrs; Hon Rl; Stu Cncl; Spn Clb;.

SEITZ, DEBORA; Carroll HS; Dayton, OH; 25/265 Band; Girl Scts; Hon Rl; NHS; Orch; Key Clb; Twrlr; College; Nuclear Physist.

SEITZ, KAREN; Oakwood HS; Dayton, OH; 5/140 Chrs; Girl Scts; Hon Rl; Sch Mus; IM Sprt; 1jth Pl In Div 2 Of Oh Tests Of Schsltc Achvmnt 78; Hon Mntn In St Fortest Above Achvmnt In Eng 78; Univ; Bus.

SEITZ, LINDA K; Beaver Local HS; Wellsville, OH; 4/242 Hon Rl; NHS; Yrbk; 4-H; OEA; 4-H Awd; Summi Dacum; Pres Busns Ofc Ed;.

SEITZ, REBECCA; St Charles HS; St Charles, MI; Cmnty Wkr; Hon Rl; NHS; 4-H; Sci Clb; Letter Bsktbl; Mgrs; Cit Awd; 4-H Awd; Natl Merit Ltr; Lake Superior St Coll; Bio Sci.

SEITZER, MARY ANN; Seton HS; Cincinnati, OH; 18/271 Chrh Wkr; Girl Scts; Hon Rl; Pres JA; Mod UN; NHS; Sec Yth Flsp; Drama Clb; Mth Clb; Pep Clb; Xavier Univ; Elem Educ.

SEIWERT, CYNTHIA; Ursuline Acad; Cincinnati, OH; Girl Scts; Lit Mag; Pol Wkr; 4-H; Univ; Eng.

SEKEL, JOSEPH M; Meadowbrook HS; Buffalo, OH; 1/175 Pres Jr Cls; Val; Band; NHS; Stu Cncl; Pres Key Clb; Pres Sci Clb; Treas Spn Clb; Bsbl; Ohio St Univ; Elec Engr.

SEKULICH, DANA; Rutherford B Hayes HS; Delaware, OH; Girl Scts; Hon Rl; Rptr Sch Nwsp; Sch Nwsp; Scr Kpr; Schltsc Achvmnt Awd 76; Bus Schl.

SELBY, BETH K; North Central HS; Indpls, IN; 139/999 Cmnty Wkr; Hon Rl; Hosp Ade; Sch Pl; Stu Cncl; Sci Clb; Letter Chrldng; Univ.

SELBY, STEVE W; Pike Central HS; Winslow, IN; Band; Hon Rl; NHS; Univ; Laser Optics.

SELBY, TINA; Engadine HS; Naubinway, MI; Cls Rep Frsh Cls; Cls Rep Soph Cls; Cl Rep Jr Cls; Pres Sr Cls; Band; Chrh Wkr; Girl Scts; Hon Rl; Lbry Ade; Stu Cncl; Achvmnt In Phys Sci 76; Outstndg Stu In World Hstry 77; Amer & Me Essay Contest 75; Bus Schl; Bus.

SELBY, TRACY; Allen East HS; Lafayette, OH; 31/114 Chrs; Sch Pl; Stu Cncl; Pep Clb; Capt Chrldng; GAA; Leg Sec.

SELEPACK, CARRIE; Ravenna HS; Ravenna, OH; Band; Girl Scts; Hon Rl; JA; Pep Clb; Chrldng; Akron Univ; Cpa.

SELESKI, LAURIE; Hilliard HS; Hilliard, OH; Cls Rep Soph Cls; Sec Jr Cls; Cl Rep Jr Cls; Chrs; Chrh Wkr; Cmnty Wkr; FCA; Girl Scts; Hon Rl; Hosp Ade; College; Elem Ed.

SELIG, DIANE; Huntington North HS; Huntington, IN; Pres Frsh Cls; Cls Rep Frsh Cls; Pres Soph Cls; Cls Rep Soph Cls; Cl Rep Jr Cls; Cls Rep Sr Cls; Chrs; Hosp Ade; Stu Cncl; 4-H; Marion Schl Of Nursing; LPN.

SELIG, ROSE MARY; Shawe Memorial HS; Lexington, IN; 6/28 VP Frsh Cls; Cls Rep Soph Cls; Sec Jr Cls; Hon Rl; Hosp Ade; Lbry Ade; NHS; Yrbk; Pep Clb; Trk; Marian Coll; Nursing.

SELIGA, JOSEPH; Stow HS; Stow, OH; Hon Rl; Quill & Scroll; Sprt Ed Sch Nwsp; Mth Clb; IM Sprt; Lion Awd; College; Engr.

SELITSKI, LINDA; Fitch HS; Youngstown, OH; 225/600 Stu Cncl; Y-Teens; OEA; PPFtbl; Youngstown St Univ; Sec.

SELL, CEDRIC; Northridge HS; Goshen, IN; Machinist.

SELL, STEVE; Hillsdale HS; Hillsdale, MI; Band; Chrh Wkr; Pol Wkr; Capt Crs Cntry; Trk; Mich Univ; Biology.

SELL, STEVEN; Hillsdale HS; Hillsdale, MI; Band; Pol Wkr; Crs Cntry; Trk; Western Michigan Univ.

SELLARS, RUTH; New Richmond HS; New Rihcmond, OH; Chrs; Chrh Wkr; Hon Rl; Fr Clb; FTA; Pep Clb; George Town Coll; Pre Law.

SELLECK, EVANGELEA; Columbia HS; Columbia Sta, OH; Hst Soph Cls; Pres Jr Cls; Aud/Vis; Stu Cncl; Pep Clb; Spn Clb; Trk; Scr Kpr; Kent St Univ; Psych.

SELLERS, DAWN; William Henry Harrison HS; Evansville, IN; Trs Soph Cls; Cl Rep Jr Cls; Hon Rl; Stu Cncl; Rptr Sch Nwsp; Pep Clb; Letter Trk; PPFtbl; Cit Awd; Deaconess Schl Of Nursing; Nursing.

SELLERS, HEIDI L; Indian Valley South HS; Gnadenhutten, OH; 12/94 Sec Soph Cls; Sec Jr Cls; Sec Sr Cls; Band; Chrs; Chrh Wkr; Hon Rl; Off Ade; Sch Pl; Stu Cncl; Mt Union Coll.

SELLERS, KATHY; Pennsboro HS; Pennsboro, WV; Hon Rl; Off Ade; FFA;.

SELLERS, ROY; Ft Frye HS; Beverly, OH; 5/122 Chrs; Hon Rl; NHS; Quill & Scroll; Sch Mus; Sch Pl; Stu Cncl; Sch Nwsp; Drama Clb; Eng Clb; Univ; Pre Med.

SELLERS, ROY A; Fort Frye HS; Beverly, OH; 4/126 Hon Rl; NHS; Quill & Scroll; Sch Mus; Sec Stu Cncl; Rptr Sch Nwsp; Drama Clb; Eng Clb; Leo Clb; Spn Clb; Univ.

SELLERS, SALLY; Prairie Hts HS; Angola, IN; 7/121 Cls Rep Soph Cls; Cl Rep Jr Cls; Cls Rep Sr Cls; Chrs; Hon Rl; NHS; 4-H; Letter Trk; Capt Chrldng; PPFtbl; Intl Bus Coll; Sec.

SELLERS, SHANNON M; Seymour HS; Seymour, IN; Am Leg Aux Girls St; Chrs; Sch Mus; Pep Clb; VP Spn Clb; Letter Gym; Letter Trk; Chrldng; Mgrs; Mat Maids; Indiana Univ; Educ.

SELLERS, STEPHEN; Madison Hts HS; Anderson, IN; Cl Rep Jr Cls; Hon Rl; Purdue Univ; Elec Engr.

SELLGREN, GREGORY J; E W Seaholm HS; Birmingham, MI; Band; Mod UN; Sch Mus; Sch Pl; Natl Merit Ltr; Natl Merit SF; Sec Of HS Bowling Leagues; Represented Schl At Computer Competition; Qualified For Mich Math Prize Test; Univ Of Michigan; Math.

SELLICK, SCOTT; Harbor Springs HS; Harbor Springs, MI; Chrh Wkr; Hon Rl; Yth Flsp; Letter Bsbl; Letter Bsktbl; Letter Ftbl; Univ.

SELLS, JAYNA; Wintersville HS; Wintersville, OH; Drl Tm; Hon Rl; Lbry Ade; Sch Pl; Stg Crw; Rptr Sch Nwsp; Drama Clb; Spn Clb; Trk; GAA; College; Sprts Brdcst.

SELTENRIGHT, LISA; Laville Jr Sr HS; Plymouth, IN; Band; Chrs; Chrh Wkr; Off Ade; Treas Yth Flsp; Pres 4-H; Fr Clb; Mat Maids; 4-H Awd; Dairy Foods Council 4 H Awd 79; Marion Coll; Sociology.

SELTZER, DEBRA; Whetstone HS; Columbus, OH; Cl Rep Jr Cls; Cmp Fr Grls; Debate Tm; Hon Rl; Lbry Ade; NHS; Fr Clb; Mth Clb; Socr; College; Psych.

SELVAGE, REBECCA; Northwestern HS; Wooster, OH; Pres Sr Cls; Band; Chrs; Girl Scts; Hon Rl; JA; NHS; Sch Mus; Yth Flsp; Sch Nwsp; Voc Schl; Modeling.

SEMAN, LANA; Struthers HS; Struthers, OH; Cmp Fr Grls; Chrh Wkr; Cmnty Wkr; Hon Rl; Yth Flsp; Drama Clb; Pep Clb; Spn Clb; 4-H Awd; Lab Tech.

SEMANS, WENDY; Worthington HS; Worthington, OH; Cls Rep Frsh Cls; Cl Rep Jr Cls; Cls Rep Sr Cls; Am Leg Aux Girls St; Cmp Fr Grls; Cmnty Wkr; Hon Rl; Miami Univ; Communications.

SEMEGEN, DAVID; Stow HS; Munroe Falls, OH; Band; Drm Bgl; Rptr Sch Nwsp; Sch Nwsp; Fr Clb; Univ; Bus Admin.

SEMER, SCOTT; North Central HS; Pioneer, OH; Pres Jr Cls; Am Leg Boys St; Band; Chrs; Hon Rl; Sch Pl; Rptr Sch Nwsp; Sch Nwsp; 4-H; 4-H Awd; Hs Chrs Pres; Bowling Green St Univ; Sociology.

SEMON, KRISTIN; Rutherford B Hayes HS; Delaware, OH; 1/294 Girl Scts; Hon Rl; JA; Jr NHS; Lit Mag; NHS; ROTC; Fr Clb; Key Clb; Natl Merit Ltr; Reserve Offcrs Assoc Awrd 78; Air Force Assoc Awrd 79; Honor Stdnt 78; Univ.

SEMPLE, CYNTHIA; Grosse Pointe South HS; Grss Pte Frm, MI; Aud/Vis; Band; Girl Scts; Swmmng; Coach Actv; IM Sprt; PPFtbl; Tmr; College; Commercial Art.

SENA, MARK; Lakeview HS; Cortland, OH; Band; Boy Scts; Chrh Wkr; Hon Rl; Sch Pl; Sct Actv; Lat Clb; Letter Ftbl; IM Sprt; Northeastern Univ; Medicine.

SENA, MONICA; Lakeview HS; Cortland, OH; Band; Chrs; Cmnty Wkr; Girl Scts; Hon Rl; Jr NHS; Sch Pl; Y-Teens; Beta Clb; Fr Clb; Kent St Univ; Bus Mgr.

SENESAC, JO; Clinton Prairie HS; Frankfort, IN; 14/90 Trs Frsh Cls; Trs Soph Cls; NHS; Sch Mus; Sch Pl; Stu Cncl; Lat Clb; Letter Trk; Letter Chrldng; Pres Awd; Purdue Univ; Math.

SENESAC, POLLY; Benton Central HS; Otterbein, IN; VP Frsh Cls; Cls Rep Frsh Cls; Drl Tm; FCA; Hon Rl; Jr NHS; NHS; Off Ade; Stu Cncl; Yrbk; College; Business.

SENFF, TRACY; Manchester HS; Barberton, OH; Letter Trk;.

SENG, MICHELE; Mona Shores HS; Muskegon, MI; Girl Scts; NHS; Pep Clb; Sci Clb; Hope Sci Academic Awd 79; Mic Comptn Schrlship 79; Hope Schlrshp 79; Hope Coll; Med Tech.

SENIOUR, CINDY; Brown Co HS; Morgantown, IN; DECA; 4-H; FHA; Jackson Coll Of Ministries.

SENN, SUSAN; Rockford Sr HS; Rockford, MI; Hon Rl; Fr Clb; Trk; Voice Dem Awd; Ctrl Michigan Univ; Acctg.

SENNISH, MARTIN; St Marys Ctrl Cath HS; Sandusky, OH; Chrs; Chrh Wkr; FCA; Off Ade; Y-

Teens; Rptr Sch Nwsp; Letter Bsbl; Letter Bsktbl; Univ.

SENSEMAN, KIMBERLY; Bethel HS; Tipp City, OH; 4/100 Band; Chrs; Hon Rl; Jr NHS; VP NHS; Stg Crw; Stu Cncl; VP Fr Clb; Letter Chrldng; Scr Kpr; Lamp Of Learning 77; Univ.

SENTELL, KEVIN; Goshen HS; Goshen, IN; 1/268 Am Leg Boys St; Chrh Wkr; Hon Rl; NHS; Crs Cntry; Glf; Letter Swmmng; Am Leg Awd; Freed Hardeman Coll; Bio Sci.

SENTERS, JENNIFER; Centerville Sr HS; Centerville, IN; Band; FCA; Hon Rl; Sch Mus; Y-Teens; FBLA; FHA; Mgrs; PPFtbl; Scr Kpr; Coll; Data Process.

SENTIVANY, DEBRA; Tri Valley HS; Dresden, OH; 12/215 Drl Tm; Hon Rl; Yrbk; FHA; Spn Clb;.

SENTKERESTY, NANCY; East Grand Rapids HS; E Grnd Rpd, MI; Hon Rl; Off Ade; Yrbk; VP Fr Clb; Bsktbl; Central Michigan Univ.

SEPEHRI, NAHID; Bloomington North HS; Bloomington, IN; Indiana Univ; Med.

SEPETA, RICHARD; Madison Heights HS; Anderson, IN; Cls Rep Frsh Cls; Cl Rep Jr Cls; Pres Sr Cls; Am Leg Boys St; Swmmng; Wrstlng; College; Engineering.

SEPTER, SHARI; Southgate HS; Southgate, MI; Chrh Wkr; Chrldng; Wayne State Univ; Phys Ther.

SEPURA, MICHAEL; Gaylord HS; Gaylord, MI; Cmnty Wkr; Hon Rl; Red Cr Ade; Rptr Yrbk; Yrbk; Ed Sch Nwsp; Rptr Sch Nwsp; Sch Nwsp; Sci Clb; Letter Ftbl; Lake Superior St Coll; Jrnlsm.

SERAFIN, PRISCILLA; Philip Barbour HS; Philippi, WV; Band; Chrh Wkr; Hon Rl; NHS; Yth Flsp; 4-H; Mth Clb; Letter Ten; Twrlr; 4-H Awd; Univ; Archt.

SERAFINI, DON; Martins Ferry HS; Martins Ferry, OH; Pres Jr Cls; Hon Rl; Fr Clb; Letter Bsbl; Letter Ftbl; College.

SERAFINI, GIA; Roosevelt Wilson HS; Anmoore, WV; 10/122 Cls Rep Soph Cls; VP Jr Cls; Cl Rep Jr Cls; Cls Rep Sr Cls; Band; Chrs; Chrh Wkr; Hon Rl; Sch Pl; Stu Cncl; Fairmont St Univ; Home Ec.

SERAFINI, L; Catholic Central HS; Steubenvll, OH; 26/204 Hon Rl; NHS; Yth Flsp; Yrbk; FNA; Pep Clb; Spn Clb; College; Physical Therapy.

SERATT, WILLIAM; Marion L Steele HS; Amherst, OH; 50/352 Hon Rl; Bsbl; Capt Wrstlng; IM Sprt; Lorain Cnty Cmnty Coll; Med.

SERBAN, JOHN; Canton South HS; Canton, OH; 35/300 Aud/Vis; Boy Scts; Chrh Wkr; Y-Teens; Rptr Yrbk; Yrbk; Fr Clb; Trk; Univ Of Cincinnati; Archt.

SERDEN, NANCY; Our Lady Of The Lakes HS; Union Lake, MI; 7/45 Hon Rl; NHS; Sch Pl; Stg Crw; Ed Yrbk; Rptr Yrbk; Drama Clb; PPFtbl; Natl Merit Ltr; Voice Dem Awd; Adrian Coll; Busns Admin.

SEREK, KATHLEEN; Pickerington HS; Pickerington, OH; Chrh Wkr; Hon Rl; NHS; Sec Spn Clb; Ohio St Univ; Comp Progr.

SERESUN, ROSE M; Meadowbrook HS; Byesville, OH; Cls Rep Frsh Cls; Cls Rep Soph Cls; Cl Rep Jr Cls; Band; Chrs; Chrh Wkr; Hon Rl; JA; Stu Cncl; Rptr Yrbk; Muskingum Coll; Jrnlsm.

SERFOZO, LINDA; Newark Sr HS; Newark, OH; Cls Rep Frsh Cls; Trs Soph Cls; Cls Rep Soph Cls; VP Jr Cls; Cl Rep Jr Cls; Chrs; Hon Rl; Hosp Ade; Jr NHS; Mdrgl; Miss Ohio Natl Teenager Pageant Schlrshp; Ohio St Univ; Phys Therapy.

SERGENT, JAY; Union Schl Corperation; Losantville, IN; Letter Glf;.

SERGENT, JOHN; Union HS; Losantville, IN; Letter Bsbl;.

SERGOTT, MARY; Ladywood HS; Livonia, MI; Cls Rep Frsh Cls; VP Soph Cls; Cl Rep Jr Cls; VP Sr Cls; Girl Scts; Hon Rl; NHS; Stu Cncl; Ed Yrbk; Sec FNA; Madonna Coll; Surgical Nursing.

SERING, JAMIE; Brownsburg HS; Brownsburg, IN; 16/314 Band; Hon Rl; NHS; Quill & Scroll; Sch Pl; Yth Flsp; Ed Sch Nwsp; Lat Clb; College; Journalism.

SERIO, RICHARD; R B Chamberlin HS; Twinsburg, OH; VP Frsh Cls; Pres Soph Cls; Pres Sr Cls; FCA; Hon Rl; Sch Mus; Stu Cncl; Wrstlng; Univ; Med.

SERMERSHEIM, MICHAEL; Jasper HS; Jasper, IN; 2/329 VP Sr Cls; Sal; Am Leg Boys St; Hon Rl; NHS; Quill & Scroll; Pres Stu Cncl; Pres 4-H; 4-H Awd; Natl Merit Schl; Indiana Univ; Pre Med.

SERR, JULIE; Owosso HS; Owosso, MI; Band; Girl Scts; Hon Rl; NHS; Y-Teens; Spn Clb; College.

SERRONE, CHERYL A; Mentor HS; Mentor, OH; 14/808 Cls Rep Frsh Cls; AFS; Girl Scts; Hon Rl; Hosp Ade; NHS; Sct Actv; Stu Cncl; Rptr Yrbk; Key Clb; Sophmr Schlrshp Awrd 77; Univ; Pre Med.

SESHER, TIMOTHY R; Ironton HS; Ironton, OH; Band; Boy Scts; Pres Ger Clb; IM Sprt; Univ; Dent.

SESSIONS, LORI; Harper Creek HS; Battle Creek, MI; 15/355 Hon Rl; NHS; Spn Clb; Chrldng; PPFtbl; Ctrl Michigan Univ; Psych.

SETHMAN, MICHELE; Heritage Christian HS; Indianapolis, IN; Trs Soph Cls; Trs Jr Cls; Band; Hosp Ade; Fr Clb; 4-H Awd; Coll; Nursing.

SETSER, ROBIN; Carlson HS; Rockwood, MI; 10/250 Band; Chrh Wkr; Hon Rl; NHS; Chrldng; Elk Awd; Mic State Univ.

SETTE, GAYLENE; Waldron Area HS; Camden, MI; 9/39 Hst Sr Cls; Band; Drm Mjrt; Hon Rl; NHS; Off Ade; Rptr Sch Nwsp; Trk; GAA;.

SETTER, CHRISTOPHER; St Josephs Ctrl HS; Huntington, WV; Boy Scts; Hon Rl; Bsktbl; Glf; Scr Kpr; Tmr; Marshall Univ; Bus.

SETTER, MICHAEL P; Sycamore HS; Cincinnati, OH; 2/470 Hon Rl; Mod UN; Scr Kpr; DAR Awd; Natl Merit SF; College; Chemistry.

SETTER, WILLIAM; Deckerville HS; Deckervll, MI; Hon Rl; NHS; Letter Bsbl; Letter Bsktbl; Letter Ftbl; Letter Trk; Univ; Engr.

SETTLE, LYNN; Gallia Academy HS; Gallipolis, OH; 38/221 Am Leg Aux Girls St; Band; Chrs; Chrh Wkr; Drl Tm; Girl Scts; Mdrgl; Sch Mus; Y-Teens; Yrbk; Ohio Youth In Govt Mbr 79; Hawaiian Music Fest Partcpt 78; Cedarville Coll; Elem Educ.

SETTLE, TRACY; South Range HS; North Lima, OH; Sec Jr Cls; Hon Rl; NHS; FTA; Chrldng; PPFtbl; Scr Kpr; Tmr; Youngstown St Univ; Acctg.

SETTLES, DANIEL L; Miamisburg Sr HS; Dayton, OH; 10/316 Pres Band; Hosp Ade; NHS; Orch; Sch Mus; Ten; JETS Awd; Wright St Univ; Pre Med.

SETTY, TERRY; Peebles HS; Peebles, OH; Pres Frsh Cls; Pres Soph Cls; Pres Jr Cls; Hon Rl; Rptr Sch Nwsp; Spn Clb; Bsbl; Bsktbl; Crs Cntry; Trk; Miami Univ; Poli Sci.

SETZLER, DAVID; Clyde Sr HS; Clyde, OH; 3/213 Band; Hon Rl; Sch Mus; Sci Clb; Ten; Scholastic C Awd; Second Yr Varsity Tennis; College; Computer Sci.

SETZLER, DONALD; Clyde HS; Clyde, OH; 5/215 Band; Hon Rl; Sch Mus; Sci Clb; Letter Socr; College; Engr.

SEUBERT, JOHN; East Central HS; Sunman, IN; Pres Frsh Cls; Pres Soph Cls; Cls Rep Sr Cls; Aud/Vis; Chrh Wkr; Cmnty Wkr; Hon Rl; JA; Off Ade; Sch Nwsp; Dekalb Schlrshp Awd; Best All Around Jr Citizenship Awd; FFA Awds; Purdue Univ; Ag.

SEVER, LISA; Brighton HS; Brighton, MI; Hon Rl; PAVAS; Michigan Univ; Modeling.

SEVERANCE, CAROL; John F Kennedy HS; York, PA; 8/400 Chrh Wkr; Hon Rl; NHS; Yth Flsp; Letter Ten; Trk; IM Sprt; Scr Kpr; Univ; Sci.

SEVERN, E THOMAS; Chelsea HS; Chelsea, MI; Am Leg Boys St; Debate Tm; Hon Rl; NHS; Letter Ten; Univ; Engr.

SEVERNS, MATTHEW; Elgin HS; Marion, OH; Chrs; Chrh Wkr; Hon Rl; Yth Flsp; Letter Bsktbl;.

SEVERT, JOHN; Coldwater Exempted Vill HS; Coldwater, OH; 16/140 Chrh Wkr; Cmnty Wkr; Hon Rl; NHS; Y-Teens; Ger Clb; Ftbl; Wrstlng; IM Sprt; Kiwan Awd; Wright State; Engineering.

SEVERT, ROY E; Shady Spring HS; Cool Ridge, WV; Treas Boy Scts; Chrh Wkr; Chmn FCA; NHS; Sct Actv; Letter Crs Cntry; Letter Ten; Letter Trk; Letter Wrstlng; Cit Awd; West Virginia Wesleyan Coll; Phys Ed.

SEVERTSON, CRYSTAL; Faithway Baptist HS; Canton, MI; 2/21 Trs Sr Cls; Chrs; Chrh Wkr; Hon Rl; Sch Pl; Chrldng; Cit Awd; Tenn Temple Univ; Music.

SEWARD, EDWARD; Hale HS; Hale, MI; 8/65 Band; Chrs; Hon Rl; NHS; Stu Cncl; Rptr Sch Nwsp; Letter Bsbl; Letter Bsktbl; Letter Crs Cntry; Letter Ftbl; Northern Michigan Univ.

SEWARD, JEANINE; All Saints Central HS; Bay City, MI; 2/187 Hst Frsh Cls; Hon Rl; Jr NHS; Lit Mag; NHS; Pol Wkr; Yrbk; HS Ltr Earned For Academic Excel 79; Univ Of Michigan; Archt.

SEWARD, JOSEPH M; Rockville HS; Rockville, IN; 1/100 Cls Rep Soph Cls; Cl Rep Jr Cls; Cls Rep Sr Cls; Hon Rl; NHS; Pres 4-H; Pres FFA; Letter Ten; DAR Awd; Natl Merit SF; Purdue Univ; Preveterinary Medicine.

SEWELL, J; Regina HS; Highland Hts, OH; Cls Rep Frsh Cls; Cls Rep Soph Cls; Cl Rep Jr Cls; Girl Scts; Hon Rl; Stu Cncl; FTA; John Carroll Univ; Special Educ.

SEWELL, JACQUELINE; Regina HS; Highland Hts, OH; Cls Rep Frsh Cls; Cls Rep Soph Cls; Cl Rep Jr Cls; Girl Scts; Hon Rl; FTA; GAA; John Carroll Univ; Spec Educ.

SEWELL, MARK J; Andrean HS; Merrillville, IN; 76/251 Chrh Wkr; Hon Rl; Stu Cncl; Mth Clb; Sci Clb; IM Sprt; Scr Kpr; Chess Club; Photog Club; Liturgy Club; Univ; Archt.

SEXTON, CHARLES; Marysville HS; Marysville, OH; 10/250 Hon Rl; NHS; Sct Actv; Rptr Sch Nwsp; Fr Clb; Mth Clb; Wrstlng; Ohio St Univ; Civil Engr.

SEXTON, DAVID; Parchment HS; Parchment, MI; 12/180 Cls Rep Frsh Cls; Cls Rep Soph Cls; Cl Rep Jr Cls; Cls Rep Sr Cls; Chrh Wkr; Hon Rl; NHS; Stu Cncl; Lat Clb; Letter Bsbl; Alma Coll; Busns.

SEXTON, JANICE; Glen Este HS; Batavia, OH; Cl Rep Jr Cls; Hon Rl; Jr NHS; Stu Cncl; Pep Clb; Spn Clb; Chrldng; College; Med.

SEXTON, KAREN; Bramwell HS; Freeman, WV; 1/33 Sec Jr Cls; Am Leg Aux Girls St; Band; Chrh Wkr; Hon Rl; NHS; Sch Pl; Stu Cncl; Ed Yrbk; Pres Drama Clb; Concord; Travel Industry Mgmt.

SEXTON, KENNETH; Northrop HS; Bradenton, FL; 19/554 FCA; Hon Rl; Red Cr Ade; Yth Flsp; Letter Trk; IM Sprt; Cit Awd; Part In The Amer Natl Red Cross Yth Ldrshp Prog 77; Achvmnt Awd In Adv Algebra Chem & Trigonometry 79; US Coast Guard Acad; Math.

SEXTON, LESLIE; Garfield HS; Hamilton, OH; Chrh Wkr; Cmnty Wkr; FCA; Hon Rl; JA; Mod UN; Letter Socr; Lee College; Finance.

SEXTON, LINDA; Portsmouth HS; Portsmouth, OH; Chrs; Chrh Wkr; Hon Rl; Sch Mus; Sch Pl; Stg Crw; Yth Flsp; Drama Clb; Spn Clb; Oho Tests Of Schlstc Achvmnt 8th Pl 76; Ohio Tests Of Sclstc Achvmnt 15th Pl Div 1 Algebra 2 77; Mt Vernon Nazarene Univ.

SEXTON, MARK; Tuslaw HS; Massillon, OH; 37/160 Band; Boy Scts; Chrh Wkr; Sct Actv; Yth Flsp; God Cntry Awd; College; Tele Communication.

SEXTON, RONALD L; Williamsburg HS; Williamsburg, OH; 8/98 Cls Rep Frsh Cls; Am Leg Boys St; Cmnty Wkr; Hon Rl; Jr NHS; NHS; Mth Clb; Pres Sci Clb; Spn Clb; Trk; Navy Tech Schl; Nuclear Engr.

SEXTONS, MICHELLE; Medina HS; Medina, OH; 38/341 Sec AFS; Hon Rl; NHS; Pres Sci Clb; Tmr; College.

SEYBOLD, ELIZABETH; Clay HS; S Bend, IN; 12/431 Hon Rl; Treas JA; NHS; Orch; ROTC; Ger Clb; Indiana Univ; CPA.

SEYBOLD, ERIN; North Side HS; Ft Wayne, IN; 51/499 Band; Drl Tm; Hon Rl; Capt Pom Pon; PPFtbl; Cit Awd; Blue Ribbons Superstar Drill Team Camps; Indiana Univ.

SEYBOLD, TAMARA; Clay HS; S Bend, IN; Pres Chrh Wkr; Cmnty Wkr; Girl Scts; Hon Rl; Rptr Sch Nwsp; Drama Clb; 4-H; 4-H Awd; Ball State Univ; Spec Ed.

SEYFERTH, PAUL; Holton HS; Holton, MI; 5/100 Cls Rep Soph Cls; Boy Scts; Hon Rl; Sct Actv; Stu Cncl; Bsbl; IM Sprt; Univ; Eng.

SEYFRED, JILL; Hart HS; Hart, MI; 17/144 Trs Soph Cls; Trs Jr Cls; VP Sr Cls; Hon Rl; Pres NHS; OEA; Elk Awd; Hope Coll; Spec Ed.

SEYFRIED, TIMOTHY; Colerain Sr HS; Cincinnati, OH; Boy Scts; Hon Rl; Sct Actv; Crs Cntry; Trk; College.

SEYMOUR, DANIELLE; Westfall HS; Orient, OH; Trs Frsh Cls; Trs Soph Cls; Band; Stu Cncl; Rptr Sch Nwsp; 4-H; Fr Clb; FNA; Key Clb; Trk; College; Comp Sci.

SEYMOUR, GLENNA; Tri Township HS; Rapid Rvr, MI; Band; Chrh Wkr; Hon Rl; Hosp Ade; Off Ade; Rptr Sch Nwsp; 4-H; Pep Clb; Bsbl; 4-H Awd; Bay De Noc Cmmty Coll; Med Tech.

SEYMOUR, KAREN; Ripley HS; Ripley, WV; 4/300 Trs Jr Cls; Trs Sr Cls; Band; Chrh Wkr; Cmnty Wkr; Hon Rl; NHS; Sch Nwsp; Drama Clb; Mth Clb; Marshall Univ; Jrnlsm.

SEYMOUR, MARY K; Olentangy HS; Powell, OH; 11/133 Band; Hon Rl; NHS; Quill & Scroll; Rptr Sch Nwsp; Drama Clb; Natl Merit SF; Miami Univ; Aero.

SEYMOUR, PATTY; Olentangy HS; Powell, OH; 2/172 Band; Hon Rl; NHS; Quill & Scroll; Rptr Sch Nwsp; Spn Clb; Letter Gym; Trk; Natl Merit Ltr; Oh Schlstc Achvmnt Test Spanish I 5th In Dist Hon Mnt In St 77; Ohio Schlshtc Achvmtn Test Spnsh II 7th 78; Miami Univ; Botany.

SEYMOUR, ROBERT; Riverdale HS; Forest, OH; 15/95 Hon Rl; NHS; Rptr Sch Nwsp; Spn Clb; Bsbl; Trk; IM Sprt; Ohio North Univ; Engr.

SEYMOUR, TAMARA; Springfield HS; Springfield, MI; Cls Rep Soph Cls; Sec Jr Cls; Cl Rep Jr Cls; Hon Rl; Off Ade; Stu Cncl; Capt Ten; PPFtbl; Am Leg Awd; Cit Awd; Voc Schl; Travel.

SFERRA, JAMES; Campbell Memorial HS; Campbell, OH; 1/205 Cls Rep Soph Cls; Cl Rep Jr Cls; Val; Am Leg Boys St; Hon Rl; NHS; Y-Teens; Key Clb; Bsbl; Ftbl; Univ; Med.

SFERRA, STEPHEN; Campbell Memorial HS; Campbell, OH; 1/210 Cls Rep Soph Cls; Val; Chrh Wkr; Hon Rl; Pres NHS; Sch Pl; Stg Crw; Stu Cncl; Y-Teens; Sprt Ed Yrbk; Bowling Green State Univ; Law.

SFERRA, THOMAS; Ursuline HS; Campbell, OH; 1/360 Chrh Wkr; Hon Rl; Sec JA; NHS; Pol Wkr; FDA; Key Clb; Lat Clb; College; Pre Med.

SGAMBELLONE, NANCY; St Peters HS; Lucas, OH; Cls Rep Frsh Cls; Rptr Yrbk; Sch Nwsp; College; Sci.

SGONTZ, DONALD L; Fairbanks HS; Plain City, OH; 7/110 Cls Rep Frsh Cls; Cls Rep Soph Cls; VP Jr Cls; Chrs; Hon Rl; NHS; Stu Cncl; FFA; Spn Clb; Bsktbl; Shclhsp Team 78; Univ; Bio.

SHACKELFORD, JAMES; Rutherford B Hayes HS; Delaware, OH; AFS; Chrh Wkr; Hon Rl; Key Clb; Letter Bsbl; Natl Merit SF; Acad Awds Tin Bronze & Silver Medals; College.

SHACKELFORD, KEN; Richmond Sr HS; Richmond, IN; Hon Rl; Pol Wkr; Purdue Univ; Comp Sci.

SHACKELFORD, MICHELLE; West Preston Sr HS; Arthurdale, WV; VP Jr Cls; Hon Rl; Stg Crw; Pep Clb; VICA; Letter Chrldng; PPFtbl; West Virginia Career Coll; Dent Asst.

SHACKELFORD, WILLIAM; Champion HS; Warren, OH; Chrh Wkr; Hon Rl; Bsktbl; IM Sprt; Mt Vernon Nazarene Univ.

SHACKLEFORD, CYNTHIA; Allen Park HS; Allen Park, MI; Chrs; Jr NHS; Off Ade; Pep Clb; Wayne Cmnty Coll; Nursing.

SHADBOLT, BRIAN; Gorham Fayette HS; Fayette, OH; 1/40 Cls Rep Soph Cls; VP Jr Cls; VP Sr Cls; Band; Hon Rl; Pres NHS; Sch Pl; Stu Cncl; Fr Clb; Letter Bsktbl; Outstndng Jr Rep Fayette HS At BGSU 79; All Amer Band Hon 79; Dir Awd For Band 79; Univ; Geology.

SHADE, ROBERT; Central HS; Columbus, OH; 17/160 Cls Rep Frsh Cls; Cls Rep Soph Cls; Pres Jr Cls; Pres Sr Cls; Chrh Wkr; Cmnty Wkr; NHS; Stu Cncl; Rptr Sch Nwsp; Spn Clb; Bowling Green St Univ; Bus Admin.

SHADE, STEVE; South Ripley Jr Sr HS; Versailles, IN; Am Leg Boys St; Band; Hon Rl; NHS; Sch Pl; Pep Clb; Glf; IM Sprt; Purdue Univ; Engr.

SHADE, VICKI D; Hedgesville HS; Martinsburg, WV; Trs Jr Cls; Letter Band; Hon Rl; Sch Pl; Rptr Sch Nwsp; Pep Clb; Chrldng; West Virginia Univ.

SHADOAN, SUSAN; Sidney HS; Sidney, OH; Hon Rl; Off Ade; FHA; Letter Scr Kpr; Wrkd With Handicpd Stdnt Tutored 78; Hocking Tech Schl; Conservation.

SHADOWEN, ROBIN; Midland Trail HS; Ansted, WV; Cls Rep Soph Cls; Sec Jr Cls; Hst Jr Cls; Cls Rep Sr Cls; Band; Chrs; Stu Cncl; Yrbk; FHA; Pep Clb; Know Your Cnty Gov Day; All Cnty Bnd; West Virginia Tech Coll; Nursing.

SHAEFFER, KATHY; Amanda Clearcreek HS; Amanda, OH; 4/105 Aud/Vis; Band; Chrs; Hon Rl; Lbry Ade; NHS; Off Ade; Ohi Univ; Bus Admin.

SHAFER, DEBBIE; Whiteoak HS; Hillsboro, OH; Hon Rl; JA; Lbry Ade; NHS; 4-H; 4-H Awd;.

SHAFER, DEBORAH; Kent City HS; Kent City, MI; Hon Rl; Bsktbl; GAA; Suomi College; Comp Progr.

SHAFER, DORENE; Penn HS; S Bend, IN; Chrs; Cmnty Wkr; Hon Rl; Sch Pl; Drama Clb; 4-H; Ger Clb; 4-H Awd; Univ; Agri.

SHAFER, HEATHER; Clearford HS; Belleville, OH; Cl Rep Jr Cls; Cls Rep Sr Cls; Chrs; Chrh Wkr; Debate Tm; Hon Rl; Stu Cncl; Yth Flsp; Yrbk; 4-H; Otterbein Univ; Nursing.

SHAFER, KRISTI; Marion Harding HS; Marion, OH; AFS; Band; Chrs; Chrh Wkr; Hon Rl; Sch Mus; Yth Flsp; Rptr Sch Nwsp; Pep Clb; Spn Clb; Mbr Of All Oh St Fair Yth Chr 78; Mbr Of Oh Uth Chr Europn Tour 79; N Cntrl Oh Dist Impact Teeam 78 &79; Mt Vernon Nazarene Coll; Music.

SHAFER, LEANNE; Strongsville Sr HS; Strongsville, OH; Band; Chrh Wkr; Girl Scts; Off Ade; Orch; Sch Mus; Stu Cncl; Y-Teens; Sch Nwsp; Spn Clb; Govr Art Show Columbus Oh Art Recgntn Awd 79; 2 Yr Orch Awd 79; Greater Clevelnd Solo & Ensmlb Awd 78 & 79; Kent St Univ; Graphic Design.

SHAFER, LISA; Archbishop Alter HS; Kettering, OH; 15/300 Chrh Wkr; Girl Scts; Hon Rl; NHS; Sct Actv; Sec Stu Cncl; Rptr Yrbk; Drama Clb; Fr Clb; Letter Trk; College; Engr.

SHAFER, LORI; Garaway HS; Baltic, OH; Band; Cmnty Wkr; Hon Rl; NHS; FTA; Letter Crs Cntry; Letter Trk; Scr Kpr; Malone; Medical Technology.

SHAFER, PENNY; La Ville Jr Sr HS; Lakeville, IN; Chrs; Girl Scts; 4-H; Pres FHA; Pep Clb; Sci Clb; Spn Clb; Am Leg Awd; 4-H Awd; Purdue Univ; Home Ec.

SHAFER, RONALD; Frank Cody HS; Detroit, MI; Boy Scts; Sct Actv; Rptr Sch Nwsp; Univ Of Mich; Physics.

SHAFER, TOM; Beavercreek HS; Xenia, OH; 48/702 Cmnty Wkr; Hon Rl; Pol Wkr; Boys Clb Am; Glf; IM Sprt; Wright State Univ; Engr.

SHAFFER, BRIAN; Clay HS; S Bend, IN; 50/390 Hst Sr Cls; Hon Rl; Pol Wkr; Ger Clb; DAR Awd; Indiana Univ; Hist.

SHAFFER, CINDY; East Preston Sr HS; Terra Alta, WV; Cls Rep Frsh Cls; Cls Rep Soph Cls; Cl Rep Jr Cls; Am Leg Aux Girls St; Hon Rl; Jr NHS; Lbry Ade; Stu Cncl; FHA; Ger Clb; GAA Letter; Pep Club Charm; West Virginia Univ; Law.

SHAFFER, DANIEL; Fredericktown HS; Fredericktown, OH; 1/113 Trs Jr Cls; Pres Sr Cls; Val; VP FCA; Pres NHS; Capt Bsbl; Letter Bsktbl; Letter Crs Cntry; Elk Awd; Rotary Awd; Embry Riddle Aeronautical Univ; Engr.

SHAFFER, DAWN; Columbia City Joint HS; Columbia City, IN; Debate Tm; Hon Rl; Natl Forn Lg; 4-H; Ger Clb; GAA; Gov Hon Prg Awd; Kiwan Awd; Ind Univ; Nurse.

SHAFFER, DIANA; Northrop HS; Ft Wayne, IN; 16/554 Cls Rep Soph Cls; Cl Rep Jr Cls; Cls Rep Sr Cls; Band; Chrs; Chrh Wkr; Cmnty Wkr; Drl Tm; Girl Scts; Hon Rl; Schlrshp With Distinction; High Honors; Riding Academy Horsemanship Instructor; College; Journalism.

SHAFFER, ERIC; Shaker Hts HS; Shaker Hts, OH; Chrs; Hon Rl; Ed Sch Nwsp; College.

SHAFFER, HAROLD W; Champion HS; Warren, OH; Band; Chrh Wkr; Hon Rl; Fr Clb; Natl Merit Ltr; Muskingum College; History.

SHAFFER, JACQUE; Whiteland Comm HS; New Whiteland, IN; 1/219 Sec Jr Cls; AFS; Chrh Wkr; FCA; Hon Rl; Key Clb; Pep Clb; Letter Trk; Chrldng; College.

SHAFFER, JOHN; Central Preston Sr HS; Fellowsvl, WV; Band; Boy Scts; Hon Rl; Sch Pl; VICA; Bsktbl;.

SHAFFER, JULIA; Northrop HS; Fort Wayne, IN; Hon Rl; VP JA; Natl Forn Lg; Pol Wkr; Sch Pl; Stu Cncl; Rptr Yrbk; Sch Nwsp; Pres 4-H; Pres Sci Clb; Whos Who Among Amer HS Stud 77; Principal Stud Advisory Bd 77 78 & 79; Ft Wayne St Hosptl Volntr 78; Univ; Educ.

SHAFFER, JULIE; Monongah HS; Idamay, WV; 6/94 Trs Jr Cls; Cl Rep Jr Cls; Chrh Wkr; Cmnty Wkr; Girl Scts; Hon Rl; Hosp Ade; NHS; Off Ade; Pol Wkr; Photography Clb Rep; Jr Sr Prom Princess; Ship Of State Awd Capt; College; Med Tech.

SHAFFER, KELLIE; Fairfield Union HS; Lancaster, OH; Cl Rep Jr Cls; Chrs; Hon Rl; Jr NHS; Stu Cncl; Rptr Yrbk; Sch Nwsp; FNA; Pep Clb; Sci Clb; Univ; Nurse.

SHAFFER, KEVIN; Barberton HS; Barberton, OH; Cls Rep Frsh Cls; Boy Scts; Hon Rl; Stu Cncl; Swmmng; Trk; Akron Univ; Pharmacies.

SHAFFER, KEVIN; Maysville HS; Zanesville, OH; Band; Hon Rl; 4-H; 4-H Awd; College.

SHAFFER, KIM; Vanlue HS; Vanlue, OH; 2/22 Sec Frsh Cls; Sec Soph Cls; Sec Jr Cls; Sec Sr Cls; Sal; Band; Chrs; Hon Rl; Lbry Ade; NHS;.

SHAFFER, LISA; Smithville HS; Marshallvl, OH; Sec Soph Cls; Hon Rl; NHS; Treas Stu Cncl; Pres Yth Flsp; Yrbk; Letter Bsktbl; Letter Trk; Letter Wrstlng; GAA; Teenager Of The Mth Chosen By Local Nwspr; Track Night Relays Queen; Girl Ath

Of The Yr; GGA Girl Of Yr; Bluffton Coll; Phys Ed.

SHAFFER, LISA; Fountain Central HS; Hillsboro, IN; Am Leg Aux Girls St; Chrs; Chrh Wkr; Girl Scts; Hon Rl; Sch Mus; Sct Actv; Stu Cncl; Y-Teens; 4-H; Business School; Accounting.

SHAFFER, LORI; Holt HS; Mason, MI; Band; Chrs; Chrh Wkr; Drm Bgl; Girl Scts; Off Ade; Sch Mus; Sct Actv; Stu Cncl; Yth Flsp; Lansing Comm Coll.

SHAFFER, LOYD; Bethel HS; New Carlisle, OH; Boy Scts; Hon Rl; Lbry Ade; Bsbl; Wright State Univ; Bus.

SHAFFER, MARK; Ursuline HS; Campbell, OH; 1/315 Am Leg Boys St; Pres Band; Boy Scts; Lbry Ade; NHS; Orch; Yrbk; FTA; Spn Clb; Scr Kpr; College; Comp Sci.

SHAFFER, NANETTE; Utica HS; Utica, MI; 3/379 Sec Jr Cls; Debate Tm; Hon Rl; NHS; Off Ade; Stu Cncl; Fr Clb; Capt Swmmng; Ten; General Motors Inst; Metallurgical.

SHAFFER, PAUL; Hannan Trace HS; Crown City, OH; Cls Rep Frsh Cls; Cls Rep Soph Cls; Pres Jr Cls; Pres Sr Cls; Hon Rl; Stu Cncl; Beta Clb; FFA;.

SHAFFER, SALLY; Northridge HS; Utica, OH; 22/130 Band; Hon Rl; Lbry Ade; Sch Mus; Rptr Yrbk; Sch Nwsp; 4-H; VP FFA; Sci Clb; Bsktbl; Ohio State; Vet Med.

SHAFFER, TERRI; Fremont Ross HS; Fremont, OH; Drl Tm; Hon Rl; NHS; Stu Cncl; Key Clb; Tmr; Bolwing Green State Univ; Comp Sci.

SHAFFER, THERESA; Penta County Vocational HS; Whitehouse, OH; Pres Jr Cls; Cmp Fr Grls; Girl Scts; Hon Rl; Drama Clb; Sec 4-H; FHA; OEA; Spn Clb; 4-H Awd; Most Likely To Succeed Awd 78; Best Sec Awd 78; Cert Of Proficiency For Highest Shorthand Dictation 78; Bowling Green Univ; Sec.

SHAFFER, THOMAS A; Pleasant HS; Marion, OH; 4/150 Hon Rl; NHS; Quill & Scroll; Sch Pl; Stg Crw; Rptr Sch Nwsp; Sch Nwsp; Drama Clb; 4-H; Crs Cntry; Thespian Soc The Intl; College; Medicine.

SHAFFER, TODD; Mogadore HS; Mogadore, OH; Boy Scts; Chrh Wkr; Sct Actv; Yth Flsp; Letter Bsbl; Letter Ftbl; Letter Wrstlng; Scr Kpr; Univ.

SHAFFNER, SANDRA A; Lakota HS; W Chester, OH; 28/500 Cls Rep Soph Cls; Cl Rep Jr Cls; Chrh Wkr; Drl Tm; Girl Scts; Hon Rl; Jr NHS; Lbry Ade; NHS; Off Ade; Cert Of Mert From Soc Of Womn Engr 79; Purdue Univ; Engr.

SHAFFRON, ANDREW; Mt View HS; Gary, WV; VP Frsh Cls; Am Leg Boys St; Hon Rl; Jr NHS; VP NHS; Yth Flsp; Rptr Sch Nwsp; Sch Nwsp; Treas Key Clb; Bsktbl; West Virginia Univ; Engr.

SHAH, KELLY; Meadowdale HS; Dayton, OH; 8/250 Hon Rl; Jr NHS; NHS; Med.

SHAHABI, MARTIN L; Zanesville HS; Zanesville, OH; Aud/Vis; Hon Rl; Lbry Ade; Ten; Univ; Law.

SHAHADEY, CHARLES; Terre Haute S Vigo HS; Terre Haute, IN; 200/630 Cls Rep Frsh Cls; Cls Rep Soph Cls; Cl Rep Jr Cls; Cls Rep Sr Cls; Boy Scts; Chrs; Chrh Wkr; Hon Rl; JA; Mdrgl; 2nd Plc Stu Of The Yr St Of Indiana; Terre Haute Stu Of The Month; Terre Haute S HS Stu Of The Yr; Indiana St Univ; Busns.

SHAHAN, CHRISTINA; Utica HS; Utica, MI; Girl Scts; Spn Clb; Wanye St Univ; Pre Med.

SHAHEEN, COLLEEN; Flint Kearsley HS; Flint, MI; Hon Rl; Sch Pl; Capt Bsktbl; Univ; Bus Admin.

SHAKER, ELLEN; John F Kennedy HS; Nilis, OH; Chrs; Hon Rl; JA; NHS; Stu Cncl; Yrbk; Fr Clb; College; Acctg.

SHAKER, MARK; John F Kennedy HS; Niles, OH; 34/186 Pres Frsh Cls; Cls Rep Soph Cls; AFS; Boy Scts; Chrs; JA; NHS; Stu Cncl; Ohio St Univ; Admin Sci.

SHALHOUB, ELIZABETH; John Glenn HS; Westland, MI; Chrs; Chrh Wkr; Hon Rl; JA; Jr NHS; Fr Clb; Treas Of Jr Achvmnt Co 76; Recommnd To The Mi Hgh Ed For A Schlrshp 79; Rcvd A Cert Of Recog Form St Of Mi; Eastern Michigan Univ; Music.

SHALLAL, JAMES; Univ Of Detroit HS; Franklin Vlg, MI; Cls Rep Soph Cls; Cl Rep Jr Cls; Pep Clb; Sci Clb; Spn Clb; College; Bus.

SHALLENBERGER, RAY; Hobart HS; Hobart, IN; 3/425 Cls Rep Soph Cls; Chrh Wkr; Hon Rl; Sch Mus; Sch Pl; Stu Cncl; Drama Clb; Pres Fr Clb; Mth Clb; IM Sprt; Ach Awrd For French; Ach Awrd For Academic Wrk; Univ Of California; Aviation.

SHALLOW, MATTHEW; Pontiac Northern HS; Pontiac, MI; Cls Rep Frsh Cls; Cls Rep Soph Cls; Aud/Vis; Chrs; Hon Rl; Sch Mus; Stu Cncl; Rptr Sch Nwsp; Am Leg Awd; Cit Awd; Univ; Bus.

SHALLOW, ZACHARY J; Brighton HS; Pontiac, MI; Cls Rep Frsh Cls; Debate Tm; Hon Rl; Pol Wkr; Ftbl; Letter Ten; IM Sprt; Natl Merit Schl; Adrian Coll; Poli Sci.

SHALVEY, JOHN; Linsly Military Inst; Wheeling, WV; Sec Frsh Cls; FCA; Hon Rl; ROTC; Bsktbl; Ftbl; Trk; Penn St Univ.

SHAMAKIAN, LORI; Brecksville Sr HS; Brecksville, OH; 1/373 Band; Cmnty Wkr; Girl Scts; Hon Rl; NHS; Ger Clb; Twrlr; John Carroll Univ; Math.

SHAMBLEN, STEVEN; Tuscarawas Valley HS; Bolivar, OH; 15/145 Aud/Vis; Band; Chrs; Chrh Wkr; Hon Rl; Sprt Ed Yrbk; Letter Crs Cntry; Letter Trk; Ohi State Univ; Med.

SHAMBLIN, BRIAN; Maysville HS; Zanesville, OH; 1/225 Band; Hon Rl; NHS; College; Med.

SHAMBLIN, DREMA; Sherman HS; Racine, WV; Sec Frsh Cls; Pres Soph Cls; Band; Chrh Wkr; Girl Scts; NHS; Off Ade; Sch Pl; Stu Cncl; Yth Flsp; Marshall Univ; Eng.

SHAMMA, JACQUELINE; Hillsdale HS; Hillsdale, MI; Hon Rl; 4-H; Chrldng; Western Michigan Univ; Interior Dsgn.

SHAMMO, BECKY; Gibsonburg HS; Gibsonburg, OH; 11/101 Trs Sr Cls; Am Leg Aux Girls St; Sec Band; Chrs; Chrh Wkr; Cmnty Wkr; Hon Rl; Lbry Ade; Orch; Sch Mus; Work.

SHAMO, KAREN; La Ville Jr Sr HS; Lakeville, IN; NHS; Stu Cncl; 4-H; Sec Fr Clb; Sci Clb; Letter Glf; Hst Frsh Cls; Univ; Nursing.

SHAMP, JEFF; Mc Cutcheon HS; Lafayette, IN; 157/260 Boy Scts; Chrs; Lbry Ade; Natl Forn Lg; Sch Mus; DECA; 4-H; FFA; Wrstlng; IM Sprt; Natl FFA Conf; Citizen Short Course; Ach Trip Chicago; Career Deve Conf Houston;.

SHANABROOK, KATHERINE; Calvert HS; Tiffin, OH; 10/99 Pres Frsh Cls; Cls Rep Soph Cls; Cl Rep Jr Cls; Cls Rep Sr Cls; Am Leg Aux Girls St; Chrh Wkr; Girl Scts; Hon Rl; NHS; Stu Cncl; Vllybl 3 Yrs Capt 1 Yrs;.

SHANAHAN, THOMAS J; Penn HS; South Bend, IN; Pres Frsh Cls; Cls Rep Frsh Cls; Hon Rl; Rptr Yrbk; Yrbk; 4-H; Fr Clb; Letter Hockey; 4-H Awd; Purdue Univ; Elec Engr.

SHAND, MARTHA; Carman HS; Flint, MI; Cls Rep Frsh Cls; Cl Rep Jr Cls; Hon Rl; Stu Cncl; Spn Clb; IM Sprt; PPFtbl; St Marys Coll.

SHANDLE, PHILIP G; Defiance HS; Defiance, OH; Band; Jr NHS; NHS; Orch; Sch Mus; Stg Crw; Letter Bsbl; Letter Ftbl; Letter Wrstlng; Am Leg Awd; Univ Schlrshp; Pi Sigma Sigma Schlstc Honor Soc; Bowling Green St Univ.

SHANE, MICHAEL; Watervliet Sr HS; Watervliet, MI; Boy Scts; Chrh Wkr; Hon Rl; Jr NHS; Bsktbl; Crs Cntry; Trk; Cit Awd; Univ; Bio.

SHANEFF, ANGELINE; Cardinal Ritter HS; Indianapolis, IN; 2/160 Chrh Wkr; Hon Rl; Treas NHS; Stu Cncl; Ed Yrbk; 4-H; Cit Awd; DAR Awd; 4-H Awd; 1st Pl In Yrbk Plan Bk At HS Jrnlms Inst In Univ 78 & 79; Natl Fdn For Humnts Gratn 78; Univ; Jrnlsm.

SHANEOUR, CHRISTINE; Hillsdale HS; Hillsdale, MI; 6/175 Cmp Fr Grls; Chrs; Hon Rl; Jr NHS; NHS; Off Ade; Fr Clb; Albion College.

SHANER, LINDA; Waynesfield Goshen HS; New Hampshire, OH; 11/46 Sec Soph Cls; Sec Band; Chrs; Chrh Wkr; Hon Rl; Jr NHS; Sec NHS; Sec Stu Cncl; Yth Flsp; Yrbk; Bus Schl; Sec.

SHANGLE, BOB; Sparta HS; Sparta, MI; Band; Chrh Wkr; Hon Rl; Yth Flsp; Spn Clb; Capt Crs Cntry; Trk; Aquinas College; Med.

SHANGLE, COLLENE M; Grand Rapids Central HS; Grand Rapids, MI; Am Leg Aux Girls St; Hon Rl; NHS; Crs Cntry; Letter Gym; Letter Trk; Scr Kpr; Tmr; Ken Cnty Chap Of March Of Dimes 78; Cntrl HS Attainded Excclnc In Amer Life 78; Univ; Tchr.

SHANGLE, KATHLEEN; Meridian Sr HS; Sanford, MI; Band; Girl Scts; Hon Rl; JA; Lbry Ade; Orch; Sch Mus; Sch Pl; Sct Actv; Yrbk; Central Michigan Univ; Poli Sci.

SHANK, DE ANNA; Fort Frye HS; Lowell, OH; 7/129 Band; Hon Rl; NHS; Orch; Sch Mus; Yth Flsp; Eng Clb; 4-H; Twrlr; Am Leg Awd; Heidelburg Coll; Child Psych.

SHANK, DEBBIE; Norwood HS; Norwood, OH; Hon Rl; Stg Crw; DECA; 3rd Pl Bus Vocab; 4th Pl Marketing Test; Cincinnati Tech Coll; Bus Mgmt.

SHANK, DEBRA; Lincolnview HS; Middle Pt, OH; Band; Chrs; Lbry Ade; VP Yth Flsp; 4-H; FHA; Crs Cntry; Trk; GAA; 4-H Awd; Miss Farm Focus Princess; Ohio Forestry Assn Camp; Voc Ag FFA Sec In Ofc; Coll; Educ.

SHANK, JAMIE; Timken HS; Canton, OH; Hon Rl; Hosp Ade; IM Sprt; Mount Union Coll; Psyc.

SHANK, KAY; Delta HS; Albany, IN; 10/298 Trs Soph Cls; Pres Jr Cls; Chrs; Chrh Wkr; Girl Scts; Hon Rl; Jr NHS; Lbry Ade; NHS; Sch Mus; Sci Fair Awd 3rd Pl 76; Univ; Anthropology.

SHANK, KEVIN; Brookville HS; Brookville, IN; Aud/Vis; Band; Hon Rl; NHS; Orch; Ger Clb; Pep Clb; Sci Clb; Voc Schl; Elec.

SHANK, MARY; Tiffin Calvert HS; Clyde, OH; Band; Hon Rl; JA; Pep Clb; IM Sprt; Twrlr; Am Leg Awd; Academic Schlrshp; Quiz Team; Mission Rep; Notre Dame Univ; Medicine.

SHANK, TAMMY; Perrysburg HS; Perrysburg, OH; Sec Frsh Cls; Chrh Wkr; Girl Scts; Hon Rl; Jr NHS; NHS; Red Cr Ade; Sct Actv; Stu Cncl; Pep Clb; Swimming St Qualifier YMCA 73 76; Grad Barbizon Modeling Schl 78; Bowling Green St Univ; Acctg.

SHANK, VICKIE E; Huntington HS; Huntington, WV; Pres Frsh Cls; Cls Rep Soph Cls; Cl Rep Jr Cls; Chrs; Chrh Wkr; Cmnty Wkr; Hon Rl; Jr NHS; NHS; Red Cr Ade; Miss Congeniality Miss Teenage Huntington Contest; 1st Runner Up Miss Teenage Huntington Contest; College.

SHANKLE, JILL; De Kalb HS; Auburn, IN; 32/287 Chrs; NHS; Orch; Sch Mus; Yth Flsp; Spn Clb; PPFtbl; Kiwan Awd; Butler Univ; Pharmacy.

SHANKLE, KIM; Massillon Washington HS; Massillon, OH; 192/482 Band; Chrh Wkr; Yth Flsp; Ger Clb; Coach Actv; IM Sprt; Stark Tech Coll; Comp Progr.

SHANKLIN, REGINA; Charleston Catholic HS; Charleston, WV; Band; Drl Tm; Drm Mjrt; Girl Scts; Hon Rl; JA; Off Ade; Yth Flsp; JA Awd; The Social Studies Achvmnt Awd 79; Hnr Roll Achvmnt Awd 79; Univ Of North Carolina; Elec Engr.

SHANKS, PAULA; Memphis HS; Smiths Crk, MI; Chrs; Hon Rl; Lbry Ade; Off Ade; 4-H; St Clair Cmnty Coll; Home Ec.

SHANNON, ANGELA; Theodore Roosevelt HS; Gary, IN; Chrh Wkr; Hon Rl; Stg Crw; VP FSA; Spn Clb; Cit Awd; Awrd Of Serv & Ded As Pres Of Fornsics Clb 79; Gary City Wide Fornsics Mt 1st Pl 78; Gnrl Schlrshp Awds 79; Univ; Pre Law.

SHANNON, BRADLEY; Anderson HS; Anderson, IN; 55/443 Cls Rep Frsh Cls; Cls Rep Soph Cls; Cl Rep Jr Cls; Band; Boy Scts; Drm Bgl; Hon Rl; Spn Clb; Spansih Hon Soc 78; Mst Outstndng Drummer 79; Purdue Univ; Engr.

SHANNON, KATHLEEN; Newark Catholic HS; Newark, OH; 6/90 Am Leg Aux Girls St; Hon Rl; NHS; Stu Cncl; Fr Clb; GAA; IM Sprt; Central Ohio Tech Coll; Radio.

SHANNON, KATHY; Indianapolis Baptist HS; Indianapolis, IN; 4/36 VP Frsh Cls; Am Leg Aux Girls St; Band; Chrs; Chrh Wkr; Cmnty Wkr; Hon Rl; Pol Wkr; Sch Mus; Sch Pl; Univ; Sci.

SHANNON, MARGIE; Loy Narrix HS; Kalamazoo, MI; Chrs; Stu Cncl; 4-H; Western Mic Univ; Eng.

SHANNON, TAMMY; Saginaw HS; Saginaw, MI; Chrs; OEA; Univ; Music.

SHANNON, THOMAS; Defiance Sr HS; Defiance, OH; Hon Rl; Letter Bsbl; Letter Trk; Univ; Engr.

SHANNON, TREVA; Brookhaven HS; Columbus, OH; 3/436 Band; Hon Rl; Jr NHS; NHS; Off Ade; Orch; Natl Merit SF; Ohio St Univ; Med Tech.

SHAPIRO, MARK; Walnut Hills HS; Cincinnati, OH; Hon Rl; Orch; Stu Cncl; Mth Clb; Natl Merit SF; Univ; Astro.

SHAPIRO, MARK; North Farmington HS; Farm Hills, MI; Band; Boy Scts; Cmnty Wkr; Hon Rl; Sct Actv; Bsktbl; Trk; Coach Actv; IM Sprt; Mic State Univ; Med.

SHAPIRO, MICHAEL; Marquette HS; Marquette, MI; Cls Rep Frsh Cls; Cls Rep Soph Cls; Band; Boy Scts; Sch Mus; Sch Pl; Sct Actv; Stu Cncl; Yth Flsp; Bsbl; College; Mech Engr.

SHARER, NANCY; Beckley HS; Berkley, MI; 92/380 Lbry Ade; Off Ade; Oakland Univ; Acctg.

SHARKEY, KEVIN; Fairview HS; Fairview Pk, OH; 44/268 Boy Scts; Hon Rl; NHS; Trk; Wrstlng; College.

SHARKEY, LORI; William G Mather HS; Munising, MI; Cls Rep Sr Cls; Letter Band; Girl Scts; Hon Rl; Stg Crw; Stu Cncl; Rptr Sch Nwsp; Bsbl; Letter Trk; Letter Chrldng; Lake Superior St Coll; Stenography.

SHARKO, SANDY; Vassar HS; Millington, MI; Chrs; Girl Scts; Hon Rl; JA; Lbry Ade; Off Ade; FHA; Letter Bsbl; Bsktbl; Gym; Vocational Schl; Nursing.

SHARNOWSKI, M; Warren Sr HS; Warren, MI; Cls Rep Soph Cls; Cl Rep Jr Cls; Cls Rep Sr Cls; Band; Drm Mjrt; NHS; Sch Pl; Stu Cncl; Drama Clb; Fr Clb; MSU; Dent Hygnst.

SHARP, CAROLA; Union County HS; Liberty, IN; 16/128 Chrs; Drl Tm; Hon Rl; Stu Cncl; Yrbk; Pres 4-H; Letter Gym; Letter Ten; Trk; Chrldng; Outsdng Bus Math Awd 78; 3rd Runner Up In NCHA St Teen Quuen Cntst 79; 1st Pl In Piano Ensemble Cntst 75; Univ; Hairstylist.

SHARP, DANIEL; Colon Cmnty HS; Colon, MI; Lbry Ade; FFA; Bsbl; Univ.

SHARP, DAVID; Rossville HS; Rossville, IN; Am Leg Boys St; Chrh Wkr; Hon Rl; Yth Flsp; Fr Clb; Bsktbl; Crs Cntry; Glf; Univ; Bus.

SHARP, FELICIA; Pocahontas Cnty HS; Marlinton, WV; 1/125 Trs Soph Cls; Val; NHS; Sec 4-H; VP FHA; C of C Awd; Univ Of Charleston; Nursing.

SHARP, JEREMY; Webster County HS; Nelsonville, OH; 7/127 Hon Rl; 4-H; Bsktbl; IM Sprt; Ohi Univ; Forensic Chem.

SHARP, JOHN; Fairmont West HS; Kettering, OH; Cls Rep Soph Cls; Band; Boy Scts; Chrh Wkr; Hon Rl; Pres Yth Flsp; Mth Clb; 4-H Awd; Natl Merit Ltr; Univ.

SHARP, JOYCE; Barnesville HS; Barnesville, OH; Chrs; Hon Rl; Lbry Ade;.

SHARP, KEVIN; Flat Rock HS; Flat Rock, MI; Band; Chrh Wkr; Hon Rl; Sch Mus; Yth Flsp; Sci Clb; Mich State Univ; Zoo Orni Bio.

SHARP, KIM; Lamphere HS; Madison Heights, MI; Band; Chrs; Hon Rl; Jr NHS; NHS; Rptr Sch Nwsp; DECA; Letter Bsbl; Cit Awd; MSU; Bio.

SHARP, LEA A; Ripley HS; Ripley, WV; 15/250 Chrh Wkr; Hon Rl; VP JA; Jr NHS; NHS; Stg Crw; Beta Clb; VP FBLA; Mth Clb; Natl Merit Ltr; Marshall Univ; Accounting.

SHARP, LINDA; South Dearborn HS; Aurora, IN; 31/265 Hon Rl; Lbry Ade; Off Ade; Sch Nwsp; IM Sprt; College; Comp Sci.

SHARP, PAULA; Ben Davis HS; Indianapolis, IN; Aud/Vis; Drl Tm; Mod UN; ROTC; Spn Clb; Purdue Univ; Data Proc.

SHARP, REBECCA; South Point HS; South Point, OH; 3/170 Trs Frsh Cls; Cl Rep Jr Cls; Sec Sr Cls; Band; Chrh Wkr; Cmnty Wkr; Hon Rl; NHS; Off Ade; Sch Pl; Univ.

SHARP, RICHARD E; Berne Union HS; Sugar Grove, OH; 1/92 Cls Rep Frsh Cls; Trs Jr Cls; Am Leg Boys St; Treas Band; Chrh Wkr; Hon Rl; NHS; Off Ade; Stu Cncl; Yth Flsp; Univ; Finance.

SHARP, SUSAN; Plymouth Salem HS; Plymouth, MI; 3/540 Chrh Wkr; Debate Tm; Girl Scts; Hon Rl; Mod UN; Natl Forn Lg; NHS; IM Sprt; Am Leg Awd; Northwestern Univ.

SHARP, SYLVIA; Withrow HS; Cincinnati, OH; Cl Rep Jr Cls; Drl Tm; Hon Rl; NHS; Fr Clb; Letter Bsbl; Cit Awd; Pres Awd; Univ Of Cincinnati; Comp Tech.

SHARPE, BETH; Highland Sr HS; Highland, IN; 11/493 Hon Rl; Lit Mag; NHS; VP Quill & Scroll; Yrbk; Ed Sch Nwsp; Scr Kpr; Natl Merit Schl; Ball St Univ; Jrnlsm.

SHARPE, VALERIE; Shortridge HS; Indianapolis, IN; Girl Scts; Hon Rl; DECA; Mth Clb; Letter Bsktbl; Letter Trk; Pom Pon; College; Animal Science.

SHARPER, RODERICK; Cass Technical HS; Detroit, MI; Hon Rl; College; Engr.

SHARRITTS, JOHN; Hilliard HS; Columbus, OH; 72/360 Band; Boy Scts; Chrs; Chrh Wkr; Hon Rl; Lbry Ade; Mdrgl; Off Ade; Orch; Sch Mus; Otterbein Coll; Music Educ.

SHASTRI, SAUMIL; Fairview HS; Fairview, OH; 65/268 Band; Hon Rl; Swmmng; Univ; Chem Engr.

SHATTUCK, LYNNE; Woodlan HS; Woodburn, IN; 6/120 Chrs; Girl Scts; Hon Rl; Quill & Scroll; Ed Yrbk; Fr Clb; FHA; Mth Clb; Scr Kpr; Coll; Law.

SHATTUCK, ROBERT; Roscommon HS; Roscommon, MI; Cls Rep Sr Cls; Band; Boy Scts; Pol Wkr; Sct Actv; Stu Cncl; Yth Flsp; Sprt Ed Sch Nwsp; Rptr Sch Nwsp; 4-H; Ferris St Coll; Archt Drafting.

SHATZER, CHARLES; Ontario HS; Ontario, OH; 21/185 VP Frsh Cls; Hon Rl; VP NHS; Red Cr Ade; ROTC; Stu Cncl; Letter Bsktbl; Letter Ftbl; Letter Trk; Cit Awd; College; Engineering.

SHAUDYS, AMY; Grandview Heights HS; Columbus, OH; Band; Cmp Fr Grls; Drm Mjrt; Sch Pl; Yrbk; Drama Clb; FHA; FTA; Pep Clb; Otterbren College; Home Ec.

SHAUGER, KEVIN; Meridian HS; Sanford, MI; 1/115 VP Frsh Cls; Pres Soph Cls; Hon Rl; Jr NHS; NHS; Sch Pl; Spn Clb; Letter Ftbl; Natl Merit SF; College; Comp Sci.

SHAUGHNESSY, KATHERINE; Bishop Borgess HS; Livonia, MI; 67/483 Chrs; Girl Scts; Hon Rl; Natl Forn Lg; NHS; Stg Crw; Sci Clb; IM Sprt; Mich State Univ.

SHAULL, KATHLEEN; Eastmoor HS; Columbus, OH; 4/290 Girl Scts; Hon Rl; NHS; Rptr Sch Nwsp; OEA; Franklin Univ; Data Processing.

SHAVER, BARBARA; Buena Vista HS; Saginaw, MI; 14/158 Hon Rl; Off Ade; Saginaw Bus Inst; Bus.

SHAVER, BETTY; Breckenridge Jr Sr HS; Wheeler, MI; 3/109 Hon Rl; Mdrgl; Treas NHS; Sch Mus; Sch Pl; Drama Clb; 4-H; PPFtbl; 4-H Awd; Alma Coll; Sci.

SHAVER, JACQUELINE R; Lewis County HS; Weston, WV; Band; Hon Rl; NHS; Rptr Sch Nwsp; Pep Clb; Natl Merit Ltr; Wv Univ; Dental Hygiene.

SHAVER, LISA; Milton HS; Milton, WV; Cl Rep Jr Cls; Sec Sr Cls; Band; Chrh Wkr; Drm Mjrt; Girl Scts; Hon Rl; Hosp Ade; NHS; Sct Actv; Marshall Univ; Medicine.

SHAVER, MARSHA; Lincoln HS; Enterprise, WV; Hon Rl; Jr NHS; NHS; Stg Crw; Drama Clb; Spn Clb; Capt Bsktbl; GAA; IM Sprt; Scr Kpr; Fairmont St Coll; Elem Educ.

SHAVER, ROBERT; Nitro HS; Charleston, WV; Cls Rep Frsh Cls; Cls Rep Soph Cls; Cl Rep Jr Cls; Am Leg Boys St; Hon Rl; Stu Cncl; Rptr Yrbk; Sprt Ed Sch Nwsp; Drama Clb; Mth Clb; Wv Univ; Dent.

SHAW, AMY; Trinity HS; Garfield Hts, OH; Hon Rl; Fr Clb; Pep Clb; Bsktbl; Kent St Univ; Bus Admin.

SHAW, BRENDA; New Washington HS; Nabb, IN; 7/49 Trs Frsh Cls; Sec Soph Cls; Sec Sr Cls; Band; Chrh Wkr; Hon Rl; Lbry Ade; NHS; Stu Cncl; Rptr Yrbk; Hoosier Schlr; Flag Corp Mrch Band;.

SHAW, BUDDY; Whiteland Cmnty HS; New Whiteland, IN; 39/200 Boy Scts; Hon Rl; VICA; Ten; Trk; Ball St Univ; Archt.

SHAW, CHARLES T; La Porte HS; La Porte, IN; 20/520 Am Leg Boys St; Band; Debate Tm; Hon Rl; MMM; Natl Forn Lg; NHS; Stu Cncl; Natl Merit SF; Univ Of Notre Dame; Law.

SHAW, CHRISTINE; Clear Fork Sr HS; Butler, OH; 3/160 Cls Rep Frsh Cls; Cls Rep Soph Cls; Cl Rep Jr Cls; Band; Sec Chrs; Hon Rl; NHS; Sch Mus; Rptr Yrbk; 4-H; Rio Grande Coll; Recreation.

SHAW, DANETTE; Immaculata HS; Detroit, MI; Chrs; Drl Tm; Girl Scts; Hon Rl; Off Ade; Pep Clb; Mas Awd; Univ Of Michigan; Acctg.

SHAW, DAVID; West Geauga HS; Chesterland, OH; VP Sr Cls; Yrbk; IM Sprt; Ohio Univ; Chef.

SHAW, DEBBIE; Firestone HS; Akron, OH; Chrs; Hon Rl; Hosp Ade; Sch Mus; Rptr Yrbk; Fr Clb;.

SHAW, JENNIE; Woodsfield HS; Woodsfield, OH; Chrs; Yth Flsp; Fr Clb; Pep Clb; Letter Bsktbl; Mgrs; Scr Kpr; Jefferson Tech Univ; Law.

SHAW, JODY; Kirtland HS; Kirtland, OH; AFS; Chrh Wkr; Hon Rl; NHS; Sch Pl; Treas Stu Cncl; Key Clb; Letter Crs Cntry; Letter Trk; Letter Wrstlng; Univ.

SHAW, JOHN; Shoals HS; Shoals, IN; 4/71 Am Leg Boys St; Band; Hon Rl; Jr NHS; Sch Mus; Sch Pl; Yrbk; Beta Clb; Drama Clb; Ball State Univ; Pre Med.

SHAW, JOHN A; Tri Valley HS; Frazeysburg, OH; 10/220 VP Jr Cls; Am Leg Boys St; Aud/Vis; Hon Rl; NHS; 4-H; Lat Clb; 4-H Awd; Univ.

SHAW, KELLY; Ashley Community HS; Ashley, MI; VP Frsh Cls; VP Jr Cls; Band; Hon Rl; NHS; FTA; Bsbl; Bsktbl; Anderson College; Comp Progr.

SHAW, KEM; Tygarts Vly HS; Mill Creek, WV; VP Soph Cls; Boy Scts; Hon Rl; NHS; Stu Cncl; Ftbl; Univ; Forestry.

SHAW, KEVIN; Greenfield Central HS; Greenfield, IN; 13/300 Band; Boy Scts; Hon Rl; NHS; Ger Clb; Mth Clb; First Pl Sci Fair; Alternate Brain Game Team; Patrol Boy Of The Year; Purdue Univ; Systems Analyst.

SHAW, MARILYN; Roosevelt HS; Gary, IN; 6/525 Trs Sr Cls; Sec Chrh Wkr; NHS; Off Ade; Stu Cncl; Rptr Yrbk; FTA; Capital Univ; Acct.

SHAW, MARSHA; Breckenridge Jr Sr HS; Breckenridge, MI; 8/109 Chrs; Chrh Wkr; Hon Rl; Lbry Ade; NHS; Spn Clb; Gods Bible Schl & Coll.

SHAW, MARSHA; Breckenridge HS; Breckenridge, MI; 8/109 Trs Soph Cls; Trs Jr Cls; Chrs; Chrh Wkr; Hon Rl; Lbry Ade; Mdrgl; NHS; Spn Clb; Gods Bible Schl; Missions.

SHAW, PAMELA; Perry HS; Cridersville, OH; Band; Chrs; Chrh Wkr; Cmnty Wkr; Hon Rl; Yth Flsp; Rptr Yrbk; 4-H; OEA; Pep Clb; Busns Schl; Comp Prog.

SHAW, PATTI D; Mississinewa HS; Marion, IN; 29/198 Am Leg Aux Girls St; Sec Chrh Wkr; Hon Rl; Hosp Ade; Off Ade; Yrbk; OEA; Pep Clb; Ten; Mgrs; Miss United Teengr Pgnt St Finlst 250 Cash Schslhp 78; OEA Dist 1st Pl St 2nd Pl Natl 4th Verb Cmnctns 78; Ball St Univ; Bus.

SHAW, PATTY; Madison Comp HS; Mansfield, OH; Cmnty Wkr; Girl Scts; Off Ade; Red Cr Ade; Rptr Sch Nwsp; 4-H; FHA; Letter Bsbl; Coach Actv; 4-H Awd; Univ; Soc Work.

SHAW, SALLY; Wm Henry Harrison HS; Evansville, IN; 8/466 Band; Chrh Wkr; FCA; Hon Rl; Off Ade; Sch Mus; Sch Pl; Stg Crw; Yth Flsp; 4-H; Mc Donald Yth Salute Progr 79; Schlrshp H 77; Univ Of Illinois; Math.

SHAW, SANDRA; New Knoxville Local HS; New Knoxville, OH; Band; Chrs; Chrh Wkr; Girl Scts; Hon Rl; Lbry Ade; Sch Pl; Yth Flsp; Rptr Sch Nwsp; 4-H; Ohio St Univ; Airline Stwrdss.

SHAW, SCOTT; Finney HS; Detroit, MI; 5/350 Hon Rl; NHS; Sct Actv; Mth Clb; Coach Actv; JETS Awd; General Motors Inst; Mech Engr.

SHAW, SUZY; Munster HS; Munster, IN; 1/425 Cls Rep Frsh Cls; Cls Rep Soph Cls; Cl Rep Jr Cls; Cls Rep Sr Cls; Val; Am Leg Aux Girls St; VP Ger Clb; Pep Clb; Capt Gym; Capt Chrldng; Purdue Univ.

SHAW, TERESA; Avon HS; Indpls, IN; 61/186 Chrs; Chrh Wkr; Girl Scts; Yth Flsp; Rptr Yrbk; Rptr Sch Nwsp; Fr Clb; FTA; OEA; Spn Clb; Olivet Nazarene Coll; Elem Educ.

SHAWD, CYNTHIA; Warren Local HS; Bartlett, OH; Band; Hon Rl; Sprt Ed Yrbk; Pep Clb; Letter Bsbl; Letter Bsktbl; Scr Kpr; Ohio St Univ.

SHAY, ANNE; Midland HS; Midland, MI; Cls Rep Frsh Cls; Cls Rep Soph Cls; Cl Rep Jr Cls; Cls Rep Sr Cls; Chrh Wkr; Jr NHS; Pol Wkr; Stu Cncl; Letter Crs Cntry; Letter Trk; Michigan Tech Univ; Med.

SHAY, DAVID; St Francis De Sales HS; Toledo, OH; 3/200 Boy Scts; Hon Rl; NHS; Sch Mus; Stg Crw; Rptr Sch Nwsp; College; Bio Chem.

SHAY, JOHN; Chaminade Julienne HS; Dayton, OH; 8/249 Band; Chrs; Hon Rl; NHS; Sch Mus; Sch Pl; Stu Cncl; Band Pres; St Ritas Church Teen Club VP; Outstndng Fresh Soph & Jr Band Mbr; College; Acctg.

SHAY, LISA; Western HS; Kokomo, IN; Band; FCA; Hon Rl; NHS; 4-H; FBLA; FHA; Pep Clb; Letter Trk; IUK; Bus.

SHAY, MATTHEW; Newark Catholic HS; Newark, OH; Pres Frsh Cls; Pres Soph Cls; Hon Rl; Fr Clb; Lat Clb; Letter Ftbl; Letter Trk; IM Sprt; Duke Univ; Eng.

SHAYES, EILEEN; Coventry HS; Akron, OH; 11/200 Band; Chrs; Hon Rl; Rptr Sch Nwsp; Akron Univ; Acctg.

SHEA, DANIEL; Rudyard HS; Kinross, MI; Cls Rep Soph Cls; Chrs; Hon Rl; Letter Ftbl; Michigan St Univ; Bio Research.

SHEA, DAVID; St Charles Prep; Whitehall, OH; Hon Rl; NHS; Letter Socr; Letter Wrstlng; Univ; Chem.

SHEA, HARRY; St Charles Preparatory HS; Whitehall, OH; NHS; Letter Socr; Letter Wrstlng; Univ; Chem.

SHEA, MARGARET; St Ursula Academy; Cincinnati, OH; Hon Rl; NHS; Spn Clb; Univ.

SHEAFFER, KIMBERLY; Buckeye Central HS; Tiro, OH; 14/89 Cl Rep Jr Cls; Band; Chrs; Chrh Wkr; Cmnty Wkr; Girl Scts; Hon Rl; Stu Cncl; Yth Flsp; Cit Awd; Bowling Green State Univ; Comp Engr.

SHEAR, VICKI; Piketon HS; Piketon, OH; Band; Chrs; Hon Rl; Lbry Ade; Off Ade; Sch Mus; Yth Flsp; FHA; OEA; Pep Clb; Shawnee St Tech Coll; Exec Sec.

SHEARER, AMY; Upper Sandusky HS; Upper Sandusky, OH; Hon Rl; NHS; Mgrs; Spec Ed Teachers Asst; Art Club; Marion Tech Coll; Acctg.

SHEARER, CONSTANCE; Munster HS; Munster, IN; AFS; Hon Rl; NHS; Treas Orch; Sch Mus; Drama Clb; Treas Ger Clb; Pep Clb; PPFtbl; Calumet Coll Almn Bk Awd 79; Outdoors Club; N W In Yth Orch; Prjct Bio; Univ; Vet Med.

SHEARER, MARY; Lewis County HS; Weston, WV; FCA; Hon Rl; Trk; PPFtbl; Cert Of Achmvnt For Crative Writng Contst 79; Glenville St Univ; Comp Sci.

SHEARER, T; Triton HS; Bourbon, IN; Chrh Wkr; FCA; Hon Rl; Off Ade; Yth Flsp; 4-H; FBLA; Purdue Univ; Amimal Tech.

SHEARER, WHITNEY L; Marysville HS; Marysville, OH; VP Frsh Cls; Cls Rep Soph Cls; Chrs; Chrh Wkr; Off Ade; Sch Mus; Stg Crw; Stu Cncl; Yth Flsp; Rptr Yrbk; Voc Schl; Cosmotology.

SHEARIN, JIM; Oregon Davis HS; Hamlet, IN; 5/60 Am Leg Boys St; Boy Scts; Hon Rl; Yrbk; Sch Nwsp; 4-H; FFA; Bsbl; Bsktbl; Glf; College; Bus Mgmt.

SHEARIN, THOMAS; Oregon Davis HS; Hamlet, IN; 2/65 Pres Sr Cls; Sal; Am Leg Boys St; Boy Scts; Hon Rl; NHS; Yrbk; 4-H; Pres FFA; Sci Clb; Purdue Univ; Engr.

SHEARS, LORI; Wirt County HS; Elizabeth, WV; Am Leg Aux Girls St; Band; Chrh Wkr; Hon Rl; NHS; FBLA; Know Your State Govt Day; Outstndng Names & Faces Of Amer; FBLA St Parliamentary Procedure Team For WV; West Virginia Univ; Medicine.

SHEARS, PENNY; Burr Oak HS; Burr Oak, MI; Chrs; Off Ade; Ed Sch Nwsp; Sprt Ed Sch Nwsp; Sch Nwsp; Trk;.

SHECKLER, GREG; Maumee Vly Cntry Day HS; Lambertville, MI; Boy Scts; Debate Tm; Hon Rl; Stg Crw; Socr; Wrstlng; Ohio Hist Day Cont; Local Art Show 3rd Pl; Toledo Art Show Hnrbl Men Acrylic Painting; Coll; Engr.

SHECKLER, KRISTYN; Huntington North HS; Huntington, IN; Cls Rep Soph Cls; Cl Rep Jr Cls; Cls Rep Sr Cls; Band; Chrh Wkr; Girl Scts; Pol Wkr; 4-H; Bsktbl; Trk; Intl Bus Coll; Acctg.

SHECKLER, SCOTT; Milan HS; Dillsboro, IN; 4-H; FFA; VICA; Letter Crs Cntry; Letter Trk; Univ; Elec.

SHEDLARZ, JODI; Fairless HS; Navarre, OH; Band; Chrs; Hon Rl; Sch Mus; Sch Pl; Y-Teens; Ed Yrbk; Drama Clb; Pep Clb; Select Choir; Sunrise Singing Ensemble; Thespians; Akron Univ; Music.

SHEEHAN, CHRISTINE; Mcnicholas HS; Cincinnati, OH; Drl Tm; Girl Scts; Hon Rl; JA; NHS; Rptr Yrbk; Trk; Pres GAA; Tmr; College.

SHEEHAN, CINDY; James A Garfield HS; Garrettsville, OH; VP Soph Cls; VP Jr Cls; Stu Cncl; Yrbk; 4-H; Pep Clb; Sci Clb; Bsktbl; Crs Cntry; Trk; Pharmacy.

SHEEHAN, ELIZABETH; Lumen Cordium HS; Maple Hts, OH; Cls Rep Frsh Cls; Pres Soph Cls; Hon Rl; Stu Cncl; Fr Clb; GAA; IM Sprt; Excllnc In Chem 78; Nursing.

SHEEHAN, KERRY; Woodrow Wilson HS; Beckley, WV; Band; Chrh Wkr; Drl Tm; Hon Rl; Hosp Ade; JA; Pol Wkr; Chrldng; Twrlr; JA Awd; Semi Finalist Miss Teenage Amer Competition; College.

SHEEHAN, MOIRA; Dominican HS; Detroit, MI; Band; Chrh Wkr; Girl Scts; Hon Rl; Lbry Ade; NHS; Orch; Natl Merit Ltr; Wayne State Univ; Pub Relations.

SHEEHY, MARK; Clarence M Kimball HS; Royal Oak, MI; Hon Rl; Boys Clb Am; General Motors Tech; Mech Engr.

SHEETS, CARINA; Arthur Hill HS; Saginaw, MI; 7/522 Chrs; Hon Rl; NHS; Fr Clb; Pep Clb; Spn Clb; Bd Of Trustees Schlrshp 300.

SHEETS, CARLA; Jefferson Union HS; Richmond, OH; VP Jr Cls; Chrs; Chrh Wkr; Girl Scts; Off Ade; Sch Mus; Sch Pl; Stg Crw; Yth Flsp; Y-Teens; Bus Schl; Legal Sec.

SHEETS, DEBBIE; Churubusco HS; Churubusco, IN; 12/102 FCA; Hon Rl; NHS; Pres Stu Cncl; FNA; Spn Clb; Letter Bsktbl; Letter Trk; Am Leg Awd; Indiana Univ; Nursing.

SHEETS, EDNA; W Union HS; W Union, OH; Drama Clb; Fr Clb; FHA; Pep Clb; Bsktbl; Scr Kpr; Rio Grande Coll; Photog.

SHEETS, JOHNETTA; Ridgewood HS; Coshocton, OH; Hon Rl; Jr NHS; NHS; Rptr Yrbk; Trk; Voice Dem Awd; Dollars For Schlrs 79; Basic Educ Opportunity Grant 79; Ohio St Univ; Engr.

SHEETS, L; Kyger Creek HS; Gallipolis, OH; Key Clb; Bsktbl; Letter Ftbl; Ten; Letter Trk; Coll; Elec.

SHEETS, RODNEY A; Ridgewood HS; Coshocton, OH; Am Leg Boys St; Hon Rl; NHS; Crs Cntry; Trk; Ohi St Univ.

SHEETS, RONALD; Buchanan HS; Buchanan, MI; Cls Rep Sr Cls; Band; Chrh Wkr; Cmnty Wkr; Hon Rl; Stu Cncl; Yth Flsp; Ftbl; Trk; Tmr; IN Univ Hnrs Course Studied Geol In MT 79; Geol Schl Grand Vly St Coll 79; BEOG 79; Grand Valley St Coll; Geology.

SHEETS, SALLIE; North Union HS; Richwood, OH; 14/138 Chrh Wkr; Cmnty Wkr; Hon Rl; Hosp Ade; NHS; Sch Nwsp; 4-H; Spn Clb; Bsbl; Bsktbl; Art Inst Of Pittsburgh; Cmmrcl Art.

SHEETS, SCOTT; Chesapeake HS; Chesapeake, OH; 1/128 Cls Rep Soph Cls; Cl Rep Jr Cls; Cls Rep Sr Cls; Val; Chrs; Chrh Wkr; Hon Rl; Pres NHS; Off Ade; Stu Cncl; Ust St In Spnsh 1 Ohio Test Of Schlstc Achvmnt 76; 8th In St Inspnsh 2 Oh Tests Of Schlstc Achvmnt 77; Marshall Univ; Econ.

SHEETS, VICKI; Rutherford B Hayes HS; Delawre, OH; Cls Rep Frsh Cls; Band; Drm Mjrt; Girl Scts; Hon Rl; Stu Cncl; Pep Clb; Spn Clb; Chrldng; Twrlr; Univ; Psych.

SHEETS, WILLIAM D; Chesterton Sr HS; Chesterton, IN; Am Leg Boys St; Boy Scts; Chrh Wkr; Hon Rl; NHS; Sct Actv; Yth Flsp; Rdo Clb; Bsbl; Bsktbl; Notre Dame Univ; ROTC.

SHEETZ, DESIREE; Mississinewa HS; Marion, IN; Chrs; Girl Scts; Sch Mus; Sch Pl; Rptr Yrbk; Treas Drama Clb; Treas Fr Clb; FTA; Pep Clb; Mgrs; Anderson Coll; Nursing.

SHEETZ, SUSAN; Rochester Comm HS; Rochester, IN; Chrs; Chrh Wkr; Hon Rl; Lbry Ade; Mdrgl; Sch Mus; Sch Nwsp; Drama Clb; 4-H; FTA; Grace Coll; Music.

SHEFFIELD, BRENDA; Little Miami HS; Goshen, OH; Girl Scts; PAVAS; 4-H; Fr Clb; 4-H Awd; JA Awd; Artists Art Stu For 3yrs Going To 4th Yr 76; Most Outsdng Art Stu 77; Univ; Artist.

SHEFFIELD, ERIC W; Adrian HS; Adrian, MI; 3/420 Hon Rl; NHS; Stu Cncl; Lat Clb; Letter Ftbl; Letter Trk; IM Sprt; Natl Merit SF; Rotary Awd; Univ Of Michigan; Engr.

SHEFFIELD, TAMMY; Olmsted Falls HS; Olmsted Falls, OH; Band; Chrs; Drl Tm; Off Ade; Sch Mus; Spn Clb; Trk; PPFtbl; Miami Univ; Sci.

SHEFFIELD, TIM; Muncie South HS; Muncie, IN; 1/327 Val; Boy Scts; Hon Rl; Jr NHS; NHS; Sct Actv; Yrbk; Treas Lat Clb; Capt Bsbl; Bsktbl; Indiana Univ; Acctg.

SHEILL, KEVEN; Bentley HS; Livonia, MI; Aud/Vis; Band; Boy Scts; Hon Rl; Orch; Stg Crw; Bsktbl; Univ Of Michigan; Engr.

SHEKEIS, TERRI; Marlington HS; Alliance, OH; Chrs; Chrh Wkr; Girl Scts; Hosp Ade; Lbry Ade; Off Ade; Sch Mus; Yth Flsp; 4-H; FFA; Tech Schl; Naturalist.

SHELBURNE, JOHN; Hampshire HS; Bloomery, WV; Cls Rep Frsh Cls; Cls Rep Soph Cls; AFS; Band; Boy Scts; Chrh Wkr; FCA; Letter Bsktbl; Letter Crs Cntry; Letter Trk; Fairmont State Univ.

SHELBY, DEBORA; Benton Harbor HS; Benton Hbr, MI; Band; Girl Scts; Hon Rl; NHS; 4-H; Spn Clb; 4-H Awd; Univ Of Michigan.

SHELBY, KAREN; R Nelson Snider HS; Ft Wayne, IN; Chrs; Hon Rl; Yrbk; 4-H; Spn Clb; College.

SHELBY JR, KENNETH; Jennings County HS; North Vernon, IN; 37/360 Aud/Vis; Hon Rl; Lbry Ade; NHS; PAVAS; Sch Mus; Sch Pl; Stg Crw; Bsbl; Bsktbl; Video Crew For Sports Studio & On Locatn Projct; Light Crew For All Plays Concerts & Spec Show; Ivy Tech Voc Schl; Disital Elec.

SHELDON, PERRY; Hardin Northern HS; Kenton, OH; 9/65 Band; Hon Rl; NHS; Orch; Yth Flsp; 4-H; Fr Clb; FFA; Capt Ftbl; Letter Trk; Findley Coll; Radiologist.

SHELDON, RAYMOND; Columbiana HS; Columbiana, OH; 30/100 Pres Sr Cls; Aud/Vis; Chrs; Chrh Wkr; Hon Rl; Sch Pl; Stu Cncl; Yrbk; Youngstown State U; Actuary.

SHELINE, BETH; Thomas A De Vilbiss HS; Toledo, OH; 22/350 Hon Rl; Jr NHS; NHS; Yrbk; Univ Of Toledo; Photo Journalism.

SHELINE, BRUCE; Calumet HS; Gary, IN; Am Leg Boys St; Debate Tm; Hon Rl; Ger Clb; Bsktbl; Alternate For Boys St; Jr Coll In Florida; Ministry.

SHELL, BARBARA D; Brownstown Central HS; Seymour, IN; 67/138 Chrh Wkr; FCA; Hon Rl; Lbry Ade; NHS; Sch Pl; Rptr Sch Nwsp; Treas FHA; Ivy Tech; Sec.

SHELL, J MICHAEL; Greenville Sr HS; Greenville, OH; Bsbl; Ftbl; Wrstlng;.

SHELL, SARAH; Croswell Lexington HS; Yale, MI; Chrs; Chrh Wkr; NHS; Off Ade; Pres 4-H; Spn Clb; Letter Crs Cntry; Letter Trk; 4-H Awd; Ferris St Univ; Dent Hygnst.

SHELL, SHERRY; Pendleton Heights HS; Anderson, IN; Band; Drl Tm; Sch Mus; Pep Clb; Spn Clb; Letter Trk; Pom Pon; Twrlr; Cit Awd; 4-H Awd; Coll; Phys Therapy.

SHELLABARGER, DIANE; Mendon Union HS; Mendon, OH; 13/35 Pres Band; Sec Chrh Wkr; Sch Pl; Pres 4-H; Sec FFA; Pep Clb; Bsktbl; Chrldng; Coach Actv; GAA;.

SHELLENBERGER, KIM; Cuyahoga Vly Christian Acad; Akron, OH; 8/57 Hon Rl; Univ; Nursing.

SHELLEY, DARCY; Summerfield HS; Petersburg, MI; Hon Rl; Michigan St Univ; Vet.

SHELLEY, JULIE; Bethesda Christian HS; Camby, IN; VP Soph Cls; Cls Rep Sr Cls; Hon Rl; Rptr Yrbk; Ed Sch Nwsp; Rptr Sch Nwsp; Voc Schl; Bus.

SHELLEY, SHANNON; Decatur Central HS; Camby, IN; 124/315 Lbry Ade; Yth Flsp; Treas 4-H; Trk; IM Sprt; PPFtbl; Treasurer & 2nd V P Of Sunshine Soc; Treasurer & Librarian Jobs Daughter; Media Club; Business Schl.

SHELLHOUSE, FRANCINE; Mohawk HS; Sycamore, OH; Sec Jr Cls; Am Leg Aux Girls St; Band; Chrs; Hon Rl; Lbry Ade; Off Ade; Stg Crw; Yth Flsp; Y-Teens; Univ.

SHELLITO, ROXANNE; St Johns HS; Dewitt, MI; Sec Frsh Cls; Sec Soph Cls; Chrs; Sch Mus; Sch Pl; Stg Crw; Chrldng; Bob Jones Univ; Theatre.

SHELLS, CRYSTAL; Cardinal Mooney HS; Youngstown, OH; 114/302 Cls Rep Frsh Cls; Cls Rep Soph Cls; Cl Rep Jr Cls; VP Sr Cls; Chrh Wkr; Hon Rl; Stu Cncl; Rptr Sch Nwsp; Lat Clb; Youngstown State; Bio.

SHELLY, KARL; John Glenn HS; Wayne, MI; 38/900 Chrh Wkr; FCA; Hon Rl; NHS; Pol Wkr; Sprt Ed Yrbk; Ftbl; Ten; Coach Actv; IM Sprt; Adrian Coll; Pre Law.

SHELTON, ANGELA; Taylor HS; Kokomo, IN; Band; Capt Drl Tm; Girl Scts; Hon Rl; VP NHS; Stu Cncl; Treas Fr Clb; Bsbl; Bsktbl; Trk; Mbr Foreign Exchange Club; Teen Writer For City Nwspr; Butler Univ; Lib Arts.

SHELTON, BETH; Harper Creek HS; Battle Creek, MI; 20/244 Cls Rep Frsh Cls; Cls Rep Soph Cls; Cl Rep Jr Cls; Cmnty Wkr; Hon Rl; NHS; Rptr Sch Nwsp; Ten; Chrldng; PPFtbl; Kellogg Comm Coll; Data Processing.

SHELTON, CYNTHIA; Lakeland HS; Davisburg, MI; Hon Rl; Sch Pl; Mercy College; Nursing.

SHELTON, DANA; Franklin HS; Franklin, OH; 16/302 Pres Soph Cls; Am Leg Aux Girls St; Chrs; Hon Rl; NHS; Stu Cncl; Rptr Yrbk; Mth Clb; Sci Clb; Letter Bsktbl; Champ Phys Fitness Awd 77; Homecoming Candidate 78 & 79; Univ; Sci.

SHELTON, DAVID B; Aiken Sr HS; Cincinnati, OH; 1/575 Band; Hon Rl; Jr NHS; VP NHS; Rptr Sch Nwsp; Ger Clb; Letter Ftbl; Capt Wrstlng; IM Sprt; Nelson Schwab Awd; Aforlang Foreign Lang Hnr Soc VP; Youth City Government; College; Law.

SHELTON, JANET S; Taft HS; Hamilton, OH; Band; Chrh Wkr; Hon Rl; Jr NHS; Yth Flsp; College.

SHELTON, JIM; River Forest HS; Hobart, IN; 6/130 Hon Rl; Quill & Scroll; Sch Pl; Ed Sch Nwsp; Most Valuable Staffer Awrd 1976; Indiana Univ N W; Jrnlsm.

SHELTON, LA; L C Mohr HS; South Haven, MI; Cls Rep Frsh Cls; Cls Rep Soph Cls; Cl Rep Jr Cls; Chrs; Girl Scts; Hon Rl; Stu Cncl; 4-H; Trk; Chrldng; Michigan St Univ; Interpretor.

SHELTON, LARRY; Scott HS; Jeffrey, WV; Hon Rl; Jr NHS; Stg Crw; Pep Clb; Bsbl; Bsktbl; Letter Ftbl; Marshall Univ.

SHELTON, NANCY; Aiken Sr HS; Cincinnati, OH; 27/576 Band; Drl Tm; Girl Scts; Hon Rl; Jr NHS; Off Ade; Rptr Yrbk; Fr Clb; Swmmng; Tmr; Univ Of Cincinnati; Ec.

SHELTON, PAM; North Adams HS; Seaman, OH; 1/91 VP Frsh Cls; Sec Jr Cls; Band; Chrs; Hon Rl; NHS; Sch Pl; Stu Cncl; VP Yrbk; Sec FHA; Cin Tech College; Med Tech.

SHELTON, RANDY; Princeton HS; Princeton, WV; Chrh Wkr; Jr NHS; VP NHS; Sci Clb; 2nd Place St Sci/engr Fair; Alternate 1st S E WV Regional Sci Fair; Most Outstanding US Air Force; Colleg; Elec Engr.

SHELTON, RENEE; Boardman HS; Youngstown, OH; Hon Rl; Univ.

SHELTON, RON; Terre Haute South Vigo HS; Terre Haute, IN; Cls Rep Soph Cls; Boy Scts; Hon Rl; Sch Pl; Sct Actv; Boys Clb Am; Lat Clb; Ftbl; Trk; Univ; Law Enforcmnt.

SHELTON, TERESA; Fayetteville HS; Fayetteville, WV; VP Frsh Cls; Sec Soph Cls; Cl Rep Jr Cls; Band; Chrs; Chrh Wkr; Hon Rl; Stu Cncl; Yrbk; Fr Clb; Majorette; Conservation Club; Stu Councils Honor Council; College.

SHEMENSKE, ROBERT; Boardman HS; Youngstown, OH; 125/597 Hon Rl; NHS; Sci Clb; Youngstown St Univ; Engr.

SHEMON, JUDE; Bishop Donahue HS; Wheeling, WV; Chrh Wkr; Cmnty Wkr; Hon Rl; NHS; Stu Cncl; Yrbk; Key Clb; West Virginia Univ; Engr.

SHENEMAN, CAROL; Green HS; N Canton, OH; 116/315 Drl Tm; Hosp Ade; Off Ade; Pep Clb; Univ.

SHENKLE, JAMIE; Canton South HS; Canton, OH; Band; Girl Scts; JA; Y-Teens; Sec 4-H; Sec OEA; JA Awd; Stark Tech College; Commputer Progra.

SHEPARD, ALAN; Brownstown Central HS; Brownstown, IN; 10/150 Am Leg Boys St; Boy Scts; Chrh Wkr; Hon Rl; NHS; Sct Actv; Lat Clb; Sci Clb; Letter Ftbl; Letter Glf; Indiana Univ; Optometry.

SHEPARD, ANN M; Elyria Catholic HS; Elyria, OH; Band; Off Ade; Trk; Chrldng; Bee County Coll.

SHEPARD, DAVID; Greenville Sr HS; Greenville, OH; 19/360 Hon Rl; NHS; Sch Mus; Sch Pl; Drama Clb; Spn Clb; College.

SHEPARD, JIM; Mississinewa HS; Marion, IN; Yth Flsp; DECA; OEA; Bsbl; Ftbl; Wrstlng; IM Sprt; Coll; Busns.

SHEPARD, ROBERT; Athens HS; Athens, MI; Hon Rl; NHS; Quill & Scroll; Sch Pl; Stu Cncl; Rptr Yrbk; Ftbl; Trk; Coach Actv; IM Sprt; Kellogg Comnty Coll; Med Asst.

SHEPARD, THOMAS; Ashtabula HS; Ashtabula, OH; 3/200 Chrs; Hon Rl; NHS; Sch Mus; Sch Pl; Drama Clb; Fr Clb; Lat Clb; Sci Clb; Univ; Psych.

SHEPARD, TINA; Groveport HS; Columbus, OH; Hon Rl; Rptr Sch Nwsp; Drama Clb; Ohio State Univ; Writer.

SHEPARDSON, DIANN; Montabella HS; Six Lks, MI; Trs Frsh Cls; Trs Soph Cls; Trs Jr Cls; Trs Sr Cls; Rptr Sch Nwsp; PPFtbl; Scr Kpr; VFW Awd; Montcalm Community; Soc Work.

SHEPECK, DAVID K; Escanaba Area HS; Escanaba, MI; Letter Ftbl; Northern Michigan Univ.

SHEPERD, KENNY; Hilltop HS; Montpelier, OH; 2/74 Pres Frsh Cls; Cls Rep Soph Cls; Cl Rep Jr Cls; Band; Hon Rl; NHS; 4-H; Spn Clb; Letter Glf; Letter Trk; Univ Of Notre Dame; Engr.

SHEPHERD, CRAIG; Centerville HS; Centerville, OH; 90/720 Boy Scts; Chrh Wkr; Hosp Ade; NHS; Orch; Sch Mus; Sct Actv; Stg Crw; Yth Flsp; Hosp Voluntter Awd 77; Orchestra Serv Awd 79; Jackson Coll; Radiology.

SHEPHERD, DUANE; Muskegon Catholic Cntrl HS; Muskegon Hts, MI; Hon Rl; NHS; Ftbl; Ten; Coach Actv; IM Sprt; Scr Kpr; Mic St Univ; Elec Engr.

SHEPHERD, JULIE; Capac HS; Capac, MI; Pres Soph Cls; Hon Rl; VP NHS; Off Ade; VP Stu Cncl; Sec OEA; Chmn Chrldng; Scr Kpr; Jackson Comm Coll; Bus.

SHEPHERD, LORI; New Richmond HS; New Richmond, OH; 35/192 VP Chrs; Hon Rl; NHS; Sch Mus; Sch Pl; VP Stu Cncl; Drama Clb; Sec Spn Clb; Scr Kpr; Univ Of Cincinnati; Speech Hear Ther.

SHEPHERD, POLLY; Paint Valley HS; Bainbridge, OH; 12/90 Sec Frsh Cls; Trs Frsh Cls; Cls Rep Soph Cls; Cl Rep Jr Cls; Hon Rl; Stu Cncl; 4-H; FHA; 4-H Awd;.

SHEPHERD, REBECCA; Greenfield Christian Schl; Mc Cordsville, IN; 2/3 Sec Sr Cls; Chrs; Chrh Wkr; Girl Scts; Hon Rl; Hosp Ade; Sch Mus; Sch Pl; Stu Cncl; Yth Flsp; Baptist Bible Coll; Sec.

SHEPHERD, ROBIN; Marshall HS; Marshall, MI; 80/250 Band; Chrh Wkr; Hon Rl; Pres JA; NHS; Sec Yth Flsp; 4-H; Fr Clb; 4-H Awd; JA Awd; Kalamazoo Coll; French.

SHEPHERD, TINA; Shelby Sr HS; Shelby, OH; Chrs; Hon Rl; Sci Clb; Chrldng; N Ctrl Tech Univ; Comp Progr.

SHEPHERD, YVONNE Y; East HS; Columbus, OH; Pres Chrs; Chrh Wkr; Debate Tm; Hon Rl; Jr NHS; Fr Clb; Ten; Trk; Chairprsn For Upward Band 78; Socialite 78 79 & 80; Univ; Chem Engr.

SHEPPARD, CHANDRA; Union HS; Gormania, WV; Hst Soph Cls; VP Jr Cls; Hon Rl; Sch Pl; Stu Cncl; Yth Flsp; Beta Clb; Pres FHA; Bsbl; Pres Awd; Potomoc State Coll; Forestry.

SHEPPARD, ELIZABETH; Black River HS; Polk, OH; 8/79 Chrs; Hon Rl; Off Ade; Yth Flsp; Rptr Yrbk; Beta Clb; 4-H; FTA; Pep Clb; Sci Clb; Bus Schl; Sec Sci.

SHEPPARD, GEORGE; Upper Arlington HS; Columbus, OH; Band; Boy Scts; Hon Rl; Jr NHS; Orch; Ger Clb; Natl Merit SF;.

SHEPPARD, MARK; Parkersburg HS; Vienna, WV; Am Leg Boys St; Chrs; Hon Rl; Lbry Ade; Mdrgl; Sch Mus; Yrbk; Sch Nwsp; Letter Gym; IM Sprt; Capt Of Ship To St 76; West Virginia Univ; Acctg.

SHEPPARD, MARK A; Northwestern HS; West Salem, OH; Wrkng With Mentally Retarded.

SHEPPARD, TAMMY; Waverly HS; Waverly, OH; Cmnty Wkr; Hosp Ade; Yth Flsp; FHA; Spn Clb; Shawnee St Univ; Reg Nurse.

SHERBURN, LELAND G; Athens HS; Fulton, MI; JA; NHS; Quill & Scroll; Sch Pl; Rptr Yrbk; IM Sprt; Univ; Meteorology.

SHERER, ANGELA; Clay Sr HS; Oregon, OH; 79/355 Chrs; Hon Rl; Hosp Ade; VP 4-H; Fr Clb; 4-H Awd; Univ Of Toledo.

SHERER, KRISTIN; Ridgedale HS; Marion, OH; 46/102 Band; Chrs; Hon Rl; Orch; Sch Mus; VP FHA; Great Lakes College; Music.

SHERER, RANDY; Eastern HS; Bloomfield, IN; 19/90 Fr Clb; Socr; Trk; IM Sprt; Indiana Univ; Bio.

SHERER, SHELLEY E; Jefferson Twp HS; Dayton, OH; 1/170 Sec Sr Cls; Val; Hon Rl; NHS; Stu Cncl; Ed Yrbk; Rptr Sch Nwsp; Twrlr; Natl Merit Ltr; Mount Holyoke Univ; Economics.

SHERFICK, J; New Palestine HS; Greenfield, IN; 42/160 Trs Sr Cls; Band; Girl Scts; JA; Yrbk; 4-H; Spn Clb; Btty Crckr Awd; JA Awd; Univ; Sci.

SHERFIELD, JOHN; Eastern Of Greene Cnty HS; Spencer, IN; Aud/Vis; Chrh Wkr; Cmnty Wkr; Lbry Ade; Bsktbl; Voc Schl; Elec.

SHERICK, KAY; Bethel Local HS; New Carlisle, OH; 7/100 Chrh Wkr; Hon Rl; NHS; Sch Mus; Yth Flsp; VICA; Bsbl; Coll; Cosmetology.

SHERIDAN, BETTE; Boardman HS; Youngstown, OH; Hon Rl; Fr Clb; Youngstown State Univ.

SHERIDAN, TERRENCE; Bloomfield HS; N Bloomfield, OH; 1/43 Cl Rep Jr Cls; Sch Mus; Stu Cncl; Rptr Yrbk; Rptr Sch Nwsp; Spn Clb; Bsktbl; Crs Cntry; Trk; Opt Clb Awd; Hiram Coll; Physics.

SHERIDAN, VINCENT; Sts Peter & Paul HS; Saginaw, MI; 10/130 Chrs; Chrh Wkr; Hon Rl; Jr NHS; NHS; Sci Clb; Spn Clb; Wrstlng; Univ; Pre Dentistry.

SHERK, ERIC; Marquette Sr HS; Marquette, MI; 1/400 Val; Am Leg Boys St; Band; Orch; Sch Mus; Yrbk; Rdo Clb; Mich Tech Univ Bd Of Cntrl Schlrshp; Kaufman Endowment Fund Schlrshp; St Of Mich Schlrshp Finalist; Michigan Tech Univ; Elec Engr.

SHERMAN, AUDREY; Monroe HS; Monroe, MI; Chrs; Hon Rl; NHS; Off Ade; Yth Flsp; Trk; College; Dental Hygenist.

SHERMAN, CYNTHIA; Utica HS; Utica, MI; Debate Tm; Hon Rl; Lbry Ade; Natl Forn Lg; Off Ade; Univ; Criminal Law.

SHERMAN, DEBRA; Brighton HS; Brighton, MI; Hon Rl; Quill & Scroll; Rptr Sch Nwsp; Sch Nwsp; Ten; Natl Merit Ltr; Univ; Jrnlsm.

SHERMAN, MICHAEL; Pike Delta York Sr HS; Delta, OH; 15/115 Am Leg Boys St; Chrs; Pres Chrh Wkr; Mdrgl; Sch Pl; Rptr Sch Nwsp; Bsbl; Ftbl; Wrstlng; Am Leg Awd; Millard E Brown Memrl Schlrshp; Soc Of Dstngshd Amer HS Stu; Great Lakes Bible Coll; Counseling.

SHERMAN, MICHAEL; Colonel Crawford Local Schl; Bucyrus, OH; 25/120 Cls Rep Sr Cls; Boy Scts; Hon Rl; Stu Cncl; 4-H; Fr Clb; Bsbl; Capt Bsktbl; Capt Crs Cntry; Trk; Pride Awd Cross Cntry 76; Univ Of Cincinnati; Archt.

SHERMAN, RAY; Greenbrier East HS; Alderson, WV; Cls Rep Frsh Cls; Chrh Wkr; Cmnty Wkr; Hon Rl; Yth Flsp; Rptr Sch Nwsp; Pres 4-H; IM Sprt; 4-H Awd; Concord Coll; Art.

SHERMAN, ROBERT; St Alphonsus HS; Dearborn, MI; Chrs; Sch Mus; Stg Crw; Stu Cncl; Cl Rep Jr Cls; Cls Rep Sr Cls; Hon Rl; Rptr Yrbk; Mgrs; College; Mech Engr.

SHERMAN, TAYLOR; Charlotte HS; Charlotte, MI; Sch Pl; Yth Flsp; Univ; Photog.

SHERMAN, WILLIAM; Taft HS; Hamilton, OH; 128/444 Chrs; Jr NHS; Stu Cncl; Yth Flsp; Boys Clb Am; Fr Clb; Bsktbl; Natl Merit Ltr, Morgan State Univ; Law.

SHERMAN, WILLIAM; Oak Park HS; Oak Park, MI; 84/355 Chrs; Lit Mag; Mdrgl; Orch; Sch Mus; Drama Clb; Eng Clb; Wayne St Univ; Music.

SHEROCK, NICHOLAS E; Girard HS; Girard, OH; 18/213 Stu Cncl; Yrbk; Treas Key Clb; Letter Ftbl; Letter Wrstlng; Youngstown St Univ; Acctg.

SHERR, CAROLYN; Carolyn Ruth Sherer HS; Richmond, IN; 104/550 Cls Rep Frsh Cls; Cls Rep Soph Cls; Cl Rep Jr Cls; Band; Chrh Wkr; Girl Scts; Hon Rl; Hosp Ade; Orch; Stg Crw; Collegef Eng.

SHERRARD, PAM; Henryville HS; Henryville, IN; Trs Frsh Cls; Trs Jr Cls; NHS; Sch Pl; Yrbk; FHA; Pep Clb; Bsktbl; Trk; Capt Chrldng; Univ Of Louisville; Dent Lab Tech.

SHERRELL, EDNA; Theodore Roosevelt HS; Gary, IN; 20/525 Pres Jr Cls; Chrh Wkr; Debate Tm; Hon Rl; Quill & Scroll; Pres Stu Cncl; Rptr Sch Nwsp; Treas FTA; Lion-Awd; Voice Dem Awd; Clark Coll; Speech Pathology.

SHERROD, ALISA J; Western Hills HS; Cincinnati, OH; Cls Rep Frsh Cls; Drl Tm; JA; Sch Mus; Sch Pl; Yrbk; Bsbl; Chrldng; Tmr; College.

SHERWIN, TOM; Cedar Lake Academy; Battle Creek, MI; Pres Frsh Cls; VP Soph Cls; Band; Chrs; Hon Rl; Mdrgl; NHS; Stu Cncl; Bsktbl; Crs Cntry; Andrews Univ; Pre Med.

SHERWOOD, DEBBIE; Toronto HS; Toronto, OH; Band; Drm Mjrt; Mod UN; Sch Mus; Sch Pl; Yrbk; Pres Fr Clb; Pep Clb; Arkon Univ; Broadcasting Prof.

SHERWOOD, GARY; Ellet HS; Akron, OH; 35/363 Hon Rl; NHS; Ftbl; Ten; Trk; Coach Actv; IM Sprt; Voice Dem Awd; Capt Of Ftbl Team 1978; Ftbl Leadrshp Awd 1977; Ellet High Schl Schlrshp Awd 1978; Ohio Univ; Acctg.

SHERWOOD, JACKIE; Newaygo HS; Newaygo, MI; Cl Rep Jr Cls; Am Leg Aux Girls St; Girl Scts; Hon Rl; Pres NHS; 4-H; Spn Clb; Letter Bsktbl; Letter Trk; 4-H Awd; College; Math.

SHERWOOD, KARELA; Dupont HS; Belle, WV; AFS; Band; Hosp Ade; JA; Orch; Sch Mus; Lat Clb; Crs Cntry; Flo College; Music.

SHERWOOD, THERESA; Pinckney HS; Pinckney, MI; 7/257 Band; Chrs; Girl Scts; Hon Rl; Jr NHS; Mdrgl; NHS; 4-H; Pep Clb; JC Awd; Top 10 Acad Awd 79; St Of Mi Comp Schlp For Outstndng Acad Achvmtn 79; Natl Ho Soc; Michigan Tech Univ; Engr.

SHERWOOD, TODD C; W Lafayette HS; W Lafayette, IN; Debate Tm; Hon Rl; Sch Pl; Univ; Law.

SHERWOOD, WILLIAM; Garrett HS; Garrett, IN; 5/130 Am Leg Boys St; Treas NHS; Yth Flsp; Letter Bsbl; Bsktbl; Butler Univ; Bus Admin.

SHETLER, KAREN; Mater Dei HS; Evansville, IN; Cls Rep Frsh Cls; Hon Rl; Jr NHS; Pol Wkr; Sch Pl; Stu Cncl; Pep Clb; Sci Clb; Mat Maids; College.

SHETZER, JUDY; Fremont Ross HS; Fremont, OH; Off Ade; Stu Cncl; 4-H; Letter Bsktbl; Letter Glf; Letter Trk; Univ; Phys Ed.

SHEW, ELLEN; S Vermillion HS; Clinton, IN; 30/180 Band; Chrh Wkr; Hon Rl; Sct Actv; Yrbk; Eng Clb; 4-H; Spn Clb; Letter Bsktbl; Letter Trk; Purdue Univ.

SHEW, SANFORD; Sandy Valley HS; Magnolia, OH; 1/171 Val; Am Leg Boys St; Pres Band; Boy Scts; Chrh Wkr; Hon Rl; Natl Forn Lg; Pres NHS; Orch; Sprt Ed Yrbk; Ohio St Univ; Bio.

SHIBLE, MARILYN; Bedford Sr HS; Temperance, MI; Cmp Fr Grls; Chrs; Girl Scts; Hon Rl; Lbry Ade; Off Ade; Drama Clb; 4-H; Lat Clb; 4-H Awd; Univ Of Toledo.

SHICK, KAREN; Cashocton HS; Coshocton, OH; Pres Frsh Cls; Pres Soph Cls; Pres Jr Cls; Pres Sr Cls; Am Leg Aux Girls St; Band; Girl Scts; Hon Rl; Pol Wkr; Red Cr Ade; Ohio St Univ; Art Tchr.

SHICK, KATHERINE; Godwin Heights HS; Wyoming, MI; 2/170 Band; Treas NHS; Off Ade; Pep Clb; Spn Clb; PPFtbl; Ferris St Coll; CPA.

SHICK, STEVEN F; Godwin Hts HS; Wyoming, MI; 28/156 Hon Rl; Pres JA; NHS; JA Awd; Grand Rapids Jr Coll; Archt.

SHICK, WENDY; Harbor HS; Ashtabula, OH; 13/199 Fr Clb; Letter Bsktbl; GAA; IM Sprt; College; Physical Education.

SHIEFLER, CINDI; Rocky River HS; Rocky Rvr, OH; Drl Tm; Hon Rl; Hosp Ade; Red Cr Ade; Rptr Yrbk; Ger Clb; Letter Swmmng; Capt Chrldng; IM Sprt; PPFtbl; Ohio St Univ; Nursing.

SHIELDS, ALAN J; Austintown Fitch HS; Younstown, OH; 10/700 Am Leg Boys St; Hon Rl; NHS; Glf; Trk; Am Leg Awd; Air Force Academy; Aviation.

SHIELDS, ALTON C; Wirt HS; Gary, IN; Band; Hon Rl; Pol Wkr; Sch Pl; Drama Clb; Pep Clb; Spn Clb; Socr; Trk; Cit Awd; College; Science.

SHIELDS, CARLA; Buckeye N HS; Brilliant, OH; 6/106 Band; Chrs; Cmnty Wkr; Girl Scts; Hon Rl; NHS; Off Ade; Stu Cncl; Yth Flsp; Drama Clb; Malone Coll; Elem Ed.

SHIELDS, DANIEL; Cheboygan Area HS; Cheboygan, MI; 5/200 Davenport College Of Bus; Acctg.

SHIELDS, GAYLA; Waynesfield Goshen HS; Waynesfield, OH; Trs Frsh Cls; Band; Chrs; Chrh Wkr; Stu Cncl; Yth Flsp; 4-H; PPFtbl; Bus Schl; Acctg.

SHIELDS, GREGORY; St Peter & Paul Area HS; Saginaw, MI; 12/116 Pres Soph Cls; Cl Rep Jr Cls; Cls Rep Sr Cls; Chrs; Hon Rl; NHS; Sch Mus; Bsbl; Ftbl; Hockey; Central Michigan Univ; Comp Prog.

SHIELDS, GREGORY; Saints Peter & Paul Area HS; Saginaw, MI; 11/116 Hon Rl; NHS; Bsbl; Ftbl; Hockey; Central Michigan Univ; Comp Sci.

SHIELDS, JULIE; Williamsburg HS; Williamsburg, OH; 5/92 Cls Rep Soph Cls; Cl Rep Jr Cls; Band; Chrs; Chrh Wkr; Girl Scts; Hon Rl; MMM; NHS; Orch; Arion Foundation Awd For Outstndng Musical Ach; Croswell Busline Music Awd; Clermont Cnty Gifted & Talented; Coll Of Mt St Joseph; Music.

SHIELDS, KAREN A; Bluefield HS; Bluefield, WV; 37/285 Sec Frsh Cls; VP Soph Cls; VP Jr Cls; Hon Rl; Jr NHS; VP Stu Cncl; Yth Flsp; Y-Teens; Rptr Yrbk; 4-H; Univ Of North Carolina; Spec Ed.

SHIELDS, KEN; North Newton HS; Demotte, IN; 10/150 Hon Rl; Treas NHS; Mth Clb; OEA; Letter Bsbl; Letter Ftbl; Purdue Univ; Engr.

SHIELDS, MIKE; Clearview HS; Lorain, OH; Chrs; Sch Pl; Stg Crw; Drama Clb; Letter Ftbl; Jackson St Univ; Interior Dec.

SHIELDS, RIKA; Doddridge County HS; West Union, WV; Pres Frsh Cls; VP Jr Cls; Band; Hon Rl; NHS; Yth Flsp; 4-H; FBLA; Chrldng; Dnfth Awd; Scholastis D High Grade 1978; Bkpng High Grades 1979; Marshall Univ; Acctg.

SHIFLEY, JULIE; Galion HS; Galion, OH; 10/275 Treas Band; Chrs; Hon Rl; Hosp Ade; Jr NHS; NHS; Orch; Sch Mus; Yth Flsp; Ohi Univ; Phy Ther.

SHIGLEY, RAY; Castle HS; Elberfield, IN; 2/360 Hon Rl; Jr NHS; NHS; Stu Cncl; Ger Clb; Pres Sci Clb; Crs Cntry; Trk; Scr Kpr; Clemson Univ; Bio Chem.

SHIKE, SCOTT; Martinsville HS; Martinsville, IN; 64/425 Band; Boy Scts; Sct Actv; DECA; Fr Clb; Letter Ftbl; Mgrs; DECA 2nd State CDC 1979; Mstr Cnslr De Molay 1979; Eagle Scout 1979; Rose Hulman Univ; Comp Sci.

SHILLING, TINA; Morgan HS; Malta, OH; Chrh Wkr; Hon Rl; Lbry Ade; NHS; Yth Flsp; Drama Clb; Spn Clb; Ohio Univ.

SHILLINGBURG, JERRI; Elk Garden HS; Elk Garden, WV; Sec Frsh Cls; Chrs; Hon Rl; Sch Pl; Ed Yrbk; Yrbk; Pep Clb; Bsktbl; Coll.

SHILLINGBURG, PATRICIA; Elk Garden HS; Keyser, WV; 10/32 VP Soph Cls; Chrs; Cmnty Wkr; Hon Rl; Off Ade; Sch Pl; Stg Crw; Stu Cncl; Yth Flsp; Rptr Yrbk;.

SHIMEL, HOLLY; Mohawk HS; Sycamore, OH; Band; Cmnty Wkr; Girl Scts; Off Ade; Orch; Red Cr Ade; Stu Cncl; Pep Clb; Spn Clb; IM Sprt; Band Awds 77 78 & 79; Orch 75 & 76; Flight Training.

SHIMKO, MICHAEL; Eastlake North HS; Eastlake, OH; 73/669 Am Leg Boys St; NHS; Yrbk; Ed Sch Nwsp; Rptr Sch Nwsp; Sch Nwsp; Spn Clb; News Photograph Scholastic Press Assoc; Press Journalism Inst;.

SHIMP, JENNIFER; Marquette Sr HS; Marquette, MI; Sec Soph Cls; Am Leg Aux Girls St; Hosp Ade; Am Leg Awd; Michigan St Univ; Busns.

SHIMP, JILL; Clay HS; South Bend, IN; Band; Chrh Wkr; Girl Scts; Hon Rl; Sct Actv; Yth Flsp; Univ.

SHIMP, RICHARD; Buchtel HS; Mogadore, OH; 15/430 Cls Rep Frsh Cls; Cls Rep Soph Cls; Chrs; Chrh Wkr; Hon Rl; NHS; PAVAS; Sch Mus; Sch Pl; Stg Crw; St & Tri St Champ Hist Day Comptn 76 77 & 78; Finlst NCTE Writing Contst 79; Mst Likly To Succedd 79; Univ; Drama.

SHINABARGAR, CARL; Carson City Crystal Area HS; Carson City, MI; Aud/Vis; Band; Hon Rl; 4-H; Letter Trk; ITT; Architecture.

SHINABERRY, THERESA; Pocahontas County HS; Frank, WV; 32/125 Band; Chrs; Drm Mjrt; Off Ade; Sch Pl; Stg Crw; Drama Clb; 4-H; Trk; Twrlr; N W Va All Area Band 77 & 78; 1st Runner Up Nov Contest NMC 78; W Virginia Inst Of Tech; Acctg.

SHINAULT, TINA; Bluefield HS; Bluefield, WV; Cls Rep Frsh Cls; Chrh Wkr; Hon Rl; Lbry Ade; Off Ade; Sch Pl; Stu Cncl; Y-Teens; 4-H; FBLA; Bluefield St Coll; Bus.

SHINAVER, PAMELA; Maumee HS; Maumee, OH; Chrs; Girl Scts; Hon Rl; Sch Mus; Yth Flsp; Eng Clb; Pres 4-H; Fr Clb; Twrlr; 4-H Awd; Ohio St Univ; Vet Med.

SHINE, JOHN; Mount Healthy HS; Cincinnati, OH; 28/562 Cl Rep Jr Cls; Cls Rep Sr Cls; Band; Hon Rl; NHS; Stu Cncl; Beta Clb; VICA; Bsbl; IM Sprt; Hugh O Brian Yth Foundation Ldrshp Awd 78; Univ Of Kentucky; Comp Progr.

SHINGLEDECKER, JANICE; Struthers HS; Struthers, OH; Cmp Fr Grls; Chrs; Y-Teens; Drama Clb; FNA; Lat Clb; Pep Clb; Univ; Nurse.

SHINGLER, DAWN; Champion Sr HS; Warren, OH; 10/226 Hon Rl; NHS; Spn Clb;.

SHINGLER, PATRICIA J; Alexander HS; Albany, OH; 16/132 Hon Rl; Stu Cncl; Ed Yrbk; Yrbk; Pres Fr Clb; Spn Clb; Hocking Tech Coll; Nursing.

SHINGLETON, CONNIE L; Beaver Local HS; Rogers, OH; 7/242 Chrh Wkr; Hon Rl; Jr NHS; NHS; Yth Flsp; Yrbk; OEA; Summi Decum 3 Years; Schl Of Christian Evangelism; Sec.

SHINGLETON, STEVEN; Buckhannon Upshur HS; Buckhannon, WV; Boy Scts; Chrs; Chrh Wkr; Yth Flsp; 4-H; Ftbl; West Virginia Univ; Poli Sci.

SHININGER, STEPHEN; Fairview HS; Defiance, OH; 12/124 Band; Chrs; Chrh Wkr; Cmnty Wkr; NHS; Orch; Red Cr Ade; Sch Mus; Pres Yth Flsp; VP FFA; John Phillip Sousa Awd 79; Natl Choral Awd 79; Ldg Roll & Best Actor Awd Schl Musical 79; Bowling Green St Univ; Music Educ.

SHINKLE, ROBERT; Clermont Northeastern HS; Goshen, OH; Band; Boy Scts; Spn Clb; Bus Schl.

SHINN, LYDIA; Licking Valley HS; Newark, OH; Sec Soph Cls; Trs Jr Cls; Band; Chrs; FCA; Hon Rl; Sch Mus; VP Stu Cncl; Sec Yth Flsp; Yrbk; Jazz Choir; 1st Cnty For Amer Legion Americanism Govt Test; Citizenship Awd; Ohio St Univ; Real Estate.

SHINN, TAMMY; William Henry Harrison HS; West Lafayette, IN; Stu Cncl; Yth Flsp; Rptr Yrbk; DECA; 4-H; Fr Clb; Pep Clb; Civic Consciousness Awd; Purdue Univ; Elem Ed.

SHIOMI, TAKEYUKI; Heath HS; Granville, OH; Pres Frsh Cls; Pres Soph Cls; Pres Jr Cls; Hon Rl; Fr Clb; Bsbl; Central Missouri St Univ; Archt.

SHIPE, PAMELA; Wadsworth Sr HS; Wadsworth, OH; Hon Rl; Off Ade; Rptr Yrbk; Sec 4-H; Lat Clb; 4-H Awd; Whos Who In Foreign Lang 77; Nominated For Natl Hon Soc 78; Nominated For Stud Of Month 78; Salem Univ; Equestrian Studies.

SHIPLEY, DEBRA R; Southport HS; Indianapolis, IN; Girl Scts; Hon Rl; Stu Cncl; Pep Clb; Spn Clb; Letter Swmmng; Trk; Chrldng; GAA; Scr Kpr; Ball St Univ; Bus.

SHIPLEY, MELINDA; Dublin HS; Columbus, OH; Sec Frsh Cls; Pres Soph Cls; Chrs; Hon Rl; Sch Mus; Letter Bsbl; Letter Bsktbl; GAA; Florida Southern Coll; Acctg.

SHIPMAN, SHARON; Bloomfield HS; N Bloomfield, OH; VP Sr Cls; Am Leg Aux Girls St; Hon Rl; Lbry Ade; Y-Teens; Yrbk; Sch Nwsp; Pres Beta Clb; Trk; Chrldng; College.

SHIPP, BRENDA; Whiteland Cmnty HS; New Whiteland, IN; 5/200 VP Soph Cls; Hon Rl; Jr NHS; Treas Key Clb; Pep Clb; Bsktbl; Trk; Chrldng; Indiana Univ; Med.

SHIRE, MARK; Prairie Heights HS; Hudson, IN; Band; Hon Rl; Stu Cncl; Yth Flsp; Letter Ftbl; Letter Trk; Letter Wrstlng; Univ.

SHIREY JR, JAMES; Hedgesville HS; Martinsburg, WV; 8/215 Trs Jr Cls; Pres Sr Cls; Am Leg Boys St; Band; Pres NHS; Stu Cncl; Sci Clb; Bsbl; Letter Ftbl; SAR Awd; Lacy I Rice Mem Schlrshp; Division Winner Region III Sci Fair; Reg VIII Bandmasters Clinic; West Virginia Univ; Dentistry.

SHIRILLA, GEORGE; Campbell Memorial HS; Campbell, OH; Boy Scts; Jr NHS; Sct Actv; Fr Clb; Mth Clb; Sci Clb; Bsbl; Bsktbl; Glf; Orthodox Youth Awd Of Yr 78; Eagle Scout 78; Univ; Engr.

SHIRK, DANIEL; Royal Oak Kimball HS; Royal Oak, MI; Boy Scts; FCA; Hon Rl; Letter Trk; Pres Awd; College; Accounting.

SHIRK, SHERRY A; Hardin Northern HS; Dunkirk, OH; Cls Rep Frsh Cls; Cls Rep Soph Cls; Cl Rep Jr Cls; Band; Drm Mjrt; Girl Scts; Sch Pl; Sct Actv; Stu Cncl; Rptr Yrbk; Ohio Northern Univ; Bsns Admin.

SHIRLEY, ANN; North Central HS; Indianapolis, IN; 390/999 Cls Rep Soph Cls; Cl Rep Jr Cls; Hon Rl; Stu Cncl; Fr Clb; Letter Trk; Letter Chrldng; Indiana Univ; Dent Hygnst.

SHIRLEY, ANTHONY D; East Edison HS; Milan, OH; Hon Rl; Sch Pl; Drama Clb; Mth Clb; Letter Bsbl; Bsktbl; IM Sprt; College; Comp Prog.

SHIRLEY, DAVID; St Stephen T Badin HS; Hamilton, OH; Aud/Vis; Chrs; Chrh Wkr; Boys Clb Am; Bsktbl; Trk; College; Elec Engr.

SHIRLEY, TERRY; Kearsley HS; Flint, MI; 12/375 Chrh Wkr; Hon Rl; JA; Jr NHS; Swmmng; Wrstlng; Cit Awd; Elk Awd; JA Awd; Natl Merit Ltr; General Motors Inst; Elec Engr.

SHISSLER, JILL; Avon Jr Sr HS; Plainfield, IN; 33/250 Cls Rep Frsh Cls; Cls Rep Soph Cls; Cl Rep Jr Cls; Cls Rep Sr Cls; Band; Drl Tm; Hon Rl; Stu Cncl; Drama Clb; 4-H; Indiana Univ; Bus.

SHIVELEY, CHRIS D; Milford HS; Milford, OH; 3/387 Am Leg Boys St; Lit Mag; NHS; Quill & Scroll; Sch Pl; Stu Cncl; Rptr Sch Nwsp; Journalism.

SHIVELY, BENJAMIN; Cadillac Sr HS; Cadillac, MI; Chrs; Chrh Wkr; Hon Rl; NHS; Sch Mus; Yth Flsp; Univ; Sci.

SHIVELY, BRIAN; Columbia City Joint HS; Columbia City, IN; 5/273 Am Leg Boys St; Chrh Wkr; Hon Rl; NHS; Yrbk; VP 4-H; Fr Clb; College; Engin Comp Sci.

SHIVELY, RENEE E; Trotwood Madison HS; Trotwood, OH; 5/450 Band; Girl Scts; Hon Rl; Jr NHS; NHS; Orch; Natl Merit SF; Opt Clb Awd; Univ; Jrnlsm.

SHIVELY, STANLEY; Ypsilanti HS; Ypsilanti, MI; 37/420 Cl Rep Jr Cls; Pres Sr Cls; Am Leg Boys St; Hon Rl; JA; Jr NHS; NHS; Stu Cncl; Chmn Bsbl; Chmn Ftbl; Hillsdale; Pre Law.

SHIVELY, TANDY; Fremont HS; Fremont, IN; 3/50 Band; Hon Rl; NHS; Sch Mus; Sch Pl; Stu Cncl; Drama Clb; 4-H; Fr Clb; Pep Clb; Purdue Univ; Pre Vet.

SHIVENER, TED; Amelia HS; Cincinnati, OH; 19/250 Hon Rl; NHS; Stu Cncl; Letter Bsbl; Letter Bsktbl; Letter Crs Cntry; Georgetown College; Teaching.

SHIVERS, RORY; Marion HS; Marion, IN; 1/710 Chrs; Hon Rl; NHS; Sch Mus; Sch Pl; Drama Clb; Kiwan Awd; Ind Univ; Musical Educ.

SHOBE, CARLA; Cass Technical HS; Detroit, MI; Cls Rep Soph Cls; Chrh Wkr; Cmnty Wkr; Hon Rl; Off Ade; Stu Cncl; OEA; Trk; Univ Of Michigan; Music.

SHOCK, WANDA J; Pickens HS; Helvetia, WV; 2/11 Trs Frsh Cls; Hon Rl; NHS;.

SHOCKEY, LAURA; Mathews HS; Vienna, OH; Chrs; Chrh Wkr; Hon Rl; Sec Yth Flsp; Y-Teens; Key Clb; Pep Clb; Spn Clb; Chrldng; Bowling Green; Fashion Merch.

SHOCKEY, TOD; Mathews HS; Vienna, OH; 55/140 Pres Soph Cls; Cls Rep Sr Cls; Boy Scts; Off Ade; Sct Actv; Stg Crw; Stu Cncl; Yth Flsp; Fr Clb; FTA; Ohi State Univ.

SHOCKLEY, CAROLYN; Chesapeake HS; Chesapeake, OH; 24/140 Hon Rl; Off Ade; Yrbk; Art.

SHOCKLEY, QUINTINA; Cleveland East HS; Cleveland, OH; Cls Rep Soph Cls; Cl Rep Jr Cls; Band; Chrs; Rptr Yrbk; Drama Clb; Fr Clb; Pep Clb; Letter Trk; Natl Merit SF; Hiram Univ; Communication.

SHOCKLEY, SHELLEY; Regina HS; E Cleveland, OH; VP Frsh Cls; Chrs; Girl Scts; Sct Actv; Rptr Sch Nwsp; Sch Nwsp; Pep Clb; Letter Bsktbl; Letter Trk; Indiana Univ; Journalism.

SHOCKLEY, TROY; East HS; Cleveland, OH; Band; Boy Scts; JA; Ed Yrbk; Sch Nwsp; Rdo Clb; Trk; Mgrs; Scr Kpr; Ohio St Univ; Bus Admin.

SHOCKNEY, AMY; Traverse City Sr HS; Traverse City, MI; Cmnty Wkr; Lbry Ade; Pep Clb; St Of Michigan Schlrshp; Masonic St Official Of Rainbow Girls; N W Michigan Coll; Nursing.

SHOEMAKER, ADAM P; Madison Plains HS; London, OH; Sch Pl; Civ Clb; 4-H; Letter Ftbl; Capt Wrstlng; Ohio St Univ; Comp Progr.

SHOEMAKER, BONNIE; Dowagiac Union HS; Dowagiac, MI; 4/217 Cls Rep Sr Cls; NHS; Sch

Mus; Sch Pl; Stu Cncl; Yrbk; Drama Clb; Univ Of Mic; Lawyer.

SHOEMAKER, BRUCE; Brownstown Central HS; Vallonia, IN; Hon Rl; 4-H; FFA; Letter Bsbl; Letter Bsktbl; Coach Actv; College; Agri.

SHOEMAKER, CINDY; Cardington Lincoln HS; Fulton, OH; 23/79 Trs Soph Cls; Sec Jr Cls; Band; Chrs; FCA; Hon Rl; Stg Crw; 4-H; Fr Clb; Bsbl; Cosmetology Schl.

SHOEMAKER, CINDY; Paint Valley HS; Chillicothe, OH; 9/75 VP Frsh Cls; Pres Sr Cls; Hon Rl; NHS; Stu Cncl; Rptr Yrbk; Drama Clb; Lat Clb; Pep Clb; Am Leg Awd; Shawnee St Univ; Nurse.

SHOEMAKER, DIANE; Hammond HS; Hammond, IN; 30/329 Chrs; Girl Scts; Hon Rl; Jr NHS; Sch Mus; Sch Pl; Drama Clb; Pom Pon; College; Interir Decorator.

SHOEMAKER, JOSEPH A; Ottawa Hills HS; Grand Rapids, MI; 1/450 Band; Boy Scts; Hon Rl; NHS; Orch; Sch Mus; Yth Flsp; Sch Nwsp; Mth Clb; Am Leg Awd; Univ; Math.

SHOEMAKER, KAREN; London HS; London, OH; 25/133 Drm Mjrt; Hon Rl; NHS; Quill & Scroll; Yth Flsp; Rptr Yrbk; Rptr Sch Nwsp; Fr Clb; Chrldng; Tmr; Major Awd 1yr Name On Plaque 78; Univ; Int Design.

SHOEMAKER, MARGARET; Reading HS; Reading, MI; 1/100 Sec Soph Cls; VP Sr Cls; Sal; Chrh Wkr; Hon Rl; NHS; Sec Stu Cncl; Rptr Yrbk; Rptr Sch Nwsp; 4-H; Western Michigan Univ; Chem.

SHOEMAKER, RHONDA; London HS; London, OH; Cls Rep Frsh Cls; Sch Pl; Drama Clb; Fr Clb; Trk; Coll.

SHOEMAKER, RHONDA; Brownstown Central HS; Vallonia, IN; 29/135 Band; Chrs; Hon Rl; Sch Mus; Stg Crw; Pres FTA; Spn Clb; Ftbl; Letter Trk; IM Sprt; Indiana State Univ; Bus Admin.

SHOEMAKER, SCOTT; Parkside HS; Jackson, MI; 12/344 Cls Rep Sr Cls; Band; Chrs; Chrh Wkr; Hon Rl; Orch; Sch Mus; Stu Cncl; Yth Flsp; Natl Merit SF; Jackson Comm Coll Recognition Schlrshp; Choral Music & Musical Theatre Dept Awds; Scholastic Honor Awd; Jackson Comm Coll; Busns Admin.

SHOEMAKER, SHERRIE; Lucas HS; Mansfield, OH; Band; FCA; Hon Rl; Lbry Ade; Yth Flsp; Letter Trk; Ashland College; Cpa.

SHOEMAKER, TODD; London HS; London, OH; 67/135 Cls Rep Frsh Cls; Pres Soph Cls; Cls Rep Soph Cls; Pres Jr Cls; Cl Rep Jr Cls; Pres Sr Cls; Cls Rep Sr Cls; Band; Chrh Wkr; Cmnty Wkr; Ohio State Univ; Poli Sci.

SHOEMAKER, TRACI; Hamilton S E HS; Indianapolis, IN; Band; Bsktbl; Trk; Ball St Univ.

SHOEMAKER, WILLIAM; Brownstown Central HS; Vallonia, IN; 25/150 Boy Scts; Chrh Wkr; Hon Rl; Yth Flsp; 4-H; FFA; IM Sprt;.

SHOFFNER, MICHAEL; Shaker Hts Sr HS; Shaker Hts, OH; Cls Rep Frsh Cls; Cls Rep Soph Cls; Cl Rep Jr Cls; Cls Rep Sr Cls; Band; Hon Rl; Orch; Sch Mus; Stu Cncl; Mgrs; Principals Awd 79; Band Awd 79; Ohio St Univ; Med.

SHOFFNER, SHEILA; Osborn HS; Detroit, MI; Girl Scts; Hon Rl; Off Ade; ROTC; Stu Cncl; Yrbk; Cit Awd; Wayne State Univ; Educ.

SHOMIN, ROBIN; Flushing HS; Flushing, MI; Band; Boy Scts; Girl Scts; Hon Rl; Sct Actv; Rdo Clb; Trk; Pom Pon; Univ Of Mich; Comp Progr.

SHONG, GAYLA; Stockbridge HS; Stockbridge, MI; Cls Rep Soph Cls; Cl Rep Jr Cls; Cls Rep Sr Cls; Hon Rl; Off Ade; Stu Cncl; Yrbk; 4-H; Trk; Chrldng; College; Psych.

SHONK, MONICA; William V Fisher Cath HS; Lancaster, OH; 10/70 Sec Soph Cls; VP Jr Cls; Cmnty Wkr; Hon Rl; Pres NHS; Stu Cncl; Letter Ten; Chrldng; GAA; JC Awd; Ohio St Univ; Fash Merch.

SHONK, SCOTT; East Kentwood HS; Kentwood, MI; Chrs; Sch Mus; Letter Ftbl; Letter Trk; IM Sprt; Univ; Bus.

SHONKWILER, PAMELA; London HS; W Jeffersn, OH; Hon Rl; Yth Flsp; Ohio St Univ; Busns.

SHOOK, B; Tiffin Calvert HS; Tiffin, OH; Chrs; Girl Scts; Sch Mus; Sdlty; 4-H; Pep Clb; Bsktbl; 4-H Awd; Bowling Green St Univ; Dent Hydnst.

SHOOK, BARBARA A; Columbian HS; Bloomville, OH; Cls Rep Frsh Cls; Chrh Wkr; Hon Rl; Yth Flsp; 4-H; Spn Clb; Coach Actv; 4-H Awd; Ohio St Univ; Psych.

SHOOK, BARBIE; Greenfield Central HS; Greenfield, IN; Boys Clb Am; Fr Clb; College; Psyco.

SHOOK, CYNTHIA; Liberty HS; Girard, OH; Chrs; Hon Rl; Yrbk; Trk; Business School; Sec.

SHOOK, DONNA; S Ripley Jr & Sr HS; Versailles, IN; 10/110 Band; Drl Tm; Hon Rl; FNA; Lat Clb; Pep Clb; Sci Clb; Bsktbl; Trk; Univ; Phys Educ.

SHOOK, GREGORY; Tiffin Calvert HS; Tiffin, OH; Boy Scts; Chrh Wkr; 4-H; Letter Ftbl; Letter Wrstlng; Coach Actv; IM Sprt; Bowling Green St Univ; Bus.

SHOOK, GWENDOLYN; Herbert Henry Dow HS; Midland, MI; 154/407 Band; Orch; Yrbk; Ed Sch Nwsp; Rptr Sch Nwsp; Sci Clb; Bsbl; Trk; Coach Actv; PPFtbl; Ball St For Jrnlsm 78; Phylosophy Workshp; Wayne St Univ; Sociology.

SHOOK, LUCILLE; Seeger Memorial HS; Williamsport, IN; Band; Chrh Wkr; Hon Rl; Sch Mus; VP Yth Flsp; Drama Clb; Sec 4-H; Mgrs; Scr Kpr; Tmr;.

SHOOKMAN, PAMELA; Huntington North HS; Huntington, IN; 2/750 Hon Rl; Ger Clb; College; Restaurant.

SHOOPMAN, JOE; West Muskingom HS; Zanesville, OH; 10/200 Pres Frsh Cls; Pres Soph Cls; Pres Jr Cls; Pres Sr Cls; Band; Chrs; Drm Mjrt; Hon Rl; NHS; Sch Mus; Student Cncl Pres 78; Most Active Key Club Membr 78; Univ; Communication.

SHOPE, BEVERLY; Bloom Local HS; South Webster, OH; Band; Chrs; Drm Mjrt; Hon Rl; Off Ade; FHA; OEA; Pep Clb; Trk; IM Sprt; Shawnee State; Secretary.

SHORE, CHRISTOPHER; Union HS; Modoc, IN; 5/85 Treas Band; Hon Rl; NHS; Spn Clb; Letter Bsbl; Letter Bsktbl; Ministry.

SHORE, RENEE; Union HS; Modoc, IN; 1/59 Pres Frsh Cls; Val; Band; Chrs; Drl Tm; Hon Rl; NHS; Professional Careers Inst; Dental As.

SHORT, ANITA; Iaeger HS; Bradshaw, WV; Band; Chrh Wkr; Hon Rl; Jr NHS; Pres Stu Cncl; Drama Clb; Fr Clb; Pres Keyettes; Pep Clb; Am Leg Awd; Marshall Univ; Med.

SHORT, BETH; South Harrison HS; Lost Creek, WV; Band; Hon Rl; NHS; Sch Pl; Stu Cncl; Rptr Yrbk; 4-H; VICA; Bsktbl; GAA; Homecoming Princess; Clarksburg Beauty Acad.

SHORT, CATHY; Archbold HS; Archbold, OH; Chrs; Yth Flsp; Letter Bsktbl; IM Sprt; College; Art.

SHORT, DOREEN; R Nelson Snider HS; Ft Wayne, IN; Cls Rep Soph Cls; Trs Jr Cls; Cl Rep Jr Cls; Hon Rl; Pol Wkr; Stu Cncl; Spn Clb; Letter Bsktbl; Top Schlr Awd 76; Vllybl Lttr Co Captain 76; Univ.

SHORT, JEFF; Upper Sandusky HS; Upper Sandusky, OH; 14/210 Cls Rep Frsh Cls; Trs Soph Cls; Pres Jr Cls; Am Leg Boys St; Band; Hon Rl; Pres NHS; Chmn Stg Crw; Stu Cncl; Ed Yrbk; Ball St Univ; Comp Engr.

SHORT, JEFFREY; Hagerstown Jr Sr HS; Economy, IN; 2/182 Chrh Wkr; Hon Rl; NHS; Sch Mus; Sch Pl; Ed Sch Nwsp; Sci Clb; Pres Spn Clb; Rotary Awd; Edwin V O Neel Journalism Awd; Ball St Univ; Journalism.

SHORT, KAREN; St Francis De Sales HS; Westerville, OH; Cls Rep Sr Cls; Rptr Yrbk; Fr Clb; Letter Gym; Letter Trk; Mat Maids; PPFtbl; Bowling Green Univ; Fashion Design.

SHORT, KOREEN; Pettisville Local HS; Wauseon, OH; Band; Chrs; Hon Rl; NHS; Yth Flsp; Rptr Yrbk; Rptr Sch Nwsp; 4-H; Spn Clb; Chrldng; Univ; Elem Ed.

SHORT, NYANA; East Detroit HS; Warren, MI; Chrs; Chrh Wkr; Girl Scts; Hon Rl; Sct Actv; Yth Flsp; Baptist Bible Coll; Missionary.

SHORT, RUSSELL; Midpark HS; Brook Park, OH; 120/636 Hon Rl; NHS; Spn Clb; Capt Ftbl; Swmmng; Trk; IM Sprt; Cleveland St Univ; Phys Ther.

SHORT, TERRI; Ainsworth HS; Flint, MI; Cls Rep Soph Cls; Cl Rep Jr Cls; Chrh Wkr; Hon Rl; NHS; Stu Cncl; Chrldng; Cit Awd; DAR Awd; Michigan State Univ.

SHORT, TODD; Coldwater HS; Coldwater, MI; VP Frsh Cls; JA; Rptr Yrbk; DECA; Glf; Ten; JA Awd; Best Short Story Of The Yr; Awd In Leadership; Western Univ; Law.

SHORT, TODD; Stryker HS; Stryker, OH; Aud/Vis; Yth Flsp; FFA; Bsbl; Truck Driver.

SHORT, TREVA; New Palestine HS; New Palestine, IN; Girl Scts; Hon Rl; Sct Actv; 4-H; Fr Clb; 4-H Awd; Univ; Nurse.

SHORT, WENDELL; Pettisville HS; Archbold, OH; Trs Jr Cls; Band; Chrs; Hon Rl; Stg Crw; Yth Flsp; FFA; Trophy For Bwlng Tm Coming In 2nd 78; Hesston Coll.

SHORT, WILLIAM; Wapakoneta Sr HS; Wapakoneta, OH; 6/322 Pres Chrs; Hon Rl; NHS; Sch Mus; Stg Crw; Drama Clb; Lat Clb; Coach Actv; 3.5 Avg For 7 Sem; Hauss Helms Foundtn Schlrshp; Hon Mention On OTSA In Chem; Bowling Green St Univ.

SHORTER, RICHARD; Athens HS; Lerona, WV; 5/70 VP Soph Cls; Pres Jr Cls; Band; Hon Rl; Lbry Ade; NHS; Sch Pl; Ed Yrbk; Pres Key Clb; Sci Clb; Concord Coll; Bio.

SHORTER, RICHARD A; Athens HS; Athens, WV; 5/70 Pres Soph Cls; Pres Jr Cls; Aud/Vis; Chrh Wkr; Hon Rl; Lbry Ade; NHS; Ed Yrbk; Pres Key Clb; Pep Clb; Marshall Univ; Med Dr.

SHORTS, DANIEL; Brooke HS; Wellsburg, WV; 110/403 Cls Rep Frsh Cls; Hon Rl; Trk; Scr Kpr; Univ; Law.

SHORTT, DAVID; Farmington Sr HS; Farmington Hls, MI; Aud/Vis; Boy Scts; Debate Tm; Hon Rl; NHS; Sct Actv; Stg Crw; Pres Mth Clb; Univ; Math.

SHOUB, CHRIS; Huntington East HS; Huntington, WV; Cl Rep Jr Cls; Am Leg Boys St; Hon Rl; Jr NHS; NHS; Stu Cncl; Yth Flsp; Boys Clb Am; VP Fr Clb; Key Clb; W V Key Clb Dstrct Otstndng Lt Gvrnr 78; Univ; Elec Engr.

SHOULDERS, JULIA; Decatur Central HS; Indnpls, IN; 6/350 Hon Rl; NHS; Quill & Scroll; Yrbk; 4-H; Lat Clb; Pep Clb; Letter Swmmng; 4-H Awd; Ind Univ; Envir Sci.

SHOULDERS, WANDA; John Hay HS; Cleveland, OH; Cls Rep Frsh Cls; Cls Rep Soph Cls; Cl Rep Jr Cls; Cls Rep Sr Cls; Hon Rl; Stu Cncl; Sch Nwsp; Drama Clb; Fr Clb; Cincinnati Univ.

SHOULTS, CARRIE; Pellston HS; Levering, MI; Band; Chrh Wkr; Hon Rl; Lbry Ade; NHS; Trk; Natl Merit SF; N Michigan Univ; Busns.

SHOULTS, CHERYL; John Glenn HS; Westland, MI; 65/660 Chrh Wkr; Hon Rl; Treas Ger Clb; IM Sprt; Eastern Mich Univ; Acctg.

SHOULTZ, ROBIN; Madison Hts HS; Anderson, IN; Chrs; Cmnty Wkr; Hon Rl; ROTC; Yth Flsp; Purdue Univ; Educ.

SHOUP, CHERYL; Marion HS; Marion, IN; 114/648 Band; Chrh Wkr; Hon Rl; Yrbk; Ed Sch Nwsp; Fr Clb; Gym; Vc Pres Of Church Yth Grp 78; Pianist For Var Singer & Daystar 78; Taylor Univ; Music.

SHOUP, KIMBERLY; Upper Valley Jt Voc Schl; Troy, OH; VP Jr Cls; Cls Rep Sr Cls; Band; Cmp Fr Grls; Chrs; Hon Rl; Hosp Ade; Drama Clb; 4-H; OEA; 4 Yrs Perfect Attndnc 79; OEA Regnl Contest Speech 1st Plc 78; OEA St Contest Speech 5th Plc 79; Clark Tech Univ; Ct Reportr.

SHOUP, SUSAN; Belleville HS; Belleville, MI; Sec Jr Cls; Sec Sr Cls; Cmnty Wkr; Hon Rl; NHS; Stu Cncl; Ed Yrbk; Yrbk; Gym; Swmmng; Henry Ford Univ; Jrnlsm.

SHOVALD, TERRI; West Iron Cnty HS; Iron River, MI; 40/130 Cls Rep Sr Cls; Band; Drl Tm; Hon Rl; Sch Pl; Ed Sch Nwsp; VICA; Pom Pon; Capt Twrlr; N Michigan Univ; Jrnslm.

SHOWALLTER, AMY; Greenville Sr HS; Greenville, OH; 71/360 Hon Rl; NHS; Orch; Yth Flsp; Letter Ten; Capt Chrldng; Wright St Univ; Poli Sci.

SHOWALTER, CATHY; Parkersburg HS; Parkersburg, WV; Chrh Wkr; Cmnty Wkr; Hon Rl; Hosp Ade; Sch Pl; Yth Flsp; Drama Clb; Letter Gym; Elk Awd; Scndry Stdnt Training Progr At Ia Univ;1st Pl In Set Design In St Drama Comp 78; Parish Councl Lectr; Wheeling Coll; Bio.

SHOWALTER, CINDY; Barr Reeve HS; Montgomery, IN; 11/66 Girl Scts; Hon Rl; Sec Jr NHS; NHS; Treas Yth Flsp; Rptr Yrbk; Beta Clb; 4-H; FHA; Pep Clb; Univ Of Evansville; Nursing.

SHOWALTER, WM E; Onekama HS; Onekama, MI; 6/58 Band; Boy Scts; Hon Rl; NHS; Sch Mus; Bsktbl; Crs Cntry; Trk; IM Sprt; Elk Awd; Mich Tech Univ; Engineering.

SHOWERMAN, WANDA; Webberville HS; Williamston, MI; Band; Hon Rl; Sch Pl; Rptr Yrbk; 4-H; Sec Fr Clb; GAA; 4-H Awd; Univ Of Tulsa; Advrtsg.

SHOWERS, PAUL; Monroe HS; Monroe, MI; 93/550 Hon Rl; VP NHS; Stu Cncl; Fr Clb; Crs Cntry; Capt Ten; IM Sprt; Natl Merit Ltr; Kalamazoo Coll; Health Sci.

SHOWMAN, JOYCE; Evergreen HS; Delta, OH; Band; Lit Mag; Sch Pl; Stg Crw; Rptr Sch Nwsp; Sch Nwsp; Drama Clb; Letter Trk; GAA; Volybl 79; Nominated To Participate In Miss Teenage Amer Contest 79; Military; Cmmrcl Art.

SHOWRONEK, JAMES; Norway HS; Norway, MI; 33/96 Boy Scts; Chrs; Chrh Wkr; Cmnty Wkr; Hon Rl; Ten; IM Sprt; Northern Michigan Univ; History.

SHRADER, SALLY; Centerville HS; Centerville, OH; 40/680 Chrs; Cmnty Wkr; Girl Scts; Sch Mus; Sch Pl; Sct Actv; Stu Cncl; Yth Flsp; Drama Clb; Fr Clb; College; Acctg.

SHRADER, TAMMY; Bluefield HS; Bluefield, WV; 1/323 Cls Rep Soph Cls; Val; Hon Rl; NHS; Quill & Scroll; Stu Cncl; Ed Sch Nwsp; Rptr Sch Nwsp; Spn Clb; Bausch & Lomb Awd; Virginia Poly Tech Inst; Engr.

SHRAMO, CHRIS; Jackson Milton HS; Lake Milton, OH; 6/111 Cls Rep Frsh Cls; VP Band; Chrs; Drm Mjrt; Girl Scts; Hon Rl; NHS; Sch Mus; Sch Pl; Sec Stu Cncl; Soc Dist Amer HS Stu SOS Club; University; Radiology.

SHRECONGOST, SUZANNE; Marion HS; Marion, IN; Chrs; Hon Rl; Jr NHS; NHS; Off Ade; Sch Mus; Rptr Yrbk; Drama Clb; Purdue Univ; Pharmacy.

SHRESTHA, DEEPIKA; Bowling Green HS; Bowling Green, OH; 9/325 Cls Rep Frsh Cls; Band; Chrs; Girl Scts; Hon Rl; Hosp Ade; Jr NHS; NHS; Stu Cncl; Sci Clb; Regents Schlrshp 79; Stud Of Month Nov 78; Runner Up Archt Design Contest 78; Schlstc Art Show Hon Mention; Cornell Univ; A rcht.

SHREVE, ED; Zane Trace HS; Chillicothe, OH; 18/95 Hon Rl; Jr NHS; NHS; Stu Cncl; Spn Clb; Letter Bsktbl; Letter Ftbl;.

SHREVE, GARY; Willard HS; New Haven, OH; Chrs; Hon Rl; Jr NHS; NHS; Orch; Sch Mus; Sch Pl; Letter Ftbl; Wrstlng; College.

SHREVE, GARY; Morgan HS; Mc Connelsville, OH; Am Leg Boys St; Chrh Wkr; Hon Rl; Jr NHS; NHS; Yth Flsp; Spn Clb; Bsbl; Bsktbl; IM Sprt; Univ.

SHREVE, JEFFERY; Arthur Hill HS; Saginaw, MI; Boy Scts; Hon Rl; Sci Clb; Delta College; Engr.

SHREVES, KRIS; Yorktown HS; Muncie, IN; Yrbk; 4-H; FBLA; FHA; Treas Spn Clb; 4-H Awd; Ivy Tech Voc Schl; Dent Asst.

SHREWSBURY, JEFFREY; Wirt County HS; Elizabeth, WV; Cls Rep Frsh Cls; Cls Rep Soph Cls; Cl Rep Jr Cls; Band; Chrs; Hon Rl; NHS; Stu Cncl; VP 4-H; Fr Clb; Bst Musicn Frsh & Soph Yr 77 & 78; West Virginia Univ; Bus.

SHREWSBURY, KAREN; Matoaka HS; Rock, WV; Band; Chrs; Hon Rl; Stu Cncl; Yth Flsp; Treas FBLA; FHA; Sftbl Team; Jr Attendant Homecoming; Natl Busns Coll; Sec.

SHREWSBURY, KATHY; Shady Spring HS; Beaver, WV; Chrh Wkr; FCA; Hon Rl; NHS; Off Ade; Sch Pl; Stg Crw; Yth Flsp; Rptr Yrbk; Rptr Sch Nwsp; Homecoming Attendant; Homecoming Queen; Marshall Univ; Special Ed.

SHREWSBURY, LORETTA S; Herndon HS; Herndon, WV; 9/45 Am Leg Aux Girls St; Hon Rl; NHS; FBLA; FHA; Pep Clb; Capt Chrldng; Am Leg Awd; 4-H Awd; Univ; Spec Educ.

SHREWSBURY, SONIA; Matonka HS; Lashmeet, WV; Cls Rep Frsh Cls; Cls Rep Soph Cls; Cl Rep Jr Cls; Band; Chrs; Chrh Wkr; Cmnty Wkr; Hon Rl; Lbry Ade; NHS; Bluefield St Univ; Jrnlsm.

SHREWSBURY, TINA; Matoaka HS; Matoaka, WV; Hon Rl; Stg Crw; Rptr Sch Nwsp; Sch Nwsp; FBLA; Bluefield St Coll.

SHRIFT, GRETCHEN; St Francis HS; Traverse City, MI; VP Frsh Cls; Chrh Wkr; Girl Scts; Hon Rl; Sch Pl; Stu Cncl; Cit Awd; Northern Mic Univ; Psych.

SHRINER, KENNETH; Stevenson HS; Livonia, MI; 12/756 Hon Rl; Lbry Ade; Off Ade; Sch Nwsp; Trk; Coach Actv; IM Sprt; U S Air Force Academy; Engr.

SHRIVER, DANIEL W; Jackson HS; North Canton, OH; Band; Boy Scts; Orch; Sch Mus; Sct Actv; VICA; Trk; Building Trades.

SHRIVER, DEBBY; Norwood HS; Norwood, OH; 52/343 Sec Band; Drm Mjrt; Hon Rl; Jr NHS; Orch; Sch Mus; Yrbk; VP Key Clb; Spn Clb; Mem Of All Ohio St Fair Band; Nominated For Mc Donalds All American HS Band; College; Music.

SHRIVER, JANET M; Triton Central HS; Fairland, IN; 8/162 Band; FCA; NHS; Sch Pl; Pres Drama Clb; Pep Clb; Sec Spn Clb; Bsktbl; Trk; Pres Awd; Voleyball 1977; Univ; Math.

SHRIVER, JEFF; Lakeview HS; Cortland, OH; Boy Scts; Hon Rl; Glf; Univ; Mech Engr.

SHRIVER, KATHERINE; Meadowbrook HS; Pleasant City, OH; Band; Chrs; Hon Rl; NHS; Stg Crw; Yth Flsp; 4-H; FBLA; FHA; Key Clb; Muskingum Area Tech Coll; Accounting.

SHRIVER, NORINE; South Charleston HS; S Charleston, WV; Chrh Wkr; Girl Scts; Hon Rl; Jr NHS; Lbry Ade; NHS; Off Ade; Trk; Univ; Botany.

SHROSBREE, BOB; Southfield HS; Southfield, MI; Pres Frsh Cls; Band; Chrs; Chrh Wkr; Drm Bgl; Hon Rl; Jr NHS; Lbry Ade; Mdrgl; NHS; Univ; Bus.

SHROYER, ANNA; Bishop Ready HS; Columbus, OH; Band; Boy Scts; Cmp Fr Grls; Hon Rl; Jr NHS; Orch; Letter Trk; Ohi St Univ; Forestry.

SHROYER, SHERI; Anderson HS; Anderson, IN; Chrs; Chrh Wkr; Girl Scts; Hon Rl; NHS; Off Ade; Sct Actv; Sec Yth Flsp; College; Scndry Educ.

SHUBITOWSKI, LISA; Arthur Hill HS; Saginaw, MI; Am Leg Aux Girls St; Band; Debate Tm; Drm Bgl; Hon Rl; NHS; Stg Crw; Yth Flsp; Fr Clb; Pep Clb; Wayne St Univ; Liberal Arts.

SHUBITOWSKI, RUSSELL; Henry Ford HS; Detroit, MI; Hon Rl; Cit Awd; Central Michigan Univ; Comp Sci.

SHUCK, ANITA; Meadow Bridge HS; Danese, WV; 2/50 Cmnty Wkr; Hon Rl; Jr NHS; NHS; Pol Wkr; 4-H; Fr Clb; FTA; Trk; Univ; Engr.

SHUEY, PAULA; Tiffin Columbian HS; Tiffin, OH; Chrh Wkr; Hon Rl; Lbry Ade; Yth Flsp; Drama Clb; Spn Clb; IM Sprt; Bowling Green St Univ; Bus Educ.

SHUFF, SHERRY; Bellbrook HS; Spring Vlly, OH; AFS; Chrs; Girl Scts; Hon Rl; 4-H; Fr Clb; Cit Awd; Univ; Earth Sci.

SHUGERT, MARGARET S; Waldron HS; Waldron, IN; Sec Soph Cls; Trs Soph Cls; Trs Jr Cls; Band; Chrh Wkr; Hon Rl; Hosp Ade; Sch Nwsp; Lat Clb; Pep Clb; Indiana Univ.

SHULEVITZ, J; Interlochen Arts Acad; Miami, FL; Aud/Vis; Lit Mag; Sch Pl; Rptr Yrbk; NCTE; Natl Merit Ltr; Natl Merit SF; Univ; History.

SHULL, CONNIE; St Ursula Academy; Toledo, OH; Cls Rep Sr Cls; Chrs; Girl Scts; Hon Rl; JA; Off Ade; Stu Cncl; Rptr Yrbk; Pep Clb; Trk; Univ Of Toledo; Marktng.

SHULL, LORI; Garrett HS; Auburn, IN; Cls Rep Sr Cls; Chrs; Hon Rl; Pres Ger Clb; Pres Pep Clb; Girls Vllybl Varsity Letter 78; Ravenscroft Univ; Cosmetologist.

SHULL, LUANE; East Noble HS; Kendallville, IN; Sec Soph Cls; Sec Jr Cls; Band; Girl Scts; Stg Crw; 4-H; OEA; Letter Chrldng; Scr Kpr; 4-H Awd; College; Busns.

SHULL, SANDY; De Kalb HS; Auburn, IN; Band; Chrs; Girl Scts; Hon Rl; Natl Forn Lg; NHS; Sch Mus; Sch Pl; Stg Crw; Sch Nwsp; Hnr Awd 79; Tri Kappa Hnr Awd 78 & 79; Manchester Coll; Art.

SHULL, TINA; Grant HS; Bailey, MI; Chrh Wkr; Yth Flsp; FBLA; Mat Maids; Bus Schl; Data Processing.

SHULTZ, BEV; Valley Local HS; Lucasville, OH; 6/110 Trs Soph Cls; Trs Jr Cls; Band; Chrh Wkr; Hosp Ade; NHS; Stu Cncl; Yrbk; 4-H; FTA; FHA; Rainbow; Jr Fair Board;.

SHULTZ, CHARLES C; Danville HS; Danville, OH; VP Soph Cls; Trs Jr Cls; Hon Rl; Sch Mus; Stg Crw; 4-H; FFA; Ftbl; 4-H Awd; Univ; Agri Farmer.

SHULTZ, DEBRA; Cedar Lake Academy; Cedar Lake, MI; VP Soph Cls; VP Jr Cls; Hon Rl; Capt Bsbl; Bsktbl; Capt Ftbl; IM Sprt; PPFtbl; Scr Kpr; Tmr; Andrews Univ.

SHULTZ, GREG; Spring Valley Acad; Lincoln, NE; Pres Jr Cls; Hst Sr Cls; Band; Hon Rl; Ftbl; Hndbl; Union College;.

SHULTZ, JUDITH; Schoolcraft HS; Schoolcraft, MI; Chrs; Chrh Wkr; Hon Rl; Lbry Ade; Off Ade; Sch Pl; Ed Sch Nwsp; Fr Clb; Bsbl; IM Sprt; College; Executive Bus Sec.

SHULTZ, MELODY L; Big Walnut HS; Sunbury, OH; Sec Frsh Cls; Sec Soph Cls; Band; Chrh Wkr; Off Ade; Yth Flsp; 4-H; FHA; Bsktbl; 4-H Awd; Bowling Green Coll; Fashion Mdse.

SHULTZ, RANDALL; Cedar Lake Academy; Cedar Lake, MI; Pres Frsh Cls; Cls Rep Frsh Cls; Pres Soph Cls; Pres Jr Cls; Pres Sr Cls; Chrs; Mdrgl; NHS; Yrbk; Bsbl; Andrews Univ; Indus Educ.

SHULTZ, SONYA; South Newton HS; Earl Park, IN; Am Leg Aux Girls St; Band; Girl Scts; Sch Mus; Sch Pl; 4-H; FBLA; FHA; Lat Clb; Pep Clb; Bus Schl; Bus.

SHUMAKER, GRETA; Amanda Clearcreek HS; Lancaster, OH; 1/109 Cls Rep Frsh Cls; Cls Rep Soph Cls; Cl Rep Jr Cls; VP Sr Cls; Val; Am Leg Aux Girls St; Hon Rl; Pres NHS; Sch Pl; Stu Cncl; Bowling Green St Univ; Med.

SHUMAN, MARLA; Hundred HS; Burton, WV; Band; Hon Rl; Stg Crw; Yrbk; Drama Clb; Pep Clb; Wv Univ; Jounalism.

SHUMATE, PAM; Pt Clinton HS; Pt Clinton, OH; Chrs; Chrh Wkr; Girl Scts; Spn Clb; Church Woker; Univ.

SHUMICK, L; Perry HS; Canton, OH; Girl Scts; JA; Sct Actv; Bsktbl; Trk; Scr Kpr; College; Bus Acctg.

SHUNESON, KEVIN; Charlotte HS; Charlotte, MI; 64/306 Pres Band; Chrh Wkr; FCA; Stu Cncl; Letter Bsktbl; Capt Ten; Dnfth Awd; Rotary Awd; St Of Mi Schlshp; Grand Rapids Baptist Coll; Elem Educ.

SHUNK, BRENDA; Fulton HS; Perrinton, MI; Band; Hon Rl; Lbry Ade; Yrbk; 4-H; Lansing Business Univ; Secretary.

SHUNTA, RANDALL; Muskegon Catholic Ctrl HS; Muskegon Hts, MI; Chrh Wkr; Cmnty Wkr; Hon Rl; Sdlty; Mth Clb; IM Sprt; Scr Kpr; Ctrl Michigan Univ; Sci.

SHUPE, BRAD; Clearcreek HS; Amanda, OH; 10/107 Am Leg Boys St; NHS; Sch Pl; Stu Cncl; Sprt Ed Yrbk; Sci Clb; Capt Bsbl; Letter Bsktbl; Crs Cntry; Am Leg Awd; Amer Schl Of Broadcasting; Disc Jock.

SHUPERT, LORI; Carlisle HS; Franklin, OH; VP Sr Cls; Chrs; Chrh Wkr; Girl Scts; Hon Rl; NHS; Wright St Univ; Comp Sci.

SHUPPE, MIKE; Lake Catholic HS; Willowick, OH; Cls Rep Soph Cls; Hon Rl; IM Sprt; JETS Awd; Coll; Bus.

SHUPTAR, DOUGLAS; Portage Northern HS; Portage, MI; 50/424 Jr NHS; NHS; Letter Bsktbl; IM Sprt; Wheaton Coll; Acctg.

SHURELL, JAYNE; Ursuline HS; Youngstown, OH; 23/330 Hon Rl; NHS; Sec FTA; Spn Clb; Youngstown State Univ.

SHURMAN, GERALD S; Chesterton HS; Chesterton, IN; 20/450 Debate Tm; Hon Rl; Jr NHS; NHS; Trk; IM Sprt; Natl Merit Ltr; Univ; Engr.

SHURTZ, FRED; Ridgewood HS; W Lafayette, OH; 9/150 Pres Jr Cls; Pres Sr Cls; Debate Tm; Hon Rl; NHS; Sch Pl; Stu Cncl; Mth Clb; Spn Clb; Letter Bsktbl; Marietta Coll; Petroleum Engr.

SHURTZ, TANE; Goshen HS; Goshen, IN; 13/268 FCA; Hon Rl; Yth Flsp; Pep Clb; Spn Clb; Lettered On Volleyball Team 78; Manchester Univ.

SHUST, BILL; Manistique HS; Manistique, MI; Chrs; Hon Rl; Sch Mus; Stg Crw; Rptr Yrbk; Sprt Ed Sch Nwsp; Drama Clb; Ger Clb; Sci Clb; Natl Merit SF; Univ Of Michigan; Aero Engr.

SHUSTA, DAVID; Gwinn HS; Skandia, MI; Band; Hon Rl; NHS; Univ Of Michigan; Aerospace Engr.

SHUSTER, ANDREW; Bishop Luers HS; Ft Wayne, IN; Hon Rl; Rptr Sch Nwsp; Bsktbl; IM Sprt; Indiana Univ; Psych.

SHUSTER, SUSAN C; Rogers HS; Toledo, OH; Hon Rl; Jr NHS; NHS; Yrbk; Spn Clb; Cit Awd; Toledo Univ; Math.

SHUSTER, TIMOTHY; Rensselaer Ctrl HS; Brook, IN; Sch Pl; Stg Crw; Ftbl; Trk; Flathead Vly Cmnty Coll; Forestry.

SHUSTER II, R; Roosevelt Wilson HS; Stonewood, WV; Boy Scts; Hon Rl; Sct Actv; Stg Crw; Bsbl; Letter Ftbl; Letter Mgrs; Fairmont State College; Cmmrcl Art.

SHUTES, ROB; Marcellus HS; Marcellus, MI; 9/73 Hon Rl; Lit Mag; Pres NHS; Rptr Yrbk; Yrbk; Letter Bsktbl; Letter Trk; Scr Kpr; W Mi Univ Acad Schlhsp 79 83; Mi Copttv Schlshp 79; Western Michigan Univ; Acctg.

SHUTICH, DANIEL; West Catholic HS; Grand Rapids, MI; Cmnty Wkr; Hon Rl; Ftbl; Letter Wrstlng; Mgrs; Univ; Mech Engr.

SHUTT, MARGARET; Princeton HS; Bluefield, WV; 16/312 Hon Rl; Treas NHS; Sch Pl; Stu Cncl; Keyettes; Pep Clb; DAR Awd; Bluefield Coll; Elem Ed.

SHUTT, PEGGY; Coshocton HS; Coshcoton, OH; Sec Frsh Cls; Trs Soph Cls; Trs Jr Cls; Trs Sr Cls; Chrs; Stu Cncl; Treas Key Clb; Pres Spn Clb; Capt Chrldng; Univ; Elem Tchr.

SHUTT, TAMI; Bluffton HS; Bluffton, IN; 15/135 Band; Chrh Wkr; Drm Bgl; Hon Rl; Sch Mus; Y-Teens; Ger Clb; OEA; Kentucky Christian Coll; Regigion.

SHUTWAY, NINA; Chippewa HS; Doylestown, OH; Girl Scts; Hon Rl; Sch Mus; Sch Pl; Drama Clb; 4-H; Spn Clb; Bsktbl; Trk; 4-H Awd; Military; Archt.

SHY, CHARLES; Buffalo HS; Lavalette, WV; Boy Scts; Hon Rl; Mod UN; Sct Actv; Spn Clb; Socr; Cit Awd; Marshall Univ; Civil Engr.

SIBBERSON, MICHAEL F; Elkhart Memorial HS; Elkhart, IN; Hon Rl; Hosp Ade; Yrbk; Rptr Sch Nwsp; Sch Nwsp; Sec Fr Clb; Spn Clb; Crs Cntry; Univ; Sci.

SIBBITT, DOUG; Carroll HS; Bringhurst, IN; Chrh Wkr; Debate Tm; Hon Rl; Yth Flsp; Sch Nwsp; 4-H; Treas FFA; Spn Clb; Bsktbl; IM Sprt; Natl Jr Historical Soc 76 80; Purdue Univ; Agri.

SIBERT, ANN; Norwood Sr HS; Norwood, OH; Hon Rl; Sch Mus; Stg Crw; Fr Clb; Pep Clb; Coach Actv; GAA; IM Sprt; Xavier Coll; Busns.

SIBERT, DANIEL; Clermont Northeastern HS; Batavia, OH; Hon Rl; FFA; VICA; IM Sprt; JA Awd; Principals Awd Outstndg Stu 75; Hnr Stu Industrial Art 1 76; Live Oaks Voc Schl; Machinist.

SIBERT, DOUG; West Carrollton Sr HS; Dayton, OH; 8/418 Chrs; Debate Tm; Hon Rl; Jr NHS; Natl Forn Lg; NHS; Spn Clb; Cit Awd; St Fnls In Debt 4th Pl 78; Summer For Exchng Stdnt To Mexico 78; Delgt To World Affairs On Africa 78; Univ Of Dayton; Intl Bus.

SIBREL, KATHY; Tell City HS; Cannelton, IN; 5/225 Hon Rl; NHS; Sch Pl; Sec Yth Flsp; Pres 4-H; Letter Bsktbl; Cit Awd; God Cntry Awd; Honor Banquet; Tri Kappa Special State Schlrshp; Optimist Clb Dinner For Outstanding Sr; Univ Of Evansville; Nursing.

SIBRIK, TERRI; Eastmoor Sr HS; Columbus, OH; 23/290 Letter Band; Hon Rl; Off Ade; Orch; PAVAS; DECA; Rdo Clb; Letter Bsbl; Graduating With Diploma With Distinction; Bowling Green Univ; Mass Comm.

SICHHART, CHRIS; George Rogers Clark HS; Hammond, IN; 101/219 Chrs; Drl Tm; Sch Mus; Pep Clb; Swmmng; Pom Pon; Tmr; Univ At Purdue; Fashion Retailing.

SICHTING, LISA ANN; Martinsville HS; Martinsville, IN; Trs Soph Cls; Trs Jr Cls; Trs Sr Cls; Off Ade; Stu Cncl; Chrldng;.

SICILIANO, JOANNE; Berkshire HS; Burton, OH; 1/130 Hon Rl; NHS; 4-H; Cit Awd; DAR Awd; 4-H Awd; Kiwan Awd; Ohi State Univ ;vet.

SICK, STEVEN; Canfield HS; Canfield, OH; 31/258 Band; Chrs; Chrh Wkr; Hon Rl; Jr NHS; Mdrgl; NHS; College; Meteorology.

SICKAFOOSE, KATHY; Sandy Valley HS; Magnolia, OH; 25/171 Chrs; Hon Rl; Hosp Ade; Natl Forn Lg; NHS; Quill & Scroll; Yrbk; Rptr Sch Nwsp; Pep Clb; Aultman Hosp Nursing Schl; RN.

SICKLES, HALDEN A; Bridgeport Sr HS; Bridgeport, WV; Band; Boy Scts; CAP; Hon Rl; DECA; Spn Clb; Bsktbl; Am Leg Awd; Amer Legion Boys St 77; West Virginia Univ; Vet Med.

SICKLESTEEL, MARY L; Saranac Community HS; Saranac, MI; Am Leg Aux Girls St; Hon Rl; NHS; Off Ade; FBLA; Natl Merit Ltr; College; Bus Admin.

SICKLING, KELLY J; Brandywine Sr HS; Niles, MI; Band; Girl Scts; Hon Rl; NHS; Sct Actv; Spn Clb; Letter Ten; Spanish Natl Honor Soc; Counselor For Brandywine Outdoor Ed Program; College.

SICKMILLER, TAMELA; North Central HS; Montpelier, OH; 5/60 Am Leg Aux Girls St; Hon Rl; NHS; Off Ade; Quill & Scroll; Sch Pl; Treas Stu Cncl; Rptr Sch Nwsp; Sch Nwsp; Drama Clb; Outstanding Sr; Jr Leadership; Most Promising Fresh FHA Awd; Northwest Tech Coll; Sec.

SIDDERS, MICHELLE; Benjamin Logan HS; Bellefontaine, OH; Chrs; Hon Rl; Rptr Yrbk; 4-H; Bsbl; Bsktbl; IM Sprt; 4-H Awd;.

SIDENBENDER, KARLA; Parkway HS; Rockford, OH; Cls Rep Frsh Cls; Cls Rep Soph Cls; Pres Jr Cls; Band; NHS; Stu Cncl; Sec Yth Flsp; Sci Clb; Letter Bsktbl; PPFtbl; Wright St Univ; Lab Tech.

SIDERS, BECKY; Millersport HS; Millersport, OH; 4/65 Am Leg Aux Girls St; Band; Chrs; Girl Scts; Hon Rl; NHS; Orch; Sch Nwsp; 4-H; FHA; Univ; Foreign Speech.

SIDES, JUDY; Northwood HS; Elkhart, IN; 30/209 Hon Rl; Hosp Ade; Sch Pl; Yth Flsp; Y-Teens; Drama Clb; Pep Clb; Messiah Coll; Psych.

SIDICK, JOAN; Plymouth Canton HS; Canton, MI; 8/440 Hon Rl; NHS; Sch Mus; Stu Cncl; Ed Sch Nwsp; Drama Clb; IM Sprt; VFW Awd; Voice Dem Awd; Univ Of Michigan; Comp Sci.

SIDLE, KRIS; Tell City HS; Tell City, IN; 7/250 Hon Rl; NHS; Sch Pl; Drama Clb; Pep Clb; Spn Clb; Crs Cntry; Trk; Le Tourneau College; Electrical Eng.

SIEBENALER, BILL; Hamilton Comm HS; Hamilton, IN; Pres Frsh Cls; VP Jr Cls; Band; Chrs; Sch Mus; Sch Pl; Stg Crw; Drama Clb; FFA; Letter Bsktbl; FFA State Band; Most Improved Runner Awd In Cross Country; 1st Pl At Regional Sci Fair Math; College.

SIEBENALER, MICHELLE; Edon HS; Edon, OH; Band; Chrh Wkr; Hon Rl; Off Ade; Yth Flsp; Rptr Sch Nwsp; Sch Nwsp; 4-H; FHA; Spn Clb; Cincinnati Bible Coll; Jrnlsm.

SIEBER, JEFFREY D; Delphi Cmnty HS; Camden, IN; Boy Scts; Chrs; Chrh Wkr; Lbry Ade; Sch Mus; Sch Pl; Sct Actv; Stg Crw; Yth Flsp; Rptr Sch Nwsp; Paper Staff Cert 79; Art Awds 77 & 78; Floristry.

SIEBERT, KAREN; Celina HS; Celina, OH; 12/283 Chrs; Hon Rl; NHS; Off Ade; VP FBLA; Lat Clb; Trk; Wrstlng; IM Sprt; College; Photo.

SIEBERT, KATHLEEN; Warren Woods HS; Warren, MI; 92/365 OEA; Macomb Cty College; Med Sec.

SIEBERT, LINDA M; Celina Sr HS; Celina, OH; Trs Sr Cls; Hon Rl; NHS; 4-H; FBLA; FTA; Pep Clb; IM Sprt; 4-H Awd; Univ; Educ.

SIEBERT, ROBERT; Hartland HS; Hartland, MI; Hon Rl;.

SIEDLECKI, BARBARA; Mona Shores HS; Muskegon, MI; NHS; Off Ade; Sci Clb; Letter Ten; Letter Trk; Grand Valley St Coll; Med.

SIEFERT, ANITA; Immaculate Conception Acad; Batesville, IN; 12/70 Chrh Wkr; Hon Rl; NHS; 4-H; Spn Clb; 4-H Awd; Univ; Envir Engr.

SIEFERT, DEBORAH; Mount Notre Dame HS; Cincinnati, OH; 18/173 Hon Rl; Drama Clb; Spn Clb; Work.

SIEFKER, LISA; Delphos Jefferson HS; Ft Jennings, OH; Chrs; Hon Rl; Lbry Ade; NHS; Fr Clb; Sci Clb; College; Occupational Ther.

SIEFKER, LISA K; Delphos Jefferson HS; Ft Jennings, OH; Chrs; Hon Rl; NHS; Fr Clb; Sci Clb; Univ; Occup Ther.

SIEFRING, DEBORAH; St Henry HS; New Weston, OH; 16/125 VP Jr Cls; Cl Rep Jr Cls; Cls Rep Sr Cls; Chrs; Hon Rl; NHS; OEA; Pep Clb;.

SIEFRING, RICHARD; Coldwater HS; Celina, OH; Chrs; Hon Rl; FFA; Wright State Univ; Engr.

SIEG, JONELLA; Bremen HS; Bremen, IN; 1/110 VP Frsh Cls; Band; Drl Tm; Hon Rl; Hosp Ade; Sch Pl; Stu Cncl; College; Pre Med.

SIEGEL, CATHRYN; Sycamore HS; Cincinnati, OH; Trk; Cert Of Merit & Key Awd 79; Univ Of Cincinnati; Archt Art.

SIEGEL, JENNIFER; West Catholic HS; Grand Rapids, MI; Chrs; Sch Pl; Pep Clb; Capt Ten; PPFtbl; Grand Rapids Junior College; Nurse.

SIEGEL, SHELLY K; Springfield HS; Holland, OH; Band; Chrh Wkr; Hon Rl; Yth Flsp; Spn Clb; Letter Bsktbl; Letter Trk; GAA; College.

SIEGEL JR, PHILLIP M; Saint Joseph Prep Seminary; Grand Rapids, MI; Cls Rep Frsh Cls; Cls Rep Soph Cls; VP Jr Cls; Boy Scts; Chrh Wkr; Hon Rl; Stu Cncl; Lat Clb; Bsktbl; IM Sprt; Michigan St Univ; Agri.

SIEGELMAN, BONNIE; Mayfield HS; Mayfield Hts, OH; AFS; Chrs; Hon Rl; Pep Clb; Univ; Law.

SIEGLAR, LISA; Union City Cmnty HS; Union City, IN; DECA; Intl Bus Coll; Legal Sec.

SIEGLE, JOSEPH; Divine Child HS; Dearborn Hts, MI; Band; FCA; Hon Rl; Orch; Letter Bsbl; Letter Ftbl; Coach Actv; Wayne St Univ.

SIEGLITZ, JOHN; Switzerland Cnty HS; Vevay, IN; 16/120 Hon Rl; Sch Pl; Stg Crw; Drama Clb; Key Clb; Glf; Scr Kpr; Rose Hulman Coll; Elec Engr.

SIEGMUNDT, MARK; St Xavier HS; Cincinnati, OH; Hon Rl; Bsbl; Univ; Engr.

SIEKIERDA, JOHN; Whitmer Sr HS; Toledo, OH; 82/810 Hon Rl; VICA; Univ Of Toledo; Elec Engr.

SIEKIERKA, MATTHEW; Walter E Stebbins HS; Dayton, OH; 3/400 Chrh Wkr; Hon Rl; Sci Clb; Jr Cncl World Affairs; Stebbins Booster Schlrshps; Polish Clb; Wright St Univ; Law.

SIEKMAN, TRACY; Wood Memorial HS; Buckskin, IN; Cl Rep Jr Cls; Cls Rep Sr Cls; Off Ade; Pres Stu Cncl; Pep Clb; Mas Awd; Evansville Univ; RN.

SIEL, BETH; Davison HS; Davison, MI; Chrs; Hon Rl; Natl Forn Lg; Orch; Sch Mus; Coll; Music.

SIELER, BRUCE; Summerfield HS; Petersburg, MI; Band; Hon Rl; Sch Pl; Treas 4-H; Monroe Comm Coll; Data Processing.

SIELSCHOTT, SHARON; Bellmont HS; Decatur, IN; 15/244 Hon Rl; NHS; Quill & Scroll; Pres Yth Flsp; Rptr Yrbk; Treas Ger Clb; Pep Clb; Letter Gym; Univ; Applied Math.

SIEMER, ANNA; Wm V Fisher Catholic HS; Lancaster, OH; Band; Hon Rl; NHS; Stu Cncl; FBLA; VP Keyettes; Bsktbl; Chrldng; PPFtbl; College; Communications.

SIEMER, JOE; La Salle HS; Cincinnati, OH; Cls Rep Soph Cls; Aud/Vis; Band; Chrs; Chrh Wkr; Hon Rl; Orch; Sch Mus; Stu Cncl; Sci Clb; Vocational Schl; Computer Tech.

SIEMER, RON; La Salle HS; Cincinnati, OH; 46/250 Band; Hon Rl; Off Ade; Sch Mus; IM Sprt; College.

SIEMERS, KIMBERLY; Central Catholic HS; Lafayette, IN; 30/96 Chrh Wkr; Y-Teens; Sprt Ed Sch Nwsp; Sch Nwsp; Pep Clb; Capt Bsktbl; Letter Trk; Pres Awd; Purdue Univ; Computer Tech.

SIEMINSKI, JULIE; Elmhurst HS; Ft Wayne, IN; 63/346 AFS; Chrs; Chrh Wkr; Hon Rl; Lit Mag; Quill & Scroll; Sch Pl; Yth Flsp; Rptr Yrbk; Drama Clb; Ind Univ; English.

SIEMS, JON; Holland HS; Holland, MI; Band; Hon Rl; Univ; Aviation.

SIEMS, T; Bridgeport HS; Bridgeprt, MI; Trs Jr Cls; Band; Chrs; Girl Scts; Hon Rl; Sch Mus; Sch Pl; Sct Actv; Stu Cncl; Rptr Sch Nwsp; Outstanding Eng; Ms J Brd Mbr; Hnrs Indiv Study Prog; Coll; Med.

SIENKIEWICZ, DONNA; St Florian HS; Detroit, MI; Cls Rep Sr Cls; Hon Rl; Off Ade; FNA; Cit Awd; Madonna Coll; Spec Educ.

SIENKIEWICZ, TERESA; Yale HS; Yale, MI; Hon Rl; Lbry Ade; 4-H; S C C C C; Educ.

SIENS, TINA; Clinton Massie HS; Wilmington, OH; 3/100 VP Frsh Cls; VP Soph Cls; Pres Jr Cls; Am Leg Aux Girls St; Band; Chrs; Drl Tm; Hon Rl; NHS; Off Ade; Schlstc Achvmnt Test 1oth In St In Geom 77; Schlstc Achvmnt Test 19th In St In 2nd Yr Alg 78; Ohio Univ; Speech Pathology.

SIERRA, TIMOTHY; Andrean HS; Valparaiso, IN; 32/251 Chrh Wkr; FCA; Hon Rl; Rptr Sch Nwsp; FBLA; IM Sprt; Univ.

SIERS, JEFFREY; Bluefield HS; Bluefield, WV; Boy Scts; Hon Rl; Sct Actv; Coll.

SIERS, REBECCA; Kimball HS; Royaloak, MI; 44/602 Girl Scts; Hon Rl; JA; Lion Awd; Center Of Creative Studies; Comm Art.

SIESS, KIM; Center Line HS; Warren, MI; 6/435 Chrs; Chrh Wkr; Hon Rl; Jr NHS; NHS; OEA; Sci Clb; College; CPA.

SIEU, LILY; Walnut Ridge Sr HS; Columbus, OH; 78/408 PAVAS; Quill & Scroll; Ed Yrbk; Fr Clb; PPFtbl; UCLA; Comm Art.

SIEVERS, RICHARD; Traverse City Sr HS; Traverse City, MI; 74/897 Cls Rep Frsh Cls; Letter Trk; Cit Awd; Michigan St Univ; Chem Engr.

SIEVERT, JEFF; Chesterton HS; Chesterton, IN; 5/400 Band; Cmnty Wkr; Hon Rl; NHS; Off Ade; Sct Actv; Yth Flsp; Mth Clb; Spn Clb; Letter Glf; Indiana Univ; Bio.

SIEVING, ROBERT P; Clear Fork HS; Fredericktown, OH; Hon Rl; NHS; 4-H; FFA; 4-H Awd; Ag Tech Inst.

SIEWERS, LEO; North Knox HS; Vincennes, IN; 10/150 Band; Hon Rl; NHS; 4-H; Vincennes Univ; Elec Engr.

SIEWERT, MELINDA; Cass Technical HS; Detroit, MI; Girl Scts; Hon Rl; Rptr Yrbk; Univ Of Michigan; Forestry.

SIEWERT, PAUL; Rochester HS; Rochester, MI; Chrh Wkr; Sch Pl; Yth Flsp; Rdo Clb; Crs Cntry; Trk; Michigan St Univ; Mech Engr.

SIEWERT, SARA; Lutheran HS North; Rochester, MI; 14/110 Chrs; Chrh Wkr; Hon Rl; Hosp Ade; Sch Pl; Yrbk; Rptr Sch Nwsp; Drama Clb; Sci Clb; Crs Cntry; Concordia Coll; Comp Sci.

SIGELMIER, JOHN; Hamilton Township Local HS; Columbus, OH; 4/189 Chrs; Chrh Wkr; Hon Rl; NHS; Sch Mus; Sch Pl; Drama Clb; Lat Clb; Natl Merit SF; Cleveland Inst Of Music; Organ Perfm.

SIGG, JANET; Napoleon HS; Napoleon, OH; Cls Rep Soph Cls; Cl Rep Jr Cls; Cls Rep Sr Cls; Band; Chrh Wkr; Hon Rl; NHS; Orch; Sch Mus; Yth Flsp; Univ; Nursing.

SIGLER, DIANNE; Woodhaven HS; Woodhaven, MI; Band; Girl Scts; Hon Rl; Treas Jr NHS; NHS; Letter Bsbl; PPFtbl; Michigan St Univ; Bus.

SIGLER, JANICE; Garrett HS; Auburn, IN; Band; Drl Tm; Hon Rl; Red Cr Ade; Sch Mus; Rptr Sch Nwsp; Sch Nwsp; Pres 4-H; Treas Ger Clb; 4-H Awd; Perfect Attendance 3 Yrs;.

SIGLER, LAUREL; Northwestern HS; Burbank, OH; Hon Rl; Lbry Ade; Off Ade; Sch Pl; Rptr Yrbk; Rptr Sch Nwsp; Drama Clb; 4-H; FHA; FTA; Ashland College.

SIGLEY, LORETTA; Mineral Ridge HS; Mineral Ridge, OH; Band; JA; Sch Pl; Stg Crw; Pep Clb; IM Sprt; PPFtbl; JA Awd; Kent State Univ; Psych.

SIGLOW, JAMES; Brookfield HS; Brookfield, OH; Pres Sr Cls; Chrh Wkr; Hon Rl; Jr NHS; NHS; Beta Clb; Letter Ftbl; IM Sprt; College; Med.

SIGLOW, KIMBERLY; Rogers HS; Toledo, OH; 43/450 Sec Frsh Cls; Pres Sr Cls; Hon Rl; JA; Jr NHS; Orch; Stu Cncl; Yrbk; Rptr Sch Nwsp; JA Awd; Univ Of Toledo Jrnlsm Awd 79; Lions Pride Teenboard 79; BGSU; Env Engr.

SIGLOWSKI, KIMBERLY S; Princeton HS; Evendale, OH; Chrs; Cmnty Wkr; Hon Rl; Natl Forn Lg; NHS; Sch Mus; Sch Pl; Rptr Yrbk; Drama Clb; Natl Merit SF; Purdue Univ; Chem Engr.

SIGMAN, BECKY; Benton Central HS; Montmorenci, IN; Chrs; Girl Scts; Off Ade; Sch Pl; Stg Crw; Drama Clb; OEA; GAA; IM Sprt; Pom Pon; 550.

SIGMAN, MARGIE; Stow HS; Munroe Fl, OH; Band; Hon Rl; Hosp Ade; Off Ade; Cert Of Mert For Basic Stds 79; Honors Awd 76; Akron Univ; Acctg.

SIGMAN, MICHELE; Poca HS; Poca, WV; Band; Chrh Wkr; Girl Scts; Hon Rl; NHS; Off Ade; Stu Cncl; Yth Flsp; Pep Clb; Chrldng; Univ; Court Reporter.

SIGNORE, MICHAEL A; St Philip Cath Cntrl HS; Battle Creek, MI; Hon Rl; Letter Bsbl; Letter Crs Cntry; Recipient Of Father Gerald Owens Awd Bsbl; Voc Schl; Electronics.

SIGRIST, MARY; Grove City HS; Grove City, OH; Cls Rep Frsh Cls; Cls Rep Soph Cls; Cl Rep Jr Cls; Pres Sr Cls; Cls Rep Sr Cls; Hon Rl; NHS; Stu Cncl; Ed Yrbk; PPFtbl; Ohio Univ; Jrnlsm.

SIGUIANI, JOE; Cardinal Mooney HS; Youngstown, OH; Aud/Vis; Boy Scts; Hon Rl; Lbry Ade; Boys Clb Am; Mth Clb; Kenyon Univ; Eng.

SIKKILA, KEVIN; L Anse HS; L Anse, MI; 3/97 Hst Soph Cls; Band; Hon Rl; NHS; Sch Pl; Stg Crw; Sch Nwsp; 4-H; Am Leg Awd; 4-H Awd; Hanna Mining Co Schlrshp; Michigan Tech Univ; Geology.

SIKORSKI, ELLEN; Garden City West Sr HS; Garden City, MI; Chrs; Hon Rl; NHS; Sch Mus; Drama Clb; Fr Clb; Pep Clb; IM Sprt; Mi Comp Schslp Progr 78; Michigan St Univ; Acctg.

SIKORSKI, JAYNE; Coldwater HS; Coldwater, MI; DECA; Ten; IM Sprt; St Of Mi Compttv Schlshp Progr 79; Western Michigan Univ; Psych.

SIKORSKI, KENT; Kimball HS; Troy, MI; Band; NHS; Orch; Mich Tech Univ; Chem Engr.

SILA, MICHAEL; Lake Michigan Catholic HS; Benton Hrbr, MI; Chrh Wkr; Hon Rl; Univ; Pathology.

SILBER, ROBERT; Norwood HS; Norwood, OH; Band; Hon Rl; JA; Jr NHS; Red Cr Ade; Stg Crw; Y-Teens; Mth Clb; Letter Swmmng; Coach Actv; Univ Of Cincinnati; Elec Engr.

SILBIGER, MARCI; Mayfield HS; Mayfield Hts, OH; 46/521 Band; Chrs; Drl Tm; Hon Rl; Y-Teens; Drama Clb; OEA; Principals List; 7th Pl In Ohio Regional Office Ed Assoc; Treas Of Voc/accounting Class; Ohio State Univ; Accounting.

SILCOX, LISA; Fairland HS; Proctorvll, OH; 11/153 Sec Jr Cls; Cl Rep Jr Cls; Cls Rep Sr Cls; Band; Chrh Wkr; Hon Rl; NHS; Stu Cncl; Mth Clb; Univ Of Ten; Nursing.

SILDERS, GUNTARS R; Kirtland HS; Kirtland, OH; Am Leg Boys St; Boy Scts; Chrs; Hon Rl; Jr NHS; IM Sprt; DAR Awd; Natl Merit SF; Georgia Inst Tech; Elec Engr.

SILECKY, MARKIAN; Lorain Catholic HS; Lorain, OH; Boy Scts; Chrs; Hon Rl; Yrbk; Sch Nwsp; Ger Clb; Spn Clb; Toledo Univ; Law.

SILER, BRIAN K; Crestview Sr HS; Ashland, OH; 35/105 Treas Boy Scts; Chrs; Hon Rl; Rptr Sch Nwsp; Treas 4-H; Fr Clb; Sec FFA; Letter Bsbl; Capt Crs Cntry; 4-H Awd; Ohio St Univ; Vet Med.

SILER, DENISE; Merrill Community School; Merrill, MI; Chrs; Hon Rl; FHA; Pep Clb; Bsktbl; Letter Trk; Mgrs; Delta Coll; Music.

SILER, KAREN; Merrill HS; Merrill, MI; Chrs; Chrh Wkr; Hon Rl; 4-H; 4-H Awd; Business Schl.

SILKWORTH, DOLORES; A D Johnston HS; Bessemer, MI; 1/81 Trs Sr Cls; Band; Chrs; Sch Pl; Ed Yrbk; Ed Sch Nwsp; Mich State Univ; Landscape.

SILL, BRIAN; Parkway HS; Rockford, OH; 23/91 Chrh Wkr; Hon Rl; Pres Yth Flsp; Huntington College; Bus Admin.

SILLIMAN, LINDA; South Central HS; Plymouth, OH; 3/65 VP Soph Cls; Cl Rep Jr Cls; Am Leg Aux Girls St; Band; Hon Rl; Sec MMM; Sec NHS; Off Ade; Univ Of Toledo; Comp Progr.

SILSKI, ROBERT; Crestwood HS; Dearborn Hts, MI; Hon Rl; Fr Clb; IM Sprt; College; Commrcl Art.

SILVA, ROLANDO; Okemos HS; Okemos, MI; 1/300 Chrs; Lit Mag; Pol Wkr; Univ; Pre Law.

SILVANI, MICHAEL; Southgate HS; Southgate, MI; 65/240 Cls Rep Frsh Cls; Boy Scts; Hon Rl; Pep Clb; Bsbl; Bsktbl; Ftbl; Hon Mntn All Lg 2nd Team All Area All Lg 78 79; Saginaw Vly St Coll; Criminal Justc.

SILVASHY, JAMES; Austintown Fitch HS; Youngstown, OH; 1/650 Chrh Wkr; JA; Pres NHS; Yth Flsp; Fr Clb; Spn Clb; Letter Ten; College; Engr.

SILVASI, MICHAEL; Bishop Noll Inst; Whiting, IN; 55/321 Hon Rl; Mth Clb; St Joseph Coll; Engr.

SILVER, JAYANA; Knightstown HS; Carthage, IN; Trs Soph Cls; Sec Jr Cls; Sec Sr Cls; Chrs; Hon Rl; NHS; Off Ade; Sch Mus; Stu Cncl; Yrbk; Voc Schl; Interior Decrt.

SILVER, MARGARET; Seeger Memorial HS; Williamsport, IN; 13/127 VP Soph Cls; Pres Jr Cls; Cls Rep Sr Cls; Sec Band; Chrs; Cmnty Wkr; Hon Rl; NHS; Off Ade; Sch Mus; Purdue Univ; Fashion Retailng.

SILVERS, NANCY; Eaton HS; Eaton, OH; Cmp Fr Grls; Chrs; Chrh Wkr; Girl Scts; Hon Rl; Yth Flsp; Pep Clb; Spn Clb; Letter Swmmng; GAA; AAU Ohio Age Group Champ; Dayton Dolphin Diving Team; Natl Jr Olympic Finalist Diving; College.

SILVERS, TERESA; Ursuline HS; Youngstown, OH; 41/289 Hon Rl; Fr Clb; Letter Ten; IM Sprt; Ohio St Univ; Med.

SILVERTHORN, CAROL; St Joseph HS; Saint Joseph, MI; 13/308 Band; FCA; Jr NHS; NHS; Stu Cncl; Lat Clb; Capt Bsktbl; IM Sprt; Central Mich Univ; Secondary Educ.

SILVERWOOD, NANCY; Heath Senior HS; Heath, OH; Drl Tm; Hon Rl; Sch Pl; Drama Clb; FHA; Columbus Business; Executive Secr.

SILVESTER, TONI; Portage Lakes Jnt Voc Schl; Akron, OH; Chrs; Hon Rl; Lbry Ade; Off Ade; Stu Cncl; 4-H; Fr Clb; OEA; Akron Univ; Exec Sec.

SILVESTKI, MARTIN; Maple Hts Sr HS; Maple Hgts, OH; Hon Rl; Pol Wkr; Bsktbl; Ten; Univ.

SILVESTRI, DAWN; Buckeye North HS; Rayland, OH; 20/106 Sec Frsh Cls; Hon Rl; NHS; Off Ade; Stu Cncl; Yrbk; Fr Clb; Bsktbl; Ftbl; Am Leg Awd; West Liberty St Coll; Med Tech.

SILVEY, RANDY; Fairmont West HS; Kettering, OH; Chrh Wkr; Hon Rl; Lbry Ade; Oral Roberts Univ; Theol.

SILVIEUS, LYNNE; Edgewood Sr HS; Kingsville, OH; 1/250 Sec NHS; Rptr Yrbk; Rptr Sch Nwsp; Treas Sci Clb; Spn Clb; Letter Bsbl; Letter Bsktbl; IM Sprt; Cit Awd; Univ.

SIM, ROWENA; Notre Dame Acad; Toledo, OH; Hon Rl; Mod UN; NHS; Spn Clb; Univ Of Michigan; Med.

SIMA, TERRIE; Solon HS; Solon, OH; 29/288 Sec Frsh Cls; Sec Soph Cls; Sec Jr Cls; Sec Sr Cls; Chrh Wkr; NHS; Letter Bsktbl; Ohi State Univ; Environmental Sci.

SIMAZ, JUDY; Lake Michigan Catholic HS; Eau Claire, MI; FCA; Sch Nwsp; 4-H; Crs Cntry; Trk; Chrldng; Mgrs; Mat Maids; Scr Kpr; Tmr; Grand Vly St Univ; Conservation.

SIMBOB, LORETTA; Kingsford HS; Quinnesec, MI; 8/170 Band; Chrs; Chrh Wkr; Hon Rl; Jr NHS; Mdrgl; NHS; Sch Mus; Natl Merit SF; Kingford Music Booster Schlrshp 74 78; Iron Mtn Womens Club Schlrhp 77; Alma Talent Award 79; Chopin Piano; Alma Coll; Music.

SIMCOX, CONNIE; Springfield Local HS; Newspringfield, OH; AFS; Band; Girl Scts; Hon Rl; Sch Mus; Sec Yth Flsp; 4-H; Pep Clb; Spn Clb; 4-H Awd; 1st Cls Girl Scout Awd 1977; Inter County Bank; Dana Schl Of Music; Music.

SIMENS, MARK; Lake Catholic HS; Solon, OH; VP Sr Cls; Hon Rl; Lit Mag; Sch Mus; Sch Pl; Stg Crw; Stu Cncl; Wrstlng; Chopin Piano Awd 78; Intl Thespian Soc 78; Carnegie Mellon Univ; Archt.

SIMERLINK, DEBBIE; Beavercreek HS; Dayton, OH; 38/702 Letter Drl Tm; Hon Rl; Pep Clb; IM Sprt; Scr Kpr; Finlst In Miss Oh Nalt Teegr Pgnt 79; Tchr Aide 79; Whos Who Among Amer HS Stdtn 77; Wright St Univ; Psych.

SIMIC, THOMAS; George Rogers Clark HS; Whiting, IN; 9/218 Am Leg Boys St; Chrs; Chrh Wkr; NHS; Sch Mus; Sch Pl; Stu Cncl; Spn Clb; Am Leg Awd; Univ; Pre Law.

SIMILE, DANIEL; St Thomas Aquinas HS; Canton, OH; 40/144 Hon Rl; Sch Mus; Sprt Ed Sch Nwsp; Spn Clb; Letter Ftbl; Letter Wrstlng; IM Sprt; Am Leg Awd;.

SIMKINS, AMY; West Jefferson HS; W Jefferson, OH; Am Leg Aux Girls St; Band; Chrs; Hon Rl; NHS; Spn Clb; Mat Maids; Natl Band Assn Outstaning Music Campers Awd 79; Band Vice Pres 79; Columbus Coll Of Art & Dsgn; Art.

SIMKINS, TANYA; Springfield Local HS; Petersburg, OH; Cls Rep Frsh Cls; Cls Rep Soph Cls; Cl Rep Jr Cls; AFS; Hon Rl; Lbry Ade; Sec Stu Cncl; Yth Flsp; FTA; Pep Clb; Volleyball Captain Lettered 1977; Univ; Tchr.

SIMKO, DAVID; Chanel HS; Bedford Hts, OH; 3/114 Pres Sr Cls; Aud/Vis; Pres NHS; Sch Mus; Letter Bsbl; Letter Ftbl; Pres Awd; Univ Of Dayton; Comp Sci.

SIMKO, WILLIAM; North Royalton HS; N Royalton, OH; Band; Orch; Sch Mus; Sch Pl; Stg Crw; Drama Clb.

SIMMERLY, ROBERT; Cardinal Mooney HS; Boardman, OH; 20/300 Hon Rl; Y-Teens; Fr Clb; Rdo Clb; IM Sprt; Youngstown St Univ; Comp Sci.

SIMMERMACHER, BRIAN; Crestline HS; Crestline, OH; 1/100 Cls Rep Sr Cls; Am Leg Boys St; Hon Rl; NHS; Stu Cncl; Capt Bsbl; Bsktbl; Capt Ftbl; Trk; 1st Pl In Fund For Animals Natl Essay Contest; Univ.

SIMMERMAKER, JENNIFER; Winamac Cmnty HS; Winamac, IN; Cls Rep Frsh Cls; Cls Rep Soph Cls; Band; Drl Tm; FCA; Hon Rl; Jr NHS; NHS; Off Ade; Sch Mus; Ball St Univ; Nursing.

SIMMERMON, DEBRA; Felicity Franklin HS; Felicity, OH; 10/86 Chrh Wkr; Drm Mjrt; Hon Rl; Hosp Ade; Sch Mus; Sch Pl; FHA; College; Med.

SIMMERS, JEFFREY L; Licking Valley HS; Nashport, OH; Am Leg Boys St; Boy Scts; Hon Rl; Sch Pl; Fr Clb; FFA; Sci Clb; Crs Cntry; Trk; Am Leg Awd; Extemporaneous & Prepared Public Speaking FFA; 10th In Dist 2 Div Hon Mentn In St For Amer History Test; College.

SIMMONS, A; Elkins HS; Elkins, WV; 4-H; FFA; VICA; Nashville Auto & Diesel College;dies.

SIMMONS, ANNETTE; Olentangy HS; Powell, OH; 12/150 Hon Rl; Lbry Ade; NHS; Fr Clb; PPFtbl; Business School; Busns.

SIMMONS, BONNIE; Elkins HS; Elkins, WV; Pep Clb; Bus Schl; Acctg.

SIMMONS, BOYD; Liberty HS; Clarksburg, WV; Hon Rl; Lbry Ade; DECA; 4-H; Fr Clb; Sci Clb; Spn Clb;.

SIMMONS, BRENDA; Ellet HS; Akron, OH; 11/365 Band; Chrh Wkr; Hon Rl; Jr NHS; NHS; Off Ade; Yth Flsp; Ger Clb; Pom Pon; Univ Of Akron; Nursing.

SIMMONS, CONNIE; Bedford N Lawrence HS; Bedford, IN; 130/400 Chrh Wkr; Girl Scts; Beta Clb; 4-H; Letter Bsktbl; Letter Trk; All Sectional 1979; Honrbl Mentn All Conf 1979; Honrary Schlrshp In Basktbl 1979; Franklin Coll; Phys Educ.

SIMMONS, DANIEL L; Shady Spring HS; White Oak, WV; Band; Boy Scts; CAP; Hon Rl; Lbry Ade; NHS; Sct Actv; 4-H; 4-H Awd; U S Air Force Acad; Aerospace Tech.

SIMMONS, DANITA; Clio Area HS; Clio, MI; Chrh Wkr; Jr NHS; NHS; OEA; Mott Comm Coll; Exec Sec.

SIMMONS, DAVID; Hauser Jr Sr HS; Columbus, IN; 5/103 Band; Hon Rl; Lbry Ade; NHS; Yth Flsp; 4-H; FFA; 4-H Awd; Perfect Attend 79; De Kalb Awd Winner FFA 79; Purdue Univ; Agri.

SIMMONS, DAVID D; Hurricane HS; Hurrican, WV; Boy Scts; Chrs; Chrh Wkr; Hon Rl; JA; Sct Actv; Yth Flsp; IM Sprt; Univ; Acctg.

SIMMONS, GRACE; Buffalo HS; Huntington, WV; 5/141 Band; Hon Rl; Lby Ade; NHS; Sch Pl; Rptr Yrbk; Yrbk; Drama Clb; Mth Clb; Marshall Univ.

SIMMONS, GREGORY; John Adams Sr HS; Cleveland, OH; Trs Jr Cls; Aud/Vis; Hon Rl; Jr NHS; Stu Cncl; Crs Cntry; Cit Awd; Univ; Elec Engr.

SIMMONS, HELYCIA; Notre Dame Academy; Toledo, OH; Chrh Wkr; Cmnty Wkr; Sch Mus; Sch Pl; Sct Actv; FDA; Lat Clb; Univ Of Toledo Frgn Lang Day For Lat Costume 2nd Pl 79; Fnd For Lfe Essay Cntst 78; Univ; Med.

SIMMONS, JEFFREY; Tiffin Calvert HS; Tiffin, OH; Hon Rl; Bsbl; Bsktbl; Ftbl; Glf; College.

SIMMONS, JEFFREY R; Rensselaer Central HS; Hereford, AZ; Pres Jr Cls; Band; Hon Rl; NHS; Orch; Pol Wkr; Sch Mus; Stu Cncl; Glf; Wabash College; Pre Law.

SIMMONS, JULIE; White Pine HS; White Pine, MI; Band; Cmp Fr Grls; Chrh Wkr; Cmnty Wkr; Girl Scts; Hon Rl; Off Ade; Y-Teens; Rptr Yrbk; Letter Bsktbl; Gogebic Cmnty Coll; LPN.

SIMMONS, KAREN; Findlay HS; Findlay, OH; Trs Soph Cls; Chrs; Chrh Wkr; Hon Rl; Lit Mag; Sch Mus; FTA; Trk; Scr Kpr; Tmr; Gods Bible Sch & Coll; Business Educ.

SIMMONS, KAY; Marshall HS; Albion, MI; Chrh Wkr; Hon Rl; VP JA; Off Ade; Yth Flsp; VP 4-H; Mi Comptn Schlrshp 78; Sr Sci Stu Of The Yr 78; Sftbl Schlrshp 79; Spring Arbor Coll; Bio.

SIMMONS, KELLY; East Noble HS; Kendallville, IN; 16/272 VP Frsh Cls; Hon Rl; Letter Bsktbl; E Noble Sci Open House 77; N E Tri St Regnl Sci Fair 77; Var Vllybl Letter; Indiana Univ; Bus.

SIMMONS, KEVIN; Pineville HS; Pineville, WV; 9/93 Jr NHS; NHS; Fr Clb; Sci Clb; W Virginia Univ; Forestry.

SIMMONS, LINDA; Bluefield HS; Blufeild, WV; 26/320 Cls Rep Frsh Cls; Band; Chrh Wkr; Hon Rl; NHS; Sch Pl; Stu Cncl; Yth Flsp; Y-Teens; Sci Clb; Bluefield St Univ; Spanish.

SIMMONS, LORI; Green HS; N Canton, OH; NHS; IM Sprt; Akron Univ; Cmmrcl Art.

SIMMONS, MARY KAY; Jennings County HS; No Vernon, IN; Band; Chrs; Chrh Wkr; Drm Mjrt; Sch Pl; Stg Crw; 4-H; College; Math.

SIMMONS, MARY T; Greenbrier East HS; Lewisburg, WV; Trs Frsh Cls; FCA; Hon Rl; Stu Cncl; Yrbk; Bsktbl; Trk; GAA; IM Sprt; Hagerstown Jr Coll; Marine Bio.

SIMMONS, MICHELLE; Wood Memorial HS; Oakland City, IN; Chrs; Hon Rl; Lbry Ade; Orch; FHA; Pep Clb; Trk; Mat Maids; Barbizon Schl; Modeling.

SIMMONS, RANDY; North Adams HS; Peebles, OH; 4-H; FFA; 4-H Awd; Ohio Vly Voc Schl; Farm Busns Mgmt.

SIMMONS, REBECCA L; North Ridgeville Sr HS; N Ridgeville, OH; Chrh Wkr; Hon Rl; Lbry Ade; Pres Ger Clb; Bsktbl; Girls Volleyball; College Escrow; Bowling Green Univ; Sec.

SIMMONS, ROBERT; Pocahontas County HS; Hillsboro, WV; 25/116 Boy Scts; Chrs; Drl Tm; Hon Rl; NHS; Sch Pl; FFA; Bsktbl; Ftbl; Trk; Cert Of Merit Math Field Day Awd Reg IV 78; West Virginia Tech Univ; Mech Engr.

SIMMONS, ROBIN; Greenview HS; So Solon, OH; Band; Chrh Wkr; Sch Mus; 4-H; FHA; 4-H Awd; Clark Tech Coll; Child Care Mgmt.

SIMMONS, ROBIN; Clawson HS; Clawson, MI; 3/300 Cls Rep Soph Cls; AFS; Hon Rl; Jr NHS; Stu Cncl; Spn Clb; Cit Awd; College; Special Educ.

SIMMONS, RUTH; Marlington HS; Paris, OH; Band; Chrs; Hon Rl; Yth Flsp; 4-H; Spn Clb; 4-H Awd; Warner Southern Univ; Psych.

SIMMONS, STEVEN; Chippewa HS; Doylestown, OH; Cls Rep Frsh Cls; Chrs; Chrh Wkr; Hon Rl; Sch Mus; Stg Crw; Letter Gym; IM Sprt; Univ Of Akron; Law.

SIMMONS, SUZAN; Cedar Springs HS; Cedar Springs, MI; 18/172 Pres Sr Cls; Band; Hon Rl; Ed Yrbk; Rptr Yrbk; Letter Ten; Pom Pon; PPFtbl; Natl Merit Ltr; Michigan St Univ; Nursing.

SIMMONS, TAMARA; Elkhart Central HS; Elkhart, IN; 15/401 Chrs; Hon Rl; Sch Mus; Sch Pl; Stg Crw; Stu Cncl; Yth Flsp; PPFtbl; Purdue Univ; Clinical Chem.

SIMMONS, TRESA L; Bronson HS; Bronson, MI; Cls Rep Frsh Cls; Cls Rep Soph Cls; Cl Rep Jr Cls; Band; Girl Scts; Hon Rl; Lbry Ade; Off Ade; Orch; Stu Cncl; 2nd Pl Dist Food Marktng Contst In DECA 1979; St Hon In Writtn Evnt Qualigyng To Go To Natls 1979; Delta Coll; Bus Mgmt.

SIMMONS, VENUS; Olentangy HS; Powell, OH; 2/145 Sal; Hon Rl; Treas NHS; Drama Clb; Fr Clb; Letter Bsbl; PPFtbl; Natl Merit Schl; Columbus Tech Inst; Elec Engr.

SIMMONS, W TOM; Greenbrier East; Alderson, WV; Chrh Wkr; FCA; Hon Rl; Yth Flsp; 4-H; Sci Clb; Letter Bsktbl; Letter Ftbl; Letter Trk; 4-H Awd; College; Engineering.

SIMMS, CATHERINE; Cardington Lincoln HS; Cardington, OH; Cl Rep Jr Cls; Hon Rl; Off Ade; Stu Cncl; Consumer Educ Bus Educ 79; OSUM; Soc Work.

SIMMS, CRAIG; Robert S Rogers HS; Toledo, OH; 33/412 Cls Rep Frsh Cls; Cls Rep Soph Cls; Cl Rep Jr Cls; Cls Rep Sr Cls; Band; Hon Rl; NHS; Orch; Sch Mus; Sci Clb; Miami Univ; Engr.

SIMMS, CRAIG; Sherman HS; Seth, WV; Band; Hon Rl; Jr NHS; Sch Pl; Stu Cncl; Yth Flsp; VICA; Cit Awd; W Vir Univ; Law.

SIMMS, LYNN; Arsenal Technical HS; Indianapolis, IN; Chrh Wkr; Cmnty Wkr; Drm Mjrt; Off Ade; Pep Clb; Sec Spn Clb; Pom Pon;.

SIMMS, TAMMY; E Liverpool HS; E Liverpool, OH; Band; Cmp Fr Grls; Chrs; Hon Rl; Sch Mus; FNA; Pep Clb; Trk; Mgrs; Pom Pon; Kent St Univ; Nursing.

SIMMS, VICKII; Oak Hill HS; Oak Hill, WV; Cls Rep Soph Cls; Pres Jr Cls; Pres Sr Cls; Hon Rl; NHS; Sch Pl; Stu Cncl; Drama Clb; Fr Clb; Pep Clb; Univ; Phys Ther.

SIMO, TERRY; Admiral King HS; Lorain, OH; Band; Chrs; Hon Rl; NHS; Sch Mus; Stg Crw; Yrbk; Ohio St Univ; Aero Engr.

SIMON, AMY; Taylor HS; Cleves, OH; Band; Cmnty Wkr; Drl Tm; Hon Rl; Sch Mus; Sch Pl; Drama Clb; Letter Ten; Letter Chrldng; CTC; Drama.

SIMON, BARBARA; Barberton HS; Barberton, OH; 82/442 Cls Rep Frsh Cls; Boy Scts; Chrs; Chrh Wkr; Girl Scts; Hon Rl; Jr NHS; Stu Cncl; Yth Flsp; Rptr Sch Nwsp; Stark Cnty Tech Voc Schl; Drafting.

SIMON, BARBARA; Versailles HS; Yorkshire, OH; Sec Jr Cls; Am Leg Aux Girls St; Band; Chrs; FCA; Girl Scts; NHS; Sch Mus; Drama Clb; 4-H; Hocking Tech Coll; Recreation.

SIMON, CAROLYN; Monroeville HS; Monroeville, OH; Pres Soph Cls; VP Band; Girl Scts; Hon Rl; VP NHS; Pres Spn Clb; Mgrs; Scr Kpr; Univ; Radiolgcl Tech.

SIMON, CHERYL; Pike Delta York Sr HS; Delta, OH; 2/121 Girl Scts; Stu Cncl; OEA; Letter Bsktbl; Toledo Univ; Acctg.

SIMON, DAVID; Chadsey HS; Detroit, MI; Chrh Wkr; Swmmng; Ten; Cit Awd; Wayne Univ; Psych.

SIMON, GLENN; Russia Local HS; Russia, OH; 3/35 Band; Chrh Wkr; Hon Rl; NHS; Pres Stu Cncl; Sci Clb; Spn Clb; Mgrs; Natl Merit Ltr; Univ Of Dayton; Elec Engr.

SIMON, GLENN; Russia Local School; Russia, OH; 3/34 Band; Hon Rl; NHS; Stg Crw; Pres Stu Cncl; Sci Clb; Spn Clb; Mgrs; Bausch & Lomb Awd; Natl Merit Ltr; Univ Of Dayton; Elec Engr.

SIMON, JAMES; Tell City HS; Tell City, IN; 21/216 Hon Rl; Pep Clb; Wrstlng; Coach Actv; IM Sprt; Indiana St Univ; Bus.

SIMON, KAREN; Ionia HS; Ionia, MI; 18/272 Cls Rep Soph Cls; Hon Rl; Jr NHS; NHS; Off Ade; Sch Mus; Stg Crw; Stu Cncl; Rptr Yrbk; Rptr Sch Nwsp; Davenport Coll Schlrshp 79; Davenport Coll Of Bus; Acctg.

SIMON, KENNETH; Thornapple Kellogg HS; Middleville, MI; 9/158 Trs Frsh Cls; Band; Jr NHS; Treas Stu Cncl; Letter Ftbl; Letter Wrstlng; Albion College; Math.

SIMON, LISA; Upper Arlington HS; Columbus, OH; AFS; Band; Chrs; Chrh Wkr; Cmnty Wkr; Girl Scts; Hon Rl; Quill & Scroll; Sch Pl; Sct Actv; Univ; Law.

SIMON, LOUIS; Lake HS; Millbury, OH; Hon Rl; NHS; Sch Nwsp; Univ Of California; Philosophy.

SIMON, MARJORIE A; Russia Local HS; Russia, OH; 1/44 Band; Chrs; Chrh Wkr; Girl Scts; Hon Rl; Lbry Ade; NHS; Stu Cncl; FTA; Pep Clb; Univ.

SIMON, MARK; Saint Patricks HS; Portland, MI; Cls Rep Sr Cls; Chrh Wkr; Cmnty Wkr; Hon Rl; NHS; Stu Cncl; Bsbl;.

SIMON, PATRICK C; Lucas HS; Perrysville, OH; 10/90 Boy Scts; Hon Rl; NHS; Sct Actv; Rptr Sch Nwsp; Sch Nwsp; Pep Clb; Letter Ftbl; Letter Trk; Mgrs; Mid Buckeye Cnfrnc All League 78; Merit Roll 75; Ohio St Univ; Bus Admin.

SIMON, RITA; Whitmer Sr HS; Toledo, OH; 12/910 Girl Scts; NHS; 4-H; Ger Clb; 4-H Awd; Univ; Indus Engr.

SIMON, ROBERT; Notre Dame HS; Bridgeport, WV; 15/64 Band; Coll.

SIMON, SHERI; Malvern HS; Malvern, OH; 4 AFS; Am Leg Aux Girls St; Band; Hon Rl; NHS; Red Cr Ade; Yrbk; Lake Erie College; Physicians.

SIMON, WILLIAM; Moutobella HS; Edmore, MI; 10/106 Band; Chrs; Chrh Wkr; Hon Rl; NHS; Yrbk; Spn Clb; Ferris State College; Bus Admin.

SIMONES, LISA; Catholic Central HS; Enon, OH; 9/150 Sec Jr Cls; Trs Sr Cls; Chrs; NHS; Stu Cncl; Letter Trk; Letter Chrldng; Eastern Kentucky Univ; Music.

SIMONIS, RUTH; Beaumont HS; E Cleve, OH; Chrh Wkr; Girl Scts; JA; Spn Clb; JA Awd; College.

SIMONS, CECILIA; Sacred Heart Academy; Mt Pleasant, MI; 12/52 Trs Sr Cls; Hon Rl; Natl Forn Lg; NHS; Rptr Yrbk; Ed Sch Nwsp; Lat Clb; Pep Clb; Bsktbl; DAR Awd; Central Michigan Univ; Journalism.

SIMONS, CHRISTINE; Shelby HS; Shelby, MI; 13/124 Pres Sr Cls; Cls Rep Sr Cls; Cls Rep Sr Cls; NHS; Sch Pl; Stu Cncl; Ten; Cit Awd; DAR Awd; Opt Clb Awd; Hope College; Law.

SIMONS, CHRISTOPHER; Almont HS; Romeo, MI; 6/100 Aud/Vis; Band; Chrh Wkr; Cmnty Wkr; Hon Rl; Lbry Ade; NHS; Mich St Univ; Hotel Restaurant Mgmt.

SIMONS MC HENRY, KATHLEEN; Nicholas Cnty HS; Summersville, WV; Chrh Wkr; Hon Rl; Hosp Ade; Sch Pl; Y-Teens; Sch Nwsp; 4-H; FBLA; Chrldng;.

SIMONYI, VICTOR; St Ignatius HS; Lyndhurst, OH; 43/312 Boy Scts; Chrh Wkr; Hosp Ade; Lit Mag; Sct Actv; Y-Teens; Lat Clb; Case Western Univ; Bio Med Engr.

SIMOTA, SUSAN; St Alphonsus HS; Detroit, MI; 35/177 Hon Rl; Sch Mus; Sch Pl; Henry Ford Comm Coll; Busns.

SIMPKINS, ANN; Benedictine HS; Detroit, MI; 80/153 Cl Rep Jr Cls; VP Sr Cls; Wayne State Univ; Journalism.

SIMPKINS, ANNETTE; Buffalo HS; Huntington, WV; 4/100 Band; Chrh Wkr; Hon Rl; Sec NHS; Off Ade; Red Cr Ade; Yth Flsp; Rptr Sch Nwsp; FBLA; Letter Trk; College; Busns.

SIMPKINS, RHONDA; Montcalm HS; Montcalm, WV; Sec Jr Cls; Band; Chrs; Chrh Wkr; Pep Clb; Bsbl; Bsktbl; Chrldng; Mgrs; Pom Pon; 2 #1 In Cls A Div Chrldrs 1978; 2nd Pl Miss MHS Beauty Pgnt 1979; Ship Of State From Sec Of St A J Manchin; Concord Coll; Phys Educ.

SIMPSON, BETH; Cass Technical HS; It, MI; 10/950 Band; Hon Rl; NHS; Off Ade; Fr Clb; OEA; Air Frc ROTC 4 Yr Schlshp 1979; Univ Of Mi Regents Almn Schlshp 1979; Mmbr Detroit Phi Assic Phi Beta Kapp; Univ Of Michigan; Bus Admin.

SIMPSON, BRETT; Penn HS; Mishawaka, IN; Hon Rl; College; Ecologist.

SIMPSON, CARYL; Eastern HS; Russellville, OH; Hon Rl; FFA; FHA; Pep Clb.

SIMPSON, DAVID; St Xavier HS; Cincinnati, OH; 92/280 Cl Rep Jr Cls; Hon Rl; Spn Clb; Bsbl; Bsktbl; Ftbl; IM Sprt; College; Aeronatuical Engineering.

SIMPSON, DENNIS; Kirtland HS; Kirtland, OH; 11/150 Am Leg Boys St; Hon Rl; NHS; Sch Pl; Spn Clb; Bsbl; Bsktbl; Ftbl; Trk; College; Dentistry.

SIMPSON, DON; Forest Park HS; Forest Park, OH; Boy Scts; Cmnty Wkr; JA; Sct Actv; Letter Socr; JA Awd; Pres Awd; Univ; Law Enforcement.

SIMPSON, DREMA; Clay Battelle HS; Wana, WV; Chrs; Chrh Wkr; Hon Rl; Jr NHS; Lbry Ade; NHS; Off Ade; Sch Pl; Stu Cncl; FHA; Fairmont St Coll; Bus.

SIMPSON, GREGORY R; Greenville HS; Greenville, OH; 4/388 Band; Hon Rl; NHS; Orch; Sch Mus; Yth Flsp; Treas Drama Clb; Key Clb; Lat Clb; Sec Sci Clb; Purdue Univ; Engr.

SIMPSON, HENRY B; Greenbrier East HS; White Sul Spgs, WV; 2/414 Am Leg Boys St; Chrh Wkr; FCA; Hon Rl; Jr NHS; NHS; Yth Flsp; Sci Clb; Ftbl; Military Youth Ldrshp Camp Natl Guard 79; VMI; Military.

SIMPSON, JOYCE; Crawfordsville HS; Crawfordsville, IN; 11/196 Band; Hon Rl; NHS; Lat Clb; OEA; Awrd For Cum Laude In Latine 76; Awrd For Otstnfng Achvmnt In OEA 78; Otstndng Undrlclssmn Bus Awrd 78; Bus Schl.

SIMPSON, KATHLEEN; Hammond HS; Hammond, IN; 48/333 Band; Drm Mjrt; Jr NHS; Orch; Stu Cncl; Rptr Yrbk; Swmmng; PPFtbl; Ball State.

SIMPSON, KATHRYN; Harper Creek Sr HS; Battle Creek, MI; Hon Rl; NHS; Schlstc Achvmnt 79; Univ; Nurse.

SIMPSON, MICHELLE; Caledonia HS; Caledonia, MI; 15/175 Chrh Wkr; Girl Scts; Drama Clb; Bsktbl; Glf; Chrldng; PPFtbl; Cit Awd; Ferris St Univ; Bus Acctg.

SIMPSON, PHILIP E; North Putnam Jr Sr HS; Bainbridge, IN; Spn Clb; Coll; Comp Engr.

SIMPSON, ROGER A; Whetstone Sr HS; Columbus, OH; Chrs; Chrh Wkr; Hon Rl; DECA; Natl Merit Ltr; Commended Stu; Sci English Math Awds; College.

SIMPSON, SARA; Milton HS; Glenwood, WV; Girl Scts; Hon Rl; Pep Clb; Clerk In Hosp.

SIMPSON, STEPHANY; Brookville HS; Brookville, OH; 24/164 Cls Rep Frsh Cls; Cmp Fr Grls; Chrs; Hon Rl; Stu Cncl; Rptr Yrbk; Capt Bsktbl; Capt Trk; Coach Actv; Tmr; Voc Schl; Elec Engr.

SIMPSON, SUSAN; Cheboygan Area Public HS; Cheboygan, MI; Band; Chrh Wkr; Cmnty Wkr; Girl Scts; Hon Rl; Sch Pl; 4-H; Fr Clb; Gym; 4-H Awd; Partial Schlrshp To Blue Lk Fine Arts Camp 77; Toured Europe With Blue Lk Intl Band 78; Michigan St Univ; Animal Health.

SIMPSON, TAMMY J; Montcalm HS; Duhring, WV; 2/35 VP Frsh Cls; VP Soph Cls; Cls Rep Soph Cls; Cl Rep Jr Cls; Chrs; Hon Rl; Pep Clb; Bsktbl; Chrldng; Scr Kpr; Bluefield St Coll; Sec.

SIMPSON, TERI R; Niles Senior HS; Niles, MI; Aud/Vis; Sec Chrh Wkr; Debate Tm; Hon Rl; Sch Mus; Sch Pl; Stg Crw; Yth Flsp; Drama Clb; Treas FFA; Mich Univ; Medicine.

SIMPSON, TERI R; Niles Sr HS; Niles, MI; Aud/Vis; Chrh Wkr; Debate Tm; Hon Rl; Sch Mus; Sch Pl; Yth Flsp; Drama Clb; Treas FFA; Lat Clb; Michigan St Univ; Med.

SIMPSON, TRACEY; Plymouth HS; Plymouth, IN; 6/225 Chrs; Chrh Wkr; Debate Tm; Hon Rl; Lit Mag; Mdrgl; MMM; NHS; Pol Wkr; Sch Mus; Indiana Univ; Journalism.

SIMPSON, TRICIA; Rochester Community HS; Rochester, IN; 16/166 Chrs; Chrh Wkr; Girl Scts; Hon Rl; Hosp Ade; NHS; Sdlty; Ger Clb; Pep Clb; Scr Kpr; College; Nursing.

SIMPSON, WILLIAM E; University HS; Morgantown, WV; 1/146 Band; Chrs; Hon Rl; Jr NHS; NHS; Sch Mus; Sci Clb; Trk; IM Sprt; West Virginia Univ; Math.

SIMS, CLAUDIA; Howland HS; Warren, OH; 1/418 Chrh Wkr; Hon Rl; Quill & Scroll; Yth Flsp; Y-Teens; Yrbk; 4-H; Pep Clb; College; Vet.

SIMS, DARCUS; University HS; Granville, WV; Hon Rl; Quill & Scroll; Yrbk; FBLA; West Virginia Univ; Tchr Blind.

SIMS, JOHN; Dublin HS; Dublin, OH; Hon Rl; Rptr Sch Nwsp; 4-H; Lat Clb; Spn Clb; Bsbl; Letter Ftbl; Letter Wrstlng; IM Sprt; OWE Mst Imprvd Stu 78; OWE Stu Of The Yr 79; Ohio St Univ.

SIMS, JOHN; Harper Creek HS; Battle Creek, MI; 20/225 Cls Rep Frsh Cls; Cls Rep Soph Cls; Cl Rep Jr Cls; Am Leg Boys St; Band; Boy Scts; Debate Tm; Hon Rl; NHS; Pol Wkr; College; Chemical Engr.

SIMS, LESLIE; Shaker Heights HS; Shaker Hts, OH; Sec Frsh Cls; Hon Rl; Stu Cncl; Yrbk; College.

SIMS, LISA; Berea HS; Brook Park, OH; Chrs; Hon Rl; Lbry Ade; NHS; Off Ade; Coll; Sci.

SIMS, RETHA; Eastmoor Sr HS; Columbus, OH; Trs Jr Cls; Chrs; OEA; Letter Chrldng; Ohio State Univ; Acctg.

SIMS, SANDRA; Calhoun Cnty HS; Big Bend, WV; Cls Rep Soph Cls; Cl Rep Jr Cls; Chrs; Hon Rl; Hosp Ade; NHS; Stu Cncl; Yrbk; 4-H; Mth Clb; Bsktbl Sweetheart Queen; Hnrble Men Stu Cncl; 1st Plc In Sci Fair Identification Of Biros & Treas; Parkersburg Comm Coll; Nursing.

SIMS, SUSAN; Douglas Mac Arthur HS; Saginaw, MI; Trs Sr Cls; Chrs; Chrh Wkr; Cmnty Wkr; Girl Scts; Hon Rl; NHS; Off Ade; Stg Crw; Stu Cncl; 2 Jr Vrsty Tennis Lttr 77; 5 Awd In 8 Yrs Of Piano 72; Appoint A Prncl Comm For The Betterment Of Tchr Asst; Univ; Bio.

SIMS, TONYA; Smithville HS; Smithvill, OH; Chrs; Girl Scts; FHA; GAA; Voc Schl.

SIMS, TRACEY; Western Hills HS; Cincinnati, OH; Chrs; Chrh Wkr; Cmnty Wkr; FCA; Girl Scts; Hon Rl; Hosp Ade; Sch Pl; Drama Clb; Spn Clb; Youngstown St Univ; Nursing.

SIMS, VICKI; Calhoun County HS; Big Bend, WV; Pres Jr Cls; Chrh Wkr; Hon Rl; Hosp Ade; Mod UN; NHS; Off Ade; Yrbk; Sch Nwsp; 4-H; Parkersburg Comm Coll; Med Tech.

SIMS, YOLANDA A; Eaton HS; Eaton, OH; 42/177 Hon Rl; Spn Clb; GAA; PPFtbl; Sinclair Cmnty Coll; Phys Ther.

SINACOLA, MICHAEL; St Charlos Prep; Whitehall, OH; Hon Rl; NHS; Letter Bsbl; Socr; Letter Wrstlng; IM Sprt; Univ; Bus.

SINACOLA, MICHAEL; St Charles Prep; Columbus, OH; Hon Rl; NHS; Letter Bsbl; Letter Wrstlng; IM Sprt; Coll; Busns.

SINACORI, VITA; Dominican HS; Detroit, MI; Pres Frsh Cls; Chrh Wkr; Cmnty Wkr; Girl Scts; Mdrgl; NHS; Sch Pl; Yrbk; Drama Clb; Natl Merit SF; Siena Heights; Artist.

SINARD, JOHN; Detroit Cntry Day HS; Farmington, MI; 1/81 Trs Frsh Cls; Val; Hon Rl; NHS; Ed Yrbk; Sci Clb; Bsktbl; Mgrs; Scr Kpr; Am Leg Awd; Harvard Univ; Bio Chem.

SINAY, STEVEN J; Cardinal Stritch HS; Oregon, OH; Am Leg Boys St; Hon Rl; NHS; IM Sprt; JETS Awd; Univ Of Toledo; Engr.

SINCLAIR, DEBORAH; Scecina Memorial HS; Indianapolis, IN; Chrs; Girl Scts; IM Sprt; IUPUI; Sec.

SINCLAIR, JOHN; Cardinal Mooney HS; Youngstown, OH; 22/302 NHS; Eng Clb; Lat Clb; Crs Cntry; Capt Ten; IM Sprt; Tmr; Youngstown State; Engineering.

SINCLAIR, KATHLEEN; Trenton HS; Trenton, MI; Cl Rep Jr Cls; Chrh Wkr; Stu Cncl; Yrbk; Mgrs; Tmr; College; Recreation Admin.

SINCLAIR, LORI; Steubenville Cath Cntrl HS; Wintersville, OH; Sec Sr Cls; Chrh Wkr; Hon Rl; Hosp Ade; Stu Cncl; 4-H; FHA; FTA; Pep Clb; 4-H Awd; Coll.

SINDELAR, CYNTHIA; Greenville Sr HS; Greenville, OH; 28/360 Cmnty Wkr; Girl Scts; Hon Rl; FHA; Capt Bsktbl; Captn Vllybl Tm 1st Tm All League 3 Letters 78; Captn Sftbl Tm 2 Letters 79; Bsktbl 1st Tm All League 79; Bluffton Univ.

SINDELAR, JODEE A; Huntley Project HS; Ballantine, MT; 12/47 Sec Soph Cls; Am Leg Aux Girls St; Band; Chrs; Chrh Wkr; Debate Tm; Girl Scts; Hon Rl; Sch Mus; Sch Pl; Eastern Montana Coll; Communications.

SINDEN, LORI; Pleasant HS; Marion, OH; 13/180 Hon Rl; Quill & Scroll; Sch Nwsp; IM Sprt; OSU; Den.

SINELLI, RICK; Harrison HS; Farmington, MI; Cls Rep Frsh Cls; Cls Rep Soph Cls; Trs Jr Cls; Chrh Wkr; Cmnty Wkr; FCA; Hon Rl; NHS; Pol Wkr; FBLA; Western Michigan Univ; Busns Mgmt.

SINES, HARLA; East Preston Sr HS; Terra Alta, WV; Chrs; Hon Rl; Lbry Ade; Off Ade; Yth Flsp; Ger Clb; Pep Clb; Univ.

SINFIELD, TIMOTHY B; Cadiz HS; Hopedale, OH; Chrh Wkr; Hon Rl; NHS; Sch Pl; Pres Yth Flsp; Spn Clb; Grove City College; Bio.

SINGER, BILL; Peebles HS; Peebles, OH; Cls Rep Soph Cls; Cl Rep Jr Cls; Band; Boy Scts; Chrh Wkr; Cmnty Wkr; Hon Rl; Sch Pl; Drama Clb; Fr Clb; Univ; Engr.

SINGER, JOHN; Alpena HS; Alpena, MI; NHS; Alpena Comm Coll; Med.

SINGER, MARTHA; Henry Ford II HS; Stelring Hts, MI; 31/438 Girl Scts; Hon Rl; NHS; Orch; Letter Bsbl; Letter Bsktbl; Univ; Med.

SINGER, MAUREEN; Regina HS; Shaker Hts, OH; Sch Pl; Stg Crw; Stu Cncl; Rptr Sch Nwsp; Sec Drama Clb; Coll; Acctg.

SINGER, SCOTT; Beachwood HS; Beachwood, OH; Pres Frsh Cls; Cls Rep Soph Cls; Cl Rep Jr Cls; Debate Tm; Natl Forn Lg; Pol Wkr; Stu Cncl; Yrbk; Bsbl; Bsktbl; College.

SINGH, PRADEEP K; Bloomington HS North; Bloomington, IN; Stg Crw; Boys Clb Am; Fr Clb; Swmmng; Univ; Physics.

SINGH, SUKWINDAR; Morgantown HS; Morgantwn, WV; Hon Rl; Jr NHS; VP 4-H; Sec Fr Clb; 4-H Awd; Harvard; Med.

SINGLER, WADE; Deckerville HS; Deckerville, MI; 7/90 Band; Debate Tm; Hon Rl; FFA; Letter Bsbl; Bsktbl; Alma Coll.

SINGLETON, CHARLES; Collinwood HS; Cleveland, OH; Chrs; Chrh Wkr; Hon Rl; Yth Flsp; Cit Awd; Anthropos Motivation Awrd 79; Oral Roberts Univ; Psych.

SINGLETON, JEFF D; Charleston HS; Charleston, WV; 1/300 Cls Rep Frsh Cls; Cls Rep Sr Cls; Am Leg Boys St; Band; Boy Scts; Chrs; Drm Mjrt; Hon Rl; JA; Jr NHS; Univ; Engr.

SINGLETON, KATHY; Washington HS; Washington, IN; 2/216 Cls Rep Soph Cls; Band; Girl Scts; Hon Rl; Red Cr Ade; Sct Actv; Stu Cncl; Beta Clb; Pep Clb; Am Leg Awd; Busns Schl.

SINGLETON, KENTON; Copley HS; Akron, OH; Band; Chrs; Hon Rl; NHS; Spn Clb; Bsktbl; Coll; Elec Engr.

SINGLETON, KRISTY; Oakland Christian School; Clarkston, MI; VP Sr Cls; Chrh Wkr; Hon Rl; Off Ade; Yth Flsp; Rptr Yrbk; Sprt Ed Sch Nwsp; Letter Bsktbl; Letter Trk; IM Sprt; Grand Rapids Univ.

SINGLETON, LEON M; Cass Technical HS; Detroit, MI; Cmnty Wkr; Hon Rl; Letter Ftbl; JETS Awd; Northrop Coll; Aero Engr.

SINICKI, JOHN; Lumen Christi HS; Jackson, MI; Hon Rl; Yth Flsp; Letter Ftbl; Letter Trk; IM Sprt; Coll; Comp Sci.

SINISHTAJ, LUKE; Warren HS; Sterling Hts, MI; Band; Hon Rl; Sch Mus; DECA; Perfect Attndnc & Hon Roll 76; Hon Roll 77 78 & 79; Oakland Univ; Doctor.

SINKO, BRIDGET; Regine HS; Euclid, OH; Chrs; Girl Scts; Hosp Ade; Sch Pl; Sct Actv; Mission Hrn Awd Mission Club 76 79; Dyke Coll; Bus.

SINLEY, CHRISTINE; Manchester HS; Clinton, OH; Trs Sr Cls; Stu Cncl; Ed Sch Nwsp; Pep Clb; Letter Bsbl; Letter Bsktbl; Akron Univ; Finance.

SINN, SUSIE; Wayne Trace HS; Haviland, OH; Pres Jr Cls; Pres Sr Cls; Chrs; Hon Rl; Lbry Ade; NHS; Off Ade; Stu Cncl; Rptr Sch Nwsp; OEA;.

SINNEMA, KIMBERLY A; Black River HS; West Salem, OH; 4/79 Chrs; Hon Rl; NHS; Ed Yrbk; Yrbk; Ed Sch Nwsp; Rptr Sch Nwsp; FTA; Sci Clb; Spn Clb; Northwestern Univ; Communctns.

SINOPOLI, LISA; Revere HS; Akron, OH; Cl Rep Jr Cls; Chrs; Chrh Wkr; Girl Scts; Hon Rl; Pep Clb; Chrldng; Univ Of Akron; Graphic Design.

SINSABAUGH, VIRGINIA; Watervliet HS; Watervliet, MI; Sec Frsh Cls; Band; Chrs; Hon Rl; Sch Mus; Rptr Yrbk; Sprt Ed Sch Nwsp; Bsktbl; PPFtbl; Central Mi Univ; Journalist.

SINSEL, BETSY; Washington Irving HS; Clarksburg, WV; Pres Frsh Cls; Cls Rep Sr Cls; Band; Drm Bgl; Hon Rl; NHS; Sch Mus; Sch Pl; Stg Crw; Stu Cncl;.

SINTIC, WILLIAM; Geneva Secondary HS; Rock Creek, OH; 45/250 PAVAS; Bsktbl; IM Sprt; Cleveland St Univ; Art.

SIPE, DOTTIE; Buckhannon Upshur HS; Tallmansville, WV; Hon Rl;.

SIPE, JOY; Centerville HS; Dayton, OH; 46/684 Band; Chrh Wkr; Hon Rl; NHS; DECA; Miami Univ; Pre Bus.

SIPE, KIM; Parkway HS; Willshire, OH; 20/83 Band; Hon Rl; Sch Pl; Stu Cncl; Sci Clb; Spn Clb; Mgrs; Scr Kpr; Voc Schl.

SIPES, RHONDA; Orrville HS; Orrville, OH; 44/166 FCA; JA; FTA; Pres JA Awd; Wayne Genrl Univ; Soc Work.

SIPOCZ, ANDREW; La Salle HS; S Bend, IN; Boy Scts; Hon Rl; JA; Sch Nwsp; JA Awd; Univ; Forestry.

SIPOS, CAROL; Aquinas HS; Southgate, MI; Hon Rl; Hosp Ade; Rptr Sch Nwsp; Sch Nwsp; Pep Clb; Ten; IM Sprt; Univ; Bus.

SIPPLE, CONSTANCE; Beaumont School For Girls; Cleve Hts, OH; Chrh Wkr; Hon Rl; Lit Mag; PAVAS; Rptr Sch Nwsp; Sch Nwsp; Socr; IM Sprt; Scr Kpr; Tmr; Outstndg Serv To Beaumont Awd 78; Beaumont Art Show & Sale 3rd Pl 78; Beaumont Art Show & Sale Hnr Mntn 78; Univ.

SIR, SUSAN; Parma Sr HS; Parma, OH; 17/780 Band; Drl Tm; Hon Rl; Lbry Ade; NHS; Stu Cncl; Rptr Yrbk; Rptr Sch Nwsp; Ger Clb; NCTE; Univ; Comp Sci.

SIRAGUSANO, JOE; Wintersville HS; Wintrvll, OH; Band; Hon Rl; Orch; Sch Pl; Rptr Yrbk; Yrbk; Drama Clb; FDA; Lat Clb; Pep Clb; Univ; Bus Ed.

SIRAGUSANO, TRACEY; Jefferson Union HS; Richmond, OH; Cls Rep Frsh Cls; Cls Rep Soph Cls; Chrs; Hon Rl; Stu Cncl; Y-Teens; Beta Clb; 4-H; FBLA; OEA; Intl Mining & Mfg Festival Qn; World Youth Festival Dancing Awd; Tony Grant Talent Unlimited Contest Awds; College; Performing Arts.

SIRBAUGH, SUSAN; Hampshire HS; Capon Bridge, WV; AFS; Hon Rl; Jr NHS; NHS; 4-H; Chrldng; GAA; Scr Kpr; 4-H Awd; Rotary Awd; Univ.

SIRHAN, JUDY; Western HS; Detroit, MI; 1/37 Chrh Wkr; Cmnty Wkr; Hon Rl; JA; NHS; Off Ade; Sch Pl; Yth Flsp; Cit Awd; JA Awd; Univ Of Michigan; Psych.

SIRLS, LARRY; George G Schafer HS; Allen Park, MI; NHS; Rptr Sch Nwsp; Capt Wrstlng; Univ Of Detroit; Med.

SISCO, LAURIE; Lexington Sr HS; Mansfield, OH; 16/266 VP Sr Cls; Am Leg Aux Girls St; Chrh Wkr; Girl Scts; Hon Rl; NHS; Sct Actv; Stu Cncl; Yrbk; Fr Clb; Univ; Spec Educ.

SISCO, SHARON; Fairmont West HS; Kettering, OH; Hon Rl; Pol Wkr; Yrbk; Pep Clb; Letter Hockey; Scr Kpr; Tmr; Univ; Med.

SISINGER, DENISE; Delphos St Johns HS; Delphos, OH; Girl Scts; Hon Rl; JA; Stg Crw; Ed Yrbk; Sprt Ed Yrbk; Rptr Yrbk; 4-H; FTA; Crs Cntry;.

SISK, MARTHA; Strongsville HS; Strongsville, OH; 19/481 Cls Rep Soph Cls; Cl Rep Jr Cls; Cls Rep Sr Cls; Chrs; Hon Rl; Lit Mag; Pres NHS; Quill & Scroll; Sch Mus; Stu Cncl; Ashland Coll; Cmnctns.

SISKA, KIM; James Ford Rhodes HS; Cleveland, OH; Chrs; JA; Univ; Archeology.

SISLER, BONNIE; West Preston HS; Masontown, WV; Pres Frsh Cls; Band; Drm Mjrt; Hon Rl; NHS; Stu Cncl; FBLA; FHA; Twrlr; Bank Work; Banking Accounting.

SISLER, DAWN; Waterloo HS; Atwater, OH; 6/126 Band; Chrh Wkr; Hon Rl; NHS; Stu Cncl; Beta Clb; 4-H; College; Acctg.

SISON, EDITHA; Terre Haute South Vigo HS; Terre Haute, IN; Chrh Wkr; Hon Rl; Off Ade; Y-Teens; Bsktbl; Indiana St Univ; Soc Wrk.

SISSON, DAWN; Ashtabula Harbor HS; Ashtabula, OH; Trs Sr Cls; AFS; Hosp Ade; Off Ade; Sch Mus; Stu Cncl; Drama Clb; Letter Chrldng; GAA; Kent State; Nursing.

SISSON, JANET; Brown County HS; Nashville, IN; 22/149 Cls Rep Frsh Cls; Trs Soph Cls; Cls Rep Soph Cls; Band; Chrh Wkr; Hon Rl; NHS; Orch; Pol Wkr; Quill & Scroll; Vincennes Univ; Journalism.

SISSON, LAURALEE; Brown County HS; Morgantown, IN; Chrh Wkr; Cmnty Wkr; Hon Rl; Treas DECA; Eng Clb; Chmn FHA; Spn Clb; DECA Achvmnt Awd 78; Univ; Fshn.

SISSON, MANDY; Meigs HS; Pomeroy, OH; Cls Rep Frsh Cls; Band; Chrs; Chrh Wkr; Drm Bgl; Hon Rl; Sch Pl; Stg Crw; Stu Cncl; Spn Clb; Tennessee Tech; Music Ther.

SISSON, SANDY; Elgin HS; La Rue, OH; 9/155 Chrs; Girl Scts; Hon Rl; Sch Pl; Sct Actv; Lat Clb; Wnr Of Dist Spelling Bee 75 & 76; Magna Cum Laude Natl Latin Test 79; Univ.

SITCH, MARK; Mount Vernon Academy; Youngstown, OH; Chrh Wkr; Debate Tm; Hon Rl; Sch Pl; Sct Actv; Boys Clb Am; Rdo Clb; Letter Bsbl; Letter Ftbl; Partcptn Keyboard Music Awd 77; Worker Of The Month Awd 77 & 78; Sr Class Pastor 78; Columbia Union Coll; Elec Tech.

SITEK, GERALD; Southgate Aquinas HS; Southgate, MI; Hon Rl; Trk; Univ.

SITES, COLLEEN; Parkway HS; Rockford, OH; 8/96 Band; Hon Rl; NHS; 4-H; Pep Clb; Bsktbl; Trk; Chrldng; PPFtbl; Univ; Phys Ther.

SITES, SHIRLEY; Parkway HS; Celina, OH; 3/82 Band; Pres NHS; Sch Pl; Yrbk; Pres FTA; Pep Clb; PPFtbl; Scr Kpr; Ohio Univ; Industrl Acctg.

SITLER, MARTIN; Leetonia HS; Salem, OH; 3/86 Sec Frsh Cls; Cl Rep Jr Cls; Cls Rep Sr Cls; Am Leg Boys St; Chrh Wkr; Hon Rl; NHS; Yth Flsp; Yrbk; Spn Clb; Marietta Coll; Petroleum Engr.

SITTASON, TRACI; Norwood HS; Norwood, OH; Am Leg Aux Girls St; Chrh Wkr; Hon Rl; Jr NHS; NHS; Pol Wkr; Sch Mus; College; Foreign Language.

SITZ, KAREN; R S Tower HS; Warren, MI; Cls Rep Sr Cls; Hon Rl; Off Ade; Rptr Sch Nwsp; OEA; South Macomb Cmnty Coll; Exec Sec.

SIVLEY, CHERYL; New Palestine HS; Greenfield, IN; 3/175 Band; Hon Rl; NHS; Yrbk; Pres 4-H; Fr Clb; Pep Clb; Univ; Bus.

SIVO, JOHN; Field HS; Kent, OH; 10/240 Hon Rl; NHS; Sch Mus; Sch Pl; Stg Crw; Yrbk; Drama Clb; Treas 4-H; VP Spn Clb; Kent St Univ; Comp Sci.

SIWOJEK, LAWRENCE; St Francis De Sales HS; Toledo, OH; 12/176 Hon Rl; Jr NHS; NHS; Stg Crw; Trk; IM Sprt; Natl Merit Ltr; College; Chem Engr.

SIX, DAVID L; Oak Glenn HS; Lisbon, OH; Hon Rl; NHS; 4-H; Letter Ftbl; Letter Trk; 4-H Awd;.

SIX, KELLY; Lima Sr HS; Lima, OH; Boy Scts; Stu Cncl; DECA; Letter Ftbl; Letter Ten; Letter Wrstlng; 1st Pl District & St Distributive Education Contest; Busns Schl; Busns Mgmt.

SIX, RICHARD; Brookhaven HS; Columbus, OH; Hon Rl; Ohio St Univ; Radio.

SIZELOVE, JEFF; Alexandria Monroe HS; Alexandria, IN; 30/185 Cls Rep Frsh Cls; Cls Rep Soph Cls; Cl Rep Jr Cls; Pres Sr Cls; Cls Rep Sr Cls; Am Leg Boys St; Hon Rl; Jr NHS; NHS; Stu Cncl; Ftbl Tm Cptn MVP 1st Tm All Conf 78; Bsktbl Mst Imprvd 78; Wrld Champ Pole Bending Mt Vernon Horses 76; Findlay Coll; Pre Vet.

SIZEMORE, ANNA; Northfork HS; Northfork, WV; 3/125 Band; Chrh Wkr; Cmnty Wkr; Hon Rl; Jr NHS; Red Cr Ade; Pres Fr Clb; Treas Keyettes; IM Sprt; All Cnty Sr HS Bnd 77 79; Bluefield St Coll; Educ.

SIZEMORE, CATHY; Bloom Local HS; So Webster, OH; Chrs; Sec Chrh Wkr; Hon Rl; Hosp Ade; Lbry Ade; Off Ade; Yth Flsp; FHA; OEA; Univ; Med Sec.

SIZEMORE, MELISSA A; Garfield Sr HS; Hamilton, OH; 12/356 Chrs; Chrh Wkr; Hon Rl; NHS; Spn Clb; Letter Bsktbl; Letter Socr; Coach Actv; Eastern Kentucky Univ; Med Tech.

SIZEMORE, SCOTT; Northfork HS; Northfork, WV; 15/135 Band; Chrh Wkr; Cmnty Wkr; Hon Rl; NHS; Pol Wkr; Sch Pl; Yth Flsp; Rptr Yrbk; Drama Clb; Ath; USAF Academy; Pilot.

SIZICK, JULIE; Bridgeport Spaudling HS; Saginaw, MI; Girl Scts; Hon Rl; JA; Letter Trk; Delta College; Arch.

SKAGGS, BETH; Grafton Sr HS; Grafton, WV; Chrs; Hon Rl; Hosp Ade; Sec NHS; Off Ade; Sch Mus; Treas Keyettes; Letter Trk; IM Sprt; PPFtbl; Fairmont St Coll; Busns.

SKAGGS, DAVE; Inland Lakes HS; Afton, MI; 32/77 Trs Sr Cls; Band; Cmnty Wkr; Stu Cncl; 4-H; FFA; Sci Clb; Letter Trk; 4-H Awd; JA Awd; Alpena Community Coll; Forestry.

SKAGGS, JENNIFER; Perkins HS; Sandusky, OH; 5/265 Chrs; Hon Rl; Pres NHS; Sch Mus; Drama Clb; Pres Fr Clb; Capt Ten; Mgrs; Bowling Green St Univ; Music.

SKAGGS, KIMBERLY; Madison Comprehensive HS; Mansfield, OH; 38/452 Band; Hon Rl; Red Cr Ade; Ger Clb; Ohio St Univ; Nursing.

SKAGGS, MACHELLE; Columbiana HS; Columbiana, OH; 5/112 Band; Hon Rl; Jr NHS; Orch; Stu Cncl; Pep Clb; Spn Clb; Gym; Letter Trk; Chrldng; College; Nursing.

SKAGGS, MARY; South Central HS; Elizabeth, IN; 20/66 Hon Rl; Sch Pl; Stg Crw; Rptr Sch Nwsp; FHA; IM Sprt; DAR Awd; Prossec Voc Schl.

SKAGGS, MICHAEL; Tuscarawas Valley HS; Dover, OH; 19/142 Band; Hon Rl; Natl Forn Lg; Kent State Univ; Pharmacist.

SKAGGS, STEVE; Waynedale HS; Fredericksburg, OH; Band; Chrs; Chrh Wkr; Hon Rl; NHS; Sch Mus; Sch Pl; Stg Crw; Rptr Yrbk; Spn Clb; Bob Jones Univ; Music.

SKALECKI, LISA; Valley Forge HS; Parma, OH; 8/777 Chrs; Hon Rl; Lbry Ade; Lit Mag; Treas NHS; Fr Clb; Spn Clb; Univ Of Cin; Aerospace Engr.

SKAPEK, STEPHEN; St Ignatius HS; Shaker Hts, OH; 14/275 Boy Scts; Hon Rl; NHS; Red Cr Ade; Capt Swmmng; Swimming Coaches Awd 80; Greek Stud Union Treas; Univ; Pre Med.

SKARBEK, ANN; St Josephs HS; South Bend, IN; Cmp Fr Grls; Hon Rl; 4-H; Fr Clb; 4-H Awd; Univ.

SKARICA, DORIS; Euclid Sr HS; Euclid, OH; Cls Rep Frsh Cls; Chrs; Hon Rl; Hosp Ade; Gym; Trk; GAA; IM Sprt; Univ; Law.

SKARSTEN, KEVIN; Pickerington HS; Pickerington, OH; Chrh Wkr; Cmnty Wkr; Hon Rl; Yth Flsp; Fr Clb; Capital Univ; Chemistry.

SKATULA, FRANK; Buckeye South HS; Dillonvale, OH; VP Frsh Cls; Am Leg Boys St; Hon Rl; Letter Bsbl; Bsktbl; Letter Ftbl; IM Sprt;.

SKEELS, DAVID; Anderson HS; Anderson, IN; 34/465 Band; Drm Bgl; Hon Rl; NHS; Orch; Sch Mus; Yth Flsp; Spn Clb; Pres Sr High Yth Grp 79; Asst Qtrmstr Of Band 79; Univ; Engr.

SKEEN, MARGARET; Stonewall Jackson HS; Charleston, WV; Mth Clb; Marshall University; Acctg.

SKEENS, E; Greenbrier East HS; Lewisburg, WV; 1/414 Band; Hon Rl; FBLA;.

SKELLEY, ELIZABETH; St Joseph HS; St Joseph, MI; 16/301 Band; Chrh Wkr; FCA; NHS; Orch; Quill & Scroll; Ed Yrbk; Sci Clb; Bausch & Lomb Awd; Kiwan Awd; Western Michigan Univ; Med.

SKELLY, LAURIE; Fairless HS; Navarre, OH; Chrs; Hon Rl; JA; Yth Flsp; FNA; Bsktbl; Hndbl; Swmmng; Ten; Chrldng; Univ; Nursing.

SKELLY, MICHAEL; Washington HS; Massillon, OH; Boy Scts; Chrs; Chrh Wkr; Hon Rl; JA; Sch Mus; Sch Pl; Sct Actv; Stg Crw; Boys Clb Am; Voc Schl; Comp Training.

SKELTIS, ANTHONY; Chesaning HS; Burt, MI; 3/241 Hon Rl; NHS; Fr Clb; Letter Bsbl; Letter Ftbl; Letter Glf; Natl Merit Ltr; Rotary Awd; College Bsbl Recruiting Honor; Awd For Acad Excellence; Chesaning Alumni Schlrshp; Alma Coll Advisory Bd; Alma Coll; Mech Engr.

SKELTON, TY; St Francis De Sales HS; Columbus, OH; 14/189 Chrh Wkr; Hon Rl; Rptr Sch Nwsp; Sch Nwsp; Bsbl; Letter Bsktbl; Letter Ftbl; IM Sprt; Univ Of Toledo; Indust Engr.

SKIBA, HOLLEE; Alpena Sr HS; Alpena, MI; 28/791 Chrs; Chrh Wkr; Cmnty Wkr; Hon Rl; Lbry Ade; NHS; PAVAS; Sch Mus; Stg Crw; Ed Sch Nwsp; French Awd; Adv Alg & Trig; Michigan St Univ; Busns.

SKIDMORE, ELIZABETH; Castle HS; Newburgh, IN; Band; Chrh Wkr; Hon Rl; Sch Mus; Sch Pl; Stg Crw; 4-H; Sci Clb; IM Sprt; 4-H Awd; Indiana St Univ; Med.

SKIDMORE, LARRY D; Gilmer County HS; Kingsport, TN; Trs Soph Cls; Hon Rl; Sch Pl; Rptr Sch Nwsp; 4-H; FBLA; Pep Clb; 4-H Awd; Univ; Bus Admin.

SKIDMORE, LESLIE; Franklin HS; Franklin, WV; Chrs; Hon Rl; NHS; Sch Pl; 4-H; FFA; 4-H Awd; West Virginia Univ; Psych.

SKIDMORE, LINDA; Dominican HS; Detroit, MI; Off Ade; PAVAS; ROTC; Sch Pl; Stg Crw; Drama Clb; OEA; Spn Clb; Gym; Montgomery Wards Miss Jr Teen Pgnt Runner Up 75; Univ; Pro Model.

SKIDMORE, RHONDA; Pennfield HS; Bellevue, MI; 1/160 Cls Rep Soph Cls; Cl Rep Jr Cls; Cls Rep Sr Cls; Val; Hon Rl; NHS; Pres Spn Clb; Natl Merit Ltr; Mich State Univ; Chem Engr.

SKIDMORE, STEPHEN E; Alexander Local HS; Athens, OH; Cls Rep Frsh Cls; VP Jr Cls; Am Leg Boys St; Hon Rl; Sch Pl; Stu Cncl; Drama Clb; FFA; Pep Clb; Letter Ftbl; College.

SKIERA, KATERI; Pellston HS; Indian River, MI; 10/53 Hon Rl; Univ; Bus.

SKILJAN, DANA; Edwardsburg HS; Edwardsburg, MI; Cl Rep Jr Cls; Chrh Wkr; Lbry Ade; Sch Mus; Stu Cncl; Ed Yrbk; Rptr Yrbk; Drama Clb; 4-H; Fr Clb; Univ.

SKILLINGS, TERESA; Wauseon HS; Wauseon, OH; Am Leg Aux Girls St; Band; Chrs; Hon Rl; NHS; Sch Mus; Sch Pl; Stu Cncl; Yth Flsp; VP Drama Clb; Wittenburg Univ; Music.

SKINDELL, MICHAEL; Brunswick HS; Brunswick, OH; Boy Scts; Lat Clb; Spn Clb; Achvmnt Awd Creatvtyy In Spnsh 78; Dipoma Of Hnr For Spnsh 79; Walsh Coll; Pre Law.

SKINNER, ALBERT; Anderson HS; Anderson, IN; Band; Hon Rl; NHS; Lat Clb; Capt Ftbl; Trk; Capt Wrstlng; Wrestling Sectnl Champ 78; Wrestling Cnty Champ 79; Wrestling NCC Tourney Champ 79; Plc 2nd In St Wrestlg; General Motors Inst; Mech Engr.

SKINNER, BETH; Harbor HS; Ashtabula, OH; 2/197 AFS; Chrs; Hon Rl; NHS; Off Ade; Yth Flsp; Yrbk; Fr Clb; Mas Awd; Kent State Univ; Nursing.

SKINNER, CAROLYN; Lake Central HS; Schererville, IN; 101/520 Cls Rep Soph Cls; Cl Rep Jr Cls; Cls Rep Sr Cls; Hosp Ade; Off Ade; Treas Stu Cncl; Pep Clb; Capt Chrldng; Ball State Univ; Nursing.

SKINNER, DEBBIE; Madison HS; Adrian, MI; Cls Rep Soph Cls; Band; Drm Mjrt; Hon Rl; NHS; VP Quill & Scroll; Stu Cncl; Ed Yrbk; Rptr Yrbk; Rptr Sch Nwsp; Softball; Adrian Coll; Bio.

SKINNER, DOUGLAS; Franklin HS; Franklin, OH; Boy Scts; Sct Actv; Bsktbl; IM Sprt; Scr Kpr; College; Tv Radio Brdcstng.

SKINNER, D S; Galion HS; Galion, OH; Am Leg Boys St; Band; Boy Scts; Hon Rl; Ten; Trk; Am Leg Awd; College; Med.

SKINNER, MARK; Theodore Roosevelt HS; Kent, OH; Chrs; Chrh Wkr; Hon Rl; NHS; Sch Pl; Stu Cncl; Yth Flsp; Spn Clb; George Washington Univ; Law.

SKINNER, MARUICE L; Bronson HS; Bronson, MI; Cl Rep Jr Cls; Am Leg Boys St; Band; Boy Scts; Stu Cncl; Yth Flsp; 4-H; Pep Clb; Letter Ftbl; Capt Wrstlng; Americanism Awd; Ath Of The Yr Awd; Hnrble Mention In All St Ftbl In Detroit Free Press & Detroit News; Adrian Coll; Poli Sci.

SKINNER, MICHAEL J; Green HS; Akron, OH; Cmnty Wkr; Hon Rl; IM Sprt; Merit Achievement Awd; Univ Of Florida; Busns.

SKINNER, PAUL D; Lincoln HS; Shinnston, WV; Am Leg Boys St; Aud/Vis; Debate Tm; FCA; Hon Rl; Jr NHS; NHS; 4-H; FDA; John Hopkins Univ; Pre Med.

SKINNER, THERESA; Arlington HS; Indianapolis, IN; 19/325 Cls Rep Frsh Cls; Cls Rep Soph Cls; Cl Rep Jr Cls; Cls Rep Sr Cls; Girl Scts; Hon Rl; Hosp Ade; NHS; Sch Mus; Stu Cncl; Indiana Univ; Marketing.

SKINNER, VALERIE; Olivet HS; Olivet, MI; Band; Chrh Wkr; Sch Mus; Sch Pl; Yth Flsp; 4-H; Chrldng; Lansing Cmnty Coll.

SKINNER, WAYNE; Flint Christian HS; Mt Morris, MI; Chrs; Chrh Wkr; FCA; Hon Rl; Sch Pl; Yth Flsp; Bsktbl; Socr; Trk; College.

SKINNER, WAYNE E; Pleasant HS; Marion, OH; 30/160 Boy Scts; Hon Rl; Quill & Scroll; Rptr Sch Nwsp; Key Clb; Letter Bsktbl; Letter Ftbl; Letter Trk; IM Sprt; College; Bus Mgmt.

SKIPPER, DAVID A; Marlington HS; Alliance, OH; Chrs; Chrh Wkr; Sch Mus; Sch Pl; IM Sprt; Akron Univ; Poli Sci.

SKIPPER, GREG; Flatrock HS; Flatrock, MI; VP Frsh Cls; Pres Soph Cls; FCA; Hon Rl; NHS; Quill & Scroll; Stu Cncl; Yrbk; Sprt Ed Sch Nwsp; Sci Clb; Univ Of Michigan.

SKIPPER, GREGORY; Flatrock HS; Flat Rock, MI; VP Frsh Cls; Pres Soph Cls; FCA; Hon Rl; NHS; Quill & Scroll; Stu Cncl; Sprt Ed Sch Nwsp; Sci Clb; Letter Bsbl; Univ.

SKIPWORTH, YALE; Fairmont West HS; Kettering, OH; Chrh Wkr; Chrs; FCA; Hon Rl; Yth Flsp; Letter Crs Cntry; Letter Trk; U S Air Force Acad; Astro Engr.

SKIRTICH, DAN; Fairless HS; Navarre, OH; VP Sr Cls; Chrh Wkr; Hon Rl; Rptr Sch Nwsp; Pres Key Clb; Letter Ftbl; Letter Wrstlng; Univ.

SKIRVIN, LISA; Jimtown HS; Elkhart, IN; 5/96 Chrh Wkr; Hon Rl; NHS; 4-H; Pep Clb; Trk; PPFtbl; 4-H Awd; Lion Awd; Ball State Univ; Bsns.

SKIVER, RITA; Randolph Southern HS; Lynn, IN; Trs Jr Cls; Am Leg Aux Girls St; Drm Mjrt; Hon Rl; NHS; Off Ade; Pep Clb; Letter Trk; Chrldng; College; Phys Educ.

SKLAR, MICHAEL; Southfield Lathrup Sr HS; Southfield, MI; Debate Tm; Hon Rl; Mod UN; IM Sprt; Natl Merit SF; Bridge Club 78 79; Explorers Club 78 79; Chess Club 78 79; Princeton Univ; Astronomy.

SKLAREK, MARIANNE; High School; Lorain, OH; Band; Chrh Wkr; Girl Scts; Hon Rl; Hosp Ade; Lbry Ade; Off Ade; Lorain County Community; Accntg.

SKLENAR, SUSIE; Shenandoah HS; Belle Valley, OH; 20/88 Chrs; Chrh Wkr; Girl Scts; Hon Rl; Lbry Ade; Sch Pl; Stg Crw; Drama Clb; 4-H; FHA; VICA Citizens Degree; Vocational Schl; Cosmetology.

SKOBRAK, JANE; Bishop Hartley HS; Columbus, OH; 26/177 Cmnty Wkr; Hon Rl; Lbry Ade; Schlrshp Ohio Domn Coll 79; Ohio Cert Supr Math 79; Pre Calculus Awd 79; Ohio Dominican Coll; Math.

SKOCELAS, JUDITH; Sault Area HS; Sault Stemarie, MI; Hon Rl; NHS; Pep Clb; Trk; IM Sprt; Natl Merit Ltr; Natl Merit SF; Natl Merit Schl; Lk Superior State College; Elem Teac.

SKOCELAS, LYNN; Gladwin HS; Gladwin, MI; Band; Girl Scts; Hon Rl; NHS; Rptr Sch Nwsp; Glf; Lion Awd; CMU; Sec.

SKOCIK, CHRIS; Niles Mckinley HS; Niles, OH; 18/420 VP Jr Cls; Am Leg Boys St; Hon Rl; NHS; Sch Pl; VP Stu Cncl; Drama Clb; Letter Ftbl; IM Sprt; Us Naval Acad.

SKOCZYLAS, DENISE M; Southwestern Community HS; Flint, MI; 8/451 Band; Drl Tm; Hon Rl; JA; NHS; Quill & Scroll; Red Cr Ade; Yrbk; Ed Sch Nwsp; JA Awd; Article In Flint Chamber Of Commerce Mag; Univ Of Michigan; Busns Admin.

SKOLASINSKI, DONALD; Wakefield HS; Wakefield, MI; Univ.

SKOMP, JOHN; John Skomp HS; Greenfield, IN; 33/350 Chrh Wkr; Hon Rl; NHS; Spn Clb; Univ; CPA.

SKONIECZNY, CYNTHIA; West Catholic HS; Grand Rapids, MI; Jr NHS; NHS; Yth Flsp; Pep Clb; Acqiuanas; Comp Sci.

SKORCZ, MARK J; Moeller HS; Cincinnati, OH; 25/250 Cls Rep Frsh Cls; VP Soph Cls; Trs Jr Cls; Pres Sr Cls; Hon Rl; Jr NHS; NHS; PAVAS; Sch Pl; Stu Cncl; Notre Dame Univ; Medicine.

SKORDOS, MOLLY; Northside HS; Ft Wayne, IN; 80/449 Band; Hon Rl; JA; NHS; OEA; Gym; Pom Pon; JA Awd; Indiana Voc Tech Coll; Computer Sci.

SKOREPA, R; Charles F Brush HS; S Euclid, OH; Cl Rep Jr Cls; Chrs; Pep Clb; College; Vet.

SKOVIRA, BOB; Revere HS; Richfield, OH; Hon Rl; Red Cr Ade; Ed Sch Nwsp; Sch Nwsp; Spn Clb; VICA; Cuyanoga Comm College; Graphic Comm.

SKOWRONSKI, ANNETTE; Dominican HS; Detroit, MI; Chrs; Cmnty Wkr; NHS; Natl Merit Schl; Univ Of Detroit; Biology.

SKRAN, CLAUDENA; Bridgeport HS; Saginaw, MI; 3/350 Band; Chrh Wkr; Treas NHS; Off Ade; Pres Yth Flsp; Ed Sch Nwsp; Rptr Sch Nwsp; Scr Kpr; Mich State Univ; Bus.

SKROBACS, TAMMIE L; N Ridgeville Sr HS; N Ridgeville, OH; Sec Frsh Cls; Trs Soph Cls; Trs Jr Cls; Trs Sr Cls; Hon Rl; Mod UN; NHS; Stu Cncl; Yth Flsp; Pep Clb; Univ Of Cincinnati; Nursing.

SKROK, LINDA; Warren Woods Public HS; Warren, MI; Cls Rep Frsh Cls; Hon Rl; NHS; Sch Pl; Stu Cncl; Yth Flsp; Ed Sch Nwsp; Sch Nwsp; Letter Bsktbl; Letter Trk; St Of Mi Comp Schlrshp 79; Cntrl Mi Univ Hon Schlrshp 79; Central Michigan Univ; Jrnlsm.

SKRUCK, JOHN; Hubbard HS; Hubbard, OH; 25/370 Band; Boy Scts; Chrh Wkr; Cmnty Wkr; Hon Rl; JA; Lit Mag; Sch Mus; Sct Actv; Civ Clb; Ohio St Univ; Med.

SKRZYNIARZ, CATHY; Center Line HS; Warren, MI; Cls Rep Frsh Cls; Cls Rep Soph Cls; Cl Rep Jr Cls; Band; Hon Rl; Jr NHS; Stu Cncl; DECA; Spn Clb; Capt Chrldng; Coll; Retailing.

SKRZYNSKI, DONALD; Jackson HS; Jackson, MI; 57/326 Boy Scts; Ger Clb; Mich State; Astro Physics.

SKRZYPCZAK, SHERRY; Fraser HS; Fraser, MI; Band; Cmnty Wkr; Jr NHS; Orch; Y-Teens; Bsbl; Michigan St Univ; Law.

SKUBBY, SUE; Parma Sr HS; Parma, OH; Chrh Wkr; Hon Rl; NHS; C of C Awd; Parisho Guitar Groups; Bus Stu Of Yr Parma Sr High; Univ; Bus.

SKULICH, SARA; Steubenville Cath Cntrl HS; Steubenvll, OH; 37/205 Chrs; Girl Scts; Hon Rl; Fr Clb; Trk; Letters In Vlybl; College; Health.

SKUTT, T; Flushing Sr HS; Flushing, MI; Band; Chrs; Drl Tm; Girl Scts; Hon Rl; Yth Flsp; Beta Clb; Fr Clb; Pom Pon; PPFtbl; Univ; Nursing.

SKUTT, VICTORIA; Northern HS; Flint, MI; 1/458 Chrh Wkr; Hon Rl; Sec NHS; Off Ade; Sec Yth Flsp; Sci Clb; Letter Ten; Kalamazoo College; Pre Med.

SKUTT, WAYNE; E A Johnson HS; Mt Morris, MI; Boy Scts; Chrh Wkr; Air Force; Mech Engr.

SKUZA, JANET; Holy Name Nazareth HS; Independence, OH; Chrh Wkr; Hon Rl; NHS; Drama Clb; Spn Clb; College.

SKVARKA, MARY E; Bishop Donahue HS; Moundsville, WV; Aud/Vis; Chrs; Chrh Wkr; Girl Scts; Hon Rl; Sch Mus; Yrbk; Sch Nwsp; 4-H; Treas Pep Clb; Bus Schl.

SKWIERA, CAROL; Cabrini HS; Allen Park, MI; Hon Rl; Sch Nwsp; Spn Clb; Bus Schl; Data Proc.

SKYE, ERIC; Pioneer HS; Ann Arbor, MI; Boy Scts; Hon Rl; Lbry Ade; Off Ade; Red Cr Ade; Sct Actv; Ftbl; Wrstlng; Coach Actv; Univ Of Mich; Sci.

SLAATS, PAUL; Jasper HS; Jasper, IN; 35/350 Am Leg Boys St; Chrh Wkr; Cmnty Wkr; Hon Rl; JA; Pol Wkr; Civ Clb; JA Awd; Univ; Engr.

SLABAUGH, BRYAN; Chippewa HS; Doylestown, OH; Hon Rl; Spn Clb;.

SLABAUGH, JEAN; John Adams HS; So Bend, IN; 34/395 Hon Rl; JA; NHS; Off Ade; 4-H; Pep Clb; Sci Clb; Letter Trk; PPFtbl; Univ; Bio.

SLABAUGH, JOAN; John Adams HS; So Bend, IN; 41/430 Girl Scts; Hon Rl; VP JA; Off Ade; Sct Actv; 4-H; Sci Clb; Swmmng; Purdue Univ; Chem Engr.

SLABAUGH, KAREN; Jackson HS; North Canton, OH; 50/400 Hon Rl; JA; Lbry Ade; NHS; Off Ade; Fr Clb; JA Awd; Outstanding Media Ctr Serv Awd 78; Awd For Accumluative A Avg For 5 Semesters 78; Akron Univ; Engr.

SLABAUGH, MARVIN; Whitmore Lake HS; Whitmore Lk, MI; 1/82 Trs Frsh Cls; Band; Hon Rl; Jr NHS; NHS; Letter Trk; Univ.

SLABICKI, CHRISTOPHER; St Ignatius HS; Cleveland, OH; 32/309 Hon Rl; Hosp Ade; NHS; Pep Clb; Ten; College; Architecture.

SLABY, T; Lumen Christi HS; Clark Lk, MI; Voc Schl.

SLACK, CAROL; Switzerland County HS; Vevay, IN; 8/140 Band; Drm Mjrt; Hon Rl; MMM; NHS; Sch Pl; 4-H; Fr Clb; Pep Clb; Twrlr; Univ.

SLACK, DALE; Hurricane HS; Hurricane, WV; Cls Rep Frsh Cls; Cls Rep Soph Cls; Cl Rep Jr Cls; Cls Rep Sr Cls; FCA; Hon Rl; Stg Crw; Stu Cncl; Capt Ftbl; Trk; Univ; Bus.

SLACK, JOANNE; Manton Consolidated Schl; Manton, MI; Cls Rep Frsh Cls; Trs Soph Cls; Band; Chrs; Cmnty Wkr; Drm Mjrt; Girl Scts; Hon Rl; Lbry Ade; Off Ade; Mercy Schl Of Prac Nursing; Nurse.

SLACK, MARK W; Engadine Con HS; Gould, MI; Hon Rl; Bsbl; Bsktbl; Ftbl; Trk;.

SLACK, STEPHANIE; East HS; Akron, OH; 31/200 Chrh Wkr; Hosp Ade; Orch; Akron Univ; Registered Nurse.

SLADE, JAMES; Escanaba Area Public HS; Escanaba, MI; Band; Orch; College; Business.

SLADEK, ROSEMARIE; West Lafayette Sr HS; W Lafayete, IN; 8/186 Chrh Wkr; Cmnty Wkr; Hon Rl; Yth Flsp; Pep Clb; Letter Gym; Univ; Sci.

SLAGEL, KATHY; Ironton HS; Ironton, OH; Cl Rep Jr Cls; Chrs; Chrh Wkr; Hon Rl; Sch Pl; Stu Cncl; Drama Clb; Pres 4-H; Lat Clb; Sci Clb; Coll.

SLAGELL, MARK H; St Johns HS; St Johns, MI; 9/350 Band; Hon Rl; Mod UN; NHS; Orch; Sch Mus; Yth Flsp; IM Sprt; Natl Merit SF; Natl Merit Schl; N Michigan Univ; Scndry Tchr.

SLAGHT, MARGARET; Magnificat HS; Rocky River, OH; Chrs; Sch Mus; Sch Pl; Stg Crw; Drama Clb; Key Clb; College.

SLAGLE, RUSSELL; Arlington HS; Indianapolis, IN; Aud/Vis; Chrs; Hon Rl; Lbry Ade; Pol Wkr; Sch Mus; Stg Crw; Yrbk; Sch Nwsp; Fr Clb; Winona Schl; Photography.

SLAIS, ROBERT; Walled Lake Central HS; Orchard Lake, MI; 67/385 Hon Rl; NHS; Off Ade; Ger Clb; Crs Cntry; Trk; Cross Cntry All Conf Jr Sr Yr 77; Cptn Cross Cntry Team Jr Sr Yr 77; St Of Mi Cmptn Schlrshp 79; Oakland Cmnty Coll; Cmmrcl Art.

SLAJUS, SUSAN; Grand Haven Sr HS; Grand Haven, MI; Hon Rl; Hosp Ade; Jr NHS; NHS; Orch; Sch Mus; Yth Flsp; Coll; Math.

SLAMAN, SARAH; Bay HS; Bay Village, OH; 42/343 Sec Frsh Cls; Sec Soph Cls; Am Leg Aux Girls St; Chrs; NHS; Sch Mus; Yrbk; Swmmng; Trk; Chrldng; College.

SLANSKY, SHERI; Gaylord HS; Gaylord, MI; Cls Rep Frsh Cls; Cls Rep Soph Cls; Trs Jr Cls; Trs Sr Cls; Debate Tm; Girl Scts; Hon Rl; Natl Forn Lg; NHS; Stu Cncl; Lk Superior St Coll; Law Enforcement.

SLAON, MARK; Princeton Community HS; Princeton, IN; 23/210 Aud/Vis; Sci Clb; Univ Of Evansville; Elec Engr.

SLAPP, TODD; Bark River Harris HS; Bark River, MI; Band; NHS; Rptr Yrbk; Natl Merit SF; Adrian Coll; Acctg.

SLATER, ALICIA; Trenton HS; Trenton, MI; Band; Chrh Wkr; Girl Scts; Hon Rl; Hosp Ade; Sct Actv; Stg Crw; Pep Clb; Tmr; Univ Of Mic; Math.

SLATER, DAWNE; Northrop HS; Ft Wayne, IN; 14/565 Chrh Wkr; Drm Bgl; Hon Rl; JA; Yth Flsp; Rptr Yrbk; Rptr Sch Nwsp; Drama Clb; Fr Clb; Pep Clb; Univ; Photo Jrnlsm.

SLATER, LINDA; St Agatha HS; Detroit, MI; Trs Sr Cls; Chrs; Girl Scts; Hon Rl; JA; Off Ade; FBLA; Bsbl; Gym; Swmmng; Dearborn Schl Of Bus; Sec.

SLATER, MICHAEL; Divine Child HS; Dearborn Ht, MI; Band; Hon Rl; Sci Clb; IM Sprt; Univ; Acctg.

SLATTER, CAROL; Mississinewa HS; Gas City, IN; 16/749 Chrs; Hon Rl; Sch Mus; Sch Pl; Stg Crw; Pres Yth Flsp; Yrbk; Drama Clb; Pres Fr Clb; Coll; Nursing.

SLATTERY, CATHERINE; Bethel Local HS; Dayton, OH; Cls Rep Frsh Cls; Band; Chrs; Hon Rl; Jr NHS; Off Ade; Stg Crw; Stu Cncl; Bsktbl; Trk;.

SLATTERY, MICHAEL; La Salle HS; Cincinnati, OH; Chrh Wkr; Hon Rl; IM Sprt; Mgrs; Scr Kpr; DAR Awd; Dayton; Acctg.

SLAUBAUGH, CAROLYN; Barr Reeve HS; Loogootee, IN; Chrs; Chrh Wkr; Hon Rl; Yth Flsp; Rptr Yrbk; Beta Clb; FHA; JA Awd; College; Educ.

SLAUBAUGH, EARL; East Preston Sr HS; Terra Alta, WV; Aud/Vis; Boy Scts; Chrs; Drl Tm; Hon Rl; Yth Flsp; Drama Clb; Gov Hon Prg Awd; JETS Awd; Fairmont St Univ; Elect.

SLAUGHTER, ANTHONY; Madison Heights HS; Anderson, IN; Am Leg Boys St; Band; Boy Scts; Chrs; Cmnty Wkr; Hon Rl; JA; Sch Mus; Stg Crw; Spn Clb; UCLA; Math.

SLAUGHTER, DANIEL K; Nitro HS; Charleston, WV; 6/275 VP Jr Cls; Cls Rep Sr Cls; Chrs; Hon Rl; NHS; Stu Cncl; Yth Flsp; Mth Clb; Natl Merit SF; Univ.

SLAUGHTER, FAY W; Buckhannon Upshur HS; Buckhannon, WV; Boy Scts; Chrs; Drama Clb; Spn Clb; Ftbl; Trk; Wrstlng; Glenville St Coll; Bus.

SLAUGHTER, JEFFREY; Caldwell HS; Caldwell, OH; Chrh Wkr; Hon Rl; Spn Clb; Crs Cntry; Trk; Wrstlng; College; Mathematics.

SLAUGHTER, KELLY E; Northridge HS; Pataskala, OH; Band; Chrh Wkr; Hon Rl; VP Yth Flsp; Pres Beta Clb; VP 4-H; Cedarville College; Elem Educ.

SLAUGHTER, TRACEY; Buckhannon Upshur HS; Buckhannon, WV; Chrs; Chrh Wkr; Stg Crw; Yth Flsp; 4-H; Pep Clb; Bsktbl; Trk; Mgrs; 4-H Awd; Wesleyan Coll; Acctg.

SLAVIK, JAMES; Fulton HS; Ashley, MI; 11/97 Cls Rep Frsh Cls; Cls Rep Soph Cls; Band; Hon Rl; Stu Cncl; Rptr Sch Nwsp; 4-H; FFA; Bsbl; Bsktbl; Michigan St Univ; Agri.

SLAVIN, MIKE; Fort Frye HS; Beverly, OH; Cls Rep Sr Cls; Boy Scts; Chrs; Sch Pl; Stu Cncl; Sci Clb; Letter Bsktbl; Letter Ftbl; Letter Trk; Coach Actv;.

SLAWSON, RICK; Lincoln HS; Vincennes, IN; 70/216 Am Leg Boys St; Chrh Wkr; FCA; Pol Wkr; Pep Clb; Ftbl; Coach Actv; Offensive Lineman Of The Yr 1978; Univ.

SLAY, TAWNEY; Heath HS; Heath, OH; 40/160 Cls Rep Soph Cls; Cl Rep Jr Cls; Cls Rep Sr Cls; FCA; Girl Scts; Stu Cncl; FHA; Key Clb; Lat Clb; Letter Gym; COTC; Comp.

SLAYBACK, KIMBERLY; South Dearborn HS; Aurora, IN; Band; Hon Rl; Off Ade; Rptr Yrbk; Rptr Sch Nwsp; 4-H; Pep Clb; Bsbl; Bsktbl; Trk; Univ; Sci.

SLEBODNIK, LISA A; Lawrence North HS; Indianapolis, IN; 44/384 Band; Cmnty Wkr; Drl Tm; Orch; Sch Mus; Yth Flsp; Drama Clb; Fr Clb; Scr Kpr; Natl Merit SF; Univ.

SLEDER, JANET; Traverse City Sr HS; Traverse City, MI; 5/780 Chrh Wkr; Cmnty Wkr; Hon Rl; NHS; Pep Clb; Natl Merit Ltr; Kenneth M Koch Schlrshp; Ferris St Coll Merit Schlrshp; Bronze Silver & Gold Keys; Ferris St Coll; Pharm.

SLEEK, S GINGER; Newark Sr HS; Newark, OH; Hon Rl; Fr Clb; DAR Awd;.

SLEEMAN, GEOFFREY; Royal Oak Dondero HS; Huntington Wds, MI; 76/400 Chrh Wkr; NHS; Sch Nwsp; Ger Clb; Letter Bsbl; Coach Actv; IM Sprt; Natl Merit Ltr; Albion Coll; Business Admin.

SLEPPY, MARK; Goshen HS; Goshen, IN; 28/274 Am Leg Boys St; Boy Scts; FCA; Hon Rl; Sct Actv; 4-H; Sci Clb; Ftbl; Letter Swmmng; Trk; Purdue Univ; Aerospace Design Engr.

SLESSMAN, DOREEN; Willard HS; Plymouth, OH; 21/176 Band; Chrh Wkr; Hon Rl; Jr NHS; NHS; Orch; Sch Mus; 4-H; Pep Clb; Trk; Band V P 78; Bowling Green St Univ; Math.

SLICKER, ROBERT; Houghton Lake HS; Houghton Lk, MI; Cmnty Wkr; Hon Rl; Yth Flsp; Rptr Yrbk; Fr Clb; Pep Clb; Ftbl; College; Law.

SLIHET, ALEX; East Detroit HS; Warren, MI; Wrstlng; UCLA; Bus.

SLIKKERS, THOMAS B; Cedar Lake Academy; Holland, MI; Chrs; Hon Rl; Mdrgl; Stu Cncl; Sch Nwsp; IM Sprt; Scr Kpr; Tmr; Andrews Univ; Bus Admin.

SLIVER, STEVEN; Warren HS; Warren, MI; Band; Hon Rl; Yth Flsp; Mic Tech; Phys Sci.

SLIVINSKI, RICHARD; Northwest HS; Clinton, OH; 10/130 Hon Rl; NHS; Stg Crw; Yrbk; Spn Clb; Letter Bsbl; Letter Glf; Coach Actv; IM Sprt; Voted By Coaches To The 79 All Senate League Bsebl Team; Miami Dade Comm Coll; Archt.

SLIWA, SUSAN; Morton Sr HS; Hammond, IN; 1/450 Cls Rep Soph Cls; Cl Rep Jr Cls; Hon Rl; Ten; PPFtbl; Univ; Fash Merch.

SLOAN, CARLA; Notre Dame Academy; Toledo, OH; Hosp Ade; JA; JA Awd; Toledo Univ; Acctg.

SLOAN, CHARLES; Lebanon Sr HS; Lebanon, IN; 61/219 Chrs; Chrh Wkr; Sch Mus; Stg Crw; Yth

Flsp; Lat Clb; Mgrs; Concert Choir Outstndng Sr Male Vocal; A Hoosier Schlr; Purdue Univ Cert Of Recognition; Purdue Univ; Vet Med.

SLOAN, LAURA; Our Lady Star Of The Sea HS; St Clair Shore, MI; Cls Rep Frsh Cls; Cls Rep Soph Cls; Sec Jr Cls; Trs Sr Cls; Cmnty Wkr; Hon Rl; NHS; PAVAS; Sch Pl; Stu Cncl; Northwood Inst; Bus Admin.

SLOAN, LINDA; Franklin Monroe HS; Greenville, OH; 12/62 Band; Chrs; Chrh Wkr; Hon Rl; Lbry Ade; Sch Pl; Rptr Sch Nwsp; FHA; Pep Clb; VICA; Wright St Univ; Nursing.

SLOAN, MARY; St Joseph HS; S Bend, IN; 15/249 Hon Rl; Hosp Ade; Rptr Sch Nwsp; Univ Of Notre Dame.

SLOAN, MARY; Gladwin HS; Gladwin, MI; VP Frsh Cls; Cls Rep Soph Cls; Hon Rl; Stu Cncl; IM Sprt; PPFtbl; Scr Kpr; Cleary College; Bus.

SLOAN, MITZI; Bosse HS; Evansville, IN; VP Frsh Cls; Cls Rep Soph Cls; Cl Rep Jr Cls; VP Sr Cls; Hon Rl; Stu Cncl; Letter Bsktbl; Letter Ten; Cit Awd; Evansville Univ; Law Enforce.

SLOAN, SHIRLEY; Kelloggville HS; Kentwood, MI; 8/130 Chrs; Chrh Wkr; Hon Rl; NHS; Rptr Yrbk; Spn Clb; Tennessee Temple Univ; Psych.

SLOCUM, JACK; Waterford Township HS; Pontiac, MI; 39/350 Band; Hon Rl; NHS; IM Sprt; Natl Merit Ltr; Michigan St Univ; Engr.

SLOCUM, LYNNE; Saginaw HS; Saginaw, MI; 2/331 Cls Rep Sr Cls; Sal; Chrs; Girl Scts; Hon Rl; Hosp Ade; Sec Jr NHS; Lbry Ade; NHS; Off Ade; Michigan St Comp Schlrshp; Amer Womens Busns Assn Schlrshp; 3 Local Schlrshps From Saginaw Schl Bd; Kalamazoo Coll; Med.

SLOCUM, SUSAN E; Marian 'S; Birmingham, MI; Cl Rep Jr Cls; Cls Rep Sr Cls; Girl Scts; Hon Rl; Mod UN; NHS; Stg Crw; Ed Yrbk; Tmr; Marquette Univ; Phys Ther.

SLOGAR, RAYMOND J; Gilmour Acad; Ft Wayne, IN; 8/82 Pres Soph Cls; Cl Rep Jr Cls; Chrs; Hon Rl; NHS; Letter Ftbl; Trk; Wrstlng; Lion Awd; Pres Awd; Univ Of Notre Dame; Econ.

SLONE, ANDREA; Springboro HS; Springboro, OH; Cls Rep Frsh Cls; Trs Jr Cls; Cls Rep Sr Cls; Cmp Fr Grls; Chrs; Girl Scts; Hon Rl; Hosp Ade; Treas NHS; Sch Pl; 1st In MAA Contest In Schl 76; Selected To Rep SHS In Warren Co Fest 79; Chosen To Take OST In Eng 77; Univ; Pre Med.

SLONE, DONNA; Richmond Sr HS; Richmond, IN; Band; Chrs; Girl Scts; Hon Rl; Hosp Ade; Treas JA; NHS; Orch; Sch Mus; Sct Actv; Coll.

SLONE, SUSAN; Shelby Sr HS; Shelby, OH; 58/259 Cls Rep Frsh Cls; Cls Rep Soph Cls; Cl Rep Jr Cls; Am Leg Aux Girls St; Band; Chrh Wkr; Cmnty Wkr; Drm Mjrt; Girl Scts; Hon Rl; Ohio St Univ; Mgmt.

SLOSSER, RUTH; Willard HS; Willard, OH; Band; Drl Tm; Hon Rl; NHS; Orch; Sch Mus; Mgrs; Bowling Green State Univ; Bus.

SLOTMAN, CINDY S; Fennville HS; Fennville, MI; Hon Rl; Lbry Ade; NHS; Sch Pl; IM Sprt; Natl Merit Ltr; Natl Merit SF; Missionary Work.

SLOTMAN, MARY; Byron Center HS; Byron Center, MI; 1/136 Val; Band; Debate Tm; Hon Rl; Jr NHS; NHS; Orch; Sch Pl; Yth Flsp; Drama Clb; Ferris St Coll; CPA.

SLOTVIK, SHERRY L; Springfield HS; Battle Crk, MI; Chrs; Hon Rl; Lit Mag; Sch Mus; Sch Pl; Stg Crw; Drama Clb; 4-H; Univ; Jrnlsm.

SLOVER, SUZANNE; Miami Trace HS; Jeffersonville, OH; 30/250 AFS; Girl Scts; Hon Rl; Stg Crw; 4-H; FTA; Columbus Busns Univ; Legal Sec.

SLOWIKOWSKI, LAURA; Tuscarawas Ctrl Catholic HS; New Phila, OH; 1/75 Band; Girl Scts; Hon Rl; NHS; Sch Pl; Rptr Sch Nwsp; 4-H; Trk; 4-H Awd; Walsh Coll; Elem Educ.

SLUDER, VICKI; Cloverdale HS; Cloverdale, IN; Chrs; Hon Rl; Rptr Sch Nwsp; Sch Nwsp; Pep Clb; Chrldng; Shop Awd 78 & 79; Univ; Drftng.

SLUSIEWICZ, JEROME; West Catholic HS; Belmont, MI; 4/267 Trs Frsh Cls; Trs Soph Cls; Cl Rep Jr Cls; Chrs; JA; NHS; Sch Mus; General Motor Inst; Mech.

SLUSSER, BETSY; Richmond Sr HS; Richmond, IN; Cls Rep Soph Cls; Cl Rep Jr Cls; Trs Sr Cls; Chrs; Hon Rl; Stu Cncl; 4-H; Gym; 4-H Awd; Univ.

SLUSSER, BRADLEY A; East Fairmount HS; Fairmont, WV; Am Leg Boys St; Chrh Wkr; Hon Rl; NHS; Stg Crw; Stu Cncl; Treas Yth Flsp; Drama Clb; VP Key Clb; Wrstlng; Fairmont St Coll.

SLUTZ, JUNE; Sandy Valley HS; Magnolia, OH; Chrs; Cmnty Wkr; Hon Rl; Rptr Yrbk; Fr Clb; Ger Clb; Pep Clb; Letter Gym; Letter Trk;.

SLUTZ, KEVIN; Timken Sr HS; Canton, OH; Aud/Vis; Chrs; Hon Rl; Sch Pl; Stg Crw; Drama Clb; Pep Clb; DAR Awd; Akron Univ.

SLUTZKER, SUSAN; Admiral King HS; Lorain, OH; Band; Hon Rl; Off Ade; Orch; Sch Mus; Univ.

SMAGACZ, KAREN; Fraser HS; Fraser, MI; 32/620 Cls Rep Sr Cls; Hon Rl; NHS; Stu Cncl; Gym; IM Sprt; Wayne State Univ; Fashion Merchd.

SMAIL, TAMMY; Lakeview HS; Cortland, OH; 32/188 Band; Chrh Wkr; Hon Rl; Hosp Ade; Red Cr Ade; Yth Flsp; Ger Clb; Spn Clb; St Board Certificate Award Of Distinction; Capital Univ; Nursing.

SMAILES, SUZANNE A; Wooster HS; Wooster, OH; Chrh Wkr; Girl Scts; NHS; Orch; Sch Mus; P res Fr Clb; God Cntry Awd; NCTE; Ohio St Univ; Phys Therapy.

SMALL, BETSY; Defiance Sr HS; Defiance, OH; Chrs; Drl Tm; Hon Rl; NHS; ROTC; Sch Pl; Rptr Yrbk; VP Fr Clb; Natl Merit Ltr; Natl Merit SF; Univ; Astronomy.

SMALL, DAVID; Grand Rapids Central HS; Grand Rapids, MI; Boy Scts; Hon Rl; Pres JA; Sct Actv; Bsbl; JC Awd; JA Awd; Pres Awd; Unites States Coast Guard; Law Engor.

SMALL, JENNIFER; Hamilton Heights HS; Arcadia, IN; 18/152 Trs Frsh Cls; Trs Jr Cls; Hon Rl; NHS; Ed Yrbk; Yrbk; 4-H; Fr Clb; FHA; FTA; Butler Univ; Elem Educ.

SMALL, JENNIFER; Regina HS; Cleve Hts, OH; Hon Rl; Hosp Ade; Sch Pl; Stg Crw; Drama Clb; College; Phy Ther.

SMALL, JENNIFER; Regina HS; Cleveland Hts, OH; Hosp Ade; Sch Pl; Stg Crw; Drama Clb; College; Phys Ther.

SMALL, KIMBERLY; Arcanum Butler HS; Arcanum, OH; Chrh Wkr; Girl Scts; Pol Wkr; Univ Of Dayton; Fine Arts.

SMALL, LISA; Our Lady Of Mercy HS; Detroit, MI; Chrs; Girl Scts; Univ Of Michigan; Soc Worker.

SMALL, PHYLLIS; Lutheran HS East; E Cleveland, OH; 7/44 Cmp Fr Grls; Chrs; Chrh Wkr; Hon Rl; JA; Lbry Ade; Stg Crw; Yrbk; Pep Clb; Sawyer Coll Of Bus; Med Sec.

SMALL, SALLY; Williamston HS; Williamston, MI; Band; Cmnty Wkr; 4-H; 4-H Awd; Michigan St Univ; Horticulture.

SMALL, XEN; Hamilton Hts HS; Atlanta, IN; Boy Scts; Chrs; Sct Actv; Spn Clb; Letter Bsktbl; Letter Crs Cntry; Letter Trk; Mgrs; Indiana Voc Tech Coll; Construction.

SMALLEGAN, DARLENE; Lee HS; Wyoming, MI; Band; Hon Rl; NHS; Stu Cncl; Capt Ten; PPFtbl; Am Leg Awd; DAR Awd; Rotary Awd; Davenport College Of Bus; Legal Sec.

SMALLEY, CARA; Tippecanoe Valley HS; Claypool, IN; Cls Rep Soph Cls; Chrs; Hon Rl; Yth Flsp; 4-H; Chrldng; IM Sprt; 4-H Awd; Ball St Univ.

SMALLEY, DARLENE; Charlevoix HS; Charlevoix, MI; 21/152 Trs Soph Cls; Trs Jr Cls; Band; Chrh Wkr; Drl Tm; Hon Rl; Olivet Nazarene College; Music.

SMALLEY, DAVID; Solon HS; Solon, OH; Boy Scts; Wrstlng; Akron; Engr.

SMALLEY, DEBRA; Wintersville HS; Steubenville, OH; 51/287 Band; Chrh Wkr; NHS; Sch Pl; Stu Cncl; Yrbk; GAA; PPFtbl; Youngstown St Univ; Nursing.

SMALLEY, ELIZABETH; Peebles HS; Peebles, OH; Band; Chrs; Chrh Wkr; Girl Scts; Hon Rl; Sch Mus; Sch Pl; Sct Actv; Yth Flsp; Drama Clb; Bible College; Music.

SMALLEY, ENITH; Eastwood HS; Perrysburg, OH; 11/180 Band; FCA; Hon Rl; Off Ade; PAVAS; Treas 4-H; FHA; Lat Clb; Pep Clb; GAA; Toledo Univ; Law.

SMALLEY, JULIA; Tri HS; Spiceland, IN; 11/85 Trs Jr Cls; Band; Girl Scts; Hon Rl; Hosp Ade; Jr NHS; Lbry Ade; NHS; Off Ade; Sch Pl; Thespian Awd Outstndng Actress 79; Jr Sr Prom Princess 79; Indiana Univ; Fshn Mdse.

SMALLEY, NANCY L; Cheboygan Area HS; Cheboygan, MI; Band; Girl Scts; Hon Rl; Rptr Yrbk; 4-H; Trk; 4-H Awd; Ferris State Univ; Legal Sec.

SMALLEY, SHERRI; Dansville Agri HS; Williamston, MI; 8/63 Trs Sr Cls; Hon Rl; NHS; Off Ade; Rptr Sch Nwsp; 4-H; Letter Bsktbl; Letter Trk; Michigan St Univ.

SMALLEY, SUSAN; Whitmer HS; Toledo, OH; Cls Rep Frsh Cls; Hon Rl; JA; Off Ade; DECA; Fr Clb; FTA; Pep Clb; Spn Clb; PPFtbl; Work.

SMALLWOOD, CAROL; Nicholas County HS; Calvin, WV; 21/213 Hon Rl; NHS; Sec FBLA; GAA; IM Sprt; Scr Kpr; Key Punch Oper.

SMALTZ, CINDY; Fitch HS; Youngstown, OH; 172/650 Band; Cmp Fr Grls; Hon Rl; Off Ade; Sch Mus; Yth Flsp; Y-Teens; Ohi State; Nurs.

SMARELLI, JAMES R; Richmond Sr HS; Richmond, IN; 5/626 Band; Chrs; Hon Rl; Jr NHS; NHS; Orch; Letter Crs Cntry; Trk; IM Sprt; Math Sci Inst At Indiana Univ 79; Notre Dame Univ; Law.

SMARRELLA, K; Catholic Central HS; Steubenvll, OH; 12/204 Cls Rep Sr Cls; Girl Scts; Hon Rl; NHS; Stu Cncl; Rptr Yrbk; Sec FHA; Sec Pep Clb; Spn Clb; College; Math.

SMART, DOUG; St Joseph HS; St Joseph, MI; Band; Boy Scts; VP JA; Sct Actv; Ger Clb; Pep Clb; Glf; JA Awd; College; Acctg.

SMART, LAURA; Highland Park Cmnty HS; Highland Pk, MI; Cls Rep Frsh Cls; Cl Rep Jr Cls; Hon Rl; Orch; Wayne St Univ; Acctg.

SMART, SALLY A; Attica HS; Attica, IN; Pres Jr Cls; Stu Cncl; Yrbk; Sch Nwsp; 4-H; FTA; Pep Clb; Spn Clb; Ten; Trk; Prom Queen Candidate 79; Girls Varsity Ltr Sweater 78; Univ; Tchr.

SMART, VICTORIA M; John R Buchtel HS; Akron, OH; Chrs; Cmnty Wkr; Debate Tm; Drl Tm; Lbry Ade; Off Ade; Rptr Sch Nwsp; Fr Clb; Coach Actv; Cit Awd; Univ; Law.

SMARTO, JANE; Crestline HS; Galion, OH; 7/120 VP Jr Cls; Am Leg Aux Girls St; Hon Rl; Pres NHS; Off Ade; Sch Pl; Stu Cncl; Rptr Yrbk; Rptr Sch Nwsp; Capt Bsktbl; Ohio St Univ; Elem Ed.

SMEAD, CHRIS; Waynesville HS; Waynesville, OH; Hon Rl; NHS; Stg Crw; Letter Crs Cntry; Ohi State; Vet.

SMEAD, REBECCA; Notre Dame Academy; Toledo, OH; Cmp Fr Grls; Drm Mjrt; Hosp Ade; JA; Jr NHS; Red Cr Ade; Yrbk; Rptr Sch Nwsp; JA Awd; Part Yth In Gov Day Progr 79; Mbr Toastmstr Yth Ldrshp 76 78; Attend Natl Jr Achvd Conf 78; Univ Of Toledo; Elem Educ.

SMEDINGHOFF, GEORGE; Muncie Northside HS; Muncie, IN; 36/286 Hon Rl; JA; NHS; Stu Cncl; Mth Clb; Letter Bsbl; Letter Bsktbl; Letter Ftbl; Letter Trk; Natl Merit Ltr; Ball State Univ; Actuarial Sci.

SMEDLEY, JODY; Salem HS; Salem, IN; 2/160 Cls Rep Frsh Cls; Cls Rep Soph Cls; Pres Jr Cls; VP Sr Cls; Pres Debate Tm; NHS; Lat Clb; Ind Univ Se; Bus.

SMEJKAL, TRACY; Lumen Cordium HS; Twinsburg, OH; Chrs; Drl Tm; Girl Scts; Hon Rl; Sch Mus; Sch Pl; Drama Clb; Music Schl; Pro Singer.

SMELKO, LORI; Greenon HS; Enon, OH; 34/280 Cl Rep Jr Cls; Trs Sr Cls; Cls Rep Sr Cls; Chrs; Chrh Wkr; Girl Scts; Hon Rl; Hosp Ade; Off Ade; Stu Cncl; Ohio State Univ; Occup Therapy.

SMELLIE, JOE; Trenton HS; Trenton, MI; Hockey; Wrstlng; IM Sprt; Univ; Law.

SMELTZER, DIANNA L; Goshen HS; Goshen, IN; 33/268 Cmp Fr Grls; Chrs; Hon Rl; Yth Flsp; Rptr Sch Nwsp; 4-H; Pep Clb; College; Art.

SMELTZER, KAREN; Hamilton Hts HS; Arcadia, IN; Hon Rl; Pep Clb; Spn Clb; Trk; Chrldng; PPFtbl; Pres Awd; Anderson Bus Schl; Sec.

SMERGLIA, CATHERINE; Field HS; Mogadore, OH; Cl Rep Jr Cls; Band; Cmp Fr Grls; Chrs; Hon Rl; Off Ade; Sch Mus; Sch Pl; Stu Cncl; Rptr Yrbk; Kent St Univ; Theater.

SMERIK, JAN; Parkway HS; Celina, OH; 7/96 Hon Rl; Yrbk; FHA; Pep Clb; College; Commercial Art.

SMERIK, JAN E; Parkway HS; Celina, OH; 7/96 Am Leg Aux Girls St; Hon Rl; Yrbk; FHA; Pep Clb; Univ; Interior Dsgn.

SMETTERS, HELEN; Madison HS; Unionville, OH; Band; Chrs; Hon Rl; Pol Wkr; Bsbl; Letter Hockey; IM Sprt; Scr Kpr; Akron Univ.

SMIDT, LUANN; Bangor HS; Bangor, MI; 3/98 Sec Frsh Cls; Trs Frsh Cls; Cl Rep Jr Cls; Am Leg Aux Girls St; Band; Cmp Fr Grls; Chrh Wkr; Pres Yth Flsp; Yrbk; Chrldng; Kalamazoo Valley Comm Coll; Drafting.

SMIENSKI, LAURA; Holy Name Nazareth HS; Parma, OH; Hon Rl; Clerical.

SMIGIELSKI, LAURA; Cousino HS; Warren, MI; Cls Rep Frsh Cls; Cls Rep Soph Cls; Girl Scts; FBLA; Rdo Clb; Chrldng; Macomb Community College; Bus Mgmt.

SMILEY, BRYAN; Southwestern HS; Detroit, MI; Cls Rep Frsh Cls; Cls Rep Soph Cls; Cl Rep Jr Cls; Cls Rep Sr Cls; Band; Chrs; Hon Rl; Sch Mus; Sch Nwsp; Sci Clb; Mi St Band & Orch Asooc 1st Pl 76 & 78; Oakland Univ; Music.

SMILEY, JERRY; Reading HS; Reading, OH; 39/219 Cls Rep Frsh Cls; Cls Rep Soph Cls; Cl Rep Jr Cls; Cls Rep Sr Cls; Aud/Vis; Hon Rl; Stu Cncl; Rptr Sch Nwsp; Rdo Clb; Univ Of Ohio; Elec Engineer.

SMILEY, MARY; Mooresville HS; Camby, IN; 75/269 AFS; Hon Rl; Lbry Ade; Spn Clb; Work.

SMILEY, TERESA; Dayton Christian HS; Dayton, OH; Cls Rep Soph Cls; Cl Rep Jr Cls; Cls Rep Sr Cls; Chrs; Hon Rl; Sch Mus; Stu Cncl; Chrldng; Cit Awd; Ldrshp Awd Chrldng Camp Bryan Coll 78; Total Person Awd DCS 79; Kettering Coll; Nursing.

SMILLIE, LYNN; Norwalk Sr HS; Norwalk, OH; Band; Drl Tm; Hon Rl; 4-H; Lat Clb; Pep Clb; GAA; Pom Pon; St English Tests; Miami Univ; Acctg.

SMILO, DEBRA; Maumee HS; Maumee, OH; 62/316 VP Jr Cls; Cmnty Wkr; Girl Scts; Hon Rl; Stu Cncl; Scr Kpr; BGSU; Psychology.

SMITH, ADAM; Shelby Sr HS; Shelby, OH; Band; Chrs; Hon Rl; Orch; Sch Mus; Fr Clb; Lat Clb; Natl Merit Ltr; Univ; Comp Sci.

SMITH, ALLISON; Cuyahoga Falls HS; Cuyahoga Falls, OH; Band; Chrs; Hon Rl; Hosp Ade; Orch; Sch Mus; Pres Yth Flsp; Rotary Awd; NHS; Miami Coll.

SMITH, ALLISON; Pontiac Northern HS; Pontiac, MI; Hon Rl; Trade Schl; Comp Tech.

SMITH, ALYCE; Shady Spring HS; Beaver, WV; Chrh Wkr; FCA; Hon Rl; JA; Lbry Ade; NHS; Off Ade; Sch Pl; Yth Flsp; Ed Yrbk; Principals List Award 79; Univ; Comp Sci.

SMITH, AMY; Continental Local HS; Continental, OH; 1/59 Cls Rep Frsh Cls; Val; Am Leg Aux Girls St; Hon Rl; NHS; Off Ade; Stu Cncl; Treas Yrbk; Spn Clb; Am Leg Awd; Defiance Coll; Med Tech.

SMITH, AMY; Mentor HS; Mentor, OH; 15/761 Am Leg Aux Girls St; Pres Jr NHS; NHS; Stu Cncl; Ed Sch Nwsp; Letter Gym; Chrldng; Cit Awd; DAR Awd; Ohio State Univ; Business Admin.

SMITH, ANDREA; Fenton HS; Fenton, MI; Band; Chrs; Debate Tm; Hon Rl; College; Sci.

SMITH, ANDREW; Portsmouth East HS; Portsmouth, OH; 6/88 Am Leg Boys St; Band; Hon Rl; Letter Ftbl; Rotary Awd; Ohio St Univ; Sci.

SMITH, ANDY; Maumee HS; Maumee, OH; 4/316 Debate Tm; Hon Rl; Natl Forn Lg; NHS; Yrbk; Fr Clb; Natl Merit Ltr; Sup Rating At 79 St Of Oh Sci Fair; St Of Oh Sup Achmvnt In Math Awd; Oh Sclstc Achvmnt Tst In Chem 78; Univ; Bus.

SMITH, ANGELA E; Cardinal Ritter HS; Indianapolis, IN; 19/147 Chrs; Chrh Wkr; Drl Tm; Hon Rl; Mod UN; NHS; Sch Mus; Rptr Yrbk; Spn Clb; Pom Pon; Cert Of Awds In World History Typing & Religion; Outstanding Rifle Mdls; Butler Univ; Business.

SMITH, ANNETTE; Flemington HS; Flemington, WV; 1/48 Pres Sr Cls; Val; Am Leg Aux Girls St; Band; NHS; Key Clb; VP VICA; Bsktbl; Scr Kpr; 4-H Awd; Marshall Univ; Pharmacy.

SMITH, ANNETTE; Meadow Bridge HS; Layland, WV; Chrs; Chrh Wkr; Hon Rl; Hosp Ade; 4-H; FHA; FNA; VICA; 4-H Awd; Nurse Asst.

SMITH, ANNETTE; Hazel Park HS; Hazel Park, MI; 1/306 Cmnty Wkr; NHS; Pol Wkr; Fr Clb; Treas Pep Clb; Letter Ten; Mgrs; Scr Kpr; Cit Awd; VFW Awd; Alma Coll; Comp Sci.

SMITH, ANN M; New Lexington HS; New Lexington, OH; 31/180 Trs Frsh Cls; Trs Soph Cls; Trs Jr Cls; Trs Sr Cls; Hon Rl; Treas NHS; Treas Stu Cncl; 4-H; VP FHA; Treas Spn Clb; Ohio St Univ; Phys Ther.

SMITH, APRIL; Triad HS; Urbana, OH; 2/77 Sec Jr Cls; Sal; Chrs; Hon Rl; Jr NHS; NHS; Sch Pl; Stu Cncl; Beta Clb; 4-H; Perpetual Schlrshp 79; PTO Schlrshp 79; Salutatoriam Of Grad Class & Sr Homecoming Attndnt 74; Wittenberg Univ; Acctg.

SMITH, APRIL; Milan HS; Milan, MI; Univ; Phys Ther.

SMITH, APRIL; Norton HS; Norton, OH; 16/300 Chrs; Chrh Wkr; Girl Scts; Hon Rl; Jr NHS; Off Ade; Yth Flsp; IM Sprt; Akron Univ; Acctg.

SMITH, ARLENE; Clinton Prairie HS; Frankfort, IN; 4/90 Chrs; Chrh Wkr; Hon Rl; NHS; Sch Mus; Rptr Sch Nwsp; Lat Clb; Bsktbl; Coll.

SMITH, BARB; Parkersburg South HS; Parkersburg, WV; Pres Frsh Cls; Cls Rep Soph Cls; Cls Rep Sr Cls; Hon Rl; Stu Cncl; Rptr Yrbk; Rptr Sch Nwsp; Stdnt Councl Awd 76; Jrnslm Awd 76; Parkersburg Beauty Coll; Beautician.

SMITH, BARBARA; Franklin Central HS; Indpls, IN; Indiana Univ; Jrnlsm.

SMITH, BARBARA; Anderson Sr HS; Anderson, IN; 89/419 Chrh Wkr; Cmnty Wkr; Hosp Ade; JA; Pres Yth Flsp; FHA; OEA; Silver Medl For Storytelling Event 79; Exec Diplomat Stateswmn & Mabassador Awds 79; Hoosier Schlr 79; Ball St Univ; Comp Sci.

SMITH, BARBARA; Waterloo HS; Atwater, OH; 4/150 Band; Hon Rl; Rptr Sch Nwsp; Beta Clb; 4-H; Mth Clb; Elk Awd; Ohio State; Comp Sci.

SMITH, BARRY; St Alphonsus HS; Detroit, MI; 12/189 VP Frsh Cls; Pres Soph Cls; Aud/Vis; Chrs; Hon Rl; NHS; Sch Mus; Sch Pl; Stu Cncl; Bsbl; Univ; Law Enfrcmt.

SMITH, BART; National Trail HS; W Manchester, OH; Sec Frsh Cls; FFA; Letter Bsbl; Letter Bsktbl; Letter Glf; Bsbl Bst Attidtd Trophy 79; Marshall For Grad 79; Farmer.

SMITH, BECKY; Clinton Central HS; Michigantown, IN; 3/106 Pres Soph Cls; Band; Drm Mjrt; NHS; 4-H; FHA; Pep Clb; Purdue Univ; Management.

SMITH, BELINDA; Wayne HS; Ft Wayne, IN; 35/321 Chrs; Chrh Wkr; Hon Rl; Off Ade; OEA; Spn Clb; Spnsh Awd; Acctg Awd; Outstndng COE Stdnt Awd & Hoosier Schlr Awd; Tomlinson Coll; Elem Educ.

SMITH, BETH; Franklin Cmnty HS; Franklin, IN; 36/300 Band; FCA; Hon Rl; Jr NHS; Stu Cncl; Eng Clb; Lat Clb; Pep Clb; Sci Clb; PPFtbl; Ball St Univ; Tchr.

SMITH, BETH; Ontario HS; Mansfield, OH; 11/198 Hon Rl; Jr NHS; Treas NHS; Stg Crw; Akron Coll; Mech Engr.

SMITH, BETSY; Terre Haute North Vigo HS; Terre Haute, IN; Chrs; Chrh Wkr; Hon Rl; Y-Teens; DECA; Bus Schl; Sec.

SMITH, BETTY; Walter P Chrysler HS; New Castle, IN; Chrh Wkr; Hon Rl; Yth Flsp; OEA; Opt Clb Awd; Tennessee Temple Coll; Acctg.

SMITH, BEVERLY; Saline HS; Saline, MI; 23/245 Sec Jr Cls; Hon Rl; Sec NHS; Letter Bsbl; Letter Bsktbl; Cert Of Recogntn From St Of Mi Comp Schlrshp Prog 79; Grad With Hon From Saline HS 79; Michigan St Univ; Nursing.

SMITH, BONITA; Chaminade Julienne HS; Dayton, OH; Cmp Fr Grls; Chrs; Chrh Wkr; Cmnty Wkr; Girl Scts; Sch Pl; Sct Actv; Yth Flsp; Y-Teens; Pep Clb; Dayton Urban League Chrmn Of Recreation Comm; Univ Of Notre Dame; Comp Sci.

SMITH, BONNIE; Andrews Acad; Berrien Sprgs, MI; Aud/Vis; Chrs; NHS; Off Ade; Rptr Sch Nwsp; Sch Nwsp; Andrews Univ; Nursing.

SMITH, BRAD; Holland Chrstn HS; Holland, MI; Chrh Wkr; Hon Rl; Mod UN; NHS; Sch Pl; Stg Crw; Letter Crs Cntry; Letter Trk; IM Sprt; Natl Merit Schl; BEOG 79; St Of Mis 79; Pres Workshp For Young Amer 79; Hope Coll; Music.

SMITH, BRADFORD; Adrian Sr HS; Adrian, MI; 33/386 Band; Debate Tm; Hon Rl; Orch; Sch Mus; Sch Pl; Drama Clb; Mth Clb; Treas JA Awd; Rotary Awd; Finalist In GTCTM 75; Outstanding Thespian 79; St Conductor For Chr & Orch & Band 77 79; Western Michigan Univ; Theater.

SMITH, BRADLEY; Addison HS; Addison, MI; 1/115 Pres Soph Cls; Val; Am Leg Boys St; Chrs; VP NHS; Pres Stu Cncl; Drama Clb; Wrstlng; Kiwan Awd; Natl Merit SF; Cornell Univ; Agri.

SMITH, BRENDA; St Marys HS; Bens Run, WV; Band; Off Ade; Sch Pl; Stg Crw; Drama Clb; Pres 4-H; FHA; Pep Clb; Capt Trk; PPFtbl; Public Speaking Pin In 4 H 77 & 78; Alderson Broaddus Coll; Nursing.

SMITH, BRENDA; Winfield HS; Scott Depot, WV; 4/130 Sec Soph Cls; Trs Soph Cls; Sec Jr Cls; Trs Jr Cls; Sec Sr Cls; Trs Sr Cls; Chrh Wkr; Hon Rl; Jr NHS; NHS; Univ.

SMITH, BRIAN; Wellsville HS; Wellsville, OH; Hon Rl; IM Sprt; College; Chem.

SMITH, BRIAN; Broad Ripple HS; Indianapolis, IN; VP Frsh Cls; Trs Soph Cls; Cl Rep Jr Cls; Chrs; Hon Rl; NHS; Sch Mus; Sch Pl; Ger Clb; Letter Bsbl; Univ; Math.

SMITH, BRIEN; Saint Alphonsus HS; Detroit, MI; 10/180 VP Soph Cls; Cl Rep Jr Cls; Pres Sr Cls; Hon

Rl; NHS; Stu Cncl; Ed Yrbk; Rptr Sch Nwsp; Bsbl; Ferris State College; Optometry.

SMITH, BRIEN J; St Alphonsus HS; Detroit, MI; 9/190 Pres Frsh Cls; VP Soph Cls; Pres Sr Cls; Hon Rl; NHS; Sch Mus; Stu Cncl; Ed Yrbk; Bsbl; Ftbl; Ferris State Univ; Optometrist.

SMITH, BRUCE; Sidney HS; Sidney, OH; 49/250 Band; Chrh Wkr; Hon Rl; NHS; Sct Actv; Fr Clb; Key Clb; Capt Crs Cntry; Trk; Bowling Green St Univ; Pre Law.

SMITH, BRUCE; Lapeer East HS; North Branch, MI; 26/265 Am Leg Boys St; NHS; Wrstlng; Am Leg Awd; Mic Tech Univ; Engr.

SMITH, BRYON D; R Nelsen Snider HS; Ft Wayne, IN; Band; Chrs; Chrh Wkr; Hon Rl; Mdrgl; NHS; Sch Mus; College.

SMITH, CAREN M; Northwest HS; Pleasant Lake, MI; Girl Scts; Hon Rl; NHS; Yrbk; Rptr Sch Nwsp; 4-H; 4-H Awd; Jackson Comm Coll.

SMITH, CAROL; Troy HS; Troy, OH; Chrh Wkr; Hon Rl; Orch; Yth Flsp; OEA; IM Sprt; Tennessee Temple Univ; Busns.

SMITH, CAROL; Bridgeport HS; Bridgeport, WV; Am Leg Aux Girls St; Band; Girl Scts; Hon Rl; Pol Wkr; Spn Clb; Kiwan Awd; Wheeling College.

SMITH, CAROL; Hilliard HS; Hilliard, OH; 66/370 Girl Scts; Off Ade; Red Cr Ade; Sch Mus; Sch Pl; Sct Actv; Stg Crw; Yth Flsp; U S Air Force.

SMITH, CAROL; Portage Northern HS; Portage, MI; 51/410 Treas Band; Hon Rl; NHS; Sch Mus; Sch Pl; Stg Crw; Rptr Yrbk; Sci Clb; IM Sprt; Natl Merit Ltr; Western Mic Uni; Engr.

SMITH, CAROL; Our Lady Of Mercy HS; Farmington Hls, MI; 79/320 Cls Rep Frsh Cls; Cls Rep Soph Cls; Cl Rep Jr Cls; Am Leg Aux Girls St; Chrs; Cmnty Wkr; Off Ade; Pol Wkr; Stu Cncl; Pom Pon; Univ Of Michigan; Poli Sci.

SMITH, CAROLYN; Woodrow Wilson HS; Beckley, WV; 32/500 Cls Rep Frsh Cls; Cls Rep Soph Cls; VP Jr Cls; Cl Rep Jr Cls; Cls Rep Sr Cls; Am Leg Aux Girls St; Hon Rl; Jr NHS; Sec NHS; Sec Stu Cncl; Social Studies Awd 1976; Homecoming Queen 1978; Prom Attendnt 1979; Virginia Tech Univ; Vet Sci.

SMITH, CAROLYN; Bishop Noll Inst; Griffith, IN; 120/331 Cls Rep Soph Cls; Chrh Wkr; Hon Rl; Sch Mus; Stg Crw; Pep Clb; Indiana Univ.

SMITH, CARRIE; London HS; London, OH; 10/161 Hon Rl; Lit Mag; NHS; Sch Pl; Drama Clb; 4-H; Fr Clb; Letter Trk; Chrldng; Kiwan Awd; Ohio St Univ; Psych.

SMITH, CARRON; St Marys HS; Hebron, WV; Aud/Vis; Ed Yrbk; Sprt Ed Yrbk; Rptr Yrbk; Yrbk; Sprt Ed Sch Nwsp; Rptr Sch Nwsp; Sch Nwsp; Letter Trk; Miss Wv Natl Teen Ager St Finalist 79; Glenville St Univ; Jrnlsm.

SMITH, CATHERINE A; Northwest HS; Pleasant Lake, MI; 3/282 Girl Scts; Hon Rl; Lbry Ade; NHS; 4-H; Jackson Community College.

SMITH, CHANCELLOR; Emerson HS; Gary, IN; Band; Hon Rl; Lbry Ade; Boys Clb Am; Fr Clb; Trk; Wrstlng; Rcvd Awrd Eng 78 79; Rcvd Awrd Library Aide 78 79; Rcvd Awrd Hnr Roll 78 79; Purdue Univ; Acctg.

SMITH, CHERYL; Lutheran HS East; Cleveland, OH; Am Leg Aux Girls St; Cmp Fr Grls; Chrh Wkr; Girl Scts; Hon Rl; Lbry Ade; Off Ade; Sct Actv; Stu Cncl; Fr Clb; Martha Holdings Jennings Awd 78; 2nd Pl St Sci Fair In Physics 77; Michigan St Univ; Corp Law.

SMITH, CHERYL; Wooster HS; Wooster, OH; 25/362 Band; Chrs; Chrh Wkr; Hon Rl; NHS; Univ Of Akron; Acctg.

SMITH, CHERYL; Ecorse HS; Ecorse, MI; Band; Hon Rl; Hosp Ade; JA; Rptr Yrbk; Drama Clb; Rdo Clb; Mi Legislature Cert Of Merit 78 & 79; Kalamazoo Coll; Med.

SMITH, CHRIS; Princeton HS; Cincinnati, OH; 3/670 Hon Rl; Lat Clb; Mth Clb; Natl Merit Schl; Washington Univ; Physn.

SMITH, CHRIS; Southside HS; Monroe Falls, OH; Lbry Ade; FBLA; OEA; Akron Univ; Acctg.

SMITH, CHRIS; Gwinn HS; Montgomery, AL; Aud/Vis; Hon Rl; Lbry Ade; Orch; Yrbk; Sci Clb; Univ Of Texas; Sci.

SMITH, CHRISTOPHER; Bishop Dwenger HS; Ft Wayne, IN; Cls Rep Frsh Cls; Hon Rl; JA; Sch Mus; Sch Pl; Stg Crw; Y-Teens; Rptr Sch Nwsp; Sch Nwsp; Crs Cntry; Hon Awd In Literature & Speech; Univ; Econ.

SMITH, CHRISTOPHER; Ovid Elsie HS; Ovid, MI; Chrh Wkr; Crs Cntry; Wrstlng; Great Lakes Bible College.

SMITH, CINDI G; Howell HS; Howell, MI; 1/396 Val; Band; Chrs; Chrh Wkr; Drl Tm; Girl Scts; Hon Rl; NHS; Orch; Sch Mus; Michigan State Univ; Acctg.

SMITH, CLAIRE; Mansfield Sr HS; Mansfield, OH; 2/309 Sal; Am Leg Aux Girls St; Chrh Wkr; Girl Scts; NHS; Red Cr Ade; Stu Cncl; Chrldng; Am Leg Awd; Outsdng Soph Girl 76; Univ Of Mi Hon Trophy Awd 78; Amer Assn Of Univ Awd 78; Univ Of Cincinnati; Surg Nurse.

SMITH, CYNTHIA; Caro Community HS; Caro, MI; VP Jr Cls; Band; Debate Tm; Hon Rl; Natl Forn Lg; NHS; Sch Mus; Sch Pl; Pep Clb; 17 Band Medals 76 79; Tri County Hon Band E Mi Univ Hon Band 76 79; Band Boosters & Musical Arts Schlrshp; Eastern Michigan Univ; Music Educ.

SMITH, CYNTHIA; Columbian HS; Tiffin, OH; 41/342 Band; Chrh Wkr; Hon Rl; NHS; Yth Flsp; Sch Nwsp; VP 4-H; Bsktbl; Ohio State Univ; Med.

SMITH, D; Marion Pleasant HS; Marion, OH; Girl Scts; Bsktbl; Trk; Coach Actv; IM Sprt;.

SMITH, D; Barnesville HS; Barnesville, OH; 1/100 Trs Jr Cls; Am Leg Boys St; Hon Rl; Treas NHS; Fr Clb; Treas Key Clb; College; Acct.

SMITH, DANE; Watkins Memorial HS; Baltimore, OH; Cls Rep Sr Cls; FCA; Hon Rl; Lbry Ade; NHS; Quill & Scroll; Rptr Sch Nwsp; Spn Clb; Capt Ftbl; Wrstlng; Honorable Mention Awd; Ohio Univ; Medicine.

SMITH, DANIEL; Nordonia HS; Macedonia, OH; 127/440 Hon Rl; Letter Socr; Letter Wrstlng; Miami Univ; Indust Educ.

SMITH, DANIEL; Central HS; Detroit, MI; Hon Rl; Fr Clb; Bsbl; Ftbl; Ten; IM Sprt; JETS Awd; Univ; Engr.

SMITH, DAUNEDA; North Miami HS; Roann, IN; 18/122 Cls Rep Soph Cls; Cl Rep Jr Cls; Cls Rep Sr Cls; Am Leg Aux Girls St; Band; NHS; Stu Cncl; 4-H; Pep Clb; Bsbl; Upper Wabash Voc Schl; Data Process.

SMITH, DAVE; Stow HS; Munroe Falls, OH; Letter Ftbl; Coach Actv; Stow Varsity Club VP 79; Univ; Sci.

SMITH, DAVID; Boonville HS; Boonville, IN; 44/265 Hst Frsh Cls; Chrh Wkr; Hon Rl; NHS; Yrbk; IM Sprt; Indiana St Univ; Engr Chem.

SMITH, DAVID; Princeton HS; Princeton, WV; 146/345 Cl Rep Jr Cls; Chrh Wkr; Hon Rl; Sch Mus; Sch Pl; Letter Crs Cntry; Letter Trk; JA Awd; Voc School; Elec.

SMITH, DAVID; Buckeye North HS; Smithfield, OH; 17/100 Chrs; Hon Rl; IM Sprt; College; Eng.

SMITH, DAVID A; Lakota HS; Westchester, OH; 15/500 Cls Rep Frsh Cls; Cls Rep Soph Cls; Band; Boy Scts; Hon Rl; NHS; Yth Flsp; Sci Clb; Letter Bsktbl; Natl Merit SF; Univ; Physcis.

SMITH, DAVID G; Douglas Mac Arthur HS; Saginaw, MI; Band; Boy Scts; Chrs; Hon Rl; Lit Mag; VP MMM; NHS; Orch; Sch Mus; Sct Actv; Chosen 1st Chair French Horn In Blue Lake Intl Band; Twice Sel For Mi All St Hnrs Orchestra; Awd For Music; College; Music.

SMITH, DEAN; Coventry HS; Barberton, OH; 47/204 Cl Rep Jr Cls; Sct Actv; Stu Cncl; Fr Clb; Spn Clb; Akron Univ; For Lang.

SMITH, DEANNA; Roosevelt HS; E Chicago, IN; 27/199 Cl Rep Jr Cls; Sec Sr Cls; Chrs; Chrh Wkr; Debate Tm; Hon Rl; Natl Forn Lg; Orch; Stu Cncl; Drama Clb; Jackson State; Speech Ther.

SMITH, DEANNE; North Central HS; Kunkle, OH; Cls Rep Frsh Cls; Cls Rep Soph Cls; Cl Rep Jr Cls; Am Leg Aux Girls St; Band; Chrs; Girl Scts; Hon Rl; Sch Pl; Sec Stu Cncl; Otstndng Sci Stud 77; Sci Fair 77; Univ; Lab Tech.

SMITH, DEBBIE; Fremont HS; Fremont, IN; 8/49 VP Jr Cls; Trs Jr Cls; VP NHS; 4-H; Pep Clb; Trk; 4-H Awd; Purdue Univ; Horticulture.

SMITH, DEBBIE; Mariemont HS; Terrace Pk, OH; 39/169 AFS; Band; Chrs; Sch Mus; Pep Clb; Letter Bsktbl; Socr; Letter Trk; Coach Actv; PPFtbl; College; Profession.

SMITH, DEBI; Cadiz HS; New Athens, OH; 30/104 Am Leg Aux Girls St; Band; Girl Scts; Hon Rl; Orch; 4-H; Lat Clb; GAA; 4-H Awd; Recv A Letter In Band; College; Nursing.

SMITH, DEBORAH; High School; Frankfort, IN; Band; Chrs; Girl Scts; Hon Rl; 4-H; Pep Clb; 4-H Awd; Modeling Schl; Model.

SMITH, DEBORAH; Lexington HS; Lexington, OH; 28/271 Band; Chrs; Hosp Ade; NHS; Y-Teens; Trk; Mgrs; Ohio St Univ.

SMITH, DEBORAH L; Wilbur Wright HS; Dayton, OH; 44/218 Sec Jr Cls; Sec Sr Cls; Cmnty Wkr; Hon Rl; Off Ade; Stu Cncl; Rptr Yrbk; Rptr Sch Nwsp; Sch Nwsp; FBLA; Sharkey Schl; Modeling.

SMITH, DEBRA; Graham HS; Urbana, OH; 5/165 Chrs; Chrh Wkr; Cmnty Wkr; Hon Rl; NHS; VP Yth Flsp; FHA; Bsktbl; Trk; GAA; Miami Univ; Art/sci.

SMITH, DEBRA; Manistique HS; Manistique, MI; 3/132 Hon Rl; NHS; IM Sprt; Rotary Awd; Lake Superior St Coll; Sec.

SMITH, DEBRA; Northwestern HS; West Salem, OH; Band; Chrs; Chrh Wkr; Sch Pl; Yth Flsp; Drama Clb; 4-H; FTA; Spn Clb; Grace College; Music.

SMITH, DEBRA; New Albany HS; New Albany, OH; Chrs; Sch Pl; Drama Clb; 4-H; Pep Clb; Bsbl; Ohio State Univ; Vet Med.

SMITH, DENISE; Decatur HS; Decatur, MI; 3/74 Hon Rl; Jr NHS; NHS; Sec 4-H; Chrldng; Mic State Univ; Interior Design.

SMITH, DENISE; Ellet Sr HS; Akron, OH; Hon Rl; NHS; Off Ade; Treas Stu Cncl; Sec OEA; Scr Kpr; Univ Of Akron; Acctg.

SMITH, DENISE; Potterville HS; Potterville, MI; 5/67 Pres Soph Cls; Pres Jr Cls; Pres Sr Cls; Band; Chrs; Drl Tm; Hon Rl; NHS; Rptr Sch Nwsp; Pep Clb; Most Dedicated Cheerleader; Home Ec Awd; Honor Roll Awd; Lansing Comm Coll; Busns Admin.

SMITH, DENISE L A; Immaculata HS; Detroit, MI; 3/93 Cls Rep Frsh Cls; Cl Rep Jr Cls; Chrh Wkr; Hon Rl; Jr NHS; Natl Forn Lg; NHS; Rptr Yrbk; Yrbk; Rptr Sch Nwsp; Univ; Poli Sci.

SMITH, DIANA; Gilmer Cnty HS; Glenville, WV; Hon Rl; Stu Cncl; Yth Flsp; Mth Clb; Pep Clb; Bsktbl; GAA; Glenville St Coll; Acctg.

SMITH, DIANA G; West Muskingum HS; Zanesville, OH; 1/161 Trs Soph Cls; Trs Jr Cls; Trs Sr Cls; Band; Chrs; Chrh Wkr; Cmnty Wkr; Girl Scts; Hon Rl; Hosp Ade; Univ.

SMITH, DIANE; Colon HS; Sherwood, MI; Band; Chrs; Capt Drl Tm; Girl Scts; Hon Rl; Sch Mus; Stg Crw; Pres Stu Cncl; Pep Clb; Chrldng; Coll; Educ.

SMITH, DIANE; Ft Recovery HS; Ft Recovery, OH; 10/73 Am Leg Aux Girls St; Band; Hon Rl; NHS; Stu Cncl; FHA; OEA; GAA; IM Sprt; PPFtbl; Bus.

SMITH, DIANE; Unionville Sebewaing HS; Sebewaing, MI; 11/113 Sec Sr Cls; Chrs; Hon Rl; NHS; Off Ade; Stu Cncl; Yth Flsp; 4-H; FHA; Bsktbl; Delta Coll; Dent Asst.

SMITH, DIANE MARIE; Our Lady Of Mt Carmel HS; Wyandotte, MI; 14/68 Hon Rl; Sch Mus; Rptr Sch Nwsp; Pep Clb; Letter Bsktbl; Chrldng; IM Sprt; Pres Awd; Schl Jr Serv Awrd 78; Michigan St Univ; Psych.

SMITH, DI ANNA; Tuslaw HS; Massillon, OH; Girl Scts; Hon Rl; Hosp Ade; Jr NHS; Natl Forn Lg; Sch Mus; 4-H; FHA; FNA; College; Nursing.

SMITH, DONNA; Harman HS; Dry Fork, WV; VP Jr Cls; Band; Chrs; Chrh Wkr; Hon Rl; Ed Yrbk; Sec FBLA; Bsktbl; Chrldng; Clerical Awd 79; Extra Office Work Plaque 79; Davis & Elkins Coll; Engr.

SMITH, DORA M; East HS; Youngstown, OH; 13/180 Band; Drm Mjrt; Treas NHS; VP Stu Cncl; DECA; Treas Key Clb; Spn Clb; Letter Trk; Pom Pon; Letter Scr Kpr; Youngstown St Univ; Med Lab Tech.

SMITH, DORCELLA J; Mifflin HS; Columbus, OH; Pres Jr Cls; Am Leg Aux Girls St; Off Ade; Red Cr Ade; Stu Cncl; Chrldng; Scr Kpr; Tmr; College; Bus Admin.

SMITH, DOROTHY; Brown County HS; Morgantown, IN; VP Band; Chrh Wkr; Hon Rl; Jr NHS; NHS; Orch; Fr Clb; Pres FHA; Inidana Univ; Nursing.

SMITH, DOUGLAS; Gibsonburg HS; Gibsonburg, OH; 6/105 VP Jr Cls; Cl Rep Jr Cls; Pres Sr Cls; Boy Scts; Hon Rl; Stu Cncl; Trk; Wrstlng; Mgrs; Scr Kpr; Greater Toledo Coun Of Tchrs Math Semi Finalist 77 79; Oh Coun Of Tchrs Math Semi Finalist 78; Univ; Comp Progr.

SMITH, DOUGLAS; Marysville HS; Marysville, OH; 28/230 Pres Soph Cls; Chrs; Debate Tm; Natl Forn Lg; NHS; IM Sprt; Univ; Comp Sci.

SMITH, DOUGLAS; Tri Valley HS; Nashport, OH; 47/220 Band; Chrh Wkr; Drm Bgl; FCA; Hon Rl; Yth Flsp; Spn Clb; Bsbl; Glf; Ohi Univ; Radio & Tv Comm.

SMITH, DOUGLAS; Padua Franciscan HS; Seven Hills, OH; Cls Rep Soph Cls; Cl Rep Jr Cls; Hon Rl; Fr Clb; Bsktbl; Glf; IM Sprt; Golf Letter; Busns Schl; Busns Mgmt.

SMITH, DUANE; De Kalb HS; Waterloo, IN; 7/292 Band; Chrh Wkr; Hon Rl; NHS; 4-H; Ger Clb; Honorary Hoosier Schlrshp; German Club Schlrshp; Dollars For Scholars Schlrshp; Huntington Coll; Busns Mgmt.

SMITH, DUANE; Lapeer East HS; Lapeer, MI; Hon Rl; NHS; Letter Wrstlng; Michigan St Univ; Pre Med.

SMITH, DUANE; Linden Mc Kinley HS; Columbus, OH; Hon Rl; IM Sprt; Winston Salem St Univ; Law Enfrcmnt.

SMITH, E; Garrett HS; Garrett, IN; 3/131 Band; Hon Rl; NHS; Ger Clb; Bsktbl; Letter Crs Cntry; Letter Trk; GAA; Natl Merit Ltr; Univ.

SMITH, EDGAR L; Catholic Central HS; Southfield, MI; Boy Scts; Cmnty Wkr; Hon Rl; JA; Sch Pl; Sct Actv; Rptr Sch Nwsp; Drama Clb; VP Sci Clb; Trk; Outstndg Yth 77; Cert Of Recogntn Comptn Schlrshp 79; Achvmnt Awds In Publc Rltns & Sci Club 77 79; Morehouse Coll; Labor Mgmt.

SMITH, EDWARD; Warren Woods HS; Warren, MI; 20/360 Hon Rl; Jr NHS; NHS; Glf; IM Sprt; Natl Merit Ltr; Natl Merit SF; Natl Merit Schl; Pres Awd; Wayne St Univ; Pre Bus.

SMITH, EFFIE M; Marian Heights Academy; Chicago, IL; Chrs; Chrh Wkr; Cmnty Wkr; Girl Scts; Hon Rl; Off Ade; PAVAS; Sch Mus; Sch Pl; Treas Sdlty; 1st Pl Music Contest Voice Soloist Dist; 1st Pl Music Contest Voice & Trio Soloist Dist & State; Talledega Coll; Busns Admin.

SMITH, ELDON; Miami Trace HS; New Holland, OH; Band; FCA; Hon Rl; Yth Flsp; FSA; Sci Clb; Crs Cntry; Trk; Mas Awd; Math.

SMITH, ELIZABETH; Mariemont HS; Terrace Pk, OH; Sec Sr Cls; Band; Chrs; Girl Scts; Sch Mus; Pep Clb; Spn Clb; Trk; Chrldng; Pom Pon; Univ; Educ.

SMITH, EVERETT; Hammond Tech Voc HS; Hammond, IN; 50/210 Hon Rl; Sprt Ed Yrbk; Rptr Yrbk; Sprt Ed Sch Nwsp; Rptr Sch Nwsp; Sch Nwsp; DECA; Letter Bsbl; Ftbl; Purdue Univ; Jrnlsm.

SMITH, FORREST C; Tucker County HS; Parsons, WV; Am Leg Boys St; Hon Rl; NHS; 4-H; Sec Key Clb; Letter Glf; Potomac State Coll; Comp Sci.

SMITH, GARY; Jennings County HS; Scipio, IN; 102/360 Boy Scts; Chrs; Chrh Wkr; Sch Mus; Sch Pl; Stg Crw; Boys Clb Am; 4-H; FTA; Spn Clb; Perfect Attendance Grades 1 12 67 79; A Hoosier Schlr 79; Govt Awd 79; Coll; Real Estate.

SMITH, GAY; Beal City HS; Weidman, MI; 1/64 Val; Aud/Vis; Band; Capt Drl Tm; Hon Rl; Pres NHS; Stg Crw; Ed Yrbk; Pres Sci Clb; Michigan St Competitive Schlrshp; Central Michigan Bd Of Trustees Schlrshp; HS Sci Awd; Central Michigan Univ; Chem.

SMITH, GERALD; Pontiac Northern HS; Pontiac, MI; 36/450 Boy Scts; Hon Rl; NHS; Orch; Yth Flsp; Mth Clb; Letter Swmmng; Coach Actv; Mgrs; God Cntry Awd; Michigan Tech Univ; Mech Engr.

SMITH, GERALD R; Buckeye North HS; Mingo Jct, OH; 10/119 Cls Rep Frsh Cls; Band; Boy Scts; Chrs; Chrh Wkr; Hon Rl; NHS; Stg Crw; Sci Clb; Ftbl; 1977 Whos Who; Mount Union Univ; Comp Tech.

SMITH, GLENDA; Mount View HS; Welch, WV; Chrh Wkr; Hon Rl; Jr NHS; Yth Flsp; Keyettes; Pep Clb; Coll.

SMITH, GLORIA; Washington Sr HS; Washington, OH; Pres Frsh Cls; Cls Rep Frsh Cls; Sec Soph Cls; Cls Rep Soph Cls; AFS; Hon Rl; Stu Cncl; Y-Teens; Chrldng; Univ; Med.

SMITH, GLORIA; Romulus HS; Romulus, MI; Sec Soph Cls; VP Sr Cls; Hon Rl; Hosp Ade; NHS; Stu Cncl; VICA; Univ Of Mic; Nursing.

SMITH, GREG; Frontier HS; Newport, OH; Cls Rep Sr Cls; Chrh Wkr; Hon Rl; Sct Actv; Stu Cncl; Yth Flsp; Letter Bsbl; 1st Pl Awd In Wrld Geography 77; 2nd Pl Awd In Bldg Ctzns 77; 2nd Pl Awd In Draft 78; Univ; Acctg.

SMITH, GREG; Highland HS; Anderson, IN; Band; Boy Scts; Cmp Fr Grls; Debate Tm; FCA; Hon Rl; Yth Flsp; Rptr Sch Nwsp; Ger Clb; Cit Awd; Anderson Coll; Comp Bus.

SMITH, GREGORY; Brooke HS; Wellsburg, WV; 62/466 Cls Rep Soph Cls; Am Leg Boys St; Hon Rl; JA; NHS; Pol Wkr; VP Fr Clb; VP Key Clb; Sci Clb; IM Sprt; West Virginia Wesleyan Coll; Dent.

SMITH, GREGORY; Yellow Springs HS; Yellow Sprg, OH; Band; Boy Scts; Sch Mus; Sct Actv; Sch Nwsp; Fr Clb; Bsbl; Bsktbl; Ten; Cit Awd; College; Med.

SMITH, GREGORY; Brooke HS; Weirton, WV; Boy Scts; Hon Rl; Sct Actv; Ftbl; Jeff Teck Steubenville Univ; Engr.

SMITH, GREGORY R; Tygarts Valley HS; Dailey, WV; 11/54 VP Frsh Cls; VP Soph Cls; Chrs; Hon Rl; NHS; Stu Cncl; VP Leo Clb; Bsbl; Bsktbl; Capt Ftbl; Potomac State Coll; Forestry.

SMITH, HAROLD; Zanesville HS; Zanesville, OH; 148/383 Boy Scts; Hon Rl; Sci Clb; Crs Cntry; Letter Trk; Mgrs; Coll.

SMITH, HEIDI; Pickerington HS; Pickerington, OH; Chrs; Chrh Wkr; Hon Rl; Lbry Ade; NHS; VP Yth Flsp; Fr Clb; Tmr; Univ; Eng.

SMITH, HEIDI A; Beaver Local HS; E Liverpool, OH; Band; Chrh Wkr; Cmnty Wkr; Hon Rl; Jr NHS; Off Ade; Pol Wkr; Sch Mus; Yth Flsp; IM Sprt; Univ; Sociology.

SMITH, IRENE; Jefferson Area HS; Jefferson, OH; 12/190 Chrs; Hon Rl; Pres Yth Flsp; FTA; Treas Spn Clb; Rotary Awd; Grace Coll; Math Educ.

SMITH, ISABELLE; Farmington HS; Northville, MI; Band; Cmnty Wkr; Hon Rl; Letter Bsktbl; Letter Swmmng; GAA; IM Sprt; PPFtbl; Twrlr; Mich State Univ; Marine Bio.

SMITH, JACKIE K; Pennfield HS; Bellevue, MI; 16/150 Chrs; NHS; Sch Mus; Sch Pl; Stu Cncl; Drama Clb; Pres Spn Clb; Mi Comp Schlrshp 79; Gifted & Talented Educ Project For Futuristic Studies Awd 79; Univ Of Michigan; Sci.

SMITH, JACQUELINE; Three Rivers HS; Three Rivers, MI; Band; Girl Scts; Hon Rl; Hosp Ade; NHS; Rptr Sch Nwsp; Fr Clb; Pep Clb; College; Bus.

SMITH, JAMES; Southgate HS; Southgate, MI; 17/400 Cls Rep Frsh Cls; Boy Scts; Hon Rl; Sct Actv; Stu Cncl; Ten; Math Awd For Highest Math Stu; Univ Of Michigan; Language.

SMITH, JAMES; National Trail HS; Eaton, OH; 10/130 Cls Rep Sr Cls; Am Leg Boys St; Boy Scts; Hon Rl; Sct Actv; Stg Crw; Stu Cncl; Am Leg Awd; DAR Awd; God Cntry Awd; Bus Schl.

SMITH, JAMES; London HS; London, OH; 18/160 Am Leg Boys St; Hon Rl; Jr NHS; NHS; Sch Pl; Rptr Sch Nwsp; Drama Clb; Bsktbl; Letter Crs Cntry; Letter Trk; College; Law.

SMITH, JAMES; Westview Jr Sr HS; Shipshewana, IN; 2/83 Sal; Band; Boy Scts; Hon Rl; NHS; Sct Actv; Yth Flsp; Trk; Letter Wrstlng; Scr Kpr; Vennard Coll; Missionary.

SMITH, JAMES H; Arlington HS; Indianapolis, IN; 11/304 Cls Rep Soph Cls; Chrs; Cmnty Wkr; Hon Rl; Jr NHS; Mdrgl; MMM; NHS; PAVAS; Sch Mus; Cert For Help In Keep Amer Beautiful; Academic Schlrshp To ISU; Indiana St Univ; Archt.

SMITH, JAMI; Lincolnview HS; Van Wert, OH; Cls Rep Frsh Cls; Cl Rep Jr Cls; Cls Rep Sr Cls; VP Stu Cncl; Bsktbl; Chrldng; GAA; Scr Kpr; Mdse.

SMITH, JAMIE; Robert S Rogers HS; Toledo, OH; Hon Rl; Hosp Ade; NHS; Off Ade; Sch Mus; Yth Fls p; Rptr Yrbk; 4-H; Treas Lat Clb; VP Sci Clb; Univ; Math.

SMITH, JAMIE; Rogers HS; Toledo, OH; Hon Rl; Hosp Ade; NHS; Sch Mus; Yth Flsp; Rptr Yrbk; Treas Lat Clb; Sci Clb; Am Leg Awd; JC Awd; College; Vet.

SMITH, JAN; Lapel HS; Lapel, IN; Band; Cmnty Wkr; Hon Rl; JA; Off Ade; Rptr Yrbk; 4-H; FHA; OEA; Pep Clb; Appex Beauty Schl; Beautician.

SMITH, JANELLE; Ravenna HS; Ravenna, OH; 9/320 Chrs; Hon Rl; Hosp Ade; Lbry Ade; Stg Crw; Yrbk; Spn Clb; Kent State Univ; Nursing.

SMITH, JANET; Broad Ripple HS; Indianapolis, IN; Cl Rep Jr Cls; Am Leg Aux Girls St; Chrs; Chrh Wkr; Hon Rl; Orch; PAVAS; Sch Mus; Sch Pl; Sec Stu Cncl; Univ; Comp Sci.

SMITH, JANETTE; Connersville Sr HS; Cincinnati, OH; 25/400 Hon Rl; NHS; Fr Clb; Letter Bsktbl; Letter Trk; GAA; IM Sprt; PPFtbl; Kiwan Awd; Univ Of Cincinnati; Med Tech.

SMITH, JANICE; Portland HS; Portland, MI; Band; Chrh Wkr; Hon Rl; Stu Cncl; Yth Flsp; Pep Clb; Chrldng; PPFtbl; Lansing Bus Inst; Sec.

SMITH, JAYNE; Hilltop HS; W Unity, OH; 8/72 Trs Frsh Cls; Trs Jr Cls; Band; Chrs; Drm Mjrt; Hon Rl; Pres Yth Flsp; 4-H; Chrldng; Scr Kpr; Vllybll Lttr Earned; Softball; Univ; Educ.

SMITH, JAYNE A; Western HS; Russiaville, IN; 32/220 Hon Rl; Drama Clb; FHA; Pep Clb; Sec Sci Clb; PPFtbl; Tmr; Indiana Univ; Art.

SMITH, J BRADLEY; Tell City HS; Tell City, IN; 40/225 Am Leg Boys St; Hon Rl; Pol Wkr; Pep Clb; Spn Clb; Bsbl; Letter Crs Cntry; IM Sprt; Rose Hulman Inst Of Tech.

SMITH, J C; Massillon Washington HS; Massillon, OH; Band; NHS; Ger Clb; Univ Of Akron; Music Educ.

SMITH, JEANNE; Brownsburg HS; Brownsburg, IN; Hon Rl; Jr NHS; NHS; Sec Lat Clb; Letter Swmmng; Ind Univ; Nurs.

SMITH, JEANNETTE; Ovid Elsie HS; Ovid, MI; Chrh Wkr; Girl Scts; Hon Rl; Hosp Ade; Sch Pl; Yrbk; 4-H; FHA; Pep Clb; Trk; Lansing Cmnty Coll; Nursing.

SMITH, JEFF; Washington Irving HS; Clarksburg, WV; Hon Rl; Bsktbl; Letter Trk; Univ; Bus Admin.

SMITH, JEFF; Lake HS; Walbridge, OH; Boy Scts; Chrs; Hon Rl; Sch Mus; Sch Pl; Stg Crw; Drama Clb; Letter Ftbl; Univ Of Toledo; Business Managment.

SMITH, JEFF; Blanchester HS; Blanchester, OH; 91/160 Cmnty Wkr; Sch Pl; Stg Crw; FFA; Bsktbl; IM Sprt; Ffa; 1st In Dairy Production 78; 1st In Acctg; 1st In Dairy Production 79; St Farmer Degree Production Agri; Tech Schl; Operating Engr.

SMITH, JEFFERSON; Northeastern HS; S Vienna, OH; 7/129 Hon Rl; JA; NHS; Ed Sch Nwsp; Drama Clb; Fr Clb; Ftbl; Bausch & Lomb Awd; JA Awd; Ohi State Univ; Chem.

SMITH, JEFFREY; Carmel HS; Carmel, IN; Hon Rl; NHS; Rdo Clb; Letter Ftbl; Trk; Wrstlng; Univ; Cmnctns.

SMITH, JEFFREY; St Peters HS; Lexington, OH; Chrh Wkr; JA; Lbry Ade; Sct Actv; Rptr Sch Nwsp; Bsbl; Ftbl; Wrstlng; IM Sprt; Ball St Univ; Jrnlsm.

SMITH, JEFFREY; Columbia City Joint HS; Columbia City, IN; Boy Scts; Sct Actv; Yrbk; Treas FTA; Letter Bsktbl; Letter Crs Cntry; Letter Trk; Univ; Archt.

SMITH, JEFFREY; Salem HS; Salem, IN; 1/150 Cl Rep Jr Cls; Am Leg Boys St; VP JA; Pres NHS; Stu Cncl; Sci Clb; Trk; Univ; Mech Engr.

SMITH, JEFFREY; Switzerland Cnty HS; Bennington, IN; 14/123 Am Leg Boys St; Hon Rl; Stg Crw; Sprt Ed Sch Nwsp; Rptr Sch Nwsp; Sch Nwsp; Drama Clb; Fr Clb; Sci Clb; Cit Awd; Vincinnes Univ; Acctg.

SMITH, JEFFREY D; Athens HS; Troy, MI; 18/470 Band; Chrh Wkr; FCA; Hon Rl; NHS; Sci Clb; Capt Glf; IM Sprt; Bausch & Lomb Awd; Natl Merit SF; Hawk Of The Yr For Golf 1978; Washington Univ; Med.

SMITH, JEFFREY T; Herbert Henry Dow HS; Midland, MI; 17/466 Hon Rl; Jr NHS; Mod UN; NHS; Yth Flsp; Mth Clb; Natl Merit SF; Purdue Univ; Aero Engr.

SMITH, JENNIFER; Barberton HS; Barberton, OH; 11/475 Band; Chrs; Chrh Wkr; Hon Rl; Lbry Ade; Red Cr Ade; Yth Flsp; FTA; Ger Clb; Sci Clb; Ohio Northern Univ; Pharmacology.

SMITH, JENNIFER; Watkins Memorial HS; Kirkersville, OH; 3/220 Band; Hon Rl; FHA; FTA; Pep Clb; Ohio St Univ; Prim Ed.

SMITH, JENNIFER; Madison HS; Madison, OH; 1/290 Band; Hon Rl; NHS; Yth Flsp; Ger Clb; Letter Bsktbl; Trk; Univ.

SMITH, JENNIFER E; Park Hills HS; Fairborn, OH; 8/366 Chrh Wkr; Cmnty Wkr; Hon Rl; NHS; Stg Crw; Drama Clb; Lat Clb; VP Sci Clb; Natl Merit SF; Washington Univ; Medicine.

SMITH, JENNIFER L; Lemon Monroe HS; Monroe, OH; Cls Rep Soph Cls; Band; Chrs; Drl Tm; Hon Rl; Hosp Ade; Stu Cncl; Rptr Sch Nwsp; Cit Awd; Triple Trio 78; Univ; Liberal Arts.

SMITH, JERIESHA; Immaculata HS; Detroit, MI; Cls Rep Soph Cls; Trs Jr Cls; Girl Scts; JA; Jr NHS; NHS; Sch Pl; Stu Cncl; Drama Clb; Letter Bsktbl; College; Pre Med.

SMITH, JERRY; Brookville HS; Brookville, IN; Band; Yth Flsp; 4-H; Letter Glf; Letter Ten; Letter Wrstlng; 4-H Awd; College; Busns Admin.

SMITH, JEWEL E; East HS; Columbus, OH; Cls Rep Frsh Cls; Cl Rep Jr Cls; Cls Rep Sr Cls; Hon Rl; Pol Wkr; Stu Cncl; Ed Sch Nwsp; Bsktbl; Central St Univ; Jrnlsm.

SMITH, JILL; Lexington HS; Mansfield, OH; 2/270 Pres Sr Cls; Band; Drl Tm; Hon Rl; NHS; Stu Cncl; Y-Teens; Fr Clb; Sec Mth Clb; Letter Trk; Recog For Acad Exc; Best Color Guard Mbr In Mrchng Bnd; Penn St Univ; Math.

SMITH, JILL; Wheelersburg HS; Wheelersburg, OH; Chrs; Hosp Ade; Stg Crw; FHA; Pep Clb;.

SMITH, JILL L; University HS; Morgantown, WV; Chrs; Hon Rl; Jr NHS; Mdrgl; Sch Mus; Rptr Yrbk; 4-H; FHA; Sci Clb; Chrldng; West Virginia Univ; Med Tech.

SMITH, JIM; Mona Shores HS; Muskegon, MI; Sec Soph Cls; Cl Rep Jr Cls; Band; Chrh Wkr; Stu Cncl; Capt Bsktbl; Cit Awd; Pres Awd; Bsktbl MVP 77; Music Awd 77; Athletic Awd 77; Schlrshp Awd 77; Participtn Awd 76; Univ; Law.

SMITH, JIM; Revere HS; Richfield, OH; 5/287 Hon Rl; Sch Pl; Ohio St Univ; Geology.

SMITH, JOANNE; Mona Shores HS; Muskegon, MI; Band; Hon Rl; Lbry Ade; Muskegon Business College; Business.

SMITH, JODI; Dunbar HS; Dunbar, WV; 1/190 Sec Soph Cls; Chrs; Chrh Wkr; Hon Rl; Jr NHS; Lit Mag; Mod UN; NHS; Off Ade; Sch Mus; Univ.

SMITH, JOEL; Tippecanoe Valley HS; Claypool, IN; Sec Jr Cls; Band; Boy Scts; Chrh Wkr; Hon Rl; Jr NHS; NHS; Orch; Sch Mus; Sct Actv; Horsemanship Cntst Riding; Purdue Univ; Civil Engr.

SMITH, JOE R; Elkins HS; Elkins, WV; Chrs; Key Clb; Crs Cntry; Trk; Wrstlng; IM Sprt; St Champ 78 Wv Cross Cntry 78; Univ; Marine Bio.

SMITH, JOHN; Mount View HS; Superior, WV; Hon Rl; Jr NHS; Key Clb; Letter Bsbl; Univ.

SMITH, JOHN; Fairmont West HS; Kettering, OH; Band; Hon Rl; NHS; Orch; Sch Mus; Trk; Florida Inst Of Tech; Oceanography.

SMITH, JOHN; Bethesda Christian HS; Lebanon, IN; Chrh Wkr; Hon Rl; Sch Pl; Letter Bsbl; Letter Bsktbl; Bob Jones Univ; Bus.

SMITH, JON; Concord HS; Albion, MI; Lbry Ade; Orch; Stu Cncl; Yrbk; Rptr Sch Nwsp; 4-H; Rdo Clb; Univ Of Michigan; Nuclear Engr.

SMITH, JONATHAN; Crestline HS; Crestline, OH; Cls Rep Sr Cls; Sal; Hon Rl; NHS; Sch Mus; Stu Cncl; Glf; Ten; Am Leg Awd; Ohio St Univ; Archt.

SMITH, JOY D; Kettering HS; Detroit, MI; Cls Rep Sr Cls; Wayne State Univ; Psychiatry.

SMITH, JUANITA; Valley HS; Lucasville, OH; Cls Rep Sr Cls; Band; Cmp Fr Grls; Chrs; Girl Scts; Sch Pl; Stu Cncl; Rptr Yrbk; Yrbk; Sch Nwsp;.

SMITH, JULIE; Huntington North HS; Huntington, IN; Trs Jr Cls; Swmmng; Trk; Chrldng; Ball St Univ; Law Enforcement.

SMITH, KAREN; La Porte HS; Laporte, IN; 2/610 Chrh Wkr; Hon Rl; MMM; NHS; Orch; Fr Clb; DAR Awd; Univ; French.

SMITH, KAREN; Regina HS; Cleveland Hts, OH; Cls Rep Soph Cls; Chrs; Hon Rl; Stu Cncl; Chrldng; Univ; Nursing.

SMITH, KAREN; Daleville HS; Daleville, IN; 6/90 Cl Rep Jr Cls; Chrh Wkr; Hon Rl; Lbry Ade; NHS; Stu Cncl; Yth Flsp; Spn Clb; Letter Gym; Trk; College; Nurse.

SMITH, KAREN S; Washington HS; Washington, IN; Cl Rep Jr Cls; Band; Debate Tm; Drl Tm; Hon Rl; NHS; Off Ade; Beta Clb; Pep Clb; Pom Pon; Indiana Univ; Health.

SMITH, KATHERINE; Olmsted Falls HS; Olmsted Falls, OH; 13/235 Pres AFS; Cmp Fr Grls; Chrs; Girl Scts; Hon Rl; NHS; Sch Mus; Fr Clb; FTA; Kiwan Awd; Miami Univ; Sociology.

SMITH, KATHY; Marlette HS; Snover, MI; 1/130 Val; Girl Scts; Hon Rl; Treas NHS; Treas Stu Cncl; Treas Yth Flsp; Treas 4-H; FTA; Ger Clb; OEA; Sanilac County 4 H Queen; 1st In Acctg I In Natl Office Ed Assoc Comp; District Winner In 4 H Gardening; Michigan Univ; Acctg.

SMITH, KATHY; Hammond Baptist HS; Chicago, IL; Chrh Wkr; Hon Rl; Sch Pl; Chrldng; Cit Awd; Jr Natl Assoc For The Deaf; Stu Council; Jr Illinois Assoc For The Deaf; Tennessee Temple Univ; Spec Ed.

SMITH, KATHY; Buffalo HS; Huntington, WV; VP Jr Cls; Band; Hon Rl; Stg Crw; Rptr Sch Nwsp; Mth Clb; Pep Clb; Trk; Chrldng; Mat Maids; Huntington Marshall Cmnty Coll.

SMITH, KATRINA; Immaculata HS; Detroit, MI; Hon Rl; Lbry Ade; Rptr Yrbk; Rptr Sch Nwsp; St Of Mi Comp Schlrshp Progr 79; Cum Laude 79; Michigan St Univ; Bus Admin.

SMITH, KAYE Y; Osborn Sr HS; Detroit, MI; 9/415 Pres Jr Cls; Pres Sr Cls; Chrs; Chrh Wkr; Hon Rl; VP NHS; Stu Cncl; Yth Flsp; Rptr Sch Nwsp; Pep Clb; Univ Of MI Regnts Alumni Schlrshp 79; Rcvd Spec Recgntn Fr Phi Beta Kappa For Acadmc 79; Univ Of Michigan; Psych.

SMITH, KEITH; Okemos HS; Okemos, MI; Chrs; Bsbl; Hockey; Mic State.

SMITH, KELLY; Euclid Sr HS; Willoughby, OH; 364/763 Band; Chrh Wkr; Drm Bgl; Hon Rl; Lbry Ade; Lit Mag; Yth Flsp; Y-Teens; Lakeland Coll; Paramedic Tech.

SMITH, KELLY; Clinton Prairie HS; Mulberry, IN; 9/97 Cl Rep Jr Cls; Hon Rl; Jr NHS; FBLA; FTA; Trk; Pres Awd; Voc Schl; Stewardess.

SMITH, KELLY; Buckeye Valley HS; Ashley, OH; 2/223 Band; Hon Rl; Sch Mus; Pres 4-H; VP FTA; Spn Clb; Am Leg Awd; 4-H Awd; Univ; Comp Sci.

SMITH, KELLY; Marion HS; Marion, IN; Girl Scts; Hon Rl; JA; Jr NHS; NHS; Drama Clb; 4-H; 4-H Awd; Univ.

SMITH, KELYN; Cass Tech HS; Detroit, MI; Cls Rep Frsh Cls; Aud/Vis; Cmnty Wkr; Pol Wkr; Sch Pl; Yth Flsp; Letter Bsktbl; Letter Ftbl; Letter Trk; Letter Mgrs; Morehouse Coll; Cmnctns.

SMITH, KENNETH; Valley HS; Lucasville, OH; 12/107 Hon Rl; Hosp Ade; Pres Lbry Ade; NHS; Sch Pl; VP 4-H; FTA; 4-H Awd; Ohio Univ; Chem.

SMITH, KENNY; Valley HS; Lucasville, OH; 12/107 Hon Rl; Hosp Ade; Lbry Ade; NHS; Sch Pl; 4-H; FTA; 4-H Awd; Ohio Univ; Chem.

SMITH, KENT R; Whiteford HS; Riga, MI; Aud/Vis; Pres Band; Boy Scts; Chrs; Chrh Wkr; Hon Rl; JA; Off Ade; Red Cr Ade; Sch Mus; E Michigan Univ; Music.

SMITH, KEVIN; Columbia City Joint HS; Columbia City, IN; Boy Scts; Hon Rl; Bsbl; Bsktbl; Crs Cntry; Swmmng; College; Marine Biology.

SMITH, KEVIN; Southeastern HS; Chillicothe, OH; Cl Rep Jr Cls; Hon Rl; Jr NHS; NHS; Stu Cncl; Fr Clb; FTA; Letter Bsbl; Bsktbl; Letter Crs Cntry; Bus Sch; Architect.

SMITH, KEVIN; Calvert HS; Republic, OH; 5/108 Hon Rl; 4-H; IM Sprt; 4-H Awd; College; Bus.

SMITH, KEVIN; Mineral Ridge HS; Mc Donald, OH; Boy Scts; Hon Rl; Quill & Scroll; Yrbk; Ed Sch Nwsp; Rptr Sch Nwsp; Beta Clb; Univ; Engr.

SMITH, KEVIN; Highland HS; Anderson, IN; 14/406 Hon Rl; NHS; Yth Flsp; Am Leg Awd; C of C Awd; Cit Awd; Ball State Univ; Pre Med.

SMITH, KIM; Jackson Milton HS; Lake Milton, OH; Hon Rl; Sch Pl; Yrbk; Key Clb; Bsktbl; Trk; Business School; Secretary.

SMITH, KIMBERLEE; Collinwood HS; Cleveland, OH; Hon Rl; Off Ade; Rptr Sch Nwsp; Sch Nwsp; Pres Drama Clb; Rdo Clb; Northwestern Univ; Mag Journalism.

SMITH, KIRSTEN L; Wyoming HS; Cincinnati, OH; 15/196 Band; Boy Scts; Hon Rl; Mod UN; NHS; Rptr Yrbk; Sch Nwsp; GAA; IM Sprt; Natl Merit SF; Univ Of Michigan; Foreign Lnguag.

SMITH, KRISTI; South Amherst HS; S Amherst, OH; Sec Frsh Cls; Cls Rep Frsh Cls; Cls Rep Soph Cls; Cl Rep Jr Cls; Cls Rep Sr Cls; Debate Tm; Hon Rl; Lbry Ade; Sec NHS; Stg Crw; Vlybl 77 78; Attend Aide 76 77; Univ; Health Care.

SMITH, KRISTINE; Hastings HS; Hastings, MI; 15/252 Cls Rep Frsh Cls; VP Soph Cls; Cl Rep Jr Cls; Cls Rep Sr Cls; NHS; Orch; Sch Mus; Stu Cncl; Pres 4-H; Mi Dstngshd Holstein Girl 79; Interlochen Natl Music Camp Schlrshp 77; Outstdng Greenhand Awrd For FFA 76; Michigan St Univ; Dairy Cmnctns.

SMITH, KURT; Troy HS; Troy, MI; Stg Crw; Socr; Gov Hon Prg Awd; Oregon St Univ; Ecology.

SMITH, LAURA; Logansport HS; Logansport, IN; 15/342 Band; Girl Scts; Hon Rl; Sch Mus; Sch Pl; Rptr Sch Nwsp; Drama Clb; Ger Clb; Ind Univ; Medical Technology.

SMITH, LAURA; Tinora Sr HS; Defiance, OH; Chrs; Hon Rl; Hosp Ade; Sch Mus; Yth Flsp; OEA; Scr Kpr; Northwest Tech Coll; Acctg.

SMITH, LAUREN; Dublin HS; Dublin, OH; 24/153 Sec Sr Cls; Band; Chrs; Jr NHS; NHS; Sch Mus; Stu Cncl; Yth Flsp; Heidelberg College; Music.

SMITH, LAURI; Sts Peter And Paul Area HS; Saginaw, MI; Hst Soph Cls; VP Jr Cls; Pres Sr Cls; Girl Scts; Hon Rl; NHS; Stg Crw; College; Architecture.

SMITH, LA VELLA; Everett HS; Lansing, MI; Off Ade; PAVAS; Lansing Comm Coll; Eng.

SMITH, LEANNE M; Tuslaw HS; Massillon, OH; 46/190 Cl Rep Jr Cls; Cls Rep Sr Cls; Cmnty Wkr; Hon Rl; Sch Mus; Sch Pl; VP Stu Cncl; Yth Flsp; Y-Teens; Pep Clb; Ohio St Univ; Theater.

SMITH, LESLIE; Flushing HS; Flushing, MI; Band; Cmnty Wkr; Drl Tm; Yth Flsp; Fr Clb; IM Sprt; Twrlr; Mas Awd; Hnr Dist 8 Sweetheart For De Molays; Hnr Open Class Champ For Marching Bands Of Amer; Univ; Psych.

SMITH, LESLIE; Stonewall Jackson HS; Charleston, WV; Cls Rep Soph Cls; Chrs; Hon Rl; NHS; Off Ade; Stu Cncl; Fr Clb; Letter Bsktbl; Letter Trk; Letter Chrldng; French Hnr Soc; Coll; Vet.

SMITH, LESLIE; North Farmington HS; Farm Hills, MI; Chrs; Stg Crw; Chrldng; College; Psych.

SMITH, LINDA; Brooke HS; Beech Bottom, WV; 28/473 Band; Chrs; Chrh Wkr; FCA; Hon Rl; NHS; Orch; Ger Clb; W Liberty State College; Flght Attdt.

SMITH, LINDA; Adrian Sr HS; Adrian, MI; Chrh Wkr; Girl Scts; Hon Rl; Off Ade; FTA; Ger Clb; Siena Heights Coll; Sec.

SMITH, LINDA; Shenandoah HS; Sarahsville, OH; 10/92 Cls Rep Sr Cls; Am Leg Aux Girls St; Band; Hon Rl; Off Ade; Sch Pl; Stu Cncl; Drama Clb; 4-H; Pep Clb; Work; Horticulture.

SMITH, LINDA; Salem Sr HS; Salem, OH; 12/250 Band; Cmnty Wkr; Hon Rl; Fr Clb; Pep Clb; Bowling Green St Univ; RN.

SMITH, LINDA; Mogadore HS; Mogadore, OH; Band; Chrh Wkr; Cmnty Wkr; Drl Tm; Girl Scts; Hon Rl; Hosp Ade; NHS; Sch Mus; Sch Pl; Univ; Math.

SMITH, LISA; Lake Central HS; Dyer, IN; 70/512 Hon Rl; NHS; VP Quill & Scroll; Y-Teens; Sprt Ed Sch Nwsp; Rptr Sch Nwsp; Letter Bsktbl; Letter Trk; Coach Actv; PPFtbl; All Star Softball Team; College; Journalism.

SMITH, LISA; Greenon HS; Fairborn, OH; Debate Tm; Hon Rl; Jr NHS; NHS; Off Ade; Red Cr Ade; Sch Mus; Sch Pl; Ed Sch Nwsp; Drama Clb; Univ.

SMITH, LISA; Gallia Academy HS; Gallipolis, OH; Ohi State Univ; Comp Sci.

SMITH, LISA; West Musingum HS; Zanesville, OH; Cls Rep Frsh Cls; Cls Rep Soph Cls; Hon Rl; Off Ade; Red Cr Ade; Y-Teens; Pep Clb; Gym; Letter Trk; Mgrs; College.

SMITH, LISA; John Hay HS; Cleveland, OH; 4/251 Hon Rl; NHS; Ger Clb; Cit Awd; Miami Univ; Bus Admin.

SMITH, LISA; Tecumseh HS; Tecumseh, MI; Cl Rep Jr Cls; Hon Rl; Hosp Ade; NHS; Stu Cncl; Yrbk; Pep Clb; Letter Gym; Univ; Med.

SMITH, LISA A; Switzerland Cnty Jr Sr HS; Florence, IN; 29/130 Sec Frsh Cls; Trs Soph Cls; Sec Jr Cls; Chrs; MMM; Sch Mus; Sch Pl; Stu Cncl; Drama Clb; FFA; Airline Personnel.

SMITH, LONNA; Coleman HS; Coleman, MI; 9/89 Sec Sr Cls; Trs Sr Cls; Band; Hon Rl; NHS; Yrbk; Drama Clb; Pep Clb; Central Michigan Univ; Comp Sci.

SMITH, LORA; Daleville HS; Daleville, IN; 9/59 Chrh Wkr; Girl Scts; Hon Rl; JA; NHS; Yth Flsp; 4-H; Spn Clb; Bsktbl; Ball State Univ; Acctg.

SMITH, LORI; Whitko HS; S Whitley, IN; 2/150 Sec Frsh Cls; Cls Rep Soph Cls; Cl Rep Jr Cls; Cls Rep Sr Cls; Sal; FCA; NHS; Rptr Yrbk; Ger Clb; Sci Clb; Hanover Coll.

SMITH, LORI; Benton Central HS; Montmorenci, IN; 2/225 Cl Rep Jr Cls; Sal; NHS; 4-H; Pres OEA; IM Sprt; Mentl Attitude Awd & Letter Vllybl 78; Jr Crop Growers Achvmnt Awd 4 H 79; Chrmn 2nd Plc Parliamentary Proc; Purdue Univ; Mgmt.

SMITH, LORI; Worthington Jefferson HS; Worthington, IN; 3/40 Band; Hon Rl; NHS; Off Ade; Beta Clb; Pep Clb; Spn Clb; GAA; Ind State Univ.

SMITH, LOU; Waldron Area Schools; Alvordton, OH; 7/55 Sec Soph Cls; Sec Jr Cls; Sch Pl; Spn Clb; GAA; Mgrs; Cosmetology Schl.

SMITH, LOU ANN; Waldron Area Schools; Alvordton, OH; 6/56 Sec Soph Cls; Sec Jr Cls; Hon Rl; Sch Pl; Spn Clb; Univ.

SMITH, LOUANNE; Lake Orion HS; Lake Orion, MI; Trs Jr Cls; Trs Sr Cls; Sec Band; Chrh Wkr; Hon Rl; VP Jr NHS; Treas NHS; Rptr Yrbk; Twrlr; St Joseph Mercy Hosp; Rad Tech.

SMITH, LUANN; Fowler HS; Fowler, MI; 10/56 Chrh Wkr; Hon Rl; NHS; 4-H; Letter Trk; GAA; IM Sprt; Mgrs; PPFtbl; 4-H Awd; Lansing Comm College; Special Ed.

SMITH, LUCIE; Ferndale HS; Ferndale, MI; Chrs; Hon Rl; Mdrgl; PAVAS; Quill & Scroll; Sch Mus; Sch Pl; Stg Crw; Rptr Sch Nwsp; Sch Nwsp; Univ; Pub Relations.

SMITH, LYNNE; Grandview Hts HS; Columbus, OH; 15/130 Sec Band; Drl Tm; Hon Rl; Orch; Yrbk; Letter Trk; Capt Chrldng; Scr Kpr; Cit Awd; Ohio Univ; Acctg.

SMITH, MARCIA; Davison HS; Davison, MI; Band; Chrs; Cmnty Wkr; Hon Rl; Lbry Ade; Sch Mus; Sch Pl; Stg Crw; Drama Clb; Univ Of Michigan; Theatre Tech.

SMITH, MARCIA M; John H Patterson Coop HS; Dayton, OH; VP Soph Cls; Pres Jr Cls; VP Sr Cls; Band; Chrs; Hon Rl; Yrbk; VICA; Pres Awd; St Clair Community Coll; Radiology.

SMITH, MARGARET; Columbia HS; Columbia Sta, OH; Band; Girl Scts; Lbry Ade; Sch Mus; Sch Pl; Sct Actv; Stg Crw; Rptr Yrbk; Yrbk; Drama Clb; Lorain Cnty Cmnty Coll; Brdcstng.

SMITH, MARGARET; Pewamo Westphalia HS; Pewamo, MI; Trs Jr Cls; Sch Pl; Rptr Sch Nwsp; Treas FHA; PPFtbl; Central Michigan Univ; Spec Educ.

SMITH, MARIANNE; St Francis Desales Cntrl HS; Morgantown, WV; Drl Tm; Hon Rl; Drama Clb; Pep Clb; Spn Clb; IM Sprt; West Vir Univ; Bus.

SMITH, MARION; Randolph Southern HS; Union City, IN; 1/75 VP Frsh Cls; VP Soph Cls; Am Leg Boys St; Band; Hon Rl; Jr NHS; NHS; 4-H; FFA; Spn Clb; Ball St Univ.

SMITH, MARK; Vinson HS; Huntington, WV; Hon Rl; Key Clb; Mgrs; Natl Merit Ltr; St Winner Amer Chem Soc Test 79; 2nd Pl Essay Marshall Univ Acad Fair 79; Schlrshp Resrch Grant 79; Univ; Chem.

SMITH, MARK; Eastern HS; Minford, OH; Cls Rep Frsh Cls; Cls Rep Soph Cls; Cl Rep Jr Cls; Am Leg Boys St; Hon Rl; Yrbk; Rptr Sch Nwsp; Pep Clb;.

SMITH, MARK; Pontiac Central HS; Pontiac, MI; 18/473 Hon Rl; NHS; Wayne St Univ; Engr.

SMITH, MARK; Clawson HS; Clawson, MI; Band; Sch Mus; Oakland Univ; Musician.

SMITH, MARK E; United HS; Salem, OH; Chrh Wkr; Hon Rl; 4-H; FFA; 4-H Awd; Farm.

SMITH, MARLENE; Reeths Puffer HS; Muskegon, MI; Band; Chrs; Chrh Wkr; Hon Rl; Hosp Ade; Yth Flsp; Rptr Sch Nwsp; Chrldng; Maskegon Cmnty Coll; Educ.

SMITH, MARSHA; Lemon Monroe HS; Middletown, OH; 24/278 Band; Chrs; Drl Tm; Hon Rl; JA; Sch Mus; Stg Crw; Rptr Sch Nwsp; Glee Clb Sec 77; Flag Unit 79; Univ; Dent.

SMITH, MARTALYN; Central Hower HS; Akron, OH; Chrs; Chrh Wkr; Hon Rl; NHS; Stu Cncl; Sch Nwsp; Sci Clb; Bsktbl; Crs Cntry; Trk; Top Schlr West Jr HS 77; Todays Youth For Christ Bible Bowl Awrd 78; MVP Central Hower Girls Trck 79; Univ; Soc Sci.

SMITH, MARY; Minster HS; Minster, OH; Girl Scts; Hon Rl; Sct Actv; Sdlty; FTA; Pep Clb; IM Sprt; Univ; Acctg.

SMITH, MARY; Lumen Christi HS; Jackson, MI; Cls Rep Frsh Cls; Sec Sr Cls; Cmnty Wkr; NHS; Sch Pl; Rptr Yrbk; Pep Clb; Spn Clb; Capt Chrldng; W Michigan Univ; Jrnlsm.

SMITH, MATTHEW; Chillicothe HS; Chillicothe, OH; Band; Chrh Wkr; Hon Rl; Jr NHS; NHS; Orch; Yth Flsp; Key Clb; Letter Bsktbl; Letter Ftbl; Univ.

SMITH, MAUREEN; Marian HS; Birmingham, MI; VP Soph Cls; Cl Rep Jr Cls; Girl Scts; Sec Mod UN; NHS; Fr Clb; Swmmng; Trk; Chrldng; Opt Clb Awd; College; Nursing.

SMITH, MELISSA; Maplewood Jr Sr HS; Cortland, OH; Girl Scts; Hon Rl; JA; Bsbl; Trk; JA Awd; Trumbull Joint Voc Schl; Surgeon.

SMITH, MELISSA; Union HS; Jasonville, IN; 1/45 Cls Rep Frsh Cls; Cls Rep Soph Cls; Sec Jr Cls; Cl Rep Jr Cls; Val; FCA; Hon Rl; NHS; Off Ade; Pres Stu Cncl; Indiana Univ; Comp Tech.

SMITH, MICHAEL; Bishop Foley HS; Hazel Pk, MI; 10/200 Band; Boy Scts; Chrh Wkr; Hon Rl; Sct Actv; Lat Clb; Sci Clb; IM Sprt; Attended Natl Sci Foundation Stu Sci Training Prog At Kalamazoo Coll; Recve Awd For Recog Outstndng Latin; Coll; Chem.

SMITH, MICHAEL D; North Vermillion HS; New Albany, IN; 2/60 Pres Soph Cls; Pres Jr Cls; Pres Sr Cls; Band; Boy Scts; Chrs; Chrh Wkr; FCA; Hon Rl; NHS; Indiana Univ; Bus.

SMITH, MICHAEL D; Medora HS; Medora, IN; 1/23 Cls Rep Soph Cls; Pres Jr Cls; VP Sr Cls; Band; Hon Rl; NHS; Stu Cncl; Ed Yrbk; Sprt Ed Sch Nwsp; Beta Clb; Selected To Be The Boys State Alternate; Univ; Med Sci.

SMITH, MICHAEL L; Traverse City HS; Traverse City, MI; 67/744 IM Sprt; Northwestern Mich College; Law.

SMITH, MICHAEL L; Ripley HS; Ripley, WV; 1/250 Am Leg Boys St; Chrh Wkr; Hon Rl; NHS; Stg Crw; Yth Flsp; Mth Clb; Letter Glf; Letter Wrstlng; Chmn IM Sprt; W Vir Univ; Med.

SMITH, MICHELLE; Ellet HS; Akron, OH; Chrh Wkr; Cmnty Wkr; Hon Rl; Civ Clb; Cit Awd; Univ Of Akron.

SMITH, MICHELLE; Marion HS; Marion, IN; Band; Hon Rl; Jr NHS; NHS; Sci Clb; Spn Clb; College; Med.

SMITH, MIKE; Chaminade Julienne HS; Dayton, OH; Cls Rep Frsh Cls; Cls Rep Soph Cls; Boy Scts; Chrh Wkr; JA; Pol Wkr; Sch Pl; Stg Crw; Sprt Ed Sch Nwsp; IM Sprt; Univ Of Dayton; Comp Progr.

SMITH, MINDY K; Landmark Christian HS; La Porte, IN; Sec Soph Cls; Sec Jr Cls; Chrs; Chrh Wkr; Hon Rl; Sch Mus; Rptr Yrbk; Sch Nwsp; Pep Clb; Chrldng; Christian Honor Society Hardest Worker Axasemic Excellence Outstanding Chritinan Character; Coll; Scndry Educ.

SMITH, MONICA; Bishop Donahue Mem HS; Benwood, WV; 26/70 Sec Frsh Cls; VP Soph Cls; VP Jr Cls; Band; Chrs; Chrh Wkr; Cmnty Wkr; Hon Rl; Stu Cncl; Pep Clb; Vocational Schl; Cosmetology.

SMITH, NANCIE; Rocky River HS; Rocky Rvr, OH; Red Cr Ade; Letter Bsktbl; Volleyball Varsity Plyr Capt 76 80; Cleveland St Univ; Phys Educ Tchr.

SMITH, NANCY; Valley Local HS; Lucasville, OH; 1/110 Am Leg Aux Girls St; Band; VP Chrs; Chrh Wkr; Cmnty Wkr; Debate Tm; Drm Mjrt; Hon Rl; NHS; Sch Pl; Ohio St Univ; Optometry.

SMITH, NELETA R; Liberty HS; Eccles, WV; Sec Sr Cls; Band; Chrs; Chrh Wkr; Cmnty Wkr; Girl Scts; JA; Quill & Scroll; Ed Yrbk; Yrbk; Beckley College.

SMITH, NORMAN; Calvert HS; Tiffin, OH; 6/98 Cls Rep Soph Cls; Hon Rl; Lbry Ade; NHS; Stu Cncl; 4-H; Bsktbl; Ftbl; Wrstlng; Cit Awd; Univ; Engr.

SMITH, O KEY; Williamson HS; Chattaroy, WV; 25/81 Pres Frsh Cls; Pres Soph Cls; Cl Rep Jr Cls; Pres Sr Cls; Hon Rl; Off Ade; Pol Wkr; Beta Clb; FBLA; Pep Clb; Mbr Whose Ya Daddy Cheering Section; Tom Charles Awd Srs; Dr Robert Tohu Schlrshp Awd; S W Virginia Cmnty Univ; Bus Ed.

SMITH, OZRO; Sault Area HS; Sault Ste Marie, MI; Hon Rl; VICA; Letter Ftbl; Letter Trk; Am Leg Awd; Var Letter For Rifld Tm 79; Michigan Tech Univ; Elec Engr.

SMITH, PAMELA; Miami Trace HS; New Holland, OH; 4/249 Hon Rl; VP Jr NHS; VP NHS; Rptr Sch Nwsp; VP FNA; FTA; VP Sci Clb; Treas Spn Clb; Mas Awd; Community Hosp Schl Of Nursing.

SMITH, PAMELA; Edgewood HS; Bloomington, IN; Chrs; Chrh Wkr; Girl Scts; Hon Rl; Lbry Ade; Sch Mus; Sec Stu Cncl; Rptr Yrbk; PPFtbl;.

SMITH, PAMELA M; Buena Vista HS; Saginaw, MI; 7/175 Boy Scts; Chrh Wkr; Hon Rl; Rptr Sch Nwsp; Scr Kpr; Saginaw Valley St Coll; Psych.

SMITH, PAT; Heritage HS; Monroeville, IN; Hon Rl; Pep Clb; PPFtbl; Internatl Bus Coll; Acctg.

SMITH, PATRICIA; Argos Cmnty School; Argos, IN; 1/58 Band; Hon Rl; Lbry Ade; NHS; Sch Mus; Sch Pl; Yrbk; Sch Nwsp; Drama Clb; FTA; IN Univ Hnrs Progr In Forgn Lang 79; Whos Who In Music 79; Geometry Awd 79; Indiana Univ; Translator.

SMITH, PATRICIA; High School; Xenia, OH; Pres Frsh Cls; Cl Rep Jr Cls; Hst Sr Cls; AFS; Am Leg Aux Girls St; Pres Band; Chrs; Chrh Wkr; Cmnty Wkr; Girl Scts; Guilford Coll.

SMITH, PATRICIA; Traverse City Sr HS; Traverse City, MI; Chrh Wkr; Cmnty Wkr; Off Ade; Sec Yth Flsp; Coach Actv; Grand Rapids Bapt Coll; Sec Sci.

SMITH, PATRICK J; Reynoldsburg HS; Reynoldsburg, OH; Am Leg Boys St; Aud/Vis; Band; Hon Rl; Yrbk; Letter Bsktbl; Letter Crs Cntry; Letter Trk; Am Leg Awd; C C & Track Capt; OCC All Confrnc Winner In High Jump Long Jump & Tripl Jump; Dayton Univ; Photog.

SMITH, PAULA; Clinton Prairie HS; Mulberry, IN; Band; Chrh Wkr; Hon Rl; Hosp Ade; Ed Yrbk; Rptr Yrbk; Rptr Sch Nwsp; 4-H; Pep Clb; College; Comp Sci.

SMITH, PEGGY; Western HS; Russiaville, IN; 7/220 Am Leg Aux Girls St; Capt Drl Tm; Treas NHS; Off Ade; VP PAVAS; Sch Pl; Mgrs; Capt Pom Pon; Tmr; Coll; Spec Ed.

SMITH, PEGGY A; Liberty HS; Salem, WV; 40/228 Pres Frsh Cls; Cls Rep Frsh Cls; Cls Rep Soph Cls; Cl Rep Jr Cls; Band; Hon Rl; NHS; Stu Cncl; Drama Clb; Pep Clb; Old Domion Univ; Physc Educ.

SMITH, PENNE; Colonel Crawford HS; Galion, OH; Band; Hon Rl; Rptr Sch Nwsp; 4-H; Bsktbl; 4-H Awd; Univ; Chem Engr.

SMITH, PETE; Northrop HS; Ft Wayne, IN; Cls Rep Frsh Cls; Hon Rl; JA; Letter Bsktbl; Capt Ten; C of C Awd; JA Awd; Natl Merit Ltr; Univ Of Notre Dame; Pre Med.

SMITH, PHIL; Liberty HS; Youngstown, OH; 26/214 Band; Rdo Clb; Letter Trk; Letter Wrstlng; College.

SMITH, PHIL; Liberty HS; Yngstn, OH; 26/214 Band; Ger Clb; Rdo Clb; Trk; Wrstlng; Univ; Physics.

SMITH, PHIL; Leelanau HS; Frankfort, MI; Cls Rep Frsh Cls; Band; Boy Scts; Chrh Wkr; Hon Rl; Sch Pl; Sct Actv; Stu Cncl; Letter Bsktbl; Letter Ftbl; College; Medicine.

SMITH, PHILIP; Wauseon HS; Wauseon, OH; Band; Sch Mus; Sch Pl; Stg Crw; Drama Clb; Sci Clb; Swmmng; Ohio Univ; Law.

SMITH, PHILIP; Edward Lee Mc Clain HS; Greenfield, OH; 1/160 Cl Rep Jr Cls; Cls Rep Sr Cls; Val; Pres NHS; Bsbl; Bsktbl; Crs Cntry; Natl Merit Schl; Ohio St Univ; Mech Engr.

SMITH, PHILLIP; Pleasant Local HS; Marion, OH; Hon Rl; Hosp Ade; Red Cr Ade; Sct Actv; Stg Crw; Yth Flsp; Ftbl; Coach Actv; IM Sprt; Mgrs; Ohio State; Profesional Aviator.

SMITH, PHILLIP; Lincoln HS; Cambridge City, IN; 1/135 Chrh Wkr; Hon Rl; NHS; Sch Pl; Stg Crw; Rptr Yrbk; Drama Clb; Treas Spn Clb; Univ; Systems Analysts.

SMITH, RANDAL; John Adams HS; So Bend, IN; Boy Scts; Hon Rl; NHS; Sct Actv; Yth Flsp; 4-H; Sci Clb; Socr; Coll; Med.

SMITH, RANDY; Alma HS; Alma, MI; 104/252 Band; Boy Scts; Sch Pl; Drama Clb; IM Sprt; Mgrs; St Of Mich Competitive Schlrshp Prog; Cntrl Michigan Univ.

SMITH, RANDY; Salem HS; Salem, OH; 41/296 Chrs; Hon Rl; Mdrgl; Pol Wkr; Sch Mus; Sch Pl; Drama Clb; Mth Clb; Ten; DAR Awd; Miami Of Ohio Univ; Math.

SMITH, RAYMOND; Ida HS; Callerton, MI; Cls Rep Soph Cls; Hon Rl; Stu Cncl; Yth Flsp; Letter Bsbl; Letter Ftbl; Letter Wrstlng; IM Sprt; Univ Of Mic; Math.

SMITH, REBECCA; Rutherford B Hayes HS; Delaware, OH; VP AFS; Am Leg Aux Girls St; Chrs; Chrh Wkr; Sch Mus; Stg Crw; Yth Flsp; Drama Clb; Letter Gym; Trk; College.

SMITH, REBECCA; Warren Central HS; Indpls, IN; Band; Hon Rl; Sch Pl; Sct Actv; Stg Crw; Drama Clb; VP 4-H; Pep Clb; Bsktbl; Trk; Nominated For Cmnty Ldrshp Awd 79; Various Ath Awd; Mbr Of Jobs Daughtrs; Univ.

SMITH, REBECCA; Port Huron Northern HS; North Street, MI; 17/410 Band; Hon Rl; NHS; 4-H; Natl Merit Ltr; St Clair Cnty Coll; Advertising Dsgn.

SMITH, RENEE; Cedar Springs HS; Cedar Spgs, MI; Cl Rep Jr Cls; Band; Hon Rl; NHS; Stu Cncl; Rptr Yrbk; Chrldng; Twrlr; Univ; Sci.

SMITH, REVE; Portsmouth HS; Portsmouth, OH; 1/225 Cls Rep Sr Cls; Val; Chrs; Chrh Wkr; Hon Rl; NHS; Sch Mus; Sch Pl; Stu Cncl; Drama Clb; Ohio Bd Of Regent Schlrshp 79; Cedarville Coll.

SMITH, RHONDA; William Henry Harrison HS; Lafayette, IN; 20/327 Band; Chrh Wkr; Hon Rl; Jr NHS; NHS; Sch Mus; Stu Cncl; Rptr Sch Nwsp; Pep Clb; Spn Clb; Purdue Univ; Soc Work.

SMITH, RHONDA; East HS; Cleveland, OH; Cls Rep Frsh Cls; Cls Rep Soph Cls; Cl Rep Jr Cls; Sal; Chrs; Drl Tm; Hon Rl; JA; Off Ade; PAVAS; Diamond Shamrock Bus Schl; Acctg.

SMITH, RICHARD; Canton South HS; Canton, OH; Aud/Vis; FCA; NHS; Lat Clb; Mth Clb; Sci Clb; Letter Glf; Coach Actv; Univ; Chem Engr.

SMITH, RICHARD; Hanover Central Jr Sr HS; Cedar Lake, IN; 12/126 Hon Rl; Jr NHS; NHS; Pol Wkr; Quill & Scroll; Sch Nwsp; Wrstlng; IM Sprt; Calumet Coll; Bus Mgmt.

SMITH, RICHARD; John Marshall HS; Indianapolis, IN; 27/427 Hon Rl; NHS; Quill & Scroll; Sch Mus; Sch Pl; Stg Crw; Rptr Yrbk; Sch Nwsp; Indiana Univ; Telecommunications.

SMITH, RICHARD M; John Adams HS; So Bend, IN; Hon Rl; 4-H Awd; Inlnd Daily Press Trphy For Hon Nwspaper Carrier 76; Carrier Of Mnth Trphy 75; IU; Bus.

SMITH, RICK; Lincolnview HS; Van Wert, OH; Hon Rl; DECA; Bsktbl; Lincoln Tech Schl; Auto Mech.

SMITH, ROBERT; Wheeling Park HS; Wheeling, WV; 164/579 Chrh Wkr; West Virginia Univ; Law.

SMITH, ROBERT; Trenton HS; Trenton, MI; Hon Rl; IM Sprt; Natl Merit Ltr; Wayne St Univ; Pharm.

SMITH, ROBIN; Amelia HS; Cincinnati, OH; Am Leg Aux Girls St; Band; Drl Tm; Hon Rl; NHS; Sch Mus; Sch Pl; Drama Clb; Ten; Bus Schl; Bus.

SMITH, ROBIN; Perrysburg HS; Perrysburg, OH; AFS; Chrs; Cmnty Wkr; Girl Scts; Off Ade; Red Cr Ade; Sct Actv; Stg Crw; Rptr Yrbk; Drama Clb; Univ; Spec Educ.

SMITH, ROBIN; George Washington HS; Indianapolis, IN; Hon Rl; Fr Clb; Ger Clb; Crs Cntry; Trk; Ind Univ; Med.

SMITH, ROBIN L; Eastmoor HS; Columbus, OH; 13/290 Cls Rep Sr Cls; Am Leg Aux Girls St; Band; Chrs; Girl Scts; Hon Rl; Orch; Sch Pl; Stu Cncl; Letter Bsktbl; Mt Holyoke Coll; Intl Law.

SMITH, ROBYN; Goshen HS; Goshen, OH; Cls Rep Frsh Cls; Cls Rep Soph Cls; Cl Rep Jr Cls; Chrs; Girl Scts; Hon Rl; Off Ade; Sch Mus; Treas Stu Cncl; Treas Yth Flsp; College; Dental Hygiene.

SMITH, RODNEY; Wapakoneta Sr HS; Cridersville, OH; 70/308 Yth Flsp; Fr Clb; Glf; Univ; Meteorology.

SMITH, RONALD; Zanesville HS; Zanesville, OH; Boy Scts; Hon Rl; NHS; Sci Clb; Natl Merit Ltr; 3.5 Club 77 78 78 79; Univ; Sci.

SMITH, ROSEMARY; Archbold Area HS; Archbold, OH; Am Leg Aux Girls St; Band; Chrs; Hon Rl; Orch; Sch Mus; Sch Pl; Treas Yth Flsp; Letter Crs Cntry; Letter Trk; College; History.

SMITH, ROXANE; Westside HS; Gary, IN; Chrs; Hon Rl; Mdrgl; Letter Bsktbl; Letter Trk; Cit Awd; 4-H Awd; Pres Awd; Most Athletic Awrd 78; Univ; Incorp Law.

SMITH, ROXANNE; Little Miami HS; Morrow, OH; 4/201 Debate Tm; Girl Scts; Hon Rl; NHS; Sct Actv; Yrbk; Fr Clb; OEA;.

SMITH, ROY; Richmond Sr HS; Richmond, IN; Pres Frsh Cls; Am Leg Boys St; Debate Tm; Hon Rl; Natl Forn Lg; NHS; Pol Wkr; Stu Cncl; Letter Crs Cntry; Letter Wrstlng; 3 Yr Sci Awd 77; Bst Spkr Debate Tm 77; All Spts Awd 77; Univ; Sci.

SMITH, RUSTY; Wynford HS; Bucyrus, OH; 8/141 Cl Rep Jr Cls; Cls Rep Sr Cls; Band; Boy Scts; Chrs; Hon Rl; Jr NHS; NHS; Sch Pl; Treas Stu Cncl; Extra Effort Awd; Top Defensive Driver Awd; Findlay Coll; Communications.

SMITH, RUTH; Jackson Center HS; Jackson Cntr, OH; Hon Rl; JA; Lbry Ade; Off Ade; Sch Pl; DECA; FHA; College; Bus.

SMITH, S; Wapakoneta Sr HS; Wapakoneta, OH; 17/308 Chrs; Hon Rl; NHS; PAVAS; Sch Pl; Ed Sch Nwsp; Drama Clb; Fr Clb; FHA; Pep Clb; Comm Coll Arts Fest Poestry Contest; Ohio Univ Wrkshp Cert Of Merit; Serv Awd; Coll; Law.

SMITH, SANDRA; St Ursula Academy; Toledo, OH; Hon Rl; Stu Cncl; Spn Clb; Univ Of Toledo.

SMITH, SANDRA; Highland HS; Highland, IN; 76/500 Hon Rl; NHS; Stu Cncl; Pep Clb; Letter Ten; GAA; Treas Mat Maids; Pom Pon; PPFtbl; Purdue Univ; Math.

SMITH, SANDY; Lasalle HS; South Bend, IN; Hon Rl; Trk; IM Sprt; Mgrs; College; Sci.

SMITH, SARA; National Trail HS; Eaton, OH; Chrs; Girl Scts; PAVAS; Yth Flsp; Yrbk; Pep Clb; Sci Clb; Univ; Psych.

SMITH, SARAH; Zanesville HS; Newark, OH; Chrs; Hon Rl; Lbry Ade; Off Ade; Red Cr Ade; Sch Mus; Bsktbl; Mgrs; Scr Kpr; Tmr; College; Registered Nursing.

SMITH, SCOTT; Buffalo HS; Huntington, WV; 7/150 Chrh Wkr; Hon Rl; Mod UN; NHS; Sch Pl; Mth Clb; West Virginia State Math Field Day; 30th Annual Math Exam Awd; College; Biochem Engr.

SMITH, SCOTT; Lapel HS; Anderson, IN; 14/99 Hon Rl; Spn Clb; College; Electronics.

SMITH, SCOTT; North Canton Hoover HS; North Canton, OH; Boy Scts; Chrh Wkr; Hon Rl; Sct Actv; Yth Flsp; Letter Glf; Ftbl; Trk; Natl Merit SF; Ohio St Univ; Forestry.

SMITH, SCOTT; Beal City HS; Weidman, MI; Band; 4-H; FFA; Ferris St Coll; Diesel Mech.

SMITH, SCOTT; Harrison HS; Harrison, MI; Band; Drm Bgl; Hon Rl; NHS; Orch; Letter Bsbl; Michigan St Univ; Wildlife Bio.

SMITH, SCOTT V; La Ville HS; Lakeville, IN; Band; Hon Rl; NHS; Sch Mus; Ger Clb; Sci Clb; Glf; IM Sprt; Univ; Engr.

SMITH, SELENA S; Fairfield HS; Fairfield, OH; 224/625 Chrs; Cmnty Wkr; Hosp Ade; Lbry Ade; Off Ade; Sch Mus; Sec Frsh Cls; Stg Crw; Civ Clb; Drama Clb; Mbrshp Internal Thespain Soc; Candidate For Ohios Girls St; College; Theatre.

SMITH, SHARON; Fraser HS; Fraser, MI; Cls Rep Soph Cls; Chrs; Girl Scts; Mdrgl; NHS; Y-Teens; Rptr Yrbk; Yrbk; Pep Clb; Chrldng; Univ.

SMITH, SHARON; John Hay HS; Cleveland, OH; Cl Rep Jr Cls; Cls Rep Sr Cls; Hon Rl; Orch; Red Cr Ade; Stu Cncl; Cuyahoga Cmnty Coll; Business Admin.

SMITH, SHARON; Glen Este HS; Cincinnati, OH; Cls Rep Frsh Cls; Hon Rl; Off Ade; Stg Crw; Stu Cncl; Yth Flsp; Pres Miami Univ; Elem Ed.

SMITH, SHAWN; Holgate Local HS; New Bavaria, OH; Cls Rep Frsh Cls; Cls Rep Soph Cls; Cl Rep Jr Cls; Hon Rl; Stu Cncl; Mth Clb; Bsbl; Bsktbl; Ftbl; Univ.

SMITH, SHEILA; Catholic Cntrl HS; Steubenville, OH; Band; Chrs; Hon Rl; FHA; Pres FNA; Trk; College; Nursing.

SMITH, SHEILA; Glen Este HS; Incinnati, OH; Band; Chrh Wkr; Hon Rl; NHS; Spn Clb; Letter Bsbl; Christ Hosp School Of Nursing; Rn.

SMITH, SHELLEY; Harbor HS; Ashtabula, OH; 5/197 AFS; Chrh Wkr; Off Ade; Fr Clb; Pep Clb; Kent Univ.

SMITH, SHELLIE; Lawrence HS; Lawrence, MI; Band; Lbry Ade; Orch; Sch Pl; Rptr Sch Nwsp; 4-H; FTA; Pep Clb; Spn Clb; Bsktbl; New York Schl Of Interior Design.

SMITH, SHELLY; Niles HS; Niles, MI; Cls Rep Frsh Cls; Hon Rl; Pol Wkr; Stu Cncl; Yrbk; Chrldng; IM Sprt; Univ; Bus Admin.

SMITH, SHERI; East HS; Columbus, OH; Hon Rl; 4-H; Bsktbl; GAA; State Honor Awd; Columbus Tech Inst; Comp Prog.

SMITH, SHERRI; Webberville HS; Webberville, MI; Trs Frsh Cls; Hon Rl; VP Stu Cncl; Rptr Yrbk; Bsktbl; Trk; College; Orthodontist.

SMITH, SHERRIE; Medina HS; Medina, OH; 38/359 Aud/Vis; Chrs; Hon Rl; NHS; Sch Mus; Lat Clb; Pep Clb; Letter Gym; Capt Chrldng; GAA; Univ Of Akron; Nursing.

SMITH, SHIRLEY; Sparlingvl Cmnty Church Schl; Brown City, MI; Chrs; Chrh Wkr; Sch Pl; Yth Flsp;.

SMITH, STEPHANIE; South HS; Youngstown, OH; Chrs; Hon Rl; JA; Off Ade; Pep Clb; Univ; Bus.

SMITH, STEVE; Roy C Start HS; Toledo, OH; Cls Rep Frsh Cls; Cls Rep Soph Cls; Cl Rep Jr Cls; Band; Hon Rl; NHS; IM Sprt; Univ Of Cincinnati; Architecture.

SMITH, STEVE; Pike Central HS; Winslow, IN; 17/200 NHS; Yth Flsp; Sprt Ed Sch Nwsp; Pep Clb; Pres Sci Clb; Letter Bsbl; Letter Ten; Univ Of Evansville; Comp Sci.

SMITH, STEVE; Trenton HS; Trenton, MI; Hon Rl; IM Sprt; Univ; Dentistry.

SMITH, STEWART; Eastmoor HS; Columbus, OH; 16/290 Chrs; Hon Rl; NHS; Stg Crw; Ftbl; Ohio St Univ; Bus Admin.

SMITH, STUART; Greenbrier East HS; Roncerverte, WV; Band; Pres Chrh Wkr; Hon Rl; NHS; VP 4-H; Letter Ftbl; Letter Trk; 4-H Awd; Greenbrier Jr Hi Scholastic Athlete; Concord Coll; Med Tech.

SMITH, SUE; St Peter And Paul HS; Saginaw, MI; Cls Rep Frsh Cls; Pres Soph Cls; Cl Rep Jr Cls; Trs Sr Cls; Chrs; Chrh Wkr; Cmnty Wkr; College; Bus.

SMITH, SUSAN; Bucyrus Sr HS; Bucyrus, OH; Yrbk; Rptr Sch Nwsp; Bsktbl; GAA; IM Sprt; Univ; Secondary Ed.

SMITH, SUSAN; Valley View HS; Germantown, OH; Band; Yrbk; 4-H; Spn Clb; 4-H Awd; Univ Of So California; Geog.

SMITH, SUSAN; Bishop Donahue Memorial HS; Glen Dale, WV; Chrh Wkr; Cmnty Wkr; Hon Rl; NHS; Red Cr Ade; Ed Yrbk; Yrbk; Sprt Ed Sch Nwsp; Rptr Sch Nwsp; 4-H; Chrstn Youth Orgnztn 76; Vrsty Vllybll 78; Nwsppr Awrd Of Apprctn 79; Univ; Eng.

SMITH, SUSAN; Eastmoor HS; Columbus, OH; 32/290 Pres Frsh Cls; Band; Chrs; Chrh Wkr; Hon Rl; NHS; Beta Clb; Sci Clb; Univ; Elem Educ.

SMITH, SUSAN D; Olmsted Falls HS; Olmsted Falls, OH; 1/250 Val; Am Leg Aux Girls St; Pres NHS; Ed Yrbk; IM Sprt; Natl Merit SF; Coll; Engr.

SMITH, SUSAN M; North HS; Youngstown, OH; 15/138 Sec Jr Cls; Drl Tm; Hon Rl; Sec NHS; Stu Cncl; Drama Clb; Sec Fr Clb; Scr Kpr; Dr Belinky Med Awrd 79; Bowling Green St Univ; Nursing.

SMITH, SUZANNE; Sandusky HS; Sandusky, MI; Chrs; Chrh Wkr; Girl Scts; Sct Actv; FFA; VP FHA; Pep Clb; Letter Trk; Letter Chrldng; Coll; Interior Design.

SMITH, SUZANNE; John Hay HS; Cleveland, OH; 250258 Cls Rep Frsh Cls; Cls Rep Soph Cls; Cl Rep Jr Cls; Cls Rep Sr Cls; Band; Chrs; Drl Tm; Drm Mjrt; Hon Rl; Sch Pl; Kent St Univ; Law.

SMITH, SUZANNE; Logan Elm HS; Laurelville, OH; Band; Chrs; Hon Rl; Hosp Ade; NHS; Red Cr Ade; Sch Pl; College; Speech Educ.

SMITH, T; Ben Davis HS; Indianapolis, IN; 27/833 Debate Tm; Natl Forn Lg; Off Ade; Fr Clb; Indiana Univ; Bus.

SMITH, TAMARA; Brookville HS; Brookville, IN; 18/196 Band; Girl Scts; Hon Rl; Sprt Ed Sch Nwsp; Spn Clb; Letter Bsktbl; Trk; GAA; Univ; Eng.

SMITH, TAMARA; Lakeland HS; Highland, MI; NHS; Stu Cncl; Yth Flsp; Ed Yrbk; Rptr Yrbk; Rptr Sch Nwsp; Pep Clb; Pom Pon; Western Michigan Univ; Spec Ed.

SMITH, TAMMY; Portage Lakes Jnt Voc Schl; Akron, OH; Cl Rep Jr Cls; Band; Chrs; Chrh Wkr; Girl Scts; Hon Rl; Hosp Ade; Lbry Ade; Sch Mus; Sch Pl; Univ Of Akron; Home Ec.

SMITH, TAMORAH; Hopewell Loudon HS; Fostoria, OH; VP Sr Cls; Band; Hon Rl; VP NHS; Yth Flsp; Capt Bsktbl; Capt Trk; Cit Awd; Bowling Green S U; Computer Progr.

SMITH, TERESA; Springfield HS; Battle Crk, MI; Cl Rep Jr Cls; Cmp Fr Grls; Chrh Wkr; Hon Rl; Lbry Ade; NHS; Stu Cncl; FHA; Pep Clb;.

SMITH, TERESA; Talcott HS; Talcott, WV; Cls Rep Frsh Cls; Sec Soph Cls; Chrh Wkr; Hon Rl; JA; Sch Pl; Stu Cncl; 4-H; FBLA; FHA; Bus Schl; Sec.

SMITH, TERI; Salem Sr HS; Salem, OH; 33/245 Band; Chrs; Hon Rl; Sch Mus; Pep Clb; Spn Clb; Kent St Univ; Bus.

SMITH, TERRENCE; St Francis De Sales HS; Erie, MI; Band; Boy Scts; Chrh Wkr; Debate Tm; Hon Rl; Natl Forn Lg; Orch; Sct Actv; IM Sprt; Bst Presdng Offc Oh HS Spch Lg St Ocngrss 79; 1st Pl OHSSL Falldebts 76; Boy Scout Life Awd 77; Univ.

SMITH, TERRI; Clawson Sr HS; Clawson, MI; Chrh Wkr; Hon Rl; Orch; Sch Mus; Mth Clb; Spn Clb; Natl Merit Ltr; Lawrence Inst Of Tech; Acctg.

SMITH, TERRI; Tyler Cnty HS; Middlebourne, WV; 19/90 Band; Hon Rl; Treas Jr NHS; Stu Cncl; Yth Flsp; VP FTA; Pep Clb; Bsktbl; Trk; Sec GAA;.

SMITH, TERRI; Tyler HS; Middlebourne, WV; 19/90 Band; Hon Rl; Jr NHS; Stu Cncl; Yth Flsp; VP FTA; Pep Clb; Bsktbl; Trk; GAA; College.

SMITH, TERRI; Logansport HS; Logansport, IN; Band; Chrs; Girl Scts; Jr NHS; Mdrgl; Natl Forn Lg; Sch Mus; Sch Pl; Sct Actv; Stg Crw; Indiana Univ; Pre Med.

SMITH, TERRILEE; Harry S Truman HS; Taylor, MI; 4/507 Am Leg Aux Girls St; VP NHS; Stu Cncl; Letter Gym; Letter Swmmng; Letter Trk; JC Awd; Eastern Mic Univ; Math.

SMITH, TERRILL; Onsted Community HS; Clayton, MI; 4/118 Cmp Fr Grls; Hon Rl; Sec NHS; Sch Pl; Sec 4-H; FHA; Chrldng; 4-H Awd; Lenawee Bankers Schlrshp 79; Mi Competitive Schlrshp 79; Ferris St Coll; Archt Drafting.

SMITH, THERESA; Marsh Fork HS; Rock Crk, WV; Cls Rep Frsh Cls; Am Leg Aux Girls St; Band; Chrs; Chrh Wkr; Girl Scts; Hon Rl; Hosp Ade; NHS; Stu Cncl; Morris Harvey Coll; Nursing.

SMITH, THERESA; Newbury HS; Chagrin Falls, OH; Hon Rl; Trs Frsh Cls; College; Elem Educ.

SMITH, THERESA; Blanchester HS; Blanchester, OH; 1/155 Sec Soph Cls; Am Leg Aux Girls St; Hon Rl; NHS; Stu Cncl; Rptr Sch Nwsp; Spn Clb; Chrldng; GAA; Am Leg Awd; Univ; Math.

SMITH, THERESA K; Brown County HS; Nashville, IN; 11/149 Am Leg Aux Girls St; VP FCA; Mod UN; Treas NHS; Quill & Scroll; Stg Crw; Rptr Sch Nwsp; Lat Clb; Spn Clb; Letter Bsktbl; NHS Schlrshp 79; Grad Hon Stud; Spanish 5 6 Awrd 79; Vincennes Univ; Paralegal.

SMITH, THOMAS; Trenton HS; Trenton, MI; Aud/Vis; Hon Rl; Jr NHS; Lat Clb; Ten; Michigan St Univ; Vet.

SMITH, THOMAS H; London HS; London, OH; 11/133 Cl Rep Jr Cls; Band; Boy Scts; Hon Rl; NHS; Orch; Sct Actv; Stu Cncl; 4-H; Letter Ftbl; Oh Test Of Schlstc Achvmnt Hon Mention; Oh Tests 7th Dist Genrl Sci 77; Oh Tests 20 Dist 1st Bio 78; Univ; Sci.

SMITH, THOMAS K; Cowan HS; Muncie, IN; 3/80 Chrh Wkr; Hon Rl; NHS; Sch Mus; Yth Flsp; 4-H; 4-H Awd; Ball St Univ; Pharmacy.

SMITH, THOMAS S; Wellsville HS; Wellsville, OH; 6/109 Am Leg Boys St; Hon Rl; NHS; FTA; Youngstown St Univ; Educ.

SMITH, TIM J; Allen Park HS; Allen Park, MI; Trs Frsh Cls; Boy Scts; Chrs; Hon Rl; Treas JA; Lbry Ade; Sch Pl; Drama Clb; Western Michigan Univ; Acctg.

SMITH, TIMOTHY; St Clement HS; Center Line, MI; Sch Pl; Drama Clb; Trk; IM Sprt; Macomb County Comm College; Engr.

SMITH, TIMOTHY L; Bellefontaine HS; Bellefontaine, OH; Band; Hon Rl; Univ.

SMITH, TODD; Au Gres Sims HS; Au Gres, MI; Cl Rep Jr Cls; Boy Scts; Natl Forn Lg; Sch Pl; Yth Flsp; Ftbl; Trk; Ferris Coll; Data Processing.

SMITH, TOM; Mona Shores HS; Muskegon, MI; Hon Rl; NHS; Capt Glf; Hockey; IM Sprt; College.

SMITH, TRACY; Prairie Heights HS; La Grange, IN; 30/138 Sec Frsh Cls; Sec Soph Cls; Sec Jr Cls; Aud/Vis; Band; Hon Rl; Off Ade; Red Cr Ade; Stu Cncl; International Bus College; Bus.

SMITH, TRACY L; Beaver Local HS; E Liverpool, OH; 14/242 Trs Sr Cls; Band; Chrs; Chrh Wkr; Hon Rl; Jr NHS; NHS; Off Ade; Sch Mus; Yth Flsp; Busns Schl; Finance.

SMITH, TRINA; Princeton HS; Princeton, WV; Cls Rep Soph Cls; Band; Hon Rl; Jr NHS; Drama Clb; Pep Clb; Spn Clb; Twrlr; College; Sciences.

SMITH, TRUDY; Zanesville HS; Zanesville, OH; Chrs; Hon Rl; NHS; Sch Mus; Letter Gym; Chrldng; Scholastic Ach Awds; College.

SMITH, VERNON; Greenfield Central HS; Greenfield, IN; Boy Scts; Hon Rl; Sct Actv; Rptr Yrbk; VICA; College; Law.

SMITH, VERONICA; East HS; Columbus, OH; Sec Soph Cls; Sec Jr Cls; Band; Chrs; Chrh Wkr; Drl Tm; Sec Stu Cncl; Rptr Sch Nwsp; Trk; Mgrs; Soc Of Dist Amer HS Stu; Ball St Univ; Broadcasting.

SMITH, VICKIE; S Spencer HS; Richland, IN; 25/146 Band; Chrs; Hon Rl; NHS; Sch Mus; Drama Clb; Trk; Twrlr; Indiana Univ; Education.

SMITH, WANDA; Mount View HS; Welch, WV; Chrh Wkr; Hon Rl; Hosp Ade; Jr NHS; NHS; Quill & Scroll; Yrbk; Keyettes; Bluefield St Coll.

SMITH, WENDY; Washington HS; E Chicago, IN; Chrh Wkr; Hon Rl; NHS; FHA; Business School.

SMITH, WES; Mohawk HS; Melmore, OH; Sch Pl; FTA; Lat Clb; Letter Bsbl; Letter Bsktbl; Letter Ftbl; Cit Awd; College; Law.

SMITH, WILLIAM; East HS; Akron, OH; Aud/Vis; Chrh Wkr; Hon Rl; Off Ade; Kent State; Forestry.

SMITH, WILLIAM; Northwestern HS; West Salem, OH; 5/150 VP Frsh Cls; Chrs; Hon Rl; NHS; Sch Pl; IM Sprt; College; Acctg.

SMITH, WILLIAM; Chillicothe HS; Chillicothe, OH; Aud/Vis; Band; Boy Scts; Chrh Wkr; Sch Pl; Stu Cncl; Rptr Sch Nwsp; Letter Trk; Ohio Univ; Cmnctns.

SMITH, WILLIAM A; Farmington HS; Farmington Hls, MI; Cls Rep Frsh Cls; Band; Drm Bgl; Hon Rl; MMM; NHS; Orch; PAVAS; Lat Clb; Mbr Mi Yth Bnd Univ Of Mi; Oakland Univ Orch Oakland Univ; Interlochen Natl Music Cmp; Univ Of Michigan; Music.

SMITH, WILLIAM H; Elwood Community HS; Elwood, IN; Cl Rep Jr Cls; Debate Tm; Jr NHS; Pol Wkr; Sch Mus; Sch Pl; Ed Yrbk; Ed Sch Nwsp; Pres Drama Clb; Pres Lat Clb; Univ; Poli Sci.

SMITH, WILLIAM W; Dekalb HS; Corunna, IN; 2/309 Band; Natl Forn Lg; NHS; Sch Pl; Ger Clb; Sci Clb; Natl Merit SF; College.

SMITH, YVONNE; Marysville HS; Marysville, OH; 35/227 Chrs; Hon Rl; Sch Mus; Sch Pl; 4-H; FFA; Capt Chrldng; IM Sprt; 4-H Awd;.

SMITHBERGER, JOE; St Charles Prep; Pataskala, OH; Chrh Wkr; Hon Rl; NHS; Univ; Engr.

SMITHBERGER, STEVEN; St Charles Prep; Pataskala, OH; 5/63 Chrh Wkr; Hon Rl; Jr NHS; NHS; Rptr Yrbk; Rptr Sch Nwsp; Letter Ftbl; Ohio St Univ; Elec Engr.

SMITHERMAN, JAMES OTIS C; St Xavier HS; Cincinnati, OH; Band; Boy Scts; Hon Rl; Hosp Ade; Red Cr Ade; Sct Actv; Hosp Volunteer; Med.

SMITHSON, JEFF; Sycamore HS; Montgomery, OH; Hon Rl; JA; Cit Awd; Coll; Cmmrcl Art.

SMITKA, CAROLYN M; Morton Sr HS; Hammond, IN; Chrs; Hon Rl; Mdrgl; Sch Mus; Sch Pl; FTA; Purdue Univ.

SMITLEY, LA NAE; Adams Central HS; Monroe, IN; 2/98 Cls Rep Frsh Cls; Cls Rep Soph Cls; Band; Chrh Wkr; FCA; Girl Scts; Hon Rl; NHS; Sch Pl; Stu Cncl; Chosen To Go To Indiana Yth Power Indianapolis; Went To Seminar For Talented Stu At ISU; College; Medicine.

SMITLEY, MARK; Bishop Nell Inst; Munster, IN; 51/321 Boy Scts; JA; Sct Actv; College; Architecture.

SMITS, PETER; Redford HS; Detroit, MI; 1/400 Val; Band; Hon Rl; NHS; Orch; Sch Mus; Ten; Bausch & Lomb Awd; Elk Awd; Natl Merit Ltr; St Of Mi Legsltv Grant 79; Mi St Univ Ohon 79; John J Muldowney Memrl Soc Std Awd 78; Michigan St Univ; Elec Engr.

SMITT, DOUGLAS; Marysville HS; Marsyville, OH; 28/230 Pres Soph Cls; Chrs; Debate Tm; Natl Forn Lg; NHS; IM Sprt; Univ; Comp Progr.

SMOCK, BRENDA; Lake Fenton HS; Linden, MI; Band; Drm Mjrt; Girl Scts; Hon Rl; NHS; Red Cr Ade; Sct Actv; Drama Clb; Letter Chrldng; Twrlr; Mi Comptn Schlrshp Awd 79; Michigan St Univ; Travel.

SMOKE, MARY; Tecumseh HS; Adrian, MI; Chrs; Chrh Wkr; Girl Scts; Hon Rl; NHS; Sch Pl; Fr Clb; Crs Cntry; Letter Trk; College.

SMOLBOSKI, SHERYL; Pershing HS; Detroit, MI; Chrs; Hon Rl; Hosp Ade; NHS; Off Ade; Swmmng; College; Med Tech.

SMOLEN, JAMES; George Rogers Clark HS; Whiting, IN; Trs Frsh Cls; JA; Sct Actv; Ger Clb; Crs Cntry; Glf; Trk; Purdue; Elec Tech.

SMOLINSKI, JEFFREY; Monroe Catholic Central HS; Monroe, MI; 1/95 Val; Hon Rl; NHS; Ed Sch Nwsp; 4-H; Glf; Trk; Bausch & Lomb Awd; Boy Scts; IM Sprt; Mic Tech Univ; Mechanical Engineer.

SMOLINSKI, MARK; Monroe Catholic Central HS; Monroe, MI; 1/100 Cls Rep Soph Cls; Cl Rep Jr Cls; Hon Rl; NHS; Sch Pl; Stg Crw; Stu Cncl; 4-H; Pep Clb; 4-H Awd; Univ Of Mic; Medicine.

SMONT, KIMBERLY; Garfield HS; Akron, OH; Hon Rl; Jr NHS; Lbry Ade; NHS; Off Ade; Treas Sct Actv; VP OEA; Pep Clb; Legal Stenog.

SMOOT, DIANA; East HS; Columbus, OH; Chrh Wkr; Hon Rl; Stu Cncl; OEA; Spn Clb; Trk; Mgrs; Math Awd; Duke Univ; Law.

SMOOT, GARY; Valley HS; Lucasville, OH; 1/107 Val; Chrs; Hon Rl; NHS; Stu Cncl; Capt Crs Cntry; Capt Trk; Ohio St Univ; Pharm.

SMOOT, JOSEPH; Hampshire HS; Romney, WV; 57/220 Cls Rep Frsh Cls; Cls Rep Soph Cls; Cl Rep Jr Cls; Cls Rep Sr Cls; AFS; Chrh Wkr; Cmnty Wkr; Hon Rl; JA; Off Ade; St Farmer Degree 79; FFA Actvty Ribbn 79; Goldn Anniv Medl Schlhp Pin & Learshp Pin FFA; WVU; Natl Resorces.

SMOOT, KATHY; Huntington East HS; Huntington, WV; Band; Hon Rl; Jr NHS; NHS; Yrbk; Mth Clb; Spn Clb; DAR Awd; Med Tech.

SMREK, JEAN; Woodrow Wilson HS; Youngstown, OH; 72/307 Y-Teens; Pres FHA;.

SMTIH, CAMILLA; Buckhannon Upshur HS; Buckhannon, WV; Sec Frsh Cls; Sec Soph Cls; Girl Scts; Off Ade; Sct Actv; Y-Teens; 4-H; Wv Career College; Secreetarial.

SMTIH, STEVEN; Kelloggsville HS; Kentwood, MI; Chrh Wkr; Hon Rl; JA; Ftbl; Ten; Trk; IM Sprt; USC; Bus Admin.

SMULO, JODY; Trinity HS; Maple Hts, OH; 1/150 Cls Rep Soph Cls; Cl Rep Jr Cls; Chrs; Hon Rl; Hosp Ade; Jr NHS; NHS; Sch Mus; Stu Cncl; Pep Clb; Appreciation Schlrshp; Ohio St Univ; Mathematics.

SMURDA, MICHAEL; Brooke HS; Follansbee, WV; 66/466 FCA; Hon Rl; NHS; Sci Clb; Crs Cntry; Wrstlng; IM Sprt; West Virginia Univ; Pharm.

SMURL, M ELIZABETH; North Central HS; Indianapolis, IN; 76/1060 Hon Rl; NHS; Sch Pl; Stu Cncl; Drama Clb; Fr Clb; Letter Trk; Univ; Dramatic Arts.

SMYCZYNSKI, STEPHEN N; Cardinal Mooney HS; Youngstown, OH; 29/288 Sal; Debate Tm; Hon Rl; Orch; Glf; Highest Avg In Bio 1 & Mech Drawing 1; Highest Avg Chem 1 Adv Placement; MIT; Nuclear Engr.

SMYLES, SHIRLEY; Lumen Cordium HS; Garfield Hts, OH; 32/106 Hon Rl; Ed Yrbk; Spn Clb; GAA; Scholastic Award 77 78; Tri Coll; Law.

SMYTH, SCOTT L; Champion HS; Warren, OH; Band; Boy Scts; Chrh Wkr; Sct Actv; Yth Flsp; DECA; Ftbl; IM Sprt; Kent St Univ; Auto Engr.

SMYTH, SHELLY; Howell Sr HS; Howell, MI; 4/407 Chrh Wkr; Cmnty Wkr; Hon Rl; NHS; Off Ade; Sch Pl; Stg Crw; VP Yth Flsp; Civ Clb; Drama Clb; Ferris Merit Schlrshp; Chem Awd; Acctg Awd; Ferris St Coll; Comp Prog.

SMYTH, WILLIAM; Gwinn HS; Skandia, MI; 13/206 Hon Rl; NHS; Ten; Natl Merit Schl; Northern Mic Univ; Agri.

SNADER, JILL; Walnut Ridge HS; Columbus, OH; Chrs; Chrh Wkr; Hon Rl; Orch; VP Yth Flsp; Treas Spn Clb; GAA; Ohio State Univ; Education.

SNAPP, BETTY; Whiteland Cmnty HS; New Whiteland, IN; 32/229 Chrs; Chrh Wkr; FCA; Girl Scts; Hon Rl; NHS; Sch Mus; Drama Clb; 4-H; FHA; Sales.

SNARE, KAREN; Ridgedale HS; Marion, OH; Chrs; Chrh Wkr; Hon Rl; Hosp Ade; Lbry Ade; Sch Mus; Yth Flsp; College; Nursing.

SNAVELY, TAMMY; Delphi Community HS; Camden, IN; 21/137 Am Leg Aux Girls St; Chrh Wkr; Girl Scts; Hon Rl; Univ.

SNEAD, MARILYN; Onsted Community HS; Onsted, MI; Chrs; Chrh Wkr; Cmnty Wkr; Hon Rl; NHS; Yth Flsp; Spn Clb; College; Acctg.

SNEAD, RONALD; East Kentwood HS; Kentwood, MI; Natl Forn Lg; Sch Mus; Spn Clb; IM Sprt; Natl Merit Ltr; Pres Awd; Young Amer Club Mbr; Black Awareness Club Treas; Univ; Tchr.

SNELL, DAVE; West Clermont Career Ctr; Amelia, OH; Chrh Wkr; Hon Rl; Yth Flsp; DECA; Letter Bsbl; Letter Ftbl; IM Sprt; Letter Mgrs; Univ Of Cincinnati; Retail Mgmt.

SNELL, KEVIN; Columbia City Joint HS; Columbia City, IN; Boy Scts; Sci Clb; Spn Clb; Letter Bsktbl; Bus Schl; Bus.

SNELL, MICHELLE; East Jackson HS; Jackson, MI; 7/120 Trs Frsh Cls; Sec Soph Cls; VP Jr Cls; VP Sr Cls; Hon Rl; VP NHS; Bsktbl; Trk; Jackson Community College; Pre Law.

SNELLMAN, JILL; Lake Ridge Acad; Strongsville, OH; Band; Chrh Wkr; Girl Scts; Hon Rl; Orch; Sch Pl; Ten; Chrldng; IM Sprt; PPFtbl; College Of Wooster; Bus Admin.

SNIDE, CINDY; Whetstone HS; Columbus, OH; Chrs; Chrh Wkr; Drl Tm; Girl Scts; Hon Rl; Jr NHS; Sch Mus; Sch Pl; Stu Cncl; Yth Flsp; UCLA; Theatre.

SNIDER, BARBARA; Buckhannon Upshur HS; French Creek, WV; Chrh Wkr; Cmnty Wkr; Hon Rl; Lbry Ade; 4-H;.

SNIDER, BELINDA S; Williamston HS; Williamston, MI; 8/154 AFS; Chrs; Girl Scts; Jr NHS; Sct Actv; Rptr Yrbk; Scr Kpr; Tmr; Natl Merit SF; Univ Of Michigan; Nursing.

SNIDER, DAVID; Glen Este HS; Cincinnati, OH; Band; Cmnty Wkr; Hon Rl; Bsktbl; Ftbl; Univ Of Cincinnati; Busns.

SNIDER, HAROLD; Lebanon HS; Lebanon, OH; Boy Scts; Chrs; Cmnty Wkr; Hon Rl; NHS; Sct Actv; Stg Crw; Sch Nwsp; Sci Clb; IM Sprt; Cert Yearly Recd For Perf Schl Attnd For 11 Yrs; Nom For Best Stu Of The Yr 76; Univ; Archt.

SNIDER, JACQUELINE; Caldwell HS; Caldwell, OH; Lbry Ade; Off Ade; 4-H; FHA; Lat Clb; Pep Clb; Letter Bsbl; College.

SNIDER, JOYCE; Notre Dame HS; Clarksburg, WV; Band; Chrs; Stg Crw; FDA; Pep Clb; IM Sprt;.

SNIDER, LISA; Lakeland Christian Academy; Winona Lake, IN; 3/18 Sec Soph Cls; Pres Jr Cls; Band; Hon Rl; NHS; Off Ade; Sch Pl; Stu Cncl; Rptr Sch Nwsp; Drama Clb; Grace Coll; Bus.

SNIDER, MARY L; Milton HS; Milton, WV; Band; Chrs; Cmnty Wkr; Pol Wkr; Red Cr Ade; Sch Mus; Stg Crw; DECA; 4-H; FBLA; Marshall Univ; Soc Work.

SNIDER, NEYSA; Western Brown HS; Mt Orab, OH; 26/220 Band; Cmp Fr Grls; Girl Scts; Hon Rl; Jr NHS; NHS; Yrbk; Drama Clb; College; Psych.

SNIDER, PAUL; Swartz Creek Community HS; Flint, MI; Univ Of Michigan.

SNIDER, RANDY; Delta HS; Albany, IN; 88/297 FFA; Lat Clb; Sci Clb; Ball St Univ Sci Fair; Delta H S Sci Fair; FFA Awds; Univ.

SNIDER, SALLY; Dexter HS; Dexter, MI; Band; Pres Girl Scts; NHS; Off Ade; Sct Actv; Treas Ger Clb; Letter Trk; 1st Cl Scout Recvd 76; Girl Scout Acknowldg Awd Recv 79; Michigan Tech; Conservation.

SNIDER, SUSAN; St Joseph Cntrl Catholic HS; Fremont, OH; 31/100 Cls Rep Soph Cls; Band; Cmp Fr Grls; Chrs; Chrh Wkr; Hon Rl; Hosp Ade; Sch Mus; Sct Actv; Stu Cncl; Univ; Nursing.

SNITZER, ROBERT; Ursuline HS; Campbell, OH; 1/350 Cl Rep Jr Cls; Hon Rl; NHS; Stu Cncl; IM Sprt; Math Lab Asst 78; Student Council 78; Univ; Pre Med.

SNIVELY, KIRBY; Harbor Springs HS; Harbor Springs, MI; Cls Rep Frsh Cls; Cls Rep Soph Cls; VP Jr Cls; Boy Scts; Chrs; Cmnty Wkr; Hon Rl; Sch Mus; Sct Actv; Stg Crw; Kendall Schl Of Design; Advrtsng.

SNIVELY, MARK; Lexington HS; Mansfield, OH; Treas Band; Chrh Wkr; Trk; Wrstlng; Mas Awd; Columbus Tech Inst; Aviation Tech.

SNODDY, JULIE; Waynesville HS; Waynesville, OH; 30/110 Girl Scts; Hon Rl; Sch Mus; Sch Pl; Yth Flsp; Rptr Sch Nwsp; Sch Nwsp; 4-H; Gym; Trk; Eastern Kentucky Univ; Spec Educ.

SNODGRASS, CARLA; Frankfort Sr HS; Frankfort, IN; 32/251 Band; Chrh Wkr; Drm Bgl; Orch; Sch Mus; Sch Pl; Yth Flsp; FTA; Univ; Music.

SNODGRASS, DARREN; Avon HS; Plainfield, IN; Band; Chrs; Chrh Wkr; Drm Mjrt; Hon Rl; Sch Mus; Sci Clb; Glf; IM Sprt; Milligan Coll; Pre Law.

SNODGRASS, KIM; South Charleston HS; South Charlestn, WV; Band; Chrs; Hon Rl; Jr NHS; NHS; Sch Mus; Pres Stu Cncl; Pres Spn Clb; Letter Ten; Cit Awd; Univ.

SNODGRASS, THOMAS; Mannington HS; Mannington, WV; Hon Rl; NHS; Letter Bsktbl; Ftbl; Letter Trk; Coach Actv; IM Sprt; Fairmont State; Math.

SNOGRASS, ERIC; Maple Hts HS; Maple Hgts, OH; Ftbl; Univ.

SNOOK, JACKLYN; Celina Sr HS; Celina, OH; NHS; Lat Clb; PPFtbl; Univ; Art.

SNOOR, RUTH L; Newark Sr HS; Newark, OH; Chrs; Hon Rl; Natl Forn Lg; NHS; Sch Nwsp; Pres DECA; Pep Clb; Sci Clb; Voice Dem Awd; Ohio State Univ; Busns Admin.

SNOPIK, TERESA; St Francis Desales HS; Columbus, OH; Cls Rep Frsh Cls; Hon Rl; Sch Mus; Stg Crw; Rptr Yrbk; Drama Clb; Coach Actv; Mat Maids; Univ Of Dayton; Criminology.

SNOW, DEBORAH; Perrysburg HS; Perrysburg, OH; 7/248 Trs Frsh Cls; Hon Rl; NHS; Stu Cncl; Spn Clb; Letter Bsktbl; College; Recreation.

SNOW, RICHARD T; Jackson HS; Jackson, MI; Band; Crs Cntry; Wrstlng; Tmr; Mic State Univ; Athletic Trainer.

SNOW, SHELLY; Springport HS; Springport, MI; Chrs; Hon Rl;.

SNOWBALL, PAUL; John Adams HS; Cleveland, OH; Jr NHS; NHS; Coll; Psych.

SNOWDEN, ANNETTE; Gallia Academy; Gallipolis, OH; Band; Yth Flsp; Y-Teens; Rptr Yrbk; 4-H; FTA; Pep Clb; Sci Clb; Spn Clb; Chrldng; Marching Band; Symphonic Band; Woodwind Choir; Job Daughters Mbr; Soph Homeroom Pres; College; Elem Ed.

SNOWDEN, ELIZABETH; Manchester HS; Akron, OH; Hosp Ade; Akron Univ; Eng.

SNOWHITE, JENNIFER; Marion HS; Marion, IN; Chrs; NHS; Quill & Scroll; Sch Mus; Sprt Ed Sch Nwsp; Sch Nwsp; Letter Gym; Letter Swmmng; Letter Ten; Rotary Awd; Univ; Med.

SNUFFER, DANIEL H; Independence HS; Coal City, WV; Boy Scts; Trs Frsh Cls; Stu Cncl; Beta Clb; Sci Clb; Letter Crs Cntry; Letter Trk; Letter Wrstlng; Scr Kpr; Eagle Scout BSA 1978; Intl Sci & Engr Fair Finlst 1978; Annapolis; Research.

SNYDER, ALICE; Bellaire HS; Bellaire, OH; 5/238 Trs Soph Cls; VP Jr Cls; Hon Rl; Jr NHS; NHS; Y-Teens; Fr Clb; Pep Clb; Bsktbl; IM Sprt; West Liberty St Coll; Dent Hygnst.

SNYDER, AMANDA; Oak Hill HS; Oak Hill, OH; Chrs; Hon Rl; Sch Mus; Sch Pl; Stg Crw; Stu Cncl; Rptr Yrbk; Rptr Sch Nwsp; Lat Clb; Pep Clb; Ohio Univ.

SNYDER, CATHY; Laville HS; Lapaz, IN; Fr Clb; Ten; GAA; Scr Kpr; College; Nursing.

SNYDER, CHARLES; Charlestown HS; Charlestown, IN; Band; Boy Scts; NHS; Drama Clb; IM Sprt; Univ; Engr.

SNYDER, CYNTHIA; Port Clinton Sr HS; Pt Clinton, OH; Band; Hon Rl; Red Cr Ade; Ger Clb; Bsktbl; Red Cross Awd For Volunteering 77; All Around Excell Perf In German I Class 78; Univ; Phys Ther.

SNYDER, DANA; Webster County HS; Webster Springs, WV; Chrh Wkr; Hon Rl; Yth Flsp; 4-H; Trk; Ohio State; Rotc.

SNYDER, DEBORAH; Bremen HS; Bremen, IN; 9/104 FCA; Hon Rl; NHS; 4-H; Bsktbl; Ten; GAA; 4-H Awd;.

SNYDER, DENISE; Whitmer HS; Toledo, OH; 17/900 Hon Rl; NHS; Stg Crw; Yth Flsp; Ger Clb; German Amer Fest Soc Schlrshp 77 79; Univ; Pre Med.

SNYDER, DONNA; Forest Park HS; Cincinnati, OH; Girl Scts; Sch Mus; Rptr Sch Nwsp; Sch Nwsp; College; Journalism.

SNYDER, DOUGLAS; Richmond Sr HS; Richmond, IN; Am Leg Boys St; Chrh Wkr; Debate Tm; Hon Rl; Jr NHS; Spn Clb; Natl Merit Ltr; Univ; Poli Sci.

SNYDER, JEFF; Harding HS; Marion, OH; 49/490 Boy Scts; NHS; Pres Yth Flsp; VP 4-H; Coach Actv; IM Sprt; Ohio St Univ; Busns.

SNYDER, JILL; Comstock Park HS; Comstock Pk, MI; Band; Hon Rl; NHS; Orch; Sch Mus; Yrbk; Bsktbl; GAA; Cit Awd; Grand Rapids Jr Coll; Bus Admin.

SNYDER, JOHN; Harry S Truman HS; Taylor, MI; Lbry Ade; GUSC; Comp Sci.

SNYDER, JOHN; Ypsilanti HS; Ypsilanti, MI; Hon Rl; Boys Clb Am; Bsbl; Glf; IM Sprt;.

SNYDER, JOSETTE; Lumen Cordium HS; Northfield, OH; Cls Rep Frsh Cls; Cls Rep Soph Cls; Cl Rep Jr Cls; Drl Tm; Hon Rl; NHS; Sch Pl; Treas Stu Cncl; Drama Clb; GAA; College.

SNYDER, JUDITH; Seymour HS; Seymour, IN; Chrh Wkr; Hon Rl; Sch Pl; Yrbk; VP Drama Clb; FFA; OEA; Pep Clb; VP Pres Ball State University; Major.

SNYDER, JULIE; Washington HS; Massillon, OH; Cls Rep Frsh Cls; Cls Rep Soph Cls; Cl Rep Jr Cls; Cls Rep Sr Cls; AFS; Girl Scts; Off Ade; Y-Teens; Pep Clb; Spn Clb; Aultman; Rn.

SNYDER, KAREN; Perry HS; Massillon, OH; Am Leg Aux Girls St; Band; Chrs; Drm Mjrt; Hon Rl; Natl Forn Lg; NHS; Off Ade; Sch Mus; Twrlr; Univ; Vocal Music.

SNYDER, KENNETH; Washington HS; Massillon, OH; College; Radiology.

SNYDER, KIMBERLY; Grafton HS; Grafton, WV; Band; Chrs; Hon Rl; Hosp Ade; Sch Mus; Sch Pl; Yrbk; Drama Clb; Chrldng; PPFtbl; Univ.

SNYDER, LEE M; Southeastern HS; Chillicothe, OH; 4/100 Am Leg Boys St; Hon Rl; Jr NHS; NHS; Treas Ger Clb; Letter Bsbl; Letter Bsktbl; Coach Actv; Am Leg Awd; Univ; Phys Educ.

SNYDER, LISA; Plymouth HS; Rochester, IN; 25 Hon Rl; NHS; Off Ade; Sch Pl; Stg Crw; College; Elem Educ.

SNYDER, MARTHA; Goshen HS; Goshen, IN; Chrs; Hon Rl; NHS; Sch Mus; Sch Pl; Drama Clb; VP Spn Clb; Crs Cntry; Trk; Univ; Engr.

SNYDER, MARY; Madison Plains HS; London, OH; Band; Chrs; Hon Rl; Lbry Ade; Mod UN; Sch Pl; 4-H; Spn Clb; Letter Trk; 4-H Awd; Salem Coll; Equestrian Studies.

SNYDER, MARY; Clay HS; South Bend, IN; 38/448 Chrh Wkr; Hon Rl; Mod UN; NHS; Sprt Ed Yrbk; Rptr Yrbk; Rptr Sch Nwsp; Lat Clb; Mgrs; Univ; Poli Sci.

SNYDER, NANCY J; Tri West Hendricks HS; Lizton, IN; 2/125 Band; Cmp Fr Grls; Chrh Wkr; FCA; Hon Rl; NHS; 4-H; Fr Clb; Pep Clb; Letter Trk; Purdue Univ; Sci.

SNYDER, PENNY; Garaway HS; Baltic, OH; Sec Sr Cls; Band; Chrs; Chrh Wkr; Hon Rl; Yth Flsp; Rptr Sch Nwsp; College.

SNYDER, REBECCA; Grace Christian School; Benton Harbor, MI; 1/5 Cl Rep Jr Cls; Val; Chrh Wkr; Hon Rl; NHS; Stu Cncl; Fr Clb; Mth Clb; DAR Awd; Highst Pace Avr Awd 79; Admin Awd 79; Grace Coll; Elem Educ.

SNYDER, REBECCA; Concordia Lutheran HS; Ft Wayne, IN; 15/187 Chrs; Hon Rl; Letter Bsktbl; Letter Trk; Univ; Phys Ed.

SNYDER, RHONDA; Our Lady Of Angels HS; Cincinnati, OH; Am Leg Aux Girls St; Chrs; Chrh

Wkr; Girl Scts; Hon Rl; Sch Pl; Ed Yrbk; Rptr Yrbk; Mgrs; Scr Kpr; Mbr Of Natl Bus Hon Soc 78; Instrmntl 78; Cincinnati Tech Coll; Law.

SNYDER, ROBERT; Southeastern HS; Londonderry, OH; Hon Rl; Yth Flsp; Spn Clb; Bsbl; IM Sprt; Univ.

SNYDER, ROBIN; Harper Creek HS; Battle Creek, MI; VP Band; Hon Rl; NHS; Sch Nwsp; Spn Clb; Bsktbl; Michigan St Univ; Sci.

SNYDER, ROSE; Edgewood HS; Ashtabula, OH; 33/275 Am Leg Aux Girls St; Chrh Wkr; Jr NHS; NHS; Ed Sch Nwsp; Bsbl; Bsktbl; GAA; Akron; Med.

SNYDER, SANDY; East HS; Akron, OH; 11/297 Chrs; Hon Rl; Natl Forn Lg; NHS; Quill & Scroll; Pres Red Cr Ade; Sch Nwsp; Univ Of Akron; Guidance Cnslr.

SNYDER, SCOTT; Sullivan HS; Sulivan, IN; 4/151 Band; Hon Rl; Lat Clb; IM Sprt; Rose Hulman Inst Of Tech; Chem.

SNYDER, SHELLY; Rogers HS; Toledo, OH; Cls Rep Soph Cls; Trs Jr Cls; Cls Rep Sr Cls; Chrh Wkr; FCA; Hon Rl; Lbry Ade; Off Ade; Pep Clb; Spn Clb; OSU Bgsu Tu; Soc Std.

SNYDER, SHERRY C; South Knox HS; Wheatland, IN; Chrs; Drl Tm; Hon Rl; FNA; IM Sprt; Pom Pon; Vincennes Jr Coll; Lab Tech.

SNYDER, STEPHANIE; Westfall HS; Williamsport, OH; Sec Frsh Cls; Sec Soph Cls; Band; NHS; Stu Cncl; Yth Flsp; Rptr Sch Nwsp; 4-H; FNA; Chrldng; Delegate Ohio Clb Conress 4 H; Capital Univ; Nursing.

SNYDER, TERESA; Allendale Public HS; Allendale, MI; 1/69 Val; Band; Chrh Wkr; FCA; Hon Rl; Lit Mag; NHS; Drama Clb; Pep Clb; Bsktbl; Western Mi Univ; Bus Admin.

SNYDER, THOMAS; Loveland Hurst HS; Loveland, OH; 20/229 Boy Scts; Hon Rl; Socr; Trk; Univ; Engr.

SNYDER, WENDY; Tiffin Columbian HS; Tiffin, OH; Band; Chrs; Hon Rl; NHS; Spn Clb; Chrldng; Wind Symphony; Concert Band; Stage Band; Vocational School.

SNYDER, WILLIAM; Jimtown HS; Elkhart, IN; Am Leg Boys St; Boy Scts; Chrh Wkr; Hon Rl; Mod UN; NHS; Yth Flsp; Fr Clb; Bsktbl; Ftbl; Summer Honors Seminar; Most Likely To Succeed; Nominee Lily Awd Schlrshp; Wabash Coll; Law.

SNYDER JR, LEWIS; Reading HS; Reading, MI; 7/85 Band; Chrh Wkr; Hon Rl; NHS; Fr Clb; Pep Clb; Crs Cntry; Liberty Baptist Coll; Elem Ed.

SOARDS, BONNIE; Mississinewa HS; Marion, IN; 31/198 Sec Jr Cls; Chrh Wkr; Hon Rl; Hosp Ade; Jr NHS; Off Ade; Rptr Yrbk; Rptr Sch Nwsp; DECA; FHA; Univ; CPA.

SOBAK, KAREN; Regina HS; Detroit, MI; 5/134 Debate Tm; Hon Rl; Hosp Ade; Natl Forn Lg; Pres NHS; FDA; Wayne State Univ; Bio.

SOBCZAK, CHRIS; Bishop Foley HS; Warren, MI; Hon Rl; Letter Glf; College; Pro Golfer.

SOBCZAK, EDWARD; St Clement HS; Detroit, MI; Boy Scts; Chrh Wkr; Hon Rl; Sch Pl; Sct Actv; Yrbk; Boys Clb Am; Drama Clb; Univ; Jrnlsm.

SOBCZYK, KEN; Bloomingdale HS; Grand Junction, MI; VP Sr Cls; Hon Rl; Ftbl; Michigan Competitive Schlrshp; Merrifield Schlrshp; Davenport Coll; Acctg.

SOBECKI, KIRK; Penn HS; Mishawaka, IN; Hon Rl; Jr NHS; NHS; Letter Ftbl; Letter Trk; Purdue Univ; Wildlife Mgmt.

SOBEL, ROCHELLE; Firestone HS; Akron, OH; Chrh Wkr; Cmnty Wkr; Yrbk; Sch Nwsp; Ohio Univ; Jrnlsm.

SOBER, LAURA; Fowlerville HS; Fowlerville, MI; 1/150 Val; Band; Cmnty Wkr; Hon Rl; NHS; Mth Clb; Am Leg Awd; DAR Awd; 4-H Awd; Compus Hdr Schlrshp Eastern Mi Univ 79; Philomathearn Schlrshp 79; Stu Coun Schlrshp 79; Eastern Michigan Univ; Acctg.

SOBESKI, MICHAEL; Shady Spring HS; Shady Spring, WV; 25/160 Pres Frsh Cls; Cls Rep Frsh Cls; Pres Soph Cls; Cls Rep Soph Cls; Cls Rep Sr Cls; Am Leg Boys St; Boy Scts; Chrh Wkr; FCA; Hon Rl; Outstndng Stu; Marshall Univ; Education.

SOBOLEWSKI, DAN; Medina HS; Medina, OH; 71/354 Aud/Vis; Band; Boy Scts; Cmnty Wkr; Off Ade; Yrbk; Key Clb; Bsbl; Ten; IM Sprt; Creighton Univ; Bus.

SOBOLEWSKI, JAMES; Ironwood Catholic HS; Ironwood, MI; 1/25 Pres Frsh Cls; Val; Am Leg Boys St; Chrh Wkr; Hon Rl; Sch Mus; Pres Stu Cncl; Pep Clb; Letter Bsktbl; Letter Trk; N Michigan Univ; Communications.

SOBOLEWSKI, JIM; Ironwood Catholic HS; Ironwood, MI; 1/25 Pres Frsh Cls; Val; Am Leg Boys St; Hon Rl; Sch Mus; Pres Stg Crw; Pep Clb; Capt Bsbl; Letter Bsktbl; Letter Trk; College; Communications.

SOBOLEWSKI, JOHN; St Edward HS; Cleveland, OH; Chrh Wkr; Hon Rl; Mod UN; NHS; Quill & Scroll; Rptr Yrbk; Ed Sch Nwsp; Rptr Sch Nwsp; Am Leg Awd; Univ.

SOBOTKA, CYNDY; Admiral King HS; Lorain, OH; Band; Chrs; Sch Mus; Rptr Yrbk; Fr Clb; Key Clb; Mth Clb; Sci Clb; Gym; Twrlr; Akron St Univ; Acctg.

SOCALL, CYNTHIA; Garden City West HS; Garden City, MI; 10/400 Chrh Wkr; Cmnty Wkr; Hon Rl; NHS; Fr Clb; Spn Clb; Tmr; Natl Merit Schl; Hope Coll; Chem.

SOCHA, STEVE; Marysville Sr HS; Marysville, MI; Cl Rep Jr Cls; Am Leg Boys St; Band; Sch Pl; Stu Cncl; Ftbl; Wayne St Univ; Mortuary Sci.

SOCIE, TAMI; Cardinal Stritch HS; Toledo, OH; Hon Rl; Sch Pl; Stu Cncl; Fr Clb; Trk; Chrldng; Bowling Green.

SODERBERG, ANGELA; Pine River HS; Le Roy, MI; Band; Hon Rl; Natl Merit Schl; College; Vet.

SODERGREN, HOLLY; Westwood HS; Ishpeming, MI; Band; Chrh Wkr; Hon Rl; Sch Mus; Sch Pl; Stg Crw; Yrbk; OEA; Pep Clb; Trk; N Michigan Univ.

SOEDEL, SVEN; West Lafayette HS; W Lafayette, IN; Hon Rl; Sch Mus; Sch Pl; Letter Swmmng; Ten; Trk; College; Med.

SOEURT, CONNIE L; Decatur Central HS; Indianapolis, IN; 88/400 Trs Soph Cls; Cl Rep Jr Cls; Off Ade; Sec Stu Cncl; Letter Bsktbl; Letter Glf; Ten; Univ; Law.

SOFIAN, MARLENE; St Frances Cabrini HS; Allen Pk, MI; Chrs; Hon Rl; Jr NHS; NHS; Spn Clb; Pres Awd; Detroit Coll Of Bus Admin; Lgl Sec.

SOFIKITIS, IRENE; Brookfield HS; Brookfield, OH; Cls Rep Frsh Cls; Band; Girl Scts; Hon Rl; NHS; Stu Cncl; Beta Clb; FDA; Spn Clb; Chrldng; NEDT Superior Perfrmnc 77; Attndnc Awd 76 & 77; Youngstown St Univ; Med Tech.

SOHMER, JEAN; Bentley HS; Burton, MI; Band; Hon Rl; Lbry Ade; NHS; Off Ade; Sch Pl; Chrldng; Cit Awd; College; Vet.

SOHNS, JACK; Bishop Gallagher HS; Harper Woods, MI; 5/350 Hon Rl; Letter Ftbl; IM Sprt; Univ; Phys Sci.

SOJA, K; Belleville HS; Belleville, MI; Band; Hon Rl; 4-H; Ger Clb; Pep Clb; Bsbl; 4-H Awd; Eastern Mich Univ.

SOKELAND, JUSTIN; Orleans HS; Orleans, IN; 8/80 Am Leg Boys St; Chrh Wkr; Cmnty Wkr; Hon Rl; Lbry Ade; Yrbk; Sec FFA; IM Sprt; Ind State; Mathamatics.

SOKOL, DAN; Meadowdale HS; Dayton, OH; 23/239 Chrh Wkr; Cmnty Wkr; Hon Rl; NHS; Sch Pl; Stg Crw; Hockey; Univ Of Wisconsin; Engr.

SOKOL, DAVID; St Edwards HS; No Olmsted, OH; Chrh Wkr; Cmnty Wkr; Hon Rl; Stu Cncl; Sch Nwsp; Pep Clb; Spn Clb; Coach Actv; IM Sprt; PPFtbl; Bowling Green Univ; Med.

SOKOLIK, MARK; Poul K Cousino HS; Warren, MI; Hon Rl; Wayne State Univ; Elec Engr.

SOKOLOSK, MARY; Saint Francis De Sales HS; Columbus, OH; 1/200 Chrs; Girl Scts; Hon Rl; Capt NHS; Quill & Scroll; Sch Nwsp; Spn Clb; Capt Trk; IM Sprt; College; Engineer.

SOKOLOSKIS, BARNEY; Bridgman HS; Bridgman, MI; Boy Scts; Chrs; Hon Rl; Lbry Ade; Sct Actv; 4-H; Trk; Wrstlng; Tmr; Michigan Tech Univ; Chem.

SOKOLOSKIS, BERNEY; Bridgman HS; Bridgman, MI; Boy Scts; Chrs; Sch Mus; Sct Actv; Stg Crw; Boys Clb Am; Bsktbl; Letter Trk; Mgrs; MTU; Electronic.

SOLAR, PATRICIA; Croswell Lexington HS; Lecington, MI; Band; Girl Scts; Hon Rl; Hosp Ade; 4-H; IM Sprt; 4-H Awd; St Clair Cnty Cmnty Coll; LPN.

SOLEM, ELIZABETH; L C Mohr HS; South Haven, MI; Band; Chrs; Chrh Wkr; Hon Rl; NHS; Sch Mus; Bsbl; Chrldng; IM Sprt; College; Health Profession.

SOLERO, NARCISO; Northrop HS; Ft Wayne, IN; 1/590 Chrh Wkr; Hon Rl; Orch; Sch Mus; Yth Flsp; Tri Kappa Pin & Cert; Music Letters; Schlrshp With Distinction Cert; Whos Who In In & Ky HS Foreign Lang; De Pauw Schl; Music Performance.

SOLGERE, VICKI; Greensburg Community HS; Greensburg, IN; 25/211 Cls Rep Soph Cls; Cl Rep Jr Cls; Trs Sr Cls; Cls Rep Sr Cls; FCA; NHS; Sch Mus; Stu Cncl; Glf; Purdue; Sch Of Bus.

SOLIK, CAROL E; Flat Rock HS; Flat Rock, MI; 5/114 Hon Rl; NHS; Off Ade; Letter Trk; Detroit Busns Inst; Exec Sec.

SOLITRO, ANTHONY; James A Garfield HS; Ravenna, OH; Cls Rep Soph Cls; Band; Boy Scts; Hon Rl; NHS; Sch Pl; Rptr Sch Nwsp; Sci Clb; Spn Clb; Letter Bsktbl; Univ; Med.

SOLLARS, CHARLES; Westfall HS; Mt Sterling, OH; 36/140 Band; Sci Clb; Bsbl; Bsktbl; Crs Cntry; Trk; College; Architect.

SOLLER, WILLIAM; Marysville HS; Marysville, OH; Hon Rl; Stg Crw; Letter Ten; IM Sprt; Ohio St Univ; Aviation.

SOLLERS, JODY; Bridgeport HS; Bridgeport, WV; 8/189 Chrs; Hon Rl; Treas NHS; Sch Mus; Sch Pl; Fr Clb; Capt Ten; Yale Univ; Economics.

SOLLMANN, DEAN; Bradford HS; Bradford, OH; 3/69 Am Leg Boys St; Band; Chrs; Hon Rl; NHS; Sch Pl; Rptr Yrbk; Drama Clb; FFA; FHA; U S Air Force Acad; Aviation Sci.

SOLLY, DEBBIE; Evergreen HS; Berkey, OH; Hon Rl; Rptr Sch Nwsp; Sch Nwsp; GAA; Findlay Coll; Communication.

SOLMEN, DAVID; Crestview Local HS; Columbia, OH; Hon Rl; Key Clb; Trk; Attended Th Wrld Affairs Inst Rot Club 79; Pittsburg Gunsmithing Schl; Gunsmith.

SOLOKO, JENINE; Holly Sr HS; Holly, MI; 7/293 VP Band; Hon Rl; Chrldng; PPFtbl; Flag Corps 1978; Michigan St Univ.

SOLOMON, CYNTHIA; Covington HS; Covington, OH; Band; Chrh Wkr; Drm Mjrt; Hon Rl; Off Ade; 4-H; Bsbl; Chrldng; Edison State College; Sec.

SOLOMON, JOHN; Weirton Madonna HS; Weirton, WV; 32/96 Chrs; Hon Rl; JA; Jr NHS; NHS; Sch Mus; Rptr Sch Nwsp; Trk; IM Sprt; Univ; Bus.

SOLOMON, KRISTINE; Mumford HS; Detroit, MI; 40/500 Chrh Wkr; Hon Rl; Lbry Ade; NHS; Beta Clb; VICA; Cit Awd; College; Commercial Artist.

SOLOMON, MARK; Central Preston Sr HS; Albright, WV; Hon Rl; Lit Mag; Yrbk; Trk; Dundalk Cmnty Univ; Pro Photog.

SOLOMON, STEVEN; Luke M Powers HS; Grand Blanc, MI; Chrs; Chrh Wkr; Drl Tm; Sch Mus; Glf; St Of Michigan Comp Schlrshp Awd; Michigan St Univ; Criminal Justice.

SOLON, LORI; Oxford West Campus HS; Oxford, MI; Cls Rep Frsh Cls; Cl Rep Jr Cls; VP Band; Pres Chrs; Hon Rl; Pres Jr NHS; Sch Mus; Sch Pl; Stu Cncl; PPFtbl; Univ; Theatre.

SOLOVEIKO, THERESA; Stow Lakeview HS; Stow, OH; 25/536 Cls Rep Frsh Cls; Sec Soph Cls; Band; Chrs; Chrh Wkr; Hon Rl; Hosp Ade; NHS; Sch Pl; Stu Cncl; Bowling Green Univ.

SOLT, TIM; Bucyrus HS; Burycus, OH; 24/200 Cls Rep Frsh Cls; Band; Boy Scts; Cmnty Wkr; Hon Rl; Jr NHS; NHS; Sct Actv; Stg Crw; Stu Cncl; Eagle Scout Boy Scouts 78; Univ; Archt.

SOLTER, JEFFREY; Wintersville HS; Wintersville, OH; FCA; Hosp Ade; Red Cr Ade; ROTC; 4-H; Gym; Trk; Letter Wrstlng; IM Sprt; Cit Awd; College; Civil Engr.

SOLTES, PATRICIA; Regina HS; Richmond Hts, OH; Cls Rep Soph Cls; Cls Rep Sr Cls; Chrs; Girl Scts; Hon Rl; Stg Crw; Stu Cncl; Chrldng; College; Business.

SOLTIS, BARBARA; Columbiana HS; N Lima, OH; 28/101 Hon Rl; JA; Rptr Sch Nwsp; Sch Nwsp; Drama Clb; Hiramor Youngstown St Univ; Med.

SOLTISZ, BENJAMIN; Nordonia Sr HS; Northfield, OH; Letter Ftbl; Letter Wrstlng; Ohio St Univ; Dentistry.

SOLYMOSI, JANICE L; North HS; Willowick, OH; 29/612 Cls Rep Frsh Cls; Hon Rl; JA; Jr NHS; Mod UN; NHS; Stu Cncl; VP Keyettes; Bus Mgmt.

SOMENSATIO, MIRNA; Aquinas HS; Southgate, MI; Sec Frsh Cls; Sec Soph Cls; Sec Jr Cls; Cmp Fr Grls; Chrh Wkr; Hon Rl; NHS; Off Ade; Fr Clb; Pep Clb; Univ Of Michigan; Law.

SOMERS, LAURIE; Ovid Elsie HS; Elsie, MI; Hon Rl; Mgrs; Univ; Child Care.

SOMERVILLE, DAVID; Wirt County HS; Elizabeth, WV; 20/106 Pres Frsh Cls; Cls Rep Soph Cls; Pres Jr Cls; Cmnty Wkr; FCA; Hon Rl; NHS; Stu Cncl; Letter Bsbl; Letter Ftbl; Wv Tech; Welder.

SOMERVILLE, JANICE; North Farmington HS; Farmington Hil, MI; Cls Rep Frsh Cls; Trs Soph Cls; Sec Sr Cls; Chrs; Chrh Wkr; Hon Rl; Natl Forn Lg; NHS; Sch Pl; Stu Cncl; Eng Awd; Public Speaking/-dram Awd; Michigan St Univ; Journalism.

SOMERVILLE, KAY; Coventry HS; Akron, OH; 5/150 Band; Chrs; Off Ade; Sch Mus; Stu Cncl; Yth Flsp; Chrldng; Twrlr; Am Leg Awd; College; Teacher.

SOMERVILLE, SUSAN; Grayling HS; Grayling, MI; VP Frsh Cls; Cls Rep Soph Cls; Pres Sr Cls; Am Leg Aux Girls St; Band; Chrh Wkr; Hon Rl; Natl Forn Lg; NHS; Stu Cncl; Univ; Pre Med.

SOMERVILLE, VICTORIA; William Henry Harrison HS; W Laf, IN; 30/350 Band; Hon Rl; NHS; Fr Clb; Letter Swmmng; Letter Trk; Tmr; College; Bus.

SOMICH, CATHY; Streetsboro HS; Streetsboro, OH; Chrs; Girl Scts; Hon Rl; Hosp Ade;.

SOMMER, ANTHONY; Rossville HS; Frankfort, IN; 4/51 Pres Frsh Cls; Natl Forn Lg; Fr Clb; Natl Merit Ltr; Opt Clb Awd; VFW Awd; Voice Dem Awd;.

SOMMER, BARBARA; Edsel Ford HS; Dearborn, MI; 83/490 Cls Rep Sr Cls; Chrh Wkr; Girl Scts; Hon Rl; NHS; Stu Cncl; Treas Pep Clb; Letter GAA; IM Sprt; Mat Maids; Detroit Coll Of Bus; Office Admin.

SOMMER, CRAIG; Solon HS; Solon, OH; Hon Rl; Stg Crw; Bsbl; Bsktbl; Ftbl; Hndbl; Hockey; Swmmng; Wrstlng; IM Sprt; Univ; Drafting.

SOMMER, DOUGLAS; Standish Sterling Cntrl HS; Standish, MI; 14/152 Cls Rep Sr Cls; Band; Hon Rl; Hnr Stu; Central Michigan Univ.

SOMMER, ELIZABETH P; Dondero HS; Royal Oak, MI; 7/400 Chrh Wkr; Debate Tm; Hon Rl; Lit Mag; Sec NHS; Quill & Scroll; Sch Pl; Ed Yrbk; Yrbk; Drama Clb; Michigan St Univ; Bus.

SOMMER, MARK; Concord HS; Albion, MI; 6/90 Hon Rl; JA; NHS; VICA; Cit Awd; Univ Of Michigan; Bus Mgmt.

SOMMERFELDT, DENISE; Hartford HS; Hartford, MI; 1/90 Sec Sr Cls; Am Leg Aux Girls St; Band; Hon Rl; NHS; Sch Pl; Stu Cncl; Chrldng; Twrlr; 4-H Awd; Perfect Attndnc Awds 77 78 & 79; Michigan St Univ; Comp Sci.

SOMMERS, DANIEL; Browsburg HS; Indianapolis, IN; Hon Rl; NHS; 4-H; Ten; IM Sprt; 4-H Awd;.

SOMMERS, LOIS; Cardinal Stritch HS; Oregon, OH; Chrs; Hon Rl; Sch Mus; Univ Of Dayton; Comp Prog.

SOMMERS, LYNN; Clarkston Sr HS; Davisburg, MI; Cmp Fr Grls; Chrh Wkr; Hon Rl; Drama Clb; Gym; Germn Awd 77; Coll.

SOMMERVILLE, DAVID; Buckhannon Upshur HS; Buckhannon, WV; Am Leg Boys St; Band; Chrh Wkr; Hon Rl; Stg Crw; Yth Flsp; 4-H; Letter Bsbl; W Va Univ; Engr.

SOMMERVILLE, TROY; South Harrison HS; Wolf Summit, WV; Trs Jr Cls; Hon Rl; Jr NHS; Pres NHS; Sch Pl; Treas Stu Cncl; Treas FTA; Math Assoc Of Amer Awd 78; Fairmont St Coll; Physician.

SON, T; Snider HS; Ft Wayne, IN; Boy Scts; Chrh Wkr; Cmnty Wkr; Hon Rl; Red Cr Ade; Fr Clb; Mth Clb; IUPU; Comp Sci.

SONCHIK, JANET; Beaumont Girls HS; Maple Hts, OH; Cls Rep Soph Cls; Chrh Wkr; Hon Rl; PAVAS; Sch Pl; Fr Clb; IM Sprt; College; Law.

SONDEREKER, DENISE; Southeast Local HS; Rootstown, OH; 1/165 Val; Band; NHS; Orch; PAVAS; Sch Pl; Stg Crw; Rptr Yrbk; Ed Sch Nwsp; Rptr Sch Nwsp; Kent State Univ; Journalism.

SONEFELD, JENNIFER; Douglas Mac Arthur HS; Saginaw, MI; Band; Chrs; Chrh Wkr; Cmnty Wkr; Drm Bgl; Drm Mjrt; Hon Rl; PAVAS; Sch Mus; Yth Flsp; Trophy For Most Valuable & Outstanding Mbr Of Saginaires Drum & Bugle Corp 2nd Plc In Vocal Reg Duet; College; Music.

SONNAD, SEEMA; Loy Norrix HS; Kalamzoo, MI; Chrs; Girl Scts; Hon Rl; Orch; Sch Mus; Stg Crw; Yth Flsp; Drama Clb; College; Med Research.

SONNEFELD, SHAWNA; Cambridge HS; Cambridge, OH; Cls Rep Frsh Cls; Cls Rep Soph Cls; Cl Rep Jr Cls; Cls Rep Sr Cls; Bsktbl; Swmmng; Ten; Trk; Coach Actv; GAA; Mic State Univ; Physch.

SONNENBERG, EDMUND J; Madison Comprehensive HS; Mansfield, OH; 8/480 Lbry Ade; Treas NHS; Sch Pl; Stg Crw; Stu Cncl; Treas Spn Clb; Century III Ldrs Award; College; English Ed.

SONNER, ANGELINE; Corydon Central HS; Mauckport, IN; 6/164 Band; Chrh Wkr; Hon Rl; NHS; Sprt Ed Sch Nwsp; Drama Clb; 4-H; Pep Clb; Spn Clb; Letter Bsktbl;.

SONNEVILLE, SHARI; Pennfield HS; Battle Creek, MI; Letter Band; Hon Rl; Letter JA; Sch Pl; Letter Chrldng; GAA; St Of Mi Competitive Schlrshp Progr 79; Cmnty Hosp Med Club Assoc With The Scout; Univ Of Michigan; Phys Ther.

SONODA, KEVIN; Cuyahoga Heights HS; Cuyahoga Hts, OH; Band; Hon Rl; Yrbk; Ftbl; Trk; Univ; Elec Engr.

SONS, ESTHER; Felicity Franklin HS; Bethel, OH; 20/74 Chrs; Chrh Wkr; Drl Tm; Sch Pl; Spn Clb; Bsktbl; College; Bus Admin Mkgt.

SONS, KAREN; Tri Jr Sr HS; Straughn, IN; Spn Clb; Bus Schl; Sec.

SOOS, MICHAEL; Trinity HS; Garfield Hts, OH; Chrs; Hon Rl; IM Sprt; Elec Tech Inst; Elec Engr.

SOPER, EDITH; Gaylord HS; Gaylord, MI; 13/182 Chrs; Chrh Wkr; Girl Scts; Hon Rl; NHS; Spn Clb; Lake Superior State College; Math.

SOPER, SCOTT A; Cedar Lake Acad; Berrien Spgs, MI; Band; Chrh Wkr; Hon Rl; Andrews Univ; Aviation Mech.

SOPER, SHARON; Norwell HS; Bluffton, IN; 9/193 Sec Soph Cls; Chrs; Chrh Wkr; Hon Rl; Jr NHS; NHS; Treas Yth Flsp; Sec 4-H; Key Clb; Pep Clb; Huntington Univ; Elem Ed.

SOPHA, JAMES; Redford Union HS; Redford, MI; Cmnty Wkr; Hon Rl; JA; Bsktbl; Ftbl; Trk; Coach Actv; Tmr; Univ; Bus.

SOPHER, MICHELLE; Galion HS; Galion, OH; Band; Chrs; Girl Scts; Hon Rl; Hosp Ade; Yth Flsp; Y-Teens; 4-H; Mat Maids; 4-H Awd; College; Comp Programing.

SORELL, JENNIFER L; Morgan HS; Mc Connelsville, OH; Trs Sr Cls; Am Leg Aux Girls St; Drm Mjrt; NHS; VP Stu Cncl; Ed Yrbk; Letter Gym; Letter Trk; Chrldng; PPFtbl; Univ.

SORENSON, DEBORAH; Hill Mccloy HS; Montrose, MI; Hon Rl; NHS; Yrbk; Sch Nwsp; Trk; Univ Of Mic.

SORENSON, STEVEN; La Salle HS; St Ignace, MI; Am Leg Boys St; Chrh Wkr; Hon Rl; Sch Pl; Stg Crw; Drama Clb; Sci Clb; Trk; Coach Actv; Letter Mgrs; Lake Superior St Coll; Med Tech.

SORENSON, STEVEN; Farmington HS; Farmington, MI; Band; Hon Rl; Rptr Sch Nwsp; Ger Clb; Natl Merit Schl; Univ Of Michigan; Engr.

SORG, CHRIS; Washington HS; Massillon, OH; Chrs; Hon Rl; Sch Mus; Civ Clb; Chrldng; Stark Tech Coll.

SORG, LORI; Heritage HS; Ft Wayne, IN; 8/175 Chrh Wkr; Hon Rl; Y-Teens; Lat Clb; Coach Actv; Univ; Med.

SORG, MARY ANN; Fremont Ross HS; Fremont, OH; 16/448 Pres Cmp Fr Grls; Drl Tm; Hon Rl; Jr NHS; MMM; NHS; Key Clb; Pom Pon; Ohio St Univ; Law.

SORG, STACY; Wheeling Cntrl Catholic HS; Wheeling, WV; Hon Rl; JA; Sch Pl; Natl Merit SF; Univ; Bio.

SORGI, SUZANNE; N Royalton HS; Broadview Hts, OH; 35/286 Drama Clb; Fr Clb; Cuyahoga Comm College; Social Work.

SORN, KEVIN; Reeths Puffer HS; Muskegon, MI; Hon Rl; Yth Flsp; Spn Clb; Bsktbl; Ftbl; Socr; Trk; Coach Actv; Pres Awd; Outstndng Off Linemn 77; All Sports Awd Trophy 74 76; Univ; Data Proc.

SOROKA, MICHAEL R; Campbell Memorial HS; Cambpell, OH; 58/205 Boy Scts; Chrh Wkr; Cmnty Wkr; Mth Clb; Spn Clb; Letter Ftbl; Letter Wrstlng; Coll; Engr.

SOROVETZ, JOHN S; Gabriel Richard HS; Southgate, MI; Hon Rl; Sch Pl; Ed Yrbk; Bsbl; Letter Bsktbl; Ftbl; IM Sprt; Mgrs; Scr Kpr; Natl Merit Ltr; St Of Mi Comp Schlrshp 79; Michigan St Univ; Mrktng Research.

SORRELL, JOE; Hagerstown Jr Sr HS; Hagerstown, IN; VP Frsh Cls; Hon Rl; Letter Bsktbl; Coach Actv; Univ.

SORRELL, MARTIN; Wellston HS; Jackson, OH; 15/126 Cls Rep Soph Cls; Cl Rep Jr Cls; VP Sr Cls; Chrh Wkr; Cmnty Wkr; Hon Rl; Lbry Ade; NHS; Sch Mus; Stu Cncl; World Affairs Delgt 78; Valparaiso Univ; Poli Sci.

SORRELL, SCOTT; Keystone HS; La Grange, OH; Chrs; Pres FTA; Letter Bsbl; Letter Bsktbl; Letter Ftbl; Letter Trk; Coach Actv; Ftbl Mr Offence Awd 79; Bsktbl Sportsmnshp Awd 79; Ashland Coll; History.

SORRELS JR, JAMES H; Lakota HS; West Chester, OH; 24/469 Band; Boy Scts; Hon Rl; Jr NHS; NHS; Orch; Yth Flsp; Spn Clb; Cit Awd; Univ Of Cincinnati; Doctor.

SORSTOKKE, LEN; Benzie Cnty Ctrl HS; Honor, MI; Band; Hon Rl; Jr NHS; 4-H; Lat Clb; Mth Clb; Univ; Elec Engr.

SOSA, MARY; West Washington HS; R R 1, IN; 3/64 Am Leg Aux Girls St; Band; Drm Mjrt; Hon Rl; NHS; Sch Mus; Sch Pl; Drama Clb; FFA; Sci Clb; Purdue Univ; Sci.

SOSNOWSKI, CAROL; Charles Stewart Mott HS; Warren, MI; 17/670 Chrh Wkr; Hon Rl; Jr NHS; NHS; Off Ade; Stg Crw; Spn Clb; Crs Cntry; Trk; Mgrs; Wayne State Univ; Bus.

SOTIROPOULOS, THOMAS J; Kettering Fairmont East HS; Kettering, OH; Cls Rep Frsh Cls; Cls Rep Soph Cls; Trs Jr Cls; AFS; Boy Scts; Chrs; Chrh Wkr; Hon Rl; Natl Forn Lg; Pol Wkr; Ohio H S Speech Lge 2nd 1979; Fairmnt E Schlstc Awds Speech & Soc Stds 1979; Soroptimist Yth Citznshp Awd; Baldwin Wallace Coll; Poli Sci.

SOTNYK, JERRY; Benton Harbor HS; Benton Hbr, MI; Band; Hon Rl; NHS; Orch; Glf; Voc Schl; Electronics.

SOTO, MICHAEL; Bettsville HS; Bettsville, OH; Pres Frsh Cls; VP Jr Cls; Am Leg Boys St; JA; Jr NHS; Bsbl; Bsktbl; Am Leg Awd; Cit Awd; College; Elec.

SOUCEK, DAVID; Normandy Sr HS; Seven Hls, OH; Cls Rep Frsh Cls; Cls Rep Soph Cls; Hon Rl; NHS; Mth Clb; Letter Ftbl; Letter Trk; Letter Wrstlng; Univ Of Cincinnati; Civil Engr.

SOUCEK, TED; Padua Franciscan HS; Cleveland, OH; Cls Rep Soph Cls; Cls Rep Sr Cls; Hon Rl; Cleveland St Univ; Bus Mgmt.

SOUCHOCK, CAROL; Fordson HS; Dearborn, MI; Cls Rep Soph Cls; Cl Rep Jr Cls; Cls Rep Sr Cls; Hon Rl; Stu Cncl; Sprt Ed Yrbk; Letter Glf; GAA; Univ Of Michigan; Busns.

SOUDER, AMY; Southern HS; Portland, OH; Cls Rep Frsh Cls; Pres Soph Cls; Am Leg Aux Girls St; Chrs; Hon Rl; Jr NHS; MMM; Stu Cncl; Yrbk; Capt Chrldng; Ohio Univ; Medical Lab Tech.

SOUDER, JEFFREY; Eastern HS; Pekin, IN; 3/91 Cls Rep Sr Cls; Am Leg Boys St; Band; Hon Rl; Pres NHS; Sch Pl; Sec FFA; Letter Bsbl; Glf; DAR Awd; Purdue Univ; Comp Sci.

SOUDER, KENNETH E; Wayne HS; Dayton, OH; 186/570 ROTC; Natl Ach Commended Stu; Natl Sci Found Project 1 Scholarship; College; Astro Engr.

SOUDERS, ANGIE; Findlay HS; Findlay, OH; 100/686 Cmp Fr Grls; Hon Rl; Quill & Scroll; Sprt Ed Sch Nwsp; Sch Nwsp; Pep Clb; Coach Actv; Ohio Univ; Jrnlsm.

SOUDERS, BARRY; Jackson HS; Jackson, OH; 96/238 Chrs; Sch Nwsp; Pres 4-H; Sci Clb; 4-H Awd; Coll; Conservation.

SOUERS, STEVEN; Northrop HS; Ft Wayne, IN; 15/589 Aud/Vis; Band; Hon Rl; Indiana Univ; CPA.

SOULE, ELIZABETH; Theodore Roosevelt HS; Kent, OH; 99/368 Band; Cmp Fr Grls; Chrs; Chrh Wkr; Hon Rl; NHS; Pres Stu Cncl; Ed Sch Nwsp; Pep Clb; Spn Clb; MAC Schools; Foreign Lang.

SOULLIER, DANIEL; East Detroit HS; E Detroit, MI; Band; Hon Rl; JA; Tex A & M; Agri Sci.

SOULLIERE, JUDY; Algonac HS; Harsens Island, MI; 3/220 Cls Rep Frsh Cls; Hst Soph Cls; Cls Rep Soph Cls; Hon Rl; Hosp Ade; NHS; Stu Cncl; Mic State Univ; Civil Engr.

SOULTS, MARY; Trenton HS; Trenton, MI; Trs Frsh Cls; Jr NHS; Sec NHS; Sch Mus; Stu Cncl; Pep Clb; Capt Chrldng; Michigan St Univ; Acctg.

SOURBECK, GREGG; Dondero HS; Royal Oak, MI; Hon Rl; Jr NHS; Spanish Achvmnt Awd 76; Univ; Comp Sci.

SOURGES, JAMES; Warren John F Kennedy HS; Warren, OH; VP Frsh Cls; Pres Soph Cls; Am Leg Boys St; Hon Rl; NHS; Sch Pl; Letter Ftbl; Letter Trk; College; Eng.

SOUTH, JULIE; Badin HS; Hamilton, OH; 4/217 Chrs; Chrh Wkr; Hon Rl; NHS; Sch Mus; Sch Pl; Ed Sch Nwsp; Drama Clb; Fr Clb; Miami Univ; English.

SOUTHERLAND, LENORE; The Rayen School; Youngstown, OH; 10/184 Cls Rep Sr Cls; Pres Band; Hon Rl; Rptr Yrbk; VP Key Clb; Lat Clb; Bsktbl; Trk; Scr Kpr; Kiwan Awd; 2nd Pl City Sci Fair 78; Schlrshp For Kiwanis 79; Broke Discus Rec In Schl For Rayen 79; Youngstown St Univ; Vet.

SOUTHERLAND, SARAH; Central HS; Evansville, IN; 18/571 Band; Capt Drm Mjrt; NHS; Stu Cncl; Yth Flsp; Twrlr; College; Commercial Art.

SOUTHERN, TINA; Clinton Prairie HS; Colfax, IN; Girl Scts; Hon Rl; Hosp Ade; Sch Nwsp; Drama Clb; FBLA; FTA; Letter Bsktbl; Letter Trk; GAA; Purdue Univ; Phys Educ.

SOUTHEY, ROBERT G; Copley HS; Akron, OH; 1/317 Hon Rl; NHS; Natl Merit Ltr; Univ; Internatl Affairs.

SOUTHGATE, CHRISTY; Unionville Sebewaing HS; Akron, MI; Chrs; Hon Rl; NHS; Drama Clb; Pep Clb; Letter Bsbl; Letter Trk; Coach Actv; Tmr; College; Florist.

SOUTHGATE, DAVID; U S A HS; Unionville, MI; Am Leg Boys St; Hon Rl; Stu Cncl; Yrbk; Bsbl; Ftbl; Am Leg Awd; Pres Awd; Univ; Construction.

SOUTHLAND, MARK; St Joseph Sr HS; St Joseph, MI; Cls Rep Frsh Cls; Cls Rep Soph Cls; VP Jr Cls; Cl Rep Jr Cls; Chrs; Hon Rl; Sch Mus; Fr Clb; IM Sprt; Tmr; Stdnt Sen Vc Pres 79; Univ; Pre Med.

SOUTHWARD, MARY; Kearsley HS; Flint, MI; Cls Rep Frsh Cls; Hon Rl; Stu Cncl; Yrbk; Chrldng; Homecoming Ct; Univ Of Michigan.

SOUTHWELL, MICHAEL; Jackson County Western HS; Parma, MI; Sec Frsh Cls; Trs Frsh Cls; Cls Rep Soph Cls; Stu Cncl; Fr Clb; Letter Trk; IM Sprt; Univ; Bio Sci.

SOUTHWICK, LESLIE; Huron HS; Ann Arbor, MI; 60/600 Chrh Wkr; Hon Rl; Lit Mag; Yth Flsp; Ger Clb; Alma Coll; Eng.

SOUTHWOOD, SCOTT; Timken HS; Canton, OH; Band; Boy Scts; Hon Rl; Yth Flsp; God Cntry Awd; College; Zoology.

SOUTHWORTH, CORINNE; Marcellus HS; Marcellus, MI; 2/100 Sec Soph Cls; Hon Rl; NHS; Yrbk; Chrldng; Mi Correctns Assoc 78; Cass Cnty Police Dept 74; Western Michigan Univ; Acctg.

SOUTHWORTH, DEBBRA; Miami Trace HS; Washington C H, OH; Sec Frsh Cls; Cls Rep Soph Cls; Cl Rep Jr Cls; AFS; Drl Tm; Hon Rl; Off Ade; Sch Pl; Stu Cncl; Drama Clb; Univ.

SOVA, ELAINE; Cardinal Mooney HS; Youngstown, OH; Cls Rep Soph Cls; Band; Sch Pl; Stg Crw; Mth Clb; Spn Clb; Univ Of Akron; Nursing.

SOVA, STEPHEN A; Bishop Watterson HS; Columbus, OH; 10/249 Boy Scts; Hon Rl; Sct Actv; Rptr Yrbk; Ed Sch Nwsp; Sprt Ed Sch Nwsp; Natl Merit Ltr; Insignis Schlrshp Univ Of Detroit 79; Battelle Memorial Ldrshp Schlrshp OSU 79; Mbr Champshp In The Know; The Ohio St Univ; Engr.

SOVIS, JOHN; Ovid Elsie HS; Elsie, MI; Cls Rep Frsh Cls; Cls Rep Soph Cls; Hon Rl; Sch Nwsp; Bsbl; Letter Ftbl; IM Sprt; Central Michigan Univ; Bus.

SOWA, CHRISTOPHER; Aquinas HS; Lincoln Park, MI; Boy Scts; Drama Clb; Natl Merit SF; Michigan St Lgsltve Awd 79; Michigan Competitive Schlrshp; Wayne St Univ.

SOWA, DIANE; St Alphonsus HS; Detroit, MI; 7/171 Girl Scts; Hon Rl; Fr Clb; Pres Awd; College.

SOWA, PAULA; Perrysburg HS; Perrysburg, OH; Chrh Wkr; Cmnty Wkr; Girl Scts; Sch Nwsp; Ger Clb; Crs Cntry; Socr; Trk; College; Environ Sci.

SOWAR, JUDITH; Archbishop Alter HS; Dayton, OH; 48/300 Letter Drl Tm; Hon Rl; NHS; Sch Nwsp; Treas Spn Clb; Letter Trk; Miami Univ; English.

SOWARDS, SHIRLEY; Peebles HS; Peebles, OH; 6/95 Sec Frsh Cls; VP Jr Cls; Hon Rl; Lbry Ade; Off Ade; FTA; Pep Clb; Southern St Univ.

SOWARDS, VALERIE; Eastern HS; Beaver, OH; 1/67 Pres Frsh Cls; Cl Rep Jr Cls; Girl Scts; Hon Rl; VP NHS; Yrbk; FHA; Pep Clb; College; Home Ec.

SOWASH, THOMAS; Anderson HS; Anderson, IN; Band; Hon Rl; Orch; 4-H; Lat Clb; 4-H Awd; Ind Univ; Optometry.

SOWDER, MICHELE; Lockland HS; Cincinnati, OH; 6/71 Chrh Wkr; Drl Tm; Hon Rl; Hosp Ade; NHS; Sch Pl; Drama Clb; Spn Clb; Scr Kpr; Univ; Phys Ther.

SOWDER, PENNY; Hinton HS; Hinton, WV; Chrh Wkr; Hon Rl; Sch Pl; FBLA; Lat Clb; Vocational School.

SOWDER, RICHARD; Edgewood HS; Bloomington, IN; 2/223 Trs Frsh Cls; Band; Hon Rl; VP JA; NHS; Ger Clb; JA Awd; Lion Awd; Indiana Univ; Pre Med.

SOWDER, RICHARD E; Edgewood HS; Bloomington, IN; 3/230 Trs Frsh Cls; Band; Hon Rl; JA; Ger Clb; JA Awd; Lion Awd; Indiana Univ; Dentistry.

SOWDERS, BETTIE; Bedford North Lawrence HS; Bedford, IN; 46/385 Cls Rep Soph Cls; Cl Rep Jr Cls; Cls Rep Sr Cls; Chrs; Chrh Wkr; Girl Scts; Hon Rl; Lbry Ade; Sct Actv; Stu Cncl; Univ; Psych.

SOWELL, DEBORAH; Pontiac Central HS; Pontiac, MI; VP Frsh Cls; Cls Rep Soph Cls; Cl Rep Jr Cls; Girl Scts; Hon Rl; Stu Cncl; Pep Clb; Letter Bsktbl; Letter Trk; PPFtbl; Coll; Engr.

SOWERS, KEVIN W; Triad HS; Cable, OH; 7/75 Pres Soph Cls; VP Jr Cls; Band; Chrs; Chrh Wkr; Cmnty Wkr; Hon Rl; Jr NHS; NHS; Off Ade; Capital Univ; Music.

SOWERS, KIM; Peterstown HS; Peterstown, WV; Sec Frsh Cls; Sec Soph Cls; Hon Rl; NHS; Fr Clb; Mth Clb; Schlrshp Awd Fr Schl 77 78 & 79; Bluefield St Coll; Comp Sci.

SOWERS, LAURA; Van Wert HS; Van Wert, OH; 18/220 Hon Rl; NHS; Sci Clb; Spn Clb; Dept Awd For Spanish 79; Awd Of Distinction 79; Lima Tech Coll; Comp Sci.

SOWERS, ROBERT J; Philo HS; Roseville, OH; Am Leg Boys St; Band; Chrh Wkr; Hon Rl; Sch Mus; Sch Pl; Yth Flsp; Ger Clb; Sci Clb; Trk; U S Military Academy; Army Officer.

SOWERS, SUZANNE; Niles Mckinley HS; Niles, OH; 15/421 AFS; Chrs; Hon Rl; Jr NHS; NHS; Sch Mus; Sch Pl; Stu Cncl; Drama Clb; Youngstown State Univ; Math.

SOWLES, GREG; Northrop HS; Ft Wayne, IN; Cls Rep Frsh Cls; Hon Rl; Stu Cncl; Wrstlng; Smmr Hnr Cert Of Achvmnt For Phys IN St Univ 79; Sertoma Freedm Awd 77; Sci Awd; Industrl Arts Awd 77; Univ; Physics.

SOWLES, LOIS; Utica HS; Utica, MI; 7/268 Cl Rep Jr Cls; Cls Rep Sr Cls; Chrh Wkr; Drl Tm; Hon Rl; NHS; Orch; Sch Mus; Stu Cncl; Pres Yth Flsp; Mt Vernon Nazarene Coll; Med Tech.

SOWRY, STEVE; Western HS; Hillsboro, OH; 11/76 Treas Band; Chrs; Hon Rl; Lbry Ade; Yrbk; Fr Clb; FTA; Pep Clb; Sci Clb; Pres Spn Clb; Univ; Radio & T V Communications.

SPACE, WILLIAM; St Charles Community HS; St Charles, MI; Cl Rep Jr Cls; Band; Chrs; Sch Mus; Voice Dem Awd; Michigan St Univ; Lit.

SPACIL, WYMAN; Vicksburg HS; Three Rivers, MI; 3/233 NHS; Bausch & Lomb Awd; Lion Awd; Rotary Awd; Michigan St Univ; Elec Engr.

SPADA, CYNTHIA; Green HS; Uniontown, OH; Band; Chrs; Chrh Wkr; Cmnty Wkr; Off Ade; Y-Teens; Pres 4-H; Pep Clb; Scr Kpr; 4-H Awd; Ohio St Univ; Nursery Mgmt.

SPADE, BRENDA; Meadow Bridge HS; Rainelle, WV; 6/60 Cls Rep Soph Cls; Cl Rep Jr Cls; Am Leg Aux Girls St; Band; Hon Rl; Mod UN; NHS; Off Ade; Sch Pl; Stu Cncl; H O Brian Ldrshp Semnr 77; U S Pilgrimage Spch Contst Wnnr 78; Concord Coll; Recreation.

SPADEMAN, THOMAS; E W Seahalm HS; Birmingham, MI; Chmn Hockey; College.

SPAETH, DOUGLAS J; Batavia HS; Batavia, OH; Am Leg Boys St; Boy Scts; Chrs; Hon Rl; Lbry Ade; NHS; Sct Actv; Sec Rptr Yrbk; Fr Clb; Sci Clb; Miami Univ; Research In Bio.

SPAETH, PENNY; Rushville Consolidated HS; Rushville, IN; Chrh Wkr; Hon Rl; Hosp Ade; FHA; OEA; Tri Kappa Voc Schlrshp 79; OEA Natl Contest Plcd 5th In Nation 78; Pro Careers Inst; Dent Asst.

SPAETH, TIM; Lebanon HS; Lebanon, OH; 56/298 Aud/Vis; Drl Tm; Hon Rl; Capt ROTC; Fr Clb; IM Sprt; Sqd Ldr Of The Yr In AFJROTC 77; Grad From AFJROTC Ldrshp Schl At Rickenbacker AFB 79; Univ; Aero Engr.

SPAHN, MIKE; Mater Dei HS; Evansville, IN; Hon Rl; Sci Clb; IM Sprt; Univ.

SPAHN, MITCHELL W; Lincoln HS; Vincennes, IN; 1/290 Am Leg Boys St; Boy Scts; FCA; Hon Rl; Yth Flsp; Bsktbl; Ftbl; Trk; Indiana Univ; Medical.

SPAHR, ROBERT; West Carrollton HS; W Carrollton, OH; Boys Clb Am; Spn Clb; Bsktbl; Letter Ftbl; Trk; Univ; Conservation.

SPAID, TAMMIE; Hampshire HS; Capon Bridge, WV; AFS; Chrs; Hon Rl; Jr NHS; Rptr Yrbk; 4-H; Pep Clb; Bsktbl; GAA; 4-H Awd;.

SPALDING, GARY; Jefferson HS; Lafayette, IN; Band; Jr NHS; Rdo Clb; Purdue Univ; Elec Engr.

SPALDING, SUSAN; Buchanan HS; Buchanan, MI; 3/123 Hon Rl; Pres NHS; Sch Mus; Sch Pl; Stg Crw; Drama Clb; Fr Clb; Univ; Theatre.

SPALL, CARLA; Columbia City Joint HS; Columbia City, IN; Chrs; Girl Scts; Hon Rl; Pep Clb; Sci Clb; Spn Clb; GAA; Ind Univ; Comp Sci.

SPALLINGER, MINDY; Cory Rawson HS; Bluffton, OH; Chrs; Hon Rl; NHS; Sch Mus; FTA; Chrldng; Fredericks Beauty Coll.

SPALSBURY, JILL; London HS; London, OH; 22/133 Chrh Wkr; Drl Tm; Hon Rl; Lbry Ade; Rptr Sch Nwsp; 4-H; Fr Clb; FHA; Bus Schl.

SPANGLER, JANET; Unioto HS; Chillicothe, OH; 3/124 Sec Sr Cls; Band; Hon Rl; NHS; Off Ade; Quill & Scroll; Stu Cncl; Ed Yrbk; Ohio Univ; Social Work.

SPANGLER, JODY; Walnut Ridge HS; Columbus, OH; Band; Chrs; Hon Rl; NHS; Orch; Sch Mus; Sec Stu Cncl; Trk; PPFtbl; Ohio St Univ; Law.

SPANGLER, KRIS; Carroll HS; Flora, IN; Cl Rep Jr Cls; Band; Hon Rl; Stu Cncl; Yth Flsp; 4-H; Pep Clb; Spn Clb; Letter Ten; Chrldng; Voc Schl; Realty.

SPANGLER, SUE; Merrillville HS; Merrillville, IN; Chrs; Girl Scts; Hon Rl; Stu Cncl; Pep Clb; Pom Pon; PPFtbl; Tmr; Indiana Univ; Medicine.

SPANN, LYNN; Beaumont School For Girls; Cleveland, OH; Hon Rl; JA; Lit Mag; Yth Flsp; Yrbk; Fr Clb; Ten; Cleveland Inst Of Art; Cmmrcl Art.

SPANOS, THOMAS; Bishop Gallagher HS; Detroit, MI; 113/333 Boy Scts; Hon Rl; Univ; Engr.

SPANTON, DAWN; E G Kingsford HS; Kingsford, MI; Band; Chrs; Hon Rl; Mdrgl; Sch Mus; Sch Pl; Drama Clb; Northern Mic Univ; Music.

SPARKMAN, LISA; Eastern HS; Salem, IN; Chrh Wkr; Hon Rl; Yth Flsp; Yrbk; Sch Nwsp; 4-H; Pep Clb; Bsktbl; GAA; IM Sprt; Univ; Law.

SPARKS, BONITA M; Rogers HS; Toledo, OH; 30/438 Pres Chrh Wkr; Cmnty Wkr; Hon Rl; Hosp Ade; JA; Jr NHS; NHS; Stu Cncl; Pres OEA; Pep Clb; Employee Of The Month; Homecoming Qn; Toledo Univ; Busns Admin.

SPARKS, CARSON; Garrett HS; Garrett, IN; Letter Crs Cntry; Letter Trk; IM Sprt; Air Force Acad; Aero.

SPARKS, DENISE; Richmond HS; Richmond, IN; 10/625 Pres Frsh Cls; Chrh Wkr; Cmnty Wkr; Hon Rl; NHS; Stu Cncl; Yth Flsp; Sec Spn Clb; Cit Awd; DAR Awd; Oral Roberts Univ.

SPARKS, JENNIFER; Danville HS; Danville, IN; 25/151 Band; Chrs; Chrh Wkr; FCA; Girl Scts; Hon Rl; Sch Mus; Sch Pl; Stg Crw; 4-H; Univ.

SPARKS, KATHERINE S; St Joseph HS; St Joseph, MI; Chrh Wkr; Cmnty Wkr; NHS; Rptr Sch Nwsp; Lat Clb; Crs Cntry; Trk; DAR Awd; College; Journalism.

SPARKS, KIM; Worthington Jefferson HS; Worthington, IN; 7/34 Sec Band; Capt Drl Tm; Hon Rl; Pres NHS; Yrbk; Sec Beta Clb; 4-H; Pep Clb; Letter Bsktbl; Capt Chrldng; Franklin Coll; Accounting.

SPARKS, MICHELLE; Watkins Memorial HS; Pataskala, OH; Band; Chrs; Scr Kpr; Ohi Univ.

SPARKS, RICHARD; Holland HS; Holland, MI; Band; Boy Scts; Hon Rl; JA; Orch; PAVAS; Rptr Yrbk; Ger Clb; JA Awd; Hope College; Acctg.

SPARKS, SALLY; Fruitport HS; Spring Lake, MI; 27/281 Sec Frsh Cls; Sec Soph Cls; Debate Tm; Off Ade; Fr Clb; Pom Pon; St Of Mi Comp Schlrshp 79; Muskegon Cmnty Coll Bd Of Trustees Schlrshp 79; Letter In Debate 79; Muskegon Cmnty Coll; Bus.

SPARKS, TERESA A; Lincoln HS; Pershing, IN; Cmnty Wkr; Girl Scts; Hon Rl; Lbry Ade; Indiana Univ; RN.

SPARKS, TYRONE; Mumford HS; Detroit, MI; Chrs; Hon Rl; NHS; Cit Awd; Wayne State Univ; Elec Engr.

SPARKS, WILLIAM; Pontiac Central HS; Pontiac, MI; Chrh Wkr; Hon Rl; NHS; Sch Pl; Ed Yrbk; Capt Bsbl; Scr Kpr; Oakland Univ; Mech Engr.

SPARLING, DANIEL J; Northfield HS; Wabash, IN; 1/120 Band; Chrh Wkr; Cmnty Wkr; Hon Rl; NHS; Sch Mus; Sch Pl; Stg Crw; Yth Flsp; Drama Clb; Purdue Sumr Music Camp Outstndg Male Musician 1978; Sociedad Honoraria Hispanica 1978; Natl Band Assn 1978; Univ; Math.

SPARLING, MARY; Marysville HS; Smiths Creek, MI; Band; Chrs; Chrh Wkr; Hon Rl; Sch Mus; Yth Flsp; Pep Clb; Letter Bsbl; Tennessee Temple Univ; Math.

SPARR, MARK; Triway HS; Shreve, OH; 21/158 Sec Frsh Cls; Hon Rl; Jr NHS; Sch Mus; Sch Pl; Stu Cncl; Drama Clb; 4-H; FFA; Bsktbl; Ohi State.

SPARROW, JENNIFER; E Lansing HS; East Lansing, MI; Chrs; Sch Mus; OEA; IM Sprt; Natl Merit Ltr; Michigan St Univ; Restaurant Mgmt.

SPASENBERG, KELLY; Muncie North HS; Muncie, IN; 1/294 Trs Frsh Cls; Trs Soph Cls; Trs Jr Cls; Debate Tm; FCA; Hon Rl; NHS; Stu Cncl; Yth Flsp; Pep Clb; Univ; Bus Mgmt.

SPATAFORE, TERESA; Liberty HS; Clarksburg, WV; 4/226 Pres Sr Cls; Band; Chrs; Hon Rl; NHS; Sch Mus; Stu Cncl; Rptr Yrbk; Sec Drama Clb; FTA; West Virginia Univ; Scndry Educ.

SPATARO, CARLA; Reeths Puffer HS; Twin Lake, MI; 38/400 Band; Chrs; Hon Rl; Sch Pl; Stg Crw; Sch Nwsp; Drama Clb; College; Music.

SPAULDING, AMY; Cardinal Stritch HS; Genoa, OH; Sec Chrs; Chrh Wkr; Cmnty Wkr; Drl Tm; Girl Scts; Hon Rl; Lbry Ade; NHS; Sch Mus; Sch Pl; TV Quiz Boql Team Letter Earned & Sec; Cnty Gifted Stu Honors In Drama & Journalism; Coll; Communications.

SPAULDING, BETTY; Portsmouth East HS; Sciotoville, OH; 10/81 Trs Frsh Cls; Trs Jr Cls; Band; Chrs; Drl Tm; Hon Rl; Mod UN; Yrbk; Pres Pep Clb; Bsktbl; Shawnee St Coll; Exec Sec.

SPAULDING, LESLIE; Bridgeport HS; Bridgeport, MI; Band; Hon Rl; NHS; Pom Pon; Univ; Med Tech.

SPAULDING, MELODY; Miami Trace HS; Washington C H, OH; 68/297 AFS; Band; Chrs; Chrh Wkr; Drl Tm; Off Ade; Sch Mus; Sch Pl; Stg Crw; Y-Teens; Otterbein College.

SPAULDING, STEVE; Breckenridge HS; Breckenridge, MI; 19/109 Cls Rep Frsh Cls; Cls Rep Soph Cls; VP Sr Cls; Am Leg Boys St; Hon Rl; NHS; Sch Mus; Sch Pl; Stu Cncl; Rptr Yrbk; Univ.

SPAULDING, SUSAN; Jennings County HS; Elizabethtown, IN; 1/420 Cl Rep Jr Cls; Chrh Wkr; Hon Rl; Pres NHS; Sch Pl; Stu Cncl; Pres Spn Clb; Natl Merit Ltr; Hanover College.

SPAULDING, YVETTE M; Northern Sr HS; Detroit, MI; Cls Rep Frsh Cls; Cls Rep Soph Cls; Trs Jr Cls; Cls Rep Sr Cls; Chrs; Girl Scts; Hon Rl; Jr NHS; NHS; Sch Pl; Awd Cheerteam Capt 79; Scshlp For Being An Actv Part In Natl Hon Soc 79; Univ Of Michigan; Med.

SPEAKMAN, DEBRA; Southeastern HS; Kingston, OH; 10/77 Am Leg Aux Girls St; Band; Hon Rl; Jr NHS; NHS; 4-H; Lat Clb; Spn Clb; Am Leg Awd; 4-H Awd; Hocking Tech Univ; Nursing.

SPEAKS, SCOTT; New Haven HS; New Haven, IN; Hon Rl; Ftbl; IM Sprt; College; History.

SPEAR, LAURIE; Bloomington HS; Gasport, IN; Band; Chrs; CAP; Cmnty Wkr; Drm Bgl; Hosp Ade; Sch Pl; Ger Clb; Pep Clb; Mgrs; Ind Univ; Bus.

SPEAR, TIMOTHY; Saints Peter And Paul HS; Saginaw, MI; Band; Jr NHS; Sch Nwsp; Trk; College; Commercial Art.

SPEARS, DAWN; West Carrollton HS; Dayton, OH; 21/418 AFS; Band; Chrs; Chrh Wkr; Girl Scts; JA; Lit Mag; NHS; Off Ade; Sch Pl; College.

SPEARS, DONNIE; Kenmore HS; Akron, OH;

SPEARS, GINA; Ellison Sr HS; Lake Station, IN; Pres Soph Cls; Hon Rl; Stu Cncl; Ed Sch Nwsp; Pep Clb; GAA; PPFtbl; Jrnslm Awd 79; Univ; Med.

SPEARS, JEANETTE; Jefferson Sr HS; Delphos, OH; Band; Chrs; Chrh Wkr; Girl Scts; Hon Rl; Sch Mus; Pres Yth Flsp; IM Sprt; Southwestern Coll Of The God.

SPEARS, MICHAEL; Jesup W Scott HS; Toledo, OH; Hon Rl; Cit Awd; Owens Tech Schl.

SPEARS, SHEILA; Ripley HS; Sandyville, WV; 22/262 Cmnty Wkr; Hon Rl; JA; Jr NHS; Off Ade; Pol Wkr; Stg Crw; 4-H; Sci Clb; Bsktbl; Muskingum Coll; Bio.

SPEARS, SUSAN; Leslie HS; Leslie, MI; Cls Rep Frsh Cls; Cls Rep Soph Cls; Cl Rep Jr Cls; Trs Sr Cls; Cls Rep Sr Cls; Band; Chrh Wkr; Cmnty Wkr; Girl Scts; Hon Rl; Michigan St Univ; Animal Husbandry.

SPEBAR, STEVEN P; Bishop Noll Institute; Whiting, IN; 75/331 Chrh Wkr; Cmnty Wkr; Hon Rl; Ger Clb; Mth Clb; Bsbl; IM Sprt; Am Leg Awd; Lion Awd; 2 Varsity Letters Starting 1st Baseman Of Regnl Finalists; Altar Boy Of Yr Awrd 75; Univ; Bus Mgmt.

SPECH, RICHARD; St Joseph HS; Cleveland, OH; Cls Rep Frsh Cls; Cls Rep Soph Cls; Sec Jr Cls; Lit Mag; NHS; Quill & Scroll; Stu Cncl; Rptr Sch Nwsp; College; Medicine.

SPECHT, BRIAN; Fairless HS; Beach City, OH; Am Leg Boys St; Boy Scts; Chrs; Chrh Wkr; Hon Rl; Sct Actv; Pep Clb; College; Comp.

SPEELMAN, KANDY; Ohio City Liberty HS; Ohio City, OH; Pres Jr Cls; Cl Rep Jr Cls; Pres Sr Cls; Band; Chrs; Chrh Wkr; Girl Scts; Off Ade; Sch Pl; Stu Cncl; Lambert Days Queen; Demolay Chptr & Dist Sweetheart; OEA Natl Ambassador Awd; Liberty Baptise Coll; Sociology.

SPEER, JEANETTA; Jennings Co HS; No Vernon, IN; 68/400 Band; Chrh Wkr; Hosp Ade; Pep Clb; Spn Clb; Bsktbl; Typing 1 Awd 78; Typing 2 Awd 79; Evansville Univ; R N.

SPEER, SCOTT; Springport HS; Springport, MI; Hon Rl; Sch Mus; Sch Pl; Drama Clb; Sci Clb; Ftbl; JA Awd; Natl Merit Ltr; College; Nuclear Physicist.

SPEER, TERRI L; E Lansing HS; E Lansing, MI; Girl Scts; 4-H; 4-H Awd; Coll; Law Enforcement.

SPEES, ANGEL; Fairlawn HS; Sidney, OH; 10/40 Hst Jr Cls; Trs Sr Cls; Band; Chrs; Hon Rl; Jr NHS; Lbry Ade; NHS; Off Ade; Sch Mus;.

SPEES, GREGORY W; Gallia Acad; Gallipolis, OH; Band; Chrh Wkr; Sch Pl; Stg Crw; Rptr Sch Nwsp; Drama Clb; Lat Clb; Sci Clb; Univ; Chem.

SPEET, SCOTT; Hamilton HS; Hamilton, MI; 18/131 Hon Rl; Stg Crw; Letter Ftbl; Scr Kpr; Natl Merit SF; Ferris St Coll; Tech Drafting.

SPEGAL, TAMMY; Madison Plains HS; London, OH; Stu Cncl; Civ Clb; Drama Clb; Pep Clb; Ch rldng; IM Sprt; Bus Schl.

SPEHAR, RICHARD; Walled Lake Western HS; Milford, MI; 26/468 Band; Boy Scts; NHS; Letter Bsktbl; Letter Crs Cntry; Letter Trk; IM Sprt; Oakland Univ; Chem Engr.

SPEICHER, JEFFREY T; Walsh Jesuit HS; Stow, OH; 4/175 Aud/Vis; Band; Boy Scts; Chrs; JA; Sch Mus; Sch Pl; Ed Sch Nwsp; Drama Clb; JA Awd; Ohio St Univ; Vet Med.

SPEICHER, JUDITH; Tuslaw HS; Massillon, OH; 20/150 Band; Drm Mjrt; Hon Rl; Pres Yth Flsp; Y-Teens; Rptr Yrbk; VP 4-H; FTA; Pep Clb; Twrlr; Cnty Princess Cntst 1st Rnnr Up 79; Kent St Univ; Fshn Mdse.

SPEICHER, MELVIN; Tuslaw HS; Massillon, OH; Chrh Wkr; Hon Rl; Otstndng Sr Boy Of Massillon Baptist Temple Youth Dept 79; 3rd Pl For Preaching In N E Oh Youth Fellowship; Massillon Baptist Coll; Ministry.

SPEICHER, MIKE; Bosse HS; Evansville, IN; Boy Scts; Hon Rl; Ger Clb; College; Sci.

SPEIDEL, CAROL; River Valley HS; Caledonia, OH; 27/218 Cls Rep Frsh Cls; Band; Chrs; Drm Mjrt; Hon Rl; Jr NHS; NHS; Sch Mus; Yrbk; 4-H; Ohio St Univ; Home Ec.

SPEIGHT, ED; Garfield HS; Akron, OH; VP Band; Orch; OEA; Coach Actv; Akron Univ; Data Processing.

SPEIGL, SANDY; Maumee HS; Maumee, OH; Hon Rl; PPFtbl; Bowling Green St Univ; Sci.

SPENCE, CELINA; Arlington HS; Indianapolis, IN; 5/300 Am Leg Aux Girls St; Girl Scts; Hon Rl; Jr NHS; NHS; Off Ade; Orch; Sch Mus; Stu Cncl; Ed Yrbk; Indiana Univ; Jrnlsm.

SPENCE, LISA M; Pine River Area HS; Le Roy, MI; Cls Rep Frsh Cls; Cls Rep Sr Cls; Band; Chrs; Hon Rl; Off Ade; Stu Cncl; Yrbk; Bsbl; Bsktbl;.

SPENCE, RONALD W; Rittman HS; Rittman, OH; 1/120 Am Leg Boys St; Hon Rl; NHS; Stu Cncl; Mth Clb; Sci Clb; Letter Bsbl; Bsktbl; Glf; Coach Actv;.

SPENCE, SHARON; Rensselaer Central HS; Wolcott, IN; Hosp Ade; Yth Flsp; Pep Clb; IUTC; Oper Rm Tech.

SPENCE, TIMOTHY E; Columbian HS; Tiffin, OH; Boy Scts; Hon Rl; Pol Wkr; Quill & Scroll; Ed Sch Nwsp; Sch Nwsp; Drama Clb; Fr Clb; VP JA Awd; Coll Of Wooster; History.

SPENCER, DARLENE; Westwood HS; Ishpeming, MI; 1/113 Val; Hon Rl; NHS; Rptr Yrbk; Ger Clb; OEA; Northern Mic Univ; Bio.

SPENCER, DAWN; Bluefield HS; Bluefield, WV; Cl Rep Jr Cls; Band; Drm Mjrt; Hon Rl; Jr NHS; Stu Cncl; Civ Clb; Fr Clb; Pep Clb; GAA; All County Band; Univ.

SPENCER, DEANNA; Du Pont HS; Belle, WV; Cls Rep Soph Cls; Hon Rl; Hosp Ade; Jr NHS; Off Ade; Rptr Sch Nwsp; Sci Clb; Chrldng; Mgrs; Morris Harvey Coll; Nursing.

SPENCER, DEREK; Aero Mechanics HS; Detroit, MI; Cmnty Wkr; Hon Rl; JA; JA Awd; Univ; Mech Engr.

SPENCER, DWAYNE J; Northfork HS; Eckman, WV; 16/131 Pres Frsh Cls; Am Leg Boys St; Hon Rl; Pol Wkr; Stu Cncl; Beta Clb; Fr Clb; FBLA; Bsktbl; Am Leg Awd; Typing II 79; Acctg I 79; Univ Of Tennessee; Bus Admin.

SPENCER, GREGORY; E E Root HS; N Royalton, OH; FFA; Agricultural Tech Inst; Forestry.

SPENCER, JEFFREY; Athens HS; Athens, WV; 4/55 VP Frsh Cls; Cls Rep Soph Cls; Sec Jr Cls; Boy Scts; Chrh Wkr; Cmnty Wkr; Hon Rl; Lbry Ade; NHS; Stu Cncl; College; Medicine.

SPENCER, JIMMIE; Kelloggsville HS; Wyoming, MI; Trs Soph Cls; Cmp Fr Grls; Hon Rl; Sch Mus; Yrbk; Pep Clb; IM Sprt; Pom Pon; PPFtbl; Tutor For 1st Grade; Cheerldr For Rocket Ftbl; Grand Rapids Jr Coll; Acctg.

SPENCER, JULIE; Waynesfield Goshen HS; Waynesfield, OH; 8/57 Am Leg Aux Girls St; Chrs; Capt Drl Tm; Hon Rl; NHS; Off Ade; Sch Pl; Stg Crw; FHA; Letter Bsktbl; Bus Schl; Legal Sec.

SPENCER, KATHLEEN B; Liberty HS; Salem, WV; 34/228 Chrh Wkr; Hon Rl; Red Cr Ade; Sch Mus; Sch Pl; Yth Flsp; FDA; Gym; Letter Trk; GAA; Pres Salem 7th Day Baptist Yth 1976; Exchange Camper S E Conf 1978; Delegate Natl SDB Conf 1978; Salem Univ; Nursing.

SPENCER, LAURA; Cedarville HS; Cedarville, OH; Band; Hosp Ade; Lbry Ade; NHS; Sdlty; Ed Sch Nwsp; 4-H; Fr Clb; Sci Clb; Glf; Natl Educ Dvlpmnt Tstng Top 6% 76 78; Excel In Eng Awd 76; Univ; Pre Med.

SPENCER, LONNIE; Morrice Area HS; Owosso, MI; Boy Scts; Chrh Wkr; Hon Rl; Lbry Ade; Yth Flsp; FFA; Leo Clb; Bsktbl; Ftbl; IM Sprt; Ferris St Univ.

SPENCER, MARY K; Our Lady Of Angels HS; Cincinnati, OH; Chrs; Chrh Wkr; Hosp Ade; Stg Crw; Spn Clb; IM Sprt; Eastern Kentucky Univ; Law Enfrcmnt.

SPENCER, MELINDA M; South HS; Youngstown, OH; 2/293 Pres Sr Cls; Sal; Hon Rl; Mod UN; NHS; Orch; Sch Pl; VP Stu Cncl; Y-Teens; Ed Sch Nwsp; Nost Outstanding French Student 77; Most Outstanding Jr 78; Youngstown St Univ; Nursing.

SPENCER, PENNY; Fairview HS; Dayton, OH; Trs Jr Cls; Yrbk; Wright State; Dent Hygiene.

SPENCER, PETER B; Lumen Christi HS; Jackson, MI; Chrh Wkr; Hon Rl; Sch Nwsp; Letter Crs Cntry; Letter Trk; IM Sprt; Univ.

SPENCER, SCOTT; Hudson HS; Hudson, OH; Band; Boy Scts; Chrs; Hon Rl; Orch; Stu Cncl; Yth Flsp; Lat Clb; Coach Actv; IM Sprt; Univ; Math.

SPENCER, SHARON; Belpre HS; Belpre, OH; Cls Rep Frsh Cls; Cls Rep Soph Cls; Cl Rep Jr Cls; Cls Rep Sr Cls; Am Leg Aux Girls St; Chrh Wkr; Hon Rl; Hosp Ade; Lbry Ade; Natl Forn Lg; Brigham Young Univ; Speech Ther.

SPENCER, SHARYN; Ursuline HS; Campbell, OH; 221/325 JA; Red Cr Ade; Yth Flsp; FTA; Key Clb; Spn Clb; IM Sprt; Youngstown State Univ; Sociology.

SPENCER, TAMMY; Little Miami HS; Morrow, OH; Hon Rl; Lit Mag; Univ; Jrnlsm.

SPENCER, TERRI; Rensselaer Central HS; Rensselaer, IN; Band; Chrh Wkr; Drl Tm; Hon Rl; Stu Cncl; Rptr Yrbk; Pep Clb; Pom Pon; College; Elem Tchr.

SPENCER, WILFRED; Martin Luther King Jr HS; Detroit, MI; Cl Rep Jr Cls; Cls Rep Sr Cls; Chrh Wkr; Hon Rl; Stu Cncl; Bsbl; Glf; Morehouse Univ; Architecture.

SPERDUTI, KAREN; Catholic Central HS; Steubenville, OH; 63/224 Cl Rep Jr Cls; Hon Rl; FHA; Pep Clb; Ohio Valley Schl; Reg Nurse.

SPERKO, SUE; Hubbard HS; Hubbard, OH; 30/330 Hon Rl; Stu Cncl; Fr Clb; Ten; PPFtbl; Univ; Forestry.

SPEROS, PAUL; Bellbrook HS; Bellbrook, OH; 12/169 Cls Rep Soph Cls; Trs Jr Cls; Trs Sr Cls; Hon Rl; NHS; FFA; Lat Clb; Sci Clb; JC Awd; Miami Univ; Pre Optometry.

SPEROW, VICKIE; Ovid Elsie HS; Ovid, MI; 27/170 Aud/Vis; Hon Rl; Lbry Ade; 4-H; FFA; 4-H Awd; St Of Mi Schlshp 79; FFA Awd Skils Contst & Schlshp 77 79; Michigan St Univ; Vet Med.

SPERR, DAVID; Mansfield Christian HS; Mansfield, OH; 1/55 Pres Soph Cls; Band; Chrh Wkr; Hon Rl; NHS; Sch Pl; Drama Clb; Rdo Clb; Letter Crs Cntry; Letter Wrstlng; Bob Jones Univ; Med.

SPERRY, ELIZABETH; Lc Mohr HS; South Haven, MI; Chrs; Chrh Wkr; Hon Rl; NHS; Sch Mus; Sch Pl; Stg Crw; Pep Clb; College; English.

SPERRY, GEORGE; Lutheran East HS; Harper Woods, MI; 23/130 Sprt Ed Sch Nwsp; Rptr Sch Nwsp; Letter Bsbl; Letter Ftbl; Wayne St Coll.

SPERRY, JEANNIE; Philip Barbour HS; Philippi, WV; Hon Rl; Stu Cncl; Rptr Yrbk; Drama Clb; FTA; Keyettes; Mth Clb; Natl Merit Ltr; Alderson Broaddus Coll; Psych.

SPERRY, RANEE; Liberty HS; Wolf Summit, WV; 3/224 Cls Rep Sr Cls; Band; Drm Mjrt; Jr NHS; NHS; Red Cr Ade; Sch Pl; Fairmont State College; Hom Ec.

SPETH, DONNA; Clay HS; S Bend, IN; 78/450 Band; Chrh Wkr; Hon Rl; Hosp Ade; NHS; Orch; PAVAS; Sch Mus; Sch Pl; Stg Crw; St Marys Coll; Nursing.

SPETZ, JANET; Wickliffe Sr HS; Wickliffe, OH; Band; Chrldng; Univ; Sci.

SPEZIALE, SHERRI; Ursuline HS; Youngstown, OH; Chrs; Hon Rl; Pres 4-H; Bsktbl; Letter Trk; IM Sprt; Mgrs; 4-H Awd; Italian Clb Sec; Vet Sci Awd 4 H & Dog Care Awd; John Bowers Schlrshp To Ursuline HS; Ohio St Univ; Vet.

SPICER, VICKIE; Whitmore Lake HS; Whitmore Lake, MI; 10/86 Cls Rep Frsh Cls; VP Soph Cls; Pres Jr Cls; Cls Rep Sr Cls; Band; Chrh Wkr; Hon Rl; Jr NHS; Pres NHS; Fr Clb; Washtenaw Comm Coll; Busns.

SPICKNALL, KRISTIN; Haslett HS; Haslett, MI; 25/154 Chrs; Chrh Wkr; Cmnty Wkr; Hon Rl; JA; Jr NHS; Sch Mus; Sch Pl; Yth Flsp; Sch Nwsp; College; Social Work.

SPIEGEL, JORDAN; Bluefield HS; Bluefld, WV; Cls Rep Frsh Cls; Cls Rep Soph Cls; Cl Rep Jr Cls; Hon Rl; Jr NHS; Stu Cncl; Sprt Ed Yrbk; Drama Clb; Pres Key Clb; Leo Clb; UCLA; Pre Law.

SPIEGEL, NANCY; George Washington HS; Charleston, WV; Cls Rep Frsh Cls; Chrh Wkr; Hon Rl; Jr NHS; Pol Wkr; Stu Cncl; Rptr Sch Nwsp; Drama Clb; Keyettes; Univ; Lib Arts.

SPIEGEL, SCOTT; Colonel Crawford HS; Sulphur Springs, OH; Cls Rep Soph Cls; Chrs; Chrh Wkr; Cmnty Wkr; Hon Rl; Stu Cncl; Key Clb; Bsbl; College; Math Teacher.

SPIEGEL, SHELLEY A; Cuyahoga Vlly Christian Acad; Akron, OH; 6/68 Chrs; Cmnty Wkr; Hon Rl; Rptr Sch Nwsp; Letter Hockey; Chrldng; Mgrs; Cit Awd; NEDT; OTSA; Listed In Society Of Distinguished Amer HS Stu; Univ; Journalism.

SPIELDENNER, LISA; Vicksburg HS; Vicksburg, MI; 6/234 Cls Rep Frsh Cls; Sec Soph Cls; Sec Jr Cls; Sec Sr Cls; NHS; Sch Mus; Chrldng; Hope College.

SPIES, JILL; Castle HS; Newburgh, IN; Hon Rl; Jr NHS; Beta Clb; Spn Clb; Schlstc C Awd 78; Spanish Diploma Of Merit 78; Univ Of Tennessee; Forestry.

SPIESS, SUSAN; Liberty Center HS; Liberty Ctr, OH; VP Frsh Cls; Sec Jr Cls; VP Sr Cls; Band; Chrs; Chrh Wkr; MMM; NHS; Sch Mus; Rptr Yrbk; College; Paralegal.

SPIGARELLI, CATHY; Kingsford HS; Kingsford, MI; VP Soph Cls; VP Jr Cls; Hon Rl; Letter Trk; Univ; Chem Engr.

SPIGNER, TORA; Port Huron Central HS; Port Huron, MI; 34/222 Cls Rep Frsh Cls; Chrs; Girl Scts; Hon Rl; Lbry Ade; NHS; Off Ade; Sch Mus; Stu Cncl; 4-H; Michigan St Univ; Vet Med.

SPIKER, KELLY; Zanesville HS; Zanesville, OH; Hon Rl; Coll; Comp Sci.

SPIKER, MELANIE; S Harrison HS; Lost Creek, WV; Band; Chrs; Hon Rl; Jr NHS; NHS; Sch Pl; Yth Flsp; 4-H; Sec FTA; Pep Clb; Coll.

SPILLER, ELISA; Fairview HS; Fairview Park, OH; 33/230 Chrs; Drl Tm; Girl Scts; Hon Rl; Orch; Sch Mus; Yth Flsp; Ger Clb; Sci Clb; Ten; 300 Shclhp To E Ky Uni 78; 3rd Pl Sci Fair Awd 79; Univ; Vocal Music.

SPINDLER, SONDRA; Mater Dei HS; Poseville, IN; 5/180 Hon Rl; NHS; 4-H; Pep Clb; Ind State Univ; Med.

SPINK, J; Mason HS; Mason, MI; Chrs; Chrh Wkr; Hon Rl; NHS; Sch Mus; 4-H; Letter Swmmng; Tmr; 4-H Awd; Pres Awd; College; Animal Tech.

SPINKLE, TERRY; Paoli HS; Hardinsburg, IN; 4-H; Fr Clb; Letter Bsktbl; Ten; Trk; GAA; Scr Kpr; 4-H Awd; College; Phys Educ.

SPIRAKUS, LISA; Strongsville Sr HS; Strongsville, OH; VP Band; Hon Rl; Chmn Jr NHS; Off Ade; Sec Y-Teens; Rptr Yrbk; Univ Of Cincinnati; Chem Engr.

SPIRES, JOANNE; Bishop Flaget HS; Chillicothe, OH; Sec Frsh Cls; Girl Scts; Hon Rl; NHS; Sch Mus; Key Clb; Pep Clb; Spn Clb; Chrldng; College; Education.

SPIRES, JO ANNE; Bishop Flaget HS; Chillicothe, OH; Sec Frsh Cls; Girl Scts; Hon Rl; Sch Mus; Key Clb; Pep Clb; Spn Clb; Chrldng; Univ; Educ.

SPIRES, MARK; William V Fisher Cath HS; Lancaster, OH; Hon Rl; Stg Crw; Key Clb; Bsbl; Bsktbl; Glf; Trk; Letter Mgrs; Scr Kpr; Tmr; Columbus Bus Univ; Acctg.

SPISAK, PATRICIA; Lowell Sr HS; Lowell, IN; Chrh Wkr; Hon Rl; Fr Clb; PPFtbl; Natl Soc Of Stu Organists 79; Univ; Music.

SPITLER, PAT; Black River HS; West Salem, OH; Letter Band; Bsktbl; GAA; Letter.

SPITLER, TINA; Mohawk HS; Mccutchenville, OH; Lbry Ade; Stg Crw; Rptr Sch Nwsp; Drama Clb; 4-H; FTA; Scr Kpr; Cit Awd; 4-H Awd; Bowling Green State; Special Educ.

SPITSNAUGLE, TIM; Mc Comb HS; Mccomb, OH; Sch Pl; FFA; Letter Bsbl; Letter Bsktbl; Letter Ftbl; Am Leg Awd; College; Forestry.

SPITSNAUGLE, TIM; Mc Comb HS; Mc Comb, OH; Sch Pl; FFA; Letter Bsbl; Bsktbl; Crs Cntry; Letter Ftbl; Am Leg Awd; Univ; Forestry.

SPITULSKI, NANCY; Roy C Start HS; Toledo, OH; 67/395 Girl Scts; Off Ade; Sct Actv; PPFtbl; Univ Of Toledo; Bus Admin.

SPITZ, ANITA; Griffith HS; Griffith, IN; 1/325 Cls Rep Soph Cls; Cl Rep Jr Cls; Sec Sr Cls; Val; Am Leg Aux Girls St; NHS; Sch Mus; Sch Pl; Pres Stu Cncl; Letter Ten; Ind Univ; Biology.

SPITZ, PAUL; Walnut Hills HS; Cincinnati, OH; AFS; Hon Rl; Hosp Ade; Lbry Ade; Lit Mag; PAVAS; Pol Wkr; Sch Mus; Sch Pl; Yth Flsp; Univ.

SPITZER, TOM; Versailles HS; Versailles, OH; 6/120 Hon Rl; Letter Bsbl; Letter Glf; Mgrs; Univ Of Cincinnati; Pharm.

SPITZLEY, JUDY; Pewamo Westphalia HS; Westphalia, MI; Cls Rep Frsh Cls; Cls Rep Soph Cls; Band; Girl Scts; 4-H; Bsktbl; Trk; Chrldng; IM Sprt;.

SPITZNAGLE, KIMBERLY; Harrison HS; Lafayette, IN; Hon Rl; Jr NHS; Lbry Ade; NHS; 4-H; Pep Clb; Spn Clb; GAA; PPFtbl; Twrlr; Ball State; Acctng.

SPITZNAGLE, MICHAEL; Central Catholic HS; Lafayette, IN; Chrh Wkr; FCA; Hon Rl; NHS; Yth Flsp; 4-H; Spn Clb; Letter Ftbl; Trk; IM Sprt; Purdue Univ; Agri.

SPLAIN, SUZANNE; St Ursula Acad; Cincinnati, OH; 5/82 Cls Rep Soph Cls; Hon Rl; Jr NHS; NHS; Stu Cncl; Ed Yrbk; Univ Of Cincinnati; Mgmt.

SPLEAR, SHEILA; George A Dondero HS; Royal Oak, MI; 21/403 Chrs; Hon Rl; NHS; Sch Pl; Drama Clb; Fr Clb; Natl Merit Ltr; Michigan St Univ; Pre Med.

SPLETZER, KAREN A; Finneytown HS; Cincinnati, OH; 2/251 Cmnty Wkr; Hon Rl; Ger Clb; Key Clb; Letter Hockey; Letter Trk; Natl Merit SF; Univ; Chem.

SPLETZER, MARLENE; Eau Claire HS; Eau Claire, MI; 1/100 Trs Jr Cls; Chrs; Chrh Wkr; Hon Rl; Sch Mus; Letter Bsktbl; Letter Ten; Monday Musical Scholarship At Interlochen; St Joe Art Cntr HS Comp Mixed Media 2nd Pl; Berrien Cnty Fair; College.

SPOELMAN, JEFFREY; Orchard View HS; Muskegon, MI; 2/175 Sal; Band; Hon Rl; NHS; Letter Bsbl; Letter Wrstlng; Elk Awd; Oral Roberts Univ.

SPOELSTRA, ROBERT; Godwin Heights HS; Wyoming, MI; Pres Jr Cls; Chrs; Sch Mus; Sch Pl; Rptr Sch Nwsp; Spn Clb; Ftbl; Trk; Voc Schl; Design.

SPOERNDLE, SANDY; East HS; Akron, OH; Letter Band; Hon Rl; Off Ade; Quill & Scroll; Rptr Yrbk; Drama Clb; Fr Clb; OEA; Pep Clb; Letter Ten; Akron Univ; Psych.

SPOHN, WENDI; Fowlerville HS; Fowlerville, MI; Cls Rep Sr Cls; Boy Scts; Chrh Wkr; Hon Rl; Pol Wkr; Stu Cncl; Yth Flsp; 4-H; FFA; Spn Clb; Cert Of Recognition St Of Mi Schlrshp Progr For Outsdng Acad Achvmnt In Mi 79; Cert Of Hon In Geom 77; LCC; Math.

SPOHR, LORRAINE; East Noble HS; Avilla, IN; Chrh Wkr; JA; VP Natl Forn Lg; NHS; Y-Teens; Sch Nwsp; Drama Clb; 4-H; FFA; Pres FHA; Purdue; Home Economics.

SPOHR, SUANNE; Aikan Senior HS; Cincinnati, OH; 29/576 Chrs; Pres Yth Flsp; FTA; Ger Clb; Swmmng; Letter Chrldng; Univ Of Evansville; Phys Ther.

SPONAUGLE, JOHN; Mingo HS; Mingo Jct, OH; 16/120 Hst Sr Cls; Am Leg Boys St; Aud/Vis; Band; Debate Tm; Hon Rl; Red Cr Ade; Yrbk; Key Clb; Lat Clb; Bethany Coll; Bio.

SPONAUGLE, STEVEN A; Tucker County HS; Hendricks, WV; VP Frsh Cls; Am Leg Boys St; Hon Rl; Yth Flsp; 4-H; Key Clb; Pep Clb; Bsktbl; Ftbl; Trk; Coll.

SPONN, ANNA; Washington Catholic HS; Washington, IN; Band; Chrs; Drl Tm; Sch Pl; Stg Crw; Drama Clb; 4-H; Pep Clb; Pom Pon; Univ; Art.

SPONSELLER, ERIC A; Jackson HS; Canton, OH; Band; Hon Rl; NHS; Ger Clb; Bsbl; Trk; College; Sci.

SPOONER, PATTY; David Anderson HS; Lisbon, OH; Hst Sr Cls; Hon Rl; Stu Cncl; Ed Sch Nwsp; OEA;.

SPOONER, RALPH; Williamston HS; Williamston, MI; Band; Hon Rl; 4-H; Letter Crs Cntry; Letter Trk; Mgrs; 4-H Awd; Natl Merit Ltr; Michigan Tech Univ; Metal Engr.

SPOONER, SHARI; Laingsburg HS; Laingsburg, MI; Hon Rl; FHA; Pep Clb; PPFtbl; Lansing Comm Coll; Sec.

SPOONER, STEVEN; Rocky River HS; Rocky Rvr, OH; Cls Rep Frsh Cls; Band; Hon Rl; Jr NHS; Rptr Yrbk; Yrbk; Sch Nwsp; Letter Glf; Trk; IM Sprt; College; Bus Mgmt.

SPORE, JOAN; Clio HS; Clio, MI; Sec Chrh Wkr; Girl Scts; Hon Rl; Fr Clb; Pep Clb; 4-H Awd; Baker Jr Coll Of Bus; Bus.

SPORNHAUER, JOE; Eastern HS; Sardinia, OH; 2/92 Sal; Band; Hon Rl; NHS; Sprt Ed Sch Nwsp; Rptr Sch Nwsp; Sch Nwsp; Fr Clb; Bsktbl; Glf; Univ Of Cincinnati; Pre Med.

SPOSATO, MICHAEL; Columbiana HS; Columbiana, OH; Sec Soph Cls; Chrh Wkr; Hon Rl; NHS; Fr Clb; Bsbl; College.

SPOTTS, CHRISTINE; Reading HS; Reading, MI; Trs Sr Cls; Hon Rl; Lbry Ade; Rptr Yrbk; Rptr Sch Nwsp; Fr Clb; FHA; FTA; PPFtbl; Univ; Secondary Ed.

SPRADLIN, BRENCIA; Columbian HS; Tiffin, OH; Band; Hon Rl; Spn Clb; College; Special Ed.

SPRADLIN, D; Waterloo HS; Mogadore, OH; Pres Sr Cls; FHA; Trk; Cpa.

SPRADLIN, SCOTT L; Midland Trail HS; Victor, WV; Am Leg Boys St; Boy Scts; Chrh Wkr; Hon Rl; NHS; Pol Wkr; Rptr Yrbk; Fr Clb; FBLA; 4-H Awd; English Awd; Chem Bowl Rep; Union Carbide Essay Awd; Georgetown Univ; Doctor.

SPRAGG, JAMES; Buckeye West HS; Adena, OH; 10/85 VP Soph Cls; VP Jr Cls; Am Leg Boys St; Hon Rl; NHS; 4-H; Sci Clb; Letter Bsbl; Letter Bsktbl; 4-H Awd; College; Engr.

SPRAGG, JIM; Buckeye West HS; Adena, OH; VP Soph Cls; VP Jr Cls; Chrh Wkr; Hon Rl; NHS; Yth Flsp; 4-H; Sci Clb; Letter Bsbl; Letter Bsktbl; College.

SPRAGUE, BETSY; South Vermillion HS; Clinton, IN; 2/182 Sal; Band; Hon Rl; NHS; Off Ade; Drama Clb; 4-H; Lat Clb; Sci Clb; DAR Awd; Century Three Schlrshp Runner Up; Varsity Volleyball Letter; Lettermans Club; Purdue Univ; Engr.

SPRAGUE, DREW; Chelsea HS; Grass Lake, MI; 3/238 Band; Debate Tm; Hon Rl; NHS; Orch; Sch Mus; Fr Clb; Glf; College; Music.

SPRAGUE, JEANNE; Madison HS; Madison, OH; 36/263 Chrs; Cmnty Wkr; Hon Rl; Stg Crw; Drama Clb; Pep Clb; Sci Clb; Spn Clb; Scr Kpr; Tmr; Univ Of Akron; Nursing.

SPRAGUE, LISA; Cadillac Sr HS; Cadillac, MI; Cls Rep Soph Cls; Cl Rep Jr Cls; Sec Sr Cls; Hon Rl; NHS; Off Ade; Stu Cncl; Chrldng; PPFtbl; Central Michigan Univ; Soc Psych.

SPRAGUE, PENNY; Harrison Cmnty HS; Harrison, MI; 25/158 Girl Scts; Hon Rl; NHS; Sch Pl; Yrbk; Sch Nwsp; Bsktbl; Coach Actv; IM Sprt; PPFtbl; Mid Michigan St Univ; Elem Ed.

SPRAGUE, SARAH; H H Dow HS; Midland, MI; Chrh Wkr; Hon Rl; Jr NHS; NHS; Yth Flsp; Y-Teens; Rptr Yrbk; Rptr Sch Nwsp; Sch Nwsp; Schlstc Schlrshp Anonymous Dnr 79; HH Dow Outstndg Stu Writer 78; Cert Of Rec Form Mi St Bd Of Ed 79; Michigan St Univ; Bus Mgmt.

SPRANG, BRYAN D; Loudonville HS; Perrysville, OH; 25/133 Am Leg Boys St; Band; Boy Scts; Chrh Wkr; Hon Rl; NHS; Sch Mus; Sch Pl; Yth Flsp; Letter Bsbl; Ohio Inst Of Tech; Elec Engr Tech.

SPRANG, JERRI; Loudonville HS; Loudonville, OH; Pres Jr Cls; Cl Rep Jr Cls; Band; Chrh Wkr; Girl Scts; Hon Rl; Hosp Ade; Off Ade; Red Cr Ade; Sch Pl; Gold Pennant Awd VICA; Parliamentary Procedure Tm Awd VICA; Univ; Med.

SPRATLEY, WENDY; East Liverpool HS; Wellsville, OH; 22/364 Hon Rl; Rptr Sch Nwsp; Pep Clb; Spn Clb; Kent State Univ.

SPRATT, KAREN; North Canton Hoover HS; North Canton, OH; 19/417 Cls Rep Frsh Cls; Cls Rep Sr Cls; Chrh Wkr; Hon Rl; JA; NHS; Pol Wkr; Stu Cncl; Rptr Yrbk; Yrbk; Univ; Bus.

SPRAY, CARLA; Lewis County HS; Roanoke, WV; FCA; Hon Rl; 4-H; FFA; Spn Clb; Letter Bsktbl; Trk; IM Sprt; Am Leg Awd; Cit Awd; Glenville; Education.

SPRAY, TERI; Cheboygan Area HS; Cheboygan, MI; Hon Rl; NHS; Sch Pl; Fr Clb; Chrldng; College; Engr.

SPRENG, WILLIAM; Loudonville HS; Perrysville, OH; 5/133 Pres Frsh Cls; Cls Rep Frsh Cls; Trs Jr Cls; Hon Rl; Pres NHS; Sprt Ed Sch Nwsp; Capt Ftbl; Trk; Cit Awd; Rotary Awd; Jr Acad Chlng Cont; Ist Tm Off Gd Ftbl; Mst Likely To Succeed; Ohio St Univ; Dairy Sci.

SPRICK, LINDA; Fairbanks HS; Marysville, OH; Band; Chrs; Chrh Wkr; Hon Rl; Drama Clb; 4-H; Spn Clb; 4-H Awd; Heidelburg; Social Services.

SPRIGG, LESLEY; Green HS; Akron, OH; 30/321 Cmnty Wkr; Hon Rl; Sec JA; Mdrgl; Off Ade; Sch Pl; Stg Crw; Rptr Yrbk; Drama Clb; Pom Pon; Akron; Interior Design.

SPRIGG, WILLIAM; Danbury HS; Marblehead, OH; Cls Rep Frsh Cls; Cls Rep Soph Cls; Pres Jr Cls; Pres Sr Cls; Hon Rl; Stu Cncl; Sci Clb; Miami Univ; Archi.

SPRIGGS, CRAIG; Kelloggsville Public HS; Wyoming, MI; 11/140 Aud/Vis; Band; Hon Rl; Lbry Ade; NHS; Orch; Rptr Sch Nwsp; Bsktbl; College; Musician.

SPRIGGS, ERIC; Carson City Crystal HS; Carson City, MI; 4/127 VP Sr Cls; Hon Rl; NHS; Off Ade; Sch Pl; Stu Cncl; Rptr Sch Nwsp; Letter Crs Cntry; Letter Trk; Bausch & Lomb Awd; Univ Of Miami; Elec Engr.

SPRIGGS, ROBIN; Dawson Bryant HS; Ironton, OH; 7/122 Hon Rl; NHS; Mth Clb; Pep Clb; Bsktbl; Morehead State Univ; Med Lab Tech.

SPRIK, CHRIS; Grand Rpds So Christian HS; Wayland, MI; Letter Band; Chrh Wkr; Hon Rl; NHS; Pol Wkr; Pep Clb; Letter Bsktbl; Letter Trk; Calvin Coll.

SPRIK, JULIE; Holland Christian HS; Holland, MI; Sec Frsh Cls; Chrh Wkr; Cmnty Wkr; Lit Mag; Ger Clb; IM Sprt; Calvin Coll; Educ.

SPRING, HEIDI; Clay HS; Oregon, OH; 3/345 Cls Rep Sr Cls; Sal; Band; Drm Mjrt; FCA; NHS; Sch Mus; Stu Cncl; Fr Clb; Twrlr; BGSU; Eng.

SPRING, JEFF; Edgewood Sr HS; Conneaut, OH; AFS; Boy Scts; Chrh Wkr; Hon Rl; Sch Pl; Stu Cncl; Sci Clb; Spn Clb; Wrstlng; Cit Awd; Coll; Med.

SPRING, RENITA; Morgan HS; Mc Connelsville, OH; 1/250 Chrh Wkr; Hon Rl; NHS; Off Ade; 4-H; FSA; Letter Bsbl; Letter Bsktbl; Trk; Ohio Univ; Medicine.

SPRING, TAMMY; William Henry Harrison HS; Evansville, IN; 25/475 Chrs; Chrh Wkr; Hon Rl; Sch Pl; Yth Flsp; Sec Civ Clb; Pep Clb; Cit Awd; Marion College; Music.

SPRING, TODD; Philo HS; Zanesville, OH; Am Leg Boys St; Boy Scts; Chrh Wkr; Hon Rl; NHS; Sch Mus; Sch Pl; Sct Actv; Ger Clb; Bsktbl; Cnty Winner Hist Shclsp Test 79; Schl Winner Math Assn Of Amer 78; Univ.

SPRINGER, ADAM; Frontier HS; New Matamoras, OH; 32/122 Aud/Vis; Sch Pl; Stg Crw; Yrbk; Mgrs; Am Leg Awd; Ohi Univ; Pre Med.

SPRINGER, D; Heritage HS; Ossian, IN; Hon Rl; Ftbl; College; Law.

SPRINGER, DIANA; Liberty HS; Bristol, WV; 18/228 FCA; Hon Rl; Jr NHS; DECA; Bsktbl; Letter Trk; Fairmont; Computer Programing.

SPRINGER, GAY; Lakeville HS; Otisville, MI; 6/186 Am Leg Aux Girls St; NHS; Treas Spn Clb; Am Leg Awd; VFW Awd; Voice Dem Awd; Detroit Coll; Acctg.

SPRINGER, JEFFREY; Jennings County HS; N Vernon, IN; Band; Chrs; CAP; Sch Mus; Sch Pl; 4-H; Pres Ger Clb; Chrldng; Ind Univ Schl Of Music; Music Ed.

SPRINGER, JERRY; Norwell HS; Ossian, IN; 63/195 Chrh Wkr; Hon Rl; Rptr Yrbk; Rptr Sch Nwsp; 4-H; Pep Clb; 4-H Awd;.

SPRINGER, JOHN; Lamphere HS; Madison Hts, MI; Band; Hon Rl; NHS; Sch Mus; IM Sprt; Wayne St Univ.

SPRINGER, JOHNNY; Northwest HS; Cincinnati, OH; Chrh Wkr; FCA; Hon Rl; Jr NHS; NHS; Spn Clb; Coach Actv; SAR Awd; Mem Of Span Hon Soc & Particip In Span Test 77; Trav To Mex & Spain 78; Rec A Book Fr Yale Univ 79; Univ Of Cincinnati; Med.

SPRINGER, JUDITH; Southmont HS; Crawfordsville, IN; Chrs; Girl Scts; FHA; Pep Clb;.

SPRINGER, MARK; Tippecanoe HS; Tipp City, OH; Boy Scts; Hon Rl; Univ; Engr.

SPRINGER, VALARIE; Central HS; Detroit, MI; Hon Rl; Lbry Ade; Off Ade; Fr Clb; College; Accgt.

SPRINGS, DEANNA; Van Wert HS; Van Wert, OH; Hon Rl; Sch Pl; Spn Clb; Letter Bsktbl; Letter Trk; IM Sprt; Scr Kpr; College.

SPRINGSTON, JOY; Roosevelt Wilson HS; Stonewood, WV; Cls Rep Soph Cls; Cl Rep Jr Cls; Band; Hon Rl; Sec Stu Cncl; Sec Y-Teens; Leo Clb; Pep Clb; Bsktbl; Swmmng; Busns Schl; Sec.

SPROUSE, GLORIA; Cardinal Ritter HS; Indianapolis, IN; 38/157 Cls Rep Sr Cls; Band; Chrs; Hon Rl; Hosp Ade; Mdrgl; MMM; NHS; Sch Mus; Stu Cncl; Butler Univ; Music.

SPROUSE, MARY P; Liberty HS; Clarksburg, WV; 35/228 Sec Frsh Cls; Band; Drm Mjrt; Hon Rl; Y-Teens; DECA; Fr Clb; Pep Clb; Fairmont St Coll; Sec.

SPROUSE, MONESA; Chillicothe HS; Chillicothe, OH; 7/235 AFS; Aud/Vis; Band; Cmnty Wkr; Hon Rl; Jr NHS; NHS; Off Ade; Sch Pl; Stu Cncl; 1st Zoology Awd & Bst Bio Prjct 77; Homcmng Ct 78; Mead Essay Contst Hon Mnt 78; Ohio St Univ; Med Tech.

SPROUT, TRACY; Roosevelt Wilson HS; Clarksburg, WV; 10/122 Sec Frsh Cls; VP Soph Cls; Hon Rl; NHS; Stu Cncl; Yth Flsp; Y-Teens; Sprt Ed Yrbk; Yrbk; 4-H; Fairmont State Univ; Education.

SPROW, REBECCA; Fairview HS; Ney, OH; Band; Chrs; Sch Mus; Sec Yth Flsp; Sec FTA; Bowling Green St Univ; Music.

SPROWLS, MICHAEL; Medina Sr HS; Medina, OH; 8/350 Band; Chrs; Hon Rl; NHS; Sch Mus; Key Clb; Letter Ten; Ohio St Univ; Math.

SPRUIT, BRENDA; High School; Comstock, MI; Chrs; Chrh Wkr; Girl Scts; Hon Rl; JA; Jr NHS; NHS; 4-H; Lat Clb; Pep Clb; Univ; Med.

SPRUIT, NANCY; Creston HS; Grand Rapids, MI; Trs Soph Cls; Cl Rep Jr Cls; Chrs; FCA; Sch Mus; Yrbk; Letter Gym; Letter Swmmng; Capt Chrldng; Tmr; Voc Schl; Cosmetology.

SPRUIT, SUSAN; Creston HS; Grand Rapids, MI; 28/432 VP Frsh Cls; FCA; Jr NHS; Mdrgl; NHS; Sch Mus; Gym; Capt Swmmng; Twrlr; Hope Coll; Math.

SPRUNGER, JULIE; Bluffton HS; Bluffton, OH; Band; Chrs; Chrh Wkr; Sch Mus; Sch Pl; Stg Crw; Yth Flsp; Drama Clb; Chrldng; Scr Kpr; Interior Design.

SPRUNGL, BARBARA; Newbury HS; Newbury, OH; Aud/Vis; Girl Scts; Hon Rl; Lbry Ade; FHA; FNA; Voc Schl; Bus.

SPURBECK, KAREN; Crooksville HS; Crooksville, OH; 25/95 Band; Chrh Wkr; Hon Rl; Off Ade; Red Cr Ade; Sch Pl; Stu Cncl; Yth Flsp; Rptr Sch Nwsp; Sch Nwsp; Bus Schl; Sec.

SPURLINO, JIM; Oakwood HS; Dayton, OH; Aud/Vis; FCA; JA; Letter Bsktbl; Letter Glf; IM Sprt; Natl Merit Ltr; Univ.

SPURLOCK, KAREN L; William A Wirt HS; Gary, IN; 9/230 Band; Chrh Wkr; Cmnty Wkr; Girl Scts; Hon Rl; Jr NHS; NHS; Red Cr Ade; Yth Flsp; Rptr Sch Nwsp; Pres Clsrm Wash Dc 78; Guidance Club Pres 79; Girls Softball Trvlng Tm 76; Ball St Univ; Prod Mgmt.

SPURLOCK, PATRICIA J; Danville HS; Danville, IN; 50/180 Band; Chrh Wkr; Cmnty Wkr; Hon Rl; Lbry Ade; Off Ade; Sct Actv; VP Yth Flsp; Rptr Sch Nwsp; 4-H; ESA Opprtnty Cottage Day Queen 79; Union Coll; Bus Admin.

SPURLOCK, ROBIN; Tippecanoe HS; Tipp City, OH; Band; Hon Rl; Trk; GAA;.

SPURLOCK, TAMI; Wheelersburg HS; Wheelersburg, OH; 21/178 Band; Chrs; Hon Rl; NHS; Sch Mus; Chrldng; Christ Hospital Schl Of Nursing; RN.

SQUANDA, GREGORY; Reese HS; Saginaw, MI; 29/130 Band; Hon Rl; NHS; Mth Clb; Bsbl; Bsktbl; Ftbl; Trk; 4-H Awd; Natl Merit Ltr; Saginaw Valley State Coll; Mech Engr.

SQUANDA, LORI; Reese HS; Saginaw, MI; 1/131 Cl Rep Jr Cls; Val; Treas Band; Hon Rl; NHS; Cit Awd; Alumni Schlshp 79; Ctrl Mi Bd Of Trustees 79; Math Awd 79; Ctrl Michigan Univ; Math.

SQUARE, JEFFERY; Madison Memorial HS; Madison, OH; 31/280 Band; Hon Rl; Ten; Ohio Inst Of Tech; Elec Engr.

SQUIER, SHIELA; Bluffton HS; Bluffton, IN; 34/135 Lbry Ade; Y-Teens; Pep Clb; Scr Kpr; Purdue Univ; Drafting Engr.

SQUIRES, EUGENE; Marion L Steele HS; Amherst, OH; 59/360 NHS; Ger Clb; Ohio State Univ.

SQUIRES, JOANN; Britton Malon Area HS; Britton, MI; Cls Rep Frsh Cls; VP Sr Cls; Am Leg Aux Girls St; Sec Band; Hon Rl; NHS; VP Stu Cncl; Yth Flsp; Sec FFA; Sci Clb; Marion Coll; Psych.

SQUIRES, MICHAEL W; Highland HS; Chesterville, OH; Am Leg Boys St; Band; NHS; 4-H; Sec FFA; Pep Clb; Bsbl; Am Leg Awd; 4-H Awd; Ffa St Degree 1978; Ffa Dist Sheep Prof 1979; Ffa Natl Lvstk Jdg Rep 1978; Ohio St Univ; Vet Med.

SQUIRES, ROCHELLE; Lewis County HS; Weston, WV; Chrs; FCA; Hon Rl; NHS; Stu Cncl; 4-H; Pep Clb; Bsktbl; Mat Maids; PPFtbl; Clarksburg Career Coll; Sec Work.

SRACKANGAST, TIM; Galesburg Augusta HS; Galesburg, MI; 33/103 Hon Rl; Yth Flsp; FFA; Bsktbl; Ftbl; Mgrs; Ferris Voc Schl; Auto Mech.

SRIVASTAVA, VANDANA; Howland HS; Warren, OH; 52/402 Chrs; Cmnty Wkr; Girl Scts; Hon Rl; Lbry Ade; Sch Pl; Stg Crw; Rptr Yrbk; Ed Sch Nwsp; Fr Clb; Kent State Univ; Law.

SROKA, CHERYLANN; St Alphonsus HS; Detroit, MI; 1/180 Chrh Wkr; Girl Scts; Hon Rl; Fr Clb; Cit Awd; Pres Awd; Fashion Design.

SROUT, MARIE; Moorefield HS; Moorefield, WV; 14/88 Drl Tm; Girl Scts; Hon Rl; Hosp Ade; Sch Pl; Sct Actv; Stg Crw; Yrbk; 4-H; FHA; Girls Scout Drill Team Cap 77; Univ.

STAAL, PAMELA; O A Carlson HS; Rockwood, MI; 17/288 Band; Chrh Wkr; Hon Rl; Hosp Ade; NHS; Yth Flsp; FNA; FTA; St Ofmi Comp Schslhp 79; Univ Of Michigan; Med Tech.

STAASHELM, KATHLEEN; Floyd Central HS; New Albany, IN; 115/389 Hon Rl; JA; Sch Pl; 4-H; Spn Clb; Pom Pon; Univ; Sci.

STAASHELM, KATHY; Floyd Central HS; New Albany, IN; Hon Rl; JA; Sch Mus; 4-H; Spn Clb; Letter Pom Pon; University; Nursing.

STAATS, BRIAN; Labrae HS; Newton Falls, OH; Cls Rep Soph Cls; Am Leg Boys St; Band; Chrh Wkr; Hon Rl; Yth Flsp; FTA; Bsktbl; Crs Cntry; College.

STAATS, DENISE; Danville HS; Danville, OH; 5/62 Pres Chrs; Hon Rl; NHS; Sch Mus; Sch Pl; Yrbk; Drama Clb; Pres FHA; Pep Clb; PPFtbl;.

STABILE, KATHERINE; Whitefish Twp HS; Paradise, MI; Sec Sr Cls; Band; Drl Tm; Girl Scts; Hon Rl; Sch Pl; Rptr Yrbk; Chrldng; Pom Pon; Univ; Lib Arts.

STABLER, NATHANIEL; Sandy Valley HS; E Sparta, OH; 6/171 Hon Rl; NHS; Bsktbl; Letter Trk; Am Leg Awd; DAR Awd; JC Awd; Lion Awd; Mas Awd; Natl Merit Ltr; Marietta Coll; Petro Engr.

STACEY, CARL; Central Catholic HS; Toledo, OH; 46/333 Cls Rep Frsh Cls; Cls Rep Soph Cls; Cl Rep Jr Cls; Cls Rep Sr Cls; Chrs; Hon Rl; NHS; Letter Bsktbl; Letter Ftbl; Letter Trk; 2 Yr Whos Who Recptn 77 79; BEOG 700 79; Morehouse Coll; Pre Dent.

STACEY, T; Delphi Cmnty HS; Delphi, IN; Chrh Wkr; Yth Flsp; Y-Teens; FHA; Pep Clb; Marion Coll; X Ray Tech.

STACH, MARK; St Joseph Ctrl HS; Huntington, WV; Cls Rep Frsh Cls; Boy Scts; Hon Rl; Jr NHS; Sch Mus; Sch Pl; Sct Actv; Stg Crw; Letter Bsbl; Letter Trk; Univ; Bus Mgmt.

STACHLER, CASSIE; Celina Sr HS; Celina, OH; Cls Rep Frsh Cls; Cls Rep Soph Cls; Band; Hon Rl; NHS; Sch Mus; Stu Cncl; Ohio State Univ; Tech Engr.

STACHOWIAK, BARBARA; Green HS; Akron, OH; 14/316 Band; Chrs; Girl Scts; Hon Rl; Sct Actv; Rptr Yrbk; Pep Clb; Bsktbl; Scr Kpr; College; Engr.

STACHOWIAK, CATHERINE; Harrison HS; Harrison, MI; 25/152 Cl Rep Jr Cls; Pres Sr Cls; Cmp Fr Grls; FCA; Hon Rl; Lbry Ade; NHS; Sch Mus; Sch Pl; Stg Crw; Patricia Stevens Schl; Flight Attndt.

STACHOWICZ, LINDA; St Ladislaus HS; Hamtramck, MI; 16/118 Hon Rl; Stu Cncl; Fr Clb; Letter Bsktbl; Letter Trk; Michigan St Univ.

STACHURSKI, FELICIA; St Ladislaus HS; Detroit, MI; Hon Rl; Chrldng; Wayne Cnty Cmnty Coll; Animal Tech.

STACHURSKI, FELICIA; Saint Ladislaus HS; Detroit, MI; 7/90 Michigan State Univ; Vet.

STACK, CHRIS; Erieview Catholic HS; Bedford, OH; 11/100 Chrs; Hon Rl; NHS; John Carroll Univ; Acctg.

STACK, GARY; St Alphonsus HS; Detroit, MI; Cls Rep Sr Cls; Hon Rl; Pep Clb; Letter Bsbl; Letter Ftbl; College; Science.

STACKHOUSE, KRISTI; Springs Valley HS; French Lick, IN; Aud/Vis; Band; Hon Rl; Pep Clb; Letter Bsktbl; Letter Trk; Indiana Univ.

STACKHOUSE, SHARON; Marian HS; Birmingham, MI; Cmnty Wkr; Hon Rl; Mod UN; NHS; Ger Clb; IM Sprt; College; Sci.

STACKHOUSE, VICKY L; Jeffersonville HS; Jeffersonville, IN; 17/601 Chrs; FCA; Hon Rl; NHS; Pep Clb; Gym; Chrldng; PPFtbl; Univ.

STACKLIN, DUANE; Buckeye Central HS; New Washington, OH; 30/90 Stu Cncl; FFA; Letter Bsktbl; Letter Ftbl; Letter Trk; Bst Def Lineman 77; 1st Team All Confrnc In Ftbl 78; 2nd Team UPI All St Ftbl 78; Univ; Bus.

STACKPOLE, KIM; Tyler County HS; Middlebourne, WV; Band; Hon Rl; JA; Jr NHS; Yrbk; Rptr Sch Nwsp; 4-H; FTA; Pep Clb; Chrldng; Coll; Bus Mgmt.

STACY, SUSAN; Tiffin Columbian HS; Tiffin, OH; Sec Frsh Cls; Am Leg Aux Girls St; Band; Hon Rl; Bsktbl; Kiwan Awd; Bowling Green St Univ; Educ.

STADDON, KATHY; Univ HS; Morgantown, WV; Aud/Vis; Hon Rl; Off Ade; Stu Cncl; Yth Flsp; Ger Clb; Pep Clb; Scr Kpr; JC Awd; W Va Univ; Bus Admin.

STADELMAN, DENNIS; Wm Henry Harrison HS; Cleves, OH; 1/200 Hon Rl; NHS; University Of Cincnnati; Elec Engr.

STADELMAYER, ROBERT; Northrop HS; Ft Wayne, IN; 89/564 Hon Rl; Rptr Yrbk; Rptr Sch Nwsp; Coll; Comp Sci.

STADER, BRIAN; Monrovia HS; Mooresville, IN; Cls Rep Frsh Cls; Cls Rep Soph Cls; Cl Rep Jr Cls; FCA; VP Stu Cncl; Bsktbl; Letter Crs Cntry; Letter Trk; Univ.

STADIUS, CLAUDIA; Hancock Central HS; Hancock, MI; 5/99 Cls Rep Soph Cls; Band; Chrs; Chrh Wkr; Hon Rl; NHS; Sch Mus; Sch Pl; Letter Bsktbl; Letter Swmmng; Suomi Coll; Pre Educ.

STADLBERGER, ALDEN; Greenville HS; Gowen, MI; Cls Rep Sr Cls; Hon Rl; Stu Cncl; Letter Ftbl; Letter Trk; IM Sprt; Grand Valley St Coll; Comp Sci.

STADLER, ALAN; North Royalton HS; N Royalton, OH; 8/286 VP Sr Cls; Am Leg Boys St; Band; Hon Rl; VP NHS; Letter Bsbl; Ftbl; Coach Actv; Mgrs; Natl Merit Ltr; Outstanding Varsity Lineman 78; Pres Lettermens Club 79; Honorary Usher For Cls Of 79; Univ; Engr.

STADTFELD, BARBARA; Chippewa Hills HS; Remus, MI; Band; Hon Rl; Orch; 4-H; Mat Maids; Scr Kpr; Tmr; 4-H Awd; Ferris State College; Radiologic.

STAEHLE, DANIEL; Andrean HS; Gary, IN; Ftbl; Wrstlng; IM Sprt; Indiana Univ; Bus Admin.

STAFFAN, LORIE; Madison Plains HS; S Solon, OH; Hon Rl; Mod UN; Civ Clb; Hon At Madison Plains Annual Hon Banquet 78; Quick Recall Tm 78; Eng 11 Schlrshp Test At Oh St Univ 78; Univ; Writer.

STAFFORD, FRACINE; Bellbrook HS; Bellbrook, OH; Cls Rep Frsh Cls; Pres Soph Cls; VP Jr Cls; Chrh Wkr; Girl Scts; Hon Rl; NHS; Stu Cncl; Lat Clb; Pep Clb; College; Medicine.

STAFFORD, K; Bluefield HS; Bluefld, WV; Chrs; Hon Rl; Y-Teens; Fr Clb; Pep Clb; Univ; Optometry.

STAFFORD, LINDA; Yale HS; Yale, MI; 1/170 Chrs; Hon Rl; NHS; Sch Mus; Ten; College; Veterinarian.

STAFFORD, MARIANNE; Northridge HS; Bristol, IN; 18/150 Band; Drm Mjrt; Hon Rl; Jr NHS; NHS; Orch; Sch Mus; Stu Cncl; Rptr Sch Nwsp; Key Clb; Ball St Univ; Elem Ed.

STAFFORD, SANDRA; Charlestown HS; Charlestown, IN; 6/155 Chrs; Hon Rl; JA; Mdrgl; NHS; Pep Clb; Spn Clb; JA Awd; Univ Of Kentucky; Comp Sci.

STAFFORD, STEVEN; Traverse City Sr HS; Traverse City, MI; Mod UN; NHS; Sch Mus; Sch Pl; Stg Crw; Pres Drama Clb; Trojan Hall Of Fame For Dramatics; Adrian Coll; Theatre.

STAFFORD, TODD; Waldron Jr Sr HS; Waldron, IN; 5/65 Hon Rl; Stu Cncl; Rptr Sch Nwsp; Fr Clb; Trk; Natl Merit Schl; Indiana Univ; Tele Cmnctns.

STAGER, JEANNINE; Trinity HS; Seven Hills, OH; Cls Rep Frsh Cls; Hon Rl; Chrldng; College; Comp Sci.

STAGGENBURG, SUSAN; Anderson Sr HS; Anderson, IN; 26/400 Chrh Wkr; Hon Rl; NHS; Fr Clb; FHA; Frech Hon Soc 78; Univ.

STAHL, ANNE M; Tri West HS; Lizton, IN; 15/120 Hon Rl; Stg Crw; Drama Clb; Voc Schl; Comp Sci.

STAHL, BETH; Coshocton HS; Coshocton, OH; 101/231 Band; Fr Clb; OEA; Katharine Gibbs Sec Schl; Exec Sec.

STAHL, CHARLES; Keyser HS; Keyser, WV; 35/260 Pres Band; Hon Rl; NHS; Stu Cncl; Letter Ten; Potomac St Coll; Pharm.

STAHL, DIANE; Dekalb HS; Kendallville, IN; 9/283 Sec Soph Cls; Sec Jr Cls; Cls Rep Sr Cls; Am Leg Aux Girls St; Band; Chrs; Drl Tm; JA; NHS; Stu Cncl; Awded Dekalbs 1st Grls Acad Athltc Awd 1977; Mmbr Of Vocal Grp 1978; Vocal & Instrmntl Trmbne 1st Pl 1976; Indiana Univ; Bus Admin.

STAHL, JEAN; Scecina Memorial HS; Indianapolis, IN; 48/211 Hon Rl; Sch Mus; Sch Pl; Sct Actv; 4-H; Spn Clb; 4-H Awd; Purdue Univ; Dietitian.

STAHL, PATRICIA; Edison HS; Lake Station, IN; 19/171 Sec Frsh Cls; Cls Rep Soph Cls; Drl Tm; Hosp Ade; Jr NHS; NHS; Off Ade; Stu Cncl; Fr Clb; Pep Clb;.

STAHL, SUZANNE; Grosse Pointe North HS; Grosse Pt Wds, MI; Aud/Vis; FCA; Girl Scts; Hon Rl; Sct Actv; Crs Cntry; Trk; PPFtbl; Tmr; God Cntry Awd; Univ; Animal Husbandry.

STAHLER, AMY; Riverside HS; Degraff, OH; VP Soph Cls; Pres Jr Cls; Band; Chrs; Hon Rl; NHS; Sch Pl; Yth Flsp; 4-H; Rdo Clb; College; Dental Tech.

STAHLER, JENNIFER; West Geauga HS; Chesterland, OH; 143/348 Cl Rep Jr Cls; Cls Rep Sr Cls; Drl Tm; Drm Bgl; Girl Scts; Hon Rl; Off Ade; Stu Cncl; Pep Clb; Chrldng; Rainbow For Girsl 5 Yrs Worth Advsr 78; Grand Immortlty In St Of Ohio Rainbow Girls 79; Lakeland Cmnty Coll; CPA.

STAINES, LENORA; Central Montcalm HS; Fenwidk, MI; 19/128 Chrs; Hon Rl; Sch Mus; Stg Crw; Drama Clb; FHA; Central Michigan Univ; Bus Admin.

STAINFIELD, ROY; Jefferson HS; Jefferson, OH; Band; 4-H; FFA; Green Hand Awd 77; Agri.

STAIRE, DAVID; Green HS; N Canton, OH; Mgrs; Univ; Comp Sci.

STAKELBECK, RON; Taylor HS; Kokomo, IN; Hon Rl; Ftbl; Univ Of N Arizona; Forestry.

STAKER, MAUREEN; Carroll HS; Dayton, OH; 8/285 Band; Chrh Wkr; Hon Rl; Hosp Ade; NHS; Key Clb; College; Nursing.

STALDER, RICHARD; East Canton HS; Louisville, OH; Debate Tm; Jr NHS; Natl Forn Lg; Sch Pl; Fr Clb; Crs Cntry; Trk; IM Sprt; Coll; Oceanographer.

STALEY, CINDY; Bedford North Lawrence HS; Bedford, IN; Hon Rl; OEA; College; Secretary.

STALEY, DENNIS; Martinsburg Sr HS; Martinsburg, WV; 22/220 Cls Rep Frsh Cls; Cls Rep Soph Cls; Cl Rep Jr Cls; Hon Rl; Sch Pl; Stu Cncl; Letter Bsktbl; Math Field Day Placed 1st Of All People In County; Outstndng Bsktbl Player On Team; All Star Baseball Team; Florida State Univ; Meteorology.

STALEY, DENNIS W; Martinsburg HS; Martinsburg, WV; 22/220 Cls Rep Frsh Cls; Cls Rep Soph Cls; Cl Rep Jr Cls; Debate Tm; Hon Rl; Sch Pl; Boys Clb Am; Letter Bsktbl; Florida St Univ; Meteorology.

STALEY, LAURA; Delaware Hayes HS; Delaware, OH; Cls Rep Frsh Cls; AFS; Am Leg Aux Girls St; Chrs; Chrh Wkr; Hon Rl; Jr NHS; Natl Forn Lg; Sch Mus; Sch Pl; Hnr Thespian 79; Univ; Math.

STALEY, LUANN; Riverdale HS; Forest, OH; Am Leg Aux Girls St; Chrs; Hon Rl; NHS; Quill & Scroll; Sch Mus; Ed Yrbk; 4-H; FHA; 4-H Awd; Ohio St Univ; Landscaping.

STALEY, SHERRI; Butler HS; Vandalia, OH; Univ; Elem Educ.

STALEY, THOMAS; John Glenn HS; Westland, MI; Debate Tm; Hon Rl; Jr NHS; NHS; Univ; Sci.

STALICA, MAUREEN; Central Catholic HS; Canton, OH; Band; Chrs; Chrh Wkr; Hon Rl; Rptr Yrbk; Sch Nwsp; Fr Clb; FTA; Pep Clb; Sci Clb; Ohio Northern Univ; Pharm.

STALLARD, BARRY K; Licking Heights HS; Reynoldsburg, OH; 2/80 Pres Jr Cls; Am Leg Boys St; Band; Hon Rl; NHS; Ger Clb; Sci Clb; Letter Bsktbl; Cit Awd; Rotary Awd; College; Electronics.

STALLARD, DEBORAH; Peru HS; Peru, IN; 3/260 Hon Rl; NHS; Manchester Coll; Phys Sci.

STALLER, JOHN; Central Catholic HS; Canton, OH; Pres Aud/Vis; Hon Rl; NHS; Sch Pl; Stg Crw; Yrbk; Natl Merit Ltr; Ohi State Univ; Engr.

STALLER, KIRK; Northrop HS; Ft Wayne, IN; CAP; JA; 4-H; JA Awd; Purdue Univ; Mech Engr.

STALNAKER, BOB; Washington Irving HS; Clarksburg, WV; Am Leg Boys St; Hon Rl; Sch Nwsp; Fr Clb; Key Clb; Bsktbl; West Virginia Univ.

STALNAKER, DEBORAH; Buckhannon Upshur HS; Buckhannon, WV; Band; Cmnty Wkr; Hosp Ade; Sch Nwsp; 4-H; FBLA; Pep Clb; 4-H Awd; Glenville; Nursing.

STALNAKER, SHERRY; Kenton Sr HS; Kenton, OH; 2/232 Am Leg Aux Girls St; Band; Hon Rl; Sec JA; NHS; Rptr Yrbk; 4-H; Fr Clb; Spn Clb; Bsktbl; Univ Of Cincinnati; Pharm.

ST AMAND, DIANE J; Petoskey Sr HS; Petoskey, MI; Trs Soph Cls; Debate Tm; Hon Rl; NHS; Yrbk; 4-H; Treas Spn Clb; Bsktbl; 4-H Awd; St Of Mi Comp Schlrshp 79; Cntrl Mi Bd Of Trustees Hon Schlrshp 79; N Cntrl Michigan Coll; Retail Mdse.

STAMATIADES, MARIA; Saint Augustine Acad; Cleveland, OH; Trs Frsh Cls; Cl Rep Jr Cls; Cls Rep Sr Cls; Chrs; Hon Rl; Sch Mus; Stu Cncl; Yrbk; Civ Clb; Crs Cntry; College.

STAMM, AMY; Liberty HS; Salem, WV; 61/231 Chrs; Chrh Wkr; Cmnty Wkr; Hon Rl; Off Ade; Orch; Sch Mus; Salem College; Bio.

STAMM, BRENDA S; L & M HS; Linton, IN; Trs Sr Cls; Am Leg Aux Girls St; Chrs; Chrh Wkr; Cmnty Wkr; Hon Rl; Off Ade; Pol Wkr; Ed Yrbk; Yrbk; IVTC; Legal Sec.

STAMM, CYNTHIA; Waldron Jr Sr HS; Waldron, IN; Cls Rep Frsh Cls; Hon Rl; Off Ade; Stu Cncl; Yth Flsp; Yrbk; Sch Nwsp; 4-H; Fr Clb; Pep Clb; Shelby Cnty Grand Champion Phtog 1st St Fair IN; Univ; Lib Arts.

STAMM, SCOTT; Harper Creek HS; Battle Creek, MI; Band; Hon Rl; Orch; Sch Mus; College; Computer Prog.

STAMMEN, CHRISTOPHER; Coldwater HS; Coldwater, OH; Chrs; Chrh Wkr; Hon Rl; FFA; FTA; Wrstlng; IM Sprt; Bowling Greene; Elec Engr.

STAMP, BRENDA; Brandon HS; Oxford, MI; Cls Rep Soph Cls; VP Jr Cls; Hon Rl; Stu Cncl; Pep Clb; Bsktbl; Trk; Univ; Phys Ther.

STAMPER, CHARMAE; Columbia HS; Columbia Sta, OH; Cl Rep Jr Cls; Chrs; Chrh Wkr; Hon Rl; Lbry Ade; Stg Crw; Stu Cncl; Ed Yrbk; Sch Nwsp; FHA; Met With Carlton Publishers To Pub Book Of Poetry 78; Won Hon Mention In Kent St Poetry Cont 78; Baldin Wallace Coll; Eng.

STAMPER, DEBRA; Randolph Southern HS; Lynn, IN; Hon Rl; NHS; Miami Jacobs Jr College; Acctg.

STAMPER, JULIE; Brown County HS; Nashville, IN; 5/100 Am Leg Aux Girls St; Band; Drl Tm; Girl Scts; Hon Rl; Mod UN; Pres NHS; Ed Sch Nwsp; 4-H; Fr Clb; Purdue; Engr.

STAMPER, ROBERT R; Bellefontaine HS; W Mansfield, OH; 1/241 Am Leg Boys St; Debate Tm; Jr NHS; Natl Forn Lg; NHS; ROTC; Ger Clb; Sci Clb; Kiwan Awd; Rotary Awd; Soph Schslrshp All A 77; Soph Hnrs A Avg 77; Jur Schlrshp 78; Univ; Med.

STANDER, TERRI; Leland Public HS; Leland, MI; 6/31 Band; Chrs; Chrh Wkr; Girl Scts; Hon Rl; Mdrgl; NHS; Sct Actv; Yth Flsp; Bsbl; Bus Schl; Le gl Sec.

STANDISH, KELLI; Centerville HS; Richmond, IN; 57/157 Pres Frsh Cls; Drl Tm; Hon Rl; Mod UN; Sch Mus; Y-Teens; Yrbk; Rptr Sch Nwsp; Trk; Pom Pon; All Amer Drill Team 79; Miss Oh Weslyan At Oh Wesltyan Drill Camp 79; Ball St Univ.

ST ANDRE, D; Gwinn HS; Gwinn, MI; Bsktbl; Ftbl; Trk; College; English.

ST ANDRE, DAVID; Gwinn HS; Gwinn, MI; Off Ade; Bsktbl; Ftbl; Trk; Univ; Eng.

ST ANDRE, JODY; Belleville HS; Belleville, MI; Sec Frsh Cls; Cls Rep Soph Cls; Cl Rep Jr Cls; Cls Rep Sr Cls; Cmnty Wkr; Hon Rl; Off Ade; Letter Chrldng; Eastern Mic Univ; Nursing.

STANDRIDGE, ELIZABETH; Ithaca HS; Ithaca, MI; Band; Chrs; Cmnty Wkr; Debate Tm; Hon Rl; Sch Mus; Fr Clb; Pep Clb; Ten; W Mich Univ; Flight Tech.

STANEK, JANICE L; Euclid Sr HS; Euclid, OH; 6/730 Boy Scts; Hon Rl; NHS; Off Ade; Red Cr Ade; Ed Sch Nwsp; Natl Merit SF; Dstngshd Honor Awd & Scholar Awd; Girls Ldrs Clb Parliamentarian; Ohio State Univ; Physical Therapy.

STANEK, JULIE; St Joseph Ctrl Catholic HS; Huntington, WV; 4/54 Girl Scts; Hon Rl; Sch Nwsp; Drama Clb; Pep Clb; College; Journalism.

STANEK, LARRY; Normandy Sr HS; Seven Hls, OH; Chrs; NHS; Spn Clb; Ftbl; Letter Ten; Academitions; Spanish Honor Soc; Univ; Art.

STANEK, LAURA; St Joseph Academy; Lakewood, OH; Chrs; Hon Rl; Pres Yth Flsp; Rptr Yrbk; Rptr Sch Nwsp; Fr Clb; Sci Clb; Ftr Med Careers Club Pres 78; E Oh Gas Co Stdnt Energy Awd 79; St Bd Awd Of Distnctn 78; Univ Of Akron; Nursing.

STANEK, PAM; Perry HS; Perry, MI; 18/176 Girl Scts; Hon Rl; FFA; Pep Clb; Letter Trk; Chrldng; Mic State; Social Work.

STANFILL, BARBARA; Dexter HS; Dexter, MI; Girl Scts; Hon Rl; Jr NHS; NHS; Stu Cncl; Yrbk; Letter Ftbl; Chrldng; Mgrs; Natl Merit Schl; Eastern Michigan Univ.

STANFORD, DARLENE; Washington HS; Massillon, OH; DECA; Ger Clb;.

STANFORD, DAVID; South HS; Youngstown, OH; 5/279 Hosp Ade; NHS; Stg Crw; Cit Awd; Youngstown St Univ; Mech Engr.

STANFORD, TERRI; Anderson HS; Anderson, IN; Rptr Sch Nwsp; Fr Clb; Sec FHA; Lat Clb; Ball State Univ; Med.

STANG, DAVID; Newbury HS; Newbury, OH; 5/80 Aud/Vis; Band; Chrs; Jr NHS; Treas NHS; Yrbk; Sci Clb; Spn Clb; Letter Bsbl; Hiram.

STANG, DOUGLAS; Brookville HS; Brookville, IN; 2/200 Am Leg Boys St; Boy Scts; Chrs; Chrh Wkr; Hon Rl; NHS; Sch Pl; VP 4-H; Spn Clb; Pres Awd; College; Optometry.

STANG, GINA; Taft Sr HS; Hamilton, OH; Band; Drm Bgl; Hon Rl; Hosp Ade; Sec Jr NHS; Lbry Ade; NHS; Off Ade; Y-Teens; Ger Clb; Ohio St Univ; Pharm.

STANG, SHARON; Brookville HS; Brookville, IN; 41/189 Cls Rep Frsh Cls; Cl Rep Jr Cls; Hon Rl; Off Ade; Stu Cncl; FHA; Chrldng; College; Secretary.

STANISH, JO ANN; Woodrow Wilson HS; Youngstown, OH; Cmp Fr Grls; Chrs; Off Ade; Pep Clb; Pres Sci Clb; Letter Trk; Letter Chrldng; IM Sprt; Youngstown St Univ; Sci.

STANKO, JOHN; Washington HS; Massillon, OH; Am Leg Boys St; Hon Rl; Jr NHS; NHS; Boys Clb Am; Spn Clb; Letter Bsbl; Univ; Archt.

STANKO, TERESA; St Francis De Sales HS; Columbus, OH; Franklin Univ; Sec.

STANKOWSKI, GARY; Gladwin HS; Gladwin, MI; Hon Rl; Letter Bsbl; Letter Bsktbl; Letter Ftbl; Coach Actv; Univ; Bus.

STANLEY, ALESIA D; Liberty HS; Mt Clare, WV; 17/228 Chrs; Cmnty Wkr; Hon Rl; Lbry Ade; Fr Clb; FBLA; Clarksburg Beauty Academy; Beautcian.

STANLEY, CHERYL; Walkerville HS; Walkerville, MI; 1/31 Sec Frsh Cls; Trs Soph Cls; Trs Jr Cls; Trs Sr Cls; Hon Rl; NHS; Sch Pl; Stu Cncl; Yrbk; 4-H; Central Michigan Univ; Poli Sci.

STANLEY, DIANE; Newton Falls HS; Newton Falls, OH; 1/153 Val; Band; Hosp Ade; NHS; Capt Stu Cncl; Ed Yrbk; VP FSA; VP GAA; Elk Awd; Miami Univ; Psych.

STANLEY, ELAINE; Big Creek HS; War, WV; Chrs; Hon Rl; Off Ade; Rptr Yrbk; FHA; Keyettes; Pep Clb; Berea College; Marketing.

STANLEY, JOHN; John F Kennedy HS; Taylor, MI; 5/550 Cls Rep Frsh Cls; Hon Rl; NHS; Ger Clb; Bsbl; Wrstlng; Cit Awd; College.

STANLEY, JOHN; Bucyrus HS; Bucyrus, OH; Crs Cntry; Trk; Ohio State Univ; Physical Education.

STANLEY, LEISA J; Northside HS; Muncie, IN; 15/259 Chrh Wkr; Debate Tm; Hon Rl; Jr NHS; Natl Forn Lg; NHS; Pol Wkr; Bob Jones Univ; Political Sci.

STANLEY, LINDA; Madison Hts HS; Anderson, IN; 20/371 Cls Rep Soph Cls; Cl Rep Jr Cls; NHS; Pres Quill & Scroll; Ed Yrbk; Rptr Yrbk; 4-H; Spn Clb; Gym; Coll; Journalism.

STANLEY, LISA; Eastbrook HS; Marion, IN; Hon Rl; Pep Clb; Univ; Bus.

STANLEY, MICHAEL; Valley HS; Flint, MI; Debate Tm; Lbry Ade; Sch Pl; Rptr Yrbk; Rptr Sch Nwsp; Drama Clb; Spn Clb; Bsbl; Bsktbl; Glf; College; Journalism.

STANLEY, PAUL; Taft HS; Hamilton, OH; 34/450 Band; Boy Scts; Debate Tm; Hon Rl; Natl Forn Lg; Orch; Sch Mus; Drake; Physics.

STANLEY, WILLIAM K; Mt View HS; Welch, WV; Am Leg Boys St; Hst Frsh Cls; Jr NHS; Yth Flsp; Concord Coll; Bus.

STANNY, MARY; Morton HS; Hammond, IN; 62/447 Pep Clb; Letter Bsktbl; IM Sprt; PPFtbl; Scr Kpr; College; Accountant.

STANO, GARY; De La Salle Collegiate HS; Detroit, MI; 8/130 Boy Scts; Hon Rl; NHS; Quill & Scroll; Sch Mus; Rptr Sch Nwsp; Letter Trk; Alma Coll; Pre Med.

STANSBERRY, JOLINNE; Georgetown HS; Georgetown, OH; 1/86 Trs Soph Cls; Cl Rep Jr Cls; Val; Am Leg Aux Girls St; Band; Chrs; Girl Scts; Hon Rl; NHS; Sch Mus; Univ Of Cincinnati; Pharm.

STANSBERRY, KAREN L; Eastmoor HS; Columbus, OH; 27/290 Cls Rep Frsh Cls; Cls Rep Soph Cls; Cl Rep Jr Cls; Cls Rep Sr Cls; Pres Chrs; Girl Scts; Hon Rl; Sch Mus; Stu Cncl; Letter GAA; Winston Salem Univ; Education.

STANSBERRY, MICHELLE; Doddridge Co HS; West Union, WV; Am Leg Aux Girls St; Hon Rl; FBLA; Pep Clb; Bsktbl; Letter Socr; Glenville St Univ; Business.

STANSBERY, SCOTT; Upper Sandusky HS; Upper Sandusky, OH; Band; Hon Rl; JA; NHS; Yth Flsp; 4-H; Sec FFA; OSU; Agri Mgmt.

STANSEL, TERI; Archbishop Alter HS; Kettering, OH; 29/348 Hon Rl; NHS; Sch Mus; Stu Cncl; Keyettes; Spn Clb; Gym; Trk; Washington Univ; Corporate Law.

STANSFIELD, SARAH; Oakwood HS; Dayton, OH; VP Soph Cls; Chrs; Chrh Wkr; FCA; Hon Rl; Red Cr Ade; Stg Crw; Stu Cncl; FDA; Hockey; College.

STANTON, BRENDA; Belding HS; Belding, MI; Cls Rep Soph Cls; Cl Rep Jr Cls; Hon Rl; Off Ade; Stu Cncl; Pep Clb; Trk; Davenport Coll.

STANTON, DEBBIE; Buchanan HS; South Bend, IN; Chrs; Hon Rl; Hosp Ade; JA; Lbry Ade; Red Cr Ade; 4-H; Pep Clb; BYU; Nursing.

STANTON, LISA; Central Catholic HS; Wheeling, WV; Hon Rl; 4-H; Trk; College; Nursing.

STANTON, PAMELA; Buckhannon Upshur HS; Buckhannon, WV; Band; Girl Scts; Hon Rl; Hosp Ade; NHS; Stu Cncl; Y-Teens; 4-H; Pep Clb; Know Youth St Govt Day; West Virginia Univ; Phys Ther.

STANTON, TIMOTHY; Plymouth Canton HS; Plymouth, MI; 16/437 Hon Rl; Spring Arbor Coll.

STAP, JOHN; Gull Lake HS; Richland, MI; 19/228 Hon Rl; Lit Mag; NHS; Rptr Sch Nwsp; Fr Clb; Awds For Schlstc Achvmnt 1976; Magician Of The Month 1978; Membr Of Soc Of Amer Magicians; Western Michigan Univ; Bus Admin.

STAPEL, TODD; Reeths Puffer HS; Muskegon, MI; 40/345 Boy Scts; Debate Tm; Natl Forn Lg; Red Cr Ade; Sch Pl; Sct Actv; Stg Crw; Muskegon Comm College.

STAPHER, BRIAN; New Albany HS; New Albany, IN; Am Leg Boys St; Band; Drm Bgl; FCA; Hon Rl; Jr NHS; NHS; Military Acad; Engr.

STAPLES, RICHARD; Ovid Elsie HS; St Johns, MI; 8/156 Aud/Vis; Band; Boy Scts; Sch Mus; Sch Pl; Drama Clb; Bsktbl; Letter Ftbl; Trk; Michigan State Univ; Research Chemis.

STAPLETON, MICHAEL; Buffalo HS; Kenova, WV; Chrh Wkr; Hon Rl; Letter Bsbl; Letter Ftbl; Trk; IM Sprt; Marshall Univ; Chem.

STAPLETON, TERIANA; Union City Cmnty HS; Union City, IN; Debate Tm; Hon Rl; Lbry Ade; DECA; Eng Clb; Deca St Off Elect 1979; Mbr Ind Deca Brd 1979; Purdue Univ; Bus.

STARCHER, DIANNE; Sissonville Sr HS; Charleston, WV; Hon Rl; JA; Jr NHS; Rptr Sch Nwsp; FTA; Pep Clb; Chrldng; Coll; Acctg.

STARCHER, GREG; Spencer HS; Spencer, WV; Hon Rl; Ftbl; Trk; College; Crimonology.

STARCHER, JEANNE; Parkersburg South HS; Washington, WV; Sec Frsh Cls; Hon Rl; Hosp Ade; Off Ade; Sch Mus; Sch Pl; Stg Crw; Ger Clb; GAA; Coll; Child Dev.

STARCHER, JOHN; Danbury Local HS; Lakeside, OH; 9/87 VP Jr Cls; VP Sr Cls; Hon Rl; NHS; Sch Pl; Yth Flsp; Sci Clb; Spn Clb; Ftbl; Letter Trk; Exc Dist Sci Fair; Ohio Test Of Schlstc Ach 12th Plc Chemistry; Carnegie Mellon Univ; Elec Tech.

STARCHER, LARRY W; Parkersburg South HS; Parkersburg, WV; 47/575 Am Leg Boys St; Band; Chrs; Hon Rl; Mdrgl; Sch Mus; Sch Pl; All St Bnd 79; WUU Invtnl Hon Bnd 78; Mid E Instrmntl Music Conf 79; West Virginia Univ; Applied Music.

STARCHER, LORNA; Washington HS; Massillon, OH; Boy Scts; Chrh Wkr; Off Ade; Red Cr Ade; Fr Clb; Massillon Community Schl; Rn.

STARCZEWSKI, KELLENE D; Andrean HS; Miller Beach, IN; Cls Rep Frsh Cls; Cls Rep Soph Cls; Cmnty Wkr; Drl Tm; Hon Rl; Jr NHS; Yth Flsp; Pep Clb; Pom Pon; Awds In Pom Pon Camp Showmanshp 77 78 & 79 Marching 78; Achvmnt 77 78 & 79; Purdue Univ; Psych.

STARE, DAWN; Howland HS; Warren, OH; 1/439 Val; Chrs; Chrh Wkr; Girl Scts; Hon Rl; NHS; Off Ade; Y-Teens; Ger Clb; Letter Glf; Soc Dstngshd Amer HS Stu; Nom To Martin Essex Schl Gifted Chldrn; Explr At Trumbull Memrl Hsp; Math Cntst; Youngstown State Univ; Med Tech.

STARGEL, MARK; Maconaquah HS; Bunker Hill, IN; 66/219 Aud/Vis; Boy Scts; Chrh Wkr; Lbry Ade; Pres Yth Flsp; VP DECA; Spn Clb; Voice Dem Awd; Hoosier Schlr By St Stdnt Asstnc Cmmssn 79; Ivy Tech Voc Schl; Comp Prgrmng.

STARK, J; Corydon Ctrl HS; Corydon, IN; Indiana S Univ; Nursing.

STARK, JILL; Whitko HS; Pierceton, IN; 43/151 Cl Rep Jr Cls; Cls Rep Sr Cls; Chrs; Debate Tm; FCA; Sch Pl; Stu Cncl; Drama Clb; Pep Clb; Trk; Indiana Coll; Communications.

STARK, JOY; Springport HS; Albion, MI; Chrs; Hon Rl; Lit Mag; Sch Mus; Sch Pl; Stu Cncl; Rptr Yrbk; Yrbk; College; Music.

STARK, KRISTY; Mason Cnty Eastern HS; Scottville, MI; 4/60 Hon Rl; Sch Pl; Stu Cncl; Pep Clb; Capt Bsktbl; Univ; Phys Ed.

STARK, MICHAEL; Lake Orion Community HS; Pontiac, MI; 3/454 Aud/Vis; Hon Rl; NHS; Rdo Clb; Univ Of Mi Regnst Almn Schlr Awd 79; St Of Mi Comp Schlshp Progr Cert Of Recngntn 79; Univ Of Michigan; Poli Sci.

STARK, RICHARD; Hilliard HS; Hilliard, OH; 21/335 Hon Rl; Jr NHS; NHS; Sch Pl; Drama Clb; Spn Clb; Ohio State Univ; Comp Progr.

STARK, ROBIN; South Harrison HS; Clarksburg, WV; 18/86 Band; Chrs; Chrh Wkr; Hon Rl; Lbry Ade; NHS; Yrbk; 4-H; FHA; 4-H Awd; Marshall Univ; Law Enforcement.

STARK, VINCE; Bryan HS; Bryan, OH; Pres Sr Cls; Sal; Chrh Wkr; Cmnty Wkr; FCA; Hon Rl; Sch Nwsp; Lat Clb; Bsktbl; Crs Cntry; Eastern Michigan Univ; Bio.

STARKE, JANICE; Merrill HS; Brant, MI; 3/119 Chrs; Hon Rl; NHS; Stg Crw; Delta Coll; Legal Sec.

STARKEY, BETTIE; Winfield HS; Scott Depot, WV; Sec Frsh Cls; Sec Soph Cls; Trs Soph Cls; Cl Rep Jr Cls; Hon Rl; Yth Flsp; Drama Clb; 4-H; Fr Clb; FHA; Marshall Coll; Journalism.

STARKEY, BRADLEY; Zanesville HS; Zanesville, OH; Band; Chrh Wkr; Hon Rl; NHS; Pres Yth Flsp; 4-H; Pep Clb; Sci Clb; 4-H Awd; God Cntry Awd; Univ; Law.

STARKEY, DIANE; Brookhaven HS; Columbus, OH; Girl Scts; Hon Rl; 4-H; Spn Clb; Letter Bsktbl; Trk; Univ; Engr.

STARKEY, DON; Malabar HS; Mansfield, OH; Aud/Vis; Band; Boy Scts; Chrh Wkr; Orch; Sct Actv; Stg Crw; Stu Cncl; Pres Yth Flsp; Ger Clb; Grove City Coll; Elec Engr.

STARKEY, KATHERINE; Warren Local HS; Vincent, OH; Sec Sr Cls; Chrh Wkr; Hon Rl; NHS; Yth Flsp; Yrbk; Pep Clb; Ohi State Univ; Elem Educ.

STARKEY, MARCIA; Bethesda Christian Schls; Brownsberg, IL; VP Soph Cls; Trs Jr Cls; Chrs; Girl Scts; Hon Rl; Sch Mus; Sch Pl; Rptr Yrbk; Cit Awd; Grace Brethern Univ; Christian Educ.

STARKEY, SUSAN; Morgantown HS; Morgantwn, WV; Band; Letter Trk; IM Sprt; Letter Mat Maids; West Virginia Univ; Wildlife Mgmt.

STARKEY, THERESA; Millersport HS; Millersport, OH; 8/65 Trs Jr Cls; Trs Sr Cls; Band; Chrs; Hon Rl; Jr NHS; NHS; Sch Mus; Keyettes; Pep Clb; CTI; Genrl Offc Skills.

STARKEY, VICKIE; Buckhannon Upshur HS; Buckhannon, WV; Cls Rep Frsh Cls; Pres Soph Cls; VP Jr Cls; Band; Girl Scts; Y-Teens; 4-H; FHA; Pep Clb; Chrldng; All Tournment Cheerleader; College; Home Ec.

STARKS, HERMAN; East HS; Youngstown, OH; Cls Rep Sr Cls; Band; Boy Scts; Chrh Wkr; JA; Yth Flsp; Fr Clb; Ftbl; IM Sprt; Opt Clb Awd; Univ Of Tennessee; Public Relations.

STARKS, JEAN; Creston HS; Grand Rpds, MI; Debate Tm; JA; Rptr Yrbk; Univ Of Michigan; Forestry.

STARKS, KAREN; West Side HS; Gary, IN; Chrh Wkr; Hon Rl; Orch; FBLA; Bsktbl; Indiana Univ; Tchr.

STARKWEATHER, LORIE; Edwardsburg HS; Edwardsburg, MI; Cmp Fr Grls; Chrs; Chrh Wkr; Hon Rl; Mdrgl; Yth Flsp; Letter Bsktbl; Univ; Park Admin.

STARLIPER, CAROL; Martinsburg HS; Martinsburg, WV; Hon Rl; Off Ade; Shepherd College.

STARMAN, LORI; Wylie E Groves HS; Birmingham, MI; VP Sr Cls; AFS; Chrs; Hon Rl; Mdrgl; NHS; Sch Mus; Sch Nwsp; Fr Clb; Cit Awd; Univ Of Mich.

STARNER, AMY; Warsaw Cmnty HS; Warsaw, IN; Sec Frsh Cls; Sec Soph Cls; VP Jr Cls; Sec Sr Cls; Stu Cncl; DECA; GAA;.

STARNER, JEFFREY; Heath HS; Heath, OH; Hon Rl; NHS; Spn Clb; Crs Cntry; Letter Ftbl; Letter Trk; Ohio St Univ; Engr.

STARNER, JERRY; Bucyrus Sr HS; Bucyrus, OH; Boy Scts; Hon Rl; Letter Crs Cntry; Letter Wrstlng; Part In St Champ Of AMUETS Driver Excllnc 79; Amer Lgn St Trapshootng Champ 75; Univ; Comp Systems Analyst.

STARON, CHERYL; Thurston HS; Redford, MI; Band; Girl Scts; Jr NHS; Off Ade; Orch; Sch Pl; Sct Actv; Stg Crw; Rptr Sch Nwsp; Drama Clb; Mic State; Dramatic Arts.

STARR, CHRIS; Muskegon Catholic Cntrl HS; Kalamazoo, MI; VP Soph Cls; Boy Scts; Sct Actv; Rptr Yrbk; Eagle Scout Awd BSA 76; Mi Competitive Schlrshp Semi Finalist 79; Michigan St Univ; Agri.

STARR, MILDRED; Magnolia HS; Delbarton, WV; Val; Hon Rl; Jr NHS; NHS; Sch Nwsp; 4-H; Fr Clb; FHA; FSA; Millitary Voc Schl; Comp Progr.

STARR, SUE; All Saints Central HS; Essxville, MI; Hon Rl; 4-H; Letter Bsktbl; Trk; Cit Awd; DAR Awd; 4-H Awd; Voice Dem Awd; College.

STARR, THOMAS; Roy C Start HS; Toledo, OH; Hon Rl; Sch Pl; Stg Crw; Ed Sch Nwsp; Sch Nwsp; FHA; Ohio Univ; Public Relations.

STARRE, JEFF; Padua Franciscan HS; Broadview Hts, OH; Cmnty Wkr; Hon Rl; NHS; Letter Bsktbl; Coach Actv; College; Bio.

START, PAULA; Ladywood HS; Livonia, MI; Girl Scts; Hon Rl; Red Cr Ade; Sch Mus; Stg Crw; Drama Clb; Michigan St Univ.

STARTS, BRENT E; Memorial HS; St Marys, OH; 30/245 VP Soph Cls; Band; Chrh Wkr; Cmnty Wkr; Hon Rl; NHS; Letter Ftbl; Letter Trk; IM Sprt; Voice Dem Awd; Ohio Northern Univ; Health.

STARY, SHIRLEY; Cleveland Central Cath HS; Cleveland, OH; 6/180 Trs Jr Cls; Capt Drl Tm; Mod UN; NHS; Quill & Scroll; Stg Crw; Ed Yrbk; Rptr Yrbk; Scr Kpr; Ashland Coll; Radio/TV Brdcstng.

STARYKOWICZ, JOANNE; George Washington HS; E Chicago, IN; 93/263 Chrs; JA; FTA; Key Clb; Spn Clb; Ten; College; Pilot.

STASA, CAMILLA; Chesaning HS; Owosso, MI; 110241 Band; Drm Mjrt; Hon Rl; NHS; Sch Mus; Sch Pl; Pres Drama Clb; Arion Awd 79; Stdnt Speaker At Commencements 79; Perf Of The Yr Awd 78; Eastern Michigan Univ; Dramatic Arts.

STASH, LAURIE; Austintown Fitch HS; Youngstown, OH; 6/700 Hon Rl; Lit Mag; NHS; Pol Wkr; Y-Teens; Pres Fr Clb; FTA; Ten; Elk Awd; Opt Clb Awd; Youngstown St Univ; Math.

STASIAK, ANNETTE; Ida HS; Ida, MI; Chrh Wkr; Hon Rl; NHS; PAVAS; Sch Pl; Stg Crw; Drama Clb; 4-H; 4-H Awd; College; Engineering.

STASSIN, LISA; Avon Jr Sr HS; Plainfield, IN; Band; Girl Scts; Hon Rl; NHS; Sch Mus; Sch Pl; Stg Crw; Ed Sch Nwsp; Sprt Ed Sch Nwsp; Rptr Sch Nwsp; Sunshine Soc 1978; Pres Corr Sec 1978; OEA 3rd & 1st Pl Prepd Verbal Ore; 1st Pl Job Intvw Ore; Volleyball; Univ; Public Reltns.

STATON, G MICHAEL; Malabar HS; Mansfield, OH; 90/280 Band; Orch; Natl Merit Ltr;.

STATON, SCOTT; Troy Athens HS; Troy, MI; 86/507 Cls Rep Frsh Cls; Aud/Vis; Hon Rl; Lbry Ade; NHS; Letter Bsktbl; Coach Actv; Mgrs; Scr Kpr; Tmr; Univ; Geology.

STATTS, JEANNE; Herbert Hoover HS; Charleston, WV; Pres Sr Cls; Hon Rl; Jr NHS; Rptr Yrbk; Rptr Sch Nwsp; Pres Fr Clb; West Virginia Wesleyan Univ; Law.

STAUBLIN, DEBBIE; Shawe Memorial HS; Madison, IN; 1/27 Sec Soph Cls; Val; Hon Rl; Treas NHS; Pol Wkr; Ed Sch Nwsp; Drama Clb; Treas Pep Clb; Chrldng; Bausch & Lomb Awd; Purdue Univ; Engr.

STAUCH, TERESA; Warren Local HS; Marietta, OH; Treas Chrs; Hon Rl; NHS; Sch Mus; Yrbk; 4-H; Treas Fr Clb; Bowling Green St Univ; Educ.

STAUCH, TREVA; Warren Local HS; Marietta, OH; Band; Chrs; Chrh Wkr; Girl Scts; Hon Rl; NHS; Sch Mus; Bowling Green State Univ; Elem Ed.

STAUD, KIM; Mother Of Mercy HS; Cincinnati, OH; 12/220 Cl Rep Jr Cls; Chrs; Hon Rl; JA; NHS; Stu Cncl; Spn Clb; Socr; GAA; IM Sprt; Univ Of Cincinnati; Engr.

STAUDT, JOSEPH E; Perry HS; Canton, OH; 50/480 Band; Chrs; Debate Tm; Hon Rl; Natl Forn Lg; Quill & Scroll; Sch Pl; Rptr Sch Nwsp; Drama Clb; Ohio Tests Of Scholastic Ach; Honorable Mention In Sci; College; Mech Engr.

STAUFENGER, MIKE; Leetonia HS; Leetonia, OH; 7/84 Band; Hon Rl; NHS; Sch Mus; Spn Clb; Dnfth Awd; Kent St Univ; Aerospace Tech.

STAUFF, LYNNE; Northwest HS; Rives Jct, MI; Cls Rep Sr Cls; Chrs; Hon Rl; Sch Mus; Sch Pl; 4-H; IM Sprt; 4-H Awd; Univ.

STAUFFER, MARTHA; Sandusky HS; Sandusky, OH; 10/400 Cls Rep Frsh Cls; Cls Rep Soph Cls; Cl Rep Jr Cls; Am Leg Aux Girls St; Treas Band; Girl Scts; Hon Rl; NHS; Orch; Stu Cncl; College; Math.

STAUFFER, ROBERT; R Nelson Snider HS; Ft Wayne, IN; 4/525 Cls Rep Frsh Cls; Hon Rl; Stu Cncl; FDA; Ger Clb; Letter Bsktbl; Glf; Trk; C of C Awd; Cit Awd; Univ Of Notre Dame; Med.

STAUFFER, SUSAN; Southeastern HS; Chillicothe, OH; Chrs; Hon Rl; Stu Cncl; Yrbk; 4-H; FTA; Mgrs; 4-H Awd; Ohio Univ; Elem Educ.

STAUNTON, CLARENCE B; Greenbrier East HS; Lewisburg, WV; Chrs; Chrh Wkr; FCA; Hon Rl; MMM; NHS; Sch Mus; Drama Clb; Mgrs; Cit Awd; Concord College; Elem Educ.

STAUNTON, DARLA; Woodward HS; Toledo, OH; Band; Pep Clb; Univ Of Toledo; Fshn Mdse.

STAUNTON, SCOTT; Lapeer East Sr HS; Metamora, MI; Cls Rep Soph Cls; Pres Jr Cls; Band; Boy Scts; Chrh Wkr; Debate Tm; Drm Bgl; Hon Rl; Stu Cncl; Ten; Albion Univ; Bus Admin.

STAVOLE, JUDY; Valley Forge HS; Parma Heights, OH; Cl Rep Jr Cls; Chrh Wkr; Girl Scts; Pol Wkr; Stu Cncl; FFA; Letter Bsbl; Bsktbl; GAA;.

STAWICKI, RENE; Garden City East HS; Garden City, MI; 64/450 Band; Cmp Fr Grls; Girl Scts; Hon Rl; Jr NHS; Stu Cncl; Drama Clb; Pep Clb; Spn Clb; Ferris St College; Respiratory Ther.

STAYER, DONNA; Timken HS; Canton, OH; Chrs; Girl Scts; Sch Mus; Sch Pl; Stg Crw; Rptr Yrbk; Rptr Sch Nwsp; Sch Nwsp; Drama Clb; Am Leg Awd; Akron Univ; Medical Tech.

ST CHARLES, ROBERT W; N Ridgeville HS; North Ridgevl, OH; Pres Frsh Cls; VP Soph Cls; Sec Jr Cls; Pres Sr Cls; Sch Pl; Stu Cncl; Capt Swmmng; Michigan St Univ; Brdcstng.

ST CLAIR, DONNA; West Preston HS; Arthurdale, WV; 15/115 Hon Rl; NHS; Sch Pl; Stg Crw; Drama Clb; Fr Clb; Mth Clb; Us Army; Med Lab.

ST CLAIR, JONA; Miami Trace HS; Jeffersonville, OH; 3/252 Cls Rep Frsh Cls; VP Soph Cls; AFS; Hon Rl; Pres NHS; Sch Pl; Yrbk; Drama Clb; 4-H; Spn Clb; Ohio State Univ; Communications.

ST CLAIR, KAREN; Fairfield Union HS; Bremen, OH; 21/150 Band; Chrs; Chrh Wkr; Hon Rl; Jr NHS; NHS; Yth Flsp; FTA; Asbury Coll.

ST CLAIR, MARTIN A; Caston Educ Center HS; Kewanna, IN; 1/70 Val; Chrs; Chrh Wkr; Pres NHS; Sch Mus; Sch Pl; Yth Flsp; Ed Yrbk; Drama Clb; VP FTA; Butler Univ; Chem.

ST DENNIS, CAROLYN M; Our Lady Of The Lakes HS; Waterford, MI; Hon Rl; Natl Forn Lg; Off Ade; Stu Cncl; Sci Clb; Spn Clb; Bsktbl; GAA; IM Sprt; Natl Merit SF; Oakland Univ; Med.

STEADMAN, SHEILA L; Huntington HS; Chillicothe, OH; 5/99 Band; Chrh Wkr; Hon Rl; NHS; Sch Mus; Fr Clb; FTA; Univ; Spec Educ Tchr.

STEAGER, SUSAN; R Nelson Snider HS; Ft Wayne, IN; Cls Rep Frsh Cls; Cls Rep Soph Cls; Band; Drl Tm; Hon Rl; JA; Stu Cncl; Pom Pon; Cit Awd; Indiana Univ; Bus.

STEARLEY, RITA; Van Buren HS; Center Pt, IN; 15/96 Cls Rep Frsh Cls; Cls Rep Soph Cls; Cl Rep Jr Cls; Cls Rep Sr Cls; Chrh Wkr; Cmnty Wkr; Hon Rl; NHS; Sprt Ed Yrbk; Yrbk; Patricia Stevens Schl; Fshn Dsgn.

STEARNS, LORI; Fostoria HS; Fostoria, OH; Am Leg Aux Girls St; Band; Chrs; Hon Rl; Jr NHS; Y-Teens; 4-H; Fr Clb; Scr Kpr; Bowling Green State Univ; Math.

STEARNS, RENEE; St Marys Cntrl Catholic HS; Sandusky, OH; 43/122 Band; Chrs; Drl Tm; Girl Scts; Hon Rl; Hosp Ade; Sch Mus; Sch Pl; Sct Actv; Pres 4-H; Akron Univ; Nursing.

STEBBENS, SHEILA; Marion HS; Marion, IN; Trs Soph Cls; Chrs; Hon Rl; Jr NHS; NHS; Sch Mus; Stu Cncl; Rotary Awd; Schlrshp Hnr Awd; Mbr Of 26th St Singers Bishop Leurs Swing Chr Cont; Whos Who Among Music Stu In Amer HS; Coll; Music.

STEBBINS, DAVID; Fruitport HS; Fruitport, MI; 70/281 Band; Hon Rl; Mich State Univ.

STEBBINS, DAVID; Stow HS; Stow, OH; Band; NHS; Ger Clb; Lat Clb; Mth Clb; Natl Merit Ltr; College.

STEBEL, LYNNE; Brookville HS; Brookville, OH; Band; NHS; Stu Cncl; Ed Yrbk; Yrbk; Pres Sci Clb; Opt Clb Awd; Univ Of Dayton; Philosophy.

STEBEL, THOMAS; Normandy HS; Seven Hls, OH; 12/659 Cls Rep Frsh Cls; Cls Rep Soph Cls; Cl Rep Jr Cls; Cls Rep Sr Cls; Hon Rl; Sch Pl; Stu Cncl; Rptr Yrbk; Drama Clb; Key Clb; Univ.

STEBELTON, KELLY; Chelsea HS; Chelsea, MI; Chrh Wkr; Hon Rl; Rdo Clb; Voice Dem Awd; Detroit Bible Coll; Voice.

STEC, KATHLEEN; Saint Alphonsus HS; Dearborn, MI; 2/181 Cls Rep Frsh Cls; Cl Rep Jr Cls; Hon Rl; Natl Forn Lg; NHS; Sch Mus; Rptr Sch Nwsp; Natl Merit SF; Univ Of Mich; Dentistry.

STECEWYCZ, ANNA; Struthers HS; Struthers, OH; 72/272 Chrh Wkr; NHS; Rptr Sch Nwsp; Pep Clb; Spn Clb; Youngstown St Univ; Radio/TV Brdcst.

STECHSCHULTE, BEVERLY; Ottawa Glandorf HS; Ottawa, OH; 37/171 Band; Hon Rl; Off Ade; Orch; Sch Mus; Yrbk; Drama Clb; FTA; N W Busns Coll; Med Ofc Asst.

STECK, PAULETTE; Owosso HS; Owosso, MI; Hon Rl; Eng Clb; FNA; Mth Clb; Sci Clb; Gym; Trk; Cit Awd; Univ; Nursing.

STECKEL, SCOTT W; Hilliard HS; Columbus, OH; 36/440 Am Leg Boys St; FCA; Hon Rl; NHS; Pol Wkr; Stu Cncl; Yth Flsp; FSA; Mth Clb; Sci Clb; Air Force Acad; Engr.

STEEBY, SUSAN; Michigan Lutheran Seminary; Bay City, MI; Band; Chrs; Hon Rl; Trk; Mgrs; PPFtbl; Mich State Univ; Vet Med.

STEED, JULIE; Napoleon HS; Napoleon, OH; NHS; Fr Clb; Bsktbl; Ten; Trk; JC Awd; Voice Dem Awd; College; Business.

STEED, TINA; Wapakoneta HS; Wapakoneta, OH; OEA; Lima Tech Univ; Med Sec.

STEEL, ELLEN; Elston Sr HS; Mich City, IN; 21/313 Band; Girl Scts; Hon Rl; Jr NHS; Sct Actv; Rptr Sch Nwsp; 4-H; Ger Clb; Tmr; Coll; Foods & Nutrition.

STEELE, ALAN; Concord Cmnty HS; Goshen, IN; Cls Rep Frsh Cls; Band; Hon Rl; Jr NHS; Orch; IM Sprt; Indiana Univ; Bus.

STEELE, ARTHUR J; Tri Valley HS; Zanesville, OH; 36/220 Boy Scts; Chrs; Hon Rl; Trk; Am Leg Awd; Amer Legions Amer Test Winner 78; Washington St Univ; Forestry.

STEELE, CHERYL; Franklin HS; Franklin, OH; Chrs; Hon Rl; Fr Clb; VP FTA; Mth Clb; Sci Clb; Univ; Exec Sec.

STEELE, CHRISTINE; Wintersville HS; Steubenvll, OH; 42/280 Band; Spn Clb; GAA; College; Data Proc.

STEELE, LINDA; Otsego HS; Grand Rapids, OH; Band; Hon Rl; Jr NHS; NHS; Sec Sci Clb; Bsktbl;.

STEELE, LINDA; Pickaway Ross Joint Voc HS; Derby, OH; 10/130 Cls Rep Soph Cls; Hon Rl; NHS; Stu Cncl; OEA; Bsktbl; Scr Kpr; Pickaway Ross Voc Schl; Comp Sci.

STEELE, LISA; Clarkston HS; Clarkston, MI; Cls Rep Frsh Cls; Cl Rep Jr Cls; Am Leg Aux Girls St; Band; Girl Scts; Hon Rl; Mdrgl; Long Beach State.

STEELE, MEG; Buckeys HS; Medina, OH; 31/173 Trs Sr Cls; Am Leg Aux Girls St; Band; Chrs; NHS; Sch Mus; Stu Cncl; Treas 4-H; Sec Ger Clb; Akron Unic; Med Tech.

STEELE, STEPHANIE; Adlai E Stevenson HS; Livonia, MI; 19/741 Cls Rep Soph Cls; Sec Jr Cls; Am Leg Aux Girls St; Chrs; Chrh Wkr; Hon Rl; Hosp Ade; Pol Wkr; Stu Cncl; Mat Maids; Mic State Univ; Law.

STEELE, TERRI; Harbor HS; Ashtabula, OH; 10/160 Trs Jr Cls; AFS; Stu Cncl; Yrbk; Spn Clb; GAA; Ohio St Univ; Paralegal Asst.

STEELE, TIMOTHY; Roseville HS; Roseville, MI; Chrh Wkr; Cmnty Wkr; Hon Rl; Chmn NHS; Stu Cncl; Pres Fr Clb; Letter Bsbl; Letter Ftbl; Capt Wrstlng; Coach Actv; Teenagers Against Smoking Awd 78; Outstndg Stu Awd 77 & 78; Univ Of Tennessee; Pre Optometry.

STEEN, CARL J; Adams HS; South Bend, IN; Band; Chrs; Chrh Wkr; Cmnty Wkr; Boys Clb Am; Bsktbl; Ftbl; IM Sprt; JETS Awd; 3 Yr Letterman Football; 2 Yr Lettermen Basketball; Drummer Of Yr; Church Awd; Purdue Univ; Engr.

STEENROD, BEVERLY; Jackson Center HS; Jackson Center, OH; 3/41 Am Leg Aux Girls St; Chrs; NHS; Off Ade; Quill & Scroll; Sch Pl; Ed Yrbk; Pres FHA; Letter Trk; Capt Chrldng; Ohio St Univ; Home Ec.

STEENWYK, LINDA; South Christian HS; Byron Center, MI; Chrh Wkr; Hon Rl; NHS; Yrbk; Sec 4-H; 4-H Awd; Calvin Coll; Nursing.

STEFANCIN, DEBBIE; Keystone HS; Grafton, OH; 25/133 Hon Rl; Pep Clb; Letter Bsbl; Letter Bsktbl; Scr Kpr; LCCC; Data Proc.

STEFANEK, JANET; Ovid Elsie HS; Bannister, MI; 11/170 Hon Rl; Sch Pl; PPFtbl; Ferris St Univ; Acctg.

STEFANEK, KENNETH; Lake Catholic HS; Willowick, OH; 30/350 Hon Rl; IM Sprt; Notre Dame Univ; Engr.

STEFANKO, DIANE; Kenmore HS; Akron, OH; Band; Ed Yrbk; Rptr Yrbk; Sch Nwsp; Chrldng; IM Sprt; JA Awd;.

STEFANKO, MARIE; St Florian HS; Detroit, MI; 4/115 Chrs; Hon Rl; NHS; Fr Clb; Pep Clb; Univ; Wildlife Conserv.

STEFANOVSKY, LUKE; Arthur Hill HS; Saginaw, MI; Hon Rl; NHS; Bsbl; Bsktbl; Ftbl; Mbr King Arthurs Court; Alma Coll; Criminology.

STEFFEN, LYNN M; Bellbrook HS; Bellbrook, OH; 3/147 Cl Rep Jr Cls; Band; Girl Scts; NHS; Stu Cncl; Rptr Yrbk; Fr Clb; Lat Clb; Univ; Bus Admin.

STEFFEN, RENEE; Berea HS; Brook Pk, OH; VP Frsh Cls; Cls Rep Soph Cls; Cl Rep Jr Cls; Cmp Fr Grls; Letter Bsbl; Letter Bsktbl; Chrldng; Coach Actv; Acad Achvmnt 77; Cleveland St Univ; Acctg.

STEFFEN JR, ALLEN E; Grand Haven HS; Grand Haven, MI; Western Mich Univ; Computer Engineer.

STEFFENS, HAZEL; Philip Barbour HS; Belington, WV; 31/260 Cls Rep Frsh Cls; Band; Debate Tm; Girl Scts; Hon Rl; Off Ade; Stu Cncl; Yth Flsp; Sch Nwsp; Pep Clb; Nursing.

STEFFENS, MARY; West Catholic HS; Grand Rapids, MI; Chrs; Chrh Wkr; Hon Rl; Lit Mag; NHS; Sch Mus; 4-H; College; Psych.

STEFFENS, SANDY; Creston HS; Grand Rpds, MI; FCA; Girl Scts; Hon Rl; NHS; Sch Pl; Letter Gym; Chrldng; Am Leg Awd; Univ; Nursing.

STEFFEY, BRETT; Warren Central HS; Indpls, IN; 34/1000 Band; Drm Bgl; Hon Rl; NHS; Orch; Sch Mus; Key Clb; Pep Clb; Rdo Clb; Letter Wrstlng; Indiana St Univ; Cmnctns.

STEGELMANN, MURRY; Goshen HS; Goshen, IN; 1/268 Pres Jr Cls; Am Leg Boys St; NHS; Pres Yth Flsp; Sci Clb; Letter Swmmng; Trk; Univ; Physics.

STEGEMAN, JAMES; Roger Bacon HS; Cincinnati, OH; 22/242 Hon Rl; NHS; IM Sprt; Cit Awd; Pres Awd; SAR Awd; Valparaiso Univ; Math.

STEGEMAN, MARK; Robert S Rogers HS; Toledo, OH; 87/612 Hon Rl; Jr NHS; Ger Clb; Sci Clb; Ftbl; Swmmng; Capt Ten; Wrstlng; Athetic Boosters Schlrshp 79; Ohio St Univ; Chem Engr.

STEGEMAN, STEVE; Pleasant HS; Marion, OH; 23/150 Hon Rl; Red Cr Ade; Rptr Sch Nwsp; Key Clb; Ftbl; Trk; Wrstlng; Univ; Engr.

STEGEMOLLER, LISA; Avon Jr Sr HS; Danville, IN; Band; Chrs; Chrh Wkr; Girl Scts; Hon Rl; Lbry Ade; Sch Mus; Yth Flsp; Pep Clb; Chrldng; Class Spirit Awd 1976 ; 1st Chair Awd In Band 1977; Lettered In Cheering 1978; Indianapolis Bus Schl; Bus Sec.

STEGENGA, LAURA; Bloomington North HS; Bloomington, IN; Debate Tm; Yrbk; Trk; PPFtbl; Ind Univ; Publications.

STEGENGA, LYNNETTE; Holland HS; Holland, MI; Off Ade; Orch; Hope College; Soci.

STEGER, DONNA; New Haven HS; New Haven, IN; 23/352 Band; Hon Rl; Orch; Pol Wkr; Ger Clb; Trk; Mat Maids; Pom Pon; Am Leg Awd; Cit Awd; Whos Who In Foreign Lang 78; Univ; Comp Sci.

STEGER, LISA; Little Miami HS; Maineville, OH; Sec Soph Cls; Trs Soph Cls; Sec Jr Cls; Trs Jr Cls; Hon Rl; Off Ade; Tech Schl; Med.

STEGER, MATTHEW J; Scecina Mem HS; Indianapolis, IN; Cl Rep Jr Cls; Cls Rep Sr Cls; Hon Rl; FBLA; Wrstlng; Univ Of Indiana; Hotel Mgmt.

STEGMANN, SHELLIE; John Glenn HS; Bay City, MI; Band; Cmnty Wkr; Girl Scts; Hon Rl; NHS; Sch Mus; Yth Flsp; Fr Clb; Chrldng; PPFtbl; Saginaw Vly St Coll; RN.

STEGNER, THOMAS M; Fairborn Baker HS; Fairborn, OH; Cls Rep Frsh Cls; AFS; Am Leg Boys St; Aud/Vis; Band; Cmnty Wkr; Hon Rl; Lbry Ade; Off Ade; Stu Cncl; World Affairs Conf In Dayton Oh; Ohio St Univ; Cmnctns.

STEIGER, DANIEL; University School; Beachwood, OH; Hon Rl; Lbry Ade; Pol Wkr; Sch Mus; Rptr Sch Nwsp; Key Clb; IM Sprt; Univ Of Michigan.

STEIGER, LAURIE; Archbishop Alter HS; Dayton, OH; Hon Rl; NHS; VP Y-Teens; VP Ger Clb; VP Pep Clb; Spn Clb; Trk; GAA; Pres Awd; Univ Of Cincinnati; Pharmacy.

STEIMEL, B; Washington Catholic HS; Washington, IN; 1/58 Hon Rl; Sch Pl; Drama Clb; Bsbl; Bsktbl; Crs Cntry; Glf; Ten; Trk; Ind St Univ; Bus Ad.

STEIN, AMY; Riverside HS; Concord, OH; 34/350 Cl Rep Jr Cls; Band; Chrh Wkr; Hon Rl; Hosp Ade; Sch Mus; Stu Cncl; 4-H; Spn Clb; Bsbl; Univ; Med.

STEIN, CHERYL; Olentangy HS; Powell, OH; Sec Frsh Cls; Sec Soph Cls; Trs Jr Cls; Pres Cmp Fr Grls; Chrs; Drl Tm; Hon Rl; Bowling Green State Univ; Journalism.

STEIN, DENISE; C S Mott HS; Warren, MI; Sec Cmp Fr Grls; Chrs; Chrh Wkr; Cmnty Wkr; Hon Rl; Lit Mag; Mdrgl; Off Ade; Sch Mus; Mic State Univ; Soc Work.

STEIN, JEFFREY; Hartland HS; Hartland, MI; Hon Rl; NHS; Yrbk; Spn Clb; Letter Bsbl; Letter Bsktbl; Letter Ftbl; Letter Trk; Natl Merit SF; Univ Of Michigan; Pre Med.

STEIN, JOEL; Wabash HS; Wabash, IN; 6/191 Am Leg Boys St; Hon Rl; JA; Jr NHS; NHS; Ger Clb; Letter Ten; IM Sprt; Marquette Univ; Chemistry.

STEIN, MARK; La Ville Jr Sr HS; Lakeville, IN; Fr Clb; Mth Clb; Bsbl; Wrstlng; Purdue Univ; Math.

STEINBACHER, PAUL; St Philip Catholic Ctrl HS; Battle Crk, MI; VP Frsh Cls; VP Soph Cls; Hon Rl; NHS; Stu Cncl; Letter Glf; Coach Actv; Sci Clb; Natl Merit Ltr; College; Engr.

STEINBACK, SABRINA; Reitz Mem HS; Evansville, IN; Hon Rl; Deacones Schl; Nursing.

STEINBECK, GARY; La Brae HS; Warren, OH; Hon Rl; Spn Clb; Bsbl;.

STEINBERG, JOAN; Manistee Catholic Cntrl HS; Manistee, MI; Yrbk; Pep Clb; Voice Dem Awd; Ferris State College; Bus.

STEINBRECHER, DEBBIE; Maple Valley HS; Nashville, MI; 18/121 Chrh Wkr; Hon Rl; Off Ade; Sch Pl; 4-H; Letter Ten; PPFtbl; 4-H Awd; Lansing Community College; Data Proc.

STEINBRUNNER, JAMES; Coldwater HS; Coldwater, OH; 26/147 Pres Frsh Cls; Cls Rep Frsh Cls; Cls Rep Soph Cls; VP Jr Cls; Pres Sr Cls; Chrs; Hon Rl; Jr NHS; NHS; Stu Cncl; Wright St Univ; Chem.

STEINBRUNNER, MARY; Bishop Luers HS; Ft Wayne, IN; Cls Rep Sr Cls; Am Leg Aux Girls St; Band; Chrs; Chrh Wkr; Hon Rl; Orch; Rptr Sch Nwsp; Fr Clb; Coach Actv; Hon Awd 77 78 & 79; Univ; Sci.

STEINER, JAYME; Hubbard HS; Hubbard, OH; Girl Scts; Off Ade; Sct Actv; Yth Flsp; DECA; Fr Clb; FBLA; Key Clb; Trk; Youngstown St Univ; CPA.

STEINER, KAREN; Harry S Truman HS; Taylor, MI; 2/550 Hon Rl; NHS; College; Comp Sci.

STEINER, KARYN; Smithville HS; Smithville, OH; 6/98 Band; Chrh Wkr; Hon Rl; NHS; Yth Flsp; 4-H; Fr Clb; GAA; 4-H Awd; Grace Coll; Home Ec.

STEINER, RANDY; Washington HS; Massillon, OH; AFS; Chrh Wkr; Hon Rl; Jr NHS; Spn Clb; Univ; Telecmnctns.

STEINER, TINA L; Huntington HS; Chillicothe, OH; 1/106 Pres Soph Cls; Hon Rl; Jr NHS; NHS; 4-H; Fr Clb; Bsktbl; Scr Kpr; 4-H Awd; Univ.

STEINES, RICHARD; John F Kennedy HS; Warren, OH; 4/180 Trs Frsh Cls; Trs Soph Cls; Am Leg Boys St; NHS; Stu Cncl; Fr Clb; Ftbl; Letter Glf; Univ; Engr.

STEINGASS, ROXANNE; Defiance Sr HS; Defiance, OH; Chrh Wkr; Cmnty Wkr; Hon Rl; Jr NHS; Stg Crw; Rptr Sch Nwsp; Chrldng; Univ; Bus.

STEINHAUSER, DAN; Mohawk HS; Tiffin, OH; Boy Scts; Chrh Wkr; Stg Crw; Bsktbl; Ftbl; Voc Schl.

STEINHOFF, SCOTT; Creston HS; Gr Rapids, MI; Band; Boy Scts; Hon Rl; NHS; Orch; College; Vet.

STEININGER, JOYCE; De Kalb HS; Auburn, IN; 42/287 Chrs; Chrh Wkr; Hon Rl; Jr NHS; Lbry Ade; NHS; Off Ade; Pol Wkr; Drama Clb; OEA; Indiana Univ; Art.

STEIN JR, CHARLES R; Clyde HS; Clyde, OH; 12/207 Cls Rep Frsh Cls; Band; Hon Rl; Sch Mus; Sch Pl; Stg Crw; Stu Cncl; Drama Clb; Ten;.

STEINKAMP, JERILYN; Crothersville Cmnty HS; Crothersville, IN; Girl Scts; Yth Flsp; FHA; Voc Schl.

STEINKE, MICHAEL; Botkins Ctrl HS; Botkins, OH; 9/49 Band; Boy Scts; Hon Rl; NHS; Sct Actv; FTA; Sci Clb; Findlay Coll; Acctg.

STEINKERCHNER, SCOTT; Wadsworth Sr HS; Wadsworth, OH; Band; Pres Chrh Wkr; Cmnty Wkr; Hon Rl; Jr NHS; NHS; PAVAS; Sch Mus; Sch Pl; Rptr Sch Nwsp; Univ Of Akron; Engr.

STEINLE, DORITA; St Joseph Central Cath HS; Fremont, OH; 4/100 Cmp Fr Grls; Hon Rl; NHS; 4-H; Bsktbl; Terra Tech Coll; Computer Prog.

STEINMAN, JOSEPH; Jefferson HS; Monroe, MI; 12/179 Band; Hon Rl; Jr NHS; NHS; Sch Mus; Pres Fr Clb; Mbr Of E Mi Univ Hon Band 79; Monroe County Cmnty Coll; Auto.

STEINMAN, LINDA; St Mary Academy; Monroe, MI; 8/130 Chrs; Chrh Wkr; Cmnty Wkr; Hon Rl; Lbry Ade; Treas NHS; Civ Clb; Pres 4-H; Key Clb; Rdo Clb; Michigan St Univ; Vet Sci.

STEINMAN, R; Brandon HS; Ortonville, MI; 1/200 Chrs; Hon Rl; VP NHS; Ed Yrbk; Ger Clb; Crs Cntry; Capt Trk; Cit Awd; College; Chem Engnr.

STEINMETZ, JILL; East Knox Local HS; Gambier, OH; Band; Chrs; Chrh Wkr; Hon Rl; Lit Mag; NHS; Quill & Scroll; Sec Stu Cncl; Rptr Sch Nwsp; Twrlr; Columbus Para Professional Inst; Med.

STEINMETZ, JULIE; Wheeling Park HS; Wheeling, WV; 160/700 AFS; Chrs; Hon Rl; Mdrgl; Natl Forn Lg; Sch Mus; Stg Crw; Drama Clb; West Virginia Univ; Music Theatre.

STEINMETZ, LINDA; Gibsonburg HS; Helena, OH; 1/100 Val; Chrh Wkr; Rptr Yrbk; FTA; Sci Clb; Spn Clb; Bowling Green St Univ; Spec Ed.

STEINMETZ, RENEE; Scecina Memorial HS; Indianapolis, IN; 45/194 Cl Rep Jr Cls; Girl Scts; Hon Rl; Fr Clb; IUPUI; Med.

STEINS, GEORGE E; Rocky River HS; Rocky River, OH; 16/308 Boy Scts; Cmnty Wkr; Hon Rl; Pres NHS; Sct Actv; Letter Socr; IM Sprt; Eagle Scout 77; Excllnc In Spanish 79; Cert Of Commendation Bio 78; Univ; Engr.

STEINS, K; Solon HS; Alliance, OH; Hon Rl; Lbry Ade; Mth Clb; Bsktbl; Trk;.

STELLHORN, DOUGLAS B; Northrop HS; Ft Wayne, IN; Boy Scts; Hon Rl; Off Ade; Pol Wkr; Ftbl; Trk; Wrstlng; Kiwan Awd; Carmel Ind St Track Meet; Lettered In Football Soph; Wrestling 1st Place In City Finals; Indiana Univ; Health.

STELLJES, ROBIN; Stebbins HS; Dayton, OH; Band; Drl Tm; MMM; Stg Crw; Trk; Mgrs; Scr Kpr; Wright St Univ; Bus.

STELLMAR, SHARON; Ursuline HS; Campbell, OH; Chrs; Chrh Wkr; Hon Rl; Hosp Ade; Jr NHS; Lbry Ade; Red Cr Ade; FTA; Spn Clb; YSU; Speech Path.

STELMA, STEVEN; Ottawa Hills HS; Grand Rapids, MI; NHS; Orch; Sch Pl; Yth Flsp; Sch Nwsp; Bsbl; IM Sprt; Natl Merit SF; Mich State Univ; Veterinary Medicine.

STELMAN, DAVID; Utica HS; Utica, MI; Hon Rl; NHS; Natl Merit Ltr; Wayne State Univ; Mech Engr.

STELZER, DEAN; Coldwater HS; Coldwater, OH; Cls Rep Soph Cls; Sch Pl; Stu Cncl; Letter Bsbl; Letter Bsktbl; Letter Ftbl; Letter Glf; Letter Trk; Coach Actv; Bowling Green St Univ; Bus Admin.

STEMEN, JUDY; Fairfield Union HS; Bremen, OH; 18/150 Chrs; Hon Rl; Hosp Ade; Jr NHS; NHS; Pres 4-H; Pres FHA; IM Sprt; 4-H Awd; Ohio Univ; Psych.

STEMITZ, SANDY; Berea HS; Berea, OH; Cls Rep Soph Cls; Band; Hon Rl; NHS; Off Ade; Ed Yrbk; Letter Gym; Letter Swmmng; Letter Chrldng; IM Sprt; Kent State; Acctg.

STEMKOWSKI, MARIE; Shadyside HS; Shadyside, OH; Band; Girl Scts; Hon Rl; Y-Teens; Spn Clb; GAA; Scr Kpr; Tmr; Univ; Lang.

STEMPEK, LAWRENCE; Pinconning Area HS; Pinconning, MI; Chrh Wkr; Hon Rl; Off Ade; Ftbl; Wrstlng; Mgrs; Mat Maids; Scr Kpr; Tmr; Auto Body.

STEMPER, MARK; Hammond Tech; Hammond, IN; Chrs; Hon Rl; Sch Mus; Sch Nwsp; Purdue Univ.

STEMPKY, ANDY; Cheboygan Catholic HS; Cheboygan, MI; Chrh Wkr; Rptr Yrbk; 4-H; Bsbl; Bsktbl; Capt Ftbl; Kalamazoo Coll.

STEMPKY, MICHELLE; Cheboygan Catholic HS; Cheboygan, MI; 6/33 Cls Rep Frsh Cls; Cl Rep Jr Cls; Pres Sr Cls; Hon Rl; Sch Pl; Stu Cncl;.

STEMPKY, MONICA; Cheboygan Catholic HS; Cheboygan, MI; Cls Rep Frsh Cls; Cls Rep Soph Cls; Pres Jr Cls; Chrs; Chrh Wkr; Debate Tm; FCA; Hon Rl; Sch Mus; Sch Pl; Univ; Bus.

STEMPLE, DAVID; E Preston Sr HS; Aurora, WV; 1/64 Band; NHS; Yth Flsp; 4-H; FFA; FFA St Farmer Degree; West Virginia Univ.

STENCEL, PHILIP; St Hedwig HS; Detroit, MI; 15/90 Trs Jr Cls; Band; Chrs; Hon Rl; NHS; Orch; Sch Mus; Yrbk; Letter Ftbl; Henry Ford C C; Law.

STENDER, BONNIE; Buffalo HS; Huntington, WV; Off Ade; Sch Pl; 4-H; FHA; Tmr; 4-H Awd; Marshall Univ; Bus.

STENGEL, DIANA; Durand HS; Lennon, MI; 24/265 Band; Chrs; Chrh Wkr; Hon Rl; NHS; Yth Flsp; Bsbl; Bsktbl; Mgrs; Scr Kpr; Spring Arbor Coll; Busns.

STENGEL, JACKIE; Northville HS; Northville, MI; Hon Rl; NHS; Ger Clb; Univ Of Mich.

STENGER, JOHN; East Central HS; Sunman, IN; Hst Frsh Cls; Pres Sr Cls; Am Leg Boys St; Hon Rl; NHS; Stu Cncl; Treas FFA; Spn Clb; Letter Ten; Chrldng; Purdue Univ; Civil Engr.

STENGER, SHERRY; Mc Auley HS; Cincinnati, OH; Cls Rep Sr Cls; Hon Rl; NHS; Sch Mus; Sch Pl; Stg Crw; Stu Cncl; Ed Sch Nwsp; Rptr Sch Nwsp; Sch Nwsp; Univ Coll; Paralegal Sec.

STENMAN, SHARI; Alpena Sr HS; Alpena, MI; Band; Drl Tm; Pep Clb; Chrldng; PPFtbl; Michigan St Univ; Math.

STENNETT, LAURA; Lamphere HS; Madison Hts, MI; VP Frsh Cls; Pres Soph Cls; Pres Jr Cls; Pres Sr Cls; Hon Rl; NHS; Stu Cncl; Yrbk; Letter Gym; Chrldng; Michigan St Univ; Bus.

STENSON, MARTHA; Newark Catholic HS; Newark, OH; Cmnty Wkr; Hon Rl; Red Cr Ade; Fr Clb; Sci Clb; Swmmng; GAA; IM Sprt; Scr Kpr; Tmr; Coll; Busns Admin.

STEPHAN, TERESA; West Clermont Career Ctr; Cincinnati, OH; Chrs; Girl Scts; Hon Rl; Hosp Ade; JA; Off Ade; Sct Actv; Pres DECA; OEA; Scr Kpr;.

STEPHANY, RAY; Old Trail School; Brecksville, OH; Chrh Wkr; Cmnty Wkr; Debate Tm; Hon Rl; Fr Clb; Ten; IM Sprt; Univ; Elec Engr.

STEPHEN, ALLGYRE; Seneca East HS; Bloomville, OH; Band; Chrh Wkr; Hon Rl; FFA; Pep Clb; Pres Awd; College; Sci.

STEPHEN, MARY A; Hill Mccloy HS; Montrose, MI; 11/133 Chrh Wkr; Hon Rl; Hosp Ade; NHS; Yrbk; FNA; Spn Clb; PPFtbl; Oakland Univ; Regist Nurse.

STEPHEN, SUSAN; Berkley HS; Berkle Y, MI; Chrh Wkr; Cmnty Wkr; Hon Rl; NHS; Eastern Michigan Univ; Occptnl Ther.

STEPHENS, BRUCE; North Knox HS; Bruceville, IN; 11/154 Hon Rl; NHS; Letter Bsbl; Letter Bsktbl; Indiana Voc Tech; Elec Tech.

STEPHENS, BRYON; Highland HS; Highland, IN; 12/494 Am Leg Boys St; Pres Natl Forn Lg; NHS; Treas Quill & Scroll; Yrbk; Treas Ger Clb; Bausch & Lomb Awd; Wabash College; Med.

STEPHENS, CINDY; Pike Central HS; Otwell, IN; 28/192 Band; Hon Rl; Jr NHS; Off Ade; Rptr Sch Nwsp; Pres FHA; Pres Pep Clb; Chrldng; IM Sprt; Mgrs; Perfect Attnd 1 4; Ban Constes 1 2; USTA & IMEA Twirling 1 2; Univ; Bus.

STEPHENS, DAN; Richmond Sr HS; Richmond, IN; 37/550 Cls Rep Frsh Cls; Cl Rep Jr Cls; Band; Chrh Wkr; Hon Rl; Jr NHS; NHS; Air Force Academy; Aeronautical Engr.

STEPHENS, ERIC; Northridge HS; Johnstown, OH; 2/118 Sal; Am Leg Boys St; Hon Rl; NHS; Sch Pl; 4-H; Fr Clb; Sci Clb; Ohio State Univ; Nuclear Engr.

STEPHENS, JAMES; Murray Wright HS; Detroit, MI; Boy Scts; Hon Rl; Jr NHS; NHS; Sch Pl; Drama Clb; Sci Clb; Mic State Univ; Psych.

STEPHENS, JEAN; Divine Child HS; Dearborn, MI; Girl Scts; Hon Rl; NHS; Sct Actv; Fr Clb; Pep Clb; Chrldng; IM Sprt; College; Bus.

STEPHENS, JONATHAN R; Sidney HS; Sidney, OH; 20/250 Hon Rl; Lbry Ade; Mdrgl; Orch; Sch Mus; Sch Pl; Stg Crw; Ger Clb; Key Clb; Spn Clb; Earlham Coll; Polylinguistics.

STEPHENS, JULIE; Boardman HS; Youngstown, OH; 52/634 Chrs; Hon Rl; Jr NHS; NHS; Quill & Scroll; Stg Crw; Sec Y-Teens; Yrbk; Ger Clb; Univ Of Cincinnati; German.

STEPHENS, KENNA; Brown County HS; Helmsburg, IN; DECA; FHA; Sci Clb; Univ; Vet Med.

STEPHENS, LINDA; Warren HS; Sterling Hts, MI; 1/520 Band; Chrs; Girl Scts; Hon Rl; NHS; Sct Actv; Stu Cncl; Univ Of Mic; Engr.

STEPHENS, LISA; Goodrich Area HS; Goodrich, MI; Band; Cmnty Wkr; Girl Scts; Hon Rl; Orch; Sch Mus; Sct Actv; Stg Crw; Yth Flsp; Fr Clb; St Finlst Miss Teen Mi 79; 1st Cls Girl Scout 78; Kendall Schl Of Design; Cmmrcl Art.

STEPHENS, LORI; Oxford HS; Oxford, MI; Band; Hon Rl; Sch Mus; Albion College.

STEPHENS, M; Davison HS; Burton, MI; Band; Orch; Spn Clb; Crs Cntry; Trk; Univ; Comp Tech.

STEPHENS, MARY R; Cleveland Cent Catholic HS; Cleveland, OH; Cmnty Wkr; Tri C.

STEPHENS, MELISSA; Rogers HS; Toledo, OH; 27/415 Sec Soph Cls; Trs Soph Cls; Chrs; Chrh Wkr; Girl Scts; Hon Rl; NHS; Harding Univ; Educ.

STEPHENS, MELISSA K; Rogers HS; Toledo, OH; 23/415 Sec Soph Cls; Trs Soph Cls; Cls Rep Sr Cls; Chrs; Chrh Wkr; Cmnty Wkr; Girl Scts; Hon Rl; NHS; Stu Cncl; Harding Coll; Art.

STEPHENS, PHIL; Napoleon HS; Napoleon, OH; Aud/Vis; Hon Rl; Pol Wkr; Stg Crw; Rptr Yrbk; Swmmng; Univ; Comp Engr.

STEPHENS, ROCHELLE; Arcanum Butler Local Schls; Arcanum, OH; 23/99 Band; Chrs; Chrh Wkr; Girl Scts; Off Ade; Sch Mus; Drama Clb; 4-H; 4-H Awd; Silver Dollar Awd Eng 78; Perfect Attendance Awd 76 77 & 79; Co Ed Of Creative Writing Bk; Wright St Univ; Writing.

STEPHENS, ROGER; Woodsfield HS; Woodsfield, OH; 15/66 Hon Rl; Stu Cncl; Fr Clb; Bsbl; Bsktbl; Glf; Scr Kpr; Am Leg Awd; Ohi Univ; History.

STEPHENS, T; Elmhurst HS; Ft Wayne, IN; 10/346 Chrs; Hon Rl; Orch; Yth Flsp; 4-H; Mth Clb; C of C Awd; 4-H Awd; Gov Hon Prg Awd; Univ Of Evansville; Engr.

STEPHENS, THOMAS L; Parkersburg South HS; Parkersburg, WV; Am Leg Boys St; Band; Boy Scts; Hon Rl; Orch; Sct Actv; Stu Cncl; Sprt Ed Yrbk; Boys Clb Am; Fr Clb; Voc Schl.

STEPHENS, TIM; Boonville HS; Newburgh, IN; 15/228 Chrs; Chrh Wkr; Debate Tm; Hon Rl; Natl Forn Lg; Sch Mus; Sch Pl; Drama Clb; Letter Glf; Univ Of Evansville; Brdcst Jrnlsm.

STEPHENS, TIMOTHY; Washington HS; South Bend, IN; Cl Rep Jr Cls; Chrs; JA; Sch Mus; Sch Pl; Stg Crw; Drama Clb; Fr Clb; FBLA; Bsbl; Univ; Tchr.

STEPHENS, TOD; Berrien Springs HS; Berrien Spgs, MI; Cls Rep Frsh Cls; Hon Rl; Lbry Ade; Mgrs; S W Michigan Coll; Acctg.

STEPHENS, WAYNE; Mc Nicholas HS; Cincinnati, OH; Hon Rl; JA; NHS; Wrstlng; Cincinnati Tech; Electronics.

STEPHENSON, CHRIS; Rochester HS; Rochester, IN; Cls Rep Frsh Cls; FCA; Hon Rl; Fr Clb; Letter Ftbl; Letter Glf; PPFtbl; College; Architecture.

STEPHENSON, DAVID; Whiteland Cmnty HS; New Whiteland, IN; 109/210 Band; Key Clb; Pep Clb; Atlanta Art Inst; Interior Dsgn.

STEPHENSON, GEOFFREY; Huron HS; Huron, OH; VP Frsh Cls; VP Soph Cls; Band; Boy Scts; Chrs; NHS; Sch Mus; Drama Clb; Arion Awd Outstanding Ach For Jr In Instrumental Music; Received Schlrshp To Fred Warning Music Workshop; Vocational Schl; Musical Theater.

STEPHENSON, JILL; John Marshall HS; Indianapolis, IN; 40/466 Hon Rl; Off Ade; Sec Quill & Scroll; Stg Crw; Rptr Sch Nwsp; Sch Nwsp; Eng Clb; NCTE; Univ Of Evansville; Paralegal.

STEPHENSON, JILL; Mississinewa HS; Jonesboro, IN; 1/200 Am Leg Aux Girls St; Cmnty Wkr; Hon Rl; Sec Jr NHS; Sec NHS; Yrbk; Capt Fr Clb; Purdue Univ; Engr.

STEPHENSON, JUDY; Salem Sr HS; Salem, OH; 56/300 VP Sr Cls; Band; Cmp Fr Grls; Hon Rl; Sch Mus; Pres Stu Cncl; Coach Actv; Scr Kpr; Kent St Univ; Nursing.

STEPHENSON, KAREN; Northwestern HS; West Salem, OH; Hon Rl; Sch Pl; Rptr Yrbk; Rptr Sch Nwsp; Pres Drama Clb; Fr Clb; VP FHA; Treas Spn Clb; Chrldng; Natl Thespian Soc V P 79; County Typing Contst 79; Spec Medal For Serv In Spirit & Pride Comm 79; Univ; Bus Admin.

STEPHENSON, LORA; Austintown Fitch HS; Youngstown, OH; 24/700 Cl Rep Jr Cls; Debate Tm; Hon Rl; Lit Mag; Natl Forn Lg; NHS; Sch Pl; Stu Cncl; Y-Teens; FTA; Youngstown St Univ.

STEPHENSON, NANCY; Marquette Sr HS; Marquette, MI; Pres Soph Cls; Cl Rep Jr Cls; Stu Cncl; Ger Clb; Capt Ten; Letter Trk; Tmr; Hon Queen Of Jobs Daughters 79; Backpack Through Europe 8 Countries 6 Wks 79; Univ; Educ.

STEPHENSON, PAULA; Parkway HS; Rockford, OH; 4/96 Trs Soph Cls; Trs Jr Cls; Band; Chrs; Chrh Wkr; Hon Rl; NHS; Pres Yth Flsp; Sci Clb; Trk; College.

STEPHENSON, TRACY; R Nelson Snider HS; Ft Wayne, IN; Letter Chrs; Chrh Wkr; Hon Rl; Sch Pl; Yth Flsp; Spn Clb; Cit Awd; Purdue Univ; Early Child Ed.

STEPIEN, BRENDA; Berea HS; Berea, OH; Girl Scts; Hon Rl; NHS; Yth Flsp; Rptr Yrbk; Rptr Sch Nwsp; Letter Bsbl; Letter Bsktbl; 2nd Pl Natl Write Off In Sportswrtng 77; Natl Art Awd From Schlstc Art Assoc 76; Univ; Jrnlsm.

STEPLETON, KIMBERLY; Van Wert HS; Van Wert, OH; 2/250 Chrs; Chrh Wkr; Hon Rl; Yth Flsp; Sch Nwsp; Lat Clb; Spn Clb; N W Dist Diving Champ 8th In St 78; N W Dist Diving Runner Up 8th In St 79; Hon Mention In St For Eng 2 79; Univ; Philosophy.

STEPNIEWSKI, CECILIA; Washington HS; South Bend, IN; 10/355 Hon Rl; Pres NHS; Stu Cncl; Yrbk; Coach Actv; Scr Kpr; Tmr; Pres Of Des Moiselles Girls Sorority 79; Notre Dame Univ.

STEPOWSKI, JAMES; Bishop Foley HS; Royal Oak, MI; Boy Scts; Hon Rl; Boys Clb Am; IM Sprt; College; Engr.

STEPP, BENJAMIN; Bluefield HS; Bluefield, WV; Hst Frsh Cls; Boy Scts; Chrh Wkr; Hon Rl; Soc Study 1st Plc 76; Bluefield St Univ; Miner Engr.

STEPRO, ANGELA; New Albany Sr HS; New Albany, IN; 57/620 Cls Rep Frsh Cls; Cls Rep Soph Cls; Am Leg Aux Girls St; Hon Rl; Stu Cncl; Ball St Univ; Archt.

STERBA, KELLY; Ovid Elsie HS; Ovid, MI; Letter Band; Girl Scts; Hon Rl; Yth Flsp; FFA; PPFtbl; Michigan St Univ; Agri.

STERK, WILLIAM; South Christian HS; Byron Center, MI; Hon Rl; Treas Stu Cncl; Ftbl; Trk; Wrstlng; Calvin College.

STERLING, CHRIS; Ashtabula Cnty Joint Voc HS; Ashtabula, OH; Hon Rl; Lbry Ade; NHS;.

STERLING, GEORGE; Lake Shore HS; St Clair Shr, MI; Boy Scts; Hon Rl; Ftbl; Trk; IM Sprt; Scr Kpr; Tmr; College; Predentistry.

STERLING, GEORGE; Lake Shore HS; St Clair Shrs, MI; Boy Scts; Hon Rl; Ftbl; Glf; Trk; Coach Actv; IM Sprt; Scr Kpr; Tmr; Albion; Pre Dent.

STERLING, JAMES J; Frankfort Sr HS; Frankfort, IN; 45/260 VP Soph Cls; Cls Rep Sr Cls; Stg Crw; Stu Cncl; Rptr Sch Nwsp; Fr Clb; Key Clb; Mth Clb; Swmmng; Natl Merit SF; Rose Hulman Inst Of Tech; Comp Sci.

STERLING, ROBERT; Loogootee HS; Loogootee, IN; Band; Chrh Wkr; 4-H; Pep Clb; Spn Clb; Bsbl; IM Sprt; Purdue Univ; Civil Engr.

STERN, JUDITH; Oak Park HS; Oak Park, MI; Hon Rl; Sch Pl; Spn Clb; Trk; Natl Merit SF; Spanish Natl Exam Outstndng Mert 79; St O Mi Cert Of Recngnt 79; Acad Achvmnt Hon Mntn 79; Mi Shclshp 79; Wayne St Univ; Med.

STERN, JUDITH L; Castle HS; Newburgh, IN; Band; Hon Rl; Jr NHS; Sch Pl; Stg Crw; Rptr Sch Nwsp; Swmmng; Mgrs; JETS Awd; Univ.

STERN, JULIE; William A Wirt HS; Gary, IN; 3/230 Debate Tm; Hon Rl; Jr NHS; NHS; Mth Clb; Letter Swmmng; Tmr; Oberlin College; Poli Sci.

STERN, MARC; Brush HS; S Euclid, OH; Bsktbl; Ohio State Univ; Bus Law.

STERN, PHILLIP; Detroit Cntry Day HS; Pontiac, MI; Cls Rep Sr Cls; Am Leg Boys St; Band; NHS; Yrbk; Ftbl; Trk; Wrstlng; Natl Merit Schl; Harvard Coll.

STERN, TERRI; Bad Axe HS; Filion, MI; Hon Rl; Off Ade; DECA; Fr Clb; Letter Bsbl; Letter Bsktbl; Coach Actv; Letter Trk; GAA; Mgrs; Vlybl Hrnble Men For Thumb B All Cnfrnce Team; Participation In Thumb B Vlybl Finalist; Medals For Thumb B; College.

STERNAD, LISA; Nordonia HS; Northfield, OH; Chrh Wkr; Cmnty Wkr; Hon Rl; Lbry Ade; Univ; Nursing.

STERNASTY, GALE; Sycamore HS; Cincinnati, OH; 37/436 Sch Mus; Drama Clb; Trk; Natl Merit Ltr; College.

STERNBERG, LISA; Unionville Sebewaing HS; Unionville, MI; 22/113 Am Leg Aux Girls St; Chrs; Chrh Wkr; Hon Rl; Yth Flsp; Cit Awd; Grand Valley State College; Theatre.

STERNBERG, STEVE; Allen Park HS; Allen Park, MI; Chrh Wkr; Cmnty Wkr; JA; JA Awd; Michigan Technical Univ; Chem Engr.

STERNER JR, ROBERT; Lutheran HS East; Roseville, MI; Ger Clb; Bsktbl; Trk; Certf From Natl Educ Development Test 78; Lawrence Inst Of Tech; Archt.

STERRETT, DEBBIE; Ehove Joint Vocational HS; Vermilion, OH; Cl Rep Jr Cls; Pres Sr Cls; Chrs; Cmnty Wkr; Hon Rl; Off Ade; Stu Cncl; Sch Nwsp; Banking.

STERRETT, MARK; Tecumseh HS; New Carlisle, OH; 15/384 Cls Rep Frsh Cls; VP Soph Cls; Am Leg Boys St; Band; Chrh Wkr; Cmnty Wkr; FCA; Hon Rl; Jr NHS; NHS; Ohio Northern Univ; Engr.

STERRETT, MATTHEW; Gallia Academy HS; Gallipolis, OH; Trs Jr Cls; Chrs; Chrh Wkr; Cmnty Wkr; Hon Rl; NHS; PAVAS; Sch Mus; Sch Pl; Miami Univ Of Oxford; Acctg.

STERRETT, RAMON; Central HS; Detroit, MI; Band; Orch; Univ Of Detroi; Computer Sci.

STERRETT, TOYIA; Central HS; Detroit, MI; Band; Hon Rl; Hosp Ade; JA; Orch; Fr Clb; JA Awd; Detroit Inst Of Commeace; Stenograph.

STETLER, BETH; Celina Sr HS; Celina, OH; Cls Rep Frsh Cls; Cls Rep Soph Cls; Cl Rep Jr Cls; Cls Rep Sr Cls; Girl Scts; NHS; Stu Cncl; FBLA; Lat Clb; Chrldng; Ohio St Univ; Dental Hygiene.

STETLER, BETH A; Celina Sr HS; Celina, OH; Band; Girl Scts; NHS; Stu Cncl; Yth Flsp; FBLA; FTA; Lat Clb; Pep Clb; Chrldng; Univ; Dent Hygiene.

STETLER, RONDA; Parkway Local HS; Willshire, OH; 3/82 Am Leg Aux Girls St; Sec Chrh Wkr; Cmnty Wkr; Hon Rl; Treas Lat Clb; Pep Clb; Pres Sci Clb; Ohio Northern Univ; Pharm.

STETTIN, JEANINE; Griffith Sr HS; Griffith, IN; Cls Rep Frsh Cls; Cl Rep Jr Cls; Cls Rep Sr Cls; Band; Chrs; Chrh Wkr; Hon Rl; Jr NHS; Off Ade; Quill & Scroll; Spec Serv Awd Pep Club 78; Jrnlsm Awd 79; Purdue Univ; Interior Dsgn.

STETZEL, DAN; Huntington North HS; Roanoke, IN; Sec Frsh Cls; Am Leg Boys St; Chrs; Chrh Wkr; Jr NHS; PAVAS; Pol Wkr; Sch Mus; Sch Pl; Am Leg Awd; College; Medicine.

STETZEL, ELIZABETH; St Joseph Cntrl CatholicHS; Fremont, OH; AFS; Cmp Fr Grls; Chrs; Hosp Ade; Rptr Yrbk; Univ; Jrnlsm.

STEUART, JENNIE K; Springfield South HS; Springfield, OH; Cls Rep Soph Cls; Cl Rep Jr Cls; VP Sr Cls; Band; Chrs; Cmnty Wkr; Drl Tm; Hon Rl; Natl Forn Lg; Off Ade; Miami Univ; Psych.

STEUK, KATHERINE; North Olmsted Sr HS; N Olmsted, OH; Pres Soph Cls; Am Leg Aux Girls St; Girl Scts; Off Ade; Sch Nwsp; Drama Clb; Natl Merit Ltr; Cleveland St Univ; Broadcasting.

STEUVER, JOSEPH; South Dearborn HS; Aurora, IN; Am Leg Boys St; Band; Boy Scts; Chrs; Chrh Wkr; Drm Mjrt; Hon Rl; Red Cr Ade; Sch Mus; Sch Pl; Tri Kappa Music Schlrshp; Swing Choir; Purdue Univ; Elec Engr.

STEUVER, THOMAS; South Dearborn HS; Aurora, IN; Band; Boy Scts; Chrs; Chrh Wkr; Drm Mjrt; Hon Rl; Sct Actv; Stg Crw; Yth Flsp; College; Computer Science.

STEVANOVIC, ZLATKO; Grosse Pointe North HS; Grosse Pte Wds, MI; Hon Rl; Off Ade; Stu Cncl; Am Leg Awd; Cit Awd; Wayne State Univ; Engr.

STEVANUS, RENEE; Garaway HS; Sugarcreek, OH; 8/101 Am Leg Aux Girls St; NHS; Yth Flsp; 4-H; Pep Clb; Spn Clb; Gym; 4-H Awd; Univ; Music.

STEVE, ANN; Archbishop Alter HS; Kettering, OH; Chrldng; College; Busns.

STEVENS, ABBY; Beachwood HS; Beachwood, OH; Bsbl; IM Sprt; Univ; Art.

STEVENS, ANGELA; Warren HS; Marietta, OH; Band; Drm Mjrt; Hon Rl; Orch; Letter Bsktbl; Twrlr; Outstndg Majorette Awd; Ohio Univ; Educ.

STEVENS, ANN M; Utica Sr HS; Utica, MI; Sec Soph Cls; Am Leg Aux Girls St; Debate Tm; Hon Rl; Natl Forn Lg; NHS; Stu Cncl; Pep Clb; Trk; Natl Merit Ltr; Michigan St Univ; Chem.

STEVENS, CATHY; Southeastern HS; Chillicothe, OH; 6/79 Am Leg Aux Girls St; Chrs; Hon Rl; Jr NHS; NHS; FTA; Lat Clb; Scr Kpr; Univ; Legal Sec.

STEVENS, COLLEEN; Springfield Local HS; New Middletown, OH; Cmp Fr Grls; Girl Scts; Hosp Ade; Sct Actv; Fr Clb; Pep Clb; Univ.

STEVENS, CRAIG; Plymouth Salem HS; Plymouth, MI; Hon Rl; Capt Glf; Capt Ten; Am Leg Awd; Cit Awd; Hough Fmly Schlrshp 79; St Of Mic Comptn Schlrshp 79; Mi St Univ Hnryb Cert Schlrshp 79; Princ Acad Awd; Hope Univ; Pre Dent.

STEVENS, DAVID; Manchester HS; Akron, OH; Cls Rep Frsh Cls; Band; Key Clb; Bsbl; Bsktbl; Glf; Coach Actv; IM Sprt; Ken St Univ; Law.

STEVENS, DAVID; Okemos HS; East Lansing, MI; Pres Sr Cls; Band; Chrh Wkr; Sch Mus; Stu Cncl; IM Sprt; Western Michigan Univ; Bio.

STEVENS, DORIS; Girard HS; Girard, OH; Band; Hon Rl; Y-Teens; Rptr Sch Nwsp; OEA; IM Sprt; Youngstown St Univ; Advertising.

STEVENS, GREG; Warsaw Community HS; Warsaw, IN; 12/370 Pres Band; Chrh Wkr; Hon Rl; Orch; Sch Mus; Sch Pl; Yth Flsp; Eng Clb; Pep Clb; Kiwan Awd; Spring Arbor Coll; Music.

STEVENS, GREGORY; Admiral King HS; Lorain, OH; Band; Hon Rl; Orch; College; Elec Engr.

STEVENS, GREGORY; West Jefferson HS; W Jefferson, OH; 22/94 Hon Rl; Ohi St Univ; Forestry.

STEVENS, JACKIE; Hudson HS; Clayton, MI; Cl Rep Jr Cls; Debate Tm; Off Ade; Stu Cncl; Bsktbl; GAA; Northwood Univ; Fshn Mdse.

STEVENS, JEFF; Dewitt HS; Dewitt, MI; Val; Hon Rl; Jr NHS; NHS; Trk; IM Sprt; Ferris State College; Accnt.

STEVENS, JOHN; Ursuline HS; Youngstown, OH; 87/320 Chrh Wkr; Hon Rl; Letter Bsbl; IM Sprt; Youngstown State Univ; Engr.

STEVENS, JOYCE; Wahama HS; New Haven, WV; Chrh Wkr; Hon Rl; FBLA; VP FHA; Keyettes; Chrldng; IM Sprt; W Virginia Inst Of Tech; Dent Hygnst.

STEVENS, KEVIN; Whiteford HS; Ottawa Lake, MI; Hon Rl; Lbry Ade; NHS; Red Cr Ade; Sch Mus; Sch Pl; Stg Crw; Rptr Sch Nwsp; Letter Bsktbl; Letter G lf; College; Comp Tech.

STEVENS, LARRY; Columbiana HS; Columbiana, OH; VP Jr Cls; Hon Rl; Bsbl; Crs Cntry; Univ.

STEVENS, LAURA; Creston HS; Grand Rapids, MI; 36/395 Chrs; Cmnty Wkr; Hon Rl; Jr NHS; NHS; Sch Mus; Fr Clb; Chrldng; Tmr; Natl Merit SF; Merit Achvmnt Awd 79; Michigan St Univ; Law.

STEVENS, LINDA; Comstock Park Secondary HS; Comstock Pk, MI; Cmp Fr Grls; Chrs; Girl Scts; Hon Rl; Natl Forn Lg; NHS; Sch Mus; Rptr Yrbk; Pep Clb; Chrldng; Univ Of Mic; Law.

STEVENS, LISA; Liberty HS; Girard, OH; Chrs; Chrh Wkr; Cmnty Wkr; Girl Scts; Red Cr Ade; Sct Actv; Yth Flsp; Fr Clb; Cit Awd; Cert Of Gratitude Girl Scouts 76; Middle Tennessee St Univ; Med Tech.

STEVENS, MARGARET; Sault Area HS; Sault Ste Marie, MI; Band; Cmnty Wkr; Hon Rl; NHS; Quill & Scroll; Sch Mus; Sch Pl; Stg Crw; Rptr Sch Nwsp; Drama Clb; Intl Thespians 79; Historian 79; Schl Nwsppr 79; Co Editor 79; KIPS VP 79; Univ.

STEVENS, MELISSA; East HS; Columbus, OH; 10/272 Hon Rl; NHS; Rptr Sch Nwsp; Sch Nwsp; Spn Clb; Capital Univ; Journalism.

STEVENS, MICHAEL; Forest Hills Central HS; Grand Rapids, MI; Hon Rl; JA; Mod UN; Sch Mus; Sch Pl; Stg Crw; Ed Yrbk; Mic St Univ; Advertising Graphic Art.

STEVENS, MICHELLE; Meadowbrook HS; Pleasant City, OH; Hon Rl; 4-H; FTA; Pep Clb; Sci Clb; Bsktbl; Trk; 4-H Awd; Univ; Phys Educ.

STEVENS, MINDI; Meadow Brook HS; Senecaville, OH; 2/185 Am Leg Aux Girls St; Am Leg Aux Girls St; Band; Chrs; Hon Rl; VP NHS; Stg Crw; Pres Yth Flsp; 4-H; Key Clb; Asbury Coll; Music.

STEVENS, RENEE; Columbus E HS; Columbus, OH; Hon Rl; College; Medicine.

STEVENS, ROBERT T; Marlington HS; Alliance, OH; 6/322 Am Leg Boys St; Chrs; Hon Rl; Pres Jr NHS; Pres NHS; Sch Mus; Letter Glf; Univ Of Mic; Bus.

STEVENS, STEPHANIE; Southmont HS; Crawfordsville, IN; 15/167 Trs Jr Cls; Trs Sr Cls; Pres Band; Chrs; Hon Rl; Jr NHS; Sec Natl Forn Lg; NHS; Sch Mus; Sch Pl; Indiana State Univ; Elem Ed.

STEVENS, TAMARA; Douglas Mac Arthur HS; Saginaw, MI; 102/302 Cmp Fr Grls; Hon Rl; Sec MMM; Orch; Pol Wkr; Sch Mus; Sch Pl; Stg Crw; Rptr Sch Nwsp; Ger Clb; Miss Michigan Of NCHA; St VP Of Michigan Teen Assn; W Kalamazoo Univ; Med Tech.

STEVENS, VICKI; Kirtland HS; Mentor, OH; 16/123 Cls Rep Soph Cls; Cl Rep Jr Cls; AFS; Chrs; Chrh Wkr; Cmnty Wkr; Hon Rl; Hosp Ade; Stu Cncl; Pep Clb; Cerr Of Outstnsng Schlstc Achvmnt; Cert Of Awd 11th Pl In 1st Yr Spansih In Kent St Dist; Univ; Bus Admin.

STEVENS, VICTORIA; Faith Christian HS; Fruitport, MI; Band; Chrs; Chrh Wkr; FCA; Hon Rl; Lbry Ade; Orch; Fr Clb; Ger Clb; Grand Rapids Baptist College; Englis.

STEVENSEN, JEFF; Van Buren HS; Findlay, OH; Am Leg Boys St; Chrs; JA; NHS; Sch Pl; Rptr Sch Nwsp; Drama Clb; Letter Bsktbl; Letter Trk; Natl Merit Ltr; Ohio St Univ; Jrnlsm.

STEVENSON, ALAN; Van Buren HS; Brazil, IN; Chrs; Hon Rl; Sch Mus; Yth Flsp; 4-H; Key Clb; Sci Clb; IM Sprt; Dnfth Awd; 4-H Awd; Purdue Univ; Agri.

STEVENSON, AMY; Carmel HS; Carmel, IN; 71/788 Band; Chrs; Drl Tm; Hon Rl; Jr NHS; NHS; Sch Mus; Stg Crw; IM Sprt; Pom Pon; De Pauw Univ; Psych.

STEVENSON, ANN; Dexter HS; Ann Arbor, MI; Hon Rl; NHS; Sch Pl; Stg Crw; Yth Flsp; Drama Clb; Ger Clb; Pres Awd; Univ.

STEVENSON, CHERYL; Hialeah Miami Lakes HS; Kalamazoo, MI; Cls Rep Soph Cls; Cl Rep Jr Cls; Cmnty Wkr; FCA; Hon Rl; Hosp Ade; Stu Cncl; Spn Clb; Chrldng; Miami Univ.

STEVENSON, JAMES; Ben Davis HS; Indianapolis, IN; 173/834 Boy Scts; Hon Rl; Sct Actv; 4-H; Spn Clb; Univ; CPA.

STEVENSON, JEFF; Wilmington HS; Martinsville, OH; 10/289 Pres Frsh Cls; Trs Jr Cls; Chrh Wkr; Jr NHS; Pres Yth Flsp; 4-H; FFA; Letter Bsbl; Letter Bsktbl; Miami Univ; Educ Field.

STEVENSON, KAREN; Baldwin HS; Baldwin, MI; Cls Rep Frsh Cls; Hon Rl; Lbry Ade; Yrbk; FHA; Ten; Trk; GAA; Pom Pon; Auto Mech.

STEVENSON, LEZLIE; Hamilton Southeastern HS; Noblesville, IN; 26/137 VP Jr Cls; VP Sr Cls; Band; NHS; Stu Cncl; Leo Clb; OEA; Spn Clb; Chrldng; 4-H Awd; Purdue Univ; Data Proc.

STEVENSON, LOREN; Washington HS; Massillon, OH; Boy Scts; Chrh Wkr; Sct Actv; Boys Clb Am; DECA; Akron Univ; Busns.

STEVENSON, MARSHALL; Van Wert HS; Van Wert, OH; 15/202 Hon Rl; Sct Actv; Yth Flsp; Univ; Elec Engr.

STEVENSON, STEPHANIE; Henry Ford HS; Detroit, MI; Chrs; Girl Scts; Hon Rl; Pol Wkr; Lat Clb; Sci Clb; IM Sprt; Cit Awd; Terrill Newman Awd Given To Stu In The Top 10% Of Their Cl 76 78; The Univ Of Michigan; Med.

STEVICK, ROBERT K; Linsly Institute; Wheeling, WV; 2/65 Pres Frsh Cls; VP Jr Cls; VP Sr Cls; Debate Tm; Hon Rl; NHS; Stu Cncl; Capt Bsbl; Letter Ftbl; Letter Wrstlng; Univ; Chem Engr.

STEVNING, MARY M; Newark HS; Newark, OH; Cls Rep Soph Cls; Cl Rep Jr Cls; Cls Rep Sr Cls; Chrs; Cmnty Wkr; Drl Tm; Hon Rl; Jr NHS; NHS; Off Ade; Ohio St Univ; Internatl Studies.

STEWARD, BARRY; North Putnam Jr Sr HS; Roachdale, IN; 16/152 Band; Boy Scts; FCA; Hon Rl; NHS; Orch; Stg Crw; Drama Clb; Sci Clb; Spn Clb; Univ; Bio.

STEWARD, BRADLEY; North Putnam Jr Sr HS; Roachdale, IN; 18/152 Band; Boy Scts; FCA; NHS; Stg Crw; Drama Clb; Sci Clb; Spn Clb; IM Sprt; Mgrs; Univ; Sci.

STEWARD, JAMES; Fremont Ross HS; Fremont, OH; 23/459 Cmnty Wkr; Hon Rl; NHS; Rptr Sch Nwsp; Ger Clb; IM Sprt; Univ Of Neb; Chem Engr.

STEWARD, JONATHAN S; Lebanon HS; Oregonia, OH; Chrh Wkr; Drl Tm; Hon Rl; ROTC; Sch Nwsp; Outstndng Drill Perfromnc 78; Hon Grad Leadrshp Schl 79; Miami Univ; Nuclear Phycist.

STEWART, ALAN; Berkley HS; Berkley, MI; Chrs; Pres JA; Mdrgl; Sch Mus; Sch Pl; Stg Crw; Stu Cncl; Drama Clb; Excel In Theatre 79; Forenics; Oakland Univ; Peace Corps.

STEWART, ANNE; Bridgeport HS; Bridgeport, WV; Pres Soph Cls; Chrh Wkr; Hon Rl; NHS; Stg Crw; Stu Cncl; Y-Teens; 4-H; Pep Clb; Sr Lifeguard; Fairmont St Coll; Medical Lab Tech.

STEWART, BARBARA; Portage Northern HS; Fayetteville, NY; Hon Rl; Off Ade; Trk; DAR Awd; 4-H Awd; Hope; Psych.

STEWART, BARBARA; Southwestern HS; Patriot, OH; 1/44 Trs Frsh Cls; Trs Soph Cls; Trs Jr Cls; Trs Sr Cls; Band; Hon Rl; Pres Stu Cncl; Pres Beta Clb; VP 4-H; FHA; Ohio St Univ; Optometry.

STEWART, BARBARA J; Southwestern HS; Patriot, OH; Trs Frsh Cls; Trs Soph Cls; Trs Jr Cls; Trs Sr Cls; Band; Hon Rl; Pres Stu Cncl; Rptr Yrbk; Pres Beta Clb; 4-H; Ohio St Univ.

STEWART, BETH; Cadiz HS; Cadiz, OH; Band; Girl Scts; Hon Rl; NHS; Sct Actv; Rptr Yrbk; 4-H; Fr Clb; Trk; IM Sprt; Whos Who In Foreign Languages In Ohio HS; Vlybl Letter Earned; Most Improved Vlybl; Ohio St Univ; Busns Admin.

STEWART, BEVERLY; Washington Irving HS; Clarksburg, WV; Band; Hon Rl; NHS; Stu Cncl; Fairmont State.

STEWART, CHRIS; New Albany HS; New Albany, OH; Letter Glf; Am Leg Awd; Univ; Psych.

STEWART, CONNIE; Oceana HS; Oceana, WV; Chrs; Chrh Wkr; Cmnty Wkr; Girl Scts; Hon Rl; NHS; Yth Flsp; FNA; VICA; VFW Awd; Concord College; Bus Admin.

STEWART, CURTIS; Pontiac Central HS; Pontiac, MI; Am Leg Boys St; Boy Scts; Chrh Wkr; Oakland Community College; Hvy Equip.

STEWART, CYNTHIA; New Albany HS; New Albany, IN; Cls Rep Frsh Cls; Chrh Wkr; Drl Tm; Hon Rl; Fr Clb; Pep Clb; Rdo Clb; Letter Coach Actv; Chrldng; IM Sprt; Univ; Phys Educ.

STEWART, CYNTHIA; Marietta Sr HS; Marietta, OH; 15/390 Cls Rep Frsh Cls; Sec Soph Cls; Trs Soph Cls; Cl Rep Jr Cls; Band; Drm Mjrt; NHS; Stu Cncl; Yth Flsp; Spn Clb; Univ; Bio.

STEWART, CYNTHIA L; Gilmer County HS; Harrisville, WV; 7/92 Pres Soph Cls; Trs Jr Cls; Hon Rl; Sprt Ed Yrbk; Pres Pep Clb; Bsktbl; Trk; Coach Actv; GAA; Mgrs; Glenville State College; Pro Trainin.

STEWART, DENNIS; Roosevelt HS; Gary, IN; Band; Boy Scts; Chrh Wkr; Cmnty Wkr; Drm Bgl; Hon Rl; JA; Jr NHS; NHS; ROTC; Purdue Univ; Aeronautic Engr.

STEWART, DONNA; Wayne HS; Dayton, OH; Girl Scts; Hon Rl; Lbry Ade; Off Ade; Red Cr Ade; ROTC; Army.

STEWART, DONNA; Stiver Patterson Coop HS; Dayton, OH; Cls Rep Frsh Cls; Cls Rep Soph Cls; Cl Rep Jr Cls; Hon Rl; OEA; Pom Pon; Sinclair Cmnty Coll; Bus Admin.

STEWART, ELIZABETH F; Wahoma HS; Mason, WV; Hon Rl; 4-H; FBLA; Sec FHA; Chrldng;.

STEWART, GINA; Clio HS; Clio, MI; Band; Hon Rl; Orch; OEA; GAA; Baker Jr Coll Of Bus; Sec.

STEWART, GWENDOLYN; Pineville HS; Pineville, WV; Band; Hon Rl; Jr NHS; Pep Clb; Spn Clb; All Area Band Awd 79; All Cnty Band 78 & 79; Jazz & Concert Awds 79; Concord Univ; Bio.

STEWART, HELEN; Union Scioto HS; Chillicothe, OH; 7/124 Am Leg Aux Girls St; Band; Hon Rl; Jr NHS; NHS; Off Ade; Ten; Trk; Chrldng; PPFtbl; Otterblen College; Nursing.

STEWART, JAMES T; Mooresville HS; Mooresville, IN; 60/265 Cls Rep Frsh Cls; Cls Rep Soph Cls; Chrs; Hon Rl; Mdrgl; Sch Mus; Sch Pl; Drama Clb; College; Elec.

STEWART, JEFF; South Range HS; Greenford, OH; Chrs; Hon Rl; Lbry Ade; Off Ade; Sch Mus; Sec Stu Cncl; Rptr Yrbk; Yrbk; Drama Clb; Trk; Hugh O Brian Youth Foundtn Internatl Leadrshp Runner Up 77; Mt Union Univ; Fshn Designer.

STEWART, JENNIFER; Bosse HS; Evansville, IN; 1/360 Band; Chrh Wkr; Hon Rl; Hosp Ade; Jr NHS; NHS; Fr Clb; Pep Clb; Cit Awd; Univ Of Evansville; Med.

STEWART, JOHN; Meigs HS; Middleport, OH; Hon Rl; Lbry Ade; Stu Cncl; Hocking Tech Schl.

STEWART, JOSEPH; Cuyahoga Falls HS; Cuyahoga Fls, OH; Hon Rl; NHS; Stu Cncl; Bsbl; Letter Ftbl; Acolyte St Joseph Parish; Vol Summit County Health Dept; Northeastern Ohio Univ; Bio.

STEWART, JOY C; Garfield HS; Hamilton, OH; 2/376 Cl Rep Jr Cls; Band; Chrs; Hon Rl; Jr NHS; NHS; Orch; Sch Mus; Rptr Sch Nwsp; Ger Clb; 3yrs Member Of The All Ohio St Fair Band 1977,78,79; Miami Univ; Acctg.

STEWART, JUDITH; Madison HS; Madison, OH; 3/295 Sec Frsh Cls; Trs Frsh Cls; Sec Soph Cls; Trs Soph Cls; Sec Jr Cls; Trs Jr Cls; Sec Sr Cls; Trs Sr Cls; Band; Hon Rl; Univ; Phys Ther.

STEWART, JULIE; Jay County HS; Portland, IN; 19/450 Hon Rl; Jr NHS; NHS; Quill & Scroll; Y-Teens; Sch Nwsp; Pep Clb; Spn Clb; Schlrshp To Attnd Jrnlsm Workshp 78; Nisbova Music Awd Piano Sup Rtngs; Ball St Univ; Sci.

STEWART, KAREN; Thomas Carr Howe HS; Indianapolis, IN; 29/580 Chrs; Hon Rl; NHS; Quill & Scroll; Stu Cncl; Yth Flsp; Ed Sch Nwsp; Sch Nwsp; DECA; Fr Clb; Univ Of Missouri; Jrnlsm.

STEWART, KAREN; Maumee HS; Maumee, OH; 5/320 Boy Scts; Chrh Wkr; Hon Rl; NHS; Sct Actv; Yth Flsp; Rptr Yrbk; Rptr Sch Nwsp; Fr Clb; Mth Clb; Mt Vernon Nazarene Coll; Math.

STEWART, KATHY; Kankakee Valley HS; Wheatfield, IN; Chrh Wkr; Hon Rl; NHS; Ed Sch Nwsp; Ger Clb; OEA; Mst Valuable Staffer Awd; Shrthnd Awd; Perfect Attend Awd; Photog Cert Of Hnr Overall Blue Ribbn For Photog; Purdue Univ; Acctg.

STEWART, KATHY; Lexington HS; Lexington, OH; Band; Drl Tm; Girl Scts; Hon Rl; Lbry Ade; Off Ade; Sch Mus; Yth Flsp; Y-Teens; Fr Clb; Univ; Acctg.

STEWART, KENNA; Eastern HS; Pekin, IN; 10/91 VP Band; Hon Rl; NHS; 4-H; Pep Clb; Indiana Univ.

STEWART, KENNETH; Southgate HS; Southgate, MI; Band; Boy Scts; CAP; Hon Rl; Pol Wkr; Sch Nwsp; Boys Clb Am; Bsbl; Crs Cntry; Swmmng; Pilots License 78; Michigan St Univ; Law.

STEWART, KIMBERLY; Cass Technical HS; Detroit, MI; Drl Tm; Hon Rl; Lbry Ade; ROTC; G M Inst; Mech Engr.

STEWART, KIMBERLY; Tri West Hendricks HS; Pittsboro, IN; 16/123 Cls Rep Soph Cls; Cl Rep Jr Cls; Hon Rl; NHS; Treas Stu Cncl; Bsktbl; Chmn Pom Pon; College; Elem Educ.

STEWART, KIMBERLY E; Woodrow Wilson HS; Beckley, WV; Cls Rep Frsh Cls; Cls Rep Soph Cls; Cl Rep Jr Cls; Band; Chrh Wkr; Hon Rl; Lbry Ade; Off Ade; Sch Pl; Stg Crw; West Virginia Univ; Guid Cnslr.

STEWART, LAWRENCE; Jefferson HS; Shepherdstown, WV; Hon Rl; Sch Pl; Yth Flsp; College; Art.

STEWART, LORI; Southmont HS; Waynetown, IN; 18/165 Band; Chrh Wkr; Hon Rl; Hosp Ade; Lbry Ade; NHS; Off Ade; Liberty Baptist College; Tchr.

STEWART, MARK; Carlisle Sr HS; Franklin, OH; 1/225 Pres Frsh Cls; Am Leg Boys St; Hon Rl; Jr NHS; NHS; Off Ade; Spn Clb; Bsbl; Bsktbl; Trk; Carlisle Educ Recog Assn; Outstanding Frosh Boy; Recipient Of Schl Algebra & Chem Awd; Indiana Univ; Engr.

STEWART, MARY; Wintersville HS; Steubenvll, OH; Cl Rep Jr Cls; Chrs; Cmnty Wkr; Debate Tm; Red Cı Ade; Sch Pl; Stu Cncl; Y-Teens; 4-H; GAA; Akron Univ; Law Enforcement.

STEWART, MELODY; Beaumont HS; E Cleve, OH; Cl Rep Jr Cls; Pres Sr Cls; Cmp Fr Grls; Chrs; Chrh Wkr; Hon Rl; JA; College; Music.

STEWART, MICHAEL; Clinton Massie HS; Wilmington, OH; 2/100 Boy Scts; Hon Rl; NHS; Sch Mus; 4-H; Bsbl; Bsktbl; Crs Cntry; Ten; 4-H Awd; Univ; Engr.

STEWART, MICKEYE; Madison Plains HS; Mt Sterling, OH; Aud/Vis; Band; Hon Rl; Mod UN; Stg Crw; Civ Clb; 4-H; Pep Clb; Bsbl; IM Sprt; CTI; Bus.

STEWART, NANCY; Bloomington HS; Bloomington, IN; Cl Rep Jr Cls; FCA; Off Ade; Pol Wkr; Letter Glf; Tmr; College; Bus.

STEWART, NANCY; Hamilton Southeastern HS; Indianapolis, IN; Cl Rep Jr Cls; Cls Rep Sr Cls; Band; Girl Scts; Hon Rl; NHS; Off Ade; Stu Cncl; Ger Clb; OEA; Bus Schl; Bus.

STEWART, PAMELA; Fitzgerald HS; Warren, MI; Cls Rep Sr Cls; Girl Scts; Hon Rl; Red Cr Ade; Bsktbl; Coach Actv; PPFtbl; Letter Letter Letter Wayne State Univ; Medicine.

STEWART, RALPH; Orange HS; Cleveland, OH; 2/250 Cls Rep Frsh Cls; Band; Boy Scts; Hon Rl; NHS; Sec Quill & Scroll; Sch Pl; Sct Actv; Stu Cncl; Rptr Yrbk; Univ; Med.

STEWART, RHONDA; Jefferson Union HS; Richmond, OH; Band; Chrh Wkr; Hon Rl; Stu Cncl; Pres Beta Clb; Pep Clb; Bsktbl; Trk; GAA; PPFtbl; Attend Awd 77 79; French Cert Awd For Excellant Work In French 78; Univ; Radiolgc Tech.

STEWART, RODNEY; Columbus Ctrl HS; Columbus, OH; Hon Rl; Jr NHS; NHS; Bsbl; Bsktbl; Ohio St Univ; Med.

STEWART, ROLAND; Central HS; Columbus, OH; Jr NHS; Am Leg Awd; Univ; Law.

STEWART, SANDRA; Southfield HS; Southfield, MI; Band; Hon Rl; Ten; Trk; Twrlr; Cit Awd; Trophy In Tennis; Trophy In Bowling; Univ Of Michigan; Busns.

STEWART, SANDRA; Switzerland Co Jr Sr HS; Florence, IN; Hst Frsh Cls; Cls Rep Frsh Cls; Band; Chrh Wkr; Cmnty Wkr; Girl Scts; Hon Rl; JA; Jr NHS; NHS; Univ; Elem Ed.

STEWART, STEPHANIE; Tippecanoe Valley HS; Akron, IN; Chrs; Chrh Wkr; Cmnty Wkr; Hon Rl; Sch Pl; Stg Crw; Yth Flsp; Rptr Yrbk; Drama Clb; Anderson Coll; Nursing.

STEWART, STEPHNI; Parkersburg HS; Parkersburg, WV; 107/735 Cls Rep Frsh Cls; Cls Rep Soph Cls; Cl Rep Jr Cls; Cls Rep Sr Cls; Aud/Vis; Band; Chrh Wkr; Girl Scts; Hon Rl; Hosp Ade; Wmns Study Club Academic Achvmnt Awd 79; West Liberty St Coll; Chem.

STEWART, STEVE; Roosevelt Wilson HS; Clarksbrg, WV; VP Frsh Cls; VP Soph Cls; Chrs; Hon Rl; Sch Pl; Sprt Ed Yrbk; Lat Clb; Bsbl; Bsktbl; Ftbl; Univ; Optometry.

STEWART, TAMERA; Zanesville HS; Zanesville, OH; Chrh Wkr; Drl Tm; Hon Rl; JA; Lbry Ade; NHS; Sct Actv; Stu Cncl; Yth Flsp; Y-Teens; College; Nursing.

STEWART, TIMOTHY A; La Salle HS; St Ignace, MI; Am Leg Boys St; Band; Hon Rl; ROTC; Sci Clb; Wrstlng; Michigan Tech Univ; Comp Sci.

STEWART, TINA; Strongsville HS; Strongsville, OH; 7/470 Trs Sr Cls; Cls Rep Sr Cls; Sec Band; Hon Rl; NHS; Orch; Stu Cncl; Civ Clb; FTA; Mth Clb; MVP Tennis 78; Exclinct Soc 78; All City Bnd 78; Univ; Acctg.

STEWART, WANDA; North Western HS; West Salem, OH; Band; Chrs; Hon Rl; Sch Mus; Sch Pl; Fr Clb; FTA; Rdo Clb; IM Sprt; Coll; Communications.

STEYER, C; Calvert HS; Tiffin, OH; Chrs; Hon Rl; NHS; Sch Mus; Ed Yrbk; Letter Bsktbl; Cit Awd; Bowling Green St Univ; Educ.

STEYER, TINA; Lakota HS; Fostoria, OH; 19/144 Cls Rep Sr Cls; Hon Rl; NHS; Stu Cncl; Drama Clb; 4-H; 4-H Awd; Bowling Green St Univ; Nursing.

ST GERMAIN, DIANA; Robert S Tower HS; Warren, MI; Hon Rl; Hosp Ade; Off Ade; Yth Flsp; Madonna Coll; Nursing.

ST GERMAIN, EILEEN; Southgate HS; Southgage, MI; Sec Sr Cls; Band; Jr NHS; NHS; Drama Clb; Fr Clb; Swmmng; Univ.

STIBAL, ROSANNE; Taylor Center HS; Taylor, MI; 5/412 Hon Rl; JA; Lit Mag; NHS; Stu Cncl; Letter Bsktbl; Letter Ten; GAA; PPFtbl; Scr Kpr; Wayne State Univ; Phys Ther.

STIBINGER, EDITH; Euclid Sr HS; Euclid, OH; 107/746 Cmp Fr Grls; Chrs; Hon Rl; Lbry Ade; Off Ade; PAVAS; Pol Wkr; Sch Mus; Sch Pl; Stu Cncl; Akron Univ; Choreography.

STICCO, CAROLYN; Madonna HS; Weirton, WV; Trs Frsh Cls; Cls Rep Sr Cls; Hon Rl; Stu Cncl; Sprt Ed Yrbk; Pep Clb; Trk; Mat Maids; Coll; Phys Educ.

STICHLER, VICKIE; Laingsburg Christian HS; Laingsburg, MI; 2/5 Sec Jr Cls; Sec Sr Cls; Sal; Chrs; Chrh Wkr; Hon Rl; Stu Cncl; Yth Flsp; Rptr Yrbk; Yrbk; Grand Rapids Baptist Coll; Sec Stds.

STICHTER, TIMOTHY; Bremen HS; Plymouth, IN; Pres Frsh Cls; Pres Soph Cls; Band; VP Chrs; FCA; Hon Rl; NHS; Sch Mus; Sch Pl;.

STICK, TAMMY; New Buffalo HS; New Buffalo, MI; 1/90 Trs Sr Cls; Hon Rl; Off Ade; Sct Actv; Placed 2nd In Natl Spanish Contest For Berrien County; Act Test Honor Letter; Am Mbr Natl Spanish Hnr Soc; College; Comp Prog.

STICKEL, KATHY; Wilbur Wright HS; Dayton, OH; Girl Scts; Off Ade; Ed Sch Nwsp; College; Law.

STICKLAND, WILLIAM; Grandville HS; Grandville, MI; Band; Hon Rl; NHS; Capt Hockey; IM Sprt; Michigan Tech Univ; Engr.

STICKNEY, MICHAELA; Rocky River HS; Rocky Rvr, OH; Chrs; Chrh Wkr; Cmnty Wkr; Hon Rl; Jr NHS; NHS; Yth Flsp; Crs Cntry; Trk; IM Sprt; One Of The Aud Win Piano Buckeye Aud 79; Elect Sec Of The Natl Hon Soc 79; Awd The Most Outsdng Lat Stu 78; Univ; Frgn Lang.

STIDD, SHARON; Southeast HS; Ravenna, OH; Sec Jr Cls; Pres Band; Hon Rl; MMM; Quill & Scroll; Stu Cncl; Rptr Yrbk; Rptr Sch Nwsp; Sec Pep Clb; Bsbl; Akron Univ; Sales & Merch.

STIDHAM, GINNY; Cedar Springs HS; Cedar Springs, MI; Hon Rl; Jr NHS; Lbry Ade; Rptr Yrbk; FHA; College; Psychologist.

STIDHAM, STEVE; Ben Davis HS; Indianapolis, IN; Cls Rep Soph Cls; Cl Rep Jr Cls; Chrh Wkr; FCA; Hon Rl; Stu Cncl; DECA; Letter Ftbl; PPFtbl; Consecutive Honor Roll 1975; Univ; Mrktng.

STIDOM, CYNTHIA A; Greenbrier East HS; Whte Slphr Spgs, WV; 15/480 Sec Soph Cls; Band; Cmnty Wkr; FCA; Hon Rl; Jr NHS; NHS; Off Ade; FBLA; Trk; Univ; Bus Mgmt.

STIEBER, CHERYL; Monroeville HS; Norwalk, OH; 5/75 Sec Frsh Cls; Pres Soph Cls; Sec Sr Cls; Band; Hon Rl; NHS; 4-H; Pep Clb; Chrldng; 4-H Awd;.

STIEBER, ELIZABETH; Monroeville HS; Norwalk, OH; Hon Rl; NHS; Off Ade; 4-H; Scr Kpr; Perfect Attendance; Univ; Brdcstng.

STIEBER, SCOT; Grosse Pointe North HS; Grosse Pt Wds, MI; Hon Rl; Rptr Sch Nwsp; IM Sprt; College; Acctg.

STIEFEL, ROBERT; Garber HS; Essexville, MI; 2/172 Cls Rep Soph Cls; Cl Rep Jr Cls; Cls Rep Sr Cls; Band; Hon Rl; Stu Cncl; IM Sprt; Mgrs; Cit Awd; Natl Merit SF; Distngshd Stdnt Sci Awrd 76; Schlrshp To Attend The HS Engr Inst 79; Dow Chem Sci Awrd 79; Univ.

STIER, LAURA; Greensburg Cmnty HS; Greensburg, IN; 22/205 Band; Chrs; Hon Rl; Jr NHS; Mdrgl; NHS; Sch Mus; Fr Clb; Pep Clb; Sci Clb; Ball St Univ; Med Tech.

STIERS, ELIZABETH; Meadowbrook HS; Salesville, OH; Chrs; Chrh Wkr; Hon Rl; Yrbk; VP 4-H; FBLA; FHA; Lat Clb; Sci Clb; 4-H Awd; Coll; Bus.

STIFFLER, DANIEL; Medina Sr HS; Medina, OH; 96/345 AFS; Aud/Vis; Sch Mus; Rptr Yrbk; Rptr Sch Nwsp; Drama Clb; Key Clb; Bsbl; Ten; Mgrs; Univ; Dent.

STIFFLER, KATHY; Shawnee HS; Springfield, OH; Sec Frsh Cls; Cls Rep Frsh Cls; VP Soph Cls; Cls Rep Soph Cls; VP Jr Cls; Cl Rep Jr Cls; Chrs; Debate Tm; Lbry Ade; Lit Mag; Clark Tech Coll; Nursing.

STIFFLER, SANDRA; Holt HS; Holt, MI; 46/285 Chrs; Hon Rl; Lbry Ade; Natl Forn Lg; NHS; Sch Mus; Sch Pl; Stg Crw; Drama Clb; Key Clb; Lansing Community Coll.

STIGDON, DARA; Jennings Cnty HS; Elizabethtown, IN; 24/367 Trs Sr Cls; Hon Rl; NHS; Stg Crw; Ger Clb; Letter Ten; Indiana Univ; Poli Sci.

STIGER, CHERIE; Canfield HS; Canfield, OH; Chrs; Girl Scts; Hon Rl; Lit Mag; Stg Crw; Rptr Sch Nwsp; Sch Nwsp; 4-H; Ger Clb; Sci Clb; Art Inst Of Pittsburgh; Art.

STIGER, PHILIP; Greencastle HS; Madeira Bch, FL; 15/150 Girl Scts; Hon Rl; Hosp Ade; JA; Jr NHS; Natl Forn Lg; Sch Mus; Sdlty; Stu Cncl; 4-H; Indiana St Univ.

STILES, BLAINE; Allen East HS; Cridersville, OH; Band; Chrs; Chrh Wkr; Mdrgl; Sch Pl; Rptr Yrbk; All Ohio St Fair Youth Choir 78; Toured Europe All Ohio St Fair Youth Choir 79; Univ; Music.

STILES, KATHLEEN RAE; Coventry HS; Uniontown, OH; Band; Chrs; Off Ade; Sch Mus; Rptr Sch Nwsp; Akron Univ; Fshn Mdse.

STILES, MARCIA L; Clay Battelle HS; Blacksville, WV; Pres Soph Cls; Hst Jr Cls; Am Leg Aux Girls St; Chrs; Hon Rl; Jr NHS; NHS; Stu Cncl; Rptr Yrbk; Rptr Sch Nwsp; Fairmont St Coll; Early Child Educ.

STILES, RICHARD; Miller HS; Shawnee, OH; 20/101 Band; Chrs; Hon Rl; NHS; Sch Pl; Ed Yrbk; Rptr Sch Nwsp; FBLA; Crs Cntry; Trk; Univ Of S Carolina; Jrnlsm.

STILKE, LYNN; Newbury HS; Newbury, OH; Cl Rep Jr Cls; Sec Sr Cls; Hon Rl; Off Ade; Kent St Branch Univ; Bus.

STILLIONS, CHRISTINE; Mitchell Sr HS; Mitchell, IN; Hon Rl; VP 4-H; FHA; OEA; Cit Awd; 4-H Awd; Schltc M; Bedford N Lawrence Schl; Data Proc.

STILLMAN, DENIS; R Nelson Snider HS; Ft Wayne, IN; Hon Rl; JA; Spn Clb; IM Sprt; Indiana Univ; Chem.

STILSON, SHERRY; Cadillac Sr HS; Cadillac, MI; 1/316 Val; Band; Hon Rl; NHS; Sch Mus; Yth Flsp; Central Michigan Univ; Acctg.

STILWELL, JEFF; Logansport HS; Logansport, IN; 45/370 Band; Hon Rl; Orch; Sch Mus; 4-H; Ger Clb; Cit Awd; DAR Awd; 4-H Awd; Whos Who In Music 1979; Band Honors Jazz Bankd Music Contest 1979; Ind St Solo & Ens Contest Awds & Medals; Purdue Univ; Sci.

STILWELL, SANDY; Pinconning Area HS; Linwood, MI; 23/254 Sec Jr Cls; Hon Rl; Sch Pl; Letter Bsktbl; Delta Comm Coll; Respiratory Therapy.

STILWELL, SUZIE; Shortridge HS; Indianapolis, IN; Cmp Fr Grls; Chrh Wkr; Hon Rl; Fr Clb; Mth Clb; Ten; College.

STIMAC, DIANE; Dominican HS; Detroit, MI; Chrs; Girl Scts; NHS; Stu Cncl; Ten; Wayne St Univ; Educ.

STIMPERT, FRED; Crestview HS; Ashland, OH; Letter Bsbl; Letter Crs Cntry; Letter Ftbl; All Area Ftbl Tm 78; Schl MVP Awd; 3 Letter; 1st Tm All Area Bsktbl 78; All N W Dist Class A Spec Mention; Univ.

STIMSON, DWIGHT; North Branch HS; Canton, MI; Band; Sct Actv; 4-H; Pep Clb; Jazz Band; Pep Band; Lake Superior St Coll; Elec Engr Tec.

STINARD, RICHARD; Wintersville HS; Wintrsvll, OH; Aud/Vis; Band; Chrs; Drm Bgl; Hon Rl; Orch; Sch Mus; Sch Pl; Yth Flsp; Lat Clb; College.

STINCHCOMB, ROBERT; Tiffin Columbian HS; Tiffin, OH; Chrs; Hon Rl; Stu Cncl; Ger Clb; Letter Bsktbl; IM Sprt; Univ.

STINCIC, KIMBERLY; Madison HS; Madison, OH; 82/295 Cls Rep Soph Cls; Cl Rep Jr Cls; Band; Cmnty Wkr; Hon Rl; Lbry Ade; Stu Cncl; Fr Clb; Pep Clb; Scr Kpr; Lakeland Cmnty Coll; Hstry Tchr.

STINEDURF, DAWN; Clinton HS; Tipton, MI; FCA; Hon Rl; Yth Flsp; Pep Clb; Spn Clb; Letter Bsbl; Letter Bsktbl; Letter Chrldng; IM Sprt; Cit Awd; College; Phys Therapy.

STINEHELFER, JODI; Wynford HS; Bucyrus, OH; Trs Jr Cls; Chrs; Chrh Wkr; Hon Rl; NHS; Off Ade; Yth Flsp; Yrbk; Drama Clb; Ohio State Univ; Elem Educ.

STINEMAN, JO; Galion Sr HS; Galion, OH; 9/279 Am Leg Aux Girls St; Band; Girl Scts; Hon Rl; NHS; Yrbk; 4-H; Fr Clb; Trk; Miami Univ; Systems Analysis.

STINEMETZ, CHARLES; North Union HS; Marysville, OH; Pres Frsh Cls; Aud/Vis; Hon Rl; NHS; Fr Clb; Lat Clb; Letter Bsktbl; Capt Ftbl; Capt Trk; IM Sprt; Ohio Weslayan Univ.

STINGER, KEVIN; Franklin HS; Franklin, OH; Am Leg Boys St; Boy Scts; Chrh Wkr; FCA; Sch Pl; Bsbl; Bsktbl; IM Sprt;.

STINGLE, KEITH A; Seeger Memorial HS; Williamsport, IN; Cls Rep Soph Cls; Trs Jr Cls; Cl Rep Jr Cls; Trs Sr Cls; Cls Rep Sr Cls; Chrh Wkr; FCA; Hon Rl; NHS; Sct Actv; Hoosier Scholr 1978; ISU Acad Schlshp 1979; Indiana St Univ; Acctg.

STINNETT, MARY; Oak Hill HS; Oak Hill, WV; Girl Scts; Hon Rl; Lit Mag; VP NHS; Stg Crw; Drama Clb; Pep Clb; Letter Trk; Letter Chrldng; Cit Awd; Treas Of Conservation Clb 78; Univ; Med.

STINNETT, SHELLY; Hurricane HS; Hurricane, WV; Cmnty Wkr; Hon Rl; Pep Clb; Univ; Beauty Stylist.

STINSON, RONALD; Shenandoah HS; Daleville, IN; Hon Rl; Yth Flsp; Beta Clb; 4-H; Mth Clb; 4-H Awd; De Molay; Mech Engr.

STINSON, SHEILA; Cass Tech HS; Detroit, MI; 32/889 Hon Rl; NHS; Y-Teens; Sci Clb; Letter Bsbl; Michigan St Univ; Chem.

STINSON, STACY; Maumee Valley Cntry Day Schl; Swanton, OH; Drm Mjrt; Girl Scts; Hon Rl; Yth Flsp; Pep Clb; Letter Bsktbl; Capt Chrldng; IM Sprt; Twrlr; Am Leg Awd; History Day Exclint 8th Pl 68 Entries 79; Lions Pride Teen Bd Model Maumee Valley Rep 79; Univ; Psych.

STINZIANO, S; Nordonia HS; Macedonia, OH; 14/442 Cls Rep Frsh Cls; Cl Rep Jr Cls; Cls Rep Sr Cls; Hon Rl; NHS; Red Cr Ade; Treas Stu Cncl; Letter Bsktbl; GAA; Univ; Engr.

STIREWALT, SHERRIE; Green HS; Uniontown, OH; Chrh Wkr; Girl Scts; Hon Rl; Jr NHS; Off Ade; Rptr Yrbk; Sch Nwsp; GAA; Moody Bible Inst; Commun.

STIRNEMANN, MICHELLE; Taylor HS; Cleves, OH; Cls Rep Soph Cls; Am Leg Aux Girls St; FCA; Hon Rl; Jr NHS; Sch Mus; Sch Pl; Stu Cncl; Yth Flsp; Capt Bsbl; College; Medical Technology.

STIS, DIANNE; Hamilton Southeastern HS; Noblesville, IN; 37/122 Girl Scts; Hon Rl; Mod UN; Sch Mus; Sch Pl; Drama Clb; Pres OEA; Scr Kpr; 1st Pl OEA Job Intervw 78; 2nd Pl OEA Prep & Verbl Cmnctsn II 3rd Pl OEA Recrds Mgr 79; Ball St Univ; Bus.

STITES, JANET; Mariemont HS; Terrace Pk, OH; 19/149 Band; Chrs; Cmnty Wkr; Hosp Ade; Sch Mus; Sprt Ed Yrbk; Pep Clb; Ten; Scr Kpr; Mt Union College; Elem Ed.

STITT, BOB; Father Wehrle Memrl HS; Columbus, OH; 20/126 Ten; JA Awd; Ohio State Univ; Aeronautics.

STITT, JOSEPH; Bishop Flaget HS; Chillicothe, OH; Chrh Wkr; Cmnty Wkr; Hon Rl; Letter Bsktbl; Crs Cntry; Letter Glf; Letter Ten; Univ Of Dayton; Acctg.

STITT, JOSEPH M; Bishop Flaget HS; Chillicothe, OH; Chrh Wkr; Cmnty Wkr; Hon Rl; NHS; Bsktbl; Glf; Ten; Dayton Univ; Bus Admin.

STITT JR, ROBERT; Wehrle HS; Columbus, OH; 20/126 Cls Rep Sr Cls; Hon Rl; JA; Jr NHS; NHS; Stu Cncl; Ten; JA Awd; Ohio St Univ; Aeronautical Engr.

STITZEL, SUSAN; Middletown HS; Middletown, OH; Chrs; Hon Rl; NHS; Sch Mus; Sch Pl; Stg Crw; Drama Clb; Capt Swmmng; Kenyon College.

STITZLEIN, JAMES; Danville HS; Glenmont, OH; Debate Tm; Stu Cncl; Yrbk; Rptr Sch Nwsp; 4-H; Fr Clb; FFA; Culinary Inst Of America; Chef.

STIVER, DAVID; Austintown Fitch HS; Youngstown, OH; Band; Chrs; Chrh Wkr; Hon Rl; NHS; Sch Pl; Stg Crw; Younstown St Univ; Voice & Comp.

STIVERS, MELINDA; Maumee HS; Maumee, OH; 31/316 Univ; Engr.

STIVERSON, ARTHUR; Hudson Area HS; Hudson, MI; Cls Rep Frsh Cls; Cls Rep Soph Cls; Cl Rep Jr Cls; Hon Rl; Stu Cncl; Rptr Sch Nwsp; Letter Ftbl; Letter Wrstlng; Scr Kpr;.

STIVERSON, JAMES; Ridgedale HS; Marion, OH; FCA; 4-H; Pres FFA; Letter Bsktbl; Letter Ftbl; IM Sprt; Most Improved Football Player; Merit Point System; Swine Efficiency Awd; Vocational Schl; Ag.

STIZMAN, ROBERT; Scecina HS; Indianapolis, IN; 43/194 Boy Scts; NHS; Letter Ftbl; Letter Wrstlng; Hnr Carrier Indianapolis Star; Pres Phys Fit Awd;.

ST JOHN, CARL; Geneva Secondary HS; Geneva, OH; 12/245 Am Leg Boys St; Band; NHS; Sch Pl; Yrbk; Fr Clb; Bsbl; Ohio St Univ; Comp Sci.

ST JOHN, PATRICIA; Notre Dame Acad; Toledo, OH; Hon Rl; Spn Clb; GAA; College.

STOCK, JAMES; Bishop Watterson HS; Columbus, OH; Hon Rl; Sch Pl; Stg Crw; Crs Cntry; Trk; Natl Merit Ltr; Kent St Univ; Archt.

STOCK, JOHN; Lapeer West HS; Lapeer, MI; 50/260 Boy Scts; Chrh Wkr; NHS; 4-H; Cit Awd; 4-H Awd; Univ Of Mich.

STOCK, LORI; Waterloo HS; Atwater, OH; 11/150 Am Leg Aux Girls St; Band; Hon Rl; NHS; Yth Flsp; Rptr Sch Nwsp; 4-H; Fr Clb; Pep Clb; Am Leg Awd; College; Med Research.

STOCK, MARIE; Marian HS; Birmingham, MI; Cls Rep Frsh Cls; Cls Rep Soph Cls; Aud/Vis; Chrs; Chrh Wkr; Hon Rl; Lbry Ade; Mod UN; PAVAS; Sch Mus; Georgetown Univ; French.

STOCK, MARTHA; Canton South HS; Canton, OH; JA; 4-H; Lat Clb; Gym; Trk; 4-H Awd; JA Awd; Univ; Animal Sci.

STOCK, PAULA; Watkins Memorial HS; Pataskala, OH; 40/226 Cls Rep Sr Cls; Hon Rl; NHS; Off Ade; Stu Cncl; Yrbk; Rptr Sch Nwsp; FTA; Scr Kpr; Chiropractic Asst.

STOCK, TOBY; Sycamore HS; Cincinnati, OH; Hon Rl; JA; Scr Kpr; Natl Merit Ltr;.

STOCKAMP, KURT; Columbia City Joint HS; Columbia City, IN; 2/300 Am Leg Boys St; FCA; Hon Rl; NHS; Spn Clb; Bsktbl; Ftbl; Med.

STOCKER, DENNIS; Gull Lake HS; Augusta, MI; 8/233 Boy Scts; Hon Rl; NHS; Sci Clb; Michigan St Univ; Chem Engr.

STOCKER, DUANE; Jay County HS; Dunkirk, IN; Am Leg Boys St; NHS; JA Awd;.

STOCKER, SUE; Newcomerstown HS; Newcomerstown, OH; 2/105 Sal; Am Leg Aux Girls St; Band; Girl Scts; Hon Rl; NHS; Stu Cncl; PPFtbl; Oh Merit Schlrshp 79; Arion Awd 79; Kent St Univ.

STOCKERO, CHERYL M; Forest Park HS; Crystal Falls, MI; 17/80 Trs Frsh Cls; Trs Soph Cls; Cls Rep Soph Cls; Trs Jr Cls; Cl Rep Jr Cls; Cls Rep Sr Cls; Band; Girl Scts; Hon Rl; Stu Cncl; Davenport Coll Of Bus; Lgl Sec.

STOCKFORD, LAURIE; Kearsley HS; Davison, MI; 17/375 Chrs; Chrh Wkr; Hosp Ade; NHS; Off Ade; Sch Pl; Stg Crw; Trk; Flgs; Y-Teens; Drama Clb; Baker Jr Coll; Exec Sec.

STOCKHAM, LAURA; Highland HS; Schekerville, IN; 21/503 Hon Rl; NHS; Pep Clb; Bsktbl; Trk; Univ Of Alabama; Oceanography.

STOCKHOUSE, CARLA; Munster HS; Munster, IN; 105/365 Band; Chrs; Drm Bgl; Drm Mjrt; Girl Scts; Off Ade; Orch; Sct Actv; Spn Clb; 22 N In Medl Of Musi C 73 79; 3 In St Music Medl 78; Indiana Univ; Music.

STOCKMAN, KAREN; Tippecanoe Vly HS; Sikeston, MO; 12/159 Chrh Wkr; Hon Rl; Lbry Ade; NHS; Fr Clb; Media Clb Treas; Future Ed Of Amer; Freed Hardeman Coll; Bio.

STOCKMAN, SHERYL; Reeths Puffer HS; Muskegon, MI; 7/330 Band; Hon Rl; NHS; Spn Clb; Letter Bsktbl; Letter Trk; GAA; Michigan Tech Univ; Civil Engr.

STOCKMAN, TERESA; Union Scioto HS; Chillicothe, OH; 18/127 Sec Frsh Cls; Chrs; Chrh Wkr; NHS; Off Ade; Yth Flsp; 4-H; Sp Clb; Chrldng; Ohio Univ; Dent Asst.

STOCKMAN, VIVIAN; Harvey S Firestone HS; Akron, OH; 60/375 Hon Rl; Lbry Ade; Lit Mag; NHS; Natl Merit Ltr; Mercyhurst Coll.

STOCKMEYER, ELIZABETH; Reese HS; Reese, MI; 2/131 Sal; Am Leg Aux Girls St; Chrh Wkr; Hon Rl; Natl Forn Lg; NHS; Ger Clb; Bsktbl; Cit Awd; Northern Mich; Nursing.

STOCKS, ANTHONY; Ursuline HS; Youngstown, OH; Capt Debate Tm; Hon Rl; Lbry Ade; Natl Forn Lg; Pres NHS; Rptr Sch Nwsp; Ger Clb; Lat Clb; Natl Merit SF;.

STOCKS, LORENA; Yale HS; Goodells, MI; Cmp Fr Grls; Debate Tm; Hon Rl; VICA; Bsbl; GAA; PPFtbl; Cit Awd; St Clair Cnty; Law.

STODOLA, GREGORY; Wahama HS; Mason, WV; 2/98 Sal; Am Leg Boys St; Hon Rl; NHS; Stu Cncl; Pres Key Clb; Rdo Clb; Bsktbl; Glf; Wrstlng; W Vir Institute Of Tech; Comp Sci.

STOEBER, ERIC; Struthers HS; Struthers, OH; Trs Jr Cls; Hon Rl; Stu Cncl; Sprt Ed Yrbk; Sprt Ed Sch Nwsp; Lat Clb; Bsbl; Bsktbl; Letter Crs Cntry; Youngstown St Univ; Chem Engr.

STOECKLIN, MELISSA; Indian Hill HS; Cincinnati, OH; 2/285 Sal; Lit Mag; NHS; Orch; Sch Mus; Sprt Ed Sch Nwsp; Rptr Sch Nwsp; Spn Clb; PPFtbl; Scr Kpr; Vanderbilt Univ; Comp Sci.

STOEFFLER, ANDREA; Warren Central HS; Indpls, IN; 29/850 Trs Frsh Cls; Cls Rep Sr Cls; Hon Rl; Jr NHS; NHS; Quill & Scroll; Sch Mus; Sch Pl; Stg Crw; Stu Cncl; Ball St Univ; Radio Brdcstng.

STOEHR, MARY E; Seton HS; Cincinnati, OH; 86/276 Cls Rep Frsh Cls; Sec Soph Cls; VP Jr Cls; Pres Sr Cls; Cmnty Wkr; Girl Scts; Hon Rl; Hosp Ade; Jr NHS; Orch; Univ Of Cincinnati; Nursing.

STOEL, SHARON; Forest Hills Northern HS; Grand Rapids, MI; 4/138 Chrh Wkr; Drl Tm; Hon Rl; JA; Pom Pon; Mich State Univ; Bus.

STOEWSAND, ROBERT J; Avondale Sr HS; Auburn Hts, MI; Hon Rl; Quill & Scroll; Rptr Sch Nwsp; Northern Michigan Univ; English.

STOFFER, LAURIE; Salem Sr HS; Salem, OH; 9/250 AFS; Chrh Wkr; Hon Rl; Yth Flsp; Univ Of Akron; Home Ec.

STOGSDILL, RICKY; George Washington HS; Indianapolis, IN; 13/405 Hon Rl; Boys Clb Am; Tmr; Air Traffic Controller.

STOHLER, MARY B; Kokomo HS; Kokomo, IN; 3/376 Am Leg Aux Girls St; Pres Chrh Wkr; Hon Rl; Jr NHS; Natl Forn Lg; NHS; VP Quill & Scroll; Stu Cncl; Rptr Sch Nwsp; 4-H; Purdue Univ; Engr.

STOKAN, CATHERINE; Denby HS; Detroit, MI; 8/350 Hon Rl; NHS; Hon Guard 79; Univ; Comp.

STOKER, KENNY; Parkside HS; Jackson, MI; Bsbl; Ftbl; Hockey; IM Sprt; Scr Kpr; Univ; Art.

STOKES, CARCILLA; Calumet HS; Gary, IN; Band; Chrh Wkr; Girl Scts; Hon Rl; Off Ade; Sch Pl; Sch Nwsp; Pep Clb; College.

STOKES, CYNTHIA; Pumatuning Valley HS; Jefferson, OH; Cls Rep Frsh Cls; VP Soph Cls; VP Sr Cls; Cls Rep Sr Cls; Chrs; Hon Rl; NHS; Stg Crw; 4-H; 4-H Awd; Austintown Beauty Acad; Cosmetology.

STOKES, DANIEL; Ironton HS; Ashland, KY; 14/184 Hon Rl; JA; Mod UN; NHS; Sch Mus; Yth Flsp; Ger Clb; Sci Clb; Univ Of Cincinnati; Architecture.

STOKES, DONNA; South Dearborn HS; Aurora, IN; 37/256 Cmnty Wkr; Girl Scts; Hon Rl; Off Ade; Yrbk; Rptr Sch Nwsp; Pep Clb; Letter Glf; GAA; DAR Awd; 2nd Plc In DAR Essay Contest For 2yrs; Yng Artist Workshop At Ball St Univ; Most Impr oved Awd Grls Golf Tm; College; Medical Illustrator.

STOKES, JEAN A; Marian HS; South Bend, IN; Pres Soph Cls; Hon Rl; Mdrgl; NHS; Sch Mus; Yrbk; Rptr Sch Nwsp; Drama Clb; Pep Clb; Spn Clb; Natl Negro Merit Commd Stu 1978; Whos Who Among HS Stu 1977; Spanish Awd I & Ii & Iii 1976; Georgetown Univ; Forgn Serv.

STOKES, RICHARD; St Joseph HS; Euclid, OH; Aud/Vis; Band; Boy Scts; Hon Rl; Lbry Ade; MMM; Orch; Sch Mus; Sct Actv; IM Sprt; Kent St Univ; Archt.

STOKES, SHARON; Carmel HS; Carmel, IN; 76/770 Pres Sr Cls; Chrh Wkr; Hon Rl; Lbry Ade; NHS; Yth Flsp; Fr Clb; Letter Swmmng; Tmr; Partcipant In IN Univ Foreign Lang Honor Prog 79; Studied & Lived France For 7 Wks; Univ.

STOLARZ, GRACE; Vicksburg HS; Vicksburg, MI; 2/236 Sal; NHS; Pol Wkr; Stg Crw; 4-H; GAA; Michigan St Univ; Chem Engr.

STOLBA, RUSSELL; Chalker HS; Southington, OH; Pres Soph Cls; Am Leg Boys St; Lbry Ade; NHS; Beta Clb; Bsbl; Bsktbl; Ftbl; Glf; Marietta College; Mass Media.

STOLICKER, TERRI; Deckerville Community School; Palms, MI; Trs Soph Cls; Cls Rep Sr Cls; Hon Rl; NHS; Off Ade; Capt Chrldng; Scr Kpr; Bus Schl; Sec.

STOLINE, ANNE; Loy Norrix HS; Kalamazoo, MI; 7/426 Band; VP Boy Scts; Hon Rl; Hosp Ade; NHS; Pol Wkr; Sch Mus; Treas Fr Clb; Letter Swmmng; Letter Trk; Kalamazoo Coll; Physn.

STOLINE, ANNE M; Loy Norrix HS; Kalamazoo, MI; 7/426 Band; Drm Mjrt; Sch Pl; Hon Rl; Hosp Ade; Pol Wkr; Fr Clb; Letter Swmmng; Natl Merit SF; Univ; Physician.

STOLL, BRIAN M; Andover HS; Orchard Lake, MI; 15/420 Debate Tm; Hon Rl; Lit Mag; Mdrgl; NHS; Orch; Sch Mus; Sci Clb; Socr; Natl Merit SF; Univ; Math.

STOLL, GREG; Edison HS; Norwalk, OH; Chrh Wkr; Hon Rl; FFA; Letter Ftbl; Letter Trk; Letter Wrstlng; Baldwin Univ; Bio.

STOLL, RHONDA; Highland HS; Wadsworth, OH; Band; Girl Scts; Hon Rl; NHS; Quill & Scroll; Sch Mus; Spn Clb; Univ; Bio Sci.

STOLL, SHARON; North Daviess Jr Sr HS; Odon, IN; 30/93 Hon Rl; Vincennes Univ.

STOLL, SUSAN; Centerville HS; Centerville, OH; 173/680 Chrs; Girl Scts; Sch Mus; Pep Clb; PPFtbl; Scr Kpr; Wright St Univ; Bus.

STOLL, SUSAN; Princeton Community HS; Princeton, IN; 26/204 Am Leg Aux Girls St; Drl Tm; DECA; Drama Clb; Spn Clb; Univ; Vet.

STOLLE, GREGORY; Tri HS; Cambridge City, IN; 15/84 Am Leg Boys St; Band; Hon Rl; NHS; Pres Fr Clb; FFA; Letter Bsbl; Bsktbl; Letter Ftbl; All Big Blue River Conf In Bsbl 78; Mst Interceptns On Ftbl Team 2 Yrs 77& 78; Univ; Agri Engr.

STOLLER, LARESA; Bryan HS; Provo, UT; .

STOLMACK, SUE; Northmont HS; Clayton, OH; Hon Rl; Jr NHS; Lbry Ade; OEA; Chrldng; Scr Kpr; Univ Of Ken; Engr.

STOLSON, BRETT; Conneaut HS; Conneaut, OH; Cls Rep Frsh Cls; Cls Rep Soph Cls; Cl Rep Jr Cls; Cls Rep Sr Cls; Am Leg Boys St; Chrh Wkr; Stu Cncl; Rptr Sch Nwsp; Rdo Clb; Trk; Ohi St Univ; Bus Admin.

STOLT, SHEILA; Harbor Springs HS; Hrbr Spgs, MI; Chrs; Hon Rl; Hosp Ade; Sch Pl; Drama Clb; Pep Clb; Spn Clb; Chrldng; College; Bus Mktg.

STOLTZ, BRENDA; Liberty Benton HS; Findlay, OH; Cl Rep Jr Cls; Cls Rep Sr Cls; VP Band; Chrh Wkr; Hon Rl; NHS; Treas Stu Cncl; Yth Flsp; Sec 4-H; College; Education.

STOLTZ, LISA; Kimball HS; Royal Oak, MI; Band; Chrs; Chrh Wkr; Girl Scts; Hon Rl; Lbry Ade; Sch Mus; Sch Pl; Sct Actv; Stg Crw; Letter For Marching Band 77; First Class Scout 76; Univ; Forestry.

STOLZ, BARBARA; North Posey HS; Evansville, IN; 52/182 Trs Jr Cls; Trs Sr Cls; Chrh Wkr; Drl Tm; Hon Rl; Off Ade; Stu Cncl; 4-H; Pep Clb; GAA; West Side Beauty Coll; Cosmetology.

STOLZ, JEANNIE; Lebanon HS; Lebanon, OH; Chrh Wkr; Girl Scts; Hon Rl; Coll; Nursing.

STOLZ, WERNER L; North Central HS; Indianapolis, IN; Boy Scts; Hon Rl; Lbry Ade; Stg Crw; Yrbk; Sch Nwsp; Ger Clb; Sci Clb; IM Sprt; Natl Merit SF; Purdue Univ; Chem.

STOLZ, WILLIAM; Alma HS; Sumner, MI; Band; Chrh Wkr; Hon Rl; Pol Wkr; Bsbl; Ftbl; Wrstlng; Alma Coll; Math.

STOLZENFELD, KATHRYN; Lutheran HS; Detroit, MI; Chrs; Chrh Wkr; Girl Scts; Hon Rl; NHS; Off Ade; Sct Actv; Yth Flsp; Rptr Sch Nwsp; Wayne State Univ; Med.

STONE, ANN; H H Dow HS; Midland, MI; 16/460 Girl Scts; Hon Rl; NHS; Letter Bsktbl; Letter Swmmng; Natl Merit SF; Hope College; Bus Admin.

STONE, BRENTON; Maumee Valley Cntry Day Schl; Toledo, OH; 3/35 Pres Frsh Cls; Trs Frsh Cls; Pres Soph Cls; Trs Soph Cls; VP Jr Cls; Trs Jr Cls; Cl Rep Jr Cls; Boy Scts; Chrs; Hon Rl; Univ.

STONE, BRIAN E; Meadowbrook HS; Pleasant City, OH; 52/201 Band; Chrh Wkr; Sch Pl; Yth Flsp; Yrbk; Sprt Ed Sch Nwsp; Key Clb; Mth Clb; Pep Clb; Ohi Univ; Engineering.

STONE, CAMBI; Bloomfield HS; Bloomfield, IN; 13/95 Pres Jr Cls; FCA; Hon Rl; NHS; Stu Cncl; Yrbk; FBLA; Pep Clb; Spn Clb; Capt Chrldng; Symposium For Tomorrows Leaders; Indiana Univ.

STONE, CLARENCE; Cass Tech HS; Detroit, MI; Band; Hon Rl; Yth Flsp; Fr Clb; Swmmng; College; Law.

STONE, CLAUDE R; Woodward HS; Toledo, OH; Hon Rl; VICA; Socr; Toledo Univ; Chem Engr.

STONE, DAPHNE; Heritage Christian Schl; Indianapolis, IN; 29/64 Band; Hon Rl; Gym; Letter Trk; Chrldng; Bob Jones Univ; Home Ec.

STONE, DAVID; Du Pont HS; Charleston, WV; Am Leg Boys St; Boy Scts; Chrh Wkr; Cmnty Wkr; Sct Actv; Lat Clb; Bsbl; Bsktbl; IM Sprt;.

STONE, DIANE; West Geauga HS; Chesterland, OH; Cls Rep Soph Cls; Cl Rep Jr Cls; Cls Rep Sr Cls; Band; Chrs; Hon Rl; Stu Cncl; 4-H; IM Sprt; PPFtbl; College; Nurse.

STONE, ERIC; Manchester HS; Akron, OH; 24/216 Cmnty Wkr; Hon Rl; NHS; Sprt Ed Sch Nwsp; Rptr Sch Nwsp; Am Leg Awd; Lion Awd; Univ Of Akron; Mass Media.

STONE, ERIC L; East HS; Columbus, OH; Am Leg Boys St; Boy Scts; Hon Rl; Letter Ftbl; Wrstlng; Jr Cadet For The Oh St Hghwy Patrol Acad 79; Univ; Coach.

STONE, FAWN; De Kalb HS; Corunna, IN; Chrs; Hon Rl; NHS; Sch Mus; Sch Pl; Spn Clb; Goddard Coll; Archt.

STONE, HEIDI; Indian Creek HS; Martinsville, IN; 7/161 FCA; Hon Rl; Stu Cncl; Yrbk; Sch Nwsp; Drama Clb; Fr Clb; Pep Clb; Letter Trk; Chrldng; College; Journalism.

STONE, JEFF; West Muskingum HS; Zanesville, OH; 6/200 Am Leg Boys St; Chrs; NHS; Pol Wkr; VP Stu Cncl; Pres Drama Clb; Pres Key Clb; Letter Trk; Washburn Univ; Poli Sci.

STONE, JOHN; Monroe HS; Monroe, MI; Jr NHS; NHS; Bsbl; Adrian Coll.

STONE, LINDA; Haslett HS; Haslett, MI; Band; Chrs; Drm Mjrt; NHS; 4-H; Letter Gym; Letter Swmmng; Letter Trk; Letter Chrldng; Univ; Bio Sci.

STONE, PAMELA B; Kiser HS; Dayton, OH; ! Sec Jr Cls; Chrs; Drl Tm; FCA; Lbry Ade; Off Ade; Sch Pl; Stu Cncl; Y-Teens; DECA;.

STONE, RAYMOND; N Newton HS; Lake Village, IN; 13/160 Am Leg Boys St; Boy Scts; Chrh Wkr; Hon Rl; NHS; Sct Actv; Coach Actv; IM Sprt; Mgrs; Hoosier Schlr 79; Purdue Univ Cert Of Recog 79; Purdue Univ; Aero.

STONE, RODGER; Whitehall HS; Muskegon, MI; Cmnty Wkr; JA; Ftbl; Cit Awd; JA Awd; College.

STONE, RONALD; Stockbridge HS; Stockbridge, MI; 18/124 Hon Rl; Rptr Sch Nwsp; Lat Clb; Sci Clb; Letter Ten; Mich State Univ; Geol.

STONE, RUTH; Franklin Hts HS; Columbus, OH; 6/300 Chrh Wkr; Cmnty Wkr; Hon Rl; Am Leg Awd; Franklin Univ; Acctg.

STONE, SCOTT; Whiteford HS; Ottawa Lk, MI; Boy Scts; Lbry Ade; Off Ade; Yth Flsp; Letter Ftbl; Letter Wrstlng; Ftbl All Lge & All Rgn 78; Outstdg Offnsv Plyr 78; Coll.

STONE, TAMARA; Clinton Central HS; Frankfort, IN; Band; Hon Rl; NHS; Quill & Scroll; Rptr Sch Nwsp; Lat Clb; Pep Clb; Vocational School; Med Records.

STONE, TRESA; Whitehall HS; Whitehall, MI; Cls Rep Frsh Cls; Sec Soph Cls; Pres Jr Cls; Chrs; Hon Rl; Sch Mus; Sch Pl; Stu Cncl; Bsktbl; PPFtbl; Coll; Photog.

STONE, WINNIE; Andrean HS; Merrillville, IN; Hst Frsh Cls; Hst Soph Cls; Hst Jr Cls; Band; Drl Tm; Drm Bgl; Hon Rl; Hosp Ade; Sch Pl; Rptr Sch Nwsp; Ind Univ; Nurse.

STONECASH, KENT E; Eaton HS; Eaton, OH; Pres Soph Cls; Pres Jr Cls; Chrs; Chrh Wkr; Hon Rl; Jr NHS; Sch Mus; Sch Pl; Stg Crw; VP Stu Cncl; Homecoming Escort Soph; Tres Hi Y Club; Music Contest; Univ Of Cincinnati; Elec Engr.

STONEKING, KAY; De Kalb HS; Corunna, IN; 4/292 Hon Rl; Pres Hosp Ade; Pres Natl Forn Lg; Sec NHS; Sch Mus; Sch Pl; Stg Crw; Drama Clb; 4-H; Pep Clb; De Pauw Univ; Nursing.

STONER, KATHERINE; Jackson HS; Canal Fulton, OH; Band; Cmnty Wkr; FCA; Girl Scts; NHS; Red Cr Ade; Yth Flsp; Y-Teens; Fr Clb; Pep Clb; College.

STONER, KEITH; Lexington Sr HS; Lexington, OH; 32/264 Am Leg Boys St; Chrs; Chrh Wkr; Mdrgl; NHS; Key Clb; Letter Ftbl; Letter Trk; Ringling Schl Of Art; Graphic Dsgn.

STONESTREET, STEVEN R; Sissonville HS; Charleston, WV; Cls Rep Frsh Cls; Cls Rep Soph Cls; Cl Rep Jr Cls; Pres Sr Cls; Am Leg Boys St; Hon Rl; Jr NHS; NHS; Stu Cncl; Fr Clb; Stu Of The Mnth 78; Hugh O Brien Yth Camp 78; West Virginia St Univ; Acctg.

STONG, CYNTHIA; Whitehall HS; Whitehall, MI; 54/150 Hon Rl; 4-H; Mat Maids; Scr Kpr; Tmr; Twrlr; Cit Awd; DAR Awd; Academic Asst 77 79; Passed 8 Basic United Stats Figure Skating Tests 77; Ferris St Coll; Ophthalmic Dispensng.

ST ONGE, SANDRA; Davison Sr HS; Davison, MI; 58/425 Chrh Wkr; Cmnty Wkr; Hon Rl; NHS; Off Ade; Red Cr Ade; Rptr Yrbk; Rptr Sch Nwsp; OEA; Letter Mgrs; Univ Of Michigan; Spec Ed.

STOOKEY, JULI; Hobart Sr HS; Hobart, IN; Hon Rl; Jr NHS; Stu Cncl; Ger Clb; Pep Clb; Trk; Mat Maids; Scholastic & Acadmc Achvmnt Awds 1976; Purdue Univ; Model.

STOOPS, JAMES; Salem HS; Salem, OH; 61/295 Mth Clb; Letter Crs Cntry; Capt Trk; Univ Of Cin; Elect Engr.

STOPAR, JUDY; Regina HS; Richmond Hts, OH; Hosp Ade; Univ; Music.

STOPHLET, MARK; Mount Healthy HS; Cincinnati, OH; Chrs; NHS; Sch Mus; Ger Clb; College; Med.

STOPPENHAGEN, DAN; Heritage HS; Monroevle, IN; 15/185 Cls Rep Soph Cls; Cl Rep Jr Cls; Cls Rep Sr Cls; Hon Rl; Orch; VP Stu Cncl; Letter Bsbl; Wrstlng; Coach Actv; Volleyball Letter 78; Football Letter 79; Lettermans Club 78; Univ; Archt.

STORACE, BRIAN; Woodhaven HS; Woodhaven, MI; Chrs; Sch Pl; Stg Crw; Drama Clb; Adrian Coll; Broadcast Journalism.

STORACI, PAUL; Tecumseh HS; Medway, OH; VP FCA; Hon Rl; Treas Jr NHS; NHS; Rptr Sch Nwsp; Drama Clb; Letter Bsbl; Wrstlng; College; Computer Sci.

STORAD, JIM; Indian Valley South HS; Tippecanoe, OH; 3/95 Pres Frsh Cls; Am Leg Boys St; Hon Rl; NHS; Yth Flsp; Yrbk; Am Leg Awd; Muskingum Coll; Geology.

STORAGE, MARK A; Lincoln HS; Shinnston, WV; Am Leg Boys St; Hon Rl; Boys Clb Am; Spn Clb; Ftbl; Trk; Wrstlng; Fairmount State College; Comp Sci.

STORBECK, MATT; Clio HS; Clio, MI; Boy Scts; Chrh Wkr; Hon Rl; Jr NHS; NHS; Sct Actv; Fr Clb; Michigan St Univ; Optometry.

STORCH, JEANNETTE; Black River HS; Sullivan, OH; 1/79 Chrh Wkr; Debate Tm; Girl Scts; Hon Rl; Rptr Yrbk; Beta Clb; 4-H; Fr Clb; Sci Clb; Letter Gym; Coll; Econ.

STORCKMAN, ERICK; Logansport HS; Logansport, IN; Band; Boy Scts; Chrs; Drm Mjrt; Natl Forn Lg; Sch Mus; Sch Pl; Sct Actv; Stu Cncl; Drama Clb; Univ; Music.

STORDAHL, KRISTIN; Marquette Sr HS; Marquette, MI; 18/440 Band; Hon Rl; Orch; Sch Mus; Rptr Yrbk; Ger Clb; Northern Michigan Univ.

STOREY, SUSAN; Ursuline HS; Girard, OH; Cl Rep Jr Cls; Hon Rl; Stu Cncl; Fr Clb; Ten; IM Sprt; College.

STOREY, TRUDIE; North Newton HS; Morocco, IN; 6/150 Aud/Vis; Chrh Wkr; Cmnty Wkr; Hon Rl; NHS; Yth Flsp; Lat Clb; Pep Clb; Trk; Chrldng; Modeling Schl; Model.

STORK, KURT F; St Johns Public HS; St Johns, MI; 3/375 Am Leg Boys St; Band; Chrh Wkr; Hon Rl; Jr NHS; NHS; Mod UN; NHS; Sch Mus; Sch Pl; Treas Yth Flsp; Hope Coll; Natural Sci.

STORK, MICHELLE; Davison Sr HS; Davison, MI; Band; Chrs; Girl Scts; Hon Rl; Off Ade; Stu Cncl; Capt Pom Pon; 1st Pl Team Trophy Orig 77; 1st Pl Team Trophy Over All 77; Chgo Natl 2nd Pl Team Trophy Orig 77; Ferris St Coll; Psych.

STORL, HEIDI; Black River HS; Spencer, OH; 1/100 Chrh Wkr; Cmnty Wkr; Hon Rl; Sch Nwsp; Beta Clb; Drama Clb; Fr Clb; Ger Clb; Sci Clb; U S Yth Conservtn Corps Best Camper 1978; Yth Sci Rep Ohio St Univ 1976; Capital Univ; Bio Chem.

STORM, REBECCA; J F Kennedy HS; Taylor, MI; Band; Girl Scts; Hon Rl; Jr NHS; Off Ade; Sch Pl; College; Math.

STORMS, AMY; High School; Indianapolis, IN; Hon Rl; Off Ade; ROTC; Key Clb; Cit Awd; Natl Merit Ltr;.

STORTI, JOAN; Cherry Hill HS; Dbn Hts, MI; Cls Rep Soph Cls; Chrh Wkr; Hon Rl; Stu Cncl; Pep Clb; Chrldng; Tmr; College; Health.

STORTI, LISA; Ishpeming HS; Ishpeming, MI; Chrs; Hon Rl; Sch Mus; Hon Rl; Swmmng; Trk; Northern Mich Univ; Medical Tech.

STORTZ, TOM L; Clear Fork HS; Butler, OH; Band; Hon Rl; Lit Mag; Fr Clb; FFA; Trk; Wrstlng; Ohio St Coll; Vet.

STORY, ROBERT M; Lake Michigan Catholic HS; Benton Hrbr, MI; Band; Boy Scts; CAP; Hon Rl; Sch Mus; Sch Pl; Stg Crw; Stu Cncl; Drama Clb; Fr Clb; Intl Thespien Society 79; Univ; Math.

STOTLER, MINDY; Paw Paw HS; Paw Paw, WV; VP Soph Cls; Drl Tm; Hon Rl; Red Cr Ade; Sch Mus; 4-H; FBLA; FHA; Pep Clb; Bsktbl; Univ; Comp.

STOTT, ALANA; Central Lake HS; Central Lake, MI; Cls Rep Frsh Cls; Cls Rep Soph Cls; Band; Hon Rl; NHS; Sch Mus; Stu Cncl; Rptr Yrbk; Rptr Sch Nwsp; Pep Clb; John Philip Sousa Awd 78; Clive B Nichols Achvmnt Awd 78; Davenport Univ; Acctg.

STOTT, MARCIA; Bethel HS; Tipp City, OH; Chrs; Lbry Ade; Ed Yrbk; Yrbk; Wright St Univ; Child Psych.

STOTTLER, JEFFREY; Barnesville HS; Barnesville, OH; Hon Rl; Rptr Yrbk; Fr Clb; Key Clb; IM Sprt; Mgrs; World Affairs Inst; Study Tour To France; College; Engr.

STOTTSBERRY, TRESA; Guernsey Noble Voc HS; Caldwell, OH; Cls Rep Frsh Cls; Girl Scts; Hon Rl; Stu Cncl; Rptr Sch Nwsp; FHA; Pep Clb; VICA; Chrldng; Vocational Schl.

STOTZ, CYNTHIA; Hilltop HS; W Unity, OH; 16/74 Am Leg Aux Girls St; Chrs; Girl Scts; Hon Rl; NHS; Stg Crw; Rptr Sch Nwsp; 4-H; FHA; 4-H Awd; Univ Of Toledo; Med Asst.

STOUDT, NANCY; North Side HS; Ft Wayne, IN; 2/425 Sec Jr Cls; Cl Rep Jr Cls; Cls Rep Sr Cls; Am Leg Aux Girls St; Band; Hon Rl; Sec NHS; Stu Cncl; Eng Clb; Letter Gym; Davidson Coll; Pre Med.

STOUGH, MEG; Lebanon HS; Kirklin, IN; 77/219 Band; Chrs; Hon Rl; Red Cr Ade; Sch Mus; Sch Pl; Civ Clb; Fr Clb; Glf; Pom Pon; Lead In South Pacific; Indiana Univ; Childhd Educ.

STOUGHTON, NANCY; Streetsboro HS; Streetsboro, OH; Cmp Fr Grls; Chrs; Yrbk; Rptr Sch Nwsp; FHA; Sec OEA; Busns Schl.

ST OURS, GERALDINE; St Francis HS; Traverse City, MI; Cls Rep Frsh Cls; Band; Chrh Wkr; Cmnty Wkr; Hon Rl; PAVAS; Sch Mus; Sch Pl; Yth Flsp; Rptr Yrbk; Art Awd 79 ; Youth Advsry Councl 79; Runner Up Miss 16 Of Jackson 78; Western Michigan Univ; Bus.

STOUT, ALAN; Southern Wells Jr Sr HS; Bluffton, IN; 1/87 Hon Rl; NHS; Voctl Schl; Farmer.

STOUT, BILL; South Christian HS; Byron Center, MI; VP Frsh Cls; Hon Rl; Jr NHS; NHS; Letter Bsktbl; Letter Ftbl; Letter Ten; IM Sprt; Mgrs;.

STOUT, CATHY; Lewis County HS; Weston, WV; Pres Soph Cls; FCA; Hon Rl; Jr NHS; Stu Cncl; Yth Flsp; Chrldng; PPFtbl; 4-H Awd; Parkersburg Career Coll.

STOUT, CHERYL; Watkins Memorial HS; Pataskala, OH; 35/211 FCA; Hon Rl; Rptr Sch Nwsp; Sch Nwsp; Letter Trk; PPFtbl; Nationwide Beauty Acad; Cosmetology.

STOUT, DEBBIE; Winfield HS; Winfield, WV; Girl Scts; Hon Rl; St Marys Schl Of Nursing; Nursing.

STOUT, JANICE; Flemington HS; Flemington, WV; 2/46 Trs Jr Cls; VP Sr Cls; Sal; Chrs; Chrh Wkr; Hon Rl; Hosp Ade; NHS; Yth Flsp; 4-H Awd; Univ; Nursing.

STOUT, LUANNE; Washington Irving HS; Clarksburg, WV; Quill & Scroll; Sch Mus; Sch Pl; Yth Flsp; Y-Teens; Rptr Yrbk; Rptr Sch Nwsp; 4-H; Fr Clb; Lat Clb; West Virginia Univ.

STOUT, RUSSELL; Brownstown Ctrl HS; Brownstown, IN; 4-H; Sci Clb; Indiana Voc Schl.

STOVALL, VICKI; Hamilton Southeastern HS; Fortville, IN; Hon Rl; JA; NHS; Drama Clb; Fr Clb; Univ; Dance.

STOVER,; Greenbrier East HS; , ; Hon Rl; Jr NHS; FBLA; Coll; Elem Ed.

STOVER, CYNTHIA; Belleville HS; Ypsilanti, MI; 16/519 Chrh Wkr; Hon Rl; NHS; Stg Crw; Rptr Sch Nwsp; French Cert Of Merit; 2 Cert Of Musical Achievement Participation In Piano Recitals; College; Medicine.

STOVER, DEBRA; Kyger Creek HS; Gallipolis, OH; Aud/Vis; Band; Chrs; Chrh Wkr; Cmnty Wkr; Lbry Ade; Sch Pl; Stg Crw; Fr Clb; Keyettes; Regnl Awd For Outstndng Command Of Scrptrs 79; Rating I In Ensmbl Voice Contst 79; Brigham Young Univ; Occupt Ther.

STOVER, JANET; Lutheran West HS; N Olmsted, OH; 21/79 Cls Rep Frsh Cls; Cls Rep Soph Cls; Chrs; Drl Tm; Hon Rl; NHS; Off Ade; Stu Cncl; Yrbk; Pep Clb; Southeastern Acad; Travel Agent.

STOVER, JEFF; Napoleon HS; Napoleon, OH; 40/262 Trs Frsh Cls; Trs Sr Cls; Chrs; Hon Rl; Stu Cncl; Fr Clb; Spn Clb; Bsktbl; Ftbl; Trk; Univ; Engr Tech.

STOVER, KEITH; Pleasant Local HS; Prospect, OH; 41/165 Rptr Sch Nwsp; Sch Nwsp; Letter Ftbl; Letter Trk; IM Sprt; College; Engr.

STOVER, MICHELLE; Teays Valley HS; Ashville, OH; Pres Frsh Cls; Cls Rep Soph Cls; Cl Rep Jr Cls; Am Leg Aux Girls St; Hon Rl; NHS; Yth Flsp; FBLA; Lat Clb; Chrldng; Univ; Med.

STOVER, SANDRA; Westfall HS; Orient, OH; Am Leg Aux Girls St; Band; Hon Rl; NHS; Ed Yrbk; FNA; FTA; Spn Clb; Twrlr;.

STOVER, SHERRY; Clear Fork HS; Colcord, WV; 6/35 Trs Jr Cls; Band; Chrh Wkr; Hon Rl; NHS; Stu Cncl; Sch Nwsp; 4-H; Voc Sch.

STOVER, TWILLA; Ripley HS; Given, WV; 6/250 Hon Rl; Jr NHS; NHS; Beta Clb; 4-H; Pres Mth Clb; Pres VICA; Natl Merit Ltr; Wv Inst Of Tech; Engr.

STOVER, WILLIAM R; Oak Hill HS; Oak Hill, WV; VP Jr Cls; Am Leg Boys St; Hon Rl; Natl Forn Lg; Stu Cncl; FBLA; Pep Clb; Letter Bsktbl; Letter Ten; Letter Trk; Pres Of Stud Body; Concord Coll; Bus Mgmt.

STOWASSER, JOSEPH W; Buffalo HS; Huntngtn, WV; Chrh Wkr; FCA; Sch Pl; Letter Crs Cntry; Letter Ftbl; Letter Trk; Letter Wrstlng; Univ.

STOWELL, JON; Hauser Jr Sr HS; Columbus, IN; Cmnty Wkr; Hon Rl; Jr NHS; Rptr Yrbk; Sci Clb; Bsktbl; Coach Actv; Indiana Coll Of Mortuary; Mort Sci.

STOWERS, ELIZABETH; Clinton Central HS; Frankfort, IN; 6/106 Am Leg Aux Girls St; Band; Chrh Wkr; FCA; NHS; Stg Crw; Rptr Yrbk; Letter Swmmng; Pom Pon; 4-H Awd; Indiana State Univ; Art Education.

STOWERS, TERESA S; Gallia Academy HS; Bidwell, OH; 55/225 Cls Rep Frsh Cls; Band; Girl Scts; Yrbk; 4-H; FFA; Key Clb; Cit Awd; DAR Awd; 4-H Awd; Ohio St Univ; Ag Educ.

STOYCHEFF, TAMMY; Cardinal Stritch HS; Oregon, OH; Cls Rep Soph Cls; Cl Rep Jr Cls; Cls Rep Sr Cls; Band; Chrh Wkr; Hon Rl; Red Cr Ade; Stu Cncl; Yrbk; Fr Clb; Red Cross Treas/sec; Head Of Council Projects; Serve As Counselor At Storer Camps; Teach Sunday Schl 2 Yrs; College; Nursing.

ST PETER, SANDEE; Newark Sr HS; Newark, OH; Band; Chrs; Drl Tm; Girl Scts; Orch; Sch Mus; Sch Pl; Drama Clb; 4-H; Fr Clb; College; Keypunch Operator.

STRAEFFER, GREGORY S; Rogers HS; Michigan City, IN; 2/484 Sal; Band; Chrs; NHS; Sch Mus; Mth Clb; Sci Clb; Ten; JETS Awd; Natl Merit Ltr; Purdue Univ; Chem Engr.

STRAFFEN, MARK; St Edward HS; Fairview Pk, OH; 32/330 Hon Rl; Jr NHS; NHS; Sch Pl; IM Sprt; Bowling Green St Univ; Cmnty Servs.

STRAH, CHRISTINA; Lumen Cordium HS; Twinsburg, OH; 20/111 Chrs; Drl Tm; Girl Scts; Hon Rl; Sch Mus; Rptr Sch Nwsp; Sch Nwsp; Drama Clb; Fr Clb; Crs Cntry; Univ; Jrnlsm.

STRAHL, DAVID; Westfield Washington HS; Westfield, IN; Rptr Sch Nwsp; Letter Ftbl; Letter Trk; Letter Wrstlng; Ind State Univ; Political Sci.

STRAIGHT, SCOTT; Belleville HS; Ypsilanti, MI; Ger Clb; Capt Bsktbl; Ftbl; Letter Trk; Univ.

STRAIN, ANNETTE; Little Miami HS; Maineville, OH; 17/200 Hon Rl; Lit Mag; NHS; Stu Cncl; VP Yth Flsp; Rptr Yrbk; GAA; Campbellsville; Art.

STRAIN, JANET; Chagrin Falls HS; Chagrin Falls, OH; 61/187 Cls Rep Frsh Cls; AFS; Chrs; Girl Scts; Hosp Ade; Sch Mus; Sct Actv; Stu Cncl; Ger Clb; PPFtbl; Univ; Nursing.

STRAIN, LAURIE; Rogers HS; Toledo, OH; Cls Rep Frsh Cls; Chrh Wkr; Hon Rl; 4-H; FHA; Sci Clb; Spn Clb; 4-H Awd; Horticulturist.

STRAINER, MARGERY; Grand Haven HS; Grand Haven, MI; Cls Rep Frsh Cls; Cls Rep Soph Cls; Chrs; NHS; Sch Mus; Sch Pl; Rptr Sch Nwsp; Drama Clb; Bsbl; Ten; Aquinas Coll; Poli Sci.

STRAIT, BRENDA; Ansonia Local HS; New Weston, OH; 23/64 Chrs; Hon Rl; Yrbk; Sch Nwsp; Drama Clb; 4-H; FHA; OEA; Pep Clb; Spn Clb; FHA Jr Degree 77; OEA Doplomt Statesman & Ambsdr Awd 79; Third Yr Chorus Awd 79; Schl Of Nursing; Nursing.

STRAIT, JEAN; Bryan HS; Bryan, OH; 13/182 Trs Sr Cls; Am Leg Aux Girls St; Sec Band; Chrs; Jr NHS; Orch; Yrbk; Chmn Crs Cntry; Chmn Trk; Eastern Ken Univ; Interior Design.

STRAIT, PATRICIA; Mendon HS; Three Rivers, MI; Red Cr Ade; Fr Clb; Spn Clb; Univ.

STRAIT, REBECCA; Owen Valley HS; Poland, IN; 1/200 Val; Jr NHS; NHS; Pol Wkr; Pep Clb; Dnfth Awd; DAR Awd; Gov Hon Prg Awd; Purdue Univ; DVM.

STRAIT, SUSANNE; Middletown HS; Franklin, OH; 6/550 Chrs; Chrh Wkr; Cmnty Wkr; Girl Scts; Hon Rl; NHS; Sch Mus; Sch Pl; Stg Crw; Ed Yrbk; De Pauw Univ; French.

STRAKA, ANTOINETTE; Father J Wehrle Mem HS; Columbus, OH; Hon Rl; Spn Clb; Amer History Honor Awd; Spanish Honor Soc; Superior Awd Cert For NEDT; Ohio St Univ.

STRAKA, DAVID; Stanton HS; Toronto, OH; Aud/Vis; Chrs; Hon Rl; Lbry Ade; NHS; Sch Mus; Pres Sci Clb; Letter Crs Cntry; Trk; Embry Riddle Univ; Aeronautical Sci.

STRAKA, DAVID A; Stanton HS; Toronto, OH; Aud/Vis; Chrs; Chrh Wkr; Hon Rl; Lbry Ade; NHS; Sch Mus; Sec Sci Clb; Letter Crs Cntry; Embry Riddle Aero Univ; Aerontcl Sci.

STRAKIS, G; Decatur Central HS; Indnpls, IN; 49/380 Coll.

STRAKOWSKI, STEVE; Northwood HS; Nappanee, IN; 4/191 VP Frsh Cls; Cls Rep Frsh Cls; Cls Rep Soph Cls; Cl Rep Jr Cls; Am Leg Boys St; FCA; Hon Rl; NHS; Stu Cncl; Letter Ftbl; Purdue Univ; Vet.

STRALEY, CHERYL; Western HS; Auburn, MI; Aud/Vis; Band; Drm Mjrt; Girl Scts; Sch Mus; Sct Actv; DECA; GAA; Twrlr; Natl Merit Schl; Delta Coll; Optometry.

STRAMAN, SALLY; Four County Joint Voc School; Defiance, OH; 1/98 Sec Jr Cls; Sec Sr Cls; Val; Band; Chrs; Hon Rl; NHS; Red Cr Ade; Sch Mus; OEA; Outstndng Jr Of Four County Jrs 1977; Northwest Tech Coll; Bus Mgmt.

STRAND, CHARLES; Luther L Wright HS; Ironwood, MI; 31/179 Am Leg Boys St; Treas Chrs; NHS; Sch Pl; Stu Cncl; Yrbk; Bogebic Comm College; Med.

STRAND, ERIC; Loveland Hurst HS; Loveland, OH; 4/230 Hon Rl; NHS; Ger Clb; Ten; Univ Of Cinn; Chemical Engineer.

STRANEY, ROSEMARY; Grand Ledge HS; Grand Ledge, MI; 54/416 Hon Rl; NHS; Treas Fr Clb; Gym; Tmr; Univ Of Michigan; Archaeology.

STRANG, CHRISTI; Gallia Acad; Gallipolis, OH; Band; Chrs; Girl Scts; Sch Pl; Stg Crw; Sch Nwsp; Lat Clb; GAA; Natl Merit Ltr; College; Art.

STRANG, JANET; William A Wirt HS; Gary, IN; Cls Rep Soph Cls; Cl Rep Jr Cls; Girl Scts; Hon Rl; Jr NHS; Lit Mag; Stu Cncl; Fr Clb; Mth Clb; Pep Clb; Who Who In Indiana & Kentucky HS; Foreign Languages; Ball St Univ; Nursing.

STRANG, TERRI; Bexley HS; Bexley, OH; Boy Scts; Girl Scts; Yrbk; Lat Clb; Rus Clb; Sci Clb; Natl Merit Schl; Ohi State Univ; Chem Engr.

STRANGE, BRADLEY; Jackson County Western HS; Spring Arbor, MI; Jackson Jr Coll; Acctg.

STRANGE, SUSAN; Immaculate Conception Acad; Batesville, IN; 13/68 Chrs; Hon Rl; JA; NHS; Sch Pl; Yrbk; Ten; Univ; Archt.

STRAPP, JOHN; Linden Mc Kinley HS; Columbus, OH; Aud/Vis; Hon Rl; Jr NHS;.

STRASBURG, HEATHER; Benton Harbor HS; Benton Hbr, MI; Chrh Wkr; Girl Scts; Hon Rl; Fr Clb; Pom Pon; College; English.

STRASER, IRENE; Girard HS; Girard, OH; 2/202 AFS; Girl Scts; Hon Rl; Fr Clb; Ger Clb; Sci Clb; Am Leg Awd; Voice Dem Awd; 1st Pl Dist Wnr Ohio Hist Day 1978; Univ; Coll Prep.

STRASSELL, JULIE; Tell City HS; Tell City, IN; 20/224 Sec Frsh Cls; Band; Hon Rl; NHS; Yth Flsp; Bsktbl; IM Sprt; Twrlr; ISU.

STRASSER, DAVID; Muskegon HS; Muskegon, MI; Band; NHS; Orch; W Michigan Univ; Elec Engr.

STRASSER, GENE; Lake Orion HS; Lake Orion, MI; 8/435 Jr NHS; NHS; Univ; Elec Engr.

STRASSER, KEVIN; Garden City W Sr HS; Garden City, MI; Ger Clb; Letter Ftbl; IM Sprt; Coll.

STRASSER, TIMOTHY; Upper Sandusky HS; Upper Sandusky, OH; Hon Rl; Letter Bsbl; Univ; Drafting.

STRATE, VICKIE; Avondale Sr HS; Bloomfield Hls, MI; 2/271 Am Leg Aux Girls St; Band; Hon Rl; Jr NHS; NHS; Off Ade; Quill & Scroll; Stu Cncl; Rptr Yrbk; Ed Sch Nwsp; Univ; Radio TV Jrnlsm.

STRATER, SUZANNE; Munster HS; Munster, IN; 42/403 Cls Rep Frsh Cls; Pres Soph Cls; Am Leg Aux Girls St; Chrs; Hon Rl; NHS; Rptr Sch Nwsp; Pres Pep Clb; Glf; IM Sprt; Purdue Univ; Communications.

STRATMAN, ANTHONY; Mater Dei HS; Evansville, IN; Boy Scts; Chrh Wkr; Hon Rl; Sct Actv; VICA; Cit Awd; DAR Awd; Elec Trades.

STRATTAN, KEITH; Perry HS; Perry, MI; 12/146 Cls Rep Frsh Cls; Hon Rl; NHS; FFA; Pep Clb; Bsktbl; Ftbl; Trk; Tmr; Natl Merit Ltr; Univ; Elec.

STRATTON, BOB; South Ripley HS; Holton, IN; Pres Frsh Cls; Cls Rep Soph Cls; Band; Chrs; Hon Rl; Spn Clb; Letter Bsbl; Letter Bsktbl; Letter Crs Cntry; Letter Trk; ISU.

STRATTON, GARY; Shelby HS; Shelby, MI; VP Jr Cls; Hon Rl; Letter Bsbl; Letter Bsktbl; Letter Ftbl; Univ; Tchr.

STRATTON, HELENE; St Johns HS; St Johns, MI; Girl Scts; Hon Rl; Drama Clb; 4-H; Bsktbl; Letter Swmmng; Letter Trk; GAA; Tmr; 4-H Awd; Brooks Coll; Fshn Dsgn.

STRATTON, JOYCE; Burch HS; Delbarton, WV; Hon Rl; Beta Clb; FTA; Pep Clb; Gym; Chrldng; Pom Pon;.

STRATTON, ROBERT; Hill Mccloy HS; Clio, MI; 1/135 Val; Band; Hon Rl; NHS; Dnfth Awd; Rose Hulman Inst Of Tech; Chem Engr.

STRAUB, LESLIE; Bellefontaine HS; Bellefontaine, OH; 1/210 Val; Am Leg Aux Girls St; Band; Hon Rl; NHS; Sch Mus; Pres Sci Clb; Am Leg Awd; Kiwan Awd; Rotary Awd; Univ Of Cincinnati; Med.

STRAUB, MARC; Northrop HS; Ft Wayne, IN; 3/600 Band; Hon Rl; VP JA; Orch; Sct Actv; Yrbk; Sch Nwsp; Letter Trk; IM Sprt; C of C Awd; Tri Kappa Awd; Commended Stu Mayor Cong; High Scor On MAA; Natl Math Test; MVP Track; N Amer Schlrshp; Drake Univ; Engr.

STRAUGHEN, SANDRA; C S Mott HS; Warren, MI; Chrs; NHS; Orch; Sch Mus; Sch Pl; Stu Cncl; Rptr Sch Nwsp; Sec Fr Clb; IM Sprt; College; Liberal Arts.

STRAUGHN, SUSAN; Central Catholic HS; Wheeling, WV; 13/132 Hon Rl; Rptr Yrbk; Rptr Sch Nwsp; Dent Hygienist.

STRAUSBAUGH, NITA; Zane Trace HS; Chillicothe, OH; 31/94 Band; Chrs; Hon Rl; Off Ade; Y-

Teens; Pep Clb; Sci Clb; Bsktbl; Mas Awd; Outstnd Bookkeeping 1979; Bus Schl.

STRAUSBAUGH, TINA; Southeastern HS; Chillicothe, OH; 4-H; FHA;.

STRAUSER, JOHN; St Francis Seminary; Lorain, OH; 2/14 Sal; Chrh Wkr; Hon Rl; Letter Bsktbl; IM Sprt; Ert Of Awd From Oh Gnrl Sci 79; Univ; Acctg.

STRAUSS, JOSEPH; Milford HS; Milford, MI; Boy Scts; Cmnty Wkr; Hon Rl; Sct Actv; Stg Crw; Bsbl; Ftbl; Mi Comptn Schlrshp 79; Hnr Cord For 3.0 GPA Through HS 79; Lawrence Inst Of Tech; Archt.

STRAUSS, SUSAN; Boardman HS; Boardman, OH; 82/593 Cls Rep Soph Cls; Cl Rep Jr Cls; Cls Rep Sr Cls; Chrs; Hon Rl; NHS; Sch Mus; Stu Cncl; Pep Clb; Chrldng; Kent St Univ; Phys Ther.

STRAUTMAN, BRIAN; South Dearborn HS; Aurora, IN; 18/250 Am Leg Boys St; Band; Hon Rl; NHS; Stu Cncl; Letter Bsbl; Letter Bsktbl; IM Sprt; Univ.

STRAW, BILL; Clarksville HS; Clarksville, IN; 27/167 Cls Rep Frsh Cls; Cls Rep Soph Cls; Chrs; Hon Rl; NHS; Quill & Scroll; Sch Mus; Sch Pl; Rptr Sch Nwsp; Sch Nwsp; Thespian Intl Soc 78; Western Kentucky Univ; Psych.

STRAW, KATHLEEN; Stow HS; Stow, OH; AFS; Am Leg Aux Girls St; Debate Tm; Natl Forn Lg; Fr Clb; Am Leg Awd; College; Law.

STRAW, LYDIA; Rockford HS; Rockford, MI; 16/450 Band; Chrh Wkr; FCA; Hon Rl; NHS; Orch; Pol Wkr; Drama Clb; Fr Clb; Sci Clb; Hope Schlrshp 79; MI Competitive Schlrshp 79; Whos Who Among Amer HS Stu 78; Hope Coll.

STRAWDERMAN, JAMES; Mathias HS; Mathias, WV; 4/18 Pres Jr Cls; Chrh Wkr; Cmnty Wkr; Jr NHS; NHS; Stu Cncl; Dnfth Awd;.

STRAWN, CHERI; Swartz Creek HS; Swartz Creek, MI; Band; Drl Tm; Hon Rl; NHS; Sch Mus; Sch Pl; Stg Crw; Drama Clb; Michigan St Univ; Law.

STRAWN, RENE; Clinton Central HS; Kirklin, IN; 10/100 Sec Soph Cls; Sec Jr Cls; Sec Sr Cls; Chrs; FCA; Hon Rl; NHS; Yrbk; Drama Clb; Pep Clb; Univ; Elem Educ.

STRAWSER, JODI; Montpelier HS; Mntpelier, OH; 18/109 Trs Sr Cls; Band; Chrs; Chrh Wkr; Girl Scts; Hon Rl; NHS; Sch Mus; Sch Pl; Sct Actv; Indiana Univ; Radiogic Tech.

STRAWSER, PATRICIA; Constantine Sr HS; Constantine, MI; 17/105 Hon Rl; Lbry Ade; NHS; Pep Clb; Sci Clb; Spn Clb; Letter Trk; Univ Of Arizona; Spanish.

STRAWSER, ROBERT; Whitmer HS; Toledo, OH; Boy Scts; Hon Rl; Treas JA; Off Ade; IM Sprt; Treas JA Awd; Univ Of Tol; Bus.

STRAYER, DIANE; Griffith Sr HS; Griffith, IN; 4/320 Cls Rep Frsh Cls; VP Soph Cls; Cl Rep Jr Cls; Am Leg Aux Girls St; Chrs; Hon Rl; Jr NHS; NHS; Stu Cncl; Pep Clb; Univ; Sci.

STRAYER, JANET; Riverside HS; De Graff, OH; 3/83 Band; Chrs; Chrh Wkr; Hon Rl; Jr NHS; Lbry Ade; Treas NHS; Sch Pl; Sec Stu Cncl; Yrbk; Prsnted Organ Cncrt 1978; Chrch Organist; Play For Weddings; Univ; Music.

STRAYER, JOANNE; Riverside HS; Degraff, OH; 19/82 Cl Rep Jr Cls; Cls Rep Sr Cls; Am Leg Aux Girls St; Band; Chrs; Chrh Wkr; Cmnty Wkr; Hon Rl; Lbry Ade; Off Ade; Lima Tech Coll; Nursing.

STRAYER, PAULA; Riverside HS; De Graff, OH; Cl Rep Jr Cls; Cls Rep Sr Cls; Am Leg Aux Girls St; Band; Chrs; Chrh Wkr; Cmnty Wkr; Hon Rl; Lbry Ade; Off Ade; Lima Tech College; Nurse.

STRAZIUSO, LISA; St Marys Cntrl Catholic HS; Sandusky, OH; Aud/Vis; Lbry Ade; Rptr Yrbk; 4-H; Trk; GAA; Scr Kpr; 4-H Awd; Firelands Campus; Med Rec Tech.

STREACKER, SARA; Terre Haute North Vigo HS; Terre Haute, IN; 32/800 Band; Chrh Wkr; Hon Rl; Y-Teens; FDA; Bsbl; Trk; GAA; PPFtbl; Pres Tmr; Indiana St Univ; Acctg.

STREBER, GREGORY; East Clinton HS; New Vienna, OH; FCA; Hon Rl; Sch Pl; Stg Crw; Pres Stu Cncl; VP FTA; Capt Bsktbl; Bluffton Coll; Bus Educ.

STREBICK, MARY; St Vincent St Mary HS; Akron, OH; 200/288 Chrh Wkr; Cmnty Wkr; Hon Rl; Hosp Ade; Mth Clb; MU Alpha Theta Awd 78; Psych Awd 79; Akron Univ; Languages.

STREET, PAMELA; Bluefield HS; Bluefield, WV; 92/285 Drl Tm; Stu Cncl; Rptr Sch Nwsp; VP Spn Clb; Capt Pom Pon; College.

STREETER, TAMMY; Manistique HS; Germfask, MI; Chrh Wkr; Hon Rl; Hosp Ade; 4-H; FHA; 4-H Awd; Bay De Noc Cmnty Coll; Reg Nurse.

STREETS, JIM; Coshocton HS; Coshocton, OH; Hon Rl; IM Sprt; Univ; Engr.

STREETS, JULIE A; School For The Deaf; Keyser, WV; Sec Sr Cls; Drm Mjrt; Girl Scts; Hon Rl; NHS; Sch Pl; Yrbk; 4-H; Bsktbl; Trk;.

STREICHER, BRENDA; Jasper HS; Jasper, IN; 29/345 Chrs; Chrh Wkr; Hon Rl; NHS; Sch Mus; Sch Pl; Drama Clb; 4-H; Pep Clb; 4-H Awd; Univ Of Evansville; Music Mgmt.

STREICHERT, SANDRA; Maumee HS; Maumee, OH; Hon Rl; Stu Cncl; Treas Y-Teens; Yrbk; Drama Clb; Spn Clb; Bsbl; Treas PPFtbl; College.

STREIFF, RICHARD; Monrovia HS; Mooresville, IN; 17/134 Hon Rl; Spn Clb; Bsktbl; Trk; Univ; Tchr.

STREIT, GLORIA J; Hobart Sr HS; Hobart, IN; Sec AFS; Letter Band; Sec Chrh Wkr; Hon Rl; Hosp Ade; Stu Cncl; Yrbk; Treas Fr Clb; Letter Bsktbl; Letter Trk; College; Languages.

STREK, JOHN; Grosse Pointe North HS; Grosse Pt Wds, MI; FCA; Hon Rl; NHS; Ten; Coach Actv; IM Sprt; Mich; Pre Med.

STRELOW, BARBARA; Plainwell HS; Plainwell, MI; Hon Rl; NHS; Yrbk; Letter Ten; Letter Trk; PPFtbl; Univ.

STRENG, LAURA; Clawson HS; Clawson, MI; Band; Chrs; Girl Scts; Hon Rl; Sch Mus; Bsbl; Bsktbl; GAA; PPFtbl; College.

STRETCH, TONYA; Granville HS; Grandville, MI; 21/339 Band; Chrh Wkr; Hon Rl; Hosp Ade; Lbry Ade; NHS; Off Ade; Ger Clb; Cedarville Coll; Sci.

STRETCHER, BRIAN N; Springs Valley HS; French Lick, IN; 2/72 Band; Hon Rl; Fr Clb; Chrldng; Rose Hulman Inst Of Tech; Chem Engr.

STRICHARCZUK, SCOTT; Solon HS; Solon, OH; Cls Rep Frsh Cls; Cls Rep Soph Cls; Cl Rep Jr Cls; Hon Rl; Key Clb; Letter Bsbl; Letter Bsktbl; Letter Ftbl; Chrldng; College; Business.

STRICKER, GREGORY; Stow HS; Stow, OH; Red Cr Ade; Glf; IM Sprt; College.

STRICKLAND, MONICA; Northern HS; Pontiac, MI; Pres Soph Cls; Cl Rep Jr Cls; Chrh Wkr; Cmnty Wkr; Hon Rl; Lit Mag; Off Ade; Stu Cncl; Yth Flsp; Chrldng; Cranbrook Upward Bound Prog 77 79; VP Of Cranbrook Horizons Upward Bound 78 79; Michigan St Univ; Scndry Educ.

STRICKLAND, PHYLLIS; East HS; Columbus, OH; Hon Rl; Jr NHS; Drama Clb; Soc Of Dist Amer HS Stu; College.

STRICKLAND, PHYLLIS; Columbus East HS; Columbus, OH; Hon Rl; Jr NHS; College; Thtr.

STRICKLER, DANIEL; Holly HS; Holly, MI; 28/265 Band; Hon Rl; NHS; 4-H; Wrstlng; AAU Cultrl Exchng Wrstlng Team To West Germny 78; AAU Cultrl Exchng Wrstlng Team To Turkey 79; Lock Haven St Coll; Phys Educ.

STRICKLER, KIMBELRY; Ontario HS; Mansfield, OH; Chrs; Drl Tm; Hon Rl; NHS; Yth Flsp; 4-H; Letter Bsktbl; Letter Trk; Mgrs; Ohio St Univ; Occup Ther.

STRICKLER, MARC; Grosse I 6 HS; Grosse Ile, MI; 11/226 Band; Chrh Wkr; Hon Rl; NHS; Orch; Bsbl; Bsktbl; IM Sprt; Michigan St Univ; Pre Med.

STRICKLER, SCOTT; Williamstown HS; Williamstown, WV; 1/160 Trs Soph Cls; Cls Rep Sr Cls; Am Leg Boys St; Chrh Wkr; Hon Rl; Pres NHS; Stu Cncl; Yth Flsp; Capt Ten; Consrvtn Club Sec; Creatb Writng Awd; Univ; Chem.

STRICKLER, SHARI; Huntington North HS; Huntington, IN; 40/576 Chrs; Chrh Wkr; Cmnty Wkr; Sch Mus; Sch Pl; Stg Crw; Yth Flsp; Rptr Yrbk; Ger Clb; Pep Clb; In St Univ Smmr Hon Semnr In Life Sci 79; Exchnge Stndt To Germn 78; Univ; Bio Sci.

STRICKLETT, PATRICIA; Madison Hts HS; Anderson, IN; Chrs; Chrh Wkr; Hon Rl; PAVAS; Sch Mus; Sch Pl; Stg Crw; Letter Bsbl; Bsktbl; Swmmng;.

STRIEBICH, LISA; Our Lady Of Angels HS; Cincinnati, OH; 7/148 Chrh Wkr; Hon Rl; NHS; Spn Clb; DAR Awd; Ten; GAA; Mgrs; College; Art.

STRIEBY, KATHY; Pine River HS; Luther, MI; Hon Rl; NHS; Bsktbl; Trk; College.

STRIGGOW, LORI; Bedford Sr HS; Temperance, MI; 27/457 Cls Rep Soph Cls; VP Jr Cls; Cl Rep Jr Cls; VP Sr Cls; Cls Rep Sr Cls; Band; Girl Scts; NHS; 4-H; Ger Clb; Western Michigan Univ; Home Ec.

STRIGHT, LINDA; Lakeshore HS; Stevensville, MI; 49/299 Band; Girl Scts; Hon Rl; Sec JA; St Of Mi Comp Schlrshp Cert Of Recogntn 79; Lake Michigan Coll.

STRIGLE, THOMAS R; Walsh Jesuit HS; Akron, OH; Chrs; Chrh Wkr; Cmnty Wkr; Hon Rl; Red Cr Ade; Sch Mus; Stg Crw; Sch Nwsp; Cit Awd; College.

STRIKER, KENT A; Cheboygan Area HS; Cheboygan, MI; 4/197 Band; Hon Rl; Sct Actv; Sci Clb; Ftbl; Hockey; Ten; IM Sprt; Michigan Tech Univ; Elec Engr.

STRIMBU, DOROTHY; Tuscarawas Cntrl Catholc HS; New Phila, OH; Girl Scts; Hon Rl; NHS; Stg Crw; Bsktbl; Schlstic Achvment Awd World Hstry & In Spnsh 77; Awds In Eng; Spnsh II Bio & Religional 78; Eng Spnsh III; Univ; Cmnctns.

STRINGER, DIANA; Samuel C Mumford HS; Detroit, MI; Val; Hon Rl; NHS; Off Ade; Wayne State Univ; Acctng.

STRINGER, FRANCES; St Marys HS; Highland Pk, MI; 17/53 Hon Rl; Lbry Ade; Sch Pl; Rptr Yrbk; Yrbk; Chrldng; Scr Kpr; Tmr; Opt Clb Awd; Off Ade; Oakland Univ; Pediatric Nursing.

STRINGER, ROBBIE; Bloom Local HS; So Webster, OH; Chrs; Hon Rl; Sch Pl; Stg Crw; Drama Clb; FFA; Treas Spn Clb; Spn Clb; Trk; IM Sprt; Voc Coll; Carpenter.

STRINGER, TAMMY; Girard HS; Girard, OH; Trs Frsh Cls; Sec Soph Cls; Cl Rep Jr Cls; Rptr Yrbk; Fr Clb; Pep Clb; Letter Gym; Chrldng; GAA; God Cntry Awd; College; Medicine.

STRINGHAM, KATHY; Lakeview Sr HS; Battle Creek, MI; Band; Chrs; Girl Scts; Hon Rl; NHS; Stg Crw; Yth Flsp; Y-Teens; Pep Clb; Am Leg Awd; Ferris St Coll; Data Proc.

STRITTO, CARL; Alter HS; Centerville, OH; Boy Scts; Chrh Wkr; Sch Mus; Sch Pl; Ftbl; Trk; IM Sprt; Univ Of Dayton; Engr.

STRIZ, BARBARA; Whitmore Lake HS; Whitmore Lk, MI; 7/82 Sec Soph Cls; Band; Hon Rl; Jr NHS; NHS; Bsbl; Capt Bsktbl; Capt Crs Cntry; Univ.

STRIZAK, BRIAN; Bellaire HS; Bellaire, OH; 18/238 Hon Rl; NHS; Beta Clb; Fr Clb; Rdo Clb; Letter Crs Cntry; Ftbl; Trk; Letter Wrstlng; IM Sprt; Univ Of Cincinnati; Aerospace Engr.

STROBACH, RUSSELL; Kenston HS; Chagrin Falls, OH; Chrs; FCA; Hon Rl; Mdrgl; Off Ade; Yth Flsp; Letter Bsbl; College; Aeronautical Engr.

STROBLE, NANCY; Reading HS; Reading, MI; Cls Rep Frsh Cls; Cls Rep Soph Cls; Trs Jr Cls; Chrs; Hon Rl; Off Ade; Stu Cncl; Rptr Yrbk; 4-H; Chrldng; St Tel Awd In Food Preservation; Selected Girls St Rep; Washington D C Citizen Shortcourse Trip 4 H; Kellogg Cmnty Coll; Med.

STROCK, KATHY; Southington Local HS; Southington, OH; Y-Teens; 4-H; Sci Clb; Bsbl; Bsktbl; 4-H Awd;.

STROCK, LEANN; Chalker HS; Southington, OH; 1/72 Pres Frsh Cls; Pres Soph Cls; Hon Rl; Beta Clb; 4-H; Spn Clb; Letter Bsbl; Letter Chrldng; 4-H Awd; Rotary Awd;.

STROGEN, BRIAN; Roosevelt Wilson HS; Stongwood, WV; Trs Frsh Cls; Trs Soph Cls; Trs Jr Cls; Chrs; Chrh Wkr; Hon Rl; NHS; Sch Pl; Stu Cncl; Leo Clb; Fairmont St Univ; Acctg.

STROGEN, EDWARD; Roosevelt Wilson HS; Clarksburg, WV; Fr Clb; Bsktbl; Ten; Mgrs; Elk Awd; Fairmont Univ; Engr.

STROGEN, EDWARD; Roosevelt Wilson HS; Stonewood, WV; Hon Rl; Fr Clb; Bsktbl; Ten; Mgrs; Elk Awd; Univ; Engr.

STROH, DIANE; Wapakoneta HS; Wapakoneta, OH; Band; Hon Rl; NHS; Yrbk; Lat Clb; Pep Clb; Tech Schl; Radiologic Tech.

STROH, ROSS; Warsaw Community HS; Warsaw, IN; 33/358 Band; Chrh Wkr; Hon Rl; Pres Yth Flsp; Ball St Univ; Architecture.

STROH, STEVE; Stivers Patterson HS; Dayton, OH; 19/428 Cls Rep Soph Cls; Chrh Wkr; Hon Rl; NHS; Yth Flsp; VICA; College; Archt.

STROHACKER, BRENDA; Tri Valley HS; Dresden, OH; Hon Rl; FHA; Spn Clb;.

STROHAUER, NANCY; John J Pershing HS; Detroit, MI; Hon Rl; OEA; Univ; Bus Admin.

STROHECKER, JOHN; Columbiana HS; Columbiana, OH; 10/98 Band; Hon Rl; Wrstlng; Youngstown Univ; Elec Engr.

STROHECKER, MELANIE N; Big Walnut HS; Galena, OH; 7/147 Band; Girl Scts; Hon Rl; Sch Pl; Stg Crw; Drama Clb; Sci Clb; Spn Clb; Univ; Music.

STROHM, DOUGLAS; Wapakoneta HS; Wapakoneta, OH; Spn Clb; Letter Ten; Cit Awd; College; Cmmrcl Retailing.

STROM, RENAY; Brandon HS; Ortonville, MI; Cmnty Wkr; Hon Rl; NHS; Rptr Yrbk; 4-H; 4-H Awd; Achvmnt Awd For History 77; Michigan St Univ; Vet.

STROMAN, JULIE; Imlay City HS; Imlay City, MI; Cl Rep Jr Cls; Cls Rep Sr Cls; Hon Rl; NHS; Yth Flsp; Delta Coll; Nursing.

STROMAN, LAURA; Capac HS; Capac, MI; Chrh Wkr; 4-H; FFA; Pres OEA; Mgrs; 4-H Awd; Bus Schl; Bus.

STROMINGER, MARK; Bishop Hartley HS; Columbus, OH; Hon Rl; Merit Awd 77; Improvmt Hon Roll 78; Ohio St Univ; Real Estate.

STROMME, JOHANNA; Maumee HS; Maumee, OH; Band; Cmp Fr Grls; Hon Rl; Y-Teens; Spn Clb; Letter Bsbl; Letter Bsktbl; Letter Trk; GAA; IM Sprt; Ohio St Univ; Nurse.

STROMSKI, RUSSELL; Wayne Memorial HS; Westland, MI; Hon Rl; JA; Jr NHS; NHS; Spn Clb; Univ; Elec.

STROMSWOLD, CAROL; Buchanan Sr HS; Buchanan, MI; Am Leg Aux Girls St; Band; Hon Rl; JA; Lbry Ade; NHS; Sch Mus; Yth Flsp; Rptr Sch Nwsp; FTA; Manchester Coll; Sec.

STRONG, ALISON; Lapeer East HS; Lapeer, MI; Am Leg Aux Girls St; Band; NHS; Spn Clb; Michigan St Univ; Vet Med.

STRONG, CANDI; Clinton Prairie School; Mulberry, IN; 22/90 Chrs; Hon Rl; Hosp Ade; Lbry Ade; 4-H; FBLA; FHA; OEA; Spn Clb; Mat Maids; Bus Schl; Bus.

STRONG, DAWN; Quincy HS; Quincy, MI; Band; Chrh Wkr; Hon Rl; 4-H; Fr Clb; 4-H Awd; Grand Rapids Baptist Univ; Elem Ed.

STRONG, GLORIA; Concord HS; Spring Arbor, MI; 1/85 Sec Frsh Cls; Band; Hon Rl; NHS; VP Stu Cncl; Yth Flsp; VP 4-H;.

STRONG, JACQUELINE; Merrill HS; Merrill, MI; 13/115 Chrh Wkr; Girl Scts; Hon Rl; Yth Flsp; 4-H; Bsktbl; Letter Trk; 4-H Awd; Voc Schl; Stewardess.

STRONG, JERRY; Michigan Lutheran Sem; Remus, MI; 8/62 Trs Jr Cls; Trs Sr Cls; Band; Chrs; Chrh Wkr; Hon Rl; Mdrgl; Sch Pl; Ed Yrbk; Dr Martin Luther College; Ed.

STRONG, JULIE; Rudyard HS; Rudyard, MI; Hon Rl; Hosp Ade; NHS; Quill & Scroll; Rptr Yrbk; Sprt Ed Sch Nwsp; Pres OEA; Letter Swmmng; Capt Pom Pon; PPFtbl; Michigan St Univ; Pre Med.

STRONG, RANDY; Ben Davis HS; Indianapolis, IN; Cls Rep Frsh Cls; Treas Boy Scts; Chrh Wkr; Cmnty Wkr; Hon Rl; Yth Flsp; Pres DECA; Treas 4-H; Pep Clb; IM Sprt; Colorado Univ; Mrktng.

STRONG, WILLIAM; Central Catholic HS; Wheeling, WV; 3/140 Trk; West Virginia Univ; Medicine.

STROPE, CINDY; Cameron HS; Cameron, WV; 9/139 Band; Hon Rl; NHS; Sch Mus; Yth Flsp; Y-Teens; 4-H; Pep Clb; West Liberty State; Acctg.

STROPKI, LORI K; Timken Sr HS; Canton, OH; Band; Hosp Ade; Off Ade; DECA; Pep Clb; Aultman Hosp Tech Schl; X Ray Tech.

STROTHER, JULIE; Stonewall Jackson HS; Chrlstn, WV; Band; Cmp Fr Grls; Chrh Wkr; Capt Debate Tm; Natl Forn Lg; Lat Clb; Sec Sci Clb; Trk; Univ; Chem.

STROTHER, MAX; Eaton HS; Eaton, OH; 4/175 Chrs; FCA; Hon Rl; NHS; Yth Flsp; 4-H; FFA; 4-H Awd; Ohio St Univ; Welding.

STROUD, JOHN; Tim Ken Sr HS; Canton, OH; Aud/Vis; Boy Scts; Hon Rl; Lbry Ade; Sct Actv; Univ Of Akron; Chem Engr.

STROUF, LINDA K; Manistee HS; Manistee, MI; 2/190 Sal; Band; Chrs; Hon Rl; Jr NHS; Pres Mdrgl; Sec NHS; Sch Mus; Yth Flsp; Sch Nwsp; Music Prize In Flute 79; St Of Mi Hon Band & Choir 78 79; Winner In Proficiency 3 At St Flute 79; Hope Coll; Instrumntl Music Educ.

STROUP, JENNIFER; Lawrence Central HS; Indianapolis, IN; 26/435 Sec Drl Tm; Girl Scts; Sec Y-Teens; Beta Clb; Sec Pom Pon; PPFtbl; Univ.

STROUSE, CARLEEN; Clare HS; Clare, MI; 6/130 Cls Rep Soph Cls; VP Jr Cls; Cls Rep Sr Cls; Debate Tm; FCA; Hon Rl; VP NHS; Off Ade; Ed Yrbk; Rptr Yrbk; Mid Michigan Comm Coll; Acct.

STROUSE, RITA; Loudonville HS; Loudonville, OH; Hon Rl; Jr NHS; NHS; Sch Pl; Stu Cncl; Yth Flsp; Sch Nwsp; Drama Clb; Lat Clb; Scr Kpr; College; Psychology.

STROVILAS, CRIS; Toronto HS; Toronto, OH; 1/150 Band; Girl Scts; Hon Rl; Sch Mus; Fr Clb; Pep Clb; Am Leg Awd; Natl Merit Ltr; Arion Awd; Schlshp Achvmnt Test In Eng Ranked In St; Ohio St Univ; Law.

STRUBLE, DEBRA; Evart HS; Mt Pleasant, MI; Hon Rl; NHS; Off Ade; Sch Pl; Sch Nwsp; Drama Clb; Treas FHA; Pep Clb; PPFtbl; DAR Awd;.

STRUBLE, DIANE; Champion HS; Warren, OH; Band; Girl Scts; Hon Rl; Orch; Pep Clb; Music S chlrshp Heidelberg Coll 79; Natl Educ Development Awd 77; Heidelberg Coll; Music Perf.

STRUBLE, MARK; Floyd Central HS; New Albany, IN; Cls Rep Frsh Cls; Cls Rep Soph Cls; Hon Rl; Mod UN; Stu Cncl; Fr Clb; Pep Clb; Ten; College; Engr.

STRUBLE, THOMAS; Ainsworth HS; Flint, MI; 17/261 Band; Boy Scts; Hon Rl; JA; NHS; Elk Awd; JA Awd; JETS Awd; 2nd Pl 30th Intl Sci Fair 79; 1st Pl USDA 79; 2nd Pl USAF; Northern Michigan Univ; Med Doctor.

STRUDAS, BRIDGET; Hobart Sr HS; Hobart, IN; Cls Rep Soph Cls; Cl Rep Jr Cls; Hon Rl; Jr NHS; Pol Wkr; Stu Cncl; Mat Maids; Pom Pon; Scr Kpr; Tmr; Ldrshp Conference 1977; Purdue Univ; Vet Med.

STRUEBING, SHERRY; East Detroit HS; Warren, MI; Chrs; Hon Rl; NHS; Bsbl; Bsktbl; Trk; PPFtbl; Macomb Cnty Com Coll.

STRUGLINSKI, JENIFER; Revere HS; Akron, OH; 3/290 AFS; VP Band; Hon Rl; Pres NHS; Sch Pl; Drama Clb; Womnhd Awd 79; Univ Of Akron Hon Progr & Schlshp 79; Bath Voluntr Fo Rserv Scshp 79; For Lang Awd 79; Univ Of Akron; Chem Engr.

STRUM, A; Fayetteville HS; Fayetteville, WV; Sec Sr Cls; Chrs; Chrh Wkr; Hon Rl; Stu Cncl; Rptr Yrbk; Rptr Sch Nwsp; Drama Clb; 4-H; FBLA; Marshall Univ; Early Childhood Ed.

STRUNAK, JANET; Valley Forge Sr HS; Parma Hts, OH; 284/777 Hon Rl; Letter Bsbl; Letter Bsktbl; IM Sprt; Cit Awd; Most Improved Player Bsktbl & Volleyball; Honorable Mention Dream Tm Bsktbl; College; Busns Mgmt.

STRUNK, SHEILA; Wood Memorial HS; Oakland City, IN; Cls Rep Frsh Cls; Cls Rep Soph Cls; Cl Rep Jr Cls; Cls Rep Sr Cls; Band; Drl Tm; FCA; Girl Scts; Hon Rl; Off Ade; Elected As Football Homecoming Queen; Stu Cncl Pres; OEA Vice Pres; Univ Of Evansville; Modeling.

STRUP, DAVID; Edgerton HS; Edgerton, OH; 1/72 Val; Boy Scts; Hon Rl; Pres NHS; Yth Flsp; Mth Clb; Pres Spn Clb; Bsbl; Pep Clb; Ten; Notre Dame Univ; Acctg.

STRUP, STEPHEN; Edgerton HS; Edgerton, OH; 1/82 Am Leg Boys St; Band; Boy Scts; Hon Rl; Pres NHS; VP Spn Clb; Letter Bsbl; Letter Bsktbl; Letter Ftbl; Coach Actv; Univ; Pre Med.

STRUP, STEVE; Edgerton HS; Edgerton, OH; 1/87 Am Leg Boys St; Band; Boy Scts; Hon Rl; NHS; Sct Actv; Yth Flsp; Spn Clb; Letter Bsbl; Letter Bsktbl; College; Medicine.

STRUSINSKI, FRANK; St Hedwig HS; Detroit, MI; 4/65 Hon Rl; Pres NHS; Voice Dem Awd; Natl Honor Soc; General Motors Inst; Engr.

STRUYK, DAVID; Comstock Park HS; Comstock Pk, MI; Pres Sr Cls; Am Leg Boys St; Aud/Vis; Band; Boy Scts; Chrs; Hon Rl; NHS; Sch Mus; Rptr Yrbk; Mi Indust Educ Soc Grad Awd Winner 77; Indust Art Awd 77 & 7; Univ Of Michigan; Elec Engr.

STRYFFELER, DANIEL; Austintown Fitch HS; Youngstown, OH; 30/655 Pres Frsh Cls; Hon Rl; NHS; Key Clb; Letter Bsbl; Letter Bsktbl; Capt Ftbl; College; Business Law.

STRYKER, BONNIE; Jenison HS; Grandville, MI; 31/341 Treas OEA; VP JA Awd; Grand Valley State College; Acctg.

STUART, ALAN; Vassar HS; Vassar, MI; Band; Drm Bgl; Sch Mus; Sch Pl; Stg Crw; Yth Flsp; Yrbk; Sch Nwsp; Drama Clb; Lion Awd; Central Michigan Univ; Music.

STUART, CAROL; Houghton HS; Houghton, MI; 1/114 Val; Chrs; Pres Girl Scts; Hon Rl; Sch Pl; Sct Actv; Pres Spn Clb; Mic State Univ.

STUART, JAMES; Highland HS; Anderson, IN; Cmnty Wkr; Hon Rl; Stg Crw; Pres OEA; Letter Ftbl; Letter Wrstlng; Cit Awd; Purdue Univ; Comp Sci.

STUART, J R; South Decatur HS; Westport, IN; Trs Frsh Cls; Cls Rep Frsh Cls; Cls Rep Soph Cls; Sec Jr Cls; Cl Rep Jr Cls; Band; Chrh Wkr; Lbry Ade; Pol Wkr; Sch Mus; Coll; Drama.

STUBBINS, TAMARA; Elmwood HS; Jerry City, OH; Cl Rep Jr Cls; Cls Rep Sr Cls; Chrs; Chrh Wkr; Hon Rl; Stu Cncl; Rptr Yrbk; Sch Nwsp; OEA; Sci Clb; Office Educ.

STUBBLEFIELD, BELINDA; Rochester HS; Rochester, MI; Cls Rep Sr Cls; Chrs; Drl Tm; Hon Rl; NHS; Stu Cncl; Trk; UCLA.

STUBBLEFIELD, CHERYL; St Ursula Academy; Toledo, OH; Pres Jr Cls; Hon Rl; Sec JA; Stu Cncl; Rptr Sch Nwsp; Fr Clb; JA Awd; Opt Clb Awd; Jr Achvmnt Of NW OH Sec Of Yr 78; Appntd Ed In Chf Fr Schl Newspr 79; Awd For Outstndg Achvmnt In Stdy 79; Univ; Jrnlsm.

STUBBLEFIELD, MICHAEL; Southwestern HS; Detroit, MI; Hon Rl; Off Ade; Yrbk; JA Awd; Natl Merit Ltr; Natl Merit Schl; Hon Roll Awd 78; Natl Mer Ltr 79; Natl Mert Schlshp 79; Michigan St Univ; Psych.

STUBBLES, DAVID; Boardman HS; Youngstown, OH; 5/558 Cl Rep Jr Cls; Cls Rep Sr Cls; Hon Rl; Pres Jr NHS; Pres NHS; Orch; Sch Mus; Stu Cncl; Yth Flsp; Pres Sci Clb; Duke; Medicine.

STUBBS, ERIC; Northern HS; Detroit, MI; 75/275 Aud/Vis; Boy Scts; Pres Chrh Wkr; Drl Tm; Pres FCA; ROTC; Treas Stu Cncl; Leo Clb; Pep Clb; Spn Clb; Eastern Mic; Law.

STUBE, KENNETH A; Charles S Mott HS; Warren, MI; NHS; College; Engr.

STUBENRAUCH, KAREN; Mc Auley HS; Cinti, OH; Hosp Ade; Sch Pl; Letter Swmmng; GAA; IM Sprt; Univ Of Cincinnati; Nursing.

STUBER, BARBARA; Williamston HS; Williamston, MI; 6/168 Chrs; Hon Rl; Off Ade; Trk; Tmr; Mic State College; Acctg.

STUCK, CURTIS; Waldron Area HS; Waldron, MI; Pres Jr Cls; Hon Rl; Sch Pl; VP Stu Cncl; Yth Flsp; Yrbk; Letter Bsbl; Letter Bsktbl; Letter Ftbl; Letter Trk; Voc Schl; Elec.

STUCK, SUSAN; Memorial HS; St Marys, OH; 22/240 Sec Band; Chrh Wkr; Hon Rl; Y-Teens; FHA; Pep Clb; Trk; GAA; IM Sprt; Natl Merit Schl; Whos Who Amng Amer HS Stu 77; Delegate To Nazarene World Yth Conf 78; Olivet Nazarene Coll; Eng Lit.

STUCKER, GARY; Edison Sr HS; Lake Station, IN; 3/180 Hon Rl; Spn Clb; JETS Awd; Perfect Attendance; Honor Roll; Purdue Univ; Engr.

STUCKER, VALORIE; Clay HS; S Bend, IN; Band; Chrh Wkr; Girl Scts; JA; Orch; Yth Flsp; 4-H; Lat Clb; Sci Clb; JA Awd; Purdue Univ; Chemistry.

STUCKEY, ANTOINETTE; Jare W Finney HS; Detroit, MI; Band; Chrs; Chrh Wkr; Hon Rl; JA; Sch Mus; Bsbl; GAA; Cit Awd; JA Awd; Bus Schl; Mgmt.

STUCKEY, DEAN; Hilltop HS; West Unity, OH; 13/69 Band; Chrs; Chrh Wkr; Cmnty Wkr; Orch; Sch Mus; Sch Pl; Stg Crw; Yth Flsp; Bsktbl; Band Serv Awd; Tech Schl.

STUCKEY, DIANE; North Central HS; Indianapolis, IN; 332/999 Band; Chrh Wkr; Girl Scts; Hon Rl; Lbry Ade; NHS; Sct Actv; OEA; Pep Clb; Pom Pon; Diplomat Awd St Women Awd & Ambassador Awd 78; Ball St Univ; Bus.

STUCKEY, DOUG; Port Clinton HS; Port Clinton, OH; Hon Rl; Crs Cntry; Capt Ten; College; Math.

STUCKEY, PAM; Hilltop HS; W Unity, OH; 7/72 Chrs; Chrh Wkr; Hon Rl; 4-H; Bsktbl; Letter Trk; Pres Awd; Volleyball; College; Math.

STUCKY, BRIAN; Valley Forge HS; Parma Hts, OH; 88/754 Cls Rep Frsh Cls; Cls Rep Soph Cls; Cl Rep Jr Cls; Cls Rep Sr Cls; Boy Scts; Chrh Wkr; Hon Rl; NHS; Sct Actv; Yth Flsp; Ohio Univ.

STUCKY, STEVEN; Goshen HS; Goshen, IN; 50/250 Band; Hon Rl; Orch; Red Cr Ade; Stg Crw; Yth Flsp; Swmmng; IM Sprt; Univ.

STUCKY, WANDA; Garaway HS; New Phila, OH; Cl Rep Jr Cls; Chrh Wkr; Hon Rl; Stu Cncl; 4-H; Pep Clb; Spn Clb; Letter Gym; Letter Trk; Chrldng; 1st Pl Algebra 78; Univ; Health Tchr.

STUCZYNSKI, KATHLEEN; Holy Name Nazareth HS; Garfield Hts, OH; 30/300 Hon Rl; Jr NHS; Bsktbl; Coach Actv; IM Sprt; Michigan St Univ; Math.

STUDEBAKER, BRENDA; Northrop HS; Ft Wayne, IN; 117/554 Band; Girl Scts; Orch; Sch Mus; Yth Flsp; Spn Clb; Ten; Trk;.

STUDENER, JEANETTE; Ferndale HS; Ferndale, MI; 3/383 Band; Hon Rl; NHS; Orch; Univ Of Michigan; Architecture.

STUDENIC, ROBERT; Norton HS; Norton, OH; Jr NHS; College; Math.

STUDER, DAN; Homestead HS; Roanoke, IN; 22/248 Chrh Wkr; Hon Rl; Jr NHS; OEA; IM Sprt; 2nd In Bus Math OEA Regional Contest 79; 2nd High Acctg I Grade 77; High Consideration In Drafting Cont 77; Data Proc.

STUDER, DOUG; Buckeye Central HS; New Washington, OH; 15/100 Boy Scts; Chrh Wkr; Hon Rl; Red Cr Ade; Sch Pl; Bsbl; Bsktbl; Letter Ftbl; Glf; IM Sprt; Ohio St Univ; Archt Engr.

STUDER, JEFFREY; Little Miami HS; Pleasant Plains, OH; Hon Rl; Pol Wkr; Fr Clb; IM Sprt; Ohio State; Bus.

STUDER, KAREN; Onsted HS; Onsted, MI; 11/129 Band; Girl Scts; Hon Rl; Hosp Ade; Off Ade; 4-H; FFA; Jackson Comm College.

STUDER, KIMBERLY; River Valley HS; Marion, OH; 1/200 Am Leg Aux Girls St; Chrh Wkr; Hon Rl; NHS; Stu Cncl; Letter Ten; Letter Trk; Chrldng; College; Pre Med.

STUDER, LAURA; Wapakoneta HS; Cridersvll, OH; Girl Scts; Hon Rl; Lbry Ade; 4-H; FHA; 4-H Awd; Ohi State; Bus.

STUDER, LOUIS O; Cardinal Ritter HS; Indianapolis, IN; Band; Chrs; Chrh Wkr; Hon Rl; Mdrgl; MMM; Sch Mus; Stg Crw;.

STUDT, TIMOTHY D; Henry Ford II HS; Sterling Hts, MI; Chrs; Chrh Wkr; Yth Flsp; Capt Socr; Trk; Ferris St Univ; Pre Med.

STUEBER, TONI; Theodore Roosevelt HS; Kent, OH; Cmp Fr Grls; Chrs; Hon Rl; Off Ade; Spn Clb; IM Sprt; Vocational School; Medical Aide.

STUERZENBERGER, RON; Solon HS; Solon, OH; AFS; Boy Scts; FCA; Ftbl; Letter Trk; IM Sprt; College.

STUHAN, JUDY; Mona Shores HS; Muskegon, MI; NHS; PAVAS; Sch Pl; Stg Crw; Sec Drama Clb; Cit Awd; College; Computer Science.

STUIVE, LAURIE; Calvin Chr HS; Wyoming, MI; Cls Rep Soph Cls; Pres Jr Cls; Pres Sr Cls; Band; Hon Rl; NHS; Orch; College; Med.

STUKEY, LORRAINE; Hilliard HS; Amlin, OH; Hon Rl; FNA; Spn Clb; Columbus Tech Inst; Med.

STULL, JOANNE; Danville HS; Glenmont, OH; Band; Debate Tm; Off Ade; Sch Mus; Sch Pl; Stg Crw; Treas Drama Clb; VP 4-H; Fr Clb; College; Graphic Art.

STULL, SANDY; Calhoun County HS; Grantsville, WV; Cls Rep Frsh Cls; Band; Cmp Fr Grls; Chrs; Chrh Wkr; Cmnty Wkr; FCA; Girl Scts; Hon Rl; Off Ade; Fairmont St Coll; Phys Ed.

STULL, SUSAN; Edward Drummond Libbey HS; Toledo, OH; 3/297 Hon Rl; NHS; Sch Nwsp; Phoenix Proj 76; Quiz Bowl 76; Explorers 76; Harvard Coll; Poli Sci.

STULLENBARGER, RITA; Elk Garden HS; Elk Garden, WV; 1/21 Sec Sr Cls; Val; Chrs; Hon Rl; Lbry Ade; Sch Pl; Drama Clb; Pep Clb; Chrldng; Voice Dem Awd; Schlrshp From D & L Coal Co 1979; Senator Robert Byrd Svngs Bond; Univ; Sec.

STULL JR, WILLIAM; Maplewood HS; Cortland, OH; Band; Boy Scts; Chrh Wkr; Cmnty Wkr; Hon Rl; Sct Actv; Beta Clb; VICA; Bsktbl; Trk; Kent State Univ; Elec Engr.

STULTS, EVAN; John Glenn HS; New Concord, OH; 1/193 Pres Frsh Cls; Cl Rep Jr Cls; AFS; VP Chrs; Hon Rl; VP NHS; Sch Mus; Stu Cncl; Yth Flsp; Fr Clb; College; Music.

STULTZ, CECIL; John Hay HS; Cleveland, OH; 2/357 Sal; Hon Rl; Sec Jr NHS; NHS; VP Stu Cncl; Yrbk; Sch Nwsp; Cit Awd; Oberlin Coll; Studio Art.

STULTZ, KENNETH R; Wayne HS; Lavalette, WV; Trs Jr Cls; Band; Chrs; Drm Mjrt; Hon Rl; NHS; Sch Mus; Glf; All St Choir 78; All St Band 78 & 79; Marshall Univ; Med Tech.

STULTZ, KIMBER; North Union HS; Magnetic Spg, OH; Band; Chrh Wkr; Hon Rl; Hosp Ade; Lbry Ade; NHS; Yth Flsp; Rptr Sch Nwsp; 4-H; Pep Clb; Marion Tech College; Rn.

STULTZ, SHIRL; North Union HS; Magnetic Spgs, OH; Band; Drm Mjrt; Hon Rl; Lbry Ade; NHS; Orch; Rptr Sch Nwsp; 4-H; 4-H Awd;.

STUMBAUGH, KELLY; Lexington HS; Lexington, OH; Band; Chrh Wkr; Cmnty Wkr; Girl Scts; Quill & Scroll; Sct Actv; Pres 4-H; Fr Clb; 4-H Awd; Massfield Symphny Soc Inc Spec Recgntn 79; Art Cls Public Disply In Massfield Mall 78 & 79; Ohio St Univ; Psych.

STUMBO, LORI; Benjamin Logan HS; W Mansfield, OH; Am Leg Aux Girls St; Band; Chrh Wkr; Cmnty Wkr; Girl Scts; Hon Rl; NHS; Sct Actv; Yth Flsp; Yrbk; Awrd Of Merit French I 77; Awrd Of Schlrshp Typing I 78; Tech Schl; Cmmrcl Art.

STUMP, ALBERT; Dunbar HS; Dunbar, WV; Hon Rl; Mod UN; NHS; Mth Clb; Bsktbl; Crs Cntry; IM Sprt; Sr Cnslr Of Herbert H Jarrett Chaptr Of De Molay 79; 1st Plc St Sheetmetal Proj 78; French Hon Soc 78; West Virginia Inst Of Tech; Cvl Engr.

STUMP, DEBBIE; Licking Cnty Joint Voc HS; Hebron, OH; Hst Jr Cls; Cmp Fr Grls; Chrh Wkr; Girl Scts; Sch Pl; Yth Flsp; Sch Nwsp; OEA; Mt Vernon Nazarene Coll.

STUMP, DEBBIE; Brookhaven HS; Columbus, OH; Band; Drm Mjrt; Girl Scts; Hon Rl; Sch Pl; Stu Cncl; Chrldng; Twrlr; Ohio St Univ; Interior Dsgn.

STUMP, DENISE; Sturgis HS; Sturgis, MI; Band; Hon Rl; NHS; Orch; Sch Mus; Sch Pl; Rotary Awd; Western Mic Univ; Music Ed.

STUMP, KYM; Northridge HS; Bristol, IN; 16/144 Cmp Fr Grls; Chrs; Chrh Wkr; Drl Tm; Hon Rl; Lbry Ade; NHS; Sch Pl; Stg Crw; Rptr Yrbk; Coll; Doctor.

STUMP, LORI; Marysville HS; Marysville, MI; 18/173 Band; Hon Rl; Hosp Ade; NHS; Stu Cncl; OEA; Spn Clb; Bsbl; Trk; Mat Maids; St Clair Co Comm Coll; Bus.

STUMP, RANDALL L; Churubusco HS; Churubusco, IN; 1/145 Am Leg Boys St; Band; Chrh Wkr; Hon Rl; NHS; Orch; Sch Mus; Sch Pl; Yth Flsp; Rptr Yrbk; 4th Dst Congressional Stdnt Prog; Perfect Attndce; St Level Nisbova Solo; Univ Of Notre Dame; Archt.

STUPICA, TERRI; Euclid HS; Euclid, OH; 56/747 Band; Hon Rl; NHS; Pep Clb; Ftbl; Mgrs; Tmr; Ohi State; Law.

STUPLIN, MARK; Holy Name HS; Brook Park, OH; Chrh Wkr; Hon Rl; JA; Cleveland Inst Of Art; Comm Art.

STURGEON, CINDY; South Point HS; South Point, OH; Cmp Fr Grls; Hon Rl; Jr NHS; Sch Pl; OEA; Pep Clb; Ohio Univ HS Schlr; College.

STURGILL, TODD; Columbia City Joint HS; Columbia City, IN; 64/256 Cls Rep Frsh Cls; Cls Rep Soph Cls; Cl Rep Jr Cls; Rptr Yrbk; Rptr Sch Nwsp; DECA; Ger Clb; Univ; Humanities.

STURIS, ILZE; Winston Churchill HS; Westland, MI; Pres Orch; Sci Clb; Swmmng; GAA; Mgrs; Soc Studies Hnr Music Hnr Alma Fresh Talent Awd In Music; Alma Pres Schlrshp; Mich Competitive Schlrshp; Alma Coll; Busns Admin.

STURM, JAMES; Crum HS; Crum, WV; 4/40 Hst Jr Cls; Band; Hon Rl; NHS; Beta Clb; IM Sprt; Navy.

STURM, NATHAN; Anderson Sr HS; Cincinnati, OH; 97/378 Band; Chrh Wkr; Lbry Ade; Lit Mag; Orch; Sch Mus; Rptr Sch Nwsp; Sch Pl; Lat Clb; Rdo Clb; Univ; History.

STURONAS, JOSEPH; Gavit HS; Hammond, IN; Hon Rl; Jr NHS; VP Sci Clb; Letter Crs Cntry; Letter Trk; Indiana Univ; Meteorology.

STURR, TOMAS; Pentwater HS; Pentwater, MI; Letter Bsbl; Letter Bsktbl; Western Mic Univ; Architecture.

STURTEVANT, BRIAN; Ravenna HS; Ravenna, MI; Boy Scts; Chrh Wkr; Sct Actv; Ftbl; Wrstlng; Michigan St Univ; History.

STURTZ, DAVID; Austintown Fitch HS; Austintown, OH; Boy Scts; Sct Actv; Ger Clb; Trk; Wrstlng; IM Sprt; U S Coast Guard Academy.

STUTER, ROBERT K; Winfield HS; Scott Depot, WV; VP Soph Cls; FCA; Hon Rl; Jr NHS; Beta Clb; Mth Clb; Pep Clb; Spn Clb; Letter Ftbl; Letter Trk; Soc Dstngshd Amer HS Stu; Tech Inst; Mech Engr.

STUTEVILLE, DAVID; Harrison HS; Evansville, IN; Cls Rep Soph Cls; Cl Rep Jr Cls; Sal; Hon Rl; Stu Cncl; Sch Nwsp; Letter Bsbl; Letter Bsktbl; Univ; Engr.

STUTEVILLE, K; Mason HS; Mason, MI; Chrs; Hon Rl; Fr Clb; Bsktbl; Trk; Tmr; Mis Univ; English.

STUTLER, BETH; Point Pleasant HS; Pt Pleasant, WV; 75/209 Cls Rep Soph Cls; Cl Rep Jr Cls; Cls Rep Sr Cls; Band; Girl Scts; Sct Actv; Stu Cncl; VP Keyettes; GAA; Twrlr; Parkersburg Cmnty Coll; Dent Asst.

STUTLER, BETH; Rockville Jr Sr HS; Rockville, IN; FCA; Hon Rl; NHS; Sch Pl; Sch Nwsp; Treas Drama Clb; Pres 4-H; VP FFA; Bsktbl; Letter Trk; 1st Dist 2nd St Frshmn Pub Speaking FFA; Blue Ribbon Grp 4 H St Pub Speaking; FFA Hoosier Farmer Degree; Purdue Univ; Agri Ed.

STUTLER, KURT; South Ripley HS; Versailles, IN; Band; Chrs; Chrh Wkr; Hon Rl; Sch Mus; Yrbk; Ed Sch Nwsp; Spn Clb; Scr Kpr; Lion Awd; College.

STUTSMAN, BECKY; Scottsburg HS; Scottsburg, IN; 8/250 NHS; Sch Pl; Drama Clb; VP Fr Clb; Pep Clb; Letter Ten; In Univ; Political Sci.

STUVEL, C; Atherton HS; Burton, MI; Band; Chrh Wkr; Girl Scts; Hon Rl; Quill & Scroll; Sch Pl; Sct Actv; Yth Flsp; Rptr Sch Nwsp; Sch Nwsp; Univ Of Michigan; Art.

STYDNICKI, CHERYL; Lorain Catholic HS; Lorain, OH; Hon Rl; DECA; Letter Chrldng; PPFtbl; Lorain Cnty Community Coll.

STYER, JOY L; Kenton Sr HS; Kenton, OH; Am Leg Aux Girls St; Chrs; Hon Rl; Lbry Ade; Stu Cncl; VP Yth Flsp; Rptr Yrbk; FHA; Pep Clb; Letter IM Sprt; Ohio St Univ; Econ.

STYERS, TAMMI; Buckeye Valley HS; Delaware, OH; Trs Jr Cls; Pres Sr Cls; Band; Chrs; Chrh Wkr; Girl Scts; Hon Rl; Jr NHS; NHS; Off Ade; Secret Spirit Awd; Most Improved Jr; Univ; Coach.

STYLES, RUSTY A; Warsaw Community HS; Warsaw, IN; 6/360 Chrh Wkr; Hon Rl; Rotary Awd; Wabash College; Math.

SUAREZ, CRISTINA; Southwestern HS; Madison, IN; 1/100 VP Soph Cls; Am Leg Aux Girls St; Band; Drl Tm; Girl Scts; Hon Rl; Sec NHS; Pres Yth Flsp; Ed Sch Nwsp; Rptr Sch Nwsp; Univ; Math.

SUAREZ, DEIDRE; Cameron HS; Cameron, WV; 39/110 FHA; Mat Maids; Scr Kpr; Belmont Tech Schl; Jrnlsm.

SUBLER, BONNIE; Covington HS; Bradford, OH; Am Leg Aux Girls St; Band; Stu Cncl; Yrbk; 4-H; 4-H Awd; Univ Of Dayton; Law.

SUBOSKI, R; Kalkaska HS; Rapid City, MI; Girl Scts; Hon Rl; Off Ade; Sch Pl; Sct Actv; Chrldng; GAA; Mich State.

SUCAET, MICHAEL; St Clement HS; Warren, MI; Sec Frsh Cls; Cl Rep Jr Cls; Hon Rl; NHS; Ed Yrbk; Beta Clb; Drama Clb; Bsktbl; Ftbl; Trk; Univ.

SUCCI, DIANA; Ashtabula Cnty Jt Voc HS; Jefferson, OH; 7/198 AFS; Band; Hon Rl; NHS; Orch; OEA; Chrldng; 4th Pl Keypunch Region II Competition; 7th Pl Keypunch St Competition; College.

SUCHECKI, TODD M; Grand Ledge HS; Lansing, MI; 29/416 Hon Rl; Jr NHS; NHS; Yrbk; Michigan Tech Univ; Elec Engr.

SUCHODOLSKI, ANTHONY; Micheal H Hamady HS; Flint, MI; NHS; Letter Bsbl; Letter Ftbl; Carpenter.

SUCHOSKI, JON; Catholic Central HS; Steubenville, OH; Chrh Wkr; FCA; Sch Mus; Letter Ftbl; IM Sprt; College; Aero Engr.

SUCHOSKI, LISA; Steubenville Cath Ctrl HS; Steubenvill, OH; 9/204 Girl Scts; Hosp Ade; NHS; Spn Clb; Bsktbl; Univ; Nursing.

SUCK, JOE; Warren Local HS; Belpre, OH; Chrs; Chrh Wkr; Hon Rl; NHS; Sch Mus; Fr Clb; Mth Clb; Pep Clb; Sci Clb; Bsktbl; Ohio Univ; Elec Engr.

SUCKOW, CHARLES; Marquette Sr HS; Marquette, MI; 18/418 Chrh Wkr; Debate Tm; Kiwan Awd; Natl Merit Ltr; L G Kaufmna Sclshp 79; Awd Eagle Scout 79; Sr Patrol Leadr 75 79; Jr Asst Scoutmaster 79; Northern Michigan Univ; Bio.

SUCKOW, PAUL; North Muskegon HS; N Muskegon, MI; 2/108 Band; Chrs; Chrh Wkr; Hon Rl; NHS; Orch; PAVAS; Sch Mus; Yth Flsp; Ger Clb; HS TV Quizbowl Team; Full Schlrshp For 4 Consecutive Yrs At Blue Lake Fine Arts; College; Aeronautical Engr.

SUCRE, YONTZ; Fairmont West HS; Kettering, OH; 47/494 Band; Hon Rl; Natl Merit Ltr; Mich St Solo 78; Chem Awd 78; Schl Math Lge Awd 1st 79; Ohio St Univ; Elec Engr.

SUCRO, MARCUS; Wayne HS; Dayton, OH; Hon Rl; Jr NHS; NHS; Ger Clb; Ohi State Univ; Pre Med.

SUDDUTH, SHERRYL; Fairmont West HS; Kettering, OH; 186/494 Chrs; Hon Rl; Sch Mus; Lat Clb; Coll.

SUDO, JONATHON; Clawson HS; Clawson, MI; 116/299 Cmnty Wkr; Hon Rl; Pep Clb; Letter Bsbl; Natl Merit Schl; St Of Michigan Competitive Schlrshp; Oakland Univ; Elec Engr.

SUESSMUTH, MARILYN; Garber HS; Essexville, MI; 30/170 Band; Chrs; Chrh Wkr; Cmnty Wkr; Hon Rl; Sch Mus; Sch Pl; Stg Crw; Yth Flsp; Bsktbl; Univ; Bus.

SUEVER, DEBRA; Quincy HS; Quincy, MI; 2/118 Cls Rep Frsh Cls; Sec Soph Cls; Cl Rep Jr Cls; Am Leg Aux Girls St; Hon Rl; NHS; Stu Cncl; Yrbk; Rptr Sch Nwsp; 4-H; Serve Exec Comm Of Natl Hon Soc 78; Comm Chrprsn Youth In Govt Convntn At St 79; Active Mbr Youth Govt 79; Indiana Univ; Health.

SUEVER, DOUG; Aulney HS; Quincy, MI; 24/127 Cls Rep Frsh Cls; Band; Sch Nwsp; 4-H; Bsktbl; Glf; Mgrs; Elk Awd; 4-H Awd; Lion Awd; Oakland Univ; Acctg.

SUEVER, JEANNE; St John HS; Delphos, OH; 1/135 Cl Rep Jr Cls; Aud/Vis; Hon Rl; Pres NHS; Sch Mus; Sch Pl; Stu Cncl; Ed Sch Nwsp; Fr Clb; Bausch & Lomb Awd; Univ Of Cincinnati; Elec Engr.

SUGG, ELIZABETH; Berkley HS; Hunt Wds, MI; Cls Rep Frsh Cls; Northern Michigan Univ; Sci.

SUGO, LOUIS; Cabrini HS; Allen Pk, MI; Hon Rl; Sct Actv; Rptr Yrbk; Pres Civ Clb; Letter Ftbl; Letter Trk; Coach Actv; IM Sprt; College; Communications.

SUHADOLNIK, JACQUELINE; Lake Catholic HS; Mentor, OH; Hon Rl; NHS; Rptr Yrbk; Pep Clb; IM Sprt; Univ Of Cincinnati; Fshn Dsgn.

SUHOVECKY, MICHAEL; Ursuline HS; Youngstown, OH; 31/300 Band; Boy Scts; Debate Tm; Hon Rl; Lbry Ade; MMM; Treas Natl Forn Lg; Ger Clb; Univ; Bus Admin.

SUHRE, KERBY; St Agatha HS; Detroit, MI; Hon Rl; Rptr Yrbk; Drama Clb;.

SUHY, PEGGY; St Clement HS; Warren, MI; 27/114 Cls Rep Frsh Cls; Cls Rep Soph Cls; Cls Rep Sr Cls; Sch Pl; Stu Cncl; Rptr Yrbk; Drama Clb; Chrldng; Mgrs; Ross Med Educ Ctr; Med Asst.

SUK CHOI, HYUN; St Ursula Acad; Toledo, OH; Chrs; Hon Rl; Sch Mus; Ed Yrbk; Ger Clb; Univ; Music.

SULIN, RICH; Nordonia Sr HS; Northfield, OH; Band; Hon Rl; Sch Mus; Ten; Voice Dem Awd; St Dept Of Ed; Ohio Cncl Of Teachers Of Math; Tennis Awds; Band Cert; College; Electronics.

SULISZ, SUSAN; Dearborn HS; Deaborn, MI; Sec Frsh Cls; Sec Soph Cls; Sec Jr Cls; Pres Sr Cls; Chrs; Cmnty Wkr; Girl Scts; Hon Rl; Alma College; Bio.

SULKO, KIMBERLY; Coloma HS; Coloma, MI; Girl Scts; NHS; Off Ade; 4-H; Pep Clb; Gym; Letter Trk; Coach Actv; Scr Kpr; Univ.

SULKOWSKI, NANCY; St Andrew HS; Detroit, MI; 1/109 Chrs; Hon Rl; NHS; Yrbk; Bsbl; Bsktbl; Coach Actv; Wayne St Univ; Vet Sci.

SULLIVAN, ANDREW; East Kentwood HS; Kentwood, MI; Letter Swmmng; Coach Actv; Univ; Poli Sci.

SULLIVAN, BARBARA; Willard HS; Willard, OH; 45/187 Cls Rep Frsh Cls; Am Leg Aux Girls St; Chrs; Chrh Wkr; Girl Scts; Sch Mus; Sch Pl; Ed Yrbk; Rptr Yrbk; Spn Clb; Wright St Univ; Theatre.

SULLIVAN, BECKY; Pt Pleasant HS; Leon, WV; Band; Cmnty Wkr; Hon Rl; NHS; Sch Mus; Civ Clb; Majorette 80; Hi Y Hist; Yth In Gvt Prog 79; St Marys Schl Of Nursing; Nursing.

SULLIVAN, CAROL; Bay HS; Bay Vil, OH; 26/375 Chrs; NHS; Quill & Scroll; Sch Mus; Stu Cncl; Ed Sch Nwsp; Sprt Ed Sch Nwsp; Sch Nwsp; Pep Clb; Capt Chrldng; Univ; Jrnlsm.

SULLIVAN, CHRIS; Tecumseh HS; Tecumseh, MI; 30/236 VP Frsh Cls; Cls Rep Soph Cls; Boy Scts; Hon Rl; NHS; Sct Actv; Stu Cncl; Letter Crs Cntry; Letter Trk; IM Sprt; Michigan Tech Univ; Forestry.

SULLIVAN, CHRIS; St Joseph HS; Euclid, OH; 35/300 Trs Jr Cls; Sec Sr Cls; Boy Scts; Hon Rl; Stu Cncl; Ger Clb; Letter Crs Cntry; Capt Wrstlng; Letter Chrldng; Cleveland St Univ; Comp Analist.

SULLIVAN, CRAIG D; Clay HS; Portsmouth, OH; 1/60 Am Leg Boys St; Band; Chrs; Chrh Wkr; Hon Rl; Lbry Ade; NHS; Rptr Yrbk; College; Acctg.

SULLIVAN, DONALD; Stryker HS; Stryker, OH; 25/58 Band; Chrh Wkr; Yth Flsp; Pep Clb; Bsbl; Bsktbl; Crs Cntry; Carpentry.

SULLIVAN, JAMES; Terre Haute North Vigo HS; Terre Haute, IN; 81/600 Key Clb; Letter Crs Cntry; Trk;.

SULLIVAN, JANET; Plymouth Salem HS; Plymouth Twp, MI; 19/540 CAP; Girl Scts; Hon Rl; Lbry Ade; NHS; Kiwan Awd; Natl Merit Ltr; Purdue Univ; Pre Med.

SULLIVAN, JERRY G; Eastern Pulaski Cmnty Schl; Winamac, IN; Cls Rep Frsh Cls; Hon Rl; Jr NHS; Sct Actv; Stu Cncl; FFA; Pep Clb; Letter Bsbl; Bsktbl; Letter Ftbl; Purdue Univ; Agri Engr.

SULLIVAN, JOHN C; Cincinnati Country Day Schl; Cincinnati, OH; Cmnty Wkr; Hon Rl; Stg Crw; Rus Clb; Univ; Bus.

SULLIVAN, JOHN J; St Xavier HS; Cincinnati, OH; 29/300 Hon Rl; Jr NHS; Mod UN; NHS; Stg Crw; Rptr Sch Nwsp; Letter Ftbl; Natl Merit SF; Med.

SULLIVAN, KATHLEEN; Turpin HS; Cincinnati, OH; 3/357 Sal; Chrh Wkr; Hon Rl; Hosp Ade; NHS; Sch Pl; FHA; Capt Chrldng; GAA; IM Sprt; Miami Univ; Psych.

SULLIVAN, KENNETH; Lake Catholic HS; Wickliffe, OH; Band; Hon Rl; Red Cr Ade; IM Sprt; Ohi State.

SULLIVAN, LORA; Father Joseph Wehrle HS; Columbus, OH; 3/137 Band; Hon Rl; Jr NHS; GAA; College; Natural Resources.

SULLIVAN, MARGARET; St Mary Of Redford HS; Detroit, MI; 15/160 Hon Rl; NHS; Stu Cncl; Sch Nwsp; Natl Merit SF; Albion Coll; Law.

SULLIVAN, MARGUERITE; Wellsville HS; Wellsville, OH; Am Leg Aux Girls St; Hon Rl; NHS; Y-Teens; FNA; FTA; Pep Clb; Am Leg Awd; Mbr 78 79 Jr Sr Prom Court 79; Nike Club 79 80; Kent St Univ; Speech.

SULLIVAN, MARY; Luther L Wright HS; Ironwood, MI; Girl Scts; Hon Rl; Fr Clb; Pep Clb; Chrldng; Gogebic Comm Coll; Phys Therapy.

SULLIVAN, MARY L; Springfld Catholic Ctrl HS; Springfield, OH; VP Frsh Cls; Cls Rep Soph Cls; Cl Rep Jr Cls; Chrh Wkr; Stu Cncl; 4-H; Lat Clb; Chrldng; IM Sprt; 4-H Awd; Univ; Nursing.

SULLIVAN, MELISSA; Taylor HS; Cleves, OH; Chrs; JA; PAVAS; Stg Crw; Rptr Sch Nwsp; Drama Clb; Pep Clb; Cit Awd; Coll Of Mt St Joseph; Art.

SULLIVAN, MOLLY; Bishop Foley HS; Royal Oak, MI; B Girl Scts; Hon Rl; Rptr Yrbk; Rptr Sch Nwsp; Fr Clb; Chrldng; Michigan State.

SULLIVAN, MONICA; L Anse HS; Lanse, MI; 10/200 Am Leg Aux Girls St; Band; Chrs; Chrh Wkr; Cmnty Wkr; Hon Rl; Natl Forn Lg; Cit Awd; DAR Awd; Voice Dem Awd; Eastern Michigan Univ; Music.

SULLIVAN, MORTIMER J; Archbishop Alter HS; Kettering, OH; Cl Rep Jr Cls; Boy Scts; Rdo Clb; Ftbl; Hockey; Trk; Georgetown Univ; MBA.

SULLIVAN, PAT; Carroll HS; Dayton, OH; Aud/Vis; Hon Rl; Stu Cncl; Sprt Ed Sch Nwsp; Letter Bsktbl; Letter Ftbl; Letter Trk; Natl Merit Ltr; College; Law.

SULLIVAN, PATRICIA; Maumee HS; Maumee, OH; 60/334 Hon Rl; Y-Teens; Spn Clb; IM Sprt; PPFtbl; Purdue Univ; Med.

SULLIVAN, PATRICIA; Scecina Memorial HS; Indianapolis, IN; Chrs; Hon Rl; Sec JA; Sch Mus; Drama Clb; College.

SULLIVAN, PETER; Bishop Watterson HS; Worthington, OH; Boy Scts; Hon Rl; Sch Nwsp; Bsktbl; Crs Cntry; Letter Trk; IM Sprt; Natl Merit Ltr; College; Bus.

SULLIVAN, ROBERT S; Portsmouth East HS; Wheelersburg, OH; Boy Scts; Chrs; Sch Mus; Sct Actv; Yrbk; Lat Clb; Ftbl; Mgrs; Coll; Med.

SULLIVAN, STEVEN; Cass Technical HS; Detroit, MI; Hon Rl; Gym; Michigan St Univ; Bus Comp Prog.

SULLIVAN, SUSAN; Churchill HS; Livonia, MI; Off Ade; Sci Clb; Swmmng; Letter Ten; Letter Trk; Univ Of Michigan; Engr.

SULLIVAN, SUSAN; Oakridge HS; Muskegon, MI; Hon Rl; Jr NHS; Bsktbl; Muskegon Comm College; Acctg.

SULLIVAN, SUSAN; Willard HS; Willard, OH; Chrs; Chrh Wkr; Girl Scts; Jr NHS; Sch Mus; Sch Pl; Stg Crw; Rptr Yrbk; Scr Kpr; Cit Awd; Nursing Schl; Nursing.

SULLIVAN, TERESA; Stryker HS; Bryan, OH; 19/50 Band; Hon Rl; 4-H; FHA; Univ.

SULLIVAN, TERRENCE; Niles HS; Niles, MI; Hon Rl; JA; Red Cr Ade; Y-Teens; Swmmng; Coach Actv; IM Sprt; Natl Merit Ltr; Natl Merit Schl; Adrian Coll; Bus Admin.

SULLIVAN, TIM; Westfall HS; Mt Sterling, OH; Band; Chrs; Chrh Wkr; Drm Bgl; Hon Rl; Lbry Ade; Orch; Stg Crw; Pep Clb; Bsbl; Ohio State Univ; Bus.

SULLIVAN, TIMOTHY; St Charles Prep; Upper Arlington, OH; Trs Jr Cls; Am Leg Boys St; Chrh Wkr; Cmnty Wkr; Hon Rl; NHS; Stu Cncl; Rptr Yrbk; Socr; Capt Ten; Univ; Pre Law.

SULLIVAN, TRESA; South Central HS; Elizabeth, IN; Band; Chrs; Drl Tm; Hon Rl; Lbry Ade; Lit Mag; Yrbk; Sch Nwsp; Pep Clb; IM Sprt; Bus Schl; Sec.

SULPIZIO, GLENN; Defiance HS; Defiance, OH; Band; Boy Scts; Hon Rl; Sch Mus; Bowling Green St Univ; Medicine.

SULT, TODD; Barr Reeve HS; Loogootee, IN; VP Soph Cls; Pres Jr Cls; Cl Rep Jr Cls; Pres Sr Cls; Cls Rep Sr Cls; Aud/Vis; Chrh Wkr; Ind State Univ; Math.

SULZER, GERTRUDE; St Augustine Acad; Cleveland, OH; 1/132 Val; NHS; Chrldng; Coach Actv; Case Western Reserve Univ; Accountin.

SUMAN, MELANIE; Onekama HS; Manistee, MI; Band; Lbry Ade; Sch Mus; Sch Pl; Stg Crw; Drama Clb; West Shore Cmnty Coll; Bus.

SUMBERA, KELLENE; Chesaning Union HS; Chesaning, MI; 7/258 Aud/Vis; Hon Rl; NHS; Rptr Sch Nwsp; Mic State; Commrcl Art.

SUMKIN, THEODORE; High School; Canton, OH; Hon Rl; Capt Ten; College; Med.

SUMMER, DAVID; Willowrun HS; Ypsilanti, MI; 8/200 Hon Rl; Letter Crs Cntry; Letter Swmmng; Capt Trk; College; Elec Engr.

SUMMERS, ALLEN; Brandywine HS; Niles, MI; Hon Rl; Pol Wkr; Letter Crs Cntry; Gym; Letter Trk; Athltc Schslhp 79; Mi Dept Of Edud Awd 79; Southwestern Michigan Univ; Forestry.

SUMMERS, BECKY; Roosevelt Wilson HS; Stonewood, WV; VP Frsh Cls; Cls Rep Soph Cls; Pres Sr Cls; Hon Rl; Sec NHS; Sch Pl; Y-Teens; Yrbk; Leo Clb; Pep Clb; Fairmont Coll; Busns.

SUMMERS, BOBBI J; Loogootee HS; Loogootee, IN; Band; Girl Scts; Hon Rl; Stu Cncl; Ed Yrbk; FHA; Pep Clb; IM Sprt; Vincennes Univ; Phys Ther.

SUMMERS, DOUGLAS; Loogootee HS; Loogootee, IN; Band; Chrh Wkr; 4-H; Pep Clb; Bsbl; Bsktbl; Mgrs; 4-H Awd; Univ Of Evansville; Mech Engr.

SUMMERS, KAREN; Tuslaw HS; No Lawrence, OH; 23/183 Band; Chrs; Hon Rl; NHS; Sch Mus; Y-Teens; General Office Work.

SUMMERS, PAMELA; Bishop Foley HS; Detroit, MI; Hon Rl; Orch; Lat Clb; Cit Awd; Univ Of Michigan; Med.

SUMMIT, PAUL; North Knox HS; Sandborn, IN; Chrh Wkr; FCA; Hon Rl; Sch Pl; Yrbk; Fr Clb; Bsbl; Oakland City College; Art.

SUMMONS, BARBARA; Hillsdale HS; Hillsdale, MI; 1/185 Val; Chrs; Girl Scts; Hon Rl; NHS; Sch Mus; Sct Actv; PPFtbl; Mic State Univ; Comp Sci.

SUMNER, LAURA; Aquinas HS; Lincoln Park, MI; Cmnty Wkr; Hon Rl; Sch Mus; Sch Pl; Stg Crw; Rptr Sch Nwsp; Sec Drama Clb; Univ Of Michigan; Phys Ther.

SUMNER, REBECCA; Castle HS; Chandler, IN; 20/429 VP Soph Cls; Girl Scts; Hon Rl; Hosp Ade; JA; NHS; Sch Mus; Sch Pl; Stg Crw; Stu Cncl; Indiana St Univ; Radiologic Tech.

SUMNER, SCOTT; Midpark HS; Middleburg Hgts, OH; Band; Boy Scts; Chrs; Chrh Wkr; Hon Rl; Orch; Sch Mus; Sch Pl; Sct Actv; Ger Clb; John Phillip Sousa Bnd Awd; Eagle Scout; College; Music.

SUMNER, TERRI; Parkersburg South HS; Parkersburg, WV; Chrs; Hon Rl; Yth Flsp; FTA; West Virginia Inst Of Tech; Engr.

SUNBERG, MICHELE; Mcnicholas HS; Cincinnati, OH; 72/218 Hon Rl; Y-Teens; Clermont Tech.

SUND, DOUGLAS; Maumee HS; Maumee, OH; Chrs; Bsbl; Bsktbl; Ftbl; Toledo Univ; Comp.

SUNDAY, BECKY; Withrow HS; Cincinnati, OH; Chrs; Off Ade; Pol Wkr; Sch Pl; Stu Cncl; Sch Nwsp; DECA; Drama Clb; Trk; Cit Awd; Univ Of Cincinnati; Drama.

SUNDBERG, JEAN; Holton HS; Twin Lake, MI; 5/80 Am Leg Aux Girls St; Hon Rl; NHS; Stg Crw; Stu Cncl; Pep Clb; Bsktbl; Trk; Chrldng; Mgrs; Alma Univ; CPA.

SUNDBERG, VAUGHN; Hubbard HS; Hubbard, OH; 9/314 Hon Rl; College; Elec Engr.

SUNDBLAD, HEIDI; Ishpeming HS; Ishpeming, MI; 6/137 Pres Frsh Cls; Cl Rep Jr Cls; Cls Rep Sr Cls; Band; Hon Rl; NHS; Letter Bsktbl; Letter Trk; Cit Awd; Pres Awd; Northern Michigan Univ; Sci.

SUNDQUIST, SUSAN; West Ottawa HS; Holland, MI; Hon Rl; Pres 4-H; Lat Clb; Swmmng; Tmr; 4-H Awd; Michigan St Univ; Vet Tech.

SUNENBERG, BERNARD; Moeller HS; Cincinnati, OH; Band; Boy Scts; Hon Rl; Stg Crw; Univ Of Cincinnati; Music Educ.

SUNNENBERG, MARCIA; Deer Park HS; Cincinnati, OH; Cmp Fr Grls; Hon Rl; NHS; Pres GAA; College.

SUN YEE, LAI SUN; Walnut Hills HS; Cincinnati, OH; Hon Rl; Pol Wkr; Sch Pl; Ed Sch Nwsp; Rptr Sch Nwsp; Sch Nwsp; Oh Achvmnt Awd French II 79; Univ; Lib Art.

SUPER, PAUL; Strongsville Sr HS; Strongsville, OH; AFS; Chrh Wkr; Hon Rl; Jr NHS; Fr Clb; Ftbl; Ten; Trk; Wrstlng; IM Sprt; Univ; Aviation.

SUPERCYNSKI, RITA; Ironwood Catholic HS; Ironwood, MI; 2/24 Cls Rep Soph Cls; Trs Jr Cls; Pres Sr Cls; Chrs; Hon Rl; Sch Mus; Stu Cncl; Rptr Yrbk; Pep Clb; Bsktbl; Gogebic Cmnty Coll; Phys Ther.

SUPPA, SHERRY; Hedgesville HS; Martinsburg, WV; 17/250 Sec Soph Cls; Band; Chrh Wkr; Hon Rl; Sch Pl; Stu Cncl; Yth Flsp; Drama Clb; Fr Clb; Pep Clb; Mbr Of Intl Thespian Soc 76; Soph Homecoming Princess 77; Shepherd Coll; Psych.

SURA, MARK; Wylie E Groves HS; Birmingham, MI; Boy Scts; Hon Rl; Jr NHS; Pol Wkr; Sct Actv; Yth Flsp; Letter Socr; Letter Trk; Univ; Pre Dentistry.

SURBER, DAVID; Whiteoak HS; Hillsboro, OH; Band; Chrh Wkr; Cmnty Wkr; Orch; Sch Mus; 4-H; Pres FFA; Mth Clb; Pep Clb; 4-H Awd; Ohio St Univ; Agri.

SURBEY, P; Taylor HS; Kokomo, IN; Chrs; Hon Rl; 4-H; FNA; Spn Clb; Coll; Nursing.

SURCH, SANDRA; Portage Central HS; Portage, MI; Hon Rl; NHS; Sct Actv; Capt Ten; Mic State; Vet Med.

SURFACE, PATTY; Talawanda HS; Oxford, OH; Jr NHS; Fr Clb; Pep Clb; Letter Bsktbl; Ftbl; Chrldng; IM Sprt; Pres Awd; Miami Univ; Sci.

SURFACE, ROBERT; Springboro HS; Springboro, OH; Boy Scts; Hon Rl; Lbry Ade; NHS; ROTC; Sct Actv; Spn Clb; Univ; Sci.

SURFUS, PATRICIA; Bluffton HS; Bluffton, IN; 11/136 Hon Rl; NHS; Sch Mus; Yth Flsp; Y-Teens; Rptr Yrbk; 4-H; Sec Ger Clb; Letter Gym; 4-H Awd; Purdue Univ; Vet Med.

SURIAN, TAMMY; Douglas Mac Arthur HS; Saginaw, MI; Hon Rl; Hosp Ade; Fr Clb; Western Michigan Univ; Dietetics.

SURIANO, ROBERT; Fairmont West HS; Kettering, OH; 108/480 Band; Orch; Sch Mus; Bsbl; Mgrs; Iow State Univ; Agric Engr.

SURLES, TRACI; Arthur Hill HS; Saginaw, MI; Cl Rep Jr Cls; Trs Sr Cls; Chrs; Chrh Wkr; Cmnty Wkr; Sch Mus; Stu Cncl; Yth Flsp; College; Nursing.

SURMA, JUDITH; Berea HS; Berea, OH; 56/540 VP Frsh Cls; Cls Rep Soph Cls; Cl Rep Jr Cls; Trs Sr Cls; AFS; Am Leg Aux Girls St; Sec Chrs; NHS; Letter Mgrs; VP Tmr; Univ Of Akron; Educ.

SURMA, MARIA; St Andrew HS; Detroit, MI; Hon Rl; NHS; Letter Bsbl; Letter Bsktbl; Chrldng; Scr Kpr; Opt Clb Awd; Univ.

SURMA, MICHELLE; North Judson San Pierre HS; N Judson, IN; 7/118 Sec Sr Cls; Jr NHS; NHS; Mth Clb; Bsktbl; Trk; Mgrs; Tri State Univ; Civil Engr.

SUROVICK, LINDA M; Warren Sr HS; Sterling Hts, MI; Cls Rep Soph Cls; Cmp Fr Grls; Chrs; Girl Scts; Hon Rl; Jr NHS; Sec NHS; Drama Clb; Bsbl; Chrldng; Univ; Clothing Mktg.

SUSALLA, JAY S; Bishop Foley HS; Royal Oak, MI; 27/193 Hon Rl; IM Sprt; Univ.

SUSALSKI, JONATHAN; Inland Lakes HS; Indian River, MI; 34/75 Cls Rep Soph Cls; Boy Scts; Chrh Wkr; Hon Rl; Stu Cncl; Sch Nwsp; Bsktbl; Ftbl; Trk; Mgrs; Lake Superior St Coll; Elec Engr.

SUSEMICHEL, STEVEN C; Ben Davis HS; Indianapolis, IN; Chrh Wkr; Boys Clb Am; Ger Clb; 24 Bwlng Trphs & Awds 68; Cmpltd H&r Blk Incme Tx Crse Still Emplyd By Them 76; Bwlng On B Davis HS Lg 78; General Motors Inst; Acctg.

SUSIN, NANCY; Gabriel Richard HS; Riverview, MI; Sec Soph Cls; Hon Rl; NHS; Stu Cncl; Letter Chrldng; Univ; Comp Progr.

SUSKOWICZ, SCOTT; Chanel HS; Solon, OH; 25/114 Cls Rep Soph Cls; Cl Rep Jr Cls; Cls Rep Sr Cls; Hon Rl; NHS; Sch Mus; Sch Pl; Ed Yrbk; IM Sprt; Miami Univ; Botany Landscp.

SUSSEX, KAREN; Lumen Christi HS; Jackson, MI; 32/242 Hon Rl; NHS; Spn Clb; Letter Gym; Letter Trk; Mic State Univ; Law.

SUSTARICH, LORI; Southwell HS; Chassell, MI; Trs Jr Cls; Band; Hon Rl; Hosp Ade; Lbry Ade; Off Ade; Bsktbl; Chrldng; IM Sprt; Mgrs; Northern Mic Univ; Acctg.

SUTER, JOANNA; Montpelier HS; Montpelier, OH; 3/109 Band; Chrs; Drl Tm; Hon Rl; Sec NHS; Sch Mus; Sch Pl; Yth Flsp; Rptr Yrbk; Sec Fr Clb; Miami Univ; Intl Studies.

SUTHERBY, CHERIE; Gobles HS; Gobles, MI; 1/70 Val; Band; Hon Rl; NHS; Sch Pl; Drama Clb; Mth Clb; Sci Clb; Letter Trk; Natl Merit Ltr; Natl Sci Foundtn Summer Prog 78; Kalamazoo Coll; Pre Med.

SUTHERLAND, BOB; Kimball HS; Royal Oak, MI; Hon Rl; Letter Bsktbl; Letter Ten; Coach Actv; Michigan St Univ; Acctg.

SUTHERLAND, ERIC; Lake Ridge Acad; Grafton, OH; Cls Rep Frsh Cls; Cls Rep Soph Cls; Cl Rep Jr Cls; AFS; Chrs; Stu Cncl; Rptr Yrbk; Letter Bsktbl; Letter Glf; Letter Trk; Bus Schl; Hist.

SUTHERLAND, JAEDS; Hurrican HS; Hurricane, WV; Trs Sr Cls; NHS; Chrldng; Dnfth Awd; West Virginia Tech Schl; Acctg.

SUTHERLAND, JERI; Whitehall HS; Whitehall, MI; 17/150 Sec Band; Chrs; Hon Rl; NHS; Orch; Sch Mus; Stg Crw; Letter Trk; Capt Chrldng; PPFtbl; W Mich Univ; Spanish French Tchr.

SUTHERLAND, KAREN; Wayne HS; Dayton, OH; Band; Hon Rl; Stu Cncl; Pep Clb; Scr Kpr; Coll; Busns Mgmt.

SUTHERLAND, LISA; Paw Paw HS; Mattawan, MI; Hon Rl; Sci Clb; Letter Trk; Chrldng; PPFtbl; Pres Awd; Nazareth Coll; Nursing.

SUTHERLAND, NANCY; Central Montcalm HS; Sheridan, MI; Trs Frsh Cls; Band; Hon Rl; Sch Mus; Sch Nwsp; Bsktbl; PPFtbl; X Alma College;.

SUTHERLAND, ROBERT; New Palestine HS; Greenfield, IN; Aud/Vis; Band; Chrh Wkr; Cmnty Wkr; Hon Rl; NHS; IM Sprt; Milligan Coll Of Tenn; Bus.

SUTHERLAND, STEVE; Walled Lake Western HS; Wixom, MI; Trs Frsh Cls; Trs Soph Cls; Trs Jr Cls; Trs Sr Cls; Chrh Wkr; Hon Rl; NHS; Rptr Yrbk; Letter Crs Cntry; Letter Trk; U S A F Acad; Aviation.

SUTLER, DENISE; Stonewall Jackson HS; Charleston, WV; Cls Rep Frsh Cls; Cmp Fr Grls; Chrh Wkr; Hon Rl; JA; Stu Cncl; VP Y-Teens; Sch Nwsp; Drama Clb; Lat Clb; Univ; Med.

SUTLER, RICHARD; Stonewall Jackson HS; Chrlstn, WV; Pres Frsh Cls; Cls Rep Soph Cls; Cl Rep Jr Cls; Pres Sr Cls; Am Leg Boys St; Jr NHS; NHS; Stu Cncl; Crs Cntry; Dnfth Awd; Mu Alpha Theta; West Virginia Tech Coll; Engr.

SUTLIFF, THOMAS J; Hammond HS; Hammond, IN; 5/245 Am Leg Boys St; CAP; NHS; Sci Clb; Mgrs; Bausch & Lomb Awd; Dnfth Awd; Rose Hillman Inst Of Tech; Mech Engr.

SUTPHEN, CATHERINE; Owosso HS; Owosso, MI; 9/406 Debate Tm; Hon Rl; Lit Mag; NHS; Sch Pl; Sch Nwsp; Drama Clb; Lat Clb; Spn Clb; Central Mich; Psych & Eng.

SUTPHIN, RONALD; Clay HS; Oregon, OH; Boy Scts; Hon Rl; Yth Flsp; Boys Clb Am; Letter Ftbl; Univ.

SUTPHIN, SARA; L & M HS; Lyons, IN; 3/34 Sec Frsh Cls; Sec Soph Cls; Band; Chrs; Chrh Wkr; Hon Rl; Yth Flsp; Sprt Ed Yrbk; FHA; Pep Clb; Vincennes Univ.

SUTTER, PHYLLIS; Coldwater HS; Coldwater, OH; Chrs; Hon Rl; Sch Mus; Drama Clb; FHA; FTA; Spn Clb; Gym; Swmmng; IM Sprt; Univ; Comm Art.

SUTTER, SANDI; Amelia HS; Amelia, OH; Hon Rl; NHS; Letter Bsbl; Socr; Letter Trk; Scr Kpr; Voc Schl; RN.

SUTTER, SUSAN; Sandusky HS; Sandusky, OH; Band; Hon Rl; NHS; Letter Gy.n; Letter Swmmng; Letter Trk; Wittenberg Univ.

SUTTINGER, SARAH; Ann Arbor Huron HS; Ann Arbor, MI; 42/568 Hon Rl; Orch; Sch Mus; Ger Clb; Swmmng; Mic State Univ; Psychology.

SUTTLE, BOBBY; Spanishburg HS; Princeton, WV; Cl Rep Jr Cls; Chrh Wkr; Hon Rl; Rptr Yrbk; 4-H; Pep Clb; Bsbl; Bsktbl; Crs Cntry; Bluefield Coll; Music.

SUTTLES, CATHY; Hilliard HS; Columbus, OH; Band; Chrh Wkr; Hon Rl; Hosp Ade; Orch; Stu Cncl; OEA; Trk; Scr Kpr; Twrlr; Bus Schl; Acctg.

SUTTMAN, LORI; Archbishop Alter HS; Dayton, OH; Hon Rl; NHS; Sch Mus; Sch Pl; Stu Cncl; Drama Clb; Fr Clb; College.

SUTTMILLER, ANITA; Chaminade Julienne HS; Dayton, OH; Hon Rl; JA; Ten; Univ; Psych.

SUTTON, BETH A; Bellaire HS; Bellaire, OH; Band; Chrs; Hon Rl; Off Ade; Y-Teens; Pres Pep Clb; GAA; IM Sprt; Belmont Tech Voc Schl; Nursing.

SUTTON, D; Brookhaven HS; Columbus, OH; Band; Hon Rl; Jr NHS; Yth Flsp; Pep Clb; Rus Clb; Ftbl; Wrstlng; Ohio Wesleyan Univ; Acctg.

SUTTON, DAVE; Brookhaven HS; Columbus, OH; Band; Hon Rl; Jr NHS; Yth Flsp; Pep Clb; Rus Clb; Ftbl; Wrstlng; IM Sprt; Ohio Wesleyan; Accountant.

SUTTON, ELLEN; Lapeer East HS; Metamora, MI; Pres Frsh Cls; VP Soph Cls; Cl Rep Jr Cls; Aud/Vis; Band; Chrh Wkr; Hon Rl; NHS; Off Ade; Sch Mus; Univ; Foreign Lang.

SUTTON, LINDA; Danville Community HS; Danville, IN; 2/160 Am Leg Aux Girls St; Chrs; Girl Scts; Hon Rl; Natl Forn Lg; NHS; Quill & Scroll; Butler Univ; Psych.

SUTTON, LINDA M; Swan Valley HS; Saginaw, MI; 28/189 Sec Frsh Cls; Cls Rep Soph Cls; Cls Rep Sr Cls; Sec NHS; Stu Cncl; Pep Clb; Bsktbl; Baker Jr College; Interior Design.

SUTTON, MARJORIE; St Ursula Academy; Toledo, OH; Chrs; JA; Lbry Ade; Sch Pl; Y-Teens; 4-H; Lat Clb; Trk; 4-H Awd; JA Awd; Air Force; Aero Engr.

SUTTON, MARK; Tipton HS; Tipton, IN; 38/173 Hon Rl; Stu Cncl; FBLA; FTA; Bsbl; Pres Of Student Council & Student Body 79 80; Indiana Univ; Cmmctns.

SUTTON, MICHAEL; Edon Northwest HS; Edon, OH; Boy Scts; Hon Rl; Bsktbl; Crs Cntry; Trk; Letter Mgrs; Ohio Univ; Amer Hist.

SUTTON, STEPHANIE; Our Lady Of Mercy HS; Detroit, MI; 32/332 Girl Scts; Off Ade; Awd For Exc In French; Winner Of Schl Spelling Bee; Univ Of Michigan; Law.

SUTTON, SUSAN; Orchard View HS; Muskegon, MI; 3/190 Hon Rl; Pres NHS; Ed Yrbk; Sprt Ed Sch Nwsp; Letter Bsktbl; Gym; Letter Trk; Scr Kpr; DAR Awd; Pres Awd; Central Michigan Univ; Elem Ed.

SUTTON, TOD; Big Rapids HS; Big Rapids, MI; Hon Rl; Jr NHS; NHS; Off Ade; 4-H; Bsbl; Bsktbl; Ftbl; Michigan Tech Univ; Chem Engr.

SVATOS, WILLIAM; Columbia HS; Columbia Sta, OH; 4/120 Cls Rep Frsh Cls; Cls Rep Soph Cls; Pres Jr Cls; Chrh Wkr; Cmnty Wkr; Hon Rl; NHS; Elec Tech Sch; Elec Engr.

SVEDA, JO ANN; Ravenna HS; Ravenna, OH; 15/327 AFS; Band; Hon Rl; Hosp Ade; Jr NHS; NHS; Sch Nwsp; Lat Clb; Kent St Univ; Sec Ed.

SVERA, LAIMA; Crestwood HS; Dearborn Hts, MI; Band; Chrs; Girl Scts; Sch Pl; Key Clb; IM Sprt; Treas Pom Pon; Michigan St Univ; Engr.

SVOBODA, SUSAN; Lumen Cordium HS; Garfield Hts, OH; 25/95 Cl Rep Jr Cls; Cls Rep Sr Cls; Sec Chrh Wkr; Cmnty Wkr; Hon Rl; Hosp Ade; NHS; Off Ade; Sec Stu Cncl; Drama Clb; Univ; Med Tech.

SVOKE, TAMMY; A D Johnston HS; Bessemer, MI; 5/80 Cls Rep Soph Cls; Cl Rep Jr Cls; Cls Rep Sr Cls; Band; Chrs; Chrh Wkr; Hon Rl; Grand Valley State Collge; Nursing.

SWABON, ANNE; Bishop Borgess HS; Plymouth, MI; Chrs; Bsktbl; Trk; IM Sprt; Univ; Art Mgmt.

SWABY, TAMARA; Petoskey HS; Petoskey, MI; 4/255 Band; Chrs; Girl Scts; Hon Rl; Jr NHS; NHS; Sch Mus; 4-H; Translvana Univ.

SWACKHAMER, ROXANNE; Reynoldsburg HS; Reynoldsburg, OH; Girl Scts; Hon Rl; Sct Actv; Fr Clb; Trk; PPFtbl; Shot Put Schl Rec 77 79; Freed Hardeman Coll.

SWADENER, RHONDA; La Porte HS; Laporte, IN; Girl Scts; Hon Rl; NHS; Fr Clb; Pres Ger Clb; VICA; Univ; Bus.

SWAFFAR, DEBBIE; Morton Sr HS; Hammond, IN; 113/447 Chrh Wkr; Drl Tm; Girl Scts; Off Ade; Sct Actv; Yrbk; 4-H; Pep Clb; Trk; Letter Chrldng; Stu Exch Prog To Spain; Purdue Univ; Travel Mgr.

SWAGER, DONNA; Cascade HS; Clayton, IN; 3/138 Band; Hon Rl; NHS; 4-H; Fr Clb; Mat Maids; Vincennes Univ; Distributive Mktg.

SWAGER, ERIC; Climax Scotts HS; Scotts, MI; 2/70 Band; Chrh Wkr; Hon Rl; Bsbl; Univ.

SWAGER, TIM; Fremont HS; Fremont, IN; Pres Frsh Cls; VP Soph Cls; Am Leg Boys St; Hon Rl; VICA; Ftbl; Trk; Pres Awd; Coll; Aviation.

SWAIM, KEVIN; Rockville HS; Rockville, IN; 6/86 Pres Jr Cls; Pres Sr Cls; Am Leg Boys St; Boy Scts;

Hon Rl; NHS; Sct Actv; Stu Cncl; 4-H; Lat Clb; Eagle Scout 78; Wabash Coll.

SWAIM, TIMOTHY; Union HS; Losantville, IN; 29/90 Band; Yrbk; Letter Bsbl; Indiana Tech Inst.

SWAIM, TRACY; Buchanan HS; Niles, MI; 1/160 Cls Rep Frsh Cls; Band; Hon Rl; NHS; Sch Mus; Yth Flsp; Rptr Yrbk; Yrbk; Fr Clb; VP FTA; St Solo & Ensemble Cornet #1 Rating; District 6 All Star Band; Quiz Bowl Team; College; Psych.

SWAIN, DARLA; Hannan Trace HS; Crown City, OH; Sec Frsh Cls; Sec Soph Cls; VP Jr Cls; Band; Chrs; Chrh Wkr; Hon Rl; Stu Cncl; Beta Clb; Drama Clb; Bus Schl; Sec.

SWAIN, ELIZABETH; Charles F Brush HS; Lyndhurst, OH; Cls Rep Frsh Cls; Cls Rep Soph Cls; Cl Rep Jr Cls; Cls Rep Sr Cls; AFS; Am Leg Aux Girls St; Band; Chrs; Girl Scts; Hon Rl; Univ; Marine Bio.

SWAIN, GWENYTH; Brown County HS; Nas Ville, IN; 1/150 Val; Band; Girl Scts; NHS; Pol Wkr; Quill & Scroll; Sch Pl; Stg Crw; Ed Sch Nwsp; 4-H; Grinnell Coll; French.

SWAIN, MICHAEL; Shelbyville Sr HS; Shelbyville, IN; Debate Tm; Rptr Sch Nwsp; VP Spn Clb; IM Sprt; Ball St Univ.

SWAIN, TERESA K; Mississinewa HS; Gas City, IN; Trs Soph Cls; Hon Rl; Hosp Ade; FNA; Pep Clb; Spn Clb; PPFtbl; Univ; Nursing.

SWALLOW, JULIE K; Pike HS; Indpls, IN; Cls Rep Soph Cls; Cls Rep Sr Cls; Band; Chrs; Hon Rl; NHS; Stu Cncl; Y-Teens; Yrbk; Beta Clb; Schlstc Achvmnt Awd 77; Athletic Awd 74; Purdue Univ; Med.

SWALLOW, STEVE; Versailles HS; Versailles, OH; Band; Boy Scts; Chrs; Chrh Wkr; FCA; Hon Rl; Sch Pl; Sct Actv; Ftbl; College.

SWALLOW, THOMAS; Harrison HS; Harrison, MI; VP Soph Cls; Chrh Wkr; Bsbl; Bsktbl; Ftbl; Most Outsdng Sr Ath Trphy Awd 79; Most Outsdng Welder 78; Voc Welding Class; Most Valuable Bsbl 79; Mid Michigan Coll; Builder.

SWAN, GINA; Wintersville HS; Steubenville, OH; 19/282 Ed Yrbk; Yrbk; Spn Clb; Chrldng; GAA; PPFtbl; Ohio Valley Schl Nursing; R N.

SWAN, GREGORY; Wheeling Park HS; Wheeling, WV; Band; Chrh Wkr; Orch; West Virginia Univ; Marine Bio.

SWAN, JILL; Clare Public School; Clare, MI; VP Soph Cls; VP Jr Cls; FCA; Hon Rl; Off Ade; Stu Cncl; Spn Clb; Letter Trk; Capt Chrldng; Archt.

SWAN, KIMBERLY; New Albany HS; New Albany, IN; 103/565 Chrs; Chrh Wkr; Debate Tm; Girl Scts; Hon Rl; Orch; PAVAS; Yth Flsp; Ger Clb; Oselected To Play With Floyd County Youth Symphony Which Performed 9 Concerts & Toured Romania For 3 Weeks; College; Elem Ed.

SWAN, KRISTA; Utica Sr HS; Utica, OH; 23/193 Band; Pres Chrs; Hon Rl; NHS; Sch Mus; Stu Cncl; Ed Sch Nwsp; Drama Clb; Fr Clb; Cincinnati Bible Coll; Jrnlsm.

SWAN, MATTHEW; Olivet HS; Olivet, MI; Hon Rl; Orch; FFA; Sci Clb; Olivet Coll; Engr.

SWAN, RUTH E; Olivet HS; Olivet, MI; Chrs; Hon Rl; Sch Pl; Fr Clb; Olivet Coll; Psych.

SWANDER, JANET; Yorktown HS; Muncie, IN; 17/172 Hon Rl; NHS; FHA; Spn Clb; Whos Who In For Lang 78 & 79; Ball St Univ; Bus.

SWANEY, JOHN; Saint Francis HS; Traverse, MI; 3/125 Cl Rep Jr Cls; NHS; Red Cr Ade; Letter Bsktbl; Letter Crs Cntry; Letter Trk; Cit Awd; Univ.

SWANEY, TONYA; Heath HS; Heath, OH; 31/151 Cls Rep Sr Cls; Treas Band; Hon Rl; NHS; Off Ade; Stu Cncl; Yrbk; Twrlr; Sec.

SWANEY, WILLIAM; Reading HS; Reading, MI; 15/99 Hon Rl; Lbry Ade; NHS; Off Ade; Letter Bsktbl; Letter Ftbl; Scr Kpr; Tmr; Western Michigan Univ; Bus Mgmt.

SWANGER, DOUGLAS; Marion Harding HS; Marion, OH; Boy Scts; Hon Rl; Jr NHS; Wrstlng; Bowling Green Univ; Writer.

SWANK, CAROL; Attica Jr Sr HS; Attica, IN; 18/70 Hon Rl; Yrbk; Pep Clb;.

SWANK, CATHI R; Clay City HS; Centerpoint, IN; 6/58 Chrs; Hon Rl; Lbry Ade; NHS; OEA; 4th Pl Typing OEA; 5th Pl Acctg OEA; Indiana Voc Tech Coll; Music.

SWANK, J; Decatur Central HS; Camby, IN; Cmp Fr Grls; Chrs; Chrh Wkr; Hon Rl; NHS; Off Ade; Stu Cncl; Yth Flsp; Pres 4-H; Mat Maids; College; Chemistry.

SWANN, GREGORY; Jackson HS; Jackson, OH; 41/228 Aud/Vis; Boy Scts; Chrs; Chrh Wkr; Hon Rl; Jr NHS; NHS; Sch Mus; Sch Pl; Yth Flsp; Schlrshp Tm Amer Hstry 79; Univ; Speech Cmnctns.

SWANN, MELISSA A; Memorial HS; Elkhart, IN; Chrs; Girl Scts; Univ; Marine Bio.

SWANN, YALONDA; Brandon HS; Ortonville, MI; Sec Soph Cls; Girl Scts; Hon Rl; Sch Pl; Stu Cncl; Sch Nwsp; Pep Clb; Crs Cntry; Letter Trk; Letter Chrldng; Mich State Univ; Social Sciences.

SWANSON, CHRISTINE; Luther L Wright HS; Ironwood, MI; 5/175 Debate Tm; Hon Rl; Hosp Ade; Off Ade; Stg Crw; Rptr Sch Nwsp; Pep Clb; Gogebic Cmnty Coll.

SWANSON, DEANDA; Rogers HS; La Porte, IN; 50/500 Hon Rl; NHS; Off Ade; Sch Pl; Stu Cncl; Yrbk; 4-H; Ger Clb; Tri St Univ; Mktg.

SWANSON, JACK D; West Iron County HS; Iron River, MI; Letter Bsbl; Michigan Competitive Schlrshp Winner; Gogebic Community Coll; Radio.

SWANSON, LINDA; Benedictine HS; Detroit, MI; Cls Rep Frsh Cls; Sec Soph Cls; Cl Rep Jr Cls; Chrh Wkr; Girl Scts; Hon Rl; Natl Forn Lg; Stu Cncl; Yrbk; Cit Awd; Mst Outstndng Girl Of The Yr Honor 77; Outstndng Serv To Class Awrd 77; Spirit Awrd 77; Univ; Psych.

SWANSON, LINDA; Carman HS; Flint, MI; 14/375 Cl Rep Jr Cls; VP Sr Cls; Chrh Wkr; Cmnty Wkr; Hon Rl; NHS; Red Cr Ade; Stu Cncl; Yth Flsp; DAR Awd; Alma Coll; Elem Educ.

SWANSON, LORI; Cadillac HS; Cadillac, MI; Cls Rep Frsh Cls; Cls Rep Soph Cls; Cl Rep Jr Cls; Cls Rep Sr Cls; Hon Rl; Stu Cncl; Bsktbl; Gym; PPFtbl; College; Psychology.

SWANSON, RICHARD A; Holly Sr HS; Davisburg, MI; Band; Hon Rl; NHS; Orch; Sch Mus; Trk; IM Sprt; Michigan St Univ; Music.

SWANSON, SAM; Magnolia HS; New Martinsvle, WV; Band; Boy Scts; Hon Rl; Sct Actv; Wrstlng; Univ; Engr.

SWANSON, SANDY; Pine River Jr Sr HS; Le Roy, MI; Cls Rep Frsh Cls; Band; Chrs; Chrh Wkr; Hon Rl; Natl Forn Lg; NHS; Stu Cncl; Chrldng; IM Sprt; Muskegon Busns Coll; Exec Sec.

SWANSON, SHERRYL; Kingsford HS; Iron Mountain, MI; Band; Drl Tm; Pres 4-H; Pres Pep Clb; Univ; Equestrian.

SWANTEK, ANNETTE; Center Line HS; Warren, MI; Chrs; Girl Scts; Hon Rl; Jr NHS; NHS; Sch Pl; Sct Actv; Yrbk; Fr Clb; OEA; Univ; Acctg.

SWARK, MIRIAM; Eaton HS; Eaton, OH; Chrs; Hon Rl; Sch Mus; Yth Flsp; Drama Clb; Sec 4-H; Pep Clb; Spn Clb; GAA; Tri Hi Yt Schslp 79; Bethel Coll; Elem Educ.

SWART, KEN; Bridgman HS; Bridgman, MI; 4/90 Trs Jr Cls; Am Leg Boys St; Band; Hon Rl; NHS; Sch Mus; Letter Glf; IM Sprt; Mgrs; Scr Kpr; College.

SWARTS, JAMES; Muskegon HS; Muskegon, MI; Debate Tm; Hon Rl; Lit Mag; NHS; Ed Sch Nwsp; Sprt Ed Sch Nwsp; Rptr Sch Nwsp; Sch Nwsp; Am Leg Awd; Voice Dem Awd; Crtfct Of Awrd In Eng 77; Crtfct Of Awrd In Civics 77; Coll; Comp Sci.

SWARTZ, BETH; Muncie Southside HS; Muncie, IN; 36/342 Hon Rl; Rptr Sch Nwsp; Fr Clb; Univ; Jrnlsm.

SWARTZ, CYNDI; Carl Brablec HS; Roseville, MI; Hon Rl; Jr NHS; Off Ade; Pol Wkr; Sch Nwsp; Spn Clb; Macomb Cnty Cmnty Coll; Comm Art.

SWARTZ, DEBBIE; Wapakoneta HS; Wapakoneta, OH; 11/332 Cl Rep Jr Cls; Am Leg Aux Girls St; Band; Drm Mjrt; Hosp Ade; NHS; Stu Cncl; Gym; Ten; Voice Dem Awd; Maimi Univ; Psych.

SWARTZ, DEBORAH; East Detroit HS; East Detroit, MI; Hon Rl; NHS; Sci Clb; Wayne State Univ; Bio.

SWARTZ, DONNA; Gallia Acad; Gallipolis, OH; Chrs; Chrh Wkr; Girl Scts; Sch Mus; Yth Flsp; Fr Clb; FHA; OEA; Pep Clb; Sci Clb; Busns Schl.

SWARTZ, GAIL; Ridgedale HS; Marion, OH; 3/75 Hon Rl; Quill & Scroll; Rptr Sch Nwsp; Sch Nwsp; Sec 4-H; Treas FHA; Bsktbl; Trk; 4-H Awd;.

SWARTZ, GAIL; Coldwater HS; Coldwater, OH; 10/145 Cls Rep Frsh Cls; Sec Soph Cls; Sec Jr Cls; Band; Chrs; Hon Rl; Jr NHS; NHS; Stu Cncl; Ger Clb; Miami Univ; Jrnlsm.

SWARTZ, JILL; Brookville HS; Metamora, IN; Hon Rl; NHS; Stu Cncl; Yth Flsp; Ed Yrbk; 4-H; FHA; Cincinnati Tech Coll; Sec.

SWARTZ, KRIS; Rossford HS; Perrysburg, OH; 1/147 Cls Rep Soph Cls; Cl Rep Jr Cls; Cls Rep Sr Cls; Val; Chrs; Hon Rl; NHS; Stu Cncl; Letter Bsbl; IM Sprt; Ohio State Univ; Medicine.

SWARTZ, LARRY; Colon HS; Sherwood, MI; Pres Frsh Cls; Pres Soph Cls; Band; Hon Rl; Orch; Rptr Yrbk; FFA; Letter Bsbl; Letter Ftbl; Univ Of Arizona; Archt Engr.

SWARTZ, LISA; Regina HS; S Euclid, OH; 1/120 Cls Rep Frsh Cls; Hon Rl; Jr NHS; NHS; Yrbk; Rptr Sch Nwsp; Sch Nwsp; Hon Mention In Bio & Algebra 2 77 78 & 79; Exccllnc In Latin 76 79; 2nd Plc In Diocesan Foreign Lang 77; Univ; Bio Chem.

SWARTZ, LORI C; Meadowdale HS; Dayton, OH; 9/250 Cmp Fr Grls; Letter Drl Tm; Hon Rl; Hosp Ade; NHS; Stg Crw; DECA; Letter Gym; Wright State Univ; Elem Ed.

SWARTZ, LYNN; Fostoria HS; Fostoria, OH; 1/200 Cls Rep Frsh Cls; Cls Rep Soph Cls; Cl Rep Jr Cls; Pres Sr Cls; Band; Chrh Wkr; Cmnty Wkr; Hon Rl; JA; Jr NHS; Olivet Nazarene Coll; Acctg.

SWARTZ, MARY; St Josephs HS; South Bend, IN; Chrh Wkr; Cmnty Wkr; Sch Mus; Sch Pl; Stg Crw; Drama Clb; Fr Clb; IM Sprt; Univ.

SWARTZ, ROGER; Mt View HS; Gary, WV; VP Jr Cls; Am Leg Boys St; Aud/Vis; Hon Rl; Pres Key Clb; Letter Bsbl; Mgrs; Scr Kpr; West Virginia Univ; Bus.

SWARTZ, SHEILA; St Ladislaus HS; Hamtramck, MI; 26/112 Hon Rl; Mth Clb; St Clair Cnty Cmnty Coll; Nursing.

SWARTZ, TERESA; Philip Barbour HS; Philippi, WV; 10/220 Band; Hon Rl; NHS; Pres Stu Cncl; Treas Fr Clb; Mat Maids; Twrlr; Cit Awd; DAR Awd; Chsn Bst Band Ctzn; Wnnr Of Merson Essay Contst; Alderson Braaddus Univ; Psych.

SWARTZ, WENDY; Smithville HS; Wooster, OH; 2/96 Sec Soph Cls; Treas Band; Hon Rl; NHS; Fr Clb; Letter Bsktbl; Letter Trk; GAA; Ohio St Univ; Med Tech.

SWARTZENTRUBER, JEFFREY; Westview Jr Sr HS; Shipshewana, IN; 5/84 Pres NHS; Pres Yth Flsp; Letter Bsktbl; Scr Kpr; Goshen Coll; Accounting.

SWARTZLANDER, BRENDA; Napoleon HS; Defiance, OH; Hon Rl; Ger Clb; Letter Swmmng; Trk; Tmr; Most Valuable Swimmer 78; Ball St Univ; Public Rel.

SWARTZLANDER, DONNA; Groveport Madison HS; Groveport, OH; Cmp Fr Grls; Chrh Wkr; Drl Tm; Girl Scts; Hon Rl; Off Ade; Sch Nwsp; Business School.

SWARY, MELANIE; Holgate HS; New Bavaria, OH; 1/50 Cls Rep Sr Cls; Band; Chrs; Chrh Wkr; Girl Scts; Hon Rl; NHS; Ohi State Univ; Comp Sci.

SWASTEK, DAVID; Catholic Central HS; Dearborn, MI; 2/207 Hon Rl; NHS; Pol Wkr; Stu Cncl; Rptr Sch Nwsp; IM Sprt; Univ Of Mich Ann Arbor; Chem.

SWASTEK, MICHELLE; St Andrew HS; Dearborn, MI; 1/99 Pres Soph Cls; Hon Rl; NHS; Pol Wkr; Stu Cncl; Rptr Yrbk; Univ; Bus Educ.

SWATHWOOD, MICHELLE; Gaylord HS; Gaylord, MI; Band; NHS; College; Med.

SWAYER, GENE; Big Bay De Noc HS; Cooks, MI; Hon Rl; Bsktbl; Ftbl; Trk; Cit Awd; Mi St Polic Acad; Law Enforcement.

SWEARINGEN, CHRISTINE; Southern Local HS; Wellsville, OH; Pres Soph Cls; Chrs; Hon Rl; Lbry Ade; NHS; Off Ade; Sch Pl; FSA; OEA; Youngstown St Univ; Speech.

SWEARINGEN, DIANA; Martins Ferry HS; Martins Ferry, OH; Sec Soph Cls; Cl Rep Jr Cls; Hon Rl; Stu Cncl; Y-Teens; Spn Clb; Letter Bsktbl; Letter Trk; GAA; Ohio St Univ; Nursing.

SWEARINGEN, DOUG; Martins Ferry HS; Martins Ferry, OH; 10/215 Am Leg Boys St; Hon Rl; NHS; Stu Cncl; Capt Bsbl; Letter Ftbl; Cit Awd;.

SWEARINGEN, GREGG; Cloverdale HS; Cloverdale, IN; 20/89 Am Leg Boys St; Band; Boy Scts; Chrs; Chrh Wkr; Cmnty Wkr; FCA; Hon Rl; NHS; Orch; Harding Univ; Archt.

SWEAT, TAMARA; Stebbins HS; Dayton, OH; Cls Rep Soph Cls; Cl Rep Jr Cls; Chrs; Sch Mus; Sch Pl; Stg Crw; Drama Clb; College; Theatre.

SWEAZY, KATE; Wehrle HS; Columbus, OH; 4/116 Cls Rep Frsh Cls; Trs Soph Cls; VP Jr Cls; VP Sr Cls; Hon Rl; Treas NHS; Sch Mus; Sec VP Soph Cls; Business School; Business.

SWEDA, LEIGH; Garden City West Sr HS; Garden City, MI; 6/450 Band; Chrh Wkr; Hon Rl; VP NHS; Sch Nwsp; Honored By Detroit Chaptr Phi Beta Kappa 79; Univ Of Mi Dearborn Chancellors Schlrshp 79; Univ Of Michigan; Bus Admin.

SWEEBE, DIANNE; Meridian Sr HS; Sanford, MI; 33/115 Girl Scts; Hon Rl; Lbry Ade; Off Ade; Stu Cncl; Stu Serv Awd; Saginaw Busns Inst; Sec.

SWEENEY, CHERYL L; Rochester HS; Rochester, IN; 25/168 FCA; Hon Rl; NHS; 4-H; Fr Clb; Capt Bsktbl; Ten; GAA; Pres 4-H Awd; Volleyball Capt MVP All Conf; Univ.

SWEENEY, COLLEEN; Redford HS; Detroit, MI; 12/350 Cls Rep Soph Cls; Cl Rep Jr Cls; Cls Rep Sr Cls; Hon Rl; Swmmng; Mic State Univ.

SWEENEY, CYNTHIA S; Lawrence North HS; Indianapolis, IN; Chrs; Pres FCA; Sch Mus; Yth Flsp; Gym; Ten; Chrldng; PPFtbl; Ball St Univ; Phys Educ.

SWEENEY, DIANNE; Traverse City HS; Traverse City, MI; 2/750 Chrs; Hon Rl; NHS; Drama Clb; Key Clb; Pep Clb; Univ Of Notre Dame; Engr.

SWEENEY, JAMES; Brebeuf Prep; Indianapolis, IN; 5/145 Trs Soph Cls; Cls Rep Sr Cls; Boy Scts; Hon Rl; Jr NHS; NHS; Sct Actv; Stu Cncl; Yrbk; Sch Nwsp; Chiefs Awd Swiming; Tomahawk Awd Ldrshp Highest Awd; Chiefs Awd Cross Cntry; Lilly Schlr Semi Finalist; U S Naval Acad.

SWEENEY, LINDA; Oxford Area Community HS; Oxford, MI; 4/218 Chrs; Hon Rl; Sec NHS; Sch Mus; Bsktbl; IM Sprt; Western Mic Univ; Pre Med.

SWEENEY, MARCIA; Sheridan HS; Somerset, OH; 25/180 Chrs; Chrh Wkr; Hon Rl; Jr NHS; Lbry Ade; NHS; Sec OEA; IM Sprt; Sec.

SWEENEY, MARK L; Culver Military Academy; Steubenville, OH; 49/218 Band; Boy Scts; Drm Bgl; ROTC; Ed Sch Nwsp; Letter Bsbl; IM Sprt; The Vedette Pen 1979; 1st Pl Edit Writing 1979; Blue Key Soc 1978; Mt Union Coll; Cmnctns.

SWEENY, TIMOTHY; Chelsea HS; Chelsea, MI; 42/210 Boy Scts; Chrh Wkr; Hon Rl; Sct Actv; Key Clb; IM Sprt; Mgrs; College; Engr.

SWEET, BOB; St Philip Catholic Cntrl HS; Battle Creek, MI; 3/48 Pres Frsh Cls; Cls Rep Soph Cls; Cl Rep Jr Cls; Boy Scts; Hon Rl; NHS; Stu Cncl; Yrbk; Pres Fr Clb; Bsbl; Aquinas Coll; Law.

SWEET, COLLEEN; Deer Park HS; Sharonville, OH; 14/210 Girl Scts; Hon Rl; NHS; Sch Pl; Drama Clb; Ger Clb; Miami Univ; Systems Anlyst.

SWEET, HOLLY; Ravenna HS; Ravenna, OH; 43/313 Cls Rep Sr Cls; Chrs; Girl Scts; Hon Rl; Quill & Scroll; Sct Actv; Rptr Yrbk; Rptr Sch Nwsp; OEA; Pep Clb; Chrprsn For Prom 77; Kent St Univ; Fashion.

SWEET, IAN; West Lafayette HS; W Lafayette, IN; 47/189 Band; Hon Rl; Orch; Letter Wrstlng; Interlochen Music Acad; Music.

SWEETERMAN, LINDA; Chaminade Julienne HS; Dayton, OH; Drl Tm; Hon Rl; Purdue Univ; Comp Sci.

SWEIGART, BARRY; Sidney HS; Sidney, OH; Cmnty Wkr; Hon Rl; Off Ade; Treas DECA; Key Clb; Coach Actv; Vocational School; Air Condition.

SWEITZER, DENISE; Marlington HS; Alliance, OH; Treas Band; Hosp Ade; Natl Forn Lg; Off Ade; Sch Mus; Sch Pl; Drama Clb; Fr Clb; FBLA; FTA; Stark Tech Bus Schl; Bus Mgmt.

SWEITZER, SUE ANN; Marlington HS; Hartville, OH; 6/320 Band; Chrs; Chrh Wkr; Hon Rl; Off Ade; Orch; PAVAS; Sch Mus; Sch Pl; Stg Crw; Univ; Bus Admin.

SWENDA, KRISTINA; Bishop Dwenger HS; Ft Wayne, IN; Chrs; Chrh Wkr; Hon Rl; Mdrgl; Pol Wkr; Sch Mus; Sdlty; Rptr Yrbk; Rptr Sch Nwsp; Fr Clb; Indiana Univ; Acctg.

SWENEY, RICHARD; Lutheran HS West; N Olmsted, OH; Chrs; Chrh Wkr; Hon Rl; NHS; Yth Flsp; Letter Bsktbl; Capt Ftbl; IM Sprt; Cuyahoga Cmnty Coll; Psych.

SWENSEN, REGINALD; Andrews Academy; Berrien Spring, MI; Aud/Vis; Chrh Wkr; Stg Crw; Yrbk; Rptr Sch Nwsp; Sch Nwsp; Andrews Univ; Elec.

SWENSKOWSKI, CYNTHIA; Saint Andrew HS; Detroit, MI; 11/109 Hon Rl; NHS; Detroit Coll Of Bus; Legl Sec.

SWERDLOW, JOHN D; Oak Park HS; Oak Park, MI; 2/350 Bsbl; Natl Merit SF; Univ.

SWERLEIN, CHRISTINA; Mohawk HS; Carey, OH; 10/122 Am Leg Aux Girls St; Band; Chrs; Chrh Wkr; Cmnty Wkr; Hon Rl; Lbry Ade; Lit Mag; NHS; Off Ade; Ohio St Univ; Voice.

SWERLEIN, TINA; Mohawk HS; Carey, OH; 10/126 Am Leg Aux Girls St; Band; Chrs; Chrh Wkr; Cmnty Wkr; Hon Rl; Lbry Ade; Lit Mag; NHS; Off Ade; Ohio St Univ; Vocal Music.

SWETT, BRIAN; Brimley HS; Brimley, MI; Hon Rl; Letter Ftbl; Letter Wrstlng; Mgrs; Lake Superior St Coll; Gen Busns.

SWETT, SHARLOTT; Onaway Area Comm HS; Onaway, MI; 3/115 Band; Girl Scts; Hon Rl; Jr NHS; Sch Pl; Yth Flsp; Sch Nwsp; 4-H; College; English.

SWFFORD, SHERMAN; Big Creek HS; Yukon, WV; Chrs; Hon Rl; Sprt Ed Yrbk; College; Comp Sci.

SWIATEK, LOUISE; Mona Shores HS; Norton Shr, MI; Cls Rep Frsh Cls; Sec Jr Cls; VP Sr Cls; Band; Boy Scts; Hon Rl; Stu Cncl; Pep Clb; Letter Ten; Cit Awd; Muskegon Cmnty Coll; Med Records.

SWICK, T; Flushing HS; Flushing, MI; 99/525 Boy Scts; Hon Rl; Yth Flsp; Crs Cntry; Letter Trk; Letter Mgrs; Michigan St Univ; Busns Admin.

SWICK, VICKI; Canton South HS; Canton, OH; Hon Rl; OEA; Bus Schl; Acctg.

SWICK, WILLIAM; South Harrison HS; Clarksburg, WV; Boy Scts; Chrh Wkr; Hon Rl; Jr NHS; NHS; Sch Pl; Stu Cncl; Sci Clb; College; Bio.

SWICKARD, DEBORAH; Clio HS; Clio, MI; Band; Chrs; Chrh Wkr; Girl Scts; Hon Rl; Hosp Ade; NHS; Key Clb; Pep Clb; Univ Of Michigan.

SWIDEREK, GLORIA; Cheboygan Catholic HS; Cheboygan, MI; 2/33 VP Sr Cls; Sal; Girl Scts; Sch Mus; Stu Cncl; 4-H; Fr Clb; Capt Bsktbl; Capt Trk; St Marys College.

SWIDEREK, WILLIAM; Cheboygan Catholic HS; Cheboygan, MI; 8/27 Hon Rl; Stg Crw; Rptr Yrbk; Rptr Sch Nwsp; 4-H; Letter Bsbl; Letter Bsktbl; Letter Ftbl; Tmr; 4-H Awd; Central Michigan Univ.

SWIDERSKI, DAWN; Lumen Cordium HS; Bedford, OH; JA; Fr Clb; Crs Cntry; GAA; Meritorious Awd Essay Contest; Part Ne Ohio Sci Fair; Red Cross Volunteer Swimming Instruction 2 Yrs; College; Archt.

SWIECKI, TAMARA; Grosse Ile HS; Grosse Ile, MI; Girl Scts; Hon Rl; Pol Wkr; Trk; IM Sprt; E Michigan Univ; Speech Therapy.

SWIEN, CYNTHIA; Marian HS; Rochester, MI; Cls Rep Soph Cls; Cls Rep Sr Cls; Mod UN; Stu Cncl; Yrbk; Fr Clb; Ten; Trk; Univ Of Michigan; CPA.

SWIERCZ, CHRISTINE; Bay City All Saints HS; Bay City, MI; Girl Scts; Hon Rl; College; Busns.

SWIERCZEK, JANINE; Bedford HS; Toledo, OH; Band; Chrh Wkr; Drm Bgl; Orch; Pol Wkr; Sch Mus; Lat Clb; College; Math.

SWIERKOSZ, JANET; Marysville HS; Smiths Creek, MI; 14/179 Cl Rep Jr Cls; NHS; Stg Crw; Letter Bsktbl; Scr Kpr; St Clair Cmnty Coll; Med Lab Tech.

SWIETER, KELLY; Forest Hills Northern HS; Grand Rapids, MI; 36/140 Sprt Ed Yrbk; Rptr Yrbk; Letter Ftbl; Letter Swmmng; GRJC; Lib Arts.

SWIFT, DEBRA; La Porte HS; Laporte, IN; Band; Hon Rl; MMM; Orch; Civ Clb; Fr Clb; Pep Clb; Hanover Coll; Bus Admin.

SWIFT, LORETTA; Franklin HS; Franklin, OH; Hon Rl; Off Ade; Sch Pl; Stg Crw; Fr Clb; Mth Clb; Sci Clb; Letter Bsbl; Letter Bsktbl; College; Vet Med.

SWIFT, ROBERTA; Comstock HS; Kalamazoo, MI; Girl Scts; Hon Rl; JA; NHS; Off Ade; DECA; Pep Clb; Western Michigan Univ; Bus.

SWIFT, TERRI; Colon HS; Bronson, MI; Hon Rl; Lbry Ade; NHS; Fr Clb; Letter Bsktbl;.

SWIGART, MARK; Wadsworth Sr HS; Rittman, OH; Boy Scts; Chrh Wkr; Natl Forn Lg; Sct Actv; Sci Clb; Spn Clb; Akron Univ; Engr.

SWIGER, JANET; Tyler Cnty HS; West Union, WV; Sec Frsh Cls; Hon Rl; Stu Cncl; Letter Bsktbl; Letter Trk; GAA; Univ.

SWIGER, STANLEY E; High School; Wallace, WV; Chrh Wkr; Cmnty Wkr; Hon Rl; NHS; Sch Pl; Stu Cncl; Ed Yrbk; Rptr Yrbk; Yrbk; 4-H; Univ; Archt.

SWIGERT, SHARON; River View HS; Coshocton, OH; 35/215 Cls Rep Frsh Cls; Cls Rep Soph Cls; Cl Rep Jr Cls; Cls Rep Sr Cls; Am Leg Aux Girls St; Band; Hon Rl; NHS; Orch; Sch Mus; Ohio St Univ; Elem Educ.

SWIGERT, TAMMY; Little Miami HS; Loveland, OH; Cls Rep Soph Cls; Hon Rl; Off Ade; Nutrition.

SWIHART, JAMES; Tippecanoe Vly HS; Argos, IN; Aud/Vis; Hon Rl; Yth Flsp; 4-H; Swmmng; College; Chiropractor.

SWIHART, RITA; National Trail HS; Lewisburg, OH; Band; Drm Mjrt; Hon Rl; Lbry Ade; NHS; Stu Cncl; Yrbk; Pres 4-H; Sec Spn Clb; Am Leg Awd; College.

SWIM, R STANLEY; North Vermillion HS; Covington, IN; Aud/Vis; Hon Rl; NHS; Bio Hnr Awd; Eng Hnr Awd 76; Eng Awd; Hstry Awd 77; Geo Awd Hnr 78; Chem Hnr Awd; Hstry Hnr Awd 79; Univ.

SWINCICKI, JONI; All Saints Catholic Cntl HS; Bay City, MI; Sec Frsh Cls; Cl Rep Jr Cls; Sec Sr Cls; Hon Rl; NHS; Stu Cncl; Pom Pon; College; Phys Ther.

SWINEFORD, DIANNA; John Marshall HS; Indianapolis, IN; Cls Rep Soph Cls; Hosp Ade; Stu Cncl; Letter Gym; Letter Trk; Chrldng; 1st Pl WIFE Radio Stn Super Summer Olympics; Sr Girls All Stars; College; Phys Ed.

SWINEFORD, LISA; Jackson Mem HS; Massillon, OH; Band; NHS; Off Ade; Yth Flsp; Y-Teens; Pep Clb; Pres Spn Clb; Letter Swmmng; Mat Maids; Bowling Green St Univ; Food Sci.

SWINEY, PATRICIA A; Herbert Hoover HS; Elkview, WV; Band; Hon Rl; JA; Jr NHS; JA Awd; Univ; Music.

SWINEY, TAMI; Herbert Hoover HS; Clendenin, WV; Band; Drl Tm; Hon Rl; Jr NHS; Letter Trk; GAA; Mgrs; Marshall Univ; Comp Prog.

SWING, BRADLEY; Northrop HS; Ft Wayne, IN; Mod UN; Indiana Univ; Space Sci.

SWINGLE, DONNA; Philo HS; Blue Rock, OH; Chrh Wkr; Hon Rl; Lit Mag; NHS; Off Ade; Yrbk; Sch Nwsp; 4-H; Lion Awd; Univ; Sec.

SWISHER, BARBARA; River Valley HS; Caledonia, OH; Chrs; Sec Yth Flsp; 4-H; IM Sprt; 4-H Awd; Ohi State Univ; Public Relations.

SWISHER, CALVIN; Calhoun Cnty HS; Munday, WV; Chrs; Hon Rl; NHS; 4-H; FFA; Bsktbl; Trk; Wrstlng; Mgrs; 4-H Awd; Voc Schl; Truck Driver.

SWISHER, DEBBIE; Gallia Academy HS; Gallipolis, OH; Trs Frsh Cls; Trs Jr Cls; Band; Chrs; Chrh Wkr; Girl Scts; Lbry Ade; Sch Mus; Sch Pl; Stu Cncl; Ohio St Univ; Fashion Designer.

SWISHER, KATHY; Lewis Cnty HS; Weston, WV; 14/268 Band; Chrh Wkr; Hon Rl; Jr NHS; NHS; 4-H; PPFtbl; Twrlr; 4-H Awd; West Virginia Univ; Vet.

SWISHER, LISA; Clay Battelle HS; Fairview, WV; Cls Rep Soph Cls; Cl Rep Jr Cls; Chrs; Hon Rl; Jr NHS; Lbry Ade; Fr Clb; FHA; Pep Clb; Chrldng; WVU; Music.

SWISHER, MICHAEL; Holy Name HS; Lakewood, OH; Boy Scts; Chrs; Chrh Wkr; Hon Rl; Sch Mus; Sct Actv; Yth Flsp; IM Sprt; God Cntry Awd; All Ohio Yth Choir 79; Univ.

SWISHER, SUSAN; Perrysburg HS; Perrysburg, OH; 40/255 Band; Chrs; Chrh Wkr; Girl Scts; Hon Rl; Hosp Ade; Sch Mus; Sch Pl; Sct Actv; Yth Flsp; Coll; Nursing.

SWITALSKI, ANGELINE; St Marys Cathedral HS; Gaylord, MI; Cl Rep Jr Cls; Band; Chrh Wkr; Cmnty Wkr; Drl Tm; Hon Rl; Hosp Ade; Lbry Ade; Off Ade; Orch; Ctrl Michigan Univ; Elem Ed.

SWITZER, BRIAN G; Clermont Northeastern HS; Batavia, OH; Cls Rep Frsh Cls; Am Leg Boys St; Boy Scts; Cmnty Wkr; Hon Rl; Jr NHS; Sct Actv; Stu Cncl; 4-H; Bsktbl; Top Soc Studies Stu 78; Principals Hnr Stu 75; Bsbl Tickets Awd For Straight A's 75; Univ Of Cincinnati; Bus Admin.

SWITZER, CAROLYN; Mt Healthy HS; Cincinnati, OH; 1/500 Am Leg Aux Girls St; Band; Hon Rl; Hosp Ade; NHS; Ed Sch Nwsp; VP Beta Clb; C of C Awd; Rotary Awd; Univ; Phys Ther.

SWITZER, SCOTT; Findley HS; Findlay, OH; 200/700 Cls Rep Frsh Cls; Hon Rl; Quill & Scroll; Sch Pl; Sch Nwsp; Drama Clb; Created Produced & Directed A Newsmagazine Show On Trojan TV; Directed & Announced Basketball Ganes; Ohio Univ; Broadcasting.

SWIX, SCOTT R; J W Sexton HS; Lansing, MI; 11/390 Am Leg Boys St; Boy Scts; Pres Chrh Wkr; Girl Scts; Pres JA; NHS; Mth Clb; Ten; VP JA Awd; Natl Merit SF; Univ; Archt.

SWOBODA, GERALD; Plainwell HS; Plainwell, MI; Hon Rl; Jr NHS; NHS; Letter Bsbl; Western Mic Univ; Chem.

SWOGGER, JUDITH; Brookfield HS; Masury, OH; 11/160 NHS; Quill & Scroll; Sch Pl; Yrbk; Ed Sch Nwsp; Sec Beta Clb; Drama Clb; Spn Clb; DAR Awd; Natl Merit Ltr; Kent St Univ.

SWOGGER, ROBIN; Brookfield HS; Masury, OH; Band; Hon Rl; NHS; Rptr Sch Nwsp; Beta Clb; Trk; Univ.

SWONGER, MARK; Wellston HS; Wellston, OH; 3/120 Cls Rep Frsh Cls; Trs Soph Cls; Cl Rep Jr Cls; Cls Rep Sr Cls; Band; Chrs; Hon Rl; NHS; Orch; Sch Mus; U S Air Force Acad; Officer USAF.

SWORDS, CHARLOTTE; Allen East HS; Lima, OH; Band; Chrh Wkr; Sch Pl; VP Yth Flsp; Ed Yrbk; Rptr Sch Nwsp; Univ; Soc Work.

SWORTWOOD, SANDY; Caledonia HS; Caledonia, MI; Cls Rep Frsh Cls; Cls Rep Soph Cls; Cl Rep Jr Cls; NHS; Pol Wkr; Sec Stu Cncl; Chrldng; PPFtbl; Scr Kpr; Ferris St Coll; Acctg.

SWOVELAND, EDWARD A; Goshen HS; Goshen, IN; 63/269 Cls Rep Frsh Cls; Cl Rep Jr Cls; Boy Scts; Hon Rl; Stu Cncl; Boys Clb Am; Sci Clb; Letter Bsbl; Letter Ftbl; IM Sprt; Mbr Of A A HS St Champ On In 78; Selectd To 2nd Tm All Confrnc In Bsbl 79; Univ; Cmmrcl Pilot.

SWOVERLAND, ROBERT; Dwight D Eisenhower HS; Saginaw, MI; 4/350 NHS; Letter Bsktbl; Delta College; Bus Mgmt.

SY, CHRISTINE; Unionvlle Sebewaing Area HS; Uninville, MI; Hon Rl; Chrldng; Bus Sch; Accounting.

SYER, TRACI; St Frances Cabrini HS; Lincoln Pk, MI; Cmp Fr Grls; Drm Bgl; Hon Rl; Bsktbl; Trk; Chrldng; Coach Actv; IM Sprt; Scr Kpr; Tmr; Bsktbl Letter 76 79 Captn 79 Allarea 79; St Of Mi Comp Schlrshp 79; Univ Of Michigan; Acctg.

SYJUD, MARY; Osborn HS; Detroit, MI; Hon Rl; NHS; Natl Merit Schl; Wayne St Univ; Pharm.

SYKES, MICHELLE; Saint Alphonsus HS; Dearborn, MI; Chrs; Chrh Wkr; Hon Rl; JA; PAVAS; Sch Mus; Sch Pl; Mic State Univ; Zoology.

SYKES, RICHARD; Springport HS; Parma, MI; Boy Scts; Chrh Wkr; Hon Rl; Stg Crw; Yrbk; 4-H; Treas FFA; Ger Clb; Crs Cntry; Trk; 3rd Prize In Jackson Dist Library Logo Contest 79; 4th Awd Ribbon In Marty Awds 79; 2 Blue Ribbons In JCEA; Cmmrcl Art.

SYKES, SUSAN; St Alphonsus HS; Dearborn, MI; Hon Rl; Jr NHS; Letter Trk; JA Awd; All As In Hist 79; Northwood Inst; Sec.

SYLER, BARBARA; Plymouth HS; Plymouth, IN; 48/225 Chrs; Hon Rl; Off Ade; Sprt Ed Sch Nwsp; Rptr Sch Nwsp; Pres FTA; Capt Bsktbl; Capt Swmmng; Ten; Mgrs; Otstndng Sr Girl Athlete 79; Hoosier Schlr; Ball St Univ; Phys Educ.

SYLWESTRZAK, THEODORE; Anchor Bay Sr HS; New Baltimore, MI; Northern Michigan Univ; Chem.

SYME, JAMES W; Chagrin Falls Exempted HS; Chagrin Falls, OH; 33/187 Band; Boy Scts; Chrh Wkr; Lit Mag; Sct Actv; Stg Crw; Ger Clb; Crs Cntry; Socr; Ten; Cornell College; Arch.

SYMKO, DAVID; Greenville Sr HS; Greenville, MI; 59/231 Quill & Scroll; Rptr Yrbk; Yrbk; 4-H; Fr Clb; Letter Ftbl; Letter Trk; IM Sprt; Mgrs; St Of Mi Schlshp 79; St Of Mi Compt Cert 78; 4 Yrs Of Perfct Attndnc 75 79; Northern Michigan Univ; Math.

SYMON, LISA; Reeths Puffer HS; Muskegon, MI; 12/352 Sec Soph Cls; Trs Sr Cls; Chrs; Chrh Wkr; Hon Rl; Jr NHS; NHS; Gym; Ten; Trk; Coll; Counseling.

SYMONS, DANIEL; Sts Peter & Paul Area HS; Saginaw, MI; Chrs; Chrh Wkr; Hon Rl; Mdrgl; NHS; Off Ade; Sch Mus; Fr Clb; Cent Mich Univ; Law.

SYMONS, LINDA; The Summit Country Day Schl; Cincinnati, OH; 2/42 Girl Scts; Hon Rl; NHS; Sch Pl; Sdlty; Sprt Ed Sch Nwsp; Bsktbl; GAA; Scr Kpr; Natl Merit Ltr; Coll Of William & Mary; Bio Sci.

SYMONS, LISA; Fennville HS; Fennville, MI; 3/96 Trs Frsh Cls; Trs Sr Cls; Cls Rep Sr Cls; Chrs; NHS; Stu Cncl; Ed Sch Nwsp; Central Mic Univ; Comp Sci.

SYMONS, SALLY; Houghton Lake HS; Houghton Lk, MI; 6/100 Cmnty Wkr; Girl Scts; Hon Rl; Jr NHS; 4-H; Swmmng;.

SYMSICK, LAURA J; Madison Comprehensive HS; Tucson, AZ; 42/452 Chrs; Chrh Wkr; Girl Scts; Sch Mus; Sct Actv; Stu Cncl; Y-Teens; Drama Clb; Eng Clb; Mth Clb; Whos Who Among Amer HS Stu 77 78 & 79; Awd Fr Schl Acad Achvmnt Awd 78; Grad In The Top 9% Of Sr Class 79; Pima Cmnty Coll; Radiologic Tech.

SYNDER, DAVID; Centerburg HS; Mt Liberty, OH; 15/75 Stu Cncl; Yth Flsp; Rptr Yrbk; Yrbk; Bsktbl; Ftbl; Trk; Coach Actv; Art School; Commercial Art.

SYNER, JOEY; Midland Trail HS; Hico, WV; Hon Rl; NHS; Stu Cncl; Rptr Sch Nwsp; Pep Clb; Coach Actv; Capt Of Hist Bwl Team 79; WVIT; Bus.

SYNER, THOMAS E; Valley HS; Powellton, WV; 15/133 Am Leg Boys St; Chrh Wkr; Hon Rl; NHS; Sch Pl; Sch Nwsp; Highest Schlstc Achievement Awd 75; Vocational Field.

SYNK, DONNA; Harry Hill HS; Lansing, MI; Chrh Wkr; Hon Rl; NHS; Natl Merit Ltr; Michigan St Univ; Social Work.

SYNK, TRACY; Berea HS; Berea, OH; 13/529 Hon Rl; Sec NHS; Pep Clb; Bsbl; Bsktbl; Capt Chrldng; PPFtbl; Tmr; College; Spec Educ.

SYNKELMA, ROBIN; A D Johnston HS; Ironwood, MI; Band; Hon Rl; Lbry Ade; Rptr Sch Nwsp; Pep Clb; Letter Trk; Cert Of Otstndng Production Work In Typewriting 79; Gogebic Cmnty Coll; Sec.

SYRIA, GERRI; Ewen Trout Creek HS; Bruce Crossing, MI; 1/43 Pres Sr Cls; Val; Band; Natl Forn Lg; Yrbk; Cit Awd; Lion Awd; Natl Merit SF; Northern Mic Univ; Speech.

SYRON, KATHLEEN; Our Lady Of Mercy HS; Livonia, MI; Cls Rep Frsh Cls; Stu Cncl; Lat Clb; Swmmng; IM Sprt; Mgrs; Scr Kpr; College; Astronautical Engr.

SYRON, LAURA; Our Lady Of Mercy HS; Livonia, MI; NHS; Capt Swmmng; Univ Of Mic; Med.

SYRONEY, JANE; Holy Name HS; Brooklyn Hts, OH; Trs Frsh Cls; Cls Rep Soph Cls; Chrs; Drl Tm; Hon Rl; Jr NHS; NHS; Sch Mus; Stu Cncl; Yrbk; College; Nurse.

SYSOL, THERESA; Almont HS; Almont, MI; Hon Rl; FFA; Spn Clb; Bsktbl; Michigan Tech Univ; Forestry.

SYTSMA, RACHELLE; South Christian HS; Grand Rapids, MI; 15/181 Chrs; Drl Tm; Hon Rl; Hosp Ade; Stg Crw; Yrbk; Rptr Sch Nwsp; Sch Nwsp; Acctg.

SZABO, ANN; Clio HS; Clio, MI; 44/392 OEA; Univ; Bus Admin.

SZABO, ANNE; West Geauga HS; Chagrin Falls, OH; Band; Chrs; Hon Rl; Orch; Fr Clb; Pep Clb; IM Sprt; Mat Maids; PPFtbl; Univ.

SZABO, STACEY; Luthern East HS; E Detroit, MI; Chrh Wkr; Hon Rl; NHS; Stu Cncl; Ger Clb; Pom Pon; Univ; Bio.

SZABO, SYLVIA; Kearsley HS; Flint, MI; 37/370 Hon Rl; Off Ade; OEA; Flint Univ; Photography.

SZAFRANSKI, CARLENE; Pinconning HS; Linwood, MI; Hon Rl; NHS; Off Ade; Yrbk; 4-H; IM Sprt; 4-H Awd; Delta Univ; Phys Ther.

SZAFRANSKI, JEREEN; Pinconning Area HS; Linwood, MI; VP Jr Cls; Hon Rl; NHS; Sct Actv; PPFtbl; College.

SZAJERSKI, KARLA; Bishop Noll Inst HS; Chicago, IL; 43/321 Hon Rl; Jr NHS; Stg Crw; Mth Clb; Letter Swmmng; Trk; Univ; Cmnctns.

SZAKACS, ANNA; Bluefield HS; Bluefield, WV; Chrh Wkr; Cmnty Wkr; Off Ade; FHA; Leo Clb; Pep Clb; Spn Clb; Bluefield State Concord; Teach.

SZAKACS, BILL; Springfield HS; Springfield, MI; FCA; Hon Rl; Ten; College; Sci.

SZAKAL, KATHERINE; Trinity HS; Cleveland, OH; 45/150 Chrs; Chrh Wkr; Cmnty Wkr; Hon Rl; Hosp Ade; Pep Clb; College; Architect.

SZAKAS, THERESA; Niles Sr HS; Niles, MI; Sec Band; Hon Rl; NHS; Sch Pl; Stu Cncl; Rptr Yrbk; Lat Clb; Ten; Opt Clb Awd; Univ; Law.

SZAKATIS, ROBERT; Hammond HS; Hammond, IN; Hon Rl; Jr NHS; NHS; Socr; Ten; Purdue Univ; Elect Engr.

SZALKOWSKI, SANDRA; Parma Sr HS; Parma, OH; 38/831 Chrs; Girl Scts; Hon Rl; Hosp Ade; Rptr Yrbk; Drama Clb; Ger Clb; Coach Actv; Mat Maids; Service Awd; Volunteer Awd Jr Volunteer Parma Comm Hosp; Cuyahoga Comm Coll; Phys Therapy.

SZALONY, ED; Donald E Gavit HS; Hammond, IN; Chrh Wkr; Quill & Scroll; Sch Pl; Ed Sch Nwsp; Socr; Swmmng; USC; Cinema Production.

SZARAFINSKI, MARY; St Agatha HS; Detroit, MI; 31/131 Hon Rl; Lat Clb; Letter Bsbl; Letter Bsktbl; Letter Trk; Saginaw Vly St Coll.

SZAROLETTA, S; Ontonagon Area HS; Ontonagon, MI; Hon Rl; Rptr Sch Nwsp; Pep Clb; GAA; Univ.

SZCYPKA, MARK; Bay City All Saints HS; Bay City, MI; Chrs; Hon Rl; Sch Mus; Letter Ftbl; Trk; Central Mic Univ.

SZCZEPANSKI, KATHLEEN; Lumen Christi HS; Jackson, MI; 85/253 Band; Chrs; Girl Scts; Hon Rl; Orch; Sch Mus; Sct Actv; Sch Nwsp; Drama Clb; Pep Clb; Grand Valley St Coll; Soc Work.

SZCZEPANSKI, ROSE; Bishop Noll Inst; E Chicago, IN; 74/337 Chrh Wkr; Cmnty Wkr; Hon Rl; NHS; Stg Crw; Mth Clb; Capt Bsktbl; Purdue; Nursing.

SZCZESNY, BRIAN; St Clement HS; Detroit, MI; Hon Rl; Ftbl; IM Sprt; Wayne State Univ; Field Broadcasting.

SZCZOTKA, EDWARD; St Alphonsus HS; Detroit, MI; Debate Tm; Hon Rl; Natl Forn Lg; Rptr Sch Nwsp; Natl Merit Ltr; Univ Of Michigan; Law.

SZCZUBLEWSKI, CONNIE; Rossford HS; Rossford, OH; 15/150 Sec Sr Cls; Chrs; Girl Scts; Hon Rl; NHS; Sch Mus; Drama Clb; Capt Bsktbl; Capt Trk; Univ Of Toledo; Math.

SZCZUBLEWSKI, MICHELLE; Notre Dame Acad; Toledo, OH; Mod UN; Pol Wkr; Red Cr Ade; Civ Clb; FDA; Lat Clb; Univ Of Tol; Psych.

SZCZUBLEWSKI, THERESA; Rossford HS; Rossford, OH; 2/150 Hon Rl; VP NHS; Sch Mus; Drama Clb; Fr Clb; Spn Clb; Letter Bsktbl; Letter Crs Cntry; Trk; Coll; Elem Ed.

SZCZUREK, ELIZABETH; Chalker HS; Southington, OH; Band; Orch; Beta Clb; 4-H; Sci Clb; Spn Clb; Trk; Chrldng; 4-H Awd; St Fair Comp Alternate 77; Yr End Awrd Champ Reining Horse 78; Reserve Champ Horsemanship Awrd 79; Univ; Equestrian.

SZEFLER, CYNTHIA; Hamtramck HS; Hamtramck, MI; 8/110 Band; Chrs; Drm Mjrt; Hon Rl; JA; NHS; Off Ade; Stu Cncl; Rptr Yrbk; Twrlr; Macomb Cmnty Coll; Sec.

SZELA, JOHN; Charles Stewart Mott HS; Warren, MI; Band; Hon Rl; Sch Mus; Univ Of Michigan; Bio.

SZEL PAL, KARL; Fairview HS; Fairview Pk, OH; Boy Scts; Hon Rl; Sct Actv; Rptr Sch Nwsp; Ger Clb; Sci Clb; Trk; Wrstlng; Cleveland St Univ; Bio.

SZEMPRUCH, MELANIE; Kenton Ridge HS; Springfield, OH; 90/147 Chrs; Sch Mus; Sch Pl; Drama Clb; FHA; Letter Bsktbl; Letter Ftbl; Letter Chrldng; GAA; Scr Kpr; Sinclair Cmnty Coll; Dent Hygnst.

SZEPIETOWSKI, TERESA; Champion HS; Cortland, OH; 6/229 Chrs; Hon Rl; Jr NHS; Mdrgl; NHS; 4-H; Spn Clb; Bsktbl; Trk; 4-H Awd; Buckeye Girls St Alt 78; Champ PTO Schlrshp 79; St Bd Of Educ Awd Of Distnctn 79; Champ High Gold Music Ad; Ohio St Univ; Vet Med.

SZETELA, ANTHONY; Aquinas HS; Dearborn Hts, MI; Boy Scts; Chrh Wkr; Hon Rl; PAVAS; Sch Mus; Sch Pl; Sct Actv; Stu Cncl; Yrbk; Drama Clb; College; Dentistry.

SZIGETHY, STEPHEN M; Lumen Christi HS; Jackson, MI; 8/231 VP Frsh Cls; Cls Rep Sr Cls; Hon Rl; Pres Soph Cls; VP Lat Clb; Trk; IM Sprt; Univ Of Michigan; Econ.

SZILAGYI, JERRY J; Solon HS; Solon, OH; Band; Chrh Wkr; Hon Rl; Yth Flsp; Rensselaer; Chem Engr.

SZILAGYI, LINDA; Ovid Elsie HS; Elsie, MI; 9/180 Hon Rl; NHS; Ed Yrbk; Rptr Sch Nwsp; 4-H; Letter GAA; PPFtbl; Michigan St Univ; Jrnlsm.

SZILVAS, ALEXANDER; Padua Franciscan HS; Middleburg Hts, OH; 1/259 Hon Rl; NHS; Fr Clb; Key Clb; Mth Clb; Letter Ten; IM Sprt; Mgrs; Am Leg Awd; Univ Of Nortre Dame; Bus.

SZMUTKO, ROBERT; Andrean HS; Gary, IN; 114/251 Cls Rep Frsh Cls; Cls Rep Soph Cls; Stu Cncl; Ger Clb; Letter Crs Cntry; Letter Glf; Letter Ten; IM Sprt; Opt Clb Awd; Coll; Psych.

SZOKA, JODI; Perry HS; Painesville, OH; Off Ade; FHA; Key Clb; Pep Clb; Bsktbl; Chrldng; GAA; Business School; Clerical.

SZOTKO, GARY; W Catholic HS; Grand Rapids, MI; Pres Frsh Cls; Pres Soph Cls; Cl Rep Jr Cls; Chrs; Hon Rl; Ftbl; Coach Actv; Coll; Busns-Admin.

SZUBINSKI, KATHLEEN; West Catholic HS; Grand Rapids, MI; Hon Rl; VP JA; Pep Clb; Spn Clb; VP JA Awd; Western Michigan Univ; Med.

SZUCH, JANET; Jefferson HS; S Rockwood, MI; 7/158 Trs Sr Cls; Hon Rl; Jr NHS; NHS; Off Ade; VP Stu Cncl; Yrbk; Sch Nwsp; Natl Merit SF; Voice Dem Awd; Monro Cnty Cmnt Coll Bd Of Trustees Schlshp 79; Jefferson HS Soc Std Dep Awd 78; Monroe Cnty Cmnty Coll; Cmnctns.

SZUCH, M; Elisabeth Ann Johnson HS; Clio, MI; Am Leg Boys St; Pres Band; Drm Mjrt; Pres NHS; Letter Ten; Blue Lake Fine Arts Camp Schlrshp; St Solo & Ensemble Soli 1 Rating; Michigan St Univ; Med.

SZUMLAS, DANIEL; Bishop Noll Inst; Hammond, IN; 47/321 Band; Chrh Wkr; Hon Rl; Orch; Sch Mus; Ten; Indiana Univ; Sci.

SZUMLAS, DAVID; Bishop Noll Inst; Hammond, IN; 3/321 Chrh Wkr; Hon Rl; Mth Clb; Indiana Univ.

SZUNKE, JEFFREY; Douglas Macarthur HS; Saginaw, MI; Hon Rl; Lbry Ade; Stu Cncl; Sch Nwsp; Mich State Univ; Bus.

SZURGOT, ROBERT; Griffith HS; Griffith, IN; Hon Rl; Jr NHS; Letter Swmmng; Univ; Optometry.

SZUTKOWSKI, NORMA J; Dominican HS; Detroit, MI; Cl Rep Jr Cls; Aud/Vis; Hon Rl; Stg Crw; Rptr Yrbk; Univ; Advertising.

SZYMANOWSKI, BRIAN R; Dowagiac Union HS; Dowagiac, MI; 24/220 Band; Hon Rl; NHS; Letter Ten; College; Engr.

SZYMANSKI, CHRISTOPHER; Yale HS; Emmett, MI; Band; Boy Scts; Sct Actv; Letter Ftbl; Eagle Scout 78; Univ; Law.

SZYMANSKI, MARY; River Valley HS; Three Oaks, MI; Band; Chrh Wkr; NHS; Rptr Yrbk; Yrbk; Sprt Ed Sch Nwsp; Drama Clb; Sci Clb; College.

SZYMANSKI, MICHELE; Center Line HS; Warren, MI; 2/435 Band; Girl Scts; Hon Rl; Jr NHS; NHS; Fr Clb; OEA; GAA; Isia Figure Skating Comp 1978 ; BOEC Reg Rec Mgmt Cont 1979; BOEC Reg Parlm Proc Team 1979; Macomb Cnty Cmnty Coll; Respiratory.

SZYMANSKI, TERESE; Cardinal Stritch HS; Northwood, OH; 3/205 Cls Rep Sr Cls; Chrh Wkr; Cmnty Wkr; Girl Scts; Hon Rl; NHS; Red Cr Ade; Sch Mus; Stu Cncl; 4-H; Toledo Univ; Busns.

SZYMARSKI, ROSLYN; North Huron HS; Pt Austin, MI; Pres Soph Cls; VP Jr Cls; Band; Girl Scts; Hon Rl; Stu Cncl; Pres FBLA; Twrlr; Pres Awd; College; Acctg.

SZYMIALIS, CARMELLA; Bishop Donahue Memorial HS; Benwood, WV; Band; Chrs; Chrh Wkr; Cmnty Wkr; Hon Rl; PAVAS; Sch Mus; Rptr Yrbk; Rptr Sch Nwsp; Art Inst Of New York; Art Tchr; Law.

SZYPERSKI, CONNIE; Meridian HS; Sanford, MI; Band; Girl Scts; Hon Rl; Orch; Sch Mus; Univ; Data Processing.

SZYSKOWSKI, KEVIN; St Francis De Sales HS; Toledo, OH; 18/200 By Scts; Chrh Wkr; Hon Rl; NHS; Sch Mus; Rptr Sch Nwsp; Ftbl; Univ; Pharm.

T

TABACHKI, GINA; Interlochen Arts Academy; Gaylord, MI; Cls Rep Frsh Cls; Cls Rep Sr Cls; Chrs; Mdrgl; Stu Cncl; Rptr Yrbk; Semi Finalist Mi Comp Schlrshp 78; Northwestern Univ.

TABACYK, EDWARD; St Marys Prep; Chicago, IL; 1/25 Cl Rep Jr Cls; VP Sr Cls; Sal; Boy Scts; Hon Rl; NHS; Sch Nwsp; Letter Ftbl; IM Sprt; Univ Of Illinois; Pre Law.

TABAKA, DEBBIE; Springfield Local HS; New Middletown, OH; 4/150 VP Frsh Cls; Drl Tm; Hon Rl; NHS; Fr Clb; Pep Clb; Trk; Pom Pon; Youngstown St Univ; Nursing.

TABAKA, SHELLI; Boardman HS; Boardman, OH; 33/558 Cmp Fr Grls; Hon Rl; NHS; Y-Teens; Fr Clb; Pep Clb; College; Med.

TABANGUIL, MARIBEL; Portage Northern HS; Portage, MI; Hon Rl; Hosp Ade; Off Ade; Opt Clb Awd; Nazareth College; Pre Nursing.

TABAR, TIMOTHY A; St Edward HS; N Olmsted, OH; 120/360 Band; Hon Rl; Key Clb; Union Carbide Washington Workshops Congressional Seminar; NEDT Superior Perf Awd; Art Culture Class Awd; Notre Dame Univ; Poli Sci.

TABELLION, SUE; Sandy Vly HS; Magnolia, OH; 30/179 Band; Chrh Wkr; Hon Rl; Rptr Yrbk; Rptr Sch Nwsp; Aultman Schl; Nursing.

TABOR, ALTHEA; Talcott Elem HS; Talcott, WV; Cls Rep Frsh Cls; Cls Rep Soph Cls; Cl Rep Jr Cls; Hon Rl; Yth Flsp; Yrbk; Bsktbl; Mgrs; College; Music Teacher.

TABOR, RHONDA; Princeton HS; Princeton, WV; Mdrgl; Sec Yth Flsp; Sch Nwsp; Pep Clb; Spn Clb; College; Art.

TABOR, VICKI; West Geauga HS; Chesterland, OH; Band; Chrh Wkr; FCA; Hon Rl; Trk; IM Sprt; PPFtbl; College; Phys Ther.

TACCOLINI, KRIS; Marquette Sr HS; Marquette, MI; 18/435 Trs Frsh Cls; Hon Rl; Capt Gym; Letter

Ten; Capt Trk; Capt Chrldng; N Michigan Univ; Bus.

TACCOLINI, NATALE; Marquette Sr HS; Marquette, MI; 11/437 Band; Hon Rl; Orch; Ten; Chrldng; IM Sprt; Univ; History.

TACEY, CATHY; Midland HS; Midland, MI; 55/486 Girl Scts; Hon Rl; JA; Pol Wkr; Yth Flsp; 4-H; Spn Clb; Crs Cntry; Swmmng; 4-H Awd; Michigan St Univ; Vet Med.

TACKE, KIM M; Michigan Luthrn Seminry; New Ulm, MN; Chrs; Hon Rl; Mdrgl; Stu Cncl; Yth Flsp; Pep Clb; Chrldng; Dr Martin Luther College; History.

TACKETT, BONNIE; Ecorse HS; Ecorse, MI; 14/169 Band; Hon Rl; Lbry Ade; NHS; Rptr Sch Nwsp; St Of Mi Schlrshp 79; Beog Grant 78; 1st Pl Shorthand Awd 76; Oakland Univ; Writer.

TACKETT, BRIAN; Madison Sr HS; Mansfield, OH; 21/500 Pres JA; NHS; IM Sprt; JA Awd; Ohio St Univ; Engr.

TACKETT, DEENA; Paint Valley HS; Lyndon, OH; 13/75 Hon Rl; FHA; Bus Schl.

TACKETT, DONNA; Eastern Local HS; Beaver, OH; Chrs; Drl Tm; Hon Rl; Sch Pl; Stg Crw; Drama Clb; FTA; Pep Clb; Letter Trk; Morehead St Univ; Elec Engr.

TACKETT, JACK; Harding HS; Marion, OH; Hon Rl; Lit Mag; Fr Clb; Sci Clb; MIT; Phys Sci.

TACKETT, PATSY; Buckeye Valley HS; Sunbury, OH; 2/184 Sal; Band; Chrs; Hon Rl; Jr NHS; NHS; Pep Clb; Bus Schl; Orthodontist Asst.

TACKETTE, ROGER; Whitehall Yearling HS; Columbus, OH; Band; Boy Scts; Hon Rl; Jr NHS; Lbry Ade; VP NHS; PAVAS; Sch Mus; Sch Pl; Stg Crw; 3.5 Or Better GPA; Otterbein Univ; Theatre.

TADSEN, KASSIE; Napoleon HS; Napoleon, OH; 3/255 Hon Rl; NHS; Stu Cncl; Fr Clb; Ger Clb; Spn Clb; Gym; Chrldng; Scr Kpr; Findlay Coll; Marketing.

TADSEN, ROBIN; Napoleon HS; Napoleon, OH; Chrs; Hon Rl; Stg Crw; Rptr Yrbk; Ger Clb; Lat Clb; College; Food Processing.

TADY, CHRISTINE; Russia Local HS; Russia, OH; 6/35 Am Leg Aux Girls St; Chrs; Hon Rl; Sec NHS; Off Ade; Stg Crw; Yrbk; Sch Nwsp; Pep Clb; Spn Clb; Edison St Commun Coll; Spec Educ.

TAFILOWSKI, ERIC; Henry Ford II HS; Sterling Hts, MI; 136/438 Michigan Tech Univ; Forestry.

TAFLAN, SHARON; Weir HS; Weirton, WV; Cls Rep Frsh Cls; Cls Rep Soph Cls; Chrh Wkr; Hon Rl; Off Ade; Stu Cncl; Y-Teens; Pep Clb; Chrldng; GAA; College; Secretary.

TAFT, KRYSTAL K; University HS; Morgantown, WV; 17/166 Band; Chrs; Drm Mjrt; Hon Rl; Lbry Ade; NHS; Orch; Quill & Scroll; Sch Mus; Stg Crw; Art Schl; Cartooning.

TAFT, MITCHELL; University HS; Morgantown, WV; 8/146 Band; Chrs; Hon Rl; Jr NHS; NHS; Sch Mus; Stu Cncl; Sci Clb; Letter Bsbl; Wrstlng; Stage Bank; Univ.

TAFT, VIRGINIA; Chagrin Falls HS; Chagrin Falls, OH; 47/189 Chrs; Pres Girl Scts; Hon Rl; Red Cr Ade; Sch Mus; Sct Actv; Crs Cntry; Trk; PPFtbl; Mas Awd; Rainbow Grand Rep To Ia 79; 1st Class Girls Scout 77; Rainbow Grand Cross Of Color 79; Univ; History.

TAIBI, PAUL; Brooke HS; Follansbee, WV; 169/403 Chrh Wkr; Hon Rl; Sct Actv; Yth Flsp; Univ; Math.

TAKACH, LATISHA; Buckeye South HS; Tiltonsville, OH; 11/139 Hst Soph Cls; Cl Rep Jr Cls; Pres Sr Cls; Am Leg Aux Girls St; Treas Band; Debate Tm; Hon Rl; NHS; Stu Cncl; Y-Teens; West Liberty St Coll; Soc Work.

TAKACS, ADRIENNE; Nazareth Acad; Parma, OH; 4 Hon Rl; Rptr Yrbk; Spn Clb; Pres Awd; John Carroll Univ; Biochem.

TAKUS, A D; Kenowa Hills HS; Grand Rapids, MI; Am Leg Boys St; Band; NHS; Natl Merit Ltr; Mich Tech Univ; Comp Sci.

TALAREK, JOHN; Ben Franklin HS; Livonia, MI; Chrh Wkr; Hon Rl; Univ Of Michigan; Dentistry.

TALARICO, IOLANDO; Lincoln West HS; Cleveland, OH; Hon Rl; Sprt Ed Yrbk; Ftbl; IM Sprt; Cit Awd; Univ; Metallurgy.

TALASKI, CAROL L; North Huron HS; Filion, MI; Band; IM Sprt; Univ; Clerk Typist.

TALASKI, CHRIS; Harbor Beach Comm HS; Harbor Beach, MI; Band; Chrh Wkr; Hon Rl; NHS; Sch Mus; FFA; Pep Clb; Vocational Schl; Cosmetology.

TALBERT, BETH; Springfield HS; Holland, OH; Cl Rep Jr Cls; Chrs; Hon Rl; Off Ade; Pep Clb; Bsbl; Letter Bsktbl; Capt Crs Cntry; Trk; GAA; College; Fashion.

TALBOT, JAMES; Bishop Foley HS; Madison Hts, MI; Boy Scts; Chrh Wkr; Cmnty Wkr; Hon Rl; Pol Wkr; Stg Crw; Bsbl; Letter Ftbl; Letter Wrstlng; Coach Actv; Cert Of Excel Span Alg Trig; Univ Of Michigan; Comp Sci.

TALBOT, LISA; Bloomington HS South; Bloomington, IN; 43/390 Chrh Wkr; FCA; Fr Clb; Pep Clb; Letter Gym; Chrldng; Scr Kpr; Tmr; Indiana Univ; Elem Educ.

TALBOT, MAUREEN; Redford Union HS; Redford, MI; VP Frsh Cls; Pres Soph Cls; Cl Rep Jr Cls; Hon Rl; JA; Sprt Ed Yrbk; Spn Clb; Michigan St Univ; Vet.

TALBOTT, CHESTER; Mitchell HS; Mitchell, IN; 8/143 VP Sr Cls; Am Leg Boys St; Chrh Wkr; Hon Rl; Jr NHS; NHS; Sch Pl; Sci Clb; Am Leg Awd; DAR Awd; Indiana Univ; Chem.

TALBOTT, CYNTHIA; Philip Barbour HS; Belington, WV; Hon Rl; Jr NHS; DECA; FTA; Sec.

TALBOTT, MARTY; Cardinal Stritch HS; Northwood, OH; 40/172 VP Frsh Cls; Pres Soph Cls; Trs Jr Cls; VP Sr Cls; Chrs; Girl Scts; Hon Rl; Hosp Ade; JA; NHS; Univ Of Toledo; Cmnctns.

TALBOTT, PENNY; East Canton HS; E Canton, OH; 8/104 Cls Rep Soph Cls; Cmp Fr Grls; Chrs; Chrh Wkr; Hon Rl; Hosp Ade; Jr NHS; Lbry Ade; Sch Pl; Stg Crw; Kent St Univ; RN.

TALBOTT, SHELLEY; Tri HS; Straughn, IN; Hon Rl; Lbry Ade; 4-H; Fr Clb; FHA; Pep Clb; Spn Clb; Mat Maids; College; R N.

TALCOTT, MARY; Berkshire HS; Burton, OH; 8/133 Band; Cmp Fr Grls; Chrh Wkr; Cmnty Wkr; Hon Rl; MMM; NHS; Pol Wkr; Red Cr Ade; Sch Mus; Mt Vernon Univ; Med Tech.

TALERICO, TINA; Liberty HS; Hepzipah, WV; Hon Rl; Pol Wkr; Spn Clb; Bsktbl; Trk; Letter Letter Letter Wv Career College; Acctg.

TALIEFERO, PAUL S; Bishop Noll Institute; Gary, IN; Hon Rl; Sch Pl; Univ; Bus Admin.

TALL, VICTOR; Shaker Heights HS; Cleveland, OH; 4/550 Boy Scts; Chrh Wkr; Cmnty Wkr; Hon Rl; Pol Wkr; Sct Actv; Yth Flsp; 4-H; FSA; Bsbl; Howard Univ; Law.

TALLANT, ELISE; Jennings County HS; N Vernon, IN; 45/377 NHS; Off Ade; Sec Stu Cncl; VP FTA; Spn Clb; Purdue Univ; Comp Progr.

TALOVICH, MICHAEL; Winston Churchill HS; Livonia, MI; Cls Rep Frsh Cls; Hon Rl; Sci Clb; Letter Bsbl; Letter Bsktbl; Ftbl; Natl Merit Ltr; Michigan St Univ; Advertising.

TALPAS, TIMOTHY; Padua Franciscan HS; Parma, OH; Hon Rl; NHS; Lat Clb; Hockey; Amer Clsscl Lg Jr Clsscl Lg Natl Latin Exasm 77; Univ; Bus.

TALSMA, CHRISTINE; Creston HS; Grand Rapids, MI; Chrh Wkr; Cmnty Wkr; FCA; Hon Rl; JA; Jr NHS; NHS; Sch Mus; Pep Clb; Letter Swmmng; Cntrl Michigan Univ; Comp Sci.

TALSMA, VALERIE; Caledonia HS; Caledonia, MI; Chrs; Chrh Wkr; Debate Tm; Hon Rl; NHS; Sch Mus; Pres Yth Flsp; Pres 4-H; Letter Bsktbl; Mgrs; Michigan St Univ; Botany.

TAMANKO, VICKIE; Forest Park HS; Cincinnati, OH; 38/356 Girl Scts; Hon Rl; Capt Gym; Chrldng; PPFtbl; Univ; Bus.

TAMBURRA, PETER; Charles F Brush HS; S Euclid, OH; Hon Rl; PAVAS; Sch Pl; Yrbk; Rptr Sch Nwsp; Drama Clb; Spn Clb; Cooper Schl Of Art; Cmmrcl Art.

TAMBURRO, PATRICK; Brooklyn HS; Brooklyn, OH; 21/170 Cls Rep Soph Cls; Cl Rep Jr Cls; Cls Rep Sr Cls; Band; Chrs; Hon Rl; NHS; Sch Pl; Stg Crw; Stu Cncl; Cleveland St Univ; Engr.

TAMBURRO, ROBERT; Boardman HS; Youngstown, OH; 1/558 Cls Rep Frsh Cls; Cls Rep Soph Cls; Pres Jr Cls; Pres Sr Cls; Am Leg Boys St; Chrh Wkr; FCA; Hon Rl; NHS; Pol Wkr; 3 Spanish Awds Westminster Tournament Champs; MVP Ohio Northern Bsktbl Camp; Essec Schl For Gifted; College; Medicine.

TAMEZ, TAMMY; Hampshire HS; Romney, WV; 10/213 Cls Rep Frsh Cls; AFS; Hon Rl; NHS; Stg Crw; Yrbk; Sch Nwsp; Drama Clb; GAA; West Virginia Univ; Psych.

TAMMELIN, BOB; Negaunee HS; Negaunee, MI; Am Leg Boys St; Boy Scts; Chrs; Chrh Wkr; Sch Nwsp; Boys Clb Am; Bsktbl; Ftbl; IM Sprt; Scr Kpr; Michigan St Univ; Forestry.

TAMMEN, MELANIE; Dexter HS; Dexter, MI; 6/170 Band; Lit Mag; NHS; Sch Mus; Sch Pl; Drama Clb; Ger Clb; Wrstlng; Rollins College; Theater Arts.

TAMPLIN, GAIL; Hale HS; Hale, MI; 2/65 Sec Jr Cls; Sec Sr Cls; Band; Chrs; Drl Tm; Drm Mjrt; Girl Scts; Hon Rl; NHS; Orch; 1st Oboe Intl Orch 78; 1st Oboe Mich Hnrs Orch 78; St I Rtgs Oboe Solo 79; Univ Of Rochester; Oboe Perf.

TAMPLIN, NANCY; Hale Area HS; Hale, MI; 5/62 Band; Hon Rl; NHS; Orch; Yrbk; 4-H; 4-H Awd; John Phillip Sousa Awd 79; U S Marines Youth Fdn Of Distngshd Musicn Awd 79; Mi Compttv Schslhp 79; Michigan St Univ; Music Ther.

TAMULEWICZ, KAREN; Valley Forge HS; Parma, OH; Chrs; Chrh Wkr; Hon Rl; Mdrgl; NHS; Off Ade; Ed Yrbk; Rptr Yrbk; Pep Clb; Spn Clb; Case Western Reserve Univ; Phys Ther.

TANCHEVSKI, MIKE; Mansfield Malabar HS; Mansfield, OH; 60/270 Sch Nwsp; 4-H; Letter Bsbl; Letter Ftbl; Wrstlng; College; Agri.

TANDY, TERRY; South Dearborn HS; Aurora, IN; 75/290 Band; Drl Tm; Hon Rl; Pep Clb; Letter Bsktbl; Letter Swmmng; Chrldng; GAA; IM Sprt; College; Bus Educ.

TANGEMAN, TRACEY; Coldwater HS; Coldwater, OH; 15/134 Chrs; Hon Rl; Sch Mus; Sch Pl; Stg Crw; Rptr Sch Nwsp; Sch Nwsp; Drama Clb; Ger Clb; Mth Clb; Coll; Acctg.

TANGUILIG, CAROLYN; George Washington HS; Charleston, WV; Cls Rep Soph Cls; Cl Rep Jr Cls; Cls Rep Sr Cls; Drl Tm; Hosp Ade; Treas JA; Stu Cncl; Fr Clb; Keyettes; Pom Pon; Univ; Comp Progr.

TANIER, PEGGY; Delta Sr HS; Delta, OH; Girl Scts; 4-H; Chrldng; Bowling Green Univ; Psych.

TANIS, KATHRYN; Vicksburg HS; Vicksburg, MI; 4/230 Cmnty Wkr; NHS; Orch; Pol Wkr; Sch Mus; Fr Clb; FTA; Spn Clb; Natl Merit Schl; Kalamazoo Coll; Poli Sci.

TANKERSLEY, THOMAS J; Independence HS; Coal City, WV; Pres Soph Cls; Am Leg Boys St; Band; Chrh Wkr; Hon Rl; NHS; Stu Cncl; Beta Clb; Pep Clb; Spn Clb; Univ.

TANKSLEY, MICHAEL; Canfield HS; Canfield, OH; Aud/Vis; Cmnty Wkr; Hon Rl; Jr NHS; NHS; Sch Mus; Stg Crw; Yth Flsp; Ger Clb; Letter Ten; Univ; Med.

TANN, R; Taft HS; Hamilton, OH; AFS; Chrs; Hon Rl; Jr NHS; Sch Pl; VP Ger Clb; College; Bus.

TANNER, ANGELA; Bexley HS; Bexley, OH; Hon Rl; Spn Clb; GAA; Ohio St Univ.

TANNER, JOHN; Winchester Cmnty HS; Winchester, IN; Cls Rep Frsh Cls; Cls Rep Soph Cls; Cl Rep Jr Cls; Cls Rep Sr Cls; Band; FCA; Hon Rl; NHS; VP Stu Cncl; Pres Yth Flsp; Model Legislature Outstndg Comm Mbr Ind 78; Miami Univ; Poli Sci.

TANNER, KRISTY L; Attica Jr Sr HS; Attica, IN; 11/83 Hon Rl; NHS; Off Ade; Drama Clb; Pep Clb; Chrldng; Ivy Tech; Dental Asst.

TANNER, MARTHA R; Cloverleaf Sr HS; Lodi, OH; 1/350 Am Leg Aux Girls St; Band; Chrs; Girl Scts; Hon Rl; VP Jr NHS; NHS; Pres Spn Clb; Letter Bsktbl; Letter Gym; Univ; Foreign Lang.

TANNER, RODNEY; Shelby HS; Shelby, MI; 1/122 Val; Band; Chrh Wkr; Hon Rl; VP NHS; Fr Clb; Bausch & Lomb Awd; Elk Awd; Opt Clb Awd; Michigan Tech Univ; Comp Sci.

TANNER, WILLIAM R; Sebring Mckinley HS; Sebring, OH; 1/75 Hst Soph Cls; VP Jr Cls; Hst Jr Cls; Am Leg Boys St; Hon Rl; NHS; Ger Clb; Ohi State Univ.

TANNOUS, ROBERT; North Canton Hoover HS; North Canton, OH; 33/427 Am Leg Boys St; Band; Chrs; Chrh Wkr; Hon Rl; NHS; Pres Pol Wkr; Sct Actv; VP Ger Clb; Mth Clb; Eagle Scout 76; Brnz Palm 78; Univ; Law.

TANSEK, MARGARET A; Carmel HS; Carmel, IN; 94/722 Trs Jr Cls; Trs Sr Cls; Aud/Vis; Girl Scts; Hon Rl; Hosp Ade; Lit Mag; NHS; Off Ade; Pol Wkr; Reg Sci Fair Awd; Honorable Mention In St Art Gold Key Competition; Gov Bowens Vlntr Service & Vicotry Awd; Yale Univ; Biology.

TANSEY, LARRY; Clinton Prairie HS; Mulberry, IN; Cmnty Wkr; Indiana Voc Tech Schl; Mech.

TANSKI, LAURA; Norton HS; Wadsworth, OH; 2/327 Cls Rep Frsh Cls; Cls Rep Soph Cls; Cl Rep Jr Cls; Cls Rep Sr Cls; Am Leg Aux Girls St; Aud/Vis; Girl Scts; Natl Forn Lg; NHS; Stu Cncl; College.

TANSKLEY, DAVID E; Southeastern HS; Detroit, MI; 18/245 Boy Scts; Chrs; Chrh Wkr; Hon Rl; ROTC; VP VICA; Cit Awd; Natl Merit Schl; St Of Mi Comp Schlrshp 79; Achvmnt Awd In Elec 79; Delta Sigma Theta Hon Awd 79; Wayne St Univ; Comp Engr.

TANSLEY, CAROL M; Southgate HS; Southgate, MI; Hon Rl; Off Ade; OEA; Mat Maids; Scr Kpr; Tmr; Detroit Coll Of Busns; Legal Sec.

TANTLINGER, RUTH; Wintersville HS; Wintersville, OH; Band; Girl Scts; Hosp Ade; Spn Clb; Trk; Univ; Sec.

TARANTINO, LISA; Canfield HS; Canfield, OH; Band; Chrs; Chrh Wkr; Hon Rl; Lit Mag; NHS; Sch Mus; Stg Crw; Rptr Sch Nwsp; Sch Nwsp; Greenville Coll; Psych.

TARANTO, KIMBERLY; Brookhaven HS; Columbus, OH; VP Jr Cls; Chrs; Chrh Wkr; Girl Scts; Hon Rl; Lbry Ade; Lit Mag; Off Ade; Sch Pl; Yth Flsp; Ohio St Univ; Bus Educ.

TARASZEWSKI, ROBERT; Cardinal Mooney HS; Youngstown, OH; 6/296 Cls Rep Soph Cls; Cl Rep Jr Cls; Cls Rep Sr Cls; Am Leg Boys St; Band; Chrs; Hon Rl; NHS; Orch; Sch Mus; Northeastern Ohio Univ; Med.

TARBET, MICHAEL; Green HS; Uniontown, OH; Band; Hon Rl; Orch; Sch Pl; Drama Clb; Ohio State Univ; Broadcast Journalis.

TARBUTTON, TODD; Miami Trace HS; Washington Ch, OH; Cls Rep Frsh Cls; Chrs; Hon Rl; VP PAVAS; Sch Nwsp; VP Drama Clb; Ftbl; Mgrs; Ohio State Univ; Med.

TARGOSZ, SYLVIA; Aquinas HS; Lincoln Park, MI; VP Soph Cls; Chrs; Hon Rl; Sch Mus; Sch Pl; Stu Cncl; Rptr Yrbk; Pep Clb; Chrldng; Kiwan Awd; Univ; Phys Ther.

TARNACKI, DIANE; Divine Child HS; Dearborn, MI; Chrs; Girl Scts; NHS; Rptr Yrbk; Ger Clb; Pep Clb; Bsktbl; Letter Trk; Capt Chrldng; IM Sprt; Mi St Schlrshp; Ferris St Univ; Dent Hygnst.

TARNAS, KEVIN; St Ladislaus HS; Detroit, MI; Chrh Wkr; Cmnty Wkr; Hon Rl; PAVAS; Rptr Yrbk; Rptr Sch Nwsp; Spn Clb; Opt Clb Awd; HS Comm Serv Awd; Cert Of Hnr In Advanced Biology; Journalism Awd; Wayne St Univ; Business Admin.

TARNER, MARK; Clay HS; South Bend, IN; 137/456 Cmnty Wkr; Hon Rl; Ger Clb; Letter Bsktbl; South Bend All Metro Tm 78; Purdue MVP Awd Camp 78; Univ; Soc Studies.

TAROLLI, ROGER; Port Clinton HS; Port Clinton, OH; Chrs; Chrh Wkr; Cmnty Wkr; FCA; Sch Nwsp; Pres DECA; Bsbl; Bsktbl; Crs Cntry; Coach Actv;.

TARPLEY, KEVIN; South HS; Youngstown, OH; 50/290 VP Frsh Cls; Pres Soph Cls; Pres Jr Cls; Pres Sr Cls; Am Leg Boys St; Band; Cmnty Wkr; Drm Mjrt; Red Cr Ade; DECA; YSU; School Counselor.

TARR, DIANE; Clay HS; Martin, OH; 17/373 Band; Chrh Wkr; Hon Rl; NHS; 4-H; Fr Clb; FTA; Heidelberg College; Pre Vet.

TARR, JAMES; Chagrin Falls HS; Chagrin Falls, OH; Cls Rep Frsh Cls; Band; Hon Rl; Orch; Ger Clb; Letter Crs Cntry; Letter Trk; JC Awd; Oh Music Educ Assoc Partiptn In Dist Solo Contest 77 78 & 79; Miami Univ; Chem.

TARSA, JULIA; St Marys HS; Maple City, MI; Trs Sr Cls; Chrh Wkr; Cmnty Wkr; Girl Scts; Hon Rl; Off Ade; Rptr Yrbk; Ed Sch Nwsp; 4-H; Cit Awd; Central Michigan Univ; Home Ec.

TARTER, KATHY; Southeast Local HS; Rootstown, OH; 1/213 Treas Band; MMM; NHS; Stu Cncl; Rptr Sch Nwsp; Treas 4-H; Treas Fr Clb; Pep Clb; Cit Awd; Sec 4-H Awd; Alternate For Hugh O Brien Participated In Typing Contest; French I Awd; Chosen For Creative Writing Cntst; College; Busns.

TARTONI, NATALIE; Franklin HS; Livonia, MI; Letter Swmmng; Trk; PPFtbl; Michigan St Univ.

TARVIN, JEFF; Lapel HS; Lapel, IN; Band; Chrs; Hon Rl; NHS; Sch Mus; Yth Flsp; Rptr Yrbk; Sci Clb; Spn Clb; Crs Cntry; Rose Hulman Inst Of Tech.

TARVIN, KIMBERLY; Taylor HS; N Bend, OH; Sec Jr Cls; Band; Girl Scts; Hon Rl; Sch Pl; Stg Crw; Stu Cncl; College; Journalism.

TASHIJAN, JOHN V; Penn HS; Mishawaka, IN; 8/489 Band; Chrh Wkr; Hon Rl; Jr NHS; Mod UN; NHS; Ger Clb; Letter Swmmng; Purdue Univ; Engr.

TASKER, CATHERINE; East Grand Rapids HS; Grand Rapids, MI; Hon Rl; Sch Mus; Sch Pl; Stu Cncl; Chrldng; PPFtbl; Tmr; Univ Of Michigan.

TASKER, RUSSELL; Allen Park HS; Allen Park, MI; IM Sprt; Whos Who 2 Yrs 77; Wayne St Univ; Chem.

TASKOTT, LISA; Jackson HS; Jackson, OH; 59/256 Band; Chrh Wkr; Girl Scts; Hon Rl; Yth Flsp; VP 4-H; Lat Clb; Sci Clb; IM Sprt; 1st Plc Arts Fest Acrostics 78; 1st Plc Arts Fest Tanka 78; 3rd Plc Arts Fest String Art 76;.

TASSELL, KAREN; Loy Norrix HS; Kalamazoo, MI; Cls Rep Frsh Cls; Hon Rl; 4-H; Letter Trk; Cit Awd; 4-H Awd; Opt Clb Awd; Kal Valley Comm Coll; Acctg.

TATARELLI, FRANCES; Carl Brablec HS; Roseville, MI; Chrh Wkr; Cmnty Wkr; Hon Rl; Hosp Ade; Jr NHS; Red Cr Ade; Sci Clb; Spn Clb; Mas Awd; Wayne State; Journalism.

TATASEO, GEORGE; Campbell Memorial HS; Campbell, OH; Y-Teens; Key Clb; Mth Clb; Spn Clb; Bsktbl; Youngstown St Univ; Chem Engr.

TATE, DEBRA L; Watersmeet HS; Watersmeet, MI; 1/13 Hst Soph Cls; Cl Rep Jr Cls; Trs Sr Cls; Val; Am Leg Aux Girls St; Band; Chrh Wkr; Hon Rl; Off Ade; Pres Stu Cncl; Northern Michigan Univ; Music Educ.

TATE, GAIL; Clarkston Sr HS; Clarkston, MI; Chrs; Girl Scts; Hon Rl; Sch Mus; Sct Actv; Drama Clb; PPFtbl; Most Otstndng In Chorus Awd 77; Central Michigan Univ; Soc Studies.

TATE, GLORIA; Kelloggsville HS; Kentwood, MI; Cls Rep Frsh Cls; VP Jr Cls; Sec Jr Cls; Sec Sr Cls; Band; Cmp Fr Grls; Chrh Wkr; Drl Tm; Hon Rl; NHS; Drama; Univ; Bus Mgmt.

TATE, KENNETH; North HS; Youngstown, OH; Chrs; Hon Rl; Spn Clb; Bsbl; Bsktbl; Ftbl; Cit Awd; Univ.

TATE, LORIN; Kelloggsville HS; Kentwood, MI; Pres Frsh Cls; Pres Soph Cls; Boy Scts; Chrh Wkr; Hon Rl; Off Ade; Sch Pl; Stu Cncl; Rptr Yrbk; Ftbl; Univ Of Southern Calif; Law.

TATE, MARY E; Hart HS; Hart, MI; 11/153 Band; Girl Scts; Hon Rl; NHS; Sch Mus; Ed Sch Nwsp; Cit Awd; 4-H Awd; Inter Scholastic Press Assn Hnrble Mention; Whos Who Among HS Musicians; Ctznshp Awd; Michigan St Univ; Journalism.

TATE, RENEE; Central HS; Detroit, MI; Sal; Chrs; Chrh Wkr; Drl Tm; Hon Rl; Off Ade; PAVAS; College; Bus.

TATE, TAMMY L; Cadillac Sr HS; Cadillac, MI; 3/310 Hon Rl; NHS; Pep Clb; Chrldng; PPFtbl; Jr Rotarian; Hmcmng Qn; Model Millikens Youth Council; Depauw Univ; Medicine.

TATLOCK, MICHAEL W; Brownstown Central HS; Crothersville, IN; 1/160 Chrh Wkr; Cmnty Wkr; Hon Rl; NHS; Sct Actv; VP 4-H; Pres FFA; Purdue Univ; Agri Ed.

TATMAN, LAURIE; Logansport HS; Logansport, IN; 59/342 Band; Chrs; Chrh Wkr; Cmnty Wkr; FCA; Girl Scts; Hon Rl; Lbry Ade; Off Ade; Orch; Intl Yr Of The Child Awd 79; Hooshier Schlr 79; Whos Who Nominee 77; Ball St Univ; Spec Educ.

TATRO, JANICE; Bishop Borgess HS; Garden City, MI; 35/482 Chrh Wkr; Debate Tm; Hon Rl; Natl Forn Lg; NHS; Stg Crw; Rptr Sch Nwsp; Sch Nwsp; Sec Spn Clb; Chanclr Schlshp Univ Of Mi 79; Regnst Schslhp Univ Of Mi Alumni Asooc 79; Mert Schslhp 79; Univ Of Michigan; Acctg.

TATUCH, MARTIN; Immaculate Conception HS; Warren, MI; Hon Rl; NHS; Rptr Sch Nwsp; Bsbl; Bsktbl; Crs Cntry; Ftbl; Scr Kpr; Opt Clb Awd; Univ Of Michigan.

TATUM, RHANDA; Groveport Madison Sr HS; Columbus, OH; Chrh Wkr; Girl Scts; Fr Clb; Scr Kpr; Tmr; Univ; Bio Chem Research.

TAUB, GAYLE; William A Wirt HS; Gary, IN; Hon Rl; Spn Clb; Swmmng; Coach Actv; Tmr; Indiana Univ; Photography.

TAUBE, ERIK K; City HS; Grand Rapids, MI; Aud/Vis; Chrh Wkr; Cmnty Wkr; Debate Tm; Hon Rl; Lit Mag; Yrbk; Univ; Med.

TAUBER, ELLEN; Groves HS; Franklin, MI; Hst Soph Cls; Hst Jr Cls; Chrs; Jr NHS; Pol Wkr; Stu Cncl; Rptr Yrbk; Scr Kpr; Chrldng; Mgrs; College; Bus.

TAULBEE, JOHN; Marysville HS; Marysville, OH; 94/230 Stg Crw; Wrstlng; Wittenburg Univ; Music.

TAURIAINEN, KARLA; Manchester Community Schools; Manchester, MI; Band; Chrh Wkr; PAVAS; Sch Mus; Sch Pl; Stg Crw; Yth Flsp; Yrbk; Letter Bsktbl; Letter Trk; Michigan St Univ; Rec Leadrshp.

TAURMAN, SUSAN; Our Lady Of Providence HS; New Albany, IN; Hon Rl; Scr Kpr; Business Ed Honor Awd; Indiana Univ; Acctg.

TAUTE, TINA M; Corunna HS; Durand, MI; 32/207 Chrh Wkr; Girl Scts; Hon Rl; JA; 4-H; FHA; GAA;

Mgrs; 4-H Awd; Club Futr Sec Assoc 77 79; Baker Jr Coll Of Bus; Bus.

TAVARES, JESSLYN; Lee M Thurston HS; Redford, MI; 22/484 Band; Jr NHS; NHS; Spn Clb; Letter Bsbl; Capt Swmmng; Letter Trk; Phi Beta Kappa Awd 79; Dept Of Educ Schlrshp 79; Western Michigan Univ.

TAVENOR, THOMAS; Harper Woods HS; Harper Woods, MI; Hon Rl; Letter Crs Cntry; Letter Trk; College; Mechanical Engineer.

TAVENS, RENEE; Charles F Brush HS; Lyndhurst, OH; PAVAS; Sch Pl; Sch Nwsp; Drama Clb; College; Chem Engr.

TAVERNIER, KEVIN; Constantine Public HS; Constantine, MI; 38/104 Hon Rl; Yth Flsp; Sprt Ed Yrbk; Rptr Yrbk; Ed Sch Nwsp; ROTC; Pres Sr Cls; Hope Coll; Busns.

TAWNEY, DAVID A; St Marys HS; Belmont, WV; Am Leg Boys St; NHS; Sch Pl; Treas Stu Cncl; Pres Key Clb; VP Spn Clb; Letter Bsbl; Bsktbl; Crs Cntry; DAR Awd; Wv Goldn Horsehoe Winner 76; All Conf Bsbl 79; Pres Clsrm Foryoung Amer Part 79; Spanish Hon 78; Univ; Pub Relations.

TAWNEY, DIANNA; Chesapeake HS; Chesapeake, OH; 15/129 Hon Rl; VP NHS; VP Beta Clb; Fr Clb; Crisco Awrd Outstndng Stu In Home Ec; Banner Awrd Outstndng Stu In Home Ec; Glenville St Coll; Accounting.

TAWNEY, S; Cedar Springs HS; Cedar Spgs, MI; 1/160 Pres Frsh Cls; Am Leg Boys St; Pres Chrh Wkr; FCA; Hon Rl; Jr NHS; NHS; Letter Bsktbl; Letter Ten; IM Sprt; Coll.

TAY, RUBY; Dover HS; Dover, OH; 20/240 Hon Rl; 4-H; FDA; Ten; IM Sprt; Scr Kpr; Tmr; College; Architecture.

TAYLOR, ALANA; Wintersville HS; Wintrsvll, OH; 15/282 Chrs; NHS; Off Ade; Pep Clb; Rus Clb; GAA; PPFtbl; William & Mary; Political Science.

TAYLOR, ALLEN; Decatur HS; Decatur, MI; Chrh Wkr; Hon Rl; NHS; Treas Yth Flsp; Treas 4-H; VP FFA; Letter Bsktbl; 4-H Awd; Mic State Univ.

TAYLOR, ANGELICA; Scott HS; Toledo, OH; Hon Rl; Most Improved Student Awd 78; Univ; Physiology.

TAYLOR, ARLA K; Edgewood HS; Ellettsville, IN; 19/194 Band; Chrh Wkr; FCA; Hon Rl; NHS; Off Ade; Stg Crw; Yth Flsp; Yrbk; Civ Clb; Over All Sr Fair Winner At Edgewood HS; 1st Alternat In Regional Sci Fair To Attend Natl Sci Fair; College; Computer Prog.

TAYLOR, ASHLEY S; Avon Lake HS; Avon Lake, OH; 1/300 Am Leg Boys St; Boy Scts; Chrh Wkr; NHS; Yth Flsp; Yrbk; Letter Bsbl; Letter Bsktbl; Capt Glf; Am Leg Awd; College; Engineering.

TAYLOR, BARBARA; Kouts HS; Kouts, IN; 4/66 Cls Rep Soph Cls; Cl Rep Jr Cls; Chrs; Girl Scts; Hon Rl; Lbry Ade; NHS; Stu Cncl; 4-H; Pep Clb; Bus Schl.

TAYLOR, BARBARA; Goodrich HS; Goodrich, MI; Band; Girl Scts; Hon Rl; Sch Pl; Fr Clb; Central Michigan Univ; CPA.

TAYLOR, BETH A; Lake Orion Sr HS; Lake Orion, MI; Cmp Fr Grls; Hon Rl; Jr NHS; Lbry Ade; Red Cr Ade; Sch Pl; Sct Actv; Stg Crw; Stu Cncl; Sec Drama Clb; College; Busns.

TAYLOR, BRENT; Danville Cmnty HS; Danville, IN; 14/180 Pres Soph Cls; Am Leg Boys St; Hon Rl; NHS; Stg Crw; Fr Clb; Ftbl; Letter Swmmng; IM Sprt; Cit Awd; Pres Social Studies Activities Club 78; Indiana Univ; Bio.

TAYLOR, BRIAN; Quincy HS; Coldwater, MI; 2/110 VP NHS; Bsbl; Bsktbl; IM Sprt; Natl Merit Ltr; Western Michigan Univ Acad Schlrshp; Outstndng Advanced Math Stu Awd; Varsity Clb Treas; Western Michigan Univ; Busns.

TAYLOR, CARLA; Northwest HS; Lucasville, OH; VP Jr Cls; VP Sr Cls; Am Leg Aux Girls St; Sec Band; Chrs; Hon Rl; NHS; Sch Pl; Stu Cncl; FTA; Band Best Marcher Best Of Class 77 79; Band John Philip Sousa Awd 79; Homecoming Attent 75 76 & 78; Capital Univ; Nursing.

TAYLOR, CATHARINE; Van Buren HS; Brazil, IN; Drl Tm; Hon Rl; VP Yth Flsp; Yrbk; Sci Clb; Letter Ten; Letter Trk; GAA; Letter.

TAYLOR, CATHY; Calumet HS; Gary, IN; PAVAS; Quill & Scroll; Sch Mus; Sch Pl; Yrbk; Drama Clb; Lat Clb; Pep Clb; Sci Clb; College; Journalism.

TAYLOR, CHERYL; Ida HS; La Salle, MI; Chrs; Stg Crw; Pep Clb; Toledo Univ; Med.

TAYLOR, CHRISTINE; Miami Trace HS; New Holland, OH; 2/247 Sal; AFS; Am Leg Aux Girls St; Band; Chrs; Hon Rl; NHS; Sch Mus; Sch Pl; Yth Flsp; Ohio St Univ; Dietetics.

TAYLOR, CORENA; Upper Valley Joint Voc Schl; Piqua, OH; Hst Sr Cls; Chrh Wkr; Hosp Ade; Lbry Ade; Off Ade; OEA; Pep Clb; Ten; OEA Exec Dplmt Stswmn & Ambssdr Awd; Dedctd Worker Awd; 1st Pl In OEA Regnl Bus Eng II; Edison St Coll; Legal Sec.

TAYLOR, CYNDA; Inkster HS; Westland, MI; 12/204 VP Jr Cls; Cmnty Wkr; Debate Tm; Hon Rl; NHS; Off Ade; Stg Crw; Pres Stu Cncl; Yth Flsp; Rptr Yrbk; Most Outstanding Co Op Stu; Miss Omega Phi Teen Gamma Phi Delta Sor; Awd Acad Trophies Wayne St Upward Pgm; Howard Univ; Comp Engr.

TAYLOR, CYNTHIA; Edison Jr Sr HS; Lake Sta, IN; 4/154 Hon Rl; Jr NHS; Fr Clb; Lion Awd;.

TAYLOR, CYNTHIA; Jesup W Scott HS; Toledo, OH; 2/273 Hon Rl; NHS; Fr Clb; Spn Clb; Graduate Schl; Law.

TAYLOR, DANNY R; Bethel HS; Nw Carlisle, OH; 17/93 Hon Rl; College; Bus.

TAYLOR, DAVID; Highland Park HS; Highland Pk, MI; 1/36 Aud/Vis; Band; Boy Scts; Chrs; Chrh Wkr; Debate Tm; Hon Rl; Orch; PAVAS; Sch Mus; Awd As Best Male Res & Presented Trophies 79; Math Trophy; Drama Trophy; Religion Trophy; Wayne St Univ; Public Rel.

TAYLOR, DAVID; St Peter & Paul Area HS; Saginaw, MI; Hon Rl; Stg Crw; FDA; FSA; Ger Clb; Sci Clb; Bsktbl; Ftbl; Trk; Univ; Bio.

TAYLOR, DAWN; Mc Bain Rural Agri School; Mc Bain, MI; Sec Soph Cls; Pres Jr Cls; VP Sr Cls; Hon Rl; NHS; Yrbk; 4-H; Trk; Chrldng; Mgrs; Univ.

TAYLOR, DEAN; Wadsworth HS; Wadsworth, OH; 150/380 Yth Flsp; Sprt Ed Yrbk; Rptr Yrbk; Key Clb; Spn Clb; Wrstlng; Cincinnati Univ; Drafting.

TAYLOR, DEBORAH; Grand Rapids Baptist HS; Omaha, NE; VP Soph Cls; Chrs; Hon Rl; Yrbk; 4-H; Bsktbl; Swmmng; IM Sprt; Grand Rapids Bapt College; Elem Educ.

TAYLOR, DEBORAH; Clio HS; Clio, MI; Band; Chrh Wkr; Hon Rl; NHS; Sch Mus;.

TAYLOR, DEBORAH; Baptist HS; Grand Rapids, MI; VP Soph Cls; Chrs; Hon Rl; Rptr Yrbk; Bsktbl; Swmmng; Chrldng; Dnfth Awd; Grand Rapids Baptist College; Educa.

TAYLOR, DELLA; Emerson HS; Gary, IN; Hon Rl; DECA; Accountant, Marketing.

TAYLOR, DENISE; Tri Valley HS; Adamsville, OH; 34/220 NHS; Off Ade; 4-H; Lat Clb; GAA; Mat Maids; 4-H Awd; Bus Schl; Fshn Mdse.

TAYLOR, DENNIS; Pontiac Northern HS; Pontiac, MI; Hon Rl; Michigan St Univ; Engr.

TAYLOR, DIANN; Anderson HS; Anderson, IN; 9/415 Am Leg Aux Girls St; Chrh Wkr; Girl Scts; Hon Rl; Hosp Ade; NHS; 4-H; Fr Clb; Letter Trk; Am Leg Awd; Purdue Univ; Educ.

TAYLOR, DORIS; Arthur Hill HS; Saginaw, MI; 22/531 Debate Tm; Hon Rl; NHS; Orch; Sci Clb; Spn Clb; Natl Merit Ltr; Chatham Scholar; Creativity Awd 8th Annual Black Honors Convocation; Chatham Coll; Medicine.

TAYLOR, DOUGLAS A; Xenia HS; Xenia, OH; 3/579 Band; Boy Scts; Chrs; Chrh Wkr; Hon Rl; NHS; Sch Mus; Sct Actv; Natl Merit SF; College; Math.

TAYLOR, DOUGLAS E; North Central HS; Indianapolis, IN; 40/1194 Cls Rep Frsh Cls; Cls Rep Soph Cls; Cl Rep Jr Cls; Cls Rep Sr Cls; Band; Hon Rl; NHS; Sch Mus; Stu Cncl; Letter Ftbl; Varsity Football Schlastic Awd; Morehouse Coll.

TAYLOR, EDWARD; Belding HS; Belding, MI; Hon Rl; NHS; 4-H; FFA; Key Clb; Bsbl; Letter Ftbl; Wrstlng; 4-H Awd; Central Michigan Univ; Acctg.

TAYLOR, ELIZABETH; Columbian HS; Tiffin, OH; 24/342 Band; Chrs; Hon Rl; Hosp Ade; Spn Clb; Bsktbl; Letter Trk; RN.

TAYLOR, ELIZABETH; Jennings County HS; No Vernon, IN; Sec Frsh Cls; VP Soph Cls; VP Jr Cls; NHS; Sch Pl; Stu Cncl; Rptr Sch Nwsp; Spn Clb; Kiwan Awd; College; Pre Law.

TAYLOR, ELIZABETH S; Carmel HS; Carmel, IN; 2/685 Cls Rep Sr Cls; Sal; Am Leg Aux Girls St; Chrs; Drama Clb; Sec Key Clb; Sec Lat Clb; Mth Clb; Sci Clb; Natl Merit SF; Univ; Chemistry.

TAYLOR, ELORA; R Nelson Snider HS; Ft Wayne, IN; Sec Jr Cls; Chrs; Chrh Wkr; Cmnty Wkr; Hon Rl; JA; Lbry Ade; Stu Cncl; Yrbk; Pep Clb; Frshmn Engr Purdue Univ 76; Gamma Phi Dalta Participant & Recipcnt For Annual Artist 79; Afro Heritage Club; Putdue Univ; Dress Dsgn.

TAYLOR, FRANCES; Richmond Sr HS; Richmond, IN; 22/720 Cls Rep Sr Cls; Hon Rl; Hosp Ade; JA; NHS; Yth Flsp; Y-Teens; Pep Clb; Spn Clb; Indiana Hoosier Schlr Awd 79; Presidential Alumni Schrshp 79; Purdue Univ Awd Of Recognition 79; Purdue Univ.

TAYLOR, G STEVEN; New Richmond HS; New Richmond, OH; Chrs; Hon Rl; Sch Mus; Sch Pl; Stg Crw; Rptr Sch Nwsp; Sch Nwsp; Pep Clb; Bsbl; Bsktbl; Best Supporting Actor 77; Best Actor 78; Jeff Nobis Memrl Fine Arts Awrd 78; Univ; Law.

TAYLOR, HENRY; Buchtel HS; Akron, OH; Band; Crs Cntry; Wrstlng; Voc Schl; Own Body Shop.

TAYLOR, HENRY F; Upper Arlington HS; Columbus, OH; Boy Scts; Hon Rl; Sct Actv; Ger Clb; Letter Wrstlng; God Cntry Awd; Eagle Scout 76; Gold Silver Bronz Pal In Scouting 78; Duty To God Awd Church Of Jesus Of Latter Day Sts 79; Ohio St Univ.

TAYLOR, JACKIE; Bridgeport Sr HS; Bridgeport, WV; Chrs; Chrh Wkr; Hon Rl; Trk; Coll; Criminal Law.

TAYLOR, JACQUELINE; Mother Of Mercy HS; Cincinnati, OH; Cl Rep Jr Cls; Band; Cmp Fr Grls; Sch Mus; Sch Pl; 4-H; Fr Clb; Chrldng; 4-H Awd; Deaconess School Of Nursing; Nursing.

TAYLOR, JAMES A; Rochester HS; Rochester, MI; Cls Rep Sr Cls; Boy Scts; Debate Tm; Hon Rl; Natl Forn Lg; NHS; Mth Clb; Sci Clb; Elk Awd; Natl Merit SF; Univ; Elec Engr.

TAYLOR, JEFFREY R; Cloverleaf HS; Medina, OH; 19/319 Am Leg Boys St; Hon Rl; NHS; Sch Mus; Sch Pl; Stg Crw; Rptr Yrbk; Yrbk; Drama Clb; Letter Trk; Ohio State Univ.

TAYLOR, JENNIFER; Greenbrier East HS; Ronceverte, WV; Trs Jr Cls; Band; Chrs; Capt Drl Tm; FCA; NHS; Treas Stu Cncl; College; Creative Writing.

TAYLOR, JODI; Edison HS; Huron, OH; 38/175 Trs Frsh Cls; Trs Jr Cls; VP Sr Cls; Chrs; Girl Scts; NHS; Sch Mus; Sch Pl; Stg Crw; Drama Clb; Univ; Educ.

TAYLOR, JOHN; Bullock Creek HS; Midland, MI; Debate Tm; Hon Rl; JA; Lit Mag; JA Awd; Sci Fair Winning Tm Trophy; Exc Debater Trophy; Cert Of Acceptance For Poetry Manuscript; Coll; Drama.

TAYLOR, JOHN M; Martinsburg Sr HS; Martinsburg, WV; 23/220 Boy Scts; Chrs; Chrh Wkr; Hon Rl; Sch Mus; Sch Pl; Yth Flsp; Treas Drama Clb; Hnrbl Mentn For Best Perfmr 77 & 79; Dir Of Sr 1 Act In My Sr Yr 79; Wake Forest Univ; Med.

TAYLOR, JOSEPH; John Adams HS; So Bend, IN; 14/395 Jr NHS; Quill & Scroll; Ed Sch Nwsp; Sprt Ed Sch Nwsp; Socr; College; Law.

TAYLOR, JULIE; Lawrence Central HS; Indianapolis, IN; 8/450 Band; Hon Rl; Mod UN; NHS; Orch; Sch Mus; Pres Yth Flsp; Rptr Sch Nwsp; Pep Clb; Univ; Accounting.

TAYLOR, JUNE; Chadsey HS; Detroit, MI; Cmp Fr Grls; Chrs; Pres Chrh Wkr; Hon Rl; Hosp Ade; Lbry Ade; Off Ade; Sch Mus; Rptr Sch Nwsp; Pep Clb; Schlstc 75; Vllybl 79; Music Piano Contst 2 1st Pl 78; Univ Of Michigan; RN.

TAYLOR, JUNE; Pocahontas Cnty HS; Dunmore, WV; Cls Rep Soph Cls; Sec Jr Cls; Band; Jr NHS; Off Ade; Stu Cncl; Bsktbl; Fairmont St Univ; Vet.

TAYLOR, KEIP L; Hyland Park HS; Highland Park, MI; 2/36 Aud/Vis; Band; Lit Mag; Red Cr Ade; Boys Clb Am; Drama Clb; FTA; Mth Clb; Spn Clb;.

TAYLOR, KENNETH; Pickerington Sr HS; Pickerington, OH; Cls Rep Frsh Cls; Trs Soph Cls; Boy Scts; Chrh Wkr; Cmnty Wkr; Hon Rl; Red Cr Ade; Sct Actv; Stu Cncl; Civ Clb; La Sertoma Yth Serv Awd; Columbus Tech Univ; Para Medic.

TAYLOR, KENNIE; Arthur Hill HS; Saginaw, MI; Cls Rep Sr Cls; Hon Rl; Sci Clb; Ftbl; Trk; Hon Awd 8th Annual Black Hon Convocation 78 & 79; Michigan St Univ; Vet Med.

TAYLOR, KEVIN; Kankakee Valley HS; De Motte, IN; 23/182 Boy Scts; Hon Rl; NHS; Sch Pl; Sct Actv; Yth Flsp; Ger Clb; Ftbl; Capt Trk; Purdue Univ; Officer In US Marines.

TAYLOR, KIM; Bishop Donahue HS; Benwood, WV; 15/56 Am Leg Aux Girls St; Chrs; Chrh Wkr; Hon Rl; NHS; Rptr Yrbk; Rptr Sch Nwsp; Pep Clb; Letter Chrldng; GAA; West Liberty St Coll; Speech Therapy.

TAYLOR, KIM; Jonathan Alder HS; Plain City, OH; 4/105 Sec Frsh Cls; Band; Lbry Ade; NHS; Quill & Scroll; Pres Y-Teens; Sprt Ed Sch Nwsp; VP Fr Clb; Treas Spn Clb; Cit Awd; Ohio State Univ; Nurse.

TAYLOR, KIMBERLY; Mc Bain Rural Agri HS; Mc Bain, MI; 1/60 Trs Frsh Cls; Trs Soph Cls; Pres Jr Cls; Pres Sr Cls; Val; Am Leg Aux Girls St; Pres Band; Chrs; Chrh Wkr; Hon Rl; Natl Presbyterian Schlrshp 79; Alma Coll Trustee Hnrs Schlrshp 79; Alma Coll Pres Schlrshp 79; Alma Coll; Law.

TAYLOR, KIP N; Grand Ledge HS; Grand Ledge, MI; 221/425 Band; Boy Scts; Hon Rl; Sch Pl; Sct Actv; Stg Crw; Boys Clb Am; IM Sprt; Scr Kpr; Tmr; Hillsdale Coll; Poli Econ.

TAYLOR, LAURA; Buckeye HS; Medina, OH; 18/173 Hon Rl; Jr NHS; NHS; Yth Flsp; Chrh Wkr; Girl Scts; Fr Clb; Pep Clb; College; Flight Attendant.

TAYLOR, LAURIE A; Port Clinton HS; Port Clinton, OH; Am Leg Aux Girls St; Band; Hon Rl; NHS; Pol Wkr; Lat Clb; Letter Bsktbl; Letter Trk; VP GAA; Miami Univ; Psych.

TAYLOR, LESLIE; Frontier HS; Nw Mtmrs, OH; Sec Frsh Cls; Cl Rep Jr Cls; Am Leg Aux Girls St; Band; Girl Scts; Lbry Ade; NHS; Sch Pl; Treas Stu Cncl; Treas Yth Flsp; Holzer Med Center; RN.

TAYLOR, LYNDON; Andrews Acad; Berrien Spgs, MI; Chrh Wkr; Natl Merit Ltr; Michigan St Univ; Music.

TAYLOR, M; Benton Harbor HS; Benton Hrbr, MI; Chrh Wkr; Debate Tm; Hon Rl; JA; Lbry Ade; OEA; Mich State College; Medicine.

TAYLOR, MARCIE; Martins Ferry HS; Martins Ferry, OH; 15/215 Band; Chrh Wkr; Hon Rl; NHS; Orch; Stu Cncl; Y-Teens; Fr Clb; Wheeling Coll; French.

TAYLOR, MARK; Hoover HS; North Canton, OH; 104/460 FCA; Jr NHS; Bsbl; Bsktbl; Ftbl; College; Law.

TAYLOR, MARTHA; Fairmont West HS; Kettering, OH; AFS; Chrs; Hon Rl; NHS; Sch Mus; Yth Flsp; Sch Nwsp; Fr Clb; Depauw Univ.

TAYLOR, MARTHA E; North Central HS; Indianapolis, IN; 79/1194 Chrh Wkr; Hon Rl; NHS; Off Ade; Sch Pl; Pep Clb; Gym; Natl Merit Ltr; Spanish Honor Soc; Scholastic Citation; Purdue Univ; Psychology.

TAYLOR, MARVIN; Union County HS; Liberty, IN; 5/128 Aud/Vis; Band; Chrs; Chrh Wkr; Hon Rl; Lbry Ade; Mdrgl; NHS; PAVAS; Sch Mus; College; Music History.

TAYLOR, N; Warren Sr HS; Troy, MI; Cls Rep Frsh Cls; Cl Rep Jr Cls; Cls Rep Sr Cls; Girl Scts; Hon Rl; NHS; Off Ade; Sch Pl; Stu Cncl; Drama Clb; Wayne St Univ; Intl Bus.

TAYLOR, NAOMI; Pocahontas Cnty HS; Dunmore, WV; 22/126 Band; Boy Scts; Chrh Wkr; Girl Scts; Yth Flsp; FFA; FHA; Pep Clb; 4-H Awd; Marshall Univ; Pre Vet.

TAYLOR, PAMELA; John Nay HS; Cleveland, OH; Cls Rep Sr Cls; Band; Chrs; Chrh Wkr; Off Ade; Orch; Stu Cncl; Yrbk; FNA; Chrldng; Kent State Univ; Nursing.

TAYLOR, PAMELA; Immaculata HS; Detroit, MI; Cls Rep Frsh Cls; Cl Rep Jr Cls; Cmnty Wkr; Drl Tm; Hon Rl; Off Ade; Stu Cncl; Pep Clb; Pom Pon; Kiwan Awd; Howard Univ.

TAYLOR, PATRICIA; Kenowa Hills HS; Grand Rapids, MI; Cmnty Wkr; JA; Lbry Ade; NHS; 4-H; Trk; PPFtbl; 4-H Awd; Treas JA Awd; Univ; Bio.

TAYLOR, PAUL; N Michigan Christian HS; Mc Bain, MI; Hon Rl; Yth Flsp; 4-H; 4-H Awd;.

TAYLOR, PAULA; South Charleston HS; S Charleston, WV; Y-Teens; FHA; Chrldng; IM Sprt; Marshal Univ; Bus.

TAYLOR, REBECCA; Osborn HS; Detroit, MI; Hon Rl; Lbry Ade; Off Ade; Y-Teens; Letter Trk; Bus Schl; Exec Sec.

TAYLOR, RENEE; Cass Technical HS; Detroit, MI; Cls Rep Frsh Cls; Chrh Wkr; Drl Tm; Off Ade; Recgngnt Savng Ones Life 78; Univ Of Detroit; Psych.

TAYLOR, RITA; Salem HS; Salme, IN; 33/170 Trs Soph Cls; Trs Jr Cls; Am Leg Aux Girls St; Aud/Vis; Girl Scts; JA; NHS; Yth Flsp; Drama Clb; Lat Clb; Honored Queen Of Jobs Daughters; Tri Hi Y Pres; Busns Schl; Acctg.

TAYLOR, ROBERT; H H Dow HS; Midland, MI; Cls Rep Soph Cls; Stg Crw; Sprt Ed Sch Nwsp; 4-H; Key Clb; Letter Bsbl; Letter Ftbl; Ariz State Univ; Bus Admin.

TAYLOR, ROBERT H; Loveland Lincoln Hurst HS; Loveland, OH; Lit Mag; Sch Mus; Sch Pl; Yth Flsp; Rptr Yrbk; Rptr Sch Nwsp; Drama Clb; Ger Clb; College; Pre Law.

TAYLOR, RUBERTHA L; East HS; Cleveland, OH; Cls Rep Frsh Cls; Stu Cncl; Bsktbl; Trk; Cit Awd; Natl Merit Ltr; Malone Coll; Archt.

TAYLOR, SAMUEL; University HS; Morgantown, WV; Sch Pl; Ed Yrbk; Sprt Ed Yrbk; Drama Clb; Letter Ftbl; Mgrs; Scr Kpr; Univ; Art.

TAYLOR, SAMUEL D; Avon HS; Indianapolis, IN; 19/188 Aud/Vis; Hon Rl; Lbry Ade; NHS; Ed Sch Nwsp; Fr Clb; Sec Sci Clb; Letter Ftbl; Glf; IM Sprt; Ind Univ; Communications.

TAYLOR, SANDRA; Osborn HS; Detroit, MI; Chrs; Chrh Wkr; Drl Tm; Hon Rl; Off Ade; Yth Flsp; FTA; Lat Clb; Bsbl; Letter Trk; Mercy Coll Schl Of Nursing; Med.

TAYLOR, SAUNDRA; Mt Hope HS; Scarbro, WV; 2/85 Sal; Band; Hon Rl; Treas NHS; Sch Pl; Rptr Sch Nwsp; FHA; Pep Clb; Spn Clb; Letter Bsktbl; Marshall Univ; Psych.

TAYLOR, SCOT; Portsmouth HS; Portsmouth, OH; Pres Frsh Cls; Cmnty Wkr; Hon Rl; Yth Flsp; Bsktbl; Rotary Awd; Miami Univ; Bus.

TAYLOR, SCOTT; Britton Macon HS; Britton, MI; Boy Scts; Hon Rl; Sct Actv; Bsbl; Ftbl; Ypsilantj Little Lg All Star Bsbl Team 77; Univ; Sports Statistition.

TAYLOR, SHEILA; Tygarts Valley HS; Mill Creek, WV; Cls Rep Frsh Cls; Pres Sr Cls; Stu Cncl; Rptr Yrbk; 4-H; FBLA; Bsktbl; Chrldng; Scr Kpr; Bus Coll.

TAYLOR, SHELLEY L; Michigan Lutheran Seminary; Saginaw, MI; VP Frsh Cls; Chrs; Sch Pl; Stu Cncl; Letter Bsktbl; IM Sprt; PPFtbl; Bus.

TAYLOR, SHERYL; Kent City HS; Casnovia, MI; 7/98 Sec Sr Cls; Band; Hon Rl; NHS; Off Ade; Rptr Sch Nwsp; Chrldng; PPFtbl; Davenport Coll Of Bus; Acctg.

TAYLOR, SONYA; St Ursula Acad; Toledo, OH; Boy Scts; Chrs; Hon Rl; JA; Lbry Ade; Stu Cncl; Yth Flsp; Boys Clb Am; Drama Clb; Lat Clb; University; Premed.

TAYLOR, STEVEN; Ainsworth HS; Flint, MI; 30/270 Hon Rl; NHS; Ftbl; Trk; Wrstlng; Lion Awd; Saginaw Vly St Coll; Econ.

TAYLOR, STEVEN R; Jackson HS; North Canton, OH; Boy Scts; Debate Tm; Hon Rl; Mod UN; Natl Forn Lg; Sch Nwsp; Ftbl; Aero Engr.

TAYLOR, SYLVIA; Jane Addams Voc HS; Cleveland , OH; Cls Rep Soph Cls; Sec Jr Cls; Chrs; Jr NHS; Stu Cncl; Rptr Sch Nwsp; Chrldng; Cit Awd; JA Awd; Coll; Secretary.

TAYLOR, TAMIE; Euclid Sr HS; Euclid, OH; 151/646 Chrs; Hon Rl; Ohio St Univ; Acctg.

TAYLOR, TAMMY; Columbia HS; Columbia Sta, OH; Hon Rl; Lbry Ade; NHS; Sch Mus; Sch Pl; Stg Crw; Drama Clb; Fr Clb; Hon Mention At Dstrct Sci Fair 78; Oh Tests Of Schlstc Achvmnt In Geometry; Univ.

TAYLOR, TAMRA; Mc Clain HS; Lyndon, OH; Chrh Wkr; Cmnty Wkr; Sec NHS; Stg Crw; Stu Cncl; Pres Yth Flsp; Yrbk; VP 4-H; Sec Spn Clb; IM Sprt; Typing I Awd; Shrthnd I Awd; Sec Of Yr; Bus Schl; Bus.

TAYLOR, TERESA; Mount Notre Dame HS; Cincinnati, OH; Chrs; Chrh Wkr Hon Rl; Mod UN; NHS; College; Sci.

TAYLOR, TERI; Newark HS; Newark, OH; 159/600 Chrs; Cmnty Wkr; Girl Scts; Hon Rl; Off Ade; Sct Actv; Yth Flsp; VP 4-H; FHA; Letter Trk; Homecoming Court; County 4 H Fashion Board; Envir Ed Camp Counselor; Central Ohio Tech Coll.

TAYLOR, TERI; Brookville HS; Brookville, IN; Hon Rl; NHS; Stu Cncl; Pep Clb; Chrldng; Indiana Central Univ; Nursing.

TAYLOR, THOMAS L; Napoleon HS; Napoleon, OH; Pres Frsh Cls; VP Soph Cls; Pres Sr Cls; Band; Stu Cncl; Letter Ftbl; Letter Trk; Letter Wrstlng; IM Sprt; VP Of Athletic Club; Will Become Pres Of Athletic Club; Ohio St Univ; Math.

TAYLOR, TIMOTHY; Quincy HS; Coldwater, MI; 5/110 Pres Frsh Cls; Hon Rl; Pres NHS; Sprt Ed Yrbk; Rptr Sch Nwsp; Letter Bsbl; Letter Bsktbl; Letter Trk; Dnfth Awd; Western Michigan Univ; Busns Admin.

TAYLOR, TINA; Gladwin HS; Gladwin, MI; 5/189 Sec Jr Cls; Chrh Wkr; Cmnty Wkr; Hon Rl; Sch Pl; 4-H; Lat Clb; Pep Clb; Trk; Chrldng; Univ; Sci.

TAYLOR, TRACY; Fairfield HS; Leesburg, OH; 1/60 Val; Drl Tm; Hon Rl; Lbry Ade; NHS; Yrbk; Pres Spn Clb; Kenyon College; Atty.

TAYLOR, WANDA R; La Salle HS; South Bend, IN; NHS; Sch Pl; Drama Clb; Purdue Univ; Psych.

TAYLOR, WILLARD; Bishop Flaget HS; Chillicothe, OH; Chrh Wkr; Cmnty Wkr; Hon Rl; Sch Mus; Stg Crw; Fr Clb; Letter Bsbl; Bsktbl; Letter Crs Cntry; Am Leg Awd; Univ; Vet.

TAYLOR, WILLIAM P; Euclid HS; Euclid, OH; Aud/Vis; Band; Boy Scts; Chrs; Off Ade; Sct Actv; West Washington Coll; Elec.

TAYLOR, ZONDRA L; Belleville HS; Ypsilanti, MI; Cmp Fr Grls; Chrs; Girl Scts; Hon Rl; JA; Off Ade; Sch Mus; Stu Cncl; Trk; Eastern Michigan Univ; Music.

TAYLOR JR, JOHN; West Branch HS; Alliance, OH; 4/231 Am Leg Boys St; Chrs; Debate Tm; Hon Rl; Natl Forn Lg; NHS; Sch Mus; Ten; Tmr; Air Force Acad; Pilot.

TAYSE, MAUREEN; Tecumseh HS; New Carlisle, OH; 19/381 AFS; Band; Chrs; Chrh Wkr; Girl Scts; Hon Rl; Jr NHS; NHS; Sch Mus; Sch Pl; Ohio St Univ.

TEACHOUT, INGRID; Hudsonville HS; Hudsonville, MI; Chrs; Hon Rl; Natl Forn Lg; NHS; Sch Mus; Rptr Sch Nwsp; Chrldng; Grand Rapids Baptist Coll; Music.

TEAGUE, KENT; Macon Eastern HS; Sardinia, OH; Chrs; Hon Rl; Stu Cncl; Pres 4-H; Pres FFA; 4-H Awd; College; Agri Bus.

TEAGUE, THOMAS E; Garfield Sr HS; Hamilton, OH; Am Leg Boys St; Band; Orch; Ger Clb;.

TEAHEN, CRAIG; Clio HS; Clio, MI; Cls Rep Frsh Cls; Pres Soph Cls; Cls Rep Soph Cls; Pres Jr Cls; Cl Rep Jr Cls; Hon Rl; Jr NHS; NHS; Sch Pl; Stu Cncl; NASA Cert Of Outstndng Ach Flint Sci Fair; U S Army Most Outstndng In Earth & Space Sci Flint Sci Fair; College; Medicine.

TEAL, BARBARA; Evergreen HS; Lyons, OH; Hon Rl; Hosp Ade; 4-H; Fr Clb; OEA; Bsktbl; Tech Coll.

TEAL, PENNY; Perry HS; Perry, MI; VP Jr Cls; NHS; Sch Pl; Letter Bsktbl; Letter Trk; Mgrs; Natl Merit SF; Univ Of Col; Engr Physics.

TEATER, TOM; Bellaire HS; Neffs, OH; 1/230 Boy Scts; VP FCA; Hon Rl; NHS; Pres Stu Cncl; Yth Flsp; Spn Clb; Letter Bsbl; Letter Ftbl; IM Sprt; College; Med.

TEBBE, ERIC; Lincoln HS; Cambridge, IN; VICA; Wyo Tech; Automotive.

TEBBE, ROBERT J; La Salle HS; Cincinnati, OH; 8/249 Cl Rep Jr Cls; Chrh Wkr; Hon Rl; Stg Crw; Yth Flsp; Rdo Clb; Ftbl; Wrstlng; K Of C Rel Award 1976; Bronz & Silver Honor Awards 1978; Xavier Univ; Commctns.

TEBBING, BONNIE; South Ripley HS; Versailles, IN; 13/112 Band; Drl Tm; Hon Rl; Yrbk; Sch Nwsp; Sec 4-H; Pep Clb; Spn Clb; Univ; Med.

TEDESCO, TONI E; Seton HS; Cincinnati, OH; 8/255 Hon Rl; JA; Jr NHS; NHS; Fr Clb; Pep Clb; Socr; Coach Actv; GAA; IM Sprt; Straight A Tickets 1974; Natl French Contest Certif 1978; 1st Pl Essay Contest Kiwanis 1973; Univ; Med Lab Tech.

TEDRICK, CATHERINE; Centerburg HS; Centerburg, OH; 11/62 Chrs; Drl Tm; Hon Rl; NHS; Yrbk; Pres 4-H; Letter Bsktbl; PPFtbl; Scr Kpr; Otterbein College; Phys Educ.

TEDROW, BARRY D; Barr Reeve HS; Loogootee, IN; Hon Rl; Beta Clb; Bsbl; Bsktbl; Univ Of Evansville; Law Enf.

TEDROW, LORI; Shelby HS; Shelby, OH; Band; Chrs; Hon Rl; JA; Red Cr Ade; Sch Pl; Sct Actv; NCTC; Med.

TEDSCHI, PETER; Valley Forge HS; Parma, OH; 47/777 Hon Rl; College; Pharmacy.

TEEGARDIN, TERRY; Penn HS; Mishawaka, IN; 35/500 Hon Rl; NHS; Sct Actv; Pep Clb; Spn Clb; Letter Crs Cntry; Letter Trk; IM Sprt; Univ; Comp Sci.

TEENIER, THOMAS; Arthur Hill HS; Saginaw, MI; Hon Rl; Chmn NHS; Cit Awd; Natl Merit Ltr; Chrmn Of Natl Hon Soc 79; Hon Roll; Univ Of Michigan; Pre Dent.

TEEPLE, KATHY; Jackson HS; North Canton, OH; 63/409 Band; Girl Scts; Hon Rl; Orch; Sch Mus; Sct Actv; Sec Yth Flsp; Y-Teens; 4-H; Fr Clb; Soc Distg Amer Stud 77 79; 1st Clss Cadet Girl Sct 76; Supr Flute Solo 78; Ohio St Univ; Med Tech.

TEER, BILLY; Boonville HS; Boonville, IN; 26/218 Aud/Vis; Debate Tm; Hon Rl; NHS; Pol Wkr; Sch Pl; Stg Crw; Ind Univ; Bio.

TEETER, LAURA; Indiana Acad; Buchanan, MI; Sec Sr Cls; Chrs; Hon Rl; Rptr Sch Nwsp; IM Sprt; Andrews Univ; Elem Educ.

TEETER, RANDY; Roscommon HS; Roscommon, MI; College; Mngmt.

TEETERS, JODY; Martinsville Sr HS; Martinsville, IN; 62/389 Chrh Wkr; Hon Rl; Off Ade; Yrbk; Sch Nwsp; 4-H; Ger Clb; OEA; Pep Clb; Trk;.

TEETERS, LINDA; Howell HS; Howell, MI; 36/395 Girl Scts; Hon Rl; NHS; Ger Clb; Letter Bsktbl; GAA; Adrian Coll; Pre Law.

TEFEND, JAMES; Flat Rock HS; Flat Rock, MI; Pres Jr Cls; Chrs; Hon Rl; Sct Actv; Pres Stu Cncl; Bsbl; Univ; Pre Law.

TEGTMEYER, CHRISTINE S; Ansonia HS; Ansonia, OH; 3/60 Trs Sr Cls; Am Leg Aux Girls St; Band; Chrs; Hon Rl; NHS; 4-H;.

TEHI, ELIZABETH; Wadsworth Sr HS; Wadsworth, OH; 1/360 AFS; Band; Chrs; Hosp Ade; Natl Forn Lg; NHS; Fr Clb; Pep Clb; Natl Merit Ltr; Univ; Optometry.

TEICHMAN, LORI; Cass City HS; Cass City, MI; 1/160 Chrh Wkr; Hon Rl; Jr NHS; NHS; Off Ade; Yth Flsp; Trk; Chrldng; Univ; Acctg.

TEIGA, TERESA; New Albany HS; New Albany, OH; 27/110 Sec Sr Cls; Girl Scts; Off Ade; Stu Cncl; Pep Clb; Chrldng; PPFtbl; Ohio St Univ; Eng.

TEISAN, ALICE; Denby HS; Detroit, MI; Chrh Wkr; Hon Rl; NHS; Orch; Letter Ten; Wayne State Univ; Youth Pastor.

TELDER, JEFF; Grandville HS; Grandville, MI; 94/340 Cls Rep Frsh Cls; Cls Rep Soph Cls; Hon Rl; VP Stu Cncl; Letter Bsktbl; Letter Ten; Mgrs; Scr Kpr; Tmr; Western Michigan Univ; Bus.

TELEK, BETH; New Richmond HS; New Richmond, OH; Chrs; Girl Scts; Hon Rl; NHS; Off Ade; PAVAS; Sch Mus; Sch Pl; Sct Actv; Stg Crw; Drama Clb Awrd High Pt Holder 78; Bus Educ Schlstc Achvmnt Awrd 78; Danced In 4 Pro Shows 1 On TV; Phoenix St Univ; Dancing.

TELEPAK, JUDITH; Holy Name Nazareth HS; Seven Hills, OH; Cls Rep Frsh Cls; Chrh Wkr; Cmnty Wkr; Hon Rl; Drama Clb; IM Sprt; Tmr; Ski Club; Univ.

TELEPAK, THEODORE A; Padua Franciscan HS; Seven Hills, OH; Chrh Wkr; Cmnty Wkr; Ftbl; Coach Actv; IM Sprt; Coll Of Steubenville; Bio.

TELFER, GAYLE; Corunna HS; Owosso, MI; 26/207 Treas Chrs; Chrh Wkr; Hon Rl; Yth Flsp; Rptr Yrbk; 4-H; Pep Clb; 4-H Awd; Christian Youth Crusaders 67 73; Spring Arbor Outside Schlrshp Grant 79; Believers Vocal Grp 76 79; Spring Arbor Coll; Psych.

TELGER, MARY; Seton HS; Cincinnati, OH; Chrs; Girl Scts; Hon Rl; JA; Sch Mus; Sct Actv; Spn Clb; Bsbl; GAA; College; Journalism.

TEMPLE, BLAIR; Belleville HS; Belleville, MI; VP Frsh Cls; Hon Rl; Bsbl; Ftbl; Trk; Wrstlng; Natl Merit Schl; Hnrble Mention All Area Ftbl; Ctr For Creative Study; Fine Arts.

TEMPLE, JAMIE; Belleville HS; Belleville, MI; Cls Rep Frsh Cls; Band; Girl Scts; Hon Rl; Sch Pl; Sct Actv; Rptr Yrbk; Rptr Sch Nwsp; Ger Clb; Pep Clb; Coll.

TEMPLE, MARIE; Chatard HS; Louisville, KY; Cl Rep Jr Cls; Cls Rep Sr Cls; Hon Rl; Jr NHS; NHS; Sch Mus; Sch Pl; Stu Cncl; Pep Clb; Swmmng; Univ Of Kentucky; Bus.

TEMPLE, MARK; St Joseph HS; Chardon, OH; 28/300 Lit Mag; NHS; Stu Cncl; Ed Yrbk; Rptr Sch Nwsp; Trk; IM Sprt; College; Marine Bio.

TEMPLETON, DONALD; Park Hills HS; Fairborn, OH; Swim On Wright Patterosn AFB Flyng Fish Swim Team 70 79; ITT Tech Schl; Tool.

TEMPLETON, RUTHANN; Margaretta HS; Castalia, OH; 35/175 Band; Chrh Wkr; Hon Rl; Orch; Sch Pl; Stg Crw; Ed Yrbk; Rptr Yrbk; Ed Sch Nwsp; Rptr Sch Nwsp; Hon Jrnslm Stdnt Awd 77; Bst Actress Awd 78; Super Rating At Solo & Ensemble Contst Piano 79; Bowling Green St Univ; Spec Educ.

TEMPLETON, THOMAS T; Hannan HS; Apple Grove, WV; VP Soph Cls; VP Jr Cls; Aud/Vis; Hon Rl; VP FFA; Letter Bsbl; Letter Ftbl; Cit Awd; DAR Awd; College.

TENAGLIA, MARY L; St Agatha HS; Detroit, MI; Hon Rl; College.

TENBARGE, LAURA; Mater Dei HS; Evansvl, IN; 9/171 Sec Sr Cls; Hon Rl; Jr NHS; NHS; Sch Pl; Pep Clb; Sci Clb; IM Sprt; Univ; Comp Sci.

TENBRINK, JAMIE; Anderson HS; Cincinnati, OH; 29/377 Band; Chrs; Drl Tm; Hon Rl; VP NHS; Pep Clb; Univ.

TENBUSCH, KAREN L; Mona Shores HS; Muskegon, MI; Hon Rl; Off Ade; Muskegon Cmnty Coll; Engr.

TENEROVE, LISA; Mentor HS; Mentor Lake, OH; Hon Rl; Off Ade; Sec DECA; 2nd Pl Winner In Dist For Apparel & Accessories; Top 10 In State For Apparel & Accesoories; Mbr Of YARC; Lakeland Comm Coll; Busns.

TEN EYCK, KAY; Bucyrus HS; Bucyrus, OH; Chrh Wkr; Cmnty Wkr; Girl Scts; NHS; Off Ade; Sch Mus; Yth Flsp; Rptr Sch Nwsp; Mas Awd; Univ; Music.

TENGEL, JEFF; Padua Franciscan HS; Brunswick, OH; 25/292 Hon Rl; NHS; Bsktbl; Coach Actv; IM Sprt; College.

TENGLER, SUSAN; Nazareth Acad; Parma, OH; Chrh Wkr; FCA; Lat Clb; Bsbl; Capt Bsktbl; Gym; Ten; Chrldng; Coach Actv; IM Sprt; Bowling Green Univ; Nursing.

TEN HAAF, SHIRLEY; Caledonia HS; Caledonia, MI; Chrh Wkr; Yth Flsp; FFA; IM Sprt; Univ; RN.

TENNANT, DAVID; Bridgeport HS; Bridgeport, WV; 4/189 Hon Rl; Jr NHS; NHS; Natl Merit SF; Natl Merit Schl; West Virginia Univ; Engr.

TENNANT, DIANA; Fairview HS; Fairview, WV; 3/54 Pres Frsh Cls; Am Leg Aux Girls St; Chrs; Hon Rl; NHS; Pres Stu Cncl; Rptr Yrbk; Sprt Ed Sch Nwsp; Capt Bsktbl; Capt Chrldng; Fairmont St Coll; Busns Admin.

TENNANT, KIMBERLY; University HS; Morgantown, WV; Band; Chrs; Hon Rl; Stu Cncl; Sprt Ed Yrbk; Rptr Sch Nwsp; Pres Pep Clb; Bsktbl; Twrlr; Univ; Law.

TENNANT, LISA; Valley HS; Reader, WV; 6/78 Cls Rep Frsh Cls; Chrs; Hon Rl; NHS; Rptr Yrbk; Drama Clb; West Virginia Univ; Bus Mgmt.

TENNANT, ROGER; Hampshire HS; Shanks, WV; 21/213 Band; Hon Rl; Rptr Sch Nwsp; Letter Ten; Wrstlng; March Of Dimes Med Schlshp 79; Schl Winner Of Patrick Henry Oratorical Contst 76; Forencisc Awd 76; Shepherd Coll; Med Tech.

TENNANT, VICKIE; Clay Battelle HS; Fairview, WV; Band; Girl Scts; Hon Rl; Lbry Ade; NHS; Off Ade; Stu Cncl; 4-H; FHA; Pep Clb; Morgantown Voc Schl; Med Ofc Asst.

TENNELL, CLAIRE; Bloomington HS; Bloomington, IN; 14/385 VP Frsh Cls; Hst Sr Cls; Chrs; Girl Scts; Hon Rl; Jr NHS; Mdrgl; NHS; Stu Cncl; Ten; Ind Univ; Med.

TENNEY, ALVIN; Philip Barbour HS; Belington, WV; .

TENNEY, DENISE; Roosevelt HS; Kent, OH; Band; Girl Scts; Hon Rl; DHO/DCHO; PTA Schlrshp; Worked At Robinson Mem Hosp; Cleveland St Univ; Occup Therapy.

TENNEY, ELIOT J; Philip Barbour HS; Philippi, WV; Am Leg Boys St; Hon Rl; Stu Cncl; Trk; Wrstlng; Natl Merit Ltr; Voc Schl; Mach.

TENNEY, JAMES; Warsaw Community HS; Warsaw, IN; 74/404 Cmnty Wkr; FCA; Hon Rl; Boys Clb Am; Bsbl; Bsktbl; Ftbl; IM Sprt; Indiana Univ; Bus.

TENNEY, MELISSA; Lehman HS; Sidney, OH; 18/75 Band; Hon Rl; NHS; Sch Mus; Stu Cncl; Yrbk; Drama Clb; Pep Clb; Spn Clb; Bsktbl; College; Nursing.

TENNEY, REBECCA; Onsted HS; Onsted, MI; Sec Frsh Cls; Pres Soph Cls; Treas Band; Hon Rl; NHS; Sch Pl; Rptr Yrbk; Michigan St Univ.

TENNIS, NANCY; Washington Catholic HS; Washington, IN; Pep Clb; Indiana Univ; Spec Ed.

TENNY, AMY L; Lima Sr HS; Lima, OH; 29/486 Cls Rep Soph Cls; Cls Rep Sr Cls; Am Leg Aux Girls St; Chrs; Chrh Wkr; Girl Scts; Hon Rl; Hosp Ade; NHS; Sch Mus; Org Pep Club Block L 78 & 79; Starring Role In Cmnty Theatre Play Diary Of Anne Frank 77; Ohio St Univ; R N.

TENPENNY, SHIELA; Withrow HS; Cincinnati, OH; 3/351 Hon Rl; NHS; Off Ade; Union Coll; Acctg.

TENSMEYER, JOHN; Broad Ripple HS; Indianapolis, IN; Trs Jr Cls; Boy Scts; Chrs; Chrh Wkr; Hon Rl; NHS; Stg Crw; Letter Crs Cntry; Letter Trk; Chrldng; BYU; Comp Tech.

TENTERIS, ED; Northwood HS; Northwood, OH; Band; Chrs; Stg Crw; 4-H; Key Clb; Letter Bsbl; Letter Bsktbl; Letter Ftbl; Univ; Sci.

TENTLER, TRACEY; Newton Falls HS; Newton Falls, OH; Cmp Fr Grls; Chrs; Drl Tm; Drm Bgl; Hon Rl; JA; Stu Cncl; Y-Teens; Sch Nwsp; Pep Clb; Kent St Univ; Mdse.

TENWALDE, THERESA; Ottoville Local HS; Ft Jennings, OH; Chrs; Chrh Wkr; Cmnty Wkr; FCA; Girl Scts; Hon Rl; Yth Flsp; Y-Teens; 4-H; FHA; Nw Bus College.

TEPE, JOHN; Elder HS; Cinn, OH; 64/382 VP Chrs; Cmnty Wkr; Hon Rl; Sch Mus; Univ Of Cincinnati; Acctg.

TEPE, MARK; Marian HS; South Bend, IN; Chrh Wkr; Hon Rl; Letter Glf; IM Sprt; DAR Awd; College; Bus Admin Acctg.

TEPE, MARK; Bellbrook HS; Bellbrook, OH; Boy Scts; Chrh Wkr; Sch Pl; Spn Clb; Letter Trk; IM Sprt; Wright St Univ.

TEPE, MICHELE; Wheeling Cntrl Catholic HS; Wheeling, WV; 37/132 Hon Rl; Sch Mus; Sch Pl; Stu Cncl; Drama Clb; Pep Clb; Letter Bsbl; Letter Bsktbl; Letter Mgrs; Letter Scr Kpr; Marshall Univ; Dietetics.

TEPE, SUSAN; Mother Of Mercy HS; Cincinnati, OH; 2/230 Sal; Chrs; Hon Rl; Mod UN; Pres NHS; Red Cr Ade; Sct Actv; Ed Yrbk; Spn Clb; Socr; Univ Of Cincinnati; Chem Engr.

TEPE, VICTORIA; Bridgeport Spaulding HS; Saginaw, MI; 7/355 Band; Cmnty Wkr; Hon Rl; Hosp Ade; NHS; Orch; PAVAS; Sch Pl; VP Pep Clb; Ten; Saginaw Vly St Coll; Psych.

TEPE, VICTORIA; Brdgprt Spaulding Cmnty HS; Saginaw, MI; 7/360 Band; Chrh Wkr; Cmnty Wkr; Hon Rl; Hosp Ade; NHS; Orch; PAVAS; Red Cr Ade; Sch Pl; Saginaw Vly Coll; Psych.

TERAMANA, LARRY; Buckeye North HS; Brilliant, OH; Hon Rl; Bsbl; Ftbl; Letter Wrstlng; College.

TERBRACK, JEAN; Ubly Community HS; Minden City, MI; 1/114 Sec Jr Cls; Sec Sr Cls; Band; Hon Rl; NHS; Sch Pl; 4-H; Mic State Univ; Rn.

TERBURGH, ANN; Saranac HS; Saranac, MI; 7/80 Hon Rl; NHS; Sch Mus; Sch Pl; Ed Sch Nwsp; FHA; Mat Maids; Western Mic Univ.

TER BURGH, ANN; Saranac HS; Saranac, MI; 7/80 Hon Rl; Jr NHS; Sch Mus; Sch Pl; Ed Sch Nwsp; FHA; Mat Maids; Western Michigan Univ; Spanish.

TERHUNE, BRENDA; North Putnam HS; Greencastle, IN; 13/102 Chrs; Chrh Wkr; Hon Rl; Hosp Ade; Jr NHS; NHS; Off Ade; Yrbk; Sch Nwsp; 4-H; Most Improvd Sr Math Stud 79; Hon Cord For Being Top 15% Of Class 79; Indiana Voc Tech Coll; Med Lab Tech.

TERHUNE, BRIAN; Harry S Truman HS; Taylor, MI; Boy Scts; Hon Rl; Lit Mag; NHS; N Woods Progr Through The Univ Of Ia 3 Crdts 79; Michigan St Univ; Sci.

TERHUNE, GINA; Franklin Community HS; Franklin, IN; 18/300 Band; Hon Rl; Lbry Ade; NHS; Orch; Fr Clb; VP Sci Clb; Trk; Univ Of Houston; Medicine.

TERMEER, ANNE; East Grand Rapids HS; Jackson, MI; 7/290 Chrs; Jr NHS; NHS; Orch; Sch Mus; Pres Yth Flsp; Treas Fr Clb; Jackson Comm College; Intl Bus.

TERNES, CINDY; Black River HS; Spencer, OH; 24/115 Hon Rl; Hosp Ade; Off Ade; Stu Cncl; 4-H; Pep Clb; Sci Clb; Spn Clb; Letter Bsktbl; Capt Chrldng; Bus Schl; Nursing.

TERNES, SUSAN; Bloomfield HS; Bloomfield, IN; 3/85 Capt Band; Boy Scts; Chrs; Chrh Wkr; Girl Scts; Hon Rl; NHS; Sch Mus; Sch Pl; Stg Crw; Indiana St Univ; Art.

TERPENING, MARK; Kingsley Area HS; Kingsley, MI; 3/56 Band; Chrh Wkr; Hon Rl; NHS; Yth Flsp; Letter Bsbl; Letter Bsktbl; Letter Ftbl; Capt Trk; Cit Awd; Ath Of Yr; Michigan Competitive Schlrshp; Bd Of Trustee Schlrshp Ctrl Mich Univ; Central Michigan Univ; Comp Sci.

TERPENNING, JAMES; Deckerville HS; Deckerville, MI; 7/80 Cls Rep Sr Cls; Band; Chrs; Chrh Wkr; Hon Rl; NHS; Sch Mus; Yth Flsp; FFA; Letter Bsbl; Mbr Of Whos Who Music 78; Suomi Coll; Law Enfrmnt.

TERRELL, ALAN; Canton South HS; Canton, OH; Cls Rep Frsh Cls; Cmnty Wkr; Hon Rl; Sch Pl; Boys Clb Am; Crs Cntry; Trk; IM Sprt; Tmr; College; Law.

TERRELL, GIGI; Benedictine HS; Detroit, MI; Aud/Vis; Chrh Wkr; Hon Rl; Hosp Ade; Lbry Ade; Off Ade; Yth Flsp; Y-Teens; Trk; GAA; Nursing Schl; Nurse.

TERRELL, KATHY; Salem HS; Salem, IN; Band; Chrs; Chrh Wkr; Hon Rl; Hosp Ade; Y-Teens; 4-H; IUS; Registered Nurse.

TERRELL, KEVIN; Crispus Ahucks HS; Indianapolis, IN; 1/218 VP Jr Cls; Am Leg Boys St; Band; Hon Rl; NHS; ROTC; Lat Clb; Ftbl; Trk; Wrstlng; Hnr Stu Academic Awd 76; Purdue Univ; Elec Engr.

TERRELL, LISA; St Johns HS; St Johns, MI; Aud/Vis; Chrs; Chrh Wkr; Cmnty Wkr; Hon Rl; Sch Mus; Y-Teens; Ten; Univ; Math.

TERRELL, MELODY; Salem HS; Salem, IN; Trs Frsh Cls; Hon Rl; 4-H; FHA; Lat Clb; GAA; 4-H Awd; Coll; Fash Merch.

TERRELL, ROBIN; Clinton Central HS; Michigantown, IN; 13/100 FCA; Hon Rl; Sdlty; Stg Crw; Drama Clb; Pep Clb; Bsktbl; Univ.

TERRES, TERESA; Negaunee HS; Negaunee, MI; Band; Cmp Fr Grls; Chrh Wkr; Cmnty Wkr; Hon Rl; Off Ade; Pep Clb; Trk; College; Criminal Justice.

TERRIAN, JANET; Mackinaw City HS; Mackinaw City, MI; Sec Frsh Cls; Sec Soph Cls; Am Leg Aux Girls St; Band; Chrh Wkr; Hon Rl; NHS; Rptr Yrbk; Drama Clb; Pep Clb; Michigan St Univ; Busns Admin.

TERRIL, JULIE; Heath HS; Heath, OH; Chrs; Girl Scts; Hon Rl; Sci Clb; Central Ohio Tech Coll; Comp Progr.

TERRILL, KATHERINE; Clare HS; Clare, MI; Girl Scts; Hon Rl; Off Ade; Fr Clb; Letter Bsktbl; Mgrs; Opt Clb Awd; College; Registered Nurse.

TERRY, BERNICE; Kettering HS; Detroit, MI; Off Ade; Y-Teens; Wayne Cnty Comm College; Law.

TERRY, HOLLY; Little Miami HS; Maineville, OH; Hon Rl; Lit Mag; NHS; Sch Mus; Sch Pl; Fr Clb; Voice Dem Awd; Hon Mention In St For Eng 2 Schlstc Achvmnt Test 79; Otstndng Performnc On Psat/nmsqt Test 92% 79; Bowling Green St Univ; Jrnlsm.

TERRY, LESLIE; Northern HS; Pontiac, MI; Band; Hon Rl; JA; College; Elec Eng.

TERRY, MICHAEL; Warren Central HS; Indianapolis, IN; FCA; Hon Rl; Jr NHS; NHS; IM Sprt; Pres Awd; Purdue Univ; Chem Engr.

TERRY, SONYA; Miami Trace HS; Wash C H, OH; AFS; Band; Chrs; Chrh Wkr; Debate Tm; Hon Rl; Orch; Sch Pl; Rptr Sch Nwsp; Drama Clb; Univ Of Dayton; Music.

TERRY, TERESA; Greenbrier East HS; Ronceverte, WV; Band; Chrs; Girl Scts; Hon Rl; Lbry Ade; Off Ade; Yth Flsp; FHA; Marshall Univ; Law.

TERRY, TIMOTHY; South Newton Jr Sr HS; Goodland, IN; Chrh Wkr; Pres Yth Flsp; VP Ger Clb; Indiana Assn Of Stu Of German St Recording & Corresponding Sec; College; Math.

TERTEL, JACK; Sylvania Southview HS; Sylvania, OH; 2/320 Cls Rep Frsh Cls; VP Soph Cls; Pres Jr Cls; Cls Rep Sr Cls; Hon Rl; NHS; Stu Cncl; Rptr Yrbk; Pep Clb; Bsktbl; Univ; Pre Med.

TERWILLIGER, TROY; Onekama Consolidated HS; Manistee, MI; 3/58 Pres Soph Cls; Band; Hon Rl; NHS; Sch Mus; Sch Pl; Stg Crw; Drama Clb; Crs Cntry; Trk; Michigan St Univ; Vet.

TESCHNER, CHARLES L; Bay Village HS; Bay Village, OH; 19/377 Band; Boy Scts; Chrh Wkr; Hon Rl; Lit Mag; NHS; Sct Actv; Yrbk; Sci Clb; Natl Merit SF; College; Chemistry.

TESSIN, MARGIE; Mendon Community HS; Mendon, MI; 5/9C Hon Rl; NHS; Stg Crw; 4-H; Spn Clb; IM Sprt; PPFtbl; 2nd Pl Mendon Bicentennial Essay; 1st Pl Amer & Me Essay Contest; Perfect Attendance Awds; Harvard Univ; Poli Sci.

TESSMAN, EDWIN K; Pine River HS; Tustin, MI; Hon Rl; Ftbl; Trk; Wrstlng; College.

TESTA, MICHAEL; Ursuline HS; Youngstown, OH; Letter Bsbl; Ftbl; Univ.

TESTAGUZZA, JAMES; Weir Sr HS; Weirton, WV; 103/395 Boy Scts; NHS; Sct Actv; Y-Teens; Sci Clb; Spn Clb; Ftbl; Wrstlng; 1st Pl US Navy Awd & US Army Awd 2nd Pl Life Sci Awd 77; BSA Order Of Arrow Ordeal 76; Brotherhood 77; Ohio St Univ; Med.

TESTMAN, TAMI; Mt Vernon Academy; Pepper Pike, OH; Band; Ed Yrbk; Rptr Yrbk; Letter Bsbl; Letter Bsktbl; Letter Ftbl; Letter Socr; Letter Trk; Natl Merit SF; Pacific Union Coll; Bio.

TESTORI, DONNA; Warren Woods HS; Warren, MI; Hon Rl; JA; Off Ade; OEA; S Macomb Comm College; Legal Asst.

TESTY, SCOTT; Edgewood HS; Ellettsville, IN; Band; Chrs; Hon Rl; Red Cr Ade; Sch Mus; Sch Pl; Stg Crw; Sch Nwsp; Drama Clb; Indiana Univ; Music.

TETER, WILLIAM D; Buckhannon Upshur HS; Buckhannon, WV; Boy Scts; Chrs; Pres 4-H; Treas VICA; 4-H Awd; College; Forestry.

TETLAK, JUDITH; Erieview Catholic HS; Middleburg Hts, OH; 6/100 Cls Rep Soph Cls; Trs Jr Cls; Chrs; Hon Rl; Mod UN; Sch Pl; Stu Cncl; Rptr Yrbk; Rptr Sch Nwsp; Bsbl; College; Communications.

TETLOW, LORI; Barnesville HS; Barnesville, OH; Cls Rep Sr Cls; Band; Hon Rl; Sec Stu Cncl; Bsktbl; Trk; Coach Actv; GAA; Ohio Univ; Med Asst.

TETRICK, DAVID; Washington Irving HS; Clarksburg, WV; 50/170 Band; Chrh Wkr; Hon Rl; Key Clb; Bsktbl; Glf; College; Bus.

TETTEH, GEORGE; Chadsey HS; Detroit, MI; Cls Rep Soph Cls; Cl Rep Jr Cls; Hon Rl; Lbry Ade; NHS; Stu Cncl; Ftbl; Cit Awd; Opt Clb Awd; De Pub Schl Reg Two Math Sem Awd 78; Western Michigan Univ; Finance.

TETTENBORN, CONNIE; Deer Park HS; Cincinnati, OH; 1/214 Val; Chrs; Chrh Wkr; Hon Rl; NHS; Stu Cncl; Yth Flsp; Natl Merit Schl; Asbury Coll; Bio.

TEUFEL, MARY; Hedgesville HS; Martinsburg, WV; Cl Rep Jr Cls; Hon Rl; Sec Yth Flsp; Pres 4-H; Pep Clb; Chrldng; Shepherd Coll; Mdse.

TEUNIS, TIMOTHY; Spring Lake HS; Spring Lake, MI; Band; Hon Rl; Muskegon Comm Coll.

TEWES, DEBRA; Pontiac Central HS; Pontiac, MI; 8/419 Cls Rep Frsh Cls; Cmp Fr Grls; Chrs; Chrh Wkr; Hon Rl; Off Ade; Sch Mus; Pres Yth Flsp; Y-Teens; Rptr Sch Nwsp; Eastern Michigan Univ; Spec Educ.

THACKER, JEFFREY; Zionsville Community HS; Zionsville, IN; 14/151 FCA; Hon Rl; Spn Clb; Letter Bsbl; Letter Bsktbl; Letter Ten; Ind State Univ; Bus Manag.

THACKER, MICHAEL S; Buffalo HS; Huntington, WV; Boy Scts; Chrh Wkr; FFA; FHA; Voc Sch; Civil Engr.

THACKER, PAM; Chillicothe HS; Chillicothe, OH; 86/380 Band; Chrh Wkr; Hon Rl; 4-H; OEA; 2nd Pl In Keypunch At Regional Office Ed Assoc; College; Acctg.

THACKER, RHONDA; Southeastern HS; Chillicothe, OH; Letter Band; Chrs; Girl Scts; Hon Rl; Pep Clb; Letter Bsktbl; Intensv Off Educ 78; Bus Schl; Recptnst.

THACKRAY, JOHN; Niles Sr HS; Niles, MI; 70/400 Band; Hon Rl; Bsbl; Hockey; Rotary Awd; Michigan St Univ; Bus Admin.

THACKSTON, JOHN M; Ben Davis HS; Indianapolis, IN; Cls Rep Frsh Cls; Cls Rep Soph Cls; Cl Rep Jr Cls; Boy Scts; Chrh Wkr; CAP; Mod UN; Natl Forn Lg; Pol Wkr; Ger Clb; Natl Leadrshp Confrnvn 79; Univ; Law.

THAGARD, NEAL; Newark Catholic HS; Newark, OH; Sch Mus; Sch Pl; Stg Crw; Rptr Yrbk; Yrbk; Drama Clb; Lat Clb; Sci Clb; Ftbl; Central Ohio Tech Coll; Elec.

THAI, TUNG H; North HS; Columbus, OH; 14/350 Jr NHS; NHS; Fr Clb; Ten; Ohio State Univ; Electronics.

THAIS, BYRAN; Lincoln HS; Vincennes, IN; 45/320 Pres Soph Cls; Pres Jr Cls; Pres Sr Cls; FCA; Yth Flsp; Letter Bsktbl; Letter Ftbl; Coach Actv; Indiana Univ; Bus Ec.

THAL, SUSAN; Berkley HS; Hunt Woods, MI; Girl Scts; Univ Of Michigan; Math.

THALER, LINDA; L C Mohr HS; South Haven, MI; FCA; Hon Rl; Pres Soph Cls; NHS; FDA; FSA; Sci Clb; Ten; Mic State; Science.

THALER, LINDA; L C Mohr HS; S Haven, MI; FCA; Hon Rl; Lbry Ade; NHS; Stu Cncl; Sci Clb; Ten; Am Leg Awd; Bausch & Lomb Awd; Mic State; Sci.

THAMAN, THERESA; Marian HS; Cincinnati, OH; Hosp Ade; NHS; Stu Cncl; Spn Clb; College; Spec Educ.

THANG, NGUYEN; Pike HS; Indianapolis, IN; Hon Rl; NHS; Fr Clb; Mth Clb; Socr; Purdue Univ; Mech Engr.

THARP, SANDRA; Clarkston HS; Clarkston, MI; 90/510 Girl Scts; Hon Rl; NHS; OEA; Letter Trk; Mgrs; PPFtbl; St Woman Awd St Level OEA 79; Ambssdr Awd Natl Level OEA 79; Michigan St Univ; Bus Admin.

THARP, SHELLEY; Webster Cnty Higlanders HS; Webster Sprg, WV; Trs Soph Cls; Girl Scts; Hon Rl; NHS; Sch Pl; 4-H; Capt Bsktbl; Letter Trk; GAA; IM Sprt; Glenville Coll.

THARP, TAMEA K; Ellet Sr HS; Akron, OH; 27/365 Cls Rep Sr Cls; Chrs; Chrh Wkr; Hon Rl; Lbry Ade; Natl Forn Lg; NHS; Off Ade; Red Cr Ade; VP OEA; Akron Univ; Busns.

THATCHER, BARB; Knox Co JVS; Mt Vernon, OH; Hon Rl; NHS; Yrbk; Pep Clb; VICA; Mt Vernon Nazarene Coll.

THATCHER, KAREN; Tipton HS; Tipton, IN; Chrh Wkr; Yth Flsp; FBLA; Pep Clb; Indiana Univ; Med Asst.

THATCHER, LYNN; Grant Public HS; Grant, MI; 2/116 Sal; Chrs; Chrh Wkr; Hon Rl; Lbry Ade; Mdrgl; Pol Wkr; Olivet College; Teach.

THATCHER, MELANIE; Lincolnview HS; Middle Pt, OH; Trs Soph Cls; Cmnty Wkr; Sch Mus; Pres 4-H; FHA; Bsktbl; Trk; Sec 4-H Awd; Vantage Joint Voc.

THATCHER, ROE; Batavia HS; Batavia, OH; Cl Rep Jr Cls; Boy Scts; Debate Tm; Sch Pl; Stg Crw; Sch Nwsp; Drama Clb; 4-H; Fr Clb; Mth Clb; Miami Univ; Bus Mgmt.

THATCHER, RONDA; Lincolnview HS; Van Wert, OH; Band; Chrs; Chrh Wkr; Lbry Ade; Yth Flsp; FHA; Crs Cntry; Trk; GAA; College.

THAXTON, BOB; Clay Sr HS; Oregon, OH; Hon Rl; VICA; Toledo Univ; Archt.

THAXTON, D; Nordonia HS; Northfield, OH; Bsbl; Crs Cntry; Univ.

THAYER, CHARLES O; Notre Dame HS; Clarksburg, WV; 3/59 Cls Rep Sr Cls; Am Leg Boys St; Band; Chrs; Chrh Wkr; Sch Mus; Sch Pl; Stu Cncl; Pres 4-H; FDA; Univ; Math.

THAYER, KATHRYN; Southmont HS; New Ross, IN; 44/167 Band; Hon Rl; Jr NHS; 4-H; FFA; FHA; Ger Clb; Purdue Univ; Vet Sci.

THAYER, THERESA; Mt Vernon Sr HS; Mt Vernon, OH; Cmnty Wkr; Hon Rl; Hosp Ade; JA; NHS; Off Ade; Red Cr Ade; OEA; Kiwan Awd; Mas Awd; Columbus Bus Univ; Exec Sec.

THEAKER, TERRY A; Lexington HS; Mansfield, OH; Band; Orch; Stg Crw; Trk; IM Sprt; Cit Awd; Ohio St Univ; Pre Med.

THEDOS, DONALD; New Albany HS; New Albany, OH; Hon Rl; Sci Clb; Letter Bsbl; Mgrs; Scr Kpr; Ohio St Univ; Acctg.

THEIS, DARLENE; Northrop HS; Ft Wayne, IN; Chrs; Chrh Wkr; Cmnty Wkr; JA; Yth Flsp; Letter Bsktbl; PPFtbl; Pres Awd; Purdue Univ; Math.

THEIS, EILEEN; Pewamo Westphalia HS; Fowler, MI; 5/117 Cls Rep Soph Cls; Sec Jr Cls; Cl Rep Jr Cls; Sec Sr Cls; Band; Chrs; Drm Bgl; Hon Rl; Hosp Ade; NHS; Michigan St Univ; Acctg.

THEIS, KELLI; St Joseph Academy; Westlake, OH; Cls Rep Soph Cls; Hon Rl; Stu Cncl; Mth Clb; Coach Actv; Honroll Achvmnt 78; Univ Of Akron; Child Psych.

THEISEN, JANE; Theodore Roosevelt HS; Wyandotte, MI; Sec Frsh Cls; Hon Rl; Tmr; Natl Merit Ltr; Natl Merit SF; Natl Merit Schl; Western Mich Univ; Speech Pathology.

THEISEN, JANET; Beal City HS; Weidman, MI; Band; Chrs; Chrh Wkr; Drl Tm; Drm Mjrt; Hon Rl; Off Ade; Rptr Yrbk; 4-H; FHA; Central Michigan Univ; Elem Educ.

THEISEN, JANIS; Dearborn HS; Dearborn, MI; Cls Rep Frsh Cls; AFS; Band; Debate Tm; Pres NHS; Orch; Sch Mus; Rptr Sch Nwsp; Sec Ger Clb; VP GAA; Univ Mich Ann Arbor; Bio Chemistry.

THEISEN, JOSEPH; Capac HS; Emmett, MI; Pres Sr Cls; Hon Rl; NHS; FFA; Letter Ftbl; Michigan St Univ; Horticulture.

THEISEN, LORI; Marietta Sr HS; Marietta, OH; 32/450 Band; Drm Mjrt; Girl Scts; Hon Rl; NHS; Off Ade; Y-Teens; Drama Clb; IM Sprt; Twrlr; Ohio St Univ; Math.

THEISEN, NANCY; St Frances Cabrini HS; Allen Pk, MI; Cmnty Wkr; Drl Tm; Girl Scts; Hon Rl; Pol Wkr; Sct Actv; Spn Clb; Pom Pon; Mi Comp Schlrshp 79; Mercy Coll; Nursing.

THEISS, HEIDI; Admiral King HS; Lorain, OH; 28/382 Band; Chrs; Chrh Wkr; Hon Rl; Hosp Ade; NHS; Lorain Cnty Community College; Stew.

THELEN, BRENDA; St Johns HS; St Johns, MI; Band; Chrh Wkr; Cmnty Wkr; Hon Rl; Jr NHS; NHS; Yth Flsp; 4-H; Bsktbl; Letter Trk; Central Michigan Univ; Elem Ed.

THELEN, CAROLYN; Pewamo Westphalia HS; Fowler, MI; Band; Hon Rl; NHS; Stg Crw; 4-H; Ferris State College; Accounting.

THELEN, CHRIS G; Fowler HS; Fowler, MI; VP Jr Cls; Cls Rep Sr Cls; Stu Cncl; Yrbk; 4-H; VICA; Michigan St Univ; Tele Cmnctns.

THELEN, KAREN; Pewamo Westphalia HS; St Johns, MI; Hon Rl; Lbry Ade; 4-H; PPFtbl; 4-H Awd; College; Sec.

THELEN, MARILYN; St Johns HS; St Johns, MI; Val; Chrh Wkr; Hon Rl; Jr NHS; NHS; 4-H; Bsktbl; IM Sprt; Michigan St Univ; Hotel & Rest Mgmt.

THELEN, STEVEN; Williamston HS; Williamston, MI; 51/165 Am Leg Boys St; Chrh Wkr; JA; Ftbl; Am Leg Awd; Class Devotion Participation Awd; Michigan Tech Univ; Engr.

THEOBALD, JANA; Frontier HS; Dart, OH; 16/122 Pres Band; Girl Scts; Hon Rl; NHS; Yth Flsp; 4-H; FNA; Sec Sci Clb; GAA; Ohio Valley Schl Of Nursing; Nurse.

THEODORE, PAULA; Catholic Central HS; Grand Rpds, MI; Chrh Wkr; Hon Rl; Off Ade; Grand Rapids Jr Coll; CPA.

THEODORE, PAULA G; Morton Sr HS; Hammond, IN; 11/419 Cls Rep Soph Cls; VP Jr Cls; Chrh Wkr; Hon Rl; Stu Cncl; Rptr Yrbk; Pep Clb; IM Sprt; PPFtbl; Sec Of Foreign Language Club; Governing Board Of Travel Club; Bookstore Aide; Indiana Univ; Accounting.

THEODORE, T J; Euclid HS; Euclid, OH; Am Leg Boys St; Band; Boy Scts; Hon Rl; NHS; Sch Mus; Sct Actv; Y-Teens; Sci Clb; Letter Crs Cntry; College; Elec.

THEODOROU, IRENE; Southfield Lathrop HS; Southfield, MI; Chrs; Chrh Wkr; Hon Rl; Lbry Ade; Orch; Cit Awd; Natl Merit Schl; Wayne State; Chem.

THEODOROU, MARIA; Southfield Lathrup HS; Southfield, MI; Chrh Wkr; Hon Rl; Orch; Natl Merit Ltr; Natl Merit SF; University; Med Tech.

THEOHARES, NICK; Madison Comp HS; Mansfield, OH; Band; Sct Actv; Fr Clb; Am Leg Awd; College.

THERBER, JOE; Crawfordsville HS; Crawfordsville, IN; 1/196 Am Leg Boys St; Chrh Wkr; Pres FCA; Hon Rl; Jr NHS; NHS; Pres Stu Cncl; Pres Key Clb; Letter Bsbl; Letter Bsktbl; Frosh Stdnt Of Year 1977; Outstndg Achvmnt Math 1977 & 1978; Wabash Coll; Comp Sci.

THERIAULT, DAVID; Clio HS; Clio, MI; Cls Rep Soph Cls; Cl Rep Jr Cls; Cls Rep Sr Cls; Sch Pl; Stg Crw; Stu Cncl; Drama Clb; Spn Clb; Rotary Awd; College; Med.

THERING, DEBRA; Sacred Heart Academy; Mt P Easant, MI; 9/54 Sec Sr Cls; Hon Rl; Natl Forn Lg; NHS; Ed Sch Nwsp; Pep Clb; Bsktbl; Central Michigan Univ; Math.

THEROFF, KELLY; Washington HS; Montgomery, IN; Chrs; Chrh Wkr; Girl Scts; Hon Rl; Off Ade; Yth Flsp; Beta Clb; 4-H; Lat Clb; Pep Clb; Indiana Univ; Law.

THERRIAN, LINDA; Calumet HS; Calumet, MI; Hon Rl; Off Ade; Letter Crs Cntry; Letter Trk; IM Sprt; Univ.

THEURING, ANDREW; Clermont Northeastern HS; Milford, OH; Cls Rep Soph Cls; Boy Scts; FCA; Yth Flsp; Capt Ftbl; Capt Trk; Univ; Engr.

THEWLIS, PATRICIA; Median Sr HS; Medina, OH; 36/360 Cmnty Wkr; Hon Rl; NHS; Red Cr Ade; Fr Clb; Miami Univ; Sociology.

THIBAULT, JILL; Fenton HS; Fenton, MI; Trs Sr Cls; Girl Scts; Hon Rl; Sch Pl; Stu Cncl; Pep Clb; Letter Ten; Letter Trk; Letter Chrldng; Mat Maids; Central Mich; Tchr.

THIBAUT, LINDA; Mt Vernon HS; Mt Vernon, OH; 1/365 Cmnty Wkr; Lit Mag; Sch Pl; Ed Sch Nwsp; Rptr Sch Nwsp; Sch Nwsp; Drama Clb; Spn Clb; PPFtbl; College; Advertising.

THIEDE, NANCY; St Florian HS; Detroit, MI; Sec Jr Cls; Trs Sr Cls; Stu Cncl; Yrbk; FBLA; FNA; Western Michigan Univ; Bio.

THIEL, BARBARA; Upper Sandusky HS; Upper Sandusky, OH; 24/212 Cls Rep Frsh Cls; Chrs; Chrh Wkr; Hon Rl; Jr NHS; NHS; Off Ade; Sch Pl; Stu Cncl; Yrbk; Toledo Univ; Social Serv Tech.

THIEL, DAVID; Deer Park HS; Cincinnati, OH; Pres Sr Cls; Band; PAVAS; Sch Mus; Sch Pl; Sct Actv; Rptr Sch Nwsp; Drama Clb; Univ; Aeronautical Engr.

THIEL, JOHN M; Upper Sandusky HS; Upper Sandusky, OH; 49/218 Cls Rep Frsh Cls; Chrs; FCA; Hon Rl; 4-H; FFA; Bsktbl; Ftbl; IM Sprt; 4-H Awd; CYO Bsktbl Player Of The Year; Sec Of The Year; 7th Cnty Hand Judging Contest FFA; Tiffin Univ; Acctg.

THIEL, KAREN; Upper Sandusky HS; Upper Sandusky, OH; Hon Rl; Sch Pl; Stg Crw; Sch Nwsp; 4-H; 4-H Awd; Ohio St Univ; Phys Ed Tchr.

THIEL, YVONDA; Edon Northwest HS; Edon, OH; Chrs; Chrh Wkr; Cmnty Wkr; Sch Mus; Sch Pl; Yth Flsp; Yrbk; FHA; Coach Actv; Bus Schl.

THIEMAN, ANNETTE; Newbury HS; Newbury, OH; Band; Cmp Fr Grls; Chrs; Chrs; Hon Rl; Hosp Ade; Orch; Sch Mus; Yth Flsp; Drama Clb; Fresh Yr Awd; Schlrshp To Trinity HS Holy Name Soc; De Paul Univ; Music Therapy.

THIEMAN, BARB; Minster HS; Minster, OH; 9/80 Am Leg Aux Girls St; Band; Chrs; Hon Rl; NHS; Sch Mus; Yrbk; FTA; Pep Clb; Twrlr; College; Acctg.

THIEMAN, CONSTANCE; East Detroit HS; E Detroit, MI; Chrh Wkr; Hon Rl; Hosp Ade; Natl Merit Ltr; Natl Merit SF; Mbr Of Juv Diabetes Fnd ADF 78 79 & 80; Mer Achiev Awd 77; Mbr Of Joslin Diabetes Fnd Boston MA; Univ Of Michigan; Nurse.

THIEMAN, POLLY; Parkway HS; Rockford, OH; 2/97 Band; Chrh Wkr; Hon Rl; Ger Clb; Lat Clb; Sci Clb; College; Language.

THIEMAN, POLLY; Parkway Local HS; Rockford, OH; 2/96 Band; Hon Rl; Ger Clb; Lat Clb; Sci Clb; Scr Kpr; Tmr; Univ; Foreign Lang.

THIEMAN, SHARON; Fairmont West HS; Kettering, OH; 50/471 Hon Rl; Quill & Scroll; Rptr Yrbk; Fr Clb; Mth Clb; Cert In Recogtn Of Superior Perfrmnc In NEDT 77; Cert For Taking Natl French Test 78; Univ; Acctg.

THIEMANN, LAURA; Mc Avley HS; Cinti, OH; 18/265 Cls Rep Sr Cls; Hon Rl; Hosp Ade; Sch Mus; Stu Cncl; Rptr Sch Nwsp; Drama Clb; 4-H; Socr; Miami University; Bus Admin.

THIEMANN, WILLIAM F; La Salle HS; Cincinnati, OH; 13/249 Hon Rl; Jr NHS; IM Sprt; Univ; Cmmrcl Art.

THIEME, CINDY; Bellmont HS; Monroeville, IN; 9/244 Hon Rl; NHS; Yth Flsp; Treas 4-H; Ger Clb; Letter Gym; PPFtbl; 4-H Awd; IU; Comp Prog.

THIEME, RONALD H; Hamilton Southeastern HS; Noblesville, IN; 4/140 Am Leg Boys St; Band; Chrh Wkr; Hon Rl; MMM; NHS; Sch Mus; 4-H; FFA; Ger Clb; John Philip Sousa Awd; Hoosier Schlr Awd; Purdue Univ; Agri Mechanics.

THIEME, TAYA; Bellmont HS; Decatur, IN; 40/244 Hon Rl; Yth Flsp; 4-H; Ger Clb; PPFtbl; 4-H Awd; Voc Schl.

THIERET, EDWARD; South Amherst HS; S Amherst, OH; Am Leg Boys St; Boy Scts; Chrh Wkr; Hon Rl; Stu Cncl; Yth Flsp; Yrbk; Letter Ftbl; Coach Actv; Am Leg Awd; Univ; Chem Engr.

THIERET, RICHARD; Berkshire HS; Burton, OH; Boy Scts; Hon Rl; Sct Actv; Sprt Ed Yrbk; Yrbk; Bsktbl; Ftbl; Trk; Gov Hon Prg Awd; Oh Gov Yth Art Exhbntn 78; Schlstc Art Awd 78; Univ; Cmmrcl Art.

THIERY, BECKY; Onsted HS; Onsted, MI; Pres Jr Cls; Band; Chrh Wkr; Hon Rl; Lit Mag; NHS; Yth Flsp; Rptr Yrbk; Sprt Ed Sch Nwsp; Letter Bsktbl; Grace Coll; Phys Ed.

THIERY, REBECCA; Onsted HS; Onsted, MI; Pres Jr Cls; Band; Chrh Wkr; Hon Rl; Lit Mag; Rptr Yrbk; Rptr Sch Nwsp; Letter Bsktbl; Letter Trk; College; Art.

THIES, CHRISTINE; High School; Fairview Park, OH; 10/280 Trs Frsh Cls; Trs Soph Cls; Trs Jr Cls; Hon Rl; NHS; Off Ade; Stu Cncl; Spn Clb; Chrldng; IM Sprt; Univ; Zoology.

THIESMEYER, DARLENE; Benedictine HS; Detroit, MI; Girl Scts; Hon Rl; JA; Cit Awd; Univ; Comp Prog.

THIESSEN, MARK; Perry HS; Navarre, OH; Jr NHS; Swmmng; College; Elec.

THILL, DONALD M; Woodhaven HS; Woodhaven, MI; Chrs; Hon Rl; Jr NHS; Sch Pl; Bsbl; Cit Awd; Coll; Med.

THILL, LYNDELL; North Muskegon HS; N Muskegon, MI; Band; Chrs; Girl Scts; Hon Rl; Sch Mus; Ger Clb; Letter Chrldng; PPFtbl; College; Lib Arts.

THILL, RHONDA; Mt Gilead HS; Mt Gilead, OH; Chrh Wkr; Capt FCA; Hon Rl; Hosp Ade; Yth Flsp; Rptr Yrbk; Capt 4-H; Capt Trk; Scr Kpr; Olivet Nazarene; Nursing.

THINES, MICHELLE; Delphos Jefferson HS; Delphos, OH; Sec Sr Cls; Band; Chrs; CAP; Hon Rl; 4-H; Chrldng; Toledo Univ; Nurse.

THIROS, MARK; High School; Merrillville, IN; 31/251 Hon Rl; Stg Crw; Drama Clb; Fr Clb; Gym; Hockey; Univ; Law.

THIRTYACRE, TOM; Walter E Stebbins HS; Dayton, OH; Hst Jr Cls; Cl Rep Jr Cls; Hst Sr Cls; Cls Rep Sr Cls; Chrs; Chrh Wkr; Hon Rl; ROTC; Sch Mus; Sch Pl; Arizona St Univ.

THOBE, PAMELA; Marion Local HS; Maria Stein, OH; Chrs; Pep Clb; Sci Clb; Trk; Chrldng; IM Sprt;.

THOBER, VICTORIA; Springfield HS; Maumee, OH; 2/245 Am Leg Aux Girls St; Chrh Wkr; Girl Scts; Hon Rl; Hosp Ade; NHS; Red Cr Ade; Rptr Yrbk; Rptr Sch Nwsp; Fr Clb; English Awd; Awds In Ohio Tests Of Scholastic Achievement; Univ Of Toledo.

THOE, LAURA; Big Rapids HS; Big Rapids, MI; 29/180 Chrs; Hon Rl; Sch Mus; Rptr Sch Nwsp; Sci Clb; Grand Valley St Coll; Nursing.

THOENNES, CONNIE; Greenville Sr HS; Greenville, MI; 3/260 Band; Hon Rl; Letter Bsktbl; PPFtbl; Univ; Pharm.

THOM, TRACY; Sandusky HS; Sandusky, OH; Chrs; Mdrgl; Off Ade; Sch Mus; Treas Stu Cncl; Yrbk; VP VICA; Mgrs; Scr Kpr; Tmr; Outstndng Stu Council Mbr; Art Institute; Commercial Art.

THOMAS, ANNE MARIE; Boardman HS; Youngstown, OH; Chrs; Chrh Wkr; Cmnty Wkr; Hon Rl; Rptr Yrbk; Pep Clb; Youngstown St Univ; Phys Ther.

THOMAS, BARBARA; Napoleon HS; Jackson, MI; Band; Chrs; Hon Rl; NHS; Sch Mus; Blue Lake Fine Arts Camp Marshall Music Schlrshp 79; World History Awd 79; Eng Awd 79; Jackson Cmnty Coll; Music Ther.

THOMAS, BARBARA; Whiteland HS; Greenwood, IN; 30/208 AFS; Hon Rl; Jr NHS; NHS; FBLA; Pep Clb; Pom Pon; Ind Univ; Political Sci.

THOMAS, BESSIE; East HS; Columbus, OH; Hon Rl; Ten; Columbus Tech Inst; Auto Mech.

THOMAS, BETH; Bucyrus HS; Bucyrus, OH; Cls Rep Frsh Cls; Am Leg Aux Girls St; Band; Chrs; Hon Rl; NHS; Stu Cncl; Y-Teens; 4-H; Fr Clb; Girls Booster Clb Pres; Ohio St Univ.

THOMAS, BOB; Fairfield Union HS; Bremen, OH; 7/150 Hon Rl; Capt NHS; Stg Crw; Stu Cncl; Yth Flsp; FFA; Key Clb; Trk; Capt Wrstlng; DAR Awd; Ohio St Univ; Agri.

THOMAS, BRENDA; Frontier HS; Newport, OH; Trs Jr Cls; Trs Sr Cls; Off Ade; Sch Pl; Rptr Yrbk; OEA; Bsktbl; GAA; Washington Tech Coll; CPA.

THOMAS, BRIAN; Madison HS; Madison, OH; Am Leg Boys St; Band; Boy Scts; Hon Rl; NHS; Letter Ftbl; Wrstlng; Pres Of Explr Post & Delgt To Wash Dc 79; 1st In Dist & 13th In St On OTSA Genrl Sci 77; OSU; Elec Engr.

THOMAS, CASSANDRA; Washington HS; South Bend, IN; 41/354 Hon Rl; NHS; Spn Clb; Capt Pom Pon; Colorado Univ; Math.

THOMAS, CATHLINE; Redford Union HS; Redford, MI; Cmp Fr Grls; Hon Rl; Henry Ford Cmnty Coll; Music.

THOMAS, CHARLES; Grosse Pointe North HS; Grosse Pt Wds, MI; AFS; Orch; Sch Mus; Rptr Yrbk; Fr Clb; Mich State Univ; Acctg.

THOMAS, CHARLES; Midland HS; Midland, MI; 115/486 Band; Boy Scts; Hon Rl; Sct Actv; DECA; Socr; Swmmng; Trk; Tmr; Michigan St Univ.

THOMAS, CHARLES K; South Charleston HS; S Charleston, WV; Aud/Vis; Hon Rl; Pep Clb; JETS Awd; Wv Tech; Mech Engr.

THOMAS, CHERYL; Twin Valley North HS; Lewisburg, OH; Sec Frsh Cls; Trs Soph Cls; Am Leg Aux Girls St; Band; Hon Rl; Stu Cncl; Pep Clb; Letter Trk; Letter Chrldng; Sinclair Comm College; Executive Sec.

THOMAS, CHRISTINE; Austintown Fitch HS; Youngstown, OH; 165/662 Cls Rep Sr Cls; Drl Tm; Hon Rl; Off Ade; Sch Pl; Stu Cncl; Y-Teens; Key Clb; PPFtbl; Youngstown St Univ; Exec Sec.

THOMAS, DALE; Greenville Sr HS; Greenville, OH; 71/380 Boy Scts; Hon Rl; Wrstlng; Univ.

THOMAS, DALE J; Gahanna Lincoln HS; Gahanna, OH; 11/469 Cls Rep Frsh Cls; Cls Rep Soph Cls; Pres Jr Cls; Am Leg Boys St; Boy Scts; Hon Rl; NHS; Off Ade; Sct Actv; Stu Cncl; OSU; Bio.

THOMAS, DEBBIE; Eastern HS; Pekin, IN; 25/91 Cls Rep Soph Cls; Cl Rep Jr Cls; Hon Rl; NHS; Off

Ade; Stu Cncl; Pep Clb; Spn Clb; Chrldng; GAA; Indiana Univ; Busns.

THOMAS, DEBRA; Lincoln HS; Shinnston, WV; 26/160 Sec Jr Cls; Band; Chrs; Drl Tm; Hon Rl; Lbry Ade; Mdrgl; NHS; Off Ade; Stg Crw; Univ; Acctg.

THOMAS, DENISE; Dixie HS; New Lebanon, OH; 4-H; Bsktbl; Chrldng; GAA; 4-H Awd; Miami Univ; Law.

THOMAS, DENISE; Covington HS; Piqua, OH; Pres Jr Cls; Trs Jr Cls; Band; Chrs; Hon Rl; OEA; Pep Clb; Bsbl; Trk; Chrldng; Edison St Coll; Sec.

THOMAS, DIXIE; Cardington Lincoln HS; Cardington, OH; Hon Rl; Lbry Ade; NHS; Off Ade; Stu Cncl; Yth Flsp; Rptr Yrbk; 4-H; Capt Chrldng; Business Schl.

THOMAS, DONALD A; Woodhaven HS; Romulus, MI; Cl Rep Jr Cls; Cls Rep Sr Cls; NHS; Stu Cncl; VICA; Letter Bsbl; Letter Ftbl; Letter Swmmng; Rotary Awd; 3rd Awd In The Detroit News Mi Industrial Educ Awds 78; Ferris St Coll; Elec Tech.

THOMAS, DONNA; Switzerland Cnty Jr Sr HS; Patriot, IN; Band; Chrs; Stu Cncl; Pep Clb;.

THOMAS, ERIC; Brookhaven HS; Columbus, OH; 59/401 Band; NHS; Ohio State.

THOMAS, FOREST; Carrollton HS; Carrollton, OH; 45/350 Band; Boy Scts; Cmnty Wkr; Hon Rl; Lit Mag; Sct Actv; Rptr Yrbk; Ed Sch Nwsp; 4-H; Lat Clb; Outstndng 4 H Boy Carroll Cnty 78; Gov Commission On Traffic Safety 76; Ed Feature Page Schl Ppr 79; Ohio Univ; Jrnlsm.

THOMAS, FRANK; Connersville HS; Connersville, IN; 100/400 Cls Rep Sr Cls; Hon Rl; Civ Clb; Spn Clb; Letter Glf; Letter Swmmng; Letter Ten; IM Sprt; Tmr; Purdue Univ; Engr.

THOMAS, FREDRICK; Meigs HS; Cheshire, OH; Cls Rep Frsh Cls; Band; Chrs; Chrh Wkr; Hon Rl; Mdrgl; NHS; Orch; Sch Mus; Sch Pl; Univ.

THOMAS, GALE; Crestwood HS; Mantua, OH; 10/238 Band; Chrh Wkr; Drm Bgl; Drm Mjrt; Hon Rl; NHS; Twrlr; Univ Of Hawaii; Travel Indust Mgmt.

THOMAS, GARY; Jackson Milton HS; Diamond, OH; Am Leg Boys St; Boy Scts; Hon Rl; Sct Actv; Univ; Pharm.

THOMAS, GARY; Emerson HS; Gary, IN; Hon Rl; Jr NHS; Boys Clb Am; Letter Ten; Trk; Chess Team Most Valuable Plyr 1977; Chess Team Cptn 1979; French Student Tchr 1978; Univ; Law.

THOMAS, GARY; Jackson Milton HS; Diamond, OH; Am Leg Boys St; Boy Scts; Hon Rl; Sct Actv; College; Pharmacy.

THOMAS, GLENDA; Cass Technical HS; Detroit, MI; Hon Rl; OEA; Univ Of Michigan; Bus Admin.

THOMAS, GLINDA J; Roosevelt HS; Gary, IN; Drl Tm; Hon Rl; NHS; ROTC; Pep Clb; Trade Schl; Welder.

THOMAS, GREG; Van Buren HS; Findlay, OH; 12/87 Aud/Vis; Band; Chrs; Chrh Wkr; Hon Rl; Jr NHS; NHS; Sch Mus; Sch Pl; Stg Crw; Voc Schl; Carpenter.

THOMAS, HOLLY; Lake Central HS; Dyer, IN; 34/503 Cls Rep Frsh Cls; Cls Rep Soph Cls; Hon Rl; NHS; Sec Quill & Scroll; Sch Pl; Stu Cncl; Ed Sch Nwsp; Rptr Sch Nwsp; 4-H; Purdue Univ; Jrnlsm.

THOMAS, JAMES; Howell HS; Howell, MI; Boy Scts; Sct Actv; Fr Clb; Univ Of Michigan; Law.

THOMAS, JAMES; Cardinal Mooney HS; Poland, OH; Boy Scts; Chrh Wkr; Hon Rl; Fr Clb; Mth Clb; Duquesne; Phar.

THOMAS, JAMES; Lake Catholic HS; Mentor, OH; Cls Rep Frsh Cls; Cls Rep Soph Cls; Cl Rep Jr Cls; VP Sr Cls; Boy Scts; Chrh Wkr; Sct Actv; Stu Cncl; Ed Sch Nwsp; Sch Nwsp; Univ; Law.

THOMAS, JAMES; George Washington HS; S Charleston, WV; Boy Scts; Jr NHS; Pres 4-H; Letter Bsbl; Letter Ftbl; IM Sprt; Wv Univ; Phys Educ.

THOMAS, JANICE; Caro HS; Caro, MI; Band; Chrh Wkr; Hon Rl; NHS; Fr Clb; Mat Maids; Coll; Sec Sci.

THOMAS, JEFFREY; Meadow Bridge HS; Layland, WV; 3/50 Band; Chrs; Hon Rl; NHS; Sch Mus; Sch Pl; Fr Clb; All Cnty Band All Area Band 76; All Cnty Band All Area Band Orch Band Awd 77; Cooper Union Coll; Archt.

THOMAS, JESSIE; Brighton HS; Brighton, MI; Band; Chrs; Hon Rl; Ger Clb; Oakland Community College; Psych.

THOMAS, JILL; Eastern HS; Pekin, IN; 2/80 Trs Jr Cls; Pres Band; Chrs; Hon Rl; NHS; Pep Clb; Spn Clb; Chrldng; Scr Kpr; College.

THOMAS, JILL; Dearborn HS; Dearborn, MI; Chrs; Hon Rl; IM Sprt; Mgrs; Scr Kpr; Tmr; Natl Merit Ltr; Michigan St Univ; Elem Educ.

THOMAS, JOANNE; Caro HS; Caro, MI; Band; Hon Rl; NHS; Sec Fr Clb; Mat Maids; Pres Awd; College.

THOMAS, JOE; Lakeview HS; Cortland, OH; Band; Hon Rl; Stu Cncl; Yrbk; Beta Clb; Mth Clb; College; Bus Admin.

THOMAS, JULIE; Arcadia Local HS; Findlay, OH; 4/63 Sec Soph Cls; VP Sr Cls; Pres Band; Hon Rl; NHS; Pres Sch Pl; Yth Flsp; Pres Drama Clb; Pres FHA; Twrlr; Findlay Coll; English.

THOMAS, KAREN; Edison HS; Milan, OH; Trs Soph Cls; Chrs; Hon Rl; NHS; Sch Mus; Sch Pl; Drama Clb; Scr Kpr; College; Business.

THOMAS, KAREN; L L Wright HS; Ironwood, MI; Band; Hon Rl; Pep Clb; Chrldng; Pom Pon; Gogebic Jr Coll; Acctg.

THOMAS, KENNETH; Indian Creek Sr HS; Morgantown, IN; 23/160 Am Leg Boys St; Band; Sch Mus; Univ.

THOMAS, KEVIN; Howland HS; Warren, OH; 17/350 Hon Rl; NHS; Letter Bsbl; Letter Bsktbl; Letter Ftbl; Letter Glf; Scr Kpr; Tmr; Youngstown St Univ; Bus Mgmt.

THOMAS, KIMBERLY; High School; Detroit, MI; Girl Scts; Hon Rl; NHS; Stu Cncl; Fr Clb; Pep Clb; College; Poli Sci.

THOMAS, LAURA; Northwest HS; Cincinnati, OH; AFS; Cmnty Wkr; Hon Rl; Sec JA; Natl Forn Lg; Sch Pl; Stg Crw; Pres Yth Flsp; Drama Clb; Fr Clb; Univ; Spec Educ.

THOMAS, LINDA; East HS; Akron, OH; Hon Rl; Lbry Ade; Off Ade; Drama Clb; FHA; Bsbl; Bsktbl; Gym; Coach Actv; GAA; Cooking.

THOMAS, LINDA; Newton Local HS; Plsnt Hl, OH; Trs Jr Cls; Pres Sr Cls; VP Sr Cls; Am Leg Aux Girls St; Band; Chrs; Drm Mjrt; Hon Rl; Lbry Ade; NHS; Miami Univ.

THOMAS, LINDA; West Side HS; Gary, IN; Cls Rep Soph Cls; Cl Rep Jr Cls; Chrh Wkr; Hon Rl; Lbry Ade; NHS; Mth Clb; Cit Awd; Voc Schl; Math.

THOMAS, LISA; Grosse Pointe North HS; Grosse Pt Wds, MI; Chrs; Chrh Wkr; FCA; Hon Rl; Lbry Ade; NHS; Orch; Sch Mus; Ger Clb; PPFtbl; MSU; Educ.

THOMAS, LISA; London HS; Columbus, OH; Chrs; Hon Rl; Orch; FHA; Voc Schl; Sec.

THOMAS, LORA; South Vermillion HS; Clinton, IN; Sec Soph Cls; VP Jr Cls; VP Sr Cls; Hon Rl; NHS; Rptr Sch Nwsp; Fr Clb; Pep Clb; Chrldng; IM Sprt; Whos Who In Foreign Languages 1977; Indiana Univ; Art.

THOMAS, LORI; Maumee HS; Maumee, OH; 46/316 Band; Off Ade; Rptr Yrbk; Spn Clb; IM Sprt; Univ; Sci.

THOMAS, LORI; Parkside HS; Jackson, MI; Band; Chrh Wkr; Hon Rl; Yrbk; Treas Ger Clb; Univ Of Mi; Bus Admin.

THOMAS, LYNNE; Ursuline HS; Girard, OH; 31/286 Cls Rep Sr Cls; Hon Rl; VP NHS; Stu Cncl; Letter Glf; Letter Trk; Tmr; Youngstown St Univ; Nursing.

THOMAS, LYNNE; Fairborn Baker HS; Wp Afb, OH; 1/330 Pres Soph Cls; Chrs; Hon Rl; Mod UN; NHS; Rptr Sch Nwsp; Drama Clb; Rice Univ; Political Sci.

THOMAS, MARK; Hazel Park HS; Hazel Park, MI; 1/354 Cl Rep Jr Cls; Val; Am Leg Boys St; NHS; Stu Cncl; Letter Crs Cntry; Capt Ten; PPFtbl; DAR Awd; Natl Merit Schl; Coll.

THOMAS, MARY; Southwestern HS; Flint, MI; Hon Rl; Mod UN; NHS; Natl Merit SF; Univ.

THOMAS, MARY; Indian Hill HS; Cincinnati, OH; 90/280 Chrs; PAVAS; Sch Mus; Sch Nwsp; Pep Clb; Trk; Capt Chrldng; PPFtbl; Southern Methodist Univ; Med.

THOMAS, MARYANN; Baldwin HS; Baldwin, MI; Girl Scts; Hon Rl; Sch Pl; Spn Clb; Univ; Archt.

THOMAS, MERI A; Portage Central HS; Portage, MI; 33/379 Chrs; Hon Rl; Off Ade; Sch Mus; Pres Pep Clb; DAR Awd; Western Michigan Univ; Spec Educ.

THOMAS, MICHAEL; Morgantown HS; Morgantwn, WV; Am Leg Boys St; Boy Scts; Hon Rl; NHS; Sct Actv; Treas Fr Clb; Pres Mth Clb; IM Sprt; Med Schl; Bio.

THOMAS, MICHAEL R; Lakota HS; Westchester, OH; Boy Scts; Chrs; Hon Rl; Sct Actv; 4-H; Spn Clb; Univ Hnr Schlrshp From Univ Of Cincinnati 79; Pres Of Explorer Post 962; Univ Of Cincinnati; Elec Engr.

THOMAS, MICHEAL; Buckeye West HS; Cadiz, OH; 8/87 Hst Sr Cls; Am Leg Boys St; Boy Scts; Hon Rl; NHS; Sch Pl; Rptr Sch Nwsp; Sci Clb; Capt Wrstlng; Am Leg Awd; College; Elec Engr.

THOMAS, MICHELE; Comstock Park HS; Comstock Pk, MI; 7/136 Pres Chrs; NHS; Sch Mus; Yrbk; Pep Clb; Sec Pom Pon; PPFtbl; Univ Of Notre Dame; Lib Arts.

THOMAS, MICHELLE; Mc Comb HS; Mccomb, OH; Sec Frsh Cls; Chrs; Hon Rl; Sch Nwsp; 4-H; FHA; College; Secretarial.

THOMAS, NADINE; Canfield HS; Canfield, OH; Letter Chrs; Chrh Wkr; Drl Tm; Girl Scts; Hon Rl; Treas JA; Lbry Ade; Lit Mag; Mdrgl; NHS; 1st Plc Westminster Coll Latin Drama Comp 79; Achvmnt Awrd 100.

THOMAS, NANCY L; Coalton HS; Coalton, WV; 1/33 Pres Soph Cls; Cls Rep Sr Cls; Val; Hon Rl; Hosp Ade; Lbry Ade; Stu Cncl; Yrbk; Rptr Sch Nwsp; Pep Clb; Soc Of Dist Amer HS Stu; Co Ed Hi Y VP; Tri Hi Y Pres; Davis & Elkins Coll; Nursing.

THOMAS, NATE; Gallia Acad; Gallipolis, OH; Cls Rep Frsh Cls; Cls Rep Soph Cls; Cl Rep Jr Cls; Cls Rep Sr Cls; NHS; Sprt Ed Sch Nwsp; Lat Clb; Letter Bsktbl; Ohi Univ; Comm.

THOMAS, PAMELA; Finneytown HS; Cincinnati, OH; VP Soph Cls; Pres Sr Cls; Chrh Wkr; Capt Drl Tm; Hon Rl; Sch Mus; Yth Flsp; Miami Univ; Psych.

THOMAS, PAMELA; Grosse Pointe North HS; Gs Pte Shores, MI; Band; Hon Rl; NHS; Orch; Tmr; Natl Merit SF; Michigan St Univ; Pre Med.

THOMAS, PAULA; Immaculata HS; Detroit, MI; Cl Rep Jr Cls; Cmnty Wkr; Hon Rl; Stu Cncl; Bsktbl; Mgrs; Univ Of Michigan.

THOMAS, PHYLLIS; George Washington HS; E Chicago, IN; 4/263 VP Soph Cls; Pres Jr Cls; Am Leg Aux Girls St; Hon Rl; NHS; Stu Cncl; Fr Clb; Pep Clb; Chrldng; Stu Sci Training Prog In Math & Computers Participant; College; Comp Sci.

THOMAS, RANDALL; Laurel Oaks JVS HS; Blanchester, OH; 41/154 Hon Rl; Red Cr Ade; Stu Cncl; VP FFA; Ftbl; Ten; Tech Schl; Wildlife Mgmt.

THOMAS, RHONDA; Tyler County HS; Lima, WV; 8/105 Sec Frsh Cls; Pres Soph Cls; Cl Rep Jr Cls; Cls Rep Sr Cls; Band; Hon Rl; NHS; Sch Pl; Stu Cncl; Rptr Sch Nwsp; Fairmont St Coll; Med Lab Tech.

THOMAS, RICHARD; Fostoria HS; Fostoria, OH; 17/177 Cls Rep Frsh Cls; Cls Rep Sr Cls; Chrs; Hon Rl; NHS; Sch Mus; Stu Cncl; Fr Clb; Ohio St Univ; Med.

THOMAS, RICHARD K; Gahanna Lincoln HS; Gahanna, OH; 2/450 Sal; Band; Boy Scts; Chrh Wkr; Natl Forn Lg; NHS; Orch; Stu Cncl; Natl Merit SF; Voice Dem Awd; Ohio St Univ; Chem.

THOMAS, ROBERT; Newbury HS; Newbury, OH; Cls Rep Frsh Cls; Cls Rep Soph Cls; Band; Hon Rl; Jr NHS; NHS; Sch Mus; Stu Cncl; Ger Clb; Mgrs; Hiram Coll; Hist.

THOMAS, ROBIN; Hudson Area HS; Osseo, MI; Cls Rep Frsh Cls; VP Soph Cls; Cl Rep Jr Cls; Am Leg Aux Girls St; Band; Hon Rl; NHS; Treas Stu Cncl; Ed Sch Nwsp; Rptr Sch Nwsp; 4 H Mi St Horse Received Gold & Two Silver Medals; Eastern Michigan Univ; Comp Sci.

THOMAS, ROBIN; Grant HS; Grant, MI; Cls Rep Sr Cls; Chrs; Hon Rl; Mdrgl; Sch Pl; Stg Crw; Stu Cncl; FNA; Natl Merit Ltr; Kalamazoo Coll; Sci.

THOMAS, ROBYN; Lebanon HS; Lebanon, OH; 40/296 Cmp Fr Grls; Hon Rl; Hosp Ade; Stu Cncl; Rptr Sch Nwsp; Fr Clb; FTA; Pep Clb; Bsbl; Univ Of Dayton; Sec Educ.

THOMAS, ROGER W; Woodrow Wilson HS; Beckley, WV; 55/700 Am Leg Boys St; Boy Scts; Hon Rl; NHS; Yth Flsp; Glf; IM Sprt; West Virginia Univ; Elec Engr.

THOMAS, RONDA; Lakeview HS; Cortland, OH; VP Band; Hon Rl; Y-Teens; Beta Clb; Fr Clb; Mth Clb; Pep Clb; Kent St Univ; Elem Ed.

THOMAS, RUSSELL R; Badin HS; Hamilton, OH; Chrh Wkr; Cmnty Wkr; Stg Crw; Ftbl; Univ Of Dayton; Mechanical Engr.

THOMAS, SALLY; Sheridan HS; Somerset, OH; 76/168 Band; Chrs; Drl Tm; Hon Rl; Lbry Ade; Sch Pl; Drama Clb; Lat Clb; Pep Clb; Gym; Muskingum Area Tech Coll; Acctg.

THOMAS, SANDRA D; Berea HS; Berea, OH; 2/520 Pres Frsh Cls; Band; Debate Tm; Natl Forn Lg; NHS; Stu Cncl; Rptr Yrbk; Ed Sch Nwsp; Fr Clb; Letter Ten; Ohio St Univ; Bus.

THOMAS, SARAH; Andrean HS; Hobart, IN; 33/270 Cl Rep Jr Cls; Hon Rl; Sch Mus; Sch Pl; Stg Crw; Drama Clb; Fr Clb; Univ; Theatre Arts.

THOMAS, SHARON; Meadowdale HS; Dayton, OH; 22/279 Cl Rep Jr Cls; Hon Rl; NHS; Off Ade; OEA; Wright St Univ; Busns Admin.

THOMAS, SHAWN; Mt Gilead HS; Mt Gilead, OH; VP Frsh Cls; VP Soph Cls; Cl Rep Jr Cls; Cls Rep Sr Cls; Am Leg Boys St; DECA; Bsbl; IM Sprt; Muskigum Univ; Med.

THOMAS, SHELLY; Concordia Luthran HS; Ft Wayne, IN; Hosp Ade; JA; Off Ade; FBLA; Lat Clb; Pep Clb; JA Awd; Ind Univ; Recordkeep.

THOMAS, SHERI; Logan Elm HS; Circleville, OH; 11/165 FCA; NHS; Sec Stu Cncl; Rptr Yrbk; GAA; Ohio St Univ; Pharm.

THOMAS, SOPHIE; Rayen HS; Youngstown, OH; Band; Chrs; Chrh Wkr; Girl Scts; Hon Rl; JA; Lbry Ade; Off Ade; Y-Teens; Univ; Med.

THOMAS, SUSAN; Warren Local HS; Cutler, OH; Band; Chrs; Lbry Ade; 4-H; OEA; 4-H Awd; Wash Cnty Voc Schl; Legal Sec.

THOMAS, SUSAN; Stonewall Jackson HS; Charleston, WV; Chrs; Chrh Wkr; Hon Rl; NHS; Off Ade; VP Sch Mus; Yth Flsp; Marshall Univ; Bus.

THOMAS, TAMARA; Portsmouth East HS; Portsmouth, OH; Hon Rl; Lbry Ade; Lat Clb; Scioto County Vo Tec; Accounting.

THOMAS, TERENCE; Shaker Hts HS; Shaker Hts, OH; Cls Rep Frsh Cls; Cls Rep Soph Cls; Cl Rep Jr Cls; Trs Sr Cls; Chrh Wkr; Stu Cncl; Ftbl; Univ; Acctg.

THOMAS, TERESA; Brookfield Sr HS; Brookfield, OH; Hon Rl; NHS; Treas Stu Cncl; Beta Clb; Treas Fr Clb; Pres FTA; Chrldng; Med Explrr Treas 79; Var Sftbl Ltr 79; Med Careers Club Vc Pres 78; Ohio St Univ; Optometrist.

THOMAS, TERRY W; Dublin HS; Plain City, OH; 13/153 Pres Frsh Cls; Am Leg Boys St; Hon Rl; Jr NHS; Lbry Ade; NHS; Quill & Scroll; Sch Nwsp; Pres Lat Clb; Sci Clb; Univ; Poli Sci.

THOMAS, THERESA; W V Fisher Catholic HS; Lancaster, OH; 10/74 Am Leg Aux Girls St; Chrh Wkr; Hon Rl; JA; NHS; Am Leg Awd; Natl Merit Ltr; Rotary Awd; Ohio Univ; Acctg.

THOMAS, TIMOTHY; Ironton HS; Ironton, OH; 24/189 Cl Rep Jr Cls; Hon Rl; NHS; Sch Mus; Drama Clb; Spn Clb; Bsktbl; Capt Crs Cntry; Letter Trk; Coach Actv; J F Grounds Memrl Athletic Awd 79; Schl Track Record Holder 79; Oh Univ Dist Schlrshp Test 7th Pl 78; Miami Of Ohio Univ; Educ.

THOMAS, TIMOTHY; Greenfield Central HS; Greenfield, IN; 55/340 Cls Rep Frsh Cls; Aud/Vis; Hon Rl; Pol Wkr; Stu Cncl; Boys Clb Am; Pres Pep Clb; Spn Clb; Bsktbl; Ftbl; Boys Clb Quiz Bowl St Champ 78; Indiana Univ; Astro.

THOMAS, TODD; Union Bible Seminary; Westfield, IN; Cls Rep Soph Cls; Pres Jr Cls; Chrs; Chrh Wkr; Hon Rl; Stu Cncl; Phys Sci Awd; Stu Of The Yr Awd; Soc Dstngshd Amer HS Stu; Union Bible Seminary; Religion.

THOMAS, VICTORIA; Engadine Consolidated HS; Engadine, MI; 2/35 Girl Scts; Sch Pl; Stu Cncl; Sprt Ed Sch Nwsp; Rptr Sch Nwsp; Sch Nwsp; FHA; Capt Bsktbl; Chrldng; Mic Tech Univ; Civil Engr.

THOMAS, VIKKI; St Ursula Academy; Cincinnati, OH; Hon Rl; Sch Pl; Stg Crw; Sch Nwsp; Fr Clb; IM Sprt; Univ Of Cincinnati; Med Tech.

THOMAS, W DANIEL; Triway HS; Wooster, OH; 78/200 Jr NHS; Stu Cncl; Crs Cntry; Trk; IM Sprt; Tmr; Kent St Univ; Indstrl Tech.

THOMAS JR, DONALD; Memorial HS; St Marys, OH; 7/219 Am Leg Boys St; Chrh Wkr; Cmnty Wkr; Hon Rl; NHS; Sch Mus; Sch Pl; Pres Yth Flsp; Drama Clb; Spn Clb; Ga Military Coll; Pre Med.

THOMASON, DANA; Lakeville Memorial HS; Otisville, MI; 23/189 Sec Soph Cls; Sec Jr Cls; Band; Drm Bgl; Girl Scts; NHS; Pres Mth Clb; Sec Spn Clb; Univ Of Mic; Pre Med.

THOMMEN, LAURA; Walkerville HS; Walkerville, MI; 3/40 Hon Rl; NHS; Bsktbl; Trk; Univ.

THOMPASON, TODD; Warsaw Community HS; Warsaw, IN; 21/400 Hon Rl; JA; JA Awd; College; Bus Admin.

THOMPSON, ALICIA J; Marian HS; Cincinnati, OH; 42/131 Chrh Wkr; Hon Rl; Pol Wkr; Yrbk; Spn Clb; Trk; GAA; Womens Alliance Inc Recognition Awd; Schmidlapp Fund; Spanish IV Hnr; Ohio Univ; Advertising Mgmt.

THOMPSON, ANNA; Paw Paw HS; Paw Paw, MI; 29/183 Band; Chrh Wkr; Hon Rl; NHS; Fr Clb; Mic State Univ; Music.

THOMPSON, BARRY; Marysville HS; W Mansfield, OH; Band; Chrs; Sch Mus; Key Clb; Bsbl; Ftbl; IM Sprt; Mic Christian.

THOMPSON, BECKY; Western Brown Sr HS; Georgetown, OH; 11/159 Am Leg Aux Girls St; Hon Rl; Jr NHS; NHS; Sch Pl; Ed Yrbk; Rptr Sch Nwsp; Treas Drama Clb; Spn Clb; Hosptl Auxillary; Advance Composition Awd; Yrbk Awd; Morehead St Univ; Jrnlsm.

THOMPSON, BECKY; Lakewood HS; Hebron, OH; Cmnty Wkr; Hon Rl; Hosp Ade; Lbry Ade; Red Cr Ade; Y-Teens; Rptr Sch Nwsp; Sch Nwsp; Trk; GAA; Univ; Nursing.

THOMPSON, BOB; Valley Forge HS; Parma Hts, OH; Cls Rep Sr Cls; Hon Rl; Stu Cncl; Y-Teens; Letter Bsktbl; Letter Ftbl; Letter Trk; Coach Actv; Cleveland State Univ; Acctg.

THOMPSON, BONNIE; Wirt County HS; Elizabeth, WV; Cls Rep Frsh Cls; Cls Rep Soph Cls; Cl Rep Jr Cls; Chrh Wkr; Cmnty Wkr; Off Ade; Yth Flsp; 4-H; FHA; 4-H Awd; Parkersburg Community; Sec Sci.

THOMPSON, BRADLEY; Vanburen HS; Carbon, IN; 9/96 Hon Rl; NHS; Yth Flsp; Key Clb; Sci Clb; Spn Clb; Capt Bsktbl; Rose Hulman Inst Of Techn; Engr.

THOMPSON, BRIAN; Marysville HS; W Mansfield, OH; Chrh Wkr; IM Sprt; Mgrs; Freed Hardeman Coll; Acctg.

THOMPSON, BRIAN; Charlevoix Sr HS; Charlevoix, MI; 15/146 Am Leg Boys St; Band; Letter Crs Cntry; Ftbl; Michigan Tech Univ; Civil Engr.

THOMPSON, BRUCE; Chesapeake HS; Chesapeake, OH; 4/140 Chrh Wkr; Hon Rl; NHS; Beta Clb; Letter Ftbl; Achievement Team English; College.

THOMPSON, CALVIN; Hamtramck HS; Hamtramck, MI; 16/90 Cl Rep Jr Cls; VP Sr Cls; Band; Chrs; Chrh Wkr; Pres JA; Jr NHS; NHS; Orch; Pres Sci Clb; Univ S California; Musical Entertnmt.

THOMPSON, CARMELLA; Gilbert HS; Baisden, WV; Band; Rptr Yrbk; Rptr Sch Nwsp; 4-H; Ger Clb; Mth Clb; Pres Pep Clb; 4-H Awd; Marshall Univ; Nursing.

THOMPSON, CAROLYN; Rutherford B Hayes HS; Delaware, OH; AFS; Band; Chrs; Stg Crw; Drama Clb; Ohio Domincan Coll; Law Enforcement.

THOMPSON, CHRIS; Pickerington HS; Pickerington, OH; Chrs; FCA; Red Cr Ade; Ger Clb; Letter Bsbl; Letter Bsktbl; Capt Ftbl; PPFtbl; Ohio St Univ; Family Physcn.

THOMPSON, CHRIS; Houston HS; Sidney, OH; Boy Scts; Hon Rl; Yth Flsp; 4-H; Sec FFA; Letter Bsbl; Bsktbl; Crs Cntry; Glf; IM Sprt; Ohio St Univ; Animal Sci.

THOMPSON, CINDY; Edgewood HS; Bloomington, IN; Cls Rep Frsh Cls; Cls Rep Soph Cls; Cl Rep Jr Cls; Band; Girl Scts; Hon Rl; Hosp Ade; Sch Mus; Sch Pl; Stg Crw; Purdue Univ; Math.

THOMPSON, CINDY; Meigs HS; Pomeroy, OH; Band; Chrs; Chrh Wkr; Girl Scts; Hon Rl; Off Ade; Stg Crw; OEA; Pep Clb; Bsktbl; Rio Grande Cmnty Coll; Sec.

THOMPSON, CONNIE; Northwestern HS; W Salem, OH; VP Soph Cls; Chrs; Hon Rl; Jr NHS; Stu Cncl; Bsktbl; Chrldng; PPFtbl; Kent St Univ; Psych.

THOMPSON, CURTIS; Buckeye West HS; Mt Pleasant, OH; Pres Frsh Cls; Sec Soph Cls; Chrs; Chrh Wkr; Hon Rl; NHS; Sch Pl; Sci Clb; Bsbl; Bsktbl; Univ; Med.

THOMPSON, CYNTHIA; Edgewood HS; Bloomington, IN; 1/196 Cls Rep Frsh Cls; Cls Rep Soph Cls; Cl Rep Jr Cls; Cls Rep Sr Cls; Am Leg Aux Girls St; Band; Hon Rl; Hosp Ade; Sch Mus; Sch Pl; Univ; Engr.

THOMPSON, D; Dominican HS; Southfield, MI; Pres Jr Cls; Band; Chrs; Chrh Wkr; Lbry Ade; Mdrgl; Treas NHS; Orch; Univ Of Michigan; Law.

THOMPSON, DALE; Northwest HS; Indianapolis, IN; 48/506 Hon Rl; NHS; Lat Clb; Opt Clb Awd; General Motors Inst; Mech Engr.

THOMPSON, DARRELL; Columbus East HS; Columbus, OH; Boy Scts; Hon Rl; Sct Actv; OEA; VICA; Natl Merit Ltr; Howard Univ; Offc Educ.

THOMPSON, DARREN; Franklin Community HS; Franklin, IN; 29/280 Pres Chrs; Chrh Wkr; Mdrgl; Sch Mus; Stg Crw; Sec Stu Cncl; Yth Flsp; Drama Clb; Pep Clb; Letter Ftbl; Indiana St Schlrshp; Rose Hulman Inst Of Tech; Chem Engr.

THOMPSON, DAVID; Lincoln HS; Shinnston, WV; 13/227 Band; Hon Rl; Univ; Chem.

THOMPSON, DAVID; Collinwood HS; Cleveland, OH; Band; Orch; Trk; Wrstlng; Cincinnati Univ; Aerospace Engr.

THOMPSON, DAVID E; Howland HS; Warren, OH; 14/430 Cls Rep Frsh Cls; Cls Rep Soph Cls; VP Sr Cls; Boy Scts; Hon Rl; Yth Flsp; Ger Clb; Wrstlng; God Cntry Awd; Pres Awd; Cincinnati Univ; Mech Engr.

THOMPSON, DEANNA; Tri West Hendricks HS; Pittsboro, IN; 8/120 Sec Soph Cls; Pres Jr Cls; Am Leg Aux Girls St; Cmp Fr Grls; Hon Rl; NHS; Off Ade; Pep Clb; Bsktbl; Scr Kpr; Univ; Bus Admin.

THOMPSON, DEBBIE; Miami Trace HS; New Holland, OH; 17/275 Trs Soph Cls; Cls Rep Soph Cls; Sec Jr Cls; Cl Rep Jr Cls; Cls Rep Sr Cls; Am Leg Aux Girls St; Chrs; Hon Rl; NHS; Sch Pl; Columbus Bus Univ; Sec.

THOMPSON, DEBRA E; Oscoda HS; Oscoda, MI; 2/249 Hon Rl; Hosp Ade; Jr NHS; NHS; Trk; Natl Merit SF; Michigan State Univ; Nursing.

THOMPSON, DEIDRE; Logan Sr HS; Logan, WV; Hon Rl; Lbry Ade; Beta Clb; Sec 4-H; FBLA; Dnfth Awd; 4-H Awd; Busns Schl.

THOMPSON, DIANE; West Carrollton Sr HS; W Carrollton, OH; 9/418 Band; Drl Tm; Hon Rl; Jr NHS; NHS; Drama Clb; Ger Clb; PPFtbl; Univ; Fshn Mdse.

THOMPSON, DON; Lakeland Christian Academy; Winona Lake, IN; VP Frsh Cls; Cls Rep Soph Cls; Pres Jr Cls; Pres Sr Cls; Band; Chrh Wkr; Ed Yrbk; Ed Sch Nwsp; Pep Clb; Capt Socr; Grace College.

THOMPSON, DONNA; Oakwood Sr HS; Dayton, OH; Chrs; Girl Scts; Hon Rl; Sch Mus; Sch Pl; Stg Crw; Gym; Mgrs; Scr Kpr; DAR Awd; Pres Phys Ftns Awd 76; Vllybl Co Capt 78; Sftbl Var Ltr 77; Univ; Dr.

THOMPSON, D THERESA; Kyger Creek HS; Cheshire, OH; Band; Hon Rl; JA; Treas NHS; Sec Stu Cncl; Rptr Sch Nwsp; FHA; Keyettes; Trk; Vllybl Team Regnl Runner Up 77; Gallipolis Bus Coll; Typing.

THOMPSON, DWAYNE; Green HS; Akron, OH; Boy Scts; Sct Actv; Letter Trk; IM Sprt; Varsity G Clb; Perfect Attendance; Copley Relays S M 1st Sub Lg 4th 440 Yd Dash; Coll; Archt.

THOMPSON, ELIZABETH A; Marion L Steele HS; Amherst, OH; 3/365 Band; Chrs; Hon Rl; Lbry Ade; NHS; Sch Pl; Stg Crw; Yth Flsp; Pres Drama Clb; Lat Clb; International Thespian Society; Academic Challenge Team Captain; Pep Band; College; Math.

THOMPSON, ERIC; Moeller HS; Silverton, OH; JA; Pol Wkr; Yth Flsp; Univ Of Toledo; Bus Adm.

THOMPSON, FLOYD G; Wilbur Wright HS; Dayton, OH; Cl Rep Jr Cls; Chrs; PAVAS; Sch Mus; Sch Pl; Stu Cncl; Rdo Clb; Univ; Fine Arts.

THOMPSON, GAYE; Maysville HS; Zanesville, OH; 11/200 Cls Rep Frsh Cls; Cls Rep Soph Cls; Cl Rep Jr Cls; Sal; Hon Rl; NHS; Rptr Yrbk; Gym; Chrldng; Coach Actv; College; Phys Educ.

THOMPSON, INGA; Edgewood HS; Bloomington, IN; 13/223 Chrs; Chrh Wkr; Hon Rl; Ger Clb; Pep Clb; Chrldng; PPFtbl; Chosen To Go To Sci Symposium At Ind St Unv 79; Mrchng Bnd Dance Corps Mbr 78; Indiana Univ; Nursing.

THOMPSON, JAMES; Anderson HS; Anderson, IN; 39/415 Hon Rl; Ball State Univ; Art.

THOMPSON, JANE; Mahoning County Jt Voc HS; North Lima, OH; Trs Jr Cls; Chrs; Girl Scts; 4-H; OEA; Trk; PPFtbl; 4-H Awd; Ohio Regnl Comp 3rd Pl Reg 1978; Ohio St Acctg Comp 1st Pl 1978; Univ; Acctg.

THOMPSON, JEANNE; Keyser HS; Keyser, WV; 45/247 Cls Rep Sr Cls; AFS; Chrs; Hon Rl; Sch Pl; Rptr Yrbk; Keyettes; Queen Of Class Night 78; Beta Sigma Phi Schlrshp 78; Keyser Garment Factory Schlrshp 78; Potomac St Coll; Soc Work.

THOMPSON, JEFF; Buckeye South HS; Tiltonsville, OH; Pres Jr Cls; Hon Rl; NHS; Drama Clb; Bsktbl; Letter Ftbl; Schlrshp Tm Sci; Ohio St Univ; Mech Engr.

THOMPSON, JENNIFER; Mullens HS; Mullens, WV; 12/87 Hon Rl; NHS; Stu Cncl; Ed Yrbk; Sprt Ed Yrbk; Rptr Sch Nwsp; Beta Clb; Ten; Concord Coll; Early Childhood Ed.

THOMPSON, JIM; Trenton HS; Trenton, MI; Boy Scts; Hon Rl; Sch Pl; Stg Crw; Stu Cncl; Rptr Yrbk; Spn Clb; Letter Ftbl; Letter Gym; IM Sprt; RETS; Elec Tech.

THOMPSON, JOANNE; Holland HS; Holland, MI; Band; Cmp Fr Grls; Hon Rl; Sch Pl; Stu Cncl; Oakland Univ; Comp Sci.

THOMPSON, JOHN; Point Pleasant HS; Pt Pleasant, WV; 15/217 Cls Rep Soph Cls; Cl Rep Jr Cls; Am Leg Boys St; Band; Drl Tm; Hon Rl; NHS; Ed Yrbk; Pres Key Clb; Dnfth Awd; Rotary Club Schlrshp 79; Neatest In Class Awd 79; Woodsman Of The Wrld Hstry Awd 78; W Virginia Inst Of Tech; Elec Engr.

THOMPSON, JOHN; Cadiz HS; Cadiz, OH; 34/138 Cls Rep Sr Cls; Am Leg Boys St; Hon Rl; NHS; Sch Mus; Sch Pl; Letter Bsbl; Letter Ftbl; Letter Wrstlng; Coach Actv; Kent State; Bus Admin.

THOMPSON, JOHN C; Brunswick HS; Brunswick, OH; 4/495 Band; Debate Tm; Natl Forn Lg; NHS; Sch Mus; Stg Crw; Natl Merit SF; Voice Dem Awd; Univ; Math.

THOMPSON, JOHN T; Rogers HS; Toledo, OH; Boy Scts; Hon Rl; Off Ade; Letter Trk; Trk; Letter Wrstlng; Univ; Prof Athl.

THOMPSON, JOYCE; Jane Addams Voc HS; Cleveland, OH; Cl Rep Jr Cls; Chrh Wkr; Cmnty Wkr; Drl Tm; JA; Jr NHS; Mod UN; Off Ade; Y-Teens; VICA; Spec Awd In Cosmtlgy Hair Style Contst 78; Perfect Attend; Barber Coll; Barber.

THOMPSON, KAREN; Carmel HS; Carmel, IN; 54/657 Hon Rl; NHS; Yth Flsp; Letter Swmmng; Letter Ten; Letter Trk; Scr Kpr; Purdue Univ.

THOMPSON, KAREN M; Barboursville HS; Huntington, WV; Pres Frsh Cls; Cls Rep Frsh Cls; Cls Rep Soph Cls; Sec Sr Cls; Band; Cmp Fr Grls; Pres FCA; Girl Scts; Hon Rl; Lbry Ade; World Affairs Inst 33sd Annual 1979; West Virginia Univ; Phys Ther.

THOMPSON, KATHY; Washington Sr HS; Washington C H, OH; 7/140 Treas AFS; Am Leg Aux Girls St; Pres Band; Chrs; Hon Rl; Sec NHS; Sch Mus; Rptr Yrbk; 4-H; Fr Clb; John Philip Sousa Band Awd 79; Mst Tlntd Cls Of 79; Pres Clsrm For Young Amer 79; Ohio Northern Univ; Soc Work.

THOMPSON, KEVIN; Plainwell HS; Kalamazoo, MI; 62/235 Hon Rl; Ftbl; Capt Wrstlng; IM Sprt; Mi Comptn Schlrshp 79; Michigan Tech Univ; Bio Sci.

THOMPSON, KEVIN; Munford HS; Detroit, MI; Band; Chrh Wkr; Debate Tm; Drl Tm; Hon Rl; JA; NHS; ROTC; Stu Cncl; JA Awd; Lawerence Inst Of Tech; Archt.

THOMPSON, KEVIN; Mumford HS; Detroit, MI; Val; Band; Boy Scts; Chrs; Chrh Wkr; Drl Tm; Hon Rl; JA; NHS; ROTC; Notre Dame Univ; Archt.

THOMPSON, LANA; River Valley HS; New Troy, MI; Cls Rep Frsh Cls; Cls Rep Soph Cls; Cl Rep Jr Cls; Cls Rep Sr Cls; Band; Girl Scts; Hon Rl; Sch Pl; Stg Crw; Stu Cncl; Judges Spec Awd 79 Blossom Fest; Designer Of Class C St Bsktbl Champ Float; Talent Show Awd 79; Univ; Law Offcr.

THOMPSON, LARRY; Bluffton Harrison HS; Bluffton, IN; Cmnty Wkr; Hon Rl; Stu Cncl; Spn Clb; Bsbl; IM Sprt; Purdue Univ; Comp Progr.

THOMPSON, LAURA; Wayne HS; Dayton, OH; Hon Rl; Jr NHS; Lbry Ade; Sch Pl; Fr Clb; Ohi State Univ; Vet Med.

THOMPSON, LEAH; Bloomington S HS; Bloomington, IN; 29/310 Chrh Wkr; Hon Rl; NHS; Sec OEA; Busns Schl; Secretary.

THOMPSON, LIBBY; Sidney HS; Sidney, OH; Cls Rep Frsh Cls; Girl Scts; Hon Rl; PAVAS; Sct Actv; Yth Flsp; Y-Teens; Pep Clb; Gym; Trk; Bowling Green Univ; Public Relations.

THOMPSON, LINDA; Coldwater HS; Coldwater, MI; Cls Rep Soph Cls; Sec Jr Cls; Band; Chrh Wkr; Stu Cncl; Letter Glf; Letter Gym; Letter Trk; 4-H Awd; Pres Awd; Michigan State Univ; Health.

THOMPSON, LISA; Gilmer Co HS; Weston, WV; Band; Hon Rl; Hosp Ade; VICA; A & B Coll; X Ray Tech.

THOMPSON, LORI A; Euclid Sr HS; Euclid, OH; 16/714 Cls Rep Soph Cls; Cl Rep Jr Cls; Am Leg Aux Girls St; NHS; Off Ade; Pres Stu Cncl; Key Clb; Letter Bsbl; Letter Ftbl; Tmr; Distngshd Scholar Awrd 76 79; Natl Athletic Schlrshp Soc 78; Univ; Law.

THOMPSON, LORIE; Buckeye North HS; Smithfield, OH; 14/100 Am Leg Aux Girls St; Hon Rl; NHS; OEA; Spn Clb; Jefferson Tech Coll.

THOMPSON, LYNN; Solon HS; Solon, OH; Drl Tm; Girl Scts; Hon Rl; NHS; Ed Sch Nwsp; Rptr Sch Nwsp; Sch Nwsp; Pep Clb; Bsbl; Swmmng; College; Communications.

THOMPSON, LYNNE; Chillicothe HS; Chillicothe, OH; 73/366 Cls Rep Soph Cls; Cl Rep Jr Cls; Cls Rep Sr Cls; Band; Hon Rl; Stu Cncl; Yrbk; Sch Nwsp; 4-H; 4-H Awd; Ohio Univ; Pub Rel.

THOMPSON, M; Highland HS; Sharon Ctr, OH; Hon Rl; Off Ade; Sch Pl; VP Key Clb; College; Art.

THOMPSON, MALCOLM; Huntington HS; Huntington, WV; 31/250 Hon Rl; Jr NHS; NHS; Orch; Yrbk; Key Clb; Mth Clb; West Virginia Univ; Industrial Engr.

THOMPSON, MARK; Bellville HS; Ypsilanti, MI; Band; Hon Rl; Sch Nwsp; IM Sprt; Univ.

THOMPSON, MARTHA; Clinton HS; Clinton, MI; Hon Rl; Treas NHS; Off Ade; Sch Mus; Treas Yth Flsp; VP 4-H; Pep Clb; Letter Bsktbl; Trk; GAA; Univ.

THOMPSON, MARY; South Knox HS; Wheatland, IN; Hon Rl; Red Cr Ade; Yth Flsp; Sec FNA; OEA; Pep Clb; Trk; Purdue Univ; Chem Engr.

THOMPSON, MARY; Garber HS; Essexville, MI; 42/176 Chrs; Cmnty Wkr; Hon Rl; Natl Forn Lg; Sch Mus; Sch Pl; Stg Crw; Y-Teens; Rptr Yrbk; Yrbk; College; Graphic Arts.

THOMPSON, MARY BETH; Danville HS; Danville, OH; 17/62 Sec Soph Cls; Trs Sr Cls; Band; Chrh Wkr; Girl Scts; NHS; Off Ade; Sch Mus; Sch Pl; Stg Crw; Ohio Bd Of Regents 1979 Acad Schlrshp 1979; Natl Hnr Soc Schlrshp 1979; DHS Awd Of Distinction; Akron Univ; RN.

THOMPSON, MARY JO; Wm Mason HS; Mason, OH; AFS; Chrs; Cmnty Wkr; Hon Rl; Sch Mus; Lat Clb; Spn Clb; Typing Awd 76; Magna Cum Laude Awd For Latin 1 77; Awd For Hghst In Spanish III 78; Univ; Music.

THOMPSON, MELANIE G; Mooresville HS; Indianapolis, IN; 58/298 Girl Scts; Hon Rl; Spn Clb; Trk; Mas Awd; Vlyball; Pioneer Hertg; Tchr Aide; Cable Disptchr.

THOMPSON, MICAH; Sharples HS; Sharples, WV; 1/28 VP Jr Cls; Trs Sr Cls; Am Leg Boys St; Chrh Wkr; Hon Rl; Jr NHS; NHS; 4-H; Key Clb; Pep Clb; West Virginia Coll; Elec Tech.

THOMPSON, MICHAEL; Buckeye South HS; Rayland, OH; Hon Rl; NHS; Stu Cncl; VP Spn Clb; 1st & 2nd Yr Spanish Schlrshp Test Schlrshp Team; Ohio St Univ; Business Admin.

THOMPSON, MICHAEL; North Farmington HS; Farmington Hls, MI; 1/400 VP Frsh Cls; Cls Rep Sr Cls; Jr NHS; Stu Cncl; Beta Clb; Mth Clb; Bsbl; Ftbl; Am Leg Awd; Univ Of Michigan.

THOMPSON, MICHAEL E; Mt Vernon HS; Mt Vernon, OH; Hon Rl; Spn Clb; Natl Merit SF; Ohio St Univ; Engr.

THOMPSON, MIRIAM; Cass Techinical HS; Detroit, MI; Chrh Wkr; Hon Rl; Off Ade; Yth Flsp; Yrbk; FDA; College; Sci.

THOMPSON, PAM; Brooke HS; Colliers, WV; 69/454 Trs Frsh Cls; Trs Soph Cls; Cls Rep Sr Cls; Chrh Wkr; Cmnty Wkr; JA; West Liberty State College; Dental.

THOMPSON, PAMELA; Columbia HS; Columbia Sta, OH; Cls Rep Frsh Cls; Band; Chrs; ROTC; Sch Pl; Stg Crw; Stu Cncl; Rptr Yrbk; College; Actress.

THOMPSON, PAMELA K; Jeffersonville HS; Jeffersonville, IN; Sec Stu Cncl; FBLA; Chrldng; Mgrs; PPFtbl; Bus.

THOMPSON, RICHARD; John F Kennedy HS; Taylor, MI; 27/483 Band; Debate Tm; Hon Rl; JA; Jr NHS; Natl Forn Lg; NHS; Orch; 3rd Pl Schl Voice Of Demcrcy Oratory Cntst 78; 4 Letters Partcptn In Band 77 79; Univ; Law.

THOMPSON, RICHARD L; Elkins HS; Elkins, WV; 32/235 Pres Soph Cls; Am Leg Boys St; Hon Rl; Bsbl; Ftbl; IM Sprt; North Carolina St Univ; Wood Tech.

THOMPSON, ROBIN; Alma HS; Alma, MI; VP Jr Cls; Chrs; Hon Rl; NHS; Sch Pl; Stu Cncl; Yth Flsp; Ed Sch Nwsp; Rptr Sch Nwsp; Kalamzaoo College; Intrnl Commerce.

THOMPSON, SCOTT; Bremen HS; Bremen, IN; Cls Rep Sr Cls; Chrh Wkr; VP FCA; Hon Rl; NHS; Sch Nwsp; Letter Bsktbl; Letter Ftbl; Letter Trk; Pres Awd; Univ; Missions.

THOMPSON, SHARI; Ludington HS; Ludington, MI; Chrs; Chrh Wkr; Hon Rl; NHS; Yth Flsp; Spn Clb; Spring Arbor College; Elem Ed.

THOMPSON, SHARI; Oregon Davis HS; Walkerton, IN; 6/60 Sec Frsh Cls; Sec Jr Cls; Am Leg Aux Girls St; FCA; Hon Rl; Yrbk; Pep Clb; Letter Bsktbl; Letter Gym; Letter Trk;.

THOMPSON, STARR; North Muskegon HS; Muskegon, MI; Chrs; Hosp Ade; JA; Lbry Ade; Off Ade; PPFtbl; Muskegon Bus Coll; Legal Sec.

THOMPSON, STELLA; Harman HS; Bowden, WV; Trs Jr Cls; Lbry Ade; Treas FHA; Business School; Bus Mngmt.

THOMPSON, STEVE; New Albany HS; New Albany, OH; 2/100 Pres Soph Cls; Pres Jr Cls; Hon Rl; Yrbk; Sci Clb; Ftbl; University; Aero Engr.

THOMPSON, STEVEN; Manistee HS; Manistee, MI; Hon Rl; Jr NHS; Sprt Ed Sch Nwsp; Coach Actv; IM Sprt; Mgrs; Scr Kpr; Mi Compttv Schlshp 79; Davenport Coll Of Bus; Acctg.

THOMPSON, SUSAN; Triton HS; Bourbon, IN; Hst Sr Cls; Cmp Fr Grls; FCA; Hon Rl; NHS; Off Ade; Yth Flsp; Drama Clb; 4-H; FBLA; Received 4th In Indiana St FBLA Contestand; Category Busns Comm; College; Busns.

THOMPSON, TAMI; East Palestine HS; East Palestine, OH; Band; Sch Pl; Letter Trk; Scr Kpr; Incentive Schlrshp; College; Nursing.

THOMPSON, TAMMY; Grand Blanc Comm HS; Grand Blanc, MI; 14/690 Band; Hon Rl; NHS; Sch Mus; Pom Pon; PPFtbl; Central Michigan Univ; Art.

THOMPSON, TARA; Maysville HS; White Cottage, OH; 1/225 Cl Rep Jr Cls; VP Chrs; FCA; Hon Rl; NHS; Sch Mus; Sec 4-H; Letter Bsktbl; Letter Trk; 4-H Awd; Most Otstndng Jr In Maysville High Choir 79; Sweetheart Ball Attendant 79; Univ.

THOMPSON, TERRI; Baker HS; Fairborn, OH; Chrs; Chrh Wkr; Hon Rl; Quill & Scroll; Yrbk; Drama Clb; Sec Sci Clb; PPFtbl; Ohio Univ; Biology.

THOMPSON, TERRY; Escanaba Sr HS; Escanaba, MI; 52/391 Hon Rl; IM Sprt; Northwestern Univ; Corporate Law.

THOMPSON, THOMAS; Albion Sr HS; Albion, MI; 31/216 Hon Rl; Rptr Sch Nwsp; Sch Nwsp; Central Michigan Univ; Bus.

THOMPSON, TOD; Monrovia HS; Mooresville, IN; 3/109 VP Frsh Cls; Trs Soph Cls; VP Jr Cls; Pres Sr Cls; Am Leg Boys St; Band; Chrh Wkr; FCA; Hon Rl; NHS; General Motors Inst; Mech Engr.

THOMPSON, TODD; Maysville HS; White Cg, OH; 12/225 Chrh Wkr; Hon Rl; VP NHS; Pres 4-H; Key Clb; Letter Wrstlng; 4-H Awd; Ohio St Univ; Animal Sci.

THOMPSON, VICKI; New Lexington Sr HS; New Lexington, OH; 1/161 Val; Band; Hon Rl; NHS; FFA; Lat Clb; Bsktbl; Trk; Wrstlng; Pres GAA; Ohio St Univ; Vet.

THOMPSON, VICTOR; University Of Detroit HS; Detroit, MI; 59/139 Hon Rl; JA; Stg Crw; Bsbl; Letter Ftbl; Coach Actv; IM Sprt; JA Awd; Natl Merit Ltr; Univ Of Michigan; Bus Admin.

THOMPSON, VICTORIA; Crawford Co Consolidated HS; Marengo, IN; Chrh Wkr; Hon Rl; Hosp Ade; NHS; Sch Mus; Stg Crw; Yth Flsp; Rptr Sch Nwsp; Vincennes Univ; Rn.

THOMPSON, WILLIAM; Marietta HS; Marietta, OH; 75/400 Cl Rep Jr Cls; Band; Sch Pl; Stu Cncl; Yth Flsp; Spn Clb; College; Ornithocogy.

THOMPSON JR, JESSE; East HS; Cleveland, OH; Boy Scts; NHS; Ten; Scr Kpr; Case Western Reserve Univ;chemist.

THOMSBERRY, TINA; West Jefferson HS; W Jefferson, OH; Chrs; Hon Rl; Drama Clb; Fr Clb; Trk; Wrstlng; Letter Chrldng; IM Sprt; Univ; Neurosurgeon.

THOMSON, BRIAN; Munster HS; Munster, IN; 52/409 Pres Frsh Cls; Cl Rep Jr Cls; Chrs; Hon Rl; NHS; Sch Mus; Stu Cncl; Letter Ftbl; Pres IM Sprt; Rotary Awd; First Alternate Hoosier Boys St 79; Univ; Bus.

THOMSPON, ROBERT; Fairfield HS; Hamilton, OH; 91/596 Band; Debate Tm; Hon Rl; Stu Cncl; Drama Clb; Mgrs; Univ; Bus.

THORBURN, ROBT; Firestone HS; Akron, OH; FCA; Hon Rl; NHS; Letter Bsbl; Letter Bsktbl; Socr; Pres Awd; Marietta College; Accounting.

THORN, CHERYL; East Canton HS; E Canton, OH; Trs Frsh Cls; Cl Rep Jr Cls; Chrh Wkr; Drl Tm; Hon Rl; Jr NHS; Sch Pl; Stg Crw; Yth Flsp; Voc Schl; Stenographer.

THORN, KRIS A; New Albany HS; New Albany, IN; Chrs; Hon Rl; Jr NHS; NHS; PAVAS; Sch Mus; Stg Crw; Drama Clb; Natl Merit SF; Wabash Coll; Theatre.

THORN, PHYLLIS L; Grand Ledge HS; Eagle, MI; 37/416 Chrh Wkr; Hon Rl; NHS; Spn Clb; Mich State Univ; Advertising.

THORN, VICKIE; Zanesville HS; Zanesville, OH; Band; Hon Rl; Hosp Ade; Lbry Ade; NHS; Sch Mus; Y-Teens; Rptr Sch Nwsp; Lat Clb; Sci Clb; Frsh Cls Varsity Sergeant At Arms 76; Ohio St Univ; Vet Med.

THORNBERRY, DOUG; Marlington HS; Alliance, OH; Hon Rl; NHS; Pres 4-H; VP FFA; 4-H Awd; Univ; Acctg.

THORNBRO, FREDRICK; Daleville HS; Daleville, IN; Chrh Wkr; Yrbk; Fr Clb; VP Pep Clb; Letter Bsbl; Letter Crs Cntry; Letter Trk; Ball State Univ; Forestry.

THORNBURG, ALICE; Winchester Comm HS; Winchester, IN; Chrh Wkr; Hon Rl; Sch Pl; Yth Flsp; 4-H; FHA; FTA; Spn Clb; Work.

THORNBURG, PAMELA J; North Posey HS; Wadesville, IN; 28/186 Band; Sec Chrs; Hon Rl; Treas 4-H; Pep Clb; Trk; GAA; 4-H Awd; Stevens Univ; Fashion Retail.

THORNBURG, SHARA; Randolph Southern Jr Sr HS; Lynn, IN; 6/70 Cls Rep Frsh Cls; Chrh Wkr; Hon Rl; NHS; Stg Crw; Stu Cncl; Rptr Yrbk; Sec Lat Clb; Pep Clb; Spn Clb; Ball St Univ; Nurse.

THORNE, BEV; Sheridan HS; Thornville, OH; 10/180 Chrs; FCA; Hon Rl; Sec NHS; Stu Cncl; Trk; Chrldng; IM Sprt; Natl Merit Ltr; Miami Univ; Psych.

THORNE, KIM; Notre Dame HS; Clarksburg, WV; 12/53 Treas Band; Chrs; Chrh Wkr; NHS; Sch Mus; Yrbk; 4-H; FDA; IM Sprt; 4-H Awd; Univ; Acctg.

THORNE, RANDALL; Wahama HS; New Haven, WV; 13/97 Cls Rep Frsh Cls; Debate Tm; Hon Rl; Natl Forn Lg; Stu Cncl; Sch Nwsp; DECA; West Virginia Univ; Genrl Std.

THORNHILL, JAMES A; Woodrow Wilson HS; Beckley, WV; 42/500 Am Leg Boys St; Chrh Wkr; Cmnty Wkr; Hon Rl; JA; NHS; Sct Actv; Yth Flsp; Sprt Ed Sch Nwsp; Key Clb; 2nd Pl In AAA Jr Earth & Space Sci Div Of The WV St Sci Fair 77; Jrnlsm Awrd 77; Univ; Bus Admin.

THORNTON, BRENDA; St Francis De Sales HS; Columbus, OH; 10/200 Am Leg Aux Girls St; Chrh Wkr; Hon Rl; NHS; Sch Mus; Sch Pl; Rptr Yrbk; Sch Nwsp; Drama Clb; Lat Clb; Coll; Journalism.

THORNTON, BYRON W; Kermit HS; Kermit, WV; 1/27 Cls Rep Frsh Cls; Cl Rep Jr Cls; Cls Rep Sr Cls; Val; Am Leg Boys St; Band; Boy Scts; Chrh Wkr; Hon Rl; Stu Cncl; Marshall Univ; Cmmnctns.

THORNTON, DARETHA M; Cheboygan Area HS; Cheboygan, MI; 17/197 Hon Rl; Sch Pl; Rptr Yrbk; Fr Clb; Cengtral Mich Univ; Mathematics.

THORNTON, DEREK; Gary Roosevelt HS; Gary, IN; Trs Frsh Cls; Cls Rep Soph Cls; Cl Rep Jr Cls; Cls Rep Sr Cls; Aud/Vis; Hon Rl; Jr NHS; Natl Forn Lg; NHS; Yrbk; Purdue Univ; Pharm.

THORNTON, DUANE; Corunna HS; Owosso, MI; 8/213 Am Leg Boys St; Band; Boy Scts; Hon Rl; Mod UN; NHS; Orch; 4-H; Rdo Clb; 4-H Awd; Michigan Tech Univ; Elec Engr.

THORNTON, ELAINE; Hurricane HS; Hurricane, WV; 3/192 Cls Rep Frsh Cls; Cls Rep Sr Cls; Hon Rl; NHS; Stu Cncl; Ed Sch Nwsp; Mth Clb; Capt Chrldng; West Virginia Tech; Chem Engr.

THORNTON, ERIC A; Blanchester HS; Midland, OH; 19/159 Chrh Wkr; Hon Rl; NHS; Pres 4-H; Treas FFA; Spn Clb; Trk; Pres 4-H Awd; Coll; Engr.

THORNTON, JANET; Seton HS; Cincinnati, OH; Cmp Fr Grls; Chrh Wkr; Cmnty Wkr; Hon Rl; Off Ade; Sch Pl; Stg Crw; College; Spec Educ.

THORNTON, KAREN; Shaker Hts HS; Shaker Hts, OH; Boy Scts; Chrs; Chrh Wkr; Girl Scts; Hosp Ade; Stu Cncl; Rptr Yrbk; Rptr Sch Nwsp; Fr Clb; Univ; Engr.

THORNTON, KARIN; Little Miami HS; Morrow, OH; 13/210 Cl Rep Jr Cls; Band; Hon Rl; Lbry Ade; Lit Mag; NHS; Sch Mus; Stu Cncl; Yrbk; Spn Clb; Schlstp Team Geom; Jazz Band & Band Council; Librarin; Geom Awd & Geom Tutor Awd; Univ.

THORNTON, MARGO J; Cheboygan Area HS; Cheboygan, MI; Hon Rl; Hosp Ade; Fr Clb; Lake Superior Univ; Acctg.

THORNTON, TAMMY; South Ripley HS; Versailles, IN; 3/112 Band; Chrh Wkr; Hon Rl; Sec Lat Clb; Lion Awd; Southern Missionary Coll; Optmtry.

THORP, MILES; Owendale Gagetown HS; Owendale, MI; Hon Rl; Sch Pl; Letter Bsbl; Letter Ftbl;.

THORPE, AIMEE; Marysville HS; Marysville, OH; 10/250 Cls Rep Soph Cls; Am Leg Aux Girls St; Band; Debate Tm; Hon Rl; Jr NHS; Natl Forn Lg; NHS; Sch Mus; Sch Pl; Univ Of Cinc; Engineer.

THORSEN, LINDA; Escanaba Area Public HS; Escanaba, MI; 19/451 Band; Hon Rl; NHS; Bay De Noc Cmnty Coll.

THORSON, CYNTHIA M; Loy Norrix HS; Kalamazoo, MI; 11/427 Band; Drl Tm; Girl Scts; Hon Rl; Orch; Sch Mus; Sct Actv; Rptr Sch Nwsp; Natl Merit Ltr; Quiz Bowl 77; 2nd Pl In Spelling Bee 77; Univ; Envrmntl Sci.

THRALL, KATHLEEN; Marlette HS; Marlette, MI; 4/130 Chrh Wkr; Hon Rl; Lbry Ade; NHS; FTA; Ger Clb; OEA; Spn Clb; Spring Arbor Coll; Bilingual Educ.

THRASHER, CHRISTY; Kokomo HS; Kokomo, IN; Chrh Wkr; Stu Cncl; Y-Teens; Lat Clb; Pep Clb; Gym; Socr; Trk; Chrldng; Coach Actv; Miss Cheerldr Of Indiana; Most Outstndng Cheerleader Of Camp; Made Natl Cheerleading Staff; Purdue Univ; Phys Ed.

THROOP, KEVIN; Edgewood HS; Ashtabula, OH; Band; Sch Pl; Sci Clb; Letter Crs Cntry; Trk; College; Aerospace.

THRUSH, BECKY T; Garrett HS; Garrett, IN; Chrs; Hon Rl; Hosp Ade; Off Ade; Yth Flsp; Y-Teens; Ger Clb; OEA; Pep Clb; Mat Maids; Ravenscroft Beauty Coll; Cosmotlgst.

THUE, JULIE; Muskegon Catholic Cntrl HS; Muskegon, MI; JA; Letter Ten; Trk; IM Sprt; PPFtbl; Western Mic Univ; Bio Sci.

THUL, BARBARA; St Ursula Acad; Cincinnati, OH; 5/101 VP Frsh Cls; VP Soph Cls; VP Sr Cls; Chrs; JA; Sch Pl; Stu Cncl; Rptr Sch Nwsp; Socr; Cit Awd; Univ; Pre Med.

THUM, MICHAEL T; Ithaca HS; Ithaca, MI; Sec Frsh Cls; Cls Rep Sr Cls; Am Leg Boys St; Hon Rl; NHS; Stu Cncl; Boys Clb Am; Bsbl; Bsktbl; Ftbl; SVSC; Elec.

THURAU, MICHAEL; Davison Sr HS; Davison, MI; 27/435 Pres Sr Cls; Boy Scts; Pres Chrs; Hon Rl; Mdrgl; NHS; Sch Mus; Stu Cncl; Drama Clb; Ger Clb; Century III Ldrshp Schl Finalist 79; Arion Awd 79; Michigan St Univ; Music.

THURMAN, ARLENE E; Anderson HS; Anderson, IN; Cl Rep Jr Cls; Chrh Wkr; Cmnty Wkr; JA; Off Ade; Stu Cncl; Yth Flsp; Sch Nwsp; Indiana Univ; Law.

THURMAN, TIM; Edison HS; Milan, OH; Aud/Vis; Boy Scts; Chrs; Chrh Wkr; Sch Pl; Sct Actv; Yth Flsp; Drama Clb; Glf; Bowling Green State Univ; Actor.

THURSTON, LORRAINE; Athens HS; Battle Crk, MI; Chrs; Chrh Wkr; Hon Rl; NHS; Off Ade; Quill & Scroll; Red Cr Ade; Yrbk; Sch Nwsp; Letter Trk;.

THURSTON, NANCY; Midland HS; Midland, MI; Band; Hon Rl; Sct Actv; Letter Bsktbl; Letter Trk; Mic State Univ; Fash Design.

THURSTON, THOMAS; St Johns HS; Saint Johns, MI; Boy Scts; Hon Rl; Sct Actv; DECA; IM Sprt; LCC; Cpa.

TIBBETS, DAN; Tippecanoe Valley HS; Mentone, IN; Band; Hon Rl; NHS; Sch Mus; Spn Clb; Swmmng; Letter Ten; College; Computer Sci.

TIBBETTS, PEGGY; Lake Central HS; St John, IN; 98/470 Chrs; Chrh Wkr; Hon Rl; Lbry Ade; Y-Teens; Pep Clb; GAA; Cit Awd; Purdue Calumet; Interior Design.

TIBBITTS, NANCY; River Valley HS; Marion, OH; 13/220 Cls Rep Sr Cls; Am Leg Aux Girls St; Cmnty Wkr; Hon Rl; Lit Mag; NHS; Red Cr Ade; Yth Flsp; Spn Clb; Ohio St Univ; Occupational Therapy.

TIBBITTS, VICKI; North Muskegon HS; Muskegon, MI; Chrs; Chrldng; PPFtbl; Muskegon Jr Coll; Acctg.

TIBBS, KAREN; Lemon Monroe HS; Monroe, OH; Cl Rep Jr Cls; Cls Rep Sr Cls; Band; Chrs; Chrh Wkr; Drl Tm; Girl Scts; Hon Rl; JA; Off Ade; College.

TIBERI, RICHARD; Saint Francis Desales HS; Columbus, OH; Cls Rep Frsh Cls; Cls Rep Soph Cls; Cl Rep Jr Cls; Hon Rl; Lbry Ade; Bsbl; Letter Bsktbl; College.

TICHENOR, JIM; Oxford Sr HS; Oxford, MI; Cl Rep Jr Cls; Band; Chrs; Drm Bgl; FCA; Hon Rl; Sch Mus; Stu Cncl; Varsity Choir Summer Camp Scholarship; Choir Awd; St Honors Choir; Taylor Univ.

TICHVON, CAROL; Portland HS; Portland, MI; 21/200 Hon Rl; Jr NHS; Lbry Ade; NHS; Sch Mus; Sch Pl; Drama Clb; Fr Clb; Mth Clb; Letter Bsktbl; Ferris Univ; Tchr.

TIDD, MARY; Greeneview HS; Jamestown, OH; 1/106 Sec Frsh Cls; Cls Rep Soph Cls; Cl Rep Jr Cls; Cls Rep Sr Cls; Am Leg Aux Girls St; Hon Rl; NHS;.

TIDD, TONI; River Valley HS; Marion, OH; VP Frsh Cls; Cls Rep Soph Cls; Cl Rep Jr Cls; Stu Cncl; Spn Clb; Crs Cntry; Trk; Chrldng; PPFtbl; Vrsty Clb 76 79; Art Clb 76 79; Jr Attendent Homecmng Crt 78; Columbus Schl Art & Dsgn; Int Dsgn.

TIDMORE, ROCHEE; Independence Jr Sr HS; Columbus, OH; 23/216 Band; Cmp Fr Grls; Drl Tm; Girl Scts; Hon Rl; Lbry Ade; NHS; Fr Clb; OEA; Pep Clb; Bowling Green St Univ; Pre Law.

TIDRICK, JESANN; Jewett Scio Sr HS; Scio, OH; Am Leg Aux Girls St; Band; Chrs; Girl Scts; Hon Rl; Sct Actv; Spn Clb; GAA; Mgrs; Perfct Attndnc 75; Math Awd 7j; Univ; Spanish.

TIEDE, DAVE; Madison HS; Adrian, MI; Cls Rep Soph Cls; Hon Rl; NHS; Quill & Scroll; Sch Pl; VP Stu Cncl; Yrbk; Rptr Sch Nwsp; Key Clb; Cit Awd; Michigan St Univ; Soc Sci.

TIEDE, JULIA R; Addison HS; Addison, MI; 1/110 Sec Frsh Cls; Sec Soph Cls; VP Jr Cls; VP Sr Cls; Band; Chrs; Hon Rl; Pres NHS; Sec Off Ade; Sch Mus; Co Vadltrn Sr Class 79; 2 Yr Schlrshp Jackson Cmnty Coll 79; Eastern Mich Univ Regents Schlrshp; Jackson Cmnty Coll; RN.

TIEDE, KATHRYN; Northfield HS; Wabash, IN; 9/117 Capt FCA; Hon Rl; NHS; Sch Mus; Rptr Yrbk; Rptr Sch Nwsp; Drama Clb; Fr Clb; Pep Clb; Swmmng; Guild Paderewski Mem Gold Medal Piano Playing Auditions; Whos Who In Foreign Languages; College.

TIEDEMAN, TYRONE; Holly HS; Holly, MI; 15/283 Aud/Vis; Debate Tm; Hon Rl; NHS; Pres 4-H; VP Sci Clb; 4-H Awd; A Mi Rep To Natl 4h Congress 78; Ctznshp Rep To Wa DC & Mn 77; St 4h Dvlpmnt Comm Mbr 79; Michigan St Univ; Pre Med.

TIEDT, KELLY L; Marysville HS; Marysville, OH; Am Leg Aux Girls St; Chrh Wkr; Hon Rl; Natl Forn Lg; NHS; Orch; Sch Mus; Yrbk; IM Sprt; Univ.

TIEK, VICKI; North Knox HS; Bicknell, IN; 1/154 Val; Capt Drl Tm; Hon Rl; VP NHS; 4-H; VP Pep Clb; Capt Pom Pon; Cit Awd; DAR Awd; Purdue Univ; Math.

TIEMAN, DAVID; Northridge HS; Middlebury, IN; 23/170 Am Leg Boys St; Band; Boy Scts; Bsbl; Bsktbl; Am Leg Awd; Univ; Comp Progr.

TIEMANN, GERALD; Portland HS; Lyons, MI; 6/170 Trs Soph Cls; Chrh Wkr; Cmnty Wkr; Hon Rl; NHS; Sch Pl; Yth Flsp; Drama Clb; Fr Clb; IM Sprt; Lawrence Inst Of Tech; Archt.

TIETZ, MARTIN; Chalker HS; Warren, OH; Trs Frsh Cls; VP Jr Cls; Am Leg Boys St; NHS; Beta Clb; Bsktbl; Crs Cntry; Univ.

TIETZ, TIMOTHY; East Kentwood HS; Kentwood, MI; Chrh Wkr; Bsbl; Bsktbl; Letter Ftbl; Coach Actv; Hope Coll; Law.

TIFFANY, JOELLA; Andrews Acad; Baroda, MI; Sec Soph Cls; VP Jr Cls; Natl Merit Schl; Andrews Univ; Nursing.

TIFFT, BILL; Spring Valley Acad; Kettering, OH; 1/27 Hst Jr Cls; Val; Chrh Wkr; Hon Rl; NHS; Stu Cncl; Rptr Yrbk; Rptr Sch Nwsp; Sch Nwsp; Bsbl; Andrews Univ; Elec Engr.

TIFT, CYNTHIA; Reading HS; Reading, MI; Am Leg Aux Girls St; Band; Chrh Wkr; Hon Rl; Rptr Sch Nwsp; FFA; PPFtbl; College.

TIGAR, DARREN; Attica Jr Sr HS; Attica, IN; 10/89 Hon Rl; NHS; Spn Clb; Bsktbl; Glf; Univ.

TIGHE, CHRISTOPHER; Cathedral Latin HS; Cleveland, OH; 8/90 Cl Rep Jr Cls; Pres Sr Cls; Cmnty Wkr; FCA; Hon Rl; NHS; Pres Stu Cncl; Bsktbl; Mount Union College; Pre Med.

TIGHE, GARY; Mississinewa HS; Marion, IN; 19/169 Am Leg Boys St; Band; Hon Rl; Jr NHS; NHS; Y-Teens; Capt Ftbl; Capt Socr; Wrstlng; IM Sprt; Taylor Univ; Medicine.

TIGHE, KATHLEEN; Stow HS; Stow, OH; Chrs; Hon Rl; Sec JA; NHS; Off Ade; Y-Teens; Wrstlng; Scr Kpr; JA Awd; Kent St Univ.

TIGNOR, MARTIN; Brebeuf Preparatory Schl; Kokomo, IN; Band; Hon Rl; Sch Mus; Ger Clb; Ten; Natl Merit Schl; Yale Univ.

TIKKANEN, KAREN; Baraga HS; Baraga, MI; Chrs; Chrh Wkr; Girl Scts; Hon Rl; Lbry Ade; Pres NHS; Chmn Chrldng; Mic Tech Univ.

TILDEN, MIRIAM; Holt Sr HS; Holt, MI; 50/319 Hon Rl; Hosp Ade; NHS; Bsktbl; Chrldng; GAA; IM Sprt; Pom Pon; PPFtbl; Lansing Cmnty Coll; Audiology.

TILFORD, LAURIE; Lanesville HS; Corydon, IN; Trs Jr Cls; FCA; Hon Rl; Stu Cncl; Yth Flsp; Yrbk; FHA; Pep Clb; Bsktbl; Trk; Univ; Rec.

TILFORD, MARY; Lumen Christi HS; Jackson, MI; Chrh Wkr; Hon Rl; JA; Sch Mus; Sch Pl; Spn Clb; Bsktbl; Chrldng; IM Sprt; Univ Of Mic; Sec.

TILICKY, JEANNE; Brooklyn HS; Brooklyn, OH; 5/173 Band; NHS; Sch Pl; Stg Crw; Eng Clb; Ger Clb; Mth Clb; Mat Maids; Ohi State Univ; Engr.

TILL, KAREN; Springfield Local HS; New Middletown, OH; 10/152 Hon Rl;.

TILLISON, JOHN; Shelbyville Sr HS; Shelbyville, IN; 3/300 VP Sr Cls; Pres JA; NHS; Boys Clb Am; Pres 4-H; Pres Lat Clb; Mth Clb; Bsbl; 4-H Awd; Opt Clb Awd; Boys Club Boy Of Yr 78; Elks Natl Schlshp 79; Verne O Cling Memrl Schlshp 79; Purdue Univ; Vet Med.

TILLMAN, DAVID; Washington Irving HS; Clarksburg, WV; 6/172 Cls Rep Frsh Cls; Am Leg Boys St; Band; NHS; Rptr Yrbk; Rptr Sch Nwsp; Drama Clb; Sci Clb; West Vir Univ; Drama.

TILLMAN, DAWN; Troy HS; Troy, OH; 32/356 Band; Chrh Wkr; Cmnty Wkr; Hon Rl; Hosp Ade; JA; Jr NHS; Lit Mag; NHS; Sch Mus; DECA Dist 18 Rep 78; Miss Ohio DECA Dist 18 3rd Pl 77; DECA Dist 18 Job Intrview 1st Pl 77 & 78; Edison St Univ; Retail.

TILLMAN, KENNETH R; Linsly Institute; Wheeling, WV; Boy Scts; FCA; ROTC; Letter Crs Cntry; Letter Ftbl; Letter Wrstlng; Linsly Inst Athltc Awd In Cross Cntry; West Virginia Univ; Engr.

TILMANN, PAMELA R; Beal City HS; Weidman, MI; Sec Soph Cls; Aud/Vis; Band; Hon Rl; 4-H; Ferris St Coll; Jrnlsm.

TILTON, NATALIE; South Newton HS; Goodland, IN; Sch Mus; Yrbk; Sch Nwsp; VP Lat Clb; Pep Clb; Sci Clb; GAA; PPFtbl; College; Art.

TILTON, TRACY; Frontier HS; New Matamoras, OH; Sec Frsh Cls; Trs Frsh Cls; VP Soph Cls; VP Jr Cls; Pres Sr Cls; NHS; Red Cr Ade; Stu Cncl; Yrbk; Sec OEA; Washington Tech Coll; Sec.

TIMBERLAKE, LORI; Attica HS; Attica, IN; Sec Jr Cls; Hon Rl; Sch Pl; Drama Clb; Pep Clb; Spn Clb; Letter Bsktbl; Letter Swmmng; Letter Ten; Letter Trk; Vocational School; Medical Assistant.

TIMBERMAN, RONALD; Clay City HS; Clay City, IN; 20/65 VP Soph Cls; Band; Yth Flsp; Sprt Ed Yrbk; 4-H; Trk; Letter Mgrs; College; Bus.

TIMBLIN, RON; Field HS; Kent, OH; Am Leg Boys St; Boy Scts; Debate Tm; Letter Ftbl; Letter Trk; Wrstlng; IM Sprt; College.

TIMBROOK, KELLY; Hampshire HS; Shanks, WV; 2/230 Cls Rep Frsh Cls; Cl Rep Jr Cls; Sec Sr Cls; Cls Rep Sr Cls; AFS; Band; Chrh Wkr; Hon Rl; NHS; Sch Pl; Eng Awd 77 78 & 79; World Cultures Awd 78; 1st In St & 4th In Natl 4 H 78; Univ.

TIMKO, SHARON; Saint Clement HS; Centerline, MI; Girl Scts; Hon Rl; NHS; Sch Nwsp; Swmmng; GAA; IM Sprt; Vrsty Vllybl Most Imp Play 78; Math Awd Top Math Stu Of Jr Class 78; Eng Awd Top Eng Stu Of Soph Class 77; Lawrence Inst Of Tech; Archt.

TIMKO, TIMOTHY L; Chaney HS; Youngstown, OH; 1/350 VP Soph Cls; Sec Jr Cls; Trs Sr Cls; Hon Rl; Jr NHS; Natl Forn Lg; Sch Mus; Sch Pl; Stg Crw; Letter Ten; Coll; Med.

TIMM, ERIC E; Troy HS; Troy, OH; Am Leg Boys St; Chrs; Stu Cncl; Rptr Sch Nwsp; Key Clb; Letter Crs Cntry; Letter Socr; Letter Trk; College; Law.

TIMM, JOHN; Grand Ledge HS; Lansing, MI; Hon Rl; Spn Clb; Trk; Lansing Comm Coll; Elec Engr.

TIMM, MELISSA A; Garber HS; Essexville, MI; Cls Rep Frsh Cls; Cls Rep Soph Cls; Band; Girl Scts; Hon Rl; Stg Crw; Stu Cncl; Yrbk; Rptr Sch Nwsp; FTA; Chosen By Grad Sr To Be Permnnt Mbr Of Stdnt Sen Very High Hon 76; Univ; Eng.

TIMM, TODD; Hesperia HS; Hesperia, MI; 1/80 Cls Rep Soph Cls; Cl Rep Jr Cls; Pres Sr Cls; Val; Band; Hon Rl; Sec Stu Cncl; Letter Ftbl; Letter Trk; Letter Wrstlng; Univ Of Minnesota; Engr.

TIMMER, JOSEPH; Lockland HS; Cincinnati, OH; Cmnty Wkr; Hon Rl; Cincinnati Tech Coll; Comp Progr.

TIMMER, MARK; Ottawa Hills HS; Grand Rapids, MI; Chrh Wkr; Hon Rl; NHS; Yth Flsp; Ftbl; Socr; Spanish Awd; College.

TIMMER, SHELLEY; South Christian HS; Grand Rapids, MI; Band; Chrs; Chrh Wkr; Drl Tm; Hon Rl; Sch Pl; Rptr Yrbk; Rptr Sch Nwsp; Ger Clb; IM Sprt; College; Medicine.

TIMMINS, SUSAN; Alma HS; Alma, MI; Girl Scts; Off Ade; Yth Flsp; Spn Clb; Swmmng; IM Sprt; Cntrl Michigan Univ; Acctg.

TIMMONS, DEAN; Chillicothe HS; Chillicothe, OH; Lbry Ade; NHS; Tmr; Ohi Univ; Engr.

TIMMONS, JOSEPH; Coshocton HS; Coshocton, OH; Hon Rl; Key Clb; IM Sprt; Univ.

TIMMONS, KAREN; Magnificat HS; Middleburg Ht, OH; Letter Bsbl; Bsktbl; IM Sprt; Univ; Acctg.

TIMMONS, LESKA; Washington Irving HS; Clarksburg, WV; Chrs; Chrh Wkr; Hon Rl; NHS; Sch Pl; Yrbk; Sch Nwsp; 4-H; Fr Clb; 4-H Awd; Marshall Univ; Journalism.

TIMMONS, MELISSA; Mt Pleasant HS; Mt Pleasant, MI; Chrh Wkr; Hon Rl; Hosp Ade; Lbry Ade; Yth Flsp; Rptr Sch Nwsp; Fr Clb; Trk; Central Michigan Univ; Phys Ther.

TIMMS, BECKY; Bridgeport HS; Bridgeport, WV; Chrs; Chrh Wkr; Hon Rl; NHS; Stu Cncl; Chrldng; College; Dance.

TIMOFF, BELINDA; Pontiac Central HS; Pontiac, MI; Band; Cmp Fr Grls; Hon Rl; Hosp Ade; NHS; Ten; Northern Michigan Univ; Nurse.

TIMS, KEVIN P; Our Lady Of Mt Carmel HS; Wyandotte, MI; 18/70 Trs Frsh Cls; VP Soph Cls; Cl Rep Jr Cls; Chrh Wkr; Hon Rl; Stg Crw; Sprt Ed Yrbk; Pep Clb; Spn Clb; Bsktbl; Volunteer Work At YMCA; Rowing Awds Silver Medal Canadian Schlboy Chmpnshpgld Mdls From Amer Competitions; College; Bsns.

TIMS, ROBERT; Warren Woods HS; Warren, MI; Ftbl; Trk; Coach Actv; College; Bus.

TINDALL, GLENN; Dayton Belmont HS; Dayton, OH; Bsbl; Bsktbl; Cit Awd; College; Architectual Drafting.

TINDALL, RODNEY; Zeeland Sr HS; Zeeland, MI; 6/190 Am Leg Boys St; Band; Boy Scts; Hon Rl; Jr NHS; Natl Forn Lg; Univ; Engr.

TINDALL, STEPHEN L; Frankfort Sr HS; Frankfort, IN; 40/250 Yth Flsp; Spn Clb; Letter Bsbl; Letter Ftbl; Letter Wrstlng; Babe Ruth Bsbl Thlt Of Yr 77; Rotary Battling Champ 77; All Confrnc Bsbl Squad 79; All Confrcn Ftbl Sqd 78; Univ; Bus.

TINELLI, JULIE; Buckhannon Upshur HS; Buckhannon, WV; Chrs; Hon Rl; Orch; Drama Clb; Eng Clb; Fr Clb; Spn Clb; London Sch Of Speech; Theatre.

TINGE, MARY J; Newbury HS; Newbury, OH; Cls Rep Frsh Cls; Pres Soph Cls; Cls Rep Soph Cls; Pres Jr Cls; VP Stu Cncl; Yrbk; Rptr Sch Nwsp; Drama Clb; Bsktbl; Chrldng; Univ; Communication.

TINGLER, DONNA; Elkins HS; Elkins, WV; Hosp Ade; Lbry Ade; 4-H; 4-H Awd; Marshall Univ.

TINGLER, DOROTHY; Linden Mc Kinley HS; Columbus, OH; Hon Rl; NHS; Off Ade;.

TINKER, DOUGLAS F; Cadillac Sr HS; Cadillac, MI; 8/300 Cls Rep Frsh Cls; Trs Jr Cls; Am Leg Boys St; Hon Rl; VP NHS; VP Stu Cncl; Letter Bsktbl; Letter Ftbl; Univ Of Michigan; Engr.

TINKEY, JOY; Southern Local HS; Salinevll, OH; Chrs; Chrh Wkr; Girl Scts; FNA; Cit Awd; God Cntry Awd; Ohio St Univ; Criminal Law.

TINSLER, JUNE; Wayland HS; Caledonia, MI; 8/193 Debate Tm; Hon Rl; Natl Forn Lg; Sch Pl; Mic Tech Univ; Civil Engr.

TINSLEY, DAVID; Dunbar HS; Charleston, WV; Band; Chrs; NHS; Sch Mus; Stg Crw; 4-H; Letter Wrstlng; 4-H Awd; Natl Merit Ltr; College; Chem.

TINSLEY, TINA; Dunbar HS; Charleston, WV; Band; Hon Rl; Stu Cncl; Drama Clb; 4-H; Letter Ten; 4-H Awd; Potomac State College; Vet Sci.

TIPP, SUSAN; Bay HS; Westlake, OH; Hon Rl; Orch; Rptr Yrbk; Yrbk; Trk; IM Sprt; PPFtbl; Tmr; College; Commercial Artist.

TIPPER, CHRISTY; Independence HS; Tams, WV; Cl Rep Jr Cls; Cls Rep Sr Cls; Chrh Wkr; Hon Rl; JA; VP NHS; Stu Cncl; VP Beta Clb; Sec Fr Clb; 3rd Runner Up To Miss Teenage Amer; Jr Attendant To Independence Snowball Queen; Best Of Show Art Awd; Vocational Schl; Commercial Art.

TIPPETT, GEORGE K; Worthington Christian HS; Westerville, OH; Pres Jr Cls; Cl Rep Jr Cls; Am Leg Boys St; Band; Hon Rl; NHS; Sch Pl; VP Stu Cncl; Pres Drama Clb; VP Mth Clb; St Sci Fair 2nd Pl 79; Music Awd 77; Hist Dept Awd 79; Univ; Archt.

TIPTON, ANTHONY; Butler HS; Vandalia, OH; 5/350 Hon Rl; Mod UN; NHS; Sch Pl; Stg Crw; Drama Clb; Sci Clb; Mgrs; Cit Awd; Martin Essex Schl 78; Univ; Lang.

TIPTON, KYLE D; Gahanna Lincoln HS; Gahanna, OH; VP Frsh Cls; Pres Sr Cls; Am Leg Boys St; FCA; Hon Rl; Hosp Ade; NHS; Quill & Scroll; Stu Cncl; Ed Sch Nwsp; Univ; Med.

TIPTON, RHONDA; Chatard HS; Indianapolis, IN; Marion Univ; Bus.

TIPTON, TRACIE; Fairfield Union HS; Bremen, OH; 13/150 Band; Chrh Wkr; Capt Drl Tm; Hon Rl; Jr NHS; Sec NHS; Yth Flsp; Rptr Sch Nwsp; Treas FBLA; OEA; Sec.

TIRAKIAN, KIRK; Charles S Mott HS; Warren, MI; Sct Actv; Swmmng; Tmr; Mic State Univ; Engr.

TIRPACK, MARYELLEN; Memorial HS; Campbell, OH; Cls Rep Frsh Cls; Cls Rep Soph Cls; Cl Rep Jr Cls; NHS; Off Ade; Drama Clb; Fr Clb; Key Clb; Ten; Chrldng; Youngstown State Univ; Nurse.

TISDEL, ELIZABETH; Sturgis HS; Sturgis, MI; Girl Scts; Hosp Ade; NHS; Sci Clb; Nazareth College; Rn.

TISHLER, KEVIN; Otsego HS; Weston, OH; VP Frsh Cls; Cls Rep Frsh Cls; Cls Rep Soph Cls; Cl Rep Jr Cls; Hon Rl; Jr NHS; NHS; VP Stu Cncl; Fr Clb; Pres Sci Clb; Univ Of Toledo; Civil Engr.

TISLOW, LISA; Sullivan HS; Carlisle, IN; 19/152 VP Frsh Cls; Am Leg Aux Girls St; Hon Rl; Off Ade; Yrbk; Sch Nwsp; VP Beta Clb; Pep Clb; Letter Chrldng; GAA; Gregg Shorthand Speed Test Awd 60 Wpm Jr Yr; Indiana St Univ; Elem Educ.

TISONE, GREG; Liberty HS; Youngstown, OH; Hon Rl; Letter Bsbl; Bsktbl; Ftbl; 1st Pl Weightlifting Tri Cnty Meet; 1st Tm All League Bsbl; Prom Ct; St Weightlifting Record; Youngstown St Univ; Engr.

TISZAI, COLLEEN; Roosevelt HS; Wyandotte, MI; Girl Scts; Hon Rl; Yth Flsp;.

TITGEMEYER, EVAN; Napoleon HS; Napoleon, OH; Cls Rep Frsh Cls; Cls Rep Soph Cls; Cls Rep Sr Cls; NHS; Sch Mus; Stu Cncl; Sprt Ed Yrbk; Yrbk; 4-H; Natl Merit Ltr; Univ.

TITGEMEYER, KURT; Clay Sr HS; Curtice, OH; 46/364 Hon Rl; NHS; Yrbk; Sec 4-H; Pres FFA; Letter Bsbl; Letter Ftbl; IM Sprt; C of C Awd; 4-H Awd; 4 H Camp Counselor 2 Yrs 78; Lucas Co Jr Fair Brd 3 Yrs 77 78 & 79; Univ; Archt.

TITI, S; Catholic Central HS; Mingo Jct, OH; 23/204 Cls Rep Frsh Cls; Cls Rep Soph Cls; Chrs; Chrh Wkr; Hon Rl; NHS; Yrbk; FHA; Pep Clb; College.

TITRAN, CAROL; Austintown Fitch HS; Austintown, OH; 143/700 Trs Frsh Cls; Drl Tm; Off Ade; Sch Pl; Y-Teens; DECA; Capt Chrldng; Letter Pom Pon; PPFtbl; Scr Kpr; Univ Of Los Angeles; Fash Merch.

TITSCH, JIM; Bellbrook HS; Bellbrook, OH; 19/175 Cls Rep Sr Cls; Aud/Vis; Hon Rl; NHS; Bsktbl; Glf; Trk; IM Sprt; Univ Of Florida; Archt.

TITTLE, KATHY; North Ridgeville HS; N Ridgeville, OH; Sec Frsh Cls; Pres Soph Cls; Pres Jr Cls; Hon Rl; Quill & Scroll; Stu Cncl; Ed Yrbk; Rptr Yrbk; Ger Clb; LCC Comnty Coll; Interior Decor.

TITUS, HOWARD; Lexington HS; Lexington, OH; Cls Rep Soph Cls; Cl Rep Jr Cls; Band; Off Ade; Fr Clb; FTA; Ger Clb; Letter Ftbl; Letter Trk; Univ; History.

TITUS, LORI; Shelby HS; Shelby, MI; 14/122 Girl Scts; Hon Rl; NHS; Sch Pl; Drama Clb; Fr Clb; Pep Clb; Ten; Trk; Mgrs; Central Michigan Univ; Bio.

TITUS, MARK; Berea HS; Brook Pk, OH; Hon Rl; NHS; Letter Bsbl; Coach Actv; IM Sprt; Spec Achvmnt Awrd GPA 3.5 Or Better 78; Univ; Engr.

TOBEREN, PATRICIA; Dublin HS; Dublin, OH; 31/153 Chrs; Sch Mus; Yrbk; Fr Clb; Pep Clb; Sci Clb; Scr Kpr; Tmr; College; Med Tech.

TOBIAS, GLORIA; North Branch HS; North Branch, MI; 6/163 Cls Rep Soph Cls; Cl Rep Jr Cls; Cls Rep Sr Cls; Band; Hon Rl; NHS; Orch; Stu Cncl; Drama Clb; Pep Clb; Michigan St Univ; Social Work.

TOBIAS, KAREN; Buena Vista HS; Sagiuaw, MI; 2/157 Girl Scts; Hon Rl; Jr NHS; NHS; Off Ade; Ger Clb; Delta Coll; Data Proc.

TOBIAS, MARIE; Brookville HS; W Alexandria, OH; 7/150 Band; Chrs; Chrh Wkr; Hon Rl; NHS; Y-Teens; Pep Clb; Spn Clb; Sinclair Comm Coll; Drafting.

TOBIAS, MARYBETH; Ursuline HS; Youngstown, OH; 24/342 Chrs; Cmnty Wkr; Debate Tm; Hon Rl; Natl Forn Lg; Sch Nwsp; Eng Clb; Keyettes; Bsbl; Gym; Kent St Univ; Speech Path.

TOBIAS, STEVEN; Olivet HS; Charlotte, MI; Rptr Sch Nwsp; Letter Crs Cntry; Letter Ten; 4-H Awd; Rotary Awd; Univ; Criminal Justice.

TOBIAS, TODD; Eaton HS; Eaton, OH; 31/171 VP Frsh Cls; VP Soph Cls; Pres Jr Cls; Pres Sr Cls; Band; Boy Scts; Chrs; Cmnty Wkr; Sch Pl; Stu Cncl; Univ Of Colorado; Archt Engr.

TOBIN, JEFFREY; St Mary Cathedral HS; Gaylord, MI; Trs Frsh Cls; Cls Rep Sr Cls; Band; Hon Rl; NHS; Sch Mus; Sch Pl; Stg Crw; Stu Cncl; Rptr Yrbk; Michigan Tech Univ; Elec Engr.

TOBLER, KEITH; Buchanan HS; Buchanan, MI; Cls Rep Frsh Cls; Cls Rep Soph Cls; Cl Rep Jr Cls; Cls Rep Sr Cls; Off Ade; VP Stu Cncl; Bsbl; Univ.

TOBOLSKI, DIANE; Edwin Denby HS; Detroit, MI; 15/341 Cls Rep Sr Cls; Chrs; Chrh Wkr; Girl Scts; Hon Rl; Pres NHS; ROTC; Sct Actv; Stu Cncl; Pep Clb; Siena Hts Coll; Guidance Cnslng.

TOCCO, ANTHONY; Servite HS; Detroit, MI; Pres Frsh Cls; Pres Soph Cls; Pres Jr Cls; Pres Sr Cls; Hon Rl; Jr NHS; NHS; Off Ade; Stu Cncl; Rptr Sch Nwsp; Detrot Coll Of Bus; Acctg.

TOCCO, JEROME; Bishop Gallagher HS; Grss Pt Wds, MI; Hon Rl; Sci Clb; Hockey; Coach Actv; IM Sprt; Mgrs; Spec Hnr Awd Hnr Roll For 3 Yrs 79; Aug Spch Fest & Genesian Interprtn Fest 78; Univ Of Dayton; Bus Admin.

TOCHMAN, LORI; Franklin HS; Livonia, MI; Trs Frsh Cls; Cls Rep Soph Cls; Trs Jr Cls; Pres Sr Cls; Chrs; Hon Rl; Sch Mus; Stu Cncl; Chrldng; Cit Awd; Mich State Univ; Vet Med.

TODARO, ZINA; Adlai Stevenson Cmnty HS; Sterling Hts, MI; Cls Rep Frsh Cls; Hon Rl; NHS; Fr Clb; OEA; Natl Merit Ltr; Western Michigan Univ Acad Schlrshp; Womens Assn For Ma Comb Cnty Cmnty Coll Schlrshp; NROTC Schlrshp Prog; Macomb Cnty Cmnty Coll; Acctg.

TODD, CARLA; North Putnam Jr Sr HS; Ladoga, IN; 10/150 Chrs; Chrh Wkr; Hon Rl; NHS; Sch Mus; Spn Clb; Spanish Awd 79; Missionary.

TODD, CHARLES K; Hagerstown Jr Sr HS; Hagerstown, IN; 8/142 Cls Rep Frsh Cls; Cls Rep Soph Cls; Hon Rl; NHS; Stu Cncl; Yrbk; Fr Clb; Letter Glf; Letter Ten; Scholastic Awd 1976 & 1977; All Conf Tennis Awd 1978; Univ; Math.

TODD, DIANE; Greenfield Central HS; Greenfield, IN; 7/350 Band; Chrs; Treas FCA; Hon Rl; Sec NHS; Pres Yth Flsp; Mth Clb; Pres Spn Clb; Trk; Mgrs; Whos Who In In & Ky HS Foreign Lang 78; Univ; Pre Dent.

TODD, DIANE; Northridge HS; Newark, OH; 1/129 Hon Rl; NHS; Stg Crw; Sch Nwsp; Spn Clb; Otterbein College; Comp Sci.

TODD, DOUG; Coshocton HS; Coshocton, OH; 13/252 Am Leg Boys St; Ed Sch Nwsp; Rptr Sch Nwsp; Spn Clb; Capt Ftbl; Letter Swmmng; Ohio State Univ; Engr.

TODD, JOHN; Archbold HS; Archbold, OH; Band; Chrs; Hon Rl; Sch Mus; Yth Flsp; Glf; Trk; IM Sprt; Voice Dem Awd; Univ; Law.

TODD, JOHN L; Stonewall Jackson HS; Charleston, WV; Am Leg Boys St; Boy Scts; Hon Rl; Sprt Ed Yrbk; Boys Clb Am; Key Clb; Sci Clb; Letter Crs Cntry; JA Awd; Jr Achvmnt Pres Of Ach Assoc 79; Mr Exec 79; Treas Of Yr 78; Mu Alpha Theta Mbr 77 80; Pres Sci Clb; Univ; Chem Engr.

TODD, MARK; John Glenn HS; New Concord, OH; 14/205 Chrh Wkr; Drl Tm; Hon Rl; Spn Clb; Trk; Ambassador Coll; Agri Bus.

TODD, MARTHA; Oakwood HS; Dayton, OH; Chrs; Chrh Wkr; Cmnty Wkr; FCA; Girl Scts; Hon Rl; Sch Mus; Sch Pl; Stg Crw; Stu Cncl; Univ; History.

TODD, MOLLY; Rochester Adams HS; Rochester, MI; Band; Hon Rl; NHS; Orch; Sch Mus; Letter Bsktbl; Mgrs; Alma Coll; Phys Ther.

TODD, RICHARD; Horace Mann HS; Gary, IN; Band; Chrh Wkr; Hon Rl; Jr NHS; Boys Clb Am; Ftbl; Sci.

TODD, SUSAN; Turpin HS; Cincinnati, OH; 1/347 Hosp Ade; Ten; Univ.

TODD, WILLIAM; Lapel HS; Anderson, IN; 17/100 Hon Rl; Yrbk; FSA; Sci Clb; Spn Clb; Bsbl; Bsktbl; Ftbl; Letter Glf; GMI; Engr.

TODDY, CONNIE; Ottawa Hills HS; Grand Rapids, MI; Band; Chrh Wkr; Girl Scts; Hon Rl; NHS; Yth Flsp; Ftbl; Central Michigan Univ; Cmnctns.

TODESSA, LIANN; Campbell Memorial HS; Campbell, OH; Cmp Fr Grls; Hon Rl; JA; Pol Wkr; Mth Clb; Sci Clb; Spn Clb; Chrldng; JA Awd; College; Law.

TODHUNTER, TINA; Marion L Steele HS; Amherst, OH; 70/365 Pres Band; Jr NHS; NHS; Sec Fr Clb; IM Sprt; Mgrs; Villa Maria College; Nurse.

TOERNER, JOSEPH; Oakwood HS; Dayton, OH; Hon Rl; IM Sprt; College; Engr.

TOERNER, KATHLEEN; Mother Of Mercy HS; Cincinati, OH; 56/220 Chrs; Chrh Wkr; Girl Scts; Hon Rl; Off Ade; Sct Actv; Yrbk; Socr; Coach Actv; Univ Of Cinc; Nursing.

TOERNER, TERRI; Stephen T Badin HS; Hamilton, OH; 8/222 Cl Rep Jr Cls; Cls Rep Sr Cls; Chrh Wkr; NHS; Sch Mus; Stu Cncl; Fr Clb; Ten; IM Sprt; Univ; Phys Ther.

TOIVONEN, SHERRY; L L Wright HS; Ironwood, MI; Trs Soph Cls; Hon Rl; NHS; Rptr Yrbk; Pep Clb; Letter Bsktbl; Letter Trk; Chrldng; Ferris St Coll; Med Tech.

TOKAR, EVA; Fairport Harding HS; Fairport Hrbr, OH; Band; Hon Rl; Sch Mus; Sch Pl; Stg Crw; Pep Clb; Letter Bsktbl; Capt Chrldng; Pres GAA; Bus Schl; Comp Tech.

TOKARCIK, PAMELA; Roosevelt Wilson HS; Stonewood, WV; Sec Jr Cls; Trs Jr Cls; Hon Rl; Y-Teens; Leo Clb; Pep Clb; Twrlr; Univ; Nursing.

TOKARSKI, ALLAN; Andrean HS; Gary, IN; 87/259 Band; Hon Rl; Sch Mus; Letter Ftbl; Letter Trk; IM Sprt; Univ; Elec Engr.

TOKARZ, GEORGE; St Alphonsus HS; Dearborn, MI; 108/270 Boy Scts; Chrh Wkr; Cmnty Wkr; Hon Rl; JA; Lbry Ade; Sch Pl; Civ Clb; JA Awd; Wayne St Univ; Bus Admin.

TOKASH, DEIDRE; Jackson Memorial HS; Canton, OH; Band; FCA; Sec Natl Forn Lg; Y-Teens; Treas Fr Clb; Pep Clb; Capt Swmmng; Miami; Psych.

TOLAN, LAURIE; Caledonia HS; Caledonia, MI; Cls Rep Sr Cls; Off Ade; Sch Mus; Sch Pl; Drama Clb; Glf; Trk; Chrldng; Coach Actv; Capt PPFtbl; Grand Rapids Jr Coll; Fashion Mdse.

TOLAN, PAT; Taylor HS; Kokomo, IN; 30/180 Aud/Vis; Hon Rl; Fr Clb; College.

TOLAN, ROBERT W; Taylor HS; Kokomo, IN; 2/210 Boy Scts; Chrs; Chrh Wkr; Hon Rl; Mod UN; NHS; Sch Pl; Sct Actv; Stu Cncl; Drama Clb; Northwestern Univ; Med.

TOLAN, TAMMI; Cascade HS; Brazil, IN; 13/148 Cls Rep Sr Cls; Band; Drl Tm; Drm Mjrt; Hon Rl; NHS; Off Ade; Stu Cncl; Spn Clb; Mat Maids;.

TOLAND, KIMBERLY; Bloom Local HS; South Webster, OH; Band; Chrs; Hon Rl; Lbry Ade; Off Ade; Pol Wkr; Red Cr Ade; Sch Nwsp; Pres OEA; Pep Clb; Ambassador Awd Foc Ed Assn;.

TOLBERT, JANICE; Pershing HS; Detroit, MI; Chrs; Chrh Wkr; Hon Rl; NHS; Pol Wkr; Sch Mus; Ed Yrbk; Yrbk; FHA; Bsktbl; Rep Pershing In Operation Bently 1978; Wayne St Univ; Psych.

TOLBERT, JOSEPH L; West Side HS; Gary, IN; 10/650 Hon Rl; NHS; Lat Clb; Ftbl; Trk; Beloit Coll; Econ.

TOLER, KIMBERLY; Zanesville HS; Zanesville, OH; 99/399 Chrh Wkr; Cmnty Wkr; Drl Tm; Hon Rl; Lbry Ade; Off Ade; Yrbk; Fresman Foundation Schlrshp Ohio St Univ 79; Ohio St Univ; Jrnlsm.

TOLER, RONNIE J; Oceana HS; Oceana, WV; Am Leg Boys St; Hon Rl; NHS; Letter Ftbl; Letter Trk; Cit Awd; Collebe.

TOLER, TERESA; Oceana HS; Lynco, WV; 3/119 Sal; Hon Rl; NHS; VP Yth Flsp; Rptr Yrbk; Treas Beta Clb; Fr Clb; Voice Dem Awd; Marshall Univ; Acctg.

TOLES, C; Elmhurst HS; Ft Wayne, IN; Sch Pl; Stg Crw; Treas DECA; Drama Clb; PPFtbl; College; Pre Med.

TOLES, SUSAN; Washington HS; Massillon, OH; 75/475 AFS; Band; Cmnty Wkr; Drm Bgl; Hon Rl; Sec JA; Lbry Ade; NHS; Off Ade; Spn Clb; Univ Of Cincinnati; Spanish.

TOLGER, KEITH; Grand Rapids North View HS; Grand Rapids, MI; 4/293 Band; Hon Rl; Jr NHS; NHS; Sch Mus; Sch Pl; Letter Swmmng; Kiwan Awd; Grand Rapids Jr Coll; Busns Admin.

TOLIVER, GALE; Niles Sr HS; Niles, MI; Hon Rl; Orch; Univ; Foreign Lang.

TOLLEFSON, JAN; Escanaba Area HS; Escanaba, MI; 61/432 Band; Boy Scts; Chrh Wkr; Hon Rl; NHS; Sct Actv; God Cntry Awd; Michigan Tech Univ; Physics.

TOLLES, SUE; Otsego HS; Grand Rapids, OH; 8/127 Band; Jr NHS; NHS; Sch Pl; Rptr Sch Nwsp; Pres Fr Clb; Ohio St Univ; Law.

TOLLEY, BRADLEY J; Hurricane HS; Hurrican, WV; Band; Chrh Wkr; Cmnty Wkr; Hon Rl; JA; JA Awd; Univ; Acctg.

TOLLEY, BRIAN; Herbert Hoover HS; Pinch, WV; Cls Rep Frsh Cls; Cls Rep Soph Cls; Cl Rep Jr Cls; Hon Rl; Sch Pl; Sprt Ed Sch Nwsp; Fr Clb; Bsbl; IM Sprt; Marshall Univ; Jrnlsm.

TOLLIVER, ALICE; Crooksville HS; Crooksville, OH; Am Leg Aux Girls St; Band; Hon Rl; Off Ade; Sch Pl; Yth Flsp; Rptr Sch Nwsp; 4-H; GAA; Scr Kpr; Muskingum Tech Univ; Sec.

TOLUSSO, LUISA; Normandy HS; Parma, OH; Hon Rl; Jr NHS; Orch; Fr Clb; Bsbl; Bsktbl; Trk; IM Sprt; Univ; CPA.

TOM, JUDY; Southfield Lathrup HS; Southfield, MI; Girl Scts; Hon Rl; Lbry Ade; Orch; Cit Awd; Natl Merit Ltr; Phi Beta Kappa 79; Wayne St Univ Merit Schlrshp 79; Schlstc Art Awd 76 78 & 79; Wayne St Univ; Library Sci.

TOM, KARMA; Northrop HS; Ft Wayne, IN; Sec Frsh Cls; Chrh Wkr; FCA; Yth Flsp; DECA; Letter Gym; PPFtbl; Cit Awd; Pres Awd;.

TOMA, GEORGE; Chippewa Valley HS; Mt Clemens, MI; 15/400 Cls Rep Sr Cls; Chrs; Hon Rl; Mdrgl; NHS; Sch Mus; Sprt Ed Yrbk; Rptr Sch Nwsp; Bsbl; 160 P Above In Phys Educ 1977; Stdnt Life Schlshp To Oakland Univ 1979; Appointmnt To US Merchnt Marn 197.; U S Merchant Marine Acad; Law.

TOMAN, MICHAEL; Thomas W Harvey HS; Painesville, OH; 10/180 Sal; Chrh Wkr; NHS; Y-Teens; Ftbl; Swmmng; Bausch & Lomb Awd; Univ Of Akron; Engr.

TOMAN, TERESA; Greenville Sr HS; Greenvile, OH; 51/380 Band; Hon Rl; Orch; Sch Mus; Yth Flsp; Drama Clb; 4-H; Spn Clb; 4-H Awd; Univ; Home Ec.

TOMAN, THERESA; Reed City HS; Hersey, MI; Cl Rep Jr Cls; Hon Rl; NHS; Ed Sch Nwsp; Pres 4-H Awd; Pres Awd; Univ.

TOMASHOT, VICKI; Carroll HS; Dayton, OH; Am Leg Aux Girls St; Drl Tm; Girl Scts; FDA; Trk; Ohi State Univ; Dent.

TOMASIC, BETH; Columbia HS; Columbia Sta, OH; Cls Rep Frsh Cls; Cls Rep Soph Cls; Cl Rep Jr Cls; Hon Rl; Stu Cncl; Pep Clb; Chrldng; College.

TOMASIK, ROBERT; Notre Dame HS; Bridgeport, WV; Chrh Wkr; Cmnty Wkr; FCA; Letter Bsbl; Bsktbl; Ftbl; WVAU; Med.

TOMASZEWSKI, CAROL A; Hanover Central Jr Sr HS; Cedar Lake, IN; 6/137 Girl Scts; Hon Rl; Jr NHS; Sec NHS; Sct Actv; Fr Clb; Pep Clb; Purdue Univ; Busns.

TOMAYKO, TERESA; Clawson HS; Clason, MI; Hon Rl; Rptr Sch Nwsp; Bsbl; Oakland; Comp Sci.

TOMBLIN, ELIZABETH; Bluefield HS; Bluefield, WV; 24/319 Cls Rep Frsh Cls; Cls Rep Soph Cls; Cl Rep Jr Cls; Cls Rep Sr Cls; Chrh Wkr; Cmnty Wkr; Hon Rl; NHS; Stu Cncl; Y-Teens; Bluefield St Coll; Comp Sci.

TOMBLIN, LUCY L; Guyan Valley HS; Ranger, WV; 7/98 Cls Rep Soph Cls; Cl Rep Jr Cls; Sec Sr Cls; Chrh Wkr; Hon Rl; NHS; Rptr Sch Nwsp; FBLA; FHA; Pep Clb;.

TOMBONI, STEVEN N; Yorktown HS; Muncie, IN; 37/180 Chrh Wkr; Hon Rl; Fr Clb; Sci Clb; Letter Ftbl; Letter Wrstlng; Mgrs; Univ Of Michigan; Earth Sci.

TOMCHIN, KENNETH; Bluefield HS; Bluefield, WV; 16/286 Band; Boy Scts; Chrs; Hon Rl; Jr NHS; Key Clb; Pep Clb; Spn Clb; Letter Bsktbl; Capt Glf; Duke Univ; Law.

TOMCZYK, MARK; Northville HS; Northville, MI; Chrh Wkr; Hon Rl; Off Ade; Ger Clb; Wrstlng; IM Sprt; Univ Of Mich; Predentristry.

TOMCZYK, MICHAEL; Swartz Creek HS; Lennon, MI; 14/400 Hon Rl; Jr NHS; NHS; Wrstlng; Michigan Tech Univ; Elec Engr.

TOME, SUSAN; Eastlake North HS; Willowick, OH; Hon Rl; Jr NHS; NHS; Key Clb; Spn Clb; College; Veterinary Medicine.

TOMEI, LISA A; Aquinas HS; Gibraltar, MI; 2/231 Cls Rep Frsh Cls; Cl Rep Jr Cls; Chrs; Hon Rl; NHS; Sch Mus; Sch Pl; Stu Cncl; Rptr Sch Nwsp; Drama Clb; Outstanding Stu Awd; Schl Spelling Bee Champ; Harvard Univ; Medicine.

TOMEY, DANITA; Whiteland HS; Whiteland, IN; 8/223 Cmp Fr Grls; Sec Chrh Wkr; FCA; Pep Clb; Voc Schl; Offc Mgmt.

TOMEY, TAMARA; North Daviess HS; Elnora, IN; Band; Chrs; Chrh Wkr; Girl Scts; Hon Rl; Sch Mus; Yth Flsp; Beta Clb; Univ; Acctg.

TOMIAK, MYROSIA; Immaculate Conception HS; Hamtramck, MI; 1/34 Trs Frsh Cls; Trs Soph Cls; Chrs; Hon Rl; NHS; Sch Pl; Fr Clb; DAR Awd; Opt Clb Awd; Wayne St Univ; Pre Med.

TOMKIES, MICHAEL C; Huntington HS; Huntington, WV; Cls Rep Frsh Cls; Cl Rep Jr Cls; Boy Scts; Chrs; Chrh Wkr; Cmnty Wkr; Hon Rl; Jr NHS; NHS; Pol Wkr; Univ; Bus.

TOMLIN, AMY; Chesapeake HS; Chesapeake, OH; 25/140 Cls Rep Frsh Cls; Cl Rep Jr Cls; Hon Rl; Stu Cncl; Treas Pep Clb; Letter Trk; Chrldng; Marshall Univ; Social Work.

TOMLIN, TANYA; Wayne HS; Dayton, OH; 25/700 Cls Rep Sr Cls; Sec Band; Chrs; Drm Bgl; Girl Scts; Hon Rl; Jr NHS; NHS; Orch; Sch Mus; Optimist O ratorical Contest 1st Pl Local & 3rd Pl Dist 77; Superior Rating I In OMEA Solo & Ensemble 76 78; Univ Of S California; Music Educ.

TOMLINSON, DEBORAH; Sault Area HS; Sault Ste Mari, MI; 25/302 Pres Band; Hon Rl; Hosp Ade; NHS; Quill & Scroll; Ed Sch Nwsp; Rptr Sch Nwsp; Mic State Univ; Clothing & Textiles.

TOMLISON, BETTY; Eastern HS; Waverly, OH; Treas Band; Chrs; Chrh Wkr; Hon Rl; VP MMM; Sec Yth Flsp; Sec 4-H; Pep Clb; 4-H Awd; Univ; Music.

TOMMAS, WENDY; Sandusky St Marys HS; Sandusky, OH; Cls Rep Frsh Cls; Cls Rep Soph Cls; Chrs; Girl Scts; 4-H; Sci Clb; Spn Clb; VP GAA; Capt IM Sprt; Scr Kpr; Grd Schl Tutor 78; Volunteer Wkr With The Mentally Difficient 78; Univ; Spec Educ.

TOMPKINS, LORI; Mineral Ridge HS; Mineral Ridge, OH; 14/45 Cmnty Wkr; Sch Mus; Sch Pl; Stg Crw; Drama Clb; Trk; Kent State; Theatre.

TONCIC, TERRY; Linsly Inst; Wheeling, WV; Trs Frsh Cls; FCA; Hon Rl; ROTC; Sch Mus; Ger Clb; Key Clb; Letter Bsbl; Letter Bsktbl; Letter Ftbl; College.

TONDIGLIA, DEAN; Ravenna HS; Ravenna, OH; Trs Frsh Cls; Trs Soph Cls; Cls Rep Soph Cls; Pres Jr Cls; Cl Rep Jr Cls; Cls Rep Sr Cls; Boy Scts; VP Chrs; Chrh Wkr; Hon Rl; Kent St Univ; Criminal Justice.

TONDU, NOREEN A; Frankfort HS; Frankfort, MI; Band; Chrs; Hon Rl; NHS; Sch Pl; Stu Cncl; Yrbk; Chrldng; Rotary Awd;.

TONER, ANITA; Mohawk HS; Tiffin, OH; 39/116 Chrs; Cmnty Wkr; Girl Scts; Lit Mag; Off Ade; Sch Mus; Sch Pl; Stg Crw; Y-Teens; Sprt Ed Sch Nwsp; Letter In Vllybll 78; Art Awrds From Fairs 77; Vrsty M 78; Navy Medical Program; Med.

TONER, KEVIN M; Columbus North HS; Edinburg, IN; 2/525 Cls Rep Frsh Cls; Cls Rep Soph Cls; Cl Rep Jr Cls; Cls Rep Sr Cls; Sal; Boy Scts; Hon Rl; Mod UN; Natl Forn Lg; Quill & Scroll; Outstanding Underclassman On Newspaper Stf 1977; Outstndng Achv Ball State Jrnlsm Workshop 1978; Indiana Univ; Jrnlsm.

TONEY, MARK; Hartford HS; Decatur, MI; Cls Rep Frsh Cls; Cls Rep Soph Cls; Pres Band; Boy Scts; Hon Rl; Mod UN; NHS; Stu Cncl; Brigham Young Univ; Acctg.

TONG VILLANUEVA, ANTHONY; Marysville HS; Marysville, OH; Band; Chrs; Chrh Wkr; Lbry Ade; Natl Forn Lg; Sch Mus; Sch Pl; Sch Nwsp; Lat Clb; IM Sprt; College; Pre Med.

TONKEL, CINDY; Camden Frontier HS; Osseo, MI; Band; Chrs; Hon Rl; Sch Pl; Stg Crw; Stu Cncl; Pres Fr Clb; Pep Clb; Letter Bsbl; Letter Trk; Manchester Coll; Music.

TONKOVICH, DARLA; Wheeling Ctrl Cath HS; Wheeling, WV; Hon Rl; Sch Pl; Stg Crw; Drama Clb; Bus Schl; Sec.

TONKOVICH, MIKE; Warren Western Reserve HS; Warren, OH; Hon Rl; Spn Clb; Letter Crs Cntry; Letter Trk; College.

TONKS, RAYMOND T; Chippewa Valley HS; Mt Clemens, MI; 10/394 Pres Soph Cls; Pres Jr Cls; Pres Sr Cls; Boy Scts; Chrs; Hon Rl; Mdrgl; NHS; Sch Mus; Univ Of Michigan; Dentistry.

TONNE, DANIEL; Colerain HS; Cincinnati, OH; 11/697 Band; Boy Scts; Hon Rl; Jr NHS; Pres 4-H; Ger Clb; 4-H Awd; Ohio St Univ; Vet.

TONNEBERGER, KAREN; Forest Hills Ctrl HS; Grand Rapids, MI; 3/256 Band; Hon Rl; JA; Mod UN; Orch; Sch Mus; Sch Pl; Stu Cncl; Letter Bsbl; Letter Ten; Princeton Univ; Intl Relations.

TONNEBERGER, KAREN L; Forest Hills Central HS; Grand Rapids, MI; 3/250 Band; Hon Rl; JA; Mod UN; Sch Pl; Yth Flsp; Fr Clb; Bsbl; Ten; Natl Merit SF; Univ; Intl Relations.

TONNEMAN, JOAN; Saint Francis Desales HS; Westerville, OH; Drl Tm; Drama Clb; Pep Clb; College; Art.

TONNESEN, DAVID; Huntington HS; Huntington, WV; Hon Rl; NHS; Yth Flsp; Fr Clb; Key Clb; Crs Cntry; Bausch & Lomb Awd; 13th Annual HS Math Comp 79; Math Field Day Cnty Rep 79; Mu Alpha Theta Honry Math Club 78; Washington Univ; Elec Engr.

TONOWSKI, JAYNE; Marian Heights Acad; Croswell, MI; Chrs; Chrh Wkr; Girl Scts; Hon Rl; Sch Mus; Sch Pl; Sdlty; Drama Clb; 4-H; Bsktbl; Mich Stae Univ; Med.

TONTI, NANCY; Cass City HS; Cass City, MI; 16/80 Hon Rl; NHS; Letter Bsbl; Letter Bsktbl; Letter Gym; PPFtbl; Rotary Awd; Mic Tech; Engr.

TOOGOOD, CYNTHIA; Big Rapids HS; Big Rapids, MI; Hon Rl; Quill & Scroll; Ed Sch Nwsp; Rptr Sch Nwsp; Lillian Palmer Memrl Schlshp 79; Keith Morford Memrl Schlshp 79; Staff Mbr Of Stdnt Jrnlsm 79; Cntrl Michigan Univ; Brdcstng.

TOOLE, CHRISTY; Philo HS; Zanesville, OH; Chrs; Hon Rl; Hosp Ade; NHS; Sch Mus; Sch Pl; 4-H; Spn Clb; GAA; 4-H Awd; Univ; Phys Ther.

TOOLEY, KATHY; Wayne HS; E Lynn, WV; 14/154 Cls Rep Sr Cls; Hon Rl; Jr NHS; NHS; Rptr Sch Nwsp; Sec Beta Clb; Cit Awd; Marshall Univ; Pre Law.

TOOLEY, THOMAS; Jackson County West HS; Spring Arbor, MI; Trs Frsh Cls; VP Soph Cls; VP Jr Cls; NHS; Bsbl; Ftbl; IM Sprt; Tmr; Jackson Comm College; Architecture.

TOOLIS, KEVIN; St Edward HS; Fairview Pk, OH; Hon Rl; Letter Wrstlng; Miami Univ; Bus.

TOOMAN, JOYCE; Arcadia Local HS; Arcadia, OH; 2/64 Cls Rep Sr Cls; Hon Rl; NHS; Stu Cncl; VP Yth Flsp; Yrbk; FHA; Pres OEA; Cit Awd; Tiffin Univ; Exec Sec.

TOOMAN, STEPHEN; West Iron County HS; Sta mbaugh, MI; Band; Boy Scts; Chrs; Chrh Wkr; Hon Rl; Trk;.

TOOMEY, JULIE; Whitehall Yearling HS; Whitehall, OH; Boy Scts; Girl Scts; Hon Rl; NHS; Red Cr Ade; Sct Actv; OEA; Spn Clb; Univ; Comp Sci.

TOONE, DEBRA; Eastmoor HS; Columbus, OH; 29/290 Cls Rep Sr Cls; Drl Tm; Hon Rl; GAA; Winston Salem St Univ; Dentistry.

TOOPS, JACQUELYN; Wehrle HS; Columbus, OH; Trs Frsh Cls; Trs Soph Cls; VP Jr Cls; Cl Rep Jr Cls; Chrs; Chrh Wkr; Cmnty Wkr; Hon Rl; JA; Off Ade; Capital Univ; Comp Sci.

TOOT, MIKE; Carrollton HS; Carrollton, OH; 42/255 Chrs; Girl Scts; Hon Rl; Sch Mus; 4-H; Fr Clb; FHA; Swmmng; Trk; Chrldng; Ohio St Univ; Fshn Dsgn.

TOOT, TERRIE; Leetonia HS; Salem, OH; 15/85 Am Leg Aux Girls St; Band; Chrh Wkr; JA; 4-H; Pep Clb; Spn Clb; Am Leg Awd; JA Awd; Youngstown Bus Coll; Sec.

TOOTHMAN, DENISE; Mannington HS; Farmington, WV; 29/118 Pres Soph Cls; Hon Rl; Stu Cncl; 4-H; FHA; Fairmont St Coll; Med.

TOOTHMAN, SHARI; Fairview HS; Fairview, WV; Cls Rep Soph Cls; Chrs; Chrh Wkr; Cmnty Wkr; Hon Rl; NHS; Stu Cncl; Yth Flsp; Drama Clb; Fr Clb; Fairmont St Univ; Nursing.

TOPASH, JENNIFER; Buchanan HS; Buchanan, MI; 30/168 Girl Scts; Hon Rl; JA; Off Ade; Sct Actv; GAA; JA Awd; Mich State Univ; Wildlife Bio.

TOPE, STEPHEN; Conotton Vly HS; Leesville, OH; 4/59 Pres Frsh Cls; Pres Soph Cls; Hon Rl; Stu Cncl; Beta Clb; Letter Bsbl; Letter Bsktbl; Ftbl; Letter Glf; Coach Actv; Took Ohio Test Of Schlstc Ach; Rep Schl In Talented Yth Seminar; Won Superintendents Awd; Ohio N Univ; Acctg.

TOPE, TAMMY; Vantage Voc HS; Latty, OH; 2/130 Trs Jr Cls; Sal; Am Leg Aux Girls St; Chrs; Chrh Wkr; Hon Rl; VP NHS; Sch Pl; Stg Crw; Yth Flsp; Patricia Stevens Coll; Fshn Mdse.

TOPHAM, SANFORD; Kenston HS; Chagrin Fl, OH; Boy Scts; Hosp Ade; Lbry Ade; Rdo Clb; Rus Clb; Coll; Busns.

TOPPIN, REGINA; Reed City HS; Reed City, MI; 37/175 Chrs; Chrh Wkr; Hon Rl; Lbry Ade; Red Cr Ade; Beta Clb; FTA; Ger Clb; Ferris St Coll; Bus Admin.

TOPPING, KENNITA G; Guyan Valley HS; West Hamlin, WV; Band; Drm Mjrt; Hon Rl; Off Ade; PAVAS; Sch Mus; Stu Cncl; Rptr Yrbk; Bsktbl; Trk; Marshall Univ; Acctg.

TOPPING, MICHELLE; Licking Valley HS; Newark, OH; Band; Chrs; Drm Mjrt; Hon Rl; Sch Mus; Stu Cncl; 4-H; Key Clb; Pep Clb; 4-H Awd; Jazz Choir; Sec & Tres Of Choir; Ohio Northern Univ; Education.

TOPY, SANDRA; Walnut Ridge HS; Columbus, OH; Chrs; Drl Tm; Jr NHS; Sch Mus; Best Drill Teamer Awd 78 79; Flight Attndt.

TORCHIA, MICHAEL; St Francis De Sales HS; Toledo, OH; 20/200 Pres Frsh Cls; Cls Rep Frsh Cls; Hon Rl; NHS; Stu Cncl; Bsbl; Letter Hockey; Trk; Univ.

TORELLO, DENISE; Marysville HS; Port Huron, MI; 6/180 Girl Scts; Hon Rl; Sct Actv; Stg Crw; Stu Cncl; 4-H; St Clair County Commumity; Data Proc.

TORGERSON, DAVID; Grove City HS; Grove City, OH; Hon Rl; Yth Flsp; Letter Bsktbl; Letter Ftbl; Letter Trk; Coach Actv; Athtl Of Wk In Ftbl 79; Dist Qualifier In Track 79; Otterbern Coll; Med.

TORMOEHLEN, SUE; Brownstown Central HS; Crothersville, IN; 1/137 Trs Soph Cls; Val; Am Leg Aux Girls St; Chrs; Hon Rl; NHS; Quill & Scroll; Sch Mus; Sch Pl; Sprt Ed Yrbk; Natl Winner Prod Demo At NJHA Convention 78; Recd Aid Assoc For Lutherans Schlrshp 79; Hortense Hurst Schr; Purdue Univ; Early Child Educ.

TORNABENE, TOM; Tuscarawas Cntrl Cathlc HS; New Phila, OH; 20/60 Cl Rep Jr Cls; Pres Sr Cls; Hon Rl; NHS; Stu Cncl; Rptr Sch Nwsp; Sch Nwsp; Bsbl; Kent State Univ Dist 1978; Capital Univ; Poli Sci.

TORNES, SHARON; Bishop Watterson HS; Columbus, OH; 25/273 Chrh Wkr; Cmnty Wkr; Debate Tm; Hon Rl; Hosp Ade; NHS; Sch Mus; Sch Pl; Drama Clb; Treas 4-H; Univ.

TOROK, KIMBERLY; Munster HS; Munster, IN; 13/404 Band; Chrs; Cmnty Wkr; Hon Rl; Hosp Ade; Jr NHS; NHS; Off Ade; Sprt Ed Yrbk; Pep Clb; Univ; Adv.

TOROK, NANCY; Austintown Fitch HS; Youngstown, OH; 112/655 Cmp Fr Grls; Hon Rl; Off Ade; Y-Teens; FSA; Chrldng; PPFtbl; College; Biological Sci.

TORP, JODIE; Mount Clemens HS; Mt Clemens, MI; Cls Rep Frsh Cls; Chrs; Hosp Ade; Off Ade; Sch Mus; Key Clb; Letter Swmmng; Tmr; Oral Roberts Univ; Registered Nurse.

TORRANCE, PATRICIA; Monroe HS; Monroe, MI; Cmp Fr Grls; Hon Rl; NHS; Stu Cncl; Y-Teens; Spn Clb; Swmmng; Mic St; Elem Educ.

TORRENCE, BRIAN; Niles Mc Kinley HS; Niles, OH; Ftbl; Trk; IM Sprt; Us Naval Acad.

TORRENCE, BRUCE; Niles Mc Kinley HS; Niles, OH; 29/420 Hon Rl; NHS; Sprt Ed Yrbk; VP Key Clb; Ftbl; Trk; U S Air Force Acad.

TORRES, ANGEL Q; Washington HS; E Chicago, IN; 45/263 Chrs; Hon Rl; Sch Pl; Boys Clb Am; Mgrs; Univ Of San Francisco; Art.

TORRES, NELLITA; West Tech HS; Cleveland, OH; Cls Rep Soph Cls; Hon Rl; Jr NHS; Lbry Ade; Off Ade; Yrbk; Spn Clb; Cit Awd; Upward Bound Case Western Reserve; Merit Roll; Perfect Attendance; Univ; Med.

TORRES, V; Washington HS; E Chicago, IN; 19/350 Chrh Wkr; Hon Rl; NHS; Off Ade; Drama Clb; Spn Clb; Univ; Drama.

TORTORELLA, LORI; Ravenna HS; Ravenna, OH; 14/313 Band; Hon Rl; NHS; Off Ade; Yrbk; OEA; Pep Clb; Capt Chrldng; Sec.

TOST, LEONARD J; Madonna HS; Weirton, WV; Hon Rl; Pol Wkr; Key Clb; Letter Ftbl; IM Sprt; Coll; Law.

TOTH, BARBARA; Our Lady Of Mercy HS; Detroit, MI; 1/320 Cls Rep Frsh Cls; Pres Soph Cls; Pres Jr Cls; Pres NHS; Stu Cncl; Pres Ger Clb; Crs Cntry; Univ; Chem Engr.

TOTH, GREGORY; John F Kennedy HS; Warren, OH; 14/160 Aud/Vis; Band; Hon Rl; Sch Mus; Stg Crw; Drama Clb; Fr Clb; Ftbl; Swmmng; Letter Ten; Natl HS Awd For Excllnc 79; Univ; Elec Engr.

TOTH, JERRY; Wickliffe HS; Wickliffe, OH; Hon Rl; Mod UN; NHS; Crs Cntry; Ftbl; Trk; Wrstlng; Kent State Univ; Aero Flight.

TOTH, JOSEPH; St Peters HS; Mansfield, OH; 33/73 Chrh Wkr; Hon Rl; Lbry Ade; Sprt Ed Sch Nwsp; Rptr Sch Nwsp; Opt Clb Awd; Bus.

TOTH, JOYCE; Orange HS; Chagrin Falls, OH; 1/225 Band; Drm Bgl; Hon Rl; NHS; Sch Mus; Natl Merit SF; Univ; Intl Bus.

TOTH, MARTIN; Phile HS; Roseville, OH; Hon Rl; Lbry Ade; FTA; Sci Clb; Elec.

TOTH, MONICA; Boardman HS; Youngstown, OH; 105/558 Hon Rl; Coll; Foreign Lang.

TOTH, PAMELA; Colerain HS; Cincinnati, OH; .

TOTH, SANDRA; Morgantown HS; Star City, WV; Mat Maids; W Va Univ; Medical.

TOTH, TIM; Monroe HS; Monroe, MI; Cls Rep Soph Cls; Cl Rep Jr Cls; Cls Rep Sr Cls; Quill & Scroll; Rptr Yrbk; Sch Nwsp; Natl Merit Ltr; Michigan State Univ; Special Ed.

TOTO, CHRISTINE; Union Local HS; Belmont, OH; 14/150 Band; Girl Scts; Hon Rl; Hosp Ade; Off Ade; Stu Cncl; Pres Fr Clb; Sci Clb; Chrldng; Voice Dem Awd; Tech Schl; Fashion.

TOTSCH, NANCY; Coshocton HS; Coshocton, OH; 9/321 Sec Frsh Cls; Sec Soph Cls; Sec Jr Cls; Pres Sr Cls; Band; Jr NHS; NHS; Sch Pl; Stu Cncl; Letter Ten; Univ Of Cincinnati; Bus.

TOUSIGNANT, TOM; Negaunee HS; Negaunee, MI; Band; Chrs; Chrh Wkr; Cmnty Wkr; Hon Rl; Lbry Ade; PAVAS; Sch Pl; Stg Crw; Drama Clb; Northern Univ.

TOUT, DEE; Fairland HS; Proctorvll, OH; Cls Rep Frsh Cls; Am Leg Aux Girls St; Hon Rl; NHS; Pres Drama Clb; Mth Clb; Mat Maids; Ohio St Univ; Psych.

TOWELL, DAVID B; Adena HS; Frankfort, OH; Cls Rep Soph Cls; VP Jr Cls; Am Leg Boys St; Band; Hon Rl; Jr NHS; NHS; Stu Cncl; Ftbl; College; History.

TOWER, CHARITY; Walter P Chrysler Mem HS; New Castle, IN; Stg Crw; Stu Cncl; Ed Yrbk; OEA; Pep Clb; Honorable Mention Copy Writing Franklin Coll; Forsco; Art Club Stu Action Comm Treas; Vincennes Coll; Art.

TOWER, HELEN; Coldwater HS; Coldwater, MI; Cmnty Wkr; PAVAS; Sci Clb; Letter Gym; IM Sprt; Michigan St Univ; Vet.

TOWER, MARY; J W Sexton HS; Lansing, MI; 1/336 Band; Chrs; Hon Rl; Mdrgl; NHS; Orch; Sch Mus; General Motors Univ; Ind Admin.

TOWER, SAMUEL; Greenville Sr HS; Gowen, MI; 10/230 Pres Frsh Cls; Am Leg Boys St; Hon Rl; Stu Cncl; Letter Bsbl; Letter Bsktbl; Coach Actv; Natl Merit Ltr; Aquinas Coll Acad Schlrshp 79; Gold Cord 79; Aquinas Coll; Acctg.

TOWERS, ANDREW; Onsted Comm HS; Clayton, MI; VP Frsh Cls; Cl Rep Jr Cls; Band; Cmnty Wkr; Hon Rl; Hosp Ade; Lit Mag; Pol Wkr; Sch Pl; Stu Cncl; Ublue Ribbon Photog Awd; Iron Man Awd In Ftbl; Central Michigan Univ; Journalism.

TOWIANSKI, STANLEY J; Henry Ford Ii HS; Steing Hts, MI; Hon Rl; IM Sprt; Univ Of Mich; Comp Sci.

TOWN, KEN; Norwood HS; Norwood, OH; Pres Soph Cls; Pres Jr Cls; Boy Scts; DECA; Letter Bsktbl; Cincinnati Tech Coll; Comp Prog.

TOWN, MARY; Ithaca HS; Ithaca, MI; Trs Jr Cls; Chrs; Hon Rl; Sch Mus; Rptr Yrbk; Rptr Sch Nwsp; Fr Clb; FTA; Pep Clb; Trk; Ctrl Michigan St Univ; Interior Dsgn.

TOWNE, ELIZABETH; Clay Sr HS; S Bend, IN; 75/430 Chrs; Hon Rl; Mdrgl; Sch Mus; Sch Pl; Stg Crw; Indiana Univ; Sci.

TOWNER, BETH; Hiland HS; Millersburg, OH; 7/61 Cl Rep Jr Cls; Cls Rep Sr Cls; Band; Chrh Wkr; Hon Rl; Treas DECA; 4-H; FHA; Pep Clb; DECA Girl Of The Year; D E Highest Grade Average; Ohio State Univ; Acctg.

TOWNER, CARLA; Orddridge Cnty HS; West Union, WV; Lbry Ade; Off Ade; Yth Flsp; Pres 4-H; Pep Clb; VICA; Pom Pon; Dnfth Awd; 4-H Awd; Salem Coll; Nursing.

TOWNLEY, JOHN; Madison Comp HS; Mansfield, OH; 44/480 Band; NHS; Orch; Sch Pl; Stg Crw; Ger Clb; Ohio St Univ; Bio Sci.

TOWNS, CHARLES A; Southern Wells HS; Warren, IN; 49/98 Band; Boy Scts; Sch Pl; Sct Actv; Stg Crw; Yth Flsp; Drama Clb; Spn Clb; Purdue Univ; Psych.

TOWNS, CHERYL; East Technical HS; Cleveland, OH; Hon Rl; Ed Sch Nwsp; Drama Clb; 4-H; Bsktbl; College; Leg Sec.

TOWNS, CORRIE; Southeastern HS; Detroit, MI; Hon Rl; Hosp Ade; Ed Sch Nwsp; Rptr Sch Nwsp; Cit Awd; Wayne St Univ; Med.

TOWNS, LANCE; Cedar Springs HS; Cedar Sprgs, MI; Band; Chrh Wkr; Hon Rl; Jr NHS; Letter Ten; Voc Schl; Diesel Mech.

TOWNSEL, MARY J; Muskegon Heights Sr HS; Muskegon Hts, MI; 3/160 Sec Frsh Cls; Band; Chrh Wkr; Cmnty Wkr; NHS; Stu Cncl; Yth Flsp; Civ Clb; FNA; Opt Clb Awd; Musk Cmnty Coll; RN.

TOWNSEL, SHERYL; Muskegon Heights HS; Muskegon Hts, MI; 10/161 Chrh Wkr; Debate Tm; Girl Scts; Hon Rl; Lbry Ade; NHS; Off Ade; Drama Clb; Fr Clb; Spn Clb; Muskegon Cmnty Coll; Bus Admin.

TOWNSEND, CARL; Manchester Community HS; Manchester, MI; 13/106 VP Band; Chrh Wkr; Hon Rl; Lbry Ade; NHS; Orch; Ger Clb; Mi St Comp Schlrshp 79; Adrian Coll; Earth Sci.

TOWNSEND, DANNY; Cardington Lincoln HS; Fulton, OH; 13/79 Hon Rl; Fr Clb; Letter Bsbl; Army; Linguistics.

TOWNSEND, JULIE; Cadillac Sr HS; Cadillac, MI; Cls Rep Frsh Cls; Cls Rep Soph Cls; Cl Rep Jr Cls; Cls Rep Sr Cls; Hon Rl; NHS; Stu Cncl; Chrldng; PPFtbl; Rotary Awd; Michigan St Univ; Medicine.

TOWNSEND, KAREN; John Hay HS; Cleveland, OH; Lbry Ade; Off Ade; Cit Awd; JA Awd; Cleveland State Univ; Comp.

TOWNSEND, LINDA; Brooke HS; Follansbee, WV; 27/403 Am Leg Aux Girls St; FCA; Spn Clb; Letter Trk; Mat Maids; West Liberty St Coll; Med Tech.

TOWNSEND, PATRICIA; Southeastern HS; Detroit, MI; Sec Cmp Fr Grls; Sec Chrh Wkr; Hon Rl; JA; Stu Cncl; Treas Fr Clb; Cit Awd; JA Awd; Florida State; Medicine.

TOWNSEND, ROBERT; Beecher HS; Mt Morris, MI; 7/275 Cls Rep Sr Cls; Band; Chrs; Chrh Wkr; NHS; Sch Mus; Pres Stu Cncl; Opt Clb Awd; Kentucky State Univ; Music.

TOWNSEND, ROBERT L; Gobles HS; Gobles, MI; 10/80 Boy Scts; NHS; Sci Clb; Spn Clb; Kalamazoo Coll; Med Doctor.

TOWNSEND, SETH; Hubbard HS; Hubbard, OH; 3/330 Boy Scts; Chrh Wkr; Hon Rl; Yth Flsp; Key Clb; Bsktbl; College.

TOWNSEND, THOR T; Celina Sr HS; Celina, OH; 1/240 Band; Chrs; Hon Rl; Mdrgl; Pres NHS; Sch Mus; VP Stu Cncl; Drama Clb; Fr Clb; Natl Merit Ltr; Ohi State Univ; Horticulture.

TOWNSHEND, MICHELLE; Union HS; Grand Rapids, MI; Debate Tm; Hon Rl; NHS; Orch; Sch Mus; Pep Clb; Letter Trk; Coll; Vet.

TOWSE, MATTHEW; St Francis De Sales; Toledo, OH; Treas Band; Hon Rl; NHS; Orch; Sch Mus; Univ Of Dayton; Civil Engr.

TOWSE, MATTHEW W; St Francis De Sales HS; Toledo, OH; 14/180 Treas Band; Hon Rl; NHS; Orch; Sch Mus; Univ Of Dayton; Bus.

TOWSON, KENNETH; Pontiac Central HS; Pontiac, MI; Boy Scts; JA; Orch; Sch Mus; Sct Actv; Yth Flsp; Coll.

TOYZAN, DINA; Whitehall Yearling HS; Columbus, OH; Band; Hon Rl; Lit Mag; Yrbk; Sch Nwsp; Fr Clb; Ohio St Univ; Photog.

TRACEY, KEVIN; Nordonia HS; Macondia, OH; VP Frsh Cls; Cls Rep Soph Cls; Pres Jr Cls; Cls Rep Sr Cls; Hon Rl; Jr NHS; Pol Wkr; Red Cr Ade; Stu Cncl; Fr Clb; Univ; Math.

TRACEY, PENELOPE; Calumet HS; Gary, IN; 14/297 Hon Rl; Jr NHS; NHS; Quill & Scroll; Y-Teens; Sch Nwsp; Fr Clb; FSA; Pep Clb; PPFtbl; College.

TRACHT, DANIEL; Huron HS; Huron, OH; 14/161 Cls Rep Sr Cls; Band; Hon Rl; NHS; Stu Cncl; Y-Teens; Mth Clb; Letter Crs Cntry; Letter Trk; Am Leg Awd; Miami Univ; Pre Law.

TRACY, BARBARA; Federal Hocking HS; Guysville, OH; Cls Rep Frsh Cls; Cls Rep Soph Cls; Cl Rep Jr Cls; Band; Girl Scts; Hon Rl; 4-H; Mth Clb; Trk; Mgrs; Hocking Tech Coll; Ceramics.

TRACY, DENISE; Clare HS; Clare, MI; 4/130 Pres Frsh Cls; Cls Rep Frsh Cls; Sec Soph Cls; Pres Jr Cls; Cl Rep Jr Cls; Cls Rep Sr Cls; Aud/Vis; Chrh Wkr; FCA; Girl Scts; Eastern Michigan Univ; Spec Educ Tch.

TRACY, JERRY; North HS; Columbus, OH; 1/300 Cls Rep Frsh Cls; Cls Rep Soph Cls; Cl Rep Jr Cls; Am Leg Boys St; Band; Boy Scts; Chrs; Chrh Wkr; FCA; Hon Rl; Univ; Engr.

TRACY, KELLI; Brownsburg HS; Brownsburg, IN; Pres Frsh Cls; NHS; Bsktbl; Trk; GAA; PPFtbl; Varsity Letter Capt Starter; Butler Univ; Acctg.

TRACY, KENDRA; Lexington Sr HS; Lexington, OH; Fr Clb; North Cntrl Tech Coll; Elec.

TRACY, M; Rocky River HS; Rocky Rvr, OH; Chrh Wkr; Cmnty Wkr; Hon Rl; Stu Cncl; Rptr Yrbk; Yrbk; Sch Nwsp; IM Sprt; Schlstc Achvmnt Awd In Theol 78; Univ; Sci.

TRACY, MARK; Webster County HS; Cowen, WV; Cls Rep Soph Cls; Cl Rep Jr Cls; Hon Rl; NHS; Stu Cncl; Rptr Sch Nwsp; Pres 4-H; Pep Clb; Ftbl; Capt Wrstlng; College; Law.

TRACY, ROBERT; Strongsville Sr HS; Strongsville, OH; Chrh Wkr; Hon Rl; Jr NHS; NHS; Pol Wkr; Sct Actv; Stu Cncl; Lat Clb; Bsktbl; Crs Cntry; Zellers Freedom Essay Awd 77; 3 Times Part In Oh Tests Of Schlstc Achvmnt 76 78; Univ; Pre Med.

TRADER, KAREN; Franklin HS; Livonia, MI; Sec Chrs; Girl Scts; Hon Rl; Mdrgl; Sch Mus; Sch Pl; Sct Actv; Stg Crw; Stu Cncl; Letter Swmmng; College; Nurse.

TRAFFORD, TAMI; Leslie HS; Leslie, MI; Cls Rep Frsh Cls; Cl Rep Jr Cls; Band; Drl Tm; Girl Scts; Hon Rl; Stu Cncl; 4-H; Trk; PPFtbl; Archt.

TRAGER, DEBORAH L; Newark Sr HS; Newark, OH; Band; Chrs; Chrh Wkr; Yth Flsp; 4-H; Fr Clb; Pep Clb; Letter Bsbl; Capt Bsktbl; Letter Trk; Wright St Univ; Phys Educ.

TRAGESSER, JULIE; Bishop Noll Inst; Hammond, IN; 36/360 Am Leg Aux Girls St; Hon Rl; Hosp Ade; NHS; Sch Nwsp; Mth Clb; IM Sprt; St Marys Coll; Bus Admin.

TRAINER, LEONA M; Southeastern HS; Chillicothe, OH; 9/79 Am Leg Aux Girls St; Hon Rl; Jr NHS; NHS; Stu Cncl; FTA; Ger Clb; Scr Kpr; Sftbl Lttr; Vllybl Lttr; Univ; Acctg.

TRAMMELL, JOAN; Plymouth Salem HS; Canton, MI; 6/540 Hon Rl; Pres JA; NHS; JA Awd; Alma Coll; Bus Admin.

TRAMMELL, KIMBERLY C; Dublin HS; Dublin, OH; Cmnty Wkr; Hon Rl; Off Ade; Stg Crw; Rptr Sch Nwsp; Lat Clb; Pep Clb; Spn Clb; West Virginia Univ; Psych.

TRAMMELL, TONY; Franklin HS; Franklin, OH; Chrs; Hon Rl; Sch Mus; Stg Crw; Ed Sch Nwsp; Fr Clb; Pep Clb; IM Sprt; All Oh St Fair Youth Chr 79; Solo & Ensemble Medl From Oh Music Educ Assoc 78; Univ; Advertising.

TRAN, THUY; North HS; Columbus, OH; Hon Rl; Jr NHS; NHS; Fr Clb; Ohio State Univ.

TRANTER, LAURA; Heritage HS; Ft Wayne, IN; Band; Hon Rl; Stg Crw; Spn Clb; College; Math.

TRAPP, AMY; River Valley HS; Sawyer, MI; Hon Rl; Drama Clb; Spn Clb; Chrldng; College; Journ.

TRAPP, PAUL; De Kalb HS; Ashley, IN; 45/289 Hon Rl; NHS; Pres FFA; Univ; Forestry.

TRAPP, VICKI; Galion Sr HS; Galion, OH; AFS; Off Ade; Yth Flsp; Y-Teens; Pep Clb; Letter Gym; Swmmng; Trk; Letter Chrldng; GAA; Eastern Michigan Univ.

TRAUGH, LESLIE; Mogadore HS; Mogadore, OH; 4/94 Hon Rl; NHS; Off Ade; FHA; Mgrs; Kent State Univ; Nursing.

TRAURIG, SCOTT; Solon HS; Solon, OH; Aud/Vis; Hon Rl; Lbry Ade; NHS; Sch Mus; Sch Pl; Stg Crw; Drama Clb; Pres Mth Clb; Natl Merit Ltr; College; Computer Science.

TRAUSCH, KAREN; Edon HS; Edon, OH; 7/64 Chrs; Hon Rl; Jr NHS; NHS; Sch Mus; FHA; OEA; Bsktbl; 4-H Awd; Bowling Green Univ; Sec.

TRAUTNER, JOEL; Arthur Hill HS; Saginaw, MI; 96/523 Cls Rep Soph Cls; Cl Rep Jr Cls; VP Sr Cls; Band; Chrh Wkr; FCA; Hon Rl; Pol Wkr; Sch Mus; Sch Pl; Outstndng De Fensive Lineman On Football Team; Represented V Pres Of St Of Michigan For Secondary Schl; Saginaw Valley St Univ; Busns.

TRAUTVETTER, DEANNA; Boonville HS; Boonville, IN; 6/218 Cmnty Wkr; Hon Rl; Lbry Ade; Off Ade; Sch Mus; Sch Pl; Stg Crw; Yth Flsp; Deaconess Hosp Schl Of Nurse; Nurse.

TRAUTWEIN, DENNIS; Upper Sandusky HS; Upper Sandusky, OH; Band; Boy Scts; Chrs; Chrh Wkr; Hon Rl; NHS; Pres 4-H; Ohio State; Vet.

TRAVER, JIM; Rossford HS; Rossford, OH; Univ Of S California; Marine Bio.

TRAVERS, DENISE; Marian HS; Birmingham, MI; Cls Rep Soph Cls; Cl Rep Jr Cls; Chrh Wkr; Cmnty Wkr; Hon Rl; Mod UN; NHS; Pres Spn Clb; IM Sprt; NCTE; College.

TRAVIS, DENISE; Woodmore HS; Woodville, OJ; Trs Frsh Cls; Off Ade; Stg Crw; Yth Flsp; Sprt Ed Yrbk; Rptr Yrbk; Pep Clb; Bsktbl; Trk; Chrldng; Owens Tech; Nursing.

TRAVIS, HOWARD; Garaway HS; Sugarcreek, OH; Aud/Vis; Hon Rl; 4-H; Ftbl; Trk; 4-H Awd; Vocational School; Electronics.

TRAVIS, TAMMY; Calumet HS; Gary, IN; 2/260 Trs Soph Cls; Cls Rep Soph Cls; Trs Jr Cls; Cl Rep Jr Cls; Am Leg Aux Girls St; Hon Rl; NHS; Stu Cncl; FSA; Flo Inst Of Tech; Aeronautical Engr.

TRAXLER, PAUL L; Quincy HS; Quincy, MI; Boy Scts; Chrs;.

TRAYER, LISA; Martinsburg Sr HS; Martinsburg, WV; Sec Frsh Cls; Sec Soph Cls; Sec Jr Cls; Chrh Wkr; Cmnty Wkr; Girl Scts; Hon Rl; Off Ade; Sch Pl; Sct Actv; West Virginia Univ; Pharm.

TRAYLOR, LYNNE; Ursuline HS; Youngstown, OH; 65/302 Hon Rl; NHS; Sch Pl; Fr Clb; FTA; Lat Clb; Pep Clb; Gym; Capt Chrldng; Natl Merit SF; Merit Achvmnt Award; Commndn Natl Achvmnt Schlrshp Award; All Star Cheerleading; Univ; Psych.

TRAYNELIS, STEPHEN; St Francis De Sales HS; Morgantown, WV; 5/78 Hon Rl; Sch Pl; Stg Crw; Drama Clb; Fr Clb; Mth Clb; Sci Clb; Ten; Gov Hon Prg Awd; Univ; Engr.

TRAYNOR, MICHAEL P; Lawrence North HS; Indianapolis, IN; 18/384 Cl Rep Jr Cls; Cmnty Wkr; FCA; Hon Rl; NHS; Pol Wkr; Stu Cncl; Yrbk; Drama Clb; Key Clb; Purdue Univ; Engr.

TREADWAY, CHERIE; Springboro HS; Franklin, OH; 17/200 Hon Rl; Hosp Ade; FTA; Bsbl; Wittenburg Univ; Pre Med.

TREADWAY, KRISTA; Clear Fork HS; Artie, WV; Chrh Wkr; Girl Scts; Hon Rl; Hosp Ade; NHS; 4-H; FBLA; 4-H Awd; Voc Schl.

TREADWAY, MARGARET A; Crown Point HS; Crown Point, IN; 19/508 Band; Hon Rl; Sch Mus; Pep Clb; Natl Merit SF; Indiana State Univ; Music Educ.

TREADWELL, LAURIE J; Harper Creek HS; Battle Creek, MI; NHS; Rptr Sch Nwsp; Kellogg Cmnty Coll; Sec.

TREBUS, PATRICIA; Woodrow Wilson HS; Youngstown, OH; 67/345 Cmp Fr Grls; Hon Rl; Hosp Ade; JA; Stg Crw; FHA; Keyettes; Pres Lat Clb; Pep Clb; Clara Barton Awd 79; X Ray Tech.

TRECHA, GREGORY; Swartz Creek HS; Swartz Creek, MI; 2/420 Sal; Am Leg Boys St; Boy Scts; Hon Rl; NHS; Crs Cntry; Trk; Univ Of Mic; Med.

TRECHA, JEFFREY; Swartz Creek HS; Swartz Creek, MI; 31/443 VP Frsh Cls; Boy Scts; Jr NHS; NHS; Pol Wkr; Letter Trk; Unif Of Mic.

TREEN, JAMES B; Lancaster HS; Lancaster, OH; Am Leg Boys St; Chrh Wkr; Debate Tm; Hon Rl; Natl Forn Lg; Yth Flsp; Ohio State; Engineering.

TREES, JOHN; Dublin HS; Dublin, OH; 34/157 Boy Scts; Hon Rl; Sct Actv; Yth Flsp; 4-H; Spn Clb; Bsktbl; Socr; IM Sprt; Univ; Engr.

TREFRY, STACEY; Eaton Rapids HS; Eaton Rapids, MI; Am Leg Aux Girls St; Band; Cmp Fr Grls; Chrs; Hon Rl; Y-Teens; Rptr Yrbk; Central Mic Coll; Psych.

TREGILGUS, MICHAEL; Milan HS; Dillsboro, IN; Cl Rep Jr Cls; VP Sr Cls; Band; NHS; Stu Cncl; Letter Bsbl; Letter Ftbl; Letter Wrstlng; College.

TREGLIA, J; Catholic Central HS; Mingo Jctn, OH; 11/230 Boy Scts; Chrh Wkr; Hon Rl;.

TREIBER, MARK; High School; Unionville, MI; VP Soph Cls; Hon Rl; Yth Flsp; 4-H; Bsktbl; Ftbl; Trk; 4-H Awd; Natl Merit Ltr; Lake Superior St Coll; Wildlife Mgmt.

TREIER, LINDA; Elmwood HS; Bloomdale, OH; 20/120 Band; Hon Rl; Sch Mus; Rptr Sch Nwsp; Sch Nwsp; FTA; GAA; Royal Lancer Flag Corp; Miss Ohio United Teenager Pageant; Coll; Elem Ed.

TREJO, JOSE; Father J Wehrle Memorial HS; Columbus, OH; Pres Frsh Cls; Pres Soph Cls; Stu Cncl; Letter Bsbl; Capt Ftbl; Letter Wrstlng; Hugh O Brian Yth Ldrshp Found 77; Outstndg Stu Qsd 78; Ohio St Univ.

TRELA, MICHELE A; Aquinas HS; Southgate, MI; Cls Rep Soph Cls; Hon Rl; NHS; Stu Cncl; Letter Trk; Chrldng; Mgrs; College; Psych.

TREMBLAY, WILLIAM; Riverside HS; Dearborn Hts, MI; 8/95 Hon Rl; Jr NHS; NHS; Off Ade; Pol Wkr; Pol Wkr; Fr Clb; Sci Clb; Bsbl; Capt Glf; Univ Of Michigan; Bus Mgmt.

TRENDEL, SUSAN; Whitmer Sr HS; Toledo, OH; FTA; Ger Clb; OEA; Toledo Univ; Data Proc.

TRENEFF, NICK; Grove City HS; Grove City, OH; VP Frsh Cls; Cls Rep Frsh Cls; VP Soph Cls; Cls Rep Soph Cls; Cl Rep Jr Cls; Cls Rep Sr Cls; Am Leg Boys St; NHS; Stu Cncl; JV Bsbll 78; Sr Clss Sargeant At Arms 79; Univ; Cmnctns.

TRENT, KAREN; Wheelersburg HS; Sciotoville, OH; 36/135 Band; Chrs; Girl Scts; Hosp Ade; Stg Crw; Yth Flsp; Fr Clb; Pep Clb; IM Sprt; Scr Kpr; Shawnee State Univ; Bus.

TRENTA, JOHN; Norton HS; Norton, OH; Cls Rep Frsh Cls; Aud/Vis; Hon Rl; Lit Mag; Sch Mus; Sch Pl; Stg Crw; Stu Cncl; Letter Ten; Voice Dem Awd; Akron Univ; Bus Mgmt.

TRETOW, ERNEST F; Wintersville HS; Wintersville, OH; Boy Scts; Fr Clb; Bsktbl; College; Journalist, Electrician.

TRETTER, BARBARA; George Washington HS; Indianapolis, IN; Cls Rep Frsh Cls; Cls Rep Soph Cls; Cl Rep Jr Cls; Girl Scts; Hon Rl; JA; Fr Clb; Capt Gym; Chrldng; 4-H Awd; Univ; Sec.

TREVARROW, WILLIAM J; Sault Area HS; Sault Ste Mari, MI; Cmnty Wkr; Drl Tm; Hon Rl; ROTC; Sch Nwsp; Am Leg Awd; Lettered On Var Rifle Tm 79; Earned Medals For Marksmanshp Events 79; Michigan Tech Univ; Forestry.

TREXLER, MARK; Harper Woods HS; Harper Woods, MI; 124/344 Cls Rep Frsh Cls; FCA; Hon Rl; Bsbl; Bsktbl; Coach Actv; IM Sprt; Natl Merit Ltr; W Michigan Univ; Engr.

TREY, VALERIE; Tippecanoe HS; Tipp City, OH; Chrldng; Univ; Child Care.

TRIAL, ALAIN; Newark Catholic HS; Newark, OH; Am Leg Boys St; Boy Scts; Hon Rl; NHS; Sct Actv; Lat Clb; Sci Clb; Univ; Geology.

TRIBBETT, CHARLES; Pioneer Regional Jr Sr HS; Monticello, IN; 2/105 Pres Frsh Cls; Pres Soph Cls; Pres Jr Cls; Pres Sr Cls; Sal; Aud/Vis; Boy Scts; Chrh Wkr; FCA; Hon Rl; Ball St Univ; Med.

TRIBBLE, CHARLIE; Winfield HS; Winfield, WV; VP Soph Cls; FCA; Hon Rl; Jr NHS; NHS; Stu Cncl; Pres Beta Clb; Letter Bsbl; Letter Bsktbl; Letter Ftbl; Univ.

TRIBBLE, DENISE; Elyria Catholic HS; Elyria, OH; Band; Chrs; Girl Scts; Hon Rl; Pep Clb; Spn Clb; Natl Hnr Soc Nom; Univ.

TRIBBLE, TAWNY; Winfield HS; Winfield, WV; Hon Rl; Jr NHS; NHS; Yth Flsp; Fr Clb; Mth Clb; Pep Clb; Letter Bsktbl; Mgrs; Scr Kpr; Univ.

TRICK, STEVEN; Ben Davis HS; Indianapolis, IN; Band; Hon Rl; NHS; Lat Clb; Ftbl; Ten; Trk; College; Med.

TRIER, MARY; Douglas Mac Arthur HS; Saginaw, MI; Hon Rl; NHS; Sch Pl; Yrbk; Ger Clb; Pep Clb; PPFtbl; Central Michigan Univ; Jrnlsm.

TRIERWEILAR, JULIE; Pervano Westphalia HS; Portland, MI; Cl Rep Jr Cls; Band; Hon Rl; Ed Sch Nwsp; Rptr Sch Nwsp; Sch Nwsp; 4-H; IM Sprt; 4-H Awd; Lansing Bus Inst; Lgl Sec.

TRIERWEILER, JOHN; High School; Lansing, MI; Hon Rl; NHS; Bsbl; Letter Glf; IM Sprt; Lansing Community Coll; Humanities.

TRIETCH, BRENDA; Trenton HS; Trenton, MI; 25/539 Sec Band; NHS; Sch Pl; Yth Flsp; Treas Ger Clb; Pep Clb; Capt Ten; DAR Awd; Mic Tech; Engr.

TRIFILETTE, LISA; Niles Mc Kinley HS; Niles, OH; AFS; Hon Rl; Drama Clb; Letter Bsbl; Letter Bsktbl; PPFtbl; Comp Tech.

TRIGG, DEBBIE; Washington HS; Massillon, OH; Chrs; Hon Rl; Off Ade; DECA;.

TRIGG, GRETCHEN; Westerville North HS; Columbus, OH; 64/450 Chrs; Capt Drl Tm; Hon Rl; NHS; Yth Flsp; PPFtbl; Trinity Univ; Engr.

TRIGGER, MARGARET; Carsonville Port Sanilac HS; Carsonville, MI; Band; Cmnty Wkr; Hon Rl; Sch Pl; Stg Crw; Drama Clb; Fr Clb; Sci Clb; Eastern Michigan Univ; Nursing.

TRIMBLE, DONNA; Unioto HS; Chillicothe, OH; 5/124 Band; Chrh Wkr; Hon Rl; Jr NHS; NHS; Yth Flsp; Spn Clb; Ohio Univ Chillicothe; Acctg.

TRIMBLE, JEFF; Sullivan HS; Carlisle, IN; Beta Clb; Pres FFA; Bsktbl; Crs Cntry; Trk; IV Tech.

TRIMBLE, MICHAEL; Buffalo HS; Huntington, WV; Trs Frsh Cls; Boy Scts; Hon Rl; Letter Bsbl; Letter Bsktbl; Letter Ftbl; Trk; Cit Awd; All Conf Basebll & Track 79; Univ.

TRIMBLE, MIKE; Philo HS; Duncan Falls, OH; Chrs; Fr Clb;.

TRIMMER, DAVE; Brooke HS; Wellsburg, WV; 90/466 Cls Rep Frsh Cls; Cls Rep Soph Cls; Cl Rep Jr Cls; Sal; Boy Scts; FCA; Hon Rl; Spn Clb; Trk; IM Sprt; West Vir Univ; Law.

TRINDLE, PAM; Poland Seminary HS; Poland, OH; Cmp Fr Grls; Chrs; Chrh Wkr; Hon Rl; NHS; Stg Crw; Sec Drama Clb; Fr Clb; Spn Clb; Honorable Mention 2nd Yr French Ohio Tests Of Schlstc Ach; Coll; Languages.

TRINE, MELINDA; Pittsford HS; Pittsford, MI; 2/60 VP Frsh Cls; VP Soph Cls; Sal; Band; Chrh Wkr; Hon Rl; NHS; Rptr Yrbk; Sprt Ed Sch Nwsp; FHA; Houghton Coll; Bio.

TRINGALI, JOSEPHINE; Lakeview HS; St Clair Shores, MI; 4/548 Hon Rl; NHS; Pres Spn Clb; Ferris State Coll; Dentistry.

TRINGALI, JOSEPHINE; Lakeview HS; St Clair Shrs, MI; 8/548 Hon Rl; NHS; Pres Spn Clb; Ferris St Coll; Dent Asst.

TRIPLETT, CHRISTINE; Tuscarawas Ctrl Cath HS; New Phila, OH; Am Leg Aux Girls St; Hon Rl; NHS; Pres Pep Clb; Spn Clb; Scr Kpr; Ohio St Univ; Dental Hygnst.

TRIPLETT, DORIS; Southeastern HS; Ray, OH; 11/80 Jr NHS; NHS; Lat Clb; Recomm For 79 Miss Oh Teen USA Pageant 79;.

TRIPLETT, LETITIA; Bluffton HS; Ada, OH; 4/96 Chrs; Chrh Wkr; Hon Rl; NHS; Sch Mus; Sch Pl; Stg Crw; Yth Flsp; Sch Nwsp; Drama Clb; Univ; Sci.

TRIPLETT, SHERMAN; Caldwell HS; Caldwell, OH; Hon Rl; FFA; Military Academy; Military Aviation.

TRIPP, DEBBIE; Westfield Washington HS; Sheridan, IN; Band; Debate Tm; 4-H; Spn Clb; Univ; Vet Med.

TRIPPEL, CHARLES; Penn HS; Mishawaka, IN; 19/468 Chrh Wkr; Hon Rl; NHS; SAR Awd; Coll; Aerospace Engr.

TRIPPEL, NANCY; Marian HS; Mishawaka, IN; Hon Rl; Hosp Ade; NHS; Orch; Sch Mus; Sch Pl; Stg Crw; IM Sprt; St Josephs Fort Wayne; Nursing.

TRISLER, LOIS; Sidney HS; Sidney, OH; Chrs; Chrh Wkr; FCA; Hon Rl; NHS; Stu Cncl; Treas Yth Flsp; Crs Cntry; Trk; Coll.

TRISLER, PAMELA; Crothersville Community HS; Crothersville, IN; 16/60 Cls Rep Frsh Cls; Cls Rep Soph Cls; Cl Rep Jr Cls; Cls Rep Sr Cls; Band; Hon Rl; NHS; Stu Cncl; Pep Clb; Chrldng; Ball St Univ; Busns.

TRISTANI, TIM; Bishop Foley HS; Detroit, MI; Boy Scts; Hon Rl; Sct Actv; Am Leg Awd; Voc Schl.

TRITCH, DEBORAH; Prairie Heights HS; Hudson, IN; Band; Sch Mus; Sch Pl; Stg Crw; Yth Flsp; Drama Clb; FTA; Pep Clb; College; Comp Sci.

TRITCH, JOHN; Prairie Hts HS; Hudson, IN; 20/136 Band; Boy Scts; Chrh Wkr; Hon Rl; 4-H; FFA; 4-H Awd; Voc Schl; Building Constr.

TRITLE, TIM; Mitchell HS; Mitchell, IN; 72/151 Band; Off Ade; 4-H; Mgrs; Scr Kpr; 4-H Awd; Rotary Awd; Vincennes Univ; Agribusiness.

TRITSCHLER, MARY C; West Lafayette Sr HS; W Lafayette, IN; 8/185 Chrs; Girl Scts; Hon Rl; Lit Mag; Sch Mus; Sct Actv; Stg Crw; Rptr Sch Nwsp; Sch Nwsp; Fr Clb; Univ.

TRITTSCHUH, CHERYL; Greenville Sr HS; Greenville, OH; Am Leg Aux Girls St; Hon Rl; Wright St Univ; Elem Ed.

TRITTSCHUH, KIM; Ansonia HS; Versailles, OH; 3/72 Cls Rep Soph Cls; Am Leg Aux Girls St; VP Band; Chrs; NHS; Stu Cncl; Pres FHA; OEA; Chrldng;.

TRITTSCHUH, LISA; Greenville HS; Greenville, OH; 27/360 Drl Tm; Hon Rl; NHS; Off Ade; Treas OEA; Edison St Coll.

TRIVISON, LISA; Solon HS; Solon, OH; 5/290 VP Jr Cls; FCA; Hon Rl; NHS; Stu Cncl; Pep Clb; Chrldng; PPFtbl; Pre Med.

TRIVUNOVIC, DANNY; Griffith Sr HS; Griffith, IN; Univ; Math.

TROCKMAN, BRETT; Harrison HS; Evansville, IN; 33/450 Chrh Wkr; Hon Rl; Ger Clb; Ftbl; Glf; Univ; Engr.

TROEHLER, BARBARA; Lake Central HS; Crown Pt, IN; Quill & Scroll; Y-Teens; Rptr Yrbk; Indiana Univ; Phys Ther.

TROJAN, STEPHEN M; Rogers Sr HS; Michigan City, IN; 123/480 NHS; 4-H; Cit Awd; 4-H Awd; Block & Bridle Club; Horticulture Asst; Purdue Univ; Agri Busns.

TROJANOWSKI, RONALD; St Josephs HS; South Bend, IN; Chrh Wkr; Hon Rl; Jr NHS; Sch Pl; Am Leg Awd; College.

TROKSA, RICHARD; Griffith HS; Griffith, IN; 2/296 VP Jr Cls; Cl Rep Jr Cls; Hon Rl; Yrbk; Sch Nwsp; Spn Clb; IM Sprt; Univ; Photog.

TROKSA, THERESE; Griffith HS; Griffith, IN; 5/311 Cls Rep Soph Cls; Hon Rl; Jr NHS; Pres NHS; Sch Mus; Sch Pl; Stg Crw; Letter Gym; GAA; Am Leg Awd; Purdue Univ; Bio.

TROMANS, TERRI; Northville HS; Northville, MI; 175/341 Sch Mus; Pep Clb; Ferris St Univ; Health Mgmt.

TROMPETER, JAMES; Bay City Western HS; Kawkawlin, MI; Cntrl Michigan Univ.

TRONTER, M; Fenwick HS; Middletown, OH; Trs Jr Cls; Trs Sr Cls; Boy Scts; Chrs; Hon Rl; Sch Mus; Sch Pl; Stg Crw; Stu Cncl; Sprt Ed Sch Nwsp; Notre Dame; Journalism.

TROOST, DAVID; John Adam HS; So Bend, IN; Cl Rep Jr Cls; Boy Scts; Chrs; JA; Sch Mus; Sch Pl; Stg Crw; Drama Clb; Sci Clb; Gym; College; Paleontology.

TROPF, APRIL; Michigan Lutheran Seminary; Monroe, MI; Chrs; Sch Mus; Sch Pl; Yth Flsp; Bsbl; Bsktbl; Trk; Chrldng; PPFtbl; Schl Talent Show; Coll.

TROPIANO, JOE; Parkside HS; Jackson, MI; Boy Scts; Hon Rl; Sct Actv; Stu Cncl; Sch Nwsp; Ger Clb; Socr; Wrstlng; IM Sprt; Univ; Engr.

TROPP, DAVID A; William A Wirt HS; Gary, IN; 4/230 Am Leg Boys St; Debate Tm; Hon Rl; Lit Mag; NHS; Sch Pl; Ed Sch Nwsp; Mth Clb; Pres Sci Clb; Scr Kpr; Maa Honors Awd 1978; City Wide Spelling Champ 1978; Memb Amer Mensa Soc; Univ; Sci.

TROPP, IRIS; William A Wirt HS; Gary, IN; Girl Scts; Hon Rl; VP Lit Mag; Drama Clb; Pres Fr Clb; Mth Clb; Pep Clb; Chrldng; Univ; Bio Sci.

TROSSEN, MARY; St Augustine Acad; Cleveland, OH; 1/143 Chrs; Hon Rl; Sch Pl; Sch Nwsp; Sci Clb; Bsbl; IM Sprt; Ohio State Univ; Botony.

TROTT, PATRICE; Seeger Memorial HS; Williamsport, IN; Hon Rl; College; Elem Education.

TROTTER, CHERYL A; North Bloomington HS; Bloomington, IN; 70/421 Drl Tm; FCA; Hon Rl; OEA; Pep Clb; Gym; Trk; Capt Chrldng; Pom Pon; Indiana Univ; Busns Mgmt.

TROTTER, NANCY; Gladstone HS; Gladstone, MI; Chrh Wkr; Hon Rl; Lbry Ade; Off Ade; Quill & Scroll; Stu Cncl; Yrbk; Rptr Sch Nwsp; Sch Nwsp; Gym;.

TROTTER, SUSAN; Colerain HS; Cincinnati, OH; Sec Jr Cls; Band; Jr NHS; NHS; Orch; Ed Sch Nwsp; Drama Clb; 4-H; Pres Awd;.

TROTTMAN, ROBERT; George Washington HS; E Chicago, IN; 36/272 Band; Hon Rl; Letter Ftbl; Wrstlng; Purdue Univ; Mech Engr.

TROUT, BROOK; Colonel Crawford HS; Bucyrus, OH; Hon Rl; NHS; College; Engr.

TROUT, CYNTHIA; Philo HS; Zanesville, OH; 3/205 Pres Frsh Cls; VP Jr Cls; Chrs; Hon Rl; NHS; Sch Mus; Stu Cncl; Ed Sch Nwsp; VP Fr Clb; FTA; Ohio Acad Of Sci Superior Awd In St Competition; Ohio Tests Of Scholastic Achv; Principals Honor List; College; Vet.

TROUT, DANIEL; Field HS; Mogadore, OH; Yrbk; Crs Cntry; Akron Univ; Elec.

TROUT, DIANE; Franklin Community HS; Franklin, IN; Chrs; Drl Tm; Capt Drm Bgl; Hon Rl; Jr NHS; NHS; Sch Mus; Stg Crw; Yth Flsp; Pep Clb; Chemistry I Awd; Regional Sci Fair Honorable Mention; Purdue Univ; Chemistry.

TROUT, DONNA; Franklin Community HS; Franklin, IN; 8/280 Chrs; Drl Tm; Capt Drm Bgl; Hon Rl; Jr NHS; NHS; Off Ade; Sch Mus; Stg Crw; Stu Cncl; Biology II Awd; Regional Sci Fair Honorable Mention; Purdue Univ; Vet.

TROUT, JAYME; Garaway HS; Sugarcreek, OH; Sec Frsh Cls; Cls Rep Soph Cls; Sec Jr Cls; Band; Cmnty Wkr; Yth Flsp; 4-H; Pep Clb; Letter Gym; Letter Trk;.

TROUT, MELANIE; Philo HS; Duncan Falls, OH; Cls Rep Soph Cls; Cl Rep Jr Cls; Cls Rep Sr Cls; Band; VP Chrs; Chrh Wkr; Girl Scts; Hon Rl; Sch Mus; Sch Pl; Ohio St Univ.

TROUT, MICHAEL V; Bishop Rosecrans HS; Zanesville, OH; Hon Rl; Rptr Yrbk; Rptr Sch Nwsp; Key Clb; Bsktbl; Letter Ftbl; Letter Trk; IM Sprt; Rotary Banquet & Club 78; All Oh Sports Banquet Track 78; Part In St Track Meets 78; Denison Univ; Hstry.

TROUT, TIMOTHY D; Nelsonville York HS; Nelsonville, OH; Am Leg Boys St; Aud/Vis; Hon Rl; NHS; Spn Clb; Spanish Hon Soc 79; Ohio Northern Univ; Pharm.

TROUTMAN, GREY; Indian Hill HS; Cincinnati, OH; Boy Scts; Chrh Wkr; Hon Rl; Mod UN; Sct Actv; Rptr Sch Nwsp; Sch Nwsp;.

TROUTWINE, TERRI; Arcanum Butler HS; Arcanum, OH; 12/99 Band; Chrs; Chrh Wkr; Girl Scts; Hon Rl; Off Ade; Sch Pl; Sct Actv; Stg Crw; Yth Flsp; Taylor Univ; Vocal Music.

TROUVE, THOMAS; Sault Area HS; Sault Ste Marie, MI; 3/306 Cl Rep Jr Cls; Hon Rl; Mdrgl; NHS; Sch Mus; Stu Cncl; Pres Drama Clb; Spn Clb; Letter Bsbl; Letter Ten; Univ.

TROVER, ANGELA; Greenbrier East HS; White Sulphur, WV; Hon Rl; Jr NHS; FBLA; Coll; Kindrgrdn Tchr.

TROXELL, LISA; Fairmont West HS; Kettering, OH; Treas Boy Scts; Letter Lbry Ade; Trs Frsh Cls; Socr; GAA; Tmr; College; Med.

TROXELL, MARK; East HS; Akron, OH; Boy Scts; Hon Rl; JA; Orch; Sch Mus; Sct Actv; Fr Clb; Univ; Theoretical Physics.

TROXELL, TONY G; Taylor HS; Kokomo, IN; Spn Clb; Indiana Univ; Bus.

TROY, JAQUELINE; Southfield HS; Southfield, MI; Band; Chrh Wkr; Girl Scts; College; Elec Tech.

TROYAN, TRACY; Loveland Hurst HS; Loveland, OH; 10/290 Cl Rep Jr Cls; Cls Rep Sr Cls; Am Leg Aux Girls St; Chrs; Girl Scts; Hon Rl; NHS; Stu Cncl; College; Pre Med.

TROYER, DON; S B John Adams HS; So Bend, IN; 73/395 Chrh Wkr; Hon Rl; Yth Flsp; Cit Awd; Goshen Coll; Pre Med.

TROYER, ERIC; Franklin Heights HS; Columbus, OH; 8/300 Am Leg Boys St; Cmnty Wkr; Hon Rl; Letter Glf; Letter Ten; Chess Tm 3 Yrs Cptn 78 76 79; In The Know Tm 1 Yr 76 77; Engr For A Day Progr Participant 78; Ohio St Univ; Civil Engr.

TROYER, JUDY; Mancelona HS; Mancelona, MI; 4/81 Pres Soph Cls; Trs Jr Cls; Band; Chrh Wkr; Hon Rl; NHS; Yth Flsp; Ferris State College; Sci.

TROYER, LINDA; Smithville HS; Smithville, OH; Fr Clb; Ger Clb; GAA; Univ; Law.

TROYER, MARLA; Goshen HS; Goshen, IN; 27/253 Trs Jr Cls; Trs Sr Cls; Chrh Wkr; FCA; 4-H; Bsktbl; Letter Trk; Letter Chrldng; Natl Merit Schl; Purdue Univ; Nursing.

TROYER, MICHAEL; Central HS; Evansville, IN; Sch Nwsp; Ten; Chrldng; College; Medicine.

TROYER, TERESA; Prarie Hts HS; La Grange, IN; 45/136 Chrs; Chrh Wkr; Stu Cncl; Crs Cntry; Trk; GAA; Scr Kpr; Tmr; Univ; Phys Ed.

TRUAN, JAMES A; Benjamin Franklin HS; Westland, MI; 20/644 Boy Scts; Hon Rl; NHS; Rptr Yrbk; Letter Ftbl; Letter Trk; Mich State Univ; Dent Med.

TRUAX, BRAD; Harrison HS; W Lafayette, IN; Band; Hon Rl; NHS; Letter Crs Cntry; Letter Wrstlng; Purdue Univ; Bio Chem.

TRUAX, DAWN; Ovid Elsie HS; Elsie, MI; 12/170 Band; Chrh Wkr; Hon Rl; Yth Flsp; 4-H; OEA; Trk; 4-H Awd; Usaf; Legal Services.

TRUAX, JACQUELINE; Loudonville HS; Loudonville, OH; Band; Hon Rl; Yth Flsp; 4-H; Spn Clb; Trk; Ohi State; Physical Ther.

TRUAX, JAMES; Shadyside HS; Shadyside, OH; Hon Rl; NHS; Stg Crw; Yth Flsp; Drama Clb; Ftbl; Gym; Trk; Scr Kpr; Tmr; NEDT Awd 76; Lab Asst Awd 79; Oh Test Of Schl Achvmnt In Eng Chem & Soc Studies; Nm Tech Hon Schlrshp; Ohio St Univ; Engr.

TRUAX, MONICA; Ovid Elsie HS; Elsie, MI; 1/180 Band; Chrh Wkr; Hon Rl; Yth Flsp; 4-H; Trk; Mi HS Forensic Assoc Cert Of Merit For Oratory 3rd Pl 79; Univ; Spec Educ.

TRUAX, PERIN; Leslie HS; Leslie, MI; Band; Hon Rl; 4-H; Crs Cntry; Letter Trk; Letter Wrstlng; 4-H Awd; Mich State Univ; Elec Engr.

TRUAX, SUZANNE; Dansville HS; Mason, MI; Chrs; Hon Rl; Yrbk; Michigan St Univ; Data Processing.

TRUCKEY, JUDY; Colon HS; Bronson, MI; 1/90 Trs Frsh Cls; Cls Rep Soph Cls; Sec Jr Cls; Sec Sr Cls; Girl Scts; Hon Rl; Lbry Ade; NHS; Stu Cncl; Fr Clb; Michigan St Univ; Bus Admin.

TRUCKEY, KATHLEEN; Mendon HS; Mendon, MI; VP Frsh Cls; VP Soph Cls; Sec Sr Cls; Hon Rl; Mod UN; Sch Pl; Stu Cncl; Letter Bsktbl; Letter Trk; Letter Chrldng; Kalamazoo Valley Comm Coll; Eng.

TRUCKLY, ROBIN; Heath HS; Heath, OH; Chrh Wkr; FCA; Hon Rl; Jr NHS; Red Cr Ade; Sch Pl; Yth Flsp; Pep Clb; Spn Clb; Bsbl; Univ Of Akron; Archt Engr.

TRUDEAU, CYNTHIA; Mason HS; Mason, MI; Chrh Wkr; Hon Rl; Hosp Ade; JA; Jr NHS; NHS; Stg Crw; Sec 4-H; Voice Dem Awd; Central Mich Univ.

TRUDEAU, MICHELLE; West Bloomfield HS; W Bloomfield, MI; NHS; Off Ade; 4-H; Pom Pon; Western Mic Univ; Acctg.

TRUDGES, JULIA; North Central HS; Indianapolis, IN; Band; Hon Rl; 4-H; Letter Swmmng; Letter Trk; Univ; Med.

TRUE, BRENDA; Bishop Flaget HS; Chillicothe, OH; Sec Soph Cls; Off Ade; Sch Mus; Sch Pl; Stu Cncl; Rptr Yrbk; Yrbk; Rptr Sch Nwsp; Sch Nwsp; Chrldng;.

TRUE, JANICE; Waldron HS; Waldron, IN; Cls Rep Frsh Cls; Band; Chrs; Drl Tm; Girl Scts; Sch Mus; 4-H; Pep Clb; Bsbl; Bsktbl; Bus Sch; Data Processing.

TRUE, WILLIAM; Shaker Hts HS; Shaker Hts, OH; Boy Scts; Orch; PAVAS; Socr; Boston Univ; Theater Arts.

TRUEBLOOD, JEFFRY D; Salem HS; Salem, IN; 43/183 Yrbk; Sci Clb; Glf; College; Meteorology.

TRUEBLOOD, THEISS; Salem HS; Salem, IN; Cls Rep Soph Cls; Band; Drl Tm; Hon Rl; JA; NHS; Orch; Sch Mus; Yth Flsp; Ed Yrbk; Coll; Comp Prog.

TRUELOVE, SHAWN; Saint Francis HS; Traverse, MI; 9/125 Boy Scts; NHS; Rptr Yrbk; Yrbk; Bsktbl; Letter Crs Cntry; Chrldng; Coach Actv; Mic Tech Univ; Engr.

TRUESDELL, DAVE; Plymouth Salem HS; Plymouth, MI; 31/531 Hon Rl; NHS; Letter Crs Cntry; Letter Trk; Univ Of Michigan; Engr.

TRUEX, ANDREA; Edgewood HS; Bloomington, IN; Am Leg Aux Girls St; Band; Chrs; Cmnty Wkr; Hon Rl; Jr NHS; Pres Stu Cncl; Drama Clb; 4-H; Spn Clb; Ind Univ Music Clinic 1977; Outstanding Bandsman & Algebra & Spanish Stdnt 1977; Superintendents Awd 1978; Univ.

TRUEX, TODD; Marion Harding HS; Marion, OH; Band; Boy Scts; Chrs; Sch Mus; Sch Pl; Letter Trk; Univ Of Cincinnati; Mech Engr.

TRUHOL, CHRISTINE; Grosse Pointe North HS; Grosse Pt Shrs, MI; Chrs; FCA; Hon Rl; NHS; Letter Swmmng; Trk; Tmr; Univ.

TRUMAN, CONNIE; Parkside HS; Jackson, MI; Chrh Wkr; Hon Rl; Off Ade; Yth Flsp; Jackson Cmnty Coll; Sec.

TRUMAN, JAMES; Kent Roosevelt HS; Kent, OH; 3/350 Hon Rl; Ger Clb; Sci Clb; Spn Clb; Socr; Univ; Law.

TRUMAN, TOM; Crown Point HS; Crown Point, IN; Beta Clb; Letter Ftbl; Purdue Univ; Acctg.

TRUMP, SCOTT; Holy Redeemer HS; Detroit, MI; 33/130 Hon Rl; Off Ade; Rptr Sch Nwsp; Ftbl; Capt Socr; Capt IM Sprt; Univ; Mech Drwng.

TRUNICK, DEBBIE; Roosevelt Wilson HS; Stonewood, WV; 14/139 Cl Rep Jr Cls; Hon Rl; Y-Teens; Yrbk; Fr Clb; Leo Clb; Davis & Elkins Coll; Interior Design.

TRUNK, CHRISTOPHER; St Edward HS; Westlake, OH; Boy Scts; Chrh Wkr; Hon Rl; Lit Mag; Mod UN; NHS; Sch Mus; Univ Of Notre Dame; Theol.

TRUSKE, CAREN; Northland HS; Columbus, OH; 5/402 Am Leg Aux Girls St; Hon Rl; NHS; Lat Clb; Bsktbl; GAA; Opt Clb Awd; Nc State Univ; Sociology.

TRUSKE, JAMES; Williamsburg HS; Williamsburg, OH; Yth Flsp; Sci Clb; Letter Ftbl; Letter Trk; Letter Wrstlng; Univ.

TRUSKOWSKI, SUZANNE; Woodhaven HS; Woodhaven, MI; 2/218 Band; Chrh Wkr; Cmnty Wkr; Girl Scts; Hon Rl; Jr NHS; NHS; Orch; Pol Wkr; Stu Cncl; Gregg Shorthand Awd 1978; Univ; Soc Work.

TRUSLER, LANCE; Staunton HS; Staunton, IN; 15/46 Sch Nwsp; Letter Trk;.

TRUSSELL, BETH; Conotton Valley Jr Sr HS; Bowerston, OH; Am Leg Aux Girls St; Hon Rl; Hosp Ade; FHA; Pep Clb; Chrldng; Ohio St Univ; RN.

TRUXTON, ROBERT; Evart HS; Marion, MI; 30/110 Hon Rl; Sch Pl; Stg Crw; Sprt Ed Sch Nwsp; 4-H; VP FFA; Letter Bsbl; Letter Ftbl; Ferris State College; Tchr.

TRYBAN, MARIANNE; Cheboygan Catholic HS; Cheboygan, MI; 4/33 Sec Soph Cls; Trs Soph Cls; Sec Jr Cls; Trs Jr Cls; Trs Sr Cls; Chrh Wkr; Hon Rl; Sch Mus; Fer State College; Acctg.

TRYON, KATHY; Perry HS; Navarre, OH; 2/480 Band; Chrh Wkr; Girl Scts; Hon Rl; Jr NHS; NHS; Orch; Natl Merit Ltr; 1st Pl In Ohio Test Of Schlstc Ach Eng; Coll; Math.

TRZASKOWSKI, JACQUELINE R; Whitmer HS; Toledo, OH; 26/910 Girl Scts; Hon Rl; Orch; Rptr Yrbk; Yrbk; Pep Clb; Spn Clb; Chrldng; PPFtbl; Business Schl; Court Reporter.

TRZECIAK, GLENN; Forest Park HS; Crystal Falls, MI; 5/90 Val; Boy Scts; Chrh Wkr; Hon Rl; College.

TSCHANNEN, REBECCA; Bellmont HS; Decatur, IN; 79/247 Chrs; Chrh Wkr; Hosp Ade; Yth Flsp; Univ.

TSCHAPPAT, ELAINE; Bellaire HS; Bellaire, OH; 16/238 Hon Rl; NHS; Y-Teens; Fr Clb; Treas FTA; Pep Clb; Natl Merit SF; Belmont Tech College; Rn.

TSCHERNE, KAREN; Cardinal Stritch HS; Toledo, OH; Cmnty Wkr; Hon Rl; Hosp Ade; Jr NHS; NHS; Spn Clb; Bsbl; Bsktbl; Coll; Nursing.

TSENG, SUE; Chaney HS; Youngstown, OH; Hon Rl; Off Ade; Pep Clb; Bsktbl; Natl Merit Ltr; Youngstown State Univ; Architectual.

TSIVITSE, PAUL; Solon HS; Solon, OH; Cls Rep Frsh Cls; Hon Rl; Stu Cncl; Rptr Sch Nwsp; OEA; Ftbl; Swmmng; Trk; Wrstlng; IM Sprt; Univ; Elec Engr.

TSOLAINOS, NICK; Charles F Brush HS; Lyndhurst, OH; Band; Chrh Wkr; Cmnty Wkr; Orch; Sch Mus; Conservatory; Music.

TUBA, NANCY; Allen Park HS; Allen Pk, MI; Hon Rl; Jr NHS; Yth Flsp; Letter Swmmng; PPFtbl; Scr Kpr; Tmr; Univ.

TUBBS, ERNEST C; Oak Hill HS; Oak Hill, WV; Band; Chrh Wkr; Hon Rl; NHS; Sch Nwsp; Sci Clb; Sci Awd 78; 3rd Pl In St Essay Contst 78; Ohio Valley Coll; Psych.

TUCCI, DENISE; Malvern HS; Malvern, OH; Trs Frsh Cls; Trs Soph Cls; Sec Jr Cls; Cls Rep Sr Cls; Chrs; Girl Scts; Lbry Ade; Sch Mus; Stu Cncl; Yrbk; Marietta Coll; Phys Ed.

TUCK, ERIC; Cardinal Stritch HS; Toledo, OH; Boy Scts; Hon Rl; Jr NHS; Pres NHS; Sch Mus; Fr Clb; Pep Clb; Letter Crs Cntry; Letter Trk; Wrstlng; Young Life Youth Organztn 78 79; Natl Hon Soc Pres 79; Right To Life Group; JV Cross Cntry Champ 77; Univ.

TUCKER, AMY; Rutherford B Hayes HS; Delawre, OH; AFS; Hon Rl; JA; Y-Teens; Sch Nwsp; Key Clb; Gym; Mgrs; Scr Kpr; Ohio Wesleyan Univ; Math.

TUCKER, ANN; Niles HS; Niles, MI; 62/388 Band; Hon Rl; NHS; Orch; Sch Mus; 4-H; Treas Ger Clb; Pep Clb; Univ Of Mic; Sci.

TUCKER, BRAD; Cloverdale HS; Cloverdale, IN; 7/88 FCA; Hon Rl; NHS; Stu Cncl; Fr Clb; Letter Bsktbl; Letter Crs Cntry; Letter Trk; Univ.

TUCKER, CARI; Central HS; Grand Rapids, MI; Chrs; Girl Scts; Hon Rl; Hosp Ade; JA; Jr NHS; NHS; Off Ade; Sch Mus; Sct Actv; Jr Coll; Natural Sci.

TUCKER, CARLA; Kyger Creek HS; Cheshire, OH; Hon Rl; Off Ade; Yrbk; Sch Nwsp; 4-H; Fr Clb; FHA; VP Keyettes; Scr Kpr; Business.

TUCKER, DARRELL; Middletown HS; Middletown, OH; Chrs; Hon Rl; Fr Clb; Ohio St Univ; Med.

TUCKER, DARREN; New Palestine HS; New Palestine, IN; 66/225 Cls Rep Sr Cls; Chrh Wkr; FCA; Hon Rl; Sprt Ed Yrbk; Rptr Sch Nwsp; Fr Clb; Bsktbl; Capt Ftbl; Glf; Indiana St Univ; Graphic Arts.

TUCKER, DAVID; Harbor HS; Ashtabula, OH; 39/197 AFS; Sch Mus; Sch Pl; Stg Crw; Yth Flsp; Drama Clb; Ger Clb; Letter Ftbl; Ten; Trk; College; Chem Engr.

TUCKER, DEBBIE; Washington HS; E Chicago, IN; 25/250 Chrs; Hon Rl; NHS; Cit Awd;.

TUCKER, ELLEN; Andrean HS; Merrillville, IN; Band; Chrs; Sch Mus; Sch Pl; Stg Crw; Drama Clb; GAA; PPFtbl; Miss Petite Bty Awd Miss Indiana Teenager Pageant; Butler Univ; Dance.

TUCKER, HARRIETT; Tiffin Columbian HS; Tiffin, OH; Chrs; Chrh Wkr; Hon Rl; Lbry Ade; Yrbk; FHA; Spn Clb; Letter Trk; IM Sprt; Bowling Green Univ; Parol Officer.

TUCKER, JONEA; Southern Wells HS; Montpelier, IN; Cls Rep Sr Cls; Band; Chrs; Hon Rl; Stu Cncl; FFA; FHA; Pep Clb; Letter Gym; Letter Trk; Purdue Univ; Forestry.

TUCKER, KATHLEEN; Whitmer HS; Toledo, OH; Hon Rl; Fr Clb; PPFtbl; Umiv Of Toledo; Nurse.

TUCKER, LESLIE; Strongsville Sr HS; Strongsville, OH; Cls Rep Frsh Cls; Cls Rep Soph Cls; Hon Rl; Stu Cncl; Yrbk; Fr Clb; Bsktbl; Trk; Capt Chrldng; Mgrs; Miss Frsh Cls 77; Homecoming Ct 77; Higbees Teen Bd 79; Univ.

TUCKER, LISA; Frankfort HS; Ridgeley, WV; AFS; Am Leg Aux Girls St; Hon Rl; NHS; VP Stu Cncl; Ten; Trk; Capt Chrldng; Fairmont Univ.

TUCKER, MIRIAM; Grandview Heights HS; Columbus, OH; 10/126 Cmp Fr Grls; Chrs; Hon Rl; JA; Jr NHS; Sch Pl; Stg Crw; Rptr Sch Nwsp; Drama Clb; Fr Clb; Ohio St Univ; Vocal Music.

TUCKER, MIRIAM A; Grandview Hgts HS; Columbus, OH; 10/120 Cmp Fr Grls; Chrs; Chrh Wkr; Hon Rl; JA; Jr NHS; Sch Pl; Stg Crw; Rptr Sch Nwsp; Fr Clb; Ohio St Univ; French.

TUCKER, SUZETTA; Holton HS; Holton, MI; Hon Rl; Lit Mag; Off Ade; Sch Nwsp; St Competitive Schlrshp 79; Grand Valley St Univ; Author.

TUCKER, THOMAS; Madison Comp HS; Mansfield, OH; Band; Cmnty Wkr; Hon Rl; Lbry Ade; NHS; Key Clb; Spn Clb; Letter Glf; Letter Wrstlng; IM Sprt; Ashland Coll; Acctg.

TUCKER, TRACY; South Ripley Jr Sr HS; Holton, IN; Pres Soph Cls; Cls Rep Soph Cls; Pres Jr Cls; Cl Rep Jr Cls; Hon Rl; Stu Cncl; Yth Flsp; Yrbk; Spn Clb; Capt Crs Cntry; Univ; Counseling.

TUCKER, WILLIAM; Frankenmuth HS; Frankenmuth, MI; Cl Rep Jr Cls; Pres Sr Cls; Cls Rep Sr Cls; Band; Chrs; Chrh Wkr; FCA; Hon Rl; NHS; Sch Mus; Concordia Teachers Coll; Theology.

TUCKERMAN, ANN M; Pike Delta York Sr HS; Delta, OH; 13/145 Trs Soph Cls; Sec Jr Cls; Chrh Wkr; NHS; Yth Flsp; Crs Cntry; Northwest Tech Coll; Forestry.

TUCKERMAN, CINDY; Pike Delta York Sr HS; Delta, OH; Rptr Sch Nwsp; 4-H; Mat Maids; Cit Awd; Univ; Comp Tech.

TUCKY, DAVID; Parma HS; Parma, OH; Band; Orch; Ohi State Univ; Jrnlsm.

TUDOR, GREGORY; Eminence Consolidated HS; Monrovia, IN; Cls Rep Frsh Cls; Cl Rep Jr Cls; Am Leg Boys St; Chrh Wkr; Hon Rl; NHS; Yrbk; 4-H; Fr Clb; Sci Clb; Univ; Comp Sci.

TUDOR, TINA; Goshen HS; Goshen, OH; 21/250 Band; Chrh Wkr; Drm Mjrt; Hosp Ade; Sch Mus; Yth Flsp; Trk; Capt Chrldng; Mat Maids; Scr Kpr; Univ; Nurse.

TUFEKCIOGLU, EMRE D; Culver Military Academy; Culver, IN; Aud/Vis; Band; Pol Wkr; ROTC; Sch Mus; Sch Nwsp; Sci Clb; Cit Awd; Natl Merit Ltr; Tulane Univ; Bio Med Engr.

TUFF, CYNTHIA; Elkhart Memorial HS; Elkhart, IN; Cls Rep Frsh Cls; Cls Rep Soph Cls; Cl Rep Jr Cls; Cls Rep Sr Cls; Chrs; Pres Chrh Wkr; Cmnty Wkr; Hon Rl; NHS; Pol Wkr; Hillsdale Coll; Busns Admin.

TUGAOEN, JEANNE; Normandy HS; Parma, OH; 34/600 Drl Tm; Hon Rl; Spn Clb; IM Sprt; Ohio St Univ; Med.

TUGGLE, ERWIN; Southwestern HS; Detroit, MI; 19/207 Cmnty Wkr; Drl Tm; FCA; Hon Rl; Bsbl; Bsktbl; Ftbl; Trk; Am Leg Awd; Cit Awd; Grambling State Univ.

TUINSTRA, CORDELIA; Zeeland HS; Hudsonville, MI; 1/180 Am Leg Aux Girls St; Hon Rl; Jr NHS; Mod UN; Pres 4-H; Ger Clb; Letter Trk; 4-H Awd; College; Vet.

TULENKO JR, JOHN; Weir HS; Weirton, WV; Hon Rl; NHS; Key Clb; Crs Cntry; Letter Ten; Trk; Grand Prize Reg Sci & Engr Fiar All Exp Paid Trip To ISEF 79; St Coll Chi Beta Awd; 1st Pl Bio Div 79; West Liberty St Coll; Chem.

TULJAK, MARIA; Cleveland Central Cath HS; Cleveland, OH; Drl Tm; Hon Rl; NHS; Chrldng; Univ.

TULLIS, BILLIE K; Leetonia HS; Washingtonville, OH; Chrh Wkr; Hon Rl; Stg Crw; Yth Flsp; Pep Clb; Mat Maids; Youngstown St Univ; Busns Mgmt.

TULLIS, KELLEE; Harry S Truman HS; Taylor, MI; Band; Orch; College; Nursing.

TULLOH, BRIAN; Shelbyville Sr HS; Shelbyville, IN; 1/287 Pres Soph Cls; Pres Jr Cls; Am Leg Boys St; FCA; NHS; Pres Stu Cncl; Rptr Sch Nwsp; Lat Clb; Pres Sci Clb; Letter Ftbl; Univ; Indus Engr.

TULLY, DONNA; Oak Hill HS; Oak Hill, WV; 24/175 Cl Rep Jr Cls; Band; Chrh Wkr; Cmnty Wkr; Hon Rl; Off Ade; VP Y-Teens; Rptr Yrbk; VP Fr Clb; Marshall Univ; French Educ.

TULLY, MATT; Tuslaw HS; Massillon, OH; Boy Scts; Hon Rl; FBLA; Stark Teach; Drafting.

TULLY, SHEILA; Lawrence Central HS; Indianapolis, IN; 35/360 VP Sr Cls; Quill & Scroll; Stu Cncl; Ed Yrbk; PPFtbl; Ind Univ; Journalism.

TUMA, JOSEPH; St Johns HS; Toledo, OH; 46/241 Chrh Wkr; Cmnty Wkr; FCA; Hon Rl; Hosp Ade; Red Cr Ade; Fr Clb; Coach Actv; IM Sprt; Univ; Pre Dent.

TUMEO II, RAYMOND P; Johnstown Monroe HS; Johnstown, OH; 4/285 Band; Boy Scts; Hon Rl; Sch Pl; Sct Actv; Drama Clb; Sci Clb; Spn Clb; California Tech Univ; Nuclear Chem.

TUNANIDIS, BARBARA; Weir HS; New Cumberland, WV; 59/400 Hon Rl; NHS; Y-Teens; 4-H; Fr Clb; Pep Clb; Sci Clb; 4-H Awd; West Virginia Univ; Chem.

TUNE, CAMMY; Morrice HS; Morrice, MI; Band; Hon Rl; NHS; College.

TUNESI, SALLY; St Clement HS; Detroit, MI; Cl Rep Jr Cls; Sal; Hon Rl; NHS; Stu Cncl; Civ Clb; Capt Chrldng; VP GAA; Pres Awd; College; Bus.

TUOMIKOSKI, SANDRA; Calumet HS; Calumet, MI; 18/143 Chrh Wkr; Hon Rl; Hosp Ade; NHS; ROTC; Sch Pl; Sec Yth Flsp; Rptr Yrbk; Pres FNA; Gogebic Community College; Courtrepo.

TURAN, CHERYL; Manistique HS; Manistique, MI; Drl Tm; Girl Scts; Hon Rl; Sct Actv; 4-H; FHA; Bsktbl; Trk; IM Sprt; 4-H Awd; Northern Michigan Univ; Acctg.

TURANCHIK, LORI; Meadowbrook HS; Pleasant Cy, OH; 23/160 Trs Jr Cls; Cl Rep Jr Cls; Band; Hon Rl; Hosp Ade; Lbry Ade; Sec NHS; Stu Cncl; Yrbk; 4-H; Univ; Nursing.

TURCHI, PAUL; Flint Holy Rosary HS; Flint, MI; Boy Scts; Sch Pl; Letter Bsbl; Letter Ftbl; Trk; Cit Awd; Michigan Tech Univ; Engr.

TURCKES, JANET; Archbishop Alter HS; Dayton, OH; 110/350 Girl Scts; Bsktbl; Chrldng; GAA; Univ Of Dayton.

TURCOTT, DARYL; Adelphian Acad; Oxford, MI; 4/49 Band; Hon Rl; Yrbk; Ed Sch Nwsp; Natl Merit Ltr; Andrews Univ; Biology.

TUREK, JAMES; Howland HS; Warren, OH; 19/430 Cl Rep Jr Cls; VP Sr Cls; Yrbk; IM Sprt; Natl Merit SF; Univ Of Cincinnati; Elec Engr.

TUREK, PETER J; Big Bay De Noc HS; Rapid River, MI; Band; Chrh Wkr; Hon Rl; Sch Mus; 4-H; OEA; Bsbl; Bsktbl; Letter Ftbl; Mgrs; Great Lakes Maritime Acad; Engr.

TURK, MICHELLE; St Mary Academy; Milan, MI; Cmnty Wkr; Debate Tm; Mod UN; Yrbk; 4-H; Key Clb; Pep Clb; Sci Clb; Letter Trk; 4-H Awd; St Of Mi Tuition Grant 79; 4 Yr Perfct Attndnc 79; Siena Hts Coll; Art.

TURKAL, JENNIFER; Eastwood HS; Pemberville, OH; 38/185 FCA; Lbry Ade; Off Ade; FHA; Ger Clb; Crs Cntry; Trk; Mgrs; Girls State CC; Winner Of SLL; Holds All Grls Eastwood CC Recrds; Bowling Green State Univ; Accounting.

TURKOVICH, MATTHEW; Lincoln HS; Shinnston, WV; Am Leg Boys St; Boy Scts; Chrh Wkr; Hon Rl; Sct Actv; Yth Flsp; Spn Clb; Glf; Art Awd 77; Fairmont St Univ; Aviation.

TURLEY, DEBBIE; Wintersville HS; Bloomingdale, OH; Spn Clb; Bsktbl; GAA; Tech; Photography.

TURLEY, ROBERT; Inkster HS; Inkster, MI; 3/200 Band; Chrh Wkr; Hon Rl; ROTC; Stg Crw; OEA; Berklee College Of Music; Musician.

TURNBAUGH, MIKE; Reitz Memorial HS; Evansville, IN; Bsktbl; Letter Ftbl; Letter Trk; IM Sprt; College; Forestry.

TURNBULL, JANE; Wirt County HS; Palestine, WV; 2/107 Trs Sr Cls; Sal; Band; Hon Rl; Pres NHS; VP Quill & Scroll; Ed Yrbk; 4-H; Pep Clb; Am Leg Awd; Berea Coll; Nursing.

TURNBULL, LISA; Wellsville HS; Wellsville, OH; 10/150 Hon Rl; NHS; Y-Teens; FNA; Pep Clb; Am Leg Awd; Walsh College; Dentist.

TURNBULL, MARK; Hale Area HS; Hale, MI; Band; Boy Scts; Chrh Wkr; Sch Nwsp; Letter Bsbl; Letter Bsktbl; Letter Ftbl; Letter Trk; Olivet Nazarene College.

TURNBULL, NANCY; Huntington HS; Huntington, WV; 40/275 Chrh Wkr; Hon Rl; NHS; Red Cr Ade; Lat Clb; Pep Clb; Gym; Chrldng; IM Sprt; Marshall Univ; Bus Mgmt.

TURNBULL, THOMAS; High School; Livonia, MI; Chrh Wkr; IM Sprt; Wayne State Univ; Bio.

TURNBULL, TODD; Brookhaven HS; Columbus, OH; 16/402 Band; Hon Rl; Jr NHS; NHS; Ohio St Univ; Elec Engr.

TURNER, ALFREDA; Mumford HS; Detroit, MI; VP Jr Cls; Hon Rl; NHS; Off Ade; Yth Flsp; Fr Clb; Cit Awd; Opt Clb Awd; Pres Of Natl Honor Society; Soc Dstngshd Amer HS Stu; Univ Of Michigan; Medicine.

TURNER, ANTHONY; Montpelier HS; Montplier, OH; 16/104 Trk; Univ.

TURNER, BARBARA; Griffith HS; Griffith, IN; 3/281 Hon Rl; Sec Jr NHS; NHS; Stu Cncl; Rptr Sch Nwsp; Pep Clb; GAA; Ball St Univ Journalism Workshop; Purdue Univ; Nursing.

TURNER, BONNIE; Austin HS; Austin, IN; 2/100 Sec Frsh Cls; Hon Rl; FTA; Pep Clb; Pres Spn Clb; Letter Ten; Univ Of Kentucky; Law.

TURNER, BRIAN; Chesterton HS; Valpairiso, IN; IM Sprt; Valparaiso Tech Schl; Comp Progr.

TURNER, CARMA; Southeastern HS; Londonderry, OH; Band; Chrs; Hon Rl; Jr NHS; NHS; Sch Pl; Rptr Yrbk; Rptr Sch Nwsp; FHA; Letter Bsktbl; Sftbll Letter 76; Intnsv Offc Educ Awrd 79; Bus.

TURNER, CAROL; Cleveland Ctrl Catholic HS; Cleveland, OH; Cls Rep Frsh Cls; Cls Rep Soph Cls; Cl Rep Jr Cls; Stu Cncl; Drama Clb; Chrldng; College; Lawyer.

TURNER, CELESTE; Central HS; Detroit, MI; Pres JA; Sec Off Ade; Sec DECA; Bus School; Secretarial.

TURNER, CHARLES; Greenfield Central HS; Greenfield, IN; 89/300 4-H; Pres FFA; 4-H Awd; Purdue Univ; Vet Med.

TURNER, CHARLIE; Greenfield Central HS; Greenfield, IN; Pres 4-H; Pres FFA; 4-H Awd; St FFA Convention Elec Proficiency; Mech Demonstration Wash Ldrshp Conference; Star Greenhand Ag Mech; Purdue Univ; Vet.

TURNER, DOLORES; Hazel Park HS; Hazel Park, MI; 21/342 Chrh Wkr; Hon Rl; Lbry Ade; NHS; Spn Clb; Letter Gym; Michigan St; Math.

TURNER, GREGG; Madison Comp HS; Mansfield, OH; Cmnty Wkr; Spn Clb; IM Sprt; Univ; Sci.

TURNER, GREGORY G; Woodrow Wilson HS; Beckley, WV; Cls Rep Frsh Cls; Pres Soph Cls; Cls Rep Soph Cls; Cl Rep Jr Cls; Cls Rep Sr Cls; Cls Rep Sr Cls; Am Leg Boys St; Band; Boy Scts; Chrh Wkr; Conservtn Club Pres Of Club Vc Pres Of St Org; Conservtn Camp George C Sharpe & Jr Leader Awds; Univ; Med.

TURNER, JACQUELINE K; Buckeye North HS; Brilliant, OH; 11/119 Sec Soph Cls; Hst Jr Cls; Hon Rl; NHS; Stg Crw; Sch Nwsp; Drama Clb; OEA; Pep Clb; Letter Bsbl; Secretary.

TURNER, JACQUELYN A; Fairfield Union HS; Pleasantville, OH; 16/158 Band; Drl Tm; Hon Rl; Yth Flsp; FTA; Sci Clb; Spn Clb; College; Sociology.

TURNER, JACQUELYN; Cass Tech HS; Detroit, MI; Chrs; Chrh Wkr; Hon Rl; Jr NHS; FHA; Marygrove Coll; Busns Mgmt.

TURNER, JERRY; Kenton HS; Kenton, OH; Hon Rl; 4-H; FFA; OSU; Farm Mgmt.

TURNER, JOHN; Ross HS; Hamilton, OH; 93/210 Pres Debate Tm; Hon Rl; Pres Natl Forn Lg; IM Sprt; College; Pol Sci.

TURNER, JUANITA; Central HS; Detroit, MI; Band; Chrh Wkr; Hon Rl; Jr NHS; Sch Mus; Stu Cncl; Sch Nwsp; FNA; Pep Clb; Spn Clb; Grambling Univ; Nursing.

TURNER, JUANITA; Edward Drummon Libbey HS; Toledo, OH; Hon Rl; Rptr Sch Nwsp; FHA; Capt Bsktbl; Letter Trk; Mat Maids; Scr Kpr; College; Psychology.

TURNER, KATHRYN; John Marshall HS; Indianapolis, IN; 2/580 NHS; Stu Cncl; Fr Clb; Pres Key Clb; Sci Clb; Ten; Rotary Awd; Purdue Univ; Eng.

TURNER, KELLIE; West Side Sr HS; Gary, IN; Band; Girl Scts; Hon Rl; PAVAS; Sch Mus; Sct Actv; Scr Kpr; Tmr; Spellman Coll; Bus.

TURNER, LA REISA; Highland Park Cmnty HS; Highland Park, MI; Band; Chrh Wkr; Drl Tm; Hon Rl; NHS; Orch; ROTC; Am Leg Awd; Univ; Music.

TURNER, LYNN; Franklin HS; Franklin, OH; Drl Tm; Hon Rl; JA; Ed Sch Nwsp; Sec DECA; Fr Clb; Pep Clb; GAA; Cit Awd; JA Awd; Bauder Univ; Model.

TURNER, MARITTA L; Northern Sr HS; Detroit, MI; Cls Rep Frsh Cls; Cls Rep Soph Cls; Cl Rep Jr Cls; Drl Tm; Hon Rl; Hosp Ade; Jr NHS; NHS; Off Ade; Stu Cncl; Natl Hnr Soc; Hospital Aide; Class Rep; Michigan Univ; Nursing.

TURNER, MICHAEL D; Richmond HS; Richmond, IN; 1/600 Cl Rep Jr Cls; Val; Pres Band; NHS; Letter Wrstlng; Elk Awd; JETS Awd; Natl Merit Schl; Indiana Univ; Pre Law.

TURNER, NANCY; De Vilbiss HS; Galesburg, MI; 44/360 Hon Rl; Fr Clb; Univ Of Michigan; Pre Med.

TURNER, NANCY; Greenville Sr HS; New Madison, OH; Chrs; Lbry Ade; Sch Mus; 4-H; Fr Clb; IM Sprt; Finlst For Miss United Teenager 78; Univ; Phys Educ.

TURNER, P; Central Baptist HS; Cincinnati, OH; Bsbl; Bsktbl; Socr; 4-H Awd; College.

TURNER, PAMELA; Greenon HS; Springfield, OH; Girl Scts; Hon Rl; Sct Actv; 4-H; Fr Clb; FHA; Ger Clb; GAA; IM Sprt; 4-H Awd; Military.

TURNER, PAMELA; Brookville HS; Harrison, OH; 11/200 Chrh Wkr; Hon Rl; Lbry Ade; NHS; Off Ade; Yrbk; Ger Clb; GAA; Mt St Joseph Coll; Chem.

TURNER, PAUL; Adrian HS; Adrian, MI; Band; Hon Rl; Adrian Coll; Sci.

TURNER, RICHARD A; Massillon Perry HS; Massillon, OH; Am Leg Boys St; Chrs; Chrh Wkr; Debate Tm; Hon Rl; Natl Forn Lg; NHS; Pol Wkr; Quill & Scroll; Sch Mus; Bowling Green St Univ; Busns Admin.

TURNER, STEPHANIE; Parkersburg HS; Vienna, WV; Chrh Wkr; Cmnty Wkr; FCA; Girl Scts; Hon Rl; Hosp Ade; Sct Actv; Yth Flsp; Swmmng; Chrldng; Fairmont St Coll; Vet Med Tech.

TURNER, STEVE; Upper Arlington HS; Columbus, OH; Boy Scts; JA; Yth Flsp; Lat Clb; Spn Clb; College; Comp Sci.

TURNER, STEWART; Mississinewa HS; Jonesboro, IN; Col St Univ; Forestry.

TURNER, SUSAN ELAINE; Laurel HS; Laurel, IN; 6/29 Chrh Wkr; Hon Rl; Jr NHS; NHS; Yth Flsp; Rptr Sch Nwsp; Sch Nwsp; Pep Clb; Spn Clb; VP Of Chrch Yth Grp 1978; Schlrshp To John Herron Art Schl 1977; Schl Mascot 1978; Univ; Med.

TURNER, SYBIL M; Henry Ford HS; Detroit, MI; Cls Rep Frsh Cls; Chrs; Hon Rl; Jr NHS; NHS; Off Ade; Sch Mus; Sch Pl; Sdlty; Yth Flsp; Schlrshp & English; Social Studies & Academic Games Awd; Spirit Of Detroit Awd; Michigan St Univ; Medicine.

TURNER, THERESA; Gladwin HS; Gladwin, MI; 35/180 Girl Scts; Hon Rl; Jr NHS; Rptr Sch Nwsp; Civ Clb; Letter Bsktbl; Central Mic Univ; Recreational Ther.

TURNER, THOMAS; Pontiac Central HS; Pontiac, MI; Band; Boy Scts; Hon Rl; JA; Sct Actv; Boys Clb Am; Bsbl; IM Sprt; Michigan St Univ; Law.

TURNER, THOMAS L; Pontiac Central HS; Pontiac, MI; Band; Boy Scts; Hon Rl; JA; Boys Clb Am; Pep Clb; Bsbl; IM Sprt; College; Law.

TURNER, TONIA; Marian HS; Cincinnati, OH; Cl Rep Jr Cls; Cls Rep Sr Cls; FHA; Psych.

TURNER, VERONICA A; Linden Mc Kinley HS; Columbus, OH; Pres Frsh Cls; Sec Frsh Cls; Cls Rep Frsh Cls; Cls Rep Soph Cls; Capt Drl Tm; Hon Rl; Jr NHS; NHS; Sch Mus; Sch Pl; Capital Univ.

TURNER, Y; Catholic Central HS; Steubenvll, OH; 132/204 Hon Rl; FTA; College; Comp Tech.

TURNER, YVONNE; Highland Park Cmnty HS; Highland Pk, MI; Chrs; Chrh Wkr; Lbry Ade; NHS; Sch Mus; OEA; Coll.

TURNER JR, ROBERT; Ontario HS; Msnfld, OH; 25/178 Cls Rep Frsh Cls; Band; Boy Scts; Cmnty Wkr; Hon Rl; Orch; Sch Mus; Sct Actv; Stu Cncl; Sch Nwsp; Akron Univ; Engr.

TURNEUR, MYRA; South HS; Akron, OH; Off Ade; Y-Teens; Akron Univ; Law.

TURNEY, CINDY; Mt Notre Dame HS; Cincinnati, OH; 30/175 Hon Rl; Letter Bsbl; Letter Bsktbl; Coach Actv; GAA; Georgetown Coll; Phys Ed.

TURNWALD, CHARLES; Ottoville Local HS; Cloverdale, OH; Pres Frsh Cls; Hon Rl; Jr NHS; NHS; Letter Bsbl; Letter Bsktbl; Univ.

TURNWALD, JANE; Ottoville Local School; Delphos, OH; Hon Rl; Lbry Ade; 4-H; FHA; Coach Actv; Scr Kpr; Tmr; 4-H Awd; Bookkeeping.

TURNWALD, NANCY; Ottoville Local HS; Ft Jennings, OH; Trs Sr Cls; Girl Scts; Hon Rl; Yrbk; Ed Sch Nwsp; Rptr Sch Nwsp; 4-H; Bsktbl; Voice Dem Awd; College; Ohio State Univ.

TURNWALD, NANCY; Ottoville Local Schl; Fort Jennings, OH; Trs Sr Cls; Cmnty Wkr; Hon Rl; JA; NHS; Rptr Sch Nwsp; 4-H; Fr Clb; Capt Bsktbl; IM Sprt; Ohio St Univ.

TUROCZY, MARY A; Flemington HS; Bridgeport, WV; VP Jr Cls; Sec Sr Cls; Band; NHS; FTA; Pep Clb; IM Sprt; Mgrs; All St Band 76 78; Fairmont St Coll; Acctg.

TURON, MARY; Farmington Local HS; W Farmington, OH; 1/22 Sec Soph Cls; Val; Am Leg Aux Girls St; Pres Band; Chrh Wkr; Girl Scts; Hon Rl; Hosp Ade; Sec NHS; Off Ade; Whos Who In Amer Stdnt 77 & 78; Whos Who In Music 1 Chair Of Amer 77 & 78; Oh Mert Schlshp 79; Hiram Coll; Dietetics.

TURPIN, BAHNI; Roeper City & Country HS; Southfield, MI; Chrs; Hon Rl; Natl Forn Lg; Orch; Sch Mus; Sch Pl; Stu Cncl; Drama Clb; Howard Univ; Actress.

TURPIN, JACKIE; Eaton HS; Eaton, OH; 13/168 Band; Chrs; Hon Rl; NHS; Fr Clb; GAA; PPFtbl; College.

TURPIN, KEVIN R; Central HS; Bloomfield, IN; 2/50 VP Sr Cls; Am Leg Boys St; Chrh Wkr; Hon Rl; NHS; Treas FFA; Spn Clb; Letter Bsbl; Letter Bsktbl; Letter Crs Cntry; I T T Tech Schl; Elec Engr.

TURPIN, TINA; Waldron HS; Shelbyville, IN; Chrs; Hon Rl; NHS; FHA; Bsktbl; GAA;.

TURRILL, DEBRA; Alexander HS; Albany, OH; Pres Frsh Cls; Hon Rl; NHS; Bsbl; Bsktbl; GAA; Mgrs; Scr Kpr; Bus.

TURSKE, SCOTT; Alpena HS; Alpena, MI; Letter Bsbl; Mi Comptty Schshp Awd 79; Athltc Schslp Bsbl 79; Acad Awd In Germn Hist 79; C S Mott Cmnty Coll; Data Proc.

TUSHMAN, DAVID; Southfield Sr HS; Southfield, MI; VP Frsh Cls; Cls Rep Frsh Cls; Pres Soph Cls; Cls Rep Soph Cls; Cl Rep Jr Cls; Cls Rep Sr Cls; Band; Hon Rl; Orch; Sch Mus; Univ; Chem Engr.

TUSON, MICHELLE; Holly HS; Davisburg, MI; 10/300 Band; Cmp Fr Grls; Chrs; Chrh Wkr; Cmnty Wkr; Hon Rl; Lbry Ade; NHS; Sci Clb; Spn Clb; Oakland Univ; Pre Med.

TUSSEL, DANE; Nordonia HS; Macedonia, OH; Hon Rl; Letter Wrstlng; Pres Awd; Coll.

TUSSING, DEANA; Watkins Memorial HS; Baltimore, OH; Cl Rep Jr Cls; Band; Chrs; Hon Rl; Jr NHS; NHS; Orch; Stu Cncl; Rptr Yrbk; Trk; Univ; Fshn Mdse.

TUSSING, WHIT; Sheridan HS; Glenford, OH; 41/186 Chrs; Hon Rl; Ed Yrbk; Sprt Ed Yrbk; Rptr Yrbk; Rptr Sch Nwsp; Sch Nwsp; Miami Univ; Archt.

TUSTIN, PHILIP; Frontier HS; New Matamoras, OH; 7/122 Hon Rl; NHS; Sch Pl; Am Leg Awd; Wash Tech Coll; Elec Eng.

TUTEN, MIKE; Fort Frye HS; Beverly, OH; Cls Rep Frsh Cls; Pres Sr Cls; Am Leg Boys St; Hon Rl; Stu Cncl; Letter Crs Cntry; Letter Trk; Univ; Engr.

TUTTERROW, MURVEL A; Hagerstown Jr Sr HS; Economy, IN; 3/150 Chrh Wkr; Hon Rl; NHS; Rptr Yrbk; Fr Clb; FFA; Sci Clb; Mgrs; Purdue Univ; Agri Sci.

TUTTLE, DAVID; Indianapolis Baptist HS; Indianapolis, IN; VP Sr Cls; Am Leg Boys St; Aud/Vis; Chrh Wkr; Lit Mag; Pol Wkr; Stu Cncl; Yth Flsp; Rptr Yrbk; Sch Nwsp; Grace Coll; Soc Stud Tchr.

TUTTLE, JODI L; Delta HS; Muncie, IN; 1/300 Am Leg Aux Girls St; Hon Rl; Jr NHS; Lbry Ade; Pres NHS; Sci Clb; Spn Clb; Bsktbl; IM Sprt; Mgrs; Regional Sci Fair Awd Fresh 76; Indiana Univ; Criminal Lawyer.

TUTTLE, LAURIE; Reeths Puffer HS; Muskegon, MI; 15/281 VP Soph Cls; VP Jr Cls; NHS; Off Ade; VP Stu Cncl; Sprt Ed Sch Nwsp; Rptr Sch Nwsp; Sch Nwsp; Spn Clb; Trk; Ferris St Coll; Advertising.

TUTTLE, ROBERT; Holt HS; Holt, MI; 18/400 Hon Rl; NHS; Bsbl; Letter Bsktbl; Ftbl; Cit Awd; General Motors Inst; Bus.

TUTTLE, ROBIN; Clay Battelle HS; Fairview, WV; Chrh Wkr; Hon Rl; Jr NHS; Treas NHS; Sch Pl; Pres Stu Cncl; Ed Yrbk; Rptr Sch Nwsp; FHA; DAR Awd; Univ; Elem Tchr.

TUTTLE, RYAN; Fremont HS; Fremont, IN; Am Leg Boys St; Boy Scts; Hon Rl; Bsbl; Bsktbl; Glf; Scr Kpr; Am Leg Awd; Univ Of Nev ; Hotel Admin.

TUTTLE, SANDRA; Athens Area HS; Athens, MI; Girl Scts; Jr NHS; Pep Clb;.

TUTTLE, TERESA; Eastern HS; Waverly, OH; 21/65 Chrs; Chrh Wkr; Drl Tm; Hon Rl; Sch Pl; Sec Stu Cncl; Yth Flsp; Rptr Yrbk; FHA; VP FTA; Shawnee St Coll.

TUTTLE, TERESA; Indian Hill HS; Cincinnati, OH; Hon Rl; NHS; Off Ade; Sch Mus; Trk; PPFtbl; Miami Univ.

TUTWILER, FRANK; Hampshire HS; Augusta, WV; 39/113 Boy Scts; Chrh Wkr; Cmnty Wkr; Hon Rl; Sct Actv; Yth Flsp; 4-H; FFA; Trk; 4-H Awd; James Rumsey Voc Schl; Machinist.

TWARDOCHLEB, MICHAEL; Saint Alphonsus HS; Detroit, MI; Band; Hon Rl; Orch; Sch Mus; Sch Pl; Fr Clb; Wayne State Univ; Dentistry.

TWEEDIE, J SCOT; Garber HS; Essexville, MI; 7/180 Pres Jr Cls; Pres Sr Cls; Band; Chrs; Hon Rl; Orch; Sch Mus; Sch Pl; Stg Crw; Stu Cncl; 3 Yr Ironman Ftbll 76; 2 Schlrshps Blue Lk Fine Arts Camp 78; Univ Of Michigan; Engr.

TWEEDIE, SCOT; Garber HS, Essexville, MI, 4/190 Pres Jr Cls; Pres Sr Cls; Band; Chrs; Chrh Wkr; Hon Rl; Sch Mus; Stg Crw; Stu Cncl; Yrbk; Univ Of Michigan; Engr.

TWEEDY, KYLE; Charles A Beard HS; Knightstown, IN; 4/145 Am Leg Aux Girls St; Chrh Wkr; VP NHS; Sch Mus; Sch Pl; Stg Crw; Stu Cncl; Yrbk; Drama Clb; Fr Clb; Depauw Univ; Busns Mgmt.

TWIGG, BETTY; Paw Paw HS; Paw Paw, WV; Trs Jr Cls; Chrs; Hon Rl; 4-H; FBLA; Pep Clb; Voc Schl; Bus.

TWIGGS, KAREN; Luther L Wright HS; Ironwood, MI; Pres Frsh Cls; Cls Rep Frsh Cls; Sec Soph Cls; Chrh Wkr; Hon Rl; Hosp Ade; Stu Cncl; Rptr Sch Nwsp; 4-H; Pep Clb; Mc Connell Univ; Tourist Guide.

TWINING, WILLIAM; Carey HS; Carey, OH; Sec Soph Cls; Cl Rep Jr Cls; Hon Rl; Stg Crw; Rptr Sch Nwsp; Mth Clb; Spn Clb; Mgrs; Ohio Tests Of Schlstc Achvmnt; Sci Day & Fair Local Level; Univ; Acctg.

TWOMLEY, JEFFREY; Indiana Acad; Berrien Spg, MI; VP Frsh Cls; Pres Soph Cls; Hst Jr Cls; Chrs; Hon Rl; Bsbl; Bsktbl; Ftbl; Andrews Univ.

TWYMAN, BRAD; Lawrence North HS; Indianapolis, IN; 12/356 Cls Rep Soph Cls; Cls Rep Sr Cls; Aud/Vis; Chrs; Hon Rl; JA; Lit Mag; Treas NHS; PAVAS; Sch Mus; Moore Schlrshp 1979; Brain Game Tm Cpn 1979; Cum Laude Soc 1976; Washington Univ; Sci.

TYE, PATRICE; Lamphere HS; Madison Hts, MI; Hon Rl; NHS; Sch Pl; Stg Crw; Drama Clb; Letter Pom Pon; Michigan St Univ; Bio.

TYE JR, HENRY; M Luther King Jr Sr HS; Detroit, MI; Aud/Vis; Hon Rl; Jr NHS; Natl Forn Lg; NHS; Off Ade; Sch Nwsp; Fr Clb; FTA; Sci Clb; Detroit Inst Of Tech; Mech Engr.

TYGRETT, CONNIE; Princeton HS; Cincinnati, OH; 70/650 Cls Rep Sr Cls; Hon Rl; NHS; Off Ade; Quill & Scroll; Stu Cncl; Ed Yrbk; Univ Of Cincinnati; Mech Engr.

TYKODI, TERI; Watkins Memorial HS; Patskala, OH; Pres Frsh Cls; Pres Soph Cls; Pres Jr Cls; Pres Sr Cls; Band; Hon Rl; Lbry Ade; Pres NHS; Letter Gym; Capt Chrldng; Univ; Med.

TYLER, ALICE; Rochester Cmnty HS; Rochester, IN; 21/166 Chrs; Cmnty Wkr; Girl Scts; Hon Rl; NHS; Sch Mus; Sch Pl; Chmn Stg Crw; Drama Clb; Sec 4-H; Voc Schl; Florist.

TYLER, DAVID; Rochester HS; Rochester, IN; 31/160 Chrh Wkr; Hon Rl; Yth Flsp; Sch Nwsp; Ger Clb; Sci Clb; Coll; Aviation.

TYLER, KATHY L; North Putnam Jr Sr HS; Bainbridge, IN; 30/158 Band; Chrh Wkr; FCA; Rptr Yrbk; Rptr Sch Nwsp; Pep Clb; Spn Clb; Trk; Chrldng; Pom Pon; Ball State Univ; Social Work.

TYLER, MELANIE; Mendon HS; Mendon, MI; Chrs; Sch Mus; Sch Pl; Stg Crw; Spn Clb; PPFtbl; College; Nurse.

TYLER, MONICA; Strongsville HS; Strongsville, OH; Band; Boy Scts; Chrh Wkr; Hon Rl; Jr NHS; NHS; Orch; Rptr Yrbk; College; Engin.

TYLER, PAMLA; Berkley HS; Hunt Woods, MI; Drl Tm; Girl Scts; Off Ade; Red Cr Ade; Trk; Pom Pon; Mich State Univ; Criminal Justice.

TYLER, ROD; Parma HS; Parma, OH; Boy Scts; Hon Rl; Letter Glf; Ten; Ohio State; Vet.

TYLER, SUSAN; Henry Ford HS; Detroit, MI; 4/454 Chrs; Chrh Wkr; Cmnty Wkr; Hon Rl; NHS; Yth Flsp; Natl Merit Ltr; Adrian Coll; Medicine.

TYLER, TANIA; Goshen HS; Goshen, IN; Cls Rep Frsh Cls; Cmp Fr Grls; Chrh Wkr; Cmnty Wkr; Stu Cncl; Ed Sch Nwsp; Fr Clb; Pep Clb; Sci Clb; Trk; Purdue; Science.

TYLER, TONYA; Jane Addams HS; Cleveland, OH; Letter Trk; Cit Awd; Cleveland State; Med Sec.

TYLER JR, RICHARD; Meadow Bridge HS; Maplewood, WV; 10/63 Yrbk; Coach Actv; IM Sprt; WVITT; Law.

TYMKIW, CHRISTINE; Holy Name Nazareth HS; Parma, OH; Girl Scts; Stg Crw; Fashion Inst Of Tech; Fashion Mdse.

TYNDALL, GREGORY; Mason Cnty Central HS; Scottville, MI; 20/118 Hon Rl; Bsktbl; Ftbl; Trk; Coach Actv; Elk Awd; Natl Merit Ltr; West Shore Comm Coll.

TYNES, SONJA; Fairhaven Christian Academy; Portage, IN; Band; Chrs; Chrh Wkr; Pres Girl Scts; Hon Rl; Ed Yrbk; Chrldng; GAA; Cit Awd; Fairhaven Coll; Sec.

TYRA, SANDRA; North Central Area HS; Wilson, MI; Band; NHS; 4-H; FHA; VP Spn Clb; 4-H Awd; Natl Merit Ltr; Univ; Eng.

TYREE, DAVID; Woodrow Wilson HS; Prosperity, WV; 6/502 Hon Rl; NHS; Off Ade; 4-H; Bsbl; Highst Grd Avrg Grades 1 Thru 6 1973; Engl Awrd 1976; Bsktball Lttr 1976; Grd Schl Bsktball Tournmnt 1973; West Virginia Univ; Engr.

TYREE, EMMA; John Adams HS; Cleveland, OH; Cl Rep Jr Cls; Hon Rl; Jr NHS; Lbry Ade; NHS; Stg Crw; Cit Awd; Case Western Reserve Univ; Med Tech.

TYREE, VIRGINIA; Romulus Sr HS; Romulus, MI; Cmp Fr Grls; Hon Rl; NHS; Off Ade; Rptr Sch Nwsp; Sch Nwsp; Fr Clb; VICA; Washtenaw Cmnty Coll; Photog.

TYRING, SCOTT A; Pike Central HS; Spurgeon, IN; Band; Boy Scts; Chrs; Hon Rl; NHS; Sch Mus; Sch Pl; Sct Actv; Stg Crw; Yth Flsp; Eagle Scout 1978; Vigil Hnr 1978; Intrnl Thespian Soc Mbr 1; Air Force Academy.

TYRRELL, CRAIG; Lake Orion HS; Lake Orion, MI; 20/450 Aud/Vis; Band; Boy Scts; Debate Tm; Hon Rl; NHS; Pol Wkr; Drama Clb; Natl Merit Ltr; Mic State Univ; Acctg.

TYRRELL, KAROLYN; Howland HS; Warren, OH; 7/418 AFS; Univ; Nurse.

TYRRELL, LORA; Crestline HS; Crestline, OH; Chrs; Girl Scts; Hon Rl; Off Ade; Sch Mus; Stg Crw; Yrbk; 4-H; Ger Clb; Bsktbl; Ohio St Univ; Psych.

TYSON, ANGIE; Elmwood HS; Wayne, OH; 21/117 Trs Sr Cls; Band; Chrs; Hon Rl; Yth Flsp; Drama Clb; FSA; FTA; Bsktbl; Letter Chrldng; College; Secondary Teaching.

TYSON, BARRINGTON C; Hubbard HS; Hubbard, OH; 22/350 Band; Hon Rl; Jr NHS; NHS; Bsktbl; Ten; Univ; Auto Engr Tech.

TYSON, KATHLEEN D; Reeths Puffer HS; Muskegon, MI; 19/351 Cls Rep Soph Cls; Boy Scts; Hon Rl; JA; NHS; Sct Actv; Natl Merit SF; College; International Relations.

TYSON, LUTHER; Washington HS; South Bend, IN ; 48/353 Cls Rep Frsh Cls; Cls Rep Soph Cls; Cl Rep Jr Cls; Cls Rep Sr Cls; Hon Rl; JA; NHS; Ed Yrbk; Spn Clb; Univ; Jrnlsm.

TYUKODY, CYNTHIA; Madison HS; Madison, OH; AFS; Band; Hon Rl; Lbry Ade; Sch Pl; Stg Crw; Y-Teens; Drama Clb; Spn Clb; Trk; Univ Of Dayton; Photography.

TYUS, EMANUEL; Cass Tech HS; Detroit, MI; Boy Scts; Chrs; Chrh Wkr; Cmnty Wkr; Pol Wkr; Sch Mus; Sct Actv; Sch Nwsp; Boys Clb Am; Inner City Creative Writing Awd Oakland Univ; Univ Of Wisconsin; Sci.

TYUS, ERICA; Buena Vista HS; Saginaw, MI; Hon Rl; Hosp Ade; Off Ade; Rptr Sch Nwsp; 4-H; Pep Clb; Natl Merit Ltr; Oakland Jr College; Reg Nurse.

TYUS, ERICA; Saginaw HS; Saginaw, MI; Chrh Wkr; Hon Rl; Ed Sch Nwsp; Pep Clb; Natl Merit Ltr; Mic State; Nursing.

TYUS, GREGORY; Cass Technical HS; Detroit, MI; 2/889 Chrh Wkr; Cmnty Wkr; Drl Tm; Hon Rl; Off Ade; ROTC; IM Sprt; Awd Of Recog By Detroit Chaptr Of Phi Beta Kappa 79; Cert Of Recog By St Of Mi Comp Schl Prog 79; General Motors Inst; Mech Engr.

U

UAHINUI, TROY; South Vigo HS; Terre Haute, IN; 82/630 Aud/Vis; Hon Rl; Mod UN; NHS; Pol Wkr; Stg Crw; Rptr Yrbk; Sch Nwsp; Rdo Clb; Sci Clb; Rose Hulman Inst Of Tech Univ; Engr.

UCHTMAN, DEBRA; Norwood HS; Norwood, OH; Drl Tm; Hon Rl; JA; Jr NHS; Rptr Yrbk; Pres Key Clb; Lat Clb; Pep Clb; College.

UEBBING, RICHARD; Athens HS; Troy, MI; Band; FCA; Hon Rl; JA; Bsbl; Ftbl; Swmmng; Trk; Natl Merit Ltr; Weamer Loyalty Awd Ftbl; Athens Ath Boosters Schlrshp; Class Spirit Awd; Central Michigan Univ; Acctg.

UEBELHOER, CHERYL; Southridge HS; Huntingburg, IN; Hon Rl; Hosp Ade; VP JA; 4-H; Treas FHA; Pep Clb; Spn Clb; PPFtbl; 4-H Awd; JA Awd; Indiana Univ; Bus.

UEBLER, JAMIE; Niles Sr HS; Niles, MI; Hon Rl; Stu Cncl; Pep Clb; Letter Chrldng; Albion Univ; Flight Attendant.

UECKER, HEATHER; Central HS; Grand Rapids, MI; 10/300 VP Jr Cls; Cls Rep Sr Cls; Chrh Wkr; Girl Scts; Hon Rl; Jr NHS; NHS; Stu Cncl; Sprt Ed Yrbk; Pres Fr Clb; Hope Coll; Eng.

UELTSCHY, JUDY; Bishop Donahue Memorial HS; Wheeling, WV; 9/54 Chrs; Hon Rl; NHS; Sch Mus; Rptr Sch Nwsp; Pep Clb; Spn Clb; Swmmng; GAA; DAR Awd; Navy; Marine Biologist.

UETRECHT, DONNA; Clinton Massie HS; Oregonia, OH; 17/125 Trs Jr Cls; Band; Drl Tm; Hon Rl; NHS; Stu Cncl; Pres 4-H; Chrldng; PPFtbl; Scr Kpr; College; Elem Ed.

UFFERMAN, FRED; Hayes HS; Delaware, OH; Band; Boy Scts; Letter Ftbl; Trk; Capt Wrstlng;.

UFFERMAN, JOHN; Hayes HS; Delaware, OH; Band; Boy Scts; Hon Rl; Ger Clb; College; Engr.

UFFINDELL, COLIN; Little Miami HS; Morrow, OH; Hon Rl; Ger Clb; Bsktbl; Crs Cntry; Socr; Trk; 4-H Awd; Univ.

UFFMAN, LISA; North Royalton HS; North Royalton, OH; Pres Soph Cls; Cl Rep Jr Cls; Girl Scts; Hon Rl; Pres Stu Cncl; 4-H; Pres OEA; Letter Chrldng; Letter Scr Kpr; Bus Schl; Bus Educ.

UFFORD, J; Regina HS; Detroit, MI; College; Comp Sci.

UGOROWSKI, PHILIP B; De La Salle Collegiate HS; St Clair Shores, MI; NHS; Sch Mus; Drama Clb; IM Sprt; JETS Awd; Natl Merit Ltr; Kalamazoo Coll; Sci.

UHER, SHARON; Trinity HS; Bedford, OH; Chrs; Hon Rl; Trk; Chrldng; PPFtbl; College; Med Sci.

UHER, THERESA; Cardinal Stritch HS; Millbury, OH; 9/210 Hon Rl; Sec NHS; Sch Mus; 4-H; Spn Clb; 4-H Awd; Atrtend Oh 4h St Conservtn Camp 78; Attend Oh 4h St Jr Ldrshp Camp 79; Co Chair Persn Of Stu Coun Scrpbk 79; Ohio St Univ; Agri.

UHLENBROCK, JIM; Urbana HS; Urbana, OH; 1/200 Trs Frsh Cls; Hon Rl; Lbry Ade; NHS; Treas 4-H; Bsbl; Letter Ftbl; Mgrs; James O Brien Schlr Ath Awd 77 & 78; Univ.

UHLER, RICHARD; Midpark HS; Brook Park, OH; Band; NHS; Orch; Sch Pl; Stg Crw; Rptr Yrbk; Drama Clb; Natl Merit Ltr; Cleveland State Univ; Music.

UHRICH, CONNIE; Hubbard HS; Hubbard, OH; Sct Actv; Yth Flsp; 4-H; Pres FHA; Pep Clb; Scr Kpr; 4-H Awd; College; Restaurant Mgmt.

UHRIG, DON; Mt Vernon Academy; Mt Vernon, OH; Cl Rep Jr Cls; Band; Chrh Wkr; Hon Rl; Sch Mus; Sch Pl; Rptr Yrbk; Yrbk; Trk; Scr Kpr; Atlantic Union Coll; CPA.

UHRIG, JACKIE; Huntington HS; Waverly, OH; Trs Sr Cls; Hon Rl; JA; Sch Pl; FHA; Pep Clb; Gym; Letter Trk; Chrldng; Pom Pon; Tech Schl; Radiologist.

UHRIG, THOMAS; Harrison HS; W Lafayette, IN; 5/286 Hon Rl; NHS; Yrbk; Fr Clb; Ten; Rotary Awd; Purdue Univ; Internatl Bus.

UHRIN, JEFF; Andrean HS; Gary, IN; 76/251 Hon Rl; IM Sprt; Univ; Bus Mgmt.

UHRMAN, CHRISTINE; Ctrl Catholic HS; Toledo, OH; 7/307 Pres Frsh Cls; Chrs; Hon Rl; NHS; Sch Pl; Trk; Univ Of Toledo; Psych.

UJCZO, DONALD; Chanel HS; Bedford, OH; 8/118 Cl Rep Jr Cls; Cls Rep Sr Cls; Aud/Vis; Hon Rl; NHS; Rptr Yrbk; Ed Sch Nwsp; Bsbl; IM Sprt; Miami Univ; Bus.

UKRAINEC, DONALD; Riverview Community HS; Riverview, MI; 7/260 Am Leg Aux Girls St; Pres Band; Jr NHS; Treas NHS; Sch Pl; Capt Crs Cntry; Letter Ten; Wayne St Merit Schlr 79; Coord Of Lcl Sccr Prog 78; Most Valuable Bandsman 79; Wayne St Univ; Scndry Educ.

ULANOWICZ, DEBBIE; West Catholic HS; Grand Rapids, MI; Cls Rep Frsh Cls; Chrs; Hon Rl; NHS; Sch Pl; Stg Crw; Rptr Yrbk; Pep Clb; Capt Gym; College; Math.

ULBRICH, REBECCA; Lehman HS; Piqua, OH; Sec Stu Cncl; Yrbk; Fr Clb; Bsktbl; Trk; Chrldng; Opt Clb Awd; Top 100 Schol 1978; Acad Team 1978; Volleyball Var 1976; Univ.

ULCH, PENNEY; Northwood HS; Northwood, OH; 7/93 Chrs; Hon Rl; VP JA; Lbry Ade; Off Ade; Sch Mus; Rptr Yrbk; College; Med Tech.

ULERY, MIKE; Lucas HS; Mansfield, OH; VP Jr Cls; NHS; Yrbk; Bsbl; Bsktbl; Am Leg Awd; College; Acctg.

ULINSKI, DIANA; Rossford HS; Perrysburg, OH; 8/152 Hon Rl; Treas NHS; Sch Pl; Ed Sch Nwsp; Drama Clb; Spn Clb; DAR Awd; Natl Merit Schl; Ohio St Univ; Journalism.

ULLMAN, D; Fort Frye HS; Beverly, OH; Pres Jr Cls; Band; Hon Rl; Quill & Scroll; Stu Cncl; Sprt Ed Sch Nwsp; 4-H; Spn Clb; Letter Bsbl; Coach Actv; Bowling Green Univ; Music.

ULLMANN, GREGORY; Clawson HS; Clawson, MI; Cmnty Wkr; Hon Rl; Ten; Natl Merit SF; Univ Of Michigan; Chem.

ULLOM, KELLEY; Milton HS; Milton, WV; Cls Rep Soph Cls; Cl Rep Jr Cls; Band; Chrs; Drm Mjrt; Girl Scts; Hon Rl; Lbry Ade; Off Ade; Red Cr Ade; Marshall Univ; Pharm.

ULMER, LISA; Mt Notre Dame HS; Cincinnati, OH; Hon Rl; NHS; Pres Spn Clb; Auto Travel Cnsltnt.

ULMER, SARAH; Grosse Pointe South HS; Grosse Pointe, MI; 37/570 Band; Hon Rl; NHS; Orch; Rptr Yrbk; Lat Clb; Letter Trk; NCTE; Natl Merit Ltr; Univ Of Michigan.

ULMER, SUSAN; Grosse Pointe South HS; Grosse Pointe, MI; 45/620 Band; Chrh Wkr; Hon Rl; NHS; Orch; Lat Clb; Bsktbl; Letter Trk; Mic State Univ.

ULMER, TERRY; Buckeye Valley HS; Delaware, OH; Hon Rl; Bsbl; Bsktbl; Glf; Ohi State; Astronomy.

ULRATH, GARY; Bridgman HS; Bridgman, MI; Cmnty Wkr; Hon Rl; Bsbl; Bsktbl; Ftbl; IM Sprt;.

ULRICH, ANDREA; Archbishop Alter HS; Kettering, OH; Chrs; Cmnty Wkr; Capt Drl Tm; Off Ade; Stu Cncl; Sinclair Comm Coll; Sec.

ULRICH, CHERYL; Floyd Central HS; Floyds Knobs, IN; Chrh Wkr; Hon Rl; PAVAS; Sch Mus; Stg Crw; 4-H; Trk; IM Sprt; Scr Kpr; 4-H Awd; Herron Schl Of Art; Commrcl Art.

ULRICH, CLIFFORD; Mona Shores HS; Muskegon, MI; Boy Scts; VP JA; NHS; Sct Actv; FSA; Mth Clb; Natl Merit Ltr; French 76; Math 76; PSAT Top 1% In Nation; ACT Top 1% In Nation; SAT Top 5% In Nation; Michigan St Univ; Comp Sci.

ULRICH, JAMES; Lake Catholic HS; Mentor, OH; Band; Hon Rl; Rptr Sch Nwsp; Socr; John Carroll Univ; Pre Med.

ULRICH, JO ANN; St Ursula Academy; Swanton, OH; Hon Rl; Lat Clb; Spn Clb; Air Force ROTC Schlrshp 4 Yrs; Univ Of Cincinnati; Medicine.

ULRICH, LISA; Ridgewood HS; W Lafayette, OH; 50/150 Hon Rl; Sprt Ed Yrbk; Bsktbl; Letter Trk; GAA; PPFtbl; Natl Merit Ltr; Voice Dem Awd; College Of Steubenville; History.

ULRICH, LUANNE; Burris HS; Muncie, IN; Band; Hon Rl; Sch Mus; Stu Cncl; Yrbk; Rptr Sch Nwsp; Sch Nwsp; Capt Bsktbl; Ten; GAA; College; Vet.

ULRICH, MARK; Maplewood HS; E Orwell, OH; 21/89 Aud/Vis; Treas Stu Cncl; Pres Yth Flsp; Sprt Ed Sch Nwsp; Beta Clb; Letter Bsbl; Letter Bsktbl; Letter Crs Cntry; Letter Glf; Letter Trk; Teenager Of The Math Trumbull Cnty 79; Ohio St Univ; Engr.

ULRICH, MICHELE; Marysville HS; St Clair, MI; Chrh Wkr; Hon Rl; Yth Flsp; Fr Clb; Scr Kpr; Univ; Psych.

ULRICH, NANCY; Sandcreek HS; Sand Creek, MI; Cls Rep Frsh Cls; Trs Sr Cls; Band; Cmp Fr Grls; Hon Rl; NHS; VP Yth Flsp; Univ.

ULRICH, TAMARA; Charlotte HS; Charlotte, MI; 20/304 Am Leg Aux Girls St; Girl Scts; NHS; Ger Clb; Pep Clb; Swmmng; Chrldng; Mat Maids; 4-H Awd; Lansing Communituy College; Acctg.

ULSH, JAY; River Vly HS; Caledonia, OH; 50/200 Band; Orch; Sch Mus; Stg Crw; Trk; Coach Actv; IM Sprt; Ohio Univ.

ULVINEN, GLENN; A D Johnston HS; Bessemer, MI; Cls Rep Frsh Cls; Cls Rep Soph Cls; Cl Rep Jr Cls; Band; Hon Rl; Stu Cncl; Rptr Yrbk; Rptr Sch Nwsp; IM Sprt; College.

UMBAUGH, ANN; Penn HS; Osceola, IN; Chrs; Hon Rl; Lit Mag; NHS; Ger Clb; Mat Maids; NCTE; Valparaiso Univ.

UMBAUGH, RANDY; Argos Community HS; Argos, IN; 4/58 Pres Frsh Cls; Cls Rep Soph Cls; Cl Rep Jr Cls; Cls Rep Sr Cls; VP NHS; Pres Stu Cncl; Pres Yth Flsp; Socr; Trk; Natl Merit SF; Ball State Univ; Acctg.

UMBS, DOUG; Sebring Mc Kinley HS; Sebring, OH; 9/100 Hon Rl; Letter Bsktbl; Letter Glf; IM Sprt; Univ; Acctg.

UMERLEY, SUSAN; Rocky River HS; Rocky Rvr, OH; Chrs; Hon Rl; Letter Bsbl; Bsktbl; Univ; Coaching.

UMLOR, DENNIS; Coopersville HS; Conklin, MI; 2/180 Hon Rl; Jr NHS; NHS; Sch Pl; Stu Cncl; 4-H; FFA; Trk; Natl Merit Schl; MSU Kent Ottawa Cnty Almni Club 79; Coopersville Stdnt Loan 79; MSU Awd For Acad Excllnc 79; Michigan St Univ; Plant Pathology.

UMLOR, LOIS; Coopersville HS; Conklin, MI; Hon Rl; NHS; Stu Cncl; Ger Clb; Bsktbl; Ten; Letter Trk; Ferris State College; Med Sec.

UMMEL, JULIE; Bishop Dwenger HS; Ft Wayne, IN; Cls Rep Frsh Cls; Hon Rl; Hosp Ade; Pep Clb; Letter Gym; Pom Pon; PPFtbl; Ball St Univ; Soc Work.

UMMEL, KRISTEN; Northwood HS; Elkhart, IN; Chrs; Chrh Wkr; FCA; Girl Scts; Hon Rl; Hosp Ade; NHS; Sch Mus; Sch Pl; Yth Flsp; Coll; Nursing.

UMPHREY, BRIAN; Standish Sterling Ctrl HS; Bentley, MI; 24/152 VP Jr Cls; Hon Rl; Capt Crs Cntry; Trk; Coach Actv; IM Sprt; Central Mic Univ; Acctg.

UMPLEBY, DAWN; Canton S HS; Canton, OH; Band; Chrs; Hon Rl; NHS; Sch Mus; Lat Clb; Scr Kpr; Choir Chaplain; College; Medicine.

UMSTEAD, LISA; Anna Local HS; Anna, OH; Cl Rep Jr Cls; Band; Chrs; Hon Rl; Jr NHS; Orch; Sch Mus; Stg Crw; Stu Cncl; Yth Flsp; Miami Jacabs Bus Schl; Fshn Mdse.

UNDERWOOD, CHARLES E; Greenbrier West HS; Rainelle, WV; 7/150 Pres Soph Cls; Pres Jr Cls; Cls Rep Sr Cls; Chrh Wkr; FCA; Hon Rl; Lbry Ade; NHS; Sch Pl; Sct Actv; Tennessee Temple Univ; Busns Admin.

UNDERWOOD, DARLENE; Pershing HS; Detroit, MI; Band; Hon Rl; Lbry Ade; NHS; Y-Teens; Letter Ten; Wayne State Univ; Reg Nurse.

UNDERWOOD, DEBORAH; Lincoln HS; Shinnston, WV; Hon Rl; FHA; VICA; Gym; Trk; Bus Schl; Cosmetology.

UNDERWOOD, JACKIE; Barboursville HS; Barboursville, WV; Cls Rep Frsh Cls; Cls Rep Soph Cls; Cl Rep Jr Cls; VP Sr Cls; Am Leg Aux Girls St; VP FCA; Stu Cncl; Sprt Ed Yrbk; Pep Clb; Capt Bsktbl; West Virginia Univ; Phys Educ.

UNDERWOOD, JEFF; Upper Arlington HS; Columbus, OH; 57/610 Band; Boy Scts; Chrh Wkr; Hon Rl; NHS; Sch Mus; Sct Actv; Fr Clb; Ten; IM Sprt; American Schl Of Broadcasting; Comm.

UNDERWOOD, JOHNNA; Inter City Christian HS; Lincoln Park, MI; 10/43 Cmp Fr Grls; Chrs; Chrh Wkr; Hon Rl; Sch Mus; Stg Crw; Yth Flsp; Rptr Yrbk; Drama Clb; FTA; Awd For Highest Avg In French; Qualified For Schlrshp From Mich Dept Of Ed; Bob Jones Univ; French.

UNDERWOOD, LINDA; Alba Public HS; Alba, MI; 5/17 Cls Rep Frsh Cls; VP Soph Cls; Chrs; Girl Scts; Hon Rl; Lbry Ade; Sch Mus; Sch Pl; Stu Cncl; 4-H; Home Ec Awrd 78; Cheerldng Sec 78; Lake Superior St Coll; Acctg.

UNDERWOOD, MIKE; West Ottawa HS; Holland, MI; FFA; College; Ornithology.

UNDERWOOD, PEGGY; Shady Spring HS; Glen Morgan, WV; Band; Drm Mjrt; Hon Rl; Off Ade; 4-H; VICA; Letter Mat Maids; College; Accounting.

UNDERWOOD, SCOT; Kalkaska HS; Mancelona, MI; Hon Rl; NHS; Mic Tech College; Engr.

UNDERWOOD, SHERRY; Shady Spring HS; Shady Spring, WV; 41/155 VP Soph Cls; Cls Rep Soph Cls; Cl Rep Jr Cls; FCA; Hon Rl; NHS; Sch Pl; Stg Crw; Stu Cncl; Drama Clb; W Va Inst Of Tech; Dental Hygiene.

UNDERWOOD, SHERRY; Fayetteville HS; Faeytteville, WV; Chrs; Hon Rl; Sch Mus; Yth Flsp; Fr Clb; FBLA; Pep Clb; Chrldng; IM Sprt; Police Acad; Police Officer.

UNDEUTSCH, SUSANNA; Upper Arlington HS; Columbus, OH; 28/610 AFS; Chrs; Girl Scts; Hon Rl; Sch Mus; Ger Clb; Spn Clb; GAA; Ohio St Univ; Med.

UNDY, STEPHEN R; Southfield Sr HS; Southfield, MI; Boy Scts; NHS; Rdo Clb; Natl Merit SF; Univ Of Michigan; Elec Engr.

UNGAR, KATHLEEN; Cabrini HS; Lincoln Pk, MI; 23/154 Hon Rl; Lit Mag; Sch Mus; Sch Pl; Stg Crw; Yrbk; Drama Clb; Ger Clb; Eng.

UNGER, DEBBIE; Walton HS; Walton, WV; Girl Scts; Hon Rl; Treas NHS; Sch Pl; Rptr Yrbk; Sec Drama Clb; Treas FHA; Treas Spn Clb; College; Architect.

UNGER, JEFFREY; South Newton Jr Sr HS; Earl Park, IN; VP Jr Cls; Chrs; Sch Pl; Letter Bsbl; Letter Ftbl; Letter Wrstlng; Univ; Comp Prog.

UNGER, JILL; South Newton Jr Sr HS; Earl Park, IN; Chrh Wkr; Cmnty Wkr; Girl Scts; Hosp Ade; Off Ade; Sch Pl; Yth Flsp; VP FBLA; Pep Clb; Ftbl; Danville Jr Coll; Nursing.

UNGER, RICKY; Mineral Ridge HS; Mineral Ridge, OH; 3/74 VP Soph Cls; Chrh Wkr; Hon Rl; Yth Flsp; Yrbk; Beta Clb; Letter Glf; Youngstown Univ; Metalurgical Engr.

UNKEFER, SHARON; East Canton HS; E Canton, OH; Chrs; Off Ade; FHA; FNA; Pep Clb; VICA; Chrldng; Salem Schl; Nursing.

UNKLESBAY, DANIEL G; Washington HS; Massillon, OH; 16/482 Cls Rep Frsh Cls; Cls Rep Soph Cls; Cls Rep Sr Cls; Hon Rl; Jr NHS; NHS; Bsktbl; Akron Univ; Bus.

UNRUH, BRENDA; Cowan HS; Muncie, IN; Hon Rl; JA; Off Ade; Yrbk; 4-H; FHA; OEA; Pep Clb; Sci Clb; Mat Maids; College.

UNTCH, JOANN; Cardinal Mooney HS; Youngstwon, OH; Band; Cmp Fr Grls; Chrs; Chrh Wkr; Cmnty Wkr; Hon Rl; Hosp Ade; Off Ade; Orch; FHA; Sr Band Awd 79; Pennsylvania Bus Schl; Off Mach.

UNTENER, JOSEPH; Stephen T Badin HS; Hamilton, OH; 40/230 VP Jr Cls; Pres Sr Cls; Boy Scts; Hon Rl; NHS; Stu Cncl; Key Clb; IM Sprt; Opt Clb Awd; Rotary Awd; General Motors Inst; Mech Engr.

UNTIED, ANTHONY; Tri Valley HS; Trinway, OH; 22/215 Boy Scts; Hon Rl; Lbry Ade; Off Ade; Sch Pl; Drama Clb; Spn Clb; Crs Cntry; Wrstlng; Pres Awd; Ohio National Guard.

UNTISZ, ANGELA; Perry HS; Perry, OH; Hon Rl; NHS; Sch Pl; VP 4-H; Spn Clb; GAA; Coll; Vet.

UPCHURCH, DAVID T; Knightstown Cmnty HS; New Castle, IN; 59/175 Chrs; Hon Rl; Sch Mus; Sch Pl; Drama Clb; 4-H; FFA; FTA; Cit Awd; 4-H Awd; Univ; Performing Arts.

UPCHURCH, STEVEN R; Hagerstown HS; Greens Fork, IN; 13/200 Cls Rep Frsh Cls; Cls Rep Soph Cls; Pres Jr Cls; Pres Sr Cls; Band; Hon Rl; Mod UN; NHS; Red Cr Ade; Pres Stu Cncl; Outstndng Comm Chairperson Model Leg 1978; Univ Of Detroit; Archt.

UPCHURCH, VICTOR; Cowan HS; Muncie, IN; 10/86 Hon Rl; Ger Clb; Bsbl; Bsktbl; Ball St Univ; Busns.

UPDIKE, JOYCE; Centerburg HS; Centerburg, OH; Pres Soph Cls; Pres Jr Cls; Chrh Wkr; NHS; Pres Stu Cncl; Yrbk; Rptr Sch Nwsp; Sec 4-H; Pres FHA; 4-H Awd; Business School.

UPDIKE, K; Theodore Roosevelt HS; Wyandotte, MI; Chrh Wkr; Cmnty Wkr; Girl Scts; Hon Rl; NHS; Red Cr Ade; Sct Actv; VP Yth Flsp; Ed Sch Nwsp; Rptr Sch Nwsp; Univ; C P A.

UPDIKE, KEITH G; Aquinas HS; Lincoln Park, MI; Hon Rl; NHS; Sct Actv; Letter Bsktbl; Univ Of Detroit.

UPDIKE, KEVIN J; Aquinas HS; Lincoln Park, MI; Aud/Vis; Boy Scts; Chrh Wkr; Hon Rl; NHS; Mgrs; Am Leg Awd; Univ Of Detroit; Engr.

UPHUES, LAURA; Eau Claire HS; Berrien Ctr, MI; Band; Hon Rl; Sch Mus; Pom Pon; U S History Awd Gerald S Sawatzki 78; Math Awd 75; Lake Michigan Coll.

UPOLE, VANESSA K; Ashtabula HS; Ashtabula, OH; 2/208 Sec AFS; Am Leg Aux Girls St; Band; Chrh Wkr; Hon Rl; Lit Mag; NHS; Sch Mus; Yth Flsp; Yrbk; Ohio Univ; Poli Sci.

UPTEGRAFT, ROGER; Manton Cons HS; Manton, MI; Cls Rep Frsh Cls; Cls Rep Soph Cls; Cl Rep Jr Cls; Cls Rep Sr Cls; Band; Boy Scts; Hon Rl; Mod UN; Sch Mus; Sch Pl; Michigan Comp Schlrshp 79; Basic Educ Opportunity Grant 79; Natl Direct Stdnt Loan 79; Ferris St Coll; Mechinist.

UPTON, ROBERT; Belleville HS; Belleville, MI; Am Leg Boys St; Hon Rl; Michigan St Univ; Nuclear Physics.

URANKAR, NANCY; Regina HS; S Euclid, OH; Hon Rl; Sch Nwsp; Notre Dame College; Medical Technolo.

URANKER, MARK; Berea HS; Berea, OH; 3/700 Cls Rep Frsh Cls; Cl Rep Jr Cls; Chrs; Hon Rl; Mdrgl; Mod UN; NHS; Sch Mus; College; Music.

URBAN, KARIN; Yale HS; Yale, MI; 4/156 Pres Jr Cls; Am Leg Aux Girls St; Hon Rl; NHS; Off Ade; Stu Cncl; Ed Sch Nwsp; Spn Clb; Bsktbl; DAR Awd; St Clair Cnty Cmnty Coll; Stewrdss.

URBAN, RAMONA; Merrillville Sr HS; Merrillville, IN; 120/601 Cmnty Wkr; Hon Rl; Lbry Ade; Rptr Yrbk; Exchng Club Yth Apprctn Awd 76; Indiana Univ; Psych.

URBAN, VICTORIA L; Tecumseh HS; Tecumseh, MI; Hon Rl; NHS; Yrbk; Drama Clb; Univ; News Media.

URBAN, WENDY; Glen Oak School; Painesville, OH; Chrs; Sch Mus; Stg Crw; Yth Flsp; Drama Clb; 4-H; Univ.

URBANIK, CATHERINE; Lorain Catholic HS; Lorain, OH; 8/132 Chrs; Hon Rl; Sec NHS; Stu Cncl; Ed Yrbk; Pep Clb; Letter Trk; Coach Actv; IM Sprt; PPFtbl; Coll; Soc Work.

URBANK, JOSEPH; Woodridge HS; Cuyhoga Fls, OH; Band; Boy Scts; Hon Rl; JA; Jr NHS; 4-H; Lat Clb; Ftbl; Wrstlng; Univ; History.

URBANOVIC, KATHLEEN; Avon HS; Danville, IN; Chrs; Chrh Wkr; CAP; Girl Scts; Hon Rl; Lbry Ade; Off Ade; Sct Actv; Beta Clb; Sci Clb; Purdue; Medicine.

URBERG, DAGNY; Concordia Lutheran HS; Ft Wayne, IN; 34/173 Chrs; Hon Rl; Hosp Ade; Yth Flsp; Ger Clb; Lat Clb; Luther Coll; Music.

URBERG, INGRID; Concordia Lutheran HS; Ft Wayne, IN; 4/181 Chrs; Hon Rl; Hosp Ade; Yth Flsp; Treas Lat Clb; Sci Clb; Luther Coll; Pre Med.

URBIEL, ALEX; Saint Andrew HS; Detroit, MI; 12/109 Boy Scts; Hon Rl; NHS; Sct Actv; Stu Cncl; Letter Bsktbl; Letter Crs Cntry; Letter Trk; Tmr; College; Sociology.

URIG, MARY B; Magnificat HS; Avon, OH; Cls Rep Soph Cls; NHS; Stu Cncl; Yrbk; Sch Nwsp; 4-H; 4-H Awd; Ohi State; Dairy Sci.

URQUHART, ROBIN; Milford HS; Holly, MI; 18/345 Cmnty Wkr; Hon Rl; NHS; Stu Cncl; Rptr Sch Nwsp; Sch Nwsp; Regnl HS Awd Estrn Mi Univ 78; Deptmnt Key Awd For Outstndg Achvmnt In Art 78; Gold Keys & 2 Cert Inart; Eastern Michigan Univ; Art Ther.

URRY, LAURIE; Olmsted Falls HS; Columbia Stn, OH; 134/250 Drl Tm; Girl Scts; Off Ade; PAVAS; Stu Cncl; 4-H; VP Ger Clb; IM Sprt; Pom Pon; 4-H Awd; Kent St Univ; Dance.

URSCHEL, HARRY; East Detroit HS; E Detroit, MI; Band; Hon Rl; Univ; Elect Tech.

URSUY, LEE; St Peter & Paul Area HS; Saginaw, MI; Chrs; Hon Rl; Pol Wkr; Sprt Ed Yrbk; FSA; Sci Clb; Univ; Dentistry.

USAK, SANDRA; Hedgesville HS; Martinsburg, WV; 12/300 Sec Frsh Cls; Band; Hon Rl; Stu Cncl; Pep Clb; Spn Clb; Twrlr; West Virginia Univ; Psych.

USHER, GLORIA; Northern Sr HS; Detroit, MI; Cmnty Wkr; Hon Rl; Hosp Ade; Jr NHS; NHS; Pol Wkr; Rptr Sch Nwsp; Sch Nwsp; OEA; VICA; N Michigan Univ; Data Processing.

USREY, LISA; Union Twp HS; Losantville, IN; Band; Chrs; Drl Tm; Hon Rl; Hosp Ade; Off Ade; FHA; Lat Clb; Pep Clb; VICA; Voc Schl; Dent Asst.

USSERY, XILLA T; Kingswood School; Birmingham, MI; 3/90 Hon Rl; Hosp Ade; NHS; Pol Wkr; Rptr Sch Nwsp; Cum Laude 79; Lincoln Esay Comp 1st Pl 78; Cranbrk Kingswd Almni Wrtng Awd 7.; Univ; Med.

UTECHT, STEVEN P; Stevenson HS; Livonia, MI; Band; Chrh Wkr; Orch; Stg Crw; St Of Mi Comptn Schlrshp Progr 79; Amer Cancer Soc 79; Univ Of Detroit; Dent.

UTHER, SUSAN; Edison HS; Milan, OH; Chrs; Hon Rl; Yth Flsp; Drama Clb; 4-H; Mth Clb; Sci Clb; 4-H Awd; Mem Of Farm Bureau Youth Council; Representative At Ohio Club Congress; N Cntrl Ohio Dist Quernsey Queen; Bowling Green St Univ; Comp Prog.

UTLEY, DAVID; Sebring Mc Kinley HS; Sebring, OH; 18/80 Chrh Wkr; Sch Pl; Drama Clb; Lat Clb; Letter Bsktbl; Letter Ftbl; Trk; Mgrs; Scr Kpr; Law.

UTLEY, MARK; Millersport HS; Millersport, OH; 5/67 Chrs; Chrh Wkr; Cmnty Wkr; Hon Rl; Jr NHS; NHS; Yth Flsp; Spn Clb; Bowling Green State Univ; Comp Sci.

UTLEY, MARY; Mc KinleyHS; Sebring, OH; 4/96 Band; Drm Mjrt; Hon Rl; Pres NHS; Quill & Scroll; Rptr Sch Nwsp; Sch Nwsp; Twrlr; Akron Univ; Med Tech.

UTRUP, STEVE; Ottawa Glandorf HS; Columbus Grove, OH; 31/172 Sec Frsh Cls; Cls Rep Soph Cls; Hon Rl; Lbry Ade; Sch Mus; Stg Crw; Pep Clb; Ftbl; IM Sprt; Toledo Univ; Elec Engr.

UTRUP, SUSAN; St John HS; Delphos, OH; 1/141 Val; Band; Chrh Wkr; Cmnty Wkr; Hon Rl; Jr NHS; NHS; Sch Mus; Ed Sch Nwsp; Sprt Ed Sch Nwsp; Univ Of Dayton; Comp Science.

UTT, JOHN; Elkins HS; Elkins, WV; Hon Rl; Rptr Yrbk; Key Clb; VICA; College; Engr.

UTTER, BRENDA; Tippecanoe Valley HS; Rochester, IN; 28/160 Hon Rl; NHS; 4-H; Spn Clb; Ball St Univ; Elem Educ.

UTTER, DANIEL; John Marshall HS; Indianapolis, IN; 9/611 Cls Rep Frsh Cls; Cmnty Wkr; Hon Rl; NHS; Stu Cncl; Fr Clb; Key Clb; Ftbl; IM Sprt; IU; Bus Admin.

UTTER, JANE; Clay Sr HS; Oregon, OH; Pres Band; Chrh Wkr; Cmnty Wkr; Hon Rl; Off Ade; Orch; Sch Mus; Coach Actv; Univ Of Toledo; Spch & Hearing Ther.

UTTER, LEIGH; Tippecanoe Valley HS; Mentone, IN; Drama Clb; 4-H; VP OEA; Pep Clb; Spn Clb; Swmmng; Internatl Jr Coll; Secretary.

UTTER, TODD; Tippecanoe Valley HS; Rochester, IN; 29/159 Cls Rep Sr Cls; Chrs; Hon Rl; NHS; Sch Mus; Sch Pl; Stu Cncl; Ed Yrbk; Rptr Yrbk; Drama Clb; Intl Thespian Society 1978; Ball St Univ; CPA.

UTZ, JON; Buckeye Central HS; New Washington, OH; Band; Hon Rl; VP Yth Flsp; 4-H; Spn Clb; Bsktbl; Letter Ftbl; Cit Awd; Ohio State Univ; Agri.

UTZ, JULIA; Beaver Local HS; Negley, OH; Band; Chrs; Hon Rl; Sch Mus; Sch Pl; Stg Crw; Sch Nwsp; Drama Clb; Eng Clb; Lat Clb; Univ; Theatre.

UTZIG, TRACY A; Solon HS; Solon, OH; 16/288 AFS; Hon Rl; Hosp Ade; NHS; Pol Wkr; Stu Cncl; Key Clb; Letter Gym; Ten; Letter Chrldng; Syracuse Univ; Home Ec.

UYEKI, ROBERT; Cleveland Hts HS; Cleveland Hts, OH; 25/800 Cls Rep Sr Cls; Chrh Wkr; Hon Rl; Lat Clb; Letter Socr; NCTE; Amherst College.

UZONI, LENA; Lamphere HS; Madison Hights, MI; Hon Rl; Lawrence Inst Of Tech; Archt.

V

VACCARO, MARY; Ottawa Hills HS; Grand Rapids, MI; Hon Rl; NHS; Orch; Sch Mus; Univ; Archt.

VADINI, MIKE; Valley Forge HS; Parma, OH; Cls Rep Frsh Cls; Cls Rep Soph Cls; Cl Rep Jr Cls; VP Sr Cls; Chrs; Hon Rl; Mdrgl; NHS; Stu Cncl; Y-Teens; Ohio Wesleyan Univ; Law.

VADNAIS, MICHAEL; Colerain Sr HS; Cincinnati, OH; Trs Frsh Cls; Cl Rep Jr Cls; Chrs; Hon Rl; Mdrgl; Sch Mus; Sch Pl; Stu Cncl; Drama Clb; Ger Clb; College; Aerospace Engr.

VAGUHN, BETTY; Southern Wells Jr Sr HS; Poneto, IN; Chrs; NHS; Pep Clb; Am Leg Awd; Awd In Home Ec 78; International Bus Coll; Acctg.

VAIA, JULIE L; Heath HS; Heath, OH; Cmnty Wkr; Hon Rl; Sch Pl; Yrbk; Ohio State Univ; Math.

VAIL, MARK; Highland HS; Highland, IN; 113/511 Debate Tm; Hon Rl; Natl Forn Lg; Sch Pl; Drama Clb; Key Clb; Best Mental Attitd Speech Team; Mmbe Of Natl Thespian Soc; Univ; Bus.

VAILLIENCOURT, ROBERT; Escanaba Area HS; Escanaba, MI; Collge.

VAILLIENCOURT, WILLIAM; Bishop Foley HS; Warren, MI; 13/183 Capt Debate Tm; Hon Rl; Pres NHS; Pol Wkr; Sch Pl; Stg Crw; Rptr Sch Nwsp; Univ Of Michigan; Poli Sci.

VAINNER, M; Lumen Christi HS; Jackson, MI; Cls Rep Frsh Cls; Cls Rep Soph Cls; Hon Rl; NHS; Stu Cncl; 4-H; Spn Clb; College; Physical Therapy.

VAJEN, DENISE; Napoleon HS; Napoleon, OH; 21/264 Cls Rep Frsh Cls; Cls Rep Sr Cls; Band; Chrs; Chrh Wkr; Hon Rl; Lit Mag; NHS; Orch; Sch Mus; Ohio St Univ; Bus.

VAJENTIC, AMY; Elyria Catholic HS; Elyria, OH; Cls Rep Soph Cls; Cl Rep Jr Cls; Chrs; Girl Scts; Hon Rl; Stu Cncl; Drama Clb; Pep Clb; Spn Clb; Letter Ten; Univ.

VALADE, JOHN; Rogers HS; Toledo, OH; Band; NHS; Sci Clb; Capt Crs Cntry; Letter Trk; College; Engr.

VALADE, JOHN W; Rogers HS; Toledo, OH; Band; Boy Scts; NHS; Sci Clb; Letter Crs Cntry; Letter Trk; JETS Awd; College; Engr.

VALAITIS, ANTHONY; Eastlake North HS; Eastlake, OH; 1/760 Hon Rl; NHS; Ger Clb; Letter Bsktbl; Spec Recogntn For 4.0 All Yr In German 3 Eng Annalysis & Amer History 79; Univ Of Dayton; Dent.

VALAN, MICHAEL; Linsly Institute; Wheeling, WV; Hon Rl; Sch Mus; Rptr Yrbk; Fr Clb; Letter Bsbl; Letter Ftbl; Univ; Contracting Law.

VALDES, CYNTHIA; Southwestern HS; Detroit, MI; Sal; Girl Scts; Hon Rl; Jr NHS; NHS; Sch Pl; Drama Clb; Wayne State Univ; Med.

VALDEZ, DAVID; Bridgeport Sr HS; Bridgeport, WV; Hon Rl; Jr NHS; Sch Pl; Stu Cncl; Eng Clb; Mth Clb; Spn Clb; Bsbl; Ftbl; Trk; Fairmont St Univ; Bus Admin.

VALDMAN, BERTRAND; Bloomington HS; Bloomington, IN; Jr NHS; NHS; Ger Clb; IM Sprt; Cit Awd; College; Poli Sci.

VALDOIS, CHRISTINA; Richmond Sr HS; Richmond, IN; 90/580 Cls Rep Frsh Cls; Cl Rep Jr Cls; Cls Rep Sr Cls; Band; Jr NHS; Natl Forn Lg; NHS; Am Leg Awd; Butler Univ; Music.

VALE, JEFF; Merrillville HS; Merrillville, IN; 130/604 Hon Rl; NEDT Cert Awd; Coll; Busns.

VALE, THOMAS; Bishop Noll Institute; Munster, IN; 38/321 Pres Frsh Cls; Pres Soph Cls; Pres Jr Cls; Pres Sr Cls; Hon Rl; NHS; Pres Stu Cncl; Mth Clb; Bsktbl; College; Law.

VALENTI, SUSAN; Brush HS; Richmond Hts, OH; Cls Rep Frsh Cls; Cls Rep Soph Cls; Cl Rep Jr Cls; Chrs; Hon Rl; Jr NHS; NHS; Stu Cncl; Yrbk; Pep Clb; John Caroll Univ; Bus Law.

VALENTINE, CARRIE; Northwest HS; Canal Fulton, OH; Chrh Wkr; Lbry Ade; Off Ade; Stg Crw; Stu Cncl; Yth Flsp; Spn Clb; College.

VALENTINE, CYNTHIA; Weir Sr HS; Weirton, WV; 7/343 Chrh Wkr; Cmnty Wkr; Hon Rl; NHS; Yth Flsp; Spn Clb; GAA; Mat Maids; Alderson Broaddus Univ; Med Asst.

VALENTINE, GERMAINE B; Boardman HS; Youngstown, OH; 67/558 Band; Hon Rl; Quill & Scroll; Y-Teens; Sch Nwsp; Fr Clb; IM Sprt; 4-H Awd; Univ.

VALENTINE, KAREN; Pinckney HS; Hamburg, MI; Cl Rep Jr Cls; Cls Rep Sr Cls; Chrh Wkr; Girl Scts; Off Ade; Treas Stu Cncl; Yrbk; Univ Of Michigan; Law.

VALENTINE, LUCINDA; Lewis County HS; Horner, WV; Band; Hon Rl; Jr NHS; NHS; Stg Crw; 4-H; Pep Clb; 4-H Awd; College; Radiologic Tech.

VALENTINE, MARY; Pickerington HS; Pickerington, OH; Cls Rep Sr Cls; Cmnty Wkr; Hon Rl; JA; Jr NHS; NHS; Stu Cncl; Am Leg Awd; Univ; Bus Mgmt.

VALENTINE, NANCY; Upper Arlington Sr HS; Columbus, OH; AFS; Hon Rl; Jr NHS; NHS; Fr Clb; Spn Clb; Letter Trk; GAA; 6th In St Of Oh In Spanish Level II 77; Vc Pres For Spanish Natl Hon Soc 78; Natl Sci Fdnt Partcpnt 79; Univ; Engr.

VALENTINE, NELSON V; Eastmoor HS; Columbus, OH; Cls Rep Frsh Cls; Cl Rep Jr Cls; Cls Rep Sr Cls; Boy Scts; Cmnty Wkr; Hon Rl; Stu Cncl; Yrbk; Boys Clb Am; Bsktbl; Morehouse Coll; Physician.

VALENTINE, PATRICK; St Joseph HS; Euclid, OH; Univ.

VALENTINO, VICTOR; Our Lady Of The Lakes HS; Clarkston, MI; Hon Rl; Natl Forn Lg; 4-H; Spn Clb; Letter Bsbl; Letter Ftbl; IM Sprt; 4-H Awd; Notre Dame Univ; Astronomy.

VALERIUS, PAUL; Theodore Roosevelt HS; Wyandotte, MI; Band; Boy Scts; Hon Rl;.

VALESANO, KATHY; Lake Ctrl HS; Dyer, IN; 10/468 Cls Rep Soph Cls; Cl Rep Jr Cls; Trs Sr Cls; Cls Rep Sr Cls; Chrs; Jr NHS; NHS; Purdue Univ; Engr.

VALIGOSKY, J; Cardinal Stritch HS; Toledo, OH; Cl Rep Jr Cls; Cls Rep Sr Cls; Hon Rl; NHS; Sch Mus;

Stu Cncl; Pep Clb; Trk; Chrldng; Owens Tech Coll; Comp Sci.

VALIGOSKY, STEVEN; St Francis De Sales HS; Toledo, OH; 3/200 Hon Rl; IM Sprt; Notre Dame Univ; Comp Systems.

VALINE, DEBRA; Baraga HS; Baraga, MI; Girl Scts; Hon Rl; NHS; Hockey; Trk; PPFtbl; College.

VALINET, GREG; Park Tudor School; Indianapolis, IN; Hon Rl; Off Ade; Stg Crw; Letter Socr; Univ; Econ.

VALK, BARBARA; Mona Shores HS; Muskegon, MI; Cl Rep Jr Cls; Band; Cmnty Wkr; Hon Rl; NHS; Stu Cncl; Letter Trk; Pom Pon; Pres Awd; Univ Of Michigan; Med Tech.

VALKIER, KIM; Hudsonville Public HS; Jenison, MI; Cmp Fr Grls; Sec Chrs; FCA; Hon Rl; JA; Lbry Ade; Mdrgl; NHS; Sch Mus; Sch Pl; Serv Awd 79; Sr Vocal Music Awd 79; Outstndng Young Amer 78; Grand Valley St Coll; Phys Ther.

VALLANCE, D; Northville HS; Northville, MI; Cls Rep Frsh Cls; Band; Hon Rl; NHS; Ger Clb; Natl Merit SF; Univ Of Michigan; Med.

VALLANCE, MARY; Milton HS; Ona, WV; Cls Rep Frsh Cls; Sec Soph Cls; VP Jr Cls; Chrs; Chrh Wkr; Hon Rl; Sch Mus; Yth Flsp; Fr Clb; FBLA; Johnson Bible Coll; Music.

VALLANDINGHAM, DEBBIE; Marsh Fork HS; Naoma, WV; Raleigh Cnty Voc Schl; Sec.

VALLEE, TROY; Crooksville HS; Crooksville, OH; 44/108 Cls Rep Frsh Cls; Cls Rep Soph Cls; Cl Rep Jr Cls; Cls Rep Sr Cls; Chrh Wkr; Hon Rl; Sch Pl; Pr es Stu Cncl; Bsbl; Bsktbl; MVP Bsktbl In Jr 79; Coll.

VALLERA, JOAN; Catholic Central HS; Steubenville, OH; 39/204 Cls Rep Frsh Cls; Cls Rep Soph Cls; Cl Rep Jr Cls; Cls Rep Sr Cls; Hon Rl; Hosp Ade; NHS; Rptr Sch Nwsp; Pep Clb; Chrldng; College; Medicine Research.

VALLERA, VALERIE; Catholic Central HS; Steubenvll, OH; 28/204 Band; Girl Scts; Hon Rl; Hosp Ade; NHS; Yrbk; FNA; Pep Clb; Spn Clb; DAR Awd; Spanish Cert For Maintaining A High Avr 76; Bishop Mussio Schltc Awd 76; 3rd Pl Poetry Awd Relgs Poem 73; Voc Schl; Cosmetology.

VALLEY, JAMES A; Saline HS; Saline, MI; Hon Rl; Crs Cntry; Ten; Trk; Coll; Drafting Engr.

VALLIE, SUE; Britton Macon HS; Britton, MI; Hon Rl; Rptr Sch Nwsp; Pres FHA; Bsktbl; Chrldng; Voice Dem Awd; Cls Homcmng Queen Jr Yr; Sr Homcmng Queen; Vllybl Team 4 Yrs; Eastern Michigan Univ.

VALLIER, MARY; Engadine Consolidated HS; Engadine, MI; Hon Rl; Lbry Ade; Sch Pl; Stg Crw; Stu Cncl; Yrbk; 4-H; FHA; Mgrs; PPFtbl; North Central Michigan Coll; Sec.

VALLIER, MICHAEL; Engadine Consolidated HS; Naubinway, MI; 4/56 Pres Frsh Cls; VP Jr Cls; Boy Scts; Hon Rl; Sct Actv; Yrbk; Letter Bsbl; Letter Bsktbl; Ftbl; Trk; Outstndng Stndt In Phys Sci 77; MVP Ftbl 79; Mst Imprvd Track 78; Michigan Tech Univ; Engr.

VALORE, PETER J; Gilmour Academy; Urbana, OH; 20/85 Hon Rl; Yrbk; Letter Bsbl; Letter Bsktbl; Letter Crs Cntry; Ohio St Univ; Law.

VANAC, MARY; Lake Catholic HS; Chardon, OH; Chrs; Cmnty Wkr; Hon Rl; JA; NHS; Pol Wkr; VP 4-H; 4-H Awd; JA Awd; Bus Admin.

VANADIA, CONCETTA; Valley Forge HS; Parma, OH; 20/777 Chrs; Cmnty Wkr; Hon Rl; NHS; Spn Clb; Mat Maids; Scr Kpr; Tmr; Ohio St Univ; Dent Hygn.

VAN AELST, TAMMIE; Mona Shores HS; Muskegon, MI; Sec Jr Cls; Cmp Fr Grls; Chrs; Hon Rl; Lbry Ade; Off Ade; Stu Cncl; Rptr Yrbk; Pep Clb; GAA; Cert Of Apprctn For Mi Wk Activits 79; Muskegon Cmnty Coll; Soc Work.

VAN ALLEN, ROSEMARY; Jonesville Community HS; Jonesville, MI; Band; Chrh Wkr; 4-H; Bsktbl; Scr Kpr; College; Herdswoman.

VAN ALST, KIMBERLY; Garber HS; Essexville, MI; Hon Rl; Lbry Ade; Cit Awd; Ferris St Coll; Data Processing.

VAN AMBURGH, MIKE; Elyria Catholic HS; Grafton, OH; Chrh Wkr; Hon Rl; 4-H; Ftbl; Wrstlng; 4-H Awd; Academic Letter GPA 3 Quarters 3.4; College; Ag.

VAN ARK, JON; Holland HS; Holland, MI; Band; Boy Scts; Hon Rl; JA; Mod UN; Stg Crw; Yrbk; Ger Clb; IM Sprt; God Cntry Awd; Hope Coll; Chem.

VAN ARSDALEN, LYNN; Hilltop HS; Alvordton, OH; VP Frsh Cls; Band; Chrh Wkr; Drl Tm; Pep Clb; Letter Bsktbl; IM Sprt; Twrlr; Univ; Music Instructor.

VAN ATTA, DEBRA; Hazel Park HS; Hazel Park, MI; Chrs; Off Ade; Michigan St Univ; Tchr.

VAN ATTA, MARSHA; Upper Arlington HS; Columbus, OH; 82/617 Chrs; Chrh Wkr; Hon Rl; Sch Mus; Spn Clb; Bsktbl; GAA; Mgrs; Coll; Med.

VAN BECK, MICHAEL; Portage Northern HS; Portage, MI; Cl Rep Jr Cls; VP Sr Cls; Hon Rl; NHS; Sci Clb; IM Sprt; Cit Awd; Univ Of Michigan; Med.

VAN BEEK, G; Holland Chr HS; Zeeland, MI; Trs Frsh Cls; Chrs; Hon Rl; NHS; Ger Clb; Letter Bsktbl; IM Sprt; Calvin Coll; Phys Ther.

VAN BENEDEN, CHRIS; Wheeling Cntrl Catholic HS; Wheeling, WV; Cl Rep Jr Cls; Chrh Wkr; Hon Rl; NHS; Stg Crw; Stu Cncl; Bsktbl; Trk; Natl Merit Ltr; Univ; Sci Bio.

VAN BRACKEL, JOE; Defiance HS; Defiance, OH; Band; Hon Rl; Jr NHS; NHS; Mth Clb; College; Business.

VAN BRUGGEN, PAM; South Christian HS; Grand Rapids, MI; Chrh Wkr; Hon Rl; Hosp Ade; Lbry Ade; Sch Pl; Stg Crw; Yrbk; Calvin Coll; Medicine.

VAN BRUGGEN, TERRIE; Portage Central HS; Portage, MI; Val; Hon Rl; OEA; Spn Clb; Natl Merit Ltr; 6th Pl In Natn Acctg 2nd Yr OEA 79; 3rd Pl In St Acctg 2nd Yr OEA 79; 1st Pl In Regnl Acctg OEA 79; Western Michigan Univ; Acctg.

VAN BUREN, CHERYL; Watkins Memorial HS; Hebron, OH; Cl Rep Jr Cls; Chrh Wkr; Hon Rl; Hosp Ade; NHS; Red Cr Ade; Stu Cncl; Pres 4-H; Ohio St Univ; Genetics.

VAN BUREN, DAVID; Lakewood HS; Vermontville, MI; 6/187 Cls Rep Frsh Cls; Chrs; FCA; Hon Rl; NHS; Stu Cncl; Ed Sch Nwsp; Mic State Univ; Math.

VAN BUREN, LESHA; Greenbrier East HS; Ronceverte, WV; Cl Rep Jr Cls; Band; Chrs; Girl Scts; Hon Rl; Sch Pl; 4-H; FHA; 4-H Awd; Business School; Sec.

VAN BUREN, LORI; Goshen HS; Goshen, IN; 52/269 Chrh Wkr; Girl Scts; Hon Rl; Fr Clb; FHA; Mth Clb; Pep Clb; Capt Chrldng; GAA; 2nd Pl Math Contst Sets & Venn Diagrams 77; 1st Pl Math Contst Geom 778; Purdue Univ; Math.

VAN BUREN, SCOT; St Johns HS; De Witt, MI; Cls Rep Frsh Cls; Cls Rep Soph Cls; Pres Jr Cls; VP Sr Cls; Hon Rl; NHS; Michigan St Univ; Chem Engr.

VAN BUREN, SUSAN; Nitro HS; Charleston, WV; VP Frsh Cls; Cls Rep Soph Cls; Cl Rep Jr Cls; Chrs; Hon Rl; Stu Cncl; Rptr Yrbk; Fr Clb; FBLA; Capt Chrldng; Univ; Acctg.

VAN CAMP, KATHY; Lake Orion Sr HS; Oxford, MI; 19/476 Band; Chrs; Hon Rl; Lit Mag; NHS; Sch Pl; Stg Crw; Ed Sch Nwsp; Drama Clb; Univ Of Michigan; Drama.

VAN CAMP, MARILYN; Jonesville HS; Jonesville, MI; 1/90 Sec Jr Cls; Am Leg Aux Girls St; Band; Hon Rl; NHS; Capt Chrldng; Rotary Awd; College; Medicine.

VAN CAMP, PEGGY; Bishop Chatard HS; Indianapolis, IN; 76/195 Hon Rl; Hosp Ade; Spn Clb; Letter Trk; Purdue Univ; Nursing.

VANCE, BARBARA; Hilliard HS; Galloway, OH; 89/324 AFS; Chrs; Cmnty Wkr; Hon Rl; PAVAS; Pol Wkr; Sch Mus; Sch Pl; Stg Crw; Yrbk; Ohio St Univ; Cmnctns.

VANCE, BRUCE; Batavia HS; Batavia, OH; Mth Clb; Spn Clb; Letter Bsbl; Letter Ftbl; Letter Trk; Kiwan Awd; Univ Of Cincinnati.

VANCE, CAROL; Lake City HS; Lake City, MI; 2/69 Sal; Lbry Ade; NHS; Stg Crw; Rptr Yrbk; Kiwan Awd; Central Mic Univ; Med Tech.

VANCE, KIMBERLY; Northwest HS; Mc Dermott, OH; 10/250 Trs Jr Cls; Chrs; Hon Rl; Hosp Ade; Treas NHS; Quill & Scroll; Sch Pl; Yrbk; VP FTA; Univ Of Cincinnati; Nursing.

VANCE, KURT; Cambridge HS; Cambridge, OH; Cmnty Wkr; Hon Rl; NHS; Pol Wkr; Key Clb; Letter Ftbl; Letter Trk; IM Sprt; Univ; Engr.

VANCE, ROBIN; Herbert Hoover HS; Charleston, WV; Off Ade; DECA; Drama Clb; Pep Clb; Chrldng; GAA; JC Awd; Marshall Univ; Med Tech.

VANCE, RONALD A; Elkins HS; Beverly, WV; Am Leg Boys St; Boy Scts; Hon Rl; NHS; Sch Pl; Sct Actv; Glf; Voice Dem Awd; Va Poly Inst; Vet Med.

VANCE, SUSAN; Pocahontas County HS; Green Bank, WV; 2/120 Trs Frsh Cls; Band; NHS; Stu Cncl; Ed Yrbk; Sec Drama Clb; VP FHA; Voice Dem Awd; College; Phys Ther.

VANCE, TAMMY; Clay County Sr HS; Lizemores, WV; Band; Chrh Wkr; FCA; Hon Rl; Jr NHS; NHS; Yth Flsp; Rptr Yrbk; Rptr Sch Nwsp; FHA; Pres Of Bible Clb 79;.

VANCE, TERESA; Wayne HS; Dayton, OH; Cls Rep Sr Cls; Band; Drm Bgl; JA; Letter Scr Kpr; Letter Twrlr; Air Force; Law Enforcement.

VANCE, TINA; Arcanum HS; Arcanum, OH; Sec Soph Cls; Hon Rl; NHS; Off Ade; Sch Pl; Yth Flsp; Chrldng; IM Sprt; Scr Kpr; Wright St Univ; Art.

VANCE, WILLIAM S; Hobart HS; Hobart, IN; 32/395 FCA; Hon Rl; NHS; Off Ade; Stu Cncl; Ger Clb; Capt Bsktbl; Trk; Indiana Univ; Bus Admin.

VANCHECK, MARLA; Marquette Sr HS; Marquette, MI; Chrs; Lbry Ade; Sct Actv; Michigan Tech Univ; Forestry.

VANDAGRIFF, RANDY; Park Hills HS; Fairborn, OH; 39/345 Hon Rl; Wrstlng; IM Sprt; College; Engr.

VANDALL, PAMELA; Brookhaven HS; Columbus, OH; Band; Chrh Wkr; Treas Drl Tm; Hon Rl; Off Ade; Stu Cncl; Pres Pep Clb; Spn Clb; Mat Maids; Mas Awd; Univ Of Southern Flo; Marine Bio.

VANDAM, DONALD; Hamilton HS; Hamilton, MI; 20/131 Boy Scts; Chrh Wkr; Hon Rl; Lat Clb; Spn Clb; Letter Bsktbl; Letter Ten; Central Michigan Univ; Med.

VANDEGRIFT, GARY; Hoover HS; North Canton, OH; 31/422 Band; Boy Scts; Chrs; Hon Rl; JA; 4-H; Ger Clb; College; Comp.

VANDEMARK, MICHAEL; Bay City Western HS; Bay City, MI; Boys Clb Am; Crs Cntry; Trk; Alma College; Chem Engr.

VANDENBERG, MICHAEL; Holland HS; Holland, MI; 17/289 Band; Boy Scts; Hon Rl; NHS; Sct Actv; Pep Clb; Sci Clb; Letter Glf; Natl Merit Schl; Mich State Univ; Premedical.

VANDENBERG, THOMAS H; Zeeland Sr HS; Zeeland, MI; 18/174 Am Leg Boys St; Hon Rl; Mod UN; NHS; Ed Sch Nwsp; Lat Clb; Letter Ftbl; Letter Trk; Natl Merit SF; Gr Rapids Baptist Univ; Mssnry Pilot.

VANDENBERGH, ANN; Elkins HS; Elkins, WV; 37/250 Cls Rep Soph Cls; Sec Jr Cls; Cl Rep Jr Cls; Trs Sr Cls; Cls Rep Sr Cls; Band; Chrh Wkr; Cmnty Wkr; Hon Rl; NHS; Univ Vir; Law.

VAN DENBURGH, PAULA; Western HS; Parma, MI; 2/171 Chrs; Debate Tm; Hon Rl; NHS; Sch Mus; Sch Pl; 4-H; Spn Clb; Mi Compttv Schlshp 79; Jackson Cmnty Coll; Data Proc.

VAN DER ARK, DAVID; South Christian HS; Grand Rapids, MI; 4/150 Band; Hon Rl; NHS; Sch Pl; Bsbl; Mgrs; Calvin Coll; Engr.

VANDER ARK, SHARON; South Christian HS; Grand Rapids, MI; Chrs; Chrh Wkr; Hon Rl; Hosp Ade; Jr NHS; Lbry Ade; Natl Forn Lg; NHS; Sch Pl; Rptr Sch Nwsp; Calvin Coll; Nursing.

VANDERBEEK, AMY; Interlochen Arts Academy; Detroit, MI; Cmnty Wkr; Hon Rl; Pol Wkr; Sch Mus; Sch Pl; Stg Crw; 5th Pl In Natl French Contst 76; Mert Schlshp In Dance & Acad 78 & 79; Univ; Dance.

VANDERCOOK, LOIS; Taylor Center HS; Taylor, MI; 15/438 Cls Rep Frsh Cls; Chrh Wkr; Hon Rl; NHS; Gym; Letter Trk; Letter Chrldng; GAA; Univ Of Mic; Nurse.

VANDERGRIFT, KELLY; Williamstown HS; Williamstown, WV; Chrs; Hon Rl; NHS; Sch Mus; Fr Clb; Trk; Letter Mgrs; Excellnt Mark At The Solo & Ensmbl Fest Regn X 78; West Liberty Univ; Educ.

VANDER HILL, JON; Muncie Central HS; Muncie, IN; 8/320 Chrh Wkr; NHS; Off Ade; Sch Pl; Stg Crw; Drama Clb; Ger Clb; Lat Clb; Ten; Kiwan Awd; Univf Comp Math.

VANDER KOOI, JOEL A; Holland Christian HS; Zeeland, MI; 22/265 Chrs; Chrh Wkr; Debate Tm; Hon Rl; Jr NHS; Natl Forn Lg; NHS; Eng Clb; Ger Clb; Calvin Coll; Poli Sci.

VANDER KOOI, STEVEN; Muskegon HS; Muskegon, MI; Am Leg Boys St; Chrh Wkr; Cmnty Wkr; NHS; Pres Stu Cncl; Sprt Ed Yrbk; Spn Clb; Ftbl; Am Leg Awd; Cit Awd; Muskegon Cnty Cmnty Found Schlrshp 79; E J Stewart Schlrshp 79; St Of Mi Competitive Schlrshp 79; Michigan St Univ; Bus Admin.

VANDER PLOEG, JUDY; Zeeland HS; Zeeland, MI; 38/193 Hon Rl;.

VANDER SCHMITT, MARK F; Washington HS; Washington, IN; 7/200 Hon Rl; Pol Wkr; ROTC; Sch Pl; Pres Beta Clb; Drama Clb; Treas 4-H; Sec Key Clb; Am Leg Awd; Voice Dem Awd; Indiana Univ; Comp Sci.

VANDER SCHUUR, DIANE; Hudsonville HS; Hudsonville, MI; 6/174 Cls Rep Soph Cls; VP Jr Cls; VP Sr Cls; Cmp Fr Grls; Chrs; FCA; Hon Rl; Mdrgl; Natl Forn Lg; NHS; Hmcmng Rep; 2nd Runner Up Miss Husdonville Pageant; Mich Busns Schls Assn Schlrshp; Davenport Coll Of Busns; Acctg.

VAN DER STEL, JODI; Kenowa Hills HS; Grand Rapids, MI; 13/250 Band; Hon Rl; NHS; 4-H; Key Clb; Spn Clb; Letter Glf; PPFtbl; 4-H Awd; Hope Coll; Pre Med.

VANDER STELT, CHRIS; Muskegon Sr HS; Muskegon, MI; Band; Girl Scts; Hon Rl; NHS; Yth Flsp; Yrbk; Coach Actv; Univ; Educ.

VANDER STELT, VICKI; Hicksville HS; Hicksville, OH; Chrs; Chrh Wkr; Hon Rl; NHS; Sch Mus; Sch Pl; Yth Flsp; Pep Clb; Spn Clb; Letter Bsbl; Coll; Interior Design.

VAN DER VEEN, LOU ANN; Warren Central HS; Indianapolis, IN; Hon Rl; NHS; OEA; Purdue Univ.

VAN DER VEEN, SHARON; Evart HS; Evart, MI; Val; Band; Chrs; Hon Rl; VP NHS; Sch Pl; Stg Crw; Yth Flsp; Mgrs; PPFtbl; Ferris St Coll; Pharm.

VAN DER VENNET, GREG; Greenville HS; Sterling, IL; 84/365 Boy Scts; Chrs; Mdrgl; Sch Mus; Sch Pl; Stg Crw; Civ Clb; Sauk Valley Jr College.

VANDER VENNET, RENE; St Agatha HS; Redford, MI; 8/134 Pres Frsh Cls; Cls Rep Soph Cls; Pres Sr Cls; Hon Rl; NHS; Yrbk; Trk; Wayne State Univ; Medicine.

VANDER WALL, KIMBERLY J; Wyoming Park HS; Wyoming, MI; Girl Scts; Hon Rl; Letter Trk; Bus Schl; Acctg.

VANDER WEFF, DENISE; Catholic Central HS; Grand Rapids, MI; Hon Rl; Hosp Ade; NHS; Drama Clb; Sec Lat Clb; Letter Bsktbl; Letter Trk; Wrstlng; Univ Of Mic; Med.

VAN DER WEIDE, LORI; South Christian HS; Middleville, MI; Band; Calvin Coll; Educ.

VANDERZALM, GLEN; Huntington E HS; Huntington, WV; 25/326 Cls Rep Soph Cls; Cl Rep Jr Cls; Am Leg Boys St; Chrs; Jr NHS; Mdrgl; NHS; Sch Mus; Letter Bsktbl; Marshall Univ; Med.

VANDER ZANDEN, LISA; Hart HS; Hart, MI; Cl Rep Jr Cls; Hon Rl; Off Ade; Stu Cncl; Rptr Yrbk; Rptr Sch Nwsp; Drama Clb; 4-H; W Shore Community; Sec.

VANDER ZEE, CARL; Kenowa Hills HS; Comstock Park, MI; 10/221 Hon Rl; Pol Wkr; Davenport Coll Of Busns; Mktg.

VAN DEUSEN, GARY; Highland HS; Medina, OH; Band; Orch; Ger Clb; Wrstlng; Ohio Inst Of Tech; Elec.

VAN DEUSEN, LORI; Ovid Elsie HS; Ovid, MI; Band; Girl Scts; Pep Clb; PPFtbl; Lansing Bus Inst; Sec.

VANDEVANDER, ANN; Meadowdale HS; Dayton, OH; 18/239 Hon Rl; NHS; Off Ade; Sch Pl; Drama Clb; Letter Gym; Socr; Mgrs; Ohio St Univ.

VAN DE VELDE, JIM; Rocky River HS; Rocky River, OH; Hon Rl; Bsbl; Bsbl; IM Sprt; College; Acctng.

VAN DEVENDER, BONNY; Canton South HS; N Industry, OH; Band; Hon Rl; JA; Mth Clb; Scr Kpr; College.

VAN DEVENTER, CRAIG; Sycamore HS; Cincinnati, OH; Boy Scts; Hon Rl; PAVAS; Sct Actv; Yth Flsp; IM Sprt; Evans Scholarship; Ohio State Univ; Aero Engr.

VAN DE VUSSE, WILLIAM; West Ottawa HS; Holland, MI; 69/323 Band; Chrs; Mdrgl; NHS; Sch Mus; Sch Pl; Stg Crw; Ed Yrbk; Rptr Sch Nwsp; Drama Clb; Principals Awd 79; Spring Arbor Coll Hon Awd Schlrshp 79; Spring Arbor Coll; Bus.

VAN DRESE, DALE; Escanaba Area HS; Escanaba, MI; 139/442 Chrh Wkr; Cmnty Wkr; Hon Rl; JA; 4-H; Bsbl; Bsktbl; Mgrs; JA Awd; Suomi Univ; Law Enforcmnt.

VAN DUZER, RICHARD; Brooklyn HS; Brooklyn, OH; Chrs; Jr NHS; NHS; Sch Mus; Fr Clb; Letter Bsbl; Bsktbl; Ftbl; College; Pre Law.

VAN DYKE, BETH M; Central HS; Grand Rapids, MI; Band; Chrs; Hon Rl; Mdrgl; Sch Mus; Sch Pl; Rptr Sch Nwsp; Fr Clb; Pep Clb; Chrldng; Jr Coll Of Grand Rapids; Jrnlsm.

VAN DYKE, BRENDA; Davison Sr HS; Davison, MI; Band; Chrh Wkr; Girl Scts; Hon Rl; Stu Cncl; Yth Flsp; Yrbk; Scr Kpr; JC Awd; Central Michigan Univ; Chld Psych.

VAN DYKE, DENISE D; Hurrican HS; Scott Depot, WV; Band; Hon Rl; NHS; Stu Cncl; Y-Teens; Letter Bsktbl; Ten; Letter Trk; Volleyball Jr & Sr Yrs; West Virginia Univ; Optometry.

VAN DYKE, JOHN J; John F Kennedy HS; Newton Falls, OH; 18/157 Boy Scts; Chrh Wkr; Hon Rl; NHS; Quill & Scroll; Sct Actv; Rptr Yrbk; Sprt Ed Sch Nwsp; Fr Clb; Sci Clb; Pope Pius The 12th 1978; Eagle Awd 1979; Univ; Physics.

VAN DYKE, MICHELLE; Brooke HS; Wellsburg, WV; 3/403 Chrs; Chrh Wkr; FCA; Hon Rl; NHS; Sec Stu Cncl; Yth Flsp; Letter Chrldng; GAA; IM Sprt; Hugh O Brian Youth Fdn 77; Chem 1 Awd Presented By BHS Chem Dept 78; Univ; Pharm.

VAN DYKE, MICHELLE; Catholic Central HS; Grand Rapids, MI; Cmnty Wkr; Hon Rl; Hosp Ade; JA; Off Ade; Pol Wkr; Red Cr Ade; Stu Cncl; Grand Rapids Jr Coll; Child Devlpmt.

VAN DYKE, SHARI; Spring Lake HS; Spring Lake, MI; 20/185 Band; Drm Mjrt; Hon Rl; NHS; Orch; Sch Mus; Trk; Twrlr; Elk Awd; Natl Merit SF; Muskegon Cmnty Coll; Acctg.

VAN DYKE, SHARON; Union HS; Grand Rapids, MI; Hon Rl; NHS; Yth Flsp; Trk; Tmr; Pres Awd; Grand Rapids Junior College.

VAN EATON, DEBORAH S; Lincoln HS; Vincennes, IN; Hon Rl; Lbry Ade; Sec Stu Cncl; 4-H; Fr Clb; FBLA; FHA; FTA; Pep Clb; Univ; Fashn Desgn.

VAN EK, DELORES J; Jenison HS; Allendale, MI; Chrs; Chrh Wkr; FCA; Hon Rl; NHS; Off Ade; Sch Mus; Yth Flsp; Grand Rapids Bapt College; Bus.

VAN EK, SHELLEY; Eastwood HS; Pemberville, OH; 13/185 Hon Rl; 4-H; VICA; GAA; 4-H Awd; Penta Cnty Voc Schl; Cmmrcl Art.

VAN ENGEN _II, RICHARD W; Hastings HS; Hastings, MI; 2/167 Am Leg Boys St; Chrs; Chrh Wkr; FCA; Hon Rl; Yth Flsp; Letter Bsbl; Letter Ftbl; IM Sprt; Hope Coll; Phys Ed.

VAN ES, TAMARA; John Adams HS; S Bend, IN; 15/350 Chrs; Chrh Wkr; Hon Rl; Lit Mag; NHS; Yth Flsp; Rptr Yrbk; 4-H; Spn Clb; Tmr; Univ Of Notre Dame.

VAN ESLEY, GREGORY J; St Alphonsus HS; Detroit, MI; Boy Scts; Chrs; Chrh Wkr; Cmnty Wkr; Debate Tm; Hon Rl; Natl Forn Lg; Off Ade; Pol Wkr; Sch Mus; Pres Of Internatl Clb; Elected Commissioner At Large; Lead Role Schl Musical Guys & Dolls; Henry Ford Cmnty Coll; Law.

VAN ESSEN, GERRI; Harrison Community HS; Harrison, MI; VP Frsh Cls; VP Soph Cls; Hon Rl; Lbry Ade; Stu Cncl; Chrldng; Pres Awd; Cntrl Michigan Univ; Acctg.

VAN ETTEN, BRADLEY; Turpin HS; Cincinnati, OH; 12/320 Band; NHS; Off Ade; Orch; Sch Pl; Treas Drama Clb; Natl Merit SF; College.

VAN ETTEN, BRADLEY T; Turpin HS; Cincinnati, OH; 20/357 Chrs; NHS; Off Ade; Orch; Sch Pl; Treas Drama Clb; Natl Merit SF; Univ; Econ.

VAN FLEET, PETER; East Kentwood HS; Kentwood, MI; Letter Hockey; Coll.

VAN FOSSAN, GAIL; Bishop Foley HS; Oak Park, MI; 24/193 Debate Tm; Girl Scts; Hon Rl; Lbry Ade; Sch Mus; Sch Pl; Stg Crw; Yth Flsp; Yrbk; PPFtbl; Oakland Univ; Nursing.

VAN FOSSEN, PEGGY; Norton HS; Norton, OH; Cls Rep Frsh Cls; Cls Rep Soph Cls; Cl Rep Jr Cls; Cmnty Wkr; Girl Scts; Hon Rl; Jr NHS; NHS; FHA; Trk; College; Special Educ.

VAN GEISON, LYNN; St Philips Cath Ctrl HS; Battle Creek, MI; Trs Frsh Cls; Cls Rep Frsh Cls; VP Sr Cls; Cls Rep Sr Cls; Hon Rl; NHS; Yrbk; Fr Clb; Lat Clb; Pep Clb; Univ.

VAN GELOFF, KENNETH; Port Clinton HS; Port Clinton, OH; 3/350 Am Leg Boys St; Chrs; Hon Rl; NHS; Mth Clb; Bsbl; Bsktbl; Am Leg Awd; Univ; Comp Sci.

VAN GENDEREN, JONI; Clawson HS; Clawson, MI; Cls Rep Soph Cls; Cl Rep Jr Cls; Hon Rl; Orch; Stu Cncl; Yrbk; Cit Awd; Univ Of Michigan; Law.

VAN GESSEL, CHRIS; East Noble HS; Kendallville, IN; Am Leg Aux Girls St; Chrh Wkr; NHS; Stg Crw; Y-Teens; Drama Clb; Trk; Am Leg Awd; Purdue; Chemical Engineering.

VAN GESSEL, DANIEL; Creston HS; Grand Rapids, MI; Boy Scts; FCA; Hon Rl; Jr NHS; NHS; Pep Clb; Sci Clb; Crs Cntry; Swmmng; Grand Rapids Jr College; Chiropactic.

VAN GIESON, KEVIN; Ovid Elsie HS; Ovid, MI; Hon Rl; Rptr Sch Nwsp; Business School; Accounting.

VAN GILDER, JAMES L; Huron HS; Huron, OH; 58/168 Am Leg Boys St; Boy Scts; Chrh Wkr; Debate Tm; FCA; Hon Rl; Yth Flsp; Lat Clb; Mth Clb; Sci Clb; Centry 6 Leadrshp Awd 79; Scotts Ppr Hi Q Team 79; Sandusky Chambr Of Commrc Econ Semnr 79; Michigan St Univ.

VAN GILDER, LOUISE; Lincoln HS; Shinnston, WV; Am Leg Aux Girls St; Band; Boy Scts; Chrs; Hon Rl; NHS; Sch Mus; Sct Actv; Drama Clb; Fr Clb; West Virginia Univ; Music.

VAN GUNDY, CHARLES; Groveport Madison HS; Columbus, OH; Chrs; Hon Rl; Sch Mus; Sch Pl; Bsbl; Ftbl; Socr; Coach Actv; IM Sprt; Cit Awd; College; Acctg.

VAN GUNDY, TAMMY; Western HS; Bainbridge, OH; 2/47 Chrs; Hon Rl; Fr Clb; Bus.

VAN HAITSMA, KENNETH; Mc Bain Rural Agri HS; Mc Bain, MI; 9/62 Hon Rl; NHS; Sch Pl; Treas FFA; Letter Bsbl; Letter Ftbl; Letter Trk; Coach Actv; Ferris St Coll; Broadcasting.

VAN HALL, PAMELA; Spring Lake HS; Spring Lake, MI; Band; Hon Rl; NHS; Sch Mus; IM Sprt; Elk Awd; Ferris St Coll; Bus Admin.

VAN HOEF, MATTHEW C; Grand Haven HS; Grand Haven, MI; Am Leg Boys St; FCA; Hon Rl; Jr NHS; NHS; Yth Flsp; Ftbl; Ten; Natl Merit SF; College; Busns Admin.

VAN HOOK, DIANA; Fountain Central HS; Hillsboro, IN; 8/150 Band; Chrh Wkr; Hon Rl; NHS; Rptr Sch Nwsp; Fr Clb; FHA; Lat Clb; DAR Awd; College; Journalism.

VAN HOOK, JEFFERY; John F Kennedy HS; Taylor, MI; 15/450 Boy Scts; Hon Rl; Jr NHS; NHS; Red Cr Ade; Yth Flsp; Capt Bsbl; Letter Ftbl; Summa Cum Laude 77; Univ.

VAN HORN, SHARON; South Charleston HS; S Charleston, WV; Band; Chrh Wkr; Girl Scts; JA; Rptr Sch Nwsp; Sch Nwsp; Spn Clb; Univ; Law.

VAN HORNE, CURT; Hubbard HS; Hubbard, OH; 27/330 Chrs; Yth Flsp; Fr Clb; Letter Swmmng; Perfect Attendence; College; Comp Sci.

VAN HOUTEN, CARRIE L; Athens HS; Athens, MI; Girl Scts; Jr NHS; Sch Pl; 4-H; Pep Clb; Bsktbl; Letter Trk; 4-H Awd; Busns Schl; Travel Agent.

VAN HOUTEN, GRETCHEN; Holy Redeemer HS; Detroit, MI; Girl Scts; Hon Rl; NHS; Rptr Sch Nwsp; Sch Nwsp; Spn Clb; College; Pre Law.

VAN HOUTEN, JUNE; Cardington Lincoln HS; Cardington, OH; Chrs; Girl Scts; Sch Pl; Yth Flsp; Rptr Sch Nwsp;.

VAN HOVE, LINDA; Whiteford HS; Riga, MI; Cmp Fr Grls; Hon Rl; NHS; Letter Bsbl; Letter Bsktbl; GAA; IM Sprt; Scr Kpr; Monroe Comm College; Acctg.

VAN HULLE, RANDY; Lincoln HS; Ferndale, MI; 9/325 Hon Rl; Jr NHS; NHS; Rptr Sch Nwsp; 3rd Pl Rgnl Mech Engr Cntst 77; 2nd Pl Macomb Univ Essy Wrtng Cntst 78; 1 Yr Full Tuition Schlrshp 78; Wayne St Univ; Pre Bus Admin.

VAN KAMPEN, KATHY; Grandville HS; Wyoming, MI; Bsktbl; PPFtbl; Univ; Phys Ther.

VAN KEPPEL, JEAN M; Kankakee Vly HS; De Motte, IN; 6/186 Cls Rep Frsh Cls; Pres Soph Cls; Cls Rep Soph Cls; Cls Rep Sr Cls; Hon Rl; NHS; Stu Cncl; Ed Yrbk; Sprt Ed Yrbk; Rptr Yrbk; Univ Of South California; Bus.

VAN KIRK, BRADLEY; Whitko HS; Warsaw, IN; Hon Rl; Fr Clb; Capt Glf; College; Architecture.

VAN KLEY, LORI; Kankakee Vly HS; De Motte, IN; 1/190 Am Leg Aux Girls St; Pres Chrh Wkr; Hon Rl; Pres NHS; Spn Clb; Capt Bsktbl; Letter Trk; GAA; Mgrs; Math Awd Geometry & Algebra; Spanish Awd; Chemistry Awd; Purdue Univ; Nursing.

VAN KOEVERING, KURTIS; Zeeland Public HS; Zeeland, MI; 111/180 Boy Scts; JA; Mod UN; Yth Flsp; Ger Clb; Ftbl; JA Awd; Bus Admin.

VAN LAAN, CATHY; South Christian HS; Caledonia, MI; Drl Tm; Hon Rl; Jr NHS; NHS; Stg Crw; St Of Mi Grant; Kendall Schl Of Design; Cmmrcl Art.

VAN LAAR, AMY; Allendale HS; Zeeland, MI; Pres Frsh Cls; Cls Rep Frsh Cls; Cls Rep Sr Cls; Sal; Band; FCA; Hon Rl; Hillsdale College; History.

VANLANDEHEM, KAREN; Lutheran HS; Detroit, MI; Band; Hon Rl; Orch; Sch Pl; Rptr Yrbk; Pep Clb Pom Pon; College; Med.

VAN LARE, PAULA; Defiance Sr HS; Defiance, OH; 1/295 Band; Chrs; Hon Rl; Jr NHS; NHS; Fr Clb; Mth Clb; Sci Clb; Univ; Engr.

VANLERBERGHE, RICHARD; L Anse Creuse HS North; Mt Clemens, MI; 95/300 Hon Rl; Jr NHS; Ftbl; St Of Mi Shclsp 79; Mi Indust Educ Awd Progr 9th Pl St 2nd Pl Local 78; Oakland Univ; Engr.

VAN LEUVEN, JULIE; North Muskegon HS; N Muskegon, MI; 4/108 Band; Hon Rl; NHS; Orch; Sch Mus; Trk; Letter Chrldng; College.

VAN LEW, DONNA; Niles HS; Niles, MI; Band; Sec Chrh Wkr; Hon Rl; Pres JA; Orch; Sec Yth Flsp; VP JA Awd; South Western Mic; Criminology.

VAN LIEROP, SUSAN S; Hartford HS; Hartford, MI; Cls Rep Soph Cls; VP Jr Cls; Band; Pres Stu Cnc l; Rptr Sch Nwsp; Pep Clb; Letter Trk; Letter Chrldng; PPFtbl; Univ.

VANLIEU, TANYA; Franklin HS; Franklin, OH; Cls Rep Frsh Cls; Cls Rep Soph Cls; Cl Rep Jr Cls; Band; Chrs; Lbry Ade; Sch Mus; Stu Cncl; Pep Clb; Scr Kpr; Miami Univ; Professional Modeling.

VAN LOO, JILL; Willard HS; Willard, OH; Cl Rep Jr Cls; Chrs; Stu Cncl; Yrbk; Tmr; Calvin Coll; Psych.

VAN LOON, ESTHER; Kentwood Public HS; Grand Rapids, MI; Cl Rep Jr Cls; Stu Cncl; Yrbk; GAA; IM Sprt; Business School; Accounting Admin.

VAN LUE, MELANIE; Niles Sr HS; Niles, MI; Cls Rep Frsh Cls; Band; Hon Rl; Stu Cncl; Yth Flsp; 4-H; Gym; Chrldng; Patricia Stevens Coll; Exec Sec.

VAN LY, NGOC; Bishop Luers HS; Ft Wayne, IN; Boy Scts; Chrh Wkr; Hon Rl; Sct Actv; Socr; Cincinnati Univ; Archt.

VAN MEERBEECK, ELIZABETH; Divine Child HS; Dearborn Ht, MI; Hon Rl; Jr NHS; NHS; Rptr Yrbk; Yrbk; Fr Clb; FTA; Pep Clb; Mic Tech Univ; Civil Engr.

VAN METER, CLAY; Park Hills HS; Fairborn, OH; Hon Rl; Fr Clb; Cit Awd; Miami Univ; Aero.

VAN METER, JOAN; North Knox HS; Bicknell, IN; 3/150 Chrh Wkr; Hon Rl; NHS; Yth Flsp; Fr Clb; ISU; Math Tchr.

VAN METER, MARK; Kent Theodore Roosevelt HS; Kent, OH; 25/346 Boy Scts; FCA; Hon Rl; NHS; Letter Bsbl; Letter Bsktbl; Letter Ftbl; Univ; Bus.

VAN METER, VICKY; Western HS; Piketon, OH; 3/76 Band; Chrh Wkr; Lbry Ade; NHS; Pol Wkr; Sec 4-H; 4-H Awd; Coll; Nursing.

VAN METRE, BRUCE; Vantage Joint Voc HS; Van Wert, OH; 28/78 Band; Hon Rl; Pres DECA; Pres 4-H; FFA; 4-H Awd; FFA Specialty Awd Dist Competition; FFA Rabbit Awds; Member Jr Fair Board;.

VAN METRE, G SCOTT; Van Wert HS; Van Wert, OH; 4/200 Hon Rl; NHS; Rptr Sch Nwsp; Fr Clb; Lat Clb; Univ Of Cin; Architecture.

VANN, KEITH; Southwestern HS; Detrit, MI; Cls Rep Frsh Cls; Cls Rep Soph Cls; Cl Rep Jr Cls; Hon Rl; College; Elec.

VANN, PATRICIA D; Columbus E HS; Columbus, OH; Hon Rl; Off Ade; Stu Cncl; Spn Clb; Bishop Univ; Fashion Mdse.

VANN, PECOLA; Horace Mann HS; Gary, IN; Chrh Wkr; Hon Rl; JA; Stu Cncl; Fr Clb; Mth Clb; Chrldng; Cit Awd; Purdue Calumet; English.

VANN, WANDA; East HS; Columbus, OH; 5/272 Girl Scts; Hon Rl; Jr NHS; Off Ade; Spn Clb; Capt Chrldng; Spanish Natl Honor Soc 1976; Univ Of Miami; Bus Admin.

VANN, WANDA L; East HS; Columbus, OH; 5/294 Hon Rl; NHS; Off Ade; Spn Clb; Capt Chrldng; Natl Merit Ltr; Natl Merit SF; Fisk Univ; Bus Admin.

VANNONI, DINO; Penn HS; Mishawaka, IN; Pres Frsh Cls; Am Leg Boys St; Boy Scts; Hon Rl; Mod UN; Natl Forn Lg; Sch Pl; Stg Crw; Stu Cncl; Drama Clb; Ball State; Acting.

VAN OCHTEN, GREG; Arthur Hill HS; Saginaw, MI; Hon Rl; Bsbl; Ftbl; Pres Awd; Univ; Optometry.

VAN OOTEGHEM, KATHY; Essexville Garber HS; Essexville, MI; 33/180 Chrs; Chrh Wkr; Hon Rl; NHS; Bsbl; Bsktbl; Cit Awd; Natl Merit Ltr; Natl Merit SF; Natl Merit Schl; Concordia Ann Arbor; Elementary Educ.

VAN ORDER, CHERYL; Olivet HS; Olivet, MI; Sec Frsh Cls; VP Soph Cls; Band; Sch Pl; Stu Cncl; Drama Clb; Lat Clb; Letter Chrldng; GAA; Calhoun Cnty Voc Cntr; Hairsyling.

VAN ORMAN, G; Pellston HS; Levering, MI; Cls Rep Frsh Cls; Cls Rep Soph Cls; Hon Rl; Stu Cncl; FTA; Letter Bsbl; Capt Bsktbl; Ftbl; Trk; College.

VANOVER, PATRICIA; Norwood HS; Norwood, OH; 35/350 Boy Scts; Drl Tm; Hon Rl; Hosp Ade; Jr NHS; Red Cr Ade; VP Lat Clb; Univ; RN.

VAN PELT, DEBBIE; South Range HS; Columbiana, OH; Am Leg Aux Girls St; Chrh Wkr; Hon Rl; Pres NHS; Stg Crw; Stu Cncl; Sec Yth Flsp; Ed Yrbk; Yrbk; Drama Clb; Eastern Mennonite College; Art.

VAN PELT, KORINNE; Reeths Puffer HS; Muskegon, MI; 1/351 Chrh Wkr; Hon Rl; JA; NHS; Sch Mus; Stu Cncl; Spn Clb; Chrldng; Michigan St Univ; Pre Vet Med.

VAN PUTTEN, JEFF; Holland HS; Holland, MI; Debate Tm; Hon Rl; Sch Nwsp; Ger Clb; Socr; Coach Actv; IM Sprt; College; German.

VAN RAVENSWAAY, JULIE; Holland HS; Holland, MI; 12/296 Hon Rl; NHS; Orch; Rptr Yrbk; Rptr Sch Nwsp; Drama Clb; FDA; FNA; Scr Kpr; Ferris State College; Mdse.

VAN REETH, LYNETTE S; John Glenn HS; Norwich, OH; 14/183 Cl Rep Jr Cls; Am Leg Aux Girls St; Band; Pres Chrs; Hon Rl; NHS; Sch Mus; Y-Teens; Fr Clb; Capt Chrldng; Bowling Green St Univ; Music Educ.

VAN RIPER, LORI; Chelsea HS; Chelsea, MI; 17/200 Band; Hosp Ade; NHS; Orch; Sch Mus; Rptr Yrbk; Pep Clb; Chrldng; PPFtbl; Natl Merit SF; Michigan St Univ; Spec Educ.

VAN ROEKEL, RONALD A; Hudsonville HS; Hudsonville, MI; Cls Rep Soph Cls; VP Jr Cls; Boy Scts; Hon Rl; NHS; Spn Clb; Letter Crs Cntry; Letter Trk; Coll; Comp Repair.

VAN ROOYEN, CINDY; Catholic Central HS; Wyoming, MI; Cmp Fr Grls; Chrs; Chrh Wkr; Hon Rl; Jr NHS; NHS; Quill & Scroll; Aquinas College; Educa.

VAN ROOYEN, ED; Catholic Central HS; Wyoming, MI; Am Leg Boys St; Boy Scts; Chrh Wkr; Hon Rl; Spn Clb; College.

VAN ROOYEN, MICHAEL; St Johns HS; St Johns, MI; Sec Soph Cls; Sec Jr Cls; Pres Sr Cls; Boy Scts; Hon Rl; Sch Pl; Sct Actv; Yth Flsp; Drama Clb; 4-H; Michigan St Univ; Pre Med.

VAN SCHAGEN, JOHN; Greenville Sr HS; Greenville, MI; 5/230 Cl Rep Jr Cls; Cls Rep Sr Cls; Am Leg Boys St; Band; Boy Scts; Orch; Stu Cncl; Rptr Sch Nwsp; IM Sprt; Natl Merit Ltr; Michigan St Univ Schlrshp For Acad Exc; R J Tower Schlrshp; Dr Bower Memorial Schlrshp; Michigan St Univ; Med.

VAN SCHOICK, TIM; Parkside HS; Jackson, MI; Cls Rep Sr Cls; Hon Rl; Bsktbl; Hope Coll; Pre Med.

VAN SCOY, KAREN; Upper Sandusky HS; La Rue, OH; 13/213 Chrs; Girl Scts; Hon Rl; NHS; Stg Crw; Stu Cncl; Yth Flsp; Pres 4-H; 4-H Awd; College; Art.

VAN SCOY, STEVE; North Miami HS; Denver, IN; PAVAS; FFA; Ftbl; Univ; Comm Art.

VAN SCOY, WILLIAM; Upper Sandusky HS; La Rue, OH; 34/215 Chrh Wkr; Hon Rl; Jr NHS; NHS; Yth Flsp; Pres 4-H; FFA; IM Sprt; 4-H Awd; Wilmington Coll; Agri.

VAN SICKLE, VICTOR; Kyger Creek HS; Gallipolis, OH; Aud/Vis; Hon Rl; Bsktbl; Ftbl; Trk;.

VAN SLAGER, CYNTHIA; George Washington HS; S Bend, IN; Pres Frsh Cls; Pres Soph Cls; NHS; Sch Mus; Sch Pl; Spn Clb; Letter Bsktbl; Letter Trk; Chrldng; Indiana Univ.

VAN SLEMBROUCK, LISA; Cheboygan Area HS; Cheboygan, MI; Girl Scts; Hon Rl; Hosp Ade; 4-H; Spn Clb;.

VAN SLYKE, DIANE; Jefferson Area HS; Jefferson, OH; AFS; Lbry Ade; Sec Stu Cncl; Sprt Ed Sch Nwsp; Fr Clb; Sec Gym; Ten; Chrldng; IM Sprt; Scr Kpr; Univ; Nurse.

VAN SLYKE, TAMARA; Lincoln HS; Shinnston, WV; 5/148 Pres Lbry Ade; NHS; Rptr Sch Nwsp; Pep Clb; Sci Clb; Spn Clb; Trk; Am Leg Awd; Dnfth Awd; JC Awd; Fairmont St Coll.

VAN SLYKE, TAMARA D; Lincoln HS; Shinnston, WV; 4/158 Hon Rl; Jr NHS; Lbry Ade; NHS; Yth Flsp; Rptr Sch Nwsp; Sch Nwsp; Pep Clb; Sci Clb; Spn Clb; Stu Of Month; Soc Dist Amer HS Stu; Fairmont St Univ; Psych.

VAN SPLINTER, SHAWN; Cedar Springs HS; Cedar Spgs, MI; Boy Scts; Hon Rl; Letter Ftbl; US Air Force.

VAN STEENKISTE, VICKI; Wadsworth HS; Wadsworth, OH; Chrs; Chrh Wkr; Hon Rl; Fr Clb; FTA; Pep Clb; Bowling Green State Univ; Elem Educ.

VAN STEENLANDT, KARIN; Lake Michigan Catholic HS; St Joseph, MI; VP Jr Cls; Chrs; Hon Rl; JA; Jr NHS; NHS; Off Ade; Sch Mus; Sch Pl; Stu Cncl; Women In Engr At Mi Tech 78; Oprtn Beritly At Olivett Coll 78; Cls C St Champ In 110 Yd Low Hurdles 78; Univ.

VAN TIFLIN, RAYMOND M; St Peter And Paul Area HS; Saginaw, MI; Band; Chrs; Hon Rl; Mdrgl; MMM; NHS; Sch Mus; Bsktbl; Trk; Coach Actv; College; Dentist.

VAN TINE, DOUG; Breckenridge Jr Sr HS; Breckenridge, MI; Chrh Wkr; Bsktbl;.

VAN TINE, DOUGLAS; Breckenridge Jr & Sr HS; Breckenridge, MI; Chrh Wkr; Hon Rl; NHS; Yth Flsp; Letter Bsktbl;.

VAN TRAN, TOM; Loveland Hurst HS; Loveland, OH; 6/239 Pres Soph Cls; Pres Jr Cls; Pres Sr Cls; Hon Rl; JA; NHS; Stu Cncl; Fr Clb; Ger Clb; Pep Clb; Univ Of Cal Of Los Angeles; Med.

VANUSKA, ERIC; Creston HS; Grand Rpds, MI; 108/434 Boy Scts; Chrh Wkr; Debate Tm; Drl Tm; Hon Rl; ROTC; Sct Actv; Spn Clb; Letter Trk; AJROTC 37 Awds; Veterans Hosp Worker; Michigan St Univ; Elec Engr.

VAN VALKENBURG, KATHERINE S; Groveport Madison Sr HS; Columbus, OH; Band; Girl Scts; Hon Rl; Red Cr Ade; Sct Actv; Lat Clb; Mat Maids; PPFtbl; Scr Kpr; Ohio St Univ; Med.

VAN VOORHIS, DANIEL; Ernest W Seaholm HS; Bloomfield Hls, MI; Red Cr Ade; ROTC; Letter Glf; Letter Swmmng; Coach Actv; IM Sprt; Tmr; Michigan St Univ; Bus Admin.

VAN VOORHIS, JILL; Canton South HS; Canton, OH; Cls Rep Soph Cls; Trs Jr Cls; Cl Rep Jr Cls; Chrs; Hon Rl; NHS; Off Ade; Sch Mus; Drama Clb; Sec Lat Clb; Schlshp Recgntn Awd 77 78 & 79; Univ; Acctg.

VAN WAGNER, LEE; Alpena HS; Alpena, MI; Aud/Vis; Ger Clb; Univ Of Michigan; Archt.

VAN WAGNER, LISA; Prairie Hts HS; Lagrange, IN; 15/140 Chrh Wkr; Hon Rl; NHS; Stu Cncl; Yth Flsp; 4-H; FTA; Pep Clb; Letter Trk; Chrldng; Coll; Phys Ed.

VAN WAGNER, LISA; Prairie Hts HS; La Grange, IN; 15/140 Cls Rep Frsh Cls; Cls Rep Soph Cls; Trs Jr Cls; Cl Rep Jr Cls; Chrh Wkr; Hon Rl; NHS; Stu Cncl; Yth Flsp; 4-H; Univ; Phys Ed.

VAN WAGONER, DEANEENE; Imlay City Community HS; Lum, MI; Band; Capt Girl Scts; Hon Rl; NHS; Sct Actv; Yrbk; Capt Sci Clb; Michigan Technology Univ; Med Tech.

VAN WINKLE, CHERYL; Rockville HS; Rockville, IN; 3/85 VP Jr Cls; NHS; Pep Clb; Sci Clb; Spn Clb; Letter Bsktbl; All Conference Basketball 1976; All Confrnce Volybll 1978; Rebounding Awrd 1977; Univ; Educ.

VAN WORMER, TAMMY; Clawson Sr HS; Clawson, MI; VP Jr Cls; VP Sr Cls; Pres Band; Girl Scts; Stu Cncl; Spn Clb; PPFtbl; Michigan St Univ; Pre Law.

VAN WYNEN, JAMES; Vicksburg HS; Vicksbrg, MI; 40/245 Boy Scts; Hon Rl; 4-H; Letter Bsbl; Letter Ftbl; Letter Trk; Letter Wrstlng; Michigan St Univ; Vet Med.

VAN ZANDT, PATRICIA; Madison Heights HS; Anderson, IN; Band; Chrs; Drm Bgl; Hon Rl; Sch Nwsp; Ger Clb; Pep Clb; Gym; Trk; Pres Awd; 1st Place Medal Solo Ensemble Contest 76; Univ; Sci.

VAN ZANT, CARMA; Dayton Christian HS; Xenia, OH; 10/97 Hon Rl; NHS; Sch Mus; Sch Pl; Stg Crw; Pres Drama Clb; Chrldng; Miami Vly Hosp Schl; Nursing.

VAN ZOEST, DAVID; South Christian HS; Grand Rapids, MI; Hon Rl; Jr NHS; NHS; Natl Merit Schl; Calvin Coll; Engr.

VARBLE, JENNIFER; South Spencer HS; Richland, IN; 31/146 Sec Soph Cls; Hon Rl; NHS; Off Ade; Pres Stu Cncl; Yrbk; Fr Clb; Pres GAA; Dnfth Awd; Indiana St Univ.

VARGA, KATHERINE; Western Reserve HS; Norwalk, OH; 22/108 Trs Sr Cls; Band; Girl Scts; Hon Rl; Lbry Ade; Off Ade; Yrbk; Sch Nwsp; Drama Clb; 4-H;.

VARGO, DENISE; Bishop Ready HS; Columbus, OH; Hon Rl; JA; Bsktbl; JA Awd; Univ.

VARGO, KATHLEEN; Cass City HS; Cass City, MI; Cmnty Wkr; Girl Scts; Hon Rl; Jr NHS; NHS; PAVAS; Sch Pl; Stg Crw; 4-H; Spn Clb; Univ; Phys Ther.

VARGO, LAURIE; Coshocton HS; Coshocton, OH; 31/230 Cls Rep Frsh Cls; Capt Band; Chrs; Chrh Wkr; Cmnty Wkr; Hon Rl; Hosp Ade; Orch; Red Cr Ade; Stu Cncl; Le Blond Music Awd 79; Fred Waring Workshp Music Sclhsp 77 & 78; Wittenberg Univ; Music Educ.

VARGO, ROBERT A; Buckeye West HS; Rayland, OH; 19/87 Yrbk; Treas Sci Clb; Letter Bsbl; Bsktbl; Am Leg Awd; Youngstown St Univ.

VARGO, ROSEANN; Hubbard HS; Hubbard, OH; 26/360 Hon Rl; Mgrs; Youngstown State Univ.

VARGULICH, LUKE; Campbell Memorial HS; Campbell, OH; Hon Rl; Jr NHS; NHS; Letter Bsbl; Bsktbl; Coll.

VARKONY, YVONNE; Buckeye W HS; Cadiz, OH; 20/85 Hst Soph Cls; Band; Chrh Wkr; Girl Scts; Hon Rl; Off Ade; Sct Actv; 4-H; OEA; Vocational Schl; Airlines.

VARLEY, JOSEPH; Warren G Harding HS; Warren, OH; 9/400 Am Leg Boys St; Chrh Wkr; Hon Rl; Jr NHS; NHS; Fr Clb; Bsbl; Capt Ftbl; Harvard Univ.

VARNADO, ARNETTA N; Roosevelt HS; Gary, IN; Chrs; Chrh Wkr; Hon Rl; JA; Mdrgl; Sch Mus; College; Business.

VARNER, CAROL; Clay Battelle HS; Pentress, WV; Band; Chrs; Chrh Wkr; Girl Scts; Hon Rl; Sec Jr NHS; Lbry Ade; Rptr Sch Nwsp; FHA; Chrldng; College; Acctg.

VARNER, HARRIETTE A; Austintown Fitch HS; Youngstown, OH; Pres Natl Forn Lg; NHS; Pol Wkr; Y-Teens; Rptr Sch Nwsp; NCTE; Natl Merit SF; Opt Clb Awd; College; Law.

VARNER, MICHAEL; Roscommon HS; Roscommon, MI; Cl Rep Jr Cls; Lbry Ade; Sch Mus; Sch Pl; Pres Stu Cncl; Bsktbl; Gif; College; Bus Admin.

VARNER, PAUL; Breckenridge HS; Merrill, MI; 29/109 Cl Rep Jr Cls; Cls Rep Sr Cls; Hon Rl; NHS; Stu Cncl; 4-H; FFA; Capt Ftbl; Mgrs; 4-H Awd; Michigan State Univ.

VARNER, PENNY; Vandalia Butler HS; Vandalia, OH; Cl Rep Jr Cls; Chrs; Sch Mus; Gym; Trk; Chrldng; PPFtbl; Western Kentucky Univ; Phys Ed.

VARNER, RICHARD; Newcomerstown HS; Newcomerstown, OH; 12/120 VP Jr Cls; VP Sr Cls; Am Leg Boys St; FCA; Hon Rl; Pres NHS; Letter Ftbl; Miami Univ.

VARNES, JACKLYN; Whitmer HS; Toledo, OH; 15/800 Hon Rl; NHS; Quill & Scroll; Ed Sch Nwsp; Pep Clb; Spn Clb; Univ Of Toledo; Jrnlsm.

VARNEY, CYNTHIA; Carey HS; Carey, OH; Hon Rl; Yrbk; FTA; Spn Clb; Trk; GAA; Natl Merit Schl; Schlstc Ach Awd Spanish; Coll.

VARNEY, KENT; Southern HS; Long Bottom, OH; Cls Rep Frsh Cls; Stu Cncl; Fr Clb; Ftbl; Voc Schl; Drafting.

VARNEY, MICHELLE; North Union HS; Richwood, OH; Trs Soph Cls; Cl Rep Jr Cls; Chrs; Hon Rl; Lbry Ade; NHS; Stu Cncl; Sec 4-H; Sec Lat Clb; Letter Trk; Univ; Tchr.

VASARHELY, KIMBERLY; Normandy HS; Parma, OH; 25/625 Hon Rl; Orch; IM Sprt; Natl Merit Ltr; Univ; Art.

VASCIL, JOHN; John Adams HS; South Bend, IN; 40/420 Cls Rep Sr Cls; Boy Scts; Hon Rl; NHS; IM Sprt; Natl Honor Soc; So Bend Tribune Honor Carrier; College; Engr.

VASEL, NANCY; Struthers HS; Poland, OH; 11/275 Cls Rep Sr Cls; Hon Rl; NHS; Y-Teens; Yrbk; Drama Clb; Spn Clb; IM Sprt; NCTE; Univ; Spec Educ.

VASICEK, SANDRA; Corunna HS; Corunna, MI; 2/213 Sal; Band; Hon Rl; NHS; Ed Yrbk; Rptr Yrbk; 4-H; GAA; 4-H Awd; Brd Of Trustees Outstndg HS Grad Schlrshp 79; Distingshd Musicians Cert Marine Awd 79; Central Michigan Univ; Comp Sci.

VASICH, SHEILA; Wintersville HS; Wintersville, OH; 7/280 Chrh Wkr; Spn Clb; Natl Merit Ltr; College; Bio.

VASSOLO, VALERIE; Seton HS; Cincinnati, OH; VP Frsh Cls; Cls Rep Soph Cls; VP Jr Cls; Pres Sr Cls; Am Leg Aux Girls St; Chrs; Chrh Wkr; Cmnty Wkr; Debate Tm; Girl Scts; Rep O Yth In City Govt 77; Univ; Elem Educ Tchr.

VASU, C; E Grand Rapids HS; Grand Rapids, MI; Cls Rep Frsh Cls; Cl Rep Jr Cls; VP Sr Cls; Hon Rl; Sch Pl; Stg Crw; Stu Cncl; Letter Glf; College; Busns.

VATTER, MICHAEL; Cass City HS; Cass City, MI; Cls Rep Frsh Cls; Trs Soph Cls; Band; Chrh Wkr; Hon Rl; Jr NHS; NHS; Sch Pl; Stu Cncl; Rptr Sch Nwsp; Michigan St Univ.

VATTER, PEGGY; Groveport Madison HS; Columbus, OH; 3/377 Hon Rl; NHS; Stu Cncl; Rptr Yrbk; Drama Clb; VP FHA; VP Mat Maids; PPFtbl; Rotary Awd; Frsh Stdnt Of Yr 1976; Perfct Attencnc 2 Yrs; Univ; Acctg.

VAUGHAN, C; Frontier HS; Newport, OH; Pres Soph Cls; Hon Rl; NHS; Sch Pl; Sec Yth Flsp; Sci Clb; College; Elec Engr.

VAUGHAN, CHARLES; Frontier HS; Newport, OH; Boy Scts; Chrh Wkr; NHS; Sch Pl; Sci Clb; College; Bio.

VAUGHAN, DANIEL; Lapeer East HS; Lapeer, MI; Cls Rep Soph Cls; Band; Chrs; Chrh Wkr; NHS; Sch Mus; Stg Crw; Drama Clb; Univ; Med.

VAUGHAN, GREGORY A; Xenia HS; Wilberforce, OH; 9/520 Band; Pres Chrs; Hon Rl; Pres NHS; Fr Clb; Letter Bsktbl; Trk; Univ Of Cincinnati; Elect Engr.

VAUGHAN, JENNIFER; Alma HS; Alma, MI; Chrs; Hon Rl; Mdrgl; NHS; Sch Mus; Stg Crw; Univ.

VAUGHAN, KAREN; East Kentwood HS; Kentw Od, MI; 6/550 Hon Rl; Treas JA; Treas Spn Clb; Letter Glf; Capt Ten; Chrldng; College; Writing.

VAUGHAN, KELLIE; Trimble Local HS; Glouster, OH; 5/97 Cls Rep Frsh Cls; Pres Soph Cls; Pres Jr Cls; Pres Sr Cls; Chrh Wkr; Cmnty Wkr; Girl Scts; Hon Rl; Jr NHS; NHS; Ohio Univ; Marine Bio.

VAUGHAN, RENEE; Catholic Central HS; Cadillac, MI; Cmp Fr Grls; Hon Rl; NHS; Yrbk; Trk; Chrldng; PPFtbl; Natl Merit Ltr; Grand Rapids Jr College; Bus Admin.

VAUGHAN, ROBERTA; Calhoun Co HS; Grantsville, WV; Sec Jr Cls; Hst Sr Cls; Band; Hon Rl; Sec Hosp Ade; VP NHS; Spn Clb; West Virginia Univ; Sci.

VAUGHAN, WILLIAM K; Rayen HS; Youngstown, OH; Pres Jr Cls; Aud/Vis; Hon Rl; Sch Mus; Sch Pl; Drama Clb; Letter Bsbl; Letter Bsktbl; Letter Ftbl; Rotary Awd; Acad All Amer 78; Mstoutsntndg Male Jr 78; Youngstown City Spch Tourn In Oratcl Intp 76; West Point Acad; Pre Med.

VAUGHN, ARNOLD; Cuyahoga Falls HS; Cuyahoga Falls, OH; Cls Rep Frsh Cls; Band; Hon Rl; Orch; Sch Pl; Mgrs; Univ Of Akron.

VAUGHN, ERIC; Greenville Sr HS; Greenville, MI; Band; Boy Scts; Chrh Wkr; Fr Clb; Eagle Scout Awd 78; Univ; Elec Engr.

VAUGHN, STEPHANY; Cascade HS; Clayton, IN; 26/150 Sec Soph Cls; Sec Jr Cls; Sec Sr Cls; Am Leg Aux Girls St; Band; FCA; Girl Scts; Hon Rl; Stu Cncl; Yth Flsp; 3d Rnnr Up Plainfld Jr Ms Contst 1978; HS Hmcmng Queen 1978; Vlybl Little Hustler Awd 1978; Southeastern Academy; Trvl Career.

VAUGHN, VICKIE; Jimtown HS; Elkhart, IN; 18/96 Hon Rl; Yrbk; Indiana Univ; Acctg.

VAUGHT, DONALD; Purcell HS; Maineville, OH; 17/171 Cmnty Wkr; Hon Rl; IM Sprt; Cincinnati Reds Straight A Stu 77; Cincinnati Stingers Perf Attend 77; Univ; Bus Admin.

VAUGHT, SALLY; Chelsea HS; Chelsea, MI; Band; Cmp Fr Grls; Chrs; Chrh Wkr; Cmnty Wkr; Debate Tm; Hon Rl; PAVAS; Sch Mus; Stg Crw; Univ; Eng.

VAUPEL, JILL; Chaney HS; Youngstown, OH; Pres Frsh Cls; Cls Rep Soph Cls; Chrh Wkr; Hon Rl; Hosp Ade; Jr NHS; Lbry Ade; NHS; Off Ade; Sch Pl; College; Bus.

VAVRA, KIM; Kearsley HS; Flint, MI; Girl Scts; Hon Rl; Off Ade; Scr Kpr; Voc Schl; X Ray Tech.

VAVRA, RHONDA; Shadyside HS; Shadyside, OH; 22/103 Sec Jr Cls; Hon Rl; Off Ade; Sch Mus; Sch Pl; Y-Teens; Drama Clb; OEA; GAA; IM Sprt; Belmont Tech Schl; Data Proc.

VAVRO, RICHARD; Swartz Creek HS; Swartz Creek, MI; 27/476 NHS; Univ Of Michigan.

VAZQUEZ, PETER A; Adrian HS; Adrian, MI; 40/387 Chrh Wkr; Debate Tm; Hon Rl; Jr NHS; Natl Forn Lg; NHS; VP Yth Flsp; VP Lat Clb; Mi Comp Schlshp 79; Outstndng Latin Stdnt 75; Michigan St Univ; Pre Law.

VECASEY, PAMELA; St Johns HS; St Johns, MI; Cls Rep Sr Cls; Hon Rl; NHS; Sch Mus; Stg Crw; Spn Clb; Letter Swmmng; IM Sprt; Tmr; Univ; Agri.

VECELLIO, FRANCIS; Ironton HS; Ironton, OH; 8/190 Cls Rep Frsh Cls; Cls Rep Sr Cls; Hon Rl; Mod UN; NHS; Sprt Ed Sch Nwsp; Pres Sci Clb; VP Spn Clb; Crs Cntry; DAR Awd; Ohio St Univ; Acctg.

VECTIRELIS, DAVE; Parma Sr HS; Parma, OH; Hon Rl; Pol Wkr; Rotary Awd; Highst Hon Achvd All 4 Qtr 78; Cleveland Inst Of Elect; Audio Desgn.

VEDRA, TIMOTHY M; Rossford HS; Rossford, OH; Am Leg Boys St; Band; Hon Rl; Sch Pl; Stg Crw; Rptr Yrbk; Drama Clb; Fr Clb; Owens Tech Coll; Radio Tech.

VEENEKER, VICKI; West Lafayette HS; W Lafayette, IN; 4/175 Trs Jr Cls; VP Sr Cls; Treas Am Leg Aux Girls St; FCA; Hon Rl; NHS; Quill & Scroll; Sch Pl; Treas Yth Flsp; Ed Yrbk; Univ.

VEENHOVEN, RICHARD; Holland HS; Holland, MI; Chrh Wkr; Hon Rl; Ger Clb; Ten; IM Sprt; Davenport Coll; Acctg.

VEGA, ALBERT; Washington HS; South Bend, IN; 1 39/350 Band; Drm Bgl; Hon Rl; Sch Mus; Rptr Sch Nwsp; Trk; Purdue Univ; Comp.

VEGA, LISA L; Harry S Truman Sr HS; Taylor, MI; Cls Rep Frsh Cls; Sec Jr Cls; Sec Sr Cls; Hon Rl; Jr NHS; Red Cr Ade; Stu Cncl; Gym; Trk; Chrldng; Grand Natl Champ On Pom Pon Sqf 78; Var Ltr In Track 78; Michigan St Univ; Child Behavior.

VEIGEL, LORRI; Tuscarawas Central Cath HS; New Phila, OH; Hon Rl; NHS; Pep Clb; Spn Clb; Univ.

VEIN, PETER; Jefferson Union HS; Richmond, OH; Pep Clb; Letter Bsbl; Letter Bsktbl; Ftbl; College; Tele Communications.

VEIT, CHRIS; Wapakoneta Sr HS; Wapakoneta, OH; Chrs; Hon Rl; Sch Mus; FBLA; OEA; Pep Clb; Spn Clb; Gym; Trk; Bus Schl; Sec.

VEIT, KATHRYN; Sacred Heart Acad; Mt Pleasant, MI; Pres Frsh Cls; Chrs; Chrh Wkr; Debate Tm; Girl Scts; Hon Rl; NHS; Off Ade; Stu Cncl; Sch Nwsp; Michigan St Univ; Interior Dsgn.

VEIT, TERESA A; Memorial HS; St Marys, OH; Hon Rl; Sch Mus; Stu Cncl; Y-Teens; Yrbk; Pres FTA; Pep Clb; Spn Clb; Sec GAA; IM Sprt; College; Stewardess.

VEITENGRUBER, CARLA; Frankenmuth HS; Bridgeport, MI; Cl Rep Jr Cls; Cls Rep Sr Cls; Debate Tm; Natl Forn Lg; NHS; PAVAS; Sch Mus; Sch Pl; College; Psychology.

VEKAS, TAMMY; Lakota HS; Fostoria, OH; 8/135 Trs Frsh Cls; Hon Rl; NHS; Sch Mus; Stg Crw; Drama Clb; State Univ; Marine Biology.

VELASQUEZ, BRENDA; Danville Comm HS; Danville, IN; 21/162 FCA; NHS; Quill & Scroll; Stu Cncl; Y-Teens; Yrbk; Pres 4-H; FHA; Chrldng; 4-H Awd; Purdue Univ; Engr.

VELDMAN, MARIA; Marian HS; Mishawaka, IN; Band; Pres Chrs; Hon Rl; NHS; Sch Mus; 4-H; 4-H Awd; Univ; Pre Med.

VELEGOL, MIKE; Brooke HS; Colliers, WV; 59/403 Hon Rl; Sprt Ed Yrbk; Sci Clb; Spn Clb; Letter Trk; Ohio St Univ; Aviation.

VELEGOL, TIM; Brooke HS; Colliers, WV; 1/466 Val; Hon Rl; Lit Mag; NHS; Quill & Scroll; Sch Mus; Stu Cncl; Ohi State Univ; Engr.

VELENYI, BOB; Charles F Brush HS; Lyndhurst, OH; Cls Rep Frsh Cls; Band; Red Cr Ade; Letter Socr; Letter Swmmng; Coach Actv; Tmr; Univ; Engr.

VELEY, DUANE; Marion Harding HS; Marion, OH; 17/460 Pres JA; Sct Actv; Sch Nwsp; Fr Clb; Mth Clb; Sci Clb; JA Awd; St Sci Fair Superior; Annual Literary Mag Staff; OSU Summer Math Prog; Coll.

VELIKOFF, JOHN; Galion HS; Galion, OH; Am Leg Boys St; Debate Tm; Hon Rl; Trk; Wrstlng; College; Chem.

VELLA, LOUISE; Allen Park HS; Marquette, MI; Band; Chrs; Chrh Wkr; Cmnty Wkr; Hosp Ade; Jr NHS; Orch; Yth Flsp; Natl Merit SF; Northern Michigan Univ; RN.

VELLANKI, MOHAN; Hoover HS; North Canton, OH; 22/434 Aud/Vis; Band; Chrh Wkr; Cmnty Wkr; Hon Rl; Hosp Ade; JA; Jr NHS; Lbry Ade; NHS; College; Medicine.

VELLIGAN, DANA; Andrean HS; St John, IN; 61/251 Chrh Wkr; Girl Scts; Hon Rl; 4-H; Fr Clb; Chmn Pep Clb; Bsktbl; GAA; Mat Maids; Pres Awd; Univ; Pre Dent.

VELTEMA, SCOTT; Hudsonville HS; Hudsonville, MI; Chrs; FCA; Mdrgl; Letter Ftbl; Letter Wrstlng;.

VELTRI, ANTHONY; Morgantown HS; Morgantown, WV; Cl Rep Jr Cls; Chrs; Stu Cncl; Letter Ftbl; Trk; IM Sprt; Pres Awd; West Virginia Univ; Bio Research.

VENABLE, GARRY; Henry Ford HS; Detroit, MI; 8/525 Cls Rep Frsh Cls; Boy Scts; Chrs; Chrh Wkr; Hon Rl; Jr NHS; Mdrgl; NHS; Pol Wkr; Red Cr Ade; Michigan All St Choir At Interlocken Arts Academy; Michigan St & District Solo & Ensemble Rating Superior; Univ Of Michigan; Health.

VENABLE, RAYMOND; Marion HS; Marion, IN; 230/715 Band; Hon Rl; Purdue Univ; Elec Engr Tech.

VENABLE, TIMOTHY; Hartland HS; Brighton, MI; Chrh Wkr; Cmnty Wkr; Yth Flsp; Rptr Yrbk; Letter Bsbl; Letter Bsktbl; Letter Ftbl; Glf; Univ.

VENDITTI, GINA; Lake Catholic HS; Painesville, OH; Pep Clb; Mgrs; College; Biology.

VENEKLASE, DAVID; Catholic Ctrl HS; Grand Rapids, MI; Boy Scts; Hon Rl; JA; Mgrs; JA Awd; Bus Schl.

VENEN, ROBIN; Otsego HS; Otsego, MI; 4/221 Cls Rep Frsh Cls; Cls Rep Soph Cls; Cl Rep Jr Cls; Trs Sr Cls; Cls Rep Sr Cls; Chrs; Hon Rl; NHS; Sch Mus; Stu Cncl; Kalamazoo Coll; Math.

VENEROSO, TONI; Ursuline HS; Youngstown, OH; Debate Tm; Hosp Ade; Natl Forn Lg; Off Ade; Red Cr Ade; Sch Pl; Sch Nwsp; FTA; Pep Clb; Trk; Youngstown St Univ.

VENHAM, TIA; Morgantown HS; Morgantwn, WV; Band; Hon Rl; West Virginia Univ; Nursing.

VENNEKOTTER, DONALD; Miller City HS; Continental, OH; Cl Rep Jr Cls; Pres Sr Cls; Band; Chrs; Hon Rl; Red Cr Ade; Stg Crw; Stu Cncl; Rptr Yrbk; IM Sprt; Boy St Alternate Amer Legion; Worked In Pathology Research Lab For Red Cross; Univ; Pre Med.

VENTIMIGLIO, TERESA; C S Mott Sr HS; Warren, MI; Cls Rep Frsh Cls; Cls Rep Soph Cls; Band; Cmnty Wkr; Hon Rl; Jr NHS; NHS; Pol Wkr; Stu Cncl; Y-Teens; Reg HS Awd From E Michigan Univ; St Of Michigan Schlrshp; St Of Michigan Cert Of Recognition Acad Ach; E Michigan Univ; Nuclear Med Tech.

VENTRESCA, ELIO; Brookhaven Sr HS; Columbus, OH; Hon Rl; Jr NHS; Lit Mag; NHS; Sch Pl; Yrbk; Rotary Awd; Columbus Tech Cncl Sci Stdnt Of Yr Awrd 78; Ohio St Univ; Chem.

VENTRESCA, ELIO; Brookhaven HS; Columbus, OH; Hon Rl; Jr NHS; Lit Mag; NHS; Sch Pl; Yrbk; Rotary Awd; Ohio State Univ; Chem.

VENUTO, GINA; Bentley HS; Livonia, MI; Cls Rep Frsh Cls; Girl Scts; Hon Rl; Stu Cncl; Bsbl; Chrldng; IM Sprt; Pom Pon; Univ Of Michigan.

VERAX, MARY ANN; Mt Notre Dame HS; Cincinnati, OH; 47/181 Am Leg Aux Girls St; Chrs; Hon Rl; JA; NHS; Pol Wkr; Sch Mus; Treas OEA; Spn Clb; IM Sprt; Univ Of Cincinnati; Comp Tech.

VER BEEK, GREG; L C Mohr HS; South Haven, MI; 24/234 Band; Hon Rl; NHS; Sch Mus; Stg Crw; Stu Cncl; Yth Flsp; Rptr Yrbk; Hope Coll; Sci.

VERBICK, LAURA; George N Bentley HS; Livonia, MI; Chrh Wkr; Hon Rl; Lit Mag; Pol Wkr; St Winner & 2nd Natl Winner Natl PTA Reflectns Contest 76; Cert Of Commndtn As Ceza Planning Mbr 79; Madonna Coll; Criminal Justice.

VERBOSKY, MARY KAY; Rossford HS; Rossford, OH; 19/147 Chrs; Hon Rl; NHS; Sch Mus; Sch Pl; Stu Cncl; Yrbk; Drama Clb; Fr Clb; Voice Dem Awd; Ftbl Hmcmng Attendant; Toledo Univ; Spec Ed.

VERBRUGGE, DAVID; East Kentwood HS; Kentwood, MI; 10/400 Cls Rep Frsh Cls; Hon Rl; NHS; Letter Crs Cntry; Letter Trk; Letter Wrstlng; Natl Merit Ltr; Calvin Coll; Elec Engr.

VER BURG, CRAIG; Holt HS; Lansing, MI; Band; Sch Pl; Ger Clb; Pep Clb; Univ; Natural Sci.

VER BURG, NANCY; Willard HS; Willard, OH; Girl Scts; Hon Rl; Hosp Ade; Off Ade; Red Cr Ade; Sct Actv; 4-H; Fr Clb; Spn Clb; Cit Awd; Ohio Pupils Readng Cir 72; Excllnc In Attndnc 78; Stdnt Cncl Awrd Home Ec 79; Schlrshp Loan Huron Cnty Med; Sandusky Provdnc Schl Of Nrsng; RN.

VERCRUYSSE, MARY ANN; Lake Shore HS; St Clair Shrs, MI; 5/600 Sec Jr Cls; Sec Sr Cls; Chrs; Hon Rl; Treas JA; Jr NHS; Pres NHS; Sch Mus; Stu Cncl; Ed Yrbk; Eggleston Memrl Foundtn Schlrshp 79; Macomb Cnty Cmnty Coll Schrs Schlrshp 79; Natl Schl Choral Awd 79; Macomb Cnty Cmnty Coll; Legal Sec.

VEREECKE, JEFFREY D; Morenci Area HS; Morenci, MI; Band; Pres Chrs; VP Jr NHS; Sch Mus; Pres Stu Cncl; Letter Crs Cntry; Trk; Grand Valley State; Bus Admin.

VEREEKE, TAMI; Zeeland HS; Holland, MI; Band; Chrh Wkr; Girl Scts; Hon Rl; Stu Cncl; Yth Flsp; Ger Clb; Pep Clb; Glf; Swmmng; Davenport Coll; Bus.

VERES, CHARLES; Frank Cody HS; Detroit, MI; 2/500 Hon Rl; NHS; Key Clb; Pres Mth Clb; Pres Sci Clb; Cit Awd; Natl Merit Ltr; College; Math.

VERHAEGHE, VICTOR; Flint Holy Rosary; Flint, MI; Chrh Wkr; Sch Pl; Crs Cntry; Trk; College.

VER HOEVEN, CINDY; Hudsonville HS; Hudsonville, MI; Sal; FCA; Hon Rl; NHS; Rptr Yrbk; Letter Ten; Chrldng; Dvnprt Sch Of Bus; Hsptlty Mngmt.

VER HOEVEN, KEVIN; Fennville HS; Fennville, MI; 11/93 Chrh Wkr; Cmnty Wkr; Hon Rl; Lbry Ade; NHS; Letter Bsbl; Letter Bsktbl; Glf; Coach Actv; Adrian College; Communication.

VERHOFF, A; Miller City HS; Continental, OH; Cl Rep Jr Cls; Cls Rep Sr Cls; Band; Drm Mjrt; Hon Rl; NHS; Pres Stu Cncl; Sch Nwsp; FHA; Chrldng; College; Mgmt.

VERHOFF, GLEN; Pandora Gilboa HS; Ottawa, OH; Am Leg Boys St; Band; Chrs; Sec Lbry Ade; NHS; Sch Mus; Sch Pl; Stu Cncl; 4-H; FFA; Univ; Comp Sci.

VERHOFF, THEODORE; St John HS; Delphos, OH; 50/149 Cls Rep Frsh Cls; Cls Rep Soph Cls; Band; Chrh Wkr; Hon Rl; Sch Mus; Sch Pl; Stu Cncl; Bsbl; Lima Tech Schl; Mech Engr.

VERHULST, JOANNE; Griffith HS; Griffith, IN; 7/281 Am Leg Aux Girls St; Hon Rl; NHS; Sec Quill & Scroll; Stg Crw; Stu Cncl; Sec Yth Flsp; Ed Sch Nwsp; Rptr Sch Nwsp;.

VER HULST, LARRY; Muskegon HS; Muskegon, MI; Hon Rl; Spn Clb; Bsbl; College; Mech.

VERHULST, SHERRY; Hanover Central HS; Cedar Lake, IN; 1/137 Hon Rl; Jr NHS; Treas NHS; Spn Clb; PPFtbl; VP Am Leg Awd; College; Commercial Art.

VERMEERSCH, SHEILA; Unionville Sebewaing HS; Unionville, MI; Hon Rl; Sch Mus; 4-H; Pep Clb; Twrlr; Delta Coll; Child Care Worker.

VERMES, WILLIAM; Strongsville HS; Strongsville, OH; Aud/Vis; Hon Rl; Jr NHS; Stg Crw; Sch Nwsp; Bsbl; Letter Bsktbl; College; Meteorology.

VERMET, EDWARD; Grosse Pointe South HS; Grosse Pt Pk, MI; 55/560 Band; Chrh Wkr; Cmnty Wkr; Hon Rl; Hosp Ade; NHS; Orch; Yth Flsp; Trk; IM Sprt; Univ Of Michigan; Med Dr.

VER MEULEN, WILLIAM K; Interlochen Arts Academy; Lake Forest, IL; Pres Frsh Cls; Cls Rep Frsh Cls; Pres Soph Cls; Chrs; Hon Rl; Mdrgl; Orch; Sch Mus; Stu Cncl; Socr; Interlochen Schlrshp 1975; Ill Fed Of Music Schlrshp 1977; Solo Winner 1979; Northwestern Univ; Music.

VERMILYEA, CHARLES; Benzie Central HS; Honor, MI; VP Jr Cls; Boy Scts; Chrs; Hon Rl; Stu Cncl; Boys Clb Am; Pep Clb; Crs Cntry; Trk; Northwestern Maritime Academy.

VERNAVA, GRACE; Our Lady Of Mercy HS; Farmington Hls, MI; Am Leg Aux Girls St; Cmnty Wkr; Hon Rl; Pol Wkr; Stg Crw; Sch Nwsp; Lat Clb; Cit Awd; Harvard Univ; Med.

VERNER, CRAIG R; Brooke HS; Wellsburg, WV; 24/403 Sec Soph Cls; Am Leg Boys St; Hon Rl; NHS; Stu Cncl; Fr Clb; Bsbl; Letter Wrstlng; Univ; Med.

VERNIER, ANNE M; Aquinas HS; Wyandotte, MI; Band; Chrs; Girl Scts; Hon Rl; NHS; Chrldng; College; Music.

VERNIER, MICHAEL; Troy HS; Troy, MI; Am Leg Boys St; Cmnty Wkr; Hon Rl; Off Ade; Bsbl; Hockey; Letter Swmmng; St Midget AA Champ Swimming 78; Univ Of Michigan; Engr.

VERNON, DANA; Laurel School; Cleveland Hts, OH; 50/55 Hon Rl; Lit Mag; Sch Pl; VP Stu Cncl; Rptr Sch Nwsp; Fr Clb; Gym; Hockey; Capt Lcrss; Natl Merit Ltr; Dartmouth Coll.

VERNON, LISA; Rogers HS; Michigan City, IN; 15/480 Cl Rep Jr Cls; Cmnty Wkr; Hon Rl; Pres JA; NHS; PAVAS; Sch Mus; Sch Pl; Stg Crw; Mth Clb; Purdue North Cntrl Univ; Comp Tech.

VERNON, TORI; East Knox HS; Mt Vernon, OH; 8/66 Cls Rep Sr Cls; Chrs; Chrh Wkr; Hon Rl; NHS; Sch Pl; Stu Cncl; Sec Drama Clb; 4-H; Sec FHA; Apostolic Bible Inst; Chrstn Educ.

VEROFF, DAVID; Ann Arbor Pioneer HS; Ann Arbor, MI; Chrs; Lat Clb; Crs Cntry; Trk; Univ; Engr.

VERON, KENNETH; New Albany HS; New Albany, IN; Band; Boy Scts; Chrh Wkr; Pol Wkr; Sct Actv; Ger Clb; Lat Clb; Mgrs; Scr Kpr; Tmr; Prosser Ivy Tech.

VERSACE, PATTI; Marion L Steele HS; Lorain, OH; 17/356 Band; Hon Rl; NHS; Spn Clb; IM Sprt; Russell A Pterson Awd Band 79; Univ Of Toledo; Clinical Psych.

VERSCHAGE, CHRIS; Everett HS; Lansing, MI; Pres Yth Flsp; Bsbl; H S Acad Letter 79; Great Lakes Bible Coll; Educ.

VERTAL, PATRICIA; St Joseph Acad; Cleveland, OH; Hon Rl; Lat Clb; Bsktbl; Mgrs; College; Nursing.

VERTEL, LAWRENCE; St Ladislaus HS; Detroit, MI; 5/110 Cl Rep Jr Cls; Trs Sr Cls; Boy Scts; Hon Rl; NHS; Sch Pl; Stu Cncl; Spn Clb; Ftbl; Natl Merit Schl; Wayne St Univ; Chem Engr.

VERTOLLI, CATHERINE; E Canton HS; E Canton, OH; Chrs; Girl Scts; Jr NHS; Sch Mus; Sch Pl; Drama Clb; FHA; Pep Clb; VICA; Trk; Tech Coll; Banking.

VERYZER, ROBERT; Seaholm HS; Birmingham, MI; Hon Rl; Jr NHS; NHS; Yrbk; Rptr Sch Nwsp; Socr; Olivet Coll.

VESCO, ANNETTE; Tuscarawas Central Cath HS; New Phila, OH; Sec Frsh Cls; Band; Chrs; Sch Pl; Stu Cncl; Drama Clb; Pep Clb; Spn Clb; Trk; Scr Kpr; College; Nurse.

VESEL, DAVID; Eastlake North HS; Willowick, OH; 30/700 Hon Rl; NHS; Rdo Clb; Letter Trk; Am Leg Awd; AAUW Amer Assoc Of Univ Women Awd 77; Cleveland St Univ; Bus Admin.

VESELENAK, ANNE; Valley Forge HS; Parma, OH; Hon Rl; Hosp Ade; Off Ade; Spn Clb; Pom Pon; 1st Pl Schlstic Art Awd 77; Hghst Hnrs Awd Vly Forge HS 78; Outstndg Achvmnt For Spnsh III 78; Ohio St Univ; Med Tech.

VESELY, DONNA; Elyria Catholic HS; Avon, OH; Sec Sr Cls; Sch Pl; Stu Cncl; Drama Clb; 4-H; Pep Clb; Capt Crs Cntry; Trk; IM Sprt; 4-H Awd; La Roche Coll; Interior Dsgn.

VESELY, LORI; Grosse Pointe South HS; Grosse Pte Farm, MI; Chrh Wkr; Drl Tm; Hon Rl; NHS; Yth Flsp; Pep Clb; Spn Clb; Mgrs; Pom Pon; PPFtbl; Oakland Univ; Psych.

VESPER, PATRICIA; St Ursula Academy; Cincinnati, OH; 17/84 Girl Scts; Hon Rl; Hosp Ade; JA; Mod UN; NHS; Sch Pl; Sct Actv; Sch Nwsp; Drama Clb; Wilmington Coll Faculty Hnr Schlrshp | Yr; Union Coll Acadmc Schlrshp; Univ Of Cincinnati; Bio.

VEST, MEG; Carroll HS; Dayton, OH; Band; Lit Mag; Rptr Sch Nwsp; Treas Rus Clb; Univ Of Cincinnati; Psych.

VETTER, DIETER; Padua HS; Parma, OH; Boy Scts; Cmnty Wkr; Sct Actv; Stg Crw; Ftbl; Trk; IM Sprt; Univ.

VETTER, REGINA; Notre Dame HS; Portsmouth, OH; 5/60 Sec Jr Cls; Trs Jr Cls; Hon Rl; Sch Nwsp; Pep Clb; Trk; Capt Chrldng; DAR Awd; Ohio St Univ; Designer.

VETTER, SCOTT; Lapeer East Sr HS; Lapeer, MI; Hon Rl; Univ; Archt.

VETTER, WILLIAM; Henryville HS; Otisco, IN; Hon Rl; FFA; Vol Sch Prosser; Elictricity.

VEYNOVICH, BRYAN; Woodrow Wilson HS; Youngstown, OH; Hon Rl; NHS; Y-Teens; Key Clb; N Eastern Ohio Educ Schlrshp; Eng Cmnctns Skill Awd; Honors Eng Class At YSU; Youngstown St Univ; Med.

VICCHIARELLI, TRACI; Regina HS; Cleveland, OH; Cls Rep Frsh Cls; VP Jr Cls; VP Sr Cls; Chrh Wkr; Girl Scts; NHS; Sch Pl; Stu Cncl; Coach Actv; GAA; 2nd & 3rd Hnrs Serv Awd 76; 2nd & 3rd Hnr 77; 2nd & 3rd Hnr Serv Awd Natl Hnr Soc 78; Univ; Bus.

VICIAN, KEVIN; Andrean HS; Crown Pt, IN; 16/251 Cls Rep Frsh Cls; Cls Rep Soph Cls; Cl Rep Jr Cls; Cls Rep Sr Cls; Am Leg Boys St; Hon Rl; Pres NHS; Treas Stu Cncl; Pep Clb; Ftbl; Univ; Archt.

VICKERS, CYNTHIA; White Cloud HS; White Cloud, MI; 1/82 Val; Band; Girl Scts; Hon Rl; NHS; Off Ade; Sct Actv; Sch Nwsp; 4-H; Pep Clb; Bessie B Slautterback Schlrshp Awd 79; Mi Bus Schls Assoc 79; Arah Beach 79; Muskegon Bus Schl; Admin Sec.

VICKERS, S; Grand Lodge HS; Lansing, MI; Michigan St Univ; Sci.

VICKERS JR, JAMES; River Valley HS; Lakeside, MI; Hon Rl; Ger Clb; Bsbl; College.

VICKERSTAFF, BONITA; Andrean HS; Gary, IN; Chrh Wkr; Hon Rl; Rptr Yrbk; Lat Clb; College; Acctg.

VICTOR, DAWN; Brookville HS; Harrison, OH; Cl Rep Jr Cls; Hon Rl; VP JA; VP Jr NHS; Off Ade; Pres Fr Clb; Sec OEA; GAA; DAR Awd; College.

VICTOR, M; Delphi Community HS; Delphi, IN; 9/150 Jr NHS; Stu Cncl; Yth Flsp; 4-H; Spn Clb; Bsktbl; Crs Cntry; Trk; Am Leg Awd; 4-H Awd; Purdue Univ; Agri.

VICTOR, SANDRA; Harper Woods Scndry School; Harper Woods, MI; Chrh Wkr; Hon Rl; Hosp Ade; NHS; Yth Flsp; Spn Clb; Ferris St Coll; Med Rcrds Admin.

VIDEAN, JILL; High School; Detroit, MI; Drl Tm; Hon Rl; Jr NHS; Off Ade; PPFtbl; Twrlr; Univ.

VIDIMOS, DAVID; Merrillville HS; Merrillville, IN; Am Leg Boys St; Hon Rl; NHS; Letter Glf; Letter Swmmng; Cit Awd; Most Valuable Swimmer; All St Swimmer Hnr Mention; Air Force Acad.

VIDISCHAK, DONNA; Lumen Cordium HS; Garfield, OH; Cls Rep Soph Cls; Trs Jr Cls; Chrh Wkr; Girl Scts; Hon Rl; Hosp Ade; NHS; Sct Actv; Stu Cncl; IM Sprt; College; Nursing.

VIDITO, CINDY; Knightstown HS; Carthage, IN; 32/147 Chrs; Chrh Wkr; Hon Rl; Lbry Ade; Sch Mus; Sch Pl; Yth Flsp; Sprt Ed Yrbk; Rptr Yrbk; Sprt Ed Sch Nwsp; Olivet Nazarene Coll; History.

VIDITO, KIMBERLY; Brownsburg HS; Brownsburg, IN; Hon Rl; Stu Cncl; Pep Clb; Chrldng; PPFtbl; Ball State Univ; Comp Tech.

VIDLER, STEPHEN; So Charleston HS; Dunbar, WV; Band; Hon Rl; Spn Clb; College; Lawyer.

VIDMAR, JEANNE; South Haven HS; South Haven, MI; Cls Rep Frsh Cls; Cl Rep Jr Cls; Cls Rep Sr Cls; FCA; Hon Rl; Lbry Ade; NHS; Rptr Sch Nwsp; Pep Clb; Trk; Univ; Jrnlsm.

VIDOLICH, JOHN; Milan HS; Ypsilanti, MI; 4/250 Boy Scts; CAP; Debate Tm; Drl Tm; Hon Rl; Stu Cncl; Trk; Mgrs; Scr Kpr; Tmr; Univ Of Michigan; Comp Sci.

VIEWEG, SCOTT; Wheeling Park HS; Wheeling, WV; Hon Rl; Rptr Yrbk; Sprt Ed Sch Nwsp; DECA; Ftbl; Wrstlng; IM Sprt; West Virginia Univ; Law.

VIEZER, STEPHEN L; High School; Chagrin Fls, OH; 1/236 Boy Scts; Debate Tm; Hon Rl; NHS; Rus Clb; Letter Trk; Natl Merit Ltr; Univ; Physics.

VIGANSKY, BETH; Bridgman HS; Bridgeman, MI; Hon Rl; Hosp Ade; NHS; Am Leg Awd;.

VIGANSKY, DAVID L; Buchanan HS; Buchanan, MI; 2/130 Sal; Band; Hon Rl; NHS; Sch Mus; 4-H; Fr Clb; Buchanan Coll Club Schlshp Grant 79; 2 S Bend Trib Carrier Schslhp 78 & 79; Arion Awd For Music; Cntrl Michigan Univ; Acctg.

VIGANSKY, GERALD; Bridgman HS; Bridgman, MI; Cls Rep Soph Cls; Cl Rep Jr Cls; VP Sr Cls; NHS; Sch Mus; Stu Cncl; Ftbl; Trk; IM Sprt; Natl Merit SF; Hope Cllege; Medical Tech.

VIGEANT, AMY; Mona Shores HS; Muskegon, MI; NHS; Rptr Sch Nwsp; Pres DECA; Muskegon Comm Coll; Busns Mgmt.

VIGGIANI, MICHELE; James A Garfield HS; Hiram, OH; Cls Rep Frsh Cls; Cls Rep Soph Cls; Pres Jr Cls; Sch Pl; Stu Cncl; Rptr Yrbk; Yrbk; Pep Clb; Cit Awd; Miami Of Ohio Univ; Art.

VILLA, JULIE; Negaunee HS; Negaunee, MI; 22/150 Band; Chrh Wkr; Hon Rl; NHS; Y-Teens; Pep Clb; PPFtbl; Northern Mic; Home Eco.

VILLAIRE, JEAN; All Saints Central HS; Bay City, MI; Chrs; Cmnty Wkr; Hon Rl; Mdrgl; Sch Mus; Pep Clb; Bsbl; Chrldng; GAA; Delta College; Business.

VILLAREAL, DONNA; John F Kennedy HS; Warren, OH; 9/185 Sec Jr Cls; VP Sr Cls; Hosp Ade; Jr NHS; Quill & Scroll; Sct Actv; Y-Teens; Rptr Yrbk; Rptr Sch Nwsp; Spn Clb; Pl Dist Ohio Scholstc Achv Spanish 1978; Natl HS Excellence 1979; Pl 2nd Alrnd St AAU Class II Gym 1977; Univ; Lib Arts.

VILLARREAL, DEBRA; Grand Ledge HS; Lansing, MI; 28/400 Band; Chrs; Hon Rl; JA; NHS; Sch Mus; Sch Pl; Stg Crw; Mic State Univ; Health Sci.

VILLELLA, TONI; Franklin HS; Farnklin, OH; Cls Rep Frsh Cls; Cls Rep Soph Cls; VP Jr Cls; Pres Sr Cls; Band; Cmnty Wkr; Girl Scts; Hon Rl; Lbry Ade; Sct Actv; Miami Univ.

VILLENEUVE, MARY; Marian HS; Troy, MI; Hosp Ade; Jr NHS; Lit Mag; NHS; Red Cr Ade; Fr Clb; Letter Swmmng; IM Sprt; Univ Of Michigan; Pre Med.

VILLERS, JANICE; Lake Central HS; Saint John, IN; 24/563 Chrs; Girl Scts; Hon Rl; Lit Mag; NHS; Sct Actv; In Univ Northwest; Acctg.

VILLERS, KAREN; Wirt County HS; Elizabeth, WV; Sec Frsh Cls; Cls Rep Soph Cls; Band; Drm Mjrt; Hon Rl; NHS; Stu Cncl; Yth Flsp; 4-H; FBLA; Gregg Shorthand Speed Contest 100 WPM 79; 3rd Pl At Regnl FBLA Conventor For Shorthand 79; Marshall Univ; Bus Educ.

VILLERS, LINDA; Lewis County HS; Weston, WV; Cls Rep Sr Cls; Chrs; Pres Hosp Ade; Lbry Ade; Stu Cncl; 500 Hr Awd Candy Strpr; Stonewall Jackson Schl; X Ray Tech.

VIMMERSTEDT, WILLIAM; Wooster HS; Wooster, OH; Cls Rep Soph Cls; Cl Rep Jr Cls; Cls Rep Sr Cls; Band; Boy Scts; Cmnty Wkr; Lit Mag; VP Stu Cncl; Yrbk; VP Ger Clb; Univ Of Colorado.

VIMR, MARK; Cabrini HS; Allen Park, MI; 1/144 Val; Chrs; Chrh Wkr; Cmnty Wkr; Hon Rl; Jr NHS; NHS; Spn Clb; Am Leg Awd; Kiwan Awd; Univ Of Detroit; Dentistry.

VINCENT, CHRISTINA; Maconaquah HS; Peru, IN; 62/219 Chrh Wkr; FCA; Hon Rl; NHS; Yth Flsp; Y-Teens; Pep Clb; Capt Chrldng;.

VINCENT, CHRISTINE; Godwin Hts HS; Wyoming, MI; 4/170 Sec Frsh Cls; Pres Soph Cls; Cl Rep Jr Cls; Cls Rep Sr Cls; Am Leg Aux Girls St; Band; Hon Rl; Pres NHS; Stu Cncl; Yrbk; Michigan St Univ.

VINCENT, JENNIFER J; Grove City HS; Orient, OH; 44/515 Cls Rep Frsh Cls; Pres Chrs; NHS; VP Orch; Sch Pl; Stg Crw; Yth Flsp; Sec Drama Clb; Pres Ger Clb; VP Pep Clb; Wittenberg Univ; Acctg.

VINCENT, KAREN; Arthur Hill HS; Saginaw, MI; Band; Girl Scts; Hon Rl; Hosp Ade; NHS; OEA; Cit Awd;.

VINCENT, MATT; Lincoln HS; Shinnston, WV; Band; Hon Rl; NHS; Ftbl; Fairmont St Univ; Music.

VINCENT, MATTHEW; Lincoln HS; Shinnston, WV; 8/153 Am Leg Boys St; Band; Hon Rl; NHS; Sci Clb; Ftbl; Am Leg Awd; Cit Awd; Fairmont St Coll; Music.

VINCENT, MAUREEN; Our Lady Of Mercy HS; Detroit, MI; Sec Chrs; Hosp Ade; Red Cr Ade; Trk; VFW Awd; Univ Of Michigan; Med.

VINCENT, MICHAEL; East Canton HS; E Canton, OH; 5/104 Sec Sr Cls; Boy Scts; Chrh Wkr; Hon Rl; Jr NHS; NHS; Sct Actv; Yth Flsp; Letter Bsbl; Ohi State Univ; Agri Eng.

VINCENT, MICHELE; Flemington HS; Simpson, WV; 3/45 Hst Jr Cls; Am Leg Aux Girls St; Band; Hon Rl; NHS; Ed Yrbk; Sec Fr Clb; Pep Clb; Chrldng; Rotary Awd; Fairmont St Univ; Journalism.

VINCENT, ROBERT; Perrysburg HS; Perrysburg, OH; Hon Rl; NHS; Fr Clb; Univ Of Michigan; Clinical Psych.

VINCENT, RONALD; Flemington HS; Flemington, WV; Cls Rep Frsh Cls; Cls Rep Soph Cls; Trs Jr Cls; Hon Rl; NHS; Sprt Ed Yrbk; Sprt Ed Sch Nwsp; Fr Clb; FTA; Pep Clb; Vocational Schl; Electronics.

VINING, TERI; Medina Sr HS; Medina, OH; Chrh Wkr; Hon Rl; NHS; IM Sprt; Univ; Sci.

VINK, GORDON; Lincoln HS; Gahanna, OH; 35/395 Band; Boy Scts; Hon Rl; NHS; Sct Actv; Fr Clb; Socr; Ohio State Univ; Med.

VINKLER, EILEEN; Cardinal Mooney HS; Youngstown, OH; 5/294 Cls Rep Soph Cls; Sec Jr Cls; Trs Sr Cls; Hon Rl; Jr NHS; NHS; Stu Cncl; Mth Clb; Carlow College; Nursing.

VINOCUR, MARCELA; Bloomington North HS; Bloomington, IN; AFS; Hon Rl; Lit Mag; Sch Pl; 4-H; Fr Clb; Indiana Univ; Med.

VINOVERSKI, JULIE; Midview HS; Grafton, OH; Girl Scts; Hon Rl; NHS; Sct Actv; Sprt Ed Yrbk; Rptr Sch Nwsp; Fr Clb; Bsktbl; Capt Crs Cntry; Trk; Univ; Intl Bus.

VINSON, BERNADETTE; R A Taft HS; Cincinnati, OH; Cls Rep Soph Cls; Sal; Hon Rl; JA; Stu Cncl; JA Awd;.

VINSON, CHRISTOPHER; Loveland Hurst HS; Loveland, OH; 7/229 Trs Frsh Cls; Am Leg Boys St; Boy Scts; FCA; Treas Stu Cncl; Yth Flsp; Key Clb; Letter Ftbl; Letter Trk; SAR Awd; College; Law.

VINSON, JENI; Waynesville HS; Waynesville, OH; Trs Sr Cls; Sec Chrs; Hon Rl; Mdrgl; Off Ade; Sch Mus; Sch Pl; VP Stu Cncl; Yrbk; Sch Nwsp; Sinclair Coll; Airline Stewardess.

VINSON, KIMBERLY; Brown County HS; Morgantown, IN; VP Frsh Cls; VP Soph Cls; VP Jr Cls; Cl Rep Jr Cls; Cls Rep Sr Cls; Chrs; Drl Tm; Off Ade; Stu Cncl; Breech Training Acad.

VINSON, SUE; Bloom Carroll HS; Carroll, OH; Sec Soph Cls; Sec Jr Cls; Debate Tm; Drl Tm; Hon Rl; Red Cr Ade; Sch Mus; Stg Crw; FFA; Mgrs; Ohio St Univ; Agriculture.

VINSON, YOLANDA; Ypsilanti HS; Ypsilanti, MI; Aud/Vis; Hon Rl; JA; Rptr Sch Nwsp; Cit Awd; Howard Univ; Journalism.

VINTZEL, JAMES; Brighton HS; Brighton, MI; Trs Jr Cls; Boy Scts; Chrs; CAP; Hon Rl; Fr Clb; Sci Clb; Bsktbl; Trk; Mich State Univ; Engineer.

VINYARD, TAMI; Calumet HS; Griffith, IN; 64/295 Off Ade; Pep Clb; Chrldng; GAA; IM Sprt; PPFtbl; College; Stewardess.

VIOLA, JOHN; Warren Western Reserve HS; Warren, OH; Hon Rl; Natl Merit Ltr; College.

VIOLA, RICHARD; St Francis De Sales HS; Westerville, OH; Hon Rl; Letter Crs Cntry; Trk; IM Sprt; Scr Kpr; Nominated For Boys St; College.

VIOX, CATHERINE; Stephen T Badin HS; Hamilton, OH; 53/223 FCA; Hon Rl; Drama Clb; IM Sprt; Miami Univ; Cmnctns.

VIRDEN, TERESA; Kktyler County HS; New Martinsvill, E; 31/101 Band; Chrh Wkr; Hosp Ade; Pres Drama Clb; VICA; Bsktbl; IM Sprt; Univ; Music.

VIRGALLITO, DAVID R; Carroll HS; Xenia, OH; Wright St Univ; Law.

VIRTUE, JANICE; Sylvania Southview HS; Toledo, OH; 7/295 Am Leg Aux Girls St; Chrs; Hon Rl; VP Natl Forn Lg; NHS; Quill & Scroll; Sch Pl; Ed Sch Nwsp; Pres Mth Clb; PPFtbl; Univ Of Toledo; Busns Admin.

VISCOGLIOSI, LORI; Dearborn HS; Dearborn Hts, MI; Hon Rl; Lit Mag; VP NHS; Treas PAVAS; Sch Pl; Stg Crw; Drama Clb; Lat Clb; Bsktbl; Natl Merit Ltr; Univ Of Michigan; Bio Chem.

VISINTINE, KAREN; Upper Arlington HS; Columbus, OH; Drl Tm; FCA; Hon Rl; Sch Mus; Pep Clb; Chrldng; GAA; Mat Maids; Alabama Univ; Mktg.

VISOCAN, ROSEMARIE; James A Garfield HS; Garrettsville, OH; Off Ade; Bsbl; Bsktbl; Bus Schl.

VISSER, BARBARA; Waverly HS; Lansing, MI; 2/366 Hon Rl; Sec NHS; Fr Clb; Pep Clb; Pom Pon; Michigan State.

VISSER, MARILOU; East Kentwood HS; Kentwood, MI; Chrs; Girl Scts; Hon Rl; NHS; Sch Mus; Stu Cncl; Natl Merit Schl; Western Mic; Bus Admin.

VISSERS, ALETHEA; St Joseph Public HS; St Joseph, MI; Band; Jr NHS; Pres Yth Flsp; Ger Clb; College; Acctg.

VITALE, JEFF; Madison HS; Madison Hts, MI; Chrs; Debate Tm; Hon Rl; Jr NHS; NHS; Pol Wkr; Sch Mus; Civ Clb; Ger Clb; Chmn Pep Clb; Harvard Summer Schl 79; Occidntl Oceanology Progr For Scndrt Stdnt 79; Michigan St Univ; Bio.

VITALE, PATRICIA; Aquinas HS; Lincoln Park, MI; Band; Hon Rl; Orch; Sch Mus; Ed Yrbk; Pep Clb; Ten; Central Mic Univ; Child Dvlmnt.

VITANYE, RHONDA; Regina HS; Cleveland, OH; 3/198 Cls Rep Frsh Cls; Hon Rl; Yrbk; Rptr Sch Nwsp; GAA; IM Sprt; Natl Merit Ltr; Summr Felllwship In Bio Resrch At Case W Reserve Univ 79; Hon Mntn Algbr II Oh Test Of Schshtc Achmnt 79; Univ; Chem.

VITARELLI, PHILLIP; Madonna HS; Follansbee, WV; Boy Scts; Hon Rl; NHS; Pep Clb; Letter Bsbl; Bsktbl; Letter Ftbl; IM Sprt;.

VITCHNER, RICH; Buckeye Local HS; Yorkville, OH; Band; Boy Scts; Hon Rl; Orch; Sch Pl; Stg Crw; Drama Clb; Voc Schl; Drafting.

VITE, JEROME; Buchanan HS; Niles, MI; 4/160 FCA; Hon Rl; NHS; Yth Flsp; Ftbl; Operation Enterprs Mgmt Course Put On By Amer Man Assocm9; Univ; Econ.

VITEK, DAVID; Muskegon HS; Muskegon, MI; Cls Rep Frsh Cls; Band; Boy Scts; Sch Mus; Sct Actv; Rptr Yrbk; Rptr Sch Nwsp; Drama Clb; Bsktbl; Trk; Muskegon Jr Coll; Hotel Management.

VITTUR, MELISSA; River Valley HS; Caledonia, OH; Cl Rep Jr Cls; Band; Chrs; Chrh Wkr; Cmnty Wkr; Mdrgl; Sch Mus; Stu Cncl; College.

VIVIAN, CHERYL; Marquette Sr HS; Marquette, MI; 9/427 Band; Hon Rl; Stg Crw; OEA; Trk; IM Sprt; L G Kaufman Endowment Fund; All Amer Hall Of Fame Bnd Hnrs; Outstndng HS Ach Bookkeeping/acctg; N Michigan Univ; Busns Admin.

VIVIO, KAREN; Norway HS; Vulcan, MI; 12/85 Hon Rl; NHS; Sec 4-H; Bsktbl; Capt Trk; GAA; 4-H Awd; Mic Tech; Comp Sci.

VIVO, ALLAN; Boardman HS; Youngstown, OH; Band; Sci Clb; VP Spn Clb; Ohio St Univ; Pre Med.

VLACK, MARY; Groveport Madison Sr HS; Columbus, OH; Band; Cmp Fr Grls; Hon Rl; Sch Pl; Spelling Bee Citizen Journal; Coll; Sec.

VLAHOS, MARGARITA; Zanesville HS; Zanesville, OH; 2/379 Cmnty Wkr; Hon Rl; Lbry Ade; NHS; Lat Clb; Pep Clb; Treas Sci Clb; Univ; Acctg.

VLARICH, CELESTE; William A Wirt HS; Gary, IN; Chrh Wkr; Girl Scts; Jr NHS; Lbry Ade; Sct Actv; Yth Flsp; Fr Clb; Sci Clb; VFW Awd; 1st Pl Wnr Gary Spelling Contest 1978; Hon Mtn Calumet Regn Sci Fair 1977; Univ; Med.

VLK, VINCENT; Fairview HS; Fairview Pk, OH; 12/280 Hon Rl; Sch Mus; Miami Univ; Acctg.

VOCATURE, TERESA; East Palestine HS; E Palestine, OH; 41/153 Band; Cmp Fr Grls; Chrs; Chrh Wkr; Sch Pl; Letter Trk; Twrlr; College; Law.

VOCK, MICHAEL; Kearsley HS; Flint, MI; CAP; Hon Rl; Letter Ftbl; Letter Trk; College; Elec Engr.

VOCKE, CRISTIAN; Lakeview HS; Battle Creek, MI; Hon Rl; Stg Crw; Bsbl; Ftbl; Wrstlng; IM Sprt; Western Michigan Univ; Bus.

VOEGTLEN, BARBARA G; Perrysburg HS; Perrysburg, OH; Girl Scts; JA; Off Ade; Sch Pl; Stg Crw; Drama Clb; Fr Clb; Pep Clb; Letter Ten; Letter Trk; Univ; Theater.

VOELKEL, DONNA; Northeast Dubois HS; Dubois, IN; Chrs; Hon Rl; Sch Mus; Stu Cncl; Yth Flsp; 4-H; Pres Fr Clb; Pres OEA; Lockyear Bus Schl; Legal Sec.

VOELKER, CHARLES; Calumet HS; Calumet, MI; Am Leg Boys St; Hon Rl; NHS; Fr Clb; Capt Crs Cntry; Ftbl; Capt Trk; IM Sprt; Michigan Tech Univ; Air Force ROTC.

VOELKER, CHARLEY; Riverside HS; Painesville, OH; Hon Rl; JA; Boys Clb Am; Spn Clb; Crs Cntry; Trk; Univ; Theatre.

VOELKER, DOW T; Grandview Hts HS; Columbus, OH; VP Frsh Cls; Pres Soph Cls; Trs Jr Cls; Cl Rep Jr Cls; Pres Sr Cls; Cls Rep Sr Cls; Am Leg Boys St; Band; Boy Scts; FCA; Univ; Pre Law.

VOELKER, DOW T; Grandview Heights HS; Columbus, OH; 10/146 VP Frsh Cls; Pres Soph Cls; Trs Jr Cls; Pres Sr Cls; Am Leg Boys St; Band; Boy Scts; Cmnty Wkr; FCA; Hon Rl; Univ; Law.

VOELKER, L; Belleville HS; Ypsilanti, MI; 4/517 Trs Soph Cls; Trs Jr Cls; Girl Scts; Hon Rl; NHS; Stu Cncl; Ger Clb; Swmmng; Chrldng; Mgrs; Univ Of Mich; Med.

VOELKER, SCOTT; Elder HS; N Bend, OH; 22/400 Hon Rl; Yth Flsp; Yrbk; Cit Awd; SAR Awd; Ohi State Univ; Vet Med.

VOELLER, SUZANNE T; Perrysburg HS; Perrysburg, OH; Hon Rl; Sch Mus; Sch Pl; Sch Nwsp; Drama Clb; Fr Clb; Mth Clb; Sci Clb; Coach Actv; IM Sprt; Coll; Med.

VOETBERG, BETTY; Holland Christian HS; Holland, MI; 1/261 Chrs; Chrh Wkr; Hosp Ade; Mod UN; NHS; Rptr Yrbk; Sch Nwsp; Mercy Central Scl Of Nrsng; Reg Nrse.

VOETBERG, LYNN; Holland Christian HS; Holland, MI; Chrs; Chrh Wkr; Yth Flsp; Yrbk; 4-H; Ger Clb; Scr Kpr; 4-H Awd; Calvin Coll; Elem Ed.

VOGEL, BARBARA; Jennings County HS; No Vernon, IN; Band; Sch Pl; 4-H; FTA; Pep Clb; College; Elem Education.

VOGEL, CATHY; Clyde HS; Clyde, OH; Aud/Vis; Hon Rl; FBLA;.

VOGEL, JULIE; H H Dow HS; Midland, MI; 5/420 Chrh Wkr; Hon Rl; NHS; Orch; Michigan St Univ; Biochem.

VOGEL, JULIE; Memorial HS; St Marys, OH; 11/220 Am Leg Aux Girls St; Band; Hon Rl; Lbry Ade; NHS; Sch Pl; Stg Crw; Yth Flsp; Ed Yrbk; Rptr Yrbk; Bowling Green Univ; Library Sci.

VOGEL, PEGGY; Memorial HS; St Marys, OH; 21/225 Am Leg Aux Girls St; Band; Chrs; Girl Scts; NHS; Sch Mus; Yth Flsp; Y-Teens; FHA; Univ; History.

VOGEL, TAMMEY; West Carrollton Sr HS; W Car rollton, OH; 35/365 Chrs; Girl Scts; Hon Rl; Jr NHS; NHS; Off Ade; Sct Actv; VFW Awd; ERA 73 79; Rainbows 75 79; Home Ec.

VOGELBACH, DALE; George Washington HS; Charleston, WV; 20/350 FCA; Hon Rl; Jr NHS; Key Clb; Letter Bsbl; Letter Bsktbl; Letter Ftbl; Guilford Coll; Phy Ther.

VOGELGESANG, CHRIS; Centerville HS; Richmond, IN; Cls Rep Frsh Cls; Band; Debate Tm; Hon Rl; Jr NHS; Sch Mus; Yrbk; Sch Nwsp; Sci Clb; Purdue; Comp Sci.

VOGELSANG, MARY; La Porte HS; Laporte, IN; Chrs; Girl Scts; Hon Rl; MMM; NHS; Orch; Spn Clb; Trk; Purdue North Cent HS.

VOGELSANG, ROBERT; Clawson HS; Clawson, MI; Pres Sr Cls; Cls Rep Sr Cls; Hon Rl; Stg Crw; Letter Ftbl; Exc In Creative Writing; Sci Key Chem; Exc In Advanced Bio; Coll; Vet.

VOGL, BARBARA A; Owosso HS; Henderson, MI; Band; Chrs; Girl Scts; Hon Rl; Lbry Ade; Rptr Yrbk; 4-H; Trk; Mgrs; Cit Awd; Delgt To Natl 4 H Ctznshp Congress In Wash Dc 79; Univ; Bus Admin.

VOGLEWEDE, LINDA; Bellmont HS; Decatur, IN; 5/250 Hon Rl; NHS; Red Cr Ade; Ger Clb; Pep Clb; Letter Bsktbl; Letter Trk; Bus Schl; Sec.

VOGRIN, GEORGE; Cardinal Mooney HS; Youngstown, OH; 41/288 Debate Tm; Hon Rl; Natl Forn Lg; NHS; Mth Clb; Trk; Natl Merit Ltr; Natl Forensic Lge Awd 79; 3rd Jr Road Race 79; U S Naval Academy; Engr.

VOGT, CONNIE; Stephen T Badin HS; Hamilton, OH; 26/223 Chrh Wkr; Cmnty Wkr; Girl Scts; Hon Rl; Sch Mus; Sct Actv; Spn Clb; Trk; Scr Kpr; Tmr; Bus Schl; Legal Sec.

VOGT, HELEN; Adelphian Academy; Pontiac, MI; Chrh Wkr; IM Sprt; Coll; Comm Art.

VOGT, JON; Ida HS; Temperance, MI; Drl Tm; FCA; Spn Clb; Bsbl; Bsktbl; IM Sprt; Monroe Cmnty Coll ; Forestry.

VOGTMANN, WALLACE; Bay City Western HS; Auburn, MI; 3/438 Boy Scts; Chrs; Chrh Wkr; Cmnty Wkr; Hon Rl; NHS; Bsktbl; Letter Ftbl; Western Michigan Univ; Comp Sci.

VOISE, MARY; Bridgeport HS; Saginaw, MI; 69/330 Letter Band; Girl Scts; Hon Rl; Hosp Ade; JA; Sch Pl; Yth Flsp; Spn Clb; Trk; Mat Maids; Flag Twirler In Marching Band; Delta Coll; Dent Hygiene.

VOISINE, CHRISTINE; Lewiston HS; Lewiston, ME; Hon Rl; Y-Teens; Univ; Acctg.

VOJTKO, SUSAN; Bangor HS; Bangor, MI; Cls Rep Frsh Cls; Pres Soph Cls; Cl Rep Jr Cls; Am Leg Aux Girls St; Band; Hon Rl; Stu Cncl; Key Clb; Letter Crs Cntry; Letter Trk; College.

VOJTUSH, GERALD; Henry Ford Ii HS; Sterling Hts, MI; College; Acct.

VOLAN, MICHAEL; Sebring Mc Kinley HS; Sebring, OH; 10/76 Am Leg Boys St; VP Band; Boy Scts; Chrs; Chrh Wkr; Hon Rl; Lbry Ade; NHS; Sch Mus; Sct Actv; Perfect Attndnc; Notre Dame Univ; Comp Sci.

VOLAND, SHERRI; Mississinewa HS; Gas City, IN; Drl Tm; FHA; Pom Pon; PPFtbl;.

VOLANDT, STEPHEN L; Kenston Sr HS; Chagrin Fls, OH; Boy Scts; Sct Actv; Letter Wrstlng; Natl Merit SF; 3rd Pl Jr Korice U S Regnl Karate Tourn 77; NROTC.

VOLK, KIMBERLY; Anderson Highland HS; Anderson, IN; Cl Rep Jr Cls; Cls Rep Sr Cls; Chrh Wkr; Cmnty Wkr; Hon Rl; Lit Mag; NHS; Off Ade; Stu Cncl; Sch Nwsp; Purdue Univ; Bio Med.

VOLK, KIMBERLY L; Highland HS; Anderson, IN; 1/500 Sch Nwsp; Bsktbl; Swmmng; Trk; Engr.

VOLK, MARITA; Niles Mc Kinley HS; Niles, OH; 3/421 AFS; Chrs; Girl Scts; Hon Rl; Hosp Ade; Lbry Ade; Natl Forn Lg; NHS; Red Cr Ade; Stu Cncl; Youngstown St Univ; Med.

VOLKERT, ALICE; Hicksville HS; Hicksville, OH; Aud/Vis; Band; Chrs; Chrh Wkr; Cmnty Wkr; Girl Scts; Hon Rl; Hosp Ade; Lbry Ade; Sch Mus; Hicksville Firemns Queen 79; Lang Camp Schlrshp To Oh U 79; St Vincents Hosp Schl; RN.

VOLKMAN, CATHERINE; Highland HS; Highland, IN; 187/514 Girl Scts; Hon Rl; Off Ade; FHA; Pep Clb; Coach Actv; GAA; IM Sprt; Tmr;.

VOLLMAR, ROBIN; Otsego HS; Tontogany, OH; 9/190 Hon Rl; Jr NHS; NHS; Drama Clb; Trk; Chrldng; Vocational School.

VOLLMAR, TONI; Unioto HS; Chillicothe, OH; 7/127 Band; Chrs; Hon Rl; Jr NHS; NHS; Quill & Scroll; Sch Mus; Rptr Sch Nwsp; Drama Clb; Spn Clb; Capital Univ; Instrmntl Music.

VOLLMER, JONATHAN; Lasalle HS; S Bend, IN; 71/473 Band; Boy Scts; Chrh Wkr; Drl Tm; Hon Rl; Sct Actv; Yth Flsp; Pep Clb; Valparaiso Univ; Aerospace Engr.

VOLLMER, VICKI; Boonville HS; Boonville, IN; Am Leg Aux Girls St; Drl Tm; Hon Rl; NHS; Off Ade; Stu Cncl; Pep Clb; Ball St Univ; Speech Pathology.

VOLTIN, RUSSELL; Ripley HS; Ripley, WV; 7/300 Hon Rl; Jr NHS; Sch Pl; Stg Crw; Drama Clb; Mth Clb; Ftbl; IM Sprt; College; Vet Med.

VOLZ, BEVERLY; Warren Central HS; Indpls, IN; 44/825 Chrs; Chrh Wkr; Cmnty Wkr; Girl Scts; Hon Rl; Mdrgl; NHS; Orch; Sch Mus; Drama Clb; Otstndng Potog Of Yr 79; Finalist In Natl Teenager Pageant 79; 2nd Plc In Phogot In In Indust Educ; Bauder Fashion Coll; Fshn Mdse.

VOLZ, MARY; St Marys Ctrl Catholic HS; Sandusky, OH; Hon Rl; Sci Clb; Spn Clb; GAA; Bowling Green St Univ; Bus Admin.

VON ASCHEN, LORI; Piqua HS; Piqua, OH; 5/335 Band; Chrs; Hon Rl; Sch Mus; Sch Pl; Ed Sch Nwsp; Rptr Sch Nwsp; Kent State Univ; Fash Merch.

VON BARGEN, TERRY; Fenwick HS; West Chester, OH; Hon Rl; Stg Crw; Letter Bsktbl; Letter Ftbl; Letter Trk; Letter Wrstlng; IM Sprt; Univ Of Cincinnati; Artist.

VON BOYD JR, DEJUAIN; North Central HS; Indianapolis, IN; Chrs; Hon Rl; VP JA; NHS; Off Ade; Quill & Scroll; Sch Mus; Sch Pl; Stg Crw; Ed Sch Nwsp; Intl Thespian Soc; Coll; Journalism.

VONDELL, JEFFREY; Battle Creek Lakeview HS; Battle Creek, MI; 29/398 Cls Rep Soph Cls; Boy Scts; Chrh Wkr; Hon Rl; Sct Actv; Yth Flsp; IM Sprt; Mgrs; Am Leg Awd; God Cntry Awd; Eagle Scout 77; Natl Hon Soc 77; Order Of The Arrow 78; Michigan Tech Voc Schl; Pulp Sci.

VONDER EMBSE, JULIA; Ottawa Glandorf HS; Ottawa, OH; 8/172 Trs Soph Cls; Hon Rl; NHS; Sch Mus; Rptr Yrbk; Ed Sch Nwsp; Drama Clb; FHA; Spn Clb; GAA; Tri St Univ; Mktg.

VONDERHEIDE, KURT; Kurt Vonderheide HS; Jasper, IN; 104/289 Letter Ftbl; Letter Wrstlng; IM Sprt; Univ.

VONDEROHE, ERIC; Warren Central HS; Indianapolis, IN; 5/760 Mdrgl; NHS; Treas Yth Flsp; Ten; IM Sprt; Kiwan Awd; Natl Merit Ltr; De Pauw Univ; Chem.

VON GLAHN, MICHAEL T; Bay HS; Bay Village, OH; Quill & Scroll; Sch Mus; Sch Pl; Stg Crw; Yrbk; Rptr Sch Nwsp; Sch Nwsp; VP Ger Clb; Natl Merit Ltr; Univ Of Iowa; Eng.

VON HOENE, KATHLEEN; St Ursula Academy; Cincinnati, OH; 2/85 Cls Rep Sr Cls; Hon Rl; NHS; Stu Cncl; Bsktbl; DAR Awd; Kiwan Awd; Capital Univ; Poli Sci.

VON HOENE, MIKE; Purcell HS; Cincinnati, OH; 24/171 Hon Rl; Bsbl; Ftbl; IM Sprt; Univ Of Cincinnati; Busns Admin.

VON HOENE, STEVE; Purcell HS; Cincinnati, OH; 13/170 Chrh Wkr; Hon Rl; Red Cr Ade; Rptr Sch Nwsp; Swmmng; Trk; IM Sprt; Univ; CPA.

VONK, RICHARD; Forest Hills Central HS; Ada, MI; 8/250 Aud/Vis; Hon Rl; Letter Ten; Natl Merit Ltr; Univ Of Mic; Bus Admin.

VON KOPIS, DONALD F M; North Miami HS; Denver, IN; 2/122 Cls Rep Sr Cls; Am Leg Boys St; Chrs; Chrh Wkr; Hon Rl; Mdrgl; NHS; PAVAS; Sch Mus; Sch Pl; Hoosier Boys St 79; Univ; Eng.

VON NEUMANN, RON; Wilbur Wright HS; Dayton, OH; 13/200 Hon Rl; Sprt Ed Yrbk; Sprt Ed Sch Nwsp; Boys Clb Am; Letter Bsbl; Letter Ftbl; Letter Socr; Letter Wrstlng; Mgrs; Scr Kpr; Univ Of Maryland.

VON PATTERSON, CARL; Ravenna HS; Ravenna, OH; 2/324 Band; Chrh Wkr; Hon Rl; NHS; Rptr Yrbk; Rptr Sch Nwsp; Sci Clb; College; Med.

VON STEENBURG, LAURA L; Ogemaw Heights HS; West Branch, MI; Cls Rep Frsh Cls; Cl Rep Jr Cls; Girl Scts; Hon Rl; Sch Pl; Ed Yrbk; Pep Clb; Bsbl; Letter Chrldng; Central Michigan Univ; Eng.

VON TRENDE, MICHAEL; Whetstone HS; Columbus, OH; Hon Rl; Lbry Ade; Sch Mus; Sch Nwsp; Voc Schl; Radio.

VOORHEES, KEN; Big Rapids HS; Big Rapids, MI; 40/188 Debate Tm; Natl Forn Lg; Sch Pl; Stu Cncl; Yrbk; Sch Nwsp; Drama Clb; Fr Clb; FBLA; Natl Merit Schl; Michigan St Univ; Pre Law.

VOORHEES, LORI; Clay HS; Granger, IN; 33/416 Cls Rep Frsh Cls; Hon Rl; Off Ade; Stu Cncl; Rptr Sch Nwsp; Fr Clb; College; Lab Tech.

VOORHEES, SUSAN; Sidney HS; Sidney, OH; Trs Soph Cls; Cl Rep Jr Cls; Chrs; Hon Rl; Hosp Ade; NHS; Orch; Sch Mus; Stg Crw; Stu Cncl; Oherbein Coll; Comp Sci.

VOORS, ANN; Bishop Luers HS; Ft Wayne, IN; Hon Rl; NHS; Letter Ten; IM Sprt; PPFtbl; Univ.

VORBROKER, ROBERT; Moeller HS; Cincinnati, OH; Hon Rl; JA; Lit Mag; Sch Mus; Spn Clb; IM Sprt; JA Awd; Evans Schlrshp 79; Natl Merit Achv Awd 78; Ohio St Univ; Law.

VORE, DIANA; Jay Cnty HS; Ridgeville, IN; 76/435 Hon Rl; NHS; Y-Teens; Rptr Sch Nwsp; Sch Nwsp; Fr Clb; OEA; Pep Clb; Coll; Acctg.

VORE, LISA; Wood Memorial HS; Oakland City, IN; 8/120 VP Sr Cls; Band; Drl Tm; Hon Rl; Off Ade; Yrbk; Sch Nwsp; OEA; Pep Clb; Chrldng; ISUE; Acctg.

VORHEES, SCOTT; Cadiz HS; Hopedale, OH; 4/133 Band; Chrs; Hon Rl; NHS; Sch Mus; Sch Pl; Rptr Sch Nwsp; Drama Clb; Muskingum Univ; Bio.

VORNHAGEN, JILL M; Herbert Henry Dow HS; Midland, MI; 104/408 Chrh Wkr; Hon Rl; NHS; Yth Flsp; Drama Clb; Pres Awd; Alma Coll; Soc Work.

VORONO, DEBORAH K; Northfork HS; Northfork, WV; 9/105 Pres Frsh Cls; Am Leg Aux Girls St; Band; Hon Rl; Jr NHS; Pres Stu Cncl; Fr Clb; Keyettes; Chrldng; Was Presented The Principals Awd; Selected Northforks Miss Jr Miss; West Virginia Univ; Veterinarian.

VORSELEN, JANET; Rivesville HS; Rivesvl, WV; 2/47 Hst Frsh Cls; Cls Rep Soph Cls; Trs Sr Cls; Sal; Hon Rl; Lbry Ade; NHS; Off Ade; Sec Stu Cncl; Y-Teens; Fairmont St Coll; Elec Data Proc.

VORTERS, DIAN; Niles HS; Niles, MI; Band; Girl Scts; Hon Rl; Pol Wkr; Stu Cncl; Ed Yrbk; Rptr Sch Nwsp; Fr Clb; Cit Awd; Opt Clb Awd; Mich St Univ; Pol Science.

VORVES, KOSTADINOS; Harry S Truman Sr HS; Taylor, MI; 6/525 Chrh Wkr; Hon Rl; Lbry Ade; NHS; St Of Mi Schlrshp 79; Otstndng Math Stud Awd 79; New Mbr Of Hon Prog 79; Henry Ford Cmnty Coll; Engr.

VOS, DAVID; Bay City Central HS; Bay City, MI; 40/464 Band; Hon Rl; Sch Mus; Stg Crw; Stu Cncl; Saginaw Valley; Cpa.

VOS, WILLIAM G; Tri County HS; Pierson, MI; 33/96 Hon Rl; Bsbl; Bsktbl; Ftbl; Glf; Var Club Pres 78; Homecoming King 78; Montcalm Cnty Mental Health Awd; Aquinas Univ; Acctg.

VOSLER, BARBARA; Brandywine HS; Niles, MI; 2/140 Trs Sr Cls; AFS; Band; Cmnty Wkr; Drl Tm; Hon Rl; NHS; Stu Cncl; Treas Spn Clb; Cit Awd; Michigan St Univ; Orthodontist.

VOSS, ESTHER; Michigan Luth Seminry HS; Frankenmuth, MI; 1/62 Val; Chrs; Mdrgl; Sch Pl; Chmn Chrldng; PPFtbl; Natl Merit Ltr; Lake Superior State College; Med.

VOSS, JONI; Schoolcraft HS; Schoolcraft, MI; Pres Soph Cls; Cl Rep Jr Cls; Hon Rl; NHS; Off Ade; 4-H; Fr Clb; Trk; Chrldng; Mic State; Psych.

VOTA, JACQUELINE R; Buckeye West HS; Dillonvale, OH; 6/92 Band; Girl Scts; Hon Rl; NHS; Sch Pl; Yth Flsp; Drama Clb; FTA; Sci Clb; Bsktbl; College; Science.

VOTAW, TY; S Range E Raiders HS; Salem, OH; Chrh Wkr; Hon Rl; Lbry Ade; ROTC; Sch Pl; Stu Cncl; Yrbk; Ed Sch Nwsp; Sprt Ed Sch Nwsp; Rptr Sch Nwsp; Kent Univ; Journalism.

VOVOS, JOHN M; Parma Sr HS; Parma, OH; Chrh Wkr; Hon Rl; Jr NHS; NHS; Capt Crs Cntry; Letter Trk; Cleveland St Univ; Comp.

VOYTECEK, BRIAN; Martins Ferry HS; Martins Ferry, OH; 38/217 Cl Rep Jr Cls; Am Leg Boys St; Sci Clb; Bsktbl; Cit Awd; Wake Forest; Optometry.

VOYTEK, KAREN; St Augustine Academy; Lakewood, OH; Chrs; Girl Scts; Orch; Sch Mus; Sch Pl; Stg Crw; Fr Clb; VP Pep Clb; Bsbl; Bsktbl; Lake Erie Coll; Bus Admin.

VOZNIAK, TRACY; Monongah HS; Fairmont, WV; Band; Drl Tm; Hon Rl; Y-Teens; Fr Clb; FHA; Pep Clb; Trk; Twrlr; 4-H Awd; Fairmont State Coll; Bus.

VRABEL, DEBORAH; Highland HS; Highland, IN; 57/510 Girl Scts; Hon Rl; Jr NHS; NHS; Off Ade; Stu Cncl; 4-H; Pep Clb; Letter Ten; Chrldng; Purdue Univ; Psych.

VRABEL, TRACY; Admiral King HS; Lorain, OH; Sec Frsh Cls; Cls Rep Frsh Cls; Cl Rep Jr Cls; Cls Rep Sr Cls; Chrh Wkr; Cmnty Wkr; Hon Rl; Sdlty; Stu Cncl; Chrldng; Young High Ideals Club Sec 77; Young High Ideals Pres 78; Coll; Cmnctns.

VRADELIS, THOMAS; Oakwood HS; Datyon, OH; 33/160 VP Jr Cls; VP Sr Cls; Hon Rl; NHS; Red Cr Ade; Stu Cncl; Rptr Yrbk; Ten; IM Sprt; Univ.

VRAHORETIS, SUSAN; Morton Sr HS; Hammond, IN; 10/419 Chrs; Girl Scts; Hon Rl; Jr NHS; Natl Forn Lg; Sch Mus; Sch Pl; FTA; College; Medicine.

VREDENBURG, KATHLEEN; Mc Bain Rural Agri HS; Tustin, MI; 3/65 Band; Hon Rl; NHS; Off Ade; Yth Flsp; Sch Nwsp; 4-H; Letter Trk; Coll.

VREDEVELD, RHONDA; Zeeland HS; Zeeland, MI; 61/193 Trs Frsh Cls; Band; Hon Rl; Yth Flsp; Bsktbl; IM Sprt; PPFtbl; Scr Kpr; Tmr; Made All Conf As Pitcher In Varsity Sftbl 78 79; Made Allconf As A Setter In Varsity Vlybl 79; Univ; Phys Educ.

VROMAN, SHERRY; Litchfield HS; Litchfield, MI; 12/52 Cls Rep Frsh Cls; Trs Sr Cls; Hon Rl; Lbry Ade; Sch Pl; Yrbk; Rptr Sch Nwsp; Gym;.

VROON, SCOTT; Holland Christian HS; Holland, MI; Band; Sch Mus; Trk; Ferris St Coll; Law Enf.

VU, HUYNH V; Harry S Truman HS; Taylor, MI; Macomb Cnty Coll; Elec Engr.

VUCKOVICH, MERLENE; Calumet HS; Gary, IN; 49/289 Sec Soph Cls; Cls Rep Soph Cls; Cl Rep Jr Cls; Cls Rep Sr Cls; Band; Chrh Wkr; Girl Scts; Hon Rl; Jr NHS; NHS; Indiana Univ; Nursing.

VUKOVICH, ROBERT JAMES; Hemlock HS; Saginaw, MI; Pres Sr Cls; NHS; Sch Pl; Yrbk; Letter Bsktbl; Letter Ftbl; Letter Trk; Mgrs; Natl Merit SF; Michigan Tech Univ; Chem Engr.

VULGAMORE, JAMES; Franklin Heights HS; Columbus, OH; Boy Scts; Cmnty Wkr; Pol Wkr; Sch Pl; Stg Crw; Ed Sch Nwsp; Sch Nwsp; Drama Clb; Fr Clb; FFA; Awd For Consrvtn Invlvmnt 76; Blue Rbbn Cnty Fair For Agri 77; Awd For Identifying Wildlife 77; Ohio St Univ; Jrnlsm.

VULICH, NADINE; Cardinal Moorey HS; Boardman, OH; Cls Rep Frsh Cls; Cls Rep Soph Cls; Cl Rep Jr Cls; Hon Rl; JA; NHS; Stu Cncl; Drama Clb; FTA; Spn Clb; Ohio St Univ; Dentistry.

VUURENS, JANET; Holland HS; Holland, MI; Boy Scts; Chrs; Chrh Wkr; Hon Rl; Stg Crw; IM Sprt; Grand Rapids Baptist Coll; Acctg.

VYHNALEK, GARY G; Valley Forge HS; Parma, OH; 1/704 Val; Hon Rl; NHS; Rptr Yrbk; Mth Clb; Letter Ten; Natl Merit SF; Purdue Univ; Aero Engr.

VYKOPAL, MICHELE; Rossford HS; Rossford, OH; 11/147 Band; Chrh Wkr; Hon Rl; Letter Bsktbl; College; Lab Tech.

W

WAACK, JEFFREY; Clarenceville HS; Livonia, MI; 24/234 Band; Hon Rl; Jr NHS; Lbry Ade; NHS; Sch Mus; Stg Crw; Drama Clb; Cit Awd; Natl Merit SF; Michigan St Univ; Comp Sci.

WAAK, SCOTT; Lutheran East HS; E Detroit, MI; FCA; Hon Rl; Lbry Ade; NHS; Capt Bsbl; Capt Bsktbl; Capt Crs Cntry; Macomb County Community College.

WACHTEL, BRENDA; Loudonville HS; Loudonville, OH; Sec Sr Cls; Trs Sr Cls; Band; Chrs; Hon Rl; Stg Crw; Letter Bsktbl; Chrldng; Volleyball Letter; Ski Club; College; Nursing.

WACHTEL, RHONDA; Eastmoor HS; Columbus, OH; 12/290 Chrs; Drl Tm; Hon Rl; Jr NHS; NHS; Sch Mus; Stu Cncl; Letter Ten; PPFtbl; Emory Univ; Child Psych.

WACHTEL, RONALD W; Orrville HS; Orrville, OH; 30/166 Cls Rep Frsh Cls; Cls Rep Soph Cls; Cl Rep Jr Cls; Cls Rep Sr Cls; Am Leg Boys St; FCA; Hon Rl; Stu Cncl; Yth Flsp; Lat Clb; Univ; Acctg.

WACHTMANN, LYNETTE; Napoleon HS; Napoleon, OH; Band; Chrs; FCA; Hon Rl; Sch Mus; Sch Pl; Stg Crw; Drama Clb; 4-H; Spn Clb;.

WACHTMANN, ROBERT; Napoleon HS; Napoleon, OH; Band; Hon Rl; Yth Flsp; 4-H; 4-H Awd; Voca Schl.

WACK, RAYMUND F; Archbishop Alter HS; Dayton, OH; 2/274 Band; Boy Scts; NHS; Stg Crw; Ed Yrbk; Key Clb; College; Vet.

WADDELL, RONALD; Olivet HS; Olivet, MI; 10/101 Trs Frsh Cls; Cls Rep Soph Cls; Am Leg Boys St; Hon Rl; Jr NHS; NHS; Off Ade; Stu Cncl; Ed Sch Nwsp; Rptr Sch Nwsp; S W Michigan Coll; Ag.

WADDINGTON, ROBERT; Start HS; Toledo, OH; Cls Rep Frsh Cls; Pres Soph Cls; Boy Scts; Debate Tm; Natl Forn Lg; Quill & Scroll; Sct Actv; Rptr Sch Nwsp; 1st Pl Amer Legion Amer Test; 1st Pl Greater Toledo Math Algebra Test; Broadcast HS Editorial; College; Journalism.

WADE, BRENDA; Highland HS; Anderson, IN; Cls Rep Sr Cls; Chrs; Drl Tm; Hon Rl; Quill & Scroll; Stu Cncl; Y-Teens; Sch Nwsp; Pres Twrlr; Pres In Voc Tech College; Legal Secretary.

WADE, CARRIE; Buckeye North HS; Mingo Junction, OH; VP Frsh Cls; Hon Rl; Off Ade; Sch Mus; 4-H; OEA; Chrldng; Jefferson Cnty Tech Inst.

WADE, CHRISTOPHER; Watkins Memorial HS; Pataskala, OH; Hon Rl; IM Sprt; Univ; Math.

WADE, CINDY; Carrollton HS; Melbourne, FL; Cls Rep Frsh Cls; Girl Scts; Hon Rl; Off Ade; Stu Cncl; Fr Clb; Busns Filing Awd; Proficiency In Typing; Tech Schl; Exec Sec.

WADE, CURTIS; Mac Kenzie HS; Detroit, MI; Aud/Vis; Boy Scts; Hon Rl; Yth Flsp; Mth Clb; Bsktbl; Gym; Trk; Univ; Comp Tech.

WADE, DEBRA; Athens HS; Princeton, WV; 9/65 FHA; FTA; Keyettes; Pep Clb; Concord Coll; Med Tech.

WADE, DEOBRA; New Albany HS; New Albany, IN; Chrh Wkr; Girl Scts; Hon Rl; DECA; Ger Clb; Trk; Twrlr; Mbr VFW; Indiana St Univ; Law.

WADE, DONNA; Lake Catholic HS; Wickliffe, OH; 130320 Cls Rep Sr Cls; Chrs; Cmnty Wkr; Hon Rl; NHS; Sch Mus; Stu Cncl; Rptr Yrbk; Drama Clb; Spn Clb; Chrstn Witnss Cert 79; Mary Rowe Moore Admssn W Distnctn To Univ Of Cincinnati 79; St Louis Univ; Nursing.

WADE, KIMMERLY; St Joseph HS; Saint Joseph, MI; 7/309 FCA; Hon Rl; Treas JA; VP NHS; Letter Bsktbl; Letter Trk; Treas Hockey; Miami Univ; System Analaysis.

WADE, LARRY; Douglas Mac Arthur HS; Saginaw, MI; 49/315 Hon Rl; NHS; Delta Coll; Archt.

WADE, LINDA; Chaminade Julienne HS; Dayton, OH; Band; Chrs; Hosp Ade; Off Ade; Orch; Sch Mus; Sch Pl; Pep Clb; Spn Clb; Perfct Attndn C77; Southern Illinois Univ; Psych.

WADE, MARK; St Albans HS; St Albans, WV; Pres Frsh Cls; Am Leg Boys St; Hon Rl; Jr NHS; NHS; Mth Clb; Spn Clb; Letter Ftbl; Vir Tech; Engr.

WADE, ROBERT; Stow HS; Stow, OH; Boy Scts; Chrs; Hon Rl; Mth Clb; Spn Clb; IM Sprt; Acclrtd Math Yr Awd 78; Univ; Eng.

WADE, ROGER; Stow HS; Munroe Fls, OH; 48/564 Band; Boy Scts; Chrs; Chrh Wkr; Hon Rl; Lbry Ade; NHS; Sct Actv; Stu Cncl; Fr Clb; Case Western Reserve Univ; Law.

WADE, SHELLY; Norwalk HS; Norwalk, OH; Girl Scts; Hon Rl; Hosp Ade; Sct Actv; 4-H; Mas Awd; Bus Schl; Bus.

WADE, SHERI; Gallia Academy; Gallipolis, OH; 1/236 Val; Am Leg Aux Girls St; Band; Hosp Ade; NHS; Sch Pl; Ed Yrbk; Drama Clb; Lat Clb; Rotary Awd; Eastern Kentucky Univ; Med Tech.

WADE, ZELEE; Jesup W Scott HS; Toledo, OH; Hon Rl; NHS; Fr Clb; FHA; Ohi State Univ; Med.

WADEL, DENISE; Copley HS; Copley, OH; Band; Chrs; Chrh Wkr; Cmnty Wkr; Girl Scts; Hon Rl; Lbry Ade; NHS; Sch Mus; Sct Actv; Univ; Nursing.

WADERKER, MICHELE; Buckeye North HS; Brilliant, OH; Am Leg Aux Girls St; Band; Hon Rl; NHS; Off Ade; Sch Mus; Sch Pl; Stu Cncl; Drama Clb; Ohi State Univ; Psych.

WADIAN, BRIAN; Jackson HS; Massillon, OH; Hon Rl; Awd For Cumulative A Avg; Stark Tech Coll; Comp Prog.

WADKINS, JIM; Calumet HS; Gary, IN; 14/295 Hon Rl; Pres NHS; FSA; Sci Clb; Ftbl; Wrstlng; Wabash College; Pre Engr.

WADLINGTON, TERRY; Logan Elm HS; Circleville, OH; Chrh Wkr; Cmnty Wkr; FCA; Hon Rl; NHS; Sec Key Clb; Bsktbl; Ohio State Univ; Engineering.

WADSWORTH, MARC; Fremont Ross HS; Fremont, OH; 1/459 Cl Rep Jr Cls; Am Leg Boys St; Band; Boy Scts; Hon Rl; Lbry Ade; NHS; Sct Actv; Stu Cncl; 4-H; Ohio St Univ; Dent.

WAFFORD, KERRY C; Broad Ripple HS; Indianapolis, IN; 59/468 Hon Rl; NHS; Sch Nwsp; Mth Clb; Sci Clb; Eli Lilly Yth Ldrshp Rep; Purdue Univ; Chem Engr.

WAGENER, KERRA D; Shortridge HS; Indianapolis, IN; 40/444 AFS; Chrh Wkr; Girl Scts; Hon Rl; Sch Mus; Sch Pl; Pres Drama Clb; Chmn Fr Clb; Mth Clb; Natl Merit Ltr; Univ; Theatre.

WAGENHOFER, LAURA; Jefferson Union HS; Toronto, OH; Chrs; Hon Rl; Off Ade; 4-H; Pep Clb; Chrldng; 4-H Awd; College; Med.

WAGENMAKER, DOUGLAS; Muskegon HS; Muskegon, MI; Hon Rl; Letter Bsbl; Electronics Engineering.

WAGG, KEVIN; Cass City HS; Cass City, MI; 6/165 Band; Chrh Wkr; Hon Rl; NHS; Yth Flsp; Letter Ftbl; Coach Actv; Univ Of Mic; Comp Sci.

WAGGONER, BETH; Marion Adams HS; Sheridan, IN; 1/86 Chrh Wkr; Sec FCA; Hosp Ade; NHS; Pres FHA; FTA; Anderson Coll; Elem Educ.

WAGGONER, CONNIE; Margaretta HS; Castalia, OH; Sec Frsh Cls; Trs Sr Cls; Drl Tm; Hon Rl; Rptr Sch Nwsp; 4-H; Fr Clb; Bsbl; Trk; Ohio St Univ; Vet.

WAGGONER, DAVID; London HS; London, OH; 25/144 Am Leg Boys St; Band; Boy Scts; Hon Rl; Jr NHS; NHS; Sch Pl; Stg Crw; Stu Cncl; Rptr Yrbk; Ohio St Univ; Comp Sci.

WAGGONER, JULIE; Northrop HS; Ft Wayne, IN; 12/589 Chrs; Debate Tm; Girl Scts; Hon Rl; Treas Natl Forn Lg; Sch Mus; VP 4-H; C of C Awd; Fort Wayne Bible Coll; Elem Educ.

WAGGONER, TAMARA; Elmhurst HS; Ft Wayne, IN; 5/400 Chrh Wkr; Drl Tm; Hon Rl; Orch; Yth Flsp; Yrbk; Sch Nwsp; 4-H; Letter Gym; Univ; Elem Educ.

WAGGONER, TERESA; Lawrence Central HS; Lawrence, IN; Girl Scts; Stg Crw; Mgrs; Scr Kpr; Indiana St Univ; Spec Ed.

WAGGONER, WANDA; Henryville HS; Otisco, IN; 5/70 Band; Hon Rl; Lbry Ade; NHS; Off Ade; Yrbk; Rptr Sch Nwsp;.

WAGGY, LINDA; Lincoln HS; Lumberport, WV; Chrs; Cmnty Wkr; Drl Tm; Off Ade; Sch Pl; Stg Crw; VICA; Ftbl; Sec.

WAGNER, AMY; Seton HS; Cincinnati, OH; Hon Rl; Sch Mus; Sch Pl; Rptr Sch Nwsp; Fr Clb; Pep Clb; Letter Swmmng; Coach Actv; GAA; IM Sprt; Swimming Awd 78; St & V Natl Qualifier Swimming 79; Natl Qualifier For Regency Dance Comp 79; Univ; Hotel Mgmt.

WAGNER, BARBARA; Benjamin Bosse HS; Evansville, IN; Band; Hon Rl; Pres NHS; Stu Cncl; Lat Clb; Letter Gym; Univ.

WAGNER, BECKY; William Henry Harrison HS; Battle Ground, IN; Band; Chrh Wkr; Hon Rl; NHS; Stg Crw; Sec Yth Flsp; Pep Clb; Spn Clb; Letter Gym; Letter Chrldng; Purdue Univ; Mgmt.

WAGNER, BILL; Dublin HS; Dublin, OH; Aud/Vis; Hon Rl; Stg Crw; Yrbk; Sch Nwsp; 4-H; Letter Ftbl; Ten; Letter Trk; Rotary Awd; Ohio St Univ; Pre Law.

WAGNER, BLAISE; Jasper HS; Jasper, IN; Chrs; Hon Rl; Sch Mus; Sch Pl; Stg Crw; Drama Clb; 4-H; Wrstlng; Hoosier Boys St Altrnt 79; Spch Team Regnl In 79; St Solo & Ensmbl Contst Perfct Score 79; Indiana Univ.

WAGNER, CARL; Princeton Community HS; Princeton, IN; 10/203 Boy Scts; Chrh Wkr; NHS; Pep Clb; Crs Cntry; Trk; Wrstlng; DAR Awd; College; Elec Engr.

WAGNER, CAROL; Fremont HS; Fremont, IN; 2/50 Trs Frsh Cls; Sec Soph Cls; Sec Sr Cls; Chrs; Girl Scts; Hon Rl; NHS; Sch Mus; Drama Clb; Treas Fr Clb; Ban St Univ; Elem Ed.

WAGNER, CHERYL; Tri Valley HS; Adamsville, OH; Hon Rl; Off Ade; Stu Cncl; Treas 4-H; Lat Clb; Bsktbl; Letter Trk; GAA; Coll; Health.

WAGNER, DAVID; Frontier HS; Brookston, IN; VP Soph Cls; Cmnty Wkr; Hon Rl; Yth Flsp; 4-H; FFA; Bsktbl; Ftbl; 4-H Awd; Vocational Schl.

WAGNER, GEORGE; Tiffin Calvert HS; Tiffin, OH; Band; Chrh Wkr; Cmnty Wkr; Hon Rl; VP JA; Lbry Ade; NHS; Sch Mus; Cit Awd; JA Awd; Univ.

WAGNER, GLENN; Elkhart Mem HS; Elkhart, IN; Chrs; Hon Rl; NHS; IM Sprt; Bus Schl; Acctg.

WAGNER, GREG; Madonna HS; Weirton, WV; 15/100 Boy Scts; Hon Rl; NHS; Sci Clb; IM Sprt; West Virginia Univ; Elec Engr.

WAGNER, J; Triway HS; Wooster, OH; 45/168 Chrs; Chrh Wkr; Girl Scts; Hon Rl; Jr NHS; Sch Mus; VP Yth Flsp; Letter Trk; Ohio State Univ; Speech Therp.

WAGNER, JANICE; Elkhart Central HS; Elkhart, IN; 58/401 Chrs; Hon Rl; NHS; Sch Mus; Drama Clb; College; Music.

WAGNER, JANIS; Whitmore Lake HS; Ann Arbor, MI; 6/90 Cls Rep Soph Cls; VP Jr Cls; Band; Chrh Wkr; Hon Rl; Sec Jr NHS; NHS; Sch Mus; Sch Pl; Pres Stu Cncl; Central Michigan Univ; Elem Ed.

WAGNER, JOSEPH; Fairmont West HS; Kettering, OH; Boy Scts; Hon Rl; Stg Crw; Wright State; Med.

WAGNER, JOY; Graham HS; St Paris, OH; 17/174 Band; NHS; Off Ade; Sec Stu Cncl; Yrbk; Rptr Sch Nwsp; 4-H; Ger Clb; VP GAA; DAR Awd; Ohio St Univ; Home Ec.

WAGNER, JOY; Graham HS; Urbana, OH; 17/165 Band; Hon Rl; NHS; Off Ade; Sec Stu Cncl; Yrbk; Rptr Sch Nwsp; 4-H; VP GAA; DAR Awd; Ohio State Univ; Home Econ.

WAGNER, JULIE; Northmont HS; Englewood, OH; Band; Hon Rl; Orch; Busns Schl; Exec Sec.

WAGNER, KAREN; Danville Community HS; Danville, IN; Cl Rep Jr Cls; Cls Rep Sr Cls; Sch Mus; Sch Pl; Stg Crw; Stu Cncl; Drama Clb; 4-H; Pep Clb; Chrldng; College; Bus.

WAGNER, KAREN; Struthers HS; Struthers, OH; Chrh Wkr; Hon Rl; OEA; Pep Clb; Spn Clb; Youngstown St Univ.

WAGNER, KAREN; St Philip Catholic Ctrl HS; Battle Creek, MI; 7/68 VP NHS; Pep Clb; Spn Clb; Bsktbl; Chrldng; PPFtbl; Natl Merit Ltr; Aquinas Coll; Comm Art.

WAGNER, KATRINA; Garrett HS; Garrett, IN; Chrs; Chrh Wkr; Hon Rl; Sch Pl; 4-H; Ger Clb; 4-H Awd; IU; Interior Dsgn.

WAGNER, KAY; Senior HS; St Joseph, MI; Chrs; Treas 4-H; 4-H Awd; Southwestern Mic College; Art.

WAGNER, KIMBERLY; James Ford Rhodes HS; Cleveland, OH; Hon Rl; NHS; Cit Awd; Kiwan Awd; Business School.

WAGNER, KIMBERLY A; La Salle HS; South Bend, IN; 29/416 Cls Rep Frsh Cls; Cls Rep Soph Cls; Cl Rep Jr Cls; Band; Chrs; Hon Rl; Mdrgl; NHS; Orch; Treas Drama Clb; De Pauw Univ; Nursing.

WAGNER, LAURA; Northwest HS; Canal Fulton, OH; 4/180 Sec Frsh Cls; Sec Soph Cls; Sec Jr Cls; Sec Sr Cls; Am Leg Aux Girls St; Hon Rl; NHS; VP Fr Clb; Pres Lat Clb; Mat Maids; Univ.

WAGNER, LAURIE; Shepherd HS; Shepherd, MI; 3/116 Band; Girl Scts; Hon Rl; Jr NHS; NHS; Yrbk; Trk; Pom Pon; Natl Merit SF; Alma Coll; Bio Chem.

WAGNER, LINDA; Our Lady Of Mercy HS; Birmingham, MI; 34/325 Mod UN; Off Ade; Sch Pl; Stu Cncl; Ger Clb; Mth Clb; Coach Actv; Western Mic Univ; Dental Hygiene.

WAGNER, LINDA; Howell HS; Howell, MI; 13/395 Band; Sec Chrs; Hon Rl; Mdrgl; NHS; Sch Mus; Treas Yth Flsp; Central Mic Univ; Fashion Mdse.

WAGNER, LOIS; Edsel Ford HS; Dearborn, MI; 10/468 Hon Rl; Hosp Ade; NHS; Ger Clb; Dearborn Bd Of Trustees Schslp 79; Henry Ford Cmnty Coll; Bus.

WAGNER, LORAINE; Edon HS; Montpelier, OH; Trs Soph Cls; Am Leg Aux Girls St; Band; Chrs; Off Ade; Sch Mus; Chmn Chrldng; IM Sprt; Scr Kpr;.

WAGNER, LORRY; Niles Sr HS; Niles, MI; Girl Scts; Hon Rl; NHS; 4-H; Ger Clb; Natl Merit Ltr; Varsity Vlbyl Ltr Earned 78; J U Bsktbl Captain Yr Of 78 77; Ushers Club 77; Michigan St Univ; Vet Med.

WAGNER, M; George Rogers Clark HS; Whiting, IN; Cmp Fr Grls; Cmnty Wkr; Girl Scts; Off Ade; Sct Actv; Stu Cncl; Key Clb; Ball State; Landscape Architecture.

WAGNER, MARY; Rock Hill Sr HS; Ironton, OH; 29/162 Band; Cmnty Wkr; Drl Tm; Hon Rl; Sct Actv; Rptr Yrbk; Rptr Sch Nwsp; Civ Clb; Sci Clb; Ohio Univ; Early Child Dev.

WAGNER, MICHELLE; Archbishop Alter HS; Kettering, OH; Spn Clb; Ten; Chrldng; Univ Of Dayton; Busns.

WAGNER, PAM; Continental Local HS; Cloverdale, OH; Chrh Wkr; Hon Rl; Jr NHS; NHS; Rptr Yrbk; FHA;.

WAGNER, PATRICIA S; Springfield Local HS; Maumee, OH; Chrs; Hosp Ade; JA; NHS; Off Ade; Red Cr Ade; Yrbk; FNA; Pep Clb; Spn Clb; Univ Of Toledo; Med.

WAGNER, RAYMOND; Mohawk HS; Mccutchenville, OH; Band; Boy Scts; Chrh Wkr; Yth Flsp; 4-H; FTA; Pep Clb; Ftbl; IM Sprt; College; Comm Pilot.

WAGNER, STEPHANIE; Greenville HS; Greenville, OH; 12/380 Cmnty Wkr; Hon Rl; PAVAS; Sch Mus; Sch Pl; Stg Crw; Rptr Sch Nwsp; Sec Drama Clb; Mia Univ; Psych.

WAGNER, STEVEN M; Bishop Ready HS; Columbus, OH; Band; Boy Scts; Chrs; Sch Mus; Sch Pl; Trk; Columbus Tech Inst.

WAGNER, SUSAN; Princeton Cmnty HS; Princeton, IN; 1/222 VP Jr Cls; Am Leg Aux Girls St; NHS; Off Ade; DECA; Pres Pep Clb; Trk; Indiana Univ; Bus.

WAGNER, TRACEY; Vassar HS; Vassar, MI; 6/200 Band; Drm Bgl; Hon Rl; Stg Crw; Spn Clb; Trk; Chrldng; PPFtbl; Central Michigan Univ; Psych.

WAGONBLAST, JEAN; Crown Point HS; Crown Point, IN; 1/500 Val; Chrh Wkr; Hon Rl; VP NHS; Fr Clb; Capt Bsktbl; Trk; IM Sprt; PPFtbl; Kiwan Awd; Valparaiso Univ; Elementary Educ.

WAGONER, CRAIG; Keyser HS; Keyser, WV; 40/248 Band; Chrh Wkr; Hon Rl; Sch Mus; Stu Cncl; Yth Flsp; 4-H; Pep Clb; VICA; Crs Cntry; Potomac St Coll; Engr.

WAGONER, DEBRA; Eastern HS; Pekin, IN; Treas FHA; Pep Clb; Spn Clb; Bsktbl; Trk; Scr Kpr; Flag Corps Letter Success Card Asst Capt; Miss Washington Cnty Queen Candidate; 4th Of July Qn Candidate; Coll; Fash Design.

WAGONER, JAMES; Columbia City Joint HS; Columbia City, IN; Am Leg Boys St; Chrh Wkr; Hon Rl; Spn Clb; Ten; IM Sprt; Rotary Awd;.

WAGONER, JONI; Evergreen HS; Swanton, OH; Cls Rep Soph Cls; Cl Rep Jr Cls; Band; Hon Rl; Stu Cncl; FTA; GAA; Pom Pon; College.

WAGONER, KENT; Frankfort HS; Ft Ashby, WV; AFS; Band; Hon Rl; NHS; Stu Cncl; Yth Flsp; FTA; Mth Clb; Sci Clb; VFW Awd; Potomac State; Hrtcltr.

WAGONER, LAURA; Bedford Sr HS; Temperance, MI; Hon Rl; NHS; Univ; Soc Sci.

WAGONER, REGINA; Calhoun Cnty HS; Big Bend, WV; Cls Rep Frsh Cls; Cls Rep Soph Cls; Chrs; Chrh Wkr; Hon Rl; NHS; Stu Cncl; Yrbk; 4-H; Mth Clb; Glenville St Coll; Education.

WAHL, CHRISTINE; Centreville HS; Centreville, MI; Hon Rl; Pep Clb; Ctrl Michigan Univ; Bus Mgmt.

WAHL, GERARD; Moeller HS; Cincinnati, OH; Boy Scts; Chrh Wkr; Cmnty Wkr; Hon Rl; JA; Spn Clb; IM Sprt; Parks College Of St Louis; Pilot.

WAHL, JON; Marysville HS; Marysville, MI; Band; Sct Actv; Yth Flsp; 4-H; Sci Clb; Glf; IM Sprt; Univ; Aero Engr.

WAHL, LORETTA J; Melvindale HS; Allen Park, MI; 1/274 Cls Rep Sr Cls; Val; NHS; Sci Clb; Letter Bsktbl; Am Leg Awd; JC Awd; Mich Tech Univ; Med Tech.

WAHL, MARY; Grass Lake HS; Grass Lk, MI; 1/81 Pres Frsh Cls; VP Jr Cls; VP Sr Cls; Val; Hon Rl; Sec NHS; Stu Cncl; Ed Yrbk; Pres 4-H; Chrldng; Michigan St Univ.

WAHL, MARY; Canfield HS; Youngstown, OH; Hon Rl; Fr Clb; Spn Clb; Lcrss; College; Languages.

WAHL, MICHAEL; Mc Nicholas HS; Cincinnati, OH; 51/218 Band; Hon Rl; Pres JA; NHS; Sch Mus; Swmmng; JA Awd; Part In Youth Incity Govt 79; Univ; Engr.

WAHLERS, GAIL; Port Clinton HS; Port Clinton, OH; Sec Frsh Cls; Trs Jr Cls; Band; Hon Rl; 4-H; Fr Clb; Swmmng; Terra Tech Coll; Acctg.

WAHR, LINDA; Bay City John Glenn HS; Bay City, MI; 40/327 Band; Chrh Wkr; Cmnty Wkr; Hon Rl; NHS; Off Ade; Red Cr Ade; Fr Clb; Letter Ten; Opt Clb Awd; March Of Dimes Schlrshp 79; Mi Comp Schlrshp Finalist 79; Whos Who In Foreign Lang 79; Univ Of Michigan; Bio Chem.

WAIBEL, HELEN; Wehrle HS; Columbus, OH; 7/109 Trs Frsh Cls; Trs Jr Cls; Hon Rl; Hosp Ade; Sch Pl; Stu Cncl; Sch Nwsp; Ten; JA Awd; VFW Awd; Ohio St Univ.

WAIDELICH, WILLIAM; Logan Elm HS; Circleville, OH; 7/185 Am Leg Boys St; Band; Cmnty Wkr; Debate Tm; Hon Rl; NHS; Pres Yth Flsp; Ed Yrbk; Rptr Yrbk; Yrbk; St & Natl FFA Band; Natl 4 H Congress Delegate; All Ohio St Fair Band; Ohio St Univ; Agric.

WAINFOR, STEPHEN; Heath HS; Heath, OH; Hon Rl; Key Clb; Spn Clb; Ohio St Univ; Vet Med.

WAINIO, JOYCE; Ursuline HS; Youngstown, OH; 16/323 Cls Rep Soph Cls; Hon Rl; Rptr Yrbk; Lat Clb; Mth Clb; Gym; College; Phys Ther.

WAIR, LISA; Eaton HS; Eaton, OH; 13/175 Sec Frsh Cls; VP Jr Cls; Hon Rl; Drama Clb; 4-H; OEA; Pep Clb; Spn Clb; Gym; Chrldng; Miami Univ; Bus.

WAITE, DONNA; Rockville Sr HS; Rockville, IN; 20/95 VP Frsh Cls; FCA; Hon Rl; Rptr Sch Nwsp; Sch Nwsp; 4-H; FHA; Pep Clb; Ten; Mat Maids; Univ.

WAITE, LISA; Brookhaven HS; Columbus, OH; Hon Rl; Jr NHS; NHS; Off Ade; VP Yth Flsp; Letter Ten; Letter Trk; IM Sprt; Univ; Med.

WAITS, LISA; Valley View HS; Germantown, OH; Am Leg Aux Girls St; Chrs; Chrh Wkr; Hon Rl; NHS; Off Ade; Sch Pl; Yth Flsp; Fr Clb; FTA; Miami Univ; Sociology.

WAITT, TAMELA; New Palestine HS; Greenfld, IN; Band; 4-H; Spn Clb; 4-H Awd; College; Math.

WAKEFIELD, CRAIG; Madiera HS; Madeira, OH; 28/110 Band; Hon Rl; Orch; Sch Mus; Lat Clb; IM Sprt; Univ; Bus.

WAKEFIELD, WENDI; Rosedale HS; Rosedale, IN; 8/55 Band; Chrh Wkr; Hon Rl; Off Ade; Pol Wkr; Pres 4-H; Pep Clb; Trk; Pom Pon; Voice Dem Awd; Parkview Methdst Schl Of Nrsng; RN.

WALAWENDER, CHESTER; C S Mott HS; Warren, MI; VP Jr Cls; Band; Boy Scts; Hon Rl; Pol Wkr; Sct Actv; Stu Cncl; Pep Clb; Socr; Ten; Mi Schls Tbl Tennis Tm Chmp Trophy 77; Awds Inn Polish Lang & Culture 77; Recogntn For Catechtl Instruct 78; St Marys Coll; Humanities.

WALBLAY, MICHELLE; Fordson HS; Dearborn, MI; Band; Hon Rl; NHS; Orch; Letter Bsbl; Letter Bsktbl; GAA; St Of Michigan Schlrshp 79 80; Bus Awd 79; Gold F Pin 76 79; Univ Of Michigan; Bus Admin.

WALBURN, SHERRY; Fort Frye HS; Beverly, OH; 16/123 Am Leg Aux Girls St; Band; Chrh Wkr; Girl Scts; Hon Rl; Off Ade; Sch Mus; 4-H; Pep Clb; 4-H Awd; Sec Work.

WALCH, TIM; Escanaba Area Public HS; Gladstone, MI; Aud/Vis; Chrs; Cmnty Wkr; Hon Rl; Pol Wkr; Sch Mus; Spn Clb; Ftbl; Trk; Loyola Univ; Busns.

WALCOTT, KIMBERLY; Huron HS; Sandusky, OH; Chrs; Chrh Wkr; Girl Scts; Hon Rl; JA; Stu Cncl; Mgrs; Mat Maids; JA Awd; College.

WALCOTT, LONNIE; Switzerland County HS; Patriot, IN; Cls Rep Frsh Cls; Aud/Vis; Hon Rl; Pep Clb; Letter Bsbl; Bsktbl; Letter Glf; Am Leg Awd; Pres Awd; College.

WALCUTT, RICHARD; Hilliard HS; Columbus, OH; 27/353 Cls Rep Frsh Cls; Cl Rep Jr Cls; Hon Rl; Jr NHS; NHS; FDA; Soroptimist; Ohi State Univ; Med.

WALD, KIMBERLY; Fairless HS; Navarre, OH; Cl Rep Jr Cls; Band; Chrh Wkr; Hon Rl; Off Ade; Treas Stu Cncl; Y-Teens; FNA; Outstdng Fresman Bandsman 76; Pres Failess HS Band 79; Nursing Schl; Nurse.

WALD, SUE; Father Joseph Wehrle HS; Columbus, OH; Hon Rl; Sch Mus; Vocational Schl; Animal Tech.

WALDBILLIG, U JOSEPH; St Xavier HS; Cincinnati, OH; Debate Tm; Pol Wkr; Letter Trk; IM Sprt; Mgrs; Natl Merit Ltr; Cert Of Educ Devlpmt Natl In Recogntn Of High NEDT Score 76; Xavier Univ.

WALDECK, NANCY; Regina HS; Cleveland Hts, OH; Cl Rep Jr Cls; Hon Rl; Stu Cncl; GAA; College; Sci.

WALDEN, DAVID; Edinburgh Community HS; Edinburgh, IN; 14/62 Band; FCA; NHS; Stu Cncl; Fr Clb; Capt Bsktbl; Ftbl; Ball State Univ; Bus.

WALDEN, DONNA; Clarkston Sr HS; Clarkston, MI; Band; Hon Rl; PPFtbl; Natl Merit Schl; Univ; Sociology.

WALDEN, RANDY; Westfield Washington HS; Westfield, IN; Jr NHS; NHS; 4-H; FFA; Spn Clb; Ftbl; Trk; Wrstlng; Cit Awd; 4-H Awd; Outstndg Jr Leader 78; Cnty Awrds 4 H Leadershp Citzenshp Recreation 78; Cnty Pres VP 78; De Pauw Univ; Psych.

WALDEN, ROBERT; Staunton HS; Brazil, IN; 5/50 Chrh Wkr; Cmnty Wkr; NHS; Off Ade; Sec Key Clb; Letter Bsbl; Letter Bsktbl; Letter Crs Cntry; Coach Actv; Purdue Univ; Mech Engr.

WALDEN, SADIE; Union HS; Bayard, WV; Treas Chrs; Pres Fr Clb; FHA; Teachers Aide Phys Ed 1979; Potomac St Univ; Lab Tech.

WALDER, BARBARA; Portages Lake Jus HS; Clinton, OH; Girl Scts; Off Ade; Stu Cncl; Yrbk; OEA; Crs Cntry; Gym;.

WALDO, REBECCA; Marlette HS; Marlette, MI; 11/130 Cls Rep Soph Cls; Sec Band; Hon Rl; NHS; Stu Cncl; Yth Flsp; Treas Spn Clb; Bsktbl; Letter Crs Cntry; Letter Trk; Univ Of Michigan; Bio Med Engr.

WALDOCK, ROBERT; Sandusky HS; Sandusky, OH; Am Leg Boys St; Chrs; Stg Crw; VP Stu Cncl; Yrbk; Ten; YMCA Youth In Govt 79; Ohio St Univ; Law.

WALDON, ALICE; Terre Haute North Vigo HS; Terre Haute, IN; VP Frsh Cls; Cl Rep Jr Cls; Hon Rl; Stu Cncl; Sch Nwsp; Cit Awd; College.

WALDON, JEFFERY; Avon Jr Sr HS; Indianapolis, IN; 35/180 Band; Boy Scts; FCA; Hon Rl; Orch; Sct Actv; Sci Clb; Spn Clb; Capt Crs Cntry; Letter Trk; Indiana Univ; Chem.

WALDRIDGE, RISA; Shenandoah HS; Middletown, IN; Band; Chrs; Chrh Wkr; Hon Rl; NHS; Off Ade; FHA; OEA; Ball St Univ; Legal Ast.

WALDRIP, BETH; Eastern HS; Solsberry, IN; 9/87 Band; Capt Drl Tm; NHS; Quill & Scroll; Sch Pl; Rptr Yrbk; Rptr Sch Nwsp; 4-H; Pom Pon; 4-H Awd; Indiana Univ; Recreation.

WALDRON, DANA; Vinton Cnty HS; Mc Arthur, OH; Sec Frsh Cls; Chrh Wkr; Cmnty Wkr; FCA; Girl Scts; Hon Rl; Lbry Ade; NHS; Sch Pl; Sct Actv; College; Fashion Merch.

WALDRON, JANE; Greenville Sr HS; Greenville, MI; 1/240 Trs Sr Cls; Band; Girl Scts; Hon Rl; Stg Crw; 4-H; Key Clb; Pep Clb; 4-H Awd; Natl Merit Ltr; Mich Tech Univ Bd Of Cntrl Schlrshp 79; Gold Cord 79; Honors Spkr 79; Michigan Tech Univ; Envrmntl Engr.

WALDRON, MARGARET; Vinton County Cnsldtd HS; Hamden, OH; Cl Rep Jr Cls; Band; Chrs; Chrh Wkr; Cmnty Wkr; Girl Scts; Hon Rl; Hosp Ade; Lbry Ade; Hocking Tech; Nurs.

WALDRON, NANCY; Central Montcalm HS; Crystal, MI; 8/127 Band; Sch Mus; Yth Flsp; Drama Clb; 4-H; FHA; Chrldng; Calvin College; Ed.

WALDRON, SUZANNE L; Turpin HS; Cincinnati, OH; 33/357 Cmp Fr Grls; Sec Chrs; Ed Yrbk; Rptr Yrbk; Spn Clb; Scr Kpr; Tmr; St Lawrence Univ; Environ Bio.

WALDROUP, LORI; Johannesburg Lewiston HS; Lewiston, MI; 3/57 Hon Rl; NHS; Quill & Scroll; Rptr Sch Nwsp; Sch Nwsp; Letter Trk; Brd Of Control Distgshd Stu Schlrshp From Lk Superior St Coll 79; Mst Outstndg Sec Stu Of The Yr Awd 79; Lake Superior St Coll; Bus Educ.

WALDRUP, PATRICIA; Clio HS; Clio, MI; 92/384 Band; Chrh Wkr; Cmnty Wkr; Girl Scts; Hon Rl; Orch; Pol Wkr; Sct Actv; Yth Flsp; IM Sprt; Michigan St Univ; Psych.

WALDUKE, DAVID; Chelsea HS; Chelsea, MI; 6/220 Am Leg Boys St; Band; Boy Scts; Debate Tm; Hon Rl; NHS; Orch; Yth Flsp; Univ Of Mic; Comp Engr.

WALDYKE, MICHAEL J; Chelsea HS; Chelsea, MI; 1/225 Band; Debate Tm; Hon Rl; NHS; Orch; Yth Flsp; Natl Merit Ltr; College; Medicine.

WALEGA, KATHLEEN; John F Kennedy HS; Taylor, MI; Hon Rl; NHS; Ten; IM Sprt; PPFtbl; Natl Merit Ltr; Eastern Univ; Art.

WALEN, PETER; Catholic Central HS; Grand Rapids, MI; 20/230 Band; Drm Bgl; Hon Rl; NHS; Orch; Red Cr Ade; Rptr Sch Nwsp; Pres Lat Clb; Capt Lcrss; Aquinas Coll; Comp Sci.

WALESCH, KATHLEEN; Fairview HS; Fairview Pk, OH; AFS; Cmp Fr Grls; Chrs; Hon Rl; Sec JA; Lbry Ade; NHS; Sci Clb; Cit Awd; JA Awd; Cuyahoga Cmnty Coll; Early Child Ed.

WALEWSKI, JOHN; Bishop Foley HS; Madison Hts, MI; Hon Rl; Rptr Sch Nwsp; Boys Clb Am; Letter Bsktbl; Ftbl; Coach Actv; IM Sprt; JC Awd; E Michigan Univ; Conservation.

WALGAMUTH, TERRI; Tippecanoe Valley HS; Akron, IN; Cls Rep Sr Cls; Hon Rl; NHS; Stu Cncl; OEA; Bsktbl; Ten; Chrldng; Clarks Beauty Academy; Hair Stylist.

WALGREN, KRISTIN L; Theodore Roosevelt HS; Kent, OH; 50/400 Chrs; Cmnty Wkr; Hon Rl; Sch Mus; Sch Pl; Stg Crw; Drama Clb; Fr Clb; Swmmng; Tmr; Mem Of Inter Thespians; Stu Director Musical; College; Law.

WALIKA, PATRICIA M; Bishop Foley HS; Detroit, MI; 11/193 Hon Rl; Wayne St Univ; Phys Therapy.

WALKER, AMY; Dekalb HS; Waterloo, IN; 16/288 Pres Frsh Cls; Cls Rep Soph Cls; Cl Rep Jr Cls; Cls Rep Sr Cls; Chrs; Girl Scts; Jr NHS; NHS; Stu Cncl; Ed Yrbk; Univ Of Notre Dame; Archt Design.

WALKER, ANDREA; Horace Mann HS; Gary, IN; Hon Rl; JA; Jr NHS; NHS; Fr Clb; FHA; Mth Clb; Cit Awd; Indiana Univ; Sec Admin.

WALKER, ANGELO A; Brookhaven HS; Columbus, OH; Am Leg Boys St; Boy Scts; Hon Rl; Rus Clb; Ftbl; Central St Univ; Acctg.

WALKER, AUDREY; Immaculata HS; Detroit, MI; Chrh Wkr; Drl Tm; Lbry Ade; PAVAS; Chrldng; Cit Awd; Cert Awds In Typing; Awd For Participation In Art Soc; Various Awds For Music Piano; Detroit Coll Of Busns; Exec Sec.

WALKER, BARBARA; Winfield HS; Fraziers Bottom, WV; Band; Chrh Wkr; Girl Scts; Hon Rl; Jr NHS; Yth Flsp; Mth Clb; Bsktbl; Univ; Bus.

WALKER, CAROL L; Wylie E Groves HS; Birmingham, MI; Cls Rep Soph Cls; Cls Rep Sr Cls; Lit Mag; PAVAS; Quill & Scroll; Sch Mus; Sch Pl; Stg Crw; VP Stu Cncl; Ed Yrbk; Schlstc Awd For Poetry; Honorable Men St Owens Festival Of The Arts For Pen & Ink Drawing; Univ Of Michigan; Studio Art.

WALKER, CAROLYN; Milford HS; Milford, MI; Hon Rl; Lbry Ade; NHS; 4-H; 4-H Awd; Michigan St Univ; Wildlife Mgmt.

WALKER, CATHERINE; Northrop HS; Fort Wayne, IN; 117/564 Chrh Wkr; Hon Rl; JA; Natl Forn Lg; Orch; Sch Mus; Sch Pl; JA Awd; Stagecraft Awd; Univ; Early Childhood Ed.

WALKER, CINDY; Harper Creek HS; Battle Creek, MI; 24/244 Hon Rl; NHS; 4-H; 4-H Awd; Kellogg Comm Coll; Mgmt.

WALKER, CINDY J; Spencer HS; Spencer, WV; Band; Girl Scts; Hon Rl; Rptr Sch Nwsp; Ten; Chrldng; Bus Schl.

WALKER, COLLEEN; Boardman HS; Boardman, OH; 55/600 Band; Cmp Fr Grls; Chrh Wkr; Girl Scts; Hon Rl; Sct Actv; Yth Flsp; Fr Clb; Spn Clb; Trk; Mst Impvd Band Membr 77; Youngstown St Univ; Creative Writng.

WALKER, DENNIS; Piqua Central HS; Piqua, OH; Chrh Wkr; Hon Rl; Jr NHS; NHS; Orch; Sch Mus; Stg Crw; 4-H; Trk; 4-H Awd; Ohio St Univ; Comp Sci.

WALKER, DWAYNE; Detroit Central HS; Detroit, MI; Hon Rl; Boys Clb Am; Cit Awd; JETS Awd; Boys Club Ctzn Of The Yr 79; Univ Of Detroit; Archt.

WALKER, EMILY; East HS; Akron, OH; Drl Tm; Orch; Letter Trk; Mas Awd; Univ Of Akron; Chem.

WALKER, GERRY; Meadowbrook HS; Senecaville, OH; Am Leg Boys St; Boy Scts; Sch Pl; Pep Clb; Sci Clb; Spn Clb; Ftbl; Capt Wrstlng; Voc Schl; Fireman.

WALKER, GREG; Meigs HS; Rutland, OH; Aud/Vis; Boy Scts; Cmnty Wkr; Hon Rl; Sct Actv; Stg Crw; 4-H; VICA; 4-H Awd; Hocking Tech Schl; Forestry Mgmt.

WALKER, J; Hartford HS; Hartford, MI; Band; Stg Crw; Wrstlng;.

WALKER, JACKIE; Northwestern Sr HS; Flint, MI; Hon Rl; Hosp Ade; Jr NHS; Lbry Ade; NHS; Red Cr Ade; Y-Teens; Rptr Sch Nwsp; Mat Maids; Michigan St Univ; Pre Med.

WALKER, JANEEN; Bishop Ready HS; Grove City, OH; 10/138 Cls Rep Soph Cls; Cl Rep Jr Cls; Cls Rep Sr Cls; Am Leg Aux Girls St; Cmp Fr Grls; Chrh Wkr; Cmnty Wkr; Hon Rl; JA; Jr NHS; Univ; Public Reltns.

WALKER, JANET; Indian Hill HS; Cincinnati, OH; Band; Capt Drm Mjrt; Girl Scts; Pres Hosp Ade; Quill & Scroll; Rptr Yrbk; Fr Clb; Pep Clb; Capt Chrldng; IM Sprt; Coll; French.

WALKER, JANICE; Lake Shore HS; St Clair Shrs, MI; 14/605 Band; Chrh Wkr; NHS; Orch; Sch Mus; Yrbk; Mich State Univ.

WALKER, JEANNE; Catholic Central HS; Grand Rapids, MI; Girl Scts; JA; Drama Clb; Lat Clb; Ten; Trk; JA Awd;.

WALKER, JED; Detroit Central HS; Detroit, MI; Band; Cmnty Wkr; Hon Rl; Off Ade; Sch Mus; Mth Clb; Am Leg Awd; Cit Awd; Opt Clb Awd; Marine Corp; Technology.

WALKER, JERRY; Maplewood HS; Cortland, OH; Hon Rl; NHS; Ger Clb; Letter Bsbl; Letter Bsktbl; Letter Crs Cntry; Letter Glf; Letter Trk;.

WALKER, JUDITH; Fowlerville HS; Fowlerville, MI; Chrs; Chrh Wkr; Girl Scts; Hon Rl; Rptr Sch Nwsp; Letter Bsbl; Letter Bsktbl; Trk; Chrldng; Univ; Jrnlsm.

WALKER, JULIE A; Solon HS; Solon, OH; 16/375 Cl Rep Jr Cls; Chrh Wkr; FCA; Hon Rl; Jr NHS; NHS; Stu Cncl; Pep Clb; Spn Clb; Gym; College.

WALKER, KATHRYN; Lynchburg Clay HS; Lynchburg, OH; Band; Chrs; Chrh Wkr; Sch Mus; Yth Flsp; 4-H; VP FHA; Pep Clb; 4-H Awd; Univ; Photog.

WALKER, KATHY; Goodrich HS; Grand Blanc, MI; 8/128 Band; Hon Rl; Hosp Ade; NHS; Sec Fr Clb; Natl Merit SF; Michigan St Univ; Nursing.

WALKER, KAYLEN; Charlestown HS; Charlestown, IN; 11/155 Hon Rl; JA; NHS; Sch Nwsp; Lat Clb; Indiana Univ; Bus Admin.

WALKER, KELLEE; Mt Clemens HS; Mt Clemens, MI; Band; Chrh Wkr; Girl Scts; Hon Rl; Sct Actv; Stu Cncl; Fr Clb; Lat Clb; Chrldng; PPFtbl; St Joseph Hospital; X Ray Tech.

WALKER, KEVIN; Blanchester HS; Blanchester, OH; 10/145 Band; Hon Rl; NHS; Sch Mus; Fr Clb; Shcslhp Team Algr I 77; Scshlhps Team Algbr II 79; Oh Test Of Schlstc Achvmnt 5th Pl In Algbr 77; Univ.

WALKER, LAURIE; Westland HS; Columbus, OH; Chrh Wkr; Cmnty Wkr; Hosp Ade; Yth Flsp; Univ; Admin Asst.

WALKER, LILLIAN M; Hughes HS; Cincinnati, OH; Cl Rep Jr Cls; Hon Rl; Jr NHS; Stu Cncl; Cit Awd; JA Awd; Natl Merit Schl; Ohio Univ; Law.

WALKER, LINDA; Lawrence Central HS; Indianapolis, IN; 15/367 Trs Frsh Cls; Cls Rep Sr Cls; NHS; Stu Cncl; Rptr Sch Nwsp; Chrldng; Capt Mat Maids; College; Pre Law.

WALKER, MARK; Bellbrook HS; Bellbrook, OH; 18/159 Pres Frsh Cls; Cls Rep Soph Cls; VP Jr Cls; Chrh Wkr; FCA; Hon Rl; Jr NHS; Pres NHS; Stu Cncl; Yth Flsp; Miami Univ; Med.

WALKER, MARY; Holland HS; Holland, MI; Chrs; Chrh Wkr; Hosp Ade; Pep Clb; Letter Bsbl; Letter Trk; Letter Mgrs; Scr Kpr; Davenport Bus Schl; Fshn Mdse.

WALKER, MARY; St Francis Desales HS; Columbus, OH; 10/200 Cls Rep Soph Cls; Hon Rl; Treas Jr NHS; Stu Cncl; Yth Flsp; Ed Sch Nwsp; Rptr Sch Nwsp; Pres Spn Clb; College; Psych.

WALKER, MARY A; Bluefield HS; Bluefield, WV; Chrh Wkr; Hon Rl; Yth Flsp; Sch Nwsp; Fr Clb; FHA; Pep Clb; Univ; Law.

WALKER, PAMELA; Hudson HS; Hudson, OH; AFS; Chrs; Cmnty Wkr; Hon Rl; NHS; PAVAS; Sch Mus; Sch Pl; New Mexico Univ; Bilingual Sec.

WALKER, PHYLLIS; City Wide Alternative School; Cincinnati, OH; Chrs; Chrh Wkr; Girl Scts; Hon Rl; Lit Mag; Red Cr Ade; Sct Actv; Rptr Sch Nwsp; Cit Awd; SAR Awd; 3 Yr Awd Upper 3% Of Cls 77; Univ; Med.

WALKER, RANDY; Mt Clemens HS; Mt Clemens, MI; Boy Scts; Hon Rl; Jr NHS; NHS; Spn Clb; Trk; IM Sprt; Mgrs; Scr Kpr; DAR Awd; Michigan St Univ; Math.

WALKER, RANDY; Berrien Springs HS; Niles, MI; 21/111 Hon Rl; JA; NHS; Lake Mic College; Cpa.

WALKER, RAYMOND; Licking Valley HS; Newark, OH; 1/154 Pres Frsh Cls; Pres Soph Cls; Pres Jr Cls; Am Leg Boys St; Hon Rl; 4-H; Bsktbl; Ftbl; Trk;.

WALKER, ROBERTA; Horace Mann HS; Gary, IN; Cls Rep Frsh Cls; Cl Rep Jr Cls; Band; Chrs; Chrh Wkr; Hon Rl; Jr NHS; NHS; Stu Cncl; Mth Clb; Band Clb Pres 79; Annual Music Fest Awds 73 79; Jazz Band Organzr 78; Univ; Music.

WALKER, ROBERTA; Bryan HS; Bryan, OH; 16/192 Am Leg Aux Girls St; Hon Rl; Jr NHS; Sec NHS; Sprt Ed Sch Nwsp; Treas Spn Clb; Bsktbl; Treas GAA; Scr Kpr; Univ Of Toledo; Retal Marketing.

WALKER, ROBIN; Plainwell HS; Plainwell, MI; Band; Hon Rl; Lbry Ade; NHS; Fr Clb; Ten; Mi St Bd Of Educ Cert Of Recogntn 79; Michigan St Univ; Bus Admin.

WALKER, ROMAIN; Mc Nicholas HS; Cincinnati, OH; 83/218 Mgrs; Univ Of Cinc.

WALKER, RUTH; Bridgman HS; Bridgman, MI; Trs Frsh Cls; Cl Rep Jr Cls; Hon Rl; NHS; Stu Cncl; IM Sprt; Mgrs; Am Leg Awd; College.

WALKER, S; Solon HS; Solon, OH; Cls Rep Frsh Cls; Chrh Wkr; FCA; Hon Rl; NHS; Pep Clb; Letter Bsktbl; Mgrs; PPFtbl; College; Sports Med.

WALKER, SCOTT; Terre Haute South HS; Terre Haute, IN; Boy Scts; Chrh Wkr; Cmnty Wkr; Hon Rl; Pol Wkr; Sct Actv; Yth Flsp; Boys Clb Am; Spn Clb; Glf; Univ; Engr.

WALKER, SHEILA; Marian Heights Academy; Washington, IN; 1/30 VP Frsh Cls; Am Leg Aux Girls St; Chrs; Hon Rl; NHS; Sch Mus; Sch Pl; Sdlty; Sec Stu Cncl; 4-H; College; Medicine.

WALKER, SHELLY; New Haven HS; New Baltimore, MI; 2/104 Pres Sr Cls; Sal; VP Band; Hon Rl; Pres NHS; Rptr Yrbk; Drama Clb; Sec OEA; Letter Trk; Eastern Mich Univ; Bus Admin.

WALKER, STEVEN; Purcell HS; Cincinnati, OH; 21/183 Aud/Vis; Boy Scts; Hon Rl; JA; Sct Actv; Glf; IM Sprt; Coll.

WALKER, SUSAN; Daleville HS; Daleville, IN; 3/70 Am Leg Aux Girls St; Chrs; Chrh Wkr; Girl Scts; Hon Rl; NHS; Off Ade; Yth Flsp; Fr Clb; Pep Clb; Ball St Univ; Math.

WALKER, TAMMY; Broad Ripple HS; Indianapolis, IN; 15/470 Hon Rl; NHS; Rptr Sch Nwsp; Mth Clb; Pep Clb; Spn Clb; Bsktbl; College; Engr.

WALKER, TERESA; Franklin Community HS; Franklin, IN; 30/265 Sec Frsh Cls; Cls Rep Soph Cls; Hon Rl; Hosp Ade; Lit Mag; NHS; Stu Cncl; Yth Flsp; Fr Clb; Lat Clb; Whos Who In Foreign Languages; Taylor Univ; Spec Ed.

WALKER, TERESA; Spanishburg HS; Spanishburg, WV; Band; Chrs; Cmnty Wkr; Hon Rl; Stg Crw; FBLA; FHA; Univ; History.

WALKER, TESS; Lancaster HS; Lancaster, OH; Cls Rep Soph Cls; Chrs; Hon Rl; Stu Cncl; Drama Clb; OEA; Chrldng; Bus Schl; Sec.

WALKER, TIMOTHY; Princeton HS; Princeton, WV; 84/350 Hon Rl; West Virginia Univ; Comp Tech.

WALKER, TINA; Westfield Washington HS; Sheridan, IN; Band; Chrh Wkr; Hon Rl; Jr NHS; Treas NHS; Orch; Sch Mus; Spn Clb; College; Draftsman.

WALKER, TONJA; Northrop HS; Ft Wayne, IN; Cls Rep Frsh Cls; Orch; Stu Cncl; OEA; Letter Gym; Chrldng; Cit Awd; Pres Awd; St Participate In Gymnastics; MVP In Gymnastics; Varsity Club; Indiana Univ; Busns.

WALKER, WAYNE; Collinwood HS; Cleveland, OH; Pres Band; Chrh Wkr; Hon Rl; Orch; Pres Yth Flsp; Drama Clb; Rdo Clb; Univ; Cmnctns.

WALKER, WILLIAM; Muskegon Hts HS; Muskegon Hts, MI; 23/160 Hon Rl; DECA; Trk; Muskegon Bus Coll; Comp Prog.

WALKLET, WENDY L; Bluefield HS; Bluefield, WV; 14/285 Chrs; Hon Rl; Jr NHS; VP NHS; Yth Flsp; Fr Clb; Pep Clb; GAA; Mgrs; Univ; Comp Sci.

WALL, ALICE; Mc Donald HS; Mc Donald, OH; Band; Drm Bgl; Hon Rl; Lbry Ade; Y-Teens; Pep Clb; Swmmng; GAA; Twrlr; College; Med.

WALL, CHRISTY; South Ripley Jr Sr HS; Madison, IN; 1/104 Pres Frsh Cls; Cls Rep Frsh Cls; Cls Rep Soph Cls; Cl Rep Jr Cls; Trs Sr Cls; Cls Rep Sr Cls; Am Leg Aux Girls St; Drm Mjrt; Girl Scts; Hon Rl; Hanover College; Music.

WALL, DANA; Onekama Consolidated HS; Manistee, MI; Band; Chrs; Hon Rl; Sch Mus; Sch Pl; Stg Crw; Yth Flsp; Drama Clb; Pep Clb; Central Mic Univ; Broadcasting.

WALL, DEE A; South Vermillion HS; Clinton, IN; 3/151 Trs Soph Cls; Am Leg Aux Girls St; Girl Scts; Hon Rl; VP JA; Sch Nwsp; Drama Clb; Pep Clb; Spn Clb; Chrldng; Who Who In Foreign Languages; Outstanding Spanish Stu; Outstndng Spanish Stu; Schlstc Ach Pins; Indiana St Univ; Nursing.

WALL, ELIZABETH; Union HS; Grand Rapids, MI; NHS; Mich State Univ; Vet.

WALL, HAROLD; Charleston HS; Charlestown, IN; 19/156 Pres Sr Cls; Band; Boy Scts; FCA; Hon Rl; JA; NHS; Pol Wkr; Sct Actv; Yth Flsp; Hooser Schlr 79; Otstndng Bandsman 77; Univ Of Oklahoma; Bus.

WALL, JESSICA; South Ripley Jr Sr HS; Madison, IN; 1/110 Pres Frsh Cls; Cls Rep Frsh Cls; Cls Rep Soph Cls; Cl Rep Jr Cls; Trs Sr Cls; Cls Rep Sr Cls; Am Leg Aux Girls St; Band; VP Chrs; Chrh Wkr; Ball St Univ; Music.

WALL, MICHAEL; North Union HS; Richwood, OH; Am Leg Boys St; Hon Rl; Jr NHS; NHS; Drama Clb; FFA; Spn Clb; Letter Bsbl; Letter Ftbl;.

WALL, PATRICIA; New Riegel HS; New Riegel, OH; 7/50 Band; Chrs; Hon Rl; VP JA; NHS; Pep Clb; Spn Clb; Am Leg Awd; Cit Awd; JA Awd;.

WALLACE, ADRIAN; Goodrich HS; Goodrich, MI; Hon Rl; JA; Ftbl; Letter Ten; St Lawrence Tech Univ; Construction.

WALLACE, AILEEN; Valley HS; Boomer, WV; 20/130 Cl Rep Jr Cls; VP Sr Cls; Band; Chrs; Chrh Wkr; Hon Rl; NHS; Stu Cncl; Yrbk; Sch Nwsp; Marshall Univ; Comp Sci.

WALLACE, BARRY; Western Brown Sr HS; Mt Orab, OH; Cls Rep Frsh Cls; Cls Rep Soph Cls; Chrh Wkr; Hon Rl; Yth Flsp; Spn Clb; Letter Bsktbl; Coach Actv; IM Sprt;.

WALLACE, BRYAN; New Albany HS; New Albany, IN; 22/570 Pres Frsh Cls; Cls Rep Soph Cls; Cl Rep Jr Cls; Band; Boy Scts; Hon Rl; Jr NHS; NHS; Sch Pl; Sct Actv; Indiana Univ; German.

WALLACE, CARLA J; Central Ohio Joint Voc HS; Columbus, OH; Cls Rep Frsh Cls; Sec Sr Cls; Cls Rep Sr Cls; Girl Scts; Stu Cncl; OEA; Chrldng; Tech; Nurse.

WALLACE, CHERYL; Cass Tech HS; Detroit, MI; Hon Rl; Trk; IM Sprt; Cit Awd; Michigan St Univ; Vet.

WALLACE, CYNTHIA M; Ben Davis HS; Indianapolis, IN; 128/926 Cls Rep Soph Cls; Cl Rep Jr Cls; Chrs; FCA; Girl Scts; Hon Rl; Orch; Stu Cncl; Spn Clb; Letter Gym; Candidate For Homecoming; Purdue Univ; Industrial Admin.

WALLACE, DANIEL; Northwest HS; Indianapolis, IN; 2/700 Aud/Vis; Chrs; Chrh Wkr; Hon Rl; JA; Lbry Ade; Mod UN; NHS; Orch; Pol Wkr; Cedarville Coll; Physics.

WALLACE, DAVID; Grosse Ile HS; Grosse Ile, MI; Band; Chrs; Hon Rl; Mdrgl; Sch Mus; Sch Pl; Stg Crw; Swmmng; Univ Of Mic; Pre Med.

WALLACE, DAVID M; Salem HS; Salem, IN; 16/165 Band; Boy Scts; Drl Tm; Jr NHS; Lbry Ade; NHS; Sch Mus; Sch Pl; Stg Crw; Yth Flsp; ISU; Comp Sci.

WALLACE, DAWN; Andrean HS; Merrillville, IN; 12/256 Girl Scts; Hon Rl; Pep Clb; Trk; Col Univ; Clinical Psychologist.

WALLACE, DEBORAH; Trenton HS; Trenton, MI; 31/537 Chrs; Chrh Wkr; Drl Tm; Hon Rl; Off Ade; Sch Mus; Pres Yth Flsp; Rptr Sch Nwsp; Fr Clb; Western Mic Univ; Occup Therapy.

WALLACE, JAN; Eastbrook HS; Upland, IN; 18/181 Chrh Wkr; Hon Rl; JA; Jr NHS; NHS; Red Cr Ade; Sch Pl; Stg Crw; Yth Flsp; Yrbk; Taylor Univ; Bio.

WALLACE, JANET; Buckhannon Upshur HS; Buckhannon, WV; Chrs; Lbry Ade; FHA; Place 3rd In St FHA Cmptn 78;.

WALLACE, JEANNETTE; West Branch HS; Beloit, OH; 10/250 AFS; Am Leg Aux Girls St; Chrh Wkr; Girl Scts; Hon Rl; Sec NHS; Off Ade; Rptr Yrbk; 4-H; FTA; Univ.

WALLACE, JULIANA; Sturgis HS; Sturgis, MI; Band; Orch; Sch Mus; Sch Pl; Stg Crw; Rptr Yrbk; PPFtbl; Western Michigan Univ; Acctg.

WALLACE, JUNE; Greencastle HS; Greencastle, IN; Chrs; Chrh Wkr; Cmnty Wkr; Girl Scts; Hon Rl; Hosp Ade; JA; Sch Mus; Sch Pl; Stg Crw; De Pauw Univ; Elem Educ.

WALLACE, LEA; North Putnam Jr Sr HS; Coatesville, IN; 20/150 NHS; VP Stu Cncl; Pres 4-H; Mth Clb; OEA; Pep Clb; Bsktbl; Capt Pom Pon; 4-H Awd; Kiwan Awd; Florida Christian Coll; Math.

WALLACE, LORI L; Alliance HS; Alliance, OH; 29/326 Hon Rl; NHS; Off Ade; Orch; Rptr Yrbk; Yrbk; Eng Clb; C of C Awd; Carntn City Poster Const 2nd Pl 78; Perfct Attndnc; Modeling.

WALLACE, MARY R; Central Catholic HS; Wheeling, WV; 10/140 Hon Rl; JA; NHS; Sch Pl; Drama Clb; 4-H; Trk; Cit Awd; 4-H Awd; JA Awd; W Virginia Wesleyan Univ; Forestry.

WALLACE, NANCY A; Turpin HS; Cincinnati, OH; 7/371 Hon Rl; Off Ade; Socr; Chrldng; Grls Varsity Soccer Team; Cheerleading Squad Freshman & Varsity; Oklahoma Univ; Medicine.

WALLACE, NORA; John Glenn HS; New Concord, OH; 2/189 Am Leg Aux Girls St; Chrs; Hon Rl; Pres Orch; Sch Mus; Y-Teens; Rptr Sch Nwsp; Drama Clb; 4-H; Fr Clb; Oberlin Coll; Music.

WALLACE, S; Elmhurst HS; Ft Wayne, IN; Aud/Vis; Band; Chrs; Hon Rl; Orch; Mth Clb; IM Sprt; Texas Tech Univ; Archt.

WALLACE, SARAH; Nitro HS; Charleston, WV; Cl Rep Jr Cls; Cls Rep Sr Cls; Chrs; Chrh Wkr; Hon Rl; JA; NHS; Berea College; Biology.

WALLACE, SHARI; Lawton HS; Lawton, MI; 3/50 Band; Chrh Wkr; Drm Mjrt; Girl Scts; Sec NHS; Sch Mus; Stu Cncl; Sci Clb; Letter Trk; Letter Chrldng; Wheaton Coll; Medicine.

WALLACE, SUSAN M; Jackson HS; Jackson, MI; Cmnty Wkr; Hon Rl; Red Cr Ade; Civ Clb; FFA; Pep Clb; Spn Clb; Adrian College; Bus.

WALLACE, TAMMRA; Brownsburg HS; Brownsburg, IN; Cls Rep Frsh Cls; Cls Rep Soph Cls; Cl Rep Jr Cls; Cls Rep Sr Cls; Am Leg Aux Girls St; Hon Rl; NHS; Stu Cncl; Bsktbl; Gym; Purdue Univ; Pharm.

WALLACE, WAYMON L; Walnut Hills HS; Cincinnati, OH; Cl Rep Jr Cls; Cls Rep Sr Cls; Boy Scts; Hon Rl; Orch; Pol Wkr; Stu Cncl; Pep Clb; IM Sprt; Natl Merit Schl; Mbr Of Cincinnati Youth Symphony Orch 77; Participated In Minority Schlrs Coll Experience 78; Univ Of Alabama; Med.

WALLAND, NANCY; St Marys Central Cath HS; Sandusky, OH; VP Frsh Cls; VP Soph Cls; Hon Rl; Stu Cncl; Spn Clb; Bsktbl; GAA; Ohio St Univ; Soc Work.

WALLAR, GINA; Defiance Sr HS; Defiance, OH; Chrs; Hon Rl; Spn Clb; Mat Maids; Vocational Schl; Cosmetology.

WALLBROWN, JOHN; Southeast HS; Deerfield, OH; Cls Rep Soph Cls; Hon Rl; VP NHS; Stu Cncl; Yth Flsp; FFA; Letter Wrstlng; Univ.

WALLE, KAREN; Douglas Mac Arthur HS; Saginaw, MI; Hon Rl; NHS; Ger Clb; Pom Pon; Cit Awd; German Awd; Bookkeeping Awd; College; Busns Admin.

WALLENHORST, MARGARET; Magnificat HS; Fairview Park, OH; Cmp Fr Grls; Chrs; Cmnty Wkr; Jr NHS; NHS; Sch Pl; Stg Crw; Mth Clb; Letter Bsktbl; Coach Actv; College; Nursing.

WALLER, JENNIFER; Clay HS; Granger, IN; Cls Rep Frsh Cls; Band; Cmnty Wkr; Hon Rl; Hosp Ade; Orch; Stu Cncl; Drama Clb; Fr Clb; Pep Clb; Univ.

WALLER, LESTER; Hughes HS; Cincinnati, OH; Cls Rep Sr Cls; Chrh Wkr; FCA; Hon Rl; Sch Pl; Boys Clb Am; Mth Clb; Bsbl; Ftbl; College; Math.

WALLER, VALERIE; Jane Addams Voc HS; Cleveland, OH; Cl Rep Jr Cls; Cls Rep Sr Cls; Drl Tm; Hon Rl; NHS; ROTC; Treas Yth Flsp; Tmr; Cit Awd; Rotary Awd; Cleveland St Univ; Med Lab.

WALLERICK, LISA; Ursuline HS; Youngstown, OH; 78/360 Spn Clb; Pom Pon; Twrlr; Youngstown St Univ; Sec.

WALLEY, JODY; Paint Valley HS; Bourneville, OH; 3/90 Chrh Wkr; Hon Rl; Hosp Ade; FHA; Lat Clb; Univ.

WALLICK, CRAIG; North Canton Hoover HS; Northcanton, OH; 143/422 Band; Hon Rl; Orch; Sch Mus; Univ Of Cincinnati; Bus Educ.

WALLIE, DAVE; Kirtland HS; Kirtland, OH; Chrs; FCA; Bsbl; Air Force.

WALLIN, JENNIFER; Merrillville Sr HS; Crown Point, IN; 122/604 Chrs; Girl Scts; Letter Glf; Purdue Univ; Spec Ed.

WALLING, DAVE; Springboro HS; Springboro, OH; Chrh Wkr; Yth Flsp; Spn Clb; Ftbl; College; Engineer.

WALLING, DAVID; Springboro HS; Springboro, OH; Chrh Wkr; FCA; Yth Flsp; Spn Clb; Letter Ftbl; Purdue Univ; Engr.

WALLING, GUY; Stow HS; Stow, OH; Ftbl; Kent St Univ; Phys Ed.

WALLINGFORD, FELICIA; Samuel Mumford HS; Detroit, MI; Chrs; Drl Tm; Hon Rl; NHS; ROTC; Fr Clb; Trk; Cit Awd; Univ Of Michigan; Aviation.

WALLINGFORD, TODD; Chillicothe HS; Chillicothe, OH; Chrs; Orch; Stu Cncl; Key Clb; Letter Bsbl; Letter Ftbl; Letter Trk; Letter Wrstlng; Voc Schl; Elec.

WALLISER, THERESA; Calvert HS; Tiffin, OH; Band; Hon Rl; 4-H; Univ.

WALLNER, JOHN; Marietta HS; Marietta, OH; Cl Rep Jr Cls; Aud/Vis; Chrs; Sec Debate Tm; NHS; Sch Pl; Stg Crw; Sec Spn Clb; College; Elec Eng.

WALLS, A; Bellville HS; Ypsilanti, MI; Chrh Wkr; Girl Scts; Hon Rl; Spn Clb; Chrldng; Ctrl Mich Univ; Eng.

WALLS, BRENDA; Central Preston HS; Albright, WV; Capt Band; Chrs; Yrbk; Sch Nwsp; FFA; Pep Clb; Sec VICA; Letter Bsktbl; Letter Chrldng; Sec GAA; Fairmont St Coll; Graphic Arts.

WALLS, G; Wapakoneta HS; Wapakoneta, OH; Boy Scts; Hon Rl; Letter Bsbl; Construction.

WALLS, J; Frankfort HS; Frankfort, MI; Chrs; Hon Rl; Jr NHS; NHS; Stu Cncl; Y-Teens; 4-H; Pep Clb; Bsktbl; 4-H Awd; Univ; Bus.

WALLS, KATHY; Aquinas HS; Westland, MI; Chrh Wkr; Cmnty Wkr; Hon Rl; Yth Flsp; Bsbl; Bsktbl; Trk; IM Sprt; Mic State; Cpa.

WALLS, LISA; Columbiana County Voc HS; East Liverpool, OH; Pres Jr Cls; Band; Chrh Wkr; NHS; Stu Cncl; Y-Teens; Rptr Sch Nwsp; OEA; Trk; Twrlr;.

WALLSKOG, KERRI; Hammond HS; Hammond, IN; Chrs; Girl Scts; Jr NHS; Univ; Nursing.

WALPOLE, JENNY; Defiance HS; Defiance, OH; Chrh Wkr; Treas Girl Scts; Hon Rl; DECA; Fort Wayne Bible Coll; Religion.

WALQUIST, HOLLY; Lamphere HS; Madison Heights, MI; 47/337 Sec Soph Cls; Sec Jr Cls; Pres Sr Cls; Natl Forn Lg; NHS; Sch Mus; Stu Cncl; Drama Clb; Capt Pom Pon; DAR Awd; DAR Good Citizen Awd For Lamphere HS; Algebra III Awd; Van Buren Leadership Camp Awd; Michigan St Univ; Vet.

WALRATH, BRETT; Edgewood HS; N Kingsville, OH; Hon Rl; Sci Clb; Spn Clb; Cit Awd; College; Dental.

WALSER, CHERYL; Flushing HS; Flushing, MI; 6/574 Cls Rep Frsh Cls; Sal; Chrs; Cmnty Wkr; Girl Scts; Hon Rl; NHS; Stg Crw; Stu Cncl; Sch Nwsp; Michigan St Univ; Med.

WALSH, CAROL; Bishop Foley HS; Madison Hts, MI; 5/193 Hon Rl; Natl Forn Lg; Off Ade; Stg Crw; Yth Flsp; Sch Nwsp; Western Michigan Univ; Sec.

WALSH, KEVIN; Bishop Foley HS; Warren, MI; Pres Jr Cls; Chrh Wkr; Debate Tm; Pres NHS; Pol Wkr; Sch Mus; Sch Nwsp; VP Sci Clb; Letter Crs Cntry; JETS Awd; College; Science.

WALSH, LAURENCE; Northwest HS; Indianapolis, IN; 10/540 Am Leg Boys St; Hon Rl; NHS; Sct Actv; Sch Nwsp; Fr Clb; Mth Clb; IM Sprt; Natl Merit Ltr; Natl Merit SF; Wabash Coll; Med.

WALSH, LORETTA; Davison Sr HS; Davison, MI; 42/455 Girl Scts; Hon Rl; NHS; Sct Actv; Eastern Michigan Univ; Comp.

WALSH, MICHAEL; Lumen Christi HS; Albion, MI; Am Leg Boys St; Boy Scts; Hon Rl; Red Cr Ade; Sct Actv; Lat Clb; Albion Coll; Chem.

WALSH, MOLLY; Notre Dame HS; Portsmouth, OH; Hon Rl; Pep Clb; Trk; Chrldng; Univ; Art.

WALSH, PAUL; Eaton HS; Eaton, OH; 84/170 Pres Band; Chrs; Cmnty Wkr; Hon Rl; Red Cr Ade; Sch Mus; Sch Pl; Sct Actv; Stg Crw; Stu Cncl; Ohio St Univ; Bus Admin.

WALSH, THOMAS; Trinity HS; Broadview Hts, OH; Cls Rep Sr Cls; Hon Rl; NHS; Stu Cncl; Ftbl; Letter Trk; Univ Of Notre Dame; Mech Engr.

WALSTON, LAURA; Pleasant HS; Marion, OH; 22/150 Hon Rl; Hosp Ade; Lbry Ade; Quill & Scroll; Rptr Sch Nwsp; FHA; IM Sprt; Mgrs; Scr Kpr; Tmr; Ohio St Univ; Jrnlsm.

WALSTON JR, W; Lawrenceburg HS; Lawrenceburg, IN; 7/175 Band; Chrs; Hon Rl; Jr NHS; NHS; Sch Mus; Sch Pl; Stg Crw; Drama Clb; Ger Clb; John Philip Sousa Awd; Annabel O Brien Schlrshp; Best Actor Drama Awd; Franklin Coll; Med Tech.

WALT, DEBBIE; Mitchell HS; Mitchell, IN; 16/143 Band; Chrs; Drm Mjrt; Sch Mus; Sch Pl; Stg Crw; Pep Clb; IN St Schlrshp 79; European Wind Band Tour With Amer Musical Ambassadors 79; Sullivan Jr Coll; Legal Sec.

WALTER, BETH; Lakeview HS; Coral, MI; 7/124 Band; Chrh Wkr; Debate Tm; Hon Rl; Natl Forn Lg; NHS; GAA; Mgrs; Dnfth Awd; Western Michigan Univ.

WALTER, CATHERINE B; Taylor HS; Cleves, OH; Chrh Wkr; FCA; Hon Rl; Letter Bsktbl; Letter Trk; Miami Univ; Home Ec.

WALTER, CATHY; Mohawk HS; Sycamore, OH; Band; Chrs; Hon Rl; NHS; Orch; VP Yth Flsp; Y-Teens; Drama Clb; Lat Clb; Cit Awd; Nursing Schl; Nurse.

WALTER, CHRISTINE; Williamsburg HS; Wiliamsburg, OH; 6/80 VP Soph Cls; Cl Rep Jr Cls; Pres Sr Cls; Am Leg Aux Girls St; Band; Hon Rl; NHS; Stu Cncl; Wrstlng; Mat Maids; Med Schl; X Ray Tech.

WALTER, CHRISTINE; Williamsburg HS; Williamsburg, OH; Cls Rep Frsh Cls; VP Soph Cls; Cl Rep Jr Cls; Aud/Vis; Cmp Fr Grls; Girl Scts; Hon Rl; NHS; Sch Mus; Sch Pl; Christ Med Schl; X Ray Tech.

WALTER, JEFFREY S; Harrison HS; Harrison, OH; 69/220 Bsbl; Bsktbl; Glf; Trk; College; Bus Admin.

WALTER, JOHN; North HS; Springfield, OH; Cls Rep Frsh Cls; Chrs; Chrh Wkr; Hon Rl; Lbry Ade; Stu Cncl; Fr Clb; Pep Clb; Bsktbl; Glf; Archery Trophies & Patches 76; NROTC; Elec Engr.

WALTER, JOHN; Lake Catholic HS; Chesterland, OH; 5/350 Boy Scts; Hon Rl; NHS; Rptr Sch Nwsp; Crs Cntry; Trk; IM Sprt; Univ.

WALTER, JUDY; Riverdale HS; Carey, OH; 1/96 Am Leg Aux Girls St; Chrs; NHS; Sch Pl; Stu Cncl; Bsktbl; Chrldng; Voice Dem Awd; Bowling Green State Univ; Diet.

WALTER, KAREN; Ypsilanti HS; Ypsilanti, MI; Spn Clb; Eastern Michigan Univ; Acctg.

WALTER, LAURIE; Hartford HS; Hartford, MI; Cl Rep Jr Cls; Trs Sr Cls; Hon Rl; Sch Pl; DECA; Chrldng; bronze Merit Awd 78; A B Pin 78; Univ; Bus.

WALTER, LISA; Chippewa Hills HS; Sears, MI; 5/240 VP Sr Cls; Band; Hon Rl; Sec NHS; Rptr Yrbk; Letter Bsktbl; Letter Trk; Womens In Engr Mi Tech Univ 79; Michigan St Univ; Engr.

WALTER, MICHAEL; Manistee HS; Manistee, MI; 40/190 Boy Scts; Hon Rl; Sct Actv; Letter Bsbl; Michigan St Univ; Comp Sci.

WALTER, TIMOTHY; Carson City Crystal HS; Carson City, MI; 5/125 Hon Rl; NHS; Bsbl; Glf; ITT; Electronics.

WALTERHOUSE, BARBARA; Firestone HS; Akron, OH; 115/350 Hon Rl; College; Business.

WALTERS, ALAN; Purcell HS; Cincinnati, OH; 30/160 Cmnty Wkr; Hon Rl; Crs Cntry; Trk; Univ; Graphic Dsgn.

WALTERS, ANITA; De Kalb HS; Auburn, IN; Chrh Wkr; Cmnty Wkr; FCA; Natl Forn Lg; VP NHS; Sch Pl; Sec Stu Cncl; 4-H; Fr Clb; Sec Ger Clb; Tri Kappa Honor Banquet; Dana Corp Schlrshp; NFL St Meet 3rd Pl In Impromptu Speaking; Indiana Univ; Medicine.

WALTERS, CHERYL; Elmwood HS; Bradner, OH; Chrs; Hon Rl; 4-H; IM Sprt; Mat Maids;.

WALTERS, CINDY; Coldwater HS; Coldwater, MI; Cls Rep Frsh Cls; Cls Rep Soph Cls; Cl Rep Jr Cls; Cls Rep Sr Cls; Boy Scts; Cmp Fr Grls; Chrs; Chrh Wkr; Cmnty Wkr; Stu Cncl; Branch County 4 H Fair Qn; Dress Revue Winner; Raised & Taught Lab Dogs For The Blind; Michigan St Univ; Fash Design.

WALTERS, DAVID; Zeeland HS; Zeeland, MI; 19/193 Cls Rep Frsh Cls; Cls Rep Soph Cls; Am Leg Boys St; Band; Chrh Wkr; Hon Rl; Stu Cncl; Ftbl; IM Sprt; Michigan State Univ; Civil Engr.

WALTERS, DAVID; Daleville HS; Daleville, IN; 4-H; Fr Clb; Bsktbl; Crs Cntry; Glf; 4-H Awd; ITT Voc Schl; Elec.

WALTERS, DAVID; Saint Edward HS; Rocky River, OH; 115/360 Fr Clb; Ftbl; College; Bus.

WALTERS, DEBRA; Zeeland HS; Zeeland, MI; 27/193 Hon Rl; 4-H; Glf; Univ.

WALTERS, DONNA G; Barboursville HS; Huntington, WV; Cls Rep Frsh Cls; Cls Rep Soph Cls; Sec Jr Cls; FCA; Hon Rl; Jr NHS; Stu Cncl; Lat Clb; Pep Clb; Chrldng; Cheerleading Awds; Vocational Schl; Nursing.

WALTERS, ELIZABETH A; John F Kennedy HS; Warren, OH; 3/180 Chrh Wkr; Cmnty Wkr; Debate Tm; Hon Rl; Lit Mag; Natl Forn Lg; NHS; Quill & Scroll; Yrbk; Drama Clb; Notre Dame College; Math.

WALTERS, JANE; Jimtown HS; Elk, IN; Cls Rep Frsh Cls; Chrs; Chrh Wkr; Drl Tm; Girl Scts; Hon Rl; JA; Sch Mus; Sch Pl; Stg Crw; Indiana Univ; Ped Nursing.

WALTERS, JANET L; Franklin Community HS; Franklin, IN; 48/250 Cls Rep Frsh Cls; Sec Soph Cls; FCA; Hon Rl; Lbry Ade; NHS; Stu Cncl; Fr Clb; Pres Pep Clb; Capt Ten; Ind State Univ; Phys Educ Tchr.

WALTERS, JIM; Clio HS; Clio, MI; Cl Rep Jr Cls; Boy Scts; Chrh Wkr; Hon Rl; Jr NHS; Treas NHS; Sch Mus; Sch Pl; Sct Actv; Stg Crw; Eagle Scout; College; Busns Mgmt.

WALTERS, LAURA; Chaminade Julienne HS; Tipp Cty, OH; Chrh Wkr; Wright State; Tchr.

WALTERS, LORI A; Bishop Donahue HS; Mc Mechen, WV; 9/64 Band; Chrs; Chrh Wkr; Drm Mjrt; Hon Rl; NHS; Pep Clb; Spn Clb; GAA; Univ.

WALTERS, LUCRETIA L; Wapahant HS; Albany, IN; Hst Frsh Cls; Chrs; Chrh Wkr; Cmnty Wkr; Hon Rl; JA; Lbry Ade; Sch Mus; Yth Flsp; Drama Clb; Miss Teen All Amer; History Essay Awd; College; Theater.

WALTERS, MARK; Loynorrix HS; Kalamazoo, MI; Western Michigan Univ; Mech Engr.

WALTERS, MICHAEL; Edon N W HS; Edon, OH; Boy Scts; Chrs; Chrh Wkr; Sch Mus; Sct Actv; Trk; College; Wildlife Conservation.

WALTERS, MICHAEL; Bishop Gallagher HS; Detroit, MI; 36/333 Cls Rep Sr Cls; Letter Ftbl; IM Sprt; Univ; Engr.

WALTERS, NANCY; St Agatha HS; Detroit, MI; 15/98 Hon Rl; Lbry Ade; Off Ade; Bsbl; Bsktbl; PPFtbl; Scr Kpr; Univ; Med.

WALTERS, RITA; John Glenn HS; Cambridge, OH; 15/162 Hon Rl; Off Ade; Sec Y-Teens; Mountain Empire Cmnty Coll; Acctg.

WALTERS, ROBERT P; Carmel HS; Carmel, IN; 70/700 Trs Sr Cls; Pres Band; Chrs; Hon Rl; NHS; Sch Mus; Wrstlng; IM Sprt; J P Sousa Band Awrd 76; Emebr Of Mrchng Spirit Pep Stage & Wind Band 77 80; Intrmrl Cross Cntry Awrd Tennis; Indiana Univ; Bus Admin.

WALTERS, SHARON; Ayersville HS; Defiance, OH; 16/82 Band; Chrs; Chrh Wkr; Hon Rl; Off Ade; NHS; Sch Pl; Stg Crw; College; Psych.

WALTERS, SINDIE; Valley View HS; Germantown, OH; FHA; Domestic Engr.

WALTERS, STARR; Rochester Cmnty HS; Rochester, IN; 5/178 Cls Rep Soph Cls; VP Jr Cls; VP Sr Cls; Band; FCA; Hon Rl; NHS; Off Ade; Stu Cncl; Yth Flsp; Ball St Univ; CPA.

WALTERS, TERRY; Lawrenceburg HS; Lawrenceburg, IN; Aud/Vis; Band; Boy Scts; Hon Rl; JA; Lat Clb; Most Otstndng Industrial Arts Stud 76; Most Otstndng Woods & Metal Stud 77; Otstndng Shop Stud 77; Univ Of Cincinnati; Bus.

WALTERS, THOMAS; St Francis De Sales HS; Rossford, OH; Cl Rep Jr Cls; Aud/Vis; Sch Mus; Stg Crw; Stu Cncl; Sch Nwsp; Univ Of Michigan; Pathologist.

WALTERS, TOM; Amelia HS; Amelia, OH; Band; Am Leg Awd; Univ; Jrnlsm.

WALTERS, WILLIAM E; Berkeley Springs HS; Berkeley Spgs, WV; 10/109 Am Leg Boys St; Band; Hon Rl; Ftbl; Trk; IM Sprt; Scr Kpr; West Virginia Univ; Ichthyology.

WALTON, ANTHONY; West Side HS; Gary, IN; Boy Scts; Hon Rl; FFA; Bsktbl; Letter Ftbl; Letter Trk; Michigan Univ; Hist.

WALTON, DAVE S; River Valley HS; Coshocton, OH; Band; Boy Scts; Chrh Wkr; Hon Rl; Lbry Ade; Sct Actv; Yth Flsp; Spn Clb; Capt Ftbl; IM Sprt; Trade Schl; Bldg Cntrctr.

WALTON, DEBORAH; Cass Tech HS; Detroit, MI; Cls Rep Frsh Cls; Cls Rep Soph Cls; Cl Rep Jr Cls; Band; Cmnty Wkr; JA; Off Ade; Stu Cncl; OEA; JETS Awd; Michigan St Univ; Acctg.

WALTON, DOUGLAS; Mohawk HS; Sycamore, OH; 7/116 Am Leg Boys St; Band; Chrh Wkr; Hon Rl; NHS; Yth Flsp; FTA; Spn Clb; Bsbl; Bsktbl; Scholarship Team; Ohio Coll; Busns.

WALTON, JOY; Walnut Hills HS; Cincinnati, OH; Chrs; Chrh Wkr; Drl Tm; Girl Scts; Pep Clb; Mgrs; Howard Univ; Art.

WALTON, KIMBERLY; William Henry Harrison HS; W Lafayette, IN; Sec Frsh Cls; Trs Frsh Cls; Band; Girl Scts; Hon Rl; Pep Clb; Swmmng; Trk; Chrldng; GAA; Purdue Univ; Math.

WALTON, LLOYD; Colon HS; Burr Oak, MI; Debate Tm; Hon Rl; Lbry Ade; FFA; Letter Bsktbl; Letter Trk; Bus Schl; Bus.

WALTON, MARIECA; Medina Sr HS; Medina, OH; 139/360 Chrh Wkr; Yth Flsp; Pep Clb; PPFtbl; Ohio St Univ; Phys Ther.

WALTON, MICHAEL; Lasalle HS; Cincinnati, OH; 72/252 Boy Scts; Chrs; Hon Rl; PAVAS; Ftbl; Trk; IM Sprt; College.

WALTON, MICHELLE; Shortridge HS; Indianapolis, IN; Girl Scts; Hon Rl; Hosp Ade; NHS; Bus Schl.

WALTON, MILTON; Oak Hill HS; Oak Hill, WV; Hon Rl; Bsktbl; West Virginia Tech Univ; Mining Engr.

WALTON, ROD; Mohawk HS; Sycamore, OH; Pres Jr Cls; Am Leg Boys St; Band; Chrs; Chrh Wkr; Hon Rl; JA; Lit Mag; NHS; Sch Mus; Univ Of Toledo; Bus Admin.

WALTZ, ALAN; Hamilton Hgts HS; Atlanta, IN; 38/104 Pres 4-H; VP FFA; Sci Clb; Trk; 4-H Awd; Purdue Univ; Agri Sci.

WALTZ, CRAIG E; Hamilton Heights HS; Cicero, IN; 2/101 Sal; Band; Chrh Wkr; Hon Rl; NHS; Sch Pl; Pres Drama Clb; Pres Lat Clb; Trk; Ball St Univ; Music.

WALTZ, TODD; Tuscarawas Valley HS; Zoar, OH; 25/145 Band; Ed Sch Nwsp; God Cntry Awd; Mount Union; Bus Admin.

WALTZER, TERESA; Benjamin Logan HS; W Mansfield, OH; Chrs; Chrh Wkr; Hon Rl; NHS; Sch Mus; Sch Pl; Yrbk;.

WALWORTH, GARRETT; Adrian HS; Adrian, MI; 81/386 Cls Rep Sr Cls; Band; Chrs; Mdrgl; Sch Mus; Sct Actv; Swmmng; Ten; Mich State Univ; Law Business.

WALWORTH, KAREN; Kearsley HS; Burton, MI; Cls Rep Sr Cls; Band; Chrs; Hon Rl; NHS; Letter Gym; Letter Trk; Tmr; Mott Coll; Sci.

WALWORTH, KURT; Chelsea HS; Chelsea, MI; Orch; Univ; Draftsman.

WALWORTH, MARY; Kearsley HS; Burton, MI; 38/375 Hon Rl; Capt Trk; Michigan St Univ; Fisheries.

WALWORTH, MICHAEL; Whittemore Prescott Area HS; Twining, MI; Pres Frsh Cls; Hon Rl; Sch Pl; Stg Crw; Drama Clb; Bsbl; Male Performer Of Yr Drama Awd; Recognition Awd Outstndng Work In Drama; College; Science.

WALZ, ANN; Pioneer HS; Ann Arbor, MI; Cmnty Wkr; Girl Scts; Lbry Ade; Off Ade; Pol Wkr; Red Cr Ade; Yth Flsp; Eastern Michigan Univ; Spec Educ.

WALZ, GEORGE; Au Gres Sims HS; Au Gres, MI; Band; Orch; Bsktbl; Letter Ftbl; Trk; Central Univ; Bus.

WALZ, JANET A; Chelsea HS; Chelsea, MI; 2/200 Trs Soph Cls; Debate Tm; Hon Rl; NHS; Natl Merit SF; College; Computer Tech.

WAMSLEY, CHET; Buckhannon Upshur HS; Buckhannon, WV; Band; Chrh Wkr; Cmnty Wkr; Hon Rl; Yth Flsp; 4-H; Bsbl; Bsktbl; IM Sprt; 4-H Awd; Athletic Recogntn W V House Of Delegates 79; Univ; Law.

WAMSLEY, JEFFREY; Pt Pleasant HS; Pt Pleasant, WV; Cls Rep Frsh Cls; Band; Boy Scts; Sch Mus; Sct Actv; Stu Cncl; Yth Flsp; Sch Nwsp; Key Clb; Univ; Music.

WAMSLEY, MARTINA; Shelbyville Sr HS; Shelbyville, IN; 226/291 Off Ade; Pep Clb; Gym; Trk; Capt Mat Maids; Scr Kpr; Tmr; Mas Awd; Vocational Schl; Cosmetology.

WANAR, LORRIE; Coldwater HS; Coldwater, MI; 32/320 Band; Chrh Wkr; Cmnty Wkr; Sec Yth Flsp; Pep Clb; C of C Awd; Spring Arbor Coll; Busns.

WANCATA, PAUL; James Ford Rhodes HS; Cleveland, OH; Band; Hon Rl; Jr NHS; NHS; Sch Mus; Stu Cncl; Rptr Sch Nwsp; Bsbl; Letter Crs Cntry; Letter Trk; College.

WANCOUR, MARY; Regina HS; St Clair Shore, MI; Trs Jr Cls; Cls Rep Sr Cls; Hon Rl; Quill & Scroll; Stu Cncl; Drama Clb; Sci Clb; Ten; Chrldng; PPFtbl; Sienna Heights Coll; Liberal Arts.

WANDER, JEFFERY; Loudonville HS; Perrysville, OH; Band; Boy Scts; Sct Actv; Spn Clb; Bsbl; Coach Actv; Am Leg Awd; Univ; Vet Med.

WANDER, JULIE; Bishop Fenwick HS; Middletown, OH; Sec Soph Cls; Drl Tm; Hon Rl; Hosp Ade; NHS; Stg Crw; Stu Cncl; Christ Hosp Schl; Sci.

WANG, BONITA; Adelphian Acad; Grand Blanc, MI; Pres Frsh Cls; Hon Rl; Stu Cncl; Rptr Yrbk; Rptr Sch Nwsp; IM Sprt; Served As Pastor Jr Yr In Kappa Delta Girls Clb; Coll; Med.

WANG, IRENE; West Ottawa HS; Holland, MI; Cls Rep Frsh Cls; Sec Soph Cls; Sec Jr Cls; Debate Tm; Hon Rl; JA; Jr NHS; Mod UN; NHS; Orch; MIT; Engr.

WANG, LINDA; West Ottawa HS; Holland, MI; 6/317 Cl Rep Jr Cls; Debate Tm; Hon Rl; JA; Mod UN; NHS; Stu Cncl; Pres Ger Clb; Sec Lat Clb; Letter Ten; Hope Coll; Pre Med.

WANGER, RHODA; Heath HS; Heath, OH; Cls Rep Frsh Cls; Cls Rep Soph Cls; Chrs; Chrh Wkr; Drl Tm; Hon Rl; Mdrgl; Sch Mus; Sprt Ed Yrbk; FTA; Cedarville Coll; Elem Ed.

WANHATALO, JOHN; Baraga HS; Pelkie, MI; Boy Scts; Chrh Wkr; Hon Rl; Sct Actv; Letter Bsktbl; Letter Trk; Pres Awd; College; Forestry.

WANKOWSKI, SANDY; St Francis De Sales HS; Columbus, OH; Cls Rep Soph Cls; Chrs; Chrh Wkr; Girl Scts; Hon Rl; Sch Pl; Stg Crw; Stu Cncl; Spn Clb; Scr Kpr; Ohio State School Of Cosmetology.

WANN, GREGORY; Jeffersonville HS; Jeffersonville, IN; 1/600 Am Leg Boys St; Chrh Wkr; FCA; Hon Rl; Stg Crw; Pep Clb; Scr Kpr; Tmr; Univ.

WANNEMACHER, DANA; Wayne Trace HS; Paye, OH; 2/119 Trs Frsh Cls; Am Leg Boys St; Band; Chrh Wkr; Hon Rl; Yth Flsp; 4-H; Letter Ftbl; Letter Trk; Capt Wrstlng; Ball St Univ; Archt.

WANNEMUEHLER, KAREN; Memorial HS; Evansville, IN; Hon Rl; NHS; Pep Clb; Ten; Chrldng; Univ Of Evansville; English.

WANNER, DONALD E; Brookhaven HS; Columbus, OH; 121/435 Chrs; Chrh Wkr; Cmnty Wkr; Fr Clb; Rus Clb; Spn Clb; Kiwan Awd; Ohio St Univ; Rec Ther.

WANSER, ELIZABETH; Kenston HS; Chagrin Fls, OH; Chrs; Chrh Wkr; Debate Tm; Drl Tm; Girl Scts; Hon Rl; Sch Mus; Sch Pl; Stg Crw; Drama Clb; Recieved Ribbons For Horseback Riding; Earned Varsity Letter For Outstndng Performance At Summer Camp; College; Law.

WANSTRATH, JANICE; Immaculate Conception Acad; Batesville, IN; 11/68 Am Leg Aux Girls St; Girl Scts; Hon Rl; NHS; IM Sprt; Coll.

WANTUCK, CHRISTINE; Marian HS; Bloomfield, MI; Chrs; Mdrgl; Sch Mus; Sch Pl; Stg Crw; Yth Flsp; Drama Clb; Fr Clb; FTA; Pep Clb; Albion Coll; Theatre.

WANTZ, SUSAN; Central Catholic HS; Massillon, OH; Band; Chrh Wkr; Cmnty Wkr; Girl Scts; Hon Rl; Sct Actv; Whos Who Among Amer HS Stud 77; Natl Cath Bandmasters Assoc 79; Hon Band Awd 79; Univ Of Akron; Nursing.

WAPLE, CHRISTOPHER; Maple Hts HS; Maple Hgts, OH; Cls Rep Frsh Cls; Cl Rep Jr Cls; Cls Rep Sr Cls; Stu Cncl; Bsbl; Wrstlng; Mert Roll Obtaind 3.3 Grd Avr 78; Mert Roll Obtained 3.0 Grd Avr 76; Univ; Math.

WAPLE, TRACY; Field HS; Mogadore, OH; 14/265 Band; Hon Rl; NHS; Yrbk; Fr Clb; Scr Kpr; Univ Of Akron; Comp Sci.

WAPPELHORST, JOE; Waynesfield Goshen HS; Waynesfield, OH; Band; Chrs; Chrh Wkr; Orch; Sch Mus; Sch Pl; Rptr Yrbk; 4-H; Crs Cntry; Trk; College; Pharmacy.

WARBERG, BARB; Penn HS; Osceola, IN; Band; 4-H; Fr Clb; Pom Pon; College; Architectural Engr.

WARBY, JANET S; Fowlerville HS; Howell, MI; Pres Sr Cls; Am Leg Aux Girls St; Chrh Wkr; Girl Scts; Sch Pl; Stu Cncl; Yth Flsp; Ed Yrbk; Rptr Yrbk; Rptr Sch Nwsp; Mi Schlrshp Awd 79; Fowlervle Alumni Schlrshp 79; Olivet Nazarene Coll; Bus Admin.

WARD, ALAN; Buchanan HS; Buchanan, MI; 4/130 Hon Rl; NHS; Off Ade; Capt Bsbl; Bsktbl; Natl Merit Ltr; Mic St Univ; Mech Engr.

WARD, ALLEN; Iaeger HS; Jolo, WV; Hon Rl; Jr NHS; NHS; Fr Clb; Letter Ftbl; Wrstlng; DAR Awd; Natl Merit Schl; West Virginia Univ; Chem.

WARD, ANN; Olentangy HS; Worthington, OH; 16/145 Chrs; Chrh Wkr; Hon Rl; Lbry Ade; NHS; Stg Crw; Rptr Yrbk; Drama Clb; 4-H; Fr Clb; College; Med.

WARD, ANTHONY L; Seeger Mem HS; Williamsport, IN; 43/144 Hon Rl; Stu Cncl; Bsktbl; Ftbl; Glf; Wrstlng; Coll; Accntg.

WARD, AUDREY; Martin Luther King HS; Detroit, MI; 15/200 Trs Jr Cls; Trs Sr Cls; Cls Rep Sr Cls; Hon Rl; NHS; Y-Teens; Capt Chrldng; Cit Awd; Eastern Michigan Univ; Nursing.

WARD, CHERYL; Western HS; Spring Arbor, MI; 6/174 Mdrgl; NHS; Stu Cncl; Sch Nwsp; Fr Clb; Spring Arbor Coll; Bio.

WARD, CHRIS; Springport HS; Springport, MI; Band; Yth Flsp; Rptr Yrbk; 4-H; VP FFA; Crs Cntry; Trk; Wrstlng; Michigan St Univ.

WARD, CINDY; Arcanum HS; Arcanum, OH; 15/99 Cl Rep Jr Cls; Off Ade; Stu Cncl; 4-H; Mgrs;.

WARD, DEBORAH; Peebles HS; Peebles, OH; Band; Chrh Wkr; Cmnty Wkr; Lbry Ade; Ed Yrbk; Treas 4-H; FHA; College.

WARD, DEBORAH; Salem HS; Salem, OH; 8/265 Band; Cmp Fr Grls; Hon Rl; Hosp Ade; Sch Mus; Sch Pl; Rptr Yrbk; Mth Clb; Pep Clb; Scr Kpr; Univ Of Akron; Nursing.

WARD, DEIRDRE; Sebring Mckinley HS; Sebring, OH; 4/76 VP Frsh Cls; Sec Soph Cls; Am Leg Aux Girls St; Hon Rl; NHS; Off Ade; Rptr Yrbk; Letter Bsktbl; College; Medicine.

WARD, DENISE; Eastwood HS; Stony Ridge, OH; 3/185 Girl Scts; Hon Rl; Lbry Ade; NHS; Sec 4-H; Sec Fr Clb; Pres Ger Clb; Wartburg Coll; Bilingual Sec.

WARD, DENISE; South Ripley Jr Sr HS; Versailles, IN; 8/106 Am Leg Aux Girls St; Chrs; Chrh Wkr; Girl Scts; Hon Rl; NHS; Quill & Scroll; Yrbk; Sch Nwsp; Drama Clb; Indiana St Univ; History.

WARD, ELDEAN; Andrews Acad; Berrien Spring, MI; VP Soph Cls; Aud/Vis; Band; Chrh Wkr; Hon Rl; NHS; Pres Stu Cncl; Andrews Univ; Physics.

WARD, ELIZABETH; Pine River Jr Sr HS; Tustin, MI; 1/109 Band; Chrs; Chrh Wkr; Hon Rl; Natl Forn Lg; NHS; Orch; Sch Mus; Stu Cncl; 4-H; Grand Rapids Baptist Univ.

WARD, GREG; Buchanan HS; Niles, MI; Chrs; Hon Rl; VP NHS; Off Ade; 4-H; Bsbl; Wrstlng; Coach Actv; 4-H Awd; Chosen To Attend Oper Enterprise 79; Most Valuable Frsh Wrst Vrsty 77; Univ; Dent.

WARD, J; Beal City HS; Weidman, MI; 1/65 Cl Rep Jr Cls; Band; Hon Rl; Stu Cncl; Sci Clb; Spn Clb; Bsktbl; College; Law.

WARD, JACQUELINE; Stivers Patterson HS; Dayton, OH; 17/500 Band; Chrh Wkr; Girl Scts; Hon Rl; NHS; Boys Clb Am; VICA; Univ.

WARD, JANIE; Pibeton HS; Lucasville, OH; Hon Rl; Off Ade; OEA;.

WARD, JOHN; Tippecanoe Valley HS; Claypool, IN; Hon Rl; Ger Clb; Letter Ftbl; Letter Wrstlng; Congrsnl Nominee To West Point & Annapolis 79; Whos Who Among Amer HS Stu 77; Purdue Univ; Poli Sci.

WARD, KATHY; Jimtown HS; Elkhart, IN; 14/100 Pres Band; Drm Mjrt; Hon Rl; Fr Clb; Pep Clb; Trk; Mat Maids; Scr Kpr; Spirit Of Jr Miss Elkhart Jr Miss Pageant; 1st Solo Contest; MVP Awd Band; Notre Dame Univ; Music.

WARD, KELLEY; Owosso HS; Owosso, MI; 68/406 Band; Chrs; NHS; Lat Clb; GAA; St Of Mi Comp Schlrshp Cert Of Recntn 79; Solo & Ensemble 1st & 2nd Div Rating Medals 76 79; Michigan St Univ; Soc Work.

WARD, KELLY; Colon HS; Colon, MI; Cls Rep Soph Cls; Trs Sr Cls; Am Leg Aux Girls St; Girl Scts; Hon Rl; Lbry Ade; Stu Cncl; Fr Clb; Pep Clb; Bsktbl; College.

WARD, KENDRA; North Gallia HS; Bidwell, OH; 6/35 Band; Chrs; Hon Rl; Off Ade; Sch Pl; Stu Cncl; Drama Clb; 4-H; Chrldng; GAA; Rio Grande Univ; Elem Ed.

WARD, KENNETH; Chanel HS; Northfield, OH; 10/115 Aud/Vis; Hon Rl; Jr NHS; NHS; Stu Cncl; Rptr Yrbk; Sch Nwsp; Bsktbl; Ftbl; IM Sprt; Bowling Green State Univ; Communicat.

WARD, KRISTEL; Mohawk HS; Sycamore, OH; 3/126 Band; Chrs; Hon Rl; NHS; Ed Yrbk; Pres 4-H; Lat Clb; Univ Of Toledo; Pre Med.

WARD, LISA; Onekama HS; Onekama, MI; Pres Frsh Cls; Cls Rep Soph Cls; Cl Rep Jr Cls; Band; Chrh Wkr; Hon Rl; Lbry Ade; Sch Mus; Sch Pl; Yth Flsp; Central Michigan Univ; Psych.

WARD, MARY; Penn HS; Osceola, IN; Cmp Fr Grls; Hon Rl; JA; NHS; Off Ade; Ger Clb; College; Bus Admin.

WARD, MICHAEL; Scecina Memorial HS; Indianapolis, IN; 77/194 IM Sprt; Ball St Univ; Law.

WARD, MICHAEL; Padua Franciscan HS; Parma, OH; Hon Rl; VP NHS; Red Cr Ade; Key Clb; Coach Actv; IM Sprt; Pres Awd; John Carroll Univ; Bus Mgmt.

WARD, MICHAEL A; Clawson HS; Clawson, MI; Hon Rl; NHS; Ftbl; Socr; Bausch & Lomb Awd; DAR Awd; Natl Merit Schl; Univ Of Mic; Chem.

WARD, NADINE; Groveport Madison HS; Groveport, OH; Cls Rep Soph Cls; FCA; Y-Teens; Spn Clb; Bsbl; Swmmng; Coll; Legal Sec.

WARD, NANCY; Romulus Sr HS; Romulus, MI; Band; Hon Rl; Stu Cncl; Fr Clb; Spn Clb; Eastern Michigan Univ; Speech Ther.

WARD, PAMELA; Clarence M Kimball HS; Royal Oak, MI; Band; Hon Rl; NHS; Drama Clb; Pep Clb; PPFtbl; College; Med.

WARD, QUENTIN; Maple Valley HS; Nashville, MI; 32/120 Hon Rl; Letter Ftbl; Letter Trk; Coach Actv; PPFtbl; Ferris St Coll; Deisel Mech.

WARD, REBECCA; Clay HS; Oregon, OH; 15/360 Chrh Wkr; FCA; Hon Rl; Jr NHS; NHS; Bsktbl; Trk; Bowling Green St Univ.

WARD, REBECCA; Ionia HS; Ionia, MI; 62/275 Band; Hon Rl; Rptr Yrbk; Rptr Sch Nwsp; Davenport Coll Of Bus; Legal Sec.

WARD, RENAE M; Marysville HS; Marysville, MI; Am Leg Aux Girls St; Band; Girl Scts; Hon Rl; Hst Frsh Cls; X Ray Tech.

WARD, RENEE; Bishop Luers HS; Ft Wayne, IN; Cls Rep Frsh Cls; Cls Rep Soph Cls; Cl Rep Jr Cls; Chrs; Hon Rl; Sch Pl; Stu Cncl; Drama Clb; Fr Clb; Letter Ten; Ariz State; Criminal Law.

WARD, ROBIN; Shady Spring HS; Glen Morgan, WV; Band; Chrh Wkr; FCA; Girl Scts; Hon Rl; NHS; Sch Pl; 4-H; FHA; Pep Clb; Home Ec Awd; Hmcmng Attendant; 3rd Pl Danc A Thon Muscular Dystrophy; Virginia Poli Inst; Interior Design.

WARD, SCOTT; Watkins Mem HS; Pataskala, OH; Hon Rl; Rptr Yrbk; Mem Of Schlrshp Team In Algebra I; Vocational Schl; Comp Tech.

WARD, SHAYNE; Andrews Acad; Berrien Springs, MI; Pres Jr Cls; Aud/Vis; Band; Chrs; Chrh Wkr; Cmnty Wkr; Lbry Ade; Sch Pl; Avondale Coll; Nurse.

WARD, SHERYLL; Shakamak HS; Jasonville, IN; 15/86 Band; Hon Rl; NHS; DECA; Letter Bsktbl; Coach Actv; Mgrs; Ind State Univ; Physical Ed.

WARD, STEPHANIE C; William A Wirt HS; Gary, IN; 51/230 Band; Chrh Wkr; Cmnty Wkr; Drm Mjrt; Hon Rl; Pres JA; Lbry Ade; Pol Wkr; ROTC; Sch Mus; Cert Of Merit For Outstanding Ach; Tobe Coburn Fash Schl; Fash Merch.

WARD, SUSAN; Sylvania Southview HS; Sylvania, OH; 28/296 Cl Rep Jr Cls; Cls Rep Sr Cls; Drl Tm;

Hon Rl; Quill & Scroll; Sch Pl; Ed Yrbk; Pep Clb; PPFtbl; C of C Awd; Wittenberg Univ; Sociology.

WARD, TAMALA; Orchard View HS; Muskegon, MI; Hon Rl; Mat Maids; Scr Kpr; Business School; Acctg.

WARD, TAMMY; Potterville HS; Potterville, MI; 6/67 Band; Ed Yrbk; Rptr Yrbk; Ger Clb; Crs Cntry; Chrldng; Mgrs; PPFtbl; Business Schl; Legal Sec.

WARD, TERRI; Orchard View HS; Muskegon, MI; Chrs; Hon Rl; NHS; Off Ade; Chrldng; Cit Awd; Muskegon Comm; Dental Assist.

WARD, THERON; Sidney HS; Sidney, OH; VP Jr Cls; Band; Boy Scts; Debate Tm; Hon Rl; NHS; Stu Cncl; Yth Flsp; Coll; Chem Engr.

WARD, TINNIE; Admiral King HS; Lorain, OH; Cls Rep Soph Cls; Cl Rep Jr Cls; Off Ade; Stu Cncl; DECA; FHA; Letter Ten; Mgrs; Ohio St Univ; Data Proc.

WARDEINER, LISA; Euclid HS; Euclid, OH; 77/747 Chrs; Chrh Wkr; Cmnty Wkr; Hon Rl; NHS; Off Ade; Ed Sch Nwsp; GAA; IM Sprt; Mgrs; John Carroll Univ; Bus Mgmt.

WARDELL, LINDA; East Lansing HS; East Lansing, MI; 103/352 Band; Chrh Wkr; Cmnty Wkr; Girl Scts; NHS; Spn Clb; Mich State Univ; Engr.

WARDEN, CYNTHIA; Southern HS; Racine, OH; Cls Rep Soph Cls; Cl Rep Jr Cls; Band; Chrs; Sch Mus; Stu Cncl; Mth Clb; Pep Clb; Chrldng; Twrlr; Univ.

WARDEN, JANICE; Rutherford B Hayes HS; Delaware, OH; Chrs; JA; Off Ade; Pres Y-Teens; 4-H; FTA; Pep Clb; Swmmng; Chrldng; IM Sprt; Girls Sftbl 3 Vrsty Lttr 77; Girls Vllybl 1 Reserve Lttr 78; Univ Of Cincinnati.

WARDLAW, LYNNE; Owen Vly HS; Spencer, IN; Quill & Scroll; Sch Mus; Stg Crw; Sch Nwsp; VP Drama Clb; Fr Clb; Glf; Indiana Univ; Sci.

WARDLE, DUANE; Brownsburg HS; Brownsburg, IN; 4/317 Band; Hon Rl; JA; Orch; Ger Clb; Spn Clb; Bsbl; Bsktbl; 6th Pl In St Math Contest 76; Rose Hulman Inst Of Tech; Nuclear.

WARDLE, LYNN; Woodrow Wilson HS; Youngstwn, OH; 50/321 Hon Rl; Off Ade; Red Cr Ade; Sdlty; Y-Teens; Keyettes; Pep Clb; Voc Schl; Radiologic Tech.

WARDLE, MICHAEL; East Canton HS; E Canton, OH; 17/108 Am Leg Boys St; Band; Boy Scts; Chrh Wkr; Cmnty Wkr; Hon Rl; VP Jr NHS; Mt Union College; Bus.

WARDLOW, SALLY; Walnut Ridge HS; Columbus, OH; Cls Rep Frsh Cls; Chrs; Chrh Wkr; Girl Scts; Hon Rl; Sch Mus; Stu Cncl; Drama Clb; Pep Clb; Spn Clb; Ohio St Univ; Bus Admin.

WARDOWSKI, DEBORAH; Bishop Foley HS; Warren, MI; 22/193 VP Sr Cls; Chrs; Hon Rl; NHS; VP Stu Cncl; Rptr Yrbk; Rptr Sch Nwsp; Letter Trk; Coach Actv; PPFtbl; Mercy Coll; Nursing.

WARE, ALICE J; Amelia HS; Cincinnati, OH; Cls Rep Frsh Cls; Girl Scts; Stu Cncl; Pres FHA; Univ Of Tex; Welding.

WARE, CYNTHIA; Cass City HS; Cass City, MI; 2/149 Sec Jr Cls; VP Sr Cls; Sal; Chrs; Drl Tm; Hon Rl; Jr NHS; NHS; Off Ade; Yth Flsp; Michigan St Univ; Sci.

WARE, DAVID; Central Preston Sr HS; Kingwood, WV; 2/167 VP Jr Cls; Pres Sr Cls; Am Leg Boys St; Boy Scts; Hon Rl; NHS; Pres Mth Clb; Ftbl; Letter Trk; IM Sprt; Prof Awd From MAA & Soc Of Actuaries 78; 5th Pl In WV St Math Field Day 78; 1st Pl In CPSHS In ATPAC; MIT; Math.

WARE, DAVID; Berea HS; Berea, OH; Letter Ftbl; Univ; Elec Engr.

WARE, LATRICE L; Redford HS; Detroit, MI; Cmnty Wkr; Hon Rl; Off Ade; FBLA; FHA; FTA; Mth Clb; Pep Clb; Coll; Busns.

WARE, SHERYL; Buckhannon Upshur HS; Buckhannon, WV; Chrs; Cmnty Wkr; Girl Scts; Hon Rl; Lbry Ade; NHS; Sch Mus; Sch Pl; Stg Crw; Y-Teens; Glenville St Univ; Sec.

WARFEL, HEIDI; Paul Harding HS; Ft Wayne, IN; Hon Rl; Mdrgl; NHS; Rptr Sch Nwsp; Drama Clb; 4-H Awd; Indiana Univ; Sing.

WARFIELD, ANTHONY A; Arsenal Tech HS; Indianapolis, IN; 3/676 Cl Rep Jr Cls; Cls Rep Sr Cls; Boy Scts; Hon Rl; Sct Actv; Stu Cncl; Rptr Sch Nwsp; Sci Clb; Spn Clb; Wrstlng; Eagle Scout Rank; Honor Carrier Awd From Indianapolis Star; Honor Stu Awd; Purdue Univ; Comp Sci.

WARFIELD, PAMELA; Perrysburg HS; Perrysburg, OH; 21/247 Cl Rep Jr Cls; Cls Rep Sr Cls; Chrs; Chrh Wkr; Cmnty Wkr; Hon Rl; Hosp Ade; Jr NHS; NHS; College; Lang.

WARGO, BETH; Fairview HS; Fairview Pk, OH; 53/286 AFS; Aud/Vis; Chrh Wkr; Hon Rl; Lbry Ade; Off Ade; Gym; Swmmng; Chrldng; Pres Awd; V P Of Fairviews Synchronette Tm 79; Miami Univ; Sci.

WARGO, ROBYN; Bay Village HS; Bay Vill, OH; Cmp Fr Grls; Hon Rl; Letter Crs Cntry; Letter Trk; IM Sprt; Univ; Agri.

WARK, SHARON; Ferndale HS; Ferndale, MI; 26/425 Hon Rl; PAVAS; College.

WARLEY, TANYA L; John F Kennedy HS; Cleveland, OH; Cls Rep Frsh Cls; Cls Rep Soph Cls; Cl Rep Jr Cls; Cls Rep Sr Cls; Cmp Fr Grls; Drl Tm; Girl Scts; Orch; DECA; FTA; Merit Roll; Coll; Fshn Mdse.

WARMOTH, MARY; Bishop Fenwick HS; Franklin, OH; Capt Band; Chrh Wkr; Hon Rl; Hosp Ade; VP JA; Mgrs; JA Awd; Dale Carnegie Schlrshp 1979; Univ; Corp Acctg.

WARMOUTH, MIKE; Madeira HS; Madeira, OH; 15/165 Chrh Wkr; Cmnty Wkr; Hon Rl; Letter Bsbl; Letter Bsktbl; Letter Glf; Coach Actv; Scr Kpr; Miami Univ; Bus.

WARNCKE, RORY; Fairview HS; Ney, OH; Am Leg Boys St; Hon Rl; NHS; Stu Cncl; Spn Clb; Glf; College; Arch.

WARNCKE, TIM; Pike Delta York Sr HS; Delta, OH; 6/140 Chrs; NHS; Rptr Yrbk; Rptr Sch Nwsp; Pres 4-H; VP Fr Clb; FTA; Bsktbl; Letter Ftbl; Letter Trk; Bowling Green St Univ; Finance.

WARNE, LORI; Cambridge HS; Cambridge, OH; Cl Rep Jr Cls; Hon Rl; Hosp Ade; NHS; Sec 4-H; Bsktbl; Trk; Mgrs; C of C Awd; 4-H Awd; Ohio Univ; Bus Admin.

WARNE, SHELLEY; Marcellus HS; Vandalia, MI; Trs Frsh Cls; Cls Rep Frsh Cls; Hon Rl; Lbry Ade; VP NHS; Treas Stu Cncl; Bsktbl; Trk; Twrlr; Voice Dem Awd; Top Salesperson Jr Cls Mag Sales 79; Univ; Eng.

WARNECK, CINDY; Barrackville HS; Fairmont, WV; Pres Jr Cls; Band; Hon Rl; NHS; Stu Cncl; Rptr Yrbk; Rptr Sch Nwsp; Chrldng; IM Sprt; Fairmont State Univ; Elem Educ.

WARNECKE, DARLENE; Lincolnview HS; Van Wert, OH; 2/81 Sec Jr Cls; Trs Sr Cls; Am Leg Aux Girls St; Chrs; Lbry Ade; NHS; Off Ade; Sch Mus; Sch Pl; Stg Crw; Ohio Northern Univ; Acctg.

WARNECKE, DELLA; Lincolnview HS; Van Wert, OH; Band; Sch Mus; Stg Crw; Yth Flsp; Letter Bsktbl; Letter Trk; Chrldng; GAA; Scr Kpr; College; Business Admin.

WARNEMENT, JULIE; Sturgis HS; Sturgis, MI; Band; Hon Rl; Jr NHS; NHS; Rptr Yrbk; Pep Clb; Letter Gym; Chrldng; Siena Heights Coll; Eng.

WARNER, ANITA; Circleville HS; Riverton, WV; 2/27 Chrs; Hon Rl; Hosp Ade; Sch Pl; Rptr Sch Nwsp; Pep Clb; VICA; Shepherdstown Univ; Nursing.

WARNER, BRETT; Pike Central HS; Petersburg, IN; Chrh Wkr; FCA; Hon Rl; NHS; Yth Flsp; Rptr Sch Nwsp; Bsktbl; Letter Trk; Univ; Sci.

WARNER, CAROLYN; Covington HS; Covington, OH; 10/98 Am Leg Aux Girls St; Chrh Wkr; Cmnty Wkr; Hon Rl; Hosp Ade; NHS; Off Ade; Sch Mus; Sch Pl; Stu Cncl; FHA Most Improved Player; FHA Schlrshp Awd; All Ohio Youth Vocational Conf Delegate; College; Speech & Hearing Therapy.

WARNER, CATHY; Arthur Hill HS; Saginaw, MI; Hon Rl; Natl Merit SF; Saginaw Vly St Coll; Elem Ed.

WARNER, CINDY L; Western Hills HS; Cincinnati, OH; Chrh Wkr; Drl Tm; Girl Scts; Hon Rl; Off Ade; Sch Pl; Sct Actv; Stg Crw; Stu Cncl; DECA; Miss DECA Western Hills; Miss DECA Dist 24; Advertising Series Event 2nd Pl;.

WARNER, DANITA; Ida HS; Petersbrg, MI; Aud/Vis; Hosp Ade; 4-H; Pep Clb; Letter Trk; Scr Kpr; 4-H Awd; St Vincent College; Nrse.

WARNER, EDWARD; Mohawk HS; Mccutchnvl, OH; Band; Chrs; Hon Rl; Lit Mag; NHS; Orch; Sch Mus; Sch Pl; Stu Cncl; Bliss Bus College; Acctg.

WARNER, GEORGE T; Lynchburg Clay HS; Lynchburg, OH; Rptr Sch Nwsp; Sch Nwsp; Pep Clb; Spn Clb; Letter Bsbl; Letter Bsktbl; Letter Crs Cntry;.

WARNER, GINA M; Flushing Sr HS; Flushing, MI; Band; Hon Rl; Orch; Sec Yth Flsp; Fr Clb; Pep Clb; Coll; Music.

WARNER, GREGORY; Liberty HS; Clarksburg, WV; Cl Rep Jr Cls; Cls Rep Sr Cls; Chrh Wkr; Hon Rl; Drama Clb; Mth Clb; Bsbl; Ftbl; Wv University.

WARNER, JEFFREY; Memorial HS; St Marys, OH; 1/224 Hon Rl; NHS; Sch Pl; Stg Crw; Drama Clb; Sci Clb; Crs Cntry; Letter Trk; Natl Merit Schl; Miami Univ; Geol.

WARNER, JOHN; Whitehall HS; Whitehall, MI; Band; Hon Rl; Yth Flsp; Yrbk; Sch Nwsp; Ger Clb; Crs Cntry; Trk; Yearbook Awd 78; Rochester Inst Of Tech; Photo Sci.

WARNER, KEN; Cambridge HS; Cambridge, OH; Cl Rep Jr Cls; Band; Hon Rl; NHS; 4-H; Bsbl; IM Sprt; 4-H Awd; College; Bus Admin.

WARNER, KENDALE; Brownstown Central HS; Seymour, IN; Chrs; Hon Rl; 4-H; Spn Clb; Bsbl; Letter Trk; IM Sprt; 4-H Awd; Elec Training.

WARNER, KEVIN; Wapakoneta Sr HS; Wapakoneta, OH; Chrs; Bsbl; Ohio St Univ; Pharm.

WARNER, KIM; Gahanna Lincoln HS; Gahanna, OH; Chrs; Cmnty Wkr; Drl Tm; Hon Rl; Off Ade; Yrbk; Pep Clb; Bsbl; Pom Pon; PPFtbl; Ohio St Univ; Fashion Mdse.

WARNER, KIMBERLY; Meigs HS; Pomeroy, OH; Cls Rep Frsh Cls; Trs Soph Cls; Band; Drl Tm; Hon Rl; NHS; Stg Crw; Rptr Yrbk; 4-H; Fr Clb; Univ; Acctg.

WARNER, LISA; Johnstown Monroe HS; Johnstown, OH; 1/141 Pres Band; Chrh Wkr; Hon Rl; NHS; Off Ade; Yth Flsp; 4-H; Pep Clb; Spn Clb; 4-H Awd; Bowling Green Univ; Spec Educ.

WARNER, PATRICIA; Harrison HS; Evansville, IN; Hon Rl; Pom Pon; PPFtbl; Cit Awd; College; Med.

WARNER, SANDRA; Covington HS; Covington, OH; 2/97 Trs Jr Cls; Trs Sr Cls; Sal; Am Leg Aux Girls St; Chrh Wkr; Cmnty Wkr; Hon Rl; Hosp Ade; NHS; Off Ade; Coll Of Mt St Joseph; Nursing.

WARNER, SARA; Arthur Hill HS; Saginaw, MI; Hon Rl; NHS; Michigan St Univ; Med.

WARNER, TERESA M; Hartland Consolidated HS; Howell, MI; 10/200 Girl Scts; Hon Rl; Off Ade; DECA; Busns Schl; Acctg.

WARNER, VICKI; Dekalb HS; Hudson, IN; 61/292 Chrh Wkr; FCA; NHS; Yth Flsp; Letter Mgrs; PPFtbl; Scr Kpr;.

WARNICK, BARBARA; Elk Garden HS; Elk Garden, WV; 2/21 Sec Frsh Cls; Trs Frsh Cls; Sal; Hon Rl; Sch Pl; Rptr Yrbk; Emerson Self Reliance Awd 79; Homecoming Queen 79; Potomac St Coll; Sec Sci.

WARNIMONT, ROD; Cory Rawson HS; Mt Cory, OH; Cls Rep Soph Cls; Aud/Vis; Drm Bgl; Hon Rl; Rptr Yrbk; Sprt Ed Sch Nwsp; FFA; Lat Clb; Letter Ftbl; Letter Wrstlng; Ohio St Univ; Vet.

WARNKE, BARBARA; Fulton HS; St Johns, MI; 4/100 Band; Hon Rl; 4-H; Mth Clb; Letter Trk; M J Murphy Beauty Coll; Make Up Art.

WARNOCK, BRIAN; Lakeshore HS; Stevensville, MI; Hon Rl; NHS; Quill & Scroll; Sprt Ed Sch Nwsp; Key Clb; Bsbl; Crs Cntry; Ftbl; Central Michigan Univ; Jrnlsm.

WARNOCK, W; Nordonia HS; Northfield, OH; Bsbl; Crs Cntry; Trk; IM Sprt; Univ; Math.

WARNSMAN, STU; Southridge HS; Huntingburg, IN; Boy Scts; FCA; Yth Flsp; Ftbl; Letter Swmmng; Trk; Summer Hnrs Seminar Indiana St Univ 79; Univ; Marine Bio.

WARREN, CHARLENE; Little Miami HS; Morrow, OH; Pres Chrs; Drl Tm; Girl Scts; Hon Rl; Lit Mag; Sch Mus; Stg Crw; Stu Cncl; Rptr Yrbk; Spn Clb; Univ; Elem Educ.

WARREN, CYNTHIA; Cory Rawson HS; Bluffton, OH; 8/64 Pres Band; Chrs; Hon Rl; NHS; Sch Mus; Sch Pl; Stu Cncl; Sprt Ed Yrbk; Rptr Sch Nwsp; Pres 4-H; Ohio State Univ; Agri Communications.

WARREN, DANA; Thomas A De Vilbiss HS; Toledo, OH; 15/350 Band; Boy Scts; Hon Rl; NHS; Sch Mus; Pres Fr Clb; Univ Of Toledo; English.

WARREN, DEBI; Hamilton Taft HS; Lawrenceburg, IN; 377/450 Cls Rep Frsh Cls; Cls Rep Soph Cls; Cl Rep Jr Cls; Cls Rep Sr Cls; Aud/Vis; Band; Chrs; Chrs; Cmnty Wkr; Girl Scts; Temple Baptist Univ; Elem Educ.

WARREN, FRANKIE; West Side HS; Gary, IN; Chrh Wkr; Hon Rl; Jr NHS; NHS; Off Ade; Pres Fr Clb; Cit Awd; Purdue Univ; Comp Progr.

WARREN, JANICE; North Vermillion HS; Perrysville, IN; 14/59 Band; Chrs; Hon Rl; Stg Crw; 4-H; OEA; Danville Jr College; Accountant.

WARREN, JO; Fulton HS; Maple Rapids, MI; 7/95 Band; Drl Tm; Girl Scts; Hon Rl; Rptr Sch Nwsp; 4-H; Pom Pon; 4-H Awd; Lansing Comm College; Court Reportng.

WARREN, JOHN J; Margaretta HS; Castalia, OH; Pres Frsh Cls; VP Soph Cls; Cls Rep Soph Cls; Cl Rep Jr Cls; Cls Rep Sr Cls; Am Leg Boys St; Hon Rl; Lbry Ade; NHS; Stu Cncl; Bowling Green St Univ; Pre Law.

WARREN, LORI; New Albany HS; New Albany, IN; 60/565 Chrs; Hon Rl; Off Ade; Yrbk; Rptr Sch Nwsp; Sch Nwsp; Ger Clb; PPFtbl; Univ; Jrnlsm.

WARREN, LUANA; Lake Fenton HS; Linden, MI; 10/179 Trs Frsh Cls; Trs Soph Cls; Trs Jr Cls; Trs Sr Cls; Am Leg Aux Girls St; Band; Hon Rl; VP NHS; Stu Cncl; Pep Clb; Homecoming Qn Cand; Natl Honor Soc Schlrshp Alternate; Adrian Coll; Hosp Admin.

WARREN, MARIA; Iron Mountain Sr HS; Iron Mountain, MI; 27/157 Band; Hon Rl; Stg Crw; Rptr Sch Nwsp; Drama Clb; Pep Clb; Spn Clb; Ten; Natl Merit Schl; Michigan Tech Univ; Bus.

WARREN, MARK A; Woodhaven HS; Woodhaven, MI; Jr NHS; FDA; Ftbl; IM Sprt; Natl Merit SF; Univ Of Michigan; Pre Med.

WARREN, SCOTT; Rapid River HS; Rapid River, MI; 1/60 Pres Jr Cls; Trs Sr Cls; Am Leg Boys St; Hon Rl; Ftbl; Am Leg Awd; DAR Awd; Univ.

WARREN, SHAWN; Highland Park Cmnty HS; Highland Pk, MI; Band; Chrh Wkr; Hon Rl; NHS; Off Ade; Sch Pl; Stu Cncl; Drama Clb; Natl Merit Ltr; Michigan St Univ; Med.

WARREN, SUSAN; Ovid Elsie HS; Ovid, MI; Chrh Wkr; Hon Rl; Off Ade; Yth Flsp; Ed Sch Nwsp; 4-H; Pep Clb; Chrldng; PPFtbl; 4-H Awd; Lansing Comm Coll.

WARREN, TERRI; Galien HS; Buchanan, MI; 1/65 Pres Frsh Cls; Pres Soph Cls; Cl Rep Jr Cls; Hon Rl; NHS; Sch Pl; Treas Stu Cncl; Yrbk; Ed Sch Nwsp; FHA; Univ.

WARREN, TRINKA M; Defiance HS; Defiance, OH; Chrs; Girl Scts; Hon Rl; JA; Stg Crw; Fr Clb; Trk; Tmr; Elk Awd; JETS Awd; College; Sec.

WARRICK, ROBIN; Mineral Ridge HS; Mineral Ridge, OH; Cmp Fr Grls; Hon Rl; JA; Off Ade; Stg Crw; Yrbk; Sch Nwsp; PPFtbl; Schlrshp Team; General Sci Awd; College; Art.

WARROW, SUSAN; Riverview Community HS; Riverview, MI; 54/250 Band; JA; Jr NHS; Sch Nwsp; Drama Clb; Sec Fr Clb; FTA; Sec Spn Clb; Wayne State Univ; Physiotherapist.

WARROW, TIMOTHY G; North Farmington HS; Farmington Hill, MI; Boy Scts; Cmnty Wkr; Hon Rl; Yth Flsp; Ftbl; Trk; Wrstlng; Coach Actv; Scr Kpr; Tmr; Univ; Engr.

WARSHAWSKY, SUSAN; S Haven HS; South Haven, MI; 1/260 Cl Rep Jr Cls; Chrs; Hon Rl; Treas NHS; Sch Mus; Stg Crw; Pep Clb; Ten; Univ Of Michigan; Busns.

WARSON, GARY; Kearsley HS; Davison, MI; Hon Rl; Bsbl; Univ; Psych.

WARTLUFT, JANET; West Branch HS; Alliance, OH; 32/240 Band; Chrs; Chrh Wkr; Hon Rl; NHS; OEA; Capt Bsktbl; Scr Kpr; Bus Schl; Sec.

WARWICK, WAYNE; Highland Sparta HS; Mt Gilead, OH; 13/125 FCA; NHS; Sch Nwsp; Bsbl; Bsktbl; Crs Cntry; Univ; Jrnlsm.

WASCH, ALLAN; Norton HS; Clinton, OH; Debate Tm; JA; Jr NHS; Ed Sch Nwsp; Lat Clb; Crs Cntry; Trk; Cit Awd; JA Awd; Bio Chem.

WASH, ANNA M; Notre Dame HS; Clarksburg, WV; 8/59 Chrs; Chrh Wkr; Hon Rl; FNA; Keyettes; Pep Clb; Chrldng; West Virginia Univ; Music.

WASH, GLENNDA M; Our Lady Of Mercy HS; Detroit, MI; Cls Rep Frsh Cls; Chrs; Hon Rl; Lbry Ade; Stg Crw; IM Sprt; College; Pre Dent.

WASH, LARRY G; Shrine HS; Oak Park, MI; 5/183 Cls Rep Soph Cls; Trs Jr Cls; Aud/Vis; NHS; Ed Yrbk; Letter Trk; Coach Actv; Wayne St Univ; Elec Engr.

WASHAM, MARY; David Anderson HS; Lisbon, OH; 12/95 Band; Chrh Wkr; Hon Rl; Hosp Ade; Lbry Ade; Off Ade; NHS; Sch Mus; Y-Teens; Pep Clb; Sci Clb; Schlrshp From Kofc In Lisbon 78; Awd Of Distnctn Form Basic Educ 78; Kent St Univ; RN.

WASHBURN, JEFF; Ridgedale HS; Morral, OH; 10/103 Hon Rl; NHS; Quill & Scroll; Stu Cncl; Yrbk; Rptr Sch Nwsp; IM Sprt; College; Elec Engr.

WASHBURN, JIM; Jennings Co HS; Crothersville, IN; FFA; Univ; Auto Mech.

WASHBURN JR, WILLIAM; St Johns HS; St Johns, MI; Band; Boy Scts; Orch; Sch Mus; Sct Actv; Mgrs; Lion Awd; Michigan St Univ; Music.

WASHENITZ, JONI L; Rivesville HS; Rivesville, WV; Chrs; Hon Rl; Hosp Ade; NHS; Off Ade; Sch Mus; Rptr Sch Nwsp; Sci Clb; Letter Chrldng; GAA; All St Chorus 1977; Accompianist Awd 1977; West Virginia Univ; Pre Med.

WASHINGTON, ARETHIA; Muskegon Heights HS; Muskegon Ht, MI; Trs Frsh Cls; Cls Rep Frsh Cls; Cls Rep Soph Cls; Trs Jr Cls; Band; Chrs; Chrh Wkr; Mic State; Occupational Ther.

WASHINGTON, CYNTHIA; Willow Run HS; Ypsilanti, MI; Hon Rl; PAVAS; 4-H; Pep Clb; Chrldng; Coll; Fashion Merch.

WASHINGTON, EDITH; East HS; Columbus, OH; Hon Rl; Stu Cncl; Pep Clb; Spn Clb; Ten; Univ; Psych.

WASHINGTON, KAREN M; Belpre HS; Belpre, OH; Sec Jr Cls; Band; Chrs; Chrh Wkr; Girl Scts; Mdrgl; Sct Actv; Ohio Valley Coll; Elem Ed.

WASHINGTON, LILLIAN; Calumet HS; Gary, IN; 16/350 Hon Rl; Data Processing Art; Univ Of N Carolina; Data Processing.

WASHINGTON, ONITA; Roosevelt HS; Gary, IN; Chrs; Chrh Wkr; Hon Rl; JA; Mdrgl; College.

WASHINGTON, PAULA; St Ursula Acad; Cincinnati, OH; Cl Rep Jr Cls; Cmp Fr Grls; Chrh Wkr; Girl Scts; Hon Rl; Hosp Ade; JA; Sch Pl; Yth Flsp; College; Med.

WASHINGTON, SHARON; Calumet HS; Gary, IN; 91/293 Chrs; Chrh Wkr; Treas JA; Boys Clb Am; Spn Clb; JA Awd; Purdue Univ; Bus Mgmt.

WASHINGTON, SHIRLEY; Emerson HS; Gary, IN; 10/140 Chrh Wkr; Hon Rl; JA; Lbry Ade; ROTC; Spn Clb; Cit Awd; Indiana Voc Tech Schl; Nursing.

WASHINGTON, VANESSA; Kingswood HS; Detroit, MI; Girl Scts; Hon Rl; Sch Mus; Mgrs; Scr Kpr; Univ.

WASHINGTON, VINCENT D; Kettering Sr HS; Detroit, MI; Cl Rep Jr Cls; Cls Rep Sr Cls; Hon Rl; Jr NHS; NHS; Stu Cncl; Eng Clb; Mth Clb; Bsktbl; Lawrence Tech; Carpentry.

WASIKOWSKI, MARK; Clay HS; S Bend, IN; 13/430 Boy Scts; Hon Rl; NHS; Sct Actv; Boys Clb Am; Ger Clb; Mth Clb; Bsbl; Letter Crs Cntry; Letter Ftbl; Purdue Univ; Engr.

WASILOFF, LISA; Madonna HS; Weirton, WV; Hon Rl; Lit Mag; Pep Clb; Pres Mat Maids; Scr Kpr; Tmr; Miss Weirton Bicentennial Ct; West Virginia Univ; Acctg.

WASINSKI, MICHAEL; Bishop Foley HS; Royal Oak, MI; Hon Rl; Lit Mag; NHS; Sch Mus; Sch Pl; Stg Crw; Rptr Sch Nwsp; Drama Clb; IM Sprt; Michigan St Univ.

WASKO, JACQUELYN; Campbell Memorial HS; Campbell, OH; 40/300 Cls Rep Frsh Cls; Cls Rep Soph Cls; VP Jr Cls; Cl Rep Jr Cls; Chrh Wkr; Cmnty Wkr; Hon Rl; Hosp Ade; JA; Lbry Ade; Ohio St Univ; Medicine.

WASOWSKI, KEVIN; John Adams HS; South Bend, IN; 36/381 VP Frsh Cls; Chrh Wkr; Hon Rl; NHS; Letter Bsbl; Letter Bsktbl; Capt Ftbl; PPFtbl; MVP Baseball; Arizona St Univ; Graphic Comm.

WASSERBAUER, THOMAS; St Edward HS; Lakewood, OH; 36/360 Hon Rl; Lit Mag; NHS; Key Clb; College; Bio.

WASSERMAN, ROSEMARY D; Delton Kellogg HS; Delton, MI; 12/126 VP Frsh Cls; Band; Hon Rl; Quill & Scroll; Ed Sch Nwsp; Rptr Sch Nwsp; OEA; Bsktbl; Trk; Chrldng; Mi Bus Schl Assoc Schlrshp 79; Ldrshp & Serv Awd Presntd By Delton Kellogg HS Faculty 79; Lansing Bus Inst; Acctg.

WASSERSTEIN, AELLA; Firestone HS; Akron, OH; 25/360 Chrh Wkr; Cmnty Wkr; Hon Rl; JA; Jr NHS; NHS; Off Ade; Yth Flsp; Yrbk; Pep Clb; Univ; Med.

WATERHOUSE, ROGER; Highland Park Community HS; Highland Pk, MI; Hon Rl; Sch Pl; Drama Clb; Letter Ftbl; Michigan St Univ.

WATERMAN, GARY; Farmington HS; Northville, MI; 3/450 Chrh Wkr; Hon Rl; Mth Clb; Bsbl; Qualified For St Of Mi Comp Schlrshp Prog 79; Partcptd In 11th Annual Sci Inst At Lawrence Tech 79; Univ; Comp Sci.

WATERN, JEFFERY; John H Patterson Co Op HS; Dayton, OH; Cls Rep Soph Cls; Hon Rl; NHS; VICA; Letter Crs Cntry; Letter Trk; Sinclair Comm Coll; Archt Tech.

WATERS, ALICE; Shady Spring HS; Shady Spring, WV; 25/155 Sec Frsh Cls; Pres Jr Cls; Chrs; Chrh Wkr; FCA; Hon Rl; Letter Ten; Capt Chrldng; Univ; Psych.

WATERS, CHRISTINE; Greenbrier East HS; Lewisburg, WV; Band; Chrh Wkr; FCA; Hon Rl; Off Ade; Yth Flsp; FHA; FTA; Letter Trk; Mas Awd; Marshall Univ; Business.

WATERS, GAYLEN; North Side HS; Ft Wayne, IN; 48/485 Chrs; Chrh Wkr; Hon Rl; NHS; Off Ade; Orch; Rptr Sch Nwsp; Sch Nwsp; DECA; Gym; Ft Wayne Bible Coll; Math.

WATERS, MARY; St Joseph Academy; Cleveland, OH; Hon Rl; NHS; Sch Mus; Sct Actv; Stu Cncl; Mth Clb; Bausch & Lomb Awd; Natl Merit SF; Baldwin Wallace Coll; Math.

WATERS, MICHAEL; Charles S Mott HS; Warren, MI; Cls Rep Frsh Cls; Cls Rep Sr Cls; Band; Ger Clb; Ftbl; IM Sprt; Aquinas Coll; Pre Med.

WATERS, MONICA; Servite HS; Detroit, MI; Hon Rl; JA; Univ Of Detroit.

WATERS, SCOTT; Tri Jr Sr HS; Straughn, IN; 7/82 Am Leg Boys St; Band; Chrh Wkr; Hon Rl; NHS; Yth Flsp; Ed Yrbk; Rptr Yrbk; Ed Sch Nwsp; Sprt Ed Sch Nwsp; Indiana Univ; Jrnlsm.

WATERS, TERESA; Frankfort Area Schools; Frankfort, MI; 2/78 Trs Frsh Cls; Trs Soph Cls; Trs Jr Cls; Trs Sr Cls; Band; Hon Rl; Sch Mus; Sch Pl; Pres Sci Clb; Letter Bsktbl; Grand Valley St Univ; Sci.

WATERSON, JULIE; Whitko HS; S Whitley, IN; FCA; Hon Rl; Stg Crw; Stu Cncl; Drama Clb; Pep Clb; Ten; De Pauw Univ; Acctg.

WATERWASH, RONALD; Northwestern HS; West Salem, OH; Trs Frsh Cls; Pres Soph Cls; Chrh Wkr; Sch Mus; Sch Pl; Stg Crw; Stu Cncl; Bsbl; Glf; Chrldng; Coll; Educ.

WATHEN, PATRICIA; Warren Woods HS; Warren, MI; 53/350 Chrh Wkr; FCA; Girl Scts; Hon Rl; Jr NHS; NHS; Bsbl; Bsktbl; IM Sprt; Mgrs; Mi Comp Schlrshp 79; Mbr Of St John & Paul Champ Bsktbl Tm 78; Varsity Letter In Girls Vllybl 77 & 79; Ferris St Coll; Dent Hygiene.

WATKINS, ALICIA; West Preston Sr HS; Newburg, WV; Band; Hon Rl; NHS; Rptr Yrbk; Pep Clb; VICA; Capt Chrldng; IM Sprt; West Virginia Univ.

WATKINS, ANN; Highland HS; Medina, OH; Chrs; Hon Rl; Sch Mus; Stu Cncl; Trk; JC Awd; Natl Merit Ltr; YFU; Internat Bus.

WATKINS, CHARISSA; Washington HS; Massillon, OH; Chrh Wkr; Girl Scts; Hon Rl; Hosp Ade; Lbry Ade; DECA; FHA;.

WATKINS, CHERYL J; South HS; Youngstown, OH; 9/327 Hosp Ade; Lbry Ade; Off Ade; Trk; IM Sprt; Pom Pon; Business School; Accounting.

WATKINS, DAVID; Wintersville HS; Steubenville, OH; 51/267 Cls Rep Frsh Cls; Cls Rep Soph Cls; Band; Fr Clb; Kent State Univ.

WATKINS, ERAINA R; Pittsford HS; Pittsford, MI; Band; Girl Scts; Lbry Ade; Stg Crw; Yrbk; 4-H; FFA; Letter Bsbl; Letter Hndbl; IM Sprt; Mich State Univ.

WATKINS, ERICA; Timken Sr HS; Canton, OH; Cls Rep Frsh Cls; Am Leg Aux Girls St; Band; Hon Rl; Sch Pl; Pep Clb; Spn Clb; IM Sprt; HS Hon Schlstc Awrd 78; HS Hon Schlstc Awrd 79; Univ; Chem Engr.

WATKINS, KAREN; Rogers HS; La Porte, IN; 56/500 Cls Rep Soph Cls; Cl Rep Jr Cls; Cls Rep Sr Cls; Chrs; Hon Rl; NHS; Rptr Yrbk; Pres Ger Clb; Pep Clb; Sci Clb; Purdue Univ; Comp Tech.

WATKINS, LISA; Stephen T Badin HS; Hamilton, OH; Band; Chrs; Drl Tm; Drm Mjrt; Hon Rl; Rptr Yrbk; DECA; Pep Clb; 2nd VP Of Distributive Ed Class 78; Ohio Univ; Soc Wrk.

WATKINS, MICHAEL; Chillicothe HS; Chillicothe, OH; 21/380 Am Leg Boys St; Band; Debate Tm; Hon Rl; Natl Forn Lg; NHS; Sct Actv; Stu Cncl; Yth Flsp; Sci Clb; Univ Of Cin; Arch.

WATKINS, PATRICK; Bangor HS; Bangor, MI; 19/98 VP Frsh Cls; Cls Rep Soph Cls; Chrh Wkr; Cmnty Wkr; FCA; Hon Rl; Stg Crw; Stu Cncl; Sch Nwsp; Key Clb; Athlt Awd 79; Outstndng Stdnt Athlt 78; Olivet Coll; Sociology.

WATKINS, PEGGY; Edgewood Sr HS; Ashtabula, OH; 1/252 AFS; Chrs; Hon Rl; NHS; Sch Mus; Oh Acad Schlshp 79; Valedictorian 79; Miami Univ; Intl Bus.

WATKINS, SARAH; Sidney HS; Sidney, OH; Sec Jr Cls; Cls Rep Sr Cls; Band; Chrh Wkr; Hon Rl; NHS; Off Ade; Orch; Sch Pl; Stu Cncl; Univ; Pre Schl Educ.

WATKINS, STACY; Beecher HS; Flint, MI; Band; Hon Rl; JA; Sch Mus; Univ; Music.

WATKINS, TROY; Huntington North HS; Huntington, IN; Cl Rep Jr Cls; Sch Mus; Yth Flsp; Fr Clb; Ball State Univ; Elem Educ.

WATSON, BARBARA J; Fairfield Union HS; Pleasantville, OH; 19/147 Drl Tm; Hon Rl; Rptr Yrbk; Rptr Sch Nwsp; 4-H; FHA; FTA; Bus Schl; Sec.

WATSON, BETH; Westerville North HS; Westerville, OH; 11/340 Cls Rep Soph Cls; Cl Rep Jr Cls; Chrs; Drl Tm; Girl Scts; Hon Rl; NHS; Sch Mus; Sch Pl; Stg Crw; College.

WATSON, CARMEN; Jonesville HS; Allen, MI; Band; Chrs; Chrh Wkr; Girl Scts; Hon Rl; JA; Yth Flsp; Ed Sch Nwsp; Rptr Sch Nwsp; Sch Nwsp; Univ; Fshn Dsgn.

WATSON, CHARLES; Edward Drummond Libbey HS; Toledo, OH; Hon Rl; JA; NHS; Sct Actv; Yrbk; Boys Clb Am; Treas Pep Clb; Cit Awd; Moorehouse; Pre Med.

WATSON, DARLENE; Celina Sr HS; Celina, OH; Hon Rl; NHS; Treas FHA; Lat Clb; Univ; Comp Sci.

WATSON, DENISE; Kent City HS; Kent City, MI; 28/95 Band; Chrh Wkr; Hon Rl; Off Ade; Yth Flsp; Ed Yrbk; Rptr Yrbk; 4-H; Trk; PPFtbl; Grand Rapids Bapt Coll; Religion.

WATSON, DONNA; North Marion HS; Monongah, WV; Chrs; Hon Rl; Fr Clb; Fairmont State College; Speech Ed.

WATSON, JEFF; Ellet HS; Akron, OH; 1/399 Hon Rl; Jr NHS; NHS; Ger Clb; Lat Clb; Letter Bsktbl; Letter Crs Cntry; Trk; Akron Univ; Engr.

WATSON, JODI; Marshall HS; Marshall, MI; 21/258 Chrs; Chrh Wkr; Cmnty Wkr; Hon Rl; JA; NHS; Yth Flsp; GAA; IM Sprt; Mgrs; Adrian Coll; Art.

WATSON, JULIE; Clay HS; S Bend, IN; 153/416 Hon Rl; Off Ade; Rptr Sch Nwsp; 4-H Awd; Past Worthy Advisor Internatl Order Rainbow For Girls 79; Article In Horse Of Course Mag; Barrel Racing Awd; New Mexico St Univ; Jrnlsm.

WATSON, K; Kalkaska Public HS; Kalkaska, MI; 7/135 Lit Mag; NHS; Quill & Scroll; Ed Yrbk; Rptr Sch Nwsp; Sch Nwsp; Letter Crs Cntry; Letter Trk; 4-H Awd; College; Dent.

WATSON, KAREN; East Detroit HS; E Detroit, MI; Band; Girl Scts; Hon Rl; NHS; Swmmng; Letter Trk; Letter Mgrs; Mich State; Vet.

WATSON, KIM; Fowlerville HS; Gregory, MI; Hon Rl; Sch Pl; Sprt Ed Yrbk; Rptr Yrbk; Spn Clb; Trk; Letter Chrldng; PPFtbl; Merrill Fshn Inst; Fshn Mdse.

WATSON, LISA; Carroll HS; Cutler, IN; 10/100 Chrs; Hon Rl; Jr NHS; NHS; 4-H; Fr Clb; Mth Clb; Pep Clb; Swmmng; Tmr; Purdue Univ; Engr.

WATSON, LYN; Lakeview HS; Battle Creek, MI; Chrs; Hon Rl; NHS; Off Ade; Stg Crw; Pres Pep Clb; Capt Chrldng; Capt IM Sprt; Mat Maids; PPFtbl; Camp Fire Awrd Crtfct Of Apprectn 77; Central Michigan Univ; Psych.

WATSON, MARGARET; Zanesville HS; Zanesville, OH; Aud/Vis; Band; Hon Rl; NHS; Rptr Sch Nwsp; Drama Clb; 4-H; Chrldng; 3.5 Club 79; News Dir Schl Radio 79; Ohio Univ; Bus Admin.

WATSON, MARK D; St Xavier HS; Bevis, OH; Boy Scts; Chrh Wkr; Hon Rl; Sct Actv; Rdo Clb; Knights Of Columbus Schlrshp 76; Pres Schlrshp 79; Ad Alatari Del Awd Boy Scouts Of Amer; Univ; Engr.

WATSON, MAX; Terre Haute North HS; Terre Haute, IN; Cls Rep Frsh Cls; Hon Rl; Boys Clb Am; Key Clb; Ftbl; Letter Glf; Ten; IM Sprt; College; Pre Law.

WATSON, MEG; Caldwell HS; Caldwell, OH; 5/109 Sec Sr Cls; Sec Band; Hon Rl; Sec NHS; Treas Stu Cncl; Pep Clb; Tmr; NCTE; Miami Univ; Med Tech.

WATSON, MICHAEL; Bishop Foley HS; Madison Hts, MI; Boy Scts; Debate Tm; Hon Rl; Sct Actv; IM Sprt; Univ; Acctg.

WATSON, PAMELA; John Glenn HS; Zanesville, OH; Chrs; Hon Rl; Off Ade; VP 4-H; Tech Schl; Sec Sci.

WATSON, REGINA; Ohio Hi Point JVS; North Lewisburg, OH; Sec Sr Cls; Chrs; Hon Rl; Orch; OEA; Gym; Trk; Ohio Hi Point JVS; Lgl Sec.

WATSON, REGINA A; Muncie Central HS; Muncie, IN; 5/350 Hon Rl; Lit Mag; VP NHS; Sch Pl; Sch Nwsp; Ger Clb; Sci Clb; Kiwan Awd; Natl Merit Ltr; Rotary Awd; Telluride Assoc Summr Progr Schlrshp 79; Tras Muncie Chptr ASTRA Clb 79; Ball St Univ Eng Achvmnt Awd 79; Univ; Lib Arts.

WATSON, ROBERT; Yale HS; Avoca, MI; Cls Rep Soph Cls; Cls Rep Sr Cls; Stu Cncl; Yth Flsp; Bsbl; Bsktbl; Ftbl; Univ; Forestry.

WATSON, ROBERT; Lake Orion HS; Pontiac, MI; Hon Rl; Bsbl; Bsktbl; Oakland Univ; Engr.

WATSON, ROBIN; Lakewood HS; Hebron, OH; Hon Rl; Bsktbl; Univ; Math.

WATSON, ROSALEE; Morrice HS; Morrice, MI; Cls Rep Frsh Cls; Hon Rl; Lbry Ade; Off Ade; Sch Pl; Stg Crw; Chrldng; Soc Work With Children.

WATSON, SUSAN; Eastern HS; Winchester, OH; Hon Rl; Stu Cncl; 4-H; Fr Clb; FFA; FHA; Pep Clb; 4-H Awd; Rep Both FFA & FHA Of Eastern HS At All Ohio Youth Conf 79; Southern St Coll; Sec.

WATSON, SUSAN J; Roosevelt Wilson HS; Stonewood, WV; Sec Frsh Cls; Trs Soph Cls; Trs Jr Cls; Hon Rl; Y-Teens; 4-H; Leo Clb; Trk; Chrldng; Grand Champ Awd ICF Cheerleading Camp; Perfect Attendance Since 3rd Grade; West Virginia Univ.

WATSON, TAMMI; Lincoln HS; Shinnston, WV; Sec Frsh Cls; Cl Rep Jr Cls; Hon Rl; NHS; Sch Pl; Stu Cncl; Drama Clb; Chrldng; Scr Kpr; Wva Univ; Pre Pharmacy.

WATSON, VIRGINIA; Coopersville Sr HS; Ravenna, MI; Band; NHS; Sch Pl; Pres Stu Cncl; 4-H; Letter Crs Cntry; Letter Trk; PPFtbl; Ctrl Michigan Univ; Secondary Ed.

WATT, JUDITH; Harrison HS; Harrison, MI; Lbry Ade; Yrbk; Trk; Mgrs; Tmr; Cit Awd; Mid Michigan Comm Coll; Sci.

WATT, KIMBERLY; Lake Shore HS; St Clair Shrs, MI; 51/688 Chrh Wkr; Hon Rl; Jr NHS; NHS; Michigan St Univ; Engr.

WATTERS, CHERYL; Sacred Heart Academy; Mt Pleasant, MI; Band; Chrs; Chrh Wkr; Cmnty Wkr; Hon Rl; NHS; Pep Clb; Crs Cntry; Trk; Michigan St Univ; Math.

WATTERS, MICHAEL; Jackson County Western HS; Jackson, MI; Boy Scts; Hon Rl; Sch Mus; Sct Actv; Spn Clb; IM Sprt; Michigan Tech Univ; Engr.

WATTERS, NEIL A; Leslie HS; Leslie, MI; Am Leg Boys St; Boy Scts; Chrs; Hon Rl; Bsbl; Bsktbl; Crs Cntry; Ftbl; Central Mic Univ; Educ.

WATTS, CONNIE; Austin HS; Austin, IN; 7/100 Sec 4-H; FTA; Pep Clb; Pres Spn Clb; Mgrs; 4-H Awd; Busns Schl; Med Sec.

WATTS, DICK; Maysville HS; So Zanesville, OH; Hon Rl; Letter Bsbl; Letter Ftbl; Trk; Univ; Aero Dynamics.

WATTS, GARY; Jackson HS; North Canton, OH; 152/409 Band; Chrh Wkr; Spn Clb; Univ Of Akron; Bus Mgmt.

WATTS, JON; Bryan HS; Bryan, OH; 21/183 Boy Scts; Chrh Wkr; Hon Rl; JA; NHS; VP Y-Teens; Lat Clb; Capt Bsbl; Bsktbl; Letter Ftbl; Adrian Coll; Dentistry.

WATTS, KATHY; Crooksville HS; Corning, OH; 8/94 Pres Sr Cls; Am Leg Aux Girls St; Chrh Wkr; Hon Rl; NHS; Sch Pl; Ed Yrbk; Yrbk; 4-H; Bus & Prof Wmns Awd 79; Ohio Univ; Elem Educ.

WATTS, KELLY; North Canton Hoover HS; North Canton, OH; Chrs; Girl Scts; Hon Rl; Lbry Ade; Sch Mus; Fr Clb; Pep Clb; Sci Clb; Swmmng; Univ.

WATTS, LINDA; Emerson HS; Gary, IN; 9/142 Cls Rep Frsh Cls; Cls Rep Soph Cls; Cl Rep Jr Cls; Cls Rep Sr Cls; Chrs; Chrh Wkr; Hon Rl; JA; Jr NHS; Natl Forn Lg; Purdue Univ.

WATTS, MARK; Gilbert HS; Justice, WV; 7/78 Chrh Wkr; Hon Rl; NHS; Rptr Sch Nwsp; Concord Coll; Bus.

WATTS, PATRICIA; Guyan Vly HS; W Hamlin, WV; 1/93 Trs Frsh Cls; Val; Hon Rl; NHS; Stu Cncl; FBLA; Huntington Coll; Stenographer.

WATTS, ROBERT; Firelands HS; Birmingham, OH; Am Leg Boys St; Band; Chrs; Chrh Wkr; Hon Rl; NHS; Sch Pl; Yth Flsp; Sprt Ed Yrbk; 4-H; Electronic Tech Inst; Elec.

WATTS, ROBIN; Gods Bible School & College; Tecumsah, MI; Chrs; Chrh Wkr; Hosp Ade; Gods Bible Schl & Coll.

WATTS, SANDRA; Caseville HS; Caseville, MI; 1/13 Cls Rep Frsh Cls; Pres Soph Cls; Sec Jr Cls; Sec Sr Cls; Val; Band; Hon Rl; Jr NHS; NHS; PAVAS; Farm Bureau Citizenship Awd Albion Coll; St Of Michigan Schlrshp; Kiwanis Schlrshp; Albion Coll; Elem Ed.

WAUGH, ANGELA; Stonewall Jackson HS; Charleston, WV; Cls Rep Frsh Cls; Cls Rep Soph Cls; Cls Rep Sr Cls; Hon Rl; Jr NHS; Stu Cncl; Yrbk; Lat Clb; Pres Sci Clb; Capt Bsktbl; Conservation Club Pres Awd Of Excel 77; Marshall Univ; Nursing.

WAUGH, MONICA L; Adena HS; Frankfort, OH; AFS; Aud/Vis; Band; Chrh Wkr; Hon Rl; Hosp Ade; Fr Clb; Concert Bnd Superior Rtng In St 76 77; Sci Fair Excellent Rtng 79; Circleville Bible Coll; Psych.

WAUGH, RANDY; Jackson HS; Jackson, OH; 60/228 Boy Scts; Chrs; Hon Rl; Sct Actv; Lat Clb; OEA; Pep Clb; 1st Pl Genrl Clercl I Regn II Oh 79; Univ; Bus Admin.

WAWOK, BRENDA A; La Porte HS; La Porte, IN; 5/500 Chrs; Pres Chrh Wkr; Yth Flsp; Fr Clb; Trinity Bible Inst; Missionary.

WAWRZYNIAK, DAVID; Yale HS; Avoca, MI; Band; Boy Scts; Chrh Wkr; Sct Actv; St Clair County Comm College; Arch.

WAY, NELSON L; Flushing Sr HS; Flushing, MI; Aud/Vis; Band; Hon Rl; Lbry Ade; MMM; Orch; Sch Mus; Spn Clb; Tmr; Mst Outstndng Jr Boy In Band 78; Band Mgr 79; Michigan St Univ; Optometry.

WAY, STACEY; Brandon HS; Ortonville, MI; 23/192 Girl Scts; Hon Rl; Off Ade; Rptr Sch Nwsp; Spn Clb; IM Sprt; Mic State Univ; Veterinarian.

WAYBRIGHT, JANETTE; Norton HS; Norton, OH; Cmnty Wkr; Girl Scts; Hon Rl; JA; Fr Clb; Trk; Akron Univ; Chem Engr.

WAYBRIGHT, VICKIE; Stow Lakeview HS; Stow, OH; Sec Band; Cmnty Wkr; Sch Pl; Stu Cncl; Drama Clb; Hammel Bus Coll; Ct Reporter.

WAYNE, GARY; Crestwood HS; Drbn Hts, MI; Bsbl; Bsktbl; College.

WEAGLEY, PAMELA; Constantine HS; Constantine, MI; 1/109 Cls Rep Sr Cls; Hon Rl; VP NHS; Pres 4-H; Ten; DAR Awd; 4-H Awd; Davenport Coll; Acctg.

WEAKLAND, KATHERINE; Bishop Borgess HS; Garden City, MI; Hon Rl; NHS; Beta Clb; Bsktbl; GAA; Natl Merit Ltr; Wayne State Univ; Phys Ther.

WEAKLAND, LAURA; Field HS; Mogadore, OH; 32/250 Hon Rl; Sec NHS; Off Ade; Orch; Yrbk; Ed Sch Nwsp; GAA; Akron Univ; Bio.

WEAKS, MARY; Huntington HS; Huntington, WV; Sec Chrs; Hon Rl; Jr NHS; NHS; Yth Flsp; Y-Teens; Fr Clb; Sec Keyettes; Pep Clb; Emory Univ; Poli Sci.

WEALAND, JOYCE; Dublin HS; Dublin, OH; 15/153 Chrs; Chrh Wkr; Hon Rl; Sch Mus; Yth Flsp; Rptr Yrbk; Rptr Sch Nwsp; College; Elem Educ.

WEAN, JON; Highland HS; Anderson, IN; 86/445 VP Sr Cls; Band; Ger Clb; Letter Gym; Letter Trk; Pres Awd; Univ Of South Florida; Marine Bio.

WEANER, MICHAEL; Napoleon HS; Napoleon, OH; 30/249 Am Leg Boys St; Band; Chrs; Chrh Wkr; Debate Tm; Hon Rl; Lbry Ade; Natl Forn Lg; NHS; Sch Mus; Captain Of HS Quiz Bowl Team 78; Awds In Eng Sci & Hstry Schlrshp Teams 77 79; Univ; Public Admin.

WEAR, GEORGIA; Berkshire HS; Hiram, OH; AFS; Chrh Wkr; Hon Rl; Lbry Ade; NHS; Yth Flsp; Natl Merit Ltr; Hon Mention In St Bio In Oh Tests Of Schlstc Achvmnt; 11th Plc In Kent St Dist In Bio In Oh Test Of Achvmnt; Univ; Pre Med.

WEAR, THOMAS H; Bishop Watterson HS; Columbus, OH; 20/260 Am Leg Boys St; Chrh Wkr; Hon Rl; NHS; Ed Yrbk; Rptr Sch Nwsp; Lat Clb; Natl Merit Schl; College; Law.

WEARDEN, JEFFREY R; St Francis D Sales Ctrl HS; Morgantown, WV; 10/70 Boy Scts; Chrh Wkr; Hon Rl; NHS; Stg Crw; Sci Clb; Spn Clb; Bsktbl; Ftbl; Coach Actv; Coll; Bio.

WEASNER, KELLY; Ridgedale HS; Marion, OH; 21/100 Band; Chrs; Girl Scts; Hon Rl; Quill & Scroll; Rptr Yrbk; Ed Sch Nwsp; 4-H; FHA; Chrldng; Bowling Green College; Journalism.

WEATHERHEAD, CHRIS; Graham HS; Conover, OH; 4/165 Band; Hon Rl; 4-H; VP OEA; 4-H Awd; Job; Sec.

WEATHERLY, JEFF; Marshall HS; Marshall, MI; Cls Rep Frsh Cls; Chrh Wkr; Hon Rl; Yrbk; Letter Bsbl; Letter Ftbl; IM Sprt; Rotary Awd; Western Michigan Univ; Bus Admin.

WEATHERS, DAVID; Culver Military Academy; San Antonio, TX; Pres AFS; Boy Scts; Trs Frsh Cls; Jr NHS; ROTC; Stu Cncl; Pres Ger Clb; Letter Trk; Natl Merit Ltr; Business.

WEATHERS, DEBRA; North Daviess HS; Elnora, IN; 5/90 Cl Rep Jr Cls; Band; Chrs; Drm Mjrt; Hon Rl; Sch Mus; Yth Flsp; Beta Clb; Pep Clb; Ten; Ball St Univ; Archt.

WEATHERS, RHONDA; Millington HS; Millington, MI; 3/200 Pres Frsh Cls; Hon Rl; NHS; Stu Cncl; Fr Clb; Mgrs; Cit Awd; University; Med.

WEATHERS, STEPHANIE A; Woodrow Wilson HS; Youngstwn, OH; 90/315 Band; Chrs; Hon Rl; JA; Off Ade; Stu Cncl; Gym; Swmmng; Ten; Chrldng; Youngstown St Univ; Nursing.

WEATHERSPOON, JAMEL; Northrop HS; Ft Wayne, IN; Am Leg Boys St; Band; Drm Bgl; Drm Mjrt; Orch; Sch Mus; Stu Cncl; Indiana Univ; Dentistry.

WEATHERUP, JON; Lakeview HS; St Clair Shrs, MI; Cls Rep Frsh Cls; Chrs; Chrh Wkr; Hosp Ade; Off Ade; Yth Flsp; Swmmng; Tmr; Mich State.

WEATHERWAX, AMY; Bridgeport HS; Bridgeport, WV; Chrh Wkr; Hon Rl; Jr NHS; NHS; Yth Flsp; Fr Clb; Bsktbl; Ten; Capt Of Bsktbl Team; All Tournament Team; 1st Team All Cnty; 2nd Team Big Ten; Honorable Mention All State; College; Special Ed.

WEAVER, BARRY E; Eastlake North HS; Willowick, OH; 1/614 Am Leg Boys St; Band; Boy Scts; Hon Rl; NHS; Northwestern Bus Coll; Auto Dsl Mech.

WEAVER, BRIAN; Little Miami HS; Blanchester, OH; 53/210 Chrh Wkr; Hon Rl; Pol Wkr; Stu Cncl; EKU; Brdcstng.

WEAVER, BRUCE; Marysville HS; Marysville, OH; 35/230 Am Leg Boys St; 4-H; Capt Ftbl; Letter Trk; Letter Wrstlng; Bowling Green Univ; Acctg.

WEAVER, CAROL; Crestview HS; Convoy, OH; Chrs; Chrh Wkr; Sch Mus; FHA; Nbc Lima Tech; Med Asst.

WEAVER, CHINA L; Erieview Catholic HS; Cleveland, OH; Chrh Wkr; Drl Tm; Hosp Ade; Lit Mag; Mod UN; Stu Cncl; Yth Flsp; Yrbk; Bsktbl; Mbr Of Black Catholic Input 78; Sec Of Ebonness Club 77; John Carroll Univ; Pre Med.

WEAVER, DAVE; North Putnam Jr Sr HS; Coatesville, IN; 7/109 Cls Rep Sr Cls; Am Leg Boys St; Chrh Wkr; Pres FCA; Hon Rl; NHS; Sch Mus; Sch Pl; Stg Crw; Stu Cncl; North Putnam Teachers Assn Schlrshp Indiana Univ; Purdue Univ; Biology.

WEAVER, DEBORAH; Monongah HS; Monongah, WV; 13/51 Cls Rep Sr Cls; Chrh Wkr; Hon Rl; Stu Cncl; Y-Teens; Fr Clb; FHA; Pep Clb; Elk Awd; Fairmont St Coll; Nursing.

WEAVER, DOUGLAS; Southeastern HS; Richmond Dale, OH; 6/60 Am Leg Boys St; Boy Scts; Hon Rl; Jr NHS; NHS; Ger Clb; Voice Dem Awd; Letter Crs Cntry; Letter Trk; Am Leg Awd; College; History.

WEAVER, DOUGLAS; Southeastern HS; Richmondale, OH; 14/82 Hst Jr Cls; Hon Rl; Jr NHS; NHS; Ger Clb; Sci Clb; Capt Crs Cntry; Trk; Am Leg Awd; Univ; Bio.

WEAVER, DOUGLAS B; Highland HS; Wadsworth, OH; 10/208 Cls Rep Frsh Cls; Band; Debate Tm; Hon Rl; Jr NHS; NHS; Orch; Quill & Scroll; Sch Mus; Stu Cncl; Oberlin Coll; Eng.

WEAVER, GAYLE; Les Cheneaux Comm HS; Cedarville, MI; Pres Frsh Cls; Cl Rep Jr Cls; Chrs; NHS; Stu Cncl; Ed Yrbk; Bsktbl; Letter Trk; Letter GAA; College; Journalism.

WEAVER, JANICE; South Range HS; Canfield, OH; AFS; Band; Girl Scts; Hon Rl; Hosp Ade; NHS; Sch Mus; 4-H; Fr Clb; Trk; School Of Nursing; R N.

WEAVER, JILL; Wintersville HS; Wintersville, OH; 7/267 Cls Rep Soph Cls; Chrs; Lbry Ade; Stu Cncl; Y-Teens; Spn Clb; Am Leg Awd; Kent State Univ; Med.

WEAVER, KAREN; South HS; Columbus, OH; 27/342 NHS; OEA; Bsbl; Letter Trk; Letter Chrldng; IM Sprt; Ohio St Univ; Comp Sci.

WEAVER, KAREN; Carlisle Sr HS; Carlisle, OH; Band; Hon Rl; Jr NHS; NHS; Yrbk; Rptr Sch Nwsp;.

WEAVER, KAREN; Carlisle HS; Carlisle, OH; Band; Hon Rl; Jr NHS; NHS; Stu Cncl; Rptr Yrbk; Sch Nwsp; Letter Bsktbl;.

WEAVER, KAREN; Carlisle Sr HS; Carlisle, OH; Band; Hon Rl; Jr NHS; NHS; Stu Cncl; Yrbk; Rptr Sch Nwsp; Bsktbl;.

WEAVER, KATHI; Belpre HS; Belpre, OH; 13/169 Band; Hon Rl; NHS; VP Stu Cncl; Yth Flsp; Lat Clb; Spn Clb; Capt Bsktbl; Capt Trk; JETS Awd; Ohio Agri Tech Inst; Agri Research.

WEAVER, KEVIN; Wheeling Central Cath HS; Wheeling, WV; 1/132 Debate Tm; Hon Rl; Pres JA; NHS; Yrbk; Sch Nwsp; Pres Key Clb; Trk; DAR Awd; JA Awd; Carnegie Mellon Univ; Chem Engr.

WEAVER, LINDA; Huntington East HS; Huntington, WV; Chrs; Chrh Wkr; Hon Rl; Sch Mus; Yth Flsp; FHA; Univ.

WEAVER, LINDA; Garaway HS; Dundee, OH; Sch Nwsp; Pep Clb; Univ.

WEAVER, M; Triway HS; Wooster, OH; 1/168 Cls Rep Soph Cls; Pres Sr Cls; Cls Rep Sr Cls; Am Leg Boys St; Hon Rl; Jr NHS; VP NHS; College Of Wooster; Law.

WEAVER, MARK; Oak Hill HS; Oak Hill, WV; Cls Rep Frsh Cls; Boy Scts; Chrh Wkr; Hon Rl; NHS; Fr Clb; Pep Clb; Letter Ftbl; Letter Ten; Schlrshp Consrvtn Camp 79; West Virginia Tech Univ; Civil Engr.

WEAVER, MARK; Canfield HS; Canfield, OH; 61/258 Band; Hon Rl; VP NHS; Spn Clb; Mount Union Coll; Comp Sci.

WEAVER, MARK; Gallia Acad; Gallipolis, OH; VP Frsh Cls; Pres Soph Cls; Cls Rep Soph Cls; Sec Jr Cls; Stu Cncl; Key Clb; Pep Clb; Letter Bsbl; Letter Bsktbl; Marshall Morehead College; Engr.

WEAVER, MYRA; Grayling HS; Grayling, MI; Hon Rl; Lbry Ade; Treas NHS; Off Ade; Pol Wkr; Pres Leo Clb; Chrldng; General Motors Inst; Engr.

WEAVER, STEPHEN; Lewis Cnty HS; Weston, WV; Cls Rep Sr Cls; Aud/Vis; Band; Boy Scts; Chrs; FCA; Hon Rl; PAVAS; Sch Pl; Stu Cncl; Ohio Inst Of Tech; Elec Tech.

WEAVER, TERRI; Herbert Hoover HS; Elkview, WV; Cl Rep Jr Cls; VP Sr Cls; Hon Rl; Jr NHS; NHS; Stu Cncl; Sch Nwsp; Fr Clb; College; Law.

WEAVER, TINA; Winfield HS; Scott Depot, WV; Chrs; Girl Scts; Hon Rl; Jr NHS; Mth Clb; Pep Clb; Letter Trk; College.

WEAVER, TONY; Martinsville HS; Martinsville, IN; 80/382 Hon Rl; DECA; Letter Ftbl; Letter Trk; IM Sprt; Gov Hon Prg Awd; DECA Dist Champ; St Runner Up; St Champ; Natl Qualif; Awds For Individual Events Track Sectional Qualif; College; Busns.

WEAVER, VALINDA; Indian Valley North HS; New Phila, OH; Pres Frsh Cls; Pres Soph Cls; Yrbk; Sch Nwsp; FTA; Spn Clb; College; Modeling.

WEAVER, WANDA; Bucyrus HS; Bucyrus, OH; Hon Rl; NHS; North Central Tech Univ; Nursing.

WEBB, ANITA; Tyler County HS; Middlebourne, WV; 7/91 Pres Soph Cls; Band; Hon Rl; JA; Yth Flsp; FTA; Pep Clb; Trk; Capt Chrldng; Scr Kpr; West Liberty Univ; Comp Proc.

WEBB, B; Buffalo HS; Lavalette, WV; Cls Rep Soph Cls; Cl Rep Jr Cls; Boy Scts; Hon Rl; Lbry Ade; Sch Pl; Sct Actv; Rptr Sch Nwsp; Crs Cntry; Socr; Aviation.

WEBB, BRENDA; Inland Lakes Schls; Indian Rvr, MI; 6/85 Hon Rl; Letter Bsktbl; Trk; Northern Michigan Univ; Jrnlsm.

WEBB, CASSANDRA; Cass Technical HS; Detroit, MI; Hon Rl; Hosp Ade; NHS; Off Ade; FHA; St Of Mi Compt Schslhp Progr Cert Of Recngtn 79; Volntr Cert Of Apprctn From Childrns Hosp Of Mi 79; Wayne St Univ.

WEBB, CHRISTINE; Whiteland Cmnty HS; Greenwood, IN; 9/250 AFS; Chrs; Drl Tm; Hon Rl; Sch Mus; Yth Flsp; Rptr Yrbk; 4-H; FHA; Pep Clb; Uni v; Public Reltns.

WEBB, DENNIS L; Firestone HS; Akron, OH; Chrs; Chrh Wkr; Cmnty Wkr; Hon Rl; NHS; Sch Mus; Yth Flsp; Ftbl; Trk; Univ Of Notre Dame; Economics.

WEBB, DONNA; Bedford North Lawrence HS; Bedford, IN; 9/417 Band; Hon Rl; NHS; Red Cr Ade; Beta Clb; Lat Clb; Mth Clb; Spn Clb; Kiwan Awd; I Rcvd A Barney G Crow Mem Schlrshp 79; I Was In The Top Ten Of My Class All Four Yrs Of HS 75 79; Indiana Univ; Phys Ther.

WEBB, JACQUELINE; Calhoun County HS; Big Springs, WV; Sec Frsh Cls; Sec Soph Cls; Chrh Wkr; Hon Rl; Treas 4-H; GAA; College; Computer Science.

WEBB, KAREN; Sherman HS; Nellis, WV; Trs Frsh Cls; Trs Jr Cls; Sec Sr Cls; Band; Hon Rl; NHS; Sch Pl; Treas Stu Cncl; Drama Clb; Sec 4-H; College.

WEBB, NANCY; Northwest HS; Canal Fulton, OH; 17/166 Hon Rl; Lbry Ade; NHS; Y-Teens; Pep Clb; Pres Spn Clb; Trk; IM Sprt; Travel Schl; Travel Agnt.

WEBB, RHONDA; Delphi Community Shs; Delphi, IN; Chrh Wkr; Hon Rl; Ger Clb; Trk; Also Active In Sunshine Soc Clbu; Univ; Phys Ther.

WEBB, RHONDA; Crestline HS; Crestline, OH; Band; Chrs; Chrh Wkr; Orch; Sch Mus; Sch Pl; 4-H; Trk; 4-H Awd; Americas Yth In Concert 79; Explorer Club 79 80; Univ.

WEBB, ROBERT; Sherman HS; Sylvester, WV; Lbry Ade; PAVAS; Sch Mus; Sch Pl; Swmmng; Wrstlng; Cit Awd; West Virginia Tech Univ; Tchr.

WEBB, ROBIN; Roosevelt HS; Gary, IN; Cls Rep Frsh Cls; Trs Soph Cls; Band; Chrh Wkr; Hon Rl; JA; Jr NHS; Treas NHS; Stu Cncl; Y-Teens; Soph/jr Schlrshp Trophy; Purdue Univ; Psych.

WEBB, SAMANTHA; Covert HS; Covert, MI; 4/38 Sec Frsh Cls; Pres Soph Cls; Band; Hon Rl; Mod UN; NHS; VP Stu Cncl; Ed Yrbk; Ed Sch Nwsp; FHA; Purdue Univ; Sci.

WEBB, SCOTT; Center Grove HS; Greenwood, IN; 11/310 VP Soph Cls; VP Jr Cls; VP Sr Cls; Hon Rl; NHS; Key Clb; Spn Clb; Letter Bsbl; Univ.

WEBB, SUSANNE; Lutheran East HS; St Clair Shores, MI; Chrh Wkr; Hon Rl; JA; NHS; Sch Pl; Drama Clb; JA Awd; College; Med Office Asst.

WEBB, TOM; Solon HS; Solon, OH; Boy Scts; Chrh Wkr; Hon Rl; Sct Actv; Crs Cntry; Trk; Natl Merit SF; Univ; Sci.

WEBB, VICKI; Hardin Northern HS; Dola, OH; 12/59 Trs Frsh Cls; Trs Jr Cls; Band; Hon Rl; Yrbk; Fr Clb; Chrldng; Sec Treas Of Band; Annual Yrbk Photor; Lima Memorial Hosp; Med Lab Tech.

WEBB, VICKY; Bellevue HS; Bellevue, OH; 44/224 Chrs; Chrh Wkr; Cmnty Wkr; Hon Rl; Yth Flsp; Rptr Yrbk; Rptr Sch Nwsp; IM Sprt; Ohi State Univ; Psych.

WEBB, WILLIAM; Wm Mason HS; Mason, OH; 23/185 Band; Boy Scts; Drm Bgl; Drm Mjrt; Hon Rl; Orch; Sch Mus; Sch Pl; Stg Crw; Drama Clb; Univ; Acctg.

WEBBER, CHERYL; Dalton Local HS; Dalton, OH; Band; Chrs; Chrh Wkr; Girl Scts; Hon Rl; NHS; Sch Pl; Stg Crw; Treas Stu Cncl; Yrbk; Univ; Law.

WEBBER, SUZANN; North Muskegon HS; North Muskegon, MI; 18/99 Cls Rep Sr Cls; Chrs; Chrh Wkr; Hosp Ade; Lit Mag; NHS; Orch; Sch Mus; Stu Cncl; Yth Flsp; Muskegon Comm College; Deaf Educ.

WEBEL, LISETTE; Malabar HS; Mansfield, OH; Hon Rl; Jr NHS; NHS; Sch Pl; Stu Cncl; Drama Clb;.

WEBER, ANTHONY; Gilmour Acad; Highland Hts, OH; Chrs; Hon Rl; NHS; Red Cr Ade; Rptr Sch Nwsp; Spn Clb; Letter Bsktbl; Letter Ftbl; Letter Trk; Coach Actv; College; Law.

WEBER, BETH; Gaylord HS; Gaylord, MI; Girl Scts; Hon Rl; NHS; Univ.

WEBER, BRUCE; Otsego HS; Otsego, MI; 23/231 Cls Rep Frsh Cls; Boy Scts; Hon Rl; Lbry Ade; NHS; Stg Crw; Sch Nwsp; Spn Clb; Ftbl; Capt Ten; Michigan St Univ; Busns Admin.

WEBER, BRYAN; Bexley HS; Columbus, OH; 34/184 Band; Hon Rl; Letter Wrstlng; College; Chem Engr.

WEBER, CAROLINE; Gwinn HS; Gwinn, MI; Sec Frsh Cls; Hon Rl; Jr NHS; NHS; Univ; Jrnlsm.

WEBER, CHRISTINA; Eaton HS; Camden, OH; 63/170 Pres Soph Cls; Chrs; Pres Stu Cncl; Fr Clb; Pep Clb; Spn Clb; Trk; Chrldng; GAA; PPFtbl; Miami Vly Schl; Nursing.

WEBER, CONDA; Eaton HS; Camden, OH; Chrs; Fr Clb; Pep Clb; Chrldng; GAA; Coll; Educ.

WEBER, CYNTHIA; St Francis HS; Kingsley, MI; 4/130 Hon Rl; NHS; 4-H; Fr Clb; Trk; 4-H Awd; College.

WEBER, DAVID; Nordonia HS; Macedonia, OH; 40/450 Band; Chrs; NHS; Sch Mus; Sch Pl; Stg Crw; Drama Clb; Letter Ten; Univ; Law.

WEBER, DAVID; Loudonville HS; Perrysville, OH; 12/135 Band; Chrs; Hon Rl; NHS; Sch Mus; Sch Pl; Stg Crw; Rptr Sch Nwsp; Bsbl; Univ Of Cincinnati; Aerospace Engr.

WEBER, DAVID; St Johns HS; St Johns, MI; Hon Rl; Yth Flsp; Coach Actv; IM Sprt; MSU; Sci.

WEBER, DAWN; Carson City Crystal HS; Sheridan, MI; 7/128 Chrh Wkr; Hon Rl; NHS; Sch Pl; Stu Cncl; FHA; Spn Clb; Am Leg Awd; DAR Awd; Outstndng Sr Girl 78; Spec HS Awrd Being Teen Editor Of Cnty Paper 78; Cntrl Michigan Univ; Intrprsnl Cmnct.

WEBER, ELIZABETH A; Pike HS; Indpls, IN; Hon Rl; Jr NHS; Lit Mag; NHS; Orch; Quill & Scroll; Lat Clb; Natl Merit SF; Univ; Eng.

WEBER, JAMIE; Hamilton HS; Dorr, MI; 7/131 Cl Rep Jr Cls; Girl Scts; Hon Rl; Sec Stu Cncl; Pres Yth Flsp; Treas Ger Clb; Bsktbl; Natl Merit SF; Mercy Ctrl Schl Of Nursing; Nursing.

WEBER, JANE; Connersville Sr HS; Connersville, IN; Cls Rep Soph Cls; Cl Rep Jr Cls; Chrs; Drl Tm; Drm Bgl; Hon Rl; Pep Clb; Spn Clb; Pom Pon; Tmr; Indiana State Univ.

WEBER, JEFFREY; Jackson HS; Massillon, OH; Boy Scts; Debate Tm; Hon Rl; Mod UN; Natl Forn Lg; NHS; Sct Actv; Natl Merit Ltr; Us Air Force Acad.

WEBER, JENNIFER; Seton HS; Cincinnati, OH; Hon Rl; NHS; Mth Clb; Socr; Natl Merit Ltr; Miami Univ; Med Tech.

WEBER, JILL; Eaton HS; Eaton, OH; Sec Frsh Cls; Am Leg Aux Girls St; Chrs; Drl Tm; Hon Rl; Jr NHS; NHS; Stu Cncl; 4-H; FHA; Univ; Own & Mgr Of Restaurant.

WEBER, JOYCE; Adams Cntrl HS; Decatur, IN; 18/110 Am Leg Aux Girls St; FCA; Hon Rl; Hosp Ade; Lbry Ade; NHS; Sch Pl; Sec Yth Flsp; Drama Clb; 4-H; Freddy Awd In Ceramics; 4 H Jr Ldrshp Conference; Indiana Univ; Interpretation.

WEBER, KAREN; Coldwater HS; Coldwater, OH; 5/147 Band; Chrs; Girl Scts; Hon Rl; NHS; Rptr Sch Nwsp; Spn Clb; Swmmng; Trk; IM Sprt; Hocking Tech Coll; Hotel Mgmt.

WEBER, KAREN; Bath HS; Lima, OH; Am Leg Aux Girls St; Chrs; Capt Drl Tm; Hon Rl; NHS; 4-H; Pres FHA; 4-H Awd; Opt Clb Awd; Voice Dem Awd; Ohio State Univ; Home Ec.

WEBER, KATHLEEN; Notre Dame Academy; Toledo, OH; Hon Rl; NHS; Off Ade; Stu Cncl; Ger Clb; Univ; Bus.

WEBER, KATHY; Eastwood HS; Pemberville, OH; Sec Frsh Cls; Cls Rep Frsh Cls; Band; Hon Rl; NHS; Off Ade; Orch; Sch Mus; Sch Pl; VP Sct Actv; Univ Of Toledo; Educ Tchr.

WEBER, LAURA; New Palestine HS; New Palestine, IN; 15/189 Am Leg Aux Girls St; Band; Chrh Wkr; Girl Scts; Hon Rl; NHS; Orch; Stu Cncl; Yth Flsp; Yrbk; Indiana Cntrl Univ; RN.

WEBER, LEIGH; Madison Hts HS; Anderson, IN; Hon Rl; Hosp Ade; Lit Mag; Off Ade; Quill & Scroll; Rptr Yrbk; Ed Sch Nwsp; Rptr Sch Nwsp; Ger Clb; Pep Clb; Mst News Story Jolly Roger Newsppr 79; Indiana Univ; Hist.

WEBER, LORI; Otsego HS; Bowling Green, OH; 8/138 Chrh Wkr; Hon Rl; Jr NHS; NHS; Great Lakes Bible College.

WEBER, LORI A; South Lake HS; St Clair Shrs, MI; 1/421 Hon Rl; Hosp Ade; Lit Mag; Sec NHS; Pol Wkr; Sch Mus; Ed Yrbk; Sci Clb; Letter Ten; IM Sprt; U Of Michigan; Medicine.

WEBER, LOUIS; La Salle HS; Cincinnati, OH; 13/252 Hon Rl; Jr NHS; NHS; Hockey; IM Sprt; Univ Of Cincinnati; Chemical Enginer.

WEBER, LYNN; Dublin HS; Dublin, OH; 26/155 Band; Chrs; Hon Rl; Lbry Ade; NHS; Sch Mus; Yth Flsp; Fr Clb; Univ; Bus.

WEBER, MARK; East Noble HS; Huntertown, IN; 32/263 Band; Hon Rl; Purdue Univ; Law Enforcement.

WEBER, MARTIN J; Kingsford HS; Iron Mtn, MI; Hon Rl; Bsbl; Ftbl; IM Sprt; Scr Kpr; Univ Of Michigan; Archt.

WEBER, MARY; Elkhart Mem HS; Elkhart, IN; 7/514 Hon Rl; Hosp Ade; NHS; Rptr Sch Nwsp; Sch Nwsp; Mth Clb; Cit Awd; Kiwan Awd; Lion Awd; Pres Awd; Univ; Comp Math.

WEBER, MICHAEL; Sts Peter & Paul HS; Dumont, NJ; 1/5 Chrs; NHS; Sch Pl; Stg Crw; Drama Clb; Pep Clb; Rdo Clb; Socr; Natl Merit Ltr; College; Religion.

WEBER, MICHAEL J; La Salle HS; Cincinnati, OH; 57/277 Band; Chrh Wkr; Hon Rl; Orch; Pol Wkr; Sch Mus; Sch Pl; Spn Clb; Univ Of Cincinnati; Chem.

WEBER, PAM; South Central Jr Sr HS; Elizabeth, IN; 1/51 Sec Soph Cls; Pres Jr Cls; Sec Sr Cls; Chrh Wkr; Hon Rl; NHS; Ed Sch Nwsp; Pres FHA; Letter Bsktbl; DAR Awd; Univ Of Evansville; RN.

WEBER, PAMELA; South Central Jr Sr HS; Elizabeth, IN; Sec Sr Cls; Val; NHS; Ed Sch Nwsp; Pres FHA; Bsktbl; Trk; DAR Awd; Univ Of Evansville; Nursing.

WEBER, PATRICK; Coldwater HS; Coldwater, OH; VP Frsh Cls; Am Leg Boys St; Band; Chrs; Hon Rl; NHS; Letter Crs Cntry; Trk; IM Sprt; Am Leg Awd; Univ; Comp Sci.

WEBER, PAUL; Ursuline HS; Youngstown, OH; Cmnty Wkr; Hon Rl; Youngstown Univ; Phys Educ.

WEBER, RANDALL; Blanchester HS; Blanchester, OH; 18/157 Hon Rl; NHS; Sec FFA; FTA; Ftbl; Letter Wrstlng; Tmr; Natl Merit SF; Algebra Schlstc Team 1977; FFA Chptr 1st 1978; S W Dist Awd FFA 1979; Annapolis; Engr.

WEBER, REBECCA; Loudonville HS; Perrysville, OH; 5/120 Aud/Vis; Band; Hon Rl; NHS; Orch; Sprt Ed Sch Nwsp; Rptr Sch Nwsp; Letter Bsktbl; Letter Trk; Notre Dame; Engineering.

WEBER, STEPHANIE; Four Cnty SVS HS; Napoleon, OH; VP Sr Cls; Cls Rep Sr Cls; Hon Rl; Lbry Ade; Stu Cncl; Yth Flsp; OEA; Trk; Northwest Tech Schl; Data Processing.

WEBER, STEPHANIE; Strongsville Sr HS; Columbia St, OH; Cls Rep Frsh Cls; Band; Chrh Wkr; Girl Scts; Hon Rl; Jr NHS; NHS; Orch; Sct Actv; Stu Cncl; Tri St Univ; Chem Engr.

WEBER, STEVE; Southfield Christian HS; Bloomfield Hls, MI; VP Soph Cls; Cl Rep Jr Cls; Am Leg Boys St; VP Chrs; Hon Rl; Sch Pl; Pres Stu Cncl; Hockey; Letter Socr; Letter Trk; College.

WEBER, TERRI; Bettsville HS; Tiffin, OH; 2/20 Sec Frsh Cls; Trs Soph Cls; Band; Chrs; Chrh Wkr; Drm Mjrt; Hon Rl; NHS; Sch Mus; Sec 4-H; Natl Machinery Citiznshp Awd 77 78 & 79; 4 H 76 79; Chorus 76 79; Univ; Spec Educ.

WEBER, THOMAS; Theodore Roosevelt HS; Wyandotte, MI; Hon Rl; Lbry Ade; NHS; Rdo Clb; Letter Bsktbl; Letter Ftbl; Letter Trk; Draftsman Of The Year; Michigan Idustrial Arts Awds; Univ Of Michigan; Archt.

WEBER, TRUDY; Glen Lake HS; Cedar, MI; Chrh Wkr; Hon Rl; NHS; Quill & Scroll; Rptr Sch Nwsp; Letter Bsbl; Trk; Letter Chrldng; Coach Actv; PPFtbl; Ctrl Mich Univ; Architect.

WEBER, WALTER; Cody HS; Detroit, MI; Band; Boy Scts; Hon Rl; Ger Clb; Mth Clb; Sci Clb; Cit Awd; Univ; Med.

WEBER, WARD; Hilliard HS; Hilliard, OH; Hon Rl; JA; Sch Pl; Drama Clb; JA Awd; Past Master Cnclr Of Order Of Demolay; Recv Meritorious Serv Awd Order Of Demolay; Coll; Engr.

WEBSTER, CHERYL; Pontiac Central HS; W Bloomfield, MI; Chrs; Hon Rl; Orch; Sch Mus; Sch Pl; Stg Crw; Drama Clb; Tmr; Univ; Engr.

WEBSTER, CINDI; Charleston HS; Charlestown, IN; Sec Frsh Cls; Sec Soph Cls; Am Leg Aux Girls St; FCA; Pres NHS; VP Stu Cncl; Yrbk; Rptr Sch Nwsp; Fr Clb;.

WEBSTER, CIRI A; Cass Technical HS; Detroit, MI; Band; Girl Scts; Hon Rl; NHS; Yth Flsp; Treas Sci Clb; Natl Merit SF; Kalamazoo Coll; Chemistry.

WEBSTER, DAN; Our Lady Of The Lakes HS; Drayton Plains, MI; Chrh Wkr; Hon Rl; Fr Clb; Bsbl; Capt Ftbl; IM Sprt; Scr Kpr; Tmr; College; Language.

WEBSTER, DANIEL; Van Buren HS; Harmony, IN; VP Frsh Cls; VP Soph Cls; Am Leg Boys St; Band; Hon Rl; NHS; Key Clb; Sci Clb; VICA; Bsbl;.

WEBSTER, JANA; Terre Haute North Vigo HS; Terre Haute, IN; Cls Rep Soph Cls; Cls Rep Sr Cls; Band; Chrs; Sec Chrh Wkr; Hon Rl; VP JA; Mod UN; Stu Cncl; Y-Teens; HS Finlst For St Marys Rose Hulman Math Test 77; ISU Smmr Hon Semnr 79; Purdue Univ; Psych.

WEBSTER, JOHN W; Univ Of Detroit HS; Detroit, MI; Chrh Wkr; Cmnty Wkr; Hon Rl; Pol Wkr; Natl Merit SF; Univ; Elec Engr.

WEBSTER, JOSEPH; Howell HS; Howell, MI; Am Leg Boys St; CAP; Cmnty Wkr; Hon Rl; NHS; Letter Ten; Mgrs; Am Leg Awd; Univ; Archt.

WEBSTER, MARK D; St Albans HS; Hurricane, WV; 45/429 Am Leg Boys St; Band; Hon Rl; Jr NHS; NHS; Sch Pl; Stu Cncl; Drama Clb; Spn Clb; Univ; Spec Med.

WEBSTER, MARTHA; Linden Cmnty HS; Linden, MI; 1/159 Val; Band; Hon Rl; Hosp Ade; NHS; Orch; Red Cr Ade; Sch Mus; Stg Crw; Drama Clb; Michigan St Univ; Sci.

WEBSTER, MICHELLE; Green HS; Akron, OH; Band; Chrs; Chrh Wkr; Yth Flsp; Bsktbl; Letter Trk; IM Sprt; Univ; Soc Sci.

WEBSTER, P; Sidney HS; Sidney, OH; Cl Rep Jr Cls; Debate Tm; Hon Rl; NHS; Sch Pl; Stu Cncl; Natl Merit Schl; College; Rsrch Bio.

WEBSTER, SUSAN; Oak Colen HS; New Cumberland, WV; 20/243 Band; Chrs; Hosp Ade; NHS; Yrbk; FNA; Pep Clb; Spn Clb; Ohio Valley Schl Of Nursing; Nursing.

WEBSTER, WADE; White Cloud HS; White Cloud, MI; 4/82 Chrh Wkr; Hon Rl; Ftbl; Trk; St Of Mi Competitive Schlrshp; Arah Beach Schlrshp; Michigan St Univ; Vet.

WECH, BARBARA; Lincoln Park HS; Lincoln Park, MI; Band; Hon Rl; NHS; Letter Ten; Cert Of Recogntn In St Of Mi Comp Schlrshp Prog 79; Wayne St Univ; Bio.

WECKLE, PENNY; Maumee HS; Toledo, OH; Cl Rep Jr Cls; Debate Tm; Hon Rl; Off Ade; Quill & Scroll; Sch Pl; Stg Crw; Pres Stu Cncl; Y-Teens; Ed Yrbk; Univ; Jrnlsm.

WEDDELL, KAY; Medora HS; Norman, IN; 2/20 Cls Rep Frsh Cls; Cls Rep Soph Cls; Chrh Wkr; Hon Rl; Sch Pl; Stu Cncl; Yrbk; Beta Clb; Bsktbl; Chrldng; Bedford Voc Schl; Bus.

WEDDLE, STEVEN; Goshen HS; Goshen, IN; 1/273 Boy Scts; Chrh Wkr; FCA; Hon Rl; NHS; Yth Flsp; Bsbl; Bsktbl; Ftbl; Coach Actv; 2nd Team All Conf Qtr 78; Hnrble Mentn All Sec Guard 78; Goshen New Schlstc Awd 77; Univ; Math.

WEDEL, LYNN; Berrien Springs HS; Berrien Ctr, MI; Sec Soph Cls; Chrh Wkr; Girl Scts; Hon Rl; Off Ade; Stu Cncl; Yth Flsp; 4-H; Pres Spn Clb; Chrldng; Ferris St Univ; Cosmetology.

WEDEL, MARTHA; Athens HS; Fulton, MI; Hon Rl; Jr NHS; 4-H; Letter Trk;.

WEDEMEYER, SHARI; Gallia Academy HS; Rio Grande, OH; 33/225 Chrs; Chrh Wkr; Girl Scts; Pres 4-H; Lat Clb; OEA; 4-H Awd; Coll.

WEDGE, TODD; East Canton HS; E Canton, OH; 30/120 Boy Scts; Spn Clb; Bsktbl; IM Sprt; Ohio State; Engineering.

WEEBER, CARLOS; Perrysburg HS; Perrysburg, OH; Boy Scts; JA; Spn Clb; Ten; College; Engineering.

WEED, KATHRYN M; Whetstone HS; Columbus, OH; 1/312 AFS; Band; Chrs; Hon Rl; NHS; JETS Awd; NCTE; Ohio St Univ; Engr Physics.

WEED, TIMOTHY; West Catholic HS; Grand Rapids, MI; Chrh Wkr; Hon Rl; Rptr Yrbk; Letter Bsbl; Capt Socr; Coach Actv; IM Sprt; Scr Kpr; Tmr; College; Doctor.

WEEDEN, GREG; Goshen HS; Goshen, IN; 35/200 Cl Rep Jr Cls; FCA; Hon Rl; Stu Cncl; Ed Yrbk; Letter Crs Cntry; Letter Trk; IM Sprt; ITT; Archt.

WEEDMAN, TERESA; Sandusky St Marys Cath HS; Sandusky, OH; 3/139 Cls Rep Frsh Cls; Cls Rep Soph Cls; Cl Rep Jr Cls; Chrh Wkr; Girl Scts; Hon Rl; Lbry Ade; Pep Clb; Spn Clb; GAA; Ohio St Univ; Sci.

WEEDON, K; Belleville HS; Belleville, MI; Sec Soph Cls; Aud/Vis; Chrs; Chrh Wkr; Girl Scts; Hon Rl; Lbry Ade; Off Ade; Yrbk; 4-H; Baptist Bible Coll; Music.

WEEKLEY, DONNA; South Harrison HS; W Milford, WV; Hon Rl; Jr NHS; NHS; Sch Pl; Pres FHA; Gym; Wv Univ; Med Tech.

WEEKLEY, ELIZABETH; Salem HS; Salem, OH; Hst Frsh Cls; Chrs; Hon Rl; JA; Drama Clb; FHA; Act Intl Ordr Of The Rainbow For Girls 77; 6th Pl Jr Div Of BOE; Youngstown Schl Of Bus; Sec.

WEEKLEY, JANICE; Washington Cnty JVS HS; Marietta, OH; Chrs; Chrh Wkr; Cmnty Wkr; OEA; Mat Maids; C of C Awd; Sec.

WEEKLEY, LINDA; Parkersburg HS; Vienna, WV; 8/785 Hon Rl; Hosp Ade; Glenville St Coll; Math.

WEEKLEY, LISA; Westerville South HS; Westerville, OH; 10/283 Cls Rep Frsh Cls; Cls Rep Soph Cls; Am Leg Aux Girls St; Pres NHS; Sch Mus; Sch Pl; Drama Clb; Marietta Coll; Law.

WEEKLEY, MELINDA; Brooke HS; Colliers, WV; 134/466 Cls Rep Frsh Cls; Cls Rep Sr Cls; Band; Hon Rl; Sec Stu Cncl; Jeff Tech Schl; Sec.

WEEKS, JEFF; Newton HS; Pleasant Hl, OH; 11/53 Pres Frsh Cls; Pres Soph Cls; VP Sr Cls; Chrh Wkr; Hon Rl; Yth Flsp; FFA; Bsktbl; Crs Cntry; Trk; College; Farmer.

WEEKS, PEGGY; Beaumont Girls HS; Univ Hts, OH; Chrs; Cmnty Wkr; Hon Rl; Sch Pl; IM Sprt; JC Awd; Kiwan Awd; College; Nurse.

WEENAN, STEVEN; Orrville HS; Orrville, OH; Hon Rl; 4-H; Crs Cntry; Trk; 4-H Awd; Agri Tech Institute.

WEENUM, NANCY; Zeeland HS; Zeeland, MI; Sec Sr Cls; Band; Chrh Wkr; Stu Cncl; Pep Clb; Chrldng; Pom Pon; Twrlr; Davenport Bus Schl; Bus Admin.

WEESE, JOHN H; Moorefield HS; Fisher, WV; Pres Frsh Cls; Pres Soph Cls; Pres Jr Cls; Chrh Wkr; Cmnty Wkr; JA; Stg Crw; Yth Flsp; Pres 4-H; Treas FFA; South Branch Voc Ctr; Electronics.

WEESE, MICHELE; Elkins HS; Elkins, WV; 36/240 Hon Rl; Hosp Ade; Sec NHS; Sch Pl; Yrbk; Sch Nwsp; VP Keyettes; Twrlr; Univ; Acctg.

WEESE, PHOEBE; Columbiana County Joint HS; East Liverpool, OH; Band; Y-Teens; 4-H; OEA; Trk;.

WEESNER, CHERYL R; Frankfort Sr HS; Frankfort, IN; 9/270 Cls Rep Sr Cls; VP Chrs; Chrh Wkr; Mdrgl; NHS; Orch; Sch Mus; Stu Cncl; F# Club Vp; Physical Ed Teachers Assistant; Piano Solo State Level 1st; Intl Jr Busns Coll; Accounting.

WEGENER, MICHAEL; Sts Peter & Paul Seminary; Coshocton, OH; 4/4 Pres Jr Cls; Pres Sr Cls; Cls Rep Sr Cls; Sch Pl; Stu Cncl; Ed Yrbk; Ed Sch Nwsp; 4-H; Letter Bsktbl; Letter Socr; Univ Of Detroit; Philosophy.

WEGER, JOSEPH; Delphos St John HS; Delphos, OH; 5/158 Pres Frsh Cls; Cls Rep Sr Cls; Am Leg Boys St; NHS; Stu Cncl; Sprt Ed Yrbk; Bsktbl; Letter Ftbl; Natl Merit SF; Bowling Green Univ Outstndng Jr Comp Finlst 79; N W Oh Chem Bowl Contst; Univ.

WEGESIN, JUDY; St Johns HS; Delphos, OH; Sec Soph Cls; Hst Jr Cls; Sch Mus; Sch Pl; Stg Crw; Rptr Yrbk; FHA; FTA; Letter Bsktbl; Trk; Univ Of Cincinati; Art.

WEGMAN, KAREN; Rochester Adams HS; Rochester, MI; Band; Cmnty Wkr; Hon Rl; Hosp Ade; Swmmng; Cit Awd; Ferris St Univ; Med Sec.

WEHERLEY, PAM; Franklin Monroe HS; Arcanum, OH; 9/78 Cls Rep Soph Cls; VP Jr Cls; Sec Sr Cls; Band; Chrs; FCA; Hon Rl; Off Ade; Sch Pl; Stu Cncl; Vlybl Letter; Sftbl All Cnty Pitcher; Stu Exec Sec Superintendents Ofc; Sinclair Coll; Sec Sci.

WEHLING, DON W; Chippewa HS; Doylestown, OH; FCA; Hon Rl; Yth Flsp; Sci Clb; Spn Clb; Letter Bsbl; Bsktbl; Letter Ftbl; Coach Actv; IM Sprt;.

WEHMEYER, ANN; Centerville HS; Centerville, OH; 9/687 Chrh Wkr; Cmnty Wkr; NHS; Yth Flsp ; Ohio Northern Univ; Pharm.

WEHMILLER, BENJIE; Crothersville Community Schl; Crothersville, IN; 6/70 Cls Rep Soph Cls; Cl Rep Jr Cls; Cls Rep Sr Cls; Band; FCA; Hon Rl; NHS; Stu Cncl; Yth Flsp; Bsbl; Band Awd For Best Non Sr Bandsmen 79; Perfect Attendence 77; Natl Hnr Soc 78; Purdue Univ; Engr.

WEHNER, ANNA; Greenfield Mc Clain HS; Lebanon, OH; Chrs; Stg Crw; Stu Cncl; 4-H; Pep Clb; Ten; Capt Chrldng; Bus Schl; Sec.

WEHNER, PAULETTE; Central Preston Sr HS; Kingwood, WV; Cls Rep Frsh Cls; Pres Jr Cls; VP Sr Cls; Am Leg Aux Girls St; Band; Girl Scts; Hon Rl; Pres NHS; Sec Stu Cncl; Pres Fr Clb; All St Band Oboe 79; All Cnty Band Oboe 77 78 & 79; Golden Horseshoe Awd 76; Univ; Med.

WEHR, DIANE; Barnesville HS; Jerusalem, OH; Chrs; Cmnty Wkr; Hon Rl; JA; Sct Actv; Drama Clb; 4-H; FHA; FTA; 4-H Awd; Business Schl; Acctg.

WEHRKAMP, BEV; St Henry HS; St Henry, OH; Chrs; Hon Rl; Yrbk; Drama Clb; OEA; Pep Clb; Trk; GAA; Sinclair Cmnty Coll; Bus.

WEHRLE, WENDY; Hammond Christian Academy; Crete, IL; Chrs; Chrh Wkr; Girl Scts; Hon Rl; Lbry Ade; Sch Mus; Sch Pl; Yth Flsp; Yrbk; Chrldng; Prairie St Coll; Social Work.

WEHRLY, SHARLA; Jay County HS; Union City, IN; 14/411 Pres AFS; Am Leg Aux Girls St; Drl Tm; Hon Rl; Jr NHS; NHS; Sch Mus; Sch Pl; Stu Cncl; Fr Clb; Wittenburg; Forestry.

WEICHHAND, GREGORY A; Lake Michigan Catholic HS; St Joseph, MI; 14/102 Pres Frsh Cls; Trs Sr Cls; Chrs; Hon Rl; NHS; Sch Mus; Sch Pl; Stg Crw; Stu Cncl; Drama Clb; W Michigan Univ; Bus.

WEIDEMAN, CHRIS; Willow Run HS; Ypsilanti, MI; 35/234 Cls Rep Sr Cls; Hon Rl; Pol Wkr; Stu Cncl; Yth Flsp; Fr Clb; Colorado St Univ; Engr.

WEIDENBENNER, JOE; Jasper HS; Jasper, IN; 2/289 Am Leg Boys St; Chrh Wkr; FCA; Hon Rl; Jr NHS; NHS; Ftbl; Trk; Cit Awd; Sr All St Ftbll 79; Univ; Mech Engr.

WEIDENDORF, BARBARA; Redford HS; Detroit, MI; Chrh Wkr; VP NHS; Stu Cncl; Letter Bsbl; Albion Coll; Amer History.

WEIDENHAMER, LAURIE; Flat Rock HS; Flat Rock, MI; VP Band; VP Girl Scts; Lbry Ade; NHS; Sch Mus; VP Yth Flsp; Letter Bsktbl; College; Math.

WEIDLE, STEVEN; Carlisle Sr HS; Carlisle, OH; Band; Chrs; Spn Clb; Ftbl; Trk; IM Sprt; Frsh MSP Track 76; 1st Highjump Dist 78; 2nd High Jump St Track & MVP 78; Univ.

WEIDMAN, ELEANOR; Wheeling Central HS; Wheeling, WV; Hon Rl; Swmmng; Trk; Chrldng; Pres Awd; West Liberty Coll.

WEIDNER, ALLEN; Ann A Local Schools; Anna, OH; 8/80 Cls Rep Frsh Cls; Hon Rl; Sch Pl; Stg Crw; Spn Clb; VICA; Trk; Amer Math Assoc Contest Winner 79; Miami Univ; Acctg.

WEIDNER, ANN; Bishop Hartley HS; Columbus, OH; Band; Capt Swmmng; Mat Maids; Univ; Phys Ther.

WEIDNER, MARY; Norwood Sr HS; Norwood, OH; Hon Rl; Y-Teens; Fr Clb; Univ; French.

WEIG, ROBERT; Lutheran HS; Washington, MI; 11/110 Aud/Vis; Chrs; Chrh Wkr; Hon Rl; Yth Flsp; Pres 4-H; 4-H Awd; Natl Merit Ltr; Michigan St Univ; Comp Sci.

WEIGAND, BECKY; Timken Sr HS; Canton, OH; Cls Rep Frsh Cls; Band; Girl Scts; Hon Rl; Sct Actv; Ger Clb; Pep Clb; Bsktbl; IM Sprt; College; Nursing.

WEIGAND, JOHN; Bishop Dwenger HS; Ft Wayne, IN; Cls Rep Frsh Cls; Cls Rep Soph Cls; Cl Rep Jr Cls; Chrh Wkr; Cmnty Wkr; Hon Rl; NHS; College; Law.

WEIGAND, KELLY; Harbor HS; Ashtabula, OH; 34/190 Trs Frsh Cls; Cls Rep Soph Cls; Sec Jr Cls; Cmnty Wkr; PAVAS; Yrbk; Sch Nwsp; College; Bus.

WEIGEL, JACULIN; Acad Of Immaculate Cncptn; Oldenburg, IN; 12/70 Chrs; Hon Rl; NHS; Orch; Sch Pl; Letter Bsktbl; GAA; IM Sprt; Univ; Corrections Admin.

WEIGOLD, LYNNETTE M; Bridgeport HS; Saginaw, MI; Chrs; Chrh Wkr; Treas Girl Scts; Hon Rl; Red Cr Ade; Sci Clb; Saginaw Bus Inst; Acctg.

WEIHROUCH, MARK; Woodmore HS; Elmore, OH; Am Leg Boys St; Band; Boy Scts; Hon Rl; Sct Actv; Yth Flsp; Pep Clb; IM Sprt; Am Leg Awd; Acad Ltr 78; Part In St Sci Fair 78; Owens Tech Coll; Comp Progr.

WEIKLE, WENDY; Edison HS; Milan, OH; 10/164 Band; Chrs; Hon Rl; NHS; Sch Mus; Sch Pl; Drama Clb; Sec Mth Clb; Scr Kpr; Ohio State Univ; Engr.

WEIL, JULIE; St Joseph HS; S Bend, IN; Hon Rl; Pep Clb; Tmr; Ball St Univ.

WEILER, JILL; Eastmoor HS; Columbus, OH; 8/290 Trs Sr Cls; Chrh Wkr; Sec Drl Tm; Girl Scts; Hon Rl; Hosp Ade; NHS; Off Ade; Rptr Yrbk; Rptr Sch Nwsp; 1st Pl Feature Writing Wkshp 1977; Homecoming Queen 1978; Hon Mtn Geometry 1976; Top 5 In Schlrshp Tsts; Scripps Univ; Humanities.

WEILER, SHELLEY; Niles Sr HS; Niles, MI; 83/388 Band; Chrh Wkr; Hon Rl; Orch; Sch Mus; Sct Actv; Yth Flsp; Natl Merit Ltr; Was Finlst In Miss Natl Teenager Of Mi 79; Kalamazoo Coll; Child Psych.

WEIMER, MARY; Madison Plains HS; London, OH; 11/146 VP Sr Cls; Band; Chrs; Hon Rl; NHS; Quill & Scroll; Rptr Sch Nwsp; Clark Tech College; Acctng.

WEIMER, TRACI; Napoleon HS; Mcclure, OH; Cl Rep Jr Cls; Am Leg Aux Girls St; Chrs; Chrh Wkr; Hon Rl; Yth Flsp; Drama Clb; Ten; Owens Tech Univ; Child Care.

WEIMERT, KIMBERLY; Memorial HS; Wapakoneta, OH; Chrs; Y-Teens; Rptr Yrbk; Pep Clb; GAA; Univ; Sociology.

WEIN, A; Norwayne HS; Sterling, OH; Cls Rep Soph Cls; VP Band; Hon Rl; VP NHS; Sch Mus; Sch Pl; Stu Cncl; Rptr Sch Nwsp; 4-H; IM Sprt; Miami Univ; Busns.

WEINBERG, KATY; Westfield Washington HS; Carmel, IN; Chrs; Hon Rl; NHS; Sch Mus; Sch Pl; Treas Drama Clb; Spn Clb; Swmmng; Trk; Chrldng; Best Supprtng Actress In Comedy, Bst New Actress, Best Singing Prfrmr 1977; Bst Actress Comedy, Bst Singng; Univ; Entertain.

WEINER, RICHARD; Walnut Ridge HS; Columbus, OH; Boy Scts; Chrh Wkr; Sch Pl; Stg Crw; Treas Fr Clb; Ten; Trk; Am Leg Awd; Pres Awd; Israel Stdy Schlrshp 79; Univ; Med.

WEINERT, LYNETTE; Marlington HS; Louisville, OH; Hon Rl; Lbry Ade; Off Ade; FFA; FHA; FSA; Pep Clb;.

WEINKAUF, JULIE; Marian HS; South Bend, IN; Cmp Fr Grls; Hon Rl; Sch Nwsp; 4-H; Pom Pon; Dnfth Awd; 4-H Awd; JA Awd; Purdue Univ; Forrestry.

WEINLE, JEROME; La Salle HS; Cincinnati, OH; 11/280 Jr NHS; NHS; Ftbl; Natl Merit Ltr; Univ; Engr.

WEINSTOCK, STAN; Anna HS; Maplewood, OH; 10/80 Am Leg Boys St; Hon Rl; Sch Mus; Sch Pl; Stg Crw; FFA; Crs Cntry; Univ; Math.

WEINZAPFEL, CYNDI; Reitz Memorial HS; Newburgh, IN; Hon Rl; Hosp Ade; Off Ade; Bsktbl; Trk; Deaconess School Of Nursing; Nursing.

WEINZAPFEL, JOY; Mater Dei HS; Evansville, IN; 2/165 Sal; Hon Rl; NHS; Sch Mus; Sch Pl; Stu Cncl; 4-H; Pep Clb; Bsktbl; Chrldng; Univ Of Evansville; Comp Sci.

WEINZAPFEL, LAURIE; Reitz Mem HS; Mt Vernon, IN; Cls Rep Frsh Cls; Cls Rep Soph Cls; Chrs; Hon Rl; Natl Forn Lg; Sch Pl; Stu Cncl; Fr Clb; Sci Clb; Indiana Univ; Law.

WEIPERT, JEFFREY J; Bishop Gallagher HS; Detroit, MI; 65/300 Rptr Sch Nwsp; IM Sprt; Univ; Civil Engr.

WEIR, ANDREW; Chelsea HS; Chelsea, MI; 71/213 Band; Boy Scts; Chrh Wkr; Hon Rl; Letter Ftbl; Letter Swmmng; Scr Kpr; Tmr; Univ; Engr.

WEIR, BETH; East Liverpool HS; E Liverpool, OH; 8/390 Chrs; Chrh Wkr; Hon Rl; VP NHS; Sch Mus; Keyettes; Pep Clb; Spn Clb; Univ; Math.

WEIR, DONALD E; Park Tudor HS; Indianapolis, IN; Cl Rep Jr Cls; Chrh Wkr; Hon Rl; Mod UN; Pol Wkr; Spn Clb; Letter Socr; C of C Awd; De Pauw Univ.

WEIR, EILEEN; Magnificat HS; Fairview Park, OH; NHS; Red Cr Ade; Sch Mus; Sch Pl; IM Sprt; College; Arts.

WEIR, KATHY L; John Marshall HS; Indianapolis, IN; 26/611 Hon Rl; Lbry Ade; Quill & Scroll; Ed Yrbk; Yrbk; Univ Of Indiana; Art.

WEIR, SUE; Centerville HS; Dayton, OH; 145/680 Band; Chrs; Chrh Wkr; Drl Tm; Girl Scts; Hon Rl; Off Ade; Orch; Sch Mus; OEA; Cert Of Merit In Spanish I Test 1975; Cert Of Mert For Spanish II Test 1977; Placed 5th In OEA Reg Cnst; Miami Univ; Speech Path.

WEIR, TRACY; Indian Valley South HS; Gnadenhutten, OH; 7/95 VP Frsh Cls; Band; Chrs; Hon Rl; NHS; Sch Pl; Stu Cncl; Sprt Ed Yrbk; Bsbl; Letter Trk; College.

WEIRICH, BECKY; Tuslaw HS; Massillon, OH; 25/175 VP Chrs; Chrh Wkr; Hon Rl; Sec NHS; Sch Mus; Y-Teens; FNA; Pep Clb; Scr Kpr; Tech School; Medicine.

WEIRICH, STEVEN; Canton Central Catholic HS; Massillon, OH; Hon Rl; NHS; IM Sprt; Akron Univ; Metalurgical Engr.

WEIRICK, LANCE; Triway HS; Wooster, OH; 7/161 Hon Rl; JA; NHS; Sct Actv; Mth Clb; Sci Clb; Crs Cntry; Trk; Wayne College; Med.

WEIR JR, DONALD E; Park Tudor School; Indianapolis, IN; Cl Rep Jr Cls; Hon Rl; Mod UN; Pol Wkr; Sch Pl; Stg Crw; Spn Clb; Letter Socr; Ten; C of C Awd; Wabash Coll; Bus.

WEIS, KAREN S; Garfield HS; Hamilton, OH; 8/369 Hon Rl; Jr NHS; Lbry Ade; NHS; Y-Teens; Spn Clb; Ten; Univ Of Cincinnati; Marketing.

WEIS, VICTORIA; Morton Sr HS; Hammond, IN; 54/465 Girl Scts; Hon Rl; Lbry Ade; NHS; Purdue Univ; Bus Admin.

WEISBARTH, WENDY; St Charles HS; Saginaw, MI; 11/130 Cls Rep Soph Cls; Cl Rep Jr Cls; Cls Rep Sr Cls; Chrh Wkr; Cmnty Wkr; Hon Rl; Jr NHS; Lbry Ade; NHS; PAVAS; Cert Of Recognition St Of Mim Comp Schl 79; Grad With High Hnrs Gld Cords 79; Grand Rapids Baptist Coll; Bus Admin.

WEISBURN, BETH; Perry HS; Massillon, OH; 1/480 Am Leg Aux Girls St; Debate Tm; FCA; Girl Scts; Hon Rl; Hosp Ade; Jr NHS; Lit Mag; Natl Forn Lg; NHS; Univ; Engr.

WEISE, BRYON; Finney HS; Detroit, MI; 21/200 Band; Boy Scts; Hon Rl; Lbry Ade; Yth Flsp; Cit Awd; Natl Merit Schl; Wayne St Univ; Mech Engr.

WEISE, DANIEL; Finney HS; Detroit, MI; Boy Scts; Hon Rl; JA; NHS; Sct Actv; Yth Flsp; Cit Awd; Oakland Univ; Mech Engr.

WEISE, PEGGY; Rosedale HS; Rosedale, IN; VP Soph Cls; Cls Rep Sr Cls; Band; Lbry Ade; Stu Cncl; 4-H; Pep Clb; Letter Bsktbl; Letter Trk; Chrldng; Indiana St Univ; Math.

WEISEL, PETER; Woodridge HS; Cuyahoga Fls, OH; Band; Hon Rl; Jr NHS; MMM; NHS; Sci Clb; Crs Cntry; IM Sprt;.

WEISENBERGER, ANNA; Rock Hill HS; Clarksville, OH; Hon Rl; 4-H; FHA; Pep Clb; Tchr Aide; Art Club;.

WEISENSTEIN, GARY; Licking Heights HS; Pataskala, OH; Hon Rl; Capt Ftbl; Capt Wrstlng; Ashland College; Art.

WEISER, MARK C; Canal Winchester HS; Canal Winchestr, OH; 10/85 Cls Rep Frsh Cls; Cl Rep Jr Cls; Band; Boy Scts; Hon Rl; NHS; Off Ade; Sct Actv; Scr Kpr; Natl Merit SF; Ohio St Univ; Art.

WEISER, MARTIN; Northeastern HS; Fountain City, IN; 77/139 Band; Rptr Sch Nwsp; College; Music.

WEISGERBER, GREGORY J; Moeller HS; Reading, OH; Band; Hon Rl; Orch; Trk; IM Sprt; Xavier Univ; Pre Med.

WEISKIRCHER, DONNA; Wheeling Park HS; Wheeling, WV; 1/600 Am Leg Aux Girls St; Band; Hon Rl; NHS; 4-H; Ten; Univ.

WEISKITTEL, BARBARA; Lumen Christi HS; Albion, MI; 1/239 Sec Band; Chrs; Pres Girl Scts; Hon Rl; VP NHS; PAVAS; Sch Mus; Sch Pl; Sct Actv; Stg Crw; St Of Mi Scshp Prgr 79; Albioncol Pres Schslhp 79; Marian Medl Awd 79; Albion Coll; Chem.

WEISKITTLE, KEITH; Riverside HS; Quincy, OH; 10/85 Cls Rep Frsh Cls; VP Jr Cls; Am Leg Boys St; Hon Rl; NHS; Sch Pl; Yth Flsp; Sprt Ed Yrbk; Rdo Clb; Letter Bsbl; College; Systems Analysis.

WEISNER, ELIZABETH; Delta HS; Muncie, IN; 11/200 VP Soph Cls; VP Jr Cls; Chrs; Chrh Wkr; FCA; Hon Rl; Hosp Ade; Off Ade; Sch Pl; Stu Cncl; Purdue Univ; Nursing.

WEISS, AMY; La Salle HS; South Bend, IN; 2/488 Band; Chrs; Chrh Wkr; Hon Rl; NHS; Sch Mus; Sch Pl; Drama Clb; Univ.

WEISS, BRIAN; Douglas Macarthur HS; Saginaw, MI; 9/320 Trs Sr Cls; Am Leg Boys St; Hon Rl; NHS; Rptr Yrbk; Pres Ger Clb; Ftbl; Ten; Trk; College; Engr.

WEISS, BRIAN E; Brethren Christian HS; Elkhart, IN; Cls Rep Frsh Cls; Cl Rep Jr Cls; Band; Chrs; Sch Pl; Stu Cncl; Fr Clb; Letter Bsbl; Letter Bsktbl; Letter Socr; Univ; Law.

WEISS, DAN; Euclid Sr HS; Euclid, OH; 216/746 Aud/Vis; Band; Boy Scts; Chrs; Hon Rl; Off Ade; Sch Mus; VP Yth Flsp; Key Clb; Rdo Clb; Univ; Recording Tech.

WEISS, JOANNE S; St Thomas Aquinas HS; Alliance, OH; 1/150 Cls Rep Frsh Cls; Cl Rep Jr Cls; Chrs; Cmnty Wkr; Hon Rl; Hosp Ade; NHS; Sch Mus; Rptr Sch Nwsp; Drama Clb; College.

WEISS, JONATHAN; Adlai E Stevenson HS; Livonia, MI; Debate Tm; ROTC; Natl Merit Schl; UCLA; Law.

WEISS, KATHRYN; All Saints Central HS; Bay City, MI; 11/167 Cmnty Wkr; Hon Rl; Jr NHS; Mdrgl; Pres NHS; Sch Mus; Sch Pl; Stg Crw; Stu Cncl; Rptr Yrbk; Delta Coll; Dent Hygiene.

WEISS, KIM; Ashland HS; Ashland, OH; Chrh Wkr; Cmnty Wkr; Hosp Ade; NHS; Off Ade; Yth Flsp; Pres FHA; Sec FTA; Pep Clb; Mat Maids; Coll; Nursing.

WEISS, LAURIE; Norwalk HS; Norwlk, OH; Chrs; Sch Pl; Ger Clb; Univ; Acctg.

WEISS, LEA; Richmond HS; Richmond, IN; 42/550 Chrs; Debate Tm; Hon Rl; NHS; Quill & Scroll; 4-H; Lat Clb; Cit Awd; Pur; Veterinarian.

WEISS, TAMMY; Mater Dei HS; Evansville, IN; 3/150 Cl Rep Jr Cls; Boy Scts; Hon Rl; Jr NHS; NHS; Stu Cncl; 4-H; Pep Clb; Pom Pon; 4-H Awd; Univ; Cmmrcl Artist.

WEISSMAN, PETER T; Walter E Stebbins HS; Centerville, OH; VP Chrs; MMM; Sch Mus; Coll; Chem.

WEISSMANN, CHRISTOPHER; St Xavier HS; Cincinnati, OH; 42/264 VP Jr Cls; Pres Sr Cls; Cmnty Wkr; Ger Clb; Trk; IM Sprt; JETS Awd; Coll; Archt.

WEIST, JAMES; Rocky River HS; Rocky Rvr, OH; 125/315 Cls Rep Frsh Cls; Cls Rep Soph Cls; Cl Rep Jr Cls; Chrh Wkr; FCA; Hon Rl; Letter Bsktbl; Letter Ftbl; Letter Trk; Coach Actv; College; Business.

WEITFLE, MIKE; Moeller HS; Cincinnati, OH; 4/263 Band; Hon Rl; JA; NHS; Stu Cncl; Rptr Yrbk; Sch Nwsp; Rdo Clb; Letter Crs Cntry; Letter Trk; Univ Of Notre Dame; Engr.

WEITHMAN, ELIZABETH; Galion HS; Galion, OH; Am Leg Aux Girls St; Chrs; Drl Tm; Hon Rl; NHS; Trk; Pres 4-H; College; Cpa.

WEITZMAN, JANE; North HS; Eastlake, OH; 127/650 Hon Rl; NHS; Spn Clb; Mgrs; Cert Of Hon Outstndng Spanish Stdnt 79; Univ Of Miami; Cmnctns.

WEKEWERT, MICHAEL; Posen HS; Posen, MI; Chrh Wkr; Cmnty Wkr; Hon Rl; Off Ade; 4-H; Letter Ftbl; Letter Trk; Ctrl Michigan Univ; Bus Admin.

WELBAUM, LISA; Twin Valley North HS; Lewisburg, OH; Cmp Fr Grls; Chrs; Drl Tm; Hon Rl; NHS; Sec Rptr Yrbk; Sec FTA; Pep Clb; Letter Trk; Chrldng; College; Vet Asst.

WELBORN, JIMMY; Union County HS; Brookville, IN; Cls Rep Frsh Cls; Cls Rep Soph Cls; Hon Rl; Stu Cncl; Yth Flsp; FFA; Letter Crs Cntry; Letter Trk; Letter Wrstlng; Connersville Area Voc Schl; Agri.

WELBOURNE, BEVERLY; Tecumseh HS; New Carlisle, OH; 5/344 AFS; Band; Hon Rl; Jr NHS; NHS; Sch Mus; Spn Clb; Trk; Wittenberg Univ.

WELCH, BRENDA; Coalton Twelve Year School; Mabie, WV; 3/33 Cls Rep Frsh Cls; Cls Rep Soph Cls; Cl Rep Jr Cls; Chrh Wkr; Cmnty Wkr; Hon Rl; Lbry Ade; Off Ade; Sch Pl; Treas Stu Cncl; Bus Schl; Sec.

WELCH, BRIAN; Lexington Sr HS; Lexington, OH; Band; Boy Scts; Chrs; Sct Actv; Ger Clb; Mth Clb; VICA; Crs Cntry; Trk; C of C Awd; Eagle Scout Letters From Gen Assembly Ohio Rep Harry E Turner; Ohio Inst Of Tech; Elec Engr.

WELCH, DEE; Wynford HS; Nevada, OH; 2/140 Aud/Vis; Sec Band; Hon Rl; NHS; Rptr Yrbk; Gym; Letter Trk; Chrldng; Letter Mgrs; Scr Kpr; Ohio St Univ; Occptnl Ther.

WELCH, JOHN; Lakeshore HS; Stevensville, MI; 3 1/292 Cls Rep Soph Cls; Band; Boy Scts; Hon Rl; NHS; Off Ade; Sch Mus; Stu Cncl; Ger Clb; Key Clb; Central Michigan Univ; Busns.

WELCH, KERRY; Green HS; Akron, OH; 15/360 VP Jr Cls; VP Sr Cls; Am Leg Aux Girls St; Chrs; NHS; Sch Mus; Stu Cncl; Y-Teens; Chrldng; Cit Awd; Ohio St Univ.

WELCH, LAWRENCE; Cathedral HS; Indianapolis, IN; Chrh Wkr; Hon Rl; IM Sprt; Mgrs; Scr Kpr; Church In The Modern World Awd 78; St Meinrad Coll; Hist.

WELCH, MARGIE; Coalton Twelve Year School; Mabie, WV; Sec Chrh Wkr; Cmnty Wkr; Hon Rl; Lbry Ade; Sch Pl; Stg Crw; Yth Flsp; Drama Clb; 4-H; Bsktbl; Univ; Basketball.

WELCH, RICHARD; Cedar Springs Public HS; Cedar Sprg, MI; Hon Rl; Jr NHS; IM Sprt; Grand Rapids Baptist Coll; Speech.

WELCH, THOMAS; Blanchester HS; Midland, OH; 15/148 Cmnty Wkr; Hon Rl; DECA; Univ; Comp Progr.

WELCH, TINA; Fulton Schools; Perrinton, MI; Mth Clb; Bsktbl; Trk; IM Sprt; Pom Pon; M J Murphy Beauty Coll; Cosmetolgy.

WELCHER, DAWN; Harper Creek HS; Battle Creek, MI; Band; Cmp Fr Grls; Chrs; Hon Rl; NHS; Sch Mus; Sch Pl; Lake Superior State; Wildlife Mgmt.

WELD, DAVID; Crestwood HS; Dearborn Hts, MI; Hon Rl; Yth Flsp; Natl Merit Ltr; Natl Merit SF; Univ Of Mich; Dentistry.

WELDON, ANNE B; Port Clinton HS; Pt Clinton, OH; 20/289 Hon Rl; Letter Bsktbl; Trk; Ohio St Univ; Dance.

WELDON, LANA; Millersport HS; Millersport, OH; 2/51 Sec Frsh Cls; Sec Soph Cls; Sec Jr Cls; Sec Sr Cls; Chrs; Hon Rl; NHS; 4-H; 4-H; Pep Clb; Ohio Univ Branch; Bus Admin.

WELDON, ROBERTA; Wyoming Park HS; Wyoming, MI; 1/257 Val; Band; NHS; Sch Pl; Fr Clb; Am Leg Awd; Univ Of Michigan; Engr.

WELDY, RUTH; Bethany Christian HS; Goshen, IN; VP Sr Cls; Cls Rep Sr Cls; Chrs; Cmnty Wkr; Hon Rl; Sch Mus; Stu Cncl; Yth Flsp; Sch Nwsp; Goshen Coll; Art Ther.

WELKER, JANET; South Vermillion HS; Clinton, IN; 25/180 Cls Rep Frsh Cls; Drl Tm; Girl Scts; Stg Crw; Stu Cncl; Yth Flsp; Drama Clb; Fr Clb; Pep Clb; Chrldng; Busns Schl.

WELKER, MELANI; Whitko HS; South Whitley, IN; Sec Soph Cls; FCA; Hon Rl; Stg Crw; Drama Clb; Fr Clb; Pep Clb; Letter Ten; Chrldng; GAA; Univ; Eng Tchr.

WELLER, DANIEL; Willard HS; Willard, OH; 30/176 Band; Chrs; Orch; Sch Mus; 4-H; Pep Clb; Glf; JC Awd; Bowling Green State Univ; Math.

WELLER, DAVID; Clay HS; S Bend, IN; Band; Chrh Wkr; Hon Rl; NHS; Sct Actv; Yth Flsp; Swmmng; Kiwan Awd; Ball St Univ; Finance.

WELLER, MICHAEL; Williamston HS; Okemos, MI; 22/180 Band; Debate Tm; Sch Pl; Am Leg Awd; Mic State Univ; Accgt.

WELLES, CHRIS; Maumee Vly Cntry Day HS; Perrysburg, OH; Cls Rep Soph Cls; Cl Rep Jr Cls; Mod UN; Pol Wkr; Rptr Sch Nwsp; Letter Bsbl; Letter Socr; Letter Trk; Univ; Law.

WELLING, DEANNA; La Brae HS; Warren, OH; 8/186 VP Sr Cls; Am Leg Aux Girls St; Hon Rl; NHS; Off Ade; Y-Teens; Sprt Ed Yrbk; FTA; College; Sociology.

WELLING, LAURIE; Eastwood HS; Perrysburg, OH; 9/186 Sec Frsh Cls; Cl Rep Jr Cls; Cmp Fr Grls; Chrh Wkr; Girl Scts; Hon Rl; Off Ade; Stu Cncl; 4-H; Pep Clb; Columbus Tech Inst; Legal Sec.

WELLING, LISA; Clay HS; Oregon, OH; 35/360 Treas Band; Chrh Wkr; Hon Rl; Hosp Ade; Sch Mus; Fr Clb; FTA; College; Music Educ.

WELLMAN, CARRIE; Northrop HS; Ft Wayne, IN; 151/587 Band; JA; Off Ade; Red Cr Ade; Pep Clb; Univ; Zoology.

WELLMAN, DEBRA; Cambridge HS; Cambridge, OH; 153/270 Cls Rep Sr Cls; 4-H; FHA; Voc Schl; Agri Bus.

WELLMAN, DEBRA; Midland Trail HS; Ansted, WV; Band; Drm Mjrt; Hon Rl; Yrbk; Fr Clb; Pep Clb; Chrldng; IM Sprt; Twrlr; W Virginia Inst Of Tech; Labor Rel.

WELLMAN, ELIZABETH; Coldwater HS; Coldwater, OH; Cls Rep Frsh Cls; Cls Rep Soph Cls; Sec Jr Cls; Sec Sr Cls; Am Leg Aux Girls St; Hon Rl; NHS; Stu Cncl; VP Ger Clb; Capt Bsktbl; Ohio St Univ; Dietetics.

WELLMAN, ELIZABETH L; Coldwater HS; Coldwater, OH; 14/155 Cls Rep Frsh Cls; Cls Rep Soph Cls; Sec Jr Cls; Sec Sr Cls; Am Leg Aux Girls St; Band; Hon Rl; Hosp Ade; Jr NHS; NHS; Ohio St Univ; Dietetics.

WELLMAN, GRETCHEN; Andrean HS; Merrillville, IN; Hon Rl; Fr Clb; IM Sprt; PPFtbl; Scr Kpr; Var Vllybl 77 80 & Captn 2 Yrs; Invited To Partcpt In Miss Teen Pageant 79; Univ; Phys Educ Tchr.

WELLMAN, MICHELE; Buffalo HS; Kenova, WV; 10/141 Cl Rep Jr Cls; Band; Chrh Wkr; Hon Rl; Mod UN; NHS; Red Cr Ade; Drama Clb; FHA; Mth Clb; College.

WELLMAN, NINA; Buffalo HS; Huntington, WV; Band; Chrs; Chrh Wkr; Hon Rl; Red Cr Ade; Sch Mus; Yth Flsp; Y-Teens; Letter Trk; Marshall Univ; Elem Educ.

WELLMAN, RHONDA; Buffalo HS; Huntington, WV; Hon Rl; Stg Crw; Mth Clb; Letter Trk; Marshall Univ; Tchr.

WELLMAN, S; Buffalo HS; Kenova, WV; FCA; Hon Rl; PAVAS; Red Cr Ade; Sch Pl; Stg Crw; Yth Flsp; Y-Teens; Civ Clb; FHA; Ohio St Univ; Busns.

WELLMEYER, CONNIE; Southridge HS; Holland, IN; Chrs; Chrh Wkr; Hon Rl; Treas Yth Flsp; Civ Clb; FHA; Pep Clb; Huntingburg Std Club 76 79; Univ; Acctg.

WELLONS, DEBRA; Lake HS; Walbridge, OH; 5/156 Sec Band; Drm Mjrt; Hon Rl; NHS; Stu Cncl; Ed Yrbk; Rptr Sch Nwsp; Bowling Green State Univ; Nurse.

WELLS, AMY; Springboro HS; Springboro, OH; Sec Jr Cls; Val; Am Leg Aux Girls St; Band; Chrh Wkr; Girl Scts; Hon Rl; NHS; Off Ade; Sch Pl; Ohio Northern Univ; Pharm.

WELLS, ANNA; Decatur Ctrl HS; Indianapolis, IN; Band; Chrh Wkr; Drl Tm; Girl Scts; Hon Rl; Off Ade; Sch Mus; Sch Pl; Sct Actv; Stu Cncl; Indiana Voc Tech Coll; Mktg.

WELLS, BARBARA; Marian HS; S Bend, IN; Girl Scts; Hon Rl; 4-H; Fr Clb; IM Sprt; Indiana Univ; Legal Asst.

WELLS, CAROL; Central Catholic HS; Canton, OH; Chrh Wkr; Girl Scts; Hon Rl; Hosp Ade; OEA;.

WELLS, CINDY; Midland Trail HS; Ansted, WV; Cls Rep Soph Cls; Pres Jr Cls; Band; Chrs; Chrh Wkr; Hon Rl; NHS; Stu Cncl; Yth Flsp; Fr Clb; W Virginia Inst Of Tech; Civil Engr.

WELLS, DARRYL; Bellbrook HS; Bellbrook, OH; NHS; Lat Clb; Bsbl; Bsktbl; Univ.

WELLS, DONALD; Timken Sr HS; Canton, OH; Cls Rep Frsh Cls; Boy Scts; Hon Rl; JA; Sch Nwsp; Boys Clb Am; Ger Clb; JA Awd; Coll; Engr.

WELLS, DONNA; Castle HS; Newburgh, IN; Chrs; Hon Rl; Mdrgl; NHS; Pep Clb; Pom Pon; Evansville Schl Hlth Occptns; LPN.

WELLS, DOUGLAS; Madison Plains HS; London, OH; Band; Sch Mus; FFA; Letter Ftbl; Letter Wrstlng; Ohio St Univ; Farming.

WELLS, ERIC; Holt Sr HS; Dimondale, MI; Jr NHS; NHS; Pepperdine Coll; Busns Admin.

WELLS, GREGORY; Central HS; Detroit, MI; 35/605 Stu Cncl; Fr Clb; Univ; Archt Dsgn.

WELLS, JAN; Bexley HS; Bexley, OH; Band; Chrs; Drm Mjrt; Fr Clb; Bsbl; Scr Kpr; Letter Twrlr; College.

WELLS, JANET; Defiance HS; Defiance, OH; Band; Hon Rl; NHS; Off Ade; Sch Mus; Rptr Yrbk; Fr Clb; Mth Clb; College; Elec Engr.

WELLS, JOHN; Delton Kellogg HS; Plainwell, MI; 17/154 VP Band; Hon Rl; Fr Clb; Bsktbl; Crs Cntry; Capt Ten; IM Sprt; Western Michigan Univ; Law.

WELLS, JOHN; Riverdale HS; Arlington, OH; Hon Rl; NHS; Sch Pl; FTA; IM Sprt; Mgrs; College; History.

WELLS, KATHERINE; Andrews HS; Painesville, OH; Cls Rep Soph Cls; Hon Rl; College; Advertising.

WELLS, KATHY; Stonewall Jackson HS; Charleston, WV; Pres Frsh Cls; Girl Scts; Hon Rl; Jr NHS; NHS; Stu Cncl; Mth Clb; Sci Clb; Spn Clb; Letter Ten; College.

WELLS, LEROY; Eastern HS; Lucasville, OH; Boy Scts; Cmnty Wkr; Hon Rl; Sct Actv; Yrbk; 4-H; Pep Clb; Letter Bsbl; Capt Bsktbl; IM Sprt; Basketball Trophy For Most Rebounds 78; Univ.

WELLS, LISA; Hamilton Township HS; Columbus, OH; 18/216 Hon Rl; Off Ade; Stu Cncl; FTA; Trk; Chrldng; PPFtbl; Milligan Christian Coll; Nurse.

WELLS, LUCINDA; Hampshire HS; Romney, WV; Cls Rep Frsh Cls; Cl Rep Jr Cls; AFS; Band; Hon Rl; Sch Pl; Stu Cncl; Drama Clb; English; Sci Coll Bio & Phys Sci; World Cultures; College; Bio Sci.

WELLS, MELISSA; Jackson Milton HS; North Jackson, OH; Hon Rl; NHS; Sch Mus; FFA; Chrldng; PPFtbl; Youngstown Coll Of Bus; Legal Sec.

WELLS, MICHELLE; Mt Clemens HS; Mt Clemens, MI; Sec Frsh Cls; Hon Rl; Off Ade; PAVAS; Fr Clb; VICA; Letter Gym; Swmmng; Tmr; Univ; Tech Illustration.

WELLS, MONICA; Utica HS; Utica, MI; Cls Rep Soph Cls; Trs Jr Cls; Hon Rl; NHS; Stu Cncl; VP Yth Flsp; Ed Sch Nwsp; Pep Clb; Tmr; Outstndng Newsppr Stndt Awd 78; Gold Key Wrtng Awd 79; Hon Mntn In Detroit News Const 79; Univ; Jrnlsm.

WELLS, NATALIE; Lutheran HS E; Willowick, OH; 5/50 Cls Rep Soph Cls; Sec Jr Cls; Trs Jr Cls; Band; Chrh Wkr; Hon Rl; Lbry Ade; Off Ade; Stu Cncl; Chrldng; Lutheran Med Ctr; Nursing.

WELLS, PATRICIA; Ferndale HS; Pleasant Ridge, MI; 17/369 Hon Rl; NHS; Stg Crw; Ger Clb; Letter Swmmng; GAA; Univ; Engr.

WELLS, REBECCA; Shaker Hts HS; Shaker Hts, OH; Band; Hon Rl; Letter Bsbl; Letter Hockey; Natl Merit Ltr; Schlrshp Key; Coll.

WELLS, SHERRY; Tippecanoe HS; Tipp City, OH; VP Band; VP Chrh Wkr; Drm Mjrt; Hon Rl; NHS; Orch; Sch Pl; 4-H; GAA; Top 70 Schlrs 78 & 79; Univ; Med Tech.

WELLS, SUSAN; Houghton Lake HS; Houghton Lk, MI; Chrh Wkr; Cmnty Wkr; Girl Scts; Sct Actv; 4-H; Univ; RN.

WELLS, WAYBON; Cass Tech HS; Detroit, MI; 15/983 Cmnty Wkr; Lbry Ade; NHS; Off Ade; FBLA; OEA; Natl Merit Schl; Western Michigan Univ; Marketing.

WELLS, WAYBON D; Cass Technical HS; Detroit, MI; Hon Rl; Lbry Ade; NHS; Off Ade; Fr Clb; FBLA; OEA; Phi Beth Kappa HS Achvmnt Certf 1979; Mim Comp Awd And Schlrshp 1979; Western Mi Univ Acad Schlrshp 1979; Western Michigan Univ; Mktg.

WELLSTEAD, WALTER; Perrysburg HS; Perrysburg, OH; Letter Bsbl; Bsktbl; Univ Of Cincinnati; Archt.

WELLY, CHRISTINA; New Riegel HS; Carey, OH; 9/51 Sec Frsh Cls; Band; Chrs; Hon Rl; Lbry Ade; NHS; Sch Mus; Sch Pl; 4-H; Pep Clb; Vocational Schl.

WELLY, THOMAS; Hicksville HS; Hicksville, OH; 31/108 Band; Boy Scts; Hon Rl; Quill & Scroll; Sch Pl; Stg Crw; Rptr Sch Nwsp; Sch Nwsp; 4-H; Lat Clb; Univ.

WELSAND, SUSAN; Brighton HS; Brighton, MI; Cls Rep Soph Cls; Aud/Vis; Debate Tm; Girl Scts; Hon Rl; Natl Forn Lg; Quill & Scroll; Sch Mus; Sch Pl; Stg Crw; Detroit News Writing Awd; Forensics Districts; Northwestern Univ; Journalism.

WELSH, BILL; Woodrow Wilson HS; Youngstown, OH; Cls Rep Soph Cls; Cl Rep Jr Cls; Cls Rep Sr Cls; Boy Scts; Sch Pl; Stu Cncl; Bsbl; Bsktbl; Ftbl; IM Sprt; Youngstown St Univ.

WELSH, DEBORAH; Jewett Scio HS; Cadiz, OH; 16/80 Chrs; Chrh Wkr; Hon Rl; Lbry Ade; Sch Mus; Drama Clb; 4-H; FHA; Spn Clb; 4-H Awd; Ohio St Univ; Med Tech.

WELSH, GREGORY; Cardinal Mooney HS; Youngstown, OH; 31/288 Hon Rl; Jr NHS; NHS; Red Cr Ade; Fr Clb; Mth Clb; IM Sprt; Univ; Med.

WELSH, IAN; Richmond HS; Richmond, IN; 15/650 Cls Rep Frsh Cls; Cls Rep Soph Cls; Cl Rep Jr Cls; Cls Rep Sr Cls; Am Leg Boys St; Hon Rl; Jr NHS; NHS; Stu Cncl; Letter Bsbl; Purdue Univ; Engr.

WELSH, JOEL; North Canton Hoover HS; Bausman, PA; 90/440 FCA; Hon Rl; NHS; Quill & Scroll; Stu Cncl; Yth Flsp; Ed Sch Nwsp; Rptr Sch Nwsp; Letter Bsktbl; Letter Ten; Grove City Coll; Bus Admin.

WELSH, KEVIN; Bishop Donahue HS; Glen Dale, WV; Hon Rl; Spn Clb; Letter Bsktbl; Ftbl; Scr Kpr; College.

WELSH, MARIANNE; Gallia Academy HS; Bidwell, OH; 9/250 Drm Mjrt; Hon Rl; Jr NHS; NHS; Sch Pl; VP Drama Clb; VP Fr Clb; Key Clb; Trk; Ohio St Univ; Pharm.

WELSH, MARY; Ursuline HS; Youngstown, OH; 1/325 Band; Debate Tm; Girl Scts; Hon Rl; Jr NHS; Natl Forn Lg; NHS; Pol Wkr; Fr Clb; FTA; Georgetown Notre Dame Univ; Pre Law.

WELSH, THERESA; Timken HS; Canton, OH; Chrs; Hon Rl; Jr NHS; NHS; Sch Mus; Sch Pl; Rptr Yrbk; Drama Clb; Mth Clb; Swmmng; College; Engnrng Comp Science.

WELSH, WILLIAM; Jewett Scio HS; Jewett, OH; Boy Scts; Cmnty Wkr; Hon Rl; Stg Crw; Letter Crs Cntry; Letter Trk; Scr Kpr;.

WELSHANS, C ROBERT; Linsly Institute; Wheeling, WV; Band; Chrs; Drm Bgl; Orch; ROTC; Sch Mus; Fr Clb; Key Clb; Pep Clb; IM Sprt; Sr Perfct Stdnt Admin 79; Univ; Optometry.

WELSHANS, SANDRA; Chelsea HS; Dexter, MI; 33/213 Band; Chrh Wkr; Hon Rl; Yth Flsp;.

WELSHANS, TINA; Madonna HS; Colliers, WV; Pep Clb; Mat Maids; West Virginia Univ.

WELSHEIMER, JOHN; Wm V Fisher Catholic HS; Lancaster, OH; Cls Rep Frsh Cls; Chrh Wkr; Cmnty Wkr; Hon Rl; Sch Pl; Stg Crw; Stu Cncl; Letter Crs Cntry; Letter Ten; College; Med Tech.

WELSHOFER JR, LEW; Fenwick HS; Middletown, OH; Am Leg Boys St; Chrh Wkr; Hon Rl; NHS; Rptr Sch Nwsp; Letter Bsktbl; Letter Crs Cntry; Letter Trk; 1st Econ In Action Progr In City 79; Miami Univ; Personnel Mgmt.

WELTON, CYNTHIA L; Hubbard HS; Hubbard, OH; 12/330 Band; Hon Rl; Sch Mus; Treas FTA; Spn Clb; Gym; Swmmng; Rotary Awd; Swimming Team Most Improved; Tri Hi Y; Youngstown Symphony Usherette; College; Phys Ed.

WELTON, EILEEN; Euclid HS; Euclid, OH; 142/700 Cls Rep Soph Cls; Cl Rep Jr Cls; Chrs; Chrh Wkr; Quill & Scroll; Stu Cncl; Rptr Yrbk; Letter Trk; Mgrs; Miami Univ Of Ohio; Retailing.

WELTON, JOHN C; Moorefield HS; Moorefield, WV; Chrs; Cmnty Wkr; Pol Wkr; Sch Pl; Yth Flsp; 4-H; FFA; VICA; Letter Ftbl; Letter Trk; Potomac St Coll; Ag.

WELTY, JILL; Kingsford HS; Kingsford, MI; Band; Hosp Ade; Lbry Ade; Micheal Reese Schl; Nursing.

WEMPLE, SUSAN; Ravenna HS; Ravenna, MI; 14/103 Girl Scts; Hon Rl; Chrldng; Muskegon Bus Schl; Sec.

WENDEL, STEVE; Brookville HS; Brookville, IN; Treas FFA;.

WENDELN, DONNA; Archbishop Alter HS; Kettering, OH; Band; Chrh Wkr; Girl Scts; Hon Rl; Lbry Ade; NHS; Univ Of Dayton; Chem Engr.

WENDLAND, HEIDI; Bridgman HS; Bridgman, MI; Band; Hon Rl; 4-H; FHA; Sci Clb; 4-H Awd; Lake Michigan Coll; Nursing.

WENDLING, D; Chesaning Union HS; Chesaning, MI; Band; Hon Rl; Jr NHS; Off Ade; Chrldng; Univ.

WENDORF, RICK; Mason HS; Mason, MI; Chrs; Chrh Wkr; Cmnty Wkr; Sch Mus; Sch Pl; Stg Crw; Stu Cncl; Yth Flsp; Y-Teens; Sci Clb; Indep Research Stu IRS; Coll; Mortician.

WENDROW, KIMBERLY; North Central HS; Indianapolis, IN; 225/999 Chrs; Chrh Wkr; Girl Scts; Hon Rl; JA; Sct Actv; Stu Cncl; Fr Clb; IM Sprt; In Univ Hon Progr 79; Top 25% Of Cls 79; Notre Dame Univ; Cmnctns.

WENDT, CYNTHIA; Napoleon HS; Napoleon, OH; Am Leg Aux Girls St; Band; Hon Rl; NHS; Orch; 4-H; Ger Clb; Letter Ten; Mgrs; Rotary Awd; Bowling Green State Univ; Acctg.

WENDT, GEORGIANN; Lockland HS; Cincinnati, OH; 3/83 Hon Rl; NHS; Stu Cncl; Ed Sch Nwsp; Chrldng; Cit Awd; College; Law.

WENDT, KATHLEEN; Perrysburg HS; Perrysburg, OH; Hon Rl; Jr NHS; Spn Clb; Univ; Acctg.

WENGER, BARBARA; Charlotte HS; Charlotte, MI; 2/386 Trs Sr Cls; Sal; Chrs; Chrh Wkr; Hon Rl; Hosp Ade; Jr NHS; Lbry Ade; NHS; Central Mic Univ; Journalism.

WENGER, JAYDON E; Northwood HS; Goshen, IN; 48/196 Am Leg Boys St; Band; Hon Rl; College; Music.

WENGER, JOYCE A; Marlington HS; Louisville, OH; Am Leg Aux Girls St; Hon Rl; NHS; 4-H; Fr Clb; FNA; Letter Bsktbl; Capt Ten; IM Sprt; Aultmun Schl Of Respiratory; Ther.

WENGER, LORI; Copley Sr HS; Copley, OH; Chrs; Cmnty Wkr; Key Clb; GAA; IM Sprt; Scr Kpr; Sftbl Vrsty 78; Vllybl Vrsty 78; Grange Rep 78; Univ; Soc Service.

WENINGER, MARK; Holy Spirit Seminary; University Hts, OH; 1/10 Cls Rep Frsh Cls; Sec Soph Cls; Pres Jr Cls; VP Jr Cls; Aud/Vis; Band; Chrs; Chrh Wkr; Hon Rl; Lbry Ade; John Carroll Univ; Communications.

WENK, LEWIS; Walsh Jesuit HS; Aurora, OH; Band; Boy Scts; Chrh Wkr; Cmnty Wkr; Hosp Ade; Orch; Red Cr Ade; Sct Actv; Ftbl; Swmmng; Eagle Scout Cert Of Rec; Highland View Hosp Volunteer Cert Of Rec; Art Award Raymond School; Case Western Reserve; Elec Engr.

WENKER, MARK; Saint Xavier HS; Cincinnati, OH; 88/278 Chrh Wkr; Cmnty Wkr; Hon Rl; Sch Pl; Coach Actv; IM Sprt; Cit Awd; College; Phys Ther.

WENMAN, FORREST; Lakeshore HS; Baroda, MI; Chrs; Hon Rl; JA; Sch Pl; Sct Actv; Spn Clb; JA Awd; Natl Merit Schl; Lakeshore Spanish Awd 77; DANK Cert Of Recgntn 79; Michigan St Univ; Forgn Lang.

WENNING, DEBORAH; Mansfield Malabar; Mansfield, OH; Cls Rep Frsh Cls; Cls Rep Soph Cls; Cl Rep Jr Cls; Cls Rep Sr Cls; Band; Chrh Wkr; Stu Cncl; Yth Flsp; Mas Awd; Bowling Green State; Occupatnl Ther.

WENNING, TIM; Marion Local HS; Yorkshire, OH; Am Leg Boys St; Hon Rl; NHS; Sci Clb; IM Sprt;.

WENNINGER, DARLA; Buckeye Central HS; Tiro, OH; Cl Rep Jr Cls; Band; Hon Rl; Stu Cncl; Sprt Ed Yrbk; Rptr Sch Nwsp; 4-H; VP FHA; Spn Clb; Mgrs; Bwlng; Chapt & Jr Degree Homemaking Degree; Miss Teen Age Amer;.

WENTMORE, CYNTHIA; Pioneer HS; Ann Arbor, MI; Univ; Math.

WENTWORTH, KATHY; Solon HS; Solon, OH; Cls Rep Frsh Cls; Cls Rep Soph Cls; FCA; Hon Rl; Gym; Ten; Letter Chrldng; Pom Pon; College; Bus Admin.

WENTWORTH, TONDA; Ansonia HS; Ansonia, OH; 3/64 Hon Rl; Jr NHS; NHS; Off Ade; Stu Cncl; Yrbk; Ed Sch Nwsp; Rptr Sch Nwsp; Sch Nwsp; FHA;.

WENTZ, DAWN; Coshocton HS; Coshocton, OH; Chrh Wkr; Girl Scts; Stu Cncl; Sprt Ed Yrbk; Rptr Sch Nwsp; 4-H; Treas Fr Clb; Sci Clb; PPFtbl; Ohio State Univ; Dental Hygiene.

WENTZ, JACQUELINE M; North Adams HS; Hillsdale, MI; 5/49 Hon Rl; Lbry Ade; Off Ade; Stu Cncl; Rptr Yrbk; Rptr Sch Nwsp; Fr Clb; Data Proc Tech.

WENTZ, PEGGY; Arlington Local School; Arlington, OH; 2/43 Sec Sr Cls; Sal; Band; Chrs; NHS; Rptr Yrbk; GAA; Lion Awd; Pensacola Christian Coll; Missions.

WENTZEL, SCOTT; Franklin HS; Franklin, OH; Hon Rl; Pep Clb; Bsbl; Letter Bsktbl; Glf; Univ; Bus Admin.

WENZ, ROBERT E; North Royalton HS; North Royalton, OH; 3/290 Pres Band; Chrh Wkr; Hon Rl; Pres NHS; Pres Orch; Sch Mus; Pres Lat Clb; Sci Clb; Bsbl; Capt Glf; Ohio Music Educ Assoc Solo & Ensmbl 1974; His Day 78 Contest 1978; 5th Pl Scripps Howard Reg Spell Bee; Case Western Reserve Univ; Bio.

WENZEL, DAWN; Baldwin HS; Baldwin, MI; 5/73 Hon Rl; Lbry Ade; NHS; Off Ade; Ed Sch Nwsp; Bus Schl; Exec Sec.

WENZEL, DAWN M; Baldwin HS; Baldwin, MI; 6/76 Hon Rl; Ed Sch Nwsp;.

WENZEL, EVELY L; St Charles HS; St Charles, MI; Girl Scts; Hon Rl; Lbry Ade; 4-H; Trk; GAA; Scr Kpr; 4-H Awd; MVP Vllybl 78; Baker Jr Coll Of Bus; Data Proc.

WENZEL, SUSAN; Lutheran West HS; Dearborn, MI; Band; Chrh Wkr; Hon Rl; NHS; Sch Mus; Yth Flsp; Sch Nwsp; Bsktbl; GAA; Mgrs; Mic State Univ; Dietetics.

WENZLAU, JANET; Rutherford B Hayes HS; Delaware, OH; Cls Rep Frsh Cls; Cls Rep Soph Cls; VP Jr Cls; Pres Sr Cls; AFS; Hon Rl; NHS; Stu Cncl; Yth Flsp; Rptr Sch Nwsp; Denison Univ; Bio.

WEPMAN, KEN; East Grand Rapids Sr HS; Grand Rapids, MI; Cmnty Wkr; Hon Rl; Sch Nwsp; IM Sprt; Michigan St Univ; Med.

WERBRICH, TIMOTHY; Miamisburg HS; Miamisburg, OH; 50/315 Am Leg Boys St; Chrh Wkr; Hon Rl; NHS; Bsktbl; Cit Awd; Univ Of Dayton; Comp Sci.

WERDEHOFF, KAREN; Whitmer HS; Toledo, OH; 5/910 Hon Rl; NHS; Ger Clb; Letter Bsktbl; Letter Trk; PPFtbl; College; Environmental Sci.

WERDMANN, NANCY; Our Lady Of Angels HS; Cincinnati, OH; 2/117 Cls Rep Frsh Cls; Cls Rep Soph Cls; Trs Jr Cls; Cmnty Wkr; Hon Rl; VP NHS; Stu Cncl; Drama Clb; Spn Clb; Letter Trk; Student Of Yr; Fest Chrmn 77; GAA Fund Raiser Chrmn 78; Natl Sci Fdtn Schlrshp; Best Def Volleyball Player; Univ; Sci.

WERKIN, ROBIN; Catholic Central HS; Steubenville, OH; Hon Rl; Spn Clb; Jefferson Tech Coll; Med Assist.

WERKING, KAREN; Shenandoah HS; Middletown, IN; 23/118 Chrh Wkr; Cmnty Wkr; FHA; FTA; Mth Clb; Glf; Purdue Univ; Math.

WERLINE, SUE; Fairmont West HS; Kettering, OH; Hon Rl; Off Ade; Miami Valley Hospital; Nursing.

WERLING, DENISE; Seton HS; Cincinnati, OH; 24/274 Chrs; Hon Rl; Sch Pl; FBLA; Univ Of Cincinnati; CPA.

WERLING, JUNE; Northrop HS; Ft Wayne, IN; Cls Rep Frsh Cls; VP Soph Cls; VP Jr Cls; VP Sr Cls; Band; Hon Rl; Stu Cncl; Trk; Pom Pon; Indiana Univ; Dent Hygnst.

WERMERT, JOHN G; Marion Local HS; Celina, OH; 1/93 Chrh Wkr; Hon Rl; Lbry Ade; NHS; Off Ade; Treas FTA; Mth Clb; Pep Clb; Sci Clb; DAR Awd; Univ Of Dayton; Acctg.

WERNER, ANNE; Barberton HS; Barberton, OH; 13/495 Am Leg Aux Girls St; Band; Hon Rl; Jr NHS; NHS; Quill & Scroll; Stu Cncl; Rptr Sch Nwsp; Spn Clb; IM Sprt; Univ Of Akron; Bus.

WERNER, ANNETTE; Streetsboro HS; Streetsboro, OH; 9/180 Band; Cmp Fr Grls; Chrs; Chrh Wkr; Hon Rl; Lit Mag; NHS; Orch; 4-H; FTA; Kent St Univ; Elem Ed.

WERNER, CAROLYN; St Joseph Cntrl Catholic HS; Fremont, OH; Aud/Vis; Cmp Fr Grls; Hon Rl; FBLA; Sec OEA; Terra Tech College; Sec.

WERNER, DENISE; Memphis HS; Memphis, MI; Band; Hon Rl; Off Ade; Yrbk; Sch Nwsp; Mgrs; Scr Kpr; Port Huron Schl Of Bus; Med Transcri.

WERNER, DUSTIN; Groveport Madison HS; Columbus, OH; 57/398 Pres Frsh Cls; Cls Rep Frsh Cls; Cls Rep Soph Cls; Cls Rep Sr Cls; Band; Boy Scts; Hon Rl; Off Ade; Sch Mus; Sch Pl; Ohio St Univ; Music Educ.

WERNER, MINDY; Groveport Madison HS; Groveport, OH; 4/370 Am Leg Aux Girls St; Chrh Wkr; Drl Tm; Hon Rl; Pres NHS; Ed Sch Nwsp; Pres 4-H; 4-H Awd; Rotary Awd; Ohio St Univ; Acctg.

WERNER, NANCY; Stevenson HS; Livonia, MI; Cls Rep Sr Cls; Band; Chrs; Hon Rl; Lbry Ade; Lit Mag; Off Ade; E Mic Univ; English.

WERNETTE, DEBORAH; Chippewa Hills HS; Weidman, MI; 4/216 Chrs; Hon Rl; NHS; Pres 4-H; Spn Clb; 4-H Awd; Ctrl Michigan Univ.

WERNETTE, GERALD; Midland HS; Midland, MI; 45/486 Band; Boy Scts; Hon Rl; Treas JA; NHS; Pol Wkr; Sct Actv; Central Mic Univ; Acctg.

WERSTLER, VICKI; Whitko HS; Pierceton, IN; Trs Frsh Cls; Band; Chrs; FCA; Sch Mus; Yth Flsp; Drama Clb; OEA; Pep Clb; GAA; Sunshine Society;

Varisty Volley Ball Lettered; Jv Volleyball; College; Sec.

WERT, DANE; Ypsilanti HS; Ypsilanti, MI; Hon Rl; Off Ade; Bsbl; Coach Actv; IM Sprt; Mgrs; Tmr; Coll.

WERT, GREGORY; Athens HS; Troy, MI; 50/500 NHS; OEA; IM Sprt; Univ Of Michigan; Busns Admin.

WERTH, CARLA A; Ogemaw Heights HS; West Branch, MI; 20/205 Trs Frsh Cls; Trs Soph Cls; Band; Chrh Wkr; Treas Girl Scts; Hon Rl; Pres NHS; Stu Cncl; Letter Chrldng; Michigan St Univ; Psych.

WERTS, JILL C; La Salle HS; South Bend, IN; 1/417 Val; Hon Rl; Lbry Ade; NHS; Orch; Sch Mus; Eng Clb; Fr Clb; Natl Merit Ltr; Natl Merit SF; Univ; Librarian.

WERTZ, HONOR; Flushing HS; Flushing, MI; Boy Scts; Cmnty Wkr; Hon Rl; Hosp Ade; JA; NHS; Red Cr Ade; Sct Actv; Spn Clb; Univ Of Michigan; Bio.

WERTZ, TRENT; Southwestern HS; Flat Rock, IN; 2/64 Pres Jr Cls; Am Leg Boys St; NHS; Sch Mus; Key Clb; Letter Bsbl; Letter Bsktbl; Letter Crs Cntry; Letter Trk; Dnfth Awd; Univ; Engr.

WESANDER, DONNA; Ontonagon Area HS; Mass City, MI; NHS; Sch Pl; Yth Flsp; Drama Clb; 4-H; GAA; 4-H Awd; Florida Inst Of Tech; Marine Sci.

WESBECHER, MARCIA; Magnificat HS; Avon, OH; Chrs; Jr NHS; NHS; Sch Mus; Sch Pl; Stg Crw; Drama Clb; College; Math.

WESEBAUM, HARRY; Highland HS; Hinckley, OH; 45/207 Hon Rl; DECA; Univ Of Akron; Bus Admin.

WESEL, MARILYN; Marietta Sr HS; Marietta, OH; Cls Rep Soph Cls; AFS; Chrh Wkr; Girl Scts; Hon Rl; NHS; Sch Pl; Stu Cncl; Spn Clb; Letter Bsktbl; Ohio St Univ; Bus.

WESER, LINDA; West Jefferson HS; W Jefferson, OH; Cls Rep Soph Cls; Sec Jr Cls; Cl Rep Jr Cls; Am Leg Aux Girls St; Treas Band; Chrs; Hon Rl; Treas NHS; Letter Bsktbl; Voc Schl; Med Tech.

WESLEY, GERALD; Marine City HS; Anchorville, MI; 1/170 Cls Rep Frsh Cls; Pres Soph Cls; Cls Rep Soph Cls; Pres Jr Cls; Cl Rep Jr Cls; Pres Sr Cls; Cls Rep Sr Cls; Val; Ferris State College; Pharmacy.

WESLEY, JULIA; Clio HS; Clio, MI; Band; Chrs; Girl Scts; Hon Rl; Hosp Ade; Red Cr Ade; Sch Mus; Sch Pl; Stg Crw; Western Michigan Univ; Occup Ther.

WESLOWSKI, MARGARET; Bay City All Saints HS; Bay City, MI; Chrs; Cmnty Wkr; Hon Rl; Hosp Ade; Mdrgl; Sch Mus; Drama Clb; Pep Clb; Pom Pon; Univ; Phys Ther.

WESNER, TONY; Brownstown Central HS; Vallonia, IN; 15/153 Boy Scts; Hon Rl; NHS; Sct Actv; Yth Flsp; FFA; 4-H Awd; Farming.

WESOLEK, KURT; Medina HS; Medina, OH; 28/350 Cls Rep Frsh Cls; Am Leg Boys St; Chrs; Cmnty Wkr; Hon Rl; NHS; Red Cr Ade; College; Lawyer.

WESORICK, LIZ; Creston HS; Grand Rpds, MI; Cl Rep Jr Cls; Hon Rl; Hosp Ade; Jr NHS; NHS; Coll; Nursing.

WESS, GREGORY W; Stonewall Jackson HS; Charleston, WV; Hon Rl; Jr NHS; Sch Pl; Mth Clb; Spn Clb; Coll; Acctg.

WESS, PATRICIA; Hubbard HS; Hubbard, OH; Hosp Ade; FTA; PPFtbl; Scr Kpr; Youngstown St Univ; Spec Ed.

WESSEL, AUDREY; Brownstown Central HS; Brownstown, IN; 5/145 Band; Chrs; Hon Rl; NHS; Sch Mus; Yrbk; FTA; Lat Clb; Sec Sci Clb; Letter Ten; Instrumental Solo & Ensemble Contest; Piano Solo Contest; Purdue Univ; Psych.

WESSEL, MICHAEL E; Lincoln HS; Vincennes, IN; 18/281 Am Leg Boys St; FCA; Hon Rl; Treas Stu Cncl; Crs Cntry; Trk; Purdue Univ; Marine Bio.

WESSEL, NANCY; Memphis HS; Smith Crk, MI; Cls Rep Frsh Cls; Chrh Wkr; Hon Rl; Stu Cncl; Rptr Sch Nwsp; Sch Nwsp; Pres 4-H; Letter Bsktbl; Letter Trk; Bus Schl; Data Proc.

WESSEL, SUE; R Nelson Snider HS; Ft Wayne, IN; 36/564 Cls Rep Frsh Cls; Cls Rep Soph Cls; Cl Rep Jr Cls; Hon Rl; Jr NHS; Fr Clb; PPFtbl; Natl Jr Hon Soc 76; Distinguished Schlr 79; Univ; Law.

WESSEL, SUSAN; North HS; Evansville, IN; 25/348 Cls Rep Soph Cls; Cl Rep Jr Cls; Chrs; Drl Tm; Hon Rl; Hosp Ade; NHS; Pol Wkr; Quill & Scroll; Sch Pl; Deaconess Schl Of Nursing; R N.

WESSELING, J; Holland Christian HS; Zeeland, MI; Chrs; Mdrgl; Sch Pl; Rptr Yrbk; Ger Clb; Trk; Natl Merit Ltr; Rotary Awd; Calvin College; Music.

WEST, BARBARA; Miller HS; Corning, OH; Band; Yrbk; Sch Nwsp; 4-H; FBLA; Capt Bsktbl; Letter Trk; Twrlr; Mas Awd; Fashion Design.

WEST, BETH; Briggs HS; Columbus, OH; 25/200 Am Leg Aux Girls St; Band; Sec Chrs; Hon Rl; Lbry Ade; NHS; Off Ade; Stu Cncl; Fr Clb; OEA; Ohio State Univ; Business Admin.

WEST, CHARLOTTE; Mooresville HS; Camby, IN; Chrs; Chrh Wkr; Cmnty Wkr; Off Ade; Sch Mus; 4-H; Pep Clb;.

WEST, CHRISTINA E; Groveport Madison HS; Groveport, OH; Sec Frsh Cls; Cls Rep Frsh Cls; Sec Soph Cls; Cls Rep Soph Cls; Sec Jr Cls; Sec Sr Cls; Cls Rep Sr Cls; Band; Girl Scts; NHS; Sears Original Girl; Basketball Hmcmng Attendant; Honored Qn Intnl Order Of Jobs Daughters; College; English.

WEST, CYNDI; Shelbyville HS; Shelbyville, IN; Cls Rep Sr Cls; Debate Tm; Hon Rl; Stu Cncl; Rptr Sch Nwsp; Lat Clb; Letter Ten; Purdue Univ; Journalism.

WEST, DEBBIE L; South Amherst HS; South Amherst, OH; 11/71 Cls Rep Frsh Cls; Cl Rep Jr Cls; Cls Rep Sr Cls; Band; Chrs; Girl Scts; Hon Rl; NHS; Sch Mus; Sch Pl; Acad Of Court Reporting; Steno.

WEST, DEBRA; Jackson HS; Jackson, MI; 51/326 Cls Rep Frsh Cls; Cls Rep Soph Cls; Hon Rl; Ger Clb; Lat Clb; Chrldng; PPFtbl; Tmr; Michigan St Univ.

WEST, DONNA; Riverside HS; Dearborn Hts, MI; Hon Rl; Bsbl; Letter Ten; Eastern Michigan Univ.

WEST, ELAINE; Portland HS; Portland, MI; Sch Pl; Sch Nwsp; Fr Clb; Grand Rapids Bapt Coll.

WEST, JACKIE; Wadsworth HS; Wadsworth, OH; 98/365 Band; NHS; Spn Clb; Bsbl; Capt Bsktbl; Crs Cntry; Akron Univ; Phys Educ.

WEST, JACQUELINE; Buckeye HS; Dillonvale, OH; Chrh Wkr; Hon Rl; Lbry Ade; NHS; Rptr Sch Nwsp; Drama Clb; Treas FHA; Treas VICA; Univ; Int Design.

WEST, JACQUELINE; Buckeye North HS; Dillonvale, OH; Hon Rl; Lbry Ade; NHS; Rptr Sch Nwsp; Sec FHA; VICA; Univ; Travel.

WEST, JANET; Lincoln HS; Cambridge City, IN; Cl Rep Jr Cls; Pres Chrh Wkr; Hon Rl; Off Ade; Pres Y-Teens; Ed Yrbk; Drama Clb; 4-H; Fr Clb; Gym; Ball St Univ; Guidance Cnslr.

WEST, JAYNE; Hilliard HS; Columbus, OH; Hon Rl; Sec JA; Jr NHS; NHS; Rptr Sch Nwsp; Sch Nwsp; Pres FHA; JA Awd;.

WEST, JEAN; West Tech HS; Cleveland, OH; Chrh Wkr; Cmnty Wkr; Hon Rl; Jr NHS; Off Ade; Stu Cncl; Yth Flsp; Cit Awd; Metro Schl; Nursing.

WEST, J KEVIN; Newton Local HS; Covington, OH; Pres Frsh Cls; Trs Soph Cls; Band; Chrs; NHS; Sch Mus; Sch Pl; Stg Crw; Stu Cncl; Rptr Yrbk; Manchester Coll; Photog.

WEST, KELLY A; Ernest W Seaholm HS; Birmingham, MI; Chrh Wkr; Cmnty Wkr; Hosp Ade; Lbry Ade; Drama Clb; Spn Clb; Albion Coll; Journalism.

WEST, KEVIN; Northwest HS; Jackson, MI; Band; Hon Rl; NHS; Sch Mus; Univ Of Michigan; Cmnctns.

WEST, KEVIN; Chatard HS; Indianapolis, IN; 93/195 Band; Chrs; Hon Rl; JA; Sch Mus; Sch Pl; Stg Crw; 4-H; Pep Clb; Sci Clb; Grant For Dance Workshop; Jr Young Churchmen Awd; Evansville Citizen Radio Leag Inc Awd; Butler Univ; Art.

WEST, LORI; Wheeling Cntrl Catholic HS; Wheeling, WV; 5/132 Hon Rl; Fr Clb; Mat Maids; West Virginia Univ; Med.

WEST, LORI; Wheeling Cent Catholic HS; Wheeling, WV; 4/134 Hon Rl; Fr Clb; Mat Maids; Wv Univ; Bio.

WEST, MICHEAL; Caldwell HS; Caldwell, OH; Chrh Wkr; Hon Rl; Spn Clb; 15th Pl In Ohio Tests Of Schlstc Achvmnt Spanish 77; 1st Pl In Ohio Tests Of Schlstc Achvmnt Spanish 78; Coll; Ministry.

WEST, PATTI; Lincoln HS; Cambridge, IN; 35/180 Cls Rep Soph Cls; Chrs; Hon Rl; Red Cr Ade; Stu Cncl; Y-Teens; 4-H; Fr Clb; Letter Gym; Lifeguard; Stud Tchr In Bio 78; Univ; Med Tech.

WEST, RANDALL; St Francis Desales HS; Columbus, OH; 73/184 Jr NHS; Spn Clb; College; Comp Sci.

WEST, SHERRI; Wayne HS; Dayton, OH; 136/590 Pres Frsh Cls; Cls Rep Soph Cls; Cl Rep Jr Cls; Cls Rep Sr Cls; Off Ade; Pres Stu Cncl; Crs Cntry; Trk; Capt Chrldng; Vincennes Univ; Exec Sec.

WEST, SHERRY; Our Lady Of Mercy HS; Southfield, MI; Chrs; Hon Rl; Capt Trk; Achvmnt For Spanish & Phys Educ 77 & 78; Cert Of Achvmnt For Sewing 77; Univ; Vet Med.

WEST, SUSAN; Bloomington HS; Bloomington, IN; Chrh Wkr; Quill & Scroll; Sch Nwsp; Journalism.

WEST, SUZANNE; Clarkston Sr HS; Clarkston, MI; Band; Chrs; Girl Scts; Hon Rl; Sch Pl; 4-H; Twrlr; Reading Aide 75 76 & 77; Otstndng Achvmnt In Eng 75 76 & 77; Univ.

WEST, TERESA; Lynchburg Clay HS; Lynchburg, OH; 1/100 Trs Jr Cls; Band; Chrs; Hon Rl; Stu Cncl; Pep Clb; Spn Clb; Chrldng; Voice Dem Awd; Ohio Test Schl Achv 1st Cnty 1977; Ohio Test Schl Ach 1st 1978; Univ.

WEST, TERRIE; Bettsville HS; Bettsville, OH; Am Leg Aux Girls St; Band; Chrs; Hon Rl; Lbry Ade; Sch Mus; FHA; Chrldng; Mgrs; Cit Awd; Tiffin Acad Of Hair Dsgn; Hair Styl.

WEST, VIRGIL; Bellaire HS; Bellaire, OH; Aud/Vis; FCA; Beta Clb; Pep Clb; Rdo Clb; Trk; Wrstlng; Belmont Tech Coll; Diesel Mech.

WEST, WANDA; Spencer HS; Spencer, WV; 12/153 Chrh Wkr; Cmnty Wkr; Girl Scts; Hon Rl; Sct Actv; Rptr Sch Nwsp; IM Sprt;.

WESTBROOK, VICTORIA; Linden Mckinley HS; Columbus, OH; Hon Rl; Hosp Ade; Lbry Ade; Off Ade; Sch Pl; Stu Cncl; Drama Clb; Spn Clb; Coach Actv; JA Awd; UCLA; Doctor.

WESTENBERG, LISA; Harbor Springs HS; Alanson, MI; Hon Rl; Off Ade; Pres 4-H; VP FHA; Ger Clb; Culinary Inst Of Amer; Chef.

WESTER, RONALD; Loy Norrix HS; Kalamazoo, MI; 1/420 Val; Hon Rl; NHS; Western Michigan Univ; Comp Sci.

WESTERFIELD, SHEILA; Batavia HS; Batavia, OH; 8/78 Chrs; FCA; Girl Scts; Hon Rl; NHS; Off Ade; Sch Pl; Stu Cncl; Yth Flsp; Drama Clb; 1st Pl In Essay Contest; Citizenship/scholarship Awd; Orthodontic Training; Assistant.

WESTERH, JOHN; St Ignatius HS; Cleveland, OH; Cleveland State College; Chem.

WESTERMAN, KAREN; Snider HS; Ft Wayne, IN; 14/564 Hon Rl; Fr Clb; Letter Ten; Mat Maids; Pres Awd; Univ; Bus.

WESTFALL, JENINE; Spencer HS; Spencer, WV; Am Leg Aux Girls St; Pres Band; Chrh Wkr; Girl Scts; Hon Rl; Jr NHS; Off Ade; Orch; Sch Pl; Stg Crw; Wv All St Band; Wv North South Honor Band; West Virginia Univ; Music.

WESTFALL, JULIE; Hill Mc Cloy HS; Montrose, MI; Chrs; Hon Rl; Off Ade; Rptr Sch Nwsp; 4-H; OEA; 4-H Awd; Genesse Area Skill Ctr; Exec Sec.

WESTFALL, KENNY; Buckhannon Upshur HS; Buckhannon, WV; Boy Scts; 4-H; Letter Ten; Letter Trk; IM Sprt; West Virginia Univ.

WESTFALL, LUAN; Edwardsburg HS; Edwardsburg, MI; 9/148 Chrs; Hon Rl; NHS; Off Ade; Yrbk; Fr Clb; Mgrs; S W Michigan Coll; Phys Ther.

WESTFALL, MARLA; Clay City HS; Cory, IN; 30/55 Cl Rep Jr Cls; Cls Rep Sr Cls; Hon Rl; Sch Nwsp; FHA; OEA; Pep Clb; Bus.

WESTFALL, MIKE; Defiance Sr HS; Defiance, OH; Band; Hon Rl; DECA; Northwest Tech Schl; Comp Sci.

WESTFALL, PATRICK; Morgan HS; Malta, OH; 18/232 Hon Rl; VICA; IM Sprt; Voc Schl.

WESTFALL JR, JAMES; Newton HS; Pleasant Hill, OH; .

WESTGERDES, CHERYL; Coldwater HS; Coldwater, OH; Band; Chrs; Hon Rl; Orch; Drama Clb; FHA; IM Sprt; Kiwan Awd; Northwestern Bus Coll; Acctg.

WESTHOVEN, KAREN; Dublin HS; Dublin, OH; Band; Chrs; Girl Scts; Sch Mus; Stg Crw; 4-H; Spn Clb; Scr Kpr; Tmr; 4-H Awd; Ohio St Univ; Animal Sci.

WESTMORELAND, GLENDA; Shortridge HS; Indianapolis, IN; 2/400 Band; Hon Rl; NHS; Fr Clb; Mth Clb; Cit Awd; Rensaleer Medl 79; Brotherhd Awd Natl Confrnc Of Chrstns & Jews 79; Math Awd 79; Butler Univ; Math.

WESTMORELAND, RANDALL; East Detroit HS; East Detroit, MI; Natl Forn Lg; Sch Pl; Stg Crw; Yth Flsp; Drama Clb; Letter Ten; Mich State.

WESTON, GREGORY; Highland HS; Anderson, IN; Hon Rl; Stg Crw; Yth Flsp; Drama Clb; Lat Clb; Capt Swmmng; Pres Awd; Ball State Univ; Architecture.

WESTON, KATHLEEN; Dearborn HS; Dearborn, MI; Chrh Wkr; Debate Tm; Girl Scts; Hon Rl; NHS; Orch; Pres Ger Clb; Natl Merit Ltr; Kalamazoo Coll.

WESTON, MICKEY; Lake Fenton HS; Fenton, MI; 20/189 Boy Scts; Chrh Wkr; Hon Rl; NHS; Stu Cncl; Capt Bsbl; Bsktbl; Ftbl; Scr Kpr; Central Michigan Univ; Busns.

WESTON, SARAH; Marian HS; Troy, MI; Cmnty Wkr; Jr NHS; Gym; Univ Of Michigan; Med Illustration.

WESTON, YVONNE; Corunna HS; Lennon, MI; Girl Scts; Hon Rl; Off Ade; Sct Actv; Y-Teens; Rptr Yrbk; 4-H; Ten; Mgrs; 4-H Awd; College; Modeling.

WESTOVER, LAURIE; Ashtabula HS; Ashtabula, OH; 26/256 Girl Scts; Hon Rl; Off Ade; Univ; Acctg.

WESTREN, DEANNA J; Ellet HS; Akron, OH; 164/365 Sec Sr Cls; Stu Cncl; OEA; Bsbl; Chrldng; Soph Homecoming Attendant; Sr Homecoming Queen;.

WESTRICH, SCOTT; Sycamore HS; Cincinnati, OH; Band; Hon Rl; Orch; Sch Mus; Natl Merit SF; Northwestern; Foreign Languages.

WESTRICK, LISA; Ayersville HS; Defiance, OH; Hon Rl; NHS; Yrbk; 4-H; Fr Clb; FHA; Mth Clb; Trk; 4-H Awd; Business School; Accounting.

WESTVEER, ANDREW; Holland HS; Holland, MI; Hon Rl; Yrbk; Natl Merit Schl; Pres Awd; Alma College; Spanish.

WESTVEER, LINDA; Union HS; Grand Rapids, MI; Cmp Fr Grls; Chrh Wkr; Girl Scts; Hon Rl; Jr NHS; NHS; Yth Flsp; Ger Clb; Pom Pon; College; Art Education.

WETHERALD, SHELLY; Franklin Cntrl HS; Indpls, IN; 44/269 Trs Soph Cls; Cl Rep Jr Cls; Girl Scts; Off Ade; Red Cr Ade; Sch Pl; Sct Actv; Stu Cncl; Rptr Yrbk; Pep Clb; Presidential Phys Fitness Awd; Homecoming Court; Prom Court; Indiana Cntrl Univ; Spanish.

WETHERELL, LORI; Buckeye North HS; Mingo Jct, OH; 21/140 Band; Chrh Wkr; Hon Rl; NHS; Off Ade; Stg Crw; Pres Yth Flsp; Drama Clb; Pres 4-H; Spn Clb; Nursing School; Rn.

WETSCH, DOUGLAS; Elkins HS; Elkins, WV; 16/256 Am Leg Boys St; Band; NHS; Sch Pl; Sch Nwsp; Bausch & Lomb Awd; Wv Univ; Pre Med.

WETTERHOLT, MARY; Mona Shores HS; Muskegon, MI; Band; Girl Scts; Hon Rl; NHS; Orch; Trk; Western Michigan Univ; Music.

WETTLIN, KAREN; Buena Vista HS; Saginaw, MI; 18/157 Band; Chrs; Chrh Wkr; Hon Rl; Lbry Ade; NHS; Quill & Scroll; Pep Clb; Cit Awd; Lion Awd; Michigan St Univ; Dentistry.

WETTLIN, ROD; Buena Vista HS; Saginaw, MI; 43/160 Cls Rep Frsh Cls; Cls Rep Soph Cls; Cls Rep Sr Cls; Band; Chrs; Hon Rl; Stg Crw; Rptr Yrbk; Yrbk; Pep Clb; Univ Of Michigan; Engr.

WETZEL, BRIAN; Elkhart Central HS; Bristol, IN; Chrs; Hon Rl; NHS; Univ Of Evansville; Acctg.

WETZEL, DON; Central Hower HS; Akron, OH; 17/330 Cmnty Wkr; Hon Rl; NHS; Sch Nwsp; Civ Clb; IM Sprt; Opt Clb Awd; Univ Of Akron; Bus Admin.

WETZEL, DOUG; Chelsea HS; Pickney, MI; 12/221 Cls Rep Sr Cls; Am Leg Boys St; Band; Hon Rl; NHS; Stg Crw; Sch Nwsp; Drama Clb; Trk; Wrstlng; Hope College; Medicine.

WETZEL, JOHN S; Medina Sr HS; Medina, OH; 13/380 Boy Scts; Hon Rl; Sct Actv; Ftbl; Natl Merit Ltr; Natl Merit SF; Commend Oh Univ Amrcn His Cntst 1978; Case Western Reserve Univ; Engr.

WETZEL, STEVE; Cedarville HS; Cedarville, OH; 2/60 Cls Rep Frsh Cls; VP Jr Cls; Band; Drm Bgl; Hon Rl; Jr NHS; NHS; Stu Cncl; Treas FBLA; Pep Clb; 2 Academic C Awds 77 79; Cedarville Coll; Law.

WEVERSTAD, SCOTT; Lakeview HS; Battle Creek, MI; Band; Chrs; Chrh Wkr; Mdrgl; 1 Rating In Fl Volal St Fest 78; Univ; Comp.

WEWER, JEAN E; Nordonia HS; , ; 14/440 Cmp Fr Grls; Hon Rl; NHS; Sci Clb; Natl Merit SF; Univ; Mech Engr.

WEYCKER, BARB; Gladstone Area HS; Gladstone, MI; Band; Hosp Ade; Lit Mag; Natl Forn Lg; NHS; VP Quill & Scroll; Stu Cncl; Ed Sch Nwsp; Fr Clb; Letter Ten; Univ; Physician.

WEYERS, CRAIG J; St Edward HS; Berea, OH; 16/360 Chrh Wkr; Cmnty Wkr; Hon Rl; Rptr Sch Nwsp; VP Key Clb; Letter Swmmng; Am Leg Awd; Kiwan Awd; Univ; Elec Engr.

WEYLER, KATHERINE; Archbishop Alter HS; Xenia, OH; Hon Rl; NHS; Drama Clb; 4-H; Key Clb; Pep Clb; Letter Trk; GAA; IM Sprt; Ohio St Univ; Vet Med.

WHALEN, ELIZABETH; Bloomington HS North; Bloomington, IN; Pres Girl Scts; VP JA; NHS; Stu Cncl; 4-H; Fr Clb; Swmmng; Univ; Lib Arts.

WHALEN, SALLY; Scecina Memorial HS; Indianpolis, IN; 47/194 Band; Chrs; Rptr Yrbk; Sec Spn Clb; Indiana St Univ; Sci.

WHALEN, TIM; Whiteford HS; Toledo, OH; VP Soph Cls; Hon Rl; NHS; Rptr Yrbk; Rptr Sch Nwsp; Bsbl; Letter Bsktbl; Letter Ftbl; Letter Trk;.

WHALEY, BRIAN; South Newton HS; Brook, IN; 13/103 Band; Orch; Ivy Tech Voc Schl; Electronics.

WHALEY, DEBRA; Cadillac HS; Cadillac, MI; 10/316 Cl Rep Jr Cls; Chrh Wkr; Hon Rl; NHS; Stu Cncl; Yth Flsp; 4-H; Letter Trk; Nw Mic College; Outdoor Ed.

WHALEY, JOAN; Bucyrus HS; Bucyrus, OH; 10/180 Girl Scts; Hon Rl; Lbry Ade; NHS; Yth Flsp; FHA; Ohio Univ; Math.

WHALEY, KIMBERLY; S Point HS; South Point, OH; 10/152 Hon Rl; Lbry Ade; Pres NHS; Off Ade; Stu Cncl; Sprt Ed Sch Nwsp; Pep Clb; Dnfth Awd; Marshall Univ.

WHALEY, LORI; Bishop Flaget HS; Chillicothe, OH; Sec Soph Cls; Chrh Wkr; Hon Rl; Sch Mus; Stu Cncl; Fr Clb; Pep Clb; Chrldng; Univ; Poli Sci.

WHALEY, MARK; Grayling HS; Grayling, MI; Am Leg Boys St; Band; Hon Rl; NHS; Sch Mus; Letter Bsktbl; Letter Crs Cntry; Letter Trk; Mic Tech; Engr.

WHALEY, TERRI; Gorham Fayette HS; Fayette, OH; 10/42 Sec Chrs; Chrh Wkr; Sch Pl; Sec Stu Cncl; Sec Yth Flsp; Yrbk; VP 4-H; Northwest Tech Schl; Med Sec.

WHARRAM, DONALD; Perry HS; Perry, OH; 13/150 Hon Rl; NHS; Key Clb; Bsbl; Ftbl; Univ.

WHARTON, JAMES R; Sandy Valley HS; Magnolia, OH; Band; Boy Scts; Chrh Wkr; Hon Rl; NHS; 4-H; IM Sprt; Univ Of Ohi; Engr.

WHARTON, JEFFREY; Marion HS; Marion, IN; 98/710 Am Leg Boys St; Hon Rl; NHS; Letter Bsktbl; Letter Ten; Letter Trk; College.

WHARTON, SHERYL; Malabar HS; Mansfield, OH; 3/251 Cls Rep Soph Cls; Cl Rep Jr Cls; Cls Rep Sr Cls; Band; Hon Rl; NHS; Orch; Mth Clb; Bsbl; Wrstlng; Bowling Green St Univ; Commiunicatio.

WHARTON, SHERYL; Malabar Sr HS; Mansfield, OH; 3/251 Cls Rep Soph Cls; Cl Rep Jr Cls; Cls Rep Sr Cls; Band; NHS; Mth Clb; Bsbl; Mat Maids; NCTE; Natl Merit Ltr; Bowling Green St Univ; Cmnctns.

WHATLEY, AMANDA R; Jane Addams Vocational HS; Cleveland, OH; Sec Frsh Cls; Trs Jr Cls; JA; 4-H; UCLA; Sec.

WHATLEY, CRAIG; E Catholic & Cass Tech HS; Detroit, MI; Cls Rep Soph Cls; Trs Jr Cls; Hon Rl; Pep Clb; Ftbl; Certificate Of Honor; Michigan State Univ; Communications.

WHEALAN, JUDITH; Calvert HS; Tiffin, OH; 11/98 Sec Band; Hon Rl; VP JA; Sch Mus; Rptr Yrbk; Sch Nwsp; Pep Clb; Firelands; Exec Sec.

WHEALDON, LORRIE; Southwestern HS; Thurman, OH; 3/42 Hon Rl; Off Ade; Ed Yrbk; Ed Sch Nwsp; OEA; Mt Vernon Nazarene Coll.

WHEALEY, DAVID; Athens HS; Athens, OH; 14/280 Cls Rep Soph Cls; Chrs; NHS; Sch Mus; Sch Pl; Rdo Clb; Letter Socr; Mgrs; Natl Merit SF; Univ Of Virginia.

WHEAT, BARBARA; Weir Sr HS; Weirton, WV; 18/350 Hon Rl; JA; Jr NHS; NHS; Pep Clb; GAA; JA Awd; J A Sclshp 79; Adv Life Sci Awd 77; Whos Who In Amer HS Sstant 77; West Virginia N Cmnty Coll; Bus Admn.

WHEATLEY, CHERYL; Evansville Data Processing; Evansville, IN; 17/432 Hon Rl; NHS; Fr Clb; FBLA; Sec OEA; Sec Sci Clb; Chrldng; Cit Awd; Pres Awd; Indiana St Univ; Data Proc.

WHEATLEY, DIANA M; St Florian HS; Highland Park, MI; 25/77 Chrs; Chrh Wkr; Debate Tm; Sch Mus; Pep Clb; Spn Clb; Voice Dem Awd; Henry Ford Coll; Music.

WHEATLEY, MICHAEL J; Brother Rice HS; Birmingham, MI; 1/260 Am Leg Boys St; Cmnty Wkr; Hon Rl; Hosp Ade; NHS; Sch Nwsp; Bsktbl; Natl Merit SF; Univ Of Michigan; Med.

WHEATON, ADAM; Charlotte HS; Charlotte, MI; Hon Rl; Yth Flsp; Pres 4-H; FFA; Letter Wrstlng;

Cit Awd; 4-H Awd; 4 H Livestock Jdgng Tm 1978; Outstndg Jr Awd FFA 1979; Michigan St Univ; Agri.

WHEATON, DENISE; Eaton Rapids HS; Eaton Rapids, MI; 10/250 Band; Girl Scts; Hon Rl; NHS; Sch Mus; Sch Pl; Stg Crw; Drama Clb; Scr Kpr; Michigan St Univ; Comp Sci.

WHEATON, JOHN; Cheboygan Cath HS; Cheboygan, MI; 14/35 Pres Jr Cls; Hon Rl; Sch Mus; Sch Pl; Stg Crw; Yrbk; Drama Clb; Natl Merit Ltr; Natl Merit SF; Natl Merit Schl; Northwestern Michigan Univ; Comm Art.

WHEATON, SHERRY; St Philip Catholic Cntrl HS; Battle Crk, MI; 2/70 Cls Rep Soph Cls; Cl Rep Jr Cls; Cls Rep Sr Cls; Sal; Am Leg Aux Girls St; NHS; Stu Cncl; Princeton Univ; Classics Major.

WHEELAND, TOM; Wadsworth HS; Wadsworth, OH; Boy Scts; Chrh Wkr; Pres JA; Akron Univ; Architecture.

WHEELER, ALAN; Hart HS; Hart, MI; 1/140 Val; NHS; Yth Flsp; 4-H; 4-H Awd; Natl Merit Schl; Michigan St Univ; Vet.

WHEELER, BARB; Mount Notre Dame HS; Montgomery, OH; Cls Rep Frsh Cls; Cls Rep Soph Cls; Cls Rep Sr Cls; Chrh Wkr; Cmnty Wkr; Hon Rl; Hosp Ade; NHS; Stu Cncl; Rptr Sch Nwsp; Univ Of Cincinnati; Special Ed.

WHEELER, CHRIS; Shelbyville HS; Shelbyville, IN; 31/297 Cls Rep Frsh Cls; Cl Rep Jr Cls; Aud/Vis; Chrh Wkr; FCA; Hon Rl; Quill & Scroll; Stu Cncl; Rptr Sch Nwsp; Sch Nwsp; Hillsdale Coll; Educ.

WHEELER, D; Fairland HS; Proctorvll, OH; Sec Frsh Cls; Trs Frsh Cls; Band; Chrh Wkr; Pep Clb; Letter Bsbl; 4-H Awd; Marshall Univ; Broadcasting.

WHEELER, DAVID; Faith Christian HS; Muskegon, MI; Chrh Wkr; Hon Rl; NHS; Spn Clb; Letter Bsktbl; Letter Ftbl; Mgrs; Scr Kpr; Century III Leaders Cert Of Recog Current Events Test; Michigan Busns Schl Assn Schlrshp; Muskegon Busns Coll; Acctg.

WHEELER, DEANNA M; Shepherd HS; Mt Pleasant, MI; Chrh Wkr; Hon Rl; Hosp Ade; Sct Actv; Spn Clb; Swmmng; CMU.

WHEELER, EMMA; Sandusky HS; Snover, MI; 28/114 Hon Rl; Lbry Ade; NHS; Rptr Yrbk; Bsktbl; Mgrs; Scr Kpr; Ctrl Michigan Univ; Educ.

WHEELER, GWEN; Olentangy HS; Delaware, OH; 40/141 Band; Sch Mus; Treas Stu Cncl; Rptr Sch Nwsp; Drama Clb; Pres 4-H; Fr Clb; Pep Clb; Trk; 4-H Awd; Whos Who In Music; Eastern Mich Univ; Music Therapy.

WHEELER, JEFF; Centerville Sr HS; Centerville, IN; Cls Rep Frsh Cls; Cls Rep Soph Cls; VP Jr Cls; Hon Rl; Stu Cncl; Sci Clb; Ftbl; Model Legislature; U S Aur Force Academy; Comp Sci.

WHEELER, JERRY; Plymouth HS; Plymouth, OH; 8/125 Boy Scts; Chrh Wkr; Hon Rl; NHS; Spn Clb; Letter Bsktbl; Letter Glf; Letter Ten; Scr Kpr; Tmr; Univ Of Virginia; Comp Sci.

WHEELER, JOHN; Pike Central HS; Petersburg, IN; 42/187 Am Leg Boys St; Chrh Wkr; NHS; Sch Pl; Rptr Sch Nwsp; Drama Clb; Sci Clb; Ftbl; Trk; Wrstlng; Most Imprvd Footbl Plyr 1978; Hnrbl Mention Offnsv Tckle PAC Confrnce 1978; Bilingual 4 Yrs Costa Rica; Univ; Marine Engr.

WHEELER, JULIANNE; Washington HS; Valparasio, IN; Chrh Wkr; Cmnty Wkr; Hon Rl; NHS; Stg Crw; 4-H;.

WHEELER, JULIE; Howell HS; Fowlerville, MI; 110/395 Cls Rep Frsh Cls; Drl Tm; Hon Rl; Jr NHS; ROTC; Sch Pl; Stg Crw; Stu Cncl; Pep Clb; Ten; Tennis Most Improved Plyr Trophy 79; US Marine Corps Meritorious Promotion 79; Certf Of Achvmnt From Mi; Univ Of New Orleans; Tchr.

WHEELER, JUNE; Groveport Madison HS; Winchester, OH; Chrs; Hon Rl; Hosp Ade; Red Cr Ade; Spn Clb; Bsbl; Bsktbl; PPFtbl; Ohio St Univ; Mental Health Rehab.

WHEELER, KATHY; Southport HS; Indianapolis, IN; Girl Scts; Hon Rl; NHS; Stu Cncl; OEA; Trk; VP GAA; St Women Awd & Ambasodor Awd From Office Education; 2nd In St In Parlimentary Procedures; Purdue Univ; Comp Prog.

WHEELER, KELLY; West Carrollton Sr HS; W Carrollton, OH; 13/418 Chrs; Hon Rl; Jr NHS; NHS; Stg Crw; Rptr Sch Nwsp; Pep Clb; Univ; Comp Sci.

WHEELER, KIMBERLY; Piqua Central HS; Piqua, OH; 6/270 Am Leg Aux Girls St; Chrh Wkr; Girl Scts; Hon Rl; Jr NHS; NHS; Sch Mus; Sch Pl; Drama Clb; 4-H; Prom Ct 79; Univ; Cmmrcl Art.

WHEELER, KRISTINA; Mason Sr HS; Mason, MI; Chrs; Hon Rl; Sec Hosp Ade; Sec Jr NHS; NHS; Pres 4-H; Sci Clb; Ten; Mason Independent Insurnc Agents Schlrshp 78; Otstndng History Stud Awd 77; Ferris St Coll; Pharm.

WHEELER, KYLE; St Ursula HS; Toledo, OH; Sec Frsh Cls; Cls Rep Soph Cls; VP Jr Cls; Pres Sr Cls; Sch Pl; Stg Crw; Stu Cncl; Yrbk; Lat Clb; Coach Actv; People Inc; Capt Of Intermural Bsktbl; Toledo Univ; Social Work.

WHEELER, LESLIE; Monrovia HS; Monrovia, IN; 10/109 Band; Hon Rl; Lit Mag; Pol Wkr; Sch Pl; Stg Crw; Drama Clb; 4-H; Spn Clb; PPFtbl; Ind Univ Indpls; Eng.

WHEELER, LINDA; Ashtabula County Jt Voc HS; Ashtabula, OH; 26/232 Girl Scts; Hon Rl; NHS; OEA; Lakeland Community College.

WHEELER, LORI; Manistee HS; Filer City, MI; 10/186 Hon Rl; NHS; Sch Pl; Rptr Yrbk; Rptr Sch Nwsp; Drama Clb; Fr Clb; Ferris Mert Schslhp 79; St Of Mi Compttv Schlshp 79; Silver Key Recpnt 79; Ferris St Coll; Legal Sec.

WHEELER, LOUISE; Kent Roosevelt HS; Kent, OH ; 17/377 AFS; Chrs; Girl Scts; Hon Rl; Hosp Ade; NHS; Sec Fr Clb; Sci Clb; Hockey; Natl Merit SF; Case Western Reserve Univ; Bio Med.

WHEELER, MARLIN S; Bridgeport HS; Lansing, OH; Boy Scts; Chrh Wkr; Spn Clb; Ten; Letter Trk; Air Force Acad; Aviation.

WHEELER, PATTI; Kent Roosevelt HS; Kent, OH; Hon Rl; Quill & Scroll; Stu Cncl; Ed Yrbk; FDA; Spn Clb; Hockey; Letter Swmmng; Univ; Med.

WHEELER, RONA; Dansville Agri Schl; Dansville, MI; Chrs; Debate Tm; Girl Scts; Hon Rl; Lbry Ade; Sch Mus; Sch Pl; Sct Actv; 4-H; Univ; Histology.

WHEELER, TERRI; New Albany HS; New Albany, IN; 23/575 Hon Rl; NHS; Ger Clb; Univ.

WHEELER, TERRY; West Branch HS; Beloit, OH; AFS; Band; Chrs; Hon Rl; Sch Mus; Yth Flsp; FHA; College.

WHEELER, WILFRED; River Rouge HS; River Rouge, MI; Cls Rep Soph Cls; Cl Rep Jr Cls; Cls Rep Sr Cls; Boy Scts; Chrs; Chrh Wkr; Hon Rl; Pol Wkr; Sct Actv; Stu Cncl; Wayne St Univ; Elec Engr.

WHEELOCK, JAMI; Greenville Sr HS; Greenville, OH; 24/360 Chrs; Hon Rl; 4-H; 4-H Awd; Missionettes Star; Missionettes Hon Star 77; Bus Schl; Acctg.

WHELAN, ELIZABETH; Pioneer HS; Ann Arbor, MI; Cmnty Wkr; Hosp Ade; Lit Mag; Yrbk; Rptr Sch Nwsp; Sch Nwsp; Fr Clb; Amax Earth Sci Schlrshp 79; Western Michigan Univ; Biomed Sci.

WHELAN, MICHAEL; Castle HS; Newburgh, IN; Pres Sr Cls; Pres NHS; Pres Drama Clb; VP Key Clb; Bsbl; Ftbl; Wrstlng; Schlstc C Awd 76 78; Castel Crest Awd Outstndng Stdnt 79; Lonnie Fisher Athtc Awd 78; Wabash Coll; Scndry Educ.

WHELAN, TRACEY; L And M HS; Lyons, IN; Pres Frsh Cls; Band; FHA; Pep Clb; Pom Pon; Butler Univ; Anthropology.

WHELCHEL, MIKE; Lincoln HS; Lumpoerport, WV; Band; Chrs; Chrh Wkr; Drm Mjrt; Hon Rl; NHS; Sch Mus; Wv Univ Invitational Hnrs Bnd; Area All Festival Hnr Bnds; Superior Rating Reg VII Solo Ensemble Festival; West Virginia Univ; Civil Engr.

WHERRY, KELLY; Nordonia Sr HS; Northfield, OH; 44/422 Cls Rep Frsh Cls; Pres Jr Cls; Hon Rl; Stu Cncl; OEA; OOEA Comp 1979; Cuyahoga Vly Jnt Voc Schl; Lgl Sec.

WHETSEL, MICHELLE; Jay County HS; Dunkirk, IN; 1/801 Band; FCA; Hon Rl; Jr NHS; Lit Mag; NHS; Stu Cncl; VP Y-Teens; Mth Clb; Sci Clb; Youth Advisory Council St Chairman; Purdue Univ; Medicine.

WHETSELL, SANDY; Central Preston Sr HS; Albright, WV; 25/168 Band; Chrs; Hon Rl; NHS; Yth Flsp; DECA; 4-H; FHA; Pep Clb; Bsktbl; Bus Schl; Bank Employee.

WHETSTONE, AMY; Northrop HS; Ft Wayne, IN; Cls Rep Frsh Cls; Band; Chrs; Girl Scts; Hon Rl; JA; Sct Actv; Stu Cncl; Sec DECA; Bsbl; Univ; Fashion Mdse.

WHETSTONE, JEFFERY; Northrop HS; Ft Wayne, IN; Cls Rep Frsh Cls; Stu Cncl; Yrbk; Sch Nwsp; Letter Bsbl; Letter Hockey; Indiana Univ; Journalism.

WHETSTONE, KELLY; High School; Berrien Spgs, MI; Cls Rep Soph Cls; Cl Rep Jr Cls; Cls Rep Sr Cls; Am Leg Aux Girls St; Chrh Wkr; Chrs; Hon Rl; Treas Stu Cncl; Ger Clb; Letter Bsktbl; College.

WHETSTONE, LAURA; Fairfield Union HS; Lancaster, OH; 21/158 Band; Drl Tm; Girl Scts; Hon Rl; Jr NHS; NHS; Orch; Yth Flsp; FDA; FTA; Sci Clb; Ohio St Univ; Marine Bio.

WHETSTONE, RHONDA; Lima Sr HS; Lima, OH; Chrh Wkr; Hon Rl; Sch Mus; Yth Flsp; Gym; Ohio St Univ; Elem Educ.

WHETZEL, CAROLYN; Hampshire HS; Romney, WV; Chrh Wkr; Cmnty Wkr; Hon Rl; Hosp Ade; Sec VICA; GAA; J Rumsey Voc Tech; LPN.

WHICKER, CAROL; Father Joseph Wehrle HS; Columbus, OH; 11/109 Cls Rep Sr Cls; Hon Rl; Sch Nwsp; Ohio St Univ; Nursing.

WHIPKEY, SHAWN; University HS; Morgantown, WV; Sec Jr Cls; Band; Chrs; Drm Mjrt; Hon Rl; Jr NHS; Yth Flsp; Twrlr; Voc Schl; Cosmetology.

WHIPKEY, SHAWN R; University HS; Morgantown, WV; 35/146 Sec Jr Cls; Band; Chrs; NHS; Sch Mus; Yth Flsp; Pep Clb; IM Sprt; Twrlr; Business Schl; Modeling.

WHIPP, ELIZBETH; Marion Local HS; Yorkshire, OH; Band; Cmnty Wkr; Hon Rl; Off Ade; Yth Flsp; Drama Clb; 4-H; FHA; OEA; Pep Clb; College; Commercial Art.

WHIPP JR, R; Elmhurst HS; Ft Wayne, IN; 39/400 Band; Hon Rl; Orch; PAVAS; Quill & Scroll; Stu Cncl; Sch Nwsp; FDA; Crs Cntry; Ten; Indiana Univ; General Sci.

WHIPPLE, LISA; Greensburg Comm HS; Greensburg, IN; Sec Band; Chrs; Chrh Wkr; FCA; Hon Rl; Mdrgl; Sch Mus; Fr Clb; Pep Clb; Sci Clb; College; Music.

WHISLER, JEFFERY; Tipton HS; Tipton, IN; 17/160 Cls Rep Frsh Cls; Cls Rep Soph Cls; Cl Rep Jr Cls; Cls Rep Sr Cls; Am Leg Boys St; Hon Rl; Stu Cncl; Pres FBLA; FFA; Univ; Bus Admin.

WHISLER, SANDRA J; Elkhart Central HS; Elkhart, IN; Chrs; Chrh Wkr; Drl Tm; Hon Rl; Orch; Stu Cncl; DECA; PPFtbl; IUSB; Bus.

WHITACRE, DIANE; Huntington North HS; Andrews, IN; Band; Chrs; Chrh Wkr; Drm Mjrt; Sch Mus; VP Yth Flsp; Pres 4-H; Ger Clb; 4-H Awd; Smtih Walbridge Bnd Camp; Perfect Attendence 3 Yrs; Ball St Univ; Busns.

WHITACRE, JEAN; Newark Catholic HS; Newark, OH; Am Leg Aux Girls St; Band; Chrs; Hon Rl; Jr NHS; NHS; Sch Mus; Sch Pl; Fr Clb; Lat Clb; Univ; Educ.

WHITAKER, COLETTE; Seton HS; Cincinnati, OH; Hon Rl; Orch; Sch Mus; Pep Clb; Socr; Chrldng; Coach Actv; Univ; Theatre.

WHITAKER, JANE; Ben Davis HS; Indianapolis, IN; Chrs; Fr Clb; Bsktbl; Ten; Coll; Commercial Art.

WHITAKER, JEANIE; Walkerville Jr Sr HS; Walkerville, MI; 1/40 Band; Chrh Wkr; Cmnty Wkr; Girl Scts; Hon Rl; NHS; Sch Pl; Stu Cncl; 4-H; Pep Clb; Univ; Data Progr.

WHITAKER, JILL; Wintersville HS; Wintersville, OH; Band; Yrbk; Fr Clb;.

WHITAKER, LISA; Parkway HS; Ohio City, OH; 17/85 Sch Pl; Yth Flsp; Yrbk; Pep Clb; Sci Clb; Spn Clb; Chrldng; PPFtbl; Northw Business College; Accntg.

WHITAKER, MARIA; Wheeling Park HS; Triadelphia, WV; Cls Rep Frsh Cls; Chrs; Chrh Wkr; Girl Scts; Natl Forn Lg; Off Ade; PAVAS; Sch Mus; Sch Pl; Stg Crw; Best Actress 79; Best Novice Inerpreter 79; Drama Award 77; Univ; Psych Jvnl Law.

WHITAKER, MARY; Fairfield Senior HS; Hamilton, OH; Chrs; Chrh Wkr; Off Ade; Stu Cncl; Yth Flsp; Fr Clb; OEA; Capt Chrldng; GAA; Mgrs; Bus Schl; Sec.

WHITAKER, MICHAEL; Eaton Rapids HS; Eaton Rapids, MI; 38/196 Hon Rl; NHS; Letter Ftbl; Letter Trk; Mi Comp Schlshp 79; Hon Mntn All Lg Ftbl 78; Bsktbl Homcmng King 79; Cntrl Michigan Univ; Bus Admin.

WHITAKER, RONDA; Lockland HS; Cincinnati, OH; 5/63 Band; Hon Rl; Sec NHS; Yrbk; Bsbl; Bsktbl; Cit Awd; Jewish Hosp Sch Of Nursing; Nursing.

WHITAKER, TODD; Tippecanoe HS; Tipp City, OH; Band; Cmnty Wkr; Hon Rl; Ftbl; Miami Univ; Dentist.

WHITAKER, TRACY; Whiteland Community HS; Greenwood, IN; 3/200 Cls Rep Soph Cls; Cl Rep Jr Cls; Pres FCA; Hon Rl; Stu Cncl; Pep Clb; Letter Bsktbl; Letter Ftbl; Coach Actv; Tmr;.

WHITCOMB, CURTIS; Clinton Central HS; Frankfort, IN; 10/101 Cls Rep Sr Cls; Am Leg Boys St; Band; Chrh Wkr; Cmnty Wkr; FCA; NHS; Sct Actv; Stu Cncl; Yth Flsp; College.

WHITE, ALFRED; Philip Barbour HS; Metz, WV; Band; Chrs; Cmnty Wkr; Hon Rl; PAVAS; Sch Pl; Stg Crw; Yth Flsp; Drama Clb; Chrldng; Marshall Univ; Music.

WHITE, ALLEN; Madison HS; Madison, OH; 48/293 FCA; NHS; Bsbl; Letter Ftbl; Univ.

WHITE, ANGELINA; Servite HS; Hale, MI; 5/93 Chrs; Cmnty Wkr; Hon Rl; JA; Jr NHS; NHS; Yrbk; IM Sprt; JA Awd; Phi Beta Kappa 79; Mi Compttv Schlshp 79; MITE Progr Purdue Univ 78; Univ; Elec Engr.

WHITE, ANNETTE; Carlson HS; Trenton, MI; 9/250 Trs Soph Cls; Cls Rep Soph Cls; Cl Rep Jr Cls; Am Leg Aux Girls St; NHS; Pres Stu Cncl; Rptr Yrbk; Pres GAA; Dnfth Awd; Siena Heights Coll; Criminal Justice.

WHITE, B; Parkside HS; Jackson, MI; Boy Scts; Hon Rl; Sct Actv; Rptr Sch Nwsp; Ger Clb; College; Bus Admin.

WHITE, BARBARA; Parkway HS; Wilshire, OH; 35/97 Chrh Wkr; Yth Flsp; Sprt Ed Yrbk; Rptr Yrbk; Yrbk; Univ; Art.

WHITE, BARBARA; John F Kennedy HS; Taylor, MI; Chrh Wkr; Sch Pl; Trk; GAA; Assoc Airline Personnel Trng Schl.

WHITE, BARBARA E; Martins Ferry HS; St Clairsville, OH; Chrs; Hon Rl; JA; Stu Cncl; Yth Flsp; Y-Teens; Fr Clb; Sci Clb; Ohio Univ Academic Ach; Gifted Stu Program; Ohio State Univ; Medicine.

WHITE, BRAIN; St Xavner HS; Cincinnati, OH; 35/264 VP Sr Cls; Cls Rep Sr Cls; Cmnty Wkr; Hon Rl; NHS; Sprt Ed Sch Nwsp; Rptr Sch Nwsp; Socr; Coach Actv; College; Journalism.

WHITE, BRIAN D; Grand Ledge HS; Lansing, MI; Hon Rl; Lat Clb; Socr; Swmmng; Univ Of Michigan; Med.

WHITE, BYRON; Bishop Ready HS; Columbus, OH; Band; Boy Scts; FCA; Jr NHS; Sprt Ed Sch Nwsp; Ftbl; Wrstlng; College.

WHITE, CALVELLA; Cass Technical HS; Detroit, MI; Hon Rl; Off Ade; ROTC; Wayne St Univ; Comp Sci.

WHITE, CARL; Jonesville HS; Jonesville, MI; Chrs; Yrbk; Letter Bsbl; Letter Ftbl; Voc Schl; Electronics.

WHITE, CAROLYN; Donald E Gavit Jr Sr HS; Hammond, IN; 21/249 Cls Rep Frsh Cls; Cls Rep Soph Cls; Cl Rep Jr Cls; Sec Sr Cls; Cls Rep Sr Cls; Am Leg Aux Girls St; Hon Rl; Jr NHS; NHS; Stu Cncl; Purdue West Lafayette Univ; Mgmt.

WHITE, CHARLENE; Roosevelt HS; Gary, IN; Chrh Wkr; Sch Pl; Yth Flsp; Y-Teens; Yrbk; Drama Clb; Fr Clb; FHA; Pep Clb; Cit Awd; Tuskegee Inst; Child Psych.

WHITE, CHARLES; Pontiac Central HS; Pontiac, MI; Swmmng; Coach Actv; East Ten State; Law.

WHITE, CHRIS; River Valley HS; Sawyer, MI; Boy Scts; Chrh Wkr; Hon Rl; Sch Pl; Sct Actv; Drama Clb; Glf; LMC; Bus Admin.

WHITE, CHRISTOPHER; Lumen Christi HS; Jackson, MI; 36/231 Cls Rep Sr Cls; Hon Rl; NHS; Letter Ftbl; Letter Wrstlng; IM Sprt; Coll; Busns.

WHITE, CRAIG C; Morgantown HS; Morgantown, WV; Debate Tm; FCA; Hon Rl; NHS; Stu Cncl; Rptr Sch Nwsp; Sch Nwsp; Fr Clb; Mth Clb; Letter Crs Cntry; Natl Sci Found; Century III Scholarship Schl Winner; Charleston Distance Run St HS Winner; College; Medicine.

WHITE, DANE C; Terre Haute South Vigo HS; Terre Haute, IN; 81/630 Cls Rep Sr Cls; Boy Scts; Chrh Wkr; Hon Rl; JA; NHS; Orch; VICA; Whos Who Among Amer HS Stud Second Yr In Row 78; Indiana St Univ; Bus.

WHITE, DARIN; Crooksville HS; Crooksville, OH; Hon Rl; Stg Crw; 4-H; Bsbl; Bsktbl; Ftbl; Trk; 4-H Awd;.

WHITE, DAVID; Princeton Community HS; Princeton, IN; 39/222 Band; Boy Scts; DECA; FFA; 4 Yr NROTC Schlshp 79; De Kalb Agri Accmplshmnt Awd 78; Future Farmers Of Amer Mbr Of Yr 78; Purdue Univ; Agri.

WHITE, DAVID; Buckeye Central HS; New Washington, OH; Cls Rep Frsh Cls; Cls Rep Soph Cls; Cl Rep Jr Cls; Hon Rl; Spn Clb; Bsbl; Bsktbl; Ftbl; Univ; Bus.

WHITE, DAVID; Shelby Sr HS; Shelby, OH; Chrs; Hon Rl; Stg Crw; Yth Flsp; Pres FFA; Pres Rdo Clb; Trk; College; Civil Engr.

WHITE, DAVID C; Trenton HS; Trenton, MI; 64/546 Band; Hon Rl; NHS; Sch Pl; Stg Crw; Ger Clb; Natl Merit SF; Natl Sci Fdn Stud Sci Training Prog NSF/SSTP 78; Alma Coll Pres Shclrshp 79; Alma Coll; Bio.

WHITE, DAVID J; Walsh Jesuit HS; Akron, OH; 1/175 Band; Boy Scts; Chrh Wkr; Cmnty Wkr; Hon Rl; Orch; Sch Mus; Sch Pl; Sct Actv; Yrbk; Univ; Engr.

WHITE, DEBBIE; Harbor HS; Ashtabula, OH; 64/201 Cls Rep Frsh Cls; Trs Soph Cls; Cls Rep Soph Cls; Cl Rep Jr Cls; Band; Girl Scts; Sch Mus; Sch Pl; Stu Cncl; Drama Clb; Univ Of Akr; Nursing.

WHITE, DELENA; Southside HS; Muncie, IN; 26/328 Chrs; Chrh Wkr; Cmnty Wkr; Hon Rl; Mdrgl; Off Ade; OEA; Scr Kpr; 2nd Pl Trophy At DEA District Contest; Ball State Univ; Office Admin.

WHITE, DENYSE; Frank Cody HS; Detroit, MI; Cmp Fr Grls; Chrs; Chrh Wkr; Cmnty Wkr; Hon Rl; FDA; Harvard Univ; Med.

WHITE, DIANA D; Ravenna HS; Ravenna, OH; 129/313 Band; Chrs; Girl Scts; Hon Rl; Off Ade; Sct Actv; OEA; Pep Clb; IM Sprt; Exec Awd 1978; Diplomatic Awd 1978; Stateswoman Awd 1978; Ambassador Awd 1978; Kent St Univ; Fshn Mdse.

WHITE, DICK; Indian Valley North HS; Uhrichsville, OH; Cls Rep Soph Cls; Hon Rl; Rptr Yrbk; Rptr Sch Nwsp; Ger Clb; IM Sprt; Ohio Inst Of Tech; Electronics.

WHITE, DONNA S; Jeffersonville HS; Jeffersonville, IN; 26/621 AFS; Chrs; Chrh Wkr; Girl Scts; Hon Rl; Hosp Ade; Jr NHS; Sch Mus; Sch Pl; Treas OEA; 1st Pl Typing In Dist OEA Contest 79; 4th Pl Typing In St OEA Contest L79; Indiana St Univ; Pblc Rltns.

WHITE, ELIZABETH; Lewis County HS; Weston, WV; FCA; Hon Rl; Jr NHS; Red Cr Ade; Pep Clb; Gym; Chrldng; PPFtbl; 4-H Awd; Natl Merit Ltr; Fairmont St Coll; Phys Educ.

WHITE, ELLEN; Princeton HS; Princeton, WV; 63/345 Cls Rep Frsh Cls; Chrs; Hon Rl; Jr NHS; Stu Cncl; Yth Flsp; VP Fr Clb; Keyettes; Pep Clb; Scr Kpr; Amer Studies Awd Curriculum Fair 78; Hnr Soc 76; Concord Coll; Soc Work.

WHITE, EMILY B; Stonewall Jackson HS; Charlston, WV; 10/275 Cls Rep Frsh Cls; Cls Rep Soph Cls; Cl Rep Jr Cls; Band; Drm Mjrt; Jr NHS; Stu Cncl; Fr Clb; Mth Clb; Pred Natl Jr Honor Soc 1976; French Honor Society 1978; Page W V House Of Delegates 1979; Univ.

WHITE, FLETCHER; Berea HS; Berea, OH; Band; Chrh Wkr; Orch; Yth Flsp; Letter Socr; IM Sprt; SMU; Wildlife Tech.

WHITE, GLADYS; Cameron HS; Glen Easton, WV; 42/120 Hon Rl; NHS; Rptr Sch Nwsp; 4-H; FHA; Pep Clb; 4-H Awd; Art Awwd 78; Bus Schl; Sec.

WHITE, GRACE; Luke M Powers HS; Mt Morris, MI; Band; Chrh Wkr; Hon Rl; Jr NHS; NHS; Fr Clb; Trk; Michigan St Univ; Bus.

WHITE, HAROLD; Harding HS; Marion, OH; Boy Scts; Debate Tm; Univ; Law.

WHITE, JACQUELINE; Monroeville HS; Monroeville, OH; Cls Rep Sr Cls; Band; Hon Rl; NHS; Sch Pl; Stg Crw; Stu Cncl; Rptr Yrbk; Drama Clb; Pep Clb; Bowling Green State.

WHITE, JACQUELINE; Kearsley HS; Burton, MI; Chrh Wkr; Cmnty Wkr; Hon Rl; Coach Actv; Ferris St Univ; Pharm.

WHITE, JACQUELINE L; Clarkston HS; Clarkston, MI; 52/500 Band; Drl Tm; Hon Rl; NHS; Twrlr; Natl Merit SF; Ferris State College; Pre Sci.

WHITE, JANDYLL; Huntington Schl; Chillicothe, OH; Chrh Wkr; Hon Rl; NHS; OEA; Cert For Plc In Typing Cntst; Awrd For Various Actvts In Voc Schl; Rcvd Hon For Typing Cntst At Voc Schl; Sec.

WHITE, JEFFREY; Grand Ledge HS; Grand Ledge, MI; Cls Rep Frsh Cls; Cls Rep Soph Cls; Aud/Vis; Band; Orch; Sch Mus; Sch Pl; Stg Crw; Stu Cncl; Yrbk; Mich State Univ; Bus Admin.

WHITE, JILL; Harding HS; Marion, OH; 26/449 Sec Sr Cls; Chrs; Hon Rl; NHS; Sch Mus; Sch Pl; Stg Crw; Yth Flsp; Drama Clb; Ohio St Univ.

WHITE, JOANN; Black River HS; Sullivan, OH; 23/107 Hosp Ade; Lbry Ade; Treas FHA; Pep Clb; Sci Clb; Spn Clb; Natl Merit Ltr; Univ; Educ.

WHITE, JOCELYN C; Seven Hills School; Cincinnati, OH; 1/50 Sec Frsh Cls; Sec Soph Cls; Sec Jr Cls; Treas Chrs; Hon Rl; Stu Cncl; Ed Sch Nwsp; Pres Fr Clb; Natl Merit SF; Univ; Bio Chem.

WHITE, JOEL; Marquette Sr HS; Marquette, MI; Am Leg Boys St; Debate Tm; Natl Forn Lg; Orch; Pol Wkr; Sch Mus; Yth Flsp; Fr Clb; Kiwan Awd; Natl Merit Schl; Univ; Poli Sci.

WHITE, JOHN; High School; Sault Ste Marie, MI; Aud/Vis; Hon Rl; Lbry Ade; VICA; Ftbl; Lake Superior State Coll.

WHITE, JOHN W; Glen Este Sr HS; Cincinnati, OH; Band; Boy Scts; Hon Rl; Stg Crw; Drama Clb; Fr Clb; Coach Actv; Scr Kpr; Tmr; Marine Phys Fitness Tm 78; Drill Tm Band 78; Bsbl Umpire 76 77 & 78; NROTC; Aero Engr.

WHITE, JONDA; Hilliard HS; Columbus, OH; 33/332 Girl Scts; Hon Rl; VP JA; Jr NHS; NHS; Yth Flsp; Sch Nwsp; Treas Spn Clb; Ohi State Univ; Bus Admin.

WHITE, JOSEPH E; Newark Senior HS; Newark, OH; Pres Frsh Cls; Cls Rep Frsh Cls; Pres Soph Cls; Cls Rep Soph Cls; Cl Rep Jr Cls; Band; Chrs; Debate Tm; FCA; Hon Rl; Univ; Physician.

WHITE, KAREN; Carroll HS; Cutler, IN; Chrs; Drl Tm; Hon Rl; Off Ade; Yth Flsp; 4-H; Spn Clb; Mat Maids; Pom Pon; 4-H Awd; Cedarville Coll; Airlines.

WHITE, KARLA; Greenville Sr HS; Greenville, OH; 8/360 Sec Frsh Cls; Sec Jr Cls; Am Leg Aux Girls St; Hon Rl; NHS; Pol Wkr; Spn Clb; Letter Trk; Chrldng; College; Poli Sci.

WHITE, KEITH; East Knox HS; Howard, OH; Hon Rl; Pep Clb; Spn Clb; Bsbl; Letter Bsktbl; Letter Ftbl; College; Communications.

WHITE, KELLEY; Oregon Davis HS; Grovertown, IN; Band; Hon Rl; 4-H; Pep Clb; Gym; 4-H Awd; Ancilla College; Business Mgmt.

WHITE, KEVIN; Princeton HS; Princeton, WV; NHS; Pol Wkr; Key Clb; Ten; Wv Univ; Phys Ther.

WHITE, KIM; Greenbrier East HS; Whte Slphr Spg, WV; 25/413 Band; Chrh Wkr; Cmnty Wkr; Drm Mjrt; Hon Rl; Jr NHS; PAVAS; Red Cr Ade; Twrlr; 3rd Plc Feature Twirler Awd; 2 2nd Plc Ribbons Corps Awd; Concord Coll; Art.

WHITE, KIMBERLEY; St Alphonsus HS; Dearborn, MI; 12/171 Hst Frsh Cls; Hst Soph Cls; Debate Tm; Hon Rl; Sch Mus; Swmmng; GAA; Opt Clb Awd; Univ.

WHITE, KIMBERLEY; James Ford Rhodes HS; Cleveland, OH; 13/310 AFS; Band; Hon Rl; NHS; Off Ade; Sch Mus; Dept Awrd For Best Spanish Stud 78; 4.0 Avrg Or Better 78; Job.

WHITE, LANA M; Manistique HS; Manistique, MI; 4-H; Glf; Chrldng; Pom Pon; 4-H Awd;.

WHITE, LAURA; Mona Shores HS; Muskegon, MI; Michigan State; Child Psychologist.

WHITE, LAURA; Columbia City Joint HS; Columbia City, IN; Band; Drl Tm; Hon Rl; Orch; Sch Mus; Fr Clb; Pom Pon; Indiana Univ; Psych.

WHITE, LENORA; Immaculata HS; Detroit, MI; 13/96 Cls Rep Frsh Cls; Hon Rl; Natl Forn Lg; NHS; Rptr Yrbk; Ed Sch Nwsp; Rptr Sch Nwsp; Pres Lat Clb; Pep Clb; Ntl Hnr Soc Awrd; Jrnlsm Schl Awrd; Latin Schlr Awrd; Mercy Coll; Nursing.

WHITE, LINDA; Jackson HS; Jackson, OH; Chrh Wkr; Girl Scts; Hon Rl; 4-H; Bsktbl; 4-H Awd; Art Fest Awd 2 1st 77; Art Fest Awd Bst Of Show 7 1st 78; AAA & Trans World Affairs Airlines Const 1st 78; Univ; Interior Design.

WHITE, LISA J; L & M HS; Lyons, IN; Drl Tm; Beta Clb; 4-H; FHA; Pep Clb; Capt Pom Pon; 4-H Awd; Univ; Vet.

WHITE, LORI; Beaver Local HS; Rogers, OH; Band; Chrs; Chrh Wkr; Sch Mus; Sprt Ed Yrbk; Eng Clb; Fr Clb; Lat Clb; Pep Clb; Letter Trk; Univ Of S Cal; Nursing.

WHITE, LUANNE; Reeths Puffer HS; Twin Lake, MI; Chrs; Hon Rl; Bus Schl; Data Proc.

WHITE, MICHAEL; New Albany HS; New Albany, IN; 10/565 Band; Boy Scts; Chrh Wkr; Hon Rl; NHS; Sch Pl; Sct Actv; Yth Flsp; Ger Clb; Socr; Univ Of Evansville; Comp Engr.

WHITE, MICHAEL A; River Valley HS; Waldo, OH; 4/196 Hon Rl; Lbry Ade; Stu Cncl; Rptr Sch Nwsp; Eng Clb; 4-H; Spn Clb; 4-H Awd; Natl Merit SF; Stu Council Mem; College; Sec Ed.

WHITE, PAULA; Milan Jr Sr HS; Milan, IN; 3/85 Cls Rep Frsh Cls; Cls Rep Soph Cls; Cl Rep Jr Cls; Cls Rep Sr Cls; Band; Hon Rl; NHS; Stu Cncl; Drama Clb; Pep Clb; Univ; Wildlife Sci.

WHITE, PAUL S; Washington HS; Massillon, OH; 218/482 Cls Rep Frsh Cls; Cls Rep Soph Cls; Cl Rep Jr Cls; Cls Rep Sr Cls; Aud/Vis; Cmnty Wkr; Pol Wkr; Boys Clb Am; Sci Clb; Spn Clb; Kent St Univ; Micro Bio.

WHITE, PHYLLIS; Beaumont For Girls HS; E Cleve, OH; 3/150 Band; Chrs; Drl Tm; Girl Scts; JA; Lbry Ade; Off Ade; Pep Clb; Univ Of Cincinnati; Fashion Mdse.

WHITE, RAYNALD; Detroit Central HS; Detroit, MI; Aud/Vis; Band; Chrs; Chrh Wkr; Hon Rl; Lbry Ade; Orch; Sch Mus; Stg Crw; C of C Awd; Grambling Coll; Music.

WHITE, REX; Jefferson Union HS; Steubenville, OH; Stg Crw; Stu Cncl; Beta Clb; VP 4-H; 4-H Awd; Honorble Mention Jefferson Cnty Bicentennial Comm 77; Univ; Bus.

WHITE, RHONDA; Snider HS; Ft Wayne, IN; 117/583 Band; Chrh Wkr; Girl Scts; Hon Rl; Yth Flsp; 4-H; Univ; Music.

WHITE, RICHARD; Danville Community HS; Danville, IN; Am Leg Boys St; Pres FCA; NHS; Sch Mus; Sch Pl; Pres Stu Cncl; Pres Yth Flsp; Letter Crs Cntry; Letter Trk; U S Air Force Acad; Radio.

WHITE, ROBERTA; Ursuline HS; Youngstown, OH; 72/350 Hon Rl; Pep Clb; Spn Clb; Beloit Coll; Envir Geol.

WHITE, ROBIN; Pontiac Central HS; Pontiac, MI; Cls Rep Frsh Cls; Cls Rep Soph Cls; Girl Scts; Hon Rl; Off Ade; Sch Mus; Sch Pl; Bsktbl; Trk; PPFtbl; Michigan St Univ; CPA.

WHITE, RONDA L; Gahanna Lincoln HS; Gahanna, OH; Cls Rep Frsh Cls; Cls Rep Soph Cls; Cl Rep Jr Cls; Band; Chrs; Drm Mjrt; Hon Rl; NHS; Orch; Sch Mus; Ohio St Univ; Comp Sci.

WHITE, SHARON; Lebanon HS; Mason, OH; 51/268 Chrh Wkr; Girl Scts; Hon Rl; NHS; Pol Wkr; Trk; Miami Univ; Art Educ.

WHITE, SHERYL; Tipton HS; Tipton, IN; 55/165 Chrs; Chrh Wkr; Off Ade; Sch Mus; FTA; VP Pep Clb; Purdue Univ; Elem Tchr.

WHITE, STEPHANIE; Bloomington South HS; Bloomington, IN; 60/360 Chrs; Mdrgl; PAVAS; Pol Wkr; Sch Mus; Sch Pl; Stg Crw; Drama Clb; Indiana Univ; Comp Sci.

WHITE, STEVE; Webster County HS; Camden On Gauly, WV; Band; Hon Rl; NHS; Pres 4-H; Sci Clb; Trk; 4-H Awd; Fairmont St Univ; Music.

WHITE, SYBYL M; Cass Technical HS; Detroit, MI; OEA; Jr Offc Traingng Soc 78; BORC 78; Mbr Of SCOTS 78; Mbr Of Co Op Progr At Schl 78; Univ Of Cincinnati; Comp Ct Reprtng.

WHITE, THERESA; North Putnam Jr Sr HS; Greencastle, IN; 19/151 Aud/Vis; Chrs; Debate Tm; Hon Rl; Lbry Ade; NHS; Sch Pl; Stg Crw; Drama Clb; 4-H;.

WHITE, THERESA; Denby HS; Detroit, MI; Hon Rl; Sch Pl; Sci Clb; Cit Awd; Michigan St Univ; Vet.

WHITE, THERESA; Lumen Christi HS; Jackson, MI; Band; NHS; Stu Cncl; Spn Clb; Letter Gym; Pres Awd; Nazareth College; Nursing.

WHITE, TRACI; Ovid Elsie HS; Lainsburg, MI; Cls Rep Frsh Cls; Sec Soph Cls; Cl Rep Jr Cls; Hon Rl; Mdrgl; VP 4-H; Treas FFA; Pep Clb; Wrstlng; Letter Mgrs; Grand Champ On Cow 79; Top Schl In FFA Chapter 78; Dist Rep For 4 H 79; LBI Bus Schl; Banking.

WHITE, TRACY; Bridgeport Sr HS; Bridgeport, WV; Hst Sr Cls; Chrs; Chrh Wkr; Hon Rl; NHS; Sch Mus; Sch Pl; Stu Cncl; Chrldng; West Virginia Wesleyan Coll.

WHITE, VICKI; Sidney HS; Sidney, OH; Trs Jr Cls; Sec Sr Cls; Band; Drl Tm; Hon Rl; Stu Cncl; OEA; Awd Of Distinction Sr 78; Class Stud Of Yr 78; Class Mbr Of Yr 77; Grad With High Hon 78; Tech Schl; Receptnst.

WHITE, VIVIAN; Jane Addams Vocational HS; Cleveland, OH; 3/218 Trs Frsh Cls; Hon Rl; Jr NHS; NHS; Sch Pl; Stg Crw; Fr Clb; OEA; Cit Awd; Rotary Awd; Legal Sec.

WHITE, WILLIAM G; Hamilton Southeastern HS; Noblesville, IN; Chrh Wkr; Hon Rl; NHS; FFA; FFA Chptr Farmer Degree; FFA Chptr Treas 78; Green Hand Degree 77; Agri Mech Proficiency Awd 78; Lincoln Tech Inst; Auto Tech.

WHITE, WILMA; Chillicothe HS; Chillicothe, OH; AFS; Chrh Wkr; Hon Rl; NHS; Pres Stu Cncl; Pep Clb; Spn Clb; Chrldng; Mgrs; Am Leg Awd; Ohio Univ; Spec Ed.

WHITED, CHRISTINE; Wm A Wirt HS; Gary, IN; Band; Hon Rl; Jr NHS; Fr Clb; Swmmng; Chrldng; Purdue Univ; Vet.

WHITED, DAN; Whitehall Yearling HS; Whitehall, OH; Cls Rep Frsh Cls; Cls Rep Soph Cls; Cl Rep Jr Cls; Stg Crw; Ohio St Univ; Sci.

WHITEHAIR, BRAD; Meadowbrook HS; Pleasant City, OH; Pres Soph Cls; Hon Rl; Pep Clb; Sci Clb; Spn Clb; Ftbl; Trk; Voc Schl.

WHITEHEAD, CINDI; Clyde HS; Clyde, OH; 31/211 Cmp Fr Grls; Chrs; Hon Rl; Sch Mus; Sch Pl; Stg Crw; Yrbk; Drama Clb; Spn Clb; Kent State Univ; Com Art.

WHITEHEAD, DONA; Perry Central HS; Rome, IN; 13/97 Band; Chrh Wkr; Hon Rl; NHS; Yth Flsp; Drama Clb; 4-H; Fr Clb; Dnfth Awd; 4-H Awd; Univ; Nurse.

WHITEHEAD, DONA; Perry Central Jr Sr HS; Rome, IN; 13/99 Band; Hon Rl; NHS; Sch Pl; Stg Crw; Yth Flsp; Rptr Sch Nwsp; Drama Clb; 4-H; Fr Clb; Univ; Nursing.

WHITEHEAD, MITCHELL; Pike Central HS; Otwell, IN; 31/192 Trs Soph Cls; FCA; Hon Rl; NHS; 4-H; FFA; Key Clb; Letter Bsktbl; Letter Ftbl; Letter Trk; Univ; Engr.

WHITEHEAD, PAMELA; University HS; Morgantown, WV; Cl Rep Jr Cls; Band; Chrs; Hon Rl; Yrbk; FBLA; Pres FHA; Pep Clb; Bsktbl; Chrldng; Miss Tomahawk; FHA Home Ec Awd; W Virginia Univ; Busns.

WHITEHOUSE, REBECCA; South Lyon HS; Northville, MI; Cl Rep Jr Cls; Cls Rep Sr Cls; Hon Rl; NHS; Stu Cncl; Ed Yrbk; Rptr Sch Nwsp; VP Pep Clb; Scr Kpr; Natl Merit Schl; Western Michigan Univ; Bus.

WHITEHURST, JESSIE A; South Charleston HS; S Charleston, WV; Am Leg Aux Girls St; Hon Rl; Jr NHS; Mod UN; NHS; Rptr Sch Nwsp; Univ; Med.

WHITE JR, GORDON; Barberton HS; Barberton, OH; 180/500 VP Frsh Cls; Cls Rep Soph Cls; Am Leg Boys St; Chrh Wkr; FCA; Jr NHS; NHS; Off Ade; Stu Cncl; Ed Yrbk; West Liberty St Coll; Spec Ed.

WHITEMAN, BRIAN; Ithaca HS; Ithaca, MI; Band; Boy Scts; Chrs; Hon Rl; Sch Mus; Rptr Sch Nwsp; Glf; Ten; Central Mich Univ; Bus.

WHITEMAN, KELLY; Roosevelt Wilson HS; Stonewood, WV; Band; Chrs; Cmnty Wkr; Hon Rl; Off Ade; Pol Wkr; Y-Teens; Pep Clb; Chrldng; Fairmont Coll; Acctg.

WHITEMAN, REBECCA G; Valley HS; Hastings, WV; Cls Rep Frsh Cls; Band; Chrs; Girl Scts; Hon Rl; Sch Pl; Stu Cncl; 4-H; FFA; Capt Bsktbl; Cosmetology School; Cosmetologist.

WHITEMAN, WILLIAM; Lincoln HS; Wallace, WV; Band; Hon Rl; NHS; Stg Crw; 4-H; 4-H Awd; Wv Univ; Comp Sci.

WHITESEL, KURT; Strongsville HS; Strongsville, OH; 75/512 Hon Rl; Yth Flsp; Ger Clb; Letter Bsktbl; Crs Cntry; Coach Actv; Walsh Coll; Acctg.

WHITESELL, BEV; Eaton HS; Camden, OH; 3/176 Trs Soph Cls; Chrs; Chrh Wkr; Drl Tm; Hon Rl; Jr NHS; NHS; Off Ade; Sch Mus; 4-H; Miami Univ; Bus Ed.

WHITESELL, BEVERLY; Eaton HS; Camden, OH; 3/176 Trs Soph Cls; Chrs; Chrh Wkr; Chmn Drl Tm; Hon Rl; Jr NHS; NHS; Miami Univ; Bus Educ.

WHITESELL, RHONDA; Northmont HS; Englewood, OH; Drl Tm; Fr Clb; Letter Univ Of Cin; Medicine.

WHITESIDES, JAMES F; Turpin HS; Cincinnati, OH; 40/405 Aud/Vis; Bsktbl; PPFtbl; Lttrd In Basketbl; All League All City Plyr Of Wk For Scrng 37 Pts 1 Night; Univ; Elec Engr.

WHITFIELD, CHIQUITA S; Pershing HS; Detroit, MI; Band; Chrh Wkr; Cmnty Wkr; Hon Rl; NHS; Sch Mus; Sch Pl; Drama Clb; Sci Clb; Swmmng; Juilliard Univ.

WHITFORD, CRAIG; Eaton Rapids HS; Eaton Rapids, MI; 42/270 Aud/Vis; Boy Scts; Hon Rl; NHS; Univ Of Ari; Med.

WHITFORD, MARY; William Henry Harrison HS; W Lafayette, IN; Chrs; Chrh Wkr; Yth Flsp; Purdue Univ; Child Dev.

WHITHAM, KAREN; Switzerland Cnty Jr Sr HS; Vevay, IN; 19/120 Treas NHS; Sch Mus; Yrbk; Treas Drama Clb; Pep Clb; Spn Clb; Letter Bsktbl; Letter Trk; Sterling Coll; Busns Mgmt.

WHITING, DONNA L; Cass Technical HS; Detroit, MI; Chrh Wkr; Girl Scts; Hon Rl; Lbry Ade; Sct Actv; Sch Nwsp; Sci Clb; Natl Merit Ltr; NASN Outstndng Negro Stu; College; Health Sci.

WHITIS, GARY; Guernsey Catholic Cntrl HS; Byesville, OH; 9/26 Val; Chrs; Hon Rl; Sch Pl; Stg Crw; Yrbk; Fr Clb; Pep Clb; Letter Bsbl; Letter Bsktbl; French Awd; Principals Awd; Atlantic Pacific HS Math League; St Bd Of Educ Awd Of Distinction; Ohio St Univ; Civil Engr.

WHITIS, RUTH; Avon HS; Plainfield, IN; 3/133 VP Sr Cls; Band; Girl Scts; Hon Rl; NHS; Sct Actv; Yth Flsp; Fr Clb; Trk; College; Computer Sci.

WHITLEY, MICHELLE; Greenon HS; Enon, OH; Chrh Wkr; Hon Rl; NHS; Stu Cncl; Fr Clb; Lat Clb; Sci Clb; GAA; Natl Merit SF; Whos Who Amont Amer HS Stud 77; Auburn Univ; Prevet Med.

WHITLOCK, VICKI L; North Ridgeville HS; N Ridgeville, OH; Bus.

WHITLOW, LISA; Lawrence Central HS; Indianapolis, IN; Chrh Wkr; Girl Scts; Off Ade; Sct Actv; Yth Flsp; Beta Clb; Key Clb; Pep Clb; Letter Bsktbl; PPFtbl; College; Bus.

WHITMAN, KAREN; Central HS; Evansville, IN; Cls Rep Frsh Cls; Cls Rep Soph Cls; Cl Rep Jr Cls; Cls Rep Sr Cls; Hon Rl; NHS; Lat Clb; Pep Clb; Ind Univ; Bio.

WHITMER, SUSAN; Ellet HS; Akron, OH; 8/399 Hon Rl; Jr NHS; NHS; Pres Pep Clb; Letter Crs Cntry; Letter Trk; Univ; Med Sci.

WHITMIRE, JEAN; Brownsburg HS; Brownsburg, IN; 2/275 Cls Rep Sr Cls; Letter Band; Hon Rl; JA; Jr NHS; NHS; Spn Clb; Letter Swmmng; Coach Actv; Scr Kpr; Natl Champion Synchronized Swimmer In Jr Olympics; Attended Summer Honors Seminar At Indiana St In Physics; College; Phys Sci.

WHITMORE, BRET S; Lake Ville Mem HS; Otter Lake, MI; 30/189 Band; Chrh Wkr; Hon Rl; NHS; Sch Mus; Sch Pl; Sct Actv; Yth Flsp; Rptr Yrbk; Rptr Sch Nwsp; Mich Comp Schlrshp 1979; Honr Cmnty Serv 1978; Forensic 3 Yr Comp Brdcst 1979; Delta Coll; Brdcstng.

WHITMORE, DAVID; Pike HS; Indpls, IN; 50/281 Boy Scts; Jr NHS; Sct Actv; Ger Clb; Letter Wrstlng; Indiana Univ; Pre Dent.

WHITMORE, KRISTINE; Kenston HS; Chagrin Fls, OH; Cls Rep Frsh Cls; Chrs; Chrh Wkr; Hon Rl; VP 4-H; Letter Gym; Mst Outstndng Stdnnt In Russiam III 79; Awd For News Prep In Media 78; Brnz & Silvr Medl Gymnastics 78 79; Univ; Cmnctns.

WHITMORE, PAULA; Fairless HS; Navarre, OH; 1/200 Band; Hon Rl; NHS; Off Ade; Yth Flsp; Fr Clb; Mth Clb; Sci Clb; Scr Kpr; Voc Schl; Nursing.

WHITMORE, ROBERT; Carmel HS; Carmel, IN; Chrs; Hon Rl; Sch Mus; 4-H; 4-H Awd; Chorus Awds 77; Purdue Univ; Aero Engr.

WHITMORE, SUE; Saint Johns HS; De Witt, MI; Band; Hon Rl; NHS; 4-H; OEA; IM Sprt; College; Bus.

WHITMORE, WENDY; Warrensville Hts HS; Warrensville, OH; 6/250 Cls Rep Frsh Cls; Hon Rl; Jr NHS; Lbry Ade; NHS; Off Ade; Sch Nwsp; Rdo Clb; Spn Clb; IM Sprt; Bus Schl; Exec Sec.

WHITNEY, ALICE; Olivet HS; Olivet, MI; 2/98 Trs Sr Cls; Sal; Band; Hon Rl; NHS; Sch Mus; Treas Stu Cncl; Ed Yrbk; Yrbk; Spn Clb; Michigan St Univ; Landscape Archt.

WHITNEY, MICHAEL M J; Lexington Sr HS; Lexington, OH; Pres Frsh Cls; Cls Rep Frsh Cls; Trs Soph Cls; Cls Rep Soph Cls; Cl Rep Jr Cls; Pres Sr Cls; Band; Drm Bgl; Hon Rl; Hosp Ade; Ross School Of Aviation; Pilot.

WHITSON, CONNIE; Delta Sr HS; Wauseon, OH; Chrh Wkr; FCA; Yth Flsp; Yrbk; FHA; Pep Clb; Voc Schl; Art.

WHITT, CAROLYN; Independence HS; Beckley, WV; Sec Jr Cls; Chrh Wkr; Girl Scts; Hon Rl; Beta Clb; 4-H; Fr Clb; Cit Awd; Beckly Coll; Nursing.

WHITT, KAREN S; Greenbrier East HS; Renick, WV; Chrh Wkr; Hon Rl; Yth Flsp; Sch Nwsp; Pep Clb; Swmmng; Chrldng;.

WHITTAKER, JUDY; Centerville HS; Centerville, IN; JA; Y-Teens; Drama Clb; FBLA; FHA; Pep Clb; Spn Clb; IM Sprt; PPFtbl; Tmr; Ball State Univ; Bus.

WHITTAKER, KAREN; Berrien Springs HS; Berrien Spring, MI; 25/106 Hon Rl; JA; 4-H; JA Awd; Western Michigan Univ; Acctg.

WHITTAKER, LINDA; Cass City HS; Cass City, MI; Band; Chrh Wkr; Hon Rl; Jr NHS; NHS; Yth Flsp; Fr Clb; Coll.

WHITTEN, DAN; Solon HS; Solon, OH; 56/288 Hon Rl; Pol Wkr; Letter Crs Cntry; Letter Trk; IM Sprt; Kent State Univ; Busns.

WHITTEN, LISA; Beaver Local HS; Lisbon, OH; Band; Chrs; Mod UN; Sch Mus; Y-Teens; Eng Clb; VP Lat Clb; Scr Kpr; Akron Univ; Nurse.

WHITTEN, MICHAEL; Westfall HS; Williamsport, OH; Pres Frsh Cls; Pres Soph Cls; Pres Jr Cls; Pres Sr Cls; Am Leg Boys St; Chrh Wkr; Cmnty Wkr; Hon Rl; NHS; Stu Cncl; Algebra Spanish Science Biology English World History Biology II Physiology Chemistry Awds; U S Air Force Academy; Medicine.

WHITTICO, WILLIAM J; Williamson HS; Williamson, WV; VP Sr Cls; Cmnty Wkr; Hon Rl; Pep Clb; VP Spn Clb; Letter Trk; IM Sprt; Wv Tech; Engr.

WHITTINGSTALL, SANDI; Hubbard HS; Hubbard, OH; 6/330 Am Leg Aux Girls St; Band; Girl Scts; Hon Rl; Keyettes; Spn Clb; Gym; Trk; Mgrs; Youngstown State Univ; Math.

WHITTINGSTALL, SANDRA; Hubbard HS; Hubbard, OH; 6/330 Band; Chrs; Chrh Wkr; Girl Scts; Hon Rl; Sct Actv; Keyettes; Spn Clb; Gym; Trk; Univ; Math.

WHITTINGTON, GAIL; Point Pleasant HS; Pt Pleasant, WV; Chrh Wkr; Girl Scts; Hon Rl; Stu Cncl; Yth Flsp; Y-Teens; Keyettes; Chrldng; GAA; Fairmont St Coll; Bus.

WHITTINGTON, LYNETA; Meigs HS; Pomeroy, OH; Pres Jr Cls; Chrs; Mdrgl; Sch Mus; Sch Pl; Roberts Univ; Voice.

WHITTLESEY, STEPHANIE; Lemon Monroe HS; Monroe, OH; Band; Boy Scts; Chrs; Drl Tm; Girl Scts; Hon Rl; Sch Mus; Sch Pl; Sct Actv; Yrbk; Indiana Univ; Music.

WHITTON, DEBRA; New Palestine HS; Greenfield, IN; Chrh Wkr; Cmnty Wkr; Hon Rl; JA; NHS; Off Ade; Fr Clb; OEA; JA Awd; Manchester Coll; Sec.

WHITTUM, LORI; Grandville HS; Grandville, MI; Cls Rep Frsh Cls; Sec Soph Cls; Cls Rep Soph Cls; Band; Chrs; Chrh Wkr; FCA; JA; Stu Cncl; Rptr Sch Nwsp; Schl Of Psych; Bio Oceanography.

WHITWORTH, W; Wayne Memorial HS; Wayne, MI; Chrh Wkr; Hon Rl; Letter Ftbl; Mich State Univ; Criminal Justice.

WHOLIHAN, KEVIN; Bethel Local HS; New Carlisle, OH; 39/95 Ftbl; Trk; College; Engineering.

WHYBRA, ERIC; Brighton HS; Brighton, MI; Hon Rl; NHS; Letter Ten; Dnfth Awd; Michigan St Univ; Busns.

WHYDE, DIANE; Margaretta HS; Castalia, OH; Stu Cncl; Yrbk; Sch Nwsp; Pres 4-H; OEA; Tmr; 4-H Awd; Top Typist In Class 79; OEA Soc Comm 79; Merit Roll 78; EHOVE Voc Schl; Mgmt.

WHYLE, WANDA; Mc Auley HS; Cincinnati, OH; Chrh Wkr; Orch; Sch Mus; Sch Pl; Stg Crw; Pres Y-Teens; Treas 4-H; Mat Maids; Scr Kpr; Tmr; Secretary.

WHYTE, DIANE; Coventry HS; Barberton, OH; Cls Rep Frsh Cls; Cls Rep Soph Cls; Cl Rep Jr Cls; Band; Hon Rl; Stu Cncl; Rptr Sch Nwsp; Pep Clb; Chrldng; Scr Kpr; Ohio Univ; Business Admin.

WHYTE, RANDY; Mason HS; Mason, MI; Band; Chrs; Orch; Sch Mus; Sch Pl; Stg Crw; Drama Clb; 4-H; Spn Clb; College; Fine Arts.

WIANT, BILLIE J; Woodrow Wilson HS; Beckley, WV; 15/508 Am Leg Aux Girls St; NHS; Pres Stu Cncl; Rptr Yrbk; Rptr Sch Nwsp; Gym; Chrldng; Girl Representative To Know Your St Government Day; Sr Graduation Committee; Emory & Henry Coll; Accounting.

WIANT, PHILLIP; North HS; Springfield, OH; 3 Band; Chrs; Hon Rl; Orch; College.

WIARD, MAXWELL; Bedford Sr HS; Temperance, MI; Cmnty Wkr; Hon Rl; Leo Clb; Capt Hockey; Capt Ten; Coach Actv; Mas Awd; Univ Of Toledo; Art.

WIATR, NOREEN; Paul Cousino HS; Warren, MI; Band; Girl Scts; Hon Rl; Jr NHS; Sct Actv; PPFtbl; Ferris St Coll; Pharm.

WIATRAK, JOHN; Rocky River HS; Rocky Rvr, OH; Cls Rep Frsh Cls; Aud/Vis; Boy Scts; Hon Rl; JA; Lbry Ade; Sch Pl; Stg Crw; Coll.

WIBERG, SVEN; West Muskingum HS; Zanesville, OH; Chrs; Hon Rl; NHS; Stu Cncl; Letter Bsbl; Capt Bsktbl; Pres Socr; IM Sprt; 3.5 Banquet 77 79; Jr Marshall For Grad 79; Univ; Engr.

WIBERT, BETHANN; Laingsburg HS; Laingsburg, MI; 20/80 Band; Girl Scts; Hon Rl; Hosp Ade; Lbry Ade; Off Ade; Sch Pl; Sct Actv; Pep Clb; Letter Chrldng; Baker Jr Coll; Med Asst.

WIBLE, MARTHA; Medina HS; Medina, OH; Cls Rep Frsh Cls; Cls Rep Soph Cls; Chrs; Girl Scts; Sch Mus; Stg Crw; Stu Cncl; Pep Clb; Letter Ten; College.

WIBLE, MICHAEL; Carroll HS; Dayton, OH; 82/266 Rus Clb; Univ; Poli Sci.

WICHMANN, MARK; North Ridgeville HS; N Ridgeville, OH; 16/373 Hon Rl; Lorain Cnty Comm Coll; Author.

WICK, DOUG; Houston HS; Sidney, OH; Am Leg Boys St; Debate Tm; Hon Rl; Lbry Ade; NHS; Off Ade; Yth Flsp; 4-H; Sci Clb; Letter Bsbl; Ohi State; Sci.

WICK, LORNA; Chalker HS; Warren, OH; Chrh Wkr; NHS; Yrbk; Sec Beta Clb; Sci Clb; Letter Bsktbl; Chrldng; Univ; Religion.

WICK, MARI; Adelphian Acad; Lk Orion, MI; Sec Jr Cls; Band; Chrs; Chrh Wkr; Hon Rl; Stu Cncl; Yrbk; Sch Nwsp; Andrews Univ; Bus.

WICKARD, VICKI; North Baltimore HS; N Baltimore, OH; Chrs; Hon Rl; Sch Mus; Yth Flsp; 4-H; Pres FHA; Pep Clb; 4-H Awd; Univ; Conservation.

WICKENHEISER, LAURIE; St Mary Academy; Carleton, MI; Chrh Wkr; Hon Rl; JA; Treas Fr Clb; Sci Clb; Monroe County Cmnty Coll; Acctg.

WICKENS, MARY; Highland Sr HS; Anderson, IN; 20/470 Band; Girl Scts; Hon Rl; 4-H; Bs Soph Musicn Awd 78; Sci Awd & Math Awd 77; Indiana Univ; Child Psych.

WICKER, DEBORA; Brookhaven HS; Gahunna, OH; Band; Chrh Wkr; Hon Rl; Jr NHS; NHS; Orch; College; Acctg.

WICKER, JOHN; Northrop HS; Ft Wayne, IN; 15/624 Letter Band; Hon Rl; Pres JA; Mod UN; Orch; Pol Wkr; Sch Mus; Crs Cntry; Trk; Wrstlng; Indiana Univ; Poli Sci.

WICKHAM, DEBBIE; Loudonville HS; Loudonville, OH; 3/138 Band; Chrs; Chrh Wkr; Cmnty Wkr; Hon Rl; Jr NHS; NHS; Off Ade; Sch Mus; Rptr Sch Nwsp; Univ; Dent Hygnst.

WICKLINE, MATT; North HS; Willowick, OH; 31/700 Hon Rl; Lbry Ade; Orch; Sch Nwsp; Pres Rdo Clb; JETS Awd; Kent St Univ; Cinematography.

WICKLINE, SHERRI; Jackson HS; Jackson, OH; 40/230 Am Leg Aux Girls St; Band; Hon Rl; NHS; Rptr Yrbk; Ed Sch Nwsp; Lat Clb; Ten; PPFtbl; Tennis Most Improved Player Awd; Sci Fair 2nd Pl Sr High Div Lung Capacity; Miami Univ; Poli Sci.

WICKS, JACQUELINE S; Oregon Davis HS; Hamlet, IN; 4/68 Cls Rep Frsh Cls; Cls Rep Soph Cls; Cl Rep Jr Cls; Cls Rep Sr Cls; Am Leg Aux Girls St; Chrs; Hon Rl; NHS; Sch Pl; Yrbk; Ball St Univ; Phys Educ.

WIDANKA, ROBIN; Reading HS; Reading, MI; 5/97 Trs Frsh Cls; Trs Soph Cls; Trs Jr Cls; Trs Sr Cls; Am Leg Aux Girls St; Hon Rl; Chrs; Treas Stu Cncl; Ed Yrbk; Rptr Sch Nwsp; Western Michigan Univ; Acctg.

WIDAS, DONNA; West Iron County HS; Stambaugh, MI; Hon Rl; Trk; Chrldng; Vocational Schl; Cosmetology.

WIDDER, ROBERT; Marysville HS; Marysville, OH; Band; Boy Scts; Hon Rl; Sct Actv; Yth Flsp; IM Sprt; California Tech Voc Schl; Bus Mgmt.

WIDEMAN, WILLIAM; Ithaca HS; Ithaca, MI; Stu Cncl; Crs Cntry; Capt Ten; Ferris St Univ; Data Proc.

WIDMAN, DOUGLAS; Galion HS; Galion, OH; Trs Jr Cls; Trs Sr Cls; Am Leg Boys St; Hon Rl; NHS; Pol Wkr; Yth Flsp; Letter Ten; God Cntry Awd; College.

WIDMAN, SALLY; Fairmont West HS; Kettering, OH; 65/478 Chrh Wkr; Cmnty Wkr; Girl Scts; Hon Rl; NHS; Pres Mth Clb; Trk; Coll Of Wooster; Geology.

WIDMAR, GERALD; Bay City Western HS; Linwood, MI; 24/447 Chrs; Chrh Wkr; Cmnty Wkr; Hon Rl; NHS; Sch Pl; Swmmng; Mic Tech; Mech Engr.

WIDON, PATRICIA; Roscommon HS; Roscommon, MI; Chrh Wkr; Hon Rl; Kirtland Comm Coll; Dietition.

WIECINSKI, SOPHIE; Bishop Noll Institute; Hammond, IN; 41/321 VP Band; Drm Mjrt; Girl Scts; Hon Rl; NHS; Orch; Cls Rep Frsh Cls; Mth Clb; IM Sprt; Scr Kpr; Ind State Univ; Educatin.

WIEDEMAN, AIMEE; Triton HS; Plymouth, IN; Chrh Wkr; Hon Rl; Hosp Ade; Pres FNA; Spn Clb; Pom Pon; Tmr; Univ; Pub Relations.

WIEDEMAN, STEAWRT; Griffith Sr HS; Griffith, IN; 45/281 Ed Yrbk; Wrstlng;.

WIEDEMANN, MARTHA; Glen Oak HS; Chagrin Falls, OH; Aud/Vis; Lit Mag; Yrbk; Sch Nwsp; Bsbl; Bsktbl; Ten; Scr Kpr; Smith Coll.

WIEDERHOLD, JEFF; Clermont Northeastern HS; Batavia, OH; 12/225 VP Jr Cls; Am Leg Boys St; FCA; Hon Rl; Lbry Ade; Pres NHS; Off Ade; Sch Pl; Stu Cncl; Drama Clb; Wilmington Coll; Bus Admin.

WIEDYK, ROGER; Garber HS; Essexville, MI; Stg Crw; Coll; Elec Engr.

WIEGAND, MARTIN; Buena Vista HS; Saginaw, MI; Cl Rep Jr Cls; Band; Boy Scts; Chrh Wkr; Sct Actv; Coach Actv; General Motors Inst; Engr.

WIEGAND, RONALD; Center Line HS; Warren, MI; 30/407 Hon Rl; Jr NHS; NHS; Fr Clb; Bsktbl; Natl Merit Schl; Lawrence Inst Of Tech; Mech.

WIEGING, TERESA; Delphos St Johns HS; Delphos, OH; Band; Hon Rl; 4-H; FTA; 4-H Awd; Coll; Comp Prog.

WIELAND, CINDY; Miami Trace HS; Washington Ch, OH; 3/300 AFS; Chrs; Sec Chrh Wkr; Hon Rl; NHS; Off Ade; Y-Teens; 4-H; Sci Clb; 4-H Awd; Ohio State.

WIELBRUDA, RICH; Liberty HS; Girard, OH; Letter Ftbl; Univ; Comp Sci.

WIELOH, PAULA; Madonna HS; Weirton, WV; 38/99 Jr NHS; Lit Mag; NHS; Rptr Yrbk; Pep Clb; West Liberty St Coll; Bus.

WIENER, LAURA; East HS; Grand Rapids, MI; Hon Rl; Stg Crw; Yth Flsp; Capt Swmmng; Coach Actv; PPFtbl; Tmr; Univ Of Colorado.

WIERDA, BRUCE; North Muskegon HS; North Muskegon, MI; 13/101 Hon Rl; Mth Clb; Ftbl; Letter Trk; Wrstlng; Coach Actv; IM Sprt; PPFtbl; Cit Awd; Michigan St Univ; Bus.

WIERENGO, JEFF; Orchard View HS; Muskegon, MI; 7/192 Band; Hon Rl; NHS; Letter Trk; Muskegon Cmnty Coll; Carpentry.

WIERSBA, ALAN A; Charles F Brush HS; Lyndhurst, OH; 9/650 Pres Chrh Wkr; Pres Debate Tm; Pres JA; Mod UN; NHS; Mth Clb; Letter Socr; Wrstlng; Natl Merit SF; Elec Engr.

WIERSMA, LORI; Caledonia HS; Caledonia, MI; 3/180 Band; Debate Tm; Hon Rl; NHS; Sch Pl; Twrlr; Michigan St Univ.

WIERSMA, LYNNETTE; South Christian HS; Grand Rapids, MI; Pres Frsh Cls; Cl Rep Jr Cls; Pres Sr Cls; Band; Chrs; Stg Crw; Stu Cncl; Yth Flsp; Sch Nwsp; Ger Clb; Calvin Coll; Occuptnl Ther.

WIERZBOWSKI, JOSEPH; Saint Florian HS; Hamtramck, MI; Trs Frsh Cls; Cls Rep Frsh Cls; VP Soph Cls; Pres Jr Cls; Hon Rl; NHS; Rptr Yrbk; Rptr Sch Nwsp; Bsktbl; Central Mic Univ; Comp Sci.

WIESE, RENEE; Brandon HS; Ortonville, MI; 8/253 Cmnty Wkr; Hon Rl; NHS; Stg Crw; Ger Clb; Trk; Mgrs; Scr Kpr; Lion Awd; Univ.

WIESE, ROSEMARY; Clay HS; S Bend, IN; 48/430 Chrh Wkr; Hon Rl; Jr NHS; Mdrgl; NHS; Orch; Sch Mus; Yth Flsp; College; Comp Progr.

WIESE, TERRI; Franklin Central HS; Indianapolis, IN; Girl Scts; NHS; Pres 4-H; Letter Bsktbl; Ten; Letter Trk; 4-H Awd; Univ.

WIESMAN, KIMBERLY; Carroll HS; Dayto, OH; 49/286 Sec Frsh Cls; Sec Soph Cls; Cmnty Wkr; Hon Rl; NHS; Fr Clb; Pep Clb; Chrldng; College; Psych.

WIETSTOCK, STEVEN; Crestwood HS; Dearborn Hts, MI; 2/410 Sal; Band; Boy Scts; Chrh Wkr; Hon Rl; NHS; Sch Mus; Sch Pl; Sec Yth Flsp; God Cntry Awd; Phi Beta Kappa Cert 79; Trustees Hon Schlrshp 79; Eagle Sct 76; Mich Math Prize Comp 79; Alma Coll; Chem.

WIEWANDT, BILL; Port Clinton HS; Port Clinton, OH; Hon Rl; NHS; DECA; Ger Clb; Bowling Green State Univ; Mrktng.

WIGGER, WENDY; Holland HS; Holland, MI; 40/200 Cls Rep Frsh Cls; Band; Hon Rl; JA; NHS; Ger Clb; Letter Gym; Letter Trk; Letter Chrldng; Twrlr; Michigan St Univ.

WIGGERLY, KIM; Daleville HS; Parker City, IN; 18/58 Aud/Vis; Band; Lbry Ade; Sch Mus; Sch Pl; Stg Crw; Rptr Yrbk; Ball St Univ; Acctg.

WIGGERSHAUS, TOM; Dayton Christian HS; Dayton, OH; VP Sr Cls; Chrs; Sch Mus; Sch Pl; Yth Flsp; Rptr Sch Nwsp; Drama Clb; Voice Dem Awd; VP Of Ensemble Life Anew 78 79; Career Devlpmnt Prog 76 77; Univ; Acting.

WIGGINGTON, EDWIN; Thomas Carr Howe HS; Indianapolis, IN; 51/600 Boy Scts; Hon Rl; Jr NHS; Lbry Ade; NHS; Twrlr; Univ; Envir Sci.

WIGGINS, ANDREA; West Geauga HS; Chesterland, OH; AFS; Hon Rl; Yrbk; College; Bus.

WIGGINS, DOROTHY G; East HS; Columbus, OH; Cls Rep Soph Cls; VP Jr Cls; Hon Rl; Jr NHS; Off Ade; Stu Cncl; OEA; Chrldng; Pom Pon; Univ; Word Proc.

WIGGINS, KIM; Mc Cutcheon HS; Lafayette, IN; 25/279 Cls Rep Frsh Cls; Cls Rep Soph Cls; Cl Rep Jr Cls; Band; Girl Scts; Hon Rl; Jr NHS; Natl Forn Lg; NHS; Sch Mus; College; Communications.

WIGGINS, NINA; Our Lady Of Mercy HS; Bloomfield Hls, MI; Cls Rep Soph Cls; Cl Rep Jr Cls; Cls Rep Sr Cls; Mod UN; NHS; Stg Crw; Rptr Sch Nwsp; Sch Nwsp; Fr Clb; Natl Merit SF; General Motors Inst; Elect Engr.

WIGGINS, PAGE; North Posey HS; Poseyville, IN; 4/170 Boy Scts; Cmnty Wkr; Debate Tm; Hon Rl; Natl Forn Lg; NHS; Ger Clb; Bsbl; Bsktbl; Ftbl; Univ; Pre Med.

WIGGINS, SHEILA; Adelphian Acad; Durand, MI; VP Soph Cls; Cl Rep Jr Cls; Chrs; Drl Tm; Hon Rl; Yrbk; 4-H; IM Sprt; 4-H Awd; Pres Awd; Mich State Univ; Agriculture.

WIGGS, JOHN W; Wood Memorial HS; Oakland City, IN; Boy Scts; Hon Rl; Sct Actv; Rptr Yrbk; Spn Clb; Vocational School; Electronics.

WIITALA, LORI; Houghton HS; Houghton, MI; Chrs; Chrh Wkr; Drl Tm; Girl Scts; Hon Rl; Sch Mus; Sch Pl; Yrbk; 4-H;.

WIITANEN, CAROL; Hancock Central HS; Hancock, MI; 6/91 Band; NHS; Off Ade; Orch; Sch Mus; Sch Pl; Yrbk; Letter Bsktbl; Letter Trk; Mich Tech Univ; Metallurgical Engr.

WIKE, KATHLEEN; Magnificat HS; Middleburg Hts, OH; Chrs; Jr NHS; NHS; Off Ade; Sch Mus; Sch Pl; Spn Clb; Gym; Chrldng; GAA; Niagara Univ; Nursing.

WILA, DONNA; Hopkins HS; Dorr, MI; Hon Rl; Jr NHS; NHS; Off Ade; Stu Cncl; Ed Yrbk; Letter Bsbl; Letter Bsktbl; Coach Actv; Scr Kpr;.

WILBER, JENNY; Bedford North Lawrence HS; Bedford, IN; Hon Rl; Hosp Ade; Sch Mus; Beta Clb; Sec Drama Clb; Mth Clb; Spn Clb; Hnr Thespianship In Intl Thespian Soc 79; Bst Tech In Scarlet & Purple Drama Club 79; Indiana Univ; Pre Med.

WILBER, KELLY; Rochester Comm HS; Rochester, IN; 2/170 Chrs; Hon Rl; NHS; Sch Mus; Sch Pl; Drama Clb; FHA; Pres Ger Clb; Pep Clb; Sci Clb; Best One Act Actress; Whos Who In Foreign Language; College; Chem Engr.

WILBER, MARY; Port Clinton HS; Port Clinton, OH; 10/280 Hon Rl; NHS; Orch; Sch Pl; Mth Clb; Spn Clb; John Carroll Coll; Acctg.

WILBORN, VONZETTA J; Princeton HS; Princeton, WV; Cls Rep Frsh Cls; Cls Rep Soph Cls; Chrs; Chrh Wkr; Cmnty Wkr; Mdrgl; Stu Cncl; Pep Clb; Spn Clb; Chrldng; Shaw College; Psych.

WILBURN, DEBBIE; Bridgeport HS; Bridgeport, WV; 15/189 Girl Scts; Hon Rl; Jr NHS; NHS; Yth Flsp; Y-Teens; Spn Clb; Glenville State College; Acctg.

WILBURN, DEBRA; William A Wirt HS; Gary, IN; Letter Band; Hon Rl; JA; Jr NHS; Pep Clb; Trk; Chrldng; College; Medicine.

WILBURN JR, THOMAS; Penn HS; Osceola, IN; 130/500 Hon Rl; Machinist.

WILCHECK, ANNE; Ontario HS; Mansfield, OH; 4/198 VP Frsh Cls; Sec Soph Cls; Sec Jr Cls; Am Leg Aux Girls St; NHS; Fr Clb; Bsktbl; Ohi State Univ; Education.

WILCHER, LYNWOOD; Buckhannon Upshur HS; Buckhannon, WV; Cls Rep Frsh Cls; Cls Rep Soph Cls; Am Leg Boys St; Chrh Wkr; Hon Rl; NHS; Bsbl; Bsktbl; Coach Actv; IM Sprt; Named 1st Team Big Ten Center In Bsktbl 79; Named Hon Ment All St In Bsktbl 79; Led Bsktbl In Scor & Rbndng; Univ.

WILCOX, CARROLL; Elmwood HS; Bloomdale, OH; 9/115 VP Soph Cls; Treas Band; VP Chrs; Chrh Wkr; Drl Tm; Hon Rl; VP MMM; NHS; Orch; Sch Mus; Owens Tech Coll; Executive Secretary.

WILCOX, CHARLES; Hilliard HS; Columbus, OH; Hon Rl; Jr NHS; Stu Cncl; Lat Clb; Letter Bsktbl; Ohio St Univ; Busns Admin.

WILCOX, DARCI; Ravenna HS; Ravenna, OH; 1/300 Chrs; Hon Rl; Hosp Ade; NHS; Sch Mus; Letter Bsbl; Univ; Nursing.

WILCOX, DAVID; Bedford HS; Temperance, MI; 35/439 Band; Chrs; FCA; Hon Rl; NHS; Sch Mus; Yth Flsp; Sprt Ed Yrbk; Yrbk; Drama Clb; Univ Of Toledo; Elec Engr.

WILCOX, DEBORAH; Clay HS; Granger, IN; 40/430 Band; Cmp Fr Grls; Chrh Wkr; Cmnty Wkr; Hon Rl; Hosp Ade; NHS; Off Ade; DECA; Indiana Univ.

WILCOX, ERIC; Piqua Central HS; Piqua, OH; 13/287 Boy Scts; Hon Rl; Jr NHS; NHS; Sct Actv; Crs Cntry; Glf; Top 100 Schlstc Awd 79; Air Force Academy.

WILCOX, KELLY; Neguanee HS; Negaunee, MI; Hon Rl; Yrbk; IM Sprt; Western Michigan Univ; Psych.

WILCOX, LISA; Morgantown HS; Morgantown, WV; Cls Rep Soph Cls; Band; Chrs; Hon Rl; JA; NHS; Stu Cncl; Mth Clb; Spn Clb; Letter Chrldng; Univ; Bus Admin.

WILCOX, MARILYN; Glen Lake HS; Empire, MI; VP Frsh Cls; Pres Soph Cls; Pres Jr Cls; Band; Girl Scts; Hon Rl; Off Ade; Yrbk; Sch Nwsp; Fr Clb; Michigan St Univ; Oceanography.

WILCOX, MOLLY; Grandview Hts HS; Columbus, OH; 1/130 Chrs; Drl Tm; Hon Rl; Jr NHS; Letter Bsktbl; Letter Hockey; Letter Trk; Univ.

WILCOX, PAM; Oakwood HS; Dayton, OH; Cmnty Wkr; Hon Rl; JA; NHS; Off Ade; Bsktbl; Chrldng; IM Sprt; Mgrs; Univ.

WILCOX, PAMELA; Oakwood HS; Dayton, OH; Hon Rl; JA; NHS; Off Ade; Rptr Yrbk; Bsktbl; Chrldng; IM Sprt; Mgrs; College.

WILCOX, RANDALL; Manton Consolidated HS; Manton, MI; Am Leg Boys St; Hon Rl; NHS; Yrbk; Sch Nwsp; Ftbl; Ferris State Univ; Sci.

WILCOXEN, RON; Belpon HS; Belpre, OH; AFS; Drl Tm; Natl Forn Lg; Sch Pl; Drama Clb; Fr Clb; Mth Clb; Sci Clb; Spn Clb; JETS Awd; Ohio St Univ; Astronomy.

WILCOXEN, VALERIE; North Vermillion HS; Perrysville, IN; 14/98 Band; Chrs; Hon Rl; NHS; 4-H; OEA; Spn Clb; 4-H Awd; Bus Schl; Sec Wrk.

WILCZEWSKI, DAVID; St Edward HS; Cleveland, OH; 14/400 Boy Scts; Chrh Wkr; Debate Tm; Hon Rl; Jr NHS; Natl Forn Lg; Sct Actv; Rptr Sch Nwsp; Key Clb; Scr Kpr; Univ; Comp Sci.

WILCZYNSKI, VINCENT; St Francis De Sales HS; Toledo, OH; 15/233 Cl Rep Jr Cls; Cls Rep Sr Cls; Chrh Wkr; Hon Rl; NHS; ROTC; Rptr Sch Nwsp; 4-H; Crs Cntry; Trk; Coast Guard Academy; Engineer.

WILD, LAURIE; Brooklyn HS; Brooklyn, OH; 38/173 Pres AFS; Band; Hon Rl; Hosp Ade; Lbry Ade; Red Cr Ade; Rptr Sch Nwsp; Capt Trk; Scr Kpr; Toledo Univ; Pre Med.

WILD, WENDY; North Vermillion HS; New Albany, IN; 2/90 Pres Frsh Cls; Band; Chrs; Chrh Wkr; Hon Rl; NHS; 4-H; Letter Trk; Letter Chrldng; GAA; Ind State Univ; Childhood Developmen.

WILDEBOER, SUE; Creston HS; Grand Rpds, MI; Cls Rep Frsh Cls; FCA; Hon Rl; Jr NHS; NHS; Bsktbl; Capt Ten; Trk; Mat Maids; Hope Univ; Phys Ed.

WILDEMAN, SHEILA; Niles Sr HS; Niles, MI; Cl Rep Jr Cls; Band; Girl Scts; Hon Rl; NHS; Off Ade; Sct Actv; Stg Crw; Stu Cncl; Sch Nwsp; Stud Council Comm 78; Michigan St Univ; Wildlife Mgmt.

WILDER, DAWN; Marion HS; Marion, IN; 74/710 Chrs; Hon Rl; NHS; Sch Pl; Stu Cncl; Drama Clb; VP Spn Clb; Taylor Univ; Major Undecided.

WILDER, GERALD; Detroit Redford HS; Detroit, MI; Cls Rep Soph Cls; Cl Rep Jr Cls; Hon Rl; NHS; Capt Ftbl; Trk; Mich State Univ; Medicine.

WILDER, LAURA; N Posey Sr HS; Poseyville, IN; Chrh Wkr; Cmnty Wkr; Hon Rl; Hosp Ade; Off Ade; Stg Crw; VP Yth Flsp; Fr Clb; OEA; Treas Pep Clb; Vincennes Univ; Bsns Ed.

WILDER, LINDA; Montpelier HS; Montpelier, OH; Band; Chrs; Chrh Wkr; Cmnty Wkr; Sch Mus; Sch Pl; 4-H; Fr Clb; Pep Clb; 4-H Awd; Tiffin Univ; Ct Reporting.

WILDER, MARION; Fruitport HS; Muskegon, MI; 27/280 Cls Rep Sr Cls; Band; Hon Rl; NHS; Pep Clb; Spn Clb; Gym; Trk; Pom Pon; PPFtbl; West Point Acad; Engr.

WILDER, STEVEN E; Montpelier HS; Montpelier, OH; 10/103 Am Leg Boys St; Chrh Wkr; Hon Rl; Fr Clb; Letter Crs Cntry; Letter Trk; Coach Actv; Acad Achvmnt Club 3 Yrs; Univ.

WILDER, SUSAN; Decatur Central HS; Indnpls, IN; Band; Chrh Wkr; College; Music.

WILDER, WILLIAM S; Lakewood HS; Lakewood, OH; 111/693 Am Leg Boys St; Band; Chrs; Chrh Wkr; Yth Flsp; Lat Clb; Ten; Citations In Music & Phys Educ; Univ.

WILDERMUTH, BRETT; Anna HS; Anna, OH; 9/83 Pres Soph Cls; Chrs; Chrh Wkr; Hon Rl; Sch Mus; Sch Pl; Drama Clb; Sci Clb; IM Sprt; Voice Dem Awd; Vocational School.

WILDERMUTH, MARLENE; Upper Valley Joint Voc Schl; Maplewood, OH; Girl Scts; Hon Rl; NHS; 4-H; OEA; Pep Clb; 4-H Awd; Typing Prodctn Awd 78;.

WILDERMUTH, MICHELLE; Allen East HS; Lima, OH; 15/109 Sec Sr Cls; Hon Rl; JA; Yth Flsp; Rptr Yrbk; Rptr Sch Nwsp; OSU Tech Schl; Acctg.

WILDEY, KENDALL; Jennings County HS; No Vernon, IN; 13/400 VP Frsh Cls; Cls Rep Frsh Cls; Trs Soph Cls; Cls Rep Soph Cls; Chrs; Treas Chrh Wkr; Hon Rl; Jr NHS; NHS; Off Ade; Free Throw Asst Awd; Univ; Optometry.

WILDFONG, BRIDGET; Gladwin HS; Gladwin, MI; 17/150 Sec Soph Cls; Sec Jr Cls; Chrh Wkr; Hon Rl; Jr NHS; Sec NHS; Off Ade; Stu Cncl; Pres Yth Flsp; Chrldng; Camp Rotary Counselor; Girls Sftbl Tm For 2 Yrs Earned Letter; Spring Arbor Coll; Med.

WILDMAN, LINDA; Fountain Central Jr Sr HS; Veedersburg, IN; 1/145 Band; Drl Tm; VP Stu Cncl; Rptr Yrbk; Lat Clb; Ten; Dnfth Awd; DAR Awd; Univ.

WILDMAN, WARD; North Union HS; Richwood, OH; 14/139 VP Soph Cls; Pres Sr Cls; Cls Rep Sr Cls; NHS; Stu Cncl; Rptr Sch Nwsp; Letter Ftbl; Ohio Northern Univ; Bus Admin.

WILDRIDGE, JEFF; Washington HS; Washington, IN; 16/216 Band; Fr Clb; Letter Glf; Univ Of Florida; Engr.

WILDS, DENISE; Sterling Heights HS; Sterling Hts, MI; Band; Cmp Fr Grls; Chrs; Hon Rl; Swmmng; Coach Actv; Tmr; Natl Merit Ltr; Oakland Univ; Engr.

WILDS, TONDA; Rock Hill HS; Ironton, OH; Cls Rep Soph Cls; Band; Chrh Wkr; Hon Rl; NHS; Stu Cncl; Rptr Sch Nwsp; Sch Nwsp; Beta Clb; 4-H;.

WILE, MICHELE; Green HS; Akron, OH; 30/316 Chrs; Yrbk; Pep Clb; GAA; Scr Kpr; Univ; Vet Asst.

WILES, BRENDA; Swanton HS; Swanton, OH; Hon Rl; NHS; Rptr Yrbk; Rptr Sch Nwsp; 4-H; Fr Clb; Pep Clb; 4-H Awd; JC Awd; Toledo Nrsg Hosp Sch; Reg Nurse.

WILES, ESTELLE; Ionia HS; Ionia, MI; 147/272 Chrs; Hon Rl; Rptr Yrbk; Rptr Sch Nwsp; Davenport Coll Of Bus; Fshn Mdse.

WILES, ESTHER; Ionia HS; Ionia, MI; 156/272 Chrs; Hon Rl; Rptr Yrbk; Rptr Sch Nwsp; Trk; Davenport Coll Of Bus; Fshn Mdse.

WILEY, BARBARA K; Western Hills HS; Cincinnati, OH; 213/800 Girl Scts; Hon Rl; Sec DECA; Scr Kpr; Treas Mas Awd; 5th Pl In Busns Vocabulary In DECA; 1st Pl In Genl Merch In DECA;.

WILEY, JAYLANE; Hazel Park HS; Hazel Park, MI; Band; Chrh Wkr; Girl Scts; Hon Rl; NHS; Ten; Univ; Fshn Dsgnr.

WILEY, JOHN; Cloverdale Community HS; Quincy, IN; Hon Rl; NHS; VP FFA; Cit Awd;.

WILEY, TINA; Bethel Local HS; Tipp City, OH; 30/97 Sec Frsh Cls; Sec Soph Cls; Sec Jr Cls; Sec Sr Cls; Hon Rl; Jr NHS; NHS; Off Ade; Sch Pl; Stu Cncl; Rptr Sch Nwsp; Univ Of Cincinnati; Elem Ed.

WILFONG, JEANIE; Monongah HS; Worthington, WV; Boy Scts; Chrh Wkr; Girl Scts; Hon Rl; Lbry Ade; Y-Teens; Rptr Yrbk; Fr Clb; Pep Clb; Gym; Fairmont St Univ; Journalism.

WILFONG, KIM; Brandon HS; Ortonville, MI; Hon Rl; Rptr Yrbk; Yrbk; Bsktbl; Univ.

WILFONG, LISA; Marsh Fork HS; Naoma, WV; Chrh Wkr; Hon Rl; Sec NHS; Drama Clb; Raleigh Co Voc & Tech Cntr; Nursing.

WILFONG, PAM; Ashtabula HS; Ashtabula, OH; Cl Rep Jr Cls; Chrh Wkr; Mod UN; Off Ade; Pol Wkr; Stu Cncl; Rptr Yrbk; Yrbk; Rptr Sch Nwsp; Sch Nwsp; Acad Of Court Reporting; Stenography.

WILGES, D; Sidney HS; Sidney, OH; Band; Hon Rl; Jr NHS; NHS; Bsktbl; Ten; Miami Univ; Engr.

WILHELM, ELIZABETH; Redford Union HS; Redford, MI; Band; Chrs; Hon Rl; Mdrgl; Pep Clb; Gym; Madonna College; Nursing.

WILHELM, ELIZABETH; Wheeling Park HS; Wheeling, WV; Cls Rep Frsh Cls; Cls Rep Soph Cls; Cl Rep Jr Cls; Pres Sr Cls; Girl Scts; Stu Cncl; Trk; Scr Kpr; Rec Enviro Educ Progr 78; Bsktbl Babe 78; Capt Bsktbl Babes 79; Univ.

WILHELM, KAREN J; Marion Harding HS; Marion, OH; AFS; Chrs; Girl Scts; Hon Rl; Sch Mus; 4-H; Show Horse Highpoint Broodmare Of Ohio In AQHA;.

WILHELM, MARY; Fairview HS; Defiance, OH; 2/104 Pres Jr Cls; Chrs; Chrh Wkr; Hon Rl; NHS; Off Ade; Sch Mus; Sch Pl; VP Yth Flsp; 4-H; Univ; Elem Educ Tchr.

WILHELM, MARY B; Saint Alphonsus HS; Detroit, MI; 15/171 Chrs; Chrh Wkr; Hon Rl; Sch Mus; Cit Awd; History Spanish Religion Geometry & Contri To Ctr Of Performing Arts Recog; College.

WILHELM, SHERRIE; Owosso HS; Owosso, MI; 33/406 Band; Chrs; Chrh Wkr; Hon Rl; Hosp Ade; NHS; Pol Wkr; Spring Arbor College; Art Ther.

WILHELM, THERESA; De Kalb HS; Ashley, IN; Letter Chrs; Girl Scts; Hon Rl; Jr NHS; NHS; Ger Clb; Sci Clb; PPFtbl;.

WILHITE, GREG; Harrison HS; Evansville, IN; Boy Scts; FSA; Ftbl; Cit Awd; College.

WILK, CHERYL; Huron HS; New Boston, MI; 6/163 Cls Rep Frsh Cls; Band; Hon Rl; Jr NHS; NHS; Stu Cncl; Fr Clb; Letter Trk; PPFtbl; Mic Tech Univ; Med Tech.

WILK, JOYCE; Unioto HS; Chillicothe, OH; 1/140 Val; Band; Chrh Wkr; Hon Rl; JA; NHS; Stu Cncl; Drama Clb; Sec FTA; Sec Spn Clb; Coll; Educ.

WILKES, CAROL; Meigs HS; Rutland, OH; 8/178 Chrs; Chrh Wkr; Hon Rl; NHS; Sch Pl; FFA; Ohio St Univ; Lab Tech.

WILKIN, CONNIE; North Daviess HS; Elnora, IN; Girl Scts; Hon Rl; Sct Actv; FHA; Pep Clb; Indiana State Univ; Secratarial.

WILKINS, DAVID; Schafer HS; Southgate, MI; 25/240 Hon Rl; NHS; Capt Bsktbl; Ftbl; Michigan St Univ; Mech Engr.

WILKINS, JAMES D; Circleville HS; Riverton, WV; 1/30 Trs Frsh Cls; Trs Soph Cls; Trs Jr Cls; Trs Sr Cls; Band; Hon Rl; Pres NHS; Ed Yrbk; Ed Sch Nwsp; Treas 4-H; FFA Schlrshp 1979; Potomac St Coll; Agri Econ.

WILKINS, LISA ANN; Roy C Start HS; Toledo, OH; 132/395 Pres Chrh Wkr; Off Ade; Sch Mus; Sch Pl; Pres DECA; FHA; Ger Clb; Ten; IM Sprt; Univ Of Toledo; Gen Mdse.

WILKINS, LOUANN; Fostoria HS; Fostoria, OH; Chrs; Chrh Wkr; Hon Rl; JA; Lbry Ade; Off Ade; Fr Clb; Geneva College; Pre Med.

WILKINS, MARCIA; Lawrence Central HS; Indianapolis, IN; 17/275 Cls Rep Frsh Cls; VP Soph Cls; Am Leg Aux Girls St; Letter Band; Drm Mjrt; NHS; Y-Teens; 4-H; Opt Clb Awd; Indiana Univ; Med.

WILKINS, MARK; Holy Redeemer HS; Detroit, MI; 2/122 Trs Sr Cls; Sal; NHS; Yrbk; Sch Nwsp; VP Drama Clb; Sci Clb; Lawrence Inst Of Tech; Elec Engr.

WILKINS, PAUL; Clarence Kimball HS; Royal Oak, MI; 42/602 Cls Rep Frsh Cls; Cls Rep Soph Cls; Cl Rep Jr Cls; Cls Rep Sr Cls; Sal; Cmnty Wkr; Hon Rl; NHS; Stu Cncl; Drama Clb; Albion Coll; Mech Engr.

WILKINS, SHERRY; Allen East HS; Lafayette, OH; 6/107 Sec Frsh Cls; Cls Rep Frsh Cls; Band; Chrs; Chrh Wkr; Hon Rl; Jr NHS; Sch Pl; College; Bus Admin.

WILKINSON, BEVERLY; Turpin HS; Cincinnati, OH; Sec AFS; Mgrs; Treas Univ Of Cincinnati; Ind ustrail Engr.

WILKINSON, CARY; Union HS; Winchester, IN; Hon Rl; NHS; Yth Flsp; Rptr Sch Nwsp; FHA; Spn Clb; Recognition For Newspapers Ad Mngr; College; Child Psych.

WILKINSON, JUANITA; Colerain HS; Cincinnati, OH; College; Comt.

WILKINSON, LORI; Elmwood HS; Bloomdale, OH; 8/120 Band; Chrh Wkr; Hon Rl; MMM; Sch Mus; Stg Crw; Drama Clb; 4-H; FTA; Sci Clb; Alt To Buckeye Girls St 79; Attnded 4 H Cong 79; Sel For All Cntry Wood Bnd 78; Ohio St Univ; Admin Sci.

WILKS, TALVIN W; The Miami Valley School; Dayton, OH; Cls Rep Soph Cls; Natl Forn Lg; Sch Mus; Sch Pl; VP Stu Cncl; Rptr Yrbk; Rptr Sch Nwsp; Letter Socr; Trk; Natl Sci Found Stu Sci Training Progr 78; Degree Of Excel Natl Forensics Lg 79; The Cum Laude Soc 79; Univ; Bio Chem.

WILL, BETH; North Posey HS; Poseyville, IN; VP Soph Cls; VP Jr Cls; Hon Rl; NHS; 4-H; Chrldng; Univ.

WILL, JEFFREY; Delphos St Johns HS; Delphos, OH; 47/145 Band; Boy Scts; Chrh Wkr; Off Ade; Sct Actv; Yrbk; Florist.

WILL, JEFFREY A; Westerville South HS; Westerville, OH; 104/284 Aud/Vis; Band; Boy Scts; Chrs; Hon Rl; Lbry Ade; Off Ade; Sch Mus; Sch Pl; Stu Cncl; Ohio Univ; Health Education.

WILL, MARILYN; Marion Local HS; Celina, OH; Chrh Wkr; Hon Rl; Sch Nwsp; Drama Clb; Mth Clb; OEA; Pep Clb; Sci Clb; IM Sprt; Scr Kpr; Bus Schl; Acctg.

WILL, TAMARA; Valley HS; Minford, OH; 6/107 Trs Soph Cls; Band; Pres Chrs; Chrh Wkr; Hon Rl; NHS; Sch Pl; Yth Flsp; Treas FTA; Cedarville Coll.

WILLAERT, KATHY; Bishop Gallagher HS; Detroit, MI; 16/322 Cls Rep Frsh Cls; Cls Rep Soph Cls; Cl Rep Jr Cls; Cls Rep Sr Cls; Chrh Wkr; Hon Rl; Sch Pl; Yrbk; Natl Merit Ltr; Natl Merit SF; Mich State Univ; Elem Educ.

WILLAIMSON, ELIZABETH; Hagerstown Jr Sr HS; Greensfork, IN; 72/176 Band; Chrh Wkr; Cmnty Wkr; Hon Rl; Off Ade; Yth Flsp; 4-H; FHA; OEA; Pep Clb; IVTC; Bus.

WILLARD, JULIE; Port Huron Northern HS; Port Huron, MI; 206/400 Cmp Fr Grls; Hon Rl; Off Ade; Y-Teens; Ed Yrbk; Trk; IM Sprt; Central Mich Univ; Journalism.

WILLARD, KAREN; Clay Sr HS; Oregon, OH; Chrh Wkr; Hon Rl; Lbry Ade; Letter Ten; Letter Trk; Univ.

WILLARD, TRICIA L; Hagerstown Jr Sr HS; Hagerstown, IN; 10/140 Cls Rep Frsh Cls; Cls Rep Soph Cls; Cl Rep Jr Cls; Chrh Wkr; VP FCA; Hon Rl; Stg Crw; Pres Stu Cncl; Fr Clb; Pep Clb; Purdue Univ; Vet Tech.

WILLAVAGE, LETA; Hamilton Southeastern HS; Noblesville, IN; Fr Clb; Ger Clb; OEA; Spn Clb; Gym; Letter Swmmng; Mgrs; Ball St Univ; Lang.

WILLCOCK, CAROL; Manistique HS; Manistique, MI; 8/160 Band; Debate Tm; Hon Rl; Natl Forn Lg; Drama Clb; 4-H; Pep Clb; 4-H Awd; Voice Dem Awd; College; Dental Asst.

WILLCOME, MARY; Grant Sr HS; Grant, MI; Aud/Vis; Chrs; Hon Rl; Off Ade; Yrbk; Crs Cntry; Hndbl; Trk; GAA; PPFtbl; Grand Vly St Coll; Spec Educ.

WILLCOX, PATRICIA; Bexley HS; Columbus, OH; Cl Rep Jr Cls; Trs Sr Cls; Chrs; Chrh Wkr; Quill & Scroll; Stu Cncl; Yth Flsp; Ed Yrbk; Rptr Yrbk; Spn Clb; Univ; Eng.

WILLEKE, TONYA; Marysville HS; Marysville, OH; 10/230 Cls Rep Soph Cls; Am Leg Aux Girls St; Band; Chrs; Chrh Wkr; Girl Scts; Hon Rl; NHS; Orch; Stu Cncl; Ohio St Univ; Dietitian.

WILLEMSTYN, BRIAN; West Ottawa HS; Holland, MI; Aud/Vis; Band; NHS; Orch; Sch Mus; Sch Pl; Crs Cntry; Trk; Hope College; Psych.

WILLER, PEGGY; Margaretta HS; Vickery, OH; Band; Chrs; Chrh Wkr; Girl Scts; Hon Rl; Sch Pl; Yth Flsp; Yrbk; Sprt Ed Sch Nwsp; Rptr Sch Nwsp; Ohio St Univ; Soc Work.

WILLETT, BRADLEY; Bishop Watterson HS; Columbus, OH; Cls Rep Soph Cls; Boy Scts; Chrh Wkr; Cmnty Wkr; Hon Rl; Stg Crw; Stu Cncl; Letter Ftbl; Letter Wrstlng; Coach Actv; Outstndng Jr In Franklin County 79; Univ.

WILLETT, RANDAL; St Johns HS; St Johns, MI; Band; Boy Scts; Chrh Wkr; Cmnty Wkr; Hon Rl; Sch Pl; Sct Actv; Stg Crw; Drama Clb; Pep Clb; Eagle Scout Awd; Rodney B Wilson Schlrshp; Michigan St Stu Schlrshp; Michigan St Univ; Comp Sci.

WILLETTE, JOHN; St Johns HS; St Johns, MI; Band; Boy Scts; Chrh Wkr; Hon Rl; NHS; Sct Actv; Voc Schl.

WILLEY, KATHLEEN; Waterloo HS; Randolph, OH; Trs Frsh Cls; Sec Soph Cls; Band; Chrh Wkr; Hon Rl; Lbry Ade; Stu Cncl; Beta Clb; Fr Clb; Pep Clb; Akron Univ; Phys Ther.

WILLEY, SHEILA; South Newton HS; Brook, IN; Hosp Ade; Lbry Ade; Off Ade; Quill & Scroll; Yrbk; FBLA; FHA; Lat Clb; Pep Clb; Voc School; Fashion Mdse.

WILLHITE, KIM; Brethren Christian HS; Mishawaka, IN; Band; Chrs; Chrh Wkr; Cmnty Wkr; Hon Rl; NHS; Orch; Sch Mus; Sch Pl; Yrbk; 2nd & 3rd Pl Go Reporter Elkhart Truth; Charger List Above Honor Roll; Grace Coll; Journalism.

WILLHITE, PAUL; Taylor HS; Kokomo, IN; 12/200 Band; Hon Rl; Off Ade; Letter Glf; Natl Merit Ltr; Indiana Univ; Bio Engr.

WILLIAMS, A; Marsh Fork HS; Packsville, WV; Cls Rep Frsh Cls; Cls Rep Soph Cls; VP Jr Cls; Cl Rep Jr Cls; Sec Band; Chrs; Hon Rl; Glenville St College.

WILLIAMS, ALAN; North Adams HS; Hillsdale, MI; 2/49 Trs Frsh Cls; Trs Soph Cls; Cls Rep Soph Cls; Trs Jr Cls; Sal; Am Leg Boys St; Hon Rl; Lbry Ade; NHS; Central Mic Univ.

WILLIAMS, ALETA Y; Southeastern HS; Detroit, MI; Chrh Wkr; Cmnty Wkr; Hon Rl; Cit Awd; Wayne St Univ; Data Proc.

WILLIAMS, AMY; Bexley HS; Columbus, OH; Cl Rep Jr Cls; Sec Sr Cls; Cls Rep Sr Cls; Hon Rl; Jr NHS; Quill & Scroll; Chmn Stu Cncl; Ed Yrbk; Spn Clb; Capt Ten; Univ Of Virginia; Psych.

WILLIAMS, AMY; Ridgedale HS; Marion, OH; Trs Soph Cls; Hst Jr Cls; Band; Chrs; Chrh Wkr; FCA; Hon Rl; Jr NHS; NHS; Off Ade; Univ Of Cincinnati; Med Tech.

WILLIAMS, AMY R; Davison Sr HS; Davison, MI; Chrs; Chrh Wkr; Hon Rl; Mdrgl; Orch; Sch Mus; Baptist Bible Coll; Music.

WILLIAMS, ANN; Walnut Hills HS; Cincinnati, OH; Hon Rl; Hosp Ade; Sch Pl; Rptr Yrbk; DAR Awd; Univ.

WILLIAMS, ANNETTE; John F Kennedy HS; Cleveland, OH; Red Cr Ade; Pep Clb; Spn Clb; College; Psych.

WILLIAMS, AVA; West Side Sr HS; Gary, IN; 47/650 Cl Rep Jr Cls; Girl Scts; Hon Rl; Pres JA; Jr NHS; Lbry Ade; NHS; Off Ade; Stu Cncl; Y-Teens; Purdue Univ; Pre Med.

WILLIAMS, BELINDA; Henry Ford HS; Detroit, MI; Chrs; Hon Rl; Lbry Ade; Sch Mus; Bsktbl; Natl Merit Ltr; Newscaster.

WILLIAMS, BETSY; Bluffton HS; Bluffton, IN; 20/133 Band; Chrh Wkr; Cmnty Wkr; Drm Bgl; Girl Scts; Hon Rl; Orch; Sch Mus; Sct Actv; Yth Flsp; Univ.

WILLIAMS, BETTY; Washington HS; Washington, IN; 36/194 Chrs; Hon Rl; Off Ade; Sch Mus; Sch Pl; Stg Crw; Rptr Yrbk; Rptr Sch Nwsp; Drama Clb; Pep Clb; Vincennes Univ; Spec Educ.

WILLIAMS, BILL; Hubbard HS; Hubbard, OH; Boy Scts; Chrh Wkr; FCA; Off Ade; Ftbl; Letter Trk; Wrstlng; Coach Actv; Scr Kpr; Tmr; Youngstown St Univ; Mach.

WILLIAMS, BILL; Stebbins HS; Dayton, OH; Boy Scts; Sch Pl; Sct Actv; Stg Crw; Rptr Yrbk; Drama Clb; Fr Clb; Spn Clb; Trk; Opt Clb Awd; Wright St Univ; Cpa.

WILLIAMS, BOB; Solon HS; Solon, OH; Cls Rep Frsh Cls; Cls Rep Soph Cls; Pres Jr Cls; Pres Sr Cls; Hon Rl; NHS; Pol Wkr; Stu Cncl; Key Clb; Letter Bsktbl; Chagrin Hearld Nwsp Player Of The Wk; All League Solon Times Nwsp 2nd Team Chagrinvly Conf; College; Busns Mgmt.

WILLIAMS, BRADFORD; Barberton HS; Barberton, OH; Cl Rep Jr Cls; Band; Hon Rl; Off Ade; Pres Stu Cncl; Rptr Sch Nwsp; College; Law.

WILLIAMS, BRENDA; Valley View HS; Germantown, OH; Band; Chrs; Girl Scts; Hon Rl; Yth Flsp; 4-H; Sci Clb; Spn Clb; Trk; Scr Kpr; College.

WILLIAMS, BRENDA; Buckhannon Upshur HS; Buckhannon, WV; Hon Rl; NHS; Yth Flsp; FBLA; Bsktbl; Trk; Mgrs;.

WILLIAMS, BRENDA; Lincoln HS; Shinnston, WV; 3/150 Cls Rep Frsh Cls; Pres Soph Cls; VP Jr Cls; Cls Rep Sr Cls; Am Leg Aux Girls St; Band; Hon Rl; NHS; Stu Cncl; Pres Sci Clb; Fairmont St Coll; Pre Pharm.

WILLIAMS, B RENEE; Lincoln HS; Shinnston, WV; 2/158 Cls Rep Frsh Cls; Pres Soph Cls; VP Jr Cls; Am Leg Aux Girls St; Band; Hon Rl; NHS; Stu Cncl; FTA; Pres Sci Clb; Fairmont St Coll; Sci.

WILLIAMS, BRIDGETTE; Saginaw HS; Saginaw, MI; Band; Cmp Fr Grls; Chrs; Chrh Wkr; Girl Scts; Hon Rl; Sch Pl; Pep Clb; Sci Clb; Trk; Vlybl 76; Bsktbl 76; Coll; Nursing.

WILLIAMS, C; Lumen Christi HS; Jackson, MI; 2/233 Band; Girl Scts; Hon Rl; Hosp Ade; NHS; Off Ade; Spn Clb; Mic State Univ; Nursing.

WILLIAMS, C; Amanda Clearcreek HS; Brandon, FL; Lat Clb; Bsktbl; Trk; GAA; IM Sprt; Univ; Phys Ed.

WILLIAMS, CARLA; Piketon HS; Piketon, OH; Sec Soph Cls; Chrs; Chrh Wkr; Hon Rl; JA; Sch Mus; Treas Stu Cncl; Yrbk; 4-H; FHA; Shawnee St Univ; Elem Educ.

WILLIAMS, CATHERINE; Clinton Massie HS; Harveysburg, OH; 8/97 Chrh Wkr; Hon Rl; NHS; Yrbk; Bsktbl; Trk; IM Sprt; Cit Awd; DAR Awd; Ohio St Univ; Advertising.

WILLIAMS, CATHLEEN; Oakwood HS; Dayton, OH; AFS; Chrs; Girl Scts; Hon Rl; JA; Stg Crw; Yth Flsp; Drama Clb; Univ; Bus Admin.

WILLIAMS, CATHY; Jackson Milton HS; Lake Milton, OH; 5/111 Trs Soph Cls; Hon Rl; NHS; Stu Cncl; Rptr Yrbk; FHA; Key Clb; Letter Trk; Chrldng; Scr Kpr; Ohio St Univ; Law.

WILLIAMS, CATHY; Wayne HS; Radnor, WV; Hon Rl; Lbry Ade; FHA; Pep Clb; Cit Awd; Busns Schl; Social Worker.

WILLIAMS, CHERYL; South Knox HS; Wheatland, IN; VP Frsh Cls; Chrs; Hon Rl; Sch Mus; FHA; Letter Trk; Chrldng; Vincennes Univ; Phys Therapy.

WILLIAMS, CHRISTINE; Caldwell HS; Caldwell, OH; Hon Rl; 4-H; Spn Clb; Mgrs; Scr Kpr; Was Tech; Accountant.

WILLIAMS, CHRISTINE; Green HS; Greensburg, OH; Trs Frsh Cls; Cls Rep Soph Cls; Cl Rep Jr Cls; Cls Rep Sr Cls; Mdrgl; Sec Y-Teens; Pres 4-H; Pep Clb; Chrldng; Pom Pon; Ohio State Univ; Nursing.

WILLIAMS, CINDY; Leo HS; Spencerville, IN; Sec Soph Cls; Sec Chrs; Drl Tm; Hon Rl; Treas NHS; Stu Cncl; Yth Flsp; Y-Teens; Pres 4-H; Sec Spn Clb; College.

WILLIAMS, CINDY; Ackson Milton HS; Lake Milton, OH; 5/113 NHS; Stu Cncl; 4-H; Pres FFA; VP OEA; Capt Bsktbl; 4-H Awd; Vocational Schl; Accounting.

WILLIAMS, CINDY J; Piketon HS; Piketon, OH; Band; Chrh Wkr; Cmnty Wkr; Hon Rl; Jr NHS; NHS; Off Ade; 4-H; OEA; 4-H Awd;.

WILLIAMS, CLARA; Washington Catholic HS; Washington, IN; Band; Chrs; Drm Mjrt; Sch Mus; Sch Pl; Stg Crw; Drama Clb; 4-H; Pep Clb; Rdo Clb; Awd Mst Imprvd Tennis Plyr 79; Univ; Pre Schl Tchr.

WILLIAMS, CRAIG; Washington HS; Massillon, OH; 100/536 Band; Hon Rl; NHS; Akron Univ; Civil Engr.

WILLIAMS, DANNY; Monongah HS; Worthington, WV; 16/104 Cls Rep Frsh Cls; Cls Rep Soph Cls; Cl Rep Jr Cls; Chrs; Hon Rl; Stu Cncl; 4-H; Bsktbl; Ftbl; Trk; All Marion Cnty & Mason Dixon Defnsv Ftbl Tm 77; Marion Cnty & Mason Dixon Offnsv & Defnsv Ftbl Tm 78; Fairmont St Coll.

WILLIAMS, DAVID; Clarkston Sr HS; Clarkston, MI; 42/571 Aud/Vis; Hon Rl; Sci Clb; Mi St Comptn Schlrshp 79; Grad Cum Laude 79; Oakland Univ; Bus.

WILLIAMS, DAVID; Ashtabula HS; Ashtabula, OH; 32/218 Hon Rl; Letter Bsktbl; Letter Glf; Ohio St Univ; Phys Ther.

WILLIAMS, DAVID; Dublin HS; Powell, OH; 25/156 Band; Hon Rl; Lit Mag; Sch Mus; Sch Pl; Yrbk; Fr Clb; Ohio St Univ; Comp Sci.

WILLIAMS, DAWN; Clay HS; Oregon, OH; 43/350 Band; Chrh Wkr; Girl Scts; Hon Rl; Sct Actv; Yth Flsp; 4-H; IM Sprt; Toledo Hosp Schl Of Nursing.

WILLIAMS, DAWN; Bristol Local HS; Bristolville, OH; Band; Hon Rl; Sch Mus; Stg Crw; Ed Yrbk; Rptr Yrbk; Yrbk; Pep Clb; Bsktbl; Trk; Ohio Univ; Photog.

WILLIAMS, DEBBIE; Edgewood HS; N Kingsville, OH; Band; Chrs; Chrh Wkr; Girl Scts; Hon Rl; Sct Actv; 4-H; Fr Clb; Mth Clb; College.

WILLIAMS, DEBORAH; Huron HS; Huron, OH; Band; Drl Tm; Girl Scts; Hon Rl; NHS; Sec Eng Clb; Sci Clb; BGSU; Bus.

WILLIAMS, DEBORAH; Flushing HS; Flushing, MI; 38/523 Hon Rl; Hosp Ade; NHS; Spn Clb; PPFtbl; Nazareth Coll; Nursing.

WILLIAMS, DEBRA; Wilmington HS; Wilmington, OH; Sec Soph Cls; Sec Jr Cls; Band; Cmnty Wkr; Girl Scts; Hon Rl; NHS; Civ Clb; VP 4-H; VP Pep Clb; Phi Delta Sigma Honor Soc 76; Finalist In Miss Ohio Natl Teenager Pagnt 79; Univ; Med.

WILLIAMS, DEBRA; Morton Sr HS; Hammond, IN; 8/436 Debate Tm; Hon Rl; Natl Forn Lg; NHS; Pep Clb; PPFtbl; Voice Dem Awd; Purdue Univ; Gen Bus.

WILLIAMS, DEBRA; Ross Sr HS; Shandon, OH; 4/220 Am Leg Aux Girls St; Chrs; Chrh Wkr; FCA; Hon Rl; NHS; Sch Pl; Stg Crw; Yth Flsp; Yrbk; Coll; Bio Sci.

WILLIAMS, DENISE; Newbury HS; Burton, OH; Aud/Vis; Chrs; Drl Tm; Girl Scts; Hon Rl; Sch Mus; Sch Pl; Stg Crw; 4-H; Spn Clb;.

WILLIAMS, DENNIS; Holgate HS; Holgate, OH; Hon Rl; Stu Cncl; Mth Clb; Bsbl; Bsktbl; Trk; Univ; Chiropractics.

WILLIAMS, DIANA; Wheeling Park HS; Wheeling, WV; AFS; Hon Rl; Lbry Ade; Off Ade; Sct Actv; Ed Sch Nwsp; Sec 4-H; Pep Clb; DAR Awd; 4-H Awd; George E Stifel Awd 73 79; West Virginia Univ; Comp Sci.

WILLIAMS, DIXIE; Indiana Academy; Logansport, IN; Sec Sr Cls; Chrs; Chrh Wkr; Girl Scts; Hon Rl; Lbry Ade; Yrbk; S Missionary Coll; Acctg.

WILLIAMS, DON; Ridgedale HS; Marion, OH; FCA; Hon Rl; Rptr Sch Nwsp; Ftbl; IM Sprt; Tmr; Sci Fair Superior 2 Cnty 1 Dist 74; Columbus Tech Coll; Elec.

WILLIAMS, DONALD; Walter E Stebbins HS; Dayton, OH; Letter Ftbl; Trk; Wrstlng; Coach Actv; Ohio St Univ; Graphic Art.

WILLIAMS, DONALD; Kimball HS; Royal Oak, MI; Aud/Vis; Hon Rl; Spn Clb; IM Sprt; Mic State Univ; Engr.

WILLIAMS, DONNA; New Riegel HS; Carey, OH; 3/48 VP Frsh Cls; Pres Jr Cls; Band; Hon Rl; Lbry Ade; NHS; Sec 4-H; FHA; Pep Clb; Sec Spn Clb; Tiffin Univ; Acctg.

WILLIAMS, DORIS; Clarkston Sr HS; Clarkston, MI; Chrs; Cmnty Wkr; Hon Rl; Mdrgl; PAVAS; Fr Clb; Oakland Univ; Music.

WILLIAMS, DOROTHY; John Adams HS; Cleveland, OH; Lbry Ade; Spn Clb; Natl Merit Ltr; Coll; Sec.

WILLIAMS, DREGORY; Theodore Roosevelt HS; E Chicago, IN; Band; Orch; Ftbl; Ind Univ.

WILLIAMS, ELANA; M L King Jr Sr HS; Detroit, MI; 7/200 Drl Tm; Hon Rl; JA; Lbry Ade; ROTC; Scr Kpr; Cit Awd; DAR Awd; Merit Awd In English; First Place In Afro American Poetry Contest; Spelling Bee Schl Champ Burroughs Jr; Wayne St Coll; Comp Sci.

WILLIAMS, ERIC; Lansing Everett Sr HS; Lansing, MI; Hon Rl; Rptr Sch Nwsp; Cit Awd; Univ; Law.

WILLIAMS, GILBERT; Kirtland HS; Waite Hill, OH; Bsbl; Ftbl; Earned A Gold St Report Card; Merit Role; Miami Univ; Elec Engr.

WILLIAMS, GLENN; Sandusky HS; Sandusky, OH; Hon Rl; VICA; Ftbl; Letter Trk; Firelands Branch Of Bgsu; Elec.

WILLIAMS, GREGGERY; Concord HS; Jackson, MI; VP Jr Cls; Stg Crw; Stu Cncl; Rptr Sch Nwsp; Sch Nwsp; 4-H; Bsbl; Letter Bsktbl; Trk; IM Sprt; Honorable Mention All Conference Basktbll; Spec Sci Awd;.

WILLIAMS, HEIDI; Grandview Heights HS; Columbus, OH; 5/120 Chrs; Hon Rl; Jr NHS; VP NHS; Rptr Yrbk; Fr Clb; Trk; Cit Awd; College; Med.

WILLIAMS, HOLLY; Martins Ferry HS; Martins Ferry, OH; Band; Hosp Ade; Y-Teens; Pres Fr Clb; Capt Swmmng; Ohio Vly Coll; Nursing.

WILLIAMS, HOWARD; The Columbus Academy; Columbus, OH; Hon Rl; Red Cr Ade; Ed Yrbk; Sprt Ed Yrbk; Rptr Yrbk; Yrbk; Rptr Sch Nwsp; Letter Bsbl; Boston Univ; Photojrnlsm.

WILLIAMS, HUNTER; Moorefield HS; Moorefield, WV; 73/88 Band; Boy Scts; Chrh Wkr; Debate Tm; NHS; Sch Pl; Stu Cncl; Yth Flsp; 4-H; FFA; State Farmer FFA; Pres Stu Council; Blue Ribbon 1st Pl Baby Beef 4 H Project Tri County Fair; West Virginia Univ; Ag.

WILLIAMS, J; Bexley HS; Bexley, OH; Cls Rep Frsh Cls; Sch Nwsp; Fr Clb; Bsbl; Bsktbl; Letter Ftbl; IM Sprt; Rotary Awd; Rotary Intl Cmp Enterprise Schl 79; Emory Univ; Acctg.

WILLIAMS, JACK; North HS; Youngstown, OH; 7/120 VP Soph Cls; Boy Scts; FCA; Hon Rl; Jr NHS; NHS; Stg Crw; Sci Clb; Bsktbl; Ohio St Univ; Aero Engr.

WILLIAMS, JAMES; Holland HS; Holland, MI; Band; Hon Rl; Yth Flsp; Rptr Yrbk; Ftbl; Swmmng; IM Sprt; College.

WILLIAMS, JAMES P; Oscar A Carlson HS; Trenton, MI; 61/358 Am Leg Boys St; Boy Scts; Hon Rl; Off Ade; Sprt Ed Yrbk; Capt Bsbl; Capt Ftbl; Am Leg Awd; Pres Varsity Clb; Homecoming King; Michigan St Univ; Cmnctns.

WILLIAMS, JANE L; Breckenridge HS; Wheeler, MI; 15/109 Sec Frsh Cls; Cls Rep Soph Cls; Cl Rep Jr Cls; Cls Rep Sr Cls; NHS; Stg Crw; Stu Cncl; Spn Clb; Letter Trk; Letter Chrldng; Alma Coll; Spanish.

WILLIAMS, JANE L; Breckenridge Jr Sr HS; Wheeler, MI; 15/109 Cls Rep Frsh Cls; Cls Rep Soph Cls; Cl Rep Jr Cls; Cls Rep Sr Cls; NHS; Stu Cncl; Drama Clb; Pres Spn Clb; Letter Trk; Chrldng; Alma Coll; Pre Dent.

WILLIAMS, JANICE; Oceana HS; Hinton, WV; Band; Chrh Wkr; Girl Scts; Hon Rl; NHS; Sch Mus; Yth Flsp; Sch Nwsp; Beta Clb; 4-H; College; Communications.

WILLIAMS, JAY; Wood Memorial HS; Oakland City, IN; Chrh Wkr; Hon Rl; Bsbl; Univ.

WILLIAMS, JAYMI; Edison Sr HS; Lake Station, IN; Trs Soph Cls; Chrs; Girl Scts; Hon Rl; Sch Mus;

Stu Cncl; Yth Flsp; Fr Clb; Pres Pep Clb; Chrldng; Bus Schl; Bus.

WILLIAMS, JEANNIE; Crestline HS; Crestline, OH; Off Ade; Sch Nwsp; Bsktbl;.

WILLIAMS, JEFFREY; River Valley HS; Three Oaks, MI; 1/165 Pres Sr Cls; Val; Band; Pres NHS; Pol Wkr; Yth Flsp; Ger Clb; Cdntral Mic Univ; Engr.

WILLIAMS, JEFFREY; Jackson HS; North Canton, OH; Ohio St Univ; Elec Engr.

WILLIAMS, JENA; Greenville Sr HS; Greenville, OH; Hst Jr Cls; Hst Sr Cls; Yth Flsp; Spn Clb; Letter Glf; Letter Trk; Continental Schl; Cosmetologist.

WILLIAMS, JENNIFER; Inkster HS; Inkster, MI; 4/165 Sec Soph Cls; Band; Hon Rl; NHS; Stu Cncl; Sec Y-Teens; Chrldng; Capt Pom Pon; Capt Twrlr; VP Elk Awd; Outstndng Serv Awd Elks #973; Congressman Ford Medal Of Merit; Michigan St Univ; Chem Engr.

WILLIAMS, JENNIFER; Northern HS; Detroit, MI; Cl Rep Jr Cls; Debate Tm; Hon Rl; JA; Lbry Ade; NHS; Stu Cncl; Drama Clb; Sci Clb; Spn Clb; Outsdng HS Jr Awd Eastern Mi Univ 79; Chrysler Awd At Completion 78; Wayne St Univ; Pediatrician.

WILLIAMS, JENNIFER; Lumen Christi HS; Jackson, MI; 1/239 Hon Rl; Jr NHS; NHS; Spn Clb; Natl Merit Ltr; College; Engr.

WILLIAMS, JERRY; Wintersville HS; Wintersville, OH; Boy Scts; Hon Rl; Sch Mus; Sch Pl; Sct Actv; Spn Clb; Bsbl; Ftbl; Trk; Wrstlng; Fresh OVAC Wrestling Champ; Brooke Wresting Classic Champ 78; Rnr Up Babe Ruth St Bsbl 75; Univ; Dent.

WILLIAMS, JIM; George Washington HS; Indianapolis, IN; 15/350 Hon Rl; JA; NHS; Quill & Scroll; Sprt Ed Sch Nwsp; Ger Clb; NCTE; Indiana Univ; German.

WILLIAMS, JIMMY; Boonville HS; Boonville, IN; 82/230 Pep Clb; Bsbl; Capt Ftbl; Wrstlng; Trvis B William Bsbl Awd 150 79; Indiana St Univ; Phys Educ.

WILLIAMS, JOANNE; Sandy Valley HS; Dellroy, OH; Hon Rl; 4-H; Pep Clb; Spn Clb; Bsktbl; Scr Kpr; 4-H Awd; Natl Merit Ltr; College.

WILLIAMS, JOHN; Shakamak HS; Jasonville, IN; 6/91 Cl Rep Jr Cls; Band; Hon Rl; Quill & Scroll; Stu Cncl; Rptr Yrbk; Yrbk; Drama Clb; College; Foreign Language.

WILLIAMS, JOHN; Elyria Cath HS; Elyria, OH; Cl Rep Jr Cls; VP Sr Cls; Chrs; Sch Mus; Sch Pl; Capt Crs Cntry; Letter Trk; Univ; Bus.

WILLIAMS, JOSEPH; Centerville Sr HS; Richmond, IN; Band; Hon Rl; FFA; Sci Clb; IM Sprt; Connersville Area Voc Schl; Ind Elec.

WILLIAMS, JOSEPH P; Maysville HS; Zanesville, OH; Am Leg Boys St; Hon Rl; NHS; College; Poli Sci.

WILLIAMS, J ROBERT; Fountain Central HS; Hillsboro, IN; 8/138 Pres Jr Cls; Cl Rep Jr Cls; Cls Rep Sr Cls; Chrh Wkr; Hon Rl; NHS; Crs Cntry; Trk; Mgrs; Scr Kpr; Univ; Acctg.

WILLIAMS, JUDY; Northwest Sr HS; Cinti, OH; Pres Soph Cls; Cmnty Wkr; Hon Rl; Jr NHS; Off Ade; Stu Cncl; Mth Clb; Letter Trk; Capt Chrldng; Coach Actv; College; Phys Ed.

WILLIAMS, JULIE; Princeton Community HS; Princeton, IN; Chrs; Chrh Wkr; Hon Rl; Jr NHS; Mdrgl; NHS; Sch Mus; Stu Cncl; College; Acct.

WILLIAMS, K; Perry HS; Canton, OH; Chrs; Chrh Wkr; Hon Rl; Lit Mag; NHS; Off Ade; Sch Mus; Rptr Sch Nwsp; Pep Clb; Tmr; College; Psych.

WILLIAMS, K; Terre Haute North Vigo HS; Terre Haute, IN; Chrs; Chrh Wkr; Hon Rl; Ind State.

WILLIAMS, KAREN; Oak Park HS; Oak Pk, MI; Stu Cncl; Sch Nwsp; DECA; VICA; Gym; Wayne St Univ; Nursing.

WILLIAMS, KARIN; Rutherford B Hayes HS; Delawree, OH; Band; Chrs; Orch; Sch Mus; Yth Flsp; Acad Hon Awd 77 78 & 79; Band Awds 76 79; Solo & Ensemble Awds 77; Columbus Tech Inst; Animal Hlth Tech.

WILLIAMS, KATHY; West Washington HS; Campbellsburg, IN; 1/98 Chrh Wkr; Hon Rl; NHS; Sch Mus; Sch Pl; Stg Crw; Drama Clb; 4-H; FHA; Pep Clb; South Cntrl Area Voc Schl; Exec Sec.

WILLIAMS, KATSUO; Genoa Area HS; Genoa, OH; Boy Scts; Cmnty Wkr; Hon Rl; Sct Actv; 4-H; Letter Bsbl; Coach Actv; College; Art.

WILLIAMS, KEITH D; Mifflin Sr HS; Columbus, OH; 15/250 Hon Rl; Letter Ftbl; Letter Wrstlng; Univ Of Akron; Avionics Engr.

WILLIAMS, KELLY JO; Lancaster HS; Lancaster, OH; Chrh Wkr; Hon Rl; Lbry Ade; Off Ade; Yth Flsp; 4-H; FHA; Capt Chrldng; 4-H Awd; 1st Grade Queen J C Mardi Gras; Modeling Schl; Model.

WILLIAMS, KENT; Woodrow Wilson HS; Youngstown, OH; Chrh Wkr; VICA; Voc Schl.

WILLIAMS, KIM; South Harrison HS; Clarksburg, WV; 19/84 Band; Lbry Ade; NHS; 4-H; Fairmont Coll; Bio.

WILLIAMS, KIMBERLY; George Washington HS; East Chicago, IN; 9/286 Cls Rep Sr Cls; Chrs; Hon Rl; NHS; Stu Cncl; Boys Clb Am; Fr Clb; FHA; Pom Pon; Cit Awd; S Illinois Univ; Public Admin.

WILLIAMS, KIRBY; Highland Park Community HS; Highland Park, MI; Boy Scts; Chrs; Hon Rl; NHS; Boys Clb Am; Letter Ten; IM Sprt; DAR Awd; Natl Act So Silver Awd In Poetry Category 79; 1st Pl In HS Honors Test In Math 79; Univ; Engr.

WILLIAMS, LATONYA; Highland Park Community HS; Highland Pk, MI; Chrh Wkr; Hon Rl; JA; Y-Teens; Rptr Yrbk; Pom Pon; Western Univ; Bus Admin.

WILLIAMS, LAURIE; Grand Blanc HS; Flint, MI; 46/690 Band; Hon Rl; Lbry Ade; NHS; Ger Clb; Sec Spn Clb; Central Michigan Univ; Spanish.

WILLIAMS, LEWIS S; Wilmington HS; Wilmington, OH; 6/300 Pres Soph Cls; VP Jr Cls; Am Leg Boys St; Band; Chrs; Chrh Wkr; NHS; Sch Mus; Bus Mgmt.

WILLIAMS, LINDA; Jackson Milton HS; No Jackson, OH; Band; Chrh Wkr; Stu Cncl; Ed Yrbk; Rptr Yrbk; FHA; VICA; Scr Kpr; Univ; Speech Ther.

WILLIAMS, LINDA; Horace Mann HS; Gary, IN; Cl Rep Jr Cls; Hon Rl; Jr NHS; Stu Cncl; Y-Teens; Rptr Yrbk; Sec Pep Clb; Natl Merit Ltr; Columbia Univ; Law.

WILLIAMS, LORI; Hubbard HS; Masury, OH; 40/356 Chrh Wkr; Girl Scts; Hon Rl; Lbry Ade; NHS; Off Ade; Stg Crw; Key Clb; Spn Clb; Coach Actv; Kent St Univ; Photo Illustrtn.

WILLIAMS, LORI; Laville HS; Plymouth, IN; Chrs; Girl Scts; 4-H; Spn Clb; Am Leg Awd; Vogue Beauty College; Beautician.

WILLIAMS, LORI; Parkersburg HS; Vienna, WV; Sec Frsh Cls; Cls Rep Soph Cls; Cl Rep Jr Cls; Cmnty Wkr; FCA; Hosp Ade; Stu Cncl; Letter Gym; Letter Chrldng; GAA; Univ; Math.

WILLIAMS, LORI; Fordson HS; Dearborn Hgts, MI; 19/575 Chrs; Hon Rl; NHS; Letter Bsbl; Letter Ten; GAA; IM Sprt; Detroit College Of Bus; Accntg.

WILLIAMS, LORYNDA M; Our Lady Of Mercy HS; Detroit, MI; 45/306 Cmnty Wkr; Boys Clb Am; Commended Stu Natl Ach Scholarship Prog; Highland Pk Awd For Boys Club; Cert Of Recognition; New York Univ; Business.

WILLIAMS, LYNN; Washington Irving HS; Clarksburg, WV; Band; Chrh Wkr; Cmnty Wkr; Hon Rl; Orch; Fr Clb; YMCA Weightlifting Cntst 4 First Rbbn 78; Music Lttr Wa Irving HS Bnd 79; Barklee Coll Of Music; Music.

WILLIAMS, LYNNARD; Southeastern HS; Detroit, MI; Cls Rep Frsh Cls; Cls Rep Soph Cls; Chrs; Mod UN; Sch Pl; Stu Cncl; Sch Nwsp; Gym; Swmmng; Ten; Drama School; Acting.

WILLIAMS, M; Hartford HS; Hartford, MI; Pres Frsh Cls; Hon Rl; Spn Clb; Letter Crs Cntry; Letter Trk; IM Sprt; Cit Awd; College; Construction.

WILLIAMS, MARILYN; Warrensville Sr HS; Warrensville, OH; 15/200 Cls Rep Frsh Cls; Cls Rep Soph Cls; Cl Rep Jr Cls; Chrs; Chrh Wkr; JA; Yth Flsp; Rptr Yrbk; Mgrs; JA Awd; Akron Univ; Prof Recording Eng.

WILLIAMS, MARK; Bishop Luers HS; Ft Wayne, IN; Hon Rl; Pol Wkr; Yrbk; Bsbl; Letter Ftbl; Trk; IM Sprt; Natl Merit Ltr; Univ; Law.

WILLIAMS, MARTHA; Gladwin HS; Gladwin, MI; Band; Chrh Wkr; Girl Scts; Hon Rl; NHS; Off Ade; Stu Cncl; Yth Flsp; Rptr Yrbk; Rptr Sch Nwsp; College.

WILLIAMS, MEGAN; Hamilton Taft HS; Hamilton, OH; 6/450 Pres Debate Tm; Jr NHS; Pres Natl Forn Lg; Pres NHS; Ger Clb; Miami Univ; Zoology.

WILLIAMS, MELINDA; Pike HS; Indianapolis, IN; 6/300 Band; Girl Scts; Hon Rl; Jr NHS; NHS; 4-H; Mth Clb; Pep Clb; Spn Clb; Indiana Univ; Pre Med.

WILLIAMS, MERRIE; Lake HS; Toledo, OH; 1/156 Val; Am Leg Aux Girls St; Girl Scts; Hon Rl; NHS; Sch Mus; Sch Pl; Stu Cncl; Drama Clb; Spn Clb; Univ Of Toledo; Engr.

WILLIAMS, MICHAEL; Bucyrus HS; Bucyrus, OH; Boy Scts; Hon Rl; NHS; Stu Cncl; Bsktbl; Letter Ftbl; College.

WILLIAMS, MICHAEL; Northern HS; Detroit, MI; Cls Rep Sr Cls; Boy Scts; Drl Tm; Hon Rl; Lbry Ade; Lit Mag; ROTC; Sch Pl; Mth Clb; Ftbl; Lawrence Inst Of Tech; Pro Archt.

WILLIAMS, MICHAEL; Reeths Puffer HS; N Muskegon, MI; Hon Rl; Western Mic Univ; Data Proc.

WILLIAMS, MICHELE D; Newark HS; Newark, OH; Cl Rep Jr Cls; Band; Girl Scts; Hon Rl; Jr NHS; Lbry Ade; NHS; Off Ade; Sch Mus; Sch Pl; Hnr Thespion 1978; Camp Entrprise Rotary 12 Jr 550 1978;.

WILLIAMS, MICHELLE; Newbury HS; Burton, OH; Aud/Vis; Chrs; Hon Rl; Jr NHS; Pres 4-H; Pres FNA; Spn Clb; Chmn Twrlr; Lakeland Community; Med Lab Tech.

WILLIAMS, PAT; Cedar Lake Academy; Wyoming, MI; Cls Rep Soph Cls; Band; Hon Rl; Ed Yrbk; Capt Bsbl; Capt Socr; IM Sprt; Most Athletic Girl 1977; Most Admirable 1978; Best All Around 1977; Sec.

WILLIAMS, PATTI; Elmhurst HS; Ft Wayne, IN; 329/400 Chrs; Pom Pon; Bus Schl; Keypunch Opr.

WILLIAMS, PAUL; John Glenn HS; Westland, MI; 65/705 Hon Rl; Jr NHS; Sch Mus; Stg Crw; Fr Clb; Ftbl; Central Mich Univ; Acctg.

WILLIAMS, PAULA; Gwinn HS; Gwinn, MI; Band; Hon Rl; Rptr Yrbk; 4-H Awd; Mich State Univ.

WILLIAMS, PAULA J; Warren G Harding Sr HS; Warren, OH; 2/399 Cls Rep Soph Cls; Sal; Band; Chrs; Hon Rl; Lit Mag; NHS; Stu Cncl; Y-Teens; Letter Ten; Wellesley Coll; Music.

WILLIAMS, PAUL W; Bloomfield HS; Orwell, OH; Pres Frsh Cls; Am Leg Boys St; Band; Sch Mus; Pres Stu Cncl; Rptr Yrbk; Rptr Sch Nwsp; VP Spn Clb; Bsktbl; Crs Cntry; Univ Of Akron; Law.

WILLIAMS, PENNY; Struthers HS; Struthers, OH; 20/276 Sec Frsh Cls; Sec Soph Cls; Sec Jr Cls; Sec Sr Cls; Cmp Fr Grls; Chrh Wkr; Hon Rl; Hosp Ade; Jr NHS; NHS; Article Pblshd Free Spirit Magzn 1978; BOE Awrds Typing 1, Diplomat Awrd 1979; Harding Coll; Sec Sci.

WILLIAMS, PETER; Catholic Central HS; Detroit, MI; Chrh Wkr; Cmnty Wkr; Sch Pl; Fr Clb; Pep Clb; Letter Crs Cntry; Trk; Letter Wrstlng; Opt Clb Awd; Won Spirit Of Detroit Awd For Civ Duty; Giv Cert Of Appreciation Wayne Cnty Bd Of Dir For Wrld 76; Univ; Bus Admin.

WILLIAMS, PHILIP; Lincoln HS; Shinnston, WV; Am Leg Boys St; Hon Rl; Jr NHS; NHS; Stu Cncl; Spn Clb; College.

WILLIAMS, PHILLIP; Upper Sandusky HS; Harpster, OH; 53/228 Hon Rl; 4-H; IM Sprt; Cit Awd; Opt Clb Awd; College; History.

WILLIAMS, RANDY; Hobart Sr HS; Hobart, IN; 1/395 Cls Rep Sr Cls; Val; AFS; Am Leg Boys St; Sec FCA; NHS; Stu Cncl; Ger Clb; Sci Clb; Capt Swmmng; Wabash Coll; Doctor.

WILLIAMS, RANDY; Wheeling Park HS; Wheeling, WV; 39/700 Boy Scts; Hon Rl; ROTC; Sct Actv; Yrbk; Rptr Sch Nwsp; Boys Clb Am; Fr Clb; Mth Clb; Letter Bsktbl; Purdue Univ; Engr.

WILLIAMS, REBECCA; Parkersburg HS; Parkersburg, WV; Band; FCA; Girl Scts; Hon Rl; Hosp Ade; Sch Pl; Sct Actv; Stg Crw; Drama Clb; Mth Clb; West Virginia Univ; Med Tech.

WILLIAMS, RICHARD; Whitehall Yearling HS; Whitehall, OH; Hon Rl; Ed Sch Nwsp; Rptr Sch Nwsp; Spn Clb; Letter Bsbl; Bsktbl; College; Aviation.

WILLIAMS, RICHARD; South Harrison HS; Lost Creek, WV; Am Leg Boys St; Chrh Wkr; Hon Rl; Sch Pl; Sct Actv; Stg Crw; Stu Cncl; Yth Flsp; 4-H; FFA; Fairmont State; Drafting.

WILLIAMS, RICHARD; Pentwater HS; Pentwater, MI; Trs Frsh Cls; Trs Jr Cls; Band; Hon Rl; Stu Cncl; 4-H; Mich State Univ; Chem Engr.

WILLIAMS, RICKY; South Charleston HS; S Charleston, WV; Am Leg Boys St; Chrh Wkr; Hon Rl; Rptr Sch Nwsp; Spn Clb; Mt Vernon Nazarene Coll; Missionary.

WILLIAMS, RITA; North HS; Youngstown, OH; Chrh Wkr; Hon Rl; NHS; NHS; ROTC; Ed Yrbk; Rptr Sch Nwsp; Pep Clb; Bsktbl; Trk; Univ Of Alabama; Sci.

WILLIAMS, ROBERT; Heritage Christian Schl; Indianapolis, IN; Hon Rl; Trk; Univ; Comp Progr.

WILLIAMS, ROBIN; Marysville HS; Marysville, OH; Chrs; Hon Rl; Sch Mus; Key Clb; Chrldng; GAA; IM Sprt; Scr Kpr; Ohio St Univ; Med.

WILLIAMS, ROBYN; Belding HS; Belding, MI; Am Leg Aux Girls St; Aud/Vis; Band; Chrh Wkr; Hon Rl; NHS; Sch Pl; Drama Clb; Pep Clb; College.

WILLIAMS, RONALD; Floyd Cntrl HS; New Albany, IN; Boy Scts; Chrh Wkr; Hon Rl; Off Ade; Sec Orch; Ftbl; Wrstlng; Opt Clb Awd; Floyd Cntrl Jr High Record Holder Best Wrestling Season; Bible Coll; Ministry.

WILLIAMS, SABRINA; Saginaw HS; Saginaw, MI; Hon Rl; JA; Jr NHS; Chrldng; JA Awd; Natl Hon Stud; Michigan St Univ; Educ.

WILLIAMS, SANDRA; East Catholic HS; Detroit, MI; 4/73 Hon Rl; Jr NHS; NHS; Sch Pl; Stu Cncl; Yth Flsp; Ed Yrbk; Ed Sch Nwsp; Pep Clb; Northwood Inst; Mdse.

WILLIAMS, SANDRA; Otsego HS; Kalamazoo, MI; Hon Rl; Mod UN; 4-H; Spn Clb; Letter Ten; College.

WILLIAMS, SCOTT; East Detroit HS; E Detroit, MI; Hon Rl; Univ; Chem Tech.

WILLIAMS, SCOTT; Clinton Massie HS; Wilmington, OH; 2/100 Sec Soph Cls; VP Jr Cls; Am Leg Boys St; Band; Hon Rl; NHS; Yth Flsp; 4-H; Bsbl; Crs Cntry; Miami Univ; Aeronautics.

WILLIAMS, SCOTT; William Henry Harrison HS; Evansville, IN; Aud/Vis; Hon Rl; Stg Crw; FSA; Crs Cntry; Trk; IM Sprt; Cit Awd; Purdue Univ; Elec Engr.

WILLIAMS, SEAN D; Turpin HS; Cincinnati, OH; 13/357 NHS; Ten; Univ; Psych.

WILLIAMS, SHARI K; Bad Axe HS; Filion, MI; 5/147 Band; Chrs; Chrh Wkr; Cmnty Wkr; Hon Rl; Jr NHS; Lbry Ade; Delta College; Secretarial.

WILLIAMS, SHARON; Warsaw Community HS; Warsaw, IN; 32/394 Band; Chrs; Girl Scts; Hon Rl; Sch Pl; Yth Flsp; Drama Clb; Spn Clb; Swmmng; College; Bus.

WILLIAMS, SHERMAN; Fairborn Pk Hills HS; Fairborn, OH; 107/344 Boy Scts; Hon Rl; ROTC; Rptr Sch Nwsp; Letter Ftbl; Wrstlng; Chrldng; IM Sprt; Am Leg Awd; Bsbl; Kent State Univ; Jrnslm.

WILLIAMS, SHERRE; Clay HS; Oregon, OH; 18/353 Cls Rep Soph Cls; Sec Jr Cls; Hon Rl; NHS; Off Ade; Stu Cncl; Fr Clb; Pep Clb; GAA; IM Sprt; Bowling Green State Univ; Nursing.

WILLIAMS, SHERYL; Chillicothe HS; Chillicothe, OH; Chrs; Lbry Ade; Orch; Sch Mus; Sch Pl; Lat Clb; Miss Hospitality 79; Best Thank You Letter For Spnshrshp 79; 2nd Pl Trophy In Womes White Belt Kata 77; Ohio St Univ; Nurse.

WILLIAMS, SONYA; Central HS; Detroit, MI; Chrs; Chrh Wkr; Cmnty Wkr; Hosp Ade; Lbry Ade; Off Ade; Pol Wkr; Sec Yth Flsp; OEA; Chrldng; Wilberforce Univ; Sec Sci.

WILLIAMS, STACEY; Benedictine HS; Detroit, MI; 12/173 Cls Rep Frsh Cls; Cls Rep Soph Cls; Cl Rep Jr Cls; Cls Rep Sr Cls; Hon Rl; NHS; Stu Cncl; Yrbk; Rptr Sch Nwsp; Bsktbl; Univ Of Michigan; Acctg.

WILLIAMS, STACI A; Tri West Hendericks HS; N Salem, IN; 6/120 Hst Frsh Cls; Hst Soph Cls; VP Jr Cls; Band; Cmp Fr Grls; FCA; Hon Rl; NHS; 4-H; Fr Clb; College; Vet.

WILLIAMS, STACI A; Tri West Hendericks HS; North Salem, IN; 6/120 Hst Soph Cls; VP Jr Cls; FCA; Hon Rl; NHS; 4-H; Trk; Capt Chrldng; Coach Actv; DAR Awd; College.

WILLIAMS, STEVE; Pinckney HS; Howell, MI; Cls Rep Sr Cls; Chrh Wkr; Hon Rl; Sch Pl; Stu Cncl; Sch Nwsp; 4-H; Key Clb; Trk; IM Sprt; Mich Tech; Fisheries Mgmt.

WILLIAMS, SUE; Jonathan Alder HS; Plain City, OH; 10/106 Am Leg Aux Girls St; Band; Chrs; Hon Rl; NHS; Sch Mus; Stg Crw; Y-Teens; Yrbk; Drama Clb; East Central Univ; Educ.

WILLIAMS, SUSAN; Lincoln HS; Shinnston, WV; Cl Rep Jr Cls; Band; Chrh Wkr; Hon Rl; Jr NHS; NHS; Stg Crw; Stu Cncl; Yth Flsp; Drama Clb; Jr Prom Princss 79; Stdnt Actv In Educ 79; West Virginia Univ; X Ray Tech.

WILLIAMS, SUSAN M; Marlington HS; Alliance, OH; Chrs; Girl Scts; Lbry Ade; Sch Mus; Yth Flsp; OEA; Swmmng; IM Sprt; The Univ Of Akron; Special Educ.

WILLIAMS, TAMMY; Ursuline HS; Youngstown, OH; 185/365 Band; Chrs; Chrh Wkr; JA; Pep Clb; JA Awd; Univ; RN.

WILLIAMS, TANYA A; Cass Tech HS; Detroit, MI; 84/901 Girl Scts; Hon Rl; Lbry Ade; Off Ade; Capt ROTC; FHA; Sci Clb; Natl Merit Ltr; College; Science.

WILLIAMS, TERESA; Chesapeake HS; Chesapeake, OH; Hst Jr Cls; Hst Sr Cls; Chrh Wkr; Hon Rl; Yth Flsp; Rptr Sch Nwsp; OEA;.

WILLIAMS, TERRI; Pike Central HS; Petersburg, IN; Girl Scts; Hon Rl; NHS; Bsktbl; Coach Actv; Coll; Elem Ed.

WILLIAMS, TERRI; Big Walnut HS; Westerville, OH; 9/230 Cl Rep Jr Cls; Trs Sr Cls; Drl Tm; Hon Rl; NHS; Sch Pl; Drama Clb; Fr Clb; Pep Clb; Trk; Acctg.

WILLIAMS, THERESA; Barr Reeve HS; Cannelburg, IN; 10/64 Cls Rep Sr Cls; Hon Rl; Sch Pl; Sec Stu Cncl; Rptr Yrbk; Beta Clb; Pep Clb; Trk; Chrldng; IM Sprt;.

WILLIAMS, THOMAS; Galion Sr HS; Galion, OH; Am Leg Boys St; Chrs; Hon Rl; Sch Mus; Y-Teens; Bsbl; Letter Bsktbl; Trk; Boys Var Club 78; Univ; Bus Admin.

WILLIAMS, THOMAS; Oscoda Area HS; Wurtsmith AFB, MI; 3/240 Debate Tm; Hon Rl; Pres Soph Cls; Lbry Ade; NHS; Letter Chrldng; Voice Dem Awd; James T Shipman Hon Phys Schslhp 79; Mi Compt Schlshp 79; Natl Jr Hon Soc Schlshp For Acad 79; Ohio Univ; Research.

WILLIAMS, THOMAS; Battle Creek Acad; Battle Creek, MI; Cls Rep Soph Cls; Pres Sr Cls; Stu Cncl; Ed Yrbk; Sch Nwsp; Bsbl; Bsktbl; Ftbl; Kellogg Comm College; Bus.

WILLIAMS, THOMAS; Colerain HS; Cincinnati, OH; Hon Rl; Jr NHS; NHS; Off Ade; Mth Clb; Trk; SAR Awd; Univ Of Cin; Engr.

WILLIAMS, TIM; Ursuline HS; Brookfield, OH; 61/340 Cmnty Wkr; Hon Rl; Fr Clb; Bsktbl; Letter Ftbl; Trk; Univ; Pre Law.

WILLIAMS, TONI; Brooke HS; Wheeling, WV; 65/450 Band; Hon Rl; Lit Mag; NHS; Orch; Quill & Scroll; Spn Clb; NCTE; Univ Of Dayton; Music.

WILLIAMS, TONY G; Lincoln HS; Shinnston, WV; Chrs; Hon Rl; Spn Clb; Wrstlng; Fairmont St Univ.

WILLIAMS, TRACY L; Paul Laurence Dunbar HS; Dayton, OH; Cls Rep Frsh Cls; Cls Rep Soph Cls; Cl Rep Jr Cls; Hst Sr Cls; Band; Drl Tm; Hon Rl; Orch; Rptr Yrbk; Howard Univ; Phamocology.

WILLIAMS, TRINNA; Buckeye Valley HS; Ostrander, OH; 19/186 Cls Rep Frsh Cls; Sec Soph Cls; Trs Soph Cls; Sec Jr Cls; VP Sr Cls; Am Leg Aux Girls St; Band; Chrs; Chrh Wkr; Drm Mjrt; Teen Of Wk City O Fde 79; Homecoming Attndnt 78; Real Estate Schl; Real Estate Assoc.

WILLIAMS, VALERIE; Everett HS; Lansing, MI; Chrh Wkr; Hon Rl; PPFtbl; Natl Merit SF; Mich State; Mech Engr.

WILLIAMS, VALERIE; Pine River HS; Tustin, MI; Trs Sr Cls; Band; Hon Rl; NHS; Fr Clb; Ferris State Coll; Nursing.

WILLIAMS, VINCENT; Redford HS; Detroit, MI; Hon Rl; NHS; Natl Merit Ltr; Magna Cum Laude Awd 79; Focus Hope Leadership Trng Progr Awd 78; Sci Lab Aide Merit Cert 79; General Motors Inst; Elec Engr.

WILLIAMS, WANDA; Buckhannon Upshur HS; French Creek, WV; Chrs; Hon Rl; Lbry Ade; NHS; Sch Mus; Mas Awd; Fairmont St Coll; Law Enforcement.

WILLIAMS, WAYNE; Kirtland HS; Mentor, OH; 36/140 Cmnty Wkr; Hon Rl; Key Clb; Pep Clb; Bsktbl; Letter Ftbl; Letter Trk; IM Sprt; PPFtbl; College; Law.

WILLIAMS, WILLIAM; Norton HS; Norton, OH; Letter Ftbl; Akron Univ; Constru Tech.

WILLIAMSON, CATHY; Linden Mc Kinley HS; Columbus, OH; 23/268 Chrs; Hon Rl; Hosp Ade; JA; Stu Cncl; Pep Clb;.

WILLIAMSON, CHRIS; Whiteoak HS; Hillsboro, OH; Pres Soph Cls; Chrs; Hon Rl; Sch Pl; 4-H; FFA; FHA; DAR Awd; Ohio St Univ; Civil Engr.

WILLIAMSON, D; Bettsville HS; Bettsville, OH; 4/21 Cls Rep Frsh Cls; Pres Soph Cls; Am Leg Aux Girls St; Band; Chrs; Chrh Wkr; Girl Scts; Hon Rl; JA; NHS; Tiffin Univ; Banking.

WILLIAMSON, DAVE; Caston Educational Center; Logansport, IN; 8/90 Hon Rl; NHS; 4-H; FFA; Letter Bsbl; Letter Bsktbl; Letter Crs Cntry; 4-H Awd; St Joseph Coll; Acctg.

WILLIAMSON, GREG; Jay Cnty HS; Ft Recovery, OH; 25/500 FCA; Hon Rl; NHS; Bsbl; Bsktbl; Univ; Engr.

WILLIAMSON, JEFFREY; Brown County HS; Nashville, IN; Pres Frsh Cls; Pres Soph Cls; Pres Jr Cls; Pres Sr Cls; Chrh Wkr; Cmnty Wkr; FCA; Pol Wkr; Red Cr Ade; Stu Cncl; Babe Ruth Pennant Awd 77; Zone Tm Bible Quiz 75; Univ.

WILLIAMSON, JOYCE; Hilliard HS; Hilliard, OH; AFS; Band; Chrh Wkr; Hon Rl; Sch Mus; Stg Crw; Spn Clb; All Sussex County Band 77; Univ; Sec.

WILLIAMSON, K; Greenbrier East HS; Lewisburg, WV; Pres Frsh Cls; FCA; Hon Rl; NHS; Stu Cncl; Yrbk; FBLA; Ten; Chrldng; IM Sprt; UNC; Comp Sci.

WILLIAMSON, MARY; Heath HS; Heath, OH; Chrs; Hon Rl; Sec Natl Forn Lg; Central Ohio Tech Coll; Comp Prog.

WILLIAMSON, MISSY; Ida HS; Monroe, MI; Cls Rep Frsh Cls; Sec Sr Cls; Hon Rl; NHS; Off Ade; OEA; GAA; IM Sprt; Scr Kpr; Central Michigan Univ; Acctg.

WILLIAMSON, MONYA Y; Eastmoor Sr HS; Columbus, OH; 19/290 Pres Sr Cls; Band; Chrs; Hon Rl; NHS; Yth Flsp; VICA; Letter Trk; IM Sprt; Univ Of Tennessee; Criminal Justice.

WILLIAMSON, PAT; Gibsonburg HS; Gibsonburg, OH; Trs Sr Cls; Chrh Wkr; Rptr Yrbk; Rptr Sch Nwsp; Sch Nwsp; Ten; Trk; College.

WILLIAMSON, PATTY; Huntington HS; Waverly, OH; Cmp Fr Grls; Hon Rl; NHS; OEA; Pep Clb; Letter Bsktbl; Trk; Sec.

WILLIAMSON, PAULA; Whitehall Yearling HS; Whitehall, OH; Band; Girl Scts; Hon Rl; Off Ade; Fr Clb; Lat Clb; IM Sprt; Mat Maids; Scr Kpr; Tmr; Capital Univ; Med.

WILLIAMSON, PENNY; Westfall HS; Orient, OH; 1/131 Band; NHS; Rptr Sch Nwsp; 4-H; FTA; Sci Clb; Mgrs; Scr Kpr; Twrlr; Voice Dem Awd; Algebra French Eng Sc Awds; Botany Awd; Typing I Awd; Amer History Awd;.

WILLIAMSON, RICHARD; Meigs HS; Rutland, OH; Am Leg Boys St; Hon Rl; Ftbl; Mgrs; Vocational School; Elec.

WILLIAMSON, SANDRA; Sistersville HS; Friendly, WV; Chrs; Chrh Wkr; Cmnty Wkr; Girl Scts; Hon Rl; Sch Mus; Sch Pl; Drama Clb; 4-H; FHA; Ohi Valley College; Home Economics.

WILLIAMSON, SUE; Boardman HS; Youngstown, OH; 61/591 Chrs; Treas Chrh Wkr; Hon Rl; Jr NHS; Treas Mdrgl; NHS; Sch Mus; Chrldng; College; Music Dir.

WILLIAMSON, VICKY; Bloom Carroll HS; Carroll, OH; Cls Rep Soph Cls; Pres Jr Cls; Cl Rep Jr Cls; Hon Rl; Red Cr Ade; Y-Teens; Rptr Sch Nwsp; 4-H; FFA; Swmmng; Ohio St Univ; Forest Ecology.

WILLIARD, JAMES; Whiteford HS; Ottawa Lk, MI; Letter Wrstlng; Monroe; Comp Operator.

WILLIFORD, LA; Southeastern HS; Detroit, MI; Hon Rl; Lbry Ade; Off Ade; Sch Pl; Stu Cncl; Rptr Sch Nwsp; Fr Clb; Pep Clb; Sci Clb; Gym; NAACP Writng 79; Upward Boung Math 78; Spelman Coll; Med.

WILLIG, MICHAEL; Goshen HS; Goshen, IN; 79/268 Aud/Vis; Boy Scts; Orch; Yrbk; Rdo Clb; IM Sprt; College; Bio.

WILLIMAN, JACK; Van Wert HS; Van Wert, OH; Band; Chrs; Chrh Wkr; Hon Rl; Stg Crw; Yth Flsp; Fr Clb; Crs Cntry; Swmmng; IM Sprt; Wright St Univ; Elec Engr.

WILLING, RHONDA; St Ursula Academy; Cincinnati, OH; Pres Frsh Cls; Stu Cncl; Spn Clb; Coach Actv; IM Sprt; Univ; Mrktg.

WILLIS, BRENDA; Logan Sr HS; Logan, WV; Band; Lbry Ade; 4-H; Bsktbl; 4-H Awd; Ralph R Willis Voc Center; Sec.

WILLIS, CYNTHIA D; South Point HS; South Point, OH; Hon Rl; Hosp Ade; Sci Clb; Ohio St Univ; Pre Med.

WILLIS, DANIELA; Utica Sr HS; Utica, MI; Girl Scts; Hon Rl; Pres Ger Clb; Pep Clb; Letter Bsbl; PPFtbl; Scr Kpr; Excellence In Written German Awd; Teaching German To Elem Children Honor; Busns Schl; Busns.

WILLIS, DEBORAH; Rutherford B Hayes HS; Delaware, OH; Band; Chrs; Fr Clb; Letter Bsbl; Letter Bsktbl; Univ; Bio.

WILLIS, DEE ANN; Eastmoor HS; Columbus, OH; Pres Jr Cls; Chrs; Chrh Wkr; Debate Tm; Hon Rl; Off Ade; Sch Pl; Stu Cncl; Pres OEA; Letter Chrldng; Miss Hattie Jackson Guild At Church 76; Coll; Law.

WILLIS, ELIZABETH; Pike Central HS; Winslow, IN; Band; Drl Tm; Jr NHS; Off Ade; Sch Pl; Drama Clb; 4-H; FHA; Pep Clb; Trk; 1st Runner Up In Miss Pk County 79; ISUE; Bus.

WILLIS, JACQUELINE; St Peter & Paul Area HS; Saginaw, MI; 72/124 Cls Rep Frsh Cls; Cls Rep Soph Cls; Cl Rep Jr Cls; Cls Rep Sr Cls; Chrs; Debate Tm; Hon Rl; JA; Jr NHS; Mdrgl; Northwestern Univ; Theater.

WILLIS, JAMES; Midland Trail HS; Lansing, WV; Band; Hon Rl; NHS; Yrbk; 4-H; 4-H Awd; Vc Pres Band Councl 78; Jr Cnslr Pres 4 H Club 78; Drum Capt 77; West Virginia Univ; Wildlife Mgmt.

WILLIS, JONATHAN; St Joseph HS; St Joseph, MI; Chrs; Letter Swmmng; Letter Trk; Scr Kpr; Tmr; Univ.

WILLIS, KAREN; Franklin HS; Franklin, WV; Band; Chrs; Chrh Wkr; Hosp Ade; Sch Pl; Civ Clb; 4-H; Pep Clb; Scr Kpr; 4-H Awd; Marshall Univ.

WILLIS, LORI; Archbishop Alter HS; Kettering, OH; Hon Rl; Hosp Ade; NHS; Stu Cncl; Yrbk; Spn Clb; Natl Merit Ltr; Knight Of Month; Nominated To Miss Ohio Teenage Pageant; College; Medicine.

WILLIS, MARCIA; Anderson HS; Anderson, IN; 50/415 Band; Chrh Wkr; Cmnty Wkr; Drl Tm; Capt Drm Bgl; FCA; Hon Rl; Off Ade; Bsktbl; GAA; Indiana Univ; Educ.

WILLIS, MARIE; Lutheran East HS; Cleveland, OH; Trs Sr Cls; Band; Chrs; Chrh Wkr; Cmnty Wkr; Hosp Ade; Pep Clb; Rdo Clb; Howard Univ; Bio Chem.

WILLIS, MARTHA; Martinsville HS; Indianapolis, IN; 54/382 Chrs; Lbry Ade; Mdrgl; Off Ade; Orch; Sch Mus; Kiwan Awd; Northwood Inst Schlrshp; Natl Schlr Choral Awd; Natl Schl Orchestra Awd; Northwood Inst Coll; Hotel Mgmt.

WILLIS, MATTHEW; Gallia Academy HS; Gallipolis, OH; 61/227 Cls Rep Frsh Cls; Cls Rep Soph Cls; Cl Rep Jr Cls; Chrh Wkr; FCA; Key Clb; Letter Bsbl; Letter Ftbl; Coach Actv; College; Mortuary Sci.

WILLIS, MICHAEL; Maumee HS; Maumee, OH; 41/316 Univ; Engr.

WILLIS, MIKE; New Albany HS; New Albany, OH; 3/100 Band; Hon Rl; Jr NHS; Ger Clb; College; Education.

WILLIS, PAM; Alexander HS; Albany, OH; Sec Soph Cls; Am Leg Aux Girls St; Hon Rl; NHS; Off Ade; Sch Pl; Ed Sch Nwsp; FHA; Lat Clb; Pep Clb; Hocking Tech Coll; Nursing.

WILLIS, PAMELA; Triad HS; North Lewisburg, OH; 1/77 Pres Jr Cls; Val; Band; Chrh Wkr; NHS; Yrbk; Drama Clb; Bowling Green State Univ; Pr Nursing.

WILLIS, PATRICK; Lake Catholic HS; Eastlake, OH; 50/300 Aud/Vis; Chrs; Hon Rl; Lit Mag; PAVAS; Crs Cntry; Trk; Edinboro St Coll; Elem Educ.

WILLIS, PHILLIP; Fairfield Sr HS; Fairfield, OH; 82/596 Band; Chrs; Hon Rl; Off Ade; Red Cr Ade; Sch Mus; Rdo Clb; Univ.

WILLIS, RANDOLPH; Normandy HS; Seven Hls, OH; Band; Debate Tm; JA; Natl Forn Lg; NHS; Sch Nwsp; Treas Spn Clb; JA Awd; Serv Awd Tchr Aide 1979f Natl Spansh Hon Soc 1978; Presdntla Sports Awd Golf 1978; Univ; Bus.

WILLIS, SHERI; Old Fort HS; Ft Seneca, OH; Hst Sr Cls; Am Leg Aux Girls St; Hon Rl; Off Ade; Sch Mus; Sch Pl; Stg Crw; Ed Yrbk; Rptr Sch Nwsp; 4-H; Tiffin Univ; Business Ed.

WILLIS, TRINA; Southwestern HS; Detroit, MI; Chrh Wkr; Hon Rl; Hosp Ade; JA; Cit Awd; Clark College; Comp Tech.

WILLIS, WENDY; Brooke HS; Wellsburg, WV; 166/466 Cmnty Wkr; Hon Rl; FHA; Mat Maids; Contestant In Miss Teen USA Pageant 79;.

WILLIS, WENDY; Lakeview HS; St Clair Shores, MI; Cl Rep Jr Cls; Hon Rl; Lit Mag; Off Ade; Sci Clb; VP Spn Clb; Michigan Tech Univ; Genetic Sci.

WILLISON, LORI; Olivet HS; Charlotte, MI; 1/97 Val; Band; Girl Scts; Natl Forn Lg; FFA; Spn Clb; Cenral Mich Univ.

WILLITS, DALE; Greenfield Central HS; Pendleton, IN; Hon Rl; NHS; Yth Flsp; FFA; Ger Clb; Mth Clb; Ball St Univ; Comp Sci.

WILLITZER, ROXANNE; Fairview HS; Defiance, OH; 16/124 Band; Chrs; Chrh Wkr; Cmnty Wkr; Hon Rl; JA; NHS; Red Cr Ade; Sch Mus; Stg Crw; Drama Awd Trophy 79; Florida Coll; Soc Work.

WILLMAN, KAREN; Urbana HS; Urbana, OH; Band; Hon Rl; Jr NHS; NHS; 4-H; Bsktbl; Gym; Ten; Twrlr; 4-H Awd; Univ.

WILLMAN, LINDA; John Glenn HS; Westland, MI; Cmp Fr Grls; Chrs; Debate Tm; Hon Rl; Jr NHS; Stg Crw; Yrbk; Sch Nwsp; Drama Clb; Pres 4-H; Serv Awd For Jr Natl Hnr Soc; Young Authors Clb Awd; Michigan St Univ; Vet.

WILLOCK, RANDI; Terre Haute S Vigo HS; Terre Haute, IN; 27/650 Cl Rep Jr Cls; Am Leg Aux Girls St; Band; Cmnty Wkr; Drl Tm; Hon Rl; Off Ade; Y-Teens; Pep Clb; Swmmng; Taylor Univ; Comp Sci.

WILLOUGHBY, CELESD; Lumen Christi HS; Jackson, MI; 5/250 Band; Boy Scts; Cmnty Wkr; Hon Rl; JA; NHS; Orch; PAVAS; Sch Mus; Stu Cncl; Acad Awd & Hon Algebra Eng & Symphony Cert 77; Eng Symphony MSBOA Solo & Ensemble Medl & Latin Cert 78; Univ; Bio.

WILLOUGHBY, GALA; Shepherd HS; Shepherd, MI; Chrh Wkr; Hon Rl; Lbry Ade; Yth Flsp; 4-H; FHA; Pep Clb; VICA; Letter Trk; Chrldng; Cntrl Mic Univ; Data Processing.

WILLOUGHBY, JULIE; Toronto HS; Toronto, OH; Band; Cmp Fr Grls; Orch; Sch Mus; Sch Pl; Fr Clb; GAA; Jefferson Tech College; Engineering.

WILLOUGHBY, TIM; Indian Valley South HS; Gnadenhutten, OH; 4/95 Hon Rl; NHS; Stu Cncl; Yrbk; Pep Clb; Letter Glf; Muskingum Coll; Math.

WILLS, BARBARA; Valley Forge Sr HS; Parma, OH; 72/777 Cls Rep Soph Cls; Chrs; Girl Scts; Hon Rl; Lbry Ade; Off Ade; Stg Crw; Stu Cncl; Drama Clb; Fr Clb; Milestone Of Freedom Awd Presntd By Exchange Club 79; Departmntl Achvmnt Awd In Phys Ed 79; Univ; Bus.

WILLS, DOUGLAS; West Washington HS; Pekin, IN; Hon Rl; NHS; VICA; Univ; Elec.

WILLS, ERIC; Lansing Everett HS; Lansing, MI; Cls Rep Frsh Cls; Hon Rl; Jr NHS; NHS; Stu Cncl; Bsktbl; Natl Merit Ltr; Pres Awd; Acad Varsity Letter 78; Michigan St Univ; Acctg.

WILLS, JACQUELINE; Independence Jr Sr HS; Columbus, OH; 1/216 Cl Rep Jr Cls; Val; Chrs; Girl Scts; Hon Rl; JA; Jr NHS; Treas NHS; Sch Mus; Sch Pl; Finalist Battelle Mem Schlrshp; Sel Outstanding Busns Woman; Reg Top Salesperson Casual Corner; COE Stu Yr; Capital Univ; Industrial Relations.

WILLS, JEFFREY; Chillicothe HS; Chillicothe, OH; Trs Sr Cls; Band; Boy Scts; Chrs; Sch Mus; Sch Pl; Received No 1 Rating On Contest Solo Voice Solo; College; Music.

WILLS, LORI; Gwinn HS; Gwinn, MI; Band; Chrh Wkr; Cmnty Wkr; Sec Soph Cls; Girl Scts; Hon Rl; Hosp Ade; Stu Cncl; 4-H; Bsktbl; West Shore Community College; Nurse.

WILLS, PATRICIA; Scecina Memorial HS; Indianapolis, IN; Girl Scts; Lbry Ade; ITT Tech Schl; Bus.

WILLS, RON; Dover HS; Dover, OH; Am Leg Boys St; Hon Rl; Ger Clb; Letter Bsbl; Letter Bsktbl; Glf; Coach Actv; Univ.

WILLY, STEVEN; Parkside HS; Jackson, MI; Band; Rptr Yrbk; Mic State Univ.

WILMER, WILLIAM; Taft Sr HS; Hamilton, OH; 20/450 Cl Rep Jr Cls; Jr NHS; Lit Mag; NHS; Stg Crw; Yrbk; Ger Clb; Letter Socr; Schlrshp From Womens Auxillary To Butter Cnty Med Soc 79; Recognzd For Acad Achvmnt By Oh Bd Of Regents 79; Wittenberg Univ; Pre Med.

WILMES, MARY; Norwood Sr HS; Norwood, OH; 3/350 Girl Scts; Hon Rl; Jr NHS; VP NHS; Stg Crw; Yrbk; Fr Clb; Pep Clb; GAA; Coll; Bio.

WILMOT, KELLY; Mt Pleasant HS; Mt Pleasant, MI; Band; Chrs; Debate Tm; Girl Scts; Hon Rl; JA; Sch Mus; Pep Clb; Chrldng; JA Awd; Univ; RN.

WILMOT, MICHELE; Montgomery County Jnt Voc Sc; Camden, OH; Hon Rl; NHS; Stu Cncl; Pres 4-H; Pres OEA; Letter Trk; IM Sprt; 4-H Awd; Pres Awd; U S Air Force; Elec Engr.

WILMOTH, JOHN; Noblesville HS; Noblesville, IN; 1/258 Val; Chrs; Natl Forn Lg; NHS; Yth Flsp; Rptr Yrbk; VP Drama Clb; Pres Lat Clb; Natl Merit SF; Rotary Awd; Univ.

WILMOTH, SUZANNA; Philip Barbour HS; Belington, WV; Band; Cmnty Wkr; Drm Mjrt; Hon Rl; Pep Clb; Chrldng; Decca Club Awd 78; Bus Schl.

WILSKINSON, LAURA L; Whitko HS; Pierceton, IN; Chrs; Chrh Wkr; Hon Rl; Sch Mus; Sch Pl; Yth Flsp; 4-H; 4-H Awd; Sec.

WILSON, AMY; New Albany HS; New Albany, IN; 118/565 Chrs; Debate Tm; Sch Mus; Sch Pl; Stg Crw; Stu Cncl; Yrbk; Drama Clb; DAR Awd; De Pauw Univ; Jrnlsm.

WILSON, ANGEL; Union Local HS; Belmont, OH; 13/144 VP Jr Cls; Hon Rl; NHS; Rptr Yrbk; Fr Clb; Pep Clb; Sci Clb; Bsbl; GAA; Univ; Elem Educ.

WILSON, ANN; Lebanon HS; Lebanon, OH; Band; Chrs; Chrh Wkr; Girl Scts; Hosp Ade; Sch Mus; Sct Actv; Sec Stu Cncl; Yth Flsp; Rptr Yrbk; Rainbow Grand Soloist Of Oh 79; Pres Of United Methodist Youth Fellowshp 79; Class Of 81 Homecmng Princess; Eastern Kentucky Univ.

WILSON, ANN; Kewanna HS; Kewanna, IN; 3/18 Trs Frsh Cls; Trs Soph Cls; Band; Chrs; Drm Mjrt; Hon Rl; Off Ade; Sch Pl; Ed Yrbk; Sch Nwsp; Indiana Univ; Optometric Tech.

WILSON, ANNE; Haslett HS; Haslett, MI; 52/171 Pres Frsh Cls; Pres Soph Cls; Cl Rep Jr Cls; Band; Pol Wkr; Sch Pl; Stu Cncl; Rptr Sch Nwsp; OEA; Chrldng; I Was 1st Stu To Be Elected To The Haslett Bd Of Ed 76; I Was Re Electd To Serv On The Haslett Bd Of Ed 77; Michigan St Univ; Psych.

WILSON, BERNADINE; Warsaw Community HS; Warsaw, IN; Chrs; Yth Flsp; Bsktbl; GAA; IM Sprt; Pres Awd; Vlybl Ltr 76 79; Music Piano 76 78 2 Gld Mdls; Muisc Voice 76 78 2 Gld Mdls; Ball St Univ; Spch Ther.

WILSON, BERNARD W; Cleveland Lutheran HS East; Cleveland Hts, OH; 6/44 NHS; Off Ade; Sch Mus; Rptr Sch Nwsp; Letter Bsbl; Capt Bsktbl; Letter Ftbl; Letter Trk; Scr Kpr; Hnrbl Mntn Basketball All Conf Hnrbl Mntn Basketball1979; Hmg King 1978; Chapel Usher 1978; Acdm Chlng 79; Baldwin Wallace Coll; Mech Engr.

WILSON, BOB; Danville HS; Danville, OH; Pres Chrh Wkr; NHS; Drama Clb; Treas FFA; Treas Ftbl; Outstndg Sr In FFA Vp 1978; Pltry Jdgng 1st Indvdl Dist 1978; Outstndg Jr In FFA Trsur 1977; Agri.

WILSON, BRENDA; Ridgewood HS; Newcomerstown, OH; Cmnty Wkr; Drl Tm; Hon Rl; Sch Mus; Sec 4-H; Treas FHA; 4-H Awd; JC Awd; Natl Merit Schl; Runner Up St Grange Spelling Contest; BEOG; Ohio Instructional Grant; Malone Coll; CPA.

WILSON, BRIAN; Decatur Central HS; Indpls, IN; 5/403 Band; Hon Rl; NHS; Lat Clb; IM Sprt; College.

WILSON, CAROL; Philip Barbour HS; Philippi, WV; Band; Drl Tm; Hon Rl; Stu Cncl; Yrbk; 4-H; Bsktbl; Letter Trk; Letter Chrldng; Mat Maids; Alderson Broaddus Coll; Phys Ed.

WILSON, CAROL; Calhoun Cnty HS; Annamoriah, WV; 1/120 Val; Band; Chrs; Hon Rl; NHS; Off Ade; Treas Yth Flsp; Pres Spn Clb; Glenville St Coll; Music.

WILSON, CAROLYN; Marlette HS; Marlette, MI; Cmp Fr Grls; Hon Rl; Ed Sch Nwsp; Rptr Sch Nwsp; 4-H; OEA; 4-H Awd; 3rd Pl Job Interview Regnl Level OEA 1979; Mbr Of Parliamentary Proc Tm 1979; Editor Of H S Newspaper; Univ.

WILSON, CATHERINE; Corunna HS; Corunna, MI; Cmnty Wkr; Hon Rl; Off Ade; Pol Wkr; Stu Cncl; Rptr Yrbk; Mgrs; Baker Jr Coll Of Bus; Legal Sec.

WILSON, CHERYL; Clinton Prairie HS; Colfax, IN; 24/99 Band; Off Ade; Sch Mus; Pres Yth Flsp; 4-H; FHA; FTA; Pep Clb; Mat Maids; 4-H Awd; Purdue Univ; Mass Cmnctns.

WILSON, CHRISTINE; Madonna HS; Weirton, WV; Cmp Fr Grls; Chrh Wkr; Cmnty Wkr; Hon Rl; Hosp Ade; NHS; Rptr Yrbk; Pep Clb; Letter Ten; Medal For Excllnc In Religion For All 4 Yrs 79; Albertus Magnus Coll; Psych.

WILSON, CHRISTY; Elston HS; Michigan City, IN; 12/308 Band; Hon Rl; NHS; Rptr Yrbk; Pep Clb; Miami Univ; Marketing.

WILSON, CHUCK; Ida HS; La Salle, MI; 30/167 Trs Frsh Cls; Am Leg Boys St; Boy Scts; Hon Rl; NHS; Stu Cncl; Letter Bsbl; Letter Bsktbl; Letter Ftbl; IM Sprt; College; Data Proc.

WILSON, CLARENCE; Ben Davis HS; Indianapolis, IN; 49/809 Band; Boy Scts; Chrs; Chrh Wkr; Cmnty Wkr; Debate Tm; Hon Rl; Cit Awd; FCC 3rd Class Radio License 79; Ctr For Ldrshp Dvlpt Yth Dvlpt Progr 78; Oral Roberts Univ; Pre Med.

WILSON, CRYSTAL L; Meadowdale HS; Dayton, OH; Cl Rep Jr Cls; Cls Rep Sr Cls; Chrh Wkr; Girl Scts; Hon Rl; Off Ade; Sprt Ed Yrbk; Yrbk; Pep Clb; Ftbl; Lucia Wiatt Spch Cntst Schl Winner; Howard Univ; Vet Med.

WILSON, CYNTHIA; Western HS; Union Lake, MI; Chrh Wkr; Girl Scts; Hon Rl; PAVAS; Stg Crw; Central Michigan Univ; Costuming Dsg.

WILSON, DANA; Marion HS; Marion, IN; Band; Chrs; Cmnty Wkr; Girl Scts; Hon Rl; Hosp Ade; NHS; Ind State; Speech Ther.

WILSON, DANIEL S; Elkhart Central HS; Elkhart, IN; Cmnty Wkr; Hon Rl; Natl Forn Lg; NHS; Orch; Pol Wkr; Stu Cncl; Natl Schl Orch Assn Orch Awd 77; Univ.

WILSON, DAVID; Chelsea HS; Chelsea, MI; 42/250 Cls Rep Soph Cls; Cl Rep Jr Cls; Hon Rl; JA; Jr NHS; Natl Forn Lg; NHS; Rptr Sch Nwsp; Key Clb; Letter Bsbl; Ferris St Univ; Auto Mech.

WILSON, DAVID; Cambridge HS; Cambridge, OH; Band; Hon Rl; Stg Crw; Wrstlng; Univ; Marine Bio.

WILSON, DEBRA J; Traverse City Sr HS; Traverse City, MI; 210/693 Girl Scts; Hon Rl; Sch Nwsp; Pep Clb; Spn Clb; Trk; Tmr; Mas Awd; Mi Comp Schlrshp 79; Cntrl Michigan Univ; Bus Retail.

WILSON, DIANE; Franklin HS; Livonia, MI; Chrh Wkr; Hon Rl; Lbry Ade; Cit Awd; Mic State Univ; Chem Bio.

WILSON, DONIAL; Clinton Massie HS; Oregonia, OH; Cmnty Wkr; Hon Rl; Bsktbl; Ftbl; Cincinnati Tech Coll; Acctg.

WILSON, DONNA; La Salle HS; South Bend, IN; 51/417 Cls Rep Soph Cls; Cl Rep Jr Cls; Chrs; Chrh Wkr; Hon Rl; Off Ade; Y-Teens; OEA; IM Sprt; Marquette Univ; Accounting.

WILSON, DOUGLAS; Newbury HS; Newbury, OH; Sec Soph Cls; Hon Rl; Jr NHS; Sci Clb; Spn Clb; Bsktbl; Univ; Engr.

WILSON, DWAYNE; Lincoln West HS; Cleveland, OH; Bsbl; Capt Bsktbl; Letter Ftbl; Letter Trk; Cit Awd; Cls Pres Of Sr Acctg Computing Cls 79; Cleveland Schlshp Finalist 79; Press Star Mr Versaliity Var Bsktbl; Jackson St Univ; Comp Sci.

WILSON, EMILEE; Pinconning Area HS; Pinconning, MI; 79/270 Chrh Wkr; Cmnty Wkr; Hon Rl; Sch Mus; Sch Pl; Yth Flsp; FNA; Treas FTA; PPFtbl; JA Awd; Exchange Stu To Japan; Jr Merit For Fitness; Delta Coll; Nursing.

WILSON, FRANK; Wheeling Park HS; Wheeling, WV; 66/500 Pol Wkr; Sch Mus; Sch Pl; Stg Crw; Rptr Yrbk; Yrbk; Rptr Sch Nwsp; Sch Nwsp; Fr Clb; Mth Clb; Univ; Sci.

WILSON, GENEVA; East HS; Columbus, OH; Capt Debate Tm; Hon Rl; Jr NHS; Natl Forn Lg; Stu Cncl; Howard Univ; Law.

WILSON, GEORGE A; Redford Catholic Central HS; Detroit, MI; Am Leg Boys St; Band; Boy Scts; Chrs; Hon Rl; Orch; PAVAS; Sch Mus; Sch Pl; Drama Clb; Univ Of Mich; Med.

WILSON, GERALD; Hackett HS; Kalamazoo, MI; Band; Chrh Wkr; Hon Rl; Pol Wkr; Sch Mus; Sch Pl; Stg Crw; IM Sprt; College.

WILSON, GINA; River Rouge HS; River Rouge, MI; 18/199 Pres Frsh Cls; Cls Rep Soph Cls; Pres Jr Cls; Pres Sr Cls; Band; Hon Rl; NHS; Stu Cncl; Mth Clb; Tuskegee Inst; Bio.

WILSON, GREGORY; Purcell HS; Cincinnati, OH; 23/171 Hon Rl; Lat Clb; Bsbl; Univ; Acctg.

WILSON, HEATHER; Gilmer County HS; Glenville, WV; Trs Soph Cls; Chrs; Chrh Wkr; Cmnty Wkr; Girl Scts; Hon Rl; Sch Pl; Sct Actv; Yth Flsp; Yrbk; Glenville St Coll; Bus.

WILSON, JAMES; Stivers Patterson Co Op HS; Dayton, OH; Cls Rep Frsh Cls; Cls Rep Soph Cls; VP Jr Cls; Boy Scts; Chrs; Hon Rl; Stu Cncl; Boys Clb Am; DECA; Ftbl; Oh Bicntl Awd Regnl Winner 1st Pl 76; 1st Pl St DECA Career Actvy 78; Whos Who 77; Univ Of Cincinnati; Engr.

WILSON, JAMES; Miami Trace HS; Washington Ch, OH; Cl Rep Jr Cls; Pres Sr Cls; Cls Rep Sr Cls; Am Leg Boys St; Hon Rl; Treas NHS; Stu Cncl; Crs Cntry; Capt Wrstlng; Univ; Engr.

WILSON, JANET; Brunswick HS; Brunswick, OH; Sec Band; Hon Rl; NHS; Sch Mus; Stg Crw; Whos Who Among Amer HS Stdnt 77; Ohio St Univ; Vet Med.

WILSON, JANNA; Madeira HS; Cincinnati, OH; 10/167 Band; Chrs; Hon Rl; Sch Mus; Drama Clb; Fr Clb; Coll; Fash Designer.

WILSON, JEFF; Park Hills HS; Fairborn, OH; Chrs; Chrh Wkr; Hon Rl; Jr NHS; Sch Pl; Stg Crw; Rptr Sch Nwsp; Sch Nwsp; Drama Clb; Morehead St Univ; Cmnctns.

WILSON, JEFF; Plainwell HS; Plainwell, MI; 8/205 Boy Scts; Hon Rl; NHS; Capt Bsbl; Bsktbl; Ftbl; Eastern Arizona Jr Coll; Engr.

WILSON, JEFF; Southern Local HS; Irondale, OH; Boy Scts; FCA; Hon Rl; ROTC; Lat Clb; Bsbl; Bsktbl; Ftbl; Trk; JC Awd;.

WILSON, JEFFREY; Garber HS; Essexville, MI; Band; Chrs; Hon Rl; Stg Crw; Rptr Sch Nwsp; Drama Clb; Trk; Delta College; Acct.

WILSON, JERILYN; South Ripley HS; Versailles, IN; 24/125 Am Leg Aux Girls St; Band; Chrs; Hon Rl; Quill & Scroll; Rptr Yrbk; Yrbk; Rptr Sch Nwsp; Sch Nwsp; VP Spn Clb; Ind Univ; Journalism.

WILSON, JERRY; Pleasant HS; Marion, OH; 23/160 Hon Rl; Keyettes; Letter Ftbl; Letter Wrstlng; IM Sprt; Univ; Vet.

WILSON, JILL; Brooke HS; Wellsburg, WV; 34/401 Cls Rep Soph Cls; Cl Rep Jr Cls; Hon Rl; Lit Mag; NHS; Stu Cncl; Sci Clb; Spn Clb; Mat Maids; College; Cmmrcl Art.

WILSON, JODI; Zanesville HS; Zanesville, OH; Chrs; Hon Rl; Hosp Ade; Lbry Ade; NHS; Sch Mus; Stu Cncl; Sch Nwsp; VP Lat Clb; Sci Clb; Otstndng Jr Choir Mbr Awd 79; All Oh Youth Choir 79; Schlrshp Recogntn Awd 77 78 & 79; Univ; Nursing.

WILSON, JOSEPH; Medina Sr HS; Medina, OH; 94/450 Cls Rep Frsh Cls; Cls Rep Soph Cls; Aud/Vis; Boy Scts; FCA; Hon Rl; Sch Pl; Sct Actv; Stg Crw; Stu Cncl; Ohio Univ; Pre Law.

WILSON, JUNE; Central Hower HS; Akron, OH; Cls Rep Frsh Cls; Hon Rl; Lbry Ade; NHS; Red Cr Ade; Sch Pl; Rptr Yrbk; Ed Sch Nwsp; Pep Clb; Spn Clb; Univ; Nursing.

WILSON, KAREN; Niles Mc Kinley HS; Niles, OH; 24/420 AFS; Hon Rl; NHS; PAVAS; Stg Crw; Rptr Yrbk; Drama Clb; Bicentennial Photg Awrd Theme Whats Good About Your Community 76; Youngstown St Univ; Math.

WILSON, KARI; Worthington HS; Worthington, OH; 74/560 Cls Rep Frsh Cls; Cls Rep Soph Cls; Chrs; Hon Rl; JA; Off Ade; Stg Crw; Stu Cncl; Rptr Yrbk; Yrbk; Ohio St Univ; Bio.

WILSON, KEITH; Northrop HS; Ft Wayne, IN; Cls Rep Frsh Cls; Band; Boy Scts; FCA; Hon Rl; Stu Cncl; Letter Bsbl; Bsktbl; Crs Cntry; Trk; Indiana Univ; CPA.

WILSON, KELLY; Buckhannon Upshur HS; Selbyville, WV; Treas FFA; FFA Greenhand Degree 79; Agri.

WILSON, KENDRA; Shenandoah HS; Summerfield, OH; 17/91 Cls Rep Frsh Cls; Chrs; Hon Rl; Sch Mus; Sch Pl; Stg Crw; Stu Cncl; Pres 4-H; Pep Clb; Mat Maids; Chatham Coll; Public Rel.

WILSON, KENT; Cory Rawson HS; Jenera, OH; Chrs; Chrh Wkr; Hon Rl; Sch Mus; FFA; Letter Ftbl; Trk; Wooster Vocational Schl; Agri.

WILSON, KEVIN; Romulus Senior HS; Romulus, MI; Hon Rl; Off Ade; Bsktbl; Trk; Mgrs; Scr Kpr; Tmr; Cit Awd; Pres Awd; Comp Progr.

WILSON, KIM; Miami Trace HS; Washington C H, OH; Band; Drl Tm; Yth Flsp; 4-H; FTA; Pep Clb; Sci Clb; Trk; Mat Maids; Ollivet Coll; Medicine.

WILSON, KIMBERLY; Tawas Area HS; Tawas City, MI; 9/200 Band; Hon Rl; NHS; Sch Pl; Voice Dem Awd; Univ; Comp Sci.

WILSON, KIMBERLY; Columbia City HS; Columbia City, IN; Chrh Wkr; Hon Rl; NHS; Pres Yth Flsp; 4-H; Pep Clb; Spn Clb; Trk; GAA; Pom Pon; Purdue Univ; Vet Tech.

WILSON, KIMBERLY; Wellsville HS; Wellsville, OH; Am Leg Aux Girls St; Hon Rl; NHS; Y-Teens; Rptr Yrbk; FTA; Letter Bsktbl; Scr Kpr; West Virginia Univ; Phys Ther.

WILSON, LAURA; Douglas Macarthur HS; Saginaw, MI; 13/354 Cls Rep Frsh Cls; Cl Rep Jr Cls; Hon Rl; NHS; Off Ade; Sch Pl; Stu Cncl; Ten; Chrldng; Natl Merit Ltr; Mich State Univ; Agri.

WILSON, LE ANN; Crooksville HS; Roseville, OH; 32/96 Cls Rep Soph Cls; Am Leg Aux Girls St; Chrh Wkr; Hon Rl; Sch Pl; Stu Cncl; Sch Nwsp; Spn Clb; Treas Chrldng; GAA; Univ; Jrnlsm.

WILSON, LESLIE; Howland HS; Waren, OH; Hosp Ade; Lbry Ade; Off Ade; 4-H; Pep Clb; Spn Clb; Trk; Ohio Univ; Psych.

WILSON, LESLIE R; Norwalk Sr HS; Norwalk, O H; 43/185 Capt Drl Tm; Hon Rl; Rptr Yrbk; Sch Nwsp; Lat Clb; Pep Clb; GAA; Ohio State Univ; Dental Hygiene.

WILSON, LINDA; London HS; London, OH; 9/160 Cls Rep Soph Cls; Hon Rl; Lit Mag; NHS; Sch Pl; Stu Cncl; Y-Teens; Rptr Yrbk; 4-H; 4-H Awd; Univ; Nursing.

WILSON, LISA; Field HS; Kent, OH; Band; Sch Pl; Sct Actv; Stg Crw; Rptr Yrbk; Fr Clb; Wrstlng; Mgrs; Akron Univ; Psych.

WILSON, LISA; Lebanon HS; Lebanon, OH; Chrs; Hon Rl; Stg Crw; Yth Flsp; Drama Clb; Pres 4-H; FHA; VP Pep Clb; Sci Clb; Spn Clb; Univ Of Cincinnati; Law.

WILSON, LYNDA; Washington Irving HS; Clarksburg, WV; 16/139 Hon Rl; Letter Bsktbl; Letter Trk; Chrldng; Natl Merit SF; West Virginia Univ; Pharmacy.

WILSON, MARGARET; St Ursula Academy; Toledo, OH; Chrs; Hon Rl; Orch; Rptr Sch Nwsp; Treas Spn Clb; Univ Of Toledo Cmnty; Food Serv Mgmt.

WILSON, MARIAN R; Lockland HS; Cincinnati, OH; 11/70 Am Leg Aux Girls St; Chrh Wkr; Cmnty Wkr; Hon Rl; Jr NHS; Lbry Ade; NHS; Off Ade; Sch Mus; Sch Pl; Univ; Educ.

WILSON, MARILYN; Salem HS; Salem, OH; 25/250 Pres AFS; Am Leg Aux Girls St; Sec Band; Pres Cmp Fr Grls; Hon Rl; Sch Mus; Ed Yrbk; Sec Fr Clb; Sec Mth Clb; Elk Awd; Adrian College; Health Sci.

WILSON, MARK; Central HS; Evansville, IN; 46/482 Cls Rep Soph Cls; Cl Rep Jr Cls; Cls Rep Sr Cls; Chrs; Chrh Wkr; Cmnty Wkr; Hon Rl; NHS; Stu Cncl; Pres Yth Flsp; Butler Univ; Pharm.

WILSON, MARK; Kalkaska HS; Mancelona, MI; Bsbl; Bsktbl; Voc Schl; Welder.

WILSON, MARLENE; Hillsdale HS; Hillsdale, MI; Band; Cmp Fr Grls; Girl Scts; 4-H; Pep Clb; 4-H Awd; Jackson Cmnty Coll.

WILSON, MARSHA; Akron Fairgrove HS; Fairgrove, MI; 1/73 Trs Sr Cls; Val; Pres Band; Chrh Wkr; Hon Rl; NHS; 4-H; Central Mic Univ; Math.

WILSON, MARY; Northside HS; Muncie, IN; 13/250 Cl Rep Jr Cls; Hon Rl; Hosp Ade; NHS; Sci Clb; Spn Clb; Ten; Purdue; Food Sci.

WILSON, MELODY; Buckhannon Upshur HS; French Creek, WV; Hon Rl; Stg Crw; Drama Clb; FHA Hero; Tchrs Aid 3 Yrs; ESEA Tutorial Aide Rdng 3yrs; ESEA Tutorial Aide; Tchr.

WILSON, MICHAEL; Hazel Park HS; Hazel Park, MI; Hon Rl; Ten; IM Sprt; Detroit Coll Of Busns.

WILSON, MICHELE; Lake Shore HS; Stclair Shores, MI; Girl Scts; Off Ade; Rptr Sch Nwsp; Central Mic Univ;scndry Educ.

WILSON, MICHELLE; Gladwin HS; Gladwin, MI; Cls Rep Soph Cls; Chrs; Girl Scts; Hon Rl; Hosp Ade; Yth Flsp; Rptr Sch Nwsp; Sch Nwsp; Civ Clb; Bsbl; Michigan St Univ; Legal Sec.

WILSON, M KEITH; Lebanon HS; Lebanon, OH; Am Leg Boys St; Hon Rl; NHS; ROTC; Yth Flsp; Yrbk; FBLA; Spn Clb; Am Leg Awd; DAR Awd; Miami Univ; Bus Mgmt.

WILSON, NANCY; Teays Valley HS; Ashville, OH; 10/203 Am Leg Aux Girls St; Band; Chrh Wkr; Hon Rl; Hosp Ade; NHS; FNA; Lat Clb; Capital Univ; Nursing.

WILSON, PAMELA; Sandusky Community HS; Sandusky, MI; Chrs; Hon Rl; Natl Forn Lg; Yth Flsp; FHA; Pep Clb; Letter Bsktbl; Gym; Letter Trk; Letter Chrldng; Siena Heights College; Occup Ther.

WILSON, PAMELA; Brownsburg HS; Brownsburg, IN; 47/314 Chrs; Chrh Wkr; Hon Rl; Lit Mag; NHS; Stg Crw; Lat Clb; Purdue Univ; Vet.

WILSON, PAMELA; North White HS; Monon, IN; 4/85 VP Soph Cls; Pres Jr Cls; Band; Hon Rl; NHS; Stg Crw; Ed Sch Nwsp; Rptr Sch Nwsp; Pres Spn Clb; Ball St Univ; Eng.

WILSON, PATRICIA S; Newark HS; Newark, OH; Pres Frsh Cls; Cmnty Wkr; Hon Rl; Jr NHS; Pres Lbry Ade; Pol Wkr; Stu Cncl; Yth Flsp; Pep Clb; Letter Bsktbl; College; Health.

WILSON, PATTY; Perry HS; Perry, OH; Am Leg Aux Girls St; Band; Chrs; Cmnty Wkr; Hon Rl; Lbry Ade; Pres NHS; Off Ade; Orch; Sch Mus; Rotary Intl Awd Best Supporting Actress; Rainbow Girls Worthy Advisor; College; Music.

WILSON, PAULA; Bucyrus HS; Bucyrus, OH; Cmp Fr Grls; Chrs; Chrh Wkr; JA; Sch Mus; Sch Pl; Stu Cncl; 4-H; Ohi State; Law.

WILSON, RICHARD; Adrian HS; Ortonville, MI; 63/385 Hon Rl; NHS; Sci Clb; Ftbl; Ten; IM Sprt; Univ Of Michigan.

WILSON, RITA; Middletown HS; Middletown, OH; Hon Rl; OEA;.

WILSON, ROBERT D; Athens HS; Fulton, MI; College; Astronomy.

WILSON, ROBIN; Wintersville HS; Wintersville, OH; 75/267 Chrs; Drl Tm; Girl Scts; Orch; Fr Clb; Trk; Letter In Band; Superior Rating In Ensemble At St Solo Ensemble Cntst; Two Superior Ratings In St Solo Ense; Akron Univ; Sales & Mdse.

WILSON, ROD; Eminence HS; Martinsville, IN; Hon Rl; NHS; Yth Flsp; VP 4-H; Fr Clb; Bsbl; Bsktbl; Crs Cntry; Trk; Ind Univ; Nuclear Engr.

WILSON, ROD; Indian Valley North HS; Uhrichsville, OH; Hon Rl; Spn Clb; Letter Ftbl; Letter Trk; IM Sprt; Univ; Electronics.

WILSON, RODNEY; Indian Valley North HS; Uhrichsville, OH; Hon Rl; Spn Clb; Letter Rdo Clb; Letter Trk; IM Sprt; College; Electronics.

WILSON, ROGER; Arsenal Technical HS; Indianapolis, IN; Boy Scts; Hon Rl; Sct Actv; Key Clb; Bsbl; Letter Ftbl; College.

WILSON, RONALD; Lawrence Central HS; Indianapolis, IN; Cls Rep Frsh Cls; Cls Rep Soph Cls; Cl Rep Jr Cls; Cls Rep Sr Cls; FCA; Stu Cncl; Fr Clb; Letter Ftbl; Letter Trk; Coach Actv; Purdue; Bus.

WILSON, RONALD K; Springfield Sr HS; Holland, OH; 10/250 Pres Soph Cls; Cls Rep Soph Cls; Pres Jr Cls; Cl Rep Jr Cls; Hon Rl; JA; Off Ade; Stu Cncl; Rptr Yrbk; Pep Clb; S Florida Univ; Data Processing.

WILSON, ROSANNE; Hobart Sr HS; Hobart, IN; 13/400 Chrh Wkr; Hon Rl; Jr NHS; NHS; Treas Fr Clb; Bsktbl; GAA; Purdue Univ; Archt.

WILSON, ROSE; Lockland HS; Cincinnati, OH; 11/71 Chrh Wkr; Hon Rl; Lbry Ade; NHS; Off Ade; Sch Pl; Stg Crw; Rptr Sch Nwsp; Drama Clb; Fr Clb; College; Education.

WILSON, ROSEMARIE; Deer Park HS; Cincinnati, OH; 20/250 Band; Chrh Wkr; Girl Scts; Hon Rl; Sct Actv; Yth Flsp; Rptr Yrbk; Rptr Sch Nwsp; Sci Clb; Univ; Humanities.

WILSON, SHANE; Crooksville HS; Crooksville, OH; 7/99 Boy Scts; Hon Rl; NHS; Fr Clb; Sci Clb; Spn Clb; Trk; Ohio St Univ; Law Enfrcmnt.

WILSON, SHARON; Philip Barbour HS; Moatsville, WV; Chrh Wkr; Cmnty Wkr; Hon Rl; NHS; Pres Yth Flsp; Pres 4-H; Pep Clb; Mgrs; Scr Kpr; Typing Awd; Alderson Broaddus Coll; Poli Sci.

WILSON, SHEILA; Northfield HS; Wabash, IN; 11/114 Trs Sr Cls; Chrh Wkr; Hon Rl; NHS; Sch Mus; Sch Pl; Stg Crw; Yth Flsp; Yrbk; Rptr Sch Nwsp; Purdue Univ; Fashion Retailing.

WILSON, SHEILA; Greensburg Commun HS; Greensburg, IN; 63/209 Band; Chrs; Hon Rl; Orch; Sch Mus; Drama Clb; 4-H; IM Sprt; Mgrs; Mat Maids; Indiana Central Univ; Nurs.

WILSON, STACI; Grand Blanc HS; Grand Blanc, MI; Chrs; Hon Rl; Stg Crw; 4-H; Chrldng; IM Sprt; Pom Pon; Univ; Atty.

WILSON, STEPHEN A; Saint Xavier HS; Cincinnati, OH; 65/289 Cl Rep Jr Cls; Band; Boy Scts; Chrh Wkr; Cmnty Wkr; Hon Rl; VP JA; NHS; Pol Wkr; Sch Pl; 2 Scholarships From Knghts Of Columbus; Attended Operatn Yth; Purdue Univ; Elec Engr.

WILSON, SUSAN; Calhoun County HS; Grantsville, WV; Cl Rep Jr Cls; Chrs; Chrh Wkr; Hon Rl; Hosp Ade; VP NHS; Stu Cncl; Sch Nwsp; Pep Clb; Hon Guard For Grad 79; Glenville St Coll; Mgmt.

WILSON, SUSAN I; Cass Tech HS; Detroit, MI; Band; Chrs; Hon Rl; NHS; Orch; Won Scholarshp To Ply Harp Interlochen Natl Mus Cmp 1979; Univ Of Michigan; Music Educ.

WILSON, SYLVIA H; Central Hower HS; Akron, OH; Chrs; Chrh Wkr; JA; Lbry Ade; Off Ade; Red Cr Ade; Pep Clb; Spn Clb; Cit Awd; DAR Awd; Univ; Nursing.

WILSON, TAMARA J; New Prairie HS; North Liberty, IN; 1/168 Am Leg Aux Girls St; Treas Band; Chrh Wkr; NHS; Sch Mus; Sec Ger Clb; Natl Merit SF; College; Elec Engr.

WILSON, TAMMY; East Liverpool HS; East Liverpool, OH; 66/366 Band; Chrs; Drm Bgl; Off Ade; Sch Mus; Sch Pl; Stg Crw; Pep Clb; Bsktbl; Mgrs; Voc Schl; Cosmetology.

WILSON, TARI; Northfield HS; Wabash, IN; Chrh Wkr; Cmnty Wkr; FCA; Girl Scts; Hon Rl; Hosp Ade; JA; Red Cr Ade; Sch Mus; Sch Pl; Taylor Univ; Nursing.

WILSON, TARI; Lebanon HS; Lebanon, OH; 53/278 Band; Chrh Wkr; Cmnty Wkr; Girl Scts; Hon Rl; Sec NHS; Sch Mus; Sch Pl; Pres Yth Flsp; Sch Nwsp; Rainbow Worthy Advsr 78; Gran Cross Of Color & Rainbow Schlshp 79; Fairboard 75 79 Sec 79; Eastern Kentucky Univ.

WILSON, TERESA; Point Pleasant HS; Pt Pleasant, WV; Cl Rep Jr Cls; Am Leg Aux Girls St; Band; Chrs; Chrh Wkr; Hon Rl; Hosp Ade; NHS; Sch Mus; Stu Cncl; 1st Pl Phys Sci Div Pt Pleasant Jr Hi; St Ldrshp Conf; Treas Of Point Pleasant Co Ed Hi T Clb; Coll; Comp Sci.

WILSON, TERRI; Martinsville HS; Martinsville, IN; 25/390 Hon Rl; DECA; Dental Lab.

WILSON, TERRY; Felicity Franklin HS; Felicity, OH; 9/72 Band; Chrs; Cmnty Wkr; Hon Rl; 4-H; FFA; Letter Bsbl; FFA 78; Agri Elec 2nd Indvdl In St 78; All Ohio Yth Choir 78; Welder.

WILSON, TERRY; Zionsville Comm HS; Zionsville, IN; Letter Ftbl; IM Sprt; Bus School; Bus.

WILSON, THOMAS; Shakamak HS; Jasonville, IN; 23/84 Am Leg Boys St; Band; Boy Scts; Chrh Wkr; FCA; Hon Rl; NHS; Quill & Scroll; Sch Nwsp; Trk; Indiana State; Computer Sci.

WILSON, THOMASINA; Regina HS; Moreland Hills, OH; Cls Rep Soph Cls; Band; Cmp Fr Grls; JA; Lbry Ade; Stg Crw; Rptr Sch Nwsp; Trk; Cit Awd; Univ Of Cincinnati; Med Tech.

WILSON, TONI R; Bloomington HS North; B loomington, IN; 6/415 FCA; Jr NHS; Ger Clb; Natl Merit Ltr; Univ; Math.

WILSON, TRACY; Columbiana HS; Columbiana, OH; Cl Rep Jr Cls; Chrs; Hon Rl; Lbry Ade; Stu Cncl; Yrbk; Fr Clb; OEA; Pep Clb; Pom Pon; Sec.

WILSON, VALERIE; Martin Luther King Sr HS; Detroit, MI; Hon Rl; Lbry Ade; NHS; Off Ade; FDA; Pep Clb; Glf; Univ; Bio Med Engr.

WILSON, VICKIE; Tecumseh HS; Tecumseh, MI; Band; NHS; Spn Clb; Michigan St Univ.

WILSON, WANDA; East Catholic HS; Detroit, MI; 2/66 VP Frsh Cls; Trs Soph Cls; VP Sr Cls; Chrh Wkr; Hon Rl; Lbry Ade; NHS; Off Ade; Y-Teens; Yrbk; College; Communications.

WILSON, WENDI; Pleasant HS; Marion, OH; Girl Scts; Lbry Ade; Sec Yth Flsp; Y-Teens; Letter Trk; IM Sprt; Sec Mat Maids;.

WILSON, WENDY; Oak Glen HS; Chester, WV; Band; Chrh Wkr; Girl Scts; NHS; Sch Mus; Yth Flsp; Sec Fr Clb; FNA; Pep Clb; College; Nursing.

WILSON, WILLIAM; Ravenna HS; Ravenna, OH; 3/313 Am Leg Boys St; Pres NHS; Stu Cncl; Rptr Sch Nwsp; Ftbl; Am Leg Awd; DAR Awd; Elk Awd; Natl Merit Ltr; Northwestern Univ; Med.

WILSON, WILLIAM T; Marysville HS; Marysville, MI; Sch Mus; Sch Pl; Stg Crw; Drama Clb; St Clair Co Comm College; Bus Mgmt.

WILSON, WILMA; River Valley HS; Marion, OH; 11/193 Girl Scts; Treas JA; NHS; VP Yth Flsp; 4-H; Spn Clb; JA Awd; Bowler Of The Month; Most Imporved Average; Ohio St Univ; Acctg.

WILSON JR, RICHARD K; Johnstown HS; Johnstown, OH; 21/140 Band; Boy Scts; FCA; 4-H; Spn Clb; Letter Ftbl; Letter Trk; 4-H Awd; Science Health Outstanding Ach; Whos Who Awd; Ohio St Univ; Law.

WILT, CINDY; Anna HS; Anna, OH; 22/84 Cls Rep Soph Cls; Trs Sr Cls; Band; Chrs; Chrh Wkr; Girl Scts; Hon Rl; Off Ade; Sch Mus; Sch Pl; Sec.

WILT, JON; Miami Trace HS; Washington C H, OH; AFS; Cmnty Wkr; Hon Rl; 4-H; FFA; IM Sprt; Cit Awd; 4-H Awd; FFA St Farmer Degree 1979; FFA Star Chap Farmer 1979; 4 H St Awd Winner Swine 1979; Farm.

WILT, LISA; Upper Sandusky HS; Upper Sandusky, OH; Cl Rep Jr Cls; Band; Chrs; Hon Rl; Sch Mus; Stu Cncl; 4-H; Bsktbl; Trk; Chrldng; College; Nursing.

WILT, MARTY; Delaware Hayes HS; Delaware, OH; Hon Rl; Sch Nwsp; Lat Clb; Ftbl; Trk; IM Sprt; Tmr; Mbr Of Winter Track Team 77; Frosh Track Most Improved Player 77; Mbr Of Undefeated Track Team 78; Univ; Corp Law.

WILT, SANDY; Triad HS; Woodstock, OH; Trs Jr Cls; Pres Sr Cls; Girl Scts; Hon Rl; Hosp Ade; Off Ade; FHA; OEA; Pep Clb; Bsbl; Ohio Hi Point JVS; Typist.

WILTING, MICHAEL; Bishop Gallagher HS; Grosse Pte Pk, MI; 78/322 Cls Rep Sr Cls; Hon Rl; NHS; Sch Pl; Stg Crw; Yrbk; Glf; IM Sprt; Gov Hon Prg Awd; Natl Merit Ltr; Wayne St Univ; Chem Engr.

WILTON, RICHARD; Stonewall Jackson HS; Charleston, WV; Sec Sr Cls; Am Leg Boys St; Chrh Wkr; Cmnty Wkr; Hosp Ade; NHS; Stu Cncl; Yth Flsp; Spn Clb; Letter Crs Cntry; Marshall Univ; Business.

WIMBERLY, PAMELA K; R Nelson Snider HS; Ft Wayne, IN; Cls Rep Soph Cls; Girl Scts; Hon Rl; Hosp Ade; Stu Cncl; Yth Flsp; Trk; Chrldng; GAA; IM Sprt; St Pauls Freindshp Guild Awd 76; Pres Of Del Teens 78; Bst Jump Chrldr Trophy 76; Univ; Sociologist.

WIMER, GARY; Green HS; Akron, OH; Boy Scts; Chrs; Chrh Wkr; FCA; Hon Rl; Mdrgl; Sch Mus; Sch Pl; Yth Flsp; Letter Ftbl; PC For Reach Out Youth Camp Ldr 79; Pres Of UMYF 79; Green HS E nsemble Mbr 79; Ohio St Univ; Optometry.

WIMER, KIM; Circleville HS; Riverton, WV; 4/30 Hon Rl; Yrbk; Rptr Sch Nwsp; FHA; Bsktbl; Fairmount St Coll; Social Work.

WIMER, LORI; Franklin HS; Franklin, WV; 7/82 Sec Frsh Cls; Chrs; Chrh Wkr; Cmnty Wkr; Hon Rl; Sec NHS; Off Ade; Stu Cncl; Pep Clb; Chrldng; James Madison Univ; Elem Ed.

WIMMER, MARCIA; Shelbyville HS; Shelbyville, IN; 43/340 Chrh Wkr; Hon Rl; NHS; Spn Clb; Indiana Bus Coll; Acctg.

WIMMER, NANCY; Spanishburg HS; Kegley, WV; 5/35 Band; Chrs; Chrh Wkr; Cmnty Wkr; Debate Tm; Hon Rl; Off Ade; Sch Mus; FHA; Sci Clb; Concord Coll; Poli Sci.

WINBIGLER, DOUGLAS; Hillsdale HS; Jeromesville, OH; Pres Sr Cls; Am Leg Boys St; Chrs; Hon Rl; Fr Clb; Bsbl; Letter Bsktbl; Ftbl; Univ.

WINCE, MARSHA; St Marys HS; St Marys, WV; Band; Drm Mjrt; Off Ade; Sch Pl; Pep Clb; Chrldng; Mat Maids; PPFtbl; Scr Kpr; Twrlr; Fairmont St Univ; RN.

WINCHELL, KIMBERLY; Pinconning Area HS; Linwood, MI; 11/260 Hon Rl; Hosp Ade; Lbry Ade; NHS; Red Cr Ade; Delta Coll; Nurse.

WIND, DEBORAH; Penn HS; South Bend, IN; 16/468 Cls Rep Frsh Cls; Cls Rep Soph Cls; Cl Rep Jr Cls; Cls Rep Sr Cls; NHS; Chrldng; PPFtbl; Miami Univ.

WINDBERG, TIMOTHY; Gwinn HS; Gwinn, MI; 25/200 Hon Rl; NHS; Bsktbl; Chmn Ftbl; Chmn Trk; Adrian College; Engr.

WINDELL, KATRINA; Corydon Central HS; Corydon, IN; 18/164 Cls Rep Frsh Cls; Cl Rep Jr Cls; NHS; Stu Cncl; Rptr Sch Nwsp; Sch Nwsp; 4-H; Fr Clb; Pep Clb; 4-H Awd; Aninal Asst.

WINDER, BRYAN; Onsted HS; Onsted, MI; Band; Boy Scts; Hon Rl; Bsktbl; Crs Cntry; Trk; Coach Actv; Scr Kpr; Saginaw Valley Coll; Law Enforcement.

WINDHAM, BRANDON; North Newton HS; Demotte, IN; 14/145 Boy Scts; Chrh Wkr; NHS; Letter Crs Cntry; Letter Swmmng; Letter Trk; DAR Awd; Fresh Biology Ach Awd; College; Vet.

WINDLE, CAROL; Northwest HS; Mc Dermott, OH; Hon Rl; NHS; Off Ade; Camp Enterprise Delegate; 3rd Typing Contest;.

WINDON, BLAIR; Eastern HS; Pomeroy, OH; 14/57 Chrh Wkr; Hon Rl; 4-H; Fr Clb; FFA; Ftbl; 4-H Awd; JC Awd; Univ.

WINE, GARY; Springfield HS; Springfield, MI; Band; Boy Scts; Hon Rl; NHS; Sct Actv; Am Leg Awd; Univ; Archt.

WINE, SARITA K; Braxton County HS; Copen, WV; 8/182 Cls Rep Frsh Cls; Cls Rep Soph Cls; VP Jr Cls; Chrh Wkr; Sec FCA; Hon Rl; Jr NHS; NHS; Stu Cncl; Yth Flsp; Jr Homecoming Princess 1977; All Tournment Plyr Dur Cls Tournments 1976; Davis & Elkins Coll; Soc Serv.

WINE, STAN; Carroll HS; Flora, IN; 34/135 Hon Rl; Sch Nwsp; Spn Clb; Coach Actv; Letter Mgrs; Tmr; Perfect Attendance 78; Received Sweater Because Of Letters 76; Indiana St Univ; Sports Brdcstng.

WINEBRENNER, SONDRA; Hardin Northern HS; Forest, OH; 6/59 Trs Sr Cls; Chrs; Hon Rl; Jr NHS; NHS; Pres Yth Flsp; Pres 4-H; Letter Bsktbl; Letter Trk;.

WINECKI, DAWN; Wylie E Groves HS; Birmingham, MI; AFS; Chrs; Hon Rl; Jr NHS; St Schlrshp Consideration For St Of Mich Schlr Pgm; Adrian Coll; Elem Ed.

WINEGAR, STEVEN; Willoughby South HS; Willoughby, OH; 1/416 Val; Capt Glf; Case Western Reserve Univ; Mech Engr.

WINEGARDNER, BECKY; Sheridan HS; Thornville, OH; 6/178 Chrs; Hon Rl; Jr NHS; Lbry Ade; NHS; Off Ade; FTA; VP OEA; Ohio Univ; Bus.

WINEGARDNER, BECKY A; Sheridan HS; Thornville, OH; 6/180 Chrs; Hon Rl; Jr NHS; Lbry Ade; NHS; Off Ade; FTA; OEA; Ohio St Univ; Bus.

WINEINGER, DELLA; Northeast Dubois HS; French Lick, IN; Band; Chrs; Drl Tm; Beta Clb; 4-H; FBLA; FHA; Pep Clb; Chrldng; Mgrs; Dental Tech.

WINELAND, JON; Midland HS; Midland, MI; 10/500 Hon Rl; Jr NHS; NHS; Univ; Engr.

WINENGER, JOHN; Argos Cmnty HS; Argos, IN; 17/60 VP Soph Cls; Am Leg Boys St; Chrh Wkr; Hon Rl; Pep Clb; Mgrs; Scr Kpr; Tmr; Univ; Meteorology.

WINES, CAROL; Howell Senior HS; Howell, MI; Am Leg Aux Girls St; Hon Rl; Mod UN; Stu Cncl; Fr Clb; Spn Clb; Trk; College.

WING, BRIAN; Cheboygan Catholic HS; Cheboygan, MI; Letter Bsbl; Letter Bsktbl; Letter Ftbl; Letter Trk; Coach Actv; Scr Kpr; Tmr; Central Michigan Univ.

WING, JENNIFER; Bellevue Comm HS; Bellevue, MI; 6/87 Pres Frsh Cls; Cls Rep Soph Cls; Sec Jr Cls; Band; Chrh Wkr; Hon Rl; NHS; Red Cr Ade; Sch Mus; Stu Cncl; Michigan St Univ; Nursing.

WING, SHERRY; Unionville Sebewaing AreaHS; Sebewaing, MI; Band; Girl Scts; Hon Rl; FHA; College.

WINGARD, HELEN; Admiral King HS; Lorain, OH; Off Ade; OEA; Gym; Trk; Business School; Major Course.

WINGARD, JULIE; Carroll HS; Flora, IN; 4/150 Chrs; Hon Rl; Sch Pl; Stg Crw; Drama Clb; Spn Clb; PPFtbl; Purdue Univ Comp Tech.

WINGATE, THOMAS; Mooresville HS; Mooresville, IN; 45/265 Aud/Vis; Boy Scts; Chrh Wkr; Cmnty Wkr; FCA; Hon Rl; NHS; Sct Actv; Yth Flsp; Bsbl; E Pulliam Mem Schlrshp For News 79; Ministerial Assoc Fpor Ctznshp & Academic Achvmnt 79; Indiana St Univ; Comp Tech.

WINGET, BRADLEY S; Memorial HS; St Marys, OH; 56/223 Cl Rep Jr Cls; Band; Boy Scts; Chrs; Hon Rl; JA; Orch; PAVAS; Sch Mus; Sch Pl; Univ; Commnctns.

WINGFIELD, LORENA; Centerville HS; Centreville, MI; Band; Drm Mjrt; Hon Rl; Hosp Ade; NHS; Fr Clb; Pep Clb; Sci Clb; Ten; Trk; Excllnc In Eng Awd 77 78 & 79; Excllnc In Art Awd 78; Hon Roll For Entire Yr Awd 78; Univ; Palentology.

WINIESDORFFER, JEFFREY; Wheeling Park HS; Wheeling, WV; Chrh Wkr; Hon Rl; NHS; Stu Cncl; Ger Clb; Key Clb; Letter Crs Cntry; Letter Trk; IM Sprt; Mgrs; Univ.

WININGER, DANIEL; Whiteland Community HS; Whiteland, IN; 48/200 Chrh Wkr; Pres 4-H; FFA; Key Clb; Pep Clb; Bsbl; 4-H Awd; New Mexico St Univ; Bus Mgmt.

WININGER, JILL; Springs Vly HS; French Lick, IN; Am Leg Aux Girls St; Chrh Wkr; Hon Rl; NHS; Yth Flsp; Pep Clb; Trk; Chrldng; Coll.

WININGER, REBECCA; Memphis HS; Memphis, MI; Hon Rl; Ed Sch Nwsp; Univ; Jrnlsm.

WININGS, DONALD E; North Putnam HS; Roachdale, IN; Band; 4-H; Spn Clb; VICA; Crs Cntry; Ftbl; Trk; Wrstlng; Vocational School; Mechanic.

WINK, PAM; South Spencer HS; Rockport, IN; VP Jr Cls; Chrs; Sch Mus; Letter Swmmng; Letter Trk; Chrldng; Indiana Univ; Electrocardiograph Tec.

WINKELMAN, GAIL; Seton HS; Cincinnati, OH; Hon Rl; Jr NHS; NHS; Pol Wkr; FBLA; Coach Actv; Coll; Busns Admin.

WINKLE, CHERYL; Winchester Community HS; Winchester, IN; Hon Rl; FHA;.

WINKLE, DAVID V; St Joseph HS; St Joseph, MI; 13/290 FCA; VP NHS; Pres Stu Cncl; Ger Clb; Lat Clb; Letter Swmmng; Tmr; Calvin Coll.

WINKLE, DAWN; Continental Local HS; Continental, OH; Trs Frsh Cls; Sec Soph Cls; Sec Jr Cls; Am Leg Aux Girls St; Band; Drm Mjrt; Hon Rl; NHS; Off Ade; Stu Cncl; MVP Awd In Track 78; Trophy For Being Highst Scrr In Runnin Event 77; Vllybl 3 Yrs 76 79; Bowling Green St Univ.

WINKLE, DEBORAH; Indian Hill HS; Cincinnati, OH; 25/280 Band; Chrs; Chrh Wkr; Hon Rl; Sch Mus; Yth Flsp; Drama Clb; Fr Clb; Pep Clb; Pres Awd; College; Social Sciences.

WINKLE, GAIL; Austintown Fitch HS; Youngstown, OH; 114/666 Hon Rl; Jr NHS; NHS; Off Ade; Y-Teens; Ger Clb; Pep Clb; Letter Chrldng; PPFtbl; Youngstown St Univ.

WINKLER, AMY; Chillicothe HS; Chillicothe, OH; Pres Jr Cls; Cl Rep Jr Cls; Band; Chrh Wkr; Drl Tm; Hon Rl; Jr NHS; NHS; Pep Clb; Chrldng; Hon Roll 73; Natl Hon Soc 77; Ohio Univ; Psych.

WINKLER, CEILANN M; Crestline HS; Crestline, OH; Am Leg Aux Girls St; Hon Rl; Sct Actv; Trk; Chrldng; Scr Kpr; Tmr; College; Phys Ther.

WINKLER, CHARLENE; Rittman HS; Sterling, OH; 25/113 Trs Jr Cls; Trs Sr Cls; Hon Rl; Lbry Ade; Sch Nwsp; 4-H; FHA; OEA; IM Sprt; 4-H Awd; Plc 2nd In Rec Mgmt At Reg Skills Cont In OEA; Received A Reading Cir Awd Every Yr For 12 Yrs; Busns Schl; Sec.

WINKLER, DONNA; Yale HS; Yale, MI; 9/162 Girl Scts; Hon Rl; Lbry Ade; NHS; Sch Nwsp; Ferris St Coll; Dent Hygn.

WINKLER, KATHARINE; Concordia Lutheran HS; Elkhart, IN; Hosp Ade; JA; Pol Wkr; Yth Flsp; Sec Lat Clb; PPFtbl; JA Awd; Ball State Univ; Education.

WINKLER, MICHELLE; Marysville HS; Marysville, MI; Cls Rep Frsh Cls; Cls Rep Soph Cls; Chrh Wkr; Girl Scts; Hon Rl; Sch Pl; Stu Cncl; Yth Flsp; Pep Clb; Trk; Pom Pon Squad Squad Ldr Varsity Letter Trophy; Band Gold Band Concert Band; Lifeguard For Schl Pool; Coll; Child Psych.

WINLAND, CHRISTIE; Buckeye North HS; Brilliant, OH; Sec Frsh Cls; Band; Girl Scts; Hon Rl; NHS; Off Ade; Sch Pl; Rptr Yrbk; Rptr Sch Nwsp; Drama Clb;.

WINLAND, PEGGY; Martins Ferry HS; Bridgeport, OH; Band; Chrh Wkr; Hon Rl; Off Ade; Orch; Yth Flsp; Sec 4-H; 4-H Awd;.

WINLAND, SIDNEY R; Wellsville HS; Wellsville, OH; 14/125 Cls Rep Frsh Cls; Pres Soph Cls; Cl Rep Jr Cls; Am Leg Boys St; Chrh Wkr; Sch Pl; Stg Crw; Stu Cncl; Rptr Yrbk; Sprt Ed Sch Nwsp; Spec Mention All Columbiana Cnty Bsktbl; Coll; Busns Admin.

WINN, D; Belleville HS; Belleville, MI; Girl Scts; Hon Rl; Sct Actv; Bus Schl; Accountant.

WINN, KAREN A; Brazil Sr HS; Brazil, IN; 3/191 Cls Rep Sr Cls; Band; Hon Rl; NHS; Sch Pl; Fr Clb; FHA; FTA; Mth Clb; Pep Clb; Indiana St Univ; Early Childhood Ed.

WINN, VANDA; Eastmoor Sr HS; Columbus, OH; 14/290 Chrs; Drl Tm; Hon Rl; Jr NHS; NHS; Swmmng; Ohio St Univ.

WINNEFELD, J D; Centerville HS; Richmond, IN; 12/169 Cls Rep Frsh Cls; Cls Rep Soph Cls; Am Leg Boys St; Hon Rl; Jr NHS; 4-H; Letter Ftbl; Letter Trk; Letter Wrstlng; College; Pre Law.

WINNER, ALYSIA; Norton HS; Clinton, OH; Chrs; Chrh Wkr; Cmnty Wkr; Hon Rl; JA; Sch Mus; Sch Pl; Yth Flsp; Sci Clb; Spn Clb; Nursing Schl; Nursing.

WINNER, SARAH; Celina Sr HS; Celina, OH; 9/240 Trs Frsh Cls; VP Jr Cls; VP Sr Cls; Band; Hon Rl; NHS; Orch; Stg Crw; Rptr Yrbk; Rptr Sch Nwsp; College; Bio.

WINSHALL, JULIE E; Berkley HS; Huntingtn Wds, MI; 1/482 Val; Hon Rl; NHS; Sch Mus; Rptr Yrbk; NCTE; Wayne St Univ Awd Writing 1979; St Schlrshp 1979; Explr Prog 1979; Univ Of Michigan; Sci.

WINSLOW, DAREL; Pinckney Community HS; Lakeland, MI; Boy Scts; Chrs; Hon Rl; Sct Actv; Yrbk; Letter Ftbl; Letter Trk; Vocational School; Photographer.

WINSLOW, FRANCEN; Salem HS; Salem, IN; Band; Drl Tm; JA; NHS; Stu Cncl; FHA; OEA; Pep Clb; College; Nursing.

WINSLOW, WILLIAM J; Indian Creek HS; Trafalgar, IN; 1/145 Cl Rep Jr Cls; Val; Am Leg Boys St; VP FCA; Pres NHS; Off Ade; Pres Stu Cncl; Ed Sch Nwsp; Sprt Ed Sch Nwsp; Rptr Sch Nwsp; College; Acct.

WINSON, ROLAND; St Alphonsus HS; Dearborn, MI; 76/177 Chrh Wkr; Cmnty Wkr; Hon Rl; Pol Wkr; Mth Clb; Trk; IM Sprt; Univ Of Michigan; Comp Engr.

WINSTEL, DEBORAH; Turpin HS; Cincinnati, OH; 31/320 Chrh Wkr; Hon Rl; Jr NHS; Stu Cncl; Rptr Yrbk; Yrbk; Fr Clb; FHA; Swmmng; Mgrs; Univ Of Cincinnati; Bus.

WINSTEL, MARY; St Francis Desales HS; Columbus, OH; 27/190 Hon Rl; Quill & Scroll; Sch Pl; Rptr Yrbk; Sch Nwsp; Drama Clb; Mat Maids; Natl Merit Ltr; College; Corp Law.

WINSTON, NAVARRO; Central HS; Detroit, MI; Band; CAP; Cit Awd; Hon Awd Schlshp 78 & 79; Hon Awd Perfct Attndnc 78; Macomb Cnty Cmnty Coll; Engr.

WINSTON, RUSTY; Colon HS; Colon, MI; Hon Rl; NHS; Letter Bsbl; Mich State Univ; Engr.

WINSTON, THORLA T; Newark Sr HS; Newark, OH; Chrs; Chrh Wkr; FCA; Hon Rl; Jr NHS; NHS; Capt Bsktbl; Letter Ftbl; Trk; Wrstlng; Miles Mc Ketric Awd 1976; Univ.

WINTER, CAROL; Marian HS; Birmingham, MI; Cls Rep Frsh Cls; Cls Rep Soph Cls; Cl Rep Jr Cls; Cls Rep Sr Cls; Hon Rl; NHS; Bsbl; Bsktbl; Sftbl Var All Cntrl Div 2nd Baseman 79; St Marys Of Notre Dame Univ.

WINTER, CAROL; Traverse City Sr HS; Traverse City, MI; Cl Rep Jr Cls; Chrs; Mdrgl; NHS; Sch Mus; Stu Cncl; Mi Compttv Schlshp 79; Hon Schlshp From CMU 79; 4 Schlshp Key Awds 76 79; Cntrl Michigan Univ; Bus.

WINTER, FRANKLIN; Upper Sandusky HS; Upper Sandusky, OH; 43/219 Band; Hon Rl; Sch Pl; Sct Actv; Yth Flsp; 4-H; Spn Clb; Ten; IM Sprt; Univ; Sci.

WINTERICH, DARLENE; Normandy HS; North Royalton, OH; Hon Rl; VICA; Cleveland St Univ; Bus.

WINTERMAN, RICHARD J; Madeira HS; Madeira, OH; Boy Scts; Hon Rl; Jr NHS; Lat Clb; Capt Ftbl; PPFtbl; Cit Awd; Pres Awd; USJC Awd; Univ; Engr.

WINTERNHEIMER, KAREN; North HS; Evansville, IN; 15/300 NHS; Quill & Scroll; Stu Cncl; Ed Sch Nwsp; Letter Mgrs; Indiana Univ; Lib Arts.

WINTERS, ALAN D; High School; Memphis, MI; Trs Frsh Cls; Hon Rl; Jr NHS; Sprt Ed Sch Nwsp; Sch Nwsp; Bsbl; Wrstlng; Coach Actv; IM Sprt; Mgrs; MSU; History.

WINTERS, BRUCE; St Johns HS; Whitehouse, OH; Aud/Vis; Band; Hon Rl; Spn Clb; Bsktbl; 1st Hon Awd 78; Speech Contest Awd 75; Univ Of Toledo; Elec Engr Tech.

WINTERS, DAVID T; West Vigo HS; W Terre Haute, IN; Sec Key Clb; Letter Ftbl; Letter Trk; Capt Wrstlng; Natl Merit Ltr; Indiana St Univ; Econ.

WINTERS, DEITRA; Perry Meridian HS; Indianapolis, IN; 21/550 Girl Scts; Hon Rl; Off Ade; Sch Mus; Yth Flsp; Fr Clb; Pep Clb; Chrldng; Univ; Art.

WINTERS, DONETTA; Logan HS; Logan, WV; Sec Frsh Cls; Chrh Wkr; Hon Rl; NHS; Ed Yrbk; Beta Clb; Fr Clb; Keyettes; Pep Clb; Chrldng; Most Outstanding Freshman; Prayer Clb Pres; Golden Circle V Pres; Univ Of Kentucky; Computer Tech.

WINTERS, JANET; Wirt Cnty HS; Elizabeth, WV; 6/100 Hon Rl; NHS; Quill & Scroll; Yth Flsp; Ed Sch Nwsp; 4-H; FHA; PPFtbl; 4-H Awd; Parkersburg Comm Coll; Comp Sci.

WINTERS, KAREN; Wayne HS; Dayton, OH; 49/600 Hon Rl; Jr NHS; NHS; Off Ade; OEA; JA Awd; St Comptn Steno 79; Coll; Bus Admin.

WINTERS, KATHY L; Montezuma HS; Montezuma, IN; FHA; Letter Bsktbl; Letter Ten; Letter Trk; Chrldng; Ivy Tech Voc Schl; Nursing.

WINTERS, MARK; Milton Union HS; Ludlow Fl, OH; Chrh Wkr; Hon Rl; Sch Pl; Sprt Ed Sch Nwsp; Drama Clb; Fr Clb; Lat Clb; Wright St Univ; Eng.

WINTERS, TAMI; Columbia City Joint HS; Columbia City, IN; 18/257 Hon Rl; Off Ade; Yth Flsp; FTA; OEA; Pep Clb; Mat Maids; Key Punch Opertr.

WINTERS, TODD; Tiffin Columbian HS; Tiffin, OH; Hon Rl; Spn Clb; Letter Bsbl; Bsktbl; Ftbl; Univ.

WINTERSTEIN, DEBRA; Arthur Hill HS; Saginaw, MI; Chrh Wkr; Girl Scts; Hon Rl; JA; Mdrgl; NHS; Red Cr Ade; Memrol Lib In Saginaw 77 79; St Of Mi Compt Schslhp 79; Triskelion Mert Sclhsp From Saginaw Coll 79; Saginaw Vly St Coll; Acctg.

WINTLE, SANDRA D; Euclid Sr HS; Euclid, OH; 77/746 Hon Rl; Off Ade; Univ; Sci.

WINTON, DARLENE; Pontiac Ctrl HS; Pontiac, MI; Cls Rep Frsh Cls; Cls Rep Soph Cls; Cl Rep Jr Cls; Cls Rep Sr Cls; Chrh Wkr; Cmnty Wkr; Hon Rl; Off Ade; Drama Clb; PPFtbl; Oakland Univ; Dent Hygnst.

WINTON, PETER; Terre Haute North Vigo HS; Terre Haute, IN; Band; Boy Scts; Hon Rl; Sct Actv; Boys Clb Am; Civ Clb; IM Sprt; College; Bus.

WINTZINGER, ROLAND; St Xavier HS; Cincinnati, OH; 25/268 Hon Rl; NHS; Glf; Swmmng; Coach Actv; IM Sprt; Pres Awd; College; Premed.

WINZELER, MICHAEL; Montpelier HS; Montpelier, OH; 24/105 Am Leg Boys St; Boy Scts; Chrh Wkr; Hon Rl; Sch Mus; Stg Crw; Yth Flsp; Rptr Yrbk; Letter Glf; Letter Trk; Univ; Engr.

WIREMAN, ERNEST; Jimtown HS; Elkhart, IN; 12/95 Boy Scts; Hon Rl; Letter Crs Cntry; Trk; Letter Wrstlng; Honor Awds; Honor Roll; Tri State Drafting Schl Runner Up; Purdue Univ; Technical Engr.

WIREMAN, KATHY; Ironton HS; Ironton, OH; 1/156 Band; Chrs; Chrh Wkr; Girl Scts; Hon Rl; JA; NHS; Sch Pl; Sct Actv; Fr Clb; NEDT Cert; Hnrbl Men In Ohio St Schlrshp Tests; St Winner In Amer Chem Soc Test; Univ Of North Carolina; Acctg.

WIRFEL, CAROLYN; Madison HS; Madison, OH; 28/300 Band; Hon Rl; NHS; Red Cr Ade; Keyettes; Letter Bsbl; Letter Bsktbl;.

WIRICK, LINDA; Chaminade Julienne HS; Dayton, OH; 63/271 Aud/Vis; Chrs; Chrh Wkr; Hon Rl; NHS; Off Ade; Typist.

WIRICK, RANDY; John F Kennedy HS; Warren, OH; Hon Rl; Lit Mag; Rptr Sch Nwsp; Bsbl; Bsktbl; Crs Cntry; Ftbl; Univ; Med.

WIRSCH, JEANNETTE; Badin HS; Hamilton, OH; Chrh Wkr; Girl Scts; Sch Mus; Fr Clb; IM Sprt; Univ; Soc Work.

WIRTH, ANGELA K; Ben Davis HS; Indianapolis, IN; Cmnty Wkr; Hon Rl; Lbry Ade; Sch Pl; Stu Cncl; Sch Nwsp; Drama Clb; Bsktbl; Gym; PPFtbl; Middle Tennessee St Univ; Philosophy.

WIRTH, BRADLEY; West Bloomfield HS; W Bloomfield, MI; Band; Cmnty Wkr; Hon Rl; Quill & Scroll; Sch Mus; Rptr Sch Nwsp; Michigan St Univ; Bus.

WIRTH, KEITH; Meridian Sr HS; Hope, MI; Chrh Wkr; Hon Rl; Univ; Archt.

WIRTH, LISA; Columbus Eastmoor Sr HS; Columbus, OH; 92/310 Cls Rep Sr Cls; Hon Rl; Capt Chrldng; PPFtbl; Ohio St Univ; Phys Ther.

WIRTH, MIKE; Lasalle HS; Cincinnati, OH; 8/277 Sec Sr Cls; Hon Rl; Jr NHS; NHS; Stu Cncl; Glf; Miami Univ; Acctg.

WIRTH, MIKE; La Salle HS; Cincinnati, OH; 8/282 Sec Sr Cls; Hon Rl; Jr NHS; NHS; Pol Wkr; Glf; IM Sprt; Miami Ohio Univ; Acctg.

WIRTH, TERRI; Kimball HS; Royal Oak, MI; Cmnty Wkr; Girl Scts; Hon Rl; Sct Actv; Yrbk; 4-H; Chrldng; IM Sprt; 4-H Awd; A Poem Was Published In The Schl Yrbk; In Competition For Michigan Competitive Schlrshp; College; Speech Pathology.

WIRTHLIN, RICHARD E; Turpin HS; Cincinnati, OH; 15/371 Hon Rl; Letter Glf; Letter Wrstlng; PPFtbl; Univ Of Texas; Bus.

WIRTZ, RUTH; Freeland HS; Freeland, MI; Band; Hon Rl; Whos Who Among Amer Stu 77;.

WISE, CATHERINE; Perrysburg HS; Perrysburg, OH; Cl Rep Jr Cls; Cls Rep Sr Cls; Girl Scts; Stu Cncl; Letter Bsktbl; College; Naturalist.

WISE, CATHI; Barnesville HS; Barnesville, OH; 33/135 Band; Chrs; Chrh Wkr; Girl Scts; Hon Rl; Hosp Ade; Lbry Ade; Orch; Sch Mus; Sch Pl; Belmont Tech Coll; Sec Tech.

WISE, CHARLES; Madison Comprehensive HS; Mansfield, OH; Cls Rep Frsh Cls; Cls Rep Soph Cls; Band; Cmnty Wkr; Hon Rl; Stu Cncl; Ger Clb; Key Clb; Bsbl; Bsktbl; Univ; Engr.

WISE, DAVID; Crestview HS; New Waterford, OH; Boy Scts; Red Cr Ade; Sct Actv; Key Clb; Spn Clb; Letter Glf; Univ.

WISE, GINNY; Jewett Scio HS; Scio, OH; 3/70 Cls Rep Frsh Cls; Cls Rep Soph Cls; Hon Rl; NHS; Stu Cncl; Spn Clb; Chrldng; Am Leg Awd; Ohio St Univ; Comp Sci.

WISE, JOHN; Bishop Donahue HS; Moundsville, WV; 5/65 Pres Jr Cls; Chrh Wkr; Hon Rl; NHS; 4-H; Key Clb; Spn Clb; Letter Bsktbl; Letter Ftbl; Carnegie Mellon Univ; Archt.

WISE, KAREN; Clyde HS; Clyde, OH; Trs Frsh Cls; Trs Soph Cls; Trs Jr Cls; Trs Sr Cls; Am Leg Aux Girls St; Chrs; Hon Rl; Stu Cncl; Trk; Scr Kpr; Ohi State Univ; Phys Ther.

WISE, KATHRYN; Northwestern HS; West Salem, OH; Band; Hon Rl; Sch Pl; Sec Stu Cncl; Sec Drama Clb; Sec 4-H; VP FFA; FTA; Pep Clb; Trk; All Amer Hall Of Frame Board Hon 78; Ohio St Univ; Animal Sci.

WISE, KELLY A; Ravenna HS; Ravenna, OH; 65/318 Girl Scts; Hon Rl; NHS; Sct Actv; Yrbk; Lat Clb; OEA; Ten; Bowling Green St Univ; Bus.

WISE, KIMBERLEE; Centerville Sr HS; Centerville, IN; 13/163 Chrs; Hon Rl; NHS; Off Ade; Sch Pl; Stg Crw; Y-Teens; Rptr Sch Nwsp; Drama Clb; Sci Clb; Ball State Univ; Criminalogy.

WISE, LESLIE; Stow HS; Stow, OH; 24/500 Boy Scts; Hon Rl; NHS; Stu Cncl; Y-Teens; VP Pep Clb; Trk; IM Sprt; College; Bio Chem.

WISE, MARY T; Bishop Ready HS; Columbus, OH; Hon Rl; VP JA; Fr Clb; Letter Trk; JA Awd; French I Outstndng Achievmnt 98 GPA; Georgetown Univ; Law.

WISE, MICHAEL; Chagrin Falls HS; Chagrin Falls, OH; Trs Soph Cls; Hon Rl; Spn Clb; Letter Bsbl; Letter Ftbl; Univ; Sci.

WISE, PATRICIA; Lexington HS; Mansfield, OH; 16/250 Band; Hon Rl; Hosp Ade; Off Ade; Pol Wkr; Stu Cncl; Y-Teens; Fr Clb; Key Clb; Chrldng; Activits Awd 79; Accptd Into Hnrs Progr At BGSU 79; Whos Who Among Oh Frgn Lang Stu 79; Bowling Green St Univ; Poli Sci.

WISE, SHARON; Northwood HS; New Paris, IN; Band; Chrs; Chrh Wkr; Hon Rl; Off Ade; Ger Clb; Capt Gym; GAA; 4-H Awd; College; Registered Nurse.

WISE, SUSAN; Chagrin Falls HS; Chagrin Falls, OH; Sec Jr Cls; Pres Sr Cls; Chrh Wkr; Hon Rl; NHS; Sprt Ed Sch Nwsp; Mth Clb; Letter Bsktbl; Letter Ten; Letter Trk; College; Education.

WISE, THOMAS J; Mohawk HS; Mc Cutchenville, OH; Hon Rl; Jr NHS; NHS; Rptr Yrbk; IM Sprt; 4-H Awd; Terra Tech; Accounting.

WISE, VIRGINIA; Jewett Scio HS; Scio, OH; 3/70 Cls Rep Frsh Cls; Cls Rep Soph Cls; Hon Rl; NHS; Stu Cncl; Spn Clb; Chrldng; Am Leg Awd; Ohio State Univ; Computer Science.

WISE, WILLIAM D; Little Miami HS; Pleasant Plain, OH; 8/200 Am Leg Boys St; Band; Hon Rl; NHS; Orch; Sch Mus; Rdo Clb; Socr; Trk; Wrstlng; Electronic Engr.

WISECUP, BENITA; Union Scioto HS; Chillicothe, OH; 30/125 Chrs; Hon Rl; NHS; 4-H; FTA; Coll; Bus.

WISECUP, LISA; Edward Lee Mc Clain HS; S Salem, OH; 23/150 Chrh Wkr; NHS; Sch Pl; Stu Cncl; Y-Teens; Yrbk; 4-H; Lat Clb; Chrldng; 4-H Awd; Ohio Univ; Med Sec.

WISEHEART, JIM; New Albany HS; New Albany, IN; 1/565 Am Leg Boys St; Chrh Wkr; Hon Rl; NHS; Yth Flsp; Sci Clb; Letter Bsbl; College.

WISEMAN, ANDRE; Cass Technical HS; Detroit, MI; 50/901 Pres Sr Cls; Hon Rl; NHS; Mth Clb; Bsbl; Ftbl; Trk; JETS Awd; Kiwan Awd; Mi Competitive Schlrshp 79; Mi Soc Of Prof Engr Whirpool Schlrshp 79; Mi Pol Yth Awd 79; Michigan St Univ; Engr.

WISEMAN, DAVID; Sheridan HS; Thornville, OH; Chrh Wkr; Hon Rl; FFA; Mgrs; GMI; Math.

WISEMAN, FRANKLIN; West Washington HS; Campbellsburg, IN; Aud/Vis; Hon Rl; NHS; Sch Nwsp; Fr Clb; Sci Clb; Purdue Univ; Elec.

WISEMAN, SUSAN; Dearborn HS; Dearborn, MI; Chrs; Hon Rl; Sch Pl; Sprt Ed Yrbk; Swmmng; IM Sprt; Mat Maids; Natl Merit Ltr; Michigan Schlrshp 1200 79; Deptmntl Music 79; Hope Schlrhsp 79; Hope Coll; Geol.

WISEN, DAVID; Bloomington HS S; Bloomington, IN; Hon Rl; Yth Flsp; Letter Swmmng; Univ; Dent.

WISIENSKI, DONALD; Carsonville Port Sanilac HS; Carsonville, MI; 2/80 Boy Scts; Hon Rl; NHS; FFA; Sci Clb; Michigan St Univ; Engr.

WISKIND, ROBERT H; Western Reserve Acad; Akron, OH; 3/86 Hon Rl; Sch Mus; Sch Pl; Rptr Sch Nwsp; Bsktbl; IM Sprt; Natl Merit SF; Pre Med.

WISNE, SUSAN; Lake Catholic HS; Chesterland, OH; 5/326 AFS; VP Band; Hon Rl; JA; Lit Mag; Soroptimist; Academic Exc Cert; Superior Rating Cal Music Editors Solo & Ensemble Contest; Super Rating Class A Music Ed; College; Bio Sci.

WISNER, BERNARD; Adams HS; Rochester, MI; Cls Rep Frsh Cls; Cls Rep Sr Cls; Cmnty Wkr; Hon Rl; Stu Cncl; N Metro Hcky Assoc Cptn Of Hcky Tm; Ldng Scorer; Tm 1st Div 2nd In Dist 77; Michigan St Univ; Bus Admin.

WISNER, FAWN; Les Cheneaux Comm HS; Cedarville, MI; Hon Rl; Business Schl.

WISNER, TERESA; Sebring Mc Kinley HS; Sebring, OH; Band; Hon Rl; Off Ade; Quill & Scroll; Rptr Sch Nwsp; Sch Nwsp; Fr Clb; Pep Clb; Trk; Scr Kpr; Scholastic Aptitude Tests Algebra 1 78; Scholastic Aptitude Tests French 11 79; Univ; Elem Schl Tchr.

WISNIEWSKI, CRAIG; Bishop Noll Institute; Chicago, IL; 47/321 Boy Scts; Hon Rl; College; Engineering.

WISNIEWSKI, DOUGLAS; Edwin Denby HS; Detroit, MI; Chrh Wkr; NHS; Rptr Yrbk; Brown Univ Assoc Alumni Awrd 79; Amvets Dodge Driver Excllnc Awrd 79; Univ; Bus Admin.

WISNIEWSKI, GREG; Bishop Foley HS; Warren, MI; Debate Tm; Hon Rl; Univ Of Michigan; Pre Law.

WISNIEWSKI, JOANN; St Alphonsus HS; Detroit, MI; Hon Rl; Univ; Sci.

WISNIEWSKI, KATHY; Oakridge Sr HS; Muskegon, MI; 33/137 Aud/Vis; Cmnty Wkr; Hon Rl; Stu

Cncl; Yrbk; 4-H; Pep Clb; Trk; Mgrs; 4-H Awd; Grand Valley St Univ; Music.

WISNIEWSKI, MICHELLE; All Saints Central HS; Bay City, MI; 1/167 Sec Frsh Cls; Val; Hon Rl; Hosp Ade; Pom Pon; Bausch & Lomb Awd; Natl Merit Ltr; Mic Tech Univ; Chem Engr.

WISNIEWSKI, PRUDENCE; Alpena Sr HS; Alpena, MI; NHS; Capt Ten; PPFtbl; Alpena Rotary Club Schlrshp 79; Alpena Cmnty Coll.

WISNIEWSKI, ROBERT; Lake Catholic HS; Willowick, OH; Gardening; Borromeo Coll; Priesthood.

WISNIEWSKI, VICKIE; St Alphonsus HS; Detroit, MI; 24/177 Trs Frsh Cls; Trs Soph Cls; Trs Jr Cls; Trs Sr Cls; Hon Rl; Hosp Ade; NHS; Wayne State Univ; Agri.

WISSINGER, TONJA; Springfield South HS; Springfield, OH; Cls Rep Frsh Cls; Sec Chrs; Drl Tm; Sch Mus; Sch Pl; Rptr Yrbk; Pep Clb; Spn Clb; Intl Thespian Soc; Outstanding Jr In Block; Outstanding Drama Awd; Wright St Univ; Sociology.

WISSMAN, SHERYL; Northville HS; Northville, MI; 3/380 VP Soph Cls; Trs Jr Cls; Pres Sr Cls; Am Leg Aux Girls St; Band; Chrh Wkr; Girl Scts; Hon Rl; NHS; Sch Mus; Michigan St Univ; Music.

WISTER, JEANNE; Liberty HS; Youngstown, OH; Cls Rep Frsh Cls; Cls Rep Soph Cls; Trs Jr Cls; Pres Sr Cls; Chrs; Hosp Ade; Off Ade; Sch Pl; Stg Crw; Stu Cncl; Bowling Green Univ.

WISTNER, LAURA; Wayne Trace HS; Haviland, OH; 20/120 Am Leg Aux Girls St; Pres Band; Hon Rl; Hosp Ade; NHS; Sch Pl; Stu Cncl; Univ Of Toledo; Educ.

WISTROM, CHERYL L; Whitehall Sr HS; Whitehall, MI; Am Leg Aux Girls St; Band; Girl Scts; Hon Rl; Hosp Ade; NHS; Sch Mus; Sch Pl; Stg Crw; Stu Cncl; Univ Of Michigan; Engr.

WISZ, DIANE; Kankakee Valley HS; Wheatfield, IN; 28/200 Chrs; Hon Rl; NHS; Sch Mus; Sch Pl; Stg Crw; 4-H; Trk; IM Sprt; Pres Awd; St Josephs Coll; Vet.

WITA, DEBRA; Lima Sr HS; Lima, OH; Cls Rep Frsh Cls; Band; Chrs; Chrh Wkr; Hon Rl; Orch; Sch Mus; Sch Pl; Yth Flsp; Lat Clb; John Philip Sousa; Sylvia Sawyer Kapp; All Amer Hall Of Fame Band Honors; Cedarville Coll; Music Ed.

WITBERGER, JEAN; Upper Arlington HS; Columbus, OH; 254/610 Cls Rep Frsh Cls; Chrh Wkr; FCA; Hon Rl; VP Ger Clb; Pep Clb; Trk; Ohi State; German.

WITCHELL, DANIEL; Laingsburg HS; Laingsburg, MI; Chrs; Chrh Wkr; Cmnty Wkr; Hon Rl; Yth Flsp; FFA; Bsktbl; Swmmng; Scr Kpr;.

WITHAM, DEBORAH; Bishop Dwenger HS; Ft Wayne, IN; Chrs; Cmnty Wkr; Girl Scts; Hon Rl; NHS; Stg Crw; Rptr Yrbk; Keyettes; Pep Clb; Purdue Univ; Computers.

WITHAM, LARRY; North Muskegon HS; N Muskegon, MI; 27/108 Cls Rep Frsh Cls; Trs Soph Cls; Hon Rl; NHS; Stu Cncl; Fr Clb; Ftbl; Ten; Trk; Wrstlng; Tennis City & Regnl Champ 5thn St 78; Tennis City & Regnl Finlst St Competitor 79; Univ; Med.

WITHERELL, WINSTON; Stonewall Jackson HS; Charleston, WV; Am Leg Boys St; Boy Scts; FCA; Hon Rl; JA; Stu Cncl; Boys Clb Am; Pres Mth Clb; Letter Ftbl; Letter Trk; Rep Med Explorers Of Genrl Div At Pres Confrnc 79; Cnslr At Kanawha Youth Camp 3 Yrs; West Virginia Univ; Orthopedic Surgn.

WITHEROW, MYRNA; Jane Addams Vocational HS; Cleveland, OH; Boy Scts; Stu Cncl; Rptr Yrbk; Beta Clb; OEA; Cit Awd; Central State Of Usc; Drama.

WITHERS, GINGER; Springfield Local HS; Petersburg, OH; 7/146 Cls Rep Frsh Cls; VP Soph Cls; Band; Chrs; Chrh Wkr; Hon Rl; Lbry Ade; Sec NHS; Ed Sch Nwsp; 4-H; Muskingum Coll; Psych.

WITHERS, JEFFREY; Buckhannon Upshur HS; Buckhannon, WV; Chrs; Hon Rl; Sch Mus; Stu Cncl; 4-H; Key Clb; Bsbl; Bsktbl; Capt IM Sprt; 4-H Awd; Univ; Data Processing.

WITHERSPOON, TERRY; Port Hope Community HS; Port Hope, MI; 4/18 VP Sr Cls; Chrh Wkr; FFA; Bsktbl; St Clair County Community; Agri.

WITHEY, CHUCK; Webberville HS; Webberville, MI; 9/63 Band; Hon Rl; Sch Pl; Pres Stu Cncl; Yrbk; FFA; Mth Clb; Letter Bsktbl; Letter Crs Cntry; Letter Ftbl; Valpariaso Coll; Civil Engr.

WITKO, LISA; Mt Healty HS; Cincinnati, OH; 70/572 Cls Rep Frsh Cls; Cls Rep Soph Cls; Band; Hon Rl; Lbry Ade; Off Ade; Stu Cncl; Raymond Walters; Animal Tech.

WITKOUSKY, ROBERT; Caro HS; Caro, MI; Boy Scts; Hon Rl; FFA; Letter Ten;.

WITKOVSKY, JERRY; Westwood HS; Ishpeming, MI; 3/108 Am Leg Boys St; Hon Rl; NHS; OEA; Letter Swmmng; Letter Ten; Kiwan Awd; Michigan St Univ; Acctg.

WITKOWSKI, JOAN; Woodhaven HS; Romulus, MI; Trs Jr Cls; Band; Chrs; Jr NHS; NHS; College.

WITKOWSKI, MARY; Schafer HS; Southgate, MI; Cls Rep Frsh Cls; Cls Rep Soph Cls; Cl Rep Jr Cls; Hst Sr Cls; Cls Rep Sr Cls; NHS; Stg Crw; Stu Cncl; Mic State Univ; Nursing.

WITMER, RHONDA; Brown City HS; Brown City, MI; 1/87 Cl Rep Jr Cls; Cls Rep Sr Cls; Val; Band; Drm Mjrt; NHS; Off Ade; Stu Cncl; FHA; DAR Awd; Bethel Coll; Sec.

WITOSZYNSKI, JAMES; Wyle E Groves HS; Birmingham, MI; 26/559 AFS; Hon Rl; NHS; Sch Mus; Rptr Yrbk; Yrbk; Rptr Sch Nwsp; Sch Nwsp; Letter Bsbl; Letter Bsktbl; Gene Hirs Schshp 79; Mi Compttv Shclhp Recognttn 79; Announcer For Girls & Boys Bsktbl 78 & 79; Michigan St Univ; Pre Vet.

WITSCHEY, GREG; Wadsworth Sr HS; Wadsworth, OH; Chrh Wkr; Jr NHS; NHS; Fr Clb; Bsktbl; Letter Crs Cntry; Letter Trk; IM Sprt; Lion Awd; Univ Of Akron; Comp Progr.

WITSKEN, KAREN A; Seton HS; Cincinnati, OH; 14/255 Girl Scts; Hon Rl; NHS; Red Cr Ade; Pep Clb; Coach Actv; GAA; Opt Clb Awd; Univ; Med Tech.

WITT, CARLA; Greenville Sr HS; Greenville, OH; 12/380 Am Leg Aux Girls St; Chrh Wkr; Hon Rl; Jr NHS; NHS; Stg Crw; Yth Flsp; Drama Clb; Spn Clb; Ten; Univ; Bus.

WITT, JERRY K; Brookville HS; Brookville, IN; Band; Rptr Yrbk; ITT Tech Inst; Elec Engr.

WITTBRODT, DAVID; Carman Sr HS; Flint, MI; 5/400 NHS; Letter Crs Cntry; Univ Of Michigan; Med.

WITTBRODT, MICHAEL; Carman Sr HS; Flint, MI; Cl Rep Jr Cls; Am Leg Boys St; Hon Rl; NHS; Letter Bsbl; Letter Bsktbl; Crs Cntry; Letter Ftbl; Letter Trk; Univ Of Michigan; Chem.

WITTBRODT, THERESA; Flushing HS; Flushing, MI; Band; Chrs; Drl Tm; Girl Scts; Hon Rl; NHS; Bsbl; College; Sci.

WITTE, CINDY; Richmond Sr HS; Richmond, IN; VP Frsh Cls; Girl Scts; Hon Rl; Off Ade; Pol Wkr; Stu Cncl; Rptr Sch Nwsp; Pep Clb; Letter Gym; Letter Swmmng; College; Phys Ed.

WITTE, DELLA; Norwood HS; Norwood, OH; 26/348 Drl Tm; NHS; Sch Mus; Sch Pl; Ed Yrbk; Mth Clb; Pep Clb; Rdo Clb; Northern Ky; Photog.

WITTE, DENISE; Fairview HS; Hicksville, OH; Chrh Wkr; Hon Rl; Coach Actv; GAA; College; Pre School Tchr.

WITTE, DEWEY; Northrop HS; Ft Wayne, IN; Natl Forn Lg; Cit Awd; College; Architect.

WITTE, NORMAN; Garber HS; Essexville, MI; 13/180 Cls Rep Soph Cls; Cls Rep Sr Cls; Am Leg Boys St; Band; Debate Tm; Hon Rl; Natl Forn Lg; Stu Cncl; Sch Nwsp; Stud Congress 77 78 & 79; 1 Act Play Forensics 77; Forensics Multiple Extemp Speaking 78; Univ; Law.

WITTENBACH, CHRIS; Belding HS; Belding, MI; Band; Chrs; Chrh Wkr; Hon Rl; NHS; Orch; College; Music.

WITTENBROOK, SUSAN; Woodsfield HS; Jerusalem, OH; Band; Chrs; Girl Scts; Hon Rl; Off Ade; Sch Mus; Sch Pl; Sprt Ed Yrbk; Rptr Yrbk; Yrbk; Voc Schl; Model.

WITTERS, MARA; Northmont HS; Englewood, OH; Chrs; Girl Scts; Letter Twrlr; Univ; Bus Educ.

WITTEVRONGEL, RENE; Reeths Puffer HS; Muskegon, MI; 7/281 Hon Rl; Jr NHS; NHS; Letter Ten; Mgrs; Muskegon Comm College; Data Proc.

WITTHOHN, MARGARET; Herbert Hoover Sr HS; Elkview, WV; Hon Rl; JA; Y-Teens; Fr Clb; Pep Clb; Chrldng; GAA; IM Sprt; Pom Pon; VP JA Awd; Elk Dist Softball 1978; Cheerleading N Y St 1977; West Virginia Univ; Med.

WITTINGEN, CAROL; Unity Christian HS; Allendale, MI; Chrh Wkr; Hon Rl; Yth Flsp; Yrbk; IM Sprt; Davenport Coll Of Bus; Acctg Asst.

WITTLINGER, DEBRA; Newbury HS; Newbury, OH; Band; Girl Scts; Hon Rl; Jr NHS; Sec NHS; Pres 4-H; Ger Clb; Letter Trk; Scr Kpr; Busns Schl; Acctg.

WITTMAN, ANNE; Archbishop Alter HS; Dayton, OH; 29/280 Chrs; Cmnty Wkr; Girl Scts; Hon Rl; NHS; Off Ade; Stg Crw; Ger Clb; Univ; Acctg.

WITTMAN, CHRIS; Archbishop Alter HS; Dayton, OH; 9/325 Cls Rep Soph Cls; Cl Rep Jr Cls; Chrs; Hon Rl; NHS; Sch Mus; Sch Pl; Stu Cncl; Drama Clb; Pres Ger Clb; Univ Of Dayton; Engr.

WITTMAN, LORI; Ashland Sr HS; Ashland, OH; 4/375 Val; Chrh Wkr; Cmnty Wkr; Hon Rl; NHS; Off Ade; Pol Wkr; Yrbk; Pres 4-H; Sec Pep Clb; Sec.

WITTUNG JR, ED; Van Wert HS; Van Wert, OH; 13/213 Band; Chrh Wkr; Hon Rl; NHS; Lat Clb; Pep Clb; Natl Merit Schl; Ohio Jr Classical Lg 2nd Pl In Mottoes Qts & Abrv 78; IMPACT Tm Dist Chrch Of Nazarene Sng Grp 78; Mt Vernon Nazarene Coll; Ministry.

WITWER, JOHN; Penn HS; Mishawaka, IN; Boy Scts; JA; Rptr Sch Nwsp; Ger Clb; Opt Clb Awd; IUSB; Sociology.

WITZENMAN, ROSE; Churubusco HS; Churubusco, IN; 14/125 Band; Girl Scts; Hon Rl; Hosp Ade; Yth Flsp; 4-H; FNA; Spn Clb; Purdue Univ; Nursing.

WITZMAN, ROBERT A; Lakota HS; West Chester, OH; 8/437 Hon Rl; NHS; Ger Clb; Letter Trk; IM Sprt; Alg Medal 75; Latin Cert 75; Geo Cert 76; Ohio St Univ; Engr.

WIWI, ROSE; Brookville HS; Brookville, IN; 15/200 Hon Rl; Rptr Yrbk; Rptr Sch Nwsp; FHA; Ger Clb; Valparaiso Univ; Soc Work.

WIXSON, DENISE; Yale HS; Avoca, MI; Chrs; Hon Rl; FHA; Pep Clb; Spn Clb; IM Sprt; Central Mich Univ; Social Work.

WIXTROM, MIKE; Republic Michigamme HS; Republic, MI; Band; Chrh Wkr; Hon Rl; Stg Crw; Yth Flsp; Sch Nwsp;.

WIZNIUK, ANDREW; Warren HS; Troy, MI; Chrh Wkr; Cmnty Wkr; Hon Rl; Natl Merit Schl; Oakland Univ; Eng.

WLOCHOWSKI, ANN; Washington HS; So Bend, IN; Cls Rep Frsh Cls; Cls Rep Soph Cls; Chrh Wkr; Girl Scts; Hon Rl; NHS; Cit Awd; God Cntry Awd; Michigan St Univ; Comp Sci.

WLODARCZAK, GREG; Bay Cty All Saints Cntrl HS; Bay City, MI; Hon Rl; Glf; Univ; Math.

WLODARCZYK, DONNA; St Alphonsus HS; Detroit, MI; 30/180 Cmp Fr Grls; Chrs; Drm Mjrt; Hon Rl; Hosp Ade; PAVAS; Sch Mus; Pep Clb; Twrlr; Pres Awd; Detroit Coll Of Bus; Acctg.

WLODKOWSKI, PATRICIA; Riverview Community HS; Riverview, MI; 27/250 Girl Scts; Hon Rl; Jr NHS; NHS; Fr Clb; Ferris State College; Pharmacy.

WNUK, MARY; Alcona Community Jr Sr HS; Barton City, MI; Band; Hon Rl; Jr NHS; NHS; Rptr Yrbk; Spn Clb; Lake Superior St Univ; Nurse.

WOBSER, DANIEL; Charleston Catholic HS; Charleston, WV; Am Leg Boys St; Chrh Wkr; Hon Rl; Sct Actv; Letter Bsktbl; Capt Ftbl; Letter Wrstlng; Univ Of Ken; Indus Engr.

WOBSER, JEFFREY; St Marys Cntrl Catholic HS; Sansuky, OH; 10/127 Cls Rep Frsh Cls; Cls Rep Soph Cls; Trs Jr Cls; Am Leg Boys St; Chrh Wkr; Hon Rl; NHS; 4-H; Letter Trk; College; Med.

WODARCYK, JULIE A; Grove City HS; Grove City, OH; Pres Jr Cls; Cls Rep Sr Cls; Chrs; Hon Rl; NHS; Stu Cncl; Ger Clb; Pep Clb; Natl Merit SF; Univ; Bus Mgmt.

WODARSKI, RICK A; Whitmer Sr HS; Toledo, OH; 33/912 Pres Sr Cls; Boy Scts; Chrs; JA; NHS; Stu Cncl; Sch Nwsp; Drama Clb; Dnfth Awd; Natl Merit Ltr; Univ; Med.

WODYKA, JAMES F; St Alphonsus HS; Detroit, MI; 65/171 Band; Chrh Wkr; Hon Rl; Orch; Coll; Engr.

WOEBER, KATHY A; Turpin HS; Cincinnati, OH; 28/371 Cls Rep Soph Cls; Girl Scts; Fr Clb; Letter Gym; Swmmng; Letter Chrldng; PPFtbl;.

WOEHNKER, JUDY; East Noble HS; Kendallville, IN; 72/242 Band; Chrh Wkr; OEA; VICA; Swmmng; Mat Maids; Indiana Central Univ; Nursing.

WOEHRLE, ANNE; Cass Tech HS; Detroit, MI; Chrh Wkr; Cmnty Wkr; Hon Rl; Orch; Pol Wkr; VP Yth Flsp; Rptr Sch Nwsp; Fr Clb; Swmmng; Coll; Liberal Arts.

WOEHRMYER, LINDA; Minster HS; Minster, OH; 17/79 Chrs; Cmnty Wkr; Hon Rl; Off Ade; Sch Mus; Sch Pl; Drama Clb; FTA; OEA; Pep Clb; Bus Schl.

WOEHRMYER, LISA; Oakwood HS; Dayton, OH; Band; Hon Rl; Lbry Ade; NHS; Orch; Univ; Tchr.

WOELFEL, DONNA; Mother Of Mercy HS; Cincinnati, OH; 22/235 Hon Rl; NHS; Lat Clb; Sci Clb; Trk; GAA; Ohio St Univ; Vet.

WOELFFER, MARY; Forest Park HS; Crystal Falls, MI; 3/90 Band; Chrs; Chrh Wkr; Hon Rl; Pres Stu Cncl; Capt Bsktbl; Letter Trk; Letter Chrldng; IM Sprt; Pres Physical Fitness Awd; A C A Youth Council V Pres Pres; Band Assistant; College.

WOELMER, THOMAS; Ida HS; Monroe, MI; Boy Scts; Chrh Wkr; NHS; Sct Actv; 4-H; Mich State Univ; Agri Tech.

WOERPEL, CRAIG; Escanaba Area HS; Escanaba, MI; 100/451 Am Leg Boys St; Band; Boy Scts; Sch Mus; Yrbk; Sch Nwsp; Michigan Tech Univ; Bus Admin.

WOERTZ, ROGER; South Central Jr Sr HS; Elizabeth, IN; VP Soph Cls; VP Jr Cls; Hon Rl; Sch Pl; Stg Crw; 4-H; FFA; Sci Clb; IM Sprt; 4-H Awd; Vocational Schl; Carpentry.

WOESTE, JOHN; Archbishop Alter HS; Kettering, OH; 2/332 Sal; Pres JA; NHS; Key Clb; IM Sprt; Natl Merit SF; Univ Of Dayton; Accounting.

WOESTE, ROBERTA; Chaminade Julienne HS; Dayton, OH; Chrs; Girl Scts; JA; Ger Clb; Trk; College; Engr.

WOHLSCHEID, LORI; Sacred Heart Academy; Mt Pleasant, MI; Chrs; Girl Scts; Hon Rl; Lat Clb; Vocational School.

WOHLSTEIN, KATHY; Athens HS; Athens, OH; Cls Rep Sr Cls; Pres Band; Chrs; MMM; NHS; Stu Cncl; Letter Trk; Capt Twrlr; Ntl Arion Award 1978; Ntl Schlstc Gold Key 1976; Superior At Dist & St Sci Fair 1978; Music.

WOIDKE, JULIE; Lutheran West HS; Lakewood, OH; 5/96 Chrs; Chrh Wkr; Hon Rl; NHS; Ger Clb; GAA; College; Environmental Tech.

WOJCIK, DENISE; Cntrl Catholic HS; Wheeling, WV; 4/132 Cls Rep Frsh Cls; Cl Rep Jr Cls; Cls Rep Sr Cls; Am Leg Aux Girls St; Cmnty Wkr; Hon Rl; Hosp Ade; Natl Forn Lg; Pres NHS; Quill & Scroll; Wheeling Univ; Bio.

WOJCIK, DIANE; Highland HS; Highland, IN; 114/494 Girl Scts; Hon Rl; Jr NHS; NHS; Pep Clb; PPFtbl; UGSI Girls Sftbl St Champ 75; In Hoosier Schlr 79; Whos Who 78; St Josephs Coll; Acctg.

WOJCIK, JEFF; Bishop Donahue HS; Wheeling, WV; Chrh Wkr; Hon Rl; Key Clb; Bsbl; Ftbl; Scr Kpr; Univ; Acctg.

WOJCIK, MIKE; St Clements HS; Detroit, MI; Hon Rl; NHS; Sci Clb; Bsbl; Ftbl; IM Sprt; Univ Of Detroit; Pre Med.

WOJCIK, TERRY; Deckerville HS; Deckervll, MI; Band; Hon Rl; Off Ade; Sch Mus; Stg Crw; College; Chem.

WOJDA, LIZABETH; St Josephs HS; South Bend, IN; 25/289 Chrh Wkr; NHS; Ger Clb; Univ Of Notre Dame; Law.

WOJKOVICH, GERALYNN; Andrean HS; Merrillville, IN; Cls Rep Frsh Cls; Cls Rep Soph Cls; Cl Rep Jr Cls; Girl Scts; Hon Rl; Sct Actv; Stu Cncl; Fr Clb; Ger Clb; Mth Clb; Valparaiso Univ; Acctg.

WOJNA, HELEN; St Florian HS; Detroit, MI; 6/109 Sec Soph Cls; VP Jr Cls; Hon Rl; NHS; Stu Cncl; Rptr Sch Nwsp; Pres FBLA; FNA; Pep Clb; Letter Bsktbl; Rep In Mission Club; Wayne St Univ; Comp Tech.

WOJNAR, ANNE; Saint Alphonsus HS; Detroit, MI; Hon Rl; College; Occupational Therapy.

WOJNAR, KEN; St Andrew HS; Detroit, MI; Cls Rep Soph Cls; Cl Rep Jr Cls; NHS; Rptr Yrbk; Yrbk; Univ Of Michigan; Comp Progr.

WOJNAR, ROSEANNE; Bishop Borgess HS; Redford Twp, MI; Chrs; Girl Scts; Hon Rl; NHS; Sch Nwsp; Spn Clb; IM Sprt; Am Leg Awd; Michigan St Univ; Jrnlsm.

WOJTALIK, ELAINE; Hamtramck HS; Hamtramck, MI; 1/70 Hon Rl; VP NHS; Quill & Scroll; Ed Sch Nwsp; Rptr Sch Nwsp; FSA; Mth Clb; Sci Clb; Michigan St Univ; Comp Sci.

WOJTAS, RICHARD; Deckerville Community HS; Deckerivlle, MI; Boy Scts; Chrh Wkr; Debate Tm; Natl Forn Lg; Off Ade; Yrbk; Ftbl; Mgrs; 4-H Awd; Voice Dem Awd; Siena Heights; Photog.

WOJTASIK, CHRIS; Lake Catholic HS; Willoughby Hs, OH; Aud/Vis; Boy Scts; Hon Rl; JA; Sct Actv; Rptr Sch Nwsp; 4-H; Lat Clb; 4-H Awd; JA Awd; Cleveland St Univ; Comp Sci.

WOJTEWILZ, ANN; Trinity HS; Maple Hts, OH; 14/143 Chrs; Hon Rl; JA; Off Ade; Yth Flsp; Pep Clb; Spn Clb; College; Airlines.

WOJTKUN, MARIANN; Erieview Catholic HS; Cleveland, OH; 2/120 Chrs; Chrh Wkr; Hon Rl; Sch Mus; Sch Pl; Rptr Sch Nwsp; Bsbl; Bsktbl; Coach Actv; IM Sprt; Univ; Acctg.

WOJTOWYCZ, JEFFREY; Fraser HS; Fraser, MI; Hon Rl; IM Sprt; Univ; Drafting.

WOJTYSIAK, BARB; A D Johnston HS; Ramsay, MI; Band; Chrs; Sch Mus; Sch Pl; Drama Clb; Pep Clb; Trk; Chrldng; PPFtbl;.

WOKEN, GREGORY; Buckeye Central HS; Chatfield, OH; 12/90 Trs Frsh Cls; Boy Scts; Chrh Wkr; Cmnty Wkr; Hon Rl; Lbry Ade; Sct Actv; Bsktbl; Ftbl; College.

WOLANCZYK, STEPHAN; Wilbur Wright HS; Dayton, OH; 4/250 Trs Jr Cls; Hon Rl; Stg Crw; Sch Nwsp; Fr Clb; Ger Clb; Bsbl; Glf; Cit Awd; Univ; Engr.

WOLANCZYK, SUSAN; Wilbur Wright HS; Dayton, OH; 2/218 Sal; Hon Rl; Jr NHS; NHS; Stu Cncl; Sch Nwsp; Fr Clb; FHA; Ger Clb; OEA; Miami Univ; Acctg.

WOLBERS, RACHELLE; Saranac HS; Clarksvle, MI; 3/90 Band; Girl Scts; Hon Rl; NHS; 4-H; Pep Clb; Letter Glf; Capt Chrldng; Btty Crckr Awd; Mercy Cntrl Schl Of Nursing; RN.

WOLCOTT, ALAN; Switzerland Cnty HS; Patriot, IN; Hon Rl; Sch Mus; Sch Pl; Rptr Sch Nwsp; Drama Clb; Fr Clb; Pep Clb; Bsbl; Bsktbl; Letter Glf; Marion Univ.

WOLF, BARRY; Zanesville HS; Zanesville, OH; 39/420 Am Leg Boys St; Band; Drm Bgl; Drm Mjrt; Hon Rl; NHS; Stg Crw; Sci Clb; Hughes Engr Schlrshp 79; 3.5 Clb 78; Ohio St Univ; Ceramic Engr.

WOLF, BRETT; Springfield Local HS; New Middletown, OH; 5/150 Trs Soph Cls; AFS; Hon Rl; Lbry Ade; NHS; Rptr Sch Nwsp; Fr Clb; Geneva College; Elec Engr.

WOLF, C; Clinton HS; Clinton, MI; Band; Girl Scts; Hon Rl; Yth Flsp; Spn Clb; Bsktbl; Trk; Western Mic Univ.

WOLF, DEBORAH; Marion HS; Marion, IN; Band; Hon Rl; Hosp Ade; Lbry Ade; NHS; Yth Flsp; 4-H; Ger Clb; Pep Clb; 4-H Awd; Univ; Bus.

WOLF, JEFFREY; Greenville HS; Greenville, MI; 6/231 Am Leg Boys St; Hon Rl; Stu Cncl; Fr Clb; Letter Ten; IM Sprt; All Confrnc In Tennis 78; Pres Schlrshp Alma Coll 79; Commndr Grow Awd; Character Awd; Mi Hon Comp Schlrshp; Notre Dame Univ.

WOLF, JOHN; Western Reserve Academy; Hudson, OH; VP Jr Cls; Lbry Ade; Stu Cncl; Ed Sch Nwsp; Letter Socr; Letter Ten; Natl Merit Ltr; Joel B Hayden Awd Top All Around Mbr Of The Jr Cl 79; Extemp Spkng Contest 1st Pl 78; Univ; Jrnlsm.

WOLF, KARIN; Hillsdale HS; Ashland, OH; 1/116 Trs Frsh Cls; Trs Soph Cls; VP Jr Cls; Pres Sr Cls; Am Leg Aux Girls St; Chrh Wkr; Cmnty Wkr; Hon Rl; NHS; Co Fair Queen 1978; Semi Finl Miss Teenage Amer 1978; Chr Publ Jr Fairbd 1977; Univ; Pre Med.

WOLF, KARYN; Allen Park HS; Allen Park, MI; Hon Rl; Gym; College; Physical Therapy.

WOLF, LARRY; E Liverpool HS; E Liverpool, OH; Band; FCA; Hon Rl; Spn Clb; Bsbl; Bsktbl; Coll Bowl & Chess Clb; Bd Of Ed Basic Studies Awd; Youngstown St Univ; Elec Engr.

WOLF, LEE; Hastings Sr HS; Hastings, MI; 26/365 Chrh Wkr; Cmnty Wkr; Hon Rl; NHS; Humanities Clb; Bio Clb VP Jr Yr; Elec By Parish To Parish Cncl; Gyman Briggs Coll; Med.

WOLF, LILLI; West Ottawa HS; Holland, MI; Band; Cmp Fr Grls; Hon Rl; Stu Cncl; 4-H; Ger Clb; Ten; Trk; 4-H Awd; Pres Awd; Univ; Vet.

WOLF, LISA A; Marlington HS; Canton, OH; 53/278 Pres Band; Chrh Wkr; Cmnty Wkr; Girl Scts; Sch Mus; Yth Flsp; 4-H; Sci Clb; Bsktbl; Trk; Akron Univ; Medicine.

WOLF, LORI; North Royalton HS; N Royalton, OH; Band; Girl Scts; Sct Actv; Drama Clb; FTA; OEA; Bsbl; GAA;.

WOLF, MARK; Southfield Lathrup HS; Southfield, MI; Hon Rl; IM Sprt; Cit Awd; Wayne St Univ; Med.

WOLF, MARY; Bishop Watterson HS; Columbus, OH; Chrs; Yth Flsp; Chrldng; College; Commercial Arts.

WOLF, PAUL; La Salle HS; Cincinnati, OH; Band; Sch Mus; Mth Clb; Univ; Comp Engr.

WOLF, RALE R; Brookville HS; Brookville, OH; 1/170 Pres Frsh Cls; Pres Soph Cls; Pres Jr Cls; Pres

Sr Cls; Am Leg Boys St; Band; Hon Rl; NHS; Sch Mus; Stu Cncl; Optimst Awd Outstndng Soph Boy; Schl Match Wits Team WKEF TV; Ohio Schlstc Ach Test 16th Plc In St Geom; Univ.

WOLF, RAY; Woodrow Wilson HS; Youngstwn, OH; 17/365 Aud/Vis; Hon Rl; NHS; Ger Clb; Key Clb; Sci Clb; Letter Bsktbl; Letter Ftbl; Recpnt Of Key Clb Awd For Otstndng Serv 77; Youngstown St Univ; Engr.

WOLF, ROBERT; Mount Clemens HS; Mt Clemens, MI; 2/300 NHS; Stu Cncl; Rptr Yrbk; Rptr Sch Nwsp; Lat Clb; Letter Glf; Letter Socr; Letter Swmmng; Letter Ten; Cit Awd; Newspaper Sports Column 3rd Pl In St Comp 78 79; Swim Team Most Vlbl Swimmer Awd 78 79; Univ Of Michigan; Pre Med.

WOLF, SCOTT; Northridge HS; Mt Vernon, OH; 15/114 Band; Hon Rl; Orch; Rptr Sch Nwsp; Sch Nwsp; Pres 4-H; Pres Spn Clb; 4-H Awd; Ohio St Univ.

WOLF, THERESA; Bishop Noll Inst; Hammond, IN; 47/321 Band; Chrs; Drl Tm; Girl Scts; Hon Rl; NHS; Sch Mus; Stu Cncl; Rptr Yrbk; Pep Clb; Coll; Engr.

WOLF, VICTORIA; David Anderson HS; Lisbon, OH; Chrs; Hon Rl; Lbry Ade; Sch Mus; Sch Pl; Lab Tech.

WOLF, WENDY; Logansport HS; Logansport, IN; 49/349 Pol Wkr; Y-Teens; Yrbk; Fr Clb; Ten; Chrldng; Ball St Univ; Art.

WOLFCALE, AMY; Canfield HS; Canfield, OH; 16/280 Sec Jr Cls; Cls Rep Sr Cls; Debate Tm; Jr NHS; Lit Mag; Sch Mus; Sch Pl; Stu Cncl; Rptr Sch Nwsp; Witenburg Univ; Law.

WOLFE, BONNIE; Quincy HS; Ray, IN; 4/110 Hst Frsh Cls; Hst Soph Cls; Hst Jr Cls; Hst Sr Cls; Band; Hon Rl; NHS; Off Ade; Pep Clb; Letter Trk; Coll; Med.

WOLFE, CONNIE; Sterling Heights HS; Warren, MI; Cl Rep Jr Cls; Cls Rep Sr Cls; Girl Scts; Hon Rl; Stu Cncl; DECA; Opt Clb Awd; Adrian Coll; Acctg.

WOLFE, CONNIE; Quincy HS; Ray, IN; 5/110 Cls Rep Soph Cls; Cl Rep Jr Cls; Band; Hon Rl; NHS; Off Ade; Stu Cncl; Trk; Capt Chrldng; Ferris State Univ; Dentistry.

WOLFE, DEBBIE; Anderson HS; Cincinnati, OH; 102/387 Band; Girl Scts; Lbry Ade; Lat Clb; Tmr; Univ; Data Process.

WOLFE, DON; Indian Valley North HS; New Phila, OH; Pres Soph Cls; Boy Scts; Hon Rl; Jr NHS; NHS; Stg Crw; Yrbk; Sch Nwsp; Spn Clb; Bsbl; Univ Of Akron; Computer Sci.

WOLFE, JIM; Fairmont Sr HS; Fairmont, WV; VP Frsh Cls; Pres Soph Cls; Cl Rep Jr Cls; Am Leg Boys St; Chrs; NHS; Pres Stu Cncl; Drama Clb; Pres Key Clb; Univ.

WOLFE, JOHN; Richmond Sr HS; Richmond, IN; 45/550 VP FCA; Hon Rl; Jr NHS; NHS; Letter Crs Cntry; Letter Trk; IM Sprt; Gannett Schlshp 79; Marine Corps Marathon Winner 77; Depauw Univ; Math.

WOLFE, JULIE; Delta HS; Albany, IN; 12/294 Cls Rep Soph Cls; Cl Rep Jr Cls; Cls Rep Sr Cls; Band; Chrh Wkr; Cmnty Wkr; Girl Scts; Hon Rl; Jr NHS; NHS; Purdue Univ; Fashion Retailing.

WOLFE, JUNIOR G; Central Preston HS; Albright, WV; 5/167 Am Leg Boys St; Boy Scts; Chrs; Chrh Wkr; Hon Rl; NHS; Sct Actv; Stu Cncl; Sch Nwsp; FFA; Chamer Gibson Awrd For Congnlty 78; B F Mc Connell Memrl Schlrshp 78; St Farmer Degree Awrd Future Farmers; West Virginia Univ; Agri Prodctn.

WOLFE, KAREN; Bedford North Lawrence HS; Avoca, IN; 122/417 Sec Jr Cls; Sec Sr Cls; Band; Drl Tm; Hon Rl; Red Cr Ade; Stu Cncl; FHA; OEA; Trk; Indiana Voc Tech Coll; Med Asst.

WOLFE, KAREN; Oberlin Sr HS; Oberlin, OH; 18/133 Chrs; Chrh Wkr; Hon Rl; NHS; Off Ade; Sch Mus; Sch Pl; Yth Flsp; Drama Clb; Letter Ten; Wittenberg Univ; Spec Ed.

WOLFE, KEVIN B; Stonewall Jackson HS; Charleston, WV; Wrstlng; Comp Ben Franklin Career & Tech Course In Elec 78; Comp In Wheels Sponsered By Firestone Tire & Rbr Co 79; Elk Career Center Voc Schl; Elec.

WOLFE, KIMBERLY; Stow HS; Stow, OH; Chrs; Chrh Wkr; Lbry Ade; Off Ade; Rptr Sch Nwsp; OEA; Gym; Chrldng; Coach Actv; IM Sprt; Kent St Univ; Dance.

WOLFE, MICHAEL; Central Preston Sr HS; Thornton, WV; 3/163 Hon Rl; Sec NHS; Pres 4-H; Sec FFA; Sci Clb; 4-H Awd; St Farmer Degree FFA 79; Otstndng Proficiency In Amer History Awd 78; Mbr Of Parliamentry Procdr Tm 79; Univ; Agri.

WOLFE, PAULA; Southern HS; Racine, OH; Sec Frsh Cls; Trs Frsh Cls; Cls Rep Soph Cls; Chrs; Hon Rl; Stu Cncl; Fr Clb; Pep Clb; Trk; Chrldng; Rio Grande College; Schl Cnslr.

WOLFE, RANDALL; Colon HS; Burr Oak, MI; Hon Rl; NHS; Sch Mus; Sch Pl; Rptr Sch Nwsp; Fr Clb; Univ.

WOLFE, STEVEN; Beaver Local HS; E Liverpool, OH; Band; Chrs; ROTC; Sch Pl; Drama Clb; Fr Clb; Crs Cntry; Wrstlng; Ohio St Univ; Sci.

WOLFE, WALTER; Martins Ferry HS; Martins Ferry, OH; 26/215 Letter Bsbl; Letter Bsktbl; Letter Crs Cntry; Ftbl; College.

WOLFE JR, REGINALD; North Miami Jr Sr HS; Mexico, IN; Chrh Wkr; Hon Rl; Yth Flsp; 4-H; FFA; Bsktbl; 4-H Awd; Natl Merit Ltr; Ivy Tech Schl; Engr.

WOLFEL, CHRISTINE; River Valley HS; Caledonia, OH; 14/196 Band; NHS; Orch; Sch Mus; Pres 4-H; Sci Clb; Scr Kpr; College; Mathematics.

WOLFER, MARY; Clermont Northeastern HS; Marathon, OH; 17/234 Pres Soph Cls; Band; FCA; Sch Pl; Stu Cncl; Drama Clb; 4-H; Spn Clb; Trk; IM Sprt; Top Hon In Instrumental Music 78; 2nd Plc Cnty Sh otput 5th Sectionals & 6th District 78; Univ; Art.

WOLFER, MICHAEL; Mcnicholas HS; Cincinnati, OH; Aud/Vis; Chrh Wkr; Cmnty Wkr; Hon Rl; Lbry Ade; Off Ade; Stg Crw; Ger Clb; Scr Kpr; Tmr; St Thomas More College; Architecture.

WOLFF, DAVID; John Adams HS; Mishawaka, IN; Cmnty Wkr; Hon Rl; Sch Nwsp; Ger Clb; Sci Clb; Gym; Trk; Univ; Sci.

WOLFF, DEBBIE; John Glenn HS; Wlakerton, IN; 14/100 Girl Scts; Hon Rl; Sch Pl; Sct Actv; Yth Flsp; 4-H; FHA; Pep Clb; Letter Gym; Trk; Robertons Schlstc Achvmnt 1978; Kodack Eastman Winner 1978; Jr Miss Miss Congenalty 1978; Univ; Fashion Mdse.

WOLFF, JAMES R; Mona Shores HS; Muskegon, MI; Sch Pl; Rptr Sch Nwsp; DECA; Letter Ftbl; Letter Wrstlng; Opt Clb Awd; Placed 2nd In St DECA Competition 78; Competed In DECA Natls 78; Muskegon Cmnty Coll; Bus Admin.

WOLFF, JEFF; Brownstown Central HS; Vallonia, IN; 30/143 Boy Scts; Yth Flsp; Treas FFA; Bsktbl; IM Sprt; Farmer.

WOLFF, SHELLY; Maple Valley HS; Nashville, MI; 1/130 Cls Rep Sr Cls; Val; Band; Hon Rl; VP NHS; Stu Cncl; Trk; Chrldng; PPFtbl; Cit Awd; Central Michigan Univ; Bus.

WOLFGANG, BONNIE; Jay Cnty HS; Dunkirk, IN; Chrh Wkr; Hon Rl; Jr NHS; NHS; Pres Yth Flsp; Y-Teens; VP 4-H; Fr Clb; Trk; GAA; Ball St Univ.

WOLFGANG, KAREN; Bridgeport HS; Bridgeport, WV; Sec Chrs; Hon Rl; NHS; Off Ade; Letter Trk; Toured Spain With Fellow Stu In Span Class 79; Also Lttrd In Track Soph Yr 78; Univ.

WOLFLIN, ROSEMARY; Marion HS; Marion, IN; Band; NHS; Orch; Bsktbl; Trk; Mgrs; Tmr; Cntrl Mi Univ Bnd Comp 76 & 77; Indiana Univ; Scndry Educ.

WOLFORD, DIANNA; Crestview HS; Greenwich, OH; Cls Rep Frsh Cls; Band; Hon Rl; Lbry Ade; Stu Cncl; Rptr Sch Nwsp; Sch Nwsp; Fr Clb; FTA; Chrldng; Ohio St Univ; Acctg.

WOLFORD, DOUGLAS D; East Fairmont HS; Fairmont, WV; Am Leg Boys St; Band; Hon Rl; Fr Clb; Key Clb; Mth Clb; Sci Clb; West Virginia Univ; Med.

WOLFORD, JANET; North Side HS; Ft Wayne, IN; 20/449 Band; NHS; PPFtbl; C of C Awd; St Francis College; Tchr For Mr.

WOLFORD, KELLE; Hurricane HS; Hurricane, WV; 1/187 Pres Jr Cls; Val; Band; NHS; Quill & Scroll; Stu Cncl; Y-Teens; Ed Yrbk; Lion Awd; Chemistry Awd; College; Engr.

WOLFORD, KEVIN; Rochester Community HS; Rochester, IN; Hon Rl; Fr Clb; Mgrs; Univ; Law.

WOLFRAM, DALE; Grand Blanc HS; Grand Blanc, MI; Chrh Wkr; Hon Rl; NHS; Sch Pl; Yrbk; FSA; FTA; Sci Clb; Glf; Univ Of Miami; Oceanographer.

WOLIN, MARK; Oak Park HS; Oak Pk, MI; Boy Scts; Cmp Fr Grls; JA; Sct Actv; FDA; Spn Clb; JA Awd; College; Med.

WOLK, KIMBERLEY; Turpin HS; Cincinnati, OH; 11/357 Cls Rep Soph Cls; Am Leg Aux Girls St; Chrs; Hosp Ade; NHS; Stu Cncl; PPFtbl; Univ Of Cincinnati.

WOLKA, CHERYL; Brownstown Central HS; Brownstown, IN; Am Leg Aux Girls St; Chrs; Girl Scts; Pol Wkr; 4-H; Spn Clb; GAA;.

WOLL, CHRISTINA; Mount Notre Dame HS; Cincinnati, OH; Cls Rep Sr Cls; Chrh Wkr; Hon Rl; Mod UN; NHS; Stu Cncl; Pep Clb; Spn Clb; Miami Univ; Acctg.

WOLL, JOHN P; Univ Of Detroit HS; Southfield, MI; 4/138 Cls Rep Soph Cls; Cl Rep Jr Cls; Cls Rep Sr Cls; Val; Boy Scts; Chrh Wkr; Debate Tm; Hon Rl; Mod UN; NHS; Princeton Univ; Law.

WOLLENBERG, PENNY; New Lexington HS; New Lexington, OH; 25/170 Cl Rep Jr Cls; Cls Rep Sr Cls; NHS; VP Stu Cncl; Ed Yrbk; Capt Bsktbl; Capt Trk; Chrldng; GAA; Bowling Green State Univ; Spec Ed.

WOLLENHAUPT, KIZ; Northmont HS; Englewood, OH; 12/560 Band; Chrh Wkr; Hon Rl; Orch; Yth Flsp; Ger Clb; Pep Clb; JC Awd; Brigham Young; Music Educ.

WOLLENZIEN, DANA; Huntington East HS; Huntington, WV; Aud/Vis; Chrs; Hosp Ade; Sch Mus; Rptr Sch Nwsp; DECA; FBLA; WVA Music Teachers Assoc Competition For Exceptional 77 & 78; Huntington Coll; Finance.

WOLLSCHLAGER, LENA; John Glenn HS; Westland, MI; Cmp Fr Grls; Hon Rl; NHS; Swmmng; Univ Of Mic; Chem.

WOLMAN, KIMBERLY; Whitehall Yearling HS; Whitehall, OH; Cls Rep Frsh Cls; Cls Rep Soph Cls; Sec Jr Cls; Drl Tm; Hon Rl; JA; Off Ade; Red Cr Ade; Sch Mus; Sch Pl; Natl Jr Achievers Conference; Cert Of Achievement US Army; Miami Univ; Busns Admin.

WOLNY, DIANE; Regina HS; Mt Clemens, MI; 7/134 Hon Rl; NHS; PPFtbl; Central Michigan Univ; Ct Reporter.

WOLTER, CYNTHIA; Chelsea HS; Chelsea, MI; Band; Debate Tm; Orch; Sch Mus; Univ Of Michigan; Music.

WOLTERS, DAWN R; Zeeland HS; Zeeland, MI; 9/180 Hon Rl; JA; Lat Clb; Natl Merit SF; Univ Of Michigan; Physical Therapy.

WOLTERS, JANE; Coldwater HS; Coldwater, OH; Band; Chrs; Hon Rl; Lbry Ade; FHA; Spn Clb; IM Sprt; College; Math.

WOLTJER, LAURIE L; South Christian HS; Caledonia, MI; Chrs; Chrh Wkr; Lbry Ade; Sec Yth Flsp; Chic Univ Of Cosmetology; Vocation.

WOLZ, MICHELLE; Floyd Central HS; Floyd Knobs, IN; Am Leg Aux Girls St; Cmnty Wkr; Hon Rl; Mod UN; NHS; Sec Stu Cncl; Pres 4-H; Sec Lat Clb; DAR Awd; 4-H Awd; Purdue Univ; Agri Engr.

WONACOTT, LAURA; Elk Rapids HS; Rapid City, MI; 1/90 VP Jr Cls; VP Sr Cls; Debate Tm; Jr NHS; NHS; Sch Pl; Rptr Yrbk; Letter Bsktbl; Letter Trk; Alma Coll; Bio.

WONDERS, JEFFREY; Jonesville HS; Jonesville, MI; Hon Rl; Sprt Ed Yrbk; Letter Bsbl; Letter Bsktbl; Letter Crs Cntry; Made All Conf & All Rgn Tm In Bsbl 79; Was Co Capt Bsbl Tm 79; Rec Bsbl Most Valuable Play Awd On Tm 79; Central Michigan Univ; Comp Progr.

WONG, AUDREY; Taylor HS; N Bend, OH; Cls Rep Soph Cls; Cl Rep Jr Cls; Sec Sr Cls; Hon Rl; Jr NHS; Stu Cncl; Pep Clb; Bsktbl; Letter Trk; SAR Awd; Univ Of Ct; CPA.

WONG, KWONG; Finney HS; Detroit, MI; 2/200 Sal; Hon Rl; Lbry Ade; NHS; Off Ade; Mth Clb; Cit Awd; Wayne State Univ; Engr.

WONKA, ELIZABETH M; Carroll HS; Dayton, OH; Chrh Wkr; Cmnty Wkr; Hon Rl; Pol Wkr; Sch Pl; Stg Crw; Rptr Sch Nwsp; Drama Clb; College; Pre Law.

WOOD, BLAKE; Lincoln Consolidated HS; Willis, MI; 6/200 Ftbl; Trk; Eastern Michigan Univ; Bio.

WOOD, BRAD; Whiteford HS; Ottawa Lk, MI; Boy Scts; Chrs; Hon Rl; Sch Pl; Stu Cncl; Glf; Wrstlng; Coll; Engr.

WOOD, BRENDA; North Putnam Jr Sr HS; Bainbridge, IN; FCA; Girl Scts; NHS; OEA; Pep Clb; Gym; Swmmng; Trk; Chrldng; Mat Maids; Indiana St Univ; Bsns.

WOOD, CAROL; Marlette HS; Marlette, MI; 20/136 Band; Chrh Wkr; Hon Rl; NHS; Stu Cncl; Yth Flsp; Yrbk; DECA; 4-H; 4-H Awd; Mi Educ Schlrshp 79; 4 H Queens Ct 78; 4 H St Dairy Foods Winner 78; Baker Jr Coll Of Bus; Leg Sec.

WOOD, CHERYL; Allen Park HS; Allen Park, MI; 2/386 Band; Chrs; Hon Rl; Jr NHS; NHS; Gym; Chrldng; Univ Of Mic; Pre Dentistry.

WOOD, CONNA; Ben Davis Sr HS; Indianapolis, IN; 42/849 Chrs; Debate Tm; Hon Rl; Natl Forn Lg; Sch Mus; Drama Clb; Lat Clb; Univ; Poli Sci.

WOOD, DARCI; Whiteland Cmnty HS; New Whiteland, IN; 28/192 Pres Sr Cls; AFS; Am Leg Aux Girls St; FCA; NHS; Stu Cncl; Pres FHA; Pep Clb; Letter Trk; DAR Awd; Indiana Univ; Pre Med.

WOOD, DENISE A; Rockville Jr Sr HS; Rockville, IN; Hon Rl; Chrldng; PPFtbl; Univ; Meteorology.

WOOD, DONALD; Southgate HS; Southgate, MI; Band; Hon Rl; Jr NHS; Sch Mus; Sch Pl; Stg Crw; Rptr Yrbk; Rptr Sch Nwsp; Univ; Bus.

WOOD, EDDIE; Madison Heights HS; Anderson, IN; 158/371 Chrh Wkr; Cmnty Wkr; Stu Cncl; Letter Crs Cntry; Letter Trk; Pres Phys Fitness Awd 74 76 & 78;.

WOOD, ELAINE; Midland Trail HS; Rainelle, WV; Hon Rl; NHS; Stu Cncl; Yrbk; IM Sprt; Bus Schl; Acctg.

WOOD, ELLEN; Clyde HS; Clyde, OH; 69/213 Capt Bsktbl; Capt Trk; GAA; West Point Academy; Engr.

WOOD, GAIL; Washington HS; South Bend, IN; 21/355 Trs Frsh Cls; Trs Soph Cls; Trs Jr Cls; Trs Sr Cls; NHS; Sch Mus; Drama Clb; Ten; Chrldng; College.

WOOD, GAIL; Rutherford B Hayes HS; Delaware, OH; AFS; Hon Rl; NHS; Ger Clb; Pep Clb; Trk; Mgrs; Scr Kpr; Ohio St Univ; Lib Arts.

WOOD, JAMES; John Glenn HS; New Concord, OH; 10/184 NHS; Letter Ftbl; Letter Trk; Voice Dem Awd; Univ.

WOOD, JAYNELLEN; Gallia Academy; Gallipolis, OH; Hon Rl; Sch Pl; Stg Crw; Yth Flsp; Yrbk; Rptr Sch Nwsp; Drama Clb; 4-H; Spn Clb; Chrldng; Miami Univ.

WOOD, JEFFERY; Winfield HS; Scott Depot, WV; 9/123 Hon Rl; Jr NHS; NHS; Beta Clb; Marshall Univ; Bio Sci.

WOOD, JENNI; Bellbrook HS; Bellbrook, OH; Cls Rep Frsh Cls; Cls Rep Soph Cls; Band; Girl Scts; Hon Rl; NHS; Treas Stu Cncl; Yth Flsp; Rptr Yrbk; Lat Clb; Softball Varsity Letter; Volleyball; Honor Seminar Finalist; College; Med Tech.

WOOD, JERRY; River Valley HS; Marion, OH; FCA; Hon Rl; NHS; Fr Clb; Sci Clb; Crs Cntry; Ten; Univ; Elec Engr.

WOOD, JERRY B; River Valley HS; Marion, OH; FCA; Hon Rl; NHS; 4-H; Fr Clb; Sci Clb; Letter Ten; Coach Actv; 4-H Awd; Univ; Elec Engr.

WOOD, JOHN; Ogemaw Heights HS; West Branch, MI; Hon Rl; Letter Ftbl; Mic State Univ; Engr.

WOOD, JONATHAN L; Tri County HS; Howard City, MI; Cl Rep Jr Cls; Chrh Wkr; Hon Rl; Yth Flsp; Natl Merit SF; VFW Awd; Voice Dem Awd; Alma Coll; Sociology.

WOOD, JULIE; Pike Delta York Sr HS; Delta, OH; FHA; FTA; Mth Clb; Pep Clb; Sci Clb; Spn Clb; Trk; GAA; Bowling Green St Univ; Mgmt.

WOOD, KENT; Richmond Dale HS; Chillicothe, OH; Boy Scts; Hon Rl; Cit Awd; God Cntry Awd; College.

WOOD, KIMBERLEY; N Montgomery HS; Crawfordsville, IN; 21/210 Sec Sr Cls; Cls Rep Sr Cls; Am Leg Aux Girls St; Cmp Fr Grls; Chrh Wkr; Drl Tm; FCA; Hon Rl; JA; Quill & Scroll; Purdue Univ; Art.

WOOD, KIMBERLY; Chelsea HS; Chelsea, MI; Hon Rl; Lbry Ade; Chmn Bsktbl; Letter Swmmng; Coach Actv; College.

WOOD, LANCE; Fulton HS; Middleton, MI; Debate Tm; Hon Rl; 4-H; Pres FFA; Bsktbl; IM Sprt; MSU; Agriculture.

WOOD, LESA; Princeton HS; Princeton, WV; Chrs; Hon Rl; Jr NHS; Pep Clb; College.

WOOD, LISA; Algonac HS; Algonac, MI; Hon Rl; NHS; Sct Actv; Letter Bsktbl; Mich State Univ; Vet.

WOOD, LISA; Mississinewa HS; Gas City, IN; 19/250 Trs Frsh Cls; Hon Rl; Jr NHS; Stu Cncl; DECA; FHA; OEA; Pep Clb; Chrldng; Pom Pon; Ball State Univ; Bus.

WOOD, LISA; Douglas Mac Arthur HS; Saginaw, MI; Hon Rl; Lit Mag; Ed Sch Nwsp; Rptr Sch Nwsp; Michigan St Univ; Journalism.

WOOD, LORI; Meigs HS; Pomeroy, OH; Cls Rep Frsh Cls; Cls Rep Soph Cls; Cl Rep Jr Cls; Cls Rep Sr Cls; Am Leg Aux Girls St; Band; Chrs; Chrh Wkr; Drm Bgl; Hon Rl; West Virginia Univ; Music Educ.

WOOD, LORIE; Shadyside HS; Shadyside, OH; Hon Rl; Sch Mus; Y-Teens; Drama Clb; Chrldng; GAA; IM Sprt; Ohio St Univ; Med Tech.

WOOD, MARY; Gallia Academy HS; Bidwell, OH; Band; Chrh Wkr; NHS; 4-H; 4-H Awd; Natl Merit Ltr; Schlrshp Tm Chem 1 6th In Dist & Geometry 3rd In Dist 76; Solo & Ensemble Contest OBOE Solo Superior 78; David Lipscomb Coll.

WOOD, MICHAEL; St Joseph HS; Lyndhurst, OH; Letter Socr; Letter Trk; IM Sprt; Ohio St Univ; Mech Engr.

WOOD, MIKE; Jackson Milton HS; North Jackson, OH; 4/102 Band; Boy Scts; Chrs; Chrh Wkr; Hon Rl; NHS; Off Ade; Sch Mus; Sct Actv; Key Clb; Ohio St Univ; Med Tech.

WOOD, PAMELA; Franklin Cmnty HS; Franklin, IN; 37/285 Drl Tm; Hon Rl; Jr NHS; Sch Mus; 4-H; Pep Clb; Sci Clb; Spn Clb; Swmmng; Chrldng; Purdue Univ; Indus Mgmt.

WOOD, RAE; Penn HS; Bremen, IN; Chrs; Hon Rl; Jr NHS; Spn Clb; Letter Bsktbl; Trk; IM Sprt; PPFtbl; Tmr; Univ; Poli Sci.

WOOD, RYAN; Columbia City Joint HS; Columbia City, IN; VP Ger Clb; Letter Ftbl; Letter Glf; IM Sprt; Qualif For St Natl Ins Yth Golf Classic 79; Univ; Bus Mgmt.

WOOD, SANDRA; Mumford HS; Detroit, MI; Hon Rl; VP JA; Jr NHS; NHS; Off Ade; ROTC; Sch Pl; Sch Nwsp; Drama Clb; JA Awd; Good Citz Awd From Cnslr 1977; Perfect Attnd Awd 1978; Univ.

WOOD, SARAH; Peru HS; Peru, IN; 16/271 Sec Frsh Cls; Sec Soph Cls; Sec Jr Cls; VP Sr Cls; Hon Rl; JA; Jr NHS; NHS; Stu Cncl; Crs Cntry; Univ Of Kentucky; Elem Ed.

WOOD, STEVEN; Hilliard HS; Hilliard, OH; 75/342 Hon Rl; Cit Awd; JC Awd; Ohio State Univ; Stocks.

WOOD, SUZANNE; Oak Hill HS; Oak Hill, WV; VP Frsh Cls; VP Soph Cls; Sch Pl; Stg Crw; Stu Cncl; Yrbk; Drama Clb; Pres 4-H; Letter Ten; Letter Trk; Schlsp To Forest Indust Camp 79; Wv St HS Drama Awd Exlln In Playwrtng 79; Oak Hill HS Psycha Wd; West Virginia Univ.

WOOD, TANYA; Parkside HS; Jackson, MI; Cl Rep Jr Cls; Chrh Wkr; Girl Scts; Hon Rl; Stu Cncl; Fr Clb; Jackson Community College; Bus Admin.

WOOD, TERA; Roosevelt Wilson HS; Clarksburg, WV; Hon Rl; Lit Mag; Sch Pl; Y-Teens; Rptr Sch Nwsp; Sch Nwsp; Fr Clb; FTA; Rdo Clb; Fairmont St Univ; Law Enforcement.

WOOD, THOMAS; Shady Spring HS; Beaver, WV; Hon Rl; Off Ade; Sch Nwsp; Pep Clb; Bsbl; Bsktbl; VICA; Ftbl; Trk; Wrstlng; W Virginia Inst Of Tech; Civil Engr.

WOOD, VALERIE; Mt Pleasant HS; Mt Pleasant, MI; Chrs; Chrh Wkr; Hon Rl; Mdrgl; Sch Pl; PPFtbl; 4-H Awd; CMU.

WOOD, VALERIE J; Manistique Area HS; Manistique, MI; 10/170 Cls Rep Frsh Cls; Trs Soph Cls; NHS; Stu Cncl; Pres 4-H; Letter Trk; Capt Chrldng; 4-H Awd; Natl Merit SF; Voice Dem Awd; Maniskique Youth Comm 1975; Student Rep Lbry Advsry Brd 1978; Mi Cmptve Schlrshp 1979; Central Michigan Univ; Communication.

WOOD, WENDY; Monsignor John R Hackett HS; Schoolcraft, MI; Many Awds In Horsemanship 77 78 79; Texas A & M Univ; Psych.

WOOD, WINNIE; L C Mohr HS; South Haven, MI; Chrs; Chrh Wkr; Girl Scts; Hon Rl; Pep Clb; Letter Bsbl; Letter Bsktbl; Wayne State; Occupational Ther.

WOODALL, ANNIE; Akron South HS; Akron, OH; 18/138 Pres Soph Cls; Pres Jr Cls; Pres Sr Cls; JA; Eng Clb; Pep Clb; Bsktbl; Trk; Coach Actv; Ore St; Sociology.

WOODARD, BETSY; Grand Ledge HS; Lansing, MI; 2/418 Pres Soph Cls; Pres Jr Cls; Sal; Am Leg Aux Girls St; Hon Rl; NHS; Stu Cncl; Mic State Univ; English Educ.

WOODARD, CHERYL L; Heritage Christian HS; Indianapolis, IN; Sec Jr Cls; Chrh Wkr; Girl Scts; Hon Rl; Lbry Ade; Sch Mus; Sch Pl; Stg Crw; Yth Flsp; Awana Timothy Awd; Sci Fair; Indiana Univ; Nursing.

WOODARD, JOHN; Bay HS; Bay Village, OH; 54/379 Am Leg Boys St; Lit Mag; Natl Forn Lg; Sch Pl; Yrbk; Letter Trk; Rotary Awd; Book Awd Brown Univ 79; Natl Thespian Soc Hd Of Publcty 79; Demolay Sr Cnslr 79; Univ; Bio.

WOODARD, TAMMY; Caro Community School; Caro, MI; Sec Frsh Cls; VP Soph Cls; Band; Chrh Wkr; Cmnty Wkr; Hon Rl; NHS; Off Ade; Yth Flsp; Ferris St Coll; RN.

WOODBRIDGE, LISA A; Huntington Pickaway Ross; Chillicothe, OH; Band; Chrh Wkr; Cmnty Wkr; Hon Rl; NHS; Sch Nwsp; 4-H; FTA; Pres OEA; Trk; Ohio Univ; Law.

WOODCOCK, STEVE; Montabella HS; Mcbride, MI; Cls Rep Frsh Cls; Pres Soph Cls; Hon Rl; NHS; Stu Cncl; Spn Clb; Letter Ftbl; Aquinas Coll; Med.

WOODFORD, JOHN; Gilmer County HS; Tanner, WV; 28/104 Chrh Wkr; Cmnty Wkr; Hon Rl; FFA; Pep Clb; VICA; Bsbl; Bsktbl; Ftbl; Trk;.

WOODFORD, SUZANNE; Hudson Area HS; Hudson, MI; 25/117 Band; Hon Rl; Lbry Ade; Off Ade; Drama Clb; Spn Clb; Trk;.

WOODFORD, THOMAS; Jefferson HS; Charles Town, WV; 2/307 Sal; Treas Am Leg Boys St; Hon Rl; NHS; 4-H; Sci Clb; Pres Spn Clb; Duke Univ; Med.

WOODFORK, JUANITA; Columbus E HS; Columbus, OH; 7/272 Girl Scts; Hon Rl; JA; Lbry Ade; NHS; Stu Cncl; Sch Nwsp; Spn Clb; VICA; Am Leg Awd; Ohio St Univ; Histotechnology.

WOOD JR, IRA LEE; Greenbrier East HS; Alderson, WV; Chrs; Chrh Wkr; Cmnty Wkr; FCA; Hon Rl; Yth Flsp; 4-H; FFA; Pep Clb; Ftbl; Univ; Law.

WOODLAND, DAN; Grand Ledge HS; Lansing, MI; Band; Chrh Wkr; Hon Rl; NHS; Treas Yth Flsp; Lat Clb; Nalt Latin Exam Cert Of Hon Mnt Magna Cum Laude 78; Alma Coll; Pre Dent.

WOODLEY, TERRI; West Side HS; Gary, IN; 48/650 Chrs; Hon Rl; NHS; Off Ade; Sch Pl; Tmr; Nassau Community College; Secr Sci.

WOODLIFF, SUSAN; Kenmore HS; Akron, OH; 5/300 Chrs; Girl Scts; Hon Rl; NHS; Sch Mus; Sch Pl; Sct Actv; Stu Cncl; Fr Clb; Pep Clb; 3rd Pl In City Champ Gymnstc Meet 79; Var Team Br 76 80; MVMP Gymnstc 79; Bowling Green St Univ; Cmnctns.

WOODRING, KURT; Mason Sr HS; Mason, MI; Cls Rep Frsh Cls; Cl Rep Jr Cls; AFS; Chrs; Sch Mus; Stu Cncl; Sci Clb; Wrstlng; Cit Awd; W Michigan Univ.

WOODRING, LORETTA J; East Preston Sr HS; Terra Alta, WV; Cls Rep Frsh Cls; Cls Rep Soph Cls; Cl Rep Jr Cls; Hon Rl; Mdrgl; FBLA; Pep Clb; Chrldng; Natl Merit Ltr; Voice Dem Awd; Busns Schl; CPA.

WOODRUFF, CONNIE; Rogers HS; Michigan City, IN; 100/483 Cls Rep Frsh Cls; Cls Rep Soph Cls; Aud/Vis; Band; Chrs; Hon Rl; NHS; PAVAS; Sch Mus; Sch Pl; Purdue Univ; Archt.

WOODRUFF, CYNTHIA; Shakamak HS; Jasonville, IN; Quill & Scroll; Treas Stu Cncl; Rptr Yrbk; Treas Drama Clb; ISU; Psych.

WOODRUFF, JACK R; Clay City HS; Clay City, IN; 9/59 Pres Soph Cls; Pres Jr Cls; Pres Sr Cls; Am Leg Boys St; Hon Rl; NHS; Stu Cncl; Yth Flsp; Pres Fr Clb; Mth Clb; Indiana St Univ; Law.

WOODRUFF, JEFF; Bridgman HS; Bridgman, MI; Boy Scts; Hon Rl; Off Ade; Mth Clb; Sci Clb; Michigan Tech Univ; Physics.

WOODRUFF, JOHN; Wood Memorial HS; Oakland City, IN; Hon Rl; Pep Clb; Glf; Vocational Schl.

WOODRUFF, LARRY; Heritage HS; New Haven, IN; 25/187 Boy Scts; Hon Rl; Mth Clb; Spn Clb; Bsbl; Ftbl; Gym; Wrstlng; IM Sprt; Purdue; Comp Sci.

WOODRUFF, MIKE; Malabar HS; Mansfield, OH; Cls Rep Sr Cls; Band; Boy Scts; Chrh Wkr; FCA; Hon Rl; Sct Actv; Crs Cntry; Letter Trk; Wrstlng; Ohio St Univ; Med.

WOODRUFF, RHONDA; Delphos Jefferson Sr HS; Delphos, OH; Chrh Wkr; Hon Rl; Y-Teens; OEA; Spn Clb; GAA; Bus Schl.

WOODRUFF, TINA; Tippecanoe Valley HS; Claypool, IN; 3/158 Cmnty Wkr; Hon Rl; Hosp Ade; NHS; FTA; Ball State Univ; Education.

WOODRUFF, WESLEY J; Point Pleasant HS; Point Pleasant, WV; 10/270 Cl Rep Jr Cls; Am Leg Boys St; Band; Capt Drl Tm; Hon Rl; Pres NHS; Stu Cncl; Fr Clb; Key Clb; Bsbl; Math Awd 10 & 11th Grd Hghst In Whole Schl 77 79; W Virginia Inst Of Tech; Mech Engr.

WOODRUM, KAREN; Elgin HS; Marion, OH; 21/155 Letter Bsktbl; Capt PPFtbl; Ohi St Univ; Bus Admin.

WOODRUM, MARK; Ironton HS; Ironton, OH; College; Engr.

WOODRUM, TAMMALA; Gabriel Richard HS; Ypsilanti, MI; 1/88 Val; Chrh Wkr; Hon Rl; NHS; PPFtbl; General Motors Inst; Mech Engr.

WOODS, ALLAYNE R; Immaculata HS; Detroit, MI; 22/94 Cls Rep Sr Cls; Band; Chrh Wkr; Hon Rl; NHS; Yrbk; Rptr Sch Nwsp; Lat Clb; Award Of Recognition 1977; Spec Honor As Newspaper Photogrphr 1978; Univ; Jrnlsm.

WOODS, ANTHONY; Jefferson HS; Shenandoah Jct, WV; Am Leg Boys St; Boy Scts; Cmnty Wkr; Hon Rl; Key Clb; Am Leg Awd; Hi Y Mbr 3 Yrs; Hi Y VP 78; Marshall Univ; Med.

WOODS, AUGUSTA; Pontiac Central HS; Pontiac, MI; Cls Rep Soph Cls; Cl Rep Jr Cls; Chrh Wkr; Girl Scts; Hon Rl; JA; Pep Clb; Univ Of Michigan; Nursing.

WOODS, C; Our Lady Of Mercy HS; Lathrup Vlg, MI; Cls Rep Frsh Cls; Aud/Vis; Lbry Ade; Stg Crw; Pep Clb; Sci Clb; Coach Actv; Tmr; Letter College; Math.

WOODS, CURTIS; Cass Technical HS; Detroit, MI; Hon Rl; ROTC; Ger Clb; Ftbl; Trk; All City Ftbl Plyr 79; Ftbl Schlrshp To Saginaw Vly St Coll 79; Marine ROTC Schlrshp 79; N Carolina Central Univ; Bio.

WOODS, DEBORAH; Warren Ctrl HS; Indpls, IN; 69/822 Band; Hon Rl; Jr NHS; Fr Clb; Pep Clb; Bob Jones Univ; Elem Ed.

WOODS, DOUGLAS; South Amherst HS; Amherst, OH; 1/70 Val; Am Leg Boys St; Band; Chrs; Hon Rl; Lbry Ade; NHS; Sch Pl; Drama Clb; 4-H; S Maurice Bostic Sclshp 79; Oh N Univ Acad Schslp 79; W O Larson Fdn Schslhp 79; Ohio Northern Univ; Pharm.

WOODS, JACK; Rose D Warwick HS; Tekonsha, MI; 3/60 Cls Rep Soph Cls; Pres Jr Cls; Pres Sr Cls; Chrs; Hon Rl; Off Ade; Sch Pl; Stu Cncl; Ed Yrbk; Rptr Yrbk; Mi St Ldrshp Fnlst 78; Camp Cncl 79; St Capital Guest 79; Univ; Bus.

WOODS, JACQUELINE; South HS; Columbus, OH; 65/342 Cl Rep Jr Cls; Hon Rl; JA; Jr NHS; Orch; Treas OEA; Univ; Acctg.

WOODS, JALENE; Pellston HS; Pellston, MI; Cls Rep Frsh Cls; Cls Rep Soph Cls; Cl Rep Jr Cls; Band; Chrs; Stu Cncl; Bsbl; Bsktbl; JA Awd; N Michigan Univ; Music.

WOODS, JENNIFER; Hampshire HS; Romney, WV; Chrh Wkr; Girl Scts; Hon Rl; 4-H; Mbr Of Yth Grp At Church; Potomac St Coll.

WOODS, JOHN; Gladwin HS; Gladwin, MI; Trs Frsh Cls; Pres Jr Cls; Band; NHS; Ed Yrbk; Yrbk; Letter Bsktbl; Capt Crs Cntry; Letter Trk; Lion Awd; College; Engineering.

WOODS, JOYCE; Eastmoor Sr HS; Columbus, OH; Aud/Vis; Chrs; Chrh Wkr; Cmnty Wkr; Hosp Ade; JA; Lbry Ade; Yth Flsp; Sprt Ed Yrbk; Sch Nwsp; Friends Unlimited 78; Gregg Typist & Shorthnd Awds 78; Ohio St Univ; Bus Admin.

WOODS, MIKE; Princeton Cmnty HS; Princeton, IN; 24/225 FCA; Sct Actv; 4-H; FFA; Pep Clb; Letter Ftbl; Letter Trk; Letter Wrstlng; 4-H Awd; Indiana St Univ; Educ.

WOODS, PEGGI; Decatur Central HS; Indnpls, IN; 22/302 Chrh Wkr; Hon Rl; Mod UN; Off Ade; Stg Crw; Drama Clb; 4-H; Lat Clb; 4-H Awd; Mas Awd; Indiana Univ; Med Tech.

WOODS, SHARON; Liberty HS; Girard, OH; 25/2 38 Chrs; Chrh Wkr; Hon Rl; Youngstown St Univ; Comp Sci.

WOODS, SUSAN; Brebeuf Preparatory HS; Indnpls, IN; Girl Scts; JA; Sch Pl; Letter Bsbl; Bsktbl; Natl Merit Ltr; Univ.

WOODS, TAMI; Wilmington HS; Wilmington, OH; Sec Frsh Cls; Trs Soph Cls; Cl Rep Jr Cls; Chrs; Lit Mag; Stg Crw; Rptr Sch Nwsp; Drama Clb; 4-H; Pep Clb; Univ Of Cincinnati; Fash Merch.

WOODS, TIMOTHY; West Lafayette HS; W Lafayette, IN; 62/185 Band; Chrs; Hon Rl; JA; Mdrgl; Orch; Sch Mus; Yth Flsp; 4-H; Fr Clb; Purdue Univ; Music.

WOODS, TODD; North Knox HS; Sandborn, IN; Boy Scts; Chrh Wkr; Cmnty Wkr; FCA; Hon Rl; Lbry Ade; Pol Wkr; Yth Flsp; 4-H; Letter Bsbl; Voc Schl.

WOODSIDE, BETH; Toronto HS; Toronto, OH; Cmp Fr Grls; Chrs; Girl Scts; Hon Rl; Lbry Ade; Sch Mus; Stg Crw; VP Fr Clb; Pep Clb; Trk; Univ.

WOODSIDE, ROBERT; Toronto HS; Toronto, OH; 10/125 Pres Soph Cls; Cls Rep Soph Cls; Am Leg Boys St; Band; VP Chrs; Hon Rl; Sch Mus; Sch Pl; Ed Sch Nwsp; Drama Clb; Duquesne Univ; Pre Law.

WOODSIDE, ROBERT V; Toronto HS; Toronto, OH; 12/125 Pres Soph Cls; Am Leg Boys St; Band; Boy Scts; VP Chrs; Hon Rl; Sch Mus; Sch Pl; Stu Cncl; Ed Sch Nwsp; Univ; Poli Work.

WOODSON, DWIGHT D; Arsenal Tech HS; Indianapolis, IN; 17/660 Cls Rep Soph Cls; Chrs; Hon Rl; Sch Mus; Rptr Yrbk; Ger Clb; OEA; Tech Legion Honor Soc 1978; Indian Univ Engr Placmnt Progm 1976; Wabash Coll; Internl Poli.

WOODSON, KIM; Scecina Memorial HS; Indianapolis, IN; IM Sprt; Cal State; Model.

WOODSON, N; Buchtel HS; Akron, OH; Chrs; Mdrgl; Sch Mus; Indiana Univ; Music.

WOODSON, NATHANIEL; Buchtel HS; Akron, OH; Chrs; Mdrgl; PAVAS; Sch Mus; Stg Crw; Bsktbl; Eastman Schl Of Music; Voice.

WOODWARD, BRIAN; Landmark Christian HS; Westville, IN; 1/20 Pres Jr Cls; Pres Sr Cls; Sprt Ed Sch Nwsp; Drama Clb; Letter Bsbl; Letter Bsktbl; Letter Crs Cntry; Letter Socr; Letter Wrstlng; Bob Jones Univ.

WOODWARD, BRUCE; Haslett HS; Haslett, MI; 25/160 Cl Rep Jr Cls; Boy Scts; 4-H; Crs Cntry; Socr; 4-H Awd; Ari St Univ; Bio Sci.

WOODWARD, GREG; Cory Rawson HS; Jenera, OH; Pres Sr Cls; Treas Chrs; Cmnty Wkr; Hon Rl; Off Ade; Sch Mus; Sch Pl; Stg Crw; Sch Nwsp; Bsbl; Bus Schl.

WOODWARD, JAMIE; Cloverdale HS; Cloverdale, IN; Band; Drl Tm; Yrbk; OEA; Pep Clb; Swmmng; Trk; Univ.

WOODWARD, K; Hartford HS; Hartford, MI; Band; Hon Rl; MMM; Sch Pl; Stg Crw; Ftbl; Coach Actv; 6 Yrs Jazz Band; Tour Europ With Blue Lake Fine Arts Camp Jazz Band; ITT Tech Schl; Aero Engr.

WOODWORTH, BRIAN; Springfield North HS; Springfield, OH; Band; Chrs; Sct Actv; 4-H; Fr Clb; Ftbl; Trk; Univ Of Dayton; Eng.

WOODWORTH, DANIEL; Union HS; Grand Rapids, MI; Cls Rep Frsh Cls; Chrh Wkr; Hon Rl; Mod UN; NHS; Stu Cncl; Trk; IM Sprt; Grand Rapids Junior College; Doctor.

WOODWORTH, MARLENE; Houghton Lake HS; Houghton Lk, MI; Band; Hon Rl; NHS; Yrbk; Spn Clb; Mgrs; E Michigan Univ; Med.

WOODWYK, LORI; Hudsonville HS; Hudsonville, MI; VP Soph Cls; Sec Sr Cls; FCA; Hon Rl; Pep Clb; Chrldng; Davenport Univ; Sec.

WOODY, CINDI; Bishop Donahue HS; Wheeling, WV; 1/54 Trs Frsh Cls; Val; NHS; Stu Cncl; Ed Yrbk; Rptr Sch Nwsp; Pep Clb; Spn Clb; GAA; West Virginia Univ; Pharm.

WOODY, JODI L; Midland Trail HS; Victor, WV; Trs Soph Cls; Cls Rep Sr Cls; Chrs; Hon Rl; NHS; Sch Pl; Stg Crw; Stu Cncl; Ed Sch Nwsp; Rptr Sch Nwsp; Marshall Univ; Anthropology.

WOODY, STEPHEN; Bishop Donahue Memorial HS; Wheeling, WV; 4/65 Cl Rep Jr Cls; Boy Scts; Hon Rl; VP NHS; Sch Mus; Sct Actv; Pres Stu Cncl; Rptr Sch Nwsp; 4-H; Key Clb; College; Engr.

WOODY, STEVE; Bishop Donahue Mem HS; Wheeling, WV; 5/75 Cl Rep Jr Cls; Boy Scts; Hon Rl; NHS; Sch Pl; Rptr Sch Nwsp; 4-H; Spn Clb; Letter Bsbl; Letter Ftbl; Univ; Dentist.

WOOFTER, KENT; Gilmer Co HS; Glenville, WV; 1/98 Pres Frsh Cls; VP Jr Cls; Val; Am Leg Boys St; Chrs; Chrh Wkr; Debate Tm; Hon Rl; NHS; Sch Pl; Glenville St Coll; Art.

WOOLDRIDGE, BRUCE; Gwinn HS; Gwinn, MI; 31/210 Aud/Vis; Chrh Wkr; Hon Rl; Jr NHS; NHS; ROTC; OEA; Ftbl; Ten; Natl Merit SF; Northern Michigan Univ; Comp Oper.

WOOLDRIDGE, LINDA; Center Line HS; Warren, MI; Chrs; Chrh Wkr; Cmnty Wkr; Hon Rl; Sch Mus; Yth Flsp; Drama Clb; OEA; Sci Clb; Cit Awd; Awrd Best Short Story In Creative Writing 79; Awrd Tchrs Essay Contest 77; Nominated For Phi Betta Cappa 79; Univ; Bus Admin.

WOOLERY, BRIAN; Cass Technical HS; Detroit, MI; Hon Rl; Yrbk; Sch Nwsp; Fr Clb; Univ Of Detroit; Poli.

WOOLERY, LISA; Brookville HS; Brookville, OH; VP Frsh Cls; Cls Rep Soph Cls; VP Jr Cls; Pres Sr Cls; Hon Rl; Yrbk; 4-H; Pep Clb; Chrldng; PPFtbl; Miami Jacobs Jr Coll; Med Asst.

WOOLEY, M; Boardman HS; Youngstown, OH; Hon Rl; Y-Teens; Rptr Sch Nwsp; Sch Nwsp; Pres 4-H; Fr Clb; 4-H Awd; Patrial Schlrshp To Villa Maria HS; Univ; Jrnlsm.

WOOLF, DAVID; John Glenn HS; New Concord, OH; 16/198 FCA; Hon Rl; Yth Flsp; 4-H; Spn Clb; Bsktbl; Letter Ftbl; Letter Trk; Univ Of Georgia.

WOOLF, EILEEN; Woodrow Wilson HS; Youngstown, OH; Hon Rl; JA; Lbry Ade; NHS; Y-Teens;.

WOOLF, KENNETH; Gull Lake HS; Richland, MI; 15/228 Cls Rep Frsh Cls; Chrh Wkr; Hon Rl; NHS; Stu Cncl; Yrbk; DECA; Ftbl; Trk; Wrstlng; College.

WOOLSEY, MICHAEL; Wood Memorial HS; Oakland City, IN; Band; Chrh Wkr; Hon Rl; Orch; Stu Cncl; Vincennes Univ; Tool & Dye Maker.

WOOLVERTON, WILLIAM; Niles HS; Niles, MI; 46/388 Am Leg Boys St; Hon Rl; NHS; Capt Ftbl; Am Leg Awd; Dnfth Awd; Rotary Awd; Purdue Univ; Biology.

WOOLWORTH, CINDY; Concord HS; Concord, MI; 4/85 Sec Sr Cls; Chrh Wkr; Hon Rl; NHS; College; Literature.

WOOSTER, PAUL; Bloom Carroll HS; Baltimore, OH; 22/143 VP Sr Cls; Cls Rep Sr Cls; Hon Rl; NHS; Stu Cncl; Yth Flsp; Pres 4-H; FFA; Letter Bsbl; Letter Bsktbl; Ohio St Univ; Jrnlsm.

WOOSTER, SCOTT; Northwest HS; Rives Jct, MI; Cls Rep Frsh Cls; Cl Rep Jr Cls; Hon Rl; NHS; Bsktbl; Glf; Tmr; Michigan St Univ; Comp Work.

WOOTEN, EUGENE; Sharples HS; Blair, WV; Boy Scts; Sct Actv; Sch Nwsp; 4-H; FHA; Pep Clb; VICA; Bsbl; Bsktbl; Trk; Track Award 1976; Voc Schl; Mech.

WOOTEN, KELLIE; Logan Sr HS; Pecks Mill, WV; Chrh Wkr; Hon Rl; Pres NHS; Sec Stu Cncl; Fr Clb; Keyettes; Pep Clb; Wrstlng; Chrldng; Concord Coll; Acctg.

WOOTEN, KEVIN; Whiteland Cmnty HS; Whiteland, IN; 6/198 Band; Chrh Wkr; Hon Rl; NHS; VP Key Clb; Mth Clb; Letter Bsktbl; Crs Cntry; Letter Glf; Trk; Western Kentucky Univ; Comp Sci.

WOOTEN, KEVIN; Whiteland Comm HS; Whiteland, IN; 5/204 Chrh Wkr; Hon Rl; NHS; VP Key Clb; Bsktbl; Crs Cntry; Glf; IM Sprt; Western Kentucky Univ; Comp Sci.

WOOTEN, LEONARD; Murray Wright HS; Detroit, MI; 40/250 Hon Rl; Lbry Ade; Off Ade; Stu Cncl; Sci Clb; Kiwan Awd; Bsc Educ Opprt Grant 79; Mi St Schshp Tuition Grant 79; St Keffrntl Grant 79; Lawrence Inst Of Tech; Elec Engr.

WOOTEN, MAVIS E; Pickens HS; Helvetia, WV; 3/11 Sec Frsh Cls; Sec Soph Cls; Sec Jr Cls; Cmnty Wkr; Hon Rl; NHS; 4-H; Pep Clb; Chrldng; Scr Kpr;.

WOOTEN, MIKE; Austin HS; Austin, IN; 13/103 Chrh Wkr; Hon Rl; Sch Pl; Yth Flsp; Drama Clb; 4-H; Lat Clb; Pep Clb; Sci Clb; Bsktbl; Indiana St Univ; Dentistry.

WOOTON, JOHN; Grosse Pointe N HS; Grosse Pt Wds, MI; Trs Soph Cls; Cl Rep Jr Cls; Stu Cncl; Ftbl; Letter Swmmng; Trk; Univ Of Michigan.

WOPSHALL, MARILYN; Central Catholic HS; Toledo, OH; 10/350 Hon Rl; JA; Sch Nwsp; Spn Clb; Univ Of Toledo Acad Schslp 7;9 St Bd Of Educ Awd For Destnctn 79; Cert Of Achvmnt In Acctg 79; Univ Of Toledo; Acctg.

WORBS, STEVE; Hilliard HS; Hilliard, OH; Chrh Wkr; Cmnty Wkr; Yth Flsp; Cert Of Achvmnt Neither Absnt Nor Tardy Awd 78; Ohio St Univ; Bus Admin.

WORDELMAN, AMY L; Interlochen Arts Academy; Windom, MN; Sal; Band; Chrs; Chrh Wkr; Hon Rl; Orch; Yth Flsp; Natl Merit Ltr; Oberlin Coll.

WORDEN, KELLY J; Southfield Christian HS; Detroit, MI; Chrh Wkr; Hon Rl; Yth Flsp; Letter Trk; Letter Chrldng; Univ; Home Ec.

WORK, JOAN; Hilliard HS; Hilliard, OH; 51/350 Pres Cmp Fr Grls; Hon Rl; Hosp Ade; NHS; Stu Cncl; Rptr Yrbk; Drama Clb; Pres FHA; Lat Clb; Pep Clb; Ohi St Univ; Scndry Educ.

WORK, RONALD; Brooke HS; Follansbee, WV; 56/500 Boy Scts; Hon Rl; Sci Clb; Spn Clb; Bsktbl; IM Sprt; Univ; Archt.

WORKLAN, JANIS; Cadiz HS; Bloomingdale, OH; 4/104 Cls Rep Soph Cls; Cl Rep Jr Cls; Hon Rl; NHS; Stu Cncl; Lat Clb; Letter Glf; Scr Kpr; Am Leg Awd; Hnrbl Men In Ohio Schlstc Ach Test US History; Journalism Latin; Amer History II; Coll; Journalism.

WORKMAN, CATHY; Clear Fork HS; Dorothy, WV; 3/35 Hst Soph Cls; Sec Jr Cls; Band; Cmp Fr Grls; Chrh Wkr; Girl Scts; Hon Rl; NHS; Sct Actv; Yrbk; Univ.

WORKMAN, JOE; Colerain Sr HS; Cincinnati, OH; Cls Rep Frsh Cls; Cls Rep Soph Cls; Boy Scts; Hon Rl; Off Ade; Stu Cncl; Cit Awd; SAR Awd; Spec Awd For Doing Well In Amer Std 75; Univ Of Cincinnati; Bus Admin.

WORKMAN, LARRY; Columbia City Joint HS; Columbia City, IN; Cls Rep Soph Cls; Cl Rep Jr Cls; Cls Rep Sr Cls; Am Leg Boys St; Debate Tm; Hon Rl; Pres Natl Forn Lg; Pol Wkr; Quill & Scroll; Stu Cncl; Indiana Univ; Poli Sci.

WORKMAN, NANCY; Danville HS; Danville, OH; Band; Chrh Wkr; Drm Mjrt; Hon Rl; NHS; Orch; Yth Flsp; Yrbk; 4-H; Pep Clb; Univ.

WORKMAN, RICK; Whiteland Community HS; New Whiteland, IN; 4/219 4-H; Bsbl; Bsktbl; Univ; Ofc Mgr.

WORKMAN, ROBERT A; Roosevelt Wilson HS; Clarksburg, WV; 29/130 Pres Frsh Cls; Am Leg Boys St; Pres Band; Hon Rl; Fr Clb; College.

WORKMAN, STEVEN; Hauser HS; Hope, IN; 7/80 Pres Frsh Cls; Am Leg Boys St; Chrs; Chrh Wkr; Hon Rl; Lbry Ade; NHS; Quill & Scroll; Yth Flsp; Ed Yrbk; College; Minister Of Music.

WORKMAN, THERESA; Center Line HS; Warren, MI; Chrs; Chrh Wkr; Hon Rl; Jr NHS; Sch Mus; Letter Tmr; Hstry Awd 77; Eng Awd 75; Medical Inst; Med.

WORKMAN, WAYNE; West Preston HS; Arthurdale, WV; Cls Rep Soph Cls; Chrh Wkr; Hon Rl; Bs bl; Letter Bsktbl; Letter Ftbl; Armed Forces.

WORLAND, MARY; Tiffin Calvert HS; Tiffin, OH; 3/99 Cls Rep Frsh Cls; Cls Rep Soph Cls; Pres Jr Cls; Chrs; NHS; Sch Mus; Stu Cncl; Sch Nwsp; Cit Awd; JC Awd; Univ; Pre Law.

WORLEY, DORISTIENE; Jane Addams Vocational HS; Cleveland, OH; Sec Jr Cls; Cmp Fr Grls; Chrs; Girl Scts; Hon Rl; Sch Pl; Yrbk; Drama Clb; Ten; Chrldng; Bowling Green Coll; Nurse.

WORLEY, LARRY D; Cuyahoga Vly Christian Acad; Akron, OH; 6/60 Pres Soph Cls; Cls Rep Soph Cls; Band; Boy Scts; Chrs; Chrh Wkr; Hon Rl; Mdrgl; Orch; Stu Cncl; Akron Univ.

WORLEY, RONALD; Kent City HS; Vanderbilt, MI; 8/95 Boy Scts; Hon Rl; Jr NHS; Pres Yth Flsp; Rptr Yrbk; Letter Crs Cntry; Letter Trk; Muskegon Busns Coll; Data Processing.

WORLEY JR, L DARYLE; Cuyahoga Vly Christian Acad; Akron, OH; 5/57 Pres Soph Cls; Cls Rep Soph Cls; Band; Boy Scts; Chrs; Chrh Wkr; Hon Rl; Mdrgl; Stu Cncl; Sch Nwsp; Univ Of Akron; Bus.

WORMAN, RICKY; New Haven HS; Fort Wayne, IN; 85/350 Band; Chrs; Debate Tm; JA; Sch Mus; Sch Pl; Stu Cncl; Drama Clb; Univ Of Mic; Math.

WORRELL, KATHLEEN; Our Lady Of The Elms HS; Akron, OH; Hon Rl; Ten; College; Business Major.

WORRELL, MICHAEL; Arthur Hill HS; Saginaw, MI; 10/550 Boy Scts; Hon Rl; NHS; Sci Clb; Mi St Univ Acad Acvhvmnt Schslhp 79; Cert Of Recgntn From Mi Compttv Schslhp Progr 79; Michigan St Univ; Engr.

WORSHAM, CARLA; Franklin HS; Westland, MI; Sec Sr Cls; Am Leg Aux Girls St; Band; Chrs; Hon Rl; Sch Mus; Stu Cncl; Yth Flsp; Swmmng; Cit Awd; Univ; Ecology.

WORSTER, HELEN; Greenville Sr HS; Greenville, OH; 51/370 Trs Frsh Cls; Cls Rep Frsh Cls; Cls Rep Soph Cls; Cl Rep Jr Cls; Hon Rl; Quill & Scroll; Yth Flsp; Ed Yrbk; 4-H; Ten; Univ; Eng.

WORTHAM, ARON; Reeths Puffer HS; Muskegon, MI; Cl Rep Jr Cls; Pres Chrs; Chrh Wkr; Hon Rl; Stu Cncl; Capt Bsktbl; Ftbl; Letter Trk; Made St Hnrs Chr In 76; Went To St In Track 78; I Was Slctd As A Cmp Cnslr For Elem Stu 79; Western Michigan Univ; Banking.

WORTHINGTON, PATTY; Taylor HS; Cleves, OH; Chrs; Lbry Ade; PAVAS; Sch Mus; Sch Pl; Stg Crw; Drama Clb; Pep Clb; Cit Awd; Univ Of Ohio; Psych.

WORTHY, JENNIFER E; Southfield HS; Southfield, MI; Trs Sr Cls; Chrh Wkr; Hon Rl; Sch Pl; Stg Crw; Yth Flsp; Fr Clb; Letter Crs Cntry; Letter Trk; College; Medicine.

WORTINGER, TODD; Galesburg Augusta HS; Galesburg, MI; 25/109 Cls Rep Frsh Cls; Cls Rep Soph Cls; Chrs; Hon Rl; Sch Pl; Stu Cncl; Bsbl; Bsktbl; Ftbl; Wrstlng; Lake Superior St Univ; Acctg.

WORTMAN, LISA E; Parkside HS; Jackson, MI; Band; Hon Rl; Orch; Rptr Sch Nwsp; Letter Ten; Sftbl 1st & 2nd Yr Jr Varsity Awd; St Of Michigan Comp Schlrshp Cert; Dist Solo & Ensamble 2nd Div Awd; Michigan St Univ; Comp Sci.

WOSNIEWSKI, GERALD; Manistee Catholic Ctrl HS; Manistee, MI; Band; Hon Rl; NHS; Orch; College.

WOTEN, RON; Southern Wells HS; Bluffton, IN; 1/97 Val; Am Leg Boys St; Hon Rl; NHS; Ftbl; Mgrs; DAR Awd; Rotary Awd; Richard Lugar Ldrshp Confrnc; Lettermns Club; Purdue Univ; Sci.

WOTRING, STANLEY; Liberty HS; Clarksburg, WV; Am Leg Boys St; Cmnty Wkr; Hon Rl; Jr NHS; NHS; Fr Clb; Mth Clb; Spn Clb; Letter Bsbl; Coach Actv; Natl Sci Fdn Coal Chem Camp 79; Pulp & Paper Resources & Enviro Seminar At W Mi Univ 79; Univ; Bus Admin.

WOTT, BRIAN; Bridgman HS; Bridgman, MI; Hon Rl; Trk; Wrstlng; IM Sprt; Univ Of Mich.

WOUDSTRA, JOHN D; Adams HS; Rochester, MI; 34/500 Cmnty Wkr; Hon Rl; NHS; VP Sci Clb; Spn Clb; Natl Merit Ltr; Natl Merit SF; Stu Of Dist Awd; Michigan Tech Univ; Physics.

WOURMS, JANE; Carroll HS; Dayton, OH; 54/305 Hon Rl; NHS; Wright State; History.

WOYTEK, BERNIE; Padau Franciscan HS; Parma, OH; 7/296 Hon Rl; NHS; Orch; Yrbk; Sch Nwsp; Pep Clb; Sci Clb; Ten; IM Sprt; Natl Merit Ltr; Played In Cleveland Dio HS Orch 78 80; Part Inthe Oh Coun Of Tchr Of Math Contest 79; Univ Of Detroit; Archt.

WOZNIAK, BARBARA; Nordonia HS; Northfield, OH; Cmp Fr Grls; Chrs; Chrh Wkr; Cmnty Wkr; Red Cr Ade; Sch Mus; Sch Pl; Stg Crw; Drama Clb; Pep Clb; Psychology.

WOZNIAK, CINDY; Sandusky HS; Sandusky, OH; Chrh Wkr; Hon Rl;.

WOZNIAK, THOMAS; Rogers HS; Michigan City, IN; 109/489 Band; Chrs; NHS; Letter Ftbl; Indiana Univ; Bus.

WRAGG, KATHLEEN J; Centreville HS; Sturgis, MI; 9/70 Pres Soph Cls; Sec Jr Cls; Pres Sr Cls; Hon Rl; Stu Cncl; 4-H; Pep Clb; Glen Oaks Comm College; Art.

WRASMAN, MICHAEL; Delphos St John HS; Delphos, OH; 90/139 Hst Sr Cls; Band; Hon Rl; Sch Mus; Sch Pl; 4-H; IM Sprt; ONU Hon Band 78; Schlstc Team Sr Yr 79; Oh Test Of Schstc Achvmtn 19in Oh 79; Ohio Northern Univ; Music Educ.

WRATHELL, ROD; Whittemore Prescott HS; Turner, MI; 19/120 Band; Hon Rl; Letter Ten; Wrstlng; Cit Awd; College.

WRAY, TONI; Jennings County HS; Scipio, IN; 18/365 Chrh Wkr; Hon Rl; NHS; Off Ade; Yth Flsp; Mert Schshp 79; Schlrs For Dollars 79; Franklin Coll; Vet Med.

WREN, JENNY; Hubbard HS; Hubbard, OH; 16/330 Cl Rep Jr Cls; Band; Girl Scts; Hon Rl; Natl Forn Lg; Stu Cncl; Swmmng; PPFtbl; College; Vet.

WRENS, BRENDA; Benton Harbor HS; Benton Harbor, MI; Band; Chrh Wkr; JA; Spn Clb; Natl Spanish Hon Soc 78; Eastern Michigan Univ; Music.

WRIGHT, AMANDA; Lake City HS; Lake City, MI; VP Jr Cls; Band; Letter Bsktbl; Letter Trk; U S Navy; Elec.

WRIGHT, AMY JO; Black River HS; West Salem, OH; 14/79 Hon Rl; Beta Clb; Capt Bsktbl; GAA; Scr Kpr; Salem Coll; Phys Educ.

WRIGHT, ANN; Gladwin HS; Gladwin, MI; Sec Frsh Cls; VP Jr Cls; Sec Sr Cls; Hon Rl; Jr NHS; NHS; PAVAS; Sch Pl; Stu Cncl; Sch Nwsp; Ctrl Michigan Univ; Interior Design.

WRIGHT, BARBARA; Baker HS; Fairborn, OH; Band; Chrs; Hon Rl; Mdrgl; Sch Mus; Sch Pl; Yth Flsp; Pres Drama Clb; Cit Awd; Univ; Music.

WRIGHT, BERNICE; Benton Harbor HS; Benton Hbr, MI; Cl Rep Jr Cls; Chrh Wkr; Hon Rl; Hon Rl; JA; Jr NHS; Stu Cncl; Lat Clb; Sci Clb; Cit Awd; Mic State Univ; Med Tech.

WRIGHT, BETH; Terre Haute South Vigo HS; Terre Haute, IN; Hon Rl; JA; Off Ade; Stu Cncl; Y-Teens; Pep Clb; Spanish Awd 76; Univ Of Louisville; Cmmrcl Design.

WRIGHT, BEVERLY; Knightstown HS; Knightstown, IN; 9/144 Cls Rep Sr Cls; VP Chrs; Hon Rl; NHS; Sch Mus; Yth Flsp; FBLA; Spn Clb; Letter Ten; GAA; Univ Of Southern California; Bus.

WRIGHT, BILL; Merrillville HS; Merrillville, IN; 85/613 Hon Rl; Trk; IM Sprt; Purdue Univ; Engr.

WRIGHT, BRENDA; Olivet HS; Olivet, MI; 2/95 Pres Frsh Cls; Trs Soph Cls; Pres Jr Cls; Chrs; Girl Scts; Hon Rl; NHS; Off Ade; Sch Mus; Sch Pl; Univ; Agri.

WRIGHT, BRIDGET; Niles Mc Kinley HS; Niles, OH; 70/490 AFS; Band; Girl Scts; Hosp Ade; Orch; Sch Mus; Sch Pl; Stg Crw; Yth Flsp; Drama Clb; Ohio St Univ; Phys Ther.

WRIGHT, CAROLYN A; Steubenville Cthlc Cntrl HS; Mingo Jct, OH; 1/226 Val; Chrh Wkr; Hon Rl; NHS; Rptr Yrbk; Fr Clb; Sec Sci Clb; C of C Awd; Vlybl Cptn 78 & 77 ; Ltr 77 & 78; Sftbl Ltr 76 79; Steubenville Cthlc Cntrl Dominician Schlrshp 79 80; Ohio Dominican Coll; Chem.

WRIGHT, CAROLYN S; Huntington HS; Chillicothe, OH; Hon Rl; Lbry Ade; NHS; Sch Nwsp; 4-H; FHA; OEA; Pep Clb; Trk; 4-H Awd;.

WRIGHT, CATHERINE; Kalamazoo Central HS; Kalamazoo, MI; Pres Chrh Wkr; Debate Tm; Hon Rl; Natl Forn Lg; Sec Ger Clb; Lat Clb; Pep Clb; Kalamazoo Coll; Law.

WRIGHT, CHRISTOPHER; Union County HS; Liberty, IN; 49/135 Am Leg Boys St; Hon Rl; Letter Bsbl; Letter Bsktbl; Letter Crs Cntry; Mbr Of Sen Richard Lugars Symposium For Tomorrows Leaders 78; Sen In Model Legislature; Univ; Law.

WRIGHT, CHUCK W; Wyoming HS; Cincinnati, OH; Chrs; Hon Rl; Sch Mus; Sch Pl; Yth Flsp; Letter Ftbl; Letter Wrstlng; Natl Merit SF; Univ; Liberal Arts.

WRIGHT, DALE; Leslie HS; Stockbridge, MI; Hon Rl; FFA; Univ; CPA.

WRIGHT, DANNY W; Jennings County HS; N Vernon, IN; 80/358 Band; Chrs; Chrh Wkr; Pol Wkr; Sch Mus; Sch Pl; Sch Nwsp; Pres Fr Clb; Letter Bsbl; Wrstlng; Pres Jr Histrcl Soc 79; Sandcreek Baptist Schlrshp.

WRIGHT, DAVID; Liberty HS; Girard, OH; Hon Rl; Letter Bsbl; University; Engineering.

WRIGHT, DAVID B; William Henry Harrison HS; Evansville, IN; 1/400 Boy Scts; Hon Rl; Hosp Ade; Off Ade; Sct Actv; Stg Crw; Glf; Coach Actv; Cit Awd; Natl Merit SF; Univ; Math.

WRIGHT, DAVID G; N Ridgeville HS; N Ridgeville, OH; Cls Rep Sr Cls; Band; Hon Rl; NHS; Letter Trk; College; Electical Engineer.

WRIGHT, DAWN; Northview HS; Grand Rapids, MI; Cls Rep Soph Cls; Drl Tm; Hon Rl; NHS; Sch Pl; Stu Cncl; Rptr Yrbk; Yrbk; Spn Clb; Pom Pon; Grand Rapids Jr Coll; Dent Asst.

WRIGHT, DEBORAH; Novi HS; Novi, MI; 16/200 Band; Chrs; Drm Bgl; Hon Rl; NHS; Sch Mus; Fr Clb; Capt Pom Pon; Natl Merit Ltr; E Mi Univ Schlrshp 79; Novi Fndtn Perf Arts Schlrshp 77; Novi Bus & Prof Wmn Schlrshp 79; Eastern Michigan Univ; Music.

WRIGHT, DEE A; North Central HS; Shelburn, IN; Cls Rep Frsh Cls; Hon Rl; Stu Cncl; Sec FBLA; FSA; Ger Clb; Pep Clb; Letter Chrldng; Letter GAA; Indiana Univ; Bus.

WRIGHT, DIANNA; West Washington HS; Palmyra, IN; 14/100 Cls Rep Frsh Cls; Hon Rl; NHS; Yrbk; DECA; FHA; Bsktbl; Mgrs; Scr Kpr; Girls Bsktbl Most Improved Player 79;.

WRIGHT, DINAH K; Cowan HS; Oakville, IN; 1/70 Trs Frsh Cls; Debate Tm; Drl Tm; Sec FCA; Hon Rl; Lbry Ade; NHS; Sch Mus; Yrbk; OEA; Ball St Univ; Business.

WRIGHT, DONNA; Huntington East HS; Huntington, WV; 50/314 Cmp Fr Grls; Chrs; Lbry Ade; NHS; Yth Flsp; Y-Teens; Fr Clb; FHA; Letter Trk; Miss Teenage Huntington; Marshall Univ; Home Ec.

WRIGHT, DOUG; Clay Battelle HS; Core, WV; Chrh Wkr; Cmnty Wkr; Yth Flsp; Rptr Sch Nwsp; Swmmng;.

WRIGHT, DOUG; Eastern HS; Solsberry, IN; Band; Boy Scts; Hon Rl; Lbry Ade; NHS; Sch Mus; Sct Actv; Yth Flsp; Ind Univ; Business.

WRIGHT, DOUGLAS; Tri Cnty Middle Sr HS; Reynolds, IN; Trs Frsh Cls; Pres Soph Cls; Pres Jr Cls; Pres Sr Cls; Am Leg Boys St; Band; Boy Scts; Chrh Wkr; Cmnty Wkr; Hon Rl; Ind Univ Band Schlrshp Psi Iota Xi Sorority; Amer Soc Of Agri Engrs Reg Sci Fair; Purdue Univ; Engr.

WRIGHT, DOUGLAS B; South Harrison HS; West Milford, WV; Am Leg Boys St; Chrh Wkr; Hon Rl; Stu Cncl; FFA; Bsktbl; Ftbl; Mgrs; College.

WRIGHT, DOUGLAS E; Southfield Christian HS; Farmington Hls, MI; Pres Jr Cls; Pres Sr Cls; Hon Rl; NHS; Stu Cncl; Letter Crs Cntry; Letter Trk; Taylor Univ; Math.

WRIGHT, ELIZABETH; Howland HS; Warren, OH; 14/440 Trs Frsh Cls; Trs Soph Cls; Trs Jr Cls; Trs Sr Cls; Am Leg Aux Girls St; Band; Debate Tm; Hon Rl; Natl Forn Lg; Hon Rl; Univ Of Virginia; Medicine.

WRIGHT, ERIC; Mt Gilead HS; Mt Gilead, OH; Cls Rep Soph Cls; Boy Scts; PAVAS; Sch Pl; Stu Cncl; Drama Clb; Univ; Art.

WRIGHT, ERIC; Arsenal Technical HS; Indianapolis, IN; Cls Rep Frsh Cls; Cls Rep Soph Cls; Cl Rep Jr Cls; Chrs; Sch Mus; Sch Pl; Stu Cncl; Drama Clb; Key Clb; Cit Awd; Bradley Univ; Communications.

WRIGHT, ERIC; East Grand Rapids HS; E Grand Rpd, MI; Boy Scts; Hon Rl; Swmmng; Natl Merit Ltr; Central Mic Univ; Sci.

WRIGHT, FRANK; Eaton Rapids HS; Eaton Rapids, MI; Band; Sch Mus; Sch Pl; Pres Yth Flsp; Ftbl; Michigan State Univ; Music.

WRIGHT, JAMES; Croswell Lexington HS; Applegate, MI; Am Leg Boys St; Chrs; Hon Rl; Sch Mus; Sch Pl; Drama Clb; FFA; Letter Crs Cntry; Trk; MSU; Mech Engr.

WRIGHT, JEFF; Claymont HS; Dennison, OH; 8/200 Cls Rep Frsh Cls; Pres Soph Cls; Cls Rep Sr Cls; Hon Rl; NHS; Stu Cncl; Yrbk; Sprt Ed Sch Nwsp; Bsktbl; Letter Glf; Kent State Univ.

WRIGHT, KELLY; Central HS; Evansville, IN; Cls Rep Frsh Cls; Cls Rep Soph Cls; Cl Rep Jr Cls; Sec Sr Cls; Chrs; Girl Scts; Hon Rl; NHS; Off Ade; Pol Wkr; Deaconess Hospital; Nurse.

WRIGHT, KIM; Madison Plains HS; South Solon, OH; 4/153 Hon Rl; NHS; Off Ade; Rptr Yrbk; Chrldng; Shorthand Awd; Bookkeeping Straight A;.

WRIGHT, KIM; Inkster HS; Westland, MI; 4/200 Pres Soph Cls; Pres Jr Cls; Hon Rl; NHS; Stu Cncl; Yth Flsp; Yrbk; Cit Awd; Univ Of Michigan; Med.

WRIGHT, KYLE P; Barnesville HS; Barnesville, OH; Chrs; Hon Rl; Rptr Sch Nwsp; Sch Nwsp; Drama Clb; Fr Clb; FTA; Ohio St Univ; Nursing.

WRIGHT, LARRY; Spencer HS; Spencer, WV; Hon Rl; Lbry Ade; Yrbk; Letter Bsbl; Letter Wrstlng;.

WRIGHT, LESA; Franklin Heights HS; Columbus, OH; Chrh Wkr; Yth Flsp; Ohio State; Teach.

WRIGHT, LINDA; Oak Hills HS; Cincinnati, OH; 47/859 Hon Rl; Quill & Scroll; Yth Flsp; Sch Nwsp; FTA; Letter Crs Cntry; Letter Trk; Tmr; Univ Of Miami; Anthropology.

WRIGHT, LISA; Brookside HS; Sheffield Lake, OH; 6/227 Hon Rl; Jr NHS; Lbry Ade; NHS; Univ Of Akron; Psych.

WRIGHT, LOIS; South Harrison HS; West Milford, WV; Chrh Wkr; Hon Rl; Jr NHS; Lbry Ade; NHS; Sch Pl; Y-Teens; FHA; Am Leg Awd; Bob Jones Univ; Elem Educ.

WRIGHT, LORI; Northfield HS; Wabash, IN; Sch Mus; Sch Pl; Stg Crw; Yth Flsp; Rptr Yrbk; Rptr Sch Nwsp; Drama Clb; VP FHA; Pep Clb; Ball St Univ; Fashion Coordinating.

WRIGHT, LORI; Henry Ford Ii HS; Sterling Hts, MI; 30/432 Band; Chrh Wkr; Hon Rl; NHS; Orch; Mich Tech Univ; Med Tech.

WRIGHT, LYNN; Wintersville HS; Steubenville, OH; 11/309 Cls Rep Frsh Cls; VP Soph Cls; VP Jr Cls; Cl Rep Jr Cls; Band; Hon Rl; NHS; Orch; Sch Pl; Stg Crw; Field Commander For Marching Band Cmptn Awd In 78 80; Best Actress In Thespian Troup #1336 78; Univ; Public Rltns.

WRIGHT, MARTHA; Shadyside HS; Jacobsburg, OH; Chrs; Debate Tm; NHS; Spn Clb; Univ; Theatre.

WRIGHT, MARTHA S; Central Preston Sr HS; Kingwood, WV; 11/169 Hon Rl; NHS; Treas Stu Cncl; Yrbk; Civ Clb; VP Fr Clb; VP FHA; Chrldng; Fairmont St Coll; Vet Asst.

WRIGHT, MARTIN; Sturgis HS; Sturgis, MI; Letter Ftbl; Letter Trk; Letter Wrstlng; IM Sprt; Western Mic Univ; Bus.

WRIGHT, MARVIN; John Glenn HS; Westland, MI; Hon Rl; DECA; Eastern Michigan Univ; Bus Admin.

WRIGHT, MARY; New Albany HS; New Albany, IN; 69/565 Band; Hon Rl; Chrldng; IM Sprt; PPFtbl; Bus.

WRIGHT, MARY; Upper Sandusky HS; Upper Sandusky, OH; Chrs; Chrh Wkr; Hon Rl; Sch Mus; Stg Crw; Drama Clb; FTA; Spn Clb; Ohio St Univ; Tchr.

WRIGHT, MARY; Kirtland HS; Kirtland, OH; 1/126 VP Soph Cls; Cl Rep Jr Cls; AFS; Am Leg Aux Girls St; Hon Rl; NHS; Spn Clb; Bsktbl; Crs Cntry; Trk; College; Education.

WRIGHT, MELANIE; Adelphian Acad; Salt Lk City, UT; Trs Soph Cls; Pres Jr Cls; Chrs; Chrh Wkr; Hon Rl; Stu Cncl; Rptr Yrbk; Rptr Sch Nwsp; Fr Clb; IM Sprt; Andrews Univ; Med.

WRIGHT, MELINDA; Tri Jr Sr HS; Spiceland, IN; 6/83 Girl Scts; Hon Rl; Lbry Ade; NHS; Pres 4-H; Fr Clb; Sec FFA; Gym; Coach Actv; 4-H Awd; FFA Star Greenhand; Indiana St Dairy Princess & Ayrshire Showman Awd; Purdue Univ; Vet.

WRIGHT, MICHAEL; Tri Valley HS; Frazeysburg, OH; 11/220 Am Leg Boys St; Chrh Wkr; Hon Rl; NHS; Yth Flsp; 4-H; Bsktbl; Glf; Letter Trk; Mgrs; Ohio State Univ; Architectural Engr.

WRIGHT, MICHAEL A; Tri Valley HS; Frazeysburg, OH; Chrh Wkr; Hon Rl; Yth Flsp; 4-H; Glf; Trk; Mgrs; Ohio St Univ; Archt Engr.

WRIGHT, MICHELE; Cameron HS; Cameron, WV; 39/115 Cls Rep Frsh Cls; Band; Hon Rl; Y-Teens; Bsktbl; Trk; Chrldng; Mat Maids; PPFtbl; Scr Kpr; Marshall Univ; Acctg.

WRIGHT, PAM; FR Gabriel Richard HS; Ann Arbor, MI; 19/82 Hon Rl; NHS; Ed Sch Nwsp; Pep Clb; Capt Bsbl; Capt Bsktbl; Western Michigan Univ; Bus Admin.

WRIGHT, PAMELA; St Charles HS; St Charles, MI; Band; Drl Tm; Hon Rl; NHS; Sch Mus; ACT Semi Finalist 79; Band Council Rep 77; Univ; Advert.

WRIGHT, PATRICIA; Indian Valley South HS; Port Washington, OH; 18/95 Am Leg Aux Girls St; Band; Chrs; Hon Rl; Off Ade; Sch Pl; Stg Crw; Rptr Yrbk; 4-H; Pep Clb; Stark Tech Coll; Comp Prog.

WRIGHT, PAUL; Bloomington South HS; Bloomington, IN; VP Jr Cls; Pres Sr Cls; Band; Drm Bgl; Orch; Sch Mus; Mst Outstndng Muscn In Jazz Bnad 78; Indiana Univ; Music.

WRIGHT, PHILLIP; Princeton HS; Bluefield, WV; 9/301 Debate Tm; Hon Rl; NHS; Sch Pl; Rptr Sch Nwsp; Drama Clb; Sec Key Clb; Spn Clb; Am Leg Awd; God Cntry Awd; Concord Coll; Pharm.

WRIGHT, RACHEL; Pike Central HS; Petersburg, IN; Chrh Wkr; FCA; Hon Rl; NHS; Sprt Ed Sch Nwsp; Pres FHA; Pep Clb; Trk; IM Sprt; Univ.

WRIGHT, RANDY; Hopkins HS; Hopkins, MI; VP Frsh Cls; Cls Rep Frsh Cls; Chrh Wkr; Hon Rl; Jr NHS; Sct Actv; Yth Flsp; Bsbl; Bsktbl; Ftbl; Voc Schl; Archt.

WRIGHT, REGINA; Muskegon HS; Muskegon, MI; Hon Rl; Hosp Ade; Orch; Stg Crw; Muskegon Comm Coll; Fshn Merch.

WRIGHT, RONALD E; Frontier HS; Marietta, OH; Band; 4-H; Ftbl;.

WRIGHT, RUDY; Mcbain Rural Agrcltrl HS; Marion, MI; 4/62 Am Leg Boys St; Hon Rl; NHS; Yrbk; Fr Clb; Letter Ftbl; Kiwan Awd; Judson College; Comp.

WRIGHT, STACIE; George Washington HS; Charleston, WV; Band; Chrh Wkr; Hon Rl; Hosp Ade; Jr NHS; Orch; Sch Mus; Keyettes; Coll; Med.

WRIGHT, STANLEY; Norwood Sr HS; Norwood, OH; Band; Cmnty Wkr; Hon Rl; JA; Pol Wkr; Stu Cncl; Key Clb; Spn Clb; Swmmng; Cit Awd; Ball St Univ; Econ.

WRIGHT, STEWART; Olivet HS; Olivet, MI; 4/98 VP Sr Cls; Hon Rl; NHS; Sch Pl; Drama Clb; Crs Cntry; Letter Ftbl; Letter Ten; Marines.

WRIGHT, SUSAN; Lake Michigan Cath HS; Stevensville, MI; 27/100 Cl Rep Jr Cls; Cls Rep Sr Cls; Stu Cncl; Sprt Ed Yrbk; Rptr Yrbk; Yrbk; Letter Trk; Chrldng; IM Sprt; Stephens Coll; Sci.

WRIGHT, SUSAN; North Vermillion HS; Cayuga, IN; 5/96 Pres Soph Cls; Pres Jr Cls; Pres Sr Cls; Band; Hon Rl; NHS; Off Ade; Sch Pl; Drama Clb; Ind Univ; Phy Ther.

WRIGHT, SUSAN; Mount View HS; Welch, WV; 72/230 Hon Rl; Lbry Ade; Stg Crw; Pep Clb; Acting School; Actress.

WRIGHT, TED; Redford HS; Detroit, MI; Cls Rep Soph Cls; Cl Rep Jr Cls; Cmnty Wkr; Drl Tm; Hon Rl; NHS; Off Ade; ROTC; Stu Cncl; Rptr Yrbk; Outstanding Ach In Stu Participation; Focus Hope Leadership Training Program; Univ Of Michigan; Elec Engr.

WRIGHT, TERRY; Vinton Co HS; Mc Arthur, OH; Chrh Wkr; FCA; Lbry Ade; Sct Actv; Fr Clb; Ten; Tennis Varsity Letter 2 Yrs MVP 2 Yrs; Jr Deccon & 1st Christian Church; Hocking Tech Coll.

WRIGHT, THERESA; Mother Of Mercy HS; Cincinnati, OH; Trs Soph Cls; Trs Jr Cls; Girl Scts; Hosp Ade; JA; Fr Clb; Raymond Walters Coll; Dent Hygnst.

WRIGHT, THOMAS; Hayes HS; Delaware, OH; Cl Rep Jr Cls; Cls Rep Sr Cls; Pol Wkr; Stu Cncl; Ftbl; Coach Actv; IM Sprt; Univ; Law Enforcement.

WRIGHT, THOMAS C; North Muskegan HS; N Muskegon, MI; 10/100 Am Leg Boys St; Boy Scts; Chrh Wkr; Hon Rl; NHS; Sch Mus; Fr Clb; FDA; Bsbl; Letter Bsktbl; Notre Dame Univ; Pre Med.

WRIGHT, TIMOTHY; Riverdale HS; Forest, OH; 1/106 Trs Frsh Cls; VP Soph Cls; Pres Jr Cls; Am Leg Boys St; Band; Hon Rl; Jr NHS; Sch Mus; Sch Pl; Stg Crw; College; Comp Progr.

WRIGHT, TONYA; Gods Bible HS; Covington, KY; Cls Rep Frsh Cls; Cl Rep Jr Cls; Cls Rep Sr Cls; Chrs; Chrh Wkr; Hon Rl; Eng Clb; FHA; Mth Clb; Spn Clb; N Ken Univ; Nursing.

WRIGHT, VALERIE; Jackson Center HS; Jackson Cntr, OH; 1/40 Trs Frsh Cls; Trs Soph Cls; Am Leg Aux Girls St; Band; Chrs; Hon Rl; NHS; Stg Crw; Sec Stu Cncl; Sch Nwsp; Oh Test Of Schlstc Acvhmnt 76; Perfct Attndnc 76 78; Univ Of Bluffton; Med Tech.

WRIGHT, VICKE; Wayne HS; Dayton, OH; 27/600 VP Soph Cls; Band; Sec FCA; Hon Rl; Jr NHS; NHS; Stu Cncl; Pres DECA; Bsktbl; Capt Chrldng; Univ Of Dayton; Finance.

WRIGHT, VIETTA; Kearsley HS; Flint, MI; Band; Chrs; Chrh Wkr; Hon Rl; Stg Crw; Fr Clb; Univ Of Michigan; Music Tchr.

WRIGHT, WILLIAM; Cedar Lake Acad; Detroit, MI; 60/83 Sal; Chrs; Drl Tm; Hon Rl; Bsktbl; IM Sprt; Scr Kpr; Tmr; Univ Of Detroit; Elec Engr.

WRIGHT, WILLIAM; Royal Oak Kimball HS; Royal Oak, MI; Boy Scts; Hon Rl; Bsktbl; Letter Swmmng; Trk; College.

WRIGHT, WILLIAM D; Cedar Lake Academy; Detroit, MI; Drl Tm; Hon Rl; Bsktbl; IM Sprt; Andrews Univ; Archt.

WRIGHTSMAN, KATHLEEN; Madison Heights HS; Anderson, IN; 10/375 Chrh Wkr; Cmnty Wkr; Hon Rl; NHS; Off Ade; Orch; Pol Wkr; 4-H; FDA; 4-H Awd; Univ; Chem.

WRIGHTT, GRAHAM; Center Grove HS; Greenwood, IN; 14/310 Boy Scts; Hon Rl; Jr NHS; NHS; Fr Clb; Key Clb; Sci Clb; JETS Awd; Natl Merit Ltr; Certifct Of Mert In French 1976; Univ; Engr.

WRISTON, BEVERLY; Clear Fork HS; Clear Creek, WV; 1/40 Pres Frsh Cls; Pres Jr Cls; Val; Band; Hon Rl; Jr NHS; NHS; Sch Pl; Ed Yrbk; Sprt Ed Yrbk; Marshall Univ; Pre Law.

WRISTON, DENISE; Clear Fork HS; Clear Creek, WV; 1/40 Pres Frsh Cls; Pres Jr Cls; Band; Hon Rl; Lbry Ade; NHS; Off Ade; Ed Yrbk; Rptr Yrbk; FBLA; Athlete Of Year 1979; Miss Fresh; Home Ec Sci Math Alg Awds; Trip To Wash; Track Eng Chrldr Amer Stds Awds; Marshall Univ; Pre Law.

WROBEL, DIANNA; St Josephs HS; South Bend, IN; Chrs; Chrh Wkr; Drl Tm; Hon Rl; Hosp Ade; Mdrgl; Stg Crw; Sec Ger Clb; IM Sprt; Butler Univ; Pharmacy.

WROBEL, KAREN; North Canton Hoover HS; North Canton, OH; 25/441 Chrh Wkr; Cmnty Wkr; Hon Rl; NHS; Y-Teens; Spn Clb; Bsktbl; Ten; Am Leg Awd; Pres Awd; Univ Of Akron; Mech Engr.

WROBEL, REBECCA; Airport HS; Newport, MI; Cmnty Wkr; Quill & Scroll; Sprt Ed Sch Nwsp; College; Law.

WROBLESKI, KAREN; St Andrew HS; Detroit, MI; Hon Rl; Bsktbl; Trk; Capt IM Sprt; Mgrs; College; Art.

WROBLEWSKI, SANDI; Beaver Creek HS; Xenia, OH; Chrs; Chrh Wkr; Cmnty Wkr; Girl Scts; Hosp Ade; Lbry Ade; Sct Actv; 4-H; Spn Clb; Bsktbl; College; Med.

WROTEN, MARK; Novi HS; Northville, MI; Hon Rl; Stg Crw; Spn Clb; Crs Cntry; Trk; Varsity Letter In Track; Perfect Attendance Through HS; Univ Of Michigan; Comp.

WRUBLE, MARC; Truman HS; Taylor, MI; Cls Rep Frsh Cls; Hon Rl; Letter Ftbl; Wayne County; Tchr.

WRZESINSKI, STEPHANIE; Manistee Catholic Cntrl HS; Manistee, MI; Cls Rep Soph Cls; Cmnty Wkr; Hon Rl; Stg Crw; Rptr Sch Nwsp; Drama Clb; 4-H; Letter Chrldng; Scr Kpr; 4-H Awd; Quill & Scroll Awd 78; Writing Awd Pin 78; Hist Awd 77; Northwestern Michigan Univ; Cmnctns.

WU, MARION; E Lansing HS; E Lansing, MI; Chrs; NHS; Pom Pon; Tmr; Michigan St Univ; Engr Arts.

WUBBELS, DARIA; Alba Public HS; Elmira, MI; 1/10 Pres Frsh Cls; Am Leg Aux Girls St; Hon Rl; Lbry Ade; Sch Pl; Pres Stu Cncl; Ed Yrbk; Rptr Sch Nwsp; 4-H; Pep Clb; Lake Superior St Coll; Liberal Arts.

WUBBELS, KATHY; Alba Public HS; Elmira, MI; Sec Frsh Cls; Trs Soph Cls; Pres Jr Cls; Am Leg Aux Girls St; Band; Chrs; Chrh Wkr; Hon Rl; Lbry Ade; Sch Mus; Ctrl Michigan Univ; Lib Arts.

WUDI, SHIRLEY; St Ursula Acad; Toledo, OH; Girl Scts; Sch Pl; Stg Crw; Ger Clb; IM Sprt; Varsity Vlybl Letter; Sftbl; Coll; Acctg.

WUEBBELING, JANE; Coldwater HS; Celina, OH; Band; Chrs; Hon Rl; Ger Clb; Trk; Chrldng; IM Sprt; Kiwan Awd; Miami Vly Schl; Nursing.

WUEBBEN, DON; Edon Northwest HS; Edon, OH; 5/65 Chrs; Chrh Wkr; Cmnty Wkr; Hon Rl; Lbry Ade; NHS; Orch; Sch Mus; Sch Pl; Ed Yrbk; Bowling Green Univ; Computer Sci.

WUEBBEN, JULIE; Carroll HS; Xenia, OH; 55/286 Hon Rl; NHS; Stu Cncl; Pep Clb; Coach Actv; IM Sprt; Mat Maids; Scr Kpr; College; Psych.

WUEBKER, SUSAN; Minster HS; Minster, OH; 1/80 Treas Band; Chrs; Hon Rl; Sec NHS; Sch Mus; FTA; Sec Pep Clb; Letter Trk; Univ; Acctg.

WUELLER, LEONA; Ottoville Local HS; Ottoville, OH; Chrs; Chrh Wkr; Hon Rl; NHS; Off Ade; Stg Crw; FHA; Trk; Coach Actv; Mgrs; Indiana Tech Bus Schl; Acctg.

WUERFEL, VIOLA; Fennville HS; Fennville, MI; 26/92 Band; Hon Rl; Orch; Shepard Wade Schlrshp 79; Hope Coll; Med Tech.

WUERTZ, MELODY; Washington HS; Montgomery, IN; 9/194 Chrs; Chrh Wkr; Hon Rl; Jr NHS; Mdrgl; NHS; Sch Mus; Sch Pl; Stg Crw; Beta Clb; St Louis Christian Coll; Music.

WUJEK, JOHN; All Saints Central HS; Bay City, MI; 18/200 Cmnty Wkr; Hon Rl; Letter Ten; Saginaw Valley St College; Bus.

WUNDERLE, NORA; Ravenna HS; Ravenna, OH; 27/315 Hon Rl; NHS; Sch Mus; Sch Pl; Lat Clb; Ohi State; Nrs.

WUNDERLY, LYNNETTE; Tecumseh HS; New Carlisle, OH; 17/328 AFS; Band; Chrs; Drm Bgl; Hon Rl; Jr NHS; NHS; Orch; Bsbl; Scr Kpr; Wright St Univ; Environmental Health.

WUNKER, FREDERICK; Terre Haute North Vigo HS; Terre Haute, IN; 1/650 Hon Rl; Hosp Ade; Orch; Sch Mus; Treas Sci Clb; Spn Clb; Swmmng; In Sci Educ Schlrshp 79; Indiana St Univ; Med.

WUOLUKKA, CHERYL; Troy HS; Troy, MI; 120/300 Chrs; Girl Scts; Hon Rl; PAVAS; Sch Pl; Stg Crw; Drama Clb; PPFtbl; Ferris State; Art Teacher.

WURM, DANIEL; Calvert HS; Republic, OH; Hon Rl; Stg Crw; Bsbl; Ftbl; Wrstlng; IM Sprt; Cit Awd; Ohio State; Architecture.

WURSTER, JULIE; Archbishop Alter HS; Kettering, OH; 17/334 Cl Rep Jr Cls; Cmnty Wkr; Hon Rl; Hosp Ade; NHS; Sch Pl; Drama Clb; Keyettes; Natl Merit Ltr; Univ Of Evansville; Psych Nursing.

WURSTER, JULIE A; Archbishop Alter HS; Kettering, OH; 17/332 Cl Rep Jr Cls; Cmnty Wkr; Hon Rl; Hosp Ade; NHS; Sch Mus; Stu Cncl; Keyettes; Natl Merit SF; Univ Of Evansville; Nursing.

WURTH, BETH; Kalida HS; Columbus Grv, OH; Band; Hon Rl; NHS; Orch; Sch Mus; 4-H; Pep Clb; IM Sprt; Scr Kpr; 4-H Awd; Univ.

WURTH, D; Kalida HS; Cloverdale, OH; Band; Chrs; Hon Rl; Orch; Sch Mus; Stg Crw; Rptr Sch Nwsp; Sch Nwsp; BGSU; Med Sci.

WURTS, JOHN M; Fairmont West HS; Kettering, OH; Boy Scts; Hon Rl; Mod UN; VP Lat Clb; Syracuse Univ; Comp Engr.

WURZEL, DONALD; Ursuline HS; Girard, OH; 100/300 Boy Scts; Chrh Wkr; Cmnty Wkr; Hon Rl; Sct Actv; Spn Clb; Elk Awd; Univ; Elec.

WURZELBACHER, MARTHA; Summit Cntry Day HS; Cincinnati, OH; 3/42 Hon Rl; Hosp Ade; Sdlty; Bsbl; Bsktbl; Hockey; IM Sprt; Mgrs; Boston Coll; Studio Art.

WYANT, ERIC; Woodrow Wilson Sr HS; Youngstown, OH; 16/346 Aud/Vis; Band; Chrh Wkr; Hon Rl; NHS; Orch; Fr Clb; Youngstown St Univ; Comp Sci.

WYANT, LARY H; Daleville HS; Yorktown, IN; Band; Spn Clb; Bsbl; Bsktbl; Scr Kpr; Tmr; Purdue Univ.

WYANT, PATRICIA; Fairfield Union HS; Lancaster, OH; 18/158 Band; Hon Rl; Jr NHS; FDA; FNA; FTA; Sci Clb; Bsktbl; IM Sprt;.

WYANT, TAMMY; Lapel HS; Lapel, IN; 7/100 VP Soph Cls; Pres NHS; Sprt Ed Yrbk; Lat Clb; Pres Sci Clb; Letter Bsktbl; Letter Trk; DAR Awd; Voice Dem Awd; Purdue Univ; Pharm.

WYANT, VALERIE; Canfield HS; Canfield, OH; Trs Jr Cls; Chrs; Girl Scts; Hon Rl; Jr NHS; NHS; Sct Actv; OEA; Spn Clb; Youngstown St Univ; Sec.

WYATT, BONITA; Scott HS; Toledo, OH; Cls Rep Frsh Cls; Cl Rep Jr Cls; Cls Rep Sr Cls; Chrh Wkr; Hon Rl; NHS; Off Ade; Stu Cncl; VP Spn Clb; Art Inst Of Atlanta; Fashion Dsgn.

WYATT, DAWN; Colon HS; Leonidas, MI; Band; Hon Rl; 4-H; Fr Clb; Trk; 4-H Awd; Ferris State; Biologist.

WYATT, JOHN; Tell City HS; Tell City, IN; Boy Scts; Hon Rl; NHS; Pep Clb; Spn Clb; Capt Crs Cntry; Trk; Western Ken; Civil Engineer.

WYATT, KATHY; Memorial HS; St Marys, OH; 35/250 Am Leg Aux Girls St; Chrs; Chrh Wkr; Cmnty Wkr; FCA; Hon Rl; Hosp Ade; NHS; Yth Flsp; Y-Teens; Coll; Chem Research.

WYATT, KRISTA; Lebanon HS; Lebanon, OH; Band; Hon Rl; Orch; Sch Mus; Sch Pl; Yth Flsp; Spn Clb; Bsktbl; Hockey; Trk; Univ; Phys Ther.

WYATT, LORI; Sandusky HS; Norwalk, OH; 39/373 Cls Rep Soph Cls; Cl Rep Jr Cls; Cls Rep Sr Cls; Chrs; Hon Rl; NHS; Yrbk; IM Sprt; Mat Maids; Bauder Fashion College; Fashion Mdse.

WYATT, RENEE; Swan Valley HS; Saginaw, MI; Band; Cmnty Wkr; Ed Yrbk; Sch Nwsp; Drama Clb; Bsbl; Bsktbl; Swmmng; Trk; IM Sprt; Delta; Elem Educ.

WYATT JR, ALFRED R; Horace Mann HS; Gary, IN; Band; Hon Rl; Jr NHS; NHS; Mth Clb; Ten; VFW Awd; Voice Dem Awd; Sec Of Sr Hnr Soc; Mbr Of Upward Bound Prog; I U Bloomington Coll; Med.

WYCHE, ANNETTE; R B Chamberlin HS; Twinsburg, OH; 23/230 Cls Rep Frsh Cls; Cls Rep Soph Cls; Cl Rep Jr Cls; Sec Sr Cls; Chrs; Chrh Wkr; Drl Tm; FCA; Hosp Ade; Lbry Ade; Akron Univ; Med Tech.

WYCOFF, THOMAS; East Liverpool HS; E Liverpool, OH; 6/366 Cls Rep Frsh Cls; Cls Rep Soph Cls; Cl Rep Jr Cls; Pres Sr Cls; Am Leg Boys St; Chrs; Hon Rl; NHS; Sch Mus; College.

WYDRINSKI, SHARON; Lake Central HS; Dyer, IN; 83/480 Drl Tm; Hon Rl; Y-Teens; Spn Clb; Pom Pon; Purdue Univ; Elec Engr.

WYGOWSKI, JULIEANNE; J F Rhodes HS; Cleveland, OH; Sec Frsh Cls; Cls Rep Frsh Cls; VP Soph Cls; Cls Rep Soph Cls; Cl Rep Jr Cls; Chrs; Girl Scts; FFA; Bsktbl; GAA; Ohio St Univ; Horticulture.

WYKA, DEBRA; Elston HS; Michigan City, IN; Chrh Wkr; Hon Rl; Sch Mus; Stu Cncl; Drama Clb; Pep Clb; Spn Clb; Capt Pom Pon; Ind Univ; Med Tech.

WYKLE, PAM; Lakeview HS; Cortland, OH; Band; Girl Scts; Hon Rl; Stg Crw; Beta Clb; Pep Clb; Spn Clb; College; Med.

WYLAND, GARY A; Elkins HS; Elkins, WV; 2/227 Am Leg Boys St; Hon Rl; Pres NHS; Sch Pl; Rptr Sch Nwsp; Sch Nwsp; Bsbl; Univ; Engr.

WYLIE, JANET; Peru HS; Peru, IN; 10/271 Chrh Wkr; Hon Rl; Yth Flsp; Pep Clb; Letter Gym; Letter Chrldng; Indiana St Univ; Phys Educ.

WYMAN, KELLEY; West Tech HS; Cleveland, OH; Band; Jr NHS; Yrbk; IM Sprt; Univ; Public Relations.

WYMER, JILL; Ravenna HS; Ravenna, OH; Lat Clb; Kent St Univ; Sci.

WYMER, SUSAN; Field HS; Mogadore, OH; 4/300 Girl Scts; Hon Rl; NHS; Spn Clb; GAA; Ltr In Vllybl Var 3 Yrs 77 79; Ltr In Sftbl Var 3 Yrs 78 80; All Suburbn Lg Sftbl Player 79; Akron Univ; Acctg.

WYND, CYNTHIA; Edward Lee Mcclain HS; Greenfield, OH; 7/148 Sec Soph Cls; Chrs; Jr NHS; Mod UN; NHS; Sch Pl; Drama Clb; Ohi State Univ; Theatre.

WYNN, K; Withrow HS; Cincinnati, OH; Hon Rl; Jr NHS; Treas NHS; Sch Mus; Pep Clb; Mgrs; C of C Awd; College; Chemical Engineer.

WYNN, RACHELLE; Kimball HS; Royal Oak, MI; Chrh Wkr; Hon Rl; JA; NHS; Orch; Sch Mus; Stg Crw; Drama Clb; Spn Clb; PPFtbl; College; Mech Engr.

WYNNE, LORI; West Side Sr HS; Gary, IN; 76/650 Chrs; Chrh Wkr; Hon Rl; JA; Lat Clb; Pep Clb; Indiana St Univ; Pre Law.

WYPASEK, MIKE; Padua Fransiscan HS; Parma, OH; Hon Rl; JA; NHS; Rptr Yrbk; Rptr Sch Nwsp; College; Creative Writing.

WYRICK, GLORIA; Ovid Elsie HS; St Johns, MI; Band; Chrh Wkr; Hon Rl; Lbry Ade; Yth Flsp; 4-H; FHA; Pep Clb; 4-H Awd; Mich State Univ; Nurse.

WYRICK, KRISTA; National Trail HS; New Paris, OH; Cls Rep Soph Cls; Cl Rep Jr Cls; Cls Rep Sr Cls; Am Leg Aux Girls St; Drl Tm; Stu Cncl; Rptr Sch Nwsp; 4-H; FTA; Trk; E Kentucky Univ; Elem Educ.

WYRICK, P; Clinton HS; Tecumseh, MI; Chrs; Hon Rl; Off Ade; Sch Mus; Stu Cncl; Pep Clb; Sec Spn Clb; Trk; Chrldng; Scr Kpr; University; Psych.

WYSE, T; Decatur Central HS; Indnpls, IN; Cmp Fr Grls; Natl Forn Lg; Off Ade; Quill & Scroll; Stu Cncl; Ed Sch Nwsp; Rptr Sch Nwsp; 4-H; Pres Fr Clb; Mat Maids; Hnr Qn Jobs Daughter; 1st Pl News Writing Marion Cnty Press Day; Coll; Eng.

WYSKIVER, CAROL; Chillicothe HS; Chillicothe, OH; Pres Frsh Cls; Trs Soph Cls; Cl Rep Jr Cls; Band; Girl Scts; Hon Rl; Jr NHS; Orch; Sch Mus; Sch Pl;.

WYSOCKI, CATHY; Henry Ford HS; Detroit, MI; Girl Scts; Hon Rl; NHS; VP Quill & Scroll; Sch Nwsp; Fr Clb; Letter Swmmng; Univ.

WYSOCKI, JEAN; Magnificat HS; N Olmsted, OH; Sec Jr Cls; Chrs; Chrh Wkr; Lit Mag; Sch Mus; Sch Pl; Stu Cncl; Rptr Sch Nwsp; Drama Clb; College; Med Sec.

WYSOCKI, LINDA; Mio Au Sable HS; Mio, MI; 2/50 Trs Frsh Cls; Trs Soph Cls; Trs Jr Cls; Trs Sr Cls; Sal; Am Leg Aux Girls St; Hon Rl; NHS; Bsktbl; Dnfth Awd; Northern Michigan Univ; Nursing.

WYSOCKI, MICHELLE; Vermilion HS; Vermilion, OH; Pres Soph Cls; Hon Rl; NHS; Sch Pl; Sch Nwsp; Treas OEA; Spn Clb; Chrldng; OEA Dist Competition 2nd Pl; Bowling Green St Univ; Busns.

WYSONG, MICHELLE; Winchester Cmnty HS; Winchester, IN; Am Leg Aux Girls St; Band; Chrh Wkr; Hon Rl; NHS; Pres Yth Flsp; Pres 4-H; Fr Clb; FDA; FHA; Manchester Coll; Phys Ther.

WYSONG, RICK L; Butler HS; Vandalia, OH; 6/300 Chrh Wkr; Hon Rl; Lbry Ade; Mod UN; NHS; Sch Pl; Stg Crw; Yth Flsp; Drama Clb; Sci Clb; College; Aerospace Engr.

WYSS, MIKE; Eastwood HS; Perrysburg, OH; 14/158 Cls Rep Frsh Cls; Cls Rep Soph Cls; Cl Rep Jr Cls; Band; Cmnty Wkr; Hon Rl; Hosp Ade; Sch Pl; Stg Crw; Yrbk; Univ; Sci.

WYSZYNSKI, CYNTHIA; River Valley HS; Caledonia, OH; Band; Chrs; Orch; Sch Mus; Pep Clb; Rdo Clb; Univ; Eng.

Y

YABLONKAI, MARIA; Woodrow Wilson HS; Youngstown, OH; Sdlty; Y-Teens; Keyettes; Pep Clb; College; Nursing.

YACTEEN, JIHANE; Maumee HS; Maumee, OH; 41/364 Fr Clb; Spn Clb; IM Sprt; Girl Scouts; Chorus; Debate; Office Aide; Tchr Aide; Red Cross Aide; Schl Plays; Scout Activities; Toledo Univ; Pre Med.

YAEGER, L; Trenton HS; Trenton, MI; Band; Chrh Wkr; Drl Tm; Girl Scts; Hon Rl; Hosp Ade; NHS; 4-H; Ger Clb; 4-H Awd; Mich State; Vet.

YAEGER, MICHELLE; St Mary Academy; Monroe, MI; 2/131 Cls Rep Frsh Cls; Cls Rep Soph Cls; Trs Jr Cls; VP Sr Cls; Hon Rl; NHS; Stg Crw; Stu Cncl; Natl Merit Ltr; Michigan St Univ; Busns.

YAEK, CINDY; Memphis HS; Memphis, MI; 7/89 Cls Rep Sr Cls; Hon Rl; Stu Cncl; PPFtbl; Scr Kpr; St Clair Cnty Comm College; Rn.

YAGER, GAYLE; Perrysburg HS; Perrysburg, OH; Chrs; PAVAS; Sch Mus; Sch Pl; Drama Clb; Ger Clb; Recognition Role For Grades Not Quite Honor Roll; College; Communications.

YAGIELA, DAVID; Bay City All Saints Ctrl HS; Essexville, MI; Hon Rl; Letter Bsbl; Letter Trk; College; Aero Engr.

YAGLEY, ANN; Bishop Gallagher HS; Harper Woods, MI; 55/322 Cls Rep Frsh Cls; Cls Rep Soph Cls; Hon Rl; Spn Clb; Chrldng; Mich State Univ.

YAGUNICH, JOHN; Roosevelt HS; E Chicago, IN; 13/199 Am Leg Boys St; Hon Rl; NHS; Treas PAVAS; Yrbk; Sch Nwsp; Spn Clb; Ftbl; Trk; Capt Wrstlng; Purdue Univ; Archt.

YAKE, AMY; Marion Harding HS; Marion, OH; Cls Rep Frsh Cls; Cls Rep Soph Cls; Cl Rep Jr Cls; Cls Rep Sr Cls; Chrs; Hon Rl; Orch; Sch Mus; Pres Stu Cncl; VP Yth Flsp; 4 H Camp Cnslr Hon 77 78 & 79; Jr Fair Bd Hon 78 79; Ohio St Univ; Pblc Rltns.

YAKUBIK, WILLIAM; Hoover HS; Belington, WV; Cls Rep Soph Cls; Boy Scts; FCA; Sct Actv; Stu Cncl; Rptr Sch Nwsp; Letter Bsbl; Letter Ftbl; Letter Trk; Letter Wrstlng; Univ; Pro Ftbl.

YAKUBOV, LYN; Struthers HS; Struthers, OH; 1/206 Band; Hon Rl; Orch; Sch Mus; FNA; Lat Clb; Glf; Ten; Trk; Akron Univ; Surgcl Nurse.

YAKUBOV, STEVEN; Struthers HS; Struthers, OH; 4/257 Hon Rl; VP NHS; DECA; VP Lat Clb; IM Sprt; Scr Kpr; Natl Merit Ltr; N E Ohio Coll Of Medicine; Doctor.

YALE, PATRICIA; Green HS; Akron, OH; Girl Scts; Letter Bsbl; Letter Bsktbl; Letter Crs Cntry; Letter Ftbl; Letter Trk; IM Sprt; 2nd Team All Subrbn Bsktbll Jr 79; Vllybll Cross Cntry Track Sftbll Bsktbll Letters 78; Univ.

YALE, PATTY; Green HS; Akron, OH; Girl Scts; Letter Bsbl; Letter Bsktbl; Letter Crs Cntry; Letter Trk; IM Sprt; Univ.

YALLUP, SUSAN; St Johns HS; St Johns, MI; Chrs; Chrh Wkr; Hon Rl; Mdrgl; NHS; Sch Pl; Yth Flsp; Drama Clb; 4-H; Grand Rapids Baptist College; Bus Ad.

YALOWITZ, DEBBIE; Munster HS; Munstr, IN; 6/441 Pres FFA; Natl Forn Lg; NHS; Yrbk; Rptr Sch Nwsp; Sch Nwsp; Treas Drama Clb; Tmr; Ind Univ; Finance.

YAMADA, JEFF; Donald E Gavit HS; Hammond, IN; Jr NHS; Stu Cncl; Sch Nwsp; DECA; Ind State Univ; Printing.

YAMAMURA, SHINKO; Edon Northwest Local School; Montpelier, OH; Chrs; Hon Rl; GAA; Univ Of Tokyo.

YAMAUCHI, LILLIAN; Ypsilanti HS; Ypsilanti, MI; Hon Rl; Ger Clb; Natl Merit Ltr; Dartmouth College; Chem.

YANCEY, MARK; Buchtel HS; Akron, OH; VICA;.

YANCY, ANGELA; Washington HS; E Chicago, IN; 49/279 Cls Rep Soph Cls; Cl Rep Jr Cls; Chrs; JA; Sch Pl; Stu Cncl; Civ Clb; Key Clb; Pep Clb; Twrlr; Wichita State Univ; Sociology.

YANICK, THOMAS A; St Alphonsus HS; Detroit, MI; Cls Rep Soph Cls; Pres Jr Cls; Hon Rl; NHS; Stu Cncl; 1st Pl School Spelling Bee 1974; 2nd Pl Essay Contest 1975; 1st Pl Schl Science Fair; Wayne State Univ; Drama.

YANKOVICH, MICHELE; Southeast HS; Rootstown, OH; 10/213 Sec Soph Cls; Sec Jr Cls; Band; Chrh Wkr; Hon Rl; MMM; NHS; Off Ade; Orch; Sch Pl; Kent St Univ; Elem Educ.

YANN, STACEY; Marian HS; Elkhart, IN; Hosp Ade; JA; Off Ade; Stg Crw; Yrbk; Sec Pep Clb; Univ Of Evansville; Bus Mgmt.

YANNON, TINA; Bishop Watterson HS; Columbus, OH; Cls Rep Frsh Cls; Band; Stu Cncl; Mat Maids; Scr Kpr; Univ; Med.

YANOS, NEAL; Tri Jr Sr HS; Cambridge City, IN; 5/81 Pres Soph Cls; Pres Jr Cls; Aud/Vis; Hon Rl; NHS; Sch Pl; Stu Cncl; 4-H; Fr Clb; Ten; Purdue Univ; Engr.

YANSSENS, TAMARA L; Buckeye North HS; Mingo Jct, OH; 5/119 Band; NHS; Off Ade; Sch Pl; Stu Cncl; Drama Clb; Pep Clb; Sci Clb; Spn Clb; Chrldng; Univ.

YANSURA, JULIE; Meadowbrook HS; Pleasant City, OH; Band; Chrh Wkr; Hon Rl; NHS; Key Clb; Mth Clb; Sci Clb; Spn Clb; Muskingum Tech Coll; Radiology.

YANTIS, JOHN; Westerville South HS; Westerville, OH; 11/275 Cls Rep Sr Cls; Am Leg Boys St; Boy Scts; Hon Rl; NHS; Stu Cncl; Letter Glf; Capt Swmmng; U S Naval Academy.

YAPP, KAY; Southfield Christian HS; Livonia, MI; 2/61 Pres Soph Cls; Sal; Chrs; Chrh Wkr; Hon Rl; NHS; Red Cr Ade; Stu Cncl; Yrbk; Gordon Coll; Psych.

YARB, DENISE; Woodrow Wilson HS; Youngstown, OH; 21/430 Cmp Fr Grls; Hon Rl; Jr NHS; NHS; Off Ade; Youngstown State Univ; Exec Sec.

YARBOROUGH, JAMES C; Woodridge HS; Cuyahoga Falls, OH; 1/150 Cls Rep Frsh Cls; Pres Soph Cls; Pres Sr Cls; Band; Chrh Wkr; Debate Tm; Hon Rl; Jr NHS; Lbry Ade; Natl Forn Lg; Miami Univ; Pulp & Paper Tech.

YARBROUGH, CHRISTINE; Emerson HS; Gary, IN; Hon Rl; Off Ade; Stu Cncl; Pres FBLA; Cit Awd; Purdue Univ; Rn.

YARBROUGH, JERI; Elmhurst HS; Huntington, IN; 26/346 AFS; Band; Drm Mjrt; Hon Rl; NHS; Pep Clb; PPFtbl; Cit Awd; Schlrshp Awds; Indiana Univ; Phys Therapy.

YARCUSKO, ALAN C; Rocky River HS; Rocky River, OH; 15/324 Am Leg Boys St; Aud/Vis; Debate Tm; Hon Rl; JA; Jr NHS; Lbry Ade; Lit Mag; Natl Forn Lg; NHS; Full 4 Yr Scslhp U S Army ROTC & U S Navy ROTC 78; 18000 Asst & Schslp Cornell Univ 78; Rose Hulman Inst Of Tech; Elec Engr.

YARDLEY, RICH; Upper Arlington HS; Columbus, OH; Band; Boy Scts; Hon Rl; Sct Actv; Rptr Yrbk; Lcrss; Letter Wrstlng; IM Sprt; IM Sprt; Ohio St Univ; Chemistry.

YARIAN, JENNIFER; Newbury HS; Newbury, OH; Girl Scts; Hosp Ade; Rptr Yrbk; Sci Clb; Spn Clb; Coach Actv; IM Sprt; Letter Mgrs; Mat Maids; Univ.

YARIAN, TRACIE; Garrett HS; Garrett, IN; Chrs; Hon Rl; Y-Teens; Ger Clb; Pep Clb; Spn Clb; Bsktbl; Trk; Coach Actv; Pres GAA; Univ; Spec Educ Tchr.

YARNELL, LOIS A; Westerville North HS; Westerville, OH; 13/425 Chrs; Hon Rl; NHS; Pres FFA; Bsktbl; Ohio St Univ; Horticulture.

YARNELL, PATRICIA; Robert Rogers HS; Toledo, OH; Chrh Wkr; Hon Rl; Lbry Ade; FHA; Lat Clb; Mth Clb; Davis Bus Coll.

YARRINGTON, KIM; Walnut Ridge HS; Columbus, OH; Girl Scts; Hon Rl; NHS; Quill & Scroll; Sch Nwsp; Spn Clb; Letter Bsbl; Wrstlng; Mat Maids; College.

YARRIS, BETH; Westlake HS; Westlake, OH; 59/300 Cls Rep Soph Cls; Am Leg Aux Girls St; Band; Jr NHS; Lit Mag; VP Stu Cncl; Pep Clb; Rdo Clb; Letter Ten; Letter Chrldng; Jr High & HS St Rep For Ohio Assoc 76 77 & 79 80; Stdnt Council Sec 78 79; Stdnt Council V P 79 80; Univ; Scndry Educ.

YASECHKO, JANET; Struthers HS; Struthers, OH; 40/272 Hon Rl; Jr NHS; Lbry Ade; NHS; Drama Clb; Fr Clb; FNA; Pep Clb; Youngstown State Univ.

YASECHKO, JOANN; Cardinal Mooney HS; New Middletown, OH; 147/308 Chrh Wkr; Hon Rl; 4-H; Fr Clb; Mth Clb; 4-H Awd; Univ Of Dayton; Comp Sci.

YASSO, THEKRA; Charle S Mott HS; Warren, MI; Lbry Ade; Rptr Yrbk; Coll.

YAST, PATRICIA; Andrean HS; Merrillville, IN; 22/272 Sec Jr Cls; Cls Rep Sr Cls; Aud/Vis; Hon Rl; NHS; Stu Cncl; Yrbk; Glf; GAA; IM Sprt; Vanderbilt Univ; Bio.

YASTE, MELANIE; Edinburg HS; Franklin, IN; Band; Chrs; Girl Scts; NHS; Drama Clb; Fr Clb; Sci Clb; Trk; GAA; Lion Awd; Ball St Univ; Music.

YATES, DANTE; Beecher HS; Mt Morris, MI; Cl Rep Jr Cls; Chrh Wkr; Hon Rl; Stg Crw; Stu Cncl; Sprt Ed Sch Nwsp; Rptr Sch Nwsp; Sch Nwsp; Pep Clb; Spn Clb; Plq Frsh Ftbl Big Nine Champs; Tennessee St Univ; Archt.

YATES, DEMETREA; J W Scott HS; Toledo, OH; Hon Rl; FHA; Spn Clb; Univ; Educ.

YATES, KIM; Hesperia HS; Hesperia, MI; Sec Jr Cls; VP Band; Hon Rl; Sch Mus; 4-H; Pres OEA; Bsbl; Letter Trk; IM Sprt; PPFtbl; Typng Ii Awd Hesperia HS 1977; OEA Reg Comp Interof Cmmntns 2nd Pl 1978; Dist Solo & Ensmbl 1st Div 1978; Muskegon Bus Coll; Bus.

YATES, MICHAEL R; Eastmoor Sr HS; Columbus, OH; 43/290 Cls Rep Frsh Cls; Band; Boy Scts; Chrh Wkr; Cmnty Wkr; Orch; Sch Mus; Letter Trk; Outstnd Instrumnt Music 1975; Commd Student Nat Achv Scholarshp Prog Outstnd Negro Stud 1978; Univ; Engr.

YATES, RANDALL; Oak Hill HS; Oak Hill, OH; 12/112 Pres Frsh Cls; Pres Soph Cls; Band; Boy Scts; Hon Rl; NHS; Stu Cncl; Beta Clb; Pep Clb; Bsbl; All League In Ftbl 2nd Tm Dist 79; Best Defensv Linemn 79; Best Rebounder Bsktbl 79; Univ.

YATES, RANDY; Green HS; Akron, OH; Boy Scts; Hon Rl; Bsktbl; IM Sprt; Scr Kpr; Tmr; Univ; Bus Admin.

YATES, WILLIAM B; Forest Park HS; Crystal Falls, MI; Hon Rl; Pep Clb; Ftbl; Trk; Coach Actv; IM Sprt; Cit Awd; Ftbl 80; Ctznshp 79; Michigan Tech Univ; Pro Ftbll.

YAU, JOHN; William A Wirt HS; Gary, IN; 36/230 Hon Rl; Letter Socr; Letter Ten; Wrstlng; Cit Awd; Purdue Univ; Mech Engr.

YAUCH, LAURA; Bishop Ready HS; Columbus, OH; 3/130 Drl Tm; Hon Rl; NHS; Sch Pl; Sci Clb; Spn Clb; Trk; Am Leg Awd; Ohio St Univ; Vet Med.

YAUGER, ANGIE; Springboro HS; Springboro, OH; AFS; Chrs; Chrh Wkr; Girl Scts; Hon Rl; Off Ade; VP Yth Flsp; Rptr Sch Nwsp; Drama Clb; Pres FTA; Anderson Coll; Elem Educ.

YAW, CONNIE; Brandywine HS; Niles, MI; Trs Soph Cls; VP Jr Cls; Pres Sr Cls; Hon Rl; NHS; Stu Cncl; Yrbk; Pep Clb; Letter Bsbl; Letter Bsktbl; Univ; Photog.

YAWORSKI, KAREN; Beaver Creek HS; Beaver Creek, OH; 64/702 Chrs; Chrh Wkr; FCA; Hon Rl; NHS; Pres Yth Flsp; Sec 4-H; Trk; 4-H Awd; 1st Pl Phys Ftnss St Team 77 79; Phys Ftnss Indv Awds 77 & 79; Phys Ftns Team 75 79; Miami Univ; Phys Educ.

YAZEL, DEBORAH; Lima HS; Lima, OH; Band; Chrh Wkr; Hon Rl; Orch; Ten Temple Univ; Elem Educa.

YBANEZ, JESSICA; Greenbrier East HS; Lewisburg, WV; Cls Rep Soph Cls; Band; Chrs; Girl Scts; Hon Rl; NHS; Sch Mus; Stu Cncl; Rptr Sch Nwsp; VP Fr Clb; Univ; Med.

YEAGER, DONALD; Lawrence Ctrl HS; Indianapolis, IN; Chrh Wkr; Quill & Scroll; Pres Yth Flsp; Sprt Ed Sch Nwsp; Rptr Sch Nwsp; Sch Nwsp; Univ; Jrnlsm.

YEAGER, KIM; Indian Hill HS; Cincinnati, OH; Cls Rep Frsh Cls; Cls Rep Soph Cls; Sec Sr Cls; Trs Sr Cls; Orch; Sch Mus; Bsktbl; Socr; Chrldng; PPFtbl; Univ.

YEAGER, MARTHA; Wickliffe HS; Wickliffe, OH; Sec Soph Cls; Sec Sr Cls; Cmp Fr Grls; Pres Chrs; Chrh Wkr; Hon Rl; Mdrgl; Orch; Sch Mus; Cit Awd; Columbia Union Coll; Social Wkr.

YEAGER, SCOTT; Brookside HS; Sheffield Vlge, OH; Aud/Vis; Band; Boy Scts; Lbry Ade; Off Ade; Stg Crw; Sch Nwsp; Mth Clb; Tmr; Natl Merit Ltr; Lorain County Community College.

YEAGER, STEVEN; Chaminade Julienne HS; Dayton, OH; Chrh Wkr; Hon Rl; Ger Clb; Trk; College; Chemistry.

YEAGLEY, BRYAN; Battle Creek Academy; Battle Creek, MI; Cls Rep Soph Cls; Sal; Pres Band; Hon Rl; Pres NHS; Yrbk; Bsbl; Hockey; Andrews Univ; Medicine.

YEAGLEY, CATHY; Salem Sr HS; Salem, OH; 1/252 Val; Rptr Yrbk; Mth Clb; Spn Clb; Capt Bsktbl; Capt Ten; Mgrs; Drake Univ; Pharm.

YEARY, JEFF; Cloverdale Clovers HS; Quincy, IN; Sch Pl; Ftbl; Trk; Wrstlng; Depaul Ind; Law Inforcement.

YEATER, BECKY; Brooke HS; Weirton, WV; Chrh Wkr; Girl Scts; Hon Rl; NHS; Y-Teens; DECA; Spn Clb; Mat Maids; Cashier.

YEATER, KEVIN; Lincoln HS; Wallace, WV; Pres Soph Cls; Hon Rl; NHS; Stu Cncl; VICA; Letter Bsbl; Crs Cntry; Letter Ftbl; Fairmont St Univ; Elec Engr.

YECKLEY, LISA; St Joseph Cntrl Catholic HS; Fremont, OH; Cls Rep Frsh Cls; Trs Jr Cls; Cmp Fr Grls; Hon Rl; Stu Cncl; Yrbk; 4-H; FBLA; Pep Clb; Bsktbl; Terra Tech Coll; Executive Sec.

YEE, ALFRED; Wheeling Park HS; Wheeling, WV; Cls Rep Soph Cls; Hon Rl; NHS; Stu Cncl; IM Sprt; Univ; Engr.

YEE, DARLENE; Magnificat HS; No Olmsted, OH; Chrs; Chrh Wkr; Girl Scts; Hosp Ade; Sch Mus; Coach Actv; Candystripping 200 Hrs 79; Perfect Attendance 79; Univ; Med Tech.

YEE, HENRY; Bishop Hartley HS; Columbus, OH; Cmnty Wkr; Hon Rl; Mth Clb; Pep Clb; Coach Actv; IM Sprt; College; Architecture.

YEE, JACK; Thomas A De Vilbiss HS; Toledo, OH; Hon Rl; JA; Jr NHS; NHS; Off Ade; Mth Clb; Sci Clb; Spn Clb; JA Awd; College; Bio Sci.

YEE, KAREN; Austintown Fitch HS; Youngstown, OH; 11/600 Band; Debate Tm; Capt Drl Tm; Hon Rl; Treas JA; Sec NHS; Sch Mus; Yth Flsp; Spn Clb; Trk; Girls Chrstn Org Awd 70 76; Solo Ensmbl Contst 1 Ratng 79; Readng Devlpmt Enrchmnt 79; Univ; Math.

YEE, NANCY; Henry Ford HS; Detroit, MI; Val; Hon Rl; NHS; Spn Clb; Bausch & Lomb Awd; Univ Of Michigan; Elec Engr.

YEE, TRACY A; Beechcroft HS; Columbus, OH; 5/213 Hon Rl; NHS; Off Ade; Sch Pl; Stu Cncl; Ed Yrbk; Drama Clb; Fr Clb; Pep Clb; Capt Trk; PTA Schlrshp Awd; 2nd Runner Up To Miss Teenage Columbus; Appeared In Movie Grease; Ohio State Univ; Psych.

YEICHNER, BARBARA; Galion Sr HS; Galion, OH; Band; Chrs; Chrh Wkr; Girl Scts; Hon Rl; NHS; Off Ade; Sch Mus; Drama Clb; Supr Rating OMEA Solo & Ensemble Contest 78; Musicial Show Tune Ensemble 78; Played Organ At Baccalaureate; Univ; Music Tchr.

YEKER, JENNIFER; Harrison HS; Evansville, IN; Cls Rep Frsh Cls; Cls Rep Soph Cls; Cl Rep Jr Cls; Cls Rep Sr Cls; Band; Drm Mjrt; Hon Rl; Stu Cncl; Pep Clb; Glf; Western Ky; Comp Sci.

YELDA, MICHAEL J; Cass Technical HS; Detroit, MI; 8/896 Band; Chrh Wkr; Cmnty Wkr; Hon Rl; Lbry Ade; MMM; NHS; Orch; PAVAS; Sch Mus; Hghst Awd In Performance St Wide Trumpet 98% Out Of 100 78; Wayne St Univ; Bus Admin.

YELEY, BRIAN; Dublin HS; Dublin, OH; 1/153 Val; Am Leg Boys St; Band; Hon Rl; Jr NHS; NHS; Orch; Sch Mus; Ed Yrbk; Ger Clb; Cls Spkr At Commencmnt 79; Sclhsp Team French 77 Chem 78 Eng 79; 4 Pt Grd Avr Jr Yr 78; Univ Of Michigan; Archt.

YELIC, SANDY; Medina HS; Medina, OH; 56/381 Cls Rep Sr Cls; Cmnty Wkr; Drl Tm; Hon Rl; Sch Mus; Stu Cncl; 4-H; Pep Clb; Trk; Chrldng; Ohi State Univ; Vet Med.

YELLSEAGLE, STANLEY; Howe Military HS; Eagle Butte, SD; 12/31 NHS; ROTC; Rptr Sch Nwsp; Fr Clb; Glf; Chrldng; Scr Kpr; Manchester College; Pre Med.

YELTON, RICK; Canfield HS; Canfield, OH; Boy Scts; Cmnty Wkr; Hon Rl; NHS; Ger Clb; Key Clb; Swmmng; Mgrs; Scr Kpr; Natl Merit Ltr; Varsity Swim Team Mst Improvd Swimmer 78; Univ; Engr.

YENCHIK, JANE; Green HS; Akron, OH; Cls Rep Frsh Cls; Cls Rep Soph Cls; Cl Rep Jr Cls; Chrs; Girl Scts; Off Ade; Yth Flsp; Y-Teens; Spn Clb; Bsbl; Akron Univ; Medicine.

YENCSO, DAVID; Davison HS; Davison, MI; 26/462 Hon Rl; Off Ade; Sch Nwsp; Fr Clb; Sci Clb; College; Elec.

YENIOR, ALLEN C; Standish Sterling Cntrl HS; Sterling, MI; 4/176 Cl Rep Jr Cls; Hon Rl; Pres Stu Cncl; IM Sprt; Natl Merit Ltr; Natl Merit SF; N Michigan Univ; Criminology.

YENKEL, TAMMY; Woodhaven HS; Flat Rock, MI; Band; Hon Rl; Hosp Ade; Lbry Ade; Off Ade; Glf; Michigan St Univ; Nurse.

YENNIE, CATHY; West Branch HS; Homeworth, OH; AFS; Letter Band; Chrs; Orch; Sch Mus; College.

YENTES, NORA; Northfield Jr Sr HS; Urbana, IN; 8/110 Band; Hon Rl; Rptr Sch Nwsp; Fr Clb; Pep Clb; Upper Wabash Career Ctr; Sec.

YENTES, TAMI; Northfield HS; Urbana, IN; 14/106 Hon Rl; NHS; Yth Flsp; FHA; Pep Clb; Spn Clb; DAR Awd; College; Phys Therapy.

YEO, CHARLES D; Lansing Eastern HS; Lansing, MI; 47/497 Band; Hon Rl; JA; Jr NHS; NHS; Rptr Sch Nwsp; Ger Clb; JA Awd; Natl Merit Ltr; Mich State Univ; Pre Vet Med.

YEOMANS, DENISE; Buena Vista HS; Saginaw, MI; 10/107 Hon Rl; Hosp Ade; Off Ade; Ed Yrbk; Rptr Sch Nwsp; Delta Coll; Bus.

YERAK, REBECCA; Willoughby South HS; Willoughby Hill, OH; 35/416 NHS; VP Stu Cncl; Sch Nwsp; Pep Clb; Spn Clb; Bsbl; Bsktbl; DAR Awd; Ohi State; Journalism.

YERDEN, DANA; Highland HS; Anderson, IN; Band; Chrh Wkr; Hon Rl; NHS; Sch Mus; Yth Flsp; Anderson Coll; Nursing.

YERIAN, DONNA; Canton South HS; Canton, OH; Cls Rep Frsh Cls; Girl Scts; Hon Rl; Hosp Ade; Lbry Ade; NHS; Stg Crw; Yrbk; Fr Clb; Pep Clb; Univ; Sci.

YERKEY, JENNIFER; Ontario HS; Mansfield, OH; Band; Hon Rl; Off Ade; Stu Cncl; Bsktbl; Ten; Mansfield Univ; Nursing.

YET, BETTY; Henry Ford HS; Detroit, MI; Cls Rep Soph Cls; Chrh Wkr; Hon Rl; Lbry Ade; NHS; Off Ade; Stu Cncl; Univ; Acctg.

YETTER, MARY; Crestline HS; Crestline, OH; Cls Rep Frsh Cls; Cls Rep Soph Cls; Cl Rep Jr Cls; Cls Rep Sr Cls; Chrs; Hon Rl; Off Ade; Sch Mus; Treas Stu Cncl; Rptr Sch Nwsp; Jr Homecoming Attndnt 78; Vllybl Var Ltr Hon Mntn 78; Vllybl Trophy 78; Spec Educ.

YETTS, NATHAN; Wintersville HS; Wintrsvll, OH; Chrh Wkr; Hon Rl; Lat Clb; IM Sprt; Ohio St Univ; Marketing.

YIESLA, SHARON; Shawe Memorial HS; Madison, IN; 2/26 Sal; Hon Rl; Pres NHS; Natl Merit SF; Purdue Univ; Agricuhure Spec Horticu.

YIM, JONATHAN; West Lafayette HS; W Lafayette, IN; 18/185 Hon Rl; NHS; Ftbl; Wrstlng; Purdue Univ.

YINGLING, CONNIE; Fairless Local HS; Navarre, OH; 10/225 Cls Rep Soph Cls; Cl Rep Jr Cls; Hon Rl; NHS; Sch Mus; Sch Pl; Stg Crw; Stu Cncl; Yth Flsp; Y-Teens; Akron Univ; Art.

YISCOGLIOSI, DIANA; Our Lady Of Mercy HS; Livonia, MI; Yrbk; Sch Nwsp; Univ; Bus.

YLIMAKI, ROSE M; Burt Township HS; Grand Marais, MI; Pres Jr Cls; Band; Chrh Wkr; Cmnty Wkr; Hon Rl; Off Ade; Stu Cncl; Yth Flsp; Rptr Yrbk; Yrbk; Poem Published In Young Amer Sings Copy Editor At Voyager Press; Teach Remedial Reading; Lake Superior State Univ; Elem Ed.

YOAKAM, DAWN; Danbury HS; Lakeside, OH; Pres Frsh Cls; Band; Girl Scts; Hon Rl; Off Ade; 4-H; Trk; Chrldng; GAA; Mgrs; Firelands Campus; Soc Work.

YOAKEM, LORI; Paint Valley HS; Bainbridge, OH; 5/90 Band; Hon Rl; Univ; Educ.

YOAKUM, JOANI; Marysville HS; Marysville, OH; Cl Rep Jr Cls; Girl Scts; Hon Rl; FHA; IM Sprt; College; Sci.

YOCHEM, LINDA; Central Catholic HS; Lafayette, IN; Chrs; Hon Rl; Sch Mus; Pres Purdue Univ; Sociology.

YOCHUM, BETH; North Knox HS; Oaktown, TN; Drl Tm; FCA; Hon Rl; NHS; Stu Cncl; 4-H; Fr Clb; FHA; Pep Clb; Vincennes Univ.

YOCHUM, DEBRA; Reitz Memorial HS; Evansville, IN; 20/200 Cl Rep Jr Cls; Chrh Wkr; Hon Rl; Hosp Ade; Lbry Ade; Off Ade; Stu Cncl; Rptr Sch Nwsp; 4-H; Sci Clb; Univ; Biology.

YOCKEY, RANDY; Eastern HS; Russellville, OH; Trs Soph Cls; Band; Chrh Wkr; Hon Rl; Pol Wkr; Stg Crw; Rptr Sch Nwsp; 4-H; Fr Clb; FFA; Southern St Cmnty Coll.

YOCUM, DEANNA M; University HS; Morgantown, WV; 5/146 Cls Rep Frsh Cls; Hon Rl; Jr NHS; Lit Mag; Quill & Scroll; Rptr Sch Nwsp; Sch Nwsp; Sci Clb; Spn Clb; Scr Kpr; West Virginia Univ; Engr.

YOCUM, JOHN G; William Henry Harrison HS; Harrison, OH; Am Leg Boys St; Boy Scts; Chrh Wkr; Cmnty Wkr; Hon Rl; Jr NHS; NHS; Pol Wkr; Sct Actv; Stu Cncl; Univ.

YOCUM, TRACEY; South Range HS; Salem, OH; Band; Boy Scts; Chrh Wkr; Orch; Sch Mus; Ger Clb; College; Bio.

YODER, ANNA; Millington HS; Vassar, MI; 12/171 Cls Rep Frsh Cls; Cls Rep Soph Cls; Cl Rep Jr Cls; Cls Rep Sr Cls; Am Leg Aux Girls St; Chrs; Chrh Wkr; Hon Rl; NHS; Sch Pl; MEA Schlrshp 79; Acad Achvmnt Awds 76 78 & 79; Bio Publshd In Otstndng Young Amer 79; Univ Of Michigan; Tch Spec Educ.

YODER, BRIAN; Bullock Creek HS; Midland, MI; 8/190 Band; Boy Scts; Debate Tm; Hon Rl; Natl Forn Lg; Sct Actv; Sec FSA; Univ; Comp Sci.

YODER, BRIAN K; West Jefferson HS; W Jefferson, OH; VP Soph Cls; Pres Jr Cls; Am Leg Boys St; VP Band; Pres Chrs; Jr NHS; Sch Mus; Stu Cncl; VP 4-H; Voice Dem Awd;.

YODER, CRAIG; Garaway HS; Sugarcreek, OH; 13/90 Sec Frsh Cls; Pres Soph Cls; VP Sr Cls; Chrh Wkr; Hon Rl; Pres Yth Flsp; Ger Clb; Letter Bsbl; Letter Ftbl; Pom Pon; Akron Univ; Elec Engr.

YODER, DAVE; Elkhart Central HS; Elkhart, IN; Band; Boy Scts; Chrs; Sch Mus; Sch Pl; Stg Crw; Ed Sch Nwsp; Ind Univ; Dentistry.

YODER, DEBORAH; White Pigeon HS; White Pigeon, MI; 9/95 Trs Sr Cls; Hon Rl; NHS; Yth Flsp; Yrbk; FHA; Pres OEA; Letter Bsktbl; Coach Actv; Natl Merit Schl; Southwestern Mic College; Data Prc.

YODER, DEIDA; Daleville HS; Daleville, IN; 13/80 Band; Drl Tm; Hon Rl; Lbry Ade; NHS; Sch Mus; Rptr Yrbk; Eng Clb; 4-H; Spn Clb; 2 Yrs Perfect Attendance Awds; Busns Schl; Modeling.

YODER, DOUGLAS K; Rocky River HS; Rocky River, OH; 9/307 Pres Band; Hon Rl; Jr NHS; NHS; Stu Cncl; Bsktbl; IM Sprt; Natl Merit SF; College; Business.

YODER, GAIL; Martins Ferry HS; Bridgeport, OH; 26/215 NHS; Y-Teens; Rptr Yrbk; Spn Clb; Chrldng; GAA; Elk Awd; Muskingum Coll.

YODER, GARY; Westview HS; Topeka, IN; Cls Rep Frsh Cls; VP Soph Cls; Cl Rep Jr Cls; Band; Hon Rl; Pol Wkr; Rptr Sch Nwsp; 4-H; FFA; Ger Clb;.

YODER, HEIDI; Brookside HS; Downers Grove, IL; Band; Chrs; Mdrgl; Sch Mus; Sch Pl; Stg Crw; Ed Sch Nwsp; Pres Drama Clb; Pep Clb; Letter Bsbl; Whos Who Among Amer Music Stu;.

YODER, JOSEPH; Pinckney HS; Pinckney, MI; Stu Cncl; Bsktbl; Ftbl; Ferris St Coll; Pre Law.

YODER, K; Pike Delta York HS; Delta, OH; 10/115 Sec Soph Cls; Cl Rep Jr Cls; Cls Rep Sr Cls; Chrh Wkr; NHS; VP Stu Cncl; Letter Trk; Mat Maids; Bowling Green Univ; Tech.

YODER, KAY; Pike Delta York HS; Delta, OH; 10/115 Sec Soph Cls; Cl Rep Jr Cls; Cls Rep Sr Cls; Chrs; Chrh Wkr; Hon Rl; NHS; Stu Cncl; 4-H; Spn Clb; Bowling Green Univ.

YODER, KEVIN; Garaway HS; Sugarcreek, OH; 3/100 Am Leg Boys St; Aud/Vis; Chrh Wkr; Hon Rl; NHS; Yth Flsp; Ger Clb; Bsktbl; Letter Glf; Coach Actv; Tied Of R1st In Cls Rank 78; Univ; Chem Engr.

YODER, KEVIN; Columbiana HS; Columbiana, OH; 11/98 VP Chrs; Chrh Wkr; Hon Rl; Mdrgl; NHS; VP Yth Flsp; 4-H; VP Spn Clb; Letter Bsktbl; Hesston College; Music.

YODER, L; Davison HS; Davison, MI; Chrs; Chrh Wkr; Hon Rl; Mdrgl; Sch Mus; Letter Trk; Letter Mgrs; Grand Rapids Baptist Coll.

YODER, RENETTE; Bethany Christian HS; Goshen, IN; Chrs; Chrh Wkr; Hon Rl; Jr NHS; Yth Flsp; Rptr Sch Nwsp; 4-H; Ger Clb; Pep Clb; 4-H Awd; Hesston Collegef Bus Admin.

YODER, ROBERT E; Rossville HS; Mulberry, IN; 13/50 Hon Rl; Fr Clb; Letter Bsktbl; Letter Crs Cntry; Letter Trk; Purdue Univ; Agri.

YODER, SARAH; Carroll HS; Flora, IN; Hon Rl; Yth Flsp; Rptr Yrbk; 4-H; FHA; Pep Clb; Spn Clb; Trk; Scr Kpr; Tmr; Fort Wayne Bus Coll; Acctg.

YODER, THOS; Goshen HS; Goshen, IN; Cls Rep Frsh Cls; Cl Rep Jr Cls; Band; Hon Rl; Jr NHS; NHS; Sct Actv; Stu Cncl; 4-H; Pep Clb; Youth Of The Month Exchange Club Goshen Indiana; U S Naval Academy; Poli Sci.

YOERGER, WILLIAM; Hilliard HS; Hilliard, OH; 53/420 Cls Rep Soph Cls; Cls Rep Sr Cls; Chrs; FCA; Hon Rl; NHS; Pres Stu Cncl; Rptr Yrbk; Spn Clb; Ohio St Univ; Bus.

YOHE, DAVID; Lake Catholic HS; Wickliffe, OH; Chrs; Chrh Wkr; Hon Rl; Pol Wkr; Sch Mus; Sch Pl; IM Sprt; Am Leg Awd; Cert Of Honor Excellence In Schlrshp; Cert Of Merit In Composition; Coll; Bio Chem Engr.

YOHO, BRIAN; Woodsfield HS; Woodsfield, OH; Cmnty Wkr; Hon Rl; Bsbl; Bsktbl; Scr Kpr; Univ; Pharm.

YOHO, KATHY; Bloom Local HS; Wheelersburg, OH; Band; Chrs; Drm Mjrt; Hon Rl; Sch Pl; Stg Crw; FHA; Treas OEA; IM Sprt; Bus Schl; Book Keeper.

YOHO, LISA; Woodsfield HS; Woodsfield, OH; Am Leg Aux Girls St; Hon Rl; NHS; Off Ade; Sch Pl; Drama Clb; Fr Clb; Pep Clb; Chrldng; Kiwan Awd; Ohio St Univ.

YOHO, MARY; Ashland Sr HS; Ashland, OH; Chrs; Chrh Wkr; Hon Rl; Hosp Ade; Off Ade; Sch Mus; Lat Clb; Pep Clb; GAA; Wright St Univ; Nursing.

YOHO, PATRICIA; Fairless HS; Navarre, OH; Cls Rep Soph Cls; Chrs; Cmnty Wkr; Girl Scts; Hosp Ade; Sch Mus; Sch Pl; Stu Cncl; Y-Teens; Drama Clb; Nursing Schl; Nurse.

YOKIE, MICHAEL; Jeffers HS; Painesdale, MI; Letter Bsktbl; Letter Crs Cntry; Letter Swmmng; Letter Trk; IM Sprt; Navy; Elec.

YOKUM, RICKY; Harman HS; Harman, WV; Sec Frsh Cls; Hon Rl; NHS; FBLA; VP FFA; Pep Clb; Bsktbl; Coll.

YONCHAK, BOB; Lake Catholic HS; Chesterland, OH; Pres Soph Cls; Hon Rl; Sch Mus; Sch Pl; Stg Crw; Stu Cncl; Rptr Sch Nwsp; Univ Of Notre Dame; Law.

YONDERS, DEBI; Copley HS; Fairlawn, OH; Chrs; Hon Rl; FHA; Pep Clb; Spn Clb; Trk; Chrldng; Most Dedicated Mbr Of Track Tm 77; Univ; Law.

YONG, KATHLEEN; Ben Davis HS; Indianapolis, IN; Debate Tm; FCA; Girl Scts; Natl Forn Lg; Off Ade; Quill & Scroll; Sprt Ed Yrbk; Letter Swmmng; Trk; Purdue Univ; Oceanography.

YONG JO, HWA; Willow Run HS; Ypsilanti, MI; Cl Rep Jr Cls; Am Leg Boys St; Chrh Wkr; Hon Rl; Stu Cncl; Fr Clb; Letter Ftbl; Coach Actv; Am Leg Awd; JETS Awd; EISP Summer Enrichment Prog; The Most Hard Working Stu Awd; EISP Schlrshp; Harvard Univ; Med.

YONKE, JEFFREY; Unionvll Sebewaing Area HS; Unionville, MI; Hon Rl; VP Yth Flsp; Letter Crs Cntry; Letter Trk; Am Leg Awd; College.

YONKER, CINDY; Hamilton HS; Hamilton, MI; 9/131 Chrh Wkr; Hon Rl; Mdrgl; Sch Mus; Sch Pl; Stg Crw; Yth Flsp; Rptr Yrbk; Rptr Sch Nwsp; Sch Nwsp; Davenport Busns Coll; Acctg.

YONKERS, PAULA; Caledonia HS; Caledonia, MI; Girl Scts; Hon Rl; Letter Bsbl; Mgrs; Natl Merit Ltr; Natl Merit SF; Natl Merit Schl; Central Mich Univ; Teaching.

YONKOVITCH, REBECCA; John F Kennedy HS; Warren, OH; Pres Soph Cls; VP Sr Cls; Am Leg Aux Girls St; Hon Rl; NHS; Stu Cncl; Rptr Yrbk; Letter Bsbl; Letter Bsktbl; Kent St Univ; Acctg.

YONKS, DAVID; Terre Haute S Vigo HS; Terre Haute, IN; Hon Rl; Boys Clb Am; Key Clb; Sci Clb; Spn Clb; Glf; Indiana Univ.

YOOKAM, JENNIE; Springboro HS; Springboro, OH; Band; Cmp Fr Grls; Chrs; Chrh Wkr; Drl Tm; Hon Rl; 4-H; Trk; Pom Pon; 4-H Awd; David Lipscomb Coll; Schl Cnslr.

YOON, MARILYN; Owosso HS; Owosso, MI; 80/406 Cls Rep Frsh Cls; Cls Rep Soph Cls; Chrs; Hon Rl; NHS; Stu Cncl; Lat Clb; GAA; PPFtbl; Mic State Univ.

YOREY, JOSEPH; Saint Josephs HS; South Bend, IN; 10/250 Chrh Wkr; Hon Rl; Sch Mus; Opt Clb Awd; Coll Of Steubenville; Acctg.

YORK, BRUCE; Fairborn Park Hills HS; Fairborn, OH; Band; Chrs; Hon Rl; NHS; Letter Trk; Wright St Univ; Engr Tech.

YORK, DAVID; St Francis De Sales Ctrl HS; Morgantown, WV; Chrs; Chrh Wkr; Hon Rl; Lbry Ade; Lit Mag; Treas Yth Flsp; Fr Clb; Mth Clb; Sci Clb; College; Biology.

YORK, DEANNA; Ansonia HS; Rossburg, OH; Band; Chrs; Rptr Yrbk; Rptr Sch Nwsp; 4-H; FHA; OEA; Pep Clb; Sci Clb; Twrlr;.

YORK, DONNA; Switz City HS; Lyons, IN; 1/52 Cls Rep Frsh Cls; Cls Rep Soph Cls; Cl Rep Jr Cls; Band; Hon Rl; Lit Mag; NHS; Ind State Univ; Educ.

YORK, GARY; Plymouth HS; Plymouth, IN; 9/225 VP Sr Cls; Hon Rl; NHS; Ed Yrbk; Mth Clb; Spn Clb; Purdue Univ; Comp Sci.

YORK, JEFFREY; Holt HS; Holt, MI; 1/332 Cls Rep Frsh Cls; Hon Rl; NHS; Stu Cncl; Fr Clb; Bsktbl; Ftbl; Ten; Coach Actv; Scr Kpr; Coll; Pre Law.

YORK, LORA; Hazel Park HS; Ferndale, MI; Sec Soph Cls; Band; Chrs; Drl Tm; Girl Scts; Hon Rl; NHS; Chrldng; Coach Actv; Pom Pon; College; Exec Sec.

YORK, STEVEN; Hartland HS; Hartland, MI; Boy Scts; Hon Rl; Boys Clb Am; Bsbl; Ftbl; Glf; IM Sprt; Pres Awd; MSU; Dentistry.

YORK, WILLIAM A; Holt Sr HS; Holt, MI; 5/360 Band; Lbry Ade; NHS; Sch Pl; Yrbk; Rptr Sch Nwsp; Sch Nwsp; Ger Clb; Crs Cntry; Trk; Michigan St Univ; Historian.

YOSHINO, DOUG; West Geauga HS; Chesterland, OH; 50/352 Band; Chrh Wkr; FCA; Hon Rl; NHS; Stu Cncl; Letter Wrstlng; IM Sprt; Jacl Schlrshp Awd 79; Serv & Particiption Awd 79; Univ Of Toledo; Pre Med.

YOSHINO, RICHARD; West Geavga HS; Chesterland, OH; Chrh Wkr; FCA; Hon Rl; Yth Flsp; Bsbl; Letter Wrstlng; IM Sprt; College.

YOSICK, DREW; Dover HS; Dover, OH; 15/243 Hon Rl; Jr NHS; Letter Glf; IM Sprt; Ohi State Univ; Engr.

YOST, CHERYL; Catholic Central HS; Bloomingdale, OH; 2/203 Hon Rl; NHS; Lat Clb; Mgrs; Scr Kpr; Univ; Med.

YOST, ROBIN; Grafton HS; Grafton, WV; Chrs; Chrh Wkr; Girl Scts; Sch Mus; Sch Pl; Stg Crw; Yth Flsp; Drama Clb; 4-H; Pep Clb; Busns Schl; Dietetics.

YOST, STEPHEN; Colonel Crawford HS; Bucyrus, OH; 4/130 Band; Chrs; NHS; Ohio Univ; Elec Engr.

YOST, WILLIAM; Princeton HS; Princeton, WV; 18/344 Chrh Wkr; Hon Rl; Jr NHS; Lbry Ade; NHS; Rptr Yrbk; Fr Clb; Cit Awd; Concord Coll; Scndry Educ.

YOUMANS, YVONNE; Millington HS; Millington, MI; 42/145 Band; Chrh Wkr; Girl Scts; Hon Rl; Hosp Ade; Lbry Ade; Sct Actv; Yth Flsp; FNA; Mott Cmnty Coll; Nursing.

YOUNCE, DANA; Sr Lakeview HS; Stow, OH; Cls Rep Frsh Cls; Cls Rep Soph Cls; Cl Rep Jr Cls; Chrs; Off Ade; Sch Mus; Stu Cncl; Sch Nwsp; Pep Clb; VICA; Stolian Awd; Kent St Univ; Busns.

YOUNG, ALAN; Canfield HS; Canfield, OH; 27/258 Aud/Vis; Chrh Wkr; Hon Rl; NHS; Sch Pl; 4-H; Ger Clb; Harding University; Civil Engineerin.

YOUNG, ALLISON; Centerville HS; Centerville, OH; 60/300 AFS; Hon Rl; Red Cr Ade; Stu Cncl; Pep Clb; Chrldng; College; Broadcasting.

YOUNG, ANNETTE; Edon HS; Edon, OH; 5/78 Band; Chrs; Hon Rl; Sch Mus; Rptr Sch Nwsp; Pep Clb;.

YOUNG, BETH; Warsaw Community HS; Warsaw, IN; 8/360 Chrh Wkr; Hon Rl; Sch Pl; Eng Clb; 4-H; Spn Clb; Rotary Awd; Brigham Young Univ; Computer Sci.

YOUNG, BETH; Amanda Clearcreek HS; Amanda, OH; Band; Cmp Fr Grls; Yth Flsp; Rptr Yrbk; 4-H; GAA; IM Sprt; Scr Kpr; 4-H Awd; Ohio Univ; Communications.

YOUNG, BEVERLY; New Lexington Sr HS; New Lexington, OH; 10/168 Am Leg Aux Girls St; Chrs; Chrh Wkr; Hon Rl; NHS; Orch; Rptr Yrbk; Spn Clb; Ohio Univ; Acctg.

YOUNG, BRENDA J; Brunswick HS; Brunswick, OH; 7/675 Cls Rep Frsh Cls; Cl Rep Jr Cls; Chrs; Chrh Wkr; Debate Tm; Hon Rl; Natl Forn Lg; NHS; Off Ade; Sch Mus; College.

YOUNG, CARTER; Shelby Sr HS; Shelby, OH; Am Leg Boys St; Boy Scts; ROTC; Sct Actv; Wrstlng; Am Leg Awd; God Cntry Awd; Univ.

YOUNG, CHARLES; Memorial HS; St Marys, OH; 35/285 VP Frsh Cls; Hon Rl; Sct Actv; Ftbl; Wrstlng; Natl Merit Ltr; College; Med.

YOUNG, CHERYL S; Wehrle HS; Columbus, OH; 8/126 Hon Rl; Off Ade; Pep Clb; Gym; Am Leg Awd; Natl Merit Ltr; SAR Awd; Vlybl Won CCL 76; Typng Awd 76; Rcvd Plque Fr Amer Lgn 78; Rcvd Awd Frm Sons Of Amer Rev 78; Cosmotology.

YOUNG, CHUCK; East HS; Akron, OH; Chrs; Hon Rl; Red Cr Ade; Sch Nwsp; DECA; Mgrs; College; Elec.

YOUNG, CINDY; Monrovia HS; Mooresville, IN; 8/134 Cls Rep Frsh Cls; Cls Rep Soph Cls; Cl Rep Jr Cls; Drl Tm; Hon Rl; Stu Cncl; Rptr Yrbk; Rptr Sch Nwsp; Pom Pon; Scr Kpr; College; Forensic Law.

YOUNG, CONNIE; Lexington HS; Mansfield, OH; Univ Of Dayton; Bus Admin.

YOUNG, DARYL; Northrop HS; Ft Wayne, IN; Band; Chrh Wkr; Drm Bgl; JA; Spn Clb; JA Awd; Mas Awd; Indiana Univ; Bus.

YOUNG, DAVID; Archbishop Alter HS; Kettering, OH; 50/350 Cmnty Wkr; Hon Rl; Jr NHS; NHS; Ftbl; Capt Wrstlng; Coach Actv; IM Sprt; All Star Ftbl & Wrestling Teams; Miami Of Ohio Coll; Busns Admin.

YOUNG, DAVID; Washington Irving HS; Clarksburg, WV; 39/139 Am Leg Boys St; Band; Chrh Wkr; Hon Rl; Orch; Fr Clb; FSA; Leo Clb; Ten; West Virginia Weslyan Univ; Bus.

YOUNG, DAVID BRUCE; Midland HS; Midland, MI; Aud/Vis; Boy Scts; Chrh Wkr; Hon Rl; Orch; Sch Mus; Sct Actv; Stg Crw; Yth Flsp; Natl Merit SF; Univ; Nuclear Physics.

YOUNG, DEBBIE; Traverse City Sr HS; Traverse City, MI; 7/698 Chrs; Chrh Wkr; Cmnty Wkr; Girl Scts; Hon Rl; Hosp Ade; Lbry Ade; NHS; Stg Crw; Drama Clb; Natl Hnr Soc Schlrshp; Acad Ach Awd; Cecchetti Meth Classical Ballet Dancing Awd; N W Michigan Coll; Math.

YOUNG, DEBBIE; Frankfort HS; Frankfort, IN; 4/256 Band; NHS; 4-H; FBLA; Pep Clb; Spn Clb; Bsktbl; College; Accounting.

YOUNG, DEBRA; Portage Central HS; Portage, MI; Cl Rep Jr Cls; Chrh Wkr; Hon Rl; Stu Cncl; Graduated With High Honors; Western Michigan Univ; Elem Ed.

YOUNG, DIANA; Pymatuning Valley HS; Andover, OH; 2/121 Hon Rl; NHS; Sch Pl; Stg Crw; Stu Cncl; Yrbk; Rptr Sch Nwsp; Pep Clb; Bsbl; College; Chemistry.

YOUNG, DISEREE; Holy Redeemer HS; Detroit, MI; Cls Rep Soph Cls; Cl Rep Jr Cls; Chrs; Hon Rl; Pres JA; NHS; Off Ade; Sch Pl; Stg Crw; Drama Clb; Actvts Awd 78; Sci & Engr Fair Spec Awd 79; Michigan St Univ; Pharm.

YOUNG, DONNA; Stephen T Badin HS; Hamilton, OH; 6/215 Chrs; Chrh Wkr; Cmnty Wkr; Girl Scts; Hon Rl; Hosp Ade; NHS; Red Cr Ade; Sch Mus; Sec Fr Clb; Amer Histry Awd 1977; Frnch Awd Overall Accomplshd 1978; Whos Who In Forgn Lang Oh St 1978; Univ; Eng.

YOUNG, DUANE D; Cannelton HS; Cannelton, IN; Am Leg Boys St; Chrh Wkr; Hon Rl; NHS; DECA; Pep Clb; Letter Trk; IM Sprt; Mgrs; Am Leg Awd;.

YOUNG, ELIZABETH; Dexter HS; Whitmore, MI; Band; Girl Scts; Hon Rl; Jr NHS; Sch Nwsp; Ger Clb; College.

YOUNG, GREGG; Clinton Prairie HS; Frnkfrt, IN; 22/90 Cls Rep Sr Cls; Band; Boy Scts; Chrh Wkr; Hon Rl; Sch Mus; Sct Actv; Stg Crw; Stu Cncl; Sec Yth Flsp; Pres Physical Fitness 77; Univ; Archt.

YOUNG, HAROLD; Saginaw HS; Saginaw, MI; Hon Rl; JA; Drama Clb; Letter Bsbl; Ftbl; Letter Wrstlng; Western Mich Univ; Architectural Eng.

YOUNG, IONA; Northwestern HS; W Salem, OH; Chrh Wkr; Cmnty Wkr; GAA; IM Sprt; PPFtbl; College; Soc Sci.

YOUNG, JACKIE; Delphos Jefferson HS; Delphos, OH; Chrs; Girl Scts; Hon Rl; Spn Clb; GAA; Univ.

YOUNG, JACQUELINE; Bishop Noll Institute; Calumet, IL; Cls Rep Soph Cls; Band; Chrh Wkr; Drl Tm; Hon Rl; Pol Wkr; Sch Nwsp; Mth Clb; Coach Actv; Pom Pon; St Marys Of Notre Dame; Engr.

YOUNG, JAMES; River Valley HS; Marion, OH; 1/208 Trs Jr Cls; Pres Sr Cls; Pres Band; VP Chrs; Pres FCA; NHS; Sch Mus; Stu Cncl; Bsbl; Depauw Univ; Engr.

YOUNG, JEANNE; Wapakoneta HS; Wapakoneta, OH; 14/308 Band; Girl Scts; Hon Rl; NHS; Sct Actv; Yth Flsp; 4-H; Spn Clb; Letter Gym; Cls Rep Frsh Cls; Purdue; Language.

YOUNG, JED; William Henry Harrison HS; W Lafayette, IN; 48/285 Band; Drm Mjrt; Hon Rl; Orch; Stg Crw; Yrbk; 4-H; Fr Clb; Sci Clb; Letter Bsbl; Purdue Univ.

YOUNG, JOAN; Sylvania Northview HS; Sylvania, OH; 1/341 Val; Girl Scts; Hon Rl; Jr NHS; Treas NHS; Sec Quill & Scroll; Sch Mus; Ed Yrbk; Rptr Yrbk; Pep Clb; College; Busns.

YOUNG, JOHN; Marion HS; Marion, IN; Chrs; Hon Rl; Sch Mus; Trk; Chrldng; Forestry.

YOUNG, JOSEPH B; Brebeuf HS; Indianapolis, IN; Trs Sr Cls; Band; Boy Scts; Chrh Wkr; Cmnty Wkr; Hon Rl; Orch; Sch Mus; Sct Actv; Stu Cncl; Exchange Stu Germany For 1 Mth; High Honor Roll; Eagle Scout; Coll; Law.

YOUNG, KANDY; Fairfield Union HS; Pleasantville, OH; 4/152 Sec Soph Cls; Hst Jr Cls; Band; Cmnty Wkr; Drl Tm; Girl Scts; Hon Rl; Jr NHS; NHS; Yth Flsp; Shawnee State Schl; Dent Hygiene.

YOUNG, KATHRYN; Mt Vernon Acad; Columbus, OH; Band; Chrs; Chrh Wkr; Cmnty Wkr; Hon Rl; Orch; Ger Clb; Pep Clb; Gym; Swmmng; Ohio St Univ; Psych.

YOUNG, KELLY; Culver Community HS; Culver, IN; Sec Jr Cls; Trs Jr Cls; Sec Sr Cls; Trs Sr Cls; Hon Rl; Ed Yrbk; Pres 4-H; Fr Clb; Pres Pep Clb; Trk; Manchester College; Special Ed.

YOUNG, KEVIN; St Clair HS; St Clair, MI; 3/205 VP Soph Cls; VP Jr Cls; Am Leg Boys St; Hon Rl; NHS; Sch Pl; VP Stu Cncl; Treas 4-H; Treas OEA; Michigan HS Footbl Coaches Schlrshp 1979; 3rd Pl In St Comp Of Bus & Ofc Educ Club 1979; Adrian Coll; Acctg.

YOUNG, KIM; Shaw HS; East Cleveland, OH; Cls Rep Frsh Cls; Hon Rl; JA; OEA; Cit Awd; College; Stenographer.

YOUNG, KIMBERLY; Lexington Sr HS; Lexington, OH; Am Leg Aux Girls St; NHS; Pol Wkr; Sch Pl; Y-Teens; Drama Clb; Fr Clb; Chrldng; Cit Awd; DAR Awd; Outstndg Soph Of The Yr Exchange Club 77; Mbr Of Girls Buckeye St 79; Univ; Pre Law.

YOUNG, KRISTI; Marietta Sr HS; Akron, OH; Girl Scts; Sct Actv; OEA; Spn Clb; Ambassador Awd OEA 78; Univ Of Akron.

YOUNG, KRISTI; Whitehall Yearling HS; Whitehall, OH; Band; Chrs; Hon Rl; Pres JA; Lit Mag; Stg Crw; Fr Clb; OEA; Spn Clb; Franklin Univ; Bus Admin.

YOUNG, KRISTINA; Jay Cnty HS; Portland, IN; 33/435 Cls Rep Frsh Cls; AFS; Band; Drl Tm; FCA; Hon Rl; Jr NHS; NHS; Off Ade; Sch Mus; Purdue Univ; Pro Photog.

YOUNG, LAURA; Brookhaven HS; Columbus, OH; Trs Jr Cls; Girl Scts; Hon Rl; Off Ade; OEA; Spn Clb; Gym; Letter GAA; Exec & Diplomat Awards 1979; Mbr Of Brookhaven Ski Club 1979; NECC; Bus.

YOUNG, LAURA; Trinity HS; Cleveland, OH; 71/150 Chrs; FCA; Girl Scts; JA; Yth Flsp; Bsbl; Bsktbl; Glf; Socr; Ten; Community College.

YOUNG, LINDA; Tuslaw HS; N Lawrence, OH; 37/183 Band; FNA; Aultman Hosp Schl Of Nursing; LPN.

YOUNG, LISA; Columbus Girls HS; Columbus, OH; Chrs; Hon Rl; Jr NHS; Lbry Ade; Lit Mag; Sch Pl; Rptr Yrbk; Fr Clb; Wheaton Coll; Archt.

YOUNG, LISA; Reading HS; Reading, OH; 21/212 Hon Rl; Jr NHS; Fr Clb; Pep Clb; Trk; Tmr; Univ Of Cincinnati; Phys Ther.

YOUNG, LORNA; Jackson HS; Jackson, OH; 24/237 Band; Hon Rl; NHS; Lat Clb; Pep Clb; IM Sprt; PPFtbl; Chem I Schlrshp Team 79; Rio Grande Coll; RN.

YOUNG, LORNE; Mott HS; Warren, MI; Boy Scts; Chrh Wkr; Hon Rl; Jr NHS; Lbry Ade; Sct Actv; Bsbl; Cit Awd; Lawrence Inst Of Tech; Archt.

YOUNG, M; Marshall HS; Marshall, MI; Cls Rep Frsh Cls; Boy Scts; Hon Rl; Sct Actv; Spn Clb; Letter Ftbl; Natl Merit Ltr; College; Comp Sci.

YOUNG, MARGARET; Allen Park HS; Allen Park, MI; Band; Chrh Wkr; Hon Rl; NHS; Coll; Soc Sci.

YOUNG, MARY; Bridgeport HS; Saginaw, MI; Cls Rep Frsh Cls; Cls Rep Jr Cls; Hon Rl; Pres NHS; Pol Wkr; Sec Stu Cncl; Rptr Yrbk; Ger Clb; Trk; Mich State Univ; Music.

YOUNG, META; Aquinas HS; Inkster, MI; Band; Hon Rl; Ten; College; Psych.

YOUNG, MINNIE; Stivers Patterson Coop HS; Dayton, OH; 86/415 Band; Chrs; Chrh Wkr; JA; Orch; Sch Pl; OEA; Wright State Univ; Acctg.

YOUNG, NOLA; Bristol Local HS; Bristolville, OH; Band; Chrs; Chrh Wkr; Girl Scts; Hon Rl; Sch Mus; Sct Actv; 4-H;.

YOUNG, PAM; Anderson HS; Cincinnati, OH; 42/377 Band; Chrs; Girl Scts; Off Ade; Stu Cncl; Sec 4-H; Capt Chrldng; PPFtbl; College; Para Legal.

YOUNG, PAMELA; Paw Paw HS; Paw Paw, MI; 4/182 Trs Frsh Cls; Chrh Wkr; Hon Rl; NHS; Off Ade; Stu Cncl; Yth Flsp; 4-H; Fr Clb; IM Sprt; Michigan St Univ; Pre Law.

YOUNG, PAMELA J; Fairless HS; Brewster, OH; 8/218 Cls Rep Frsh Cls; Pres Jr Cls; Chrs; Hon Rl; Jr NHS; NHS; Stu Cncl; Sch Nwsp; FHA; OEA; Stu Sec 2 Yrs; Stu Of Yr; Gregg Awds For Typing & Shorthand Prod; College; Nursing.

YOUNG, PATRICIA L; Parma Sr HS; Parma, OH; 2/710 Hon Rl; Jr NHS; NHS; Off Ade; Y-Teens; Rptr Sch Nwsp; Sci Clb; Spn Clb; Natl Merit SF; Century III Ldrs Prog Schl Wnr 1978; Univ; Bus.

YOUNG, PAULA; Salem HS; Salem, OH; 6/225 Chrh Wkr; Hon Rl; Yth Flsp; Yrbk; Fr Clb; Treas OEA; Letter IM Sprt; Kent St Univ; Bus Admin.

YOUNG, PAULA; Bristol Local HS; Bristolville, OH; Band; Boy Scts; Chrs; Chrh Wkr; Girl Scts; Sch Mus; Sct Actv; 4-H; Trk; 4-H Awd; College.

YOUNG, PETER; St Ignatius HS; Fairview Pk, OH; 60/306 IM Sprt; Univ; Acctg.

YOUNG, POLLY; West Side HS; Gary, IN; Cls Rep Frsh Cls; Cls Rep Soph Cls; Chrh Wkr; Hon Rl; Jr NHS; Stu Cncl; Y-Teens; Spn Clb; Ind Univ; Pl Therapy.

YOUNG, R; Garrett HS; Garret, IN; Chrs; Girl Scts; Hon Rl; Off Ade; Y-Teens; Sch Nwsp; Ger Clb; Pep Clb; Bsbl; Bsktbl; College; Mgmt.

YOUNG, RAMONA; Prairie Hts HS; Wolcottville, IN; 13/155 Band; Chrs; Hon Rl; Stu Cncl; Drama Clb; 4-H; Pep Clb; Trk; GAA; Letter Mgrs; Univ; Med Tech.

YOUNG, RAMONA; George Washington HS; Charleston, WV; Band; Chrh Wkr; FCA; Girl Scts; Hon Rl; Hosp Ade; Sch Mus; 4-H; Keyettes; IM Sprt; Univ; Med.

YOUNG, RANDAL; Whiteland Comm HS; Greenwood, IN; 10/216 FCA; Hon Rl; Pres 4-H; Pres FFA; Pep Clb; Bsktbl; Letter Crs Cntry; Letter Trk; IM Sprt; Purdue Univ; Agric.

YOUNG, ROBERT; Upper Sandusky HS; Upper Sandusky, OH; 40/220 Chrh Wkr; Hon Rl; Sch Pl; 4-H; Ten; IM Sprt; Univ; Comp Sci.

YOUNG, ROBERT A; Niles Sr HS; Niles, MI; Hon Rl; Letter Wrstlng; Scr Kpr; Tmr; N Michigan Univ; Wildlife Bio.

YOUNG, ROBIN; Peru Sr HS; Peru, IN; 61/298 Aud/Vis; Chrs; JA; MMM; Sch Pl; Ger Clb; Indiana Univ; Sec.

YOUNG, ROBYN; Mona Shores HS; Muskegon, MI; Band; Chrs; Cmnty Wkr; Sch Mus; Trk; Chrldng; Muskegon Community College; Rn.

YOUNG, RODNEY; Mumford HS; Detroit, MI; Hon Rl; NHS; Key Clb; Letter Bsktbl; Letter Crs Cntry; Letter Trk; Opt Clb Awd; Purdue Univ; Engr.

YOUNG, RUTH; West Washington HS; Salem, IN; Trs Frsh Cls; Trs Soph Cls; Trs Jr Cls; Band; Hon Rl; Stu Cncl; Yrbk; 4-H; Pep Clb; Bsktbl; Butler Coll; Sci.

YOUNG, SHEILA; Nitro HS; Charleston, WV; JA; Trk; Marshall Univ; Poli Sci.

YOUNG, SHERYL; Amanda Clearcreek HS; Amanda, OH; Band; Cmp Fr Grls; Chrh Wkr; Hon Rl; Rptr Yrbk; Sec 4-H; Sci Clb; Treas GAA; IM Sprt; Scr Kpr; Univ; Forsenic Chem.

YOUNG, SHERYL; Lexington HS; Mansfield, OH; 86/275 Band; Chrs; Chrh Wkr; Cmnty Wkr; Mdrgl; Sch Mus; Yth Flsp; Y-Teens; Fr Clb; Mas Awd; All Oh Youth Chr 78; Adrian Hon Workshop 78; Univ; Music.

YOUNG, STEPHANIE; Madison Hts HS; Anderson, IN; 14/371 Cls Rep Frsh Cls; Pres Soph Cls; VP Boy Scts; Chrs; Hon Rl; NHS; Red Cr Ade; FDA; Ger Clb; Purdue Univ; Comp Sci.

YOUNG, TERESA; Hammond HS; Hammond, IN; Girl Scts; Capt Bsktbl; IM Sprt; Purdue; Modeling.

YOUNG, TERESA; Stonewall Jackson HS; Charleston, WV; Chrs; Chrh Wkr; Hon Rl; Jr NHS; Lbry Ade; NHS; Off Ade; Sch Pl; Stg Crw; Yth Flsp; Univ; Comp Sci.

YOUNG, TIMOTHY; Roosevelt HS; Gary, IN; Boy Scts; Chrs; Chrh Wkr; Hon Rl; Sch Mus; Sch Pl; VP Yth Flsp; Pres Y-Teens; Bsktbl; Crs Cntry; Pre Med.

YOUNG, TIMOTHY; Martin Public HS; Martin, MI; Hon Rl; Sch Pl; Stu Cncl; Rptr Yrbk; Sprt Ed Sch Nwsp; Rptr Sch Nwsp; Sch Nwsp; Bsbl; Hope College.

YOUNG, VICKIE; West Jefferson HS; W Jefferson, OH; Spn Clb; Bsktbl; Univ; Phys Educ.

YOUNG, VICKI S; Warren County Joint Voc Schl; Morrow, OH; Girl Scts; Hon Rl; NHS; Off Ade; OEA; Mat Maids; Parliamentarian For Jr Acctg Comp OOEA Club 1979; Parlaimentarian For OOEA Chap 1979; Perf Attendance Awd; Univ; Comp Progr.

YOUNG, YORK; Knox Sr HS; Knox, IN; 48/158 Chrh Wkr; Cmnty Wkr; Hon Rl; 4-H; Letter Crs Cntry; Letter Trk; 4-H Awd; Ancilla Coll; Astronomy.

YOUNG, YVONNE; Mumford HS; Detroit, MI; Cls Rep Frsh Cls; Hst Sr Cls; Chrh Wkr; FCA; Hon Rl; Jr NHS; Lbry Ade; NHS; Off Ade; Sch Pl; Univ Of Michigan; Archt.

YOUNGBLOOD, GARY; Martinsburg HS; Martinsburg, WV; 6/204 Hon Rl; NHS; Rptr Yrbk; Key Clb; Letter Crs Cntry; Letter Trk; College; Vet.

YOUNGER, CRAIG; Whitehall Yearling HS; Whitehall, OH; Hon Rl; Ftbl; Ohi State Univ; Bus.

YOUNGER, LISA C; Fitzgerald HS; Warren, MI; Chrh Wkr; Lit Mag; NHS; Rptr Sch Nwsp; Pep Clb; Trk; Univ Of Michigan; Jrnlsm.

YOUNGERT, PATRICIA; Manton Consolidated HS; Manton, MI; Band; Chrs; Hon Rl; Lbry Ade; NHS; FTA; Trk; College.

YOUNG JR, PAUL J; Whitehall HS; Whitehall, MI; 36/150 Sch Pl; Spn Clb; Bsbl; Bsktbl; Ftbl; Glf; IM Sprt;.

YOUNGKIN, DONALD F; Walsh Jesuit HS; Cuyahoga Falls, OH; 16/163 Cls Rep Frsh Cls; Band; Chrh Wkr; Hon Rl; Orch; Sch Mus; Yth Flsp; Sprt Ed Sch Nwsp; Univ; Chem.

YOUNGLOVE, D; Parkside HS; Jackson, MI; Band; College; Architectural Engr.

YOUNGLOVE, SARAH; Britton Macon Area Schools; Britton, MI; Cmp Fr Grls; Chrs; Hon Rl; Lbry Ade; Stg Crw; Yth Flsp; Univ; Acctg.

YOUNGPETER, BRUCE; Delphos Jefferson HS; Delphos, OH; 2/120 Trs Soph Cls; Trs Sr Cls; Am Leg Boys St; Boy Scts; Chrs; Hon Rl; Sec NHS; Sch Mus; Sct Actv; Spn Clb; Univ; Math.

YOUNGPETER, SUE; Delphos St Johns HS; Delphos, OH; 10/141 Am Leg Aux Girls St; Aud/Vis; Hon Rl; NHS; Stg Crw; Rptr Sch Nwsp; 4-H; FTA; Bsktbl; Letter Trk; Univ Of Dayton; Cmnctn Arts.

YOUNGS, LYNN; Meadowbrook HS; Pleasant City, OH; Band; Hon Rl; VP JA; Orch; VP Key Clb; Mth Clb; VP Sci Clb; Am Leg Awd; Univ; Physics.

YOUNKER, DAVE; Margaretta HS; Vickery, OH; 3/200 Am Leg Boys St; Band; Chrh Wkr; Cmnty Wkr; Hon Rl; NHS; Yth Flsp; IM Sprt; Natl Merit Ltr; Univ; Comp Progr.

YOUNKER, DAVID R; Margaretta HS; Vickery, OH; 3/150 Am Leg Boys St; Band; Chrh Wkr; Hon Rl; NHS; Yth Flsp; Natl Merit Ltr; Bowling Green State Univ; Comp Sci.

YOUNKER, RICK; Brookside HS; Sheffield Lke, OH; Wrstlng; Lorain Cnty Cmnty Coll; Engr.

YOUNKVICH, AUDREY; Trinton HS; Shelbyville, IN; 5/167 Sec Frsh Cls; Chrh Wkr; Yth Flsp; Fr Clb; FHA; Mat Maids; Scr Kpr; Tmr; College; Science.

YOURKOVICH, ED; Wheeling Park HS; Wheeling, WV; Hon Rl; Wv Univ; Accgt.

YOVANOVICH, CAROL; Cadiz HS; Cadiz, OH; Trs Soph Cls; Am Leg Aux Girls St; Chrs; Hon Rl; NHS; Off Ade; Stu Cncl; 4-H; Lat Clb; Chrldng; Coll; Dent Asst.

YUN, ELISE H; Midland HS; Midland, MI; Chrh Wkr; Hon Rl; NHS; Orch; Yth Flsp; Yrbk; Solost With Mi Youth Symphny Youth Arts Fest 78; Winner Of Mi Music Tchr Assoc St Contst HS Div 77; Coll.

YURICEK, LAURA; Warren G Harding HS; Warren, OH; 4/381 Chrs; Girl Scts; Hon Rl; Mdrgl; NHS; Yth Flsp; Y-Teens; Ed Yrbk; Pep Clb; Member Of Academic Challenge Tm For WEWS Tv; Miami Univ; English.

YURKEWYCZ, CATHY; Cardinal Mooney HS; Youngstown, OH; 43/280 Hon Rl; NHS; Mth Clb; College; Bio.

YURKO, MICHAEL; Andrean HS; Gary, IN; Hon Rl; Jr NHS; NHS; Off Ade; Yrbk; Ger Clb; Rdo Clb; Univ; Physics.

YUSCHIK, ANDREA; Lakeland HS; Milford, MI; Chrs; Cmnty Wkr; Drl Tm; Girl Scts; 4-H; Ger Clb; Pom Pon; 4-H Awd; SW Oakland Voc Ctr; Med Asst.

Z

ZABRISKIE, ROBERT S; Caro Community HS; Vassar, MI; Band; Debate Tm; Hon Rl; Swmmng; 1st Div Rating Awd For Solo Cornet 79; 1st Div Rating Awd For Brass Quartet 79; 2nd Div Rating Awd For Solo; Univ; Comp Sci.

ZACCAGNI, MICHAEL J; Bishop Gallagher HS; Harper Woods, MI; 14/332 Hon Rl; Ftbl; Trk; College; Accounting.

ZACCAGNI, PAUL; Bishop Gallagher HS; Harper Wds, MI; 59/333 Cmnty Wkr; FCA; Bsktbl; Ftbl; IM Sprt; Mgrs; Scr Kpr; Tmr; JETS Awd; Coll.

ZACHARIAS, JULI D; Indiana Acad; Arcadia, IN; 13/57 Trs Frsh Cls; Trs Soph Cls; Chrs; Chrh Wkr; Cmnty Wkr; Hon Rl; Mdrgl; Stu Cncl; Ed Sch Nwsp; Rptr Sch Nwsp; Southern Missionary; Sec.

ZACHARIAS, KELLEY; Addison HS; Cement, MI; 21/109 Trs Frsh Cls; Trs Soph Cls; Cl Rep Jr Cls; Chrs; Hon Rl; Stu Cncl; Capt Bsktbl; Coach Actv; W Michigan Univ; Psych.

ZACHARIAS, STEPHEN; Saint Agatha HS; Redford, MI; 26/145 Hon Rl; Bsktbl; Trk; IM Sprt; College; Business.

ZACHARY, DAWN; Bedford Sr HS; Bedford, OH; 59/580 Chrs; Hon Rl; JA; Jr NHS; Off Ade; Spn Clb; Univ Of Cincinnati; Busns.

ZACHARY, MARK; Walled Lake Western HS; Walled Lake, MI; 32/459 Cls Rep Frsh Cls; Cls Rep Soph Cls; Cl Rep Jr Cls; Band; Hon Rl; Lbry Ade; NHS; Sch Mus; Stu Cncl; College; Physics.

ZACHEA, MARINA; Normandy HS; Parma, OH; 40/570 Am Leg Aux Girls St; Hon Rl; Off Ade; Pol Wkr; OEA; Pep Clb; IM Sprt; Public Relations.

ZADIK, DAVID; Bedford Sr HS; Temperance, MI; Chrs; FCA; Sch Mus; Sch Pl; Letter Ftbl; Letter Ten; Univ Of Toledo; Bio.

ZAFIROFF, KAREN; Holy Rosary HS; Flint, MI; Sec Frsh Cls; Sec Soph Cls; Sec Jr Cls; Pres Sr Cls; Hon Rl; Hosp Ade; Sch Pl; Chrldng; IM Sprt; Medicine.

ZAFT, DEBORAH R; Clarenceville HS; Livonia, MI; 1/250 Cls Rep Sr Cls; Am Leg Aux Girls St; Chrs; Jr NHS; NHS; Sch Mus; Drama Clb; Letter Swmmng; DAR Awd; Natl Merit SF; Univ Of Michigan; Liberal Arts.

ZAGONE, PETER; Dondero HS; Royal Oak, MI; Hon Rl; NHS; Sch Mus; Sch Pl; Drama Clb; Rdo Clb; Natl Merit SF; Mich Univ; Engr.

ZAHEL, KEVIN; Margaretta HS; Castalia, OH; 20/170 Hon Rl; NHS; Quill & Scroll; Sch Pl; Sprt Ed Sch Nwsp; Drama Clb; Rdo Clb; Capt Bsktbl; Univ.

ZAHM, KAREN; Huntington Catholic HS; Huntington, IN; 2/33 VP Frsh Cls; Pres Sr Cls; Am Leg Aux Girls St; Hon Rl; NHS; Sch Pl; Rptr Yrbk; Pres Sr Cls; Vocational Schl; Dent Hygenist.

ZAHN, JOHN; Tiffin Calvert HS; Tiffin, OH; 15/98 Hon Rl; NHS; Stg Crw; Capt Bsktbl; Ftbl; Ithaca College; Physical Therapy.

ZAHNER, KENNETH; Garaway HS; Sugarcreek, OH; Aud/Vis; Chrs; Hon Rl; Eng Clb; 4-H; Ger Clb; Trk; 4-H Awd; Ohio St Univ; Dentistry.

ZAHRNDT, RUTH; Highland HS; Highland, IN; 29/503 Girl Scts; Hon Rl; NHS; Stu Cncl; Pep Clb; GAA; Ball State Univ; Business.

ZAINA, LISA; Saint Thomas Aquinas HS; Alliance, OH; 2/175 Pres Frsh Cls; Cls Rep Soph Cls; VP Jr Cls; Am Leg Aux Girls St; Boy Scts; Chrh Wkr; Hon Rl; Lit Mag; NHS; Sch Mus; Univ Of Notre Dame; Pre Med.

ZAJAC, RICHARD; Southgate HS; Southgate, MI; Trs Sr Cls; Chrh Wkr; Hon Rl; Stu Cncl; Yrbk; Mth Clb; Crs Cntry; Hockey; Socr; Trk; Michigan St Univ; Dietetics.

ZAJACK, RENEE; Madison Comprehensive HS; Mansfield, OH; Lbry Ade; Sch Pl; Drama Clb; VICA; Perfect Attendance For 3 Yrs 1976; Acting Schl; Actress.

ZAJACZKOWSKI, KENNETH; Chanel HS; Maple Hts, OH; 2/115 Cl Rep Jr Cls; Cls Rep Sr Cls; Sal; Hon Rl; NHS; Yrbk; Ed Sch Nwsp; Letter Bsbl; IM Sprt; Pres Awd; John Carroll Univ; Acctng.

ZAJC, CATHERINE; Regina HS; Euclid, OH; Aud/Vis; Hon Rl; Sci Clb; Univ.

ZAK, ANN M; Euclid Sr HS; Euclid, OH; 5/710 Hon Rl; Lbry Ade; Pres NHS; Off Ade; Rptr Yrbk; Rptr Sch Nwsp; Ger Clb; Sci Clb; Ten; GAA; Dstngshd Scholar; Outstndng Female Science Stu; YWCA Future Career Woman; Case Western Reserve Univ; Engr.

ZAK, DEAN; Northwest HS; Jackson, MI; Band; Hon Rl; NHS; Crs Cntry; Trk; College; Engr.

ZAK, KENNETH A; Parma Sr HS; Parma, OH; 5/784 Cl Rep Jr Cls; Hon Rl; Pres NHS; Stu Cncl; Letter Swmmng; YMCA All Amer Waterpolo Plyrs High Scrr At Natl YMCA Chanmp 76; Waterpolo MVP & High Scrr 77; Univ; Bus.

ZALEHA, MICHAEL; Wadsworth HS; Wadsworth, OH; Chrh Wkr; Cmnty Wkr; FCA; NHS; Pol Wkr; Key Clb; Spn Clb; Letter Ftbl; Letter Trk; College; Pk Department.

ZALESKI, BARB; Tuscarawas Valley HS; East Sparta, OH; 32/143 Hon Rl; Drama Clb; 4-H; Fr Clb; FHA; Pep Clb; Chrldng; 4-H Awd; College; Vet.

ZALESKI, DIANNE; Divine Child HS; Detroit, MI; Girl Scts; Hon Rl; Ger Clb; Sci Clb; Voice Dem Awd;.

ZALEWSKI, JANE; Newaygo HS; Newaygo, MI; 4/100 VP Frsh Cls; Cl Rep Jr Cls; Am Leg Aux Girls St; Chrh Wkr; Cmnty Wkr; Hon Rl; NHS; Sch Pl; Stu Cncl; Yrbk; W Michigan Univ; Occup Therapy.

ZALEWSKI, KAREN; T Roosevelt HS; Wyandotte, MI; Sec Jr Cls; Chrh Wkr; Hon Rl; NHS; Sch Mus; Pep Clb; Letter Ten; Letter Trk; PPFtbl; Cit Awd; Western Michigan Univ; Speech Path.

ZALEWSKI, LINDA; Buckeye West HS; Adena, OH; Hon Rl; NHS; Off Ade; Rptr Yrbk; Drama Clb; FHA; OEA; Ftbl; IM Sprt;.

ZALEWSKI, ROBERT; Eastlake North HS; Willowick, OH; 50/706 Boy Scts; Cmnty Wkr; Hon Rl; Pol Wkr; Civ Clb; Key Clb; Ftbl; Coach Actv; Pres JC Awd; Kiwan Awd; Coll; Busns Admin.

ZALIAGIRIS, MARGARET; Our Lady Of Mercy HS; Livonia, MI; Stg Crw; Rptr Yrbk; Univ.

ZALUD, DEIRDRE; St Josephs HS; Mishawaka, IN; 5/300 Cmnty Wkr; Hon Rl; NHS; Sch Nwsp; Fr Clb; Pep Clb; Letter Trk; Chrldng; PPFtbl; Univ Of Notre Dame; Pre Law.

ZAMARRON, JENNIFER; Wyoming Park HS; Wyoming, MI; Band; Drl Tm; Hon Rl; NHS; Yth Flsp; Trk; Grand Rapids Jr Coll; Banking.

ZAMBETIS, M; Regina HS; Detroit, MI; 28/248 Trs Jr Cls; Cmp Fr Grls; NHS; Michigan St Univ.

ZAMBO, STEPHEN; Hanover Ctrl HS; Cedar Lake, IN; 3/137 Jr NHS; NHS; FSA; Spn Clb; IM Sprt; Letter Mgrs; Scr Kpr; Purdue Univ; Engr.

ZAMBON, MARY; West Catholic HS; Grand Rapids, MI; Cmnty Wkr; Hon Rl; Spn Clb; Trk; Coach Actv; Mic State Univ; Natural Resources.

ZAMMIT, ANDREW; Holy Redeemer HS; Detroit, MI; Cls Rep Frsh Cls; Cls Rep Soph Cls; VP Jr Cls; Hon Rl; Jr NHS; NHS; Stu Cncl; Rptr Sch Nwsp; Sch Nwsp; Socr; Univ; Archt.

ZAMORA, JONATHAN; Maysville HS; Zanesville, OH; Band; Hon Rl; Letter Wrstlng; Ohio Univ; Dent.

ZAMPINI, MARIA; Perry HS; Perry, OH; Band; Drm Mjrt; Jr NHS; Off Ade; Sch Pl; Yrbk; 4-H; Pep Clb; Spn Clb; Twrlr; Univ; Nursery Oper.

ZAMPONI, TRINA; Lanse Creuse HS; Mt Clemens, MI; Trs Frsh Cls; Cls Rep Soph Cls; Trs Jr Cls; Cls Rep Sr Cls; Girl Scts; Hon Rl; NHS; The Center For Creative Studies;inds.

ZANATH, THOMAS; Padua Franciscan HS; Seven Hills, OH; Chrh Wkr; Hon Rl; JA; Rptr Yrbk; Sci Clb; JA Awd; Univ Of Cincinnati; Engr.

ZANDBERGEN, RANDALL; Grandville HS; Grandville, MI; 34/349 Cls Rep Frsh Cls; Cls Rep Soph Cls; Cl Rep Jr Cls; Cls Rep Sr Cls; Hon Rl; NHS; Stu Cncl; Pep Clb; Bsktbl; Cit Awd; Central Michigan Univ; Acctg.

ZANE, ELLEN; Center Line HS; Warren, MI; Letter Band; Hon Rl; Jr NHS; NHS; Sch Pl; Drama Clb; Capt Twrlr; Business School; Cosmetology.

ZANE, MARTHA; Allen Park HS; Allen Park, MI; Chrs; Off Ade; Pol Wkr; Rptr Sch Nwsp; FNA; Pep Clb; Letter Swmmng; GAA; IM Sprt; PPFtbl; Univ; Sci.

ZANETTI, JEFFREY; Trenton HS; Trenton, MI; 42/550 Trs Jr Cls; Trs Sr Cls; Am Leg Boys St; Hon Rl; Pres NHS; Capt Crs Cntry; Capt Trk; Natl Merit SF; Stdnt Govt Day Cncl Prsn 78 Mayor 79; All Area Cross Cntry & Track 79; Homecoming Escort 79; Teen Of Week; Univ Of Michigan; Pre Dent.

ZANNER, HEIDI; Au Gres Sims HS; Au Gres, MI; 15/60 Sec Jr Cls; Band; Chrh Wkr; Hon Rl; Off Ade; Yrbk; Letter Bsbl; Letter Bsktbl; Chrldng; 4-H Awd; Outstndng Young Amer 79; St Finalist Miss Natl Teenager 79; Sci Fair Awd 77; Michigan St Univ; Travel Agent.

ZANON, SCOTT; Indian Valley North HS; Tuscarawas, OH; 7/79 Cls Rep Frsh Cls; Cls Rep Soph Cls; Trs Jr Cls; Hon Rl; NHS; Stu Cncl; Rptr Yrbk; FTA; Ger Clb; Bsbl; Ohio State Univ; Agronomy.

ZANONA, WENDY; Norway HS; Vulcan, MI; 21/88 Chrh Wkr; Hon Rl; Yrbk; GAA; Natl Merit Ltr; Michigan Tech Univ; Pre Med.

ZANOUDAKIS, MARY ANN; Harvey S Firestone Sr HS; Wadsworth, OH; Chrs; Hon Rl; NHS; Yth Flsp; Tmr; Univ; Pre Med.

ZAPALSKI, DAVID; St Alphonsus HS; Detroit, MI; Chrs; Mercy College Of Detroit; Respiritor.

ZAPIECKI, THOMAS; St Francis De Sales HS; Bowling Green, OH; Hon Rl; Yrbk; Bowling Green State Univ; Communicat.

ZARA, LYNN M; Crestline HS; Crestline, OH; Sec Frsh Cls; Band; Chrh Wkr; Cmnty Wkr; Hon Rl; NHS; Off Ade; Sch Mus; Sch Pl; Yrbk; Bowling Green Univ; Soc Work.

ZARCZYNSKI, DIANE; James Ford Rhodes HS; Cleveland, OH; 134/358 Cls Rep Frsh Cls; Aud/Vis; Chrh Wkr; Girl Scts; Hon Rl; Pres JA; Lbry Ade; Sch Mus; Sch Pl; Stu Cncl; Univ; Engr.

ZARELLA, JOHN CARL; Brookfield HS; Masury, OH; 3/165 Cls Rep Soph Cls; Band; Chrh Wkr; Cmnty Wkr; Hon Rl; NHS; Sch Pl; Bsbl; General Motors Inst; Engr.

ZAREMBA, CARRIE; St Marys Cathedral HS; Elmira, MI; Sec Soph Cls; Cls Rep Soph Cls; Cls Rep Sr Cls; Band; Hon Rl; NHS; Stu Cncl; Drama Clb; 4-H; Mic Tech Univ; Engr.

ZAREMBA, JEROME; St Marys Cathedral HS; Elmira, MI; Chrh Wkr; Hon Rl; NHS; Sch Mus; Sch Pl; Sprt Ed Sch Nwsp; Rptr Sch Nwsp; Sec Drama Clb; Pep Clb; Bsbl; College; Law.

ZAREMBA, SUZY; Lawrence Central HS; Indianapolis, IN; Chrs; Chrh Wkr; Cmnty Wkr; Girl Scts; NHS; Fr Clb; Key Clb; Mat Maids; Scr Kpr; Indiana Univ; Frgn Lang.

ZARN, BETTY J; Strongsville HS; Strongsville, OH; Hon Rl; Sch Pl; Rptr Sch Nwsp; Drama Clb; 4-H; Treas OEA; 4-H Awd; Bus Educ.

ZARONAS, LAUREL; Lexington HS; Mansfield, OH; 24/240 Hosp Ade; NHS; Off Ade; Sch Pl; Stg Crw; Ed Yrbk; Spn Clb; Ten; Ohio St Univ; Medicine.

ZARSKA, BRENDA; Mt Vernon Acad; Mt Vernon, OH; Chrs; Chrh Wkr; Hon Rl; Off Ade; Sch Mus; Southern Missionary Univ; Home Ec.

ZARTMAN, SUSAN; Dayton Christian HS; Dayton, OH; 2/125 Cls Rep Frsh Cls; Sec Soph Cls; VP Jr Cls; Sec Band; Chrs; Girl Scts; Hon Rl; Sch Mus; Sct Actv; Stu Cncl; Univ; Music.

ZARZECKI, MARGARET; Central HS; Grand Rapids, MI; Hon Rl; NHS; Stu Cncl; 4-H; Swmmng; Cit Awd; 4-H Awd; Kiwan Awd; Acad Achvmnt Lt Dist By Schl Eng Dept 79; Grand Rapids Jr Coll; Bus.

ZATARAIN, S BETSY; Fairmont West HS; Kettering, OH; Chrs; Stu Cncl; Sprt Ed Yrbk; Ed Sch Nwsp; Ger Clb; Univ; Math.

ZATEZALO, DOUG; Shadyside HS; Shadyside, OH; Y-Teens; Rdo Clb; Bsktbl; Belmont Tech Schl; Construction.

ZATEZALO, MYRA; Buckeye South HS; Rayland, OH; 15/124 Am Leg Aux Girls St; Debate Tm; Hon Rl; Hosp Ade; Jr NHS; VP NHS; Pres Off Ade; Sch Pl; Stu Cncl; Y-Teens; Muskingum Coll; Cmnctns.

ZAUNER, LINDA; Berkley HS; Berkley, MI; Crs Cntry; Trk; College.

ZAUTNER, BRENDA; Jackson Milton HS; Diamond, OH; 35/114 Hon Rl; Off Ade; Youngstown Coll; Exec Sec.

ZAVATSKY, CATHERINE; Wintersville HS; Steubenville, OH; 1/280 Am Leg Aux Girls St; Band; Girl Scts; Hon Rl; Hosp Ade; NHS; Sch Pl; Sct Actv; Rptr Yrbk; Sec Drama Clb; Stu Of The Month Awd; 6 Superior Ratings At Solo Ensemble Contest; Bowling Green St Univ; Optometry.

ZAVODNIK, LOUIS; St Joseph HS; Wickliffe, OH; Boy Scts; Hon Rl; Capt Crs Cntry; Capt Trk; IM Sprt; Cleveland State Univ; Chem Engr.

ZAVODNY, ROGER; Rocky River HS; Rocky Rvr, OH; Bsbl; IM Sprt; Ohio State; Bus Admin.

ZAWACKI, RONALD; Franklin HS; Livonia, MI; Band; Hon Rl; IM Sprt; Cit Awd; General Motors Inst; Auto Engr.

ZAWADIWSKY, LUBA; Nazareth Acad; Parma, OH; Chrs; Chrh Wkr; Cmnty Wkr; Girl Scts; Hon Rl; NHS; Sct Actv; Sdlty; Fr Clb; Coach Actv; Varsity Vlybl Letter GCCGAC All Star; Track Tm; USVBA U S Vlybl Assn; Coll.

ZAYAC, TERESA; Meadowbrook HS; Senecaville, OH; 18/179 Hon Rl; Lbry Ade; Pres NHS; Yrbk; Rptr Sch Nwsp; Sci Clb; Spn Clb; College; Nursing.

ZAYNOR, LESLIE; Theodore Roosevelt HS; Kent, OH; Spn Clb; Univ; Psych.

ZAZO, STEPHEN; Arthur Hill HS; Saginaw, MI; Hon Rl; Rptr Yrbk; Swmmng; Northwood Inst; Advertising.

ZDEB, THOMAS; Bishop Borgess HS; Dearborn Hts, MI; Hon Rl; NHS; Fr Clb; Letter Bsktbl; Trk; IM Sprt; College.

ZDINAK, PAUL; Stanton HS; Stratton, OH; 26/62 Trs Sr Cls; Band; Chrs; Cmnty Wkr; Hon Rl; Pol Wkr; Sch Mus; Stg Crw; Stu Cncl; Rptr Yrbk; Jefferson Tech Coll; Elec Engr.

ZDYBEL, NANCY; Alpena HS; Alpena, MI; Hon Rl; Michigan Comp Awd 79; Muskegon Bus Coll; Comp Prog.

ZEBERKIEWICZ, SANDRA; Calvin M Woodward HS; Toledo, OH; Hon Rl; JA; Jr NHS; 4-H; 4-H Awd; JA Awd; Toledo Univ; Bus.

ZECCHIN, KENNETH; Bishop Borgess HS; Detroit, MI; Hon Rl; Jr NHS; NHS; Ftbl; IM Sprt; Natl Merit SF; Natl Merit Schl; Mi BEOG; Michigan St Univ; Wildlife Bio.

ZECK, CYNTHIA; Whetstone Sr HS; Columbus, OH; Chrs; Cmnty Wkr; Girl Scts; Pol Wkr; Stu Cncl; Spn Clb; Bsbl; Univ; Eng.

ZECK, JAMES; Sandusky St Marys Cntrl HS; Castalia, OH; 7/136 Cls Rep Sr Cls; Am Leg Boys St; Band; Chrh Wkr; Hon Rl; NHS; Sch Mus; Rptr Sch Nwsp; Sci Clb; Letter Ftbl; Sci Fairs Johnny Clearwater Awd 77; Stud Of Month Dec 78; Ohio St Univ; Vet.

ZEDDIES, CLARK A; Ottawa Hills HS; Grand Rapids, MI; 7/450 Am Leg Boys St; VP Chrs; Chrh Wkr; Hon Rl; Mdrgl; Treas NHS; Sch Mus; Stu Cncl; Ed Yrbk; Letter Ftbl; Jr Revue Annual Varty Show 1978; Kalamazoo Coll; Health.

ZEEDYK, MICHAEL; Oakridge HS; Muskegon, MI; 21/165 Debate Tm; Jr NHS; Sch Pl; Stg Crw; Sch Nwsp; Drama Clb; Trk; Cit Awd; Ferris St Univ; Drafting.

ZEEK, RANDY; Badin HS; Hamilton, OH; 13/219 Cls Rep Soph Cls; Pres Jr Cls; Hon Rl; NHS; Stu Cncl; Letter Ftbl; Opt Clb Awd; Univ; Acctg.

ZEFFER, MIKE; Wadsworth Sr HS; Wadsworth, OH; Spn Clb; Letter Swmmng; Letter Trk; Coach Actv; IM Sprt; Business School; Business.

ZEGER, DONALD; Conotton Vly HS; Scio, OH; 5/59 Aud/Vis; Hon Rl; NHS; Rptr Yrbk; Ed Sch Nwsp; Sprt Ed Sch Nwsp; Rptr Sch Nwsp; Beta Clb; OEA; Rotary Awd; 1st Plc Acctg & Related I OEA Reg VIII; 2nd Plc Acctg & Related II OEA Reg VIII; Prfct Attendance Awd; Buckeye Joint Voc Schl; Comp Prog.

ZEHNER, MICHAEL; Central HS; Evansville, IN; Cls Rep Frsh Cls; Cls Rep Soph Cls; Cmnty Wkr; Off Ade; Pol Wkr; Stu Cncl; Civ Clb; IM Sprt; Cit Awd; Univ Of Evansville; Acctg.

ZEHR, CLINT; Centreville Public HS; Centreville, MI; Cl Rep Jr Cls; Chrs; Hon Rl; NHS; Pres Stu Cncl; Pres Yth Flsp; Yrbk; FFA; Ftbl; 4-H Awd; Univ.

ZEHR, ROBERT; Avon Jr Sr HS; Plainfield, IN; 53/166 Band; Chrs; Sch Mus; Stg Crw; Glf; IM Sprt; Indiana St Univ; Math.

ZEHR, SANDY; Bedford North Lawrence HS; Bedford, IN; 15/420 Cls Rep Frsh Cls; Am Leg Boys St; Pres Chrs; VP NHS; Pres Yth Flsp; Beta Clb; VP Spn Clb; Letter Bsbl; Letter Swmmng; Opt Clb Awd; Goshen Coll; Pre Dental.

ZEHR, SHARON; Clay City HS; Clay City, IN; 1/65 Sec Soph Cls; Val; NHS; VP Stu Cncl; Treas Fr Clb; Sci Clb; Letter Bsbl; Letter Trk; GAA; Voice Dem Awd; Indiana St Univ; Comp Prog.

ZEHR, SHARON L; Clay City HS; Clay City, IN; 1/60 Sec Soph Cls; Hon Rl; NHS; Treas Stu Cncl; Treas Fr Clb; Sci Clb; Letter Bsktbl; Letter Trk; GAA; Voice Dem Awd; Franklin Univ; Comp Sci.

ZEIDER, MARY; Garrett HS; Garrett, IN; Am Leg Aux Girls St; Hon Rl; NHS; Stu Cncl; Y-Teens; 4-H; Ger Clb; Pep Clb; Mgrs; Univ; Speech Ther.

ZEIGER, MARK; Tiffin Calvert HS; Tiffin, OH; 30/99 Aud/Vis; Chrh Wkr; JA; Ten; IM Sprt; JA Awd; Tiffin Univ; Bus.

ZEIGLER, LEE; Hauser HS; Hope, IN; 25/99.

ZEIGLER, TIMOTHY; Ann Arbor Huron HS; Ann Arbor, MI; Hon Rl; Mic Tech Univ; Comp Engr.

ZEIGLER, YVETTE; Warrensville Heights HS; Warrensvl Hts, OH; VP Frsh Cls; Pres Soph Cls; Cls Rep Soph Cls; Drl Tm; Hon Rl; Jr NHS; NHS; Stu Cncl; Business School; Airlines.

ZEISER, PHILIP; La Salle HS; Cincinnati, OH; 18/250 Cls Rep Sr Cls; Boy Scts; Hon Rl; Jr NHS; NHS; Wrstlng; College; Engineering.

ZELASKO, SERENE; Marcellus HS; Marcellus, MI; Hon Rl; Pep Clb; Letter Trk; Letter Chrldng; Univ; Eng.

ZELDER, MARTIN; Kalamazoo Loy Norrix HS; Kalamazoo, MI; 2/426 Band; Chrs; Hosp Ade; NHS; Orch; Letter Ten; Natl Merit Schl; Kalamazoo College; Pre Med.

ZELDER, MARTIN R; Kalamazoo Loy Norrix HS; Kalamazoo, MI; 2/425 Band; Chrs; Hon Rl; Mdrgl; NHS; Orch; Sch Mus; Letter Ten; Natl Merit Ltr; Natl Merit SF; Oberlin Coll; Psych.

ZELEK, MARK; George G Schafer HS; Southgate, MI; Cls Rep Sr Cls; Band; Hon Rl; NHS; Orch; Comp Sci.

ZELESNIK, PAULA; Magnificat HS; Fairview Pk, OH; Boy Scts; Mod UN; Sct Actv; Bsktbl; IM Sprt; Univ Of Cinn; Chem.

ZELICHOWSKI, WALTER; Vicksburg HS; Fulton, MI; Band; Hon Rl; Lit Mag; Bsbl; Univ; Acctg.

ZELINKA, TINA; Struthers HS; Struthers, OH; Chrs; Hon Rl; JA; Off Ade; Y-Teens; Drama Clb; Stg Crw; Pep Clb; Spn Clb; Letter Trk; Youngstown St Univ; Computer Sci.

ZELINSKI, ALAN; Traverse City St Francis HS; Traverse City, MI; 26/126 VP Soph Cls; JA; NHS; Stu Cncl; Letter Crs Cntry; Letter Ten; Coach Actv; IM Sprt; Cit Awd; JA Awd; Perfect Attendance Awd 77; Northwestern Michigan Coll; Law.

ZELINSKI, LOIS; Bishop Donahue HS; Glendale, WV; 16/52 Hon Rl; Spn Clb; West Virginia Univ; Govt Researcher.

ZELKOWSKI, KIM; St Anne HS; Warren, MI; Aud/Vis; Rptr Yrbk; IM Sprt; Univ; Pro Photog.

ZELLER, MARY; R B Hayes HS; Delawre, OH; 20/300 AFS; Band; Hon Rl; Rptr Yrbk; Yrbk; Scr Kpr; Miami State Univ; Engr.

ZELLER, MAUREEN; Beaumont HS; University Ht, OH; 2/130 Trs Frsh Cls; VP Sr Cls; Hon Rl; Fr Clb; GAA; Pres Awd; Univ Of Notre Dame.

ZELLERS, DEAN; Theodore Roosevelt HS; E Chicago, IN; Band; NHS; Orch; Sch Nwsp; Letter Glf; Cit Awd; Valparaiso Univ; Dent.

ZELLO, NICHOLAS; Bluffton HS; Bluffton, IN; 16/132 Pres Frsh Cls; Cls Rep Frsh Cls; Pres Soph Cls; Pres Jr Cls; Pres Sr Cls; Am Leg Boys St; Hon Rl; Stu Cncl; Ed Yrbk; Spn Clb; Univ; Mech Engr.

ZELLTE, MARTHA; Ogemaw Heights HS; West Branch, MI; Girl Scts; Stu Cncl; Chrldng; College; Medicine.

ZEMAN, TRISH; Nordonia HS; Macedonia, OH; Band; Chrs; Hosp Ade; Off Ade; Sch Mus; Sch Pl; PPFtbl; Univ; Nursing.

ZEMANEK, MICHELE; Marion L Steele HS; Amherst, OH; Hosp Ade; Sch Pl; Drama Clb; Ger Clb; Sci Clb; Spn Clb; Trk; Letter Chrldng; Tmr; Ohio St Univ; Medicine.

ZEMELKA, ROBERT; Field HS; Kent, OH; Aud/Vis; Boy Scts; Hon Rl; Lbry Ade; Sch Pl; Sct Actv; Yth Flsp; Spn Clb; Bsktbl; Ftbl; College; Atheletic Trainer.

ZEMKO, MARILYN; Clare HS; Clare, MI; FCA; Girl Scts; Hon Rl; NHS; Letter Bsbl; Letter Bsktbl; GAA; Aquinas Coll; Phys Educ.

ZEMONICK, SUZANNE; Garfield HS; Akron, OH; 35/403 Band; Chrs; Chrh Wkr; Girl Scts; Hon Rl; NHS; Off Ade; Sch Pl; Fr Clb; Sci Clb; Univ Of Akron.

ZENDER, JON A; Celina Sr HS; Celina, OH; 16/240 VP NHS; Stu Cncl; Lat Clb; Letter Bsbl; Capt IM Sprt; Miami Univ; Acctg.

ZENDER, VERONICA; New Riegel HS; New Riegel, OH; 8/48 Trs Frsh Cls; VP Jr Cls; Band; Chrs; Hon Rl; NHS; Stg Crw; Pres 4-H; FHA; FTA; Ohio State Univ; Accounting.

ZENEBERG, PENNY; Sacred Heart Academy; Mt Pleasant, MI; 12/55 Sec Soph Cls; Cmnty Wkr; Girl Scts; Hon Rl; Lbry Ade; Natl Forn Lg; NHS; Off Ade; Sch Pl; Stg Crw; Central Michigan Univ; Acctg.

ZENGEL, ANN; Archbishop Alter HS; Dayton, OH; 16/350 Chrs; Girl Scts; Hon Rl; JA; NHS; Sch Mus; Treas Stu Cncl; Trk; GAA; JA Awd; St Josephs Univ; Acctg.

ZENN, RICHARD D; Grosse Pointe North HS; Grosse Pt Woods, MI; Treas Chrs; Rptr Yrbk; Capt Bsktbl; Letter Glf; Coach Actv; Natl Merit SF; Univ; Chem Engr.

ZENOBI, MICHAEL S; Solon HS; Solon, OH; 53/288 VP Frsh Cls; Cls Rep Frsh Cls; VP Soph Cls; Cls Rep Soph Cls; VP Jr Cls; Cl Rep Jr Cls; Boy Scts; Stu Cncl; Ftbl; Trk; Akron Univ; Banking.

ZENZ, CONNIE; Liberty Center HS; Liberty Cntr, OH; Sec Sr Cls; NHS; Sch Mus; Rptr Yrbk; Bsktbl; 4-H Awd; Voice Dem Awd; Ohi State Univ; Agricultural Comm.

ZEOLLA, LYNN; Girard HS; Girard, OH; Lbry Ade; Natl Forn Lg; Stg Crw; Rptr Sch Nwsp; Fr Clb; Univ; Art.

ZERBONIA, MARIE; Austintown Fitch HS; Youngstown, OH; 98/659 Chrh Wkr; Hon Rl; Off Ade; Y-Teens; Rptr Yrbk; Pep Clb; Chrldng; Youngstown State Univ; Teach Span.

ZERFAS, PATRICIA; Hopkins HS; Dorr, MI; Sec Soph Cls; Chrs; Hon Rl; Jr NHS; NHS; Fr Clb; FHA; Trk; Chrldng; Voc Schl; Cosmetology.

ZERKOWSKI, CRISTINA; Valley Forge HS; Parma, OH; 18/777 Chrs; Chrh Wkr; Hon Rl; NHS; Rptr Sch Nwsp; Spn Clb; Cit Awd; Cuyahoga Cmnty Coll; Sci.

ZERNICK, CHRISTINE B; Canfield HS; Canfield, OH; 17/258 Cls Rep Frsh Cls; Cls Rep Soph Cls; Cl Rep Jr Cls; Hon Rl; NHS; Stu Cncl; Y-Teens; Fr Clb; Letter Swmmng; College; Acctg.

ZERR, KARIN; Valley Forge Sr HS; Parma Heights, OH; 26/704 Boy Scts; Chrh Wkr; Cmnty Wkr; Hon Rl; Lit Mag; NHS; Ger Clb; Pep Clb; IM Sprt; Natl Merit SF; Nominee NCTE Achvmnt Awards In Writing; Univ; Bus Admin.

ZERRUDO, PHOEBE; Parkersburg Catholic HS; Parkersburg, WV; 16/44 Cls Rep Frsh Cls; Trs Jr Cls; Am Leg Aux Girls St; Chrh Wkr; Cmnty Wkr; Hon Rl; Jr NHS; Lbry Ade; NHS; Off Ade; Wheeling Coll; Nursing.

ZESZOTEK, MARCY; West Jefferson HS; W Jefferson, OH; Band; Chrs; Hon Rl; Quill & Scroll; Rptr Yrbk; Ed Sch Nwsp; Sch Nwsp; University; Photo Journalism.

ZETTLE, DANIEL; East Palestine HS; E Palestine, OH; VP Frsh Cls; Pres Soph Cls; Cls Rep Soph Cls; Cl Rep Jr Cls; Boy Scts; Hosp Ade; Sct Actv; Stu Cncl; Y-Teens; Key Clb; Silver Key Schlrshp Awd; Incentive Schlrshp Awds; God & Cntry Awd; Eagle Scout Awd; Notre Dame Univ; Engr.

ZETTLER, CONSTANCE; Stephen T Badin HS; Hamilton, OH; Trs Frsh Cls; Trs Soph Cls; Trs Jr Cls; Chrh Wkr; Hon Rl; Treas Stu Cncl; Drama Clb; Fr Clb; FHA; Swmmng; Univ.

ZETTLER, TERI; Springfield Cathlc Cntrl HS; Springfield, OH; Trs Frsh Cls; Cls Rep Soph Cls; Trs Jr Cls; Cls Rep Sr Cls; Chrs; NHS; Sch Mus; Capt Chrldng; GAA; IM Sprt; Bus Sec.

ZETZL, LAWRENCE J; Cardinal Ritter HS; Speedway, IN; 6/147 Cls Rep Sr Cls; Pres Band; Chrs; Hon Rl; Mdrgl; VP MMM; NHS; Sch Mus; Stg Crw; Yth Flsp; Honor Awrd Eng 77; Honor Awrd Acctg 78; Cntrl Ind Regnl Music Cntst 1st Pl 78; Butler Univ; Pre Med.

ZETZL, MARY A; Cardinal Ritter HS; Speedway, IN; 21/186 Cl Rep Jr Cls; Band; Chrs; Girl Scts; Hon Rl; Hosp Ade; Sec MMM; NHS; Sch Mus; Stu Cncl; Cntrl Ind Music Contest Piano & Voice 1st 77; Teen Tonics Awrd 78; Butler Univ; Occptnl Ther.

ZEUG, DOUGLAS; Schoolcraft HS; Schoolcraft, MI; 8/165 Hon Rl; Stu Cncl; Letter Bsktbl; Letter Glf; Letter Trk; Western Michigan Univ; Law.

ZEUNIK, ROBERT; Parkside HS; Jackson, MI; Boy Scts; Sch Mus; City Table Tennis Champ Jackson Rec 75 76 & 77 City Champ Softball Team 75 76 & 77;.

ZEYEN, ELIZABETH; St Wendelin HS; Fostoria, OH; Cls Rep Soph Cls; Band; Hon Rl; Pep Clb; Twrlr; Providence Hospital Schl Of Nrsg; Rn.

ZGODA, HELEN; Our Lady Of Mt Carmel HS; Wyandotte, MI; 1/75 Chrs; Hon Rl; NHS; Sch Mus; College; Med Tech.

ZIBAS, JURA; Walnut Hills HS; Cincinnati, OH; Boy Scts; Cmp Fr Grls; Chrh Wkr; Hon Rl; Hosp Ade; Lit Mag; Sct Actv; Yth Flsp; Rptr Sch Nwsp; Ger Clb; Univ; Med.

ZICARELLI, MILVA; Fraser HS; Fraser, MI; Hon Rl; Off Ade; College.

ZICHERMAN, DAVID L; Parkersburg HS; Vienna, WV; 18/785 Cls Rep Sr Cls; AFS; Am Leg Boys St; Boy Scts; Chrh Wkr; Cmnty Wkr; Debate Tm; Hon Rl; Hosp Ade; Lbry Ade; Univ; Med.

ZICKA FOOSE, BRENT; Huntington HS; Chillicothe, OH; 31/104 Pres Frsh Cls; Cl Rep Jr Cls; Hon Rl; Yrbk; Letter Bsbl; Letter Bsktbl; Crs Cntry; Coach Actv; Am Leg Awd; Univ.

ZIDONIS, ANDREA; Maplewood HS; Cortland, OH; 22/86 VP Soph Cls; Am Leg Aux Girls St; Boy Scts; Chrs; Cmnty Wkr; Hon Rl; Hosp Ade; Beta Clb; Drama Clb; 4-H; Kent St Univ; Nursing.

ZIEBART, RICHARD; Covington HS; Veedersburg, IN; Cls Rep Frsh Cls; Hon Rl; Stu Cncl; 4-H; Agric.

ZIEBARTH, BRENDA; Muskegon HS; Muskegon, MI; VP Sr Cls; Trs Sr Cls; Band; Hon Rl; NHS; Stu Cncl; Yth Flsp; Fr Clb; Am Leg Awd; Cit Awd; Univ.

ZIEBERT, THOMAS; St Ingnatius HS; Parma, OH; Band; Hosp Ade; Bsbl; Ftbl; Socr; Wrstlng; Coach Actv; Mgrs; Scr Kpr; Tmr; Embry Riddle Aeron Univ; Sci.

ZIEGE, ELIZABETH; Ben Davis HS; Indianapolis, IN; 12/840 Cls Rep Frsh Cls; Am Leg Aux Girls St; Band; Chrs; Girl Scts; Hosp Ade; Natl Forn Lg; NHS; Sch Mus; Stg Crw; Oral Roberts Univ; Music.

ZIEGELMAN, SHARON; North Farmington HS; Farmington Hill, S ; Chrs; Girl Scts; Hon Rl; Hosp Ade; Natl Forn Lg; Rptr Yrbk; Fr Clb; Scr Kpr; Rotary Awd; Temple Youth Grp Pres & Sec 77 & 78; Univ Of Michigan; Psych.

ZIEGLER, CHERYL L; Princeton Sr HS; Cincinnati, OH; Cls Rep Sr Cls; Am Leg Aux Girls St; Chrs; Chrh Wkr; Cmnty Wkr; Hon Rl; Jr NHS; Natl Forn Lg; NHS; John Hopkins Univ; Pre Law.

ZIEGLER, DENISE; North Royalton HS; N Royalton, OH; Chrs; Girl Scts; Off Ade; OEA; IM Sprt; Ohio State Univ; Law.

ZIEGLER, DENISE; Cuyahoga Vly Jt Voc HS; N Royalton, OH; Girl Scts; Off Ade; OEA; IM Sprt; Ohio St Univ; Law.

ZIEGLER, DONNA; Reading HS; Reading, OH; Sec Soph Cls; Trs Jr Cls; VP Sr Cls; Chrs; Girl Scts; Hon Rl; Stu Cncl; Fr Clb; Pep Clb; Chrldng; College; Med Asst.

ZIEGLER, GREG; Niles Mc Kinley HS; Niles, OH; Am Leg Boys St; Boy Scts; Hon Rl; Lat Clb; GMI; Elec Engr.

ZIEGLER, GREG; Niles Mckinley HS; Nils, OH; Am Leg Boys St; Boy Scts; Hon Rl; Lat Clb; GMI; Elec Eng.

ZIEGLER, LAYNE; Loudonville HS; Loudonville, OH; 30/130 Chrh Wkr; Cmnty Wkr; Hon Rl; Red Cr Ade; 4-H; 4-H Awd; Univ; Law.

ZIEGLER, ROBERT; Caro Cmnty Sr HS; Caro, MI; Band; Boy Scts; Hon Rl; NHS; Sct Actv; Stg Crw; Bnd Lttr 77; Michigan Tech Univ; Frst Fire Off.

ZIEGLER, STEPHEN; Laville HS; Plymouth, IN; 1/129 NHS; Mth Clb; Sci Clb; IM Sprt; Am Leg Awd; Bausch & Lomb Awd; Ind Univ; Fine Arts.

ZIELASKO, JANET; Lakeland Christian Academy; Winona Lake, IN; Pres Frsh Cls; Pres Soph Cls; Sec Jr Cls; Sec Sr Cls; Chrs; Chrh Wkr; Sch Pl; Stg Crw; Sec Stu Cncl; Drama Clb; Grace Coll; Phys Ed.

ZIELASKO, RICHARD; Anderson HS; Cincinnati, OH; 33/350 Pres Band; Boy Scts; Hon Rl; Jr NHS; NHS; Sch Mus; Sct Actv; Ohio State Univ; Elec Engr.

ZIELASKO, TRACY; Hoover HS; North Canton, OH; Band; Chrs; Girl Scts; Hon Rl; Off Ade; Orch; Pol Wkr; Sch Mus; Yth Flsp; Rptr Yrbk; Miami Univ; Spec Educ.

ZIELENBACH, KAREN; Hilliard HS; Hilliard, OH; 31/400 AFS; Chrs; Hon Rl; Mdrgl; NHS; Off Ade; Sch Mus; Sch Pl; Yth Flsp; Rptr Yrbk; Miami Univ; Intrntl Studies.

ZIELINSKI, DIANE; St Alphonsus HS; Dearborn Hts, MI; Hon Rl; Yrbk; Detroit Coll Of Busns; Acct g.

ZIELINSKI, JAMES; Washington HS; South Bend, IN; 120/355 Boy Scts; Chrh Wkr; Debate Tm; Hon Rl; Sct Actv; Letter Trk; Ball St Univ; Archt.

ZIELINSKI, JOHN; Washington HS; South Bend, IN; 3/355 Chrh Wkr; Hon Rl; Jr NHS; NHS; Sch Mus; Sch Pl; Stg Crw; Drama Clb; Bsktbl; Mgrs; Mr Congeniality At Purdue Acad Leasdrshp Seminar 78; Univ; Anthropology.

ZIELINSKI, SUZANNE; St Clement HS; Sterling Hts, MI; Pres Frsh Cls; Sec Chrh Wkr; Cmnty Wkr; Hon Rl; Mdrgl; Off Ade; Sch Mus; Sch Pl; Stg Crw; Stu Cncl; Congeniality Awd 76; Ath Awd Vlybl 76; Schl Serv Awd 78; Coll; Educ.

ZIELKE, RON; Carey HS; Carey, OH; 1/95 Band; Chrh Wkr; Hon Rl; NHS; Off Ade; Yrbk; Letter Bsbl; Letter Ftbl; Letter Wrstlng; Ohi St Univ; Engr.

ZIELONKA, SUSAN; Regina HS; Detroti, MI; Chrh Wkr; Cmnty Wkr; Hon Rl; Off Ade; Pol Wkr; JETS Awd; Wayne St Univ; Lib Arts.

ZIEMNICK, LINDA; Lake Linden Hubbell HS; Lake Linden, MI; 9/52 Trs Jr Cls; Band; Hon Rl; Off Ade; Sch Pl; Stu Cncl; Ed Yrbk; Rptr Sch Nwsp; Drama Clb; 4-H; Michigan Tech Univ; Elec Engr.

ZIEMS, TODD; Gladstone Area HS; Gladstone, MI; 31/203 Band; Boy Scts; Chrh Wkr; Hon Rl; Orch; Bsktbl; Ftbl; Trk; IM Sprt; Michigan Tech Univ; Comp Sci.

ZIENTA, SUZETTE; St Joseph Central Cathlc HS; Fremont, OH; Cmp Fr Grls; Chrh Wkr; Cmnty Wkr; Hon Rl; Sprt Ed Yrbk; Yrbk; 4-H; Letter Bsktbl; Letter Chrldng; Ohio St Univ.

ZIENTAK, ROBERT; St Clement HS; Warren, MI; Boy Scts; Hon Rl; Letter Bsbl; IM Sprt; College; Accounting.

ZIENTARA, CONNIE; Lake Central HS; Dyer, IN; 115/486 Cls Rep Soph Cls; Cl Rep Jr Cls; Band; Chrs; Hon Rl; Off Ade; Sch Mus; Sch Pl; Y-Teens; Drama Clb; Thornton Commiunity; Rn.

ZIFZAL, DAVE; Buckeye North HS; Smithfield, OH; Sec Jr Cls; Band; Hon Rl; NHS; Sch Pl; Letter Bsbl; Letter Ftbl; Letter Wrstlng; IM Sprt;.

ZIGENFUS, ROBIN; Mater Dei HS; Evansvl, IN; Hon Rl; Sct Actv; Rptr Sch Nwsp; Pep Clb; Univ; Marine Bio.

ZIGLER, TAMMY; Jay County HS; Dunkirk, IN; JA; Y-Teens; 4-H; Fr Clb; OEA; Pep Clb; Gym; GAA; 4-H Awd; JA Awd; Ball State Univ; Bus.

ZIGMOND, MICHAEL; St Marys Cntrl Catholic HS; Sandusky, OH; Aud/Vis; Ger Clb;.

ZIGTERMAN, MARC; Holland HS; Holland, MI; Chrs; Debate Tm; Hon Rl; Mod UN; NHS; Rptr Sch Nwsp; Sch Nwsp; IM Sprt; Natl Merit Ltr; Kalamazoo Coll.

ZIKOWITZ, JULIE; Carroll HS; Dayton, OH; Chrh Wkr; Red Cr Ade; Sch Pl; Drama Clb; Pep Clb; Spn Clb; Coach Actv; Mgrs; Univ; Paralegal.

ZILE, RONNIE; Vinton Co HS; West Union, OH; Cls Rep Sr Cls; Band; Chrs; Chrh Wkr; Cmnty Wkr; FCA; Hon Rl; NHS; Sch Mus; Sch Pl; Ohio Northern Univ; Pre Med.

ZILICH, DAWN; Cardinal HS; Huntsburg, OH; 11/104 Sec Frsh Cls; Trs Frsh Cls; VP Jr Cls; Sch Pl; 4-H; Bsktbl; Crs Cntry; Trk; Chrldng; GAA; College; Psych.

ZILKA, BRIAN; Clearview HS; Lorain, OH; Hon Rl; Sci Clb; Spn Clb; IM Sprt; College; Band.

ZILLANDI, MIKE A; Louisville HS; Louisville, OH; Cls Rep Frsh Cls; Stu Cncl; Letter Wrstlng; 2nd Plc In Art Show; Kent St Univ; Bus Admin.

ZIMMER, JILL; Vanlue HS; Carey, OH; 6/36 Pres Sr Cls; Hon Rl; NHS; Sch Pl; Bsbl; Letter Bsktbl; Letter Trk; College; Math.

ZIMMER, MARY; Marietta Sr HS; Whipple, OH; Band; Chrs; Chrh Wkr; Hon Rl; 4-H; 4-H Awd; 1st Pl In Solo Concert While With Sr High Chr 75; Ohio Univ; Early Child Educ.

ZIMMER, MICHAEL; Marysville HS; St Clair, MI; 16/173 Cls Rep Soph Cls; Cl Rep Jr Cls; VP Sr Cls; Cls Rep Sr Cls; Sch Pl; Stu Cncl; 4-H; Ftbl; Mgrs; 4-H Awd; Michigan St Univ; Comp Sci.

ZIMMER, MONICA; Wadsworth Sr HS; Wadsworth, OH; JA; DECA; Pep Clb; Spn Clb; Natl Merit Ltr; Ohio St Univ.

ZIMMERLY, ELLIOT; Groveport Madison HS; Obetz, OH; Hon Rl; Crs Cntry; Trk; U S Air Force Acad; Aero Engr.

ZIMMERMAN, AMY; Fostoria HS; Fostoria, OH; VP Sr Cls; Hon Rl; NHS; Y-Teens; Yrbk; Fr Clb; Chrldng; Univ; Nursing.

ZIMMERMAN, CHRIS; Wayne Goshen HS; Waynesfield, OH; Bsbl; Ftbl;.

ZIMMERMAN, CONSTANCE; Chaminade Julienne HS; Kettering, OH; Hon Rl; JA; Coll; Nursing.

ZIMMERMAN, DEBRA; North Muskegon HS; Muskegon, MI; Cls Rep Sr Cls; Hon Rl; NHS; Off Ade; Stu Cncl; Ger Clb; Mth Clb; Muskegon Community College; Doctor.

ZIMMERMAN, FRED; Alexander HS; Athens, OH; 7/132 Hon Rl; Yth Flsp; 4-H; FFA; 4-H Awd; Hocking Tech Coll; Bus.

ZIMMERMAN, JAMES; Greencastle HS; Greencastle, IN; Hon Rl; Rptr Sch Nwsp; Spn Clb; JC Awd; Opt Clb Awd; De Pauw Univ; Math.

ZIMMERMAN, JAMES; Edsel B Ford HS; Dearborn, MI; 7/468 Cls Rep Soph Cls; Hon Rl; Rptr Sch Nwsp; Ftbl; Letter Glf; Socr; Coach Actv; IM Sprt; Natl Merit Ltr; General Motors Inst; Mech Engr.

ZIMMERMAN, JON; Bently HS; Livonia, MI; Hon Rl; Albion.

ZIMMERMAN, KAREN; Columbia City Joint HS; Columbia City, IN; Band; Chrs; Chrh Wkr; Cmnty Wkr; Girl Scts; Hon Rl; Sct Actv; Yth Flsp; Asbury Coll; Music Ed.

ZIMMERMAN, KATHY; Pike County Joint Voc Schl; Piketon, OH; Chrs; Girl Scts; Hon Rl; Sch Mus; Sct Actv; FHA; Pep Clb; VICA; Pom Pon; Shawnee St Coll; Nurse.

ZIMMERMAN, KAYELLEN; Kalamazoo Central HS; Kalamazoo, MI; Hon Rl; Lit Mag; Drama Clb; Western Mic; Anthropology.

ZIMMERMAN, LINDA; Regina HS; Detroit, MI; 20/134 Cl Rep Jr Cls; Cls Rep Sr Cls; Chrs; Hon Rl; NHS; Stg Crw; Stu Cncl; Drama Clb; Sci Clb; Wayne St Univ; Nursing.

ZIMMERMAN, LISA; Southmont Jr Sr HS; Ladoga, IN; 54/200 Chrh Wkr; Drl Tm; Hon Rl; Lbry Ade; Pep Clb; Sci Clb; Tmr; Indiana St Univ; Psych.

ZIMMERMAN, LYNDA; Erieview Catholic HS; Cleveland, OH; 10/92 Chrs; Hon Rl; Hosp Ade; NHS; Sch Mus; Drama Clb; Sec.

ZIMMERMAN, MARCUS; Bethany Christian HS; Goshen, IN; Band; Boy Scts; Chrh Wkr; Hon Rl; Orch; Pol Wkr; Sct Actv; Yth Flsp; Rptr Yrbk; Sprt Ed Sch Nwsp; St 4 H & FFA Demo Contests 77; St Christian HS Athletic Mile Record Holder 77; 4 Yr Var Letter In Bsktbl; Grace Coll; Cnstrctn Elec.

ZIMMERMAN, MARK; Shepherd HS; Shepherd, MI; 6/116 Pres Soph Cls; Pres Jr Cls; Hon Rl; NHS; Letter Bsbl; Letter Bsktbl; Letter Ftbl; Dnfth Awd; Natl Merit SF; St Of Mi Schlrshp 79; Achvmnt Awd Shepherd HS 79; Ferris St Coll; BS Surveying.

ZIMMERMAN, MARK; Marion Harding HS; Marion, OH; Am Leg Boys St; Chrh Wkr; Hon Rl; Ten; IM Sprt; Sci Fair Superioer 77; Oh Schlstc Achvmnt Test Hon Mntn 77; Univ; Engr.

ZIMMERMAN, MARK; North Canton Hoover HS; North Canton, OH; 96/425 Boy Scts; Hon Rl; Sct Actv; Treas Ger Clb; Letter Bsktbl; Cit Awd; Us Naval Acad.

ZIMMERMAN, MICHAEL; Woodridge HS; Cuyahoga Fls, OH; Band; Chrh Wkr; Hon Rl; Yth Flsp; Lat Clb; Crs Cntry; IM Sprt; Rochester Inst Of Tech; Graphic Arts.

ZIMMERMAN, MICHELLE; Kenowa Hills HS; Grand Rapids, MI; Band; Cmp Fr Grls; Chrh Wkr; Cmnty Wkr; Hosp Ade; JA; Pol Wkr; Red Cr Ade; Rptr Yrbk; Rptr Sch Nwsp; Cheerleaders Awd Pep Stik; Jr Ach Company Of The Yr; Awd Of Battered Boot A Walk A Thon For March Of Dimes; Grand Rapids Jr Coll; Educ.

ZIMMERMAN, PEGGY; Norwood HS; Norwood, OH; 4/350 Chrh Wkr; Cmnty Wkr; Drl Tm; Hon Rl; Jr NHS; NHS; Yrbk; Rptr Sch Nwsp; Sec Key Clb; Lat Clb; College; Bus Mgmt.

ZIMMERMAN, REBECCA J; Archbishop Alter HS; Kettering, OH; 9/278 Girl Scts; Hon Rl; NHS; Sct Actv; Stu Cncl; Keyettes; IM Sprt; Mgrs; Univ; Comp Sci.

ZIMMERMAN, SHELLEY; Northrop HS; New Haven, IN; 58/500 Cls Rep Frsh Cls; Chrs; Girl Scts; Hon Rl; Off Ade; Stu Cncl; Rptr Yrbk; Rptr Sch Nwsp; Pep Clb; Gym; Schlstc Ach Awd; Vlybl Team; Oral Roberts Univ; Nursing.

ZIMMERMAN, STEVEN; Defiance Sr HS; Defiance, OH; VP Frsh Cls; Chrs; Hon Rl; Mdrgl; Quill & Scroll; Sch Pl; Sprt Ed Sch Nwsp; Letter Crs Cntry; Trk; Art Club 78; Pres Phys Fitness Awd 2 77 79; Schlr Ath 78; Univ.

ZIMMERMAN, THERESA; Roscommon HS; Roscommon, MI; Cls Rep Frsh Cls; Cls Rep Soph Cls; Chrs; Hon Rl; Stu Cncl; Trk; Kirtland Community Coll; Acctg.

ZIMMERMANN, BETH; Grosse Ile HS; Grosse Ile, MI; Girl Scts; Hon Rl; Hosp Ade; NHS; Sch Mus; Drama Clb; 4-H; Pep Clb; Gym; 4-H Awd; Univ.

ZIMOVAN, JOSEPH; Maple Hts Sr HS; Maple Hts, OH; 31/438 Chrh Wkr; Hon Rl; VP Jr NHS; Treas Yth Flsp; Fr Clb; JA Awd; Kent St Univ; Pharm.

ZINGRONE, MARIANGELA; Central Catholic HS; Massillon, OH; 47/250 Cls Rep Sr Cls; Band; Cmnty Wkr; Drl Tm; Hon Rl; NHS; Sch Mus; Rptr Yrbk; Drama Clb; Spn Clb; John Carroll Univ; Translator.

ZINK, ANNE; Lapel HS; Anderson, IN; 1/100 VP Jr Cls; VP Sr Cls; Am Leg Aux Girls St; JA; NHS; Rptr Yrbk; Pres Lat Clb; Dnfth Awd; Natl Merit Ltr; Opt Clb Awd; College; Doctor.

ZINK, JOHN; Wadsworth Sr HS; Wadsworth, OH; Cls Rep Frsh Cls; Cl Rep Jr Cls; Stu Cncl; Yrbk; Capt Swmmng; Coach Actv; College.

ZINK, LAWRENCE; Bridgeport HS; Bridgeport, OH; 12/112 Hon Rl; NHS; Spn Clb; Letter Bsktbl; Scr Kpr; College.

ZINK, SUSAN; Salem HS; Salem, IN; Lat Clb; Pep Clb; Mgrs; Scr Kpr; Univ; Elem Educ.

ZINKE, SHANE; Bay Rockets HS; Bay Vill, OH; Hon Rl; Ftbl; Hockey; College; Engr.

ZINKIVACH, BONNI; Osborn HS; Detroit, MI; Chrs; Hon Rl; Sch Pl; Ed Yrbk; Rptr Sch Nwsp; Rdo Clb; Oakland Community College.

ZINN, JENNIFER A; Grosse Pointe S HS; Grosse Pointe, MI; 10/540 Hon Rl; NHS; Orch; Sch Mus; Treas Stu Cncl; Sec Lat Clb; Natl Merit SF; Spoke At Ldrshp Comference 1978; 1st Pl Mythology For 2nd Yr Stus In Mi Jr Classical League 1977; Williams Coll.

ZINNI, SYLVIA S; Buckeye South HS; Rayland, OH; Am Leg Aux Girls St; Band; Capt Drl Tm; Girl Scts; Hon Rl; NHS; Sch Pl; Stu Cncl; Y-Teens; Drama Clb; Univ; Vet Sci.

ZINS, RICHARD; Brookville HS; Brookville, IN; Band; Sch Pl; Stg Crw; Drama Clb; Sci Clb; Bsbl; Band Concert 1st Pl Awd 79; Drama 76; Serv; Photog.

ZIOLO, ROSE; Paw Paw HS; Paw Paw, MI; 53/194 Hon Rl; Natl Forn Lg; NHS; Sch Pl; Western Mic Univ; Spec Ed.

ZIRGER, MELANIE; Fostoria HS; Fostoria, OH; Chrh Wkr; Hon Rl; Red Cr Ade; Y-Teens; Yrbk; Fr Clb; Bsktbl; Trk; Chrldng; Ohi State Univ; Dentistry.

ZIRK, SUSAN; Hampshire HS; Romney, WV; Hon Rl; Off Ade; FBLA; FHA;.

ZIRKEL, STEVE; St Francis Desales HS; Westerville, OH; 23/200 Chrh Wkr; Hon Rl; Spn Clb; Letter Bsbl; Bsktbl; JA; Ftbl; Coach Actv; Bowling Green Univ; Political Sci.

ZIRKER, CHRIS; Notre Dame Academy; Toledo, OH; Band; Cmnty Wkr; Orch; Stu Cncl; Fr Clb; IM Sprt; Univ Of Toledo; Bus.

ZISKIND, PENNY; Oak Park HS; Oak Park, MI; 64/300 Pres Frsh Cls; Treas Stu Cncl; Spn Clb; Pom Pon; Michigan St Univ; Interior Dsgn.

ZISSLER, JENNY; Engadine Consolidated School; Birch Run, MI; Girl Scts; Hon Rl; Off Ade; Acad Awd 75 & 77; Bus Schl; Legal Sec.

ZITTEL, JOHN; Waterford Mott HS; Pontiac, MI; Hon Rl; NHS; Rptr Yrbk; Bsktbl; Ftbl; Dnfth Awd; Michigan St Univ; Engr.

ZIVIAN, ROBERT J; Cranbrook HS; Oak Park, MI; Trs Frsh Cls; Sec Soph Cls; Band; Orch; Sch Mus; Rptr Sch Nwsp; Letter Bsktbl; Letter Socr; Letter Ten; Natl Merit SF; Univ; Law.

ZIZZI, ANNETTE; Elkins HS; Elkins, WV; 4/217 VP Soph Cls; VP Jr Cls; VP Sr Cls; Am Leg Aux Girls St; NHS; Off Ade; Stu Cncl; Keyettes; Letter Trk; Chrldng; Coll; Comp Sci.

ZLOMAK, TIM; Merrill Community HS; Merrill, MI; Pres Jr Cls; VP Sr Cls; Band; Chrs; Hon Rl; Hosp Ade; NHS; Sch Pl; Univ Of Michigan; Music.

ZNIDARSIC, DAVID; St Joseph HS; Euclid, OH; 11/295 Chrh Wkr; Hon Rl; Pres NHS; Sch Mus; Sch Pl; Stg Crw; Chmn Stu Cncl; Rptr Sch Nwsp; Sch Nwsp; Mth Clb; College; Math.

ZNIDARSIC, JOHN; St Ignatius HS; Euclid, OH; 30/252 Sec Frsh Cls; Cls Rep Frsh Cls; Cls Rep Soph Cls; Cl Rep Jr Cls; Sec Sr Cls; Band; Boy Scts; Chrs; Chrh Wkr; Cmnty Wkr; John Carroll Univ; Liberal Arts.

ZOBEL, JAMES F; Greensburg Community HS; Greensburg, IN; Band; Boy Scts; Chrh Wkr; Hon Rl; Sct Actv; Univ; Sci.

ZOELLER, JEFFREY R; East Lansing HS; E Lansing, MI; Mod UN; Pol Wkr; Natl Merit SF; Kalamazoo Coll.

ZOFKIE, TIM; Archbishop Alter HS; Kettering, OH; 12/300 Pres Soph Cls; Cls Rep Soph Cls; VP Jr Cls; Chrs; Chrh Wkr; Cmnty Wkr; Jr NHS; NHS; Stu Cncl; Ger Clb; College; Medicine.

ZOFKO, MARY; Niles Mc Kinley HS; Niles, OH; 21/425 VP Soph Cls; Pres Jr Cls; Chrs; Hon Rl; Mdrgl; Natl Forn Lg; VP NHS; Sch Mus; Sec Stu Cncl; Drama Clb; Univ; Elem Tchr.

ZOGLIO, MICHAEL; Anderson HS; Cincinnati, OH; 20/370 Treas Band; Hon Rl; Jr NHS; Orch; Sch Mus; Case Western Reserve Univ; Pysch.

ZOGLMAN, ANN; Jasper HS; Jasper, IN; 48/289 Cl Rep Jr Cls; Hon Rl; Sec JA; Lbry Ade; NHS; Stu Cncl; 4-H; Pep Clb; 4-H Awd; JA Awd; Acctg.

ZOHN, AIMEE; Magnolia HS; New Martinsvle, WV; Band; Girl Scts; Hon Rl; Treas Stu Cncl; DECA; Twrlr; College; Bus.

ZOHOURY, RICHARD; Upper Sandusky HS; Upper Sandusky, OH; Boy Scts; Hon Rl; Sch Pl; Yrbk; Ftbl; Wrstlng; IM Sprt; College; Med.

ZOLDAK, DAVID; Edward Lee Mcclain HS; Greenfield, OH; 3/155 VP Frsh Cls; Cls Rep Soph Cls; Pres Jr Cls; Am Leg Boys St; Band; Boy Scts; Chrs; College; Pre Law.

ZOLDAN, SANDRA; Clarenceville Sr HS; Livonia, MI; 1/225 Sec Frsh Cls; Hon Rl; Jr NHS; NHS; Stg Crw; Fr Clb; Letter Gym; IM Sprt; Cit Awd; Natl Merit Ltr; Univ Of Michigan; Acctg.

ZOLEN, BERNADETTE; South Haven HS; S Haven, MI; Cls Rep Frsh Cls; Cls Rep Soph Cls; Cl Rep Jr Cls; Cmp Fr Grls; Chrh Wkr; Girl Scts; Hon Rl; Stu Cncl; Ed Sch Nwsp; 4-H; Ferris; Bus.

ZOLLINGER, JAY; Millersport HS; Millersport, OH; 8/69 Cls Rep Sr Cls; Am Leg Boys St; Chrh Wkr; Debate Tm; Hon Rl; Jr NHS; NHS; Stg Crw; Pres Stu Cncl; Yth Flsp; Bowling Green St Univ; Comp Prog.

ZOLO, CAROLYN; Newark HS; Newark, OH; Cls Rep Frsh Cls; Cls Rep Soph Cls; Cl Rep Jr Cls; Cls Rep Sr Cls; Band; Chrs; Hon Rl; NHS; Stu Cncl; Eng Clb; Ltr Varsity 1978; Res Envrn Educ Counslr 1978; Mbr PRIDE Comm St 1978; Wittenburg Univ; History.

ZOLPER, DIANE J; Delphi Comm HS; Delphi, IN; 10/144 AFS; Am Leg Aux Girls St; Band; NHS; Pres Yth Flsp; Rptr Sch Nwsp; VP 4-H; Pres Fr Clb; Capt Swmmng; GAA; Coll; History.

ZOMERMAN, IRENE; Potterville HS; Potterville, MI; 2/66 Sec Jr Cls; Cls Rep Sr Cls; Sal; Aud/Vis; Band; Sec Frsh Cls; Hon Rl; Mic Tech Univ; Engr.

ZOMPARELLI, GINO; St Ignatius HS; Cleveland, OH; Cmnty Wkr; Mth Clb; Capt IM Sprt; Eng Wrtng Contst 78; 2nd Hon 76 78; Univ; Pre Law.

ZONARAS, THOMAS; Fairmont West HS; Kettering, OH; Cls Rep Frsh Cls; Hon Rl; Stu Cncl; Bsktbl; Coach Actv; IM Sprt; Scr Kpr; College; Acctg.

ZONDOR, ANN; Munster HS; Munster, IN; Sec AFS; Chrs; Hon Rl; Stg Crw; Pres 4-H; IM Sprt; Mat Maids; Tmr; Ball St Univ; Elem Ed.

ZONKER, JANET; Woodsfield HS; Woodsfield, OH; Trs Soph Cls; Trs Jr Cls; Trs Sr Cls; Band; Chrs; Hon Rl; Sch Pl; Drama Clb; 4-H; Fr Clb; Pulmonary Lab.

ZOOG, PETE; Cathedral HS; Indianapolis, IN; 1/150 Val; Hon Rl; Jr NHS; NHS; Rptr Yrbk; Rptr Sch Nwsp; Bsktbl; Letter Crs Cntry; Letter Trk; IM Sprt; 4 Yr Lennox Industries Inc Natl Merit Spec Schlrshp; Phi Beta Kappa Awd Indianna Alpha Chapter; Purdue Univ; Acctg.

ZOPFF, THOMAS E; Godwin Hts HS; Wyoming, MI; 10/170 Band; Hon Rl; Letter Swmmng; Trk; Michigan Tech Univ; Engr.

ZORKO, JACQUELINE; Euclid Sr HS; Euclid, OH; 30/747 Pres Debate Tm; Hon Rl; NHS; Off Ade; Quill & Scroll; Sct Actv; Rptr Sch Nwsp; Sch Nwsp; Keyettes; College; Medicine.

ZORN, MARY; Beaumont Girls Schl; Clevelnd, OH; Cmnty Wkr; Lbry Ade; FNA; FTA; Spn Clb; Coach Actv; GAA; Natl Merit Ltr; Univ; Pre Med.

ZORNES, RONNIE; Sharples HS; Clothier, WV; VP Frsh Cls; Pres Soph Cls; Cls Rep Soph Cls; Pres Jr Cls; Cl Rep Jr Cls; Boy Scts; Hon Rl; Stu Cncl; Yth Flsp; Sprt Ed Sch Nwsp;.

ZORNOW, CLAUDIA; Thomas A De Vilbiss HS; Toledo, OH; Band; Hon Rl; Hosp Ade; Sch Mus; Univ; Math.

ZORZA, CATHY; Gwinn HS; Skandia, MI; Drm Bgl; Hon Rl; Treas 4-H; Crs Cntry; Letter Trk; 4-H Awd; Northern Michigan Univ.

ZORZA, WAYNE P; Gwinn Cmnty HS; Gwinn, MI; 10/206 Cls Rep Frsh Cls; Band; Boy Scts; NHS; Key Clb; Capt Crs Cntry; Letter Swmmng; Letter Trk; Natl Merit Ltr; Schlrshp Officers Wives Club 79; 1st Pl 100 Yd Breast Stroke U P Finals 79; 1st Alto Sax 78 Stage Band 79; Univ Of Michigan; Pre Med.

ZOTOS, MICHAEL; East Detroit HS; Utica, MI; 90/800 Cls Rep Soph Cls; Cl Rep Jr Cls; Cls Rep Sr Cls; Aud/Vis; Boy Scts; Debate Tm; Hon Rl; Stu Cncl; IM Sprt; Cit Awd; Oakland Univ; Mgmt.

ZOTT, BRIAN; Centerline Sr HS; Center Line, MI; 34/417 Hon Rl; Lbry Ade; VICA; Letter Bsbl; Letter Ftbl; IM Sprt; Western Michigan Univ; Engr.

ZOUCK, FREDERICK; Springfield Local HS; New Springfield, OH; 44/145 Treas AFS; Chrh Wkr; Pres Yth Flsp; Fr Clb; FTA; Pep Clb; Scr Kpr; Miami Univ Ohio; Pulp & Paper Tech.

ZOX, HOLLY; Bexley HS; Columbus, OH; Hon Rl; Lit Mag; Sch Nwsp; 4-H; Fr Clb; Hockey; Trk; GAA; IM Sprt; Awds For Paints Getting Them Accptd In Juried Art Shows; Art Club Metro Art League; Write Schl Lit Mag; College; Art.

ZOYHOFSKI, SHARRON; Glen Lake Community HS; Empire, MI; Hon Rl; NHS; Fr Clb; Letter Bsktbl; Letter Trk; Homestead Schslhp & Empire Nalt Bank Sclshp 79; Loren Richardson Memrl Athltc Awd 79; Ferris St Coll; Auto Serv.

ZUBAL, VICTORIA; Holy Name Nazareth HS; Parma, OH; 16/360 Cls Rep Soph Cls; Hon Rl; Hosp Ade; Lit Mag; NHS; Sch Mus; Sch Pl; Stg Crw; Stu Cncl; Rptr Yrbk; Univ; Dent Surgery.

ZUBECK, LINDA; George Rogers Clark HS; Whiting, IN; 59/218 Cmp Fr Grls; Chrs; Drl Tm; Stu Cncl; Spn Clb; Trk; GAA; PPFtbl; Univ.

ZUBER, GREGORY N; Interlochen Arts Academy; Chicago, IL; Cl Rep Jr Cls; Band; Chrs; Hon Rl; Orch; Sch Mus; Sch Pl; Stg Crw; Stu Cncl; IM Sprt; Univ Of Illinois; Music.

ZUBER, LISA; Avon Lake HS; Avon Lake, OH; 84/279 Trs Jr Cls; Cls Rep Sr Cls; Am Leg Aux Girls St; Hon Rl; Stu Cncl; Pep Clb; Bsktbl; Capt Ten; Chrldng; Muskingum College; Business.

ZUBER, MARY L; Northrop HS; Ft Wayne, IN; Band; Hon Rl; Sec JA; Off Ade; Pom Pon; Scr Kpr; JA Awd; Sec JETS Awd; Purdue Univ; Micro Bio.

ZUCKERMAN, J; Culver Military Acad; La Jolla, CA; 3/197 Band; Drm Bgl; Hon Rl; ROTC; Lat Clb; Mth Clb; Sci Clb; Swmmng; Cit Awd; Univ; Chem Engr.

ZUELCH, HOLLY; Crestwood HS; Aurora, OH; Hon Rl; Off Ade; OEA; Typing 1 50 Wds Per Mn 77; Intensv Off Educ 78; Kent St Univ; Art.

ZUFFELATO, SCOTT; St Joseph Ctrl Cath HS; Huntington, WV; 7/50 Am Leg Boys St; Band; Chrh Wkr; Hon Rl; Pres Key Clb; Bsbl; Letter Bsktbl; Univ; Pre Med.

ZUFFELATO, SCOTT E; St Joseph Central HS; Huntington, WV; 7/50 Am Leg Boys St; Band; Chrh Wkr; Hon Rl; Pres Key Clb; Letter Bsbl; Letter Bsktbl; Univ; Pre Med.

ZUIDERVEEN, JEFFREY; Allegan HS; Allegan, MI; 3/193 Trs Sr Cls; Band; Chrh Wkr; Hon Rl; NHS; Stu Cncl; Lat Clb; Grand Rapids Baptist College; Bioche.

ZUKOWSKI, LAURA; Bishop Foley HS; Sterling Hts, MI; 4/294 Hon Rl; Fr Clb; Oakland Univ.

ZULCH, THOMAS; Clawson HS; Clawson, MI; Cls Rep Frsh Cls; Cls Rep Soph Cls; Pres Jr Cls; Cmnty Wkr; Hon Rl; Sch Mus; Sch Pl; Stg Crw; Stu Cncl; Rptr Sch Nwsp; Univ; Engr.

ZULL, JO ANN; Lakeview HS; Battle Creek, MI; 60/398 Hon Rl; NHS; Mgrs; Lakeview Ed Assn Schlrshp; St Of Mich Schlrshp; W Michigan Univ; Busns.

ZUMACK, BRIAN; Black River HS; West Salem, OH; 24/90 Trs Jr Cls; Hon Rl; NHS; Sch Pl; Drama Clb; Fr Clb; Sci Clb; Letter Bsbl; Letter Ftbl; Voc Schl.

ZUMBRUN, ANDREA; Churubusco HS; Albion, IN; 6/135 Sec Band; Hon Rl; NHS; FNA; Lat Clb; Parkview Methodist Univ; Nursing.

ZUMKEHR, JENIFER; Kent Roosevelt HS; Kent, OH; Sec Sr Cls; Hon Rl; Lit Mag; Stu Cncl; Sch Nwsp; Hockey; Swmmng; Ten; Outstndg Art Stu Awd 77; Westminster Univ; Eng.

ZUMRICK, JANET; Ursuline HS; Youngstown, OH; 21/342 Hon Rl; Mdrgl; Quill & Scroll; Ger Clb; Capt IM Sprt; University; Nursing.

ZUPI, JOSEPH T; Bishop Flaget HS; Chillicothe, OH; 3/36 VP Jr Cls; AFS; Chrh Wkr; Hon Rl; Jr NHS; NHS; Sch Mus; Sch Pl; Stg Crw; Ten; Xavier Univ.

ZUPIN, KEVIN; Onekama HS; Manistee, MI; Cls Rep Frsh Cls; VP Soph Cls; Boy Scts; Pres Yth Flsp; Rptr Yrbk; Drama Clb; Letter Trk; College; English.

ZUPPA, SHARON; Allen Park HS; Allen Pk, MI; Band; Chrs; Chrh Wkr; Cmnty Wkr; Girl Scts; Hon Rl; Jr NHS; College; Med.

ZUR, RANDALL; Willoughby South HS; Will Hills, OH; Band; NHS; Glf; Pro Bowler.

ZURASKI, JEFF; Menominee HS; Menominee, MI; Am Leg Boys St; Boy Scts; Hon Rl; Jr NHS; Letter Ftbl; Trk; Michigan Tech Univ; Engr.

ZURBRIGGEN, DIANE M; Our Lady Of The Lakes HS; Waterford, MI; 1/45 Hon Rl; Hosp Ade; NHS; Yrbk; Spn Clb; IM Sprt; Natl Merit SF; College.

ZURBRIGGEN, EILEEN L; Our Lady Of Lakes HS; Waterford, MI; 1/45 Hon Rl; Sec NHS; Sch Mus; Rptr Yrbk; Sec Fr Clb; Chrldng; Coach Actv; IM Sprt; PPFtbl; Natl Merit SF; College.

ZURBRUGG, DOROTHY; R Nelson Snider HS; Ft Wayne, IN; Chrh Wkr; Hon Rl; Off Ade; Fr Clb; Ind Univ; Bus.

ZURCA, ANTHONY; Kenston HS; Chagrin Fl, OH; Hon Rl; Letter Bsbl; Letter Ftbl; PPFtbl; Bowling Green State Univ; Acctg.

ZURCHER, MELODY; Firelands HS; Oberlin, OH; 2/148 Sal; Pres Band; Chrs; Chrh Wkr; Hon Rl; NHS; Ashland Coll; Math.

ZUREK, JOHN; Bishop Borgess HS; Redford, MI; Hon Rl; NHS; Pol Wkr; IM Sprt; Mgrs; Univ Of Mich Dearborn; Eng.

ZURSCHMIEDE, ERIC; Floyd Central HS; Floyd Knobs, IN; 61/462 Chrs; NHS; Swmmng; Perdue Univ; Engr.

ZUSMANIS, VALDIS; Central HS; Grand Rapids, MI; 1/360 Val; Band; Chrh Wkr; Hon Rl; Mod UN; NHS; Sch Mus; Ger Clb; Pep Clb; Am Leg Awd; Harvard Book Awd; Class 1926 Awd; Edward F Snell Awd; Outstndng Chem Stu; Michigan St Univ; Landscape Archt.

ZUTTER, ANDREW; John Adams HS; So Bend, IN; 12/395 Sec Frsh Cls; Jr NHS; Bsbl; IM Sprt; Natl Merit Ltr; College.

ZUZEK, JOHN; Madison HS; Madison, OH; 15/295 Band; Hon Rl; NHS; Ger Clb; Key Clb; Crs Cntry; Trk; Wrstlng; Ohio St Univ; Forestry.

ZUZEK, JOHN E; Lake Catholic HS; Willoughby, OH; 2/305 Aud/Vis; Hon Rl; Lit Mag; NHS; Pol Wkr; Ed Sch Nwsp; Rptr Sch Nwsp; Lat Clb; Am Leg Awd; Natl Merit Ltr; Cleveland St Univ; Elec Engr.

ZWICK, COLLEEN A; Minerva HS; East Rochester, OH; 12/241 Chrs; Chrh Wkr; Girl Scts; Hon Rl; Off Ade; FHA; Letter Trk; Exec Sec.

ZWICKER, NANCY; Aiken Sr HS; Cincinnati, OH; 11/525 Cls Rep Soph Cls; Band; Drl Tm; Jr NHS; NHS; Rptr Sch Nwsp; Fr Clb; Ger Clb; Chrldng; IM Sprt; Mercantile Library Mbr; Language Honor Society; Univ Of Cincinnati; Journalism.

ZWICKL, KEVIN M; John Adams HS; South Bend, IN; 29/391 Hon Rl; Jr NHS; NHS; Sct Actv; Bsbl; Letter Glf; Butler Univ; Pharmacy.

ZWIER, JOAN; West Catholic HS; Grand Rapids, MI; 3/264 Cls Rep Frsh Cls; Cls Rep Soph Cls; Chrs; Hon Rl; NHS; Rptr Sch Nwsp; Sch Nwsp; Fr Clb; Pep Clb; Letter Trk; Mich State Univ; Vet.

ZWILLER, DONNA; Monroe HS; Monroe, MI; 75/585 Band; Chrs; Chrh Wkr; Hon Rl; PAVAS; Sch Mus; Sch Pl; Stg Crw; Drama Clb; Rdo Clb; Monroe Comm Coll; Drama.

ZWOLINSKI, JOSEPH; John J Pershing HS; Detroit, MI; Band; Boy Scts; Chrs; Hon Rl; NHS; Off Ade; Orch; Sch Mus; Sct Actv; Letter Ftbl; Lawrence Inst Of Tech; Engr.

ZWYGHUIZEN, KAREN; Zeeland HS; Zeeland, MI; 15/193 Chrh Wkr; Debate Tm; Hon Rl; Mod UN; Natl Forn Lg; NHS; Yth Flsp; 4-H; Glf; PPFtbl; Northwestern Coll; Elem Ed.

ZYCH, JOSEPH; Osborn HS; Detroit, MI; Drl Tm; Hon Rl; ROTC; Lat Clb; Am Leg Awd; Cit Awd; Univ Of Det; Aero Engr.

ZYCH, SUSAN; Osborn HS; Detroit, MI; Hon Rl; ROTC; OEA; Am Leg Awd; Cit Awd; Detroit Inst Of Tech.

ZYCHOWSKI, ED; Norway HS; Vulcan, MI; Chrh Wkr; Hon Rl; Key Clb; Michigan Tech Univ; Elec Engr.

ZYCK, PATRICIA A; Lake Catholic HS; Willowick, OH; 55/320 Chrh Wkr; Hon Rl; Sch Pl; Stg Crw; Pep Clb; Bsktbl; Chrldng; Coach Actv; IM Sprt; PPFtbl; College; Medical Field.

ZYGMUNT, CHRISTINA; Lake Central HS; St John, IN; 33/512 Chrs; Chrh Wkr; Hon Rl; Hosp Ade; NHS; 4-H; Ger Clb; Spn Clb; 4-H Awd; Valparaiso Univ; Nursing.

ZYGMUNT, STAN; Munster HS; Munster, IN; 1/420 Cl Rep Jr Cls; Pres Sr Cls; Am Leg Boys St; Hon Rl; Natl Forn Lg; NHS; Mth Clb; IM Sprt; College; Physics.

ZYLKA, LYDIA; Standish Sterling Cntrl HS; Standish, MI; 6/175 Cls Rep Frsh Cls; Cls Rep Soph Cls; Cl Rep Jr Cls; Band; Hon Rl; Sch Pl; Stu Cncl; Drama Clb; Keyettes; Pep Clb; Most Improved Player Awd For Sftbl 78; Homecoming Queen 78; Sr Schlstc Athlete Awd 79; Cntrl Michigan Univ.

ZYSKI, MICHAEL; Fremont St Joseph Ctrl HS; Fremont, OH; Cls Rep Frsh Cls; Key Clb; Ftbl; College; Comp Sci.

ZYWIEC, POLLY; Bishop Noll Inst; E Chicago, IN; 70/336 Cls Rep Sr Cls; Hon Rl; NHS; Yrbk; Mth Clb; Am Leg Awd; Purdue Univ; Pre Vet.

A

Abbott April
Marietta Sr HS
Marietta OH

Abbott John
Norton HS
Norton OH

Abbott Suzanne
Cambridge HS
Cambridge OH

Abbott William
Eastwood HS
Pemberville OH

Abel Joseph R
Buckhannon Upshur HS
Buckhannon WV

Abell Jeffrey A
Carroll HS
Dayton OH

Aber Donald M
Morgan HS
Malta OH

Aber Evelyn
Bellbrook HS
Bellbrook OH

Abernathy Darwyn
George Washington HS
E Chicago IN

Abney Bruce
Fountain Central Jr Sr HS
Hillsboro IN

Abraham Frank
Lincoln HS
Shinnston WV

Abraham Gregory
Liberty HS
Reynoldsville WV

Abraham Julie
Niles Mc Kinley HS
Niles OH

Abrahamson Clayton
Ludington HS
Ludington MI

Abrams Eric
Springboro HS
Lebanon OH

Abusamra Gary
Mishawaka HS
Mishawaka IN

Acheson Terry
Perry HS
Lima OH

Achkar Antonio A
Liberty HS
Youngstown OH

Ackerman Roderick C
Brookside HS
Sheffield Lake OH

Ackerson Cathy
South Range Raiders HS
Salem OH

Ac Moody Kevin
Coldwater HS
Coldwater MI

Acre James
Adelphian Academy
Otter Lk MI

Acre Scott
Adelphian Acad
Otter Lk MI

Acton Maryanna
Bloom Carroll HS
Lancaster OH

Adams Alice
Bremen HS
Bremen IN

Adams Belinda
Immaculata HS
Detroit MI

Adams Cheri L
Glen Este HS
Batavia OH

Adams Debra
Wardensville HS
Wardensville WV

Adams Diana L
Patrick Henry HS
Grelton OH

Adams Edward A
Mariemont HS
Cincinnati OH

Adams Elizabeth
Hamilton Township HS
R A F B OH

Adams Fred
Hammond Baptist HS
Omaha NE

Adams Jeffery A
Lewis County HS
Weston WV

Adams Jill
West Iron County HS
Princeton MI

Adams John
Padua Franciscan HS
Brunswick OH

Adams John Q
Arthur Hill HS
Vassar MI

Adams Karen
Dominican HS
Mt Clemens MI

Adams Keri L
Chesterton HS
Chesterton IN

Adams Kimberly
Chaminade Julienne HS
Dayton OH

Adams Marvin
Elgin HS
La Rue OH

Adams Matthew D
Parkersburg HS
Vienna WV

Adams Michael
Greenville Sr HS
Greenville OH

Adams Pamela
Madison Heights HS
Anderson IN

Adams Patricia
Baldwin HS
Idlewild MI

Adams Sally
Eau Claire HS
Eau Claire MI

Adams Sharon
Wirt County HS
Palestine WV

Adams Susan
Streetsboro HS
Streetsboro OH

Adams Susan K
Independence HS
Coal City WV

Adams Tamara
Laingsburg HS
Dewitt MI

Adams Tammy
Point Valley HS
Bainbridge OH

STUDENTS
PHOTOGRAPH
SCHEDULED
FOR PUBLI-
CATION HERE
COULD NOT
BE REPRO-
DUCED

Adams William
Logan Elm HS
Kingston OH

Adamson Melody
Kenowa Hills HS
Grand Rapids MI

Adamy Paul
Buckhannon Upshur HS
Buckhannon WV

Adastik Bethanne
Forest Hills Northern HS
Ada MI

Addams John S
Marysville HS
Marysville OH

Adelsberger Annette
London HS
West Jefferson OH

Aden Janet
Warrensville Heights HS
Warrensville OH

Adkins Alanna
Guyan Valley HS
Branchland WV

Adkins Barry
South Point HS
South Point OH

Adkins Kathleen J
Valley Local HS
Lucasville OH

Adkins Mark
Vermilion HS
Vermilion OH

Adkins Randy
Winfield HS
Pliny WV

Adkins Ronda
Nordonia HS
Macedonia OH

Adkins Susan
Greenfield Central HS
Wilkinson IN

Adkins Timothy
Washington HS
Massillon OH

Adkins Tina
Gallia Acad
Gallipolis OH

Adkins Todd
Huntington HS
Huntington WV

Adorjan Sharon
Morton Sr HS
Hammond IN

Adrianowycz Sonia
James Ford Rhodes HS
Parma OH

Adrine Ethel
Shaker Heights Sr HS
Shaker Hts OH

Adsit Susan
Douglas Mac Arthur HS
Sagianaw MI

Ady Kelly
Perry HS
Massillon OH

Aeder Rebecca
Waverly HS
Lansing MI

Aeling James
Minerva HS
Minerva OH

Aeschliman Kim
Bluffton HS
Bluffton IN

Affholter James E
Woodhaven HS
Woodhaven MI

Agatep Maria R C
St Florian HS
Detroit MI

Agatep Merileen
St Florian HS
Detroit MI

Agne Brian
Lakeview HS
Battle Creek MI

Ahle Cindy
Old Fort HS
Tiffin OH

Ahlquist Anne
West Carrollton Sr HS
Dayton OH

Ahmed Jerry
Maple Hts HS
Maple Hgts OH

Ahrens Shari
Plainwell HS
Plainwell MI

STUDENTS
PHOTOGRAPH
SCHEDULED
FOR PUBLI-
CATION HERE
COULD NOT
BE REPRO-
DUCED

Aikens Crystal
Hedgesville HS
Hedgesville WV

Ake Shirley
Whitehall HS
Whitehall MI

Akins Millicent
Mansfield Malabar HS
Mansfield OH

STUDENTS
PHOTOGRAPH
SCHEDULED
FOR PUBLI-
CATION HERE
COULD NOT
BE REPRO-
DUCED

Alasti Isabella
Richmond Sr HS
Richmond IN

Albaneso Virginia
Wellsville HS
Wellsville OH

Albaugh Anita
Columbia City Joint HS
Columbia City IN

Alber Margaret
Huntington North HS
Warren IN

Albers Lynne
Strongsville Sr HS
Strongsville OH

Albert Penny
Martins Ferry HS
Martins Ferry OH

Albert Shauna
Hardin Northern School
Dola OH

Albert Ted
Belding HS
Belding MI

Alberts Marianne
Imlay City HS
Attica MI

Albright Barbara
Kelloggsville HS
Kentwood MI

Albright Katrina
Logan Sr HS
Logan WV

Albus David
Madison HS
Madison OH

Alcorn Janet
Broad Ripple HS
Indianapolis IN

Alcorn Raymond S
New Albany Sr HS
New Albany IN

Aldrich Sharise
Chesanina HS
Oakley MI

Aldridge Kemi J
Ripley HS
Kenna WV

Alessi Vincent
Pontiac Central HS
Pontiac MI

Alexander Chris
Walnut Ridge HS
Columbus OH

Alexander Doncella D
Independence Jr Sr HS
Columbus OH

Alexander Fred
Washington HS
Massillon OH

Alexander Josilyn
Roosevelt HS
Gary IN

Alexander Katrina
West Side Sr HS
Gary IN

Alexander Kendall
Lexington HS
Mansfield OH

Alexander Laurie A
John Hay HS
Cleveland OH

Alexander Ruth
Berkeley Springs HS
Berkeley Spgs WV

Alexander Sharon
John Adams HS
Cleveland OH

Alexander William P
Barberton HS
Barberton OH

Alflen Elizabeth
Wayland Union HS
Wayland MI

Alford Dena
Switzerland Co Jr Sr HS
Vevay IN

Alford Robin
Stivers Patterson Co Op HS
Dayton OH

Alfrey Steve
Little Miami HS
Morrow OH

Alfultis Charles
North Ridgeville HS
N Ridgeville OH

Ali Duncan C
Reeths Puffer HS
Muskegon MI

Alicea Annette
Washington HS
E Chicago IN

Alicox Linda
Elmhurst HS
Ft Wayne IN

Allard Jennifer
Lebanon HS
Lebanon OH

Allbright Angela
Rock Hill Sr HS
Pedro OH

Alleman James
Point Pleasant HS
Pt Pleasant WV

Allen Andre
Warrensville Hts HS
Warrensville OH

STUDENTS PHOTOGRAPH SCHEDULED FOR PUBLICATION HERE COULD NOT BE REPRODUCED

Allen Boyd
Hubbard HS
Hubbard OH

Allen Cheryl
Wilbur Wright HS
Dayton OH

Allen Curt
Southmont HS
New Market IN

Allen Debbie
Beallsville HS
Clarington OH

Allen Donna
Frank Cody HS
Detroit MI

Allen Fawn
Warrensville Hts HS
Warrensville OH

Allen James
Loy Norrix HS
Kalamazoo MI

STUDENTS PHOTOGRAPH SCHEDULED FOR PUBLICATION HERE COULD NOT BE REPRODUCED

Allen Kimberly
Bishop Noll Inst
Gary IN

Allen Kimberly
John Glenn HS
Bay City MI

Allen Mary
Penn HS
Osceola IN

Allen Michael
Terre Haute North Vigo HS
Terre Haute IN

Allen Michael
Oak Hill HS
Oak Hill WV

Allen Michael J
Lawton Comm HS
Lawton MI

Allen Michelle
Toronto HS
Toronto OH

Allen Patricia
East Technical HS
Cleveland OH

Allen Richard L
Bridgeport Sr HS
Bridgeport WV

Allen Robert M
Plainwell HS
Plainwell MI

Allen Shari
Johannesburg Lewiston
HS
Lewiston MI

Allen Sharon L
Emerson HS
Gary IN

Allen Tammy
Parkersburg South HS
Parkersburg WV

Allen Todd
Jefferson HS
Dayton OH

Allensworth Gary L
Jewett Scio HS
Uhrhichsville OH

Allison Henry
Gallia Academy
Gallipolis OH

Allison Leslie
Carroll HS
Dayton OH

Allison Stephanie A
Rogers HS
Toledo OH

Allman Michael
Buckhannon Upshur HS
Buckhannon WV

Allmon Bill
Grove City HS
Orient OH

Allwine David
Shelby Sr HS
Shelby OH

Almon Joseph C
Decatur Central HS
Indnpls IN

Almond Ted
Woodrow Wilson HS
Beckley WV

Alouf Maurice
Fayetteville HS
Fayetteville WV

Alsman Jacky
North Knox HS
Oaktown IN

Alspaugh Cynthia
Benjamin Logan HS
Zanesfield OH

Alspaugh Pattie
Westerville South HS
Westerville OH

Altenburger Larry
Ottoville HS
Ottoville OH

Altenhof Michael
United Local HS
Kensington OH

Althardt John
Warren Central HS
Indianapolis IN

Altizer Treva
Centerburg HS
Centerburg OH

Altman Cynthia S
New Buffalo HS
New Buffalo MI

Altschuld Matthew
James Ford Rhodes HS
Cleveland OH

Altstaetter Jon
Mc Comb Local School
Mc Comb OH

Alvarado Victor
Harbor Springs HS
Cross Vlg MI

Alvey Richard
Sturgis HS
Sturgis MI

Alvey Terry
Mater Dei HS
Evansvl IN

Aman Anita
Lewis County HS
Camden WV

Amari Francesca
Lakeview HS
Battle Creek MI

Amaro Debora
Delton Kellogg HS
Delton MI

STUDENTS
PHOTOGRAPH
SCHEDULED
FOR PUBLI-
CATION HERE
COULD NOT
BE REPRO-
DUCED

Ameli Stephen D
Brother Rice HS
Birmingham MI

Amell Lane
Holly HS
Holly MI

Amerman David
Clay City HS
Clay City IN

Ames Stanley
Hudson Area HS
Hudson MI

Ammar Douglas
Charleston HS
Charleston WV

Ammons Beverly J
St Johns Public HS
St Johns MI

Amon Elizabeth
Canfield HS
Canfield OH

Amonett Teresa
Yorktown HS
Muncie IN

Amor Andrew
Grand Haven Sr HS
Grand Haven MI

Amos Debra
The Andrews School
Painesville OH

Amrhein Mary C
Immaculate Conception
Acad
Brookville IN

Amsler Diamantina
Marshall HS
Marshall MI

Amundson Paul
Greenfield Central HS
Greenfield IN

Anders Sheryl
Madison Plains Local HS
Mt Sterling OH

Andersen Todd
Mooresville HS
Mooresville IN

Anderson Cynthia
Arsenal Technical HS
Indianapolis IN

Anderson David
Bear Lake HS
Bear Lake MI

Anderson Donna K
Charlestown HS
Charlestown IN

Anderson Jay
Tippecanoe Valley HS
Mentone IN

STUDENTS PHOTOGRAPH SCHEDULED FOR PUBLICATION HERE COULD NOT BE REPRODUCED

Anderson Jeff
Hammond Baptist HS
Hobart IN

Anderson Jeffery
North HS
Willoughby Hls OH

Anderson Jeffrey
Negaunee HS
Negaunee MI

Anderson John
Osborn HS
Detroit MI

Anderson Karen
Winchester Comm HS
Winchester IN

Anderson Keith
Mid Peninsula HS
Rapid River MI

Anderson Kelly
Wayne Mem HS
Westland MI

Anderson Kelly L
Liberty HS
Clarksburg WV

Anderson Kimberly D
Liberty HS
Clarksburg WV

Anderson Laura
Niles HS
Niles MI

Anderson Lisa
Upper Vly HS
Troy OH

Anderson Marie
Fairless HS
Brewster OH

Anderson Peggy
Arch Bishop Alter HS
Kettering OH

Anderson Robert
Waverly HS
Waverly OH

Anderson Robert
Toronto HS
Toronto OH

Anderson Scott
Mooresville HS
Mooresville IN

Anderson Sheila
Spencer HS
Spencer WV

Anderson Sherry
La Salle HS
South Bend IN

Anderson Sue E
Laker HS
Pigeon MI

Anderson Susan
Chassell HS
Houghton MI

Anderson Terri
St Francis Central HS
Morgantown WV

Anderson Thomas
Lake City Area HS
Lake City MI

Anderson Yolanda
Osborn HS
Detroit MI

Andreatta Dale A
Claymont HS
Uhrichsville OH

Andreatta Susan
Claymont HS
Uhrichsville OH

Andrejczuk Joseph
Lawrence Public HS
Lawrence MI

Andres Deborah
Trinity HS
Seven Hills OH

Andrews Billy F
Floyd Central HS
Floyd Knobs IN

Andrews Darryl
John F Kennedy HS
Cleveland OH

Andrews Don
Stephen T Badin HS
Oxford OH

Andrews Jeffrey
Wilbur Wright HS
Dayton OH

Andrews John
Jackson HS
Massillon OH

Andujar Gloria
Bowling Green HS
Tulsa OK

Angel Timothy B
Portsmouth HS
Portsmouth OH

Angelo Linda
Williamston HS
Williamston MI

Angelo Terri
Williamston HS
Williamston MI

Angelo Tom
Warren Western Reserve HS
Warren OH

Angotti John D
Notre Dame HS
Clarksburg WV

Angotti Mary J
Hinton HS
Hinton WV

Ankrapp Sandra
St Clair HS
Richmond MI

Ankrom Ernest
Bloom Carroll HS
Carroll OH

Anson Elizabeth
Walnut Hills HS
Cincinnati OH

Antaya Kathy
Our Lady Of Mercy HS
Detroit MI

Anteau Sandra K
St Mary Academy
Newport MI

Anter Mary Jo
Port Huron HS
Mount Clemens MI

Anthony Mary A
Mount View HS
Gary WV

Anzevino Harry
Boardman HS
Youngstown OH

Apel Cheri
Wheelersburg HS
Sciotoville OH

Apicella Suzanne
Salem Sr HS
Salem OH

Apitz Wendy
Akron East HS
Akron OH

Appel Barbara
East Clinton HS
Sabina OH

Appelbaum Todd
Charles F Brush HS
Lyndhurst OH

Appledorn Scott
Holland HS
Holland MI

Arbogast Natalie
Harman HS
Harman WV

Archambault Jeffrey
Farwell Area HS
Clare MI

Archer Martha
Regina HS
Highland Hts OH

Archer Scott
Green HS
Uniontown OH

Archie Corinne
Southeastern HS
Detroit MI

Areford Wendy K
Univ HS
Morgantown WV

Arend Julie A
Jackson County Western HS
Jackson MI

Arendt Anita
Parma Sr HS
Parma OH

Arevalo Deborah
Mendon Jr Sr HS
Mendon MI

Argeline Barbara
Howell HS
Howell MI

Argyle Jennifer
Kulkaska HS
Graham TX

Arizmendi Wanda
Marshall HS
Marshall MI

STUDENTS
PHOTOGRAPH
SCHEDULED
FOR PUBLI-
CATION HERE
COULD NOT
BE REPRO-
DUCED

Arko Andrea
Tuslaw HS
Massillon OH

Armeni Mark
Boardman HS
Youngstown OH

Armes Robbyn
Charlestown HS
Charlestown IN

Arminio Lisa M
Fairfield HS
Fairfield OH

Armstrong Bonnie
Shenandoah HS
New Castle IN

Armstrong Frank
Holy Name Nazareth HS
Maple Hts OH

Armstrong Jeffrey K
Turpin HS
Cincinnati OH

Armstrong Kyle
East Kentwood HS
Kentwood MI

Armstrong Nancy
Alcona HS
Lincoln MI

Armstrong Paula
Highland HS
Anderson IN

Armstrong Randolph
Turpin HS
Cincinnati OH

Armstrong Rebecca
Jefferson Area HS
Jefferson OH

Armstrong Rhea
New Haven HS
New Haven MI

Armstrong Rodney
Portsmouth East HS
Sciotoville OH

Arndt Shel
Bethesda Christian HS
Indianapolis IN

Arnett Larry
Waverly HS
Waverly OH

Arnett Peggy
Sullivan HS
Merom IN

Arnold Don M
Mt Vernon HS
Fortville IN

Arnold Kim
South Putnam HS
Cloverdale IN

Arnold Larin
Jackson HS
Jackson MI

Arnold Matthew
Au Gres Sims HS
Augres MI

Arnold Pamela
Field HS
Kent OH

Arnold Roderick
Kettering HS
Detroit MI

Arnold Terry
Chadsey HS
Detroit MI

Arnold Tracy
Vinson HS
Huntington WV

Aronhalt David
Elk Garden HS
Elk Garden WV

Arrendondo Felice M
Merrillville Sr HS
Merrillville IN

Arrington Roderick T
Oscoda Area HS
Oscoda MI

Arrowood Jacqueli
Southwestern HS
Fenton MI

Arsic Sinisa
Lincoln West HS
Cleveland OH

Artemik Edward
Niles Sr HS
Niles MI

STUDENTS
PHOTOGRAPH
SCHEDULED
FOR PUBLI-
CATION HERE
COULD NOT
BE REPRO-
DUCED

Artibee Janet
Carman HS
Flint MI

Artman J Curtis
Jefferson Union HS
Toronto OH

Artzner Thais
Sandy Valley HS
Waynesburg OH

Arvin Doug
Loogootee HS
Loogootee IN

Ash Jennifer
Liberty HS
Clarksburg WV

Ash Judith
Liberty HS
Bristol WV

Ashbrook Bambi L
Revere Sr HS
Akron OH

Ashby Karen
Warren Western Reserve HS
Warren OH

Ashby Regina
Washington Catholic HS
Washington IN

Ashley Angela
Hudson Area HS
Hudson MI

Ashley James
Holly HS
Holly MI

Ashley Saundra
Ripley Union Lewis HS
D OH

Ashman Michael D
St Albans HS
St Albans WV

Ashman Rod
Jay County HS
Portland IN

Ashmore Kathryn
Stockbridge HS
Stockbridge MI

Askren Tracy
Attica HS
Attica IN

STUDENTS
PHOTOGRAPH
SCHEDULED
FOR PUBLI-
CATION HERE
COULD NOT
BE REPRO-
DUCED

Aston Charles
Warren G Harding HS
Warren OH

Atkins Phyllis
Emerson HS
Gary IN

Atkins Stephen J
Maysville HS
So Zanesville OH

Atkins Teigha
Princeton HS
Princeton WV

Atkinson Kenneth
Adlai Stevenson HS
Sterling Hgts MI

Atkinson Steve
Struthers HS
Struthers OH

STUDENTS
PHOTOGRAPH
SCHEDULED
FOR PUBLI-
CATION HERE
COULD NOT
BE REPRO-
DUCED

Augsburger Joan
Cory Rawson HS
Bluffton OH

Augustein Tawnee
Sebring Mc Kinley HS
Sebring OH

Augustine Judith
Trenton HS
Trenton MI

Augustus Carla
Sandusky HS
Sandusky OH

Aukerman Bruce
North Vermillion HS
Newport IN

Aukerman Robin
Eaton HS
Eaton OH

Aull Jackie
Pike Central HS
Petersburg IN

Ault Bobbi
Switz City Central HS
Lyons IN

Ault William
Rossford HS
Perrysburg OH

Ausenheimer Ann
Bucyrus HS
Bucyus OH

Aust Lisa
Pike Central HS
Stendal IN

Austerman Robert
William Mason HS
Mason OH

Austin Bradley
Cloverdale HS
Cloverdale IN

Austin Susan
New Richmond HS
New Richmond OH

Autry J Eric
Southeast HS
Diamond OH

Auvenshine Jeffrey
Mason Sr HS
Mason MI

Auvil David
Winfield HS
Scott Depot WV

Avason Anthony
East Detroit HS
East Detroit MI

Avedisian Paul
Southfield Christian HS
Southfield MI

Averesch Marlene
Kalida HS
Kalida OH

Avery Judy
Mio Au Sable HS
Mio MI

Avery Lance N
Anderson HS
Anderson IN

Avery Timothy
Cedar Springs HS
Cedar Springs MI

Avis Todd
Valley Forge HS
Parma Hts OH

Axelberg John T
La Ville HS
Lakeville IN

Aydent Lori
Lake Catholic HS
Chardon OH

Ayers Chris
Moorefield HS
Moorefield WV

Ayers Regina
Holly Sr HS
Holly MI

Ayres Carrie
Carroll HS
Bringhurst IN

Azbell Paula
Westfall HS
Williamsport OH

Azer Audrey
St Peters HS
Mansfield OH

B

Baar David
Grand Rapids Christian
HS
Holland MI

Babcock Brenda
Anderson HS
Cincinnati OH

Babcock Jeff
Port Clinton Sr HS
Port Clinton OH

Babcock Regina
Napoleon HS
Mc Clure OH

Babicka Gregory P
Andrean HS
Crown Point IN

Bacak Alice
Port Clinton HS
La Carne OH

Bacchi Joe
Euclid HS
Euclid OH

Bachanov Arlene
Jared W Finney Sr HS
Detroit MI

Bachtel Martha
Canfield HS
Canfield OH

Back Steven F
Highland HS
Wadsworth OH

Backus Jacqueline
Berrien Springs HS
Berrien Spgs MI

Bacon Debbie
Rockville HS
Rockville IN

Bacon Ronald
Rockville HS
Rockville IN

Badour Jacquelyn
Bullock Creek HS
Midland MI

Bady Shelton
Buena Vista HS
Saginaw MI

Baer Mary
Carroll HS
Dayton OH

Baer Jr Richard
Paint Valley HS
Bainbridge OH

Bagal Ujjvala A
Centerville HS
Centerville OH

Bahensky Susan
Lumen Cordium HS
Bedford OH

Bahler Lisa J
Marlington HS
Louisville OH

Bailey Andrea
Cedarville HS
Yellow Spgs OH

Bailey Beverly
Withrow HS
Cincinnati OH

Bailey Bonnie
Carmel HS
Inidanapolis IN

Bailey Cindy
Loudonville HS
Loudonville OH

Bailey Deanna
Lychburg Clay HS
Lynchburg OH

Bailey Gregory L
Montcalm HS
Rock WV

Bailey Jacob
Northfork HS
Mc Dowell WV

Bailey James
West Side HS
Gary IN

Bailey Jennifer
Iaeger HS
Panther WV

Bailey John
Harper Creek HS
Battle Creek MI

Bailey Kelli
Green HS
N Canton OH

Bailey Kimberly S
Guyan Valley HS
Branchland WV

Bailey Lonnie
Bloomfield HS
Bloomfield IN

Bailey Patrick H
Poca HS
Poca WV

Bailey Phil
Jay County HS
Portland IN

Bailey Sandy
Austintown Fitch HS
Youngstown OH

Bailey Sharon S
Lewis County HS
Weston WV

Bailey Susan
Upper Sandusky HS
Forest OH

Bailey Tom
Goshen HS
Goshen IN

Bair Bruce A
New Philadelphia HS
New Phila OH

Bajko Donna
Trinity HS
Seven Hills OH

Bakeman Craig
White Pigeon HS
White Pigeon MI

Baker Bruce M
Jefferson Area HS
Jefferson OH

Baker Carla
Upper Sandusky HS
Upper Sandusky OH

Baker Cheryl
New Albany HS
New Albany OH

Baker Christine
New Miami HS
Overpeck OH

Baker Cindy
Twin Valley North HS
Lewisburg OH

Baker Cynthia
Paul Lawrence Dunbar HS
Dayton OH

Baker Dale A
Edison HS
Berlin Hts OH

Baker Deanna
Port Clinton HS
Port Clinton OH

Baker Doris
Shaw HS
East Cleveland OH

Baker Douglas
Lakeview HS
Battle Creek MI

Baker Douglas
Crooksville HS
Nw Lexington OH

Baker Elizabeth
Woodridge HS
Stow OH

Baker Faye
Central HS
Detroit MI

Baker Judy
Southgate HS
Southgate MI

Baker Kathy
Little Miami HS
Morrow OH

Baker Kelly
Lake HS
Walbridge OH

Baker Laurie
Turpin HS
Cincinnati OH

Baker Lorry
Rogers HS
Michigan City IN

Baker Mike
Worthington Jefferson HS
Worthington IN

Baker Nancy
Conotton Valley HS
Sherrodsville OH

Baker Ronnie
Peebles HS
Peebles OH

Baker Roxanne
Carrollton HS
Saginaw MI

Baker Sandra
Harrison HS
Evansville IN

Baker Sheila
Calumet HS
Gary IN

Baker Steve
Salem HS
Salem IN

Baker Steven
N Putnam Jr Sr HS
Greencastle IN

Baker Vincent
Kenmore HS
Akron OH

Bakich Denise
Weir Sr HS
Weirton WV

Bakita Todd
St Johns Public HS
St Johns MI

Bakker Margie
Zeeland HS
Zeeland MI

Balagrin James
Northwood HS
Northwood OH

Balash Evan M
John Glenn HS
Bay City MI

Balazowich Denise
Green HS
Akron OH

Baldinger Rick
Elgin Local Marion Cnty HS
Marion OH

Baldwin Cathy
Bennett HS
Marion IN

Baldwin Robin
Jennings County HS
Butlerville IN

Baldwin Thomas
Cadillac HS
Cadillac MI

Balensiefer Kim
Benton Central HS
Fowler IN

Balentine Steven
Traverse City Sr HS
Traverse City MI

Bales Bruce
Randolph Southern HS
Winchester IN

Bales Cindy
John Marshall HS
Indianapolis IN

Bales Gary L
Southeast HS
Atwater OH

Balfour Valerie
Stephen T Badin HS
Hamilton OH

Ball Greg
Scott HS
Ramage WV

Ball Janell
Central HS
Switz City IN

Ball Jeff
Norwood HS
Norwood OH

Ball Lena
Sherman HS
Ashford WV

Ball Thomas
Onaway HS
Onaway MI

Ballas Tracey
Zanesville HS
Zanesville OH

Ballinger Edward
Bexley HS
Bexley OH

Ballert Kelly
High School
Toledo OH

Ballester Sandra
Reeths Puffer HS
Muskegon MI

Ballew David
Bosse HS
Evansville IN

Ballien Elizabeth A
Swan Valley HS
Saginaw MI

Ballinger Cheryl
Licking Valley HS
Newark OH

Ballinger Randy
National Trail HS
New Paris OH

Ballo Judith
C S Mott HS
Warren MI

Ballou Amy
Wayne HS
Dayton OH

Balogh Rebecca W
La Ville Jr Sr HS
Plymouth IN

Balster Tina
St Henry HS
St Henry OH

Balzhiser Jeni
Clermont Northeastern
HS
Batavia OH

Bammert Linda
Lake Linden Hubbell HS
Lake Linden MI

Banchich Robert S
Donald E Gauit Jr Sr HS
Hammond IN

Bandelow Patricia
The Andrews School
Eastlake OH

Banes Trudi J
North White HS
Monon IN

Banet Duane
Floyd Central HS
Floyd Knobs IN

Banhart John E
Calumet HS
Gary IN

Banks Susan D
Cass Tech HS
Detroit MI

Bankston Earnestine E
East HS
Columbus OH

Bannhard David
Carsonville Port Sanilac
HS
Pt Sanilac MI

Bannister Jackie
Wadsworth HS
Wadsworth OH

Bapst Richard
Hammond Tech Voc HS
Hammond IN

Baranouski Cynthia J
Quincy HS
Quincy MI

Baranowski Mike
Kalkaska HS
Maneiona MI

Barber Maryann
Logan HS
Logan WV

Barber Mike
Madison Comprehensive
HS
Mansfield OH

Barber Susan
Sylvania Southview HS
Sylvania OH

Barbera Margie
Villa Angela Academy
Cleveland OH

Barchfeld Joy
Marion L Steele HS
Amherst OH

Barclay Curt
Highland HS
Anderson IN

Barcus Jeffrey
Gallia Acad
Gallipolis OH

Barczykowski Sandra
Washington HS
So Bend IN

Bardar Jill
Lorain Cath HS
Lorain OH

Barholomai James G
Jeffersonville HS
Jeffersonville IN

Barhorst Mark
Sidney HS
Sidney OH

Barhorst Nancy
Sidney HS
Sidney OH

Barido Richard
Herber Hoover HS
Elkvw WV

Barkel Barbara S
W Michigan Christian HS
Muskegon MI

Barker Bradley
Mc Comb HS
Mc Comb OH

Barker Katherine
Bay HS
Bay Vill OH

Barker Kimberly
Vinton County Consldtd HS
Ray OH

Barker Marianna
Crestline HS
Crestline OH

Barker Stephanie
Amelia HS
Cincinnati OH

Barker Steve
Piketon HS
Piketon OH

Barker Tim
Martinsville HS
Martinsville IN

Barkey Elisa
Copley Sr HS
Barberton OH

Barkheimer Sandy
Perry HS
Navarre OH

Barkley Ann
Heritage HS
Ft Wayne IN

Barlay Cynthia
St Joseph Acad
Cleveland OH

Barlay Kathleen
St Joseph Academy
Cleveland OH

Barlekamp Harold C
Fostoria HS
Fostoria OH

Barlett Doug
Streetsboro HS
Streetsboro OH

Barlow Roberta
Wintersville HS
Wintersville OH

Barlow Vickie
Benedictine HS
Detroit MI

Barmore Matthew
Marion HS
Marion IN

Barnard Douglas
Rossville HS
Rossville IN

Barner Leanne
Everett HS
Lansing MI

Barnes Alice E
Delphos St Johns HS
Delphos OH

Barnes Douglas
Madison Heights HS
Anderson IN

Barnes Eric
Knightstown Community HS
Knightstown IN

Barnes Evelyn
Jane Addons Voc
Cleveland OH

Barnes Kelly S
Crestview Local HS
Leetonia OH

Barnes Laurie
Paulding Exempted Vllg Schl
Paulding OH

Barnes Susan
Morgan HS
Mc Connelsville OH

Barnes Teresa
Rutherford B Hayes HS
Delaware OH

Barnes Thomas
Cascade HS
Clayton IN

Barnes Toni
Edwin Denby HS
Detroit MI

Barnett Kevin
Jackson HS
Jackson OH

Barnett Kevin
Franklin Comm HS
Franklin IN

Barnett Valerie
Lorain Catholic HS
Lorain OH

Barnett Veta
Marion HS
Marion IN

Barnfield Andrea K
Carroll HS
Huntertown IN

Barnhard Doris J
Fruitport HS
Fruitport MI

Barnhart Karla
Middletown HS
Middletown OH

Barnhart Kent T
Ewen Trout Creek HS
Ewen MI

Barnhart Kimberly
Lynchburg Clay HS
Hillsboro OH

Barnhart Rose
Benjamin Logan HS
Rushsylvania OH

Barnhart Steve
Deerfield HS
Deerfield MI

Barnthouse Brenda
Lebanon HS
Mason OH

Baron Debra
Admiral King HS
Lorain OH

Barone Angelo
Southgate HS
Southgate MI

Barr Melody
Candiz HS
Cadiz OH

Barr Rhonda
Buffalo HS
Kenova WV

Barr Richard
R B Chamberlin HS
Twinsburg OH

Barr Scott
Muskegon HS
Muskegon MI

Barrass Carla
Niles Mc Kinley HS
Niles OH

Barren Joe
Revere HS
Richfield OH

Barrett Kenneth C
Padua Franciscan HS
Seven Hills OH

Barrick April
Notre Dame HS
Bridgeport WV

Barrick Christopher
Yorktown HS
Muncie IN

Barricklow Lana
Eastern HS
Sardina OH

Barrier Gerrlyn
Penn HS
Mishawaka IN

Barrish Donna
Eastlake North HS
Willowick OH

Barron Chris
Monroe Catholic Central
HS
Monroe MI

Barron Peggy
Kings HS
Loveland OH

Barror Sherri L
Pike Delta York Sr HS
Delta OH

Barrow Diana
Fremont HS
Fremont IN

Barrow Kimberly
Corydon Central HS
Corydon IN

Barrow Samuel
Dunbar HS
Dayton OH

Barry Cindy
Hillsdale HS
Hillsdale MI

Bartaway Ruth
Central HS
Grand Rapids MI

Bartels David
Watterson HS
Columbus OH

Barthel Linda
Freeland HS
Freeland MI

Bartholomew Barbara
Highland Sr HS
Highland IN

Bartlett Charles
Shaken Heights HS
Shaker Hts OH

Bartlett Twila
Lincoln HS
Lumberport WV

Barto Kristine
Lockland HS
Lockland OH

Bartolin Laura J
Hubbard HS
Hubbard OH

Bartoo Michael
Jackson HS
Massillon OH

Bartos Jonathan
Hill Mc Cloy HS
Flushing MI

Bartosik Cynthia
Lumen Cordium HS
Walton Hills OH

Bartrom Melo
Marion HS
Marin IN

Barwick Grant W
Westerville North HS
Westerville OH

Basco Rene
Andrean HS
Hobart IN

Basham Ken
East Liverpool HS
E Liverpool OH

Bashian Jack
Solon HS
Solon OH

Basiger Cynthia
Whitko HS
So Whitley IN

Basista Karen E
Struthers HS
Struthers OH

Bass John
Morton Sr HS
Hammond IN

Bass Meeta
Catholic Ctrl HS
Steubenvll OH

Bass Monica
Niles Sr HS
Niles MI

Bassett Gregory
Alexandria Monroe HS
Alexandria IN

Bassett Jena L
Rogers HS
Toledo OH

Basso Joseph
Owosso HS
Owosso MI

Bastin Kevin
Roosevelt Wilson HS
Mt Clare WV

Batchelor Gregory
Pontiac Central HS
Pontiac MI

Bateman Christopher
West Jefferson HS
W Jefferson OH

Bates Barbara A
Ben Davis HS
Indianapolis IN

Bates Beverly
Southwestern HS
Detroit MI

Bates Joe
Princeton Community HS
Princeton IN

Bates Laura
Centerville HS
Centerville OH

Bates Linda
South Sr HS
Columbus OH

Bates Richard
Fowlerville HS
Fowlerville MI

Bath Annette
Washington HS
Washington IN

Batson Robert
Niles Mc Kinley HS
Niles OH

Battisfore Dona
Charlotte HS
Potterville MI

Battle Ramone
Muskegon Hts HS
Muskegon MI

Battle Shelley
Clare HS
Clare MI

Bauer Julie
Reese HS
Reese MI

Bauer Lori
Haslett HS
Haslett MI

Bauer Paul
Champion HS
Warren OH

Bauerle Heidi
Snider HS
Ft Wayne IN

Bauermeister Caryn
Northrop HS
Ft Wayne IN

Baugher Bobbi Jo
Triton HS
Bourbon IN

Baughman David
Lucas HS
Perrysville OH

Baughman J
Decatur Central HS
Indnpls IN

Baughman Julie
Mathews HS
Cortland OH

Bauman James
Heritage Christian Schl
Indianapolis IN

Baumann Robert E
Cuyahoga Hts HS
Brklyn Hts OH

Baumgardner Dave
Tri West HS
Jamestown IN

Baurley Janet
South Ripley Jr Sr HS
Holton IN

Baxter Kent
Pontiac Central HS
Pontiac MI

Baxter Susin
Glen Lake Cmnty
Schools
Glen Arbor MI

Baxter Tami W
Hamilton S Eastern HS
Noblesville IN

STUDENTS
PHOTOGRAPH
SCHEDULED
FOR PUBLI-
CATION HERE
COULD NOT
BE REPRO-
DUCED

Bayer Mary
St Annes HS
Warren MI

Bayes Brenda
Taylor HS
Cleves OH

Bayless Paul N
Corunna HS
Corunna MI

Bayless R
Fairmont West HS
Kettering OH

Bayless Rosann
Brooke HS
Wellsburg WV

Bayliss Rick
Harbor Springs HS
Hrbr Spgs MI

Bays James M
Gallia Academy
Gallipolis OH

Bays Lorie
Midland Trail HS
Hico WV

Bazzarelli Robert
Collinwood HS
Cleveland OH

Beach Simone
Floyd Central HS
Floyd Knobs IN

Beadle Andrea
Traverse City Sr HS
Traverse City MI

Beadle Brian
Peck HS
Melvin MI

Beadle Dianne
Fremont HS
Fremont IN

Beadle Mirtha
Ottawa Hills HS
Grand Rapids MI

Beal Nadine
Franklin Central HS
Indpls IN

Beall Donald
Hedgesville HS
Hedgesville WV

Beals Shauna
Hilltop HS
W Unity OH

Beals Theresa
Tecumseh HS
New Carlisle OH

Beamont Teresa
Stryker HS
Stryker OH

Bean Jim
Connersville Sr HS
Connersville IN

Beard Lorna T
Lutheran East HS
Detroit MI

Bearss Glenda
Clawson HS
Clawson MI

Beasley Judy
Mitchell HS
Mitchell IN

Beatty D
Triton HS
Bourbon IN

Beatty James
Williamstown HS
Williamstown WV

Beatty Trina A
Athens HS
Athens MI

Beaudrie John
River Rouge HS
River Rouge MI

Beauman Jeff
Monroe HS
Monroe MI

Beaven Theresa
Reitz Mem HS
Evansville IN

Becerra Frank
Elkins HS
Elkins WV

Bechtel Gloria
Almont HS
Almont MI

Bechtler Stu
Mansfield Christian
School
Mansfield OH

Beck Carter
David Anderson HS
Lisbon OH

Beck Dwain
Lapeer East HS
Metamora MI

Beck Elizabeth
Western Boone Jr Sr HS
Lebanon IN

Beck Kimberly
Whiteford Agricultural
HS
Ottawa Lk MI

Beck Kristi
Brooke HS
Wellsburg WV

Beck Rhonda
Dunbar Sr HS
Dunbar WV

Beck Sally
St Johns HS
St Johns MI

Beck Steve
Moeller HS
Edgewood KY

Becker Mike
Marian HS
S Bend IN

Becker Sandra
Stow HS
Stow OH

Beckert Richard
Cadiz HS
Cadiz OH

Beckett Michael
Battle Creek Central HS
Battle Creek MI

Beckholt Kenneth
Mt Vernon Academy
Mt Vernon OH

Beckley Mary Beth
Muskegon HS
Muskegon MI

Beckmeyer Madge M
Seton HS
North Bend OH

Beckwith Ann M
Swan Valley HS
Saginaw MI

Becraft Max
Stivers Patterson Co Op
HS
Dayton OH

Bedell Harold
Cheboygan Area HS
Cheboygan MI

Bedell Paul
Riverside HS
Dearborn Hts MI

Bednard Walter A
Charles S Mott HS
Warren MI

Bedson Jay A
Princeton HS
Springdale OH

Beech Donald
Clinton Central HS
Forest IN

Beeghley Julia
Dublin HS
Dublin OH

Beegle Kevin
Walsh Jesuit HS
Univ Heights OH

Beels Denise
Lakeview Sr HS
St Clair Shore MI

Begeot Paula
Hubbard HS
Hubbard OH

Beggs Dianne
Port Clinton Sr HS
Port Clinton OH

Behnke Anne Jane
Westerville South HS
Westerville OH

Behroozi Yasmin
Shortridge HS
Indianapolis IN

Bein Cary
Highland HS
Highland IN

Beindorf Robin
Hudson Area HS
Hudson MI

Belak Michael
Padua Franciscan HS
Parma OH

Belanger Jay
Redford Union HS
Redford MI

Belcher Kathy L
Eastmoor Sr HS
Columbus OH

Belkowski Deborah
Northville HS
Northville MI

Bell Andre
Ypsilanti HS
Ypsilanti MI

Bell Charles
Decatur Central HS
Indpls IN

Bell Charles
West Preston HS
Newburg WV

Bell Darrell
Staunton HS
Brazil IN

Bell Deborah L
Terre Haute N Vigo HS
Terre Haute IN

Bell Diatricia
Mt View HS
Anawalt WV

Bell Jeffrey
Niles HS
Niles MI

Bell Jo
Cadillac Sr HS
Cadillac MI

Bell Joseph K
Doddridge County HS
Salem WV

Bell Julie
John Glenn HS
Walkerton IN

Bell Nina
Morton Sr HS
Hammond IN

Bell Pamela
Holt HS
Holt MI

Bell Saundra Sue
Walter P Chrysler Memrl
HS
New Castle IN

Bell Shanna D
Mc Kinley HS
Sebring OH

Bell Teena
Arlington HS
Indianapolis IN

Bell Willard
Solon HS
Solon OH

Bellamah Laura
St Ursula Academy
Cincinnati OH

Bellamy James
Little Miami HS
Morrow OH

Bellinger Timothy
Sacred Heart Academy
Lake MI

Bellot Terrence
Andrean HS
Lake Station IN

Bellotte Justina
Notre Dame HS
Clarksburg WV

Beloat Greg
North Posey HS
Poseyville IN

Belson Tamara
Mendon HS
Mendon MI

Belton Michael
Benedictine HS
Cleveland OH

Beltz Lisa
Washington HS
Massillon OH

Bemenderfer Joy
Indianapolis Baptist HS
Indianapolis IN

Bender Kathryn
Boonville HS
Boonville IN

Bender Ronald
Goshen HS
Goshen IN

Bene Richard
William Mason HS
Mason OH

Benedict Dawn
Winchester Comm HS
Winchester IN

Benefield Bellandra
Beecher HS
Mt Morris MI

Benefield John
Flint S W HS
Flint MI

Bengry Alan
Evart HS
Evart MI

Benifield Robin
East HS
Youngstown OH

Benjamin Keith
Riverdale HS
Mt Blanchard OH

Benjamin Lisa
Loogootee HS
Loogootee IN

Benjamin Ted
Piqua Ctrl HS
Piqua OH

Benn Lavita
Jane Addams Vocational
HS
Cleveland OH

Bennell Kimberly
Edison Sr HS
Lake Station IN

Benner Mike
Dekalb HS
Auburn IN

Bennett Andrew
Benzie Cnty Cntrl HS
Beulah MI

Bennett Angela D
Jefferson Twp Local HS
Dayton OH

Bennett Arla
Negaunee HS
Neagunee MI

Bennett Carol
Niles Sr HS
Niles MI

Bennett Darrell
Philip Barbour HS
Philippi WV

Bennett Frank
Harper Creek HS
Battle Creek MI

Bennett Gray
Eaton HS
Eaton OH

Bennett Jacqueline L
Federal Hocking HS
Stewart OH

Bennett Janeen
Terre Haute North Vigo
HS
Terre Haute IN

Bennett Jo
Buckhannon Upshur HS
Buckhannon WV

Bennett Joanna
New Lexington Sr HS
New Lexington OH

Bennett Kimberly
Rose D Warwick HS
Tekonsh MI

Bennett Laura
Union Scioto Loc Schls
Chillicothe OH

Bennett Mike
Portsmouth East HS
Portsmouth OH

Bennett Randy
North Newton HS
Morocco IN

Bennett Renea
Midland HS
Midland MI

Bennett Renee
Jackson HS
Jackson OH

Bennett Sharon
Immaculata HS
Detroit MI

Benninghofen Fredrick
Heath HS
Heath OH

Bennington Michelle
Bridgeport HS
Bridgeport OH

Bennington Patricia
Shadyside HS
Shadyside OH

Benoy Deborah
Lemon Monroe HS
Monroe OH

Bensley Robert
Mt Pleasant HS
Mt Pleasant MI

Benson Beth
Salem Sr HS
Salem OH

Benson Dennis
Southridge HS
Huntngbrg IN

Benson Tammy
North Central Area HS
Powers MI

Bentley Jody
Southwood HS
La Fontaine IN

Benton Karen
Toronto HS
Toronto OH

Benton Sharon
Cass Tech HS
Detroit MI

Berciunas Harold
Ben Davis HS
Indianapolis IN

Beres Kevin
Marquette HS
Michigan City IN

Berg Michael
Shaker Heights HS
Shaker Hts OH

Berghoff Jeff
Bishop Dwenger HS
Ft Wayne IN

Bergman Catherine
Cardinal Stritch HS
Genoa OH

Bergman Doug
Tipton HS
Atlanta IN

Bergner Pamela
Walled Lake Central Sr
HS
Union Lake MI

Bergstrom Kurt
Kingsford HS
Iron Mtn MI

Berkemer Angela
Fort Frye HS
Beverly OH

Berkenkemper Mitch
Webster County HS
Webster Sprgs WV

Berman Robert
Bishop Watterson HS
Columbus OH

Bernard Jean A
Andrean HS
Gary IN

Bernard Richard J
Eastlake North HS
Eastlake OH

Berndt Debra
Merrillville HS
Hobart IN

Bernosky Dave
Watterson HS
Columbus OH

Bernthisel Jeffrey
Otsego HS
Bowling Grn OH

Beroske Kristin
Evergreen HS
Delta OH

Berry Bonnie K
Midland Trail HS
Danese WV

Berry Bronwyn
Harper Creek HS
Battle Creek MI

Berry Cindy
Berea HS
Berea OH

Berry Dawn
Milan HS
Milan MI

Berry Dena
Groveport Madison Sr
HS
Columbus OH

Berry Terri Lynne
Licking Valley HS
Newark OH

Berry Valgenia
Princeton Community H
Princeton IN

Berryman Bradley
Standish Sterling Cntrl
HS
Alger MI

Berryman Debbie
Rosedale HS
Terre Haute IN

Bert Tammy
Sebring Mc Kinley HS
Sebring OH

Bertling William M
Clarkston HS
Clarkston MI

Bertoldi Paul
Kingsford HS
Kingsford MI

Bertsche Karen
Woodlan HS
Woodburn IN

Best Kathy L
Marietta Sr HS
Marietta OH

Bethel Kimberly J
Huntington HS
Chillicothe OH

Bethel Steve
Hanover Horton HS
Horton MI

Bethke Carrie
Pioneer HS
Ann Arbor MI

Beto Michele
Notre Dame HS
Clarksburg WV

Betonte Amy
Harbor HS
Ashtabula OH

Bette Kathryn
Bishop Gallagher HS
Detroit MI

Better William E
Western Reserve
Academy
Warren OH

Betterly Teresa
Dansville HS
Webberville MI

Bettross Mary Louise
Mahoning County Jnt
Voc HS
Campbell OH

Betts David
Watkins Memorial HS
Pataskala OH

Betz Alan
Ovid Elsie HS
Bannister MI

Beucler Pam
Liberty Benton HS
Findlay OH

Beutter Elizabeth
Penn HS
S Bend IN

Beveridge Kimberly
Niles Mckinley HS
Niles OH

Bewley Marc
Hammond Baptist HS
Crown Point IN

Bezek David
Milan HS
Maybee MI

Bezzarro Teresa
Ursuline HS
Youngstown OH

Bhardwaj Anu
Roosevelt HS
Kent OH

Bhargava Vivek
Clay Sr HS
Oregon OH

Bhirdo Teresa
Bridgeport HS
Bridgeport MI

Bianco Barrie L
Wheeling Park HS
Wheeling WV

Bianco John
St Edward HS
Lakewood OH

Bias Gary
Milton HS
Milton WV

Bible Diane
Montpelier HS
Montpelier OH

Bible Pam
Kelloggsville HS
Wyoming MI

Bican Sue
Erieview Catholic HS
Cleveland OH

Bickel Carolyn S
Anderson HS
Anderson IN

Bickel Joseph
Bishop Luers HS
Ft Wayne IN

Bickel Kimberly Jo
East Clinton HS
New Vienna OH

Bidinger Tandy
Brandon HS
Ortonville MI

Biedenbender Mike
Elyria Catholic HS
Elyria OH

Bielec Thomas
Flint Northern HS
Flint MI

Bielski Karen
Bishop Foley HS
Madison Hts MI

Biery Michele
Hicksville HS
Hicksville OH

Bigam Robyn
Westfall HS
Mt Sterling OH

Bigelow Cheryl
Highland HS
Anderson IN

Bigelow Sandra
Pinconning Sr HS
Linwood MI

Biggers Kevin
Talcott HS
Talcott WV

Biggs Robert L
Woodrow Wilson HS
Beckley WV

Bigler Cathy
Augres Sims HS
Au Gres MI

Bigna Michael A
Taylor HS
Kokomo IN

Bilas Roger B
North Olmsted Sr HS
North Olmsted OH

Bilby Laura
Douglas Mac Arthur HS
Saginaw MI

Bilby Paula
Rochester HS
Rochester IN

Bilger Laura J
Bad Axe HS
Filion MI

Bilkovsky Margie
Brighton HS
Brighton MI

Billerman Donna
Coldwater HS
Coldwater OH

Billeter Brian
Carrollton HS
Saginaw MI

Billman Anita
Buckeye Valley HS
Ostrander OH

Bills Deborah
Lake Shore HS
St Cl Shores MI

Bills Terrence
Kalamazoo Loy Norrix HS
Kalamzoo MI

Bing Robert
Southeastern HS
Highland Pk MI

Bingaman Bradford L
Fountain Central HS
Hillsboro IN

Bingman Sarah E
Eastmoor HS
Columbus OH

Binion Wade
Tri HS
Spiceland IN

Binius Corrina
West Branch HS
Alliance OH

Binsbacher Kathy
Warren Central HS
Indianapolis IN

Birkenberger Lori
Lake Catholic HS
Mentor OH

Birkhoff Josephine
Grandview Hts HS
Columbus OH

Birman Karen
Gull Lake HS
Battle Creek MI

Bishop David
Fairfield Union HS
Bremen OH

Bishop Deborah
Daleville HS
Daleville IN

Bishop Irma
Onaway HS
Onaway MI

Bishop Lee
Gilbert HS
Gilbert WV

Bittikofer Renee
Willard HS
Plymouth OH

Bitzinger Lynne
Concordia Lutheran HS
Ft Wayne IN

Bixler Brian
Canfield HS
Canfield OH

Bizic Christine M
Buckeye West HS
Adena OH

Bizon Sheila M
St Hedwig HS
Detroit MI

Black Jeanne
Stryker HS
Stryker OH

Black Pat
Muncie Southside HS
Muncie IN

Black Paul
Cooley HS
Detroit MI

Black Renita
Harman HS
Harman WV

Black Scot
Meadowbrook HS
Byesville OH

Black Troy
Princeton HS
Cincinnati OH

Black Yolanda M
Warrensville Hts HS
Warrensville Hts OH

Blackburn Deanna
Southern Local HS
Salineville OH

Blackburn Greg
Tippecanoe Valley HS
Mentone IN

Blackenberry Angela M
Marion Franklin HS
Columbus OH

Blackwell Brian D
Bedford North Lawrence HS
Bedford IN

Blackwell Jr Jan D
Muncie Central HS
Muncie IN

Bladuf Kathy
Pt Clinton HS
Pt Clinton OH

Blain Suzette
St Clement HS
Detroit MI

Blair Carol
George Washington HS
Charleston WV

Blair F Ward
Lakota HS
W Chester OH

Blair Rebecca
Delta HS
Dunkirk IN

Blair Sheila
Wilbur Wright HS
Dayton OH

Blake Peggy
Rosedale HS
Rosedale IN

Blake Richard
Lincoln Sr HS
Warren MI

Blake Trent
Milton HS
Ona WV

Blakeman Teresa
Columbiana HS
Columbiana OH

Blaney Kathleen
Newark Catholic HS
Newark OH

Blanken Celeste
Tecumseh Sr HS
Medway OH

Blankenberger Maria
North Posey HS
Cynthiana IN

Blankenship Sherry
Tippecanoe Valley HS
Warsaw IN

Blanks Shawn
Inkster HS
Westland MI

Blasco Virginia
Lew Wallace HS
Gary IN

Blatt Joan
Buffalo HS
Huntington WV

Blazejewski Gail
Our Lady Of Mercy HS
Livonia MI

Blazer William E
Barboursville HS
Barboursville WV

Bleecker James
Adrian Sr HS
Clayton MI

Bleitz Beth
Avondale Sr HS
Bloomfield Hls MI

Blevins Lana
De Kalb HS
Auburn IN

Blevins Mandy
De Kalb HS
Auburn IN

Blevins Twana
Jonathan Alder HS
Plain City OH

Blinn Lorie
Southern Wells HS
Warren IN

Bliss Daniel
Owosso HS
Owosso MI

Blizzard Kyle
Buckeye South HS
Rayland OH

Bloch Phillp
Bexley HS
Columbus OH

Block Sandra
Hamtramck HS
Hamtramck MI

Blodgett Bruce
Charlotte HS
Charlotte MI

Blome Elizabeth
Mother Of Mercy HS
Cincinnati OH

Bloodgood Linda
Greenfield Central HS
Greenfield IN

Blosser Sharon
Bridgman HS
Bridgman MI

Blosser Terrance
Morgantown HS
Morgantown WV

Blough Robert
Lynchburg Clay HS
Lynchburg OH

Blount Patricia
Franklin Heights HS
Grove City OH

Bloxsom Jerry
Gaylord HS
Gaylord MI

Bloxsom Julie A
Stevenson HS
Livonia MI

Bloyer Jill
Boardman HS
Poland OH

Blubaugh Laura M
Sullivan HS
Sullivan IN

Blue John G
Morgantown HS
Morgantown WV

Blue Kimberly
North Union HS
Richwood OH

Blue Steve
Edon Northwest HS
Edon OH

Blumenschein Gaynell L
Holly HS
Holly MI

Bluntschly Thomas
Onsted HS
Onsted MI

Board David
Lawrence Central HS
Indianapolis IN

Bobo Valerie F
Springfield HS
Holland OH

Bobovecz Mary B
Struthers HS
Struthers OH

Bobowski Brad
Morton Sr HS
Hammond IN

Bobroski Michael
Riverside HS
Painesville OH

Bock Richard
Lincoln HS
Shinnston WV

Bockover William
Anderson Highland HS
Anderson IN

Bodak Kimberly
Admiral King HS
Lorain OH

Boden Lorrie
Field HS
Suffield OH

Bodenbender Linda
Continental Local HS
Cloverdale OH

Bodenmiller Dan
Vandalia Butler HS
Vandalia OH

Bodkins I Randall
Coalton HS
Norton WV

Bodner David
Guernsey Catholic Cntrl
HS
Cambridge OH

Boedecker Diana
Linden Sr HS
Fenton MI

Boemker Terri
St Ursula Academy
Cincinnati OH

Boerema Douglas
Landmark Christian HS
La Porte IN

Bogan Daren D
Clinton Massie HS
Wilmington OH

Boggs Debora A
Lewis County HS
Weston WV

Boggs Patsy
Pocahontas County HS
Hillsboro WV

Boggs Terry
Perrysburg HS
Perrysburg OH

Boglin Lori
Withrow HS
Cincinnati OH

Boguslawski William
Grand Rapids Central HS
Grand Rapids MI

Bohaychyk Crystal L
Marlington HS
Hartville OH

Bohman Deb
Coldwater HS
Coldwater OH

Bolalek Diane
Bishop Noll Inst
Munster IN

Boldoser Todd
Logan Elm HS
Laurelville OH

Bolen Deborah J
Upper Scioto Valley HS
Mc Guffey OH

Bolen Julia
Independence HS
Crab Orchard WV

Bolenbaugh Gary
R Nelson Snider HS
Ft Wayne IN

Boles K
La Ville Jr Sr HS
Lakeville IN

Boley Laura J
Lancaster HS
Lancaster OH

Bolinger Candis
Shakamak HS
Jasonville IN

Bolinger Nancy
Randolph Southern HS
Winchester IN

Bollaert Michelle
Capac Jr Sr HS
Capac MI

Bollenbacher Bruce
Parkway HS
Rockford OH

Bollenbacher James
Laker HS
Bay Port MI

Bollenbacher Mary
Champion HS
Warren OH

Bolles Danna
Kirtland HS
Kirtland OH

Bollhoefer Debra
Tippecanoe Valley HS
Rochester IN

Bolton Brenda
Niles Sr HS
Niles MI

Bolton Kathleen
Archbishop Alter HS
Dayton OH

Bolton Tami
Ovid Elsie HS
Ovid MI

Bometch John
Marion Harding HS
Marion OH

Bonanni Linda
Belleville HS
Belleville MI

Bonardi Tim
Harper Creek HS
Ceresco MI

Bond Glenn
South Harrison HS
Mt Clare WV

Bonds Rita
East HS
Cleveland OH

Bone John
Nitro HS
Charleston WV

Bone Tom
Woodrow Wilson HS
Beckley WV

Bonhart Wilkes
St Johns HS
Toledo OH

Bonifer Tom
St Philip Catholic Cntrl
HS
Battle Crk MI

Bonner Pam
Ellet HS
Akron OH

Bonnette Robin
Streetsboro HS
Streetsboro OH

Bontempo Scott
North Ridgeville HS
N Ridgeville OH

Bontrager Gregory
Owosso HS
Owosso MI

Bontrager Roger
Bethany Christian HS
Middlebury IN

Bontvager Gary
Bethany Christian HS
Goshen IN

Booker Cheryl
Fayetteville HS
Fayetteville WV

Booker Rudolph E
Stivers Patterson Co Op
HS
Dayton OH

Booker Stephanie
Du Pont HS
Charleston WV

Boon Brian
Port Clinton Sr HS
Port Clinton OH

Boone Monica
Warrensville Hts HS
Warrensvl Hts OH

Boone Shari
Carman HS
Flint MI

Boos Sharon
Huron HS
Sandusky OH

Booth Rick
Washington County Voc
HS
Wingett Run OH

Boothe Carleen
Collinwood HS
Cleveland OH

Boothe Lori
Ellet HS
Akron OH

Booton Anita
Fairland HS
Proctorvll OH

Borck Barb
Woodward HS
Toledo OH

Bordonaro Stephanie
Beaumont School For Girls
Morelnd Hls OH

Borek Michael
Lee HS
Wyoming MI

Borgs Dace
Columbia HS
Columbia Sta OH

Boris Barbara
Villa Angela Academy
Euclid OH

Born Deborah
Perrysburg HS
Perrysburg OH

Borntrager Annetta
Northridge HS
Middlebury IN

Boroski Lisa
Buckeye South HS
Rayland OH

Borowski John
St Stephens HS
Saginaw MI

Borton Elizabeth
West HS
Columbus OH

Borton Gregory
Tecumseh HS
Tecumseh MI

Boruch Alan V
Hobart Sr HS
Hobart IN

Boruff Janell
Bloomfield HS
Bloomfield IN

Bosecker Connie
South Spencer HS
Rockport IN

Boskovic Christine
Villa Angela Academy
Euclid OH

Boss James
Cuyahoga Falls HS
Cuyahoga Falls OH

Bossert Melinda
Acad Immaculate Conception
Batesville IN

Bostdorff Jim
Otsego HS
Bowling Green OH

Boster Kris
Hurricane HS
Hurricane WV

Bostick James
Shady Springs HS
Daniels WV

Bostick Timothy R
Du Pont HS
Charleston WV

Boston Bonnie
Southern Local HS
Salineville OH

Botbyl Jeffrey
North Muskegon HS
N Muskegon MI

Botsko Karen
Brooklyn HS
Brooklyn OH

Botson Pam
Magnificat HS
N Olmsted OH

Bottoms Charles W
St Ignatius HS
Cleveland OH

Bottorff Arthur
Washington HS
So Bend IN

Botts Kathy
South HS
Columbus OH

Bouchonnet Sandra
Scarlet Oaks HS
Cincinnati OH

Boudrie Terri
Jefferson HS
Monroe MI

Bouldin Debra
Peterstown HS
Peterstown WV

Boulton Jeffrey
Fostoria HS
Fostoria OH

Bourdeau Jodi
Harbor HS
Ashtabula OH

Bourdon Richard L
La Salle HS
South Bend IN

Bourn Robert
Braxton County HS
Rosedale WV

Bourne Lisa
Jay County HS
Redkey IN

Bouschor Amy
Traverse City Sr HS
Traverse City MI

Boutcher Barb
Morton Sr HS
Hammond IN

Boutyard Trina
Martinsburg HS
Martinsburg WV

Bowen Denise
South Point HS
Chesapeake OH

Bowen Thomas R
Yorktown HS
Muncie IN

Bower Vicki
Malvern HS
Malvern OH

Bowerman Nancy
Quincy HS
Quincy MI

Bowers James E
Coldwater HS
Coldwater MI

Bowers Linda
Philip Barbour HS
Philippi WV

Bowersock Doug
Perry HS
Cridersville OH

Bowersox Jonathan W
Xenia HS
Xenia OH

Bowles Kim
Belleville HS
Ypsilanti MI

Bowles Robin
Corunna HS
Owosso MI

Bowles Steve
Chaminade Julienne HS
Dayton OH

Bowling Kathy R
Mt View HS
Tuscaloosa AL

Bowling Tamara
Fairborn Park Hills HS
Fairborn OH

Bowman C David
W Carrollton Sr HS
Dayton OH

Bowman David
Waterford Twp HS
Union Lake MI

Bowman Donald
Decatur Central HS
Indnpls IN

Bowman Greg
Kings Mills HS
S Lebanon OH

Bowman Jeffrey
Patterson Co Op HS
Dayton OH

Bowman Joan
Logan Elm HS
Laurelville OH

Bowman Stanley
Northfield HS
Lagro IN

Bowser Margie
Hubbard HS
Masury OH

Bowser Rosemary
Fairborn Park Hills HS
Fairborn OH

Boyce Christina
Grafton HS
Grafton WV

Boyd Anita
Cascade HS
Clayton IN

Boyd Beth Anne
Hedgesville HS
Hedgesville WV

Boyd Clement W
Patterson Co Operative
HS
Dayton OH

Boyd Linda
Shady Spring HS
White Oak WV

Boyd Stephanie
Immaculata HS
Detroit MI

Boyd William
Shakamak HS
Jasonville IN

Boyer Carrie
Van Wert HS
Van Wert OH

Boyer Lisa
Hillsdale HS
Hayesville OH

Boyer Steven
Castle HS
Newburgh IN

Boyer Suzanne M
Aquinas HS
Taylor MI

Boyer Terry
Holy Rosary HS
Flint MI

Boyle Barbara
New Richmond HS
New Richmond OH

Boyles Glenna
Matoaka HS
Matoaka WV

Bracey Jill
Grosse Ile HS
Grosse Ile MI

Brackett Susan
Berrien Springs HS
Berrien Spgs MI

Brackin Pamela
Princeton Community HS
Hazleton IN

Braddock Laurie
Fredericktown HS
Fred OH

Bradfield Blair
Our Lady Of Mercy HS
Detroit MI

Bradfield James
Elk Rapids HS
Elk Rapids MI

Bradfield Susan
Indian Hill HS
Cincinnati OH

Bradford Celesta
Frontier HS
Nw Mtmrs OH

Bradford Donna
Avon Jr & Sr HS
Danville IN

Bradley Mary
Warren Wshngtn Cnty
Voc Schl
Marietta OH

Bradley Melissa
Mansfield Christian HS
Mansfield OH

Bradley Michael
Garfield HS
Akron OH

Bradley Peter
Lee M Thurston HS
Redford MI

Bradley Rebecca
Barr Reeve HS
Montgomery IN

Bradley Sherry
Chaminade Julienne HS
Dayton OH

Bradley Susan
Bedford HS
Bedford OH

Bradley Walter A
Tell City HS
Tell City IN

Bradshaw Deborah
Cathedral HS
Indianapolis IN

Bradshaw Rita
Clinton Central HS
Frankfort IN

Brady Jill
North Canton Hoover HS
North Canton OH

Brady V Wayne
Carrollton HS
Saginaw MI

Bragg Forrest
Midland Trail HS
Ansted WV

Bragg Stanley
Shady Spring HS
Shady Spring WV

Brainard Richard
Swan Valley HS
Saginaw MI

STUDENTS
PHOTOGRAPH
SCHEDULED
FOR PUBLI-
CATION HERE
COULD NOT
BE REPRO-
DUCED

Braker Glen
Rensselaer Cntrl HS
Rensselaer IN

Brandt Dorine
Arthur Hill HS
Saginaw MI

Braniff Emiley
Brooke HS
Wellsburg WV

Brankamp Rob
William Henry Harrison
HS
Harrison OH

Brankle Nancy
Warren Central HS
Indianapolis IN

Brannon Thomas J
Field HS
Mogadore OH

Branson Daniel
River Valley HS
Harbert MI

Brantley Drake A
Central HS
Detroit MI

Branz Marie
Kingsford HS
Iron Mtn MI

Brasch Birch
Sycamore HS
Blue Ash OH

Brashaw Cheri
Bay City Central HS
Bay City MI

Brasic Gregory
Sparta HS
Sparta MI

Brasseur John
Penn HS
Mishawaka IN

Bratcher Alexis
Gladwin HS
Gladwin MI

Brawner Tim
Southwestern HS
Hanover IN

Bray Andrew P
Hawken HS
Pepper Pike OH

Bredehoeft Jeff
Leland Public HS
Lake Leelanau MI

Breedlove Candy
Marion HS
Marion IN

Breedlove Coralee
Southern Wells HS
Bluffton IN

Breen Dennis
Brooke HS
Follansbee WV

Brekrus Susan
La Salle HS
South Bend IN

Brennan Kerrin J
St Joseph HS
South Bend IN

Brennan Robert
Zanesville HS
Zanesville OH

Brennan Stephanie
Lehman HS
Sidney OH

Breslin Kelly
Tecumseh HS
New Carlisle OH

Bresnahan Maureen
Grosse Ile HS
Grosse Ile MI

Bressette Julie
Marquette Sr HS
Marquette MI

Brett Kimberly
John Glenn HS
Westland MI

Bretz Kathlene
Little Miami HS
Morow OH

Brewer Catherine
Clyde Sr HS
Clyde OH

Brewer Chris
Linton Stockton HS
Linton IN

Brewer Cindy
Wilmington HS
Wilmington OH

Brewer Darrin
Jennings County HS
No Vernon IN

Brewer Elvis
Hammond Technical Voc
HS
Hammond IN

Brewer Sandra
Canton South HS
Canton OH

Brewer Sandra L
Beechcroft Sr HS
Columbus OH

Brewer Steven
Salem HS
Salem IN

Brewer Terry
Clinton Massie HS
Waynesville OH

Brewton Charles A
Princeton HS
Cincinnati OH

Bricker Barbara
Big Walnut HS
Sunbury OH

Bricker Sara
Boyne City HS
East Jordan MI

Bridenstine Janice
Ridgedale HS
Morral OH

Bridge Lisa
Frontier HS
Monticello IN

Bridges Gina
Lake HS
Walbridge OH

Brigandi Joseph
Garfield HS
Akron OH

Briggs Cynthia J
Highland HS
Wadsworth OH

Bright Carl P
Benzie Central HS
Empire MI

Bright Melissa
South Charleston HS
S Charleston WV

Brill Michelle
Griffith HS
Griffith IN

Brincefield Thomas L
Lincolnview HS
Elgin OH

Brindiar John
Mahoning Cnty Jnt Voc HS
Lowellville OH

Brinker Deborah L
Carmel HS
Carmel IN

Brinkerhoff Scott
Wooster HS
Wooster OH

Brinkman Lynn
Bedford Sr HS
Temperance MI

Brinkmoeller Lisa
Immaculate Conception Acad
Batesville IN

Briske Kirby J
Manistee HS
Manistee MI

Brislinger Christy
Fisher Catholic HS
Logan OH

Bristow Michael E
Bloomington HS North
Bloomington IN

Britigan Robert D
Gull Lake HS
Richland MI

Brittain Randy
Northmont HS
Dayton OH

Britton Annette
Atlanta Community HS
Atlanta MI

Britton Sabrina
Carroll HS
Flora IN

Brnilovich Robert
Nordonia HS
Macedonia OH

Broadway Nola
Western HS
Spring Arbor MI

Brock Byron
Marysville HS
Marysville MI

Brock Denise C
Lebanon HS
Lebanon OH

Brock Donna
West Carrollton Sr HS
Dayton OH

Brockman Stephen R
Floyd Central HS
New Albany IN

Brockman Vicki
Battle Creek Cntrl HS
Battle Crk MI

Broderick Lisa
Cathedral HS
Indianapolis IN

Brodzinski Kelly
La Ville Jr Sr HS
Lakeville IN

Brogdon Bonita
Mount View HS
Thorpe WV

Bromley Elizabeth
West Muskingum HS
Brownsville OH

Bronish Louise
Lakewood HS
Lakewood OH

Bronner Darryl
Cass Technical HS
Detroit MI

Brooks Edwin
North Muskegon HS
North Muskegon MI

Brooks Gary
Northrop HS
Ft Wayne IN

Brooks George
Roosevelt HS
Gary IN

Brooks Gina
Alexandria Monroe HS
Alexandria IN

Brooks Jacquelyn R
Crispus A Hucks HS
Indpls IN

Brooks James
Frankfort HS
Ridgeley WV

Brooks Janet
Pineville HS
Pineville WV

Brooks Jeff
Lewis County HS
Weston WV

Brooks Jo L
Ironton HS
Ironton OH

Brooks K
Northeastern HS
Fountain Cy IN

Brooks Laura
Scottsburg Sr HS
Scottsburg IN

Brooks Penny R
Independence HS
Pemberton WV

Brooks Susan
Clyde Sr HS
Green Spg OH

Brooks Suzie
Philip Barbour HS
Belington WV

Broome Cheryl L
Washington Co Voc HS
Warner OH

Brophey Joseph
East Liverpool HS
E Liverpool OH

Brophey Marsha
East Liverpool HS
E Liverpool OH

Brophy Shawne
Bishop Ready HS
Columbus OH

Brosey Mary
Ursuline Academy
Cincinnati OH

Brosius Diane
Beaver Local HS
E Liverpool OH

Broski Joseph
Holy Name Nazareth HS
Maple Hts OH

Brosko Kathryn
Springfield Local HS
New Midd OH

STUDENTS
PHOTOGRAPH
SCHEDULED
FOR PUBLI-
CATION HERE
COULD NOT
BE REPRO-
DUCED

Bross Cathy
Seton HS
Cincinnati OH

Brothers Teresa
Southern Local HS
Salineville OH

Brothers Theresa
Centreville HS
Sturgis MI

Broughton Ronald V
Monroe Catholic HS
Monroe MI

Brousseau James
Imlay City Cmnty HS
Imlay City MI

Brower Laurie
Tri Jr Sr HS
Cambridge IN

Brower William C
Tri Jr Sr HS
Cambridge IN

Brown Angela
Cass Tech HS
Detroit MI

Brown Camille
Williamstown HS
Williamstown WV

Brown Carla
Marian HS
Detroit MI

Brown Carlie
Kent Roosevelt HS
Kent OH

Brown Cedric M
Belmont HS
Dayton OH

Brown Chandra
Romulus Sr HS
Romulus MI

Brown Charles
Du Pont Sr HS
Belle WV

Brown Charles A
Shortridge HS
Indianapolis IN

Brown Cynthia
Churubusco HS
Churubusco IN

Brown Cynthia
Cass Tech HS
Detroit MI

Brown David
Grove City HS
Orient OH

Brown David
Westfield Washington
HS
Westfield IN

Brown Debra P
Our Lady Of Angels HS
Cincinnati OH

Brown Decelia
East Knox HS
Howard OH

Brown Denise
John F Kennedy HS
Taylor MI

Brown Donna K
Fort Frye HS
Lowell OH

Brown Douglas
Gladwin HS
Gladwin MI

Brown Eddie L
Garaway HS
Sugarcreek OH

Brown Elizabeth A
Jonesville HS
Jonesville MI

Brown Gail R
Lakola HS
W Chester OH

Brown Glenn
Brighton HS
Brighton MI

Brown Inge
Bluefield HS
Bluefield WV

Brown Janet
Rockville HS
Rockville IN

Brown Janice
Hamilton Southeastern
HS
Noblesville IN

Brown Janie C
Emerson HS
Gary IN

Brown Jennifer
Oceana HS
Oceana WV

Brown Jill
Morgan HS
Mc Connelsville OH

Brown Jim
Jackson HS
Wellston OH

Brown Kim
Pendleton Heights HS
Anderson IN

Brown Kimberly
Maumee HS
Toledo OH

Brown Kimberly
Grafton HS
Graftan WV

Brown Kirsten C
Norwalk HS
Norwalk OH

Brown Kurt
Morgantown HS
Morgantwon WV

Brown Laura
Marshall HS
Marshall MI

Brown Leslie
Shaker Heights HS
Shaker Hts OH

Brown Leslie
Clinton Massie HS
Harveysburg OH

Brown Leslie J
Buckeye North HS
Smithfield OH

Brown Linda
Reynoldsburg HS
Reynoldsburg OH

Brown Linda
Battle Creek Central HS
Battle Creek MI

Brown Lisa K
Cardinal Ritter HS
Indianapolis IN

Brown Lorelle R
William A Wirt HS
Gary IN

Brown Lori S
Edison Sr HS
Merriville IN

Brown Melanie D
Lewis County HS
Weston WV

Brown Pamela
Tipton HS
Tipton IN

Brown Payne
Northrop HS
Ft Wayne IN

Brown Richard
Madison Plains HS
Mt Sterling OH

Brown Robert
Stow HS
Munroe Falls OH

Brown Robin
Wayne HS
Dayton OH

Brown Rochelle
East HS
Columbus OH

Brown Rowena
Eastern HS
Waverly OH

Brown Sally
Perry HS
Massillon OH

Brown Sandra
Buckhannon Upshur HS
Rock Cave WV

Brown Stanley
Madison Hts HS
Anderson IN

Brown Stefan
Yellow Springs HS
Yellow Sprg OH

Brown Susan
Crestview HS
Ohio City OH

Brown Tamara
Mater Dei HS
Evansvl IN

Brown Tammy
Hillsdale HS
Ashland OH

Brown Tammy
Indianapolis Baptist HS
Indianapolis IN

Brown Tania
Columbus East HS
Columbus OH

Brown Tessy
North Adams HS
Seaman OH

Brown Tina
Champion HS
Warren OH

Brown Tonya
Pittsford HS
Osseo MI

Brown Tracy
Greenville Sr HS
Greenville OH

Brown William
Midland Trail HS
Lansing WV

Browning Bill
Aiken HS
Cincinnati OH

Brown Jr Michael
Warren Sr HS
Troy MI

Brownlee Wendi
Hartland HS
Fenton MI

Brownsword Sue
Perry HS
Canton OH

Broyles Tamara
Watkins Mem HS
Pataskala OH

Brozenick Norman J
St Joseph Prep
Vienna WV

Brual Barb
Ursuline Academy
Celina OH

Brubaker Paul
Austintown Fitch HS
Youngstown OH

Brueck Corinne
Lake Shore HS
Baroda MI

Bruening Daniel
Moeller HS
Deer Pk OH

Bruhn Tim
Whiteland Comm HS
Greenwood IN

Brumfield Cynthia D
Barboursville HS
Le Sage WV

Brumfield Joyce
Fairland HS
Proctorville OH

Brummett Robin
Martinsville HS
Martinsville IN

Brundza Joseph
Bloomington N HS
Bloomington IN

Brune John
Brighton HS
Brighton MI

Brunfield Thomas
Huntington HS
Huntington WV

Brunn Bob
Jackson Memorial HS
Canton OH

Bruno Christina
Grandville HS
Wyoming MI

Bruns Ronald
Chaminade Julienne HS
Dayton OH

Brush Chris
Celina Sr HS
Celina OH

Brusseau Kimberley
Inter City Christian HS
Allen Park MI

Brusso James
Calumet HS
Laurium MI

Bryan La Mar
Colon HS
Colon MI

Bryan Sue
Merrill Community HS
St Charles MI

Bryant Charalena
West Union HS
W Union OH

Bryant Douglas
Carroll Sr HS
Cutler IN

Bryant Evon
East HS
Youngstown OH

Bryant Karen
Elkins HS
Elkins WV

Bryenton Elisabeth
Fairview HS
Fairview Pk OH

Brzezicki Mike
Deer Park HS
Cincinnati OH

Brzezinski Terese
Bay City All Sts Central
HS
Bay City MI

Bublitz Stephen
Bridgeport HS
Bridgeport MI

Bucata Diane
Aquinas HS
Dearborn Hts MI

Bucci Enrico
Rocky River HS
Rocky Rvr OH

Buchanan Larry
Cascade HS
Coatesville IN

Buckingham Darlene
Willard HS
Willard OH

Buckley Cindy
Franklin HS
Farnklin OH

Buckman John
Patterson Co Op HS
Dayton OH

Buckman Julia
Marquette Sr HS
Marquette MI

Buckmaster Dennis R
De Kalb HS
Ashley IN

Buckner A
Brookhaven HS
Columbus OH

Buckner Cynthia
John F Kennedy HS
Cleveland OH

Buckner Stacy
Brownsburg HS
Brownsbrg IN

Buczkowski Lisa
Washington HS
South Bend IN

Budd Jimmy R
Brandon HS
Goodrich MI

Buddelmeyer Waneta
Northridge HS
Johnstown OH

Budny Tracy
Bloomfield HS
Bloomfield IN

Budzinski Cindy
Cleveland Central Cath
HS
Cleveland OH

Buehler Sue
Clay HS
Oregon OH

Buffaloe Chris
Decatur Central HS
Indpls IN

Buffington Steve
Anderson HS
Anderson IN

Bugai Alan
Traverse City Sr HS
Traverse City MI

Bugh David
Bedford N Lawrence HS
Bedford IN

Buick David
Kearsley HS
Flint MI

Buie Sylvia A
Immaculata HS
Detroit MI

Bukovcik Ronald
Ovid Elsie HS
Henderson MI

Buletko Andy
Canfield HS
Canfield OH

Bulla Dwayne
Highland Sr HS
Highland IN

Bumgardner Eric
Wahama HS
New Haven WV

Bumgarner Lisa
Spencer HS
Spencer WV

Bundy Paula
Weir HS
Weirton WV

Bundy Roger
Salem HS
Salem IN

Bunemann L
Trenton HS
Trenton MI

Bunsey Laura
Nordonia HS
Northfield OH

Bura Robert
Padua Franciscan HS
Parma OH

Burch Betsy J
Turpin HS
Cincinnati OH

Burch Edward A
Eastmoor Sr HS
Columbus OH

Burcham Lisa
South Ripley Jr Sr HS
Versailles IN

Burchett Jimmy
North Vermillion HS
Cayuga IN

Burd Terri
Lawrence Cnty Joint Voc
Schl
Proctorville OH

Burdette Tamie
Perry HS
Canton OH

Burdsall Paul
Clermont Northeastern
HS
Batavia OH

Burean Melissa
Jackson Center HS
Jackson Cntr OH

Burge Annette
Everett HS
Lansing MI

Burgess Cindy
Shady Spring HS
Daniels WV

Burgess Dianne
Newberry HS
Newberry MI

Burgess Edward
Our Lady Of Mt Carmel
HS
Taylor MI

Burgess Kathy
West Branch HS
Beloit OH

Burgess Marilyn
Brown City HS
Brown City MI

Burgess Pam
Bridgeport HS
Bridgeport WV

Burgess T Robin
Carlisle Sr HS
Carlisle OH

Burgos Eva
Logansport HS
Logansport IN

Burich Ray
Streetsboro HS
Streetsboro OH

Burk Daniel
Fremont HS
Fremont MI

Burke Brian P
Fairmont W HS
Kettering OH

Burke Dennis
Orleans HS
Orleans IN

Burkett Billie
Princeton HS
Princeton WV

Burkey Kerry
Monroe Cath Central HS
Monroe MI

Burkhammer Jill
Lewis County HS
Weston WV

Burkhart Julia A
Tri West Hendricks HS
North Salem IN

Burkhart Julie
Lexington HS
Mansfield OH

Burkholder Robert
Tri Village HS
Greenville OH

Burkholder Sarah
Elston Sr HS
Mich Cit IN

Burking Brook C
Pike HS
Indianapolis IN

Burks Leonard
Mount View HS
Welch WV

Burks Pamela
Whiteland Cmnty HS
New Whiteland IN

Burner Jamie
Philip Barbour HS
Philippi WV

Burnett Gregory
Parkside HS
Jackson MI

Burney Joel
John Adams HS
Cleveland OH

Burns Mary A
Coleman HS
Coleman MI

Burns Paula
Salem HS
Salem IN

Burns Sherrie
Gaylord HS
Gaylord MI

Burns Tammy
Wilbur Wright HS
Dayton OH

Burns Tammy
Austin HS
Austin IN

Burns William
Loy Norrix HS
Kalamazoo MI

Burnside Beth
Bridgeport Sr HS
Bridgeport WV

Burnside Sandra K
Lewis County HS
Weston WV

Burnsworth Kathy
Southern Wells
Bluffton IN

Burr Diane
Marlington HS
Alliance OH

Burr Ronda
Anchor Bay HS
New Haven MI

Burrell Pamela D
William A Wirt HS
Gary IN

Burris Brian D
Toronto HS
Toronto OH

Burris Susan
Eastmoor Sr HS
Columbus OH

Burriss David M
Waverly HS
Waverly OH

Burroughs Dave
Barberton HS
Barberton OH

Burroughs Sherry
Hinton HS
Jumping Branch WV

Burroway James
Portsmouth HS
Portsmouth OH

Burrus Gina M
Jefferson HS
Newport MI

Burrus James
Jefferson HS
Newport MI

Burskey Judith
Walled Lake Central HS
Union Lake MI

Burslem Jeffrey G
Jackson HS
Massillon OH

Burt Ann
Lake Orion Comm HS
Lake Orion MI

Burt Jeffrey S
A D Johnston HS
Bessemer MI

Burtch Michelle
Chesaning Union HS
Burt MI

Burton Donnie
Lockland HS
Cincinnati OH

Burton Drenna
Hundred HS
Wileyville WV

Burton Gregory K
Mumford Sr HS
Detroit MI

Burton Gwendolyn D
South HS
Cleveland OH

Burton Jackie
Henryville HS
Jeffersonville IN

Burton Kelly
Salem HS
Salem IN

Burton Latanya
John Adams HS
Cleveland OH

Burton Lucinda
Wirt County HS
Elizabeth WV

Burton Ricky
Lockland HS
Lockland OH

Burwinkel James
St Francis Sem
Cincinnati OH

Bury Diana
Benton Harbor HS
Benton Hbr MI

Busack Frederick L
St Joseph Central Cath HS
Fremont OH

Busby Joanna
Oak Hill HS
Oak Hill WV

Busche Marsha
Eastside Jr Sr HS
Hicksville OH

Bush Beverly A
Mona Shores HS
Muskegon MI

Bush Cynthia
Norwood HS
Norwood OH

Bush Deanna
Morgantown HS
Westover WV

Bush Joseph
Padua Franciscan HS
Cleveland OH

Bush Julie
John Marshall HS
Indianapolis IN

Bush Pamela
Central Hower HS
Akron OH

Bush Richard
Seeger Mem HS
Wlmsprt IN

Bush Russell
Southwestern HS
Flat Rock IN

Bush Vivian
Franklin Central HS
Indianapolis IN

Bushman Brenda
Eastwood HS
Pemberville OH

Busick Karmen
Bellmont HS
Decatur IN

Buskey John
Centerville HS
Centerville IN

Buskirk Carla
Diamond Oaks Career Dvlpmnt
Harrison OH

Busler Susan
Carrollton HS
Carrollton OH

Busse Bob
Milton Union HS
Ludlow Fl OH

Bussman Debbie
Grove City HS
Grove City OH

Busson Julie
St Vincent St Mary HS
Akron OH

Buswell Alan
South Newton HS
Kentland IN

Butcher Jean
Bentley HS
Livonia MI

Butcher Letha
Lewis County HS
Weston WV

Butler Audrey
Larel Oaks Career Dev Cmps
Hillsboro OH

Butler Donald
Pike Central HS
Winslow IN

Butler Jeannine A
St Marys Of Redford Sr HS
Detroit MI

Butler Julie
Marian HS
Cincinnati OH

Butler Kenneth
St Francis De Sales HS
Toledo OH

Butler Tenia L
Godwin Heights HS
Wyoming MI

Butler Valerie
Gabriel Richard HS
Wyandotte MI

Butner Tom
St Edward HS
Cleveland OH

Butters Fred
Homer Cmnty HS
Homer MI

Butts Barbara J
Chippewa Hills HS
Remus MI

Butts Charles L
Lima Sr HS
Lima OH

Butts Robert J
Western Brown Sr HS
Georgetown OH

Buxton James
John Glenn HS
Westland MI

Buzek Donna M
Cloverleaf Sr HS
Spencer OH

Buzzell Dianna
Beaverton HS
Beaverton MI

Byard Sandra
Pellston Public HS
Levering MI

Byerly Cheryl
Madison Plains HS
London OH

Byers Cheron
Marion L Steele HS
Amherst OH

Byers Donna
Toronto HS
Toronto OH

Byers Michele
Steubenville Cath Ctrl HS
Mingo Junction OH

Byers Paul
Madison Hts HS
Anderson IN

Byndon Elaine
Our Lady Of Angels HS
Cincinnati OH

Byrd Cheryl M
Oak Park HS
Oak Park MI

Byrd Darla D
East Sr HS
Akron OH

Byrne Joan
Regina HS
E Cleveland OH

Byrum Beth
Greenville Sr HS
Greenville OH

C

Cabacungan Genevie R
Taft Sr HS
Hamilton OH

Cabacungan Guillermo R
Taft Sr HS
Hamilton OH

Cable Deena
Toronto HS
Toronto OH

Cabot John
West Geauga HS
Chesterland OH

Cabrera Juan
Harrison HS
Evansville IN

Cadiente Eileen
Indiana Academy
Indpls IN

Cady Christine
Gladwin Comm HS
Gladwin MI

Cairo Tania R
Thomas A De Vilbiss HS
Toledo OH

Calabro Deborah J
Port Huron Northern HS
Port Huron MI

Calamita Lisa
Mayfield HS
Mayfield Hts OH

Caldemyer Mark
Southridge HS
Holland IN

Caldwell Carla
Jackson HS
Massillon OH

Caldwell Charma R
John Marshall HS
Brookly OH

Caldwell Jennifer
St Ursula Academy
Toledo OH

Caldwell Kristy
Princeton HS
Princeton WV

Caldwell Teisha K
Bloom Local HS
Wheelersburg OH

Caley Janie B
Schoolcraft HS
Vicksburg MI

Calhoon Sarah S
Hilliard HS
Hilliard OH

Calhoun Lynn
Greenville Sr HS
Greenville MI

Calhoun Nathaniel
Buena Vista HS
Saginaw MI

Callahan Alta
Lockland HS
Cincinnati OH

Callahan Brian S
Morristown HS
Shelbyville IN

Callahan Deborah
Westfall HS
Orient OH

Callahan Lisa
Green HS
N Canton OH

Callender Judy
Port Huron Northern HS
North Street MI

Calvert Debra
Decatur Central HS
Indianapolis IN

Calvin Christine D
Highland HS
Highland IN

Cameron Dana
George Washington HS
Indianapolis IN

Cameron Jeffrey
Gladwin HS
Gladwin MI

Camp Kathryn L
Waverly HS
Waverly OH

Campau Roxanne
Zeeland HS
Zeeland MI

Campbell Ben
Gallia Academy HS
Gallipolis OH

Campbell Beverly
Put In Bay Schl
Put In Bay OH

Campbell Carla
Niles Mc Kinley HS
Niles OH

Campbell David H
Linsly Military Inst
Toronto OH

Campbell Diane
Penn Township HS
Mishawaka IN

Campbell Elizabeth
Barnesville HS
Barnesville OH

Campbell Jackie
Marion Harding HS
Marion OH

Campbell James H
George Washington Sr
HS
Charleston WV

Campbell Kathleen M
Villa Angela Academy
Cleveland OH

Campbell Kristen
Fenton Sr HS
Fenton MI

Campbell Lee A
Ursuline Academy
Golf Manor OH

Campbell Lisa
Beaumont Schl For Girls
Cleveland OH

Campbell Marianna
Upper Scioto Valley HS
Alger OH

Campbell Monique
Jefferson Area HS
Rock Creek OH

Campbell Richard M
Dayton Christian HS
Miamisburg OH

Campbell Rosemary
Springboro HS
Springboro OH

Campbell Russell K
Rockville HS
Rockville IN

Campbell Tamara
Eastside Jr/sr HS
Butler IN

Campbell William
Wirt County HS
Palistine WV

Campeau Steven
Cheboygan Area HS
Cheboygan MI

Campensa Ross
Euclid Sr HS
Euclid OH

Camperman Richard
Donald E Gavit HS
Hammond IN

Canada Barbara
Reading Community HS
Cincinnati OH

Canaday Bonnie
Wood Memorial HS
Oakland City IN

Canaday Connie
Wood Memorial HS
Oakland City IN

Canady Irvin
Ben Davis HS
Indianapolis IN

Canady Jr Albert
Shakamak HS
Midland IN

Cannon Carol
Taylor HS
Kokomo IN

Cannon Kayetta
Hinton HS
Hinton WV

Cannon Mike
Solon HS
Solon OH

Canter Pat
Troy HS
Troy OH

Canterbury Jeff
Green HS
Uniontown OH

Cantrell William K
Grand Ledge HS
Grand Ledge MI

Capen Mary Ann
Ursuline HS
Canfield OH

Capes Lisa
Jennings County HS
No Vernon IN

Caplis Therese M
Chesterton HS
Valpariaso IN

Capouch Patricia
Kankakee Vly HS
Rensselaer IN

Cappa Tina M
Fairfield Sr HS
Fairfield OH

Cappas Constance
Grosse Pointe North HS
Grosse Pt Shrs MI

Cappocciami Toni
Grove City HS
Grove City OH

Caprez Raphael
Akron North HS
Akron OH

Capuano Bettina
Mc Kinley Sr HS
Carton OH

Caputo Felicia
Bridgeport Sr HS
Bridgeport WV

Caraballo Arturo
Washington HS
E Chicgo IN

Caraballo Daniel
Theodore Roosevelt HS
E Chicago IN

Caraboolad Cynthia
St Augustine Academy
Cleveland OH

Caraway Christine
Everett HS
Lansing MI

Carbary Roxianne
Whitmore Lake HS
Whitmore Lk MI

Card Kathy
Kearsley Community HS
Flint MI

Carder Alicia A
Covington HS
Covington OH

Carder Jackquelyn
Liberty HS
Salem WV

Carducci Laura
Mount Vernon Academy
Ashtabula OH

Carey Arthur M
Chalker HS
Southington OH

Carey Lisa
Springfield HS
Springfield MI

Carino Teresa
Marian HS
Troy MI

Carleton Allison
Delaware Hayes HS
Delaware OH

Carlini Thomas
Jackson HS
Canton OH

Carlisle Joyce
Mt View HS
Vivian WV

Carlisle Lori C
Grandview Heights HS
Columbus OH

Carlisle Marcy
Jonesville HS
Jonesville MI

Carlock Michael
Hartford HS
Hartford MI

Carlson Cathy
South Newton Jr Sr HS
Brook IN

Carlson Mark
Princeton Community HS
Princeton IN

Carlson Pete
Pine River HS
Tustin MI

Carlson Raine
Merrillville HS
Merrillville IN

Carlson Raymond
Decatur HS
Dowagiac MI

Carlson Raymond
Canfield HS
Canfield OH

Carlson Scott
Flushing Sr HS
Flushing MI

Carlson Susanmarie
Belleville HS
Belleville MI

Carlson Tracy
Calumet HS
Mohawk MI

Carman Brad
Fort Frye HS
Beverly OH

Carman Charles D
Stow HS
Stow OH

Carmichael Amy
East Liverpool HS
E Liverpool OH

Carnegie Jyme
Bloomington HS N
Bloomington IN

Carnes Bruce
Tippecanoe Valley HS
Rochester IN

Carnes Shirley E
Heath HS
Heath OH

Carney Gary
Cardinal HS
Middlefield OH

Carney Lance
Dunbar HS
Dunbar WV

STUDENTS
PHOTOGRAPH
SCHEDULED
FOR PUBLI-
CATION HERE
COULD NOT
BE REPRO-
DUCED

Caro Joseph
Huntington HS
Huntington WV

Carolen Carolyn
Highland Park Comm HS
Highland Pk MI

Carpenter Brian
Amanda Clearcreek HS
Lancaster OH

Carpenter Buddy
Windham HS
Windham OH

Carpenter Carmen
Plymouth Centon HS
Canton MI

Carpenter Caroline
Upper Arlington HS
Columbus OH

Carpenter Diane
John Glenn HS
Bay City MI

Carpenter Donna
Wayne Memorial HS
Westland MI

Carpenter Julie
Chillicothe HS
Chillicothe OH

Carpenter Kimberly
Bloomfield School
District
Newberry IN

Carpenter Nina
Hagerstown Jr Sr HS
Hagerstown IN

Carpenter Regenia
Cedar Lake Academy
South Haven MI

Carpenter Ronald
Webster County HS
Webstersprg WV

Carpenter Vicki
Willard HS
Willad OH

Carpenter Wesley
Independence HS
Coal City WV

STUDENTS
PHOTOGRAPH
SCHEDULED
FOR PUBLI-
CATION HERE
COULD NOT
BE REPRO-
DUCED

Carr Cathy D
Southport HS
Indianapolis IN

Carr James
Switzerland Co Jr Sr HS
Vevay IN

STUDENTS
PHOTOGRAPH
SCHEDULED
FOR PUBLI-
CATION HERE
COULD NOT
BE REPRO-
DUCED

Carr Michele S
Beecher HS
Mt Morris MI

STUDENTS
PHOTOGRAPH
SCHEDULED
FOR PUBLI-
CATION HERE
COULD NOT
BE REPRO-
DUCED

Carr Vernon
Bluefield HS
Bluefield WV

Carrasco Richard
Norwalk Sr HS
Norwalk OH

Carrauthers Michael B
Cass Technical HS
Detroit MI

Carreathers Eva
Aquinas HS
Inkster MI

Carrier Joseph
East Detroit HS
E Detroit MI

Carrier Lisa
South Amherst HS
Elyria OH

Carroll Charles E
Mumford HS
Detroit MI

Carroll Dave
Clear Fork HS
Butler OH

Carroll Deborah
Bloom Carroll HS
Carroll OH

Carroll Karen
Huntington North HS
Warren IN

Carroll Kimilen
Logan HS
Logan WV

Carroll Stephanie
Warren Central HS
Indpls IN

Carroll Susan
West Branch HS
Beloit OH

Carrow Steven
Braxton County HS
Gassaway WV

Carson Betsy
Ben Davis Sr HS
Indianapolis IN

Carson Carmela
Collinwood HS
Cleveland OH

Carson David
Little Miami HS
Loveland OH

Carson Lynn
Port Huron HS
Port Huron MI

Carson Patti
Garfield Hts Sr HS
Garfield Hts OH

Carson Patti
Garfield Heights Sr HS
Garfield Hts OH

Carter Allison
Benedictine HS
Detroit MI

Carter Douglas
Tippecanoe HS
Tipp City OH

Carter Emily A
Dayton Christian HS
Dayton OH

Carter Jill
Reynoldsburg HS
Reynoldsburg OH

Carter Karen
Marlette HS
Marlette MI

Carter Mimi
Wellsville HS
Wellsville OH

Carter Robbi
Clare HS
Clare MI

Carter Robyn
Elmwood HS
Cygnet OH

Carter Walter
Milton HS
Milton WV

Cartwright Janice
East Canton HS
E Canton OH

Cartwright Sharon
Scottsburg HS
Scottsburg IN

Caruso Thomas
Notre Dame HS
Clarksburs WV

Carver Caroline
South Vigo HS
Terre Haute IN

Carver Lora
Valley Local HS
Lucasville OH

Carver Rick
Oxford HS West Campus
Oxford MI

Casbar Deborah
Amelia HS
Amelia OH

Casey Deborah
Medina Sr HS
Medina OH

P—33

Casey Jeffery B
North Baltimore HS
N Baltimore OH

Casey Linda
Catholic Central HS
Grand Rpds MI

Casey Lorraine K
Bay HS
Bay Vill OH

Casillas Terri
Libbey HS
Toledo OH

Casity Janet L
Springfield Local HS
New Springfield OH

Caskey James
Madison Plains HS
London OH

Caslavka Sharon
Catholic Central HS
Grand Rpds MI

Casner Kathy
Zanesville HS
Zanesville OH

Caspers Janet
Bay City Ctrl HS
Bay City MI

Cassel Keith
Roosevelt HS
Gary IN

Cassidy Kevin
Eminence HS
Stilesville IN

Castanier Kari
John Glenn HS
Bay MI

Casteel Carla
Buckeye West HS
Adena OH

Casteel Ellen D
Hagerstown Jr Sr HS
Hagerstown IN

Casteel Jacqueline
Woodridge HS
Cuyahoga Fls OH

Caster Melvin
South Decatur HS
Greensburg IN

Castilow Kathryn
Bishop Donahue HS
Glendale WV

Castle Brad
North Newton HS
Demotte IN

Castle David
Southeastern HS
Londonderry OH

Castle Lon
West Geauga HS
Novelty OH

Casto Alice
David Anderson HS
Lisbon OH

STUDENTS
PHOTOGRAPH
SCHEDULED
FOR PUBLI-
CATION HERE
COULD NOT
BE REPRO-
DUCED

Casto Joan
Marion Harding HS
Marion OH

Casto Laurie
Barberton HS
Barberton OH

Castor Roger
Elwood Community HS
Elwood IN

Castronovo David P
Chesterton HS
Valparaiso IN

Caswell Bob
Seaholm HS
Troy MI

Caswell Christine
Walled Lake Central HS
Union Lake MI

Catanzaro Joenett
Seton HS
Cincinnati OH

Cate Andrew E
Lawrence North HS
Indianapolis IN

Cathell Jeff
Bridgeport HS
Bridgeport WV

Cather Mary Lou
Medina County Voc Schl
Wellington OH

Cato Angie
Pike Central Middle HS
Velper IN

Cato Terrence
Adelphian Academy
W Bloomfield MI

Catoline Marybeth
Ursuline HS
Youngstown OH

Cattledge Andrea
Hammond HS
Hammond IN

Cattrell Jody
Southern Local HS
Wellsville OH

Cauble Denise
Orleans HS
Orleans IN

Caudel Debra
Grosse Ile HS
Grosse Ile MI

Caudill Julia
Sandy Valley HS
Sandyville OH

Caudill Julie A
Dundee Community HS
Maybee MI

STUDENTS
PHOTOGRAPH
SCHEDULED
FOR PUBLI-
CATION HERE
COULD NOT
BE REPRO-
DUCED

Caudill La Verta
Peru HS
Peru IN

Caulk David
Ben Davis HS
Indianapolis IN

Causby Barb
Conotton Valley HS
Sherrodsville OH

Cavadeas Susanne
Escanaba Area Public HS
Cornell MI

Cavalli Cathy C
Eastlake North HS
Willowick OH

Cavanaugh Darren
Stow Lakeview HS
Stow OH

Cave Kim
Madison Plains HS
London OH

Cavell Judith
Beachwood HS
Beachwood OH

Caven Bob
Hubbard HS
Hubbard OH

Cawley Galen
Bridgeman HS
Buchanan MI

Caylor Patricia
East Palestine HS
E Palestine OH

Cayton Bobby
Lewis County HS
Weston WV

Cayton Teresa
Pontiac Central HS
Pontiac MI

Cebak Kathy
Struthers HS
Struthers OH

Cecelones Catherine S
Catholic Central HS
Steubenville OH

Cecelones Mariann
Catholic Central HS
Steubenville OH

Cech Michael
Saginaw HS
Saginaw MI

Celarek Joseph
Bishop Luers HS
Ft Wayne IN

Celeste Jose
Gilmour Acad
Mayfield Hts OH

Cencelewski Caryle
Washington HS
South Bend IN

Centlivre Cynthia
Bishop Dwenger HS
Ft Wayne IN

Cerar Mary
Galion HS
Galion OH

Cerbin Heidi
Euclid Sr HS
Euclid OH

Cervantes Phillip
St Francis De Sales HS
Oregon OH

Chacalos Michele
Bridgeport HS
Bridgeport OH

Chadd Doris
Calumet HS
Gary IN

Chadda Jyoti
Trenton HS
Trenton MI

STUDENTS
PHOTOGRAPH
SCHEDULED
FOR PUBLI-
CATION HERE
COULD NOT
BE REPRO-
DUCED

Chadwick David
Mt Vernon Sr HS
Butler OH

Chaffin Barry
Ithaca HS
Ithaca MI

Chalker Robert H
Girard HS
Girard OH

Chaloupka Frank J
Walsh Jesuit HS
Northfield OH

Chamberlain Amy
Franklin HS
Franklin OH

Chamberlain Judy
Belleville HS
Belleville MI

Chamberlain Lynda
Lamphere HS
Madisonheights MI

Chamberlain Sandra
Walter P Chrysler Mem
HS
New Castle IN

Chamberlin Gayla
Northwestern HS
Wooster OH

Chambers Arnese
Beaumont School For
Girls
Clevelnd OH

STUDENTS
PHOTOGRAPH
SCHEDULED
FOR PUBLI-
CATION HERE
COULD NOT
BE REPRO-
DUCED

Chambers Keith
Kyger Creek HS
Gallipolis OH

Chambers Teresa
Kyger Creek HS
Gallipolis OH

Champer Lesa
Madison Plains HS
London OH

Chan Susan
Dublin HS
Dublin OH

Chance Janis
Richmond Sr HS
Richmond IN

Chandler Colleen
Bedford Sr HS
Toledo OH

Chandler Constance
Pontiac Northern HS
Pontiac MI

Chandler Deborah
North Putnam HS
Coatesville IN

Chandler Deborah
North Putnam HS
Coatesville IN

Chandler Lisa J
Bridgeport Sr HS
Bridgeport WV

Chandler Michelle
Brookhaven HS
Columbus OH

Chandler Mike
Decatur Jr Sr HS
Lawton MI

Chandler William E
Tri West Hendricks HS
Pittsboro IN

Chaney Larry L
Paint Valley HS
Chillicothe OH

Chaparian Michael
Edsel B Ford HS
Dearborn MI

Chapin Timothy
Walled Lake Central HS
Union Lake MI

Chapin Toni L
Springfield HS
Toledo OH

Chapman Bert
Marion HS
Marion IN

Chapman Jennifer L
Richwood HS
Richwood WV

Chapman J Rodrick
Lewis Cnty HS
Roanoke WV

Chapman Mark
Milton HS
Milton WV

Chapman Michelle
Columbian HS
Tiffin OH

Chapman Richard
Port Clinton HS
Pt Clinton OH

Chapman Sandra C
North Ridgeville HS
N Ridgeville OH

Chapman Vicki
Beechcroft Jr Sr HS
Columbus OH

Chappell Kitty
Pike Central HS
Petersburg IN

Chapple Rebecca
Kenston HS
Chagrin Fls OH

Charles Christopher
Princeton HS
Princeton WV

Charme Michael
Meadowdale HS
Dayton OH

Charr Jeffrey S
View HS
Anawalt WV

Chase Dennis
Highland HS
Fredericktown OH

Chase Lawrence R
Switzerland Cnty Jr Sr HS
Vevay IN

Chase Penny
Amanda Clearcreek HS
Lancaster OH

Chatfield David
Normandy HS
Parma OH

Chattin Lori
South Knox HS
Vincennes IN

Cheatham Sheryl
Daleville HS
Daleville IN

Cheatum Ty
Broad Ripple HS
Indianapolis IN

Checkley Mark
Blissfield HS
Howell MI

Cheek Keith E
Bloom Carroll HS
Lancaster OH

Cheek Kimberlee
Alma HS
Alma MI

Chenault James C
St Francis De Salles HS
Temperance MI

Cheney Susan M
Sidney HS
Sidney OH

Cherry Steven
Northwestern HS
Burbank OH

Cherryholmes Shara
Waynesville HS
Waynesville OH

Chesser Charles
Alexander HS
Athens OH

Chew Connie
Tri HS
New Castle IN

Chian Chao In
Ravenna HS
Solon OH

Chick Greg
Fairborn Park Hills HS
Xenia OH

Childers Brenda
Springfield North HS
Springfield OH

Childers Glenn
Lawrenceburg HS
Lawrenceburg IN

Childers Jennifer
Arsenal Tech HS
Indianapolis IN

Childs Kellie
Central HS
Detroit MI

Chioldi Mario
St Edward HS
Middleburg Hts OH

STUDENTS PHOTOGRAPH SCHEDULED FOR PUBLICATION HERE COULD NOT BE REPRODUCED

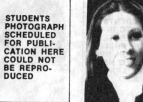
STUDENTS PHOTOGRAPH SCHEDULED FOR PUBLICATION HERE COULD NOT BE REPRODUCED

Chitwood Kimberly
Culver Girls Academy
Louisville KY

Chizmadia Gerald L
Lakeville Memorial HS
Columbiaville MI

Cho Peggy
East Kentwood HS
Kentwood MI

Choban Gary
Buckannon Upshur HS
Buckhannon WV

Choi Chul
Greenville Sr HS
Greenville MI

Choison Jerri J
Bishop Noll Inst
Gary IN

Choitz Carolyn
Gladwin HS
Gladwin MI

Choler Debbie
Walled Lake Central HS
Union Lake MI

Christensen Jo Ann
East Kentwood HS
Kentwood MI

Christensen Karen
Lake City Area HS
Lake City MI

Christensen Richard
Hartland HS
Hartland MI

Christensen Robert
Westfall HS
Orient OH

Christian Kent C
Cascade HS
Clayton IN

Christian Schondra
South HS
Youngstown OH

Christian Thomas
North Dickinson HS
Sagola MI

Christiansen Lisa
Williamston HS
Williamston MI

Christiansen Todd
St Marys Central Cath
HS
Sandusky OH

Christin Amy
Anderson Sr HS
Cincinnati OH

Christmas Christina
Mason Cnty Cntrl HS
Scottville MI

Christmon Kevin
Pontiac Central HS
Pontiac MI

Christofield Joanna
Indian Hill HS
Cincinnati OH

Christoforidis John
St Johns HS
Toledo OH

Chriswell Karen
Ravenna HS
Ravenna OH

Chudakoff Robert
Charles F Brush HS
Lyndhurst OH

Chumley Gina
Trenton HS
Trenton MI

Chumley Jonathan
Broad Ripple HS
Indianapolis IN

Church Amanda
Meadow Bridge HS
Meadowbrdg WV

Church J C
Marion Harding HS
Marion OH

Churness Emory
Robert S Rogers HS
Toledo OH

Ciabattoni Carol
Maplewood HS
Cortland OH

Ciamacco Bridget
Brookhaven HS
Columbus OH

Cielensky Amy
Ravenna HS
Ravenna OH

Cimini Tina
Union Local HS
Belmont OH

Cimperman Anthony J
Lake Catholic HS
Mentor OH

Ciofani Terri
Bellaire HS
Bellaire OH

Cisarik Kimberly
Andrean HS
Hobart IN

Citron Gregg
Southfield HS
Southfield MI

Clampitt Cort
New Palestine HS
New Palestine IN

Clancy Deirdre T
Shrine HS
Royal Oak MI

Clapp Tamara L
Montezuma HS
Montezuma IN

Clark Beth E
Belleville HS
Wayne MI

Clark Catherine
Flushing Sr HS
Flint MI

Clark Charlene
Bristol HS
Bristolville OH

Clark Craig
Milton HS
Milton WV

Clark David
Carmel HS
Carmel IN

Clark Deirdre
Davison Sr HS
Davison MI

Clark Denise
Cathedral HS
Indianapolis IN

Clark Gina
Stanton HS
Irondale OH

Clark Gregory
Bishop Chatard HS
Indianapolis IN

Clark James R
Madison Heights HS
Anderson IN

Clark Janet
Doddridge County HS
Salem WV

Clark Jeff
Grand Ledge HS
Grand Ledge MI

Clark Jeffrey
Belleville HS
Belleville MI

Clark Julie
Bloomington HS South
Bloomington IN

Clark Kathleen M
Servite HS
Detroit MI

Clark Linda
Mc Bain Rural Agri
School
Mc Bain MI

Clark Lora R
Hurricane HS
Hurricane WV

Clark Maggie
Gallia Academy HS
Gallipolis OH

Clark Michael
Northrop HS
Ft Wayne IN

STUDENTS
PHOTOGRAPH
SCHEDULED
FOR PUBLI-
CATION HERE
COULD NOT
BE REPRO-
DUCED

Clark Richard
Princeton Community HS
Princeton IN

Clark Steven
Jackson HS
North Canton OH

Clark Todd R
Oak Hills HS
Cincinnati OH

Clarkson David
Croswell Lexington HS
Croswell MI

Claton Lori
Tri County HS
Remington IN

Clatworthy Sandra
Huntington East HS
Huntington WV

Clay Charles E
Pennfield HS
Battle Creek MI

Clay Jeffery
Pineville HS
Saulsville WV

Clay Patricia E
Mid America Christian
HS
Barboursville WV

Clayton Connye
Southeastern HS
Detroit MI

Clear Bradley
John Adams HS
South Bend IN

Cleary R Michael
Washington Sr HS
Washington C H OH

Cleavenger Brigetta
Philip Barbour HS
Philippi WV

Clegg Mark
Ida HS
Petersbrg MI

Clemans Lori
Madison Plains HS
London OH

Clemens Margery
Normandy HS
Seven Hills OH

Clement Jim
Hammond Baptist HS
Merrillville IN

Clement Michael D
Sand Creek HS
Adrian MI

Clemente Diane
Niles Mckinley HS
Niles OH

Clemmons Cindy
Paint Valley HS
Bainbridge OH

Clemons Barry
North Miami HS
Macy IN

Clemons Brent
North Miami HS
Macy IN

Clemons Paul
Mahoning Cnty Joint Voc
Schl
Lake Milton OH

Clevenger Cynthia
Jefferson Union HS
Steubenville OH

Clevenger Debra K
North Ridgeville Sr HS
N Ridgeville OH

Clevenger Kevi M
Lima Sr HS
Lima OH

Clevenger Mike
Portsmouth East HS
Sciotoville OH

Clifford Marsha
Davison Sr HS
Davison MI

Clime Mary
Marcellus HS
Marcellus MI

Cline Bonita
Independence HS
Sophia WV

Cline Michelle
Greencastle HS
Greencastle IN

Cline Patricia
Mt View HS
Welch WV

Cline Robin
Grandview Hts HS
Columbus OH

Cline Susan
Jennings Cnty HS
N Vernon IN

Clingan Linda C
Hedgesville HS
Martinsburg WV

Clingenpeel Julie
Lincoln HS
Cambridge IN

Clinkenbeard Cindi
Snider HS
Ft Wayne IN

Clore Krista
Davison HS
Davison MI

Close Tammy
Loudonville HS
Loudonville OH

Clossman L
Tri Valley HS
Nashport OH

Closson Nena
Roosevelt Wilson HS
Clarksburg WV

STUDENTS
PHOTOGRAPH
SCHEDULED
FOR PUBLI-
CATION HERE
COULD NOT
BE REPRO-
DUCED

Clough Deborah
Fordson HS
Dearborn MI

Clouse Anthony
A Leon Clouse HS
Losantville IN

Clouse Julia
Brookhaven HS
Columbus OH

Clouse Kevin
Monrovia HS
Martinsville IN

Clouse Saralynn
North Central HS
Farmersbg IN

Clovesko Anita
Rocky River HS
Rocky Rvr OH

Clunk David
Whitmer Sr HS
Toledo OH

Clutter Angie
Boonville HS
Boonville IN

Clutter Kevin
Toronto HS
Toronto OH

Coates Douglas
Tuscarawas Valley HS
E Sparta OH

Coatsolonia Dina
Kouts HS
Kouts IN

STUDENTS
PHOTOGRAPH
SCHEDULED
FOR PUBLI-
CATION HERE
COULD NOT
BE REPRO-
DUCED

Cobb Janelle
Aquinas HS
Westland MI

Cobb Katherine
Thomas A De Vilbiss HS
Toledo OH

Cobb Patty
Herbert Hoover HS
Clendenin WV

Cobb Tammy
West Side Sr HS
Gary IN

Coberly Thomas
Summerfield HS
Petersburg MI

Coblentz Kristi
Greenville Sr HS
Greenville OH

Coburn Deborah
Mannington HS
Farmington WV

Coburn Timothy J
Fremont HS
Fremont IN

Coby Charles
Moorefield HS
Moorefield WV

Cochenour Dave
N Canton Hoover HS
North Canton OH

Cocherl Donna
Marion Harding HS
Marion OH

STUDENTS
PHOTOGRAPH
SCHEDULED
FOR PUBLI-
CATION HERE
COULD NOT
BE REPRO-
DUCED

Cochran Lynn
Mason Sr HS
Mason MI

Cochran Paul
Peru Sr HS
Peru IN

Cocking Lloyd
Trenton HS
Trenton MI

Coeburn Patricia
Reading HS
Reading MI

Coffer Karen L
Indianapolis Baptist HS
Indianapolis IN

Coffey Jacqueline
Mount Vernon HS
Indianapolis IN

Coffey Sondra
Sidney HS
Sidney OH

Coffey Teresa
Warren Ctrl HS
Indpls IN

Coffindaffer Donna
Winfield HS
Scott Depot WV

Coffindaffer Terry
Scott HS
Madison WV

Coffman Lisa
Ben Davis HS
Indianapolis IN

Cohen Cathy J
Thomas A De Vilbiss HS
Toledo OH

Cohn Morton
Summerfield HS
Petersburg MI

Colaner Vicki
Huron HS
Ann Arbor MI

Colbert Angela
Southeast HS
N Benton OH

Colby Craig
Houston HS
Houston OH

Colchagoff Wick R
Rogers HS
Toledo OH

Cole Alicia
Admiral King HS
Lorain OH

Cole Julie
Avondale Sr HS
Auburn Hts MI

Cole Marylee
Houghton Lake HS
St Helen MI

Cole Nancy
Concord HS
Concord MI

Cole Patty
Clermont Northeastern
HS
Marathon OH

Cole Randy
L & M HS
Lyons IN

Cole Shelia
Mooresville HS
Mooresville IN

Cole Vicki L
Bridgeport Sr HS
Bridgeport WV

Cole Walter
Gwinn HS
Sawyer Afb MI

Cole Jr James
West Side HS
Gary IN

STUDENTS PHOTOGRAPH SCHEDULED FOR PUBLICATION HERE COULD NOT BE REPRODUCED

Coleman Jack D
North Ridgeville HS
N Ridgeville OH

Coleman Jacqueline
Cass Technical HS
Detroit MI

Coleman J Todd
L & M HS
Lyons IN

Coleman Shawna L
John Glenn HS
New Concord OH

Coles Gregory E
Hawken HS
Cleveland Hts OH

Collier Betsy
Lexington HS
Lexington OH

Collier Mark A
Valparaiso HS
Valparaiso IN

Collier Mary R
Mifflin Sr HS
Columbus OH

Collins Cathy L
Wm H Harrison HS
Evansville IN

Collins Charles
Windham HS
Windham OH

Collins Charles W
Brookhaven HS
Columbus OH

Collins Christy
Union Local HS
Bethesda OH

Collins Dawn
Hobart HS
Hobart IN

Collins Jacqueline
Rutherford B Hayes HS
Delaware OH

Collins Kathryn S
Buffalo HS
Prichard WV

Collins Mary Jo
Clear Fork
Beckley WV

Collins Michael
Pontiac Central HS
Pontiac MI

Collins Robert
Northrop HS
Ft Wayne IN

Collins Robert
Beaverton HS
Beaverton MI

Collins Rosanna
Saginaw HS
Saginaw MI

Collins Roxane
Wellston HS
Wellston OH

Collins Sheila R
Upper Sandusky Sr HS
Upper Sandusky OH

Collison Charlotte
Arthur Hill HS
Saginaw MI

Colucci Ella
Ashtabula HS
Ashtabula OH

Colvin Edward
Medina Sr HS
Medina OH

Coman Pam
Fairview HS
Fairview Park OH

Combes Laura
Beaumont Girls HS
Shaker Hts OH

Comito Carla M
Our Lady Of Mercy HS
Redford MI

Comodeca James A
Normandy HS
Parma OH

Conder Steven
Goshen HS
Goshen IN

Condon Celeste
St Marys Cntrl Cath HS
Sandusky OH

Condon Jan M
Clay Sr HS
Oregon OH

Condon Timothy
Moelled HS
Cincinnati OH

Congleton Jill
Washington Cnty Voc
School
Belpre OH

Conigliaro Joyce
Crestwood HS
Hiram OH

Conkle Karen
Garrett HS
Garrett IN

Conklin Leanne
Geneva HS
Geneva OH

STUDENTS PHOTOGRAPH SCHEDULED FOR PUBLICATION HERE COULD NOT BE REPRODUCED

Conley Lori
Jackson HS
Jackson OH

Conley Lyn
Lake Central HS
Dyer IN

STUDENTS PHOTOGRAPH SCHEDULED FOR PUBLICATION HERE COULD NOT BE REPRODUCED

Conley Teresa
Birmingham Seaholm HS
Troy MI

Conley Tobin P
Traverse City St Francis
HS
Traverse City MI

Conley Yale
Parkersburg HS
Vienna WV

STUDENTS PHOTOGRAPH SCHEDULED FOR PUBLICATION HERE COULD NOT BE REPRODUCED

Connair Brian
Archbishop Alter HS
Kettering OH

Connell Jefferey
Everett HS
Lansing MI

Connell Kathleen
Nordonia HS
Northfield OH

Conner Buddy
Benjamin Bosse HS
Evansville IN

Conner Rhonda
Bath Sr HS
Lima OH

Conner Thomas
Wheeling Park HS
Wheeling WV

Conner Timothy
Bluffton HS
Bluffton IN

Conner Tracy L
Barboursville HS
Huntington WV

Conners Kevin
Hayes HS
Delaware OH

Connolly John R
Purcell HS
Cincinnati OH

Connolly Joline
Defiance Sr HS
Defiance OH

Connor David
Pontiac Northern HS
Pontiac MI

Connor Keith
Shaker Heights Sr HS
Shaker Hts OH

STUDENTS
PHOTOGRAPH
SCHEDULED
FOR PUBLI-
CATION HERE
COULD NOT
BE REPRO-
DUCED

Connor Tim
Wilmington HS
Wilmington OH

Conomea Jamie
Brooklyn HS
Brooklyn OH

Conrad Carlin
Springs Valley HS
French Lick IN

Conrad Dennis
Spencer HS
Reedy WV

Conrad James
Whiteland Community
HS
Franklin IN

Conrad Kevin
South Dearborn HS
Aurora IN

Conrad Lynn V
Liberty HS
Bristol WV

Conrad Ralph
Sandy Valley HS
E Sparta OH

Conrad Ron
Garrett HS
Garrett IN

Conroy Karen
Catholic Central HS
Steubenville OH

Conroy Kathy
Utica HS
Utica MI

Contino Michael S
Circleville HS
Circleville OH

Contreraz Raimundo
Paulding HS
Paulding OH

Conway Joanne
Bloomfield HS
Bloomfield IN

Conway Kathleen
Clarkston HS
Drayton Plns MI

Conway Ruchelle
Struthers HS
Struthers OH

Conyngham Pam
Magnificat HS
North Olmsted OH

Cook Belinda
Southridge HS
Huntingburg IN

Cook Cari
Lake HS
Walbridge OH

Cook David
Mullens HS
Mullens WV

Cook David
Little Miami HS
Blanchester OH

Cook Deborah
Lumen Cordium HS
Cleveland OH

Cook Eric
Allen Park HS
Allen Park MI

Cook Fleming
Cass Technical HS
Detroit MI

Cook Leisa
Vandalia Butler Sr HS
Vandalia OH

Cook Randy
Norwood HS
Norwood OH

Cook Rick
De Kalb HS
Ashley IN

Cook Rodney A
Ravenna HS
Ravenna OH

Cook Tim
Pike Central HS
Winslow IN

Cooke Phillip
Pineville HS
Pineville WV

Cooley Gary
North Union HS
Richwood OH

Coon Christina L
Westland HS
Columbus OH

Cooper Austin
Lutheran HS East
Cleveland Hts OH

Cooper Bill
Chillicothe HS
Chillicothe OH

Cooper Elecca
Harman HS
Harman WV

Cooper Jeffrey L
Wauseon HS
Ostrander OH

Cooper Kevin
Elkins HS
Elkins WV

Cooper Margaret
Edison Sr HS
Lk Station IN

Cooper Mary J
Madison HS
Madison OH

Cooper Robin
Cardington Lincoln HS
Cardington OH

Cooper Tari
Taft Sr HS
Hamilton OH

Cooper Tracy
Tippecanoe HS
Tipp City OH

Cooper Tris T
Eastern HS
Winchester OH

Copas Christina
Wehrle HS
Columbus OH

Copeland Barbara
Lakeland HS
Milford MI

Copeland Roberta
Henry Ford HS
Detroit MI

Coppernoll Richard
Peru Sr HS
Peru IN

Coppock Tammy
Pickaway Ross Joint Voc Schl
Waverly OH

Corazzi Susan
R Nelson Snider HS
Ft Wayne IN

STUDENTS
PHOTOGRAPH
SCHEDULED
FOR PUBLI-
CATION HERE
COULD NOT
BE REPRO-
DUCED

Corcoglioniti Michele
Roosevelt Wilson HS
Stonewood WV

Corder Dolly
Clay Battelle HS
Blacksville WV

Cordle Cathy
St Charles Cmnty HS
St Charles MI

Cordova Daniel
Baker HS
Dayton OH

Cords Laura
Frank Cody HS
Detroit MI

Corley Steven B
Coalton HS
Coalton WV

Corley Walter
Elkins HS
Elkins WV

Corlson Robert
Walled Lake Central HS
Union Lake MI

Cormany Jill
Marysville HS
Marysville OH

Cornachione Jill
Chippewa HS
Doylestown OH

Cornelis Carol
St Joseph HS
South Bend IN

Cornelison Loree
Morton Sr HS
Hammond IN

Cornell James
New Richmond HS
New Richmond OH

Cornell Keith
Kenton HS
Kenton OH

Cornett Donald R
Marlington HS
Minerva OH

Cornett Marissa
Eaton HS
Eaton OH

Cornwell Julia
North Central HS
Indianapolis IN

Cornwell Karen
Upper Arlington HS
Columbus OH

Correll Jeffrey
Central Catholic HS
Canton OH

Corrigan Jeffrey
Carlisle Sr HS
Carlisle OH

Cortopassi Johnna
La Salle HS
San Clemente CA

Corzatt Rob
Miami Trace HS
Leesburg OH

Cosma Catherine
St Joseph Academy
Cleveland OH

Coss Pamela J
Lordstown HS
Warren OH

Costa Stephen
Ursuline HS
Youngstown OH

Costello Kyle
Washington Irving HS
Clarksburg WV

Costello Robert W
St Joseph HS
Cleveland OH

Costick Mike
Hubbard HS
Hubbard OH

Costin Belinda M
Notre Dame Academy
Perrysburg OH

Cotcher Deborah
Fenton Sr HS
Fenton MI

Cote Diane
Upper Arlington HS
Columbus OH

Cotter Lorie
Howell Sr HS
Howell MI

Cotton Beth
Bishop Donahue HS
Glen Dale WV

Cotton Dianna
United Local HS
Kensington OH

Cotton Donna L
Marlington HS
Alliance OH

Cotton Jed
Big Rapids HS
Big Rapids MI

Cotton Pamela
Ashtabula Harbor HS
Ashtabula OH

Cottongim Ed
Plainfield Jr Sr HS
Plainfield IN

Cottrell Kazuo O
Fenwick HS
Middletown OH

Cottrill Carol A
Huntington HS
Chillicothe OH

Cottrill Kathryn
Stonewall Jackson HS
Charleston WV

Cottrill Reona
Washington Irving HS
Clarksburg WV

Cottrill Sheila
Gilmer County HS
Shock WV

Cotts Cheryl
Zeeland HS
Hudsonville MI

Couch Mark
Huntington North HS
Huntington IN

Couch Nancy
Rosedale HS
Rosedale IN

Couch Pamela
Fitzgerald HS
Warren MI

Coughlin Carolyn
Ursuline HS
Youngstown OH

Coulter Shawn
Whitehall Yearling HS
Columbus OH

Court Denise
Harper Creek HS
Battle Creek MI

Courter Thomas
Bullock Creek HS
Midland MI

Courtney Carol
Alexandria Monroe HS
Alexandria IN

Courtney Kim
Staunton HS
Brazil IN

Cousino Colleen S
Notre Dame Acad
Erie MI

Cousins Brenda
George Washington HS
East Chicago IN

Covault Vicki
Sidney HS
Sidney OH

Coventry Rhonda
Lapeer West Sr HS
Columbiaville MI

Coventry Sharon
Lapeer West HS
Columbiaville MI

Covert Yvonne
West Sr HS
Garden City MI

Covington Dawn
River Rouge HS
River Rouge MI

Covington Zenara
Ecorse HS
Ecorse MI

Covy Dale
Bishop Borgess HS
Livonia MI

Coward Rhoda
Quincy HS
Quincy MI

Cowles Jack D
Battle Creek Central HS
Battle Creek MI

Cox A
Brookhaven HS
Columbus OH

Cox Darrell
Warsaw Comm HS
Warsaw IN

Cox Mark A
Charlestown HS
Charlestown IN

Cox Monica
Mc Auley HS
Cincinnati OH

Cox Robbin J
West Branch Sr HS
Beloit OH

Cox Robin
Muskegon Sr HS
Muskegon MI

Cox Sandy
Lebanon HS
Lebanon OH

Cox Tammy
Midland Trail HS
Ramsey WV

Coyne Kelly S
Newark Sr HS
Newark OH

Coyne Kimberly
Eastlake North HS
Timberlake OH

Crable Rhonda P
St Francis De Sales HS
Columbus OH

Crabtree David
Kyger Creek HS
Addison OH

Crabtree Doug
Stow HS
Stow OH

Crabtree Judith
Hartford HS
Hartford MI

Crabtree Sandy
Walter P Chrysler Memrl HS
New Castle IN

Crabtree Jr Glenn
Hampshire HS
Romney WV

Crackel Daniel
Owosso HS
Owosso MI

Craft Cheryl
Portsmouth E HS
Portsmouth OH

Craft Lloyd E
Fairmont Sr HS
Fairmont WV

Craig Diane
Akron Fairgrove HS
Fairgrove MI

Craig Kimberly
Norton HS
Norton OH

Craig Lisa A
Marion Franklin Sr HS
Columbus OH

Crain Ruth
Benjamin Logan HS
West Mansfield OH

Crall Martha
Bullock Creek HS
Midland MI

Crane Cindy
Ross Beatty HS
Cassopolis MI

Crane Michael
Cass Tech HS
Detroit MI

Crankshaw Marc
Lapeer East HS
Lapeer MI

Crase Sheena
Galion Sr HS
Galion OH

Craven Markham
Mt Gilead HS
Mt Gilead OH

STUDENTS
PHOTOGRAPH
SCHEDULED
FOR PUBLI-
CATION HERE
COULD NOT
BE REPRO-
DUCED

Crawford Bianca M
Bishop Noll Institute
Gary IN

Crawford Dan
Felicity Franklin HS
Bethel OH

Crawford Doug
Lima Sr HS
Lima OH

Crawford Jeff
Waverly HS
Lansing MI

Crawford Kathi
Champion HS
Warren OH

Crawford Kevin
Highland HS
Anderson IN

Crawford Michael
Hazel Park HS
Ferndale MI

Crea Donna J
Hubbard HS
Hubbard OH

Creagan Karen
Decatur Jr Sr HS
Decatur MI

Creagan Robert
Decatur HS
Decatur MI

Creasap Laura B
River Valley HS
Marion OH

Creasey Errol
Wood Memorial HS
Oakland City IN

Crecelius Sara
Central HS
Newberry IN

Creech Tracy
Western Brown Sr HS
Willmsbrg OH

Creed Lawrence
Hubbard HS
Hubbard OH

Crelin James W
Boardman HS
Boardman OH

Cremeans Shanda R
Crown Point HS
Crown Point IN

Crew Sharon
Wilbur Wright HS
Dayton OH

Crews Amy
Southern Local HS
Wellsville OH

Crickenberger Katherine
Pocahontas County HS
Hillsboro WV

Crider Rex A
Shawnee Sr HS
Lima OH

Cridge Michael
Madison Heights HS
Anderson IN

Crihfield Diannia
Walton Jr Sr HS
Harmony WV

Criminski Scott
Linsly Institute
Wheeling WV

Criner Brian
Roscommon HS
Roscommon MI

Cripliver Tom
Thomas A Edison HS
Lake Station IN

Crislip Michelle
Wellsville HS
Wellsville OH

Crist Natalie
Edon HS
Edon OH

Crites Dennis
Bloomfield HS
Bloomfield IN

Crnarich Mariann
Mahoning County JVS
HS
Poland OH

Croce Suzanne
Westerville North HS
Westerville OH

STUDENTS
PHOTOGRAPH
SCHEDULED
FOR PUBLI-
CATION HERE
COULD NOT
BE REPRO-
DUCED

Crone Laurie
Van Wert HS
Van Wert OH

Croniger Colleen
Regina HS
Euclid OH

Crooks Merriam
Olivet Comm HS
Olivet MI

Crooks Shelly
Benzie County Central
HS
Benzonia MI

Crookston Fred
Gull Lake HS
Kalamazoo MI

Crosby Jerilyn
Fairview HS
Dayton OH

Crosby K Sue
Bellaire HS
Bellaire OH

Cross Claudia
Shadyside HS
Shadyside OH

Cross Lisa
Stow Sr HS
Stow OH

Cross Patricia A
Walter P Chrysler Memm HS
New Castle IN

Cross Rhonda
Shaker Heights HS
Shaker Hts OH

Crossfield Rosemie
Culver Girls Academy
Oyster Bay NY

Crouch Mary
John Marshall HS
Indianapolis IN

Crouch Teresa
Bedford N Lawrence HS
Bedford IN

Crouse Terry
Hampshire HS
Romney WV

Crow Glenn
L C Mohr HS
South Haven MI

Crow Lisa
Herbert Henry Dow HS
Midland MI

Crowder Dorrine
John Adams HS
Cleveland OH

Crowder Joy
Springs Valley HS
French Lick IN

Crowdus Dana
North Central HS
Indianapolis IN

Crowe Alvin J
Northeastern HS
Williamsburg IN

Crowe David
Rock Hill Sr HS
Kitts Hill OH

Crowe Laura
Heritage Christian School
Indianapolis IN

Crowe Richard
Bosse HS
Evansville IN

Crowell Sheila K
Hedgesville HS
Martinsburg WV

Crowl Harold S
Lewis County HS
Weston WV

Crum Scott
Cardington Lincoln HS
Cardington OH

Crum Tim
Kermit HS
Kermit WV

Crumback Tracy
Caledonia HS
Caledonia MI

Csizi Edward
Morrison R Waite HS
Toledo OH

Cubia Perry E
Pontiac Central HS
Pontiac MI

Culey Andrew
Manistique Ctrl HS
Manistique MI

Culp Kendell
Rennsselaer Central HS
Rensselaer IN

Culter Ronald
Marysville HS
Smith Creek MI

Cummings Anita
Muskegon Hts HS
Muskegon Ht MI

Cummings Brian
Hillman HS
Hillman MI

Cummings Christine
Dwight D Eisenhower HS
Saginaw MI

Cummings Joe
Barr Reeve HS
Cannelburg IN

Cummings Mary
Wheeling Park HS
Triadelphia WV

Cunningham Brent
Orrville HS
Orrville OH

Cunningham Deborah
Delphi Community HS
Delphi IN

Cunningham Diana
Lincoln HS
Lumberport WV

Cunningham Joan
Dexter HS
Dexter MI

Cunningham Michelle
Edward Lee Mc Clain HS
Greenfield OH

Cunningham Robert
Wheelensburg HS
Wheelersubrg OH

Cunningham Sally S
Covington Comm HS
Covington IN

Curley Carolyn G
Highland HS
Wadsworth OH

Curlin Paul
Switzerland Cnty HS
Vevay IN

Curnow Thomas
Harbor Springs HS
Harbor Springs MI

Curran Michael
Orchard View HS
Muskegon MI

Curran Randy
South Ripley Jr Sr HS
Versailles IN

Curren Camilla
North Ridgeville HS
N Ridgeville OH

Currie Maxine
Kettering Sr HS
Detroit MI

Curry Anita
Cardinal HS
Middlefield OH

Curry David
Buckhannon Upshur HS
Buckhannon WV

Curry David A
West Lafayette HS
W Lafayette IN

Curry Debra
Westfall HS
Orient OH

Curry Sandy
Hamlin HS
Hamlin WV

Curtis Craig
Wilmington HS
Wilmington OH

Curtis James D
East Clinton HS
New Vienna OH

Curtis Kim
Bedford HS
Bedford OH

Cushman Kathy J
West Liberty Salem HS
West Liberty OH

Custer James
United Local HS
Hanoverton OH

Custer Kathleen
Andrean HS
Valparaiso IN

Custodio Bambi
De Kalb HS
Auburn IN

Cuthrell Randy
Clawson HS
Clawson MI

Cutler Anne
Central HS
Evansville IN

Cutteridge Ronda
Central HS
Evansville IN

Cvengros Jospeh
Center Line HS
Warren MI

Cygan Christopher
Warren Woods HS
Warren MI

Cygan David M
Warren Woods HS
Warren MI

Cyrus Pamela
Milton HS
Milton WV

Cyrus Sherry D
Buffalo HS
Prichard WV

Cyrus Tressa
Milton HS
Milton WV

Czarnik Mary
St Florian HS
Detroit MI

Czarnota Jan
Paul K Cousino Sr HS
Warren MI

Czuchran Denny
Buckeye South HS
Rayland OH

D

Dadaian Michelle
Fairview HS
Fairview Pk OH

D Agostino Jeffery
St Francis Central HS
Morgantown WV

Dagostino Lisa
Canfield HS
Canfield OH

Dague Tammy
Johnstown Monroe Sr HS
Johnstown OH

Dahl Kevin
Coopersville HS
Coopersville MI

Dahm Maureen
Bishop Dwenger HS
Ft Wayne IN

Dailey James
Columbiana HS
Columbiana OH

Dailey N
Mississinewa HS
Jonesboro IN

Dailey W H
Culver Military Acad
Shreveport LA

Daily Marcia
Loogootee HS
Loogootee IN

Dakin Maureen
Plainfield HS
Plainfield IN

Dakin Susan J
Middletown HS
Middletown OH

Dale Larry
Northfork HS
Mc Dowell WV

STUDENTS
PHOTOGRAPH
SCHEDULED
FOR PUBLI-
CATION HERE
COULD NOT
BE REPRO-
DUCED

Dales Eldon
Lebanon HS
Lebanon OH

Daley Lisa
Lexington Sr HS
Lexington OH

Daller Joseph
Belding HS
Belding MI

Dalley Jeffrey
Taylor Center HS
Taylor MI

Dalton Daphne
Marion HS
Marion IN

Dalton Doug
Sidney HS
Sidney OH

Dalton Freddie
Rock Hill Sr HS
Ironton OH

Dalton John
Madison Heights HS
Anderson IN

Dalton Terry
Monrovia HS
Mooresville IN

Dalverny Carly
Winamac Community HS
Winamac IN

Damiani Paul
Grandview HS
Columbus OH

D Amico Beverly
Mayfield HS
Highland Hts OH

D Amour James C
Sparta HS
Sparta MI

Dandar Mary
Cardinal Stritch HS
Toledo OH

Danesten Mandana
Andrews School
Cleveland OH

Dangelo Nicholas
Morton Sr HS
Hammond IN

Dangler Chris
Crestview HS
Convoy OH

Dangler Patricia
Springfield HS
Battle Crk MI

Daniel Cynthia
Tippecanoe Valley HS
Akron IN

Daniel Elizabeth D
Liberty HS
Lester WV

Daniel Frankie
Perry Central Comm HS
Rome IN

Daniel Kelley
Fairfield Union HS
Thornville OH

Daniel Mark
Mannington HS
Mannington WV

Daniel Rachel
Avon Jr Sr HS
Danville IN

Daniell Julia A
Tyler County HS
Middlebourne WV

Daniels James
Maysville HS
Zanesville OH

Daniels Kim
Springport HS
Albion MI

Daniels Rinda
East HS
Akron OH

Daniels Steve
Bellevue HS
Nashville TN

Danneffel Tina
Hartford HS
Watervliet MI

Dantimo Julie
Nordonia HS
Northfield OH

Darby Pam
Shady Spring
Beaver WV

Darling Doris J
Linden Mc Kinley HS
Columbus OH

Darling Kevin
Dublin HS
Dublin OH

Darling Rose
Central HS
Grand Rapids MI

Darr Linda
Dublin HS
Dublin OH

Darrah Linda
Canton South HS
Canton OH

Darrall Michele
Fairview Park HS
Fairview Pk OH

Dasen Sue
Corunna HS
Corunna MI

Dasher Michael
Elkins HS
Elkins WV

Datte Steven
Bay City Western HS
Auburn MI

Datz Terri
Hilliard HS
Amlin OH

Daugherty Caralee
South Lake HS
St Clair Shore MI

Daugherty Julia A
Highland HS
Anderson IN

Daugherty Regina
Belmont HS
Dayton OH

Daugherty Rhonda
Cascade HS
Clayton IN

Dault Karen
Chelsea HS
Grass Lk MI

Daum Krista
Marion Harding HS
Marion OH

D Aurora Robert M
St Joseph Prep Seminary
Follansbee WV

Davet Bob
R B Chamberlin HS
Twinsburg OH

David Michelle
Miami Valley School
Centerville OH

Davids Robert M
John Marshall HS
Indpls IN

Davidson James
Milton HS
Culloden WV

Davidson Peggie A
Southeast HS
Ravenna OH

Davidson Peter S
Greenwood Comm HS
Greenwood IN

Davidson Terry
Lynchburg Clay HS
Hillsboro OH

Davies Cathy
Washington HS
Massillon OH

Davis Allison
University HS
Morgantown WV

Davis Beth
Charleston HS
Charleston WV

Davis Beverly C
Williamson HS
Williamson WV

Davis Brenda
River Valley HS
Three Oaks MI

Davis Brenda D
Stivers Patterson Coop
HS
Dayton OH

Davis Bryan
Madison HS
Madison OH

Davis Carla
Franklin HS
Franklin OH

Davis Carol
N Central Area HS
Powers MI

Davis Carolyn
Southeastern HS
Detroit MI

Davis Catherine
Guernsey Noble Voc
School
Caldwell OH

Davis Charles
Morgantown HS
Morgantown WV

Davis Cheryl
St Clair HS
St Clair MI

Davis Clarence
Clear Fork HS
Artie WV

Davis Danna
Oak Hill HS
Oak Hill WV

Davis David
Princeton Community HS
Princeton IN

Davis De Ann
Liberty HS
Salem WV

Davis Douglas
Ironton HS
Ironton OH

Davis Drema
Webster County HS
Webster Spgs WV

Davis Gail
Maplewood Area Joint
Voc Sch
Kent OH

Davis George
Beechcroft HS
Columbus OH

Davis Harvey
Pontiac Central HS
Pontiac MI

Davis John
Hubbard HS
Hubbard OH

Davis Joni
Girard HS
Girard OH

Davis Karen
Ripley HS
Kentuck WV

Davis Karen
Ashtabula HS
Ashtabula OH

Davis Karen
Turpin HS
Cincinnati OH

Davis Karen
Ashtabula Cnty Joint Voc
HS
Jefferson OH

Davis Kevin
Woodsfield HS
Woodsfield OH

Davis Kevin
Madison Comprehensive
HS
Mansfield OH

Davis Kimberly
Laingsburg HS
Laingsburg MI

Davis Lee
Lincoln HS
Shinnston WV

Davis Mark
Liberty HS
Wilsonburg WV

Davis Martha
South Christian HS
Caledonia MI

Davis Michelle
Greenfield Central HS
Pendleton IN

Davis Mitchell
Merrillville HS
Merrillville IN

Davis Pamela
Brookside HS
Sheffield Lake OH

Davis Penny
Newcomerstown HS
Guernsey OH

Davis Priscilla
Onekama HS
Onekama MI

Davis Rogena
Glen Este HS
Cincinnati OH

Davis Ruby
Buena Vista HS
Saginaw MI

Davis Sandra
West Sr HS
Garden City MI

Davis Stacie
Park Hills HS
Fairborn OH

Davis Stephan C
Liberty HS
Clarksburg WV

Davis Sue
Notre Dame Academy
Toledo OH

Davis Susan
Colerain HS
Cincinnati OH

Davis Suzanne
East Canton HS
E Canton OH

Davis Verniece
George Washington HS
Indianapolis IN

Davis Vicki
Newcomerstown HS
Newcomerstown OH

Davis Wendy
Harbor HS
Ashtabula OH

Davis William K
Lebanon HS
Lebanon OH

Dawkins Gregory J
Cass Tech HS
Detroit MI

Dawson Angela
Magnificat HS
Bayvillage OH

Dawson Charles J
Hampshire HS
Romney WV

Dawson Doug
Ashtabula County Jt Voc
Schl
Dorset OH

Dawson George
Buckhannon Upshur HS
French Creek WV

Day April
Princeton HS
Princeton WV

Day Debbie
Salem HS
Salem IN

Day James
Mason HS
Mason MI

Day Robert
Mason Sr HS
Mason MI

Deahl Steve
Heritage HS
Ft Wayne IN

Deal Nancy
Hubbard HS
Hubbard OH

Dean Andrea
Henry Ford HS
Detroit MI

Dean Edward
Michigan Center HS
Michigan Cente MI

Dean Joseph
Niles Mc Kinley HS
Niles OH

Dean Kimberly
Franklin HS
Livonia MI

Dean Tonya
Buckhannon Upshur HS
Buckhannon WV

Deary Sandra
Western HS
Detroit MI

Deason Diane
Huron HS
New Boston MI

Deaton Todd
Switzerland Co Jr Sr HS
Vevay IN

De Barge Mary
Munster HS
Munster IN

De Bee Rex A
Oak Glen HS
Chester WV

Debelak Maureen

North HS
Willowick OH

Debo Dona
Madison Comprehensive
HS
Mansfield OH

De Busk Gerald
Oak Hill HS
Oak Hill WV

De Cato Deborah A
Cardinal Mooney HS
Boardman OH

De Celles Cindy
Chesterton HS
Chesterton IN

De Cesaro Mary
Upper Arlington HS
Middletown OH

STUDENTS
PHOTOGRAPH
SCHEDULED
FOR PUBLI-
CATION HERE
COULD NOT
BE REPRO-
DUCED

De Christofaro Carmen
Niles Mc Kinley HS
Niles OH

De Christofaro Lou
Niles Mc Kinley HS
Niles OH

Deckard Debbie
Randolph Southern Jr Sr
HS
Winchester IN

Deckard Pamela S
Danville Community HS
Danville IN

Decker Karen
Warsaw Community HS
Claypool IN

Decker William
Bridgeport Sr HS
Bridgeport WV

De Cooman Laura
Fenton HS
Fenton MI

Decot Kevin Dale
Bloom Carroll HS
Carroll OH

De Crane Tricia
Tuscarawas Ctrl Catholic
HS
New Phila OH

Deeks Melissa J
Cuyahoga Falls HS
Cuyahoga Falls OH

Deem Joan
Lincoln HS
Fairmont WV

Deen Steven C
Corydon Central HS
Corydon IN

Deer Lisa
New Palestine HS
New Palestine IN

Dees Konda
Richmond Sr HS
Richmond IN

Dees Mitch
Northwest Sr HS
Fairfield OH

De Graff Rhonda
Pickerington HS
Pickerington OH

De Grandchamp Paul
Mt Pleasant Sr HS
Mount Pleasant MI

De Groot James
Olivet HS
Olivet MI

De Guzman Maria N
Highland Park Cmnty HS
Highland Park MI

Deibel Jill
Ridgewood HS
Fresno OH

Deichler Karen
Brookfield HS
Brookfield OH

Deiters Julie
Anna HS
Anna OH

Deitzen Vincent
Hillsdale HS
Osseo MI

Dejanovich Michael J
Bishop Noll Inst
Chicago IL

De Julian Michele
Trenton HS
Trenton MI

De Jute David
St Johns HS
Toledo OH

De Kemper Donna
Princeton Cmnty HS
Princeton IN

De Klerk Hilda
Lapeer East Sr HS
Lapeer MI

De Kock Sharon
Kankakee Valley HS
Fair Oaks IN

Delaine Valerie
Western Hills HS
Cincinnati OH

Delaplaine Chris
Bedford North Lawrence
HS
Bedford IN

Delauder Sherri L
Morgantown HS
Morgantwn WV

De Lavern Donna
Bridgeport HS
Saginaw MI

Del Camp Dinah D
Newton HS
Plesant Hill OH

De Leon Tammy
Jonathan Alder HS
Plain City OH

Dellinger John
Hedgesville HS
Falling Wtrs WV

De Long Elizabeth
Mt Pleasant HS
Mt Pleasamt MI

De Long Susan
New Richmond HS
Bethel OH

Del Signore Thomas
Struthers HS
Struthers OH

Del Valle Elena
Marian HS
Blmfld Hls MI

Demak Ronald
Berkley HS
Oak Park MI

De Marco Kathy
Euclid Sr HS
Euclid OH

De Matas Lisa G
Immaculata HS
Detroit MI

Dembczynski Patricia
Eau Claire HS
Sodus MI

Demechko Edward A
Woodrow Wilson HS
Youngstwn OH

Demidovich Jill
Van Wert HS
Van Wert OH

De Moss Rose M
Shelbyville Sr HS
Shelbyville IN

De Mott Doug
Northwest HS
Jackson MI

Dempsey Kelly
William Henry Harrison
HS
Evansville IN

Demshar Denise
North Royalton HS
N Royalton OH

De Mundo Melinda L
Notre Dame HS
Clarksburg WV

Denbow Jamie
Morgan HS
Mc Connelsville OH

Dendler Jeffrey
Central Baptist HS
Sharonville OH

Denisi Laura
Niles Sr HS
Niles MI

Denney David
Watkins Memorial HS
Pataskala OH

Denning Jackie
Southport HS
Indianapolis IN

Dennis Brent
Clearview HS
Lorain OH

Dennis Connie
Loudonville HS
Loudonville OH

Dennis Robert R
Claymont HS
Uhrichsville OH

Dennis Scott
Elk Rapids HS
Elk Rapids MI

Dennis Susan
Marlette Comm HS
Marlette MI

Dennison Kimberly
Lewis Cnty HS
Camden WV

Denny Allen
Catholic Central HS
Grand Rapids MI

Denny Cynthia
Cooley HS
Detroit MI

Densford Brian
Crothersville HS
Austin IN

Denson Laverne
George Washington HS
E Chicago IN

Denstedt William F
Hale HS
Hale MI

De Paepe Denise
Penn HS
Mishawaka IN

De Pew Sterling
Northrop HS
Ft Wayne IN

De Pugh Tracy A
Huntington HS
Waverly OH

Deralas Dean
Barberton HS
Barberton OH

De Raud Michele
Plymouth Salem HS
Canton MI

Derda Julie
La Salle HS
South Bend IN

Deremer Diana
Canton South HS
Canton OH

Dericko Deborah
Grandview Heights HS
Columbus OH

Derisi Tom
Crown Point HS
Crown Point IN

Derks Douglas
Sparta HS
Conklin MI

De Ronghe Beth
Dominican HS
Detroit MI

Derr Jeffrey W
Huntington North HS
Huntington IN

Derr Vickie
Tuslaw HS
No Lawrnece OH

Derrickson Mike
Tri Jr Sr HS
New Lisbon IN

Derse Jayne
Groves HS
Birmingham MI

De Santis Anne
Bishop Gallagher HS
Harper Woods MI

De Sellem Marlene
Southern Local HS
Salineville OH

Desero Tina
Richmond HS
Richmond MI

Deskins Debbie
Big Creek HS
Coalwood WV

Detrick Tammy
Dublin HS
Dublin OH

Detwiler Scott
Marcellus Community HS
Decator MI

Detwiler Sharon
Tippicanoe Valley HS
Warsaw IN

Deuitch Matt
Greenfield Central HS
Greenfield IN

Deuley Robert
Calhoun HS
Mt Zion WV

De Vault Liz
Lowell HS
Lowell IN

De Vries Lexie
Fairmont West HS
Kettering OH

Dewaters Ronald
Hartland HS
Brighton MI

De Weese Margy
Fairlawn HS
Sidney OH

Dewey Elizabeth
Maumee Valley Cntry
Day Schl
Lambertville MI

De Wind John
Reeths Puffer Sr HS
Muskegon MI

De Witt Michael S
Rowlesburg HS
Rowlesburg WV

De Wolff Dea
Kalamazoo Christian HS
Kalamazoo MI

Dexter David
Muskegon Sr HS
Muskegon MI

Dey Lori
Oscoda Area HS
Saginaw MI

De Zarn Charles
La Salle HS
Cincinnati OH

Di Angelis Tammy
Weir HS
Weirton WV

Dian Moore Lisa
Van Buren HS
Brazil IN

Diaz Jose
Calumet HS
Gary IN

Di Cesare Francis
Steubenville Cath Ctrl HS
Wintersville OH

Dick Steve
Lincoln HS
Cambrid E IN

Dickerson Barbara
Kenton Sr HS
Kenton OH

Dickerson Natalie
Taylor HS
Cincinnati OH

Dickey Michael G
Anderson HS
Anderson IN

Dickinson Joseph
Wadsworth Sr HS
Wadsworth OH

Dickson Andrew C
Port Huron Northern HS
Port Huron MI

Dickson Everett J
Union HS
Jasonville IN

Di Domenico Kevin
Wintersville HS
Wintersville OH

Didomizio Tina
Hazel Park HS
Detroit MI

Diederick June
Midview HS
Elyria OH

Dieffenbaugher Lori
Jackson HS
North Canton OH

Diegel Vicki
Belleville HS
Belleville MI

Diehl Michael
Milton HS
Ona WV

Dieker Larry
St Charles Prep HS
Upper Arlington OH

Diener Dawn
Kearsley HS
Flint MI

Diener Jonathan
Bedford HS
Temperance MI

Dierna John S
Elyria Cath HS
Elyria OH

Dieterich Roy
Hedgesville HS
Falling Waters WV

Dietz Dale
Warren Central HS
Indianapolis IN

Dietz Hope L
Ft Frye HS
Beverly OH

Diez David C
Malabar HS
Mansfield OH

Diggins Sha Rea
Horace Mann HS
Gary IN

Di Gregorio Marianna C
East Detroit HS
East Detroit MI

Di Labio Lisa
Grosse Pointe N HS
Grosse Pt Fms MI

Di Lisio Geraldine M
Woodrow Wilson HS
Youngstown OH

Dill Lee Ann K
Holt HS
Holt MI

Dill Susan
Vandalia Butler HS
Dayton OH

Diller Karen
Cuyahoga Falls HS
Cuyahoga Fls OH

Dilley Donna
Pocahontas County HS
Marlinton WV

Dilley Gary
Riley HS
Clrksbrg WV

Dilley Pamela
Pocahontas County HS
Marlinton WV

Dillman Mitchell F
Lawrence Central HS
Indianapolis IN

Dillon Julia
St Peters HS
Mansfield OH

Dillon Mary E
Bedford Sr HS
Temperance MI

Dillon Samuel
Woodsfield HS
Woodsfield OH

Dillon Tony
Princeton Cmnty HS
Princeton IN

Dilts William
Philo HS
Ironsport OH

Diltz Lora
Bradford HS
Covington OH

Din Naveed A
Linsly Military Institute
Bethlehem Whlng WV

Dinka John
Grosse Pointe South HS
Grosse Pointe MI

Di Orio K
Kettering Fairmont West
HS
Kettering OH

Diorka Sandra
Essexville Garber HS
Essexville MI

Di Persi Renee
Liberty HS
Youngstown OH

Di Pietrantonio
Antoinette
St Ursula Academy
Cincinnati OH

Di Renzo Teresa
Boardman HS
Youngstown OH

Dirig Scott
Elmhurst HS
Ft Wayne IN

Dirksen Teresa
Marion Local HS
Maria Stein OH

Dirlam Dana
Delta HS
Muncie IN

Dirlam John E
Delta HS
Muncie IN

Dismore Terri
Henryville HS
Henryville IN

Dissinger Julie
Heath HS
Heath OH

Dittenber Susan
Au Gres Sims HS
Au Gres MI

Dittmer Terri M
Firelands HS
Berlin Heights OH

Dix Kevin
Paulding HS
Paulding OH

Dixon Charlotte L
Saginaw HS
Saginaw MI

Dixon Daniel
Waverly HS
Waverly OH

Dixon Hebrew L
Stivers Patterson HS
Dayton OH

Dixon Paul
Lincolnview Local HS
Van Wert OH

Dixon Sara
Lincolnview HS
Van Wert OH

Dobler Steve
Peru HS
Peru IN

Dobson Beth
Wellsville HS
Wellsville OH

Dobson Cathy
Vassar HS
Vassar MI

Dockery Ramona
North HS
Evansville IN

Dodd Cheryl
Jesup W Scott HS
Toledo OH

Dodd Lee A
Roosevelt Wilson HS
Clarksburg WV

Dodd Tonia
Whetstone HS
Columbus OH

Doerfler Kevin
Mc Comb HS
Mccomb OH

Doerfler Michael
Northwestern HS
Wooster OH

Dogan John
Coldwater HS
Coldwater MI

Doherty Colleen
Amelia HS
Amelia OH

Dokes Jennifer
Buckeye North HS
Smithfield OH

Dolan James
Pocahontas County HS
Arbovale WV

Doll Lynn
Bath HS
Dewitt MI

Doll Mary Beth
Mother Of Mercy HS
Cincinnati OH

Dolph Deborah K
Chesterton HS
Chesterton IN

Dolsen Ronald
Au Gres Sims HS
Au Gres MI

Dombrosky Patricia
Brooke HS
Wellsburg WV

Dominick Carlos
Collinwood HS
Cleveland OH

Donley Donna
Martins Ferry HS
Bridgeport OH

Donlin Colleen
Madison HS
Madison OH

Donnellon Dan
Moeller HS
Cincinnati OH

Donnelly Chris
Whiteford School
Ottawa Lk MI

Donohoe Lisa
Tuscarawas Cntrl Cath HS
Uhrichsville OH

Donohue Trina
West Branch HS
Homeworth OH

Donovan Angela
Holy Name Nazareth HS
Parma OH

Doolan Jean
Lakeshore HS
St Joseph MI

Doperalski Nora
Elston HS
Michigan City IN

Dorcey William J
Swan Valley HS
Saginaw MI

Doria Dawn
St Vincent St Mary HS
Akron OH

Dorich Annette
Madonna HS
Weirton WV

Dorotinsky William
John F Kennedy HS
Taylor MI

Dorris Lorrie
Shadyside HS
Shadyside OH

Dorris Teresa
Holly HS
Holly MI

Dorsey Linda
Tippecanoe Valley HS
Warsaw IN

Dorsten Peg
St Henry HS
Celina OH

Dortch Robin
London HS
W Jefferson OH

Dorton Vanessa A
Independence Jr Sr HS
Columbus OH

Dosa John J
Marlington HS
Alliance OH

Doseck Kevin
Memorial HS
St Marys OH

Dosmann Cathy
Brethren Christian HS
South Bend IN

Dosmann Rosemarie
Penn HS
Granger IN

Doss Cathy
Baptist Academy
Indianapolis IN

Doss Cheryl
Fairland HS
Proctorvll OH

Doster Dawn
Wayne Trace HS
Paulding OH

Doswald Caroline S
Kent Roosevelt HS
Kent OH

Dotson Cristal
Franklin Heights HS
Columbus OH

Dotson Kelly
South Charleston HS
S Charleston WV

Dotson Kim
Wayne Memorial HS
Wayne MI

Dotson Melissa
Groveport Madison Sr
HS
Groveport OH

Doughman J Shane
Gallia Academy HS
Gallipolis OH

Douglas Beth E
Fairview HS
Fairview Pk OH

Douglas Deana
Edison HS
Lake Station IN

Douglas Kelly
Clio Area HS
Clio MI

Douglas Valerie
Libbey HS
Toledo OH

Douthit Dorothy
Interlochen Arts
Academy
Concord MI

Douthitt Phil
Frankfort HS
Fort Ashby WV

Dove Lorri
Hedgesville HS
Hedgesville WV

Dovichi Lori
Marian HS
Blmfld Hls MI

Dowdell Jennifer
Yellow Springs HS
Yellow Sprg OH

Dowell Gregory
Clermont N E HS
Goshen OH

Dowler Bob
Groveport Madison HS
Groveport OH

Dowler Lynn
Groveport Madison HS
Groveport OH

Dowler Sandra
Heritage Jr Sr HS
New Haven IN

Dowling Cynthia D
West Technical HS
Cleveland OH

Dowling Dennis
Adrian Sr HS
Adrian MI

Dowmont Dineen
United HS
Salem OH

STUDENTS
PHOTOGRAPH
SCHEDULED
FOR PUBLI-
CATION HERE
COULD NOT
BE REPRO-
DUCED

Downer Rosalind F
Ecorse HS
Ecorse MI

Downey Carol
Berea HS
Berea OH

Downey Debra J
Berea HS
Berea OH

Downey Mark J
City HS
Grand Rapids MI

Downing Tami
Margaretta HS
Vickery OH

Downs Alan
Anderson HS
Cincinnati OH

Doyle Carolyn
Scecina Memorial HS
Indianapolis IN

Doyle Kyle
Loogootee HS
Loogootee IN

Doyle Sarah M
R Nelson Snider HS
Ft Wayne IN

Drabek Scott
Padua Franciscan HS
Parma OH

Drabick R Steven
Canton South HS
Canton OH

Draeger Sue
Clay Sr HS
Oregon OH

Drak Gerald J
Fruitport HS
Nunica MI

Drake Connie
Seeger HS
Williamsport IN

Drake James
Oregon Davis HS
Hamlet IN

Drake Karen
University HS
Morgantown WV

Drake Thomas J
Yorktown HS
Yorktown IN

Drakos Linda
Weir Sr HS
Weirton WV

Draper Jeffrey
Northfield HS
Roann IN

Draper Treva
Whitehall Yearling HS
Whitehall OH

Drazga Michael
Hamilton J Robichaud
HS
Dearborn Hts MI

Drennan III John F
Sts Peter & Paul Area
HS
Saginaw MI

Dresbach Norman
Teays Valley HS
Circleville OH

Dresbach jj Joe N
Southeastern Ross HS
Chillicothe OH

Drew Katie
Cathedral HS
Indianapolis IN

Driggers Troy
Carey HS
Carey OH

Driscoll Patrick
Moeller HS
Cincinnati OH

Driver Julia
Kalamazoo Central HS
Kalamazoo MI

Droll Lisa
St Wendelin HS
Fostoria OH

Droz Stephen B
Franklin HS
Westland MI

Drozdowski Katrina
Pinckney HS
Pinckney MI

Dubay Thomas W
Douglas Mac Arthur HS
Saginaw MI

Dubberly Steven
East Liverpool HS
E Liverpool OH

Dubbert Frederick R
Port Clinton HS
Port Clinton OH

Dubinin Peter
Goshen HS
Goshen IN

STUDENTS
PHOTOGRAPH
SCHEDULED
FOR PUBLI-
CATION HERE
COULD NOT
BE REPRO-
DUCED

Ducey James
Belleville HS
Belleville MI

Duch Terri
James A Garfield HS
Garrettsville OH

Du Chaine Julie
Escanaba Area Pub HS
Escanaba MI

Duck Terri
Southern Local HS
Wellsville OH

Duco Michael P
Steubenville Cath Cntrl
HS
Steubenvll OH

Duddles Kimberly
Lake Orion HS
Pontiac MI

Dudek Denise
Richmond HS
Richmond MI

Dudley Todd
Franklin Central HS
Indianapolis IN

Duff Gil
Deer Park HS
Cincinnati OH

Duff Robert
Walnut Ridge HS
Columbus OH

Duffey Erin
John Adams HS
So Bend IN

Duggan Joan K
Briggs HS
Columbus OH

Duggan Maureen
L Anse Creuse North HS
Mount Clemens MI

Dugger Dennis
Benton Harbor HS
Benton Hrbr MI

Du Hamel Kathryn L
Rochester Sr HS
Rochester MI

Duke James F
Milton Sr HS
Culloden WV

Duke Robert A
Winston Churchill HS
Livonia MI

Dukelow Scott R
Holt HS
Holt MI

Dula Jeffrey J
Solon HS
Solon OH

Du Laney Kevin D
John Marshall HS
Moundsville WV

Dular Janet
Kirtland HS
Kirtland OH

Dulberger Kehley
Park Tudor HS
Indianapolis IN

Dull Richard
John F Kennedy HS
Taylor MI

Dumford Dianna
Hagerstown Jr Sr HS
Hagerstown IN

Dumke Kimberly
Our Lady Of The Elms
HS
Stow OH

Du Moulin Robert
da HS
Monroe MI

Dunaway Joel
Brookville HS
Brookville IN

Dunaway Patrick
Connersville Sr HS
Connersville IN

Dunbar Theresa
Ben Davis HS
Indianapolis IN

STUDENTS
PHOTOGRAPH
SCHEDULED
FOR PUBLI-
CATION HERE
COULD NOT
BE REPRO-
DUCED

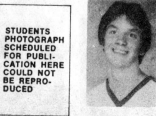
Duncan Casey E
Waldo J Wood Memorial
HS
Oakland City IN

Duncan Julie
Anderson HS
Anderson IN

Duncan Linda
Hundred HS
Hundred WV

Duncan Sandy
Peterstown HS
Ballard WV

Duncan Sharon
Parkersburg South HS
Washington WV

Dunham Denise
Winchester Community
HS
Winchester IN

Dunham Shelley
Van Wert HS
Van Wert OH

Dunigan Danette
Pike Central HS
Petersburg IN

Dunkel Erika
Berea HS
Berea OH

Dunlap Lloyd
Whitmore Lake HS
Whitmore Lk MI

Dunlap Valerie
Admiral King HS
Lorain OH

Dunn Brian
Van Wert HS
Van Wert OH

Dunn Joni J
North Knox HS
Bicknell IN

Dunn Lori
East Clinton HS
Sabina OH

Dunn Nancy
Norwood HS
Norwood OH

Dunnington Lee Ann
Buffalo HS
Huntington WV

Dunseth Colleen
Eisenhower HS
Utica MI

Dupler Micke
Frankfort Sr HS
Frankfort IN

Du Pree Deborah
Dowagiac Union HS
Dowagiac MI

Du Rant Debra
Watkins Memorial HS
Pataskala OH

Durbin Lori
Winchester Community
HS
Winchester IN

Durcanin Cynthia
Firestone HS
Akron OH

Duremdes Gene B
Princeton HS
Princeton WV

Duress Scott
Upper Sandusky HS
Upper Sandusky OH

Durham Dawn
Napoleon HS
Napoleon OH

Duricek Beth A
Notre Dame Academy
Rossford OH

Durkos Duane M
Pike HS
Lebanon IN

Durr Tracy
Bucyrus HS
Bucyrus OH

Durst Duane
Lakota HS
Burgoon OH

Durst Sandra
Ripley HS
Cottageville WV

Duska Geralyn
Catholic Central HS
Mingo Junction OH

Dussel Kathleen
Field HS
Kent OH

Dusseljee Mary
Holland Christian HS
Holland MI

Du Tiel Suzanne
Alexander HS
Amesville OH

Dutton Michael
Marion Harding HS
Marion OH

Du Vall Gregory
Greenville Sr HS
Greenville OH

Dvorscak Robert
George Rogers Clark HS
Whiting IN

Dye Keith
Hannan HS
Glenwood WV

Dye Mark A
Parkersburg HS
Vienna WV

Dye Sherry
Stanton HS
Salineville OH

Dyer Lounette
Orchard View HS
Muskegon MI

Dyer Patty
Meigs HS
Bidwell OH

Dygert Sally
Meadowdale HS
Dayton OH

Dyka Samuel M
Divine Child HS
Dearborn Hts MI

Dysert Deanna
Wellsville HS
Wellsville OH

Dziatkowicz Richard
Madonna HS
Weirton WV

Dzieciehowicz Mary
Nicholas County HS
Mt Nebo WV

Dzugan Paul
Crestline HS
Crestline OH

E

Eads Danette
Fergus HS
Lewistown MT

Eads Vicky
Bedford North Lawrence
HS
Bedford IN

Eagle Charles E
Newark Sr HS
Newark OH

Eagles Marc
Douglas Mac Arthur HS
Saginaw MI

Eakins Bryan
Penn HS
Osceola IN

Eakins Sharon
Rushville Consolidated
HS
Rushville IN

Earhart Cynthia
Lincoln West HS
Cleveland OH

Earley Pam
N Putnam Jr Sr HS
Greencastle IN

Eash Beverly
Pettisville HS
Wauseon OH

Kimberly S
North Posey Jr Sr HS
Poseyville IN

Easterday Craig
Wadsworth HS
Wadsworth OH

Easterlin Colleen
De Sales HS
Columbus OH

Eastin William
Carsonville Pt Sanilac HS
Pt Sanilac MI

Eastman Amy
River Valley HS
Caledonia OH

Eastman Tammy
Everett HS
Lansing MI

Eastwood Carol
Medina Sr HS
Medina OH

Eastwood Ronald
Medina Sr HS
Medina OH

Eaton Bruce
Portage Northern HS
Portage MI

Eaton James
Central HS
Evansville IN

Ebbesmier Rhonda
Ottawa Glandorf HS
Ottawa OH

Ebe Bill
Owosso HS
Owosso MI

Eberhard Laura
Wheeling Park HS
Wheeling WV

Eberhard Mark
Lutheran E HS
Detroit MI

Eberhart James R
East Liverpool HS
East Liverpool OH

Eberst Mary E
Westerville N HS
Westerville OH

Eblin Scott
Unioto HS
Chillicothe OH

Ebright Lori
Brookhaven HS
Columbus OH

Eckart Julie
Union County HS
Liberty IN

Ecker Kimberly
Forest Park HS
Cincinnati OH

Eckerle Sheila
Jasper HS
Jasper IN

Eckerman Robert C
Swan Valley HS
Saginaw MI

Eckert Debra A
Princeton Community HS
Princeton IN

Eckhart Barbara
Parkersburg South HS
Parkersburg WV

Eckley Joseph P
Stivers Patterson Co Op
HS
Dayton OH

Eckman Denise
Lansing Christian HS
Lansing MI

Economou Jennifer
Turpin HS
Cincinnati OH

Eddy Brenda
Parkersburg HS
Vienna WV

Eddy Debra
Frontier HS
Reno OH

Eddy Joseph
Sistersville HS
Friendly WV

Edens Jeff
Peterstown HS
Ballard WV

Edgar Tim
Wadsworth Sr HS
Wadsworth OH

Edgecomb Julie
Yale HS
Yale MI

Edmond Tim
Tiffin Columbian HS
Tiffin OH

Edmonds Christopher
Thomas A De Vilbiss HS
Toledo OH

Edmonds Jonathan
Ravenna City HS
Ravenna OH

Edmondson James A
Manistee Catholic Cntrl
HS
Manistee MI

Edwards Angela
Immaculata HS
Detroit MI

Edwards Cynthia
Roy C Start HS
Toledo OH

Edwards Danice
South Lyon HS
So Lyon MI

Edwards Daniel B
Woodrow Wilson HS
Beckley WV

Edwards Douglas Pike Central HS Petersburg IN	Edwards Elizabeth Bedford N Lawrence HS Bedford IN	Edwards John Greenfield Central HS Greenfield IN	Edwards Marilyn Chesapeake HS Chesapeake OH	Edwards Mary B Cardinal Mooney HS Youngstown OH	Edwards Monica Covington HS Covington IN	Edwards Percola Cass Tech HS Detroit MI

Edwards Rebecca
Eastern Local HS
Long Bottom OH

Edwards Steve
Pinconning HS
Pinconning MI

Egert Debbie
Genoa Area HS
Millbury OH

Egg Laura
Marion Harding HS
Marion OH

Eggeman Catherine
Delphos St John HS
Delphos OH

Egnew Teresa
Central HS
Evansville IN

Egtvedt Richard T
Comstock Park HS
Comstock Pk MI

Ehrhart Jeffrey
Salem Sr HS
Salem OH

Ehrman Brian
Buckeye Central HS
New Washington OH

Ehrman Joanne
Nordonia HS
Macedonia OH

Ehrnsberger Mark
Margaretta HS
Bay View OH

Ehrsam Eric
Cascade HS
Danville IN

Eib Larry
Springfield HS
Springfield MI

Eichenauer Todd
Sidney HS
Sidney OH

Eichenberger William
New Albany HS
New Albany IN

Eicher Melissa J
Catholic Central HS
Steubenvll OH

Eichorst John P
Clay HS
South Bend IN

Eiken Amy
West Carrollton HS
Dayton OH

Eisbrenner Laura
Watervliet HS
Watervliet MI

Eisenach Randall
Northrop HS
Ft Wayne IN

Eisenman Willia
Marietta Sr HS
Marietta OH

Eisenmann Cheryl
Summerfield HS
Petersburg MI

Eisenmann Deborah L
Summerfield HS
Petersburg MI

Eisentrout Sylvia J
University HS
Morgantown WV

Eitniear Vicki
Hesperia HS
Hesperia MI

Eix Laura
Northrop HS
Ft Wayne IN

El Campbell Theresa E
Hammond HS
Hammond IN

Elder Patrice
Oak Hill HS
Oak Hill WV

Eldridge Ambra
Van Buren HS
Brazil IN

Eldridge Kevin
Lakota HS
W Chester OH

Elek Marcia
Midview HS
Elyria OH

Eley Linda
Niles Sr HS
Niles MI

Eliachevsky Andrew
Paul K Cousino Sr HS
Warren MI

Eliopoulos Janet
Andrean HS
Cary IN

Elkins Garry
Medora HS
Medora IN

Elkins Sandra
Oak Hill HS
Oak Hill WV

Eller Kathy
Ashtabula HS
Ashtabula OH

Eller Kevin
Belleville HS
Belleville MI

Ellert Ted
De Kalb HS
Waterloo IN

Ellington Jeffery
Wilbur Wright HS
Dayton OH

Elliott Gregory
Garfield HS
Akron OH

Elliott Jennifer
Ashtabula Harbor HS
Ashtabula OH

Elliott Karen S
Bellefontaine HS
Bellefontaine OH

Elliott Laura E
Solon HS
Solon OH

Elliott Lesley
Sidney HS
Sidney OH

Elliott Lori
West Washington HS
Fredericksburg IN

Elliott Valerie
Loogootee HS
Loogootee IN

Ellis Alan M
Washington HS
So Bend IN

Ellis Courtenay F
Seven Hills HS
Lexington KY

Ellis David
Norton HS
Norton OH

Ellis David
Carey HS
Carey OH

Ellis Ella
Pike Central HS
Spurgeon IN

Ellis Jana
Chesapeake HS
Chesapeake OH

Ellis Kelly
Chesaning Union HS
Chesaning MI

Ellis Kimberly
Southmont HS
Crawfordsville IN

Ellis Linda
Niles Mc Kinley HS
Niles OH

Ellis Lynn
Jeffersonville HS
Jeffersonville IN

Ellis Rebecca
Twin Lakes HS
Monticello IN

Ellis Theresa
Michigan Ctr HS
Michigan Center MI

Ellis Vernon
Sheridan HS
Somerset OH

Ellis William
Park Hills HS
Wp Afb OH

Ellison Brenda
Madison Heights HS
Anderson IN

Ellison Deanne L
Spencer HS
Spencer WV

Ellison Patricia S
Hoover HS
North Canton OH

Elliston Cindy
Maple Valley HS
Nashville MI

Elmore Rhonda
Jefferson HS
Newport MI

Elowsky Beth
Bay City Western HS
Bay City MI

Elrod Brenda
Northfield HS
Wabash IN

Elston Donna
Eau Claire HS
Riverside MI

Elswick Joetta
St Francis Cabrini HS
Ecorse MI

Eltzroth Cynthia
Peru HS
Peru IN

Ely Jon
Charleston HS
Charleston WV

Elzinga Darryl
West Ottawa HS
Holland MI

Embrey David
Farwell HS
Farwell MI

Emerson Sandra
Wapakoneta Sr HS
Wapakoneta OH

Emery Mary
Roscommon HS
Roscommon MI

Emigh Kevin D
Elisabeth Johnson HS
Mt Morris MI

Emmanoelides Demetrios
Washington HS
E Chicago IN

Emmel Shannon
Lincoln HS
Gypsy WV

Emmons Donna
New Albany HS
New Albany OH

Emmons Monica R
Springfield South HS
Springfield OH

Endel Barbara
Waynesfield Goshen HS
Wapokoneta OH

Endelman Julie
Algonac HS
Algonac MI

Endelman Karen
Marysville HS
Marysville MI

Enderle Allison
Columbus North HS
Columbus OH

Endres Lucy
Talawanda HS
Oxford OH

Engelbach Kirk
Timken Sr HS
Canton OH

Engelhardt David
Arthur Hill HS
Saginaw MI

England Brian
Heath HS
Heath OH

England Cynthia
Heath HS
Newark OH

England Julie
Manchester HS
Manchester MI

England Lori
Manchester HS
Manchester MI

England Terri
Herbert Hoover HS
Elkview WV

Engle Melinda
Bellmont HS
Decatur IN

Engler James
Washington HS
Massillon OH

Englert Michael
Shenandoah HS
Middletown IN

English Elizabeth
Nitro HS
Charleston WV

Ensign Mark
Austin Town Fitch HS
Youngstown OH

Ensinger Becky
River HS
Sardis OH

Epling Scot A
Spencer HS
Spencer WV

Epperson Terry
Covington HS
Covington IN

Ercoline Laura
Bluefield HS
Bluefield WV

Erdmann Lisa
Linton Stockton HS
Linton IN

Erdos Joseph
Cadiz HS
New Athens OH

Erhardt Julie
Spring Lake HS
Spring Lake MI

Erich Janet
Willoughby South HS
Will Hills OH

Erickson Kathy J
Reed City HS
Reed City MI

Erisman Jeffrey
Valley View HS
Frmrsvl OH

Ernst Barbara
Western Brown Sr HS
Bethel OH

Ernst Lisa
Archbishop Alter HS
Centerville OH

Ervin Laura
Miami Trace HS
Wash C H OH

Eschleman Michael
Wintersville HS
Bloomingdale OH

Esper Laura
Clarenceville HS
Livonia MI

Esper Linda
Miami Trace HS
Washington Ch OH

Espinosa Paul A
Jefferson HS
Charles Town WV

Esposito Carmela
Fenwick HS
Middletown OH

Essex Alicia
Walnut Ridge HS
Columbus OH

Essex David
Walnut Ridge HS
Columbus OH

Estadt Michael
Zanesville Rosecrans HS
Zanesville OH

Estep Diane
Ontario HS
Mansfield OH

Estes Pamela
Central Hower HS
Akron OH

Eubank Glenda
Addison HS
Addison MI

Eurich Dawn
Arthur Hill HS
Saginaw MI

Evanowski Letitia
St Francis Cabrini HS
Allen Park MI

Evans Beth
Westlake HS
Westlake OH

Evans Jami
Brandon HS
Ortonville MI

Evans Jane
Newark Sr HS
Newark OH

Evans Karen
Monroe HS
Monroe MI

Evans Kelly
Dunbar HS
Dunbar WV

Evans Laura E
Van Wert HS
Van Wert OH

Evans Laurel
Benzie Central HS
Frankfort MI

Evans L Tanya C
Newark Sr HS
Newark OH

Evans Margaret
Bluefield HS
Bluefield WV

Evans Michael
Clarkston Sr HS
Clarkston MI

Evans Nora
Manistique HS
Manistique MI

Evans Pam
Southport HS
Indianapolis IN

Evans Robert
Woodrow Wilson HS
Dunbar WV

Evans Sally
Chardon HS
Chardon OH

Evans Suzanne M
Vassar HS
Millington MI

Evans Teresa
Allen E HS
Harrod OH

Evans Valerie
Lakeview Sr HS
St Clair Shores MI

Eveland Cathy
Hilligard HS
Hilliard OH

Evens David
North Putnam HS
Fillmore IN

Evens Lynne
Reeths Putter HS
Muskegon MI

Evens Mark A
Lewis County HS
Weston WV

Everett Camille
Chesapeake HS
Cheaspeake OH

STUDENTS
PHOTOGRAPH
SCHEDULED
FOR PUBLI-
CATION HERE
COULD NOT
BE REPRO-
DUCED

Everman Diana L
East Clinton HS
Sabina OH

Everman Jan M
Celina Sr HS
Celina OH

Eversole Jami
Franklin HS
Franklin OH

Everson Mary
T L Handy HS
Bay City MI

Everts Duana
North Putnam Jr Sr HS
Greencastle IN

Evoy Kerry
Marion Adams HS
Sheridan IN

Ewart Glenn
Springfield Township HS
Akron OH

Ewart Kathleen
London HS
London OH

Ewell Timothy
Concordia Lutheran HS
Ft Wayne IN

Ewin Karen
Boonville HS
Boonville IN

Ewing Amy
Greenfield Cntrl HS
Greenfield IN

Ewing Kelly
Scott HS
Toledo OH

Ewing Robert L
Brebeuf Preparatory HS
Indianapolis IN

Exner Ellen
Avondale HS
Bloomfield Hil MI

Exum Marc H
William A Wirt HS
Gary IN

Eyster Jeffrey
Northwest HS
Indianapolis IN

Ezzo Dawn
Liberty HS
Hubbard OH

F

Fabian Henry
Lutheran HS West
Clveland OH

Fabian Lisa
Bishop Dwenger HS
Ft Wayne IN

Fabian Mary B
Campbell Memorial HS
Campbell OH

Fabyan Peter
Bad Axe HS
Bad Axe MI

Fadero Stephen
Bluefield HS
Bluefield WV

Fadil Gary
St Edward HS
Middleburg Hts OH

Faflick Lori
Fairview HS
Fairview Pk OH

Fagen Peggy
Lake Central HS
Dyer IN

Fagerlund Marcia
Mt Pleasant HS
Mt Pleasant MI

Fair Elaine
Beechcroft Sr HS
Columbus OH

Fair Eugene
Federal Hocking HS
Athens OH

Fairchild Greg
Hesperia HS
Hesperia MI

Fairchild John
Green HS
Uniontown OH

Fairchild Linda
Mother Of Mercy HS
Cincinnati OH

Faire Michelle
Merrillville Sr HS
Merrillville IN

Fairfield Holly
Western Boone Jr Sr HS
Thorntown IN

Fairfull Harold
Western Reserve
Academy
Mountain View CA

Falconberry Wade
Lockland HS
Cincinnati OH

Fallen Robin
Wirt County HS
Palestine WV

Faller Shelly
Cuyahoga Falls HS
Cuyahoga Fls OH

Fallon Ann
St Joseph Academy
Cleveland OH

Falls Ralph L
Ironton HS
Ironton OH

Falstad Todd
Quincy HS
Quincy MI

Falter Marilyn
Seneca East HS
Bellevue OH

Fant Linnea
Chesterton HS
Chesterton IN

Farkas David
Barberton HS
Barberton OH

Farlee Lenny
Brown Cnty HS
Nashville IN

Farley Amy
Hoover HS
North Canton OH

Farley Cathy
Princeton HS
Princeton WV

Farley Roger
Princeton HS
Princeton WV

Farlie Brenda
Garden City West Sr HS
Gardencity MI

Farmer Betsy
Mathews HS
Cortland OH

Farmer Dwight
Terre Haute South Vigo
HS
Terre Haute IN

Farmer Ed
New Haven HS
New Haven MI

Farmer Kathryn
Gods Bible HS
Huntington WV

Farmer Mary
Mount View HS
Pageton WV

Farnalcher Teresa
Marysville HS
Marysville OH

Farnan Eva M
Sacred Heart Academy
Shepherd MI

Farno Dawn
Upper Valley JVS
Pleasant Hill OH

Farnsworth Jewell
Buckhannon Upshur HS
Buckhannon WV

Farr Scott
Hamilton Southeastern
HS
Noblesville IN

Farrell Christopher
St Xavier HS
Cincinnati OH

Farrell Dianne
South Newton Jr Sr HS
Kentland IN

Farrell Kathy
Magnificat HS
Bay Village OH

Farrell Patricia
Northwood HS
Northwood OH

Farrell Rhonda
Pennsboro HS
Pennsboro WV

Farrens Candy
East Canton HS
E Canton OH

Farris Scott
Bloomfield HS
Bloomfield IN

Farrow Gary L
Benton Carroll Salem HS
Oak Harbor OH

Farrow Greg
North Putnam HS
Roachdale IN

Farrow Michael
Brookville HS
New Trenton IN

Farruggia Mary
Independence HS
Rhodell WV

Fassler Curtis
Pleasant HS
Marion OH

Faulkens Robert
South Bend La Salle HS
South Bend IN

Faulkner Beth
Wayne HS
Ft Wayne IN

Faulkner Cheryl
Gavit Jr Sr HS
Hammond IN

Faulkner Pamela
Brownsburg HS
Brownsburg IN

Faurote Beth
Bellmont HS
Decatur IN

Faust Kathleen
Peru Sr HS
Peru IN

Fayne Priscilla
East HS
Cleveland OH

Fazio Ann M
Bishop Gallagher HS
Detroit MI

Fazio Frank
Cloverleaf HS
Seville OH

Feasel Nick
Elmwood HS
Bloomdale OH

Feathers Paul
Delphos Jefferson HS
Delphos OH

Federspiel Holly
Arthur Hill HS
Saginaw MI

Feierstein Bryan
Greenville Sr HS
Greenville OH

Felcyn Wendy
Dwight D Eisenhower HS
Rochester MI

Feldman Becky
Waldo J Wood Memorial
HS
Oakland City IN

Feldt Charles
Mona Shores HS
Muskegon MI

Felger Mark
Garrett HS
La Otto IN

Felix Dawn
William Henry Harrison
HS
W Lafayette IN

Fellows Chris
Anchor Bay HS
New Baltimore MI

Felten Brian
New Haven HS
New Have IN

Feltman John W
Shepherd Public HS
Shepherd MI

Fenderson Audrey
Malabar HS
Mansfield OH

Fennell Andrew
Gladwin HS
Gladwin MI

Fennell James C
Pleasant Local HS
Marion OH

Fennell Margaret
Warren Woods HS
Warren MI

Fenstermacher Bruce
Edwardsburg HS
Edwardsburg MI

Fenton Kim
Bloom Local HS
So Webster OH

Feranchak Catherine
Trinity HS
Youngstown OH

Ferber Mark
Edison HS
Berlin Heights OH

Ferdinand Victor
Jackson HS
Canal Fulton OH

Ferguson Juli
Brownstown Central HS
Freetown IN

Ferguson Kim
Ft Frye HS
Beverly OH

Ferguson Lana
Warsaw Community HS
Warsaw IN

Ferguson Marianne
Graham HS
St Paris OH

Ferguson Melodie
Fredericktown HS
Mtvernon OH

Ferguson Norman
Maumee HS
Maumee OH

Ferguson V Wayne
Alcona HS
Hubbard Lake MI

Ferkany James
Grand Blanc HS
Grand Blanc MI

Fernandez Mildred
Adelphian Academy
Flint MI

Fernandez Miriam
Adelphian Academy
Flint MI

Fernett Larry K
Stonewall Jackson HS
Charleston WV

Ferrare Micci
South Vermillion HS
Clinton IN

Ferrell Shawn
Southeastern HS
Richmondale OH

Ferrell Tammy
Grove City HS
Orient OH

Ferreri Anthony M
Chaney HS
Youngstown OH

Ferri Barbara
Mifflin Sr HS
Columbus OH

Ferrier Victoria
St Marys HS
St Marys WV

Ferris Tamara
Ionia HS
Lyons MI

Ferry Carole
Theodore Roosevelt HS
Kent OH

Ferry Tom
Linton Stockton HS
Linton IN

Fesmire Roy
Marquette Sr HS
Marquette MI

Fessier Renee
South Dearborn HS
Aurora IN

Fetters Mike
Hilliard HS
Lexington OH

Fetty Candy
East Liverpool HS
E Liverpool OH

Fetty Margaret
Buckhannon Upshur HS
Buckhannon WV

Feutz Douglas
Eminence Consolidated
HS
Quincy IN

Fiber Charles
Lincoln HS
Lumberport WV

Fieberkorn Karla
Burr Oak HS
Sturgis MI

Fiedler Kim
Logansport HS
Logansport IN

Fiedler Roy W
Vermilion HS
Vermilion OH

Field Elizabeth A
Lawrence N HS
Indianapolis IN

Fields Byron
Decatur Central HS
Indnpls IN

Fields Edward D
Madison Comprehensive
HS
Mansfield OH

Fields Gregory
Grosse Pte North HS
Grosse Pt Wds MI

Fields Jody
Eastern HS
Owensburg IN

Fields Kathy
Kouts HS
Kouts IN

Fields Kim
Anderson HS
Anderson IN

Fields Lorri
Marion HS
Marion IN

Fields Teresa L
Austin HS
Austin IN

Figlar Edward
St Edward HS
Lakewood OH

Figuracion Angeli
L C Mohr HS
South Haven MI

Filiccia Barri
Holy Redeemer HS
Detroit MI

Filippi Douglas
Buckeye North HS
Smithfield OH

Filisznowski Debra
Grafton HS
Clarksburg WV

Filson Loran
Greenfield Central HS
Greenfield IN

Fincel David A
Lakota Sr HS
Middletown OH

Finchio Lillian
Jenison HS
Jenison MI

Finders Janice
Calumet HS
Goodland KS

Findley Jeffrey
Lorain Catholic HS
Lorain OH

Fineran Marcella
Lewis County HS
Ireland WV

Finfrock Gregory
Martinsburg HS
Martinsburg WV

Finley Jon
Greensburg Community
HS
Greensburg IN

Finley Lee
Sandy Valley HS
E Sparta OH

Finley Leonard
Calumet HS
Gary IN

Finn Grant
Water Ford Kettering HS
Drayton Plains MI

Finnessy Lynn M
Northwestern HS
West Salem OH

Finney Devenia
Lutheran HS East
Cleveland OH

Finstrom Kathleen
Cadillac Sr HS
Cadillac MI

Finzer Steve
Turpin HS
Cincinnati OH

Fiore Maria
Clay HS
S Bend IN

Fiorilli Robert
St Ignatius HS
S Euclid OH

Firestone Deborah
Pathfinder HS
Northport MI

Fischbach Leslie
Nazareth Acad
Parma OH

Fischer Lori
Brandon HS
Ortonville MI

Fish Deborah
Rochester Cmnty HS
Rochester IN

Fish Rhonda
Brownstown Central HS
Brownstown IN

Fisher Barbara
Bluffton HS
Bluffton OH

Fisher Brian
Cascade HS
Clayton IN

Fisher Debbie
Belpre HS
Little Hockng OH

Fisher Denver S
Dunbar HS
Dunbar WV

Fisher Jackie
Martinsville HS
Martinsville IN

Fisher Jeffrey B
Princeton Community HS
Princeton IN

Fisher Kelli
Chillicothe HS
Chillicothe OH

Fisher Laura
Rutherford B Hayes HS
Delaware OH

Fisher Loman T
Warren County Joint Voc
HS
Franklin OH

Fisher Marcy
Fulton HS
Perrinton MI

Fisher Mark
Grove City HS
Grove City OH

Fisher Mary Beth
Bishop Luers HS
Ft Wayne IN

Fisher Michael
Mason HS
Erie MI

Fisher Rebecca
Tippecanoe Vly HS
Mentone IN

Fisher Sandra
Immaculate Conception
Acad
Batesville IN

Fisher Shawn A
St Martin De Porres HS
Detroit MI

Fitch Caroline
Mc Auley HS
Cinti OH

Fitzgerald Craig
Shepherd HS
Mt Pleasant MI

Fitzgerald Kellee
Poland Seminary HS
Poland OH

Fitzgerald Pamela L
Washington HS
Washington IN

Fitz Gerald Sean
Bishop Borgess HS
Detroit MI

Fitzpatrick Jackie
Carson City Crystal HS
Fowler MI

Fitzwater Margaret
Philip Barbour HS
Philippi WV

Fix Lucinda J
Shelbyville Sr HS
Shelbyville IN

Fix Richard
Rossford HS
Perrysburg OH

Flaherty Mary V
Liberty HS
Clarksburg WV

STUDENTS
PHOTOGRAPH
SCHEDULED
FOR PUBLI-
CATION HERE
COULD NOT
BE REPRO-
DUCED

Flake James
Portsmouth East HS
Portsmouth OH

Flanders Lauren L
Federal Hocking HS
Guysville OH

Flanigan Dana
Lawrence Central HS
Indianapolis IN

Flannery Jill
Bad Axe HS
Bad Axe MI

Flannery Kelly
Summit Country Day HS
Batavia OH

Flannery Patrick O
Hamilton Taft HS
Hamilton OH

Flannery Sharon
Glen Este HS
Cincinnati OH

Flaugher Roger
Beal City HS
Weidman MI

Fleck Debra A
Celina Sr HS
Celina OH

Fleck Tony
Liberty Benton HS
Findlay OH

Fleener Todd
Martinsville HS
Martinsville IN

Fleenor Paula
Chalker HS
Southington OH

Fleer Liane
Maysville HS
Zanesville OH

Flegel Richard
Ithaca HS
Ithaca MI

Fleischer David
Withrow Sr HS
Cincinnati OH

Fleming Chris
Gull Lake HS
Augusta MI

Fleming Dawn
Lansing Everett HS
Lansing MI

Fleming Nancy
Bellmont HS
Decatur IN

Fleming Robert L
William Henry Harrison
HS
Evansville IN

Flennoy Lalah
Immaculata HS
Detroit MI

Fletcher Carol
Forest Hills Central HS
Grand Rapids MI

Fletcher John
East HS
Akron OH

Fletcher Karen
Cameron HS
Glen Easton WV

Fletcher Tina
North White HS
Monon IN

Flewelling Thomas
Niles Sr HS
Niles MI

Flick Mindy
Kankakee Vly HS
Rensselaer IN

Flinn Anne
Grandview Heights HS
Columbus OH

Flinn Carol
Schoolcraft HS
Schoolcraft MI

Flockenhaus Michael
Rossford HS
Rossford OH

Florea Richard W
Elwood Cmnty HS
Elwood IN

Florence Kimberly
Goshen HS
Goshen OH

Flowers Barry
Frankfort HS
Ft Ashby WV

Flowers Karen M
Horace Mann HS
Gary IN

Flowers Kenneth
Cass Technical HS
Detroit MI

Floyd Candace
Brooke HS
Follansbee WV

Floyd James M
Greenbrier East HS
Lewisbrg WV

Floyd Kathy
Eastmoor Sr HS
Columbus OH

Floyd Rosalind
Highland Park Comm HS
Highland Pk MI

Fluegge Veronica
Michigan Lutheran
Seminary
Elkton MI

Fluharty Kimberly J
Fairview HS
Fairview WV

Fluharty Lisa
Mannington HS
Mannington WV

Fluharty Rebecca A
Lincoln HS
Wallace WV

Flynn Frank
Heath HS
Heath OH

Flynn Marra
Springfield Catholic HS
London OH

Focke Julie
Archbishop Alter HS
Kettering OH

Fogle De Lynn
Southfield Christian HS
Orchard Lake MI

Fogle Tammy L
Dayton Christian HS
Dayton OH

Fogleman Gary
Woodrow Wilson HS
Beckley WV

Fogt Eldon G
Madison Heights HS
Anderson IN

Foland Sheila
Mississinewa HS
Marion IN

Foltz Chris
Southern Wells HS
Geneva IN

Foltz Donald
Mathias HS
Mathias WV

Foltz Timothy C
South Vermillion HS
Clinton IN

Fonner Thomas
Magnolia HS
New Martinsvle WV

Fonte Leisa
Sandy Valley HS
Magnolia OH

Ford Darlene M
Immaculata HS
Detroit MI

Ford David
Harper Creek HS
Battle Creek MI

Ford Eugene
Monroe HS
Monroe MI

Ford Illice
Highland Park
Community HS
Highland Park MI

Ford Kevin
Pike Delta York Sr HS
Delta OH

Ford Lisa
Licking Valley HS
Newark OH

Ford Lula
Federal Hocking HS
Amesville OH

Ford Matthew
Moeller HS
Cincinnati OH

Ford Ramona
Benton Harbor Sr HS
Benton Hrbr MI

Foreman Brad
Maumee HS
Maumee OH

Foreman David
Southern HS
Portland OH

Forker Brad
Garrett HS
Garrett IN

Forkert Richard
Elmhurst HS
Ft Wayne IN

Forman Angela
Hopewell Loudon HS
Fostoria OH

Forman Mindy
Oak Hill HS
Oak Hill WV

Forney Myrna
Regina HS
Cleveland Hts OH

Forrest L Arick
Dublin HS
Columbus OH

Forry Sandra
L C Mohr HS
S Haven MI

Forth Laura
Dawson Bryant HS
Coal Grove OH

Fortier Virginia
Davison Sr HS
Davison MI

Fortner Guy R
Western Hills HS
Cincinnati OH

Forton Jennifer
Lanse Creuse HS
Mt Clemens MI

Fortuna Nancy
Perry Meridian HS
Indianpolis IN

Forward Sheryl
Western HS
Jackson MI

Fosdick Karen
St Marys Cathedral HS
Gaylord MI

Fosheim Lisa
Fairborn Baker HS
Fairborn OH

Foss John
Delton Kellog HS
Delton MI

Fossnock Doreen
Clinton Prairie HS
Frankfort IN

Foster Audrey
New Haven HS
New Haven MI

Foster Carol
Southgate HS
Southgate MI

Foster Kathy
Kenowa Hills HS
Grand Rapids MI

Foster Kevin N
Robert S Rogers HS
Toledo OH

Foster Mark
Oak Hill HS
Oak Hill WV

Foster Regina
Gauley Bridge HS
Gauley Bridge WV

Foster Shelley
Fountain Cntrl HS
Hillsboro IN

Fountain Carol
Ida HS
Ida MI

Fournier Serge
John Glenn HS
Canton MI

Foust Alice
Parkside HS
Jackson MI

Foust Cindy
Poland Seminary HS
Poland OH

Fout Eric
Hobart Sr HS
Hobart IN

Fout William
Riverdale HS
Forest OH

Fouts Debbie
N Miami HS
Deedsville IN

Fouty Douglas
Columbia Central HS
Clark Lake MI

Fouty Terria
Spencer HS
Spencer WV

Foutz Jim
Greenville Sr HS
Greenville OH

Fowler Anita
North Putnam HS
Bainbridge IN

Fowler Gary
Mt Healthy HS
Cincinnati OH

Fowler Nina
South Vigo HS
Terre Haute IN

Fowler Tracey
Coventry HS
Akron OH

Fowler William R
Highland Park Comm HS
Highland Park MI

Fowlkes Ronda M
Immaculata HS
Detroit MI

Fowlkes Tonya
Immaculata HS
Detroit MI

Fox Beth
Lansing Catholic Ctrl HS
Lansing MI

Fox Diane
Lakeview HS
Cortland OH

Fox Elaine
Otsego HS
Tontogany OH

Fox Frank
Lake Michigan Catholic
HS
Sodus MI

Fox Fred
Bishop Noll Inst
Hammond IN

Fox Janet
Doddridge Cnty HS
West Union WV

Fox Kathy
Franklin Community HS
Franklin IN

Fox Kimberly A
Independence HS
Sophia WV

Fox Melissa
Westerville North HS
Westerville OH

Fox Steven
Douglas Mac Arthur HS
Saginaw MI

Foxworth Mary
Northwestern HS
Flint MI

Foy Mary
Holt HS
Holt MI

Fraley Anita
Shady Spring HS
Shady Spring WV

Fraley Charles
Fort Gay HS
Ft Gay WV

Fraley Kathleen D
Clear Fork HS
Dorothy WV

Fralich Rebecca
Beecher HS
Flint MI

Frame Denise M
Northeastern HS
Williamsburg IN

Frame K
Calhoun County HS
Millstone WV

Frame Ted
North Central HS
Pioneer OH

Frampton Tracey
Culver Girls Academy
Columbus OH

Francis Deborah
Liberty HS
Clarksburg WV

Francis Vicki
Zane Trace HS
Chillicothe OH

Frank Carrie
Traverse City Sr HS
Traverse City MI

Frank Denise E
Stryker HS
Stryker OH

Frank Lynn
Southfield Christian HS
Birmingham MI

Frank Robert M
Euclid Sr HS
Euclid OH

Frank Teresa
Marlington HS
Louisville OH

Frank William E
Perry HS
Massillon OH

Franklin Beth
Harding HS
Marion OH

Franklin Harriet
Point Pleasant HS
Pt Pleasant WV

Franklin Stanley E
Brookfield HS
Brookfield OH

Franks Donna
Hillsdale HS
Jeromesville OH

Franks Laurie
Liberty Benton HS
Findlay OH

Franks Melanie
Olivet HS
Olivert MI

Franks Richard
Columbia City Joint HS
Columbia City IN

Frantz Neal
Whitko HS
Sidney IN

Frantz Wendy
Eaton HS
Eaton OH

Franz Toni
Chippewa Hills HS
Stanwood MI

Franze Jeff
Bellmont HS
Decatur IN

Franze Linda
East HS
Akron OH

Fraser Elizabeth
Washington Irving HS
Clarksburg WV

Frasure Lisa D
Fairfield Union HS
Bremen OH

Fratino Philip
Lake Catholic HS
Willoughby OH

Fravel David
Groveport Madison HS
St Paul MN

Frazier Beverly
Amelia HS
Amelia OH

Frazier Donna
Hilliard HS
Columbus OH

Frazier Julie A
Watervliet HS
Watervliet MI

Fredeking William
Princeton HS
Princeton WV

Fredenburg Catherine
Mason Sr HS
Mason MI

Frederick Karen
Lumen Christi HS
Jackson MI

Frederick Karla
Crestline HS
Crestline OH

Frederick Nina
Calhoun County HS
Nobe WV

Frederickson Sydney
Nordonia HS
Northfield OH

Free Almena
Rogers HS
Michigan City IN

Freed Pamela
Ithaca HS
Sumner MI

Freehling Donna
Au Gres Sims HS
Au Gres MI

STUDENTS PHOTOGRAPH SCHEDULED FOR PUBLICATION HERE COULD NOT BE REPRODUCED

Freeland Linda
Benton Central HS
Fowler IN

Freels Jed
Northrop HS
Ft Wayne IN

Freeman Christie
Hamilton Southeastern HS
Noblesville IN

Freeman Dell
South Point HS
South Point OH

Freeman Douglas
Clyde Sr HS
Fremont OH

Freeman Douglas J
Creston HS
Grand Rapids MI

Freeman L
Triway HS
Wooster OH

Freeman Marie
Scott HS
Madison WV

Freeman Tina
Arsenal Tech HS
Indianapolis IN

Freemon Doug
The Miami Valley Schl
Kettering OH

Freer Janet
Eaton Rapids Sr HS
Eaton Rapids MI

Freer Rebecca
Muskegon HS
Muskegon MI

Freese Carolyn
Washington Irving HS
Clarksburg WV

Freeze John
Peebles HS
Peebles OH

Freiburger Julie
Bishop Dwenger HS
Ft Wayne IN

French Brenda
Cardington Lincoln HS
Cardington OH

French Gregory
Shortridge HS
Indianapolis IN

Frens Gregory
Fremont Public HS
Newaygo MI

Frerichs Donald J
East Kentwood HS
Hudsonville MI

Freshwater Michael
Brooke HS
Wellsburg WV

Frey Russell
Napoleon HS
Jackson MI

Frichtl Kathleen
Bishop Noll Institute
Calumet City IL

Friddle Kevin
Alcona HS
Barton City MI

Friedrichs Necia M
Wheeling Park HS
Wheeling WV

Friend Laura
Brookville HS
Connersville IN

Friend Melinda
Keyser HS
Keyser WV

Fries Joel
Monroeville HS
Monroeville OH

Friesenborg Trudy
Fairmont West HS
Kettering OH

Friess Brent
Corunna HS
Corunna MI

Frink Carla
Fountain Central HS
Kingman IN

Frischkorn Mary
Anderson HS
Anderson IN

Fritinger Amy
Lake Catholic HS
Pnsvl OH

Fritz Beth
Beaver Local HS
E Liverpool OH

Fritz Kaye
Centennial HS
Columbus OH

Frizzell Regina
Eastern HS
Pekin IN

Frizzell Sue
Hammond Baptist HS
Hammond IN

Froehlich Paul M
Barnesville HS
Barnesville OH

Frohriep Denise C
Colon HS
Colon MI

Fronczek Andrew
Eastlake North HS
Eastlake OH

Frontiero Rose
Fraser HS
Fraser MI

Frost Ann E
Timken Sr HS
Canton OH

Frost Susan
Norton HS
Norton OH

Frum Michele
Flemington HS
Rosemont WV

Frush Candace
South Harrison HS
W Milford WV

Frush Sandra
South Harrison HS
W Milford WV

Fry Charles
Springboro HS
Springboro OH

Fry Debbie
Springboro HS
Franklin OH

Fry Melissa K
Edon Northwest HS
Edon OH

Fry Paula
Timken Sr HS
Canton OH

Frye Cindi
Walnut Ridge Sr HS
Columbus OH

Frye Rodger
Cloverdale Clovers HS
Poland IN

Frymier Mark
London HS
London OH

Fuhrhop Brenda
Patrick Henry HS
Hamler OH

STUDENTS
PHOTOGRAPH
SCHEDULED
FOR PUBLI-
CATION HERE
COULD NOT
BE REPRO-
DUCED

Fuleki Shari
Canal Winchester HS
Canal Winch OH

Fulk Gina C
Martinsburg HS
Martinsburg WV

Fulks Mary
Chalker HS
Southington OH

Fuller Daniel
Padua Franciscan HS
Broadview Hts OH

Fuller Jill
Lincoln HS
Vincennes IN

Fuller Karen
Bay HS
Bay Village OH

Fuller Lisa
Maysville HS
Zanesville OH

Fulton Doris
Four County Joint Voc
HS
Berkey OH

Fulton Douglas
Jefferson HS
Jefferson OH

Fulton Eunice
Union Bible Seminary
Westfield IN

Fultz Betty
Dodd Ridge Cnty HS
Salem WV

Funk Kimberly
Crooksville HS
Corning OH

Funk Richard
Rossford HS
Rossford OH

Funkhouser Vicki
William Henry Harrison
HS
Lafayette IN

Furbee Richard
Southern HS
Racine OH

Furrow Donna S
Shady Spring HS
Shady Spring WV

Furry Jodi A
North Ridgeville Sr HS
N Ridgeville OH

Furstenau Gayle
Ovid Elsie HS
Elsie MI

Furto Toni
Bishop Noll Institute
Hammond IN

Fusilier Mike
Pinckney HS
Pinckney MI

Fuson Cynthia
Terre Haute North Vigo
HS
Terre Haute IN

Fusselman Robin
Farmington Local HS
W Farmington OH

Futhey Tracy
Wheeling Park HS
Wheeling WV

G

Gaar Diana
Anderson Highland HS
Anderson IN

Gable John
New Lexington HS
New Lexington OH

Gabriel Jasmine
Penn HS
Mishawaka IN

Gabriel Kim
Franklin Heights HS
Columbus OH

Gacetta Jami
Archbishop Alter HS
Centervll OH

Gach Susan M
Elyria Catholic HS
Elyria OH

Gadd Amy
Farmington Local HS
W Farmington OH

Gaertner Barbara
Trenton HS
Trenton MI

Gagle Cindy
Jay County HS
Portland IN

STUDENTS
PHOTOGRAPH
SCHEDULED
FOR PUBLI-
CATION HERE
COULD NOT
BE REPRO-
DUCED

Gaich Sharon
Genoa Area HS
Curtice OH

Gaines Cynthia
Loudonville HS
Loudonville OH

Gaines Michele
Dominican HS
Detroit MI

Gainey Wesley R
John Marshall HS
Indianapolis IN

Galasso Michael J
Jimtown HS
Elkhart IN

Gale Todd
Owosso HS
Owosso MI

Galford Tom
Harrison HS
Gladwin MI

Galko Patty
Trenton HS
Trenton MI

Gall Vincent
Lincoln HS
Shinnston WV

Gallardo John D
Williamson HS
Williamson WV

Gallimore Lecia L
Princeton HS
Princeton WV

Gallion Shauni
Brownstown Central HS
Brownstown IN

Galloway Brian
Portsmouth HS
Portsmouth OH

Galloway Cynthia L
University HS
Morgantown WV

Galloway Greg
Franklin Hts HS
Grove City OH

Gamble Janet
Pine River HS
Reed City MI

Gamble Lydia
Carrollton HS
Carrollton OH

Gampel Carl
Bridgman HS
Bridgman MI

Gamponia Jessica
Spencer HS
Spencer WV

Gandee David L
Walton HS
Gandeeville WV

Gang Lesa
Perry HS
Canton OH

Gannon Alfred
Oak Hill HS
Oak Hill WV

Gannon E Michael
University Liggett School
Detroit MI

Ganshorn Rebecca
La Ville Jr Sr HS
Warsaw IN

Ganthier Stanley
St Francis De Sales HS
Toledo OH

Ganzel Pete
St Francis De Sales HS
Toledo OH

Garbe Connie
Norton HS
Norton OH

Garcia Carmen
Pike Delta York HS
Delta OH

Garcia Domingo G
Walsh Jesuit HS
Pepper Pike OH

Garcia Linda
Saginaw HS
Saginaw MI

Garcia Nelly
Lincoln West HS
Cleveland OH

Gardner Carol
Bishop Noll Institute
Chicago IL

Gardner Mark
David Anderson HS
Lisbon OH

Garey Lory
Miller HS
Crooksville OH

Gargano Patricia
St Mary Academy
Monroe MI

Garland Amanda
Garfield HS
Akron OH

Garland Jeff
Eau Claire HS
Sodus MI

Garland Kimberly
Zanesville HS
Zanesville OH

Garlick Joseph
Richmond HS
Richmond MI

Garnett Valerie
Garden City East HS
Garden City MI

Garno Carl
Utica Sr HS
Newark OH

Garofalo Julie
Solon HS
Solon OH

Garozzo John
De La Salle Collegiate HS
East Detroit MI

Garrabrant Terri
Northridge HS
Johnstown OH

Garren Mike
Barberton HS
Barberton OH

Garretson Reggie
Guyan Valley HS
Branchland WV

Garrett Deborah
Pontiac Central HS
Pontiac MI

Garrett Debra
Davison Sr HS
Davison MI

Garrett Gordon
John R Buchtel Univ HS
Akron OH

Garrett Jon
Culver Military Academy
Lacon IL

Garrett Maribeth
Eaton HS
Camden OH

Garrett Pam
Tecumseh HS
New Carlisle OH

Garrett Ryan
Stockbridge HS
Stockbridge MI

Garringer Layne
Miami Trace HS
Jamestown OH

Garrison David
Southwestern HS
Edinburg IN

Garrison Denise R
Hillsboro HS
Hillsboro OH

Garritano Ann Marie L
Divine Child HS
Dearborn Hgts MI

Garrod Paul F
Lawrence HS
Lawrence MI

Garrod Scott
Lawrence HS
Lawrence MI

Garsteck Christine
Strongsville HS
Strongsville OH

Garver Kim
Northwestern HS
W Salem OH

Garvin James
Tecumseh HS
Pt Clinton OH

Gary Kenneth
Fremont HS
Fremont IN

Gary Sheri
Perry HS
Lima OH

Garza Rosanne
Bishop Noll Inst
Hammond IN

Gascho Lonnie
Fairview Area Schools
Fairview MI

Gaskell Kenneth
Winston Churchill HS
Livonia MI

Gaskins Charles R
Point Pleasant HS
Point Pleasant WV

Gaspar Teresa
Parchment HS
Parchment MI

Gasparovic Deborah
Owosso HS
Owosso MI

Gasper Sharon
Clay HS
South Bend IN

Gasper Susan
Martinsburg HS
Martinsburg WV

Gasser Cindy
Salem HS
Scottsburg IN

Gastineau Edward A
Stonewall Jackson HS
Charleston WV

Gastineau Jeff
Tecumseh HS
New Carlisle OH

Gaston Kathryn M
Lordstown HS
Warren OH

Gaston Lou
Buckhannon Upshur HS
Buckhannon WV

Gaston Sharon
Chaminade Julienne HS
Dayton OH

Gates Betsy
Columbia City Joint HS
Columbia City IN

Gatica Mark
Michael Hamady Comm
HS
Flint MI

Gatte Pamela
Brownstown Central HS
Brownstown IN

Gauker Vikki
Richmond HS
Richmond IN

Gaul Nancy
Berrien Springs HS
Berrien Springs MI

Gault Toynia
Jennings Co HS
No Vernon IN

Gaunt Mitchell
Point Pleasant HS
Pt Pleasant WV

Gauthier James
St Xavier HS
Cincinnati OH

Gavigan Kim
Rochester HS
Rochester MI

Gavrun Andrea
Hopkins HS
Hopkins MI

Gawart Chris
Harper Creek HS
Battle Creek MI

Gawron Mary L
Technical Voc HS
Hammond IN

Gay Lisa
Milan HS
Milan IN

Gay Michelle
Canfield HS
Canfield OH

Gaydos Mary R
Holy Name Nazareth HS
Parma OH

Gaydosh Mary L
Lordstown HS
Warren OH

Gaylord Heidi
Whitmer HS
Toledo OH

Gaylord J Eric
Cardinal Ritter HS
Indianapolis IN

Gearhart Karen
Bluefield HS
Bluefld WV

Gearhart Leslie J
Eastlake North HS
Eastlake OH

Gearheart Gary
Bluefield HS
Bluefield WV

Gebert Dawn
Griffith HS
Griffith IN

Gebert Ed
Whitko HS
Pierceton IN

Gebhardt Samuel L
Cedar Springs HS
Cedar Spgs MI

Geerinck Kathryn M
Richmond Sr HS
Richmond IN

Gehlmann Gregory
Lorain Catholic HS
Lorain OH

Gehring Kelly
Perry HS
Massillon OH

Geick Timothy
Port Huron HS
Marysville MI

Geiger Christine
East Canton HS
E Canton OH

Geiger Steve
Clermont Northeastern
HS
Batavia OH

Geiger Vivian
Delta Sr HS
Delta OH

Geiselman Tracy
Sycamore HS
Cincinnati OH

Geiss Gloria
Reitz Memorial HS
Evansville IN

Gelios Dave
Archbold HS
Archbold OH

Gellner Gregory A
John Marshall HS
Wheeling WV

Gendron Pamla M
Kingsford HS
Iron Mtn MI

Gengnagel Susan
Dekalb HS
Auburn IN

Gensler Diana R
Robert S Rogers HS
Toledo OH

Gentis Rhonda
Southern Wells HS
Bluffton IN

Gentry Chet
Center Line HS
Warren MI

Gentry Kimberly
Southmont Jr Sr HS
New Market IN

Gentz Christine
Lutheran HS North
Fraser MI

Genwright Raul
Buena Vista HS
Saginaw MI

George Anthony
Clinton Massie HS
Wilmington OH

George Carole L
Zanesville HS
Zanesville OH

George Christopher
Franklin Community HS
Franklin IN

George Julie
Otsego HS
Kalamazoo MI

George Kim
Elmwood HS
Bloomdale OH

George Molly
Pleasant HS
Caledonia OH

George Susan M
Thomas A De Vilbiss HS
Toledo OH

George Terri L
South Knox HS
Vincennes IN

Georgiou Electra
Kearsley HS
Burton MI

Geozeff Jerilyn
New Castle Chrysler HS
New Castle IN

Gepford Andrea
John Glenn HS
New Concord OH

Geraci Mark
Moeller HS
Cincinnati OH

Gerard Twila
Grafton HS
Grafton WV

Gerardot Chris
Woodlan HS
New Haven IN

Gerardot Ernest
Heritage HS
Monroeville IN

Gerardot Paul J
Bishop Luers HS
Ft Wayne IN

Gerber Cynthia F
Shenandoah HS
Middletown IN

Gerber Jan
Forest Park HS
Ferdinand IN

Gerfen Darrell
Elgin HS
Prospect OH

Gerfen Lorri
Elgin HS
Prospect OH

Gericke Jennifer
Dover HS
Dover OH

Gerken Kathy
Napoleon HS
Napoleon OH

Gerken Mary A
Holgate HS
New Bavaria OH

Gerks Richard C
Lakewood HS
Sunfield MI

Gerland Robert
Mentor HS
Mentor OH

Germann Gayle L
Lincolnview HS
Delphos OH

Gerrits Linda
Holland Christian HS
Holland MI

Gerulski Michael
Bay City Western HS
Auburn MI

Gerwig Mark
Bellmont HS
Decatur IN

Geschwind Pamla
Cedar Lake Acad
Gobles MI

Gesing Richard G
Boardman HS
Youngstown OH

Gesing Robert G
Boardman HS
Boardman OH

Gessler Carol
Euclid Sr HS
Euclid OH

Geswein Bev
Benton Central HS
Fowler IN

Geyer Lore
Parma Sr HS
Parma OH

Ghaphery Nick
Linsly HS
Wheeling WV

Ghearing Larry L
Jackson HS
Jackson OH

Giaconia Joseph
Kirtland HS
Kirtland OH

Giangrande John
Cleveland Central Cathlc
HS
Cleveland OH

Gibbons Douglas
Taylor HS
Cleves OH

Gibbs Douglas F
Arthur Hill HS
Saginaw MI

Gibbs Lora
Avon Jr Sr HS
Danville IN

Gibbs Pete
Fairmont West HS
Blacksburg VA

Gibbs Tammy
R B Chamberlin HS
Twinsburg OH

Gibler Misty
Kingsford HS
Kingsford MI

Giblin Clare
St Augustine Academy
Lakewood OH

Giblin Cornelius J
Culver Military Academy
Yardley PA

Gibney Patty
Grosse Pointe South HS
Grss Pte Pk MI

Gibson Bruce
Matewan HS
Meador WV

Gibson Catherine
Lakota HS
Rising Sun OH

Gibson Joyce
Ontario HS
Crestline OH

Gibson Ken
Norwood HS
Norwood OH

Gick Debbie
Clinton Prairie HS
Colfax IN

Gidley Donna
Calumet HS
Gary IN

Gifford David
Buckhannon Upshur HS
Buckhannon WV

Gifford Sharon
Liberty HS
Poland OH

Gilbert Cynthia A
Turpin HS
Cincinnati OH

Gilbert Cynthia J
Comstock Park HS
Comstock Park MI

Gilbert Daniel
Holy Rosary HS
Flint MI

Gilbert David
De Witt HS
Dewitt MI

Gilbert Patricia
New Washington HS
Marysville IN

Gilbert Scott
Bellaire HS
Bellaire OH

Giles Daniel P
Brebeuf Preparatory
School
Zionsville IN

Giles Gregory S
Jefferson Union HS
Steubenville OH

Giles Stephen
Webster Cnty HS
Cowen WV

Giles Valerie
Cass Technical HS
Detroit MI

Gilkerson Misty L
Huntington E HS
Huntington WV

Gill Mary
All Saints Central HS
Bay City MI

Gill Steve
Shelbyville HS
Shelbyville IN

Gilleland Judith
Northmont HS
Dayton OH

Gillenwater Thomas S
Matoaka HS
Lashmeet WV

Gilles Cheryl
William Wirt HS
Gary IN

Gillespie Crystal
Oak Glen HS
Chester WV

Gillespie David
Danville Community HS
Danville IN

Gillespie Jeremy
Mariemont HS
Cincinnati OH

Gilliam Sarah J
William Mason HS
Mason OH

Gillian Noran
Donald E Gavit Jr Sr HS
Hammond IN

Gilligan John
St Xavier HS
Cincinnati OH

Gillispie Debbie
Southeastern Indiana
Voc HS
Milan IN

Gillispie Gregory
Montpelier HS
Montpelier OH

Gilmore Brent
Elkhart Memorial HS
Elkhart IN

Gilmore Daniel
Western Reserve Acad
Hudson OH

Gilmore Jack
Princeton HS
Princeton WV

Gilmore Kimberlee A
Briggs HS
Columbus OH

Gilreath Rodney P
Aquinas HS
Inkster MI

Gilreath Stephen W
Bethel Local HS
Tipp City OH

Gilson Leslie
Triway HS
Wooster OH

Gilvary Claire
Archbishop Alter HS
Kettering OH

Ginderske Gerald W
Swan Valley HS
Saginaw MI

Gineman Tamara
Liberty Center HS
Liberty Cntr OH

Gingrich Mitchell
Bluffton HS
Bluffton OH

Ginther Ronald
Washington HS
Massillon OH

Giroux John
Servite HS
Grosse Pointe MI

STUDENTS
PHOTOGRAPH
SCHEDULED
FOR PUBLI-
CATION HERE
COULD NOT
BE REPRO-
DUCED

Gissinger Jacqueline
Norton HS
Clinton OH

Giudici Sandra A
Adlai E Stevenson HS
Sterling Hts MI

Givens Timothy W
East Canton HS
Louisville OH

Gladen Renee
Elmhurst HS
Ft Wayne IN

Glancy Linda
Little Miami HS
Morrow OH

Glaros George
Jackson HS
Massillon OH

Glascock Jane
Fountain Central HS
Kingman IN

Glass Janice
Eastbrook HS
Upland IN

Glatt Cheri
Merrillville HS
Merrillville IN

Glaub Kenneth
Yorktown HS
Yorktown IN

Glaze Dolletta
Ross Beatty HS
Cassopolis MI

Gleason Penny
Danville HS
Danville IN

Gleason Susan L
Hathaway Brown HS
Cleveland OH

STUDENTS PHOTOGRAPH SCHEDULED FOR PUBLICATION HERE COULD NOT BE REPRODUCED

Gleitz Ellen
Niles Sr HS
Niles MI

Glenn John
Washington HS
Massillon OH

Glick Loveta
Hauser Jr Sr HS
Hope IN

Gloden Shawn
Climax Scotts HS
Battle Creek MI

Glover Clinton
Bethel HS
New Carlisle OH

Gloyd Douglas
Meigs HS
Dexter OH

Glugla Celeste
St Florian HS
Detroit MI

Glynn Sara
Dansville Agricultural Schl
Webberville MI

Goble C Jane
O A Carlson HS
Gibraltar MI

Gobol John A
Oak Glen HS
Newell WV

Gocke Karen
Cascade HS
Coatesville IN

Goddard Jill R
Howell HS
Howell MI

Godlew Scott
Bangor HS
Bangor MI

Godlewski Randy
Escanaba Area Public HS
Cornell MI

Goebel David
Padua Franciscan HS
Parma OH

Goehler Mark
Norton HS
Norton OH

Goering Jr Gene
Pittsford Area HS
Hudson MI

Goettemoeller Cheryl
Versailles HS
Versailles OH

Goff Natalie
Philip Barbour HS
Belington WV

Going Mark
Gods Bible School
Greenfield IN

Golba Denise
Adams HS
So Bend IN

Goldberg Daniel P
Hawken HS
Hunting Valley OH

Golden Marchell
Hamilton Township HS
R A F B OH

Golden Roy
Bethel Tate HS
Bethel OH

Goldey Ellen
Talawanda HS
Oxford OH

Goldie Wendy
Garrett HS
Garrett IN

Goldsberry Lisa
South Spencer Rebels HS
Newburgh IN

Goldsby Teresa
Mitchell HS
Mitchell IN

Goldsmith Becky
Doddridge County HS
Greenwood WV

Goldstein Andrew
West Geauga HS
Chesterland OH

Golias David
Trinity HS
Garfield Hts OH

Goll Stacey
Ferndale HS
Pleasant Ridge MI

Goltz James
Lawrenceburg HS
Lawrenceburg IN

Gonos Audrey
South Amherst HS
S Amherst OH

Gonser Todd
Olivet HS
Olivet MI

Gonzales Carmen
Wayland Union HS
Wayland MI

Gonzales Cristella
Defiance Sr HS
Defiance OH

Gonzales Lesley
Oak Hill HS
Oak Hill WV

Gonzales Jr Ronald
Douglas Mac Arthur HS
Saginaw MI

Gonzalez Cynthia
Carroll HS
Flora IN

Gonzalez Diana
Boardman HS
Canfield OH

Gooch Rebecca
Wellsville HS
Wellsville OH

Good Danny
Clermont N E HS
Batavia OH

Good Todd
Western HS
Parma MI

Goode L Tonya
Emerson Sr HS
Gary IN

Gooden Darnell
Buchtel Univ HS
Akron OH

Goodenough Beth
Paulding HS
Paulding OH

Goodgion Toni
Lincoln HS
Cambridge IN

Gooding Deborah
St Albans HS
St Albans WV

Goodman Cheryl
Brookville HS
Brookville IN

Goodman Jayne
West Washington HS
Fredericksbg IN

Goodnite Judy
Point Pleasant HS
Point Pleasant WV

Goodpaster Cynthia
Union HS
Economy IN

STUDENTS
PHOTOGRAPH
SCHEDULED
FOR PUBLI-
CATION HERE
COULD NOT
BE REPRO-
DUCED

Goolsby Rosalyn
Scott HS
Toledo OH

Goonen Kathy
Avon HS
Plainfld IN

Gorbett Lisa
Brownstown Central HS
Freetown IN

Gordley Beth
Brookville HS
Brookville OH

Gordon Christine
Wayne HS
Ft Wayne IN

Gordon Diana
Chelsea HS
Chelsea MI

Gordon Dorinda
Wayne HS
Dayton OH

Gordon Keith
Van Wert HS
Van Wert OH

Gordon Linne
Quincy HS
Quincy MI

Gordon Lori L
North Putnam Jr Sr HS
Roachdale IN

Gordon Rodney
Federal Hocking HS
Coolville OH

Gordon Sherman
Sandusky HS
Sandusky OH

Gordon Sherry
Dowagiac Union HS
Dowagiac MI

Gordon Terrance G
South Spencer HS
Rockport IN

Gordon Thomas
St Edwards HS
N Olmsted OH

Gore Jeff
Richmond Sr HS
Richmond IN

Gore Natalie
Arsenal Technical HS
Indianapolis IN

Gorges Suzanne
Loveland Horst HS
Loveland OH

Gorgonio Suzanne C
Notre Dame HS
Clarksburg WV

Gorski Jeffrey
St Francis Desales HS
Toledo OH

Gorski Joseph
Cody HS
Detroit MI

Gort Kathy
Hudsonville HS
Hudsonville MI

Gorwitz Rachel
Interlochen Arts
Academy
Oshkosh WI

Goshorn Mark
Alma HS
Alma MI

Goslin Duane
Unionville Sebewaing HS
Unionville MI

Gossett Dean
Oscar A Carlson HS
Rockwood MI

Gossman Karen
New Albany HS
Westerville OH

Gottschalk Ingo
Zeeland HS
Hudsonville MI

Gough Austin R
Licking Cnty Joint Voc
HS
Newark OH

Gould Gregory
Whitmer Sr HS
Toledo OH

Goulding James
Otsego HS
Otsego MI

Gouldsherry Alice
David Anderson HS
Columbiana OH

Goundrill Dale
High School
Battle Crk MI

Gourlay Tim
Niles Sr HS
Niles MI

Gower Denise
Coalton HS
Ellamore WV

Gowright Tanya J
Middletown HS
Middletown OH

Graber Bob
Barr Reeve HS
Cannelburg IN

Graber Bret N
Barr Reeve HS
Montgomery IN

Graber Mark
Rittman HS
Rittman OH

Grabham Jill
Zionsville Community HS
Zionsville IN

Grady Philip L
Solon HS
Solon OH

Graham Alice J
Southern Wells Jr Sr HS
Keystone IN

Graham Brenda
University HS
Morgantown WV

Graham Brenda L
University HS
Albright WV

Graham Cheryl
Western HS
Kokomo IN

Graham Crystal L
Lawrence County Jt Voc Schl
Chesapeake OH

Graham Jodi
Ursuline Acad
Cincinnati OH

Graham Juliana
Bishop Hartley HS
Columbus OH

Graham Monica D
Norwalk HS
Norwalk OH

Graham Susan
Andrean HS
Merrillville IN

Gralak Sherry
St Ursula Academy
Toledo OH

Grandberry Sybil M
Immaculata HS
Detroit MI

Granich Jodi
Bloomington HS South
Bloomington IN

Grant J Kevin
Roosevelt Wilson HS
Stonewood WV

Grant Marshall
Bloomington South HS
Bloomington IN

Grant Monique A
Dayton Christian HS
Dayton OH

Grant Taryn
Roosevelt HS
Gary IN

Grant Tom
Jefferson Union HS
Toronto OH

Grant Valorie A
Aiken HS
Cincinnati OH

Grassman Deanne
Wooster HS
Wooster OH

Grata Karen
Wm A Wirt HS
Gary IN

Grate Steven
New Hope Christian School
Camden MI

Grater Cynthia
Fairview HS
Fairview Pk OH

Gravely Kathy
Southwestern HS
Shelbyville IN

Graves Cherrie
Bexley Sr HS
Bexley OH

Graves Shannon
Lewis County HS
Jane Lew WV

Gray Elizabeth
Holland HS
Holland MI

Gray Fredonna
Fayetteville HS
Fayetteville WV

Gray James H
Dublin HS
Plain City OH

Gray Kim
Pike Central HS
Otwell IN

Gray Linda
Rogers HS
Michigan City IN

Gray Lori
Gull Lake HS
Battle Creek MI

Gray Steven
Huntington North HS
Andrews IN

Greaser F Christophr
St Josephs Prep Sem
Tunnelton WV

Greathouse Michael
East HS
Columbus OH

Greathouse William
Flemington HS
Rosemont WV

Greco Mary
Madonna HS
Weirton WV

Green De Ann
Philip Barbour HS
Philippi WV

Green Diana L
Mc Cutcheon HS
Lafayette IN

Green Gerald
Henry Ford HS
Detroit MI

Green Gregory
Jennings County HS
No Vernon IN

Green Judy
Madison Plains HS
London OH

Green Lance
Coloma HS
Coloma MI

Green Laura
Marion HS
Marion IN

Green Lorinda
Cass Tech HS
Detroit MI

Green Mark A
Oak Hills HS
Cincinnati OH

Green Marklin
Mt Vernon Acad
Gallipolis OH

Green Randy
Marion Harding HS
Marion OH

Green Rebecca L
De Kalb HS
Ashley IN

Green Robert
Hartland HS
Brighton MI

Green Scott
Fowlerville HS
Howell MI

Green Sherry
Withrow HS
Cincinnati OH

Green Stephanie
South Ripley HS
Versailles IN

Green Veronica M
Buena Vista HS
Saginaw MI

Greenan Joseph
John Marshall HS
Moundsville WV

Greene Becky
Lemon Monroe HS
Monroe OH

Greene Lisa
Northwest HS
Clinton OH

Greene Rebecca
Webster Co HS
Cowen WV

Greenough Deborah
Lansing Everett HS
Lansing MI

Greenwalt Pamela
Ursuline HS
Youngstown OH

Greenwood Kevin L
Bellaire HS
Bellaire OH

Greenwood Rodney A
Coshocton HS
Coshocton OH

Greer Doug
Glen Este HS
Cincinnati OH

Greer Gregory
Indiana Acad
Indianapolis IN

Greer Mark
Richwood HS
Richwood WV

Greer Susan
Ben Davis HS
Indianapolis IN

Gregg Cheryl A
Bellbrook HS
Bellbrook OH

Gregg Jennifer
Triad HS
Cable OH

Gregg Mary
Yellow Springs HS
Yellow Sprg OH

Gregg Paula
Fairview HS
Bryan OH

Gregory John
Hurricane HS
Hurricane WV

Gregory John
Belding HS
Belding MI

Gregory Lois J
Rocky River HS
Rocky River OH

Gregory Stephanie
Field HS
Suffield OH

Greiwe Douglas
Purcell HS
Cincinnati OH

Gresak Tom
Bishop Donahue HS
Wheeling WV

Gresham Susan
Brookhaven HS
Columbus OH

Gricewich Mark
Bridgeport Sr HS
Bridgeport WV

Grier Karen L
Washington HS
Massillon OH

Griesinger Jeanne
Adrian HS
Adrian MI

Griffin Glen
Holt HS
Holt MI

Griffin Grant
Watervliet Public
Schools
Watervliet MI

Griffin Jill
Wickliffe HS
Wickliffe OH

Griffin Ruth E
Scecina Mem HS
Indianapolis IN

Griffin Stacie
Field HS
Kent OH

Griffin William
Wayland HS
Dorr MI

Griffing Kathleen
Plymouth Canton HS
Plymouth MI

Griffin III Herbert E
Bedford North Lawrence HS
Bedford IN

Griffith Brian
Robert S Rogers HS
Toledo OH

Griffith Kathleen M
Flushing HS
Flushing MI

Griffith Kathryn
Walnut Hills HS
Cincinnati OH

Griffith Laura
Bluefield HS
Bluefield WV

Griffith Sharon S
Terre Haute North Vigo HS
Terre Haute IN

Griffiths Jana
Oak Hill HS
Oak Hill OH

Griffiths Patricia
Danbury HS
Marblehead OH

Grigereit Todd
Hammond HS
Hammond IN

Griggs Susan
Decatur Jr Sr HS
Decatur MI

Grigsby Sandra
Wayland Union HS
Dorr MI

Grime Penny
Liberty Center HS
Liberty Center OH

Grimm Mary B
Sistersville HS
Sistersville WV

Grimm Stephen
Lawton HS
Lawton MI

Grimm Steven
Whitmer HS
Toledo OH

Grimmett Donald
Lenore HS
Dingess WV

Grimmett Melvin
Crooksville HS
Crooksville OH

Grimshaw Rhonda
Grosse Pointe South HS
Grss Pte Park MI

Grissom Gary
Union Cnty HS
Liberty IN

Grit Jonathan
Willard HS
Willard OH

Groewa Eric
Solon HS
Solon OH

Groewa Lori M
Solon HS
Solon OH

Grof Shirley
Portage Lakes Jt Voc HS
Akron OH

Grogan Kathy
Upper Arlington HS
Columbus OH

Grogg Debrah
Tecumseh HS
Donnelsville OH

Groleau Phillip
Big Bay De Noc HS
Rapid River MI

Groleau Vicki
Big Bay De Noc HS
Rapid River MI

Groner John
Ursuline HS
Girard OH

Groomer Ann E
Brownsburg HS
Brownsburg IN

Groover David A
Elwood Community HS
Elwood IN

Gross Cara
East Noble HS
Laotto IN

Gross Geoffrey
Elmhurst HS
Ft Wayne IN

Gross Gordon K
Pontiac Central HS
Pontiac MI

Gross Kathy
Douglas Mac Arthur HS
Rochester MI

Gross Laurel
Chesaning HS
St Charles MI

Gross Nathan
Columbia Central HS
Brooklyn MI

Gross Richard
Elwood Community HS
Elwood IN

Gross Rosetta
Liberty HS
Salem WV

Grossman Marsha
Madeira HS
Cincinnati OH

Grounds Lori
Bloomington HS South
Bloomington IN

Grous Albin
St Marys Preparatory HS
Philadelphia PA

Grove June
Berkeley Springs HS
Berkeley Spg WV

Grove Sally
Frankfort Sr HS
Frankfort IN

Grove Shelly
Van Wert HS
Van Wert OH

Groves Jana
Avon HS
Danville IN

Groves William
Barnesville HS
Barnesville OH

Grubb Katherine
John Adams HS
S Bend IN

Grubb Kim
Mc Comb HS
Mccomb OH

Grube Kathleen
Kankakee Valley HS
Wheatfield IN

Gruber David J
Columbus West HS
Columbus OH

Gruber Debra
Copley HS
Akron OH

Gruber Joseph
Moeller HS
Cincinnati OH

Gruber Karey
Reese HS
Reese MI

Gruen Tami
West Lafayette Sr HS
West Lafayette IN

Gruhl Tami
Zionsville Comm HS
Zionsville IN

Grumman Teresa A
Westland HS
Columbus OH

Grunder Shelly
Minerva HS
Minerva OH

Gruscinski Thomas
Catholic Central HS
Grand Rapids MI

Gruskiewicz Jackie
Pymatuning Valley HS
Williamsfield OH

Grygier Barbara
Capac Jr Sr HS
Emmett MI

Grygier Kathleen
Capac Jr Sr HS
Emmett MI

Grys Gregory
Trinity HS
Garfield Hts OH

Grywalski Aimee
Garfield HS
Akron OH

Grzechowski Raymond
St Alphonsus HS
Detroit MI

Grzelak Keith
Houghton HS
Dollar Bay MI

Guadiana Jesus
Washington HS
East Chicago IN

Guarino Catherine
Royal Oak Dondero HS
Berkley MI

Gucker Jim
Mohawk HS
Mc Cutchenville OH

Gude Brook
Loveland Hurst HS
Loveland OH

Guenterberg Brian
Adelphian Acad
Plymouth MI

Guernsey Brian
Henryville HS
Henryville IN

Guertin Judy
Mt Healthy HS
Mt Healthy OH

Guffy Patricia
Lumen Christi HS
Jackson MI

Guice Bettina
Washington Irving HS
Clarksburg WV

Guidi Terry
Morgantown HS
Westover WV

Guirlinger Christoher
Pleasant HS
Marion OH

Gulan Richard J
Catholic Central HS
Steubenville OH

Gulutz Annalisa
East Liverpool HS
E Liverpool OH

Gumkowski John
La Salle HS
South Bend IN

Gummere Peggy
Van Buren HS
Brazil IN

Gumowski Alex B
George Washington HS
Charleston WV

Gundy Kimberly
Reeths Puffer HS
Muskegon MI

Gunn Belinda
Benedictine HS
Detroit MI

Gunn Michelle
Immaculate Conception
Acad
Dayton OH

Gunn Roger
Benjamin Bosse HS
Evansville IN

Gunnoe Donna
Meadow Bridge HS
Danese WV

Gunnoe Marsha
H H Dow HS
Midland MI

Gunsell Debra
Durand Area HS
Swartz Crk MI

Gunther David
Sts Peter & Paul Area
HS
Saginaw MI

Gunyula Kathy
Mineral Ridge HS
Mineral Ridge OH

Gupta Latha
Bluefield HS
Bluefield WV

Gurgos Michele
Boardman HS
Youngstown OH

Gursal Jihan D
Fairview HS
Fairview Park OH

Gurtner Jolenna
Vantage Joint Voc HS
Van Wert OH

Gustafson Dale A
Bishop Noll Inst
Chicago IL

Gustafson Gregg
Negaunee HS
Negaunee MI

Gustafson Rosemary
La Salle HS
St Ignace MI

Guster Rodney
Cass Technical HS
Chelsea MI

Guthrie Julie
Springboro HS
Miamisburg OH

Gutmann Anne
Lehman HS
Piqua OH

Gutridge Michele R
Licking Valley HS
Newark OH

Gutschenritter Victoria M
St Josephs HS
South Bend IN

Gutzwiller Kirk W
East Central HS
Harrison OH

Guy Geri
Columbiana HS
Columbiana OH

Guyer Cheryl
Hubbard HS
Hubbard OH

Guyer Dawn
Linden HS
Linden MI

Guyer Julia A
Munster HS
Munster IN

Gwin Ric
Gahanna Lincoln HS
Gahanna OH

Gyorgyi Sandra
John Adams HS
So Bend IN

H

Haak C
Holland Christian HS
Holland MI

Haar Lori
Michigan Lutheran
Seminary
Saginaw MI

Haas Bethany S
Arenac Eastern HS
Omer MI

Haataja Gerrie
Ewen Trout Creek HS
Bruce Crossing MI

Habermas Ronald
South Lake HS
St Clair Shore MI

Habian George
Rocky River HS
Rocky River OH

Habig Todd
De Kalb Central United
HS
Auburn IN

Hackenbracht Jeffrey
Marion Harding HS
Marion OH

STUDENTS
PHOTOGRAPH
SCHEDULED
FOR PUBLI-
CATION HERE
COULD NOT
BE REPRO-
DUCED

Hackett Matthew
Avondale Sr HS
Rochester MI

Hackett Pamela
Our Lady Of Mercy HS
Detroit MI

Hackman Darla
Brownstown Central HS
Brownstown IN

Hackmann Lesli
Carroll HS
South Bend IN

Haddix Cristina
Buckhannon Upshur HS
Buckhannon WV

Haddow William
Woodridge HS
Peninsula OH

Hadley Laura
Bridgman HS
Bridgman MI

Haffner Deneen
Perry HS
Canton OH

Haffner Sandi
Merrill HS
Merrill MI

Haffner Teresa
Jay County HS
Portland IN

Hafler David
Westfall HS
Orient OH

Hafner Deborah
Millersport HS
Millersport OH

Hafner Mark
Rogers HS
Toledo OH

Hagen Laurie
Pt Huron Northern HS
Marysville MI

Hagen Susanne
Lake Orion Comm HS
Lake Orion MI

Hagenbuch Jon
Mendon Jr Sr HS
Three Rivers MI

Hager Robert
Padva Franciscan HS
Burnswick OH

Hager Scott A
Streetsboro HS
Streetsboro OH

Hagood Cathy
Flat Rock HS
Flat Rock MI

Hague Thomas
Earnest W Seaholm HS
Bloomfield Hls MI

Hahn Karla
Greensburg Cmnty HS
Greensburg IN

Hahn Sharon
Northside HS
Muncie IN

Haines Diane
Arthur Hill HS
Saginaw MI

Haines Mary L
High School
Sabina OH

Hainline Nora M
Marian HS
Redford MI

Hairston Donald G
Williamson HS
Williamson WV

Haker Heather
Solon HS
Solon OH

Hale Beckie
Pike Central HS
Petersburg IN

Hale Caroline M
Decatur Central HS
Indpls IN

Hale John
Toronto HS
Toronto OH

Hale Karen
Sandusky HS
Sandusky MI

Hale Lisa
Charleston Catholic HS
Charleston WV

Hale Robin
Independence HS
Coal City WV

Hale Sandra
Buffalo HS
Huntingtn WV

Hale Wendy
Zanesville HS
Zanesville OH

Halfacre Vincent
Patterson Cooperative
HS
Dayton OH

Halkoski Jackie
St Ladislaus HS
Detroit MI

Hall Brad
Washington Irving HS
Clarksburg WV

Hall Darrell R
Buffalo HS
Kenova WV

Hall Debi Lynn
Williamsburg HS
Williamsburg OH

Hall Edward
Fruitport HS
Muskegon MI

Hall Jacqualine M
S Newton Jr Sr HS
Goodland IN

Hall Jennifer
Shelby Sr HS
Shelby OH

Hall Joey J
Coshocton HS
Coshocton OH

Hall Julius
Jefferson Area HS
Jefferson OH

Hall Kenneth
Pike Central HS
Winslow IN

Hall Lynnette
Elyria Cath HS
Fairview Park OH

Hall Mary
East HS
Akron OH

Hall Paula D
South Amherst HS
South Amherst OH

Hall Rick V
Cowan HS
Muncie IN

Hall Sarah
Northwestern HS
Detroit MI

Hall Stephanie
Turpin HS
Cincinnati OH

Hall T
Federal Hocking HS
Coolville OH

Hall Teresa
Lenore HS
Williamson WV

Hall Terrilyn
Lake Fenton HS
Grand Blanc MI

Hall Theresa
Oxford Area Cmnty HS
Oxford MI

Hall William P
Huntington East HS
Huntington WV

Haller Barbara
Wyoming Park HS
Wyoming MI

Haller John G
Bloomfield Hills Andover
HS
West Bloomfield MI

Hallock Jeffery
Owendale Gagetown HS
Owendale MI

Halwes Suzanne
Wood Memorial HS
Elberfeld IN

Ham Douglas K
Bridgeprt Spauldng
Cmnty HS
Bridgeport MI

Hamad Camille
St Vincent St Mary HS
Akron OH

Hamaide Cindy
Genoa Area HS
Genoa OH

Hamann Julie
Adrian Sr HS
Adrian MI

Hamberg James
Marion Local HS
Saint Henry OH

Hamby Joan
Solon HS
Solon OH

Hamer Lisa M
Greensburg Cmnty HS
Greensburg IN

Hamilton Beth
Cedarville HS
Cedarvl OH

Hamilton Carol
Clay Battelle HS
Fairview WV

Hamilton Christopher
Culver Military Academy
Ft Wayne IN

Hamilton Juliana
Central HS
Evansville IN

Hamilton Kristina
Onekama HS
Kaleva MI

Hamilton Mary
La Ville Jr Sr HS
Lakeville IN

Hamilton Mindy
Cadillac Sr HS
Cadillac MI

Hamilton Teri
South Newton HS
Kentland IN

Hamlin Carol
Andrews Acad
Berrien Spgs MI

Hamlin Elizabeth
Chesapeake HS
Chesapeake OH

Hamlin Gary
Barberton HS
Barberton OH

Hamlin Jill
Norwalk HS
Norwalk OH

Hammel Jane
North HS
Bloomington IN

Hammer Blaine A
Indian Hill Sr HS
Cincinnati OH

Hammer Doris
Lutheran HS West
Southgate MI

Hammer Jeffrey
Wintersville HS
Wintersville OH

Hammer Rita
Magnificat HS
Bay Village OH

Hammerbacher Neil
Sts Peter & Paul HS
Saginaw MI

Hammon Jeff
Defiance Sr HS
Defiance OH

Hammond Russ
Canfield HS
Canfield OH

Hammons Jeanette
Keyser HS
Keyser WV

Hampshire Larry D
Versailles HS
Versailles OH

Hampton Joy
B H Sr HS
Benton Hbr MI

Hampton Kathy
New Palestine HS
New Palestine IN

Hampton Sherman
Big Creek HS
Bishop VA

Hamrick Karen
George Washington HS
Charleston WV

Hamstra Corinna
Kouts HS
Kouts IN

Hanaway Malissa
Hammond Tech Voc HS
Hammond IN

STUDENTS PHOTOGRAPH SCHEDULED FOR PUBLICATION HERE COULD NOT BE REPRODUCED

Hancock Robert
Bluffton HS
Beaverdam OH

Handler Robin
Monroe HS
Monroe MI

Handley Carl F
Hurricane HS
Hurricane WV

STUDENTS PHOTOGRAPH SCHEDULED FOR PUBLICATION HERE COULD NOT BE REPRODUCED

Haney Kim
Clarkston HS
Drayton Pln MI

Haney Tim
Franklin HS
Franklin OH

Hange Elizabeth
Black River HS
Spencer OH

Hankenhof Jane
Notre Dame Academy
Toledo OH

Hanlin Frank
Weirton Madonna HS
Slovan PA

Hanna Mary
Our Lady Star Of The Sea HS
Detroit MI

Hanner Gregory
Brownstown Central HS
Norman IN

Hannett Laura
Muskegon Sr HS
Muskegon MI

Hanselman Laurey
Ubly Community School
Minden City MI

Hansen Holli
Indian Hill HS
Cincinnati OH

Hansen Michelle
Lakeview HS
Coral MI

Hansen Randall
Mason County Central HS
Ludington MI

Hanshue Scott
Grant HS
Grant MI

Hanson David
Alpena HS
Alpena MI

Hanson Lisa
Pendleton Heights HS
Pendleton IN

Hanson Robert
Morgan Local HS
Malta OH

Hantzis Charles W
Northwest HS
Indianapolis IN

Hap Tonia
Union City Comm HS
Union City IN

Harber Ronald G
Bishop Dwenger HS
Fort Wayne IN

Harbick Mark
Marquette Sr HS
Marquette MI

Harbison Roger
Floyd Central HS
New Albany IN

Harbour Paula
Milton HS
Milton WV

Harbour Stephen
Washington HS
E Chicago IN

Harclerode Kris
La Brae Sr HS
Leavittsburg OH

Harden Pam
Southern Local HS
Racine OH

Harden Randy
Haslett HS
Williamston MI

Harden Ruth
Concord HS
Concord MI

Hardesty Kimberly
Edgewood HS
Bloomington IN

Hardiek Teri
Fremont HS
Fremont IN

Harding Bonnie K
Arsenal Technical HS
Indianapolis IN

Harding Cathy
Lowell Sr HS
Lowell IN

Harding Cheryl
West Side HS
Gary IN

Hardman Karen
Newbury HS
Chardon OH

Hardman Page L
Charleston HS
Charleston WV

Hardwick Frank
Pennfield HS
Battle Creek MI

Hardwick Susan
Washington HS
Massillon OH

Hardy Kevin D
Stonewall Jackson HS
Charleston WV

Hardy Terry
Fremont HS
Fremont MI

Hare John M
Carmel HS
Carmel IN

Hargitt Macy
Ben Davis HS
Indianapolis IN

Haris Daphine
Monrovia HS
Mooresville IN

Harkenrider Kristi
Bishop Dwenger HS
Ft Wayne IN

Harker Penny
Zane Trace HS
Chillicothe OH

Harless Jr Jim
Jackson HS
Jackson OH

Harman Rebecca
Portsmouth East HS
Sciotoville OH

Harman Rick
Warsaw Community HS
Claypool IN

Harmeyer Jackie
Reading Community HS
Reading OH

Harmon Anna
Big Creek HS
Warriormines WV

Harmon Tammy
Waldron HS
Waldron MI

Harner Dianne
La Porte HS
La Porte IN

Harper Bob
Norwood HS
Norwood OH

Harper Elizabeth A
Circleville HS
Riverton WV

Harper Kim
Our Lady Of The Lakes
HS
Ortonville MI

Harper Randall
South Harrison HS
Lost Creek WV

Harpest Rosalie
Greenville Sr HS
Greenville OH

Harpster Dayna
Huron HS
Huron OH

Harrell David
Northfield HS
Wabash IN

Harrigan Diana
Taylor Center HS
Taylor MI

Harrington Janice
Theodore Roosevelt HS
Kent OH

Harrington Tony
Anderson HS
Anderson IN

Harris Alan
Cuyahoga Falls HS
Cuyahoga Fls OH

Harris Angie
Cardinal Stritch HS
Toledo OH

Harris Arvanders
John Hay HS
Cleveland OH

Harris Beverly
Benzie Central HS
Beulah MI

Harris Catherine
St Joseph HS
Lakeville IN

Harris Donna
Ecorse HS
Ecorse MI

Harris Greg
Cuyahoga Falls HS
Cuyahoga Falls OH

Harris Lynette
East HS
Columbus OH

Harris Michael
Kearsley HS
Flint MI

Harris Phronda
Philip Barbour HS
Century WV

Harris Robert
Midland HS
Midland MI

Harris Ron
Southport HS
Southport IN

Harris Stewart L
Rochester Adams HS
Rochester MI

Harris Susan
Martin Luther King Jr Sr
HS
Detroit MI

Harris Teandre
William A Wirt HS
Gary IN

Harris Tracy
Jefferson Union HS
Steubenville OH

Harris Jr Clyde A
Central Hower HS
Akron OH

Harrison Brent
Croswell Lexington HS
Jeddo MI

Harrison Cynthia
Pontiac Northern HS
Pontiac MI

Harrison David
Wapakoneta HS
Wapakoneta OH

Harrison Gregory
Wapakoneta Sr HS
Wapakoneta OH

Harrison Joseph
Jewett Scio HS
Scio OH

Harrison Karlene
Riverview Community HS
Riverview MI

Harrison Kelley
Bishop Donahue HS
Mc Mechen WV

Harrison Larry
Kyger Creek HS
Gallipolis OH

Harrison Lori
St Clement HS
Centerline MI

Harrison Misty
Brown County HS
Nashville IN

Harrison Sherry
Kyger Creek HS
Gallipolis OH

Harrison Tami
Clay Sr HS
Oregon OH

Harrison Thomas L
Northwest HS
Indianapolis IN

Harry Tina
Flushing HS
Flushing MI

Harsha William
Plymouth Salem HS
Plymouth MI

Harshe Darla
Liberty Benton HS
Findlay OH

Harsin Jeff
Switzerland Cnty HS
Vevay IN

Hart Christine
West Wood Heights HS
Flint MI

Hart Joan E
Vermilion HS
Vermilion OH

Hart Melanie
Greensburg Cmnty HS
Greensburg IN

Hart Norman
De Kalb HS
Waterloo IN

Hart Rebecca A
Berea HS
Berea OH

Hart Rian
Pickens HS
Pickens WV

Hart Ron
Wadsworth Sr HS
Wadsworth OH

Hart Roxanne
Greenville Sr HS
Greenville OH

Hart Sandra
Franklin HS
Franklin OH

Hart Steven
Highland Park HS
Highland Pk MI

Hart Tina
Athens HS
East Leroy MI

Harte Brian
West Bloomfield HS
Westbloomfield MI

Harter Gary D
Valley HS
Smithfield WV

Hartieroad Melanie
Lewis County HS
Weston WV

Hartley Debbie
Madison Hts HS
Anderson IN

Hartley Jon
Pendleton Heights HS
Anderson IN

Hartley Timothy
Butler HS
Vandalia OH

Hartman Debra
Ionia HS
Ionia MI

Hartman Diane
Vicksburg HS
Vicksburg MI

Hartman Jerry
Plymouth HS
Plymouth OH

Hartman Kelly L
Fairmont West HS
Kettering OH

Hartman Kevin
North Putnam Jr Sr HS
Bainbridge IN

Hartman Sherry
North Wood HS
Elkhart IN

Hartman Steven
St Joseph Sr HS
Saint Joseph MI

Hartmann Jeffery
La Salle HS
Cincinnati OH

Hartnell Loretta
Farwell Area HS
Farwell MI

Hartnett Patrick
Riverside HS
Dearborn Hts MI

Hartsell Lisa
Wayne Memorial HS
Westland MI

Hartshorn Amy
Northridge HS
Johnstown OH

Hartsough Debora
Chillicothe HS
Chillicothe OH

Hartwig Deeanna
Rapid River HS
Rapid River MI

Hartzell John
Bridgeport HS
Bridgeport WV

Hartzler Rob
Warsaw Comm Sr HS
Warsaw IN

Hartzog Joseph
Bluefield HS
Bluefield WV

Harvan Michele
Holy Name Nazareth HS
Cleveland OH

Harvey Amy L
Whitko HS
S Whitley IN

Harvey Cyndra
Magnolia HS
New Martinsvle WV

Harvey Dave
Cardington Lincoln HS
Cardington OH

Harvey Dorothy M
Lake Catholic HS
Mentor OH

Harvey James B
Logan Sr HS
Chauncey WV

Harvey Jeffrey
Stow Sr HS
Stow OH

Harvey Patricia
Buena Vista HS
Saginaw MI

Harvey Stephen B
Walnut Ridge HS
Columbus OH

Haskins Lori
Midland HS
Midland MI

Haskins Pamela
Catholic Central HS
Steubenvll OH

Haslinger Kimberly
Old Trail School
Bath OH

Hassan Ronald G
Brooke HS
Bethany WV

Hassen Robert
Chippewa Hills HS
Chippewa Lake MI

Hasser Monica
Benton Central Jr Sr HS
Earl Park IN

Hastedt Victoria
Fairview HS
Mark Center OH

Hastings Candy
Lutheran HS West
Rocky River OH

Hastings Darlene
Marion L Steele HS
Elyria OH

Hastings Laurie
Chelsea HS
Chelsea MI

Hatfield Barry
Streetsboro HS
Streetsboro OH

Hatfield James
Clay Sr HS
Curtice OH

Hatfield Michael
Willard HS
Willard OH

Hatfield Nancy
Xenia HS
Xenia OH

Hathaway Jonathan
Liberty HS
Salem WV

Hathaway Kathryn
Otsego HS
Kalamazoo MI

Hathaway Pamela
Garfield HS
Akron OH

Hathcock Lisa A
Interlochen Arts
Academy
Ft Smith AR

Hathorn Tamara
Watkins Memorial HS
Balt OH

Hatley Mitzi
Wellston HS
Wellston OH

Hatten Lisa
Buffalo HS
Kenova WV

STUDENTS
PHOTOGRAPH
SCHEDULED
FOR PUBLI-
CATION HERE
COULD NOT
BE REPRO-
DUCED

Hatten Terri
Whetstone HS
Columbus OH

Hattle Jimmy
Eastern HS
Lucasville OH

Hatzell Julie
Jay County HS
Redkey IN

Hauer Dee
Brownstown Central HS
Vallonia IN

Haughn James
Wabash HS
Wabash IN

Haught Kenneth
Lincoln HS
Lumberport WV

Hausbeck Mary
Bridgeport HS
Saginaw MI

Hauter Kay
Crestview HS
Van Wert OH

Havanas John
Chamberlin HS
Twinsburg OH

Havens Kevin
Madison Plains HS
Mt Sterling OH

Havens Linda
Belding HS
Belding MI

Havens Sharon
Zane Trace HS
Kingston OH

Havenstein Paul
Flat Rock Sr HS
Flat Rock MI

Havey Glenna S
Kalkaska HS
Kalkaska MI

Hawarny Amy
Milan HS
Milan MI

Hawes Glenda
Salem HS
Salem IN

Hawk Sheryl
West Carrollton HS
W Carrollton OH

Hawkins Crystal L
Bridgeport Sr HS
Bridgeport WV

Hawkins Deb
Westerville North HS
Westerville OH

Hawkins Gwendolyn
Henry Ford HS
Detroit MI

Hawkins Karen
Buckhannon Upshur HS
Buckhannon WV

Hawkins Pamela
Princeton HS
Princeton WV

Hawkins Rebecca
Cadiz HS
Hopedale OH

Hawkins Verneda
Lumen Cordium HS
Cleveland OH

Hawley Theresa
Brookhaven HS
Zanesfield OH

Hawthorne Sydna
Plainwell HS
Plainwell MI

Hay Angie
Anderson HS
Anderson IN

Hay Donna M
Beaver Local HS
E Liverpool OH

Hay Kathleen
Morley Stanwood HS
Morley MI

Hayden Robin
Cuyahoga Falls HS
Cuahoga Fls OH

Haye Dawn
Millington HS
Millington MI

Hayes Christine
Westerville North HS
Westerville OH

Hayes Diana
North Posey Sr HS
Wadesville IN

Hayes James
Plainwell HS
Plainwell MI

Hayes Jeffrey
Cambridge HS
Cambridge OH

Hayes Jo L
Monrovia HS
Monrovia IN

Hayes Michelle
Northville HS
Northville MI

Hayes Tammy
East HS
Akron OH

Hayes Terri
Franklin Comm HS
Franklin IN

Hayford Kathy
Springfield HS
Battle Crk MI

Haynes Gregory H
George Washington HS
Charleston WV

Haynes Nancy
Dayton Christian HS
Dayton OH

Haynes Stephan
Warren Local HS
Little Hocking OH

Haynes Steve
Jackson HS
Jackson OH

Haynes Voras
Tygarts Vly HS
Valley Bend WV

Hays Debra
Hanover Central HS
Cedar Lake IN

Hazel Juliee
Harper Creek HS
Battle Creek MI

Hazelett Sonya
West Side HS
Gary IN

Hazlett Laura M
Decatur Central HS
Indnpls IN

Hazlewood Mike
Princeton HS
Princeton WV

Head Dana
Providence HS
Lanesville IN

P—87

Heady Warren
Hammond Baptist HS
Dyer IN

Heald Philip
Ironton HS
Ironton OH

Healey Rhonda
De Kalb HS
Ashley IN

Healy Richard
John Marshall HS
Glen Dale WV

Heater Karen
Flemington HS
Bridgeport WV

Heath Dan
Mineral Ridge HS
Mc Donald OH

Heath Deborah A
Mendon Community
School
Mendon MI

Heath Lisa
Lincolnview HS
Van Wert OH

Heath Sally
Black River HS
Sullivan OH

Heaton Sarah
Elwood Cmnty HS
Elwood IN

Heatwole David
Hampshire HS
Romney WV

Heavenridge Ruth
Waverly HS
Waverly OH

Heavilin Brooke
Cadiz HS
Cadiz OH

Hebden Pamela
Central Lake Public HS
Central Lake MI

Hebel Scott R
North Central HS
Indianapolis IN

Heberlie Susan
Erieview Catholic HS
Cleveland OH

Heckathorn M Robert
Wellsville HS
Wellsville OH

Hedington Tina
Warsaw Community HS
Warsaw IN

Hedrick Diane J
Greencastle HS
Greencastle IN

Hedrick Jason
Northwestern HS
Kokomo IN

Heerspink Donna
Holland Christian HS
Holland MI

Heffernan Julia
Washington Catholic HS
Washington IN

Hefner Kammi
Bridgeport Sr HS
Bridgeport WV

Heidger Sally
Douglas Mac Arthur HS
Saginaw MI

STUDENTS
PHOTOGRAPH
SCHEDULED
FOR PUBLI-
CATION HERE
COULD NOT
BE REPRO-
DUCED

Heil Karen
Morral Ridgedale HS
Marion OH

Heilman David
Grove City HS
Grove City OH

Heilman Laurie
Carrollton HS
Carrollton OH

Heilman Ted
Saranac HS
Saranac MI

Hein Natalie
Adlai E Stevenson HS
Sterling Hts MI

Heineman Lee Ann
Mc Clain HS
Leesburg OH

Heinemann Norma
Coldwater HS
Coldwater MI

Heiner Beth
Huntington HS
Huntington WV

Heinlein Daniel
Indiana Academy
Plymouth IN

Heinold Tammy
Whitko HS
Pierceton IN

Heins William A
Firestone HS
Eau Claire WI

Heintz David
Lake Central HS
Schererville IN

Heishman Mark
Hurricane HS
Hurricane WV

Heistand Dan
Oakridge HS
Twin Lk MI

Held Jennifer
Rutherford B Hayes HS
Delaware OH

Heldreth Nancy
Dunbar HS
Charleston WV

Heleski Margo
Ubly HS
Bad Axe MI

Heller Charles
Washington HS
Washington IN

Helm Cathy
Brownsburg HS
Brownsburg IN

Helm Steven
Andrews Academy
Berrien Spring MI

Helm Tonya R
East HS
Columbus OH

Helman Carol
Houston HS
Sidney OH

Helmer Camille
Parkway HS
Rockford OH

Helmkamp Elaine
East Noble HS
Kendallville IN

Helms Athena
Western HS
Russiaville IN

Helms Dave A
Buckeye South HS
Tiltonsville OH

Helmuth Ron
Findlay HS
Findlay OH

Helt Randy
Mt Gilead HS
Mt Gilead OH

Helton Andrea L
Zane Trace HS
Chillicothe OH

Helton Teresa
Greenfield Central HS
Greenfield IN

Hemker Debra
Delphos St John HS
Delphos OH

Hemmer Tamela
Warsaw Community HS
Warsaw IN

Hemmer Tracy
Seton HS
Cincinnati OH

Hemmerich Lynda
Morton Sr HS
Hammond IN

Hempfling Anita
Liberty Benton HS
Findlay OH

Hendershot Julie
Bexley HS
Columbus OH

Henderson Cherryl
Buena Vista HS
Saginaw MI

Henderson Cynthia
Wakefield HS
Wakefield MI

Henderson Douglas L
Lake Orion Cmnty HS
Lake Orion MI

Henderson Greggory
Delaware Hayes HS
Delaware OH

Henderson James
Pt Pleasant HS
Henderson WV

Henderson Pat
Bishop Watterson HS
Worthington OH

Henderson Pippa
Glen Oak School
Cleveland OH

Henderson Shari
Walnut Hills HS
Cincinnati OH

Henderson Terri
Gull Lake HS
Augusta MI

Henderson Timothy
Brooke HS
Wellsburg WV

Henderson Walter
Elkhart Memorial HS
Elkhart IN

Hendricks John
Lake Ridge Academy
N Olmsted OH

Hendricks Michael
Sparta Sr HS
Sparta MI

Henkener Elizabeth
Anderson HS
Cincinnati OH

Henkle Kenneth C
London HS
S Vienna OH

Hennen Janet
Wirt County HS
Elizabeth WV

Hennessee Emily
Dayton Christian HS
Enon OH

Hennis Jody
Jewett Scio HS
Jewett OH

Henry Carrie
Olivet HS
Olivet MI

Henry Colleen
Magnificat HS
Rocky River OH

Henry Le Anne
Central Catholic HS
Canton OH

Henry Mark
Northrop HS
Ft Wayne IN

Henry Nancy
Caro HS
Caro MI

Henry Sharon R
Martinsburg Sr HS
Martinsburg WV

Hensil Christina
Elkins HS
Elkins WV

Hensley Brenda
Vinson HS
Huntington WV

Henson Kimberly
Franklin HS
Franklin OH

Henthorn Daniel M
Magnolia HS
New Martinsvle WV

Hentosh Gina
Hubbard HS
Hubbard OH

Hepp Brian
Southfield Lathrup Sr HS
Southfield MI

Herendeen Catherine
Clay HS
S Bend IN

Hergenrather Ken
Roy C Start HS
Toledo OH

Herm Valerie
Douglas Mac Arthur HS
Saginaw MI

Herman Glen
Riverside HS
Dearborn Hts MI

Herman Mary
La Salle HS
South Bend IN

Hernan Noreen
Euclid Sr HS
Euclid OH

Herport Tina
Clinton Central HS
Frankfort IN

Herr Shari
Bluffton HS
Pandora OH

Herrera Karen A
Park Hills HS
Fairborn OH

Herrgord Deann
Reeths Putter HS
Muskegon MI

Herring Dennis
Columbus North HS
Columbus OH

Herring Sheila
Crispus Attucks HS
Indianapolis IN

Herrington Sheila
Glen Este HS
Cincinnati OH

Herriott Betty
Marion Harding HS
Marion OH

Herron Denise
Salem Sr HS
Salem OH

Herron Lisa
Madonna HS
Follansbee WV

Hersey Tommijuana
Lake Michigan Catholic HS
Benton Hrbr MI

Hershberger Jane
Newton HS
Pleasant HI OH

Hertenstein Teresa
Carroll HS
Camden IN

Herzog Debbie
Port Clinton HS
Pt Clinton OH

Herzog Luann
Reading HS
Reading OH

Hesch Crhistine
Pickerington HS
Pickeringtn OH

Hescott Mark
Kearsley HS
Burton MI

Heshelman Angie
N Daviess Jr Sr HS
Plainville IN

Heslin Bruce
West Lafayette HS
W Lafayette IN

Hess Debbie
Graham HS
De Graff OH

Hess Gail
Morton Sr HS
Hammond IN

Hess James C
Shenandoah HS
Middletown IN

Hess Kelly
Elmwood HS
Wayne OH

Hess Lora
Lemon Monroe HS
Middletown OH

Hess Paul
Centerville HS
Centerville OH

Hester Julie G
New Buffalo HS
New Buffalo MI

Hestwood Jefferey
Parkside HS
Jackson MI

Hetherington Anna
Gladwin HS
Gladwin MI

Hetrick Dana
Vicksburg HS
Vicksburg MI

Hetson Greg
Hubbard HS
Hubbard OH

Hetzler Scott D
Franklin HS
Franklin OH

Hewett Lisa
West Carrollton Sr HS
W Carrollton OH

Hewitt Christine A
Westerville North HS
Westerville OH

Heyd Delvita
J A Garfield HS
Garrettsville OH

Heyman Diana
Eastmoor HS
Columbus OH

Hiatt Debra
Danville Community HS
Danville IN

Hiatt Margie
Churubusco HS
Churubusco IN

Hiatt Melissa
Eastbrook HS
Upland IN

Hickerson Linda
Mt Vernon HS
Mt Vernon OH

Hickman Jason
Champion Sr HS
Warren OH

Hicks David
Shady Spring HS
Cool Ridge WV

Hicks Felicia
Lakota HS
W Chester OH

Hicks Henry W
Pickens HS
Pickens WV

Hicks Jon E
Memorial HS
Elkhart IN

Hicks Kenneth L
U S Grant Joint Vocl Schl
Bethel OH

Hicks Michelle
Westerville S HS
Westerville OH

Hicks Terry
Jefferson HS
Ranson WV

Hidalgo Ana
St Ursula Academy
Cincinnati OH

Hietala Robert
Harvey HS
Painesville OH

Hiett Barbara
S Vermillion HS
Clinton IN

Higbea Cheryl A
Delphos Jefferson Sr HS
Delphos OH

Higginbotham Annette
Henryville HS
Henryville IN

Higginbotham Rebecca
Poca HS
Nitro WV

Higginbotham Robin
Noblesville HS
Noblesville IN

Higgins Ann
Trimble Local HS
Glouster OH

Higgins William
Struthers HS
Struthers OH

Higgs Linda
Martins Ferry HS
Martins Ferry OH

High Steve
William Henry Harrison
HS
W Lafayette IN

Highlander Pam
Margaretta HS
Castalia OH

Hight Michelle
Adelphian Academy
Vassar MI

Hightower Whitney
River Rouge HS
River Rouge MI

Hilbert Thomas
Jonathan Alder HS
Plain City OH

Hill Barbara
Scott HS
Chapmanville WV

Hill Barbara
Crown Point HS
Crown Point IN

Hill Damita J
Madison Heights HS
Anderson IN

Hill David
Williamstown HS
Williamstown WV

Hill Dean
Richmond Sr HS
Richmond IN

Hill Deborah
Princeton HS
Princeton WV

Hill Debra
Montrose Hill Mc Cloy
HS
Montrose MI

Hill Joanna
Scott HS
Turtle Ck WV

Hill John A
Moeller HS
Silverton OH

Hill John L
South Point HS
South Point OH

Hill Julia
Philip Barbour HS
Philippi WV

Hill La
Cass Technical HS
Detroit MI

Hill Lisa
Dunbar HS
Dunbar WV

Hill Lisa
Federal Hocking HS
Amesville OH

Hill Melanie
Washington Irving HS
Clarksburg WV

Hill Richard
Northrop HS
Ft Wayne IN

Hill Tammy
Bellbrook HS
Cookeville TN

Hill Teri
Winfield HS
Winfield WV

Hill Tina
Mt Vernon Academy
Orlando FL

Hill Vata C
Lutheran HS E
Cleveland OH

Hilliard Michael
Bishop Foley HS
Hazel Pk MI

Hillstead Steven
Muskegon Sr HS
Muskegon MI

Hillyard Julie
Philip Barbour HS
Junior WV

Hiltbrand Robert
Jackson HS
North Canton OH

Hilty Jacqueline
Wintersville HS
Wintersville OH

Hiltz Linda
Lapeer East HS
Lapeer MI

Hindi Michael
Clay Sr HS
Oregon OH

Hindman Fred
Magnolia HS
New Martinsvle WV

Hinen Laura
Columbia City Jt HS
Ft Wayne IN

Hines Gregory
Pleasant HS
Prospect OH

Hines James L
Benton Harbor HS
Benton Harbor MI

Hinkle James
Cody HS
Detroit MI

Hinkle Kathy
Moorefield HS
Old Fields WV

Hinkle Laurie
Calumet HS
Gary IN

Hinman Brian
Manton Consolidated
Schools
Manton MI

Hinnegan Patricia
Wayne HS
Dayton OH

Hinsky Doug
Bellmont HS
Decatur IN

Hipple Jacqueline S
Howland Sr HS
Warren OH

Hirzel Kathy
Northwood HS
Nothwood OH

Hise Joe
Lincoln HS
Wallace WV

Hisek Thomas
Padua Franciscan HS
Seven Hls OH

Hiser Kathy A
Morgantown HS
Morgantown WV

Hishon Chris
Anchor Bay HS
Anchorville MI

Hisle Gregory C
Williamsburg HS
Williamsburg OH

Hitchcock Kelly
Madison Comprehensive
HS
Mansfield OH

Hitchens Joseph
Mt Clemens HS
Mt Clemens MI

Hite Jerry
Greenville HS
Greenville OH

Hite Mike
Plymouth HS
Plymouth IN

Hite Stephen
Columbian HS
Tiffin OH

Hite Ty
Greenfield Central HS
Greenfield IN

Hites Thomas
Madison HS
Madison OH

Hitt Ray
Stryker HS
Stryker OH

Hittie Deanne
Struthers HS
Struthers OH

Hittle Carrie
Kankakee Valley HS
Wheatfield IN

Hjortsberg Frederick
Maumee HS
Maumee OH

Hlad Sandy
Morton Sr HS
Hammond IN

Hluck George
Padua Franciscan HS
N Royalton OH

Hoag John
Ida HS
Monroe MI

Hoag John C
Wadsworth Sr HS
Wadsworth OH

Hoaglin Russell
Concord Community HS
Concord MI

Hoard Steven F
Breckenridge Jr Sr HS
St Louis MI

Hobba Holly
Green HS
Akron OH

Hobba William J
Green HS
Akron OH

Hobbs Jody
Madison Hts HS
Anderson IN

Hobbs Mark
Clinton Massie HS
Clarksville OH

Hobbs Melissa
Brookhaven HS
Columbus OH

Hobbs Tara
Robert S Rogers HS
Toledo OH

Hobbs Varna M
Patterson Co Op HS
Dayton OH

Hobson Mark
Orleans HS
Orleans IN

Hock Teresa
Freeland HS
Freeland MI

Hodder Tanya
Sault Area HS
Slt Ste Marie MI

Hodge Debbie
Greenbrier East HS
Ronceverte WV

Hodge Jennifer
Warrensville Hts HS
Warrensvl Hts OH

Hodge Paul
Allegan HS
Allegan MI

Hodge Stephen
Princeton HS
Princeton WV

Hodges Tim D
Carmel HS
Carmel IN

Hodoval Jodi
Marshall HS
Marshall MI

Hoefel Roseanne
Buchtel Univ HS
Akron OH

Hoeffel Cynthia
Napoleon HS
Napoleon OH

Hoeffler Chris
Reading HS
Cincinnati OH

Hoeft Roberta
Pioneer HS
Ann Arbor MI

Hoehner Paul J
North Lutheran HS
Rochester MI

Hoenie Jane
Carroll HS
Dayton OH

Hofer Kristine
East Detroit HS
East Detroit MI

Hoffman E Julianne
Jeffersonville HS
Jeffersonville IN

Hoffman Gatha
Philip Barbour HS
Galloway WV

Hoffman Kevin S
Malabar HS
Mansfield OH

Hoffman Lori
Griffith Sr HS
Griffith IN

Hoffman Roxanne
Crooksville HS
Crooksville OH

Hoffman Steve
Madeira HS
Cincinnati OH

Hoffmann Donna
Colerain Sr HS
Cincinnati OH

Hoffmann Karen
Traverse City Sr HS
Traverse City MI

Hoffmeister Bruce
Purcell HS
Cincinnati OH

Hofman Nancy
Zeeland HS
Zeeland MI

Hofmann Cynthia
Scecina Mem HS
Indianapolis IN

Hogan Alan
Washington Catholic HS
Washington IN

Hogan Cindy
Terre Haute North Vigo
HS
Terre Haute IN

Hogle Tamara
Charlotte HS
Charlotte MI

Hogrefe Jayne
Lorain Catholic HS
Lorain OH

Hogsten Thomas
Brecksville HS
Brecksville OH

Hogue Melinda L
Warren Central HS
Indianapolis IN

Hoh Robert
New Richmond HS
New Richmond OH

Hohler Molly
Monroeville HS
Norwalk OH

Hoke Tim
Terre Haute South Vigo
HS
Terre Haute IN

Holbrook Alisa
Valley View HS
Germantown OH

Holbrook Bobbie
Willow Run HS
Ypsilanti MI

Holcomb Jay M
George Washington HS
Charleston WV

Holcomb Richard
North Muskegon HS
N Muskegon MI

Holder Angela C
Park Tudor HS
Indianapolis IN

Holderman Patricia
Colon HS
Colon MI

Holdren Todd
Zane Trace HS
Chillicothe OH

Holen Kathy
Saint Joseph Acad
Cleveland OH

Holfinger Mark
Madison Comprehensive
HS
Mansfield OH

Holiday Steve
New Albany HS
New Albany IN

Holl Blair
Talawanda HS
Oxford OH

Holland Gary A
Newark Sr HS
Newark OH

Holland Isabel B
Seaholm HS
Troy MI

Holland John
Hazel Park HS
Hazel Park MI

Holland Leona
Watervliet HS
Watervliet MI

Holland Martin C
Seaholm HS
Troy MI

Hollandbeck Mike
Warren Central HS
Indianapolis IN

Hollar Pam
Miami Trace HS
Washington C H OH

Holleman Eric
St Francis De Sales HS
Columbus OH

Holley Brian
Brookside HS
Sheffield Lke OH

Hollins Richard
Zanesville HS
Zanesville OH

Hollis Thomas
Bishop Flaget HS
Chillicothe OH

Hollister Robin
Niles Sr HS
Niles MI

Holloway Mark
Miami Trace HS
Bloomingburg OH

Holmes Tom
Bishop Dwenger HS
Ft Wayne IN

Holmes Jr Richard
Bellbrook HS
Bellbrook OH

Holohan Colette
Immaculate Conception
Acad
Cabery IL

Holscher Brenda
South Knox HS
Vincennes IN

Holt Cynthia
Matoaka HS
Matoaka WV

Holt Denise
Chaminade Julienne HS
Dayton OH

Holt Karen
Smithville HS
Smithville OH

Holt Kelly
Cardinal Mooney HS
Youngstown OH

Holt Roger D
Temple Christian School
Canton MI

Holter Edward
Eastern Meigs HS
Pomeroy OH

Holtvoigt James
Archbishop Alter HS
Miamisbrg OH

Holtzhauer Chip
Memorial HS
St Marys OH

Holub Don
Solon HS
Solon OH

Holzmer Lucy
Hobart Sr HS
Hobart IN

Hom Harold
Fairview Park HS
Fairview Pk OH

Homeister Raymond
Grosse Ile HS
Grosse Ile MI

Homer Cameron
Northeastern HS
Fountain City IN

Honaker Arthur
South Charleston HS
S Charleston WV

Honaker Denny E
Big Creek HS
English WV

Honbaum Debbie
Chelsea HS
Chelsea MI

Hood Charles C
Andover HS
Birmingham MI

Hood Robert
Gallia Academy HS
Gallipolis OH

Hooker Kevin
Madison HS
Adrian MI

Hoops Chris
Meadowbrook HS
Pleasant City OH

Hoose Troy
Hill Mc Cloy HS
Montrose MI

Hoover Anthony C
Marlington HS
Louisville OH

Hoover Laura
Anderson HS
Anderson IN

Hoover La Vonda
Imlay City Community
HS
Imlay City MI

Hoover Mark
Summerfield HS
Petersburg MI

Hoover Tanya
Penn HS
Oceola IN

Hopkins Eric
Warren Central HS
Indpls IN

Hopkins Serretha
Horace Mann HS
Gary IN

Hoppe Dominique
Dearborn HS
Dearborn MI

Hoppe Ronald
St Francis Cabrini HS
Detroit MI

Hopper Christie
Olentangy HS
Delaware OH

Hopper Howard
Highland HS
Hinckley OH

Hopper Kent
Northwest HS
Indianapolis IN

Hopper Lisa
Springs Valley HS
French Lick IN

Hopper Pat
Seeger Memorial HS
Pine Village IN

Hopping Bradley M
Madeira HS
Madeira OH

Hoptry David
Lexington HS
Lexington OH

Horanyi Anna
Belmont HS
Dayton OH

Horlocker Jacki
Westerville South HS
Westerville OH

Hormuth Sarah
William Henry Harrison
HS
Evansville IN

Horn David
Moellen HS
Cincinnati OH

Horn George
Sturgis HS
Sturgis MI

Horn John
Pineville HS
Pineville WV

Horn Judy
North White HS
Monon IN

Horne Nancy D
Cassopolis Ross Beatty
HS
Cassopolis MI

STUDENTS
PHOTOGRAPH
SCHEDULED
FOR PUBLI-
CATION HERE
COULD NOT
BE REPRO-
DUCED

Horner Dawn E
Loudonville HS
Loudonville OH

Horner Elizabeth
Magnolia HS
Proctor WV

Hornes Brenda
Benton Harbor HS
Benton Hrbr MI

Horning Mike
Sebring Mckinley HS
Sebring OH

Hornung Judith A
Eudid Sr HS
Euclid OH

Hornyak Margaret
Cardinal Stritch HS
Oregon OH

Horsch Shirley
Parkside HS
Jackson MI

Horsfall Patricia
Climax Scotts HS
Scotts MI

Horsford Julie
Jackson County Western
HS
Jackson MI

Horsley Karen
William Henry Harrison
HS
Harrison OH

Horton Jeff
Portsmouth East HS
Portsmouth OH

Horton Laverne
Washington HS
E Chicago IN

Horton Marnita
Wirt HS
Gary IN

Horvat Diane M
Fairmont West HS

Horvath James
Stow Sr HS
Kent OH

Horvath Kimberley
Bellbrook HS
Bellbrook OH

Horvath Rob
Haslett HS
E Lansing MI

Hosaflook Theodore
Buckhannon Upshur HS
Buckhannon WV

Hoskins Tina
Pontiac Northern HS
Pontiac MI

Hostelley Greg
St Ignatius HS
Parma Hts OH

Hottois Michael
Normandy HS
Parma OH

Houchins Mark
Pike Central HS
Winslow IN

Houck Bonnie
Alma HS
Riverdale MI

Houck Tom
Hicksville HS
Hicksville OH

Hough Whitney
Rochester HS
Rochester MI

Hough William J
Upper Arlington HS
Upper Arlington OH

House Janet
St Joseph HS
Niles MI

Houser Susan
Kearsley HS
Flint MI

Houseworth Kim
Martinsville HS
Martinsville ID

Houston Craig
Rensselaer Central HS
Rensselaer IN

Houston Joyce
Brookville HS
Brookville IN

Houston Kay A
Swan Valley HS
Saginaw MI

Houston Melanie
Bishop Noll Institute
E Chicago IN

Houts Randal
Boardman HS
Boardman OH

Hovanec Mike
Hubbard HS
Hubbard OH

Hovarter Shari
De Kalb HS
Corunna IN

Hove Jeff
Crown Point HS
Crown Point IN

Hoven Mary J
Saint Augustine Acad
Cleveland OH

Hoverman Daniel
Midland HS
Midland MI

Howard Elizabeth
Little Miami HS
Morrow OH

Howard Jeffrey
East Grand Rapids HS
Grand Rapids MI

Howard John
John F Kennedy HS
Taylor MI

Howard Joseph
Woodrow Wilson HS
Youngstown OH

Howard Joseph
Whitko HS
Pierceton IN

Howard Karen
Madison Plains HS
London OH

Howard Michael
Castle HS
Newburgh IN

Howard Roger
Jewett Scio HS
Jewett OH

Howe Amy
Napoleon HS
Napoleon OH

Howell Ann
Hedgesville HS
Shepherdstown WV

Howell Rhonda
Marion HS
Marion IN

Howell Steven
River Valley HS
Three Oaks MI

Howells Bronwen
North Royalton HS
Broadview Ht OH

Howison Rebecca
J W Sexton HS
Lansing MI

Hoy Colleen
Windham HS
Windham OH

Hoy Mary J
Whetstone HS
Columbus OH

Hoy Russell
Riverdale HS
Forest OH

Hoyle Dawn
Brighton HS
Brighton MI

Hoyt Ralph
Little Miami HS
Morrow OH

Hoyt Robert
Otsego HS
Otsego MI

Hrdlicka Leigh A
Bellaire HS
Bellaire OH

Hricovsky Marianne
Rossford HS
Rossford OH

Hrometz Janet
East Canton HS
E Canon OH

Hrvatin Diane
Salem Sr HS
Salem OH

Hubbard David
Jimtown HS
Elkhart IN

Hubbard Sonia
South Dearborn HS
Moores HI IN

Hubbard Troy
Salem HS
Salem IN

Hubbell Bradley
Mattawan HS
Kalamazoo MI

Hubbell Tim
Turpin HS
Cincinnati OH

Huber Richard
Woodlan HS
New Haven IN

Hubhard Troy
Salem HS
Salem IN

Huckleberry Jamie
New Albany HS
New Albany IN

Huckstep Bruce
Western Boone Jr Sr HS
Jamestown IN

Huddleston Kellie
Bethesda Christian HS
Indianapolis IN

Hudson Earl
West Side Sr HS
Gary IN

Hudson James
Richmond HS
Richmond IN

Hudson Julia
Lapel HS
Lapel IN

Hudson Nancy
Byron Area HS
Byron MI

Huelsman Fred
Sidney HS
Maplewood OH

Huettner Mary
Bishop Dwenger HS
Ft Wayne IN

Huff Bruce A
Gods Bible HS
Robinson IL

Huff Carol A
Cadillac Sr HS
Cadillac MI

Huff Dave
Cambridge HS
Cambridge OH

Huff Patrick
Hampshire HS
Romney WV

Huffer Brett
Clinton Central HS
Forest IN

Huffman Deborah
St Ursula Academy
Cincinnati OH

Huffman Donna
Sherman HS
Seth WV

Huffman Joyce
Tri Jr Sr HS
Lewisville IN

Huffman Lisa
Fairfield Union HS
Hide A Way HIs OH

Huffman Pamela
Spanishburg HS
Kegley WV

Huffman Robert S
Fairfield Union HS
Hide A Way Hill OH

Huffman Vicki
South Harrison HS
Clarksburg WV

Hufnagel Nancy
Seton HS
Cincinnati OH

Hufstetler Guy
Perry HS
Massillon OH

Huggins Bruce P
West Preston HS
Reedsville WV

Hughes John
Du Pont HS
Belle WV

Hughes Keith G
Lake Orion Comm HS
Lake Orion MI

Hughes Lisa
Spencer HS
Spencer WV

Hughes Robert
Clay Battelle HS
Fairview WV

Hughes Roberta
Edgewood HS
Hamilton OH

Huguenard Jeannette
Bishop Luers HS
Ft Wayne IN

Huguenin Michele
Galion Sr HS
Galion OH

Huibrechts Marion
Orchard View HS
Muskegon MI

Hukari Terri
James A Garfield HS
Garrettsville OH

Hulbert Heidi
Westerville North HS
Columbus OH

Hulin Cynthia
Whitehall Sr HS
Whitehall MI

Huling Catherin
Summerfield HS
Petersburg MI

Hull Brenda
East Knox HS
Howard OH

Hull Denise
Lewis Co HS
Jane Lew WV

Hull John
Greenwood Comm HS
Greenwood IN

Hull Phyllis
South Ripley HS
Holton IN

Humbarger Gary
Clay HS
Oregon OH

Humbaugh Kraig E
Washington HS
Washington IN

Hume Maggie
St Philip Cath Central HS
Battle Creek MI

Hume Melody
Dayton Christian HS
Dayton OH

Humphress Sonjia
Danville Community HS
Danville IN

Humphreys Shirlee L
Walton HS
Walton WV

Humphries Venita
Alexandria Monroe HS
Alexandria IN

Hunley John
Bexley HS
Columbus OH

Hunley Peggy
N Knox HS
Oaktown IN

Hunsucker Keith
Mogadore HS
Mogadore OH

Hunt Angela
Connersville Sr HS
Milton IN

Hunt Chuck
Oceana HS
Oceana WV

Hunt Kimberly A
Van Buren Local HS
Findlay OH

Hunt Monica
Upper Scioto Valley HS
Kenton OH

STUDENTS
PHOTOGRAPH
SCHEDULED
FOR PUBLI-
CATION HERE
COULD NOT
BE REPRO-
DUCED

Hunter Bradley
Brownsburg HS
Brownsbrg IN

Hunter Donnie
Greenbrier East HS
Alderson WV

Hunter Francis
Anderson HS
Anderson IN

Hunter Gregory
Morgantown HS
Morgantown WV

Hunter Sherry
Fairfield Sr HS
Fairfield OH

Hunter Valeria L
Cass Tech HS
Detroit MI

Huntzinger Maria
Nitro HS
Charleston WV

Hunziker Raymond E
Lake Catholic HS
Wickliffe OH

Hupp Michael
Clear Fork HS
Bellville OH

Hura Douglas
Ursuline HS
Youngstown OH

Hurley Jeremiah L
Elder HS
Cincinnati OH

Huron Robert A
Chesapeake HS
Chesapeake OH

Hursong Lisa
Mt Healthy HS
Cincinnati OH

Hurst Andrew
Benton Harbor HS
Benton Harbor MI

Hurst Scott M
Logan Sr HS
Logan WV

Hurth Jenni
High School
Gladstone MI

Hussar Susan
St Thomas Aquinas HS
Canton OH

Huston Rhea
Dunbar HS
Dunbar WV

Hutchings Karla
Dexter HS
Dexter MI

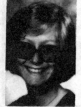
Hutchinson Rose A
Richwood HS
Tioga WV

Hutchinson Tim
Buffalo HS
Kenova WV

Hutchison James R
East Liverpool HS
E Liverpool OH

Hutchison Thomas E
Brighton Area HS
Brighton MI

Hutson Mike
Franklin HS
Franklin OH

Hyatt Diane
Brandon HS
Ortonville MI

Hyldahl Carol
Davison HS
Davison MI

Hymes Barbara
East HS
Columbus OH

Hynes Cynthia
Ben Davis HS
Indianapolis IN

Hysell Eric
Lakota HS
Middletown OH

I

Ice Jeffrey K
Madison Heights HS
Anderson IN

Ice William
Wellsville HS
Wellsville OH

Ickes Christopher
Washington HS
Massillon OH

Ide Jeanne
Greenbrier West HS
Smoot WV

Iden Pamela
Zanesville HS
Zanesville OH

Iezzi Julie
Olentangy HS
Galena OH

Ignazzitto Gina
Valley Forge HS
Parma OH

Iker Teresa
Central Baptist HS
Cincinnati OH

Iles Rhonda
Quincy Cmnty Schl
Quincy MI

Illes Mary
Archbishop Alter HS
Dayton OH

Ilstrup Thomas G
Calvin M Woodward HS
Toledo OH

Imber Thomas
Wadsworth HS
Wadsworth OH

Imbody Denyse
River Valley HS
Marion OH

Imel Diana
George Washington HS
Indianapolis IN

Imhoff Judith
Clay HS
Oregon OH

Immarino Thomas
Ledgemont HS
Thompson OH

Imray Dina
Cardinal Stritch HS
Perrysburg OH

Incropera Terri
Harrison HS
W Laf IN

Ingle Deborah
Lincoln West HS
Cleveland OH

Ingraham Sally
Mason County Central
HS
Scottville MI

Ingraham Susan
Rockford HS
Muskegon MI

Ingram Kadeejah W
Immaculata HS
Detroit MI

Ingram Pamela
Jennings Co HS
Butlerville IN

Ingram Steven
Midland Trail HS
Ansted WV

Inman Matthew
East Palestine HS
E Palestine OH

Inman Shelly
Jefferson Area HS
Jefferson OH

Iorgulescu Daniela
Pleasant HS
New Berlin WI

Irby Sheryl
Emerson HS
Gary IN

Irish Debra
Ovid Elsie HS
Ovid MI

Irish Lee
Hartland HS
Howell MI

Irvin Bonnie
Zanesville HS
Zanesville OH

Irvine Deborah
New Albany HS
New Albany OH

Irwin Cathy S
Garfield Sr HS
Hamilton OH

Irwin Kent
Terre Haute South Vigo
HS
Terre Haute IN

Irwin Michael D
Padua HS
Strongsville OH

Isaacs Gregory B
Gallia Academy HS
Vinton OH

Isabella Mark S
Notre Dame HS
Bridgeport WV

Isler Carolyn
Stephen T Badin HS
Okeana OH

Isler William P
Windham HS
Windham OH

Ison Scott
Clermont Northeastern
HS
Batavia OH

Isonhood Robin
F J Reitz HS
Evansville IN

Israel Carolyne
Mt Vernon Academy
Worthington OH

Istrabadi Feisal A
Bloomington HS South
Bloomington IN

Ivanovich Rocco
Jackson County Western
HS
Albion MI

Ivens Keith
Dowagiac Union HS
Dowagiac MI

Ivens Sandra K
Marcellus HS
Marcellus MI

Ivers Rebecca
Amelia HS
Cincinnati OH

STUDENTS
PHOTOGRAPH
SCHEDULED
FOR PUBLI-
CATION HERE
COULD NOT
BE REPRO-
DUCED

Ives Lisa
Tecumseh HS
Tecumseh MI

Ivey Sheri
Belpre HS
Belpre OH

Ivory Audrey
George Washington HS
E Chicago IN

J

Jabs Susan
Elkhart Memorial HS
Elkhart IN

Jack Carol
Medina Sr HS
Medina OH

Jackson Bradley D
Parchment HS
Parchment MI

Jackson Checita V
East HS
Columbus OH

Jackson David
Edwardsburg HS
Edwardsburg MI

Jackson Deborah
Franklin Hts HS
Columbus OH

Jackson Glory
Southwestern HS
Detroit MI

Jackson H Warn
Parkside HS
Jackson MI

Jackson James
Western Boone Jr Sr HS
Jamestown IN

Jackson Jodi
Atherton HS
Burton MI

Jackson Karen G
Warrensville Hts HS
Warrensville OH

Jackson Kimberly
Dayton Christian HS
Dayton OH

Jackson Lori
Merrillville HS
Merrillville IN

Jackson Lynda B
Jesup W Scott HS
Toledo OH

Jackson Lynn D
Mogadore HS
Mogadore OH

Jackson Michael
Laville HS
Lakeville IN

Jackson Michele
United Local HS
Medina OH

Jackson Morgann
Buena Vista HS
Saginaw MI

Jackson Paula J
Southwestern HS
Hanover IN

Jackson Richard
Harding HS
Marion OH

Jackson Richard
Elk Garden HS
Elk Garden WV

Jackson Robert
Edwardsburg HS
Edwardsburg MI

Jackson Rochelle
Highland HS
Anderson IN

Jackson Ruth
Oakwood HS
Dayton OH

Jackson Tamara
East HS
Columbus OH

Jackson Thomas
Eaton HS
Camden OH

Jackson Tina
Brooke HS
Weirton WV

Jackson Tom
Spencer HS
Spencer WV

Jackson Valarie
Northern Sr HS
Detroit MI

Jackson Venas
Lakeview HS
Howard City MI

Jacobs Amy
Durand Area HS
Durand MI

Jacobs Linette
St Johns HS
St Johns MI

Jacobs Lori
Algonac HS
Algonac MI

Jacobs Michael
Rockford Sr HS
Rockford MI

Jacobs Roger
Springs Valley HS
West Baden IN

Jacquay Justina
Northrop HS
Ft Wayne IN

Jaffe Carrie
Oak Hill HS
Jackson OH

Jaggers Sandra
Edon HS
Edon OH

Jaggers Steven
Frankfort Sr HS
Frankfort IN

Jahrman Christopher
Carroll HS
Cutler IN

Jaje Stephen
Garden City West Sr HS
Garden City MI

Jakacki Peter A
Bishop Borgess HS
Livonia MI

Jakary Susan
John Glenn HS
Westland MI

Jakee Keith
Lutheran East HS
Detroit MI

Jakes Lori
Douglas Mac Arthur HS
Saginaw MI

Jaksetic Daniel
Cardinal Stritch HS
Toledo OH

Jakubik Paul
Catholic Central HS
Northville MI

James Deborah
Floyd Central HS
Georgetown IN

James George
Walter P Chrysler Memrl HS
New Castle IN

James Jeff
Prairie Hts HS
Wolcottville IN

James Karlos
Martin Luther King Jr Sr HS
Detroit MI

James Katrina
Central HS
Detroit MI

James Michael
Hampshire HS
Augusta WV

James Robert
Miami Trace HS
Greenfield OH

Jameson Mary
Tippecanoe Valley HS
Rochester IN

Jamieson Scott
Andrean HS
Gary IN

Jamiot Marilyn
Cleveland Cntrl Cath HS
Cleveland OH

Jamison Rodger
John Hay HS
Cleveland OH

Jamison Vanesse
Jane Addams Voc HS
Cleveland OH

Jammer Brenda
Bay City Western HS
Auburn MI

Janes Brian
Grand Rapids Union HS
Grand Rapids MI

Janes Duane
University HS
Morgantown WV

Janezic Patricia
Streetsboro HS
Streetsboro OH

Janis Linda
Lumen Cordium HS
Solon OH

Jankowski Jeffery J
St Francis De Sales HS
Toledo OH

Janos Cynthia
Lake Catholic HS
Painesville OH

Janosko Stephan
Keystone HS
La Grange OH

Janota Lorrie
Nordonia HS
Northfield OH

Janovec John
Norton HS
Norton OH

Janus Jon
Newton Falls HS
Newton Falls OH

Janush Rachelle
Bishop Foley HS
Detroit MI

Janz Robert
Clinton Prairie HS
Frankfort IN

Janz Roger
Clinton Prairie HS
Frankfort IN

Jara Julie
Austintown Fitch HS
Youngstown OH

Jarc Christopher
Willoughby South HS
Eastlake OH

Jarrell Donald
Sylvania Northview HS
Toledo OH

Jarrett Debra A
West Side Sr HS
Gary IN

Jarrett James
Southfield Lathrup Sr HS
Southfield MI

Jarvie David
Ironton HS
Ironton OH

Jarvis Carlita A
Hurricane HS
Hurricane WV

Jarvis Rachel
Southeast HS
Rootstown OH

Jarzab Shawn
High School
Maple Hgts OH

Jaworsky Anna M
Corunna HS
Corunna MI

Jay Anne Marie
Marian Heights Academy
Washburn IL

Jefferies Mark K
Lincoln HS
Shinnston WV

Jeffers Aaron
Gallia Acad
Gallipolis OH

Jefferson Ann
John R Buchtel High
Univ
Akron OH

Jeffery Dennis
Lebanon HS
Lebanon OH

Jeffries Bonnie
Salem HS
Salem IN

Jeffries Chauncey
Mckinley HS
Canton OH

Jeffries John
Reed City Sr HS
Reed City MI

Jeffries Rita
North Putnam HS
Roachdale IN

Jenkin Dave L
Bloomington HS South
Bloomington IN

Jenkins Brian
Ironton HS
Ironton OH

Jenkins Casandra
Ridgedale HS
Marion OH

Jenkins Cornella
Barberton HS
Barberton OH

Jenkins James R
Bishop Hartley HS
Whitehall OH

Jenkins Kelly
Watkins Memorial HS
Pataskala OH

Jenkins Kimberly
Regina HS
Cleveland OH

Jenkins Mark
Jackson HS
Jackson OH

Jenkins Robin D
Liberty HS
Clarksburg WV

Jenkins Tami
Woodrow Wilson HS
Youngstown OH

Jennings Burton K
Brooke HS
Wellsburg WV

Jennings Chris
Colon HS
Colon MI

Jennings Derek
Amelia HS
Cincinnati OH

Jennings Lori A
Shelbyville HS
Shelbyville IN

Jennings Walter
North HS
Youngstown OH

Jensen Charles
Negaunee HS
Negaunee MI

Jerge Martin
St Joseph Prep Seminary
St Clairsville OH

Jerome Gregory A
Barberton HS
Barberton OH

Jerred Richard
Clare HS
Clare MI

Jesitus Robert
Maple Hts Sr HS
Maple Hgts OH

Jesse Peg
Margaretta HS
Castalia OH

Jeter Jennifer K
Central Hower HS
Akron OH

Jett Paula D
Batavia HS
Batavia OH

Jewel Douglas L
De Kalb Central HS
Auburn IN

Jewell Lisa
North Central HS
Shelburn IN

Jimenez Michelle
Holy Name Nazareth HS
Middleburg Ht OH

Jira Paul
N Royalton HS
N Royalton OH

Jividen Kimberly
Gallia Academy
Gallipolis OH

Jobe Kimberly
Dunbar HS
Dunbar WV

Jochen Marsha
Hill Community HS
Lansing MI

Jochum Francis E
Euclid Sr HS
Euclid OH

Jocius Jerrold
Wirt HS
Gary IN

Johannigman Jeffrey D
St Xavier HS
Cincinnati OH

John Sharon
Waldron Jr Sr HS
Shelbyville IN

John Thomas A
Olentangy HS
Powell OH

Johns Terri
Philip Barbour HS
Philippi WV

Johnson Bernie
Big Creek HS
Coalwood WV

Johnson Brenda
Washington Irving HS
Clarksburg WV

Johnson Burley W
West Preston HS
Kingwood WV

Johnson Carl
Chesterton HS
Chesterton IN

Johnson Carol R
Pioneer HS
Ann Arbor MI

Johnson Cathy
La Ville Jr Sr HS
Plymouth IN

Johnson Christine M
John R Buchtel Univ HS
Akron OH

Johnson Curt
Northmont HS
Dayton OH

Johnson David
La Porte HS
Laporte IN

Johnson Dawn
T Roosevelt HS
E Chicago IN

Johnson Deborah
Hackett HS
Kalamazoo MI

Johnson Derek V
Wayne HS
Dayton OH

Johnson Devona
Patterson Coop HS
Dayton OH

Johnson Enoch
Central Preston HS
Tunnelton WV

Johnson Georgia A
Hammond Tech Voc HS
Hammond IN

Johnson Greg
Park Hills HS
Fairborn OH

Johnson James
Kingsford HS
Quinnesec MI

Johnson Jay
Parkersburg HS
Vienna WV

Johnson Jeffrey
Heritage Christian School
Carmel IN

Johnson Jeffrey
Miami Trace HS
Washington Ch OH

Johnson Jeffrey
Western Boone Jr Sr HS
Thorntown IN

Johnson Jennifer
Anderson HS
Anderson IN

Johnson John K
Walnut Hills HS
Cincinnati OH

Johnson Joseph
Cadillac Sr HS
Cadillac MI

Johnson Juanita
Prairie Heights HS
Pleasant Lk IN

Johnson Julie
Turpin HS
Cincinnati OH

Johnson Julie
Midland Trail HS
Ansted WV

Johnson Karen
Brownstown Central HS
Brownstown IN

Johnson Kathy M
North Ridgeville HS
N Ridgeville OH

Johnson Keith E
Thomas M Cooley HS
Detroit MI

Johnson Kellie
Edgerton HS
Bryan OH

Johnson Kimberly
Heath HS
Heath OH

Johnson Kimberly
Arthur Hill HS
Saginaw MI

Johnson Korree
Allegan HS
Allegan MI

Johnson Lance L
Horace Mann HS
Gary IN

Johnson Lauren J
Highland HS
Anderson IN

Johnson Leisha
Groveport Madison HS
Groveport OH

Johnson Lisa
Henry Ford II HS
Sterling Hts MI

Johnson M
Decatus Central HS
Indnpls IN

Johnson M
Fairland HS
Proctorvll OH

Johnson Mark
Algonac HS
Algonac MI

Johnson Mark R
Brandon HS
Ortonville MI

Johnson Marsha L
Indiana Academy
Alexandria IN

Johnson Mary
Rutherford B Hayes HS
Delaware OH

Johnson Pam
Posen Consolidated HS
Posen MI

Johnson Patricia
A D Johnston HS
Bessemer MI

Johnson Salli
Northridge HS
Johnstown OH

Johnson Sandra
Horace Mann HS
Gary IN

Johnson Sandra
Cass Tech HS
Detroit MI

Johnson Shane
Maysville HS
Zanesville OH

Johnson Shannon
Northrop HS
Ft Wayne IN

Johnson Sherry
Decatur Central HS
Indnpls IN

Johnson Steven
Orleans HS
Orleans IN

Johnson Susan J
Jackson Milton HS
North Kackson OH

Johnson Tenna
Clay Battelle HS
Pentress WV

Johnson Teresa
Bluefield HS
Bluefield WV

Johnson Timothy
Harry S Truman HS
Taylor MI

Johnson Virginia F
Marion HS
Marion IN

Johnson Zavaan
Grove City HS
Urbancrest OH

Johnston Cheryl
Pike HS
Indianapolis IN

Johnston Jill
Celina Sr HS
Celina OH

Johnston Joseph
Milton HS
Ona WV

Johnston Laura
Milton HS
Ona WV

Johnston Lydia
Wilbur Wright HS
Dayton OH

Johnston Marlene
Lake Orion HS
Lake Orion MI

Johnston Matt
Sebring Mc Kinley HS
Sebring OH

Johnston Stephen A
Walnut Hills HS
Cincinnati OH

Johnston Terry J
Jackson Center HS
Maplewood OH

Joiner Frederick
Waterford Township HS
Pontiac MI

Jonas William
Parkersburg HS
Vienna WV

Jonaus Mary C
Grand Haven Sr HS
Grand Haven MI

Jones Alisa
Robert S Rogers HS
Toledo OH

Jones Andrea
Fennville HS
Fennville MI

Jones Angela
Carlisle HS
Franklin OH

Jones Anita
Shady Spring HS
Shady Spring WV

Jones Cathy
Withrow HS
Cincinnati OH

Jones Cheryl L
Atherton Sr HS
Burton MI

Jones Chris
Archbishop Alter HS
Dayton OH

Jones Darek
Marine City HS
Marine City MI

Jones Deborah
Carson City Crystal Area
HS
Carson City MI

Jones Deborah
Piqua Central HS
Piqua OH

Jones Dennis
Garaway HS
Dundee OH

Jones Diana
Houghton HS
Houghton MI

Jones Dwayne K
Greenville Sr HS
Greenville OH

Jones Earl
Washington HS
Massillon OH

Jones Eric
Rutherford B Hayes HS
Delaware OH

Jones Ernie
South Spencer HS
Richland IN

Jones Gregory
Kearsley HS
Usaf Academy CO

Jones Gregory
Glen Este HS
Cincinnati OH

Jones Jami
Edward Lee Mc Clain HS
Greenfield OH

Jones Janet
Chapmanville HS
Harts WV

Jones Jeff
Washington Irving HS
Clarksburg WV

Jones Jeffery W
Detroit Northern Sr HS
Detroit MI

Jones Jennifer
Canfield HS
Canfield OH

Jones Jesse J
New Haven HS
New Haven MI

Jones Joseph
Rochester Comm HS
Rochester IN

Jones Julie
Hartland HS
Milford MI

Jones Katherine
Shelbyville Sr HS
Shelbyville IN

Jones Kelly
Bremen HS
Bremen IN

Jones Kimberly
Elkins HS
Elkins WV

Jones Leigh
Firestone HS
Akron OH

Jones Lori
Cardington Lincoln HS
Marengo OH

Jones Lyndon
William H Harrison Sr HS
Harrison OH

Jones Marlena
Flint Open Schl
Flint MI

Jones Maryellen
Anderson HS
Anderson IN

Jones Michael
Beaver Local HS
E Liverpool OH

Jones Mona
Solon HS
Solon OH

Jones Priscella
Cleveland Central Cath
HS
Cleveland OH

Jones Scott
Ontario HS
Mnsfld OH

Jones Scott
Indian Creek HS
Morgantown IN

Jones Shelli
Continental Local HS
Continental OH

Jones Sherry
Our Lady Of Angels HS
Cincinnati OH

Jones Stephen
Northwest HS
Indianapolis IN

Jones Susan
Decatur HS
Decatur MI

Jones Susan
Tekonsha HS
Tekonsha MI

Jones Tandra
Du Pont HS
Charleston WV

Jones Teresa
Springboro HS
Springboro OH

Jones Teresa
Milton Union HS
W Milton OH

Jones Teresa
Switzerland Cnty Jr Sr
HS
Canaan IN

Jones Trent
Peebles HS
Peebles OH

Jones Ursula
Wehrle HS
Columbus OH

Jones Valerie
John Hay HS
Cleveland OH

Jones Veronica
Immaculata HS
Detroit MI

Jones William
Buchanan HS
Buchanan MI

Jones Jr Sam
Park Tudor HS
Indianapolis IN

Jordan Chrystal
Urbana HS
Urbana OH

Jordan Denise
Canfield HS
Youngstown OH

Jordan Denise
Grant HS
Grant MI

Jordan Denise
Euclid Sr HS
Euclid OH

Jordan Marie
Benton Harbor HS
Benton Hbr MI

Jordan Quintin
Woodward HS
Cincinnati OH

Jordan Ralph
Alexander HS
Pomeroy OH

Jordan Rebecca L
Jennings County HS
No Vernon IN

Jordan Susan A
Jackson HS
Massillon OH

Jordon Brenda
Tecumseh HS
New Carlisle OH

Jorgensen Linda
Wayne HS
Dayton OH

Jorgenson Janet
New Lexington Sr HS
New Lexington OH

Josef Ernest
Ripley HS
Ripley WV

Joseph Maria
Our Lady Of Mercy HS
W Bloomfield MI

Josey Richard
Highland Park Commty
HS
Highland Park MI

Jovanovich Ray W
Hammond HS
Hammond IN

Joyce Debbie
South Knox HS
Vincennes IN

Joyner Angela
Watkins Memorial HS
Pataskala OH

Jozwiak Johanna
Midland HS
Midland MI

Jrososky Roger
Newbury HS
Newbury OH

Juday David
William G Mather HS
Wetmore MI

Judd John
Kiser HS
Dayton OH

Judge Patricia
Otsego HS
Bowling Gren OH

Judis Janet
Rockford Sr HS
Belmont MI

Judson Timm
University HS
Gates Mills OH

Jueckstock Diane
Kimball HS
Royal Oak MI

Julian Debbie
Valparaiso HS
Valparaiso IN

Julian Gail
Jackson HS
North Canton OH

Jung Chris
Brush HS
S Euclid OH

Jungclas Daniel
Roseville HS
Roseville MI

Junge Daniel
Napoleon HS
Napoleon OH

Junkins Brenda
Liberty HS
Bristol WV

Juratovac Evanne
Nordonia HS
Sagamore Hls OH

Justice Frelon
Willow Run HS
Ypsilanti MI

Justice Jackie
Crestview HS
Mansfield OH

Justice Ronnie
Logan HS
West Logan WV

Justo Emilio
Andrean HS
Crown Pt IN

K

Kacho Brenda
Greeneview HS
Jamestown OH

Kacik Richard
Morgantown HS
Morgantwn WV

Kaczmarek David A
Greenfield Central HS
Greenfield IN

Kaczmarek Lori
Manistee Public HS
Manistee MI

Kadiyala Rajendra K
West Lafayette Sr HS
W Lafayette IN

Kaelber Mark
Jackson HS
Massillon OH

Kafer Karen
Upper Arlington HS
Columbus OH

Kafker Roger
Cincinnati Country Day
Schl
Cincinnati OH

Kafton Joyce
Cameron HS
Cameron WV

Kage Theresa
Willard HS
Willard OH

Kahl Sherri L
Austin HS
Austin IN

Keifesh Mark
Mott Sr HS
Warren MI

Kail Connie
Canton South HS
E Sparta OH

Kaiser Janice
Sullivan HS
Carlisle IN

Kaiser Kirk
Upper Valley J V S HS
Piqua OH

Kaiser Michael G
North Farmington HS
Farmington Hls MI

Kaji Reiko
Rogers HS
Toledo OH

Kalaycioglu Matt
Lincoln HS
Shinnston WV

Kale Tracey
North Union HS
Richwood OH

Kalil Kim
Magnificat HS
N Olmsted OH

Kalis Pam
Lakewood HS
Lakewood OH

Kall Philip F
Benedictine HS
Chesterland OH

Kalmbach Anna
Cadillac Sr HS
Cadillac MI

Kelsen Susan
La Salle HS
S Bend IN

Kalt Loren
New Philadelphia HS
New Phila OH

Kaminski Karol
Magnificat HS
Middleburg Hts OH

Kaminski Lisa M
Marian HS
Royal Oak MI

Kammann Ellen
Bishop Gallagher HS
Detroit MI

Kamody Steve
Marion L Steele HS
Amherst OH

Kamp Andrea L
Dearborn HS
Dearborn Hts MI

Kampman Kimberly A
Beaumont School For
Girls
Chagrin Falls OH

Kamprath Paul H
Monroe HS
Monroe MI

Kandel Mara
West Branch Local HS
Salem OH

Kane Carmel
Immaculate Conception
Acad
No Vernon IN

Kane Joan
Harbor HS
Ashtabula OH

Kanne Gregg
Rensselaer Central HS
Fair Oaks IN

Kanott Frances
Oceana HS
Lynco WV

Kantor Susan
Maplewood HS
Cortland OH

Kantzer Kim
Marion Pleasant HS
Marion OH

Kapalka David
Munster HS
Munster IN

Kapelka Kathleen
Tiffin Calvert HS
Tiffin OH

Kaplan David R
Clarenceville HS
Livonia MI

Kaplan Sheri
North Farmington HS
Farm Hills MI

Kappel Gregory
Fairview HS
Fairview Pk OH

Karadin Kimberly
Our Lady Of The Elms
HS
Akron OH

Karam Brian
Timken Sr HS
Canton OH

Karandos Pamela
Warren Central HS
Indpls IN

Karboske Letha
Mason County Central
HS
Ludington MI

Karnes Linda
Nitro Sr HS
Nitro WV

Karns Leslie
North Daviess HS
Odon IN

Karr Diane
Edsel Ford HS
Dearborn MI

Karrick Mark
Eastern Local HS
Beaver OH

Karrick Mark W
Eastern Local HS
Beaver OH

Karst Larry A
Marion Franklin HS
Columbus OH

Kartholl Nancy
Bishop Dwenger HS
Ft Wayne IN

Kasmar Judee
Niles Mc Kinley HS
Niles OH

Kaspryzycki Elizabeth
St Florian HS
Detroit MI

Kassebaum Jeanette
Hamilton S E HS
Noblesville IN

Kastner Michael
Tiffin Calvert HS
Tiffin OH

Katschke Karen
Fitch HS
Youngstown OH

Katter Karen
Wilmington HS
Wilmington OH

Katter Shana
Martinsville HS
Martinsville IN

Kattus Tara
Colerain Sr HS
Cincinnati OH

Kauffman Audrey
Columbiana HS
Columbiana OH

Kaufman Lisa
Mineral Ridge HS
Mineral Ridge OH

Kaufmann Paul E
Eastlake N HS
Willowick OH

Kaurich Thomas
North HS
Columbus OH

Kautz Margaret G
Zanesville HS
Zanesville OH

Kava Cathy J
Winston Churchill HS
Livonia MI

Kayafas Gus
Wintersville HS
Wintersville OH

Kayla Deborah
Lake HS
Uniontown OH

Kays Mark
North Putnam HS
Bainbridge IN

Kearney Bryan
James A Garfield HS
Garrettsville OH

Kearns Kevin
Madison Comp HS
Mansfield OH

Kearns Thomas
Padua Franciscan HS
Cleveland OH

Keasling B
Union County HS
Liberty IN

Kee Donald E
Green HS
Clinton OH

Kee Donna
Franklin HS
Franklin WV

Keebler Cynthia G
Loveland Hurst HS
Loveland OH

Keefe Lisa
Niles HS
Niles MI

Keegan Lisa
Ehove Joint Voc HS
Vickery OH

Keeler Marian
Withrow HS
Cincinnati OH

Keeler Rebecca
Waterford Township HS
Pontiac MI

Keeling Nora
Danville Community HS
Danville IN

Keen Sandi K
Mt Vernon Sr HS
Mt Vernon OH

Keene Pearl C
Iaeger Sr HS
Jolo WV

Keeslar Paul
Hackett HS
Kalamazoo MI

Keesler Sharla J
Gods Bible HS
Nebraska City NE

Keesucker Kathy
South Harrison HS
Jane Lew WV

Keeton Cathleen L
Southwestern HS
Franklin IN

Keilitz Robert
Caro Community HS
Caro MI

Keisler Mark
North Newton HS
Demotte IN

Keister Matthew
Churubusco HS
Albion IN

Keith Betty
Charlestown HS
Charlestown IN

Keith Richard
Peebles HS
Peebles OH

Keizer Jackie
Wayland HS
Wayland MI

Kellam Mark
Tri HS
Spiceland IN

Kellar Sharon
Wintersville HS
Wintersville OH

Kellas George
Bridgeport HS
Barton OH

Kellenberger Lori
Merrillville HS
Merrillville IN

Keller Deborah
Cadillac Sr HS
Cadillac MI

Keller Donna
Southgate HS
Southgate MI

Keller Dusty
Father Wehrle Memorial
HS
Columbus OH

Keller Eileen
Boardman HS
Youngstown OH

Keller Letia A
Berkley HS
Oak Park MI

Keller Lisa
Northland HS
Columbus OH

Keller Mary
Jennings County HS
Commiskey IN

Keller Nancy
Millersport HS
Millersport OH

Keller Pamela
Clay Sr HS
Oregon OH

Keller Paul
Worthington Jefferson
HS
Worthington IN

Keller Stephen
Chesterton HS
Chesterton IN

Kelley Beth
Prairie Hts HS
Hudson IN

Kelley Connie
Tyler County HS
Middlebourne WV

Kelley Deborah
Mentor HS
Willoughby OH

Kelley Kathy
Eastern HS
Haslett MI

Kelley Le Anne
Franklin Community HS
Franklin IN

Kelley Michael
Kyger Creek HS
Gallipolis OH

Kelley Wanda
Bruceton HS
Bruceton Mills WV

Kelly Adrianne
Cardinal HS
Huntsburg OH

Kelly Anne
Carroll HS
Xenia OH

Kelly Bill
Caseville HS
Caseville MI

Kelly David M
Chesterton HS
Porter IN

Kelly Donna
Barberton HS
Barberton OH

Kelly James
St Joseph Prep Seminary
Vienna WV

Kelly Jana
Riverside HS
De Graff OH

Kelly Kathy
Miami Trace HS
Washington Ch OH

Kelly Kim
Fremont Ross HS
Fremont OH

Kelly Lisa
Dominican HS
Detroit MI

Kelly Lisa
Cuyahoga Falls HS
Cuyahoga Fls OH

Kelly Patrick
Coldwater HS
Coldwater MI

Kelly Robin
Lake Central HS
Schererville IN

Kelly Suzanne
Fairmont West HS
Dayton OH

Kelly Terri
St Peter & Paul Area HS
Saginaw MI

Kelm Jeanie
Salem HS
Campbellsburg IN

Kemmerlin Laura R
Watervliet HS
Watervliet MI

Kemp Kimberly
Washington HS
Massillon OH

Kemp Tammy
West Washington HS
Campbellsburg IN

Kemper Karen
St Francis De Sales HS
Columbus OH

Kemper Rickena
Millersport HS
Thornville OH

Kendall Richard
Spencer HS
Spencer WV

Kendrick Teresa
Albion Sr HS
Albion MI

Kendricks Camille Jo
Andrean HS
Gary IN

Kenerson John E
Eastlake North HS
Willowick OH

Kenne Deborah
Alpena HS
Alpena MI

Kennedy Cheryl
Wheelersburg HS
Wheelersburg OH

Kennedy Christopher
St Joseph Central HS
Huntington WV

Kennedy Jo Lynne
Caro Community HS
Caro MI

Kennedy Kenny
Cloverdale Community
Schools
Cloverdale IN

Kennedy Mark
Northwest HS
Lucasville OH

Kennedy Martha J
Ironton HS
Ironton OH

Kennedy Matthew
Culver Military Academy
De Motte IN

Kennedy Stephen
Culver Military Academy
Maumee OH

Kennedy Thomas
Washington Irving HS
Clarksburg WV

Kennedy Tim
Griffith HS
Griffith IN

Kenney Jayne
Hampshire HS
Levels WV

Kent Andre
Cass Technical HS
Detroit MI

Kent Kari
William Henry Harrison
HS
Evansville IN

Kent Teresa
Morrice HS
Bancroft MI

Kenworthy Kelly
Randolph Southern Jr Sr
HS
Lynn IN

Kenyon Brad
La Porte HS
Laporte IN

Kerbleski Gerard
T L Handy HS
Bay City MI

Kerby Deb
Barberton HS
Barberton OH

Kerekes Rodney A
Bishop Donahue HS
Moundsville WV

Kerlin Chris
Rensselaer Central HS
Rensselaer IN

Kern Christopher
Cardinal Ritter HS
Indianapolis IN

Kern Pam
Vincennes Lincoln HS
Vincennes IN

Kerner David
Solon HS
Solon OH

Kerns Becky
Springs Vly Comm HS
French Lick IN

Kerns Hugh
North Putnam Jr Sr HS
Roachdale IN

Kerns Vicky
Wirt County HS
Elizabeth WV

Kerns Vicky A
Indian Lake HS
Huntsville OH

Kerpsack Heidi
Canfield HS
Canfield OH

Kerr Barbara
St Johns HS
St Johns MI

Kerrigan Michael J
Badin HS
Hamilton OH

Kersjes Timothy C
East Kentwood HS
Kentwood MI

Kerst Kina
Ontario HS
Mansfield OH

Kerstetter David J
Garden City West Sr HS
Garden City MI

Keschl Lisa
Bishop Gallagher HS
Detroit MI

Kesecker Shelly
Martinsburg Sr HS
Martinsburg WV

Keshner Glenn
Oak Park HS
Oak Pk MI

Kesling Scott
Springboro HS
Lebanon OH

Kesner Teresa
Keyser HS
Keyser WV

Kessel Emily
Wellsville HS
Wellsville OH

Kessel Melinda J
Keyser HS
Keyser WV

Kessler Laura
Archbishop Alter HS
Dayton OH

Kessler Mary
Wellston HS
Wellston OH

Kessler Tracy
Greenfield Central HS
Greenfield IN

Kesteloot Jo Ann
Grayling HS
Grayling MI

Kesterson J
Cambridge HS
Cambridge OH

Ketchem Mark
Ishpeming HS
Ishpeming MI

Kettel Keith
Ironton HS
Ironton OH

Ketten Elizabeth
Msgr John R Hackett HS
Richland MI

Kettler Michelle
St Ursula Academy
Toeldo OH

Key Debra
Andrean HS
Gary IN

Key Jeanine
Martin Luther King Jr Sr
HS
Detroit MI

Keyes Katrina
Keyser HS
Piedmont WV

Keyes Tanya
Linden Mc Kinley Sr HS
Columbus OH

Keylor Hyde
East Palestine HS
Columbiana OH

Keys Brenda
Bluefield HS
Bluefld WV

Keys Kathleen
Big Rapids HS
Big Rapids MI

Keyser Terry
Bullock Creek HS
Midland MI

Kharbas Vijay
Northrop HS
Ft Wayne IN

Kibbey Martha
Brookhaven HS
Columbus OH

Kibbey Warren
Ludington HS
Ludington MI

Kibellus Carlton
Concordia Lutheran HS
Ft Wayne IN

Kick Virginia
Loundonville HS
Loudonville OH

Kidd Stephanie
Northrop HS
Ft Wayne IN

Kidder Cynthia
Bullock Creek HS
Midland MI

Kiefer Todd
Shelby Sr HS
Shelby OH

Kien Joyce
Lowell HS
Lowell IN

Kies Cathy
Anna HS
Anna OH

Kiger Daniel
Mineral Ridge HS
Mineral Ridge OH

Kiger Matthew
Doddridge County HS
Ctr Point WV

Kihm Jeannie
Hackett HS
Kalamazoo MI

Kilbourne Pamela
Wayne Memorial HS
Wayne MI

Kilburn Lori A
Anderson HS
Anderson IN

Kile Charlene
Franklin HS
Upper Tract WV

Kilian Lori
Southridge HS
Huntngbrg IN

Kilps Rhonda D
Washington HS
Washington IN

Kimball Walter C
Cadiz HS
Cadiz OH

Kimbrough Valerie
Oak Park HS
Oak Park MI

Kime Patricia A
Colon HS
Colon MI

Kimler Alicia
St Joseph Central HS
Huntington WV

Kimmel Dave
Bishop Watterson HS
Columbus OH

Kimpel Beth A
Columbiana HS
Columbiana OH

Kincaid Dean
Columbia City Joint HS
Columbia City IN

Kinch Teresa
Michigan Center HS
Jackson MI

Kindervator John
Rossford HS
Perrysburg OH

Kindred Don
Anderson HS
Anderson IN

Kinemond Treva
Minerva HS
Minerva OH

King Andrew
Moeller HS
Reading OH

King Beverly
Princeton HS
Princeton WV

King Beverly
Williamstown HS
Williamstown WV

King Charlotte
Wadsworth Sr HS
Wadsworth OH

King Deborah
Terre Haute N Vigo HS
Terre Haute IN

King Denna
Corydon Central HS
Corydon IN

King Dennis
Princeton HS
Princeton WV

King Jeff
Wehrle HS
Columbus OH

King Joan
Bishop Foley HS
Royal Oak MI

King Joan
Upper Arlington HS
Columbus OH

King Kevin
Meigs HS
Middleport OH

King Laurie
Mendon HS
Three Rivers MI

King Leslie
Warrensville Heights HS
Warrensville OH

King Linda
Terre Haute North Vigo
HS
Terre Haute IN

King Marthlena A
Lewis County HS
Alum Bridge WV

King Mary
Clay Battelle HS
Burton WV

King Michael D
Lewis County HS
Alum Bridge WV

King Michelle
Perry HS
Painesville OH

King Michelle
Bridgman Sr HS
Bridgman MI

King Mike
Mc Nicholas HS
Cincinnati OH

King Sherry
Shenandoah HS
Middletown IN

King Sherry
Henryville HS
Henryville IN

King Tuesday
Northrop HS
Ft Wayne IN

King Venice Lynn
Bishop Hartley HS
Columbus OH

King Wilmer W
Adena HS
Clarksburg OH

King Ii Darrell H
Tippecanoe Vly HS
Mentone IN

Kingstrom David R
Pontiac Northern HS
Pontiac MI

Kinkead Brenda
Marion Adams HS
Sheridan IN

Kinnett Gayle
New Palestine HS
Greenfield IN

Kinney Michael
Liberty HS
Clarksburg WV

Kinsey Paul
St Clairsville HS
St Clairsville OH

Kinzie Beth
Andrean HS
Merrillville IN

Kipp Kathy
Chesapeake HS
Chesapeake OH

Kipp Kristopher M
Walsh Jesuit HS
Akron OH

Kirbitz Craig
Atherton HS
Davison MI

Kirby Jennifer
Franklin HS
Franklin OH

Kirby Kathy
Rochester HS
Rochester IN

Kirchner David
Anderson HS
Anderson IN

Kirincic Helen A
Morton HS
Hammond IN

Kirk Janice
North Knox HS
Bicknell IN

Kirkham Kay
Daleville HS
Daleville IN

Kirkland Eugene A
Columbus East HS
Columbus OH

Kirkpatrick Brad
Dayton Christian HS
New Carlisle OH

Kirkpatrick Kay L
Wawasee HS
Syracuse IN

Kirkpatrick Sheri
Frontier HS
Nw Mtmrs OH

Kirsch Matthias J
Cousino Sr HS
Warren MI

Kiser Kelly
Frontier HS
Chalmers IN

Kisner Donna
Waldron Area Schools
Pittsford MI

Kisner Fleeta
Grafton HS
Grafton WV

Kissee Konnie
Highland HS
Highland IN

Kissick Rick
Manchester HS
Manchester OH

Kistner John
Delta Sr HS
Delta OH

Kittell Vickey L
Solon HS
Solon OH

Kittle Laura
Morrice HS
Morrice MI

Kittle Rhonda
Grafton HS
Flemington WV

Kittle Tonya K
Buffalo HS
Huntington WV

Klaffke Doris
Northrop HS
Ft Wayne IN

Klain Ronald A
North Central HS
Indianapolis IN

Klann Karen
Nordonia HS
Macedonia OH

Klapko Charles
Hamady HS
Flint MI

Klawinski Chris
Colon HS
Colon MI

Klay Jeanine
Bluffton HS
Bluffton OH

Klein Alan
Brooke HS
Wellsburg WV

Klein Kay
Sylvania Northview HS
Sylvania OH

Kleinbauer Chris
Bloomington HS
Bloomington IN

Kline Camille
Columbia City Joint HS
Columbia City IN

Kline Cathy
De Kalb HS
Waterloo IN

Kline Don
Kalkaska HS
Alden MI

Kline John
Kenston HS
Chagrin Falls OH

Kline Julie
Roscommon HS
Higgins Lake MI

Kline Keith
Memorial HS
Bristol IN

Kline Martine
Liberty Benton HS
Findlay OH

Kline Timothy
Perry HS
Painesville OH

Klingenberg Janice
Bedford HS
Temperance MI

Klinker Janet
Heritage HS
Monroeville IN

Kloeckner Blaine
Grand Ledge HS
Eagle MI

Klompmaker Anita
Holland Chr HS
Holland MI

Klosowski Julie
All Saints Central HS
Bay City MI

Klueg Shelly
Central HS
Evansville IN

Klug Brian
River Valley HS
Buchanan MI

Kmonk Janet
Rossford HS
Rossford OH

Knape Tracy
Forest Hills Central Sr
HS
Grand Rapids MI

Knapke Dorothy
Marion Local HS
Chickasaw OH

Knapp Elizabeth M
Highland HS
Hinckley OH

Knecht Mary
Miami Trace HS
Washington OH

Kneebone James
Yale HS
Yale MI

Kneisley Jennifer
North Central HS
Indianapolis IN

Knepp Robert
Grayling HS
Grayling MI

Knezetic James
Admiral King HS
Lorain OH

Knickerbocker Brad
Chelsea HS
Chelsea MI

Kniffen Michael
Houghton Lake HS
Merritt MI

Knight Brad
Inland Lakes HS
Afton MI

Knight Rebecca
Old Trail HS
Akron OH

Knight Rick
Elkins HS
Elkins WV

Knisely Barbara
Sylvania Northview HS
Sylvania OH

Knobb Kim
Washington HS
Massillon OH

Knol David
Jenison Public HS
Jenison MI

Knol Susi
Jenison HS
Jenison MI

Knoll Kay
Niles Sr HS
Niles MI

STUDENTS
PHOTOGRAPH
SCHEDULED
FOR PUBLI-
CATION HERE
COULD NOT
BE REPRO-
DUCED

Knoop Annette
Sidney HS
Sidney OH

Knop Julie
Walled Lake Central HS
Union Lake MI

Knopf Chris
Kenston HS
Chagrin Fls OH

Knopp Laurie
S Range HS
Salem OH

Knous Tom
Memorial HS
St Marys OH

Knouse Todd
Upper Arlington HS
Columbus OH

Knowles Robert S
Charleston HS
Charleston WV

Knue Susan
Edinburgh HS
Edinburgh IN

Knuff Christine
Boardman HS
Boardman OH

Knuff Edward
Ursuline HS
Hubbard OH

Knych Carol
Cathedral HS
Indianapolis IN

Kobasic Mary
Escanaba Area Public HS
Escanaba MI

Kobasko Mike
Bishop Donahue HS
Moundsville WV

Kober Ann
Hubbard HS
Hubbard OH

Koch Julia
Bay City Western HS
Midland MI

Koch Kenneth
Springfield Local HS
Petersburg OH

Kocher Linda
William Henry Harrison
HS
Cleves OH

Kock Rex
Garrett HS
Garrett IN

Kocks Carl
Arthur Hill HS
Saginaw MI

Kocon Robert
Donald E Gavit Jr Sr HS
Hammond IN

Kocsis Jeff
Wyoming Park HS
Wyoming MI

Koehler Jackie
Washington HS
Massillon OH

Koeler Robert
Eastern HS
Russellville OH

Koenig Matthew
Northville HS
Northville MI

Koenig Scott
Lima Central Catholic HS
Lima OH

Koewler James L
F J Reitz HS
Evansville IN

Kohl Scott
Cambridge HS
Cambridge OH

Kohls Sharon
St Ursula Academy
Cincinnati OH

Kohn David
Calumet HS
Calumet MI

Kojac Diana
Morgantown HS
Westover WV

Kokalari Susan
Edwin Denby HS
Detroit MI

Kokenge Dawn J
Valley View HS
Farmersville OH

Koker Kimberly
Revere HS
Las Vegas NV

Kolarik Matthew
Hoover HS
N Canton OH

Kolb Beverly
Brookville HS
Brookville IN

Kolean Timothy
West Ottawa HS
Holland MI

Kolesar Edward
Strongsville Sr HS
Strongsville OH

Kolettis George J
Andrean HS
Merrillville IN

Kolettis Georgia
Andrean HS
Merrillville IN

Koliser Darla
Austintown Fitch HS
Austintown OH

Koliser Darra
Austintown Fitch HS
Youngstown OH

Kollasch Kristen
Lake Orion Cmnty HS
Lake Orion MI

Kollenberg Judith
Southfield Lathrup Sr HS
Southfield MI

Kolmetz Jane E
Center Line HS
Warren MI

Kolosionek Mark
James Ford Rhodes HS
Cleveland OH

Koltyk Gregory
Adlai Stevenson HS
Livonia MI

Koman Steve
Lincoln Park HS
Lincoln Park MI

Komisarcik Ed
Andrean HS
Merrillvle IN

Konal Christopher
Notre Dame HS
East Detroit MI

Konchesky Michael
University HS
Morgantown WV

Konczal Joseph C
Oxford Area Cmnty HS
Oxford MI

Kondik Norma
Bedford HS
Bedford Hts OH

Koolstra Gordon
Mc Bain Rural Agri HS
Lake City MI

Koontz David
Marian HS
Clearwater FL

Koontz Douglas A
Warsaw Community HS
Warsaw IN

Koowtz Charles
Harbor Springs HS
Hoarbor Spgs MI

Kopchak Dena M
Port Clinton HS
Port Clinton OH

Kopf Ronald
Forest Park HS
Crystal Falls MI

Koppenhofer Laura
Oregon Davis HS
Grovertown IN

Koppes K C
Wadsworth HS
Wadsworth OH

Korchyk Jerome
Northrop HS
Ft Wayne IN

Koren Gregory J
Rutherford B Hayes HS
Delawre OH

Kornowski Ronald
Padua Franciscan HS
Brunswick OH

Korosec Tim
Solon HS
Lexington KY

Korotko Charles
Bishop Foley HS
Warren MI

Korytkowski Barbara
Bishop Borgess HS
Detroit MI

Kos Greg
Niles Mc Kinley Sr HS
Niles OH

Kosak Lindy
Marian HS
Bloomfield Hl MI

Kosar Leonard
Ursuline HS
Youngstown OH

Koscielniak Kimberly
Frank Cody HS
Detroit MI

Kosich Todd
Glen Oak HS
Canton OH

Koster Daniel G
Ottawa Hills HS
Grand Rapids MI

Kostohryz Denice
Brecksville HS
Broadview Hts OH

Kostrevagh Elisabeth
Monsignor J R Hackett
HS
Kalamazoo MI

Kotnik Joe
W Geavga HS
Chesterlands OH

Kovach Catherine
Regina HS
S Euclid OH

Kovach Judith M
George Rogers Clark HS
Whiting IN

Kovach Marjorie L
Oakridge Sr HS
Muskegon MI

Kovalchik Gary
Meadowbrook HS
Pleasant City OH

Kowalewski Karen
Rochester HS
Rochester MI

Kowalski Kenneth P
Catholic Central HS
Redford MI

Kowatch Lori
Northwestern HS
West Salem OH

Kozan Frances
Cass City HS
Cass City MI

Kozinski Michael E
Perry HS
Massillon OH

Kozlowski Lori
Solon HS
Solon OH

Kraegel Randy
Elida HS
Elida OH

STUDENTS PHOTOGRAPH SCHEDULED FOR PUBLICATION HERE COULD NOT BE REPRODUCED

Krafty Sandy
St Marys Cntrl Cath HS
Sandusky OH

Kragerud Tammy
Brownsburg HS
Brownsburg IN

Kragt Daniel
Kent City HS
Casnovia MI

Krajnik Mike
Traverse City St Francis HS
Traverse City MI

Krall Karen
Parkway HS
Willshire OH

Krall Martha
Linden HS
Fenton MI

Kramer Kelley
Thomas Carr Howe HS
Indianapolis IN

STUDENTS PHOTOGRAPH SCHEDULED FOR PUBLICATION HERE COULD NOT BE REPRODUCED

Kramer Paula
Huntington North HS
Huntington IN

Kramer Stephen A
Ft Wayne R Nelson Snider HS
Ft Wayne IN

Krauss Mike
Ben Davis HS
Indianapolis IN

Krebs Bernd
Coloma HS
Coloma MI

Kreeger Lisa
Theodore Roosevelt HS
Kent OH

Kreft Maria
La Porte HS
Laporte IN

Kreh Gloria
Peru HS
Peru IN

Kreher Colleen
Douglas Mac Arthur HS
Saginaw MI

Kreher Tasha
Douglas Mac Arthur HS
Saginaw MI

Kreider Ladonna
Whitko HS
Pierceton IN

Kreigbaum Julie
Midpark HS
Middleburg Hts OH

Krenrick Mary
Loudonville HS
Loudonville OH

Kress Jane M
Perry HS
Massillon OH

Krick Todd
Bishop Flaget HS
Chillicothe OH

Krigline Kathy
N Canton Hoover HS
North Canton OH

Kriser Lynn A
Coldwater HS
Coldwater MI

Krispin Lorette
Algonac HS
Harsens Island MI

Kristin Matthew L
Ithaca HS
Ithaca MI

Kriuthoff Theresa
Zeeland HS
Zeeland MI

Krochmalny Michael
Divine Child HS
Dearborn Hts MI

Kroeger Craig
Rossford HS
Rossford OH

Krofft Lishs S
Sheridan HS
Mt Perry OH

Kroger Richard J
La Salle HS
Cincinnati OH

Kromer Donna
Chalker HS
Southington OH

Kropka Judi
Buckeye South HS
Smithfield OH

Krozal Robert
Adlai E Stevenson HS
Livonia MI

Krueck Margie
South Amherst HS
So Amherst OH

Krueger Cheri
Fruitport HS
Fruitport MI

Krueger Diane
Williamston HS
Williamston MI

Kruger Kathy
West Central Jr Sr HS
Francesville IN

Kruger Robert
Vinton Cnty Consolidated HS
Mc Arthur OH

Kruk Diane
Marian HS
S Bend IN

Krumback Linda
Alcona Comm HS
Harrisville MI

Krupinski Alice
St Florian HS
Detroit MI

Krushinski Matthew
St Johns HS
Toledo OH

Kruzan Joseph
Bishop Noll Institute
E Chicago IN

STUDENTS PHOTOGRAPH SCHEDULED FOR PUBLICATION HERE COULD NOT BE REPRODUCED

Krystek Christopher
Warren Sr HS
Warren MI

Kubit Nancy
Lamphere HS
Mt Clemens MI

Kuchinic Kara
Herbert Henry Dow HS
Midland MI

Kuczynski Michelle
Kenston HS
Chagrin Fl OH

Kuehn Kelly
South Spencer HS
Rockport IN

Kugler Thomas
Coloma HS
Coloma MI

Kuhn Holly
Northrop HS
Ft Wayne IN

Kuklo Jane
Perry HS
Canton OH

Kukura Linda
Woodrow Wilson HS
Youngstown OH

Kulback Tracy
Scottsburg HS
Scottsburg IN

Kulczak Barbara
Scecina Mem HS
Indianapolis IN

Kulek Karen
Arenac Eastern HS
Omer MI

Kumar Sanjay
Park Hills HS
Fairborn OH

Kumm Michelle
Walled Lake Western HS
Milford MI

Kummer Teresa
Huntington North HS
Roanoke IN

Kummerer Michelle
Tiffin Columbian HS
Tiffin OH

Kunard Douglas
Perry Central HS
Tell City IN

Kuniewicz Theresa
Sebring Mc Kinley HS
Sebring OH

Kunkle Timothy
Gorham Fayette HS
Fayette OH

Kunter Drew
Bellefontaine Sr HS
Bellefontaine OH

Kupec Janet
Cleveland Central Cath HS
Cleveland OH

Kurker Chris
Cardinal Ritter HS
Indianapolis IN

Kursey Michael
Martinsburg HS
Martinsburg WV

Kurtz Lisa
East Canton HS
E Canton OH

Kurtz Steven
Mc Nicholas HS
Cincinnati OH

Kurylo Valerie
East Kentwood HS
Grand Rapids MI

Kurzer Ann
Meadowdale HS
Dayton OH

Kurzhals Karen
John Adams HS
S Bend IN

Kusch David
Kalkaska HS
Williamsbrg MI

Kushnak Karen
Munster HS
Munster IN

Kussy Leisa
Washington Catholic HS
Washington IN

L

Kustron Edward
Lake Catholic HS
Mentor OH

Kutay Mike
Bishop Donahue HS
Moundsville WV

Kutie Janet
Lake Catholic HS
Painesville OH

Kuzak Deborah
Marion L Steele HS
Amherst OH

Kuznar Carla
Valley Forge HS
Parma OH

Labasan Janet
Greenon HS
Fairborn OH

Labeots Laura
Munster HS
Munster IN

Labis Frank
Lorain Catholic HS
Lorain OH

Labuda Pamela
Trinity HS
Seven Hills OH

La Bumbard Kevin J
Tri Township Schools
Rapid River MI

Lach Patricia
Grandview HS
Columbus OH

Lackey Constance C
Vinson HS
Huntington WV

Lackey Scott W
Walnut Hills HS
Cincinnati OH

Laconis Janine
Berkley HS
Hunt Woods MI

Lacoste Helene
Brishton HS
Howell MI

Lacy Anne
Zionsville Comm HS
Zionsville IN

Ladd Bruce
Summerfield HS
Petersburg MI

Ladd Geralyn
Muskegon Catholic Cntrl
HS
Muskegon MI

Ladd Karen
Wooster HS
Wooster OH

Ladegaard Kevin
Avon HS
Avon OH

Ladermann Joann
Greenville Sr HS
Greenville MI

La Duke Michael
South Central HS
Elizabeth IN

Laffoon Laura
Northridge HS
Bristol IN

La Fleur David
Flushing Sr HS
Flushing MI

La Forge Lori
Saline HS
Saline MI

La Fountain Kim
Miller City HS
Continental OH

La Framboise Jeffrey
Romulus Sr HS
Romulus MI

La Freniere Patrick
Manistee Catholic Cntrl
HS
Manistee MI

Lagae Mike
Grosse Pointe N HS
Grosse Pt Wds MI

Lageveen Kathy
Kankakee Valley HS
De Motte IN

La Gorin Mark W
Bedford North Lawrence
HS
Saginaw MI

La Grou James
Fremont Ross HS
Fremont OH

Lahm Michele
Garaway HS
Sugarcreek OH

Lahti Mya
White Pine HS
White Pine MI

Lail Cindy
Hammond Baptist HS
Cedar Lake IN

Lain Teresa
Bay HS
Bay Vill OH

Laing Lori
Harper Creek HS
Battle Creek MI

Lainhart Sandra
Fairfield HS
Hamilton OH

Lakatos Brian
Chesterton HS
Chesterton IN

Lake Brian
Canton South HS
Canton OH

Lake Jerry
Lebanon HS
Lebanon OH

Lake Kimberly
Mona Shores HS
Muskegon MI

Lakos Winona
Cuyahoga Falls HS
Cuyahoga Falls OH

Lalain Marcia
Taylor Center HS
Taylor MI

La Londe Anna
S Amherst HS
So Amherst OH

La Londe Rosemarie
Midland HS
Midland MI

La Mantia Joe
Lake Catholic HS
Euclid OH

Lamb Eleanor
R B Chamberlin HS
Twinsburg OH

Lamb Greg
South Dearborn HS
Aurora IN

Lamb Pamela N
Huntington HS
Huntington WV

Lambert Doug
Hampshire HS
Slanesville WV

Lambert Gregory
Crown Point HS
Crown Point IN

Lambert Jerry
Grafton HS
Grafton WV

Lambert Jonathan
Princeton HS
Princeton WV

Lambert Ricky
Pineville HS
Pineville WV

Lambke Mary P
Marian HS
Blmfld Hls MI

Lambros Mary J
Hamilton Taft Sr HS
Hamilton OH

Lamer Deb
Zeeland HS
Zeeland MI

Lammott Trudy
Twin Valley North HS
Fairfax VT

Lamoreaux Wayne
Elk Rapids Sr HS
Elk Rapids MI

Lampen Lowell
Portland HS
Lyons MI

Lampkin Ramona
Monongah HS
Carolina WV

Lampkin Thalia
Buckhannon Upshur HS
French Creek WV

Lancaster Cindy
Springs Valley HS
Paoli IN

Lancaster Robert N
Greenon HS
Enon OH

Lancaster Susan
Wintersville HS
Wintersville OH

Lancendorfer Patricia A
Southwestern HS
Detroit MI

Lancy Sherri A
Struthers HS
Poland OH

Land Rebecca
Lincoln HS
Vincennes IN

Landaker Beverly
Tri Valley HS
Adams Mills OH

Landfried Barbara
Harbor HS
Ashtabula OH

Landrum Jennifer R
Heath HS
Heath OH

Landry Martha
Highland HS
Wadsworth OH

Landry Mary
St Ursula Acad
Toledo OH

Lane Dawn
Greenfield Central HS
Greenfield IN

Lane Jeffrey S
Sharples HS
Sharples WV

Lane Kimberly
George Washington HS
East Chicago IN

Lane Nicolette
Greenville Sr HS
Greenville OH

Lane Randy
Southern Wells HS
Poneto IN

Lane Susan
South Knox HS
Vincennes IN

Lanford Dave
Ben Davis HS
Clermont IN

Lang Brian E
Maplewood Jr Sr HS
Cortland OH

Lang Joyce
North Farmington HS
Farm Hills MI

Langdon Therese
St Augustine Academy
Lakewood OH

Lange Carla
Whittemore Prescott HS
Whittemore MI

Lange Caroline
Traverse City Sr HS
Traverse City MI

Lange William
Minerva HS
Minerva OH

Langenderfer Beth
Evergreen HS
Swanton OH

Langenkamp Michael J
Versailles HS
Yorkshire OH

Langston Shelley M
Lorain County Joint Voc
Ctr
Amherst OH

Lanham James
Morgantown HS
Morgntwn WV

La Nier Lori
Washington HS
Massillon OH

STUDENTS
PHOTOGRAPH
SCHEDULED
FOR PUBLI-
CATION HERE
COULD NOT
BE REPRO-
DUCED

Lanigan Robert A
Madison Plains HS
London OH

Lannan Michael B
Linton Stocton HS
Linton IN

Lannigan Lois
Belmont HS
Dayton OH

Lantz Denise
Goshen HS
Goshen IN

Lantz Loretta
New Haven HS
New Haven IN

Lanzy Fabian
Redford Union HS
Redford MI

Lao Norman
Upper Arlington HS
Columbus OH

La Pan Roslee
Paulding HS
Cecil OH

Lapham David
Wayland Union HS
Shelbyville MI

Lapham Kathleen
Wayland Union HS
Wayland MI

Lapham Nancy
Kearsley HS
Flint MI

La Pine Jill
East Clinton HS
Lees Creek OH

Lapinsky Marc T
Swartz Creek HS
Swartz Creek MI

La Pointe Beth
Ionia HS
Ionia MI

La Porte Mark
Hemlock HS
Hemlock MI

Larch Melanie
Herbert Hoover HS
Charleston WV

Large Duane
Rochester HS
Rochester IN

Larger Mary C
Ft Loramie HS
Ft Loramie OH

Larimer Myron
Hammond Tech Voc HS
Hammond IN

Larrick Lori
Western Hills HS
Cincinnati OH

Larrick Scott
West Grauga HS
Chesterland OH

Larsen Douglas D
Swan Valley HS
Saginaw MI

Larsen Fredrick A
Decatur Central HS
Indianapolis IN

Larsen Jill
Grand Haven Sr HS
Grand Haven MI

Larsen Lynn
Hamilton Southeastern HS
Noblesville IN

Larsen Randy
Detroit Catholic Central HS
Southfield MI

Larson Gladys
Stephenson HS
Stephenson MI

Larson Ingrid
Romulus HS
Romulus MI

Larson Kimberly
Muskegon Sr HS
Muskegon MI

Larson Todd
North Putnam Jr Sr HS
Bainbridge IN

Larzelere Shannon
North Newton HS
Fair Oaks IN

Lasher Michelle
Chaminade Julienne HS
Dayton OH

Laster Alphonso
Pontiac Northern HS
Pontiac MI

Lata Susan
Bishop Foley HS
Madison Hts MI

Latham Lisa
Staunton HS
Staunton IN

Lather J B
Traverse City HS
Traverse City MI

Latimer Jeff
Riverside HS
Quincy OH

Latimer Kevin
Lutheran HS West
Inkster MI

Latreille Carolyn
Howell HS
Howell MI

Latshaw Michael K
Nordonia HS
Macedonia OH

STUDENTS
PHOTOGRAPH
SCHEDULED
FOR PUBLI-
CATION HERE
COULD NOT
BE REPRO-
DUCED

Lattimore Scott
Danbury Local HS
Lakeside OH

Laudeman Teresa
Marion HS
Marion IN

Laudenshlager David L
North Miami HS
Peru IN

Lauer Elizabeth
Loy Norrix HS
Kalamazoo MI

Laughlin Richard
Brooke HS
Wellsburg WV

Laurell Dennis
Northwood HS
Northwood OH

Laurianti Donna
Nordonia HS
Northfield OH

Lautenschlager Phillip E
Upper Scioto Valley HS
Belle Ctr OH

Lautenschlegar Brent
Loveland Hurst HS
Loveland OH

Lauterbach David
Lutheran HS
N Olmsted OH

Lautermitch Tim
Upper Sandusky HS
Upper Sandusky OH

Law Bruce A
Mooresville HS
Mooresville IN

Law Jeffrey A
Dayton Christian HS
Dayton OH

Law John C
Bluefield HS
Bluefield WV

Law Lori
Carlisle Sr HS
Carlisle OH

Law Raeta A
Cambridge HS
Cambridge OH

Lawes Carol
St Peters HS
Mansfield OH

Lawless Mark
Princeton HS
Princeton WV

Lawrence Deborah
Sherman HS
Seth WV

Lawrence Lisa
Jefferson Union HS
Toronto OH

Lawrence Melissa
Indianapolis Baptist HS
Greenwood IN

Lawrence Pamela
Perry HS
Laingsburg MI

Lawrence Stacy
Arlington HS
Indianapolis IN

Lawson Cheri
Blanchester HS
Blanchester OH

Lawson Debbie
Sidney HS
Sidney OH

Lawson Diane
Cascade HS
Clayton IN

Lawson Robin
St Johns HS
De Witt MI

Lay Ronald
Holt HS
Lansing MI

Layfield Jeffrey
Wirt County HS
Elizabeth WV

Layne Kimberly A
Tecumseh HS
New Carlisle OH

Layton Deanna
Whitehall Yearling HS
Whitehall OH

Layton Don
Point Pleasant HS
Pt Pleasant WV

Lazarus Beth
Wheeling Park HS
Wheeling WV

Lazarus Jewel
Carson City Crystal HS
Crystal MI

Lazarus Jill
Homer HS
Homer MI

Le Tin T
Pontiac Northern HS
Pontiac MI

Leabu Dana
Belleville HS
Ypsilanti MI

STUDENTS
PHOTOGRAPH
SCHEDULED
FOR PUBLI-
CATION HERE
COULD NOT
BE REPRO-
DUCED

Leach Michelene
Olmsted Falls HS
Olmsted Falls OH

Leach Robin
Jackson HS
Jackson OH

Leahy Kelly
Columbian HS
Tiffin OH

Leamer Jerry L
Westfield Washington
HS
Westfield IN

Lear Genia
Point Pleasant HS
Gallipolis Ferr Y

Lease Gene
Riverdale HS
Mt Blanchard OH

Leath Andre M
Northfork HS
Northfork WV

Leathers Marilee
Climax Scotts Jr Sr HS
Climax MI

Leavens Pamela K
Pinconning Area HS
Linwood MI

Lebednick Mark
Grand Rapids Cath Cntrl
HS
Wyoming MI

Le Blanc Regina
Romulus Sr HS
Romulus MI

Lech Leo
Bishop Noll Inst
Hammond IN

Le Claire Dena
North Vermillion HS
Cayuga IN

Le Cocq Sherri
Shakamak HS
Jasonville IN

Le Cureux Susan
North Branch HS
Columbiaville MI

Ledford Chris
West Central HS
Winamac IN

Ledington Tammy
Fayetteville Perry HS
Fayetteville OH

STUDENTS
PHOTOGRAPH
SCHEDULED
FOR PUBLI-
CATION HERE
COULD NOT
BE REPRO-
DUCED

Lee Gregory
H.H Dow HS
Midland MI

Lee Marchelle
Edgerton HS
Montpelier OH

Lee Marianne
Southern Local HS
Lisbon OH

Lee Nancy
Elmwood HS
Bloomdale OH

Lee Robert
Detroit Catholic Ctrl HS
Dearborn Heigh MI

Lee Roger
Canton South HS
Canton OH

Lee Tim
Fostoria HS
Fostoria OH

Leeber Angela
Woodrow Wilson HS
Mabscott WV

Leesburg Jayne
Portsmouth East HS
Wheelersburg OH

Leesburg Sheri
Portsmouth East HS
Wheelesburg OH

Leeson Caroline
Bridgeport Sr HS
Bridgeport WV

Le Fevre Lynne
Edwin Denby HS
Detroit MI

Le Fort Michael
Taylor Center HS
Taylor MI

Leftrict Fred T
Nettie Lee Roth HS
Dayton OH

Legg Patricia
Fairland HS
Proctorville OH

Legg William L
Poca HS
Poca WV

Le Gros Sandra L
Southeast HS
Deerfield OH

Lehigh Elizabeth A
Tuscarawas Central Cath HS
Zoar OH

Lehman Brent
Lima Perry HS
Lima OH

Lehman Jill
Evart Public Schools
Evart MI

Lehman Terri
Hilltop HS
W Unity OH

Lehman Tonya
Northwest HS
Jackson MI

Lehmann Pamela
Berrien Springs HS
Berrien Spgs MI

Lehmkuhl Catherine A
Versailles HS
Versailles OH

Lehner Daniel
Pleasant HS
Marion OH

Lehner Sandra
Liberty HS
Yngstn OH

Lehnhart Kevin
Lucas HS
Lucas OH

Leidy Rae
North Central HS
Pioneer OH

Lein Johnathan
Brethren HS
Kaleva MI

Leinbach Earl T
Oregon Davis HS
Hamlet IN

Leirstein Kevin
Livonia Franklin HS
Westland MI

Leishmann Vanessa
Sandy Valley HS
Waynesburg OH

Leising Charlene
Connersville Sr HS
Connersville IN

Leitch Carmen
Churubusco HS
La Otto IN

Leitch David
Jackson Milton HS
N Jackson OH

Leitch Mary A
Central Noble HS
Albion IN

Leite Joseph
Fremont Ross HS
Fremont OH

Leitman Mindy
Southfield HS
Southfield MI

Lekas Constantine
Pontiac Central HS
Pontiac MI

Lekson Jeff
Eastlake North HS
Willowick OH

Leland John
Loudonville HS
Loudonville OH

Le Master Laurel
Wheelersburg HS
Wheelersburg OH

Le Master Paul
Ayersville HS
Defiance OH

Le Masters Diana
Wellsville HS
Wellsville OH

Le Masters Noreen J
Tyler County HS
Middlebourne WV

Le May Diane
William V Fisher Cath HS
Lancaster OH

Le May Marlene A
Grove City HS
Grove City OH

Le May Renee
Westfall HS
Circleville OH

Lemcke Belinda J
N Royalton HS
Cleveland OH

Le Mieux Theresa
Reeths Puffer HS
Muskegon MI

Lemna Jill
Northrop HS
Ft Wayne IN

Le Mon Anita
Spencer HS
Spencer WV

Le Mon David
Taylor Center HS
Taylor MI

Len Douglas
Ovid Elsie HS
Ovid MI

Lenegar Chris
Vinton Cnty Consolidated HS
Mc Arthur OH

Lengerlioglu Gulferi
Bluefield HS
Bluefield WV

Lenhart Gary
Winfield HS
Scott Depot WV

Lenk Daniel
Edgewood Sr HS
Ashtabula OH

Lensing Pamela
Harrison HS
Evansville IN

Lents Dana
Loogootee HS
Loogootee IN

Lents Debbie
Marysville HS
Marysville MI

Lentz Marjorie
Avon HS
Indianapolis IN

Leonard Christine
Lorain Catholic HS
Amherst OH

Leonard James
Norton HS
Norton OH

Leonard Kathryn
Niles Mc Kinley Sr HS
Niles OH

Leonard Patricia
Port Huron Northern HS
Port Huron MI

Leonard Timothy
Greenfield Cntrl HS
Greenfield IN

Leonard Todd
Shelbyville Sr HS
Shelbyville IN

Leonhardt Mary
Shelby Sr HS
Shelby OH

Le Page Michele
Bishop Foley HS
Rochester MI

Leruth Michael
St Francis De Sales HS
Toledo OH

Leskuski Dona
Buckhannon Upshur HS
Buckhannon WV

Leslie Carol
Charles F Brush HS
Lyndhurst OH

Leslie Dorothy
Solon HS
Solon OH

Leslie Lisa
Kenton Ridge HS
Springfield OH

Leslie Terry
Edwardsburg HS
Niles MI

Lester Charla
Lewis County HS
Weston WV

Lester Jayne
Marquette Sr HS
Marquette MI

Lester Michael P
Hurricane HS
Hurricane WV

Lester Rebecca
Sullivan HS
Sullivan IN

Lester Vanessa
Shenandoah HS
Pleasant City OH

Lesti Christine
Stow HS
Stow OH

Letcavits Joi
Washington HS
Massillon OH

Letcher Laura
Fowlerville HS
Fowlerville MI

Letizia Donald
Bishop Dwenger HS
Ft Wayne IN

Letizia Lori A
Garrett HS
Garrett IN

Letteney Neal
Martinsville HS
Martinsville IN

Leuteritz Robert
Arlington HS
Indianapolis IN

Levacy Beth
William V Fisher Cath HS
Lancaster OH

Levelle Randy
Clay Battelle HS
Core WV

Levely Melissa E
Beaverton HS
Beaverton MI

Leveranz Linda
James Ford Rhodes HS
Cleveland OH

Levin Michelle P
Donald E Gavit Jr Sr HS
Hammond IN

Leviner Donna
Calumet HS
Gary IN

Levinson Ralph
Linsly Inst
Steubenville OH

Lewandowski Lisa
Bishop Donahue HS
Wheeling WV

Lewandowski Michelle
Norwell HS
Roanoke IN

Lewe Robert
Fostoria HS
Fostoria OH

Lewis Antoinette
Northeastern HS
Detroit MI

Lewis Bell
Clay Battelle HS
Fairview WV

Lewis Brenda
Perrysburg HS
Perrysburg OH

Lewis Christopher
Kearsley Community HS
Flint MI

Lewis Chuck
Barberton HS
Barberton OH

Lewis Deborah
Farmington HS
W Farmington OH

Lewis Duane S
Bellefontaine Sr HS
Bellefontaine OH

Lewis J
Bellaire HS
Neffs OH

Lewis Jeffrey
United Local HS
Hanoverton OH

Lewis Jenny
Point Pleasant HS
Pt Pleasant WV

Lewis Kelly
Lakeland HS
La Grange IN

Lewis Laura
Elmhurst HS
Ft Wayne IN

Lewis Lee Ann
Escanaba Public HS
Escanaba MI

Lewis Lee R
Pocahontas County HS
Marlinton WV

Lewis Lisa
Regina HS
Cleveland Hts OH

Lewis Nita L
Emmerigh Manual HS
Indianapolis IN

Lewis Pamela
Crothersville HS
Crothersville IN

Lewis Regina
Immaculata HS
Detroit MI

Lewis Renee
Creston HS
Grand Rapids MI

Lewis Sandy
Huntington HS
Huntington WV

Lewis Scott
Linsly Institute
Wheeling WV

Lewis Susan
Fairland HS
Proctorvll OH

Lewis Terri B
Linton Stockton HS
Linton IN

Lewis Timothy
Park Hills HS
Fairborn OH

Lewis Tracey
Kettering Sr HS
Detroit MI

Lewter Abbe
Speedway HS
Speedway IN

Leyrer Kelley
Gladwin HS
Gladwin MI

Liadis Diane
Adlai E Stevenson HS
Livonia MI

Liaskos Violet
Hammond HS
Hammond IN

Libb Cindy
Rising Sun HS
Rising Sun IN

STUDENTS
PHOTOGRAPH
SCHEDULED
FOR PUBLI-
CATION HERE
COULD NOT
BE REPRO-
DUCED

Licata Antonio
Weirton Madonna HS
Weirton WV

Licause Gail
Wadsworth Sr HS
Wadsworth OH

Lichney Jean
Boardman HS
Youngstown OH

Licht Donald
Escanaba HS
Escanaba MI

Lichte Lori
Brownsburg HS
Pittsboro IN

Lico Isabella
Our Lady Star Of The
Sea HS
Grse Pt Shr MI

Lieber Kathleen
Mayville HS
Millington MI

Lieberman Kathy
Stonewall Jackson HS
Charleston WV

Liebetrau Kurt
Cadillac Sr HS
Cadillac MI

Liepack Karen
Whitehall Yearling HS
Whitehall OH

Lieser Carl
Buckeye Central HS
Tiro OH

Lifer J David
Clearfork HS
Butler OH

Lifer Steven T
Clear Fork HS
Butler OH

Liggett Jo Dee
Brooke HS
Wellsburg WV

STUDENTS
PHOTOGRAPH
SCHEDULED
FOR PUBLI-
CATION HERE
COULD NOT
BE REPRO-
DUCED

Lightcap Daniel
Pontiac Northern HS
Pontiac MI

Lightfoot Chandrea D
Broad Ripple HS
Indianapolis IN

Lightfoot Mark A
Bluefield HS
Bluefield WV

Lightle Timothy R
Highland HS
Fredericktown OH

Lihani Teresa
Parma Sr HS
Parma OH

Like Julie
Lincoln HS
Vincennes IN

Lilly Carl
Chesapeake HS
Chesapeake OH

Lilly Kevin
Talcott HS
Hinton WV

Lilly Richard D
Shady Spring HS
Daniels WV

Lim David J
W Lafayette HS
W Lafayette IN

Limonoff Lawrence
Fowlerville HS
Webberville MI

Linabury Lisa
Southfield Christian HS
Birmingham MI

Linch Arnetta
Rooseevlet Wilson HS
Stonewood WV

Lincoln Stephen
Okemos HS
Okemos MI

Lindauer Kelvin
Perry Central HS
St Meinrad IN

Lindeman James
Henry Ford II HS
Sterling Hts MI

Lindemann Allan
Ann Arbor Pioneer HS
Ann Arbor MI

Lindemann Dana
Lansing Everett HS
Lansing MI

Linder Cindy
Woodridge HS
Hudson OH

Linderman Karen
Huron HS
Ann Arbor MI

Lindh Cindy A
Clinton HS
Clinton MI

Lindke Gary
Gaylord HS
Gaylord MI

Lindley Patrick
Tipton HS
Tipton IN

Lindsay Brenda
Tygarts Valley HS
Valley Bend WV

Lindsey James J
Cuyahoga Falls HS
Cuyahoga Falls OH

Lindsly Terri
Lakota HS
W Chester OH

Lindstead Mark
Parkersburg HS
Parkersburg WV

Line Jenni
Heritage Christian HS
Anderson IN

Linebaugh Michelle
Belding Area HS
Belding MI

Linedecker Angie
Mc Cutcheon HS
Clarks Hill IN

Linger Darlene
Lewis County HS
Buckhannon WV

Linger Jane
Beaver Local HS
Negley OH

Linger Linda
Bridgeport Sr HS
Bridgeport WV

Linger Marilyn
Buckhannon Upshur HS
Buckhannon WV

Link David
Bowsher HS
Toledo OH

Linson Richard E
W Lafayette HS
W Lafayette IN

Linton Michael D
Circleville HS
Circleville OH

Linton Richard
Hedgesville HS
Martinsburg WV

Lio Suzanne
L C Mohr HS
South Haven MI

Liotti Jennifer A
Carmel HS
Carmel IN

Lippencott Jon
Graham HS
Urbana OH

Lippert Cindy
Cedar Lake Academy
Alma MI

Lippiatt Lorie
West Branch HS
Salem OH

Lippincott Roger
Connersville Sr HS
Connersville IN

Lipps Jackie J
Union City Community
HS
Union City IN

Lipscomb Susan
Federal Hocking HS
Coolville OH

Liptak Lisa
Pocahontas County HS
Arbovale WV

Litteral Brian
Emmerich Manual HS
Indianapolis IN

Litteral David
Loveland Hurst HS
Loveland OH

Little Camille
Bishop Hartley HS
Columbus OH

Little Carol
Cass City HS
Cass City MI

Little Carolyn
Bay City Central HS
Bay City MI

Little Cindy
Teays Valley HS
Grove Port OH

Little David B
Swan Valley HS
Saginaw MI

Little Deborah
Elgin HS
La Rue OH

Little Jean
Elgin HS
Larue OH

Little Kim
North Putnam Jr Sr HS
Greencastle IN

Little Shelly
St Johns HS
St Johns MI

Littlefield David
North Olmsted H3
N Olmsted OH

Liverett Michael A
Charles Stewart Mott Sr
HS
Warren MI

Livernois James L
Vandercook Lake HS
Jackson MI

Livezey Kelly
Walter P Chrysler Mem
HS
New Castle IN

Livingston Jeff
Pt Pleasant HS
Leon WV

Livingston Lisa
Lawrence Central HS
Lawrence IN

Livingston Mary
Clay City HS
Center Point IN

Livingston Pamela
Wadsworth Sr HS
Wadsworth OH

Lixey Cheryl
Lamphere HS
Madison Height MI

Locke Cynthia A
Charlotte HS
Charlotte MI

Lockett Patricia
Osborn HS
Detroit MI

Lockhart Dyke
Chesapeake HS
Chesapeake OH

Lockhart Gerald
Parkersburg South HS
Mineral Wells WV

Lockhart Kevin
Belpre HS
Belpre OH

Lockhart Lisa
Avon HS
Plainfield IN

Lockwood Charla
Carroll HS
Ft Wayne IN

Lockwood Joan
Skeels Northern Chrstn
HS
Harrison MI

Lockwood Laura
Lima Perry HS
Lima OH

Logan Carol J
Marion Harding HS
Marion OH

Logan David
Deerfield HS
Deerfield MI

Logan Kendra K
North Putnam Jr Sr HS
Russellville IN

Logan Linda
Roosevelt HS
Gary IN

Logan Michele
Archbishop Alter HS
Kettering OH

Logsdon Brenda
Penn HS
Granger IN

Logsdon Brian
Teays Valley HS
Ashville OH

Logsdon Cynthia A
Upper Sandusky HS
Upper Sandusky OH

Logsdon Lynn
Bedford North Lawrence
HS
Bedford IN

Loh Judy
Andrean HS
Gary IN

Loher Suellen
Warsaw Comm HS
Warsaw IN

Lohr Melanie
Vandalia Butler HS
Dayton OH

Lombardo Pina
Warren Sr HS
Sterling Hts MI

Lonchar Michelle
Euclid Sr HS
Euclid OH

Long Angela
Archbishop Alter HS
Dayton OH

Long Brian
Tecumseh HS
Tecumseh MI

Long Doug
Reitz Memorial HS
Boonville IN

Long G
Northeastern HS
Williamsburg IN

Long Jay
Connersville HS
Glenwood IN

Long Jeff
Princeton HS
Cincinnati OH

Long Karen
Cleveland Cntrl Catholic
HS
Cleveland OH

Long Kim
Lincolnview HS
Middle Pt OH

Long Margaret
Lakeshore HS
St Joseph MI

Long Mark
Brown County HS
Nineveh IN

Long Susan
Marietta Sr HS
Marietta OH

Longanacre Timothy
Mullens HS
Mullens WV

Longenberger Sheryl
Bluffton HS
Bluffton IN

Longhi Pat
Madonna HS
Weirton WV

Longley Patty
Hubbard HS
Hubbard OH

Longmire Jr Wilbert
Hughes HS
Cincinati OH

Longpre Carole
Atlanta Community
School
Atlanta MI

Longwell Rona
Hundred HS
Littleton WV

Loniewski Edward
Detroit Catholic Cntrl HS
Detroit MI

Loomis Kim
Waterloo HS
Atwater OH

Loomis Mark
Old Trail School
Medina OH

Loomis Tina
Heath HS
Heath OH

Loos Cynthia
West Washington HS
Hardingsburg IN

Lopez Suzanne
Lincoln HS
Vincennes IN

Loraff Richard
Eau Claire HS
Eau Claire MI

Lorenger Peter M
Univ Of Detroit HS
Detroit MI

Lorick Jerard
Arsenal Technical HS
Indianapolis IN

Lorton Sherri
Ursuline Academy
Cincinnati OH

Loscalzo Beth
Kalamazoo Central HS
Kalamazoo MI

Lothridge Kevin
South Dearborn HS
Aurora IN

Lott Naja
Whitehall Yearling HS
Whitehall OH

Louchart Lisa
Clio HS
Mt Morris MI

Louden Lawrence
Edgewood HS
Kingsville OH

Loudenslager Bonnie
Colon HS
Burr Oak MI

Louderback Darla
Western Brown Sr HS
Bethel OH

Louderback Ronald
Felicity Franklin HS
Felicity OH

Loudin Melinda
Buckhannon Upshur HS
Buckhannon WV

Lough Philip H
Lewis County HS
Jane Lew WV

Love Tammy L
Stow HS
Stow OH

Loveday John A
Walter P Chrysler Memrl HS
New Castle IN

Lovegrove Norman
Frankfort HS
Elberta MI

Lovejoy Paula
Jonathan Alder HS
Plain City OH

Loveless Andrea
Robert A Taft HS
Cincinnati OH

Lovse Valerie
Waterford Twp HS
Union Lake MI

Low Nancy
Newark HS
Newark OH

Lowe Alice
Huron HS
Huron OH

Lowe Deirdre
West Side HS
Gary IN

Lowe Jeffre
Clerance M Kimball HS
Royal Oak MI

Lowe Kimberly
Liberty HS
Bristol WV

Lowe Linda
H H Dow HS
Midland MI

Lowe Lisa
Wirt County HS
Elizabeth WV

Lowe Renee
Dominican HS
Detroit MI

Lowe Scott
Seeger Memorial HS
Williamsport IN

Lowe Thomas
Pinconning Area HS
Linwood MI

Lower Diane
Beaver Local HS
Negler OH

Lowery Lisa
Shady Spring HS
Daniels WV

Lowrey Shane
East HS
Akron OH

Lowry Eric
Scottsburg HS
Scottsburg IN

Lowry Linda S
Eastwood HS
Perrysburg OH

Loy Tracy
Roosevelt Wilson HS
Clarksburg WV

Lozano Paul
Upper Sandusky HS
Upper Sandusky OH

Lozier Ida
Marlington HS
Paris OH

Lubahn Deborah
Fulton HS
Ashley MI

Lubeck Jeffrey
East Detroit HS
East Detroit MI

Lubecky David
West Geauga HS
Novelty OH

Lubinski Annette
Springfield HS
Holland OH

Lubkowski Leona
Carl Brablec HS
Roseville MI

Lucas Beverly
Brown County HS
Nashville IN

Lucas J Bradley
Bloomfield HS
Bloomfield IN

Lucas Jim D
Port Clinton HS
Port Clinton OH

Lucas Kevin
Union Local HS
Belmont OH

Lucas Marilyn D
Arsenal Technical HS
Indianapolis IN

Lucas Pamela
Willard HS
Willard OH

Luchetti Adelaide
Wheeling Park HS
Triadelphia WV

Luck Tina
New Richmond HS
Bethel OH

Lucke Janice
Delphos St Johns HS
Delphos OH

Luckel Mark
Hammond Baptist HS
Lowell IN

Lucken Beverly
Taft HS
Hamilton OH

Luckiewicz James
Andrean HS
Merrillville IN

Luczkowski Mary
Washington HS
South Bend IN

Ludwig Paula K
Plymouth HS
Plymouth IN

Luedtke Robin
Lee M Thurston HS
Redford MI

Luehrmann Paul
Moeller HS
Cincinnati OH

Luft Di Ann
Owosso HS
Owosso MI

Luginbill Deanna F
Parkway HS
Rockford OH

Lukas Suzanne
Cardinal HS
Middlefield OH

Lukaschewski Melanie
S Lyon HS
New Hudson MI

Luking Robert B
Rivet HS
Vincennes IN

Lukotch Deborah
Lorain Catholic HS
Lorain OH

Lulko Debora
Adlai E Stevenson HS
Livonia MI

Lumb Mary
Ursuline Academy
Cincinnati OH

Lummer Cheryl
Bellbrook HS
Bellbrook OH

Lund Julie
Cedar Springs HS
Cedar Spgs MI

Lundberg Donald
Rapid River HS
Rapid River MI

Lundberg Thomas
St Francis De Sales HS
Toledo OH

Luneke Patricia
Tecumseh HS
New Carlisle OH

Lungaro Joan
Cody HS
Detroit MI

Lunsford Ellen C
Shawe Memorial HS
Madison IN

Lunsford Gina
Brookville HS
Laurel IN

Lusby Doug
Mt Healthy HS
Cincinnati OH

Lusk Tracy
Princeton HS
Princeton WV

Luta Jacquelyn J
Bridgeport Cmnty HS
Bridgeport MI

Lutes Cynthia J
Lawrence Central HS
Lawrence IN

Lutes Pamela G
Brownstown Central HS
Brownstown IN

Lutterbach Lisa
Memorial HS
Evansville IN

Lutz Lawrence
Central HS
Evansville IN

Lutz Lori
Memorial HS
St Marys OH

Luu Daniel
Carmel HS
Indianapolis IN

Lyden Thomas
Turpin HS
Cincinnati OH

Lykins Sandra
Utica HS
Utica MI

Lyles Mary
Salem HS
Salem IN

Lynam Edward P
Brookfield Sr HS
Hubbard OH

Lynch James
Pineville HS
Pineville WV

Lynch Laura
Floyd Central HS
Floyd Knobs IN

Lynch Richard H
St Xavier HS
Maineville OH

Lynn Dawn
Bloomington HS N
Bloomington IN

Lyonette John
Boardman HS
Youngstown OH

Lyons Brian
Northfield HS
Roann IN

Lyons Daniel
Central HS
Grand Rapids MI

Lyons Regina
Elk Garden HS
Elk Garden WV

Lyons Shelli A
Northside HS
Muncie IN

Lyons Wilbur M
Bluefield HS
Bluefield WV

Lysyj Martha
North Royalton HS
N Royalton OH

M

Maanika David
Calumet HS
Laurium MI

Mac Michelle
Wayne Memorial HS
Wayne MI

MacDonald Heather
Algonac HS
Algonac MI

MacDonald Scott
Allendale HS
Allendale MI

Mace Sherry
Vinton County HS
Mc Arthur OH

Maceyko Ronald
Campbell Memorial HS
Campbell OH

MacGregor Jana
Southfield Lathrup Sr HS
Southfield MI

Machiela Jeff
Zeeland Public HS
Zeeland MI

Machuca Angelo
Bishop Noll Institute
E Chicago IN

Mack Michele L
Cadillac Sr HS
Cadillac MI

MacKall Lynn
West Muskingum HS
Zanesville OH

MacKey Helen
Cadillac Sr HS
Cadillac MI

MacKey John
Yale HS
Avoca MI

MacKey Joseph
Yale HS
Avoca MI

MacKey Tammy
Okemos HS
East Lansing MI

Mackie Hugh
Sault Area HS
Sault Ste Marie MI

Mackin Ann
Alpena Sr HS
Alpena MI

Macmain R
Flushing HS
Flushing MI

MacNaughton Elizabeth
R B Chamberlin HS
Twinsburg OH

MacNeill David G
Clay HS
Niles MI

MacQueen Lynette M
Springfield Local HS
Holland OH

Madden Jerry
Deer Park HS
Cincinnati OH

Maddox Denise
Baldwin HS
Idlewild MI

Maddox Sharon
Cassopolis Ross Beatty
HS
Cassopolis MI

Madeka John P
Hammond Tech
Vocational HS
Hammond IN

Madsen Lisa
Cascade HS
Coatesville IN

Madsen Tim
St Johns HS
St Johns MI

Madura Michele
Hammond HS
Hammond IN

Magdich Leslie
Northville HS
Northville MI

Maggiano Holly
Howland HS
Warren OH

Magill Monte
Park Hills HS
Fairborn OH

Magnacca David
St Francis De Sales HS
Columbus OH

Magyaros Barry R
Salem Sr HS
Salem OH

Mahar Lorraine
Fordson HS
Dearborn MI

Mahoney Darlene
Gods Bible School HS
Milton KY

Maiorana Barbara
Ursuline HS
Youngstown OH

Majerczak Doris R
Wooster HS
Wooster OH

Majeski Peter V
Penn HS
Mishawaka IN

Majnaric Lidija
Mt Vernon Academy
Akron OH

Maker Ronald
Clawson HS
Clawson MI

Makowski Joel
Bluffton HS
Bluffton IN

Makowski Mary
Berkshire HS
Burton OH

Makra Melissa
Green HS
Uniontown OH

P—127

Malarkey Dawn S
Lemon Monroe HS
Monroe OH

Malburg Martha
Hart HS
Hart MI

Malcomb Charles R
Pickens HS
Helvetia WV

Malinar Drina
Elyria Catholic HS
N Ridgeville OH

Malinowski Robert
Divine Child HS
Dearborn Hts MI

Mallernee Kimberly
Cadiz HS
Cadiz OH

Mallis Marcia
Bedford HS
Bedford OH

Mallory Crystal B
Huntington East HS
Huntington WV

Malloy Jim
Washington Irving HS
Clarksburg WV

Malloy Susan
Wintersville HS
Steubenville OH

Malone Daphne
South Point HS
South Point OH

Malone John
New Albany HS
New Albany IN

Malone Kathleen
George Washington HS
Charleston WV

Maloney Janet
Wheeling Ctrl Catholic
HS
Wheeling WV

Maloney Kathleen
Tiffin Calvert HS
Tiffin OH

Maloney Lawrence
Admiral King HS
Lorain OH

Malotte Michelle
Pike Central HS
Petersburg IN

Mamakos Joanne
Wheeling Park HS
Wheeling WV

Mance Charity K
Park Tudor HS
Indianapolis IN

Mancinelli Corrie
St Francis Desales HS
Morgantown WV

Mancini Leo
Schafer HS
Southgate MI

Mandzia Lesia
Holy Name Nazareth HS
Cleveland OH

Manenti John
Girard HS
Girard OH

Manfredi John
Troy Athens HS
Troy MI

Mangold Julie
Wayne HS
Dayton OH

Manko Dennis
Waterford Township HS
Pontiac MI

Mann Kimberly
Warren Central HS
Indpls IN

Manner Jan
Marshall HS
Marshall MI

Manners Wendy
Columbiana HS
Columbiana OH

Manning Tammy
Fairbanks HS
Plain City OH

Manning Thomas
East Lansing HS
East Lansing MI

Mannion Randolph
Bishop Noll Institute
Hammond IN

Mannon Cynthia
Hamlin HS
W Hamlin WV

Manolovich George
Crown Point HS
Crown Point IN

Manolukas John
Boardman HS
Youngstown OH

Manske Roger
Knox Sr HS
Knox IN

Mansour Jennifer
Carman Sr HS
Flint MI

Manudhane Pradeep
Turpin HS
Cincinnati OH

Manuel Carla
North Vigo HS
Terre Haute IN

Manuel Carmen J
Southern Local HS
Racine OH

Manuel Marcia
Cass Technical HS
Detroit MI

Manusakis Jr Nicholas
Western Reserve HS
Warren OH

Manwell Lori
Midland HS
Midland MI

Manzano Melody
Eastern HS
Lansing MI

Maraney Donald
St Francis HS
Star City WV

Marazita Elizabeth
Waverly HS
Lansing MI

March Linda
Green HS
Uniontown OH

March Richard
Buchanan HS
Buchanan MI

Marciniak Penny
Elston Sr HS
Mich City IN

Marckel Karen
Whiteford HS
Ottawa Lk MI

Marcotte Ron
Bishop Fenwick HS
West Chester OH

Marcum Allen M
Barboursville HS
Huntington WV

Marcum Cindie
Oceana HS
Kopperston WV

Marcy Bryan
Edgewood Sr HS
Kingsville OH

Mardones Daniel
Liberty HS
Clarksburg WV

Marek John
Port Clinton HS
Gypsum OH

Marentette Stephen
Whittemore Prescott HS
Prescott MI

Margolis J
Springfield North HS
Springfield OH

Marheineke Mark
R S Tower HS
Warren MI

Mariner Shari
Hoover HS
North Canton OH

Marjomaki Dana L
Gwinn HS
Gwinn MI

Mark David P
E A Johnson HS
Clio MI

Markley Julie
Kewanna HS
Kewanna IN

Markley Michael
Bishop Luers HS
Ft Wayne IN

Marks Debbie
Gilmer County HS
Orlando WV

Marks Jerri
Parkersburg South HS
Washington WV

Marks Jim
Manchester HS
N Manchester IN

Marlatt Margot S
Interlochen Arts Acad
Klamath Falls OR

Marlett Christine
Grand Rapids HS
Grand Rapids MI

Marley Jon
Western HS
Russiaville IN

Marlow Barry
Otsego HS
Grand Rpds OH

Marlow Tracy
William Mason HS
Mason OH

Marlowe Wanda M
Holly HS
Holly MI

Marmaduke Anita
Greenwood Community
HS
Greenwood IN

Marmaduke Elizabeth
St Vincent St Mary HS
Akron OH

Marmilick Diane
Gladstone Area HS
Gladstone MI

Marple Cheryl
Buckhannon Upshur HS
Buckhannon WV

Marquart Todd
Maumee HS
Toledo OH

Marquez Rodolfo
Plymouth HS
Plymouth IN

Marra Robert A
Bridgeport HS
Bridgeport WV

Marriage Eldina
Ovid Elsie HS
Ovid MI

Marsee Sharon
Monrovia HS
Martinsville IN

Marsh Douglas J
Oregon Davis HS
Hamlet IN

Marsh Iwanda K
Oregon Davis HS
Hamlet IN

Marsh Marla
Akron East Sr HS
Akron OH

Marsh Monica
Akron East Sr HS
Akron OH

Marsh Shelley R
Owosso HS
Owosso MI

Marshall Barbara
Northview HS
Grand Rapids MI

STUDENTS
PHOTOGRAPH
SCHEDULED
FOR PUBLI-
CATION HERE
COULD NOT
BE REPRO-
DUCED

Marshall Bryan
Richmond Sr Shs
Richmond IN

Marshall Carol
Eastern HS
Salem IN

Marshall Denise
Graham HS
St Paris OH

Marshall Dorothy K
Centennial HS
Columbus OH

Marshall Jean
Athen HS
Troy MI

Marshall Karen A
East Technical HS
Cleveland OH

Marshall Kristine K
Rochester Sr HS
Utica MI

Marshall Sandra
Wilmington Sr HS
Wilmington OH

Marsolf Chris
Rosedale HS
Rockville IN

Marsteller Lynne D
Lakota HS
W Chester OH

Martensen Lisa
George Rogers Clark HS
Whiting IN

Martin Anita
Bloomfield HS
N Bloomfield OH

Martin Anne
Culver Girls Academy
Laredo TX

Martin Annette
Morgantown HS
Morgantown WV

Martin Brenda
Watkins Memorial HS
Pataskala OH

Martin Carol
Brookville HS
Oxford OH

Martin Cathy
Northrop HS
Ft Wayne IN

Martin Christina
London HS
London OH

Martin Daniel
David Anderson HS
Leetonia OH

Martin Darlene
Toronto HS
Toronto OH

Martin David
Wayland HS
Wayland MI

Martin David
Bluefield HS
Freeman WV

Martin Dean
La Ville Jr Sr HS
Plymouth IN

Martin Deborah
Northeastern HS
Fountain Cy IN

Martin Deborah
Adrian HS
Blissfield MI

Martin Denise
M L King HS
Detroit MI

Martin Eddie
Marsh Fork HS
Dry Creek WV

Martin Elizabeth
Sullivan HS
Shelburn IN

Martin James A
George Washington HS
Charleston WV

Martin James K
Princeton HS
Princeton WV

Martin Jeff
Kings HS
Loveland OH

Martin Jim
Warsaw Community HS
Warsaw IN

Martin Jim
Father Joseph Wehrle
Mem HS
Columbus OH

Martin Kenneth
Jefferson Area Local HS
Jefferson OH

Martin Kevin
Northmont HS
Englewood OH

Martin Linda
Little Miami HS
Loveland OH

Martin Lynn
Cedar Springs HS
Cedar Spgs MI

Martin Marjorie M
Warren Sr HS
Warren MI

Martin Mary
St Marys Ctrl Catholic
HS
Castalia OH

Martin Michelle
Clay HS
S Bend IN

Martin Mitchell
Lincoln HS
Shinnston WV

Martin Nancy
Gabriel Richard HS
Ann Arbor MI

Martin Robert
Lincoln HS
Shinnston WV

Martin Sheila
Wirt County HS
Elizabeth WV

Martin Stephen
Salem HS
Salem IN

Martin Wendy
Western HS
Auburn MI

Martindale Christine
Greenville Sr HS
Gettysburg OH

Martinez Abelina
River Rouge HS
River Rouge MI

Martinez Alicia
Hammond Voc Tech HS
Hammond IN

Martinez Maria
South Dearborn HS
Aurora IN

Martinez Mary F
George Washington HS
East Chicago IN

Marting Peggy
Cuyahoga Falls HS
Cuyahoga Fls OH

Martini Betty A
Seton HS
Cincinnati OH

Martino Joseph J
Brooke HS
Follansbee WV

Marvel Stephen
William Henry Harrison
HS
Evansville IN

Marvig Jeff
Cheboygan HS
Cheboygan MI

Marvin Brenda
Evergreen HS
Swanton OH

Marvin Shirley
Fredericktown Sr HS
Fredericktown OH

Marzolino Gregory
Aquinas HS
Southgate MI

Masnyk Michael
Rossford HS
Rossford OH

Mason Jody
Port Clinton HS
Port Clinton OH

Mason Michelle
Yellow Springs HS
Yellow Sprg OH

Mason Rhonda A
Walnut Ridge HS
Columbus OH

Mason Richard L
Dover HS
Dover OH

Massey Karen
Indian Creek HS
Martinsvll IN

Massey W
Midland Trail HS
Ansted WV

Massie B
Buffalo HS
Prichard WV

STUDENTS
PHOTOGRAPH
SCHEDULED
FOR PUBLI-
CATION HERE
COULD NOT
BE REPRO-
DUCED

Massie Kimberly
Libbey HS
Toledo OH

Massie William
Port Clinton HS
Pt Clinton OH

Massoglia David
Calumet HS
Laurium MI

Mast David
Avon Jr Sr HS
Indianapolis IN

Mastel Jon P
Walnut Township HS
Millersport OH

Masterson Wayne
Eau Claire HS
Eau Cliare MI

Mata Mary
Jefferson HS
La Salle MI

Matanguihan Gregorio
Moeller HS
Cincinnati OH

Matesich Mark
Newark Catholic HS
Newark OH

Matheny Scott
Wauseon HS
Wauseon OH

Mather Cynthia
Salem Sr HS
Salem OH

Matherly Anita
Independence HS
Sophia WV

Mathews Danna
Columbiana HS
Columbiana OH

Mathews Julie A
Richwood HS
Nettie WV

Mathews Lisa
Harbor Springs HS
Hrbr Spgs MI

Mathews Terri
Whetstone HS
Columbus OH

Mathey Laurie
Perry HS
Massillon OH

Mathias Virginia
North Miami HS
Roann IN

Mathis Lisa
Brazil Sr HS
Brazil IN

Mathis Sally
Hamilton Southeastern
HS
Noblesville IN

Mathis William
Goodrich HS
Goodrich MI

Mattaliano Virginia
Philip Barbour HS
Philippi WV

Mattern Norman
Beaver Local HS
Wellsville OH

Matthews Cindy
South Spencer HS
Rockport IN

Matthews John
Montpelier HS
Montpelier OH

Matthews Melanie
Hale Area HS
Hale MI

Matthews Pamela
William Henry Harrison
HS
Evansville IN

Matthews Tami
Martinsburg HS
Martinsburg WV

Mattiello Joseph
Ferndale HS
Oak Park MI

Mattis Julia
Millersport HS
Thornville OH

Matuja Leslie
Bishop Gallagher HS
Roseville MI

Mauch Cynthia
Glen Este HS
Cincinatti OH

Mauk Debbie
Ehove Vocational School
Sandusky OH

Mauren Mark
St Joseph Prep Seminary
Portland MI

Maurer Carolyn
Elmhurst HS
Ft Wayne IN

Maurer Karen L
Grove City HS
Grove City OH

Maurice Keith
Melvindale HS
Allen Park MI

Maust Marietta
North Daviess Jr Sr HS
Montgomery IN

Mauzy Timothy J
Circleville HS
Riverton WV

Mavis Charles
Deckerville Community
School
Sandusky MI

Maxcy Jeffrey
Marion HS
Marion IN

Maxie Sheila
Crothersville HS
Crothersville IN

Maxson Crystal
Bridgeport HS
Bridgeport WV

Maxson Lois
Elkins HS
Elkins WV

Maxwell Trisha
Claymont HS
Uhrichsville OH

Maxwell Jr Glenn E
Bellaire HS
Bellaire OH

May Bruce A
Pontiac Central HS
Clarkston MI

May Charles J
Dayton Christian HS
Arcanum OH

May David P
Sandy Valley HS
Magnolia OH

May Jacqueline
Mississinawa Vly HS
New Weston OH

May Kathleen
Edgewood HS
Bloomington IN

May Michael P
Northwest HS
Cincinnati OH

May Renetta
Point Pleasant HS
Pt Pleasant WV

May Yelandra
Marian HS
Cincinnati OH

Mayberry Dale
Norwayne HS
Sterling OH

Mayberry Jane E
Highland Sr HS
Highland IN

Maye Brenda
Withrow HS
Cincinnati OH

Mayeda Mary Lynn
Loy Norrix HS
Kalamazoo MI

Mayer Ed
St Xavier HS
Cincinnati OH

Mayer Mark W
Wheeling Park HS
Wheeling WV

Mayernik Shawn
Lake Catholic HS
Eastlake OH

Mayers Stephanie
Delta Sr HS
Delta OH

Mayes Jane
Mt Pleasant HS
Mt Pleasant MI

Mayhew Julie
S Newton Jr/sr HS
Kentland IN

Mayhugh Rexine
Ida Public HS
Petersbrg MI

Mayle Joy
Canton South HS
Canton OH

Mayle Roger L
Warren Local HS
Belpre OH

Maynard Gregory
Muncie Southside HS
Muncie IN

Maynard Kevin
Lenore HS
Lenore WV

Mayo Allen
Zanesville HS
Zanesville OH

Mays Celestia L
Immaculata HS
Detroit MI

Mays Eric
Montgomery Cnty Jnt
Voc Schl
Trotwood OH

Mays Meledy
E Liverpool HS
E Liverpool OH

Mays Sandra L
North Ridgeville HS
N Ridgeville OH

Mays Waneta
Ainsworth Sr HS
Flint MI

Mazezka George
Brooke HS
Follansbee WV

Mazik Pat
Solon HS
Solon OH

Mazza Larry
Notre Dame HS
Clarksburg WV

Mazzone John
Weirton Madonna HS
Weirton WV

McAfee Bonita
Eau Claire HS
Eau Claire MI

McAllister Karen
Anderson Sr HS
Cincinnati OH

McAlpin Chuck
Vandalia Butler HS
Dayton OH

McAndrews Sandra
Whiteland Cmnty HS
Greenwood IN

McBride Barry
West Geauga HS
Novelty OH

McBride Cynthia
Lexington Sr HS
Mansfield OH

McBride Lorraine
New Haven HS
New Haven IN

McBride Terry
Tri HS
Lewisville IN

McCain Annette
Clarkston Sr HS
Drayton Plns MI

STUDENTS
PHOTOGRAPH
SCHEDULED
FOR PUBLI-
CATION HERE
COULD NOT
BE REPRO-
DUCED

McCall Lisa
Warsaw Comm HS
Warsaw IN

McCall Pam
Seton HS
Cincinnati OH

McCan Scott
Laville Jr Sr HS
Plymouth IN

McCann Edna
Hebron HS
Hebron IN

McCann Kathy
Regina HS
Cleveland Hts OH

McCarthy Corrine
Bishop Foley HS
Madison Heights MI

McCarthy Steven
La Salle HS
Cincinnati OH

McCartney Brenda
Lewis County HS
Weston WV

McCartney Jill
Calhoun HS
Grantsville WV

McCauley Jody
Zanesville HS
Zanesville OH

STUDENTS
PHOTOGRAPH
SCHEDULED
FOR PUBLI-
CATION HERE
COULD NOT
BE REPRO-
DUCED

McCaw Lisa
Gahanna Lincoln HS
Gahanna OH

McChancy Claudia
Euclid Sr HS
Euclid OH

McChristy Suzanne
Fowlerville HS
Fowlerville MI

McClain Connie
Miller HS
Shawnee OH

McClain Heather
Talawanda HS
Oxford OH

McClain Robert
Wintersville HS
Wintrvl OH

McClary Andrew S
Heritage Christian HS
Indianapolis IN

McClary Juanita
Ironton HS
Ironton OH

McClaskey Katherine S
Huntington East HS
Huntington WV

McCleery Bonnie
Struthers HS
Struthers OH

McCleery Michael
Flat Rock Sr HS
Flat Rock MI

McClelland Kelly
Mt Gilead HS
Mt Gilead OH

McClincuck Kelly
Perry HS
Navarre OH

McClintock Cathy
The Andrews School
Madison OH

McClorey Anne M
Our Lady Of Mercy HS
Novi MI

McCloskey Darlene
Bishop Borgess HS
Detroit MI

McClung Karen
Parkersburg South HS
Parkersburg WV

McClung Tina R
Richwood HS
Leivasy WV

McClung Tonya
Lewis County HS
Weston WV

McClure Dennis D
Bishop Dwenger HS
New Haven IN

McClure Elizabeth
Rivet HS
Vincennes IN

McComas Angela L
Hannan HS
Pliny WV

McCombs Karen
Sycamore HS
Cincinnati OH

McConiga David
Northrop HS
Ft Wayne IN

McConkey Crystal A
Tippecanoe Valley HS
Rochester IN

McConnell Marjorie
Quincy HS
Quincy MI

McConnell Mark
Warsaw Cmnty HS
Warsaw IN

McConnell Thomas
South Vigo Terre Haute
HS
Terre Haute IN

McCorkle Steve
Port Huron N HS
North Street MI

McCormick Danny
Green HS
No Canton OH

McCormick David
Green HS
North Canton OH

McCormick Jennifer
Princeton HS
Princeton WV

McCormick John
Stivers Patterson Coop HS
Dayton OH

McCormick Leshia
Anderson HS
Cincinnati OH

McCormick Tim
Groveport Madison HS
Groveport OH

STUDENTS PHOTOGRAPH SCHEDULED FOR PUBLICATION HERE COULD NOT BE REPRODUCED

McCorry Tracey L
Warrensville Heights HS
Warrensvlle Hts OH

McCowan Melody
Jay County HS
Redkey IN

McCoy David R
Washington HS
Washington IN

McCoy Erin
Lima Sr HS
Lima OH

McCoy Katy
Piketon HS
Waverly OH

McCoy Thomas
Ridgewood HS
Fresno OH

McCoy Toni
Henry Ford HS
Detroit MI

McCoy Valerie J
Cass Tech HS
Detroit MI

McCracken Sherri
Lincolnview HS
Middle Point OH

McCraken Mary
North Royalton HS
N Royalton OH

McCreary David F
Brooke HS
Wellsburg WV

McCree Cedric
Cass Tech HS
Detroit MI

McCreery Beth
Fort Frye HS
Lowell OH

McCreery Jim
Grand River Academy
Poland OH

McCreight Kathleen
Hillsboro HS
Hillsboro OH

McCrone Tami
Andrew School
Painesvll OH

McCubbin Lawrence W
Covington HS
Covington IN

McCullough Evelyn
River Rouge HS
River Rouge MI

McCullough Linda
Morton Sr HS
Hammond IN

McCullough Pamela
Parkway HS
Rockford OH

McCumber Eric
Cadillac HS
Cadillac MI

McCummins Ronald
Mathews HS
Fowler OH

McCutchen Cindy
Lawrence Central HS
Lawrence IN

McCutcheon Mary J
Woodrow Wilson HS
Beckley WV

McDaniel Ginny A
Hedgesville HS
Martinsburg WV

McDaniel Jill
Manton HS
Manton MI

McDaniel Lena E
Mount Hope HS
Beckley WV

McDaniels Jacqueline A
Buckhannon Upshur HS
Buckhannon WV

McDermitt Eric
Memorial HS
St Marys OH

McDermott Kelly
Ursuline HS
Youngstown OH

McDonald Cheryl
Washington HS
Washington IN

McDonald Cynthia
Adelphian Academy
Holly MI

McDonald Jerry E
Sacred Heart Academy
Mt Pleasant MI

McDonald Karen
Cass Technical HS
Detroit MI

McDonald Kim
Calumet HS
Laurium MI

McDonald Lisa
Knightstown HS
Knightstown IN

McDonald Maria
Lake Michigan Cath HS
Benton Hrbr MI

McDonald Nadine
Warren HS
Warren MI

McDonough William
Beaver Island HS
St James MI

McDowell Kim
Muncie Central HS
Muncie IN

McElroy Amber
Univ HS
Westover WV

McElroy Debbie
Elgin HS
Green Camp OH

McElroy Jr Robert
Leslie HS
Onondasa MI

McEuen Scott
Hobart Sr HS
Hobart IN

McFadden Cathy
New Albany HS
Westerville OH

McFarland Charla
New Richmond HS
New Richmond OH

McFarland David W
Bucyrus HS
Bucyrus OH

McFarland Terri
West Ottawa HS
Holland MI

McFarland Yolanda J
East HS
Columbus OH

McGee Marlana
Brookhaven HS
Columbus OH

McGeorge Susan
Traverse City Sr HS
Traverse City MI

McGinnis Terry M
Tippecanoe HS
Tipp City OH

McGlothen Yvette
Ursuline HS
Youngstown OH

STUDENTS
PHOTOGRAPH
SCHEDULED
FOR PUBLI-
CATION HERE
COULD NOT
BE REPRO-
DUCED

McGonagle Molly Ann
W V Fisher Catholic HS
Lancaster OH

McGowan Rhonda
Warrensville Heights HS
Warrensville OH

McGrane Mary
Bishop Gallagher HS
Detroit MI

McGrath Rhonda
Meadowbrook HS
Zanesville OH

McGraw Deborah
Athens HS
Athens WV

McGraw James
Midland Trail HS
Ansted WV

McGregor Dane S
Midland HS
Midland MI

McGrew Steve
Moeller HS
W Chester OH

McGrew Tamra
Dunbar HS
Charleston WV

McHenry Daniel S
Tyler Co HS
Middlebourne WV

McHenry Darla
Tyler County HS
Middlebourne WV

McHugh Kelly
Maysville Sr HS
Zanesville OH

McInerney Lori
Mt Clemens HS
Mt Clemens MI

McInerney Patricia
Bishop Noll Inst
Highland IN

McInerney Thomas
Notre Dame HS
Mt Clemens MI

McInerny Dave
St Josephs HS
S Bend IN

McIntire Cheryl
Hillsdale HS
Jeromesville OH

McIntosh Antoinette
Jane Addams Voc HS
Cleveland OH

McIntyre Kathleen
Kalamazoo Central HS
Kalamazoo MI

McIntyre Mark
Columbiana HS
Columbiana OH

McKamey Lisa A
Cloverdale HS
Cloverdale IN

McKanna Jeff
Columbus Grove HS
Columbus Grove OH

McKay Lisa
Alcona HS
Black River MI

McKay Timothy
L C Mohr HS
S Haven MI

McKee Bryan
Groveport Madison Sr
HS
Columbus OH

McKee Joan
Vassar HS
Vassar MI

McKee Pam
Bowling Green HS
Lima OH

McKee Sue
Delphos Jefferson Sr HS
Delphos OH

McKeethen Constance
George Washington HS
E Chicago IN

McKenna Karen
Fenton HS
Fenton MI

McKenney Timothy
Holly HS
Holly MI

McKenzie Craig
Shelby Senior HS
Shelby OH

McKenzie Darlene
Ravenna HS
Ravenna OH

McKim Pamela
North Huron HS
Kinde MI

McKinley Jeffrey
West Carrollton HS
Dayton OH

McKinley Mark S
New Haven HS
Fort Wayne IN

McKinley Michelle
Jenison HS
Jenison MI

McKinley Robert
Ridgemont HS
Kenton OH

McKinney Derrick
John F Kennedy HS
Cleveland OH

McKinney Evelyn
Tecumseh Sr HS
Tecumseh MI

McKinney Gerri
Madison HS
Adrian MI

McKinney Jacqueline V
Glen Oak School
Cleveland OH

McKinney James
Medora HS
Norman IN

McKinney Karen
Mt Gilead HS
Mt Gilead OH

McKinney Melanie
Jackson HS
Jackson OH

McKinney Patrick S
Pineville HS
New Richmond WV

McKinney Paula
Gleneste HS
Cincinnati OH

McLane Joline
William G Mather HS
Munising MI

McLaughlin Dawn
Meridian Sr HS
Sanford MI

McLaughlin Elizabeth
Williamston HS
Williamston MI

STUDENTS
PHOTOGRAPH
SCHEDULED
FOR PUBLI-
CATION HERE
COULD NOT
BE REPRO-
DUCED

McLaughlin Jeffrey
Brooke HS
Wellsburg WV

McLaughlin Kelly
Mogadore HS
Mogadore OH

McLaughlin Tracy
South Vigo HS
Terre Haute IN

McLavy Mark
Elizabeth Ann Johnson Sr
HS
Mt Morris MI

McLemore Kimberly J
Logan HS
Logan WV

McLemore Lisa
Frankton HS
Anderson IN

McLenithan John
Tri Township Tribune HS
Rapid Rvr MI

McLeod Dean
Houghton Lake HS
Houghton Lkae MI

McLimore John R
Heritage Christian School
Indianapolis IN

McMahon Theresa A
Carroll HS
Dayton OH

McManus William L
Colon Comm HS
Colon MI

McMillan Laurena
North Newton HS
Morocco IN

McMillen Bill
Malvern HS
Malvern OH

McMillen Brad
Tecumseh HS
Medway OH

McMillion Donna J
Woodrow Wilson HS
Beckley WV

McMillion Sheila
Liberty HS
Fairdale WV

McMullen Sandy
Peru HS
Peru IN

McMullen Tamalyn
Rockville Jr Sr HS
Rockville IN

McMurtry Troy
Rockville HS
Rockville IN

McNabb Michael
Grosse Ile HS
Grosse Ile MI

McNamara Nancy
St Mary Academy
Indianapolis IN

McNash Robbin
Morton Sr HS
Hammond IN

McNeal Rose L
Southwestern HS
Oak Hill OH

McNeely Eileen
Logan Sr HS
Peach Creek WV

McNeely Karen K
Park Hills HS
Fairborn OH

McNeice Barbara
Inland Lakes HS
Indian River MI

McNeill Carol A
Pocahontas County HS
Buckeye WV

McNichols Kim
Zane Trace HS
Laurelville OH

McNulty Jennifer
Livonia Franklin HS
Westland MI

McPeak Barbara
Sandusky HS
Sandusky OH

McPeek David
Watkins Memorial HS
Pataskala OH

McPhillips Michael
Lake Catholic HS
Chesterland OH

McPike Jeffrey D
Medora HS
Medora IN

McQuaid Jeanie
Chesapeake HS
Chesapeake OH

McQuaid Pam
Lincoln HS
Lumberport S WV

McQuain Crystal
Grafton HS
Grafton WV

McQuarters Regina
Cass Tech HS
Detroit MI

McQuiston Marilou
Ashley Community HS
Brant MI

McRae Joseph
Quincy HS
Quincy MI

McRoberts Lori
Danville Comm HS
Danville IN

McVay Randall R
Ripley HS
Ripley WV

McVety Steven
Minster Local HS
Minster OH

Mead Lonnie
Pymatuning HS
Andover OH

Mead Michele
Alcona HS
Lincoln MI

Mead Patricia
Adrian HS
Adrian MI

Meade Drexel
Chapmanville HS
Chapmanville WV

Meade Michael
Tecumseh HS
Medway OH

Meador Cheryl
Charlestown HS
Otisco IN

Meador Connie
Willow Run HS
Ypsilanti MI

Meadows Archie
Hannan Trace HS
Crown City OH

Meadows Deborah
Pt Pleasant HS
Henderson WV

Meadows Jacqueline
South Charleston HS
S Charleston WV

Meadows Karen
Lemon Monroe HS
Middletown OH

Meadows Kristina Jo
Independence HS
Crab Orchard WV

Meadows Linette
Ovid Elsie HS
Ovid MI

Meadows Pamela J
Athens HS
Athens WV

Mealey Shawn
Midland HS
Midland MI

Meaney Leo
Ashtabula County Jt Voc HS
Jefferson OH

Means Karen
Marysville HS
Marysville OH

Means Lawretta
Warrensville Heights HS
Warrensvl Hts OH

Mears Roger
Avon HS
Indianapolis IN

Medar Melissa
Berea HS
Berea OH

Medellin Mary
Roosevelt HS
E Chicago IN

Medler Greg
Berkley HS
Berkley MI

Medley Carol
Fort Frye HS
Lower Salem OH

Medley James
Cadiz HS
Cadiz OH

Medley Todd
Shelby Sr HS
Shelby OH

Medlicott Carol
Franklin Community HS
Franklin IN

Medors Scott
Westerville S HS
Westerville OH

Medved Annette
Sandy Valley HS
Waynesburg OH

Medvez Mary
Ursuline HS
Campbell OH

Medwick Lori
Champion Sr HS
Warren OH

Meece Anna
Valparaiso HS
Valparaiso IN

Meehan Barbara
Rudyard HS
Rudyard MI

Meek Christine
Galion Sr HS
Kingsport TN

Meek Teresa
Coshocton HS
Coshocton OH

Meeker Brian
Fraklin HS
Franklin OH

Meeks Jeryl A
Orrville Sr HS
Marshallville OH

Meeks Linda
Kokomo HS
St Mary Of Wds IN

Mees Pam
Meigs HS
Pomeroy OH

Mehnert Dana
Alliance HS
Alliance OH

Meier Steven
R B Chamberlin HS
Twinsburg OH

Meier Steven F
Wickliffe Sr HS
Wickliffe OH

Meighen Martin
Norwood HS
Norwood OH

Meininger Michele
Fairmont West HS
Kettering OH

Meiring Grace
Pike Delta York Sr HS
Delta OH

Meister Patricia
R B Chamberlin HS
Twinsburg OH

Meitz Phillip
Cedar Springs HS
Cedar Spgs MI

Meleski Kevin
Swan Valley HS
Saginaw MI

Melinis Cathy
Brecksville Sr HS
Broadview Hts OH

Mellott Lynn
Lakeview HS
Cortland OH

Melton Elizabeth
Magnolia HS
New Martinsvle WV

Mendez Diane
Hudson HS
Lyons OH

Mendez Michelle
South Harrison HS
Mt Clare WV

Mendick Maureen
Floyd Central HS
Lanesville IN

Mendoza Laura
Notre Dame HS
Clarksburg WV

Menningen Linda
Carey HS
Carey OH

Mentel Michael
Bishop Ready HS
Columbus OH

Menzel Tom
Owendale Gagetown HS
Sebewaing MI

Meranda Dona
Avon Jr Sr HS
Danville IN

Mercer Mike
Kings HS
South Lebanon OH

Merck Mary
Westerville North HS
Westerville OH

Meredith William V
Brookhaven HS
Columbus OH

Mergel Carol A
Shrine HS
Royal Oak MI

Merical Steve
Beaver Local HS
East Liverpool OH

Merillat Barbara
Waldron HS
Waldron MI

Merkle Terry
Loy Norrix HS
Kalamazoo MI

Merriam Daniel
Tri Valley HS
Adamsville OH

Merrill Brad
Bentley HS
Burton MI

Merrill Glenn
Montabella Community
HS
Blanchard MI

Merriman Randal
Maysville HS
So Zanesville OH

Merry Michael
North Vermilion HS
Cayuga IN

Merryman Christe
Tri Valley HS
Adamsville OH

Mertz Barbara
Lewis Cnty HS
Jan Lew WV

Mertz Edward
Marysville HS
Marysville MI

Merullo Karen A
Whetstone HS
Columbus OH

Meschen Ronald E
Rockville Jr Sr HS
Montezuma IN

Meskunas Brenda
Eastlake North HS
Willowick OH

Messer Brenda K
Penn HS
Mishawaka IN

Messinger David
Clay HS
Granger IN

Messner Daniel R
Southfield Christian HS
Pontiac MI

Metcalf Richard
Tawas Area HS
E Tawas MI

Metiva Randy C
Bridgeport HS
Bridgeport MI

Mettert Jon
Brandywine HS
Niles MI

Metz Elizabeth
Calhoun Co HS
Mtzion WV

Metzger Delores
Perry HS
Canton OH

Metzner Cheryl
Jefferson Area HS
Rock Crk OH

Meurer Dave
North Daviess Cougars
HS
Plainville IN

Meyer Christopher
Toronto HS
Toronto OH

Meyer Jenny
Bridgeport HS
Bridgeport WV

Meyer Kurt
Kiser HS
Dayton OH

Meyer Peggy
Robert S Rogers HS
Toledo OH

Meyer Sandra
Decatur Central HS
Indianapolis IN

Meyer Thomas
Carroll HS
Dayton OH

Meyer Thos
Highland HS
Highland IN

Meyers Colleen
Salem Sr HS
Salem OH

Meyers Patti
Circle HS
Circle MT

Michael Dianne
Hicksville HS
Hicksville OH

Michael Maureen
Admiral King HS
Lorain OH

Michael Richmond
The Leelanau School
Cadillac MI

Michaelis Kim
Otsego HS
Bowling Grn OH

Michaelson Margaret
Huntington North HS
Huntington IN

Michailenko Ann
Holy Name Nazareth HS
Parma OH

Michel Ann
Sandusky HS
Sandusky OH

Michel Matthew
Sandusky HS
Sandusky OH

Micheli Mario
Fordson HS
Dearborn MI

Mick Elizabeth
Jefferson Area HS
Jefferson OH

Mick Judy
Fairless HS
Navarre OH

Mick William
Defiance Sr HS
Defiance OH

Middleton Beth
Crown Point HS
Crown Point IN

Middleton Dorann
North Central HS
Indianapolis IN

Middleton Scott
Lebanon HS
Lebanon OH

Midkiff Andrea
Watkins Memorial HS
Pataskala OH

Miele Sheri
Kearsley HS
Davison MI

Miesiak Stephen
Troy HS
Troy MI

Miesner John
Washington Irving HS
Clarksburg WV

Mieszkowski Julia
Utica HS
Utica MI

Mietla Helen M
Swan Valley HS
Saginaw MI

Mifflin Karl A
Nordonia Sr HS
Macedonia OH

Mignano Antonina M
St Mary Academy
Monroe MI

Mihalyo Michael P
Mingo HS
Mingo Jct OH

Mijares Patsy
Springfield HS
Holland OH

Mika Richard
Bay City All Saints HS
Bay City MI

Miklis Ellen
Charles F Brush HS
Lyndhurst OH

Mikolajczak Mary
Bay City All Saints Ctrl
HS
Bay City MI

Milano Mark
Clarence M Kimball HS
Royal Oak MI

Milbauer Kristina
Beaver Local HS
E Liverpool OH

Miles Henry G
Lake HS
Hartville OH

Miles Janet E
Northland HS
Columbus OH

Miles John T
Beavercreek HS
Fairborn OH

Miles Theresa
Shortridge HS
Indianapolis IN

Milewski Greg
East Detroit HS
E Detroit MI

Milionis W Kelly
Douglas Mac Arthur HS
Saginaw MI

Millen Susan
Whitmore Lake HS
Whitmore Lake MI

Miller Alan
Jackson HS
Jackson OH

Miller Amy
Crown Point HS
Crown Point IN

Miller Beth
Hiland HS
Millersburg OH

Miller Billy
Huntington E HS
Huntington WV

Miller Bonnie L
Vanlue Local School
Carey OH

Miller Brent
John Glenn HS
New Concord OH

Miller Brian
Mona Shores HS
Muskegon MI

Miller Candy
Green HS
Greensburg OH

Miller Cheryl
Eisenhower HS
Saginaw MI

Miller Christian
Decatur Jr Sr HS
Decatur MI

Miller Cindy
Maplewood HS
Cortland OH

Miller Cynthia
Flint Central HS
Flint MI

Miller Darrell
Norwood Sr HS
Norwood OH

Miller David
Walsh Jesuit HS
Akron OH

Miller Deborah
Henry Ford II HS
Sterling Hts MI

Miller Diane
Arthur Hill HS
Saginaw MI

Miller Donna S
Defiance Sr HS
Defiance OH

Miller Douglas S
Hastings HS
Bedford MI

Miller Emily M
University HS
Westover WV

Miller Eric
Bullock Creek HS
Midland MI

Miller Gary J
Centreville HS
Centreville MI

Miller Gordon
Field HS
Mogadore OH

Miller James
Rossford HS
Rossford OH

Miller James R
Linsly Institute
Wheeling WV

Miller Jeannie
Medina Sr HS
Medina OH

Miller Jeff
Buckeye HS
Valley City OH

Miller Jerry L
Breckenridge Jr Sr HS
Breckenridge MI

Miller Judy
West Branch HS
Salem OH

Miller Julie
Perrysburg HS
Perrysburg OH

Miller Julie
S Newton Jr/sr HS
Kentland IN

Miller Karen
N Canton Hoover HS
North Canton OH

Miller Karen
Washington Catholic HS
Washington IN

Miller Kathy
Logan HS
Logan OH

Miller Kenneth M
Warren G Harding HS
Warren OH

Miller Kurt
Northwood HS
Northwood OH

Miller Lamoni R
East HS
Cleveland OH

Miller Laura
South Spencer HS
Richland IN

STUDENTS
PHOTOGRAPH
SCHEDULED
FOR PUBLI-
CATION HERE
COULD NOT
BE REPRO-
DUCED

Miller Linda
Cass Tech HS
Detroit MI

Miller Linda
Four County Joint Voc
HS
Swanton OH

Miller Linda
Niles Mc Kinley HS
Niles OH

Miller Lisa
Waynesfield Goshen HS
Waynesfield OH

Miller Lori
Oakridge HS
Muskegon MI

Miller Lori A
River Rouge HS
River Rouge MI

Miller Marcellus
Cleveland Cntrl Catholic
HS
Cleveland OH

Miller Marian
Lumen Christi HS
Jackson MI

Miller Marvin
Fairview Area Schools
Fairview MI

Miller Mary A
St Joseph Central Cath
HS
Fremont OH

Miller Mary B
Washington Irving HS
Clarksburg WV

Miller Melissa
R Rogers HS
Toledo OH

Miller Michael
Washington Irving HS
Clarksburg WV

Miller Michele
Allegan Sr HS
Allegan MI

Miller Pamela
Greenville Sr HS
Greenville OH

Miller Phil
Lakewood HS
Hebron OH

Miller Rebecca
Sidney HS
Sidney OH

Miller Renee
Bedford HS
Bedford Hts OH

Miller Richard
Brooke HS
Follansbee WV

Miller Robert
Tecumseh HS
Medway OH

Miller Roma
Piketon HS
Piketon OH

Miller Roxane
Jackson County Western HS
Spring Arbor MI

Miller Russell B
Clay City HS
Clay City IN

Miller Sandra L
Archbold HS
Archbold OH

Miller Scot
Henry Ford II HS
Sterling Hts MI

Miller Shannon
Shakamak HS
Jasonville IN

Miller Starr B
London HS
London OH

Miller Stephen
Lima Sr HS
Lima OH

Miller Sue
Copley HS
Copley OH

Miller Susan
Charlevoix HS
Charlevoix MI

Miller Tammy
Father Joseph Wehrle Mem HS
Columbus OH

Miller Tammy
Blissfield HS
Blissfield MI

Miller Theresa
Rensselaer Central HS
Rensselaer IN

Miller Thomas
St Johns HS
Lambertville MI

Miller Thomas
Pontiac Northern HS
Pontiac MI

Miller Timothy
Calvin Christian HS
Grandville MI

Miller Tony
Spencer HS
Spencer WV

Miller Tracy
Pike Central HS
Stendal IN

Miller Tracy
Wheeling Park HS
Wheeling WV

Miller Valorie
Sissonville HS
Sissonville WV

Miller William E
Hubbard HS
Hubbard OH

Millett Michael
Stivers Patterson Co Op HS
Dayton OH

Milliron David
Marion Harding HS
Marion OH

Mills Jeffery
Lake Fenton HS
Lake Fenton MI

Mills Nelson
Brooke HS
Colliers WV

Mills Robert
Wintersville HS
Steubenville OH

Mills Roy
Penn HS
Bremen IN

Mills Teresa
Union HS
Losantville IN

Milne Jeffrey
North Branch HS
North Branch MI

Milner Lisa Y
Cincinnati Country Day Schl
Cincinnati OH

Milner Marla
Rossville HS
Frankfort IN

Milnes Beth
Perry HS
Canton OH

Milosevic Jane
James Ford Rhodes HS
Cleveland OH

Milton Joe
Cleveland Ctrl Catholic HS
Cleveland OH

Milum Raymond L
Malabar HS
Mansfield OH

Min Janet
Mt Clemens HS
Mt Clemens MI

Minamyer Tami
Canfield HS
Canfield OH

Mincey Kathy
Benedictine HS
Detroit MI

Minch Richard
St Ignatius HS
Euclid OH

Minchella Michael
Northwood HS
Northwood OH

Minda Michele
Admiral King HS
Lorain OH

Minderman Lori
Lincoln HS
Vincennes IN

Minge Deborah
Springboro HS
Springboro OH

Mingle Michelle
Fairborn Bakes HS
Fairborn OH

Mingle Thomas
Highland HS
Middletown IN

Mingus Dean
Edison HS
Berlin Heights OH

Minner Elizabeth
Delta HS
Eaton IN

Minnich Eugene
Lorain Catholic HS
Lorain OH

Minniear Julie
Northfield HS
Wabash IN

Minton Clay
Williamstown HS
Williamstown WV

Minton Ellen
Point Pleasant HS
Pt Pleasant WV

Minton Sherry
Milan HS
Milan MI

Minx Russell D
East HS
Akron OH

Miramonti Steve
Mt Clemens HS
Mt Clemens MI

Mirich Michele
Andrean HS
Crown Pt IN

Miron Ronald
Atherton HS
Holly MI

Misak Eric
Bluefield HS
Bluefield WV

Mischler Fred
Oakwood HS
Dayton OH

Misciskia Annette
Liberty HS
Girard OH

Miskinis Donald J
Lake Catholic HS
Chesterland OH

Missler Susan
Lima Ctrl Cath HS
Lima OH

Mister Meloney A
West Side Sr HS
Gary IN

Mitchell David D
Huntington HS
Waverly OH

Mitchell Jane M
Newton HS
Pleasant Hill OH

Mitchell Jim
Delta HS
Eaton IN

Mitchell John
Rapid River HS
Rapid Rvr MI

Mitchell Kevin
Colonel Crawford HS
Buryrus OH

Mitchell Kevin
Eau Claire HS
Eau Claire MI

Mitchell Mark
Madison HS
Madison OH

Mitchell Marsha
Clinton Central HS
Frankfort IN

Mitchell Ovie H
Withrow HS
Cincinnati OH

Mitchell Robin
Whiteland Community
HS
Franklin IN

Mitchell Shannon
Elmhurst HS
Ft Wayne IN

Mitchell Terri L
Hurricane HS
Hurricane WV

Mitchell Tobin
Lowell HS
Lowell IN

Mitchell Yvonne
Griffith HS
Griffith IN

Mitchem Shari
North Dickinson HS
Iron Mtn MI

Miteff Ganie
Lansing Eastern HS
Lansing MI

Mitro Kathie M
Merrillville Sr HS
Merrillville IN

Mitten Mary
Maumee HS
Toledo OH

Mittower Marvin A
Taylor HS
Kokomo IN

Mitzo Karen
Nordonia HS
Northfield OH

Mix Doug
Fairview HS
Sherwood OH

Mix Scott C
Jackson Milton HS
Berlin Center OH

Mix Steve
New Albany HS
New Albany IN

Mize William
Fairview HS
Fairview Pk OH

M Jones Teno D M
Buena Vista HS
Saginaw MI

Moberg Nancy
Kankakee Vly HS
Wheatfield IN

Mobley Anthony
George Washington HS
E Chicago IN

Mobley Norma
Parkside HS
Jackson MI

Mociulewski Lisa
Henry Foro Ii HS
Sterling Hts MI

Mock Dale
Union City Community
HS
Union City IN

Modos Maryann
Clay HS
South Bend IN

Moeder Jim
Coldwater HS
Celina OH

Moeller Donna
Bellbrook HS
Bellbrook OH

Moeller Mary M
Lansing Catholic Ctrl HS
Lansing MI

Moff Donnette
Columbiana HS
Columbiana OH

Mohlmaster Wendy
Ellet HS
Akron OH

Mohr Kim A
Sebring Mc Kinley HS
Sebring OH

Mohrfield Ginni
Goshen HS
Pleasant Plain OH

Mohsenzadeh
Mohammad
Richmond Sr HS
Richmond IN

Moine Jo Dee
Wadsworth Sr HS
Wadsworth OH

Molchan William
Padua Franciscan HS
Parma OH

Moles Bruce E
Calhoun County HS
Nicut WV

Molina Brenda
Theodore Roosevelt HS
E Chicago IN

Molina Michael D
Notre Dame HS
Anmoore WV

Mollaun Kelly
Lawrenceburg HS
Lawrenceburg IN

Molle Catherine
Bishop Noll Institute
Hammond IN

Mollohan Sue
Woodrow Wilson HS
Beckley WV

Momany Sharon
Davison HS
Davison MI

Momyer Gene
Gorham Fayette HS
Fayette OH

Monachino Thomas
Thomas W Harvey HS
Painesville OH

Monczynski Angela
Lumen Cordium HS
Macedonia OH

Mondora Christina
Struthers HS
Poland OH

Money Derek
Horace Mann 'S
Gary IN

Money Janis
Milford Christian
Academy
Goshen OH

Monroe Alison
Paint Valley HS
Bourneville OH

Monroe Joseph T
Martinsburg Sr HS
Martinsburg WV

Montagnese Renee
Licking Valley HS
Newark OH

Monteleone Marc
Notre Dame HS
Clarksburg WV

Montemurro Michelle
Robert S Rogers HS
Toledo OH

Montgomery Bonita S
Perry HS
Massillon OH

Montgomery Carolyn
Kalkaska HS
Rapid City MI

Montgomery Dodie
Brooke HS
Follansbee WV

Montgomery Gena
Yellow Springs HS
Yellow Sprg OH

Montgomery Jill
Green HS
N Canton OH

Montgomery Kathy
Hamilton Hts HS
Cicero IN

Montgomery Kenneth
Danville HS
Danville IN

STUDENTS
PHOTOGRAPH
SCHEDULED
FOR PUBLI-
CATION HERE
COULD NOT
BE REPRO-
DUCED

Montgomery Michael
Toronto HS
Toronto OH

Montgomery Michelle
Concord HS
Jackson MI

Montgomery Sherry
James Ford Rhodes HS
Cleveland OH

Montri Patty
Ida HS
Ida MI

Moody Marla K
South Ripley Jr Sr HS
Versailles IN

Moody Robin L
Springfield HS
Akron OH

Mook Julie
Floyd Central HS
Floyds Knobs IN

Moon Susan
Alma HS
Alma MI

Moore Adrienne
Broad Ripple HS
Indianapolis IN

Moore Brian
Redford Union HS
Redford MI

Moore Dana
West Branch HS
Damascus OH

Moore Daniel
Merrillville HS
Merrillville IN

Moore Daniel
Monroe HS
Monroe MI

Moore Debbie
Elyria Catholic HS
Elyria OH

Moore Diedra
Linden Mc Kinley HS
Columbus OH

Moore Don
Grove City HS
London OH

Moore Duane A
Woodhaven HS
Woodhaven MI

Moore Elisabeth J
Minerva HS
Minerva OH

Moore Elizabeth M
Bluefield HS
Bluefield WV

Moore Frances
Bay HS
Bay Village OH

Moore Gary
New Richmond HS
New Richmond OH

Moore Gina G
Charleston HS
Charleston WV

Moore Glenn
Northrop HS
Ft Wayne IN

Moore Judith A
Arthur Hill HS
Saginaw MI

Moore Kathy
Triton Central HS
Indianapolis IN

Moore Kimberley
Clermont Northeastern
HS
Batavia OH

Moore Kimberly
Northrop HS
Ft Wayne IN

Moore Kimberly
Hartland HS
Holly MI

Moore Larry
Shenandoah HS
Quaker City OH

Moore Lori
Cannelton Jr Sr HS
Cannelton IN

Moore Michael
Horace Mann HS
Gary IN

Moore Michael
St Johns HS
St Johns MI

Moore Mike
Johnstown Monroe HS
Johnstown OH

Moore Nancy
Parkersburg South HS
Parkersburg WV

Moore N Kent
Wintersville HS
Steubenvi OH

Moore Penny
Ithaca HS
Ithaca MI

Moore Phillip
Emerson HS
Gary IN

Moore Robin
Garfield HS
Akron OH

Moore Robyn
John Adams HS
So Bend IN

Moore Sally E
Fairfield Sr HS
Fairfield OH

Moore Sharon E
Benedictine HS
Detroit MI

Moore Shelby
Jonesville HS
Jonesville MI

Moore Terry
Fairmont West HS
Kettering OH

Moore Tom
Terre Haute So Vigo HS
Terre Haute IN

Moore Valerie
West Lafayette HS
W Lafayette IN

Moore Walter
Creston HS
Grand Rpds MI

Moorhead Jane
South Ripley Jr Sr HS
Versailles IN

Moorman Charisse
Chaminade Julienne HS
Dayton OH

Morad Helen
Ripley HS
Ripley WV

Moraja Laura
Eaton HS
Eaton OH

Morales Monica
Kankakee Valley HS
De Motte IN

Moran Kay
Jefferson Union HS
Toronto OH

Moran Leslie
Liberty HS
Reynoldsville WV

Moran Patrick
Lamphere HS
Madison Hts MI

Moran Tim
Jefferson Union HS
Toronto OH

Morand Mary C
St Ursula Acad
Cincinnati OH

Morandy Deborah L
Novi Sr HS
Novi MI

Morbitzer Mary T
Seton HS
Cincinnati OH

Morehouse Denise
Delta HS
Muncie IN

Morehouse Kim
Stockbridge HS
Stockbridge MI

Moreland Becky
Licking Valley HS
Newark OH

Morell Thomas
Vassar HS
Vassar MI

Moreno Jorge
Andrean HS
Schererville IN

Morgan Andrea
Madison Comprehensive
HS
Mansfield OH

Morgan Beverly
Mount View HS
Wilcoe WV

Morgan Bridgett
William Henry Harrison
HS
Harrison OH

STUDENTS
PHOTOGRAPH
SCHEDULED
FOR PUBLI-
CATION HERE
COULD NOT
BE REPRO-
DUCED

Morgan Dreama K
Mount View HS
Hemphill WV

Morgan Lesa
Pineville HS
Pineville WV

Morgan Lisa
Herbert Hoover HS
Clendenin WV

Morgan Paula
Stanton HS
Hammondsville OH

Morgan Phillip
Elwood Community HS
Elwood IN

Morgan Scott
Parkersburg HS
Parkersburg WV

Morgan Scott E
Jay County HS
Portland IN

Morgan Steven R
Milton Union HS
W Milton OH

Morgan Susan
Our Lady Of Mercy HS
W Bloomfield MI

Morgan Vickie
John Glenn HS
Bay City MI

Morgenroth Lori
Calumet HS
Gary IN

Morgenstern M
North Eastern HS
Richmond IN

Morikis Pete
Thomas A Edison Sr HS
Lake Station IN

Mormol Leslie
Bexley HS
Columbus OH

Morokoff Carol
Arlington HS
Indianapolis IN

Moron Michael
Chippewa Valley HS
Mt Clemens MI

Morony Catherine
Eastlake North HS
Willowick OH

Morris Connie
Grandview Hts HS
Columbus OH

Morris Gregory
Parkersburg HS
Vienna WV

Morris Heidi
Chaminade Julienne HS
Brookville OH

Morris John
Claymont HS
Uhrichsville OH

Morris Laura
Lee M Thurston HS
Redford MI

Morris Linda
Marietta Sr HS
Marietta OH

Morris Michael
Coshocton HS
Coshocton OH

Morris Robin
John Glenn HS
Westland MI

Morris Sharon
Carlisle HS
Carlisle OH

Morris Sorona
Franklin Cmnty HS
Franklin IN

Morris Steve
Utica HS
Utica MI

Morris Steven
Canton South HS
Canton OH

Morris Tammy
Groveport Madison Sr
HS
Columbus OH

Morris Tracy
Oak Hill HS
Oak Hill WV

Morrison Cindy
Milton Sr HS
Milton WV

Morrison Theodore
Hughes HS
Cincinnati OH

Morrison Troy
Philo HS
Philo OH

Morrow Craig A
Castle HS
Newburg IN

Morse Sheri
Fennville HS
Fennville MI

Morton Ellen
Andrean HS
Merrillville IN

Morton Thomas
George Washington HS
Charleston WV

Morton Valerie D
Triway HS
Wooster OH

Morvai Ann
Barberton HS
Barberton OH

Morway William M
St Hedwig HS
Detroit MI

Mosbaugh Laura
Marion Adams HS
Sheridan IN

Moschel James
Lutheran N HS
Warren MI

Moses Regina
Chippewa Valley HS
Mt Clemens MI

Moses Robert
Oak Hill HS
Thurman OH

Mosher Scott C
Michigan Lutheran
Seminary
Webberville MI

Moshier Amy
Oxford Area Community
HS
Oxford MI

Moskosky James
Campbell Memorial HS
Campbell OH

Mosley Cheryl
Pickerington HS
Pickerington OH

Mosley Diane
Adelphian Academy
Detroit MI

Mosley Lynne
Archbishop Alter HS
Dayton OH

Mospens Catherine
Tippecanoe HS
Tipp City OH

Moss Charles
William Henry Harrison
HS
Evansville IN

Moss Jerri
West Branch HS
Salem OH

Moss Kellie
Atlanta HS
Atlanta MI

Moss Theron
Patterson Co Op HS
Dayton OH

Mossbarger Teresa L
Chillicothe HS
Chillicothe OH

Mossburg Robert E
Summerfield HS
Petersburg MI

Mossor Gary
Buckeye North HS
Rayland OH

Most Kimberly
St Louis HS
St Louis MI

Mostrom Cheryl
Centreville HS
Sturgis MI

Mothersbaugh Amy
Our Lady Of The Elms
HS
Akron OH

Motl Mark
South Spencer HS
Grandview IN

Motley Norma B
Saint Thomas Aquinas
HS
Canton OH

Motsinger Nancy
Eastern HS
Salem IN

Mott Martha
Richmond HS
Richmond MI

Mott Sylvia
Olivet HS
Olivet MI

Mottes Deborah
Gwinn HS
Gwinn MI

Mottonen Tammy
Calumet HS
Laurium MI

Mouhlas Cynthia
Trinity HS
Parma OH

Moulden Rebecca
N Daviess Jr Sr HS
Elnora IN

Moulds Brenda
North Muskegon HS
North Muskegon MI

Mounsey Tori A
Southern Wells HS
Montpelier IN

Mountain Donald
Streetsboro HS
Streetsboro OH

Mounts Brenda G
Guyan Valley HS
Ranger WV

Mouser Michael S
Lakeview Sr HS
Stow OH

Mowery Gail
Southwood HS
Wabash IN

Mowery Julie
Waynesfield Goshen HS
Wapakoneta OH

Mowery Teresa
Eastbrook HS
Marion IN

Moxley Denise
Mio Au Sable HS
Mio MI

Moye Angela
Michigan Lutheran
Seminary
Detroit MI

Moye Paula
Pontiac Central HS
Pontiac MI

Moyer Diane
Cory Rawson HS
Mt Cory OH

Moyer Sheelah
Chaminade Julienne HS
Dayton OH

Moyer T
Roosevelt Wilson HS
Clarksbrg WV

Moyer Terry
Regina HS
S Euclid OH

Moyers Pamela
Bridgeport HS
Bridgeport WV

Moyzis Elizabeth J
Fairmont East HS
Kettering OH

Mozdian Rayanne
Van Wert HS
Van Wert OH

Mrocka Sandra
Hartland HS
Brighton MI

Mroz Richard
Andrean HS
Gary IN

Muck Pete
Southern Local HS
Summitvll OH

Muelle Mary
Marquette Sr HS
Marquette MI

Mueller George
Reading HS
Reading MI

Mueller Rita
Garfield HS
Akron OH

Mueller Shelley
East Kentwood HS
Kentwood MI

Mugford Rebecca L
Zanesville HS
Zanesville OH

Muldoon Marlene
Southwestern HS
Edinburgh IN

Mulholland Cheryl
Lima Perry HS
Lima OH

Mullally Mary
Holy Rosary HS
Mt Morris MI

Mullally Tom
Holy Rosary HS
Mt Morris MI

Mullen Jennifer
Floyd Central HS
Georgetown IN

Mullen Julia
Ben Davis HS
Indianapolis IN

Mullen Roger
Floyd Central HS
Georgetown IN

Mullen Sheila
Alter HS
Dayton OH

Mullenix Deborah
Goshen HS
Goshen OH

Mullens Pam
Shakamak HS
Jasonville IN

Mullet David
Groveport Madison Sr
HS
Columbus OH

Mullett Amy
Magnolia HS
New Martinsvle WV

Mulligan Joseph
Theodore Roosevelt HS
Wyandotte MI

Mullikin John
Jennings County HS
No Vernon IN

Mullins Cindy
Bucyrus HS
Bucyrus OH

Mullins Clinton L
Iaeger HS
Paynesville WV

Mullins Meloney
Philip Barbour HS
Galloway WV

Mullins Stephen
Gallia Academy
Gallipolis OH

Mullins Tammy
Attica HS
Attica IN

Mumaw John
Whetstone HS
Columbus OH

Muncy Paula
Shelbyville HS
Shelbyville IN

Mundy Rhonda
Meadowdale HS
Dayton OH

Munger Julie
Penn HS
Mishawaka IN

Munguia Randy
Brother Rice HS
Birmingham MI

Munro James
James A Garfield HS
Akron OH

Munson Andrea
Arthur Hill HS
Saginaw MI

Munson Mary
Portland HS
Portland MI

Murchake Jennifer
Upper Arlington HS
COlumbus OH

Murchland Shari
Weir Sr HS
Weirton WV

Murdock Kira
Forest Park HS
Forest Park OH

Murdock Randy
Anderson HS
Anderson IN

Murin Melissa
Munster HS
Munster IN

Murphy Cathy
Bay City All Saints Ctrl
HS
Bay City MI

Murphy Christy
Shawe Mem HS
Madison IN

Murphy Debra
Pennsboro HS
Pennsboro WV

Murphy Kathleen K
Huron HS
Huron OH

Murphy Kevin
Lake Catholic HS
Painesvl OH

Murphy Mary Anne
Cadillac Sr HS
Cadillac MI

Murphy Pamela
Shawe Memorial HS
Madison IN

Murphy Richard L
Moeller HS
Cincinnati OH

Murphy Sandra
Groveport Madison Sr
HS
Obetz OH

Murr Dave
Springboro HS
Springboro OH

Murr Kendra
Memorial HS
St Marys OH

Murray Amy
Plainwell HS
Plainwell MI

Murray Andy
Tuscarawas Valley HS
Bolivar OH

Murray Jacqueline
Warren Central HS
Indpls IN

Murray Julie
New Lexington Sr HS
New Lexington OH

Murray Kathryn
Elyria Catholic HS
Elyria OH

Murray Kelvin
John Marshall HS
Indianapolis IN

Murray Kenneth
Penn HS
Osceola IN

Murray Lisa
Gallia Academy
Gallipolis OH

Murray Marla
De Kalb HS
Auburn IN

Murray Michael D
Morton Sr HS
Schererville IN

Murray Renee
Tippecanoe Valley HS
Rochester IN

Musacchia Beth
Fairless HS
Brewster OH

Muse Yvonne S
Tri Valley HS
Trinway OH

Musgrave Mark
Hayes HS
Delaware OH

Musick Douglas
Watkins Memorial HS
Pataskala OH

Musrock William
Valley HS
Hastings WV

Musselman Beverly
Westfall HS
Orient OH

Musselman Kriss A
Charlotte HS
Charlotte MI

Muster Kellie
Thomas W Harvey HS
Canton OH

Mutschler Jacqueline
Tecumseh HS
New Carlisle OH

Muzio Nancy
Cuyahoga Vlly Christian
Acad
Akron OH

Muzzin Michael
Northville HS
Northville MI

Myaard Bruce
Grand Haven Sr HS
Spring Lake MI

Myatt Franklin J
Northrop HS
Ft Wayne IN

Myatt Gregory
Brandon HS
Ortonville MI

Myer Tamma
Dansville Agricultural HS
Mason MI

Myers Amy
Ravenna HS
Ravenna OH

Myers Anne
Willard HS
Willard OH

Myers Brad A
Miami Valley HS
Dayton OH

Myers Bret S
Washington HS
Washington IN

Myers Grant
Prairie Hts HS
Angola IN

Myers Jeff
Columbus E Sr HS
Columbus IN

Myers Jeffrey W
North Knox HS
Freelandville IN

Myers John
Gallia Academy HS
Gallipolis OH

Myers John
St Peters HS
Mansfield OH

Myers Jonathan
Whitko HS
S Whitley IN

Myers Lorena
Pleasant HS
Marion OH

Myers Martin H
Beachwood HS
Beachwood OH

Myers Mary
Willard HS
Willard OH

Myers Michael
Ellet HS
Akron OH

Myers Michael
Paden City HS
Paden City WV

Myers Philip
Evergreen HS
Berkey OH

Myers Randall J
Park Hills HS
Fairborn OH

Myers Richard
Rossville Consolidated
Schl
Rossville IN

Myers Sharon
Andrews Acad
Berrien Center MI

Myers Steve
Adams Central HS
Monroe IN

Myers Tammy
Prairie Heights HS
Mongo IN

Myers Teena
Sandusky HS
Sandusky OH

Myers Todd
Wauseon HS
Wauseon OH

Myers Tyrone
Wauseon HS
Wauseon OH

Myllyla Mary
Escanaba Area Public HS
Escanaba MI

Myszenski Patricia
Robert S Tower HS
Warren MI

N

Nachbar Sharon
Upper Sandusky HS
Upper Sandusky OH

Naeyaert Gary
Carl Brablec HS
Roseville MI

Nagle Cathleen
Meridian Sr HS
Sanford MI

Nagy David
Bedford HS
Bedford OH

Nagy Lynne
Valley Forge HS
Parma Hts OH

Nagy Steven M
Flat Rock Sr HS
Flat Rock MI

Nakagawa James
Wickliffe Sr HS
Wickliffe OH

Nakashige Suzanne
Lutheran West HS
Parma OH

Nakfoor Gus
Okemos HS
Okemos MI

Nallenweg Richard M
Morton Sr HS
Hammond IN

Nalley Patrick T
Miami Valley School
Farnklin OH

Nalley Tamela
Wood Memorial HS
Oakland City IN

Naltner L Scott
Bishop Luers HS
Ft Wayne IN

Nameroff Natalie B
Indian Hill HS
Cincinnati OH

Nanni Susan
Carl Brablec HS
Roseville MI

Napier George H
Univ Of Detroit HS
Detroit MI

Napier Nicki
Twin Valley South HS
W Alexandria OH

Napier Regina
New Lexington Sr HS
New Lexington OH

Napier Valoria
Central Baptist HS
Reading OH

Nash Alicia
Warren Western Reserve
HS
Warren OH

Nash Becky
Gladwin HS
Gladwin MI

Nash Connie S
Cardinal Ritter HS
Indianapolis IN

Nash Diane
Bethany Christian HS
Sterling Hts MI

Nash Tonya
Allegan Sr HS
Allegan MI

Naumann Sara
Bay HS
Bay Vill OH

Navarra Jose
Finney HS
Detroit MI

Naville Robert J
Floyd Central HS
Floyds Knobs IN

Navy Patty
Struthers HS
Struthers OH

Nay Lesa
Lincoln HS
Shinnston WV

Neal Brian
Barberton HS
Barberton OH

Neal Kimberly
Blue River Valley Jr Sr
HS
Mooreland IN

Neal Ronald
Indian Creek HS
Columbus IN

Neal Sue
Pike Central HS
Petersburg IN

Neal Wallace
Upper Scioto Valley HS
Alger OH

Nebel Charles
Mather HS
Munising MI

Neblett James
Crispus Attucks HS
Indianapolis IN

Neeb Douglas A
Midland HS
Hope MI

Neeb Robin
Freeland HS
Freeland MI

Needler Gloria
Newton Falls HS
Newton Falls OH

Neeley Steven
Lebanon HS
Lebanon OH

Neely Lisa D
Worthington HS
Worthington OH

Neese Quintanna
Brownsburg HS
Brownsburg IN

Neeson Joseph
Oxford Area Community HS
Oxford MI

Neff Gary
Mio Au Sable HS
Mio MI

Neff Sandra
Washington HS
Washington IN

Neftzer Connie
Amelia HS
Amelia OH

Negri Mary
Adrian Sr HS
Adrian MI

Nehrig Kay P
Clinton Prairie HS
Mulberry IN

Neibert Trudy
Indian Valley North HS
New Phila OH

Neidert Jeff
Garfield HS
Akron OH

Neil Tammy
Rock Hill Sr HS
Kitts Hill OH

Neilson Jeanna L
Bluefield HS
Bluefld WV

Neilson William S
Charles F Brush HS
South Euclid OH

Neiswinger Michael
Morton Sr HS
Hammond IN

Nelson Carri
Ripley HS
Essex Jct VT

Nelson Connie
Mississinewa HS
Gas City IN

Nelson Dottie
Circleville HS
Seneca Rocks WV

Nelson Greg
Walnut Ridge HS
Edmond OK

Nelson Joyce
Fruitport HS
Nunica MI

Nelson Julie
Crestwood HS
Dearborn Hts MI

Nelson Julie G
Central Catholic HS
Massillon OH

Nelson Keith
Howell HS
Howell MI

Nelson Marjianne
Upper Arlington Sr HS
Columbus OH

Nelson Marjorie C
Crooksville HS
Crooksville OH

Nelson Mark R
Madison Heights HS
Anderson IN

Nelson Vicki
Mississinewa HS
Marion IN

Nemanic Shelley
Douglas Mac Arthur HS
Saginaw MI

Nero Judith
Solon HS
Solon OH

Nesbit Larry
Bellbrook HS
Bellbrook OH

Ness Suzanne
Huntington Catholic HS
Huntington IN

Nester Bryan
Salem HS
Salem IN

Nethers Mary L
Licking County Jt Voc HS
Nashport OH

Nethers Mike
Newark Sr HS
Newark OH

Nettle Lisa
Northwest HS
Clinton OH

Netzley Lori L
Swan Valley HS
Saginaw MI

Neu Dale
Allen East HS
Lima OH

Neuhart Charles
Shenandoah HS
Quaker City OH

Neuman Mary
Rocky River HS
Rocky Rvr OH

Neumeyer Judy
Western HS
Saginaw MI

Neutzling Connie
Madison Comp HS
Mansfield OH

Nevels Lois
Bishop Luers HS
Ft Wayne IN

Neville Myron
Broad Ripple HS
Indianapolis IN

Neviska Timothy
Brookhaven HS
Columbus OH

Nevitt Jeri
Hamilton Southeastern HS
Noblesville IN

Nevitt Melinda
South Newton Jr Sr HS
Goodland IN

Nevius Mary
Chaminade Julienne HS
Dayton OH

Newborn Mary
Lawrence Central HS
Indianapolis IN

Newbrough Avis
Lakeview HS
Cortland OH

Newburg Julia L
Cathedral HS
Indianapolis IN

Newburn Delano
Lasalle HS
South Bend IN

Newburn Sandra
Jefferson Union HS
Bloomingdale OH

Newcomb Patricia
Morgantown HS
Morgantwn WV

Newell Ryan
Frontier HS
Newport OH

Newkirk David
Mumford HS
Detroit MI

Newman Charles L
North Adams HS
Seaman OH

Newman Frederick
Clare HS
Clare MI

Newman Jon
R Nelson Snider HS
Ft Wayne IN

Newman Krista
Sacred Heart Academy
Clare MI

Newman Laura
Big Creek HS
Caretta WV

Newman Tammy
Old Fort HS
Old Fort OH

Newport Alan
William Henry Harrison HS
Harrison OH

Newton Bill R
Turpin HS
Cincinnati OH

Nguyen Hung
Lasalle HS
Mont Clair CA

Nicholas Caroline
Beaumont HS For Girls
Lyndhurst OH

Nicholas Tammy
Hagerstown Jr Sr HS
Hagerstown IN

Nicholl John
Annapolis HS
Dearborn Hgts MI

Nichols Debbie
Spencer HS
Reedy WV

Nichols Jennifer
Cloverdale HS
Poland IN

Nichols Luella J
Braxton Co HS
Ireland WV

Nichols Sandra Y
Mendon HS
Three Rivers MI

Nicholson Douglas
Greensburg Community HS
Greensburg IN

Nickerson Lynda
Cloverdale HS
Boca Raton FL

Niday Kim
Lewis County HS
Weston WV

Nidini Kelly
St Charles HS
St Charles MI

Niebauer Linda
Clarkston HS
Clarkston MI

Niederer William G
Rochester Cmnty HS
Rochester IN

Niedermeyer Cheryl
St Alphonsus HS
Detroit MI

Nielsen Paul
Lamphere HS
Madison Hts MI

Niemann Suzanne
Central Baptist HS
Loveland OH

Niemenski Laurie
St Alphonsus HS
Livonia MI

Niemeyer Paul
Norwood HS
Cincinnati OH

Niemi Loraine
Calumet HS
Copper City MI

Niemiec Frank
Bishop Noll Institute
Griffith IN

Nieto Michael
Andrean HS
Gary IN

Nightenhelser Stuart
Hamilton Heights HS
Atlanta IN

Niles Matthew
Brighton HS
Brighton MI

Nippes Cindy
Wayne Memorial HS
Westland MI

Nisevich Lisa
Munster HS
Munster IN

Nixon Charles
Cadillac HS
Cadillac MI

Noack Brenda
Flushing Sr HS
Flushing MI

Noack Mary B
Coloma Sr HS
Coloma MI

Noble Cherri L
Chesapeake HS
Chesapeake OH

Noble Shelly
Garfield HS
Akron OH

Noe Donald A
Wadsworth Sr HS
Wadsorth OH

Noel Alice
Maysville Sr HS
Zanesville OH

Noel Eric
Worthington Jefferson
HS
Worthington IN

Noffsinger Steve
Wadsworth Sr HS
Wadsworth OH

Nofs Denise
Harper Creek HS
Battle Creek MI

Noftz Dawn
Columbian HS
Tiffin OH

Nolan Charlotte
Bridgman HS
Bridgman MI

Nolan Paul
William Henry Harrison
HS
Harrison OH

Nolan Scott
Lincolnview HS
Van Wert OH

Nolan Timothy
Maysville HS
Zanesville OH

Noll Susan
Amanda Clearcreek HS
Lancaster OH

Nommay Nancy
North Central HS
Indianapolis IN

Norander John
Aquinas HS
Detroit MI

Norlander Catherine
John Glenn HS
Westland MI

Norman Andrea
Anthony Wayne HS
Whitehouse OH

Norman Sheri
Point Pleasant HS
Pt Pleasant WV

Norris Andrew
Sycamore HS
Cincinnati OH

Norris Carole
Upper Arlington HS
Columbus OH

Norris Cheryl
Sandusky HS
Sandusky OH

Norris George
High School
Huntngbrg IN

Norris Gloria J
Parkside HS
Jackson MI

Norris James
New Palestine HS
New Palestine IN

Norris Kevin
Vinson HS
Huntington WV

Norris Tammy
Springfield HS
Springfield MI

Norris Terry L
Reeths Puffer HS
Muskegon MI

North Lori D
East Noble HS
Wolcottville IN

Northrop Sherri
Marcellus HS
Marcellus MI

Northrup Lori
Montpelier HS
Montpelier OH

Norton Diane
Licking Cnty Joint Voc
HS
Newark OH

Norton Marci
Keystone HS
Elyria OH

Noss Julie
Pike Delta York Sr HS
Delta OH

Nossett Darin
Wood Memorial HS
Oakland City IN

Nouss Linda
Hamilton Twp HS
Papillion NE

Novak Ann
Polaris Joint Voc HS
Olmsted Township OH

Novak Genevieve A
La Porte HS
Laporte IN

Novak Natalie
Our Lady Of Mt Carmel
HS
Wyandotte MI

Novak Natalie J
Flint Central HS
Flint MI

Novick Toni
St Francis Cabrini HS
Dearborn Hts MI

Novosel Linda
Hubbard HS
Hubbard OH

Novotny Jeff
Clay HS
S Bend IN

Nowak Marilyn
Ravenna HS
Ravenna OH

Nowak Renea
Perrysburg HS
Perrysburg OH

Nowell Keith T
Dunbar HS
Dunbar WV

Nowels Debra K
East Noble HS
Kendallville IN

Nowing Rebecca
Crothersville HS
Crothersville IN

Nuber Timothy
Columbus N HS
Columbus OH

Nugent David
Kouts HS
Kouts IN

Nuhring Carol
Southridge HS
Huntngbrg IN

Nunez Sylvia
Union City Cmnty HS
Union City IN

Nunn Laura
La Porte HS
La Porte IN

Nurenberg Sue
Pewamo Westphalia HS
Pewamo MI

Nuss Kathy
New Knoxville HS
New Knoxville OH

Nussbaum Steven
Central Christian HS
Smithville OH

Nussel Carole
Mayfield HS
Mayfield Hts OH

Nutter Jan
Bridgeport Sr HS
Bridgeport WV

Nutter Stephen A
Plainwell HS
Allegan MI

Nuzum Brian
Hundred HS
Hundred WV

Nuzum Ronda J
Fairview HS
Farmington WV

Nye Gary
River Valley HS
Three Oaks MI

Nye Nicki
West Carrollton Sr HS
Dayton OH

Nye Patti
Napoleon HS
Napoleon OH

Nykiel Steve
La Ville Jr Sr HS
Bremen IN

Nyland Brian
Cadillac Sr HS
Cadillac MI

O

O Jacqueline J
Philip Barbour HS
Flemington WV

Oakes Angela K
South Charleston HS
S Charleston WV

Oakley Richard
Marysville HS
Marysville OH

Oancea David M
Louisville Sr HS
Louisville OH

O Barrios Juana
Culver Girls Academy
Los Angeles CA

Obee Pamela
Notre Dame Academy
Toledo OH

Oberholtzer Tracy
Western HS
Russiaville IN

Obermiller Reed
Crestline HS
Crestline OH

O Bernard Ronald
Seneca East HS
Attica OH

O Brien Michael
De La Salle Collegiate HS
Harper Woods MI

O Brien Sandy
Vandercook Lake HS
Jackson MI

Obrzut Susan
Bishop Noll Inst
Munster IN

O Bunker Jeffrey
Wintersville HS
Wintersville OH

Ocko Susanne
Engadine Consolidated
HS
Engadine MI

O Connell Timothy
Hedgesville HS
Martinsburg WV

O Connor Janet
Barr Reeve HS
Montgomery IN

O Connor Lary E
Cros Lex HS
Jeddo MI

O Connor Mary
St Mary Cathedral HS
Gaylord MI

O Connor Michael
Athens HS
Troy MI

O Connor Raymond
Chesterton Sr HS
Chesterton IN

Odom Kevin
Waverly HS
Lansing MI

Odom Marlette
Southwestern HS
Detroit MI

O Donnell Kathleen
Holland HS
Holland MI

O Donnell Mary S
Carroll HS
Dayton OH

O Donnell Patricia
Chaminade Julienne HS
Englewood OH

Oesterle Tracie
Washington Sr HS
Wash C H OH

Offenberger Brenda
Belpre HS
Belpre OH

Ogan Scott F
Edgewood HS
Bloomington IN

Ogden Suzanne
Ypsilanti HS
Ypsilanti MI

Ogle Daniel
Rensselaer Central HS
Rensselaer IN

Ogle Mark R
Perry Meridian HS
Greenwood IN

Oglesbee Joyce
Lima Sr HS
Lima OH

Ogletree Glendal
Independence HS
Columbus OH

O Grady Colleen
Armada HS
Richmond MI

Ogston Elizabeth
Eaton Rapids Sr HS
Eaton Rapids MI

O Hara Joseph
Ursuline HS
Youngstown OH

O Hara Kathleen
Grosse Pointe N HS
Grosse Pte Shr MI

O Hatt Douglas
Allen Park HS
Allen Park MI

Ohm Michael D
Cuyahoga Falls HS
Cuyahoga Falls OH

Oko Kathryn
Maple Hts Sr HS
Maple Hgts OH

Olashuk Mary
Madonna HS
Weirton WV

Olbrich Carl
Milford HS
Milford MI

Olds Tenitia
North Central HS
Indpls IN

Olenik Jacqueline
St Augustine Academy
N Olmsted OH

Olenik Michelle
Parma Sr HS
Parma OH

Olgy Walter C
William A Wirt HS
Gary IN

STUDENTS
PHOTOGRAPH
SCHEDULED
FOR PUBLI-
CATION HERE
COULD NOT
BE REPRO-
DUCED

Oliver Karin K
Jackson HS
Jackson OH

Oliver Michelle
Coleman HS
Coleman MI

Olney Deanna
Carman Sr HS
Flint MI

Olrich Tracy
Vestaburg HS
Edmore MI

Olson Catherine
Detour Area HS
Goetzville MI

Olson Kirk
Ithaca HS
Ithaca MI

Olson Warren
Bay HS
Bay Village OH

Olson William
Lake Orion HS
Pontiac MI

Olszewski Gregory
Padua HS
Berea OH

O Malley Christopher
St Josephs HS
S Bend IN

Oman Leslie
Highland HS
Highland IN

O Neil Kahn Maura
Shawe Memorial HS
Madison IN

O Neill Eugene R
Valparaiso HS
Valparaiso IN

O Neill James T
Charleston Catholic HS
Charleston WV

O Neill Penny
Marietta Sr HS
Marietta OH

Oney Mark
Whitehall Yearling HS
Whitehall OH

Oney Melinda
Tecumseh Sr HS
New Carlisle OH

Onstott Lisa D
Cuyahoga Vly Christian
Acad
Cuyahoga Falls OH

Ontko Karen
Woodrow Wilson HS
Younstwn OH

Oprisch Beth
Toronto HS
Toronto OH

Oprisch Karl
Toronto HS
Toronto OH

Orchard Steve J
Clear Fork HS
Danville OH

Orcutt Brian
Divine Heart Seminary
Chicago IL

O Reilly Christopher
Tecumseh HS
New Carlisle OH

O Reilly Patrick
Orange HS
Pepper Pike OH

Orlando Roselle
Edgewood Sr HS
N Kingsville OH

Orlando Rose Marie
St Ladislaus HS
Detroit MI

Orr Cindy
Medina Sr HS
Medina OH

Orr David
Zane Trace HS
Chillicothe OH

Orr John
Pinckney HS
Pinckney MI

Orr Randy
Gallia Academy HS
Gallipolis OH

Orr Tamara
Bridgeport HS
Bridgeport WV

Orsini Tonette
Steubenville Cath Cntrl
HS
Mingo Jct OH

Ortegon Caroline
Hammond Tech Voc HS
Hammond IN

Ortman Kimberly
Calumet HS
Gary IN

Osborn David
United Local HS
Salem OH

Osborn Dee
Truman HS
Taylor MI

Osborn Phil
Brownsburg HS
Brownsburg IN

Osborne Jean
Parkersburg South HS
Parkersburg WV

Osborne Joe
Licking Valley HS
Newark OH

Osborne Kim
Washington Irving HS
Clarksburg WV

Osborne Stephanie
Bluefield HS
Bluefield WV

Osburn Cynthia
Lincolnview HS
Van Wert OH

O Schrock Russell
Pleasant HS
Marion OH

Osendott Bill
Kermit HS
Kermit WV

Osentoski Anna
Cass City HS
Cass City MI

Oshinsky Colleen K
Streetsboro HS
Streetsboro OH

Osmon Cindy
Yorktown HS
Muncie IN

Oster Robert
Ontario HS
Ontario OH

Ostermann Judith
St Philip Catholic Cntrl
HS
Battle Creek MI

O Stewart Christopher
Princeton Cmnty HS
Princeton IN

Osting Cindy
Tri Jr Sr HS
Lewisville IN

Ostrenga Greg
Menominee HS
Wallace MI

Ostric Elizabeth
Clay Sr HS
S Bend IN

Oswald Frederick
Bark River Harris HS
Bark River MI

Oswald Richard E
South Lake HS
St Clair Shores MI

Otcasek Juliet
Euclid Sr HS
Euclid OH

Othersen Connie
Eaton HS
Eaton OH

Otman Michael
Southgate HS
Southgate MI

Ott Arline
Mc Nicholas HS
Cincinnati OH

Ott Kevin
La Porte HS
La Porte IN

Ottney Cheryl
Wheelersburg HS
Sciotoville OH

Ouellette Barry
Northville HS
Northville MI

Oughton John
Brooke HS
Follansbee WV

Ousley Jill
Clinton Massie HS
Wilmington OH

Ousley Kent
Clinton Massie HS
Wilmington OH

Ousley Ladora
Tuslaw HS
W OH

Overholt David H
Ridgewood HS
West Lafayette OH

Overley Beth
Reeths Puffer HS
Twin Lake MI

Overly Jana
Miami Trace HS
Washington Ch OH

Overton Tina
Washington Catholic HS
Washington IN

O Wachner Howard
Buena Vista HS
Saginaw MI

Owen Christine
Lakeville Memrl HS
Otisville MI

Owen Craig
Cedar Lake Academy
Gobles MI

Owen Judy
Davison Sr HS
Davison MI

Owens Dianna R
Tyler County HS
Jacksonburg WV

Owens Jenie L
Father Joseph Wehrle
Mem HS
Columbus OH

Owens Kelli
Dayton Christian HS
Dayton OH

Owens Lorraine
Western Hills HS
Cincinnati OH

Owens Richard
Port Huron HS
Smiths Creek MI

Owens Sheree
De Vilbiss HS
Toledo OH

P

Owens William A
Bluefield HS
Bluefld WV

Oxier Sandra J
Toronto HS
Toronto OH

Oyer Danny
North Central HS
Pioneer OH

Ozburn Rodger
South Harrison HS
Lost Creek WV

Paauwe Lisa
Holland HS
Holland MI

Pace Teresa
William Mason HS
Mason OH

Pack Dora
Portsmouth E HS
Portsmouth OH

Packard Stanley R
Athens HS
Athens MI

Packert Richard C
Port Clinton HS
Port Clinton OH

Paczewitz Dean
Woodhaven HS
Wyandotte MI

Padgett Pamela
Clinton Prairie HS
Frankfort IN

Paduan Mark
Houghton HS
Houghton MI

Paesano Debra
Brooke HS
Follansbee WV

Paff David A
Penn HS
South Bend IN

Pafford Tamara S
Oceana HS
Oceana WV

Page Elizabeth
Coldwater HS
Coldwater MI

Page Terri
Marietta HS
Marietta OH

Pahl Cheryl
Gladwin HS
Gladwin MI

Painter Denise
Lincoln HS
Shinnston WV

Painter Lauri
Southeast HS
Ravenna OH

Paisley Debi
Cambridge HS
Cambridge OH

Pak Grace
Plainfield HS
Plainfield IN

Paksi Kimberly
St Johns HS
Saint Johns MI

Palfrey Deborah A
Strongsville Sr HS
Strongsville OH

Paliwoda Jeffrey W
Valley Forge HS
Parma Heights OH

Pallant Susan
Jefferson Area HS
Rock Creek OH

Palmer Dean
Milan HS
Milan IN

Palmer Dennis
Milan Jr Sr HS
Milan IN

Palmer Karen
Benedictine HS
Detroit MI

Palmer Kelly G
Pioneer HS
Ann Arbor MI

Palmer Kim
Sebring Mc Kinley HS
Sebring OH

Palmer Michael
Pontiac Central HS
Pontiac MI

Palmer Robert J
Champion HS
Warren OH

Palo Deborah
Engadine HS
Engadine MI

Palovich Becky
Hubbard HS
Hubbard OH

Pancher Jim
Tuscarawas Central Cath HS
Uhrichsville OH

Pangle Jennifer
Caldwell HS
Caldwell OH

Panico Mindy
Bridgman HS
Bridgman MI

Pankow Kathy
Jefferson HS
Charles Town WV

Pantone Michael
Magnolia HS
New Martinsvle WV

Papacella Michael
Norton HS
Norton OH

Papas Costa
Wadsworth Sr HS
Wadsworth OH

Papouras Katherine S
Regina HS
Cleve Hts OH

Papp Laurie
Orange HS
Chagrin Falls OH

Pappas Mala
Dexter HS
Whitemore Lk MI

Paradise Robert
Hammond Tech Voc HS
Hammond IN

Parady Elizabeth A
Walnut Hills HS
Cincinnati OH

Paragas David
Normandy Sr HS
Parma OH

Pareja Jaime G
Dublin HS
Columbus OH

Paris Mary
Catholic Central HS
Mingo Jctn OH

Parise Jerry
Niles Mc Kinley HS
Niles OH

Parisi Lisa
Arthur Hill HS
Saginaw MI

Park Cheryl
South Spencer HS
Rockport IN

Parke Evan
Shaker Hts HS
Shaker Hts OH

Parker Craig
Martinsburg HS
Martinsburg WV

Parker Dawn
Robert S Rogers HS
Toledo OH

Parker Doug
Farmington HS
Farmington Hls MI

Parker Gary
Springfield North HS
Springfield OH

Parker Kirk
Central HS
Grand Rapids MI

Parker Lauren
Anderson HS
Cincinnati OH

Parker Lisa
Jesup W Scott HS
Toledo OH

Parker Paula
Stanton HS
Toronto OH

Parker Peg
Tippecanoe Valley HS
Claypool IN

Parker Roselee
West Union HS
W Union OH

Parker Sandra K
Washington HS
Washington IN

Parker Susan G
Talawanda HS
Oxford OH

Parker Suzy
Margaretta HS
Castalla OH

Parker Terrance L
Valley HS
Montgomery WV

Parker Timothy T
Kalamazoo Cntrl HS
Kalamazoo MI

Parks Annette
West Side Sr HS
Gary IN

Parks Gail
Norwood HS
Norwood OH

Parks Lynnette
Ontario HS
Mansfield OH

Parks Pam
Huntington East HS
Huntington WV

Parks Rhonda
West Jefferson HS
W Jefferson OH

Parlin Deborah
Colon HS
Leonidas MI

Parmenter Kyle
Bloomington South HS
Bloomington IN

Paro Elaine
Barberton HS
Barberton OH

Parr Rebecca
Marysville HS
Marysville OH

Parrish Cynthia
Mannington HS
Mannington WV

Parrish Kathleen
Hemlock HS
Saginaw MI

Parrish Rory
Archbishop Alter HS
Dayton OH

Parrish Vida
Lee HS
Wyoming MI

Parrott Elizabeth
Olivet HS
Olivet MI

Parrott Terry
Inland Lakes HS
Indian River MI

Parsell Patricia
Peck Community HS
Peck MI

Parshall Diana
Niles Mc Kinley HS
Niles OH

Parsley Robin E
Brown County HS
Nashville IN

Parsons Melody
North Daviess HS
Odon IN

Parsons Roberta
Hubbard HS
Hubbard OH

Parsons Robert L
University HS
Morgantown WV

Parsons Sandy
Fremont Ross HS
Fremont OH

Parsons Susan
Magnolia HS
New Martinsvle WV

Partain Diana
Bloomfield HS
Bloomfield IN

Partin Gary
Romulus HS
Romulus MI

Partozoti Elizabeth
North Judson San Pierre HS
Knox IN

Partridge Dale
Clio HS
Clio MI

Pasanen Wendy
Harbor HS
Ashtabula OH

Pasche Thomas
Kearsley HS
Burton MI

Pascual Felino A
Clarenceville HS
Farmington MI

Pasman Jerry W
Harper Creek HS
Battle Creek MI

Paspek Andrea
St Augustine Academy
Cleveland OH

Pasquale Alicia
North HS
Willoughby OH

Pasqualone Renee
Geneva HS
Geneva OH

Pastor Jeffrey
Malabar HS
Mansfield OH

Pastre Renee
Buckeye North HS
Smithfield OH

Patch David
Hilliard HS
Amlin OH

Patchen Eduardo
West Geauga HS
Chesterland OH

Patchett Becky
Clinton Central HS
Frankfort IN

Patchimrat Sittirat
Mount Clemens HS
Mount Clemens MI

Pate Chris
Madison Plains HS
So Solon OH

STUDENTS
PHOTOGRAPH
SCHEDULED
FOR PUBLI-
CATION HERE
COULD NOT
BE REPRO-
DUCED

Patel Rohane
Athens HS
Troy MI

Pathak Swati
Normandy HS
Seven Hls OH

Patrick Raymond
Milton HS
Milton WV

Patrick Richard
Vinton County Cnsldtd
HS
New Plymouth OH

Patterson Cassaundra
Anderson HS
Anderson IN

Patterson Chris
Washington Catholic HS
Washington IN

Patterson Gregory
St Francis De Sales HS
Toledo OH

Patterson Heather
Parkersburg HS
Parkersburg WV

Patterson Joni
West Holmes HS
Millersburg OH

Patterson Kelvin
Norwood HS
Norwood OH

Patterson Lisa
Norwayne HS
Creston OH

Patterson Scott
Wilbur Wright HS
Dayton OH

Patterson Susan J
Bluefield HS
Bluefield WV

Pattison Tracy
Wayne Mem HS
Wayne MI

Patton Linda K
Arcadia Local Schl
Arcadia OH

Patton Rodney
Shady Spring HS
Shady Spring WV

Patton Sally
Garfield HS
Akron OH

Paugh Scott
Grafton HS
Grafton WV

Paul Cheryl J
Shady Spring HS
Shady Spring WV

Paul Diane
North Miami HS
Macy IN

Paul Joseph
Jefferson Area HS
Rome OH

Paul Karen
Cass Technical HS
Detroit MI

Paul Terry
Beaverton HS
Beaverton MI

Pauley Jo
Columbiana HS
Columbiana OH

Paulsin Michael
Andrean HS
Merrillville IN

Paulson Mary
Adelphian Academy
Mt Vernon OH

Paulus Carol
Littlefield Public Schools
Oden MI

Pauly Michael
Tahota HS
W Chester OH

Paurazas Ruth
Bloomington HS South
Bloomington IN

Pauszek David J
John Adams HS
South Bend IN

Pavella Cheryl
Brighton HS
Brighton MI

Pavkov Lynora
Manchester HS
Akron OH

Pavlov Don
Springfield Local HS
New Springfield OH

Pawelski Daniel
Dayton Christian HS
Dayton OH

Pawinski Monica
George Rogers Clark HS
Hammond IN

Pawlak Eugene
Andrean HS
Merrillville IN

Pawley Rhonda
Wilmington HS
Wilmington OH

Pawlyszyn Nadia
Holy Name Nazareth HS
Severn Hills OH

STUDENTS PHOTOGRAPH SCHEDULED FOR PUBLICATION HERE COULD NOT BE REPRODUCED

Payich Todd
Liberty HS
Yngstn OH

Payment Michele M
De Tour Area HS
Drummond Is MI

Payne Deborah L
Sissonville HS
Elkview WV

Payne Eugenia
Inkster HS
Westland MI

Payne Gary
Herbert Hoover HS
Clendenin WV

Payne Iris
West Side Sr HS
Gary IN

Payne Judith A
Philip Barbour HS
Volga WV

Payne Patricia J
Traverse City HS
Traverse City MI

Payne Richard A
Rutherford B Hayes HS
Delaware OH

Payne Suetta
Lawrence North HS
Indianapolis IN

Payne Tamera L
South Spencer HS
Grandview IN

Payne Teri
Rosedale HS
Rosedale IN

Payne Tracy
Rogers HS
Rockford MI

Payton Beverly
Bloom HS
Wheelersburg OH

Pazdzior John
Ida HS
Ida MI

Peacock Kenneth
Shortridge HS
Indianapolis IN

Peacock Kim
Norwayne HS
Creston OH

Peacock Rebecca E
Brandon HS
Ortonville MI

Peak Christine
Clinton Central HS
Frankfort IN

Pearsall C Robert
Patrick Henry HS
Deshler OH

Pearson Marie
Sidney HS
Sidney OH

Pearson Natalie
Columbus Eastmoor Sr HS
Columbus OH

Pearson Vickie
Massillon Christian HS
Waynesburg OH

Peart Jamie
Madison Plains HS
London OH

Peavly Jon
Mt View HS
Welch WV

Pecenica Nick
Washington HS
E Chicago IN

Peck David
Rochester HS
Rochester MI

Peck Debra I
Villa Angela Academy
Cleveland OH

Peck Denise
West Lafayette HS
W Lafyt IN

Peck John A
Mount Clemens HS
Mt Clemens MI

Peck Rebecca E
Fruitport HS
Muskegon MI

Peck Terri
Clarkston Sr HS
Clarkston MI

Peck Todd
Muskegon HS
Muskegon MI

Peddie Julie
Bridgman HS
Bridgman MI

Pedigo Susan
Plainfield Jr Sr HS
Plainfield IN

Peery Tina
Lumen Cordium HS
Cleveland OH

Peiffer Bamberlee
Litchfield HS
Janesville MI

Peirce Marc
Bishop Noll Institute
Whiting IN

Pelfrey Robbin
Spencer HS
Spencer WV

Pelkey Gary
Jennings County HS
No Vernon IN

Pelkie Mark
Gwinn HS
Gwinn MI

Pellegrini Guy
Calumet HS
Calumet MI

Pelly Jonathan
Lutheran HS East
Cleveland OH

Pemberton Susie
Orleans HS
Orleans IN

Pemberton Traci A
Wapakoneta HS
Wapakoneta OH

Pena Miriam
Hammond Technical Voc HS
Hammond IN

Pence Michael
Marion Adams HS
Sheridan IN

Penczak Michelle J
Donald E Gavit Jr Sr HS
Hammond IN

Pendleton Jeff
Franklin HS
Franklin OH

Pendry Carolyn Jean
Greeneview HS
Sabina OH

Penhorwood Troy
Liberty Union HS
Baltimore OH

Penix Teresa
London HS
London OH

Penkowski Blasine
Lake Catholic HS
Mentor OH

Penland Howard
John Hay HS
Cleveland OH

Penn Crystal
Saint Ursula Acad
Toledo OH

Pennington Lori
Athens HS
Princeton WV

Pennington Phyllis A
Southfield Lathrup Sr HS
Southfield MI

Pennington Ricky
Fayetteville Perry HS
Fayetteville OH

Pennington Rita
East Clinton HS
Wilmington OH

Pennisten Donald E
South Point HS
South Point OH

Pennycuff Vickie
Wayne HS
Dayton OH

Pennza Jill
Eastlake N HS
Willowick OH

Pepin Mike
Mona Shores HS
Muskegon MI

Pepmeier Karen
North Knox HS
Sandborn IN

Pepple Kimberly J
Western Boone Jr Sr HS
Jamestown IN

Perdew Lori
Ogemaw Heights HS
West Branch MI

Perdue Janie
Vinson HS
Huntington WV

Perdue Leda
Matoaka HS
Matoaka WV

Perez Ernie
Gavit HS
Hammond IN

Perez Gloria
Theodore Roosevelt HS
Wyandotte MI

Perkins Cheryl
Western Boone HS
Lebanon IN

Perkins Shelley
Onaway HS
Onaway MI

Perrin Cinda
Millington HS
Millington MI

Perry Amy
Mohawk HS
Tiffin OH

Perry Anthony
Cardinal Mooney HS
Boardman OH

Perry Cynthia A
Whitko HS
Pierceton IN

Perry Douglas
Belleville HS
Belleville MI

Perry John
Wayne HS
Wayne WV

Perry Kimberly
Bedford Sr HS
Temperance MI

Perry Lisa D
Mifflin Sr HS
Columbus OH

Perry Michael
East Kentwood HS
Kentwood MI

Perry Michele M
Vinson HS
Huntington WV

Perry Paul
Bramwell HS
Bramwell WV

Perry Steven D
West Lafayette HS
West Lafayette IN

Perry Tammy
Watkins Memorial HS
Pataskala OH

Petch Adrienne
James Ford Rhodes HS
Cleveland OH

Peterlin Susan
Holy Name Nazareth HS
Parma OH

Peterman Sally J
Indian Valley North HS
New Phila OH

Peters Kimberly
Walnut Hills HS
Cincinnati OH

Peters Nicholas
Brookville HS
Brookville IN

Peters Ray
Brownstown Central HS
Vallonia IN

Peters Sara
Tecumseh HS
New Carlisle OH

Peters Steven
Port Huron Northern HS
Pt Huron MI

Peters Stormy
Elmwood HS
N Baltimore OH

Peters Therese
Lake Cath HS
Mentor OH

Petersen Annette
Patrick Henry HS
Hamler OH

Peterson Amy
Elkhart Memorial HS
Elkhart IN

Peterson Bonni
Lawrenceburg HS
Lawrenceburg IN

Peterson Erich
Archbold HS
Archbold OH

Peterson Lance
Haslett HS
Haslett MI

Peterson Larry
East Kentwood HS
Kentwood MI

Peterson Ronald
Airport Comm HS
S Rockwood MI

Peterson Sheri
Fenton Sr HS
Fenton MI

Peterson Susan
David Anderson HS
Lisbon OH

Peterson Thomas
Novi HS
Novi MI

Petitto Michael
South Harrison HS
Clarsbury WV

Petiya Sharon
John F Kennedy HS
Warren OH

Petriella Anthony
Flushing HS
Flushing MI

Petro Christine
Strongsville Sr HS
Strongsville OH

Petteys Kimberly
Dexter HS
Pinckney MI

Pettway Patricia
Highland Park
Community HS
Highland Pk MI

Petty Kevin
Stonewall Jackson HS
Christn WV

Petzke Ann
Berrien Springs HS
Berrien Spring MI

Pever Dan
Findlay HS
Findlay OH

Peyatt Pamela
Mt View HS
Capels WV

Pezzutti Mark
Bishop Hartley HS
Pickerington OH

Pfabe Valinda
Jefferson Union HS
Steubenville OH

Pfaff Becky J
Springfield HS
Holland OH

Pfarrer Barbara
Northwestern HS
Kokomo IN

Pfau Cindy
Bexley HS
Bexley OH

Pfau Constance
Bekley HS
Bexley OH

Pfeifer Candy
Tri West Hendricks H
Pittsboro IN

Pfeifer Elizabeth
Cardinal Ritter HS
Indianapolis IN

Pfeiffer Carol
Henry Ford II HS
Sterling Hgts MI

Pfeiffer Geoffrey
Fraser HS
Fraser MI

Pfingston Patti
Pike Central Middle HS
Winslow IN

Pflueger Jonathan J
Loudonville HS
Loudonville OH

STUDENTS
PHOTOGRAPH
SCHEDULED
FOR PUBLI-
CATION HERE
COULD NOT
BE REPRO-
DUCED

Phagan Lisa
Madison Heights HS
Anderson IN

Pham Chan
Jefferson HS
Lafayette IN

Phelps Charles
Fairless HS
Canton OH

Phelps Julie
Greenville HS
Greenville MI

Phelps Marsha
Seeger Memorial HS
Attica IN

Phillabaum Mitchell
Valley View HS
Germantown OH

Phillips Albert
Jesup W Scott HS
Toledo OH

Phillips Alison
Tecumseh Sr HS
Tecumseh MI

Phillips Amy
Greenfield Central HS
Greenfield IN

Phillips Barbara A
Dayton Christian HS
Dayton OH

Phillips Bradley
Buckhannon Upshur HS
Buckhannon WV

Phillips Chris J
Miamisburg Sr HS
Dayton OH

Phillips Connie A
Lewis County HS
Weston WV

Phillips Deanna
Bluefield HS
Bluefield WV

Phillips Denise
Clarence Kimball HS
Royal Oak MI

Phillips Eric R
Shady Spring HS
Beaver WV

Phillips Jodi
Eastside HS
Butler IN

Phillips Joy
Shelby Sr HS
Shelby OH

Phillips Karen
Michigan Center HS
Michigancenter MI

Phillips Kelly
Central Hower HS
Akron OH

Phillips Kenneth
Forest Park HS
Crystal Falls MI

Phillips Laura
Magnificat HS
Westlake OH

Phillips Laurie
Champion HS
Warren OH

Phillips Lisa
Port Austin Public HS
Hickam AFB HI

Phillips Mark
Cuyahoga Falls HS
Cuyahoga Fls OH

Phillips Mary F
Greenfield Central HS
Greenfield IN

Phillips Nicholas
Canfield HS
Canfield OH

Phillips Regina
Winfield HS
Scott Depot WV

Phillips Susan
Concord HS
Concord MI

Phillips Terri
Pineville HS
Pineville WV

Phillipson Jacquline
Jefferson Union HS
Toronto OH

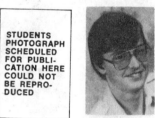
STUDENTS
PHOTOGRAPH
SCHEDULED
FOR PUBLI-
CATION HERE
COULD NOT
BE REPRO-
DUCED

Philson Richard
River Valley Sr HS
Three Oaks MI

Pia Rick
Mona Shores HS
Muskegon MI

Piaseczny Keith
St Ladislaus HS
Hamtramck MI

Pickel Sharon K
Unioto HS
Chillicothe OH

Pickell Bruce
North Adams Public HS
Jerome MI

Pickell Gregory
Leslie HS
Leslie MI

Pickenpaugh Julia
Shenandoah HS
Quaker City OH

Pickerill Theodore
Jackson HS
North Canton OH

Pickering John
Wellsville HS
Wellsville OH

Pickering Kathy
Houston HS
Houston OH

Pickett Jerry
Grandview Heights HS
Columbus OH

Pickett Tracey
Pinckney HS
Brighton MI

Pieratt Anne
Cuyahoga Falls HS
Kent OH

Pierce Bill
Alexandria Monroe HS
Alexandria IN

Pierce Deanna
Wilmington Sr HS
Wilmington OH

Pierce Jeanne
Danville Community HS
Danville IN

Pierce Robert T
Portsmouth HS
Portsmouth OH

Pierce Scott
New Albany HS
New Albany OH

Pierce Thomas D
Eastlake North HS
Willowick OH

Pierce Ty
Celina Sr HS
Celina OH

Pilney Diane
Buckeye South HS
Yorkville OH

Pine Denise
Whitmore Lake HS
Whitmore MI

Pinkerton Pam
Sebring Mc Kinley HS
Sebring OH

Pinkowski John L
Walsh Jesuit HS
Northfield Ctr OH

Pinnell Wade
John F Kennedy HS
Taylor MI

Pinnell William
Garden City East Sr HS
Garden City MI

Pinner Kevin L
Turpin HS
Cincinnati OH

Pinney Melissa
Woodlan HS
New Haven IN

Pino Donna
Highland HS
Highland IN

Piper Lawrence
Holt HS
Lansing MI

Pisarsky Paula
Swartz Creek HS
Swartz Creek MI

Pitcher Brian
Richmond Sr HS
Richmond IN

Pitt Jim
Newark HS
Newark OH

Pittenger Kelli L
Muncie Northside HS
Muncie IN

Pittman Diana
Jewett Scio HS
Scio OH

Pittman Gregoire
Muskegon Heights HS
Muskegon Hts MI

Pitts Brian
Wilbur Wright HS
Dayton OH

Pitts Danette
Parma Sr HS
Parma OH

Pitts Kevin
Collinwood HS
Cleveland OH

Pitts M
Perry HS
Massillon OH

Pitts Reva L
Wilbur Wright HS
Dayton OH

Pitzer Cindy
Eastern HS
Long Bottom OH

Pitzer Dwain
Clinton Central HS
Kirklin IN

Pizzaia Michael J
Linden Community HS
Linden MI

Pizzino Shawn
Shady Spring HS
Shady Spring WV

Pizzuti John
Brooke HS
Follansbee WV

Placke Lyn
Archbishop Alter HS
Kettering OH

Pladars Elizabeth
Columbus North HS
Columbus OH

Plak Karen
Cardinal Mooney HS
Youngstown OH

Plant Jacqueline
North Royalton HS
N Royalton OH

Plant Patricia
Northfield HS
Wabash IN

Plantamura Charles
Greenville Sr HS
Greenville MI

Plante John
Iron Mountain HS
Iron Mountain MI

Plantz Kimberly
Milton HS
Milton WV

Plass Susan
Princeton HS
Princeton WV

Plath Fred
Tri County HS
Coral MI

Platt Pamela
Copley Sr HS
Copley OH

Plavsity Ann
Barberton HS
Barberton OH

Plear Monica
Aiken Sr HS
Cincinnati OH

Pledger Robin
Gavit HS
Hammond IN

Plichta Dean
Fruitport HS
Muskegon MI

Ploetner John
Jasper HS
Jasper IN

Pluimer Karen
Benton Central Jr Sr HS
Oxford IN

Plumley Carl
Tucker Cnty HS
Parsons WV

Plummer Diana
New Albany HS
New Albany IN

Plummer Elizabeth
Aquinas HS
Allen Park MI

Plummer Kevin D
North Knox HS
Edwardsport IN

Plummer Patti
Martinsville HS
Martinsville IN

Plummer Robert
Brownstown Central HS
Vallon A IN

Plummer Robin
Shenandoah HS
Middletown IN

Plummer Sandra J
Clinton Massie HS
Wilmington OH

Plyler Jonathan
Faith Christian HS
Muskegon MI

Pocisk Sheri
Maumee HS
Maumee OH

Podlasiak Steve
Woodsfield HS
Woodsfield OH

Podsedly Judy
Geneva HS
Geneva OH

Poe Michael G
Mid America Christain HS
Huntington WV

Pogany Perry J
Austintown Fitch HS
Austintown OH

Poggemeyer Laurie
Eastwood HS
Luckey OH

Poiry Scott
Clay HS
Oregon OH

Poit T Kevin
Lapeer West Sr HS
Lapeer MI

Pokorski Nadine
St Annes HS
Sterling Hts MI

Polega Deborah
North Huron HS
Kinde MI

Polen Stephen
Southern Local HS
Salineville OH

Polhe Joseph W
Bedford HS
Temperance MI

Poling Deborah
Pittsford HS
Pittsford MI

Poling Diana
Houston HS
Piqua OH

Poling Donald
Shady Spring HS
Beaver WV

Poling Karen
Perry HS
Perry OH

Poling Polly
Urbana HS
Urbana OH

Poling Sherry
Ridgemont HS
Mt Victory OH

Poling Susan
Buckhannon Upshur HS
Buckhannon WV

Polite Lee
Culver Military Academy
Munster IN

Politzer Julie
Mentor HS
Concord OH

Polk Doug
Shady Spring HS
Daniels WV

Polley Audrey
Washington HS
Massillon OH

Polley Tammy
Windham HS
Windham OH

Pollock Susan M
Highland HS
Hinckley OH

Pollock Walter
Brooke HS
Wellsburg WV

Polomcak Annette
Decatur Jr Sr HS
Decatur MI

Polson Craig
West HS
Cincinnati OH

Polyak Mike
Munster HS
Munster IN

Pombier Philip R
Everett HS
Lansing MI

Pomeroy Debra E
Greenbrier West HS
Asbury WV

Pomeroy Lori
North Muskegon HS
N Muskegon MI

Pomeroy Randall
Hartford HS
Hartford MI

Pomorski John
Kelloggsville HS
Wyoming MI

Pond Arlene
West Liberty Salem HS
Urbana OH

Pontius Brian W
Bay HS
Bay Village OH

Ponzani William S
Eastlake North HS
Willowick OH

Pool Cynthia
Madison Heights HS
Anderson IN

Poole Nadine
Osborn HS
Detroit MI

Poole Tami
Franklin Central HS
Indianapolis IN

Poole Tammy
Jennings County HS
North Vernon IN

Poor Stephen
Elwood Cmnty HS
Elwood IN

Poore Tim
R Nelson Snider HS
Ft Wayne IN

Poort Shirley
Culver Community HS
Monterey IN

Pope James
Greenfield Central HS
Greenfield IN

Pope John
Fostoria HS
Fostoria OH

Pope Mary
Lewis County HS
Camden WV

Pope Tonya
Washington HS
Massillon OH

Popplewell Judi
Walter P Chrysler Mem HS
New Castle IN

Porsoska Mary
Marquette HS
Michigan City IN

Portaro Ross
St Edward HS
Westlake OH

Porter Brian
Madison Hts HS
Anderson IN

Porter Deborah
Royal Oak C M Kimball
HS
Royal Oak MI

Porter Jeff
Shelbyville Sr HS
Shelbyville IN

Porter Joy
Carroll HS
Flora IN

Porter Kelly
Stow Sr HS
Stow OH

Porter Patricia A
Catholic Central HS
Wintersville OH

Porter Rachael
Rutherford B Hayes HS
Dealware OH

Porter Regina
Indian Creek HS
Trafalgar IN

Porter Ron
Carey HS
Carey OH

Porter Wanda
Henry Ford HS
Detroit MI

Porterfield Gregory
Peterstown HS
Lindside WV

Posey Gail
North Knox HS
Freelandville IN

Post Jacqueline
South Harrison HS
Lost Creek WV

Post Tamara
Cheboygan Area HS
Cheboygan MI

Postel Greg
Hoover HS
Canton OH

Postels Douglas
North Central HS
Indianapolis IN

Poterack Karl A
West Catholic HS
Grand Rapids MI

Potrafke Diana
Batavia HS
Batavia OH

Potteiger Dana
Eastmoor HS
Columbus OH

Potter John T
Lutheran HS West
Cleveland OH

Potter Julia A
Westerville North HS
Westerville OH

Potts Paulisa
North Daviess Jr Sr HS
Odon IN

Poulos Nicholas
Orange HS
Pepper Pike OH

Poulson Linda
Anderson HS
Anderson IN

Povinelli Kathleen
Magnificat HS
Westlake OH

Povroznik Stephen
Washington Irving HS
Clarksburg WV

Powell Alva B
Holly HS
Royal Oak MI

Powell Cynthia
Walled Lake Central HS
W Bloomfield MI

Powell Desiree
Lutheran HS East
Cleveland OH

Powell Judy
West Muskingum HS
Hopewell OH

Powell Lionel
Flint Northwestern HS
Flint MI

Powell Stephanie
Buena Vista HS
Sagimaw MI

Power Rolfe
St Philip Catholic Cntrl
HS
Battle Crk MI

Powers Denise
New Haven HS
New Haven IN

Powers Jerri
Indianapolis Baptist HS
Indianapolis IN

Poynter Brent
William Henry Harrison
HS
Harrison OH

Prasek Pam
West Geauga HS
Chesterland OH

Prater Anita
Vinton County Consoldtd
HS
Hamden OH

Prater Joseph
John Glenn HS
Westland MI

Prather Dorian
Servite HS
Detroit MI

Pratt Barb
Tippecanoe Valley HS
Rochester IN

Pratt Gregory
Everett HS
Lansing MI

Pratt Ken
New Bremen Local HS
New Bremen OH

Pratt Kim
Grand Ledge HS
Mulliken MI

Pratt Michelle
Harman HS
Harman WV

Pratt William
Lewis County HS
Weston WV

Prebenda Michael
Catholic Central HS
Livonia MI

Preece Dianna
Wayne HS
Wayne WV

Presnell Jenny
Olmsted Falls HS
Olmsted Falls OH

Pressler Edna
Bloomington HS South
Bloomington IN

Preston Robert J
Houston HS
Piqua OH

Preston Thomas
Moeller HS
Cincinnati OH

Prewitt Claudia
Blanchester HS
Blanchester OH

Price Barbara
Plymouth Salem HS
Plymouth MI

Price Carol
Forest Hills Central HS
Ada MI

Price Denise
Bremen HS
Bremen IN

Price Denise
Vermillon HS
Vermilion OH

Price Dixie
Terre Haute N Vigo HS
Terre Haute IN

Price Dorothy G
Pike Central HS
Stendal IN

Price Faith A
Hardin Northern HS
Dunkirk OH

Price G Joseph
Rietz Mem HS
Newburgh IN

Price Gregory
Edwardsburg HS
Edwardsburg MI

Price Harold
South Haven HS
S Haven MI

Price Jeffrey
Hardin Northern HS
Dunkirk OH

Price Jeffrey
Jackson County Western
HS
Spring Arbor MI

Price Kevin
Hardin Northern HS
Dunkirk OH

Price Kevin
East HS
Sciotoville OH

Price Kim
Zanesville HS
Zanesville OH

Price Kimberley
Warren Central HS
Indianapolis IN

Price Laurie
Durand HS
Bancroft MI

Price Mark
Columbia City Joint HS
Columbia City IN

Price Mark
North HS
Evansville IN

Price Michael J
Morton Sr HS
Hammond IN

Price Paula
Mannington HS
Mannington WV

Price Teresa
North Union HS
Richwood OH

Prichard Mary E
Wayne HS
Wayne WV

Pricing Linda
Frankenmuth HS
Frankenmuth MI

Priebe Laura
St Clement HS
Detroit MI

Prielipp Harold
Deerfield Public HS
Deerfield MI

Prince Evelyn
Park Hills HS
Wp Afb OH

Prince Janice
John Hay HS
Cleveland OH

Prince Mark
Western Boone HS
Thorntown IN

Prince Thomas A
North Harrison HS
Palmyra IN

Pringle Fred J
Mifflin HS
Columbus OH

Printz Marcia
Crooksville HS
Crooksville OH

Prinzbach Mary
Princeton HS
Princeton WV

Pritchard Heather
Delaware Hayes HS
Delaware OH

Pritchard John
R Nelson Snider HS
Ft Wayne IN

Pritchard Linda
R B Chamberlin HS
Twinsburg OH

Pritchard Marchelle
Northwood HS
Northwood OH

Pritchett Alesia
Roosevelt HS
Gary IN

Pritt Debbie
East Preston HS
Terra Alta WV

Probst Kimberly
South Dearborn HS
Aurora IN

Probst Michele
Martinsburg HS
Martinsburg WV

Prochko Robert M
Midpark HS
Middleburg Hts OH

Proto Julie
Windham HS
Windham OH

Prough Jean A
Huntington North HS
Huntington IN

Provencher Renee
Kingsford HS
Kingsford MI

Provins Byron A
United Local HS
Hemet CA

Provitt Jenniffer
Warren G Harding HS
Warren OH

Pruett Debbie
Madison Hts HS
Anderson IN

Pruett Kara
Oceana HS
Oceana WV

Pruett Keith
Bluefield HS
Bluefield WV

Pruitt Arlon
Bluefield HS
Bluefield WV

Pruitt Dreama
Big Creek HS
Yukon WV

Pruitt Michael
Calumet HS
Gary IN

Pruitt Perry
Whiteland Comm HS
New Whiteland IN

Pruitt Rodney
Buena Vista HS
Saginaw MI

Prus Bob
Elwood Community HS
Elwood IN

Pryor Charlene
Columbus East HS
Columbus OH

Pryor Charlene D
East HS
Columbus OH

Pryor Cynthia M
Grafton HS
Bridgeport WV

Pryor Deborah
Chaminade Julienne HS
Dayton OH

Pryor Janelle
Morgan HS
Mc Connelsville OH

Pryor Lynette
Fostoria HS
Fostoria OH

Pryor Monica
Shortridge HS
Indianapolis IN

Pryor Rodney E
Woodrow Wilson HS
Beckley WV

Prysock Christine
Toronto HS
Toronto OH

Przebienda Theresa
Divine Child HS
Dearborn Hts MI

Przeslica Jane F
Fordson HS
Dearborn Hts MI

Puchala Maryann
John Adams HS
So Bend IN

Puckett Bruce
Bluefield HS
Bluefield WV

Puckett Carla L
Bluefield HS
Bluefield WV

Puckett David M
Redford Union HS
Novi MI

Puckett Roddy M
Gods Bible School
Goshen OH

Pudelko Shelly
Sandusky HS
Sandusky MI

Pugh Gary
Mineral Ridge HS
Mineral Ridge OH

Pugsley Thomas J
Dondero HS
Royal Oak MI

Pulfer Tony
Lehman HS
Pt Jeffersn OH

Pulley Linda J
Southfield Christian HS
Southfield MI

Pullins Terri
Eastern HS
Long Bottom OH

Pumford Angelique
Bullock Creek HS
Midland MI

Pupel Margaret M
Catholic Central HS
Grand Rapids MI

Purdy Raymond
Oscoda Area HS
Oscoda MI

Purdy Thomas
Parkside HS
Annandale VA

Purple Lisa
Covington Cmnty HS
Covington IN

Purviance James
Bishop Dwenger HS
Ft Wayne IN

Purvlicis Elza
North Central HS
Indianapolis IN

Pustay Teresa
Wadsworth HS
Wadsworth OH

Putala Connie
Hancock Central HS
Hancock MI

Puthoff David F
La Salle HS
Cincinnati OH

Putnam Nancy A
Cheboygan Area HS
Cheboygan MI

Putt Maria
Bay City Western HS
Auburn MI

Putz Lori F
Aquinas HS
Melvindale MI

Pyle Gregory
Euclid Sr HS
Euclid OH

Pyle Jennifer R
Talawanda HS
Oxford OH

Pyle Rise
Huntington Catholic HS
Huntington IN

Pyles Glenda
Arcanum Butler HS
Castine OH

Pytel Mark
De La Salle Collegiate HS
Detroit MI

Quallen John
Wilmington HS
Wilmington OH

Qualls Paula
East HS
Akron OH

Qualls Sylvia
Immaculata HS
Detroit MI

Quandt Linda
Lutheran HS East
Roseville MI

Quarles Jacqueline E
Broad Ripple HS
Indianapolis IN

Quattro Anthony
Williamson HS
Williamson WV

Queen Kimberly
Bluefield HS
Bluefld WV

Queen Norma
Wayne HS
Wayne WV

Queener Peggy
Wayne HS
Dayton OH

Quellette Sarah
Carrollton HS
Saginaw MI

Query Dan
Owen Valley HS
Coal City IN

Quince Tanya
Pontiac Central HS
Pontiac MI

Quinn Kevin
Highland HS
Chesterfield IN

Quisenberry Jeffrey J
Austintown Fitch HS
Austintown OH

Quivey Kathie
Meigs HS
Shade OH

Raak Christine
Otsego HS
Kalamazoo MI

Raasch Lorraine
Jefferson HS
Monroe MI

Racketa Martha
Medina Sr HS
Medina OH

Rada Christopher
Heath HS
Heath OH

Radcliff Joyce
Lewis Cnty HS
Weston WV

Radcliff Tonya
Liberty HS
Clarksburg WV

Radcliffe Lynne
Terre Haute S Vigo HS
Terre Haute IN

Raddatz Marie
Summerfield HS
Petersburg MI

Rade Jeffrey J
Cardinal Mooney HS
Youngstown OH

Rademacher Stratton
Chelsea HS
Chelsea MI

Raden Jonathan
Culver Military Academy
Dallas TX

Rader Elizabeth A
Newark Sr HS
Newark OH

Radermacher Tina
Anchor Bay HS
New Baltimore MI

Raehl Crystal
Merrillville Sr HS
Merrillville IN

Ragan Christina
Salem HS
Salem OH

Ragan Nikola
Kearsley HS
Burton MI

Rahn William G
John Glenn HS
Bay City MI

Raiff Julie
Dayton Chaminade
Julienne
Dayton OH

Rains Richard
Highland HS
Anderson IN

Raivzee Dolores
Timken Sr HS
Canton OH

Rake Carrie
Washington County Jt
Voc HS
Marietta OH

Ralston David
Boonville HS
Newburgh IN

Ralston Pamela
Marine Cty Ward Cottrell
HS
Marine City MI

Rambo Angela
Bridgman HS
Bridgman MI

Ramey Debbie
Williamson HS
Williamson WV

Ramey Debbie
Walnut Ridge HS
Columbus OH

Ramey Tammy
Jackson HS
Jackson OH

Ramm Brian
Boardman HS
Boardman OH

Ramona David N
Euclid Sr HS
Euclid OH

Ramsdell Deann
Hammond Baptist HS
Hammond IN

Ramsey B
Lewis Cnty HS
Weston WV

Ramsey Bonnie
Defiance Sr HS
Defiance OH

Ramsey Curtis
William Henry Harrison
HS
W Laf IN

Ramsey Lisa
Mogadore HS
Mogadore OH

Ramsey Luanne
Portsmouth East HS
Portsmouth OH

Ramsey Rollie C
Waterford HS
Waterford OH

Ramsey Susan
Warren Central HS
Indianapolis IN

Randall David J
Austintown Fitch HS
Youngstown OH

Randazzo Ross J
Bedford HS
Bedford OH

Randle Carol
Clare HS
Clare MI

Randolph Delores
Thomas M Cooley HS
Detroit MI

Randolph Rex E
Medina Sr HS
Medina OH

Randolph Robert
Mississinewa HS
Jonesboro IN

Rank Joseph
Defiance HS
Defiance OH

Rankinen Todd
Republic Michigamme
HS
Republic MI

Ranney Charles G
Heritage HS
New Haven IN

Ransburgh Twila
Grove City HS
Grove City OH

Ranzinger Yvonne
Adelphian Academy
Union Lake MI

Rapaport Sonia
Athens HS
Athens OH

Rapp Beth
Miami Trace HS
Washington C H OH

Rappley Kim
Michigan Lutheran
Seminary
Saginaw MI

Ratcliff Charles
Baker HS
Fairborn OH

Ratcliff Elizabeth
Regina HS
Cleveland OH

Rathje Kenneth W
Arthur Hill HS
Saginaw MI

Raths Michele
St Joseph Central Cath
HS
Clyde OH

Ratliff Cheryl
Martin Luther King HS
Detroit MI

Ratliff Eric
Valley Local HS
Lucasville OH

Ratliff Karl
Indiana Academy
Bloomington IN

Ratliff Keith
Valley Local HS
Lucasville OH

Rau David W
Worthington HS
Worthington OH

Rauch Elaine
Warren Local HS
Little Hocking OH

Rausch Kelly
Buckeye Valley HS
Ostrander OH

Rausch Kenneth
Buckeye Valley HS
Ostrander OH

Rauser Doris
Fairview HS
Fairview Pk OH

Ravai Kelly
Munster HS
Munster IN

Raver Bernard
Highland HS
Anderson IN

Rawles Michael
Western HS
Russiaville IN

Rawson Julie
Toronto HS
Toronto OH

Rawson Kelly
Farwell HS
Farwell MI

Rawson Shirley
Jefferson Union HS
Toronto OH

Ray Alisa
Belleville HS
Belleville MI

Ray Daniel
Gilmour Academy
Chardon OH

Ray Greg
Jackson HS
Ray OH

Ray Jamie
Alexander HS
Albany OH

Ray Lisa
Union Local HS
Bethesda OH

Rayburn Ethel
Green HS
Uniontown OH

Raymond Dawn
Bullock Creek HS
Midland MI

Razzano Janice L
Port Clinton HS
Port Clinton OH

Rch Russell D Bu
Greenfield Central HS
Greenfield IN

Rea Julia
Firestone Sr HS
Akron OH

Read Jeffrey
Anderson Sr HS
Anderson IN

Read Lynn
Lincoln HS
Vincennes IN

Readd Sally
Hilliard HS
Hilliard OH

Reale Debra
Brooke HS
Colliers WV

Reaman Renee
Goshen HS
Rockford IL

Reasoner Laura
Marian HS
Birmingham MI

Reaver Brian
Pontiac Northern HS
Pontiac MI

Rebandt Dorothy
Gladwin HS
Gladwin MI

Reck Daryl
Covington HS
Covington OH

Reckart Carmen
Bruceton HS
Bruceton WV

Recknagel Jeffrey
Mona Shores HS
Muskegon MI

Recznik Denise
Kent Roosevelt HS
Kent OH

Redden Ronald
Griffith HS
Griffith IN

Reder Clifford
Bay City Western HS
Kawkawlin MI

Redman Darcy
South Vermillion HS
Dana IN

Redman Pamela
Miami Trace HS
Goodhope OH

Reece Catherine
Marion HS
Marion IN

Reece John
Westland HS
Galloway OH

Reece Virginia
Marion HS
Marion IN

Reed James
Centreville HS
Constantine MI

STUDENTS
PHOTOGRAPH
SCHEDULED
FOR PUBLI-
CATION HERE
COULD NOT
BE REPRO-
DUCED

Reed Karen
Peebles HS
Peebles OH

Reed Kelley
Concord HS
Goshen IN

Reed Kevin
Elkins HS
Elkins WV

Reed Kimberly D
Princeton HS
Princeton WV

Reed Lisa
Ridgewood HS
West Lafayette OH

Reed Marsha
Jefferson County HS
Shepherdstown WV

Reed Michael
Philip Barbour HS
Junior WV

Reed Mike
Wilbur Wright HS
Dayton OH

Reed Mike
Napoleon HS
Napoleon MI

Reed Robin L
Harman HS
Whitmer WV

Reed Stace
Bellmont HS
Decatur IN

Reed Sue
Shelby Sr HS
Shelby OH

Reed Tim
Centreville HS
Constantine MI

Reed Wendy
Lucas HS
Lucas OH

Reedy Dianne
Leetonia HS
Washingtonville OH

Rees Donald T
Gallia Academy
Gallipolis OH

Reese Cecylia
Mumford HS
Detroit MI

Reese Christopher
Lorain HS
Lorain OH

Reese Dennis
Lowell Sr HS
Hebron IN

Reeves Joni M
Wayne HS
Dayton OH

Reeves Karen
Walled Lake Western HS
Walled Lk MI

Reeves Mark
Waterford Kettering HS
Drayton Plains MI

Reeves Philip
Norton HS
Norton OH

Regan Kathryn
Marian HS
Birmingham MI

Reger Janet
Lincoln HS
Shinnston WV

Regillo Nicky
Mannington HS
Mannington WV

Regrut Mary
Dublin HS
Dublin OH

Regrut Tom
Dublin HS
Dublin OH

Rehard Nancy
Newcomerstown HS
Newcomerstown OH

Rehfeld Ruth
D D Eisenhower HS
Saginaw MI

Rehling Carolyn A
St Francis De Sales HS
Westerville OH

Rehmann Kimberly
Chesaning Union HS
Chesaning MI

Reibel Lisa
Mater Dei HS
Evansville IN

Reichley John
New Lexington HS
New Lexington OH

Reid Darla J
Owosso HS
Owosso MI

Reid Jayne
Hinton HS
Hinton WV

Reid John
Manistique HS
Gulliver MI

Reid Londa
River Rouge HS
Rivr Rouge MI

Reid Robert
Marlette HS
Marlette MI

Reiger Jeannine
Brooklyn HS
Brooklyn OH

Rein Deborah
Pinckney Cmnty HS
Pinckney MI

Rein Monika
Normandy HS
Seven Hills OH

Reinard Kathryn
Streetsboro HS
Streetsboro OH

Reincke Blake
Forest Hills Central HS
Ada MI

Reiner William R
Bloom Carroll HS
Carroll OH

Reinhard Curtis
Fostoria HS
Fostoria OH

Reinhart Rosemary
Anderson HS
Cincinnati OH

Reis Christine
Bedford Sr HS
Temperance MI

Reisdorf William C
Baraga HS
Baraga MI

Reiter Nancy A
Trenton HS
Trenton MI

Reiva Judi
Monrovia HS
Mooresville IN

Relyea Kathy
Fairview HS
Ney OH

Relyea Kim
Fairview HS
Ney OH

Remias Kathy
Champion HS
Warren OH

Remick Mark
Monsignor Hackett HS
Kalamazoo MI

Remlinger Thomas R
Delphos Saint Johns HS
Delphos OH

Remmell Edward C
Indian Hill HS
Cincinnati OH

Remus Kathie
Avondale Sr HS
Auburn Heights MI

Renicker Joann
Fredericktown HS
Fredericktown OH

Reninger Fred
Field HS
Mogadore OH

Renner Cindy
Sheridan HS
Thornville OH

Renner Melinda
Elyria HS
Elyria OH

Rentz Tom
Patrick Henry HS
Malinta OH

Repic Teresa
North Branch HS
North Branch MI

Repka Anthony M
Genoa Area HS
Genoa OH

Replogle Lisa D
South Vermillion HS
Clinton IN

Repo James R
Kaleva Norman Dickson
Schls
Brethren MI

Requa Robin
Jefferson Area HS
Jefferson OH

Ressler Darla
Chesterton HS
Chesterton IN

Rettke Reuben
Okemos HS
Okemos MI

Revalee Richard
Centerville HS
Centerville IN

Revere Brenda
Maple Hts Sr HS
Maple Heights OH

Revock Russ
Padua Franciscan HS
Cleveland OH

Reyelts Fredric
St Clair HS
St Clair MI

Reyes Elizabeth
Northwood HS
Wakarusa IN

Reynolds Gerard J
Bishop Dwenger HS
Ft Wayne IN

Reynolds Janice
Port Clinton HS
Port Clinton OH

Reynolds Michael
Williamstown HS
Williamstown WV

Reynolds Patricia
Brownstown Central HS
Brownstown IN

Reynolds Richard
Waterford Twp HS
Union Lake MI

Reynolds Susan
Seeger Metropolitan HS
W Lebanon IN

Reynolds Terri
Frontier HS
Newport OH

Reynolds Twila
St Albans HS
St Albans WV

Reyome Patty
Anthony Wayne HS
Waterville OH

Reznik Sue
Polaris Voc Center
Middleburg Hts OH

Rhoad Tim
Fostoria HS
Fostoria OH

Rhoades Christine
Tippecanoe Valley HS
Silver Lake IN

Rhoades Ronald
Notre Dame HS
Clarksburg WV

Rhoades Rose
Philo HS
Roseville OH

Rhoads Edward R
Huntington HS
Chillicothe OH

Rhoads Gary
Peebles HS
Hillsboro OH

Rhodeback Karla A
St Bernard Elmwood Pl
HS
St Bernard OH

Rhodes Dan
Brooke HS
Follansbee WV

Rhodes David W
Tippecanoe Valley HS
Akron IN

Rhodes Julie
Belding HS
Belding MI

Rhodes Lance
Ripley HS
Ripley WV

Rhodes Megan
Crestview HS
Columbiana OH

Rhodes Nancy
Newark Sr HS
Newark OH

Rhodes Todd
Versailles HS
Versailles OH

Rhodes Virginia
Solon HS
Solon OH

Rhone Evette
Mumford HS
Detroit MI

Rhudy Vaughn
Woodrow Wilson HS
Beckley WV

Riccitelli Keith
St Francis De Sales HS
Toledo OH

Rice Duane
Sycamore HS
Cincinnati OH

Rice Elizabeth
Edison HS
Milan OH

Rice John
Sherman HS
Prenter WV

Rice Kelly
Austintown Fitch HS
Youngstown OH

Rice Lisa C
De Vilbiss HS
Toledo OH

Rice Steven
Covington HS
Covington OH

Rich Linda
George C Schafer HS
Southgate MI

Richards Barb
Houston HS
Covington OH

Richards Daniel L
Greenville Sr HS
Greenville OH

Richards Janine
Perry Meridian HS
Indianapolis IN

Richards Karen
Bloomington HS South
Bloomington IN

Richards Kenneth
Champion HS
Warren OH

Richards Thomas
Boardman HS
Boardman OH

Richardson Donna
Bucyrus HS
Buryrus OH

Richardson Jennifer J
Richmond Sr HS
Richmond IN

Richardson Latangia
Memphis HS
Smth Crk MI

Richardson Leslie
Stivers Patterson Coop
HS
Dayton OH

Richardville Craig
Monroe Catholic Central
HS
Monroe MI

Richey Brenda
Crestview HS
Wren OH

Richey William K
Xenia HS
Xenia OH

Richhart Deborah
Decatur Central HS
Indpls IN

Richman Rebecca
Floyd Central HS
Floyd Knobs IN

Richmond Lisa
London HS
London OH

Richmond Pamella
Centreville HS
Sturgis MI

Richmond Steven T
Jackson Cnty Western
HS
Parma MI

Rickard Layne
Teays Valley HS
Circleville OH

Rickel Cheryl
Ashland HS
Ashland OH

Rickman Marcel
Mt Clemens HS
Mt Clemens MI

Rickner Peggy
Van Wert HS
Van Wert OH

Riddle Nadine
Edwin Denby HS
Detroit MI

Riddle Rebecca
Owosso HS
Owosso MI

Riddle Renee
Amanda Clearcreek HS
Stoutsville OH

Ridenour Carolyn
Bridgeport HS
Bridgeport WV

Rider Denise
Champion HS
Bristolville OH

Rider Dwayne
Greenbrier East HS
Alderson WV

Ridley Stephen
E A Johnson HS
Clio MI

Riedel Herbert
Walled Lake Central HS
Union Lake MI

Riedel Kelly R
Geneva Secondary
School
Geneva OH

Rieger Bridget
Strongsville HS
Strongsville OH

Riegler Jonathan
Mona Shores HS
Muskegon MI

Riehl Lori
Nordonia HS
Northfield OH

Ries Roger
Mt Vernon Sr HS
Mt Vernon IN

Rieske Michael D
Fairmont West HS
Kettering OH

Riester Dean
North Knox HS
Bicknell IN

Rife Barbara
St Albans HS
St Albans WV

Rife Charles
Jay County HS
Dunkirk IN

Rife Penny
Kyger Creek HS
Cheshire OH

Riffe Andrew
Pendleton Hts HS
Middletown IN

Riffle Donna
Morgantown HS
Morgantwn WV

Rifkin Wendy
Dublin HS
Dublin OH

Rigdon Debra
Rockville Jr Sr HS
Rockville IN

Rigdon Lisa
Greensburg Community
HS
Greensburg IN

Rigg Michael
Richmond Sr HS
Richmond IN

Riggs Martin
Tyler County HS
Middlebourne WV

Riggs Paula
South Spencer HS
Rockport IN

Riggs Shari
Hilltop HS
W Unity OH

Riley Angela R
Barboursville HS
Barboursville WV

Riley Brian M
Caro HS
Caro MI

Riley Cassandra
Warrensville Hts Sr HS
Warrensville Hts OH

Riley Levenna
Lincoln HS
Shinnston WV

Riley Lori
Washington HS
Massillon OH

Riley Michael
Mount Vernon Academy
Proctorville OH

Riley Teri
Avon Jr Sr HS
Danville IN

Rillema Tammy
Reeths Puffer HS
Muskegon MI

Rinehart Susan
Shady Spring HS
Shady Spring WV

Rink Michael
Clay HS
S Bend IN

Rinke Gordon
St Anne HS
Warren MI

Rinkel Tony
Edgerton HS
Bryan OH

Rinkevich Sharon
Lapeer East Sr HS
Metamora MI

Rinyo Anita
Madison HS
Madison OH

Riordan Timothy
Grosse Ile HS
Grosse Ile MI

Ripepi Linda
Valley Forge HS
Parma OH

Ripley Pam
Gahanna Lincoln HS
Gahanna OH

Rippel Linda
Rudyard HS
Rudyard MI

Rishel Michele
Vinton County HS
Mc Arthur OH

Risner Holly
Fostoria HS
Fostoria OH

Ritchie Kim
Franklin Central HS
Indianapolis IN

Ritter Laura
New Haven HS
New Haven IN

Ritter Rhonda
Grandview Hts HS
Columbus OH

Ritter Richard
North Daviess HS
Washington IN

Ritz George
Trenton HS
Trenton MI

Rivard Ray
Mater Dei HS
Evansville IN

Rivard Russ
Mater Dei HS
Evansville IN

Rivas Laura
Bishop Noll Inst
E Chicago IN

Rivir Kelly
Huntington North HS
Huntington IN

Rix James
Park Hills HS
Fairborn OH

Rizk Bob
Groves HS
Birmingham MI

Rizor Tracy
Northport HS
Northport MI

Rizzuto Pamela
Brunswick HS
Brunswick OH

Roach Julie
East Lansing HS
East Lansing MI

Roach Veronica
Linton Stockton Jr Sr HS
Linton IN

Roach Jr Gerald
Gallia Academy HS
Gallipolis OH

Roark Darlene
Lowell HS
Lowell IN

Roark Janice
Brookville HS
Brookville IN

Robbins Darryl R
Terre Haute South Vigo
HS
Terre Haute IN

Robbins Marilyn
St Marys Cathedral HS
Highland Park MI

Robbins Ruth
Yale HS
Goodells MI

Roberts Cathy
Stow Sr HS Lakeview
Bldg
Stow OH

Roberts Cheryl
Tri Jr Sr HS
Lewisville IN

Roberts Connie S
East Clinton HS
Sabina OH

Roberts Dan
Ross HS
Hamilton OH

Roberts Deidra
Carson City Crystal HS
Carson City MI

Roberts James
Heath HS
Heath OH

Roberts Jeff
Madison Comprehensive
HS
Mansfield OH

Roberts Kimberle
Roosevelt HS
Gary IN

Roberts Kimberly
Webster Cnty HS
Webster Springs WV

Roberts Linda
Rockford Sr HS
Belmont MI

Roberts Lois Ann
North Ridgeville HS
N Ridgeville OH

Roberts Madolyn
Teays Valley HS
Ashville OH

Roberts Pam
Jonesville HS
Jonesville MI

Roberts Penny
Croswell Lexington HS
Croswell MI

Roberts Rita
Scott HS
Foster WV

Roberts Theodore
Madison Comprehensive
HS
Mansfield OH

Robertson Julie A
Belpre HS
Parkersburg WV

Robeson Bryan
Ontonagon Area HS
Ontonagon MI

Robinette Deann
Shelby HS
Shelby OH

Robins Carey
Crestview HS
New Waterford OH

Robinson Denise
Bellaire HS
Bellaire OH

Robinson Diane
St Vincent HS
Akron OH

Robinson Elizabeth
Lockland HS
Cincinnati OH

Robinson Frankie J
Wilmington HS
Wilmington OH

Robinson George
Miami Trace HS
Washington Ch OH

Robinson Harlescia
Lutheran East HS
Cleveland OH

Robinson Isaac
Bluefield HS
Bluefld WV

Robinson Janelle
Southern Local HS
Wellsville OH

Robinson Jill
Bentley Sr HS
Davison MI

Robinson Kathy
North Liberty HS
North Liberty IN

Robinson Kevin
Cameron HS
Cameron WV

Robinson Lana
West Jefferson HS
W Jefferson OH

Robinson Michael
Cardington Lincoln HS
Cardington OH

Robinson Phillip
Linsly Institute
Wheeling WV

Robinson Robert
Washington HS
Massillon OH

Robinson Robin
Washington HS
Massillon OH

Robinson Scott
Jackson HS
North Canton OH

Robinson Sharon
Brilliant Buckeye HS
Smithfield OH

Robinson Sheri
North Farmington HS
Farm Hills MI

Robinson Terri
Rockhill Sr HS
Kitts Hill OH

Robinson Veda
South Bend La Salle HS
South Bend IN

Robinson Vincent P
Bishop Luers HS
Fort Wayne IN

Rocchio Vincent
Hackett HS
Kalamazoo MI

Rocheleau Susan
Ithaca HS
Ithaca MI

Rochester Christie
Tiffin Columbian HS
Bloomville OH

Rockstraw Dave
Chesterton HS
Chesterton IN

Rodammer Mark
Frankenmuth HS
Frankenmuth MI

Rodeck Deborah
Negaunee HS
Negaunee MI

Roderick Dawn
Chelsea HS
Chelsea MI

Rodewald Beth
Reeths Puffer HS
Muskegon MI

Rodewald Bonnie
Reeths Puffer HS
Muskegon MI

Rodfong Tami S
E Liverpool HS
E Liverpool OH

Rodgers Kelly
Davison Sr HS
Davison MI

Rodgers Kenneth
Tecumseh HS
Tecumseh MI

Rodino Holly
William A Wirt HS
Gary IN

Rodkey Virginia
Rossville HS
Rossville IN

Rodman Mary
North Central Area
School
Hermansville MI

Rodriguez Doreen
Finney HS
Detroit MI

Rodriguez Michael
John Adams HS
South Bend IN

Roe Brian
Sand Creek HS
Adrian MI

Roe Kristin
Clare HS
Clare MI

Roe Terry
Ithaca HS
Pompeii MI

Roeder Scott A
Penn HS
Mishawaka IN

Roemer Daniel
Bishop Luers HS
Ft Wayne IN

Roesch Douglas C
Galion Sr HS
Galion OH

Rogan Narvetta
Mt Clemens HS
Mount Clemens MI

Rogers Charles R
Pt Pleasant HS
Pt Pleasant WV

Rogers Chris
Warsaw Community HS
Warsaw IN

Rogers Christine
Shenandoah HS
Caldwell OH

Rogers Darryl
Greenville HS
Greenville MI

Rogers Dave
Hammond Baptist HS
Hammond IN

Rogers Jacqueline
Ridgemont HS
Ridgeway OH

Rogers Janeen
Rock Hill HS
Pedro OH

Rogers Michael
Huntington North HS
Huntington IN

Rogers Randy
Washington Irving HS
Clarksburg WV

Rogers Rose
Lowellville HS
Lowellville OH

Rogers Scott
Oakridge HS
Muskegon MI

Rogers Terri F
Bedford HS
Temperance MI

Rogge Kimberly
Walnut Ridge Sr HS
Columbus OH

Rohrbacher Charles
Delphos St John HS
Delphos OH

Rohrbacher Colleen
Clyde HS
Clyde OH

Rohrer Kathy
John Glenn HS
Walkerton IN

Rohrer Rebekah
Olmsted Falls HS
Olmsted Falls OH

Rohweder Robert
Clay Sr HS
Granger IN

Rolf Cheryl
Kenston HS
Chagrin Fls OH

Rolka Yvonne
Fitzgerald HS
Sterling Hts MI

Roll Kim
Eastern HS
Pekin IN

Rollett Patricia
Mater Dei HS
Evansville IN

Rollison Kris
Bloomfield HS
Bloomfield IN

Rollyson Connie
Lewis County HS
Weston WV

Rollyson Mike
Parkersburg HS
Parkersburg WV

Romain Francine R
Liberty HS
Clarksburg WV

Roman Bridgette
Canfield HS
Canfield OH

Roman Felisa
George Washington HS
East Chicago IN

Roman Santita
Horace Mann HS
Gary IN

Rome Jo Ann
Garfield Sr HS
Hamilton OH

Rome Ruth
Okemos HS
E Lansing MI

Romer Lydia
Carlisle HS
Carlisle OH

Romeu Kathleen
St Joseph Sr HS
St Joseph MI

Romie Joan
Centerville HS
Centerville OH

Romig Amy S
Claymont HS
Dennison OH

Romlein Jenny
Pontiac N Sr HS
Pontiac MI

Roney Sharon
Jackson HS
Massillon OH

Rood John R
Lumen Christi HS
Jackson MI

Rood Theresa
Huntington HS
Huntington WV

Rookstool Robert J
Meadow Bridge HS
Meadow Bridge WV

Rooney Kelly
Stonewall Jackson HS
Chrlstn WV

Roose Anne M
Center Line HS
Warren MI

Root Christine
Black River HS
Spencer OH

Root Laura J
Black River HS
Spencer OH

Rorabacher Sheila
Plymouth Canton HS
Plymouth MI

Rose Crystal
Centerville HS
Centerville OH

Rose David
Mt Vernon Academy
Clyde OH

Rose Dawn
C S Mott HS
Warren MI

Rose Dick
Sandy Valley HS
Magnolia OH

Rose Hilary
Rochester HS
Rochester MI

Rose Kurt
Oakridge Sr HS
Muskegon MI

Rose Lori
Wapakoneta Sr HS
Wapakoneta OH

Rose Myra
Franklin HS
Franklin OH

Roseboom Patrick
Portage Central HS
Portage MI

Rosebrock Annette M
Fairview HS
Mark Center OH

Rosekelly George
Edison HS
Huron OH

Rosenbaum Deborah
Haworth HS
Kokomo IN

Rosenberg Craig
Hartford HS
Hartford MI

Ross Angela
Wood Memorial HS
Oakland City IN

Ross Douglas
Centreville HS
Centreville MI

Ross Elizabeth
Galion HS
Galion OH

Ross Gayle
Ravenna HS
Ravenna OH

Ross Jennie
Greeneview HS
Jamestown OH

Ross Kay
Terre Haute North Vigo HS
Terre Haute IN

Ross Kristina A
Triton Central HS
Indianapolis IN

Ross Laura
Castle HS
Newburgh IN

Ross Melody
Olentangy HS
Galena OH

Ross Michael
Fairmont West HS
Kettering OH

Ross Pamela
Centreville HS
Centreville MI

Ross Rosalyn
West Side HS
Gary IN

Ross Starla D
Lakewood HS
Newark OH

Ross Tim
Heritage Jr Sr HS
Ft Wayne IN

Rossi Dina
Niles Mc Kinley HS
Niles OH

Rosskopf Reba
Norwood Sr HS
Cincinnati OH

Rotenberg Tracey
Morton Sr HS
Hammond IN

Roth Bryan
Sandusky Sr Marys Cntrl HS
Sandusky OH

Roth Connie
Indian Valley North HS

Roth Eric
Broad Ripple HS
Indianapolis IN

Roth Sarah
Columbus North HS
Columbus OH

Roth Scott
Lorain Catholic HS
Lorain OH

Rothbauer Patricia
Southridge HS
Huntngbrg IN

Rothwell Michael
Parkersburg HS
Vienna WV

Rotruck Margo
Elk Garden HS
Elk Garden WV

Roudebush Jennifer
Anderson HS
Anderson IN

Rourk Ronald
Bishop Hartley HS
Columbus OH

Rousell Doug
Mona Shores HS
Muskegon MI

Roush Mike
Wahama HS
New Haven WV

Rousher Thomas
Boardman HS
Youngstown OH

Routh Michael
West Washington HS
Campbellsbg IN

Rowand Timothy M
Grafton HS
Grafton WV

Rowe Kenneth E
Stevenson HS
Livonia MI

Rowell Darwin
Patterson Co Op HS
Dayton OH

Rowland Carma J
Adena HS
Frankfort OH

Rowles Jan
Washington HS
Massillon OH

Rowlett Ann
Cuyahoga Falls HS
Cuyahoga Fls OH

Rowlett Benita
La Salle HS
South Bend IN

Rowley Leslie
Jefferson Union HS
Steubenville OH

Rowley Michael
Ironton HS
Ironton OH

Rowse Julie
Bellevue 'S
Bellevue MI

Roy Stephen
Cheboygan Area HS
Cheboygan MI

Royalty John
Corydon Central HS
Elizabeth IN

Royce Janice
La Salle HS
South Bend IN

Rozeboom Brenda
Holland Christian HS
Hollad MI

Rozic Roseanne
Malabar HS
Mansfield OH

Rozman Martin L
Maple Hts Sr HS
Maple Hgts OH

Rpse Lambert
Elkins HS
Elkins WV

Ruark Becky
Eastern Local HS
Beaver OH

Ruark Debra A
South Putnam HS
Fillmore IN

Rubcich Marta
Shadyside HS
Shadyside OH

Rubel Douglas
Pemberville Eastwood
HS
Pemberville OH

Rubio James
Washington HS
Massillon OH

Ruble Lynda
Merrillville HS
Merrillville IN

Ruch Patrick
Mooresville HS
Mooresville IN

Ruckel Dwain
Mansfield Christian HS
Mansfield OH

Rucker Danita
Collinwood HS
Cleveland OH

Rudloff William
Newbury HS
Newbury OH

Ruff Dawn
Plymouth HS
Plymouth IN

Ruff Michael
Monroe HS
La Salle MI

Ruffing Christopher
Huron HS
Huron OH

Ruggirello Maria
Carl Brablec HS
Roseville MI

Ruggles David
Central Preston Sr HS
Tunnelton WV

Ruhl Carole
Fredericktown HS
Fredericktown OH

Ruiz Arlene
Ashtabula Cnty Joint Voc
Sch
Pierpont OH

Ruiz Cynthia
Hammond Technical Voc
HS
Hammond IN

Ruiz Herman
Theadore Roosevelt HS
E Chicago IN

Ruiz Phyllis
E Hammond HS
Hammond IN

Rule Andrew
Clinton Central HS
Michigantown IN

Rumbaugh Greg
Wapakoneta Sr HS
Cridersville OH

Rumph Charlene
Buchtel Univeristy HS
Akron OH

Rumple Cynthia
Mississihewa HS
Marion IN

Runnells Kathleen
Tippecanoe Valley HS
Warsaw IN

Runnels Tony
Highland Park
Community HS
Highland Pk MI

Runyan Colleen
Mason HS
Mason MI

Runyan Lee Ann
Zionsville HS
Zionsville IN

Runyan Suzanne M
Rutherford B Hayes HS
Delaware OH

Rupert Laura
South Range HS
Salem OH

Rupp Mary
Gorham Fayette HS
Fayette OH

Rusch Laurie
Freeland HS
Saginaw MI

Rusche Rosalie
Castle HS
Newburgh IN

Rush Denise
Union HS
Grand Rapids MI

Rush Karen
John Fitzgerald Kennedy
HS
Cleveland OH

Rushton Jeannette
Holy Rosary HS
Davison MI

Rushton William
Onaway HS
Onaway MI

Rusin Thomas
L C Mohr HS
South Haven MI

Russell Albert
Whitehall Yearling HS
Whitehall OH

Russell Dean E
Richwood HS
Cottle WV

Russell Donn M
Yorktown HS
Muncie IN

Russell Errol
Kyger Creek HS
Cheshire OH

Russell Jeffrey
New Lexington HS
New Lexington OH

Russell Jill Ann
North Knox HS
Bicknell IN

Russell Kathryn S
Noblesville HS
Noblesville IN

Russell Kelly
Western HS
Latham OH

Russell Kimberly
Crothersville HS
Crothersville IN

Russell Linda
Monroe HS
Monroe MI

Russell Pamela
Lima Sr HS
Lima OH

Russell Sidney
Mt Vernon Academy
Cleveland OH

Russell Uretta
Bedford Sr HS
Oakwood Village OH

Russo Ron
La Salle HS
Cincinnati OH

Russo Vincent
Carroll HS
Dayton OH

Rutherford Shannon S
Eastern HS
Pekin IN

Rutherford Sue
Cannelton HS
Cannelton IN

STUDENTS
PHOTOGRAPH
SCHEDULED
FOR PUBLI-
CATION HERE
COULD NOT
BE REPRO-
DUCED

Ruttan Beverlee
Michigan Lutheran
Seminary
Kawkawlin MI

Ruzicka Frank
Holy Rosary HS
Flint MI

Ryan Becky
Tri Rivers Joint Voc HS
Marion OH

Ryan Dan
Fredericktown HS
Fred OH

Ryan Deborah
Lincoln HS
Warren MI

Ryan Glenda
Brownstown Central HS
Norman IN

Ryan Jeanne
Grosse Pointe South HS
Grosse Pte MI

Ryan Peggie
Bork River Horris HS
Harris MI

Ryan William G
Green HS
Akron OH

Rybicki Cynthia
Byron Center HS
Byron Center MI

Rybicki Grace
Hazel Park HS
Hazel Park MI

Ryder Beth
Milton HS
Ona WV

Rygiel Suzette
Franklin HS
Westland MI

Rytiewski Karen
Bay City Western HS
Auburn MI

S

Saalman Gary
Coldwater Exempted Vlg
HS
Coldwater OH

Sabatula Annette
Lumen Cordium HS
Shaker Hts OH

Sabau Georgene
Morton Sr HS
Hammond IN

Saber Debra
Jewett Scio HS
Scio OH

Sabo Richard
Melvindale HS
Melvindale MI

Sabo Tamara A
Washington HS
East Chicago IN

Sackenheim Joseph
Stephen T Badin HS
Fairfield OH

Sacks Valerie
Lakeview HS
Cortland OH

Sadowski Joan
Menominee HS
Menominee MI

Safar Julie
Coventry HS
Akron OH

Sage Doug
Matheus HS
Vienna OH

Sager Catherine
Clay Sr HS
Oregon OH

Sager Cheryl
Hagerstown Jr Sr HS
Hagerstown IN

Sager Kathryn
Big Walnut HS
Jhnstn OH

Sager Rebecca
Lapel HS
Anderson IN

Sagraves Daniel E
Portsmouth HS
Portsmouth OH

Sakalosky Paul
Lumen Christ HS
Jerome MI

Salach Pamela
St Joseph Sr HS
Saint Joseph MI

Salermo Patzi
Lincoln HS
Shinnston WV

Salge William
Kenmore HS
Akron OH

Saling Daniel
Southern Local HS
Lisbon OH

Sallak Rex A
Grace Baptist Church HS
Niles MI

Salmons Ronald
Guyan Valley HS
W Hamlin WV

Salo Tina
Grand Ledge HS
Grand Ledge MI

Saltzman Joyce
Vanlue Local HS
Alvada OH

Saltzmann Kimberly
Bristol HS
Bristolville OH

Salyer T
Heritage HS
New Haven IN

Samples J Robert
Liberty HS
Salem WV

Sampson Connie
Southeast HS
Ravenna OH

Sanborn Sharon
White Cloud HS
White Cloud MI

Sandahl Edward
Allegan Sr HS
Allegan MI

Sandefer Kelly
Lansing Everett HS
Lansing MI

Sander Lorrie
Mt Healthy HS
Cincinnati OH

Sanders Charlotte
East Chicago Roosevelt
HS
E Chicago IN

Sanders Juanita
Roosevelt HS
Gary IN

Sanders Pamela
Green HS
Akron OH

Sanders Paul C
Summit Country Day
Schl
Cincinnati OH

Sanders Sandra
Lansing Everett HS
Lansing MI

Sanders Stephen
Clarkston Sr HS
Clarkston MI

Sanders Terri
Kankakee Valley HS
Wheatfield IN

Sanderson Deborah J
Tiffin Columbian HS
Bloomville OH

Sanderson Susan
Montabella HS
Millbrook MI

Sandling Heidi
Ferndale HS
Plsnt Rdg MI

Sandor Mary
Jewett Scio HS
Jewett OH

Sandy Vickie L
Roosevelt Wilson HS
Mt Clare WV

Sanford Carolyn
Andrews Girls HS
Clevelnd Hts OH

Sangalang Sandra
Chatard HS
Indianapolis IN

Sankovich Sharron
Canton South HS
E Sparta OH

Sanner Karen
Erieview Catholic HS
Cleveland OH

Sanor Karen
West Branch HS
Salem OH

Santoro Randajo
Campbell Memorial HS
Campbell OH

Santucci Kathleen
Howland HS
Warren OH

Sapiano John
Grosse Ile HS
Grosse Ile MI

Saporito Frank A
Fairmont Sr HS
Fairmont WV

Sapp Kimberly D
Monongah HS
Fairmont WV

Sapp Pamela
Lutheran HS East
Detroit MI

Sara Sarah
Bloomington HS
Bloomington IN

Sargent Crystal
Clinton Massie HS
Clarksville OH

Sargent Troy A
Hobart Sr HS
Hobart IN

Sari Tina
Margaretta HS
Bellevue OH

Sarisky John
Woodrow Wilson Sr HS
Youngstown OH

Sasaki Patty A
West Geauga HS
Chesterland OH

Sather Tamie
Clio HS
Clio MI

Satkowiak Suzanne
Clay Sr HS
Oregon OH

Satterwhite Kenneth
Mt Healthy HS
Cincinnati OH

Sattler Richard
Quincy HS
Quincy MI

Sauceda James
Lansing Eastern HS
Lansing MI

Saucedo Annabel
Roosevelt HS
E Chicago IN

Sauls Mark D
Tippecanoe HS
Tipp City OH

Saunders Denise
Lumen Cordium HS
Bedford OH

Saunders Valerie
Du Pont HS
London WV

Saus Joe
Lake Catholic HS
Mayfield OH

Sautins Iveta
Perrysburg HS
Perrysburg OH

Sauto James W
Eastlake North HS
Willowick OH

Savage Denise
Avon HS
Indianapolis IN

Savelli Brenda
Kirtland HS
Kirtland OH

Savoie Eileen
North Central Area HS
Powers MI

Sawayda Cynthia
Champion HS
Warren OH

Sawicki Leslie
Maumee HS
Maumee OH

Sawyer Cynthia L
Richmond Sr HS
Richmond IN

Sawyer Lisa
Princeton HS
Sharonville OH

Saxton Jay
Gallia Academy
Gallipolis OH

Saxton Sharon
Petoskey HS
Petoskey MI

Sayers Susan P
Federal Hocking HS
Millfield OH

Sayles Martha
Midview HS
Grafton OH

Sayre Sherrie
Floyd Central HS
Georgetown IN

Sazima Kim
Bedford Sr HS
Bedford OH

Scafe Judith
Southwestern HS
Detroit MI

Scali Geralyn M
North HS
Eastlake OH

Scamahorn Amy
South Spencer HS
Rockport IN

Scarberry Christine
Comstock HS
Kalamazoo MI

Scarberry Gary
Mt View HS
Welch WV

Scarbrough Gary
Olentangy HS
Delaware OH

Scarbrough Karen
Kenmore HS
Akron OH

Scarbrough Roxanne E
John Adams HS
So Bend IN

Schaefer David G
Benedictine HS
Cleveland OH

Schaefer Jonathan T
Oakridge HS
Muskegon MI

Schaefer Kenneth
Fowler HS
Fowler MI

Schaeffer James
Clare HS
Clare MI

Schaeper James D
Mt Healthy HS
Cincinnati OH

Schafer Rebecca L
Winchester Comm HS
Winchester IN

Schafer Sheryl
Lake Catholic HS
Krtlnd Hls OH

Schafer Todd
Lumen Christi HS
Jackson MI

Schalk Catherine
Hopewell Loudon HS
New Riegel OH

Schalk Gregory H
Euclid Sr HS
Euclid OH

Schalk Patricia
Hopewell Loudon HS
New Riegel OH

Schantz Robert
Allen East HS
Lima OH

Scharnitzke Lydia
Garden City Sr HS East
Garden City MI

Scheafnocker Linda
Benjamin Bosse HS
Evansville IN

Scheck Richard W
Triway HS
Shreve OH

Schecter Martin
Bexley HS
Bexley OH

Scheer Denise
River Valley HS
Three Oaks MI

Scheessele Mike
South Spencer HS
Rockport IN

Scheinberg Jeff
Beachwood HS
Beachwood OH

Scheiner Jacqueline
Bishop Luers HS
Woodburn IN

Schell Frank
Sandusky HS
Sandusky MI

Schell Kyle
Newark Catholic HS
Newark OH

Schell Michael
Pike HS
Indpls IN

Schell Sandra
New Albany Sr HS
New Albany IN

Schellbacher Emil
Cabrini HS
Allen Pk MI

Schember Stephanie
Elkton Pigeon Bay Port
HS
Pigeon MI

Schemine Steven
Rutherford B Hayes HS
Delaware OH

Schenck Barbara
Canfield HS
Canfield OH

Schenck Jennifer
Deer Park HS
Cincinnati OH

Schendel Martin
Plymouth Canton HS
Plymouth MI

Schenkel Susan
Northfield HS
Andrews IN

Schenks Pamela
Wood Memorial HS
Oakland City IN

Scher Cynthia
Huntington Catholic HS
Huntington IN

Scherzinger Michael
Garfield HS
Hamilton OH

Scheuer David
Coloma HS
Coloma MI

Schiemann Lonnie
Gladwin HS
Gladwin MI

Schilling Gloria J
Greenbrier E HS
Frankford WV

Schilling Lisa
Princeton HS
Cincinnati OH

Schilling Robert
Northwest HS
Clinton OH

Schilling Sheryl L
Westfall HS
Orient OH

Schillman Laurey
Davison Sr HS
Davison MI

Schiltges Catherine
Bishop Foley HS
Warren MI

Schindel Dianne
Jackson Ctr HS
Maplewood OH

Schinderle Mary Jo
Kingsford HS
Kingsford MI

Schindler James R
Dayton Christian HS
Dayton OH

Schipper Phil
Hammond Baptist HS
Merrillville IN

Schirmann Ernest
Muskegon HS
Muskegon MI

Schirtzinger Karen
Westerville N HS
Westerville OH

Schlager Jr Barry
Swartz Creek HS
Swartz Creek MI

Schleyer Colleen
Port Huron HS
Port Huron MI

Schlosser Cindy
Memorial HS
St Marys OH

Schlosser D Andra
Litchfield HS
Litchfield MI

Schmaltz Betty
Bentley Sr HS
Davison MI

Schmedding Karen
Anderson Sr HS
Anderson IN

Schmeltzer Kathryn
Gwinn HS
Gwinn MI

Schmett Brad
Southridge HS
Huntingburg IN

Schmidike Cynthia
Schoolcraft HS
Schoolcraft MI

Schmidt Brenda
Laporte HS
Laporte IN

Schmidt Catherine M
Perry HS
Canton OH

Schmidt Cynthia
Beechwood HS
Beachwood OH

Schmidt Debra
Marian HS
S Bend IN

Schmidt Jonna Leigh
Plymouth Salem HS
Plymouth MI

Schmidt Lauri A
Perry HS
Canton OH

Schmidt Margo
Elizabeth Ann Johnson
HS
Mt Morris MI

Schmidt Melissa
Mt Healthy HS
Cincinnati OH

Schmidt Vicki
Mount Healthy HS
Cincinnati OH

Schmitmeyer Karen
Anna HS
Anna OH

Schmitt John
North Posey HS
Evansville IN

Schmitt Marc
Mariemont HS
Terr Pk OH

Schmitt Michael
Charles F Brush HS
S Euclid OH

Schmitt Sally
Canal Winchester HS
Cnl Winchester OH

Schmitt Suzanne
Port Clinton HS
Port Clinton OH

Schmitt Winfield
Vinson HS
Huntington WV

Schmitz Matthew
Imlay City Cmnty HS
Imlay City MI

Schmucker Cheri
Eastside HS
Spencerville IN

Schmuhl Karen S
Parma Sr HS
Parma OH

Schnaiter Bradley
Martinsville HS
Martinsville IN

Schnarr Sherry
Loogootee HS
Loogootee IN

Schneck Melody
Salem HS
Little York IN

Schneider Beth
Indian Hill HS
Cincinnati OH

Schneider Kim
Western Brown Sr HS
Hamersvil OH

Schneider Sandra
John Marshall HS
Cleveland OH

Schnell Stephen
Our Lady Of Providence
HS
Jeffersonville IN

Schnelle Robert
Walda J Wood Memorial
HS
Lynnville IN

Schnorr Michael
Kenston HS
San Diego CA

Schoeck Daniel
Padua Franciscan HS
Parma OH

Schoellkopf Betsy
Walnut Hills HS
Cincinnati OH

Schoener David
Ironton HS
Ironton OH

Schofner Keith
Morristown Jr Sr HS
Shelbyville IN

Scholten Karen
Gull Lake HS
Galesburg MI

Scholz Rhonda
Wickliffe HS
Wicklffe OH

Schoning Jeff
Ravenna HS
Ravenna OH

Schoonard Timothy
Battle Creek Central HS
Battle Creek MI

Schoonover Kathy
Elkins HS
Elkins WV

Schoonover Kenneth
Elkins HS
Elkins WV

Schopneyer Lori
Clay City HS
Center Point IN

Schork Carolyn R
William Mason HS
Mason OH

Schott Joan
Colonel Crawford HS
Bucyrus OH

Schoumacher Valerie
Greenbrier East HS
Lewisburg WV

Schrack M Beth
Newton Falls HS
Newton Falls OH

Schrack Ronald
Loudonville HS
Loudonville OH

Schrader Melinda
Bloom Local HS
S Webster OH

Schramke Mary
John Glenn HS
Bay City MI

Schrand Steve
Southside HS
Muncie IN

Schreiber Debbie
Loveland Hurst HS
Loveland OH

Schreiner Jackie
Brookville HS
Brookville IN

Schroeder Barbara
Pioneer Joint Vocational
HS
Shelby OH

Schroeder Craig
Chagrin Falls HS
Chagrin Falls OH

Schroeder Robert G
New Buffalo HS
New Buffalo MI

Schroeder Sheila Mie
Cathedral HS
Indianapolis IN

Schroer Kathy I
Defiance Sr HS
Defiance OH

Schroll Kathryn
Bishop Borgess HS
Detroit MI

Schroyer Diana
Heath HS
Heath OH

Schrutt Jim
Pittsford HS
Pittsford MI

Schueller Dean
Fraser HS
Fraser MI

Schuster Robert
Troy HS
Troy MI

STUDENTS
PHOTOGRAPH
SCHEDULED
FOR PUBLI-
CATION HERE
COULD NOT
BE REPRO-
DUCED

Schuette Linda
Elkton Pigeon Bay Port
HS
Pigeon MI

Schuler Pamela
Centerville HS
Spring Valley OH

Schulte Donald
Grosse Pointe North HS
Grosse Pte Wds MI

Schulte Kurt
St Marys Cathedral HS
Saginaw MI

Schultz Brian
Oakridge Sr HS
Muskegon MI

Schultz Denise
Piqua Central HS
Piqua OH

Schultz Gary K
Van Buren HS
Brazil IN

Schultz Laura
Midland Trail HS
Clifftop WV

Schultz Robert A
Maple Hts Sr HS
Maple Hgts OH

Schultz Suzanne
Rensselaer Central HS
Rensselaer IN

Schulz Donata
Euclid HS
Euclid OH

Schulze Danette
Charlotte HS
Charlotte MI

Schumacher Lynda
Woodsfield HS
Woodsfield OH

Schuman Larilee
East Noble HS
Del Norte CO

Schurko Steve
Woodrow Wilson HS
Youngstown OH

Schurr Denise
L C Mohr HS
South Haven MI

Schuster Barbara
Fairmont West HS
Kettering OH

Schuster Mark W
Fremont Ross HS
Fremont OH

Schutte Kelly
Ross Sr HS
Hamilton OH

Schuyler Gregory
William Mason HS
Mason OH

Schwab Raymond
Linden Mc Kinley HS
Columbus OH

Schwab Theresa
Lakota HS
Cincinnati OH

Schwankhaus Karen
Norwood HS
Norwood OH

Schwartz Laurie
Centreville HS
Centreville MI

Schwarz Debbie
Columbiana HS
Columbiana OH

Schweifler Rebecca
Muskegon Sr HS
Muskegon MI

Schweikert Judy
Anderson Sr HS
Cincinnati OH

Schweitzer Mary
Crown Pt HS
Crown Point IN

Schwerzler Andrew
Jackson HS
Massillon OH

Schwieterman James
Marion Local HS
Maria Stein OH

Schwind Tami
Chagrin Falls HS
Chagrin Falls OH

Sciranko Deborah
Trinity HS
Maple Hts OH

Scites Eric
Meigs HS
Pomeroy OH

Scobbo James
Stow Sr HS
Stow OH

Scobey Robert
Wayland HS
Wayland MI

Scopel Annette
Crestline HS
Crestline OH

Scopel Babette M
Crestline HS
Crestline OH

Scott Barbara A
Cloverleaf HS
Seville OH

Scott Barbara F
Cloverdale HS
Quincy IN

Scott Cynthia
Oak Hill HS
Fayetteville WV

Scott David
Mansfield Christian HS
Mansfield OH

Scott David L
Gilmer County HS
Linn WV

Scott Donna
Wood Memorial HS
Francisco IN

Scott James
Watkins Memorial HS
Pataskala OH

Scott Janet
Woodward HS
Cincinnati OH

Scott Karen
Midland Trail HS
Rainelle WV

Scott Laura
Waterloo HS
Atwater OH

Scott Martha
Springfield Cathlc Ctrl HS
San Antonio TX

Scott Randy
Colonel Crawford HS
Bucyrus OH

Scott Robert
Pineville HS
Pineville WV

Scott Robert
North White School Corp
Buffalo IN

Scott Robin
Maplewood Jr Sr HS
Cortland OH

Scott Tammi
Clinton Central HS
Frankfort IN

Scott Todd
St Johns HS
De Witt MI

Scott William R
Woodrow Wilson HS
Beckley WV

Scowden Cindy
William Henry Harrison HS
Lafayette IN

Scripter Michael
North Newton HS
Lake Village IN

Scroggs Brenda
Grafton Sr HS
Grafton WV

Scrogham Loveda
Blue River Valley HS
New Castle IN

Scully Dawn I
Berkeley Springs HS
Berkeley Spgs WV

Seals Judith
Morgantown HS
Morgantwn WV

Seals Sarah
Fraser HS
Fraser MI

Seamon Lisa
Middletown HS
Middletown OH

Searfoss Lois
Ben Davis HS
Indianapolis IN

Searing Rhonda
Rosedale HS
Rosedale IN

Sears Diane
Trinity HS
N Randall OH

Sears Jeff
Centerburg HS
Mt Liberty OH

Seawood Bruce
Indiana Academy
Indianpls IN

Sedlar Jeffrey
Chesaning Union HS
Chesaning MI

Sedlarik Teresa
Mendon HS
Three Rivers MI

STUDENTS
PHOTOGRAPH
SCHEDULED
FOR PUBLI-
CATION HERE
COULD NOT
BE REPRO-
DUCED

Seebohm Monica
North College Hill Jr Sr HS
Cincinnati OH

Seedorf Lora
Liberty Center HS
Liberty Cntr OH

Seely Dave
Barberton HS
Barberton OH

Seen Harry
Gwinn HS
Gwinn MI

Seevers Bill
Frontier HS
Marietta OH

Sefjord Mona
London HS
London OH

Sefton Kathleen R
Catholic Central HS
E Grand Rapids MI

Segaard Elizabeth
Port Clinton HS
Port Clinton OH

Seger Gaylord
Danville Comm HS
Danville IN

Segert Kathy
Crown Point HS
Crown Point IN

Segretario Diana
Struthers HS
Struthers OH

Seguine Gloria
Whiteford HS
Ottawa Lk MI

STUDENTS
PHOTOGRAPH
SCHEDULED
FOR PUBLI-
CATION HERE
COULD NOT
BE REPRO-
DUCED

P—185

Sehl Randy
Bedford Senior HS
Temperance MI

Seibert Anita
Frankfort Sr HS
Frankfort IN

Seibert Jamie
Philip Barbour HS
Philippi WV

Seibert Paula
Hoover HS
North Canton OH

Seigley Lynette
Tiffin Columbian HS
Tiffin OH

Seipel Charles K
Bishop Ready HS
Columbus OH

Seipel George
Wm V Fisher Catholic HS
Lancaster OH

Seitz Karen
Oakwood HS
Dayton OH

Seitz Linda K
Beaver Local HS
Wellsville OH

Seiwert Cynthia
Ursuline Acad
Cincinnati OH

Selby Tina
Engadine HS
Naubinway MI

Seleski Laurie
Hilliard HS
Hilliard OH

Selig Diane
Huntington North HS
Huntington IN

Selig Rose Mary
Shawe Memorial HS
Lexington IN

Sellars Ruth
New Richmond HS
New Rihcmond OH

Sellers Dawn
William Henry Harrison HS
Evansville IN

Sellgren Gregory J
E W Seaholm HS
Birmingham MI

Seltenright Lisa
Laville Jr Sr HS
Plymouth IN

Semans Wendy
Worthington HS
Worthington OH

Semer Scott
North Central HS
Pioneer OH

Semon Kristin
Rutherford B Hayes HS
Delaware OH

Sena Mark
Lakeview HS
Cortland OH

Sena Monica
Lakeview HS
Cortland OH

Senff Tracy
Manchester HS
Barberton OH

Seng Michele
Mona Shores HS
Muskegon MI

Seratt William
Marion L Steele HS
Amherst OH

Serfozo Linda
Newark Sr HS
Newark OH

Sesher Timothy R
Ironton HS
Ironton OH

Settle Lynn
Gallia Academy HS
Gallipolis OH

Setzler David
Clyde Sr HS
Clyde OH

Setzler Donald
Clyde HS
Clyde OH

Seubert John
East Central HS
Sunman IN

Severance Carol
John F Kennedy HS
York PA

Seward Jeanine
All Saints Central HS
Bay City MI

Sewell Mark J
Andrean HS
Merrillville IN

Sexton Kenneth
Northrop HS
Bradenton FL

Sexton Linda
Portsmouth HS
Portsmouth OH

Sexton Ronald L
Williamsburg HS
Williamsburg OH

Seybold Erin
North Side HS
Ft Wayne IN

Seyfried Timothy
Colerain Sr HS
Cincinnati OH

Seymour Danielle
Westfall HS
Orient OH

Shackelford Michelle
West Preston Sr HS
Arthurdale WV

Shadbolt Brian
Gorham Fayette HS
Fayette OH

Shade Vicki D
Hedgesville HS
Martinsburg WV

Shadowen Robin
Midland Trail HS
Ansted WV

Shafer Dorene
Penn HS
S Bend IN

Shafer Kristi
Marion Harding HS
Marion OH

Shafer Penny
La Ville Jr Sr HS
Lakeville IN

Shaffer Cindy
East Preston Sr HS
Terra Alta WV

Shaffer Dawn
Columbia City Joint HS
Columbia City IN

Shaffer Diana
Northrop HS
Ft Wayne IN

Shaffer Julia
Northrop HS
Fort Wayne IN

STUDENTS
PHOTOGRAPH
SCHEDULED
FOR PUBLI-
CATION HERE
COULD NOT
BE REPRO-
DUCED

Shaffer Lisa
Smithville HS
Marshallvl OH

Shaffer Lori
Holt HS
Mason MI

Shaffer Mark
Ursuline HS
Campbell OH

Shaffer Nanette
Utica HS
Utica MI

Shaffer Theresa
Penta County Vocational
HS
Whitehouse OH

Shaffner Sandra A
Lakota HS
W Chester OH

Shahadey Charles
Terre Haute S Vigo HS
Terre Haute IN

Shahan Christina
Utica HS
Utica MI

Shalhoub Elizabeth
John Glenn HS
Westland MI

Shallenberger Ray
Hobart HS
Hobart IN

Shamp Jeff
Mc Cutcheon HS
Lafayette IN

Shanahan Thomas J
Penn HS
South Bend IN

Shandle Philip G
Defiance HS
Defiance OH

Shaneff Angeline
Cardinal Ritter HS
Indianaplis IN

Shangle Kathleen
Meridian Sr HS
Sanford MI

Shank Debra
Lincolnview HS
Middle Pt OH

Shank Tammy
Perrysburg HS
Perrysburg OH

Shank Vickie E
Huntington HS
Huntington WV

Shankle Kim
Massillon Washington
HS
Massillon OH

Shanklin Regina
Charleston Catholic HS
Charleston WV

Shannon Angela
Theodore Roosevelt HS
Gary IN

Shannon Kathy
Indianapolis Baptist HS
Indianapolis IN

Sharkey Lori
William G Mather HS
Munising MI

Sharp Carola
Union County HS
Liberty IN

Sharp Felicia
Pocahontas Cnty HS
Marlinton WV

Sharp Linda
South Dearborn HS
Aurora IN

Shaudys Amy
Grandview Heights HS
Columbus OH

Shaver Jacqueline R
Lewis County HS
Weston WV

Shaw Brenda
New Washington HS
Nabb IN

Shaw Charles T
La Porte HS
La Porte IN

Shaw Kevin
Greenfield Central HS
Greenfield IN

Shaw Patti D
Mississinewa HS
Marion IN

Shaw Sally
Wm Henry Harrison HS
Evansville IN

Shay John
Chaminade Julienne HS
Dayton OH

Shearer Amy
Upper Sandusky HS
Upper Sandusky OH

Shearer Constance
Munster HS
Munster IN

Shears Lori
Wirt County HS
Elizabeth WV

Sheehan Elizabeth
Lumen Cordium HS
Maple Hts OH

Sheehan Kerry
Woodrow Wilson HS
Beckley WV

Sheets Carina
Arthur Hill HS
Saginaw MI

Sheets Debbie
Churubusco HS
Churubusco IN

Sheets Johnetta
Ridgewood HS
Coshocton OH

Sheets Ronald
Buchanan HS
Buchanan MI

Sheets Scott
Chesapeake HS
Chesapeake OH

Sheets William D
Chesterton Sr HS
Chesterton IN

Sheetz Susan
Rochester Comm HS
Rochester IN

Sheffield Brenda
Little Miami HS
Goshen OH

Sheffield Eric W
Adrian HS
Adrian MI

Sheffield Tammy
Olmsted Falls HS
Olmsted Falls OH

Shelby Jr Kenneth
Jennings County HS
North Vernon IN

Sheldon Raymond
Columbiana HS
Columbiana OH

Sheline Beth
Thomas A De Vilbiss HS
Toledo OH

Shell J Michael
Greenville Sr HS
Greenville OH

Shellabarger Diane
Mendon Union HS
Mendon OH

Shelley Shannon
Decatur Central HS
Camby IN

Shelton Angela
Taylor HS
Kokomo IN

Shelton Dana
Franklin HS
Franklin OH

Shelton David B
Aiken Sr HS
Cincinnati OH

Shelton La
L C Mohr HS
South Haven MI

Shelton Nancy
Aiken Sr HS
Cincinnati OH

Shelton Randy
Princeton HS
Princeton WV

Shelton Ron
Terre Haute South Vigo
HS
Terre Haute IN

STUDENTS
PHOTOGRAPH
SCHEDULED
FOR PUBLI-
CATION HERE
COULD NOT
BE REPRO-
DUCED

Shepard Alan
Brownstown Central HS
Brownstown IN

Shepard Ann M
Elyria Catholic HS
Elyria OH

Shepard Thomas
Ashtabula HS
Ashtabula OH

Shepeck David K
Escanaba Area HS
Escanaba MI

Shepherd Craig
Centerville HS
Centerville OH

Shepherd Robin
Marshall HS
Marshall MI

Shepherd Tina
Shelby Sr HS
Shelby OH

Shepherd Yvonne Y
East HS
Columbus OH

Sheppard Elizabeth
Black River HS
Polk OH

Sheppard Mark
Parkersburg HS
Vienna WV

Sheppard Mark A
Northwestern HS
West Salem OH

Sheppard Tammy
Waverly HS
Waverly OH

Sherer Angela
Clay Sr HS
Oregon OH

Sherk Eric
Marquette Sr HS
Marquette MI

Sherman Audrey
Monroe HS
Monroe MI

Sherman Debra
Brighton HS
Brighton MI

Sherman Michael
Pike Delta York Sr HS
Delta OH

Sherman Ray
Greenbrier East HS
Alderson WV

Sherrard Pam
Henryville HS
Henryville IN

Sherwood Gary
Ellet HS
Akron OH

Sherwood Theresa
Pinckney HS
Pinckney MI

Shible Marilyn
Bedford Sr HS
Temperance MI

Shields Julie
Williamsburg HS
Williamsburg OH

Shields Ken
North Newton HS
Demotte IN

Shields Rika
Doddridge County HS
West Union WV

Shike Scott
Martinsville HS
Martinsville IN

Shillingburg Patricia
Elk Garden HS
Keyser WV

Shimko Michael
Eastlake North HS
Eastlake OH

Shimp Jennifer
Marquette Sr HS
Marquette MI

Shimp Richard
Buchtel HS
Mogadore OH

Shinaberry Theresa
Pocahontas County HS
Frank WV

Shine John
Mount Healthy HS
Cincinnati OH

Shingler Patricia J
Alexander HS
Albany OH

Shingleton Connie L
Beaver Local HS
Rogers OH

Shininger Stephen
Fairview HS
Defiance OH

Shinn Lydia
Licking Valley HS
Newark OH

Shinn Tammy
William Henry Harrison
HS
West Lafayette IN

Shiomi Takeyuki
Heath HS
Granville OH

Shipe Pamela
Wadsworth Sr HS
Wadsworth OH

Shirley Ann
North Central HS
Indianapolis IN

Shirley Anthony D
East Edison HS
Milan OH

Shively Benjamin
Cadillac Sr HS
Cadillac MI

Shockley Shelley
Regina HS
E Cleveland OH

Shockney Amy
Traverse City Sr HS
Traverse City MI

Shoemaker Adam P
Madison Plains HS
London OH

Shoemaker Cindy
Cardington Lincoln HS
Fulton OH

Shoemaker Karen
London HS
London OH

Shoemaker Scott
Parkside HS
Jackson MI

Shoffner Michael
Shaker Hts Sr HS
Shaker Hts OH

Shook Gwendolyn
Herbert Henry Dow HS
Midland MI

Shoopman Joe
West Muskingom HS
Zanesville OH

Short Beth
South Harrison HS
Lost Creek WV

Short Karen
St Francis De Sales HS
Westerville OH

Short Russell
Midpark HS
Brook Park OH

Short Todd
Coldwater HS
Coldwater MI

Short William
Wapakoneta Sr HS
Wapakoneta OH

Shoub Chris
Huntington East HS
Huntington WV

Shoup Cheryl
Marion HS
Marion IN

Shoup Kimberly
Upper Valley Jt Voc Schl
Troy OH

Shoup Susan
Belleville HS
Belleville MI

Showalter Cathy
Parkersburg HS
Parkersburg WV

Showalter Cindy
Barr Reeve HS
Montgomery IN

Showman Joyce
Evergreen HS
Delta OH

Shrader Sally
Centerville HS
Centerville OH

Shramo Chris
Jackson Milton HS
Lake Milton OH

Shrestha Deepika
Bowling Green HS
Bowling Green OH

Shreve Ed
Zane Trace HS
Chillicothe OH

Shrewsbury Kathy
Shady Spring HS
Beaver WV

Shrewsbury Loretta S
Herndon HS
Herndon WV

Shrewsbury Tina
Matoaka HS
Matoaka WV

Shriner Kenneth
Stevenson HS
Livonia MI

Shriver Debby
Norwood HS
Norwood OH

Shriver Janet M
Triton Central HS
Fairland IN

Shriver Jeff
Lakeview HS
Cortland OH

Shriver Katherine
Meadowbrook HS
Pleasant City OH

Shull Lori
Garrett HS
Auburn IN

Shull Sandy
De Kalb HS
Auburn IN

Shultz Charles C
Danville HS
Danville OH

Shultz Randall
Cedar Lake Academy
Cedar Lake MI

Shuneson Kevin
Charlotte HS
Charlotte MI

Shust Bill
Manistique HS
Manistique MI

Shuster II R
Roosevelt Wilson HS
Stonewood WV

Shutt Peggy
Coshocton HS
Coshocton OH

Sibberson Michael F
Elkhart Memorial HS
Elkhart IN

Sibert Daniel
Clermont Northeastern
HS
Batavia OH

Sibrel Kathy
Tell City HS
Cannelton IN

Sibrik Terri
Eastmoor Sr HS
Columbus OH

Sickles Halden A
Bridgeport Sr HS
Bridgeport WV

Sickling Kelly J
Brandywine Sr HS
Niles MI

Sickmiller Tamela
North Central HS
Montpelier OH

Siders Becky
Millersport HS
Millersport OH

Sidle Kris
Tell City HS
Tell City IN

Siebenaler Bill
Hamilton Comm HS
Hamilton IN

Sieber Jeffrey D
Delphi Cmnty HS
Camden IN

Siegel Cathryn
Sycamore HS
Cincinnati OH

Siekierka Matthew
Walter E Stebbins HS
Dayton OH

Siekman Tracy
Wood Memorial HS
Buckskin IN

Siens Tina
Clinton Massie HS
Wilmington OH

Siers Jeffrey
Bluefield HS
Bluefield WV

Sievert Jeff
Chesterton HS
Chesterton IN

Sigler Janice
Garrett HS
Auburn IN

Siglow Kimberly
Rogers HS
Toledo OH

Sigman Becky
Benton Central HS
Montmorenci IN

Sigman Margie
Stow HS
Munroe Fl OH

Signore Michael A
St Philip Cath Cntrl HS
Battle Creek MI

Sikkila Kevin
L Anse HS
L Anse MI

Sikorski Ellen
Garden City West Sr HS
Garden City MI

Silders Guntars R
Kirtland HS
Kirtland OH

Silecky Markian
Lorain Catholic HS
Lorain OH

Silvani Michael
Southgate HS
Southgate MI

Silvers Nancy
Eaton HS
Eaton OH

Silverthorn Carol
St Joseph HS
Saint Joseph MI

Silvester Toni
Portage Lakes Jnt Voc
Schl
Akron OH

Simbob Loretta
Kingsford HS
Quinnesec MI

Simcox Connie
Springfield Local HS
Newspringfield OH

Simens Mark
Lake Catholic HS
Solon OH

Simerlink Debbie
Beavercreek HS
Dayton OH

Simkins Amy
West Jefferson HS
W Jefferson OH

Simkins Tanya
Springfield Local HS
Petersburg OH

Simmermacher Brian
Crestline HS
Crestline OH

Simmermon Debra
Felicity Franklin HS
Felicity OH

Simmers Jeffrey L
Licking Valley HS
Nashport OH

Simmons Bonnie
Elkins HS
Elkins WV

Simmons Boyd
Liberty HS
Clarksburg WV

Simmons David
Hauser Jr Sr HS
Columbus IN

Simmons Helycia
Notre Dame Academy
Toledo OH

Simmons Jeffrey R
Rensselaer Central HS
Hereford AZ

Simmons Karen
Findlay HS
Findlay OH

Simmons Kay
Marshall HS
Albion MI

Simmons Kelly
East Noble HS
Kendallville IN

Simmons Rebecca L
North Ridgeville Sr HS
N Ridgeville OH

Simmons Robert
Pocahontas County HS
Hillsboro WV

Simmons Robin
Greenview HS
So Solon OH

Simmons Tresa L
Bronson HS
Bronson MI

Simms Catherine
Cardington Lincoln HS
Cardington OH

Simms Lynn
Arsenal Technical HS
Indianapolis IN

Simms Tammy
E Liverpool HS
E Liverpool OH

Simms Vickii
Oak Hill HS
Oak Hill WV

Simon Cheryl
Pike Delta York Sr HS
Delta OH

Simon Karen
Ionia HS
Ionia MI

Simones Lisa
Catholic Central HS
Enon OH

Simpkins Rhonda
Montcalm HS
Montcalm WV

Simpson Beth
Cass Technical HS
It MI

Simpson Henry B
Greenbrier East HS
White Sul Spgs WV

Simpson Roger A
Whetstone Sr HS
Columbus OH

Simpson Sara
Milton HS
Glenwood WV

Simpson Susan
Cheboygan Area Public
HS
Cheboygan MI

Sims John
Dublin HS
Dublin OH

STUDENTS
PHOTOGRAPH
SCHEDULED
FOR PUBLI-
CATION HERE
COULD NOT
BE REPRO-
DUCED

Sims Susan
Douglas Mac Arthur HS
Saginaw MI

Sinden Lori
Pleasant HS
Marion OH

Singh Pradeep K
Bloomington HS North
Bloomington IN

Singleton Charles
Collinwood HS
Cleveland OH

Singleton Kenton
Copley HS
Akron OH

Sinishtaj Luke
Warren HS
Sterling Hts MI

Sinko Bridget
Regine HS
Euclid OH

Sinsel Betsy
Washington Irving HS
Clarksburg WV

Sipe Kim
Parkway HS
Willshire OH

Sipos Carol
Aquinas HS
Southgate MI

STUDENTS
PHOTOGRAPH
SCHEDULED
FOR PUBLI-
CATION HERE
COULD NOT
BE REPRO-
DUCED

Siragusano Tracey
Jefferson Union HS
Richmond OH

Sison Editha
Terre Haute South Vigo
HS
Terre Haute IN

Sisson Lauralee
Brown County HS
Morgantown IN

Sisson Sandy
Elgin HS
La Rue OH

Sitch Mark
Mount Vernon Academy
Youngstown OH

Sitek Gerald
Southgate Aquinas HS
Southgate MI

Sivley Cheryl
New Palestine HS
Greenfield IN

Sivo John
Field HS
Kent OH

Six David L
Oak Glenn HS
Lisbon OH

Six Kelly
Lima Sr HS
Lima OH

Sizelove Jeff
Alexandria Monroe HS
Alexandria IN

Sizemore Anna
Northfork HS
Northfork WV

Sizemore Melissa A
Garfield Sr HS
Hamilton OH

Sizemore Scott
Northfork HS
Northfork WV

Skaggs Beth
Grafton Sr HS
Grafton WV

Skarbek Ann
St Josephs HS
South Bend IN

Skarica Doris
Euclid Sr HS
Euclid OH

Skatula Frank
Buckeye South HS
Dillonvale OH

Skeels David
Anderson HS
Anderson IN

Skeltis Anthony
Chesaning HS
Burt MI

Skiba Hollee
Alpena Sr HS
Alpena MI

Skidmore Larry D
Gilmer County HS
Kingsport TN

Skidmore Linda
Dominican HS
Detroit MI

Skinner Albert
Anderson HS
Anderson IN

Skinner Beth
Harbor HS
Ashtabula OH

Skinner Debbie
Madison HS
Adrian MI

Skinner Maruice L
Bronson HS
Bronson MI

Skinner Michael J
Green HS
Akron OH

Skinner Wayne
Flint Christian HS
Mt Morris MI

Sklenar Susie
Shenandoah HS
Belle Valley OH

Skoczylas Denise M
Southwestern
Community HS
Flint MI

Skomp John
John Skomp HS
Greenfield IN

Skrok Linda
Warren Woods Public HS
Warren MI

Skrzyniarz Cathy
Center Line HS
Warren MI

Skrzypczak Sherry
Fraser HS
Fraser MI

Skubby Sue
Parma Sr HS
Parma OH

Skulich Sara
Steubenville Cath Cntrl
HS
Steubenvll OH

Skutt Wayne
E A Johnson HS
Mt Morris MI

Slabaugh Jean
John Adams HS
So Bend IN

Slabaugh Joan
John Adams HS
So Bend IN

Slagel Kathy
Ironton HS
Ironton OH

Slais Robert
Walled Lake Central HS
Orchard Lake MI

Slaman Sarah
Bay HS
Bay Village OH

Slaon Mark
Princeton Community HS
Princeton IN

Slater Alicia
Trenton HS
Trenton MI

Slawson Rick
Lincoln HS
Vincennes IN

Sleek S Ginger
Newark Sr HS
Newark OH

Slessman Doreen
Willard HS
Plymouth OH

Slivinski Richard
Northwest HS
Clinton OH

Sloan Charles
Lebanon Sr HS
Lebanon IN

Slocum Lynne
Saginaw HS
Saginaw MI

Slone Donna
Richmond Sr HS
Richmond IN

Slotman Cindy S
Fennville HS
Fennville MI

Slotman Mary
Byron Center HS
Byron Center MI

Sluder Vicki
Cloverdale HS
Cloverdale IN

Small Jennifer
Hamilton Heights HS
Arcadia IN

Smalley Julia
Tri HS
Spiceland IN

Smarelli James R
Richmond Sr HS
Richmond IN

Smart Sally A
Attica HS
Attica IN

Smead Rebecca
Notre Dame Academy
Toledo OH

Smerglia Catherine
Field HS
Mogadore OH

Smiley Mary
Mooresville HS
Camby IN

Smiley Teresa
Dayton Christian HS
Dayton OH

Smith Alyce
Shady Spring HS
Beaver WV

Smith Andy
Maumee HS
Maumee OH

Smith Angela E
Cardinal Ritter HS
Indianapolis IN

Smith April
Triad HS
Urbana OH

Smith Barb
Parkersburg South HS
Parkersburg WV

Smith Barbara
Franklin Central HS
Indpls IN

Smith Barbara
Anderson Sr HS
Anderson IN

Smith Bart
National Trail HS
W Manchester OH

Smith Belinda
Wayne HS
Ft Wayne IN

Smith Beth
Franklin Cmnty HS
Franklin IN

Smith Beverly
Saline HS
Saline MI

Smith Bonita
Chaminade Julienne HS
Dayton OH

Smith Brad
Holland Chrstn HS
Holland MI

Smith Bradford
Adrian Sr HS
Adrian MI

Smith Bradley
Addison HS
Addison MI

Smith Brenda
St Marys HS
Bens Run WV

Smith Carolyn
Woodrow Wilson HS
Beckley WV

Smith Carron
St Marys HS
Hebron WV

Smith Chancellor
Emerson HS
Gary IN

Smith Cheryl
Lutheran HS East
Cleveland OH

Smith Cheryl
Wooster HS
Wooster OH

Smith Cheryl
Ecorse HS
Ecorse MI

Smith Christopher
Bishop Dwenger HS
Ft Wayne IN

Smith Claire
Mansfield Sr HS
Mansfield OH

Smith Cynthia
Caro Community HS
Caro MI

Smith Dane
Watkins Memorial HS
Baltimore OH

Smith Dave
Stow HS
Munroe Falls OH

Smith David
Boonville HS
Boonville IN

Smith David G
Douglas Mac Arthur HS
Saginaw MI

Smith Dean
Coventry HS
Barberton OH

Smith Deanne
North Central HS
Kunkle OH

Smith Debi
Cadiz HS
New Athens OH

Smith Denise
Decatur HS
Decatur MI

STUDENTS
PHOTOGRAPH
SCHEDULED
FOR PUBLI-
CATION HERE
COULD NOT
BE REPRO-
DUCED

Smith Diane
Colon HS
Sherwood MI

STUDENTS
PHOTOGRAPH
SCHEDULED
FOR PUBLI-
CATION HERE
COULD NOT
BE REPRO-
DUCED

Smith Donna
Harman HS
Dry Fork WV

Smith Douglas
Gibsonburg HS
Gibsonburg OH

Smith Duane
De Kalb HS
Waterloo IN

Smith Edgar L
Catholic Central HS
Southfield MI

Smith Effie M
Marian Heights Academy
Chicago IL

Smith Gary
Jennings County HS
Scipio IN

Smith Gerald R
Buckeye North HS
Mingo Jct OH

Smith Glenda
Mount View HS
Welch WV

Smith Gloria
Washington Sr HS
Washington OH

Smith Greg
Frontier HS
Newport OH

Smith Gregory
Brooke HS
Wellsburg WV

Smith Gregory R
Tygarts Valley HS
Dailey WV

Smith Jackie K
Pennfield HS
Bellevue MI

Smith James
Southgate HS
Southgate MI

Smith Jeannette
Ovid Elsie HS
Ovid MI

Smith Jeff
Washington Irving HS
Clarksburg WV

Smith Jeff
Lake HS
Walbridge OH

Smith Jeff
Blanchester HS
Blanchester OH

Smith Jeffrey D
Athens HS
Troy MI

Smith Jennifer L
Lemon Monroe HS
Monroe OH

Smith Jerry
Brookville HS
Brookville IN

Smith Jill
Lexington HS
Mansfield OH

Smith Jim
Mona Shores HS
Muskegon MI

Smith Joel
Tippecanoe Valley HS
Claypool IN

Smith Joe R
Elkins HS
Elkins WV

Smith John
Mount View HS
Superior WV

Smith Julie
Huntington North HS
Huntington IN

Smith Kathy
Marlette HS
Snover MI

Smith Kathy
Hammond Baptist HS
Chicago IL

Smith Katrina
Immaculata HS
Detroit MI

Smith Kaye Y
Osborn Sr HS
Detroit MI

Smith Kelly
Euclid Sr HS
Willoughby OH

Smith Kevin
Columbia City Joint HS
Columbia City IN

Smith Kristi
South Amherst HS
S Amherst OH

Smith Kristine
Hastings HS
Hastings MI

Smith La Vella
Everett HS
Lansing MI

Smith Leanne M
Tuslaw HS
Massillon OH

Smith Leslie
Flushing HS
Flushing MI

Smith Leslie
Stonewall Jackson HS
Charleston WV

Smith Linda
Brooke HS
Beech Bottom WV

Smith Linda
Adrian Sr HS
Adrian MI

Smith Lisa
Lake Central HS
Dyer IN

Smith Luann
Fowler HS
Fowler MI

Smith Lynne
Grandview Hts HS
Columbus OH

Smith Marcia M
John H Patterson Coop HS
Dayton OH

Smith Margaret
Columbia HS
Columbia Sta OH

Smith Mark
Vinson HS
Huntington WV

Smith Marsha
Lemon Monroe HS
Middletown OH

Smith Martalyn
Central Hower HS
Akron OH

Smith Michael
Bishop Foley HS
Hazel Pk MI

Smith Michael L
Traverse City HS
Traverse City MI

Smith Michael L
Ripley HS
Ripley WV

Smith Nancie
Rocky River HS
Rocky Rvr OH

Smith O Key
Williamson HS
Chattaroy WV

Smith Ozro
Sault Area HS
Sault Ste Marie MI

Smith Pat
Heritage HS
Monroeville IN

Smith Patricia
Argos Cmnty School
Argos IN

Smith Patrick J
Reynoldsburg HS
Reynoldsburg OH

Smith Paula
Clinton Prairie HS
Mulberry IN

Smith Randy
Alma HS
Alma MI

Smith Rebecca
Rutherford B Hayes HS
Delaware OH

Smith Rebecca
Warren Central HS
Indpls IN

Smith Rick
Lincolnview HS
Van Wert OH

Smith Robin
Amelia HS
Cincinnati OH

Smith Ronald
Zanesville HS
Zanesville OH

Smith Rosemary
Archbold Area HS
Archbold OH

Smith Roxane
Westside HS
Gary IN

Smith Roy
Richmond Sr HS
Richmond IN

Smith Rusty
Wynford HS
Bucyrus OH

Smith Ruth
Jackson Center HS
Jackson Cntr OH

Smith Sara
National Trail HS
Eaton OH

Smith Scott
Buffalo HS
Huntington WV

Smith Scott V
La Ville HS
Lakeville IN

Smith Selena S
Fairfield HS
Fairfield OH

Smith Sheila
Catholic Cntrl HS
Steubenville OH

Smith Shelly
Niles HS
Niles MI

Smith Sheri
East HS
Columbus OH

Smith Stephanie
South HS
Youngstown OH

Smith Susan
Bucyrus Sr HS
Bucyrus OH

STUDENTS
PHOTOGRAPH
SCHEDULED
FOR PUBLI-
CATION HERE
COULD NOT
BE REPRO-
DUCED

Smith T
Ben Davis HS
Indianapolis IN

Smith Terrence
St Francis De Sales HS
Erie MI

Smith Terrilee
Harry S Truman HS
Taylor MI

Smith Terrill
Onsted Community HS
Clayton MI

Smith Theresa
Marsh Fork HS
Rock Crk WV

Smith Thomas H
London HS
London OH

Smith Thomas S
Wellsville HS
Wellsville OH

Smith Trudy
Zanesville HS
Zanesville OH

Smith Veronica
East HS
Columbus OH

Smith Vickie
S Spencer HS
Richland IN

Smith Wanda
Mount View HS
Welch WV

Smith Wes
Mohawk HS
Melmore OH

Smitherman James Otis
C
St Xavier HS
Cincinnati OH

Smitley La Nae
Adams Central HS
Monroe IN

Smits Peter
Redford HS
Detroit MI

Smoot Diana
East HS
Columbus OH

Smoot Joseph
Hampshire HS
Romney WV

Smulo Jody
Trinity HS
Maple Hts OH

Smyczynski Stephen N
Cardinal Mooney HS
Youngstown OH

Smyles Shirley
Lumen Cordium HS
Garfield Hts OH

Smyth Scott L
Champion HS
Warren OH

Smyth Shelly
Howell Sr HS
Howell MI

Snavely Tammy
Delphi Community HS
Camden IN

Snead Ronald
East Kentwood HS
Kentwood MI

Snider Harold
Lebanon HS
Lebanon OH

Snider Mary L
Milton HS
Milton WV

Snider Randy
Delta HS
Albany IN

Snider Sally
Dexter HS
Dexter MI

Snitzer Robert
Ursuline HS
Campbell OH

Snively Mark
Lexington HS
Mansfield OH

Snodgrass Darren
Avon HS
Plainfield IN

Snodgrass Kim
South Charleston HS
South Charlestn WV

Snoor Ruth L
Newark Sr HS
Newark OH

Snowden Annette
Gallia Academy
Gallipolis OH

Snuffer Daniel H
Independence HS
Coal City WV

Snyder Cynthia
Port Clinton Sr HS
Pt Clinton OH

Snyder Dana
Webster County HS
Webster Springs WV

Snyder Denise
Whitmer HS
Toledo OH

STUDENTS
PHOTOGRAPH
SCHEDULED
FOR PUBLI-
CATION HERE
COULD NOT
BE REPRO-
DUCED

Snyder Mary
Madison Plains HS
London OH

Snyder Penny
Garaway HS
Baltic OH

Snyder Rebecca
Grace Christian School
Benton Harbor MI

Snyder Rhonda
Our Lady Of Angels HS
Cincinnati OH

Snyder William
Jimtown HS
Elkhart IN

Sobczyk Ken
Bloomingdale HS
Grand Junction MI

Sober Laura
Fowlerville HS
Fowlerville MI

Sobeski Michael
Shady Spring HS
Shady Spring WV

Sofikitis Irene
Brookfield HS
Brookfield OH

Sokeland Justin
Orleans HS
Orleans IN

Solero Narciso
Northrop HS
Ft Wayne IN

Solmen David
Crestview Local HS
Columbia OH

Soloko Jenine
Holly Sr HS
Holly MI

Solomon Steven
Luke M Powers HS
Grand Blanc MI

Solter Jeffrey
Wintersville HS
Wintersville OH

Somerville Janice
North Farmington HS
Farmington Hil MI

Sommer Douglas
Standish Sterling Cntrl
HS
Standish MI

Sommerfeldt Denise
Hartford HS
Hartford MI

Sommers Daniel
Browsburg HS
Indianapolis IN

Sommers Lynn
Clarkston Sr HS
Davisburg MI

Sommerville Troy
South Harrison HS
Wolf Summit WV

Sonefeld Jennifer
Douglas Mac Arthur HS
Saginaw MI

Sonnenberg Edmund J
Madison Comprehensive
HS
Mansfield OH

Sonner Angeline
Corydon Central HS
Mauckport IN

Sonneville Shari
Pennfield HS
Battle Creek MI

Sorg Chris
Washington HS
Massillon OH

Sorg Lori
Heritage HS
Ft Wayne IN

Sorg Mary Ann
Fremont Ross HS
Fremont OH

Sorovetz John S
Gabriel Richard HS
Southgate MI

Sorrell Martin
Wellston HS
Jackson OH

Sorrell Scott
Keystone HS
La Grange OH

Sotiropoulos Thomas J
Kettering Fairmont East
HS
Kettering OH

Soto Michael
Bettsville HS
Bettsville OH

Soucek David
Normandy Sr HS
Seven Hls OH

Souchock Carol
Fordson HS
Dearborn MI

Souders Angie
Findlay HS
Findlay OH

Soule Elizabeth
Theodore Roosevelt HS
Kent OH

Soulliere Judy
Algonac HS
Harsens Island MI

Southerland Lenore
The Rayen School
Youngstown OH

Southland Mark
St Joseph Sr HS
St Joseph MI

Southward Mary
Kearsley HS
Flint MI

Southworth Debbra
Miami Trace HS
Washington C H OH

Sova Stephen A
Bishop Watterson HS
Columbus OH

Sovis John
Ovid Elsie HS
Elsie MI

Sowar Judith
Archbishop Alter HS
Dayton OH

Sowders Bettie
Bedford North Lawrence
HS
Bedford IN

Sowers Kim
Peterstown HS
Peterstown WV

Sowers Laura
Van Wert HS
Van Wert OH

Sowles Greg
Northrop HS
Ft Wayne IN

Spade Brenda
Meadow Bridge HS
Rainelle WV

Spaeth Penny
Rushville Consolidated
HS
Rushville IN

Spaeth Tim
Lebanon HS
Lebanon OH

Spalding Gary
Jefferson HS
Lafayette IN

Spallinger Mindy
Cory Rawson HS
Bluffton OH

STUDENTS
PHOTOGRAPH
SCHEDULED
FOR PUBLI-
CATION HERE
COULD NOT
BE REPRO-
DUCED

Sparkman Lisa
Eastern HS
Salem IN

Sparks Bonita M
Rogers HS
Toledo OH

Sparks Sally
Fruitport HS
Spring Lake MI

Sparling Daniel J
Northfield HS
Wabash IN

Sparling Mary
Marysville HS
Smiths Creek MI

Spatafore Teresa
Liberty HS
Clarksburg WV

Spaulding Amy
Cardinal Stritch HS
Genoa OH

Speakman Debra
Southeastern HS
Kingston OH

Spears Gina
Ellison Sr HS
Lake Station IN

Specht Brian
Fairless HS
Beach City OH

STUDENTS
PHOTOGRAPH
SCHEDULED
FOR PUBLI-
CATION HERE
COULD NOT
BE REPRO-
DUCED

Speer Jeanetta
Jennings Co HS
No Vernon IN

Speer Terri L
E Lansing HS
E Lansing MI

Speicher Melvin
Tuslaw HS
Massillon OH

Spencer Dawn
Bluefield HS
Bluefield WV

Spencer Dwayne J
Northfork HS
Eckman WV

Spencer Jeffrey
Athens HS
Athens WV

Spencer Jimmie
Kelloggsville HS
Wyoming MI

Spencer Kathleen B
Liberty HS
Salem WV

Spencer Lonnie
Morrice Area HS
Owosso MI

Spencer Scott
Hudson HS
Hudson OH

Spencer Sharyn
Ursuline HS
Campbell OH

Spencer Wilfred
Martin Luther King Jr HS
Detroit MI

Sperow Vickie
Ovid Elsie HS
Ovid MI

Spiegel Scott
Colonel Crawford HS
Sulphur Springs OH

Spiegel Shelley A
Cuyahoga Vlly Christian
Acad
Akron OH

Spiker Kelly
Zanesville HS
Zanesville OH

Spiker Melanie
S Harrison HS
Lost Creek WV

Spiller Elisa
Fairview HS
Fairview Park OH

Spisak Patricia
Lowell Sr HS
Lowell IN

Spitsnaugle Tim
Mc Comb HS
Mccomb OH

Spohn Wendi
Fowlerville HS
Fowlerville MI

Sponaugle Steven A
Tucker County HS
Hendricks WV

Sponn Anna
Washington Catholic HS
Washington IN

Spooner Patty
David Anderson HS
Lisbon OH

Sposato Michael
Columbiana HS
Columbiana OH

Spradlin Scott L
Midland Trail HS
Victor WV

Sprague Sarah
H H Dow HS
Midland MI

Sprang Jerri
Loudonville HS
Loudonville OH

Sprigg William
Danbury HS
Marblehead OH

Sprik Julie
Holland Christian HS
Holland MI

Spring Tammy
William Henry Harrison HS
Evansville IN

Springer Jerry
Norwell HS
Ossian IN

Springer Johnny
Northwest HS
Cincinnati OH

Sprouse Mary P
Liberty HS
Clarksburg WV

Sprouse Monesa
Chillicothe HS
Chillicothe OH

Sprout Tracy
Roosevelt Wilson HS
Clarksburg WV

Sprowls Michael
Medina Sr HS
Medina OH

Sprungl Barbara
Newbury HS
Newbury OH

Spurlock Karen L
William A Wirt HS
Gary IN

Spurlock Patricia J
Danville HS
Danville IN

Squires Michael W
Highland HS
Chesterville OH

Srout Marie
Moorefield HS
Moorefield WV

Staal Pamela
O A Carlson HS
Rockwood MI

Staats Denise
Danville HS
Danville OH

Stacey Carl
Central Catholic HS
Toledo OH

Stackhouse Vicky L
Jeffersonville HS
Jeffersonville IN

Stacklin Duane
Buckeye Central HS
New Washington OH

Staddon Kathy
Univ HS
Morgantown WV

Stadlberger Alden
Greenville HS
Gowen MI

Stadler Alan
North Royalton HS
N Royalton OH

Staffan Lorie
Madison Plains HS
S Solon OH

Stafford Steven
Traverse City Sr HS
Traverse City MI

Stahl Diane
Dekalb HS
Kendallville IN

Stahler Jennifer
West Geauga HS
Chesterland OH

Stainfield Roy
Jefferson HS
Jefferson OH

Stalder Richard
East Canton HS
Louisville OH

Staley Dennis
Martinsburg Sr HS
Martinsburg WV

Staley Laura
Delaware Hayes HS
Delaware OH

Stalnaker Sherry
Kenton Sr HS
Kenton OH

St Amand Diane J
Petoskey Sr HS
Petoskey MI

Stamm Amy
Liberty HS
Salem WV

Stamm Cynthia
Waldron Jr Sr HS
Waldron IN

Stamper Charmae
Columbia HS
Columbia Sta OH

Stander Terri
Leland Public HS
Leland MI

Standish Kelli
Centerville HS
Richmond IN

Stanek Janice L
Euclid Sr HS
Euclid OH

Stanek Laura
St Joseph Academy
Lakewood OH

Stanford Terri
Anderson HS
Anderson IN

Stanley Alesia D
Liberty HS
Mt Clare WV

Stanley Linda
Madison Hts HS
Anderson IN

STUDENTS
PHOTOGRAPH
SCHEDULED
FOR PUBLI-
CATION HERE
COULD NOT
BE REPRO-
DUCED

Stansbery Scott
Upper Sandusky HS
Upper Sandusky OH

Stanton Pamela
Buckhannon Upshur HS
Buckhannon WV

Stap John
Gull Lake HS
Richland MI

Stapleton Michael
Buffalo HS
Kenova WV

Stapleton Teriana
Union City Cmnty HS
Union City IN

Starcher John
Danbury Local HS
Lakeside OH

Starcher Larry W
Parkersburg South HS
Parkersburg WV

Starczewski Kellene D
Andrean HS
Miller Beach IN

Stare Dawn
Howland HS
Warren OH

Stergel Mark
Maconaquah HS
Bunker Hill IN

Stark Robin
South Harrison HS
Clarksburg WV

Starkey Marcia
Bethesda Christian Schls
Brownsberg IL

Starkey Vickie
Buckhannon Upshur HS
Buckhannon WV

Starks Karen
West Side HS
Gary IN

Starkweather Lorie
Edwardsburg HS
Edwardsburg MI

Starr Chris
Muskegon Catholic Cntrl
HS
Kalamazoo MI

Starts Brent E
Memorial HS
St Marys OH

Stasa Camilla
Chesaning HS
Owosso MI

Stassin Lisa
Avon Jr Sr HS
Plainfield IN

Staton G Michael
Malabar HS
Mansfield OH

Staudt Joseph E
Perry HS
Canton OH

Staufenger Mike
Leetonia HS
Leetonia OH

Stavole Judy
Valley Forge HS
Parma Heights OH

Stebelton Kelly
Chelsea HS
Chelsea MI

Steckel Scott W
Hilliard HS
Columbus OH

Steed Tina
Wapakoneta HS
Wapakoneta OH

Steele Cheryl
Franklin HS
Franklin OH

Steele Terri
Harbor HS
Ashtabula OH

Steele Timothy
Roseville HS
Roseville MI

Steen Carl J
Adams HS
South Bend IN

Stefanovsky Luke
Arthur Hill HS
Saginaw MI

Steffen Renee
Berea HS
Brook Pk OH

Steffens Hazel
Philip Barbour HS
Belington WV

Steffey Brett
Warren Central HS
Indpls IN

Stegemoller Lisa
Avon Jr Sr HS
Danville IN

Steger Donna
New Haven HS
New Haven IN

Stegmann Shellie
John Glenn HS
Bay City MI

Stegner Thomas M
Fairborn Baker HS
Fairborn OH

Stein Amy
Riverside HS
Concord OH

Stein Jeffrey
Hartland HS
Hartland MI

Steinbrunner Mary
Bishop Luers HS
Ft Wayne IN

Steiner Jayme
Hubbard HS
Hubbard OH

Steins George E
Rocky River HS
Rocky River OH

Stellhorn Douglas B
Northrop HS
Ft Wayne IN

Stellmar Sharon
Ursuline HS
Campbell OH

Stempek Lawrence
Pinconning Area HS
Pinconning MI

Stemper Mark
Hammond Tech
Hammond IN

Stemple David
E Preston Sr HS
Aurora WV

Stenger Sherry
Mc Auley HS
Cincinnati OH

Stephens Bryon
Highland HS
Highland IN

Stephens Cindy
Pike Central HS
Otwell IN

Stephens Kenna
Brown County HS
Helmsburg IN

Stephens Lisa
Goodrich Area HS
Goodrich MI

Stephens Rochelle
Arcanum Butler Local
Schls
Arcanum OH

Stephens Thomas L
Parkersburg South HS
Parkersburg WV

Stephenson Geoffrey
Huron HS
Huron OH

Stephenson Jill
John Marshall HS
Indianapolis IN

Stephenson Karen
Northwestern HS
West Salem OH

Stephenson Nancy
Marquette Sr HS
Marquette MI

Stepien Brenda
Berea HS
Berea OH

Stepleton Kimberly
Van Wert HS
Van Wert OH

Stepp Benjamin
Bluefield HS
Bluefield WV

Stepro Angela
New Albany Sr HS
New Albany IN

Sterner Jr Robert
Lutheran HS East
Roseville MI

Sterrett Debbie
Ehove Joint Vocational
HS
Vermilion OH

Sterrett Ramon
Central HS
Detroit MI

Sterrett Toyia
Central HS
Detroit MI

Stetler Beth
Celina Sr HS
Celina OH

Stettin Jeanine
Griffith Sr HS
Griffith IN

Stetzel Elizabeth
St Joseph Cntrl
CatholicHS
Fremont OH

Steuk Katherine
North Olmsted Sr HS
N Olmsted OH

Stevens Angela
Warren HS
Marietta OH

Stevens Craig
Plymouth Salem HS
Plymouth MI

Stevens Laura
Creston HS
Grand Rapids MI

Stevens Lisa
Liberty HS
Girard OH

Stevens Tamara
Douglas Mac Arthur HS
Saginaw MI

Stevensen Jeff
Van Buren HS
Findlay OH

Stevenson Amy
Carmel HS
Carmel IN

Stevenson James
Ben Davis HS
Indianapolis IN

Steward Barry
North Putnam Jr Sr HS
Roachdale IN

Steward Bradley
North Putnam Jr Sr HS
Roachdale IN

Steward Jonathan S
Lebanon HS
Oregonia OH

Stewart Alan
Berkley HS
Berkley MI

Stewart Anne
Bridgeport HS
Bridgeport WV

Stewart Beverly
Washington Irving HS
Clarksburg WV

Stewart Cynthia
New Albany HS
New Albany IN

Stewart Elizabeth F
Wahoma HS
Mason WV

Stewart John
Meigs HS
Middleport OH

Stewart Joseph
Cuyahoga Falls HS
Cuyahoga Fls OH

Stewart Kathy
Kankakee Valley HS
Wheatfield IN

Stewart Kenneth
Southgate HS
Southgate MI

Stewart Kimberly
Cass Technical HS
Detroit MI

Stewart Lawrence
Jefferson HS
Shepherdstown WV

Stewart Mark
Carlisle Sr HS
Franklin OH

Stewart Rhonda
Jefferson Union HS
Richmond OH

Stewart Sandra
Southfield HS
Southfield MI

Stewart Stephni
Parkersburg HS
Parkersburg WV

Stewart Tamera
Zanesville HS
Zanesville OH

STUDENTS
PHOTOGRAPH
SCHEDULED
FOR PUBLI-
CATION HERE
COULD NOT
BE REPRO-
DUCED

Stibinger Edith
Euclid Sr HS
Euclid OH

Stick Tammy
New Buffalo HS
New Buffalo MI

Stickney Michaela
Rocky River HS
Rocky Rvr OH

Stidham Steve
Ben Davis HS
Indianapolis IN

Stieber Elizabeth
Monroeville HS
Norwalk OH

Stigdon Dara
Jennings Cnty HS
Elizabethtown IN

Stiles Kathleen Rae
Coventry HS
Uniontown OH

Stiles Marcia L
Clay Battelle HS
Blacksville WV

Stillions Christine
Mitchell Sr HS
Mitchell IN

Stilwell Jeff
Logansport HS
Logansport IN

Stimson Dwight
North Branch HS
Canton MI

Stinnett Mary
Oak Hill HS
Oak Hill WV

Stinnett Shelly
Hurricane HS
Hurricane WV

Stinson Ronald
Shenandoah HS
Daleville IN

Stinson Stacy
Maumee Valley Cntry
Day Schl
Swanton OH

Stis Dianne
Hamilton Southeastern
HS
Noblesville IN

Stitzel Susan
Middletown HS
Middletown OH

Stiverson Arthur
Hudson Area HS
Hudson MI

Stiverson James
Ridgedale HS
Marion OH

Stizman Robert
Scecina HS
Indianapolis IN

Stocker Duane
Jay County HS
Dunkirk IN

Stocker Sue
Newcomerstown HS
Newcomerstown OH

Stockhouse Carla
Munster HS
Munster IN

Stockman Karen
Tippecanoe Vly HS
Sikeston MO

Stodola Gregory
Wahama HS
Mason WV

Stokes Donna
South Dearborn HS
Aurora IN

Stokes Sharon
Carmel HS
Carmel IN

Stoll Greg
Edison HS
Norwalk OH

Stolt Sheila
Harbor Springs HS
Hrbr Spgs MI

Stolz William
Alma HS
Sumner MI

Stone Cambi
Bloomfield HS
Bloomfield IN

STUDENTS
PHOTOGRAPH
SCHEDULED
FOR PUBLI-
CATION HERE
COULD NOT
BE REPRO-
DUCED

Stone Heidi
Indian Creek HS
Martinsville IN

Stone Raymond
N Newton HS
Lake Village IN

Stone Scott
Whiteford HS
Ottawa Lk MI

Stone Tresa
Whitehall HS
Whitehall MI

Stonecash Kent E
Eaton HS
Eaton OH

Stoneking Kay
De Kalb HS
Corunna IN

Stonestreet Steven R
Sissonville HS
Charleston WV

Stong Cynthia
Whitehall HS
Whitehall MI

Stookey Juli
Hobart Sr HS
Hobart IN

Stoppenhagen Dan
Heritage HS
Monroevle IN

Storage Mark A
Lincoln HS
Shinnston WV

Stork Michelle
Davison Sr HS
Davison MI

Storl Heidi
Black River HS
Spencer OH

Story Robert M
Lake Michigan Catholic HS
Benton Hrbr MI

Stott Alana
Central Lake HS
Central Lake MI

Stottler Jeffrey
Barnesville HS
Barnesville OH

Stough Meg
Lebanon HS
Kirklin IN

St Ours Geraldine
St Francis HS
Traverse City MI

Stout Cathy
Lewis County HS
Weston WV

STUDENTS PHOTOGRAPH SCHEDULED FOR PUBLICATION HERE COULD NOT BE REPRODUCED

Stout Luanne
Washington Irving HS
Clarksburg WV

Stover Cynthia
Belleville HS
Ypsilanti MI

Stover Debra
Kyger Creek HS
Gallipolis OH

Stover Keith
Pleasant Local HS
Prospect OH

Stover Michelle
Teays Valley HS
Ashville OH

STUDENTS PHOTOGRAPH SCHEDULED FOR PUBLICATION HERE COULD NOT BE REPRODUCED

Stover William R
Oak Hill HS
Oak Hill WV

Stowell Jon
Hauser Jr Sr HS
Columbus IN

Stowers Teresa S
Gallia Academy HS
Bidwell OH

Stoycheff Tammy
Cardinal Stritch HS
Oregon OH

Strait Brenda
Ansonia Local HS
New Weston OH

Straka Antoinette
Father J Wehrle Mem HS
Columbus OH

Strang Janet
William A Wirt HS
Gary IN

Strasburg Heather
Benton Harbor HS
Benton Hbr MI

STUDENTS PHOTOGRAPH SCHEDULED FOR PUBLICATION HERE COULD NOT BE REPRODUCED

Stratman Anthony
Mater Dei HS
Evansville IN

Stratton Robert
Hill Mccloy HS
Clio MI

Strauser John
St Francis Seminary
Lorain OH

Strauss Joseph
Milford HS
Milford MI

Straw Bill
Clarksville HS
Clarksville IN

Straw Lydia
Rockford HS
Rockford MI

Strayer Diane
Griffith Sr HS
Griffith IN

Strayer Joanne
Riverside HS
Degraff OH

Strayer Paula
Riverside HS
De Graff OH

Straziuso Lisa
St Marys Cntrl Catholic HS
Sandusky OH

Streber Gregory
East Clinton HS
New Vienna OH

Strebick Mary
St Vincent St Mary HS
Akron OH

Street Pamela
Bluefield HS
Bluefield WV

Strickland Monica
Northern HS
Pontiac MI

Strickler Daniel
Holly HS
Holly MI

Strickler Scott
Williamstown HS
Williamstown WV

Strickler Shari
Huntington North HS
Huntington IN

Striggow Lori
Bedford Sr HS
Temperance MI

Stringer Tammy
Girard HS
Girard OH

Stroble Nancy
Reading HS
Reading MI

Strom Renay
Brandon HS
Ortonville MI

Strominger Mark
Bishop Hartley HS
Columbus OH

Strong Alison
Lapeer East HS
Lapeer MI

Strong Randy
Ben Davis HS
Indianapolis IN

Strouf Linda K
Manistee HS
Manistee MI

Strovilas Cris
Toronto HS
Toronto OH

Struble Diane
Champion HS
Warren OH

Struble Thomas
Ainsworth HS
Flint MI

Strudas Bridget
Hobart Sr HS
Hobart IN

Struglinski Jenifer
Revere HS
Akron OH

Strunak Janet
Valley Forge Sr HS
Parma Hts OH

Strunk Sheila
Wood Memorial HS
Oakland City IN

Struyk David
Comstock Park HS
Comstock Pk MI

Stuart J R
South Decatur HS
Westport IN

STUDENTS
PHOTOGRAPH
SCHEDULED
FOR PUBLI-
CATION HERE
COULD NOT
BE REPRO-
DUCED

Stubblefield Cheryl
St Ursula Academy
Toledo OH

Stubblefield Michael
Southwestern HS
Detroit MI

Stuck Susan
Memorial HS
St Marys OH

Stuckey Dean
Hilltop HS
West Unity OH

Stuckey Diane
North Central HS
Indianapolis IN

Stuckey Pam
Hilltop HS
W Unity OH

Stucky Wanda
Garaway HS
New Phila OH

Studer Dan
Homestead HS
Roanoke IN

Stueber Toni
Theodore Roosevelt HS
Kent OH

Stukey Lorraine
Hilliard HS
Amlin OH

Stull Susan
Edward Drummond
Libbey HS
Toledo OH

Stullenbarger Rita
Elk Garden HS
Elk Garden WV

Stultz Kenneth R
Wayne HS
Lavalette WV

Stumbaugh Kelly
Lexington HS
Lexington OH

Stump Kym
Northridge HS
Bristol IN

Stupica Terri
Euclid HS
Euclid OH

Sturgeon Cindy
South Point HS
South Point OH

Sturis Ilze
Winston Churchill HS
Westland MI

Sturm James
Crum HS
Crum WV

Sturm Nathan
Anderson Sr HS
Cincinnati OH

Sturonas Joseph
Gavit HS
Hammond IN

Stuter Robert K
Winfield HS
Scott Depot WV

Styer Joy L
Kenton Sr HS
Kenton OH

Styers Tammi
Buckeye Valley HS
Delaware OH

Styles Rusty A
Warsaw Community HS
Warsaw IN

Suarez Deidre
Cameron HS
Cameron WV

Succi Diana
Ashtabula Cnty Jt Voc
HS
Jefferson OH

Suchecki Todd M
Grand Ledge HS
Lansing MI

Suckow Charles
Marquette Sr HS
Marquette MI

Suckow Paul
North Muskegon HS
N Muskegon MI

Sudo Jonathon
Clawson HS
Clawson MI

Suk Choi Hyun
St Ursula Acad
Toledo OH

Sulisz Susan
Dearborn HS
Deaborn MI

Sullivan Becky
Pt Pleasant HS
Leon WV

Sullivan Chris
Tecumseh HS
Tecumseh MI

Sullivan Chris
St Joseph HS
Euclid OH

Sullivan Jerry G
Eastern Pulaski Cmnty
Schl
Winamac IN

Sullivan Kenneth
Lake Catholic HS
Wickliffe OH

Sullivan Marguerite
Wellsville HS
Wellsville OH

Sullivan Melissa
Taylor HS
Cleves OH

Sullivan Molly
Bishop Foley HS
Royal Oak MI

Sullivan Mortimer J
Archbishop Alter HS
Kettering OH

Sullivan Pat
Carroll HS
Dayton OH

Sullivan Patricia
Maumee HS
Maumee OH

Sullivan Susan
Churchill HS
Livonia MI

Summers Allen
Brandywine HS
Niles MI

Summers Bobbi J
Loogootee HS
Loogootee IN

Sunday Becky
Withrow HS
Cincinnati OH

Sundberg Vaughn
Hubbard HS
Hubbard OH

Sun Yee Lai Sun
Walnut Hills HS
Cincinnati OH

Suppa Sherry
Hedgesville HS
Martinsburg WV

Surbey P
Taylor HS
Kokomo IN

Surface Patty
Talawanda HS
Oxford OH

Susemichel Steven C
Ben Davis HS
Indianapolis IN

Sutherby Cherie
Gobles HS
Gobles MI

Sutherland Lisa
Paw Paw HS
Mattawan MI

Sutler Richard
Stonewall Jackson HS
Chrlstn WV

Sutphin Sara
L & M HS
Lyons IN

Suttmiller Anita
Chaminade Julienne HS
Dayton OH

Sutton Beth A
Bellaire HS
Bellaire OH

Sutton Mark
Tipton HS
Tipton IN

Sutton Stephanie
Our Lady Of Mercy HS
Detroit MI

Svera Laima
Crestwood HS
Dearborn Hts MI

Svoke Tammy
A D Johnston HS
Bessemer MI

Swackhamer Roxanne
Reynoldsburg HS
Reynoldsburg OH

Swaffar Debbie
Morton Sr HS
Hammond IN

Swaim Kevin
Rockville HS
Rockville IN

Swaim Tracy
Buchanan HS
Niles MI

Swallow Thomas
Harrison HS
Harrison MI

Swan Jill
Clare Public School
Clare MI

Swan Kimberly
New Albany HS
New Albany IN

Swander Janet
Yorktown HS
Muncie IN

Swann Gregory
Jackson HS
Jackson OH

Swann Yalonda
Brandon HS
Ortonville MI

Swanson Jack D
West Iron County HS
Iron River MI

Swanson Linda
Benedictine HS
Detroit MI

Swanson Sherryl
Kingsford HS
Iron Mountain MI

Swark Miriam
Eaton HS
Eaton OH

Swartz Jill
Brookville HS
Metamora IN

Swartz Teresa
Philip Barbour HS
Philippi WV

Swartzentruber Jeffrey
Westview Jr Sr HS
Shipshewana IN

Swartzlander Brenda
Napoleon HS
Defiance OH

Sweat Tamara
Stebbins HS
Dayton OH

Sweda Leigh
Garden City West Sr HS
Garden City MI

Sweebe Dianne
Meridian Sr HS
Sanford MI

Sweeney Cheryl L
Rochester HS
Rochester IN

Sweeney James
Brebeuf Prep
Indianapolis IN

Sweeney Mark L
Culver Military Academy
Steubenville OH

Sweeny Timothy
Chelsea HS
Chelsea MI

Sweeterman Linda
Chaminade Julienne HS
Dayton OH

Sweney Richard
Lutheran HS West
N Olmsted OH

Swiatek Louise
Mona Shores HS
Norton Shr MI

Swiderski Dawn
Lumen Cordium HS
Bedford OH

Swigert Sharon
River View HS
Coshocton OH

Swihart James
Tippecanoe Vly HS
Argos IN

Swim R Stanley
North Vermillion HS
Covington IN

Swineford Dianna
John Marshall HS
Indianapolis IN

Swing Bradley
Northrop HS
Ft Wayne IN

Swisher Debbie
Gallia Academy HS
Gallipolis OH

Swisher Kathy
Lewis Cnty HS
Weston WV

Swisher Michael
Holy Name HS
Lakewood OH

Switzer Brian G
Clermont Northeastern
HS
Batavia OH

Switzer Scott
Findlay HS
Findlay OH

Swoveland Edward A
Goshen HS
Goshen IN

Syer Traci
St Frances Cabrini HS
Lincoln Pk MI

Sykes Richard
Springport HS
Parma MI

Syler Barbara
Plymouth HS
Plymouth IN

Symko David
Greenville Sr HS
Greenville MI

Symons Daniel
Sts Peter & Paul Area
HS
Saginaw MI

STUDENTS
PHOTOGRAPH
SCHEDULED
FOR PUBLI-
CATION HERE
COULD NOT
BE REPRO-
DUCED

Synder David
Centerburg HS
Mt Liberty OH

Syner Joey
Midland Trail HS
Hico WV

Syner Thomas E
Valley HS
Powellton WV

Synkelma Robin
A D Johnston HS
Ironwood MI

Szakal Katherine
Trinity HS
Cleveland OH

Szel Pal Karl
Fairview HS
Fairview Pk OH

Szepietowski Teresa
Champion HS
Cortland OH

Szigethy Stephen M
Lumen Christi HS
Jackson MI

Szuch Janet
Jefferson HS
S Rockwood MI

Szuch M
Elisabeth Ann Johnson
HS
Clio MI

Szumlas Daniel
Bishop Noll Inst
Hammond IN

Szumlas David
Bishop Noll Inst
Hammond IN

Szymanski Christopher
Yale HS
Emmett MI

Szymanski Michele
Center Line HS
Warren MI

T

Tabachki Gina
Interlochen Arts
Academy
Gaylord MI

Tabar Timothy A
St Edward HS
N Olmsted OH

Tabor Rhonda
Princeton HS
Princeton WV

Tacey Cathy
Midland HS
Midland MI

Tackett Bonnie
Ecorse HS
Ecorse MI

Tackett Jack
Harding HS
Marion OH

Tackette Roger
Whitehall Yearling HS
Columbus OH

Taft Mitchell
University HS
Morgantown WV

Taibi Paul
Brooke HS
Follansbee WV

Talbot James
Bishop Foley HS
Madison Hts MI

Taliefero Paul S
Bishop Noll Institute
Gary IN

Tall Victor
Shaker Heights HS
Cleveland OH

Talpas Timothy
Padua Franciscan HS
Parma OH

Talsma Valerie
Caledonia HS
Caledonia MI

Tamburro Robert
Boardman HS
Youngstown OH

Tamez Tammy
Hampshire HS
Romney WV

Tamplin Gail
Hale HS
Hale MI

Tamplin Nancy
Hale Area HS
Hale MI

Tanguilig Carolyn
George Washington HS
Charleston WV

Tanner John
Winchester Cmnty HS
Winchester IN

Tanner Martha R
Cloverleaf Sr HS
Lodi OH

Tannous Robert
North Canton Hoover HS
North Canton OH

Tansek Margaret A
Carmel HS
Carmel IN

Tanskley David E
Southeastern HS
Detroit MI

Tarnacki Diane
Divine Child HS
Dearborn MI

Tarnas Kevin
St Ladislaus HS
Detroit MI

Tarner Mark
Clay HS
South Bend IN

Tashijan John V
Penn HS
Mishawaka IN

Taskott Lisa
Jackson HS
Jackson OH

Tassell Karen
Loy Norrix HS
Kalamazoo MI

Tate Gail
Clarkston Sr HS
Clarkston MI

Tate Kenneth
North HS
Youngstown OH

Tate Mary E
Hart HS
Hart MI

Tate Tammy L
Cadillac Sr HS
Cadillac MI

Tatman Laurie
Logansport HS
Logansport IN

Tatro Janice
Bishop Borgess HS
Garden City MI

Taurman Susan
Our Lady Of Providence
HS
New Albany IN

Tavares Jesslyn
Lee M Thurston HS
Redford MI

Tawney David A
St Marys HS
Belmont WV

Tawney Dianna
Chesapeake HS
Chesapeake OH

Taylor Angelica
Scott HS
Toledo OH

Taylor Arla K
Edgewood HS
Ellettsville IN

Taylor Beth A
Lake Orion Sr HS
Lake Orion MI

Taylor Brian
Quincy HS
Coldwater MI

Taylor Carla
Northwest HS
Lucasville OH

Taylor Christine
Miami Trace HS
New Holland OH

Taylor Corena
Upper Valley Joint Voc
Schl
Piqua OH

Taylor David
Highland Park HS
Highland Pk MI

Taylor Elizabeth
Columbian HS
Tiffin OH

Taylor Elizabeth
Jennings County HS
No Vernon IN

Taylor Elora
R Nelson Snider HS
Ft Wayne IN

Taylor G Steven
New Richmond HS
New Richmond OH

Taylor Jackie
Bridgeport Sr HS
Bridgeport WV

Taylor John
Bullock Creek HS
Midland MI

Taylor John M
Martinsburg Sr HS
Martinsburg WV

Taylor Julie
Lawrence Central HS
Indianapolis IN

Taylor June
Chadsey HS
Detroit MI

Taylor Kenneth
Pickerington Sr HS
Pickerington OH

Taylor Kennie
Arthur Hill HS
Saginaw MI

Taylor Kimberly
Mc Bain Rural Agri HS
Mc Bain MI

Taylor Leslie
Frontier HS
Nw Mtmrs OH

Taylor Martha E
North Central HS
Indianapolis IN

Taylor Marvin
Union County HS
Liberty IN

Taylor Renee
Cass Technical HS
Detroit MI

Taylor Rita
Salem HS
Salme IN

Taylor Robert H
Loveland Lincoln Hurst
HS
Loveland OH

Taylor Sandra
Osborn HS
Detroit MI

Taylor Scott
Britton Macon HS
Britton MI

Taylor Sheila
Tygarts Valley HS
Mill Creek WV

Taylor Sylvia
Jane Addams Voc HS
Cleveland OH

Taylor Tammy
Columbia HS
Columbia Sta OH

Taylor Teri
Newark HS
Newark OH

Taylor Thomas L
Napoleon HS
Napoleon OH

Taylor Tina
Gladwin HS
Gladwin MI

Taylor William P
Euclid HS
Euclid OH

Taylor Zondra L
Belleville HS
Ypsilanti MI

Teachout Ingrid
Hudsonville HS
Hudsonville MI

Teague Thomas E
Garfield Sr HS
Hamilton OH

Teahen Craig
Clio HS
Clio MI

Teater Tom
Bellaire HS
Neffs OH

Tedesco Toni E
Seton HS
Cincinnati OH

Tedrow Barry D
Barr Reeve HS
Loogootee IN

Teenier Thomas
Arthur Hill HS
Saginaw MI

Teeple Kathy
Jackson HS
North Canton OH

Teeters Linda
Howell HS
Howell MI

Teichman Lori
Cass City HS
Cass City MI

Telek Beth
New Richmond HS
New Richmond OH

Telepak Judith
Holy Name Nazareth HS
Seven Hills OH

Temple Blair
Belleville HS
Belleville MI

Temple Jamie
Belleville HS
Belleville MI

Temple Marie
Chatard HS
Louisville KY

Templeton Donald
Park Hills HS
Fairborn OH

Templeton Ruthann
Margaretta HS
Castalia OH

Templeton Thomas T
Hannan HS
Apple Grove WV

Tenerove Lisa
Mentor HS
Mentor Lake OH

Ten Eyck Kay
Bucyrus HS
Bucyrus OH

Tengel Jeff
Padua Franciscan HS
Brunswick OH

Tennant David
Bridgeport HS
Bridgeport WV

Tennant Kimberly
University HS
Morgantown WV

Tennant Roger
Hampshire HS
Shanks WV

Tenney Eliot J
Philip Barbour HS
Philippi WV

Tenney James
Warsaw Community HS
Warsaw IN

Tenny Amy L
Lima Sr HS
Lima OH

Tentler Tracey
Newton Falls HS
Newton Falls OH

Teramana Larry
Buckeye North HS
Brilliant OH

Terhune Brenda
North Putnam HS
Greencastle IN

Terhune Brian
Harry S Truman HS
Taylor MI

Termeer Anne
East Grand Rapids HS
Jackson MI

Terpening Mark
Kingsley Area HS
Kingsley MI

Terrell Alan
Canton South HS
Canton OH

Terrell Kevin
Crispus Ahucks HS
Indianapolis IN

Terrell Robin
Clinton Central HS
Michigantown IN

STUDENTS
PHOTOGRAPH
SCHEDULED
FOR PUBLI-
CATION HERE
COULD NOT
BE REPRO-
DUCED

Terry Michael
Warren Central HS
Indianapolis IN

Terry Teresa
Greenbrier East HS
Ronceverte WV

Terry Timothy
South Newton Jr Sr HS
Goodland IN

Tessin Margie
Mendon Community HS
Mendon MI

Testa Michael
Ursuline HS
Youngstown OH

Testaguzza James
Weir Sr HS
Weirton WV

Tetrick David
Washington Irving HS
Clarksburg WV

Teufel Mary
Hedgesville HS
Martinsburg WV

Tewes Debra
Pontiac Central HS
Pontiac MI

Thacker Michael S
Buffalo HS
Huntington WV

Thacker Pam
Chillicothe HS
Chillicothe OH

Thacker Rhonda
Southeastern HS
Chillicothe OH

Tharp Sandra
Clarkston HS
Clarkston MI

Tharp Shelley
Webster Cnty Higlanders
HS
Webster Sprg WV

Thatcher Melanie
Lincolnview HS
Middle Pt OH

Thatcher Ronda
Lincolnview HS
Van Wert OH

Thaxton Bob
Clay Sr HS
Oregon OH

Theis Darlene
Northrop HS
Ft Wayne IN

Theisen Janet
Beal City HS
Weidman MI

Theisen Nancy
St Frances Cabrini HS
Allen Pk MI

Thelen Chris G
Fowler HS
Fowler MI

Thelen Steven
Williamston HS
Williamston MI

Theodore Paula G
Morton Sr HS
Hammond IN

Therber Joe
Crawfordsville HS
Crawfordsville IN

Thiel Karen
Upper Sandusky HS
Upper Sandusky OH

Thieman Annette
Newbury HS
Newbury OH

Thieman Constance
East Detroit HS
E Detroit MI

Thieman Polly
Parkway HS
Rockford OH

Thieme Ronald H
Hamilton Southeastern
HS
Noblesville IN

Thieme Taya
Bellmont HS
Decatur IN

Thieret Richard
Berkshire HS
Burton OH

Thill Lyndell
North Muskegon HS
N Muskegon MI

Thober Victoria
Springfield HS
Maumee OH

Thom Tracy
Sandusky HS
Sandusky OH

P—208

Thomas Anne Marie
Boardman HS
Youngstown OH

Thomas Barbara
Napoleon HS
Jackson MI

Thomas Brian
Madison HS
Madison OH

Thomas Denise
Dixie HS
New Lebanon OH

Thomas Donald A
Woodhaven HS
Romulus MI

Thomas Fredrick
Meigs HS
Cheshire OH

Thomas James
Howell HS
Howell MI

Thomas Jeffrey
Meadow Bridge HS
Layland WV

Thomas Lora
South Vermillion HS
Clinton IN

Thomas Maryann
Baldwin HS
Baldwin MI

Thomas Michael R
Lakota HS
Westchester OH

Thomas Nadine
Canfield HS
Canfield OH

Thomas Nancy L
Coalton HS
Coalton WV

Thomas Phyllis
George Washington HS
E Chicago IN

Thomas Richard
Fostoria HS
Fostoria OH

Thomas Richard K
Gahanna Lincoln HS
Gahanna OH

Thomas Robin
Hudson Area HS
Osseo MI

Thomas Robyn
Lebanon HS
Lebanon OH

Thomas Russell R
Badin HS
Hamilton OH

Thomas Susan
Warren Local HS
Cutler OH

Thomas Susan
Stonewall Jackson HS
Charleston WV

Thomas Terence
Shaker Hts HS
Shaker Hts OH

Thomas Teresa
Brookfield Sr HS
Brookfield OH

Thomas Timothy
Ironton HS
Ironton OH

Thomas Timothy
Greenfield Central HS
Greenfield IN

Thomas Vikki
St Ursula Academy
Cincinnati OH

Thompson Alicia J
Marian HS
Cincinnati OH

Thompson Becky
Western Brown Sr HS
Georgetown OH

Thompson Bob
Valley Forge HS
Parma Hts OH

Thompson Bruce
Chesapeake HS
Chesapeake OH

Thompson Chris
Pickerington HS
Pickerington OH

Thompson D
Dominican HS
Southfield MI

Thompson Darren
Franklin Community HS
Franklin IN

Thompson Deidre
Logan Sr HS
Logan WV

Thompson D Theresa
Kyger Creek HS
Cheshire OH

Thompson Dwayne
Green HS
Akron OH

Thompson Elizabeth A
Marion L Steele HS
Amherst OH

Thompson Floyd G
Wilbur Wright HS
Dayton OH

Thompson Inga
Edgewood HS
Bloomington IN

Thompson Jane
Mahoning County Jt Voc
North Lima OH

Thompson Jeanne
Keyser HS
Keyser WV

Thompson Jeff
Buckeye South HS
Tiltonsville OH

Thompson John
Point Pleasant HS
Pt Pleasant WV

Thompson John T
Rogers HS
Toledo OH

Thompson Joyce
Jane Addams Voc HS
Cleveland OH

Thompson Karen M
Barboursville HS
Huntington WV

Thompson Kathy
Washington Sr HS
Washington C H OH

Thompson Kevin
Plainwell HS
Kalamazoo MI

Thompson Linda
Coldwater HS
Coldwater MI

Thompson Mark
Bellville HS
Ypsilanti MI

Thompson Mary Beth
Danville HS
Danville OH

Thompson Mary Jo
Wm Mason HS
Mason OH

Thompson Melanie G
Mooresville HS
Indianapolis IN

Thompson Michael
Buckeye South HS
Rayland OH

Thompson Richard L
Elkins HS
Elkins WV

Thompson Steve
New Albany HS
New Albany OH

Thompson Victor
University Of Detroit HS
Detroit MI

Thomsberry Tina
West Jefferson HS
W Jefferson OH

Thomspon Robert
Fairfield HS
Hamilton OH

Thorn Cheryl
East Canton HS
E Canton OH

Thorn Vickie
Zanesville HS
Zanesville OH

Thornton Duane
Corunna HS
Owosso MI

Thornton Elaine
Hurricane HS
Hurricane WV

Thornton Karen
Shaker Hts HS
Shaker Hts OH

Thorson Cynthia M
Loy Norrix HS
Kalamazoo MI

Thrasher Christy
Kokomo HS
Kokomo IN

Thurau Michael
Davison Sr HS
Davison MI

Tibbets Dan
Tippecanoe Valley HS
Mentone IN

Tibbitts Vicki
North Muskegon HS
Muskegon MI

Tichenor Jim
Oxford Sr HS
Oxford MI

Tidd Toni
River Valley HS
Marion OH

Tiede Julia R
Addison HS
Addison MI

Tiede Kathryn
Northfield HS
Wabash IN

Tiedeman Tyrone
Holly HS
Holly MI

Tighe Christopher
Cathedral Latin HS
Cleveland OH

Till Karen
Springfield Local HS
New Middletown OH

Tillison John
Shelbyville Sr HS
Shelbyville IN

Tillman Dawn
Troy HS
Troy OH

Tilton Tracy
Frontier HS
New Matamoras OH

Timbrook Kelly
Hampshire HS
Shanks WV

Timm Melissa A
Garber HS
Essexville MI

Timmons Leska
Washington Irving HS
Clarksburg WV

Timoff Belinda
Pontiac Central HS
Pontiac MI

Tims Kevin P
Our Lady Of Mt Carmel HS
Wyandotte MI

Tinge Mary J
Newbury HS
Newbury OH

Tingler Donna
Elkins HS
Elkins WV

Tipper Christy
Independence HS
Tams WV

Tisdel Elizabeth
Sturgis HS
Sturgis MI

Tishler Kevin
Otsego HS
Weston OH

Tislow Lisa
Sullivan HS
Carlisle IN

Titgemeyer Kurt
Clay Sr HS
Curtice OH

Tittle Kathy
North Ridgeville HS
N Ridgeville OH

Titus Howard
Lexington HS
Lexington OH

Tobias Todd
Eaton HS
Eaton OH

Tobler Keith
Buchanan HS
Buchanan MI

Tocco Jerome
Bishop Gallagher HS
Grss Pt Wds MI

Todaro Zina
Adlai Stevenson Cmnty
HS
Sterling Hts MI

Todd Carla
North Putnam Jr Sr HS
Ladoga IN

Todd Charles K
Hagerstown Jr Sr HS
Hagerstown IN

Todd Diane
Greenfield Central HS
Greenfield IN

Todd John L
Stonewall Jackson HS
Charleston WV

Todd William
Lapel HS
Anderson IN

Tokarcik Pamela
Roosevelt Wilson HS
Stonewood WV

Tokarski Allan
Andrean HS
Gary IN

Toland Kimberly
Bloom Local HS
South Webster OH

Toler Kimberly
Zanesville HS
Zanesville OH

Toler Ronnie J
Oceana HS
Oceana WV

Toler Teresa
Oceana HS
Lynco WV

Toles C
Elmhurst HS
Ft Wayne IN

Toles Susan
Washington HS
Massillon OH

Tolley Brian
Herbert Hoover HS
Pinch WV

Tom Judy
Southfield Lathrup HS
Southfield MI

Tom Karma
Northrop HS
Ft Wayne IN

Toma George
Chippewa Valley HS
Mt Clemens MI

Tomblin Lucy L
Guyan Valley HS
Ranger WV

Tomkies Michael C
Huntington HS
Huntington WV

Tomlin Tanya
Wayne HS
Dayton OH

Tomlison Betty
Eastern HS
Waverly OH

Tommas Wendy
Sandusky St Marys HS
Sandusky OH

Toncic Terry
Linsly Inst
Wheeling WV

Toner Kevin M
Columbus North HS
Edinburg IN

Tong Villanueva Anthony
Marysville HS
Marysville OH

Tonnesen David
Huntington HS
Huntington WV

Toogood Cynthia
Big Rapids HS
Big Rapids MI

Toole Christy
Philo HS
Zanesville OH

Toot Mike
Carrollton HS
Carrollton OH

Tope Stephen
Conotton Vly HS
Leesville OH

Toppin Regina
Reed City HS
Reed City MI

Topping Michelle
Licking Valley HS
Newark OH

Torgerson David
Grove City HS
Grove City OH

Tormoehlen Sue
Brownstown Central HS
Crothersville IN

Tornabene Tom
Tuscarawas Cntrl Cathlc
HS
New Phila OH

Torok Kimberly
Munster HS
Munster IN

Torres Nellita
West Tech HS
Cleveland OH

Toth Barbara
Our Lady Of Mercy HS
Detroit MI

Toto Christine
Union Local HS
Belmont OH

Tower Charity
Walter P Chrysler Mem
HS
New Castle IN

Tower Samuel
Greenville Sr HS
Gowen MI

Towers Andrew
Onsted Comm HS
Clayton MI

Towner Beth
Hiland HS
Millersburg OH

Towner Carla
Orddridge Cnty HS
West Union WV

Townsend Carl
Manchester Community
HS
Manchester MI

Townsend Linda
Brooke HS
Follansbee WV

Townsend Robert L
Gobles HS
Gobles MI

Townsend Seth
Hubbard HS
Hubbard OH

Towson Kenneth
Pontiac Central HS
Pontiac MI

Tracy Kelli
Brownsburg HS
Brownsburg IN

Tracy M
Rocky River HS
Rocky Rvr OH

Trainer Leona M
Southeastern HS
Chillicothe OH

Trammell Joan
Plymouth Salem HS
Canton MI

Trautner Joel
Arthur Hill HS
Saginaw MI

Trautwein Dennis
Upper Sandusky HS
Upper Sandusky OH

Travis Denise
Woodmore HS
Woodville OJ

Trayer Lisa
Martinsburg Sr HS
Martinsburg WV

Traylor Lynne
Ursuline HS
Youngstown OH

Treadwell Laurie J
Harper Creek HS
Battle Creek MI

Trebus Patricia
Woodrow Wilson HS
Youngstown OH

Treier Linda
Elmwood HS
Bloomdale OH

Trejo Jose
Father J Wehrle
Memorial HS
Columbus OH

Trendel Susan
Whitmer Sr HS
Toledo OH

Treneff Nick
Grove City HS
Grove City OH

Trevarrow William J
Sault Area HS
Sault Ste Mari MI

Tribbett Charles
Pioneer Regional Jr Sr
HS
Monticello IN

Tribble Denise
Elyria Catholic HS
Elyria OH

Trifilette Lisa
Niles Mc Kinley HS
Niles OH

Trimble Michael
Buffalo HS
Huntington WV

Trimble Mike
Philo HS
Duncan Falls OH

Triplett Doris
Southeastern HS
Ray OH

Trisler Lois
Sidney HS
Sidney OH

Tritch John
Prairie Hts HS
Hudson IN

Trittschuh Lisa
Greenville HS
Greenville OH

Trivison Lisa
Solon HS
Solon OH

Trojan Stephen M
Rogers Sr HS
Michigan City IN

Trompeter James
Bay City Western HS
Kawkawlin MI

Tronter M
Fenwick HS
Middletown OH

Tropf April
Michigan Lutheran
Seminary
Monroe MI

Tropp David A
William A Wirt HS
Gary IN

Tropp Iris
William A Wirt HS
Gary IN

Trotter Cheryl A
North Bloomington HS
Bloomington IN

Trottman Robert
George Washington HS
E Chicago IN

Trout Cynthia
Philo HS
Zanesville OH

STUDENTS
PHOTOGRAPH
SCHEDULED
FOR PUBLI-
CATION HERE
COULD NOT
BE REPRO-
DUCED

Trout Donna
Franklin Community HS
Franklin IN

Trout Michael V
Bishop Rosecrans HS
Zanesville OH

Troyer Eric
Franklin Heights HS
Columbus OH

Troyer Michael
Central HS
Evansville IN

Truax Dawn
Ovid Elsie HS
Elsie MI

Truax James
Shadyside HS
Shadyside OH

Truax Monica
Ovid Elsie HS
Elsie MI

Truckey Kathleen
Mendon HS
Mendon MI

Truckly Robin
Heath HS
Heath OH

Truex Andrea
Edgewood HS
Bloomington IN

Truman Connie
Parkside HS
Jackson MI

Truman Tom
Crown Point HS
Crown Point IN

Truskowski Suzanne
Woodhaven HS
Woodhaven MI

Trusler Lance
Staunton HS
Staunton IN

Tryon Kathy
Perry HS
Navarre OH

Tscherne Karen
Cardinal Stritch HS
Toledo OH

Tsolainos Nick
Charles F Brush HS
Lyndhurst OH

Tubbs Ernest C
Oak Hill HS
Oak Hill WV

Tuck Eric
Cardinal Stritch HS
Toledo OH

Tucker Ann
Niles HS
Niles MI

Tucker Ellen
Andrean HS
Merrillville IN

Tucker Leslie
Strongsville Sr HS
Strongsville OH

Tucker Suzetta
Holton HS
Holton MI

Tucker William
Frankenmuth HS
Frankenmuth MI

Tuckerman Ann M
Pike Delta York Sr HS
Delta OH

Tudor Tina
Goshen HS
Goshen OH

Tufekcioglu Emre D
Culver Military Academy
Culver IN

Tulenko Jr John
Weir HS
Weirton WV

Tuljak Maria
Cleveland Central Cath
HS
Cleveland OH

Tullis Billie K
Leetonia HS
Washingtonville OH

Tulloh Brian
Shelbyville Sr HS
Shelbyville IN

Tuma Joseph
St Johns HS
Toledo OH

Turk Michelle
St Mary Academy
Milan MI

Turkal Jennifer
Eastwood HS
Pemberville OH

Turkovich Matthew
Lincoln HS
Shinnston WV

Turnbull Mark
Hale Area HS
Hale MI

Turner Barbara
Griffith HS
Griffith IN

Turner Brian
Chesterton HS
Valpairiso IN

Turner Carol
Cleveland Ctrl Catholic
HS
Cleveland OH

Turner Celeste
Central HS
Detroit MI

Turner Charlie
Greenfield Central HS
Greenfield IN

Turner Gregory G
Woodrow Wilson HS
Beckley WV

Turner Jacquelyn A
Fairfield Union HS
Pleasantville OH

Turner Maritta L
Northern Sr HS
Detroit MI

Turner Nancy
De Vilbiss HS
Galesburg MI

Turner Nancy
Greenville Sr HS
New Madison OH

Turner Susan Elaine
Laurel HS
Laurel IN

Turner Sybil M
Henry Ford HS
Detroit MI

Turner Yvonne
Highland Park Cmnty HS
Highland Pk MI

Turoczy Mary A
Flemington HS
Bridgeport WV

Turon Mary
Farmington Local HS
W Farmington OH

Turpin Kevin R
Central HS
Bloomfield IN

Turske Scott
Alpena HS
Alpena MI

Tuttle Jodi L
Delta HS
Muncie IN

Tuttle Robin
Clay Battelle HS
Fairview WV

Tweedie J Scot
Garber HS
Essexville MI

Twyman Brad
Lawrence North HS
Indianapolis IN

Tyler David
Rochester HS
Rochester IN

Tyler Kathy L
North Putnam Jr Sr HS
Bainbridge IN

Tyler Rod
Parma HS
Parma OH

Tyler Tania
Goshen HS
Goshen IN

Tyree Virginia
Romulus Sr HS
Romulus MI

Tyring Scott A
Pike Central HS
Spurgeon IN

Tyson Barrington C
Hubbard HS
Hubbard OH

Tyson Luther
Washington HS
South Bend IN

Tyus Gregory
Cass Technical HS
Detroit MI

U

Uebbing Richard
Athens HS
Troy MI

Uebler Jamie
Niles Sr HS
Niles MI

Uetrecht Donna
Clinton Massie HS
Oregonia OH

Uher Theresa
Cardinal Stritch HS
Millbury OH

Uhlenbrock Jim
Urbana HS
Urbana OH

Uhrich Connie
Hubbard HS
Hubbard OH

Uhrig Don
Mt Vernon Academy
Mt Vernon OH

Uhrin Jeff
Andrean HS
Gary IN

Ukrainec Donald
Riverview Community HS
Riverview MI

Ulbrich Rebecca
Lehman HS
Piqua OH

Ullom Kelley
Milton HS
Milton WV

Ulrich Clifford
Mona Shores HS
Muskegon MI

Ulrich James
Lake Catholic HS
Mentor OH

Ulrich Mark
Maplewood HS
E Orwell OH

Ulrich Nancy
Sandcreek HS
Sand Creek MI

Umlor Dennis
Coopersville HS
Conklin MI

Ummel Julie
Bishop Dwenger HS
Ft Wayne IN

Umpleby Dawn
Canton S HS
Canton OH

Underwood Charles E
Greenbrier West HS
Rainelle WV

Underwood Johnna
Inter City Christian HS
Lincoln Park MI

Underwood Peggy
Shady Spring HS
Glen Morgan WV

Underwood Sherry
Shady Spring HS
Shady Spring WV

Underwood Sherry
Fayetteville HS
Faeytteville WV

Untch Joann
Cardinal Mooney HS
Youngstwon OH

Upchurch Steven R
Hagerstown HS
Greens Fork IN

Updike Keith G
Aquinas HS
Lincoln Park MI

Uphues Laura
Eau Claire HS
Berrien Ctr MI

Upton Robert
Belleville HS
Belleville MI

Urban Ramona
Merrillville Sr HS
Merrillville IN

Urbanovic Kathleen
Avon HS
Danville IN

Urquhart Robin
Milford HS
Holly MI

Usak Sandra
Hedgesville HS
Martinsburg WV

Ussery Xilla T
Kingswood School
Birmingham MI

Utecht Steven P
Stevenson HS
Livonia MI

Uther Susan
Edison HS
Milan OH

Utrup Susan
St John HS
Delphos OH

Utter Jane
Clay Sr HS
Oregon OH

Utz Julia
Beaver Local HS
Negley OH

V

Vadini Mike
Valley Forge HS
Parma OH

Vadnais Michael
Colerain Sr HS
Cincinnati OH

Vaguhn Betty
Southern Wells Jr Sr HS
Poneto IN

Valaitis Anthony
Eastlake North HS
Eastlake OH

Valan Michael
Linsly Institute
Wheeling WV

Valenti Susan
Brush HS
Richmond Hts OH

Valentine Carrie
Northwest HS
Canal Fulton OH

Valentine Karen
Pinckney HS
Hamburg MI

Valigosky Steven
St Francis De Sales HS
Toledo OH

Valinet Greg
Park Tudor School
Indianapolis IN

Valkier Kim
Hudsonville Public HS
Jenison MI

Vallance Mary
Milton HS
Ona WV

Vallera Joan
Catholic Central HS
Steubenville OH

Valley James A
Saline HS
Saline MI

Vallie Sue
Britton Macon HS
Britton

Vallier Michael
Engadine Consolidated
HS
Naubinway MI

Van Amburgh Mike
Elyria Catholic HS
Grafton OH

Van Bruggen Terrie
Portage Central HS
Portage MI

Van Buren Lori
Goshen HS
Goshen IN

Vance Barbara
Hilliard HS
Galloway OH

Vance Kurt
Cambridge HS
Cambridge OH

Vance Tammy
Clay County Sr HS
Lizemores WV

Vance Teresa
Wayne HS
Dayton OH

Vandenberg Thomas H
Zeeland Sr HS
Zeeland MI

Vander Kooi Steven
Muskegon HS
Muskegon MI

Vander Schuur Diane
Hudsonville HS
Hudsonville MI

Vander Stelt Vicki
Hicksville HS
Hicksville OH

Van Der Vennet Greg
Greenville HS
Sterling IL

Van Devender Bonny
Canton South HS
N Industry OH

Van Deventer Craig
Sycamore HS
Cincinnati OH

Van De Vusse William
West Ottawa HS
Holland MI

Van Dyke Brenda
Davison Sr HS
Davison MI

Van Dyke Denise D
Hurrican HS
Scott Depot WV

Van Dyke John J
John F Kennedy HS
Newton Falls OH

Van Dyke Michelle
Brooke HS
Wellsburg WV

Van Esley Gregory J
St Alphonsus HS
Detroit MI

Van Genderen Joni
Clawson HS
Clawson MI

Van Gilder James L
Huron HS
Huron OH

Van Gilder Louise
Lincoln HS
Shinnston WV

Van Hook Jeffery
John F Kennedy HS
Taylor MI

Van Horn Sharon
South Charleston HS
S Charleston WV

Van Kley Lori
Kankakee Vly HS
De Motte IN

Van Laan Cathy
South Christian HS
Caledonia MI

Vanlerberghe Richard
L Anse Creuse HS North
Mt Clemens MI

Van Loo Jill
Willard HS
Willard OH

Van Metre Bruce
Vantage Joint Voc HS
Van Wert OH

Vann Wanda
East HS
Columbus OH

Vanover Patricia
Norwood HS
Norwood OH

Van Roekel Ronald A
Hudsonville HS
Hudsonville MI

Van Schagen John
Greenville Sr HS
Greenville MI

Van Scoy William
Upper Sandusky HS
La Rue OH

Van Slyke Tamara D
Lincoln HS
Shinnston WV

Van Voorhis Jill
Canton South HS
Canton OH

Van Winkle Cheryl
Rockville HS
Rockville IN

Van Zandt Patricia
Madison Heights HS
Anderson IN

Vargo Roseann
Hubbard HS
Hubbard OH

Vargo Laurie
Coshocton HS
Coshocton OH

Varnado Arnetta N
Roosevelt HS
Gary IN

Varner Carol
Clay Battelle HS
Pentress WV

Varney Cynthia
Carey HS
Carey OH

Vascil John
John Adams HS
South Bend IN

Vasicek Sandra
Corunna HS
Corunna MI

Vassolo Valerie
Seton HS
Cincinnati OH

Vasu C
E Grand Rapids HS
Grand Rapids MI

Vaughan Kellie
Trimble Local HS
Glouster OH

Vaughan William K
Rayen HS
Youngstown OH

Vaughn Eric
Greenville Sr HS
Greenville MI

Vaughn Stephany
Cascade HS
Clayton IN

Vaughn Vickie
Jimtown HS
Elkhart IN

Vaught Donald
Purcell HS
Maineville OH

Vega Albert
Washington HS
South Bend IN

Vega Lisa L
Harry S Truman Sr HS
Taylor MI

Velenyi Bob
Charles F Brush HS
Lyndhurst OH

Vellanki Mohan
Hoover HS
North Canton OH

Velligan Dana
Andrean HS
St John IN

Venable Garry
Henry Ford HS
Detroit MI

Venable Timothy
Hartland HS
Brighton MI

Venham Tia
Morgantown HS
Morgantwn WV

Ventimiglio Teresa
C S Mott Sr HS
Warren MI

Verbick Laura
George N Bentley HS
Livonia MI

Verbosky Mary Kay
Rossford HS
Rossford OH

Vercruysse Mary Ann
Lake Shore HS
St Clair Shrs MI

Vermet Edward
Grosse Pointe South HS
Grosse Pt Pk MI

Ver Meulen William K
Interlochen Arts
Academy
Lake Forest IL

Vernava Grace
Our Lady Of Mercy HS
Farmington Hls MI

Verschage Chris
Everett HS
Lansing MI

Vesel David
Eastlake North HS
Willowick OH

Vetter William
Henryville HS
Otisco IN

Veynovich Bryan
Woodrow Wilson HS
Youngstown OH

Vicchiarelli Traci
Regina HS
Cleveland OH

Vician Kevin
Andrean HS
Crown Pt IN

Vickers Cynthia
White Cloud HS
White Cloud MI

Vickerstaff Bonita
Andrean HS
Gary IN

Victor Dawn
Brookville HS
Harrison OH

Vidimos David
Merrillville HS
Merrillville IN

Villarreal Debra
Grand Ledge HS
Lansing MI

Villella Toni
Franklin HS
Farnklin OH

Villers Karen
Wirt County HS
Elizabeth WV

Villers Linda
Lewis County HS
Weston WV

Vincent Matt
Lincoln HS
Shinnston WV

Vincent Maureen
Our Lady Of Mercy HS
Detroit MI

Vinoverski Julie
Midview HS
Grafton OH

Vinson Jeni
Waynesville HS
Waynesville OH

Viscogliosi Lori
Dearborn HS
Dearborn Hts MI

Vitale Jeff
Madison HS
Madison Hts MI

Vitarelli Phillip
Madonna HS
Follansbee WV

Vitchner Rich
Buckeye Local HS
Yorkville OH

Vite Jerome
Buchanan HS
Niles MI

Vivian Cheryl
Marquette Sr HS
Marquette MI

Vlarich Celeste
William A Wirt HS
Gary IN

Voelker Charles
Calumet HS
Calumet MI

Vogel Tammey
West Carrollton Sr HS
W Carrollton OH

Vogtmann Wallace
Bay City Western HS
Auburn MI

Voise Mary
Bridgeport HS
Saginaw MI

Volan Michael
Sebring Mc Kinley HS
Sebring OH

Volk Kimberly L
Highland HS
Anderson IN

Vollmer Jonathan
Lasalle HS
S Bend IN

Volz Beverly
Warren Central HS
Indpls IN

Von Boyd Jr Dejuain
North Central HS
Indianapolis IN

Von Patterson Carl
Ravenna HS
Ravenna OH

Von Steenburg Laura L
Ogemaw Heights HS
West Branch MI

Vorbroker Robert
Moeller HS
Cincinnati OH

Vornhagen Jill M
Herbert Henry Dow HS
Midland MI

Vorono Deborah K
Northfork HS
Northfork WV

Vorters Dian
Niles HS
Niles MI

Vorves Kostadinos
Harry S Truman Sr HS
Taylor MI

Vos William G
Tri County HS
Pierson MI

Votaw Ty
S Range E Raiders HS
Salem OH

Vovos John M
Parma Sr HS
Parma OH

Vrabel Tracy
Admiral King HS
Lorain OH

Vrahoretis Susan
Morton Sr HS
Hammond IN

Vredeveld Rhonda
Zeeland HS
Zeeland MI

Vukovich Robert James
Hemlock HS
Saginaw MI

Vulgamore James
Franklin Heights HS
Columbus OH

Vyhnalek Gary G
Valley Forge HS
Parma OH

Vykopal Michele
Rossford HS
Rossford OH

W

Waak Scott
Lutheran East HS
E Detroit MI

Wachtel Brenda
Loudonville HS
Loudonville OH

Waddington Robert
Start HS
Toledo OH

Wade Carrie
Buckeye North HS
Mingo Junction OH

Wade Christopher
Watkins Memorial HS
Pataskala OH

Wade Cindy
Carrollton HS
Melbourne FL

Wade Donna
Lake Catholic HS
Wickliffe OH

Wade Linda
Chaminade Julienne HS
Dayton OH

Wade Mark
St Albans HS
St Albans WV

Wade Zelee
Jesup W Scott HS
Toledo OH

Wadian Brian
Jackson HS
Massillon OH

Wafford Kerry C
Broad Ripple HS
Indianapolis IN

Waggoner Connie
Margaretta HS
Castalia OH

Waggy Linda
Lincoln HS
Lumberport WV

Wagner Amy
Seton HS
Cincinnati OH

Wagner Barbara
Benjamin Bosse HS
Evansville IN

Wagner Blaise
Jasper HS
Jasper IN

Wagner Cheryl
Tri Valley HS
Adamsville OH

Wagner J
Triway HS
Wooster OH

Wagner Karen
Danville Community HS
Danville IN

Wagner Kimberly A
La Salle HS
South Bend IN

Wagner Lois
Edsel Ford HS
Dearborn MI

Wagner Lorry
Niles Sr HS
Niles MI

Wagner Mary
Rock Hill Sr HS
Ironton OH

Wagner Patricia S
Springfield Local HS
Maumee OH

Wagner Steven M
Bishop Ready HS
Columbus OH

Wagoner Debra
Eastern HS
Pekin IN

Wagoner Regina
Calhoun Cnty HS
Big Bend WV

Wahl Gerard
Moeller HS
Cincinnati OH

Wahl Michael
Mc Nicholas HS
Cincinnati OH

Wahr Linda
Bay City John Glenn HS
Bay City MI

Waidelich William
Logan Elm HS
Circleville OH

Waite Lisa
Brookhaven HS
Columbus OH

Walawender Chester
C S Mott HS
Warren MI

Wald Kimberly
Fairless HS
Navarre OH

Walden Randy
Westfield Washington
HS
Westfield IN

Walden Sadie
Union HS
Bayard WV

Waldock Robert
Sandusky HS
Sandusky OH

Waldron Dana
Vinton Cnty HS
Mc Arthur OH

Waldron Jane
Greenville Sr HS
Greenville MI

Waldron Suzanne L
Turpin HS
Cincinnati OH

Waldroup Lori
Johannesburg Lewiston
HS
Lewiston MI

Walega Kathleen
John F Kennedy HS
Taylor MI

Walesch Kathleen
Fairview HS
Fairview Pk OH

Walgren Kristin L
Theodore Roosevelt HS
Kent OH

Walker Carol L
Wylie E Groves HS
Birmingham MI

Walker Colleen
Boardman HS
Boardman OH

Walker Dwayne
Detroit Central HS
Detroit MI

Walker Jed
Detroit Central HS
Detroit MI

Walker Kevin
Blanchester HS
Blanchester OH

Walker Mary
Holland HS
Holland MI

Walker Phyllis
City Wide Alternative
School
Cincinnati OH

Walker Randy
Mt Clemens HS
Mt Clemens MI

Walker Roberta
Horace Mann HS
Gary IN

Walker Robin
Plainwell HS
Plainwell MI

Walker Sheila
Marian Heights Academy
Washington IN

Walker Shelly
New Haven HS
New Baltimore MI

Walker Teresa
Franklin Community HS
Franklin IN

Walker Timothy
Princeton HS
Princeton WV

Walker Tonja
Northrop HS
Ft Wayne IN

Wall Alice
Mc Donald HS
Mc Donald OH

Wall Dee A
South Vermillion HS
Clinton IN

Wall Harold
Charleston HS
Charlestown IN

Wallace Cynthia M
Ben Davis HS
Indianapolis IN

Wallace Janet
Buckhannon Upshur HS
Buckhannon WV

Wallace Lori L
Alliance HS
Alliance OH

Wallace Mary R
Central Catholic HS
Wheeling WV

Wallace Nancy A
Turpin HS
Cincinnati OH

Wallace Tammra
Brownsburg HS
Brownsburg IN

Wallace Waymon L
Walnut Hills HS
Cincinnati OH

Walland Nancy
St Marys Central Cath
HS
Sandusky OH

Wallar Gina
Defiance Sr HS
Defiance OH

Walle Karen
Douglas Mac Arthur HS
Saginaw MI

Walley Jody
Paint Valley HS
Bourneville OH

Wallingford Todd
Chillicothe HS
Chillicothe OH

Walls Brenda
Central Preston HS
Albright WV

Walls Lisa
Columbiana County Voc
HS
East Liverpool OH

Walrath Brett
Edgewood HS
N Kingsville OH

Walsh Laurence
Northwest HS
Indianapolis IN

Walston Jr W
Lawrenceburg HS
Lawrenceburg IN

Walt Debbie
Mitchell HS
Mitchell IN

Walter John
North HS
Springfield OH

Walter Laurie
Hartford HS
Hartford MI

Walters Anita
De Kalb HS
Auburn IN

Walters Donna G
Barboursville HS
Huntington WV

Walters Elizabeth A
John F Kennedy HS
Warren OH

Walters Jim
Clio HS
Clio MI

Walters Lucretia L
Wapahant HS
Albany IN

Walters Michael
Edon N W HS
Edon OH

Walters Robert P
Carmel HS
Carmel IN

Walters Terry
Lawrenceburg HS
Lawrenceburg IN

Walters William E
Berkeley Springs HS
Berkeley Spgs WV

Walton Anthony
West Side HS
Gary IN

Walton Douglas
Mohawk HS
Sycamore OH

Waltz Craig E
Hamilton Heights HS
Cicero IN

Wamsley Chet
Buckhannon Upshur HS
Buckhannon WV

Wamsley Jeffrey
Pt Pleasant HS
Pt Pleasant WV

Wang Bonita
Adelphian Acad
Grand Blanc MI

Wanger Rhoda
Heath HS
Heath OH

Wanser Elizabeth
Kenston HS
Chagrin Fls OH

Wanstrath Janice
Immaculate Conception
Acad
Batesville IN

Wantuck Christine
Marian HS
Bloomfield MI

Wantz Susan
Central Catholic HS
Massillon OH

Warby Janet S
Fowlerville HS
Howell MI

Ward Allen
Iaeger HS
Jolo WV

Ward Anthony L
Seeger Mem HS
Williamsport IN

Ward Denise
Eastwood HS
Stony Ridge OH

Ward Greg
Buchanan HS
Niles MI

Ward John
Tippecanoe Valley HS
Claypool IN

Ward Kathy
Jimtown HS
Elkhart IN

Ward Kelley
Owosso HS
Owosso MI

Ward Kenneth
Chanel HS
Northfield OH

Ward Nadine
Groveport Madison HS
Groveport OH

Ward Robin
Shady Spring HS
Glen Morgan WV

Ward Scott
Watkins Mem HS
Pataskala OH

Ward Stephanie C
William A Wirt HS
Gary IN

Ward Theron
Sidney HS
Sidney OH

Ward Tinnie
Admiral King HS
Lorain OH

Wardell Linda
East Lansing HS
East Lansing MI

Warden Cynthia
Southern HS
Racine OH

Warden Janice
Rutherford B Hayes HS
Delaware OH

Wardle Duane
Brownsburg HS
Brownsburg IN

Ware David
Central Preston Sr HS
Kingwood WV

Warfield Anthony A
Arsenal Tech HS
Indianapolis IN

Warfield Pamela
Perrysburg HS
Perrysburg OH

Wargo Beth
Fairview HS
Fairview Pk OH

Warley Tanya L
John F Kennedy HS
Cleveland OH

Warmoth Mary
Bishop Fenwick HS
Franklin OH

Warne Lori
Cambridge HS
Cambridge OH

Warne Shelley
Marcellus HS
Vandalia MI

Warner Brett
Pike Central HS
Petersburg IN

Warner Carolyn
Covington HS
Covington OH

Warner Cindy L
Western Hills HS
Cincinnati OH

Warner Kendale
Brownstown Central HS
Seymour IN

Warner Sandra
Covington HS
Covington OH

STUDENTS
PHOTOGRAPH
SCHEDULED
FOR PUBLI-
CATION HERE
COULD NOT
BE REPRO-
DUCED

Warnick Barbara
Elk Garden HS
Elk Garden WV

Warnimont Rod
Cory Rawson HS
Mt Cory OH

Warnsman Stu
Southridge HS
Huntingburg IN

Warren Debi
Hamilton Taft HS
Lawrenceburg IN

Warren Frankie
West Side HS
Gary IN

Warren Luana
Lake Fenton HS
Linden MI

Warren Susan
Ovid Elsie HS
Ovid MI

Warrick Robin
Mineral Ridge HS
Mineral Ridge OH

Warson Gary
Kearsley HS
Davison MI

Wash Anna M
Notre Dame HS
Clarksburg WV

Washam Mary
David Anderson HS
Lisbon OH

Washenitz Joni L
Rivesville HS
Rivesville WV

STUDENTS
PHOTOGRAPH
SCHEDULED
FOR PUBLI-
CATION HERE
COULD NOT
BE REPRO-
DUCED

Wasiloff Lisa
Madonna HS
Weirton WV

Wasserman Rosemary D
Delton Kellogg HS
Delton MI

Waterhouse Roger
Highland Park
Community HS
Highland Pk MI

Waterman Gary
Farmington HS
Northville MI

Waters Christine
Greenbrier East HS
Lewisburg WV

Waters Monica
Servite HS
Detroit MI

Wathen Patricia
Warren Woods HS
Warren MI

Watkins Ann
Highland HS
Medina OH

Watkins Erica
Timken Sr HS
Canton OH

Watkins Karen
Rogers HS
La Porte IN

Watkins Lisa
Stephen T Badin HS
Hamilton OH

Watkins Patrick
Bangor HS
Bangor MI

Watkins Peggy
Edgewood Sr HS
Ashtabula OH

Watson Darlene
Celina Sr HS
Celina OH

Watson Julie
Clay HS
S Bend IN

Watson Kim
Fowlerville HS
Gregory MI

Watson Lyn
Lakeview HS
Battle Creek MI

Watson Margaret
Zanesville HS
Zanesville OH

Watson Mark D
St Xavier HS
Bevis OH

Watson Michael
Bishop Foley HS
Madison Hts MI

Watson Regina
Ohio Hi Point JVS
North Lewisburg OH

Watson Regina A
Muncie Central HS
Muncie IN

Watson Robert
Yale HS
Avoca MI

Watson Susan
Eastern HS
Winchester OH

Watson Susan J
Roosevelt Wilson HS
Stonewood WV

Watts Kathy
Crooksville HS
Corning OH

Watts Robin
Gods Bible School &
College
Tecumsah MI

Waugh Angela
Stonewall Jackson HS
Charleston WV

Waugh Monica L
Adena HS
Frankfort OH

Waybright Vickie
Stow Lakeview HS
Stow OH

Wean Jon
Highland HS
Anderson IN

Weatherhead Chris
Graham HS
Conover OH

Weathers David
Culver Military Academy
San Antonio TX

Weathers Debra
North Daviess HS
Elnora IN

Weatherwax Amy
Bridgeport HS
Bridgeport WV

Weaver Barry E
Eastlake North HS
Willowick OH

Weaver Dave
North Putnam Jr Sr HS
Coatesville IN

Weaver Linda
Huntington East HS
Huntington WV

Weaver Mark
Oak Hill HS
Oak Hill WV

Weaver Stephen
Lewis Cnty HS
Weston WV

Weaver Tony
Martinsville HS
Martinsville IN

Weaver Valinda
Indian Valley North HS
New Phila OH

Webb Cassandra
Cass Technical HS
Detroit MI

Webb Donna
Bedford North Lawrence
HS
Bedford IN

Webb Jacqueline
Calhoun County HS
Big Springs WV

Webb Rhonda
Delphi Community Shs
Delphi IN

Webb Rhonda
Crestline HS
Crestline OH

Webb Robin
Roosevelt HS
Gary IN

Webb Vicki
Hardin Northern HS
Dola OH

Webber Cheryl
Dalton Local HS
Dalton OH

Weber Cynthia
St Francis HS
Kingsley MI

Weber David
Nordonia HS
Macedonia OH

Weber Jennifer
Seton HS
Cincinnati OH

Weber Jill
Eaton HS
Eaton OH

Weber Joyce
Adams Cntrl HS
Decatur IN

Weber Leigh
Madison Hts HS
Anderson IN

Weber Mark
East Noble HS
Huntertown IN

Weber Randall
Blanchester HS
Blanchester OH

Weber Stephanie
Four Cnty SVS HS
Napoleon OH

Weber Steve
Southfield Christian HS
Bloomfield Hls MI

Weber Thomas
Theodore Roosevelt HS
Wyandotte MI

Weber Ward
Hilliard HS
Hilliard OH

Webster Ciri A
Cass Technical HS
Detroit MI

Webster Daniel
Van Buren HS
Harmony IN

Webster Martha
Linden Cmnty HS
Linden MI

Webster Wade
White Cloud HS
White Cloud MI

Wech Barbara
Lincoln Park HS
Lincoln Park MI

Weddle Steven
Goshen HS
Goshen IN

Wedemeyer Shari
Gallia Academy HS
Rio Grande OH

Weekley Donna
South Harrison HS
W Milford WV

Weekley Elizabeth
Salem HS
Salem OH

Weese John H
Moorefield HS
Fisher WV

Weese Michele
Elkins HS
Elkins WV

Weese Phoebe
Columbiana County Joint
HS
East Liverpool OH

Weesner Cheryl R
Frankfort Sr HS
Frankfort IN

Weherley Pam
Franklin Monroe HS
Arcanum OH

Wehmiller Benjie
Crothersville Community
Schl
Crothersville IN

Wehrly Sharla
Jay County HS
Union City IN

Weidner Allen
Ann A Local Schools
Anna OH

Weig Robert
Lutheran HS
Washington MI

Weigand Becky
Timken Sr HS
Canton OH

Weigand Kelly
Harbor HS
Ashtabula OH

Weigold Lynnette M
Bridgeport HS
Saginaw MI

Weiler Jill
Eastmoor HS
Columbus OH

Weiler Shelley
Niles Sr HS
Niles MI

Weinberg Katy
Westfield Washington
HS
Carmel IN

Weiner Richard
Walnut Ridge HS
Columbus OH

Weir Sue
Centerville HS
Dayton OH

Weirick Lance
Triway HS
Wooster OH

Weis Victoria
Morton Sr HS
Hammond IN

Weisbarth Wendy
St Charles HS
Saginaw MI

Weisburn Beth
Perry HS
Massillon OH

Weise Peggy
Rosedale HS
Rosedale IN

Weisenberger Anna
Rock Hill HS
Clarksville OH

Weiser Mark C
Canal Winchester HS
Canal Winchestr OH

Weiskittel Barbara
Lumen Christi HS
Albion MI

Weiss Joanne S
St Thomas Aquinas HS
Alliance OH

Weitzman Jane
North HS
Eastlake OH

Welborn Jimmy
Union County HS
Brookville IN

Welch John
Lakeshore HS
Stevensville MI

Welch Thomas
Blanchester HS
Midland OH

Welch Tina
Fulton Schools
Perrinton MI

Welker Janet
South Vermillion HS
Clinton IN

STUDENTS
PHOTOGRAPH
SCHEDULED
FOR PUBLI-
CATION HERE
COULD NOT
BE REPRO-
DUCED

Wellman Gretchen
Andrean HS
Merrillville IN

Wellman Michele
Buffalo HS
Kenova WV

Wellman Nina
Buffalo HS
Huntington WV

Wellmeyer Connie
Southridge HS
Holland IN

Wells Barbara
Marian HS
S Bend IN

Wells Cindy
Midland Trail HS
Ansted WV

Wells Douglas
Madison Plains HS
London OH

Wells Eric
Holt Sr HS
Dimondale MI

Wells John
Delton Kellogg HS
Plainwell MI

Wells John
Riverdale HS
Arlington OH

Wells Kathy
Stonewall Jackson HS
Charleston WV

Wells Leroy
Eastern HS
Lucasville OH

Wells Lucinda
Hampshire HS
Romney WV

Wells Patricia
Ferndale HS
Pleasant Ridge MI

Wells Sherry
Tippecanoe HS
Tipp City OH

Wells Waybon D
Cass Technical HS
Detroit MI

Welsand Susan
Brighton HS
Brighton MI

Welsh Bill
Woodrow Wilson HS
Youngstown OH

Welshans C Robert
Linsly Institute
Wheeling WV

Welshans Tina
Madonna HS
Colliers WV

Welshofer Jr Lew
Fenwick HS
Middletown OH

Welton Cynthia L
Hubbard HS
Hubbard OH

Wendland Heidi
Bridgman HS
Bridgman MI

Wendorf Rick
Mason HS
Mason MI

Wendrow Kimberly
North Central HS
Indianapolis IN

Wenger Lori
Copley Sr HS
Copley OH

Wenk Lewis
Walsh Jesuit HS
Aurora OH

Wenman Forrest
Lakeshore HS
Baroda MI

Wentz Dawn
Coshocton HS
Coshocton OH

Wenz Robert E
North Royalton HS
North Royalton OH

Wenzel Evely L
St Charles HS
St Charles MI

Werdmann Nancy
Our Lady Of Angels HS
Cincinnati OH

Werling Denise
Seton HS
Cincinnati OH

Werling June
Northrop HS
Ft Wayne IN

Werstler Vicki
Whitko HS
Pierceton IN

Wesel Marilyn
Marietta Sr HS
Marietta OH

Wessel Audrey
Brownstown Central HS
Brownstown IN

Wessel Michael E
Lincoln HS
Vincennes IN

Wessel Sue
R Nelson Snider HS
Ft Wayne IN

West Barbara
Miller HS
Corning OH

West Christina E
Groveport Madison HS
Groveport OH

West Debra
Jackson HS
Jackson MI

West Jacqueline
Buckeye HS
Dillonvale OH

West Kelly A
Ernest W Seaholm HS
Birmingham MI

West Kevin
Northwest HS
Jackson MI

West Kevin
Chatard HS
Indianapolis IN

West Patti
Lincoln HS
Cambridge IN

West Sherry
Our Lady Of Mercy HS
Southfield MI

West Suzanne
Clarkston Sr HS
Clarkston MI

West Teresa
Lynchburg Clay HS
Lynchburg OH

West Virgil
Bellaire HS
Bellaire OH

Westfall Jenine
Spencer HS
Spencer WV

Westfall Kenny
Buckhannon Upshur HS
Buckhannon WV

Westfall Marla
Clay City HS
Cory IN

Weston Yvonne
Corunna HS
Lennon MI

Westover Laurie
Ashtabula HS
Ashtabula OH

Westren Deanna J
Ellet HS
Akron OH

Wetherald Shelly
Franklin Cntrl HS
Indpls IN

Wetzel John S
Medina Sr HS
Medina OH

Wetzel Steve
Cedarville HS
Cedarville OH

Weverstad Scott
Lakeview HS
Battle Creek MI

Wharton James R
Sandy Valley HS
Magnolia OH

Wheeler David
Faith Christian HS
Muskegon MI

STUDENTS PHOTOGRAPH SCHEDULED FOR PUBLICATION HERE COULD NOT BE REPRODUCED

Wheeler Jeff
Centerville Sr HS
Centerville IN

Wheeler John
Pike Central HS
Petersburg IN

Wheeler Julie
Howell HS
Fowlerville MI

Wheeler Kathy
Southport HS
Indianapolis IN

Wheeler Kimberly
Piqua Central HS
Piqua OH

Wheeler Kristina
Mason Sr HS
Mason MI

Wheeler Kyle
St Ursula HS
Toledo OH

Wheeler Lori
Manistee HS
Filer City MI

Wheelock Jami
Greenville Sr HS
Greenville OH

Whelan Michael
Castle HS
Newburgh IN

Whelan Tracey
L And M HS
Lyons IN

Whelchel Mike
Lincoln HS
Lumpoerport WV

Wherry Kelly
Nordonia Sr HS
Northfield OH

Whetsel Michelle
Jay County HS
Dunkirk IN

Whetstone Amy
Northrop HS
Ft Wayne IN

Whetstone Jeffery
Northrop HS
Ft Wayne IN

Whetstone Laura
Fairfield Union HS
Lancaster OH

Whipkey Shawn R
University HS
Morgantown WV

Whitacre Jean
Newark Catholic HS
Newark OH

Whitaker Mary
Fairfield Senior HS
Hamilton OH

Whitaker Michael
Eaton Rapids HS
Eaton Rapids MI

White Angelina
Servite HS
Hale MI

White Barbara E
Martins Ferry HS
St Clairsville OH

White Charlene
Roosevelt HS
Gary IN

White Christopher
Lumen Christi HS
Jackson MI

White Craig C
Morgantown HS
Morgantown WV

White Darin
Crooksville HS
Crooksville OH

White David
Princeton Community HS
Princeton IN

White David C
Trenton HS
Trenton MI

White Delena
Southside HS
Muncie IN

White Diana D
Ravenna HS
Ravenna OH

White Dick
Indian Valley North HS
Uhrichsville OH

White Donna S
Jeffersonville HS
Jeffersonville IN

White Ellen
Princeton HS
Princeton WV

White Emily B
Stonewall Jackson HS
Charlston WV

White John W
Glen Este Sr HS
Cincinnati OH

White Karla
Greenville Sr HS
Greenville OH

White Kevin
Princeton HS
Princeton WV

White Kim
Greenbrier East HS
Whte Slphr Spg WV

White Lenora
Immaculata HS
Detroit MI

White Linda
Jackson HS
Jackson OH

White Paul S
Washington HS
Massillon OH

White Rex
Jefferson Union HS
Steubenville OH

White Rhonda
Snider HS
Ft Wayne IN

White Richard
Danville Community HS
Danville IN

White Sybyl M
Cass Technical HS
Detroit MI

White Theresa
North Putnam Jr Sr HS
Greencastle IN

White Traci
Ovid Elsie HS
Lainsburg MI

White Vicki
Sidney HS
Sidney OH

White Vivian
Jane Addams Vocational
HS
Cleveland OH

White William G
Hamilton Southeastern
HS
Noblesville IN

Whitehead Pamela
University HS
Morgantown WV

Whiteman William
Lincoln HS
Wallace WV

Whitesides James F
Turpin HS
Cincinnati OH

Whitfield Chiquita S
Pershing HS
Detroit MI

Whiting Donna L
Cass Technical HS
Detroit MI

Whitlock Vicki L
North Ridgeville HS
N Ridgeville OH

Whitmire Jean
Brownsburg HS
Brownsburg IN

Whitmore Bret S
Lake Ville Mem HS
Otter Lake MI

Whitmore David
Pike HS
Indpls IN

Whitmore Robert
Carmel HS
Carmel IN

Whitney Alice
Olivet HS
Olivet MI

Whittaker Linda
Cass City HS
Cass City MI

Whitten Lisa
Beaver Local HS
Lisbon OH

Whitten Michael
Westfall HS
Williamsport OH

Whyde Diane
Margaretta HS
Castalia OH

Wiant Billie J
Woodrow Wilson HS
Beckley WV

Wiatrak John
Rocky River HS
Rocky Rvr OH

Wibert Bethann
Laingsburg HS
Laingsburg MI

Wible Martha
Medina HS
Medina OH

Wible Michael
Carroll HS
Dayton OH

Wick Doug
Houston HS
Sidney OH

Wickard Vicki
North Baltimore HS
N Baltimore OH

Wickens Mary
Highland Sr HS
Anderson IN

Wickline Sherri
Jackson HS
Jackson OH

Wiegand Martin
Buena Vista HS
Saginaw MI

Wierda Bruce
North Muskegon HS
North Muskegon MI

Wietstock Steven
Crestwood HS
Dearborn Hts MI

Wiggershaus Tom
Dayton Christian HS
Dayton OH

Wiggins Kim
Mc Cutcheon HS
Lafayette IN

Wiggins Sheila
Adelphian Acad
Durand MI

Wilber Jenny
Bedford North Lawrence
HS
Bedford IN

Wilborn Vonzetta J
Princeton HS
Princeton WV

Wilcher Lynwood
Buckhannon Upshur HS
Buckhannon WV

Wilcox Charles
Hilliard HS
Columbus OH

Wilcox Eric
Piqua Central HS
Piqua OH

Wilcox Kelly
Neguanee HS
Negaunee MI

Wilcox Marilyn
Glen Lake HS
Empire MI

STUDENTS
PHOTOGRAPH
SCHEDULED
FOR PUBLI-
CATION HERE
COULD NOT
BE REPRO-
DUCED

Wilder Susan
Decatur Central HS
Indnpls IN

Wildermuth Marlene
Upper Valley Joint Voc
Schl
Maplewood OH

Wildermuth Michelle
Allen East HS
Lima OH

Wildey Kendall
Jennings County HS
No Vernon IN

Wildfong Bridget
Gladwin HS
Gladwin MI

Wilds Tonda
Rock Hill HS
Ironton OH

Wiles Estelle
Ionia HS
Ionia MI

Wiles Esther
Ionia HS
Ionia MI

Wiley Barbara K
Western Hills HS
Cincinnati OH

Wilhelm Karen J
Marion Harding HS
Marion OH

Wilkins James D
Circleville HS
Riverton WV

Wilkins Lisa Ann
Roy C Start HS
Toledo OH

Wilkinson Cary
Union HS
Winchester IN

Wilkinson Lori
Elmwood HS
Bloomdale OH

Wilks Talvin W
The Miami Valley School
Dayton OH

Will Jeffrey
Delphos St Johns HS
Delphos OH

Will Jeffrey A
Westerville South HS
Westerville OH

Willemstyn Brian
West Ottawa HS
Holland MI

Willett Bradley
Bishop Watterson HS
Columbus OH

Willhite Kim
Brethren Christian HS
Mishawaka IN

Williams Ava
West Side Sr HS
Gary IN

Williams Betsy
Bluffton HS
Bluffton IN

Williams Bill
Hubbard HS
Hubbard OH

Williams Bob
Solon HS
Solon OH

Williams B Renee
Lincoln HS
Shinnston WV

Williams Bridgette
Saginaw HS
Saginaw MI

Williams Cindy
Leo HS
Spencerville IN

Williams Clara
Washington Catholic HS
Washington IN

Williams David
Clarkston Sr HS
Clarkston MI

Williams Debra
Wilmington HS
Wilmington OH

Williams Diana
Wheeling Park HS
Wheeling WV

Williams Dixie
Indiana Academy
Logansport IN

Williams Don
Ridgedale HS
Marion OH

Williams Donald
Walter E Stebbins HS
Dayton OH

Williams Hunter
Moorefield HS
Moorefield WV

Williams James P
Oscar A Carlson HS
Trenton MI

Williams Janice
Oceana HS
Hinton WV

Williams Jeffrey
River Valley HS
Three Oaks MI

Williams Jena
Greenville Sr HS
Greenville OH

Williams Jennifer
Inkster HS
Inkster MI

Williams Jennifer
Northern HS
Detroit MI

Williams Jerry
Wintersville HS
Wintersville OH

Williams Jimmy
Boonville HS
Boonville IN

Williams Judy
Northwest Sr HS
Cinti OH

Williams Karin
Rutherford B Hayes HS
Delawree OH

Williams Keith D
Mifflin Sr HS
Columbus OH

Williams Kelly Jo
Lancaster HS
Lancaster OH

Williams Kent
Woodrow Wilson HS
Youngstown OH

Williams Lewis S
Wilmington HS
Wilmington OH

Williams Lori
Hubbard HS
Masury OH

Williams Lori
Laville HS
Plymouth IN

Williams Lorynda M
Our Lady Of Mercy HS
Detroit MI

Williams Lynn
Washington Irving HS
Clarksburg WV

Williams Marilyn
Warrensville Sr HS
Warrensville OH

Williams Mark
Bishop Luers HS
Ft Wayne IN

Williams Martha
Gladwin HS
Gladwin MI

Williams Melinda
Pike HS
Indianapolis IN

Williams Michael
Bucyrus HS
Bucyrus OH

Williams Michele D
Newark HS
Newark OH

Williams Pat
Cedar Lake Academy
Wyoming MI

Williams Paul W
Bloomfield HS
Orwell OH

Williams Penny
Struthers HS
Struthers OH

Williams Peter
Catholic Central HS
Detroit MI

Williams Richard
Whitehall Yearling HS
Whitehall OH

Williams Richard
South Harrison HS
Lost Creek WV

Williams Ricky
South Charleston HS
S Charleston WV

Williams Ronald
Floyd Cntrl HS
New Albany IN

Williams Sabrina
Saginaw HS
Saginaw MI

Williams Sean D
Turpin HS
Cincinnati OH

Williams Sheryl
Chillicothe HS
Chillicothe OH

Williams Sonya
Central HS
Detroit MI

Williams Susan
Lincoln HS
Shinnston WV

Williams Tanya A
Cass Tech HS
Detroit MI

Williams Terri
Pike Central HS
Petersburg IN

Williams Thomas
Galion Sr HS
Galion OH

Williams Tim
Ursuline HS
Brookfield OH

Williamson Jeffrey
Brown County HS
Nashville IN

Williamson Joyce
Hilliard HS
Hilliard OH

Williamson Paula
Whitehall Yearling HS
Whitehall OH

Williamson Richard
Meigs HS
Rutland OH

Willis Brenda
Logan Sr HS
Logan WV

Willis Daniela
Utica Sr HS
Utica MI

Willis Dee Ann
Eastmoor HS
Columbus OH

Willis Elizabeth
Pike Central HS
Winslow IN

Willis James
Midland Trail HS
Lansing WV

Willis Karen
Franklin HS
Franklin WV

Willis Lori
Archbishop Alter HS
Kettering OH

Willis Marcia
Anderson HS
Anderson IN

Willis Martha
Martinsville HS
Indianapolis IN

Willis Wendy
Brooke HS
Wellsburg WV

Willits Dale
Greenfield Central HS
Pendleton IN

Willitzer Roxanne
Fairview HS
Defiance OH

Willman Karen
Urbana HS
Urbana OH

Willman Linda
John Glenn HS
Westland MI

Wills Barbara
Valley Forge Sr HS
Parma OH

Wills Eric
Lansing Everett HS
Lansing MI

Wills Jacqueline
Independence Jr Sr HS
Columbus OH

Wilmot Kelly
Mt Pleasant HS
Mt Pleasant MI

Wilmoth Suzanna
Philip Barbour HS
Belington WV

Wilskinson Laura L
Whitko HS
Pierceton IN

Wilson Angel
Union Local HS
Belmont OH

Wilson Ann
Lebanon HS
Lebanon OH

Wilson Anne
Haslett HS
Haslett MI

Wilson Bernard W
Cleveland Lutheran HS
East
Cleveland Hts OH

Wilson Bob
Danville HS
Danville OH

Wilson Brenda
Ridgewood HS
Newcomerstown OH

Wilson Brian
Decatur Central HS
Indpls IN

Wilson Carol
Philip Barbour HS
Philippi WV

Wilson Carolyn
Marlette HS
Marlette MI

Wilson Cheryl
Clinton Prairie HS
Colfax IN

Wilson Christine
Madonna HS
Weirton WV

Wilson Clarence
Ben Davis HS
Indianapolis IN

Wilson Crystal L
Meadowdale HS
Dayton OH

Wilson Daniel S
Elkhart Central HS
Elkhart IN

Wilson Debra J
Traverse City Sr HS
Traverse City MI

Wilson Dwayne
Lincoln West HS
Cleveland OH

Wilson Emilee
Pinconning Area HS
Pinconning MI

Wilson Geneva
East HS
Columbus OH

Wilson Gina
River Rouge HS
River Rouge MI

Wilson Gregory
Purcell HS
Cincinnati OH

Wilson James
Stivers Patterson Co Op
HS
Dayton OH

Wilson Janet
Brunswick HS
Brunswick OH

Wilson Jeff
Park Hills HS
Fairborn OH

Wilson Jodi
Zanesville HS
Zanesville OH

Wilson Karen
Niles Mc Kinley HS
Niles OH

Wilson Kelly
Buckhannon Upshur HS
Selbyville WV

Wilson Leslie R
Norwalk Sr HS
Norwalk OH

Wilson Melody
Buckhannon Upshur HS
French Creek WV

Wilson Michelle
Gladwin HS
Gladwin MI

Wilson Ronald K
Springfield Sr HS
Holland OH

Wilson Staci
Grand Blanc HS
Grand Blanc MI

Wilson Stephen A
Saint Xavier HS
Cincinnati OH

Wilson Susan
Calhoun County HS
Grantsville WV

Wilson Susan I
Cass Tech HS
Detroit MI

Wilson Tari
Northfield HS
Wabash IN

Wilson Tari
Lebanon HS
Lebanon OH

Wilson Teresa
Point Pleasant HS
Pt Pleasant WV

Wilson Terry
Felicity Franklin HS
Felicity OH

Wilson Wilma
River Valley HS
Marion OH

Wilson Jr Richard K
Johnstown HS
Johnstown OH

Wilt Jon
Miami Trace HS
Washington C H OH

Wilt Lisa
Upper Sandusky HS
Upper Sandusky OH

Wilt Marty
Delaware Hayes HS
Delaware OH

Wince Marsha
St Marys HS
St Marys WV

Windham Brandon
North Newton HS
Demotte IN

Windle Carol
Northwest HS
Mc Dermott OH

Windon Blair
Eastern HS
Pomeroy OH

Wine Sarita K
Braxton County HS
Copen WV

Winecki Dawn
Wylie E Groves HS
Birmingham MI

Wineinger Della
Northeast Dubois HS
French Lick IN

Wingate Thomas
Mooresville HS
Mooresville IN

Wingfield Lorena
Centerville HS
Centerville MI

Winings Donald E
North Putnam HS
Roachdale IN

Wink Pam
South Spencer HS
Rockport IN

Winkler Amy
Chillicothe HS
Chillicothe OH

Winkler Charlene
Rittman HS
Sterling OH

Winkler Michelle
Marysville HS
Marysville MI

Winland Sidney R
Wellsville HS
Wellsville OH

Winner Alysia
Norton HS
Clinton OH

Winshall Julie E
Berkley HS
Huntingtn Wds MI

Winston Thorla T
Newark Sr HS
Newark OH

Winter Carol
Marian HS
Birmingham MI

Winter Carol
Traverse City Sr HS
Traverse City MI

Winter Franklin
Upper Sandusky HS
Upper Sandusky OH

Winters Bruce
St Johns HS
Whitehouse OH

Winters Donetta
Logan HS
Logan WV

Winters Karen
Wayne HS
Dayton OH

Winters Tami
Columbia City Joint HS
Columbia City IN

Winterstein Debra
Arthur Hill HS
Saginaw MI

Wintzinger Roland
St Xavier HS
Cincinnati OH

Wireman Ernest
Jimtown HS
Elkhart IN

Wireman Kathy
Ironton HS
Ironton OH

Wirick Randy
John F Kennedy HS
Warren OH

Wirth Terri
Kimball HS
Royal Oak MI

Wirtz Ruth
Freeland HS
Freeland MI

Wise Charles
Madison Comprehensive
HS
Mansfield OH

Wise David
Crestview HS
New Waterford OH

Wise Kathryn
Northwestern HS
West Salem OH

Wise Mary T
Bishop Ready HS
Columbus OH

Wise Patricia
Lexington HS
Mansfield OH

Wise Sharon
Northwood HS
New Paris IN

Wisecup Benita
Union Scioto HS
Chillicothe OH

Wiseheart Jim
New Albany HS
New Albany IN

Wiseman Andre
Cass Technical HS
Detroit MI

Wiseman David
Sheridan HS
Thornville OH

Wiseman Susan
Dearborn HS
Dearborn MI

Wisne Susan
Lake Catholic HS
Chesterland OH

Wisner Bernard
Adams HS
Rochester MI

Wisniewski Douglas
Edwin Denby HS
Detroit MI

Wisniewski Greg
Bishop Foley HS
Warren MI

Wisniewski Prudence
Alpena Sr HS
Alpena MI

Wisniewski Robert
Lake Catholic HS
Willowick OH

Wissinger Tonja
Springfield South HS
Springfield OH

Witham Larry
North Muskegon HS
N Muskegon MI

Witherell Winston
Stonewall Jackson HS
Charleston WV

Witherow Myrna
Jane Addams Vocational
HS
Cleveland OH

Withey Chuck
Webberville HS
Webberville MI

Witkowski Joan
Woodhaven HS
Romulus MI

Witoszynski James
Wyle E Groves HS
Birmingham MI

Witte Norman
Garber HS
Essexville MI

Wittingen Carol
Unity Christian HS
Allendale MI

STUDENTS
PHOTOGRAPH
SCHEDULED
FOR PUBLI-
CATION HERE
COULD NOT
BE REPRO-
DUCED

Wixson Denise
Yale HS
Avoca MI

Woelffer Mary
Forest Park HS
Crystal Falls MI

Wohlstein Kathy
Athens HS
Athens OH

Wojna Helen
St Florian HS
Detroit MI

Wolf Barry
Zanesville HS
Zanesville OH

Wolf Jeffrey
Greenville HS
Greenville MI

Wolf John
Western Reserve
Academy
Hudson OH

Wolf Karin
Hillsdale HS
Ashland OH

Wolf Larry
E Liverpool HS
E Liverpool OH

Wolf Lee
Hastings Sr HS
Hastings MI

Wolf Mary
Bishop Watterson HS
Columbus OH

Wolf Robert
Mount Clemens HS
Mt Clemens MI

Wolf Scott
Northridge HS
Mt Vernon OH

Wolfe Jim
Fairmont Sr HS
Fairmont WV

Wolfe John
Richmond Sr HS
Richmond IN

Wolfe Junior G
Central Preston HS
Albright WV

Wolfe Karen
Bedford North Lawrence
HS
Avoca IN

Wolfe Kevin B
Stonewall Jackson HS
Charleston WV

Wolfe Kimberly
Stow HS
Stow OH

Wolfe Randall
Colon HS
Burr Oak MI

Wolfer Mary
Clermont Northeastern
HS
Marathon OH

Wolfer Michael
Mcnicholas HS
Cincinnati OH

Wolff David
John Adams HS
Mishawaka IN

Wolff Debbie
John Glenn HS
Wlakerton IN

Wolff James R
Mona Shores HS
Muskegon MI

Wolfgang Karen
Bridgeport HS
Bridgeport WV

Wolflin Rosemary
Marion HS
Marion IN

Wolford Douglas D
East Fairmont HS
Fairmont WV

Wolford Janet
North Side HS
Ft Wayne IN

Wolford Kelle
Hurricane HS
Hurricane WV

Wolford Kevin
Rochester Community
HS
Rochester IN

Woll John P
Univ Of Detroit HS
Southfield MI

Wollenzien Dana
Huntington East HS
Huntington WV

Wolman Kimberly
Whitehall Yearling HS
Whitehall OH

Wood Carol
Marlette HS
Marlette MI

Wood Eddie
Madison Heights HS
Anderson IN

Wood Jenni
Bellbrook HS
Bellbrook OH

Wood Jonathan L
Tri County HS
Howard City MI

Wood Lori
Meigs HS
Pomeroy OH

Wood Mary
Gallia Academy HS
Bidwell OH

Wood Rae
Penn HS
Bremen IN

Wood Ryan
Columbia City Joint HS
Columbia City IN

Wood Suzanne
Oak Hill HS
Oak Hill WV

Wood Valerie J
Manistique Area HS
Manistique MI

Wood Wendy
Monsignor John R
Hackett HS
Schoolcraft MI

Woodard Cheryl L
Heritage Christian HS
Indianapolis IN

Woodcock Steve
Montabella HS
Mcbride MI

Woodford John
Gilmer County HS
Tanner WV

Wood Jr Ira Lee
Greenbrier East HS
Alderson WV

Woodliff Susan
Kenmore HS
Akron OH

Woodruff Cynthia
Shakamak HS
Jasonville IN

Woodruff Wesley J
Point Pleasant HS
Point Pleasant WV

Woods Allayne R
Immaculata HS
Detroit MI

Woods Anthony
Jefferson HS
Shenandoah Jct WV

Woods Augusta
Pontiac Central HS
Pontiac MI

Woods Curtis
Cass Technical HS
Detroit MI

Woods Douglas
South Amherst HS
Amherst OH

Woods Jack
Rose D Warwick HS
Tekonsha MI

Woods Jennifer
Hampshire HS
Romney WV

Woods Joyce
Eastmoor Sr HS
Columbus OH

Woods Tami
Wilmington HS
Wilmington OH

Woodson Dwight D
Arsenal Tech HS
Indianapolis IN

Woofter Kent
Gilmer Co HS
Glenville WV

Wooldridge Linda
Center Line HS
Warren MI

Woolery Lisa
Brookville HS
Brookville OH

Wooley M
Boardman HS
Youngstown OH

Wooster Scott
Northwest HS
Rives Jct MI

Wooten Eugene
Sharples HS
Blair WV

Wopshall Marilyn
Central Catholic HS
Toledo OH

Worbs Steve
Hilliard HS
Hilliard OH

Work Ronald
Brooke HS
Follansbee WV

Worklan Janis
Cadiz HS
Bloomingdale OH

Workman Cathy
Clear Fork HS
Dorothy WV

Worrell Michael
Arthur Hill HS
Saginaw MI

Wortham Aron
Reeths Puffer HS
Muskegon MI

Wortman Lisa E
Parkside HS
Jackson MI

Woten Ron
Southern Wells HS
Bluffton IN

Wotring Stanley
Liberty HS
Clarksburg WV

Woudstra John D
Adams HS
Rochester MI

Woytek Bernie
Padau Franciscan HS
Parma OH

Wray Toni
Jennings County HS
Scipio IN

Wrens Brenda
Benton Harbor HS
Benton Harbor MI

Wright Beth
Terre Haute South Vigo
HS
Terre Haute IN

Wright Brenda
Olivet HS
Olivet MI

Wright Carolyn A
Steubenville Cthlc Cntrl
HS
Mingo Jct OH

Wright Christopher
Union County HS
Liberty IN

Wright Chuck W
Wyoming HS
Cincinnati OH

Wright Danny W
Jennings County HS
N Vernon IN

STUDENTS
PHOTOGRAPH
SCHEDULED
FOR PUBLI-
CATION HERE
COULD NOT
BE REPRO-
DUCED

Wright Dianna
West Washington HS
Palmyra IN

Wright Dinah K
Cowan HS
Oakville IN

Wright Donna
Huntington East HS
Huntington WV

Wright Douglas
Tri Cnty Middle Sr HS
Reynolds IN

Wright Douglas B
South Harrison HS
West Milford WV

Wright Kelly
Central HS
Evansville IN

Wright Kim
Madison Plains HS
South Solon OH

Wright Kim
Inkster HS
Westland MI

Wright Lynn
Wintersville HS
Steubenville OH

Wright Martha S
Central Preston Sr HS
Kingwood WV

Wright Melinda
Tri Jr Sr HS
Spiceland IN

Wright Pamela
St Charles HS
St Charles MI

Wright Randy
Hopkins HS
Hopkins MI

Wright Regina
Muskegon HS
Muskegon MI

Wright Rudy
Mcbain Rural Agrcltrl HS
Marion MI

Wright Stacie
George Washington HS
Charleston WV

Wright Stanley
Norwood Sr HS
Norwood OH

Wright Ted
Redford HS
Detroit MI

Wright Terry
Vinton Co HS
Mc Arthur OH

Wrightt Graham
Center Grove HS
Greenwood IN

Wriston Denise
Clear Fork HS
Clear Creek WV

Wrobel Dianna
St Josephs HS
South Bend IN

Wrobel Karen
North Canton Hoover HS
North Canton OH

Wroten Mark
Novi HS
Northville MI

Wrzesinski Stephanie
Manistee Catholic Cntrl
HS
Manistee MI

Wu Marion
E Lansing HS
E Lansing MI

Wudi Shirley
St Ursula Acad
Toledo OH

Wunderly Lynnette
Tecumseh HS
New Carlisle OH

11881471

Wunker Frederick
Terre Haute North Vigo
HS
Terre Haute IN

Wyant Lary H
Daleville HS
Yorktown IN

Wyatt Kathy
Memorial HS
St Marys OH

Wyatt Krista
Lebanon HS
Lebanon OH

Wyatt Jr Alfred R
Horace Mann HS
Gary IN

Wyche Annette
R B Chamberlin HS
Twinsburg OH

Wylie Janet
Peru HS
Peru IN

Wymer Jill
Ravenna HS
Ravenna OH

Wymer Susan
Field HS
Mogadore OH

Wynne Lori
West Side Sr HS
Gary IN

Wyrick Krista
National Trail HS
New Paris OH

Wyse T
Decatur Central HS
Indnpls IN

Wysocki Michelle
Vermilion HS
Vermilion OH

Y

Yacteen Jihane
Maumee HS
Maumee OH

Yager Gayle
Perrysburg HS
Perrysburg OH

Yagunich John
Roosevelt HS
E Chicago IN

Yake Amy
Marion Harding HS
Marion OH

Yakubik William
Hoover HS
Belington WV

Yansura Julie
Meadowbrook HS
Pleasant City OH

Yantis John
Westerville South HS
Westerville OH

Yarbrough Jeri
Elmhurst HS
Huntington IN

Yarcusko Alan C
Rocky River HS
Rocky River OH

Yardley Rich
Upper Arlington HS
Columbus OH

Yarian Jennifer
Newbury HS
Newbury OH

Yarris Beth
Westlake HS
Westlake OH

Yaste Melanie
Edinburg HS
Franklin IN

Yates Dante
Beecher HS
Mt Morris MI

Yates Kim
Hesperia HS
Hesperia MI

Yates Randall
Oak Hill HS
Oak Hill OH

Yates William B
Forest Park HS
Crystal Falls MI

Ybanez Jessica
Greenbrier East HS
Lewisburg WV

Yeager Kim
Indian Hill HS
Cincinnati OH

Yee Darlene
Magnificat HS
No Olmsted OH

Yee Karen
Austintown Fitch HS
Youngstown OH

Yee Tracy A
Beechcroft HS
Columbus OH

Yeichner Barbara
Galion Sr HS
Galion OH

Yelda Michael J
Cass Technical HS
Detroit MI

Yeley Brian
Dublin HS
Dublin OH

Yelton Rick
Canfield HS
Canfield OH

Yenkel Tammy
Woodhaven HS
Flat Rock MI

Yet Betty
Henry Ford HS
Detroit MI

Yetter Mary
Crestline HS
Crestline OH

Yetts Nathan
Wintersville HS
Wintrsvll OH

Yingling Connie
Fairless Local HS
Navarre OH

Ylimaki Rose M
Burt Township HS
Grand Marais MI

Yoakam Dawn
Danbury HS
Lakeside OH

Yockey Randy
Eastern HS
Russellville OH

Yocum John G
William Henry Harrison
HS
Harrison OH

Yoder Anna
Millington HS
Vassar MI

Yoder Craig
Garaway HS
Sugarcreek OH

Yoder Deida
Daleville HS
Daleville IN

Yoder Heidi
Brookside HS
Downers Grove IL

Yoder Thos
Goshen HS
Goshen IN

Yohe David
Lake Catholic HS
Wickliffe OH

Yoho Mary
Ashland Sr HS
Ashland OH

Yonders Debi
Copley HS
Fairlawn OH

Yong Jo Hwa
Willow Run HS
Ypsilanti MI

Yonks David
Terre Haute S Vigo HS
Terre Haute IN

Yookam Jennie
Springboro HS
Springboro OH

Yorey Joseph
Saint Josephs HS
South Bend IN

York Gary
Plymouth HS
Plymouth IN

Yoshino Doug
West Geauga HS
Chesterland OH

Yost Stephen
Colonel Crawford HS
Bucyrus OH

Youmans Yvonne
Millington HS
Millington MI

Younce Dana
Sr Lakeview HS
Stow OH

Young Annette
Edon HS
Edon OH

Young Cheryl S
Wehrle HS
Columbus OH

Young Cindy
Monrovia HS
Mooresville IN

Young David
Archbishop Alter HS
Kettering OH

Young Debbie
Traverse City Sr HS
Traverse City MI

Young Debra
Portage Central HS
Portage MI

Young Diseree
Holy Redeemer HS
Detroit MI

Young Duane D
Cannelton HS
Cannelton IN

Young Gregg
Clinton Prairie HS
Frnkfrt IN

Young Jacqueline
Bishop Noll Institute
Calumet IL

Young Jed
William Henry Harrison HS
W Lafayette IN

Young Joan
Sylvania Northview HS
Sylvania OH

Young Joseph B
Brebeuf HS
Indianapolis IN

Young Kevin
St Clair HS
St Clair MI

Young Kimberly
Lexington Sr HS
Lexington OH

Young Laura
Brookhaven HS
Columbus OH

Young Laura
Trinity HS
Cleveland OH

Young Lorna
Jackson HS
Jackson OH

Young Minnie
Stivers Patterson Coop HS
Dayton OH

Young Pam
Anderson HS
Cincinnati OH

Young Pamela J
Fairless HS
Brewster OH

Young Patricia L
Parma Sr HS
Parma OH

Young Robert A
Niles Sr HS
Niles MI

Young Robin
Peru Sr HS
Peru IN

Young Ruth
West Washington HS
Salem IN

Young Sheila
Nitro HS
Charleston WV

Young Sheryl
Amanda Clearcreek HS
Amanda OH

Young Sheryl
Lexington HS
Mansfield OH

Young Stephanie
Madison Hts HS
Anderson IN

Young Timothy
Roosevelt HS
Gary IN

Young Vickie
West Jefferson HS
W Jefferson OH

Young Vicki S
Warren County Joint Vo Schl
Morrow OH

Younger Craig
Whitehall Yearling HS
Whitehall OH

Youngkin Donald F
Walsh Jesuit HS
Cuyahoga Falls OH

Yuricek Laura
Warren G Harding HS
Warren OH

Yurko Michael
Andrean HS
Gary IN

Yuschik Andrea
Lakeland HS
Milford MI

Z

Zabriskie Robert S
Caro Community HS
Vassar MI

Zaccagni Michael J
Bishop Gallagher HS
Harper Woods MI

Zajack Renee
Madison Comprehensive
HS
Mansfield OH

Zak Ann M
Euclid Sr HS
Euclid OH

Zak Kenneth A
Parma Sr HS
Parma OH

Zamarron Jennifer
Wyoming Park HS
Wyoming MI

Zamponi Trina
Lanse Creuse HS
Mt Clemens MI

Zanetti Jeffrey
Trenton HS
Trenton MI

Zanner Heidi
Au Gres Sims HS
Au Gres MI

Zara Lynn M
Crestline HS
Crestline OH

Zarczynski Diane
James Ford Rhodes HS
Cleveland OH

Zarn Betty J
Strongsville HS
Strongsville OH

Zarzecki Margaret
Central HS
Grand Rapids MI

Zatezalo Myra
Buckeye South HS
Rayland OH

Zavatsky Catherine
Wintersville HS
Steubenville OH

Zawadiwsky Luba
Nazareth Acad
Parma OH

Zaynor Leslie
Theodore Roosevelt HS
Kent OH

Zdinak Paul
Stanton HS
Stratton OH

Zecchin Kenneth
Bishop Borgess HS
Detroit MI

Zeck James
Sandusky St Marys Cntrl
HS
Castalia OH

Zeddies Clark A
Ottawa Hills HS
Grand Rapids MI

Zeek Randy
Badin HS
Hamilton OH

Zehr Clint
Centreville Public HS
Centreville MI

Zehr Sharon L
Clay City HS
Clay City IN

Zelichowski Walter
Vicksburg HS
Fulton MI

Zeller Maureen
Beaumont HS
University Ht OH

Zello Nicholas
Bluffton HS
Bluffton IN

Zeman Trish
Nordonia HS
Macedonia OH

Zerr Karin
Valley Forge Sr HS
Parma Heights OH

Zettler Teri
Springfield Cathlc Cntrl
HS
Springfield OH

Zetzl Lawrence J
Cardinal Ritter HS
Speedway IN

Zetzl Mary A
Cardinal Ritter HS
Speedway IN

Zeunik Robert
Parkside HS
Jackson MI

Ziegler Cheryl L
Princeton Sr HS
Cincinnati OH

Ziegler Layne
Loudonville HS
Loudonville OH

Ziegler Robert
Caro Cmnty Sr HS
Caro MI

Zielasko Tracy
Hoover HS
North Canton OH

Zielinski Suzanne
St Clement HS
Sterling Hts MI

Zienta Suzette
St Joseph Central Cathlc
HS
Fremont OH

Zigenfus Robin
Mater Dei HS
Evansvl IN

Zile Ronnie
Vinton Co HS
West Union OH

Zimmerly Elliot
Groveport Madison HS
Obetz OH

Zimmerman Lynda
Erieview Catholic HS
Cleveland OH

Zimmerman Marcus
Bethany Christian HS
Goshen IN

Zimmerman Mark
Shepherd HS
Shepherd MI

Zimmerman Michael
Woodridge HS
Cuyahoga Fls OH

Zimmerman Michelle
Kenowa Hills HS
Grand Rapids MI

Zimmerman Steven
Defiance Sr HS
Defiance OH

Zinkivach Bonni
Osborn HS
Detroit MI

Zins Richard
Brookville HS
Brookville IN

Zissler Jenny
Engadine Consolidated
School
Birch Run MI

Zizzi Annette
Elkins HS
Elkins WV

Zofko Mary
Niles Mc Kinley HS
Niles OH

Zoldan Sandra
Clarenceville Sr HS
Livonia MI

Zolo Carolyn
Newark HS
Newark OH

Zoog Pete
Cathedral HS
Indianapolis IN

Zorko Jacqueline
Euclid Sr HS
Euclid OH

Zornes Ronnie
Sharples HS
Clothier WV

Zorza Wayne P
Gwinn Cmnty HS
Gwinn MI

Zotos Michael
East Detroit HS
Utica MI

Zoyhofski Sharron
Glen Lake Community
HS
Empire MI

Zuber Mary L
Northrop HS
Ft Wayne IN

Zull Jo Ann
Lakeview HS
Battle Creek MI

Zumkehr Jenifer
Kent Roosevelt HS
Kent OH

Zusmanis Valdis
Central HS
Grand Rapids MI

Zwicker Nancy
Aiken Sr HS
Cincinnati OH

Zwier Joan
West Catholic HS
Grand Rapids MI

Zylka Lydia
Standish Sterling Cntrl
HS
Standish MI

Zywiec Polly
Bishop Noll Inst
E Chicago IN